WEBSTER'S NEW WRLD™

Concise French Dictionary

Second Edition

WILEY

Wiley Publishing, Inc.

Library of Congress Control Number: 2005938172

ISBN-13 978-0-471-74831-1
ISBN-10 0-471-74831-5

Designed and typeset by Chambers Harrap Publishers Ltd., Edinburgh.

Manufactured in the United States of America

10 9 8 7 6 5 4 3 2 1

Project Editors / Directeurs de projet
Gearóid Cronin
Kate Nicholson

Editors / Rédacteurs
Isabelle Elkaim
Laurence Larroche

American English Editors / Rédacteurs anglais américain
Paige Weber
Peter Weisman
John Wright

with / avec
Pat Dunn
Georges Pilard
Anna Stevenson

Publishing Manager / Direction éditoriale
Patrick White

Prepress Manager / Direction prépresse
Clair Simpson

Prepress / Prépresse
Isla MacLean
Clair Simpson

Trademarks
Words considered to be trademarks have been designated in this dictionary by the symbol ®. However, no judgement is implied concerning the legal status of any trademark by virtue of the presence or absence of such a symbol.

Marques déposées
Les termes considérés comme des marques déposées sont signalés dans ce dictionnaire par le symbole ®. Cependant, la présence ou l'absence de ce symbole ne constitue nullement une indication quant à la valeur juridique de ces termes.

Contents
Table des Matières

Preface

This new edition of *Webster's New World French Concise Dictionary* provides comprehensive coverage of the basic vocabulary of both languages, including a wide range of idiomatic expressions and slang. In this dictionary you will also find many neologisms such as **altermondialisme, blog, clonage thérapeutique, dégâts collatéraux, instant messaging** and **metrosexual**. While the English-French side focuses on American English, the French-English side provides coverage of Canadian, Belgian and Swiss French terms as well as standard French.

As the dictionary will have a wide variety of users, at school, at home and in the workplace, it contains a broad range of vocabulary. In addition to good coverage of the French and American English spoken today, the dictionary features technical terms from such diverse fields as computing, finance, politics, education, the media and business, as well as encyclopedic information such as proper and geographical names.

The cultural boxes in the text are a novel feature of this dictionary. Almost a hundred of these notes can be found on the French side of the dictionary, dealing with culture-specific topics which require more explanation than a simple translation can provide. This information will give American users an insight into such uniquely French concepts as **le baccalauréat, la fête de la musique, Pacs**, and **verlan**.

Finally, the supplement contains information on French verbs, as well as a bilingual Communication Guide. The guide contains model letters and advice on how to correspond in both languages, as well as examples of résumés and sections on e-mail, telephone calls and newspaper ads, which can often be indecipherable to non-native speakers due to their extensive use of abbreviations.

Préface

Cette nouvelle édition du *Webster's New World French Concise Dictionary* présente un panorama très complet du vocabulaire de base de l'anglais et du français et comprend de nombreuses expressions idiomatiques, ainsi qu'une grande quantité de mots d'argot. Vous trouverez également dans cet ouvrage de nombreux néologismes ; nous pouvons citer comme exemples les termes **altermondialisme, blog, clonage thérapeutique, dégâts collatéraux, instant messaging** et **metrosexual**. Tandis que le côté anglais-français du dictionnaire porte essentiellement sur l'anglais américain, le côté français-anglais contient, en plus des mots courants en France, de nombreux termes issus du français du Canada, de Belgique et de Suisse.

Afin de satisfaire aux besoins des utilisateurs au collège et au lycée comme à la maison ou au bureau, cet ouvrage offre au lecteur un très large éventail de vocabulaire. Le français et l'anglais américain parlés aujourd'hui y sont traités en profondeur. Vous y trouverez également un abondant vocabulaire de spécialité provenant de domaines aussi divers que l'informatique, la finance, la politique, l'enseignement, les médias ou le monde des affaires. Ce dictionnaire contient en outre des noms propres et des noms de lieux.

Cet ouvrage propose une centaine d'encadrés culturels intégrés dans le texte du côté français-anglais. Ils concernent des thèmes propres à la culture francophone qui ne seront pas nécessairement connus de l'utilisateur américain. Des explications y sont données lorsqu'une traduction ou une glose ne suffisent pas à fournir les informations nécessaires. Ces encadrés permettront ainsi à l'utilisateur américain de comprendre des concepts typiquement français tels que **le baccalauréat, la fête de la musique, le Pacs,** ou **le verlan**.

Enfin, le supplément contient des informations sur la conjugaison des verbes français, ainsi qu'un guide de correspondance bilingue. Ce guide comprend des modèles de lettres et des conseils pour correspondre de façon efficace dans l'autre langue, ainsi que des exemples de CV et des explications sur le courrier électronique et les appels téléphoniques. Des petites annonces sont également données comme exemples car elles posent souvent des problèmes de compréhension en raison des nombreuses abréviations qui y sont utilisées.

Structure of Entries
Structure des entrées

Indicateurs de champ sémantique pour les termes spécialisés
Field labels indicate senses belonging to a particular subject area

major ['meɪdʒə(r)] **1** *n* (**a**) *Mil* (*in air force*) ≃ commandant *m*, *Can & Belg* ≃ major *m*; (*in infantry*) chef *m* de bataillon; (*in cavalry*) chef *m* d'escadron; **m. general** général *m* de division (**b**) *Univ* (*subject*) matière *f* principale; **she's a physics m.** elle fait des études de physique
    2 *adj* (**a**) (*important*) majeur(e); (*most important*) principal(e); (*accident, illness*) très grave; **of m. importance** de la plus haute importance (**b**) *Mus* majeur(e)
    3 *vi Univ* **to m. in sth** se spécialiser en qch

Seule l'initiale du mot traité apparaît dans l'exemple
Headword abbreviated to first letter only in phrases

La phonétique complète est donnée pour chaque entrée
IPA shown in full for all headwords

management ['mænɪdʒmənt] *n* (**a**) (*activity*) (*of company, project*) gestion *f*, direction *f*; (*of economy, resources, store, hotel*) gestion; **m. consultant** conseiller(ère) *m,f* en gestion; **m. studies** études *fpl* de gestion (**b**) (*managers, employers*) direction *f*; **under new m.** (*sign*) changement de propriétaire; **m. buyout** = rachat d'une société par la direction; **m. team** équipe *f* dirigeante

Les composés sont traités sous le premier élément et classés alphabétiquement
Compounds placed under first element; listed in alphabetical order

Chaque nouvelle catégorie grammaticale est traitée à la ligne et précédée d'un numéro en gras
New grammatical category introduced by bold numeral, placed on new line

managing director ['mænɪdʒɪŋdaɪ'rektə(r)] *n* directeur(trice) *m,f* général(e)

Indique que la traduction fonctionne aussi au sens figuré
This label means that the translation also works in figurative contexts

melt [melt] **1** *vt also Fig* faire fondre
    2 *vi* fondre; **to m. into thin air** s'évaporer, disparaître; **to m. into the crowd** se fondre dans la foule
▸**melt away** *vi* (*of snow*) fondre; (*of clouds, vapor*) se dissiper; (*of crowd*) se disperser; (*of objections, opposition*) s'évanouir
▸**melt down** *vt sep* (*metal*) fondre

Les verbes à particule sont précédés du signe ▸
Phrasal verbs introduced by ▸

Le genre des noms donnés en traduction est indiqué en italiques
Gender of noun translations shown in italic

minute¹ ['mɪnɪt] **1** *n* (**a**) (*of time*) minute *f*; **ten minutes past/to three** trois heures dix/moins dix; **wait a m.!** attendez une minute!; **go downstairs this m.!** descends immédiatement!; **just a m.** une minute; **the m. my back was turned** dès que j'ai eu le dos tourné; **any m.** d'une minute à l'autre; **in a m.** dans une minute; **at the last m.** à la dernière minute; **m. hand** (*of watch*) grande aiguille *f*; **m. steak** steak *m* minute (**b**) (*note*) note *f*; **minutes** (*of meeting*) compte rendu *m*
    2 *vt* (*make note of*) inscrire au procès-verbal
minute² [maɪ'njuːt] *adj* (**a**) (*small*) infime, minuscule (**b**) (*detailed*) minutieux(euse)

Les homographes sont numérotés
Superscript number marks homographs

Les indicateurs sémantiques apparaissent en italiques et entre parenthèses
Sense indicators shown in italic in brackets

La forme développée des abréviations est donnée systématiquement ; chaque abréviation est traduite
Full form of abbreviation given consistently; all abbreviations have translations

MMS [emem'es] *n Tel* (*abbr* **multimedia message service**) MMS *m*

Le féminin est donné systématiquement
Feminine inflections shown consistently

viii

académie [akademi] *nf* (**a**) *(des lettres, des sciences, d'art)* academy; **l'A. française** = learned society responsible for promoting the French language and imposing standards (**b**) *(école)* school, academy; **a. de musique/dessin** music/art school (**c**) *(dans l'Éducation nationale)* ≃ school district

académique [akademik] *adj* (**a**) *Scol* = relating to a local education authority (**b**) *Péj (style)* conventional (**c**) *Belg, Suisse & Can* **l'année a.** the academic year

acquiescer [16] [akjese] *vi* to acquiesce (**à** to); **a. d'un signe de tête** to nod in agreement

aider [ede] **1** *vt* to help; *(sujet: gouvernement)* to aid; **que puis-je faire pour vous a.?** how may I help you?**; je me suis fait a. par un ami** I got a friend to help me; **a. qn à faire qch** to help sb to do sth; **a. qn à monter/sortir** to help sb up/out; *Ironique* **tu veux que je t'aide?** stop that!; **elle n'aide jamais** she never helps (out)

2 aider à *vt ind* to contribute toward; **a. à faire qch** to help to do sth

3 s'aider *vpr* (**a**) *(soi-même)* **s'a. de qch** to use sth; **marcher en s'aidant d'une canne/de béquilles** to walk with the aid of a stick/crutches; *Prov* **aide-toi et le ciel t'aidera** God helps those who help themselves (**b**) *(l'un l'autre)* to help each other

amnistier [66] [amnistje] *vt* to grant an amnesty to

arrière-plan (*pl* **arrière-plans**) [arjɛrplɑ̃] *nm aussi Fig* background; **à l'a.** in the background

arrière-train (*pl* **arrière-trains**) [arjɛrtrɛ̃] *nm (d'un animal)* (hind)quarters; *Fam (d'une personne)* rump, rear

artériosclérose [arterjɔskleroz] *nf* hardening of the arteries, *Spéc* arteriosclerosis

aérobic [aerɔbik] *nm* aerobics *(singulier)*

avril [avril] *nm* April; **le premier a.** *(jour des farces)* April Fools' Day; *Prov* **en a., ne te découvre pas d'un fil** ne'er cast a clout till May is out; *voir aussi* **janvier**

English Phonetic Symbols
Symboles phonétiques de l'anglais

Consonnes/Consonants

[b]	but [bʌt]
[d]	dab [dæb]
[dʒ]	jam [dʒæm]; gem [dʒem]
[f]	fat [fæt]
[g]	go [gəʊ]
[h]	hat [hæt]
[j]	yet [jet]
[k]	cat [kæt]
[l]	lad [læd]
[m]	mat [mæt]
[n]	no [nəʊ]
[ŋ]	bang [bæŋ]
[p]	pat [pæt]
[r]	rat [ræt]
[(r)]	(seulement prononcé en cas de liaison avec le mot suivant) far [fɑː(r)]
[s]	sat [sæt]
[ʃ]	sham [ʃæm]
[t]	tap [tæp]
[tʃ]	chat [tʃæt]
[θ]	thatch [θætʃ]
[ð]	that [ðæt]
[v]	vat [væt]
[w]	wall [wɔːl]
[z]	zinc [zɪŋk]
[ʒ]	pleasure ['pleʒə(r)]
[χ]	loch [lɒχ]

Voyelles/Vowels

[æ]	bat [bæt]
[ɑː]	art [ɑːt]
[e]	bet [bet]
[ɜː]	curl [kɜːl]
[ə]	amend [ə'mend]
[iː]	bee [biː]
[ɪ]	bit [bɪt]
[ɒ]	wad [wɒd]
[ɔː]	all [ɔːl]
[ʊ]	put [pʊt]
[uː]	shoe [ʃuː]
[ʌ]	cut [kʌt]

Diphtongues/Diphthongs

[aɪ]	life [laɪf]
[aʊ]	house [haʊs]
[eə]	there [ðeə(r)]
[eɪ]	date [deɪt]
[əʊ]	low [ləʊ]
[ɪə]	beer [bɪə(r)]
[ɔɪ]	boil [bɔɪl]
[ʊə]	poor [pʊə(r)]

Symboles phonétiques du français
French Phonetic Symbols

Consonants/Consonnes

[b]   beau [bo]
[d]   donner [dɔne]
[f]   feu [fø]
[g]   garde [gard]
[ʒ]   gilet [ʒilɛ]
[k]   camp [kɑ̃]
[l]   lait [lɛ]
[m]   mon [mɔ̃]
[n]   né [ne]
[ŋ]   parking [parkiŋ]
[ɲ]   campagne [kɑ̃paɲ]
[p]   pain [pɛ̃]
[r]   rare [rar]
[s]   six [sis]
[ʃ]   chose [ʃoz]
[t]   table [tabl]
[v]   vie [vi]
[z]   zéro [zero]

Vowels/Voyelles

[a]   chat [ʃa]
[ɑ]   âge [ɑʒ]
[e]   été [ete]
[ə]   le [lə]; devin [dəvɛ̃]
[ø]   feu [fø]
[œ]   seul [sœl]
[ɛ]   père [pɛr]
[i]   vite [vit]
[ɔ]   donner [dɔne]
[o]   chaud [ʃo]
[u]   tout [tu]
[y]   cru [kry]
[ɑ̃]   enfant [ɑ̃fɑ̃]
[ɛ̃]   vin [vɛ̃]
[ɔ̃]   bon [bɔ̃]
[œ̃]   un [œ̃]

Semi-vowels/Semi-voyelles

[w]   noir [nwar]
[j]   yoga [jɔga]; rail [raj]
[ɥ]   huit [ɥit]

Abbreviations
Abréviations

English	Abbr	Français
gloss	=	glose
[introduces an explanation]		[introduit une explication]
cultural equivalent	≃	équivalent culturel
[introduces a translation which has a roughly equivalent status in the target language]		[introduit une traduction dont les connotations dans la langue cible sont comparables]
abbreviation	*abbr, abrév*	abréviation
adjective	*adj*	adjectif
adverb	*adv*	adverbe
agriculture	*Agr*	agriculture
anatomy	*Anat*	anatomie
architecture	*Archit*	architecture
article	*art*	article
astrology	*Astrol*	astrologie
astronomy	*Astron*	astronomie
cars	*Aut*	automobile
auxiliary	*aux*	auxiliaire
aviation	*Aviat*	aviation
Belgian French	*Belg*	belgicisme
botany	*Bot*	botanique
Canadian French	*Can*	canadianisme
chemistry	*Chem, Chim*	chimie
cinema	*Cin*	cinéma
commerce	*Com*	commerce
computing	*Comput*	informatique
conjunction	*conj*	conjonction
construction	*Constr*	construction
cooking	*Culin*	cuisine
economics	*Econ, Écon*	économie
electricity, electronics	*Elec, Élec*	électricité, électronique
European Union	*EU*	Union européenne
euphemism	*Euph*	euphémisme
exclamation	*exclam*	exclamation
feminine	*f*	féminin
familiar	*Fam*	familier
figurative	*Fig*	figuré
finance	*Fin*	finance
geography	*Geog, Géog*	géographie
geology	*Geol, Géol*	géologie
grammar	*Gram*	grammaire
history	*Hist*	histoire

humorous	*Hum*	humoristique
industry	*Ind*	industrie
invariable	*inv*	invariable
journalism	*Journ*	journalisme
law	*Jur*	droit
linguistics	*Ling*	linguistique
literary	*Lit, Litt*	littéraire
masculine	*m*	masculin
medicine	*Med, Méd*	médecine
weather	*Met, Météo*	météorologie
military	*Mil*	militaire
music	*Mus*	musique
noun	*n*	nom
shipping	*Naut*	nautisme
feminine noun	*nf*	nom féminin
feminine plural noun	*nfpl*	nom féminin pluriel
masculine noun	*nm*	nom masculin
masculine and feminine noun [same form for both genders]	*nmf*	nom masculin et féminin [formes identiques]
masculine and feminine noun [different form in the feminine]	*nm,f*	nom masculin et féminin [formes différentes]
masculine plural noun	*nmpl*	nom masculin pluriel
plural noun	*npl*	nom pluriel
proper noun	*npr*	nom propre
officially approved term	*Offic*	recommandation officielle
computing	*Ordinat*	informatique
parliament	*Parl*	parlement
pejorative	*Pej, Péj*	péjoratif
photography	*Phot*	photographie
physics	*Phys*	physique
plural	*pl*	pluriel
politics	*Pol*	politique
past participle	*pp*	participe passé
prefix	*pref, préf*	préfixe
preposition	*prep, prép*	préposition
proper noun	*pr n*	nom propre
pronoun	*pron*	pronom
proverb	*Prov*	proverbe
psychology	*Psy*	psychologie, psychiatrie
past tense	*pt*	prétérit
something	*qch*	quelque chose
somebody	*qn*	quelqu'un
registered trademark	®	marque déposée
radio	*Rad*	radio
rail	*Rail*	chemins de fer
religion	*Rel*	religion
somebody	*sb*	quelqu'un
school	*Sch, Scol*	domaine scolaire
specialist term	*Spec, Spéc*	vocabulaire de spécialité
formal	*Sout*	soutenu

something	*sth*	quelque chose
suffix	*suff*	suffixe
technical term	*Tech*	terme technique
telecommunications	*Tel, Tél*	télécommunications
textiles	*Tex*	textile
theater	*Theat, Théât*	théâtre
very familar	*très Fam*	très familier
television	*TV*	télévision
typography, printing	*Typ*	typographie, imprimerie
European Union	*UE*	Union européenne
university	*Univ*	domaine universitaire
verb	*v*	verbe
very familar	*very Fam*	très familier
intransitive verb	*vi*	verbe intransitif
reflexive verb	*vpr*	verbe pronominal
transitive verb	*vt*	verbe transitif
transitive verb used with a preposition [e.g. **parvenir à** (to reach); **ils sont parvenus à un accord** (they reached an agreement)]	*vt ind*	verbe transitif indirect [par exemple: **parvenir à; ils sont parvenus à un accord**]
inseparable transitive verb [phrasal verb where the verb and the adverb or preposition cannot be separated, e.g. **look after**; **he looked after the children**]	*vt insep*	verbe transitif à particule inséparable [par exemple: **look after** (s'occuper de); **he looked after the children** (il s'occupait des enfants)]
separable transitive verb [phrasal verb where the verb and the adverb or preposition can be separated, e.g. **send back**; **she sent the present back** or **she sent back the present**]	*vt sep*	verbe transitif à particule séparable [par exemple: **send back** (rendre); **she sent the present back** ou **she sent back the present** (elle a rendu le cadeau)]
vulgar	*Vulg*	vulgaire
zoology	*Zool*	zoologie

All other labels are written in full.
Toutes les autres indications d'usage sont données en entier.

Français-Anglais
French-English

A

A¹, a¹ [ɑ] *nm inv* A, a; **connaître un sujet de A à Z** to know a subject inside out; **prouver qch par A plus B** to prove sth in a logical *or* scientific fashion

A² [ɑ] *nf* (*abrév* **autoroute**) A1 ≃ I1

a² [ɑ] *voir* **avoir¹**

à [a] *prép*

> **à + le** contracts to form **au** [o], **à + les** contracts to form **aux** [o].

(a) *(indique la direction)* to; **aller/venir à Paris** to go/to come to Paris; **aller à la pêche** to go fishing; **partir au Venezuela** to leave for Venezuela; **rentrer à la maison** to go/to come home; **au lit!** off to bed!

(b) *(indique la position)* at; **être à la maison/à la campagne/à Marseille** to be at home/in the countryside/in Marseilles; **j'habite au 3, place des Cardeurs** I live at number 3, place des Cardeurs; **à la page deux** on page two; **à huit kilomètres/dix minutes d'ici** ≃ five miles/ten minutes from here; **à la télévision** on television; **un livre à la main** with a book in his/her hand

(c) *(dans l'expression du temps)* **à huit heures** at eight (o'clock); **au vingtième siècle** in the twentieth century; **à la tombée de la nuit** at nightfall; **au printemps** in the spring; **à mon arrivée** when I arrive/arrived; **le 2 au soir** on the evening of the 2nd; **à lundi!/ce soir!** see you Monday!/tonight!

(d) *(avec de)* to; **de Paris à Lyon** from Paris to Lyons; **du lundi au vendredi** from Monday to Friday, Monday through *or* to Friday; **de 2 à 4** *(heure)* from 2 till *or* to 4; **de 10 à 15 pour cent** *(environ)* between 10 and 15 percent

(e) *(introduit le complément d'objet indirect)* to; **donner/prêter qch à qn** to give/lend sth to sb, to give/lend sb sth; **penser à qn/qch** to think of *or* about sb/sth

(f) *(indique l'appartenance)* **c'est à lui/à Paul** it's his/Paul's; *Fam* **un ami à moi** a friend of mine; **c'est à vous de...** *(il vous incombe de)* it's up to you to...; *(c'est votre tour de)* it's your turn to...; **à toi!** your turn!

(g) *(indique le moyen, la manière)* **à bicyclette** by bicycle; **à pied/cheval** on foot/horseback; **au crayon** in pencil; **à la française** in the French style; **fonctionner à l'électricité** to run on electricity; **jouer un air au violon** to play a tune on the violin

(h) *(distributif)* **faire qch à deux/trois** to do sth in twos/threes; **se mettre à plusieurs pour faire qch** to team up to do sth; **80 km à l'heure** ≃ 50 miles an *or* per hour; **être payé à l'heure** to be paid by the hour

(i) *(indique la caractéristique)* **l'homme à la barbe/aux lunettes noires** the man with a beard/with the dark glasses; **un timbre à un euro** a one-euro stamp

(j) *(indique le but)* **maison à vendre** house for sale; **à louer** *(sur panneau)* to rent; **j'ai une lettre à écrire/des courses à faire** I've got a letter to write/some errands to run

(k) *(indique la conséquence)* **c'était à mourir de rire** it was hilarious; **laid à faire peur** hideously ugly; **c'est à se demander si...** you begin to wonder if...

abaisser [abese] **1** *vt* **(a)** *(levier, manette, pont-levis)* to lower; *(store)* to pull down **(b)** *(prix, coût, pression)* to reduce **(c)** *Litt (humilier)* to humble, to abase **(d)** *Culin (pâte)* to roll out

2 s'abaisser *vpr* **(a)** *(descendre)* to slope down **(b)** **s'a. à faire qch** to lower oneself to do sth

abandon [abɑ̃dɔ̃] *nm* **(a)** *(d'un enfant, d'un projet)* abandonment; **exiger l'a. des hostilités** to call for an end to hostilities; *Jur* **a. du domicile conjugal** desertion; *Mil* **a. de poste** desertion of one's post **(b)** *(en sport)* **gagner par a.** to win by default; **être contraint à l'a.** to be forced to withdraw **(c)** *(d'un lieu)* neglect; **être à l'a.** to be neglected; **laisser qch à l'a.** to neglect sth **(d)** *(nonchalance)* abandon **(e)** *Ordinat* abort

abandonner [abɑ̃dɔne] **1** *vt* **(a)** *(personne, village)* to desert, to abandon; *(voiture)* to abandon; **a. le navire** to abandon ship; **a. le domicile conjugal** to desert the marital home; **mes forces m'abandonnent** my strength is failing me **(b)** *(privilège, pouvoir, combat)* to give up; *(projet)* to abandon; *(course)* to withdraw from; **a. ses études** to drop out (of school/college); **a. ses études de médecine** to give up medicine; *aussi Fig* **a. la partie** to throw in the sponge *or* towel; **j'abandonne** I give up **(c)** *(céder)* to give (**à** to) **(d)** *Ordinat* to abort

2 s'abandonner *vpr* *(se laisser aller)* to let oneself go; **s'a. au sommeil** to drift off to sleep

abasourdi, -e [abazurdi] *adj* stunned

abat-jour [abaʒur] *nm inv* lampshade

abats [aba] *nmpl* variety meat; *(de volaille)* giblets

abattage [abataʒ] *nm* **(a)** *(d'animal)* slaughter, slaughtering **(b)** **avoir de l'a.** *(acteur, politicien)* to be full of go

abattant [abatɑ̃] *nm* *(d'une table)* flap; *(des toilettes)* lid

abattement [abatmɑ̃] *nm* **(a)** *(physique)* exhaustion **(b)** *(moral)* dejection, depression **(c)** *Fin* **a. (fiscal)** tax exemption

abattis [abati] *nmpl* **(a)** *(de volaille)* giblets **(b)** *Fam* **numéroter ses a.** to start saying one's prayers

abattoir [abatwar] *nm* slaughterhouse, abattoir; *Fig* **envoyer qn à l'a.** to send sb to the slaughter

abattre [11] [abatr] **1** *vt* **(a)** *(faire tomber)* *(mur, cloison)* to knock down, to pull down; *(arbre)* to fell, to cut down; *(avion)* to bring down; *(sujet: vent)* *(arbre)* to blow down; **a. de la besogne** to get through a lot of work

(b) *(tuer)* *(personne)* to kill; *(animal de boucherie)* to slaughter; *(animal malade ou dangereux)* to destroy; *Fig* **c'est l'homme à a.** he needs to be removed

(c) *Fig (fatiguer)* *(sujet: maladie)* to lay low; **la chaleur nous a complètement abattus** the heat drained us of all energy

(d) *Fig (démoraliser)* to dishearten, to depress; **ne vous laissez pas a.!** keep your chin up!

(e) *aussi Fig* **a. ses cartes** *ou* **son jeu** to lay one's cards on the table

2 s'abattre *vpr* *(arbre, mur)* to crash down (**sur** on); *(pluie)* to pour down (**sur** on); *(oiseau)* to swoop down (**sur** on)

abattu, -e [abaty] *adj* dejected, depressed

abbaye [abei] *nf* abbey

abbé [abe] *nm* (**a**) *(d'une abbaye)* abbot (**b**) *(prêtre)* priest; **j'en parlerai à Monsieur l'a.** I'll mention it to the priest; **l'a. Martin** Father Martin

abc [abese] *nm inv (rudiments)* basics

abcès [apsɛ] *nm* abscess; *Fig* **crever** *ou* **vider l'a.** to resolve the situation

abdiquer [abdike] *vt (trône)* to abdicate; *(droits)* to renounce, to surrender; **être contraint d'a.** to be forced to abdicate

abdomen [abdɔmɛn] *nm* abdomen

abdominal, -e, -aux, -ales [abdɔminal, -o] **1** *adj* abdominal

    2 *nmpl* **abdominaux** *(muscles)* stomach muscles; **faire des abdominaux** to do exercises for the stomach muscles

abdos [abdo] *nmpl Fam (muscles)* stomach muscles; **faire des a.** to do exercises for the stomach muscles

abécédaire [abesedɛr] *nm* ABC, alphabet book

abeille [abɛj] *nf* bee

aberrant, -e [abɛrɑ̃, -ɑ̃t] *adj* (**a**) *(insensé)* absurd (**b**) *Biol* aberrant

aberration [abɛrasjɔ̃] *nf* aberration; **c'est une a.!** it's absurd!

abêtir [abetir] **1** *vt* **a. qn** to dull sb's mind

    2 s'abêtir *vpr* to become stupid

abêtissant, -e [abetisɑ̃, -ɑ̃t] *adj* mind-numbing

abhorrer [abɔre] *vt Litt* to abhor

Abidjan [abidʒɑ̃] *n* Abidjan

abîme [abim] *nm (de l'océan)* abyss, depths; *Fig (entre deux personnes)* gulf; *Fig* **être au bord de l'a.** to be on the brink of disaster

abîmer [abime] **1** *vt (objet)* to spoil, to damage; *(vêtement, chaussures)* to ruin

    2 s'abîmer *vpr* (**a**) *(fruit)* to go bad; *(objet)* to get damaged; *(vêtement, chaussures)* to get ruined (**b**) **s'a. les yeux** to ruin one's eyesight (**c**) *Litt* **s'a. en mer** to be engulfed by the sea

abject, -e [abʒɛkt] *adj Péj* contemptible, despicable

abjurer [abʒyre] *vt (religion)* to abjure

ablation [ablasjɔ̃] *nf* removal

ablette [ablɛt] *nf* bleak *(fish)*

ablutions [ablysjɔ̃] *nfpl Litt ou Hum* **faire ses a.** to perform one's ablutions

abnégation [abnegasjɔ̃] *nf* abnegation, self-sacrifice

aboiement [abwamɑ̃] *nm* bark; **des aboiements** barking

abois [abwa] *nmpl* **être aux a.** *(cerf)* to be at bay; *Fig* **il est aux a.** *(personne)* the net's closing in on him

abolir [abɔlir] *vt* to abolish

abolition [abɔlisjɔ̃] *nf* abolition

abominable [abɔminabl] *adj (temps)* appalling, abominable; *(crime)* heinous; *(odeur)* foul; **l'a. homme des neiges** the abominable snowman

abominablement [abɔminabləmɑ̃] *adv* abominably; *(laid)* hideously

abomination [abɔminasjɔ̃] *nf* abomination; *Litt* **avoir qn/qch en a.** to loathe sb/sth

abondamment [abɔ̃damɑ̃] *adv (parler, critiquer)* at length; *(pleuvoir)* heavily; *(manger, illustrer)* copiously; **se servir a.** to help oneself to a generous portion of food

abondance [abɔ̃dɑ̃s] *nf* abundance; *(d'informations, de détails)* wealth; **il y avait des fruits en a.** there was plenty of fruit; **vivre dans l'a.** to live a life of ease

abondant, -e [abɔ̃dɑ̃, -ɑ̃t] *adj* abundant, plentiful; *(repas)* hearty; *(pluie)* heavy; *(saignement)* profuse; **une chevelure abondante** a thick head of hair; **peu a.** *(récolte, chevelure)* poor; *(pluie)* light; *(repas)* frugal

abonder [abɔ̃de] *vi* (**a**) *(foisonner)* to be plentiful; **a. en qch** to abound in sth (**b**) **a. dans le sens de qn** to agree entirely with sb

abonné, -e [abɔne] **1** *nm,f (d'une revue)* subscriber; *(du gaz, de l'électricité)* consumer; *(de la SNCF, d'un théâtre)* season-ticket holder; **il n'y a pas d'a. au numéro que vous avez demandé** ≃ the number you dialed is invalid

    2 *adj* **être a. à qch** *(revue)* to have a subscription to sth; *(SNCF, théâtre)* to have a season ticket to sth; *Fam (être sujet à)* to be prone to sth

abonnement [abɔnmɑ̃] *nm (à une revue)* subscription (**à** to); *(de train, de théâtre)* season ticket; *(au téléphone)* line rental; **prendre un a.** *(à une revue)* to take out a subscription; *(pour le train, pour le théâtre)* to buy a season ticket

abonner [abɔne] **1** *vt* **a. qn à une revue** to take out a subscription to a magazine for sb

    2 s'abonner *vpr (à une revue)* to take out a subscription (**à** to); *(au théâtre)* to buy a season ticket (**à** for)

abord [abɔr] *nm* (**a**) *(d'un lieu)* **l'île est d'un a. difficile** the island is not easily accessible (**b**) **abords** *(d'un bâtiment)* surroundings; *(d'une ville)* outskirts (**c**) *(d'une personne)* **être d'un a. facile/difficile** to be approachable/unapproachable; **au premier a., de prime a.** at first sight (**d**) **d'a., tout d'a.** *(pour commencer)* at first, to begin with; *(premièrement)* first (and foremost), in the first place; *Fam* **toi, d'a., je ne te parle plus!** I'm not talking to you, so there!

abordable [abɔrdabl] *adj* (**a**) *(lieu)* accessible (**b**) *(prix)* affordable (**c**) *(personne)* approachable

abordage [abɔrdaʒ] *nm (pour attaquer)* boarding; *(pour s'amarrer)* coming alongside; **monter à l'a.** to board a ship

aborder [abɔrde] **1** *vt* (**a**) *(personne)* to approach; **se faire a.** to be approached (**b**) *(question)* to deal with; *(virage)* to approach (**c**) *(navire)* to board; *(se mettre le long de)* to come alongside

    2 *vi* to land

aborigène [abɔriʒɛn] **1** *nmf (d'un pays)* native; **les aborigènes d'Australie** the (Australian) Aborigines

    2 *adj (indigène)* native, indigenous (**de** to); *(des peuplades australiennes)* Aboriginal

abortif, -ive [abɔrtif, -iv] *adj voir* **pilule**

abouler [abule] *Fam* **1** *vt* to hand over

    2 s'abouler *vpr* to turn up, to show up; **alors, tu t'aboules?** well, are you coming or not?

aboutir [abutir] *vi* (**a**) *(réussir)* to be successful; **ne pas a.** to fall through (**b**) *(dans l'espace)* **a. à/dans** *(sujet: personne)* to end up at/in; **a. à** *(sujet: chemin, escalier)* to lead to; *Fig (sujet: efforts, recherches)* to result in; **n'a. à rien** *(personne)* to get nowhere; *(efforts, recherches)* to come to nothing

aboutissants [abutisɑ̃] *nmpl voir* **tenant**

aboutissement [abutismɑ̃] *nm* result, outcome

aboyer [32] [abwaje] *vi* to bark

abracadabrant, -e [abrakadabrɑ̃, -ɑ̃t] *adj Fam (histoire)* cock-and-bull

abrasif, -ive [abrazif, -iv] *adj & nm* abrasive

abrégé [abreʒe] *nm* (**a**) *(livre)* **un a. d'histoire de France** a short history of France; **un a. de philosophie** a short guide to philosophy (**b**) **écrire en a.** to write in abbreviated form

abréger [59] [abreʒe] *vt (article, exposé)* to shorten, to cut down; *(visite)* to cut short; *(mot)* to abbreviate; *Fam* **allez, abrège!** come on, get to the point!

abreuver [abrœve] **1** *vt (chevaux, bétail)* to water; *Fig* **a. qn d'injures** to shower sb with insults

    2 s'abreuver *vpr (cheval, bétail)* to drink

abreuvoir [abrœvwar] *nm (dans une rivière)* watering place; *(baquet)* drinking trough

abréviation [abrevjasjɔ̃] *nf* abbreviation

abri [abri] *nm* shelter; **mettre qn/qch à l'a.** to shelter sb/sth; **se mettre à l'a.** to (take) shelter; **être à l'a. (de qch)** to be sheltered *(from sth)*; **être à l'a. du besoin** to have no financial worries; **personne n'est à l'a. d'une erreur** anybody can make a mistake; **a. antiatomique** fallout shelter; **a. à vélos** bike shed

abribus® [abribys] *nm* bus shelter

abricot [abriko] **1** *nm* apricot

2 *adj inv* apricot-colored

abricotier [abrikɔtje] *nm* apricot tree

abrier [66] [abrije] *Can* **1** *vt* to wrap up (well)

2 s'abrier *vpr* to wrap oneself up (well)

abriter [abrite] **1** *vt* (**a**) *(protéger)* to shelter (**de** from) (**b**) *(loger) (personnes)* to house, to accommodate; *(société, machine)* to house

2 s'abriter *vpr* **s'a. (de la pluie)** to (take) shelter (from the rain); **s'a. (du soleil)** to shade oneself (from the sun)

abrogation [abrɔgasjɔ̃] *nf (d'une loi)* repeal

abroger [45] [abrɔʒe] *vt (loi)* to repeal

abrupt, -e [abrypt] *adj (rocher, pente)* steep; *Fig (manière)* abrupt, blunt; **d'un ton a.** abruptly

abruti, -e [abryti] **1** *nm,f Fam* idiot, fool

2 *adj* (**a**) *(hébété)* stupefied, dazed; **a. par l'alcool** stupefied with drink (**b**) *Fam (bête)* stupid, idiotic

abrutir [abrytir] **1** *vt* (**a**) *(hébéter)* to daze; **a. qn de travail** to work sb to the point of exhaustion (**b**) *(abêtir)* to stultify

2 s'abrutir *vpr* **s'a. de travail** to work oneself to the point of exhaustion; **on s'abrutit à trop regarder la télévision** too much television numbs the brain

abrutissant, -e [abrytisã, -ãt] *adj (travail)* stultifying, mind-numbing; *(bruit)* wearing

ABS [abeɛs] *nm Aut* **(système)** **A.** ABS

abscisse [apsis] *nf Math* x-axis

abscons, -e [apskɔ̃, -ɔ̃s] *adj Litt* abstruse

absence [apsɑ̃s] *nf* (**a**) *(d'une personne)* absence; **en** *ou* **pendant mon a.** in *or* during my absence, while I am/was/*etc.* away (**b**) *(manque)* lack (**c**) **avoir des absences** to be prone to absent-mindedness; **dans un moment d'a.** in a moment of absent-mindedness

absent, -e [apsã, -ãt] **1** *adj* (**a**) *(qui n'est pas présent)* absent (**de** from) (**b**) *(inexistant)* missing (**c**) *(distrait)* **avoir un air a.** to be miles away

2 *nm,f* absentee; **les absents ont toujours tort** it's always those who aren't there who get the blame

absentéisme [apsɑ̃teism] *nm* absenteeism

absenter [apsɑ̃te] **s'absenter** *vpr (sortir)* to go away (**de** from); **elle a dû s'a. quelques minutes** she had to go out for a few minutes

absinthe [apsɛ̃t] *nf* absinthe

absolu, -e [apsɔly] **1** *nm* **l'a.** the absolute; **dans l'a.,...** in principle,...

2 *adj* absolute; *(règle)* hard-and-fast; **être dans l'impossibilité absolue de faire qch** to be quite unable to do sth

absolument [apsɔlymɑ̃] *adv* (**a**) *(complètement)* absolutely; **a. pas!** absolutely not! (**b**) *(sans faute)* **vous devez a. y aller!** you simply MUST go!

absolution [apsɔlysjɔ̃] *nf Rel* absolution

absolvais *etc. voir* **absoudre**

absorbant, -e [apsɔrbɑ̃, -ãt] *adj* (**a**) *(matériau)* absorbent (**b**) *(livre, tâche)* absorbing

absorber [apsɔrbe] *vt* (**a**) *(liquide)* to absorb, to soak up (**b**) *(nourriture)* to eat; *(boisson)* to drink; *(médicament)* to take (**c**) *(entreprise)* to take over (**d**) *(sujet: lecture)* to absorb, to engross; **son travail l'absorbe** she is absorbed *or* engrossed in her work; **être absorbé dans ses pensées** to be lost in thought

absorption [apsɔrpsjɔ̃] *nf* (**a**) *(de liquide)* absorption (**b**) *(de nourriture)* eating; *(d'une boisson)* drinking; *(d'un médicament)* taking (**c**) *(d'une entreprise)* takeover

absoudre [3a] [apsudr] *vt Litt ou Rel* **a. qn de qch** to forgive sb sth

abstenir [70] [apstənir] **s'abstenir** *vpr (ne pas voter)* to ab-

stain (from voting); **s'a. de faire qch** to refrain from doing sth; **dans le doute, abstiens-toi** when in doubt, don't; **pas sérieux s'a.** *(dans une petite annonce)* serious applications only

abstention [apstɑ̃sjɔ̃] *nf* abstention

abstentionniste [apstɑ̃sjɔnist] *nmf* abstainer

abstinence [apstinɑ̃s] *nf* abstinence

abstraction [apstraksjɔ̃] *nf* (**a**) **faire a. de qch** to disregard sth; **a. faite de cette dépense** leaving aside this expense (**b**) *(idée abstraite)* abstract idea, abstraction

abstrait, -e [apstrɛ, -ɛt] **1** *adj* abstract

2 *nm* **dans l'a.** in the abstract

absurde [apsyrd] **1** *adj* absurd

2 *nm* **l'a.** *(d'une situation, d'une remarque)* absurdity; **démonstration par l'a.** reductio ad absurdum

absurdité [apsyrdite] *nf* (**a**) *(caractère absurde)* absurdity (**b**) *(chose absurde)* absurdity, piece of nonsense; **dire des absurdités** to talk nonsense

abus [aby] *nm* (**a**) *(excès)* overindulgence (**de** in); **l'a. d'alcool** alcohol abuse; **l'a. de médicaments est dangereux** taking too much medication is dangerous (**b**) *(pratique)* abuse; *Fam* **il y a de l'a.!** that's going too far! (**c**) *Jur* **a. de biens sociaux** misappropriation of funds; **a. de confiance** breach of trust; **a. de pouvoir** abuse of power

abuser [abyze] **1** *vt Litt* to deceive

2 abuser de *vt ind (exploiter, violer)* to take advantage of; **a. du tabac** to smoke too much; **a. de ses forces** to overexert oneself; **il ne faut pas a. des bonnes choses** good things should be enjoyed in moderation; **je ne voudrais pas a. I** don't want to cause you any inconvenience; **alors là, vous abusez!** this is a bit much!

3 s'abuser *vpr* **si je ne m'abuse** if I'm not mistaken

abusif, -ive [abyzif, -iv] *adj* (**a**) *(emploi d'un mot)* incorrect (**b**) *(excessif)* excessive; *(mère)* possessive

abysse [abis] *nm* abyssal zone

acabit [akabi] *nm Péj* **du même a.** of that type

académicien, -enne [akademisjɛ̃, -ɛn] *nm,f* = member of the "Académie française"

académie [akademi] *nf* (**a**) *(des lettres, des sciences, d'art)* academy; **l'A. française** = learned society responsible for promoting the French language and imposing standards (**b**) *(école)* school, academy; **a. de musique/dessin** music/art school (**c**) *(dans l'Éducation nationale)* ≃ school district

> ### Académie française
> This was originally a group of men of letters who were encouraged by Cardinal Richelieu in 1635 to become an official body. Consisting of forty distinguished writers ("les Quarante" or "les Immortels"), the Académie's chief task was, and is, to produce a definitive dictionary and to be the ultimate authority in matters concerning the French language.

académique [akademik] *adj* (**a**) *Scol* = relating to a local education authority (**b**) *Péj (style)* conventional (**c**) *Belg, Suisse & Can* **l'année a.** the academic year

acajou [akaʒu] **1** *nm* mahogany

2 *adj inv* reddish-brown

a cap(p)ella [akapela] *adv* a cappella

acariâtre [akarjɑtr] *adj* cantankerous

acarien [akarjɛ̃] *nm* dust mite

accablant, -e [akablɑ̃, -ãt] *adj* (**a**) *(responsabilités)* overwhelming; *(chaleur)* oppressive (**b**) *(témoignage)* damning

accablement [akabləmɑ̃] *nm* dejection, depression

accabler [akable] *vt (sujet: chaleur, malheur)* to overwhelm; **a. qn de travail** to overload sb with work; **a. qn de reproches** to heap criticism on sb (**b**) *(sujet: témoignage)* to damn

accalmie [akalmi] *nf* lull

accaparer [akapare] *vt (personne, conversation)* to monopolize; *(places, morceaux de choix)* to grab

accéder [34] [aksede] **accéder à** *vt ind* (**a**) *(atteindre)* to reach, to get to (**b**) *Fig (responsabilités, rang)* to gain; **a. au trône** to accede to the throne (**c**) *(requête)* to comply with (**d**) *Ordinat (programme)* to access

accélérateur [akseleratœr] *nm (de voiture, d'ordinateur)* accelerator; **appuyer sur l'a.** to step on the gas pedal; *Ordinat* **a. graphique** graphic(s) accelerator; *Phys* **a. de particules** particle accelerator

accélération [akselerasjɔ̃] *nf* acceleration

accéléré, -e [akselere] **1** *nm Cin* **en a.** in speeded-up motion **2** *adj* quick, fast; *(mouvement)* accelerated; **cours a.** crash course

accélérer [34] [akselere] **1** *vt* to speed up; *Fig* **a. le mouvement** to get a move on **2** *vi (en voiture)* to accelerate **3** **s'accélérer** *vpr* to accelerate, to speed up

accent [aksɑ̃] *nm* (**a**) *(sur une lettre)* accent; **a. aigu/grave/circonflexe** acute/grave/circumflex (accent); **e a. circonflexe** e circumflex (**b**) *(en phonétique)* stress; **a. tonique** (primary) stress (**c**) *(prononciation)* accent; **elle parle anglais sans a.** she speaks English without an accent (**d**) *Fig (inflexion)* **avoir des accents de vérité** to have a ring of truth; **mettre l'a. sur qch** to stress *or* to emphasize sth

accentuation [aksɑ̃tɥasjɔ̃] *nf* (**a**) *(en phonétique)* stress (**b**) *(à l'écrit)* accentuation (**c**) *(d'un phénomène)* intensification

accentué, -e [aksɑ̃tɥe] *adj* (**a**) *(syllabe)* stressed (**b**) *(lettre)* accented (**c**) *Fig (net)* pronounced, marked

accentuer [aksɑ̃tɥe] **1** *vt* (**a**) *(syllabe)* to stress (**b**) *(lettre)* to put an accent on (**c**) *Fig (renforcer)* to emphasize; *(avance)* to increase **2** **s'accentuer** *vpr* to become more pronounced *or* marked

acceptable [akseptabl] *adj* (**a**) *(recevable)* acceptable (**b**) *(passable)* satisfactory

acceptation [akseptasjɔ̃] *nf* acceptance

accepter [aksepte] *vt* to accept; **a. de faire qch** to agree to do sth; **il est hors de question que j'accepte** I can't possibly accept; **allez, accepte!** go on, say yes!

acception [aksepsjɔ̃] *nf Sout* (**a**) *(d'un mot)* meaning, sense (**b**) **sans a. de race/de sexe** irrespective of race/sex

accès [aksɛ] *nm* (**a**) *(approche)* access, approach (**à** to); **être facile/difficile d'a.** to be easy/hard to reach; **avoir a. à qch** to have access to sth; **donner a. à qch** *(sujet: porte, chemin)* to lead to sth; *(sujet: ticket)* to allow entry to sth; **a. aux quais** *(sur panneau)* to the trains (**b**) *(d'une personne)* **être d'un a. facile/difficile** to be approachable/unapproachable (**c**) *(poussée)* fit, attack; **a. de colère** fit of anger; **a. de fièvre** bout of fever; **a. de toux** coughing fit (**d**) *Ordinat* access; *(sur Internet)* hit; **avoir a. à** to be able to access

accessible [aksesibl] *adj* (**a**) *(lieu, livre)* accessible; *(prix)* affordable (**b**) *(personne)* approachable

accession [aksesjɔ̃] *nf* **a. au pouvoir/au trône** accession (to power)/to the throne; **l'a. à la propriété** home ownership

accessoire [akseswar] **1** *nm (d'appareil ménager, de mode)* accessory; *Can* **a. électrique** domestic electrical appliance; *Théât* **accessoires** props **2** *adj* minor; **c'est a.** it's a minor detail

accessoirement [akseswarmɑ̃] *adv* if necessary, if need be; *(en plus)* also

accessoiriste [akseswarist] *nmf Théât* prop man, *f* prop woman

accident [aksidɑ̃] *nm* (**a**) *(collision, malheur)* accident; **a. d'avion** plane *or* air crash; **a. de chemin de fer** train crash; **a. de la circulation** traffic accident; **a. de la route** road accident; **a. du travail** industrial accident; **a. de voiture** car

accident *or* crash (**b**) *(événement inattendu)* mishap; **par a.** by accident, by chance; **a. de parcours** hitch (**c**) **a. de terrain** *(bosse)* bump; *(trou)* hole

accidenté, -e [aksidɑ̃te] **1** *nm,f* accident victim; **accidentés de la route** road accident victims **2** *adj* (**a**) *(terrain)* uneven (**b**) *(voiture)* damaged

accidentel, -elle [aksidɑ̃tɛl] *adj* accidental

accidentellement [aksidɑ̃tɛlmɑ̃] *adv (par hasard)* accidentally, by chance; *(mourir)* (mourir) in an accident

acclamation [aklamasjɔ̃] *nf* cheer; **sous les acclamations de la foule** to the cheers of the crowd

acclamer [aklame] *vt* to cheer

acclimatation [aklimatasjɔ̃] *nf* acclimation, acclimatization (**à** to)

acclimater [aklimate] **1** *vt* to acclimate, to acclimatize (**à** to) **2** **s'acclimater** *vpr* to become *or* to get acclimated *or* acclimatized (**à** to)

accointances [akwɛ̃tɑ̃s] *nfpl* contacts

accolade [akɔlad] *nf* (**a**) *(embrassade)* (formal) embrace; **donner l'a. à qn** to embrace sb (**b**) *(signe typographique)* bracket, brace

accoler [akɔle] *vt (mettre côte à côte)* to put side by side

accommodant, -e [akɔmɔdɑ̃, -ɑ̃t] *adj* accommodating

accommoder [akɔmɔde] **1** *vt (nourriture)* to prepare; *(restes)* to use up **2** *vi (œil)* to focus **3** **s'accommoder** *vpr* **s'a. de qch** to put up with sth

accompagnateur, -trice [akɔ̃paɲatœr, -tris] *nm,f* (**a**) *(pianiste)* accompanist (**b**) *(d'un voyage organisé)* courier, tour guide; *(d'une sortie scolaire)* accompanying adult (**c**) *Belg* **a. de train** ticket inspector

accompagnement [akɔ̃paɲmɑ̃] *nm* (**a**) *(de morceau de musique)* accompaniment; **chanter sans a.** to sing unaccompanied (**b**) *(légumes)* side dish

accompagner [akɔ̃paɲe] **1** *vt* (**a**) *(venir avec)* to come with, to accompany; *(aller avec)* to go with, to accompany; **il est venu accompagné d'une amie** he came with a friend (**b**) *(conduire)* **a. qn à la gare** to take sb to the station (**c**) *(chanteur)* to accompany (**à** on) (**d**) *(ajouter à)* **il a accompagné ses mots d'un sourire** he said it with a smile; **elle a accompagné son exposé de diapositives** she complemented her talk with a slide show; **un rôti accompagné de légumes** a roast served with vegetables **2** **s'accompagner** *vpr* (**a**) **s'a. au piano** to accompany oneself on the piano (**b**) *(se produire simultanément)* **s'a. de qch** to be accompanied by sth

accompli, -e [akɔ̃pli] *adj (excellent)* accomplished

accomplir [akɔ̃plir] **1** *vt* (**a**) *(tâche)* to carry out; *(bonne action)* to do; *(exploit)* to accomplish; *(souhait, promesse)* to fulfill (**b**) *(terminer)* to complete, to finish **2** **s'accomplir** *vpr (souhait)* to come true

accord [akɔr] *nm* (**a**) *(traité)* agreement; *(non formel)* understanding; *(pour résoudre un conflit)* settlement; **arriver** *ou* **parvenir à un a.** to come to *or* to reach an agreement (**b**) *(entente)* agreement (**sur** on); **être d'a. avec qn** to agree with sb; **se mettre d'a.** *ou* **tomber d'a. avec qn** to come to an agreement with sb; **(c'est) d'a.!** all right!, OK!; **d'un commun a.** by common consent, by mutual agreement; **faire qch en a. avec qn** to do sth in agreement with sb (**c**) *(autorisation)* consent (**d**) *Gram* agreement (**avec** with) (**e**) *(en musique)* chord; **a. parfait** common chord

accord-cadre *(pl* **accords-cadres**) [akɔrkadr] *nm* outline agreement

accordéon [akɔrdeɔ̃] *nm* accordion; *Fig* **en a.** *(chaussettes)* wrinkled

accordéoniste [akɔrdeɔnist] *nmf* accordionist, accordion player

accorder [akɔrde] **1** *vt* (**a**) **a. qch à qn** *(faveur)* to grant sb sth; *(augmentation, dommages-intérêts)* to award sb sth; *(prêt, découvert bancaire)* to authorize sth to sb; **a. son pardon à qn** to pardon sb; **a. la plus grande importance à qch** to attach the utmost importance to sth; **pouvez-vous m'a. quelques minutes?** can you spare me a few minutes?; *Sout* **je ne l'aime pas, je vous l'accorde** I don't like him, I must admit (**b**) *Gram* **a. qch avec qch** to make sth agree with sth (**c**) *(instrument de musique)* to tune; *Fig* **il faudrait a. nos violons** we'd better get our story straight (**d**) *(harmoniser) (couleurs)* to coordinate

2 s'accorder *vpr* (**a**) *(se mettre d'accord)* to agree, to come to an agreement (**avec/sur** with/on); **on s'accorde à penser que...** there is a general belief *or* it is generally believed that... (**b**) *(couleurs)* to go together (**c**) *Gram* to agree (**avec** with) (**d**) *(à soi-même)* **s'a. qch** to allow *or* to give oneself sth

accordeur [akɔrdœr] *nm* (piano) tuner

accoster [akɔste] **1** *vt (personne)* to approach

2 *vi Naut* to dock

accotement [akɔtmɑ̃] *nm (d'une route, d'une voie ferrée)* shoulder; **accotements non stabilisés** *(sur panneau)* soft shoulder

accouchement [akuʃmɑ̃] *nm* childbirth, delivery; **avoir un a. difficile** to have a difficult birth; **a. sans douleur** = childbirth made less painful by the use of relaxation techniques

accoucher [akuʃe] **1** *vt* **a. qn** to deliver sb's baby

2 *vi* (**a**) *(avoir un bébé)* to have a baby, to give birth; **elle doit a. dans un mois** her baby's due in a month (**b**) *Fam* **accouche!** come on, spit it out!

3 accoucher de *vt ind* (**a**) *(enfant)* to give birth to (**b**) *Fam (produire)* to come up with, to produce; **il a accouché de deux minables paragraphes** he produced two measly paragraphs

accoucheur [akuʃœr] *nm* **(médecin) a.** obstetrician

accoucheuse [akuʃøz] *nf* midwife

accouder [akude] **s'accouder** *vpr* **s'a. à** *ou* **sur qch** to lean one's elbow(s) on sth

accoudoir [akudwar] *nm* armrest

accouplement [akupləmɑ̃] *nm (d'animaux)* pairing, mating

accoupler [akuple] **s'accoupler** *vpr (animaux)* to mate

accourir [22] [akurir] *vi* to run up, to rush up

accoutrement [akutrəmɑ̃] *nm* rig-out, get-up

accoutrer [akutre] **1** *vt* to get out (**de** in)

2 s'accoutrer *vpr* to get oneself out (**de** in)

accoutumance [akutymɑ̃s] *nf (adaptation)* familiarization (**à** with); *(à l'alcool, à la drogue)* addiction; **créer une a.** to be addictive

accoutumé, -e [akutyme] *adj* usual; **comme à l'accoutumée** as usual

accoutumer [akutyme] **1** *vt* **a. qn à qch** to accustom sb to sth, to get sb used to sth

2 s'accoutumer *vpr* **s'a. à** to get used *or* accustomed to

accréditer [akredite] *vt* (**a**) *(ambassadeur, journaliste)* to accredit (**b**) *(rendre plausible)* to substantiate

accro [akro] *adj Fam (drogué) & Fig* addicted (**à** to), hooked (**à** on)

accroc [akro] *nm* (**a**) *(à un tissu)* tear, catch (**b**) *Fig* hitch, snag; **sans a.** without a hitch

accrochage [akrɔʃaʒ] *nm* (**a**) *(accident)* minor accident (**b**) *(dispute)* row; *Mil* skirmish

accroche [akrɔʃ] *nf* slogan

accroche-cœur *(pl* accroche-cœurs*)* [akrɔʃkœr] *nm* spit curl

accrocher [akrɔʃe] **1** *vt* (**a**) *(suspendre)* to hang up (**à** on); *(wagon)* to hitch on, to couple; *Fig* **une robe qui accroche**

le regard an eye-catching dress; **avoir le cœur bien accroché** to have strong nerves *or* a strong stomach (**b**) *(abîmer) (vêtement)* to catch (**à** on); *(pare-chocs)* to clip

2 *vi (achopper)* to hit a stumbling block; **un titre qui accroche** an eye-catching title; *Fam* **ça n'a pas du tout accroché entre eux** they didn't hit it off at all; *Fam* **je n'accroche pas du tout en maths** I just can't get into math at all

3 s'accrocher *vpr* (**a**) *aussi Fig (s'agripper)* **s'a. à qn/qch** to cling to sb/sth; *Fam* **accroche-toi, tu n'as pas tout entendu!** brace yourself, you haven't heard everything yet! (**b**) *Fam (persévérer)* to stick at it (**c**) *(voitures)* to crash into each other (**d**) *Fam (se disputer)* to have a row (**avec** with) (**e**) *(se fixer)* to fasten

accrocheur, -euse [akrɔʃœr, -øz] *adj* (**a**) *(tenace)* tenacious, stubborn (**b**) *(titre, slogan)* catchy

accroissement [akrwasmɑ̃] *nm* increase (**de** in)

accroître [akrwatr] [4a] **1** *vt* to increase, to enlarge

2 s'accroître *vpr* to increase, to grow

accroupir [akrupir] **s'accroupir** *vpr* to squat (down), to crouch (down); **être accroupi** to be squatting *or* crouching

accu [aky] *nm* battery

accueil [akœj] *nm (façon d'accueillir)* reception, welcome; *(lieu)* reception (desk); **faire bon a. à qn** to welcome sb; **faire mauvais a. à qn** to give sb a cool reception

accueillant, -e [akœjɑ̃, -ɑ̃t] *adj* welcoming

accueillir [5] [akœjir] *vt* (**a**) *(personne, proposition)* to greet; **bien a. qn** to give sb a warm welcome; **nous avons été mal accueillis** we weren't given a very warm welcome; **le film a été mal accueilli par le public** the movie was badly received by the public (**b**) *(loger) (sujet: ami)* to put up; *(sujet: hôtel)* to accommodate

acculer [akyle] *vt* to drive back (**contre** against); *Fig* **a. qn à faire qch** to give sb no choice but to do sth; *Fig* **être acculé à la faillite** to be forced into bankruptcy

accumulateur [akymylatœr] *nm Élec* battery

accumulation [akymylasjɔ̃] *nf* accumulation; *(d'énergie)* storage; **chauffage par a.** storage heating

accumuler [akymyle] **1** *vt* to accumulate, to amass; *(énergie)* to store; **a. les erreurs** to make a series of mistakes

2 s'accumuler *vpr* to accumulate; *(nuages)* to gather, to build up; *Fin (intérêts)* to accrue; **les preuves s'accumulent contre elle** the evidence against her is growing

accusateur, -trice [akyzatœr, -tris] **1** *adj (regard, doigt)* accusing

2 *nm,f* accuser

accusation [akyzasjɔ̃] *nf* accusation; **lancer** *ou* **porter une a. contre qn** to make an accusation against sb; *Jur* **mettre qn en a.** to commit sb for trial

accusé, -e [akyze] **1** *adj (trait)* prominent, pronounced

2 *nm,f (d'un crime)* accused; *(au tribunal)* defendant

3 *nm* **a. de réception** *(pour une lettre)* acknowledgment (of receipt); *Ordinat* acknowledge, acknowledgment

accuser [akyze] **1** *vt* (**a**) *(incriminer)* to accuse; **a. qn de qch/de faire qch** to accuse sb of sth/of doing sth (**b**) *(tendance, baisse)* to show; **a. le coup** to be obviously shaken (**c**) **a. réception de qch** to acknowledge (receipt of) sth

2 s'accuser *vpr* (**a**) *(se déclarer coupable)* to confess (**de** to) (**b**) *(se renforcer)* to become more pronounced *or* marked

acerbe [aserb] *adj* acerbic; **d'un ton a.** sharply

acéré, -e [asere] *adj (lame)* sharp; *Fig (remarque)* cutting

acériculteur [aserikyltœr] *nm Can* maple-syrup and sugar producer

acériculture [aserikyltyr] *nf Can* production of maple syrup and sugar

acétone [asetɔn] *nf* acetone

ACF [aseef] *nm (abrév* **Automobile Club de France**) = French automobile organization

achalandé, -e [aʃalɑ̃de] *adj Fam* **magasin bien/mal a.** well/poorly stocked shop

achaler [aʃale] *vt Can* to annoy, to bother

acharné, -e [aʃarne] *adj (lutte, concurrence)* fierce; *(travail)* relentless; *(joueur)* inveterate

acharnement [aʃarnəmɑ̃] *nm* relentlessness; **avec a.** relentlessly; **se battre avec a.** to fight tooth and nail

acharner [aʃarne] **s'acharner** *vpr* **s'a. après** *ou* **contre** *ou* **sur qn** *(persécuter)* to be always after sb; **s'a. sur qn** *(sujet: meurtrier)* to savage sb; *(sujet: examinateur)* to give sb a hard time; **s'a. sur qch** to work away at sth; **s'a. à faire qch** to try very hard to do sth

achat [aʃa] *nm* **(a)** *(action)* purchase, buying; **faire un a.** to make a purchase, to buy something; **faire l'a. de qch** to buy sth **(b)** *(ce qu'on a acheté)* purchase; **achats** *(provisions, paquets)* shopping; **aller faire ses achats** to go shopping; **achats par Internet** online shopping

acheminement [aʃminmɑ̃] *nm (de troupes)* transportation (**sur** *ou* **vers** to); *(de marchandises)* shipping (**sur** *ou* **vers** to); **a. du courrier** mail handling

acheminer [aʃmine] **1** *vt (troupes)* to transport (**sur** *ou* **vers** to); *(marchandises)* to ship (**sur** *ou* **vers** to); *(courrier)* to handle
2 s'acheminer *vpr* **s'a. vers** *(endroit)* to make one's way toward; *Fig (accord, solution)* to move toward; *(victoire)* to head toward

acheter [aʃte] **1** *vt* **(a)** *(acquérir)* to buy, to purchase; **a. qch à qn** *(faire une transaction)* to buy sth from sb; *(en cadeau)* to buy sb sth; **je vais lui a. un livre** I'm going to buy him/her a book; **j'ai acheté ce livre huit euros** I bought this book for eight euros **(b)** *Fam (corrompre)* to buy off
2 s'acheter *vpr* **(a)** *(pour soi-même)* **je vais m'a. une glace** I'm going to buy (myself) an ice cream **(b)** *(être acheté)* **ça s'achète en pharmacie** you can buy it/them in any pharmacy; **l'amour, ça ne s'achète pas** love can't be bought

acheteur, -euse [aʃtœr, -øz] *nm,f* buyer, purchaser; **je suis a.!** I'm interested!

achevé, -e [aʃve] *adj (artiste, style)* accomplished; *(travail)* perfect; **c'est d'un ridicule a.!** it's utterly ridiculous!

achèvement [aʃɛvmɑ̃] *nm* completion

achever [46] [aʃve] **1** *vt* **(a)** *(finir) (discours)* to end, to conclude; *(travail)* to complete **(b)** *(tuer) (personne, proie)* to finish off; *(animal malade ou blessé)* to put out of its misery; *Fam* **ça m'a achevé!** that really finished me (off)!
2 s'achever *vpr (finir)* to end

achigan [aʃigɑ̃] *nm Can* (black) bass

achoppement [aʃɔpmɑ̃] *nm voir* **pierre**

acide [asid] **1** *adj* acid(ic); *(au goût)* sour; *Fig (propos)* acid, caustic
2 *nm* acid

acidité [asidite] *nf* acidity; *(au goût)* sourness; *Fig (de propos)* acidity

acidulé, -e [asidyle] *adj* slightly acid; **bonbons acidulés** acid drops

acier [asje] *nm* steel; **a. inoxydable** stainless steel

aciérie [asjeri] *nf* steelworks *(singulier)*

acné [akne] *nf* acne; **a. juvénile** acne

acolyte [akɔlit] *nm Péj* accomplice

acompte [akɔ̃t] *nm* deposit, down payment; **recevoir un a.** to receive something on account; **verser un a.** to make a down payment

acoquiner [akɔkine] **s'acoquiner** *vpr Péj* **s'a. avec qn** to team up with sb; *Fig* to cosy up to sb

Açores [asɔr] *nfpl* **les A.** the Azores

à-côté *(pl* **à-côtés)** [akote] *nm* **(a)** *(élément secondaire)* side issue **(b)** *(financier)* extra

à-coup *(pl* **à-coups)** [aku] *nm* jolt; **travailler par à-coups** to work in fits and starts; **le moteur a des à-coups** the engine sputters

acoustique [akustik] **1** *adj* acoustic
2 *nf (discipline)* acoustics *(singulier)*; *(qualité)* acoustics *(pluriel)*

acquéreur [akerœr] *nm* purchaser, buyer; **notre voiture n'a pas trouvé a.** we couldn't find a buyer for our car

acquérir [7] [akerir] *vt* **(a)** *(obtenir, prendre)* to acquire; **nous avons acquis la certitude de son innocence** we have established beyond doubt that he/she is innocent; **a. de la valeur** to increase in value **(b)** *(acheter)* to purchase, to buy

acquière, acquiers, *etc. voir* **acquérir**

acquiescer [16] [akjese] *vi* to acquiesce (**à** to); **a. d'un signe de tête** to nod in agreement

acquis, -e [aki, -iz] **1** *pp voir* **acquérir**
2 *adj (savoir, caractères)* acquired; **tenir qch pour a.** to take sth for granted; **son aide nous est acquise** we can take it for granted that he will help us; **cela est a.** that's been established
3 *nm (connaissances)* knowledge; **il ne fonctionne que sur ses acquis** he gets by on what he knows already; **les a. sociaux** social benefits

acquisition [akizisjɔ̃] *nf* **(a)** *(action)* acquisition; **faire l'a. de qch** *(acheter)* to purchase sth **(b)** *(bien acheté)* purchase

acquit [aki] *nm Com* receipt; **pour a.** received (with thanks), paid; **par a. de conscience** to ease one's conscience

acquittement [akitmɑ̃] *nm* **(a)** *Jur* acquittal **(b)** *(d'une dette)* payment

acquitter [akite] **1** *vt* **(a)** *(accusé)* to acquit **(b)** *(dette, facture)* to pay
2 s'acquitter *vpr* **s'a. d'une obligation/d'un devoir** to fulfill an obligation/a duty; **s'a. envers qn** to repay sb

acre [akr] *nm ou nf Can* acre

âcre [ɑkr] *adj (goût)* bitter; *(odeur)* acrid

acrobate [akrɔbat] *nmf* acrobat

acrobatie [akrɔbasi] *nf (art)* acrobatics *(singulier)*; **faire des acrobaties** to perform acrobatics; **a. aérienne** aerobatics *(singulier)*

acrobatique [akrɔbatik] *adj* acrobatic

acronyme [akrɔnim] *nm* acronym

Acropole [akrɔpɔl] *nf* **l'A.** the Acropolis

acrylique [akrilik] *adj & nm* acrylic

acte [akt] *nm* **(a)** *(action)* act; **faire a. d'autorité** to exercise one's authority; **faire a. de candidature à un emploi** to apply for a job; **faire a. de présence** to put in an appearance; **passer aux actes** to take action; **c'était peut-être un a. manqué** maybe subconsciously I/he/*etc.* did it deliberately; **a. de terrorisme** terrorist act
(b) *Jur* deed, title; **dont a.** duly noted *or* acknowledged; **prendre a. de qch** to take note of sth; *Sout* **nous prenons a. de votre candidature** we acknowledge your application; **a. d'accusation** bill of indictment, charges; **a. de propriété** title deed; **a. unique européen** Single European Act; **a. de vente** bill of sale
(c) *(certificat)* record; **a. de décès** death certificate; **a. d'état civil** = certificate of birth, marriage or death; **a. de mariage** marriage certificate; **a. de naissance** birth certificate
(d) **actes** *(d'un procès, d'un colloque)* proceedings; *(d'un organisme scientifique)* transactions
(e) *Théât* act

acter [akte] *vt Belg (noter)* to take a note of, to note; *Jur* to record

acteur [aktœr] *nm* **(a)** *(artiste)* actor; **a. de cinéma/de théâtre** movie/stage actor **(b)** *(d'un événement)* **les différents acteurs de la négociation** the different participants in *or* parties involved in the negotiations; **a. économique** economic player; **les acteurs sociaux** = employers, workers and trade unions

actif, -ive [aktif, -iv] **1** *adj* **(a)** *(défenseur, participation, sub-*

stance) active; **femme active** working woman (**b**) *(énergique)* *(personne)* active (**c**) *Gram* active

2 *nm* (**a**) *Com* assets; *Fig* **avoir qch à son a.** to have sth to one's name; **il faut mettre sa patience à son a.** you have to give him/her credit for patience (**b**) *Gram* **verbe à l'a.** verb in the active voice

action [aksjɔ̃] *nf* (**a**) *(acte)* action, act; **bonne/mauvaise a.** good/bad deed (**b**) *(influence, effet) (d'une substance)* action, effect (**sur** on) (**c**) *(activité)* **entrer en a.** *(loi)* to come into force; **mettre qch en a.** to put sth into operation; **passer à l'a.** to take action, to act; **homme d'a.** man of action (**d**) *(histoire)* action; *TV & Cin* **a.!** action! (**e**) *Fin* stock, share (**f**) *Jur* action; **intenter une a. judiciaire** *ou* **en justice contre** to take legal action against (**g**) *Mil* action (**h**) *Suisse (vente promotionnelle)* sale, special offer

actionnaire [aksjɔnɛr] *nmf Fin* stockholder, shareholder

actionner [aksjɔne] *vt (mettre en marche)* to start up, to turn on; *(faire fonctionner)* to operate, to drive

activement [aktivmɑ̃] *adv* actively

activer [aktive] **1** *vt* (**a**) *(accélérer)* to speed up; *(feu)* to stoke (**b**) *Ordinat* to activate; **a. une option** to select an option

2 *vi Fam* to get a move on

3 s'activer *vpr* to be busy

activiste [aktivist] *adj & nmf* activist

activité [aktivite] *nf* activity; **en a.** *(volcan)* active; *(usine)* in production; *(personne)* working

actrice [aktris] *nf* actress

actualisation [aktɥalizasjɔ̃] *nf (d'un texte, d'une méthode de travail)* updating

actualiser [aktɥalize] *vt (texte, méthode de travail)* to update

actualité [aktɥalite] *nf* **l'a.** the news, current affairs; **l'a. politique française** the current French political scene; **cette question est toujours d'a.** this is still a topical question; **les actualités** *(à la télé, à la radio)* the news; **les actualités télévisées** the television news

actuel, -elle [aktɥɛl] *adj* (**a**) *(présent)* present, current; **dans la situation actuelle** as things are *or* stand at the moment (**b**) *(d'actualité)* topical

actuellement [aktɥɛlmɑ̃] *adv* at present, at the present time

acuité [akɥite] *nf (de la douleur)* acuteness; *(d'un argument)* pointedness; *(d'un son)* shrillness; **a. visuelle/auditive** keenness of vision/hearing

acuponcteur, -trice [akypɔ̃ktœr, -tris] *nm,f* acupuncturist

acuponcture [akypɔ̃ktyr] *nf* acupuncture

acupressing [akypresiŋ] *nm* acupressure

acupuncteur, -trice = acuponcteur, -trice

acupuncture = acuponcture

adage [adaʒ] *nm* adage, (common) saying; **selon l'a.** as the saying goes

adaptateur, -trice [adaptatœr, -tris] **1** *nm (dispositif)* adapter

2 *nm,f (d'une œuvre)* adapter

adaptation [adaptasjɔ̃] *nf* (**a**) *(à une situation)* adaptation (**à** to); **faire un effort d'a.** to try to adapt; **faculté d'a.** adaptability (**b**) *(d'une œuvre)* adaptation; **a. théâtrale** stage adaptation

adapter [adapte] **1** *vt* (**a**) *(ajuster)* to adapt (**à** to); **est-ce vraiment adapté à la situation?** is it really suitable for the situation? (**b**) *(œuvre)* to adapt

2 s'adapter *vpr* (**a**) *(s'acclimater)* to adapt (**à** to); **savoir s'a.** to be very adaptable *or* flexible (**b**) *(être compatible)* **la prise s'adapte à toutes les télévisions** the plug fits all types of television

Addis-Abeba [adisabeba] *n* Addis Ababa

additif [aditif] *nm* (**a**) *(ajout)* addition (**b**) *(substance)* additive; **sans additifs** additive-free

addition [adisjɔ̃] *nf* (**a**) *(fait d'ajouter)* addition, adding (**à** to);

(pour faire un total) adding up; **faire une a.** to do a sum (**b**) *(extension)* addition, extension (**c**) *(au restaurant)* check

additionnel, -elle [adisjɔnɛl] *adj* additional, extra; *Ordinat* add-on

additionner [adisjɔne] **1** *vt* to add (up); **lait additionné d'eau** watered-down milk; **café additionné d'eau-de-vie** coffee laced with brandy

2 s'additionner *vpr* to add up; **aux longues heures de travail s'additionnent celles passées dans le métro** along with the long working hours, there are those spent in the subway

adduction [adyksjɔ̃] *nf Tech* admission, intake; *Constr* **a. d'eau** canalization

adepte [adɛpt] *nmf (d'une doctrine, d'une personnalité)* follower; *(d'une activité)* enthusiast; **faire des adeptes** to attract a following

adéquat, -e [adekwa, -at] *adj (personne, lieu, expression, méthode)* appropriate, suitable; *(montant, quantité)* adequate

adéquation [adekwasjɔ̃] *nf* appropriateness, suitability

adhérence [aderɑ̃s] *nf* adhesion, adherence; *(de pneus)* grip

adhérent, -e [aderɑ̃, -ɑ̃t] **1** *adj (substance, propriétés)* adhesive

2 *nm,f* member

adhérer [34] [adere] *vi* (**a**) *(coller)* to adhere, to stick (**à** to); **a. à la route** *(pneus)* to grip the road (**b**) **a. à** *(opinion, doctrine)* to subscribe to (**c**) *(s'inscrire)* **a. à un parti** to join a party

adhésif, -ive [adezif, -iv] **1** *adj* adhesive, sticky

2 *nm* (**a**) adhesive (**b**) Scotch® tape

adhésion [adezjɔ̃] *nf* (**a**) *(accord)* support (**à** for) (**b**) *(inscription)* joining (**à** of)

ad hoc [adɔk] *adj & adv* ad hoc

adieu, -x [adjø] **1** *exclam* goodbye!, farewell!; **dire a. à qn** to say goodbye to sb; *Fam Fig* **dire a. à qch** to kiss *or* to say goodbye to sth

2 *nm* farewell; **faire ses adieux** to say one's goodbyes; **faire ses adieux à qn** to say goodbye to sb

adipeux, -euse [adipø, -øz] *adj (tissu)* adipose; *(visage)* fat

adjacent, -e [adʒasɑ̃, ɑ̃t] *adj* adjacent (**à** to)

adjectif [adʒɛktif] *nm* adjective

adjoint, -e [adʒwɛ̃, -ɛ̃t] **1** *adj* assistant, deputy

2 *nm,f* assistant; **a. au maire** deputy mayor

adjonction [adʒɔ̃ksjɔ̃] *nf* addition; **produit sans a. de sucre** product with no added sugar

adjudant [adʒydɑ̃] *nm* warrant officer (junior grade); **a.-chef** chief warrant officer

adjudication [adʒydikasjɔ̃] *nf* sale by auction

adjuger [45] [adʒyʒe] **1** *vt* **a. qch à qn** *(prix, contrat)* to award sth to sb; *(aux enchères)* to knock sth down to sb; **une fois, deux fois, trois fois, adjugé, vendu!** going, going, gone!

2 s'adjuger *vpr* **s'a. qch** to appropriate sth

ADM [adeɛm] *nfpl (abrév* **armes de destruction massive)** WMD

admettre [47] [admɛtr] *vt* (**a**) *(accueillir)* **a. qn** to admit sb, to let sb in; **les chiens ne sont pas admis** *(sur la porte d'un magasin)* no dogs allowed; **être admis à l'université** to get into college; **être admis à un concours** to pass an examination (**b**) *(accepter)* to allow; **je n'admets pas qu'on me mente** I won't tolerate being lied to; **cette règle n'admet aucune exception** there can be no exceptions to this rule (**c**) *(reconnaître)* to admit, to accept; **admettons que ce soit possible** assuming it's possible; **admettons que j'ai tort** *(pour clore une discussion)* I stand corrected

administrateur, -trice [administratœr, -tris] *nm,f* (**a**) *(d'une société, d'une banque)* director (**b**) *(de fondation)* trustee

administratif, -ive [administratif, -iv] *adj* administrative

administration [administrasjɔ̃] *nf* (**a**) *(d'affaires)* administration, management; *(d'un pays)* governing; **a. électronique** e-government (**b**) *(ensemble des directeurs)* board of directors; *(d'une institution)* governing body (**c**) **l'A.** *(service public)* ≃ the Civil Service; *(fonctionnaires)* civil servants

administré, -e [administre] *nm,f* citizen

administrer [administre] *vt* (**a**) *(propriété)* to administer, to manage; *(pays)* to govern (**b**) *(justice)* to dispense; *Rel (sacrements)* to administer; *(remède)* to administer; **je vais lui a. une bonne correction** I'm going to give him/her a good hiding

admirable [admirabl] *adj* admirable; *(très compétent)* wonderful; **elle a été a. de courage** she showed admirable courage

admirablement [admirabləmã] *adv* admirably; *(très bien)* wonderfully; **a. bien** wonderfully

admirateur, -trice [admiratœr, -tris] *nm,f* admirer

admiratif, -ive [admiratif, -iv] *adj* admiring

admiration [admirasjɔ̃] *nf* admiration; **avoir de l'a. pour qn** to admire sb; **être en a. devant qch** to be filled with admiration for sth; **tomber en a. devant qch** to be stopped in one's tracks by the beauty of sth; **faire l'a. de tous** to be universally admired

admirer [admire] *vt* to admire

admis, -e [admi, -iz] **1** *adj* (**a**) *(autorisé à entrer)* admitted, allowed (in) (**b**) *(accepté)* allowed, accepted
    2 *nm,f (à un examen)* successful candidate

admissible [admisibl] *adj (excuse, preuve, conduite)* admissible, allowable; (**candidats**) **admissibles** candidates who have qualified for the oral examination

admission [admisjɔ̃] *nf* (**a**) *(entrée)* admission (**à/dans** to) (**b**) *Tech* intake; *Aut* induction

ADN [adeɛn] *nm (abrév* **acide désoxyribonucléique**) DNA

ado [ado] *nmf Fam* teen, teenager

adolescence [adɔlesãs] *nf* adolescence; **pendant mon a.** when I was a teenager

adolescent, -e [adɔlesã, -ãt] **1** *nm,f* adolescent, teenager
    2 *adj* adolescent, teenage

adon [adɔ̃] *nm Can Fam* coincidence

adonner [adɔne] **s'adonner** *vpr* **s'a. à qch** to devote oneself to sth; **s'a. à la boisson** to be an alcoholic

adopter [adɔpte] *vt* (**a**) *(enfant)* to adopt (**b**) *(accepter)* to accept (**c**) *(choisir)* to adopt (**d**) *(projet de loi, résolution)* to adopt, to pass

adoptif, -ive [adɔptif, -iv] *adj (enfant)* adopted; *(parent)* adoptive

adoption [adɔpsjɔ̃] *nf* (**a**) *(d'un enfant)* adoption (**b**) *(d'une idée, d'une mode)* adoption; **mon pays d'a.** my adopted country (**c**) *(d'un projet de loi)* adoption, passing

adorable [adɔrabl] *adj* adorable, charming

adoration [adɔrasjɔ̃] *nf aussi Fig* adoration; **être en a. devant qn** to worship sb

adorer [adɔre] **1** *vt aussi Fig* to love, to adore; **j'adore monter à cheval** I love horseback riding
    2 **s'adorer** *vpr* to adore each other

adosser [adose] **1** *vt* **a. qch à** *ou* **contre qch** to lean sth (with its back) against sth
    2 **s'adosser** *vpr* **s'a. à** *ou* **contre qch** to lean (back) against sth; **le village est adossé à la colline** the village stands at the foot of the hill

adoucir [adusir] **1** *vt* (**a**) *(voix, eau, linge, peau)* to soften; *(contraste, couleur)* to tone down; **sa nouvelle coiffure adoucit son visage** her new haircut softens her face (**b**) *(douleur, chagrin)* to ease
    2 **s'adoucir** *vpr* (**a**) *(voix, ton)* to soften (**b**) *(personne, caractère)* to mellow

adoucissant, -e [adusisã, ãt] **1** *adj* softening
    2 *nm (pour le linge)* fabric softener

adoucisseur [adusisœr] *nm* (water) softener

adr. *(abrév* **adresse**) address

adrénaline [adrenalin] *nf* adrenalin(e)

adresse [adrɛs] *nf* (**a**) *(coordonnées)* address; **changer d'a.** to change one's address; *Fig* **tu te trompes d'a.** you've come to the wrong person; **il connaît de bonnes adresses** *(de restaurants, de magasins)* he knows all the good places to go to; **je l'ai dit à l'a. de ceux qui…** I said it for the benefit of those who… (**b**) *(habileté)* skill; *(savoir-faire)* diplomacy; **avec a.** skillfully (**c**) *Ordinat* address; **a. électronique,** *Can* **a. de courriel** e-mail address; **a. Internet** Internet address; **a. URL** URL; **a. virtuelle** virtual address

adresser [adrese] **1** *vt* (**a**) *(lettre)* to address; **a. qch à qn** to send sth to sb (**b**) *(personne)* **on m'a adressé à vous** I have been referred to you (**c**) **a. qch à qn** *(compliments, remerciements)* to present sth to sb; **cette remarque était adressée à Martin** that remark was aimed at *or* meant for Martin; **a. un sourire à qn** to smile at sb; **a. la parole à qn** to speak to sb
    2 **s'adresser** *vpr* **s'a. à qn** *(sujet: personne)* to speak to sb; *(pour un renseignement)* to ask sb; *(sujet: remarque, recommandation)* to apply to sb; **s'a. ici** *(sur écriteau)* inquire within

Adriatique [adrijatik] *nf* **l'A.** the Adriatic

adroit, -e [adrwa, -at] *adj* (**a**) *(habile)* skillful; **être a. de ses mains** to be good with one's hands (**b**) *(réponse, diplomate)* shrewd, clever

adroitement [adrwatmã] *adv* (**a**) *(avec des gestes habiles)* skillfully (**b**) *(astucieusement)* cleverly

ADSL [adeɛsɛl] *nm Ordinat & Tél (abrév* **Asymmetric Digital Subscriber Line**) ADSL; **est-ce que tu as l'A. chez toi?** do you have broadband at home?

aduler [adyle] *vt* to worship

adulte [adylt] **1** *adj (personne)* adult, grown-up; *(plante, animal)* fully-grown
    2 *nmf* adult, grown-up

adultère [adyltɛr] *nm* adultery

advenir [70] [advənir] *v impersonnel (aux être)* to happen; **or, il advint que…** it so happened that…; **quoi qu'il advienne** no matter what happens; **advienne que pourra** come what may; **qu'est-il advenu de lui?** whatever became of him?

adverbe [advɛrb] *nm* adverb

adverbial, -e, -aux, -ales [advɛrbjal, -o] *adj* adverbial

adversaire [advɛrsɛr] *nmf* opponent; *(dans un conflit, dans une guerre)* enemy

adverse [advɛrs] *adj (équipe)* opposing; *Jur* **la partie a.** the other side

AELE [aɛlə] *nf (abrév* **Association européenne de libre-échange**) **l'A.** EFTA

aérateur [aeratœr] *nm* ventilator

aération [aerasjɔ̃] *nf (d'une pièce)* ventilation

aéré, -e [aere] *adj* (**a**) *(chambre)* airy, well-ventilated (**b**) *(présentation, texte)* well-spaced

aérer [34] [aere] **1** *vt* (**a**) *(pièce, linge)* to air (**b**) *(texte, exposé)* to lighten
    2 **s'aérer** *vpr* to get some fresh air

aérien, -enne [aerjɛ̃, -ɛn] *adj* (**a**) *(défense, attaque, transport)* air (**b**) *(texture)* (light and) airy; *(grâce, allure)* ethereal (**c**) *(câble)* overhead; *(voie ferrée)* elevated

aérobic [aerɔbik] *nm* aerobics *(singulier)*

aérodrome [aerɔdrom] *nm* airfield

aérodynamique [aerɔdinamik] *adj (forme, voiture)* streamlined

aérogare [aerɔgar] *nf* (air) terminal

aéroglisseur [aerɔglisœr] *nm* hovercraft

aérogramme [aerɔgram] *nm* aerogram(me), airmail letter

aéromodélisme [aerɔmɔdelism] *nm* making model aircraft

aéronautique [aerɔnotik] **1** *adj* aeronautic(al)
    2 *nf* aeronautics *(singulier)*

aéronaval, -e, -als, -ales [aerɔnaval] **1** *adj (forces)* air and sea
    2 *nf* **l'Aéronavale** ≃ the Naval Air Service

aéronef [aerɔnɛf] *nm* aircraft

aérophagie [aerɔfaʒi] *nf* flatulence; **avoir** *ou* **faire de l'a.** to suffer from flatulence

aéroport [aerɔpɔr] *nm* airport

aéroporté, -e [aerɔpɔrte] *adj* airborne

aérosol [aerɔsɔl] *nm* aerosol; **vendu en a.** sold in spray form

aérospatial, -e, -aux, -ales [aerɔspasjal, -o] **1** *adj* aerospace

2 *nm (science)* aerospace science; *(industrie)* aerospace industry

aérostat [aerɔsta] *nm (montgolfière)* hot-air balloon; *(dirigeable)* airship; *(non rigide)* blimp

affabilité [afabilite] *nf* affability

affable [afabl] *adj* affable

affabulation [afabylasjɔ̃] *nf* fabrication

affabuler [afabyle] *vi* to make things up

affaiblir [afeblir] **1** *vt* **(a)** *(sujet: maladie)* to weaken **(b)** *(réduire)* to lessen, to reduce

2 s'affaiblir *vpr (personne)* to get weaker; *(vue, ouïe)* to get worse, to deteriorate; *(sentiment)* to wane; *(son)* to grow fainter; **le sens du mot s'est affaibli** the word has lost much of its meaning

affaiblissement [afeblismɑ̃] *nm (d'une personne, d'un gouvernement, de l'économie)* weakening; *(d'un sentiment)* waning; *(d'une lumière, d'un son)* fading

affaire [afɛr] *nf* **(a)** *(occupation)* business, concern; **ce n'est pas votre a.** it's none of your business; **j'en fais mon a.** I'll handle it; **c'est une a. de goût** it's a matter *or* question of taste; **c'est l'a. d'une minute** it won't take a minute; **ça, c'est une autre a.** that's another matter; **avoir a. à qn** *(s'adresser à quelqu'un)* to be dealt with by sb; **s'il continue à mentir, il aura a. à moi!** if he carries on lying, he'll have me to deal with!

(b) *(usage)* **cela fera parfaitement l'a.** that will do nicely; *Fam* **faire son a. à qn** to do sb in

(c) *(histoire, problème)* affair, business; **une a. de pots-de-vin** a bribery scandal; **a. de cœur** love affair; **ça n'a pas été une mince a.** it wasn't easy; **c'est toute une a.** it's quite a business; **la belle a.!** big deal!; **ça ne change rien à l'a.** that doesn't change anything; **tirer qn d'a.** to get sb out of trouble; **ce n'est pas une a. d'État!** it's no big deal!

(d) *(transaction)* deal; *(achat à bon marché)* bargain; **il a fait une a. en achetant cette voiture** he got a bargain when he bought that car; **faire a. avec qn** to make a deal with sb; **une a. en or** the bargain of the century

(e) *(entreprise)* firm, business

(f) affaires *(effets personnels)* things, belongings

(g) les affaires *(activités commerciales)* business *(singulier)*; **comment vont les affaires?** how's business?; **il est dur en affaires** he's a hard-headed businessman; **les affaires sont les affaires** business is business

(h) les Affaires étrangères ≃ the State Department

affairé, -e [afere] *adj* busy

affairer [afere] **s'affairer** *vpr* to busy oneself; **s'a. autour de qn** to fuss around sb

affairiste [aferist] *nmf* wheeler-dealer

affaissement [afɛsmɑ̃] *nm (de terrain)* subsidence; *(du plancher, d'une poutre)* sagging

affaisser [afese] **s'affaisser** *vpr* **(a)** *(s'enfoncer) (terrain)* to subside; *(poutre, fauteuil)* to sag **(b)** *(tomber, s'écrouler)* to collapse

affalé, -e [afale] *adj* **être a. dans un fauteuil** to be slumped in an armchair

affaler [afale] **s'affaler** *vpr* to collapse

affamé, -e [afame] *adj* starving

affectation [afɛktasjɔ̃] *nf* **(a)** *Péj (pose)* affectation, affectedness; *(simulacre)* pretense, affectation; **avec a.** affectedly; **sans a.** unaffectedly **(b)** *(de fonds, de crédits, de locaux)* assignment, allocation *(à* to*)* **(c)** *(à un poste)* appointment *(à* to*)*; *(d'un soldat)* posting *(à* to*)* **(d)** *Ordinat (de touche)* assignment; **a. de mémoire** memory allocation

affecté, -e [afɛkte] *adj Péj (personne, manière)* affected

affecter [afɛkte] *vt* **(a)** *(fonds, crédits, locaux)* to assign *(à* to*)*, to allocate *(à* to*)* **(b)** *(employé)* to appoint *(à* to*)*; *(soldat)* to post *(à* to*)* **(c)** *(feindre)* to affect; **a. de faire qch** to pretend to do sth **(d)** *(émouvoir)* to affect, to move **(e)** *(frapper) (carrière, santé)* to affect, to have an effect on; **la grève a affecté plusieurs usines** the strike has affected *or* hit several factories

affectif, -ive [afɛktif, -iv] *adj* emotional, *Spéc* affective

affection [afɛksjɔ̃] *nf* **(a)** *(attachement)* affection (**pour** for); **prendre qn en a.** to become fond of sb; **avoir de l'a. pour qn** to be fond of sb **(b)** *Litt (maladie)* ailment

affectionner [afɛksjɔne] *vt* to be fond of; **votre cousin affectionné** *(dans une lettre)* your affectionate cousin

affectivité [afɛktivite] *nf* feelings

affectueusement [afɛktɥøzmɑ̃] *adv* affectionately; *(dans une lettre)* love (from)

affectueux, -euse [afɛktɥø, -øz] *adj* affectionate

afférent, -e [aferɑ̃, -ɑ̃t] *adj* **a. à** *(concernant)* relating to

affermir [afɛrmir] **1** *vt* **(a)** *(muscles, chairs)* to tone (up) **(b)** *(pouvoir, position, autorité)* to strengthen, to consolidate

2 s'affermir *vpr (chairs, muscles)* to tone up; *(pouvoir, position, autorité)* to be strengthened

affichage [afiʃaʒ] *nm* **(a)** *(pose d'affiches)* billposting; **a. interdit** *(sur panneau)* post no bills **(b)** *Ordinat* display; **montre à a. numérique** digital watch; **a. à cristaux liquides** liquid crystal display

affiche [afiʃ] *nf* notice; *(de publicité)* poster; **être à l'a.** *(spectacle)* to be on; **être en tête d'a.** to top the bill; **a. électorale** election poster

afficher [afiʃe] **1** *vt* **(a)** *(annonce, poster)* to put up; *(prix, horaires, résultats)* to display; **défense d'a.** *(sur panneau)* post no bills; **a. complet** *(spectacle)* to be sold out **(b)** *(mépris, indifférence)* to show, to display; *(savoir)* to flaunt; *(déficit, excédent)* to show **(c)** *Ordinat (message)* to display

2 s'afficher *vpr* **(a)** *(personne)* to flaunt oneself **(b)** *(sur un écran)* to be displayed

affichette [afiʃɛt] *nf* small notice; *(publicitaire)* poster

afficheur [afiʃœr] *nm (personne)* billboard sticker; *(société)* publicity company

affilée [afile] **d'affilée** *adv* in a row; **cinq heures d'a.** five hours in a row

affiler [afile] *vt* to sharpen

affiliation [afiljasjɔ̃] *nf* joining (**à** of)

affilier [66] [afilije] **s'affilier** *vpr* to join; **s'a. à un parti** to join a party

affiner [afine] **1** *vt* **(a)** *(métal)* to refine; *(fromage)* to mature **(b)** *(esprit)* to sharpen; *(goût)* to refine

2 s'affiner *vpr (goût)* to become more refined; *(visage)* to get thinner; *(traits)* to become better defined; *(esprit)* to become sharper

affinité [afinite] *nf* affinity (**entre** between)

affirmatif, -ive [afifirmatif, -iv] **1** *adj* **(a)** *(réponse)* affirmative, positive; **faire un signe a. de la tête** to nod in agreement **(b)** *(personne)* positive

2 *nf* **dans l'affirmative** if so, if the answer is yes; **répondre par l'affirmative** to answer yes

3 *exclam* affirmative!

affirmation [afirmasjɔ̃] *nf* assertion

affirmer [afirme] **1** *vt* **(a)** *(soutenir)* to maintain; **il affirme vous connaître** he maintains that he knows you **(b)** *(manifester)* to assert; **a. sa volonté de faire qch** to declare one's willingness to do sth

2 s'affirmer *vpr (personnalité)* to assert itself; *(tendance, talent)* to be confirmed

affleurer [aflœre] *vi (récif)* to be near the surface; *Géol (filon)* to outcrop; *Fig (mépris, racisme)* to come to the surface

affliction [afliksjɔ̃] *nf* affliction

affligé, -e [afliʒe] *adj* (a) **être a. de** *(atteint)* to be afflicted with (b) *(peiné)* distressed

affligeant, -e [afliʒɑ̃, -ɑ̃t] *adj (nouvelle, vision)* distressing; *(bêtise, ignorance, résultats)* appalling

affliger [45] [afliʒe] **1** *vt* (a) *(atteindre)* to afflict; **région affligée par le choléra** area afflicted with cholera; **la nature l'a affligé d'un grand nez** nature has cursed him with a big nose (b) *(peiner) (sujet: nouvelle, événement)* to distress

2 s'affliger *vpr* to be distressed (**de** about)

affluence [aflyɑ̃s] *nf (de personnes)* crowd; *(de marchandises)* abundance

affluent [aflyɑ̃] *nm* tributary

affluer [aflye] *vi (liquide)* to flow (**vers/dans** to/into); *(sang)* to rush (**à** to); *(foule)* to flock (**vers** to)

afflux [afly] *nm (de sang)* rush; *(de visiteurs)* flood; *(de capitaux)* influx

affolant, -e [afɔlɑ̃, -ɑ̃t] *adj (spectacle, nouvelle)* distressing; *Fam* **c'est a.!** it's incredible!

affolé, -e [afɔle] *adj (personne)* panic-stricken

affolement [afɔlmɑ̃] *nm* panic; **pas d'a.!** don't panic!

affoler [afɔle] **1** *vt* to throw into a panic

2 s'affoler *vpr* (a) *(paniquer)* to panic (b) *(aiguille de boussole)* to spin (c) *(machine)* to race

affranchir [afrɑ̃ʃir] **1** *vt* (a) *(lettre, colis)* to put a stamp/stamps on; *(avec une machine)* to frank (b) *(esclave)* to free

2 s'affranchir *vpr* (a) *(peuple, personne)* to free oneself (**de** from) (b) *Belg (prendre de l'assurance)* to become (more) self-confident

affranchissement [afrɑ̃ʃismɑ̃] *nm* (a) *(montant payé) (de lettre, paquet)* postage (b) *(d'un esclave)* freeing

affres [afr] *nfpl Litt (du doute, de la jalousie, de la faim)* pangs; **les a. de la mort** death throes

affréter [34] [afrete] *vt* to charter

affreusement [afrøzmɑ̃] *adv* horribly; **a. laid** hideously ugly; **il parle a. mal l'anglais** his English is awful

affreux, -euse [afrø, -øz] *adj* (a) *(laid)* hideous (b) *(atroce) (nouvelle, pauvreté, crime)* dreadful (c) *Fam (épouvantable) (temps, migraine)* awful, terrible; **qu'est-ce que ça a augmenté, c'est a.!** it's terrible how the price has gone up!; **un a. jojo** a little horror

affriolant, -e [afrijɔlɑ̃, -ɑ̃t] *adj* alluring

affront [afrɔ̃] *nm* affront, insult; **faire un a. à qn** to affront or to insult sb

affrontement [afrɔ̃tmɑ̃] *nm* clash, confrontation

affronter [afrɔ̃te] **1** *vt (adversaire, danger, mort)* to face, to confront; **a. la colère de qn** to brave the wrath of sb

2 s'affronter *vpr (ennemis)* to clash; *(équipes, joueurs)* to clash; **deux thèses s'affrontent** there are two conflicting theories

affubler [afyble] **1** *vt* **a. qn de qch** to attire sb in sth

2 s'affubler *vpr* **s'a. de qch** to get oneself up in sth

affût [afy] *nm (pour les chasseurs)* blind; **être à l'a.** *(à la chasse)* to lie in wait; *Fig* **être à l'a. de qch** to be on the lookout for sth

affûter [afyte] *vt* to sharpen

afghan, -e [afgɑ̃, -an] **1** *adj* Afghan

2 *nm,f* **A., Afghane** Afghan

3 *nm (langue)* Afghan

Afghanistan [afganistɑ̃] *nm* **l'A.** Afghanistan

afin [afɛ̃] *adv* **a. de faire qch** (in order) to do sth, so as to do sth; **a. que** + *subjunctive* so that; **a. que les autres puissent le voir** so that the others may see it

AFNOR [afnɔr] *nf (abrév* **Association française de normalisation**) = French industrial standards authority, ≃ ANSI

a fortiori [afɔrsjɔri] *adv* all the more so

AFP [aɛfpe] *nf (abrév* **Agence France-Presse**) = French international news agency

africain, -e [afrikɛ̃, -ɛn] **1** *adj* African

2 *nm,f* **A., Africaine** African

Afrique [afrik] *nf* **l'A.** Africa; **l'A. noire** Black Africa; **l'A. du Nord** North Africa; **l'A. du Sud** South Africa

afro-américain, -e *(mpl* **afro-américains,** *fpl* **afro-américaines)** [afroamerikɛ̃, -ɛn] **1** *adj* Afro-American, African American

2 *nm,f* **A., Afro-Américaine** Afro-American, African American

after [aftœr] *nm* after-party

after-shave [aftœrʃɛv] **1** *nm inv* aftershave

2 *adj* **lotion a.** aftershave (lotion)

A.G. [aʒe] *nf (abrév* **assemblée générale**) Annual Meeting of Shareholders

agaçant, -e [agasɑ̃, -ɑ̃t] *adj* annoying, irritating

agacer [16] [agase] *vt* (a) *(énerver)* to annoy, to irritate; **il m'agace avec ses questions** he's getting on my nerves with all his questions (b) *(dents, nerfs)* to set on edge

agapes [agap] *nfpl Litt ou Hum* feast; **faire des a.** to have a feast

agate [agat] *nf (pierre)* agate; *(bille)* marble

âge [aʒ] *nm* (a) *(d'une personne)* age; **quel â. avez-vous?** how old are you?; **à ton â., je travaillais** when I was your age, I was working; **à l'â. de six ans** at the age of six; **on ne lui donne pas son â.** he/she doesn't look his/her age; **faire son â.** to look one's age; **un homme d'un grand â.** a very old man; **entre deux âges** middle-aged; **être en â. de faire qch, être d'â. à faire qch** to be old enough to do sth; **ce n'est plus de mon â.** I'm too old for that type of thing; **un whisky de quinze ans d'â.** a fifteen-year-old whiskey; **l'â. adulte** adulthood; **l'â. bête** *ou* **ingrat** the awkward *or* difficult age; **â. mental** mental age; **une femme d'â. mur** a mature woman; **avoir l'â. de raison** to have reached the age of reason (b) *(époque)* age; **l'â. de (la) pierre** the Stone Age; **l'â. d'or du cinéma muet** the golden age of silent movies

âgé, -e [aʒe] *adj* (a) *(qui a tel âge)* **être â. de dix ans** to be ten years old; **un enfant â. de deux ans** a two-year-old child (b) *(vieux)* old; **être plus/moins â. que qn** to be older/younger than sb

agence [aʒɑ̃s] *nf* agency; *(de banque)* branch; **a. immobilière** real estate agency; **a. d'intérim** temping agency; **a. matrimoniale** marriage bureau; **A. nationale pour l'emploi** = French national employment bureau; **a. de presse** press or news agency; **a. de recrutement** recruitment agency; **a. de voyages** travel agent's or agency

agencé, -e [aʒɑ̃se] *adj Suisse (cuisine)* fitted

agencement [aʒɑ̃smɑ̃] *nm (d'éléments)* arrangement; *(d'une maison, d'une pièce)* layout

agencer [16] [aʒɑ̃se] **1** *vt (éléments)* to arrange; *(maison, pièce)* to lay out, to design

2 s'agencer *vpr* **les parties du discours s'agencent bien/mal** the different parts of the speech fit/don't fit together well

agenda [aʒɛ̃da] *nm* diary, datebook; **a. électronique** personal organizer

agenouiller [aʒnuje] **s'agenouiller** *vpr* to kneel (down) (**devant** in front of)

agent [aʒɑ̃] *nm* (a) *(employé, espion)* agent; **a. (de police)** police officer; **pardon, Monsieur l'a.** excuse me, officer; **a. d'assurance(s)** insurance broker; **a. de change** stockbroker; **a. de la circulation** traffic policeman; **a. double** double agent; *Belg* **a. du quartier** community policeman; **a. immobilier** realtor; **a. secret** secret agent (b) *(facteur)* factor (c) *Gram* agent

agglomération [aglɔmerasjɔ̃] *nf (ville)* city, built-up area; **l'a. lyonnaise/parisienne** Lyons/Paris and its suburbs

aggloméré [aglɔmere] *nm* chipboard

agglomérer [34] [aglɔmere] **1** *vt* to bind together
2 s'agglomérer *vpr* to bind together

agglutiner [aglytine] **s'agglutiner** *vpr (personnes)* to congregate, to gather

aggravant, -e [agravã, -ãt] *adj* aggravating

aggravation [agravasjɔ̃] *nf (d'une maladie)* aggravation; *(du temps, d'un conflit)* worsening

aggraver [agrave] **1** *vt (situation, état de santé)* to make worse; *(difficultés)* to increase; **pour a. les choses** to make matters worse
2 s'aggraver *vpr (situation)* to get worse; *(état de santé)* to deteriorate; *(difficultés)* to increase

agile [aʒil] *adj* agile, nimble

agilement [aʒilmã] *adv* agilely, nimbly

agilité [aʒilite] *nf* agility

agios [aʒjo] *nmpl* bank charges

agir [aʒir] **1** *vi* (**a**) *(faire quelque chose)* to act; **bien/mal a. envers qn** to behave well/badly toward sb; **je n'aime pas sa façon** *ou* **manière d'a.** I don't like his/her behavior (**b**) *(produire un effet) (médicament, substance)* to act (**sur** on); **a. sur le moral** to have a demoralizing effect (**c**) *Jur* **a. au nom de qn** to act on behalf of sb
2 s'agir de *v impersonnel* (**a**) *(être question de)* **de quoi s'agit-il?** what's it about?; **l'affaire dont il s'agit** the matter in hand; **il ne s'agit pas d'argent** it's not a question of money; **quand il s'agit d'aider, il est toujours occupé!** when it comes to helping, he always seems to be busy! (**b**) *(falloir)* **il s'agit de prendre une décision** we have to make a decision; **il s'agirait de savoir si...** the question is whether...; **il s'agirait de se dépêcher** we've got to hurry

agissements [aʒismã] *nmpl* dealings

agitateur, -trice [aʒitatœr, -tris] *nm,f Pol* agitator

agitation [aʒitasjɔ̃] *nf (inquiétude)* agitation; *(bougeotte)* restlessness; *(troubles)* unrest

agité, -e [aʒite] *adj (mer)* rough, choppy; *(patient, nuit)* restless; *(sommeil)* troubled; *(enfant)* fidgety; *(époque)* unsettled; *(vie)* hectic

agiter [aʒite] **1** *vt* (**a**) *(mouchoir, drapeau, bras)* to wave; *(bouteille)* to shake; *(sujet: vent) (arbre, branches)* to sway; **a. la queue** *(chien)* to wag its tail; *(cheval)* to flick its tail (**b**) *(inquiéter)* to trouble; *(malade)* to excite
2 s'agiter *vpr* (**a**) *(bouger)* to fidget; *(s'affairer)* to bustle about; **s'a. dans son sommeil** to toss and turn in one's sleep (**b**) *(s'énerver)* to get excited

agneau, -x [aɲo] *nm* lamb; **(peau d')a.** lambskin

agnelle [aɲɛl] *nf* ewe lamb

agnostique [agnɔstik] *adj & nmf* agnostic

agonie [agɔni] *nf aussi Fig* death throes; **être à l'a.** to be at death's door; *Fig (régime)* to be in its death throes

agonisant, -e [agɔnizã, -ãt] **1** *adj* dying
2 *nm,f* dying person

agoniser [agɔnize] *vi* to be dying; *Fig (régime)* to be in its death throes

agoraphobie [agɔrafɔbi] *nf Méd* agoraphobia; **souffrir d'a.** to be agoraphobic

agrafe [agraf] *nf* (**a**) *(de bureau)* staple; *(de robe)* hook; *Méd* clip (**b**) *Constr* cramp (iron)

agrafer [agrafe] *vt* (**a**) *(avec une agrafeuse)* to staple; *(robe)* to fasten (**b**) *Fam (arrêter)* to catch, to bust; **se faire a.** to get busted

agrafeuse [agraføz] *nf* stapler

agraire [agrɛr] *adj (économie, société)* agrarian

agrandir [agrãdir] **1** *vt* (**a**) *(rendre plus grand)* to enlarge; *(maison, influence)* to extend; *(cercle de relations)* to widen (**b**) *(sujet:*

loupe, microscope) to magnify; **ce papier peint agrandit la pièce** this wallpaper makes the room look bigger
2 s'agrandir *vpr (ville)* to grow, to get bigger; *(nombre, influence)* to increase; *(entreprise)* to expand

agrandissement [agrãdismã] *nm* (**a**) *(d'une maison)* extension; *(d'une ville)* growth; *(d'une entreprise)* expansion (**b**) *(cliché)* enlargement

agréable [agreabl] *adj (personne, endroit, journée)* nice, pleasant; *(apparence)* pleasing; **a. au goût** tasty; **a. à regarder** nice to look at

agréablement [agreablɔmã] *adv* pleasantly

agréer [24] [agree] *vt (fournisseur, équipement)* to approve; **veuillez a. l'expression de mes sentiments distingués** sincerely yours

agrégation [agregasjɔ̃] *nf* **(le concours de) l'a.** = competitive examination for positions on the teaching staff of lycées and universities

> **Agrégation**
> This is a prestigious professional qualification for teachers in France. Those who pass the challenging competitive exam for the "agrég" become teachers in lycées or universities and are entitled to higher pay and a less onerous schedule than those who have passed the **CAPES** *(see box at this entry).*

agrégé, -e [agreʒe] **1** *adj* = who has passed the "agrégation" examination
2 *nm,f* = graduate who has passed the "agrégation" examination

agrément [agremã] *nm* (**a**) *(plaisir)* **voyage d'a.** pleasure trip (**b**) *(charme)* **une ville sans a.** an unattractive town (**c**) *(accord)* approval, consent

agrémenter [agremãte] *vt* **a. qch de** *(décorer)* to adorn sth with; **texte agrémenté de citations** text laced with quotations

agrès [agrɛ] *nmpl* (**a**) *Sport* (gymnastics) apparatus; **faire des a.** to do apparatus work (**b**) *Naut* tackle

agresser [agrese] *vt* to attack, to assault; *(en paroles)* to attack; *(tympans)* to assault; *(yeux)* to hurt; *(peau)* to damage; **se faire a.** to be attacked; *(pour son argent)* to be mugged

agresseur [agresœr] *nm* attacker

agressif, -ive [agresif, -iv] *adj* aggressive

agression [agresjɔ̃] *nf (d'une personne)* attack, assault; *(pour son argent)* mugging; *(d'un pays)* act of aggression; **être victime d'une a.** to be attacked; *(pour son argent)* to be mugged; **les agressions de la vie moderne** the stresses of modern life; **a. sexuelle** sexual assault

agressivement [agresivmã] *adv* aggressively

agressivité [agresivite] *nf* aggressiveness

agricole [agrikɔl] *adj* agricultural; *(population)* farming; *(produits)* farm

agriculteur, -trice [agrikyltœr, -tris] *nm,f* farmer

agriculture [agrikyltyr] *nf* farming, agriculture

agripper [agripe] **1** *vt* to clutch
2 s'agripper *vpr* to cling on (**à** to)

agroalimentaire [agroalimãtɛr] **1** *adj (industrie, secteur)* food
2 *nm* **l'a.** the food-processing industry

agronome [agronɔm] *nmf* agronomist

agronomie [agronɔmi] *nf* agronomy

agrotourisme [agroturism] *nm* agrotourism

agrume [agrym] *nm* citrus fruit

aguets [agɛ] **aux aguets** *adv* on the lookout; **être** *ou* **se tenir aux a.** to be on the lookout

aguichage [agiʃaʒ] *nm (technique publicitaire)* teaser advertising

aguichant, -e [agiʃã, -ãt] *adj* seductive

aguiche [agiʃ] *nf Mktg* teaser

aguicher [agiʃe] *vt* to seduce

ahuri, -e [ayri] **1** *adj* astounded
2 *nm,f* numbskull

ahurissant, -e [ayrisɑ̃, -ɑ̃t] *adj* astounding

aide [ɛd] **1** *nf* help, assistance; **demander de l'a. à qn** to ask sb for help; **venir en a. à qn** to help sb; **appeler à l'a.** to call for help; **à l'a.!** help!; **à l'a. de qch** with the aid of sth; *Ordinat* **a. à la césure** hyphenation help; **a. de l'État** government aid; **a. humanitaire** aid; **a. judiciaire** legal aid; *Ordinat* **a. en ligne** on-line help; **a. sociale** welfare
2 *nmf* assistant; **un a. de camp** an aide-de-camp; **une a. familiale** a home help; **une a. ménagère** a home helper

aide-mémoire [ɛdmemwar] *nm inv* aide-mémoire

aider [ede] **1** *vt* to help; *(sujet: gouvernement)* to aid; **que puis-je faire pour vous a.?** how may I help you?; **je me suis fait a. par un ami** I got a friend to help me; **a. qn à faire qch** to help sb to do sth; **a. qn à monter/sortir** to help sb up/out; *Ironique* **tu veux que je t'aide?** stop that!; **elle n'aide jamais** she never helps (out)
2 aider à *vt ind* to contribute toward; **a. à faire qch** to help to do sth
3 s'aider *vpr* **(a)** *(soi-même)* **s'a. de qch** to use sth; **marcher en s'aidant d'une canne/de béquilles** to walk with the aid of a stick/crutches; *Prov* **aide-toi et le ciel t'aidera** God helps those who help themselves **(b)** *(l'un l'autre)* to help each other

aide-soignant, -e *(mpl* **aides-soignants,** *fpl* **aides-soignantes)** [ɛdswaɲɑ̃, -ɑ̃t] *nm,f* nurse's aid

aïe [aj] *exclam (cri de douleur)* ow!, ouch!; *Fig* **a., j'ai fait une gaffe!** oh no, I put my foot in my mouth!

AIEA [aiɛa] *nf (abrév* **Agence internationale de l'énergie atomique)** IAEA

aïeul, -e [ajœl] *nm,f Vieilli* grandfather, *f* grandmother; **aïeuls** grandparents

aïeux [ajø] *nmpl Litt* ancestors

aigle [ɛgl] *nm* eagle; *Fig* **ce n'est pas un a.** he's no genius; **avoir un œil d'a.** to be eagle-eyed

aiglefin [ɛgləfɛ̃] *nm* haddock

aigre [ɛgr] *adj (goût, lait)* sour; *Fig (propos)* cutting; **d'un ton a.** sharply

aigre-doux, -douce *(mpl* **aigres-doux,** *fpl* **aigres-douces)** [ɛgrədu, -dus] *adj (sauce)* sweet-and-sour; *Fig (remarque)* snide

aigrelet, -ette [ɛgrəlɛ, -ɛt] *adj (vin, goût)* (rather) sour; *(son, voix)* shrill

aigrette [ɛgrɛt] *nf* **(a)** *(d'un oiseau)* crest **(b)** *(panache)* plume

aigreur [ɛgrœr] *nf* **(a)** *(d'un goût)* sourness; *(d'une remarque)* sharpness, bitterness **(b)** *Méd* **aigreurs (d'estomac)** heartburn

aigri, -e [ɛgri] *adj* embittered

aigu, -uë [egy] *adj* **(a)** *(douleur)* acute, sharp; *(regard)* penetrating; *(esprit)* keen; **avoir un sens a. de qch** to have a keen sense of sth **(b)** *(instrument)* sharp; *(angle)* acute **(c)** *(son)* high-pitched **(d)** *Méd* acute

aigue-marine *(pl* **aigues-marines)** [ɛgmarin] *nf* aquamarine

aiguillage [egɥijaʒ] *nm* **(a)** *(manœuvre)* switching; *(appareil)* switches **(b)** *Fig* **faire une erreur d'a.** to take the wrong direction

aiguille [egɥij] *nf* **(a)** *(instrument, objet pointu)* needle; *Fig* **chercher une a. dans une botte de foin** to look for a needle in a haystack; **a. à coudre/repriser/tricoter** sewing/darning/knitting needle; *Méd* **a. hypodermique** hypodermic needle; **a. de pin** pine needle **(b)** *(de boussole, de compteur de vitesse)* needle; *(de montre, d'horloge)* hand; **petite a.** hour hand; **grande a.** minute hand **(c)** *(d'une église)* spire **(d)** *(sommet)* sharp peak

aiguiller [egɥije] *vt (train)* to switch; *Fig* **a. qn vers** *(profession)* to steer sb toward; **a. ses recherches vers** to direct one's investigations toward; **a. la police sur une fausse piste** to put the police off the scent; **il a été mal aiguillé dans ses études** he was badly advised about his studies

aiguilleur [egɥijœr] *nm (de trains)* signalman, switchman; **a. du ciel** air-traffic controller

aiguillon [egɥijɔ̃] *nm* **(a)** *(pique-bœuf)* goad; *Fig* spur **(b)** *(d'une guêpe)* sting

aiguiser [egize] *vt* **(a)** *(outil, couteau)* to sharpen **(b)** *Fig (curiosité, jalousie)* to arouse; *(appétit)* to whet

aïkido [ajkido] *nm* aikido; **faire de l'a.** to do aikido

ail [aj] *(pl* **ails** [aj], *Vieilli* **aulx** [o]) *nm* garlic; *Can* **a. des bois** wild garlic

aile [ɛl] *nf* **(a)** *(d'oiseau, de papillon)* wing; *Fig* **battre de l'a.** to be struggling; **la peur nous donnait des ailes** fear gave or lent us wings; *Fam* **avoir un coup dans l'a.** to have had a bit too much to drink **(b)** *(d'une voiture)* fender; *(d'un bâtiment)* wing; *(d'une armée)* flank **(c)** *(d'un avion)* wing; *(d'un moulin)* sail; *(d'une hélice, d'une turbine)* blade **(d)** *(au football)* wing

ailé, -e [ele] *adj* winged

aileron [ɛlrɔ̃] *nm* **(a)** *(d'oiseau)* pinion; *(de requin)* fin **(b)** *Aviat* aileron

ailette [ɛlɛt] *nf (d'une turbine, d'un ventilateur)* blade; *(d'une bombe, d'un missile)* wing, fin

ailier [elje] *nm (au football)* winger; *(au basket)* wing

aille *etc. voir* **aller¹**

ailler [aje] *vt* to put garlic in

ailleurs [ajœr] *adv* **(a)** *(à un autre endroit)* elsewhere, somewhere else; *Fig* **être a., avoir l'esprit a.** to be miles away; **partout a.** everywhere else; *(n'importe où)* anywhere else; **nulle part a.** nowhere else; **vous mangerez ici comme nulle part a.** you'll eat better here than anywhere else; *Fam* **va voir a. si j'y suis!** take a hike! **(b)** **d'a.** *(de plus)* besides, anyway; *(au fait)* by the way **(c)** **par a.** *(par d'autres côtés)* in other respects; *(d'autre part)* moreover

ailloli [ajɔli] = **aïoli**

aimable [ɛmabl] *adj (gentil)* kind, nice; **vous êtes bien a., c'est très a. de votre part** it's very kind of you; **peu a.** *(personne)* not very nice; *(propos)* unkind

aimablement [ɛmabləmɑ̃] *adv* kindly

aimant¹ [ɛmɑ̃] *nm* magnet

aimant², -e [ɛmɑ̃, -ɑ̃t] *adj (personne)* loving

aimanter [ɛmɑ̃te] *vt* to magnetize

aimer [eme] **1** *vt* **(a)** *(d'amour)* to love **(b)** *(apprécier, avoir de l'affection pour)* to like; **a. beaucoup qn/qch** to like sb/sth a lot, to be very fond of sb/sth; **a. bien qn/qch** to like sb/sth; **a. faire qch** to like doing sth; **j'aurais aimé le voir** I would like to have seen him; **je n'aime pas que tu fréquentes ces gens** I don't like you mixing with those people; **j'aime(rais) autant rester ici** I would just as soon stay here; **j'aime autant qu'il ne m'attende pas** I would rather he didn't wait for me; **a. mieux** to prefer; **ah, j'aime mieux ça!** now that's more like it!; **j'aime mieux lui en parler moi-même** I'd rather talk to him/her about it myself; *Fam* **j'aime mieux pas** I'd rather not; **je vais prendre un pot – qui m'aime me suive!** I'm going for a drink – anyone want to join me?
2 aimer à *vt ind Litt* **a. à faire qch** to take pleasure in doing sth; **j'aime à croire que...** I like to think (that)...
3 s'aimer *vpr* **(a)** *(l'un l'autre)* to love each other **(b)** *(être fier de soi)* to be in love with oneself; **je ne m'aime pas dans cette veste** I don't like myself in this jacket

aine [ɛn] *nf* groin

aîné, -e [ene] **1** *adj (de deux enfants)* elder; *(de plus de deux enfants)* eldest
2 *nm,f (de deux enfants)* elder (child); *(de plus de deux enfants)* eldest (child); **nos aînés** our elders; **il est mon a.** he is older

than me; **il est mon a. de deux ans** he is two years older than me

aînesse [ɛnɛs] *nf voir* **droit**[3]

ainsi [ɛ̃si] *adv* (**a**) *(de cette façon)* like this, in this way; **c'est a. qu'il est devenu soldat** that's how he became a soldier; **et a. de suite** and so on, and so forth; **pour a. dire** so to speak, as it were; *Rel* **a. soit-il** amen (**b**) **a. (donc)** *(alors)* so; **a. vous ne venez pas?** so you're not coming? (**c**) *(par exemple)* for example, for instance (**d**) **a. que** *(et)* as well as, and

aïoli [ajɔli] *nm Culin* garlic mayonnaise

air [ɛr] *nm* (**a**) *(gaz)* air; **cela manque d'a. ici** it's stuffy in here; **faire de l'a.** to let some air in; **sortir prendre l'a.** to go out for some fresh air; **laisser qch à l'a.** to leave sth uncovered; **au grand a.** in the fresh air; **en plein a., à l'a. libre** outside; **concert en plein a.** open-air concert; **activités de plein a.** outdoor pursuits; *Fam* **allez, de l'a.!** go on, clear off!; **a. comprimé** compressed air; **avoir l'a. conditionné** to have air-conditioning

(**b**) *(ciel)* **l'a.** the air; **s'élever dans les airs** to rise into the air; **regarder en l'a.** to look up

(**c**) *Fig (atmosphère)* **changer d'a.** to have a change of scene; **il y a de la dispute/de l'orage dans l'a.** there's an argument/a storm brewing

(**d**) *(vent)* **il y a** *ou* **il fait de l'a.** there's a breeze

(**e**) *(allure)* look; *(mine)* expression; **avoir un drôle d'a.** to look odd *or* funny; **avoir l'a. fatigué/de s'ennuyer** to look tired/bored; *Fam* **avoir l'a. fin** to look stupid; **tu as l'a. de ne pas comprendre** you look as if you don't understand; **n'avoir l'a. de rien** *(travail)* to look (deceptively) easy; **il n'a l'a. de rien, mais...** he doesn't look much, but...; **sans avoir l'a. de rien** inconspicuously; **se donner** *ou* **prendre des airs** to give oneself airs; **ne prends pas tes grands airs!** don't get on your high horse!; **a. de famille** family likeness; *Can* **avoir l'a. de qn** to look like sb

(**f**) *(musique)* tune; **un a. d'opéra** an (operatic) aria

(**g**) *(locutions) Fam* **ficher qch en l'a.** to mess sth up; **mettre qch en l'a.** *(en désordre)* to make a terrible mess of sth; **c'est dans l'a. du temps** it's the in thing

air-air [ɛrɛr] *adj inv Mil* air-to-air

Airbag® [ɛrbag] *nm* (**a**) *Aut* Airbag® (**b**) *Fam* **airbags** *(seins)* tits, boobs

aire [ɛr] *nf* (**a**) *(surface plane)* area; **a. (de battage)** threshing floor; **a. d'atterrissage** *(pour avions)* landing strip; *(pour hélicoptères)* helipad; **a. de jeux** play area; **a. de lancement** *(de fusée)* launch pad; **a. de repos** *(sur l'autoroute)* rest area; **a. de stationnement** parking area (**b**) *(d'un champ, d'un triangle, d'un bâtiment)* area; *Fig* **a. d'influence** sphere of influence (**c**) *(d'un aigle)* eyrie

airelle [ɛrɛl] *nf (rouge)* cranberry

air-sol [ɛrsɔl] *adj inv Mil* air-to-ground

aisance [ɛzɑ̃s] *nf* (**a**) *(facilité, grâce)* ease (**b**) *(financière)* **vivre dans l'a.** to live comfortably

aise [ɛz] **1** *nf* **être à l'a.** *(bien installé)* to be comfortable; *(avoir beaucoup de place)* to have plenty of room; *(financièrement)* to be comfortably off; *(dans une situation)* to feel comfortable *or* at ease; **on tient à l'a. à six dans cette voiture** this car holds six comfortably; *Fam* **à l'a.!** *(c'est facile)* easy!; **ne pas être à son a.**, **se sentir mal à l'a.** to feel uncomfortable; **il me met mal à l'a.** he makes me feel uneasy *or* uncomfortable; **mettre qn à l'a.** to put sb at his *or* her ease; **se mettre à l'a.** to make oneself comfortable; *Ironique* **elle peut en parler à son a.!** it's easy (enough) for her to say that!; **à ton a.!** suit yourself!; **prendre ses aises** to make oneself at home

2 *adj Litt* **être bien** *ou* **tout a. de faire qch** to be delighted to do sth

aisé, -e [eze] *adj* (**a**) *(financièrement)* comfortably off (**b**) *(tâche, mouvements)* easy

aisément [ezemɑ̃] *adv* easily

aisselle [ɛsɛl] *nf* armpit

Aix-la-Chapelle [ɛkslaʃapɛl] *n* Aachen, Aix-la-Chapelle

AJ [aʒi] *nf (abrév* **auberge de jeunesse)** youth hostel

ajonc [aʒɔ̃] *nm* gorse

ajouré, -e [aʒure] *adj (pull)* loose-knit; *(broderie, en architecture)* openwork

ajourner [aʒurne] *vt (réunion, décision, voyage)* to postpone, to put off; *(après le début de la séance)* to adjourn; *Scol (candidat)* to refer

ajout [aʒu] *nm* addition (**à** to)

ajouter [aʒute] **1** *vt* to add (**à** to); *Ordinat (à une base de données)* to append

2 ajouter à *vt ind* to add to

3 s'ajouter *vpr* **s'a. à** to be added to; **à ceci viennent s'a. les frais de déplacement** on top of this there are travel expenses (to be added)

ajustable [aʒystabl] *adj* adjustable

ajustage [aʒystaʒ] *nm* fitting

ajuster [aʒyste] **1** *vt* (**a**) *(régler) (appareil, outil)* to adjust; *(chapeau, coiffure)* to adjust; **a. le tir** to aim (**b**) *(adapter)* to fit (**à** to); *(vêtement)* to alter; **veste ajustée** fitted jacket

2 s'ajuster *vpr* (**a**) *(personne)* to straighten one's clothes (**b**) *(s'adapter)* **s'a. à** to fit; **s'a. sur** to fit onto

ajusteur [aʒystœr] *nm* fitter

alaise [alɛz] *nf* undersheet

alambic [alɑ̃bik] *nm* still

alambiqué, -e [alɑ̃bike] *adj* convoluted

alangui, -e [alɑ̃gi] *adj* languid

alarmant, -e [alarmɑ̃, -ɑ̃t] *adj* alarming; **son état est a.** his condition is giving serious cause for concern

alarme [alarm] *nf* alarm; **donner/sonner l'a.** to give/to sound the alarm; **une fausse a.** a false alarm; **a. antivol** car alarm; **a. incendie** fire alarm

alarmer [alarme] **1** *vt* to alarm

2 s'alarmer *vpr* to get alarmed; **il n'y a pas lieu de s'a.** there is no cause for alarm

albanais, -e [albanɛ, -ɛz] **1** *adj* Albanian

2 *nm (langue)* Albanian

3 *nm,f* **A., Albanaise** Albanian

Albanie [albani] *nf* **l'A.** Albania

albâtre [albɑtr] *nm* alabaster

albatros [albatros] *nm* albatross

albinos [albinos] *adj & nmf* albino

album [albɔm] *nm* album; **a. de timbres/de photos** stamp/photo album

albumen [albymɛn] *nm Biol* albumen

albumine [albymin] *nf Chim* albumin

alcalin, -e [alkalɛ̃, -in] *adj Chim* alkaline

alchimie [alʃimi] *nf* alchemy

alchimiste [alʃimist] *nm* alchemist

alcolo [alkɔlo] *Fam* **1** *nmf* drunk, alky

2 *adj* **être a.** to be a drunk

alcool [alkɔl] *nm* (**a**) *Chim* alcohol; **a. à 90°** rubbing alcohol; **a. à brûler** methylated spirits (**b**) *(digestif)* liqueur; **l'a.** *(boissons alcoolisées)* alcohol; **il ne tient pas l'a.** he can't hold his drink; **l'a. au volant** drunk-driving; **a. de poire** pear brandy

alcoolémie [alkɔlemi] *nf* **taux d'a.** blood alcohol level

alcoolique [alkɔlik] **1** *nmf* alcoholic

2 *adj* alcoholic; **être a.** to be an alcoholic

alcoolisé, -e [alkɔlize] *adj* alcoholic

alcoolisme [alkɔlism] *nm* alcoholism

alcopop [alkɔpɔp] *nm* alcopop

Alcotest® [alkɔtɛst] *nm* breath test; **faire passer un A. à qn** to breathalyze sb

alcôve [alkov] *nf* recess *(for bed)*

aléa [alea] *nm* hazard

aléatoire [aleatwar] *adj* random; *(résultat)* uncertain

alémanique [alemanik] *adj* **la Suisse a.** German-speaking Switzerland

ALENA [alena] *nm (abrév***Accord de libre-échange nord-américain**) **l'A.** NAFTA

alentour [alãtur] **1** *adv* around; **les villages a.** the surrounding villages

2 alentours *nmpl (voisinage)* surroundings; **aux alentours** in the vicinity; **aux alentours de la ville/300 euros** in the vicinity of the town/300 euros; **aux alentours de midi** *(some time)* around noon

Aléoutiennes [aleusjɛn] *adj & nfpl* **les (îles) A.** the Aleutian Islands

alerte [alɛrt] **1** *nf* **(a)** *(avertissement)* alarm; **donner/sonner l'a.** to give/sound the alarm; **a. à la bombe** bomb scare **(b)** *(menace)* threat; *(problème de santé)* scare; **à la première a.** at the first sign of danger; **fausse a.** false alarm

2 *adj (personne) (physiquement)* sprightly; *(mentalement)* alert; *(esprit, style)* lively; **d'un pas a.** at a brisk pace

3 *exclam* look out!

alerter [alɛrte] *vt* to alert (**sur** to)

alèse [alɛz] = **alaise**

alevin [alvɛ̃] *nm* young fish

Alexandre [alɛksãdr] *npr* **A. le Grand** Alexander the Great

Alexandrie [alɛksãdri] *n* Alexandria

alexandrin [alɛksãdrɛ̃] *nm* alexandrine

alezan, -e [alzã, -an] **1** *adj (cheval)* chestnut

2 *nm* chestnut (horse)

algèbre [alʒɛbr] *nf* algebra

algébrique [alʒebrik] *adj* algebraic

Alger [alʒe] *n* Algiers

Algérie [alʒeri] *nf* **l'A.** Algeria

algérien, -enne [alʒerjɛ̃, -ɛn] **1** *adj* Algerian

2 *nm,f* **A., Algérienne** Algerian

algérois, -e [alʒerwa, -az] **1** *adj* of Algiers

2 *nm,f* **A., Algéroise** person from Algiers

algorithme [algoritm] *nm Math & Ordinat* algorithm; *Ordinat* **a. de tri** sorting algorithm

algothérapie [algoterapi] *nf* = alternative medicine based on marine plant extracts

algue [alg] *nf* piece of seaweed; **algues** seaweed

alias [aljas] *adv* alias

alibi [alibi] *nm* alibi

aliénation [aljenasjɔ̃] *nf* **(a)** *(de l'esprit)* alienation; *Psy* **a. mentale** insanity **(b)** *(de liberté)* loss; *Jur (des droits, de biens)* alienation

aliéné, -e [aljene] **1** *adj* insane

2 *nm,f* insane person

aliéner [34] [aljene] **1** *vt* **(a)** *(personne)* to alienate; **ce commentaire vous a aliéné la sympathie de l'auditoire** you lost the audience's sympathy when you made that comment **(b)** *Jur (biens, droits)* to alienate

2 s'aliéner *vpr* **s'a. la sympathie de l'électorat** to lose the goodwill of the electorate; **s'a. un ami** to alienate a friend

alignement [aliɲəmã] *nm* **(a)** *(opération)* alignment, aligning; *Pol (sur un pays, une politique)* alignment (**sur** with) **(b)** *(ligne)* line; **être dans l'a. de qch** to be in line with sth **(c)** *(de monolithes)* = line of standing stones

aligner [aliɲe] **1** *vt* **(a)** *(mettre en ligne)* to align, to line up; *(politique, monnaie)* to align (**sur** with) **(b)** *(mettre à la suite) (arguments)* to reel off; **je passe ma journée à a. des chiffres** I spend my day producing lists of figures

2 s'aligner *vpr (se mettre en rang)* to line up; *Pol (sur un pays, une politique)* to align oneself (**sur** with); *Fam* **tu peux toujours t'a.!** not a chance!

aliment [alimã] *nm* **(a)** *(nourriture)* food **(b)** *Jur* **aliments** alimony

alimentaire [alimãtɛr] *adj* **(a)** *(plante)* edible; **habitudes alimentaires** eating habits; **l'industrie a.** the food industry **(b)** *Fig* **ce n'est qu'un travail a.** I just do this job to make ends meet

alimentation [alimãtasjɔ̃] *nf* **(a)** *(régime alimentaire)* diet; **avoir une a. équilibrée** to have a balanced diet; **(magasin d')a.** grocery store; **(rayon) a.** grocery department **(b)** *(action) (de personne, de plante, d'animal)* feeding; *(d'une ville, d'un marché)* supply; **l'a. d'une ville en eau** the water supply to a town **(c)** *Tech (d'une chaudière)* feeding; *(en électricité)* power supply; **a. papier** *(d'une imprimante)* sheetfeed, paper feed

alimenter [alimãte] **1** *vt (personne, plante, animal, chaudière)* to feed; *(cours d'eau)* to flow into; *Fin (compte)* to pay money into; *Fig (conversation)* to keep going; *(sentiment)* to fuel; **a. une usine en courant** to supply a factory with power

2 s'alimenter *vpr* to eat

alinéa [alinea] *nm* **(a)** *(renfoncement)* indent **(b)** *(texte)* paragraph

aliter [alite] **s'aliter** *vpr* to take to one's bed; **être alité** *(temporairement)* to be confined to one's bed; *(grabataire)* to be bedridden

alizé [alize] *adj & nm* **les (vents) alizés** the trade winds

Allah [ala] *npr* Allah

allaitement [alɛtmã] *nm* feeding; *(d'un animal)* suckling; **a. au biberon** bottle-feeding; **a. maternel** breast-feeding

allaiter [alete] *vt (enfant)* to breast-feed; *(sujet: animal)* to suckle; **est-ce que vous allaitez?** are you breast-feeding?

allant [alã] *nm* **avoir de l'a., être plein d'a.** to be full of energy

alléchant, -e [aleʃã, -ãt] *adj (offre)* tempting; *(odeur, plat)* appetizing

allécher [34] [aleʃe] *vt* to tempt

allée [ale] *nf* **(a)** *(dans un jardin)* path; *(devant une résidence)* driveway; *(dans une ville)* avenue; *(dans un supermarché, un cinéma)* aisle **(b)** **allées et venues** coming(s) and going(s); **faire des allées et venues** to go back and forth

allégation [alegasjɔ̃] *nf* allegation

allégé, -e [aleʒe] *adj (en matières grasses)* low-fat; *(en sucre)* low-sugar

allègement [alɛʒmã] *nm* **(a)** *(d'impôts, de charges)* reduction; *(des emplois du temps scolaires)* streamlining; **a. fiscal** tax relief **(b)** *(d'un véhicule, d'un fardeau)* lightening

alléger [59] [aleʒe] *vt* **(a)** *(impôts, charges)* to reduce; *(douleur, chagrin)* to soothe **(b)** *(véhicule, fardeau)* to lighten; *(emploi du temps scolaire)* to streamline

allégorie [alegori] *nf* allegory

allégorique [alegorik] *adj* allegorical

allègre [alɛgr] *adj* lively, cheerful; **d'un ton a.** cheerfully, light-heartedly; **d'un pas a.** with a spring in one's step

allègrement [alɛgrəmã] *adv* cheerfully; *(marcher)* with a spring in one's step; **il m'a a. refilé ses enfants pour le week-end** he blithely palmed his children off on me for the weekend

allégresse [alegrɛs] *nf* joy; **a. générale** general rejoicing

alléluia [aleluja] *nm & exclam Rel* hallelujah

Allemagne [alman] *nf* **l'A.** Germany; *Anciennement* **l'A. de l'Ouest/de l'Est** West/East Germany

allemand, -e [almã, -ãd] **1** *adj* German

2 *nm (langue)* German

3 *nm,f* **A., Allemande** German; *Anciennement* **A. de l'Est/de l'Ouest** East/West German

aller¹ [8] [ale] *(aux être)* **1** *vi* **(a)** *(se déplacer)* to go; **a. à Toulon** to go to Toulon; **ce train va à Lille** this train goes to Lille; **a. à la pêche** to go fishing; **a. et venir** to come and go

(b) *(sujet: chemin, route)* **a. à** to go to

(c) *(arriver)* **a. jusqu'à** *(dans l'espace)* to go as far as; *(dans le* *temps*) to last until; **jusqu'où ira-t-il?** (*pour atteindre son but*) to what lengths will he go?; **a. jusqu'à faire qch** to go so far as to do sth

(**d**) (*fonctionner*) to go; (*bien fonctionner*) to go well; **si tu touches à mes affaires, ça va a. mal!** touch my things and there'll be trouble!; **ça va (comme ça), merci** (*à table*) that's enough, thanks; **je vous en offre 100 euros, ça va?** I'll give you 100 euros for it, OK?; *Fam* **non mais ça va pas(, la tête)!** are you crazy?

(**e**) (*se porter*) **a. bien/mal** to be well/ill; **comment allez-vous?** how are you?; **ça va? – ça va!** how's it going? – OK!

(**f**) (*indique le but*) **a. faire qch** to go and do sth; **a. se coucher** to go to bed; **a. se promener** to go for a walk; **va voir!** go and see!; **n'allez pas vous imaginer que...** don't you go thinking that...; **cet imbécile est allé tout lui raconter** that idiot went and told him/her everything

(**g**) (*convenir*) **a. à qn** to suit sb; **a. bien à qn** (*vêtement, couleur*) to look good on sb; **a. (bien) avec qch** (*vêtement, couleur*) to go (well) with sth, to match sth; *Fam* **ça lui va mal de donner des conseils** he's a fine one to be giving advice

(**h**) (*se ranger, s'adapter*) **où vont les couteaux?** where do the knives go *or* belong?; **un plat qui va au four** an ovenproof dish

(**i**) (*agir*) **il est allé un peu vite dans cette affaire** he was a bit hasty; *Fam* **vas-y doucement** take it easy; *Fam* **comme tu y vas!** don't overdo it!

(**j**) (*locutions*) **y a.** (*partir*) to go; (*commencer*) to get going; **allez!** (*pour encourager*) come on!; (*pour consoler*) come now!; **allons!** (*pour encourager, réprimander*) come on!; **ça passera, va** don't worry, you'll get over it; *Fam* **va pour 1000 euros/mardi prochain** 1,000 euros/next Tuesday, that's fine; **a. de soi** to be obvious; **a. sur ses quarante ans** to be nearing *or* pushing forty

2 *v aux* (**a**) (*indique le futur proche*) **a. faire qch** to be going to do sth; **il va s'en occuper** he's going to deal with it; **j'allais m'endormir quand...** I was about to fall asleep when...

(**b**) (*indique la progression*) **a. en empirant** to be getting worse and worse

3 *v impersonnel* **il en va de même pour moi/lui** it's the same for me/him

4 s'en aller *vpr* (**a**) (*personne*) to go (away)

(**b**) (*tache*) to come out; (*couleur*) to fade; (*peinture*) to flake off

aller² [ale] *nm* (**a**) (*trajet*) outward journey; **à l'a.** on the way there (**b**) (*billet*) **a. (simple)** one-way ticket; **a. (et) retour** round-trip (ticket); *Fam Fig* **un a. et retour** (*gifle*) a slap in the face

allergie [alɛrʒi] *nf* allergy; **avoir** *ou* **faire une a. à qch** to be allergic to sth

allergique [alɛrʒik] *adj aussi Fig* allergic (**à** to)

allergologiste [alɛrɡɔlɔʒist], **allergologue** [alɛrɡɔlɔɡ] *nmf Méd* allergist

alliage [aljaʒ] *nm* (*métallique*) alloy

alliance [aljɑ̃s] *nf* (**a**) (*entente*) alliance; (*d'un couple*) marriage; **parent par a.** relative by marriage (**b**) (*bague*) wedding ring (**c**) (*combinaison*) (*de parfums, de couleurs*) combination (**d**) **l'A. française** = organization promoting French language and culture abroad

> ### Alliance française
> The Alliance française is a non-profit private body with over 1100 branches in 132 countries worldwide. It organizes classes in French language and civilization and hosts lectures, exhibitions, other cultural events, scholarships and so on.

allié, -e [alje] **1** *nm,f* (*partisan*) ally; **parents et alliés** extended family; *Hist* **les Alliés** the Allies

2 *adj* (**a**) (*nation*) allied (**b**) *Hist* Allied

allier [66] [alje] **1** *vt* (**a**) (*pays*) to ally; (*familles*) to unite by mar-

riage (**b**) (*métaux*) to alloy; (*couleurs*) to combine; **a. l'intelligence à la beauté** to combine intelligence and beauty

2 s'allier *vpr* (**a**) (*s'unir*) to become allies (**avec** with); **s'a. contre qn/qch** to unite against sb/sth (**b**) (*goûts, parfums, couleurs*) to combine

alligator [aligatɔr] *nm* alligator

allitération [aliterasjɔ̃] *nf* alliteration; **a. en s** alliteration of the letter s

allô, allo [alo] *exclam* hello!

allocation [alɔkasjɔ̃] *nf* (**a**) (*d'argent, de terres*) allocation; (*de titres financiers*) allotment (**b**) (*prestation financière*) welfare; **les allocations (familiales)** welfare; **a. (de) chômage** unemployment compensation; **a. (de) logement** rent subsidy

allocs [alɔk] *nfpl Fam* welfare

allocution [alɔkysjɔ̃] *nf* address

allongé, -e [alɔ̃ʒe] *adj* (**a**) (*forme, silhouette*) elongated; **avoir le visage a.** to have a long face (**b**) (*couché*) **être a.** to be lying down

allongement [alɔ̃ʒmɑ̃] *nm* (**a**) (*agrandissement*) lengthening (**b**) (*dans le temps*) extension; **a. de l'espérance de vie** increase in life expectancy

allonger [45] [alɔ̃ʒe] **1** *vt* (**a**) (*rendre plus long*) to lengthen; (*vêtement*) to let down; (*sauce*) to thin (down); **cette robe allonge la silhouette** this dress makes you look taller

(**b**) (*bras*) to stretch out; (*cou*) to crane; **a. le pas** to quicken one's pace; *Sport* **a. l'allure** to increase the pace

(**c**) (*personne*) to lie down

(**d**) (*vacances, délai*) to extend

(**e**) *Fam* **a. une gifle à qn** to give sb a slap; **a. le fric/1000 euros** to hand over the dough/1,000 euros

2 *vi* (*jours*) to get longer

3 s'allonger *vpr* (**a**) (*ombres, jours*) to get longer; *Fig* (*enfant*) to grow (**b**) (*se coucher*) to lie down; *Fam* **s'a. (par terre)** (*tomber*) to fall flat on the ground

allopathie [alɔpati] *nf Méd* allopathy

allouer [alwe] *vt* **a. qch à qn** (*salaire, indemnité, délai*) to grant sb sth; (*actions, ration*) to allocate sb sth

allumage [alymaʒ] *nm* (*d'un feu*) lighting; (*d'une lampe*) switching on; (*d'un moteur*) ignition

allume-cigare (*pl* **allume-cigares**) [alymsigar] *nm* cigar lighter

allume-gaz [alymgaz] *nm inv* gas lighter

allumer [alyme] **1** *vt* (**a**) (*cigarette, briquet, feu*) to light; (*lampe, télévision, électricité*) to switch on, to turn on; (*incendie*) to start; **a. (la lumière)** to switch *or* to turn the light on; **a. le salon** to switch *or* to turn the light on in the living room; **laisser la cuisinière allumée** to leave the stove on (**b**) *Fig* (*passions*) to arouse; *Fam* (*séduire*) to tease

2 s'allumer *vpr* (*lumière, lampe, téléviseur*) to come on; **où est-ce que ça s'allume?** where does it switch *or* turn on?

allumette [alymɛt] *nf* match

allumeuse [alymøz] *nf Fam* tease

allure [alyr] *nf* (**a**) (*vitesse*) speed; **à toute a.** at top speed (**b**) (*démarche*) walk, gait; (*manière de se tenir*) bearing; **avoir de l'a.** to be stylish; **avoir fière a.** to cut a fine figure; **avoir une drôle d'a.** to look funny; **avoir des allures de malfrat** to look like a crook; *Belg* **n'avoir pas d'a.** to be unsophisticated (**c**) *Can* **avoir d'a.** (*être vraisemblable*) to be likely

allusion [alyzjɔ̃] *nf* allusion (**à** to); **faire a. à** to refer to, to allude to

alluvial, -e, -aux, -ales [alyvjal, -o] *adj* alluvial

alluvions [alyvjɔ̃] *nfpl* alluvium

almanach [almana] *nm* almanac

aloès [alɔɛs] *nm* aloe

aloi [alwa] *nm* **de bon a.** (*succès*) deserved; (*plaisanterie*) in good taste; **de mauvais a.** (*succès*) undeserved; (*plaisanterie*) in bad taste

..lor] *adv* (**a**) *(à ce moment-là)* then; *(dans ce cas)* then, in ...ase; **jusqu'a.** (up) until then; **le ministre d'a.** the min-ister at the time; **et a.?** so what?; **et a., qu'est-ce qu'il a ré-pondu?** so what did he say?; *Fam* **a., tu viens?** so are you coming?; *Fam* **non mais a., pour qui il se prend, celui-là?** really, just who does he think he is?; *Fam* **ça a.!** jeez!; **a. là, il exagère!** he's overdoing it a bit there! (**b**) *(donc)* so; **il n'était pas là, a. je suis revenu** he wasn't there, so I came back (**c**) **a. que** *(au moment où)* when; *(bien que)* even though; **il a une maison, a. que moi j'habite dans un appartement** he's got a house, whereas I live in an apartment

alouette [alwɛt] *nf* lark

alourdir [alurdir] **1** *vt (chose)* to make heavier; *Fig (phrase)* to make cumbersome; *(charges sociales)* to increase

  2 s'alourdir *vpr* to get heavy; *(taille)* to get bigger

aloyau, -x [alwajo] *nm* sirloin

alpaga [alpaga] *nm* alpaca

alpage [alpaʒ] *nm* mountain pasture

alpaguer [alpage] *vt très Fam* to collar, to bust; **se faire a.** to get busted

Alpes [alp] *nfpl* **les A.** the Alps; **les A. suisses** the Swiss Alps

alphabet [alfabɛ] *nm* alphabet

alphabétique [alfabetik] *adj* alphabetical

alphabétiquement [alfabetikmɑ̃] *adv* alphabetically

alphabétisation [alfabetizasjɔ̃] *nf* teaching of literacy

alphanumérique [alfanymerik] *adj* alphanumeric

alphapage [alfapaʒ] *nm* bleeper

alpin, -e [alpɛ̃, -in] *adj* alpine

alpinisme [alpinism] *nm* mountaineering, climbing; **faire de l'a.** to go mountaineering *or* climbing

alpiniste [alpinist] *nmf* mountaineer, climber

Alsace [alzas] *nf* **l'A.** Alsace

alsacien, -enne [alzasjɛ̃, -ɛn] **1** *adj* of Alsace, Alsatian

  2 *nm,f* **A., Alsacienne** Alsatian

altercation [altɛrkasjɔ̃] *nf* altercation

alter ego [altɛrego] *nm inv* alter ego

altérer [34] [altere] **1** *vt* (**a**) *(détériorer) (viande, vin)* to spoil; *(santé)* to damage (**b**) *(changer)* to affect

  2 s'altérer *vpr (denrée)* to spoil, to go bad; *(sentiment, amitié)* to deteriorate

altermondialisme [altɛrmɔ̃djalism] *nm* alterglobalism, ethical globalization movement

altermondialiste [altɛrmɔ̃djalist] *adj & nmf* alterglobalist

alternance [altɛrnɑ̃s] *nf* alternation; *Pol* change of govern-ment; **en a.** alternately

alternateur [altɛrnatœr] *nm Élec* alternator

alternatif, -ive [altɛrnatif, -iv] **1** *adj* (**a**) *(successif)* & *Élec* al-ternating (**b**) *(de remplacement)* alternative

  2 *nf* **alternative** alternative

alternativement [altɛrnativmɑ̃] *adv* alternately, in turn

alterner [altɛrne] **1** *vt (cultures)* to rotate

  2 *vi (se succéder)* to alternate (**avec** with); *(personnes)* to take turns (**avec** with)

altesse [altɛs] *nf* **son A. royale** His/Her Royal Highness

altier, -ère [altje, -ɛr] *adj* haughty

altimètre [altimɛtr] *nm* altimeter

altitude [altityd] *nf* altitude; **à basse/haute a.** at low/high altitude; **à 100 mètres d'a.** at an altitude of 100 meters; **en a.** at altitude; **prendre de l'a.** to climb

alto [alto] *Mus* **1** *nm (instrument)* viola

  2 *nf (chanteuse)* alto

altruisme [altryism] *nm* altruism

altruiste [altryist] *adj* altruistic

aluminium [alyminjɔm] *nm* aluminum

alunir [alynir] *vi* to land on the moon

alunissage [alynisaʒ] *nm* moon landing

alvéole [alveɔl] *nf (de ruche)* cell; *(pulmonaire)* alveolus; *(de dent)* socket

amabilité [amabilite] *nf* kindness; **auriez-vous l'a. de me le faire savoir?** would you be so kind as to let me know?

amadouer [amadwe] *vt* to coax

amaigrir [amɛgrir] **1** *vt* to make thin; **la maladie l'a beau-coup amaigri** he's much thinner following his illness

  2 s'amaigrir *vpr* to get thinner

amaigrissant, -e [amɛgrisɑ̃, -ɑ̃t] *adj (régime)* slimming

amaigrissement [amɛgrismɑ̃] *nm (involontaire)* weight loss; *(volontaire)* slimming

amalgame [amalgam] *nm* combination

amalgamer [amalgame] *vt (confondre)* to lump together

amanché, -e [amɑ̃ʃe] *adj Can* **mal a.** badly dressed

amande [amɑ̃d] *nf (fruit)* almond; *(dans un noyau)* kernel; **des yeux en a.** almond(-shaped) eyes

amandier [amɑ̃dje] *nm* almond tree

amanite [amanit] *nf* **a. phalloïde** death cap; **a. tue-mouches** fly agaric

amant [amɑ̃] *nm* lover

amarrage [amaraʒ] *nm Naut* mooring

amarre [amar] *nf Naut* (mooring) rope; **rompre ses amarres** to break its moorings

amarrer [amare] *vt Naut* to moor

amaryllis [amarilis] *nf* amaryllis

amas [ama] *nm* heap, pile

amasser [amase] **1** *vt* to amass

  2 s'amasser *vpr (preuves, foule)* to build up; *(neige)* to pile up; *(troupes)* to mass

amateur [amatœr] **1** *nm* (**a**) *(passionné)* **a. de tennis/de jar-dinage** tennis/gardening enthusiast; **a. d'art** art lover; **a. de bons vins** connoisseur of fine wines; *Fig* **est-ce qu'il y a des amateurs?** any takers?; **avis aux amateurs?** anyone inter-ested? (**b**) *(non professionnel)* amateur; **faire de la photo en a.** to be an amateur photographer; *Péj* **c'est du travail d'a.** it's amateurish work

  2 *adj* amateur; **photographe a.** amateur photographer

amateurisme [amatœrism] *nm* amateurism

Amazone [amazon] *nf* **l'A.** the Amazon

amazone [amazon] *nf* (**a**) *(dans la mythologie)* **les Amazones** the Amazons (**b**) *(cavalière)* horsewoman; **monter en a.** to ride sidesaddle

Amazonie [amazoni] *nf* **l'A.** the Amazon (Basin)

amazonien, -enne [amazonjɛ̃, -ɛn] *adj* Amazonian; *(forêt)* Amazon

ambages [ɑ̃baʒ] **sans ambages** *adv* without beating around the bush

ambassade [ɑ̃basad] *nf* embassy; **l'a. de France au Japon** the French embassy in Japan

ambassadeur, -drice [ɑ̃basadœr, -dris] **1** *nm,f* ambas-sador; **l'a. de France au Japon** the French ambassador to Japan; *Fig* **être l'a. de son pays** to be an ambassador for one's country

  2 *nf* **ambassadrice** *(épouse)* ambassador's wife

ambiance [ɑ̃bjɑ̃s] *nf* atmosphere, ambience; *Fam* **mettre de l'a.** to liven things up; *Fam* **il y a de l'a. ici** there's a good atmo-sphere here

ambiant, -e [ɑ̃bjɑ̃, -ɑ̃t] *adj (gaieté, enthousiasme)* pervading; **température ambiante** room temperature

ambidextre [ɑ̃bidɛkstr] *adj* ambidextrous

ambigu, -uë [ɑ̃bigy] *adj* ambiguous

ambiguïté [ɑ̃biguite] *nf* ambiguity; **répondre sans a.** to give an unambiguous answer

ambitieux, -euse [ɑ̃bisjø, -øz] **1** *adj* ambitious

  2 *nm,f* ambitious person

ambition [ɑ̃bisjɔ̃] *nf* ambition; **avoir de l'a.** to be ambitious;

j'ai l'a. de devenir médecin my ambition is to be a doctor

ambitionner [ãbisjɔne] *vt* (**a**) *(poste)* to aspire to; **il ambitionne de gagner le Tour de France** his ambition is to win the Tour de France (**b**) *Can (exagérer)* to overdo it

ambivalent, -e [ãbivalã, -ãt] *adj* ambivalent

ambre [ãbr] *nm (résine)* amber

ambulance [ãbylãs] *nf* ambulance

ambulancier, -ère [ãbylãsje, -ɛr] *nm,f* ambulance man, *f* ambulance woman

ambulant, -e [ãbylã, -ãt] *adj* itinerant, traveling; *Fam* **c'est un dictionnaire a.** he's a walking dictionary

AME [aɛmə] *nm (abrév* **accord monétaire européen)** EMA

âme [ãm] *nf* (**a**) *Rel & Phil* soul; *Fig (animateur)* moving spirit; **être artiste dans l'â.** to have an artistic temperament; **rendre l'â.** to give up the ghost; **aller comme une â. en peine** to wander around like a lost soul; **trouver l'â. sœur** to find one's soul mate; **de toute mon â.** with all my heart; **en mon â. et conscience** to the best of my knowledge and belief (**b**) *(personne)* **une bonne â.** a kind soul; **ils ne rencontrèrent â. qui vive** they didn't meet a (living) soul; **un hameau de cinquante âmes** a hamlet of fifty inhabitants; **â. damnée** devoted servant; *Hum* partner in crime (**c**) *(d'un câble)* core

amélioration [ameljɔrasjõ] *nf* improvement; **apporter des améliorations à qch** to make improvements to sth

améliorer [ameljɔre] **1** *vt* to improve

2 s'améliorer *vpr* to improve; **ça ne s'améliore pas** it's not getting any better

amen [amɛn] *nm inv* amen; *Fig* **dire a. à qch** to go along with sth

aménagement [amenaʒmã] *nm (changement)* adjustment; *(d'une pièce)* conversion (**en** into); *(d'une ville, d'une région)* development; **a. du temps de travail** flexibility of working hours; **a. du territoire** regional development

aménager [45] [amenaʒe] *vt (changer)* to adjust; *(pièce, maison)* to convert (**en** into)

amende [amãd] *nf* (**a**) *(contravention)* fine; **avoir 200 euros d'a.** to get a 200-euro fine (**b**) **faire a. honorable** to apologize

amendement [amãdmã] *nm Pol* amendment

amender [amãde] **1** *vt* (**a**) *(loi, texte)* to amend (**b**) *Suisse (mettre une amende à)* to fine

2 s'amender *vpr* to turn over a new leaf

amener [46] [amne] **1** *vt* (**a**) *(apporter)* to bring; **a. l'eau à ébullition** to bring the water to the boil; **a. qn à faire qch** to get sb to do sth; *(sujet: circonstances)* to lead sb to do sth; **…ce qui nous amène à parler du chômage** …which brings us to the issue of unemployment (**b**) *(occasionner)* to bring about (**c**) *(tirer à soi)* to pull in; *(voile)* to lower

2 s'amener *vpr Fam (arriver)* to turn up; **amène-toi!** come here!

amenuiser [amənɥize] **1** *vt* to wear down

2 s'amenuiser *vpr* to dwindle; *(écart)* to get smaller

amer, -ère [amɛr] *adj* bitter

amèrement [amɛrmã] *adv* bitterly

américain, -e [amerikɛ̃, -ɛn] **1** *adj* American

2 *nm (langue)* American (English)

3 *nm,f* **A., Américaine** American

4 *nf* **américaine** *Culin* **homard à l'américaine** = lobster cooked in a tomato, white wine and brandy sauce

américaniser [amerikanize] **1** *vt* to Americanize

2 s'américaniser *vpr* to become Americanized

américanisme [amerikanism] *nm Ling* Americanism

amérindien, -enne [amerɛ̃djɛ̃, -ɛn] **1** *adj* Amerindian, American Indian

2 *nm,f* **A., Amérindienne** Amerindian, American Indian

Amérique [amerik] *nf* **l'A.** America; **l'A. centrale** Central America; **l'A. latine** Latin America; **l'A. du Nord/du Sud** North/South America

Amerloque [amɛrlɔk] *nmf Fam* Yank

amerrir [amerir] *vi* to make a landing at sea; *(vaisseau spatial)* to splash down

amerrissage [amerisaʒ] *nm* landing at sea; *(d'un vaisseau spatial)* splashdown

amertume [amɛrtym] *nf* bitterness

améthyste [ametist] *nf* amethyst

ameublement [amœbləmã] *nm* (**a**) *(action de meubler)* furnishing (**b**) *(meubles)* furniture; **magasin d'a.** furniture store

ameuter [amøte] *vt (gens)* to bring out; **elle va a. tout le voisinage si elle continue à hurler comme ça!** she'll have the whole neighborhood out if she carries on shouting like that!

ami, -e [ami] **1** *nm,f* friend; **(petit) a.** *(amant)* boyfriend; **(petite) amie** *(maîtresse)* girlfriend; **a. d'enfance** childhood friend; **a. intime** close friend; **les amis des bêtes** animal lovers

2 *adj* friendly; **être a. avec qn** to be friends with sb

amiable [amjabl] *Jur* **1** *adj* amicable

2 à l'amiable *adv* out of court

amiante [amjãt] *nm* asbestos

amical, -e, -aux, -ales [amikal, -o] **1** *adj* friendly; **peu a.** unfriendly

2 *nf* **amicale** association

amicalement [amikalmã] *adv* in a friendly way; *(en fin de lettre)* yours

amidon [amidõ] *nm* starch

amidonner [amidɔne] *vt* to starch

amieuter [amjøte] **s'amieuter** *vpr Can* to improve, to get better

amincir [amɛ̃sir] **1** *vt* to make thinner; **cette robe t'amincit** that dress makes you look thinner

2 s'amincir *vpr* to get thinner

amincissant, -e [amɛ̃sisã, -ãt] *adj (produit, crème)* slimming

amincissement [amɛ̃sismã] *nm (d'une personne)* slimming

aminé, -e [amine] *adj Chim* **acide a.** amino acid

amiral, -aux [amiral, -o] *nm* admiral

amitié [amitje] *nf* (**a**) *(sentiment)* friendship; **avoir de l'a. pour qn** to like sb; **se lier d'a. avec qn** to make friends with sb; **prendre qn en a.** to befriend sb (**b**) *(dans les formules de politesse)* **faites-moi l'a. de le lui dire** would you be so kind as to tell him?; **mes amitiés à votre sœur** my best wishes to your sister; **amitiés, Luc** *(en fin de lettre)* regards *or* yours, Luc

amitieux, -euse [amitjø, -øz] *adj Belg* friendly

ammoniaque [amɔnjak] *nf* ammonia

amnésie [amnezi] *nf* amnesia; **souffrir d'a.** to have amnesia

amnésique [amnezik] **1** *adj* amnesic; **être a.** to have amnesia

2 *nmf* amnesiac

amniocentèse [amnjosɛ̃tɛz] *nf Méd* amniocentesis

amniotique [amnjɔtik] *adj* amniotic

amnistie [amnisti] *nf* amnesty

> ### Amnistie
> Parking fines as well as some prison sentences are traditionally waived by the French president immediately after a presidential election. The latter is known as "la grâce présidentielle".

amnistier [66] [amnistje] *vt* to grant an amnesty to

amocher [amɔʃe] *Fam* **1** *vt (personne)* to beat up; *(objet)* to ruin; **se faire (sérieusement) a.** to get (badly) beaten up

2 s'amocher *vpr* to smash oneself up

amoindrir [amwɛ̃drir] **1** *vt* to diminish

2 s'amoindrir *vpr* to diminish

amollir [amɔlir] **1** *vt* to soften

2 s'amollir *vpr* to soften

amonceler [11] [amɔ̃sle] **1** *vt* to pile up; *(preuves)* to accumulate

2 s'amonceler *vpr* to pile up; *(preuves)* to accumulate

amoncellement [amɔ̃sɛlmɑ̃] *nm (pile)* heap, pile

amont [amɔ̃] *nm* upstream section; *aussi Ind* **en a. (de)** upstream (from); **la Seine en a. de Paris** the Seine above Paris; **les étapes en a. de la production** the pre-production stages

amoral, -e, -aux, -ales [amɔral, -o] *adj* amoral

amorçage [amɔrsaʒ] *nm* **(a)** *Ordinat* booting; **système d'a.** *(d'une bombe)* detonating system **(b)** *(pour pêcher)* baiting

amorce [amɔrs] *nf* **(a)** *(commencement)* beginning **(b)** *(détonateur)* detonator; *(d'une petite arme)* cap; **pistolet à amorces** cap gun **(c)** *(appât)* bait

amorcer [16] [amɔrse] **1** *vt* **(a)** *(commencer)* to begin **(b)** *Ordinat* to boot (up); **a. de nouveau** to reboot **(c)** *(bombe)* to arm **(d)** *(hameçon)* to bait

2 s'amorcer *vpr* **(a)** *(commencer)* to begin; *(tendance)* to develop **(b)** *Ordinat* to boot (up)

amorphe [amɔrf] *adj* lifeless, apathetic

amortir [amɔrtir] *vt* **(a)** *(bruit)* to deaden; *(chute)* to break; *(choc)* to absorb; *(au football)* to trap; *(au tennis)* to kill **(b)** *Fin (dette)* to pay off **(c)** *(rentabiliser)* **il a amorti sa nouvelle voiture en six mois** he recouped the cost of his new car in six months; **le matériel a été amorti dès la première année** the equipment started to pay for itself after the first year

amortissement [amɔrtismɑ̃] *nm* **(a)** *(de matériel)* depreciation **(b)** *(d'un bruit)* deadening; *(d'une chute)* breaking; *(d'un choc)* absorption **(c)** *Fin (d'une dette)* paying off

amortisseur [amɔrtisœr] *nm (d'une voiture)* shock absorber

amour [amur] **1** *nm* **(a)** *(sentiment)* love; **avec a.** lovingly; **être fou d'a. pour qn** to be madly in love with sb; **faire qch par a. pour qn** to do sth out of love for sb; **faire l'a. (avec)** to make love (with); **pour l'a. du Ciel!** for heaven's sake!; **l'a. maternel/filial** a mother's/child's love; **l'a. du prochain** love of one's neighbor; **le grand a.** true love **(b)** *(personne)* **mon a.** my love, my darling; **tu es un a.!** you're an angel!; **quel a. d'enfant!** what an adorable child!

2 *nfpl* **amours** *(vie amoureuse)* love life; **à tes amours!** *(en buvant)* your health!, cheers!; *(quand on éternue)* bless you!

amouracher [amuraʃe] **s'amouracher** *vpr* **s'a. de qn** to become infatuated with sb

amourette [amurɛt] *nf* fling

amoureusement [amurøzmɑ̃] *adv* lovingly

amoureux, -euse [amurø, -øz] **1** *nm,f (amateur)* **un a. de** a lover of; **un a. de la nature** a nature lover

2 *nm,f (petit ami, petite amie)* boyfriend, *f* girlfriend; **un couple d'a.** a pair of lovers

3 *adj (soin, regard)* loving; **vie amoureuse** love life; **tomber a. (de)** to fall in love (with); **être a. de qn** to be in love with sb

amour-propre [amurprɔpr] *nm* self-respect, pride; **elle est blessée dans son a.** her pride is hurt

amovible [amɔvibl] *adj* detachable, removable; *Ordinat (disque dur)* removable

ampère [ɑ̃pɛr] *nm Élec* ampere

amphés [ɑ̃fe] *nfpl Fam* speed

amphétamine [ɑ̃fetamin] *nf* amphetamine

amphi [ɑ̃fi] *nm Fam* lecture hall

amphibie [ɑ̃fibi] *adj* amphibious

amphibien [ɑ̃fibjɛ̃] *nm Zool* amphibian

amphithéâtre [ɑ̃fiteatr] *nm* **(a)** *(d'université)* lecture hall **(b)** *Archit* amphitheater; **en a.** in a semicircle

amphore [ɑ̃fɔr] *nf* urn

ample [ɑ̃pl] *adj (robe, jupe)* full; *(geste)* sweeping; *Fig* **de plus amples renseignements** more detailed information; **jusqu'à plus a. informé** until further information is available

amplement [ɑ̃pləmɑ̃] *adv* amply, fully; **nous avons a. le temps** we have plenty of time; **c'est a. suffisant** it's more than enough

ampleur [ɑ̃plœr] *nf* **(a)** *(d'un vêtement)* fullness; *(d'un geste)* expansiveness **(b)** *(importance)* scale, extent; **prendre de l'a.** to grow in size

ampli [ɑ̃pli] *nm Fam* amp

amplificateur [ɑ̃plifikatœr] *nm* amplifier

amplification [ɑ̃plifikasjɔ̃] *nf (d'un son)* amplification; *(d'une tendance, d'un phénomène)* intensification

amplifier [66] [ɑ̃plifje] **1** *vt (son)* to amplify; *(tendance, phénomène)* to intensify

2 s'amplifier *vpr (son)* to increase; *(tendance, phénomène)* to intensify

amplitude [ɑ̃plityd] *nf* **(a)** *(d'un désastre)* magnitude, scale **(b)** *(d'un geste)* expansiveness **(c)** *(variation)* range; **a. thermique** temperature range **(d)** *(d'une oscillation)* amplitude

ampoule [ɑ̃pul] *nf* **(a)** *(d'une lampe)* (light) bulb; **a. à baïonnette/vis** bayonet/screw-in light bulb **(b)** *(sur la peau)* blister **(c)** *(fiole)* phial

ampoulé, -e [ɑ̃pule] *adj* bombastic

amputation [ɑ̃pytasjɔ̃] *nf* amputation

amputer [ɑ̃pyte] *vt* to amputate; *Fig* to slash; **il fut amputé du bras gauche** his left arm was amputated

Amsterdam [amstɛrdam] *n* Amsterdam

amulette [amylɛt] *nf* amulet

amusant, -e [amyzɑ̃, -ɑ̃t] **1** *adj* amusing, funny; *(divertissant)* entertaining; *(bizarre)* weird

2 *nm* **le plus a., c'est que...** the funniest thing is that...

amuse-gueule [amyzgœl] *nm inv* appetizer

amusement [amyzmɑ̃] *nm* amusement

amuser [amyze] **1** *vt* to amuse; **cette histoire m'a beaucoup amusé** I found the story very amusing; **si tu crois que ça m'amuse!** do you think I enjoy it?

2 s'amuser *vpr (se distraire)* to amuse oneself; **bien s'a.** to have a good time; **s'a. avec qn** to play with sb; **s'a. à faire qch** to amuse oneself doing sth; **faire qch pour s'a.** to do sth for the fun of it

amuseur, -euse [amyzœr, -øz] *nm,f* entertainer

amygdales [amidal] *nfpl* tonsils; **se faire opérer des a.** to have one's tonsils out

an [ɑ̃] *nm* year; **l'an passé** *ou* **dernier** last year; **l'an prochain** next year; **tous les ans** every year; **tous les trois ans** every three years; **en l'an 2000** in the year 2000; **en l'an de grâce 1172** in the year of Our Lord 1172; **dans trois ans** in three years' time, three years from now; **par an** per year; *Fin* per annum; **avoir dix ans** to be ten (years old); **bon an, mal an** on average over the years

anabolisant [anabɔlizɑ̃] *nm* anabolic steroid

anachronique [anakrɔnik] *adj* anachronistic

anachronisme [anakrɔnism] *nm* anachronism

anagramme [anagram] *nf* anagram

anal, -e, -aux, -ales [anal, -o] *adj* anal; *Psy* **stade a.** anal stage

analgésique [analʒezik] *nm* analgesic

anallergique [analɛrʒik] *adj* hypoallergenic

analogie [analɔʒi] *nf* analogy; **par a. avec** by analogy with

analogique [analɔʒik] *adj* **(a)** *(dictionnaire)* analogical **(b)** *Élec* analog

analogue [analɔg] *adj* similar (**à** to)

analphabète [analfabɛt] **1** *adj* illiterate

2 *nmf* illiterate person

analyse [analiz] *nf* **(a)** *(étude)* analysis; **en dernière a.** in the final analysis; **faire l'a. de qch** to analyze sth **(b)** *Méd* test; **a. de sang/d'urine** blood/urine test; **faire une a. de sang** to have a blood test **(c)** *Psy* (psycho)analysis; **faire une a.** to undergo analysis

analyser [analize] *vt* to analyze; *Méd (sang, urine)* to test

analyseur [analizœr] *nm Ordinat* **a. logique** logic analyzer; *Ordinat* **a. syntaxique** parser

analyste [analist] *nmf Ordinat* analyst; *Psy* (psycho)analyst

analyste-programmeur, -euse (*mpl* **analystes-programmeurs**, *fpl* **analystes-programmeuses**) [analist-prɔgramœr, -øz] *nm,f Ordinat* systems analyst

analytique [analitik] *adj* analytical

ananas [anana(s)] *nm* pineapple

anarchie [anarʃi] *nf aussi Fig* anarchy

anarchique [anarʃik] *adj aussi Fig* anarchic

anarchisant, -e [anarʃizɑ̃, -ɑ̃t] *adj* (*discours*) advocating anarchy

anarchisme [anarʃism] *nm* anarchism

anarchiste [anarʃist] *adj & nmf* anarchist

anatomie [anatɔmi] *nf* anatomy

anatomique [anatɔmik] *adj* anatomical

ancestral, -e, -aux, -ales [ɑ̃sɛstral, -o] *adj* ancestral

ancêtre [ɑ̃sɛtr] *nmf* ancestor; *Fam* (*vieillard*) granddad, *f* grandma

anche [ɑ̃ʃ] *nf Mus* reed

anchois [ɑ̃ʃwa] *nm* anchovy

ancien, -enne [ɑ̃sjɛ̃, -ɛn] **1** *adj* (**a**) (*vieux*) old; **livre a.** antiquarian book; **meubles anciens** antique furniture; **dans l'a. temps** in the old days; **je suis plus a. que vous dans la profession** I've been in the profession longer than you (**b**) (*d'autrefois*) (*professeur, voisin*) former, old; (*voiture, maison*) old; **c'est un a. boxeur** he used to be a boxer; **a. combattant** veteran; **a. élève** former student, alumnus, *f* alumna; *Hist* **l'A. Régime** the Ancien Régime
  2 *nm* (**a**) *Rel & Pol* elder (**b**) **l'a.** (*meubles*) antiques; (*immobilier*) old(er) buildings
  3 *nm,f* (*par l'expérience*) **c'est un a. de la maison** he's been with the firm a long time

anciennement [ɑ̃sjɛnmɑ̃] *adv* formerly

ancienneté [ɑ̃sjɛnte] *nf* (**a**) (*âge*) age (**b**) (*expérience*) seniority; **avoir quinze ans d'a.** to have fifteen years' service; **être promu à l'a.** to be promoted by seniority

ancrage [ɑ̃kraʒ] *nm Naut* anchoring

ancre [ɑ̃kr] *nf* anchor; **lever l'a.** to weigh anchor; **jeter l'a.** to anchor

ancrer [ɑ̃kre] **1** *vt* (*navire*) to anchor; **cette idée est profondément ancrée en lui** this idea is firmly rooted in his mind
  2 s'ancrer *vpr Fig* (*idée, concept*) to become rooted

andalou, -se [ɑ̃dalu, -uz] **1** *adj* Andalusian
  2 *nm,f* **A., Andalouse** Andalusian

Andalousie [ɑ̃daluzi] *nf* **l'A.** Andalusia

Andes [ɑ̃d] *nfpl* **les A.** the Andes

andorran, -e [ɑ̃dɔrɑ̃, -an] **1** *adj* Andorran
  2 *nm,f* **A., Andorrane** Andorran

Andorre [ɑ̃dɔr] *nf* Andorra; **la principauté d'A.** the Principality of Andorra

Andorre-la-Vieille [ɑ̃dɔrlavjɛj] *n* Andorra la Vella

andouille [ɑ̃duj] *nf* (**a**) *Culin* chitterlings sausage (**b**) *Fam* (*imbécile*) fool, jerk; **faire l'a.** to play the fool

andouillette [ɑ̃dujɛt] *nf Culin* = small chitterlings sausage

androgyne [ɑ̃drɔʒin] *adj* androgynous

âne [ɑn] *nm* (**a**) (*animal*) donkey; **à dos d'â.** by donkey (**b**) *Fam* (*idiot*) ass; (*ignare*) dunce

anéantir [aneɑ̃tir] *vt* (*ville*) to destroy; (*armée*) to crush; (*espoirs*) to shatter; **la nouvelle l'a anéantie** she was staggered by the news

anéantissement [aneɑ̃tismɑ̃] *nm* (**a**) (*d'une ville, d'un empire*) destruction; (*d'un espoir*) shattering (**b**) (*abattement*) **dans un état d'a. total** completely crushed

anecdote [anɛkdɔt] *nf* anecdote

anecdotique [anɛkdɔtik] *adj* anecdotal

anémie [anemi] *nf* anemia; **faire de l'a.** to have anemia

anémique [anemik] *adj* anemic; *Fig* feeble, weak

anémone [anemɔn] *nf* anemone; **a. de mer** sea anemone

ânerie [ɑnri] *nf* (*paroles*) stupid remark; (*acte*) stupid act; **dire des âneries** to talk nonsense; **faire des âneries** to behave stupidly

ânesse [ɑnɛs] *nf* she-ass

anesthésie [anɛstezi] *nf* anesthesia; **être sous a.** to be under anesthetic; **a. générale/locale** general/local anesthetic

anesthésier [66] [anɛstezje] *vt* to anesthetize

anesthésiste [anɛstezist] *nmf* anesthesiologist

aneth [anɛt] *nm* dill

ange [ɑ̃ʒ] *nm aussi Fig* angel; **un visage d'a.** an angelic face; **mon a.** my darling *or* angel; **être aux anges** to be in seventh heaven; **un a. passe** someone must have walked over my grave; **a. gardien** guardian angel

angélique [ɑ̃ʒelik] **1** *adj* angelic
  2 *nf Culin* angelica

angine [ɑ̃ʒin] *nf* sore throat; **a. de poitrine** angina (pectoris)

angiome [ɑ̃ʒjom] *nm Méd* angioma

anglais, -e [ɑ̃glɛ, -ɛz] **1** *adj* English; (*britannique*) British
  2 *nm* (*langue*) English
  3 *nm,f* **A.** Englishman; (*Britannique*) British man; **Anglaise** Englishwoman; (*Britannique*) British woman; **les A.** the English; (*Britanniques*) the British
  4 *nf* **anglaise** (**a**) *Fam* **filer à l'anglaise** to slip away (**b**) **anglaises** (*boucles*) ringlets

angle [ɑ̃gl] *nm* (**a**) (*d'une pièce, d'une rue, d'une table*) corner; **elle fait l'a. avec la rue du Bac** it intersects the rue du Bac; **la maison qui fait l'a.** the house on the corner (**b**) (*point de vue*) angle (**c**) (*en géométrie*) angle; **a. droit** right angle; **se couper à angles droits** to cross at right angles; *Aut* **a. mort** blind spot

Angleterre [ɑ̃glətɛr] *nf* **l'A.** England; (*Grande-Bretagne*) Britain

anglican, -e [ɑ̃glikɑ̃, -an] *adj & nm,f* Anglican

anglicisme [ɑ̃glisism] *nm* Anglicism

anglo-américain, -e (*mpl* **anglo-américains**, *fpl* **anglo-américaines**) [ɑ̃gloamerikɛ̃, -ɛn] *adj* Anglo-American

anglo-irlandais, -e (*mpl* **anglo-irlandais**, *fpl* **anglo-irlandaises**) [ɑ̃gloirlɑ̃dɛ, -ɛz] *adj* Anglo-Irish

anglo-normand, -e (*mpl* **anglo-normands**, *fpl* **anglo-normandes**) [ɑ̃glonɔrmɑ̃, -ɑ̃d] *adj voir* **île**

anglophone [ɑ̃glofɔn] **1** *adj* English-speaking
  2 *nmf* English speaker

anglo-saxon, -onne (*mpl* **anglo-saxons**, *fpl* **anglo-saxonnes**) [ɑ̃glosaksɔ̃, -ɔn] **1** *adj* (**a**) *Hist* Anglo-Saxon (**b**) (*culture, civilisation etc*) Anglo-American, British and American
  2 *nm,f* **A., Anglo-Saxonne** Anglo-Saxon; **les Anglo-Saxons** (*peuples*) British and American people; *Hist* the Anglo-Saxons

---

Anglo-saxon

Note that the adjective "anglo-saxon" and the noun "Anglo-Saxon" are often used in French to refer to British and American people, culture, customs, etc.: "la musique anglo-saxonne", "la littérature anglo-saxonne".

---

angoissant, -e [ɑ̃gwasɑ̃, -ɑ̃t] *adj* (*nouvelle*) distressing; (*attente*) agonizing; (*film, livre*) frightening; (*situation*) alarming

angoisse [ɑ̃gwas] *nf* anguish, distress; *Méd* **une crise d'a.** an anxiety attack; *Fam* **c'est l'a.!** what a drag!

angoissé, -e [ɑ̃gwase] **1** *adj* anxious
  2 *nm,f* anxious person

angoisser [ɑ̃gwase] **1** *vt* **a. qn** to make sb anxious
  2 *vi Fam* to worry, to get worked up
  3 s'angoisser *vpr* to get anxious; **s'a. pour un rien** to get worked up over nothing

Angola [ãgɔla] *nm* l'A. Angola

angolais, -e [ãgɔlɛ, -ɛz] **1** *adj* Angolan

   2 *nm,f* A., **Angolaise** Angolan

angora [ãgɔra] **1** *nm* (**a**) *(lapin)* angora rabbit; *(chat)* Persian cat (**b**) *(laine)* angora (wool)

   2 *adj* angora

anguille [ãgij] *nf* eel; *Fig* **il y a a. sous roche** there's something going on

angulaire [ãgylɛr] *adj* angular

anguleux, -euse [ãgylø, -øz] *adj (visage)* angular; *(contours)* rugged

anicroche [anikrɔʃ] *nf* hitch, snag; **sans a.** without a hitch

animal, -e, -aux, -ales [animal, -o] **1** *nm aussi Fig* animal; **animaux de boucherie** animals raised for slaughter; **a. domestique** pet; **a. sauvage** wild animal

   2 *adj* animal

animalerie [animalri] *nf Can* pet shop

animalier, -ère [animalje, -ɛr] *adj* **parc a.** safari park; **peintre a.** wildlife painter

animateur, -trice [animatœr, -tris] *nm,f* (**a**) *(des informations)* newscaster; *(d'un jeu télévisé, de variétés)* host; *(d'un débat)* moderator (**b**) *(dans un club)* leader

animation [animasjɔ̃] *nf* (**a**) *(vie)* life; **une ville pleine d'a.** a lively town; **parler avec a.** to speak animatedly; **mettre de l'a. dans une soirée** to liven up a party (**b**) *(divertissement)* event; **faire de l'a.** *(d'une émission de télévision)* to host (**c**) *Cin* animation (**d**) *Météo* **a. satellite** satellite picture

animé, -e [anime] *adj (personne, discussion)* lively, animated; *(rue, quartier)* busy, bustling

animer [anime] **1** *vt* (**a**) *(sujet: désir, ambition)* to drive; **être animé des meilleures intentions** to have the best of intentions (**b**) *(conversation, quartier, soirée)* to liven up (**c**) *(débat)* to moderate; *(jeu télévisé)* to host

   2 s'animer *vpr (personne)* to come to life; *(conversation, soirée)* to get more lively; *(visage)* to light up

animisme [animism] *nm* animism

animosité [animozite] *nf* animosity (**contre** towards), hostility (**contre** towards); **dire qch sans a.** to say sth calmly

anis [ani(s)] *nm (plante)* anise; **(sirop d')a.** aniseed cordial; **(graine d')a.** *(en cuisine)* aniseed; **à l'a.** aniseed-flavored

anisette [anizɛt] *nf* anisette

Ankara [ãkara] *n* Ankara

ankylose [ãkiloz] *nf* stiffness, *Spéc* ankylosis

ankyloser [ãkiloze] **1** *vt* **être ankylosé** to be stiff

   2 s'ankyloser *vpr* to get stiff; *Fig (dans un métier, des habitudes)* to get into a rut

annales [anal] *nfpl* annals; **les a. du bac** = past baccalauréat examination papers (with sample answers); **a. de géographie/littéraires** geographical/literary review; *Fig* **ça restera dans les a.** it will go down in history

anneau, -x [ano] *nm* (**a**) *(cercle, bague)* ring; *(de chaîne)* link; **a. nuptial** *ou* **de mariage** wedding ring *or* band; **a. de rideau** curtain ring; **les anneaux** *(en gymnastique)* the rings (**b**) *(d'un serpent)* coil (**c**) *Astron* ring

année [ane] *nf* year; **Bonne A.!** Happy New Year!; **une a. de vacances** a year's vacation; **d'a. en a.** year by year; **les années 80** the 80s; **en quelle a....?** in what year...?; **l'a. prochaine/dernière** next/last year; **elle entre dans sa trentième a.** she's just turned thirty; **entrer en troisième a. de médecine** to start one's third year at medical school; **a. civile** calendar year; **a. comptable** fiscal year; **a. scolaire** school year; **a. universitaire** academic year

année-lumière *(pl* **années-lumière)** [anelymjɛr] *nf* light year; **à des années-lumière** *(étoile, planète)* light years away; *Fig* **nous sommes à des années-lumière l'un de l'autre** we're light years apart

annexe [anɛks] **1** *nf* (**a**) *(bâtiment)* annex (**b**) *(de lettre)* enclo-

sure; *(de livre, de rapport)* appendix; *(de projet de loi)* rider; *(de loi)* schedule; **en a. veuillez trouver...** please find enclosed...

   2 *adj* (**a**) *(complémentaire)* *(pièces)* enclosed; *(revenus)* supplementary; *(industries)* subsidiary (**b**) *(mineur)* secondary

annexer [anɛkse] **1** *vt* (**a**) *(territoire)* to annex (**b**) *(document)* to append (**à** to); **pièces annexées** *(à une lettre)* enclosures

   2 s'annexer *vpr* **s'a. qch** to get hold of sth for oneself

annexion [anɛksjɔ̃] *nf* annexation

annihilation [aniilasjɔ̃] *nf (d'une ville, d'une armée)* annihilation; *(d'efforts, d'espoirs)* destruction

annihiler [aniile] *vt (ville, armée)* to annihilate; *(efforts, espoirs)* to destroy

anniversaire [anivɛrsɛr] **1** *nm (d'une naissance)* birthday; *(d'une victoire, d'une mort)* anniversary; **bon** *ou* **joyeux a.!** happy birthday!; **gâteau/carte d'a.** birthday cake/card; **a. de mariage** wedding anniversary

   2 *adj* anniversary; **date a.** anniversary

annonce [anɔ̃s] *nf* (**a**) *(déclaration)* announcement; *(par écrit)* notice; *(aux cartes)* declaration, bid; *Fig* sign, indication (**de** of) (**b**) *(publicitaire, de vente)* ad, advertisement; **passer une (petite) a. dans un journal** to put an ad in a newspaper; **petites annonces** want ads; **annonces classées** classified ads

annoncer [16] [anɔ̃se] **1** *vt* (**a**) *(déclarer)* to announce; **a. la nouvelle à qn** to tell sb the news (**b**) *(dans la presse)* *(soldes, exposition)* to advertise (**c**) *(indiquer)* to herald; **cela n'annonce rien de bon** things aren't looking too good (**d**) **a. qn** *(visiteur)* to show sb in; *(lors d'une occasion officielle)* to announce sb; **se faire a.** to give one's name

   2 s'annoncer *vpr* (**a**) *(prévenir de sa visite)* to announce one's arrival (**b**) *(situation)* **cela s'annonce bien/mal** things aren't looking too bad/good; **les négociations s'annoncent difficiles** the negotiations look like they're going to be difficult; **l'avènement de la démocratie s'annonce dans plusieurs pays** there are signs in several countries that democracy is on the way

annonceur [anɔ̃sœr] *nm (de publicité)* advertiser

annonciateur, -trice [anɔ̃sjatœr, -tris] *adj* **signes annonciateurs de crise** signs that a crisis is on the way

Annonciation [anɔ̃sjasjɔ̃] *nf* l'A. the Annunciation

annoncier [anɔ̃sje] *nm Can (feuille d'annonces)* advertisements page

annotation [anɔtasjɔ̃] *nf* annotation; **faire des annotations dans un texte** to annotate a text

annoter [anɔte] *vt* to annotate

annuaire [anɥɛr] *nm (d'un organisme)* yearbook; *(liste d'adresses)* directory; **l'a. du téléphone** *ou* **téléphonique** the telephone directory; **je suis dans l'a.** I'm in the phone book; **a. électronique** electronic telephone directory; **a. des marées** tide table

annuel, -elle [anɥɛl] *adj* annual, yearly

annuellement [anɥɛlmã] *adv* annually, yearly

annuité [anɥite] *nf* (**a**) *(sur un emprunt)* annual repayment (**b**) *Can & Suisse (rente)* annuity

annulaire [anɥlɛr] **1** *nm* ring finger

   2 *adj* annular, ring-shaped

annulation [anylasjɔ̃] *nf* (**a**) *(d'une commande, d'un rendez-vous, de vacances)* cancellation; *(d'une dette)* writing off; *(d'un mariage, d'un contrat)* annulment; *(d'un jugement)* quashing (**b**) *Ordinat* deletion; **a. d'entrée** *(commande)* cancel entry

annuler [anyle] **1** *vt* (**a**) *(commande, rendez-vous, vacances)* to cancel; *(dette)* to write off; *(mariage, contrat)* to annul; *(jugement)* to quash (**b**) *(remplacer)* to supersede (**c**) *Sport (but, essai)* to disallow

   2 s'annuler *vpr* to cancel each other out

anoblir [anɔblir] *vt* to ennoble

anode [anɔd] *nf Élec* anode

anodin, -e [anɔdɛ̃, -in] *adj (remarque)* harmless; *(personne)* insignificant; *(blessure, changement)* slight, minor; *(infection)* mild

anomalie [anɔmali] *nf* anomaly; *Méd* abnormality

ânon [ɑnɔ̃] *nm* little donkey

ânonner [ɑnɔne] *vt* to stumble through; **il a lu le poème en ânonnant** he read the poem haltingly

anonymat [anɔnima] *nm* anonymity; **garder l'a.** to remain anonymous

anonyme [anɔnim] *adj* anonymous; *Fig (décor, intérieur)* impersonal

anorak [anɔrak] *nm* anorak

anorexie [anɔrɛksi] *nf* anorexia; **faire de l'a.** to suffer from anorexia; **a. mentale** anorexia nervosa

anorexique [anɔrɛksik] *adj & nmf* anorexic

anormal, -e, -aux, -ales [anɔrmal, -o] **1** *adj* **(a)** *(non conforme)* abnormal; *(mentalement)* educationally subnormal; **il fait une chaleur anormale** it's abnormally hot **(b)** *(injuste)* unfair; **il est a. que tu sois si peu payé** it's unfair that you're paid so little

    2 *nm,f (mentalement)* educationally subnormal person

anormalement [anɔrmalmã] *adv* abnormally

ANP [aɛnpe] *nm (abrév* **assistant numérique personnel***)* PDA

ANPE [aɛnpeø] *nf (abrév* **Agence nationale pour l'emploi***)* = French state employment agency; **pointer à l'A.** to register as unemployed

anse [ɑ̃s] *nf* **(a)** *(d'une cruche, d'un panier)* handle **(b)** *(crique)* cove

antagonisme [ãtagɔnism] *nm* antagonism

antagoniste [ãtagɔnist] **1** *nmf* antagonist

    2 *adj (opinions, parties)* antagonistic

antalgique [ãtalʒik] *adj & nm Méd* analgesic

antan [ãtã] **d'antan** *adj Litt* of yesteryear

antarctique [ãtarktik] **1** *nm* **l'A.** the Antarctic, Antarctica

    2 *adj* Antarctic

antécédent [ãtesedã] *nm* **(a)** **antécédents** *(d'une personne)* previous history, past record; **il y a des antécédents cancéreux dans ma famille** my family has a history of cancer; **avoir de bons/mauvais antécédents** to have a good/bad record; **antécédents médicaux** medical history **(b)** *Ling* antecedent

Antéchrist [ãtekrist] *nm* Antichrist

antédiluvien, -enne [ãtedilyvjɛ̃, -ɛn] *adj Hum* **ma télévision est antédiluvienne** my television is an antique

anténatal, -e, -als, -ales [ãtenatal] *adj Méd* prenatal, antenatal

antenne [ãtɛn] *nf* **(a)** *(de radio, d'un satellite, d'un robot)* antenna; **être à l'a.** to be on the air; **passer à l'a.** *(émission)* to be broadcast; *(personne)* to be on the television/radio; **rendre l'a.** to hand over; **à vous l'a.** over to you; **hors a.** off the air; **a. parabolique** (satellite) dish **(b)** *(d'un insecte)* antenna, feeler; *Fig* **avoir des antennes** *(de l'intuition)* to have a sixth sense **(c)** *Mil* **a. chirurgicale** field hospital **(d)** *(de société)* branch

antépénultième [ãtepenyltjɛm] *adj* antepenultimate

antérieur, -e [ãterjœr] *adj* **(a)** *(période)* former; *(date)* earlier; *(année)* previous; *(engagement)* prior; **tous ces événements sont antérieurs à la révolution** all these events took place before the revolution; **dans une vie antérieure** in a previous life **(b)** *(muscle)* anterior; *(membre)* fore

anthologie [ãtɔlɔʒi] *nf* anthology

anthracite [ãtrasit] **1** *nm* **(a)** *(minerai)* anthracite **(b)** *(couleur)* charcoal gray

    2 *adj inv* charcoal gray

anthropologie [ãtrɔpɔlɔʒi] *nf* anthropology

anthropologiste [ãtrɔpɔlɔʒist], **anthropologue** [ãtrɔpɔlɔg] *nmf* anthropologist

anthropophage [ãtrɔpɔfaʒ] **1** *nmf* cannibal

    2 *adj* cannibalistic

anti- [ãti] *préf (contre)* anti-

antiacnéique [ãtiakneik] **1** *adj* anti-acne

    2 *nm* acne treatment

antiadhésif, -ive [ãtiadezif, -iv] **1** *adj (revêtement, poêle)* nonstick

    2 *nm* antiadhesive

antiaérien, -enne [ãtiaerjɛ̃, -ɛn] *adj* anti-aircraft

anti-âge [ãtiɑʒ] *adj inv* anti-ageing

antialcoolique [ãtialkɔlik] *adj (ligue)* temperance

antiatomique [ãtiatɔmik] *adj* antinuclear

antiavortement [ãtiavɔrtəmã] *adj inv* pro-life, anti-abortion

antibactérien, -enne [ãtibakterjɛ̃, -ɛn] *adj* antibacterial

antibiotique [ãtibjɔtik] **1** *nm* antibiotic; **être sous antibiotiques** to be on antibiotics

    2 *adj* antibiotic

antiblocage [ãtiblɔkaʒ] *adj inv Aut* **système a. (des roues)** anti-lock brakes

antibrouillard [ãtibrujar] *adj inv & nm Aut* **(phare) a.** fog light

antibruit [ãtibrɥi] *adj inv (mur)* soundproof; **lutte a.** noise-reduction campaign

antibuée [ãtibɥe] *adj inv & nm Aut* **(dispositif) a.** defroster

anticalcaire [ãtikalkɛr] *adj inv* **produit a.** *(pour machine à laver)* water softener

anticancéreux, -euse [ãtikãserø, -øz] *adj* **centre/sérum a.** cancer hospital/serum

anticasseurs [ãtikasœr] *adj inv* **loi a.** = law banning violent behavior during demonstrations

antichambre [ãtiʃãbr] *nf* waiting room, antechamber; *Fig* **dans les antichambres du pouvoir** on the fringes of power

antichar [ãtiʃar] *adj Mil* anti-tank

antichoc [ãtiʃɔk] *adj inv* shock-proof

anticipation [ãtisipasjɔ̃] *nf* anticipation; **payer par a.** to pay in advance; **littérature d'a.** science fiction; **film d'a.** science-fiction movie

anticipé, -e [ãtisipe] *adj (paiement)* advance; *(départ, retour)* early; **avec mes remerciements anticipés** thanking you in advance

anticiper [ãtisipe] **1** *vt (réaction, réponse)* to anticipate; *(action)* to forestall; *(tendance, résultat d'élections)* to forecast; **j'anticipais déjà le pire** I was expecting the worst

    2 *vi* to anticipate, to look *or* to think ahead; *(en sport, aux échecs)* to anticipate what one's opponent will do next; **n'anticipons pas** let's not look too far ahead; **a. sur qch** to anticipate sth

anticlérical, -e, -aux, -ales [ãtiklerikal, -o] *adj & nm,f* anticlerical

anticoagulant, -e [ãtikɔagylã, -ãt] *adj & nm* anticoagulant

anticolonialiste [ãtikɔlɔnjalist] *adj* anti-colonialist

anticommunisme [ãtikɔmynism] *nm* anti-communism

anticommuniste [ãtikɔmynist] *adj & nmf* anti-communist

anticonceptionnel, -elle [ãtikɔ̃sɛpsjɔnɛl] *adj (pilule)* contraceptive

anticonformiste [ãtikɔ̃fɔrmist] *adj & nmf* nonconformist

anticonstitutionnel, -elle [ãtikɔ̃stitysjɔnɛl] *adj* unconstitutional

anticorps [ãtikɔr] *nm* antibody

anticyclone [ãtisiklon] *nm Météo* anticyclone

antidater [ãtidate] *vt* to backdate, to antedate

antidémocratique [ãtidemɔkratik] *adj* undemocratic

antidépresseur [ãtidepresœr] *adj m & nm* antidepressant; **être sous antidépresseurs** to be on antidepressants

antidérapant, -e [ãtiderapã, -ãt] *adj (pneu, route)* non-skid; *(semelle, tapis)* non-slip

anti-discriminatoire [ãtidiskriminatwar] *adj (mesures, politique)* anti-discriminatory

antidopage [ãtidɔpaʒ], **antidoping** [ãtidɔpiŋ] *adj inv Sport* **contrôle a.** drug test

antidote [ãtidɔt] *nm aussi Fig* antidote (**contre** for)

antidumping [ãtidœmpiŋ] *adj inv (loi, législation)* antidumping

antiémeute [ãtiemøt] *adj inv* antiriot; **brigade a.** riot squad

antiesclavagiste [ãtiɛsklavaʒist] **1** *adj* anti-slavery; *Hist* abolitionist
   2 *adj* opponent of slavery; *Hist* abolitionist

antifasciste [ãtifaʃist] *adj & nmf* antifascist

antifongique [ãtifɔ̃ʒik] **1** *adj* fungicidal
   2 *nm* fungicide

antigel [ãtiʒɛl] *nm* antifreeze

antigrippal, -e, -aux, -ales [ãtigripal, -o] *adj* anti-flu

antihéros [ãtiero] *nm* antihero

antihistaminique [ãtiistaminik] *adj & nm Méd* antihistamine

anti-inflammatoire [ãtiɛ̃flamatwar] *adj & nm Méd* anti-inflammatory

anti-inflationniste [ãtiɛ̃flasjɔnist] *adj* anti-inflationary

antillais, -e [ãtijɛ, -ɛz] **1** *adj* West Indian
   2 *nm,f* **A., Antillaise** West Indian

Antilles [ãtij] *nfpl* **les A.** the West Indies

antilope [ãtilɔp] *nf* antelope

antimatière [ãtimatjɛr] *nf Phys* antimatter

antimilitariste [ãtimilitarist] *adj & nmf* antimilitarist

antimite [ãtimit] **1** *adj inv (produit)* moth-repellent; **bombe a.** moth spray
   2 *nm* mothkiller

antimondialisme [ãtimɔ̃djalizasjɔ̃] *nm Pol* antiglobalization

antimondialiste [ãtimɔ̃djalist] *adj & nmf* antiglobalist

antinazi, -e [ãtinazi] *adj & nm,f* anti-Nazi

antinomie [ãtinɔmi] *nf* antinomy

antinucléaire [ãtinyklɛɛr] *adj* anti-nuclear

Antiope® [ãtjɔp] *n* = French teletext system, providing subtitles for the deaf

antioxydant, -e [ãtiɔksidã, -ãt] *adj & nm* antioxidant

antipathie [ãtipati] *nf* antipathy; **avoir** *ou* **éprouver de l'a. pour qn** to dislike sb

antipathique [ãtipatik] *adj* unpleasant; **il m'est très a.** I don't like him at all

antipelliculaire [ãtipelikylɛr] *adj* **shampooing a.** dandruff shampoo

antiphrase [ãtifraz] *nf Ling* antiphrasis

antipodes [ãtipɔd] *nmpl Géog* antipodes; **être aux a. de** to be on the other side of the world from; *Fig* to be the exact opposite of

antipoison [ãtipwazɔ̃] *adj inv Méd* **centre a.** poison-treatment center

antiprotéase [ãtiprɔteaz] *nf Méd* protease inhibitor

antiquaire [ãtikɛr] *nmf* antique dealer

antique [ãtik] *adj (de l'Antiquité)* ancient; *(mobilier)* antique; *Hum (voiture, télévision)* antiquated; **la Grèce/la Rome a.** ancient Greece/Rome

antiquité [ãtikite] *nf* **(a)** *Hist* **l'a. grecque/romaine** ancient Greek/Rome **(b)** **antiquités** *(meubles et objets anciens)* antiques; **magasin d'antiquités** antique store **(c)** **antiquités** *(dans un musée)* antiquities

antirabique [ãtirabik] *adj Méd* anti-rabies

antiracisme [ãtirasism] *nm* anti-racism

antiraciste [ãtirasist] *adj & nm,f* anti-racist

antiradar [ãtiradar] *nm* anti-radar device

antireflet [ãtirəflɛ] *adj inv* non-reflecting; *Ordinat* non-reflecting, antiglare

antirides [ãtirid] *adj inv* anti-wrinkle

antirouille [ãtiruj] **1** *adj inv* rustproofing
   2 *nm* rustproofing agent

antiroulis [ãtiruli] *adj Aut* **barre a.** anti-roll bar

anti-scintillements [ãtisɛ̃tijmã] *adj inv Ordinat* flicker-free

antisèche [ãtisɛʃ] *nf Fam* cheat sheet, pony

antisémite [ãtisemit] **1** *adj* anti-Semitic
   2 *nmf* anti-Semite

antisémitisme [ãtisemitism] *nm* anti-Semitism

antiseptique [ãtisɛptik] *adj & nm* antiseptic

antisocial, -e, -aux, -ales [ãtisɔsjal, -o] *adj* antisocial

antispasmodique [ãtispasmɔdik] *adj & nm Méd* antispasmodic

antitabac [ãtitaba] *adj inv* **lutte** *ou* **campagne a.** anti-smoking campaign

antiterroriste [ãtitɛrɔrist] *adj* anti-terrorist

antithèse [ãtitɛz] *nf* antithesis; *Fig* **être l'a. de** to be the opposite of

antitrust [ãtitrœst] *adj inv* anti-trust

antivariolique [ãtivarjɔlik] *adj Méd* **vaccin a.** smallpox vaccine

antivenimeux, -euse [ãtivənimø, -øz] *adj Méd* antivenin

antivieillissement [ãtivjɛjismã] *nm (produit qui ralentit le vieillissement)* anti-ageing product; **traitement a.** anti-ageing treatment

antivol [ãtivɔl] **1** *adj inv (dispositif)* anti-theft
   2 *nm* anti-theft device

antre [ãtr] *nm (caverne)* cave, cavern; *(d'animaux, de brigands)* den, lair; *Fig (d'une personne)* den

anus [anys] *nm* anus

Anvers [ãvɛr(s)] *n* Antwerp

anxiété [ãksjete] *nf* anxiety; **éprouver de l'a.** to feel anxious; **avec a.** anxiously

anxieux, -euse [ãksjø, -øz] **1** *adj* anxious, worried; **a. de faire qch** anxious to do sth
   2 *nm,f* worrier

anxiolytique [ãksjɔlitik] *Méd* **1** *adj* anxiety-reducing
   2 *nm* tranquillizer

AOC [aɔsɛ] *nf (abrév* **appellation d'origine contrôlée**) = official label guaranteeing the origin and quality of French wine

aorte [aɔrt] *nf* aorta

août [u(t)] *nm* August; **le quinze a.** *(fête)* Assumption Day; *voir aussi* **janvier**

aoûtat [auta] *nm* chigger

aoûtien, -enne [ausjɛ̃, -ɛn] *nm,f* August vacationer

apache [apaʃ] **1** *nm* **A.** Apache
   2 *adj* Apache

apaisant, -e [apɛzã, -ãt] *adj* soothing, calming

apaisement [apɛzmã] *nm (de la douleur)* alleviation; *(calme)* calm

apaiser [apeze] **1** *vt (personne)* to calm (down); *(douleur)* to soothe; *(faim)* to satisfy; *(soif)* to quench; *(craintes)* to allay
   2 s'apaiser *vpr (personne)* to calm down; *(vent, douleur, craintes)* to subside

apanage [apanaʒ] *nm* prerogative; **elle croit avoir l'a. de la sagesse** she thinks she has a monopoly on wisdom

aparté [aparte] *nm* **(a)** *Théât* aside; **en a.** in an aside **(b)** *(entre deux personnes)* private conversation; **en a.** in private

apartheid [apartɛd] *nm* apartheid

apathie [apati] *nf* apathy, listlessness

apathique [apatik] *adj* apathetic, listless

apatride [apatrid] **1** *adj* stateless
   2 *nmf* stateless person

APEC [apɛk] *nf (abrév* **Association pour l'emploi des cadres**) = employment agency for executives and managers

apercevoir [60] [apɛrsəvwar] **1** *vt* to see; *(soudain, rapidement)* to catch sight of; **laisser a. qch** to let sth show

2 s'apercevoir *vpr* **s'a. de qch** *(comprendre, réaliser)* to realize *or* to notice sth; **s'a. que...** to realize *or* to notice that...; **sans s'en a.** inadvertently, without realizing it

aperçu [apɛrsy] *nm (idée générale)* general idea; *Ordinat* **a. avant impression** print preview

apéritif [aperitif] *nm* aperitif; **prendre l'a.** to have a drink before the meal

> ### Apéritif
> In France, the "apéritif", or "apéro", is an informal social ritual. It is quite usual to invite people for before-dinner drinks without actually providing dinner, or to arrange to meet someone in a café "pour l'apéritif" before going out for a meal.

apéro [apero] *Fam* = **apéritif**

apesanteur [apəzɑ̃tœr] *nf* weightlessness; **en (état d')a.** in weightless conditions

à-peu-près [apøprɛ] *nm inv* vague approximation; **il y a trop d'à. dans votre exposé** there is too much vagueness in your report

apeuré, -e [apœre] *adj* frightened, scared

apeurer [apœre] *vt* to frighten, to scare

aphasie [afazi] *nf Méd* aphasia

aphasique [afazik] *adj & nmf Méd* aphasic

aphone [afɔn] *adj Méd* voiceless; **elle était a. d'avoir trop crié** she'd lost her voice because she'd been shouting too much

aphorisme [afɔrism] *nm* aphorism; *Péj* platitude

aphrodisiaque [afrɔdizjak] *adj & nm* aphrodisiac

aphte [aft] *nm* mouth ulcer

aphteux, -euse [aftø, -øz] *adj* **fièvre aphteuse** foot-and-mouth disease

à-pic [apik] *nm inv* sheer face

apiculteur, -trice [apikyltœr, -tris] *nm,f* beekeeper

apiculture [apikyltyr] *nf* beekeeping

apitoiement [apitwamɑ̃] *nm* pity; **pas d'a.!** *(ne sois pas indulgent)* don't feel sorry for him/her/etc!; *(sois sans pitié)* show no mercy!

apitoyer [32] [apitwaje] **1** *vt* **a. qn** to move sb to pity

2 s'apitoyer *vpr* **s'a. sur (le sort de) qn** to feel sorry for sb; **s'a. sur soi-même** *ou* **sur son sort** to feel sorry for oneself

APL [apeɛl] *nf (abrév* **Aide personnalisée au logement)** rent subsidy

aplanir [aplanir] **1** *vt (bois)* to plane; *(route)* to level; *Fig (difficultés)* to iron out

2 s'aplanir *vpr (sol)* to level out

aplati, -e [aplati] *adj (ballon, nez)* flat; *(figure géométrique)* oblate

aplatir [aplatir] **1** *vt (objet)* to flatten; **a. qch à coups de marteau** to hammer sth flat

2 s'aplatir *vpr (coiffure)* to go flat; *(chapeau)* to get flattened; **s'a. contre un mur** to flatten oneself against a wall; *Fig* **s'a. devant qn** to grovel to sb

aplomb [aplɔ̃] *nm* **(a)** *(ligne droite)* perpendicularity; **mettre qch d'a.** to stand sth up straight; **les étagères ne sont pas d'a.** the shelves aren't level; **je ne me sens pas d'a. aujourd'hui** I'm feeling out of sorts today; **remettre qn d'a.** to perk sb up **(b)** *(assurance)* (self-)confidence; *Péj* nerve; *Péj* **il ne manque pas d'a.** he really has a nerve

apnée [apne] *nf* **plonger en a.** to dive without breathing apparatus

apocalypse [apɔkalips] *nf* apocalypse; **l'A.** *(dans la Bible)* the Book of Revelation; *Fig* **une vision d'a.** an apocalyptic vision

apocalyptique [apɔkaliptik] *adj* apocalyptic

apogée [apɔʒe] *nm Astron* apogee; *Fig* **être à l'a. de sa carrière** to be at the height of one's career

apolitique [apɔlitik] *adj* apolitical

apollon [apɔlɔ̃] *nm (bel homme)* Adonis

apologie [apɔlɔʒi] *nf (défense)* apologia (**de** for); *(éloge)* eulogy; **faire l'a. de** *(défendre)* to (seek to) justify; *(louer)* to eulogize

apoplectique [apɔplɛktik] *adj & nmf Méd* apoplectic

apoplexie [apɔplɛksi] *nf Méd* apoplexy; **attaque d'a.** apoplectic seizure, stroke

a posteriori [apɔsterjɔri] *adv* with hindsight

apostolat [apɔstɔla] *nm (métier)* vocation

apostrophe [apɔstrɔf] *nf* **(a)** *(signe, figure de style)* apostrophe **(b)** *(interpellation)* rude remark

apostropher [apɔstrɔfe] **1** *vt (pour attirer l'attention)* to shout to; *(être impoli envers)* to shout at

2 s'apostropher *vpr* to shout at one another

apothéose [apɔteoz] *nf (consécration)* crowning glory; **finir en a.** to end spectacularly

apothicaire [apɔtikɛr] *nm Vieilli* apothecary; *Fig* **tenir des comptes d'a.** to know where every penny goes

apôtre [apotr] *nm* apostle; *Fig* **se faire l'a. de qch** to become an advocate of sth

Appalaches [apalaʃ] *nmpl* **les (monts) A.** the Appalachians

apparaître [20] [aparɛtr] *(aux être)* **1** *vi* **(a)** *(devenir visible)* to appear; **il m'est apparu en rêve** he came *or* appeared to me in a dream **(b)** *(phénomène, espèce)* to appear **(c)** *(vérité, solution)* to become apparent **(d)** *(sembler)* to seem; **il m'apparaît comme le seul capable d'y parvenir** he seems to me to be the only person capable of doing it

2 *v impersonnel* **il apparaît que...** it appears (that)...

apparat [apara] *nm* pomp, show; **tenue d'a.** ceremonial dress; **en grand a.** with great pomp and ceremony

appareil [aparɛj] *nm* **(a)** *(instrument)* apparatus; **a. (dentaire)** *(correctif)* brace; *(dentier)* dentures; **appareils ménagers** household appliances; **a. (photographique), a. photo** camera; **a. photo numérique** digital camera

(b) *(téléphone)* telephone; **Paul à l'a.** Paul speaking; **qui est à l'a.?** who's speaking?

(c) *(avion)* aircraft, plane

(d) *(structure, système)* apparatus; **l'a. de la justice** the legal system; *Pol* **l'a. du parti** the party machine; **a. de production** *(industriel)* production facilities

(e) *Anat* system; **a. digestif/respiratoire** digestive/respiratory system

(f) *Litt ou Hum* **dans le plus simple a.** in one's birthday suit

appareillage [aparɛjaʒ] *nm* **(a)** *Naut* getting under way **(b)** *(matériel)* equipment; *Ind* plant

appareiller [apareje] *vi Naut* to get under way

apparemment [aparamɑ̃] *adv* apparently

apparence [aparɑ̃s] *nf* **(a)** *(aspect extérieur)* appearance, look; **un homme à l'a. négligée/soignée** an untidy-looking/a tidy-looking man; **en dépit des apparences** in spite of appearances **(b)** *(aspect trompeur)* **il ne faut pas se fier aux apparences** appearances can be deceptive; **il a l'air gentil, mais ce n'est qu'une a.** he seems nice, but it's only a façade; **en a.** outwardly; **pour sauver les apparences** to keep up appearances

apparent, -e [aparɑ̃, -ɑ̃t] *adj* **(a)** *(visible)* visible, apparent; **peu a.** hardly noticeable; **sans raison apparente** for no apparent reason **(b)** *(prétendu)* apparent; **sous cette apparente bonté se cache un grand égoïsme** beneath that kind exterior there lies great selfishness

apparenté, -e [aparɑ̃te] *adj* **(a)** *(par le mariage)* related; *(en rapport)* related, connected **(b)** *Pol* **candidat a. à un parti** = candidate who, though not a member of a party, can count on its support in an election

apparenter [aparɑ̃te] **s'apparenter** *vpr (ressembler)* to have something in common (**à** with)

appariteur [aparitœr] *nm (d'université)* campus policeman

apparition [aparisjɔ̃] *nf* (**a**) *(manifestation)* appearance; **faire son a.** *(personne)* to make one's appearance (**b**) *(fantôme)* apparition; **avoir des apparitions** to see things

appartement [apartəmɑ̃] *nm* apartment; *(dans un hôtel)* suite; **vivre en a.** to live in an apartment; **les grands appartements** *(d'un château)* the state apartments

appartenance [apartənɑ̃s] *nf* belonging (**à** to); *(à un parti)* membership (**à** of)

appartenir [70] [apartənir] **appartenir à 1** *vt ind* (**a**) *(être possédé par)* to belong to (**b**) *(faire partie de) (club, parti, espèce)* to belong to, to be a member of; **elle appartient à une famille très riche** she comes from a very wealthy family

2 *v impersonnel* **il appartient au comité de prendre la décision** it is up to the committee to decide

appât [apɑ] *nm (de pêche)* bait; *Fig (du succès)* lure; **l'a. du gain** the lure of money

appâter [apɑte] *vt* (**a**) *(animaux)* to lure; *Fig (personne)* to entice (**b**) *(hameçon)* to bait

appauvrir [apovrir] **1** *vt* to impoverish

2 s'appauvrir *vpr* to get poorer; *(sol, langue)* to become impoverished

appeau, -x [apo] *nm* birdcall *(instrument)*

appel [apɛl] *nm* (**a**) *(invitation, sollicitation)* appeal; **faire a. à qn** to appeal to sb; *(plombier, médecin)* to send for sb; **faire a. à la générosité de qn** to appeal to sb's generosity; **cette formation fait a. à des connaissances commerciales** this training course calls for some knowledge of business; **faire a. à ses souvenirs** to search one's memory; **un a. à la révolte** a call to revolt; *Com* **lancer un a. d'offres** to invite bids

(**b**) *(cri)* call; **a. au secours** call for help; **faire un a. de phares à qn** to blink one's headlights at sb; *Fig* **a. du pied** veiled hint

(**c**) *(attirance)* call; **l'a. du large/de la nature** the call of the sea/of the wild; **a. d'air** *(courant d'air)* draft

(**d**) **a. (téléphonique)** (tele)phone call; **a. gratuit** toll-free call; **a. en PCV,** *Can* **a. à frais virés** collect call

(**e**) *(pour vérifier) Mil & Scol* **faire l'a.** to call the roll call; **manquer/répondre à l'a.** to be absent/present

(**f**) *Jur* appeal; **faire a. d'une décision** to appeal (against) a decision; *Fig* **être sans a.** *(décision)* to be final

(**g**) *Typ* **a. de note** reference figure

(**h**) *(pour sauter)* take-off

(**i**) *Ordinat* call; *(de commande)* selection

appelé [aple] *nm* (**a**) *Mil* conscript (**b**) *Fig* **il y a beaucoup d'appelés, mais peu d'élus** many are called, but few are chosen

appeler [9] [aple] **1** *vt* (**a**) *(personne, chien)* to call (to); *(taxi)* to hail; **a. (qn) au secours** to call (to sb) for help; **il arrive qu'il appelle la nuit** he sometimes calls out during the night

(**b**) **a. qn (au téléphone)** to call sb (up); **a. un taxi/un médecin** to call (for) a taxi/a doctor; **laisse-la a. la première** wait for her to call you

(**c**) *(faire venir)* to send for; *(ascenseur)* to call; **faire a. un médecin** to send for a doctor; **a. qn à faire qch** *(inviter)* to call on sb to do sth; *aussi Hum* **le devoir t'appelle** duty calls

(**d**) *(désigner)* to call

(**e**) **être appelé à faire qch** *(être destiné à)* to be destined to do sth; *(avoir l'obligation de)* to be called upon to do sth

(**f**) *(demander, réclamer) (solution, mesures)* to call for; *(critique)* to invite

2 en appeler à *vt ind* to appeal to

3 s'appeler *vpr* (**a**) *(avoir pour nom)* to be called; **comment vous appelez-vous?** what's your name?; **je m'appelle David** my name's David (**b**) *(se téléphoner)* to call each other; **alors, on s'appelle, hein?** talk to you on the phone, okay?

appellation [apɛlasjɔ̃] *nf* name; *(de produit)* designation; **a. contrôlée** *(de vin)* guaranteed quality; **a. d'origine** = official guarantee of wine origin and quality

appendice [apɛ̃dis] *nm* (**a**) *Anat* appendix; *Zool & Bot* appendage (**b**) *(d'un livre)* appendix

appendicite [apɛ̃disit] *nf* appendicitis; **avoir l'a.** *ou* **une crise d'a.** to have appendicitis; **se faire opérer de l'a.** to have one's appendix out

appesantir [apəzɑ̃tir] **1** *vt (démarche)* to slow down; **les paupières appesanties par le sommeil** eyes heavy with sleep

2 s'appesantir *vpr (démarche)* to slow down; *Fig* **s'a. sur qch** *(sujet)* to dwell at length on sth

appétissant, -e [apetisɑ̃, -ɑ̃t] *adj (nourriture)* appetizing, tempting; *Hum (personne)* attractive

appétit [apeti] *nm* (**a**) *(de nourriture)* appetite; **couper l'a. à qn** to spoil sb's appetite; **donner de l'a. à qn, mettre qn en a.** to give sb an appetite; **perdre l'a.** to lose one's appetite; **manger de bon a.** to tuck in; **avoir un a. d'oiseau** to have a poor appetite; **avoir bon** *ou* **un gros a.** to have a good appetite; **bon a.!** enjoy your meal!; *Prov* **l'a. vient en mangeant** = it's only when you start eating that you realize you're hungry (**b**) *(désir) (de culture, de connaissances)* appetite (**de** for)

applaudimètre [aplodimɛtr] *nm* applause meter

applaudir [aplodir] **1** *vt* to applaud

2 *vi* to applaud, to clap

3 applaudir à *vt ind (décision, changement)* to applaud

applaudissements [aplodismɑ̃] *nmpl* applause, clapping; **un tonnerre** *ou* **une tempête d'a.** thunderous applause

applicable [aplikabl] *adj* applicable (**à** to)

applicateur [aplikatœr] *nm (dispositif)* applicator

application [aplikasjɔ̃] *nf* (**a**) *(de peinture, de pommade)* application (**b**) *(d'un règlement) (de la loi, d'une peine)* enforcement; **mettre une théorie en a.** to put a theory into practice; **mettre une loi en a.** to enforce a law; **entrer en a.** to come into force (**c**) *(emploi)* application (**d**) *(assiduité)* application; **travailler avec a.** to apply oneself to one's work (**e**) *Ordinat* application

applique [aplik] *nf (lampe)* wall light

appliqué, -e [aplike] *adj* (**a**) *(personne)* hard-working, diligent; *(écriture)* careful (**b**) *(sciences)* applied

appliquer [aplike] **1** *vt* (**a**) *(mettre)* to apply (**sur** to) (**b**) *(utiliser)* to apply (**à** to); *(loi, peine)* to enforce

2 s'appliquer *vpr* (**a**) *(se concentrer)* to apply oneself (**à** to); **s'a. à faire qch** to take pains to do sth (**b**) **s'a. à** *(concerner)* to apply to (**c**) *(se placer)* to be applied; **cette crème doit s'appliquer avant le coucher** this cream should be applied before going to bed

appoint [apwɛ̃] *nm* (**a**) *(monnaie)* exact money *or* change; **faire l'a.** to give the exact money (**b**) *(revenu supplémentaire)* extra income; **d'a.** *(chauffage, éclairage)* additional

appointements [apwɛ̃tmɑ̃] *nmpl* salary

apport [apɔr] *nm* (**a**) *(contribution)* contribution (**à** to); *Fin* **a. en capital/numéraire** capital/cash contribution; **a. calorique** *(d'un aliment)* calorie content

apporter [apɔrte] *vt* (**a**) *(porter)* to bring (**à** to); *(capitaux)* to bring in; **je t'ai apporté le DVD** I brought you the DVD (**b**) *(mettre)* **a. du soin à faire qch** to exercise care in doing sth (**c**) *(bonheur, soulagement)* to bring (**à** to); *(preuve)* to provide; *(changements)* to bring about; **ce travail ne m'apporte pas grand-chose** I don't get very much out of this work

apposer [apoze] *vt (affiche)* to put up; *(signature, scellés, sceau)* to affix (**à** to)

apposition [apozisjɔ̃] *nf* (**a**) *(d'un sceau, de scellés, de signature)* affixing (**à** to) (**b**) *Gram* apposition; **en a.** in apposition

appréciable [apresjabl] *adj* (**a**) *(visible)* appreciable, noticeable (**b**) *(non négligeable)* considerable, appreciable (**c**) *(agréable) (qualités)* praiseworthy; *(changement)* welcome

appréciation [apresjasjɔ̃] nf (**a**) (évaluation) valuation (**b**) (opinion) judgment, opinion; (sur devoir scolaire) comment; **laisser qch à l'a. de qn** to leave sth to sb's discretion (**c**) (augmentation de valeur) appreciation

apprécier [66] [apresje] **1** vt (**a**) (température, distance, son) to estimate; (différences, nuances) to appreciate; **tu ne l'apprécies pas à sa juste valeur** you don't appreciate her true worth (**b**) (aimer) to like; Fam **elle n'a pas apprécié** she wasn't too pleased

2 s'apprécier vpr (**a**) (personnes) to like each other (**b**) (monnaie) to appreciate

appréhender [apreɑde] vt (**a**) Jur (arrêter) to arrest, to apprehend (**b**) (craindre) to dread; **a. de faire qch** to dread doing sth (**c**) (comprendre) to grasp

appréhensif, -ive [apreɑsif, -iv] adj apprehensive

appréhension [apreɑsjɔ̃] nf (crainte) apprehension (**de** about); **avoir une a.** to be apprehensive

apprendre [58] [aprɑ̃dr] **1** vt (**a**) (leçon, langue, instrument de musique) to learn; **a. à faire qch** to learn how to do sth; **a. vite/lentement** to be a fast/slow learner

(**b**) (nouvelle) to hear; (mort, mariage) to hear of; **a. que...** to hear that...

(**c**) (enseigner) **a. qch à qn** to teach sb sth; **a. à qn à faire qch** to teach sb how to do sth; Fam **je t'apprendrai à me parler sur ce ton!** I'll teach you to speak to me like that!; Fam **ça vous apprendra!** that'll teach you!

(**d**) (informer de) **a. qch à qn** to tell sb sth; **vous ne m'apprenez rien!** you're telling me!

(**e**) Belg (former) to train

2 s'apprendre vpr **ça s'apprend vite** it can be learned quickly; **ça s'apprend facilement** it's easy to learn

apprenti, -e [aprɑ̃ti] nm,f apprentice; **a. menuisier** carpenter's apprentice; Fig **jouer les apprentis sorciers** to bite off more than one can chew

apprentissage [aprɑ̃tisaʒ] nm (**a**) (professionnel) training; (chez un artisan) apprenticeship; **être en a. chez qn** to be apprenticed to sb (**b**) (d'une matière, d'une langue) **l'a. de qch** learning sth; Fig **faire l'a. de qch** to learn about sth

apprêté, -e [aprete] adj (style, attitude) affected

apprêter [aprete] **1** vt (**a**) (repas) to prepare (**b**) (tissu, cuir) to finish

2 s'apprêter vpr (se préparer) to get ready; **s'a. à faire qch** to get ready to do sth

apprivoisé, -e [aprivwaze] adj tame

apprivoiser [aprivwaze] **1** vt (animal) to tame; Fig (personne) to win over

2 s'apprivoiser vpr (animal) to become tame; Fig (personne) to become more sociable

approbateur, -trice [aprɔbatœr, -tris] adj approving

approbation [aprɔbasjɔ̃] nf approval (**de** of); **soumettre qch à l'a. de qn** to submit sth to sb for approval; **le film a reçu l'a. du public** the movie was well received by the public; **pour a.** (sur document) for approval

approchant [aprɔʃɑ̃] adj m **je n'ai jamais rien vu d'a.** I've never seen anything like it; **voilà ce qu'il a dit ou quelque chose d'a.** that's what he said, or something similar

approche [aprɔʃ] nf (**a**) (dans le temps) approach; **à l'a. de la vieillesse** as old age draws/drew near; **aux approches de la trentaine elle a voulu avoir des enfants** as she approached thirty she wanted children (**b**) (dans l'espace) **à son a.** as she approached; Fig **d'une a. difficile** (personne) unapproachable; (livre) hard to understand (**c**) (d'une question, d'un problème) approach (**de** to) (**d**) **approches** (d'une ville, d'un village) outskirts (**e**) Aviat approach

approcher [aprɔʃe] **1** vt (**a**) (mettre plus près) to bring closer; **a. qch de qn/qch** to bring sth near (to) sb/sth (**b**) (venir près de) to approach, to get closer to; (aborder) to go up to

2 vi (**a**) (dans l'espace, dans le temps) to approach, to get closer;

l'heure ou le moment approche it will soon be time; **la nuit approchait** it was beginning to get dark; **approche, je vais te montrer quelque chose** come (over) here, I've got something to show you; **a. de qn/qch** to approach sb/sth; **a. du but** to be nearing one's goal; **il approche de la trentaine** he's nearing thirty (**b**) Fig **a. de qch** (être semblable à) to be close to sth

3 s'approcher vpr to approach, to get closer; **s'a. de qn/qch** to approach sb/sth; Fig **s'a. de qch** (être semblable à) to be close to sth

approfondi, -e [aprɔfɔ̃di] adj (recherche) detailed, extensive; (connaissances, enquête) thorough, in-depth

approfondir [aprɔfɔ̃dir] vt (examiner) to go into thoroughly

approprié, -e [aprɔprije] adj appropriate (**à** for)

approprier [66] [aprɔprije] **1** vt Belg (nettoyer) to clean; (ranger) to tidy

2 s'approprier vpr **s'a. qch** to appropriate sth

approuver [apruve] vt (**a**) (décision, choix) to approve of; **a. qn (d'avoir fait qch)** to think sb is right (to have done sth) (**b**) (facture, contrat, projet de loi) to approve

approvisionnement [aprɔvizjɔnmɑ̃] nm (**a**) (ravitaillement) (d'une ville, d'une armée) supplying (**en** with); (d'un magasin) stocking (**en** with) (**b**) **approvisionnements** (stocks) supplies

approvisionner [aprɔvizjɔne] **1** vt (**a**) (ville, armée, personne) to supply (**en** with); (magasin) to stock (**en** with) (**b**) (compte bancaire) to deposit money into; **son compte en banque n'est plus approvisionné** his/her bank account is no longer in credit

2 s'approvisionner vpr to get in supplies (**en** of); **s'a. chez qn** to get one's supplies from sb; (faire ses courses) to shop at sb's

approximatif, -ive [aprɔksimatif, -iv] adj (calcul, estimation) approximate; **dans un anglais a.** in broken English

approximation [aprɔksimasjɔ̃] nf approximation

approximativement [aprɔksimativmɑ̃] adv approximately

appt (abrév **appartement**) apartment

appui [apɥi] nm (**a**) (support) support; **prendre a. sur qch** (personne) to lean on sth; **prendre a. sur le pied gauche** (pour sauter) to take off from the left foot; **a. de fenêtre** window ledge or sill (**b**) (moral) support, backing; **à l'a. de qch** in support of sth; **preuves à l'a.** with supporting evidence

appui-tête (pl **appuis-tête**) [apɥitɛt] nm headrest

appuyé, -e [apɥije] adj (plaisanterie, ironie) labored; **il lui lançait des regards appuyés** he stared at him intently

appuyer [32] [apɥije] **1** vt (**a**) (poser) to lean, to rest (**contre** against) (**b**) (appliquer) **a. qch sur qch** to press sth on sth; **a. le pied sur la pédale de frein** to put one's foot on the brake (**c**) Fig (demande, pétition, candidat) to support, to back; (proposition) to second

2 vi (**a**) (presser) to press; **a. sur un bouton** to press a button (**b**) **a. sur** (accentuer) (mot, syllabe) to stress; Fig (insister) to emphasize, to stress

3 s'appuyer vpr (**a**) (reposer) **s'a. sur/contre** to lean on/against; Fig **s'a. sur qch** (être basé sur) to be based on sth; (se servir de) to draw on sth (**b**) Fam **s'a. qch** (corvée) to get saddled with sth

âpre [ɑpr] adj (**a**) (aigre) bitter; (vin) rough (**b**) (vent) raw (**c**) (concurrence) fierce; **être â. au gain** to be money-grubbing

âprement [ɑprəmɑ̃] adv fiercely

après [apre] **1** prép (**a**) (dans le temps, dans l'espace) after; **jour a. jour** day after day; **a. s'être rasé** after shaving; **a. vous, Monsieur/Madame!** after you!; Fam **courir a. qn** to run after sb; Fig (faire la cour à) to chase sb; **il est toujours a. moi** he's always nagging me; Fam **en avoir a. qn** to have it in for sb; **a. coup** after the event; **a. tout** after all (**b**) **d'a.** (selon) according to; **d'a. moi** in my opinion; **d'a. l'article 12** under article 12

2 *adv* afterward; **six semaines a.** six weeks later; **a. que** after, when; **avec lui, la famille, ça passe a.** his family takes second place; **le jour d'a.** the next *or* following day; **et a.?** *(que s'est-il passé?)* what happened next?; *Fam* **et (puis) a.?** so what?

après- [aprɛ] *préf* post-; **l'a.-68** the post-1968 period; **l'a.-Gorbatchev** the post-Gorbachev era

après-demain [aprɛdəmɛ̃] *adv* the day after tomorrow

après-guerre *(pl* **après-guerres)** [aprɛgɛr] *nm* postwar period

après-midi [aprɛmidi] *nm inv ou nf inv* afternoon; **trois heures de l'a.** three (o'clock) in the afternoon

après-rasage *(pl* **après-rasages)** [aprɛrazaʒ] *nm & adj inv* aftershave

après-ski *(pl* **après-skis)** [aprɛski] *nm* snowboot

après-soleil [aprɛsɔlɛj] *adj inv voir* **lait**

après-vente [aprɛvɑ̃t] *adj inv* Com **service a.** aftersales service

âpreté [ɑprəte] *nf* **(a)** *(aigreur)* bitterness; *(du vin)* roughness **(b)** *(du vent)* rawness **(c)** *(de la concurrence)* fierceness

a priori [aprijɔri] **1** *adv* in principle

2 *nm inv* preconception; **avoir des a. (contre/en faveur de qch)** to be prejudiced (against/in favor of sth); **être sans a.** to be impartial

apr. J.-C. *(abrév* **après Jésus-Christ)** AD; **en 55 apr. J.-C.** in 55 AD

à-propos [aprɔpo] *nm (d'une remarque, d'une réaction)* appropriateness; **avoir l'esprit d'à.** to have presence of mind; **répondre avec à.** to give an appropriate reply

apte [apt] *adj* **a. à qch/à faire qch** fit for sth/for doing sth; *Mil* **a. au service** fit for military service

aptitude [aptityd] *nf (capacité)* aptitude, ability (**à** *ou* **pour** for)

Aquagym® [akwaʒim] *nf* aquarobics *(singulier)*

aquaplanage [akwaplanaʒ], **aquaplaning** [akwaplaniŋ] *nm Aut* aquaplaning

aquarelle [akwarɛl] *nf* watercolor; **peindre à l'a.** to paint in watercolors

aquarelliste [akwarelist] *n* watercolorist

aquarium [akwarjɔm] *nm* aquarium

aquatique [akwatik] *adj* aquatic

aqueduc [akədyk] *nm* aqueduct

aqueux, -euse [akø, -øz] *adj Anat & Chim* aqueous; *(soupe)* watery

aquilin, -e [akilɛ̃, -in] *adj* aquiline

Aquitaine [akitɛn] *nf* l'A. Aquitaine

arabe [arab] **1** *adj (monde, littérature, pays)* Arab, Arabic; *(chiffres, langue)* Arabic; *(cheval)* Arab; *(coutumes, civilisation)* Arabian, Arabic

2 *nm (langue)* Arabic

3 *nmf* A. Arab

> **Arabe**
> Note that in a French context this word usually refers to people from the former colonies of North Africa, who make up the largest ethnic minority in France.

arabesque [arabɛsk] *nf* arabesque

arabica [arabika] *nm* arabica

Arabie [arabi] *nf* l'A. Arabia; l'A. **saoudite** Saudi Arabia

arable [arabl] *adj* arable

arachide [araʃid] *nf (plante)* peanut; **huile d'a.** peanut oil

araignée [arɛɲe] *nf* spider; *Fam* **avoir une a. au plafond** to have a screw loose; **a. de mer** spider crab

Aral [aral] *n voir* **mer**

arbalète [arbalɛt] *nf* crossbow

arbitrage [arbitraʒ] *nm* **(a)** *(au tennis)* umpiring; *(au football)* refereeing **(b)** *(dans un conflit)* arbitration

arbitraire [arbitrɛr] *adj* arbitrary

arbitrairement [arbitrɛrmɑ̃] *adv* arbitrarily

arbitre [arbitr] *nm* **(a)** *(au tennis)* umpire; *(au football)* referee **(b)** *(dans un conflit)* arbitrator **(c)** *Phil* **libre a.** free will

arbitrer [arbitre] *vt* **(a)** *(match de tennis)* to umpire; *(match de football)* to referee **(b)** *(dans un conflit)* to arbitrate

arborer [arbore] *vt (porter, exhiber)* to wear, to sport

arborescence [arborɛsɑ̃s] *nf Math & Ordinat* tree diagram

arborescent, -e [arborɛsɑ̃, -ɑ̃t] *adj* **(a)** *Bot* arborescent **(b)** *Math & Ordinat* **structure arborescente** tree diagram

arboriculteur, -trice [arborikyltœr, -tris] *nm,f* tree grower

arboriculture [arborikyltyr] *nf* tree growing

arbre [arbr] *nm* **(a)** *(végétal)* tree; *Fig* **les arbres cachent la forêt** you can't see the wood for the trees; **a. fruitier** fruit tree; **a. de Noël** Christmas tree **(b)** **a. généalogique** family tree; **faire son a. généalogique** to trace one's family tree **(c)** *Tech* shaft; **a. à cames** camshaft; **a. de transmission** transmission shaft

arbrisseau, -x [arbriso] *nm* shrub

arbuste [arbyst] *nm* shrub

arc [ark] *nm* **(a)** *(arme)* bow **(b)** *Archit & Anat* arch; **a. de triomphe** triumphal arch **(c)** *(de cercle)* arc; **assis en a. de cercle** sitting in a semicircle

arcade [arkad] *nf* **(a)** *Archit* archway; **arcades** *(d'une place)* arcade **(b)** *Anat* **a. sourcilière** arch of the eyebrows

arc-bouter [arkbute] **s'arc-bouter** *vpr* to brace oneself

arceau, -x [arso] *nm* **(a)** *(d'une voûte)* arch **(b)** *(au croquet)* hoop **(c)** *Aut* **a. de sécurité** roll bar

arc-en-ciel *(pl* **arcs-en-ciel)** [arkɑ̃sjɛl] *nm* rainbow

archaïque [arkaik] *adj* archaic

archaïsme [arkaism] *nm* archaism

archange [arkɑ̃ʒ] *nm* archangel

arche[1] [arʃ] *nf* **l'a. de Noé** Noah's ark

arche[2] [arʃ] *nf (d'un pont)* arch

archéologie [arkeɔlɔʒi] *nf* archeology, archaeology

archéologique [arkeɔlɔʒik] *adj* archeological, archaeological

archéologue [arkeɔlɔg] *nmf* archeologist, archaeologist

archer [arʃe] *nm* archer

archet [arʃɛ] *nm* bow *(for violin)*

archétype [arketip] *nm* archetype; **c'est l'a. du père de famille** he is the archetypal father figure

archevêque [arʃəvɛk] *nm* archbishop

archiconnu, -e [arʃikɔny] *adj Fam* very well-known

archiduc [arʃidyk] *nm* archduke

archiduchesse [arʃidyʃɛs] *nf* archduchess

archifaux, -fausse [arʃifo, -fos] *adj Fam* dead wrong

Archimède [arʃimɛd] *npr* Archimedes

archipel [arʃipɛl] *nm* archipelago

architecte [arʃitɛkt] *nm* architect; *Ordinat* **a. de réseaux** network architect

architectural, -e, -aux, -ales [arʃitɛktyral, -o] *adj* architectural

architecture [arʃitɛktyr] *nf aussi Ordinat* architecture; *Fig* structure

architecturé, -e [arʃitɛktyre] *adj Ordinat* **a. autour de** with its architecture built around

archiver [arʃive] *vt (documents officiels)* to archive; *(factures)* to file

archives [arʃiv] *nfpl* archives, records; **les a. nationales** ≃ the National Archives

archiviste [arʃivist] *nmf* archivist; *(employé de bureau)* filing clerk

arçon [arsɔ̃] *nm* saddlebow

arctique [arktik] **1** *adj* arctic
2 *nm* **l'A.** the Arctic

ardemment [ardamɑ̃] *adv (aimer)* passionately; **désirer a. qch** to long for sth

ardent, -e [ardɑ̃, -ɑ̃t] *adj* (a) *(braises, soleil)* scorching, blazing; *(soif, fièvre)* raging (b) *(tempérament, jeunesse)* fiery; *(désir)* burning; *(lutte, défenseur)* fierce; *(admirateur)* ardent, fervent

ardeur [ardœr] *nf* (a) *(enthousiasme)* ardor, fervor; **travailler avec a.** to work enthusiastically (b) *(du soleil, du feu)* intense heat

ardoise [ardwaz] *nf* (a) *(matière, plaque, pour écrire)* slate; **toit d'ardoises** slate roof (b) *Fam (compte)* tab; **il a des ardoises dans tous les bars de la ville** he owes money in every bar in town

ardu, -e [ardy] *adj* arduous
are [ar] *nm* are, = 100 m²

aréna [arena] *nf Can* = sports center including an ice rink

arène [arɛn] *nf (d'amphithéâtre)* arena; *(de tauromachie)* bull-ring; **arènes** *(antiques)* amphitheater; *Fig* **descendre dans l'a.** to enter the fray; *Fig* **l'a. politique** the political arena

arête [arɛt] *nf* (a) *(de poisson)* bone; **sans arêtes** boneless; **enlever les arêtes d'un poisson** to fillet a fish (b) *(du nez)* bridge (c) *(d'un solide)* edge (d) *Géog* ridge

argent [arʒɑ̃] **1** *nm* (a) *(métal)* silver; **bracelet d'a.** *ou* **en a.** silver bracelet (b) *(monnaie)* money; **en avoir pour son a.** to get one's money's worth; *Fig* **prendre qch pour a. comptant** to take sth at face value; *Prov* **l'a. ne fait pas le bonheur** money can't buy you happiness; *Prov* **l'a. n'a pas d'odeur** it's all money; **a. liquide** cash; **a. de poche** pocket money; **a. électronique, a. virtuel** e-cash, electronic money (c) *(couleur)* silver
2 *adj inv* silver

argenté, -e [arʒɑ̃te] *adj* (a) *(couleur)* silver (b) *(plaqué)* silver-plated

argenterie [arʒɑ̃tri] *nf* (silver) plate, silverware

argentin, -e [arʒɑ̃tɛ̃, -in] **1** *adj* Argentinian
2 *nm,f* **A., Argentine** Argentinian

Argentine [arʒɑ̃tin] *nf* **l'A.** Argentina

argile [arʒil] *nf* clay

argileux, -euse [arʒilø, -øz] *adj* clayey

argot [argo] *nm* slang

> **Argot**
> This term can refer both to "la langue verte" (the slang of the underworld) or the jargon of particular social or professional groups (such as butchers, soldiers, students, etc.). Some "argot" has evolved from being part of the secret language of a select group to becoming part of everyday speech, while other terms have become obsolete, supplanted by **verlan** (*see box at this entry*), the slang used by young people in the suburbs of big cities.

argotique [argɔtik] *adj* slang, slangy

arguer [arge, argɥe] **arguer de** *vt ind Litt* **a. de qch** to give sth as a reason

argument [argymɑ̃] *nm* argument; **a. de vente** selling point

argumentaire [argymɑ̃tɛr] *nm* sales blurb

argumentation [argymɑ̃tasjɔ̃] *nf (arguments)* argument

argumenter [argymɑ̃te] *vi* to argue (**contre/en faveur de** against/for)

argus [argys] *nm* = guide to used car prices

aria [arja] *nf Mus* aria

aride [arid] *adj (pays)* arid, barren; *(œuvre, sujet)* dry

aridité [aridite] *nf* aridity, barrenness

aristocrate [aristɔkrat] *nmf* aristocrat

aristocratie [aristɔkrasi] *nf* aristocracy

aristocratique [aristɔkratik] *adj* aristocratic

Aristote [aristɔt] *npr* Aristotle

arithmétique [aritmetik] **1** *adj* arithmetical
2 *nf (matière, calculs)* arithmetic

arlequin [arləkɛ̃] *nm Théât* Harlequin

armagnac [armaɲak] *nm* Armagnac

armateur [armatœr] *nm* shipowner

armature [armatyr] *nf* framework; *(dans le béton)* reinforcement; *(de tente, d'abat-jour)* frame; *(de soutien-gorge)* underwiring

arme [arm] *nf* (a) *(de combat)* arm, weapon; *Fig* weapon; **peuple/ville en armes** nation/town in arms; **prendre les armes** to take up arms (**contre** against); **aux armes!** to arms!; **le métier** *ou* **la carrière des armes** the military profession; **passer qn par les armes** to send sb to the firing squad; *Fam* **passer l'a. à gauche** to kick the bucket, to buy the farm; **faire ses premières armes** to earn one's spurs; **à armes égales** on equal terms; **avec armes et bagages** with bag and baggage; **a. biologique** biological weapon; **a. blanche** knife; **armes de destruction massive** weapons of mass destruction; **a. à feu** firearm; **a. nucléaire** nuclear weapon (b) *(section de l'armée)* service (c) **armes** *(blason)* (coat of) arms

armé, -e [arme] *adj* (a) *(muni d'une arme)* armed; **a. jusqu'aux dents** armed to the teeth; *aussi Fig* **être a. de qch** to be armed with sth; *Fig* **être a. pour qch** *(préparé)* to be equipped for sth (b) *(renforcé)* fortified, strengthened

armée [arme] *nf aussi Fig* army; **être dans l'a.** to be in the army; **être à l'a.** to be doing one's military service; **l'a. de l'air** the air force; **a. de métier** professional army; **a. régulière** *ou* **active** regular army; **a. de réserve** reserves; **l'A. du salut** the Salvation Army; **l'a. de terre** the army

armement [arməmɑ̃] *nm* (a) *(action) (d'un pays, d'une région)* armament; *(d'une armée)* arming (b) **armements** *(armes)* armaments, weaponry (c) *(d'une arme à feu)* cocking; *(d'un appareil photo)* setting (d) *(de navire)* commissioning, fitting out

Arménie [armeni] *nf* **l'A.** Armenia

arménien, -enne [armenjɛ̃, -ɛn] **1** *adj* Armenian
2 *nm (langue)* Armenian
3 *nm,f* **A., Arménienne** Armenian

armer [arme] **1** *vt* (a) *(munir d'armes)* to arm (**de** with); **je sors toujours armé** I always carry a weapon when I go out (b) *(navire)* to commission, to fit out (c) *(arme à feu)* to cock; *(appareil photo)* to set
2 **s'armer** *vpr* to arm oneself; **s'a. de courage/de patience** to summon up (one's) courage/patience

armistice [armistis] *nm* armistice

armoire [armwar] *nf* closet; **a. à glace** mirrored closet; *Hum* **c'est une a. à glace** he's built like a tank; **a. de toilette** *ou* **de salle de bain** bathroom cabinet

armoiries [armwari] *nfpl* (coat of) arms

armure [armyr] *nf* armor

armurier [armyrje] *nm* (a) *(vendeur)* gun dealer (b) *(dans une caserne)* armorer

ARN [aɛrɛn] *nm (abrév* **acide ribonucléique**) RNA

arnaque [arnak] *nf Fam* rip-off, scam; **c'est de l'a.!** what a rip-off!

arnaquer [arnake] *vt Fam* to rip off; **se faire a.** to get ripped off

arnaqueur, -euse [arnakœr, -øz] *nm,f Fam* rip-off merchant

arnica [arnika] *nm ou nf* arnica

arobase [arobaz] *nf Ordinat* at (sign)

aromate [arɔmat] *nm (herbe)* herb; *(épice)* spice

aromathérapie [arɔmaterapi] *nf* aromatherapy

aromatique [arɔmatik] *adj* aromatic

aromatisé, -e [arɔmatize] *adj* flavored; **a. à la vanille** vanilla-flavored

arôme [arom] *nm (parfum)* aroma; *(goût)* flavor; **crème gla-cée, a. vanille** vanilla ice-cream

arpège [arpɛʒ] *nm Mus* arpeggio

arpent [arpɑ̃] *nm* = former land measurement approximately equivalent to one acre

arpenter [arpɑ̃te] *vt* **(a)** *(mesurer)* to survey, to measure **(b)** *(parcourir)* to pace up and down

arqué, -e [arke] *adj (sourcils)* arched; *(nez)* hooked; **jambes arquées** bow legs

arquer [arke] **s'arquer** *vpr* to bend, to curve

arrachage [araʃaʒ] *nm (de plantes)* uprooting; *(de pommes de terre)* lifting; *(d'une dent, d'un clou, de piquets)* pulling out

arraché [araʃe] *nm (en haltérophilie)* snatch; *Fig* **gagner à l'a.** to snatch victory; *Fig* **ils ont obtenu le contrat à l'a.** it was a struggle for them to get the contract

arrachement [araʃmɑ̃] *nm (peine)* wrench

arrache-pied [araʃpje] **d'arrache-pied** *adv* relentlessly

arracher [araʃe] **1** *vt* **(a)** *(arbre)* to uproot; *(légumes)* to lift; *(dent, mauvaises herbes, piquets)* to pull out; *(page)* to tear out; *(affiche)* to tear down; *(vêtement, membre, toit)* to tear off; **se faire a. une dent** to have a tooth pulled; **a. qch à qn/des mains de qn** to snatch sth from sb/from sb's hands; *Fig* **je vais lui a. les yeux!** I'll scratch his/her eyes out!

(b) *(obtenir)* **a. qch à qn** *(argent)* to get sth off sb; *(secret)* to drag sth out of sb; *(promesse, sourire)* to force sth out of sb; *Fig* **nous sommes finalement parvenus à lui a. quelques mots** we did eventually manage to get a few words out of him/her

(c) *(séparer)* **a. un enfant à sa mère** to take a child away from its mother; **a. qn à la mort** to snatch sb from the jaws of death; **a. qn à son travail** to tear *or* to drag sb away from his/her work

(d) *Fam (sujet: alcool, piment)* **ça arrache!** it brings tears to your eyes!

2 *vi Can* **en a.** to have a hard time (of it)

3 s'arracher *vpr* **(a)** *(se disputer)* **s'a. qn/qch** to fight over sb/sth

(b) *(se retirer)* **c'est à s'a. les cheveux!** it's enough to make you tear your hair out!; **s'a. à son travail** to tear oneself away from one's work

(c) *très Fam (partir)* to hit the road

arracheur [araʃœr] *nm* **mentir comme un a. de dents** to lie through one's teeth

arraisonner [arɛzɔne] *vt* to stop and examine

arrangeant, -e [arɑ̃ʒɑ̃, -ɑ̃t] *adj* helpful

arrangement [arɑ̃ʒmɑ̃] *nm* **(a)** *(fait de disposer)* arranging; *(manière d'être disposé)* arrangement **(b)** *(accord)* agreement, settlement **(c)** *Mus* arrangement

arranger [45] [arɑ̃ʒe] **1** *vt* **(a)** *(meubles, fleurs)* to arrange; *(pièce, maison)* to put in order; *(cravate, col)* to straighten

(b) *(réparer)* to repair

(c) *(organiser)* to arrange, to organize; **j'ai tout arrangé** I've made all the arrangements

(d) *(régler) (problème)* to settle; **cela n'arrangera rien** that won't help things; *Ironique* **pour tout a., il s'est mis à pleuvoir** just to help matters, it started to rain

(e) *Fam* **a. qn** *(maltraiter)* to give sb a going over; *(critiquer)* to tear sb to pieces

(f) *(convenir à)* to suit; **faire qch pour a. qn** to do sth to help sb out

(g) *Mus* to arrange

2 s'arranger *vpr* **(a)** *(s'organiser)* to manage; **arrangez-vous pour être là/finir à temps** make sure you're there/you finish on time; *Fam* **je ne sais pas comment tu t'arranges, tu es toujours en retard** I don't know how you manage it, but you're always late

(b) *(s'améliorer)* to work out; **ça ne s'arrange pas!** things aren't any better!

(c) *(rectifier son apparence)* to tidy oneself up

(d) *(se mettre d'accord)* to come to an agreement (**avec** with); **ça ne me regarde pas, arrange-toi avec elle** it's got nothing to do with me, work it out with her

(e) *(se contenter)* **s'a. de qch** to make do with sth

arrestation [arɛstasjɔ̃] *nf* arrest; **en état d'a.** under arrest

arrêt [arɛ] *nm* **(a)** *(interruption) (des combats, des hostilités, de la production)* stop; **Clermont-Ferrand, dix minutes d'a.** *(en train)* this is Clermont-Ferrand, there will be a ten-minute stop; **sans a.** continuously; **tomber en a. devant qn/qch** to stop and stare at sb/sth; **marquer un temps d'a.** to pause; **a. du cœur** heart failure; *Ordinat* **a. de défilement** scroll lock; *TV & Cin* **a. sur image** freeze frame; **a. de jeu** *(au football)* injury time; **jouer les arrêts de jeu** to play injury time; **a. de travail** sick leave; **être en a. de travail** to be on sick leave

(b) *(de véhicule)* stop; **ne pas descendre avant l'a. complet du train** *(sur la portière)* do not get off before the train has come to a complete stop; **le train est sans a. jusqu'à Hendaye** the train is non-stop to Hendaye; **je descends au prochain a.** I'm getting off at the next stop; **a. de bus** bus stop; **a. facultatif** flag stop

(c) *Jur* judgment; *aussi Fig* **a. de mort** death sentence

arrêté, -e [arete] **1** *adj (idées)* fixed

2 *nm (décret)* order, decree; **a. ministériel** ministerial order; **a. municipal** ≃ ordinance; **a. préfectoral** ≃ ordinance *(issued by a "préfecture")*

arrêter [arete] **1** *vt* **(a)** *(personne, animal, véhicule)* to stop; *(machine, moteur, musique)* to turn off; *(fuite)* to stem; *(études)* to give up; **là je vous arrête, je ne suis pas d'accord!** hold it right there, I don't agree!; **arrête-moi au carrefour** drop me off at the intersection; **rien ne l'arrête** nothing will stop him; **a. de faire qch** to stop doing sth; **elle n'arrête pas de me déranger** she keeps disturbing me; **ce détail arrêta mon attention** this detail caught my attention **(b)** *(criminel)* to arrest **(c)** *(déterminer)* to decide; *(date, prix)* to fix

2 *vi* to stop; **arrête!** stop it!

3 s'arrêter *vpr* **(a)** *(cesser, s'immobiliser)* to stop; **s'a. de faire qch** to stop doing sth; **s'a. chez qn** to stop off at sb's house **(b)** **s'.a. à qch** *(faire attention à)* to pay attention to sth

arrhes [ar] *nfpl* deposit

arrière [arjɛr] **1** *adj inv* back; **feu a.** rear light; **roue a.** rear *or* back wheel

2 *nm* **(a)** *(d'une maison, d'un avion)* back; *(d'un bateau)* stern; **à l'a. de la voiture** in the back of the car **(b)** *Mil* **l'a.** the rear; *Fig* **protéger ses arrières** to leave oneself a way out **(c)** *(au football)* fullback

3 *exclam* stand back!

4 en arrière *adv* **(a)** *(derrière)* behind; **rester en a.** to lag behind; **en a. de qn/qch** behind sb/sth **(b)** *(dans la direction inverse)* backward; **pencher la tête en a.** to lean one's head back; **retourner en a.** to go *or* to turn back **(c)** *Suisse* **il y a un siècle en a.** a century ago

arriéré, -e [arjere] **1** *adj* **(a)** *(paiement)* overdue **(b)** *(dans ses idées, son développement)* backward

2 *nm* arrears

arrière-boutique (*pl* **arrière-boutiques**) [arjɛrbutik] *nf* **dans l'a.** in the back of the store

arrière-cour (*pl* **arrière-cours**) [arjɛrkur] *nf* backyard

arrière-garde (*pl* **arrière-gardes**) [arjɛrgard] *nf* rearguard

arrière-goût (*pl* **arrière-goûts**) [arjɛrgu] *nm aussi Fig* aftertaste

arrière-grand-mère (*pl* **arrière-grands-mères**) [arjɛrgrɑ̃mɛr] *nf* great-grandmother

arrière-grand-père (*pl* **arrière-grands-pères**) [arjɛrgrɑ̃pɛr] *nm* great-grandfather

arrière-grands-parents [arjɛrgrɑ̃parɑ̃] *nmpl* great-grandparents

arrière-pays [arjɛrpei] *nm inv* hinterland

arrière-pensée (*pl* **arrière-pensées**) [arjɛrpɑ̃se] *nf* ulterior motive

arrière-petite-fille (*pl* **arrière-petites-filles**) [arjɛrpətitfij] *nf* great-granddaughter

arrière-petit-fils (*pl* **arrière-petits-fils**) [arjɛrpətifis] *nm* great-grandson

arrière-petits-enfants [arjɛrpətizɑ̃fɑ̃] *nmpl* great-grandchildren

arrière-plan (*pl* **arrière-plans**) [arjɛrplɑ̃] *nm aussi Fig* background; **à l'a.** in the background

arrière-saison (*pl* **arrière-saisons**) [arjɛrsɛzɔ̃] *nf* late fall *or* autumn

arrière-train (*pl* **arrière-trains**) [arjɛrtrɛ̃] *nm* (*d'un animal*) (hind)quarters; *Fam* (*d'une personne*) rump, rear

arrimer [arime] *vt* (**a**) *Naut* (*cargaison*) to stow (**b**) (*fixer*) to secure *or* to fasten (**à** to)

arrivage [arivaʒ] *nm* consignment

arrivant, -e [arivɑ̃, -ɑ̃t] *nm,f* arrival; **les nouveaux arrivants** the new arrivals, the newcomers

arrivé, -e [arive] **1** *adj* **être a.** (*socialement*) to have arrived, to have made it
2 *nm,f* (*personne*) **le premier/dernier a.** the first/last (person) to arrive

arrivée [arive] *nf* (**a**) (*venue*) arrival; **depuis son a. au pouvoir** since he came to power; **à mon a.** when I arrive/arrived; **arrivées** (*sur panneau*) arrivals (**b**) *Tech* inlet (**c**) (*d'une course*) winning post, finish

arriver [arive] (*aux être*) **1** *vi* (**a**) (*venir*) to arrive; **a. à Lyon/en France** to arrive in Lyons/in France; **a. le premier/dernier** (*à une soirée*) to arrive first/last; **a. premier/second** (*dans un concours, une course*) to come first/second; **j'arrive!** (I'm) coming!; **c'est à cette heure-là que tu arrives?** do you have any idea what time it is?; **nous sommes presque arrivés** we're almost there
(**b**) (*atteindre*) **l'eau m'arrive aux chevilles** the water reaches my ankles; **ses cheveux lui arrivent aux épaules** her hair comes down to her shoulders *or* is shoulder-length
(**c**) **a. à faire qch** to get to the stage of doing sth; **c'est malheureux d'en a. là** it's a shame it's got to that stage; **elle en arrive même à ne plus le souhaiter** she's even starting to hope it won't happen; **j'en arrive à penser que.../me demander si...** I'm beginning to think.../wonder if...
(**d**) (*socialement*) to arrive, to make it
(**e**) (*parvenir*) **a. à un résultat** to achieve a result; **a. à faire qch** to manage to do sth; **je n'arrive pas à l'ouvrir** I can't get it open; **il n'arrivera jamais à rien** he'll never make anything of himself
(**f**) (*se produire*) to happen (**à** to)
2 *v impersonnel* **quoi qu'il arrive** whatever happens; **il lui est arrivé quelque chose** something's happened to him/her; **il m'arrive d'y penser** I sometimes think about it; **il arrive à tout le monde de se tromper** anyone can make a mistake; **qu'est-ce qu'il t'arrive?** what's wrong (with you)?

arrivisme [arivism] *nm* pushiness, ambition

arriviste [arivist] *nmf* social climber

arrobas [arɔbas], **arrobase** [arɔbaz] *nf Ordinat* (*dans une adresse électronique*) at (sign); **'gdupont arrobas xmail, point, com'** 'gdupont, at, xmail, dot, com'

arrogance [arɔgɑ̃s] *nf* arrogance; **avec a.** arrogantly

arrogant, -e [arɔgɑ̃, -ɑ̃t] *adj* arrogant

arroger [45] [arɔʒe] **s'arroger** *vpr* **s'a. un droit/un privilège** to claim a right/a privilege; **s'a. le droit de faire qch** to assume the right to do sth

arrondi, -e [arɔ̃di] **1** *adj* (*objet, visage*) round
2 *nm* (**a**) (*forme*) roundness, rounded form (**b**) (*d'une jupe*) hemline

arrondir [arɔ̃dir] **1** *vt* (**a**) (*forme*) **a. qch** to make sth round; **cette coiffure lui arrondit le visage** that haircut makes her face look round; *Fig* **a. les angles** to smooth things over (**b**) (*chiffre, somme*) to round off; (*vers le haut*) to round up; (*vers le bas*) to round down; *Fam* **a. ses fins de mois** to supplement one's income; **a. à l'euro supérieur/inférieur** to round up/down to the nearest euro
2 **s'arrondir** *vpr* (*corps, visage*) to fill out

arrondissement [arɔ̃dismɑ̃] *nm* = administrative subdivision of Paris, Lyons and Marseilles

---

Arrondissement
In Paris, Lyons and Marseilles, the number of the "arrondissement" corresponds to the last two figures in a zip code: thus, you can tell from the postcode 75012 that it refers to the 12th arrondissement of Paris.

---

arrosage [arozaʒ] *nm* (*des plantes, du sol*) watering; (*des rues*) spraying; (*d'une pelouse*) sprinkling

arroser [aroze] **1** *vt* (**a**) (*plantes, sol*) to water; (*pelouse*) to sprinkle; (*rues*) to spray; (*rôti*) to baste; **région très peu arrosée** area with little rainfall; **a. qch d'essence** to douse sth with gas (**b**) (*fêter*) to drink to; **un repas bien arrosé** a meal washed down with plenty of alcohol (**c**) (*sujet: rivière*) to flow through
2 **s'arroser** *vpr* (*se fêter*) **ça s'arrose!** that calls for a drink!

arroseur [arozœr] *nm* (*appareil*) sprinkler

arrosoir [arozwar] *nm* watering can

arsenal, -aux [arsənal, -o] *nm* (**a**) *Mil* arsenal; **a. maritime** *ou* **de la marine** naval dockyard (**b**) *Fam* (*attirail*) gear

arsenic [arsənik] *nm* arsenic

art [ar] *nm* (**a**) (*esthétique*) art; **c'est du grand a.!** it's a work of art!; **le septième a.** movies; **a. dramatique** drama, dramatic art; **les arts graphiques** graphic arts; **l'a. lyrique** opera; **arts martiaux** martial arts; **arts plastiques** fine art; **les arts du spectacle** the performing arts (**b**) (*savoir-faire*) **l'a. de faire qch** the art of doing sth; **cultiver l'a. de vivre** to enjoy the finer things in life; **préparer le café, c'est tout un a.** there's quite an art to making coffee; *Fig* **avoir l'a. de faire qch** to have a knack for doing sth

Arte [arte] *n* = French-German TV channel showing cultural programs

artère [arter] *nf* (**a**) (*vaisseau*) artery (**b**) (**grande**) **a.** (*route*) main road; (*en ville*) main thoroughfare

artériel, -elle [arterjɛl] *adj* (*système, maladie*) arterial

artériosclérose [arterjoskleroz] *nf* hardening of the arteries, *Spéc* arteriosclerosis

arthrite [artrit] *nf* arthritis

arthrose [artroz] *nf* osteoarthritis

Arthur [artyr] *npr Fam* **je vais me faire appeler A.!** I'm going to get a real telling-off!

artichaut [artiʃo] *nm* artichoke

article [artikl] *nm* (**a**) *Com* item; **articles de toilette** toiletries; **faire l'a.** to make a sales pitch (**b**) *Journ* article; (*de dictionnaire*) entry (**c**) (*d'un traité, d'un règlement*) article (**d**) *Gram* article; **a. défini/indéfini** definite/indefinite article (**e**) **être à l'a. de la mort** to be on the point of death (**f**) *Ordinat* (*dans base de données*) record; (*commande*) command

articulaire [artikylɛr] *adj Anat* articular, articulatory

articulation [artikylasjɔ̃] *nf* (**a**) *Anat & Tech* joint (**b**) (*prononciation*) articulation (**c**) (*organisation*) structure

articuler [artikyle] **1** *vt* (**a**) (*idées, arguments*) to link (**b**) (*mots*) to articulate; **articule!** speak clearly!
2 **s'articuler** *vpr* (*pièces, idées*) to be linked; **les différentes parties du texte s'articulent bien** the different parts of the text fit well together; **s'a. autour de qch** (*théorie*) to center on sth

artifice [artifis] *nm* trick

artificiel, -elle [artifisjɛl] *adj* (a) *(non naturel)* artificial; *Fig (personne)* false; *(rire)* forced (b) *(arbitraire)* arbitrary

artificiellement [artifisjɛlmɑ̃] *adv* (a) *(de façon non naturelle)* artificially (b) *(arbitrairement)* arbitrarily

artificier [artifisje] *nm (fabricant)* firework manufacturer; *(dans un feu d'artifice)* master of ceremonies

artillerie [artijri] *nf* artillery; **a. légère/lourde** light/heavy artillery; **pièce d'a.** artillery cannon

artilleur [artijœr] *nm* artilleryman

artisan [artizɑ̃] *nm* craftsman, *f* craftswoman; *Fig* architect

artisanal, -e, -aux, -ales [artizanal, -o] *adj* traditionally-made; *(à la main)* hand-made; **métier a.** craft

artisanat [artizana] *nm* craft industry

artiste [artist] **1** *adj (tempérament, style)* artistic; **se donner un genre a.** to cultivate an arty image
  2 *nmf* (a) *(personne créative)* artist (b) *(interprète) (musicien)* performer; *(acteur)* actor, *f* actress; *(chanteur)* singer; *(danseur)* dancer; **a. (peintre)** artist

artistique [artistik] *adj* artistic

as¹ [a] *voir* **avoir¹**

as² [ɑs] *nm* (a) *(aux cartes)* ace; *(aux dominos, aux dés)* one; *Fam* **être ficelé** *ou* **fichu comme l'as de pique** to look like a bum; **être plein aux as** to be rolling in it; *Fam* **passer à l'as** to go out the window (b) *Fam (champion)* whiz; **as du volant** crack race driver; **un as du bricolage** a home-improvement expert

ascendance [asɑ̃dɑ̃s] *nf (ancêtres)* ancestry

ascendant, -e [asɑ̃dɑ̃, -ɑ̃t] **1** *adj (échelle)* rising; *(mouvement, courant)* upward
  2 *nm* (a) *(influence)* influence; **avoir de l'a. sur qn** to have influence over sb (b) **ascendants** *(ancêtres)* ancestry

ascenseur [asɑ̃sœr] *nm* (a) *(dans un bâtiment)* elevator; *Fig* **je lui renverrai l'a.** I'll return the favor (b) *Ordinat* scroll box

ascension [asɑ̃sjɔ̃] *nf* (a) *(escalade)* ascent; **faire l'a. d'une montagne** to climb a mountain (b) *(progression)* **a. sociale** social climbing (c) *Rel* **(la fête** *ou* **le jeudi de) l'A.** Ascension Day

> ### Ascension
> Ascension Day is on the fortieth day after Easter and is a public holiday in France. Many people take an extended weekend break during this period.

ascensionnel, -elle [asɑ̃sjɔnɛl] *adj (mouvement)* upward

ascète [asɛt] *nmf* ascetic

ASCII [aski] *nm (abrév* **American Standard Code for Information Interchange)** **(code) a.** ASCII (code)

ascorbique [askɔrbik] *adj (acide)* ascorbic

aseptique [asɛptik] *adj* aseptic

aseptiser [asɛptize] *vt (blessure)* to sterilize; *(pièce)* to disinfect; *Fig & Péj* **un univers aseptisé** a sterile environment

asexué, -e [asɛksɥe], **asexuel, -elle** [asɛksɥɛl] *adj aussi Fig* asexual

ashkénaze [aʃkenaz] *adj & nmf* Ashkenazi

asiatique [azjatik] **1** *adj* Asian, oriental
  2 *nmf* **A.** Asian, Oriental

> ### Asiatique
> This word tends to refer to Oriental people (i.e. from countries such as China, Japan, Laos, etc.), rather than Asia as a whole.

Asie [azi] *nf* **l'A.** Asia; **l'A. centrale** Central Asia; **l'A. du Sud-Est** Southeast Asia

asile [azil] *nm* (a) *(abri)* refuge; *Vieilli* **a. (d'aliénés)** mental hospital; **a. de nuit** night shelter; **a. de vieillards** old people's home (b) *(statut)* **a. politique/diplomatique** political/diplomatic asylum; **demander l'a. politique** to ask for political asylum

asocial, -e, -aux, -ales [asɔsjal, -o] **1** *adj* asocial
  2 *nm, f* asocial person

aspartam(e) [aspartam] *nm* aspartame

aspect [aspɛ] *nm* (a) *(air)* appearance, look; **un bar d'a. louche** a shady-looking bar (b) *(angle)* angle, point of view; **sous tous ses aspects** from every angle, from all points of view (c) *Gram* aspect

asperge [aspɛrʒ] *nf* (a) *(plante)* asparagus (b) *Fam (personne)* beanpole

asperger [45] [aspɛrʒe] **1** *vt (linge, plante)* to spray with water; **a. qn de qch** to splash sb with sth; **se faire a.** to get splashed
  2 **s'asperger** *vpr* (a) *(soi-même)* **s'a. de qch** to splash oneself with sth (b) *(mutuellement)* to splash *or* to spray one another

aspérité [asperite] *nf* (a) *(d'une surface)* rough part (b) *(d'un caractère)* harshness

aspersion [aspɛrsjɔ̃] *nf* spraying

asphalte [asfalt] *nm* asphalt

asphyxiant, -e [asfiksjɑ̃, -ɑ̃t] *adj* asphyxiating, suffocating; *Fig* stifling, suffocating; **gaz a.** poison gas

asphyxie [asfiksi] *nf* asphyxiation

asphyxier [66] [asfiksje] **1** *vt* (a) *(personne, animal)* to asphyxiate (b) *Fig (économie, industrie)* to paralyze
  2 **s'asphyxier** *vpr (suffoquer)* to choke; *(se suicider)* to gas oneself

aspirateur [aspiratœr] *nm* vacuum cleaner; **passer l'a. dans la maison** to vacuum the house

aspiration [aspirasjɔ̃] *nf* (a) *(inhalation)* inhalation; *Tech (d'eau dans une pompe)* suction (b) *(désir)* yearning (**à** for); *(ambition)* aspiration (**à** for) (c) *Ling* aspiration

aspiré, -e [aspire] *adj Ling* aspirate(d)

aspirer [aspire] **1** *vt* (a) *(air, parfum)* to inhale, to breathe (in) (b) *(liquide)* to suck up (c) *Ling* to aspirate
  2 **aspirer à** *vt ind* to aspire to; **a. à faire qch** to aspire to do sth

aspirine [aspirin] *nf* aspirin; **un cachet d'a.** an aspirin; **blanc comme un cachet d'a.** white as a ghost

assagir [asaʒir] **1** *vt* to quiet down
  2 **s'assagir** *vpr* to settle down

assaillant, -e [asajɑ̃, -ɑ̃t] *nm, f* assailant, attacker

assaillir [67] [asajir] *vt* to assault, to attack; *Fig (sujet: difficultés, remords, doute)* to beset; **a. qn de questions** to bombard sb with questions; **il a été assailli par les journalistes** he was set upon by the journalists

assainir [asenir] *vt (maison, rivière)* to clean up; *(atmosphère)* to purify; *(marais)* to drain; *(économie)* to stabilize

assainissement [asenismɑ̃] *nm (d'une maison, d'une rivière)* cleaning up; *(de l'atmosphère)* purifying; *(d'un marais)* drainage; *(de l'économie)* stabilization

assaisonnement [asɛzɔnmɑ̃] *nm (de plat)* seasoning; *(de salade)* dressing

assaisonner [asɛzɔne] *vt (plat)* to season (**de** with); *(salade)* to dress; *Fam Fig* **se faire a.** to get a good dressing-down

assassin, -e [asasɛ̃, -in] **1** *nm* murderer; *(d'une personnalité politique)* assassin; **à l'a.!** murder!
  2 *adj* (a) *(méchant) (regard)* murderous; *(remarque)* crushing (b) *(provocant) (sourire, œillade)* provocative

assassinat [asasina] *nm* murder; *(d'une personnalité politique)* assassination

assassiner [asasine] *vt* to murder; *(personnalité politique)* to assassinate; *Fig (chanson, texte)* to murder; *(sujet: critique)* to crucify

assaut [aso] *nm (attaque)* assault, attack; *Mil* charge; **donner l'a. à** to storm, to launch an attack on; **monter à l'a.** to attack; **prendre qch d'a.** *Mil* to storm sth; *Fig (buffet, guichets)* to make a run for sth

assèchement [asɛʃmɑ̃] *nm (d'un terrain, d'un marécage)* drainage; *(d'un cours d'eau)* drying out

assécher [34] [aseʃe] **1** *vt (terrain, marécage)* to drain; *(cours d'eau)* to dry out
   2 s'assécher *vpr* to dry up

ASSEDIC [asedik] *nfpl (abrév* **Association pour l'emploi dans l'industrie et le commerce)** = French welfare agency; **toucher les A.** to get welfare

assemblage [asɑ̃blaʒ] *nm* **(a)** *(de pièces détachées)* assembly; *(en menuiserie)* joint; *(en couture)* making up; *(de feuillets)* collating **(b)** *(structure)* assembly

assemblée [asɑ̃ble] *nf* **(a)** *(réunion)* assembly; *(plus petite)* meeting; **a. générale** annual general meeting **(b)** *Pol* **l'A. nationale** the National Assembly, ≃ the House of Representatives **(c)** *(foule)* crowd

> ### Assemblée nationale
> The French parliament has two chambers: the National Assembly and the Senate. The members of the National Assembly (the "députés") are elected in the "élections législatives" held every five years.

assembler [asɑ̃ble] **1** *vt* **(a)** *(machine, meuble en kit)* to assemble, to put together; *(feuillets)* to collate **(b)** *(pièces)* to join **(c)** *Ordinat (programme)* to assemble; *(modules)* to link
   2 s'assembler *vpr (foule)* to gather

assembleur [asɑ̃blœr] *nm Ordinat* assembler

asséner [34] [asene] *vt* **a. qch à qn** *(coup)* to deliver sth to sb; *(remarque)* to hurl sth at sb

assentiment [asɑ̃timɑ̃] *nm* assent

asseoir [10a] [aswar] **1** *vt* **(a)** *(installer) (personne)* to seat, to sit; **être assis** to be sitting **(b)** *Fig (autorité, réputation)* to establish
   2 *vi* **faire a. qn** to ask sb to sit down *or* to take a seat
   3 s'asseoir *vpr* to sit (down); *(depuis la position allongée)* to sit up; **s'a. sur une chaise/dans un fauteuil** to sit on a chair/in an armchair; *Fam Fig* **ses problèmes, je m'assois dessus!** I don't give a damn about his/her problems!

assermenté, -e [asermɑ̃te] *adj* sworn (in); *(témoin)* under oath; **fonctionnaire a.** sworn official

assertion [asɛrsjɔ̃] *nf* assertion

asservir [asɛrvir] *vt* to enslave; *Tech* **moteur asservi** servomotor

asservissement [asɛrvismɑ̃] *nm* enslavement; **a. à qn/qch** subjection to sb/sth

assesseur [asesœr] *nm* assessor

asseyais *etc. voir* **asseoir**

assez [ase] *adv* **(a)** *(suffisamment)* enough; **a. grand/intelligent (pour faire qch)** big/clever enough (to do sth); **a. bien** well enough; *(appréciation scolaire)* fair; **tu as a. mangé** you've eaten enough; **a.!** that's enough!; **a. parlé!** enough talk!; **nous sommes a. de trois** three of us are enough **(b)** **a. de** enough; **il y a a. de pain/de pâtes** there's enough bread/pasta; **j'en ai a.** *(suffisamment)* I've got enough; *(je suis agacé)* I've had enough **(c)** *(plutôt)* quite, rather

assidu, -e [asidy] *adj* **(a)** *(toujours présent)* regular; **être a. aux cours** to attend classes regularly **(b)** *(appliqué)* diligent; **un soin a.** painstaking care **(c)** *(attentionné)* **être a. auprès de qn** to be attentive to sb; **faire une cour assidue à qn** to pay constant court to sb

assiduité [asiduite] *nf* **(a)** *(présence régulière)* regularity; **a. aux cours** regular attendance at classes **(b)** *(zèle)* diligence **(c)** **poursuivre qn de ses assiduités** to force one's attentions on sb

assidûment [asidymɑ̃] *adv* **(a)** *(régulièrement)* regularly **(b)** *(avec application)* diligently

assied *etc. voir* **asseoir**

assiéger [59] [asjeʒe] *vt aussi Fig* to besiege

assiéra *etc. voir* **asseoir**

assiette [asjɛt] *nf* **(a)** *(vaisselle)* plate; *(contenu)* plateful; *Culin* **a. anglaise** cold cuts; **a. creuse** soup plate; **a. à dessert** dessert plate; **a. plate** dinner plate **(b)** *(d'un impôt, d'un taux)* base **(c)** *(d'un cavalier)* seat **(d)** **ne pas être dans son a.** to be out of sorts

assiettée [asjete] *nf* plateful

assignation [asiɲasjɔ̃] *nf* **(a)** *(d'une tâche)* assignment (**à** to); *(de fonds, d'une part)* allotment (**à** to) **(b)** *Jur* summons; **a. à résidence** house arrest

assigner [asiɲe] *vt* **(a)** *(tâche)* to assign (**à** to); *(fonds, part)* to allot (**à** to) **(b)** *Jur (témoin)* to summon; **a. qn en justice** to issue a writ against sb; **a. qn à résidence** to place sb under house arrest

assimilable [asimilabl] *adj (comparable)* comparable (**à** to)

assimilation [asimilasjɔ̃] *nf* **(a)** *(absorption)* & *Fig* assimilation **(b)** *(comparaison)* comparison (**à** with)

assimilé, -e [asimile] *adj (de même nature)* similar; **cadres et assimilés** executives and those in similar categories

assimiler [asimile] **1** *vt* **(a)** *(aliment, connaissances, immigrés)* to assimilate; **un élève qui a du mal à a.** a pupil who finds it hard to take things in **(b)** *(comparer)* to compare (**à** with)
   2 s'assimiler *vpr* **(a)** *(immigré)* to assimilate **(b)** *(être comparable)* to be comparable (**à** with)

assis, -e [asi, -iz] **1** *pp voir* **asseoir**
   2 *adj* sitting, seated; **je travaille a. toute la journée** I spend the whole day at work sitting down; *Fig* **une situation/réputation bien assise** a secure job/an established reputation

assise [asiz] *nf (d'une théorie)* basis, foundation

assises [asiz] *nfpl* **(a)** *(congrès)* conference **(b)** *Jur* **les a.** ≃ circuit court

assistanat [asistana] *nm* assistantship

assistance [asistɑ̃s] *nf* **(a)** *(public)* audience **(b)** *(aide)* assistance; **prêter a. à qn** to give sb assistance; *Méd* **a. médicale à la procréation** assisted conception **(c)** **être à l'A. (publique)** to be a foster child

assistant, -e [asistɑ̃, -ɑ̃t] *nm,f* assistant; *(de langue)* language assistant; **a. metteur en scène** assistant director; **assistante maternelle** daycare-center worker; **a. personnel** personal assistant; **a. social** social worker

assisté, -e [asiste] **1** *nm,f Péj* person living on handouts
   2 *adj* **a. par ordinateur** computer-aided

assister [asiste] **1** *vt (personne)* to assist
   2 assister à *vt ind* to be (present) at, to attend; *(accident)* to witness; **je ne peux pas vous répondre, je n'ai pas assisté à la scène** I can't give you an answer, I wasn't there

associatif, -ive [asɔsjatif, -iv] *adj* **mouvement a.** associations; **la vie associative est tres développée dans ce pays** a lot of people in this country belong to clubs and associations

association [asɔsjasjɔ̃] *nf* **(a)** *(groupe, société)* association; *Com* partnership; **a. à but non lucratif** non-profit organization; **A. européenne de libre-échange** European Free Trade Association; **a. de parents d'élèves** parent-teacher association; **a. sportive** sports club **(b)** *(de mots, d'idées)* association; *(d'aliments, de substances, de couleurs)* combination **(c)** *Jur* **a. de malfaiteurs** criminal conspiracy

associé, -e [asɔsje] **1** *nm,f* associate; *Com* partner
   2 *adj* **membre a.** associate member

associer [66] [asɔsje] **1** *vt* **(a)** *(lier)* to combine (**à** with) **(b)** *(mentalement)* to associate (**à** with)
   2 s'associer *vpr* **(a)** **s'a. à un projet** to join in a project; **s'a. à** *ou* **avec qn** *(dans une lutte)* to join forces with sb; *Com* to enter into partnership with sb; **je m'associe à votre douleur** I share your grief **(b)** *(se mêler)* to combine (**à** with)

assoiffé, -e [aswafe] *adj* thirsty; *Fig* **a. de sang** bloodthirsty; **a. de savoir** thirsty for knowledge

assolement [asɔlmã] *nm* crop rotation

assombrir [asɔ̃brir] **1** *vt* to darken; *(avenir)* to cast a shadow over

2 s'assombrir *vpr (ciel, visage)* to darken, to cloud over; *(personne)* to become gloomy

assommant, -e [asɔmã, -ãt] *adj* deadly boring

assommer [asɔme] *vt* **a. qn** *(étourdir)* to knock sb senseless; *(engourdir)* to make sb lethargic; *(ennuyer)* to bore sb to death

Assomption [asɔ̃psjɔ̃] *nf* **(la fête de) l'A.** (the feast of) the Assumption

> ### Assomption
> The Feast of the Assumption, on August 15th, is a Catholic feast day and an important holiday in France.

assonance [asɔnãs] *nf* assonance

assorti, -e [asɔrti] *adj* **(a)** *(en harmonie)* matching; **bien a.** well-matched; **mal a.** ill-matched; **pull avec jupe assortie** sweater with matching skirt; **le pull n'était pas a. à la jupe** the sweater didn't match the skirt **(b)** *(bonbons)* assorted, mixed **(c) bien a.** *(magasin)* well-stocked **(d)** *(accompagné)* **a. de** accompanied by

assortiment [asɔrtimã] *nm (de produits)* assortment

assortir [asɔrtir] *vt* **(a)** *(couleurs)* to match (**à** to) **(b)** *Com* to restock

assoupir [asupir] **s'assoupir** *vpr* to doze off

assouplir [asuplir] **1** *vt (chaussures, cuir, corps)* to make supple; *Fig (réglementation)* to relax

2 s'assouplir *vpr (chaussures, cuir, corps)* to get supple; *(personne)* to loosen up

assouplissant [asuplisã] *nm* fabric softener

assouplissement [asuplismã] *nm (du corps)* making supple; *Fig (de la réglementation)* relaxing; **exercices d'a., assouplissements** limbering-up exercises

assourdir [asurdir] *vt* **(a)** *(personne)* to deafen **(b)** *(son)* to deaden

assourdissant, -e [asurdisã, -ãt] *adj* deafening

assouvir [asuvir] *vt (faim, désir)* to satisfy

assouvissement [asuvismã] *nm (de la faim, du désir)* satisfaction

assoyant *voir* **asseoir**

assujettir [asyʒetir] *vt* **(a)** *(province)* to subjugate **(b)** *(soumettre)* **a. qn à qch** to subject sb to sth; **être assujetti à l'impôt** to be liable for tax **(c)** *(objet)* to fix, to fasten (**à** to)

assujettissement [asyʒetismã] *nm* **(a)** *(dépendance)* subjection (**à** to) **(b)** *(à l'impôt)* liability (**à** for)

assumer [asyme] **1** *vt* **(a)** *(responsabilité)* to assume, to take on; *(risque)* to take **(b)** *(accepter) (conséquences)* to take; *Fam* **tu vas devoir a.** you'll have to live with it

2 s'assumer *vpr* to come to terms with oneself

assurance [asyrãs] *nf* **(a)** *(confiance)* (self-)assurance **(b)** *(garantie)* assurance; **je vous donne l'a. que tout sera fini demain** I assure you that everything will be finished tomorrow; **demander/recevoir des assurances** to ask for/to receive assurance **(c)** *(contre le vol, les accidents)* insurance; **prendre une a.** to take out insurance; *Fam* **je vais écrire à mon a.** I'm going to write to my insurance company; **a. auto** car insurance; **a. maladie** health insurance; **a. au tiers** third-party insurance; **a. tous risques** comprehensive insurance; **a. sur la vie, a.-vie** life insurance; **a. vieillesse** retirement pension

assuré, -e [asyre] **1** *adj* **(a)** *(pas, voix)* firm; *(air, personne)* assured, confident; **d'une voix mal assurée** in an unsteady voice **(b)** *(succès, victoire)* guaranteed, certain

2 *nm,f* **l'a.** the insured; **les assurés sociaux** ≃ people who pay social security

assurément [asyremã] *adv Vieilli* certainly

assurer [asyre] **1** *vt* **(a)** *(garantir)* to insure, to guarantee; **a. une rente à qn** to settle an annuity on sb; **ma retraite m'as-**

sure de quoi vivre my pension gives me enough to live on; **a. ses arrières** to leave oneself a way out

(b) *(certifier)* **a. qch à qn, a. qn de qch** to assure sb of sth; **a. qn que** to assure sb that; **c'est bien vrai, je t'assure** it's absolutely true, I assure you; **mais si, je t'assure!** yes, I swear!

(c) *(se charger de)* to be in charge of; **a. les fonctions de directeur de la production** to be production manager; **un service régulier est assuré entre Paris et New York** there is a regular service between Paris and New York; **j'assure la permanence ce matin** I'm on duty this morning; **a. la défense de qn** *(sujet: avocat)* to defend sb

(d) *(immobiliser)* to steady; *(attacher)* to secure

(e) *(par contrat d'assurance)* to insure (**contre** against)

2 *vi Fam* **a. en maths** to be brilliant at math; **à l'entretien, j'ai assuré un max** I did brilliantly at the interview

3 s'assurer *vpr* **(a)** **s'a. de qch** *(vérifier)* to make sure of sth; **s'a. que** to make sure *or* to check (that); **je vais m'en a.** I'll check

(b) *(par contrat d'assurance)* to insure oneself (**contre** against); **s'a. au tiers/sur la vie** to take out third-party/life insurance

(c) *(se procurer)* **s'a. la collaboration de qn** to secure sb's collaboration; **les Allemands se sont assuré la victoire** the Germans are assured of victory

assureur [asyrœr] *nm* insurer

astérisque [asterisk] *nm* asterisk

astéroïde [asterɔid] *nm* asteroid

asteure, astheure [astœr] *Can Fam* **1** *adv* now

2 asteure que *conj* now that

asthmatique [asmatik] *adj & nmf* asthmatic

asthme [asm] *nm* asthma; **avoir de l'a.** to have asthma; **crise d'a.** asthma attack

asticot [astiko] *nm* maggot

asticoter [astikɔte] *vt Fam* to bug

astigmate [astigmat] *adj & nmf* astigmatic

astiquer [astike] *vt (faire briller)* to polish; *(récurer)* to scour; **a. sa maison** to get one's house spotlessly clean

astrakan [astrakã] *nm* astrakhan

astre [astr] *nm* star; **beau comme un a.** radiantly handsome *or* beautiful

astreignant, -e [astrɛɲã, -ãt] *adj* exacting, demanding

astreindre [54] [astrɛ̃dr] **1** *vt* **a. qn à faire qch** to compel *or* to oblige sb to do sth

2 s'astreindre *vpr* **s'a. à un régime sévère** to strictly follow a diet; **s'a. à faire qch** to force oneself to do sth

astreinte [astrɛ̃t] *nf* constraint

astrologie [astrɔlɔʒi] *nf* astrology

astrologique [astrɔlɔʒik] *adj* astrological

astrologue [astrɔlɔg] *nmf* astrologer

astronaute [astronot] *nmf* astronaut

astronautique [astronotik] *nf* astronautics *(singulier)*

astronome [astronɔm] *nmf* astronomer

astronomie [astronɔmi] *nf* astronomy

astronomique [astronɔmik] *adj aussi Fig* astronomical

astrophysique [astrofizik] *nf* astrophysics *(singulier)*

astuce [astys] *nf* **(a)** *(finesse)* shrewdness **(b)** *(truc)* trick; *(conseil)* tip; **il doit y avoir une a.** there must be a trick to it **(c)** *(plaisanterie)* witticism; *(jeu de mots)* pun; **je ne saisis pas l'a.** I don't get it

astucieusement [astysjøzmã] *adv* shrewdly

astucieux, -euse [astysjø, -øz] *adj (personne)* shrewd; *(solution)* clever

asymétrie [asimetri] *nf* asymmetry

asymétrique [asimetrik] *adj* asymmetrical

asynchrone [asɛ̃kron] *adj Ordinat* asynchronous

ataca [ataka] *nm Can* cranberry

atavisme [atavism] *nm* atavism; **faire qch par a.** to do sth because it's in one's genes

atchoum [atʃum] *exclam* atchoo!

atelier [atəlje] *nm* (**a**) *(lieu)* workshop; *(dans une maison)* workroom; *(d'artiste)* studio; **a. de carrosserie** bodyshop; **a. de montage** assembly shop; *TV & Cin* **a. de production** production studio; **a. de réparations** repair shop (**b**) *(personnel)* workshop staff (**c**) *(groupe de travail)* workgroup

atermoiements [atɛrmwamɑ̃] *nmpl* procrastination

athée [ate] **1** *adj* atheistic
  2 *nmf* atheist

athéisme [ateism] *nm* atheism

athénée [atene] *nm Belg* secondary *or* high school

Athènes [atɛn] *n* Athens

athénien, -enne [atenjɛ̃, -ɛn] **1** *adj* Athenian
  2 *nm,f* **A., Athénienne** Athenian

athlète [atlɛt] *nmf* athlete

athlétique [atletik] *adj* athletic

athlétisme [atletism] *nm* track and field; **épreuves d'a.** track-and-field events

atlantique [atlɑ̃tik] **1** *adj* Atlantic
  2 *nm* **l'A.** the Atlantic (Ocean)

atlas [atlas] *nm (livre)* atlas

atmosphère [atmosfɛr] *nf aussi Fig* atmosphere

atmosphérique [atmosferik] *adj* atmospheric

atoca [atɔka] *nm Can* cranberry

atoll [atɔl] *nm* atoll

atome [atom] *nm* atom; *Fig* **avoir des atomes crochus avec qn** to hit it off with sb; **elle n'a pas un a. de bon sens** she doesn't have an iota of common sense

atomique [atɔmik] *adj* atomic

atomiser [atɔmize] *vt* (**a**) *(pulvériser)* to atomize (**b**) *(ville, région)* to destroy with nuclear weapons

atomiseur [atɔmizœr] *nm* atomizer, spray; **parfum en a.** perfume spray

atone [atɔn] *adj* (**a**) *(inerte)* lackluster (**b**) *(voyelle)* unstressed

atours [atur] *nmpl Litt ou Hum* finery; **parée de ses plus beaux a.** in all her finery

atout [atu] *nm (aux cartes)* trump; *Fig* asset; **a. carreau** diamonds are trumps; **a. maître** master trump; *Fig* trump card; *aussi Fig* **avoir tous les atouts dans son jeu** to hold all the winning cards

âtre [ɑtr] *nm Litt* hearth; **au coin de l'â.** by the fireplace

atriqué, -e [atrike] *adj Can* **mal a.** badly dressed

atroce [atrɔs] *adj (crime)* atrocious; *(douleur)* excruciating; *(odeur, cauchemar, repas)* dreadful, horrible; **j'avais une peur a. de le rencontrer** I dreaded meeting him

atrocement [atrɔsmɑ̃] *adv (cruellement)* atrociously; *(très mal)* dreadfully, horribly; **avoir a. mal** to be in dreadful pain; **sentir a. mauvais** to smell really bad

atrocité [atrɔsite] *nf* atrocity

atrophie [atrɔfi] *nf* atrophy

atrophier [66] [atrɔfje] **1** *vt* to atrophy
  2 s'atrophier *vpr* to atrophy

attabler [atable] **s'attabler** *vpr* to sit down at the/a table

attachant, -e [ataʃɑ̃, -ɑ̃t] *adj* engaging

attache [ataʃ] *nf* (**a**) *(lien)* fastener; *Fig* **attaches** *(amis)* links; *Fig* **sans attaches** unattached; **je n'avais plus aucune a. dans cette ville** there was nothing to keep me in the town (**b**) **avoir les attaches fines** *(chevilles et poignets)* to have delicate wrists and ankles

attaché, -e [ataʃe] **1** *adj* (**a**) *(fixé)* fastened; *(chien)* chained up (**b**) *(affectivement)* **a. à** attached to (**c**) *(dépendant)* **les avantages attachés à une fonction** the benefits attached to a position
  2 *nm,f* attaché; **a. d'ambassade** attaché; **a. culturel** cultural attaché; **a. militaire** military attaché; **a. de presse** press officer

attaché-case (*pl* **attachés-cases**) [ataʃekɛz] *nm* attaché case

attachement [ataʃmɑ̃] *nm* attachment (**à** to)

attacher [ataʃe] **1** *vt* (**a**) **a. qch à qch** *(fixer)* to fasten sth to sth; *(avec de la ficelle, avec une corde)* to tie sth to sth; *(avec une chaîne)* to chain sth to sth; **a. ses cheveux** to tie one's hair back; **a. ses lacets** *ou* **chaussures** to tie one's shoelaces (**b**) *(accorder)* **a. de l'importance/de la valeur à qch** to attach importance/great value to sth
  2 *vi (dans une poêle, une casserole)* to stick to the pan; **une casserole qui n'attache pas** a non-stick saucepan
  3 s'attacher *vpr* (**a**) *(se fixer)* to be fastened (**à** to); **cette jupe s'attache par derrière** this skirt does up at the back (**b**) *(affectivement)* **s'a. à qn/qch** to get attached to sb/sth; **je ne veux pas m'a.** I don't want to commit myself (**c**) *(se concentrer)* **s'a. aux faits** to stick to the facts; **s'a. à faire qch** to strive to do sth (**d**) *(s'assurer)* **s'a. les services de qn** to procure sb's services

attaquant, -e [atakɑ̃, -ɑ̃t] **1** *nm,f Sport* attacker
  2 *adj* attacking

attaque [atak] *nf* (**a**) *(agression, en sport)* attack; *aussi Fig* **passer à l'a.** to go on the offensive; **à l'a.!** attack!; **a. aérienne** air raid; **a. à main armée** armed robbery (**b**) *Fam* **être d'a.** to be in top form; **se sentir d'a. pour faire qch** to feel up to doing sth (**c**) *Méd (crise)* attack; **une a.** *(apoplexie)* a stroke; *(crise cardiaque)* a heart attack

attaquer [atake] **1** *vt* (**a**) *(physiquement, verbalement)* to attack; *(sujet: acide)* to attack; *Jur* **a. qn en justice** to bring an action against sb (**b**) *(repas, sujet, travail)* to tackle; *Fam* **on attaque?** *(à table)* shall we dig in? (**c**) *Mus (morceau)* to strike up; *(note)* to attack
  2 s'attaquer *vpr* **s'a. à** *(adversaire)* to attack; *(problème)* to tackle; **s'a. à plus fort que soi** to bite off more than one can chew

attardé, -e [atarde] **1** *nm,f* **a. (mental)** (mentally) retarded person
  2 *adj* (**a**) *(qui flâne)* **il ne restait plus que quelques passants attardés** there were only a few people still around (**b**) *(vieux)* old-fashioned (**c**) *(mentalement)* (mentally) retarded

attarder [atarde] **s'attarder** *vpr* to linger; **s'a. à des détails** to dwell over details; **ne nous attardons pas sur ce point** let's not dwell on this point

atteignais *etc. voir* **atteindre**

atteindre [54] [atɛ̃dr] **1** *vt* to reach; *(cible)* to hit; **être atteint d'une maladie** to be suffering from a disease; **il a été atteint dans son amour-propre** his pride has been wounded; **le poumon est atteint** the lung is affected; *Fig* **rien ne l'atteint** nothing affects him; *Fam* **il est très atteint** *(fou)* he's completely cracked
  2 atteindre à *vt ind* **a. à la perfection** to be close to perfection

atteinte [atɛ̃t] *nf (attaque)* **a. à** attack on; **porter a. à** to undermine

attelage [atəlaʒ] *nm (animaux)* team

atteler [9] [atəle] **1** *vt (chevaux)* to harness; *(bœufs)* to yoke; **a. une voiture** to hitch up horses to a carriage
  2 s'atteler *vpr* **s'a. à une tâche** to buckle down to a task

attelle [atɛl] *nf* splint

attenant, -e [atənɑ̃, -ɑ̃t] *adj* adjoining; **a. à** adjoining

attendre [atɑ̃dr] **1** *vt* to wait for; **a. son tour** to wait one's turn; **a. un bébé** to be expecting (a baby); **se faire a.** *(personne)* to keep people waiting; **la réponse ne s'est pas fait a.** the reply wasn't long in coming; **je l'attends d'une minute à l'autre** I'm expecting him/her any minute now; **a. qch de qn/qch** to expect sth from sb/sth; **qu'est-ce que tu attends pour le lui dire?** what are you waiting for? go and tell him; **a. que qn fasse qch** to wait for sb to do sth; **attends**

de lui avoir parlé avant de prendre une décision wait until you've spoken to him/her before you take a decision; *Fig* **a. qn au tournant** to be waiting to pounce on sb

2 *vi* to wait; **a. une heure** to wait (for) an hour; **sans plus a.** without further ado; **faire a. qn** to keep sb waiting; *Fam* **on ne va pas a. cent sept ans** we're not going to wait forever; **en attendant** meanwhile; *(néanmoins)* all the same; **en attendant son arrivée** until he arrives/arrived

3 s'attendre *vpr* **s'a. à qch** to expect sth; **je m'attends à tout** I'm ready for anything; **je m'y attendais** I expected as much; **il fallait s'y a.** it was only to be expected; **je m'attendais à ce que tu le lui dises** I was expecting you to tell him/her

attendrir [atɑ̃driʀ] **1** *vt* **(a)** *(émouvoir)* to move; *(rendre indulgent)* to soften **(b)** *(viande)* to tenderize

2 s'attendrir *vpr* to be moved (**sur** by)

attendrissant, -e [atɑ̃drisɑ̃, -ɑ̃t] *adj* moving

attendu, -e [atɑ̃dy] **1** *adj* expected; **le jour tant a. est arrivé** the long-awaited day has arrived

2 *prép Sout* **a. les circonstances** considering the circumstances

3 attendu que *conj Sout* considering that; *Jur* whereas

attentat [atɑ̃ta] *nm* attack; **a. à la bombe** bombing; **a. à la pudeur** indecent assault; **a. à la sûreté de l'État** high treason; **a. à la voiture piégée** car-bomb attack

attentat-suicide [atɑ̃tasɥisid] *nm* suicide attack; **a. à la bombe** suicide bomb (attack)

attente [atɑ̃t] *nf* **(a)** *(fait d'attendre)* waiting; *(période)* wait; **être dans l'a. de qch** to be waiting for sth; **en a.** *(au téléphone)* on hold; *Ordinat* **liste de fichiers à imprimer en a.** print queue **(b)** *(espoir)* expectations; **contre toute a.** against all expectations; **répondre à l'a. ou aux attentes de qn** to live up to sb's expectations; **dans l'a. de votre réponse/de vous rencontrer** *(dans une lettre)* I look forward to receiving your reply/to meeting you

attenter [atɑ̃te] **attenter à** *vt ind* to make an attempt on; **a. à ses jours** to attempt suicide

attentif, -ive [atɑ̃tif, -iv] *adj* attentive; **être a. aux autres** to be attentive to others; **être a. à qch** to pay attention to sth; *(ses intérêts, sa santé)* to look after sth; **écouter d'une oreille attentive** to listen attentively

attention [atɑ̃sjɔ̃] *nf* **(a)** *(soin)* attention; **écouter avec a.** to listen attentively; **faire a. à qch** to pay attention to sth; *(sa santé, ses intérêts)* to look after sth; **il a fait a. de ne pas la blesser** he took care not to hurt her; **ne pas prêter la moindre a. à** to take no notice of; **(faites) a.!** look out!; **a. si je t'attrape!** if I catch you there'll be trouble!; **a., peinture fraîche** *(sur écriteau)* wet paint; **a. à la fermeture des portières, a. au départ!** stand clear of the doors, the train is about to depart!; **à l'a. de qn** *(sur une lettre)* for the attention of sb **(b)** *(amabilité)* attention; **être plein d'attentions envers qn** to be very attentive toward sb

attentionné, -e [atɑ̃sjɔne] *adj* attentive (**auprès de** toward)

attentisme [atɑ̃tism] *nm* wait-and-see policy

attentiste [atɑ̃tist] **1** *adj* **attitude a.** wait-and-see attitude

2 *nmf* **les attentistes** those who play a waiting game

attentivement [atɑ̃tivmɑ̃] *adv* attentively

atténuation [atenɥasjɔ̃] *nf* *(d'un effet, de la douleur)* reduction; *(d'une lumière)* dimming; *(d'une couleur)* toning down; *(d'une chute)* breaking

atténuer [atenɥe] **1** *vt* *(effet, douleur)* to reduce; *(couleur)* to tone down; *(chute)* to break

2 s'atténuer *vpr* *(douleur)* to ease; *(lumière, couleurs, bruit)* to fade

atterrant, -e [atɛrɑ̃, -ɑ̃t] *adj* appalling

atterrer [atere] *vt* to appall

atterrir [aterir] *vi* to land; **a. en catastrophe** to make an emergency landing; *Fam* **a. dans un bar/en prison** to wind up in a bar/in prison

atterrissage [aterisaʒ] *nm* landing; **a. en douceur** soft landing; **a. forcé** forced landing

attestation [atɛstasjɔ̃] *nf* certificate

attester [atɛste] *vt* *(témoigner)* to testify to; **a. que** to testify that; **aucun dictionnaire n'atteste l'existence de ce mot** this word is not attested in any dictionary

attifer [atife] *Fam* **1** *vt* to dress (**de** in)

2 s'attifer *vpr* to dress; **s'a. de qch** to put sth on

attirail [atiraj] *nm* paraphernalia

attirance [atirɑ̃s] *nf* attraction; **éprouver de l'a. pour** *ou* **envers qn** to be attracted to sb

attirant, -e [atirɑ̃, -ɑ̃t] *adj* attractive

attirer [atire] **1** *vt* **(a)** *(sujet: aimant, planète)* to attract; *Fig* **a. qn dans un piège** to lure sb into a trap; **a. qn dans un coin** to take sb into a corner; **a. l'attention de qn** *(sujet: chose)* to catch sb's attention; **a. l'attention de qn sur qch** to draw sb's attention to sth; **a. les regards** to catch the eye **(b)** *(séduire)* to attract; *(sujet: matière, pays)* to appeal to

2 s'attirer *vpr* **(a)** *(mutuellement)* to be attracted to each other **(b)** *(sur soi)* **s'a. des critiques** to come in for criticism; **s'a. des ennuis** to get oneself into trouble; **s'a. la colère de qn** to incur sb's anger

attiser [atize] *vt* **(a)** *(feu)* to poke **(b)** *Fig* *(désir, colère, racisme)* to stir up

attitré, -e [atitre] *adj* **(a)** *(habituel)* usual **(b)** *(chargé d'une fonction)* appointed

attitude [atityd] *nf* **(a)** *(conduite, position)* attitude (**envers** *ou* **à l'égard de** toward); **tu as eu une a. déplorable** your behavior was appalling **(b)** *(maintien)* bearing, demeanor **(c)** *(affectation)* pose

attouchement [atuʃmɑ̃] *nm* fondling; **se livrer à des attouchements sur qn** to fondle sb

attraction [atraksjɔ̃] *nf* **(a)** *(d'un aimant)* attraction; **l'a. terrestre** the earth's gravitational pull **(b)** *aussi Fig* *(spectacle)* attraction

attrait [atrɛ] *nm* attraction

attrape [atrap] *nf* *(farce)* trick

attrape-nigaud *(pl* **attrape-nigauds)** [atrapnigo] *nm* con, scam

attraper [atrape] **1** *vt* **(a)** *(capturer, saisir)* to catch; **se faire a.** to get caught; *Fam* **a. qn à faire qch** to catch sb doing sth **(b)** *(maladie)* to catch; **a. froid** to catch cold; **a. mal** to catch a chill **(c)** *(tromper)* **a. qn** to take sb in; **là, tu es bien attrapé** you fell for it hook, line and sinker **(d)** *Fam (gronder)* **se faire a.** to get a dressing-down

2 s'attraper *vpr* *(maladie)* to be caught; *(habitude)* to be picked up

attrapeur de rêves [atrapœrdərɛv] *nm* dreamcatcher

attrayant, -e [atrɛjɑ̃, -ɑ̃t] *adj* attractive; **peu a.** unattractive

attribuable [atribɥabl] *adj* attributable (**à** to)

attribuer [atribɥe] **1** *vt* **(a)** *(allouer)* to assign, to allot (**à** to); *(prix, récompense, bourse)* to award (**à** to) **(b)** *(œuvre, crime, erreur)* to attribute (**à** to); **a. de l'importance à qch** to attach importance to sth

2 s'attribuer *vpr* **s'a. qch** to claim sth; **il s'en est attribué tout le mérite** he claimed *or* took all the credit for it

attribut [atriby] **1** *nm* attribute

2 *adj* attributive

attribution [atribysjɔ̃] *nf* **(a)** *(allocation)* assigning, allocation (**à** to); *(d'un prix, d'une récompense, d'une bourse)* awarding (**à** to); **attributions** *(fonctions)* duties; **entrer dans les attributions de qn** to be part of sb's duties **(b)** *(d'une œuvre, d'un crime, d'une erreur)* attribution (**à** to)

attristant, -e [atristɑ̃, -ɑ̃t] *adj* depressing

attrister [atriste] **1** *vt* to sadden; **cela m'attriste** it makes me sad
  2 s'attrister *vpr* to be saddened (**de** by)
attroupement [atrupmɑ̃] *nm* crowd; **provoquer un a.** to draw a crowd
attrouper [atrupe] **s'attrouper** *vpr* to gather
atypique [atipik] *adj* atypical
au [o] *voir* **à**
aubaine [obɛn] *nf* godsend; **profiter de l'a.** to take advantage of one's good luck; *Can* **à prix d'a.** at a reduced price
aube [ob] *nf* (**a**) *(matin)* dawn; **à l'a.** at dawn; *Fig* **l'a. de la civilisation** the dawn of civilization (**b**) *Rel* alb
aubépine [obepin] *nf* hawthorn; **fleurs d'a.** may blossom
auberge [obɛrʒ] *nf* inn; *Fig* **ici, c'est l'a. espagnole** you have to bring everything yourself here; *Fam* **on n'est pas sorti de l'a.** we're not out of the woods yet; **a. de jeunesse** youth hostel
aubergine [obɛrʒin] *nf* (**a**) *(plante)* eggplant (**b**) *Fam (contractuelle)* meter maid
aubergiste [obɛrʒist] *nmf* innkeeper
auburn [obœrn] *adj inv* auburn
aucun, -e [okœ̃, -yn] **1** *pron indéfini* (**a**) *(personne, rien)* none; **a. des deux** neither (of them); **a. d'entre eux** none of them; **je ne me fie à a. d'entre eux** I don't trust any of them (**b**) *Litt* **d'aucuns** some people
  2 *adj indéfini* (**a**) *(négatif)* no, not any; **je n'en ai aucune idée** I have no idea; **sans aucune exception** without any exception; **sans a. doute** without a doubt (**b**) *(positif)* any; **plus rapide qu'a. autre coureur** faster than any other runner
aucunement [okynmɑ̃] *adv* not at all, not in the least
audace [odas] *nf* (**a**) *(courage)* boldness, daring (**b**) *(culot)* audacity, impudence (**c**) *(originalité)* boldness (**d**) *(action audacieuse)* **avoir toutes les audaces** to do the most daring things
audacieusement [odasjøzmɑ̃] *adv* (**a**) *(avec courage)* boldly, daringly (**b**) *(avec culot)* impudently
audacieux, -euse [odasjø, -øz] *adj* (**a**) *(courageux)* bold, daring (**b**) *(culotté)* impudent (**c**) *(original)* bold
au-dedans [odədɑ̃] *adv* inside; **a. de** inside
au-dehors [odəɔr] *adv* outside; **a. de** outside
au-delà [odəla] **1** *nm* **l'a.** the next world
  2 *prép* **a. de** beyond
  3 *adv* beyond; **jusqu'à une certaine somme mais pas a.** up to a certain sum but no more
au-dessous [odəsu] *adv* below, underneath; *(à l'étage inférieur)* downstairs; **on en trouve à huit euros et même a.** you can get them for eight euros or even less; **a. de** *(dans l'espace)* below, under; *(nombre, somme)* under; *(dans une hiérarchie)* below; **15 degrés a. de zéro** 15 degrees below zero; *Fig* **être a. de tout** to be beneath contempt
au-dessus [odəsy] *adv* above; *(à l'étage supérieur)* upstairs; **une terrasse avec une marquise a.** a terrace with an awning over it; **1000 euros et a.** 1,000 euros and upward; **a. de** *(dans l'espace, dans une hiérarchie)* above; *(nombre, somme)* over; **a. de nos têtes** *(dans le ciel)* overhead; **c'est a. de mes forces** it's beyond me; **vivre a. de ses moyens** to live beyond one's means; *Fig* **je suis a. de ça** I'm above all that
au-devant [odəvɑ̃] **au-devant de** *prép* **aller/courir a. de qn** to go/run to meet sb; **aller a. des désirs de qn** to anticipate sb's wishes; **aller a. du danger** to court danger
audible [odibl] *adj* audible
audience [odjɑ̃s] *nf* (**a**) *(entrevue)* audience; *Jur* hearing; **l'a. est suspendue** the case is adjourned (**b**) *(intérêt)* **trouver a. auprès des jeunes** to find a following among young people (**c**) *(public)* audience
Audimat® [odimat] *nm (appareil)* = device for calculating television audience ratings; *(résultats)* audience ratings; **faire de l'A.** to increase audience ratings

audioconférence [odjokɔ̃ferɑ̃s] *nf* audioconference
audioguide [odjogid] *nf (lors d'une visite de musée)* audio guide, headset *(providing recorded commentary on exhibit etc.)*
audionumérique [odjonymerik] *adj* digital audio; **disque a.** compact disk
audiovisuel, -elle [odjovizɥɛl] **1** *adj* (**a**) *(méthodes)* audiovisual (**b**) *TV & Rad* television and radio
  2 *nm TV & Rad* **l'a.** television and radio
auditeur, -trice [oditœr, -tris] *nm,f* (**a**) *(d'un programme de radio)* listener (**b**) *Univ* **suivre un cours en a. libre** to audit a course
auditif, -ive [oditif, -iv] *adj (nerf)* auditory; *(troubles)* hearing
audition [odisjɔ̃] *nf* (**a**) *(faculté)* hearing (**b**) *(de chanteur, d'acteur)* audition; **passer une a.** to have an audition (**c**) *Jur* **a. des témoins** examination of the witnesses
auditionner [odisjone] *vt & vi* to audition
auditoire [oditwar] *nm* (**a**) *(public)* audience (**b**) *Belg & Suisse (amphithéâtre)* auditorium; *(salle de cours)* lecture hall or theater
auditorium [oditɔrjɔm] *nm* auditorium; *Rad & TV* recording studio
AUE [aye] *nm (abrév* **acte unique européen**) SEA
auge [oʒ] *nf (mangeoire)* trough
augmentation [ɔgmɑ̃tasjɔ̃] *nf* (**a**) *(accroissement)* increase (**de** in); **a. (de salaire)** raise; **demander une a.** to ask for a raise; **être en a.** to be on the increase (**b**) *Ordinat* **a. de puissance** upgrade
augmenter [ɔgmɑ̃te] **1** *vt* to increase; **édition augmentée** enlarged edition; **a. qn** to raise sb's salary, to give sb a raise
  2 *vi* to increase (**de** by)
augure [ogyr] *nm* (**a**) *(devin)* augur (**b**) *(présage)* omen; **de bon a.** auspicious; **de mauvais a.** ominous
augurer [ogyre] *vt* **a. bien/mal de qch** to augur well/ill for sth
auguste [ogyst] *adj* august
aujourd'hui [oʒurdɥi] *adv* (**a**) *(ce jour)* today; **le journal d'a.** today's paper; *Fam* **c'est pour a. ou pour demain?** I/we haven't got all day! (**b**) *(à l'heure actuelle)* nowadays, today; **les jeunes gens d'a.** young people today; **l'Europe d'a.** present-day Europe
aulne [on] *nm* alder
aumône [omon] *nf* alms; **demander l'a.** to ask for charity; **faire l'a. à qn** to give alms to sb
aumônier [omonje] *nm* chaplain
aune [on] *nm* alder
auparavant [oparavɑ̃] *adv (avant)* before(hand); *(d'abord)* first
auprès [oprɛ] **auprès de** *prép* (**a**) *(près de)* by, next to; **ambassadeur a. des Nations unies** ambassador to the United Nations (**b**) *(en comparaison de)* compared with (**c**) *(en s'adressant à)* **se renseigner a. de qn** to ask sb
auquel [okɛl] *voir* **lequel**
aura[1] *etc. voir* **avoir**[1]
aura[2] [ɔra] *nf* aura
auréole [ɔreɔl] *nf* (**a**) *(d'un saint, d'un astre)* halo; *Fig* **parer qn d'une a.** to idolize sb (**b**) *(trace)* ring
auréoler [ɔreɔle] *vt* **tout auréolé de gloire** crowned with glory
auriculaire [ɔrikylɛr] *nm* little finger, pinky
aurifère [ɔrifɛr] *adj* gold-bearing; **gisement a.** goldfield
Aurigny [ɔriɲi] *n* Alderney
aurore [ɔrɔr] *nf* dawn, daybreak; **à l'a.** at dawn; *Fam* **aux aurores** at the crack of dawn; **a. boréale** aurora borealis, northern lights
auscultation [ɔskyltasjɔ̃] *nf* auscultation
ausculter [ɔskylte] *vt (malade, cœur)* to listen to

auspices [ɔspis] *nmpl* **sous les a. de** *(sous l'égide de)* under the auspices of; **sous d'heureux a.** auspiciously; **sous de fâcheux a.** inauspiciously

aussi [osi] **1** *adv* **(a)** *(également)* too, as well; **lui a. il sait le faire** he, too, knows how to do it, he knows how to do it as well **(b)** *(tellement)* so; **une a. belle journée** such a nice day **(c)** *(dans les phrases comparatives)* as; **a. grand que moi** as tall as me; **pas a. gros que** not as big as, not so big as; **a. bien que moi** as well as me **(d)** *(quelque)* however; **a. bizarre que cela soit** however odd it may be **2** *conj* therefore, so

aussitôt [osito] **1** *adv* immediately, straight away; **a. avant/après** immediately before/after; **a. après son retour je suis parti** as soon as he returned I left; **a. l'argent reçu je vous paierai** as soon as I get the money I'll pay you; **a. dit, a. fait** no sooner said than done **2** *conj* **a. que** as soon as

austère [ostɛr] *adj (vie, style)* austere; *(vêtement)* severe; *(expression)* stern

austérité [osterite] *nf (de la vie, d'un style)* austerity; *(d'un vêtement)* severity; *(d'une expression)* sternness; **mesures d'a.** austerity measures

austral, -e, -als *ou* **-aux** [ostral, -o] *adj* southern

Australasie [ostralazi] *nf* **l'A.** Australasia

Australie [ostrali] *nf* **l'A.** Australia

australien, -enne [ostraljɛ̃, -ɛn] **1** *adj* Australian **2** *nm,f* **A., Australienne** Australian

autant [otɑ̃] *adv* **(a)** *(tellement)* so much; **a. de** *(quantité)* so much; *(nombre)* so many; **je n'avais jamais vu a. de neige/de bateaux** I had never seen so much snow/so many boats **(b)** *(la même quantité, le même nombre)* **remettez-m'en encore a.** give me the same again; **il m'en veut, mais je lui en veux tout a.** he's angry with me, but I'm just as angry with him; **le coût de la vie a augmenté de cinq pour cent mais les salaires n'ont pas augmenté d'a.** the cost of living has increased by five percent but salaries have not risen by the same amount; **a. que** *(quantité)* as much as; *(nombre)* as many as; **a. que possible** as far as possible; **a. de... que** *(quantité)* as much... as; *(nombre)* as many... as; **ils ont a. de terrain/d'amis que vous** they have as much land/as many friends as you **(c)** *(de même)* **on ne peut pas en dire a. de tout le monde** you can't say the same for everybody; **essaie un peu d'en faire a.** try to do the same **(d)** *(locutions)* **a. elle est expansive, a. il est réservé** she's as extroverted as he is shy; **a. pour moi!** I stand corrected!; **(pour) a. que je sache** as far as I know, to the best of my knowledge; **ce sera a. de moins à payer** it will be that much less to pay; **a. rester ici** we may as well stay here; **a. dire que...** which amounts to saying that...; **j'aimerais a. aller au cinéma** I'd rather go to the movies; **j'aime a. te dire que je n'étais pas contente!** I wasn't too happy, I can tell you!; **d'a. (plus) que...** especially since...; **d'a. plus/moins que** all the more/less because; **cela vous sera d'a. plus facile que vous êtes jeune** it will be that much easier for you since you are young; **pour a.** *(malgré cela)* for all that

autarcie [otarsi] *nf Pol* autarky; **vivre en a.** to be self-sufficient

autel [otɛl] *nm aussi Fig* altar; **conduire sa fille à l'a.** to give one's daughter away

auteur [otœr] *nm* **(a)** *(de livre)* author, writer; *(de chanson)* composer; *(de tableau)* painter **(b)** *(responsable)* author; *(d'un crime)* perpetrator; *(d'un projet)* instigator

authenticité [otɑ̃tisite] *nf* authenticity

authentification [otɑ̃tifikasjɔ̃] *nf* authentication

authentifier [66] [otɑ̃tifje] *vt* to authenticate

authentique [otɑ̃tik] *adj* authentic, genuine; *(fait, histoire)* true

authentiquement [otɑ̃tikmɑ̃] *adv* authentically, genuinely

autisme [otism] *nm* autism

autiste [otist] **1** *adj* autistic **2** *nmf* autistic person

auto [oto] *nf* car; **autos tamponneuses** bumper cars; **petite a.** *(jouet)* toy car

auto- [oto] *préf* auto-, self-

autoaccusation [otoakyzasjɔ̃] *nf* self-accusation

autobiographie [otobjografi] *nf* autobiography

autobiographique [otobjografik] *adj* autobiographical

autobronzant, -e [otobrɔ̃zɑ̃, -ɑ̃t] **1** *adj* self-tanning **2** *nm* self-tan, self-tanning cream

autobus [otobys] *nm* bus; **a. à impériale** double-decker (bus)

autocar [otokar] *nm* bus

autocassable [otokasabl] *adj* **ampoule a.** break-open phial

autocensurer [otosɑ̃syre] **s'autocensurer** *vpr* to practice self-censorship

autochtone [otɔkton] **1** *nmf aussi Hum* native **2** *adj* native

autocollant, -e [otokɔlɑ̃, -ɑ̃t] **1** *adj* self-adhesive; *(enveloppe)* self-sealing **2** *nm* sticker

autocorrecteur, -trice [otokɔrɛktœr, -tris] *adj Ordinat* self-correcting

autocouchette(s) [otokuʃɛt] *adj inv voir* **train**

autocrate [otokrat] *nmf* autocrat

autocratie [otokrasi] *nf* autocracy

autocratique [otokratik] *adj* autocratic

autocritique [otokritik] *nf* self-criticism; **faire son a.** to criticize oneself

autocuiseur [otokɥizœr] *nm* pressure cooker

autodafé [otodafe] *nm Hist* auto-da-fé

autodéfense [otodefɑ̃s] *nf* self-defense

autodestructeur, -trice [otodɛstryktœr, -tris] *adj* self-destructive

autodestruction [otodɛstryksjɔ̃] *nf* self-destruction

autodétermination [otodetɛrminasjɔ̃] *nf Pol* self-determination

autodidacte [otodidakt] **1** *adj* self-taught **2** *nmf* self-taught person

autodrome [otodrom] *nm* motor-racing track; *(pour les essais)* car-testing track

auto-école (*pl* **auto-écoles**) [otoekɔl] *nf* driving school

autofinancement [otofinɑ̃smɑ̃] *nm* self-financing

autofinancer [45] [otofinɑ̃se] **s'autofinancer** *vpr* to be self-financing

autofocus [otofɔkys] *adj & nm Phot* autofocus

autogéré, -e [otoʒere] *adj* self-managed

autogestion [otoʒɛstjɔ̃] *nf* self-management

autographe [otograf] *nm & adj* autograph

automate [otomat] *nm* **(a)** *(robot) aussi Fig* automaton **(b)** *Suisse (machine)* vending machine; *(à billets)* ATM

automation [otomasjɔ̃] *nf* automation

automatique [otomatik] **1** *adj* automatic; **il est absent tous les lundis, c'est a.** he's off every Monday without fail **2** *nm* **(a)** *Tél* direct dialing **(b)** *(pistolet)* automatic

automatiquement [otomatikmɑ̃] *adv* automatically

automatisation [otomatizasjɔ̃] *nf* automation

automatiser [otomatize] *vt* to automate

automatisme [otomatism] *nm* **(a)** *(réflexe)* automatism; **agir par a.** to act automatically; **fermer la porte à double tour est devenu un a.** double-locking the door has become automatic **(b)** *(dispositif)* automatic device

automédication [otomedikasjɔ̃] *nf* self-medication

automitrailleuse [otomitrajøz] *nf* armored car

automnal, -e, -aux, -ales [otɔnal, -o] *adj* autumnal

automne [otɔn] *nm* fall, autumn; **en a., à l'a.** in the fall, in autumn; **une soirée d'a.** a fall *or* an autumn evening; *Fig* **à l'a. de sa vie** in the autumn of his/her life

automobile [otomɔbil] **1** *nf* (**a**) *(voiture)* car, automobile (**b**) *(industrie)* **l'a.** the automobile industry
 2 *adj* (**a**) *(véhicule)* self-propelling (**b**) *(industrie, accessoires)* car, automobile

automobiliste [otomɔbilist] *nmf* motorist

autoneige [otonɛʒ] *nf Can* snowmobile

autonettoyant, -e [otonetwajã, -ãt] *adj* **four a.** self-cleaning oven

autonome [otonɔm] *adj (état, région)* autonomous, self-governing; *(appareil)* self-contained; *(personne)* self-sufficient; *Ordinat* **calculateur a.** stand-alone (computer)

autonomie [otonɔmi] *nf* (**a**) *Pol* autonomy, self-government (**b**) *(de personne)* self-sufficiency (**c**) *(de voiture)* range; *(de batterie)* life; *Aviat* **a. (de vol)** range

autonomiste [otonɔmist] *nmf Pol* separatist

autoportrait [otopɔrtrɛ] *nm* self-portrait

autopsie [otɔpsi] *nf* autopsy, post-mortem; *Fig* **faire l'a. d'une œuvre** to dissect a work

autopsier [66] [otɔpsje] *vt* to perform an autopsy *or* a post-mortem on

autopunition [otopynisjɔ̃] *nf* self-punishment

autoradio [otoradjo] *nm* car radio

autorail [otoraj] *nm* railcar

autorégulation [otoregylasjɔ̃] *nf* self-regulation

autoreverse [otorivœrs] *adj* **appareil a.** auto-reverse

autorisation [otɔrizasjɔ̃] *nf* (**a**) *(permission)* authorization, permission; **donner à qn l'a. de faire qch** to give sb permission to do sth; **demander (à qn) l'a. de faire qch** to ask (sb) permission to do sth; *Ordinat* **a. d'accès** access authorization; **a. de sortie du territoire** = parental authorization for a minor to travel abroad; *Aviat* **a. de vol** flight clearance (**b**) *(document)* authorization

autorisé, -e [otɔrize] *adj* (**a**) *(qualifié)* **tenir qch de source autorisée** to have sth from an authoritative source; **les milieux autorisés** official circles (**b**) *(permis)* permitted, allowed

autoriser [otɔrize] *vt* (**a**) *(permettre à)* **a. qn à faire qch** to authorize *or* to permit sb to do sth; **je ne vous autorise pas à me parler sur ce ton** I won't allow you to talk to me like that (**b**) *(permettre)* **ces découvertes (nous) autorisent à penser que…** these discoveries entitle us to believe that…

autoritaire [otɔritɛr] *adj* authoritarian

autoritairement [otɔritɛrmã] *adv* in an authoritarian manner

autoritarisme [otɔritarism] *nm* authoritarianism

autorité [otɔrite] *nf* (**a**) *(domination, fermeté)* authority; **avoir de l'a. sur qn** to have authority over sb; **faire qch d'a.** to do sth on one's own authority (**b**) *(poids)* **faire a. en qch** *(personne)* to be an authority on sth; **ce livre fait a.** this book is the authoritative work (**c**) *(gouvernement)* **les représentants de l'a.** the representatives of authority; **les autorités** the authorities (**d**) *(personne respectée)* authority

autoroute [otorut] *nf* (**a**) *Aut* freeway; **a. à péage** turnpike (road) (**b**) *Ordinat* **a. de l'information** information superhighway

autoroutier, -ère [otorutje, -ɛr] *adj* **réseau a.** freeway system

autosatisfaction [otosatisfaksjɔ̃] *nf* self-satisfaction

auto-stop [otostɔp] *nm* hitchhiking, hitching; **faire de l'a.** to hitchhike, to hitch; **prendre qn en a.** to give sb a lift; **faire le tour de l'Europe en a.** to hitchhike around Europe

auto-stoppeur, -euse *(mpl* **auto-stoppeurs,** *fpl* **auto-stoppeuses)** [otostɔpœr, -øz] *nm,f* hitchhiker, hitcher

autosuggestion [otosygʒɛstjɔ̃] *nf* autosuggestion

autour [otur] *adv* around; **une ville avec des murs tout a.** a town with walls all around it; **a. de** *(dans l'espace)* around; *(environ)* about; *Fig* **discuter qch a. d'un verre** to discuss sth over a drink

autre [otr] **1** *adj indéfini* (**a**) *(différent)* other; **l'a. côté** the other side; **un a. jour** another day; **as-tu d'autres questions?** do you have any other questions?; **les choux et autres légumes** cabbages and other vegetables; **je l'ai vu l'a. jour/soir** I saw him the other day/evening
 (**b**) *(avec un pronom personnel)* **nous autres Français** we French (people); *Fam* **eh, vous autres, venez par ici!** hey, you guys, come over here!
 (**c**) *(locutions)* **a. chose** something else; **avez-vous a. chose à faire?** do you have anything else to do?; *Fig* **il est assez bon musicien, mais sa femme c'est a. chose!** he's not a bad musician, but his wife's in a different league!; **a. part** somewhere else

 2 *pron indéfini* (**a**) **l'a.** *(personne, chose)* the other (one); *Fam* **et l'a. qui se plaint tout le temps!** and then there's him and his constant complaining!; *Fam* **comme dit l'a.** as the saying goes, as they say; **un a.** *(personne, chose)* another (one); **il n'est pas plus bête qu'un a.** he is no more stupid than anyone else; **c'était un touriste comme un a.** he was just an ordinary tourist; **c'est une raison comme une a.** it's as good a reason as any; **les autres** *(personnes, choses)* the others, the other ones; **tu devrais penser un peu aux autres** you should think of others; *Fam* **à d'autres!** who do you think you're kidding?; *Fam* **j'en ai vu d'autres** I've seen worse than that
 (**b**) *(avec l'un, les uns)* **l'un et l'a.** both; **l'un dit ceci, l'a. dit cela** one says this and the other says that; **les uns disent ceci, les autres disent cela** some say this and others say that; **les uns et les autres** *(deux groupes)* both parties; **l'un ou l'a.** either; **c'est l'un ou l'autre** *(il faut choisir)* it's one or the other; **ni l'un ni l'a.** neither; **je ne les connais ni l'un ni l'a.** I don't know either of them; **ni les uns ni les autres** none of them; **je n'ai vu ni les uns ni les autres** I didn't see any of them; **l'un l'a.** each other, one another; **les uns les autres** one another; **ils dépendent l'un de l'a.** they depend on each other; *Fig* **l'un dans l'a.** on the whole
 (**c**) *(avec de)* **quelque chose d'a.** something else; *(dans les questions)* anything else; **rien d'autre** nothing else; **il n'y en a pas d'a.** there aren't any others; **personne d'a.** nobody else; **quelqu'un d'a.** somebody else; *(dans les questions)* anyone else; **que pouvait-il faire d'a.?** what else could he do?; **qui d'a. sera là?** who else will be there?

autrefois [otrəfwa] *adv* in the past, once; **d'a.** of long ago

autrement [otrəmã] *adv* (**a**) *(différemment)* differently; **il ne put faire a. que d'obéir** he had no alternative but to obey; **a. dit** in other words (**b**) *(sinon)* otherwise (**c**) *(bien plus)* far more; **a. plus dangereux (que)** far more dangerous (than) (**d**) **pas a.** not particularly; **cela ne me surprend pas a.** that doesn't particularly surprise me

Autriche [otriʃ] *nf* **l'A.** Austria

autrichien, -enne [otriʃjɛ̃, -ɛn] **1** *adj* Austrian
 2 *nm,f* **A., Autrichienne** Austrian

autruche [otryʃ] *nf* ostrich; **sac en a.** ostrich-skin handbag; *Fig* **avoir un estomac d'a.** to have a stomach of steel; **pratiquer la politique de l'a., faire l'a.** to bury one's head in the sand

autrui [otrɥi] *pron indéfini* others, other people; **ne fais pas à a. ce que tu ne voudrais pas qu'on te fît** do unto others as you would have others do unto you

auvent [ovã] *nm (toit)* porch roof; *(de tente)* canopy, awning

auvergnat, -e [ovɛrɲa, -at] **1** *adj* of the Auvergne
 2 *nm,f* **A., Auvergnate** person from the Auvergne

aux [o] *voir* **à**

auxiliaire [ɔksiljɛr] **1** *adj* auxiliary
 2 *nmf (aide)* assistant; *(dans les hôpitaux)* auxiliary; *(dans l'ad-*

ministration) temporary worker; **a. familiale** mother's helper

3 *nm Gram* auxiliary verb

auxquels, auxquelles [okɛl] *voir* **lequel**

av. *(abrév* **avenue)** Ave.

avachi, -e [avaʃi] *adj* **(a)** *(vêtement, bottes, canapé)* misshapen **(b)** *(personne, muscles)* flabby; **être a. dans un fauteuil** to be slumped in an armchair

avachir [avaʃir] **s'avachir** *vpr* **(a)** *(vêtement, bottes, canapé)* to lose its shape **(b)** *(personne) (physiquement)* to get flabby; *(moralement)* to let oneself go; **s'a. dans un fauteuil** to flop into an armchair

avais *etc. voir* **avoir¹**

aval¹, -als [aval] *nm Fin (d'un effet de commerce)* endorsement; **a. bancaire** bank guarantee; *Fig* **donner son a. à un projet** to give a project one's backing *or* support

aval² [aval] *nm (d'un cours d'eau)* downstream section; *aussi Ind* **en a. (de)** downstream (from); **la Seine en a. de Paris** the Seine below Paris; **les étapes en a. de la production** the post-production stages

avalanche [avalɑ̃ʃ] *nf* avalanche; *Fig (d'injures)* shower; *(de lettres, de compliments)* flood

avaler [avale] *vt (a) (goulûment) (nourriture)* to bolt; *(boisson)* to gulp down; *Fig (livre)* to devour; *(croire)* to swallow; **j'ai avalé de travers** it went down the wrong way; **je meurs de faim, je n'ai rien avalé depuis hier** I'm starving, I haven't had a thing to eat since yesterday; **on lui fait avaler n'importe quoi** he's very gullible, he believes anything you tell him; **a. la fumée** to inhale; *Fig* **a. ses mots** to mumble; **a. une carte de crédit** *(distributeur automatique)* to swallow a credit card; **a. les kilomètres** to eat up the miles; **tu as avalé ta langue?** have you lost your tongue?

avaleur [avalœr] *nm* **a. de sabres** sword-swallower

avance [avɑ̃s] *nf* **(a)** *(progression)* advance; **a. rapide** *(sur magnétophone)* fast-forwarding

(b) *(avantage)* lead; **avoir de l'a. sur qn** to be ahead of sb; **prendre de l'a. sur qn** to take the lead over sb; **avoir deux minutes/1 km d'a. sur qn** ≃ to have a two-minute/half-mile lead over sb; **avoir un but/point d'a. (sur qn)** to be one goal/point ahead (of sb); *Scol* **avoir un an d'a.** to be a year ahead; **arriver avec cinq minutes d'a.** to arrive five minutes early; **d'a., à l'a., par a.** in advance; **d'a. merci** *(dans une lettre)* thanking you in advance; *(dans une conversation)* thanks; **en a.** early; **être en a. d'une demi-heure** to be half an hour early; **être en a. pour son âge** to be advanced for one's age; **être en a. sur son temps** to be ahead of one's time

(c) *(d'argent)* advance; **faire une a. à qn** to give sb an advance

(d) **faire des avances à qn** *(chercher à séduire)* to make advances to sb

avancé, -e [avɑ̃se] *adj* **(a)** *(dans l'espace)* advanced **(b)** *(précoce)* **être a. pour son âge** to be advanced for one's age **(c)** *(idées, technologie)* advanced **(d)** *(tardif)* **à une heure avancée de la nuit** late in the night; **à un âge a.** at an advanced age **(e)** *(presque à terme)* **à un stade a.** at an advanced stage; **mon travail est bien a.** I'm making good progress with my work; *Fig* **vous voilà bien a.!** a lot of good that's done you!

avancée [avɑ̃se] *nf* **(a)** *(saillie)* projection; *Constr* **a. du toit** eaves **(b)** *(de troupes, de la recherche)* advance

avancement [avɑ̃smɑ̃] *nm* **(a)** *(d'un projet)* progress; **état d'a. des travaux** progress report **(b)** *(promotion)* promotion; **avoir** *ou* **obtenir de l'a.** to be promoted **(c)** *Ordinat* **a. automatique** automatic feed; **a. ligne par ligne** line feed; **a. du papier** paper feed; **a. par friction** friction feed

avancer [16] [avɑ̃se] **1** *vt* **(a)** *(mettre en avant)* to move forward; *(pion)* to advance; *(présenter) (main, verre, assiette)* to hold out; *Sout ou Hum* **l'automobile de Monsieur est avancée** Sir, your car awaits you

(b) *Fig (thèse)* to advance, to put forward

(c) *(dans le temps)* to bring forward; **a. sa montre d'une heure** to put one's watch forward one hour

(d) *(argent)* **a. qch à qn** to advance sb sth; *(prêter)* to lend sb sth

(e) *(faire progresser)* **à quoi cela vous avancera-t-il?** what good will that do you?; **ça ne t'avancera à rien de te mettre en colère** losing your temper won't get you anywhere; **ses réponses ne m'ont pas beaucoup avancé** his/her answers didn't leave me much the wiser

2 *vi* **(a)** *(aller de l'avant)* to move forward; *(armée)* to advance; **a. d'un pas** to take a step forward; **faire a. qn** to move sb along; **allez, avance! on va être en retard** come on, move it! we're going to be late

(b) *(faire des progrès)* to progress; **alors, ça avance?** so how's it coming along?; **faire a. les choses** to get things moving

(c) *(montre)* to be fast; **ma montre avance d'une minute par jour** my watch gains a minute a day; **vous avancez de dix minutes** your watch is ten minutes fast

(d) *(promontoire, toit)* to jut out

3 s'avancer *vpr* **(a)** *(aller devant)* to move forward; **s'a. vers qch** to head toward sth; **s'a. d'un pas** to take a step forward

(b) *(faire son travail à l'avance)* to get ahead

(c) *Fig (s'engager hâtivement)* to commit oneself

avant [avɑ̃] **1** *prép* **(a)** *(dans le temps, dans l'espace)* before; **a. une heure** by one o'clock; *(dans moins d'une heure)* within an hour; **800 a. Jésus-Christ** 800 BC; **a. impôt** before tax; **je vous reverrai a. de partir** I'll see you before I leave; **ne fais rien a. d'être tout à fait sûr** don't do anything until you are absolutely sure; **je vous reverrai a. que vous (ne) partiez** I'll see you before you leave; **je serai parti a. que vous ayez fini** I'll have left by the time you've finished; **ne partez pas a. qu'on vous le dise** don't go until you are told; *Fam* **celle-là, a. qu'elle se décide!** she takes forever to make her mind up!

(b) *(par ordre de priorité)* before; **faire passer qch a. le reste** to put sth before everything else; **pour lui, la famille passe a. tout** for him, (the) family comes first; **a. tout** *(surtout)* above all; **a. toute chose** before anything else

2 *adv* **(a)** *(auparavant)* before; *(d'abord)* beforehand; **a. j'avais les cheveux longs** I used to have long hair; **tu ferais mieux de téléphoner a.** you'd better phone first; **le jour d'a.** the day before

(b) *(dans l'espace)* **vous voyez l'église? sa maison est juste a.** you see the church? his/her house is just before you get to it

(c) *Litt (loin)* far; *(tard)* late; *Fig* **poussons plus a. notre enquête** let's take our investigation(s) further

(d) **en a.** *(devant les autres)* in front, ahead; *(se pencher, tomber)* forward; *Mil* **en a., marche!** forward march!; **partir en a.** to go on ahead; **faire deux pas en a.** to take two steps forward; *Fig* **se mettre en a.** to push oneself forward; **en a. de** in front of

3 *adj inv* front

4 *nm* **(a)** *(d'un véhicule, d'une salle)* front; **à l'a.** *(d'un véhicule)* in the front; **aller de l'a.** to move forward

(b) *(en sport)* forward; **jouer a.** to be a forward

avantage [avɑ̃taʒ] *nm* **(a)** *(intérêt)* advantage; **cette solution a** *ou* **présente l'a. d'être rapide** this solution has the advantage of being quick **(b)** *(supériorité)* advantage (**sur** over); **être à son a.** *(physiquement)* to look one's best **(c)** *(profit)* advantage; **tu aurais a. à être poli** you'd do well to be polite; **être/tourner à l'a. de qn** to be/to turn to sb's advantage; **tirer a. de qch** to turn sth to one's advantage; **avantages complémentaires** perks; **a. fiscal** tax incentive; **a. en nature** payment in kind; **avantages sociaux** welfare benefits **(d)** *Sport* advantage; **prendre/conserver l'a.** to gain/to retain the advantage

avantager [45] [avɑ̃taʒe] *vt* **(a)** *(favoriser)* **a. qn (par rapport à)** to give sb an advantage (over); **être avantagé par rapport**

à qn to have an advantage over sb (**b**) *(physiquement)* **a. qn** to show sb off to advantage; **il n'a pas été avantagé par la nature** he hasn't been favored by nature

avantageux, -euse [avɑ̃taʒø, -øz] *adj* (**a**) *(offre)* attractive; *(conditions)* favorable; *(prix)* reasonable; *(produit)* good value (**b**) *(vaniteux) (ton)* superior

avant-bras [avɑ̃bra] *nm inv* forearm

avant-centre (*pl* **avants-centres**) [avɑ̃sɑ̃tr] *nm (au football)* center forward

avant-coureur (*pl* **avant-coureurs**) [avɑ̃kurœr] *adj m voir* **signe**

avant-dernier, -ère (*mpl* **avant-derniers**, *fpl* **avant-dernières**) [avɑ̃dɛrnje, -ɛr] **1** *adj* last but one, second to last; **l'avant-dernière fois** the time before last
2 *nm,f* last but one, second to last

avant-garde (*pl* **avant-gardes**) [avɑ̃gard] *nf* (**a**) *Mil* advance guard (**b**) **l'a.** *(modernité)* the avant-garde; **d'a.** *(œuvre, théâtre)* avant-garde; **être à l'a. de la mode** to be at the cutting edge of fashion

avant-goût (*pl* **avant-goûts**) [avɑ̃gu] *nm* foretaste (**de** of)

avant-guerre (*pl* **avant-guerres**) [avɑ̃gɛr] *nm ou nf* pre-war period

avant-hier [avɑ̃tjɛr] *adv* the day before yesterday; **a. au soir** the evening before last

avant-midi [avɑ̃midi] *nm inv ou nf inv Belg & Can* morning

avant-plan [avɑ̃plɑ̃] *nm Belg* foreground

avant-poste (*pl* **avant-postes**) [avɑ̃pɔst] *nm Mil* outpost

avant-première (*pl* **avant-premières**) [avɑ̃prəmjɛr] *nf* preview; (**présenté**) **en a.** *(film, pièce)* previewed

avant-propos [avɑ̃prɔpo] *nm inv* foreword, preface

avant-scène (*pl* **avant-scènes**) [avɑ̃sɛn] *nf Théât* apron

avant-toit (*pl* **avant-toits**) [avɑ̃twa] *nm* eaves

avant-veille (*pl* **avant-veilles**) [avɑ̃vɛj] *nf* **l'a.** (**de qch**) two days before (sth)

avare [avar] **1** *adj* miserly; *Fig* **il n'est pas a. de compliments** he's generous with his compliments
2 *nmf* miser, skinflint

avarice [avaris] *nf* miserliness, avarice

avarie [avari] *nf* damage; **subir une a.** to be damaged

avarié, -e [avarje] *adj (nourriture)* rotten

avarier [66] [avarje] **s'avarier** *vpr (nourriture)* to go bad

avatar [avatar] *nm* (**a**) *(incarnation)* incarnation (**b**) *Fam (mésaventure)* mishap, misadventure

avec [avɛk] **1** *prép* (**a**) *(en compagnie de)* with; **être gentil/méchant a. qn** to be nice/nasty to sb; **être bien/mal a. qn** *(s'entendre bien/mal)* to get along well/badly with sb; **je suis a. vous** *(je vous soutiens)* I'm right behind you; *Fam* **et a. ça?** *(chez le marchand)* anything else?
  (**b**) *(indique la manière)* **a. enthousiasme** enthusiastically, with enthusiasm; **a. beaucoup de gentillesse** very kindly, with great kindness; **c'est a. émotion que j'accepte** I'm thrilled to accept
  (**c**) *(indique la simultanéité)* **diminuer a. l'âge** to decrease with age; **cela viendra a. le temps** it will come in time
  (**d**) *(indique le moyen)* with; **ouvrir qch a. une clef** to open sth with a key; **j'ai eu un accident a. cette voiture** I had an accident in this car
  (**e**) *(à cause de)* **a. tous les ennuis que j'ai en ce moment...** with all the problems I have at the moment...; **impossible de sortir a. cette pluie** it's impossible to go out in this rain
  (**f**) *(en ce qui concerne)* **a. elle, on ne sait jamais** you never can tell with her
  (**g**) *(divorcer)* **divorcer d'a. qn** to divorce sb
2 *adv* **je suis venu a.** *(mon parapluie, mes gants)* I came with it/them; **il faut bien faire a.** I'll/we'll/*etc.* just have to put up with it

avenant, -e [avnɑ̃, -ɑ̃t] **1** *adj (personne, manières)* pleasant
2 *nm* (**a**) *(de police d'assurance)* additional clause (**b**) **le bâtiment est beau et le jardin est à l'a.** the building is beautiful and the garden is in keeping with it

avènement [avɛnmɑ̃] *nm (du Christ, d'une ère)* advent; *(d'un roi)* accession

avenir [avnir] *nm* future; **assurer l'a. de qn** to make provision for sb; **dans un très proche a.** in the very near future; **avoir de l'a.** *(personne, technique)* to have a future; **un métier d'a.** a career with good prospects; **un avocat d'a.** a lawyer with a great future; **à l'a.** in future

Avent [avɑ̃] *nm* **l'A.** Advent

aventure [avɑ̃tyr] *nf* (**a**) *(histoire)* adventure; **pour trouver des fruits en hiver, c'est tout une a.** it's quite a job finding fruit in winter (**b**) *(liaison)* (love) affair (**c**) **l'a.** *(le risque)* adventure; **tenter l'a.** to seek adventure; **partir à l'a.** to set off in search of adventure; *(sans préparation)* to set out without making plans (**d**) **dire la bonne a. à qn** to tell sb's fortune

aventurer [avɑ̃tyre] **s'aventurer** *vpr* to venture (**dans** into); **je ne m'aventurerai pas à dire que...** I wouldn't go so far as to say (that)...

aventureux, -euse [avɑ̃tyrø, -øz] *adj (vie, personne)* adventurous; *(projet)* risky

aventurier, -ère [avɑ̃tyrje, -ɛr] *nm,f* adventurer

avenue [avny] *nf* avenue

avérer [34] [avere] **s'avérer** *vpr (se révéler)* to prove to be; **il s'est avéré que...** it turned out that...

averse [avɛrs] *nf* shower; *Can* **a. de neige** snow flurry

aversion [avɛrsjɔ̃] *nf* aversion (**pour** to), dislike (**pour** of); **prendre qn en a.** to take a dislike to sb

averti, -e [avɛrti] *adj (bien informé)* (well-)informed; **vous voilà a.!** don't say I didn't warn you!; *Prov* **un homme a. en vaut deux** forewarned is forearmed

avertir [avɛrtir] *vt* **a. qn de qch** *(informer)* to inform sb of sth; *(d'un danger)* to warn sb of sth; **je vais me mettre en colère, je t'avertis!** I'm going to get angry, I'm warning you!

avertissement [avɛrtismɑ̃] *nm* (**a**) *(avis préalable)* warning; **a. (au lecteur)** foreword (**b**) *(réprimande)* warning; *Sport (de l'arbitre)* warning, caution (**c**) *(signal)* warning sign

avertisseur [avɛrtisœr] *nm (dispositif)* alarm; *(Klaxon®)* horn; **a. d'incendie** fire alarm

aveu, -x [avø] *nm* confession; **passer aux aveux** to make a confession; **je dois vous faire un a...** I must confess...; **de l'a. de tout le monde...** it is commonly acknowledged that...

aveuglant, -e [avœglɑ̃, -ɑ̃t] *adj* blinding, dazzling; *Fig (preuve)* blindingly obvious

aveugle [avœgl] **1** *adj aussi Fig* blind; **a. d'un œil** blind in one eye; **avoir une confiance a. en qn** to trust sb implicitly
2 *nmf* blind man, *f* blind woman; **les aveugles** the blind

aveuglement [avœgləmɑ̃] *nm (moral, mental)* blindness

aveuglément [avœglemɑ̃] *adv* blindly

aveugle-né, -e (*mpl* **aveugles-nés**, *fpl* **aveugles-nées**) [avœgləne] **1** *adj* blind from birth
2 *nm,f* person blind from birth

aveugler [avœgle] *vt aussi Fig* to blind; **aveuglé par la colère** blind with rage

aveuglette [avœglɛt] **à l'aveuglette** *adv* blindly; **aller à l'a.** to grope one's way

aviateur, -trice [avjatœr, -tris] *nm,f* aviator

aviation [avjasjɔ̃] *nf* (**a**) *(activité)* flying; **faire de l'a.** to go flying (**b**) *(secteur)* aviation; **a. civile/commerciale** civil/commercial aviation; **a. de tourisme** civil aviation (**c**) *Mil* air force

aviculteur, -trice [avikyltœr, -tris] *nm,f (de volailles)* poultry farmer

aviculture [avikyltyr] *nf (de volailles)* poultry farming

avide [avid] *adj* (**a**) *(passionné)* eager (**de** for); **a. de sang** bloodthirsty (**b**) *Péj (cupide)* greedy

avidement [avidmã] *adv (voracement)* greedily; *(avec passion)* eagerly

avidité [avidite] *nf (voracité, cupidité)* greed; *(passion)* eagerness; **avec a.** *(manger)* greedily; *(écouter, regarder)* eagerly

aviez *voir* avoir[1]

Avignon [aviɲɔ̃] *nf* Avignon; *Théât* **le festival d'A.** the Avignon festival

Le festival d'Avignon

Founded by Jean Vilar in 1947 and held every summer in Avignon in the South of France, this arts festival is a showcase for new theater and dance performances: "La pièce sera donnée d'abord en Avignon". Along with the program of official shows ("le in") performed in prestigious venues such as the Court of Honor of the "Palais des Papes", a program comprising numerous fringe shows, referred to as "le off", has also been performed since the 1970s.

avilir [avilir] **1** *vt (dégrader)* to degrade, to demean

2 s'avilir *vpr (personne)* to demean oneself

avilissant, -e [avilisã, -ãt] *adj* degrading

avilissement [avilismã] *nm (dégradation)* degradation

aviné, -e [avine] *adj (personne)* inebriated; *(haleine)* reeking of wine

avion [avjɔ̃] *nm* plane, airplane; **par a.** *(sur lettre)* airmail; **voyager en a.** to travel by plane *or* by air; **a. charter** charter plane; **a. de chasse** fighter (plane); **a. furtif** stealth plane; **a. gros-porteur** jumbo jet; **a. de ligne** airliner; **a. à réaction** jet (plane); **a. supersonique** supersonic plane; **a. de tourisme** private plane

avion-cargo *(pl* **avions-cargos)** [avjɔ̃kargo] *nm* freight plane, cargo plane

avion-espion *(pl* **avions-espions)** [avjɔ̃ɛspjɔ̃] *nm* spy plane

avions *voir* avoir[1]

aviron [avirɔ̃] *nm* (**a**) *(rame)* oar; *Can* paddle (**b**) *(sport)* **l'a.** rowing; **faire de l'a.** to row

avironner [avirɔne] *vi Can* to paddle

avis [avi] *nm* (**a**) *(opinion)* opinion; **changer d'a.** to change one's mind; **les a. sont partagés** opinion is divided; **à mon a.** in my opinion; **tu vas accepter? – à ton a.?** are you going to accept? – what do you think?; **être de l'a. de qn** to be of the same opinion as sb; **de l'a. de tous...** the general opinion is that...; **être d'a. de faire qch** to be of a mind to do sth; *Prov* **deux a. valent mieux qu'un** two heads are better than one (**b**) *(conseils)* advice; **suivre l'a. de qn** to follow sb's advice (**c**) *(avertissement)* notice; **jusqu'à nouvel a.** until further notice; **sauf a. contraire** unless I/you/*etc.* hear to the contrary; **a. de livraison** delivery note; **a. de prélèvement** direct debit advice; **a. de réception** acknowledgment of receipt

avisé, -e [avize] *adj (sage)* sensible, wise; *(acheteur, consommateur)* shrewd; **tu serais bien/mal a. de...** you'd be well-/ill-advised to...

aviser [avize] **1** *vt* (**a**) *(informer)* **a. qn de qch** to inform sb of sth; **a. qn que...** to inform sb that... (**b**) *Fam (entrevoir)* to spot

2 *vi (prendre une décision)* to make up one's mind

3 s'aviser *vpr* (**a**) *(se rendre compte)* **s'a. que** to notice that (**b**) *(oser)* **s'a. de faire qch** to get it into one's head to do sth; **et ne t'avise pas de recommencer!** don't you dare start again!

aviver [avive] *vt (couleurs)* to brighten up; *(passion, querelle, feu)* to stir up; *(appétit)* to sharpen

av. J.-C. *(abrév* **avant Jésus-Christ)** BC; **en 106 av. J.-C.** in 106 BC

avocat[1], -e [avɔka, -at] *nm,f* (**a**) *Jur* lawyer, attorney; **a. d'affaires** business lawyer; **a. général** prosecuting attorney; **a.**

plaidant trial attorney (**b**) *Fig* advocate; **se faire l'a. du diable** to play devil's advocate

avocat[2] [avɔka, -at] *nm (fruit)* avocado (pear)

avocette [avɔsɛt] *nf* avocet

avoine [avwan] *nf* (**a**) *(céréale)* oats (**b**) *Fam (argent)* dough

avoir[1] [1] [avwar] **1** *v aux* to have; **je ne l'ai pas encore fini** I haven't finished it yet; **je te l'ai dit hier** I told you yesterday; **j'avais déjà vu ce film** I had already seen the movie; **il faut que je l'aie fini pour demain** I have to finish it by tomorrow; **est-ce que tu auras terminé ce soir?** will you get it finished tonight?; **il aurait réussi s'il avait travaillé plus** he would have passed if he had worked harder

2 *vt* (**a**) *(posséder)* to have; **il a une fille** he has a daughter; **a. les yeux bleus** to have blue eyes; **a. une drôle de forme** to have a funny shape; **a. un rhume** to have a cold; **a. du diabète** to be diabetic; **a. mal au cœur** to feel nauseous; **j'ai le nez qui pique** I've got an itchy nose; **a. de l'ambition** to be ambitious; **a. de l'humour** to have a sense of humor; **a. 20 ans** to be 20 (years old); **elle a Guy pour voisin** Guy is her neighbor; **qui as-tu comme prof de math?** who's your math teacher?

(**b**) *(obtenir)* to get; **a. qn au téléphone** to speak to sb on the telephone; **a. son train** to catch one's train; **je l'ai eu pour 50 euros** I bought it for 50 euros; **j'ai eu mon bac en 1995** I passed my "bac" in 1995

(**c**) *(porter) (vêtement)* to wear; *(objet)* to carry

(**d**) *(faire)* **il a eu un sourire étrange** he smiled strangely

(**e**) *(atteindre) (cible)* to hit

(**f**) *Fam (duper) (personne)* to take for a ride, to con; **tu nous a bien eus!** you really fooled us!; **se faire a.** to be conned; **se faire a. de 100 euros** to be conned out of 100 euros

(**g**) *(locutions)* **a. faim/froid** to be hungry/cold; **a. quelque chose à faire** to have something to do; **j'ai à faire** I've got things to do; **j'ai à lui parler** I've got to talk to him; **tu n'as qu'à le lui dire** just tell her; **tu en as pour combien de temps?** how long will you be?; **j'en ai pour dix minutes** I'll be ten minutes; **je n'en ai pas pour longtemps** I won't be long; **qu'est-ce que tu as?** what's wrong?; **j'ai que je suis fatigué** I'm tired, that's all; **qu'est-ce qu'il a à se plaindre sans arrêt?** why is he complaining all the time?; **on les aura!** we'll get them!

3 il y a *v impersonnel* there is/are; **il y a un problème** there's a problem; **il y a des problèmes** there are some problems; **il y a six ans** six years ago; **il y a un mois que je suis ici** I've been here for a month; **il n'y a qu'à le faire** we'll just have to do it; **il n'y a pas que ça dans la vie** there's more to life than that; **il n'y a pas de quoi!** don't mention it!; **qu'y a-t-il?, qu'est-ce qu'il y a?** what is it?, what's wrong?; **il y a que j'en ai assez** I've had enough, that's all

avoir[2] [avwar] *nm (d'une compagnie)* assets; *(d'un compte)* credit; *(dans un magasin)* voucher

avoisinant, -e [avwazinã, -ãt] *adj* neighboring, nearby

avoisiner [avwazine] *vt* **une somme avoisinant les 500 euros** a sum in the neighborhood of 500 euros

avons *voir* avoir[1]

avortement [avɔrtəmã] *nm* (**a**) *(chez une femme)* **a. (provoqué)** abortion; **a. spontané** miscarriage; **a. thérapeutique** termination for medical reasons (**b**) *(chez un animal)* casting (**c**) *Fig (d'un projet)* failure

avorter [avɔrte] **1** *vi* (**a**) *(subir une IVG)* to have an abortion; *(faire une fausse couche)* to miscarry (**b**) *(animal)* to cast (**c**) *Fig (projet)* to fall through

2 *vt (sujet: médecin)* to abort; **se faire a.** to have an abortion

avorteur, -euse [avɔrtœr, -øz] *nm,f* abortionist

avorton [avɔrtɔ̃] *nm Péj* runt

avoué[1] [avwe] *nm Jur* ≃ attorney

avoué[2], -e [avwe] *adj* (**a**) *(auteur, partisan)* confessed (**b**) *(but)* declared

avouer [avwe] **1** *vt (faute, crime)* to confess to, to own up to; **il a fini par a.** he finally confessed; **a. que** to admit that; **ceci me surprend, je l'avoue** this surprises me, I must confess; **il faut bien a. que...** it must be admitted that...
2 s'avouer *vpr* **s'a. coupable** to admit one's guilt; **s'a. vaincu** to acknowledge defeat

avril [avril] *nm* April; **le premier a.** *(jour des farces)* April Fools' Day; *Prov* **en a., ne te découvre pas d'un fil** ≃ ne'er cast a clout till May is out; *voir aussi* **janvier**

axe [aks] *nm* **(a)** *(géométrique)* axis; **a. des abscisses/des ordonnées** x-/y-axis; **être dans l'a. de qch** to be in line with sth; **(grand) a.** *(routier)* main road; *Fig* **les grands axes de sa politique** the main thrust of his/her policy **(b)** *(de machine, de roue de vélo)* axle **(c)** *Hist* **l'A. (Rome-Berlin)** the (Rome-Berlin) Axis

axer [akse] *vt* to center; **être axé sur** *ou* **autour de** to center on

axiome [aksjom] *nm* axiom

ayant *etc. voir* **avoir**¹

ayant droit *(pl* **ayants droit***)* [εjᾱdrwa] *nm Jur* beneficiary

ayatollah [ajatɔla] *nm* ayatollah

azalée [azale] *nf* azalea

Azerbaïdjan [azεrbajdʒᾱ] *nm* **l'A.** Azerbaijan

azerbaïdjanais, -e [azεrbajdʒanε, -εz] **1** *adj* Azerbaijani
2 *nm,f* **A., Azerbaïdjanaise** Azerbaijani

azéri, -e [azeri] **1** *adj* Azeri
2 *nm,f* **A., Azérie** Azeri

azimuts [azimyt] *nmpl Fam* **une campagne électorale tous a.** an all-out electoral campaign

azote [azɔt] *nm* nitrogen

AZT® [azεdte] *nm Méd (abrév* **azidothymidine***)* AZT

aztèque [aztεk] **1** *adj* Aztec
2 *nmf* **A.** Aztec

azur [azyr] *nm Litt* **(a)** *(couleur)* azure **(b)** **l'a.** *(ciel)* the sky

azyme [azim] *adj m voir* **pain**

B

B, b [be] *nm inv* B, b

baba¹ [baba] *nm* **b. au rhum** rum baba; *Fam* **elle l'a dans le b.** she's been had

baba² [baba] *adj inv Fam* flabbergasted; **j'en suis resté b.** I was flabbergasted

baba cool (*pl* **babas cool**) [babakul] *nmf* hippie

Babel [babɛl] *n* **la tour de B.** the Tower of Babel

babil [babil] *nm (d'un enfant)* prattling; *(des oiseaux)* twittering; *(d'un ruisseau)* babbling

babillard [babijar] *nm Ordinat* bulletin board, BBS

babiller [babije] *vi (enfant)* to prattle; *(oiseau)* to twitter; *(ruisseau)* to babble

babines [babin] *nfpl aussi Hum* chops; **d'avance, je m'en lèche les b.** my mouth's watering in anticipation

babiole [babjɔl] *nf* (a) *(bibelot)* knick-knack, trinket (b) *(broutille)* trifle

bâbord [babɔr] *nm* port (side); **à b.** to port

babouche [babuʃ] *nf* Turkish slipper

babouin [babwɛ̃] *nm* baboon

baboune [babun] *nf Can Fam* **faire la b.** to sulk

baby-boom (*pl* **baby-booms**) [bebibum] *nm* baby boom

baby-foot [babifut] *nm inv* foosball

baby-sitter (*pl* **baby-sitters**) [bebisitœr] *nmf* baby-sitter

baby-sitting [bebisitiŋ] *nm* baby-sitting; **faire du b.** to baby-sit

bac¹ [bak] *nm* (a) *(bateau)* ferry(-boat) (b) *(récipient)* tank; *(d'imprimeur, de photographe)* tray; *Ordinat* **b. d'alimentation** sheet feed; **b. à glace** ice tray; **b. à légumes** salad drawer; *Belg* **b. à ordures** garbage can; **b. de** *ou* **à papier** *(d'imprimante)* paper tray; **b. à sable** sandbox

bac² [bak] *Fam* = **baccalauréat**

baccalauréat [bakalɔrea] *nm* = secondary-school examination qualifying for entry to university, ≃ high-school diploma; **b. L** *ou* **littéraire** = humanities-based "baccalauréat"; **b. S** *ou* **scientifique** = science-based "baccalauréat"

Baccalauréat

The "baccalauréat", or "bac", is taken by students who have completed their final year at the "lycée"; successful candidates may go to university. Depending on which subjects pupils choose to study at "lycée", they prepare for a "baccalauréat général", "technologique" (vocational) or "professionnel" (vocational and including professional training). Since the last major reform, in 1995, there have been three main types of "baccalauréat général", each corresponding to a specific field: "bac L" (humanities subjects), "bac ES" (economics and social studies) and "bac S" (sciences).

---

bacchantes [bakɑ̃t] *nfpl Hum* mustache

bâche [baʃ] *nf (toile)* tarpaulin

bachelier, -ère [baʃəlje, -ɛr] *nm,f* = student who has passed the "baccalauréat"

bâcher [baʃe] *vt* **b. qch** to cover sth with a tarpaulin

bachot [baʃo] *Fam Vieilli* = **baccalauréat**

bachotage [baʃɔtaʒ] *nm Fam Vieilli* cramming, boning up

bachoter [baʃɔte] *vi Fam Vieilli* to cram, to bone up

bacille [basil] *nm Biol* bacillus

bâcler [bɑkle] *vt Fam* to botch

bacon [bekɔn] *nm* (a) *(viande)* bacon (b) *Can Fam* **avoir du b.** to be loaded

bactérie [bakteri] *nf* bacterium

bactériologique [bakterjɔlɔʒik] *adj* bacteriological; **guerre b.** germ warfare

badaboum [badabum] *exclam Fam* crash!; **et b., il est tombé!** he fell down with a crash

badaud [bado] *nm (promeneur)* stroller; *(curieux)* rubberneck

badge [badʒ] *nm* (a) *(insigne, d'identité)* button (b) *(carte magnétique)* swipe card

badigeonner [badiʒɔne] *vt* (a) *(surface)* to daub (**de** with); *(mur)* to whitewash; *Culin* to brush (**de** with) (b) *(gorge, plaie)* to paint (**de** with)

badin, -e¹ [badɛ̃, -in] *adj* playful

badinage [badinaʒ] *nm* banter

badine² [badin] *nf* switch

badiner [badine] *vi* to jest, to joke; **il ne badine pas avec la ponctualité** he's very strict about punctuality

badinerie [badinri] *nf* jest

badminton [badmintɔn] *nm* badminton

bâdrant, -e [bɑdrɑ̃, -ɑ̃t] *adj Can* bothersome

bâdrer [bɑdre] *vt Can* to bother

baffe [baf] *nf Fam* clout, smack; **flanquer une b. à qn** to give sb a smack in the face

baffle [bafl] *nm* baffle

bafouer [bafwe] *vt (personne)* to jeer at; *(règlement, autorité)* to flout

bafouiller [bafuje] *vt & vi* to stammer

bâfrer [bɑfre] *vi très Fam* to stuff oneself

bagage [bagaʒ] *nm* (a) *(sac, valise)* **bagages** luggage, baggage; **faire ses bagages** to pack one's bags; **b. à main** piece of hand luggage (b) *Fig (connaissances)* knowledge (**en** of)

bagagiste [bagaʒist] *nm* baggage handler

bagarre [bagar] *nf* fight, brawl; **chercher la b.** to look for a fight

bagarrer [bagare] **se bagarrer** *vpr Fam* to fight

bagarreur, -euse [bagarœr, -øz] *Fam* **1** *adj (personne, caractère)* aggressive
2 *nm,f* brawler

bagatelle [bagatɛl] *nf (chose sans importance)* trifle; **pour la b. de 400 euros** for a mere 400 euros

Bagdad [bagdad] *n* Baghdad

bagnard [baɲar] *nm* convict

bagne [baɲ] *nm Hist (prison)* convict prison; *(peine)* penal servitude; *Fig* **c'est le b., ici!** they work you to death in this place!

bagnole [baɲɔl] *nf Fam* car

bagou(t) [bagu] *nm* glibness; **avoir du b.** to have the gift of the gab

bague [bag] *nf* (**a**) *(bijou)* ring; *Fig* **passer la b. au doigt à qn** to marry sb; **b. de fiançailles** engagement ring (**b**) *(d'une boîte de conserve)* ring-pull; *(de cigare)* band (**c**) *(d'oiseau)* ring (**d**) *Tech* bush, ring; **b. de serrage** jubilee clip

baguenauder [bagnode] **1** *vi* to saunter around

2 se baguenauder *vpr* to saunter around

baguer [bage] *vt (oiseau, arbre)* to ring

baguette [bagɛt] *nf (tige)* stick; *(de chef d'orchestre)* baton; *(pain)* baguette, French loaf; **baguettes** *(pour manger)* chopsticks; **mener** *ou* **faire marcher qn à la b.** to rule sb with a rod of iron; **b. magique** magic wand; **d'un coup de b. magique** with a wave of my/his/*etc.* magic wand; **baguettes de tambour** drumsticks; **avoir des cheveux raides comme des baguettes de tambour** to have poker straight hair

bah [ba] *exclam* bah!

Bahamas [baamas] *nfpl* **les B., l'archipel des B.** the Bahamas

Bahreïn [barajn], **Bahrayn** [barɛ̃] *n* Bahrain

bahut [bay] *nm* (**a**) *(coffre)* chest; *(buffet)* sideboard (**b**) *Fam (collège, lycée)* school (**c**) *Fam (camion)* truck

bai, -e[1] [bɛ] *adj (cheval)* bay

baie[2] [bɛ] *nf Géog* bay; **la b. d'Hudson** Hudson Bay

baie[3] [bɛ] *nf* **b. vitrée** picture window

baie[4] [bɛ] *nf (fruit)* berry

baignade [bɛɲad] *nf* (**a**) *(activité)* swimming; **b. interdite** *(sur panneau)* no swimming (**b**) *(endroit)* swimming place

baigner [beɲe] **1** *vt (pieds, œil, blessure, bébé, chien)* to bathe; *(sujet: mer)* to wash; *(sujet: rivière)* to water; **être baigné de sueur** to be bathed in sweat; **visage baigné de larmes** face streaming with tears; **baigné de lumière** bathed in light

2 *vi (tremper)* to soak, to steep (**dans** in); **les légumes baignent dans la sauce** the vegetables are swimming in sauce; **il baignait dans son sang** he was lying in a pool of his own blood; *Fam* **ça baigne (dans l'huile)!** everything's hunky dory!

3 se baigner *vpr* (**a**) *(se laver)* to take a bath (**b**) *(nager)* to go for a swim

baigneur, -euse [bɛɲœr, -øz] **1** *nm,f* swimmer

2 *nm (poupée)* doll

baignoire [bɛɲwar] *nf* (**a**) *(dans la salle de bains)* bathtub (**b**) *Théât* ground-floor box

Baïkal [bajkal] *voir* **lac**

bail [baj] *(pl* **baux** [bo]*) nm* lease; *Fam* **ça fait un b. que je ne l'ai pas vu** I haven't seen him for ages

bâillement [bajmɑ̃] *nm* yawn

bâiller [baje] *vi* (**a**) *(personne)* to yawn; *Fam* **b. à s'en** *ou* **se décrocher la mâchoire** to yawn one's head off (**b**) *(coutures, col)* to gape; *(porte)* to be ajar

bâillon [bajɔ̃] *nm* gag; **mettre un b. à qn** to gag sb

bâillonner [bajɔne] *vt aussi Fig* to gag

bain [bɛ̃] *nm* (**a**) *(pour se laver)* bath; **prendre un b.** to take a bath; *Fam Fig* **être/se mettre dans le b.** to be in/get into the swing of things; **b. de bouche** mouthwash; **faire un b. de bouche** to use mouthwash; **b. de boue** mud bath; **prendre un b. de foule** *(personnalité)* to press the flesh; **b. moussant** bubble bath; **prendre un b. de pieds** to soak one's feet; **prendre un b. de soleil** to sunbathe; **b. turc** Turkish bath; **b. de vapeur** steam bath (**b**) *Can (baignoire)* bathtub (**c**) *(à la piscine)* **petit/grand b.** small/large pool (**d**) *(à la mer, en rivière)* swim; *Vieilli* **bains de mer** swimming in the sea (**e**) *Phot* bath (**f**) *Tex* dye

bain-marie [bɛ̃mari] *(pl* **bains-marie**) *nm* bain-marie *(cooking pan set over second pan of boiling water)*; **faire cuire qch au b.** to cook sth in a bain-marie

baïonnette [bajɔnɛt] *nf* bayonet

baisemain [bɛzmɛ̃] *nm* **faire le b. à qn** to kiss sb's hand

baiser[1] [beze] **1** *vt* (**a**) *Litt (embrasser)* to kiss (**b**) *Vulg (coucher avec)* to fuck, to screw (**c**) *Vulg (tromper)* to screw; **se faire b.** to get screwed

2 *vi Vulg* to fuck, to screw

baiser[2] [beze] *nm* kiss; **gros baisers** *(dans une lettre)* love and kisses

baisse [bɛs] *nf* fall, drop (**de** in); **être en b.** *(température, actions)* to be falling; *(popularité)* to be on the decline

baisser [bese] **1** *vt* (**a**) *(rideau, store, vitre de voiture)* to lower; **b. la tête** to lower one's head; *(de honte, de découragement)* to hang one's head; **b. les yeux** to look down; *Fig* **b. les bras** to give in (**b**) *(lumière, son, chauffage)* to turn down; *(prix)* to lower; **b. la voix** to lower one's voice; **je vous prie de b. le ton!** please keep your voice down!

2 *vi* (**a**) *(diminuer) (température, niveau de l'eau, prix)* to fall; *(marée)* to ebb; **elle a baissé dans mon estime** she's gone down in my esteem (**b**) *(s'affaiblir) (malade)* to get weaker; *(enthousiasme)* to fall off; *(feu)* to burn low; *(vue, mémoire)* to fail; **le jour baisse** night is falling

3 se baisser *vpr* (**a**) to bend down; *(pour éviter un coup)* to duck; *Fig* **il n'y a qu'à se b. pour les ramasser** there are loads of them around

baissier [besje] *adj m voir* **marché**

bajoues [baʒu] *nfpl (d'animal)* chops; *Péj (d'une personne)* flabby cheeks

Bakou [baku] *n* Baku

bal (*pl* **bals**) [bal] *nm (populaire)* dance; *(élégant)* ball; **b. costumé** *ou* **masqué** fancy-dress ball; **b. musette** = dance to accordion music; **b. populaire** = dance, usually outdoors, open to the public

balade [balad] *nf Fam (à pied)* walk; *(en voiture)* drive; *(à bicyclette, à moto)* ride; **faire une b.** *(à pied)* to go for a walk; *(en voiture)* to go for a drive; *(à bicyclette, à moto)* to go for a ride

balader [balade] *Fam* **1** *vt (personne, chien)* to take for a walk; *(avoir avec soi) (objet)* to drag around

2 *vi* **envoyer b. qn** to send sb packing

3 se balader *vpr (à pied)* to go for a walk; *(en voiture)* to go for a drive; *(à bicyclette, à moto)* to go for a ride

baladeur, -euse [baladœr, -øz] **1** *adj Fam* **avoir les mains baladeuses** to have wandering hands

2 *nm* personal stereo, Walkman®

3 *nf* **baladeuse** *(lampe)* inspection lamp

baladin [baladɛ̃] *nm* strolling player

balafre [balafr] *nf* (**a**) *(coupure)* gash (**b**) *(cicatrice)* scar

balafré [balafre] *nm* scarface

balafrer [balafre] *vt* to gash; **visage balafré** scarred face

balai [balɛ] *nm* (**a**) *(de ménage)* broom; **passer le b.** to give the floor a sweep; **donner un coup de b.** *(balayer)* to give the floor a sweep; *Fig (dans une entreprise)* to have a shakeout; **du b.!** clear off!; **b. mécanique** carpet sweeper (**b**) *Aut (d'essuie-glace)* blade (**c**) *(percussion)* brush (**d**) *Fam (an)* **avoir quarante/cinquante balais** to be forty/fifty

balai-brosse (*pl* **balais-brosses**) [balɛbrɔs] *nm* long-handled scrub brush

balaise [balɛz] = **balèze**

balalaïka [balalaika] *nf* balalaika

balance [balɑ̃s] *nf* (**a**) *(appareil)* (pair of) scales; *(publique)* weighing machine; *Fig* **ce facteur pèse dans la b.** this factor carries some weight; **faire pencher la b.** to tip the scales (**b**) *Astron & Astrol* **la B.** Libra; **être B.** to be a Libran (**c**) *Écon* balance; **b. commerciale** balance of trade; **b. des paiements** balance of payments (**d**) *Fam (mouchard)* squealer

balancé, -e [balɑ̃se] *adj Fam* **être bien b.** *(personne)* to have a good figure

balancelle [balɑ̃sɛl] *nf (de jardin)* glider

balancement [balãsmã] *nm* swaying

balancer [16] [balãse] **1** *vt* (**a**) *(bras, jambes, trompe, pendule)* to swing; *(hanches)* to sway (**b**) *Fam (projectile, objet)* to chuck, to throw; **b. des vannes** to make snide *or* unpleasant remarks (**c**) *Com (compte)* to balance (**d**) *Fam (se débarrasser de) (objet)* to chuck *or* to throw out; **b. qn** to give sb the gate; **elle a tout balancé** *(tout abandonné)* she's given it all up (**e**) *Fam (dénoncer)* to squeal on

2 *vi Litt (hésiter)* to waver

3 se balancer *vpr* (**a**) *(arbres, blés)* to sway; **se b. sur sa chaise** to rock backward and forward on one's chair; **se b. d'un pied sur l'autre** to rock from one foot to the other (**b**) *(sur une balançoire)* to swing (**c**) *très Fam* **je m'en balance!** I don't give a rat's ass! (**d**) *Fam* **il s'est balancé du haut de la tour Eiffel** he threw himself off the top of the Eiffel Tower

balancier [balãsje] *nm* (**a**) *(d'un funambule)* balancing pole (**b**) *(d'horloge)* pendulum

balançoire [balãswar] *nf (suspendue)* swing; *(bascule)* seesaw

balayage [baleja3] *nm* (**a**) *(pour nettoyer)* sweeping (**b**) *Rad, Élec & TV* scanning

balayer [53] [baleje] *vt* (**a**) *(nettoyer)* to sweep; *(saletés)* to sweep up; *Fig (objections, obstacles)* to brush aside; **le vent a balayé les nuages** the wind has swept the clouds away; *Fig* **b. devant sa porte** to put one's own house in order (**b**) *Rad, Élec & TV* to scan; *(sujet: projecteurs)* to sweep

balayette [balejɛt] *nf* small brush; *(des WC)* toilet brush

balayeur, -euse [balejœr, -øz] **1** *nm,f* street cleaner

2 *nf* **balayeuse** *Can (aspirateur)* vacuum cleaner

balbutiement [balbysimã] *nm* (**a**) *(en parlant)* stammering (**b**) **balbutiements** *(d'une science, d'une discipline)* early stages

balbutier [66] [balbysje] **1** *vi* to stammer

2 *vt* to stammer (out)

balcon [balkɔ̃] *nm* (**a**) *(d'édifice)* balcony (**b**) *(dans un théâtre)* circle; **premier/deuxième b.** dress/upper circle

baldaquin [baldakɛ̃] *nm* canopy

Bâle [bal] *n* Basel

Baléares [balear] *nfpl* **les (îles) B.** the Balearic Islands

baleine [balɛn] *nf* (**a**) *(animal)* whale; **b. blanche/bleue** white/blue whale (**b**) *(d'un parapluie)* rib; *(d'un corset)* (whale)-bone

baleineau, -x [baleno] *nm* whale calf

baleinière [balɛnjɛr] *nf* whaleboat

balèze [balɛz] *adj Fam (grand et fort)* hefty; *(intelligent)* brainy; **b. en maths** brilliant at math

balisage [baliza3] *nm* (**a**) *(signaux)* *Naut & Rad* beacons; *Aviat* lights (**b**) *(action)* *Naut & Rad* beaconing; *Aviat* lighting

balise [baliz] *nf Naut & Rad* beacon; *Aviat* light; *(de piste de ski, d'épave)* marker; *Ordinat* tag; *Naut* **b. flottante** buoy; *Rad* **b. radar** radar beacon

baliser [balize] *vt (chenal)* to beacon; *(aéroport)* to equip with lights; *(route)* to mark out with beacons; *(piste de ski)* to mark out

balistique [balistik] **1** *adj (missile)* ballistic

2 *nf* ballistics *(singulier)*

balivernes [balivɛrn] *nfpl* twaddle

balkanisation [balkanizasjɔ̃] *nf aussi Fig* Balkanization

Balkans [balkã] *nmpl* **les B.** the Balkans

ballade [balad] *nf* ballad

ballant, -e [balã, -ãt] *adj (bras, jambes)* dangling; **ne reste pas là, les bras ballants** don't just stand there like an idiot

ballast [balast] *nm* (**a**) *Constr (d'une route, d'une voie ferrée)* ballast (**b**) *Naut* ballast tank

balle¹ [bal] *nf* (**a**) *(pour jouer)* ball; **jouer à la b.** to play ball; *Fig* **prendre** *ou* **saisir la b. au bond** to seize the opportunity; *Fig* **se renvoyer la b.** to pass the buck; *Fig* **la b. est dans votre camp** the ball's in your court; **b. de golf/de tennis** golf/tennis ball; **b. de break/de match** break/match point (**b**)

(d'arme) bullet; **b. à blanc** blank; **b. perdue** stray bullet (**c**) *Anciennement Fam* **balles** *(francs)* francs

balle² [bal] *nf (de coton, de laine)* bale

balle³ [bal] *nf (de blé)* husk

ballerine [balrin] *nf* (**a**) *(danseuse)* ballerina (**b**) *(chaussures)* **ballerines** flats

ballet [balɛ] *nm* ballet

ballon [balɔ̃] *nm* (**a**) *(aéronef)* balloon; **b. d'essai** pilot balloon (**b**) *(balle)* ball; **jouer au b.** to play with a ball; **b. de football** soccer ball; **le b. ovale** rugby; **le b. rond** soccer (**c**) *(pour boire)* **(verre) b.** round wine glass (**d**) **b. (de baudruche)** balloon; **souffler dans le b.** *(d'alcootest)* to be breathalyzed, to blow into the bag; **b. d'oxygène** oxygen tank; *Fig* lifesaver (**e**) *Suisse (petit pain)* (bread) roll

ballonné, -e [balone] *adj (ventre, personne)* bloated

ballon-panier [balɔ̃panje] *nm inv Can Sport* basketball

ballon-sonde (*pl* **ballons-sondes**) [balɔ̃sɔ̃d] *nm Météo* sounding balloon

ballot [balo] *nm* (**a**) *(paquet)* bundle (**b**) *Fam (imbécile)* twit

ballottage [balota3] *nm Pol* **il y a b.** there will be a second round of voting

ballottement [balotmã] *nm (de train)* rocking; *(des passagers)* shaking; *(de navire)* tossing

ballotter [balote] **1** *vt (bateau)* to toss about; *(passagers)* to shake about; *Fig* **un enfant ballotté entre son père et sa mère** a child passed backward and forward between its father and mother

2 *vi (bagages, bateau)* to be tossed about; *(poitrine)* to bounce up and down

ball-trap (*pl* **ball-traps**) [baltrap] *nm (sport)* clay-pigeon shooting

balluchon [balyʃɔ̃] *nm Fam (de vêtements)* bundle; **faire son b.** to pack one's bags

balnéaire [balneɛr] *adj voir* **station**

balourd, -e [balur, -urd] **1** *adj (personne)* oafish

2 *nm,f* clumsy oaf

balsa [balza] *nm* balsawood

balte [balt] **1** *adj* Baltic; **les pays baltes** the Baltic states

2 *nmf* Balt

Baltique [baltik] *nf* **la (mer) B.** the Baltic (Sea)

baluchon [balyʃɔ̃] = **balluchon**

balustrade [balystrad] *nf* (**a**) *Archit* balustrade (**b**) *(clôture)* railing

bambin [bãbɛ̃] *nm Fam* toddler

bambou [bãbu] *nm (plante)* bamboo; *Fam* **c'est le coup de b.!** it's a rip-off!

bamboula [bãbula] *nf Fam* spree; **faire la b.** to live it up

ban [bã] *nm* (**a**) *(applaudissements)* round of applause (**b**) **bans** *(de mariage)* banns; **publier les bans** to publish the (wedding) banns (**c**) **être au b. de la société** to be an outcast from society; **le b. et l'arrière-b.** *(tout le monde)* the world and his wife (**d**) *Suisse* **mettre qch au b.** to forbid access to sth

banal, -e, -als, -ales [banal] *adj (objet, gens, occupation)* ordinary; *(idée, remarque, style)* trite, banal; *(accident, exemple)* common; **pas b.** unusual

banalisation [banalizasjɔ̃] *nf (généralisation)* spread; *Péj (perte d'originalité)* trivialization; **la b. des transports aériens** the fact that air travel has become commonplace *or* an everyday phenomenon

banaliser [banalize] **1** *vt (rendre commun)* to trivialize; **véhicule banalisé** unmarked police car

2 se banaliser *vpr* to become more common

banalité [banalite] *nf* (**a**) *(d'un objet, de gens, d'une occupation)* ordinariness; *(d'une idée, d'une remarque, d'un style)* triteness, banality; *(d'un accident, d'un exemple)* commonness (**b**) **banalités** *(propos banals)* platitudes

banane [banan] *nf* (**a**) *(fruit)* banana; **b. plantain** plantain (**b**) *(coiffure)* quiff (**c**) *(petit sac)* fanny pack

bananier, -ère [bananje, -ɛr] **1** *adj (plantation, production)* banana

2 *nm (arbre)* banana tree

banc [bã] *nm* (**a**) *(siège)* bench; **ils se sont connus sur les bancs de l'école** they got to know each other at school; **b. des accusés** dock; **b. d'église** pew; **b. des témoins** witness stand (**b**) *(de roche)* layer; *Can* **b. de neige** snowdrift; *(entassé mécaniquement)* bank of snow; **b. de sable** sandbank (**c**) *(de poissons)* shoal; **b. d'huîtres** oyster bed (**d**) *(établi)* (work)bench (**e**) **b. d'essai** *Ind* test bed; *Ordinat* benchtest; *Fig* testing ground; *Ordinat* **b. de mémoire** memory bank

bancaire [bãkɛr] *adj (opération)* banking; *(chèque, compte)* bank

bancal, -e, -als, -ales [bãkal] *adj (meuble)* wobbly; *Fig (raisonnement, projet)* unsound

bandage [bãdaʒ] *nm (pansement)* bandage; *(action)* bandaging

bandana [bãdana] *nm* bandana

bande¹ [bãd] *nf* (**a**) *(de tissu, de papier, de terre)* strip; *(motif)* stripe; **b. dessinée** comic strip (**b**) *(pansement)* bandage; **b. Velpeau®** crêpe bandage (**c**) *(magnétique)* tape; *(pellicule)* film; *Ordinat* **b. en cassettes** cassette tape; *Ordinat* **b. de défilement** scroll bar; *Ordinat* **b. de données** data tape; **b. originale** *(d'un film)* original soundtrack; **b. sonore** soundtrack (**d**) *Aut* **b. d'arrêt d'urgence** emergency lane, shoulder; **b. médiane** *(sur la route)* central line; **b. de roulement** *(de pneu)* tread (**e**) *Rad* **b. (de fréquence)** (frequency) band (**f**) *(d'une mitrailleuse)* cartridge belt (**g**) *Naut* **donner de la b.** to list

bande² [bãd] *nf (de personnes)* band, group; *(de voleurs)* gang, band; **faire b. à part** *(agir seul)* to do one's own thing; **viens avec nous, ne fais pas b. à part** come with us, don't stay all on your own; **faire qch en b.** to do sth in a group; **une b. d'incapables/d'imbéciles** a bunch of incompetents/idiots

bande-annonce (*pl* **bandes-annonces**) [bãdanõs] *nf* trailer (**de** for)

bandeau, -x [bãdo] *nm* (**a**) *(pour les cheveux)* headband (**b**) *(sur les yeux)* blindfold; **mettre un b. à qn** to blindfold sb (**c**) *Ordinat (dans un site Web)* banner

bandelette [bãdlɛt] *nf (de tissu)* strip; **bandelettes** *(de momie)* bandages

bander [bãde] **1** *vt* (**a**) *(blessure, main)* to bandage; **b. les yeux à qn** to blindfold sb (**b**) *(ressort)* to tighten; *(arc)* to bend; *(muscles)* to flex

2 *vi Vulg* to have a hard-on

banderille [bãdrij] *nf* banderilla

banderole [bãdrɔl] *nf* banner

bande-son (*pl* **bandes-son**) [bãdsõ] *nf* soundtrack

bandit [bãdi] *nm (escroc)* crook; *Vieilli (brigand)* bandit; **b. de grand chemin** highwayman

banditisme [bãditism] *nm* crime; **le grand b.** organized crime

bandoulière [bãduljɛr] *nf (d'un sac)* shoulder strap; **en b.** over one's shoulder

bang [bãg] *nm inv Aviat* sonic boom; *Astron* **le big b.** the big bang

Bangkok [bãkɔk] *n* Bangkok

Bangladesh [bãgladɛʃ, bɛ̃gladɛʃ] *nm* **le B.** Bangladesh

banjo [bãdʒo] *nm* banjo

banlieue [bãljø] *nf* suburbs; **la b. parisienne/marseillaise** the suburbs of Paris/Marseilles; **la grande/proche b.** the outer/inner suburbs; **vivre en b.** to live in the suburbs; **de b.** suburban

Banlieue

In France the word "banlieue" often refers not to the upmarket areas of a city – as the word "suburbia" suggests in English-speaking countries – but to the disadvantaged suburban areas on the outskirts of some cities. These neighborhoods are culturally and ethnically diverse and are frequently associated with social problems such as delinquency, unemployment and unrest.

banlieusard, -e [bãljøzar, -ard] *nm,f* suburbanite

bannière [banjɛr] *nf* (**a**) *(drapeau)* banner; **la b. étoilée** the Star-Spangled Banner (**b**) *Ordinat (dans un site Web)* banner

bannir [banir] *vt (personne, idée)* to banish (**de** from); *(sujet de conversation)* to ban (**de** from); **vous devez b. le sucre de votre alimentation** you must exclude sugar from your diet

bannissement [banismã] *nm* banishment

banque [bãk] *nf* (**a**) *(établissement)* bank; **la b.** *(activité)* banking; **employé/directeur de b.** bank clerk/manager; **b. d'affaires** investment bank; **b. centrale** central bank; **B. centrale européenne** European Central Bank; **B. européenne pour la reconstruction et le développement** European Bank for Reconstruction and Development; **la B. de France** the Bank of France; **B. internationale pour la reconstruction et le développement** International Bank for Reconstruction and Development; **la B. mondiale** the World Bank; **b. à domicile** telebanking, home banking (**b**) *(au jeu)* bank; **faire sauter la b.** to break the bank (**c**) *Ordinat* **b. de données** data bank; *Méd* **b. de sang/d'organes/du sperme** blood/organ/sperm bank

banquer [bãke] *vi Fam* to cough up

banqueroute [bãkrut] *nf Jur* bankruptcy; **faire b.** to go bankrupt

banquet [bãkɛ] *nm* banquet

banquette [bãkɛt] *nf* (**a**) *(siège)* seat; **la b. arrière** *(d'une voiture)* the back seat (**b**) *(d'un couloir d'autobus)* = curb separating a bus lane from the rest of the roadway

banquier, -ère [bãkje, -ɛr] *nm,f* banker

banquise [bãkiz] *nf* ice floe

bantou, -e [bãtu] **1** *adj* Bantu

2 *nm,f* **B., Bantoue** Bantu

baobab [baobab] *nm* baobab (tree)

baptême [batɛm] *nm* (**a**) *Rel* baptism, christening; **donner le b. à qn** to baptize *or* to christen sb (**b**) *(d'un navire)* naming; *(d'une cloche)* blessing (**c**) **b. de l'air** inaugural flight; **b. du feu** baptism of fire (**d**) *Belg* = **bizutage**

baptiser [batize] *vt* (**a**) *Rel* to baptize, to christen (**b**) *(nommer)* to name; *(surnommer)* to christen (**c**) *(navire)* to name; *(cloche)* to bless

baptismal, -e, -aux, -ales [batismal, -o] *adj* baptismal

baptistère [batistɛr] *nm Rel* baptistry

baquet [bakɛ] *nm (cuve)* tub

bar¹ [bar] *nm (café, comptoir)* bar; **b. à thème** theme bar

bar² [bar] *nm (poisson)* bass

bar³ [bar] *nm Phys* bar

barachois [baraʃwa] *nm Can (dans une rivière)* sandbar

baragouiner [baragwine] *Fam* **1** *vt (langue étrangère)* to speak badly; **qu'est-ce qu'il baragouine?** what's he jabbering about?

2 *vi* to jabber

baraque [barak] *nf* (**a**) *(cabane)* hut, shack; *(de forain)* stall, stand (**b**) *Fam (maison)* place

baraqué, -e [barake] *adj Fam* hefty

baraquement [barakmã] *nm* shacks; *Mil* camp

baratin [baratɛ̃] *nm Fam* (**a**) *(d'un vendeur)* sales talk, patter; *(d'un séducteur)* smooth talk (**b**) *(verbiage)* waffle

baratiner [baratine] *Fam* **1** *vt (sujet: vendeur)* to give the sales talk to; *(sujet: séducteur)* to hit on

2 *vi* to waffle

baratineur, -euse [baratinœr, -øz] *nm,f Fam* smooth talker

baratte [barat] *nf* churn

Barbade [barbad] *nf* **la B.** Barbados

barbant, -e [barbɑ̃, -ɑ̃t] *adj Fam* boring

barbare [barbar] **1** *adj (cruel, sauvage)* barbaric
2 *nmf* barbarian

barbarie [barbari] *nf* **(a)** *(cruauté)* barbarity **(b)** *(manque de civilisation)* barbarism

barbarisme [barbarism] *nm* barbarism

barbe [barb] *nf* **(a)** *(d'homme)* beard; **b. de trois jours** stubble; *Fig* **à la b. de qn** right under sb's nose; **parler dans sa b.** to mutter, to mumble; **rire dans sa b.** to laugh up one's sleeve; *Fam* **la b.!** what a pain or drag!; *Fam* **quelle b.!** what a drag!; **b. à papa** cotton candy **(b)** *(de chèvre, d'épi)* beard; *(de plume, d'hameçon)* barb **(c)** *Tech (de métal)* burr; *(de papier)* ragged edge

barbecue [barbəkju] *nm* barbecue; **faire un b.** to have a barbecue

barbelé [barbəle] **1** *adj m voir* **fil**
2 *nmpl* **barbelés** barbwire

barber [barbe] *Fam* **1** *vt* **b. qn** to bore sb stiff
2 se barber *vpr* to be bored stiff

barbeuc, barbeuk [barbœk] *nm Fam (barbecue)* BBQ

barbeux, -euse [barbœ, -øz] *adj Can Fam* **être b.** to be a pain in the neck

barbiche [barbiʃ] *nf* goatee (beard)

barbichette [barbiʃɛt] *nf Fam* small goatee (beard)

barbier [barbje] *nm* **(a)** *Vieilli* barber **(b)** *Can (coiffeur pour hommes)* (men's) hairdresser

barbiturique [barbityrik] *nm* barbiturate

barboter [barbɔte] **1** *vi* to splash about
2 *vt Fam (voler)* to pinch

barboteuse [barbɔtøz] *nf* **(a)** *(vêtement)* rompers **(b)** *Can (piscine gonflable)* wading pool

barbouiller [barbuje] *vt* **(a)** *(salir)* to smear **(de** with); *(peindre)* to daub **(b)** *Fam* **b. l'estomac** *ou* **le cœur à qn** to make sb feel queasy; **se sentir barbouillé** to feel queasy

barbouze [barbuz] *nf Fam (agent secret)* secret agent

barbu, -e [barby] **1** *adj* bearded
2 *nm* bearded man

Barcelone [barsəlɔn] *n* Barcelona

barda [barda] *nm Fam* **(a)** *(affaires)* gear; *Mil* kit **(b)** *Can (pagaille)* shambles **(c)** *Can (bruit)* **faire du b.** to make a racket

barde¹ [bard] *nf Culin (sur un rôti)* bard

barde² [bard] *nm* bard

barder¹ [bard] *v impersonnel Fam* **ça va b.!** there's going to be trouble!

barder² [barde] *vt* **(a)** *Culin* to bard **(b)** **bardé de fer/cuir** steel-/leather-clad; **être bardé de décorations** to be covered with decorations; **être bardé de diplômes** to have a whole string of qualifications

barème [barɛm] *nm* **(a)** *(de notes, de salaires, de prix)* scale **(b)** *(pour calcul rapide)* ready reckoner

barge [barʒ] *nf (péniche)* barge

baril [baril] *nm (de vin, de pétrole)* barrel; *(de poudre)* keg; *(de lessive)* drum

barillet [barijɛ] *nm (de revolver)* cylinder

bariolé, -e [barjɔle] *adj* multicolored

barjo(t) [barʒo] *adj Fam* nuts

barman [barman] *(pl* **barmans** *ou* **barmen** [barmɛn]*) nm* bartender

baromètre [barɔmɛtr] *nm aussi Fig* barometer

baron [barɔ̃] *nm (seigneur)* baron; *Fig* **les barons de la finance/de l'industrie** financial/industrial tycoons

baronne [barɔn] *nf* baroness

baroque [barɔk] **1** *adj (architecture, art, musique)* baroque; *(idées)* bizarre, odd
2 *nm* **le b.** the Baroque

baroud [barud] *nm* **b. d'honneur** last stand

barouder [barude] *vi Fam (voyager)* to knock about

baroudeur [barudœr] *nm Fam* **(a)** *(combattant)* fighter **(b)** *(voyageur)* keen traveler

barouf [baruf]**, baroufle** [barufl] *nm Fam* din, row

barque [bark] *nf* boat; *Fig* **bien mener** *ou* **bien conduire sa b.** to manage one's affairs well; *Fig* **c'est elle qui mène la b.** she's the boss

barquette [barkɛt] *nf* **(a)** *(pour plat à emporter)* container; *(de fruits)* small basket **(b)** *(gâteau)* pastry boat

barrage [baraʒ] *nm (sur l'eau)* dam; **b. de police** police roadblock; **b. routier** roadblock

barre [bar] *nf* **(a)** *(de métal)* bar, rod; *(de bois)* rod; **b. d'appui** *(d'une fenêtre)* handrail; **b. de céréales** cereal or muesli bar; **b. de chocolat** *ou* **chocolatée** candy bar; **b. à mine** = metal bar used for breaking stone surfaces
(b) *(pour la danse)* barre; *Sport* **barres asymétriques** asymmetric bars; **b. fixe** horizontal bar; **barres parallèles** parallel bars; **b. transversale** *(de but)* crossbar; *Fig* **placer la b. trop haut** to set too high a standard
(c) *(trait)* line, stroke; *(d'un t)* cross; **b. oblique** oblique, slash; *Mus* **b. de mesure** bar (line)
(d) *Naut (à l'arrière)* tiller; *(volant)* helm; *aussi Fig* **être à** *ou* **tenir la b.** to be at the helm
(e) *Jur (de tribunal)* bar; **b. des témoins** witness stand; **être appelé à la b.** to be called to the stand
(f) *(de clavier)* **b. d'espacement** space bar
(g) *Ordinat* **b. d'outils** tool bar; **b. de sélection** menu bar; **b. de titre** title bar
(h) **b. HLM** large apartment building on a housing project
(i) *Can* **la b. du jour** dawn, daybreak

barreau, -x [baro] *nm* **(a)** *(d'une fenêtre, d'une cage)* bar; *(d'une échelle, d'une chaise)* rung; *Fig* **b. de chaise** fat cigar; **être derrière les barreaux** to be behind bars **(b)** *Jur* **le b.** the bar

barrer [bare] **1** *vt* **(a)** *(route, passage, chemin)* to block off; *(porte, fenêtre)* to bar; *Can (fermer à clef)* to lock; **route barrée** *(sur panneau)* road closed; **b. le passage** *ou* **la route à qn** to bar sb's way **(b)** *(chèque)* to cross **(c)** *(mot, paragraphe)* to cross out **(d)** *Naut (bateau)* to steer; *(à l'aviron)* to cox **(e)** *Fam* **on est mal barrés** things don't look good
2 se barrer *vpr Fam* to clear off, to beat it

barrette [barɛt] *nf* **(a)** *(pour les cheveux)* barrette **(b)** *(broche)* brooch **(c)** *(de haschich)* thin strip **(d)** *Ordinat* **b. de mémoire vive** RAM module

barreur [barœr] *nm Naut* helmsman; *(à l'aviron)* cox

barricade [barikad] *nf* barricade

barricader [barikade] **1** *vt (rue, porte)* to barricade
2 se barricader *vpr* to barricade oneself in

barrière [barjɛr] *nf (obstacle)* barrier; *(clôture)* fence; *(d'un passage à niveau)* gate; *Aut* **b. de dégel** = ban on the use of a road by heavy traffic during a thaw; *Com* **barrières douanières** trade barriers; *Belg* **b. Nadar** crowd barrier; **b. Vauban** security barrier; **la Grande B. de Corail** the Great Barrier Reef

barrique [barik] *nf* barrel; *Fam Fig* **plein** *ou* **rond comme une b.** blind drunk

barrir [barir] *vi (éléphant)* to trumpet

barrissements [barismɑ̃] *nmpl (d'un éléphant)* trumpeting

bar-tabac *(pl* **bars-tabacs)** [bartaba] *nm* = bar that also sells cigarettes and tobacco

baryton [baritɔ̃] *nm Mus* baritone

baryum [barjɔm] *nm Chim* barium

bas¹ [bɑ]**, basse** [bɑs] **1** *adj* **(a)** *(dans l'espace, en quantité, en intensité)* low; *(marée)* out, low; **à b. prix** cheaply; **avoir la vue basse** to be nearsighted
(b) *(dans une hiérarchie)* low; *Péj ou Hum* **le b. peuple** (the) hoi polloi; **les b. quartiers** the poor districts
(c) *(note)* low; *(instrument de musique)* bass

(**d**) *(dans le temps)* late; **le b. Moyen Âge** the late Middle Ages

(**e**) *Péj (acte)* mean, low; *(besognes)* menial

2 *adv* (**a**) *(dans l'espace)* low (down); **voir plus b.** *(dans un article)* see below; *Fig* **mettre qn plus b. que terre** to treat sb like dirt; **tomber b.** *(température, prix d'une action)* to plummet; *Fam* **b. les mains** *ou* **les pattes!** hands off!, keep your paws off!

(**b**) *(dans une hiérarchie)* low

(**c**) *(parler)* quietly; *(chanter) (dans le registre)* low; *(doucement)* softly; **rire tout b.** to chuckle to oneself

(**d**) **en b.** at the bottom; *(à l'étage inférieur)* downstairs; **les gens d'en b.** the people below *or* downstairs; **la tête en b.** upside down; **en b. de** at the bottom of

(**e**) **à b. la dictature/la police!** down with dictatorship/ the police!

3 *nm (partie inférieure)* bottom; **l'étagère du b.** the bottom shelf; **le b. du dos** the small of the back; **au b. de** at the bottom of; **de b. en haut** upward

4 *nf* **basse** *Mus* (**a**) *(partie)* bass part; *(voix, chanteur)* bass (**b**) *(contrebasse)* (double) bass; *(guitare)* bass (guitar)

bas² [bɑ] *nm (vêtement)* stocking; *Can* sock; **b. de contention** elastic stocking; *Fig* **b. de laine** nest egg; **b. nylon** nylons; **b. résille** fishnet stockings; **b. à varices** support stocking

basalte [bazalt] *nm* basalt

basané, -e [bazane] *adj (bronzé)* tanned; *(tanné)* weatherbeaten; *(naturellement)* swarthy

bas-côté *(pl* **bas-côtés)** [bɑkote] *nm* (**a**) *(d'une route)* shoulder (**b**) *(d'une église)* (side) aisle

basculant, -e [baskylɑ̃, -ɑ̃t] *adj* **benne basculante** *(de camion)* dumper; **pont b.** drawbridge

bascule [baskyl] *nf* (**a**) *(balançoire)* seesaw (**b**) *(balance)* weighing machine (**c**) *Can* **donner la b. à qn** to give sb the bumps

basculer [baskyle] **1** *vt* (**a**) *(brouette, charrette)* to tip up; *(chargement)* to tip over (**b**) *Ordinat* to toggle

2 *vi* (**a**) *(tomber)* to topple over; **faire b.** *(personne)* to knock over; *(chargement)* to tip over; **le pays a basculé dans l'anarchie** the country slid into anarchy (**b**) *Ordinat* to toggle

base [bɑz] *nf* (**a**) *(partie inférieure)* base; *Fig (d'un syndicat, d'un parti politique)* rank and file; **b. de maquillage** foundation (**b**) *Mil (d'opérations)* base; **b. aérienne/navale** air/naval base; **b. de lancement** launch site (**c**) *(principe)* basis; **jeter** *ou* **poser les bases de qch** to lay the foundations for sth; **de b.** basic; **denrées de b.** staple commodities; **à b. d'amidon/de gin** starch-/gin-based (**d**) *Math & Chim* base (**e**) *Ordinat* **b. de données** database

base-ball [bɛzbol] *nm* baseball

baser [baze] **1** *vt* to base; **être basé sur qch** to be based on sth

2 se baser *vpr* **se b. sur qch** *(sujet: personne)* to base one's argument on sth; **sur quoi te bases-tu pour dire que…?** what basis do you have for saying that…?

bas-fond *(pl* **bas-fonds)** [bafɔ̃] *nm (dans la mer, la rivière)* shallow; **les bas-fonds** *(d'une ville)* the rough areas

basic [bazik] *nm Ordinat* BASIC

basilic [bazilik] *nm (plante)* basil

basilique [bazilik] *nf* basilica

basket [baskɛt] **1** *nm ou nf (chaussure)* **baskets** sneakers; *Fam* **être bien dans ses baskets** to be very together

2 *nm (sport)* basketball

basket-ball [baskɛtbol] *nm* basketball

basketteur, -euse [baskɛtœr, -øz] *nm, f* basketball player

basque¹ [bask] **1** *adj* Basque

2 *nm (langue)* Basque

3 *nmf* **B.** Basque

basque² [bask] *nf (d'une veste)* tail; *Fig* **être toujours pendu aux basques de qn** to be always at sb's heels

bas-relief *(pl* **bas-reliefs)** [barəljɛf] *nm* bas-relief

basse [bɑs] *voir* **bas¹**

basse-cour *(pl* **basses-cours)** [bɑskur] *nf* (**a**) *(cour)* farmyard (**b**) *(volaille)* poultry

bassement [bɑsmɑ̃] *adv* **être b. intéressé** to have one's own interests at heart

bassesse [bɑsɛs] *nf* (**a**) *(d'une action, d'un caractère)* lowness (**b**) *(action)* low act

basset [bɑsɛ] *nm (chien)* basset (hound)

bassin [bɑsɛ̃] *nm* (**a**) *(récipient)* basin, bowl; **b. (hygiénique)** bedpan (**b**) *(dans un jardin)* ornamental lake; *(de fontaine)* basin; *(réservoir)* tank; **petit b.** *(de la piscine)* children's pool; **grand b.** *(de la piscine)* large pool (**c**) *(d'un port)* dock, basin (**d**) *Géol* basin; **b. houiller** coal basin; **b. minier** mining area; **le B. parisien** the Paris Basin (**e**) *(partie du corps)* pelvis

bassine [bɑsin] *nf* (**a**) *(en plastique)* basin, bowl; *(contenu)* basinful, bowlful (**b**) *(en cuivre)* pan; *(contenu)* panful

bassiner [bɑsine] *vt Fam (ennuyer)* to bore stiff

bassiste [basist] *nmf (contrebassiste)* double-bass player; *(guitariste)* bass guitarist

basson [bɑsɔ̃] *nm* (**a**) *(instrument)* bassoon (**b**) *(joueur)* bassoonist

basta [basta] *exclam Fam* enough already!

bastide [bastid] *nf* (**a**) *(maison)* country house; *(ferme)* farm (**b**) *Hist (ville fortifiée)* fortified town

bastille [bastij] *nf* fortress; *Hist* **la B.** the Bastille; **la prise de la B.** the storming of the Bastille

bastingage [bastɛ̃gaʒ] *nm Naut (garde-corps)* ship's rail

bastion [bastjɔ̃] *nm aussi Fig* bastion

baston [bastɔ̃] *nm ou nf Fam* fistfight

bastonner [bastɔne] **se bastonner** *vpr Fam* to fight

bastringue [bastrɛ̃g] *nm Fam* (**a**) *(dancing)* (seedy) dance hall (**b**) *(affaires)* gear, stuff; **et tout le b.** and the whole caboodle

bas-ventre *(pl* **bas-ventres)** [bɑvɑ̃tr] *nm* lower abdomen

bât [bɑ] *nm* packsaddle; *Fig* **c'est là que le b. blesse** there's the rub

bataclan [bataklɑ̃] *nm Fam (affaires)* stuff, gear; **et tout le b.** and the whole caboodle

bataille [batɑj] *nf* (**a**) *(lutte)* battle, fight; *(électorale)* contest; **b. terrestre/aérienne/navale** land/air/naval battle; **cheveux en b.** disheveled hair (**b**) *(jeu de cartes)* beggar-my-neighbor

batailler [batɑje] *vi Fam* **b. pour faire qch** to battle to do sth

batailleur, -euse [batɑjœr, -øz] *adj* aggressive

bataillon [batɑjɔ̃] *nm Mil* battalion; *Fam* **un b. de** a troop of

bâtard, -e [bɑtar, -ard] **1** *adj (enfant)* illegitimate; *Péj* bastard; *(style, solution)* hybrid

2 *nm,f (enfant)* illegitimate child; *Péj* bastard

3 *nm (chien)* mongrel; *(pain)* = small baguette *or* French loaf

batavia [batavja] *nf* batavia lettuce

bateau, -x [bato] **1** *nm* (**a**) *(embarcation)* boat; **faire du b.** to go boating; **prendre le b.** to go/come by boat; **en** *ou* **par b.** by boat; *Fam Fig* **mener qn en b., monter un b. à qn** to take sb for a ride; **b. de croisière** cruise ship; **b. à moteur** motorboat; **b. de pêche** fishing boat; **b. de plaisance** pleasure boat; **b. à vapeur** steamboat, steamer; **b. à voiles** sailboat (**b**) *(sur le trottoir)* driveway entrance (**c**) **encolure b.** boat neck

2 *adj inv Fam (banal)* hackneyed

bateau-mouche *(pl* **bateaux-mouches)** [batomuʃ] *nm* riverboat *(on the Seine)*

bateleur, -euse [batlœr, -øz] *nm,f Vieilli (jongleur)* juggler; *(acrobate)* acrobat

batelier, -ère [batəlje, -ɛr] *nm,f* boatman, *f* boatwoman; *(sur un bac)* ferryman, *f* ferrywoman

bat-flanc [baflɑ̃] *nm inv (dans un dortoir, une prison)* wooden partition

bâti, -e [bɑti] **1** *adj (personne)* **être bien b.** to be well-built; **être mal b.** to have an odd shape

2 *nm* (**a**) *Constr* frame, framework (**b**) *(en couture)* tacking, basting

batifoler [batifole] *vi Fam* to lark about

batik [batik] *nm* batik

bâtiment [batimã] *nm* (**a**) *(immeuble)* building; **b. d'habitation** residential building (**b**) *(secteur)* **le b.** building; **être dans le b.** to be in the building trade; **bâtiments et travaux publics** building and civil engineering (**c**) *Naut* ship; **b. de guerre** warship, battleship

bâtir [batir] **1** *vt* (**a**) *(maison, ville)* to build; *Fig (fortune, hypothèse)* to build (up); **(se) faire b. une maison** to have a house built; **terrain bâti** developed *or* built-up site (**b**) *(en couture)* to tack, to baste
 2 se bâtir *vpr* **se b. une réputation (de)** to build up a reputation (as)

bâtisse [batis] *nf* ugly building

batiste [batist] *nf* batiste

bâton [batɔ̃] *nm* (**a**) *(en bois, de colle, de craie)* stick; *(d'agent de police)* nightstick; *(de majorette)* baton; **mener une vie de b. de chaise** to lead a wild life; **mettre des bâtons dans les roues à qn** to put a spoke in sb's wheel; **parler à bâtons rompus** to talk about this and that; **conversation à bâtons rompus** rambling conversation; **b. de rouge à lèvres** lipstick; **bâtons de ski** ski poles (**b**) *(trait vertical)* vertical line (**c**) *Can & Suisse* **b. (de hockey)** hockey stick

bâtonnet [batɔnɛ] *nm* stick

batracien [batrasjɛ̃] *nm Zool* amphibian

battage [bataʒ] *nm* (**a**) *Fam (publicité)* hype; **faire du b. autour de qch** to hype sth up (**b**) *(du blé)* threshing

battant, -e [batã, -ãt] **1** *adj (pluie)* lashing; **le cœur b.** with a pounding heart
 2 *nm,f (personne combative)* fighter
 3 *nm* (**a**) *(d'une cloche)* clapper, tongue (**b**) *(d'une porte, d'un volet)* leaf; **porte à double b.** double door

batte [bat] *nf* bat; **b. de base-ball** baseball bat

battement [batmã] *nm* (**a**) *(de tambour)* beat, beating; *(de mains)* clapping; *(d'ailes, de voiles)* flapping; *(de porte)* banging; **j'entendais les battements de son cœur** I could hear his/ her heart beating (**b**) *(entre deux événements)* gap; **deux heures de b.** a two-hour gap

batterie [batri] *nf* (**a**) *(dans un orchestre)* drums; **être à la b.** to be on drums (**b**) *Mil* battery; *Fig* **dévoiler ses batteries** to show one's hand; **b. antiaérienne/antichars** anti-aircraft/ antitank battery (**c**) *(ensemble, groupe)* battery; *(de tests, de questions)* series; **élevage en b.** factory farming; **poulet de b.** battery hen; **b. de cuisine** kitchen utensils (**d**) *Élec* battery; **fonctionner sur b.** to be battery-operated *or* battery-powered; **b. de secours** emergency battery

batteur [batœr] *nm* (**a**) *(dans un groupe)* drummer (**b**) *(au baseball)* batter (**c**) *(de cuisine)* mixer

batteuse [batøz] *nf (machine agricole)* threshing machine, thresher

battoir [batwar] *nm* (**a**) *(pour les tapis)* (carpet) beater; *(pour le linge)* beetle (**b**) *Fam (grande main)* great paw *or* mitt

battre [11] [batr] **1** *vt* (**a**) *(frapper)* (personne, chien, tapis) to beat; *(blé)* to thresh; *(métal)* to hammer; **b. qn à coups de poing** to punch sb; **b. le tambour** to beat the drum; **b. le rappel** *Mil* to call to arms; *Fig* to call everyone together; **b. la campagne** to scour *or* to comb the countryside; *(esprit)* to wander; *Prov* **il faut b. le fer quand il** *ou* **pendant qu'il est chaud** strike while the iron is hot
 (**b**) *(cartes)* to shuffle; *(beurre)* to churn; *(œufs, préparation culinaire)* to beat, to whisk; **b. les blancs en neige** to beat the whites stiffly
 (**c**) *(adversaire)* to beat; *(record)* to break; **b. qn à plate(s) couture(s)** to beat sb hollow; *Fig* **b. tous les records** to take some beating

(**d**) *Mus* **b. la mesure** to beat time
 (**e**) *Naut* **b. pavillon français/américain** to fly the French/American flag
 2 *vi* (**a**) *(cœur)* to beat; *(porte, volet)* to bang; *(voile)* to flap; **il a le cœur qui bat** *(d'émotion)* his heart is pounding
 (**b**) **b. en retraite** to beat a retreat
 3 battre de *vt ind* **b. des mains** to clap one's hands; **b. des cils** to flutter one's eyelashes
 4 se battre *vpr aussi Fig* to fight (**avec/contre** with/ against); **se b. comme des chiffonniers** to fight like cat and dog; **se b. au couteau** to fight with knives; *très Fam* **je m'en bats l'œil** I don't give a rat's ass

battu, -e [baty] *adj (femme, enfant)* battered; **un air** *ou* **regard de chien b.** a hangdog look; **avoir les yeux battus** to have dark circles under one's eyes

battue [baty] *nf (à la chasse)* beat; *(pour retrouver quelqu'un)* search

batture [batyr] *nf Can* sandbank

baud [bo] *nm Tél & Ordinat* baud

baudet [bodɛ] *nm* ass, donkey; **chargé comme un b.** loaded down like a packhorse

baudrier [bodrije] *nm* shoulder strap; *(pour épée)* baldric; *(d'escalade)* harness

baudroie [bodrwa] *nf* monkfish

baudruche [bodryʃ] *nf* **(ballon de) b.** balloon

baume [bom] *nm aussi Fig* balm; **mettre du b. au cœur de qn** *(événement)* to be a consolation for sb; **b. pour les lèvres** lip balm

baux [bo] *voir* **bail**

bauxite [boksit] *nf* bauxite

bavard, -e [bavar, -ard] **1** *adj* (**a**) *(qui parle beaucoup)* chatty; *(style, essai)* wordy; **il est b. comme une pie** he'd talk the hind legs off a donkey (**b**) *(indiscret)* indiscreet
 2 *nm,f* (**a**) *(qui parle beaucoup)* chatterbox (**b**) *(indiscret)* gossip

bavardage [bavardaʒ] *nm* (**a**) *(action)* chatting; *(commérage)* gossiping (**b**) *Ordinat (sur Internet)* chat (**c**) **bavardages** *(paroles)* chat; *(commérage)* gossip

bavarder [bavarde] *vi* (**a**) *(parler)* to chat; *(commérer)* to gossip (**b**) *Ordinat (sur Internet)* to chat

bavardoir [bavardwar] *nm Can Ordinat* chat room

bavarois, -e [bavarwa, -az] **1** *adj* Bavarian
 2 *nm Culin* bavarois, = dessert consisting of set custard and whipped cream mixed with fruit purée
 3 *nm,f* **B., Bavaroise** Bavarian

bave [bav] *nf (de personne)* dribble; *(de chien)* slaver; *(de cheval, de chien enragé)* froth, foam; *(d'escargot)* slime; *(de crapaud)* spittle

baver [bave] *vi (personne)* to dribble; *(chien)* to slaver; *(chien enragé)* to foam at the mouth; *(stylo)* to leak, to run; *(encre)* to smudge; *Fam* **en b. (des ronds de chapeaux)** to have a hard time of it; *Fam* **en faire b. (des ronds de chapeaux) à qn** to give sb a hard time

bavette [bavɛt] *nf* (**a**) *(d'un bébé, d'un tablier)* bib (**b**) *Culin* skirt (of beef) (**c**) *Fam* **tailler une b.** to have a chat

baveux, -euse [bavø, -øz] **1** *adj (bouche, enfant)* dribbling; *(omelette)* runny
 2 *nm,f Can (morveux)* pain, pest

Bavière [bavjɛr] *nf* **la B.** Bavaria

bavoir [bavwar] *nm* bib

bavure [bavyr] *nf* (**a**) *(tache)* smudge, smear (**b**) *(erreur)* slip-up; **sans bavure(s)** faultless; **b. policière** case of police misconduct

bayer [53] [baje] *vi* **b. aux corneilles** to stare into space

bazar [bazar] *nm* (**a**) *(marché)* bazaar (**b**) *(magasin)* general store (**c**) *Fam (désordre)* shambles *(singulier)*; *(bruit)* racket; *(affaires)* stuff, gear; **et tout le b.** and the whole caboodle; **mettre du** *ou* **le b. dans qch** to make a shambles of sth (**d**) *Belg Fam (chose)* thing, thingy

bazarder [bazarde] *vt Fam (se débarrasser de)* to get rid of; *(jeter)* to chuck out; *(vendre)* to junk

bazooka [bazuka] *nm* bazooka

BCBG [besebeʒe] *adj inv (abrév* **bon chic bon genre)** ≃ preppy

BCE [beseα] *nf (abrév* **Banque centrale européenne)** European Central Bank

BCG® [beseʒe] *nm Méd* BCG

BD [bede] *nf* (a) *(abrév* **bande dessinée)** comic strip, cartoon (b) *Ordinat (abrév* **base de données)** dbase

> ### ßD
> This is a common abbreviation for "bande dessinée", or "comic book". Considered a serious and important art form in France, the comic book has become popular among teenagers and intellectuals alike. An annual festival of comic book art is held in Angoulême.

bd *(abrév* **boulevard)** Blvd.

beach-volley [bitʃvɔlɛ] *nm Sport* beach volleyball

béant, -e [beᾶ, -ᾶt] *adj (bouche, porte)* wide-open; *(blessure, gouffre)* gaping

béat, -e [bea, -at] *adj Rel* blessed; *(heureux)* blissful; *Péj (niais)* inane; **être b. d'admiration** to be open-mouthed in admiration; **elle nous observait d'un air b.** she watched us open-mouthed

béatement [beatmᾶ] *adv (sourire)* inanely

béatifier [66] [beatifje] *vt Rel* to beatify

béatitude [beatityd] *nf* (a) *Rel* beatitude (b) *(bonheur parfait)* bliss

beau, belle [bo, bɛl]

> **bel** is used before masculine singular nouns beginning with a vowel or h mute.

1 *adj* (a) *(d'apparence) (femme, enfant)* beautiful, good-looking; *(homme)* handsome, good-looking; *(objet, maison)* lovely, beautiful; **b. comme un dieu** like a Greek god; **ce n'est pas b. à voir** it's not a pretty sight; **se faire b.** to smarten oneself up (b) *(de qualité) (œuvre, spectacle, discours)* fine; **avoir une belle situation** to have a good job (c) *(moralement)* fine, noble; **un b. geste** a noble gesture; **ce n'est pas b. de mentir** it isn't nice to tell lies (d) *(bien)* **c'est trop b. pour être vrai** it's too good to be true; **ce serait trop b.!** that would be too much (to hope for)!; **le plus b. jour de ma vie** the best day of my life (e) *Ironique* **une belle grippe** a nasty case of the flu; **une belle correction** a good thrashing; **te voilà b.!** you're in a fine mess!; **te voilà dans un bel état!** look at the state of you!; **j'ai eu une belle peur** I had a terrible scare; **vous avez fait du b. travail!** well done!; *très Fam* **un b. salaud** a real *or* total bastard; **j'en ai entendu de belles sur votre compte!** I've heard some unpleasant things about you!; **il en a fait de belles** he got up to some real tricks (f) *(intensif)* **au b. milieu de la rue** right *or* bang in the middle of the road; **une belle somme** a tidy sum; **un b. poulet** a nice big chicken (g) *(locutions)* **bel et bien** *(complètement)* well and truly; **il est bel et bien venu** he really did come; **il s'est bel et bien trompé** he has indeed made a mistake; **de plus belle** with a vengeance; **il reprit l'entraînement de plus belle** he resumed training with a vengeance *or* more enthusiastically than ever

2 *adv* **il fait b.** the weather's fine; **il ferait b. voir ça!** that'll be the day!; **j'ai b. le lui expliquer...** no matter how many times I explain it to him...; **j'ai b. pousser, la porte ne bouge pas** no matter how hard I push *or* try as I might, I can't get the door to open

3 *nm* **le b.** *(beauté)* beauty; **mais le plus b., c'est que...** but

the best part is that ...; *Fam Ironique* **c'est du b.!** that's great!; **le temps est au b. (fixe)** the weather is set fair; *Fig* **avoir le moral au b. fixe** to be permanently in a good mood; **un vieux b.** an old roué; **faire le b.** *(chien)* to sit up and beg; *Can (homme)* to strut about

4 *nf* **belle** (a) *(partie)* deciding game (b) *Hum (amie)* lady friend (c) *Fam (locutions)* **se faire la b.** to run away; *(de prison)* to escape; *Belg* **avoir b. à faire qch** to have no trouble doing sth

beaucoup [boku] *adv* (a) *(intensément, en grande quantité)* a lot; **ça te plaît? – pas b.** do you like it? – not much *or* not a lot (b) *(une grande quantité, un grand nombre)* **il reste encore b. à faire** there's still a lot to do; **c'est déjà b. qu'il veuille bien vous parler** it's already something that he condescended to speak to you; **il y est pour b.** he has had a lot *or* a great deal to do with it; **b. pensent que...** a lot of *or* many people think that...; **b. d'entre nous** a lot *or* many of us; **de b.** *(de loin)* by far; **il s'en faut de b. que je sois riche** I'm far from rich (c) **b. de** *(quantité)* a lot of; *(nombre)* a lot of, many; **b. de vin/chance** a lot of wine/luck; **b. de fautes** a lot of *or* many mistakes; **pas b. de** *(argent, courage)* not much; *(gens, problèmes)* not many; **avec b. de soin** with great care, very carefully; **j'en veux b.!** I want a lot! (d) *(avec des comparatifs)* a lot, much; **b. moins/plus vite** a lot *or* much slower/faster; **il parle b. trop** he talks far too much; **b. moins d'enfants** a lot *or* many fewer children; **b. moins de temps** a lot *or* much less time

beauf [bof] *Fam* **1** *adj Péj* **il est un peu b.** he's a bit of a narrow-minded average Frenchman **2** *nm* (a) *(beau-frère)* brother-in-law (b) *Péj* = stereotypical narrow-minded, average Frenchman

beau-fils *(pl* **beaux-fils)** [bofis] *nm* (a) *(gendre)* son-in-law (b) *(après remariage)* stepson

beau-frère *(pl* **beaux-frères)** [bofrɛr] *nm* brother-in-law

beaujolais [boʒɔlɛ] *nm* Beaujolais

beau-père *(pl* **beaux-pères)** [bopɛr] *nm* (a) *(père du conjoint)* father-in-law (b) *(après remariage)* stepfather

beaupré [bopre] *nm Naut* bowsprit

beauté [bote] *nf* beauty; **être en b.** to be looking magnificent; **de toute b.** magnificent; **finir en b.** to end on a high note; **faire qch pour la b. du geste** to do sth for the sake of it; **se refaire une b.** to put one's face on

beaux-arts [bozar] *nmpl* fine art; **école des b., B.** art school

beaux-parents [boparᾶ] *nmpl* parents-in-law

bébé [bebe] *nm* (a) *(nourrisson)* baby; **faire le b.** to behave like a baby; **être très b.** to be very babyish (b) *(animal)* **b. gazelle/lapin** baby gazelle/rabbit

bébé-éprouvette *(pl* **bébés-éprouvette)** [bebeepruvɛt] *nm* test-tube baby

bébelle [bebɛl] *nf Can (gadget)* gadget; *(bibelot)* ornament; *(jouet)* toy

bébête [bebɛt] *Fam* **1** *adj* silly **2** *nf* creepy-crawler

bec [bɛk] *nm* (a) *(d'oiseau, de tortue, de pieuvre)* beak (b) *Fam (bouche)* mouth; **il n'a pas ouvert le b. de la journée** he hasn't opened his mouth all day; **la clope au b.** with a smoke in one's mouth; **rester le b. dans l'eau** to be left high and dry; **b. fin** gourmet; *Can* **faire le b. fin** to be picky (c) *(de pot)* *(de cafetière)* spout; *(d'instrument à vent)* mouthpiece; **b. Bunsen** Bunsen burner; **b. de gaz** *(réverbère)* gas lamp; **b. verseur** spout (d) *Belg, Suisse & Can (baiser)* **donner un b. à qn** to give sb a kiss

bécane [bekan] *nf Fam (vélo)* bike; *(machine, ordinateur)* machine

bécarre [bekar] *adj & nm Mus* natural

bécasse [bekas] *nf* (a) *(oiseau)* woodcock (b) *Fam (idiote)* silly thing

bec-de-lièvre (*pl* **becs-de-lièvre**) [bɛkdəljɛvr] *nm* harelip

béchamel [beʃamɛl] *nf* (**sauce**) **b.** béchamel sauce

bêche [bɛʃ] *nf* spade

bêcher [beʃe] *vt* to dig, to turn over

bêcheur, -euse [beʃœr, -øz] *nm,f Fam* (*snob*) stuck-up person

bécosses [bekɔs] *nfpl Can Fam* john

bécoter [bekɔte] *Fam* **1** *vt* to neck
2 se bécoter *vpr* to neck

becqueter [42] [bɛkte] **1** *vt* (*sujet: oiseau*) to peck at
2 *vi très Fam* (*personne*) to eat

becter [bɛkte] = **becqueter**

bedaine [bədɛn] *nf Fam* pot(-belly), paunch; **prendre de la b.** to get a pot(-belly) *or* a paunch

bédé [bede] *nf Fam* comic strip, cartoon

bedeau, -x [bədo] *nm* verger

bedon [bədɔ̃] *nm Fam* pot(-belly), paunch

bedonnant, -e [bədɔnɑ̃, -ɑ̃t] *adj Fam* pot-bellied, paunchy

bédouin, -e [bedwɛ̃, -in] **1** *adj* Bedouin
2 *nm,f* **B., Bédouine** Bedouin

bée [be] *adj f* **bouche b.** open-mouthed; **j'en suis restée bouche b.** I was speechless; **regarder qch bouche b.** to gape at sth

beffroi [befrwa] *nm* belfry

bégaiement [begɛmɑ̃] *nm* stuttering, stammering

bégayer [53] [begeje] **1** *vi* to stutter, to stammer
2 *vt* to stammer (out)

bégonia [begɔnja] *nm* begonia

bègue [bɛg] **1** *adj* **être b.** to stutter, to stammer
2 *nmf* stutterer, stammerer

bégueule [begœl] *adj* prudish

béguin [begɛ̃] *nm Fam* (*personne*) crush; **avoir le b. pour qn** to have a crush on sb; **avoir le b. pour qch** to have a thing about sth

BEI [beəi] *nf* (*abrév* **Banque européenne d'investissement**) EIB

beige [bɛʒ] *adj & nm* beige

beigne[1] [bɛɲ] *nf Fam* clout; **filer une b. à qn** to give sb a clout

beigne[2] [bɛɲ] *nm Can* donut

beignet [bɛɲɛ] *nm* (*salé*) fritter; (*au sucre, à la confiture*) donut; **b. de** *ou* **aux pommes** apple fritter

bel [bɛl] *voir* **beau**

bêlement [bɛlmɑ̃] *nm aussi Fig* bleat; **des bêlements** bleating

bêler [bele] *vi aussi Fig* to bleat

bel-étage, bel étage [bɛletaʒ] (*pl* **beaux-étages**) [bozetaʒ] *nm Belg* (**a**) (*rez-de-chaussée surélevé*) mezzanine first floor (**b**) (*maison*) house with mezzanine first floor

belette [bəlɛt] *nf* weasel

belge [bɛlʒ] **1** *adj* Belgian
2 *nmf* **B.** Belgian

belgicisme [bɛlʒisism] *nm* (*mot*) Belgian-French word; (*tournure*) Belgian-French expression

Belgique [bɛlʒik] *nf* **la B.** Belgium

bélier [belje] *nm* (**a**) (*animal*) ram (**b**) *Mil* battering ram (**c**) *Astron & Astrol* **le B.** Aries; **être B.** to be (an) Aries

Belize [beliz] *nm* **le B.** Belize

belladone [beladɔn] *nf* belladonna, deadly nightshade

bellâtre [bɛlɑtr] *nm Péj* smooth talker

belle [bɛl] *voir* **beau**

belle-famille (*pl* **belles-familles**) [bɛlfamij] *nf* in-laws

belle-fille (*pl* **belles-filles**) [bɛlfij] *nf* (**a**) (*épouse du fils*) daughter-in-law (**b**) (*après remariage*) stepdaughter

belle-mère (*pl* **belles-mères**) [bɛlmɛr] *nf* (**a**) (*mère du conjoint*) mother-in-law (**b**) (*après remariage*) stepmother

belle-sœur (*pl* **belles-sœurs**) [bɛlsœr] *nf* sister-in-law

belligérant, -e [beliʒerɑ̃, -ɑ̃t] **1** *adj* belligerent
2 *nm* **les belligérants** the warring nations

belliqueux, -euse [belikø, -øz] *adj* (*pays, peuple*) warlike; (*personne, humeur*) aggressive

belote [bəlɔt] *nf* = card game

bélouga [beluga], **béluga** [belyga] *nm* beluga whale

belvédère [bɛlvedɛr] *nm* (**a**) (*construction*) belvedere, gazebo (**b**) (*sur un site naturel*) viewpoint

bémol [bemɔl] *Mus* **1** *nm* flat; *Fam Fig* **mettre un b.** to tone it down
2 *adj* flat; **mi b.** E flat

ben [bɛ̃] *adv Fam* **b. oui!** well, yes!; **b. voilà, euh…** yeah, well, er…

bénédictin, -e [benediktɛ̃, -in] *adj, nm,f & nf* Benedictine

bénédiction [benediksjɔ̃] *nf Rel* blessing, benediction; (*d'une église*) consecration; *Fig* blessing

bénéfice [benefis] *nm* (**a**) (*gain*) profit; **b. d'exploitation** operating profit (**b**) (*avantage*) benefit, advantage; **tirer un certain b. de qch** to derive some benefit *or* advantage from sth; **avoir le b. de l'âge** to have the benefit of age; **accorder** *ou* **laisser le b. du doute à qn** to give sb the benefit of the doubt; **au b. de** (*œuvre charitable*) in aid of

bénéficiaire [benefisjɛr] **1** *adj Com* (*entreprise*) profit-making; (*compte*) in credit
2 *nmf* (*d'un chèque*) payee; *Jur* beneficiary

bénéficier [66] [benefisje] **bénéficier de** *vt ind* (**a**) (*profiter de*) to benefit from; **faire b. qn de son expérience** to give sb the benefit of one's experience (**b**) (*avoir*) to have; **cette carte d'abonnement vous fait b. d'une remise de 20 pour cent** this season ticket entitles you to a 20-percent reduction

bénéfique [benefik] *adj* beneficial (**à** to)

Benelux [benelyks] *nm* **le B.** Benelux

benêt [bənɛ] **1** *adj m* simple
2 *nm* simpleton

bénévolat [benevɔla] *nm* voluntary work

bénévole [benevɔl] **1** *adj* (*travail, infirmière*) voluntary
2 *nmf* volunteer, voluntary worker

Bengale [bɛ̃gal] *nm* **le B.** Bengal

Bénin [benɛ̃] *nm* **le B.** Benin

bénin, -igne [benɛ̃, -iɲ] *adj* (*accident, opération*) minor; (*tumeur*) benign

béninois, -e [beninwa, -az] **1** *adj* Beninese
2 *nm,f* **B., Béninoise** Beninese

bénir [benir] *vt aussi Fig* to bless; (*église*) to consecrate; (**que**) **Dieu vous bénisse!** (may) God bless you!; **être béni des dieux** to have been touched by God

bénit, -e [beni, -it] *adj voir* **eau, pain**

bénitier [benitje] *nm Rel* holy-water stoup

benjamin, -e [bɛ̃ʒamɛ̃, -in] *nm,f* (**a**) (*le plus jeune*) youngest (**b**) *Sport* junior (*10-12 years old*)

benjoin [bɛ̃ʒwɛ̃] *nm* (*gum*) benzoin, benjamin

benne [bɛn] *nf* (*de camion*) dump body; (*dans une mine*) tub, truck; (*de téléphérique*) (cable) car; **b. à ordures** Dumpster

benzine [bɛ̃zin] *nf* benzine

BEP [beəpe] *nm Scol* (*abrév* **brevet d'études professionnelles**) = vocational diploma taken at age eighteen

BEPC [beəpese] *nm Anciennement Scol* (*abrév* **brevet d'études du premier cycle**) = school diploma taken at age fifteen

béquille [bekij] *nf* (**a**) (*pour marcher*) crutch; **marcher avec des béquilles** to be on crutches (**b**) (*d'un vélo, d'une moto*) stand

berbère [bɛrbɛr] **1** *adj* Berber
2 *nm* (*langue*) Berber
3 *nmf* **B.** Berber

bercail [bɛrkaj] *nm* (*de l'Église*) fold; *Hum* **rentrer au b.** to return to the fold

berçante [bɛrsɑ̃t] *adj f & nf Can* (**chaise**) **b.** rocking chair
berce [bɛrs] *nf Belg & Suisse (berceau)* cradle
berceau, -x [bɛrso] *nm (de bébé)* cradle; *Fig (d'une civilisation, d'un mouvement)* birthplace; **dès le b.** from the cradle, from birth; *Fam* **il les prend au b.** he's a cradle-snatcher
bercer [16] [bɛrse] **1** *vt* (**a**) *(bébé, passager)* to rock; *Fig* **mon enfance a été bercée par la musique de Debussy** I was brought up listening to Debussy (**b**) *Fig* **b. qn de promesses** to delude sb with promises
  2 se bercer *vpr* **se b. d'illusions** to delude oneself
berceuse [bɛrsøz] *nf* (**a**) *(chanson)* lullaby (**b**) *Can (fauteuil à bascule)* rocking chair
BERD [bɛrd] *nf (abrév* **Banque européenne pour la reconstruction et le développement**) EBRD
béret [berɛ] *nm* beret
bergamote [bɛrgamɔt] *nf* bergamot; **thé à la b.** bergamot-flavored tea
berge¹ [bɛrʒ] *nf (bord)* bank
berge² [bɛrʒ] *nf Fam (an)* **il a quarante berges** he's forty
berger, -ère [bɛrʒe, -ɛr] **1** *nm,f* shepherd, *f* shepherdess
  2 *nm (chien)* **b. allemand** German shepherd; **b. des Pyrénées** Pyrenean mountain dog
  3 *nf* **bergère** *(fauteuil)* wing chair
bergerie [bɛrʒəri] *nf* sheepfold
bergeronnette [bɛrʒərɔnɛt] *nf* wagtail
Béring [beriŋ] *voir* **détroit**
berk [bɛrk] *exclam* yuk!
Berlin [bɛrlɛ̃] *n* Berlin; *Hist* **B.-Ouest/-Est** West/East Berlin
berline [bɛrlin] *nf Aut* (four-door) sedan
berlingot [bɛrlɛ̃go] *nm* (**a**) *(bonbon)* hard candy (**b**) *(de lait)* carton; *(de produit d'entretien)* pack
berlinois, -e [bɛrlinwa, -az] **1** *adj* from Berlin
  2 *nm,f* **B., Berlinoise** Berliner
berloque [bɛrlɔk] *nf Belg* **battre la b.** to beat *or* to pound wildly
berlue [bɛrly] *nf Fam* **avoir la b.** to be seeing things
berme [bɛrm] *nf Belg & Suisse (terre-plein)* **b. centrale** median (strip)
bermuda [bɛrmyda] *nm* Bermuda shorts, Bermudas
Bermudes [bɛrmyd] *nfpl* **les (îles) B.** Bermuda
bernard-l'(h)ermite [bɛrnarlɛrmit] *nm inv* hermit crab
Berne [bɛrn] *n* Bern
berne [bɛrn] **en berne** *adj Naut* at half staff; *Mil* furled
berner [bɛrne] *vt* to fool
bernois, -e [bɛrnwa, -az] **1** *adj* Bernese
  2 *nm,f* **B., Bernoise** Bernese
berzingue [bɛrzɛ̃g] **à tout(e) b.** *adv Fam* at full speed, double quick
besace [bəzas] *nf (de mendiant)* bag; *(de pèlerin)* scrip; **sac b.** = large, soft handbag
bésef [bezɛf] = **bézef**
besogne [bəzɔɲ] *nf* job, task; **aller vite en b.** to get things done quickly; *Fig & Péj* to jump the gun
besoin [bəzwɛ̃] *nm* (**a**) *(nécessité)* need (**de qch** for sth); **avoir b. de qn/qch** to need sb/sth; **avoir b. de faire qch** to need to do sth; **j'ai b. que tu m'aides** I need you to help me; **éprouver le b. de faire qch** to feel the need to do sth; **pour les besoins de la cause** for the sake of the cause; **au b.** if necessary, if need be; **en cas de b.** if need be; **si b. est** if necessary, if need be (**b**) **faire ses besoins** *(personne)* to relieve oneself; *(animal)* to do its business (**c**) *(misère)* **être dans le b.** to be in need
bestial, -e, -aux, -ales [bɛstjal, -o] *adj* bestial
bestiaux [bɛstjo] *nmpl* livestock
bestiole [bɛstjɔl] *nf* small animal; *(insecte)* creepy-crawler
best-seller (*pl* **best-sellers**) [bɛstsɛlœr] *nm* best-seller

bêta, -asse [bɛta, -as] *Fam* **1** *adj* silly
  2 *nm,f* silly-billy
bêtabloquant [betablɔkɑ̃] *nm Méd* beta-blocker
bétail [betaj] *nm* livestock; **gros b.** cattle and horses
bétaillère [betajɛr] *nf* cattle truck
bêta-test (*pl* **bêta-tests**) [betatɛst] *nm Ordinat* beta test
bête [bɛt] **1** *adj* stupid, dumb; **c'est b., on a loupé le film!** what a shame, we missed the movie!; **ce n'est pas b.** *(suggestion)* that's not a bad idea; **rester tout b.** *(décontenancé)* to be open-mouthed; *Fam* **être b. comme ses pieds** to be as dumb as they come; **être b. à pleurer** to be pathetically stupid; **c'est b. comme chou, c'est tout b.** it's as easy as pie
  2 *nf* (**a**) *(animal)* animal; **travailler comme une b.** to work flat out; **elle m'a regardé comme une b. curieuse** she looked at me as if I was from another planet; *Péj* **b. à concours** grind; **b. à cornes** horned animal; **b. fauve** big cat; **b. féroce** wild animal; **b. noire** *(personne)* bête noire; *(chose)* pet hate; *Can* **b. puante** skunk; **b. de somme** beast of burden (**b**) *(insecte)* insect; *Fig* **chercher la petite b.** to nitpick; **b. à bon Dieu** ladybug
bêtement [bɛtmɑ̃] *adv (rire, regarder)* stupidly; **mourir b.** to die senselessly; **tout b.** quite simply, purely and simply
bêtifier [66] [betifje] *vi (avec un enfant)* to use baby talk
bêtise [betiz] *nf* (**a**) *(manque d'intelligence)* stupidity, silliness (**b**) *(action idiote)* stupid thing (to do); *(parole idiote)* stupid thing to say; **dire/faire une b.** to say/to do something stupid; **dire des bêtises** to talk nonsense (**c**) *(chose sans importance)* trivial thing; **se disputer pour des bêtises** to argue over nothing (**d**) *Can* **bêtises** *(injures)* insults (**e**) **bêtises de Cambrai** ≃ hard mint candies
bêtisier [betizje] *nm (écrit)* collection of howlers; *(à la télévision)* collection of humorous outtakes
béton [betɔ̃] *nm* (**a**) *(matériau)* concrete; *Fig* **des muscles en b.** rock-hard muscles; **un alibi en b.** an ironclad alibi; **b. armé** reinforced concrete (**b**) *Fam* **laisse b.!** drop it!
bétonner [betɔne] *vt* to concrete
bétonneuse [betɔnøz], **bétonnière** [betɔnjɛr] *nf* cement mixer, concrete mixer
bette [bɛt] *nf* (Swiss) chard
betterave [bɛtrav] *nf* **b. (rouge)** beet; **b. fourragère** mangel-wurzel; **b. sucrière** sugar beet
beuglement [bøgləmɑ̃] *nm (d'une vache)* moo; *(d'un taureau)* bellow; *(de la radio, de la télé)* blaring; **des beuglements** mooing/bellowing; **pousser des beuglements** *(personne)* to bellow
beugler [bøgle] **1** *vi (vache)* to moo; *(taureau, personne)* to bellow; *(radio, télé)* to blare
  2 *vt (chanson)* to bawl out, to bellow out
beur [bœr] **1** *nmf* = North African born in France of immigrant parents
  2 *adj inv* = of North Africans born in France of immigrant parents
beurre [bœr] *nm* butter; **au b.** *(pâtisserie)* made with butter; *Fam* **ça compte pour du b.** that doesn't count; *Fam* **faire son b.** to make a pile; **ça mettra du b. dans les épinards** that will make life a bit easier; **elle veut le b. et l'argent du b.** she wants to have her cake and eat it; **b. d'anchois** anchovy paste; **b. d'arachides** peanut butter; **b. de cacao** cocoa butter; **b. salé/demi-sel** salted/slightly salted butter
beurré, -e [bœre] *adj très Fam (ivre)* plastered, bombed
beurrer [bœre] *vt* to butter
beurrier [bœrje] *nm* butter dish
beuverie [bøvri] *nf* binge, drinking session
bévue [bevy] *nf* slip-up
Beyrouth [berut] *n* Beirut
bézef [bezɛf] *adv Fam* **il n'y en a pas b.** *(pain, confiture)* there's

not much *or* a lot (of it); *(légumes, livres)* there aren't many *or* a lot (of them)

Bhoutan [butɑ̃] *nm* **le B.** Bhutan

bi [bi] *adj inv Fam (bisexuel)* bi

bi- [bi] *préf* bi-

biais [bjɛ] *nm* (**a**) *(d'un mur)* slant; **regarder qn de b.** to look sideways at sb; **en b.** at an angle; **tailler un tissu dans le b.** to cut material on the bias (**b**) *(moyen)* way; **par le b. de** through (**c**) *(aspect)* angle; **par quel b. envisager la chose?** from what angle should we look at the issue?

biaiser [bjeze] *vi (ruser)* to dodge the issue

biathlon [biatlɔ̃] *nm* biathlon

bibande [bibɑ̃d] *adj Tél* dual-band

bibelot [biblo] *nm* curio, knick-knack

biberon [bibrɔ̃] *nm* (baby's *or* feeding) bottle; **nourrir** *ou* **élever un enfant au b.** to bottle-feed a child; **c'est l'heure du b.** it's the baby's feeding time

bibi[1] [bibi] *nm (chapeau)* (woman's) hat

bibi[2] [bibi] *pron Fam (moi)* yours truly; **la vaisselle, c'est encore pour b.!** yours truly gets stuck doing the dishes again!

bibine [bibin] *nf Fam (boisson)* dishwater

bibite [bibit] *nf Can Fam* bug, insect

bible [bibl] *nf aussi Fig* bible; **la B.** the Bible

bibliographie [bibliografi] *nf* bibliography

bibliographique [bibliografik] *adj* bibliographical

bibliophile [bibliofil] *nmf* booklover

bibliothécaire [bibliotekɛr] *nmf* librarian

bibliothèque [bibliotɛk] *nf* (**a**) *(bâtiment, salle)* library; **b. municipale** public library; **b. de prêt** lending library; **b. universitaire** university library (**b**) *(meuble)* bookcase

biblique [biblik] *adj* biblical

Bic® [bik] **1** *adj* **stylo B., pointe B.** ballpoint (pen) **2** *nm* ballpoint (pen)

bicarbonate [bikarbɔnat] *nm Chim* bicarbonate; **b. de soude** bicarbonate of soda

bicentenaire [bisɑ̃tnɛr] *nm* bicentennial

biceps [bisɛps] *nm* biceps; *Fam* **avoir des b.** to have big biceps

biche [biʃ] *nf* (**a**) *(animal)* hind, doe (**b**) *Fam* **ma b.** darling

bicher [biʃe] *vi Fam Vieilli (se réjouir)* to be tickled pink

bichonner [biʃɔne] **1** *vt* (**a**) *(préparer)* to doll up (**b**) *(soigner)* to pamper **2 se bichonner** *vpr* to doll oneself up

bicolore [bikɔlɔr] *adj* two-color(ed)

bicoque [bikɔk] *nf Fam (maison)* house, place

bicorne [bikɔrn] *nm* cocked hat

bicyclette [bisiklɛt] *nf* bicycle; **aller en ville à** *ou* **en b.** to cycle into town, to go into town by bicycle; **faire de la b.** to go cycling; **il ne sait pas faire de la b.** he can't ride a bicycle

bidasse [bidas] *nm très Fam* G.I.

bide [bid] *nm Fam* (**a**) *(ventre)* belly; **avoir/prendre du b.** to have/to develop a belly (**b**) *(échec)* flop, washout; **faire un b.** to bomb

bidet [bidɛ] *nm* (**a**) *(de toilette)* bidet (**b**) *Hum (cheval)* nag

bidimensionnel, -elle [bidimɑ̃sjɔnɛl] *adj* bidimensional

bidoche [bidɔʃ] *nf très Fam* meat

bidon [bidɔ̃] **1** *adj inv Fam (excuse, argument)* phony, fake; *(élections)* rigged **2** *nm* (**a**) *(d'huile, d'essence)* can; *(de lait)* churn; *(gourde)* water bottle; **b. d'essence** gas can, jerry can (**b**) *Fam (ventre)* belly (**c**) *Fam (bluff)* **c'est du b.** it's a load of bunk (**d**) *Belg Fam* **bidons** *(vêtements)* gear, threads; *(affaires)* gear

bidonnant, -e [bidɔnɑ̃, -ɑ̃t] *adj Fam* hilarious

bidonner [bidɔne] **se bidonner** *vpr Fam* to laugh one's head off

bidonville [bidɔ̃vil] *nm* shantytown

bidouiller [biduje] *vt Fam* to patch up; *Ordinat (programme)* to modify

bidule [bidyl] *nm Fam* thingamajig, thingumajig, whatsit; **B.** *(personne)* what's-his-name, *f* what's-her-name

bielle [bjɛl] *nf Aut* connecting rod, con-rod

biélorusse [bjelɔrys] **1** *adj* Byelorussian **2** *nmf* **B.** Byelorussian

Biélorussie [bjelɔrysi] *nf* **la B.** Belarus

bien [bjɛ̃] **1** *adv* (**a**) *(convenablement)* well; **un livre b. écrit** a well-written book; **écoutez-moi b.** listen carefully; *Ironique* **ça commence b.!** that's a good start!

(**b**) *(moralement)* right; **se conduire** *ou* **se tenir b.** to behave (well); **vous avez b. fait** you did the right thing; **tu fais b. de me le dire** it's a good thing you told me; **tu ferais b. de te méfier** you would be wise to beware

(**c**) *(emphatique)* **regarder qn b. en face** to look sb right in the face; **c'est b. cela** that's right; **c'est b. une erreur** that's definitely a mistake; **est-ce b. le train pour Paris?** is this the right train for Paris?; **j'ai b. dû lire dix de ses livres** I must have read at least ten of his/her books; **j'irais b. avec vous mais...** I'd love to go with you but...; **j'y suis b. obligé** I just have to; **je sais b.** I'm well aware of it; **je vous l'avais b. dit!** I told you so!; **c'est b. ce que je pensais** that's what I thought; **nous verrons b.!** we'll see!; **qu'est-ce que ça peut b. être/vouloir dire?** what on earth can it be/mean?; **est-ce b. raisonnable?** is that really reasonable?; **B. à vous** *(dans une lettre)* Yours

(**d**) *(très)* very; **vous arrivez b. tard** you're very late; **que ce soit b. clair, je...** let's get this clear, I...

(**e**) *(beaucoup)* *(réfléchir, changer)* a lot, a great deal; **b. plus** much *or* a lot more; **b. moins** much *or* a lot less; **b. des gens** a lot of people; **b. d'autres** many others; **b. des fois** often; **avoir b. de la peine** *ou* **du mal à faire qch** to have a lot of difficulty doing sth; **tu as b. de la chance!** you're really lucky!

(**f**) *(locutions)* **b. que** although, though; **b. que je le sache** although I know it; **b. entendu, b. sûr, b. évidemment** of course; **b. sûr que je viendrai** of course I'll come; **b. sûr que non!** of course not!

2 *exclam* **eh b.!** well!; **b.! je vous appelle demain!** OK, I'll call you tomorrow!

3 *adj inv* (**a**) *(satisfaisant)* good; **c'est b.!** *(bravo)* good! (**b**) *(à l'aise)* comfortable; **être b. avec qn** *(en bons termes)* to be on good terms with sb; **se mettre b. avec qn** to get into sb's good books; *Fam* **nous voilà b.!** we're in a real mess! (**c**) *(en forme)* well (**d**) *(moral)* decent; **ce n'est pas b. de vous moquer de lui** it's not nice *or* kind of you to make fun of him (**e**) *(beau)* *(personne)* good-looking, attractive; **elle est b. sur cette photo** she looks good in this photo

4 *nm* (**a**) *Phil & Rel* good; **le b. et le mal** good and evil, right and wrong; **faire le b.** to do good; **faire du b. à qn** to do sb good; **grand b. vous fasse!** much good may it do you!; **dire du b. de qn** to speak well of sb; **c'est pour ton b.** it's for your own good; **c'était en tout b. tout honneur** it was quite innocent

(**b**) *(chose matérielle)* possession; *Jur* assets; **biens** possessions, property; **avoir du b.** to have property; *Prov* **b. mal acquis ne profite jamais** ill-gotten gains never prosper; **biens de consommation** consumer goods; **biens immobiliers** *ou* **immeubles** real estate *or* property

bien-aimé, -e *(mpl* **bien-aimés,** *fpl* **bien-aimées)** [bjɛ̃neme] *adj* beloved

bien-être [bjɛ̃nɛtr] *nm* well-being

bienfaisance [bjɛ̃fəzɑ̃s] *nf* **œuvre de b.** charity, charitable organization

bienfaisant, -e [bjɛ̃fəzɑ̃, -ɑ̃t] *adj* (**a**) *(personne)* charitable (**b**) *(remède)* beneficial; *(vent, pluie)* refreshing

bienfait [bjɛ̃fɛ] *nm* (**a**) *(acte)* kindness (**b**) *(avantage)* benefit

bienfaiteur, -trice [bjɛ̃fɛtœr, -tris] *nm,f* benefactor, *f* benefactress

bien-fondé [bjɛ̃fɔ̃de] *nm* validity; *Jur* cogency

bienheureux, -euse [bjɛ̃nørø, -øz] *adj* blissful; *Rel* blessed

biennal, -e, -aux, -ales [bjenal, -o] *adj* biennial

bien-pensant, -e (*mpl* **bien-pensants,** *fpl* **bien-pensantes**) [bjɛ̃pɑ̃sɑ̃, -ɑ̃t] *adj & nm,f* conformist

bienséance [bjɛ̃seɑ̃s] *nf* propriety, decorum

bientôt [bjɛ̃to] *adv* soon; **il est b. deux heures** it's nearly two o'clock; **on est b. arrivés?** will we soon be there?; *Fam* **tu n'as pas b. fini?** are you done?; **à b.!** see you soon!

bienveillance [bjɛ̃vɛjɑ̃s] *nf* kindness; **avec b.** kindly

bienveillant, -e [bjɛ̃vɛjɑ̃, -ɑ̃t] *adj* kind

bienvenu, -e [bjɛ̃vny] **1** *adj (remarque)* apposite; *(repas, explication)* welcome
2 *nm,f* **soyez le b.!** welcome!; **vous serez toujours la bienvenue** you're always welcome

bienvenue [bjɛ̃vny] **1** *nf* welcome; **souhaiter la b. à qn** to welcome sb
2 *exclam* welcome! (à to); *Can (de rien)* you're welcome!

bière¹ [bjɛr] *nf (boisson)* beer; *Fam* **ce n'est pas de la petite b.** it's no small thing; **b. blonde** lager; **b. brune** dark beer; **b. pression** draft beer

bière² [bjɛr] *nf (cercueil)* coffin; **assister à la mise en b.** to be present when the body is placed in the coffin

biffer [bife] *vt* to cross out; **b. un nom d'une liste** to cross a name off a list

biffure [bifyr] *nf* crossing out

bifidus [bifidys] *nm* live culture

bifocal, -e, -aux, -ales [bifɔkal, -o] *adj (lentille)* bifocal; **lunettes bifocales** bifocals

bifteck [biftɛk] *nm* (beef)steak; **b. haché** ground meat; *Fam* **gagner son b.** to bring home the bacon

bifurcation [bifyrkasjɔ̃] *nf* fork

bifurquer [bifyrke] *vi (route, chemin)* to fork; *(automobiliste)* to turn off; **bifurquez à droite** take the right fork

bigame [bigam] *adj* bigamous

bigamie [bigami] *nf* bigamy

bigarré, -e [bigare] *adj (tissu)* multicolored; **une foule bigarrée** a motley crew

bigarreau, -x [bigaro] *nm* = type of cherry

bigler [bigle] *Fam* **1** *vi* (a) *(loucher)* to have a squint (b) **b. sur qch** to have a good look at sth
2 *vt (personne)* to eye up

bigleux, -euse [biglø, -øz] *adj Fam (qui louche)* cross-eyed; *(myope)* nearsighted

bigophone [bigɔfɔn] *nm Fam* horn

bigorneau, -x [bigɔrno] *nm* winkle

bigot, -e [bigo, -ɔt] **1** *nm,f* (religious) bigot
2 *adj* sanctimonious

bigoterie [bigɔtri] *nf* (religious) bigotry

bigoudi [bigudi] *nm* (hair) curler *or* roller; **se mettre des bigoudis** to put one's hair in curlers

bigre [bigr] *exclam Fam Vieilli* gosh!

bigrement [bigrəmɑ̃] *adv Fam (très)* awfully; *(beaucoup)* a heck of a lot

bihebdomadaire [biɛbdɔmadɛr] *adj* twice-weekly

bijou, -x [biʒu] *nm* jewel; *Fig* gem; **des bijoux** jewelry, jewels; **b. de famille** family jewel; **un b. fantaisie** a piece of costume jewelry

bijouterie [biʒutri] *nf (boutique)* jewelry store; *(commerce, fabrication)* jewelery trade

bijoutier, -ère [biʒutje, -ɛr] *nm,f* jeweler

bikini® [bikini] *nm* bikini

bilan [bilɑ̃] *nm* (a) *Fin* balance sheet; **faire** *ou* **dresser un b.** to draw up a balance sheet; *Com* **déposer son b.** to declare bankruptcy; *Com* **faire un dépôt de b.** to file for bankruptcy; **b. comptable** balance sheet (b) *(appréciation) (d'une situation, de faits)* assessment, evaluation; *(résultats)* results; *(d'une catastrophe)* toll; **faire le b. de la situation** to take stock of the situation; **accident sur l'autoroute, b. quatre morts** *(titre)* freeway accident, four dead; **b. de santé** complete check-up

bilatéral, -e, -aux, -ales [bilateral, -o] *adj* bilateral

bilboquet [bilbɔkɛ] *nm* cup-and-ball

bile [bil] *nf* bile; **décharger sa b. sur qn** to vent one's spleen on sb; *Fam* **se faire de la b. (pour)** to fret (about)

biler [bile] **se biler** *vpr Fam* to fret

biliaire [biljɛr] *adj* biliary

bilingue [bilɛ̃g] *adj* bilingual

billard [bijar] *nm* (a) *(jeu)* billiards; **b. américain** pool; **b. électrique** pinball; **faire un b.** to play billiards; *(billard américain)* to shoot some pool (b) *(table)* billiard table (c) *Fam* **passer sur le b.** to go under the knife

bille¹ [bij] *nf* (a) *(de verre)* marble; *Fig* **reprendre ses billes** to pull out; *Fam* **toucher sa b. en qch** to know a thing or two about sth (b) *(de billard)* (billiard) ball; *Fig* **y aller b. en tête** not to beat around the bush (c) *Tech* ball (d) *très Fam (visage)* mug; **avoir une bonne b.** to look pleasant enough

bille² [bij] *nf (pièce de bois)* billet

billet [bijɛ] *nm* (a) *(argent)* bill; **un b. de 100 euros** a 100-euro bill; **un faux b.** a forged bill; **le b. vert** the dollar; *Fam* **je te fiche mon b. qu'il ne viendra pas!** I bet my bottom dollar he won't come! (b) *(pour voyager, pour le cinéma)* ticket; **b. d'avion/de train** plane/train ticket; **b. de première/de seconde** first-/second-class ticket; **b. aller (et) retour** round-trip ticket; **b. électronique** e-ticket; **b. simple** one-way ticket (c) *Com & Fin (effet)* bill; **b. au porteur** payable to bearer (d) *Litt (lettre)* note; *Scol* **b. d'absence** absence slip; **b. doux** love letter; *Scol* **b. de retard** = note given to student who is late, specifying the time of arrival

billetterie [bijɛtri] *nf* (a) *(lieu)* ticket office (b) *(de billets de transport)* **b. automatique** ticket machine

billion [biljɔ̃] *nm* trillion

billot [bijo] *nm* block

bimensuel, -elle [bimɑ̃sɥɛl] **1** *adj* semimonthly
2 *nm* semimonthly magazine

bimestriel, -elle [bimɛstriɛl] *adj & nm* bimonthly

bimoteur [bimɔtœr] *adj & nm (avion)* **b.** twin-engine aircraft

binaire [binɛr] *adj Math* binary; **langage b.** binary notation

biner [bine] *vt* to hoe

binette¹ [binɛt] *nf (outil)* hoe

binette² [binɛt] *nf très Fam (visage)* mug

binette³ [binɛt] *nf Can Ordinat* smiley, emoticon

biniou [binju] *nm* Breton bagpipes

binoclard, -e [binɔklar, -ard] *nm,f Fam* four-eyes

binocle [binɔkl] *nm* pince-nez *inv*; *Fam* **binocles** *(lunettes)* specs, glasses

binôme [binom] *nm* (a) *Math* binomial (b) *Scol (étudiant)* partner; **travailler en b.** to work in pairs *or* twos

binouze [binuz] *nf Fam (bière)* beer, brew; **on va se boire une b.?** want to go for a beer?

bio [bjo] *adj inv Fam (produit, yaourt)* organic

biocarburant [bjokarbyrɑ̃] *nm* biofuel

biochimie [bjoʃimi] *nf* biochemistry

biodégradable [bjodegradabl] *adj* biodegradable

biodiversité [bjodivɛrsite] *nf* biodiversity

biographe [bjograf] *nmf* biographer

biographie [bjografi] *nf* biography

biographique [bjografik] *adj* biographical

bio-industrie (*pl* **bio-industries**) [bjoɛ̃dystri] *nf* biotechnology industry

biologie [bjɔlɔʒi] *nf* biology

biologique [bjɔlɔʒik] *adj* biological; *(sans engrais chimiques)* organic

biologiste [bjɔlɔʒist] *nmf* biologist

biomasse [bjɔmas] *nf* biomass

biophysique [bjɔfizik] *nf* biophysics *(singulier)*

biopsie [bjɔpsi] *nf* biopsy

biorythme [bjɔritm] *nm* biorhythm

biosphère [bjɔsfɛr] *nf* biosphere

biotechnique [bjɔtɛknik], **biotechnologie** [bjɔtɛknɔlɔʒi] *nf* biotechnology

bioterrorisme [bjɔtɛrɔrism] *nm* bioterrorism

bioterroriste [bjɔtɛrɔrist] *adj & nmf* bioterrorist

bip [bip] **1** *exclam* beep!
2 *nm* (**a**) *(son)* beep; **faire b.** to beep (**b**) *(appareil)* beeper, pager

biparti, -e [biparti], **bipartite** [bipartit] *adj* bipartite

bipède [bipɛd] *adj & nm* biped

biper [bipe] *vt* to page

biplace [biplas] *adj & nm Aut & Aviat* two-seater

biplan [biplɑ̃] *nm* biplane

bipolaire [bipɔlɛr] *adj Élec & Phys* bipolar

bique [bik] *nf Fam* (**a**) *(chèvre)* nanny goat (**b**) *Péj (femme)* **vieille b.** old bag

biquet, -ette [bikɛ, -ɛt] *nm,f* (**a**) *(chevreau)* kid (**b**) *Fam* **mon b.** my pet

bircher [birʃɛr] *nm Suisse* muesli

BIRD [bird] *nf (abrév* **Banque internationale pour la reconstruction et le développement**) IBRD

biréacteur [bireaktœr] *nm* twin-engine jet

birman, -e [birmɑ̃, -an] **1** *adj* Burmese
2 *nm (langue)* Burmese
3 *nm,f* **B., Birmane** Burmese

Birmanie [birmani] *nf* **la B.** Burma

bis¹, -e [bi, biz] *adj* grayish-brown

bis² [bis] *adv* (**a**) *Théât* encore; *Mus* repeat (**b**) *(d'une adresse)* **10 b.** ≃ 10A

bisaïeul, -e [bizajœl] *nm,f Litt* great-grandfather, *f* great-grandmother

bisannuel, -elle [bizanɥɛl] *adj* biennial

bisbille [bisbij] *nf Fam* squabble; **être en b. avec qn** to be at odds with sb

bisbrouille [bisbruj] *nf Belg* squabble

biscornu, -e [biskɔrny] *adj* (**a**) *(chapeau)* misshapen; *(bâtiment, objet)* oddly shaped (**b**) *Fam (idées)* cranky; *(raisonnement, esprit)* tortuous

biscoteaux [biskɔto] *nmpl Fam* biceps; **avoir des b.** to have bulging biceps

biscotte [biskɔt] *nf* rusk

biscuit [biskɥi] *nm* (**a**) *(gâteau)* cookie; **b. à la cuiller** lady finger; **biscuits salés** crackers (**b**) *(porcelaine)* biscuit

bise¹ [biz] *nf (vent)* north wind

bise² [biz] *nf Fam (baiser)* kiss; **donner** *ou* **faire une b. à qn** to give sb a kiss; **se faire la b.** to give each other a kiss (on the cheek); **grosses bises** *(sur une lettre)* lots of love

biseau, -x [bizo] *nm* (**a**) *(bord)* bevel; **taillé en b.** bevel-edged (**b**) *(outil)* bevel

biseauter [bizote] *vt* (**a**) *(tailler)* to bevel (**b**) *(cartes à jouer)* to mark

bisexualité [bisɛksɥalite] *nf* bisexuality

bisexuel, -elle [bisɛksɥɛl] *adj* bisexual

bismuth [bismyt] *nm* bismuth

bison [bizɔ̃] *nm* bison

Bison Futé [bizɔ̃fyte] *n* = organization which advises drivers of driving conditions on French highways

bisou [bizu] *nm Fam* kiss

bisque [bisk] *nf Culin* **b. de homard** lobster bisque

bisquer [biske] *vi Fam* **faire b. qn** to rile sb

bissectrice [bisɛktris] *nf* bisector

bisser [bise] *vt* (**a**) *(sujet: artiste) (chanson)* to give an encore of (**b**) *(sujet: spectateur) (chanson)* to call for an encore of; **b. un chanteur** to call on a singer to give an encore (**c**) *Belg Scol (redoubler)* to repeat

bissextile [bisɛkstil] *adj* **année b.** leap year

bistouri [bisturi] *nm* lancet

bistro(t) [bistro] *nm Fam (bar)* café; *(restaurant)* restaurant

---

Βistrot

This word can refer either to a small café or to a cozy restaurant, especially one frequented by regulars. These establishments are usually less classy than bistros in English-speaking countries. The "style bistrot" refers to a style of furnishing inspired by the chairs, tables and zinc countertops typical of the traditional "bistrot".

BIT [beite] *nm (abrév* **Bureau international du travail**) ILO

bit [bit] *nm Ordinat* bit; **b. d'arrêt** stop bit; **b. de contrôle** control bit; **b. de départ** start bit

bite [bit] *nf Vulg* cock

bitoniau [bitɔnjo] *nm Fam* thingamajig, thingumajig, whatsit

bitte¹ [bit] = **bite**

bitte² [bit] *nf Naut* **b. d'amarrage** bollard

bitture [bityr] *nf très Fam* **prendre une b.** to get wasted

bitturer [bityre] **se bitturer** *vpr très Fam* to get wasted

bitume [bitym] *nm (revêtement)* asphalt

bitumer [bityme] *vt (route)* to asphalt

bitumeux, -euse [bitymø, -øz], **bitumineux, -euse** [bityminø, -øz] *adj* bituminous

biture [bityr] = **bitture**

biturer [bityre] = **bitturer**

bivouac [bivwak] *nm* bivouac

bivouaquer [bivwake] *vi* to bivouac

bizarre [bizar] *adj* strange, odd

bizarrement [bizarmɑ̃] *adv* strangely, oddly

bizarrerie [bizarri] *nf (d'une situation, d'une idée, d'une attitude)* strangeness, oddness; **bizarreries** oddities; *(d'une personne)* eccentricities

bizarroïde [bizarɔid] *adj Fam* weird

bizut [bizy] *nm Fam Scol & Univ* = first-year student on whom practical jokes are played

bizutage [bizytaʒ] *nm Fam Scol & Univ* = practical jokes played on first-year students, ≃ hazing

---

Βizutage

In some French schools and colleges, students in fancy-dress take to the streets and play practical jokes, sometimes of a very cruel nature, on each other and on passers-by at the beginning of the school year. This is part of the traditional initiation ceremony known as "bizutage". As a consequence of the excessive behavior to which it has often led, a law was passed in 1998 to make it an offense.

---

bizuter [bizyte] *vt Fam Scol & Univ (étudiant)* to play practical jokes on, ≃ to haze

bizuth [bizy] = **bizut**

bla-bla [blabla] *nm Fam* claptrap

black [blak] *Fam* **1** *adj* black
2 *nmf* **B.** Black

blackbouler [blakbule] *vt Fam (à un examen)* to fail; **se faire b.** to fail, to flunk

blafard, -e [blafar, -ard] *adj* pallid

blague [blag] *nf* (**a**) *(plaisanterie)* joke; **faire une b. à qn** to play a joke on sb; **b. à part** joking apart; **sans b.?** no kidding? (**b**) *(mensonge)* **raconter des blagues** to lie

blaguer [blage] *vi Fam* to joke; **aimer b.** to like a joke

blagueur, -euse [blagœr, -øz] *Fam* **1** *adj* **il est très b.** he really likes a joke

2 *nm,f (qui dit des blagues)* joker; *(qui fait des blagues)* practical joker

blair [blɛr] *nm très Fam* schnozzle

blaireau, -x [blɛro] *nm* (**a**) *(animal)* badger (**b**) *(pinceau)* shaving brush (**c**) *Fam Pej (personne)* jerk

blairer [blere] *vt* **je ne peux pas le b.** I can't stand him

blâme [blɑm] *nm* (**a**) *(reproche)* blame (**b**) *(sanction)* reprimand

blâmer [blɑme] *vt* (**a**) *(désapprouver)* to blame (**b**) *(sanctionner)* to reprimand

blanc, blanche [blɑ̃, blɑ̃ʃ] **1** *adj* (**a**) *(couleur)* white; **b. comme neige** snow-white, as white as snow; *Fig* (as) pure as the driven snow

(**b**) *(peau)* pale; *(pas bronzé)* white; **b. comme un linge** as white as a sheet

(**c**) *(page)* blank

(**d**) *(sourd)* **d'une voix blanche** in a toneless voice

2 *nm* (**a**) *(couleur)* white; **le b. est à la mode** white is in; **b. cassé** off-white

(**b**) *(partie blanche) (d'une cible)* bull's-eye; **le b. des yeux** the whites of the eyes; **regarder qn dans le b. des yeux** to look sb straight in the eye; **b. d'œuf** egg white; **b. de poulet** chicken breast

(**c**) *(espace)* blank

(**d**) *(aux dominos)* blank

(**e**) **chauffé à b.** white-hot; **tirer à b.** to fire a blank/blanks

(**f**) *(linge)* **(articles de) b.** linen; **je lave le b. séparément** I wash my whites separately

(**g**) *(vin)* white wine

3 *nm,f* **B.** White (man); **Blanche** White (woman); **les Blancs** the Whites

4 *nf* **blanche** *Mus* half note

blanc-bec *(pl* **blancs-becs**) [blɑ̃bɛk] *nm* total novice

blanchâtre [blɑ̃ʃɑtr] *adj* whitish

blanche [blɑ̃ʃ] *voir* **blanc**

Blanche-Neige [blɑ̃ʃnɛʒ] *npr* Snow White

blancheur [blɑ̃ʃœr] *nf* whiteness

blanchiment [blɑ̃ʃimɑ̃] *nm (d'argent)* laundering

blanchir [blɑ̃ʃir] **1** *vt* (**a**) *(rendre blanc)* to whiten; *(linge)* to launder; **b. à la chaux** to whitewash (**b**) *(disculper)* to clear (**c**) *(argent)* to launder (**d**) *Culin* to blanch

2 *vi* (**a**) *(devenir blanc)* to turn *or* to go white (**b**) *(pâlir)* to blanch

blanchissage [blɑ̃ʃisaʒ] *nm* (**a**) *(du linge)* laundering (**b**) *Can Sport* shutout

blanchissement [blɑ̃ʃismɑ̃] *nm* whitening

blanchisserie [blɑ̃ʃisri] *nf* laundry

blanchisseur, -euse [blɑ̃ʃisœr, -øz] *nm,f* laundryman, *f* laundrywoman

blanchon [blɑ̃ʃɔ̃] *nm Can* whitecoat *(seal pup)*

blanquette¹ [blɑ̃kɛt] *nf Culin* **b. (de veau)** = veal stew in a white sauce

blanquette² [blɑ̃kɛt] *nf* **b. de Limoux** = sparkling white wine from Limoux

blasé, -e [blɑze] *adj* blasé

blason [blazɔ̃] *nm* coat of arms

blasphème [blasfɛm] *nm* blasphemy

blasphémer [34] [blasfeme] *vi* to blaspheme

blatte [blat] *nf* cockroach

blazer [blazɛr, blazœr] *nm* blazer

bld *(abrév* **boulevard**) Blvd.

blé [ble] *nm* (**a**) *(céréale)* wheat; **b. dur** durum wheat; **b. en herbe** wheat in the blade; *Fig* **manger son b. en herbe** to

eat one's seed corn; *Can* **b. d'Inde** (Indian) corn (**b**) *Fam (argent)* bread

bled [blɛd] *nm* (**a**) *(en Afrique du Nord)* **le b.** the interior of the country (**b**) *Fam (lieu isolé)* dump, hole; **dans un b. perdu** in the middle of nowhere

blême [blɛm] *adj (personne, matin)* pale; **b. de colère** livid with anger; **devenir b.** to turn *or* to go pale

blêmir [blemir] *vi* to turn *or* to go pale; **b. de colère** to turn livid with anger

blennorragie [blɛnoraʒi] *nf* gonorrhea

blessant, -e [blesɑ̃, -ɑ̃t] *adj* hurtful

blessé, -e [blese] **1** *adj (par arme)* wounded; *(dans un accident)* injured; *(moralement)* hurt; **être b. dans son amour-propre** to have had one's pride hurt; **êtes-vous b.?** are you hurt?

2 *nm,f (victime d'un accident)* injured person; *(victime d'une agression)* wounded person; **les blessés** the injured/wounded

blesser [blese] **1** *vt* (**a**) *(par arme)* to wound; *(dans un accident)* to injure, to hurt; *(sujet: chaussures)* to hurt; **il a été blessé au bras** *(par arme)* he was wounded in the arm; *(dans un accident)* his arm was injured (**b**) *(moralement)* to hurt

2 se blesser *vpr (avec une arme)* to wound oneself; *(accidentellement)* to hurt *or* to injure oneself (**avec** with); **se b. à la tête** *(avec une arme)* to wound oneself in the head; *(accidentellement)* to hurt one's head

blessure [blesyr] *nf (par arme)* wound; *(dans un accident)* injury; *Fig (morale)* wound, hurt

blette [blɛt] = **bette**

bleu, -e [blø] **1** *adj* blue; *(bifteck)* very rare; **b. de froid** blue with cold

2 *nm* (**a**) *(couleur)* blue; **le b. est à la mode** blue is in; **b. canard** peacock blue; **b. ciel** sky blue; **b. électrique** electric blue; **b. marine** navy (blue); **b. nuit** midnight blue; **b. de Prusse** Prussian blue; **b. roi** royal blue

(**b**) *(ecchymose)* bruise; **se faire un b.** to bruise oneself; **couvert de bleus** black and blue

(**c**) *Fam (novice)* novice; *Mil* rookie

(**d**) *(fromage)* blue cheese; **b. d'Auvergne/de Bresse** = blue cheese from Auvergne/Bresse

(**e**) **b. (de chauffe** *ou* **de travail)** coveralls; *(salopette)* overalls

(**f**) *Suisse Fam (permis de conduire)* driver's license

bleuâtre [bløɑtr] *adj* bluish

bleuet [bløɛ] *nm* (**a**) *(plante)* cornflower (**b**) *Can (baie)* blueberry

bleuetière [bløtjɛr] *nf Can* blueberry field

bleuté, -e [bløte] *adj* bluish; *(verres)* blue-tinted

blindage [blɛ̃daʒ] *nm Mil* armor-plating

blinde [blɛ̃d] **à toute blinde** *adv Fam* at full speed, like lightning

blindé, -e [blɛ̃de] **1** *adj* (**a**) *(véhicule militaire)* armored, armor-plated; *(voiture)* bulletproof; **porte blindée** steel security door

(**b**) *Fam* **je suis b.** I'm hardened to it

2 *nm Mil* armored vehicle

blinder [blɛ̃de] *vt* (**a**) *(véhicule)* to armor-plate; *(porte)* to reinforce with steel (**b**) *Fam (personne)* to harden (**contre** to)

blini [blini] *nm* blini

blizzard [blizar] *nm* blizzard

bloc [blɔk] *nm* (**a**) *(de bois, de pierre)* block

(**b**) *(pâté de maisons)* block

(**c**) *Pol* bloc; **faire b. (avec/contre qn)** to join forces (with/against sb); *Écon* **b. monétaire** monetary bloc

(**d**) *(de papier)* pad; **b. de papier à lettres** writing pad

(**e**) *(ensemble d'éléments)* unit; **b. opératoire** operating room

(**f**) *très Fam (prison)* clink; **être au b.** to be in the clink

(**g**) *Ordinat* block; **b. d'alimentation secteur** mains power unit; **b. de données** data block; **b. de touches** keypad

(**h**) *(locutions)* **tout refuser en b.** to reject everything in its entirety; **serrer qch à b.** to screw sth as tightly as possible

blocage [blɔkaʒ] nm (**a**) (d'un mécanisme) jamming; (des freins) locking; (des prix, des salaires) freezing; Psy (mental) block; Psy **faire un b.** to get a (mental) block (**b**) Ordinat (dans réseau) lockout; **b. majuscule** caps lock

bloc-appartement (pl **blocs-appartements**) [blɔka- partəmɑ̃] nm Can apartment building

blockhaus [blɔkos] nm blockhouse

bloc-moteur (pl **blocs-moteurs**) [blɔkmɔtœr] nm engine block

bloc-notes (pl **blocs-notes**) [blɔknɔt] nm notepad, scratchpad

blocus [blɔkys] nm blockade; **lever/forcer le b.** to raise/to run the blockade

blog [blɔg] nm Ordinat (abrév **weblog**) blog

bloggeur, -euse [blɔgø, -øz] nm,f Ordinat blogger

blogging [blɔgiŋ] nm Ordinat blogging

blond, -e [blɔ̃, -ɔ̃d] **1** adj (cheveux) fair, blond; (personne) fairhaired, blond; (sable, blés) golden; **être b. comme les blés** (sujet: personne) to have golden-blond hair

2 nm,f (personne) **un b.** a fair-haired man; **une blonde** a blonde, a fair-haired woman; **une blonde décolorée** a peroxide blonde

3 nm (couleur) **b. cendré** ash blond; **b. platine** platinum blond; **b. vénitien** strawberry blond

4 nf **blonde** (**a**) (bière) beer (**b**) (cigarette) Virginia cigarette (**c**) Can Fam (amie) girlfriend

blondinet, -ette [blɔ̃dinɛ, -ɛt] nm,f fair-haired child

blondir [blɔ̃dir] **1** vt (cheveux) to bleach

2 vi (cheveux, personne) to go or to turn blond; **faire b. des oignons** to cook onions until they turn pale yellow

bloquer [blɔke] **1** vt (**a**) (mécanisme, porte) to jam; **il m'a bloqué contre un mur** he jammed me up against a wall; Fam **je suis bloqué à l'hôpital** I'm stuck in the hospital

(**b**) (réunir) to group together; (jours de congé) to lump together

(**c**) (compte en banque) to block; (prix, salaires) to freeze

(**d**) (route, ballon) to block; **b. le chemin** ou **le passage à qn** to block sb's way

(**e**) Belg Fam (sujet) to bone up on

(**f**) Can Fam (examen) to fail

(**g**) Psy **ça me bloque de me sentir observé** I get a (mental) block if I feel I'm being watched; **être bloqué** to have a (mental) block

2 se bloquer vpr (**a**) (machine, ascenseur) to get stuck (**b**) Psy to get a (mental) block

blottir [blɔtir] **se blottir** vpr to snuggle up; **se b. contre qn/dans les bras de qn** to snuggle up to sb/in sb's arms; **blottis les uns contre les autres** huddled up together

blousant, -e [bluzɑ̃, -ɑ̃t] adj loose-fitting

blouse [bluz] nf (**a**) (tablier) overall; **b. de laboratoire/ blanche** lab/white coat; **les blouses blanches** doctors and nurses (**b**) (de femme) blouse

blouser [bluze] **1** vt Fam (personne) to con

2 vi (corsage) to be loose-fitting

blouson [bluzɔ̃] nm jacket; **b. en** ou **de cuir** leather jacket; **b. d'aviateur** bomber jacket; Fam Vieilli **b. noir** young hoodlum (wearing a black leather jacket)

blue-jean [bludʒin] (pl **blue-jeans**) [bludʒins] nm Vieilli jeans

blues [bluz] nm blues

Bluetooth® [blutuθ] nm Tél Bluetooth®

bluff [blœf] nm bluff; **y aller au b.** to try and bluff

bluffer [blœfe] **1** vt (aux cartes) to bluff; Fam (personne) to take in

2 vi (aux cartes) & Fam to bluff

blush [blœʃ] nm blusher

BN [beɛn] nf (abrév **Bibliothèque nationale**) = the former French national library

BNF [beɛnɛf] nf (abrév **bibliothèque nationale de France**) = French national library, comprising the "Bibliothèque de France" and the "Bibliothèque nationale"

BO [beo] **1** nf (abrév **bande originale**) (original) soundtrack

2 nm (abrév **bulletin officiel**) = official listing of all new laws and decrees

boa [bɔa] nm (**a**) (serpent) boa; **b. constricteur** boa constrictor (**b**) (en plumes) boa

boat people [botpipœl] nmpl boat people

bob [bɔb] nm Fam (chapeau) sunhat

bobard [bɔbar] nm Fam tall story

bobine [bɔbin] nf (**a**) (de ruban, de fil) reel; (de machine à coudre) bobbin; (de machine à écrire, d'appareil photo) spool; (de film, de papier) roll (**b**) Élec coil (**c**) Fam (visage) mug

bobo [bobo] nm (langage enfantin) boo-boo; **ça fait b.?** does it hurt?; **se faire b.** to hurt oneself

bobsleigh [bɔbslɛ(g)] nm bobsled

bocage [bɔkaʒ] nm bocage (countryside with many hedges, trees and small fields)

bocal, -aux [bɔkal, -o] nm jar; (aquarium) (fish)bowl

Boche [bɔʃ] nmf Fam Péj Kraut, = offensive term referring to a German

bock [bɔk] nm beer glass

body [bɔdi] nm (vêtement) body

body-building [bɔdibildiŋ] nm body building; **faire du b.** to do body building

bœuf [bœf, pl bø] **1** nm (**a**) (animal) bullock; (de trait) ox; Fam **on n'est pas des bœufs** we're not superhuman (**b**) (viande) beef; **b. bourguignon** bœuf bourguignon; **b. (à la) mode** beef à la mode (**c**) Fam (improvisation) jam session; **faire un b.** to jam

2 adj inv Fam **avoir un succès b.** to be incredibly successful; **faire un effet b.** to make a really big impression

bof [bɔf] exclam Fam **ça te plaît? – b., pas tellement** do you like it? – not really, no; **il est chouette, hein, mon nouveau pull? – b.** my new sweater's great, isn't it? – I guess

Bogota [bogota] n Bogota

bogue [bɔg] nf (**a**) (de châtaigne) shuck (**b**) Ordinat bug; **dépourvu/plein de bogues** bug-free/-ridden; **b. de l'an 2000** millennium bug; **b. de logiciel** software bug

bohème [bɔɛm] **1** adj bohemian

2 nmf **mener une vie de b.** to lead a bohemian life

Bohême [bɔɛm] nf **la B.** Bohemia

bohémien, -enne [bɔemjɛ̃, -ɛn] nm,f gypsy

boire¹ [12] [bwar] **1** vt (**a**) (sujet: personne) to drink; Fig **b. les paroles de qn** to drink in sb's every word (**b**) (sujet: plante, matière poreuse) to soak up, to absorb

2 vi (personne) to drink; (plante) to soak up or to absorb water; Can (bébé) to feed; **b. comme un trou** to drink like a fish; **b. à la bouteille** to drink from the bottle; **b. au succès de qn/ qch** to drink to the success of sb/sth; **donner à b. à qn** to give sb a drink; **faire b. qn** to give sb something to drink; **faire b. les chevaux** to water the horses; Fig **il y a à b. et à manger là-dedans** it's a bit of a mixed bag; Prov **qui a bu boira** old habits die hard

3 se boire vpr to be drunk

boire² [bwar] nm **le b. et le manger** food and drink

bois [bwa] nm (**a**) (forêt) wood (**b**) (matériau) wood; **des meubles en b.** wooden furniture; Fig **elle n'est pas de b.** she's only human; Fig **je vais leur faire voir de quel b. je me chauffe!** I'll show them (what I'm made of)!; **petit b.** kindling; **b. de charpente** ou **de construction** lumber; **b. de chauffage** firewood; **b. mort** deadwood; Can **b. de poêle** firewood; Can **b. rond** log; **b. de rose** rosewood (**c**) (de chaise, de raquette) frame; **faire un b.** (au tennis) to hit the ball off the frame; **b. de lit** bed frame (**d**) Mus **les b.** the woodwind (**e**) **les b.** (d'un cerf) the antlers

boisé, -e [bwaze] *adj (région)* wooded; *(vin)* woody

boisement [bwazmɑ̃] *nm* afforestation

boiseries [bwazri] *nfpl* paneling

boisson [bwasɔ̃] *nf* drink; *Can (spiritueux)* hard liquor, spirits; **b. alcoolisée/non alcoolisée** alcoholic/soft drink; **b. chaude** hot drink; **b. gazeuse** carbonated drink, soda

boîte [bwat] *nf* (a) *(récipient)* box; **des haricots en b.** canned beans; **mettre qch en b.** *(marchandises)* to box sth; *(aliments)* to can sth; *Fam* **mettre qn en b.** to pull sb's leg; **b. d'allumettes** *(pleine)* box of matches; *(vide)* matchbox; **b. à bijoux** jewel box; **b. de conserve** can; **b. à couture** *ou* **ouvrage** sewing box; *Ordinat* **b. de dialogue** dialog box; **b. à gants** glove compartment; **b. à** *ou* **aux lettres** mailbox; *Ordinat* **b. à lettres électronique** mailbox; **b. à musique** music box; *Aviat* **b. noire** black box; **b. à outils** toolbox; **b. postale** Post Office Box; *Ordinat* **b. de réception** inbox; *Aut* **b. de vitesses** transmission; *Ordinat* **b. vocale** voice mail (b) *Fam (entreprise)* firm; *(école)* school (c) **b. (de nuit)** nightclub; **aller** *ou* **sortir en b.** to go to a nightclub, to go clubbing

boiter [bwate] *vi* to limp

boiteux, -euse [bwatø, -øz] *adj (personne, cheval, explication)* lame; *(raisonnement)* shaky; *(phrase)* badly constructed

boîtier [bwatje] *nm* case; *Phot* (camera) body; *Ordinat* **b. de commande** command box; *Ordinat* **b. commutateur** data switch

boitiller [bwatije] *vi* to limp slightly

boive *etc. voir* **boire**[1]

bol [bɔl] *nm* (a) *(récipient)* bowl (b) *(contenu)* bowl(ful); **prendre un b. d'air frais** *ou* **pur** to get a good breath of fresh air (c) *Fam (chance)* luck; **avoir du b.** to be lucky; **ne pas avoir de b.** to be unlucky; **manque de b., il avait déjà demandé!** just my luck, he'd already asked! (d) **le B. d'or** = 24-hour motorcycle race

bolchevique [bɔlʃəvik, bɔlʃevik] *adj & nmf* Bolshevik

bolduc [bɔldyk] *nm* gift-wrap ribbon

bolée [bɔle] *nf* bowl(ful)

boléro [bɔlero] *nm (vêtement, pièce musicale)* bolero

bolet [bɔlɛ] *nm* boletus

bolide [bɔlid] *nm (voiture)* racing car; **comme un b.** like a rocket

Bolivie [bɔlivi] *nf* **la B.** Bolivia

bolivien, -enne [bɔlivjɛ̃, -ɛn] **1** *adj* Bolivian **2** *nm,f* **B., Bolivienne** Bolivian

bolognais, -e [bɔlɔɲɛ, -ɛz] *adj* Bolognese; *Culin* **spaghetti bolognaise** spaghetti bolognese

Bologne [bɔlɔɲ] *n* Bologna

bombage [bɔ̃baʒ] *nm Fam* (aerosol) graffiti; **faire des bombages sur un mur** to spray-paint a wall with graffiti

bombance [bɔ̃bɑ̃s] *nf Fam* **faire b.** to feast

bombardement [bɔ̃bardəmɑ̃] *nm (avec des obus)* shelling; *(avec des bombes)* bombing; **b. aérien** air raid

bombarder [bɔ̃barde] *vt* (a) *(avec des obus)* to shell; *(avec des bombes)* to bomb; **b. qn de questions/de lettres** to bombard sb with questions/letters (b) *Fam* **on l'a bombardé ministre** he's been catapulted into a ministerial post

bombardier [bɔ̃bardje] *nm (avion)* bomber; *(aviateur)* bombardier

bombe [bɔ̃b] *nf* (a) *(explosif)* bomb; *Fig* **faire l'effet d'une b.** to be a bombshell; **b. atomique** atom(ic) bomb; **b. à eau** water bomb; *Culin* **b. glacée** bombe glacée; **b. H** H bomb; **b. à hydrogène** hydrogen bomb; **b. incendiaire** incendiary device, fire bomb; **b. lacrymogène** tear-gas grenade; **b. à retardement** time bomb (b) *(atomiseur)* spray, aerosol (c) *(chapeau)* riding hat (d) *Can (bouilloire)* kettle (e) *Fam* **faire la b.** to live it up

bombé, -e [bɔ̃be] *adj* bulging

bomber [bɔ̃be] **1** *vt (gonfler)* **b. qch** to cause sth to bulge; **b. le torse** to throw out one's chest; *Fig* to swagger (about) (**b**) *(slogan)* to spray, to spray-paint **2** *vi (mur)* to bulge; *(planche)* to warp

bombeur, -euse [bɔ̃bœr, -øz] *nm,f* graffiti artist *(who uses spray paint)*

bombonne [bɔ̃bɔn] = **bonbonne**

bôme [bom] *nf Naut* boom

bon[1]**, bonne** [bɔ̃, bɔn] **1** *adj* (a) *(agréable)* good; **passer une bonne soirée** to spend a pleasant evening; **l'eau est bonne** *(en se baignant)* the water's great; **de bons petits plats** nice little meals; **souhaiter une** *ou* **la bonne année à qn** to wish sb a happy New Year; **bonnes vacances!** have a great vacation!

(**b**) *(satisfaisant) (travail, qualité)* good; **c'est b.** *(d'accord)* that's fine; **c'est b., j'ai compris** all right *or* OK, I understand

(**c**) *(correct)* right; **c'est la bonne réponse/le b. bus** that's the right answer/bus; **un intellectuel, au b. sens du terme** an intellectual in the true sense of the word

(**d**) *(compétent)* good (**en** at); **un b. médecin/père** a good doctor/father

(**e**) *(profitable) (investissement, conseil, idée)* good; **cet exercice est b. pour le dos** this exercise is good for the back; **c'est b. à savoir** it's worth knowing; **il serait b. que vous lui en parliez** it would be a good idea if you spoke to her about it; **à quoi b.?** what's the point *or* the use?; **à quoi b. se plaindre?** what's the point *or* the use of complaining?; **quand b. vous semble** whenever you like

(**f**) *(apte)* **b. à manger** fit *or* safe to eat; **b. pour le service** *Mil* fit for duty; *Fig* serviceable; **elle n'est bonne à rien** she's useless; **tu es b. pour une contravention** you're in for a fine

(**g**) *(valable) (billet, abonnement)* valid; **la balle est bonne** *(au tennis)* the ball is in *or* good; **les yaourts sont-ils encore bons?** are the yoghurts still all right to eat?

(**h**) *(moralement)* good; *(généreux)* good, kind (**envers** *ou* **avec** to)

(**i**) *(en intensif)* good; **j'ai attendu deux bonnes heures** I waited for a good two hours; **il m'a fallu un b. moment pour comprendre** it took me a while to understand; **un b. rhume** a bad cold

(**j**) *(locutions)* **elle est bien bonne!** that's a good one!; **il en a de bonnes!** he must be joking *or* kidding!; *Fam* **avoir qn à la bonne** to have a soft spot for sb; **pour de b.** *(partir, revenir)* for good

2 *exclam (d'accord)* right!, fine!; **b., on y va?** right, shall we go?; **allons b.!** what!; **ah b., je ne le savais pas** really? I didn't know; **sors d'ici! – b., b., c'est pas la peine de crier!** get out of here! – OK, OK, no need to shout!

3 *adv (sentir)* good, nice; **il fait b.** it's lovely; **un pays où il fait b. vivre** a country that's good to live in

4 *nm,f* **les bons et les méchants** *(dans un film)* the good guys and the bad guys; **un b. à rien** a good-for-nothing

5 *nm* **cela a du b.** it has some good points

bon[2] [bɔ̃] *nm* (a) *(papier)* voucher, coupon; **b. d'achat** gift voucher; **b. de commande** order form; **b. de garantie** guarantee; **b. de livraison** delivery slip; **b. de réduction** money-off coupon (b) *Fin* bond; **b. du Trésor** treasury bond

bonard, -e [bɔnar, -ard] *adj Fam* **c'est b.!** that's pretty good!

bonasse [bɔnas] *adj* soft; **d'un ton b.** meekly

bonbon [bɔ̃bɔ̃] **1** *nm* (a) *(sucrerie)* candy; **b. à la menthe** mint (**b**) *Belg* cookie **2** *adv Fam* **coûter b.** to cost an arm and a leg *or* a bundle

bonbonne [bɔ̃bɔn] *nf* demijohn; *(de gaz)* cylinder

bonbonnière [bɔ̃bɔnjɛr] *nf* candy box

bond [bɔ̃] *nm* (a) *(saut)* leap, jump; **faire un b.** to leap up; *Fig* to shoot up; **faire un b. en avant/en arrière** to leap forward/back; **franchir qch d'un b.** to clear sth at one leap; **se lever d'un b.** to jump to one's feet (**b**) *(d'une balle)* bounce; **faire faux b. à qn** to leave sb in the lurch

bonde [bɔ̃d] nf (a) (bouchon) (d'un évier, d'une baignoire) plug; (d'un tonneau) bung; (d'un bassin) sluice gate (b) (trou) (d'un évier, d'une baignoire) plughole; (d'un tonneau) bunghole; (d'un bassin) drainage hole

bondé, -e [bɔ̃de] adj packed, crammed

bondir [bɔ̃diʀ] vi to leap, to jump; **b. sur** to pounce on; Fig **cela me fait b.** it makes me hopping mad

bon enfant [bɔnɑ̃fɑ̃] adj inv easy-going

bonheur [bɔnœʀ] nm (a) (bien-être) happiness; **faire le b. de qn** to make sb happy (b) (chance) good fortune, (good) luck; **j'ai le b. de la connaître** I have the good fortune to know her; **porter b. à qn** to bring sb (good) luck; **il ne connaît pas son b.** he doesn't know how lucky he is; **par b.** luckily; **au petit b. (la chance)** at random (c) Litt (réussite) **avec b.** felicitously

bonhomie [bɔnɔmi] nf good-naturedness; **avec b.** good-naturedly

bonhomme [bɔnɔm] (pl **bonshommes** [bɔ̃zɔm]) nm Fam (a) (homme) fellow, guy; **c'est un sacré b.** he's a hell of a guy; **on se retrouvera, mon b.!** I'll get even with you, my friend!; **aller son petit b. de chemin** to be jogging along nicely; **b. de neige** snowman (b) (figure) man; **dessiner des bonshommes** to draw little men or people

boniche [bɔniʃ] nf Fam maid

bonification [bɔnifikasjɔ̃] nf (a) (d'une terre, d'un vin) improvement (b) Com bonus (c) Sport advantage

bonifier [66] [bɔnifje] **1** vt (terre, caractère) to improve
  2 se bonifier vpr to improve

boniment [bɔnimɑ̃] nm (a) (discours) sales talk, patter; Fam **faire du b. à qn** to hit on sb (b) Fam (mensonges) tall story; **tout ça, c'est du b.** that's all baloney

bonite [bɔnit] nf bonito

bonjour [bɔ̃ʒuʀ] nm hello; (le matin) good morning; (l'après-midi) good afternoon; **dire b. à qn** to say hello/good morning/good afternoon to sb; **dis b. à ta mère de ma part** say hello to your mother for me; **facile ou simple comme b.** easy as pie; Fam **b. l'ambiance!** there was one hell of an atmosphere!; Fam **b. la soirée!** what an evening!; Fam **le périphérique à six heures du soir, b.!** the beltway at six o'clock at night, forget it!

bon marché [bɔ̃maʀʃe] adj inv cheap; **acheter/vendre qch (à) b.** to buy/to sell sth cheap(ly)

bonnard, -e [bɔnaʀ, -aʀd] = **bonard, -e**

bonne [bɔn] **1** voir **bon¹**
  2 nf (domestique) maid, Vieilli maidservant; Fam **dis-donc, je ne suis pas ta b.!** I'm not your maid, you know!; **b. à tout faire** maid, Vieilli maidservant; **b. d'enfants** nanny

Bonne-Espérance [bɔnɛsperɑ̃s] voir **cap**

bonne-main (pl **bonnes-mains**) [bɔnmɛ̃] nf Suisse tip

bonnement [bɔnmɑ̃] adv **tout b.** simply

bonnet [bɔnɛ] nm (a) (coiffure) hat; **c'est b. blanc et blanc b.** it's six of one and half a dozen of the other; **b. d'âne** dunce's cap; **b. de bain** bathing cap; **b. de nuit** nightcap; Fig Péj wet blanket; **b. de ski** ski cap (b) (d'un soutien-gorge) cup; **quelle profondeur de b.?** what size cup?

bonneterie [bɔnɛtri] nf (a) (bas) hosiery (b) (commerce) hosiery trade; (magasin) hosier's (shop)

bonniche [bɔniʃ] = **boniche**

bonsaï [bɔnzaj, bɔ̃zaj] nm bonsai

bonsoir [bɔ̃swaʀ] nm good evening; (quand on se quitte tard, quand on se couche) goodnight; **dire b. à qn** to say good evening/goodnight to sb

bonté [bɔ̃te] nf (a) (gentillesse) kindness, goodness; **une femme d'une grande b.** a very kind woman; **un sourire plein de b.** a kind smile; **avoir la b. de faire qch** to be so good as to do sth; **faire qch par b. d'âme** to do sth out of the goodness of one's heart; Vieilli **b. divine!** good heavens!

(b) (acte) **remercier qn pour ses bontés** to thank sb for his/her kindness

bonus [bɔnys] nm (a) (prime de salaire) bonus; (d'assurance) no-claims bonus (b) (sur un DVD) special feature

bon vivant [bɔ̃vivɑ̃] adj m **être b.** to enjoy life

bonze [bɔ̃z] nm Buddhist priest

bookmaker [bukmɛkœʀ] nm bookmaker

booléen, -enne [buleɛ̃, -ɛn] adj Math & Ordinat Boolean

boom [bum] nm boom

boomerang [bumʀɑ̃g] nm boomerang

booter [bute] vi Ordinat **b. (sur le lecteur B)** to boot up (off the B drive)

boots [buts] nmpl ankle boots

borborygmes [bɔʀbɔʀigm] nmpl rumbling

bord [bɔʀ] nm (a) (limite) edge; (d'un chapeau) brim; (d'une tasse, d'un verre) rim; **un chapeau à larges bords** a wide-brimmed hat; **le b. du trottoir** the curb; **sur le ou au b. de** (route) at the side of; (lac, rivière) beside; **aller au b. de la mer** to go to the seaside; **une maison en b. de mer** a house beside the sea; Can **l'autre b.** (outre-Atlantique) Europe; **au b. des larmes/de la catastrophe** on the verge of tears/of disaster; Fam **un peu voleur sur les bords** a bit light-fingered; **b. à b.** edge to edge; Ordinat **b. de reliure** inside margin (b) **à b. de** (bateau, avion) on board; **prendre qn à son b.** to take sb on board; **par-dessus b.** overboard; Fig **être du même b.** to be on the same side

bordages [bɔʀdaʒ] nmpl Can (glace) inshore ice

bordeaux [bɔʀdo] **1** nm Bordeaux (wine); **b. rouge** claret
  2 adj inv maroon

bordée [bɔʀde] nf (a) Naut (de coups de feu) broadside; Fig **b. de jurons** torrent of swearwords (b) Fam **être en b.** to be on a binge (c) Can **b. (de neige)** heavy snowfall

bordel [bɔʀdɛl] nm très Fam (hôtel de passe) brothel; (désordre) mess; (vacarme) racket; **mettre ou foutre le b. dans qch** to make a mess of sth; **mettre ou foutre le b. en classe** to create mayhem in the classroom; **et tout le b.** and the whole damn lot; Vulg **b.!** shit!

bordelais, -e [bɔʀdəlɛ, -ɛz] **1** adj of Bordeaux
  2 nm,f **B., Bordelaise** = person from Bordeaux
  3 nm **le B.** (région) the Bordeaux region

bordélique [bɔʀdelik] adj Fam (pièce, organisation) messy, chaotic; **être b.** (personne) to be a slob; **ta chambre est b.** your room's a pigsty

border [bɔʀde] vt (a) (garnir) **b. qch de** to edge sth with (b) (sujet: arbres) (route) to line; (sujet: bateau) (côte) to skirt (c) (lit, draps) to tuck in; **b. qn (dans son lit)** to tuck sb in

bordereau, -x [bɔʀdəʀo] nm (liste) schedule; **b. de livraison** delivery slip

bordure [bɔʀdyʀ] nf (a) (bord) edge; (d'un vêtement) border; **en b. de route/de mer** by the roadside/the sea (b) (d'un miroir, d'un tableau) frame

boréal, -e, -als ou **-aux, -ales** [bɔʀeal, -o] adj northern

borgne [bɔʀɲ] **1** adj (a) (personne) one-eyed; (mur) blind; (fenêtre) obstructed (b) (louche) shady
  2 nmf one-eyed man, f one-eyed woman

borne [bɔʀn] nf (a) (limite) boundary marker; (pierre) boundary stone; Fig **sans bornes** boundless; **b. d'incendie** fire hydrant; **b. kilométrique** kilometer marker, ≃ milestone; Fam (kilomètre) kilometer (c) Élec terminal (d) Ordinat **b. (interactive)** terminal

borné, -e [bɔʀne] adj (esprit) narrow; (personne) narrow-minded

borne-fontaine (pl **bornes-fontaines**) [bɔʀnfɔ̃tɛn] nf Can (bouche d'incendie) fire hydrant

borner [bɔʀne] **1** vt (terrain) to mark out
  2 se borner vpr (a) **se b. à qch/à faire qch** (personne) to restrict oneself to sth/to doing sth (b) **se b. à qch** (choses) to be limited to sth

borsalino [bɔrsalino] *nm* fedora

bosniaque [bɔsnjak] **1** *adj* Bosnian
  2 *nmf* **B.** Bosnian

Bosnie [bɔsni] *nf* **la B.** Bosnia; **la B.-Herzégovine** Bosnia-Herzegovina

bosquet [bɔskɛ] *nm* copse, grove

bosse [bɔs] *nf* (**a**) *(d'un bossu, d'un chameau)* hump; *Fig* **avoir la b. du commerce/des maths** to have a good head for business/math; *Fam* **il a roulé sa b.** he's knocked around a bit (**b**) *(sur la tête)* bump, lump; *(sur le sol)* bump; *(sur une piste de ski)* mogul; **se faire une b.** to get a bump

bosselé, -e [bɔsle] *adj (casserole, pare-chocs)* dented

bosser [bɔse] *Fam* **1** *vi* to work
  2 *vt Scol* to bone up on

bosseur, -euse [bɔsœr, -øz] *Fam* **1** *adj* hardworking
  2 *nm,f* hard worker

bossu, -e [bɔsy] **1** *adj (personne)* hunchbacked; *(animal)* humped
  2 *nm,f* hunchback

bot [bo] *adj m voir* **pied**

botanique [bɔtanik] **1** *adj* botanical
  2 *nf* botany

botaniste [bɔtanist] *nmf* botanist

Botox® [bɔtɔks] *nm Pharm* Botox®

Botswana [bɔtswana] *nm* **le B.** Botswana

botte¹ [bɔt] *nf (de fleurs, de carottes, de radis)* bunch; *(de foin, de paille)* bale

botte² [bɔt] *nf (chaussure)* boot; *Fig* **sous la b. de** under the heel of; *Fam* **en avoir plein les bottes de** to be sick and tired of; **bottes de ou en caoutchouc** galoshes, rubber boots; **bottes de cavalier ou de cheval** riding boots

botte³ [bɔt] *nf (en escrime)* thrust; **porter une b. à qn** to make a thrust at sb; *Fig* **b. secrète** secret weapon; *Fam* **il lui a proposé la b.** he asked her straight out to sleep with him

botter [bɔte] *vt* (**a**) *(chausser)* **botté de cuir** wearing leather boots (**b**) *Fam* **les fesses ou le derrière à qn** to give sb a kick in the backside (**c**) *Fam (plaire à)* **ça me botte** I dig it (**d**) *Sport* **b. la balle en touche** to kick the ball into touch; *Fig* to dodge the issue

bottier [bɔtje] *nm* bootmaker

bottillon [bɔtijɔ̃] *nm* ankle boot

Bottin® [bɔtɛ̃] *nm (annuaire téléphonique)* phone book, telephone directory; **B. mondain** ≃ Who's Who

bottine [bɔtin] *nf* ankle boot

botulisme [bɔtylism] *nm Méd* botulism

boubou [bubu] *nm* = long traditional African robe

bouc [buk] *nm (animal)* (billy) goat; *(barbe)* goatee (beard); *Fam* **puer comme un b., puer le b.** to stink to high heaven; **b. émissaire** scapegoat

boucan [bukɑ̃] *nm Fam* row, din; **faire du b.** to kick up a row

boucane [bukan] *nf Can* smoke

boucané, -e [bukane] *adj (teint)* weatherbeaten

boucanier [bukanje] *nm* buccaneer

bouche [buʃ] *nf* (**a**) *(de personne, d'animal)* mouth; **avoir/parler la b. pleine** to have/to talk with one's mouth full; **une pipe à la b.** with a pipe in his/her mouth; *Fig* **faire la fine b.** to be fussy; **c'est une fine b.** he's a gourmet; **elle n'a pas ouvert la b. de la soirée** she didn't say a word all evening; **b. cousue!** not a word to anyone!; **de b. à oreille** by word of mouth (**b**) *(d'une rivière, d'un cratère, d'un four)* mouth; *(d'un fusil, d'un canon)* muzzle; **b. d'égout** manhole; **b. d'incendie** fire hydrant; **b. de métro** subway entrance

bouché, e [buʃe] *adj (conduite, rue)* blocked; *(temps)* cloudy, overcast; **j'ai le nez b.** my nose is stuffed (up) *or* stuffy; **j'ai les oreilles bouchées** my ears are blocked up; *Fam* **être b. (personne)** to be dense; *Fam* **être b. à l'émeri** to be a complete moron

bouche-à-bouche [buʃabuʃ] *nm inv* mouth-to-mouth resuscitation; **faire du b. à qn** to give sb mouth-to-mouth resuscitation

bouchée [buʃe] *nf* (**a**) *(quantité)* mouthful; *Fig* **ne faire qu'une b. de qn/qch** to make short work of sb/sth; **acheter qch pour une b. de pain** to buy sth for a song; **mettre les bouchées doubles** to really get a move on (**b**) *Culin* **b. (au chocolat)** chocolate; **b. à la reine** chicken vol-au-vent

boucher¹ [buʃe] **1** *vt (fente, trou)* to fill in; *(conduite, fenêtre)* to block up; *(vue)* to block; *(bouteille)* to cork; **b. le passage à qn** to block sb's way; *Fam* **elle/ça m'en a bouché un coin** she/that took the wind out of my sails
  2 se boucher *vpr (conduite)* to get blocked up; **se b. le nez** to hold one's nose; **se b. les oreilles** to put one's fingers in one's ears

boucher², -ère¹ [buʃe, -ɛr] *nm,f aussi Fig* butcher

bouchère² [buʃɛr] *nf Suisse* cold sore

boucherie [buʃri] *nf (boutique)* butcher's (shop); *(activité)* butchery; *Fig (massacre)* slaughter; **b. chevaline** horse butcher's (shop)

bouche-trou *(pl* bouche-trous*)* [buʃtru] *nm Fam* stopgap; **servir de b.** to act as a stopgap

bouchon [buʃɔ̃] *nm* (**a**) *(à vis)* cap, top; *(d'un tonneau)* stopper; **b. (de liège)** cork; **vin qui sent le b.** corked wine; *Aut* **b. de réservoir** fuel cap (**b**) *(embouteillage)* traffic jam; **cinq kilomètres de b.** ≃ a three-mile back-up (**c**) *(d'une ligne de pêche)* float (**d**) *(de paille)* wisp (**e**) *Fam* **tu pousses le b. un peu loin!** you're going a little too far!

bouchonné, -e [buʃɔne] *adj (vin)* corked

bouchonner [buʃɔne] **1** *vt (cheval)* to rub down
  2 *vi Fam* **ça bouchonne** *(sur la route)* there's congestion *or* heavy traffic

bouchot [buʃo] *nm* mussel bank

boucle [bukl] *nf* (**a**) *(de ceinture, de chaussure, de harnais)* buckle; **b. d'oreille** earring (**b**) *(nœud, méandre, looping)* loop; **faire une b.** *(en marchant, en voiture)* to loop back (**c**) *(de cheveux)* curl (**d**) *Sport* lap (**e**) *Ordinat* loop

bouclé, -e [bukle] *adj (cheveux)* curly; *(personne)* curly-haired; *Ordinat* **système b.** looped system

boucler [bukle] **1** *vt* (**a**) *(ceinture, valise)* to buckle; *Fam (dossier, travail)* to finish off; **b. sa valise** *(se préparer à partir)* to pack one's bags; **avoir du mal à b. ses fins de mois** to find it hard to make ends meet at the end of the month; *Fam* **boucle-la!** shut it! (**b**) *(quartier)* to seal off; *Fam (chambre, maison, prisonnier)* to lock up (**c**) **b. la boucle** *Aviat* to loop the loop; *Fig* to come full circle
  2 *vi (cheveux)* to be curly; *(personne)* to have curly hair

bouclette [buklɛt] *nf (de cheveux)* small curl; *(de laine, de moquette)* curl

bouclier [buklije] *nm aussi Fig* shield; **b. atomique** *ou* **nucléaire** nuclear shield; **b. humain** human shield; **b. thermique** *(d'engin spatial)* heat shield

Bouddha [buda] *npr* Buddha

bouddhisme [budism] *nm* Buddhism

bouddhiste [budist] *adj & nmf* Buddhist

bouder [bude] **1** *vi* to sulk
  2 *vt* **b. qn/qch** to refuse to have anything to do with sb/sth; **en été, les Parisiens boudent les salles de cinéma** Parisians stay away from the movies in summer

boudeur, -euse [budœr, -øz] **1** *adj* sulky
  2 *nm,f* sulky person

boudin [budɛ̃] *nm* (**a**) *(charcuterie)* **b. noir** blood sausage; **b. blanc** white sausage (**b**) *(de pâte à modeler, de terre)* roll (**c**) *(traversin)* bolster (**d**) *Fam Péj (femme)* fatso

boudiné, -e [budine] *adj* (**a**) **je suis b. dans ce pantalon** I'm bursting out of these pants (**b**) *(doigts)* pudgy

boudoir [budwar] *nm* (**a**) *(salon)* boudoir (**b**) *(biscuit)* lady finger

boue [bu] *nf* (**a**) *(terre détrempée)* mud; *Fig* **traîner qn dans la b.** to drag sb through the mud (**b**) *(dans une rivière)* silt; *(dans l'océan)* ooze; *Méd* **boues activées** activated sludge

bouée [bwe] *nf Naut* buoy; *(pour nager)* rubber ring; **b. de sauvetage** life preserver; *Fig* lifeline

boueux, -euse [buø, -øz] **1** *adj* muddy
2 *nm Fam* garbage collector

bouffant, -e [bufã, -ãt] **1** *adj (manche)* puff(ed); *(jupe)* full; *(pantalon)* baggy; **cheveux bouffants** bouffant hair-do
2 *nm (des cheveux)* body

bouffe [buf] *nf Fam (nourriture)* grub; *(repas)* meal; **on se fait une b. samedi?** how about getting together for a meal on Saturday?

bouffée [bufe] *nf* (**a**) *(de fumée)* puff; *(de parfum)* whiff; *(d'air)* breath; *aussi Fig* **une b. d'air pur** a breath of fresh air; *Méd* **b. de chaleur** hot flash (**b**) *(d'éloquence, de colère)* outburst; *(d'orgueil)* fit

bouffer [bufe] **1** *vt Fam* (**a**) *(manger)* to eat; *Fig* **je l'aurais bouffé** I could have killed him; **elle se laisse b. par ses enfants/son travail** she has no time for anything but her children/her work; **b. du curé** to rant against the clergy; **elle a bouffé du lion!** she's full of pep! (**b**) *(argent, économies)* to blow; **b. de l'essence** *(voiture)* to be a gas-guzzler
2 *vi* (**a**) *Fam (manger)* to eat (**b**) *(manche, jupe)* to puff out; *(cheveux)* to have body; **faire b. ses cheveux** to give body to one's hair
3 se bouffer *vpr Fam* **se bouffer le nez** *(une fois)* to go for one another; *(constamment)* to be at each other's throats

bouffi, -e [bufi] *adj (yeux, visage)* puffy, swollen; **b. d'orgueil** puffed up with pride

bouffon, -onne [bufõ, -ɔn] **1** *nm* buffoon; *Hist* jester
2 *adj* farcical

bouge [buʒ] *nm Péj (maison)* hovel; *(bar)* dive

bougeoir [buʒwar] *nm (plat)* candleholder; *(haut)* candlestick

bougeotte [buʒɔt] *nf Fam* **avoir la b.** to be fidgety; *(envie de voyager)* to have itchy feet

bouger [45] [buʒe] **1** *vt* to move, to shift
2 *vi (remuer, se déplacer)* to move; **rester sans b.** to keep still; **ne bougeons plus!** *(pour une photo)* hold still!; **je n'ai pas bougé (de chez moi) pendant deux jours** I haven't been out for two days; *Fig* **ce chemisier ne bouge pas au lavage** *(ne déteint pas)* this blouse doesn't run in the wash; *(ne rétrécit pas)* this blouse doesn't shrink in the wash; *Fam* **ça bouge pas mal, dans cette ville** there's a lot going on in this town
3 se bouger *vpr Fam (se déplacer)* to move; *(s'activer)* to get a move on; **bouge-toi de là!** move your butt!

bougie [buʒi] *nf* (**a**) *(en cire)* candle; **s'éclairer à la b.** to use candles for lighting (**b**) *Aut* **b. (d'allumage)** spark plug

bougnat [buɲa] *nm Fam Vieilli* coal merchant

bougnoul(e) [buɲul] *nmf* = racist term referring to a North African person

bougon, -onne [bugõ, -ɔn] *Fam* **1** *adj* grumpy
2 *nm,f* grumbler

bougonner [bugɔne] *vi Fam* to grumble

bougre [bugr] *nm Fam* (**a**) *Vieilli (individu)* **le pauvre b.** the poor devil; **ce n'est pas un mauvais b.** he's not a bad fellow (**b**) **b. d'imbécile** damn(ed) fool

bougrement [bugrəmã] *adv* damn(ed)

boui-boui *(pl* **bouis-bouis**) [bwibwi] *nm Fam* dingy café

bouillabaisse [bujabɛs] *nf* bouillabaisse *(Provençal fish soup)*

bouillant, -e [bujã, -ãt] *adj* (**a**) *(qui bout)* boiling; *(très chaud, fiévreux)* boiling hot (**b**) *Fig (ardent)* fiery

bouille [buj] *nf Fam (visage)* mug; **il a une bonne b.** he looks like a nice guy

bouilleur [bujœr] *nm* **b. de cru** home distiller

bouilli, -e [buji] **1** *adj* boiled
2 *nm* boiled meat; *Can* = beans, cabbage, potatoes, salt pork and ham cooked together for several hours; **b. de bœuf** boiled beef

bouillie [buji] *nf (pour bébés)* baby food; *(à base de céréales)* baby cereal; **b. de légumes** mashed vegetables; **réduire qch en b.** *(légumes, fruits)* to purée sth; *(au mixer)* to liquidize sth; *Fam (voiture, visage)* to smash sth up; *Fam* **mettre ou réduire qn en b.** to beat sb to a pulp

bouillir [13] [bujir] *vi* to boil; **faire b. qch** to boil sth; **b. de colère** to seethe with anger; **b. d'impatience** to burst with impatience; **cela me fait b.** that makes my blood boil

bouilloire [bujwar] *nf* kettle

bouillon [bujõ] *nm* (**a**) *(d'un liquide en ébullition)* bubble; **bouillir à gros bouillons** to boil hard; **le sang sortait à gros bouillons** the blood was gushing out (**b**) *Culin (liquide)* stock; *Fam* **boire un b.** *(en nageant)* to get a mouthful; *(professionnellement)* to come to grief; **b. cube** stock cube; **b. de culture** culture medium; **b. de légumes** vegetable stock

bouillonnant, -e [bujɔnã, -ãt] *adj* bubbling; *(torrent)* foaming; *Fig* **b. de colère** seething; *Fig* **b. de vie/d'idées** bubbling over with life/ideas

bouillonner [bujɔne] *vi (eau, soupe, bain)* to bubble; *(torrent)* to foam; **b. de colère** to seethe with anger; **b. d'idées** to bubble over with ideas

bouillotte [bujɔt] *nf* hot-water bottle

boul. *(abrév* **boulevard)** Blvd.

boulanger, -ère [bulãʒe, -ɛr] *nm,f* baker

boulangerie [bulãʒri] *nf (magasin)* bakery; *(industrie)* bakery trade; **b.-pâtisserie** bakery and confectionery shop

boule [bul] *nf* (**a**) *(sphère)* ball; *Fam (tête)* nut; **se rouler ou se mettre en b.** *(animal)* to roll up into a ball; *Fig* **se mettre en b.** *(en colère)* to fly off the handle; *Fam* **avoir la b. à zéro** to be a skinhead; *Fam* **avoir les boules** *(être énervé)* to be pissed off; *(être déprimé)* to be down in the dumps; *Fam* **foutre les boules à qn** *(faire peur à)* to scare the pants off sb; *(énerver)* to upset sb; *Fam* **perdre la b.** to lose it; *Suisse* **b. de Berlin** donut; **b. à neige** *(décoration)* snowdome, snowglobe; **b. de neige** snowball; *Fig* **faire b. de neige** to snowball; **c'est une b. de nerfs** he's/she's a bundle of nerves; **b. puante** stink bomb; **b. Quiès®** earplug (**b**) *(de pétanque)* steel bowl; *(de bowling)* bowling ball; *(de billard)* ball; **jouer aux boules** to play bowls (**c**) *(de machine à écrire)* golf ball

bouleau, -x [bulo] *nm* (silver) birch; *(bois)* birch(-wood)

bouledogue [buldɔg] *nm* bulldog

bouler [bule] *vi Fam* **envoyer b. qn** to send sb packing

boulet [bulɛ] *nm* (**a**) *(projectile)* **b. (de canon)** cannonball; **passer comme un b. (de canon)** to hurtle past; **tirer à boulets rouges sur qn** to go for sb hammer and tongs (**b**) *(de bagnard)* ball and chain; *Fig* **c'est un b. qu'il traînera toute sa vie** it'll be a millstone around his neck all his life

boulette [bulɛt] *nf* (**a**) *(de papier, de pâte)* small ball (**b**) *Culin* meatball (**c**) *Fam (gaffe)* boo-boo; **faire une b.** to blunder, to put one's foot in one's mouth

boulevard [bulvar] *nm* boulevard; **les Grands Boulevards** *(à Paris)* the main boulevards; **b. périphérique** beltway

bouleversant, -e [bulvɛrsã, -ãt] *adj (émouvant)* deeply moving; *(perturbant)* distressing

bouleversement [bulvɛrsəmã] *nm* (**a**) *(de projets, d'habitudes)* disruption; **bouleversements politiques/économiques** political/economic upheavals (**b**) *(d'une personne)* emotion

bouleverser [bulvɛrse] *vt* (**a**) *(projets, habitudes)* to disrupt; *(vie)* to turn upside down (**b**) *(émouvoir)* to move deeply; *(perturber)* to distress

boulier [bulje] *nm* abacus

boulimie [bulimi] *nf Méd* bulimia

boulimique [bulimik] *adj & nmf Méd* bulimic; **être b.** to be bulimic, to have bulimia

bouliste [bulist] *nmf* bowls player

boulocher [buloʃe] *vi (vêtement)* to pill

boulodrome [bulodrom] *nm* bowling alley

boulon [bulɔ̃] *nm* bolt

boulonner [bulɔne] **1** *vt* to bolt
2 *vi Fam (travailler)* to slog away

boulot¹, -otte [bulo, -ɔt] *adj Fam* pudgy

boulot² [bulo] *Fam* **1** *nm (travail, lieu de travail)* work; *(emploi)* job; **allez, au b.!** come on, get to work!; **refaire les peintures dans une maison, c'est du b.** to repaint a whole house is some job; *Fig* **faire le sale b.** to do the dirty work
2 *adj inv* **être b. b.** to be a workaholic

boum [bum] **1** *exclam* bang!
2 *nm Fam* **(a)** *(bruit)* bang **(b)** *(succès)* **le b. du multimédia/ de l'informatique** the multimedia/computer boom; **en plein b.** in full swing
3 *nf Fam (fête)* party *(for young people)*

boumer [bume] *vi Fam Vieilli* **ça boume?** how's it going?

bouquet¹ [bukɛ] *nm* **(a)** *(fleurs)* bunch of flowers; *(imposant)* bouquet; *(petit)* posy; *(d'arbres)* clump; **un b. de roses** a bunch/bouquet of roses; **le b. de la mariée** the bride's bouquet; *Culin* **b. garni** bouquet garni *(bunch of mixed herbs)* **(b)** *(d'un vin)* bouquet, nose **(c)** *(d'un feu d'artifice)* **b. (final)** grand finale; *Fam Fig* **ça, c'est le b.!** that takes the cake! **(d)** *TV* (multichannel) package; **b. numérique** digital package

bouquet² [bukɛ] *nm (crevette)* prawn

bouquetin [buktɛ̃] *nm* ibex

bouquin [bukɛ̃] *nm Fam* book

bouquiner [bukine] *vi Fam* to read

bouquiniste [bukinist] *nmf* second-hand bookseller

bourbeux, -euse [burbø, -øz] *adj* muddy

bourbier [burbje] *nm aussi Fig* quagmire

bourbon [burbɔ̃] *nm (whisky)* bourbon

bourde [burd] *nf Fam* **(a)** *(balivernes)* fib **(b)** *(gaffe)* blunder; **faire une b.** to put one's foot in one's mouth

bourdon [burdɔ̃] *nm* **(a)** *(insecte)* bumblebee; *Fam* **avoir le b.** to be down (in the dumps) **(b)** *(cloche)* great bell

bourdonnement [burdɔnmɑ̃] *nm (d'insectes)* buzz(ing); *(de machine, de moteur)* hum(ming); **avoir des bourdonnements d'oreilles** to have a buzzing *or* ringing in one's ears

bourdonner [burdɔne] *vi (insectes, oreilles)* to buzz; *(machine, moteur)* to hum

bourg [bur] *nm* market town

bourgade [burgad] *nf* village

bourge [burʒ] *Fam* **1** *adj* **(a)** *(de la bourgeoisie)* upper-class **(b)** *Péj* snobby
2 *nmf* **(a)** *(de la bourgeoisie)* upper-class person **(b)** *Péj* snob

bourgeois, -e [burʒwa, -az] **1** *adj* **(a)** *(personne)* middle-class; **cuisine bourgeoise** home cooking **(b)** *Péj (conventionnel)* middle-class, bourgeois
2 *nm,f* **(a)** *(de la classe moyenne)* middle-class person; **les grands/petits b.** the upper/lower middle class **(b)** *Hist (roturier)* commoner **(c)** *Suisse (citoyen)* citizen

bourgeoisie [burʒwazi] *nf* middle class, bourgeoisie; **la haute/petite b.** the upper/lower middle class

bourgeon [burʒɔ̃] *nm* bud; **en bourgeons** in bud

bourgeonner [burʒɔne] *vi* **(a)** *(plante, arbre)* to bud **(b)** *Fam (avoir des boutons)* to come out in pimples

bourgmestre [burgmɛstr] *nm* burgomaster

Bourgogne [burgɔɲ] **1** *nf* **la B.** Burgundy
2 *nm* burgundy

bourguignon, -onne [burgiɲɔ̃, -ɔn] **1** *adj* Burgundian
2 *nm,f* **B., Bourguignonne** Burgundian

bourlinguer [burlɛ̃ge] *vi (personne) (naviguer)* to sail the seven seas; *Fam (voyager)* to knock about, to bum around

bourrade [burad] *nf* push, shove

bourrasque [burask] *nf* squall, gust (of wind); **b. de neige** snow flurry; **souffler en bourrasques** to gust

bourratif, -ive [buratif, -iv] *adj Fam* stodgy

bourre [bur] *nf* **(a)** *(pour rembourrer)* stuffing, padding; *(de coton, de soie)* waste **(b)** *(des bourgeons)* down **(c)** *(d'arme à feu)* wad **(d)** *Fam* **de première b.** first-rate; **à la b.** in a rush

bourré, -e [bure] *adj* **(a)** *(plein)* packed, crammed (**de** with); **b. à craquer** full to bursting; *Fam* **être b. de complexes** to be full of hang-ups; *Fam* **être b. de fric** to be loaded, to be rolling in money **(b)** *très Fam (ivre)* plastered, bombed

bourreau, -x [buro] *nm* **(a)** *(exécuteur)* executioner; *(qui pend)* hangman; *(tortionnaire)* torturer **(b)** *Fig* tormentor; **b. des cœurs** ladykiller; **b. d'enfants** child-beater; *Hum* child tormentor; **b. de travail** workaholic

bourrée¹ [bure] *nf (danse)* bourrée

bourrée² [bure] *nf Suisse* **(a)** *(grande affluence)* crowd **(b)** *(grande quantité)* **une b. de** masses of, loads of

bourrelé, -e [burle] *adj* **b. de remords** stricken with remorse

bourrelet [burlɛ] *nm* **(a)** *Fam* **b. (de graisse)** *(au ventre)* spare tire **(b)** *(contre les courants d'air)* weather strip

bourrer [bure] **1** *vt* **(a)** *(chaise, coussin)* to stuff, to pad **(b)** *(placard, sac)* to cram (**de** with); *(pipe)* to fill; **ça bourre** *(aliment)* it's filling; **b. qn de qch** *(gaver)* to fill sb up with sth; **b. qn de coups** to beat sb up; *Fam* **b. le crâne à qn** *(élève)* to stuff sb's head with facts; *(politiquement)* to brainwash sb; *Fam* **b. le mou à qn** to pull the wool over sb's eyes
2 se bourrer *vpr* **(a) se b. de qch** *(se gaver)* to stuff oneself with sth **(b)** *très Fam* **se b. la gueule** to get plastered, to tie one on

bourriche [buriʃ] *nf (d'huîtres)* basket

bourrichon [buriʃɔ̃] *nm Fam* **se monter le b.** to get worked up

bourricot [buriko] *nm (small)* donkey

bourrin [burɛ̃] *nm Fam (cheval)* nag

bourrique [burik] *nf (ânesse)* she-ass; *Fam (personne têtue)* pigheaded person; **faire tourner qn en b.** to drive sb crazy

bourru, -e [bury] *adj* surly

bourse [burs] *nf* **(a)** *(porte-monnaie)* purse; **la b. ou la vie!** your money or your life!; **sans b. délier** without spending a cent; **faire b. commune** to pool one's money **(b)** *Scol & Univ* **b. (d'études)** grant **(c)** *Fin* **la B. (des valeurs)** the Stock Exchange, the Stock Market; **jouer à la B.** to play the market; **b. de commerce** commodities exchange **(d)** *Anat* **bourses** scrotum

boursicoter [bursikɔte] *vi* to dabble on the Stock Market

boursier, -ère [bursje, -ɛr] **1** *adj* **(a)** *Fin* Stock Exchange, Stock Market **(b)** *Scol & Univ* **étudiant b.** grant holder
2 *nm,f* **(a)** *Scol & Univ* grant holder **(b)** *Fin* (Stock Exchange) operator **(c)** *Suisse* treasurer

boursouflé, -e [bursufle] *adj (visage, yeux)* swollen, puffy; *(peinture)* blistered; *Fig (style, discours)* turgid

bous *voir* **bouillir**

bousculade [buskylad] *nf (agitation)* pushing and shoving; **être pris dans la b.** to be caught up in the rush

bousculer [buskyle] **1** *vt* **(a)** *(pousser)* to jostle; *Fig (habitudes)* to overturn **(b)** *(presser)* to rush
2 se bousculer *vpr (foule)* to push and shove; **les idées se bousculaient dans sa tête** his/her head was buzzing with ideas; *Fig* **les candidats ne se bousculent pas au portillon** applicants aren't exactly lining up for the job

bouse [buz] *nf* **de la b. (de vache)** cow dung; **une b.** a cowpie

bouseux [buzø] *nm Fam Péj* yokel

bousiller [buzije] *Fam* **1** *vt (voiture, appareil photo)* to wreck; *(travail)* to botch (up), to bungle
2 se bousiller *vpr* **se b. la santé** to ruin one's health

boussole [busɔl] *nf* compass; **s'orienter à la b.** to use a compass to get one's bearings; *Fam Fig* **perdre la b.** to lose one's mind

boustifaille [bustifaj] *nf très Fam* grub

bout[1] [bu] *voir* **bouillir**

bout[2] [bu] *nm* (a) *(extrémité)* end; **b. à b.** end to end; **de b. en b., d'un b. à l'autre** *(dans l'espace)* from one end to the other; *(reprendre un travail, lire)* from start to finish; **à l'autre b., au b. du fil** *(au téléphone)* on the other end; *Fig* **je n'en vois pas le b.** I'm nowhere near the end of it; *Fig* **voir le b. du tunnel** to see the light at the end of the tunnel; **au b. de la rue** at the end of the street; **aller au b. du monde** to go to the ends of the earth; *Fig* **ce n'est pas le b. du monde** it's not exactly difficult; **au b. d'une heure/de quelques jours** after an hour/a few days

    (b) *(du doigt, du nez)* tip, end; *(d'une pipe)* mouthpiece; *(d'une chaussure)* toe; **b. filtre** *(d'une cigarette)* filter tip; **b. du sein** nipple

    (c) *(morceau)* bit; **elle en connaît un b. sur la question** she knows a thing or two about it; **faire un b. de chemin** to go part of the way; **un b. de temps** a little while; **ça fait un bon b. de temps que je ne l'ai pas vu** I haven't seen him for quite a while; *Fig* **b. de chou** little child; *Cin & TV* **b. d'essai** screen test

    (d) *(locutions)* **être à b.** *(épuisé)* to be exhausted; *(exaspéré)* to be at the end of one's patience; **pousser qn à b.** to push sb too far; **être à b. d'arguments** to have run out of arguments; **venir à b. de qch** *(travail)* to get through sth; *(obstacle)* to overcome sth; **à b. de bras** at arm's length; *Fig* **porter une entreprise à b. de bras** to carry a firm; **à b. portant** point-blank; **on ne sait jamais par quel b. le prendre** it's hard to know how to handle him; **avoir un mot sur le b. de la langue** to have a word on the tip of one's tongue; **tenir le bon b.** to be well on the way to success

boutade [butad] *nf (trait d'esprit)* quip

boute-en-train [butɑ̃trɛ̃] *nm inv* live wire

bouteille [butɛj] *nf* bottle; *(de gaz, d'oxygène)* cylinder; *(contenu)* bottle(ful); **c'est une bonne b.** it's a good bottle of wine; **mettre du vin en bouteilles** to bottle wine; *Fam* **prendre de la b.** to be getting long in the tooth

boutique [butik] *nf* store; **parler b.** to talk shop; **b. hors taxes** duty-free store; **b. (de mode)** fashion store, boutique

boutiquier, -ère [butikje, -ɛr] *nm,f* storekeeper

bouton [butɔ̃] *nm* (a) *(de fleur)* bud; **b. de rose** rosebud; **en b.** in bud (b) *(sur un vêtement)* button; *(de col)* stud; **boutons de manchette** cufflinks (c) *(de porte, de radio)* knob; *(qu'on pousse) & Ordinat* button; *(interrupteur)* switch; *Ordinat* **b. de réinitialisation** reset button (d) *(sur le visage)* pimple

bouton-d'or *(pl* **boutons-d'or)** [butɔ̃dɔr] *nm* buttercup

boutonnage [butɔnaʒ] *nm* buttoning (up); **veste à double b.** double-breasted jacket

boutonner [butɔne] **1** *vt (vêtement)* to button (up), to fasten (up)

    2 se boutonner *vpr (vêtement)* to button (up)

boutonneux, -euse [butɔnø, -øz] *adj* pimply

boutonnière [butɔnjɛr] *nf (de vêtement)* buttonhole; **porter une fleur à la b.** to wear a boutonnière

bouton-pression *(pl* **boutons-pression)** [butɔ̃presjɔ̃] *nm* snap fastener

bouture [butyr] *nf* cutting; **faire des boutures** to take cuttings

bouturer [butyre] *vt* to propagate by cuttings

bouvier, -ère [buvje, -ɛr] **1** *nm,f* cowherd

    2 *nm (chien)* sheepdog

bouvreuil [buvrœj] *nm* bullfinch

bovin, -e [bɔvɛ̃, -in] **1** *adj aussi Fig* bovine

    2 *nm Zool* bovine

bowling [buliŋ] *nm* (a) *(jeu)* (tenpin) bowling (b) *(lieu)* (tenpin) bowling alley

box *(pl* **boxes)** [bɔks] *nm (dans un dortoir)* cubicle; *(dans une écurie)* stall; *(dans un garage)* private parking space; *Jur* **b. des accusés** dock

boxe [bɔks] *nf* boxing; **faire de la b.** to box; **b. anglaise** boxing; **b. française** kick boxing

boxer[1] [bɔkse] **1** *vi* to box

    2 *vt Fam (frapper)* to punch

boxer[2] [bɔksɛr] *nm (chien)* boxer

boxeur [bɔksœr] *nm* boxer

box-office *(pl* **box-offices)** [bɔksɔfis] *nm* box office; **être en tête du b.** to be a box-office hit

boyau, -x [bwajo] *nm* (a) *(d'animal)* gut; *(corde)* (cat)gut (b) *(de vélo)* tubular tire (c) *(allée)* narrow alleyway; *(de mine)* narrow gallery; *Mil* communication trench

boycott [bɔjkɔt], **boycottage** [bɔjkɔtaʒ] *nm* boycott(ing)

boycotter [bɔjkɔte] *vt* to boycott

boys band [bɔjzbɑ̃d] *nm* boy band

boy-scout *(pl* **boy-scouts)** [bɔjskut] *nm Vieilli* boy scout; *Fig* **mentalité de b.** boy-scout mentality

BP [bepe] *nf (abrév* **boîte postale)** PO Box

bracelet [braslɛ] *nm* (a) *(bijou)* bracelet; *(rigide)* bangle; *(de montre)* strap; **b. électronique** *ou* **de détention** electronic tag (b) *(élastique)* rubber band

bracelet-montre *(pl* **bracelets-montres)** [braslɛmɔ̃tr] *nm* wristwatch

braconnage [brakɔnaʒ] *nm* poaching

braconner [brakɔne] *vi* to poach

braconnier [brakɔnje] *nm* poacher

brader [brade] *vt (solder)* to sell off

braderie [bradri] *nf (liquidation)* clearance sale; *(vente par des particuliers)* ≃ garage sale, yard sale; *(magasin)* discount store

braguette [bragɛt] *nf* fly *(on pants)*

braille [braj] *nm* Braille; **lire en b.** to read Braille

braillements [brajmɑ̃] *nmpl* yelling; *(d'enfant)* howling

brailler [braje] **1** *vi* to yell; *(enfant)* to howl

    2 *vt (chanson)* to bawl out; *(slogan)* to chant

braire [28] [brɛr] *vi (âne)* to bray; *Fam Fig* to yell

braise [brɛz] *nf (charbons)* (glowing) embers; **des yeux de b.** glowing eyes

braiser [brɛze] *vt Culin* to braise

bramer [brame] *vi (cerf)* to bell; *Fig (hurler)* to howl

brancard [brɑ̃kar] *nm* (a) *(d'une civière, d'une charrette)* shaft; *Fig* **ruer dans les brancards** to kick over the traces (b) *(civière)* stretcher

brancardier, -ère [brɑ̃kardje, -ɛr] *nm,f* stretcher bearer

branchage [brɑ̃ʃaʒ] *nm (des arbres)* branches; **branchages** *(coupés)* cut branches

branche [brɑ̃ʃ] *nf* (a) *(d'un arbre)* branch; *(de céleri)* stick; *Fig (de l'industrie, de la science, d'une famille)* branch; *(professionnelle)* line of business; **la b. maternelle** the mother's side; *Fam* **vieille b.** old buddy (b) *(d'un compas)* leg; *(de lunettes)* side piece; *(d'un chandelier)* branch (c) *Suisse Univ (matière)* subject

branché, -e [brɑ̃ʃe] *adj Fam (à la mode)* trendy, hip; **il est b. tennis/jazz** he's really into tennis/jazz

branchement [brɑ̃ʃmɑ̃] *nm (sur un réseau)* connecting (up) *(sur* to); *(à une prise)* plugging in; *(assemblage de fils)* connection

brancher [brɑ̃ʃe] **1** *vt* (a) *(à un réseau)* to connect (up) *(sur* to); *(à une prise)* to plug in; *Fig* **b. qn sur un sujet** to get sb onto a subject (b) *Fam (plaire à)* **l'art moderne, ça ne me branche pas tellement** I'm not really into modern art; **on se fait un resto ce soir, ça te branche?** how about going to a restaurant tonight?

    2 se brancher *vpr* (a) *(appareil électrique)* to plug in (b)

Can Fam (personne) to decide, to make up one's mind (**c**) **se b. sur** *(une station de radio)* to tune in to

branchie [brɑ̃ʃi] *nf* gill

branchitude [brɑ̃ʃityd] *nf Fam* hipness, trendiness; **cette boîte est l'un des hauts lieux de la b. parisienne** this club is one of the coolest *or* hippest in Paris

brandade [brɑ̃dad] *nf Culin* **b. (de morue)** = salt cod puréed with garlic, oil and cream

brandebourg [brɑ̃dbur] *nm* frog *(on uniform)*

brandir [brɑ̃dir] *vt* to brandish

brandy [brɑ̃di] *nm* brandy

branlant, -e [brɑ̃lɑ̃, -ɑ̃t] *adj (dent)* loose; *(chaise, escalier)* rickety

branle [brɑ̃l] *nm* **mettre qch en b.** *(processus)* to set sth in motion; **se mettre en b.** *(partir)* to get moving; *(entrer en fonctionnement)* to get going

branle-bas [brɑ̃lba] *nm inv* **b. (de combat)** *(agitation)* commotion

branlée [brɑ̃le] *nf Fam* thrashing; **prendre** *ou* **recevoir une b.** to get a thrashing

branler [brɑ̃le] **1** *vt Vulg (masturber)* to jerk off; *Fig* **mais qu'est-ce qu'il branle?** what the hell's he up to?
2 *vi (dent)* to be loose; *(chaise, escalier)* to be rickety
3 se branler *vpr Vulg (se masturber)* to jerk off; *Fig* **je m'en branle!** I don't give a shit!

branleur, -euse[1] [brɑ̃lœr, -øz] *nm,f Vulg (bon à rien)* jerk

branleux, -euse[2] [brɑ̃lø, øz] *adj Can Fam (qui hésite)* dithering; *(lâche)* cowardly

branque [brɑ̃k] *Fam* **1** *adj* bonkers, nuts
2 *nmf (imbécile)* dope, jerk; *(fou)* headcase

braquage [brakaʒ] *nm* (**a**) *Aut (des roues)* turning; **(angle de) b.** steering lock (**b**) *Fam (vol)* hold-up; **faire un b.** to do a hold-up

braque [brak] *nm (chien)* pointer

braquer [brake] **1** *vt* (**a**) *(diriger)* to point (**sur** at); *(regard)* to fix (**sur** on) (**b**) *(rendre hostile)* **b. qn contre qn/qch** to turn sb against sb/sth (**c**) *Fam (banque)* to hold up
2 *vi Aut* to turn the (steering) wheel; **b. à fond** to apply full lock; **voiture qui braque mal** car that has a poor lock
3 se braquer *vpr* to dig one's heels in; **se b. contre qn** to turn against sb

braquet [brakɛ] *nm* gear ratio; **changer de b.** to change gear

bras [brɑ] *nm* (**a**) *(membre)* arm; **donner le b. à qn** to give sb one's arm; **un panier au b.** with a basket on one's arm; **les b. croisés** with one's arms folded; *Fig* **rester les b. croisés** *(être passif)* to stand by with one's arms folded; **b. dessus, b. dessous** arm in arm; **être le b. droit de qn** to be sb's right-hand man/woman; **accueillir qn à b. ouverts** to welcome sb with open arms; *Fam* **tomber sur qn à bras raccourcis** to lay into sb; *Fig* **avoir le b. long** to have a lot of influence; *Fig* **avoir qn/qch sur les b.** to have sb/sth on one's hands; **les b. m'en tombent!** I'm flabbergasted!; **en b. de chemise** in (one's) shirtsleeves; **une partie de b. de fer** an arm-wrestling match; *Fig* **un b. de fer entre la direction et les syndicats** a tug-of-war between the management and the unions; **faire un b. d'honneur à qn** ≃ to flip sb the bird (**b**) *(d'un fauteuil, d'un levier, d'une ancre)* arm; *(d'une grue)* jib; *(d'une croix)* limb; *Can* **b. d'escalier** banister; **b. de lecture** pickup arm
(**c**) *(de fleuve)* arm; **b. de mer** arm of the sea; *Can* **b. de vitesse** stick shift

brasero [brazero] *nm* brazier

brasier [brazje] *nm (incendie)* blaze, inferno

Brasilia [brazilja] *n* Brasilia

bras-le-corps [brɑlkɔr] **à bras-le-corps** *adv* **saisir qn à b.** to seize sb around the waist; **prendre un problème à b.** to come to grips with a problem

brassage [brasaʒ] *nm* (**a**) *(de la bière)* brewing (**b**) *(mélange)* mixing

brassard [brasar] *nm* armband; **b. de deuil** black armband

brasse [bras] *nf Sport (style)* breaststroke; *(mouvement)* stroke; **nager la b.** to swim breaststroke; **b. coulée** = breaststroke in which face is submerged; **b. papillon** butterfly (stroke)

brassée [brase] *nf* armful

brasser [brase] *vt* (**a**) *(bière)* to brew (**b**) *(mélanger)* to mix; *Fig* **b. de l'argent** to handle large amounts of money; **b. de l'air** *ou* **du vent** to work without getting anything done

brasserie [brasri] *nf* (**a**) *(fabrique)* brewery; *(industrie)* brewing (**b**) *(restaurant)* brasserie

brasseur, -euse [brasœr, -øz] *nm,f* (**a**) *(fabricant de bière)* brewer (**b**) *Fig* **b. d'affaires** big businessman

brassière [brasjɛr] *nf* (**a**) *(de bébé)* undershirt (**b**) *Can (soutien-gorge)* bra

bravade [bravad] *nf* bravado; **par b.** out of bravado

brave [brav] **1** *adj* (**a**) *(courageux)* brave, courageous (**b**) *(bon)* good; **de braves gens** good people (**c**) *Péj* **il est bien b.** *(pas futé)* he means well
2 *nm* (**a**) *(héros)* brave man (**b**) *Vieilli* **mon b.** my good man

bravement [bravmɑ̃] *adv* (**a**) *(courageusement)* bravely, courageously (**b**) *(avec résolution)* boldly

braver [brave] *vt (mort, danger)* to brave; *(personne, lois, règlements)* to defy

bravo [bravo] **1** *exclam* bravo!; *(dans un débat)* hear, hear!; *Ironique* well done!
2 *nm* **un grand b. à toute l'équipe technique** a big hand for all the technical crew; **des bravos** cheers

bravoure [bravur] *nf* bravery, courage

break[1] [brɛk] *nm (voiture)* station wagon

break[2] [brɛk] *nm (pause) & Sport* break

brebis [brəbi] *nf* (**a**) *(animal)* ewe; *Fig* **b. galeuse** black sheep (**b**) *Rel* sheep

brèche [brɛʃ] *nf (dans un mur, une haie)* gap; *(dans la coque d'un bateau)* hole; *Mil* breach; *Fig* **être toujours sur la b.** to be always on the go; **battre qch en b.** to demolish sth

bréchet [breʃɛ] *nm* breastbone

bredouille [brəduj] *adj* empty-handed

bredouiller [brəduje] *vt & vi* to mumble, to mutter

bref, -ève [brɛf, brɛv] **1** *adj* brief, short; *Ling (voyelle)* short; **soyez b.!** be brief!
2 *adv* in short; **une cousine ou une tante, enfin b., quelqu'un de sa famille** a cousin or an aunt, well anyway, one of his/her relatives; **l'actualité en b.** the news in brief
3 *nf* **brève** *(nouvelle)* short news item

brelan [brəlɑ̃] *nm* three of a kind; **b. d'as** three aces

breloque [brələk] *nf (sur un bracelet)* charm

brème [brɛm] *nf* bream

Brême [brɛm] *n* Bremen

Brésil [brezil] *nm* **le B.** Brazil

brésilien, -enne [breziljɛ̃, -ɛn] **1** *adj* Brazilian
2 *nm,f* **B., Brésilienne** Brazilian

Bretagne [brətaɲ] *nf* **la B.** Brittany

bretelle [brətɛl] *nf* (**a**) *(de soutien-gorge, de robe)* (shoulder) strap; **(paire de) bretelles** *(pour pantalon)* (pair of) suspenders (**b**) *(lanière)* strap; *(de fusil)* sling (**c**) *(route)* **b. (d'accès)** access road; **b. (d'autoroute)** ramp

breton, -onne [brətɔ̃, -ɔn] **1** *adj* Breton
2 *nm (langue)* Breton
3 *nm,f* **B., Bretonne** Breton

bretzel [brɛdzɛl] *nm* pretzel

breuvage [brœvaʒ] *nm (potion)* potion; *Hum (boisson)* concoction

brève [brɛv] *voir* **bref**

brevet [brəvɛ] *nm (certificat)* certificate; *(diplôme)* diploma; *Scol*

b. (des collèges) = general exam taken at age 15; **b. d'études professionnelles** = vocational diploma; **b. (d'invention)** patent; **b. de pilote** *Aviat* pilot's license; *Mil* wings; **b. de technicien supérieur** = advanced vocational training certificate

breveter [42] [brəvte] *vt (invention)* to patent; **faire b. qch** to take out a patent on sth

bréviaire [brevjɛr] *nm Rel* breviary

briard [brijar] *nm (chien)* Briard

bribes [brib] *nfpl* **b. de conversation** snatches of conversation; **des b. de finlandais** a few scraps of Finnish

bric-à-brac [brikabrak] *nm inv (vieux objets)* odds and ends, bric-à-brac; *(mélange)* jumble (**de** of); **(boutique de) b.** second-hand shop

bric et de broc [brikedəbrɔk] **de bric et de broc** *adv* haphazardly

brick [brik] *nm (carton)* carton

bricolage [brikɔlaʒ] *nm* **(a)** *(travail)* home improvement **(b)** *Péj (réparation)* patch-up

bricole [brikɔl] *nf (objet)* trinket; *(chose sans importance)* trifle; *Fam* **il va lui arriver des bricoles** he's going to get into a mess

bricoler [brikɔle] **1** *vt (construire)* to put together; *(réparer)* to tinker with
2 *vi* to do home improvement; **j'ai passé la matinée à b. dans la maison** I spent the morning doing odd jobs about the house

bricoleur, -euse [brikɔlœr, -øz] **1** *adj* **être b.** to be good with one's hands
2 *nm,f* handyman, *f* handywoman

bride [brid] *nf* **(a)** *(de harnais)* bridle; *Fig* **lâcher la b. à qn** to give sb his/her head; *Fig* **avoir la b. sur le cou** to have a free rein; **aller à b. abattue** to ride full tilt **(b)** *(de boutonnière)* bar

bridé, -e [bride] *adj (yeux)* slanting

brider [bride] *vt (cheval)* to bridle; *(personne, passions, impulsion)* to curb, to restrain

bridge [bridʒ] *nm (jeu, prothèse)* bridge

brie [bri] *nm* Brie

brièvement [brijɛvmã] *adv* briefly

brièveté [brijɛvte] *nf* brevity, briefness

brigade [brigad] *nf* **(a)** *Mil* brigade; *(de police, de gendarmerie)* squad; **b. antigang** organized crime squad; *Hist* **les Brigades internationales** the International Brigades; **b. des stupéfiants** *ou Fam* **des stups** drug squad **(b)** *(d'ouvriers)* team

brigadier [brigadje] *nm* **(a)** *Mil* corporal; *(d'artillerie)* bombardier **(b)** **b. (de police)** (police) sergeant

brigand [brigã] *nm (bandit)* brigand; *(personne malhonnête)* crook; **petit b.!** *(enfant)* little rascal *or* rogue!

briguer [brige] *vt (honneur, poste)* to solicit

brillamment [brijamã] *adv* brilliantly

brillant, -e [brijã, -ãt] **1** *adj* **(a)** *(lumière, couleur)* bright, brilliant; *(pierre précieuse)* sparkling; *(cheveux, chaussures, cuir)* shiny; **les yeux brillants de fièvre** eyes bright with fever **(b)** *(carrière, élève, avenir)* brilliant; *(conversation)* sparkling
2 *nm* **(a)** *(d'un métal)* brilliance, brightness; *(d'une pierre précieuse)* sparkle; *(d'un papier, d'un tissu, de cheveux)* shininess **(b)** *(diamant)* brilliant **(c)** **b. à lèvres** lip gloss

brillantine [brijãtin] *nf* brilliantine

briller [brije] *vi* **(a)** *(soleil, étoiles, yeux)* to shine; *(bougie)* to glimmer; *(pierre précieuse)* to sparkle; *(eau, satin)* to shimmer; *(braises)* to glow; **faire b. ses chaussures** to shine *or* to polish one's shoes; **des yeux qui brillent de colère/de joie** eyes shining with anger/happiness; **b. de mille feux** to sparkle brilliantly; *Prov* **tout ce qui brille n'est pas or** all that glitters is not gold **(b)** *(exceller)* to shine; **b. par son absence** to be conspicuous by one's absence; **elle ne brille pas par sa ponctualité** she's not noted for her punctuality

brimade [brimad] *nf* instance of bullying; **faire subir des brimades à qn** to bully sb

brimbaler [brɛ̃bale] = **bringuebaler**

brimer [brime] *vt* to bully; **se sentir brimé** to feel victimized

brin [brɛ̃] **1** *nm* **(a)** *(de persil, de romarin)* sprig; *(de mimosa, de muguet)* spray; *(de paille)* wisp; **un b. d'herbe** a blade of grass **(b)** *Fam (petite quantité)* **un b. de qch** a bit of sth; **un b. d'ironie/de jalousie** a touch of irony/jealousy; **faire un b. de toilette** to quickly freshen up; **un beau b. de fille** a fine-looking girl **(c)** *(de laine, corde, fil)* strand
2 *adv Fam* **un b.** *(un peu)* a bit

brindille [brɛ̃dij] *nf* twig

bringue¹ [brɛ̃g] *nf Fam* **grande b.** *(fille)* beanpole

bringue² [brɛ̃g] *nf Fam (fête)* binge; **faire la b.** to go on a binge

bringue³ [brɛ̃g] *nf Suisse* **(a)** *(querelle)* row **(b)** *(rengaine)* refrain

bringuebaler [brɛ̃gbale], **brinquebaler** [brɛ̃kbale] *vt & vi Fam* to shake about

brio [brijo] *nm* brilliance; **avec b.** brilliantly

brioche [brijɔʃ] *nf* brioche; *Fam Fig* **avoir/prendre de la b.** to have/to develop a paunch

brioché, -e [brijɔʃe] *adj* **pain b.** brioche bread

brique [brik] **1** *nf* **(a)** *(de construction)* brick; **mur de** *ou* **en briques** brick wall **(b)** *Anciennement très Fam (10 000 francs)* 10,000 francs
2 *adj inv* **(rouge) b.** brick-red

briquer [brike] *vt* **(a)** *(nettoyer)* to scrub down; *(pont de navire)* to holystone **(b)** *Suisse (briser)* to break, to smash

briquet [brikɛ] *nm (cigarette)* lighter

briqueterie [brikɛtri] *nf* brickyard

briquette [brikɛt] *nf* **(a)** *(petite brique)* small brick **(b)** *(de jus de fruit)* small carton **(c)** *(de charbon)* briquette

bris [bri] *nm (de verre, de scellés)* breaking; **b. de glaces** broken windows

brisant [brizã] *nm (écueil)* reef; **brisants** *(vagues)* breakers

brise [briz] *nf* breeze; *Naut* **forte b.** stiff breeze

brise-glace [brizglas] *nm inv* **(a)** *(navire)* ice breaker **(b)** *(d'une pile de pont)* ice breaker; *(d'un navire)* ice beam

brise-lames [brizlam] *nm inv* breakwater

briser [brize] **1** *vt (casser)* to break; *(opposition, résistance, espérances)* to crush; *(carrière)* to wreck; *(grève)* to break; **b. qn** *(sujet: effort, marche)* to wear sb out; **brisé par la douleur** crushed by grief; **la voix brisée par l'émotion** his/her voice choked with emotion; **cela me brise le cœur** it breaks my heart
2 **se briser** *vpr (vagues, porcelaine, verre)* to break; *(voix)* to break; *Fig (espoirs)* to be shattered

brise-tout [briztu] *nmf inv* clumsy person *(who is always breaking things)*

briseur, -euse [brizœr, -øz] *nm,f* **b. de grève** strike breaker

brise-vent [brizvã] *nm inv* windbreak

bristol [bristɔl] *nm* Bristol board; *(carte de visite)* visiting card

britannique [britanik] **1** *adj* British; **les îles Britanniques** the British Isles
2 *nmf* **B.** Briton; **les Britanniques** the British

broc [bro] *nm* pitcher, jug

brocante [brɔkãt] *nf (commerce)* second-hand trade; *(magasin)* second-hand store; *(marché aux puces)* flea market

brocanteur, -euse [brɔkãtœr, -øz] *nm,f* second-hand dealer

brocarder [brɔkarde] *vt Litt* to gibe at

brocart [brɔkar] *nm* brocade

broche [brɔʃ] *nf* **(a)** *(pour rôtir)* spit; **faire cuire qch à la b.** to spit-roast sth **(b)** *(bijou)* brooch **(c)** *Tech, Élec & Méd* pin

brocher [brɔʃe] *vt* **(a)** *(livre)* to stitch **(b)** *(tissu)* to brocade

brochet [brɔʃɛ] *nm* pike

brochette [brɔʃɛt] *nf (broche)* skewer; *(plat)* kebab

brochure [brɔʃyr] *nf* brochure, pamphlet

brocoli [brɔkɔli] *nm* broccoli; **des brocolis** broccoli

brodequin [brɔdkɛ̃] *nm* laced boot

broder [brɔde] *vt & vi aussi Fig* to embroider

broderie [brɔdri] *nf* **(a)** *(ouvrage)* piece of embroidery; **broderies** embroidery; **b. anglaise** broderie anglaise **(b)** *(activité)* embroidery

broie *voir* **broyer**

bromure [brɔmyr] *nm* bromide

bronche [brɔ̃ʃ] *nf* bronchial tube; **être fragile des bronches** to have a weak chest

broncher [brɔ̃ʃe] *vi* **(a)** *(réagir)* **sans b.** without batting an eyelid; **il n'a pas bronché** he didn't bat an eyelid **(b)** *(cheval)* to stumble

bronchite [brɔ̃ʃit] *nf* bronchitis; **avoir une b.** to have bronchitis

broncho-pneumonie *(pl* **broncho-pneumonies)** [brɔ̃kɔpnømɔni] *nf Méd* bronchopneumonia

bronzage [brɔ̃zaʒ] *nm (activité)* tanning; *(hâle)* (sun)tan; **b. intégral** all-over tan

bronze [brɔ̃z] *nm (métal, objet d'art)* bronze

bronzé, -e [brɔ̃ze] *adj (peau)* (sun)tanned; *Euph ou Péj (personne)* colored

bronzer [brɔ̃ze] *vi (personne)* to go brown, to tan

bronzette [brɔ̃zɛt] *nf Fam* sunbathing; **faire b.** to do a bit of sunbathing

brosse [brɔs] *nf* **(a)** *(ustensile)* brush; **donner un coup de b. à qch** to give sth a brush; **donner un coup de b. à qn** *(coiffer)* to give sb's hair a brush; **avoir les cheveux en b.** to have a crew cut; *Can Fam* **être en b.** to be smashed; *Fig* **manier la b. à reluire** to bow and scrape; **b. à cheveux** hairbrush; **b. à dents** toothbrush; **b. à habits** clothes brush; **b. à ongles** nailbrush **(b)** *(pinceau large)* (paint)brush

brosser [brɔse] **1** *vt* **(a)** *(tapis, manteau, cheveux)* to brush; *(sol)* to scrub; *(cheval)* to brush down; *Belg* **b. un cours** to cut a class **(b)** *(décrire)* **b. un tableau optimiste de la situation** to paint an optimistic picture of the situation

2 se brosser *vpr (se nettoyer)* to brush oneself down; **se b. les dents/les cheveux** to brush one's teeth/one's hair; *Fam* **tu peux toujours te b.!** not a chance!

brou [bru] *nm* **(a)** *(enveloppe)* shuck **(b)** *(teinture)* **b. de noix** walnut stain

broue [bru] *nf Can* froth; *très Fam Fig* **faire** *ou* **péter de la b.** to talk big

brouette [bruɛt] *nf* wheelbarrow

brouhaha [bruaa] *nm* hubbub

brouillard [brujar] *nm* fog; **il y a du b.** it's foggy; *Fig* **être dans le b.** to be in a fog; **b. givrant** freezing fog

brouille [bruj] *nf* quarrel, disagreement

brouillé, -e [bruje] *adj* **(a)** *(teint)* blotchy **(b)** **être b. avec qn** to have fallen out with sb; **être b. avec les dates/la grammaire** to be hopeless at dates/grammar

brouiller [bruje] **1** *vt* **(a)** *(rendre trouble)* *(idées)* to muddle up; *(vue)* to blur; **yeux brouillés de larmes** eyes blurred with tears; *Fig* **b. les cartes** to confuse the issue; *Fig* **b. les pistes** to cover one's tracks **(b)** *(fâcher)* **b. qn avec qn** to set sb against sb **(c)** *Rad & Élec (accidentellement)* to cause interference to; *(intentionnellement)* to jam

2 se brouiller *vpr* **(a)** *(idées, dates)* to get muddled up **(b)** *(vue)* to get blurred **(c)** *(se détériorer)* **le temps se brouille** it's clouding over **(d)** *(se disputer)* to fall out **(avec qn** with sb)

brouillon, -onne [brujɔ̃, -ɔn] **1** *adj (mal organisé)* disorganized, unmethodical; *(mal présenté)* untidy

2 *nm (ébauche)* (rough) draft; **(papier) b.** scratch paper; **faire un exercice au b.** to do a rough version of an exercise;

(cahier de) b. scratchpad; *Ordinat* **version b.** draft version

broussaille [brusaj] *nf* **broussailles** scrub; **en b.** *(cheveux)* tousled; *(sourcils)* bushy

broussailleux, -euse [brusajø, -øz] *adj (terrain)* scrubby; *(cheveux)* tousled; *(sourcils)* bushy

brousse [brus] *nf* **la b.** the bush

brouter [brute] **1** *vt (herbe)* to graze

2 *vi* **(a)** *(animal)* to graze **(b)** *(embrayage)* to jerk, to shake

broutille [brutij] *nf* trifle

broyer [32] [brwaje] *vt (pierre, aliments, couleurs)* to grind; *(membre, main, personne)* to crush; *Fig* **b. du noir** to be down in the dumps

broyeur, -euse [brwajœr, -øz] **1** *adj (appareil)* grinding

2 *nm (machine)* grinder; **b. à ordures** garbage-disposal unit

bru [bry] *nf* daughter-in-law

brugnon [brynɔ̃] *nm* nectarine

bruine [bruin] *nf* drizzle

bruiner [bruine] *v impersonnel* to drizzle

bruire [bruir] *vi Litt (feuilles, étoffe)* to rustle; *(ruisseau, vent)* to murmur

bruissement [bruismã] *nm (des feuilles, d'une étoffe)* rustle, rustling; *(d'un ruisseau, du vent)* murmur(ing)

bruit [brui] *nm* **(a)** *(son)* sound, noise; **b. de pas** (sound of) footsteps; **des bruits de voix** the sound of voices; **sans b.** without a sound **(b)** *(vacarme)* noise; **faire du b.** *(être bruyant)* to make a noise; *Fig (affaire, histoire)* to cause a sensation; **b. de fond** background noise; **beaucoup de b. pour rien** a lot of fuss over nothing **(c)** *(rumeur)* rumor; **faire courir un b.** to spread a rumor; **le b. court que...** rumor has it that...

bruitage [bruitaʒ] *nm* sound effects

bruiteur, -euse [bruitœr, -øz] *nm,f* sound-effects man, *f* woman

brûlant, -e [brylã, -ãt] *adj (plat, casserole)* red-hot; *(café)* boiling (hot); *(soleil)* scorching; *Fig* **b. de désir** burning with desire; **question brûlante** burning question; **le sujet est d'une actualité brûlante** it's one of the burning issues of the day

brûlé, -e [bryle] **1** *nm,f (accidenté)* burns victim; *Méd* **les grands brûlés** people with third-degree burns

2 *nm* **sentir le b.** to smell burnt; **une odeur de b.** a burnt smell; **avoir un goût de b.** to taste burnt

brûle-parfum *(pl* **brûle-parfums)** [brylparfœ̃] *nm* perfume burner

brûle-pourpoint [brylpurpwɛ̃] **à brûle-pourpoint** *adv* point-blank

brûler [bryle] **1** *vt* **(a)** *(sujet: flamme, acide)* to burn; *(sujet: eau bouillante)* to scald; *(sujet: fer à repasser)* to scorch; *(café)* to roast; **gazon brûlé par le soleil** lawn scorched by the sun; **être brûlé vif** *(dans un accident)* to be burnt alive; *(être supplicié)* to be burnt at the stake; **l'argent lui brûle les doigts** money burns a hole in his/her pocket **(b)** *(consommer)* *(électricité, combustible)* to use; *(calories)* to burn **(c)** **b. un feu rouge** to go through a red light; **b. un stop** to go straight past a stop sign

2 *vi* **(a)** *(flamber, être carbonisé)* to burn; *(être très chaud)* to be red-hot; *(liquide)* to be boiling (hot); *(blessure)* to smart; **attention, ça brûle!** careful, it's hot!; **tu brûles** *(dans un jeu)* you're getting warm **(b)** *Fig* **b. de faire qch** to be burning to do sth; **b. d'impatience** to be bursting with impatience; **b. de désir** to be burning with desire

3 se brûler *vpr (par accident)* to burn oneself **(avec** on); **se b. la langue/la main** to burn one's tongue/hand

brûleur [brylœr] *nm* burner

brûlot [brylo] *nm* **(a)** *(article polémique)* scathing article **(b)** *Can (moustique)* gnat, midge

brûlure [brylyr] *nf (blessure)* burn; *(sensation)* burning; **b. de cigarette** cigarette burn; **brûlures d'estomac** heartburn

brume [brym] *nf* mist, haze; **b. de chaleur** heat haze

brumeux, -euse [brymø, -øz] *adj* misty, hazy; *Fig (idées, explication)* hazy

Brumisateur® [brymizatœr] *nm* atomizer, spray *(containing Evian mineral water)*

brun, -e [br̃œ, bryn] **1** *adj (cheveux)* dark, brown; *(peau, personne) (naturellement)* dark; *(bronzé)* brown; **être b. de peau** to be dark-skinned; *Can* **il fait b.** it's getting dark
2 *nm,f (personne)* dark-haired man, *f* dark-haired woman
3 *nm (couleur)* brown
4 *nf* **brune (a)** *(bière)* dark beer **(b)** *(cigarette)* dark-tobacco cigarette **(c)** *Litt* **à la brune** at dusk

brunante [bryñat] *nf Can* dusk

brunâtre [brynɑtr] *adj* brownish

brunch [brœntʃ] *nm* brunch

bruncher [3] [brœntʃe] *vi* to have brunch

Brunei [brynei] *nm* **le B.** Brunei

brunir [brynir] *vi (peau, personne)* to tan; *(cheveux)* to darken

bruschetta [brysketa] *nf Culin* bruschetta

brushing® [brœʃiŋ] *nm* blow-dry; **se faire un b.** to blow-dry one's hair; **se faire faire un b.** to have a blow-dry, to have one's hair blow-dried

brusque [brysk] *adj* abrupt

brusquement [bryskəm̃a] *adv* abruptly

brusquer [bryske] *vt* **(a) b. qn** *(être impoli envers)* to be abrupt with sb; *(maltraiter)* to treat sb harshly **(b)** *(hâter) (décision)* to rush; **il ne faut rien b.** we mustn't rush things

brusquerie [bryskəri] *nf* abruptness; **avec b.** abruptly

brut, -e[1] [bryt] **1** *adj* **(a)** *(pétrole, minerai)* crude; *(sucre)* unrefined; *(pierre précieuse)* uncut; *(champagne)* extra-dry; *(cidre)* dry; **à l'état b.** in its raw state **(b)** *(bénéfice, poids, salaire)* gross
2 *nm* **(a)** *(pétrole)* crude (oil) **(b)** *(champagne)* extra-dry champagne
3 *adv* gross

brutal, -e, -aux, -ales [brytal, -o] *adj* **(a)** *(personne, paroles, manières)* brutal; *(choc)* violent; **être b. avec qn** to be rough with sb **(b)** *(changement)* abrupt

brutalement [brytalm̃a] *adv (violemment)* brutally; *(avec brusquerie)* roughly; *(soudainement)* abruptly

brutaliser [brytalize] *vt* to maltreat

brutalité [brytalite] *nf (violence, brusquerie)* brutality; *(soudaineté)* abruptness; **brutalités** brutality

brute[2] [bryt] *nf (personne violente)* brute; *(personne grossière)* boor; **taper sur qch comme une b.** to bang on sth like a madman; **une b. épaisse** a great brute; **grosse b.!** you big brute!

Bruxelles [brysɛl, bryksɛl] *n* Brussels

bruxellois, -e [brysɛlwa, -az, bryksɛlwa, -az] **1** *adj* of Brussels
2 *nm,f* **B., Bruxelloise** = person from Brussels

bruyamment [brɥijam̃a] *adv (parler, rire)* loudly; *(manger)* noisily

bruyant, -e [brɥij̃a, -̃at] *adj (rue, voisin)* noisy; *(rire, applaudissements)* loud

bruyère [brɥijɛr] *nf (plante)* heather; *(terre)* heath; **pipe de b.** briar pipe; **terre de b.** peat

BTP [betepe] *nm (abrév* **bâtiment et travaux publics**) construction industry

BTS [beteɛs] *nm (abrév* **brevet de technicien supérieur**) = advanced vocational training certificate

bu, -e *pp voir* **boire**[1]

buanderette [bɥ̃adrɛt] *nf Can* Laundromat®

buanderie [bɥ̃adri] *nf* **(a)** *(pièce)* laundry (room) **(b)** *Can (laverie)* (dry) cleaner's, laundry

bubonique [bybɔnik] *adj voir* **peste**

Bucarest [bykarɛst] *n* Bucharest

buccal, -e, -aux, -ales [bykal, -o] *adj* buccal; **par voie buccale** orally

bûche [byʃ] *nf* **(a)** *(morceau de bois)* log; **b. de Noël** Yule log **(b)** *Fam (chute)* fall; **prendre une b.** to come a cropper

bûcher[1] [byʃe] **1** *nm* **(a)** *(pour le bois)* woodshed **(b)** *(de supplice)* stake **(c)** *(funéraire)* (funeral) pyre
2 *vt Can (arbre)* to fell, to cut down

bûcher[2] [byʃe] *Fam Scol* **1** *vt* to bone up on
2 *vi* to grind

bûcheron [byʃr̃ɔ] *nm* woodcutter, lumberjack

bûcheur, -euse [byʃœr, -øz] *Fam Scol* **1** *adj* hard-working
2 *nm,f* grind

bucolique [bykɔlik] *adj* pastoral

Budapest [bydapɛst] *n* Budapest

budget [bydʒɛ] *nm* budget

budgétaire [bydʒetɛr] *adj (dépenses, contrôle)* budgetary; *(année)* fiscal; **déficit/excédent b.** budget deficit/surplus

buée [bɥe] *nf (sur les vitres)* condensation; *(sur un miroir)* mist

Buenos Aires [bɥenɔzɛr] *n* Buenos Aires

buffet [byfɛ] *nm* **(a)** *(meuble) (bas)* sideboard; *(haut)* dresser **(b)** *(repas)* buffet; **b. campagnard** = cold buffet made with country produce; **b. froid** cold buffet **(c)** *Fam (ventre)* belly

buffle [byfl] *nm* buffalo

building [bildiŋ] *nm* high-rise

buis [bɥi] *nm (arbre)* box (tree); *(bois)* box(wood)

buisson [bɥis̃ɔ] *nm* bush

buissonnière [bɥisɔnjɛr] *adj f voir* **école**

bulbe [bylb] *nm* **(a)** *Bot* bulb **(b)** *Anat* **b. pileux** hair bulb; **b. rachidien** medulla oblongata **(c)** *Archit* onion dome

bulgare [bylgar] **1** *adj* Bulgarian
2 *nm (langue)* Bulgarian
3 *nmf* **B.** Bulgarian

Bulgarie [bylgari] *nf* **la B.** Bulgaria

bulldozer [byldozœr] *nm* bulldozer

bulle [byl] *nf* **(a)** *(d'air, de savon, stérile)* bubble; *(de bandes dessinées)* balloon; **faire des bulles** to blow bubbles; *Fam* **coincer la b.** to sleep; *Ordinat* **b. d'aide** help pop-up **(b)** *(lettre du pape)* (papal) bull

buller [byle] *vi Fam* to laze around

bulletin [bylt̃ɛ] *nm (communiqué)* bulletin; *(d'entreprise)* newsletter; *(formulaire)* form; *Scol* **b. (scolaire)** report card; **b. blanc** blank ballot paper; **b. d'informations** news bulletin; **b. météorologique** weather report; **b. officiel** official listing of all new laws and decrees; **b. de paie** *ou* **de salaire** pay slip; *Méd* **b. de santé** medical bulletin; **b. trimestriel** periodic report card; *Suisse* **b. de versement** money order; **b. de vote** ballot paper; **b. (de vote) nul** spoiled ballot paper

bulletin-réponse *(pl* **bulletins-réponse**) [byltɛ̃repɔs] *nm* reply form

bungalow [b̃œgalo] *nm* bungalow

bunker [bunkœr] *nm Mil* bunker; *(en golf)* bunker, sand trap

buraliste [byralist] *nmf* **(a)** *(de bureau de tabac)* tobacconist **(b)** *(dans un bureau)* clerk

bure [byr] *nf (étoffe)* frieze; *(habit religieux)* frock

bureau, -x [byro] *nm* **(a)** *(meuble)* desk **(b)** *(lieu)* office; *(à la maison)* study **(c)** *(comité)* committee **(d)** *(agence)* office; **b. de change** bureau de change; **b. d'études** design office; *(de recherche)* R & D department; **B. international du travail** International Labor Organization; **b. de poste** post office; **b. de tabac** tobacconist's (shop) **(e)** *(organisme)* **b. d'aide sociale** welfare office

bureaucrate [byrokrat] *nmf* bureaucrat

bureaucratie [byrokrasi] *nf (système)* bureaucracy; *(ensemble des fonctionnaires)* bureaucrats

bureaucratique [byrokratik] *adj* bureaucratic

Bureautique® [byrotik] *nf* office automation

burette [byrɛt] *nf* **(a)** *(pour l'huile)* oilcan; *(de chimiste)* burette **(b)** *très Fam* **burettes** *(testicules)* balls

burin [byrɛ̃] *nm* (**a**) *(de graveur)* burin (**b**) *(pour découper)* (cold) chisel

buriné, -e [byrine] *adj (visage)* deeply lined

Burkina [byrkina] *nm* **le B.** Burkina Faso

burkinabé [byrkinabe] **1** *adj* of Burkina Faso
  2 *nmf* **B.** = person from Burkina Faso

burlesque [byrlɛsk] **1** *adj* (**a**) *(ridicule)* ludicrous, ridiculous (**b**) *(film, genre)* burlesque
  2 *nm (genre)* **le b.** the burlesque

burqa [burka] *nf* burka, burqa

Burundi [burundi] *nm* **le B.** Burundi

bus [bys] *nm (autobus) & Ordinat* bus

buse [byz] *nf* (**a**) *(oiseau)* buzzard (**b**) *(conduit)* duct (**c**) *Belg (échec)* failure

busqué, -e [byske] *adj (nez)* hook(ed)

buste [byst] *nm (torse)* chest; *(seins, sculpture)* bust

bustier [bystje] *nm (corsage)* bustier; *(soutien-gorge)* strapless bra

but [by, byt] *nm* (**a**) *(objectif)* aim, goal; *(intention)* purpose; *(d'un trajet)* destination, goal; **dans ce b.** with this aim in view; **dans le b. de faire qch** with the aim of doing sth; **c'est le b. de l'opération** that's the point of the operation; **errer sans b.** to wander about aimlessly (**b**) *Sport* goal; **marquer un b.** to score a goal; **gagner/perdre (par) trois buts à un** to win/to lose by three goals to one; **les buts** *(zone)* the goal (**c**) **demander/dire qch de b. en blanc** to ask/to say sth straight out

butane [bytan] *nm* butane

buté, -e [byte] *adj* stubborn, obstinate

butée [byte] *nf* (**a**) *(pièce)* **b. (d'arrêt)** stop (**b**) *Archit* abutment

buter [byte] **1** *vt* (**a**) *(braquer)* **b. qn** to get sb's back up (**b**) *très Fam (tuer)* to bump off
  2 *vi* **b. contre qch** *(cogner)* to bump into sth; *(trébucher)* to stumble over sth; **b. sur un problème/une difficulté** to come up against a problem/a difficulty
  3 se buter *vpr (s'entêter)* to dig one's heels in

buteur [bytœr] *nm (au football)* goalscorer

butin [bytɛ̃] *nm* (**a**) *(d'une armée)* booty; *(de pillards)* spoils; *(de voleur)* loot (**b**) *Can Fam (affaires personnelles)* gear, stuff

butiner [bytine] **1** *vi (abeille)* to gather pollen
  2 *vt (sujet: abeille)* to gather pollen from; *(renseignements)* to gather

butineur [bytinœr] *nm Ordinat* browser

butoir [bytwar] *nm Rail* buffer; *(de porte)* door stop; **date b.** deadline

butte [byt] *nf (colline)* hillock; *Fig* **être en b. à qch** to be exposed to sth

buvable [byvabl] *adj* (**a**) *(potable)* drinkable (**b**) *(médicament)* to be taken orally

buvard [byvar] *nm (feuille)* sheet of blotting paper; *(sous-main)* blotter; **(papier) b.** blotting paper

buvette [byvɛt] *nf (dans une gare, à une fête)* refreshment bar

buveur, -euse [byvœr, -øz] *nm,f* drinker; **un gros b.** a heavy drinker

buviez *etc. voir* **boire**[1]

Byzance [bizɑ̃s] *n* Byzantium; *Fam* **c'est B.** it's the last word in luxury; *Fam* **ce n'est pas B.** it's not exactly luxurious

C

C¹, c [se] *nm inv* C, c; **c cédille** c cedilla
C² *(abrév* **Celsius)** C
c' *voir* **ce¹**
C4 [sekatr] *nm inv Belg* = official document given to an employee who is being laid off by his or her employer
CA [sea] *nm* **(a)** *Élec (abrév* **courant alternatif)** AC **(b)** *Com (abrév* **chiffre d'affaires)** turnover
ça [sa] *pron démonstratif* **(a)** *(en désignant) (cela)* that; *(ceci)* this; **donne-moi ça** give that to me; **c'est bien vrai ça!** that's very true!; **écoute-moi ça!** just listen to this!; **ce n'est pas si facile que ça** it isn't as easy as that; **ça oui!** oh yes!; **à part ça** apart from that; **qui/quand/où ça?** who/when/where?; **c'est ça!** that's right!; *Ironique* if you say so!; **comment ça, elle est partie?** what do you mean she's gone?; **ça alors!, ça par exemple!** my goodness!; **ça y est, j'ai fini** that's it, I'm finished; **et insolent avec ça!** AND you're/he's/she's/*etc.* rude!
  (b) *(sujet indéterminé)* it; **ça m'ennuie/me choque** it annoys/shocks me; **ça m'amuse** I find it funny; **ça me ferait plaisir** I'd enjoy it
  (c) *Fam* **ça criait dans tous les coins** there was shouting going on everywhere; *Hum* **ça travaille là-dedans!** you're not just a pretty face!
çà [sa] **çà et là** *adv* here and there
cabale [kabal] *nf* **(a)** *(complot, comploteurs)* cabal; **monter une c. contre qn** to plot against sb **(b)** *Rel* cabbala
cabalistique [kabalistik] *adj* cabbalistic
caban [kabɑ̃] *nm* reefer, pea jacket
cabane [kaban] *nf* **(a)** *(baraque)* hut; *(en rondins)* cabin; *(à outils)* shed; **c. à lapins** rabbit hutch; *Can* **c. à sucre** sugar shack **(b)** *très Fam (prison)* **en c.** in the slammer; **faire de la c.** to do time
cabanon [kabanɔ̃] *nm* **(a)** *(petite cabane)* hut, shed **(b)** *(en Provence) (maison de campagne)* (country) cottage
cabaret [kabarɛ] *nm* cabaret
cabas [kaba] *nm* shopping bag
cabestan [kabɛstɑ̃] *nm* capstan
cabillaud [kabijo] *nm* (fresh) cod
cabine [kabin] *nf* **(a)** *(de bateau, de vaisseau spatial)* cabin; **c. de pilotage** *(de petit avion)* cockpit; *(de gros avion)* flight deck **(b)** **c. de douche** *(pièce)* shower room; *(installation)* shower cubicle; **c. de bain(s)** *(de plage)* beach hut; *(de piscine)* changing cubicle; **c. d'essayage** fitting room; **c. Internet** Internet booth **(c)** *(de grue, de locomotive, de camion)* cab; *(d'ascenseur)* car; **c. téléphonique** phone booth
cabinet [kabinɛ] *nm* **(a)** *(petite pièce)* small room; *Fam* **les cabinets** the john; **c. noir** cubbyhole; **c. de toilette** (small) bathroom; **c. de travail** study **(b)** *(de pub)* agency; *(d'architectes, de notaire, de médecin)* office; **c. dentaire** dentist's office **(c)** *(entreprise)* **c. conseil** consultancy; **c. juridique** law firm **(d)** *Pol (d'un ministre)* departmental staff
câble [kɑbl] *nm* **(a)** *(fil)* cable; **c. métallique** wire cable **(b)** *TV* **le c.** cable TV; **avoir le c.** to have cable TV **(c)** *Vieilli (message)* cable

câblé, -e [kɑble] *adj* **(a)** *TV (ville, région)* with cable television; *Ordinat & Tél* hard-wired; **réseau c.** cable (TV) network; **l'immeuble est c.** the building is wired for cable TV **(b)** *(à fonctionnement fixe)* cabled
câbler [kɑble] *vt* **(a)** *TV (ville, quartier)* to install cable television in **(b)** *Vieilli (message)* to cable
câblo-opérateur *(pl* **câblo-opérateurs)** [kɑbloɔperatœr] *nm* cable company
cabochard, -e [kabɔʃar, -ard] *Fam* **1** *adj* pigheaded **2** *nm,f* pigheaded person
caboche [kabɔʃ] *nf Fam (tête)* nut; **mets-le-toi dans la c.!** get that into your thick skull!
cabosser [kabɔse] *vt (métal, voiture)* to bash up; *(chapeau)* to bash in; **un vieux chapeau cabossé** a battered old hat
cabot [kabo] *nm Fam* **(a)** *(chien)* pooch **(b)** *(acteur)* ham (actor)
cabotage [kabɔtaʒ] *nm Naut* coasting
caboteur [kabɔtœr] *nm Naut* coaster
cabotin, -e [kabɔtɛ̃, -in] **1** *adj (acteur)* ham **2** *nm,f* **(a)** *(acteur)* ham (actor, *f* actress) **(b)** *(vantard)* show-off
cabrer [kabre] **se cabrer** *vpr (cheval)* to rear (up); *Fig (personne)* to recoil
cabriole [kabrijɔl] *nf (saut, bond)* caper; *(en danse)* cabriole; *(en équitation)* capriole; *(de gymnaste)* somersault; **faire des cabrioles** to caper about
cabriolet [kabrijɔlɛ] *nm* **(a)** *(auto)* convertible **(b)** *(voiture à cheval)* cabriolet
CAC [kak] *n (abrév* **Compagnie des agents de change)** **le C.-40** = the Paris Stock Exchange index
caca [kaka] *nm (langage enfantin) (excrément)* poop; **faire c.** to poop; **c. d'oie** yellowish green
cacah(o)uète [kakawɛt] *nf* peanut
cacao [kakao] *nm (boisson, poudre)* cocoa; *(fève)* cocoa bean
cacaoui [kakawi] *nm Can* long-tailed duck
cacatoès [kakatɔɛs] *nm* cockatoo
cacatois [kakatwa] *nm Naut (voile)* royal sail; **(mât de) c.** royal mast
cachalot [kaʃalo] *nm* sperm whale
cache [kaʃ] **1** *nf* hiding place; **c. d'armes** arms cache **2** *nm (sur un texte)* masking card
caché, -e [kaʃe] *adj* hidden; *(sentiment)* secret
cache-cache [kaʃkaʃ] *nm* **jouer à c.** to play hide-and-seek
cache-col [kaʃkɔl] *nm inv Vieilli* scarf
Cachemire [kaʃmir] *nm* **le C.** Kashmir
cachemire [kaʃmir] *nm (laine)* cashmere; **à impression c.** paisley
cache-nez [kaʃne] *nm inv* scarf
cache-pot [kaʃpo] *nm inv* flowerpot holder
cacher [kaʃe] **1** *vt* to hide; **il ne cache pas que...** he makes no secret of the fact that...; **c. qch à qn** *(omettre de lui dire)* to hide sth from sb; **pour ne rien te c.** to be completely open with you; **je ne vous cache pas que j'ai été surpris** I won't

pretend (that) I wasn't surprised; **le mur nous cache la vue** the wall hides our view

2 se cacher *vpr (personne, soleil)* to hide; **se c. de qn** to hide from sb; **sa timidité se cache derrière une certaine rudesse** his shyness is hidden behind a bluff exterior; **je ne m'en cache pas** I make no secret of it; **en se cachant** secretly; **sans se c.** openly

cache-sexe [kaʃsɛks] *nm inv* G-string; *(d'indigène)* apron

cachet [kaʃɛ] *nm* **(a)** *(médicament)* tablet, pill **(b)** *(tampon)* stamp; *(sceau)* seal; *(de fabricant)* (trade)mark; **c. de la poste** postmark **(c)** *(style) (d'un endroit)* character; *(d'un vêtement)* style **(d)** *(salaire)* fee

cacheter [42] *[kaʃte] vt* to seal

cachette [kaʃɛt] *nf* **(a)** hiding place; **en c.** secretly; **boire en c.** *(habituellement)* to be a secret drinker; **faire qch en c. de qn** to do sth without sb's knowing **(b)** *Can* **jouer à la c.** to play hide-and-seek

cachot [kaʃo] *nm* **(a)** *(cellule)* dungeon **(b)** *(isolement)* solitary confinement

cachotterie [kaʃɔtri] *nf* **faire des cachotteries** to be secretive

cachottier, -ère [kaʃɔtje, -ɛr] **1** *adj* secretive **2** *nm,f* secretive person; **petit c.!** you secretive little thing!

cachou [kaʃu] *nm (bonbon)* cachou *(liquorice sweet)*

cacophonie [kakɔfɔni] *nf* cacophony

cactus [kaktys] *nm* cactus

c-à-d. *(abrév* **c'est-à-dire***)* i.e.

cadastre [kadastr] *nm (registre)* cadastre; *(administration)* cadastral survey office

cadavérique [kadaverik] *adj (teint)* deathly pale; *Méd* cadaveric

cadavre [kadavr] *nm* **(a)** *(de personne)* corpse, (dead) body; *(d'animal)* carcass, body; *Fam* **c'est un c. ambulant** he's a walking skeleton **(b)** *Fam (bouteille)* empty

caddie [kadi] *nm* **(a)** *Sport* caddy **(b)** *(chariot)* cart

cadeau, -x [kado] *nm* present, gift; *(avec un achat)* free gift; **en c.** as a present; **en c. avec** *(achat)* free with; **faire un c. à qn** to give sb a present; **faire c. de qch à qn** *(donner)* to make sb a present of sth; *Fam Fig* **il ne lui a pas fait de cadeaux** he didn't spare him/her; *Fam* **ton frère, ce n'est pas un c.** your brother's a real pain; **c'est un c. empoisonné** it's more trouble than it's worth

cadenas [kadna] *nm* padlock

cadenasser [kadnase] **1** *vt (porte, pièce)* to padlock **2 se cadenasser** *vpr (personne)* to lock oneself away

cadence [kadãs] *nf (rythme régulier)* rhythm; *(vitesse)* rate; **en c.** in time; **c. de production** rate of production; **c. de tir** rate of fire

cadencé, -e [kadãse] *adj* **(a)** *(rythmé)* rhythmic(al); **marcher au pas c.** to walk in time **(b)** *Ordinat* **c. à** running at

cadet, -ette [kadɛ, -ɛt] **1** *adj (de deux)* younger; *(de plus de deux)* youngest

2 *nm,f* **(a)** *(de deux)* younger (one); *(de plus de deux)* youngest (one); **il est mon c. de deux ans** he's two years younger than I am; **c'est le c. de mes soucis** that's the least of my worries **(b)** *Sport* junior *(16 to 18 years old)* **(c)** *Hist & Mil* cadet

cadrage [kadraʒ] *nm Cin & Phot (de l'image)* centering; *(plan)* frame; *Ordinat* positioning

cadran [kadrã] *nm (d'horloge, de baromètre)* face; *(d'instrument, de téléphone)* dial; *Fig* **faire le tour du c.** *(dormir)* to sleep round the clock; *Aut* **cadrans (de bord)** display panels; **c. solaire** sundial

cadre [kadr] *nm* **(a)** *(de tableau, de porte, de vélo)* frame

(b) *(domaine)* limits; *(structure)* framework; **dans le c. de** within the framework of

(c) *(décor)* setting; **c. (de vie)** environment

(d) *(dans un formulaire)* box; *Ordinat (pour graphique)* box; **c.**

réservé à l'administration *(sur formulaire)* for official use only

(e) *(dans une entreprise)* executive, manager; **les cadres** the management; *Mil* the officers; **c. moyen** middle manager; **c. supérieur** senior executive; **jeune c. dynamique** dynamic young executive

(f) **être rayé des cadres** to be dismissed

(g) *Can (tableau)* painting, picture

> ### Cadre
> In French companies, employees are divided into two categories, "employés" and "cadres". "Cadres", who are better qualified, tend to occupy more senior posts and consequently enjoy higher salaries, more benefits and more prestige. They are also expected to work longer hours.

cadre-adresse *(pl* **cadres-adresses***)* [kadradrɛs] *nm* address space

cadrer [kadre] **1** *vt (photo)* to center; *(plan)* to frame; *Ordinat* to position

2 *vi (correspondre)* to tally *(***avec** with)

cadreur [kadrœr] *nm TV & Cin* cameraman

caduc, caduque [kadyk] *adj* **(a)** *(feuille)* deciduous **(b)** *Jur (accord)* lapsed; *(loi)* null and void

caducée [kadyse] *nm* caduceus

CAF [seaɛf] *(abrév* **Caisse d'allocations familiales***)* = welfare office

cafard [kafar] *nm* **(a)** *(insecte)* cockroach **(b)** *Fam* **avoir le c. ou un coup de c.** to feel down *or* low **(c)** *Fam (rapporteur)* sneak

cafarder [kafarde] *vi Fam* **(a)** *(rapporter)* to sneak **(b)** *(avoir le cafard)* to feel down *or* low

cafardeur, -euse[1] [kafardœr, -øz] *nm,f Fam* sneak

cafardeux, -euse[2] [kafardø, -øz] *adj Fam* **se sentir ou être c.** to feel down *or* low

café [kafe] **1** *nm* **(a)** *(produit, boisson)* coffee; **glace au c.** coffee ice-cream; **c. crème** ≃ latte; **c. décaféiné** decaffeinated coffee; **c. en grains** coffee beans; **c. au lait** ≃ latte; **c. liégeois** = coffee ice-cream topped with whipped cream; **c. moulu** ground coffee; *Suisse* **c. nature** black coffee; **c. noir** black coffee; **c. en poudre ou instantané** instant coffee **(b)** *(bar)* café *(also serving alcoholic drinks)*; **c. tabac** = bar that also sells cigarettes and tobacco

2 *adj inv (couleur)* **c. (au lait)** coffee-colored

> ### Café
> In French cafés, a small cup of strong black coffee is called "un (petit) café", "un express" or, colloquially, "un petit noir". This may be served "serré" (extra-strong), "léger" (weak) or "allongé" (diluted with hot water). An "express" with a tiny amount of milk added is called "une noisette". A large cup of black coffee is called "un grand café", "un double express" or, colloquially, "un grand noir". Coffee with frothy, steamed milk is called "un (grand/petit) crème". The term "café au lait" is almost never used in cafés.

caféine [kafein] *nf* caffeine

cafétéria [kafeterja] *nf* cafeteria

cafetier [kaftje] *nm* café owner

cafetière [kaftjɛr] *nf (récipient)* coffee pot; *(électrique)* coffee machine; **c. à piston** cafetiere; **c. à pression** percolator

cafouillage [kafujaʒ] *nm Fam* **(a)** *(confusion)* muddle, shambles **(b)** *(de moteur de voiture)* misfiring

cafouiller [kafuje] *vi Fam* **(a)** *(personne)* to get into a muddle; *(projet)* to fall apart **(b)** *(moteur de voiture)* to misfire; *(poste de télévision)* to be on the blink

cafter [kafte] *vi Fam* to snitch, to tell tales

cage [kaʒ] *nf* (**a**) *(pour oiseaux, dans un zoo)* cage; *(pour poules)* coop; *(pour lapins)* hutch; **mettre un oiseau en c.** to put a bird in a cage; *Fam Fig* **c. à lapins** rabbit hutch (**b**) *(de foot)* goal (**c**) **c. d'ascenseur** elevator shaft; **c. d'escalier** stairwell (**d**) **c. à poules** *(pour enfants)* jungle gym (**e**) *Anat* **c. thoracique** rib cage

cageot [kaʒo] *nm* (**a**) *(caisse)* crate (**b**) *Fam Péj (femme)* dog, moose

cagette [kaʒɛt] *nf* crate

cagibi [kaʒibi] *nm Fam* storage room

cagnard [kaɲar] *nm Fam* blazing sunshine

cagneux, -euse [kaɲø, -øz] *adj* **avoir les genoux c.** to have knock-knees

cagnotte [kaɲɔt] *nf (caisse commune)* kitty; *(de jeux)* pool; *(économies)* nest egg

cagoule [kagul] *nf (de moine)* cowl; *(de pénitent, de terroriste)* hood

cahier [kaje] *nm* (**a**) notebook; **c. de brouillon** rough book; **c. de textes** homework book (**b**) *Typ* signature (**c**) *(d'un journal)* section (**d**) **Cahiers de...** *(revue)* Journal of... (**e**) *Com* **c. des charges** *(d'un contrat)* terms and conditions; *(de fabrication)* specifications

cahin-caha [kaɛ̃kaa] *adv Fam* **aller c.** *(se déplacer)* to struggle along; **ça va, la santé? – ça va, c.** how are you keeping? – oh, so-so

cahot [kao] *nm (secousse)* jolt

cahoter [kaɔte] **1** *vt* **être cahoté** *(dans un véhicule)* to be jolted about
2 *vi* to jolt along

cahoteux, -euse [kaɔtø, -øz] *adj* bumpy

cahute [kayt] *nf* shack

caïd [kaid] *nm Fam (chef de bande)* gang leader; **un c. de la drogue** a drug baron; **faire le c., jouer les caïds** to act high and mighty

caillasse [kajas] *nf Fam* loose stones

caille [kaj] *nf* quail; *Fam* **ma petite c.** my little dove

caillé [kaje] *nm* curds

caillebotis [kajbɔti] *nm* (**a**) *Naut* grating (**b**) *(plancher)* duckboard

caillebotte [kajbɔt] *nf* curds

cailler [kaje] **1** *vt (lait)* to curdle; *(sang)* to clot
2 *vi* (**a**) *(lait)* to curdle; *(sang)* to clot; **faire c. du lait** to curdle milk (**b**) *Fam* **ça caille** it's freezing
3 se cailler *vpr Fam* **on se (les) caille** it's freezing

caillot [kajo] *nm (de sang)* clot

caillou, -x [kaju] *nm* (**a**) *(petite pierre)* stone; *(sur la plage)* pebble (**b**) *Fam (pierre précieuse)* stone (**c**) *Fam (tête)* nut, pebble; **il n'a plus un poil sur le c.** he's as bald as a coot

caillouteux, -euse [kajutø, -øz] *adj (route)* stony; *(plage)* pebbly

caïman [kaimɑ̃] *nm* cayman

Caire [kɛr] *voir* **Le Caire**

cairote [kɛrɔt] **1** *adj* of Cairo
2 *nmf* **C.** person from Cairo, Cairene

caisse [kɛs] *nf* (**a**) *(pour marchandises)* case; *(à outils)* box; *(de champagne, de vin)* case; *(pour plantes)* tub; *(de fruits)* crate
(**b**) *Com & Fin (coffre)* cash box; *(d'une caisse enregistreuse)* till; *(où l'on paie) (dans un magasin)* cash desk; *(dans un supermarché)* checkout; **les caisses de l'État** the State coffers; **tenir la c.** *(dans un restaurant, dans un magasin)* to be the cashier; **passer à la c.** *(se faire licencier)* to be paid off; *Fam (payer)* to pay; *Fam (se faire payer)* to be paid; **c. (enregistreuse)** cash register; *Pol* **c. noire** slush fund
(**c**) *(argent)* cash (in hand); **faire la** *ou* **sa c.** to do the till
(**d**) *(organisme)* **c. d'allocations familiales** = welfare office; **c. d'épargne** savings bank; *Can* **c. populaire** credit union; **c. primaire d'assurance maladie** = French govern-

ment department dealing with health insurance; **c. de retraite** pension fund
(**e**) *Mus* **c. claire** snare drum; **c. de résonance** sound box
(**f**) *(de piano, d'horloge)* case; *(de véhicule)* body
(**g**) *très Fam (voiture)* car

caissette [kɛsɛt] *nf* small box

caissier, -ère [kɛsje, -ɛr] *nm,f* cashier; *(dans un supermarché)* checkout clerk

caisson [kɛsɔ̃] *nm* (**a**) *très Fam* **se faire sauter le c.** to blow one's brains out (**b**) *Archit* **plafond à caissons** coffered ceiling (**c**) *(de plongée)* caisson

cajoler [kaʒɔle] *vt* to cuddle

cajolerie [kaʒɔlri] *nf* cuddle

cajou [kaʒu] *nm voir* **noix**

cake [kɛk] *nm* fruit cake

cal (*pl* **cals**) [kal] *nm (durillon)* callus

calamar [kalamar] = **calmar**

calamine [kalamin] *nf (dépôt)* carbon deposits

calamité [kalamite] *nf (fléau)* calamity; *(malheur)* great misfortune; *Fam* **ce mec, c'est une vraie c.!** this guy is a real disaster!

calamiteux, -euse [kalamitø -øz] *adj* calamitous

calancher [kalɑ̃ʃe] *vi très Fam* to croak, to kick the bucket

calandre [kalɑ̃dr] *nf* (**a**) *(machine)* calender (**b**) *Aut* radiator grille

calanque [kalɑ̃k] *nf* deep narrow creek *(in the Mediterranean)*

calao [kalao] *nm* hornbill

calcaire [kalkɛr] **1** *adj (sol, terrain)* chalky; *(roche)* calcareous; *(eau)* hard
2 *nm* (**a**) *Géol* limestone (**b**) *(dépôt)* fur

calcification [kalsifikasjɔ̃] *nf Méd* calcification

calciner [kalsine] **1** *vt (brûler)* to char; **calciné** *(trop cuit)* burnt to a cinder
2 se calciner *vpr* to burn

calcium [kalsjɔm] *nm* calcium

calcul¹ [kalkyl] *nm* (**a**) *(compte)* calculation; **faire un c.** to make a calculation (**b**) *Scol* **le c.** arithmetic; **c. mental** mental arithmetic (**c**) *Math* **c. différentiel/intégral** differential/integral calculus (**d**) *(prévision)* calculation; **agir par c.** to act from selfish motives; **faire un mauvais c.** to miscalculate

calcul² [kalkyl] *nm Méd* stone, *Spéc* calculus; **c. biliaire/rénal** gall/kidney stone

calculateur, -trice [kalkylatœr, -tris] **1** *adj (personne, politique)* calculating
2 *nm Ordinat* (desktop) calculator; **c. (électronique)** (electronic) computer
3 *nf* **calculatrice (de poche)** (pocket) calculator

calculé, -e [kalkyle] *adj (insulte, risque)* calculated; *(méchanceté)* premeditated; *(insolence)* deliberate

calculer [kalkyle] **1** *vt (compter) (prix, superficie)* to work out; to calculate; *(comportement, propos)* to plan; *(conséquences, chances)* to weigh (up); **tout bien calculé** taking everything into account
2 *vi* to calculate; *Péj (économiser)* to count every cent

calculette [kalkylɛt] *nf* (pocket) calculator

Calcutta [kalkyta] *n* Calcutta

caldoche [kaldɔʃ] **1** *adj* White New Caledonian
2 *nmf* **C.** New Caledonian

cale¹ [kal] *nf Naut* (**a**) *(de navire)* hold; **à fond de c.** down in the hold (**b**) *(rampe)* **c. sèche** dry dock

cale² [kal] *nf (pour meuble, pour porte)* wedge; *(pour bloquer une roue)* chock

calé, -e [kale] *adj Fam* (**a**) *(personne)* **être c. en qch** to be good at sth (**b**) *(problème, question, devoir)* tough (**c**) *Belg (prêt)* ready

calebasse [kalbas] *nf* calabash

calèche [kalɛʃ] *nf* barouche

calecif [kalsif] *nm Fam* (boxer) shorts

caleçon [kalsɔ̃] *nm* boxer shorts; *(de femme)* leggings; *Vieilli* **c. de bain** swimming shorts; *Vieilli* **c. long** long johns

calédonien, -enne [kaledɔnjɛ̃, -ɛn] **1** *adj* Caledonian
2 *nm,f* **C., Calédonienne** Caledonian

calembour [kalãbur] *nm* pun, play on words; **faire des calembours** to make puns

calendes [kalãd] *nfpl* **renvoyer qch aux c. grecques** to put sth off indefinitely

calendrier [kalãdrije] *nm* **(a)** *(système, tableau)* calendar **(b)** *(de voyage, de travail)* schedule

cale-pied (*pl* cale-pieds) [kalpje] *nm* toe clip

calepin [kalpɛ̃] *nm* **(a)** *(carnet)* notebook **(b)** *Belg (serviette)* briefcase

caler[1] [kale] **1** *vt* **(a)** *(meuble, porte)* to wedge; *(roue)* to chock; *(chargement)* to secure; **c. un malade avec des coussins** to prop up a patient with cushions **(b)** *Fam (remplir)* **ça cale (l'estomac)** it fills you up; **je suis calé** I'm full up
2 *vi (moteur)* to stall
3 se caler *vpr (dans un fauteuil)* to settle oneself comfortably

caler[2] [kale] *vi* **(a)** *Fam (abandonner)* to give up **(b)** *Can (se dégarnir)* to have a receding hairline

calfater [kalfate] *vt Naut* to caulk

calfeutrer [kalføtre] **1** *vt* **(a)** *(brèches)* to block up **(b)** *(pièce, fenêtre)* to draft-proof
2 se calfeutrer *vpr (pour avoir chaud)* to make oneself snug; *(pour être seul)* to shut oneself away

calibre [kalibr] *nm* **(a)** *(d'arme à feu, de tuyau, de balle)* caliber; *(d'œufs, de fruits)* grade; *Fig* **sa sœur est d'un autre c.** his sister is of quite a different caliber **(b)** *(outil)* gauge **(c)** *très Fam (revolver)* shooter

calibrer [kalibre] *vt (pièce)* to gauge; *(instrument de mesure)* to calibrate; *Com (œufs, fruits)* to grade

calice[1] [kalis] *nm Rel* chalice; *Fig* **boire le c. jusqu'à la lie** to drain the cup to the dregs

calice[2] [kalis] *nm Bot* calyx

calife [kalif] *nm* caliph

Californie [kalifɔrni] *nf* **la C.** California

californien, -enne [kalifɔrnjɛ̃, -ɛn] **1** *adj* Californian
2 *nm,f* **C., Californienne** Californian

califourchon [kalifurʃɔ̃] **à califourchon** *adv* astride; **se mettre à c. sur qch** to sit astride sth

câlin, -e [kɑlɛ̃, -in] **1** *adj* affectionate
2 *nm* cuddle; **faire un c. à qn** to give sb a cuddle

câliner [kaline] *vt* to cuddle

calisson [kalisɔ̃] *nm* = lozenge-shaped candy made of marzipan

calleux, -euse [kalø, -øz] *adj* callous

call-girl (*pl* call-girls) [kolgœrl] *nf* call girl

calligramme [kaligram] *nm* calligram

calligraphe [kaligraf] *nmf* calligrapher

calligraphie [kaligrafi] *nf* calligraphy

calmant, -e [kalmã, -ãt] *Méd* **1** *adj (pour les nerfs)* sedative; *(pour la douleur)* painkilling
2 *nm (pour les nerfs)* sedative; *(pour la douleur)* painkiller; **sous calmants** under sedation

calmar [kalmar] *nm* squid

calme [kalm] **1** *adj* **(a)** *(personne) (qui garde son sang-froid)* calm; *(tranquille)* quiet **(b)** *(mer)* calm; *(ciel)* clear; **les affaires sont calmes en août** business is quiet in August
2 *nm (absence d'agitation)* calm, calmness; *(sang-froid)* composure; *(du paysage)* peace and quiet; **être au c.** to have peace and quiet; **du c.!** *(taisez-vous)* keep quiet!; *(ne vous affolez pas)* keep calm!; **garder/perdre son c.** to keep/to lose one's composure; *Naut* **c. plat** dead calm; **c'est le c. plat dans ma vie sentimentale** my love life is in the doldrums

calmement [kalməmã] *adv* calmly

calmer [kalme] **1** *vt (personne)* to calm (down); *(craintes)* to calm; *(douleur)* to soothe; *(fièvre)* to reduce; *(soif)* to quench; *(faim)* to appease; *(ardeur, passion)* to cool; *Fig* **c. le jeu** to calm things down
2 se calmer *vpr (personne)* to calm down; *(tempête, vent)* to die down; *(mer)* to become calm; *(pluie)* to ease off; *(douleur, fièvre)* to subside

calmos [kalmos] *exclam Fam* chill (out)!, take it easy!

calomnie [kalɔmni] *nf (en paroles)* slander; *(par écrit)* libel

calomnier [66] [kalɔmnje] *vt (en paroles)* to slander; *(par écrit)* to libel

calomnieux, -euse [kalɔmnjø, -øz] *adj (paroles)* slanderous; *(écrits)* libelous

calorie [kalɔri] *nf* calorie; **régime basses calories** low-calorie diet

calorifère [kalɔrifɛr] **1** *adj* heat-conveying
2 *nm Vieilli* (slow-combustion) stove; *Can* radiator

calorifique [kalɔrifik] *adj* calorific

calorifuge [kalɔrifyʒ] **1** *adj* (heat-)insulating
2 *nm* heat insulation; *(pour chaudière, tuyau)* lagging

calorique [kalɔrik] *adj* calorific

calot [kalo] *nm (coiffure militaire)* garrison cap

calotte [kalɔt] *nf* **(a)** *(chapeau rond)* skullcap; *Rel* calotte; *(de chapeau)* crown; *très Fam Péj* **la c.** (le clergé) the clergy **(b)** *Fam (gifle)* clout **(c)** *Anat* **c. crânienne** skullcap **(d)** *Géol* **c. glaciaire** ice cap

calque [kalk] *nm (copie)* tracing; *Fig (de poème, de portrait)* exact copy; *(traduction)* calque; **prendre un c. de qch** to make a tracing of sth; **(papier) c.** tracing paper

calquer [kalke] *vt (reproduire)* to trace; *Fig* to copy exactly; **expression calquée sur l'anglais** expression copied from the English; **il calque sa conduite sur celle de son frère** he models his behavior on his brother's

calumet [kalymɛ] *nm* peace pipe; *Fig* **fumer le c. de la paix** to bury the hatchet

calvados [kalvados] *nm* Calvados

calvaire [kalvɛr] *nm* **(a)** *(du Christ)* calvary; *Fig (épreuve pénible)* ordeal **(b)** *(croix)* calvary

calviniste [kalvinist] *adj & nmf* Calvinist

calvitie [kalvisi] *nf* baldness; **avoir un début de c.** to be starting to go bald; **c. précoce** premature baldness

camaïeu, -x [kamajø] *nm (peinture)* monochrome; *(gravure)* tint drawing; **un c. de bleu** *(papiers peints, vêtements)* different shades of blue

camarade [kamarad] *nmf* friend; *Pol (terme d'adresse)* comrade; **c. de chambre** roommate *(at university, college)*; **c. de classe** classmate; **c. d'école** school friend

camaraderie [kamaradri] *nf* camaraderie

camber [kãbe] *vt Suisse* to stride over

cambiste [kãbist] *nmf Fin* foreign-exchange dealer

Cambodge [kãbɔdʒ] *nm* **le C.** Cambodia

cambodgien, -enne [kãbɔdʒjɛ̃, -ɛn] **1** *adj* Cambodian
2 *nm,f* **C., Cambodgienne** Cambodian

cambouis [kãbwi] *nm* dirty oil

cambré, -e [kãbre] *adj (pied)* with a high instep; *(personne)* with an arched back

cambrer [kãbre] **1** *vt (dos, pied)* to arch; **c. la taille** *ou* **les reins** to arch one's back
2 se cambrer *vpr* to arch one's back

cambrien, -enne [kãbrijɛ̃, -ɛn] *Géol* **1** *adj* Cambrian
2 *nm* **le C.** the Cambrian period

cambriolage [kãbrijolaʒ] *nm* burglary, break-in

cambrioler [kãbrijole] *vt (maison, personne)* to burglarize

cambrioleur, -euse [kãbrijolœr, -øz] *nm,f* burglar

cambrousse [kãbrus], **cambrouse** [kãbruz] *nf Fam*

country; **en pleine c.** in the middle of nowhere

cambrure [kãbryr] *nf (du pied, du dos)* arch; **c. des reins** small of the back

cambuse [kãbyz] *nf* (a) *Naut* storeroom (b) *Fam Vieilli (chambre, maison)* dump

came¹ [kam] *nf Tech* cam

came² [kam] *nf très Fam (drogue)* dope

camé, -e¹ [kame] *très Fam* **1** *adj* high
2 *nm,f* junkie

camée² [kame] *nm* cameo

caméléon [kameleõ] *nm aussi Fig* chameleon

camélia [kamelja] *nm* camellia

camelote [kamlɔt] *nf Fam* (a) *(pacotille)* junk (b) *(marchandise)* stuff

camembert [kamãbɛr] *nm* (a) *(fromage)* Camembert (b) *(diagramme)* pie chart

camer [kame] **se camer** *vpr très Fam* to do drugs; **se c. à l'héroïne** to do heroin

caméra [kamera] *nf Cin & TV* camera; **c. cachée** *ou* **invisible** *(émission)* candid camera; **c. de télévision** television camera; **c. infrarouge** infrared camera; **c. Internet** webcam; **c. numérique** digicam; **c. vidéo** video camera

cameraman [kameraman] *(pl* **cameramans** *ou* **cameramen** [kameramɛn]*) nm Cin & TV* cameraman

Cameroun [kamrun] *nm* **le C.** Cameroon

camerounais, -e [kamrunɛ, -ɛz] **1** *adj* Cameroonian
2 *nm,f* **C., Camerounaise** Cameroonian

Caméscope® [kameskɔp] *nm* camcorder

camion [kamjõ] *nm* truck; **c. à benne** dump truck; **c. de déménagement** moving van; **c. de dépannage** tow truck, wrecker; **c. frigorifique** *ou* **réfrigéré** refrigerated truck

camion-benne *(pl* **camions-bennes)** [kamjõbɛn] *nm* dumper truck

camion-citerne *(pl* **camions-citernes)** [kamjõsitɛrn] *nm* tanker

camionnette [kamjɔnɛt] *nf* van; **c. de livraison** delivery van

camionneur [kamjɔnœr] *nm* (a) *(conducteur)* truck driver (b) *(transporteur)* trucker

camisole [kamizɔl] *nf* (a) *Can (tricot de corps)* undershirt (b) *(chemise de nuit)* nightshirt (c) **c. de force** straitjacket

camomille [kamɔmij] *nf* camomile; *(tisane)* camomile tea

camouflage [kamuflaʒ] *nm Mil* camouflage; *(de la vérité, d'intentions)* disguising; *(de bénéfices)* concealment

camoufler [kamufle] **1** *vt Mil* to camouflage; *(vérité, intentions)* to disguise; *(bénéfices)* to conceal; **c. un meurtre en suicide** to make a murder look like suicide
2 **se camoufler** *vpr* to camouflage oneself

camp [kã] *nm* (a) *(campement)* camp; **établir un c.** to pitch camp; **lever le c.** to strike camp; *Fam Fig (partir)* to hit the road; **c. (de vacances)** summer camp; **c. de concentration** concentration camp; **c. de loisirs** vacation camp; **c. de prisonniers** prison camp; **c. de réfugiés** refugee camp (b) *(parti)* camp, side (c) *(de jeux)* side; **faire deux camps** to form two teams

campagnard, -e [kãpaɲar, -ard] *adj* country

campagne [kãpaɲ] *nf* (a) *(par opposition à la ville)* country; *(paysage)* countryside; **à la c.** in the country; **en pleine c.** deep in the countryside; **en rase c.** in the open country (b) *Mil, Pol & Com* campaign; *Pol* **entrer en c.** to go on the campaign trail; **faire c. pour/contre** to campaign for/against; **partir en c. contre le tabac** to launch an anti-smoking campaign; **c. électorale** election campaign; **c. de presse** press campaign; **c. publicitaire** *ou* **de publicité** advertising campaign

campanile [kãpanil] *nm Archit* bell tower

campanule [kãpanyl] *nf* campanula

campement [kãpmã] *nm (installation)* camp; *(lieu)* camping place; **établir un c.** to pitch camp

camper [kãpe] **1** *vi* (a) *(faire du camping)* to camp (b) *Fig (chez quelqu'un)* to camp out
2 *vt* (a) *Vieilli* **c. son chapeau sur sa tête** to plant one's hat on one's head (b) *(décrire)* to put in context; **c. un personnage** *(sujet: acteur)* to play a part effectively
3 **se camper** *vpr* **se c. devant qn** to plant oneself in front of sb

campeur, -euse [kãpœr, -øz] *nm,f* camper

camphre [kãfr] *nm* camphor

camphré, -e [kãfre] *adj* camphorated

camping [kãpiŋ] *nm* (a) *(activité)* camping; **faire du c.** to go camping; **c. à la ferme** farm camping; **c. sauvage** unauthorized camping (b) *(lieu)* camp site; **c. aménagé** camp site with facilities

camping-car *(pl* **camping-cars)** [kãpiŋkar] *nm* camper

camping-caravaning [kãpiŋkaravaniŋ] *nm* camping-caravanning

Camping-Gaz® [kãpiŋgaz] *nm inv* camping stove

campus [kãpys] *nm* campus; **habiter sur le c.** to live on campus

camus [kamy] *adj m (nez)* flat

Canada [kanada] *nm* **le C.** Canada

Canadair® [kanadɛr] *nm* fire-fighting plane

canadianisme [kanadjanism] *nm Ling* Canadianism

canadien, -enne [kanadjɛ̃, -ɛn] **1** *adj* Canadian
2 *nm,f* **C., Canadienne** Canadian
3 *nf* **canadienne** *(veste)* sheepskin jacket; *(tente)* ridge tent

canaille [kanaj] **1** *adj (chanson, paroles)* vulgar; *(air)* roguish
2 *nf (crapule)* scoundrel; **petite c.!** *(à un enfant)* you little devil!

canal, -aux [kanal, -o] *nm* (a) *(cours d'eau)* canal; **c. d'irrigation** irrigation canal; **le c. de Panama/de Suez** the Panama/Suez Canal (b) *(conduite)* conduit (c) *Anat & Bot* duct (d) *Rad & TV* channel; *TV* **C.+** = French pay-television channel (e) *Fig (moyen)* channel; **par le c. de la poste** through the mail (f) *Com* channel; **c. de distribution** distribution channel

> ### Canal+
>
> Canal+, France's first private television channel, was established in 1982 and started broadcasting in 1984. It broadcasts programs that have to be unscrambled using a special decoding unit, although for part of the day its programs can be seen without this device. Canal+ also plays a prominent role in funding international films.

canalisation [kanalizasjõ] *nf* (a) *(conduite)* pipe; *(pour pétrole)* pipeline (b) *(de rivière)* canalization

canaliser [kanalize] *vt* (a) *(région, rivière)* to canalize (b) *(énergie)* to channel; *(trafic, foule)* to direct

canapé [kanape] *nm* (a) *(meuble)* sofa, couch; **c. convertible** sofa bed; **c. deux places** two-seater sofa (b) *(pour l'apéritif)* canapé

canapé-lit *(pl* **canapés-lits)** [kanapeli] *nm* sofa bed

canaque [kanak] **1** *adj* Kanak *(of New Caledonia)*
2 *nmf* **C.** Kanak *(from New Caledonia)*

canard [kanar] *nm* (a) *(oiseau)* duck; *(mâle)* drake; *Fam* **mon petit c.** my pet; **marcher en c.** to walk with one's feet turned out; **c. laqué** Peking duck; **c. à l'orange** duck à l'orange; **c. sauvage** wild duck (b) *Fam (journal)* rag (c) *(morceau de sucre)* = sugar lump dipped in coffee or alcoholic drink (d) *Mus* false note (e) *Can (bouilloire)* kettle

canarder [kanarde] *vt Fam* to snipe at

canari [kanari] *nm* canary

Canaries [kanari] *nfpl* **les (îles) C.** the Canary Islands

canasson [kanasõ] *nm Fam (cheval)* nag

cancan [kãkã] *nm* (a) **cancans** *(ragots)* gossip (**sur** about) (**b**) *(danse)* cancan

cancaner [kãkane] *vi* (a) *(médire)* to gossip (**sur** about) (**b**) *(canard)* to quack

cancanier, -ère [kãkanje, -ɛr] *Fam* **1** *adj* gossipy
   2 *nm,f* gossip

cancer [kãser] *nm* (a) *Méd & Fig* cancer; **c. du poumon/du sein** lung/breast cancer; **avoir un c.** to have cancer (**b**) *Astron & Astrol* **le C.** Cancer; **être C.** to be (a) Cancer

cancéreux, -euse [kãserø, -øz] **1** *adj (tumeur)* cancerous
   2 *nm,f* cancer sufferer

cancérigène [kãserizɛn] *adj* carcinogenic; **produit c.** carcinogen

cancérologie [kãserɔlɔʒi] *nf* cancerology

cancérologue [kãserɔlɔg] *nmf* cancer specialist

cancre [kãkr] *nm Fam* dunce

cancrelat [kãkrəla] *nm* cockroach

candélabre [kãdelabr] *nm (chandelier)* candelabra

candeur [kãdœr] *nf* guilelessness; **un regard plein de c.** a guileless look

candi [kãdi] *adj m voir* **sucre**

candidat, -e [kãdida, -at] *nm,f (à un poste)* applicant (**à** for); *(à un examen)* candidate (**à** for); **être c. aux élections** to run for election

candidature [kãdidatyr] *nf (aux élections)* candidacy; *(à un poste)* application (**à** for); **poser sa c. à un poste** to apply for a position; **c. spontanée** unsolicited application

candide [kãdid] *adj* guileless

candidement [kãdidmã] *adv* guilelessly

candidose [kãdidoz] *nf Méd* candidiasis

cane [kan] *nf (female) duck*

caneton [kantɔ̃] *nm* (male) duckling

canette¹ [kanɛt] *nf (petite cane)* (female) duckling

canette² [kanɛt] = **cannette**

canevas [kanva] *nm* (a) *(trame)* canvas (**b**) *(de film, de roman)* outline

caniche [kaniʃ] *nm* poodle

caniculaire [kanikylɛr] *adj (temps)* baking, scorching

canicule [kanikyl] *nf* heatwave

canif [kanif] *nm* penknife

canin, -e [kanɛ̃, -in] **1** *adj* canine; **exposition canine** dog show
   2 *nf* **canine** canine (tooth)

caniveau, -x [kanivo] *nm* gutter

cannabis [kanabis] *nm* cannabis

cannage [kanaʒ] *nm (partie en rotin)* canework

canne [kan] *nf* (a) *(tige)* cane; **c. à pêche** fishing rod; **c. à sucre** sugar cane (**b**) *(pour s'appuyer)* (walking) stick, cane; **c. blanche** white cane (**c**) *très Fam (jambe)* leg (**d**) *Suisse (au hockey sur glace)* hockey stick

canné, -e [kane] *adj (chaise)* cane

canneberge [kanbɛrʒ] *nf* cranberry

cannelé, -e [kanle] *adj (colonne)* fluted; *(pneu)* grooved

cannelle [kanɛl] *nf* cinnamon; **bâton de c.** cinnamon stick; **à la c.** cinnamon(-flavored)

cannelloni [kanɛlɔni] *nmpl* cannelloni

cannelure [kanlyr] *nf (rainure)* groove; *(de colonne)* fluting

cannette [kanɛt] *nf* (a) *(petite bouteille)* bottle; *(boîte)* can (**b**) *Tex* spool

cannibale [kanibal] **1** *nmf* cannibal
   2 *adj (pratiques)* cannibalistic; **tribu c.** tribe of cannibals

cannibalisme [kanibalism] *nm* cannibalism

canoë [kanɔe] *nm* canoe; **faire du c.** to go canoeing

canoë-kayak [kanɔekajak] *nm* canoeing

canon¹ [kanɔ̃] *nm* (a) *(pièce d'artillerie)* gun; *Hist* cannon (**b**) *(de carabine)* barrel (**c**) *Anciennement (mesure)* wine measure, $\simeq$ 1.7 fluid ounces; *Fam* **boire un c.** to have a glass of wine

canon² [kanɔ̃] **1** *nm* (a) *Rel & Fig (règle)* canon (**b**) *Mus* canon; **c. à deux/trois voix** canon for two/three voices; **chanter qch en c.** to sing sth in canon (**c**) *Fam (personne)* babe
   2 *adj inv Fam (beau)* gorgeous

canonique [kanɔnik] *adj* canonical; *Fig* **être d'un âge c.** to be advanced in years

canoniser [kanɔnize] *vt Rel* to canonize

canonnade [kanɔnad] *nf* gunfire; **une c.** a burst of gunfire

canot [kano] *nm Naut* (a) *(petit bateau)* boat; **c. pneumatique** rubber dinghy; **c. de sauvetage** lifeboat (**b**) *Can (canoë)* canoe

canotage [kanɔtaʒ] *nm* boating; *Can (en canoë)* canoeing; **faire du c.** to go boating/canoeing

canoter [kanɔte] *vi Naut* to go boating; *Can (en canoë)* to go canoeing

canotier [kanɔtje] *nm* (a) *(rameur)* rower (**b**) *(chapeau)* boater

cantal, -als [kãtal] *nm* Cantal

cantate [kãtat] *nf* cantata

cantatrice [kãtatris] *nf (chanteuse d'opéra)* opera singer; *(de concert)* (concert) singer

cantine [kãtin] *nf* (a) *(réfectoire)* cafeteria; **déjeuner à la c.** *(de l'école)* to have school meals (**b**) *(malle)* trunk (**c**) *Suisse (boîte)* lunchbox (**d**) *Suisse (tente)* marquee

cantique [kãtik] *nm Rel* hymn; **le C. des cantiques** the Song of Solomon

canton [kãtɔ̃] *nm (en France)* canton *(administrative division of a department)*; *(en Suisse)* canton *(semi-autonomous administrative region of Switzerland)*; *Can* **les cantons de l'Est** the Eastern Townships

cantonade [kãtonad] **à la cantonade** *adv* to everybody present; *(au théâtre)* off

cantonais, -e [kãtonɛ, -ɛz] **1** *adj* Cantonese
   2 *nm (langue)* Cantonese
   3 *nm,f* **C., Cantonaise** Cantonese

cantonal, -e, -aux, -ales [kãtonal, -o] *adj* cantonal; **les (élections) cantonales** the cantonal elections

cantonnement [kãtonmã] *nm Mil (des troupes)* quartering; *(lieu)* quarters

cantonner [kãtone] **1** *vt* (a) *Mil (troupes)* to billet (**b**) **c. qn dans/à** to confine sb to
   2 se cantonner *vpr (se limiter)* **se c. dans/à** to confine oneself to

cantonnier [kãtonje] *nm* roadman; *Rail* trackman

canular [kanylar] *nm Fam* hoax; **monter un c.** to play a hoax

canule [kanyl] *nf Méd* cannula

canyon [kanjɔn] *nm* canyon; **le Grand C.** the Grand Canyon

canyoning [kanjɔniŋ] *nm* canyoning

canyoniste [kanjɔnist] *nmf* canyoner

CAO [seao] *nf Ordinat (abrév* **conception assistée par ordinateur***)* CAD

caoutchouc [kautʃu] *nm* (a) *(substance)* rubber; **c. Mousse®** foam rubber; **c. synthétique** synthetic rubber (**b**) *(plante)* rubber plant

caoutchouteux, -euse [kautʃutø, -øz] *adj Péj* rubbery

CAP [seape] *nm (abrév* **certificat d'aptitude professionnelle***)* = vocational training certificate

Cap [kap] *voir* **Le Cap**

cap [kap] *nm* (a) *Géog* cape, headland; **passer** *ou* **franchir** *ou* **doubler un c.** to round a cape; **quand on a franchi le c. de la quarantaine** when you've turned forty; **notre usine va passer le c. des mille employés** our factory will soon pass the thousand-employee mark; **le c. de Bonne-Espérance** the Cape of Good Hope; **le c. Horn** Cape Horn (**b**) *Naut & Aviat (direction)* course; **mettre le c. sur…** to set course for…

capable [kapabl] *adj* (a) *(susceptible)* **être c. de qch** to be capable of sth; **être c. de faire qch** to be capable of doing sth, to be able to do sth; **il est c. de tout** he's capable of anything; **c.**

du meilleur comme du pire capable of the best as well as the worst; **elle est bien c. d'oublier les clefs!** she's quite capable of forgetting the keys! (**b**) *(compétent)* capable, able (**c**) *Jur* competent (**de faire** to do)

capacité [kapasite] *nf* (**a**) *(contenance)* capacity; **c. d'accueil** *(d'un hôtel)* accommodation capacity (**b**) *(aptitude)* ability, capability; **de grandes capacités (intellectuelles)** great intellectual abilities; *Ordinat* **c. d'adressage** address capability; **c. de concentration** attention span; *Ordinat* **c. de mémoire** memory capacity (**c**) *Jur* capacity; **avoir c. pour faire qch** to be (legally) entitled to do sth (**d**) *Univ* **c. en droit** = certificate entitling the holder to practice in some branches of the legal profession

cape [kap] *nf (vêtement)* cape; *(plus longue)* cloak; **film/roman de c. et d'épée** swashbuckling movie/novel; *Fig* **rire sous c.** to laugh up one's sleeve

capeline [kaplin] *nf (chapeau)* floppy hat

CAPES [kapɛs] *nm (abrév* **certificat d'aptitude au professorat de l'enseignement du second degré)** = postgraduate teaching certificate

> **CAPES**
>
> This is a required qualification for state teachers in France. Candidates who pass this competitive exam become "professeurs certifiés" and are entitled to teach in high schools.

CAPET [kapɛt] *nm (abrév* **certificat d'aptitude au professorat de l'enseignement technique)** = postgraduate technical teaching certificate

capétien, -enne [kapesjɛ̃, -ɛn] **1** *adj* Capetian
2 *nmpl* **les Capétiens** the Capetians

capharnaüm [kafarnaɔm] *nm Fam (pièce en désordre)* pigsty; *(désordre)* mess

capillaire [kapilɛr] **1** *adj* capillary
2 *nm* (**a**) *(plante)* maidenhair (fern) (**b**) *Anat* capillary

capillarité [kapilarite] *nf Phys* capillarity

capilotade [kapilɔtad] **en capilotade** *adv* **j'ai le dos en c.** my back's killing me

capitaine [kapitɛn] *nm* (**a**) *Mil & Naut* captain; *Aviat* captain; **c. de gendarmerie** police superintendent; **c. des pompiers** fire chief; **c. de port** harbor master (**b**) *Sport* captain

capitainerie [kapitɛnri] *nf* harbor master's office

capital, -e, -aux, -ales [kapital, -o] **1** *adj* (**a**) *(essentiel)* major; **il est c. qu'il soit présent à la réunion** it is essential for him to be at the meeting (**b**) *Typ* **lettre capitale** capital letter
2 *nm Fin* capital; *Fig (culturel, artistique)* wealth; **posséder un c.** to have some capital; **capitaux propres** equity; **c. social** (issued) share capital
3 *nf* **capitale** (**a**) *(ville)* capital (city) (**b**) *Typ* capital; **écrire en capitales d'imprimerie** to write in block letters

capitalisable [kapitalizabl] *adj (intérêts)* capitalizable

capitalisation [kapitalizasjɔ̃] *nf (d'intérêts)* capitalization

capitaliser [kapitalize] **1** *vt (intérêts)* to capitalize
2 *vi* (**a**) *Fin* to save (**b**) **c. sur qch** *(jouer sur)* to capitalize on sth

capitalisme [kapitalism] *nm* capitalism; **c. sauvage** ruthless capitalism

capitaliste [kapitalist] *adj & nmf* capitalist

capite [kapit] *nf Suisse (dans un vignoble, un jardin)* shed

capiteux, -euse [kapitø, -øz] *adj (vin, parfum)* heady; *(charme)* sensuous; *(femme)* alluring

capitonnage [kapitɔnaʒ] *nm (action, matière)* padding, stuffing

capitonné, -e [kapitɔne] *adj (siège, cellule)* padded

capitulation [kapitylasjɔ̃] *nf* surrender; **c. sans conditions** unconditional surrender

capituler [kapityle] *vi* to surrender

caporal, -aux [kapɔral, -o] *nm Mil* private first class

capot[1] [kapo] *nm Aut* hood; *Aviat (de moteur d'avion)* cowl; *Naut (bâche)* tarpaulin; *Ordinat* **c. d'imprimante** printer hood

capot[2] [kapo] *adj inv* **être c.** *(aux cartes)* to have made no tricks at all

capote [kapɔt] *nf* (**a**) *Aut (de décapotable)* top; **baisser la c.** to put the hood down (**b**) *Mil (manteau)* greatcoat (**c**) *Fam* **c. (anglaise)** rubber, condom

capoté, -e [kapɔte] *adj Can Fam* annoyed

capoter [kapɔte] *vi Naut* to capsize; *Aut & Aviat* to overturn; *Fig (échouer) (projet)* to fall through

cappuccino [kaputʃino] *nm* cappuccino

câpre [kɑpr] *nf* caper

caprice [kapris] *nm* (**a**) *(fantaisie)* whim, caprice; **on lui passe tous ses caprices** they indulge his/her every whim; **par un c. du destin** by a whim of fate (**b**) *(crise de colère)* tantrum; **faire un c.** to throw a tantrum

capricieux, -euse [kaprisjø, -øz] *adj (personne, courant, vent)* capricious; *(moteur)* temperamental; *(temps)* changeable

capricorne [kaprikɔrn] *nm* (**a**) *(insecte)* capricorn beetle (**b**) *Astron & Astrol* **le C.** Capricorn; **être C.** to be (a) Capricorn

caprin, -e [kaprɛ̃, -in] *adj Zool* goat, *Spéc* caprine

capsule [kapsyl] *nf* (**a**) *Anat, Bot & Méd* capsule (**b**) *(de bouteille)* cap, top (**c**) **c. (spatiale)** (space) capsule

capter [kapte] *vt* (**a**) *(l'attention de quelqu'un)* to gain, to capture (**b**) *(courant électrique)* to pick up; *(eaux)* to harness (**c**) *Rad & Tél (messages, station)* to pick up

capteur [kaptœr] *nm Phys* sensor; *Ordinat* **c. photosensible** photosensitive sensor; **c. solaire** solar panel

captif, -ive [kaptif, -iv] *adj & nm, f* captive

captivant, -e [kaptivɑ̃, -ɑ̃t] *adj* captivating

captiver [kaptive] *vt* to captivate

captivité [kaptivite] *nf* captivity; **en c.** in captivity

capture [kaptyr] *nf* (**a**) *(d'un ennemi, d'un animal)* capture (**b**) *(proie)* catch (**c**) *Ordinat* **c. vidéo** video capture

capturer [kaptyre] *vt* to capture

capuche [kapyʃ] *nf* hood; *(de poche)* rainhood; **un sweat-shirt à c.** a hooded sweatshirt

capuchon [kapyʃɔ̃] *nm* (**a**) *(de manteau)* hood; *(de moine)* cowl (**b**) *(de stylo, de tube de dentifrice)* cap, top; *(de cheminée)* cowl

capucine [kapysin] *nf* nasturtium

capverdien, -enne [kapvɛrdjɛ̃, -ɛn] **1** *adj* of Cape Verde
2 *nm, f* **C., Capverdienne** = person from Cape Verde

Cap-Vert [kapvɛr] *nm* **le C., les îles du C.** Cape Verde

caquelon [kaklɔ̃] *nm* fondue dish

caquet [kakɛ] *nm* (**a**) *(de poules)* cackle (**b**) *Fam (bavardage)* chatter, prattle; **quel c. elle a!** does she ever stop chattering?; **rabattre** *ou* **rabaisser le c. à qn** to shut sb up

caqueter [42] [kakte] *vi* (**a**) *(poule)* to cackle (**b**) *Fam (bavarder)* to prattle

car[1] [kar] *conj* for, because

car[2] [kar] *nm (véhicule)* bus; **c. de police** police van; **c. de ramassage scolaire** school bus

carabine [karabin] *nf* rifle; **c. à air comprimé** BB gun

carabiné, -e [karabine] *adj Fam (vent)* stiff; *(orage, fièvre)* violent; *(rhume)* stinking

carabinier [karabinje] *nm* (**a**) *(en Espagne)* frontier guard (**b**) *(en Italie)* carabiniere (**c**) *Hist* carabineer

Caracas [karakas] *n* Caracas

caraco [karako] *nm* camisole

caracoler [karakɔle] *vi (cheval)* to caracole; *Fam (sautiller)* to prance about; **c. en tête des sondages** to be riding high in the opinion polls

caractère [karaktɛr] *nm* **(a)** *(nature)* character, nature; *(détermination, style)* character; **avoir du c.** to have character; **avoir bon c.** to be good-natured; **avoir mauvais** *ou* **sale c.** to be bad-tempered; *Fam* **avoir un c. de cochon** to have a foul temper; **ce n'est pas dans son c. de…** it's not in his/her nature to…

(b) *(attribut)* characteristic, feature; *(aspect)* nature, character; **publication à c. officiel** publication of an official nature; *Biol* **c. héréditaire/acquis** hereditary/acquired characteristic

(c) *(signe)* character, letter; *Typ* **caractères** *(en métal)* type; **en petits caractères** in small print; **écrivez en caractères d'imprimerie** *(sur formulaire)* write in block letters

(d) *Ordinat* character; **c. de changement de ligne** line feed character; **c. de changement de page** page break character; **c. de contrôle** control character; **c. d'effacement** delete character; **c. imprimable** printable character; **c. d'interruption** break character; **c. en mode point** bitmap character; **c. de retour arrière** backspace character; **c. à sept bits** seven-bit character

caractériel, -elle [karakterjɛl] *Psy* **1** *adj (troubles)* emotional; **enfant c.** problem child

2 *nm,f* emotionally disturbed person; *(enfant)* problem child

caractérisé, -e [karakterize] *adj* **une rougeole caractérisée** a clear case of measles; **c'est de la méchanceté caractérisée** it's sheer spite

caractériser [karakterize] **1** *vt* to characterize; **avec la bonté qui la caractérise, elle…** with characteristic kindness, she…

2 se caractériser *vpr* **se c. par** to be characterized by

caractéristique [karakteristik] **1** *adj* characteristic (**de** of)

2 *nf (particularité)* characteristic, feature; **caractéristiques** *(d'une voiture, d'un avion)* specifications

carafe [karaf] *nf* **(a)** *(pour le vin, l'eau)* carafe, pitcher; *(pour le whisky)* decanter **(b)** *Fam* **rester en c.** to be (left) stranded

carafon [karafɔ̃] *nm (pour le vin)* small carafe or pitcher; *(pour le whisky)* small decanter

Caraïbes [karaib] *nfpl* **les C.** the Caribbean

carambolage [karɑ̃bɔlaʒ] *nm* (multiple) pile-up

caramboler [karɑ̃bɔle] **se caramboler** *vpr Fam* to collide

caramel [karamɛl] *nm (sucre brûlé)* caramel; **des caramels** *(mous)* fudge; *(durs)* taffy

caraméliser [karamelize] **1** *vt* **(a)** *(sucre)* to caramelize **(b)** *(mets, moule)* to coat with caramel

2 *vi* to caramelize

3 se caraméliser *vpr (sucre, oignons)* to caramelize

carapace [karapas] *nf aussi Fig* shell

carapater [karapate] **se carapater** *vpr Fam* to beat it

carat [kara] *nm (or, carat)*; **or (à) 18 carats** 18-carat gold; *Fam* **tu as jusqu'à trois heures, dernier c.** you've got until three o'clock at the latest

caravanage [karavanaʒ] = **caravaning**

caravane [karavan] *nf* **(a)** *(de tourisme)* trailer **(b)** *(du désert)* caravan

caravaning [karavaniŋ] *nm* **faire du c.** to go trailering

carbonate [karbɔnat] *nm Chim* carbonate; **c. de soude** sodium carbonate; *(dans le commerce)* washing soda

carbone [karbɔn] *nm Chim* carbon; **c. 14** carbon-14; **datation au c. 14** carbon dating; **(papier) c.** carbon (paper)

carbonique [karbɔnik] *adj* carbonic; **gaz c.** carbon dioxide; **neige c.** dry ice

carbonisé, -e [karbɔnize] *adj (nourriture)* burnt to a cinder; *(corps)* charred; **mourir c.** to burn to death

carburant [karbyrɑ̃] *nm* fuel

carburateur [karbyratœr] *nm Aut* carburetor

carbure [karbyr] *nm Chim* carbide; **c. d'hydrogène** hydrogen carbide

carburer [karbyre] *vi* **(a)** *(moteur)* **mal c.** to be badly tuned **(b)** *Fam* **ça carbure ici** everyone here's working like mad; **il carbure au café** coffee keeps him going

carcajou [karkaʒu] *nm* wolverine

carcan [karkɑ̃] *nm Fig* yoke; **le c. des horaires** scheduling constraints; **le c. des conventions** the straitjacket of convention

carcasse [karkas] *nf* **(a)** *(d'animal mort)* carcass; *Fam (de personne)* body **(b)** *(de maison, de bateau)* shell; **à c. radiale** *(pneu)* radial-ply

carcéral, -e, -aux, -ales [karseral, -o] *adj* prison

carcinogène [karsinɔʒɛn] *adj Méd* carcinogenic

cardan [kardɑ̃] *nm* universal joint

carder [karde] *vt* to card

cardiaque [kardjak] **1** *adj (arrêt, massage)* cardiac; **être c.** to have a heart condition

2 *nmf* person with a heart condition

cardigan [kardigɑ̃] *nm* cardigan

cardinal, -e, -aux, -ales [kardinal, -o] **1** *adj (point, nombre, vertu)* cardinal

2 *nm (religieux)* cardinal

cardiologie [kardjɔlɔʒi] *nf* cardiology

cardiologue [kardjɔlɔg] *nmf* cardiologist

cardio-training [kardjotrɛniŋ] *nm* cardio-training, CV training

cardio-vasculaire *(pl* **cardio-vasculaires)** [kardjɔvaskylɛr] *adj* cardiovascular

carême [karɛm] *nm* **(a)** *(période)* **le c.** Lent **(b)** *(jeûne)* fast; **faire c.** to fast

carence [karɑ̃s] *nf (manque)* deficiency; **c. en vitamine B** vitamin B deficiency; **c. alimentaire** nutritional deficiency; **c. affective** emotional deprivation

carène [karɛn] *nf* hull

caréner [34] [karene] *vt* **(a)** *Naut* to careen **(b)** *Aviat & Aut* to streamline

caressant, -e [karɛsɑ̃, -ɑ̃t] *adj* affectionate; **d'une voix caressante** affectionately

caresse [karɛs] *nf* caress; **faire des caresses à** *(personne)* to caress; *(animal)* to stroke

caresser [karese] *vt (personne)* to caress; *(animal)* to stroke; *Fig (espoir, rêve)* to cherish

car-ferry *(pl* **car-ferrys)** [karferi] *nm* car ferry

cargaison [kargɛzɔ̃] *nf* cargo; *Fam* **il est arrivé avec une c. de cadeaux** he arrived weighed down with presents

cargo [kargo] *nm Naut* freighter

cariatide [karjatid] *nf* caryatid

caribou [karibu] *nm* caribou

caricatural, -e, -aux, -ales [karikatyral, -o] *adj (récit, description)* caricatured

caricature [karikatyr] *nf* caricature

caricaturer [karikatyre] *vt* to caricature

caricaturiste [karikatyrist] *nmf* caricaturist

caricole [karikɔl] *nf Belg* periwinkle

carie [kari] *nf* **c. (dentaire)** tooth decay, *Spéc* dental caries; **avoir une c.** to have a cavity

carié, -e [karje] *adj* decayed

carier [66] [karje] **se carier** *vpr* to rot, to decay

carillon [karijɔ̃] *nm* **(a)** *(sonnerie)* chimes; **c. électrique** doorbell **(b)** *(ensemble de cloches)* bells **(c)** *(horloge)* chiming clock

carillonner [karijɔne] **1** *vi (cloches)* to chime; **c. à la porte** to ring the (door)bell loudly

2 *vt (air)* to chime; *(fête religieuse)* to announce with a peal of bells

carioca [karjɔka] **1** *adj* of Rio de Janeiro

2 *nmf* **C.** person from Rio de Janeiro

caritatif, -ive [karitatif, -iv] *adj* charitable; **association caritative** charity

carlingue [karlɛ̃g] *nf* (**a**) *Aviat* cabin (**b**) *Naut* keelson

carmélite [karmelit] *nf* Carmelite (nun)

carmin [karmɛ̃] **1** *nm* carmine
2 *adj inv* (**rouge**) **c.** carmine, crimson

carnage [karnaʒ] *nm* carnage

carnassier, -ère [karnasje, -ɛr] **1** *adj (animal)* flesh-eating; *Fig (sourire)* cruel
2 *nm* carnivore

carnaval, -als [karnaval] *nm* carnival; **un masque de c.** a carnival mask

carnet [karnɛ] *nm* (**a**) *(cahier)* notebook; *(de tickets de métro)* = book of ten tickets; *Scol* **c. (de notes)** report card; **c. d'adresses** address book; **c. de chèques** checkbook; *Scol* **c. de correspondance** = book of forms to be completed by parents of schoolchildren in the event of absence; *Journ* **c. mondain** society column; *Journ* **c. rose** births column; **c. de santé** health record; **c. de timbres** book of stamps (**b**) *Fin* **c. de banque** bankbook; *Belg & Suisse* **c. d'épargne** *(livret d'épargne)* savings account

carnivore [karnivɔr] **1** *adj (animal)* carnivorous
2 *nm* carnivore

Caroline [karɔlin] *nf* **la C. du Nord/du Sud** North/South Carolina

carolingien, -enne [karɔlɛ̃ʒjɛ̃, -ɛn] **1** *adj* Carolingian
2 *nmpl* **les Carolingiens** the Carolingians

carotène [karɔtɛn] *nm* carotene

carotide [karɔtid] *nf* carotid

carotte [karɔt] **1** *nf* (**a**) *(légume)* carrot; *Suisse* **c. rouge** beet; **la c. et** *ou* **ou le bâton** the carrot and the stick; *Fam* **les carottes sont cuites** you've/he's/*etc.* had it (**b**) *(enseigne)* tobacconist's sign
2 *adj inv* **cheveux (roux) c.** carroty hair

carotter [karɔte] *vt Fam (objet, argent)* to filch; **il m'a carotté 50 euros** he finagled me out of 50 euros

caroube [karub] *nf* carob (bean)

Carpates [karpat] *nfpl* **les C.** the Carpathians

carpe¹ [karp] *nm Anat* carpus

carpe² [karp] *nf* carp

carpette [karpɛt] *nf* rug; *Fam Péj* **c'est une vraie c.** he's a real doormat

carquois [karkwa] *nm* quiver

carre [kar] *nf (de patin, de ski)* edge

carré, -e [kare] **1** *adj* (**a**) *(figure, jardin, visage)* square; *(épaules)* square, broad (**b**) *Math* **10 mètres carrés** ≃ 32 square feet (**c**) *(tranché)* *(personne)* straightforward; **être c. en affaires** to be straightforward in one's business dealings
2 *nm* (**a**) *(forme)* square; *Can (place)* (public) square; **c. de soie** silk scarf; *Naut* **c. des officiers** wardroom; **c. de valets** *(aux cartes)* four jacks; **avoir une coupe au c.** *ou* **un c.** to wear one's hair in a bob; *Fam* **faire la tête au c. à qn** to smash sb's face in (**b**) *Math (d'un nombre)* square; **élever au c.** to square; **le c. de six, six au c.** six squared (**c**) *Culin* **c. d'agneau** rack of lamb

carreau, -x [karo] *nm* (**a**) *(motif)* square; *(sur du tissu)* check; **tissu à carreaux** check(ed) material (**b**) *(de céramique)* tile (**c**) *(vitre)* (window) pane; *Fam* **carreaux** *(lunettes)* specs, glasses (**d**) *(carte)* diamond; *(couleur)* diamonds; *Fam* **se tenir à c.** to keep a low profile (**e**) *(locutions)* *Fam* **rester sur le c.** *(être tué)* to get killed; *(être blessé)* to be badly injured; *(être éliminé)* to get the boot

carreauté, -e [karote] *adj Can (chemise)* check(ed)

carrefour [karfur] *nm* (**a**) *(croisement)* intersection; *Fig* **être à un c.** to be at a crossroads (**b**) *(réunion)* forum

carrelage [karlaʒ] *nm (carreaux)* tiles; *(sol)* (tiled) floor

carreler [9] [karle] *vt* to tile

carrelet [karlɛ] *nm* plaice

carreleur [karlœr] *nm* tiler

carrément [karemɑ̃] *adv Fam* (**a**) *(franchement)* straight out; **vas-y c.** get on with it (**b**) *(très)* really; **c'était c. immangeable** it was absolutely inedible; **t'as c. raison** you're absolutely right; **c'est c. du vol/de la corruption** it's highway robbery/blatant corruption

carrière¹ [karjɛr] *nf (profession)* career; **faire c. (dans)** to make a career (in)

carrière² [karjɛr] *nf (lieu)* quarry

carriériste [karjerist] *nmf Péj* careerist

carriole [karjɔl] *nf* (**a**) *(petite charrette)* light cart (**b**) *Can* sleigh, sled

carrossable [karosabl] *adj (chemin, route)* suitable for motor vehicles

carrosse [karos] *nm* (**a**) *(véhicule)* (horse-drawn) coach (**b**) *Can (voiture d'enfant)* baby carriage

carrosser [karose] *vt* to fit the body to; **une voiture bien carrossée** a sturdily built car

carrosserie [karosri] *nf (de voiture)* bodywork

carrossier [karosje] *nm* coachbuilder

carrousel [karuzɛl] *nm* (**a**) *(d'une aérogare)* carousel (**b**) *Can, Belg & Suisse (manège)* merry-go-round

carrure [karyr] *nf (de personne)* build; *(de vêtement)* width across the shoulders; **un homme à la forte c.** a broad-shouldered man; *Fig* **un homme d'une c. exceptionnelle** a man of exceptional qualities; **elle est d'une autre c. que son prédécesseur** she is of quite a different caliber from her predecessor

cartable [kartabl] *nm* school bag

carte [kart] *nf* (**a**) *(géographique)* map; *Naut* chart; **faire la c. d'une région** to map (out) an area; *Astrol* **c. du ciel** astronomical chart; **c. d'état-major** ≃ Geological Survey map; **c. routière** road map
(**b**) *(carton)* card; **c. (à jouer)** (playing) card; **jouer aux cartes** to play cards; **donner les cartes** to deal (the cards); *Fig* **donner c. blanche à qn** to give sb carte blanche; *Fig* **jouer cartes sur table** to put one's cards on the table; **c. d'anniversaire** birthday card; **c. à gratter** scratchcard; **c. maîtresse** trump card; **c. postale** postcard; **c. de visite** calling card; **c. de vœux** greeting card
(**c**) *(document officiel)* card; **c. d'abonnement** *(de bibliothèque)* library card; *(de transports, de théâtre)* season ticket; **c. d'adhérent** membership card; **c. d'électeur** voter-registration card; **c. d'embarquement** boarding pass; **c. d'étudiant** student card; **c. de fidélité** rewards card; *Aut* **c. grise** ≃ (vehicle) registration document; **c. d'identité** identity card; *Rail* **c. Jeunes** = reduced-rate railcard for young people, valid in certain European countries; **C. Orange** *(à Paris)* = combined monthly season ticket for the subway, bus and suburban train lines; **c. de presse** press card; **c. de Sécurité sociale** = Social Security Card; **c. de séjour** residence permit; *Rail* **C. Vermeil** = reduced-rate railcard for people over sixty within France; *Aut* **c. verte** certificate of insurance
(**d**) *(document informatisé)* card; **c. bancaire** bank card; **c. Bleue®** debit card; **c. de crédit** credit card; **c. de paiement** payment card; *Tél* **c. prépayé** prepaid card **c. à puce** smart card; *Tél* **c. de recharge** prepaid card; **c. de téléphone** phonecard; **c. VITALE** = smart card on which patient information is recorded, used when making payments to a doctor or chemist for purposes of reclaiming medical expenses
(**e**) *(de restaurant)* menu; **manger à la c.** to eat à la carte; **c. des vins** wine list
(**f**) *Ordinat* card; *(de clavier)* map; **c. accélératrice** accelerator card; **c. à circuit imprimé** *ou* **de circuits imprimés** printed circuit board, PCB; **c. à circuit(s) intégré(s)** integrated circuit card, IC card; **c. d'extension** expansion card *or* board; **c. mémoire** memory card; **c. mère** motherboard; **c. modem** modem card; **c. de polices de caractères** font card; **c. processeur** processor card; **c. réseau** network card;

c. SCSI SCSI card; **c. son** *ou* **sonore** sound card; **c. unité centrale** CPU board; **c. vidéo** video card; **c. vocale** voice card

carte-adaptateur (*pl* **cartes-adaptateurs**) [kartadaptatœr] *nf Ordinat* **c. réseau** network adapter card

cartel [kartɛl] *nm Écon* cartel; **c. de l'acier/de la drogue** steel/drug cartel

carte-lettre (*pl* **cartes-lettres**) [kartəlɛtr] *nf* letter-card

carter [kartɛr] *nm* (*d'engrenages*) casing; (*de bicyclette*) chain guard; *Aut* (*de vilebrequin*) crankcase

carte-réponse (*pl* **cartes-réponses**) [kartrepɔ̃s] *nf* reply card

carterie [kartəri] *nf* card shop

cartésien, -enne [kartezjɛ̃, -ɛn] *adj* (a) *Math* Cartesian (b) (*logique*) logical

carte-vue (*pl* **cartes-vues**) [kartəvy] *nf Belg* (picture) postcard

cartilage [kartilaʒ] *nm* cartilage

cartilagineux, -euse [kartilaʒinø, -øz] *adj* cartilaginous; (*viande*) gristly

cartographe [kartɔgraf] *nmf* cartographer

cartographie [kartɔgrafi] *nf* cartography

cartomancien, -enne [kartɔmɑ̃sjɛ̃, -ɛn] *nm,f* fortune-teller (*who uses cards*)

carton [kartɔ̃] *nm* (a) (*matière*) cardboard; (*feuille*) piece of cardboard; **c. d'invitation** invitation (card); **c. jaune/rouge** (*au football*) yellow/red card (b) (*boîte*) (cardboard) box; **faire des cartons** to pack one's things up in cardboard boxes; **c. à chapeau(x)** hatbox (c) *Art* (*dessin*) cartoon, sketch; **c. à dessin** portfolio (d) (*locutions*) **faire un c.** (*au tir*) to take a shot; *Fam* (*sur quelqu'un*) to shoot somebody; *Fam* (*à un examen*) to pass with flying colors; *Fam Scol* (**se**) **prendre un c.** (*une mauvaise note*) to get a bad grade

cartonner [kartɔne] **1** *vt* (*livre*) to case; **livre cartonné** hardback (book)
2 *vi Fam* (a) (*à l'école*) to get excellent grades (**en** in) (b) (*musique*) to be mind-blowing

cartonneux, -euse [kartɔnø, -øz] *adj* like cardboard

carton-pâte [kartɔ̃pat] *nm* pasteboard

cartouche [kartuʃ] *nf* (*de fusil, de stylo, d'imprimante*) cartridge; (*de cigarettes*) carton; *Ordinat* **c. Zip®** Zip® disk

cartouchière [kartuʃjɛr] *nf* cartridge belt

caryatide [karjatid] = **cariatide**

cas [kɑ] *nm* (a) (*situation*) case, situation; *Jur & Méd* case; **c. particulier** exception; **envisager tous les c. possibles** to consider all the possibilities; **examiner qch au c. par c.** to examine sth on a case-by-case basis; **c'est le c. de le dire** you can say that again; **en pareil c.** in a similar situation; **si tel est votre c.** if that applies to you; **il parle trois langues mais ce n'est pas mon c.** he speaks three languages but I don't; *Fam* **c'est un c.!** he is a case!; **un c. social** a person with social problems
(b) *Gram* case
(c) (*locutions*) **en aucun c.** under no circumstances, on no account; **en tout c., dans tous les c.** in any case, anyway; **dans ce c.** (*puisqu'il en est ainsi*) in that case; **dans tous les c. de figure** in all cases; **le c. échéant** if necessary, if need be; **selon le c.** as the case may be; **en c. d'urgence** in an emergency; **en c. de besoin** if need be; **j'ai pris un pull supplémentaire en c. de besoin** I took an extra sweater just in case; **au c. où il viendrait** in case he comes; *Fam* **je te le laisse au c. où** I'll leave it for you just in case; **faire grand c. de qn/qch** to have a high opinion of sb/sth; **faire peu de c. de qch** to have a low opinion of sth; **ne faire aucun c. de qch** to take no notice of sth

Casablanca [kazablᾶka] *n* Casablanca

casanier, -ère [kazanje, -ɛr] *adj* home-loving; *Péj* stay-at-home

casaque [kazak] *nf* (*de jockey*) blouse; *Fig* **tourner c.** (*partir*) to turn tail; (*changer d'opinion*) to switch sides

cascade [kaskad] *nf* (a) (*chute d'eau*) waterfall; *Fig* **des rires en c.** peals of laughter; *Ordinat* **ouvrir des fenêtres en c.** to cascade windows (b) (*au cinéma*) stunt

cascadeur, -euse [kaskadœr, -øz] *nm,f* stuntman, *f* stuntwoman

case [kɑz] *nf* (a) (*de tiroir*) compartment; (*de formulaire*) box; (*de mots croisés, de damier*) square; *Fam* **il lui manque une c., il a une c. de vide** he's got a screw loose; **c. départ** (*dans les jeux*) start; *Fig* **retour à la c. départ** back to square one (b) (*hutte*) hut (c) *Ordinat* button; (*en forme de boîte*) box (d) *Suisse* **c. (postale)** postbox

casemate [kazmat] *nf* blockhouse

caser [kɑze] **1** *vt* (a) (*placer*) to fit in (b) *Fam* **c. qn** (*établir*) to fix sb up with a job; (*marier*) to marry sb off
2 se caser *vpr Fam* (*trouver un emploi*) to get oneself a job; (*se marier*) to get married and settle down

caserne [kazɛrn] *nf* barracks; **c. de pompiers** fire station

cash [kaʃ] *adv Fam* **payer c.** to pay cash (down)

cash-flow (*pl* **cash-flows**) [kaʃflo] *nm Com* cash flow

casier [kɑzje] *nm* (a) (*compartiment*) compartment; (*pour le courrier*) pigeonhole; (*à vêtements*) locker; **c. à bouteilles** bottle rack (b) *Jur* **c. judiciaire** police *or* criminal record; **avoir un c. (judiciaire)** to have a record (c) (*pour pêcher*) pot; **casiers à homards** lobster pots

casino [kazino] *nm* casino

Caspienne [kaspjɛn] *adj f voir* **mer**

casque [kask] *nm* (a) (*de soldat, de pompier*) helmet; (*de motocycliste*) (crash) helmet; **le port du c. est obligatoire** (*sur panneau*) safety helmets must be worn; **c. intégral** full-face crash helmet; **les Casques bleus** the Blue Berets (b) (*écouteurs*) headphones, headset (c) (*de salon de coiffure*) hood hairdryer

casqué, -e [kaske] *adj* helmeted

casquer [kaske] *vi Fam* (*payer*) to fork out

casquette [kaskɛt] *nf* cap

cassable [kasabl] *adj* breakable

cassant, -e [kasᾶ, -ᾶt] *adj* brittle; *Fig* (*personne, ton*) brusque

cassation [kasasjɔ̃] *nf Jur* annulment

casse¹ [kas] *nf Typ* case; **bas/haut de c.** lower/upper case

casse² [kas] *nf* (a) (*action de casser*) **il va y avoir de la c.** something will get broken; *Fam* (*des ennuis*) there'll be trouble; **aller ou partir à la c.** (*voiture*) to go for scrap (b) (*objets cassés*) breakages

casse³ [kas] *nm très Fam* (*cambriolage*) break-in

cassé, -e [kase] *adj* (*objet, jambe*) broken; (*voix*) cracked; *très Fam* (*ivre*) smashed, plastered; (*drogué*) stoned

casse-cou [kasku] **1** *adj inv* (*personne*) reckless
2 *nmf inv* (*personne*) daredevil

casse-croûte [kaskrut] *nm inv* (a) *Fam* (*repas*) snack, bite (b) *Can* (*snack*) snack bar

casse-cul [kasky] *très Fam* **1** *adj inv* damn annoying
2 *nmf inv* pain in the ass

casse-gueule [kasgœl] *très Fam* **1** *adj inv* (*endroit*) dangerous; (*entreprise*) risky
2 *nm inv* (*endroit*) danger spot; (*entreprise*) risky business

casse-noisettes [kasnwazɛt] *nm inv* nutcrackers

casse-noix [kasnwa] *nm inv* nutcrackers

casse-pieds [kaspje] *Fam* **1** *adj inv* damn annoying; **ce qu'il peut être c.!** he can be a real pain (in the neck)!
2 *nmf inv* pain (in the neck)

casse-pipe [kaspip] *nm inv Fam* **aller au c.** to go to the front

casser [kase] **1** *vt* (a) (*briser*) to break; (*noix*) to crack; (*voix*) to strain; (*chaussures*) to break in; *Fam* (*personne*) to humiliate; **c. les prix** to slash prices; *aussi Fig* **c. le moral des troupes** to discourage the ranks; *Fig* **c. du sucre sur le dos de qn** to talk about sb behind his/her back; *Fam* **c. la croûte** *ou* **la graine** to have a bite to eat; *Fam* **ça ne casse pas trois pattes à un canard, ça ne casse pas des briques** it's nothing to write home about; *Fam* **c. la baraque** *(pièce, acteur)* to bring the house down; *Fam* **à tout c.** *(au maximum)* at the very most

(b) *Fam (locutions avec parties du corps)* **c. les pieds à qn** *(ennuyer)* to bore sb stiff; *(agacer)* to get on sb's nerves; **ça fait deux mois qu'elle me casse les pieds pour que j'y aille** she's been bugging me to go for two months now; **c. les oreilles à qn** to deafen sb; **c. la figure** *ou très Fam* **la gueule à qn** to smash sb's face in; *Fam* **c. sa pipe** to kick the bucket, to buy the farm; *Vulg* **il nous casse les couilles, il nous les casse** he's a real pain in the ass

(c) *Jur (verdict)* to quash; *(mariage)* to annul; *(fiançailles)* to break off

2 *vi* (a) *(se briser)* to break; **attention, ça casse!** be careful, it's fragile!

(b) *Fam (se séparer)* to break up

3 se casser *vpr* (a) *(se briser)* to break

(b) **se c. une** *ou* **la jambe** to break one's leg; *Fig* **se c. le nez** to fail; *Fig* **se c. la tête** to rack one's brains; *Fam* **se c. la figure** *ou très Fam* **la gueule** *(tomber)* to fall flat on one's face; *(échouer)* to fail

(c) *Fam (se fatiguer)* **il ne s'est pas cassé pour m'aider** he didn't exactly go out of his way to help me; *Vulg* **se c. le cul à faire qch** to bust a gut trying to do sth

(d) *Fam (partir)* to split, to clear out; **tu viens? on se casse** we're splitting, you coming?; **casse-toi!** get lost!

casserole [kasrɔl] *nf* (a) *(de cuisine)* (sauce)pan; *très Fam* **passer à la c.** *(sexuellement)* to get laid; *(être tué)* to get bumped off (b) *Fam* **chanter comme une c.** to be a lousy singer

casse-tête [kastɛt] *nm inv* (a) *(jeu)* puzzle (b) *(problème)* headache

cassette [kasɛt] *nf* (a) *(magnétique)* cassette, tape; **enregistrer qch sur c.** to tape sth; **c. vidéo** video (cassette) (b) *Ordinat* **c. à bande magnétique** mag tape cassette

casseur, -euse [kasœr, -øz] *nm,f* (a) *(manifestant)* rioter (b) *très Fam (cambrioleur)* burglar

cassis [kasis] *nm* (a) *(baie)* blackcurrant (b) *(arbuste)* blackcurrant bush (c) *(liqueur)* blackcurrant liqueur (d) *Fam (tête)* nut, noggin

cassonade [kasɔnad] *nf* brown sugar

cassoulet [kasulɛ] *nm* cassoulet *(stew of beans, pork, goose, etc., a specialty of Languedoc)*

cassure [kasyr] *nf* break; *Géol* fault

castagne [kastaɲ] *nf Fam* fighting; **aimer la c.** *(la bagarre)* to like fighting

castagnettes [kastaɲɛt] *nfpl* castanets; *Fam Fig* **ses dents/ genoux jouaient des castagnettes** his teeth were chattering/knees were knocking

caste [kast] *nf* caste

castillan, -e [kastijɑ̃, -an] **1** *adj* Castilian

2 *nm (langue)* Castilian

3 *nm,f* **C., Castillane** Castilian

Castille [kastij] *nf* **la C.** Castile

casting [kastin] *nm Cin & Théât* casting

castor [kastɔr] *nm* beaver

castrat [kastra] *nm Mus* castrato

castrer [kastre] *vt* to castrate; *(chat, chien)* to neuter

cata [kata] *nf Fam* **c'est la c.** it's a disaster

cataclysme [kataklism] *nm* cataclysm

cataclysmique [kataklismik] *adj* cataclysmic

catacombes [katakɔ̃b] *nfpl* catacombs

catadioptre [katadjɔptr] *nm (de véhicule)* reflector; *(sur la route)* cat's-eye®

catafalque [katafalk] *nm* catafalque

catalan, -e [katalɑ̃, -an] **1** *adj* Catalan

2 *nm (langue)* Catalan

3 *nm,f* **C., Catalane** Catalan

Catalogne [katalɔɲ] *nf* **la C.** Catalonia

catalogue [katalɔg] *nm* catalog; **faire le c. de** to catalog; **acheter sur c.** to buy things from a catalog

cataloguer [katalɔge] *vt* to catalog; *Fig & Péj* to label

catalyser [katalize] *vt aussi Fig* to catalyze

catalyseur [katalizœr] *nm aussi Fig* catalyst

catalytique [katalitik] *adj Chim* catalytic

catamaran [katamarɑ̃] *nm Naut* catamaran

Cataphote® [katafɔt] = **catadioptre**

cataplasme [kataplasm] *nm* poultice

catapulte [katapylt] *nf* catapult

catapulter [katapylte] *vt* to catapult; *Fig* **c. qn à un poste** to catapult sb into a position

cataracte [katarakt] *nf (maladie, chute d'eau)* cataract

catastrophe [katastrɔf] *nf* disaster, catastrophe; **c. ferroviaire/aérienne** rail/air disaster; **c'est la c.!** it's a disaster!; **c.! il est déjà là!** horrors! he's here already!; **en c.** *(à toute vitesse)* in a mad rush *or* panic

catastrophé, -e [katastrɔfe] *adj Fam* stunned

catastrophique [katastrɔfik] *adj* disastrous, catastrophic

catch [katʃ] *nm* wrestling; **faire du c.** to wrestle

catcheur, -euse [katʃœr, -øz] *nm,f* wrestler

catéchisme [kateʃism] *nm* catechism

catégorie [kategɔri] *nf* category, type; *(d'hôtel, de personnel)* grade; *(de boxeur)* class; **c. sociale** social class; **c. socioprofessionnelle** socio-professional group

catégorique [kategɔrik] *adj (réponse, refus)* categoric(al); **je suis absolument c., c'est lui** I'm absolutely positive it's him

catégoriquement [kategɔrikmɑ̃] *adv* categorically

catégoriser [kategɔrize] *vt* to categorize

Cathares [katar] *nmpl Hist* **les C.** the Cathars

catharsis [katarsis] *nf* catharsis

cathédrale [katedral] *nf* cathedral

cathéter [katetɛr] *nm Méd* catheter

catho [kato] *adj Fam* Catholic

cathode [katɔd] *nf Élec* cathode

cathodique [katɔdik] *adj Élec* cathodic; **tube c.** cathode ray tube

catholicisme [katɔlisism] *nm* (Roman) Catholicism

catholique [katɔlik] **1** *adj* (Roman) Catholic; *Fam* **ce n'est pas très c.** it's not kosher

2 *nmf* (Roman) Catholic

catimini [katimini] **en catimini** *adv* on the sly

catin [katɛ̃] *nf* (a) *Vieilli (prostituée)* trollop, slut (b) *Can (poupée)* doll

catogan [katɔgɑ̃] *nm (nœud)* hair ribbon *(for ponytail)*; *(queue de cheval)* ponytail

Caucase [kokaz] *nm* **le C.** the Caucasus

caucasien, -enne [kokazjɛ̃, -ɛn] *adj* Caucasian

cauchemar [koʃmar] *nm aussi Fig* nightmare; **une vision de c.** a nightmarish vision; **faire un c.** to have a nightmare

cauchemarder [koʃmarde] *vi* to have nightmares

cauchemardesque [koʃmardɛsk] *adj* nightmarish

causal, -e, -als *ou* **-aux, -ales** [kozal, -o] *adj* causal

causant, -e [kozɑ̃, -ɑ̃t] *adj Fam* chatty

cause [koz] *nf* (a) *(origine)* cause; **quelle est la c. de son départ?** why is he leaving?; **il s'est mis en colère, et pour c.** he got angry, and with good reason; **fermé pour c. d'inventaire/de décès** *(sur panneau)* closed for inventory/due to bereavement; **à c. de** because of (b) *Jur* case; *Fig* **la c. est entendue** there's nothing more to be said; **être en c.** *(sujet à caution)* to be in question; **mettre qch en c.** to doubt sth, to question sth; **mettre qn en c.** *(impliquer)* to implicate sb;

mettre qn hors de c. to clear sb; **en tout état de c.** in any case (**c**) (parti) cause; **faire c. commune avec qn** to join forces with sb; **c'est pour une bonne c.** it's for a good cause

causer[1] [koze] vt (provoquer) to cause; **c. des ennuis à qn** to cause sb problems

causer[2] [koze] vi (**a**) (parler) to chat, to talk (**de** about); **c. affaires** to talk business; **c. avec** ou **à qn** to chat with sb; Fam **je ne lui cause plus!** I'm not talking to him!; Ironique **cause toujours(, tu m'intéresses)!** yeah, yeah(,whatever)! (**b**) (cancaner) to talk, to gossip; **on en cause au village** it's the talk of the village

causerie [kozri] nf (**a**) (discussion) chat, talk (**b**) (conférence) (informal) talk

causette [kozɛt] nf Fam little chat; **faire la c.** ou **un brin de c. avec qn** to have a little chat with sb

causse [kos] nm = limestone plateau in central and southern France

caustique [kostik] adj aussi Fig caustic

cautériser [koterize] vt to cauterize

caution [kosjɔ̃] nf (**a**) (pour appartement) deposit; Jur bail; Fig (appui) support, backing; Jur **sous c.** on bail; **sujet à c.** (information) unconfirmed (**b**) (personne) guarantor

cautionner [kosjone] vt (personne) to stand surety for; Jur to stand bail for; Fig (approuver) to support, to back

cavalcade [kavalkad] nf Fam (bousculade) stampede

cavale [kaval] nf Fam (évasion) escape; **être en c.** to be on the run or on the lam

cavaler [kavale] vi Fam (se démener) to rush around; (fuir) to run off; **c. après qn** to chase after sb

cavalerie [kavalri] nf Mil cavalry

cavaleur, -euse [kavalœr, -øz] Fam **1** adj (homme) womanizing; (femme) man-chasing
2 nm,f (homme) skirt-chaser; (femme) man-chaser

cavalier, -ère [kavalje, -ɛr] **1** adj (manière, personne) cavalier
2 nm,f (**a**) (à cheval) rider, horseman, f horsewoman (**b**) (de bal) partner; Fig **faire c. seul** to go it alone
3 nm (**a**) (aux échecs) knight (**b**) (accompagnateur) escort (**c**) Can (amoureux) boyfriend (**d**) Ordinat jumper

cavalièrement [kavaljɛrmɑ̃] adv in a cavalier manner

cave[1] [kav] adj (joues, yeux) hollow, sunken

cave[2] [kav] nf (**a**) (cellier) cellar; **c. à charbon/vin** coal/wine cellar; Fig **de la c. au grenier** from top to bottom (**b**) Can (sous-sol) basement

caveau, -x [kavo] nm (**a**) (petite cave) small cellar (**b**) (funéraire) burial vault

caverne [kavɛrn] nf cave, cavern; **homme des cavernes** caveman

caverneux, -euse [kavɛrnø, -øz] adj (voix) deep

caviar [kavjar] nm caviar

caviarder [kavjarde] vt to censor

caviste [kavist] nm cellarman

cavité [kavite] nf cavity, hollow; **c. buccale** oral cavity

Cayenne [kajɛn] n (**a**) (ville) Cayenne (**b**) **poivre de C.** cayenne pepper

CB [sibi] nf (abrév **citizen band**) CB

CC [sese] nm (abrév **compte courant**) CA

CCI [sesei] nf (abrév **Chambre de commerce et d'industrie**) Chamber of Commerce and Industry

CCP [sesepe] nm (abrév **compte courant postal, compte chèque postal**) ≃ Post Office checking account

CD [sede] nm (**a**) (abrév **compact disc**) CD (**b**) (abrév **corps diplomatique**) CD

CDD [sedede] nm (abrév **contrat à durée déterminée**) fixed-term contract

CDI [sedei] nm inv (**a**) (abrév **centre des impôts**) tax office (**b**) (abrév **contrat à durée indéterminée**) permanent contract (**c**) (abrév **centre de documentation et d'informa-**

tion) school library (with special resources on how to find information)

CD-I [sedei] Ordinat (abrév **compact disc interactif**) CDI

CD-R [sedeɛr] nm inv (abrév **compact disc recordable**) CD-R

CD-ROM [sederɔm] nm inv Ordinat (abrév **compact disc read-only memory**) CD-ROM; **C. interactif** interactive CD-ROM

CD-RW [sedeɛr] nm inv (abbr **compact disc rewritable**) CD-RW

CE [seə] **1** nm (**a**) (abrév **Conseil de l'Europe**) Council of Europe (**b**) (abrév **cours élémentaire**) **CE1** = second year of primary school; **CE2** = third year of primary school
2 nf (abrév **Communauté européenne**) EC

ce[1] [sə] pron démonstratif

> **ce** becomes **c'** before a vowel.

(**a**) (pour désigner) **c'est mon père** that's my father; (au téléphone) it's my father; **ce sont** ou Fam **c'est mes amis** those are my friends; (qui arrivent) there are my friends; **c'était mon idée** it was my idea; **c'est le plus beau jour de ma vie** this is the best day of my life; **c'est moi** it's me; **qui est-ce?**, Fam **qui c'est?** who is it?; **c'est lui qui l'a écrit** HE wrote it; **qui a fait ça? – c'est moi!** who did that? – I did!; **c'est un bon traducteur** he's a good translator; **c'est la première voiture que j'aie eue** that was my first car; **c'est ici que je suis né** this is where I was born, I was born here; **c'est jeudi aujourd'hui** today's Thursday, it's Thursday today; **c'était il y a longtemps** it was a long time ago

(**b**) (pour qualifier ou pour expliquer) **c'est facile/joli** it's easy/nice; **c'est exact!** that's right!; **c'est que maman est déjà partie** the thing is, Mom already left; **s'il chante, (alors) c'est qu'il est de bonne humeur** if he's singing, it means he's in a good mood; Fam **c'est bizarre qu'il n'ait pas appelé!** it's strange that he hasn't called!; Fam **ce qu'il est pénible!** he's such a pain!

(**c**) (avec des pronoms relatifs) **ce qui..., ce que...** what...; **je sais ce qui s'est passé** I know what happened; **ce que je crois, c'est que...** what I think is...; **voici ce dont il s'agit** this is what it's all about; **voilà ce à quoi j'avais pensé** this is what I thought of; **ce qui compte, c'est que...** what counts is that...; **j'ai appris tout ce qui se trouve dans le chapitre quatre** I've learned everything in chapter four; **j'ai oublié tout ce qu'elle m'a dit** I've forgotten everything she told me; **pour ce qui est de la qualité** with regards to or as regards quality

(**d**) (locutions) **ce faisant** in so doing, while doing so; **il y est allé, et ce malgré mon interdiction** he went despite the fact that I had forbidden him; **sur ce, je m'en vais** on that note, I'm leaving; **...et, sur ce, il sortit son album de photos** ...whereupon he brought out his photo album

ce[2]**, cet, cette, ces** [sə, sɛt, se] adj démonstratif

> **cet** is used before a masculine singular noun or adjective beginning with a vowel or mute h.

(**a**) (par référence) **ce garçon** this boy; **cet enfant** this child; **cette fille** this girl; **ces gens/animaux/couleurs** these people/animals/colors (**b**) (en désignant) **ce vin-ci** this wine; **ce vin-là** that wine; **ces voitures-ci** these cars; **ces voitures-là** those cars (**c**) Fam (intensif) **alors, cette lettre, tu me la montres?** so do I get to see this or that letter of yours?; **et ce café, il arrive?** is that coffee on its way or what?; **je lui ai envoyé une de ces lettres!** I wrote him/her such a letter!; **j'ai une de ces faims!** I'm SO hungry!

CEA [seəa] nm (abrév **commissariat à l'énergie atomique**) = French atomic energy commission, ≃ AEC

ceci [səsi] pron démonstratif this; **c. (étant) dit** having said that; **c. n'explique pas cela** that's no explanation

cécité [sesite] *nf* blindness; **être atteint de c.** to be blind

CED [seəd] *nf* (*abrév* **Communauté européenne de défense**) EDC

céder [34] [sede] **1** *vt* (**a**) (*donner*) (*objet, droit*) to give up (**à** to); (*dans un testament*) to leave (**à** to); **c. sa place à qn** to give up one's seat to sb; **c. du terrain** to give ground; **cédez le passage** (*sur panneau*) yield (**b**) (*vendre*) to sell; **à c.** (*sur panneau*) for sale

2 *vi* (**a**) (*plancher, branche*) to give way (**b**) (*se soumettre*) to give in (**devant** to)

3 céder à *vt ind* (*personne, tentation, revendication*) to give in to

cédérom [sederɔm] *nm Ordinat* CD-Rom

Cedex [sedɛks] *nm* (*abrév* **Courrier d'entreprise à distribution exceptionnelle**) = zip code ensuring rapid delivery of business mail

cédille [sedij] *nf* cedilla

cédrat [sedra] *nm* (*fruit*) citron

cèdre [sɛdr] *nm* (*arbre, bois*) cedar; **c. du Liban** cedar of Lebanon

CEE [seəə] *nf* (*abrév* **Communauté économique européenne**) EEC

CEEA [seəəa] *nf* (*abrév* **Communauté européenne de l'énergie atomique**) Euratom

cégep [seʒɛp] *nm Can* (*abrév* **collège d'enseignement général et professionnel**) = college of adult education

CEI [seai] *nf* (*abrév* **Communauté d'États indépendants**) CIS

ceindre [54] [sɛ̃dr] *vt Litt* (**a**) (*épée*) to strap on (**b**) (*sujet: couronne*) to encircle

ceinture [sɛ̃tyr] *nf* (**a**) (*accessoire*) belt; **être c. noire de judo** to be a black belt in judo; *Fam* **se serrer la c., faire c.** to tighten one's belt; **c. de chasteté** chastity belt; **c. de sécurité** seat belt, safety belt; **attacher sa c. (de sécurité)** to fasten one's seat belt *or* safety belt (**b**) (*taille*) (*de vêtement*) waistband; (*d'une personne*) waist; **frapper au-dessous de la c.** to hit below the belt (**c**) **la petite C.** = circular bus route around the center of Paris

ceinturer [sɛ̃tyre] *vt* to grab around the waist

ceinturon [sɛ̃tyrɔ̃] *nm* belt

cela [səla, sla] *pron démonstratif* that; **c'est cela!** (*c'est exact*) that's right!; **c'est pour c. que je viens** that's what I've come for *or* why I've come; **il y a deux ans de c.** that was two years ago; **et pourquoi c.?** why is that?; **s'il n'y avait que c.** if that were the only problem; **et avec c.?** (*dans un magasin*) (will there be) anything else?; **c. (étant) dit** having said that

célébration [selebrasjɔ̃] *nf* celebration

célèbre [selɛbr] *adj* famous (**pour** for); **se rendre c. par qch** to become famous for sth; **tristement c.** notorious

célébrer [34] [selebre] *vt* (**a**) (*fêter*) (*anniversaire, victoire, messe*) to celebrate (**b**) (*vanter*) **c. les mérites/le talent de qn** to extoll sb's merits/talent

célébrité [selebrite] *nf* (*notoriété*) fame; (*personne*) celebrity

céleri [sɛlri] *nm* celery; *Culin* **c. rémoulade** = grated celeriac in mayonnaise

céleri-rave (*pl* **céleris-raves**) [sɛlrirav] *nm* celeriac

céleste [selɛst] *adj* (**a**) (*du firmament*) (*phénomènes, corps*) celestial, heavenly (**b**) *Rel* heavenly

célibat [seliba] *nm* single life; (*des prêtres*) celibacy

célibataire [selibatɛr] **1** *adj* (*non marié*) unmarried, single

2 *nm* bachelor; **un c. endurci** a confirmed bachelor

3 *nf* single woman

celle [sɛl] *voir* **celui**

cellier [selje] *nm* storeroom; (*cave*) cellar

Cellophane® [selofan] *nf* cellophane®; **sous C.** cellophane-wrapped

cellulaire [selylɛr] **1** *adj* (**a**) *Biol* cell (**b**) *Jur* **régime c.** solitary confinement (**c**) *Tél* cellular

2 *nm Can Tél* cellphone

cellule [selyl] *nf* (**a**) (*d'une prison, d'un couvent*) cell; *Hum* **il a passé la nuit en c. de dégrisement** he spent the night in the cells to sober up (**b**) *Biol* cell; **c. nerveuse** nerve cell; **c. souche** stem cell (**c**) *Fig* (*élément*) unit; (*de parti politique*) cell; **c. (terroriste) dormante** *ou* **en sommeil** sleeper cell (**d**) *Élec* **c. photoélectrique** photoelectric cell

cellulite [selylit] *nf* cellulite

Celluloïd® [selyloid] *nm* celluloid®

cellulose [selyloz] *nf* cellulose

celte [sɛlt] **1** *adj* Celtic

2 *nmf* **C.** Celt

celtique [sɛltik] *adj & nm* Celtic

celui, celle [səlɥi, sɛl] (*mpl* **ceux** [sø], *fpl* **celles**) *pron démonstratif* the one; **mon livre et c. de Paul** my book and Paul's; **mes livres et ceux de Paul** my books and Paul's; **c. que t'ai donné** the one I gave you; **celles dont je t'ai parlé** the ones I talked to you about; **c.-ci** this one; (*ce dernier*) the latter; **c.-là** that one; (*le premier*) the former; **ceux-ci** these ones; (*ces derniers*) the latter; **ceux-là** those ones; (*les premiers*) the former; **ah, c.-là, quel idiot!** he's such an idiot, that one!; **autre exemple, plus technique c.-là** another example, a more technical one this time; **elle est bien bonne, celle-là!** that's a good one!

cendre [sɑ̃dr] *nf* ash(es); **faire cuire des pommes de terre sous la c.** to roast potatoes in the ashes; **réduire qch en cendres** to reduce sth to ashes; **cendres** (*après incinération*) ashes; *Rel* **le mercredi des Cendres** Ash Wednesday

cendré, -e[1] [sɑ̃dre] *adj voir* **blond**

cendrée[2] [sɑ̃dre] *nf Sport* (*piste*) cinder track; (*mâchefer*) cinders

cendrier [sɑ̃drije] *nm* ashtray

Cendrillon [sɑ̃drijɔ̃] *npr* Cinderella

Cène [sɛn] *nf* **la C.** the Last Supper

censé, -e [sɑ̃se] *adj* **être c. faire qch** to be supposed to do sth

censeur [sɑ̃sœr] *nm* (**a**) *Scol* (*d'un lycée*) assistant principal (**b**) (*dans les médias*) censor (**c**) *Litt* (*juge*) critic

censure [sɑ̃syr] *nf* (*activité*) censorship; (*personnes*) (board of) censors

censurer [sɑ̃syre] *vt* (**a**) (*film, livre, scène*) to censor (**b**) *Litt* (*critiquer*) to censure

cent[1] [sɑ̃] **1** *adj* a *or* one hundred; **deux cents hommes** two hundred men; **deux c. cinquante** two hundred and fifty; **je te l'ai dit c. fois** I've told you a hundred times; **vous avez c. fois raison** you're absolutely right; *Fam* **je ne vais pas t'attendre (pendant) c. sept ans** I'm not going to wait for you forever; **faire les c. pas** to pace up and down; *Fam* **être aux c. coups** to be frantic; *Fam* **faire les quatre cents coups** to get up to all sorts of tricks

2 *nm* (**a**) (*nombre*) hundred; **pour c.** per cent; **c. pour c.** a hundred per cent; *voir aussi* **trois** (**b**) (*division de l'euro*) cent

cent[2] [sɛnt] *nm* (*d'euro, de dollar*) cent

centaine [sɑ̃tɛn] *nf* **une c. (de)** about a hundred, a hundred or so; **des centaines de livres** hundreds of books; **plusieurs centaines de personnes** several hundred people

centaure [sɑ̃tɔr] *nm* centaur

centenaire [sɑ̃tnɛr] **1** *adj* (*personne, arbre*) hundred-year-old; **être c.** (*avoir cent ans*) to be a hundred (years old); (*avoir plus de cent ans*) to be over a hundred (years old); **plusieurs fois c.** hundreds of years old

2 *nmf* (*vieillard*) centenarian

3 *nm* (*anniversaire*) centennial

centième [sɑ̃tjɛm] **1** *nmf, nm & adj* hundredth; *voir aussi* **cinquième**

2 *nf Théât* hundredth performance

centigrade [sãtigrad] *adj* **degré c.** degree centigrade

centigramme [sãtigram] *nm* centigram

centilitre [sãtilitr] *nm* centiliter

centime [sãtim] *nm* centime; **je ne lui donnerai pas un c.!** I won't give him/her a cent!

centimètre [sãtimɛtr] *nm* **(a)** *(unité de mesure)* centimeter **(b)** *(ruban)* tape measure

centrafricain, -e [sãtrafrikɛ̃, -ɛn] **1** *adj* of the Central African Republic

2 *nm,f* **C., Centrafricaine** person from the Central African Republic

central, -e, -aux, -ales [sãtral, -o] **1** *adj* **(a)** *(au centre)* central **(b)** *(principal)* central, main **(c)** **(l'École) Centrale** = "Grande École" specializing in engineering

2 *nm* **c. téléphonique** telephone exchange

3 *nf* **centrale (a)** *(usine)* **centrale (électrique)** power station; **centrale thermique/nucléaire** thermal/nuclear power station **(b)** *(prison)* county jail **(c)** *(groupement)* **centrale (syndicale)** group of affiliated trade unions; *Com* **centrale d'achat** (central) purchasing group

centralisation [sãtralizasjɔ̃] *nf* centralization

centraliser [sãtralize] *vt* to centralize

centralisme [sãtralism] *nm Pol* centralism

centre [sãtr] *nm* **(a)** *(milieu)* center; **il se prend pour le c. du monde** he thinks the world revolves round him; **cette question est au c. du débat** this question is at the heart of the debate; *Phys* **c. de gravité** center of gravity; **c. d'intérêt** center of interest

(b) *Pol* center; **le c. droit/gauche** the center right/left

(c) *(au football) (passe)* cross; **faire un c.** to make a cross

(d) *(organisme, lieu)* center; **les grands centres urbains** large conurbations; **c. aéré** outdoor activity center; **c. d'appels** call center; **c. commercial** shopping mall; **c. culturel** arts center; **c. hospitalier** hospital complex; **c. des impôts** tax office; **c. de loisirs** leisure center; **c. de tri** sorting office

centré, -e [sãtre] *adj Suisse (magasin, appartement)* central

centrer [sãtre] *vt (ballon, mécanisme)* to center; **c. une discussion sur un sujet** to focus a discussion on a subject

centre-ville *(pl* **centres-villes)** [sãtrǝvil] *nm* city center; *(d'une grande ville)* downtown area; **aller au c.** to go downtown; **habiter au c.** to live in the city center, to live downtown

centrifuge [sãtrifyʒ] *adj* centrifugal

centrifuger [45] [sãtrifyʒe] *vt* to centrifuge

centrifugeur [sãtrifyʒœr] *nm*, **centrifugeuse** [sãtrifyʒøz] *nf (en chimie, en biologie)* centrifuge; *(pour jus de fruits)* juice extractor, juicer

centripète [sãtripɛt] *adj* centripetal

centrisme [sãtrism] *nm Pol* centrism

centriste [sãtrist] *adj & nmf Pol* centrist

centuple [sãtypl] *nm* **le c. de dix** a hundred times ten; **je te le rendrai au c.** I'll repay you a hundred times over

cep [sɛp] *nm* **c. (de vigne)** vine-stock

cépage [sepaʒ] *nm* variety of vine

cèpe [sɛp] *nm* cep, porcini

cependant [sǝpãdã] **1** *conj* however, nevertheless; **le directeur, c., n'est pas d'accord** the manager, however, does not agree; **c., vous ne m'avez pas averti** nevertheless, you didn't tell me

2 *adv Litt* meanwhile; **c. que** while

céphalée [sefale] *nf Méd* headache, *Spéc* cephalalgia

céramique [seramik] *nf (art)* ceramics *(singulier)*; *(matière, objet)* ceramic

cerceau, -x [sɛrso] *nm* hoop

cercle [sɛrkl] *nm* **(a)** *(figure)* circle; **en c.** in a circle; **c. vicieux** vicious circle; **décrire des cercles** *(avion, oiseau)* to circle **(b)** *(groupe de personnes)* circle **(c)** *(association)* club; **c. littéraire** literary society **(d)** *(objet circulaire)* hoop, ring **(e)** *Géog* **c. (polaire) arctique** Arctic Circle

cerclé, -e [sɛrkle] *adj* **lunettes cerclées d'écaille** horn-rimmed glasses; **un tonneau c. de fer** a barrel with iron hoops

cercueil [sɛrkœj] *nm* coffin

céréale [sereal] *nf* cereal, grain; **céréales** *(au petit déjeuner)* cereal

céréalier, -ère [serealje, -ɛr] *adj (production, culture)* cereal; *(région)* cereal-growing

cérébral, -e, -aux, -ales [serebral, -o] *adj* cerebral; **hémorragie cérébrale** brain hemorrhage

cérémonial, -als [seremɔnjal] *nm* ceremonial

cérémonie [seremɔni] *nf* ceremony; **habit de c.** dress suit; **uniforme de c.** dress uniform; *Fig* **sans cérémonies** *(réception, repas)* informal; *(recevoir quelqu'un)* informally; *(renvoyer quelqu'un)* unceremoniously; **faire des cérémonies** to stand on ceremony; **sans plus de c.** without further ado

cérémonieux, -euse [seremɔnjø, -øz] *adj* ceremonious

cerf [sɛr] *nm* stag

cerfeuil [sɛrfœj] *nm* chervil

cerf-volant *(pl* **cerfs-volants)** [sɛrvɔlã] *nm* **(a)** *(jouet)* kite **(b)** *(insecte)* stag beetle

cerise [sǝriz] **1** *nf* cherry

2 *adj inv* **(rouge) c.** cherry(-red)

cerisier [sǝrizje] *nm (arbre)* cherry tree; *(bois)* cherrywood

CERN [sɛrn] *nm (abrév* **Conseil européen pour la recherche nucléaire)** CERN

cerne [sɛrn] *nm* ring

cerné, -e [sɛrne] *adj* **avoir les yeux cernés** to have rings under one's eyes

cerner [sɛrne] *vt* **(a)** *(encercler)* to surround **(b)** *(définir) (problème)* to identify; **une personne difficile à c.** a difficult person to figure out

certain, -e [sɛrtɛ̃, -ɛn] **1** *adj (sûr)* certain; **il viendra, c'est c.** he'll definitely come; **être c. de qch** to be certain of sth; **aller à une mort certaine** to be heading for certain death

2 *adj indéfini (avant le nom)* certain; **il a un c. charme** he has a certain charm; **un c. temps** a while; **jusqu'à un c. point** up to a (certain) point; **d'une certaine façon** in a way; **dans une certaine mesure** to a certain extent; **dans certaines circonstances** in some *or* certain circumstances; **d'un c. âge** elderly; **avoir un c. âge** to be getting on; **cela demande un c. culot/courage** it takes some nerve/courage; **une certaine Martine** someone called Martine

3 *pron indéfini* **certains pensent que...** some (people) think (that)...; **certaines d'entre nous/vous** some of us/you

certainement [sɛrtɛnmã] *adv (probablement)* most probably; **c.!** *(bien sûr)* of course!; **c. pas!** certainly not!

certes [sɛrt] *adv* certainly; **il n'est pas sans défauts, c., mais...** he has his faults, certainly, but...; **c. oui!** yes indeed!; **c. non!** certainly not!

certificat [sɛrtifika] *nm* certificate; **c. d'assurance** insurance certificate; **c. de garantie** certificate of guarantee; **c. médical** medical certificate; **c. de scolarité** school attendance record; **c. de travail** certificate of employment

certifié, -e [sɛrtifje] *adj* **professeur c.** = qualified (graduate) teacher

certifier [66] [sɛrtifje] *vt* **(a)** *(authentifier)* to certify; *(signature)* to witness **(b)** *(assurer)* **c. à qn que...** to assure sb that...

certitude [sɛrtityd] *nf* certainty; **j'en ai la c.** I'm certain of it

cérumen [serymɛn] *nm* earwax, *Spéc* cerumen

cerveau, -x [sɛrvo] *nm Anat & Fig* brain; *(esprit)* mind, brains; *Fam (personne intelligente)* brainy person; *(d'un projet)* mastermind

cervelas [sɛrvəla] *nm* saveloy

cervelet [sɛrvəlɛ] *nm Anat* cerebellum

cervelle [sɛrvɛl] *nf Anat (substance)* brain; *Culin* brains; **se brûler** *ou* **se faire sauter la c.** to blow one's brains out; **il n'a rien dans la c.** he's got nothing between his ears; **avoir une c. de moineau** to be bird-brained; *Culin* **c. d'agneau** lamb's brains

cervical, -e, -aux, -ales [sɛrvikal, -o] *adj Anat* cervical

CES [seøɛs] *nm* (**a**) *(abrév* **contrat emploi-solidarité)** = short-term contract subsidized by the government (**b**) *(abrév* **collège d'enseignement secondaire)** = former high school for pupils aged 12 to 15

ces [se] *voir* **ce²**

César [sezar] 1 *npr* **Jules C.** Julius Caesar
2 *nm Cin* = French film award

césarienne [sezarjɛn] *nf* Caesarean (section)

cessant, -e [sɛsɑ̃, -ɑ̃t] *adj* **toutes affaires cessantes** forthwith

cessation [sɛsasjɔ̃] *nf* cessation; **c. des hostilités** cease-fire; **c. de paiements** suspension of payments

cesse [sɛs] *nf* (**a**) **sans c.** constantly, continually (**b**) *Litt* **il n'aura (pas) de c. qu'il ne réussisse** he won't rest until he has succeeded

cesser [sese] 1 *vi* to stop, to cease; *(vent)* to die down; **faire c. qch** to put a stop to sth; **il faudra que ça cesse** this has to stop
2 *vt (interrompre)* to stop; *Mil* **cessez le feu!** cease fire!; **c. de faire qch** to stop doing sth; **il ne cesse de me contredire** he's forever contradicting me

cessez-le-feu [seselfø] *nm inv* cease-fire

cession [sɛsjɔ̃] *nf Jur* transfer

c'est-à-dire [sɛtadir] *conj* that is (to say); **vous l'avez prévenu? – eh bien, c. que non** did you let him know? – well, actually, no; **c. que je n'étais pas au courant** the thing is that no one told me; **il faut aller de l'avant! – c.?** we must forge ahead! – what do you mean by that?

césure [sezyr] *nf (en poésie)* caesura; *Ordinat* break, hyphenation

cet [sɛt] *voir* **ce²**

cétacé [setase] *nm* cetacean

cette [sɛt] *voir* **ce²**

ceux [sø] *voir* **celui**

Ceylan [selɑ̃] *n* Ceylon

cf *(abrév* **confer)** cf

CFA [seɛfa] *(abrév* **Communauté financière africaine)** **franc C.** CFA franc

CFAO [seɛfao] *nf (abrév* **conception et fabrication assistées par ordinateur)** CADCAM

CFC [seɛfse] *nm (abrév* **chlorofluorocarbone)** CFC

CFDT [seɛfdete] *nf (abrév* **Confédération française démocratique du travail)** = French labor union

CFTC [seɛftese] *nf (abrév* **Confédération française des travailleurs chrétiens)** = French labor union

CGC [seʒese] *nf (abrév* **Confédération générale des cadres)** = French labor union for managerial staff

CGT [seʒete] *nf (abrév* **Confédération générale du travail)** = French labor union

chacal, -als [ʃakal] *nm* jackal; *Fig* vulture

chacun, -e [ʃakœ̃, -yn] *pron indéfini* (**a**) *(chaque personne)* each (one), every one; **trois euros c.** three euros each; **nous avons pris c. notre chapeau** each of us took our hat (**b**) *(tout le monde)* everyone, everybody; **c. pour soi** every man for himself; **c. ses goûts** everyone to their own taste; **c. son tour** *(dans une file d'attente)* each in turn; **c. son tour!** wait your turn!; **tout un c.** everyone

chagrin, -e [ʃagrɛ̃, -in] 1 *nm (peine)* grief, sorrow; **avoir du c.** to be upset; **avoir un gros c.** *(langage enfantin)* to be very

unhappy; **faire du c. à qn** to distress sb; **un c. d'amour** an unhappy love affair
2 *adj Litt* woeful; **esprits chagrins** malcontents

chagriner [ʃagrine] 1 *vt (peiner)* to grieve; *(contrarier)* to bother
2 **se chagriner** *vpr Can* **le temps se chagrine** it's getting cloudy

chahut [ʃay] *nm Fam* racket, din; **faire du c.** to make a racket

chahuter [ʃayte] *Fam* 1 *vi (faire du tapage)* to make a racket; *(jouer brutalement)* to be rowdy
2 *vt (professeur)* to bait; *(orateur)* to heckle; **se faire c.** *(professeur)* to get baited; *(orateur)* to get heckled

chai [ʃɛ] *nm* wine and spirits storehouse

chaîne [ʃɛn] *nf* (**a**) *(pour attacher, pour décorer)* chain; **faire la c.** to form a chain; **chaînes** *Aut* (snow) chains; *Fig (contraintes)* chains, shackles (**b**) *(de transmission)* chain; **c. de vélo** bicycle chain (**c**) *(série)* *(d'hôtels, de magasins)* chain; **c. alimentaire** food chain; **c. de montagnes** range *or* chain of mountains (**d**) *TV* channel; **c. de télévision** television channel (**e**) *(dans l'industrie)* **c. (de montage)** assembly line, production line; **travail à la c.** assembly-line work; **travailler à la c.** to work on the assembly line (**f**) *Tex* warp (**g**) *Ordinat* string; **c. de caractères** character string; **c. de recherche** search string (**h**) *(c.* **(hi-fi)** hi-fi (**i**) *Can* **c. du trottoir** curb

chaînette [ʃɛnɛt] *nf* small chain

chaînon [ʃɛnɔ̃] *nm* link; *Fig* **le c. manquant** the missing link

chair [ʃɛr] 1 *nf (d'humain, d'animal, de fruit)* flesh; **en c. et en os** in the flesh; **être bien en c.** to be plump; **la c. est faible** the flesh is weak; **c. à canon** cannon fodder; **avoir la c. de poule** to have goose bumps; **donner la c. de poule à qn** to give sb goose bumps; **c. à saucisse** sausage meat; *Fam Fig* **je vais en faire de la c. à saucisse** I'll make mincemeat of him/her
2 *adj inv* **(couleur) c.** flesh-colored

chaire [ʃɛr] *nf* (**a**) *(dans une église)* pulpit (**b**) *Univ (fonction, tribune)* chair; **être titulaire d'une c.** to hold a chair

chaise [ʃɛz] *nf* chair; *Fig* **être assis** *ou* *très Fam* **avoir le cul entre deux chaises** to be in an awkward position; *Can* **c. berçante** rocking chair; **chaises musicales** musical chairs; **c. électrique** electric chair; **c. haute** high chair; **c. longue** deckchair; **c. à porteurs** sedan chair; **c. roulante** wheelchair

chaland [ʃalɑ̃] *nm* barge

châle [ʃɑl] *nm* shawl

chalet [ʃalɛ] *nm* (**a**) *(de montagne)* chalet (**b**) *Can* cottage

chaleur [ʃalœr] *nf* (**a**) *(température)* heat; **les grandes chaleurs** the hot season; **il fait une c. terrible** it's terribly hot; **coup de c.** heatstroke (**b**) *(d'une personne, d'une couleur, d'une voix, d'un accueil)* warmth; **c. humaine** human warmth; **avec c.** warmly (**c**) *Zool* **être en c.** to be in heat

chaleureusement [ʃalørøzmɑ̃] *adv* warmly

chaleureux, -euse [ʃalørø, -øz] *adj (accueil, atmosphère)* warm; *(paroles)* glowing

challenge [ʃalɑ̃ʒ] *nm* (**a**) *Sport* tournament (**b**) *(défi)* challenge

challenger [tʃalɑ̃dʒœr] *nm* challenger

chaloupe [ʃalup] *nf* (**a**) *Naut* launch; *(à rames)* rowboat; **c. à moteur** motor launch; **c. de sauvetage** lifeboat (**b**) *Can (couvre-chaussure)* rubber overshoe

chaloupé, -e [ʃalupe] *adj* swaying

chalumeau, -x [ʃalymo] *nm* (**a**) *Tech* blowtorch (**b**) *Can* spout *(for collecting sap of maple tree)*

chalut [ʃaly] *nm* trawl; **pêcher au c.** to trawl

chalutier [ʃalytje] *nm* trawler

chamade [ʃamad] *nf* **battre la c.** to beat wildly

chamailler [ʃamaje] **se chamailler** *vpr* to squabble

chamailleur, -euse [ʃamajœr, -øz] 1 *adj* quarrelsome
2 *nm,f* squabbler

chamarré, -e [ʃamare] *adj* richly colored

chambardement [ʃɑ̃bardəmɑ̃] *nm Fam* upheaval

chambarder [ʃɑ̃barde] *vt Fam (projets, maison)* to turn upside down

chambouler [ʃɑ̃bule] *vt Fam (projets, maison)* to turn upside down

chambranle [ʃɑ̃brɑ̃l] *nm (d'une porte, d'une fenêtre)* frame

chambre [ʃɑ̃br] *nf* (**a**) *(pièce)* bedroom; *(d'un hôtel)* room; **c. à un lit/deux lits** single/twin room; **vous auriez une c. (de) libre?** do you have any vacancies?; **faire c. à part** to sleep in separate rooms; **faire sa c.** to tidy (up) one's room; **garder la c.** to keep to one's room; **sportif/policitien en c.** armchair athlete/politician; **c. d'amis** spare room; **c. de bonne** maid's room; **c. à coucher** *(pièce)* bedroom; *(mobilier)* bedroom furniture; **c. forte** strongroom; **c. frigorifique** *ou* **froide** cold store; **c. à gaz** gas chamber; **c. d'hôte** ≃ guest house; **c. meublée** furnished room

(**b**) *Jur (d'un tribunal)* division; **c. d'accusation** Court of Criminal Appeal; **C. de commerce** Chamber of Commerce

(**c**) *Pol* **la C.** the House; **siéger à la C.** to sit in the House; **C. des députés** = lower chamber of Parliament

(**d**) *Tech (d'un fusil, d'un appareil photo)* chamber; **c. à air** inner tube

chambrée [ʃɑ̃bre] *nf* (**a**) *(occupants d'une chambre)* room(ful) (**b**) *Mil* barrackroom

chambrer [ʃɑ̃bre] *vt* (**a**) **c. qch** *(bouteille, vin)* to bring sth to room temperature (**b**) *Fam* **c. qn** to pull sb's leg

chambreur, -euse [ʃɑ̃brœr, -øz] *nm,f Can & Suisse* lodger

chameau, -x [ʃamo] *nm* (**a**) *(animal)* camel (**b**) *Fam (homme)* bastard; *(femme)* cow

chamelier [ʃaməlje] *nm* camel-driver

chamelle [ʃamɛl] *nf* she-camel

chamois [ʃamwa] *nm* (**a**) *(animal)* chamois (**b**) *Sport* **c. d'or/ d'argent/de bronze** = gold/silver/bronze skiing proficiency medal

chamoisette [ʃamwazɛt] *nf Belg* duster

champ [ʃɑ̃] *nm* (**a**) *(étendue)* field; **c. de blé** field of wheat, wheatfield; **prendre** *ou* **couper à travers champs** to cut across country; **à tout bout de c.** at every possible opportunity; *Fig* **laisser le c. libre à qn** to leave the field free for sb; **c. de bataille** battlefield; **c. de courses** racetrack; **c. de foire** fairground; **mort** *ou* **tombé au c. d'honneur** killed in action; **c. de mines** minefield; **c. de tir** rifle range; *Mil* practice ground; *(d'un fusil)* field of fire

(**b**) *Fig (portée)* scope; **c. d'action** field of activity; **élargir le c. de ses activités** to extend the scope of one's activities

(**c**) *Phot* shot, picture; *(d'un instrument optique)* field; **être dans le c.** to be in shot; **c. visuel** field of vision

(**d**) *Élec & Rad* field; **c. magnétique** magnetic field; **c. numérique** numeric field; **c. de texte** text field

champagne [ʃɑ̃paɲ] *nm* champagne

champenois, -e [ʃɑ̃pənwa, -az] **1** *adj* (**a**) *(de la région)* of Champagne (**b**) **méthode champenoise** champagne method

2 *nm,f* **C., Champenoise** person from Champagne

champêtre [ʃɑ̃pɛtr] *adj* rustic, rural

champignon [ʃɑ̃piɲɔ̃] *nm* (**a**) *(plante)* mushroom; *Fig* **pousser comme un c.** *(enfant)* to shoot up; *(ville)* to mushroom; **c. atomique** mushroom cloud; **c. hallucinogène** magic mushroom; **c. de Paris** button mushroom; **c. vénéneux** poisonous mushroom, toadstool (**b**) *Méd* fungus (**c**) *Fam (accélérateur)* **appuyer sur le c.** to step on the gas

champion, -onne [ʃɑ̃pjɔ̃, -ɔn] **1** *nm,f* (**a**) *(dans une discipline)* champion; **le c. du monde d'escrime** the world fencing champion; *Fam* **c'est un c. du bricolage** he's a real handyman (**b**) *(d'une cause)* champion

2 *adj* (**a**) *Sport* **l'équipe championne du monde** the

world champions (**b**) *Fam* great; **pour les gaffes, il est c.!** he's a real pro at putting his foot in his mouth!

championnat [ʃɑ̃pjɔna] *nm* championship; **le championnat du monde d'athlétisme** the world track-and-field championships

champlure [ʃɑ̃plyr] *nf Can (robinet)* faucet

chance [ʃɑ̃s] *nf* (**a**) *(sort favorable)* (good) luck; **souhaiter bonne c. à qn** to wish sb luck; **bonne c.!** good luck!; **quelle c.!** what a stroke of luck!; **avec un peu de c....** with a bit of luck...; **avoir de la c.** to be lucky *or* fortunate; **ne pas avoir de c.** to be unlucky; **porter c. à qn** to bring sb luck; **c'est mon jour de c.** it's my lucky day; **c'est bien ma c.!** just my luck!; **pas de c.!** hard luck!; **par c.** luckily, fortunately (**b**) *(possibilité)* chance; **avoir des chances de faire qch** to stand a (good) chance of doing sth; **avoir peu de chances de faire qch** to have little chance of doing sth; **donner une** *ou* **sa c. à qn** to give sb a chance; **elle a une c. sur deux de gagner** she has a fifty-fifty chance of winning; *Fam* **il y a des chances** probably; **il y a de grandes** *ou* **fortes chances (pour) qu'on le lui propose** there's every chance that he/she will be offered it

chancelant, -e [ʃɑ̃slɑ̃, -ɑ̃t] *adj (pas)* unsteady; *(mémoire)* shaky; *(santé)* delicate; *(pouvoir, gouvernement)* tottering; *(détermination)* wavering

chanceler [42] [ʃɑ̃sle] *vi (personne)* to stagger, to totter; *(objet)* to wobble; *(régime, gouvernement)* to totter; **l'uppercut le fit c.** the uppercut sent him reeling

chancelier [ʃɑ̃səlje] *nm Pol* chancellor; *(d'ambassade)* chief secretary

chancellerie [ʃɑ̃sɛlri] *nf* (**a**) *(d'une ambassade)* chancery (**b**) *(ministère de la Justice)* ≃ Department of Justice

chanceux, -euse [ʃɑ̃sø, -øz] *adj* lucky

chancre [ʃɑ̃kr] *nm Méd & Fig* canker

chandail [ʃɑ̃daj] *nm* sweater

Chandeleur [ʃɑ̃dlœr] *nf* **la C.** Candlemas

chandelier [ʃɑ̃dəlje] *nm (à une branche)* candlestick; *(à plusieurs branches)* candelabra

chandelle [ʃɑ̃dɛl] *nf* (**a**) *(bougie)* candle; **s'éclairer à la c.** to use candlelight; **un dîner aux chandelles** a candlelit dinner; **faire des économies de bouts de c.** to make penny-pinching economies; **brûler la c. par les deux bouts** to burn the candle at both ends; **le jeu n'en vaut pas la c.** the game is not worth the candle; **tenir la c.** to feel like a fifth wheel; **voir trente-six chandelles** to see stars; **devoir une fière c. à qn** to owe sb a great debt (**b**) *(en gymnastique)* **faire la c.** to do a shoulder stand; *Aviat* **(montée en) c.** vertical climb

chanfrein [ʃɑ̃frɛ̃] *nm (de cheval)* nose

change [ʃɑ̃ʒ] *nm* (**a**) *Fin* exchange; **le c. est avantageux** the exchange rate is good; *Fig* **gagner/ne pas perdre au c.** to gain on/not to lose on the exchange (**b**) *Fig* **donner le c. à qn** to put sb off the scent (**c**) *(couche-culotte)* **c. (complet)** disposable diaper

changeant, -e [ʃɑ̃ʒɑ̃, -ɑ̃t] *adj (temps)* unsettled; **d'humeur changeante** moody

changement [ʃɑ̃ʒmɑ̃] *nm* (**a**) *(modification)* change; **ça va te faire un drôle de c.** it'll be quite a change for you; **c. de décor** *ou Théât* scene change; *Fig* change of scenery; **c. de direction** *(sur un écriteau)* under new management (**b**) *(dans les transports)* change; **il y a un c. à Valence** you have to change at Valence (**c**) **c. de vitesse** *(action)* change of gear; *(levier)* gear shift; *Ordinat* **c. de ligne** line feed

changer [45] [ʃɑ̃ʒe] **1** *vt* (**a**) *(remplacer) (draps, couche de bébé, roue)* to change; **c. qch contre qch** to change *or* to exchange sth for sth

(**b**) *(enfant, bébé)* to change

(**c**) *(convertir) (argent)* to change (**en** into)

(**d**) *(transformer)* **c. qn/qch en** to change sb/sth into (**e**) *(modifier)* to change, to alter; **ça va les c.!** that'll be a change for them!; **ça lui changera les idées** that'll take his/her mind off things; **ça nous change du café du coin!** that makes a change from the corner eatery!; **cela ne change rien à l'affaire** that makes no difference; **sa nouvelle coiffure la change** she looks different with her new hairstyle; **mais cela change tout!** that changes everything!; **c. qch de place** to move sth

2 *vi* (**a**) *(se modifier)* to change; **c. en bien** *ou* **en mieux** to change for the better; **c. en mal** *ou* **en pire** to change for the worse; *Ironique* **pour c.** for a change

(**b**) *(dans les transports)* to change

3 changer de *vt ind* to change; **c. de train/de travail** to change trains/jobs; **c. de place avec qn** to change places with sb; **c. de coiffure** to change one's hairstyle; **c. de vêtements** to change (one's clothes), to get changed; **c. de couleur** to change color; *Aut* **c. de vitesse** to change gear; **je te prie de c. de ton!** don't talk to me in that tone of voice!; *Fam Fig* **change de disque!** give me/us a break!, just drop it!

4 se changer *vpr* (**a**) *(mettre d'autres vêtements)* to change

(**b**) **se c. les idées** to change one's ideas

(**c**) *(se transformer)* **se c. en** to change *or* to turn into

chanoine [ʃanwan] *nm Rel* canon

chanson [ʃɑ̃sɔ̃] *nf* (**a**) *(air)* song; **la c. française** French songs; *Fam* **c'est toujours la même c.!** it's always the same old story!; *Fam* **on connaît la c.!** I've heard that one before!; **c. d'amour** love song; **c. à boire** drinking song (**b**) *(genre littéraire)* song; **c. de geste** chanson de geste

chansonnette [ʃɑ̃sɔnɛt] *nf* ditty

chansonnier [ʃɑ̃sɔnje] *nm* satirical cabaret singer

chant [ʃɑ̃] *nm* (**a**) *(chanson)* song; *(d'un instrument de musique, de la mer, du vent)* sound; *(d'un oiseau)* singing; *(du grillon, de la cigale)* chirping; *(du coq)* crowing; **au c. du coq** at cockcrow; *Fig* **c. du cygne** swan song; **c. funèbre** dirge; **c. de Noël** Christmas carol; **c. sacré** hymn (**b**) *(art)* singing; **leçon/professeur de c.** singing lesson/teacher; **apprendre le c.** to take singing lessons; **c. choral** choral singing; **c. grégorien** Gregorian chant (**c**) *(d'un poème)* canto

chantage [ʃɑ̃taʒ] *nm* blackmail; **faire du c. à qn** to blackmail sb; **il lui fait du c. au suicide** he's blackmailing her with suicide threats

chantant, -e [ʃɑ̃tɑ̃, -ɑ̃t] *adj (musique, air)* tuneful; *(accent, voix)* lilting

chanter [ʃɑ̃te] **1** *vt (chanson)* to sing; *Fam* **qu'est-ce que vous me chantez là?** what are you talking about?; *Fam* **elle le chante sur tous les tons** she's always going on about it

2 *vi* (**a**) *(personne, oiseau)* to sing; *(coq)* to crow; *(grillon, cigale)* to chirp; **c. juste/faux** to sing in tune/out of tune (**b**) **faire c. qn** *(exercer un chantage sur)* to blackmail sb (**c**) *(plaire)* **viens, si ça te chante** come along, if you like the idea; **il vient quand ça lui chante** he comes when he feels like it

chanterelle¹ [ʃɑ̃tʀɛl] *nf Mus (corde)* top string

chanterelle² [ʃɑ̃tʀɛl] *nf (champignon)* chanterelle

chanteur, -euse [ʃɑ̃tœʀ, -øz] *nm,f* singer; **c. de charme** crooner; **c. des rues** street singer

chantier [ʃɑ̃tje] *nm* (**a**) *(lieu de construction)* construction site; *(sur la route)* roadwork; **c. interdit au public** *(sur panneau)* no admittance to the public; **mettre qch en c.** to get sth under way; **c. naval** shipyard (**b**) *(projet d'envergure)* major project *or* piece of work (**c**) *Fam (désordre)* **quel c.!** what a shambles!; **ils ont tout laissé en c.** they left the place in a complete shambles

chantilly [ʃɑ̃tiji] *nf* **(crème) c.** whipped cream

chantonner [ʃɑ̃tɔne] *vt & vi* to sing softly; *(sans paroles)* to hum

chantre [ʃɑ̃tʀ] *nm (défenseur)* champion

chanvre [ʃɑ̃vʀ] *nm* hemp; **c. indien** Indian hemp

chaos [kao] *nm* chaos

chaotique [kaɔtik] *adj* chaotic

chaparder [ʃaparde] *vt Fam* to pinch, to swipe

chapardeur, -euse [ʃapardœr, -øz] *nm,f Fam* thief

chape [ʃap] *nf (de béton)* screed; *(d'un pneu)* tread; **la chaleur pèse sur la ville comme une c. de plomb** the heat lies on the town like a lead weight

chapeau, -x [ʃapo] *nm* (**a**) *(coiffure)* hat; *Fig* **porter le c.** to take the rap; *Fig* **tirer son c. à qn** to take off one's hat to sb; **c.!** well done!; **c. de cowboy** cowboy hat; **c. melon** derby hat; **c. mou** fedora; **c. de paille** straw hat (**b**) *(d'un champignon)* cap (**c**) *(partie supérieure) (de vol-au-vent, de bouchée à la reine)* lid; **prendre un virage sur les chapeaux de roues** to take a corner at top speed; **démarrer sur les chapeaux de roues** *(projet, soirée)* to get off to a flying start (**d**) *Typ & Journ* lead-in

chapeauter [ʃapote] *vt (contrôler)* to head

chapelain [ʃaplɛ̃] *nm Rel* chaplain

chapelet [ʃaplɛ] *nm (de prière)* rosary; *Fig (d'invectives, d'insultes)* stream; *(d'objets)* string; **dire son c.** to say the rosary

chapelier, -ère [ʃapəlje, -ɛr] *nm,f* hatter

chapelle [ʃapɛl] *nf* (**a**) *Rel* chapel; **c. ardente** chapel of rest (**b**) *Belg (café)* café

chapelure [ʃaplyr] *nf* breadcrumbs

chaperon [ʃaprɔ̃] *nm* (**a**) *(personne)* chaperon (**b**) **le Petit C. rouge** Little Red Riding Hood

chaperonner [ʃaprɔne] *vt aussi Fig* to chaperon

chapiteau, -x [ʃapito] *nm* (**a**) *Archit (d'une colonne)* capital (**b**) *(d'un cirque)* big top; **sous c.** in a marquee

chapitre [ʃapitr] *nm* (**a**) *(d'un livre)* chapter; *(d'un budget)* item; **inscrire une somme au c. des recettes/dépenses** to enter a sum under revenue/expenditure; **elle est sévère sur le c. de la discipline** she is strict in the matter of discipline; **en voilà assez sur ce c.** that's enough of that; **et maintenant, au c. des faits divers…** and now for the news in brief… (**b**) *Rel (assemblée)* chapter; *Fig* **avoir voix au c.** to have a say in the matter

chapitrer [ʃapitre] *vt* **c. qn** *(réprimander)* to tell sb off; *(faire la morale à)* to lecture sb

chapon [ʃapɔ̃] *nm (coq)* capon

chaptaliser [ʃaptalize] *vt* to chaptalize

chaque [ʃak] *adj indéfini* each, every; **c. femme doit pouvoir travailler et élever ses enfants** every woman should be able to work as well as bring up her children; **ces livres coûtent 15 euros c.** these books cost 15 euros each; **c. chose à sa place** everything in its place; **c. chose en son temps** all in good time; **c. fois qu'il vient** every time *or* whenever he comes; **j'y pense à c. instant** I think about it all the time

char [ʃar] *nm* (**a**) *Mil* **c. (d'assaut** *ou* **de combat)** tank (**b**) *(romain)* chariot (**c**) **c. de carnaval** float (**d**) *Can Fam (voiture)* car (**e**) *Sport* **c. à voile** sand yacht; **faire du c. à voile** to go sand yachting (**f**) *Fam* **arrête ton c.!** come off it!

charabia [ʃarabja] *nm Fam* gibberish, nonsense

charade [ʃarad] *nf* (**a**) *(devinette)* riddle (**b**) *(mime) (game of)* charades

charançon [ʃarɑ̃sɔ̃] *nm* weevil

charbon [ʃarbɔ̃] *nm* (**a**) *(combustible)* coal; **c. (de bois)** charcoal; **chauffage au c.** coal-fired heating; *Fig* **être sur des charbons ardents** to be on tenterhooks (**b**) *Art* charcoal; **dessin au c.** charcoal drawing (**c**) *Méd (médicament)* charcoal

charbonnage [ʃarbɔnaʒ] *nm* (**a**) *(exploitation)* coal mining (**b**) **charbonnages** *(houillères)* collieries

charbonneux, -euse [ʃarbɔnø, -øz] *adj (noir)* coal-black; *(yeux)* smoky *(with dark make-up)*

charbonnier, -ère [ʃarbɔnje, -ɛr] **1** *adj (industrie)* coal

2 *nm,f* (**a**) *(marchand de charbon)* coal merchant; *Prov* **c. est**

maître dans sa maison *ou* **chez soi** a man is master in his own home (**b**) *Naut* coaler

3 *nf* **charbonnière** *(mésange)* great tit

charcuter [ʃarkyte] *Fam* **1** *vt* **c. qn** to butcher sb

2 se charcuter *vpr* to cut oneself to ribbons; **se c. le menton/le doigt** to cut one's chin/finger to ribbons

charcuterie [ʃarkytri] *nf* (**a**) *(magasin)* pork butcher's (shop) (**b**) *(activité)* delicatessen trade (**c**) *(produits)* delicatessen meats

> **Charcuterie**
>
> A "charcuterie" sells mainly food prepared with pork: sausages, pâtés, ham, etc., collectively also known as "charcuterie". Ready-prepared dishes to take out are usually also sold.

charcutier, -ère [ʃarkytje, -ɛr] *nm,f* (**a**) *(commerçant, fabricant)* pork butcher (**b**) *Fam Péj (chirurgien)* butcher

chardon [ʃardɔ̃] *nm (plante)* thistle

chardonneret [ʃardɔnrɛ] *nm* goldfinch

charentais, -e [ʃarɑ̃tɛ, -ɛz] **1** *adj* of Charente

2 *nm,f* **C., Charentaise** person from Charente

3 *nf* **charentaise** *(chausson)* slipper

charge [ʃarʒ] *nf* (**a**) *(poids)* load; *(sur bateau)* cargo; *Fig* **être une c. pour qn** to be a burden to sb; **c. utile** *(d'un véhicule)* capacity

(**b**) *(responsabilité)* responsibility; **être en c. de qch** to be in charge of sth; **prendre qn/qch en c.** to take charge of sb/sth; **se prendre en c.** to be responsible for oneself

(**c**) *(fonction)* office; *(d'avoué)* practice

(**d**) *(obligation financière)* **être à la c. de qn** *(personne)* to be dependent on sb; *(appel, transport, réparations)* to be chargeable to sb; **avoir deux enfants à c.** to have two dependent children; **prendre un client en c.** *(taxi)* to pick up a fare; **être pris et c. à cent pour cent par la Sécurité sociale** to have all one's medical expenses paid by Social Security; **charges (locatives)** *(d'un appartement)* maintenance charges; **charges d'exploitation** operating costs; **charges sociales** social-security charges *(paid by the employer)*

(**e**) *(d'une arme, d'explosifs)* charge

(**f**) *Constr (pression)* load

(**g**) *Élec (d'une batterie, d'une particule)* charge

(**h**) *Mil* charge; *Fig* **revenir à la c.** to return to the attack

(**i**) *Jur (preuve)* charge

> **Charges**
>
> Householders and tenants in apartment blocks are required to pay "charges", a monthly contribution to pay for the general maintenance of the building. In real estate agencies, rent is expressed either including this sum ("charges comprises" or "cc") or excluding it ("hors charges" or "charges en sus"). Sometimes, the "charges" include heating costs.

chargé, -e [ʃarʒe] **1** *adj* (**a**) *(camion, navire)* loaded, laden (**de** with); *(revolver, appareil photo)* loaded; *Fig (style)* ornate; **la voiture est trop chargée** the car is overloaded; **être c. comme un bourricot** *ou* **un mulet** to be loaded down; **avoir la langue chargée** to have a furred tongue; **un regard c. de reconnaissance** a look full of gratitude (**b**) *(occupé) (journée, programme)* full (**c**) *(responsable)* **être c. de qch** *(mission)* to be entrusted with sth; *(tâche)* to be responsible for sth; **être c. de famille** to have family responsibilities; **être c. de faire qch** to be responsible for doing sth (**d**) *Phys* charged

2 *nm* **c. d'affaires** chargé-d'affaires; **c. de mission** official representative

3 *nm,f* *Univ* **c. de cours** = part-time lecturer; *Can* lecturer

chargement [ʃarʒəmɑ̃] *nm* (**a**) *(action)* loading; *Élec (d'une batterie)* charging; **machine à laver à c. frontal** front-loading washing machine (**b**) *(marchandises)* load; *(sur bateau)* cargo

charger [45] [ʃarʒe] **1** *vt* (**a**) *(camion, navire, marchandises)* to load (**b**) *(remplir)* to fill (**de** with) (**c**) *(fusil, appareil photo)* to load; *Élec (batterie)* to charge; *Ordinat* to load (up) (**d**) *(donner une responsabilité à)* **c. qn de qch** to entrust sb with sth; **c. qn de faire qch** to give sb the responsibility for doing sth; **il m'a chargé de vous transmettre un message** he asked me to give you a message (**e**) *(attaquer)* to charge (at)

2 *vi* (**a**) *Ordinat* to load up (**b**) *Mil* to charge

3 se charger *vpr* (**a**) *(s'alourdir)* to weigh oneself down (**b**) **se c. de qn/qch** *(prendre la responsabilité de)* to take care of sb/sth; **se c. de faire qch** to undertake to do sth; **laisse tomber, je m'en charge** don't worry about it, I'll take care of it

chargeur [ʃarʒœr] *nm (d'arme)* magazine; *Phot* cartridge; *Élec* (battery) charger; *Ordinat* loader

chariot [ʃarjo] *nm (petite charrette)* wagon; *(de supermarché)* cart; *(pour diapositives)* cartridge; *(pour la manutention)* truck; *(d'hôpital)* gurney; *(d'une machine à écrire)* carriage; *Cin* dolly; **c. à bagages** luggage cart

charismatique [karismatik] *adj* charismatic

charisme [karism] *nm* charisma

charitable [ʃaritabl] *adj* charitable (**envers** towards); *(conseil)* friendly

charité [ʃarite] *nf* (**a**) *(altruisme)* charity; **faites-moi** *ou* **ayez la c. de...** please be kind enough to...; *Prov* **c. bien ordonnée commence par soi-même** charity begins at home (**b**) *(don)* charity; **faire la c. à qn** to give money to sb; **demander la c.** to ask for charity; **la c., Messieurs Dames** *(dans la rue)* can you spare some change, please?

charlatan [ʃarlatɑ̃] *nm Péj (mauvais médecin)* quack; *(escroc)* charlatan

Charles [ʃarl] *npr* **C. Quint** Charles the Fifth

charlot [ʃarlo] *nm Fam (personne peu sérieuse)* clown

charlotte [ʃarlɔt] *nf Culin* charlotte; **c. aux poires/au chocolat** pear/chocolate charlotte

charmant, -e [ʃarmɑ̃, -ɑ̃t] *adj (personne, chose, soirée)* charming, delightful; *Ironique* **et voilà qu'il pleut, ah, c'est c.!** now it's raining, that's just wonderful!

charme¹ [ʃarm] *nm* (**a**) *(attrait)* charm; **avoir du c.** to have charm; **c'est ce qui en fait le c.** that's what makes it so attractive; **faire du c. à qn** to turn on the charm with sb; **charmes** *(d'une femme)* charms; **vivre de ses charmes** to sell one's charms (**b**) *(magie)* spell; **être/tomber sous le c.** to be/fall under the spell; *Fig* **se porter comme un c.** to be as fit as a fiddle

charme² [ʃarm] *nm (arbre)* hornbeam

charmer [ʃarme] *vt* (**a**) *(plaire à)* to charm; **j'ai été charmé de vous rencontrer** it's been a pleasure to meet you (**b**) *(envoûter)* to charm

charmeur, -euse [ʃarmœr, -øz] **1** *nm,f* charmer; **c. de serpents** snake charmer

2 *adj (regard, sourire)* charming

charnel, -elle [ʃarnɛl] *adj* carnal

charnier [ʃarnje] *nm* mass grave

charnière [ʃarnjɛr] *nf (de porte, de fenêtre)* hinge; *Fig* **à la c. de deux grandes périodes** at the junction of two great eras; **époque/œuvre c.** transitional period/work

charnu, -e [ʃarny] *adj (partie du corps, lèvres)* fleshy; *(fruit)* pulpy; *Hum* **la partie charnue de son anatomie** his posterior

charognard [ʃarɔɲar] *nm* (**a**) *Zool* carrion-eater (**b**) *(exploiteur)* vulture

charogne [ʃarɔɲ] *nf* (**a**) *(d'animal)* carrion (**b**) *Fam (homme)* bastard; *(femme)* bitch

charpente [ʃarpɑ̃t] *nf (d'un bâtiment, d'un roman)* framework; *(du corps)* frame; **avoir une solide c.** *(personne)* to be solidly built

charpenterie [ʃarpɑ̃tri] *nf (métier)* carpentry

charpentier [ʃarpɑ̃tje] *nm* carpenter

charpie [ʃarpi] *nf* **mettre qch en c.** to tear sth to shreds; *Fam* **mettre qn en c.** to make mincemeat out of sb

charretier [ʃartje] *nm* **jurer comme un c.** to swear like a trooper

charrette [ʃarɛt] *nf* (a) *(véhicule)* cart (b) *(de licenciements)* round of layoffs (c) *Suisse Fam* **c. de Paul!** goddamn Paul!

charrier [66] [ʃarje] **1** *vt* (a) *(transporter)* to cart (b) *(entraîner)* to carry along (c) *Fam (se moquer de)* **c. qn** to put sb on; **se faire c.** to be put on
2 *vi Fam (exagérer)* to go too far; **faut pas c.!** *(n'exagère pas)* come off it!

charrue [ʃary] *nf* (a) *(pour labourer)* plow; *Fig* **mettre la c. avant les bœufs** to put the cart before the horse (b) *Can* snowplough

charte [ʃart] *nf* charter

charter [ʃartɛr] *nm* **(avion) c.** charter plane

chartreux, -euse [ʃartrø, -øz] **1** *nm,f Rel* Carthusian
2 *nf* **chartreuse** (a) *(couvent)* Carthusian monastery (b) *(alcool)* Chartreuse

chas [ʃa] *nm* eye *(of a needle)*

chasse [ʃas] *nf* (a) *(activité)* hunting; *(au fusil)* shooting; **aller à la c.** to go hunting/shooting; **la c. est ouverte/fermée** the shooting season has begun/ended; *Prov* **qui va à la c. perd sa place** = if you leave your place someone will take it; **c. à courre** hunting; **c. au lapin** rabbit shooting (b) *(événement)* hunt; *(au fusil)* shoot (c) *(réserve)* **c. gardée** private game preserve; *Fig (domaine)* preserve (d) *(poursuite)* chase; **donner la c. à qn/qch, prendre qn/qch en c.** to give chase to sb/sth; **c. à l'homme** manhunt; *Pol* **c. aux sorcières** witch hunt; **c. au trésor** treasure hunt (e) **c. (d'eau)** flush; **tirer la c. (d'eau)** to flush the toilet (f) **être en c.** *(chienne, chatte)* to be in heat

châsse [ʃas] *nf Rel* shrine

chassé-croisé *(pl* **chassés-croisés)** [ʃasekrwaze] *nm (de personnes)* comings and goings; *(de conversations)* babble

chasse-neige [ʃasnɛʒ] *nm inv* (a) *(engin)* snowplow (b) *(en ski)* snowplow; **descendre une piste en c.** to snowplow down a ski slope

chasser [ʃase] **1** *vt* (a) *(animaux)* to hunt; **c. le renard/la perdrix** to go foxhunting/partridge shooting (b) *(expulser)* to drive *or* to chase away (**de** from); *(employé)* to dismiss; *(mouches)* to brush away; *(sujet: vent) (nuages)* to blow away; *(idées noires)* to forget; **je ne veux pas vous c. mais il est tard** I'm not trying to get rid of you but it's getting late; *Fig* **c. qn/qch de son esprit** to dismiss sb/sth from one's thoughts
2 *vi* (a) *(aller à la chasse)* to hunt, to go hunting; *(au fusil)* to shoot, to go shooting (b) *Aut* to skid

chasseur, -euse [ʃasœr, -øz] **1** *nm,f* hunter; **c. de primes** bounty hunter; *aussi Fig* **c. de têtes** headhunter
2 *nm* (a) *(dans un hôtel)* bellboy, bellhop (b) *(avion de chasse)* fighter (c) *Mil* **les chasseurs alpins** the mountain light infantry

châssis [ʃasi] *nm* (a) *(charpente)* frame (b) *Art* stretcher (c) *(de jardin) (cold)* frame (d) *Aut* chassis (e) *Can (fenêtre)* window

chaste [ʃast] *adj* chaste

chastement [ʃastəmɑ̃] *adv* chastely

chasteté [ʃastəte] *nf* chastity

chasuble [ʃazybl] *nf* (a) **(robe) c.** jumper (b) *Rel* chasuble

chat¹, chatte [ʃa, ʃat] *nm,f* cat; **petit c.** kitten; *Fam* **mon petit c., ma petite chatte** my pet; *Fig* **il n'y avait pas un c.** there wasn't a soul there; **appeler un c. un c.** to call a spade a spade; **avoir un c. dans la gorge** to have a frog in one's throat; **jouer au c. et à la souris avec qn** to play cat-and-mouse with sb; *Prov* **c. échaudé craint l'eau froide** once bitten, twice shy; **quand le c. n'est pas là, les souris dansent** when the cat's away the mice will play; **c. de gouttière**

alley cat; **c. persan** Persian (cat); **c. sauvage** wildcat; *Can (raton laveur)* raccoon; **c. siamois** Siamese (cat)
2 *nf* **chatte** *Vulg (sexe féminin)* pussy

chat² [tʃat] *nm Ordinat (sur Internet)* chat

châtaigne [ʃatɛɲ] *nf* (a) *(fruit)* (sweet) chestnut (b) *très Fam (coup de poing)* thump; **flanquer une c. à qn** to thump sb; **se prendre une c.** *(décharge)* to get a shock

châtaignier [ʃatɛɲe] *nm (arbre, bois)* chestnut

châtain [ʃatɛ̃] **1** *adj (cheveux)* (chestnut-)brown; *(personne)* brown-haired
2 *nm* chestnut brown

château, -x [ʃato] *nm* (a) *(forteresse)* castle; *(manoir)* mansion; *(de famille aristocratique)* stately home; *(palais)* palace; **les châteaux de la Loire** the châteaux of the Loire; *Fig* **bâtir des châteaux en Espagne** to build castles in the air; **c. de cartes** house of cards; **c. d'eau** water tower; **c. fort** castle; **c. gonflable** inflatable castle (b) *(exploitation vinicole)* château; **mis en bouteille au c.** *(sur bouteille)* = indicates that wine was bottled at source

châtelain [ʃatlɛ̃] *nm (au Moyen Âge)* lord of the manor; *(propriétaire d'un château)* château owner

châtelaine [ʃatlɛn] *nf (au Moyen Âge)* lady of the manor; *(propriétaire d'un château)* (woman) château owner; *(épouse du propriétaire)* wife of a château owner

chat-huant *(pl* **chats-huants)** [ʃayɑ̃] *nm* tawny owl

châtié, -e [ʃatje] *adj (style)* polished; *(langage)* refined

châtier [66] [ʃatje] *vt Litt (personne)* to chastise; *Prov* **qui aime bien châtie bien** spare the rod and spoil the child

chatière [ʃatjɛr] *nf* (a) *(pour chat)* cat flap (b) *(pour aération)* ventilation hole

châtiment [ʃatimɑ̃] *nm* (a) *Litt* chastisement (b) **c. corporel** corporal punishment

chaton¹ [ʃatɔ̃] *nm* (a) *(petit chat)* kitten (b) *Bot* catkin

chaton² [ʃatɔ̃] *nm* (a) *(d'une bague)* bezel (b) *(pierre)* stone

chatouille [ʃatuj] *nf* **faire des chatouilles à qn** to tickle sb; **craindre les chatouilles** to be ticklish

chatouiller [ʃatuje] *vt* to tickle; *Fig (curiosité)* to arouse; *(amour-propre)* to flatter; **ah, ça chatouille!** oh, that tickles!

chatouilleux, -euse [ʃatujø, -øz] *adj* ticklish; *Fig* sensitive (**sur** about)

chatoyant, -e [ʃatwajɑ̃, -ɑ̃t] *adj* shimmering; *(pierre, imagination)* sparkling

chatoyer [32] [ʃatwaje] *vi* to shimmer; *(pierre)* to sparkle

châtrer [ʃatre] *vt (homme, taureau)* to castrate; *(étalon)* to geld; *(chat)* to neuter

chatte [ʃat] *nf voir* **chat**

chatterton [ʃatɛrtɔn] *nm* friction tape

chaud, -e [ʃo, ʃod] **1** *adj* (a) *(modérément)* warm; *(intensément)* hot; *Fig (voix)* sultry; *(couleur)* warm; **la soupe est toute chaude** the soup is piping hot; **l'été va être c.** it'll be a hot summer; *Fig* there'll be a lot of unrest this summer; **l'alerte fut chaude** it was a close call; **une nouvelle toute chaude** some hot news (b) *(passionné) (discussion)* heated; *(partisan)* keen; **elle n'est pas chaude pour le projet** she's not keen on the plan; **je ne suis pas très c. pour aller au cinéma** I don't really feel like going to the movies
2 *adv* **j'aime manger c.** I like my food hot
3 *nm (modéré)* warmth; *(intense)* heat; **garder** *ou* **tenir qch au c.** to keep sth warm; **chez soi, au c.** at home, in the warmth; **avoir c.** to be *or* to feel hot; *Fam (échapper de justesse)* to have a narrow escape; **il fait c.** it's hot; *Fig* **cela ne me fait ni c. ni froid** it's all the same to me; **interroger les spectateurs à c.** to question the audience on the spot; **attraper un c. et froid** to catch a chill

chaudement [ʃodmɑ̃] *adv (s'habiller, féliciter, recommander)* warmly

chaudière [ʃodjɛr] *nf* (a) *(de chauffage)* boiler; **c. à mazout/à gaz** oil-fired/gas boiler (b) *Can (seau)* bucket

chaudron [ʃodrɔ̃] *nm* cauldron

chaudronnier, -ère [ʃodrɔnje, -ɛr] *nm,f* boiler maker

chauffage [ʃofaʒ] *nm (d'une pièce, d'un bâtiment)* heating; *(appareils)* heating (system); *(dans une voiture)* heater; **c. à l'électricité/au gaz/au mazout** electric/gas/oil-fired heating; **c. central** central heating

chauffagiste [ʃofaʒist] *nm* heating engineer

chauffant, -e [ʃofɑ̃, -ɑ̃t] *adj voir* **couverture, plaque**

chauffard [ʃofar] *nm* reckless driver

chauffe-biberon (*pl* **chauffe-biberons**) [ʃofbibrɔ̃] *nm* bottle-warmer

chauffe-eau [ʃofo] *nm inv* water heater; **c. électrique** immersion heater

chauffe-plat (*pl* **chauffe-plats**) [ʃofpla] *nm* hot plate

chauffer [ʃofe] **1** *vt (pièce, bâtiment)* to heat (up); *(moteur)* to warm up; **c. une maison au gaz** to heat a house with gas; **la chambre n'est pas chauffée** there's no heating in the bedroom; *Fig* **c. la salle** to warm up one's audience
2 *vi* **(a)** *(devenir chaud)* to heat up; **ce radiateur chauffe bien/mal** this radiator gives out/doesn't give out a lot of heat; **faire c. qch, mettre qch à c.** to heat sth up **(b)** *(s'échauffer) (moteur)* to overheat **(c)** *Fam* **ça va c. s'il est en retard!** there'll be trouble if he's late!; **tu chauffes!** *(dans un jeu)* you're getting warmer!
3 se chauffer *vpr* to warm oneself; **se c. (les muscles)** to warm up; **se c. au mazout/à l'électricité** to have oil-fired/electric heating

chaufferette [ʃofrɛt] *nf (pour les pieds)* footwarmer

chaufferie [ʃofri] *nf* boiler room

chauffeur [ʃofœr] *nm (de voiture, de bus)* driver; *(employé)* chauffeur; **c. de camion** truck driver; **c. de taxi** taxi driver

chauffeuse [ʃoføz] *nf (fauteuil)* low armless chair

chauler [ʃole] *vt (murs)* to whitewash; *(terres)* to treat with lime

chaume [ʃom] *nm* **(a)** *(pour toits)* thatch **(b)** *(des céréales)* stubble

chaumière [ʃomjɛr] *nf (maison pauvre)* cottage; *(maison à toit de chaume)* thatched cottage

chaussée [ʃose] *nf (route)* roadway

chausse-pied (*pl* **chausse-pieds**) [ʃospje] *nm* shoehorn

chausser [ʃose] *vt* **1** **(a)** *(chaussures, lunettes, skis)* to put on; **chaussé de pantoufles** wearing slippers; **elle chausse du 37** she takes a size 37 **(b)** *(mettre des chaussures à)* to put shoes on **(c)** *(aller à)* to fit; **souliers qui chaussent bien** shoes that fit well
2 se chausser *vpr (mettre ses chaussures)* to put one's shoes on

chausses [ʃos] *nfpl (vêtement)* breeches

chaussette [ʃosɛt] *nf* sock; **en chaussettes** in one's socks; **laisser tomber qn comme une vieille c.** to cast sb aside like an old rag

chausseur [ʃosœr] *nm (magasin)* shoe store; *(fabricant)* shoe maker

chausson [ʃosɔ̃] *nm* **(a)** *(pantoufle)* slipper; *(de danse)* ballet shoe; *(de bébé)* bootee **(b)** *Culin* **c. aux pommes** apple turnover

chaussure [ʃosyr] *nf* shoe; **(l'industrie de) la c.** the shoe industry; **chaussures de ville/de sport/habillées** city/sports/dress shoes; **chaussures à lacets** lace-up shoes; **chaussures de marche** *ou* **de montagne** walking boots; **chaussures montantes** ankle boots; **chaussures de ski** ski boots; **chaussures à talons** high-heeled shoes; *Fig* **trouver c. à son pied** to find the right woman/man

chauve [ʃov] **1** *adj* bald
2 *nm* bald(-headed) man

chauve-souris (*pl* **chauves-souris**) [ʃovsuri] *nf* bat

chauvin, -e [ʃovɛ̃, -in] **1** *adj* chauvinistic
2 *nm,f* chauvinist

chauvinisme [ʃovinism] *nm* chauvinism

chaux [ʃo] *nf* lime; **blanchir un mur à la c.** to whitewash a wall; **c. vive** quicklime

chavirer [ʃavire] **1** *vi* **(a)** *(bateau)* to capsize; **faire c. un bateau** to capsize a boat **(b)** *(tourner)* **tout chavire autour de moi** everything's spinning
2 *vt (bouleverser)* to overwhelm

check-up [tʃɛkœp] *nm inv Méd* check-up; **se faire faire un c.** to have a check-up

chef [ʃɛf] *nm* **(a)** *(d'un parti politique, d'une bande)* leader; *(d'une tribu)* chief; *Fam (patron)* boss; **ingénieur/rédacteur en c.** chief engineer/editor; **se débrouiller comme un c.** to be doing very well; **c. d'atelier** (shop) foreman; **c. comptable** chief financial officer; **c. d'entreprise** company head; **c. d'État** head of state; **c. de famille** head of the family; **c. de file** leader; **c. de gare** station manager; **le c. du gouvernement** the head of government; **c. d'orchestre** conductor; **c. de service** departmental head; *Belg Univ* **c. de travaux** ≃ assistant professor **(b)** *(cuisinier)* chef **(c)** *Jur* **c. d'accusation** charge, count **(d)** *(tête)* head; **faire qch de son propre c.** to do sth on one's own authority

chefaillon [ʃefajɔ̃] *nm Fam Péj* little Hitler

chef-garde (*pl* **chefs-gardes**) [ʃɛfgard] *nm Belg Rail* ticket inspector

chef-d'œuvre (*pl* **chefs-d'œuvre**) [ʃɛdœvr] *nm* masterpiece

chef-lieu (*pl* **chefs-lieux**) [ʃɛfljø] *nm* = administrative center of a "département"

cheik(h) [ʃɛk] *nm* sheik(h)

chelem [ʃlɛm] *nm Sport* **grand c.** grand slam

chelou [ʃəlu] *adj inv Fam* shady, seedy

chemin [ʃəmɛ̃] *nm* **(a)** *(route étroite)* path, track; **c. de grande randonnée** hiking trail; **c. de ronde** parapet walk; **c. de terre** track; **c. de traverse** path across the fields
(b) *(itinéraire)* way **(de** to); *Fig (de la gloire, du bonheur)* road **(de** to); **sur le c. du retour** on the way back; **en c.** on the way; **se mettre en c.** to set out *or* off; **nous ne pouvons pas nous arrêter en si bon c.** we can't give up now when we're doing so well; **ne pas y aller par quatre chemins** to get straight to the point; **prendre le c. des écoliers** to take the long way around; **suivre le droit c.** to stay on the straight and narrow
(c) *(distance)* way; *aussi Fig* **avoir beaucoup de c. à faire** to have a long way to go; **nous avons fait la moitié du c. ensemble/à pied** we went half the way together/on foot; *Fig* **faire son c.** *(idée)* to gain ground
(d) *Ordinat* path; **c. d'accès** path

chemin de fer (*pl* **chemins de fer**) [ʃəmɛ̃dfɛr] *nm* railroad; *Ordinat (affichage)* thumbnail; **les chemins de fer** *(société d'exploitation)* the railroad company

cheminée [ʃəmine] *nf* **(a)** *(dans une maison)* fireplace; *(dessus)* mantelpiece **(b)** *(conduit) (de maison, d'usine)* chimney; *(de bateau à vapeur)* funnel **(c)** *Géol* chimney

cheminement [ʃəminmɑ̃] *nm (de personnes)* movement; *Fig* **le c. de la pensée** the development of thought

cheminer [ʃəmine] *vi (personne)* to make one's way; *Fig (idée)* to gain ground

cheminot [ʃəmino] *nm* railroad worker

chemise [ʃəmiz] *nf* **(a)** *(vêtement)* shirt; **c. à manches longues/courtes** long-/short-sleeved shirt; *Fig* **changer de qch comme de c.** to change sth at the drop of a hat; **c. de nuit** *(de femme)* nightdress; *(d'homme)* nightshirt **(b)** *(classeur)* folder

chemisette [ʃəmizɛt] *nf (d'homme)* short-sleeved shirt

chemisier [ʃəmizje] *nm* **(a)** *(corsage)* blouse **(b)** *(fabricant)* shirt-maker; *(marchand)* men's outfitter

chenal, -aux [ʃənal, -o] *nm (d'une rivière, d'un port)* channel

chenapan [ʃənapɑ̃] *nm Vieilli* scoundrel

chêne [ʃɛn] *nm* oak; **table en c. massif** solid oak table; **c. vert** holm oak

chêne-liège (*pl* **chênes-lièges**) [ʃɛnljɛʒ] *nm* cork oak

chenet [ʃənɛ] *nm* firedog

chenil [ʃənil] *nm* (**a**) (*niche*) doghouse (**b**) (*élevage*) kennel (**c**) *Suisse* (*désordre*) shambles

chenille [ʃənij] *nf* (**a**) (*insecte*) caterpillar (**b**) (*de char, d'auto-neige*) caterpillar track; **véhicule à chenilles** tracked vehicle (**c**) (*tissu*) chenille

chenu, -e [ʃəny] *adj Litt* (*personne, tête*) hoary; (*arbre*) leafless

cheptel [ʃɛptɛl] *nm* (*d'un agriculteur*) livestock

chèque [ʃɛk] *nm* **c.** (*bancaire*) check; **c. de 60 euros** check for 60 euros; **faire un c. à qn** to write sb a check; **payer qch par c.** to pay for sth by check; **c. de banque** cashier's check; **c. barré** crossed check; **c. en blanc** blank check; *Fam* **c. en bois** rubber check; **c. sans provision** bad check; **j'ai fait un c. sans provision** my check bounced; **c. de voyage** traveler's check

chèque-cadeau (*pl* **chèques-cadeaux**) [ʃɛkkado] *nm* gift token

chèque-repas (*pl* **chèques-repas**) [ʃɛkrəpa], **chèque-restaurant** (*pl* **chèques-restaurant**) [ʃɛkrɛstɔrɑ̃] *nm* meal ticket

chéquier [ʃekje] *nm* checkbook

cher, -ère [ʃɛr] **1** *adj* (**a**) (*coûteux*) expensive; *Fam* **pas c.** cheap; **la vie est chère en ville** it's expensive to live in town (**b**) (*aimé*) dear; *Litt* **être c. à qn** to be dear to sb; **c'est mon vœu le plus c.** it's my dearest wish; **il a retrouvé sa chère maison/son c. bureau** he's back in his beloved house/office; **C. Monsieur** (*dans une lettre*) Dear Mr. X; (*officiel*) Dear Sir

2 *adv* **payer qch c./trop c.** to pay a high price/too much for sth; *Fam* **je l'ai eu pour pas c.** I got it cheap; **coûter c.** to cost a lot; **je donnerais c. pour savoir ce qu'il leur a dit** I'd give anything to know what he said to them

3 *nm,f* **mon c., ma chère** my dear

chercher [ʃɛrʃe] **1** *vt* (**a**) (*objet, personne, emploi, solution*) to look for; (*dans un dictionnaire*) to look up; (*dans ses souvenirs*) to try to think of; **c. qn du regard** to look around for sb; **c. ses mots** to search for words; **cherche!** (*à un chien*) fetch!; *Fig* **où va-t-il donc c. tout cela?** where on earth does he get that from?; **il l'a bien cherché** he was asking for it; **c. midi à quatorze heures** to look for problems where there are none (**b**) (*prendre*) **aller/venir c. qn/qch** to (go/come and) collect sb/sth (**c**) (*essayer*) **c. à faire qch** to try to do sth (**d**) *Fam* (*atteindre*) **cela va c. dans les 10 000 euros** you're talking about something like 10,000 euros (**e**) *Fam* (*provoquer*) to get at; **tu me cherches?** are you looking for a fight?

2 se chercher *vpr* (*chercher son identité*) to try to find oneself

chercheur, -euse [ʃɛrʃœr, -øz] *nm,f* (**a**) (*scientifique*) researcher (**b**) **c. d'or** gold digger

chère [ʃɛr] *nf Litt* **aimer la bonne c.** to be a lover of good food

chèrement [ʃɛrmɑ̃] *adv* **vendre c. sa peau** to sell one's life dearly

chéri, -e [ʃeri] **1** *adj* dear; **à notre grand-mère chérie** (*sur une couronne mortuaire*) to our beloved grandmother

2 *nm,f* darling; **mon c., ma chérie** darling

chérir [ʃerir] *vt Litt* to cherish

cherra *etc. voir* **choir**

cherry (*pl* **cherrys** *ou* **cherries**) [ʃeri] *nm* cherry brandy

cherté [ʃɛrte] *nf* high cost; **la c. de la vie** the high cost of living

chérubin [ʃerybɛ̃] *nm aussi Fig* cherub

chétif, -ive [ʃetif, -iv] *adj* (*personne*) puny, sickly; (*arbuste*) stunted

cheval, -aux [ʃəval, -o] *nm* (**a**) (*animal*) horse; *Péj* (*femme*) carthorse; **à c.** on horseback; **monter à c.** to ride; *aussi Fig* **être à c. sur qch** to straddle sth; **être à c. sur l'étiquette** to be a stickler for etiquette; *Fam* **ce n'est pas un mauvais c.** he's not such a bad guy; **monter sur ses grands chevaux** to get on one's high horse; **petits chevaux** = type of board game; **c. d'arçons** (vaulting) horse; **c. à bascule** rocking horse; **c'est son c. de bataille** that's her hobbyhorse; **chevaux de bois** merry-go-round; **c. de course** racehorse; **c. de labour** workhorse; **c. de trait** draft horse (**b**) *Aut* horsepower; **une automobile de 20 chevaux** a 20-horsepower car

chevalerie [ʃəvalri] *nf* (**a**) (*dignité*) knighthood (**b**) (*institution*) chivalry

chevalet [ʃəvalɛ] *nm* (**a**) (*de peintre*) easel; (*de menuisier, de charpentier*) trestle (**b**) *Mus* (*de violon*) bridge

chevalier [ʃəvalje] *nm* (**a**) (*seigneur*) knight; **c. servant** faithful admirer (**b**) (*de la Légion d'honneur*) chevalier

chevalière [ʃəvaljɛr] *nf* signet ring

chevalin, -e [ʃəvalɛ̃, -in] *adj* equine; *Fig* (*traits*) horsey

cheval-vapeur [ʃəvalvapœr] (*pl* **chevaux-vapeur** [ʃəvova-pœr]) *nm* horsepower

chevauchée [ʃəvoʃe] *nf* (*course*) ride

chevaucher [ʃəvoʃe] **1** *vt* (*mur, chaise*) to straddle; *Litt* (*cheval, âne*) to ride

2 *vi Litt* to ride

3 se chevaucher *vpr* to overlap

chevelu, -e [ʃəvly] *adj Péj* long-haired

chevelure [ʃəvlyr] *nf* (head of) hair; **femme à la c. rousse/blonde** red-haired/blonde woman

chevet [ʃəvɛ] *nm* (**a**) (*tête de lit*) bedhead; **rester au c. de qn** to stay at sb's bedside (**b**) *Archit* (*d'une église*) chevet

cheveu, -x [ʃəvø] *nm* (**a**) (*poil*) hair; **avoir le c. terne** to have dull hair; **un c. blanc** a gray hair; **arriver comme un c. sur la soupe** to come at an awkward moment; **il s'en est fallu d'un c. qu'il n'éclate de rire** he very nearly burst out laughing; **rater qch d'un c.** to miss sth by a whisker; **à un c. près, je ratais mon train** I caught my train by a hair's breadth (**b**) **cheveux** hair; **avoir les cheveux longs/courts** to have long/short hair; **un vieillard à cheveux blancs** a white-haired old man; **argument tiré par les cheveux** far-fetched argument; **cheveux d'ange** (*pâtes*) angel-hair pasta

cheville [ʃəvij] *nf* (**a**) (*partie du corps*) ankle; *Fig* **il ne vous arrive pas à la c.** he can't hold a candle to you; *Fam Péj* **tu as les chevilles qui enflent** you're getting too big for your breeches (**b**) (*pour accrocher*) peg; (*pour boucher un trou*) plug; (*de violon, de guitare*) peg; *Fam* **être en c. avec qn** to be in cahoots with sb; *Fig* **c. ouvrière** mainspring

chèvre [ʃɛvr] **1** *nf* goat; *Fam* **devenir c.** to go around the bend; *Fam* **rendre qn c.** to drive sb around the bend

2 *nm* goat's cheese

chevreau, -x [ʃəvro] *nm* kid; **gants en c.** kid gloves

chèvrefeuille [ʃɛvrəfœj] *nm* honeysuckle

chevreuil [ʃəvrœj] *nm* roe deer; *Can* (*gibier*) venison

chevron [ʃəvrɔ̃] *nm* (**a**) *Constr* (*d'un toit*) rafter (**b**) *Mil* stripe, chevron (**c**) (*motif*) **tissu à chevrons** herringbone-pattern material

chevronné, -e [ʃəvrɔne] *adj* (*qui a de l'expérience*) experienced

chevrotant, -e [ʃəvrɔtɑ̃, -ɑ̃t] *adj* (*voix*) quavering

chevroter [ʃəvrɔte] *vi* (*voix*) to quaver

chevrotine [ʃəvrɔtin] *nf* buckshot

chewing-gum (*pl* **chewing-gums**) [ʃwiŋgɔm] *nm* chewing gum

chez [ʃe] *prép* (**a**) *(dans la maison de)* **il n'est pas c. lui** he's not at home, he's not in; **elle est rentrée c. elle** she's gone home; **faites comme c. vous** make yourself at home; **je vais c. ma sœur** I'm going to my sister's; **venez c. nous** come to our place; **il vit c. nous** he lives with us; **aller c. le dentiste** to go to the dentist; **chez...** *(sur une lettre)* c/o... (**b**) *(en, dans)* **c'est devenu une habitude c. moi** it's become a habit with me; **ce que j'admire c. cet homme, c'est...** what I admire about the man is...; **c. les Espagnols, on dîne tard** the Spanish have dinner late (**c**) *(au temps de)* during the time of (**d**) *(parmi)* among; **cette expression est courante c. les jeunes** this expression is common among young people

chez-soi [ʃeswa] *nm inv* **son petit c.** one's own little home

chialer [ʃjale] *vi très Fam* to blubber

chiant, -e [ʃjɑ̃, -ɑ̃t] *adj très Fam* damned annoying

chianti [kjɑ̃ti] *nm* Chianti

chiasse [ʃjas] *nf Vulg* **avoir la c.** *(la diarrhée)* to have the runs; *(avoir peur)* to be shit-scared

chic [ʃik] **1** *adj inv* (**a**) *(élégant)* stylish, smart; **les gens c.** the smart set (**b**) *Fam Vieilli (aimable)* decent

2 *nm* (**a**) *(savoir-faire)* **avoir le c. pour faire qch** to have the knack of doing sth (**b**) *(élégance)* style; **bon c. bon genre** ≃ preppy

3 *exclam Fam Vieilli* **c. (alors)!** great!

Chicago [ʃikago] *n* Chicago

chicaner [ʃikane] **1** *vt (chercher querelle à)* to quibble with (**sur** about)

2 chicaner sur *vt ind* to quibble over

3 se chicaner *vpr* to squabble

chicaneur, -euse [ʃikanœr, -øz], **chicanier, -ère** [ʃikanje, -ɛr] *nm,f* quibbler

chiche [ʃiʃ] *adj (repas)* scanty; *(personne)* mean; **être c. de louanges** to be sparing in one's praise; *Fam* **tu n'es pas c. d'y aller!** I bet you don't go!; *Fam* **c.!** *(pour défier)* I dare you!; *(pour relever le défi)* you're on!

chichement [ʃiʃmɑ̃] *adv* meanly

chichi [ʃiʃi] *nm Fam* **faire du c.** *ou* **des chichis** *(se donner des airs)* to put on airs; *(compliquer les choses)* to make a fuss; **repas sans c.** informal meal

chicorée [ʃikɔre] *nf* (**a**) *(plante)* chicory (**b**) *(en poudre)* chicory

chicos [ʃikos] *adj Fam* smart

chicot [ʃiko] *nm (dent)* stump

chié, -e[1] [ʃje] *adj Fam (culotté)* **il est c., lui!** he's got a nerve!

chiée[2] [ʃje] *nf très Fam* **(toute) une c. de** a hell of a lot of

chien, chienne [ʃjɛ̃, ʃjɛn] **1** *nm,f* dog, *f* bitch; **jeune c.** puppy, pup; **(attention) c. méchant** *(sur écriteau)* beware of the dog; **traiter qn comme un c.** to treat sb like a dog; *Fam* **quel temps de c.!** what foul weather!; *Fam* **vie de c.** dog's life; *Fam* **chienne de vie!** life's a bitch!; **être comme c. et chat** to fight like cat and dog; **entre c. et loup** at dusk; **se regarder en chiens de faïence** to stare at one another; **c. d'arrêt** pointer; **c. d'aveugle** seeing-eye dog; **c. de berger** sheepdog; **c. de chasse** retriever; **c. de garde** guard dog; **c. policier** police dog; **c. de race** pedigree dog; **c. savant** *(dans un cirque)* performing dog; *Fig* performing monkey; **c. de traîneau** husky, sled dog

2 *nm* (**a**) *Fam (style)* **avoir du c.** to have a certain something (**b**) *(d'un fusil)* hammer; **dormir en c. de fusil** to sleep curled up

chiendent [ʃjɛ̃dɑ̃] *nm* couch grass; **brosse en** *ou* **de c.** scrub brush; **pousser comme du c.** to sprout up

chien-loup *(pl* **chiens-loups)** [ʃjɛ̃lu] *nm* wolfhound

chienne [ʃjɛn] *nf voir* **chien**

chier [66] [ʃje] *vi Vulg* to shit, to crap; **faire c. qn** *(énerver)* to piss sb off; *(ennuyer)* to bore sb shitless; **se faire c.** *(s'ennuyer)* to be bored shitless; **se faire c. (à faire qch)** *(avoir du mal)* to

bust a gut (doing sth); **je me suis fait c. à l'attendre** I did myself in waiting for him/her

chiffe [ʃif] *nf Fam* **c'est une c. molle** he's a drip

chiffon [ʃifɔ̃] *nm* rag; **c. à poussière** dust cloth; **passer un coup de c.** to dust; **passer un coup de c. sur qch** to dust sth off; *Fam* **parler chiffons** to talk clothes

chiffonner [ʃifɔne] **1** *vt* (**a**) *(robe, morceau de papier)* to crumple (**b**) *Fam (ennuyer)* to bother

2 se chiffonner *vpr* to crumple

chiffonnier, -ère [ʃifɔnje, -ɛr] **1** *nm,f* rag picker; **se disputer comme des chiffonniers** to go at it hammer and tongs

2 *nm (meuble)* chiffonier

chiffrable [ʃifrabl] *adj* **facilement/difficilement c.** easy/difficult to calculate; **ne pas être c.** to be impossible to calculate

chiffre [ʃifr] *nm* (**a**) *(nombre)* figure, number; **chiffres arabes/romains** Arabic/Roman numerals; **nombre à trois chiffres** three-figure number; *Ordinat* **c. binaire** binary digit; *Ordinat* **c. ASCII** ASCII number (**b**) *(total)* total; **c. d'affaires (annuel)** (annual) turnover; **faire un c. d'affaires de 4 millions d'euros** to have a turnover of 4 million euros

chiffrement [ʃifrəmɑ̃] *nm Ordinat* **c. de données** data encryption

chiffrer [ʃifre] **1** *vt* (**a**) *(montant, coût)* to work out, to calculate; *(réparations)* to assess (**b**) **message chiffré** coded message

2 se chiffrer *vpr* **se c. à** to add up to, to amount to

chignole [ʃiɲɔl] *nf* hand drill; *(électrique)* electric drill

chignon [ʃiɲɔ̃] *nm* bun, chignon; **se faire un c.** to put one's hair in a bun

chihuahua [ʃiwawa] *nm* chihuahua

chiite [ʃiit] *adj & nmf Rel* Shiite

Chili [ʃili] *nm* **le C.** Chile

chili (con carne) [ʃili(kɔnkarne)] *nm Culin* chil(l)i (con carne)

chilien, -enne [ʃiljɛ̃, -ɛn] **1** *adj* Chilean

2 *nm,f* **C., Chilienne** Chilean

chimère [ʃimɛr] *nf (monstre)* chimera; *Fig (rêve)* pipe dream

chimie [ʃimi] *nf* chemistry

chimio [ʃimjo] *nf Fam Méd (abrév* **chimiothérapie***)* chemo; **faire une c.** to have chemo

chimiothérapie [ʃimjoterapi] *nf Méd* chemotherapy; **faire une c.** to have chemotherapy

chimique [ʃimik] *adj* chemical

chimiste [ʃimist] *nmf* chemist; **ingénieur c.** chemical engineer

chimpanzé [ʃɛ̃pɑ̃ze] *nm* chimpanzee

chinchilla [ʃɛ̃ʃila] *nm (animal, fourrure)* chinchilla; **veste en c.** chinchilla jacket

Chine [ʃin] *nf* **la C.** China

chiné, -e [ʃine] *adj (tissu)* flecked

chiner [ʃine] **1** *vt Fam (personne)* to kid

2 *vi* to hunt for second-hand goods

chinetoque [ʃintɔk] *nmf très Fam* Chink, = racist term used to refer to a Chinese

chinois, -e [ʃinwa, -az] **1** *adj* Chinese

2 *nm,f* **C., Chinoise** Chinese; **les C.** the Chinese

3 *nm* (**a**) *(langue)* Chinese; *Fam Fig* **c'est du c.** it's all Greek to me (**b**) *(ustensile)* conical strainer

chinoiserie [ʃinwazri] *nf* (**a**) *(objet)* Chinese curio (**b**) *Fam* **chinoiseries** *(complications)* pointless complications

chintz [ʃints] *nm* chintz; **des rideaux en c.** chintz curtains

chiot [ʃjo] *nm* puppy, pup

chiottes [ʃjɔt] *nfpl très Fam* john; *Vulg* **aux c., l'arbitre!** the referee's a jerk!

chiper [ʃipe] *vt Fam* to pinch, to swipe

chipie [ʃipi] *nf Fam* minx

chipolata [ʃipɔlata] *nf* chipolata (sausage)

chipoter [ʃipɔte] *vi* (a) *(picorer)* to pick at one's food (b) *(contester)* to quibble (**sur** about)

chips [ʃips] *nf* chip; **des (pommes) c.** (potato) chips

chique [ʃik] *nf* (a) *(de tabac)* quid (b) *Fam* **avoir la c.** *(la joue enflée)* to have a swollen cheek *(due to toothache)* (c) *Belg* candy

chiqué [ʃike] *nm Fam* **faire du c.** to put on an act; **c'est du c.** it's all put on

chiquenaude [ʃiknod] *nf* flick; **d'une c., il l'envoya sur le bureau** he flicked it onto the desk

chiquer [ʃike] **1** *vt* to chew
2 *vi* to chew tobacco

chiromancien, -enne [kirɔmɑ̃sjɛ̃, -ɛn] *nm,f* palmist

chirurgical, -e, -aux, -ales [ʃiryrʒikal, -o] *adj* surgical

chirurgie [ʃiryrʒi] *nf* surgery; **c. esthétique** plastic surgery; **c. au laser** laser surgery

chirurgien [ʃiryrʒjɛ̃] *nm* surgeon

chirurgien-dentiste (*pl* **chirurgiens-dentistes**) [ʃiryrʒjɛ̃dɑ̃tist] *nm* dental surgeon

chiure [ʃjyr] *nf* **c. de mouche** fly-speck

ch-l. *(abrév* **chef-lieu**) = administrative center of a "département"

chleuh, -e [ʃlø] *adj & nm,f très Fam* Kraut, = offensive term used to refer to a German

chlinguer [ʃlɛ̃ge] *vi très Fam* to stink

chlorate [klɔrat] *nm Chim* chlorate

chlore [klɔr] *nm* chlorine

chlorer [klɔre] *vt* to chlorinate

chlorhydrique [klɔridrik] *adj (acide)* hydrochloric

chlorofluorocarbure [klɔrɔflyɔrɔkarbyr] *nm Chim* chlorofluorocarbon

chloroforme [klɔrɔfɔrm] *nm* chloroform

chloroformer [klɔrɔfɔrme] *vt* to chloroform

chlorophylle [klɔrɔfil] *nf* chlorophyll

chlorure [klɔryr] *nm Chim* chloride; **c. de sodium** sodium chloride

chnoque [ʃnɔk] = **schnock**

choc [ʃɔk] *nm* (a) *(coup)* impact; *Fig (conflit)* clash; *(forte impression)* impact; *Écon* **c. pétrolier** oil crisis (b) *Méd* shock; **c. opératoire** post-operative shock (c) *(émotion brutale)* shock; **faire un c. à qn** to give sb a shock; **être en état de c.** to be in a state of shock; **être sous le c.** to be in shock (d) **équipe de c.** team of troubleshooters; **troupes de c.** shock troops

-choc [ʃɔk] *suff* **image-c.** shocking image; **prix-chocs** *(sur une vitrine)* drastic reductions

chochotte [ʃɔʃɔt] *nf Fam Péj* stuck-up person; *(homme)* wimp; **faire sa c.** to put on airs

chocolat [ʃɔkɔla] **1** *nm* (a) *(produit)* chocolate; **gâteau au c.** chocolate cake; **c. blanc** white chocolate; **un c. (chaud)** a hot chocolate; **c. à cuire** cooking chocolate; **c. au lait** milk chocolate; **c. noir** *ou* **à croquer** dark *or* bittersweet chocolate; **c. aux noisettes** hazelnut chocolate; **c. en poudre** drinking chocolate (b) *(bonbon)* chocolate
2 *adj inv* chocolate-colored; *Fam* **être c.** to have lost out

chocolaté, -e [ʃɔkɔlate] *adj* chocolate

chocolatier, -ère [ʃɔkɔlatje, -ɛr] **1** *nm,f (fabricant)* chocolate-maker; *(vendeur)* chocolate-seller
2 *adj (industrie)* chocolate

chocottes [ʃɔkɔt] *nfpl Fam* **avoir les c.** to have the jitters

chœur [kœr] *nm* choir; *(d'opéra)* chorus; **les chœurs** the chorus; **chanter en c.** to sing in chorus; **répétez tous en c.** repeat all together now

choir [14] [ʃwar] *vi (aux être) Litt (tomber)* to fall; **se laisser c.** to sink down; *Fam* **laisser c. qn** to drop sb

choisi, -e [ʃwazi] *adj* (a) *(sélectionné)* **morceaux choisis de...** selected extracts from... (b) *(langage, termes)* careful

choisir [ʃwazir] *vt* to choose, to pick; **c. de faire qch** to choose to do sth; **il a bien choisi son moment!** he really picked his moment!; **à toi de c., cette fois** it's your turn to choose now

choix [ʃwa] *nm* choice; **un grand c. de cravates** a wide choice *or* selection of ties; **avoir le c.** to have a choice; **faire son c.** to take one's pick; **faire le bon c.** to make the right choice; **mon c. est fait** I've made my choice; **laisser le c. à qn** to let sb choose; **viande ou poisson au c.** *(sur un menu)* choice of meat or fish; **de premier c.** top-grade; **de second c.** second-grade

choléra [kɔlera] *nm* cholera; **avoir le c.** to have cholera

cholestérol [kɔlɛsterɔl] *nm* cholesterol; **taux de c.** cholesterol level; *Fam* **avoir du c.** to have a high cholesterol level

cholestérolémie [kɔlɛsterɔlemi] *nf Méd* cholesterol level

chômage [ʃomaʒ] *nm* unemployment; **être au c.** to be unemployed, to be out of work; **toucher le c.** to claim unemployment compensation; **s'inscrire au c.** to register as unemployed; **le c. des jeunes** youth unemployment; **être en c. technique** to have been laid off; **c. de longue durée** long-term unemployment

chômé, -e [ʃome] *adj* **jour c.** public holiday

chômedu [ʃomdy] *nm Fam* unemployment; **être au c.** to be unemployed

chômer [ʃome] *vi* **vous n'avez pas chômé!** you haven't been idle!

chômeur, -euse [ʃomœr, -øz] *nm,f* unemployed person; **les chômeurs** the unemployed; **les chômeurs de longue durée** the long-term unemployed

chope [ʃɔp] *nf (récipient)* beer mug, tankard; *(contenu)* ≃ pint

choper [ʃɔpe] *vt Fam* (a) *(arrêter, prendre)* to bust; **se faire c.** to get busted (b) *(maladie)* to catch

chopine [ʃɔpin] *nf Fam (bouteille)* = bottle holding about a pint; **tu viens boire une c.?** are you coming for a drink?

choquant, -e [ʃɔkɑ̃, -ɑ̃t] *adj* shocking

choquer [ʃɔke] *vt* (a) *(indigner)* to shock (b) *(traumatiser)* **c. qn** to shake sb badly

choral, -e, -aux *ou* **-als, -ales** [kɔral, -o] **1** *adj* choral
2 *nf* **chorale** *(club)* choral society; *(chanteurs)* choir

chorégraphe [kɔregraf] *nmf* choreographer

chorégraphie [kɔregrafi] *nf* choreography; **faire la c. d'un spectacle** to choreograph a show

chorégraphier [66] [kɔregrafje] *vt* to choreograph

chorégraphique [kɔregrafik] *adj* choreographic

choriste [kɔrist] *nmf* choir member; *(d'église)* chorister; *(d'opéra)* chorus member; *(d'un chanteur)* backing singer

chorizo [tʃorizo] *nm* chorizo

chorus [kɔrys] *nm (de jazz)* chorus

chose [ʃoz] **1** *nf* (a) *(objet, parole, événement)* thing; **il s'est passé une c. incroyable** something unbelievable has happened; **je vais te dire une c.** I'm going to tell you something; **il a très bien pris la c.** he took it very well
(b) *(locutions)* **avant toute c.** first of all; **les choses étant ce qu'elles sont** with things as they are; **aller au fond des choses** to get to the heart of the matter; **bien faire les choses** to do things in style; **il ne fait pas les choses à moitié** he doesn't do things by halves; **parler de choses et d'autres** to talk about this and that; **c'est c. faite** it's done; **de deux choses l'une, soit il parle, soit...** either he talks or...; **c. curieuse, personne n'en savait rien** curiously enough, nobody knew anything about it; **et, c. rare, il a demandé pardon** he apologized for once; **dites bien des choses de ma part à...** remember me to...
2 *nm Fam (truc)* thingamajig, thingumajig, whatsit; **Monsieur/Madame C.** Mr./Mrs. thingamajig *or* thingumajig
3 *adj inv Fam* **se sentir tout c.** to feel a bit funny

chou¹, -x [ʃu] *nm* (a) *(légume)* cabbage; **faire ses choux gras**

de qch to have a field day with sth; **faire c. blanc** to draw a blank; **mon petit c.** darling; **c. de Bruxelles** Brussels sprout; **c. rouge** red cabbage (**b**) *(gâteau)* **c. à la crème** cream puff

chou² [ʃu] *adj inv Fam (mignon)* cute; *(gentil)* nice, kind

chouchou, -oute [ʃuʃu, -ut] **1** *nm,f Fam* **c'est le c. (de la maîtresse)** he's the teacher's pet; **c'est le c. de sa maman** he's his mother's little blue-eyed boy
2 *nm (pour les cheveux)* scrunchie

chouchouter [ʃuʃute] *vt Fam* to pamper; **elle aime se faire c.** she enjoys being pampered

choucroute [ʃukrut] *nf (chou)* sauerkraut; **c. (garnie)** = sauerkraut served with different types of sausages and bacon

chouette¹ [ʃwɛt] *nf* owl; **c. hulotte** tawny owl; *Fam Péj* **une vieille c.** an old shrew

chouette² [ʃwɛt] *Fam* **1** *adj* great, terrific; **il a été très c. avec elle** he's been really nice to her
2 *exclam* great!, terrific!

chou-fleur *(pl* **choux-fleurs***)* [ʃuflœr] *nm* cauliflower; **oreille en c.** cauliflower ear

chouia [ʃuja] *nm Fam* **un c. (de qch)** a tiny bit (of sth)

chouraver [ʃurave], **chourer** [ʃure] *vt très Fam* to swipe, to pinch; **se faire c. qch** to have sth swiped *or* pinched

choyer [32] [ʃwaje] *vt* to pamper

CHR [seaʃɛr] *nm (abrév* **centre hospitalier régional***)* regional hospital

chrétien, -enne [kretjɛ̃, -ɛn] *adj & nm,f* Christian

chrétienté [kretjẽte] *nf* Christendom

Christ [krist] *nm* (**a**) **le C.** Christ (**b**) *(crucifix)* **c.** crucifix

christianisme [kristjanism] *nm* Christianity

chromatique [krɔmatik] *adj* (**a**) *(des couleurs) & Mus* chromatic (**b**) *Biol* chromosomal

chrome [krom] *nm Chim* chromium; **chromes** *(d'une voiture)* chrome

chromé, -e [krome] *adj* chromium-plated; **acier c.** chrome steel

chromosome [krɔmozom] *nm* chromosome

chromosomique [krɔmozomik] *adj* chromosomal

chronique¹ [krɔnik] *adj* chronic

chronique² [krɔnik] *nf* (**a**) *Journ* column; **tenir la c. sportive** to write the sports column (**b**) *(annale)* chronicle

chroniqueur, -euse [krɔnikœr, -øz] *nm,f Journ* columnist; **c. sportif** sports reporter

chrono [krɔno] *nm Fam* stopwatch; **faire du 220 km/h c.** to be timed at 220 kph

chronologie [krɔnɔlɔʒi] *nf* chronology

chronologique [krɔnɔlɔʒik] *adj* chronological

chronomètre [krɔnɔmɛtr] *nm (montre de précision)* chronometer; *(pour le sport)* stopwatch

chronométrer [34] [krɔnɔmetre] *vt Sport* to time

chrysalide [krizalid] *nf* chrysalis

chrysanthème [krizɑ̃tɛm] *nm* chrysanthemum

Chrysanthèmes
Chrysanthemums are often associated with funerals in France, and so are never given as gifts. They are traditionally used to decorate graves, especially on All Saints' Day.

ch'timi [ʃtimi] **1** *nmf Fam* Northerner *(from Northern France)*
2 *nm (patois)* = dialect spoken in Northern France

CHU [seaʃy] *nm inv (abrév* **centre hospitalo-universitaire***)* teaching hospital

chu *voir* **choir**

chuchotement [ʃyʃɔtmɑ̃] *nm* whisper; **des chuchotements** whispering

chuchoter [ʃyʃɔte] *vt & vi* to whisper

chuintement [ʃɥɛ̃tmɑ̃] *nm* hissing

chuinter [ʃɥɛ̃te] *vi (siffler)* to hiss

chut [ʃyt] *exclam* sh!, hush!

chute [ʃyt] *nf* (**a**) *(fait de tomber) & Fig* fall; *(diminution)* drop, fall; **faire une c. (de cheval/moto)** to take a spill (from one's horse/motorcycle); **prévenir la c. des cheveux** to prevent hair loss; **il m'a entraîné dans sa c.** he has dragged me down with him; **c. libre** free fall; **descendre en c. libre** to be in free fall; **c. de neige** snowfall (**b**) **c. d'eau** waterfall; **les chutes Victoria** the Victoria Falls (**c**) *(d'histoire drôle)* punchline (**d**) *(de tissu, de métal)* scrap; *(de bois)* off-cut

chuter [ʃyte] *vi (diminuer)* to fall, to drop; *Fam (tomber)* to fall (down)

Chypre [ʃipr] *n* Cyprus

chypriote [ʃiprijɔt] **1** *adj* Cypriot
2 *nmf* **C.** Cypriot

ci¹ [si] *adv* **ce livre-ci** this book; **ces jours-ci** these days; **de-ci de-là** here and there; **par-ci par-là** here and there

ci² [si] *pron démonstratif Fam* **faire ci et ça** to do this and that

CIA [seia] *nf* **la C.** the CIA

ciao [tʃao] *exclam Fam* ciao!

ci-après [siaprɛ] *adv* below; *Jur* hereinafter

cibiste [sibist] *nmf* CB user

cible [sibl] *nf aussi Fig* target

ciblé, -e [sible] *adj* well-targeted

ciboire [sibwar] *nm Rel* ciborium

ciboulette [sibulɛt] *nf* chives

ciboulot [sibulo] *nm très Fam (tête)* nut, noggin; **il n'a rien dans le c.** he doesn't have much upstairs; **se creuser le c.** to rack one's brains

cicatrice [sikatris] *nf aussi Fig* scar

cicatrisant, -e [sikatrizɑ̃, -ɑ̃t] *adj* healing

cicatrisation [sikatrizasjɔ̃] *nf* healing

cicatriser [sikatrize] **1** *vt & vi* to heal
2 se cicatriser *vpr* to heal

ci-contre [sikɔ̃tr] *adv* opposite

ci-dessous [sidəsu] *adv* below

ci-dessus [sidəsy] *adv* above

ci-devant [sidəvɑ̃] *adv Vieilli* formerly

CIDEX [sidɛks] *nm (abrév* **courrier individuel à distribution exceptionelle***)* = system grouping mail boxes in country areas

CIDJ [seideʒi] *nm (abrév* **centre d'information et de documentation de la jeunesse***)* = library offering careers information and literature to young people

cidre [sidr] *nm* hard cider; **c. bouché** = traditionally-made hard cider, fermented twice; **c. doux/brut** sweet/dry cider

Cie *(abrév* **compagnie***)* Co.

ciel [sjɛl] *nm* (**a**) *(air)* sky; **les ciels de Turner** Turner's skies; **à c. ouvert** open-air; **sous d'autres cieux** in other climes; **lever les bras/les yeux au c.** to raise one's arms/one's eyes heavenwards; *Fam* **être au septième c.** to be in seventh heaven; *Fam* **tomber du c. (à qn)** *(héritage)* to be a godsend (to sb); *(solution)* to come (to sb) out of the blue (**b**) *(pl* **cieux** [sjø]*)* *(paradis)* heaven; **il est au c.** he's in heaven; **notre Père qui êtes aux cieux** our Father which art in Heaven (**c**) **c. de lit** canopy

cierge [sjɛrʒ] *nm Rel* candle; **brûler un c.** to light a candle; **c. magique** sparkler

cigale [sigal] *nf* cicada

cigare [sigar] *nm* (**a**) *(à fumer)* cigar (**b**) *très Fam (tête)* **ne rien avoir dans le c.** to be completely brainless

cigarette [sigarɛt] *nf* cigarette; *Culin* **c. russe** = shortcake cookie shaped like a cigarette

ci-gît [siʒi] *voir* **gésir**

cigogne [sigɔɲ] *nf* stork

ciguë [sigy] *nf* hemlock

ci-inclus, -e (*mpl* **ci-inclus**, *fpl* **ci-incluses**) [siɛ̃kly, -yz] **1** *adj* **la copie ci-incluse** the enclosed copy

    2 *adv* (**vous trouverez**) **c. copie de votre lettre** please find enclosed a copy of your letter

ci-joint, -e (*mpl* **ci-joints**, *fpl* **ci-jointes**) [siʒwɛ̃, -ɛ̃t] **1** *adj* **les pièces ci-jointes** the enclosed documents

    2 *adv* (**vous trouverez**) **c. copie de votre lettre** please find enclosed a copy of your letter

cil [sil] *nm* eyelash; **faux cils** false eyelashes

ciller [sije] *vi* to blink; *Fig* **il n'a pas cillé** he didn't bat an eyelid

cime [sim] *nf* (*d'une montagne*) summit; (*pic*) peak; (*d'un arbre, d'un mât*) top

ciment [simɑ̃] *nm* cement

cimenter [simɑ̃te] *vt aussi Fig* to cement

cimetière [simtjɛr] *nm* cemetery; (*d'église*) graveyard; **c. de voitures** scrapyard

ciné [sine] *nm Fam* movies; **se faire un c.** to go to the movies

cinéaste [sineast] *nmf* movie maker

ciné-club (*pl* **ciné-clubs**) [sineklœb] *nm* movie club

cinéma [sinema] *nm* (**a**) (*art, industrie*) movies; **faire du c.** to be a movie actor, to act in movies; *Fam* (*faire semblant*) to put on an act; *Fam* **c'est du c.** it's all an act; *Fam* **arrête ton c.!** stop making such a fuss!; **c. d'art et d'essai** art films; **c. muet** silent movies; **c. parlant** talking movies (**b**) (*salle*) movie theater; **aller au c.** to go to the movies

CinémaScope® [sinemaskɔp] *nm* CinemaScope®

cinémathèque [sinematɛk] *nf* movie library

cinématographie [sinematɔgrafi] *nf* cinematography

cinématographique [sinematɔgrafik] *adj* movie

ciné-parc (*pl* **cinés-parcs**) [sinepark] *nm Can* drive-in movie theater

cinéphile [sinefil] **1** *adj* **être c.** to be a movie buff

    2 *nmf* movie enthusiast

cinéraire [sinerɛr] *adj* (*urne*) cinerary

cinétique [sinetik] *adj* (*énergie*) kinetic

cinglant, -e [sɛ̃glɑ̃, -ɑ̃t] *adj* (*pluie*) lashing; (*vent, remarque*) cutting

cinglé, -e [sɛ̃gle] *Fam* **1** *adj* crazy

    2 *nm,f* loony

cingler¹ [sɛ̃gle] *vi Naut* **c. vers** to make for

cingler² [sɛ̃gle] *vt* (*frapper*) to lash; **la grêle lui cinglait le visage** the hail was stinging his/her face

cinoche [sinɔʃ] *nm Fam* movie theater

cinq [sɛ̃k] **1** *adj inv* five

    2 *nm inv* five; **recevoir qn c. sur c.** to receive sb loud and clear; *Fam* **c'était moins c.** it was a close call; *voir aussi* **trois**

cinquantaine [sɛ̃kɑ̃tɛn] *nf* **une c. de personnes** about fifty people, fifty or so people; **avoir la c.** to be about fifty

cinquante [sɛ̃kɑ̃t] *adj & nm inv* fifty; *voir aussi* **trois**

cinquantenaire [sɛ̃kɑ̃tnɛr] **1** *nm* (*anniversaire*) fiftieth anniversary, golden jubilee

    2 *adj* **être c.** to be fifty years old

cinquantième [sɛ̃kɑ̃tjɛm] *nmf, nm & adj* fiftieth; *voir aussi* **cinquième**

cinquième [sɛ̃kjɛm] **1** *adj* fifth; **le c. jour** the fifth day; **arriver c.** to finish fifth

    2 *nmf* fifth; **le c. en partant de la droite** the fifth from the right; **arriver le c.** to finish fifth

    3 *nm* (**a**) (*fraction*) fifth (**b**) (*étage*) fifth floor; **habiter au c.** to live on the sixth floor (**c**) (*arrondissement*) fifth arrondissement

    4 *nf* (**a**) (*classe*) ≃ sixth grade (**b**) (*vitesse*) fifth (gear); **passer la c.** to go into fifth (gear)

cinquièmement [sɛ̃kjɛmmɑ̃] *adv* fifthly

cintre [sɛ̃tr] *nm* (coat)hanger

cintré, -e [sɛ̃tre] *adj* (*veste*) fitted; (*taille*) nipped-in

CIO [seio] *nm* (*abrév* **Comité international olympique**) IOC

cirage [siraʒ] *nm* (shoe) polish; *Fam* **être dans le c.** to be feeling woozy

circoncire [sirkɔ̃sir] *vt* to circumcise

circoncision [sirkɔ̃sizjɔ̃] *nf* circumcision

circonférence [sirkɔ̃ferɑ̃s] *nf* circumference; **avoir cinq centimètres de c.** ≃ to have a circumference of two inches

circonflexe [sirkɔ̃flɛks] *adj voir* **accent**

circonlocution [sirkɔ̃lɔkysjɔ̃] *nf* circumlocution; **parler par circonlocutions** to speak in a roundabout way

circonscription [sirkɔ̃skripsjɔ̃] *nf* division, district; **c. électorale** (*au niveau municipal*) district; (*au niveau national*) constituency

circonscrire [30] [sirkɔ̃skrir] *vt Math* to circumscribe; (*encercler*) to encircle; (*incendie*) to contain

circonspect, -e [sirkɔ̃spɛ, -ɛkt] *adj* circumspect, cautious

circonstance [sirkɔ̃stɑ̃s] *nf* circumstance; **dans les circonstances actuelles** in the present circumstances; **en pareille c.** under such circumstances; **être à la hauteur des circonstances** to be equal to the occasion; **des paroles de c.** appropriate words; **habillé pour la c.** appropriately dressed; **circonstances aggravantes** aggravating circumstances; *Jur* **circonstances atténuantes** extenuating *or* mitigating circumstances

circonstancié, -e [sirkɔ̃stɑ̃sje] *adj* detailed

circonstanciel, -elle [sirkɔ̃stɑ̃sjɛl] *adj voir* **complément**

circonvolution [sirkɔ̃vɔlysjɔ̃] *nf* convolution

circuit [sirkɥi] *nm* (**a**) (*chemin*) way; (*boucle*) tour; *Fig* **ça fait longtemps que je ne suis plus dans le c.** I've been out of circulation for ages; **c. touristique** (organized) tour (**b**) (*de course automobile, de cyclisme*) circuit; **c. automobile** racing circuit (**c**) *Élec* circuit (**d**) *Tech* **c. de refroidissement** cooling system (**e**) *Ordinat* **c. de commande** command circuit; **c. imprimé** printed circuit; **c. intégré** integrated circuit; **c. de liaison** link circuit; **c. logique** logic circuit (**f**) *Écon* **c. de distribution** distribution network; **circuits de vente** commercial channels

circulaire [sirkylɛr] **1** *nf* circular

    2 *adj* circular; **billet c.** round-trip ticket

circulation [sirkylasjɔ̃] *nf* (**a**) (*d'autos, d'avions*) traffic; **c. interdite** (*sur panneau*) no thoroughfare; **c. aérienne** air traffic; **c. routière** road traffic (**b**) (*du sang, de l'information, des marchandises*) circulation; *Méd* **avoir une mauvaise c.** to have bad circulation; **mettre qch en c.** to put sth into circulation; **retirer un produit de la c.** to take a product off the market (**c**) *Fin* (*des billets, des capitaux*) circulation (**d**) *Pol & Écon* **libre c. des personnes et des biens** free movement of persons and goods

circulatoire [sirkylatwar] *adj* circulatory

circuler [sirkyle] *vi* (**a**) (*sang, air, rumeur*) to circulate; **faire c. un plat** to pass *or* to hand a dish around; **faire c. une pétition** to circulate a petition (**b**) (*voyageur*) to travel; (*train, autobus*) to run; **on circule très mal dans Paris** it's very difficult to drive about in Paris; **circulez, il n'y a rien à voir!** keep moving, there's nothing to see!

cire [sir] *nf* wax; (*pour le bois*) polish; (*dans l'oreille*) (ear)wax; **c. d'abeille** beeswax; **c. à cacheter** sealing wax; **personnage en c.** waxwork (model)

ciré [sire] *nm* oilskin

cirer [sire] *vt* (*chaussures, meubles*) to polish; *Fam* **c. les pompes à qn** to lick sb's boots; *très Fam* **il en a rien à c. (de tes histoires)** he doesn't give a damn (about your stories)

cireur, -euse [sirœr, -øz] **1** *nm,f* (*de chaussures*) shoeblack

    2 *nf* **cireuse** (*machine*) (floor) polisher

cireux, -euse [sirø, -øz] *adj* waxy

cirque [sirk] *nm* (**a**) (*spectacle*) circus; *Fam* **quel c. dans ce bureau!** it's like a zoo in this office!; *Fam* **faire tout un c.** to make a scene; **c. médiatique** media circus (**b**) *Géol* corrie

cirrhose [siroz] *nf* **c. (du foie)** cirrhosis (of the liver); **avoir une c.** to have cirrhosis

cisaille [sizɑj] *nf* **c., cisailles** *(de jardinier)* shears

cisailler [sizɑje] *vt (branches, haie)* to prune

ciseau, -x [sizo] *nm* **(a)** *(de jardin)* shears; **(une paire de) ciseaux** *(pour papier, pour tissu)* (a pair of) scissors; **des ciseaux à ongles** nail scissors **(b)** *Sport* **sauter en ciseaux** to do a scissors jump **(c)** *Tech* chisel

ciseler [39] [sizle] *vt (or, argent)* to chase; *(marbre)* to chisel; *(bijou)* to engrave a design on

Cisjordanie [sisʒɔrdani] *nf* **la C.** the West Bank

cisjordanien, -enne [sisʒɔrdanjɛ̃, -ɛn] **1** *adj* from the West Bank

2 *nm,f* **C., Cisjordanienne** person from the West Bank

cistercien, -enne [sistɛrsjɛ̃, -ɛn] *adj & nm Rel* Cistercian

citadelle [sitadɛl] *nf* citadel

citadin, -e [sitadɛ̃, -in] **1** *nm,f* city-dweller

2 *adj* city

citation [sitasjɔ̃] *nf* **(a)** *(extrait)* quotation; **fin de c.** unquote **(b)** *Jur* **c. à comparaître** *(d'un accusé)* summons; *(d'un témoin)* subpoena

cité [site] *nf* **(a)** *(ville)* city **(b)** *(groupe d'immeubles)* (housing) development; **c. universitaire** dormitory complex

cité-dortoir *(pl* **cités-dortoirs)** [sitedɔrtwar] *nf* bedroom community

citer [site] *vt* **(a)** *(rapporter)* to quote; *(auteur)* to quote (from); **c. qn en exemple** to quote sb as an example; **il a dit, je cite...** he said, and I quote,... **(b)** *(énumérer)* to name **(c)** *Jur (personne en justice)* to summons; *(témoin)* to subpoena **(d)** *Mil* **c. qn (à l'ordre du jour)** to mention sb in dispatches

citerne [sitɛrn] *nf* tank; **c. à mazout** oil tank

cithare [sitar] *nf (instrument moderne)* zither

citizen band [sitizənbɑ̃d] *nf* Citizens' Band, CB

citoyen, -enne [sitwajɛ̃, -ɛn] *nm,f* citizen; **c. d'honneur** freeman *(of a city)*

citoyenneté [sitwajɛnte] *nf* citizenship; **la c. française** French citizenship

citrique [sitrik] *adj (acide)* citric

citron [sitrɔ̃] *nm* **(a)** *(fruit)* lemon; **un c. givré** = lemon sherbet served inside the skin of a whole lemon; **un c. pressé** lemonade; **c. vert** lime **(b)** *Fam (tête)* nut, noggin

citronnade [sitrɔnad] *nf* lemonade

citronnelle [sitrɔnɛl] *nf (plante, huile)* citronella

citronnier [sitrɔnje] *nm* lemon tree

citrouille [sitruj] *nf* **(a)** *(plante)* pumpkin **(b)** *Fam (tête)* nut, noggin

civelle [sivɛl] *nf* elver

civet [sive] *nm Culin* **c. de lapin** rabbit stew; **c. de lièvre** ≃ jugged hare

civière [sivjɛr] *nf* stretcher

civil, -e [sivil] **1** *adj* **(a)** *(du citoyen, non ecclésiastique)* civil **(b)** *(non militaire)* civilian; **dans la vie civile** in civilian life **(c)** *Litt (courtois)* civil

2 *nm* **(a)** *(personne) (non ecclésiastique)* layman, civilian **(b)** **dans le c.** in civilian life; **en c.** *(policier)* in plain clothes; *(militaire)* in civilian clothes **(c)** *Jur* **poursuivre qn au c.** to bring a civil action against sb

civilement [sivilmɑ̃] *adv* **(a)** *Jur* **se marier c.** to have a civil wedding **(b)** *Litt (avec courtoisie)* civilly

civilisation [sivilizasjɔ̃] *nf* civilization

civilisé, -e [sivilize] *adj* civilized

civilité [sivilite] *nf Litt* **(a)** *(courtoisie)* civility **(b)** **civilités** *(politesses)* courtesies

civique [sivik] *adj* civic; **avoir le sens c.** to have a sense of civic responsibility

civisme [sivism] *nm* sense of civic responsibility

cl *(abrév* **centilitre(s))** cl

clac [klak] *exclam (d'un fouet)* crack!; *(d'un objet qui se casse)* snap!; *(d'une porte)* slam!

clafoutis [klafuti] *nm* clafoutis *(fruit, usually cherries, baked in a dish of batter)*

claie [klɛ] *nf* **(a)** *(treillis)* rack **(b)** *(clôture)* fence

clair, -e [klɛr] **1** *adj* **(a)** *(transparent) (eau, teint, voix)* clear; **par temps c.** on a clear day **(b)** *(pièce, couleur)* light **(c)** *(sens, explication)* clear; **il a été très c. là-dessus** he was very clear about it; **il est c. qu'il a tort** he's clearly wrong; **être c. comme de l'eau de roche** to be crystal clear; **avoir les idées claires** to have a clear head; **c'est c. et net** there are no two ways about it; *Fam* **un individu pas très c.** kind of a shady character **(d)** *(soupe)* thin

2 *adv* clearly; **il fait c.** it's light; *Fig* **je commence à y voir c.** I'm beginning to understand

3 *nm* **(a)** *(lumière)* **c. de lune** moonlight; **au c. de lune** in the moonlight **(b)** **en c.** *(autrement dit)* in plain language; **émission en c.** unscrambled broadcast **(c)** *Fig* **tirer une affaire au c.** to clear a matter up; **passer le plus c. de son temps à faire qch** to spend the better part of one's time doing sth

clairement [klɛrmɑ̃] *adv* clearly

claire-voie *(pl* **claires-voies)** [klɛrvwa] *nf* **(a)** *(treillage)* **à c.** open-work **(b)** *Archit* clerestory

clairière [klɛrjɛr] *nf* clearing, glade

clair-obscur *(pl* **clairs-obscurs)** [klɛrɔpskyr] *nm (en peinture)* chiaroscuro

clairon [klɛrɔ̃] *nm* **(a)** *(instrument)* bugle; **sonner le c.** to sound the bugle **(b)** *(joueur)* bugler

claironner [klɛrɔne] *vt (nouvelle)* to trumpet forth

clairsemé, -e [klɛrsəme] *adj (population, cheveux, gazon)* sparse; *(arbres)* scattered

clairvoyant, -e [klɛrvwajɑ̃, -ɑ̃t] *adj* perceptive

clamer [klame] *vt* to proclaim

clameur [klamœr] *nf* clamor; **une c. de joie** a shout of joy; **les clameurs de la foule** the clamor of the crowd

clamser [klamse] *vi très Fam (mourir)* to kick the bucket, to buy the farm

clan [klɑ̃] *nm (tribu)* clan; *Péj (groupe)* clique

clandestin, -e [klɑ̃dɛstɛ̃, -in] **1** *adj (réunion, atelier)* clandestine; *(travailleur, immigré)* illegal; *(mouvement)* underground

2 *nm,f (voyageur)* stowaway; *(immigré)* illegal immigrant; *(travailleur)* illegal worker

clandestinement [klɑ̃dɛstinmɑ̃] *adv (secrètement)* clandestinely; *(illégalement)* illegally

clandestinité [klɑ̃dɛstinite] *nf* **dans la c.** *(secrètement)* clandestinely; *(illégalement)* illegally; **entrer dans/sortir de la c.** to go into/to come out of hiding

clap [klap] *nm Cin* clapboard, clapperboard; **c. de fin** end board

clapet [klapɛ] *nm* **(a)** *Tech* valve; **téléphone à c.** flip-top cellphone **(b)** *Fam* **ferme ton c.!** shut your trap!

clapier [klapje] *nm (rabbit)* hutch

clapoter [klapɔte] *vi* to lap

clapotis [klapɔti] *nm* lapping

claquage [klakaʒ] *nm (blessure)* pulled muscle; **se faire un c.** to pull a muscle

claque¹ [klak] *nf* **(a)** *(gifle)* slap; **donner une c. à qn** to give sb a slap; *Fam Fig* **il va se prendre une c.** it'll be a slap in the face for him; **une paire de claques** a slap **(b)** *Fam* **j'en ai ma c.** I've had it up to here **(c)** *Can* **claques** galoshes

claque² [klak] *nm très Fam (maison de passe)* cathouse

claqué, -e [klake] *adj Fam (fatigué)* bushed

claquement [klakmɑ̃] *nm (de porte)* slam(ming); *(de dents)* chattering; *(d'un fouet)* crack(ing); *(d'un drapeau)* flap(ping); *(de doigts)* snap(ping); *(de talons, de la langue)* click(ing); *(de sabots)* clatter(ing)

claquer [klake] **1** vt (**a**) (porte) to slam; **c. la langue** to click one's tongue (**b**) Fam (dépenser) to blow; **il claque un fric monstre chez le coiffeur** he spends a fortune at the barber's
2 vi (**a**) (porte) to slam; (drapeau) to flap; (talons) to click; (sabots) to clatter; **c. des mains** to clap; **c. des doigts** to snap one's fingers; **elle claque des dents** her teeth are chattering; **faire c. sa langue** to click one's tongue (**b**) (ampoule électrique) to go; (élastique) to snap; Fam (personne) to kick the bucket, to buy the farm
3 se claquer vpr **se c. un muscle** to pull a muscle

claquettes [klakɛt] nfpl tap dancing; **faire des c.** to do tap dancing; **danseur de c.** tap dancer

clarification [klarifikasjɔ̃] nf aussi Fig clarification

clarifier [66] [klarifje] **1** vt (liquide, situation) to clarify
2 se clarifier vpr (situation) to become clear

clarinette [klarinɛt] nf clarinet

clarinettiste [klarinɛtist] nmf clarinettist

clarté [klarte] nf (**a**) (lumière) light (**b**) (transparence) clearness (**c**) Fig (du style) clarity; **avec c.** clearly; **manquer de c.** (personne) not to make oneself clear; (texte, argument) to be unclear

classe [klas] **1** nf (**a**) (catégorie) class; (dans une hiérarchie) grade; **c. affaires/économique** business/economy or coach class; **c. d'âge** age group; **la c. dirigeante** the ruling class; **les classes moyennes** the middle class(es); **la c. ouvrière** the working class(es); **c. sociale** social class
(**b**) (qualité) class; **un sportif de c. internationale** a world-class athlete; **avoir de la c.** (personne) to have class; (objet, vêtement) to be classy; Fam **ce type, c'est la c.!** he's got real class!
(**c**) (à l'école) (niveau) year; (groupe d'élèves) class; **les grandes classes, les classes supérieures** the senior school; **les petites classes** the junior school; **c. de mer/de neige** school field trip to the seaside/to the mountains; **partir en c. de mer** to go on a school field trip to the seaside; **c. préparatoire (aux grandes écoles)** = preparatory class for the entrance examinations for the Grandes Écoles; **c. unique** = class where pupils belonging to different years are taught together by one teacher; **c. verte** school field trip to the countryside
(**d**) (leçon) class; **la c. de français** the French class; **aller en c.** to go to school; **être en c.** (à l'école) to be at school; (en cours) to be in class; **faire la c.** to teach
(**e**) (pièce) (salle de) **c.** classroom
(**f**) Mil (de conscrits) levy; **faire ses classes** to undergo basic training
2 adj inv Fam classy

Classes préparatoires

This term refers to the two years of intensive preparation required for students who have passed their **baccalauréat** (see box at this entry) and wish to enter the "grandes écoles". These two years of study are extremely competitive and highly demanding. Students are completely immersed in their subject, which can be in humanities, economics or the sciences, and do little other than study for the "grandes écoles" exams. For students who are not successful in these exams, two years of "prépas" are considered equivalent to a **DEUG** (see box at this entry), and these students often go on to study at a university.

---

classé, -e [klase] adj (monument) landmarked

classement [klasmã] nm (**a**) (dans une classe ou une course) position, place; (liste d'équipes, de concurrents) classification, ranking; (au football) table; (des plantes) classification; **être troisième au c.** to be in third place, to rank third; **c. général** overall classification or ranking (**b**) (rangement) (de documents) filing; (d'articles) sorting out; **faire du c.** to do some filing; **c. (par ordre) alphabétique** alphabetical classification

classer [klase] **1** vt (**a**) (classifier) to classify, to rank; (étudiants) to grade; **être classés par pays** to be classified or ranked according to country (**b**) (ranger) (documents) to file;

(articles) to sort out; **c. une affaire** to consider a matter closed; **c'est une affaire classée** the matter's closed
2 se classer vpr **se c. parmi les meilleurs** to rank among the best; Sport **se c. troisième** to be placed third

classeur [klasœr] nm (**a**) (dossier) ring binder (**b**) (meuble) filing cabinet (**c**) Ordinat filer

classicisme [klasisism] nm classicism

classification [klasifikasjɔ̃] nf classification; Chim **c. périodique des éléments** periodic table

classifier [66] [klasifje] vt to classify

classique [klasik] **1** adj (**a**) (période) classical; (beauté) classic (**b**) (conventionnel) (vêtement, style, exemple, plaisanterie) classic; (arme, guerre) conventional; Fam **c'est le coup c.** it's the same old story
2 nm (**a**) (auteur) classical author; **connaître ses classiques** to be well-read (**b**) (œuvre, film, chanson) classic; **c'est un c. du genre** it's a classic of its kind (**c**) (style musical) **le c.** classical music

claudication [klodikasjɔ̃] nf limp

clause [kloz] nf Jur clause; **c. d'exclusivité** exclusivity clause; **c. de la nation la plus favorisée** most-favored-nation status

claustrophobe [klostrɔfɔb] adj claustrophobic

claustrophobie [klostrɔfɔbi] nf claustrophobia

clavecin [klavsɛ̃] nm harpsichord

claveciniste [klavsinist] nmf harpsichordist

clavicule [klavikyl] nf collarbone, Spéc clavicle

clavier [klavje] nm keyboard; Ordinat **c. multifonction** multifunctional keyboard; **c. numérique** numerical or numeric keypad

claviste [klavist] nmf Ordinat keyboarder; Typ typesetter

clé [kle] = clef

clean [klin] adj inv Fam (**a**) (BCBG) clean-cut (**b**) (qui ne se drogue pas) clean

clébard [klebar], **clebs** [klɛps] nm Fam pooch

clef [kle] **1** nf (**a**) (d'une porte, d'un cadenas) key; **fermer qch à c.** to lock sth; **tenir/mettre qch sous c.** to keep/put sth under lock and key; **usine clefs en main** turnkey factory; **prix clefs en main** (d'une voiture) sticker price; (d'une maison) all-inclusive price; Fig **mettre la c. sous la porte** to move away; (commerçant) to close the store; **prendre la c. des champs** (prisonnier) to make a bid for freedom; **c. de contact** ignition key; **c. passe-partout** passkey, master key
(**b**) (outil) wrench; **c. anglaise** monkey wrench; **c. à molette** adjustable wrench; **c. plate** open-end wrench
(**c**) Mus (d'un instrument à cordes) peg; (d'un instrument à vent) key; **c. de sol/de fa** treble/bass clef; **il y a une forte somme d'argent à la c.** there is a large sum of money at the end of it
(**d**) (moyen d'accès, solution) key; **la c. du mystère** the key to the mystery
(**e**) **c. de voûte** (d'une arche) keystone; Fig cornerstone
(**f**) Ordinat key; (du DOS) switch; **c. de contrôle** control key; **c. gigogne** dongle; **c. à puce** computerized key; **c. USB** flash drive, pen drive
2 adj (vital) key; **un secteur(-)c. de la recherche** a key area of research

clématite [klematit] nf clematis

clémence [klemãs] nf (**a**) (de la température) mildness (**b**) (d'un juge, d'un maître) clemency (**envers** towards)

clément, -e [klemã, -ãt] adj (**a**) (température) mild (**b**) (juge, maître) clement (**envers** towards)

clémentine [klemãtin] nf clementine

Cléopâtre [kleɔpatr] npr Cleopatra

cleptomane [klɛptɔman] adj & nmf kleptomaniac

cleptomanie [klɛptɔmani] nf kleptomania

clerc [klɛr] nm (**a**) (dans un bureau) **c. de notaire** ≃ lawyer's clerk (**b**) Rel cleric (**c**) Litt **il n'est pas besoin d'être grand c. pour...** you don't have to be a rocket scientist to...

clergé [klɛrʒe] *nm* clergy

clérical, -e, -aux, -ales [klerikal, -o] *adj* clerical

clic [klik] *nm* **(a)** *(bruit)* click; **faire c.** to click **(b)** *Ordinat* click; **double c.** double click

clic-clac [klikklak] *nm inv* **(a)** *(d'un appareil photo)* click; *(des talons)* click-clack **(b)** *(canapé)* spring-action sofa bed

cliché [kliʃe] *nm* **(a)** *(photo)* photo; *(négatif)* negative **(b)** *(lieu commun)* cliché

client, -e [klijɑ̃, -ɑ̃t] *nm,f (d'un magasin, d'une entreprise)* customer; *(d'un médecin)* patient; *(d'un avocat)* client; *(d'un hôtel)* guest; *(d'un taxi)* fare; **ici, le c. est roi** the customer is always right

clientèle [klijɑ̃tɛl] *nf* **(a)** *(d'un magasin, d'une entreprise)* customers; *(d'un médecin, d'un avocat)* practice; *(d'un hôtel)* clientèle; *(d'un taxi)* fares; **c. de passage** passing trade **(b)** *(fait d'acheter)* custom; **accorder sa c. à** to give one's custom to

cligner [kliɲe] *vi* **c. des yeux** to blink; **c. de l'œil** to wink

clignotant, -e [kliɲɔtɑ̃, -ɑ̃t] **1** *adj (étoile)* twinkling; *(lumière)* flashing
  2 *nm (de voiture)* turn signal; **mettre son c. (à gauche/droite)** to signal one is turning (left/right)

clignoter [kliɲɔte] *vi (étoile)* to twinkle; *(lumière, voyant)* to flash; *Ordinat (marqueur)* to flash, to blink

clignoteur [kliɲɔtœr] *nm Belg Aut* turn signal

clim [klim] *nf Fam (climatisation)* aircon, air-conditioning

climat [klima] *nm aussi Fig* climate; **sous des climats plus ensoleillés** in sunnier climes; **c. de détente** relaxed climate

climatique [klimatik] *adj (conditions)* climatic

climatisation [klimatizasjɔ̃] *nf* air-conditioning

climatisé, -e [klimatize] *adj* air-conditioned

climatiser [klimatize] *vt* to air-condition

climatiseur [klimatizœr] *nm* air-conditioner

clin d'œil [*pl* **clins d'œil**] [klɛ̃dœj] *nm* wink; **faire un c. à qn** to wink at sb; **en un c.** in a flash

clinique [klinik] **1** *nf* **(a)** *(hôpital privé)* clinic **(b)** *(médecine)* clinical medicine
  2 *adj* clinical

clinquant, -e [klɛ̃kɑ̃, -ɑ̃t] **1** *adj* flashy
  2 *nm (éclat trompeur)* flashiness

clip [klip] *nm* **(a)** *(vidéo)* (music) video **(b)** *(bijou)* clip

clipart [klipart] *nm Ordinat* clip art

cliquable [klikabl] *adj Ordinat* clickable; **une icône c.** a clickable icon

clique [klik] *nf* **(a)** *Fam (gang)* clique, gang; **et toute la c.** and the rest of the gang **(b)** *(d'une fanfare militaire)* drum-and-bugle band

cliquer [klike] *vi Ordinat* to click (**sur** on); **c. deux fois** to double-click

cliques [klik] *nfpl Fam* **prendre ses c. et ses claques** to pack one's bags and go

cliqueter [42] [klikte] *vi (chaînes)* to rattle; *(épées, aiguilles à tricoter)* to click; *(monnaie, clefs)* to jingle

cliquetis [klikti] *nm (de chaînes)* rattling; *(de pièces de monnaie, de clefs)* jingling; *(d'épées, d'aiguilles à tricoter)* clicking

clitoris [klitɔris] *nm* clitoris

clivage [klivaʒ] *nm (dans la société)* divide; *(dans un parti politique)* split

cloaque [klɔak] *nm aussi Fig* cesspool

clochard, -e [klɔʃar, -ard] *nm,f* bum, hobo

clochardiser [klɔʃardize] **1** *vt* to turn into a tramp
  2 se clochardiser *vpr* to turn into a tramp

cloche [klɔʃ] **1** *nf* **(a)** *(d'église, de bétail)* bell; **déménager à la c. de bois** to blow town at night; *Fig* **entendre plusieurs sons de c.** to hear several different versions of events **(b)** *(pour couvrir)* *Chim* bell jar; *(pour cultures)* cloche; *(pour garder au chaud)* dish cover; **c. à fromage(s)** covered cheese dish; **c. à**

plongeur diving bell **(c)** *Fam (imbécile)* dork **(d)** **(chapeau)** c. cloche (hat) **(e)** *Fam* **être de la c.** *(être clochard)* to be a bum *or* hobo **(f)** *Belg Méd* blister
  2 *adj Fam* dumb

cloche-pied [klɔʃpje] **à cloche-pied** *adv* **sauter à c.** to hop

clocher¹ [klɔʃe] *nm (d'une église)* bell tower, steeple

clocher² [klɔʃe] *vi Fam* **il y a quelque chose qui cloche** there's something wrong somewhere; **il y a quelque chose qui cloche dans son histoire** there's something not quite right about his/her story

clochette [klɔʃɛt] *nf* **(a)** *(petite cloche)* small bell **(b)** *(fleur)* bell-flower; *(corolle)* bell-shaped flower

clodo [klodo] *nm Fam* bum, hobo

cloison [klwazɔ̃] *nf* **(a)** *(entre des pièces)* partition **(b)** *Anat* **c. nasale** nasal septum

cloisonner [klwazɔne] *vt (pièce)* to partition (off); *Fig* to compartmentalize

cloître [klwatr] *nm* **(a)** *(partie d'un monastère)* cloister **(b)** *(bâtiment)* *(pour moines)* monastery; *(pour religieuses)* convent

cloîtrer [klwatre] **1** *vt Rel* to cloister; *Fig* to shut up *or* away; **nonne cloîtrée** nun in an enclosed order
  2 se cloîtrer *vpr (moine)* to enter a monastery; *(religieuse)* to enter a convent; *Fig* to shut oneself away

clonage [klɔnaʒ] *nm Biol* cloning; **c. humain** human cloning; **c. thérapeutique** therapeutic cloning

clone [klɔn] *nm Biol* clone

cloner [3] [klɔne] *vt* to clone

clope [klɔp] *nf Fam* smoke, cig

clopin-clopant [klɔpɛ̃klɔpɑ̃] *adv* **aller c.** to hobble along; *Fig (commerce)* to struggle along

clopiner [klɔpine] *vi* to hobble

clopinettes [klɔpinɛt] *nfpl Fam* **des c.** zilch; **travailler pour des c.** to work for peanuts

cloporte [klɔpɔrt] *nm (insecte)* woodlouse

cloque [klɔk] *nf* **(a)** *(sur la peau, sur la peinture)* blister; **faire des cloques** to blister **(b)** *très Fam* **être en c.** *(enceinte)* to be knocked up

clore [15] [klɔr] **1** *vt (réunion, discussion)* to conclude, to end; *(débat, compte)* to close; *Ordinat* **c. une session** to log off, to log out
  2 se clore *vpr (réunion, film, livre)* to end (**sur** with)

clos, -e [klo, kloz] **1** *pp voir* **clore**
  2 *adj* **(a)** *(fermé) (porte, volets)* closed **(b)** *(achevé)* finished, concluded; **l'incident est c.** the matter is closed; **les inscriptions seront closes le 5 mars** the closing date for applications is March 5 **(c)** *(clôturé) (jardin)* enclosed
  3 *nm* enclosure; **c. (de vigne)** vineyard

clôture [klotyr] *nf* **(a)** *(barrière)* fence **(b)** *(d'une réunion, d'une discussion)* conclusion, end; *(d'un débat, d'un compte)* closing; **c. des inscriptions le 3 mars** closing date for applications is March 3; **c. de la chasse** close of the hunting season; *Fin* **c. de l'exercice** end of the fiscal year **(c)** *(à la Bourse)* close; **à la c.** at the close **(d)** *Ordinat* close; **c. de session** logging off

clôturer [klotyre] **1** *vt* **(a)** *(champ, terrain)* to enclose, to fence in **(b)** *(session, débats)* to close **(c)** *Fin (comptes)* to close
  2 *vi (valeur, indice)* **c. à** to close at

clou [klu] *nm* **(a)** *(pointe)* nail; **être maigre comme un c.** to be as thin as a rake; *Fam* **ça ne vaut pas un c.** it's not worth a cent; *Fam* **des clous!** zilch!; *Fam* **travailler pour des clous** to work for peanuts **(b)** *Culin* **c. de girofle** clove **(c)** *(d'un spectacle)* main attraction; **ça a été le c. de la soirée** it was the highlight of the evening **(d)** **les clous** *(passage piéton)* the crosswalk **(e)** *Fam* **(vieux) c.** *(voiture)* old jalopy; *(vélo)* old boneshaker **(f)** *Fam* **mettre qn au c.** *(en prison)* to lock sb up; *Vieilli* **mettre qch au c.** *(en gage)* to pawn sth

clouer [klue] vt (**a**) *(au mur)* to nail up; *(ensemble)* to nail together; *(caisse)* to nail down; *Fam* **c. le bec à qn** to shut sb up (**b**) *Fig (immobiliser)* **c. qn au sol** to pin sb down; **rester cloué sur place** to be rooted to the spot; **être cloué au lit** to be stuck in bed

clouté, -e [klute] *adj (chaussures)* studded

clown [klun] *nm aussi Fig* clown; **faire le c.** to clown around

club [klœb] *nm* (**a**) *(culturel, sportif, politique)* club; **c. automobile** car club; **c. de foot** soccer club; **c. d'investissement** investment club; **c. de vacances** vacation center (**b**) *(canne de golf)* club

CM [seɛm] *nm (abrév* **cours moyen***)* **CM1** = fourth year of primary school; **CM2** = fifth year of primary school

cm *(abrév* **centimètre(s)***)* cm

CNPF [seɛnpeɛf] *nm Anciennement (abrév* **Conseil national du patronat français***)* = national employers' association

CNRS [seɛnɛrɛs] *nm (abrév* **Centre national de la recherche scientifique***)* = national organization for scientific research

coach [kotʃ] *nm (entraîneur)* coach; **c. personnel** life coach

coagulant, -e [kɔagylɑ̃, -ɑ̃t] **1** *adj* coagulating
  2 *nm* coagulant

coagulation [kɔagylasjɔ̃] *nf* coagulation

coaguler [kɔagyle] **1** *vt & vi (sang)* to clot; *(lait)* to curdle
  2 se coaguler *vpr (sang)* to clot; *(lait)* to curdle

coaliser [kɔalize] **se coaliser** *vpr* to unite; *(partis, pays)* to form a coalition

coalition [kɔalisjɔ̃] *nf* (**a**) *(alliance)* coalition (**b**) *Fig & Péj* conspiracy; **former une c. contre** to join forces against

coaltar [koltar] *nm* coaltar; *Fam* **être dans le c.** to be in a daze

coasser [kɔase] *vi (grenouille)* to croak

coassurance [kɔasyrɑ̃s] *nf* mutual assurance

coauteur [kootœr] *nm* (**a**) *(d'un livre)* co-author (**b**) *Jur* accomplice

COB [kɔb] *nf Fin (abrév* **Commission des opérations de Bourse***)* = French Stock Exchange watchdog

cobalt [kɔbalt] *nm* cobalt

cobaye [kɔbaj] *nm aussi Fig* guinea pig

cobol [kɔbɔl] *nm Ordinat* COBOL

cobra [kɔbra] *nm* cobra

Coca® [kɔka] *nm inv Fam (boisson)* Coke®

coca [kɔka] **1** *nm (plante)* coca
  2 *nf (feuilles)* coca

Coca-Cola® [kɔkakɔla] *nm inv* Coca-Cola®

cocagne [kɔkaɲ] *nf voir* **mât, pays**

cocaïne [kɔkain] *nf* cocaine

cocaïnomane [kɔkainɔman] *nmf* cocaine addict

cocarde [kɔkard] *nf (insigne)* rosette; *Hist (sur un chapeau)* cockade

cocasse [kɔkas] *adj Fam* comical

coccinelle [kɔksinɛl] *nf* (**a**) *(insecte)* ladybug (**b**) *(voiture)* beetle

coccyx [kɔksis] *nm* coccyx

coche [kɔʃ] *nm Vieilli* stagecoach; *Fam* **rater** *ou* **louper le c.** to miss the boat

cochenille [kɔʃnij] *nf* cochineal

cocher¹ [kɔʃe] *nm* coachman

cocher² [kɔʃe] *vt* to check, to tick

cochère [kɔʃɛr] *adj f voir* **porte**

cochon, -onne [kɔʃɔ̃, -ɔn] **1** *nm* (**a**) *(animal, personne sale)* pig; *(viande)* pork; **sale comme un c.** filthy; **gros** *ou* **gras comme un c.** as round as a barrel; **manger comme un c.** to eat like a pig; **tu écris comme un c.** your writing's an absolute mess; *Fig* **nous n'avons pas gardé les cochons ensemble!** but we hardly know each other!; *Fam Fig* **eh ben,**

mon c.! you old devil!; **c. de lait** suck(l)ing pig (**b**) **c. d'Inde** guinea pig (**c**) *(personne malfaisante)* swine (**d**) *(personne grivoise)* dirty devil; **un vieux c.** a dirty old man (**e**) *Can (tirelire)* piggy bank
  2 *adj (histoire, film)* dirty

cochonner [kɔʃɔne] *vt Fam (travail)* to bungle, to botch

cochonnerie [kɔʃɔnri] *nf* (**a**) *(chose sans valeur)* trash, rubbish (**b**) *(nourriture de mauvaise qualité)* muck (**c**) *(saleté)* mess; **faire des cochonneries** to make a mess (**d**) *(obscénité)* filthy remark; **dire des cochonneries** to say filthy things

cochonnet [kɔʃɔnɛ] *nm* (**a**) *(petit cochon)* piglet (**b**) *(aux boules)* jack

cocker [kɔkɛr] *nm* cocker spaniel

cockpit [kɔkpit] *nm Naut & Aviat* cockpit

cocktail [kɔktɛl] *nm (boisson) & Fig* cocktail; *(soirée)* cocktail party; **c. de fruits** fruit cocktail; **c. Molotov** Molotov cocktail

coco¹ [koko] *nm* (**a**) *(plante)* coconut (**b**) *Fam* **mets-toi ça dans le c.!** *(dans la tête)* get that into your thick skull!; *(dans l'estomac)* get that inside you!

coco² [koko] *nm* (**a**) *Fam (type)* **un drôle de c.** a strange character; **toi, mon c., je t'ai à l'œil** just watch it, buster (**b**) *(terme d'affection)* **mon petit c.** my pet

coco³ [koko] *adj & nmf Fam (communiste)* commie

cocon [kɔkɔ̃] *nm aussi Fig* cocoon; *Fig* **le c. familial** the family nest

cocorico [kɔkɔriko] **1** *exclam* cock-a-doodle-doo!
  2 *nm (cri du coq)* cock-a-doodle-doo; *aussi Fig* **faire c.** to crow

cocoter [kɔkɔte] *vi Fam* to stink

cocotier [kɔkɔtje] *nm (arbre)* coconut palm

cocotte [kɔkɔt] *nf* (**a**) *(marmite)* large casserole dish (**b**) *(poule)* hen (**c**) *(pliage)* paper bird (**d**) *(terme d'affection)* **ma c.** darling (**e**) *Fam* **hue, c.!** giddy up! (**f**) *Fam Vieilli (femme)* hooker (**g**) *Can (de pin)* pine cone

Cocotte-Minute® *(pl* **Cocottes-Minute***)* [kɔkɔtminyt] *nf* pressure cooker

cocu, -e [kɔky] **1** *adj* **un mari c.** a cuckold; **je suis c./cocue** my wife's/husband's cheating on me
  2 *nm* cuckold; **faire son mari c.** to cheat on one's husband

cocufier [66] [kɔkyfje] *vt* to be unfaithful to

coda [kɔda] *nf Mus* coda

codage [kɔdaʒ] *nm* coding

code [kɔd] *nm* (**a**) *(symboles)* code; **mettre qch en c.** to put sth into code; **c. confidentiel** security code; *(d'une carte bancaire)* PIN; **c. postal** zip code
  (**b**) *Ordinat* **c. abrégé** shortcode; **c. d'accès** access code; **c. d'arrêt** stop code; **c. d'autorisation d'accès** access authorization code; **c. de caractère** character code; **c. de commande** command code; **c. de contrôle** control code; **c. de départ** start code; **c. d'erreur** error code; **c. d'imprimante** printer code; **c. natif** source code; **c. objet** object code; **c. source** source code
  (**c**) *(ensemble de lois, livre)* code; **passer le c.** *(du permis de conduire)* to take the written part of one's driving test; **c. civil** civil code, ≃ common law; **c. de la nationalité** = laws governing French nationality; **c. pénal** penal code; **c. de la route** rules of the road; **c. du travail** employment legislation
  (**d**) *(phare)* **codes** low beams; **se mettre en codes** to switch on one's low beams; **rouler en codes** to drive with low beams
  (**e**) *Biol* **c. génétique** genetic code

Code postal

In France, the first two numbers of a given zip code correspond to the administrative code number of the relevant **département** *(see box at this entry)*. Thus all zip codes for Paris begin with 75.

code-barres (*pl* **codes-barres**) [kɔdbar] *nm* bar code

codéine [kɔdein] *nf* codeine

coder [kɔde] *vt* to code

codétenu, -e [kɔdetny] *nm,f* fellow prisoner

CODEVI [kɔdevi] *nm* = type of government savings account

codicille [kɔdisil] *nm Jur* codicil

codification [kɔdifikasjɔ̃] *nf Ordinat* **c. binaire** binary code; **c. décimale** decimal coding

codifier [66] [kɔdifje] *vt* to codify

codirecteur, -trice [kodirɛktœr, -tris] *nm,f* joint manager

coéditer [koedite] *vt* to copublish

coéditeur, -trice [koeditœr, -tris] *nm,f* copublisher

coédition [koedisjɔ̃] *nf* (*procédé*) copublishing; (*livre*) joint publication

coefficient [kɔefisjɑ̃] *nm* coefficient; *Aut* **c. aérodynamique** *ou* **de pénétration dans l'air** drag coefficient

coentreprise [koɑ̃trəpriz] *nf* joint venture

coéquipier, -ère [koekipje, -ɛr] *nm,f* teammate

coercitif, -ive [kɔɛrsitif, -iv] *adj* coercive

coercition [kɔɛrsisjɔ̃] *nf* coercion

cœur [kœr] *nm* (**a**) (*organe*) heart; **être malade du c.** to have a weak heart; **être opéré à c. ouvert** to have open-heart surgery; **recevoir une balle en plein c.** to get a bullet right in the heart; **en (forme de) c.** heart-shaped

(**b**) (*poitrine*) **serrer** *ou* **presser qn contre son c.** to hold sb close

(**c**) (*estomac*) **avoir mal au c.** to feel nauseous; **soulever le c. à qn** to turn sb's stomach; *Fig* **avoir le c. solide** *ou* **bien accroché** to have a strong stomach

(**d**) (*symbole de la bonté*) **avoir bon c.** to be kind-hearted; **ne pas avoir de c.** to be heartless; **avoir un c. d'or/de pierre** to have a heart of gold/stone; **avoir le c. sur la main** to be very generous; **à votre bon c., M'sieurs Dames** can you spare a few coins?

(**e**) (*siège des sentiments*) **donner son c. à qn** to lose one's heart to sb; **de tout (son) c.** with all one's heart; **aller droit au c. de qn** to go straight to sb's heart; **avoir le c. brisé** to be broken-hearted; *Fig* **ça (me) fait mal au c.** it's sickening; **faire qch le c. léger** to do sth with a light heart; **avoir le c. gros** *ou* **serré** to have a heavy heart; **si tu aimes les pâtes, tu vas t'en donner à c. joie** if you like pasta, you'll be able to eat it to your heart's content; **ne pas porter qn dans son c.** to be not very fond of sb; **du fond du c.** from the bottom of one's heart; **au fond de mon c.** in my heart of hearts; *Prov* **le c. a ses raisons que la raison ne connaît point** the heart has its reasons

(**f**) (*pensées intimes*) **dire ce qu'on a sur le c.** to say what's on one's mind; **en avoir le c. net** to get to the bottom of it; **ouvrir son c. à qn** to open one's heart to sb

(**g**) **par c.** by heart; *Fam* **connaître qn par c.** to know sb inside out

(**h**) (*courage*) courage; **ne pas avoir le c. de faire qch** not to have the heart to do sth; *Fam* **avoir du c. au ventre** to have plenty of guts

(**i**) (*envie, désir*) **ils n'ont pas le c. à l'ouvrage** their hearts aren't in it; **le c. n'y est pas** his/my/*etc.* heart isn't in it; **elle n'a plus le c. à rien** she doesn't have the heart for anything any more; **avoir le c. à rire** to be in the mood for laughing; **si le c. vous en dit** if you feel like it; **avoir à c. de faire qch** to have one's heart set on doing sth; **ce projet lui tient à c.** this project is close to his/her heart; **de bon c.** (*volontiers*) willingly; (*rire*) heartily; **y aller de bon c.** to get down to it

(**j**) (*personne*) **c'est un c. d'or** she has a heart of gold; **merci, mon c.** thank you, darling

(**k**) (*centre*) heart; (*d'un réacteur nucléaire*) core; **fromage fait à c.** ripe cheese; **au c. de l'hiver/l'été** in the depths of winter/height of summer; **au c. de la ville** in the heart of the town;

au c. du débat at the heart of the debate; **c. d'artichaut** artichoke heart; *Fig* **avoir un c. d'artichaut** to be always falling in love; **c. de palmier** palm heart

(**l**) (*objet en forme de cœur*) heart; (*carte*) heart; (*couleur*) hearts

cœur-poumon [kœrpumɔ̃] *nm inv Méd* **c. artificiel** (artificial) heart-lung machine

coexistence [kɔɛgzistɑ̃s] *nf* coexistence (**avec** with); *Pol* **c. pacifique** peaceful coexistence

coexister [kɔɛgziste] *vi* to coexist (**avec** with)

coffrage [kɔfraʒ] *nm* (*pour ouvrages en béton*) formwork

coffre [kɔfr] *nm* (**a**) (*meuble*) chest; **c. à jouets** toy box; **c. à linge** linen chest (**b**) (*pour objets de valeur*) safe; (*à la banque*) safe-deposit box; **les coffres de l'État** the coffers of the State (**c**) *Fam* **avoir du c.** (*avoir du souffle*) to have a lot of lung power; (*avoir de la voix*) to have a powerful voice (**d**) (*d'une voiture*) trunk; **c. à bagages** (*d'un avion*) baggage compartment

coffre-fort (*pl* **coffres-forts**) [kɔfrəfɔr] *nm* safe

coffrer [kɔfre] *vt Fam* (*mettre en prison*) to put away *or* inside; **se faire c.** to get put away *or* inside

coffret [kɔfrɛ] *nm* (**a**) (*petit coffre*) box; **c. à bijoux** jewelry box (**b**) (*de livres, de disques*) box; **c. cadeau** gift box (**c**) *Ordinat* case

cogérant, -e [koʒerɑ̃, -ɑ̃t] *nm,f* joint manager, *f* joint manageress

cogestion [koʒɛstjɔ̃] *nf* joint management

cogitation [kɔʒitasjɔ̃] *nf Hum* cogitation

cogiter [kɔʒite] *vi Hum* to cogitate

cognac [kɔɲak] *nm* cognac

cognement [kɔɲəmɑ̃] *nm* (*bruit*) banging; (*d'un moteur*) knocking

cogner [kɔɲe] **1** *vt* (**a**) (*heurter*) to knock (**b**) *Fam* (*battre*) to knock around

2 *vi* (**a**) (*buter*) to bang (**sur/contre** on); **sa tête a cogné contre le mur** he/she banged his/her head on the wall; **c. du poing sur la table** to bang (one's fist) on the table; **c. à une porte** to bang on a door (**b**) *Fam* (*frapper*) **il cogne dur** he's handy with his fists; **se faire c. dessus** to get knocked around (**c**) *Fam* **ça cogne** (*il fait chaud*) it's scorching (**d**) (*moteur*) to knock

3 se cogner *vpr* to bang oneself; **se c. à** *ou* **contre qch** to bang into sth; **se c. la tête contre qch** to bang one's head on sth; *Fig* **se c. la tête contre les murs** to bang one's head against a brick wall

cohabitation [koabitasjɔ̃] *nf* living together, cohabitation; *Pol* cohabitation

> ### Cohabitation
> Originally, this term refers to the period (1986–1988) during which the socialist President (François Mitterrand) had a right-wing Prime Minister (Jacques Chirac), following the victory of the RPR in the legislative elections and Mitterrand's decision not to resign as President. It has since been used to refer to the similar situation which arose following the 1993 elections (with Édouard Balladur as Prime Minister) and more recently the 1997 elections (with the left-wing government of Lionel Jospin co-ruling with the President Jacques Chirac).

cohabiter [koabite] *vi* to live together; **c. avec qn** to live with sb

cohérence [kɔerɑ̃s] *nf* (*d'une argumentation, d'un discours*) coherence; (*d'une attitude*) consistency

cohérent, -e [kɔerɑ̃, -ɑ̃t] *adj* (*argumentation, discours*) coherent; (*attitude*) consistent

cohéritier, -ère [kɔeritje, -ɛr] *nm,f* joint heir, *f* joint heiress

cohésion [kɔezjɔ̃] *nf* cohesion

cohorte [kɔɔrt] *nf* (*de gens*) horde

cohue [kɔy] *nf* crowd

coi, coite [kwa, kwat] *adj* **se tenir c.** to keep quiet; **en rester c.** to be speechless

coiffe [kwaf] *nf (coiffure régionale, religieuse)* headdress

coiffé, -e [kwafe] *adj* **(a)** **je ne suis pas encore coiffée** I haven't done my hair yet; **elle est bien coiffée** her hair is lovely; **il est mal c.** his hair's a mess **(b)** **être c. de qch** to be wearing sth *(on one's head)*

coiffer [kwafe] **1** *vt* **(a)** *(peigner)* **c. qn** to do sb's hair; **il coiffe bien** he's a good hairdresser; **se faire c. (chez/par qn)** to have one's hair done (at sb's/by sb) **(b)** *(mettre un chapeau à)* **c. qn de qch** to put sth on sb's head; *Fig* **c. sainte Catherine** to be twenty-five and still unmarried **(c)** *(service)* to head **(d)** *Sport & Fig* **se faire c. (au poteau)** to be nosed out
  2 se coiffer *vpr* **(a)** *(se peigner)* to do one's hair **(b)** *(mettre)* **se c. de qch** to put sth on

coiffeur, -euse [kwafœr, -øz] **1** *nm,f* hairdresser
  2 *nf* **coiffeuse** *(meuble)* dressing-table

coiffure [kwafyr] *nf* **(a)** *(coupe de cheveux)* hairstyle **(b)** *(activité)* hairdressing **(c)** *(chapeau)* headgear; *(de costume régional)* headdress

coin [kwɛ̃] *nm* **(a)** *(angle)* corner; **faire le c.** to be on the corner; **à tous les coins de rue** on every street corner; **aux quatre coins du monde** in all corners of the earth; **mettre un enfant au c.** *(pour le punir)* to make a child stand in the corner; *Fig* **rester dans son c.** to keep to oneself; **les coins et les recoins de qch** the nooks and crannies of sth; **je ne voudrais pas le rencontrer au c. d'un bois** I wouldn't like to meet him on a dark night; *Aviat & Rail* **c. fenêtre/couloir** window/aisle seat; **au c. du feu** by the fire(side); **lancer un regard en c. à qn** to give sb a sidelong glance; **sourire en c.** half smile; **regarder qn du c. de l'œil** to look at sb out of the corner of one's eye
  (b) *(endroit quelconque)* spot, place; **un petit c. tranquille** a quiet little spot; *Euph* **le petit c.** the john; **dans un c. de ma mémoire** in a corner of my mind; **j'ai dû le mettre dans un c.** I must have put it somewhere; **chercher qch dans tous les coins** to look high and low for sth
  (c) *(voisinage)* **du c.** local; **il habite dans le c.** he lives around here
  (d) *(parcelle)* patch; **c. de ciel bleu** patch of blue sky
  (e) *(cale)* wedge

coincé, -e [kwɛ̃se] *adj* **(a)** *(fermeture, porte, mécanisme)* jammed, stuck
  (b) *Fam (inhibé)* hung up
  (c) *(acculé)* **il faut que je paie, je suis c.** I'll have to pay, I've got no choice

coincer [16] [kwɛ̃se] **1** *vt* **(a)** *(accidentellement) (tiroir, clef)* to jam; **j'ai coincé mes cheveux dans ma fermeture Éclair®** I got my hair caught in my zipper; **la voiture est coincée entre deux camions** *(en stationnement)* the car is boxed in by two trucks; **être coincé** *(personne) (dans un embouteillage, un endroit)* to be stuck; *(être occupé)* to be tied up
  (b) *(volontairement) (porte)* to wedge; **elle l'a coincé dans le couloir** she cornered him in the corridor; **il m'a coincé** *(je n'ai pas su répondre)* he had me cornered
  (c) *Fam (arrêter)* to pinch; **se faire c.** to get pinched
  2 *vi (tiroir, mécanisme)* to jam, to stick; *Fam* **ça coince** there's a snag
  3 se coincer *vpr (tiroir, mécanisme)* to jam, to stick; **se c. le doigt dans la porte** to catch one's finger in the door; **je me suis coincé le dos** my back's seized up

coïncidence [kɔɛ̃sidɑ̃s] *nf* coincidence

coïncider [kɔɛ̃side] *vi (événements, versions)* to coincide (**avec** with); **leurs intérêts coïncident** they have similar interests; **tous les témoignages coïncident** the witnesses all bear each other out

coin-coin [kwɛ̃kwɛ̃] **1** *nm inv (des canards)* quacking
  2 *exclam* quack! quack!

coin-cuisine *(pl* **coins-cuisines)** [kwɛ̃kɥizin] *nm* kitchen area

coïnculpé, -e [kɔɛ̃kylpe] *nm,f* co-defendant

coing [kwɛ̃] *nm* quince

coin-repas *(pl* **coins-repas)** [kwɛ̃rəpa] *nm* dining area

coït [kɔit] *nm* coitus

coite [kwat] *voir* **coi**

coke [kɔk] **1** *nm (combustible)* coke
  2 *nf Fam (cocaïne)* coke

col [kɔl] *nm* **(a)** *(d'une robe, d'une chemise)* collar; **c. de fourrure/de dentelle** fur/lace collar; **c. blanc** *(employé de bureau)* white-collar worker; **c. bleu** *(ouvrier)* blue-collar worker; **c. cheminée** *ou* **montant** mock turtleneck; **c. ras le** *ou* **du cou** crew neck; **c. rond** round neck; **c. roulé** turtleneck; **c. en V** V-neck; **faux c.** false collar **(b)** *(d'une bouteille)* neck **(c)** *Géog* col **(d)** *Anat (d'un os)* neck; **c. de l'utérus** cervix

colchique [kɔlʃik] *nm* autumn crocus

coléoptère [kɔleɔptɛr] *nm* beetle

colère [kɔlɛr] *nf* anger; **être en c. (contre qn)** to be angry (with sb); **mettre qn en c.** to make sb angry; **se mettre en c.** to get angry; **se mettre dans une c. bleue** *ou* **noire** to fly into a towering rage; **piquer une c.** to fly into a rage; **passer sa c. sur qn** to take one's anger out on sb; **avec c.** angrily; *Litt* **la c. de Dieu** the wrath of God; **c. froide** cold fury

coléreux, -euse [kɔlerø, -øz], **colérique** [kɔlerik] *adj (personne)* quick-tempered; *(disposition)* irritable

colibri [kɔlibri] *nm* hummingbird

colifichet [kɔlifiʃɛ] *nm* trinket, knick-knack

colimaçon [kɔlimasɔ̃] *nm voir* **escalier**

colin [kɔlɛ̃] *nm (merlu)* hake; *(lieu noir)* coley

colin-maillard [kɔlɛ̃majar] *nm* blind man's buff *or* bluff; **jouer à c.** to play blind man's buff *or* bluff

colique [kɔlik] *nf* **(a)** *(diarrhée)* diarrhea; **avoir la c.** to have diarrhea **(b)** *(douleur)* **coliques** stomach pains, colic; **c. néphrétique** renal colic

colis [kɔli] *nm* package; **par c. postal** by parcel post

Colisée [kɔlize] *nm* **le C.** the Coliseum

colistier, -ère [kɔlistje, -ɛr] *nm,f Pol* fellow candidate

colite [kɔlit] *nf Méd* colitis

collabo [kɔlabo] *nmf Fam Hist* collaborator

collaborateur, -trice [kɔlabɔratœr, -tris] *nm,f* **(a)** *(aide)* assistant **(b)** *Journ* contributor (**de** to) **(c)** *Hist* collaborator

collaboration [kɔlabɔrasjɔ̃] *nf* **(a)** *(aide)* collaboration (**à** on); **travailler en étroite c. (avec qn)** to work closely (with sb) **(b)** *Journ* contribution **(c)** *Hist* collaboration

collaborer [kɔlabɔre] *vi* **(a)** *(travailler ensemble)* to collaborate (**avec** with); **c. à qch** *(projet)* to take part in sth; *(journal)* to contribute to sth **(b)** *Hist* to collaborate

collage [kɔlaʒ] *nm* **(a)** *(d'affiches)* sticking up; *(de bois)* gluing; *(de papier)* pasting **(b)** *(composition)* collage

collagène [kɔlaʒɛn] *nm* collagen

collant, -e [kɔlɑ̃, -ɑ̃t] **1** *adj* **(a)** *(adhésif)* sticky **(b)** *(poisseux)* sticky **(c)** *(moulant)* skin-tight **(d)** *Fam (personne)* **qu'est-ce qu'il est c.!** you just can't shake him off!
  2 *nm* **(a)** *(bas)* pantyhose; **c. de danse** dance tights **(b)** *Can* **c. à mouches** flypaper

collation [kɔlasjɔ̃] *nf (repas)* light meal, snack

colle [kɔl] *nf* **(a)** *(transparente)* glue; *(blanche)* paste; **c. à bois** wood glue; **c. forte** strong glue; **de la c. en pot/stick/tube** a pot/stick/tube of glue **(b)** *Fam (question difficile)* poser; **là, tu me poses une c.** you've got me there **(c)** *Fam (punition)* detention **(d)** *Fam (examen oral)* oral test **(e)** *très Fam* **vivre** *ou* **être à la c.** to be shacked up together

collecte [kɔlɛkt] *nf* collection; **faire une c. (au profit de)** to make a collection (in aid of)

collecter [kɔlɛkte] *vt* to collect

collecteur, -trice [kɔlɛktœr, -tris] **1** *nm,f* collector; **c. d'impôts** tax collector

2 *nm* (**a**) *(d'eaux pluviales)* main sewer (**b**) *Aut* **c. d'échappement** exhaust manifold

collectif, -ive [kɔlɛktif, -iv] **1** *adj (action, travail, responsabilité)* collective; *(billet)* group; *(licenciements)* mass

   2 *nm* (**a**) *Fin* **c. budgétaire** interim budget (**b**) *(association)* collective

collection [kɔlɛksjɔ̃] *nf* (**a**) *(action)* collecting; **faire la c. de qch** to collect sth (**b**) *(série) (de timbres, de papillons, d'œuvres d'art)* collection; *(de périodiques)* series; *(d'échantillons)* line; **j'en ai toute une c.** I've got a whole collection of them (**c**) *(de haute couture, de prêt-à-porter)* collection

collectionner [kɔlɛksjɔne] *vt* to collect

collectionneur, -euse [kɔlɛksjɔnœr, -øz] *nm,f* collector

collectivisme [kɔlɛktivism] *nm Écon* collectivism

collectivité [kɔlɛktivite] *nf* (**a**) *(groupe)* community (**b**) **collectivités locales** local communities (**c**) **c. d'outre-mer** = French overseas collectivity

collège [kɔlɛʒ] *nm* (**a**) *(école)* school; **c. d'enseignement secondaire** = former secondary school for pupils aged 12 to 15; **c. d'enseignement technique** technical school; **le C. de France** the Collège de France *(prestigious higher-education institution)* (**b**) *Pol* **c. électoral** electoral college

collégial, -e, -aux, -ales [kɔleʒjal, -o] **1** *adj* collegiate

   2 *nf* **collégiale** collegiate church

collégien, -enne [kɔleʒjɛ̃, -ɛn] *nm,f* schoolboy, *f* schoolgirl; **je me suis fait avoir comme un c.** I fell for it like a fool

collègue [kɔlɛg] *nmf* **c. (de travail)** colleague; *Fam* **salut, c.!** how's it going?

coller [kɔle] **1** *vt* (**a**) *(faire adhérer)* to stick (**à/sur** to/on); **il avait les cheveux collés par la sueur/la peinture** his hair was matted with sweat/paint; **il est resté collé à la télé toute la soirée** he was glued to the TV all evening

   (**b**) *(appuyer)* **c. qch à** *ou* **contre qch** to press sth against sth

   (**c**) *Fam (mettre)* **colle ton sac là** stick *or* dump your bag over there; **ils ont collé le bébé à la grand-mère** they dumped the baby on the grandmother; **on m'a collé à la comptabilité sans que j'aie dit oui** I got shoved into accounts without any say in the matter; **c. une gifle à qn** to slap sb in the face; **si tu continues, je t'en colle une!** if you don't stop, I'll sock you one!; **c. une contravention à qn** to slap a fine on sb

   (**d**) *Fam (retenir en punition)* to keep in; **se faire c.** to be kept in

   (**e**) *(refuser) (candidat)* to fail; **se faire c.** to fail

   (**f**) *Fam (suivre)* to follow closely; **il me colle!** he sticks to me like glue!

   (**g**) *Ordinat* to paste

   2 *vi Fam* (**a**) *(coïncider)* to tally (**avec** with) (**b**) *(aller bien)* **ça colle!** that's OK!; **ça ne va pas c. pour mercredi** it's no go for Wednesday; **ça ne colle pas entre eux** they don't hit it off

   3 coller à *vt ind aussi Fig* to stick to; *Fam* **c. aux fesses à qn** to stick to sb's tail; **sa réputation lui colle à la peau** he/she can't shake off his/her reputation

   4 se coller *vpr* (**a**) *(adhérer les uns aux autres)* to stick (**b**) *(s'aplatir)* **se c. contre un mur** to flatten oneself against a wall; **se c. contre qn** to cling to sb; *Fam* **se c. devant la télé** to plunk oneself down in front of the TV; *Fam* **c'est encore toi qui t'y colles** you're landed with it again

collerette [kɔlrɛt] *nf* (**a**) *(de vêtement)* collar; *Hist (fraise)* ruff (**b**) *Bot (de champignon)* annulus (**c**) *(de tuyau)* flange

collet [kɔlɛ] *nm* (**a**) *(de vêtement)* collar; **saisir** *ou* **prendre qn au c.** to grab sb by the scruff of the neck; **mettre la main au c. à qn** *(l'arrêter)* to get hold of sb; **être c. monté** to be straitlaced (**b**) *(piège)* snare

colleter [42] [kɔlte] **se colleter** *vpr Fam* to tussle (**avec qn** with sb); **se c. avec qch** to grapple with sth

collier [kɔlje] *nm* (**a**) *(bijou)* necklace; **c. de perles** pearl necklace; **c. de fleurs** garland of flowers (**b**) *(de chien)* collar; *Fig*

donner un coup de c. to put one's back into it (**c**) *(barbe)* **c. (de barbe)** fringe of beard (**d**) *Culin (de bœuf, de mouton)* neck (**e**) *Tech* collar; **c. de serrage** clamp collar (**f**) *Zool (d'oiseau)* collar

collimateur [kɔlimatœr] *nm Fig* **avoir qn dans le c.** to keep one's eye on sb

colline [kɔlin] *nf* hill

collision [kɔlizjɔ̃] *nf (entre véhicules, entre objets)* collision; **entrer en c. avec qch** to collide with sth; *Aut* **c. frontale/latérale** head-on/side-on collision

colloque [kɔlɔk] *nm (conférence)* seminar

collusion [kɔlyzjɔ̃] *nf* collusion

collutoire [kɔlytwar] *nm* throat spray

collyre [kɔlir] *nm* eyewash

colmater [kɔlmate] *vt* to fill in

colo [kɔlo] *nf Fam* summer camp

colocataire [kɔlɔkatɛr] *nmf* roommate *(sharing an apartment)*

Colomb [kɔlɔ̃] *npr* **Christophe C.** Christopher Columbus

colombage [kɔlɔ̃baʒ] *nm Constr* half-timbering; **maison à colombages** half-timbered house

colombe [kɔlɔ̃b] *nf* dove

Colombie [kɔlɔ̃bi] *nf* **la C.** Colombia

Colombie-Britannique [kɔlɔ̃bibritanik] *nf* **la C.** British Columbia

colombien, -enne [kɔlɔ̃bjɛ̃, -ɛn] **1** *adj* Colombian

   2 *nm,f* **C., Colombienne** Colombian

colombier [kɔlɔ̃bje] *nm (pigeonnier)* dovecote

colon [kɔlɔ̃] *nm* (**a**) *(pionnier)* settler, colonist (**b**) *(dans une colonie de vacances)* child (at camp)

côlon [kolɔ̃] *nm* colon

colonel [kɔlɔnɛl] *nm* colonel

colonial, -e, -aux, -ales [kɔlɔnjal, -o] **1** *adj* colonial

   2 *nf* **la coloniale** *Hist* the Colonial Army

colonialisme [kɔlɔnjalism] *nm* colonialism

colonialiste [kɔlɔnjalist] *adj & nmf* colonialist

colonie [kɔlɔni] *nf* (**a**) *(territoire, immigrés)* colony; *(occupation)* settlement (**b**) **c. (de vacances)** summer camp; **envoyer ses enfants en c.** to send one's children to camp

> ### Colonie de vacances
>
> The "colonie de vacances" or "colo" is an integral part of childhood for many French people. The children's parents do not stay with them at the "colonie", the group being supervised by "moniteurs" or "animateurs" (similar to camp counselors), who organize games and activities.

colonisation [kɔlɔnizasjɔ̃] *nf* colonization

coloniser [kɔlɔnize] *vt* to colonize

colonnade [kɔlɔnad] *nf* colonnade

colonne [kɔlɔn] *nf* (**a**) *(pilier)* column, pillar; **c. Morris** = pillar used to advertise forthcoming events (**b**) *(file)* column; **en c. par deux/trois** in columns of two/three (**c**) *(d'un dictionnaire, d'un journal)* column (**d**) *(de fumée, de mercure)* column (**e**) *Anat* **c. vertébrale** spine, spinal column (**f**) *Aut* **c. de direction** steering column

coloquinte [kɔlɔkɛ̃t] *nf (plante)* bitter apple

colorant, -e [kɔlɔrɑ̃, -ɑ̃t] **1** *adj* coloring

   2 *nm* (**a**) *(pour teindre)* colorant (**b**) *(alimentaire)* coloring; **sans colorants** *(sur étiquette)* no artificial coloring

coloration [kɔlɔrasjɔ̃] *nf* (**a**) *(fait de colorer)* coloring; **se faire faire une c.** to have one's hair dyed (**b**) *(de la peau)* coloring (**c**) *Fig* **c. politique** political color

coloré, -e [kɔlɔre] *adj* colored; *(teint)* ruddy; *Fig (style)* colorful

colorer [kɔlɔre] **1** *vt* to color; *Fig (récit)* to lend color to; **c. qch en vert** to color sth green

   2 se colorer *vpr (visage)* to become flushed

coloriage [kɔlɔrjaʒ] *nm (action)* coloring; *(dessin)* drawing; **album** *ou* **livre de c.** coloring book

colorier [66] [kɔlɔrje] *vt* to color

coloris [kɔlɔri] *nm* shade

coloriser [kɔlɔrize] *vt Cin* to colorize

colossal, -e, -aux, -ales [kɔlɔsal, -o] *adj* colossal, huge

colosse [kɔlɔs] *nm (homme)* giant; *Fig* **un c. aux pieds d'argile** a giant with feet of clay

colostomie [kɔlɔstɔmi] *nf Méd* colostomy

colporter [kɔlpɔrte] *vt (marchandises)* to hawk; *(nouvelle, rumeurs)* to spread

colporteur, -euse [kɔlpɔrtœr, -øz] *nm,f* hawker

colt [kɔlt] *nm* Colt®

coltiner [kɔltine] **se coltiner** *vpr Fam* **se c. qn/qch** to get landed with sb/sth

colvert [kɔlvɛr] *nm* mallard

colza [kɔlza] *nm* colza, rape

COM [kɔm] *nf (abrév* **collectivité d'outre-mer)** = French overseas collectivity

coma [kɔma] *nm* coma; **être/tomber dans le c.** to be in/go into a coma

comateux, -euse [kɔmatø, -øz] **1** *adj* comatose

2 *nm,f* patient in a coma

combat [kɔba] *nm (a) Mil (bataille)* fight; *(activité)* combat; **c. aérien** dog fight; *aussi Fig* **c. d'arrière-garde** rearguard action; **c. naval** naval engagement **(b)** *(dispute)* fight; **c. de boxe** boxing match; **c. de coqs** cockfight **(c)** *Fig (lutte)* fight (**contre** against)

combatif, -ive [kɔbatif, -iv] *adj* combative

combativité [kɔbativite] *nf* combativeness

combattant, -e [kɔbatɑ̃, -ɑ̃t] **1** *nm,f* combatant; **anciens combattants** veterans

2 *adj (troupes, unité)* fighting

combattre [11] [kɔbatr] **1** *vt (ennemi)* to fight (against); *(maladie, inflation, racisme)* to fight

2 *vi* to fight (**pour/contre** for/against)

combi [kɔbi] *nm Belg* police van

combien [kɔbjɛ̃] **1** *adv (a) (comme)* how (much); **j'ai pu constater c. tu avais changé** I could see how much you'd changed **(b)** *(en nombre)* how many; **c. sont-ils?** how many (of them) are there?; **c. de** how many; **c. de gens furent tués dans cette guerre!** what a lot of people were killed in that war! **(c)** *(en quantité, en poids)* how much; **ça fait c.?** *(d'argent)* how much is that?; **c. y a-t-il d'ici à Boston?** how far is it to Boston?; **à c. sommes-nous de Paris?** how far are we from Paris?; **c. mesure-t-il?** how tall is he?; **elle est enceinte – de c.?** she's pregnant – how far along is she?; **c. de** how much; **c. de temps** how long

2 *nm inv Fam* **le c. sommes-nous?** what's the date (today)?; **il y a un car tous les c.?** how often do the buses run?; **tu chausses du c.?** what size shoe do you take?

combientième [kɔbjɛ̃tjɛm] *Fam* **1** *nmf* **c'est le c. sur la liste?** where is it on the list?

2 *adj* **tu as été reçu c. à l'examen?** where did you place on the exam?; **c'est la c. fois que tu viens?** how often have you been here?

combinaison [kɔbinɛzɔ̃] *nf (a) (assemblage)* combination; **la c. gagnante** *(au tiercé)* the winning combination; *Ordinat* **c. de touches** key combination **(b)** *(vêtement) (de travail)* coveralls; *Aviat* flying suit; *(de femme)* catsuit; *(sous-vêtement)* slip; **c. de plongée** wet suit; **c. de ski** ski suit; **c. spatiale** space suit

combine [kɔbin] *nf Fam* trick; **il a une c. pour entrer sans payer** he knows a way of getting in without paying; **mettre qn dans la c.** to let sb in on it

combiné, -e [kɔbine] **1** *adj (action, efforts)* combined

2 *nm (a)* **c. (téléphonique)** receiver **(b)** *(en ski)* **c. alpin** alpine competition

combiner [kɔbine] **1** *vt (a) (unir)* to combine **(b)** *Fam (plan)* to concoct; **qu'est-ce que tu combines encore?** what are you cooking up now?

2 se combiner *vpr* to combine

comble [kɔbl] **1** *adj* (jam-)packed; **faire salle c.** *(au théâtre)* to have a full house

2 *nm (a) (maximum)* **le c. de** the height of; *(du désespoir)* the depth of; **ça, c'est le** *ou* **un c.!** that's the last straw!; **être au c. de la joie** to be overjoyed **(b)** *Archit (en bois)* roof timbers; *(en métal)* roof structure; **les combles** *(grenier)* the attic; **loger sous les combles** to live in an attic

combler [kɔble] *vt (a) (puits, fossé, trou)* to fill in; *(perte)* to make good; *(découvert)* to pay off; *(lacune)* to fill; **c. son retard** to make up for lost time **(b)** *(satisfaire)* to satisfy; **c. qn de cadeaux** to shower sb with gifts; **un mari comblé** a happily married man

combustible [kɔbystibl] **1** *nm* fuel; **c. fossile** fossil fuel

2 *adj* combustible

combustion [kɔbystjɔ̃] *nf* combustion

comédie [kɔmedi] *nf (pièce, film, genre)* comedy; **jouer** *ou* **faire la c.** to act; *Fig* to put on an act; **allons, pas de c.!** *(caprice)* come on, stop your nonsense!; **c'est une vraie c. quand il faut aller à l'école** it's a real fuss when it's time to go to school; **c. de mœurs** comedy of manners; **c. musicale** musical

---

Comédie-Française

This state-subsidized company dates back to the seventeenth century; the theatre itself, officially called "le Théâtre-Français" or "le Français", is situated in the rue Richelieu in Paris. Its repertoire consists mainly of classical works, although modern plays are sometimes staged. Actors who perform in the Comédie-Française fall into two categories: the "sociétaires" who are full-fledged members of the company, and the "pensionnaires" who work with the company on a fixed salary but are not shareholders in it.

Comédie-Française [kɔmedifrɑ̃sɛz] *nf* **la C.** = state-run theater company presenting plays from the established repertoire

comédien, -enne [kɔmedjɛ̃, -ɛn] **1** *nm,f (acteur)* actor, *f* actress; *Fig* **c'est une comédienne** she's always putting on an act; **comédiens ambulants** strolling players

2 *adj* **elle est très comédienne** she's always putting on an act

comédon [kɔmedɔ̃] *nm* blackhead

comestible [kɔmɛstibl] *adj* edible; **denrées comestibles** foodstuffs

comète [kɔmɛt] *nf* comet; *Fig* **tirer** *ou* **faire des plans sur la c.** to build castles in the air

comice [kɔmis] *nm* **c. agricole** agricultural association; **comices agricoles** *(foire)* agricultural show

comique [kɔmik] **1** *adj (a) (acteur, film, rôle)* comedy; **le genre c.** comedy **(b)** *(amusant)* comical, funny

2 *nm (a) (genre)* comedy; **c. de situation** situation comedy **(b)** *(acteur)* comic actor; *Péj (bouffon)* comedian **(c)** **le c. de l'histoire, c'est que…** the funny part is that…

comité [kɔmite] *nm* committee; **faire partie d'un c.** to sit on a committee; *Fig* **nous serons en petit c.** we'll just have a small get-together; **c. d'entreprise** works council; **C. international olympique** International Olympic Committee

---

Comité d'entreprise

The "Comité d'entreprise" or "CE" looks after the general welfare of company employees and organizes subsidised leisure activities, outings, vacations, etc. It also deals with industrial problems.

---

commandant [kɔmɑ̃dɑ̃] *nm* (**a**) *(officier) (d'unité)* commander; *(de camp, de base)* commandant; *(de bateau)* captain *(whatever his rank)*; *Aviat* **c. de bord** captain; **c. en chef** commander-in-chief; *Naut* executive officer (**b**) *(rang) (dans l'armée de terre)* major; *(dans l'armée de l'air)* major

commande [kɔmɑ̃d] *nf* (**a**) *Com* order; **faire** *ou* **passer une c.** to put in *or* to place an order; **sur c.** *aussi Fig* to order; **on ne peut pas rire sur c.** you can't laugh to order; **ouvrage de c.** commissioned work (**b**) *(action, manette)* control; *(mécanisme)* drive; **c. à distance** remote control; **commandes** *(d'un avion)* controls; **prendre les commandes** *(d'un avion)* to take over the controls; *(d'une société)* to take control (**c**) *Ordinat* command; **c. d'annulation/d'effacement** undo/delete command; **à c. vocale** voice-activated

commandement [kɔmɑ̃dmɑ̃] *nm* (**a**) *(ordre)* *Mil* command; **à mon c.** when I give the command; *Rel* **les dix commandements** the Ten Commandments (**b**) *(pouvoir)* command; **avoir/prendre le c.** to be in/to take command; **c. suprême, haut c.** high command

commander [kɔmɑ̃de] **1** *vt* (**a**) *(diriger, ordonner)* to command; *Fam* **sans vous c., est-ce que vous pourriez fermer la fenêtre?** I wonder if you'd mind closing the window (**b**) *(marchandises, dîner)* to order; *(peinture, ouvrage)* to commission; **c. qch à qn** to order/commission sth from sb (**c**) *(mouvement, valve)* to control; *(machine)* to drive (**d**) *Ordinat* to drive; **commandé par menu** menu-driven

2 *vi* **c. à qn de faire qch** to order sb to do sth; **qui est-ce qui commande ici?** who's in charge here?

3 se commander *vpr* **ces choses-là ne se commandent pas** *(sont incontrôlables)* these things are beyond our control

commanditaire [kɔmɑ̃ditɛr] *adj & nm Com* (**associé**) **c.** silent partner; **les commanditaires de l'attentat** the people behind the attack

commandite [kɔmɑ̃dit] *nf Com* (**société en**) **c.** mixed liability company

commandité [kɔmɑ̃dite] *adj & nm Com* (**associé**) **c.** active partner

commanditer [kɔmɑ̃dite] *vt Com* to finance; *(meurtre, attentat)* to be behind

commando [kɔmɑ̃do] *nm (groupe)* commando (unit)

comme [kɔm] **1** *adv* (**a**) *(devant un nom, un pronom)* like; **il n'est pas c. les autres** he isn't like the others; **c. ça** like that; *(du coup)* that way; **c'est c. ça, un point c'est tout!** too bad, that's the way it is!; **alors c. ça, vous venez de Paris?** you come from Paris, don't you?; *Fam* **c. ça!** *(formidable)* great!; **quelque chose c. deux cents personnes** something like two hundred people

(**b**) *(devant une proposition)* as; **il écrit c. il parle** he writes as he speaks; **insolent c. il est...** insolent as he is...; **il leva la main c. pour me frapper** he lifted his hand as if *or* as though to strike me; **c. il faut** *(se conduire)* properly; **des gens très c. il faut** very respectable people; **c. si** as if, as though; **c. si je ne le savais pas!** as if I didn't know!

(**c**) *(dans des images)* as; **doux c. un agneau** (as) gentle as a lamb

(**d**) *(et)* **les femmes c. les hommes** men and women alike; **tout le monde fera la vaisselle, toi c. les autres** everyone's going to do the dishes, and you're no exception

(**e**) *(tel que)* such as, like; **les bois durs c. le chêne** hard woods like *or* such as oak; **P c. pomme** P as in pomme

(**f**) *(en tant que)* as; **je l'ai eue c. professeur** she was my teacher; **qu'est-ce que vous avez c. desserts?** what have you got in the way of desserts?; **ce n'est pas mal c. film** it's not a bad movie

(**g**) *(en quelque sorte)* **elle a eu c. une hésitation** she seemed to hesitate; **j'étais c. hypnotisé** it was as if *or* as though I was hypnotized

(**h**) *(comment)* how; **tu sais bien c. il est** you know what he's like; *Fam* **elle a fait les carreaux, faut voir c.!** you should see the way she's done the windows!

(**i**) *(exclamatif)* how; **c. tu as grandi!** how you've grown!; **c. elle est bête!** she's so stupid!; **c. elle a de beaux cheveux!** what lovely hair she has!

(**j**) *Fam (locutions)* **c'est tout c.** it amounts to the same thing; **c. ci c. ça** so-so; **c. qui dirait** as it were; **c. quoi** *(disant que)* to the effect that; *(ce qui prouve que)* which goes to show that; **drôle c. tout** as funny as anything

2 *conj* (**a**) *(puisque)* as, since; **c. vous êtes mon ami, je vais tout vous dire** as you're my friend I'll tell you everything (**b**) *(alors que)* **c. il allait frapper, la porte s'ouvrit** he was just about to knock when the door opened

commémoratif, -ive [kɔmemɔratif, -iv] *adj (plaque, cérémonie)* commemorative; *(service)* memorial; **monument c.** memorial

commémoration [kɔmemɔrasjɔ̃] *nf* commemoration; **en c. de** in commemoration of

commémorer [kɔmemɔre] *vt* to commemorate

commencement [kɔmɑ̃smɑ̃] *nm* beginning, start; **au c.** at the beginning *or* start; **il faut un c. à tout** you've got to start somewhere; *Fam* **c'est le c. de la fin** it's the beginning of the end

commencer [16] [kɔmɑ̃se] **1** *vt* (**a**) *(entreprendre)* to begin, to start; *(traitement, régime)* to go on, to start; **nous avons mal commencé l'année** we've made a bad start to the year (**b**) *(être au début de)* to begin, to start

2 *vi* to begin, to start; **pour c., je dois vous dire...** to begin with, I must tell you...; *Ironique* **ça commence bien!** that's a good start!; **c. par qch/par faire qch** to begin *or* to start with sth/by doing sth; **par où c.?** where shall I begin?; **à c. par...** beginning with...

3 commencer à *vt ind* **c. à faire qch** to begin *or* to start to do sth, to begin *or* to start doing sth; *Fam* **je commence à en avoir assez!** I've had just about enough!; *Fam* **ça commence à bien faire** my patience is wearing thin

comment [kɔmɑ̃] **1** *adv* how; **c. allez-vous?** how are you?; **c.?** *(pour faire répéter)* I beg your pardon?; **c. ça, tu ne veux pas?** what do you mean, you don't want to?; **c. faire?** what can I/we*/etc.* do?; **c. est-il, ce garçon?** what's this young man like?; **elle me dira c. faire** she'll tell me how to do it

2 *exclam* what!; **mais c. donc!** why, of course!; *Fam* **ça vous a plu? – et c.!** did you like it? – you bet!

commentaire [kɔmɑ̃tɛr] *nm* (**a**) *(remarque)* comment, remark; **faire des commentaires** to make comments; **cela se passe de c.** it speaks for itself; *Fam* **sans c.!** no comment!; *Scol* **c. de texte** textual commentary (**b**) *(à la radio, à la télévision)* commentary; **c. sportif** sports commentary

commentateur, -trice [kɔmɑ̃tatœr, -tris] *nm,f (à la radio, à la télévision)* commentator; **c. sportif** sports commentator

commenter [kɔmɑ̃te] *vt (expliquer, donner son avis sur)* to comment on; *(à la radio, à la télévision) (compétition)* to commentate on; **c. l'actualité** to comment on current affairs

commérage [kɔmeraʒ] *nm* (piece of) gossip; **commérages** gossip

commerçant, -e [kɔmɛrsɑ̃, -ɑ̃t] **1** *nm,f* trader; *(qui tient un magasin)* storekeeper; **petits commerçants** small storekeepers

2 *adj* **quartier c.** shopping area; **rue très commerçante** busy shopping street; **il n'est pas très c.** he doesn't look after his customers very well

commerce [kɔmɛrs] *nm* (**a**) **le c.** *(activité, secteur)* trade; *(affaires)* business; **ça se trouve dans le c.** you can buy it in stores; **faire du c. avec** to do business with; **hors c.** not for (general) sale; **c. électronique** e-commerce; **c. équitable** fair trade; **c. en** *ou* **de gros/de détail** wholesale/retail trade; **c. intérieur/extérieur** home/foreign trade; **c. interna-**

tional world trade; **c. maritime** seaborne trade; **le petit c.** small businesses (**b**) *(magasin)* business

commercer [16] [kɔmɛrse] *vi* to trade (**avec** with)

commercial, -e, -aux, -ales [kɔmɛrsjal, -o] **1** *adj (rapports, pratiques)* business, commercial; *(embargo, tribunal)* trade; *(droit)* commercial; *Péj (film, chanson)* commercial; **suivre une formation commerciale** to take business courses

2 *nm,f* salesman, *f* saleswoman

3 *nf* **commerciale** *(voiture)* station wagon

commercialisation [kɔmɛrsjalizasjɔ̃] *nf* marketing

commercialiser [kɔmɛrsjalize] *vt (produit)* to market

commère [kɔmɛr] *nf* gossip

commettre [47] [kɔmɛtr] **1** *vt* (**a**) *(crime, péché, injustice)* to commit; *(erreur)* to make; *Hum* **il a déjà commis deux pièces de théâtre** he's already to blame for two plays (**b**) *Jur* **avocat commis d'office** counsel appointed by the court

2 se commettre *vpr Litt* **se c. avec qn** to compromise oneself by associating with sb

commis¹, -e [kɔmi, -iz] *voir* **commettre**

commis² [kɔmi] *nm* (**a**) *(employé)* clerk; *(dans un magasin)* salesclerk (**b**) *Vieilli* **c. voyageur** commercial traveler

commisération [kɔmizerasjɔ̃] *nf* commiseration; **témoigner de la c. à qn** to commiserate with sb

commissaire [kɔmisɛr] *nm* (**a**) **c. (de police)** ≃ (police) captain (**b**) *Fin* **c. aux comptes** government auditor (**c**) *(membre d'une commission)* commissioner (**d**) *Sport* steward (**e**) *(d'une exposition)* organizer

commissaire-priseur *(pl* **commissaires-priseurs)** [kɔmisɛrprizœr] *nm* auctioneer

commissariat [kɔmisarja] *nm* (**a**) **c. (de police)** police station (**b**) *(fonction)* commissionership (**c**) *(service)* commission; **le C. à l'énergie atomique** the Atomic Energy Commission

commission [kɔmisjɔ̃] *nf* (**a**) *(course)* **faire les commissions** to go shopping (**b**) *(service)* errand; *(message)* message; **faire une c.** to run an errand; **faire une c. à qn** to give sb a message (**c**) *(comité)* commission, committee; **c. d'enquête** fact-finding committee; **C. européenne** European Commission; **C. des opérations de Bourse** = French Stock Exchange watchdog (**d**) *(pourcentage)* *Com* commission; *Fin* brokerage; **être payé à la c.** to be paid on a commission basis; **c. bancaire** bank commission (**e**) *Fam* **la petite/grosse c.** number one/two

commissionnaire [kɔmisjɔnɛr] *nm* (**a**) *(messager)* messenger; *(à l'hôtel, au théâtre)* doorman (**b**) *Com* (commission) agent

commissionner [kɔmisjɔne] *vt* to commission

commissures [kɔmisyr] *nfpl* **c. des lèvres** *ou* **de la bouche** corners of the mouth

commode [kɔmɔd] **1** *adj* (**a**) *(heure, lieu)* convenient; *(outil, système)* handy (**b**) **pas c.** *(difficile)* tricky; *(peu aimable)* awkward

2 *nf* chest of drawers

commodément [kɔmɔdemɑ̃] *adv (assis, installé)* comfortably

commodité [kɔmɔdite] *nf* (**a**) *(facilité)* convenience; **pour plus de c.** for greater convenience; **les commodités de la vie moderne** the comforts of modern life (**b**) *Vieilli* **commodités** *(toilettes)* restroom

commotion [kɔmosjɔ̃] *nf* (**a**) *Méd* **c. cérébrale** concussion (**b**) *(émotion)* shock

commotionner [kɔmosjɔne] *vt* (**a**) *Méd* to concuss (**b**) *(choquer)* to shake (up)

commuer [kɔmɥe] *vt Jur (peine)* to commute (**en** to)

commun, -e [kɔmœ̃, -yn] **1** *adj* (**a**) *(non exclusif)* common (**à** to); *(travail)* joint; *(ami)* mutual; **jardin c. à deux maisons** garden shared by two houses; **en c.** *(travailler)* together; *(vivre)* communally; **avoir des choses en c.** *(se ressembler)* to have

things in common; **nous n'avons aucun point c.** we have nothing in common; **se mettre** *ou* **mettre de l'argent en c. pour acheter un cadeau** to club together to buy a present (**b**) *(répandu)* common; **il est d'une force peu commune** he's unusually strong (**c**) *(vulgaire)* common

2 *nm* (**a**) *(majorité)* **le c. des mortels** the ordinary man; **hors du c.** out of the ordinary (**b**) **communs** *(dépendances)* outbuildings

communal, -e, -aux, -ales [kɔmynal, -o] *adj (de la commune)* *(terrain, salle)* ≃ district; **école communale** ≃ local grade school; *Belg* **maison communale** town hall

communautaire [kɔmynotɛr] *adj (en commun)* communal; *(de la Communauté européenne)* Community

communauté [kɔmynote] *nf* (**a**) *(collectivité)* & *Rel* community; *(de hippies)* commune; **vivre en c.** to live in a commune; **la C. économique européenne** the European Economic Community; **la C. d'États indépendants** the Commonwealth of Independent States (**b**) *(d'intérêts, d'idées)* similarity; *Jur* **être mariés sous le régime de la c.** to be married on the basis of a joint settlement of property

commune [kɔmyn] *nf* (**a**) *(municipalité)* commune *(smallest territorial division)* (**b**) *(administration)* local authority (**c**) *Hist* **la C. (de Paris)** the Commune *(in 1789 and 1871)*

Commune

There are over 36,000 "communes" or administrative districts in France, some with fewer than 25 inhabitants. Each "commune" has an elected mayor and a town council.

---

communément [kɔmynemɑ̃] *adv* commonly

communiant, -e [kɔmynjɑ̃, -ɑ̃t] *nm,f Rel* communicant; **premier c.** person taking his first communion

communicatif, -ive [kɔmynikatif, -iv] *adj* (**a**) *(qui parle)* communicative; **peu c.** uncommunicative (**b**) *(rire, bonne humeur)* infectious

communication [kɔmynikasjɔ̃] *nf* (**a**) *(échange)* communication; **entrer** *ou* **se mettre en c. avec qn** to get in touch *or* in contact with sb; **toutes les communications sont coupées** all lines of communication are cut; **c. de masse** mass communication (**b**) *Tél* **c. (téléphonique)** (telephone) call; **je vous passe la c.** I'll put you through; **la c. est mauvaise** the line is bad (**c**) *(message)* communication, message; **faire une c.** *(dans un colloque)* to read a paper

communier [66] [kɔmynje] *vi Rel* to receive Communion

communion [kɔmynjɔ̃] *nf* (**a**) *(communauté)* communion; **être en c. avec la nature** to commune with nature (**b**) *Rel* Communion; **première c.** first Communion; **c. solennelle** solemn Communion; **faire sa c.** to make one's first/solemn Communion

communiqué [kɔmynike] *nm* communiqué; **c. de presse** press release

communiquer [kɔmynike] **1** *vt* to communicate (**à** to); *(maladie)* to pass on (**à** to)

2 *vi* (**a**) *(être en relation)* to communicate (**avec** with) (**b**) *(pièce)* to communicate (**avec** with); **porte qui communique avec le jardin** door that leads into the yard

3 se communiquer *vpr (se transmettre)* to spread (**à** to)

communisme [kɔmynism] *nm* communism

communiste [kɔmynist] *adj* & *nmf* communist

commutateur [kɔmytatœr] *nm Élec (bouton)* switch; *Ordinat* **c. de données** data switch

commutation [kɔmytasjɔ̃] *nf* (**a**) *Jur (de peine)* commutation (**b**) *(changement)* & *Gram* substitution; *(entre documents)* switching (**c**) *Ordinat* **c. de message/de paquets** message/ packet switching

Comores [kɔmɔr] *nfpl* **les C., l'archipel des C.** the Comoros

comorien, -enne [kɔmɔrjɛ̃, -ɛn] **1** *adj* Comoran
  2 *nm,f* **C., Comorienne** Comoran
compact, -e [kɔ̃pakt] **1** *adj* (**a**) *(de petit format)* compact (**b**) *(masse, terre)* compact; *(foule)* dense
  2 *nm (CD)* compact disk
Compact Disc® *(pl* **Compact Discs**) [kɔ̃paktdisk] *nm* compact disk
compacter [kɔ̃pakte] *vt* Ordinat *(fichier, données)* to compress; *(base de données)* to pack
compacteur [kɔ̃paktœr] *nm* Ordinat **c. de données** data compressor; **c. d'exécutables** execute file compressor
compagne [kɔ̃paɲ] *nf* (**a**) *(camarade)* companion; **mes compagnes de captivité** my fellow captives (**b**) *(concubine)* partner
compagnie [kɔ̃paɲi] *nf* (**a**) *(présence)* company; **tenir c. à qn** to keep sb company; **en c. de qn** with sb (**b**) *(groupe)* **et toute la c.** and everybody; *Fam* **salut, la c.!** hi, guys or everybody! (**c**) *Com & Théât* company; *Com* **Thomas et C.** Thomas and Company; **c. aérienne** airline; **c. d'assurances** insurance company; **c. maritime** shipping line; **c. pétrolière** oil company; **c. de transports** carrier (**d**) *Mil* company (**e**) *(de perdrix)* covey
compagnon [kɔ̃paɲɔ̃] *nm* (**a**) *(camarade)* companion; **c. de voyage** traveling companion (**b**) *(ouvrier)* journeyman (**c**) *(concubin)* partner
comparable [kɔ̃parabl] *adj* comparable (**à** *ou* **avec** to *or* with); **ce n'est pas c.** there's no comparison
comparaison [kɔ̃parɛzɔ̃] *nf* (**a**) *(action de comparer)* comparison; **faire la c. entre** to make a comparison between; **c'est sans c. avec...** it can't be compared with...; **il est sans c. le plus grand** he is by far the tallest; **en c. de...** in comparison with...; **par c.** by comparison; **par c. avec** *ou* **à** compared with *or* to (**b**) *(figure de style)* simile
comparaître [50a] [kɔ̃parɛtr] *vi* Jur **c. (en justice)** to appear (in court); **être appelé à c.** to be summoned to appear
comparatif, -ive [kɔ̃paratif, -iv] **1** *adj* comparative
  2 *nm* Gram **c. de supériorité/d'infériorité** comparative of greater/lesser degree
comparativement [kɔ̃parativmɑ̃] *adv* comparatively
comparé, -e [kɔ̃pare] *adj (anatomie, histoire, littérature)* comparative; **c. à** compared with *or* to
comparer [kɔ̃pare] **1** *vt* to compare (**à** *ou* **avec** to *or* with)
  2 se comparer *vpr* (**a**) *(soi-même)* **se c. à** *ou* **avec** to compare oneself to *or* with (**b**) *(être comparé)* **Händel ne peut pas se c. à Mozart** Handel can't be compared with Mozart
comparse [kɔ̃pars] *nmf* Péj associate
compartiment [kɔ̃partimɑ̃] *nm (de wagon, de boîte, de tiroir)* compartment; **c. fumeurs** smoking compartment, smoker; **c. non-fumeurs** no-smoking compartment, non-smoker; **c. à bagages** *(d'autocar)* luggage compartment
compartimenter [kɔ̃partimɑ̃te] *vt (diviser en espaces)* to partition; *Fig* **une société compartimentée** a compartmentalized society
comparution [kɔ̃parysjɔ̃] *nf* Jur appearance
compas [kɔ̃pa] *nm* (**a**) *Math* (pair of) compasses; *Fig* **avoir le c. dans l'œil** to have an accurate eye; **c. à pointes sèches** dividers (**b**) *Naut* compass
compassé, -e [kɔ̃pase] *adj* stiff, starchy
compassion [kɔ̃pasjɔ̃] *nf* compassion; **avec c.** compassionately
compatibilité [kɔ̃patibilite] *nf* compatibility
compatible [kɔ̃patibl] *adj aussi* Ordinat compatible (**avec** with)
compatir [kɔ̃patir] *vi* to sympathize; **c. au chagrin de qn** to sympathize with sb in his/her grief
compatissant, -e [kɔ̃patisɑ̃, -ɑ̃t] *adj* compassionate, sympathetic

compatriote [kɔ̃patriɔt] *nmf* compatriot
compensable [kɔ̃pɑ̃sabl] *adj (chèque)* clearable
compensation [kɔ̃pɑ̃sasjɔ̃] *nf* (**a**) *(d'une perte, d'un inconvénient)* compensation; **en c. de qch** as compensation for sth (**b**) *(de chèque)* clearing
compensé, -e [kɔ̃pɑ̃se] *adj* **chaussures à semelles compensées** platform shoes
compenser [kɔ̃pɑ̃se] **1** *vt* (**a**) *(perte, défaut)* to compensate for, to make up for (**b**) *(chèque)* to clear
  2 se compenser *vpr* to make up for each other
compère [kɔ̃pɛr] *nm* Vieilli *(camarade)* friend
compétence [kɔ̃petɑ̃s] *nf* (**a**) *(capacité)* competence; **compétences** *(connaissances)* ability; **cela n'entre pas dans mes compétences** it's beyond my capabilities (**b**) *Jur (d'un tribunal, d'un maire)* competence; **cela n'est pas de sa c.** that doesn't come within her province
compétent, -e [kɔ̃petɑ̃, -ɑ̃t] *adj* (**a**) *(capable)* competent; **c. en qch** conversant with sth (**b**) *Jur (tribunal, autorité)* competent; **adressez-vous au service c.** apply to the relevant department
compétitif, -ive [kɔ̃petitif, -iv] *adj* competitive
compétition [kɔ̃petisjɔ̃] *nf* (**a**) *(rivalité)* competition; **être en c. avec qn** to compete with sb (**b**) *Sport (épreuve)* **c. (sportive)** (sporting) event; **faire de la c.** to take part in competitive sports
compétitivité [kɔ̃petitivite] *nf* competitiveness
compilateur [kɔ̃pilatœr] *nm* Ordinat compiler; **c. croisé** cross-compiler
compilation [kɔ̃pilasjɔ̃] *nf* compilation
compiler [kɔ̃pile] *vt aussi* Ordinat to compile
complaire [55a] [kɔ̃plɛr] **se complaire** *vpr* **se c. dans qch/à faire qch** to delight *or* to revel in sth/in doing sth
complaisance [kɔ̃plɛzɑ̃s] *nf* (**a**) *(bienveillance)* kindness; **faire qch par c.** to do sth out of kindness (**b**) *Péj (indulgence)* indulgence; **certificat médical de c.** = medical certificate to which one is not entitled (**c**) *(autosatisfaction)* complacency, smugness
complaisant, -e [kɔ̃plɛzɑ̃, -ɑ̃t] *adj* (**a**) *(bienveillant)* obliging, kind (**envers** towards) (**b**) *Péj (indulgent)* indulgent (**c**) *(satisfait)* complacent, smug
complément [kɔ̃plemɑ̃] *nm* (**a**) *(reste)* rest, remainder; **demander un c. d'information** to ask for further information (**b**) *Gram* complement; **c. d'attribution** indirect object; **c. circonstanciel de temps/de manière** adverbial phrase of time/of manner; **c. de nom** possessive phrase; **c. d'objet direct/indirect** direct/indirect object
complémentaire [kɔ̃plemɑ̃tɛr] *adj (couleur)* complementary; **pour tout renseignement c., s'adresser à...** for further information, apply to...
complet, -ète [kɔ̃plɛ, -ɛt] **1** *adj* (**a**) *(entier, intégral) (tenue, service)* complete, whole; **deux jours complets** two full *or* whole days; **formation très complète** thorough training; *Fam* **c'est c.!** that's the last straw! (**b**) *(détaillé)* full (**c**) *(absolu)* complete; **un c. abruti** a complete moron; **ce fut un échec c.** it was a complete failure (**d**) *(bus, salle de théâtre)* full; **c.** *(sur panneau) (parking)* full; *(pension, hôtel)* no vacancies (**e**) *(pain, pâtes)* wholewheat; *(riz)* brown
  2 *nm* (**a**) **c.(-veston)** suit (**b**) **est-ce que nous sommes au c.?** are we all here?; **j'ai invité la famille au (grand) c. pour Noël** I've invited the whole family for Christmas
complètement [kɔ̃plɛtmɑ̃] *adv* (**a**) *(terminé, guéri)* completely, totally; **je n'ai pas c. fini** I haven't quite finished (**b**) *(vraiment) (perdu, idiot)* completely, totally
compléter [34] [kɔ̃plete] **1** *vt (collection, formation)* to complete; *(somme)* to make up; *(formulaire)* to complete, to fill out
  2 se compléter *vpr* to complement one another
complexe [kɔ̃plɛks] **1** *adj (compliqué)* complex

2 *nm* (**a**) *(ensemble de bâtiments, d'industries)* complex; **c. hôtelier** hotel complex; **c. sportif** sports complex (**b**) *(gêne)* hang-up; *Psy* complex; **avoir des complexes (à cause de qch)** to have a hang-up (about sth); **être sans c.** to have no hang-ups; **c. d'infériorité** inferiority complex; **c. d'Œdipe** Oedipus complex

complexé, -e [kɔ̃plɛkse] *adj* hung up (**par** about)

complexer [kɔ̃plɛkse] *vt* **c. qn** to give sb a hang-up

complexité [kɔ̃plɛksite] *nf* complexity

complication [kɔ̃plikasjɔ̃] *nf* (**a**) *(ennui)* complication; **faire des complications** to create complications (**b**) *(complexité)* complexity (**c**) *Méd* **complications** complications

complice [kɔ̃plis] **1** *nmf* accomplice
2 *adj (regard, sourire)* knowing; **être c. de qch** to be party to sth

complicité [kɔ̃plisite] *nf* complicity; **agir en c. avec qn** to act in collusion with sb; **accusé de c. de meurtre** accused of being an accessory to murder

compliment [kɔ̃plimã] *nm* compliment; **faire des compliments à qn (sur qch)** to pay sb compliments (on sth); **(je vous fais) mes compliments!** I congratulate you!; *Ironique* **mes compliments!** congratulations!

complimenter [kɔ̃plimãte] *vt* **c. qn pour** *(courage, présence d'esprit)* to congratulate sb on; **c. qn sur** *(toilette, coiffure)* to compliment sb on

compliqué, -e [kɔ̃plike] *adj* complicated; **ce n'est pourtant pas c.!** it's quite simple!

compliquer [kɔ̃plike] **1** *vt* to complicate; **c. les choses** to complicate matters
2 se compliquer *vpr (situation, problème)* to get complicated; **se c. l'existence** to make life complicated for oneself

complot [kɔ̃plo] *nm* plot, conspiracy

comploter [kɔ̃plɔte] **1** *vt* to plot; **c. de faire qch** to plot to do sth
2 *vi* to plot (**contre** against)

comportement [kɔ̃pɔrtəmã] *nm* behavior; *Écon* **c. d'achat** buying behavior

comporter [kɔ̃pɔrte] **1** *vt* (**a**) *(être constitué de)* to consist of, to be made up of (**b**) *(contenir)* to contain (**c**) *(difficultés, inconvénients)* to involve
2 se comporter *vpr* (**a**) *(agir)* to behave (**vis-à-vis de** *ou* **envers** towards) (**b**) *(fonctionner) (voiture)* to handle

composant [kɔ̃pozã] *nm* component

composante [kɔ̃pozãt] *nf* component

composé, -e *adj & nm* compound

composer [kɔ̃poze] **1** *vt* (**a**) *(symphonie, poème)* to compose, to write; *(bouquet)* to make up (**b**) *(faire partie de)* to make up; **être composé de qch** to be made up *or* composed of sth (**c**) *(numéro de téléphone)* to dial (**d**) *Typ* to set (**e**) **c. son visage** to compose one's features
2 *vi* (**a**) *(s'entendre)* to compromise (**avec** with) (**b**) *Scol* to take a test
3 se composer *vpr* (**a**) **se c. de qch** to be made up *or* composed of sth (**b**) **se c. un visage de circonstance** to put on a suitable expression

composite [kɔ̃pozit] *adj* composite

compositeur, -trice [kɔ̃pozitœr, -tris] *nm,f* (**a**) *Mus* composer (**b**) *Typ* typesetter

composition [kɔ̃pozisjɔ̃] *nf* (**a**) *(d'une symphonie, d'un poème)* composition, writing; **un poème de ma c.** a poem I wrote (myself); *Cin & Théât* **rôle de c.** character part (**b**) *(éléments)* composition; *(d'un aliment)* ingredients; **la c. des équipes n'est pas encore connue** the teams haven't been announced yet (**c**) *(œuvre musicale, littéraire)* composition (**d**) *(rédaction)* essay; *(examen)* test (**e**) *(caractère)* **être de bonne c.** to be good-natured (**f**) *Typ* typesetting

compost [kɔ̃pɔst] *nm* compost

composter [kɔ̃pɔste] *vt* (**a**) *(pour dater)* to date-stamp (**b**) *(pour valider)* to punch

Composter
Rail passengers in France are required to insert their ticket into a special punching machine ("composteur") on the platform before beginning their journey. The words "à composter" printed across the ticket mean that the passenger must do this before getting on the train.

compote [kɔ̃pɔt] *nf* compote, stewed fruit; **c. de pommes** applesauce; *Fam* **j'ai les jambes en c.** my legs feel like Jell-O

compotier [kɔ̃pɔtje] *nm* fruit dish

compréhensible [kɔ̃preãsibl] *adj* (**a**) *(clair)* comprehensible (**par** to) (**b**) *(justifié)* understandable

compréhensif, -ive [kɔ̃preãsif, -iv] *adj* understanding

compréhension [kɔ̃preãsjɔ̃] *nf* (**a**) *(fait de comprendre)* comprehension, understanding (**b**) *(bienveillance)* understanding

comprendre [58] [kɔ̃prãdr] **1** *vt* (**a**) *(par l'esprit)* to understand; **dois-je c. que…?** am I to understand that…?; **mal c. qn/qch** to misunderstand sb/sth; **je ne le comprends pas** *(il est étrange, il n'articule pas)* I can't understand him; **il faut la c.** you have to see things from her point of view; **je n'y comprends rien** I can't make head nor tail of it; **c'est à n'y rien c.** it's incomprehensible; **ne cherche pas, il n'y a rien à c.** don't even try to understand; **va y c. quelque chose!** YOU try to make head or tail of it!; **faire c. à qn que…** to give sb to understand that…; *(avec autorité)* to make it clear to sb that…; **se faire c.** to make oneself understood; **me suis-je bien fait c.?** have I made myself clear?; **elle comprend vite** she's quick on the uptake; **ça va, j'ai compris!** OK, I understand!; **tu comprends…** you see… (**b**) *(être composé de)* to consist of, to be made up of (**c**) *(inclure)* to include
2 se comprendre *vpr (l'un l'autre)* to understand each other; **ça se comprend** it's understandable; **je me comprends!** I know what I mean!

comprenure [kɔ̃prənyr] *nf Belg & Can Fam* **être dur de c.** to be slow on the uptake

compresse [kɔ̃prɛs] *nf* compress

compresser [kɔ̃prɛse] *vt* to compress; *Ordinat* to zip

compresseur [kɔ̃prɛsœr] *nm* (**a**) *Tech (de gaz, de vapeur)* compressor; *(de moteur)* supercharger (**b**) *Ordinat* **c. de données** data compressor

compression [kɔ̃prɛsjɔ̃] *nf* (**a**) *(de gaz, de vapeur)* compression (**b**) *(réduction)* reduction; **c. des dépenses** spending cuts

comprimé, -e [kɔ̃prime] **1** *adj (gaz)* compressed
2 *nm (médicament)* tablet; **un c. d'aspirine** an aspirin

comprimer [kɔ̃prime] *vt* (**a**) *(gaz, artère, fichier informatique)* to compress; **cette jupe me comprime la taille** this skirt is too tight around my waist (**b**) *Fig (dépenses)* to reduce (**c**) *Ordinat (données)* to compress

compris, -e [kɔ̃pri, -iz] **1** *pp voir* **comprendre**
2 *adj* (**a**) *(enregistré)* **bien c.** (fully) understood; **mal c.** misunderstood; **alors, c'est c.?** so, do you understand?; *Fam* **tu fais tes devoirs immédiatement, c.?** you'll do your homework right now, (is that) understood? (**b**) *(inclus)* included; **service non c.** service not included; **tout c.** all in; **y c.** including (**c**) *(situé)* **être c. entre** to be between

compromettant, -e [kɔ̃prɔmɛtã, -ãt] *adj* compromising

compromettre [47] [kɔ̃prɔmɛtr] **1** *vt* (**a**) *(personne, réputation)* to compromise; **être compromis dans qch** to be implicated in sth (**b**) *(sécurité, vacances, chances)* to jeopardize
2 se compromettre *vpr* to compromise oneself; **se c. dans qch** to be implicated in sth

compromis [kɔ̃prɔmi] *nm (arrangement)* compromise

compromission [kɔ̃prɔmisjɔ̃] *nf Péj* compromise

comptabiliser [kɔ̃tabilize] *vt (recettes, dépenses)* to enter in the accounts; *(points)* to count

comptabilité [kɔ̃tabilite] *nf* (a) *(livres)* accounts; *(technique)* bookkeeping, accounting; **tenir la c.** to keep the accounts (b) *(service)* accounts department

comptable [kɔ̃tabl] **1** *adj (travail, technique)* bookkeeping, accounting
2 *nmf* accountant; **c. agréé** certified public accountant

comptage [kɔ̃taʒ] *nm* counting

comptant [kɔ̃tɑ̃] **1** *adv* **payer c.** to pay (in) cash
2 *nm* cash; **payer/acheter au c.** to pay (in)/buy for cash

compte [kɔ̃t] *nm* (a) *(dans une banque, chez un commerçant)* account; **comptes** *(comptabilité)* accounts; **tenir les comptes** to keep the accounts; **faire ses comptes** to do one's accounts; **verser une somme sur son c.** to deposit a sum into one's account; **se mettre** *ou* **s'installer à son c.** to start one's own business; **faire qch pour le c. de qn** to do sth on sb's behalf; **c. en banque** *ou* **bancaire** bank account; **c. chèques** checking account; **c. chèques postal** = account held at the Post Office; **c. courant** checking account; **c. de dépôt** deposit account; **c. épargne** savings account; **c. épargne logement** savings account *(for purchasing real estate)*; **c. étranger** non-resident *or* foreign account; **c. joint** joint account
(b) *(calcul)* calculation; **faire le c. de** *(dépenses)* to add up; *(temps restant)* to calculate; *(objets, personnes)* to count; **le c. y est** *(somme)* it's the right amount; *(objets, personnes)* they're all here; **c. à rebours** countdown
(c) *(explication)* **demander des comptes à qn** to ask sb for an explanation; **rendre des comptes** to explain oneself; **je n'ai de comptes à rendre à personne** I'm not answerable to anyone; **rendre c. de qch** to account for sth
(d) *(locutions)* Fam **avoir son c.** to have had enough; **être loin du c.** *(se tromper)* to be wide of the mark; Fam **régler son c. à qn** to give sb a piece of one's mind; **on réglera nos comptes plus tard** we'll settle scores later; **apprendre qch sur le c. de qn** to learn sth about sb; **j'en ai appris de belles sur son c.!** I heard some fine things about him/her!; Fam **son c. est bon** he's/she's done for; **tenir c. de qch** to take sth into account; **il n'a tenu aucun c. de mes conseils** he took no heed of my advice; **c. tenu de** considering; **s'en tirer à bon c.** to get off lightly; **y trouver son c.** to get something out of it; **à ce c.-là** in that case; **au bout du c., en fin de c.** in the end; **tout c. fait** all things considered; Prov **les bons comptes font les bons amis** pay your debts and keep your friends

compte-gouttes [kɔ̃tgut] *nm inv* dropper; Fig **au c.** in dribs and drabs

compter [kɔ̃te] **1** *vt* (a) *(dénombrer)* to count; **on ne compte plus les mécontents** we've lost count of the malcontents; Fig **c. les points** to watch from the sidelines (b) *(donner avec parcimonie)* **il compte chaque sou** he begrudges every cent he spends; **ses jours sont comptés** his days are numbered (c) *(inclure)* to include; **sans c....** not counting...; **sans c. que...** besides the fact that...; **je le compte parmi mes meilleurs amis** I number him among my best friends (d) *(prévoir)* to allow; **j'ai compté 200 grammes par personne** I've allowed 200 grams per person; **c. faire qch** *(espérer)* to expect to do sth; *(avoir l'intention de)* to intend to do sth (e) *(facturer)* **c. qch à qn** to charge sb for sth (f) Can *(marquer)* to score
2 *vi* (a) *(calculer)* to count; **dépenser sans c.** *(dépenser trop)* to spend money like water; **à c. du 1er janvier** (with effect) from January 1st (b) *(être parcimonieux)* to count the pennies (c) *(être important)* to count, to matter; **il compte beaucoup pour elle** he means a lot to her; **c. double** to count double; **à table, il compte pour deux** he eats enough for two (d) *(figurer)* **c. parmi les meilleurs** to rank among the best (e) **c. avec qn/qch** to reckon with sb/sth (f) **c. sur qn/qch** to count *or* to rely on sb/sth; **j'y compte bien!** I should hope so!; Fam **compte là-dessus et bois de l'eau!** you'll be lucky!
3 se compter *vpr* **les membres de cette secte se**

comptent par milliers this sect has thousands of members

compte rendu *(pl* **comptes rendus)** [kɔ̃trɑ̃dy] *nm* report; *(d'un roman, d'un film)* review; *(d'une réunion)* minutes

compte-tours [kɔ̃ttur] *nm inv* tachometer

compteur [kɔ̃tœr] *nm* meter; **c. d'eau/d'électricité/à gaz** water/electricity/gas meter; **c. (de) Geiger** Geiger counter; Aut **c. kilométrique** odometer; Can **c. de stationnement** parking meter; Aut **c. de vitesse** speedometer

comptine [kɔ̃tin] *nf* nursery rhyme

comptoir [kɔ̃twar] *nm* (a) *(dans un magasin)* counter; *(dans un bar)* bar; **prendre une consommation au c.** to have a drink at the bar; **c. d'enregistrement** check-in desk; **c. d'information** information desk; **c. de réception** reception desk; **c. de vente** sales counter (b) *(dans un pays éloigné)* trading post

compulser [kɔ̃pylse] *vt (documents, livres)* to consult

comte [kɔ̃t] *nm* count; *(en Grande-Bretagne)* earl

comté [kɔ̃te] *nm* (a) Hist earldom (b) *(subdivision administrative)* county (c) *(fromage)* = type of hard cheese (d) Can Pol riding

comtesse [kɔ̃tɛs] *nf* countess

con, conne [kɔ̃, kɔn] **1** *adj très Fam* (a) *(stupide)* goddamn stupid; Fam **être c. comme la lune** *ou* **un balai** to be as dumb as they come; **c'est pas c.!** that's pretty smart! (b) *(facile)* **c'est tout c.!** it's a snap!
2 *nm,f très Fam* stupid bastard; **faire le c.** to act like a jerk; **pauvre c.!** poor schmuck!; **à la c.** *(ordinateur, voiture)* crappy, goddamn useless; *(idée, histoire)* goddamn stupid
3 *nm Vulg (sexe)* cunt

conard [kɔnar] *nm très Fam* stupid asshole

conasse [kɔnas] *nf très Fam* stupid bitch

concasser [kɔ̃kase] *vt (roche)* to crush; *(poivre)* to grind

concave [kɔ̃kav] *adj* concave

concéder [34] [kɔ̃sede] *vt* (a) *(privilège, droit, terrain, concession)* **c. qch à qn** to grant sb sth, to grant sth to sb (b) *(reconnaître)* **c. qu'on a tort** to admit that one is wrong; **il fait chaud, je vous le concède** it's warm, I grant you (c) Sport *(point, but, victoire)* to concede

concentration [kɔ̃sɑ̃trasjɔ̃] *nf* concentration

concentrationnaire [kɔ̃sɑ̃trasjɔnɛr] *adj* of concentration camps; **la vie c.** life in a concentration camp

concentré, -e [kɔ̃sɑ̃tre] **1** *adj* (a) *(solution)* concentrated; *(lait)* condensed (b) *(intellectuellement)* **il était très c.** he was concentrating hard
2 *nm Chim & Culin* concentrate; **c. de tomate** tomato purée

concentrer [kɔ̃sɑ̃tre] **1** *vt (troupes, forces, efforts)* to concentrate; *(rayons du soleil)* to focus
2 se concentrer *vpr* (a) *(être attentif)* to concentrate (**sur** on) (b) *(s'assembler) (foule)* to gather; **la population se concentre dans les grandes villes** the population is concentrated in the big cities

concentrique [kɔ̃sɑ̃trik] *adj* concentric

concept [kɔ̃sɛpt] *nm* concept

concepteur, -trice [kɔ̃sɛptœr, -tris] *nm,f* designer; **c. graphiste** graphic designer; Ordinat **c. de sites Web** Web designer

conception [kɔ̃sɛpsjɔ̃] *nf* (a) *(d'un enfant, d'une idée)* conception (b) *(idée)* concept (c) *(création)* design; **c. assistée par ordinateur** computer-aided *or* -assisted design; **c. graphique** graphic design; **c. de sites Web** Web design

concernant [kɔ̃sɛrnɑ̃] *prép* concerning

concerner [kɔ̃sɛrne] *vt* to concern; **en ce qui me concerne** as far as I am concerned; **cela ne vous concerne pas** *(cela ne vous regarde pas)* it's none of your business; *(vous n'êtes pas visé)* it doesn't concern you

concert [kɔ̃sɛr] *nm* (a) *(de musique)* concert (b) *(accord)* **agir de c. avec qn** to act jointly with sb

concertation [kɔ̃sɛrtasjɔ̃] *nf* consultation

concerté, -e [kɔ̃sɛrte] *adj (action)* concerted

concerter [kɔ̃sɛrte] **1** *vt (projet)* to devise together
   2 se concerter *vpr* to consult together

concertiste [kɔ̃sɛrtist] *nmf* concert performer

concerto [kɔ̃sɛrto] *nm* concerto; **c. pour violon** violin concerto

concession [kɔ̃sesjɔ̃] *nf* (a) *(compromis)* concession; **faire des concessions** to make concessions; **sans concessions** uncompromising (b) *(attribution) (de terrain)* granting (c) *(terrain)* concession; *(au cimetière)* plot (d) *(droit exclusif de vente)* dealership

concessionnaire [kɔ̃sesjɔnɛr] *nmf* dealer

concevable [kɔ̃səvabl] *adj* conceivable

concevoir [60] [kɔ̃səvwar] **1** *vt* (a) *(enfant, plan, idée)* to conceive; *(produit)* to design (b) *(comprendre)* to understand; **je conçois que tu sois fâché, mais...** I can understand *or* see why you're angry, but...; **c'est ainsi que je conçois l'amour** this is my idea of love (c) *(éprouver)* **c. de l'amitié pour qn** to take a liking to sb
   2 se concevoir *vpr* **ça se conçoit** that's understandable

concierge [kɔ̃sjɛrʒ] *nmf (d'immeuble) & Scol* janitor; *(d'appartements)* superintendent; *(dans un hôtel)* concierge; *Fam* **c'est une vraie c.** she's a terrible gossip

concile [kɔ̃sil] *nm Rel* council

conciliabule [kɔ̃siljabyl] *nm (conversation)* confab

conciliant, -e [kɔ̃siljɑ̃, -ɑ̃t] *adj* conciliatory

conciliation [kɔ̃siljasjɔ̃] *nf* reconciliation

concilier [66] [kɔ̃silje] **1** *vt (deux choses)* to reconcile; **c. sa vie professionnelle et sa vie de famille** to combine one's professional life with one's family life
   2 se concilier *vpr* (a) *(être compatible)* **se c. avec** to go with (b) **se c. qn** *ou* **la faveur de qn** to win sb's goodwill

concis, -e [kɔ̃si, -iz] *adj* concise

concision [kɔ̃sizjɔ̃] *nf* conciseness; **avec c.** concisely

concitoyen, -enne [kɔ̃sitwajɛ̃, -ɛn] *nm,f* fellow citizen

concluant, -e [kɔ̃klyɑ̃, -ɑ̃t] *adj* conclusive; **peu c.** inconclusive

conclure [17a] [kɔ̃klyr] **1** *vt* (a) *(terminer)* to conclude, to end (**par** with) (b) *(accord, pacte)* to finalize; *(marché)* to clinch; **marché conclu!, affaire conclue!** (it's a) deal! (c) *(déduire)* to conclude (**de** from); **dois-je en c. que...?** am I to conclude that...?
   2 conclure à *vt ind* **ils ont conclu au suicide/meurtre** they concluded it was suicide/murder

conclusion [kɔ̃klyzjɔ̃] *nf* (a) *(fin) (d'un discours, d'une réunion)* conclusion, end (b) *(déduction)* conclusion; **tirer une c. de qch** to draw a conclusion from sth; *Fam* **c., l'échafaudage s'est écroulé** the result was that the scaffolding collapsed

concocter [kɔ̃kɔkte] *vt Fam* to concoct

concombre [kɔ̃kɔ̃br] *nm* cucumber

concordance [kɔ̃kɔrdɑ̃s] *nf* (a) *(de preuves, de témoignages, de dates)* tallying (b) *Gram* **c. des temps** sequence of tenses

concorder [kɔ̃kɔrde] *vi (preuves, dates, témoignages)* to tally (**avec** with)

concourir [22] [kɔ̃kurir] *vi* (a) *Sport* to compete (b) *(lignes)* to converge
   2 concourir à *vt ind* **c. à qch/à faire qch** to contribute to sth/to doing sth

concours [kɔ̃kur] *nm* (a) *(compétition)* competition, contest; *(examen)* competitive examination; **c. agricole/hippique** agricultural/horse show; **c. de beauté** beauty contest; **c. d'entrée (à)** entrance examination (to) (b) *(aide)* aid, assistance; **avec le c. de** with the participation of, in association with (c) **c. de circonstances** combination of circumstances; **par un heureux c. de circonstances** by a lucky coincidence

---

Concours

Unlike an ordinary examination, passing a "concours" does not lead to a degree, but rather to a teaching post in the state education system (for example the **CAPES** and **agrégation** - *see boxes at these entries*), an appointment or promotion in the civil service, or a place in a **Grande École** ("ENA", "Centrale", "ENS", etc). "Concours" are extremely competitive examinations, and the quota of successful candidates is determined in advance. They are usually held over a period of several days, and comprise a series of written and oral examinations requiring a high level of preparation.

---

concret, -ète [kɔ̃krɛ, -ɛt] **1** *adj* concrete
   2 *nm* **ce que je veux, c'est du c.** what I want is something concrete *or* something I can get my teeth into

concrètement [kɔ̃krɛtmɑ̃] *adv* in concrete terms

concrétiser [kɔ̃kretize] **1** *vt (rêve)* to realize; *(projet, promesse)* to carry out
   2 se concrétiser *vpr* to materialize

conçu, -e *voir* **concevoir**

concubin, -e [kɔ̃kybɛ̃, -in] *nm,f Jur* cohabitant

concubinage [kɔ̃kybinaʒ] *nm* cohabitation; **vivre en c.** to cohabit

concupiscent, -e [kɔ̃kypisɑ̃, -ɑ̃t] *adj* concupiscent

concurrence [kɔ̃kyrɑ̃s] *nf* (a) *(rivalité, concurrents)* competition; **faire c. à** to compete with; **faire jouer la c.** to shop around (b) **jusqu'à c. de...** up to...

concurrencer [16] [kɔ̃kyrɑ̃se] *vt* to compete with

concurrent, -e [kɔ̃kyrɑ̃, -ɑ̃t] **1** *adj (industries, produits)* competing, rival
   2 *nm,f* (a) *Com* competitor (b) *(dans une épreuve, un concours)* competitor

concurrentiel, -elle [kɔ̃kyrɑ̃sjɛl] *adj* competitive

condamnation [kɔ̃danasjɔ̃] *nf* (a) *Jur (jugement)* conviction (**pour** for); *(peine)* sentence (**à** to); **c. à mort** death sentence (b) *(critique)* condemnation

condamné, -e [kɔ̃dane] **1** *adj (malade)* terminally ill
   2 *nm,f* convicted person; **un c. à mort** a condemned man

condamner [kɔ̃dane] *vt* (a) *Jur* to sentence (**à** to); **c. qn à 1000 euros d'amende** to fine sb 1,000 euros (b) *(obliger à)* **c. qn à qch** to force sb into sth; **être condamné à la solitude** to be condemned to loneliness; **je suis condamnée à les attendre** I have to wait for them (c) *(blâmer)* to condemn (d) *(porte)* to block up; *(pièce)* to seal up (e) *(interdire)* to forbid

condensateur [kɔ̃dɑ̃satœr] *nm Élec* condenser

condensation [kɔ̃dɑ̃sasjɔ̃] *nf* condensation

condensé, -e [kɔ̃dɑ̃se] **1** *adj* condensed
   2 *nm* digest

condenser [kɔ̃dɑ̃se] **1** *vt (article, récit)* to condense
   2 se condenser *vpr* to condense

condescendant, -e [kɔ̃desɑ̃dɑ̃, -ɑ̃t] *adj* condescending

condescendre [kɔ̃desɑ̃dr] *vi* **c. à faire qch** to condescend to do sth

condiment [kɔ̃dimɑ̃] *nm* condiment

condisciple [kɔ̃disipl] *nmf Univ* fellow student; *Scol* schoolmate

condition [kɔ̃disjɔ̃] *nf* (a) *(stipulation)* condition; **sans c.** unconditionally; **à une c....** on one condition...; **à c. que tu viennes avec moi** providing that *or* on condition that you come with me; **tu peux y aller à c. de rentrer pour minuit** you can go providing that *or* on condition that you're home by midnight
   (b) **conditions** *(circonstances)* conditions; *(d'une vente, d'un accord)* terms; **dans ces conditions, je n'y vais pas** if that's the way it is, I'm not going; **conditions atmosphériques** atmospheric conditions; **conditions de paiement** terms of

payment; **conditions de vie/travail** living/working conditions

(**c**) *(état)* condition; **être en bonne/mauvaise c. physique** to be in good/bad shape

(**d**) *(sort)* condition; **la c. humaine** the human condition; **la c. des ouvriers/des paysans** the workers'/farmers' lot

(**e**) *(classe sociale)* station, status; **une personne de c. modeste** a person from a humble background

conditionnel, -elle [kɔ̃disjɔnɛl] **1** *adj* conditional

2 *nm Gram* conditional

conditionnement [kɔ̃disjɔnmã] *nm* (**a**) *(fait d'emballer, emballage)* packaging (**b**) *Psy* conditioning

conditionner [kɔ̃disjɔne] *vt* (**a**) *(être la condition de)* to govern (**b**) *(emballer)* to package (**c**) *Psy (personne)* to condition

condoléances [kɔ̃dɔleãs] *nfpl* condolences; **présenter ses c. à qn** to offer one's condolences to sb; **toutes mes c.** (please accept) my condolences

condominium [kɔ̃dɔminjɔm] *nm Pol* condominium

condor [kɔ̃dɔr] *nm* condor

conducteur, -trice [kɔ̃dyktœr, -tris] **1** *nm,f (d'une voiture, d'un train)* driver; *(de machine)* operator; **c. de travaux** foreman

2 *nm Élec & Phys* conductor

3 *adj Élec & Phys* conductive

conduction [kɔ̃dyksjɔ̃] *nf Élec* conduction

conductivité [kɔ̃dyktivite] *nf Élec* conductivity

conduire [18] [kɔ̃dɥir] **1** *vt* (**a**) *(emmener)* to take; *(en voiture)* to drive, to take (**b**) *(mener) (troupeau, aveugle)* to lead (**c**) *(entraîner)* **c. qn à faire qch** to lead sb to do sth; **c. qn au désespoir/suicide** to drive sb to despair/suicide (**d**) *(voiture, camion)* to drive; *(moto)* to ride; *(bateau)* to steer (**e**) *(acheminer) (eau, gaz)* to carry (**f**) *(diriger) (opérations)* to manage, to run

2 *vi* (**a**) *(en voiture)* to drive; *(en moto)* to ride; **elle conduit bien** she's a good driver (**b**) *(sujet: porte, couloir, études)* **c. à** to lead to

3 se conduire *vpr (se comporter)* to behave; **se c. mal** *(d'un enfant)* to misbehave; **se c. bien/mal avec qn** to behave well/badly toward sb

conduit [kɔ̃dɥi] *nm* (**a**) *(tuyau)* conduit, pipe; **c. d'aération** air duct; **c. de ventilation** ventilation shaft (**b**) *Anat* **c. auditif** auditory canal

conduite [kɔ̃dɥit] *nf* (**a**) *(de voiture, de camion)* driving; *(de moto)* riding; **leçons de c.** driving lessons; **c. à gauche/droite** *(position du volant)* left-/right-hand drive; *(sur la route)* driving on the left/right; **c. accompagnée** = learning to drive accompanied by someone holding a full driver's license; **c. en état d'ivresse** drunk-driving; **c. intérieure** sedan; **c. sur route** driving on the open road (**b**) *(des affaires, des opérations)* management, running; *(d'une armée)* command; *(de travaux)* supervision (**c**) *(comportement)* behavior, conduct; *Hum* **s'acheter une c.** to turn over a new leaf (**d**) *(tuyau)* pipe; **c. d'eau/de gaz** water/gas main

cône [kon] *nm* cone

confection [kɔ̃fɛksjɔ̃] *nf* (**a**) *(d'un vêtement, d'un repas)* making (**b**) *(industrie)* (ready-made) clothing industry; **vêtements de c.** ready-made clothes

confectionner [kɔ̃fɛksjɔne] *vt* to make

confédération [kɔ̃federasjɔ̃] *nf* confederation; **la C. helvétique** the Swiss Confederation

conférence [kɔ̃ferãs] *nf* (**a**) *(congrès, colloque)* conference; **c. de presse** press conference; **c. au sommet** summit (conference) (**b**) *(exposé)* lecture; **faire une c. sur...** to give a lecture on...

conférencier, -ère [kɔ̃ferãsje, -ɛr] *nm,f* lecturer

conférer [34] [kɔ̃fere] **1** *vt (titre)* to confer (**à** on); **l'âge confère certains privilèges** age brings with it certain privileges

2 *vi* to confer (**avec** with)

confesser [kɔ̃fese] **1** *vt* (**a**) *Rel* to confess (**b**) *(reconnaître)* to confess, to admit

2 se confesser *vpr* to confess; **(aller) se c.** to go to confession

confession [kɔ̃fesjɔ̃] *nf* (**a**) *Rel & Fig* confession; *Fam* **on lui donnerait le bon Dieu sans c.** he/she looks as though butter wouldn't melt in his/her mouth (**b**) *(croyance)* denomination

confessionnal, -aux [kɔ̃fesjɔnal, -o] *nm* confessional

confetti [kɔ̃feti] *nm* (piece of) confetti; **confettis** confetti

confiance [kɔ̃fjãs] *nf* (**a**) *(foi)* trust, confidence; **avoir c. en qn/qch, faire c. à qn/qch** to trust sb/sth, to have confidence in sb/sth; **faites-moi c.** trust me; *Fam (croyez-moi)* believe me; **se sentir en c. (avec qn)** to feel safe (with sb); **digne de c.** trustworthy; **de c.** *(mission)* of trust; *(personne)* trustworthy (**b**) *(assurance)* confidence; **c. en soi** self-confidence; **avoir c. en soi** to be self-confident

confiant, -e [kɔ̃fjã, -ãt] *adj* (**a**) *(qui fait confiance)* trusting (**b**) *(optimiste)* confident (**dans** in) (**c**) *(qui a confiance en soi)* self-confident

confidence [kɔ̃fidãs] *nf* confidence; **faire une c./des confidences à qn** to confide in sb; **mettre qn dans la c.** to let sb into the secret

confident, -e [kɔ̃fidã, -ãt] *nm,f* confidant, *f* confidante

confidentiel, -elle [kɔ̃fidãsjɛl] *adj* confidential

confidentiellement [kɔ̃fidãsjɛlmã] *adv* confidentially

confier [66] [kɔ̃fje] **1** *vt* (**a**) *(laisser)* **c. qch à qn** to entrust sb with sth; **je leur ai confié les enfants** I left the children with them (**b**) *(dire)* **c. qch à qn** to confide sth to sb; **c. un secret à qn** to share a secret with sb

2 se confier *vpr* **se c. à qn** to confide in sb

configuration [kɔ̃figyrasjɔ̃] *nf* (**a**) *(disposition)* configuration; *(de bâtiment)* layout; **la c. du terrain** the lie of the land (**b**) *Ordinat* configuration; **c. matérielle** hardware configuration

configurer [kɔ̃figyre] *vt Ordinat* to configure

confiné, -e [kɔ̃fine] *adj* (**a**) *(atmosphère)* enclosed; *(air)* stale (**b**) *(enfermé)* shut up

confiner [kɔ̃fine] **1** *vt (enfermer)* to confine, to shut up

2 confiner à *vt ind* to border on

3 se confiner *vpr* **se c. chez soi** to shut oneself up indoors

confins [kɔ̃fɛ̃] *nmpl (de région, d'État)* confines, borders; **aux c. de** on the edge of

confire [19a] [kɔ̃fir] *vt (dans du sucre)* to preserve, to candy; *(dans du vinaigre)* to pickle

confirmation [kɔ̃firmasjɔ̃] *nf* confirmation

confirmer [kɔ̃firme] **1** *vt (nouvelle, jugement)* to confirm; **c. qn dans son opinion** to confirm sb in his/her opinion

2 se confirmer *vpr (nouvelle, bruit)* to be confirmed; *(tendance)* to continue

confiserie [kɔ̃fizri] *nf* (**a**) *(magasin)* candy store (**b**) *(confiseries) (bonbons)* candy (**c**) *(secteur)* confectionery

confiseur, -euse [kɔ̃fizœr, -øz] *nm,f* confectioner

confisquer [kɔ̃fiske] *vt* to confiscate; **c. qch à qn** to confiscate sth from sb

confit, -e [kɔ̃fi, -it] **1** *adj (fruits)* crystallized, candied

2 *nm* **c. d'oie/de canard** goose/duck confit

confiture [kɔ̃fityr] *nf* jam, jelly; **c. de fraises** strawberry jam; **c. d'oranges** (orange) marmalade; *Fig* **ce serait donner de la c. aux cochons** that would be throwing pearls before swine

conflictuel, -elle [kɔ̃fliktɥɛl] *adj (témoignages, intérêts)* conflicting; **situation conflictuelle** situation of potential conflict; **ils ont des rapports conflictuels** they have a tempestuous relationship

conflit [kɔ̃fli] *nm* conflict; **c. armé** armed conflict; **conflits sociaux** job action

confluent [kɔ̃flyɑ̃] *nm* confluence; **au c. du Cher et de la Loire** where the Cher and the Loire meet

confondre [kɔ̃fɔ̃dr] **1** *vt* (**a**) *(personnes, noms, dates)* to confuse, to mix up; **je l'ai confondu avec son frère** I mistook him for his brother; **toutes catégories confondues** all categories taken together (**b**) *(sidérer)* to astound (**c**) *(démasquer)* to confound

2 se confondre *vpr* (**a**) *(couleurs, formes)* to merge, to blend (**en** into) (**b**) *(être similaire)* *(intérêts)* to merge (**c**) *(se répandre)* **se c. en excuses** to apologize profusely; **se c. en remerciements** to be profuse in one's thanks

conforme [kɔ̃fɔrm] *adj* (**a**) *(identique)* **copie c. à l'original** exact copy; **pour copie c.** *(sur document)* certified true copy; *Fig* **c'est la copie c. de sa mère** she's the image of her mother (**b**) *(qui correspond)* **être c. à** to be in accordance with

conformément [kɔ̃fɔrmemɑ̃] **conformément à** *prép* in accordance with

conformer [kɔ̃fɔrme] **1** *vt* to model (**à** on)
2 se conformer *vpr* **se c. à qch** to conform to sth

conformisme [kɔ̃fɔrmism] *nm* conformism

conformiste [kɔ̃fɔrmist] *adj & nmf* conformist

conformité [kɔ̃fɔrmite] *nf* *(d'un produit aux normes)* compliance (**à** with); **en c. avec** in accordance with

confort [kɔ̃fɔr] *nm* comfort; **maison/hôtel tout c.** house/hotel with every modern convenience; **améliorer le c. d'écoute** to improve the sound quality; **c. d'emploi** *(d'un ordinateur)* user-friendliness

confortable [kɔ̃fɔrtabl] *adj* comfortable

confortablement [kɔ̃fɔrtabləmɑ̃] *adv* comfortably; **installe-toi c.** make yourself comfortable

conforter [kɔ̃fɔrte] *vt* *(position, avance)* to consolidate; **c. qn dans son opinion** to confirm sb's opinion

confrère [kɔ̃frɛr] *nm* *(de profession)* colleague; *(de société)* fellow member

confrérie [kɔ̃freri] *nf Rel* brotherhood

confrontation [kɔ̃frɔ̃tasjɔ̃] *nf* (**a**) *(face-à-face)* confrontation; *Fig (d'opinions, d'idéaux)* clash, conflict (**b**) *(comparaison)* comparison

confronter [kɔ̃frɔ̃te] *vt* (**a**) *(personnes)* to confront; **être confronté à** to be confronted with (**b**) *(comparer)* to compare

confucianisme [kɔ̃fysjanism] *nm* Confucianism

confus, -e [kɔ̃fy, -yz] *adj* (**a**) *(indistinct) (masse, explication, idées)* confused; *(bruit)* indistinct; *(style, texte)* obscure (**b**) *(embarrassé)* embarrassed

confusément [kɔ̃fyzemɑ̃] *adv* vaguely

confusion [kɔ̃fyzjɔ̃] *nf* (**a**) *(désordre)* confusion; **jeter la c. dans les esprits** to confuse people (**b**) *(méprise)* mix-up, confusion (**c**) *(gêne)* embarrassment

congé [kɔ̃ʒe] *nm* (**a**) *(vacances)* vacation; **en c.** on vacation; **un jour/une semaine de c.** a day/a week off; **congés payés** paid vacation (**b**) *(arrêt de travail)* leave; **c. de maladie** sick leave; **c. de maternité** maternity leave; **c. de paternité** paternity leave; **être en c. de maladie/maternité** to be on sick/maternity leave; **c. sans solde** unpaid leave (**c**) *(avis de renvoi)* notice; **donner son c. à qn** to give sb his/her notice; **demander son c.** to hand in one's notice (**d**) **prendre c. de qn** to take one's leave of sb

congédier [66] [kɔ̃ʒedje] *vt* to dismiss

congélateur [kɔ̃ʒelatœr] *nm* freezer

congélation [kɔ̃ʒelasjɔ̃] *nf* freezing

congeler [39] [kɔ̃ʒle] **1** *vt* *(aliments)* to freeze
2 se congeler *vpr* to freeze

congénital, -e, -aux, -ales [kɔ̃ʒenital, -o] *adj* congenital

congère [kɔ̃ʒɛr] *nf* snowdrift

congestion [kɔ̃ʒɛstjɔ̃] *nf* congestion; **c. cérébrale** stroke; **c. pulmonaire** congestion of the lungs

congestionné, -e [kɔ̃ʒɛstjɔne] *adj (visage)* flushed; *(routes)* congested

conglomérat [kɔ̃glɔmera] *nm* conglomerate

Congo [kɔ̃go] *nm* **le C.** the Congo

congolais, -e [kɔ̃gɔlɛ, -ɛz] **1** *adj* Congolese
2 *nm (pâtisserie)* coconut cake
3 *nm,f* **C., Congolaise** Congolese

congratuler [kɔ̃gratyle] **1** *vt* to congratulate
2 se congratuler *vpr* to congratulate each other

congre [kɔ̃gr] *nm* conger (eel)

congrégation [kɔ̃gregasjɔ̃] *nf Rel* congregation

congrès [kɔ̃grɛ] *nm* conference; **le C.** *(aux États-Unis)* Congress

congru, -e [kɔ̃gry] *adj voir* **portion**

conifère [kɔnifɛr] *nm* conifer

conique [kɔnik] *adj* conical

conjecture [kɔ̃ʒɛktyr] *nf* conjecture

conjecturer [kɔ̃ʒɛktyre] *vi* to conjecture

conjoint, -e [kɔ̃ʒwɛ̃, -ɛ̃t] **1** *adj* joint
2 *nm* spouse; **les conjoints** the husband and wife

conjointement [kɔ̃ʒwɛ̃tmɑ̃] *adv* jointly

conjonctif, -ive [kɔ̃ʒɔ̃ktif, -iv] *adj* (**a**) *Gram* conjunctive (**b**) *Anat* connective

conjonction [kɔ̃ʒɔ̃ksjɔ̃] *nf* (**a**) *(union)* union; **la c. de nos efforts** our combined efforts (**b**) *Gram* conjunction; **c. de coordination/subordination** coordinating/subordinating conjunction

conjonctivite [kɔ̃ʒɔ̃ktivit] *nf* conjunctivitis

conjoncture [kɔ̃ʒɔ̃ktyr] *nf* *(situation)* circumstances, situation; **dans la c. actuelle** in the present circumstances

conjugaison [kɔ̃ʒygɛzɔ̃] *nf* (**a**) *(d'un verbe)* conjugation (**b**) *(union)* combination

conjugal, -e, -aux, -ales [kɔ̃ʒygal, -o] *adj (devoir)* conjugal; **bonheur c.** wedded bliss; **le domicile c.** the matrimonial home; **le lit c.** the marital bed; **la vie conjugale** married life

conjuguer [kɔ̃ʒyge] *vt* (**a**) *(verbe)* to conjugate (**b**) *(unir)* to combine

conjurer [kɔ̃ʒyre] **1** *vt* (**a**) *(implorer)* **c. qn de faire qch** to beg or to implore sb to do sth; **je t'en conjure** I beg you (**b**) *(écarter) (danger, mauvais sort)* to avert, to ward off
2 se conjurer *vpr* to conspire (**contre** against)

connaissance [kɔnɛsɑ̃s] *nf* (**a**) *(fait de connaître)* knowledge; **avoir c. de qch** to be aware of sth; **prendre c. de qch** to acquaint oneself with sth; **à ma c.** to my knowledge; **en (toute) c. de cause** with full knowledge of the facts (**b**) *(contact)* **faire la c. de qn** to make sb's acquaintance; **faire c. avec qn** to get to know sb; **quelqu'un de ma c.** someone I know, an acquaintance of mine (**c**) *(personne)* acquaintance (**d**) *(savoir)* knowledge; **elle a de bonnes connaissances en astronomie** she has a good knowledge of astronomy (**e**) *(conscience)* consciousness; **sans c.** unconscious

connaisseur, -euse [kɔnɛsœr, -øz] **1** *nm,f* connoisseur, expert
2 *adj* expert

connaître [20] [kɔnɛtr] **1** *vt* (**a**) *(personne, détails, endroit)* to know; **c. qn de nom/de vue** to know sb by name/by sight; **il n'y connaît rien** he doesn't know anything about it; **c'est ce livre qui l'a fait c.** this is the book that made her name; **tu connais la nouvelle?** have you heard the news?; **c'est mal le c.** you/they/etc. don't know him; *Fam* **je connais la musique** *ou* **la chanson** I've heard it all before; *Fam* **si tu fais ça, je ne te connais plus** if you do that, I'll have nothing more to do with you (**b**) *(rencontrer)* to meet (**c**) *(éprouver) (famine, guerre civile)* to experience; *(amour, peur, faim)* to know; **c. des moments difficiles** to go through some difficult times; **c. un destin tragique** to have a tragic fate; **c. un succès consi-**

dérable to enjoy considerable success (**d**) *(avoir)* **ne pas c. de limites** to know no bounds

 2 se connaître *vpr* (**a**) **se c. (soi-même)** to know oneself (**b**) **s'y c. en qch** to know a lot about sth (**c**) *(mutuellement)* to know each other (**d**) *(se rencontrer)* to meet

connard [kɔnar] = **conard**

conne [kɔn] *voir* **con**

connecter [kɔnɛkte] *vt Élec* to connect; *Ordinat* **connecté** *(sur Internet)* on line; **connecté en anneau/bus/étoile** in a ring/bus/star configuration

connerie [kɔnri] *nf très Fam* (**a**) *(acte stupide)* **faire une c./des conneries** to do a goddamn stupid thing/some goddamn stupid things (**b**) *(remarque stupide)* goddamn stupid thing; **dire** *ou* **raconter des conneries** to talk bullshit (**c**) *(caractère stupide)* stupidity

connexion [kɔnɛksjɔ̃] *nf* connection

connivence [kɔnivɑ̃s] *nf* connivance; **agir/être de c. avec qn** to act/to be in connivance with sb; **des regards de c.** conniving looks

connotation [kɔnɔtasjɔ̃] *nf* connotation

connu, -e [kɔny] **1** *adj (écrivain, chanteur)* well-known; **c'est bien c.!** everyone knows that!

 2 *pp voir* **connaître**

conquérant, -e [kɔ̃kerɑ̃, -ɑ̃t] **1** *adj (air)* triumphant

 2 *nm,f* conqueror

conquérir [7] [kɔ̃kerir] *vt (pays, territoire, sommet)* to conquer; *(marché)* to capture; **ils ont été conquis par son charme** they were won over by his/her charm

conquête [kɔ̃kɛt] *nf* conquest; **faire la c. de** *(pays)* to conquer; *(personne)* to make a conquest of; **se lancer à la c. de** *(pouvoir)* to make a bid for; *(sommet)* to set out to conquer

conquis, -e *voir* **conquérir**

conquistador [kɔ̃kistadɔr] *nm* conquistador

consacré, -e [kɔ̃sakre] *adj (coutume)* established; **selon l'expression consacrée** as the saying goes; **c. par l'usage** sanctioned by usage

consacrer [kɔ̃sakre] **1** *vt* (**a**) *Rel* to consecrate (**b**) *(temps, énergie)* **c. qch à** to devote sth to; **combien de temps pouvez-vous me c.?** how much time can you spare me? (**c**) *(entériner) (coutume)* to establish; *(usage)* to sanction

 2 se consacrer *vpr* **se c. à son travail/sa famille** to devote oneself to one's work/family

consanguin, -e [kɔ̃sɑ̃gɛ̃, -in] *adj* **frère c.** half-brother *(on the father's side)*; **sœur consanguine** half-sister *(on the father's side)*; **mariage c.** intermarriage

consciemment [kɔ̃sjamɑ̃] *adv* consciously

conscience [kɔ̃sjɑ̃s] *nf* (**a**) *(esprit)* consciousness; **perdre/ reprendre c.** to lose/to regain consciousness; **avoir/ prendre c. de qch** to be/to become aware *or* conscious of sth (**b**) *(morale)* conscience; **avoir bonne/mauvaise c.** to have a clear/bad conscience; **se donner bonne c.** to ease one's conscience; **avoir la c. tranquille, avoir sa c. pour soi** to have a clear conscience; **avoir qch sur la c.** to have sth on one's conscience (**c**) **c. professionnelle** professional integrity

consciencieusement [kɔ̃sjɑ̃sjøzmɑ̃] *adv* conscientiously

consciencieux, -euse [kɔ̃sjɑ̃sjø, -øz] *adj* conscientious

conscient, -e [kɔ̃sjɑ̃, -ɑ̃t] *adj* (**a**) *(décision, choix)* conscious; **être c. de qch** to be aware *or* conscious of sth (**b**) *(lucide)* conscious

consécration [kɔ̃sekrasjɔ̃] *nf* (**a**) *(d'une église, d'un évêque)* consecration; *(d'un prêtre)* ordination (**b**) *(aboutissement) (des efforts, d'une œuvre)* recognition; *(d'une carrière)* crowning moment

consécutif, -ive [kɔ̃sekytif, -iv] *adj* consecutive; **c. à** resulting from

consécutivement [kɔ̃sekytivmɑ̃] *adv* consecutively; **c. à** following

conseil [kɔ̃sɛj] *nm* (**a**) *(recommandation)* piece of advice; **des conseils** advice; **donner un c. à qn** to give sb a piece of advice; **être de bon c.** to give good advice

 (**b**) *(assemblée)* council, committee; *(d'une entreprise)* board; *(réunion)* meeting; **c. d'administration** board of directors; **c. de classe** = staff meeting with participation of class representatives to discuss school matters; **C. constitutionnel** = independent body which pronounces on the constitutionality of government decisions; **c. de discipline** disciplinary committee; **C. d'État** Council of State; **C. de l'Europe** Council of Europe; *Can* **C. Exécutif** ≃ Cabinet; **C. général** regional council; **c. de guerre** *(réunion)* council of war; *(tribunal)* court martial; **le c. des ministres** ≃ the Cabinet; *UE* the (European) Council of Ministers; **c. municipal** city council; *Can* **C. national des autochtones du Canada** Native Council of Canada; **C. de sécurité** *(de l'ONU)* Security Council

 (**c**) *(personne)* consultant (**en** in); **c. en recrutement** recruitment consultant

---

Conseil de classe

The French school year is divided into three terms. In high schools, a "conseil de classe", or staff meeting, is held at the end of each term to discuss the progress made by pupils in a given class. A report containing the grades obtained during the term with teachers' comments is filled out for each pupil. The "conseil de classe" is initially held behind closed doors, attended by the teachers of a given class and the principal and then with two elected class representatives present. During the last "conseil de classe" of the year, decisions are taken as to which pupils should repeat a year and which should change courses.

---

conseiller¹ [kɔ̃seje] *vt* (**a**) *(guider) (personne)* to advise; **il m'a bien conseillé** he gave me good *or* sound advice (**b**) *(recommander)* **c. qch à qn** to recommend sth to sb; **c. à qn de faire qch** to advise sb to do sth; **il est conseillé de ne pas fumer** it is advisable not to smoke

conseiller², -ère [kɔ̃seje, -ɛr] *nm,f* (**a**) *(spécialiste)* adviser, consultant; **c. en gestion** management consultant; **c. d'orientation** career counselor; **c. technique** technical adviser (**b**) *Pol (d'un chef d'État)* advisor; **c. général** regional councillor; **c. municipal** city councilor

consensuel, -elle [kɔ̃sɑ̃sɥɛl] *adj* consensual

consensus [kɔ̃sɛ̃sys] *nm* consensus (of opinion)

consentant, -e [kɔ̃sɑ̃tɑ̃, -ɑ̃t] *adj* consenting; **être c.** to consent

consentement [kɔ̃sɑ̃tmɑ̃] *nm* consent; **donner son c. à qch** to give one's consent to sth; **divorce par c. mutuel** divorce by mutual consent

consentir [64a] [kɔ̃sɑ̃tir] **1** *vi* to consent, to agree (**à qch/à faire qch** to sth/to do sth); **je consens (à ce) qu'il vienne** I consent to his coming

 2 *vt* **c. un prêt à qn** to grant sb a loan; **c. une remise à qn** to allow sb a discount

conséquence [kɔ̃sekɑ̃s] *nf* consequence; **une erreur sans c.** an inconsequential mistake; **tirer les conséquences de qch** to draw conclusions from sth; **la baisse des taxes a eu pour c. de créer des emplois** the tax reduction resulted in the creation of jobs; **agir en c.** to take appropriate action; **en c. (de quoi)** consequently

conséquent, -e [kɔ̃sekɑ̃, -ɑ̃t] *adj* (**a**) *(cohérent)* consistent (**b**) *Fam (somme)* tidy (**c**) **par c.** consequently

conservateur, -trice [kɔ̃sɛrvatœr, -tris] **1** *adj Pol* Conservative

 2 *nm,f* (**a**) *(de musée)* curator; *(de bibliothèque)* librarian (**b**) *Pol* Conservative

 3 *nm (alimentaire)* preservative; **sans c.** *(sur emballage)* free of preservatives

conservation [kɔ̃sɛrvasjɔ̃] *nf (de fruits, de viande)* preserving; *(de bâtiments)* preservation; *(d'archives)* keeping

conservatoire [kɔ̃sɛrvatwar] *nm (de musique, d'art dramatique)* school, academy; **le C. (de Paris)** the (Paris) Conservatoire; **le C. des arts et métiers** = museum and college of applied sciences

conserve [kɔ̃sɛrv] *nf (aliment)* canned food; *(en bocal)* preserve; *(boîte)* can; **en c.** canned; *(en bocal)* preserved; **mettre qch en c.** to can sth; *(en bocal)* to preserve sth

conserver [kɔ̃sɛrve] **1** *vt* (**a**) *(aliment)* to keep; *(dans le sel, le vinaigre)* to preserve; **c. à l'abri de la lumière** *(sur emballage)* keep away from direct sunlight; **c. au froid** *(sur emballage)* keep in a cold place; **être bien conservé** *(personne)* to be well preserved (**b**) *(garder) (objet, emploi, sang-froid)* to keep; *(droits)* to retain; **c. un bon souvenir de qch** to have good memories of sth

   2 se conserver *vpr (aliment)* to keep

considérable [kɔ̃siderabl] *adj* considerable

considérablement [kɔ̃siderabləmɑ̃] *adv* considerably

considération [kɔ̃siderasjɔ̃] *nf* (**a**) *(examen)* **prendre qch en c.** to take sth into consideration; *(offre, demande d'emploi)* to consider sth (**b**) *(estime)* regard, esteem; **agir avec/sans c.** to act considerately/inconsiderately; **jouir d'une grande c.** to be highly regarded (**c**) **considérations (sur)** *(observations)* observations (on); **je ne peux pas entrer dans ces considérations** I can't go into that

considérer [34] [kɔ̃sidere] **1** *vt* (**a**) *(étudier, regarder)* to consider; **tout bien considéré** all things considered (**b**) *(estimer)* **c. que** to consider that; **c. qn/qch comme...** to regard sb/sth as...

   2 se considérer *vpr* **se c. désavantagé** to consider oneself disadvantaged; **se c. comme un artiste/un révolutionnaire** to consider oneself an artist/a revolutionary

consigne [kɔ̃siɲ] *nf* (**a**) *(ordres)* orders; **avoir pour c. de...** to have orders to...; **passer la c.** to pass on the orders; **consignes en cas d'incendie** fire notice (**b**) *(punition)* Mil confinement to barracks; Scol detention (**c**) *(pour les bagages)* **c. (à bagages)** checkroom; **c. automatique** lockers (**d**) *(de bouteille)* deposit

consigner [kɔ̃siɲe] *vt* (**a**) *(bouteille, emballage)* to charge a deposit on; **bouteille consignée** returnable bottle (**b**) *(noter)* to record (**c**) *(punir) (soldat)* to confine to barracks; *(élève)* to keep in (**d**) *(laisser à la consigne)* to check

consistance [kɔ̃sistɑ̃s] *nf (d'un corps)* consistency; **sans c.** *(pâte, fromage)* too soft; Fig *(personne)* bland; *(personnage de fiction)* insubstantial

consistant, -e [kɔ̃sistɑ̃, -ɑ̃t] *adj (substance)* firm; *(sauce, soupe)* thick; *(repas)* substantial; *(argument)* sound

consister [kɔ̃siste] *vi* **c. en qch** to consist of sth; **c. à faire qch** to consist in doing sth

consœur [kɔ̃sœr] *nf (female)* colleague

consolation [kɔ̃sɔlasjɔ̃] *nf* consolation, comfort

console [kɔ̃sɔl] *nf* console; **c. de jeux** games console; **c. de visualisation** (visual) display unit

consoler [kɔ̃sɔle] **1** *vt* to console, to comfort; **si ça peut te c.** if that's any consolation to you

   2 se consoler *vpr* to console oneself; *(l'un l'autre)* to console each other; **se c. d'une perte/d'un échec** to get over a loss/a failure; **elles se sont consolées mutuellement** they consoled each other

consolidation [kɔ̃sɔlidasjɔ̃] *nf* (**a**) *aussi Fig (renforcement)* strengthening (**b**) *Méd (d'une fracture)* knitting

consolider [kɔ̃sɔlide] **1** *vt* (**a**) *aussi Fig (renforcer)* to strengthen (**b**) *Méd (fracture)* to knit (**c**) *Fin (dette)* to fund; *(bilan)* to consolidate

   2 se consolider *vpr* (**a**) *(régime)* to strengthen its position; *(amitié, liens)* to become stronger (**b**) *(fracture)* to knit

consommateur, -trice [kɔ̃sɔmatœr, -tris] *nm,f* Écon consumer; *(dans un restaurant, un café)* customer; **je suis un grand c. de café** I'm a big coffee drinker; Écon **c. final** end-user

consommation [kɔ̃sɔmasjɔ̃] *nf* (**a**) *(d'électricité, de pétrole, de nourriture)* consumption; *(d'une voiture)* (fuel) consumption; **faire une grande c. de qch** to consume great quantities of sth (**b**) *(dans un café)* drink (**c**) *(du mariage)* consummation

consommé, -e [kɔ̃sɔme] **1** *nm* Culin consommé

   2 *adj (accompli)* consummate

consommer [kɔ̃sɔme] **1** *vt* (**a**) *(électricité, pétrole, nourriture)* to consume; **à c. avant fin novembre** *(sur emballage)* best before end November; **cette voiture consomme trop (d'essence)** this car uses too much gas; **c. au bar** to drink at the bar (**b**) *(mariage)* to consummate

   2 se consommer *vpr* **ce plat se consomme froid** this dish is eaten cold

consonance [kɔ̃sɔnɑ̃s] *nf* Mus & Ling consonance; **langue à c. germanique** German-sounding language

consonne [kɔ̃sɔn] *nf* consonant

consortium [kɔ̃sɔrsjɔm] *nm* Com & Fin consortium

conspirateur, -trice [kɔ̃spiratœr, -tris] **1** *nm,f* conspirator

   2 *adj* conspiratorial

conspiration [kɔ̃spirasjɔ̃] *nf* conspiracy, plot

conspirer [kɔ̃spire] *vi* (**a**) *(comploter)* to conspire, to plot (**contre** against) (**b**) *(contribuer)* to conspire (**à faire qch** to do sth)

constamment [kɔ̃stamɑ̃] *adv* constantly

constance [kɔ̃stɑ̃s] *nf* (**a**) *(dans une tâche)* perseverance; *(en amour)* constancy; **travailler avec c.** to work steadily (**b**) *(de la température, d'un phénomène)* constancy

constant, -e [kɔ̃stɑ̃, -ɑ̃t] **1** *adj* (**a**) *(souci, température, va-et-vient)* constant; *(effort)* persistent; *(amitié, intérêt)* steady (**b**) *(personne)* **être c. dans ses opinions** to stick to one's opinions; **être c. dans ses amitiés** to be faithful to one's friends

   2 *nf* **constante** (**a**) *(en sciences)* constant (**b**) *(caractéristique)* stable *or* permanent trait

constat [kɔ̃sta] *nm* (**a**) *Jur* official report; **dresser un c. d'accident** to write out an accident report; **c. amiable** = report of road accident agreed upon by parties involved (**b**) *(bilan)* assessment; **faire un c. d'échec** to acknowledge failure

constatation [kɔ̃statasjɔ̃] *nf* (**a**) *(observation)* observation; **c'est une simple c.** it's a simple statement of fact (**b**) **constatations** *(d'une enquête)* findings

constater [kɔ̃state] *vt* (**a**) *(observer)* to note (**que** that); **vous pouvez c. vous-même qu'elle est partie** you can see for yourself that she's gone (**b**) *Jur (enregistrer)* to record; *(décès)* to certify; *(dégâts)* to assess

constellation [kɔ̃stelasjɔ̃] *nf* constellation

constellé, -e [kɔ̃stele] *adj* **un ciel c. d'étoiles** a star-studded sky; **c. de taches** spattered with stains

consternant, -e [kɔ̃stɛrnɑ̃, -ɑ̃t] *adj (nouvelle)* dismaying; **d'une bêtise consternante** appallingly stupid

consternation [kɔ̃stɛrnasjɔ̃] *nf* dismay, consternation; **jeter la c. dans/parmi** to fill with dismay; **à la c. générale** to everyone's dismay

consterner [kɔ̃stɛrne] *vt* to dismay

constipation [kɔ̃stipasjɔ̃] *nf* constipation

constipé, -e [kɔ̃stipe] *adj* constipated; Fam *(mal à l'aise)* ill at ease

constituer [kɔ̃stitɥe] **1** *vt* (**a**) *(composer)* to make up; **être constitué de** to be made up of (**b**) *(équivaloir à)* to constitute (**c**) *(comité, gouvernement, équipe)* to form; *(bibliothèque, fortune, stocks)* to build up; **c. une rente/une dot à qn** to settle an annuity/a dowry on sb

   2 se constituer *vpr* (**a**) *(devenir)* **se c. prisonnier** to give oneself up; *Jur* **se c. partie civile** to sue for damages (**b**) *(se*

réunir) **se c. en commission/en association** to form a committee/an association

constitution [kɔ̃stitysjɔ̃] *nf* (**a**) *(physique, d'un pays)* constitution; **avoir une bonne c.** to have a sound constitution (**b**) *(de comité, de société, de gouvernement)* formation; *(de stocks, de bibliothèque)* building up

constitutionnel, -elle [kɔ̃stitysjɔnɛl] *adj* constitutional

constructeur [kɔ̃stryktœr] *nm (bâtisseur)* builder; **c. automobile** car manufacturer; **c. naval** shipbuilder

constructif, -ive [kɔ̃stryktif, -iv] *adj* constructive

construction [kɔ̃stryksjɔ̃] *nf* (**a**) *(d'une maison, d'une route, d'un voilier)* building, construction; *(d'une phrase)* structure; **en c.** under construction; **c. navale** shipbuilding (**b**) *(bâtiment)* building

construire [18] [kɔ̃strɥir] **1** *vt* to build, to construct; *(roman, phrase, théorie)* to construct

2 se construire *vpr Gram* **"après que" se construit avec l'indicatif** "après que" takes the indicative

consul [kɔ̃syl] *nm* consul; **le c. de France** the French consul; **c. général** consul general

consulaire [kɔ̃sylɛr] *adj* consular

consulat [kɔ̃syla] *nm (lieu)* consulate; *(charge)* consulship

consultant, -e [kɔ̃syltɑ̃, -ɑ̃t] **1** *nm,f* consultant

2 *adj* consulting; **médecin c.** consultant

consultation [kɔ̃syltasjɔ̃] *nf* (**a**) *(d'un expert, d'un médecin)* consultation; **le médecin est en c.** the doctor is with a patient; **heures de c.** consulting hours (**b**) *(de livre)* consultation (**c**) *Pol* **c. populaire** consultation of the people

consulter [kɔ̃sylte] **1** *vt* to consult

2 *vi (docteur)* to see patients

3 se consulter *vpr* to consult each other

consumer [kɔ̃syme] **1** *vt (brûler)* to consume; *Fig* **consumé par le remords** consumed with remorse

2 se consumer *vpr (brûler)* to burn; *Fig* **se c. d'inquiétude/de chagrin** to be consumed with worry/with grief

contact [kɔ̃takt] *nm* (**a**) *(relation, personne)* contact; **garder/perdre le c. avec qn** to keep in touch/lose touch with sb; **prendre c. ou se mettre en c. avec qn** to get in touch or in contact with sb; **être/entrer en c. avec qn** to be in/come into contact with sb; **être d'un c. facile/difficile** to be approachable/unapproachable; **il a changé à mon c.** he's changed since he met me (**b**) *(toucher)* contact; **au c. agréable** pleasant to the touch; **être/entrer en c. avec qch** to be in/come into contact with sth; **au c. de qch** on contact with sth (**c**) *Élec* contact (**d**) *Aut* contact; **mettre/couper le c.** to switch the ignition on/off

contacter [kɔ̃takte] *vt* to contact

contagieux, -euse [kɔ̃taʒjø, -øz] *adj (maladie, virus, personne)* contagious; *(rire, enthousiasme)* infectious

contagion [kɔ̃taʒjɔ̃] *nf Méd* contagion

container [kɔ̃tɛnɛr] *nm* container

contamination [kɔ̃taminasjɔ̃] *nf (pollution)* contamination; *Méd* infection

contaminer [kɔ̃tamine] *vt (polluer)* to contaminate; *Méd* to infect

conte [kɔ̃t] *nm* story, tale; **c. de fées** fairy tale; *Fig* **elle vit un c. de fées** her life is a fairy tale

contemplatif, -ive [kɔ̃tɑ̃platif, -iv] *adj & nm,f* contemplative

contemplation [kɔ̃tɑ̃plasjɔ̃] *nf* contemplation; **être en c. devant qch** to gaze at sth

contempler [kɔ̃tɑ̃ple] **1** *vt* to contemplate, to gaze at

2 se contempler *vpr (soi-même)* to gaze at oneself

contemporain, -e [kɔ̃tɑ̃pɔrɛ̃, -ɛn] **1** *adj* (**a**) *(moderne)* contemporary (**b**) *(du même âge)* contemporary (**de** with); **être c. de qn** to be a contemporary of sb; **ils sont contemporains** they are contemporaries

2 *nm,f* contemporary

contenance [kɔ̃tnɑ̃s] *nf* (**a**) *(d'un récipient)* capacity (**b**) *(allure)* attitude, bearing; **faire qch pour se donner une c.** to do sth to give an impression of composure; **faire bonne c.** to put on a bold front; **perdre c.** to lose one's composure

contenant [kɔ̃tnɑ̃] *nm* container

conteneur [kɔ̃tnœr] *nm* container

contenir [70] [kɔ̃tnir] **1** *vt* (**a**) *(renfermer)* to contain; **le théâtre contient mille places** the theater holds or seats a thousand (**b**) *(foule, ennemi)* to contain, to keep in check; *(colère)* to curb; *(larmes)* to hold back

2 se contenir *vpr* to contain oneself

content, -e [kɔ̃tɑ̃, -ɑ̃t] **1** *adj (satisfait)* happy, content (**de** with); *(joyeux)* glad (**de faire** to do); **je suis très c. de vous voir** I'm very pleased or glad to see you; **être c. de soi** to be pleased with oneself; **tu peux être c. de toi, tu as vu ce que tu as fait!** I hope you're happy, just look what you've done!; **non c. de mentir, il vole!** not content with lying, he steals as well!; **je suis vraiment c. que vous soyez venu** I'm so glad you came; *Fam* **et si tu n'es pas c., c'est pareil** you can like it or lump it

2 *nm* **manger tout son c.** to eat one's fill; **avoir son c. de qch** to have had one's fill of sth

contentement [kɔ̃tɑ̃tmɑ̃] *nm (état)* satisfaction, contentment; **un sourire de c.** a contented smile

contenter [kɔ̃tɑ̃te] **1** *vt (personne)* to satisfy, to please

2 se contenter *vpr* **se c. de qch/de faire qch** to content oneself with sth/with doing sth; **se c. de peu** to be easily satisfied; **je me contenterai de faire remarquer que...** I will merely point out that...

contentieux, -ieuse [kɔ̃tɑ̃sjø] *nm (querelle)* dispute; *Jur* litigation; *(service)* legal department; **avoir un c. avec qn** to be in dispute with sb

contention [kɔ̃tɑ̃sjɔ̃] *nf Méd (d'un os)* setting; *(d'un malade)* restraint; **bas ou chaussettes de c.** support socks, flight socks

contenu, -e [kɔ̃tny] **1** *nm (d'un paquet, d'une bouteille, d'une boîte)* contents; *(d'une lettre, d'un livre)* content

2 *adj (émotion)* restrained

conter [kɔ̃te] *vt* to tell; **elle ne s'en laisse pas c.** you can't fool her

contestataire [kɔ̃testatɛr] **1** *adj Pol* anti-establishment; *(mécontent)* rebellious

2 *nmf Pol* protester; *(mécontent)* rebel

contestation [kɔ̃testasjɔ̃] *nf* (**a**) *(protestation)* protest; **il y a matière ou sujet à c.** there are grounds for dispute; **sans c. possible** beyond dispute (**b**) *Pol* protest

conteste [kɔ̃tɛst] **sans conteste** *adv* indisputably

contester [kɔ̃tɛste] *vt* to dispute; **je lui conteste le droit de...** I dispute his/her right to...; **elle est très contestée** she is very controversial; **faire qch sans c.** to do sth without protest

conteur, -euse [kɔ̃tœr, -øz] *nm,f* storyteller

contexte [kɔ̃tɛkst] *nm* context; **dans le c. de** in the context of; **hors c.** out of context

contextualiser [3] [kɔ̃tɛkstɥalize] *vt* to contextualize

contigu, -ë [kɔ̃tigy] *adj (maisons, pièces)* adjoining; **c. à qch** adjoining sth

continent [kɔ̃tinɑ̃] *nm* (**a**) *(étendue)* continent; **l'Ancien/le Nouveau C.** the Old/the New World (**b**) *(par rapport à une île)* mainland

continental, -e, -aux, -ales [kɔ̃tinɑ̃tal, -o] **1** *adj (climat, plateau)* continental; *(par rapport à une île)* mainland

2 *nm,f* mainlander

contingent [kɔ̃tɛ̃ʒɑ̃] *nm* (**a**) *Mil* contingent; **les soldats du c.** the conscripted soldiers (**b**) *(quota)* quota

continu, -e [kɔ̃tiny] *adj (ligne, effort)* continuous; *(soin, attention)* constant; **en c.** continuously; *Ordinat* **papier en c.** continuous paper

continuation [kɔ̃tinɥasjɔ̃] *nf* continuation; **bonne c.!** all the best!

continuel, -elle [kɔ̃tinɥɛl] *adj (ininterrompu)* continuous; *(qui se répète)* continual

continuellement [kɔ̃tinɥɛlmɑ̃] *adv (de façon ininterrompue)* continuously; *(de façon répétitive)* continually

continuer [kɔ̃tinɥe] **1** *vt (études, efforts, politique)* to continue (with), to carry on with; *(trait, route)* to continue; **c. sa route** *ou* **son chemin** to continue on one's way; **continuez!** carry on!; **si tu continues comme ça,...** if you carry on like that,...

2 *vi* to continue

3 continuer à *ou* **de** *vt ind* **c. à** *ou* **de faire qch** to continue doing sth, to carry on doing sth; **si tu continues à m'embêter, je vais me fâcher** if you carry or keep on annoying me I'm going to get mad; **je continue à** *ou* **de me demander si...** I keep wondering if...

4 se continuer *vpr* to continue

continuité [kɔ̃tinɥite] *nf (d'une action)* continuity; *(d'une tradition, d'une politique)* continuation

contondant, -e [kɔ̃tɔ̃dɑ̃, -ɑ̃t] *adj* blunt

contorsion [kɔ̃tɔrsjɔ̃] *nf* contortion

contorsionner [kɔ̃tɔrsjɔne] **se contorsionner** *vpr* to contort oneself

contorsionniste [kɔ̃tɔrsjɔnist] *nmf* contortionist

contour [kɔ̃tur] *nm* **(a)** *(silhouette)* outline **(b)** *Suisse (virage)* bend

contourner [kɔ̃turne] *vt* to go around; *Fig (loi, difficulté)* to get around

contraceptif, -ive [kɔ̃trasɛptif, -iv] *Méd* **1** *adj* contraceptive **2** *nm* contraceptive; **c. oral** oral contraceptive

contraception [kɔ̃trasɛpsjɔ̃] *nf* contraception; **c. d'urgence** emergency contraception

contractant, -e [kɔ̃traktɑ̃, -ɑ̃t] *adj Jur (partie)* contracting

contracté, -e [kɔ̃trakte] *adj* **(a)** *(muscles, visage, personne)* tense **(b)** *Ling* contracted

contracter¹ [kɔ̃trakte] *vt* **(a)** *(alliance, dette)* to contract; *(assurance)* to take out **(b)** *(habitude, goût, manie)* to acquire; *(maladie)* to contract

contracter² [kɔ̃trakte] **1** *vt (muscles, visage)* to tense; **visage contracté par la douleur** face drawn with pain

2 se contracter *vpr* **(a)** *(cœur, muscle)* to contract; *(personne)* to tense (up) **(b)** *Ling* to contract

contraction [kɔ̃traksjɔ̃] *nf* **(a)** *(d'un muscle, d'un gaz, d'un mot)* contraction; **contractions** *(à l'accouchement)* contractions **(b)** *Scol* **c. de texte** précis; **faire une c. de texte** to summarize a text

contractuel, -elle [kɔ̃traktɥɛl] **1** *adj (obligations)* contractual; **agent c.** = contractor working for the city council **2** *nm,f (auxiliaire de police)* ≃ traffic policeman, *f* traffic policewoman

contracture [kɔ̃traktyr] *nf Méd* spasm

contradiction [kɔ̃tradiksjɔ̃] *nf* **(a)** *(opposition)* contradiction; **avoir l'esprit de c.** to be contrary; **il ne supporte pas la c.** he can't stand being contradicted **(b)** *(illogisme)* contradiction; **être en c. avec qch** to contradict sth; **être en c. avec soi-même** to contradict oneself

contradictoire [kɔ̃tradiktwar] *adj* contradictory (**avec** to); **débat c.** debate

contraignant, -e [kɔ̃trɛɲɑ̃, -ɑ̃t] *adj* restricting

contraindre [23] [kɔ̃trɛ̃dr] **1** *vt (obliger)* **c. qn à faire qch** to force or to compel sb to do sth; **être contraint de faire qch** to be forced or compelled to do sth; **contraint et forcé** under duress

2 se contraindre *vpr* **se c. à faire qch** to force oneself to do sth

contrainte [kɔ̃trɛ̃t] *nf* **(a)** *(obligation, limitation, retenue)* con-

straint; **parler sans c.** to speak freely **(b)** *(force)* force; **obtenir qch par la c.** to get sth by force; **faire qch sous la c.** to do sth under duress **(c)** *Tech* stress

contraire [kɔ̃trɛr] **1** *adj* **(a)** *(opposé) (intérêts, avis)* conflicting; **vent c.** headwind; **c. à** contrary to; **en sens c.** in the opposite direction **(b)** *(défavorable)* **le sort nous/m'est c.** fate is against us/me

2 *nm* opposite; **le c. de** the opposite of; **sa sœur est tout le c. de lui** his sister is the exact opposite of him; **(bien) au c.** on the contrary

contrairement [kɔ̃trɛrmɑ̃] **contrairement à** *prép* contrary to; **c. à moi,...** unlike me,...

contralto [kɔ̃tralto] *nm Mus* contralto

contrariant, -e [kɔ̃trarjɑ̃, -ɑ̃t] *adj* **(a)** *(personne)* contrary; **elle n'est pas contrariante** she's easy-going; *Péj* she says yes to everything **(b)** *(situation)* annoying, irritating

contrarier [66] [kɔ̃trarje] *vt* **(a)** *(ennuyer)* to annoy, to irritate **(b)** *(contrecarrer) (projets, desseins)* to thwart, to frustrate

contrariété [kɔ̃trarjete] *nf* annoyance; **éprouver une vive c.** to feel extremely annoyed

contraste [kɔ̃trast] *nm* contrast; **faire c. (avec)** to contrast (with); **par c. avec** in contrast to; **effet de c.** contrasting effect

contrasté, -e [kɔ̃traste] *adj* **(a)** *(différencié)* contrasting; **photo bien/mal contrastée** photo with the right amount of/with not enough contrast **(b)** *Ordinat* highlighted

contraster [kɔ̃traste] *vi* to contrast (**avec** with)

contrat [kɔ̃tra] *nm* **(a)** *(accord)* contract, agreement; **passer un c. (avec qn)** to enter into an agreement (with sb); **c. d'assurance** insurance policy; **c. collectif** collective agreement; **c. à durée déterminée/indéterminée** fixed-term/permanent contract; **c. emploi-solidarité** = short-term contract subsidized by the government; **c. de mariage** marriage contract, prenuptial agreement; **c. de travail** labor contract **(b)** *(au bridge)* contract

contravention [kɔ̃travɑ̃sjɔ̃] *nf (envers un règlement)* contravention; *(amende)* fine; *(pour stationnement non autorisé) (amende)* parking fine; *(avis)* (parking) ticket; **être en c.** to be in breach of the law

contre [kɔ̃tr] **1** *prép* **(a)** *(se battre, jouer)* against; **se fâcher c. qn** to get mad at sb; **la campagne c. l'avortement** the anti-abortion campaign; **je suis c.!** I'm against it!; **je n'ai rien c., je ne suis pas c.** I've got nothing against it; **par c.** on the other hand

(b) *(pour se protéger de)* **sirop c. la toux** cough syrup; **être assuré c. le vol** to be insured against theft

(c) *(en échange de)* (in exchange) for; **échanger une chose c. une autre** to exchange one thing for another

(d) *(en proportion de)* to; **parier à cinq c. un** to bet five to one; **dix voix c. deux** ten votes to two

(e) *(en contact avec)* against; **s'appuyer c. qch** to lean against sth; **leur maison est tout c. la mienne** their house is right next to mine; **joue c. joue** cheek to cheek; **le radiateur est allumé, assieds-toi tout c.** the heater is on, sit right next to it

(f) *(en dépit de)* **c. toute logique** against all logic; **c. toute attente** against all expectations

(g) *(en comparaison de)* compared to; **le dollar était à 1,2 euros c. 1,5 euros le mois précédent** the dollar stood at 1.2 euros compared to 1.5 euros the previous month

2 *nm* **(a)** **peser le pour et le c.** to weigh (up) the pros and cons **(b)** *(au volley, au basket)* block

contre-allée *(pl* **contre-allées)** [kɔ̃trale] *nf* side-road

contre-attaque *(pl* **contre-attaques)** [kɔ̃tratak] *nf* counter-attack

contre-attaquer [kɔ̃tratake] *vi* to counter-attack

contrebalancer [16] [kɔ̃trəbalɑ̃se] **1** *vt (poids)* to counterbalance; *(inconvénient)* to offset

2 se contrebalancer *vpr Fam* se c. de qch not to give a damn about sth

contrebande [kɔ̃trəbɑ̃d] *nf* (a) *(activité)* smuggling; **faire de la c.** to smuggle goods; **faire entrer des marchandises en c.** to smuggle in goods; **de c.** smuggled (b) *(marchandises)* contraband

contrebandier, -ère [kɔ̃trəbɑ̃dje, -ɛr] *nm,f* smuggler

contrebas [kɔ̃trəbɑ] **en contrebas** *adv* (down) below; **en c.** de below

contrebasse [kɔ̃trəbɑs] *nf (instrument)* (double) bass; *(musicien)* (double) bass player

contrebassiste [kɔ̃trəbasist] *nmf* (double-)bass player

contre-braquer [kɔ̃trəbrake] *vi Aut* to steer into the skid

contrecarrer [kɔ̃trəkare] *vt* to thwart

contrechamp [kɔ̃trəʃɑ̃] *nm Cin* reverse shot

contre-chant *(pl* **contre-chants)** [kɔ̃trəʃɑ̃] *nm Mus* counterpoint

contrecœur [kɔ̃trəkœr] **à contrecœur** *adv* reluctantly, unwillingly

contrecoup [kɔ̃trəku] *nm (conséquence)* repercussions

contre-courant [kɔ̃trəkurɑ̃] **à contre-courant** *adv (nager)* against the current; *(sur la route)* in the wrong direction; *Fig* **aller à c. de qch** to go against the current of sth

contredanse [kɔ̃trədɑ̃s] *nf Fam (amende)* parking fine; *(avis)* (parking) ticket; **flanquer une c. à qn** to give sb a (parking) ticket

contredire [27b] [kɔ̃trədir] **1** *vt* to contradict
2 se contredire *vpr (soi-même)* to contradict oneself; *(l'un l'autre)* to contradict each other

contrée [kɔ̃tre] *nf Litt (région)* region; *(pays)* land

contre-emploi *(pl* **contre-emplois)** [kɔ̃trɑ̃plwa] *nm Théât & Cin* miscasting; **utiliser qn à c.** to miscast sb

contre-enquête *(pl* **contre-enquêtes)** [kɔ̃trɑ̃kɛt] *nf Jur* counter-inquiry

contre-espionnage [kɔ̃trɛspjɔnaʒ] *nm* counter-espionage

contre-exemple *(pl* **contre-exemples)** [kɔ̃trɛgzɑ̃pl] *nm* counter-example

contre-expertise *(pl* **contre-expertises)** [kɔ̃trɛkspɛrtiz] *nf* second opinion

contrefaçon [kɔ̃trəfasɔ̃] *nf* (a) *(pratique)* counterfeiting; *(de signature)* forging (b) *(produit)* fake, imitation

contrefaire [36] [kɔ̃trəfɛr] *vt* (a) *(voix, écriture)* to disguise (b) *(pièce, produit de marque)* to counterfeit; *(signature)* to forge

contrefait, -e [kɔ̃trəfɛ, -ɛt] *adj* (a) *(difforme)* deformed, misshapen (b) *(falsifié) (signature, argent)* counterfeit, forged

contreficher [kɔ̃trəfiʃe] **se contreficher** *vpr très Fam* **se c. de qch** not to give a damn about sth

contre-filet *(pl* **contre-filets)** [kɔ̃trəfilɛ] *nm Culin* sirloin

contrefort [kɔ̃trəfɔr] *nm* (a) *Archit* buttress (b) *Géog* **contreforts** foothills (c) *(de chaussure)* stiffener

contre-indication *(pl* **contre-indications)** [kɔ̃trɛ̃dikasjɔ̃] *nf* contraindication

contre-interrogatoire *(pl* **contre-interrogatoires)** [kɔ̃trɛ̃terɔgatwar] *nm Jur* cross-examination

contre-jour *(pl* **contre-jours)** [kɔ̃trəʒur] *nm Art, Cin & Phot* backlighting; **à c.** against the light

contre-la-montre [kɔ̃trəlamɔ̃tr] *nm inv Sport* time trial

contremaître, -maîtresse [kɔ̃trəmɛtr, -mɛtrɛs] *nm,f* foreman, *f* forewoman

contre-manifestation *(pl* **contre-manifestations)** [kɔ̃trəmanifɛstasjɔ̃] *nf* counter-demonstration

contremarche [kɔ̃trəmarʃ] *nf (d'un escalier)* riser

contremarque [kɔ̃trəmark] *nf (au spectacle)* pass

contre-mesure *(pl* **contre-mesures)** [kɔ̃trəməzyr] *nf* countermeasure

contre-offensive *(pl* **contre-offensives)** [kɔ̃trɔfɑ̃siv] *nf* counter-offensive

contrepartie [kɔ̃trəparti] *nf (compensation)* compensation; **en c. (de)** in return (for)

contre-performance *(pl* **contre-performances)** [kɔ̃trəpɛrfɔrmɑ̃s] *nf* substandard performance

contrepèterie [kɔ̃trəpɛtri] *nf* spoonerism

contre-pied [kɔ̃trəpje] *nm* (a) **prendre le c. de qch** *(faire le contraire)* to do the opposite of sth; *(dire le contraire)* to take the opposite view to sth (b) *Sport* **prendre son adversaire à c.** to wrong-foot one's opponent; **prendre la balle à c.** to take the ball on the wrong foot

contreplaqué [kɔ̃trəplake] *nm* plywood

contre-plongée *(pl* **contre-plongées)** [kɔ̃trəplɔ̃ʒe] *nf Cin & TV* low-angle shot; **filmer qch en c.** to film sth from below

contrepoids [kɔ̃trəpwɑ] *nm aussi Fig* counterbalance; *Fig* **faire c. à qch** to counterbalance sth

contre-poil [kɔ̃trəpwal] **à contre-poil** *adv* the wrong way; *Fam* **prendre qn à c.** to rub sb the wrong way

contrepoison [kɔ̃trəpwazɔ̃] *nm* antidote

contre-pouvoir *(pl* **contre-pouvoirs)** [kɔ̃trəpuvwar] *nm* anti-establishment force

contre-proposition *(pl* **contre-propositions)** [kɔ̃trəprɔpozisjɔ̃] *nf* counterproposal

contrer [kɔ̃tre] *vt* (a) *(attaque, argument, personne)* to counter (b) *(au volley, au basket)* to block (c) *(aux cartes)* to double

contre-révolution *(pl* **contre-révolutions)** [kɔ̃trərevɔlysjɔ̃] *nf* counterrevolution

contre-révolutionnaire *(pl* **contre-révolutionnaires)** [kɔ̃trərevɔlysjɔnɛr] *adj & nmf* counterrevolutionary

contresens [kɔ̃trəsɑ̃s] *nm* (a) *(mauvaise compréhension)* misinterpretation; *(mauvaise traduction)* mistranslation; **faire un c.** *(mal comprendre)* to make a mistake in interpretation; *(mal traduire)* to make a mistake in translation (b) *Aut* **à c.** the wrong way; **prendre une rue à c.** to go the wrong way down a street

contresigner [kɔ̃trəsiɲe] *vt* to countersign

contretemps [kɔ̃trətɑ̃] *nm* (a) *(ennui)* hitch, mishap (b) *Mus* offbeat; **à c.** off the beat; *Fig* at the wrong moment

contre-ténor *(pl* **contre-ténors)** [kɔ̃trətenɔr] *nm* countertenor

contre-torpilleur *(pl* **contre-torpilleurs)** [kɔ̃trətɔrpijœr] *nm* destroyer

contrevenant, -e [kɔ̃trəvənɑ̃, -ɑ̃t] *nm,f* offender

contrevenir [70] [kɔ̃trəvənir] **contrevenir à** *vt ind* to contravene

contrevent [kɔ̃trəvɑ̃] *nm (volet)* (outside) shutter

contrevérité [kɔ̃trəverite] *nf* untruth, falsehood

contribuable [kɔ̃tribɥabl] *nmf* taxpayer

contribuer [kɔ̃tribɥe] **contribuer à** *vt ind* to contribute to; **c. financièrement à qch** to contribute (money) to sth; **c. à faire qch** to help (to) do sth

contribution [kɔ̃tribysjɔ̃] *nf* (a) *(impôt)* tax; **contributions** *(à l'État)* taxes; *(à la collectivité locale)* local taxes; **(bureau des) contributions** tax office, Internal Revenue; **contributions directes/indirectes** direct/indirect taxation; **c. sociale généralisée** = income-based tax deducted at source (b) *(collaboration, aide financière)* contribution (à to); **mettre qn à c.** to call on sb's services

contrit, -e [kɔ̃tri, -it] *adj* contrite

contrôle [kɔ̃trol] *nm* (a) *(vérification)* checking; *Scol* test; *Scol & Univ* **c. des connaissances** assessment; *Univ* **c. continu** continuous assessment; **c. douanier** customs control; **c. fiscal** tax inspection; **c. d'identité** identity check; **c. des passeports** passport control; **c. de police** police check; **c. radar** *(sur la route)* radar speed check; *Aut* **c. technique** test of roadworthiness
(b) *(surveillance) (d'opérations)* monitoring; *Fin* **c. des**

changes exchange control; **sous c. judiciaire** on probation; **sous c. médical** under medical supervision; **c. des prix** price control

(**c**) *(maîtrise)* control; **avoir le c. de qch** to have control of sth, to be in control of sth; **perdre le c. de son véhicule** to lose control of one's vehicle; **prendre le c. d'une entreprise** to take over a company; **c. de soi** self-control; **sous c. américain** under American control; **c. des naissances** birth control

(**d**) *Ordinat* **touche c.** control key; **c. d'accès** access control; **faire un c. croisé de** to cross-check

contrôler [kɔ̃trole] **1** *vt* (**a**) *(vérifier)* to check (**b**) *(surveiller) (opérations)* to monitor (**c**) *(maîtriser)* to control (**d**) *Ordinat* **contrôlé par le logiciel** software-controlled; **contrôlé par menu** menu-driven, menu-controlled

2 se contrôler *vpr* to control oneself

contrôleur, -euse [kɔ̃trolœr, -øz] **1** *nm,f (dans les trains, les bus)* conductor; **c. aérien** air-traffic controller; **c. des impôts** tax inspector

2 *nm Ordinat* **c. d'affichage** display *or* screen controller

contrordre [kɔ̃trɔrdr] *nm* countermand; **il y a c.** the orders have been changed; **sauf c.** unless otherwise directed

controverse [kɔ̃trɔvɛrs] *nf* controversy; **prêter à c.** to be controversial

controversé, -e [kɔ̃trɔvɛrse] *adj* controversial

contumace [kɔ̃tymas] **par contumace** *adv Jur* in absentia

contusion [kɔ̃tyzjɔ̃] *nf* bruise, *Spéc* contusion

contusionné, -e [kɔ̃tyzjɔne] *adj* bruised

convaincant, -e [kɔ̃vɛ̃kɑ̃, -ɑ̃t] *adj* convincing

convaincre [68] [kɔ̃vɛ̃kr] *vt* (**a**) *(persuader)* to convince (**de/ que** of/that); **c. qn de faire qch** to persuade sb to do sth; **se laisser c.** to let oneself be persuaded (**b**) *(prouver la culpabilité de)* **être convaincu de meurtre** to be convicted *or* found guilty of murder

convaincu, -e [kɔ̃vɛ̃ky] *adj* convinced; *(pacifiste, partisan)* committed; **être c. de/que** to be convinced of/that; **d'un ton c.** with conviction

convalescence [kɔ̃valɛsɑ̃s] *nf* convalescence; **être en c.** to be convalescing

convalescent, -e [kɔ̃valɛsɑ̃, -ɑ̃t] *adj & nm,f* convalescent

convecteur [kɔ̃vɛktœr] *nm* convector (heater)

convenable [kɔ̃vnabl] *adj* (**a**) *(décent)* decent, respectable; **il n'est pas c. de faire du bruit en mangeant** it is not polite to make a noise when eating (**b**) *(acceptable) (salaire, délai)* decent (**c**) *(approprié)* appropriate, suitable

convenablement [kɔ̃vnabləmɑ̃] *adv* decently

convenance [kɔ̃vnɑ̃s] *nf* (**a**) *(fait de convenir)* **pour (des raisons de) c. personnelle** for personal reasons; **trouver qch à sa c.** to find sth to one's liking; **il le fera à sa c.** he'll do it at his own convenience (**b**) **les convenances** the proprieties; **contraire aux convenances** improper

convenir [70] [kɔ̃vnir] **1 convenir à** *vt ind (aller à, plaire à)* to suit; **il est difficile de trouver le mot qui convient** it's hard to find the right word

2 convenir de *vt ind* (**a**) *(reconnaître)* to admit; **j'ai eu tort, j'en conviens** I was wrong, I admit it; **il convient qu'il a eu tort** he admits that he was wrong (**b**) *(décider de)* to agree on; **c. de faire qch** to agree to do sth

3 *v impersonnel* (**a**) **il convient de...** *(il est souhaitable de)* it is advisable to...; *(il est de bon ton de)* it is proper to... (**b**) *(être décidé)* **il fut convenu qu'ils le feraient venir** it was agreed that they would send for him

convention [kɔ̃vɑ̃sjɔ̃] *nf* (**a**) *(accord)* agreement; **c. collective** collective agreement (**b**) *(règle arbitraire)* convention; **les conventions (sociales)** the (social) conventions; *Péj* **amabilité/sourire de c.** superficial courtesy/smile (**c**) *Pol*

(assemblée) assembly; *Hist* **la C.** the French National Convention *(1792-95)*

conventionné, -e [kɔ̃vɑ̃sjone] *adj (médecin, clinique)* attached to the health system; **médecin non c.** private doctor

conventionnel, -elle [kɔ̃vɑ̃sjonɛl] *adj* (**a**) *(style, personne, armes)* conventional (**b**) *Jur (clause)* contractual

convenu, -e [kɔ̃vny] *adj* (**a**) *(décidé)* agreed; **comme c.** as agreed (**b**) *Péj (peu original)* conventional

convergence [kɔ̃vɛrʒɑ̃s] *nf* convergence

convergent, -e [kɔ̃vɛrʒɑ̃, -ɑ̃t] *adj* convergent

converger [45] [kɔ̃vɛrʒe] *vi (routes, lignes)* to converge (**vers** on); **c. vers** *(efforts)* to be focused on; **leurs opinions convergent** they are of like mind

conversation [kɔ̃vɛrsasjɔ̃] *nf* (**a**) *(discussion)* conversation; **être en grande c. (avec qn)** to be deep in conversation (with sb); **engager la c.** to start a conversation; **faire la c. (à qn)** to make conversation (with sb); **n'avoir aucune c.** to be a poor conversationalist; **c. téléphonique** telephone conversation (**b**) *(pourparlers)* **conversations diplomatiques** diplomatic talks *or* negotiations

conversationnel, -elle [kɔ̃vɛrsasjonɛl] *adj Ordinat* **mode c.** conversational *or* interactive mode

converser [kɔ̃vɛrse] *vi Sout* to converse (**avec** with)

conversion [kɔ̃vɛrsjɔ̃] *nf* (**a**) *(changement)* conversion (**en** into); *Ordinat* **c. de fichier** file conversion (**b**) *(à une doctrine)* conversion (**à** to)

converti, -e [kɔ̃vɛrti] **1** *nm,f Rel* convert; *Fig* **prêcher un c.** to preach to the converted

2 *adj* converted

convertibilité [kɔ̃vɛrtibilite] *nf Fin* convertibility

convertible [kɔ̃vɛrtibl] **1** *adj* convertible (**en** into)

2 *nm (canapé)* sofa bed

convertir [kɔ̃vɛrtir] **1** *vt* (**a**) *(changer)* to convert (**en** into) (**b**) *(à une doctrine)* to convert (**à** to)

2 se convertir *vpr* (**a**) *(à une doctrine)* to be converted (**à** to) (**b**) **se c. en** *(se changer en)* to be converted into

convertisseur [kɔ̃vɛrtisœr] *nm Tech* converter; *Ordinat* **c. analogique numérique** digitizer

convexe [kɔ̃vɛks] *adj* convex

conviction [kɔ̃viksjɔ̃] *nf* (**a**) *(certitude)* conviction; **avoir la c. que...** to be convinced that... (**b**) **convictions** *(opinions)* convictions

convier [66] [kɔ̃vje] *vt Sout (inviter)* to invite (**à** to); **c. qn à faire qch** to invite sb to do sth

convive [kɔ̃viv] *nmf* guest

convivial, -e, -aux, -ales [kɔ̃vivjal, -o] *adj* convivial; *Ordinat* user-friendly

convivialité [kɔ̃vivjalite] *nf* conviviality; *Ordinat* user-friendliness

convocation [kɔ̃vokasjɔ̃] *nf* (**a**) *(lettre)* notice to attend; *Jur* summons; **c. à un examen** notification of an examination (**b**) *(d'une assemblée)* convening

convoi [kɔ̃vwa] *nm* (**a**) *(de véhicules, de troupes, de prisonniers)* convoy; **c. exceptionnel** *(sur un camion) (dangereux)* dangerous load; *(large)* wide load (**b**) *(train)* train; **c. de marchandises** freight train; **c. postal** mail train (**c**) *(cortège)* **c. funèbre** funeral procession

convoiter [kɔ̃vwate] *vt (poste, richesse)* to covet; *(femme)* to lust after

convoitise [kɔ̃vwatiz] *nf* covetousness; **regarder qch avec c.** to look covetously at sth; **exciter les convoitises** to excite envy

convoler [kɔ̃vole] *vi Hum* **c. (en justes noces)** to marry

convoquer [kɔ̃voke] *vt* (**a**) *(assemblée)* to convene; **c. les actionnaires** to call the shareholders to a meeting (**b**) *(témoin)* to summon; *(employé)* to call in; **c. qn à un examen** to notify sb of an examination

convoyer [32] [kɔ̃vwaje] *vt (troupes)* to convoy; *(fonds)* to transport under armed guard

convoyeur [kɔ̃vwajœr] *nm* (**a**) *(personne)* **c. de fonds** security guard (**b**) *Ind* conveyer

convulser [kɔ̃vylse] **1** *vt* to convulse
2 se convulser *vpr* to be convulsed

convulsif, -ive [kɔ̃vylsif, -iv] *adj* convulsive

convulsion [kɔ̃vylsjɔ̃] *nf* convulsion; **être pris de convulsions** to go into convulsions

convulsivement [kɔ̃vylsivmɑ̃] *adv* convulsively

cookie [kuki] *nm* (**a**) *(biscuit)* cookie (**b**) *Ordinat* cookie

cool [kul] *adj inv Fam* cool

coopérant, -e [kɔɔperɑ̃, -ɑ̃t] **1** *nm,f (à l'étranger)* aid worker
2 *nm (pendant le service militaire)* = man doing voluntary work overseas instead of military service

coopératif, -ive [kɔɔperatif, -iv] **1** *adj (société, personne)* co-operative
2 *nf* **coopérative** *(association, magasin)* cooperative, co-op; **coopérative d'achat** wholesale co-operative

coopération [kɔɔperasjɔ̃] *nf* (**a**) *(appui)* cooperation; **en c. avec qn** in cooperation with sb (**b**) *Pol* overseas development; *Anciennement (comme alternative au service militaire)* = voluntary work overseas instead of military service

coopérer [34] [kɔɔpere] *vi* to cooperate (**à** in)

cooptation [kɔɔptasjɔ̃] *nf* cooption; **par c.** by co-option

coordinateur, -trice [kɔɔrdinatœr, -tris] = **coordonnateur**

coordination [kɔɔrdinasjɔ̃] *nf (d'un projet, des mouvements)* coordination

coordonnateur, -trice [kɔɔrdɔnatœr, -tris] *nm,f* coordinator

coordonné, -e [kɔɔrdɔne] **1** *adj (mouvement, efforts)* coordinated; *(draps, vêtements)* matching
2 *nmpl* **coordonnés** *(vêtements)* coordinates
3 *nfpl* **coordonnées** (**a**) *Math, Géog & Astron* coordinates (**b**) *(d'une personne)* address and phone number

coordonner [kɔɔrdɔne] *vt* to coordinate (**à** *ou* **avec** with)

copain, copine [kɔpɛ̃, kɔpin] *Fam* **1** *nm,f* (**a**) *(camarade)* buddy, pal; **salut les copains!** *(en arrivant)* hi, guys!; *(en partant)* see you, guys!; **c. de classe** classmate (**b**) *(fiancé)* **(petit) c.** boyfriend; **(petite) copine** girlfriend
2 *adj* **ils sont très copains** they're great buddies; **être copains comme cochons** to be thick as thieves; **ils sont très c.-c.** they're very buddy-buddy

coparent [kɔparɑ̃] *nm* coparent

coparentalité [kɔparɑ̃talite] *nf* coparenthood

copeau, -x [kɔpo] *nm (de bois, de chocolat)* shaving; *(de métal)* cutting

Copenhague [kɔpɛnag] *n* Copenhagen

copie [kɔpi] *nf* (**a**) *(double, manuscrit)* copy (**b**) *Scol (d'examen)* paper; **rendre c. blanche** to hand in a blank paper; *Fig* **revoir sa c.** to go back to the drawing board; **c. simple/double** single/double sheet of paper (**c**) *(d'une œuvre d'art)* copy, reproduction; *(d'un roman, d'un style)* imitation (**d**) *TV & Cin* copy (**e**) *Ordinat* **c. sur papier** hard copy, printout; **c. de sauvegarde** *ou* **de secours** backup (copy), security copy

copier [66] [kɔpje] *vt* (**a**) *(texte, musique, document informatique)* to copy; **c. qch au propre** *ou* **au net** to make a fair copy of sth, to copy sth out neatly (**b**) *(œuvre d'art)* to copy, to reproduce; *(personne, style)* to imitate (**c**) *(à un devoir sur table)* to copy (**sur** from)

copier-coller [kɔpjekɔle] *nm inv Ordinat* copy-and-paste

copieur, -euse [kɔpjœr, -øz] *nm,f (élève)* copier
2 *nm (photocopieuse)* (photo)copier

copieusement [kɔpjøzmɑ̃] *adv (manger, boire)* copiously; **il s'est servi c.** he took a generous helping; **un repas c. arrosé**

a meal washed down with plenty of wine; **je me suis fait c. insulter** I got a whole stream of insults thrown at me

copieux, -euse [kɔpjø, -øz] *adj (repas)* copious; *(portion, part, pourboire)* generous

copilote [kopilɔt] *nmf (d'avion)* co-pilot; *(de rallye automobile)* navigator

copinage [kɔpinaʒ] *nm Fam* **obtenir un poste par c.** to get a job through one's connections

copiste [kɔpist] *nmf (scribe)* copyist

coprésentateur, -trice [koprezɑ̃tatœr, -tris] *nm,f* co-presenter

coprésidence [koprezidɑ̃s] *nf* co-chairmanship

coprésident, -e [koprezidɑ̃, -ɑ̃t] *nm,f* co-chairman, *f* co-chairwoman

coprocesseur [koprɔsesœr] *nm Ordinat* co-processor; **c. arithmétique** maths co-processor

coproducteur, -trice [koprɔdyktœr, -tris] *nm,f Cin & TV* coproducer

coproduction [koprɔdyksjɔ̃] *nf Cin & TV* coproduction

coproduire [18] [koprɔdɥir] *vt Cin & TV* to coproduce

copropriétaire [koprɔprijetɛr] *nmf* co-owner, joint owner; *(d'un appartement)* condo owner

copropriété [koprɔprijete] *nf* co-ownership, joint ownership; **acheter/posséder une maison en c.** to buy/to own a house jointly; **appartement en c.** condominium, condo

copte [kɔpt] **1** *adj* Coptic
2 *nmf* **C.** Copt

copulation [kɔpylasjɔ̃] *nf* copulation

copuler [kɔpyle] *vi* to copulate

copyright [kɔpirajt] *nm* copyright

coq¹ [kɔk] *nm* (**a**) *(oiseau)* cock, rooster; **jeune c.** cockerel; *Fig* young upstart; **le c. gaulois** the French cockerel; *Fig* **le c. du village** the local Casanova; *Fig* **passer** *ou* **sauter du c. à l'âne** to jump from one subject to another; **être comme un c. en pâte** to be in clover; **c. de bruyère** capercaillie; **c. de combat** fighting cock; *Culin* **c. au vin** coq au vin *(chicken cooked in red wine)* (**b**) *(girouette)* weathercock

coq² [kɔk] *nm Naut* (ship's) cook

coq-à-l'âne [kɔkalan] *nm inv* **faire un c.** to jump from one subject to another

coquard, coquart [kɔkar] *nm Fam* shiner

coque [kɔk] *nf* (**a**) *(d'une noix, d'un fruit)* shell; *Fig* **c. de noix** flimsy craft (**b**) *(d'un navire)* hull; *(d'un avion)* fuselage; *(d'une voiture)* body (**c**) *(mollusque)* cockle

coquelet [kɔklɛ] *nm* cockerel

coquelicot [kɔkliko] *nm* (red) poppy

coqueluche [kɔklyʃ] *nf (maladie)* whooping cough; **avoir la c.** to have whooping cough; **il est devenu la c. de ces dames** he's become a heartthrob

coquet, -ette [kɔkɛ, -ɛt] **1** *adj (ville, intérieur)* charming; **elle est coquette** she's very clothes-conscious; *Fam* **une coquette somme** a tidy sum
2 *nf* **coquette** *Vieilli* coquette

coquetier [kɔktje] *nm* eggcup; *Fam* **gagner** *ou* **décrocher le c.** to hit the jackpot

coquetterie [kɔketri] *nf* (**a**) *(vestimentaire)* consciousness of one's appearance; *Vieilli (désir de plaire)* coquetry; **avec c.** *(s'habiller)* stylishly (**b**) *Fam* **avoir une c. dans l'œil** to have a cast in one's eye

coquillage [kɔkijaʒ] *nm* (**a**) *(mollusque)* shellfish; **manger des coquillages** to eat shellfish (**b**) *(coque vide)* shell

coquille [kɔkij] *nf* (**a**) *(de mollusque, d'œuf, de noix)* shell; *Fig* **rentrer dans/sortir de sa c.** to withdraw into/to come out of one's shell; *Fig* **c. de noix** flimsy craft; **c. d'œuf** *(couleur)* eggshell; **c. Saint-Jacques** *Culin* scallop; *(coquillage)* scallop shell (**b**) *Typ* misprint

coquillettes [kɔkijɛt] *nfpl* pasta shells

coquin, -e [kɔkɛ̃, -in] **1** *adj (sourire, air)* mischievous; *(sous-vêtement)* sexy; *(histoire)* risqué

2 *nm,f (garnement)* rascal; **petit c.!** little rascal *or* scamp!

cor [kɔr] *nm* **(a)** *(instrument)* horn; **c. de chasse** hunting horn; **sonner du c.** to sound the horn; *Fig* **réclamer qch à c. et à cri** to clamor for sth **(b)** *(durillon)* corn

corail, -aux [kɔraj, -o] **1** *nm* coral

2 *adj inv* **(rouge) c.** coral(-red)

Coran [kɔrɑ̃] *nm* **le C.** the Koran

coranique [kɔranik] *adj* Koranic

corbeau, -x [kɔrbo] *nm* **(a)** *(oiseau)* crow **(b)** *(auteur de lettres anonymes)* poison-pen letter writer

corbeille [kɔrbɛj] *nf* **(a)** *(panier)* basket; **c. à linge** laundry basket; **c. de mariage** wedding presents; **c. à ouvrage** work-basket; **c. à pain** breadbasket; **c. à papier** wastepaper basket, wastebasket **(b)** *(à la Bourse de Paris)* trading floor **(c)** *Théât* dress circle **(d)** *Ordinat* wastebasket, trash; **c. d'arrivée** inbox; **c. de départ** outbox

corbillard [kɔrbijar] *nm* hearse

cordage [kɔrdaʒ] *nm* *(corde)* rope; *(d'une raquette)* stringing; *Naut* **cordages** rigging

corde [kɔrd] *nf* **(a)** *(lien)* rope; **échelle de c.** rope ladder; **c. à linge** clothesline; **c. lisse** climbing rope; **c. à nœuds** knotted climbing rope; **c. raide** tightrope; *Fig* **être sur la c. raide** to be walking a tightrope; **c. à sauter** jump rope; **il ne vaut pas la c. pour le pendre** hanging's too good for him **(b)** *(d'instrument, de raquette)* string; **les cordes** *(d'un orchestre)* the strings; *Fig* **avoir plus d'une c. à son arc** to have more than one string to one's bow; *Fig* **j'ai dû toucher la c. sensible** I must have hit a raw nerve **(c)** *Sport* **tenir la c.** *(coureur)* to be on the inside; *(cheval)* to hug the rails; **les cordes** *(d'un ring)* the ropes **(d)** *Anat* **cordes vocales** vocal cords; *Fig* **ce n'est pas dans mes cordes** it's not in my line

cordeau, -x [kɔrdo] *nm (corde)* string; *Fig* **tiré au c.** as straight as a die

cordée [kɔrde] *nf (d'alpinistes)* roped party; **premier de c.** leader

cordelette [kɔrdəlɛt] *nf* cord

cordelière [kɔrdəljɛr] *nf (ceinture)* cord

cordial, -e, -aux, -ales [kɔrdjal, -o] **1** *adj (accueil, personne)* cordial

2 *nm (médicament)* tonic

cordialement [kɔrdjalmɑ̃] *adv* cordially; **détester c. qn** to heartily dislike sb; **bien c.** *(dans une lettre)* best wishes

cordier [kɔrdje] *nm (de violon)* tailpiece

cordillère [kɔrdijɛr] *nf* mountain range; **la c. des Andes** the Andes

cordon [kɔrdɔ̃] *nm* **(a)** *(lien)* cord, string; *Fig* **tenir les cordons de la bourse** to hold the purse strings; *Anat* **c. ombilical** umbilical cord; *aussi Fig* **couper le c. (ombilical)** to cut the umbilical cord **(b)** *(de policiers, de soldats)* cordon

cordon-bleu *(pl* **cordons-bleus)** [kɔrdɔ̃bløø] *nm Fam* cordon bleu (cook)

cordonnerie [kɔrdɔnri] *nf* **(a)** *(métier)* shoe repairing **(b)** *(boutique)* shoe-repair store

cordonnier, -ère [kɔrdɔnje, -ɛr] *nm,f* shoe repairer; *Prov* **les cordonniers sont toujours les plus mal chaussés** the shoemaker's wife is always the worst shod

Corée [kɔre] *nf* **la C. du Nord/du Sud** North/South Korea

coréen, -enne [kɔreɛ̃, -ɛn] **1** *adj* Korean

2 *nm,f* **C., Coréenne** Korean

Corfou [kɔrfu] *n* Corfu

coriace [kɔrjas] *adj* **(a)** *(viande)* tough **(b)** *(personne, adversaire)* tough

coriandre [kɔrjɑ̃dr] *nf Bot & Culin* coriander, cilantro

Corinthe [kɔrɛ̃t] *n voir* **raisin**

cormoran [kɔrmɔrɑ̃] *nm* cormorant

corne [kɔrn] *nf* **(a)** *(d'animal)* horn; **c. d'abondance** horn of plenty, cornucopia; **la C. de l'Afrique** the Horn of Africa; *Fam Fig* **avoir** *ou* **porter des cornes** to be a cuckold; *Fam Fig* **faire porter des cornes à qn** to cuckold sb, to cheat on sb **(b)** *(matériau)* horn; **peigne de c.** horn comb **(c)** *(d'un croissant)* end; **faire une c. à une page** to turn down the corner of a page **(d)** *(aux pieds, aux mains)* hard skin

cornée [kɔrne] *nf* cornea

cornéen, -enne [kɔrneɛ̃, -ɛn] *adj* corneal

corneille [kɔrnɛj] *nf* crow

cornemuse [kɔrnəmyz] *nf* bagpipes

corner¹ [kɔrne] *vt* **(a)** *(page)* to turn down the corner of; *(abîmer)* to make dog-eared **(b)** *Fam* **c. qch aux oreilles de qn** to shout sth into sb's ear

corner² [kɔrnɛr] *nm (au football)* corner; **tirer un c.** to take a corner

cornet [kɔrnɛ] *nm* **(a)** *(de papier)* cone; *(de marrons, de frites)* cornet; **mettre les mains en c.** to cup one's hands together; **c. (à pistons)** cornet; **c. de glace** ice-cream cone **(b)** *Suisse (sac en papier)* paper bag; *(sac en plastique)* plastic bag

cornette [kɔrnɛt] *nf (coiffe)* cornet

cornettiste [kɔrnɛtist] *nmf* cornetist

corn flakes [kɔrnflɛks] *nmpl* cornflakes

corniaud [kɔrnjo] *nm* **(a)** *(chien)* mongrel **(b)** *Fam (personne)* jerk

corniche [kɔrniʃ] *nf* **(a)** *(de bâtiment)* cornice **(b)** *(de rochers)* ledge; *(de glace, de neige)* cornice; **(route de) c.** coast road

cornichon [kɔrniʃɔ̃] *nm* gherkin, pickle

Cornouailles [kɔrnwaj] *nf* **la C.** Cornwall

cornu, -e [kɔrny] *adj (animal, diable)* horned

corollaire [kɔrɔlɛr] *nm (suite)* consequence

corolle [kɔrɔl] *nf* corolla

coron [kɔrɔ̃] *nm* mining village

coronaire [kɔrɔnɛr] *adj* coronary

coronarien, -enne [kɔrɔnarjɛ̃, -ɛn] *adj* coronary

corporation [kɔrpɔrasjɔ̃] *nf* corporate body

corporatiste [kɔrpɔratist] *adj* corporatist

corporel, -elle [kɔrpɔrɛl] *adj (punition)* corporal; *(besoins)* bodily; *(hygiène)* personal

corps [kɔr] *nm* **(a)** *(organisme)* body; **trembler de tout son c.** to tremble all over; **lutter c. à c.** to fight hand to hand; *Fig* **faire qch à son c. défendant** to do sth reluctantly; *Fig* **se jeter à c. perdu dans qch** to throw oneself into sth; *Fig* **se donner c. et âme à qn/qch** to give oneself body and soul to sb/sth

(b) *(cadavre)* body, corpse

(c) *Chim & Phys* body; *Astron* **c. céleste** heavenly body; **c. composé** compound; **c. gras** fat; **c. simple** element

(d) *(consistance)* **avoir du c.** *(vin)* to have body; *Fig* **prendre c.** *(projet, idée)* to take shape

(e) *(partie principale)* main part; *(d'un texte)* body; *Naut* **perdu c. et biens** lost with all hands; *Jur* **le c. du délit** the corpus delicti

(f) *(groupe)* **c. d'armée** army corps; **c. de ballet** corps de ballet; **c. diplomatique** diplomatic corps; **c. électoral** electorate; **plaisanterie de c. de garde** barrackroom joke; **le c. médical/enseignant** the medical/teaching profession; **c. de métier** trade; *Hist* corporation; **les grands c. de l'État** = the highest sections of the French administration *(Conseil d'État, Cour des comptes, etc.)*

corpulence [kɔrpylɑ̃s] *nf* stoutness, corpulence

corpulent, -e [kɔrpylɑ̃, -ɑ̃t] *adj* stout, corpulent

corpus [kɔrpys] *nm Jur & Ling* corpus

corpuscule [kɔrpyskyl] *nm* corpuscle

correct, -e [kɔrɛkt] *adj* **(a)** *(sans fautes)* correct **(b)** *(courtois)* *(personne)* correct; **cela n'est pas c. de sa part** that's not right of him; **elle a été correcte avec moi** she behaved properly toward me (**c**) *Fam (acceptable) (repas, travail, salaire)* reasonable

correctement [kɔrɛktəmɑ̃] *adv* (**a**) *(sans faire d'erreur, décemment)* correctly (**b**) *Fam (de façon acceptable)* reasonably; **gagner c. sa vie** to make a reasonable living

correcteur, -trice [kɔrɛktœr, -tris] **1** *nm,f (de copies d'examen)* grader; *(en typographie)* proofreader; *(dans la presse)* copy reader

2 *nm Ordinat* checker; **c. liquide** correcting fluid; *Ordinat* **c. d'orthographe** *ou* **orthographique** spellchecker

3 *adj (verres)* correcting

correction [kɔrɛksjɔ̃] *nf* (**a**) *(d'une faute)* correction; *Scol (d'un exercice)* correcting, grading; *Typ (d'épreuves)* proofreading (**b**) *(punition)* beating (**c**) *(décence, courtoisie)* correctness

correctionnel, -elle [kɔrɛksjɔnɛl] *Jur* **1** *adj* **peine correctionnelle** = penalty of more than five days' (but less than five years') imprisonment; **tribunal c.** criminal court

2 *nf* **correctionnelle** criminal court; **passer en correctionnelle** to go before the criminal court

corrélation [kɔrelasjɔ̃] *nf* correlation; **être en c. étroite** to be closely connected *or* related

correspondance [kɔrɛspɔ̃dɑ̃s] *nf* (**a**) *(lettres, échange de lettres)* correspondence (**b**) *(entre trains, avions)* connection; **assurer la c. avec...** *(train, bateau)* to connect with... (**c**) *(entre deux choses)* correspondence; *(d'idées, de principes)* conformity

correspondant, -e [kɔrɛspɔ̃dɑ̃, -ɑ̃t] **1** *adj* corresponding (**à** to)

2 *nm,f* (**a**) *(journaliste)* correspondent; **c. de guerre** war correspondent; **c. permanent à Londres** London correspondent (**b**) *(au téléphone)* caller; *(par lettre)* pen pal; **le numéro de votre c. a changé** *(au téléphone)* the number you have dialed has been changed

correspondre [kɔrɛspɔ̃dr] *vi* (**a**) *(être conforme, équivaloir)* **c. à qch** to correspond to sth; **les vis et les écrous qui correspondent** the screws and the nuts that go with them (**b**) *(par lettres)* **c. avec qn** to correspond with sb

corrida [kɔrida] *nf* bullfight; *Fam (problèmes)* hassle

corridor [kɔridɔr] *nm* corridor

corrigé, -e [kɔriʒe] **1** *adj* corrected; **en données corrigées des variations saisonnières** seasonally adjusted

2 *nm Scol (d'un exercice)* correct answers (**de** to); *(à la fin d'un ouvrage)* key (**de** to)

corriger [45] [kɔriʒe] **1** *vt* (**a**) *(erreur, faute d'orthographe, myopie, défauts)* to correct; *(exercice, examen)* to correct, to grade; *(épreuves typographiques)* to read; *(article de journal)* to sub-edit; **c. qn de qch** to cure sb of sth (**b**) *(pour punir)* **c. qn** to give sb a beating

2 se corriger *vpr (personne)* to mend one's ways; **se c. de qch** to cure oneself of sth

corroborer [kɔrɔbɔre] *vt* to corroborate

corroder [kɔrɔde] *vt* to corrode

corrompre [kɔrɔ̃pr] *vt* (**a**) *(personne, goût)* to corrupt (**b**) *(soudoyer)* to bribe

corrompu, -e [kɔrɔ̃py] *adj* corrupt

corrosif, -ive [kɔrozif, -iv] *adj* corrosive; *Fig (propos, humour)* caustic

corrosion [kɔrozjɔ̃] *nf (d'un métal)* corrosion

corruption [kɔrypsjɔ̃] *nf (perversion)* corruption; *(fait de soudoyer)* bribery

corsage [kɔrsaʒ] *nm* blouse

corsaire [kɔrsɛr] **1** *nm* (**a**) *Hist (navire, homme)* corsair (**b**) *(pantalon)* (pair of) capri pants

2 *adj* **pantalon c.** capri pants

Corse [kɔrs] *nf* **la C.** Corsica

corse [kɔrs] **1** *adj* Corsican

2 *nm (langue)* Corsican

3 *nmf* **C.** Corsican

corsé, -e [kɔrse] *adj (vin)* full-bodied; *(sauce, plat)* spicy; *(café)* full-flavored; *Fig (histoire)* spicy

corser [kɔrse] **1** *vt (plat)* to spice up; *Fig (récit)* to liven up

2 se corser *vpr (intrigue)* to thicken; **ça se corse** things are getting complicated; **l'histoire se corse** the plot thickens

corset [kɔrsɛ] *nm* corset; **c. orthopédique** surgical corset

cortège [kɔrtɛʒ] *nm* procession; *Fig* **la vie de famille et son c. de problèmes** family life and its attendant problems; **c. funèbre** funeral cortège

cortex [kɔrtɛks] *nm Anat & Bot* cortex

corticoïde [kɔrtikɔid] *nm* corticoid

cortisone [kɔrtizɔn] *nf* cortisone

corvée [kɔrve] *nf* (**a**) *(obligation pénible)* chore; **je suis de c. de vaisselle ce soir** I'm on dishwashing duty tonight; **quelle c.!** what a drag! (**b**) *Mil* fatigue duty; **être de c.** to be on fatigue duty (**c**) *Hist* corvée

corvette [kɔrvɛt] *nf* corvette

coryza [kɔriza] *nm* head cold

cosaque [kɔzak] *nm* cossack

cosignataire [kosiɲatɛr] *adj & nmf* cosignatory

cosinus [kɔsinys] *nm* cosine

cosmétique [kɔsmetik] *adj & nm* cosmetic

cosmique [kɔsmik] *adj* cosmic

cosmologie [kɔsmɔlɔʒi] *nf* cosmology

cosmonaute [kɔsmɔnot] *nmf* cosmonaut

cosmopolite [kɔsmɔpɔlit] *adj* cosmopolitan

cosmos [kɔsmos] *nm (univers)* cosmos; *(espace)* outer space

cosse [kɔs] *nf (de petits pois)* pod

cossu, -e [kɔsy] *adj (maison, intérieur)* opulent; *(personne)* well-to-do

costard [kɔstar] *nm Fam* suit; **tailler un c. à qn** to badmouth sb

Costa Rica [kɔstarika] *nm* **le C.** Costa Rica

costaud, -e [kɔsto, -od] *Fam* **1** *adj* (**a**) *(fort, solide) (personne)* sturdy (**b**) *(problème)* tough (**c**) *(alcool, café)* strong

2 *nm,f* sturdy man, *f* woman

costume [kɔstym] *nm (habit)* costume; *(complet)* suit

costumé, -e [kɔstyme] *adj voir* **bal**

costume-cravate [kɔstymkravat] *(pl* **costumes-cravates)** *nm Fam* **un (homme en) c.** a guy in a suit

costumier, -ère [kɔstymje, -ɛr] *nm,f (de théâtre)* wardrobe master, *f* wardrobe mistress; *(de cinéma)* costume supervisor

cotation [kɔtasjɔ̃] *nf* **c. (en Bourse)** quotation (on the Stock Exchange)

cote [kɔt] *nf* (**a**) *(d'une action) (valeur)* quotation; *(liste)* share index; *(d'un cheval)* odds; **hors c.** *(actions)* unlisted; *(marché)* over-the-counter; **c. de popularité** popularity rating; *Fam* **avoir la c. (avec** *ou* **auprès de)** to be popular (with) (**b**) *(servant à classer)* classification mark (**c**) *(altitude)* altitude; **at-**

teindre la c. d'alerte *(fleuve)* to reach danger level; *Fig* to reach crisis point

coté, -e [kɔte] *adj* **(a)** *(estimé)* **bien/très/mal c.** highly/very highly/not highly thought of **(b) action cotée en Bourse** share quoted on the Stock Exchange; **être c. à 100 euros** to be trading at 100 euros; **être c. à l'argus** to be listed in the car buyer's guide

côte [kot] *nf* **(a)** *(os)* rib; **c. à c.** side by side; *Fam* **on lui voit les côtes** he's nothing but skin and bone; **c. d'agneau/de porc** lamb/pork chop; **c. de bœuf** rib of beef **(b)** *(de melon, de feuille)* rib; **tissu à côtes** ribbed material **(c)** *(d'une montagne)* slope; **monter/descendre une c.** to go up/down a hill **(d)** *(rivage)* coast; **la C. (d'Azur)** the (French) Riviera

côté [kote] *nm* **(a)** *(du corps humain)* side; **couché sur le c.** lying on one's side; *Fig* **être aux côtés de qn** to be at sb's side **(b)** *(d'une route, d'un triangle, d'une feuille)* side; **de l'autre c. (de qch)** on the other side (of sth); **siège c. couloir/fenêtre** aisle/window seat; *Théât* **c. jardin/cour** on stage left/right **(c)** *(aspect)* side; **il a de bons côtés** he's got a good side to him; **prendre la vie du bon c.** to look on the bright side of life **(d)** *(endroit)* **de tous côtés** *(cerné)* on all sides; *(affluer)* from all directions; **du c. de** *(près de)* near; **ils s'en allèrent chacun de son c.** they went their separate ways; **de quel c.?** *(direction)* which way?; *(position)* which side?; *Fig* **être du c. de qn** to be on sb's side; **ma tante du c. maternel** my aunt on my mother's side; **d'un c...., d'un autre c....** on the one hand…, on the other hand… **(e)** *(en ce qui concerne)* *Fam* **c. argent, ça va** things are OK moneywise; **de ce c., il n'y a rien à craindre** there's nothing to worry about on that score **(f)** **à c.** *(près)* nearby; **à c. de** *(près de)* next to; *(comparé à)* compared with; **les voisins d'à c.** the next-door neighbors; **à c. l'un de l'autre** side by side; *Fig* **passer à c. de qch** to miss out on sth **(g) faire un saut de c.** to leap to one side *or* aside; *Fig* **mettre qch de c.** to put sth aside; *Fig* **laisser qn/qch de c.** to leave sb/sth out

coteau, -x [kɔto] *nm (versant)* hillside; *(colline)* hill

Côte d'Ivoire [kotdivwar] *nf* **la C.** the Ivory Coast

côtelé, -e [kotle] *adj voir* **velours**

côtelette [kotlɛt, kɔtlɛt] *nf* chop; **c. d'agneau/de porc** lamb/pork chop

coter [kɔte] *vt* **(a)** *(prix, actions)* to quote **(b)** *(documents)* to classify

côtier, -ère [kotje, -ɛr] *adj (fleuve, navigation)* coastal; *(pêche)* inshore

cotillon [kɔtijɔ̃] *nm* **accessoires de c., cotillons** party novelties

cotisation [kɔtizasjɔ̃] *nf* **(a)** *(à une caisse)* contribution; **cotisations de Sécurité Sociale** Social Security contributions **(b)** *(à un club)* membership dues

cotiser [kɔtize] **1** *vi (à une caisse de retraite, à une mutuelle)* to contribute (**à** to)
2 se cotiser *vpr* to club together

coton [kɔtɔ̃] **1** *nm* **(a)** *(plante, tissu)* cotton; **chemise 100% c.** 100% cotton shirt; *Fam* **filer un mauvais c.** *(financièrement, physiquement)* to be in a bad way **(b) c. (hydrophile)** absorbent cotton; **un c.** a piece of absorbent cotton; *Fig* **élever un enfant dans du c.** to wrap a child in cotton wool; *Fam* **j'ai les jambes en c.** my legs feel like Jell-O
2 *adj Fam* tough, tricky

cotonnade [kɔtɔnad] *nf* cotton fabric

cotonneux, -euse [kɔtɔnø, -øz] *adj (feuille)* downy; *(nuage)* fluffy; *(fruit)* mushy

Coton-Tige® *(pl* **Cotons-Tiges)** [kɔtɔ̃tiʒ] *nm* Q-tip®

côtoyer [32] [kotwaje] *vt* **(a)** *(personnes)* to mix with **(b)** *(rivière, forêt)* to border on

cotte [kɔt] *nf* **c. de mailles** coat of mail

cou [ku] *nm* neck; **tendre le c.** to crane one's neck; **avoir un c. de taureau** to have a neck like a bull; **se jeter au c. de qn** to throw one's arms around sb's neck; *Fam* **endetté jusqu'au c.** up to one's eyes in debt

couac [kwak] *nm (fausse note)* false note; *Fig* discordant note; **faire un c.** to play a false note; *(chanteur)* to sing a false note

couchage [kuʃaʒ] *nm voir* **sac**¹

couchant, -e [kuʃɑ̃, -ɑ̃t] **1** *adj* **le soleil c.** the setting sun
2 *nm (ouest)* west; **dans la direction du c.** in a westerly direction

couche [kuʃ] *nf* **(a)** *(de peinture)* coat; *(de beurre, de crème, de poussière)* layer; *(classe sociale)* level; *Géol* layer, stratum; **la c. d'ozone** the ozone layer; *Fam* **il en tient une c.!** he's really stupid! **(b)** *(de bébé)* diaper **(c)** *Vieilli* **femme en couches** woman in labor; **mourir en couches** to die in childbirth **(d)** *Litt (lit)* bed

couché, -e [kuʃe] *adj* **(a)** *(allongé)* lying (down); *(au lit)* in bed **(b)** *(écriture)* slanting, sloping

couche-culotte *(pl* **couches-culottes)** [kuʃkylɔt] *nf* disposable diaper

coucher¹ [kuʃe] *nm* **(a)** *(fait d'aller au lit)* **l'heure du c.** bedtime; **prendre deux comprimés au c.** take two tablets at bedtime **(b)** *(gîte)* accommodations **(c)** *(du soleil)* setting; **un superbe c. de soleil** a magnificent sunset; **au c. du soleil** at sunset

coucher² [kuʃe] **1** *vt* **(a)** *(mettre au lit)* **c. qn** to put sb to bed **(b)** *(allonger, poser)* to lay down **(c)** *(écrire)* **c. qn sur son testament** to mention sb in one's will
2 *vi* **(a)** *(passer la nuit)* to sleep; *Fig* **c. sous les ponts** to sleep on the streets **(b)** *Fam* **c. avec qn** to sleep with sb; **c. ensemble** to sleep together **(c)** *(à un chien)* **couché!** (lie) down!
3 se coucher *vpr* **(a)** *(au lit)* to go to bed; **aller se c.** to go to bed; *Fam* **se c. avec les poules** to go to bed early; *Prov* **comme on fait son lit, on se couche** as we make our bed, so we must lie in it **(b)** *(s'allonger)* to lie down; **se c. à plat ventre** to lie flat on one's stomach **(c) se c. sur le flanc** *(navire)* to keel over **(d)** *(soleil, lune)* to set, to go down

coucheries [kuʃri] *nf Fam* sleeping around

couchette [kuʃɛt] *nf (de navire)* bunk; *(de train)* couchette

coucheur [kuʃœr] *nm Fam* **c'est un mauvais c.** he's an awkward customer

couci-couça [kusikusa] *adv Fam* so-so

coucou [kuku] **1** *nm* **(a)** *(oiseau)* cuckoo **(b)** *(horloge)* cuckoo clock **(c)** *(plante)* cowslip **(d)** *Fam (avion)* old crate
2 *exclam (langage enfantin)* peekaboo!; *(bonjour)* yoo-hoo!

coude [kud] *nm* **(a)** *(articulation)* elbow; **être au c. à c.** to be neck and neck; **jouer des coudes** to push and shove; *Fig* to maneuver; *Fig* **se serrer les coudes** to stick together; *Fig* **garder qch sous le c.** to hold on to sth; *Fam* **lever le c.** to booze **(b)** *(tournant)* sharp bend; *(de barre, de tuyau)* bend; *(d'arbre)* crank

coudé, -e¹ [kude] *adj* bent

coudée² [kude] *nf* **avoir les coudées franches** to have plenty of elbow room

cou-de-pied *(pl* **cous-de-pied)** [kudəpje] *nm* instep

coudre [21] [kudr] *vt (ourlet)* to sew; *(bouton)* to sew on; *(deux morceaux d'étoffe)* to sew together; *(jupe, plaie)* to sew up; **c. un bouton à une robe** to sew a button on a dress; **je ne sais pas c.** I can't sew

coudrier [kudrije] *nm* hazel (tree); **baguette de c.** hazel stick *or* switch

couenne [kwan] *nf* rind

couette¹ [kwɛt] *nf (édredon)* comforter

couette² [kwɛt] *nf (coiffure)* pigtail; **se faire des couettes** to put one's hair in pigtails

couille [kuj] *nf Vulg (testicule)* ball; *(problème)* ball-up

couillon, -onne [kujɔ̃, -ɔn] *très Fam* **1** *adj* goddamn stupid **2** *nm,f* stupid asshole

couillonner [kujɔne] *vt très Fam (personne)* to con; **se faire c.** to be conned

couiner [kwine] *vi (animal)* to squeak; *(enfant)* to whine

coulant, -e [kulɑ̃, -ɑ̃t] *adj (fromage)* runny; *Fig (style)* flowing; *Fam (personne)* easy-going

coulée [kule] *nf* **c. de boue** mudslide; **c. de lave** lava flow

coulemelle [kulmɛl] *nf* parasol mushroom

couler [kule] **1** *vt* **(a)** *(liquide, cire, ciment)* to pour; *(métal, statue)* to cast **(b)** *(navire)* to sink; *Fig* **c. qn** to bring sb down **(c)** *(passer)* **c. des jours heureux** to lead a happy life; *Fam* **se la c. douce** to take it easy
2 *vi* **(a)** *(liquide, rivière)* to flow, to run; *(fromage, maquillage)* to run; *(style)* to flow; **la sueur coule sur son front** sweat is trickling down his/her forehead; **cette affaire a fait c. beaucoup d'encre** a lot has been written about this affair; **faire c. un bain à qn** to run a bath for sb; *Fig* **c. de source** to be obvious **(b)** *(navire)* to sink, to go down; *(entreprise)* to go under **(c)** *(tonneau, stylo)* to leak; *(nez)* to run; **avoir le nez qui coule** to have a runny nose
3 se couler *vpr (se glisser)* to slip

couleur [kulœr] **1** *nf* **(a)** *(teinte, orientation politique)* color; **de quelle c. est…?** what color is…?; **de c.** colored; **de c. jaune/verte** yellow-/green-colored; **une personne de c.** a colored person; **télévision/photographie en c.** *ou* **couleurs** color television/photography; **les couleurs** *(linge)* coloreds; *Fig* **pour faire c. locale** to add a bit of local color; *Fam* **elle nous en a fait voir de toutes les couleurs** she gave us a hard time; *Fam* **je n'en ai pas encore vu la c.** I've seen no sign of it yet
(b) *(teint)* **prendre des couleurs** to get some color in one's cheeks
(c) *Mil* **couleurs** *(drapeau)* colors
(d) **couleurs** *(d'un club, d'une écurie)* colors; **défendre les couleurs de** to represent
(e) *(peinture)* paint; **une boîte de couleurs** a paintbox
(f) *(aux cartes)* suit; **annoncer la c.** to call (trumps); *Fam* to lay one's cards on the table
(g) *(en coiffure)* dye; **se faire une c.** to dye one's hair; **se faire faire une c.** to have one's hair dyed
2 *adj inv (télévision, pellicule)* color; **une chevelure c. de feu** flame-colored hair

couleuvre [kulœvr] *nf* **c. (à collier)** grass snake; *Fig* **avaler des couleuvres** *(se faire humilier)* to eat humble pie; *(être naïf)* to swallow anything

coulis [kuli] *nm* **c. de tomates/framboises** tomato/raspberry coulis

coulissant, -e [kulisɑ̃, -ɑ̃t] *adj* sliding

coulisse [kulis] *nf* **(a)** *(glissière)* runner; **porte à c.** sliding door **(b)** *Théât* **les coulisses** the wings; **en coulisses, dans les coulisses** in the wings; *Fig* behind the scenes

coulisser [kulise] *vi* to slide

couloir [kulwar] *nm* **(a)** *(de maison)* corridor, passage; *(de train)* corridor; *(en athlétisme, en natation)* lane; *(au tennis)* alley; **c. aérien** air corridor; **c. d'autobus** bus lane; **c. à vélos** bicycle lane **(b)** *Géog* gully

coulommiers [kulɔmje] *nm* = type of soft cheese

coulon [kulɔ̃] *nm Belg* pigeon

coulpe [kulp] *nf* **battre sa c.** to beat one's breast

coup [ku] *nm* **(a)** *(choc)* blow; **donner un c. à qn** to hit sb; **se donner un c. contre qch** to knock against sth; **j'ai pris un coup sur la tête** I got a knock *or* a bang on the head; **donner un c. de bâton à qn** to hit sb with a stick; **donner un c. de coude à qn** to nudge sb; **donner un c. de couteau à qn** to knife sb; **donner un c. de griffe à qn/qch** to claw at sb/sth; **c. de pied** kick; **donner un c. de pied à qn/qch** to kick sb/

sth; **c. de poing** punch; **donner un c. de poing à qn** to punch sb; **c. de poing américain** knuckle-duster; *Fig* **donner un c. de pouce à qn** to push sb; **c. de tête** header; *Fam* **faire qch sur un c. de tête** to do sth on the spur of the moment; **rendre c. pour c.** to give as good as one gets; *Fig* **tous les coups sont permis** there are no holds barred; *Fig* **c'était un c. bas** that was below the belt; *Jur* **coups et blessures** assault and battery
(b) *(choc émotionnel)* blow; **ça m'a fait un c.** *(émotion)* it gave me a shock; *(déception)* it was a blow; **accuser le c.** to show that one has been affected; *Fam* **tenir le c.** to hold out; *Fam* **en prendre un c.** to be devastated; **un c. dur** a setback
(c) *(action soudaine, événement soudain)* **c. de vent** gust of wind; *Fam* **passer en c. de vent** to pay a flying visit; **donner un c. de frein** to brake; **donner un c. de volant** to turn the wheel sharply; **donner un c. d'arrêt à qch** to call a halt to sth; *Fam* **prendre un c. de vieux** to age; *Fam* **avoir un c. de barre** *ou* **de pompe** to have the munchies; **c. de chance** *ou* *Fam* **de bol** *ou* **de pot** stroke of luck; *Fam* **avoir un c. de cœur pour qch** to absolutely love sth; **c. d'État** coup (d'État); *Fig* **ça a été le c. de foudre** it was love at first sight; **avoir le c. de foudre pour qn** to fall head over heels in love with sb; **attraper un c. de froid** to catch a cold; *Fam* **pousser un c. de gueule** to yell; *Fam* **un c. de pub** a publicity stunt; **prendre un c. de soleil** to get sunburned; **c. de théâtre** coup de théâtre; *(dans la vie)* sudden turn of events
(d) *(bruit)* **c. de feu** shot; **c. de fusil** shot; **c. de sifflet** whistle; **c. de sonnette** ring; **c. de tonnerre** clap of thunder; **tirer deux coups** to fire twice; **l'horloge sonna trois coups** the clock struck three; *Fig* **sur le c. de midi** on the stroke of twelve; **les trois coups** *(au théâtre)* = the three knocks given just before the curtain rises
(e) *(influence)* **sous le c. de la colère** in a fit of anger; **tomber sous le c. de la loi** to be an offense
(f) *(essai)* attempt, go; *Fig* **réussir son c.** to be a great success; **d'un seul c.** in one go; **du premier c.** at the first attempt; *Fam* **à tous les coups, le patron va nous repérer** the boss is bound to see us; **il n'en est pas à son c. d'essai** it's not the first time he's done it; **c. de maître** masterstroke
(g) *(au golf)* stroke; *(aux échecs)* move; **c. droit** *(au tennis)* forehand; *Fig* **faire c. double** to kill two birds with one stone; **c. d'envoi** *(au football)* kickoff; *Fig* **donner le c. d'envoi de qch** to launch sth; **c. franc** *(au football)* free kick; **c. de pied de réparation** penalty kick
(h) *Fam (tour, combine)* **réussir un bon c.** to do well for oneself; **faire un sale c. à qn** to play a dirty trick on sb; **être sur un c.** to be on to a good thing; **être dans le c.** *(impliqué)* to be involved; *(à la mode)* to be trendy; **c. fourré, c. de Jarnac** dirty trick; **c. monté** put-up job
(i) *Vulg* **tirer un c.** to get laid
(j) *(locutions)* **tout à c., tout d'un c.** suddenly, all of a sudden; **à c. sûr** for certain, definitely; **au c. par c.** step by step; **c. sur c.** one after the other; **après c.** after the event; *Fam* **du c.** and so; **pleurer un bon c.** to have a good cry; **mourir sur le c.** to die on the spot; **sur le c., je n'ai pas compris** at the time I didn't understand; **faire les quatre cents coups** to sow one's wild oats; **donner le c. de grâce à qn** to finish sb off; **avoir le c. de main (pour faire qch)** to have the knack (of doing sth); **donner un c. de main à qn** to give sb a hand; *Fam* **boire un c.** to have a drink; *Fam* **avoir un c. dans le nez** to be smashed; *Fam* **valoir le c.** to be worth it; *Fam* **il va falloir en mettre un c.** we're going to have to pull out all the stops

coupable [kupabl] **1** *adj (personne)* guilty (**de** of); *(action, négligence)* culpable; *(faiblesse)* reprehensible; **se sentir c. (de faire qch)** to feel guilty (about doing sth)
2 *nmf* culprit

coupant, -e [kupɑ̃, -ɑ̃t] *adj* sharp

coupe¹ [kup] *nf* (**a**) *(récipient)* bowl; **c. à champagne** champagne glass; *Fig* **la c. est pleine** that's the limit; *Prov* **il y a loin de la c. aux lèvres** there's many a slip 'twixt cup and lip (**b**) *(trophée)* cup; **la C. du monde de football** the Soccer World Cup; **la c. Davis** the Davis Cup

coupe² [kup] *nf* (**a**) *(action) (du blé)* cutting; *(de tissu)* cutting out; *(d'arbres)* cutting down; **c. (de cheveux)** haircut; **acheter du fromage à la c.** to buy cheese from the fresh cheese counter; **c. sombre** *(dans une forêt)* slight thinning; *(du personnel, des dépenses)* drastic cut (**b**) *(d'un vêtement)* cut (**c**) *(plan)* section (**d**) *(aux cartes)* cut; *Fig* **être sous la c. de qn** to be under sb's thumb; **tomber sous la c. de qn** to fall into sb's clutches

coupé, -e [kupe] **1** *adj* (**a**) *(taillé)* cut; **un costume mal c.** a badly cut suit (**b**) *(au tennis)* **une balle coupée** a slice (**c**) *(castré) (chat)* neutered; **c. sombre** *(dilué)* **c. d'eau** watered down, diluted
2 *nm (voiture)* coupé; **c. sport** sports coupé

coupe-coupe [kupkup] *nm inv* machete

coupe-faim [kupfɛ̃] *nm inv* appetite suppressant

coupe-feu [kupfø] *nm inv* firebreak; *Ordinat* **mur c.** firewall; **porte c.** fire door

coupe-gorge [kupgɔrʒ] *nm inv* dangerous back alley

coupe-légumes [kuplegym] *nm inv* vegetable slicer

coupelle [kupɛl] *nf* (**a**) *(petite coupe)* small dish (**b**) *(de laboratoire)* cupel

coupe-ongles [kupɔ̃gl] *nm inv* nail clippers

coupe-papier [kuppapje] *nm inv* paper knife, letter opener

couper [kupe] **1** *vt* (**a**) *(trancher)* to cut; *(arbre)* to cut down; *(vêtement)* to cut out; **c. qch en morceaux** to cut sth up (into pieces); **c. qch en trois** to cut sth into three; **c. les cheveux à qn** to cut sb's hair; **c. la tête à qn** to cut off sb's head; **c. les cheveux en quatre** to split hairs; **un brouillard à c. au couteau** fog you could cut with a knife; **j'en donnerais ma main** *ou* **ma tête à c.** I'd stake my life on it
(**b**) *(supprimer, raccourcir)* to cut; **c. dans le vif** to take drastic measures
(**c**) *(traverser)* to cut across; **c. la route à qn** to cut in front of sb; **c. à travers champs** to cut across country; **c. par le jardin** to cut through the garden
(**d**) *(séparer)* to divide (**en deux** in two); **être coupé du monde** to be cut off from the outside world
(**e**) *(interrompre) (personne)* to cut in on; *(son)* to turn right down; **c. l'eau** *(pour réparation)* to turn off the water; *(pour non-paiement)* to cut off the water; **c. le courant** *ou* **l'électricité** *(pour réparation)* to switch off the current; *(pour non-paiement)* to cut off the power; **c. le téléphone à qn** to cut off sb's telephone; **nous avons été coupés, la communication a été coupée** we were cut off; **c. le contact** *(d'une voiture)* to switch off the ignition; **c. l'appétit à qn** to spoil sb's appetite; **ces bas me coupent la circulation** these stockings are cutting off my circulation; *Fam* **ça te la coupe!** that's taken the wind out of your sails!
(**f**) *(châtrer) (chat)* to neuter
(**g**) **c. du vin** *(en mélangeant)* to blend wine; *(avec de l'eau)* to water down wine
(**h**) *(paquet de cartes)* to cut; *(prendre avec l'atout)* to trump; **à toi de c.** it's your turn to cut; **c. à carreau** to trump with a diamond
(**i**) *(au tennis) (balle)* to slice
2 *vi (être tranchant)* to be sharp; **le couteau coupe bien** the knife cuts well
3 couper à *vt ind* (**a**) *Fam* **c. à qch** *(se dérober)* to get out of sth (**b**) **c. court à qch** to cut sth short
4 se couper *vpr* (**a**) *(se blesser)* to cut oneself; **se c. le** *ou* **au doigt** to cut one's finger; **se c. les veines** to slash one's wrists (**b**) *(tailler)* **se c. les ongles/les cheveux** to cut one's nails/hair (**c**) *(routes)* to intersect, to cross

(**d**) **se c. de qn** to cut oneself off from sb

couper-coller [kupekɔle] *nm inv Ordinat* cut and paste

couperet [kupRɛ] *nm* (**a**) *(pour la viande)* cleaver (**b**) *(de la guillotine)* blade

couperose [kupRoz] *nf* blotches

couperosé, -e [kupRoze] *adj* blotchy

coupe-vent [kupvã] *nm inv* (**a**) *(dispositif)* windbreak (**b**) *(blouson)* Windbreaker®

couple [kupl] *nm (de personnes)* couple; *(d'animaux)* pair; **vivre en c.** to live together; **un c. sans enfants** a childless couple

couplet [kuplɛ] *nm (de chanson)* verse; *Fam* tirade (**sur** about)

coupole [kupɔl] *nf* dome, cupola

coupon [kupɔ̃] *nm* (**a**) *(ticket)* **c. de réduction** money-off coupon (**b**) *(de tissu)* remnant (**c**) *Fin* **c. d'action** coupon

coupon-réponse *(pl* **coupons-réponse)** [kupɔ̃Repɔ̃s] *nm* reply coupon

coupure [kupyR] *nf* (**a**) *(blessure)* cut (**b**) *(suppression)* cut (**c**) **c. (de courant)** power cut (**d**) *Fig (séparation)* break (**e**) *(pause)* break (**f**) **c. de journal** *ou* **de presse** newspaper *or* press clipping (**g**) *Fin* denomination; **50 000 euros en petites coupures** 50,000 euros in small bills *or* denominations

cour [kuR] *nf* (**a**) *(de maison, de ferme)* yard; *Can* **c. à bois** lumber yard; **c. d'honneur** main courtyard; **c. de récréation** schoolyard; *Fig* **jouer dans la c. des grands** to be up there with the leaders (**b**) *(de souverain)* court; **vivre à la c.** to live at court (**c**) *(tribunal)* court; **Messieurs, la C.!** all rise!; **Haute C.** High Court *(for impeachment of president or ministers)*; **c. d'appel** court of appeal; **c. d'assises** court of assizes; **c. de cassation** ≃ Supreme Court of Appeal; **la C. des comptes** the Audit Office; **la C. internationale de justice** the International Court of Justice; **c. martiale** court martial; **passer en c. martiale (pour qch)** to be court-martialled (for sth); *Can* **la C. suprême** the Supreme Court (**d**) **faire la c. à qn** to court sb

courage [kuraʒ] *nm* courage, bravery; **avec c.** bravely, courageously; **perdre c.** to lose heart; **prendre son c. à deux mains** to pluck up courage; **avoir/se sentir le c. de ses opinions** to have the courage of one's convictions; **avoir/se sentir le c. de faire qch** to be/to feel up to doing sth; **bon c.!** good luck!

courageusement [kuraʒøzmã] *adv (bravement)* courageously, bravely; *(résolument)* with a will

courageux, -euse [kuraʒø, -øz] *adj* (**a**) *(brave)* courageous, brave (**b**) *(énergique)* energetic

courailler [kuRaje] *vi Can Fam* to chase women

courailleur [kuRajœR] *nm Can Fam* womanizer

couramment [kuRamã] *adv* (**a**) *(parler)* fluently (**b**) *(généralement)* commonly; **ce mot s'emploie c.** this word is in common use

courant, -e [kuRã, -ãt] **1** *adj* (**a**) *(commun)* common; **dans la vie courante** in everyday life (**b**) *(en cours)* current; **le 5 c.** the 5th inst.
2 *nm* (**a**) *(dans une rivière)* current; *Fig (tendance)* trend; **suivre/remonter le c.** to go with/against the current; **c. d'air** draft; **c. de pensée** way of thinking (**b**) *Élec* **c. (électrique)** electric current; **c. continu/alternatif** direct/alternating current; *Fig* **le c. ne passe pas** we're/they're/you're not on the same wavelength (**c**) *(durée)* **dans le c. de** in the course of; **c. janvier** during the month of January (**d**) **être au c. (de qch)** to know (about sth); **mettre qn au c. (de qch)** to tell sb (about sth); **tenir qn au c. (de qch)** to keep sb up to date (on sth)
3 *nf* **courante** *Fam* **avoir la courante** to have the runs

courbatu, -e [kurbaty] *adj* aching (all over)

courbature [kurbatyr] *nf* ache; **avoir des courbatures** to be aching (all over)

courbaturé, -e [kurbatyre] *adj* aching (all over)

courbe [kurb] **1** *adj* curved

2 *nf* curve; *(graphe)* graph; **c. de niveau** contour (line); **c. des prix/des salaires** price/salary curve; **c. de température** temperature curve

courber [kurbe] **1** *vt* to bend; **c. la tête** to bow *or* to bend one's head; *Fig* **c. l'échine** to submit

2 *vi* to bend

3 se courber *vpr (personne)* to bend down, to stoop; **se c. en deux** to bend double

courbette [kurbɛt] *nf (salut)* bow; *Fig* **faire des courbettes (à qn)** to bow and scrape (to sb)

courbure [kurbyr] *nf (d'une surface, d'une ligne)* curvature; *(d'un morceau de bois, du dos)* curve

coureur, -euse [kurœr, -øz] **1** *nm,f (à pied)* runner; **c. (automobile)** (racing) driver; **c. (cycliste)** (racing) cyclist

2 *adj (homme)* womanizing; *(femme)* manhunting

3 *nm* **c. (de jupons)** womanizer

4 *nf* **coureuse** *(dévergondée)* manhunter

courge [kurʒ] *nf (a) (plante)* squash **(b)** *Fam (imbécile)* dummy

courgette [kurʒɛt] *nf* zucchini

courir [22] [kurir] **1** *vi (a) (personne)* to run; **monter/descendre la colline en courant** to run up/down the hill; **arriver en courant** to come running (up); **je cours le prévenir** I'll run and warn him; **c. après qn/qch** to run after sb/sth; **c. après la gloire** to chase after glory; **c. à sa perte** to be heading for disaster; **l'assassin court toujours** the murderer is still at large; *Fam* **tu peux toujours c.!** not a chance!; *Fam* **laisse c.!** forget it!; *Prov* **rien ne sert de c., il faut partir à point** slow and steady wins the race

(b) *(se propager)* **le bruit court que…** rumor has it that…; **faire c. un bruit** to spread a rumor

(c) *(eau, ruisseau)* to rush

(d) *(participer à une course) (à pied)* to run; *(automobile)* to drive; *(cycliste)* to ride

2 *vt (a) (tenter)* **c. un risque** to run a risk

(b) *Sport* **c. le 100 mètres** to run the 100 meters

(c) *(parcourir, fréquenter)* **c. le monde** to roam the world; **c. les théâtres** to go to the theater all the time; **ça ne court pas les rues** *(personnes)* they're few and far between; *(objets)* you don't see that every day

(d) *(chasser)* **c. les filles** to chase women; *Fig* **c. deux lièvres à la fois** to have two irons in the fire

3 *v impersonnel* **il court des bruits sur lui** there are rumors going around about him

courlis [kurli] *nm* curlew

couronne [kurɔn] *nf (a) (de fleurs, de lauriers)* wreath; **c. funéraire** *ou* **mortuaire** (funeral) wreath **(b)** *(de souverain)* crown; *(de noble)* coronet; **la C. d'Angleterre** the English Crown **(c)** *(monnaie)* crown **(d)** *(pain)* ring-shaped loaf; *(de dent)* crown; **se faire poser une c.** to have a tooth capped

couronnement [kurɔnmɑ̃] *nm (de souverain)* coronation; *Fig (réussite)* crowning achievement

couronner [kurɔne] *vt (a) (sacrer)* to crown; *Fig* **mes efforts furent couronnés de succès** my efforts were crowned with success; **et pour c. le tout…** and to crown it all… **(b)** *(dent)* to cap

courra *etc. voir* **courir**

courre [kur] *voir* **chasse**

courriel [kurjɛl] *nm Can Ordinat* e-mail

courrier [kurje] *nm (a) (lettres)* mail; **c. électronique** electronic mail, e-mail; *Fam* **c. escargot** snail mail; **c. interne** internal mail **(b)** *Journ* **c. du cœur** advice column; **c. des lecteurs** letters to the Editor **(c)** *Vieilli (messager)* courier

courroie [kurwa] *nf (a) (de cuir, de toile)* strap **(b)** *Méc* belt; **c. de transmission** driving belt; **c. de ventilateur** fanbelt

courroucé, -e [kuruse] *adj Litt* incensed

courroux [kuru] *nm Litt* ire, wrath

cours[1] [kur] *nm (a) (leçon)* Univ lecture; *Scol* lesson; *(ensemble des leçons)* course; **aller en c.** *Univ* to go to class; *Scol* to go to school; **prendre** *ou* **suivre un c.** to take a course; **donner des c.** *Univ* to give lectures; *Scol* to give classes; **c. par correspondance** correspondence course; **c. intensif** crash course; **c. magistral** lecture; **c. particulier** private lesson; **c. du soir** evening class

(b) *(classe)* **c. élémentaire** = second and third years of primary school; **c. moyen** = fourth and fifth years of primary school; **c. préparatoire** = first year of primary school

(c) *(de rivière, d'un astre)* course; **suivre le c. de ses pensées** to follow one's train of thought; **donner libre c. à qch** to give free rein to sth; **c. d'eau** waterway

(d) *(évolution)* course; **suivre son c.** to run its course; **en c.** *(affaires)* in hand; *(travaux)* in progress; *(année)* current; **en c. de route** on the way; **au c. de qch** in the course of sth

(e) *(d'une monnaie)* currency; **avoir c.** *(monnaie)* to be legal tender; *(pratique)* to be current

(f) *Fin (d'une action)* price; *(de devises)* rate; **c. des changes** exchange rate; **c. pivot** central rate

cours[2] [kur] *voir* **courir**

course [kurs] *nf (a) Sport (épreuve)* race; *(discipline)* racing; **faire la c. avec qn** to race with sb; **les courses (de chevaux)** the races; *Fam* **ça va encore être la c.** it's going to be another mad rush; **la c. aux armements** the arms race; **c. automobile** motor race; *(discipline)* motor racing; **c. de chevaux** horse race; *Sport & Fig* **c. contre la montre** race against the clock; **c. cycliste** cycling race; **c. de haies** *(en athlétisme)* hurdles; *(course de chevaux)* steeplechase; **c. d'obstacles** steeplechase; **c. d'orientation** orienteering; **c. à pied** race; *(discipline)* running; **c. de taureaux** *(corrida)* bullfight

(b) *(action de courir)* running

(c) *(achat)* **faire une c.** to go and buy something; **courses** shopping; **faire des courses** to go shopping

(d) *(trajet en taxi)* journey; *(prix)* fare

(e) *(de planète, de projectile)* course

(f) *Suisse (trajet)* trip *(by train or boat)*; *(excursion)* excursion

courser [kurse] *vt Fam* to chase after

coursier, -ère [kursje, -ɛr] *nm,f* messenger; *(en moto)* motorcycle courier; **envoyer qch par c.** to send sth by courier

coursive [kursiv] *nf Naut* gangway

court[1], **-e** [kur, kurt] **1** *adj* short; *Fam* **15 euros, c'est un peu c.** 15 euros, that's not very much

2 *adv* short; **pour faire c.** to cut a long story short; **on l'appelle Charles tout c.** people just call him Charles; **prendre qn de c.** *(en lui laissant peu de temps)* to give sb short notice; *(sans le prévenir)* to catch sb unawares; **à c. de** short of

court[2] [kur] *nm* **c. (de tennis)** (tennis) court

court[3] [kur] *voir* **courir**

court-bouillon *(pl* **courts-bouillons)** [kurbujɔ̃] *nm* court-bouillon

court-circuit *(pl* **courts-circuits)** [kursirkɥi] *nm* short circuit

court-circuiter [kursirkɥite] *vt Élec & Fam Fig* to short-circuit

courtier, -ère [kurtje, -ɛr] *nm,f* broker; **c. d'assurances** insurance broker

courtisan [kurtizɑ̃] *nm (a) Hist* courtier **(b)** *Péj (flatteur)* sycophant

courtisane [kurtizan] *nf Litt* courtesan

courtiser [kurtize] *vt (a) (femme)* to court **(b)** *(flatter)* to fawn on

courtois, -e [kurtwa, -az] *adj (poli)* courteous (**envers** *ou* **avec** towards)

courtoisement [kurtwazmɑ̃] *adv* courteously

courtoisie [kurtwazi] *nf* courtesy (**envers** towards)

court-vêtu, -e (*mpl* **court-vêtus**, *fpl* **court-vêtues**) [kurvety] *adj* in a short skirt; **être c.** to be wearing a short skirt

couru, -e [kury] *adj* (**a**) (*lieu, spectacle*) popular (**b**) *Fam* **c'est c. (d'avance)** it's a sure thing

cousais *etc. voir* **coudre**

couscous [kuskus] *nm* couscous

cousin¹, -e [kuzɛ̃, -in] *nm,f* cousin; **c. germain** first cousin

cousin² [kuzɛ̃, -in] *nm* (*insecte*) mosquito

coussin [kusɛ̃] *nm* (**a**) (*de siège*) cushion; *Belg & Suisse* (*oreiller*) pillow (**b**) **c. d'air** air cushion

coussinet [kusinɛ] *nm* (**a**) (*coussin*) small cushion (**b**) (*d'animal*) pad

cousu, -e [kuzy] **1** *adj* sewn; **c. (à la) main** hand-sewn; *Fam Fig* **c'est du c. main** it's first-rate; **une histoire cousue de fil blanc** a blatant lie
    2 *pp voir* **coudre**

coût [ku] *nm aussi Fig* cost; **le c. de la vie** the cost of living

coûtant [kutɑ̃] *adj m voir* **prix**

couteau, -x [kuto] *nm* (**a**) (*ustensile*) knife; **être à couteaux tirés (avec qn)** to be at daggers drawn (with sb); *Fig* **avoir le c. sous la gorge** to have a gun to one's head; **c. de cuisine** kitchen knife; **c. à fromage** cheese-knife; **c. à pain** bread-knife; **c. suisse** Swiss army knife (**b**) (*mollusque*) razor shell (**c**) *Fig* **deuxième** *ou* **second c.** (*en politique, dans la Mafia*) minion

couteau-scie (*pl* **couteaux-scies**) [kutosi] *nm* serrated knife

coutelas [kutlɑ] *nm* large knife

coûter [kute] *vi* to cost; **combien ça coûte?** how much is it?, how much does it cost?; **ça coûte 100 euros** it costs 100 euros, it's 100 euros; **c. les yeux de la tête** to cost a fortune; **ça ne coûte rien d'essayer** there's no harm in trying; **c. cher** to cost a lot, to be expensive; **cela vous coûtera cher** it'll cost you a lot; *Fig* you'll pay for that; **c. la vie à qn** to cost sb his/her life; **ça m'a beaucoup coûté** it was very painful for me; **coûte que coûte** at all costs

coûteux, -euse [kutø, -øz] *adj* costly, expensive; **peu c.** inexpensive

coutume [kutym] *nf* (**a**) (*habitude*) custom; **avoir c. de faire qch** to be accustomed to doing sth; **plus aimable que de c.** nicer than usual; **comme de c.** as usual; **une fois n'est pas c.** it won't hurt for once (**b**) (*tradition*) custom

coutumier, -ère [kutymje, -ɛr] *adj* (**a**) (*habituel*) customary, usual (**b**) (*personne*) **il est c. du fait** it's not the first time he's done that (**c**) *Jur* **droit c.** common law

couture [kutyr] **1** *nf* (**a**) (*de vêtement*) seam; *Fig* **examiner qn/qch sous toutes les coutures** to examine sb/sth from every angle (**b**) (*activité*) sewing, needlework; **faire de la c.** to sew
    2 *adj inv* designer (*avant n*)

couturier [kutyrje] *nm* fashion designer, couturier; **grand c.** big fashion designer

couturière [kutyrjɛr] *nf* dressmaker

couvaison [kuvɛzɔ̃] *nf* incubation

couvée [kuve] *nf* (**a**) (*œufs*) clutch (**b**) (*d'oisillons, d'enfants*) brood

couvent [kuvɑ̃] *nm* (**a**) (*communauté religieuse*) (*de femmes*) convent; (*d'hommes*) monastery (**b**) (*pensionnat*) convent school

couver [kuve] **1** *vt* (**a**) (*œufs*) to sit on; *Fig* (*personne*) to mollycoddle; **c. qn des yeux** to look fondly at sb (**b**) (*maladie*) to be coming down with
    2 *vi* (*poule*) to brood; (*feu, passion*) to smolder; (*émeute*) to be brewing

couvercle [kuvɛrkl] *nm* lid; (*qui se visse*) cap, top

couvert¹, -e [kuvɛr, -ɛrt] **1** *adj* (**a**) (*allée, marché*) covered; (*piscine*) indoor; (*ciel*) overcast (**b**) (*jonché, plein*) **c. de** covered with

or in (**c**) (*habillé*) covered up; **chaudement** *ou* **bien c.** warmly dressed (**d**) (*ciel*) overcast
    2 *pp voir* **couvrir**

couvert² [kuvɛr] *nm* (**a**) (*ustensiles*) **un c. en argent** a silver knife, fork and spoon; **couverts** cutlery (**b**) (*pour chaque convive*) place setting; **mettre le c.** to set the table; **mettre trois couverts** to set the table for three; **mets deux couverts de plus** set two extra places (**c**) **sous le c. de** (*sous l'apparence de*) under the cover of

couverture [kuvɛrtyr] *nf* (**a**) (*de lit*) blanket; *Fig* **tirer la c. à soi** to take all the credit; **c. chauffante** electric blanket (**b**) (*d'un livre, d'un magazine, d'un cahier*) cover; **en c.** on the cover (**c**) (*protection*) **c. sociale** social security cover (**d**) (*d'un bâtiment*) roofing (**e**) (*d'un événement médiatique*) coverage

couveuse [kuvøz] *nf* (**a**) (*pour nouveau-nés*) incubator (**b**) (*poule*) brooder

couvre-chef (*pl* **couvre-chefs**) [kuvrəʃɛf] *nm Hum* hat

couvre-feu (*pl* **couvre-feux**) [kuvrəfø] *nm Mil* curfew

couvre-lit (*pl* **couvre-lits**) [kuvrəli] *nm* bedspread

couvre-pied(s) (*pl* **couvre-pieds**) [kuvrəpje] *nm* quilt

couvreur [kuvrœr] *nm* roofer

couvrir [52] [kuvrir] **1** *vt* (**a**) (*casserole, meuble, livre*) to cover (**de** with) (**b**) **c. qn de** (*cadeaux, honneurs, compliments*) to shower sb with (**c**) (*protéger, justifier*) to cover; **être couvert par ses supérieurs** to be acting with the authority of one's superiors (**d**) (*parcourir, englober*) & *Journ* to cover (**e**) (*bruit, voix*) to drown (out) (**f**) (*sujet: assurance*) to cover (**g**) *Zool* (*femelle*) to cover
    2 se couvrir *vpr* (**a**) (*pour sortir*) to wrap up; (*pour cacher sa nudité*) to cover oneself; (*mettre son chapeau*) to put on one's hat (**b**) (*ciel*) to cloud over; **le temps** *ou* **ça se couvre** it's clouding over (**c**) **se c. de** (*honte, ridicule*) to cover oneself with; **se c. de feuilles** (*arbre*) to come into leaf; **se c. de boutons** (*visage*) to come out or to become covered in pimples

covoiturage [kɔvwatyraʒ] *nm* car pooling (*for commuting to the workplace*)

cow-boy (*pl* **cow-boys**) [kɔbɔj] *nm* cowboy

coyote [kɔjɔt] *nm* coyote

CP [sepe] *nm* (*abrév* **cours préparatoire**) = first year of primary school

CPAM [sepeaɛm] *nf* (*abrév* **caisse primaire d'assurance maladie**) = French government department dealing with health insurance

cpp *Ordinat* (*abrév* **caractères par pouce**) cpi

cps *Ordinat* (*abrév* **caractères par seconde**) cps

crabe [krab] *nm* crab; **marcher en c.** to walk sideways

crac [krak] **1** *exclam* (*bruit de cassure*) crack!; *Fam* **et c., elle est tombée malade!** and what do you know, she got sick!
    2 *nm* crack

crachat [kraʃa] *nm* gob of spit; **crachats** spit

craché, -e [kraʃe] *adj Fam* **c'est sa mère tout c., c'est le portrait (tout) c. de sa mère** he's the spitting image of his mother; **c'est lui tout c.!** that's just like him!

cracher [kraʃe] **1** *vi* (**a**) (*personne*) to spit; **c. sur qn** to spit at sb; *Fam Fig* **ne pas c. sur qch** not to say no to sth; *Fam Fig* **c. dans la soupe** to bite the hand that feeds one (**b**) (*stylo*) to splutter (**c**) (*haut-parleur, téléphone, radio*) to crackle
    2 *vt* (**a**) (*chewing-gum, nourriture*) to spit out; **c. du sang** to spit blood (**b**) (*fumée*) to belch out (**c**) *très Fam* (*somme d'argent*) to cough up

cracheur, -euse [kraʃœr, -øz] *nm,f* **c. de feu** fire-eater

crachin [kraʃɛ̃] *nm* (fine) drizzle

crachoir [kraʃwar] *nm* spittoon; *Fam Fig* **tenir le c.** to monopolize the conversation; *Fam Fig* **tenir le c. à qn** to listen to sb rambling on and on

crachoter [kraʃɔte] *vi* (*feu*) to splutter; (*radio, téléphone*) to crackle

crack [krak] *nm* (**a**) *Fam (personne)* ace (**en** at) (**b**) *(drogue)* crack

cracker [krakœr] *nm* cracker

Cracovie [krakɔvi] *n* Cracow

cracra [krakra] *adj inv Fam* filthy

crade [krad], **cradingue** [kradɛ̃g], **crado** [krado] *adj Fam* filthy

craie [krɛ] *nf (matière)* chalk; *(bâtonnet)* stick of chalk

craignais *etc. voir* **craindre**

craignos [krɛɲos] *adj Fam (laid)* hideous; *(louche)* shady

craindre [23] [krɛ̃dr] **1** *vt* (**a**) *(redouter)* to fear, to be afraid of; **ne craignez rien!** *(n'ayez pas peur)* don't be frightened!; *(ne vous inquiétez pas)* don't worry!; **je crains qu'il (ne) soit parti** I'm afraid he's left; **c. de faire qch** to be afraid of doing sth (**b**) *(ne pas supporter)* **ces plantes craignent le gel** these plants don't like frost; **craint l'humidité/la chaleur** *(sur emballage)* keep dry/cool
2 *vi Fam* **ça craint!** *(c'est ennuyeux)* what a pain!; *(c'est très laid)* it's hideous!; *(c'est louche)* it's shady!

craint, -e¹ *voir* **craindre**

crainte² [krɛ̃t] *nf* fear; **de c. de tomber** for fear of falling; **de c. qu'on ne l'entende** for fear of being overheard; **soyez sans c., n'ayez c.** have no fear

craintif, -ive [krɛ̃tif, -iv] *adj* timid

cramer [krame] *Fam* **1** *vi & vt* to burn
2 se cramer *vpr* to burn oneself; **se c. les doigts** to burn one's fingers

cramoisi, -e [kramwazi] *adj* crimson

crampe [krɑ̃p] *nf* cramp; **j'ai une c. au pied** I've got a cramp in my foot; **crampes d'estomac** stomach cramps

crampon [krɑ̃pɔ̃] *nm* (**a**) *(de chaussure de sport)* cleat; *(pour alpinisme)* crampon; **crampons** *(chaussures)* boots with cleats (**b**) *Constr* cramp (iron) (**c**) *Fam (personne)* leech

cramponner [krɑ̃pɔne] **se cramponner** *vpr* to hold on; **se c. à** to hold on to; *Fig (vie, espoir)* to cling to; *(fonction)* to hang on to

cran [krɑ̃] *nm* (**a**) *(entaille)* notch; *(de ceinture)* hole; **serrer sa ceinture d'un c.** to take one's belt in a notch; **c. de sûreté** *ou* **d'arrêt** safety catch; **(couteau à) c. d'arrêt** switchblade (**b**) *Fig (degré)* **avancer/reculer d'un c.** to go up/to come down a notch (**c**) *Fam* **être à c.** to be wound up (**d**) *Fam (courage)* guts; **avoir du c.** to have guts (**e**) *(dans les cheveux)* crimp

crâne [krɑn] *nm* skull, *Spéc* cranium; *Fam* **avoir mal au c.** to have a headache; *Fam* **mets-toi ça dans le c.!** get that into your skull!

crâner [krɑne] *vi Fam* to swagger, to show off

crâneur, -euse [krɑnœr, -øz] *Fam* **1** *adj* swaggering; **être c.** to be a show-off
2 *nm,f* show-off

crânien, -enne [krɑnjɛ̃, -ɛn] *adj Anat* cranial

crapahuter [krapayte] *vi Fam* (**a**) *(marcher)* to traipse about (**b**) *Mil (soldat)* to trudge along

crapaud [krapo] *nm* (**a**) *(animal)* toad (**b**) *(défaut)* flaw

crapule [krapyl] *nf* scoundrel, villain

crapuleux, -euse [krapylø, -øz] *adj voir* **crime**

craquant, -e [krakɑ̃, -ɑ̃t] *adj Fam (personne)* gorgeous

craque [krak] *nf Fam (mensonge)* fib, lie

craqueler [42] [krakle] **1** *vt* to crack
2 se craqueler *vpr* to crack

craquement [krakmɑ̃] *nm (de branche)* crack; *(d'escalier, de plancher)* creak; **des craquements** cracking/creaking

craquer [krake] **1** *vi* (**a**) *(branche)* to crack; *(escalier, plancher)* to creak; **faire c. ses doigts** to crack one's fingers (**b**) *(se déchirer)* to rip (**c**) *(se casser)* to snap (**c**) *(perdre le contrôle de soi)* to crack up (**d**) *Fam (succomber)* **c. pour qn** to fall for sb; **ce mec me fait c.** I'm crazy about this guy
2 *vt* (**a**) *(allumette)* to strike (**b**) *(déchirer)* to rip

crasse [kras] **1** *adj (ignorance)* crass
2 *nf* (**a**) *(saleté)* filth (**b**) *Fam (mauvais tour)* dirty trick; **faire une c. à qn** to play a dirty trick on sb

crasseux, -euse [krasø, -øz] *adj* filthy

cratère [kratɛr] *nm* crater

cravache [kravaʃ] *nf (riding)* crop; *Fig* **mener qn à la c.** to rule sb with a rod of iron

cravacher [kravaʃe] **1** *vt (cheval)* to use the crop on
2 *vi Fam (travailler vite)* to work like crazy

cravate [kravat] *nf (neck)*tie; *Fam* **s'en jeter un derrière la c.** to knock back a drink

crawl [krol] *nm* crawl; **nager le c.** to do the crawl

crayeux, -euse [krɛjø, -øz] *adj (matière, teint)* chalky

crayon [krɛjɔ̃] *nm* (**a**) *(pour écrire)* pencil; **écrire au c.** to write in pencil; **c. de couleur** pencil-crayon; **c. gras** soft lead pencil; *Ordinat* **c. lumineux** *ou* **optique** light pen (**b**) *(bâton)* stick; **c. à lèvres** lip pencil (**c**) *(œuvre)* pencil-drawing

créance [kreɑ̃s] *nf* debt; **c. douteuse** bad debt

créancier, -ère [kreɑ̃sje, -ɛr] *nm,f* creditor

créateur, -trice [kreatœr, -tris] **1** *adj (génie)* creative; **industrie créatrice d'emplois** job-creating industry
2 *nm,f* creator; **c. (de mode)** *(fashion)* designer; *Rel* **le C.** the Creator

créatif, -ive [kreatif, -iv] *adj* creative

création [kreasjɔ̃] *nf* (**a**) *(fait de créer)* creation; **c. d'emplois** job creation (**b**) *(produit)* new product; *(d'un couturier)* creation (**c**) *(univers)* **la c.** creation (**d**) *(première représentation)* *(d'une pièce)* first production; *(d'un rôle)* creation; *(d'une œuvre musicale)* first performance

créativité [kreativite] *nf* creativity

créature [kreatyr] *nf* (**a**) *(être vivant)* creature; *Hum* **une c. de rêve** *(femme)* a magnificent woman (**b**) *Péj (protégé)* creature

crécelle [kresɛl] *nf* rattle; **une voix de c.** a rasping voice

crèche [krɛʃ] *nf* (**a**) *(garderie)* day-care center (**b**) *(de Noël)* crèche

---

Crèche

State-subsidized care for children under three years of age for working families is well established in France, although this is subject to the availability of places.

---

crécher [34] [kreʃe] *vi Fam (habiter)* to live; *(temporairement)* to crash

crédibilité [kredibilite] *nf* credibility

crédible [kredibl] *adj* credible

crédit [kredi] *nm* (**a**) *(prêt)* credit; **à c.** on credit; **faire c. à qn** to give sb credit; **la maison ne fait pas c.** *(sur panneau)* we do not give credit; **c. à la consommation** consumer credit; **c. gratuit** interest-free credit; **c. immobilier** home loan, mortgage (**b**) *(en comptabilité)* credit side; **porter une somme au c. de qn** to credit sb with a sum (**c**) **crédits** *(somme d'argent)* funds (**d**) *Litt (influence)* credit

crédit-bail *(pl* **crédits-bails**) [kredibaj] *nm* leasing

créditer [kredite] *vt* (**a**) *Fin (compte)* to credit (**de** with) (**b**) *Fig* **c. qn de qch** to give sb credit for sth

créditeur, -trice [kreditœr, -tris] *adj (solde, compte)* credit; **être c.** to be in credit

crédit-relais *(pl* **crédits-relais**) [kredirəlɛ] *nm* bridging loan

credo [kredo] *nm inv* credo, creed

crédule [kredyl] *adj* credulous

crédulité [kredylite] *nf* credulity

créer [24] [kree] **1** *vt* (**a**) *(emplois, poste)* to create; *(entreprise)* to set up (**b**) *(œuvre, nouveau produit, vêtement)* to create (**c**) *(difficultés, problème)* to create (**à** for) (**d**) *(interpréter pour la première fois)* *(rôle)* to create; *(pièce de théâtre)* to produce for the first time; *(œuvre musicale)* to perform for the first time
2 se créer *vpr* (**a**) *(être créé)* to be created (**b**) *(pour soi-même)*

se c. une clientèle to build up a clientèle; se c. des problè-mes to create problems for oneself

crémaillère [kremajɛr] nf (dans la cheminée) trammel (hook); pendre la c. to have a housewarming (party)

crémant [kremɑ̃] nm slightly sparkling wine

crémation [kremasjɔ̃] nf cremation

crématoire [krematwar] adj voir **four**

crématorium [krematɔrjɔm] nm crematory

crème [krɛm] 1 nf (a) (du lait, dessert) cream; Fig c'est la c. des hommes he's the best of men; c. anglaise = light custard sauce; c. au beurre = butter, sugar, eggs and cream, baked together and used as a cake filling; c. brûlée crème brûlée; c. (au) caramel caramel custard, crème caramel; c. Chantilly whipped cream (with sugar added); c. fouettée whipped cream; c. fraîche crème fraîche; c. glacée ice-cream; c. pâtissière confectioner's custard; c. renversée crème caramel (turned out of its mold) (b) (produit cosmétique) cream; c. anti-rides anti-wrinkle cream; c. hydratante moisturizing cream; c. à raser shaving cream; c. solaire sun cream, sun-tan cream (c) (liqueur) c. de menthe crème de menthe; c. de cassis blackcurrant liqueur
2 nm Fam un grand c. ≃ a latte
3 adj inv cream(-colored)

crémerie [krɛmri] nf (magasin) dairy; Fam changer de c. to go somewhere else, to move on

crémeux, -euse [kremø, -øz] adj creamy

crémier, -ère [kremje, -ɛr] nm,f dairyman, f dairywoman

crémone [kremɔn] nf espagnolette

créneau, -x [kreno] nm (a) (de rempart) crenel; Fig monter au c. to step into the breach (b) (manœuvre) faire un c. to reverse into a (parking) space (c) Com niche (d) (dans un programme, un emploi du temps) slot; c. horaire time slot

crénelé, -e [krenle] adj crenelated

créole [kreɔl] 1 adj Creole
2 nm (langue) Creole
3 nmf C. Creole
4 nfpl créoles (boucles d'oreille) hoop earrings

crêpe [krɛp] 1 nf pancake
2 nm (a) (tissu) crêpe (b) (caoutchouc) crêpe (rubber); semelles (de) c. crêpe soles

crêper [krepe] 1 vt (a) (cheveux) to backcomb (b) (tissu) to crimp
2 se crêper vpr Fam Fig se c. le chignon to have a cat-fight

crêperie [krɛpri] nf pancake restaurant

crépi, -e [krepi] adj & nm Constr roughcast

crépir [krepir] vt Constr to roughcast

crépitement [krepitmɑ̃] nm (du feu) crackling

crépiter [krepite] vi (feu) to crackle

crépon [krepɔ̃] nm (papier) crêpe paper

crépu, -e [krepy] adj frizzy

crépuscule [krepyskyl] nm aussi Fig twilight; au c. at twilight

crescendo [kreʃɛndo] 1 adv crescendo; aller c. to get louder and louder; Fig (difficultés) to get worse and worse
2 nm crescendo

cresson [kresɔ̃, krɔsɔ̃] nm watercress

crétacé, -e [kretase] Géol 1 adj Cretaceous
2 nm le C. the Cretaceous period

Crète [krɛt] nf la C. Crete

crête [krɛt] nf (a) (d'oiseau) crest; (de coq) comb (b) (de montagne, de vague, de toit) crest

crétin, -e [kretɛ̃, -in] nm,f Fam cretin

crétois, -e [kretwa, -az] 1 adj Cretan
2 nm,f C., Crétoise Cretan

cretonne [krətɔn] nf cretonne

cretons [krətɔ̃] nmpl Can potted pork

creuser [krøze] 1 vt (a) (trou, tranchée, puits) to dig; Fig c. l'écart entre to widen the gap between; Fig c. un abîme entre deux personnes to create a gulf between two people (b) (évider) to hollow (out); c. la terre to dig (c) (problème, question) to look into (d) (donner faim à) c. qn to give sb an appetite; le grand air, ça creuse the fresh air gives you an appetite (e) (cambrer) c. les reins to arch one's back (f) (amaigrir) il avait le visage creusé par la fatigue/la maladie his face was gaunt with exhaustion/illness
2 vi to dig
3 se creuser vpr (a) (s'agrandir) (écart) to widen (b) se c. (la tête ou la cervelle) (pour faire qch) to rack one's brains (to do sth) (c) (visage) to grow hollow

creuset [krøze] nm (a) Chim crucible (b) Fig melting pot

creux, -euse [krø, krøz] 1 adj (a) (vide) (arbre, mur, dent) hollow; (chemin) sunken; Fig avoir le ventre c. to be hungry (b) (période, heures) off-peak (c) (joues) hollow; (visage) gaunt (d) Péj (débat, discours, personne) hollow
2 adv sonner c. to sound hollow; Fig to sound empty
3 nm (a) (de la main, dans le sol, sur une route) hollow; le c. des reins the small of the back (b) (d'une vague, d'une courbe) trough; Fig être au c. de la vague to have hit rock bottom (c) Fam avoir un (petit) c. to be feeling (a bit) snackish

crevaison [krəvɛzɔ̃] nf (d'un pneu) flat (tire)

crevant, -e [krəvɑ̃, -ɑ̃t] adj Fam (a) (fatigant) exhausting (b) (drôle) priceless

crevasse [krəvas] nf (a) (sur la peau) crack; avoir des crevasses aux mains to have chapped hands (b) (dans un mur, le sol) crack; (dans un glacier) crevasse

crevé, -e [krəve] adj (a) (éclaté) (ballon, pneu) burst (b) Fam (fatigué) dead beat (c) très Fam (mort) dead

crève [krɛv] nf très Fam avoir la c. (gros rhume) to have a stinking cold; attraper la c. to catch one's death of cold

crève-cœur [krɛvkœr] nm inv heartbreak; c'est un c. de partir it's heartbreaking to leave

crève-la-faim [krɛvlafɛ̃] nm inv Fam down-and-out

crever [46] [krəve] 1 vt (a) (ballon, sac, pneu) to burst; c. un œil à qn to put sb's eye out; ça me crève le cœur I'm heart-broken about it; Fig ça crève les yeux it sticks out a mile; Fig c. l'écran to have great screen presence (b) Fam (épuiser) to wear out (c) très Fam c. la dalle to be totally starving
2 vi (a) (éclater) to burst; mon pneu a ou Fam j'ai crevé I have a flat (tire); c. de (jalousie, orgueil) to be bursting with (b) (mourir) (bête, plante) to die; très Fam (personne) to kick the bucket, to buy the farm; Fam il fait une chaleur à c. it's boiling hot; Fam c. d'envie de faire qch to be dying to do sth; Fam c. de faim (mourir) to starve to death; (avoir faim) to be starving; Fam c. de soif to be parched; Fam c. de froid/de chaud to be freezing/boiling; Fam c. de rire to split one's sides laughing; Fam qu'il crève! he can go to hell!; Fam plu-tôt c.! I'd rather die!
3 se crever vpr Fam to wear oneself out

crevette [krəvɛt] nf c. (rose) prawn; c. grise shrimp

cri [kri] nm (a) (d'une personne) cry, shout; (perçant) scream; j'ai entendu des cris I heard shouting; Fig pousser les hauts cris to kick up a fuss; c'est le c. du cœur it's a cry from the heart; Mil c. de guerre war cry (b) (d'un animal, d'un oiseau) cry

criailler [kriaje] vi (a) (crier sans arrêt) to bawl (b) (faisan, pintade) to cry; (oie) to honk

criant, -e [krijɑ̃, -ɑ̃t] adj (erreur) glaring; (preuve, contraste) striking; (vérité) obvious; (abus, injustice) blatant; c. de vérité (témoignage, reportage) obviously true

criard, -e [krijar, -ard] adj (a) (aigu) (voix) shrill (b) (couleur) loud (c) (enfant) noisy

crible [kribl] nm sieve; Fig passer qch au c. to go through sth with a fine-tooth comb

criblé, -e [krible] *adj* **c. de** *(trous, balles)* riddled with; *Fig* **être c. de dettes** to be up to one's eyes in debt

cric [krik] *nm* jack

cricket [krikɛt] *nm* cricket

criée [krije] *nf (vente)* (sale by) auction; *(salle)* auction room; *(dehors)* auction area; **à la c.** by auction

crier [66] [krije] **1** *vi* **(a)** *(personne)* to yell, to cry (out); *(fort)* to scream; *(parler très fort)* to shout; **c. de douleur** to cry out *or* to scream with pain; **c. contre** *ou* **après qn** to yell at sb; **c. au secours** to yell for help; **c. au scandale** to protest, to be up in arms; **c. qch sur les toits** to shout sth from the rooftops **(b)** *(souris)* to squeak; *(oiseau)* to call
2 *vt (ordre, injures)* to shout, to yell (**à** at); **c. à qn de faire qch** to shout to sb to do sth; **c. son innocence** to protest one's innocence

crime [krim] *nm* **(a)** *Jur & Fig* crime; **ce n'est pas un c.!** it's not a crime!; **c. crapuleux** crime committed for financial gain; **c. d'État** treason; **crimes de guerre** war crimes; **c. contre l'humanité** crime against humanity **(b)** *(meurtre)* murder; **c. passionnel** crime of passion

criminalité [kriminalite] *nf* crime

criminel, -elle [kriminɛl] **1** *adj (acte)* criminal; *Fam* **ce serait c. de la jeter** it would be criminal to throw it away
2 *nm,f* **(a)** *(malfaiteur)* criminal; **c. de guerre** war criminal **(b)** *(assassin)* murderer

criminologie [kriminɔlɔʒi] *nf* criminology

crin [krɛ̃] *nm* horsehair; *Fig* **à tout c., à tous crins** out-and-out

crinière [krinjɛr] *nf aussi Fig* mane

crinoline [krinɔlin] *nf* crinoline

crique [krik] *nf* creek

criquet [krikɛ] *nm* locust

crise [kriz] *nf* **(a)** *(marasme, période d'instabilité)* crisis; **c. de l'énergie** energy crisis; **c. du logement** housing crisis *or* shortage **(b)** *(d'une maladie)* attack; **c. cardiaque** heart attack; **c. de foie** bilious attack **(c)** *(accès)* **c. de colère** fit of anger; **c. de conscience** attack of conscience; **c. de larmes** crying fit; **c. de nerfs** attack of nerves, fit of hysterics; *Fam* **la c. (de rire)!** what a hoot! **(d)** *Fam (colère)* fit of rage; **piquer** *ou* **faire une c.** to throw a fit

crispant, -e [krispɑ̃, -ɑ̃t] *adj Fam* irritating, annoying

crispé, -e [krispe] *adj (visage, personne)* tense; *(sourire, rire)* forced

crisper [krispe] **1** *vt* **(a)** *(poings, mains)* to clench; *(corps)* to tense **(b)** *(énerver)* to irritate, to annoy
2 se crisper *vpr (muscle, visage)* to tense; *(sourire)* to become strained; *(personne)* to get tense

crissement [krismɑ̃] *nm (de la craie sur le tableau)* squeak; *(des pneus, des freins)* squeal; *(du gravier, de la neige)* crunch

crisser [krise] *vi (pneus, freins)* to squeal; *(gravier, neige)* to crunch; *(craie)* to squeak

cristal, -aux [kristal, -o] *nm* crystal; **c. de roche** rock crystal; **cristaux** *(verre)* crystal(ware); *(de sel, de glace)* crystals; *Tech* **cristaux liquides** liquid crystal

cristallin, -e [kristalɛ̃, -in] **1** *adj* **(a)** *(roche)* crystalline **(b)** *Fig (eau, voix)* crystal-clear; *(son, note)* ringing
2 *nm (de l'œil)* crystalline lens

cristalliser [kristalize] **1** *vi* to crystallize
2 se cristalliser *vpr* to crystallize

critère [kritɛr] *nm* criterion; *Ordinat* **c. de tri** sort criterion; *UE* **critères de convergence** convergence criteria

critérium [kriterjɔm] *nm Sport* heat

critique¹ [kritik] *adj (décisif, crucial)* critical

critique² [kritik] **1** *adj (esprit, personne, édition)* critical
2 *nmf* critic; **c. d'art/de cinéma** art/movie critic; **c. gastronomique** restaurant critic
3 *nf* **(a)** *(condamnation)* criticism; **si je peux me permettre de vous faire une c.,...** if I could just make one criticism,...; **il n'accepte pas la c.** he can't take criticism **(b)** *(article)* critical article; *Théât & Cin* review; **faire la c. de qch** to review sth **(c)** **la c.** *(l'ensemble des critiques)* the critics

critiquer [kritike] *vt (personne, attitude)* to criticize (**pour** for); **ce n'est pas pour te c., mais...** I don't mean to criticize, but...; **c'est facile de c.** it's easy to criticize

croassement [krɔasmɑ̃] *nm* caw; **des croassements** cawing

croasser [krɔase] *vi* to caw

croate [krɔat] **1** *adj* Croatian
2 *nmf* **C.** Croat, Croatian

Croatie [krɔasi] *nf* **la C.** Croatia

croc [kro] *nm* **(a)** *(de loup, de chien)* fang; *Fam* **avoir les crocs** to be starving **(b)** *(crochet)* hook

croc-en-jambe *(pl* **crocs-en-jambe)** [krɔkɑ̃ʒɑ̃b] *nm* trip; **faire un c. à qn** to trip sb up

croche [krɔʃ] *nf Mus* eighth note

croche-pied *(pl* **croche-pieds)** [krɔʃpje] = **croc-en-jambe**

crochet [krɔʃɛ] *nm* **(a)** *(pour accrocher)* hook; *Fig* **vivre aux crochets de qn** to live off sb **(b)** *(pour tricoter)* crochet hook; *(technique)* crochet; **faire du c.** to (do) crochet **(c)** *(détour)* **faire un c. (par)** *(personne)* to make a detour (through) **(d)** *Typ* square bracket; **entre crochets** in square brackets **(e)** *(coup de poing)* **c. du gauche/du droit** left/right hook **(f)** *(d'un serpent)* fang

crocheter [39] [krɔʃte] *vt (serrure)* to pick; *(porte)* to pick the lock on

crochu, -e [krɔʃy] *adj (nez, bec)* hooked; *(doigts)* claw-like

crocodile [krɔkɔdil] *nm* crocodile; **en c.** *(sac, chaussures)* crocodile(-skin)

crocus [krɔkys] *nm* crocus

croire [25] [krwar] **1** *vt* **(a)** *(accepter, faire confiance à)* to believe; *Fam Ironique* **c'est ça, je te crois!** is that so?; *Fam* **faut pas c.!** don't you believe it!; **croyez-moi, ce n'était pas facile** believe (you) me, it wasn't easy; **à l'en c.,...** to hear him, you'd think...; **si on en croit la rumeur,...** if the rumor is to be believed,...; **je n'en croyais pas mes yeux/mes oreilles** I couldn't believe my eyes/my ears
(b) *(penser)* to think; **je crois que oui** I think so; **je crois que non** I don't think so; **je ne crois pas** I don't think so; **vous croyez?** do you really think so?; **je vous croyais anglais/riche** I thought you were English/rich; **j'ai cru nécessaire de...** I thought it necessary to...; **j'ai cru bien faire** I thought *or* believed I was doing the right thing; **elle ne croyait pas si bien dire** she didn't know how right she was; **je n'aurais pas cru cela de lui** I would never have thought it of him; **on croirait qu'il dort** you'd think he was asleep
2 *vi (avoir la foi)* to be a believer
3 croire à *vt ind* **(a)** *(envisager)* **le médecin crut à une rougeole** the doctor thought it was measles
(b) *(accepter)* to believe; **veuillez c.** *ou* **je vous prie de c. à l'expression de mes sentiments distingués** sincerely yours
(c) *(avoir confiance en, adhérer à)* to believe in
4 croire en *vt ind (personne, talent, Dieu)* to believe in
5 se croire *vpr* **il se croit intelligent** he thinks he's clever; **il se croit tout permis** he thinks he can get away with anything; **on se serait cru en octobre** it felt like October; *Fam* **se c. sorti de la cuisse de Jupiter** to think a lot of oneself; *Fam* **il s'y croit** he thinks a lot of himself

croisade [krwazad] *nf Hist & Fig* crusade; **partir en c.** to go on a crusade

croisé, -e [krwaze] **1** *adj (manteau, veste)* double-breasted
2 *nm Hist* crusader

croisement [krwazmã] *nm* (**a**) *(carrefour)* intersection (**b**) *(d'animaux)* crossing; *(animal)* cross (**entre** between)

croiser [krwaze] **1** *vt* (**a**) *(couper) (ligne, route)* to cross; **c. le regard de qn** to meet sb's gaze (**b**) *(passer à côté de) (véhicule, personne)* to pass (**c**) *(mettre l'un sur l'autre)* **c. les jambes** to cross one's legs; **c. les bras** to fold one's arms; *Fig* **c. les doigts** to keep one's fingers crossed; **je croise les doigts** fingers crossed (**d**) *(animaux, espèces)* to cross(breed)
2 *vi (navire)* to cruise
3 se croiser *vpr* (**a**) *(lignes, routes)* to cross, to intersect; *(regards)* to meet (**b**) *(personnes) (dans la rue)* to walk past each other; *(se voir rapidement)* to meet briefly; *(lettres)* to cross

croiseur [krwazœr] *nm Naut* cruiser

croisière [krwazjɛr] *nf* cruise; **faire une c.** to go on a cruise

croisillon [krwazijɔ̃] *nm* (**a**) *(de croix)* crosspiece (**b**) **croisillons** *(de fenêtre, de barrière)* latticework; *(sur une tarte)* lattice

croissais *etc. voir* **croître**

croissance [krwasãs] *nf (d'un enfant) & Écon* growth; **en pleine c.** growing rapidly; **finir sa c.** *(enfant)* to stop growing

croissant[1], -e [krwasã, -ãt] *adj (plante, tendance, angoisse)* growing; *(ordre)* ascending; *(chaleur, température)* increasing

croissant[2] [krwasã] *nm* (**a**) *(arc de cercle)* crescent; **un c. de lune** a crescent moon; **en c.** crescent-shaped (**b**) *(pâtisserie)* croissant; **c. au beurre/ordinaire** croissant made with/ without butter

croissant[3] [krwasã] *voir* **croître**

croître [4b] [krwatr] *vi* (**a**) *(enfant, plantes)* to grow (**b**) *(vente, chiffre)* to grow, to increase (**de** by); *(jours)* to get longer; *(lune)* to wax; **aller croissant** *(succès)* to grow and grow; *(suspense)* to get worse and worse

croix [krwa] *nf* cross; **signer d'une c.** to make one's mark; *Fam Fig* **faire une c. sur qch** to say goodbye to sth; **en (forme de) c.** cross-shaped; **les bras en c.** with one's arms stretched out at the sides; **c. de bois c. de fer, si je mens je vais en enfer** cross my heart and hope to die; **c'est la c. et la bannière** it's one hell of a job; **c. gammée** swastika; **la c. de Lorraine** the cross of Lorraine *(symbol of the Gaullist movement)*; **la C.-Rouge** the Red Cross

croquant, -e [krɔkã, -ãt] *adj* crisp, crunchy

croque-au-sel [krɔkosɛl] **à la croque-au-sel** *adv* = raw and seasoned only with salt

croque-madame [krɔkmadam] *nm inv* = toasted cheese and ham sandwich topped with fried egg

croque-monsieur [krɔkməsjø] *nm inv* = toasted cheese and ham sandwich

croque-mort (*pl* **croque-morts**) [krɔkmɔr] *nm Fam* undertaker, mortician

croquer [krɔke] **1** *vt* (**a**) *(pomme, bonbon)* to crunch; *Fig (fortune, héritage)* to squander; **à sucer ou à c.** *(sur boîte de médicaments)* may be sucked or chewed; *Fig* **c. la vie à belles dents** to make the most of life; **il est à c.** *(enfant)* he looks good enough to eat; **joli** *ou* **mignon à c.** as pretty as a picture (**b**) *(faire un croquis de)* to sketch
2 *vi* (**a**) *(pomme, salade)* to be crunchy (**b**) *(mordre)* **c. dans** to bite into

croquet [krɔkɛ] *nm (jeu)* croquet

croquette [krɔkɛt] *nf (de pomme de terre, de viande, de poisson)* croquette; **croquettes** *(pour chien, chat)* dry food

croquis [krɔki] *nm* sketch; **faire un c. de qch** to make a sketch of sth

cross [krɔs] *nm (sport)* cross-country (running); *(événement)* cross-country race

crosse [krɔs] *nf* (**a**) *(de fusil)* butt; *(de pistolet)* grip; *(d'évêque)* crook (**b**) *(de hockey)* stick; *Fam Fig* **chercher des crosses à qn** to try to pick a fight with sb (**c**) *Can (jeu)* lacrosse

crotte [krɔt] *nf* (**a**) *(de cheval, de mouton, de lapin)* dung, droppings; **une c. de chien** dog poop; **c. de nez** booger; *Fam* **c.!**

darn! (**b**) **une c. de chocolat** a chocolate (**c**) *Vieilli (boue)* mud

crotter [krɔte] **1** *vt (chaussures, manteau)* to cover in mud
2 se crotter *vpr* to get covered in mud

crottin [krɔtɛ̃] *nm* (**a**) *(excrément) (de cheval)* dung (**b**) *(fromage)* small goat's-milk cheese

croulant, -e [krulã, -ãt] **1** *adj (bâtiment)* crumbling
2 *nm,f très Fam* (**vieux**) **c.** old fossil

crouler [krule] *vi (bâtiment)* to crumble; **c. sous le poids de qch** to give way under the weight of sth; **c. sous le travail** to be snowed under with work; **la salle croulait sous les applaudissements** the audience brought the house down

croupe [krup] *nf* rump; **monter en c.** to ride behind

croupi, -e [krupi] *adj (eau)* stagnant

croupier [krupje] *nm* croupier

croupion [krupjɔ̃] *nm (d'oiseau)* rump; *(d'une volaille)* pope's nose

croupir [krupir] *vi* (**a**) *(eau)* to stagnate (**b**) *(végéter)* **c. en prison** to rot in jail

croupissant, -e [krupisã, -ãt] *adj (eau, vie)* stagnant

CROUS [krus] *nm (abrév* **Centre régional des œuvres universitaires et scolaires**) = organization responsible for student accommodations and meals etc.

croustillant, -e [krustijã, -ãt] *adj* (**a**) *(biscuit, pâte)* crisp; *(pain)* crusty (**b**) *Fig (histoire, détails)* juicy

croustiller [krustije] *vi (biscuit, pâte)* to be crisp; *(pain)* to be crusty

croustilles [krustij] *nfpl Can* (potato) chips

croûte [krut] *nf* (**a**) *(de pain, de tarte)* crust; *(de fromage)* rind; *(d'une plaie)* scab; **la c. terrestre** the earth's crust; *Fam* **gagner sa c.** to earn one's bread and butter (**b**) *Fam (mauvaise peinture)* daub

croûton [krutɔ̃] *nm* (**a**) *(de pain)* end (**b**) *(dans la soupe, les salades)* crouton (**c**) *Fam* (**vieux**) **c.** old fossil

croyable [krwajabl] *adj* believable, credible; **ce n'est pas c.!** it's unbelievable!, it's incredible!

croyais *etc. voir* **croire**

croyance [krwajãs] *nf* belief (**en** in)

croyant, -e [krwajã, -ãt] **1** *adj* **être c.** to be a believer
2 *nm,f* believer

CRS [seeres] *nm (abrév* **compagnie républicaine de sécurité**) = French riot policeman; **les C.** = French riot police

> **CRS**
> The CRS is the Minister of the Interior's police force, whose primary responsibility is to ensure public order at demonstrations and to quell riots. They have been criticized for certain strong-arm tactics.

cru[1], -e [kry] *adj* (**a**) *(viande, poisson, légumes)* raw; *(lait)* unpasteurized (**b**) *(couleur, lumière)* garish (**c**) *(licencieux) (langage)* crude (**d**) *(direct) (réponse, personne)* blunt (**e**) **monter à c.** to ride bareback (**f**) *Belg, Can & Suisse (temps, bâtiment)* damp and cold

cru[2] [kry] *nm (terroir)* vineyard; *(vin)* wine; **un grand c.** a vintage wine; **du c.** local; *Fig* **une histoire de son (propre) c.** a story of his/her own invention

cru[3], -e [kry] *voir* **croire**

cruauté [kryote] *nf* (**a**) *(dureté)* cruelty (**envers** to) (**b**) *(acte)* (act of) cruelty

cruche [kryʃ] **1** *nf* (**a**) *(récipient, contenu)* pitcher; *Prov* **tant va la c. à l'eau qu'à la fin elle se casse** the pitcher has gone to the well once too often (**b**) *Fam (imbécile)* ass
2 *adj Fam (bête)* dumb, stupid

cruchon [kryʃɔ̃] *nm (récipient, contenu)* small pitcher

crucial, -e, -aux, -ales [krysjal, -o] *adj* crucial

crucifier [66] [krysifje] *vt* to crucify

crucifix [krysifi] *nm* crucifix

crucifixion [krysifiksjɔ̃] *nf* crucifixion

cruciforme [krysifɔrm] *adj* cruciform; **vis/tournevis c.** Phillips® screw/screwdriver

cruciverbiste [krysivɛrbist] *nmf* crossword enthusiast

crudité [krydite] *nf* (a) **crudités** (*légumes*) assorted raw vegetables (b) (*d'une couleur, d'une lumière*) garishness (c) (*d'une expression*) crudeness

crue [kry] *nf* (*montée*) swelling; (*inondation*) flood; **rivière en c.** river in flood

cruel, -elle [kryɛl] *adj* cruel (**envers** *ou* **avec** to)

cruellement [kryɛlmɑ̃] *adv* cruelly; **être c. éprouvé** to be deeply affected; **faire c. défaut** to be sadly lacking

crûment [krymɑ̃] *adv* (a) (*parler*) (*sans détours*) bluntly; (*grossièrement*) crudely (b) **éclairé c.** garishly lit

crustacé [krystase] *nm Zool* crustacean; **crustacés** crustaceans; *Culin* seafood

cruzado [kruzado] *nm* cruzado

cryogénie [krijoʒeni] *nf* cryogenics (*singulier*)

cryogénique [krijoʒenik] *adj* cryogenic

cryothérapie [krijoterapi] *nf* cryotherapy

cryptage [kriptaʒ] *nm* encoding

crypte [kript] *nf* crypt

crypté, -e [kripte] *adj* (*message*) & *TV* coded

crypter [kripte] *vt* to encode

CSA [seɛsa] *nm* (*abrév* **Conseil supérieur de l'audiovisuel**) = organization regulating French broadcasting

CSG [seɛsʒe] *nf* (*abrév* **Contribution sociale généralisée**) = income-based tax deducted at source

Cuba [kyba] *n* Cuba

cubain, -e [kybɛ̃, -ɛn] **1** *adj* Cuban
2 *nm,f* **C., Cubaine** Cuban

cube [kyb] **1** *nm* cube; (*de jeu*) building block; **élever un nombre au c.** to cube a number
2 *adj* (*mètre, centimètre*) cubic

cubique [kybik] *adj* cubic

cubisme [kybism] *nm* cubism

cubiste [kybist] *adj* & *nmf* Cubist

cubitus [kybitys] *nm* ulna

cucul [kyky] *adj inv Fam* **c. (la praline)** (*personne, décoration*) twee; (*film, livre*) corny

cueillette [kœjɛt] *nf* (*action*) gathering, picking; (*fruits, noisettes, baies*) harvest

cueillir [5] [kœjir] *vt* (*fleurs, fruits*) to gather, to pick; *Fig* **la mort l'a cueilli en pleine jeunesse** he was cut down in his prime; *Fam* **c. qn** to pick sb up

cui-cui [kɥikɥi] **1** *nm* cheeping
2 *exclam* cheep!

cuiller, cuillère [kɥijɛr] *nf* (a) (*couvert*) spoon; (*contenu*) spoon(ful); *Fam Fig* **il n'y va pas avec le dos de la c.** he doesn't go in for half measures; *Fam Fig* **en deux** *ou* **trois coups de c. à pot** in two shakes (of a lamb's tail); *Fam* **être à ramasser à la petite c.** (*épuisé*) to be all in; (*déprimé*) to be down in the dumps; **c. à café, petite c.** teaspoon; **c. à soupe,** *Can* **c. à table** soup spoon; (*pour mesurer*) tablespoon (b) (*pour la pêche*) spoon (bait); **pêcher la truite à la c.** to troll for trout

cuillerée [kɥijere] *nf* spoonful; **une c. à café** a teaspoonful; **une c. à soupe** a tablespoonful

cuir [kɥir] *nm* (a) (*matière*) leather; (*veste*) leather jacket; **chaussures/pantalon en c.** leather shoes/trousers (b) (*d'un éléphant, d'un rhinocéros*) hide (c) **c. chevelu** scalp

cuirasse [kɥiras] *nf* (a) (*protection*) breastplate; *Fig* **trouver le défaut dans la c. de qn** to find the chink in sb's armor (b) (*d'un navire de guerre, d'un blindé*) armor (plating)

cuirassé [kɥirase] *nm* battleship

cuirassier [kɥirasje] *nm* cuirassier

cuire [18] [kɥir] **1** *vt* (a) (*aliment*) to cook; **c. qch à l'eau** to boil sth; **c. qch à la vapeur** to steam sth; **c. qch au four** to bake sth (b) (*briques, poterie*) to fire (c) (*chauffer*) (*sujet: soleil*) to bake
2 *vi* (a) (*aliments, plat*) to cook; **faire trop c. qch** to overcook sth; **faire c. qch à feu doux** to cook sth over a low heat (b) (*brûler*) **les joues me cuisent** my cheeks are burning (c) *Fam* (*avoir très chaud*) to be boiling
3 *v impersonnel* **il vous en cuira** you'll regret it

cuisais *etc. voir* **cuire**

cuisant, -e [kɥizɑ̃, -ɑ̃t] *adj* (*douleur*) burning; (*froid*) biting; (*déception, échec*) bitter

cuisine [kɥizin] *nf* (a) (*pièce*) kitchen; (*sur un navire*) galley (b) (*art*) cooking; **faire la c.** to do the cooking; **bien faire la c.** to be a good cook; **c. au beurre/à l'huile** cooking with butter/oil; **la c. française/chinoise** French/Chinese cooking *or* cuisine (c) (*meubles*) kitchen (furniture); **c. intégrée,** *Suisse* **c. agencée** built-in kitchen (d) *Fam* (*magouilles*) scheming; **c. électorale** vote-rigging

cuisiner [kɥizine] **1** *vi* to cook; **bien c.** to be a good cook
2 *vt* (a) (*préparer*) to cook; **plats cuisinés** ready-cooked meals (b) *Fam* (*interroger*) to grill

cuisinette [kɥizinɛt] *nf Offic & Can & Suisse* kitchenette

cuisinier, -ère [kɥizinje, -ɛr] **1** *nm,f* cook
2 *nf* **cuisinière** stove, range; **cuisinière électrique/à gaz** electric/gas stove; **c. mixte** combined gas and electric stove

cuissardes [kɥisard] *nfpl* (*bottes de femme*) thigh boots; (*de pêche*) waders

cuisse [kɥis] *nf* thigh; **cuisses de grenouilles** frogs' legs; **c. de poulet** chicken leg

cuisson [kɥisɔ̃] *nf* (a) (*d'aliments*) cooking; (*de pain, de gâteau*) baking; **temps de c.** cooking time; **c. à la vapeur** steaming (b) (*des briques, de la porcelaine*) firing

cuissot [kɥiso] *nm* (*de venaison*) haunch

cuistot [kɥisto] *nm Fam* cook

cuit, -e [kɥi, kɥit] *adj* (a) (*aliment*) cooked; **bien c.** well done; **c. à point** done to a turn; **trop c.** overcooked; **pas assez c.** undercooked; **c. au four** baked; **c. à la vapeur** steamed (b) *Fam Fig* **être c.** to have had it; **c'est c.!** we've had it!; **c'est du tout c.** it's a piece of cake

cuite [kɥit] *nf Fam* **avoir/prendre une c.** to be/to get plastered

cuivre [kɥivr] *nm* (a) (*métal*) **c. (rouge)** copper; **c. jaune** brass; **les cuivres** (*objets*) copper(ware); (*en cuivre jaune*) brasses (b) *Mus* **les cuivres** the brass (section)

cuivré, -e [kɥivre] *adj* (*peau, teint*) (*naturellement*) copper-colored; (*par le soleil*) bronzed

cul [ky] **1** *nm* (a) *Fam* (*d'une personne*) ass, butt; **en rester** *ou* **tomber sur le c.** to be flabbergasted; **c'est à se taper le c. par terre** it's an absolute scream; **de c.** (*magazine, film*) porn; **être comme c. et chemise** to be as thick as thieves; *Vulg* **l'avoir dans le c.** to be screwed; *Vulg* **en avoir plein le c.** to be pissed off; **avoir qn au c.** to have sb on one's tail (b) *Fam* (*chance*) **avoir du c.** to be damn lucky (c) (*d'un sac, d'un tonneau, d'une bouteille*) bottom; **boire c. sec** to down one's drink in one go; **c. sec!** bottoms up!
2 *adj Fam* (*personne, décoration*) twee; (*livre*) corny

culasse [kylas] *nf* (a) (*de fusil, de pistolet*) breech (b) (*de moteur*) cylinder head

culbute [kylbyt] *nf* (a) (*cabriole*) somersault; **faire la c.** to do a somersault (b) (*chute*) tumble; **faire la c.** to take a tumble

culbuter [kylbyte] **1** *vi* (*vase, statue*) to topple over; (*personne*) to take a tumble; (*voiture*) to overturn
2 *vt* (*objet*) to knock over

cul-de-jatte (*pl* **culs-de-jatte**) [kydʒat] *nmf* legless person

cul-de-poule [kydpul] *nm* **avoir la bouche en c.** to have pursed lips

cul-de-sac (*pl* **culs-de-sac**) [kydsak] *nm* dead end, cul-de-sac; *Fig* dead end

culinaire [kylinɛr] *adj* culinary

culminant, -e [kylminã, -ãt] *adj* **point c.** (*d'une chaîne de montagnes*) highest point; (*de la gloire, d'une carrière*) height, peak

culminer [kylmine] *vi* (**a**) **le mont Blanc culmine à 4807 mètres** Mont Blanc is 4,807 meters at its highest point (**b**) (*crise, tension*) to peak

culot [kylo] *nm* (**a**) *Fam* (*audace*) cheek, nerve; **il a un de ces culots!** he's got a nerve!; **y aller au c.** to brazen it out (**b**) (*de douille, de cartouche*) base

culotte [kylɔt] *nf* (**a**) (*sous-vêtement*) panties (**b**) (*pantalon*) **c. courte** short pants; **c. de cheval** jodhpurs; **c. de golf** plus fours; *Fam Fig* **c'est elle qui porte la c.** she's the one who wears the pants; *Fam* **faire dans sa c.** to dirty one's pants; *Fig* to wet oneself (**c**) (*de bœuf*) rump

culotté, -e [kylɔte] *adj Fam* cheeky

culpabiliser [kylpabilize] **1** *vt* **c. qn** to make sb feel guilty
2 *vi* to feel guilty

culpabilité [kylpabilite] *nf* guilt

culte [kylt] *nm* (**a**) (*vénération*) worship; *Fig* cult; *Fig* **vouer un c. à qn** to (hero-)worship sb; **c. de la personnalité** personality cult (**b**) (*religion*) religion; **liberté du c.** freedom of worship (**c**) (*service protestant*) (church) service

cul-terreux (*pl* **culs-terreux**) [kytɛrø] *nm Fam Péj* hick, yokel

cultivable [kyltivabl] *adj* suitable for cultivation

cultivateur, -trice [kyltivatœr, -tris] **1** *nm,f* farmer; **petits cultivateurs** small farmers
2 *nm* (*machine*) cultivator

cultivé, -e [kyltive] *adj* (**a**) (*terre, champs*) cultivated (**b**) (*personne*) cultured, cultivated

cultiver [kyltive] **1** *vt* (**a**) (*sol, champ*) to cultivate, to farm; (*plantes*) to grow (**b**) (*art, relations, amitié, image*) to cultivate
2 se cultiver *vpr* to improve one's mind

culture [kyltyr] *nf* (**a**) (*du sol*) cultivation; (*de plantes*) growing; **cultures** land under cultivation (**b**) (*espèce cultivée*) crop (**c**) (*connaissances*) culture; **un homme d'une grande c.** a highly cultured man; **c. générale** general knowledge (**d**) (*civilisation*) culture (**e**) *Biol* **c. microbienne/de tissus** bacteria/tissue culture (**f**) **c. physique** physical training

culturel, -elle [kyltyrɛl] *adj* cultural

culturisme [kyltyrism] *nm* bodybuilding

culturiste [kyltyrist] *nmf* bodybuilder

cumin [kymɛ̃] *nm* cumin

cumul [kymyl] *nm* **c. des fonctions** plurality of offices; **c. des traitements** drawing of more than one salary

cumulable [kymylabl] *adj* (*fonctions*) which can be held concurrently; (*traitements*) which can be drawn concurrently

cumulatif, -ive [kymylatif, -iv] *adj* cumulative

cumuler [kymyle] *vt* **c. des fonctions** to hold more than one office; **c. plusieurs traitements** to draw several salaries; **c. plusieurs emplois** to have several jobs

cumulo-nimbus [kymylonɛ̃bys] *nm inv* cumulo-nimbus

cumulus [kymylys] *nm inv* cumulus

cupide [kypid] *adj* avaricious

cupidité [kypidite] *nf* cupidity

Cupidon [kypidɔ̃] *npr* Cupid

curable [kyrabl] *adj* (*maladie*) curable

curaçao [kyraso] *nm* curaçao (liqueur)

curage [kyraʒ] *nm* cleaning out

curare [kyrar] *nm* curare

cure [kyr] *nf* (**a**) (*traitement*) (course of) treatment; **c. d'amaigrissement** (course of) slimming treatment; **faire une c. de désintoxication** (*alcoolique*) to receive treatment for alcohol dependency; (*toxicomane*) to receive treatment for drug depen-

dency; **faire une c. de vitamines** to go/to be on a course of vitamins; **faire une c. de fruits** to eat a lot of fruit; **faire une c. de repos/de sommeil** to go/to be on a rest cure/sleep cure (**b**) (*dans une ville d'eau*) **c. (thermale)** spa cure; **faire une c.** to take the waters (**c**) (*fonction de curé*) office of a parish priest

curé [kyre] *nm* parish priest; **aller à l'école chez les curés** to be educated by priests

cure-dents [kyrdã] *nm inv* toothpick

curée [kyre] *nf* (*lutte*) scramble; **ce fut la c. entre les héritiers** the heirs started to fight over the spoils

cure-pipe (*pl* **cure-pipes**) [kyrpip] *nm* pipe-cleaner

curer [kyre] **1** *vt* to clean out
2 se curer *vpr* **se c. les ongles/les oreilles** to clean one's nails/one's ears

curetage [kyrtaʒ] *nm* (*en chirurgie*) D&C

curieusement [kyrjøzmã] *adv* (*bizarrement*) curiously (enough)

curieux, -euse [kyrjø, -øz] **1** *adj* (**a**) (*intéressé*) curious; **je serais c. de voir cela** I'd be curious to see that (**b**) (*indiscret*) curious, inquisitive (**c**) (*étrange*) curious, strange; **chose curieuse,...** curiously enough,...
2 *nm,f* inquisitive person; (*badaud*) onlooker

curiosité [kyrjozite] *nf* (**a**) (*intellectuelle*) curiosity; **avec c.** curiously (**b**) (*indiscrétion*) curiosity, inquisitiveness; **par c.** out of curiosity; *Prov* **la c. est un vilain défaut** curiosity killed the cat (**c**) (*objet*) curio; **les curiosités d'une ville** the interesting sights of a town

curiste [kyrist] *nmf* = patient taking a spa cure

curriculum vitae [kyrikylɔmvite] *nm inv* résumé, curriculum vitae

curry [kyri] *nm* curry; **poulet au c., c. de poulet** chicken curry

curseur [kyrsœr] *nm aussi Ordinat* cursor

cursif, -ive [kyrsif, -iv] *adj* (*écriture*) cursive

cursus [kyrsys] *nm Univ* degree course

customiser [3] [kœstɔmize] *vt* to customize

cutané, -e [kytane] *adj* skin, *Spéc* cutaneous

cuti [kyti] *nf* skin test; **virer sa c.** to have a positive skin test; *Fam Fig* to change radically

cuti-réaction (*pl* **cuti-réactions**) [kytireaksjɔ̃] *nf* skin test

cutter [kœtœr, kytɛr] *nm* Stanley knife®

cuve [kyv] *nf* (*réservoir*) (storage) tank; (*de machine à laver*) tub; (*pour la fermentation des alcools, du vin*) vat; (*en photographie*) tank

cuvée [kyve] *nf* (**a**) (*quantité*) vatful (**b**) (*produit*) vintage; *Fig* batch

cuver [kyve] *vt Fam* **c. (son vin)** to sleep it off

cuvette [kyvɛt] *nf* (**a**) (*récipient*) basin, bowl (**b**) (*de W.-C.*) bowl (**c**) *Géog* basin

CV¹ [seve] *Aut* (*abrév* **cheval-vapeur**) hp

CV² [seve] *nm* (*abrév* **curriculum vitae**) résumé, CV

cyanure [sjanyr] *nm* cyanide

cybercafé [sibɛrkafe] *nm* cybercafé

cyberespace [sibɛrɛspas] *nm Ordinat* cyberspace

cyberharcèlement [sibɛrarsɛlmã] *nm Ordinat* cyberstalking

cybernétique [sibɛrnetik] *Ordinat* **1** *adj* cybernetic
2 *nf* cybernetics (*singulier*)

cybersexe [sibɛrsɛks] *nm Ordinat* cybersex

cyberterrorisme [sibɛrtɛrɔrism] *nm Ordinat* cyberterrorism

cyberterroriste [sibɛrtɛrɔrist] *nmf Ordinat* cyberterrorist

cyclable [siklabl] *adj voir* **piste**

cyclamen [siklamɛn] *nm* cyclamen

cycle [sikl] *nm* (**a**) (*suite, mouvement*) cycle; **c. menstruel** menstrual cycle (**b**) (*dans l'éducation*) **premier/second c.** *Scol* lower/upper classes *(in secondary school)*; *Univ* first/last two years *(of degree course)*; *Univ* **troisième c.** postgraduate studies; **c. I/II/III** = subdivisions of primary school (between the ages of 2 and 4, 5 and 7, and 8 and 10 respectively) **(c)** *(bicyclette)* cycle

cyclique [siklik] *adj* cyclical

cyclisme [siklism] *nm* cycling

cycliste [siklist] **1** *nmf* cyclist
     2 *adj voir* **coureur, course**

cyclo-cross [siklokrɔs] *nm inv* cyclo-cross

cyclomoteur [siklomɔtœr] *nm* moped

cyclone [siklon] *nm* cyclone

cyclope [siklɔp] *nm* cyclops

cyclothymique [siklotimik] *adj Psy* manic-depressive

cyclotourisme [sikloturism] *nm* bicycle touring

cygne [siɲ] *nm* swan

cylindre [silɛ̃dr] *nm* **(a)** *aussi Aut* cylinder; **une quatre cylindres** a four-cylinder car **(b)** *(rouleau)* roller

cylindrée [silɛ̃dre] *nf* (cubic) capacity; **petite/grosse c.** *(moto)* motorcycle with a small/large engine; *(voiture)* car with a small/large engine

cylindrique [silɛ̃drik] *adj* cylindrical

cymbale [sɛ̃bal] *nf* cymbal

cynique [sinik] **1** *adj* cynical
     2 *nmf* cynic

cyniquement [sinikmɑ̃] *adv* cynically

cynisme [sinism] *nm* cynicism

cyprès [siprɛ] *nm* cypress (tree)

cypriote [siprijɔt] **1** *adj* Cypriot
     2 *nmf* **C.** Cypriot

cyrillique [sirilik] *adj (alphabet, caractères)* Cyrillic

cystite [sistit] *nf* cystitis

cytomégalovirus [sitomegalovirys] *nm Méd* cytomegalovirus, CMV

cytoplasme [sitɔplasm] *nm Biol* cytoplasm

D

D¹, **d** [de] *nm inv* D, d

D² [de] *nf* (*abrév* **route départementale**) = designation of secondary road

DAB [deabe] *nm* (*abrév* **distributeur automatique de billets**) ATM

dactylo [daktilo] **1** *nmf* (*abrév* **dactylographe**) typist
2 *nf* (*abrév* **dactylographie**) typing

dactylographe [daktilograf] *nmf* typist

dactylographie [daktilografi] *nf* typing

dactylographier [66] [daktilografje] *vt* to type

dada [dada] *nm* (**a**) (*langage enfantin*) (*cheval*) horsie; **à d.** on horseback (**b**) *Fam* (*sujet favori*) hobbyhorse

dadais [dadɛ] *nm Fam* **un grand d.** a great gawk

dague [dag] *nf* (*épée*) dagger

dahlia [dalja] *nm* dahlia

daigner [deɲe] *vt* **d. faire qch** to deign to do sth

daim [dɛ̃] *nm* (**a**) (*animal*) (fallow) deer; (*mâle*) buck (**b**) (*peau*) suede; **gants/veste en d.** suede gloves/jacket

dais [dɛ] *nm* canopy

Dakar [dakar] *n* Dakar

dalaï-lama [dalailama] *nm* Dalai Lama

dallage [dalaʒ] *nm* (*action, revêtement*) paving

dalle [dal] *nf* (**a**) (*de pierre*) paving stone; (*de marbre*) slab; (*de moquette, de lino*) tile (**b**) *Fam* **que d.** (*rien*) not a damn thing; **j'y vois que d.** I can't see a damn thing (**c**) *Fam* **avoir** *ou* **crever la d.** to be starving

daller [dale] *vt* to pave

dalmatien, -enne [dalmasjɛ̃, -ɛn] *nm,f* (*chien*) Dalmatian

daltonien, -enne [daltɔnjɛ̃, -ɛn] **1** *adj* color-blind
2 *nm,f* color-blind person

daltonisme [daltɔnism] *nm* color blindness

dam [dɑ̃] *nm* **au grand d. de qn** to sb's great displeasure

damage [damaʒ] *nm* (*de la terre, de la neige*) packing down

Damas [damas] *n* Damascus; *Fig* **trouver son chemin de D.** to see the light

damas [damas] *nm* damask

damassine [damasin] *nf Suisse* (*fruit*) plum; (*eau de vie*) plum brandy

dame [dam] *nf* (**a**) (*femme*) lady; **d. de compagnie** lady's companion; **d. d'honneur** lady-in-waiting (**b**) (*aux cartes, aux échecs*) queen; (*au jeu de dames*) king (**c**) **dames** (*jeu*) checkers

damer [dame] *vt* (**a**) *Fam Fig* **d. le pion à qn** to get one over on sb (**b**) (*terre, neige*) to pack down

dameuse [damøz] *nf* piste basher

damier [damje] *nm* checkerboard; **tissu à damiers** checked material

damnation [dɑnasjɔ̃] *nf* damnation

damné, -e [dɑne] **1** *adj* damned
2 *nm,f* damned soul; *Fig* **souffrir comme un d.** to suffer sheer torture

damner [dɑne] **1** *vt* to damn

2 se damner *vpr* to damn oneself; **il se damnerait pour...** he'd sell his soul to the devil for...

Damoclès [damɔklɛs] *n voir* **épée**

dancing [dɑ̃siŋ] *nm Vieilli* dance hall

dandinement [dɑ̃dinmɑ̃] *nm* waddle

dandiner [dɑ̃dine] **se dandiner** *vpr* to waddle; **se d. d'un pied sur l'autre** to shift from one foot to the other

dandy [dɑ̃di] *nm* dandy

Danemark [danmark] *nm* **le D.** Denmark

danger [dɑ̃ʒe] *nm* danger; **être en d.** to be in danger; **mettre en d. la vie de qn** to endanger sb's life; **d. de mort** (*sur panneau*) danger of death; **hors de d.** out of danger; **d. public** public menace

dangereusement [dɑ̃ʒrøzmɑ̃] *adv* dangerously

dangereux, -euse [dɑ̃ʒrø, -øz] *adj* dangerous

danois, -e [danwa, -az] **1** *adj* Danish
2 *nm* (**a**) (*langue*) Danish (**b**) (*chien*) Great Dane
3 *nm,f* **D., Danoise** Dane

dans [dɑ̃] *prép* (**a**) (*à l'intérieur de*) in; **d. une boîte** in(side) a box; **il est d. sa chambre** he's in his room; **lire qch d. un journal** to read sth in a newspaper; **tomber d. l'escalier** to fall down the stairs; **il pleut d. tout le pays** it's raining all over the country; **être d. le commerce/l'informatique** to be in business/computers; **travailler d. le bruit/la saleté** to work in noisy/dirty surroundings
(**b**) (*avec mouvement*) into; **il est entré d. leur chambre** he went into their room
(**c**) (*exprime la temporalité*) in; **d. vingt ans** in twenty years, in twenty years' time; **d. peu de temps** soon, shortly
(**d**) (*indique une provenance*) out of; **boire d. un verre** to drink out of a glass; **découper un article d. le journal** to cut an article out of the paper
(**e**) (*indique une approximation*) **d. les quarante ans/les 3000 euros** about forty (years old)/3,000 euros
(**f**) (*pour indiquer un état*) in; **d. mon excitation/ma hâte** in my excitement/hurry

dansant, -e [dɑ̃sɑ̃, -ɑ̃t] *adj voir* **soirée, thé**

danse [dɑ̃s] *nf* (*ensemble de mouvements, musique*) dance; **la d.** (*art*) dancing; **d. classique** ballet; **d. contemporaine** contemporary dance; **d. folklorique** folk dance/dancing; *Méd* **d. de Saint-Guy** St Vitus's dance; **d. aux tables** table dancing; **la d. du ventre** belly dancing

danser [dɑ̃se] **1** *vi* to dance; **le bouchon/le bateau danse sur l'eau** the cork/the boat is bobbing up and down on the water; *Fig* **avec lui je ne sais jamais sur quel pied d.** I never know where I am with him
2 *vt* (*valse, tango*) to dance

danseur, -euse [dɑ̃sœr, -øz] *nm,f* dancer; **d. (classique** *ou* **de ballet)** ballet dancer; **d. étoile** lead dancer; **danseuse étoile** prima ballerina; **être en danseuse** (*en cyclisme*) to stand on the pedals

Danube [danyb] *nm* **le D.** the Danube

dard [dar] *nm* (*d'insecte, de scorpion*) sting

darder [darde] *vt* **il a dardé sur moi un regard furieux** he shot me a furious look; **le soleil darde ses rayons** the sun is beating down

dare-dare [dardar] *adv Fam* on the double

darne [darn] *nf (de poisson)* steak

dartre [dartr] *nf* dry patch of skin

darwinisme [darwinism] *nm* Darwinism

datation [datasjɔ̃] *nf* dating

date [dat] *nf* date; **prendre d. pour qch** to fix a date for sth; **faire d.** to be a landmark; **amitié de fraîche/longue d.** recent/long-standing friendship; **je la connais de longue d.** I've known her (for) a long time; **d. limite** deadline; **d. limite de consommation/de vente/de fraîcheur** use-by/pull/best-before date; **d. de naissance** date of birth

dater [date] **1** *vt (lettre)* to date
  2 *vi* **à d. du 15** as from the 15th; **ça date un peu** it's a bit dated; **ça ne date pas d'hier** that's nothing new

dateur [datœr] *adj m* **tampon** *ou* **timbre d.** date stamp

dation [dasjɔ̃] *nf* giving, conferring; **d. en paiement** payment in kind

datte [dat] *nf* date

dattier [datje] *nm* date palm

dauphin [dofɛ̃] *nm* **(a)** *(animal)* dolphin **(b)** *Hist* **D.** Dauphin **(c)** *Fig (successeur)* heir apparent

daurade [dɔrad] *nf* sea bream

davantage [davɑ̃taʒ] *adv* more; **elle est jolie, mais tu l'es bien d.** she's pretty, but you're even prettier; **nous ne resterons pas d.** we won't stay any longer

DCA [desea] *nf Mil (abrév* **Défense contre avions***)* anti-aircraft defense

DD *Ordinat (abrév* **disque dur***)* HD

DDASS [das] *nf (abrév* **Direction départementale de l'action sanitaire et sociale***)* = local social-work department, one of whose tasks is to deal with children who have been abandoned or ill-treated

DDT [dedete] *nm (abrév* **dichloro-diphényl-trichloréthane***)* DDT

de [də]

> **de** becomes **d'** before vowel and h mute; **de** + **le** contracts to form **du**, and **de** + **les** to form **des**.

1 *prép* **(a)** *(indique l'origine)* from; **venir/être de** to come/to be from; **sortir de chez soi** to leave the house; **l'idée est de vous** it's your idea; **de vous à moi…** between you and me…
  (b) *(indique une progression)* **de… à…** from… to…; **du matin au soir** from morning till night; **de vingt à trente per-sonnes** between twenty and thirty people; **de… en…** from… to…; **errer de ville en ville** to go from town to town
  (c) *(introduit l'agent, l'auteur)* by; *(introduit l'instrument)* with; **accompagné de ses amis** accompanied by his friends; **la statue est de Rodin** the statue is by Rodin; **un concerto de Beethoven** a Beethoven concerto; **armé de pierres** armed with stones; **couvert de puces** covered in fleas
  (d) *(indique la manière)* **d'un air amusé** with an amused expression; **d'une voix douce** gently, in a gentle voice
  (e) *(indique la cause)* **sauter de joie** to jump for joy; **resplendissant de santé** blooming with health
  (f) *(introduit une mesure)* **un enfant de dix ans** a child of ten, a ten-year-old child; **il est plus grand que moi de 5 cm** ≃ he's 2 inches taller than I am; **une pièce d'un euro** a 1-euro coin; **la terrasse fait 20 mètres de long** ≃ the terrace is 65 feet long; **20 euros de l'heure** 20 euros an hour
  (g) *(indique l'appartenance)* of; **le livre de Pierre** Pierre's book; **le toit de la maison** the roof of the house; **le règlement de l'école** the school rules
  (h) *(pour préciser la nature, la matière)* **un problème d'algèbre** an algebra problem; **un hôtel de la rive gauche** a hotel

on the left bank; **le journal d'hier** yesterday's paper; **à quatre heures de l'après-midi** at four (o'clock) in the afternoon; **une robe de soie** a silk dress; **un verre de vin** a glass of wine
  (i) *(dans, parmi)* of; **l'un d'eux** one of them; **le meilleur élève de la classe** the best pupil in the class; **la moitié de ses économies** half (of) her savings
  (j) *(pendant)* **je ne l'ai pas vu de la soirée** I haven't seen him all evening; **de nuit** by night
  (k) *(introduit un infinitif)* **il est honteux de mentir** it is shameful to lie; **j'aime mieux attendre que de me faire mouiller** I would rather wait than get wet
  (l) *(pour insister)* **c'est d'un ridicule!** it's totally ridiculous!
  (m) *(dans un titre)* **de l'amour** (on) love
2 *art partitif* some; **je bois du café tous les matins** I drink coffee every morning; **donnez-moi du vin** give me some wine; **c'est du Bach** it's Bach; **avez-vous du pain?** do you have any bread?
3 *art indéfini* **je n'ai plus d'amis/de problèmes** I don't have any friends/problems any more

dé¹ [de] *nm (pour joueur)* dice; **joueur aux dés** to play dice; **couper qch en dés** *(légumes)* to dice sth

dé² [de] *nm* **dé (à coudre)** thimble

DEA [deəa] *nm (abrév* **diplôme d'études approfondies***)* = postgraduate qualification which is a prerequisite for PhD candidates

dealer [dilœr] *nm Fam (de drogue)* dealer

déambulateur [deɑ̃bylatœr] *nm* walker

déambuler [deɑ̃byle] *vi* to stroll (about)

débâcle [debɑkl] *nf* **(a)** *(d'un cours d'eau gelé)* breaking up **(b)** *Mil* rout; *Fig (d'une affaire, d'une monnaie)* collapse

déballage [debalaʒ] *nm* **(a)** *(action)* unpacking **(b)** *Fam (aveu)* outpouring

déballer [debale] *vt* **(a)** *(affaires, produits, caisses)* to unpack **(b)** *Fam (sa vie privée, ses sentiments)* to pour out

débandade [debɑ̃dad] *nf (d'une armée, d'une équipe)* rout; **c'est la d. dans l'entreprise** the company's in disarray

débaptiser [debatize] *vt (personne, rue)* to rename

débarbouillage [debarbujaʒ] *nm* face wash

débarbouiller [debarbuje] **1** *vt* **d. qn** to wash sb's face
  2 se débarbouiller *vpr* to wash one's face

débarbouillette [debarbujɛt] *nf Can* washcloth, face cloth

débarcadère [debarkadɛr] *nm* landing stage; *(pour les marchandises)* wharf

débardeur [debardœr] *nm* **(a)** *(vêtement) (en coton)* tank top; *(en laine)* sweater vest **(b)** *(personne)* stevedore, longshoreman

débarquement [debarkəmɑ̃] *nm* **(a)** *(de cargaison)* unloading; *(de passagers)* landing **(b)** *(de troupes)* landing; *Hist* **le D.** the D-Day landings

débarquer [debarke] **1** *vt (cargaison)* to unload; *(passagers)* to land
  2 *vi* **(a)** *(d'un bateau, d'un avion)* to disembark **(b)** *Fam Fig (arriver)* to turn up; **il a toujours l'air de d.** he never seems to know what's going on

débarras [debara] *nm* **(a)** *(endroit)* junk room **(b)** *Fam* **bon d.!** good riddance!

débarrasser [debarase] **1** *vt (table, bureau, pièce)* to clear; **d. qn de qch** to relieve sb of sth; **d. qn de qn** to rid sb of sb; *Fam Fig* **d. le plancher** to clear out
  2 se débarrasser *vpr* **se d. de** to get rid of

débat [deba] *nm* debate; *Pol* **débats (parlementaires)** (parliamentary) proceedings

débattre [11] *vt (discuter)* to debate, to discuss; **prix à d.** price negotiable
  2 débattre de *vt ind* to discuss
  3 se débattre *vpr* to struggle; **se d. contre les difficultés** to be up against difficulties

débauche [deboʃ] *nf* debauchery; **lieu de d.** den of vice; *Fig* **une d. de couleurs** a riot of color

débauché, -e [deboʃe] **1** *adj* debauched
2 *nm,f* debauchee

débaucher [deboʃe] *vt* (**a**) *(inciter à la débauche)* to corrupt (**b**) *(licencier)* to lay off

débecter [debɛkte] *vt très Fam* to sicken, to make nauseous; **ça me débecte** it makes me want to puke

débile [debil] **1** *adj* (**a**) *(qui manque de vigueur) (enfant)* sickly; *(corps)* weak; *(santé)* poor (**b**) *Fam (stupide)* stupid
2 *nmf* **d. mental** mental defective; *Fam Fig* complete idiot

débilitant, -e [debilitɑ̃, -ɑ̃t] *adj* debilitating; *Fig* demoralizing

débilité [debilite] *nf* (**a**) *(faiblesse)* debility; **d. mentale** mental deficiency (**b**) *Fam (stupidité)* stupidity

débiliter [debilite] *vt* to debilitate

débiner [debine] *Fam* **1** *vt* to run down
2 se débiner *vpr* to clear off

débit [debi] *nm* (**a**) *Fin* debit (**b**) *(ventes)* turnover (**c**) *(commerce)* **d. de boissons** bar; **d. de tabac** tobacco store (**d**) *(de bois)* cutting up (**e**) *(d'une rivière, de liquide)* flow; *(d'une machine)* output (**f**) *(d'un orateur)* delivery; *Fam* **il a un de ces débits!** he really has the gift of the gab! (**g**) *Ordinat* rate; **à haut d.** broadband; **d. de données** data throughput

débitant, -e [debitɑ̃, -ɑ̃t] *nm,f* **d. de boissons** bar owner; **d. de tabac** tobacconist

débiter [debite] *vt* (**a**) *(sujet: usine)* to produce; *(sujet: cours d'eau)* to have a flow rate of (**b**) *Fin (somme, compte)* to debit; **d. une somme d'un compte** to debit an account with an amount, to debit an amount to an account (**c**) *(bois, viande)* to cut up (**d**) *(vendre)* to sell (**e**) *Péj (dire)* to spout

débiteur, -trice [debitœr, -tris] **1** *adj (compte)* debit
2 *nm,f* debtor

déblaiement [deblɛmɑ̃] *nm* clearing

déblatérer [34] [deblatere] *vi Fam* **d. contre** *ou* **sur qn/qch** to rail against sb/sth

déblayage [deblɛjaʒ] *nm* clearing

déblayer [53] [debleje] *vt* (**a**) *(terre, gravats, neige)* to clear (**b**) *(terrain)* to clear; *Fig* **d. le terrain** *(faire des préparatifs)* to prepare the ground

déblocage [deblɔkaʒ] *nm* *(d'une porte, d'un tiroir, d'un mécanisme)* unjamming; *(des prix, des salaires)* unfreezing

débloquer [deblɔke] **1** *vt* (**a**) *(porte, tiroir, mécanisme)* to unjam; *(prix, salaires)* to unfreeze; **d. des fonds** to release funds (**b**) *Psy* **d. qn** *(lui ôter ses complexes)* to rid sb of his/her hangups; *(le rendre moins timide)* to make sb less inhibited
2 *vi Fam (être fou)* to be off one's rocker; *(raconter n'importe quoi)* to talk drivel; *(être gâteux)* to be gaga

déboguer [debɔge] *vt Ordinat* to debug

débogueur [debɔgœr] *nm Ordinat* debugger

déboires [debwar] *nmpl (déceptions)* disappointments; *(ennuis)* problems; **essuyer des d.** to suffer disappointments *or* setbacks

déboisement [debwazmɑ̃] *nm* deforestation

déboiser [debwaze] *vt* to deforest

déboîtement [debwatmɑ̃] *nm* (**a**) *(d'un membre, d'une articulation)* dislocation (**b**) *(en voiture)* pulling out

déboîter [debwate] **1** *vt* (**a**) *(objets encastrés)* to disconnect (**b**) *(articulation, membre)* to dislocate
2 *vi (en voiture)* to pull out
3 se déboîter *vpr (articulation, membre)* to become dislocated; **se d. l'épaule/le genou** to dislocate one's shoulder/knee

débonnaire [debɔnɛr] *adj (personne)* good-natured, easygoing; **répondre d'un ton d.** to answer good-naturedly

débordant, -e [debɔrdɑ̃, -ɑ̃t] *adj (activité)* tireless; *(imagination)* boundless; **d. de santé/d'enthousiasme** bursting with health/with enthusiasm

débordé, -e [debɔrde] *adj* **d. (de travail)** snowed under (with work)

débordement [debɔrdəmɑ̃] *nm* (**a**) *(d'une rivière)* overflowing; *Fig (d'enthousiasme, de joie)* outburst (**b**) **débordements** *(excès)* excesses (**c**) *Mil (de l'ennemi)* outflanking

déborder [debɔrde] **1** *vi* (**a**) *(liquide, rivière, baignoire)* to overflow; **l'eau déborde du vase** the vase is overflowing; **les papiers débordent de la corbeille** the wastepaper basket is overflowing with paper; **d. sur le temps prévu** to overrun (**b**) *Fig* **d. de vie** to be bursting with vitality; **d. d'imagination** to have boundless imagination
2 *vt (dépasser) (alignement)* to stick out from; *(limite)* to go beyond; *Mil (l'ennemi)* to outflank; *Sport (coureur)* to overtake; **cela déborde le cadre de...** that is beyond the scope of...

débouchage [debuʃaʒ] *nm* (**a**) *(d'un tuyau, d'un évier)* unblocking (**b**) *(d'une bouteille)* uncorking

débouché [debuʃe] *nm (professionnel)* opening, job opportunity; *Com* outlet

déboucher [debuʃe] **1** *vt* (**a**) *(tuyau, évier)* to unblock (**b**) *(bouteille)* to uncork
2 *vi* (**a**) *(dans l'espace) (personne, voiture)* to emerge (**de** from), to come out (**de** of); **d. dans/sur** to lead to (**b**) *Fig* **d. sur qch** *(avoir pour résultat)* to lead to sth
3 se déboucher *vpr (tuyau, évier, oreilles)* to clear; **la bouteille se débouche facilement** the bottle is easy to open

débouler [debule] *Fam* **1** *vt* **d. l'escalier** to race down the stairs
2 *vi* (**a**) *(descendre)* to race down (**b**) *(arriver)* to turn up

déboulonner [debulɔne] *vt* (**a**) *Tech* to unbolt; *(statue)* to take down (**b**) *Fam Fig (critiquer)* to debunk; *(de son poste)* to kick out

débourser [deburse] *vt (argent)* to lay out; **sans rien d.** without spending a cent

déboussoler [debusɔle] *vt Fam* to disorient

debout [dəbu] *adv* (**a**) *(verticalement) (chose)* upright; *(personne)* standing; **cent ans plus tard, la maison est encore d.** the house is still standing a hundred years later; **elle est d. toute la journée** she's on her feet all day; **mettre qch d.** to stand sth up; **se mettre d.** to stand up; **rester d.** to stand; **tenir d.** *(objet)* to stay upright; *(personne)* to stay on one's feet; **il ne tient plus d.** *(fatigué)* he's dead on his feet; *(ivre)* he's blind drunk; *Fig* **un argument qui ne tient pas d.** an argument that won't stand up; **se tenir d.** to stand; **conte** *ou* **histoire à dormir d.** cock-and-bull story (**b**) *(hors du lit)* **être d.** to be up; **allons, d.!** come on, get up!

débouter [debute] *vt Jur* to nonsuit

déboutonner [debutɔne] **1** *vt* to unbutton
2 se déboutonner *vpr (personne)* to undo one's coat/jacket/etc.; *(vêtement)* to unbutton; *Fig (se confier)* to open up

débraillé, -e [debraje] *adj* slovenly

débrancher [debrɑ̃ʃe] *vt (appareil électrique)* to unplug; *(tuyau)* to diconnect; *Fam* **d. un malade** to turn off a patient's life support machine

débrayage [debrɛjaʒ] *nm* (**a**) *Aut* declutching (**b**) *(grève)* stoppage

débrayer [53] [debrɛje] *vi* (**a**) *Aut* to release the clutch (**b**) *(se mettre en grève)* to stop work

débridé, -e [debride] *adj (passion)* unbridled; *(imagination)* vivid

débriefer [3] [debrife] *vt* to debrief

débriefing [debrifiŋ] *nm Mktg* debriefing

débris [debri] **1** *nmpl (d'un avion, d'une voiture)* debris, wreckage; *(de verre, de bois)* fragments; **d. de métal** scrap (metal)
2 *nm Fam* **un vieux d.** an old wreck

débrouillard, -e [debrujar, -ard] *Fam* **1** *adj* resourceful
2 *nm,f* resourceful person

débrouillardise [debrujardiz] *nf* resourcefulness

débrouiller [debruje] **1** vt (fil, mystère) to unravel

2 se débrouiller vpr to manage, to cope; (dans une langue, un domaine) to get by; **débrouillez-vous!** you'll just have to manage!; **elle s'est débrouillée pour rencontrer le directeur** she worked it so that she got to meet the director; **débrouille-toi pour arriver à l'heure** make sure you get there on time

débroussailler [debrusaje] vt to clear of undergrowth; Fig (question) to clarify

débusquer [debyske] vt to flush out

début [deby] nm **(a)** (commencement) beginning, start; **au d. (de)** at the start or beginning (of); **au tout d., tout au d.** at the very start or beginning; **dès le d.** from the start; **je le savais depuis le d.** I knew all along; **du d. à la fin** from start to finish; **en d. de** at the start of; Hum **il faut** ou **il y a un d. à tout** there's a first time for everything **(b)** **débuts** (d'un acteur, d'un chanteur) debut, first appearance; **faire ses débuts** to make one's debut; **faire des débuts prometteurs** to get off to a promising start; **en être à ses débuts** (société, projet) to be in its early stages **(c)** Ordinat home; **aller au d.** (commande) go top

débutant, -e [debytã, -ãt] **1** adj novice

2 nm,f (dans une discipline) beginner; **grand d.** complete beginner

débuter [debyte] **1** vi **(a)** (commencer) to begin, to start (**par** with) **(b)** (dans le spectacle) to make one's debut; (dans la vie professionnelle) to start out; **mal/bien d. dans la vie** to get off to a bad/good start in life

2 vt Fam to start, to begin (**par** with)

deçà [dəsa] **en deçà de** prép (dans l'espace) (on) this side of; **rester (très) en d. de la vérité** to be (very) short of the truth

déca [deka] nm Fam (café) decaf

décacheter [42] [dekaʃte] vt to unseal, to open

décadenasser [dekadnase] vt to take the padlock off

décadence [dekadãs] nf (état) decadence; (processus) decline; **tomber en d.** to go into decline

décadent, -e [dekadã, -ãt] adj decadent

décaféiné [dekafeine] **1** adj m (café) decaffeinated

2 nm decaffeinated coffee

décagonal, -e, -aux, -ales [dekagɔnal, -o] adj decagonal

décagone [dekagon] nm Math decagon

décalage [dekalaʒ] nm **(a)** (désaccord) gap **(b)** (dans le temps) time lag; **d. horaire** time difference; **souffrir du d. horaire** to have jet lag

décalaminer [dekalamine] vt to decoke

décalcification [dekalsifikasjɔ̃] nf Méd decalcification

décalcifier [66] [dekalsifje] Méd **1** vt to decalcify

2 se décalcifier vpr to become decalcified

décalcomanie [dekalkɔmani] nf (procédé) decal; (image) decal; **faire de la d.** to do decals

décalé, -e [dekale] adj (humour, style) offbeat, quirky

décaler [dekale] **1** vt **(a)** (dans l'espace) to move, to shift (**de** from) **(b)** (dans le temps) (avancer) to bring forward (**de** by); (reculer) to put back (**de** by)

2 se décaler vpr to move, to shift; **pourriez-vous vous d. d'un rang/vers la gauche?** could you move up a row/move to the left?

décalitre [dekalitr] nm decaliter

décalquer [dekalke] vt to trace

décamètre [dekamɛtr] nm decameter

décamper [dekãpe] vi Fam to clear off

décan [dekã] nm = one of three divisions of each sign of the zodiac

décaniller [dekanije] vi Fam to clear off

décanter [dekãte] **1** vt (vin) to decant

2 se décanter vpr (vin) to settle; Fig (situation) to become clearer

décapage [dekapaʒ] nm (avec un produit) stripping; (au papier de verre) sanding (down); (d'un four) cleaning

décapant, -e [dekapã, -ãt] **1** adj **(a)** **produit d.** (pour vernis, peinture) paint stripper; (pour four) oven cleaner **(b)** Fig (humour) caustic

2 nm (pour vernis, peinture) paint stripper; (pour four) oven cleaner

décaper [dekape] vt **(a)** (avec un produit) to strip; (au papier de verre) to sand (down); (four) to clean **(b)** Fam Fig **ça décape!** (alcool) it takes the roof of your mouth off!

décapeuse [dekapøz] nf scraper

décapitation [dekapitasjɔ̃] nf decapitation

décapiter [dekapite] vt (personne) to decapitate; (arbre) to pollard

décapotable [dekapɔtabl] **1** adj convertible

2 nf convertible

décapoter [dekapɔte] vt to lower the top of

décapsuler [dekapsyle] vt to take the top off

décapsuleur [dekapsylœr] nm bottle opener

décarcasser [dekarkase] **se décarcasser** vpr Fam to sweat blood (**pour faire** to do)

décasyllabe [dekasilab] **1** adj decasyllabic

2 nm decasyllable

décathlon [dekatlɔ̃] nm decathlon

décati, -e [dekati] adj (visage) age-worn; (personne) decrepit

décatir [dekatir] **se décatir** vpr to become decrepit

décédé, -e [desede] adj deceased

décéder [34] [desede] vi to die

décelable [deslabl] adj detectable

déceler [39] [desle] vt **(a)** (découvrir) to detect **(b)** (indiquer) to indicate

décélération [deselerasjɔ̃] nf deceleration

décélérer [34] [deselere] vi to decelerate

décembre [desãbr] nm December; voir aussi **janvier**

décemment [desamã] adv **(a)** (convenablement) (se comporter) properly; (s'habiller) decently **(b)** (passablement) reasonably well **(c)** (raisonnablement) reasonably; **je ne pouvais pas d. refuser** I couldn't reasonably refuse

décence [desãs] nf **(a)** (bienséance) (de comportement) propriety; (d'habillement) decency **(b)** (tact) decency; **avoir la d. de faire qch** to have the decency to do sth

décennal, -e, -aux, -ales [desenal, -o] adj ten-year

décennie [deseni] nf decade

décent, -e [desã, -ãt] adj **(a)** (comportement) proper; (vêtements) decent; **peu d.** improper/indecent **(b)** (passable) reasonable

décentralisation [desãtralizasjɔ̃] nf decentralization

décentraliser [desãtralize] vt to decentralize

décentré, -e [desãtre] adj **(a)** **être d.** to be off-center **(b)** Suisse (quartier, endroit) outlying

décentrer [desãtre] **1** vt to move off center

2 se décentrer vpr to move off center

déception [desɛpsjɔ̃] nf disappointment; **d. sentimentale** disappointment in love

décerner [deserne] vt (prix, médaille) to award (**à** to)

décès [desɛ] nm death; **fermé pour cause de d.** (sur la porte d'un magasin) closed due to bereavement

décevant, -e [desəvã, -ãt] adj disappointing

décevoir [60] [desəvwar] vt to disappoint; **il/ce voyage m'a beaucoup déçu** I was very disappointed in him/with the trip

déchaîné, -e [deʃene] adj (passion) unbridled; (mer, vent) raging; (personne) wild

déchaînement [deʃenmã] nm (des éléments) fury; (des passions) outburst

déchaîner [deʃene] **1** vt (passions, colère) to unleash; **d. l'hilarité** to provoke laughter

2 se déchaîner *vpr (tempête, vent)* to rage; *(personne)* to fly into a rage (**contre** with)

déchanter [deʃɑ̃te] *vi Fam* to become disillusioned

décharge [deʃarʒ] *nf* (**a**) *(tirs)* discharge (**b**) **d. (électrique)** (electric) shock; **prendre une d.** to get an electric shock; **d. d'adrénaline** rush of adrenaline (**c**) *(d'ordures)* **d. (publique)** garbage dump; **d. interdite** *(sur panneau)* no dumping (**d**) *Jur (d'un accusé)* acquittal; *(d'une obligation)* discharge; *Fig* **dire qch à la d. de qn** to say sth in sb's defense

déchargement [deʃarʒəmɑ̃] *nm* unloading

décharger [45] [deʃarʒe] **1** *vt* (**a**) *(vider) (camion, bateau, cargaison)* to unload; *(sujet: camion) (sable, gravier)* to dump; *(arme à feu)* to fire, to discharge; *Fig* **d. sa conscience** to unburden one's conscience (**de** of) (**b**) *(soulager)* **d. qn de qch** *(tâche, responsabilité)* to relieve sb of sth; *Jur (d'une accusation)* to acquit sb of sth

2 se décharger *vpr* (**a**) *(personne)* **se d. d'une tâche/ d'une responsabilité sur qn** to offload a task/a responsibility onto sb (**b**) *(pile, batterie)* to go flat

décharné, -e [deʃarne] *adj (corps, membres, visage)* emaciated; *Fig (arbre)* bare

déchaussé, -e [deʃose] *adj* (**a**) *(sans chaussures)* barefoot (**b**) *(dent)* loose

déchausser [deʃose] **1** *vt (enlever ses chaussures à)* **d. qn** to take off sb's shoes; **d. ses skis** to take off one's skis

2 se déchausser *vpr* (**a**) *(enlever ses chaussures)* to take off one's shoes (**b**) *(dent)* to work loose

dèche [dɛʃ] *nf Fam* **être dans la d.** to be flat broke; **c'est la d.** I'm/we're/*etc.* flat broke

déchéance [deʃeɑ̃s] *nf* (**a**) *(physique, morale)* decline (**b**) *Jur (de droits)* forfeiture; **d. de l'autorité parentale** loss of parental rights

déchet [deʃɛ] *nm* (**a**) **déchets** waste; **déchets radioactifs/ industriels** radioactive/industrial waste (**b**) *(perte)* **il y a du d.** there's some wastage (**c**) *Péj (personne)* down-and-out; **un d. de la société** a social outcast

déchiffrable [deʃifrabl] *adj* decipherable

déchiffrage [deʃifraʒ] *nm Mus* sight-reading

déchiffrement [deʃifrəmɑ̃] *nm* deciphering; *Ordinat* decryption

déchiffrer [deʃifre] *vt* (**a**) *(inscription, écriture, message)* to decipher; *(signaux)* to interpret; *Fig (pensées, sentiments, mystère)* to fathom (**b**) *(musique)* to sight-read

déchiqueté, -e [deʃikte] *adj* (**a**) *(irrégulier)* jagged (**b**) *(vêtements, papiers)* torn to shreds; *(corps) (dans une explosion)* blown to pieces

déchiqueter [42] [deʃikte] *vt (vêtements, papiers)* to tear to shreds; *(sujet: explosion) (corps)* to blow to pieces

déchirant, -e [deʃirɑ̃, -ɑ̃t] *adj (spectacle, adieux)* heartrending

déchiré, -e [deʃire] *adj aussi Méd & Fig* torn; **être d. entre deux personnes** to be torn between two people

déchirement [deʃirmɑ̃] *nm (peine)* heartbreak

déchirer [deʃire] **1** *vt* (**a**) *(accidentellement)* to tear; *(volontairement)* to tear up; *(enveloppe)* to tear open (**b**) *Fig (famille, pays)* to tear apart; *(silence)* to pierce; **des sons qui déchirent le tympan** ear-splitting sounds

2 se déchirer *vpr* (**a**) *(tissu, papier)* to tear (**b**) *Méd* **se d. un muscle** to tear a muscle (**c**) *Fig (couple)* to tear each other apart

déchirure [deʃiryr] *nf (dans un tissu) & Méd* tear; *Fig (peine)* heartbreak; **se faire une d. musculaire** to tear a muscle

déchoir [14] [deʃwar] *vi* **ce serait d. (que de...)** it would be demeaning (to...); **par ce mariage il déchoit de son rang** he is marrying beneath him

déchu, -e [deʃy] *adj (dépossédé) (roi)* deposed; **être d. de qch** *(droit, nationalité)* to be stripped of sth

décibel [desibɛl] *nm* decibel

décidé, -e [deside] *adj* (**a**) *(fixé)* settled (**b**) *(caractère, personne, manière)* determined; **d'un ton d.** in a decisive tone; **être d. à faire qch** to be determined to do sth

décidément [desidemɑ̃] *adv* really; **d. je n'ai pas de chance!, je n'ai d. pas de chance!** I really don't have any luck!

décider [deside] **1** *vt* (**a**) *(déterminer)* **d. que/quand/si** to decide that/when/if; **il fut décidé qu'on attendrait** it was decided that we/they/*etc.* should wait; **c'est moi qui décide ici** I'm the one who makes the decisions here; **je déciderai pour toi** I'll decide for you (**b**) *(convaincre)* **d. qn à faire qch** to persuade sb to do sth

2 décider de *vt ind* **d. de qch** to decide on sth; **un événement qui a décidé de sa carrière** an event that determined his/her career; **d. de faire qch** to decide to do sth

3 se décider *vpr* (**a**) *(prendre une décision)* to make up one's mind, to come to a decision; **bon, décide-toi!** OK, make up your mind!; **se d. à faire qch** to make up one's mind to do sth; **je ne peux pas me d. à le faire** I can't bring myself to do it; *Fig* **il ne se décide pas à faire beau** the weather can't make up its mind whether to be nice or not; **se d. pour qn/qch** to decide on sb/sth (**b**) *(problème, question)* to be settled

décideur, -euse [desidœr, -øz] *nm,f* decision-maker

décigramme [desigram] *nm* decigram

décilitre [desilitr] *nm* deciliter

décimal, -e, -aux, -ales [desimal, -o] **1** *adj* decimal

2 *nf* **décimale** decimal

décimer [desime] *vt* to decimate

décimètre [desimɛtr] *nm* decimeter; **double d.** *(règle)* ruler *(20 cm long)*

décisif, -ive [desizif, -iv] *adj (bataille, argument)* decisive; *(preuve)* conclusive; *(moment)* critical

décision [desizjɔ̃] *nf* (**a**) *(choix)* decision; *Jur* ruling; **arriver à/ prendre une d.** to come to/to make a decision; **prendre la d. de faire qch** to decide to do sth; **la d. ne m'appartient pas** it's not my decision (**b**) *(détermination)* determination; **avec d.** decisively; **esprit de d.** decisiveness

déclamation [deklamasjɔ̃] *nf (éloquence)* declamation

déclamatoire [deklamatwar] *adj Péj (style)* declamatory; *(discours)* bombastic

déclamer [deklame] *vt (discours, vers)* to declaim; *Péj* to spout

déclaration [deklarasjɔ̃] *nf* (**a**) *(annonce orale, écrite)* statement; **d. (d'amour)** declaration of love; **faire une ou sa d. à qn** to declare one's love to sb; **le chef de l'État a une importante d. à faire** the President has an important announcement to make; **faire une d. à la police** to make a statement to the police; **D. des droits de l'homme** Declaration of Human Rights; **d. de guerre** declaration of war; *Hist* **D. d'indépendance** Declaration of Independence; **d. de principe** statement of principle (**b**) *(acte officiel) (de naissance, de décès)* registration; *(à une compagnie d'assurances)* claim (**de** for); *(à la police)* report; **d. en douane** customs declaration; **d. d'impôts** tax return; **faire sa d. d'impôts** to file one's tax return; **d. de revenus** income-tax return (**c**) *Ordinat* **d. de champ** field definition

Déclaration d'impôts

People in France are required to declare their taxable earnings at the beginning of the year. Thrice-yearly tax payments ("tiers provisionnels") are based on one third of the previous year's total, the final payment being adjusted according to the actual tax owed. It is also possible to pay tax on a monthly basis. This is known as "mensualisation".

déclaré, -e [deklare] *adj (ennemi, intention)* declared; *(partisan)* avowed

déclarer [deklare] **1** *vt (annoncer)* to declare; *(revenus, décès, naissance)* to register; *(à une compagnie d'assurances)* to make a claim for; *(à la police)* to report; **d. que** to declare (that); **d. forfait** *(en sport)* to scratch; **d. la guerre à qn** to declare war on sb; **rien à d.** *(en douane)* nothing to declare; **être déclaré coupable** to be found guilty

2 se déclarer *vpr* (a) *(feu, maladie, guerre)* to break out (b) *(se prononcer)* **se d. pour/contre qch** to declare oneself in favor of/against sth (c) *(se dire)* **se d. satisfait/surpris** to declare oneself satisfied/surprised; **se d. coupable** to admit one's guilt (d) *(faire une déclaration d'amour)* to declare one's love (**à** to)

déclasser [deklase] *vt* (a) *(faire changer de classe)* Sport to relegate; *(hôtel)* to downgrade; *(passagers)* to transfer from one class to another (b) *(déranger)* to get out of order

déclenchement [deklãʃmã] *nm (d'un appareil)* starting; *(d'un mécanisme)* activation; *(d'une sonnerie)* setting off; *(d'un événement)* triggering

déclencher [deklãʃe] **1** *vt (appareil)* to start; *(mécanisme)* to activate; *(sonnerie)* to set off; *(événement, critiques, questions)* to trigger; *Mil (attaque)* to launch

2 se déclencher *vpr* (a) *(sonnerie, sirène, bombe)* to go off (b) *(commencer) (douleur, incendie)* to start

déclencheur [deklãʃœr] *nm Phot* shutter release

déclic [deklik] *nm (bruit)* click; **la vue de cette photo a été pour elle un véritable d.** when she looked at the photo things fell into place

déclin [deklɛ̃] *nm (du talent, de la santé, d'une civilisation)* decline; *(de la beauté)* fading; *(du jour)* close; **être en d.** to be in decline; **le soleil est à son d.** the sun is setting; **au d. de sa vie** in her declining years

déclinaison [deklinɛzɔ̃] *nf* (a) *Gram* declension (b) *Mktg* **d. de gamme** range extension

déclinant, -e [deklinã, -ãt] *adj (beauté, lumière)* fading; *(pouvoirs)* declining

décliner [dekline] **1** *vi (jour)* to draw to a close; *(talent, santé)* to decline; *(beauté)* to fade

2 *vt* (a) *Sout (refuser) (offre, invitation)* to decline; **d. toute responsabilité** to accept no liability (b) *Gram* to decline (c) *(réciter) (identité)* to state

3 se décliner *vpr Gram* to be declined

déclivité [deklivite] *nf* slope, incline

décloisonnement [deklwazɔnmã] *nm* decompartmentalization

décloisonner [deklwazɔne] *vt* to decompartmentalize

déco [deko] *nf Fam (d'une pièce)* décor; *(métier)* (interior) decorating; **j'aime beaucoup faire de la d.** I love decorating

décocher [dekɔʃe] *vt* (a) *(flèche)* to shoot; **d. un coup/une ruade à qn** to hit out at/to kick sb (b) *Fig (remarque)* to fire off (**à** at); *(sourire, œillade)* to flash (**à** at)

décoction [dekɔksjɔ̃] *nf* decoction

décodage [dekɔdaʒ] *nm* decoding

décoder [dekɔde] *vt* to decode

décodeur [dekɔdœr] *nm TV* decoder; **d. numérique** set-top box *(for receiving digital signal)*

décoiffer [dekwafe] **1** *vt (ébouriffer)* **d. qn** to mess up sb's hair; **tu es tout décoiffé** your hair's in a mess; *Fam Fig* **un film qui décoiffe** a mind-blowing movie

2 se décoiffer *vpr* (a) *(se dépeigner)* to mess up one's hair (b) *(ôter son chapeau)* to remove one's hat

décoincer [16] [dekwɛ̃se] **1** *vt (tiroir, mécanisme)* to loosen; *Fam Fig (personne)* to loosen up

2 se décoincer *vpr (tiroir, mécanisme)* to loosen; *Fam Fig (personne)* to loosen up

déçois *etc. voir* **décevoir**

décolérer [34] [dekɔlere] *vi* to calm down; **il ne décolérait pas** he was still angry; **il n'a pas décoléré depuis huit jours** he's been angry for a week

décollage [dekɔlaʒ] *nm* (a) *aussi Fig (démarrage)* takeoff (b) *(d'un timbre, de papier peint, d'une affiche)* peeling off

décollement [dekɔlmã] *nm* (a) *Méd* **d. de la rétine** detachment of the retina (b) *(d'un timbre, de papier peint, d'une affiche)* peeling off

décoller [dekɔle] **1** *vt (timbre, papier peint, affiche)* to peel off; **d. une enveloppe à la vapeur** to steam open an envelope; *Fam Fig* **d. qn de la télé/du bar** to tear sb away from the TV/the bar

2 *vi* (a) *(avion, fusée, économie)* to take off (b) *Fam (partir)* to leave; **bon, on décolle?** shall we get moving?; **je ne décollerai pas d'ici tant que...** I'm not budging until...; *Sport* **d. du peloton** to pull away from the pack

3 se décoller *vpr (se détacher)* to peel off; *Méd (rétine)* to become detached

décolleté, -e [dekɔlte] **1** *adj (vêtement)* low-cut; **une femme très décolletée** a woman in a very low-cut dress; **robe décolletée dans le dos** dress cut low at the back

2 *nm (de vêtement)* low neckline; *(haut des seins)* cleavage

décolonisation [dekɔlɔnizasjɔ̃] *nf* decolonization

décoloniser [dekɔlɔnize] *vt* to decolonize

décolorant, -e [dekɔlɔrã, -ãt] **1** *adj* bleaching

2 *nm* bleaching agent

décoloration [dekɔlɔrasjɔ̃] *nf (d'un tissu)* fading; *(des cheveux)* bleaching; **se faire faire une d.** to have one's hair bleached

décolorer [dekɔlɔre] **1** *vt (tissu)* to fade; *(cheveux)* to bleach

2 se décolorer *vpr (tissu)* to fade; **se d. les cheveux** to bleach one's hair

décombres [dekɔ̃br] *nmpl* ruins, debris

décommander [dekɔmãde] **1** *vt (réunion, dîner)* to cancel, to call off; *(invité)* to put off

2 se décommander *vpr* to cancel

décompacter [3] [dekɔ̃pakte] *vt Ordinat (données)* to unpack

décomplexer [dekɔ̃plɛkse] *vt Fam* **d. qn** to cure sb of his/her hang-ups

décomposer [dekɔ̃poze] **1** *vt* (a) *(élément chimique)* to decompose; *(problème, phrase, mouvement)* to break down (**en** into) (b) *(matière organique)* to decompose (c) *(traits, visage)* to distort; **il est arrivé complètement décomposé** *(par l'émotion)* he arrived quite distraught

2 se décomposer *vpr* (a) *(corps, viande, feuilles)* to decompose; *Fig (tomber en décadence)* to decay (b) *(visage, traits)* to become distorted

décomposition [dekɔ̃pozisjɔ̃] *nf* (a) *(d'un élément chimique)* decomposition; *(d'un problème, d'une phrase, d'un mouvement)* breaking down (**en** into) (b) *(de viande, de feuilles, de corps)* decomposition; *Fig (décadence)* decay; **en d.** *(cadavre)* decomposing; *Fig (société)* decaying

décompresser [dekɔ̃prese] **1** *vt Tech* to decompress; *Ordinat* to decompress, to unzip

2 *vi Fam* to unwind

décompression [dekɔ̃presjɔ̃] *nf* decompression; *Ordinat* decompression, unbundling; **avoir un accident de d.** *(plongeur)* to get the bends

décompte [dekɔ̃t] *nm (sur une somme à payer)* deduction; *(calcul)* calculation; **faire le d. des voix** to count the votes; **faire le d. des points** to add up the score

décompter [dekɔ̃te] *vt* to deduct (**de** from)

déconcentrer [dekɔ̃sãtre] **1** *vt* (a) *(pouvoirs, administration)* to devolve, to decentralize (b) *(distraire)* to distract

2 se déconcentrer *vpr* to lose concentration

déconcertant, -e [dekɔ̃sɛrtã, -ãt] *adj* disconcerting

déconcerté, -e [dekɔ̃sɛrte] *adj* disconcerted

déconcerter [dekɔ̃sɛrte] *vt* to disconcert

déconfit, -e [dekɔ̃fi, -it] *adj (personne, mine)* crestfallen

déconfiture [dekɔ̃fityr] *nf (échec)* defeat

décongeler [39] [dekɔ̃ʒle] *vt* to defrost, to thaw

décongestionner [dekɔ̃ʒɛstjɔne] *vt aussi Fig* to relieve congestion in

déconnecter [dekɔnɛkte] *vt (fil)* to disconnect; *Fig* **déconnecté de la réalité** out of touch with the real world

déconner [dekɔne] *vi très Fam* (**a**) *(dire des bêtises)* to talk crap; *(faire des bêtises)* to mess around; **faire qch pour d.** *(pour rire)* to do sth for a laugh; **sans d., c'était super** no kidding, it was great; **sans d.!** *(en réponse)* no kidding! (**b**) *(mal fonctionner)* to play up

déconneur, -euse [dekɔnœr, -øz] *nm,f très Fam* clown, joker

déconseiller [dekɔ̃seje] *vt* **d. qch à qn** to advise sb against sth; **d. à qn de faire qch** to advise sb against doing sth; **un livre à d. aux jeunes** an unsuitable book for young people; **il est déconseillé de…** it is inadvisable to…

déconsidérer [34] [dekɔ̃sidere] **1** *vt* to discredit
  2 se déconsidérer *vpr* to bring discredit on oneself

décontamination [dekɔ̃taminasjɔ̃] *nf* decontamination

décontaminer [dekɔ̃tamine] *vt* to decontaminate

décontenancer [16] [dekɔ̃tnɑ̃se] **1** *vt* to disconcert
  2 se décontenancer *vpr* to become disconcerted

décontracté, -e [dekɔ̃trakte] *adj (ambiance, attitude, personne)* relaxed; *(vêtement)* casual; *Péj (désinvolte)* casual

décontracter [dekɔ̃trakte] **1** *vt (muscle)* to relax; *(personne)* to put at ease
  2 se décontracter *vpr* to relax

décontraction [dekɔ̃traksjɔ̃] *nf* relaxation; **faire qch avec d.** to do sth casually

déconvenue [dekɔ̃vny] *nf Sout* disappointment; **quelle ne fut pas ma d. quand…** I was so disappointed when…

décor [dekɔr] *nm* (**a**) *(d'une maison, d'un restaurant)* décor (**b**) *Théât, Cin & TV* **décors** set, scenery; **en d. naturel** on location; *Fam* **aller/envoyer qn dans le d.** *(en voiture)* to go/to knock sb off the road (**c**) *(environnement)* surroundings; *Fig* **il aurait besoin d'un changement** *ou* **de changer de d.** he needs a change of scene

décorateur, -trice [dekɔratœr, -tris] *nm,f* (**a**) *(d'intérieur)* (interior) decorator (**b**) *Théât* set designer

décoratif, -ive [dekɔratif, -iv] *adj* decorative; *(arbre)* ornamental; *Péj* **n'avoir qu'un rôle d.** to have a purely decorative role

décoration [dekɔrasjɔ̃] *nf* (**a**) *(d'une maison, d'un restaurant)* decoration; **faire de la d.** to decorate; **d. d'intérieur** interior decorating; **décorations de Noël** Christmas decorations (**b**) *(médaille)* decoration

décorer [dekɔre] *vt* (**a**) *(pièce, maison)* to decorate (**de** with) (**b**) *(médailler)* to decorate (**de** with)

décorticage [dekɔrtikaʒ] *nm (de crevettes, de noisettes)* shelling; *(de riz, d'orge)* hulling; *Fig (d'un texte, d'un auteur)* detailed analysis

décortiquer [dekɔrtike] *vt (crevettes, noisettes)* to shell; *(riz, orge)* to hull; *Fig (texte)* to analyze in detail

décorum [dekɔrɔm] *nm* decorum

découcher [dekuʃe] *vi* to stay out all night

découdre [21] [dekudr] **1** *vt (vêtement, poche, ourlet)* to unpick, to unstitch; *(bouton)* to take off
  2 *vi* **en d.** to fight
  3 se découdre *vpr (vêtement, poche, ourlet)* to come unstitched; *(bouton)* to come off

découler [dekule] *vi* to follow (**de** from); **il en découle que…** it follows that…

découpage [dekupaʒ] *nm* (**a**) *(de gâteau)* cutting up; *(de viande)* carving; *(de métaux, du cuir)* punching; *Ordinat (de fichier, d'image)* splitting; *Pol* **d. électoral** division into constituencies (**b**) *(image découpée)* cutout; **faire du d.** *ou* **des découpages** to do some cutting out (**c**) *Fig (d'un texte)* division (**en** into); *Cin (scénario)* shooting script

découpé, -e [dekupe] *adj (irrégulier)* jagged

découper [dekupe] **1** *vt* (**a**) *(gâteau, papier)* to cut up; *(viande)* to carve; *(métaux, cuir)* to punch; *Ordinat (fichier, image)* to split; *(disque dur)* to partition; **d. un article dans un journal** to cut an article out of a newspaper (**b**) *Fig (texte)* to divide (**en** into)
  2 se découper *vpr* se **d. sur** to stand out against

décourageant, -e [dekuraʒɑ̃, -ɑ̃t] *adj (nouvelle, situation, travail)* disheartening; *(personne)* hopeless

découragement [dekuraʒmɑ̃] *nm* discouragement

décourager [45] [dekuraʒe] **1** *vt* (**a**) *(démoraliser)* to discourage, to dishearten; **se laisser d.** to be discouraged *or* disheartened (**b**) *(dissuader)* to discourage; **d. qn de faire qch** to discourage sb from doing sth
  2 se décourager *vpr* to get discouraged *or* disheartened

décousu, -e [dekuzy] *adj (ourlet, poche, vêtement)* unstitched; *Fig (phrases, idées)* disjointed; *(conversation)* rambling; *(travail)* unmethodical

découvert, -e [dekuvɛr, -ɛrt] **1** *adj (épaules)* bare; *(terrain)* open; **dormir d.** to sleep without any covers; **la tête découverte** bareheaded
  2 *nm* (**a**) *Fin* **d. (bancaire)** overdraft; **être à d. (de 200 euros)** *(personne, compte)* to be overdrawn (by 200 euros) (**b**) **agir à d.** to act openly; **s'avancer à d.** to move forward without cover

découverte [dekuvɛrt] *nf* discovery; **aller** *ou* **partir à la d. de qch** to go off to explore sth; **faire une d.** to make a discovery; *Hum* **ce n'est pas une d.!** that's nothing new!

découvrir [52] [dekuvrir] **1** *vt* (**a**) *(trouver)* to discover (**b**) *(mettre à jour) (secret, complot)* to uncover; **d. qch à qn** *(projets, secrets)* to disclose *or* to reveal sth to sb (**c**) *(apprendre à connaître) (domaine, art, sentiment)* to discover; *(personne)* to get to know (**d**) *(casserole, statue)* to uncover; *(dents, bras)* to bare; **une robe avec un décolleté qui découvre les épaules** an off-the-shoulder dress; *aussi Fig* **d. son jeu** to show one's hand (**e**) *(apercevoir)* to have a view of
  2 se découvrir *vpr* (**a**) *(enlever son chapeau)* to take off one's hat (**b**) *(en dormant)* **le malade s'est découvert** the patient threw off his bedclothes (**c**) *(ciel)* to clear (**d**) *(se trouver)* to discover; **se d. des parents éloignés** to discover some distant relatives; **il s'est découvert une passion pour le jardinage** he discovered he had a passion for gardening

décrasser [dekrase] **1** *vt* to clean; *Fam Fig* **d. qn** to knock the rough edges off sb
  2 se décrasser *vpr* to clean oneself up; *Fig (en faisant de l'exercice)* to clean out one's system

décrêper [dekrepe] *vt (cheveux)* to straighten; **se faire d. les cheveux** to have one's hair straightened

décrépit, -ite [dekrepi, -it] *adj (maison, mur, personne)* decrepit

décrépitude [dekrepityd] *nf* decrepitude; *(décadence)* decay; **tomber en d.** *(civilisation)* to decay; *(institution)* to become obsolete

décret [dekrɛ] *nm* decree

décréter [34] [dekrete] *vt* (**a**) *Jur (état d'urgence, nomination)* to decree (**b**) *(décider)* **d. que** to vow (that)

décrié, -e [dekrije] *adj* disparaged

décrire [30] [dekrir] *vt* (**a**) *(représenter)* to describe (**b**) **d. un cercle** to circle; **d. une courbe** to curve

décrispation [dekrispasjɔ̃] *nf Pol* détente

décrisper [dekrispe] **1** *vt (personne)* to relax; *(atmosphère)* to lighten
  2 se décrisper *vpr* to relax

décrocher [dekrɔʃe] **1** *vt* (**a**) *(détacher) (vêtement d'une patère, rideaux, tableau)* to take down (**de** from); *(wagons)* to uncouple; *(combiné)* to pick up; **d. (le téléphone)** *(pour répondre)* to pick up the phone; *(pour ne pas être dérangé)* to take the phone off the hook; **décrochez** *(dans cabine téléphonique)* lift the receiver (**b**) *(recevoir) (poste, prix, contrat)* to land; *Fam* **d. la timbale** to hit the jackpot

2 *vi Fam* (**a**) *(ne plus se concentrer)* to switch off; *(être à la traîne)* to fail to keep up (**b**) *(arrêter de se droguer)* to kick the habit

3 se décrocher *vpr (rideau, tableau)* to come unhooked (**de** from); *(vêtement)* to fall down (**de** from); *(collier)* to come undone; *(wagon)* to come uncoupled (**de** from); **se d. la mâchoire** to dislocate one's jaw

décrocheur, -euse [dekrɔʃœr, -øz] *nm,f Can* dropout

décroiser [dekrwaze] *vt (jambes, bras)* to uncross

décroissant, -e [dekrwasã, -ãt] *adj* decreasing; **par ordre d.** in descending order

décroître [4a] [dekrwatr] *vi (forces, population, nombre, intensité)* to decrease; *(journées)* to draw in, to get shorter; *(lune)* to wane; *(eaux)* to subside; **aller (en) décroissant** to be decreasing

décrotter [dekrɔte] *vt (chaussures, semelles)* to clean the mud off; *Fam Fig (personne)* to knock the rough edges off

décrue [dekry] *nf (de rivière)* drop in level

décrypter [dekripte] *vt* to decipher

déçu, -e [desy] **1** *pp voir* **décevoir**

2 *adj* disappointed; *Fig & Ironique* **elle ne va pas être déçue (du voyage)** she's in for a disappointment

déculottée [dekylɔte] *nf Fam* hammering

déculotter [dekylɔte] **1** *vt* **d. qn** *(enlever son slip)* to take sb's underpants off; *(enlever son pantalon)* to take sb's pants off

2 se déculotter *vpr (enlever son slip)* to take off one's underpants; *(enlever son pantalon)* to take off one's pants; *Fig (s'abaisser)* to grovel (**devant** to)

déculpabiliser [dekylpabilize] **1** *vt* **d. qn** to stop sb feeling guilty

2 se déculpabiliser *vpr* to stop feeling guilty

décuple [dekypl] *nm* **le d. de qch** ten times sth

décupler [dekyple] **1** *vt* to increase tenfold; *Fig* **la terreur décupla ses forces** terror gave her the strength of ten people

2 *vi* to increase tenfold

dédaigner [dedɛɲe] *vt (offre)* to scorn; *(injure, conseil, gloire)* to disregard; *(personne)* to despise; **il ne dédaigne pas un cigare de temps en temps** he is not averse to the occasional cigar

dédaigneusement [dedɛɲøzmã] *adv* scornfully, disdainfully

dédaigneux, -euse [dedɛɲø, -øz] *adj* scornful, disdainful (**de** of)

dédain [dedɛ̃] *nm* scorn, disdain (**pour qn/de qch** for sb/sth); **avec d.** scornfully, with disdain

dédale [dedal] *nm aussi Fig* maze

dedans [dədã] **1** *adv* inside; **la lettre est d.** the letter is inside; **c'est un bon film mais il y a trop de violence d.** it's a good movie but there's too much violence in it; **de d.** *(depuis l'intérieur)* from inside; **en d.** *(d'un objet)* (on the) inside; *(en son for intérieur)* inwardly; **marcher les pieds en d.** to be pigeon-toed; **en d. de** inside

2 *nm (d'une maison, d'une boîte)* inside; **du d.** *(depuis l'intérieur)* from inside

dédicace [dedikas] *nf* (**a**) *(de livre, de photo)* dedication (**b**) *(à la radio)* dedication

dédicacer [16] [dedikase] *vt* (**a**) *(signer)* to sign (**à** for); *(écrire dans) (livre)* to write a dedication in (**à** to); *(photo)* to write a dedication on (**à** to) (**b**) *(chanson)* to dedicate (**à** to)

dédier [66] [dedje] *vt* to dedicate (**à** to)

dédire [27b] [dedir] **se dédire** *vpr* **se d. d'une déclaration** to retract *or* to withdraw a statement; **se d. d'une promesse** to go back on one's word

dédommagement [dedɔmaʒmã] *nm* compensation; **500 000 euros de d.** 500,000 euros (in) compensation; **en d. de qch** in compensation for sth

dédommager [45] [dedɔmaʒe] *vt (financièrement)* to compensate (**de** for); **pour me d., il m'a invité au restaurant** he took me out for a meal to make up for it

dédouanement [dedwanmã] *nm* clearance through customs

dédouaner [dedwane] **1** *vt (marchandise)* to clear (through customs); *Fig (personne)* to clear

2 se dédouaner *vpr* to clear one's name

dédoublement [dedublǝmã] *nm* **d. de la personnalité** split personality

dédoubler [deduble] **1** *vt (partager)* to divide *or* to split into two

2 se dédoubler *vpr Psy* to have a split personality; *Hum* **je ne peux pas me d.** I can't be in two places at once

dédramatiser [dedramatize] *vt* **d. qch** to make sth less dramatic

déductible [dedyktibl] *adj* deductible; **d. des impôts** tax-deductible

déduction [dedyksjɔ̃] *nf* (**a**) *(soustraction, abattement)* deduction; **d. faite des frais d'essence** after deduction of gasoline costs (**b**) *(conclusion)* deduction

déduire [18] [deduir] *vt* (**a**) *(enlever)* to deduct (**de** from) (**b**) *(conclure)* to deduce, to infer (**de** from)

déesse [deɛs] *nf* goddess

défaillance [defajãs] *nf* (**a**) *(insuffisance) (morale)* failing; *(physique)* deficiency; *(d'une machine)* failure; **avoir des défaillances en** *(intellectuelles)* to have problems with; **courage sans d.** unfailing courage; **d. cardiaque** heart failure (**b**) *(évanouissement)* fainting fit; *(faiblesse)* feeling of weakness; **avoir une d.** *(s'évanouir)* to faint; *(se sentir faible)* to feel weak

défaillant, -e [defajã, -ãt] *adj* (**a**) *(forces, mémoire, santé)* failing; *(cœur)* weak; *(voix)* faltering (**b**) *(qui s'évanouit)* faint

défaillir [35] [defajir] *vi* (**a**) *(faiblir) (mémoire, forces)* to fail; **à cette nouvelle, son cœur défaillit** her heart sank at the news (**b**) *(s'évanouir)* to faint; **d. de faim/de bonheur** to feel faint with hunger/happiness

défaire [36] [defɛr] **1** *vt* (**a**) *(ouvrir, détacher)* to undo; *(valise)* to unpack; **d. le lit** *(enlever les draps)* to strip the bed; *(le mettre en désordre)* to rumple the bedclothes; **d. ses cheveux** to let one's hair down (**b**) *(désassembler) (puzzle)* to take apart; *(ourlet)* to undo

2 se défaire *vpr* (**a**) *(se dénouer) (vêtement, nœud)* to come undone; *(cheveux)* to come down (**b**) *(se désagréger) (puzzle)* to come apart; *(ourlet)* to come undone; *Fig (alliance, mariage)* to break up (**c**) **se d. de qn/qch** to get rid of sb/sth; **je ne veux pas m'en d.** I don't want to part with it (**d**) *(s'altérer) (visage)* to drop

défait, -e [defɛ, -ɛt] *adj (traits, visage)* haggard; **il est arrivé à l'hôpital, complètement d.** he arrived at the hospital in a state of great distress

défaite [defɛt] *nf* defeat

défaitisme [defɛtism] *nm* defeatism

défaitiste [defɛtist] *adj & nmf* defeatist

défalquer [defalke] *vt* to deduct (**de** from)

défausser [defose] **se défausser** *vpr (aux cartes)* to discard; **se d. à cœur** to discard a heart/some hearts; **se d. d'un dix** to discard a ten

défaut [defo] *nm* (**a**) *(imperfection) (d'une personne)* fault, shortcoming; *(d'une pierre précieuse, d'un verre, d'un tissu)* flaw; *(d'une machine)* defect; *(d'un raisonnement)* flaw; *(inconvénient)* drawback; **c'est là son moindre d.** that's the least of his/her faults; **sans d.** faultless, flawless; **prendre qn en d.** to catch sb napping; **d. de fabrication** manufacturing fault; **d. de prononciation** *ou* **d'élocution** speech impediment

(**b**) *(manque)* lack; **le courage lui a fait d.** his/her courage failed him/her; **l'argent lui fait cruellement d.** he/she is very short of money; **le bon sens lui fait cruellement d.**

he/she is sadly lacking in common sense; **ou à d.,...** or, failing that,...; **à d. de qch** for lack of sth; **à d. d'un salaire important, elle a au moins un travail intéressant** she might not have a very good salary, but at least her work is interesting

(c) *Jur* default; **faire d.** to default; **d. de paiement** default on payment

(d) *Math* **total approché par d.** total rounded down; *Ordinat* **lecteur/clavier par d.** default drive/keyboard

défaveur [defavœr] *nf* **être en d. (auprès de qn)** to be in disfavor (with sb); **s'attirer la d. de qn** to incur sb's disfavor

défavorable [defavɔrabl] *adj* unfavorable (**à** to)

défavorisé, -e [defavɔrize] *adj (milieu, pays)* underprivileged

défavoriser [defavɔrize] *vt* to put at a disadvantage (**par rapport à** compared to)

défectif, -ive [defɛktif, -iv] *adj* defective

défection [defɛksjɔ̃] *nf* (a) *(d'un espion, d'un soldat)* defection (b) *(annulation)* cancellation

défectueux, -euse [defɛktɥø, -øz] *adj* defective, faulty

défendable [defɑ̃dabl] *adj* defensible

défendre [defɑ̃dr] **1** *vt* (a) *(soutenir)* to defend (**contre** against) (b) *(protéger) (personne, pays, propriété)* to defend (**contre** against *ou* from); *(intérêts)* to protect; **d. qn contre le froid** *ou* **du froid** to protect sb from the cold; *Fig* **d. son bifteck** to look after number one; *Sport* **Durant défendra les buts de l'équipe d'Aix** Durant will be in goal for Aix (c) *(interdire)* to forbid, to prohibit; **ce médicament est défendu aux enfants** this medicine must not be given to children; **d. à qn de faire qch** to forbid sb to do sth; **il m'est défendu de fumer** I'm not allowed to smoke; **il est défendu de fumer** smoking is prohibited

2 se défendre *vpr* (a) *(se protéger)* to defend oneself (**de** *ou* **contre** against); **se d. comme un beau diable** to fight like a mad thing (b) *Fam (se débrouiller)* **je me défends (en anglais/en tennis)** I can hold my own (in English/at tennis) (c) *(se justifier)* **ça se défend** there's something to be said for it (d) *(s'empêcher)* **se d. de faire qch** to refrain from doing sth; **on ne peut se d. de les aimer** you can't help liking them

défenestrer [defənɛstre] **1** *vt* **d. qn** to to throw sb out of a window

2 se défenestrer *vpr* to jump out of the window

défense¹ [defɑ̃s] *nf* (a) *(soutien) (d'une théorie, d'une politique, d'un accusé)* defense; **prendre la d. de qn** to come to sb's defense; **sans d.** defenseless; *Jur* **assurer la d. de qn** to defend sb; **qu'avez-vous à dire pour votre d.?** what do you have to say in your defense?; **d. des consommateurs** consumer protection (b) *(protection) (d'une personne, d'un pays, en sport)* defense; **d. aérienne/nationale/passive** air/national/civil defense; *Méd* **défenses immunitaires** immune defenses (c) *(interdiction)* **d. d'entrer/de fumer** *(sur panneau)* no entry/smoking; **et d. d'en parler à ton père!** don't go telling your father about it!

défense² [defɑ̃s] *nf* *(d'éléphant, de sanglier)* tusk

défenseur [defɑ̃sœr] *nm* (a) *(d'une personne, d'une ville, d'une cause, en sport)* defender; **jouer les défenseurs de la veuve et de l'orphelin** to protect the weak and oppressed (b) *Jur* counsel for the defense

défensif, -ive [defɑ̃sif, -iv] **1** *adj* defensive

2 *nf* **être** *ou* **se tenir sur la défensive** to be on the defensive

déféquer [34] [defeke] *vi* to defecate

déférence [deferɑ̃s] *nf* deference (**pour** for)

déférer [34] [defere] *vt* *Jur* **d. une affaire à un tribunal** to refer a case to a court; **d. qn à la justice** to hand sb over to the police

déferlante [defɛrlɑ̃t] *adj f & nf* **(vague) d.** breaker; *Fig* tidal wave

déferlement [defɛrləmɑ̃] *nm* *(des vagues)* breaking; *Fig (de*

personnes) invasion; *(d'enthousiasme, de violence, de racisme)* wave

déferler [defɛrle] *vi (vagues)* to break; **la foule déferle dans les rues** the crowd is surging along the streets; **les vacanciers déferlent sur les routes** vacationers are taking to the roads in droves

défi [defi] *nm* (a) *(acte de provocation)* challenge (**à** to); **lancer** *ou* **jeter un d. à qn** to throw out a challenge to sb; **mettre qn au d. de faire qch** to defy sb to do sth; **relever un d.** to take up a challenge (b) *(bravade)* defiance

défiance [defjɑ̃s] *nf* mistrust

déficience [defisjɑ̃s] *nf* deficiency; **d. immunologique** immune deficiency

déficient, -e [defisjɑ̃, -ɑ̃t] **1** *adj* deficient; *(raisonnement, théorie)* weak

2 *nm,f* **d. moteur** person with motor deficiency; **d. mental** mentally deficient person

déficit [defisit] *nm* (a) *Fin* deficit; **être en d.** to be in deficit; **d. budgétaire/commercial** budget/trade deficit (b) *Méd (mental)* deficiency; **d. immunitaire** immunodeficiency

déficitaire [defisiter] *adj (entreprise)* loss-making; *(compte)* in debit; *(budget)* in deficit

défier [66] [defje] **1** *vt* (a) *(provoquer)* to challenge; **d. qn aux échecs** to challenge sb to a game of chess (b) *(inciter)* **d. qn de faire qch** to defy sb to do sth (c) *(braver) (personne, danger, mort)* to defy (d) *(résister à)* **d. l'imagination** to defy the imagination; **des prix qui défient toute concurrence** unbeatable prices

2 se défier *vpr Litt* **se d. de** to mistrust

défigurer [defigyre] *vt (personne, paysage)* to disfigure; *Fig (vérité, sens)* to distort; *(pensée, intentions)* to misrepresent

défilé [defile] *nm* (a) *Géog* (mountain) pass (b) *(de manifestants)* march; *(de chars de carnaval)* procession; *Mil* parade; **un d. ininterrompu de touristes/voitures** an endless stream of tourists/cars; **d. aérien** flyby, flyover; **d. de mode** fashion show

défilement [defilmɑ̃] *nm* *Ordinat* scrolling

défiler¹ [defile] **se défiler** *vpr Fam (se dérober)* to slip away

défiler² [defile] *vi* (a) *(manifestants)* to march; *(chars de carnaval)* to drive in procession; *(touristes, voitures)* to stream; *Mil* to parade (b) *(avancer) (bande)* to wind on; *Ordinat* **faire d. un document** to scroll through a document; *Ordinat* **d. vers le bas/le haut** to scroll down/up (c) *(se succéder) (images, souvenirs)* to pass; **le paysage défile à toute vitesse** the countryside is speeding past

défini, -e [defini] *adj* (a) *(précis)* definite; **bien d.** clearly defined; *Ordinat* **d. par l'utilisateur** user-defined (b) *Gram* definite

définir [definir] **1** *vt* to define

2 se définir *vpr* (a) *(concept)* **se d. comme** to be defined as (b) *(soi-même)* to describe oneself (**comme** as)

définissable [definisabl] *adj* definable

définitif, -ive [definitif, -iv] *adj* (a) *(irrévocable) (jugement, décision, version)* final (b) *(pour toujours) (séparation, fermeture)* permanent (c) *(qui fait autorité)* definitive (d) **en définitive** *(à la fin)* in the end

définition [definisjɔ̃] *nf* (a) *(d'un mot, de conditions)* definition; *(de mots croisés)* clue; **par d.** by definition (b) *(d'une image sur écran)* definition

définitivement [definitivmɑ̃] *adv (décider)* definitely; *(partir, s'installer)* for good; *(nommé)* permanently

défiscaliser [defiskalize] *vt* to exempt from tax

déflagration [deflagrasjɔ̃] *nf (explosion)* explosion

déflation [deflasjɔ̃] *nf Écon* deflation

déflecteur [deflɛktœr] *nm (d'une voiture)* vent

déflocage [deflɔkaʒ] *nm* removal of asbestos

déflorer [deflɔre] *vt* (a) *(vierge)* to deflower (b) *Fig (sujet)* to spoil

défoliant [defɔljɑ̃] *nm* defoliant

défonce [defɔ̃s] *nf Fam* **la d.** getting high

défoncé, -e [defɔ̃se] *adj* (**a**) *(chemin)* bumpy (**b**) *Fam (drogué)* high (**à** on)

défoncer [16] [defɔ̃se] **1** *vt (boîte, porte)* to smash in; *(matelas)* to ruin; *(mur)* to knock down; *(tonneau, bateau)* to stave in; *(chaussée)* to break up
   2 se défoncer *vpr Fam* (**a**) *(se droguer)* to get high (**à** on) (**b**) *(faire un grand effort)* to sweat blood (**pour faire qch** to do sth)

déforestation [defɔrɛstasjɔ̃] *nf* deforestation

déformant, -e [defɔrmɑ̃, -ɑ̃t] *adj (glace)* distorting

déformation [defɔrmasjɔ̃] *nf (d'un membre)* deformation; *(d'un vêtement, de chaussures)* putting out of shape; *(de métal)* buckling; *(de bois)* warping; *(des traits, d'une image, des faits)* distortion; *(de propos)* twisting; **d. professionnelle** = habits acquired through the type of work one does; *Hum* **ne fais pas attention, c'est la d. professionnelle!** don't worry, it's just my job!

déformer [defɔrme] **1** *vt (membre)* to deform; *(vêtement, chaussures)* to put out of shape; *(métal)* to buckle; *(bois)* to warp; *(traits, image, faits)* to distort; *(propos)* to twist; *(pensée)* to misrepresent
   2 se déformer *vpr (corps, vêtement, chaussures)* to get out of shape; *(bois)* to warp; *(métal)* to buckle

défoulement [defulmɑ̃] *nm Fam* letting off steam; **avoir besoin de d.** to need to let off steam

défouler [defule] *Fam* **1** *vt (agressivité)* to vent (**sur** on); **d. qn** to help sb let off steam; **ça défoule** it helps you let off steam
   2 se défouler *vpr* to let off steam; **se d. sur qn** to take it out on sb

défraîchi, -e [defrɛʃi] *adj (fleur, beauté)* faded; *(vêtement)* shabby

défrayer [53] [defreje] *vt* (**a**) *(rembourser)* **d. qn** to pay sb's expenses (**b**) **d. la chronique** to be widely talked about

défrichage [defriʃaʒ], **défrichement** [defriʃmɑ̃] *nm (de terrain)* clearing

défricher [defriʃe] *vt* to clear; *Fig (domaine)* to open up; *Fig* **d. le terrain** to prepare the ground

défriser [defrize] *vt (cheveux)* to straighten; *Fam Fig (agacer)* to bug

défriseur [defrizœr] *nm (pour les cheveux)* hair straighteners

défroisser [defrwase] *vt* to smooth out

défroqué, -e [defrɔke] *adj* defrocked

défunt, -e [defœ̃, -œ̃t] **1** *adj* **mon d. mari** my late husband; *Litt* **des amours défuntes** lost loves
   2 *nm,f* deceased; **prier pour les défunts** to pray for the dead

dégagé, -e [degaʒe] *adj (ton, air)* casual; *(ciel, route)* clear; *(vue)* open; **une coupe avec la nuque très dégagée** a haircut that is very short at the back

dégagement [degaʒmɑ̃] *nm* (**a**) *(d'une route, des poumons)* clearing (**b**) *(au football)* clearance (**c**) *(de vapeur, de gaz, de chaleur)* emission

dégager [45] [degaʒe] **1** *vt* (**a**) *(libérer)* to free (**de** from); *(d'une voiture accidentée, de décombres)* to pull clear (**de** of); **une robe qui dégage les épaules** an off-the-shoulder dress (**b**) *(désencombrer) (route, passage)* to clear; *Fam* **dégage!** clear off! (**c**) *Fam (enlever)* to clear away; **tu vas me d. toutes ces bricoles de tes étagères** I want you to clear all these odds and ends off your shelves (**d**) *(laisser échapper) (vapeur, odeur, chaleur)* to emit; *Fig (impression)* to give off (**e**) *(au football)* **d. (le ballon) en touche** to kick the ball into touch (**f**) *Fin (crédits)* to release; *(profit)* to show
   2 se dégager *vpr* (**a**) *(se libérer)* to free oneself (**de** from); *(d'une situation difficile)* to extricate oneself (**de** from) (**b**) *(se débloquer) (ciel, nez)* to clear (**c**) *(gaz, odeur, chaleur)* to be given

off (**de** by); *Fig* **le magnétisme qui se dégage d'elle** the magnetism she radiates

dégaine [degɛn] *nf Fam (démarche)* awkward way of walking; *(apparence)* strange appearance

dégainer [degene] *vt (arme)* to draw

dégarni, -e [degarni] *adj (personne)* balding; **avoir le front d.** to have a receding hairline

dégarnir [degarnir] **1** *vt (frigidaire, rayons)* to empty
   2 se dégarnir *vpr (personne)* to go bald; *(arbre)* to lose its leaves; *(salle)* to empty; *(rayons)* to be emptied

dégât [dega] *nm* damage; **faire du d.** *ou* **des dégâts** to cause damage; *Fig* **limiter les dégâts** to limit the damage; *Mil* **dégâts collatéraux** collateral damage; **dégâts des eaux** water damage; **dégâts matériels** material damage

dégel [deʒɛl] *nm Météo & Pol* thaw; *Écon (des prix, des salaires, des crédits)* unfreezing

dégeler [39] [deʒle] **1** *vt* (**a**) *(réchauffer)* to thaw; *(surgelé)* to defrost; *Fig (public)* to warm up; **d. l'atmosphère** to make the atmosphere less chilly (**b**) *Écon (prix, salaires, crédits)* to unfreeze
   2 *vi (étang, surgelé)* to thaw; **faire d. qch** *(surgelé)* to defrost sth
   3 *v impersonnel* to thaw
   4 se dégeler *vpr* (**a**) *(étang)* to thaw (**b**) *Fig (atmosphère)* to become less chilly; *(personne)* to thaw out, to relax

dégénératif, -ive [deʒeneratif, -iv] *adj* degenerative

dégénéré, -e [deʒenere] **1** *adj* (**a**) *(arriéré)* mentally defective (**b**) *(dépravé)* degenerate
   2 *nm,f* (**a**) *(arriéré)* mental defective (**b**) *(dépravé)* degenerate

dégénérer [34] [deʒenere] *vi (mal tourner) (situation, conversation)* to degenerate (**en** into); **son rhume a dégénéré en bronchite** his cold developed into bronchitis

dégénérescence [deʒeneresɑ̃s] *nf Méd & Fig* degeneration

dégingandé, -e [deʒɛ̃gɑ̃de] *adj* gangling, lanky

dégivrage [deʒivraʒ] *nm* (**a**) *(action) (d'un pare-brise)* de-icing; *(d'un réfrigérateur)* defrosting (**b**) *(dispositif) (d'un pare-brise)* de-icer; *(d'un réfrigérateur)* defroster

dégivrer [deʒivre] *vt (pare-brise)* to de-ice; *(réfrigérateur)* to defrost

déglacer [16] [deglase] *vt Culin (poêle à frire)* to deglaze

déglinguer [deglɛ̃ge] *Fam* **1** *vt (appareil)* to bust; **ma moto est toute déglinguée** my motorcycle is falling to pieces
   2 se déglinguer *vpr (appareil)* to go wrong; *(véhicule)* to fall to pieces

déglutir [deglytir] *vi* to swallow

déglutition [deglytisjɔ̃] *nf* swallowing

dégobiller [degɔbije] *très Fam* **1** *vi* to puke
   2 *vt* to puke up

dégonflé, -e [degɔ̃fle] **1** *adj* (**a**) *(pneu, ballon)* flat (**b**) *Fam (lâche)* chicken
   2 *nm,f Fam* chicken

dégonfler [degɔ̃fle] **1** *vt (pneu, ballon)* to let the air out of, to deflate
   2 *vi (partie du corps)* to go down
   3 se dégonfler *vpr* (**a**) *(pneu, ballon)* to go flat (**b**) *Fam (personne)* to chicken out

dégorger [45] [degɔrʒe] **1** *vt* (**a**) *(évacuer)* to discharge; **la rue a dégorgé un flot de gens** a crowd of people surged from the street (**b**) *(passage, tuyau, évier)* to unblock
   2 *vi* **faire d. des concombres** = to remove water from cucumbers by sprinkling them with salt

dégot(t)er [degɔte] *vt Fam* to dig up

dégouliner [deguline] *vi (liquide)* to trickle; **je dégouline** I'm dripping wet

dégoupiller [degupije] *vt (grenade)* to pull the pin out of

dégourdi, -e [degurdi] **1** *adj* smart, bright
   2 *nm,f* **c'est un d.** he's a smart one

dégourdir [degurdir] **1** *vt (membres)* to remove the stiffness from; *Fig* **d. qn** to teach sb a thing or two

2 se dégourdir *vpr* (**a**) *(membres)* **se d. les jambes** to stretch one's legs (**b**) *Fig* to learn a thing or two

dégoût [degu] *nm* (**a**) *(aversion)* disgust, distaste; **éprouver du d. pour qch** to be disgusted by sth; **prendre qch en d.** to take a strong dislike to sth (**b**) *(lassitude)* weariness; **le d. de la vie** world-weariness

dégoûtant, -e [degutɑ̃, -ɑ̃t] **1** *adj* disgusting

2 *nm,f* disgusting person; **un vieux d.** a dirty old man

dégoûté, -e [degute] **1** *adj* (**a**) *(écœuré)* *(air)* disgusted; *Ironique* **vous n'êtes pas d.!** you're not fussy! (**b**) *(choqué)* disgusted (**c**) *(las)* weary; **être d. de qch** to be weary *or* sick of sth

2 *nm,f* **faire le d.** to turn up one's nose

dégoûter [degute] *vt* **d. qn** *(physiquement)* to turn sb's stomach; *(moralement)* to disgust sb, to make sb sick; **d. qn de qch** to put sb off sth; **c'est à vous d. de l'Espagne/des hommes!** it's enough to put you off Spain/men for life!

dégoutter [degute] **dégoutter de** *vt ind (laisser couler)* to drip with

dégradant, -e [degradɑ̃] *adj* degrading

dégradation [degradasjɔ̃] *nf (d'un monument)* defacement; *(de matériel scolaire, de l'environnement)* damage (**de** to); *Fig (de la santé, de relations, d'une situation)* deterioration

dégradé [degrade] *nm (de couleurs)* gradation; **un d. de bleus** blues shading off into each other; **se faire faire un d.** *(chez le coiffeur)* to have one's hair layered; *Ordinat* **d. de couleur** color scale

dégrader [degrade] **1** *vt* (**a**) *(abîmer)* *(monument)* to deface; *(matériel, maison)* to damage; *Ordinat (données)* to corrupt (**b**) *Fig (humilier)* to degrade (**c**) *Mil* to demote

2 se dégrader *vpr* (**a**) *(se détériorer)* *(santé, relations, situation)* to deteriorate; *(bâtiment)* to fall into disrepair (**b**) *(s'abaisser)* to degrade oneself

dégrafer [degrafe] **1** *vt (vêtement, bracelet)* to undo

2 se dégrafer *vpr* (**a**) *(vêtement, bracelet)* to come undone (**b**) *(femme)* to undo one's dress

dégraffitage [degrafitaʒ] *nm* graffiti removal

dégraissage [degrɛsaʒ] *nm (d'une entreprise)* downsizing

dégraisser [degrese] **1** *vt (bouillon)* to skim the fat off; *Fig (entreprise)* to downsize; **d. les effectifs** to cut back on staff

2 *vi (entreprise)* to downsize

degré [dəgre] *nm* (**a**) *(d'un angle, de chaleur)* degree; *(de boisson alcoolisée)* proof; **combien de degrés fait ce whisky?** what proof is this whiskey?; **d. Celsius** degree Celsius; **d. Fahrenheit** degree Fahrenheit (**b**) *(stade, niveau)* stage; **d. de parenté** family relationship; **cousins au second d.** second cousins; **brûlure au deuxième/troisième d.** second-/third-degree burn; **au plus haut d.** *(extrêmement)* in the extreme; **jusqu'à un certain d.** up to a point; **par degrés** by degrees; **prendre une plaisanterie au premier d.** to take a joke seriously (**c**) *(d'escalier)* step; *(d'échelle)* rung

dégressif, -ive [degresif, -iv] *adj* **tarif d.** tapering rate; **impôt d.** degressive taxation

dégrèvement [degrɛvmɑ̃] *nm* **d. (fiscal)** tax relief

dégriffé, -e [degrife] **1** *adj (vêtement)* = with its designer label removed and reduced in price

2 *nm* = reduced-price designer item with its label removed

dégringolade [degrɛ̃ɡɔlad] *nf Fam (chute)* tumble; *Fig (d'une entreprise)* collapse; *(des prix, des cours)* slump (**de** in)

dégringoler [degrɛ̃ɡɔle] *Fam* **1** *vt* to rush down

2 *vi (personne)* to tumble; *Fig (entreprise)* to collapse; *(prix, cours)* to slump

dégripper [degripe] *vt (mécanisme)* to unjam

dégriser [degrize] **1** *vt* to sober up; *Fig* to bring down to earth

2 se dégriser *vpr* to sober up

dégrossir [degrosir] *vt (bois)* to trim; *(pierre)* to roughhew; *Fig*

(travail) to rough out; **d. qn** to knock the rough edges off sb; **être mal dégrossi** to be uncouth

dégrouper [degrupe] *vt* to divide into groups

déguenillé, -e [degənije] *adj* ragged

déguerpir [degɛrpir] *vi* to clear off; **faire d. qn** to chase sb away

dégueulasse [degœlas] *très Fam* **1** *adj (sale)* filthy; *(mauvais, désagréable)* disgusting; **c'est pas d.** *(bon)* it's not bad at all; **être d. avec qn** to be mean to sb; **se balader en d.** to go around in sloppy old clothes

2 *nmf* **un gros d.** *(sale)* a filthy pig; *(débauché)* a filthy swine

dégueulasser [degœlase] *vt très Fam* to mess up

dégueuler [degœle] *vi très Fam* to puke

dégueulis [degœli] *nm très Fam* puke

déguisé, -e [degize] *adj (pour tromper)* disguised; *(pour s'amuser)* dressed up; **avec une joie non déguisée** with unconcealed delight

déguisement [degizmɑ̃] *nm (pour tromper)* disguise; *(pour s'amuser)* fancy dress

déguiser [degize] **1** *vt* (**a**) *(costumer)* to dress up; **d. qn en clown** to dress sb up as a clown (**b**) *(voix, écriture, vérité, pensée)* to disguise

2 se déguiser *vpr (pour tromper)* to disguise oneself; *(pour s'amuser)* to dress up; **se d. en pompier** to dress up as a fireman

dégurgiter [degyrʒite] *vt aussi Fig* to regurgitate

dégustation [degystasjɔ̃] *nf* tasting; **d. de vin** wine tasting; **d. d'huîtres** *(panneau devant un restaurant)* oysters served here

déguster [degyste] *vt* (**a**) *(tester)* *(vin, alcool)* to taste (**b**) *(savourer)* *(aliment, livre)* to savor (**c**) *très Fam* **toute sa vie, elle a dégusté** *(souffert)* she's had a rough time of it all her life; **tu vas d.!** you're in for it!

déhanché, -e [deɑ̃ʃe] *adj* lopsided

déhanchement [deɑ̃ʃmɑ̃] *nm (en marchant)* swaying of the hips; *(à l'arrêt)* standing with one's weight on one foot

déhancher [deɑ̃ʃe] **se déhancher** *vpr (en marchant)* to sway one's hips; *(à l'arrêt)* to stand with one's weight on one foot

dehors [dəɔr] **1** *adv (à l'extérieur)* outside; *(en plein air)* outdoors, out of doors; *(pas chez soi)* out; *Fam* **ficher** *ou* **foutre qn d.** to kick sb out; **ne pas mettre le nez** *ou* **les pieds d.** not to set foot outside; **en d.** *(s'ouvrir, tourner)* outward; **marcher les pieds en d.** to walk with one's feet turned out; **en d. de** *(à l'extérieur de)* outside; *(à part)* apart from; **rester en d. d'une dispute** to keep out of an argument; **en d. du sujet** *(remarque)* irrelevant

2 *nm* (**a**) *(extérieur)* outside; **au d.** on the outside; *(se pencher, se répandre)* out (**b**) *(apparence)* **une maison aux d. imposants** a house with an imposing exterior; **sous des d. aimables** under a pleasant exterior

déhoussable [deusabl] *adj (canapé, siège)* with removable covers

déjà [deʒa] *adv* (**a**) *(dès maintenant)* already; *(si tôt)* yet; **il est d. trois heures** it's already three o'clock; **faut-il que vous partiez d.?** must you go so soon? (**b**) *(auparavant)* before; **j'avais d. lu ce livre** I'd read that book before; **d. en 1900** as early as 1900 (**c**) *(intensif)* **j'aurais dû le faire il y a d. trois jours** I should have done it three days ago as it is; **c'est d. ça!, c'est d. pas mal!** that's not bad at all!; **vous avez d. trop de travail** you have too much work as it is; **d. que je n'en ai pas beaucoup, si tu m'en prends la moitié…** I haven't got much as it is, so if you take half… (**d**) *(interrogatif)* **qu'est-ce que vous faites, d.?** what did you say your job was?; **c'est quoi, d., ton nom?** what was your name again?

déjanté, -e [deʒɑ̃te] *adj très Fam* **être (complètement) d.** to be off one's rocker

déjanter [deʒɑ̃te] **1** vi très Fam (être fou) to be off one's rocker; (devenir fou) to crack up
 2 se déjanter vpr (pneu) to come off the rim

déjà-vu [deʒavy] nm inv **une impression de d.** a feeling of déjà vu; **c'est du d.** (ce n'est pas original) it's the same old thing

déjeuner [deʒœne] **1** nm (**a**) (repas de midi) lunch; **prendre son d.** to have lunch; **d. d'affaires/de travail** business/working lunch (**b**) (repas du matin) **(petit) d.** breakfast (**c**) (tasse et soucoupe) breakfast cup and saucer
 2 vi (**a**) (le matin) to have breakfast (**b**) (à midi) to have lunch; **nous avons les Dupont à d. dimanche** the Duponts are coming for lunch on Sunday; **d. d'un sandwich** to have a sandwich for lunch

déjouer [deʒwe] vt (complot, plans) to foil

délabré, -e [delabre] adj (bâtiment, meuble) dilapidated; (santé) ruined

délabrement [delabrəmɑ̃] nm (d'un bâtiment, d'un meuble) dilapidated state; (d'une entreprise) ruin; **dans un état de grand d.** (bâtiment) in a state of total disrepair

délabrer [delabre] **se délabrer** vpr (bâtiment) to fall into disrepair; (meuble) to fall to pieces; (entreprise) to go to rack and ruin; (santé) to deteriorate

délacer [16] [delase] **1** vt (chaussures) to untie; (corset) to unlace
 2 se délacer vpr (chaussures) to come untied; (corset) to come unlaced; (femme) to unlace one's corset

délai [delɛ] nm (**a**) (laps de temps) time allowed; **dans un d. de dix jours** within ten days; **il faut compter un d. de dix jours** you should allow ten days; **respecter** ou **tenir les délais** to meet the deadline; **dans les délais** on time; **dans les plus brefs délais** as soon as possible; **lundi dernier d.** by Monday at the very latest; **d. de livraison: un mois** allow one month for delivery; **d. de paiement** (fixé par contrat) term of payment (**b**) (prolongation) extension; **laisser à qn un d. de réflexion** to give sb time to think; **sans d.** without delay, immediately

délaisser [delese] vt (abandonner) to desert, to abandon; (négliger) to neglect

délassant, -e [delɑsɑ̃, -ɑ̃t] adj (bain, massage) relaxing; (lecture) entertaining

délassement [delɑsmɑ̃] nm relaxation

délasser [delɑse] **1** vt to relax
 2 se délasser vpr to relax

délateur, -trice [delatœr, -tris] nm,f informer

délation [delasjɔ̃] nf denouncement

délavé, -e [delave] adj (tissu, jean) faded; (couleur) watery

délayage [delɛjaʒ] nm Péj padding

délayer [53] [deleje] vt (**a**) (poudre) to add water to; (peinture) to thin; (liquide) to water down; **d. de la farine dans du lait** to mix flour with milk (**b**) Fig (discours, texte) to pad out

Delco® [delko] nm Aut distributor

délectable [delɛktabl] adj delectable

délecter [delɛkte] **se délecter** vpr **se d. de qch/à faire qch** to take delight in sth/in doing sth

délégation [delegasjɔ̃] nf (**a**) (action de déléguer) (de représentants) delegation; **agir par d.** to act on the authority invested in one; **d. de pouvoir** delegation of authority (**b**) (groupe) delegation

délégué, -e [delege] nm,f delegate; Scol **d. (de classe)** class representative (at class meetings); **d. du personnel** staff representative; **d. syndical** union representative; (d'usine) shop steward

déléguer [34] [delege] vt (**a**) (personne) to delegate (**b**) (transmettre) (pouvoirs) to delegate (**à** to); **savoir d.** to know how to delegate

délestage [delɛstaʒ] nm (d'un navire, d'un ballon) unballasting; **pour assurer le d. des grandes artères** to relieve congestion on the main roads; **itinéraire de d.** bypass

délester [delɛste] vt (navire, ballon) to unballast; (voie de communication) to relieve congestion on; aussi Hum **d. qn de qch** to relieve sb of sth

délibération [deliberasjɔ̃] nf (**a**) (débat) deliberation; **être en d.** to be under discussion (**b**) (réflexion) deliberation; **après mûre d.** after careful consideration

délibéré, -e [delibere] **1** adj (intentionnel) deliberate
 2 nm Jur (de juges) consultation

délibérément [deliberemɑ̃] adv deliberately

délibérer [34] [delibere] vi (**a**) (discuter) to deliberate (**de** ou **sur** on); Jur (jury) to consider its verdict (**b**) (réfléchir) to deliberate

délicat, -e [delika, -at] adj (**a**) (fragile, fin, difficile) delicate; (peau) sensitive; (travail) fine (**b**) (raffiné) (goûts) refined; (gestes) graceful; (plat) sophisticated; **avoir le palais d.** to have a discerning palate (**c**) (plein de tact) tactful; **quelle attention délicate!** how thoughtful!; **peu d.** (peu scrupuleux) unscrupulous (**d**) (exigeant) fussy; **faire le d.** turn up one's nose

délicatement [delikatmɑ̃] adv (légèrement) gently; (finement) finely

délicatesse [delikatɛs] nf (**a**) (d'un objet) fragility; (d'une fleur, d'un tissu, d'un coloris) delicacy; (de la peau) sensitivity; (de la santé) frailty (**b**) (des goûts) refinement; (des gestes) gracefulness; (d'un plat) sophistication; **avec d.** (légèrement) gently; (finement) finely (**c**) (difficulté) delicacy (**d**) (tact) tact; **avec d.** tactfully

délice [delis] nm (plaisir) delight; **cette tarte est un vrai d.** this pie is absolutely delicious

délices [delis] nfpl Litt ou Hum delights; **faire ses d. de qch** to delight in sth

délicieusement [delisjøzmɑ̃] adv (agréablement) delightfully; **d. bon** (plat) absolutely delicious

délicieux, -euse [delisjø, -øz] adj (nourriture, sensation, chaleur) delicious; (personne, robe) delightful

délictueux, -euse [deliktɥø, -øz] adj Jur **acte d.** offense

délié, -e [delje] **1** adj (taille) slim; (doigts) nimble
 2 nm (de l'écriture) thin stroke

délier [66] [delje] **1** vt to untie; **d. qn d'une promesse** to release sb from a promise; Fig **le vin lui a délié la langue** the wine loosened his/her tongue
 2 se délier vpr (se défaire) to come untied; Fig **sa langue s'est déliée** she found her tongue

délimiter [delimite] vt (territoire) to demarcate; (responsabilité, sujet) to define

délinquance [delɛ̃kɑ̃s] nf delinquency; **d. juvénile** juvenile delinquency; **la petite d. des banlieues** petty crime in the suburbs

délinquant, -e [delɛ̃kɑ̃, -ɑ̃t] **1** adj delinquent
 2 nm,f offender; **d. juvénile** juvenile delinquent; **d. sexuel** sex offender

déliquescence [delikesɑ̃s] nf Péj (d'une civilisation, des mœurs) decay; **tomber en d.** to fall into decay

déliquescent, -e [delikesɑ̃, -ɑ̃t] adj Péj (civilisation, mœurs) decadent

délirant, -e [delirɑ̃, -ɑ̃t] adj Méd delirious; Fig (joie, imagination) frenzied; **c'est du d. de leur demander de tout payer!** it's crazy asking them to pay for everything!

délire [delir] nm (**a**) Méd delirium; **avoir le d.** to be delirious; Fig **c'est du d.!** it's crazy!; **d. de grandeur** delusions of grandeur; **d. de persécution** persecution complex (**b**) (frénésie) frenzy; **foule en d.** frenzied crowd; Fam **cette soirée, c'est le d.!** it's a wild party!

délirer [delire] vi (être malade) to be delirious; (dire n'importe quoi) to rave

delirium tremens [delirjɔmtremɛ̃s] nm delirium tremens; **avoir le d.** to have delirium tremens

délit [deli] *nm* offense; **d. de fuite** failure to report an accident; **un accident avec d. de fuite** a hit-and-run accident; **d. d'initié** insider dealing *or* trading

délivrance [delivrɑ̃s] *nf* (a) (*soulagement*) relief; **leur départ fut une vraie d.** it was a real relief when they left (b) (*accouchement*) delivery (c) (*d'un certificat, d'un passeport, d'un permis*) issue

délivrer [delivre] **1** *vt* (a) (*libérer*) (*captif, otage*) to rescue; (*ville*) to liberate; (*peuple*) to set free; **d. qn de ses liens** to free sb from his bonds (b) (*soulager*) **d. qn d'un secret trop lourd** to share the burden of a secret with sb; **d. qn d'un grand poids** to take a weight off sb's shoulders (c) (*remettre*) (*marchandises*) to deliver; (*certificat, passeport, permis*) to issue
2 se délivrer *vpr* to free oneself (**de** from)

délocalisation [delɔkalizasjɔ̃] *nf* relocation

délocaliser [delɔkalize] *vt* to relocate

déloger [45] [delɔʒe] *vt* (*envahisseur*) to drive out (**de** from); (*locataire*) to evict; (*objet coincé*) to dislodge (**de** from)

déloyal, -e, -aux, -ales [delwajal, -o] *adj* (*ami*) disloyal, unfaithful; (*adversaire, pratique, concurrence*) unfair; (*coup*) illegal

delta [dɛlta] *nm* (a) (*d'un fleuve*) delta (b) *Aviat* (**aile**) **d.** delta wing

deltaplane [dɛltaplan] *nm* hang-glider; **faire du d.** to go hang-gliding

deltiste [dɛltist] *nmf* hang-glider (*person*)

déluge [delyʒ] *nm* (*de pluie*) downpour; (*d'injures*) torrent; (*de larmes*) flood; *Rel* **le D.** the Flood; **noyer qn sous un d. de compliments** to shower sb with compliments; **après moi le d.!** when I'm gone I don't care what happens!

déluré, -e [delyre] *adj* (*vif*) sharp, smart; *Péj* (*provocant*) forward

démagogie [demagɔʒi] *nf* demagogy

démagogique [demagɔʒik] *adj* demagogic

démagogue [demagɔg] *nmf* demagogue

demain [dəmɛ̃] **1** *adv* tomorrow; **d. soir** tomorrow evening; **d. en huit** a week from tomorrow; **à d.!** see you tomorrow!; **le journal de d.** tomorrow's paper; *Fam* **ce n'est pas pour d., ce n'est pas d. la veille** that won't happen for a long time yet; *Fig* **d. il fera jour** tomorrow is another day; *Fig* **de d.** (*de l'avenir*) of tomorrow
2 *nm* tomorrow; **tu as tout d. pour y réfléchir** you've got all tomorrow to think about it

demande [dəmɑ̃d] *nf* (a) (*requête*) request (**de** for); (*formulaire*) application form; **faire une d. de qch** (*de permis, de prêt*) to apply for sth; **faire qch à** *ou* **sur la d. de qn** to do sth at sb's request; **à la d. générale** by popular demand; **sur d.** on request; **demandes d'emploi** (*titre de rubrique*) situations wanted; **d. (en mariage)** proposal (of marriage); **faire sa d. (en mariage)** to propose; **d. de rançon** ransom demand (b) *Écon* demand; **d. des consommateurs** consumer demand (c) *Jur* **faire une d. en divorce** to file for divorce; **d. de dommages-intérêts** claim for damages (d) (*besoin*) (*de soins, d'affection*) need

demander [dəmɑ̃de] **1** *vt* (a) (*réclamer*) (*augmentation, addition, preuves*) to ask for; (*dommages et intérêts*) to claim; **d. qch à qn** to ask sb for sth; (*service*) to ask sb sth; **d. à qn de faire qch** to ask sb to do sth; **d. à manger/boire** to ask for something to eat/drink; **d. son avis à qn** to ask sb's opinion; **d. le divorce** to file for divorce; **d. la main de qn** to ask for sb's hand (in marriage); **d. qn en mariage** to propose to sb; **d. la parole** to ask to speak; **d. la permission de faire qch** to ask (for) permission to do sth; **combien demandez-vous de l'heure?** how much do you charge an hour?; **combien en demande-t-elle?** how much is she asking for it?; **je ne demande pas mieux que de vous aider** I'll be only too pleased to help you; **il ne demande que ça** he'd be only too

pleased; *Hum* **que demande le peuple?** what more could I/he/*etc.* ask?; **je ne demande qu'une seule chose: qu'on me laisse tranquille** all I ask is to be left alone; **on demande un maçon** (*dans une petite annonce*) builder wanted; **être très demandé** to be in great demand; **il n'y a qu'à** *ou* **il suffit de d.** you/he/*etc.* only have/has to ask
(b) (*nécessiter*) (*tact, réflexion, attention*) to require; **ça demande de gros sacrifices** great sacrifices are called for
(c) (*exiger*) to demand; **en d. trop à qn** to ask too much of sb; **d. l'impossible** to ask the impossible
(d) (*s'enquérir de*) (*prix, cause, raison*) to ask; **d. qch à qn** to ask sb sth; **il m'a demandé de tes nouvelles** he asked after you; *Fam* **je ne t'ai rien demandé!** I didn't ask for your advice!; **je vous (le) demande, je vous demande un peu!** I ask you!
(e) (*appeler*) (*médecin, prêtre*) to ask for; **on vous demande** you're wanted; **on vous demande au téléphone** there's a call for you
2 demander à *vt ind* **d. à faire qch** to ask to do sth; **les suspects ne demandaient qu'à parler** the suspects were only too willing to speak; **demande à ce qu'on vienne te chercher** ask someone to come and pick you up
3 se demander *vpr* to wonder, to ask oneself; **je me demande pourquoi elle a dit ça** I wonder why she said that; **c'est à se d. si…** it makes you wonder whether…; **des choses comme ça, ça ne se demande pas!** you don't ask that sort of question!

demandeur, -euse [dəmɑ̃dœr, -øz] *nm,f* **d. d'asile** asylum seeker, refugee; **d. d'emploi** job seeker

démangeaison [demɑ̃ʒɛzɔ̃] *nf* itch; **avoir une d.** to have an itch, to be itching; **j'ai des démangeaisons dans les jambes** my legs are itchy

démanger [45] [demɑ̃ʒe] *vi* to itch; **l'épaule me démange** my shoulder's itching; *Fig* **méfie-toi, la main me démange!** (*à un enfant*) watch out or you'll feel the back of my hand!; **ça me démange de lui dire ce que je pense** I'm itching to tell him/her what I think

démantèlement [demɑ̃tɛlmɑ̃] *nm* breaking up

démanteler [39] [demɑ̃tle] *vt* to break up

démantibuler [demɑ̃tibyle] *Fam* **1** *vt* to break up
2 se démantibuler *vpr* to come to pieces

démaquillage [demakijaʒ] *nm* removal of make-up

démaquillant, -e [demakijɑ̃, -ɑ̃t] **1** *adj* cleansing
2 *nm* cleanser; **d. pour les yeux** eye make-up remover

démaquiller [demakije] **1** *vt* **d. qn** to remove sb's make-up
2 se démaquiller *vpr* to remove one's make-up; **se d. les yeux** to remove one's eye make-up

démarcation [demarkasjɔ̃] *nf* demarcation

démarchage [demarʃaʒ] *nm* (*porte-à-porte*) door-to-door selling; **d. électoral** canvassing; **d. par téléphone** telesales

démarche [demarʃ] *nf* (a) (*allure*) gait, walk (b) (*requête*) step; **faire une d. auprès de qn** to approach sb; **faire les démarches nécessaires pour faire qch** to take the necessary steps to do sth (c) *Fig* (*cheminement*) process; **d. intellectuelle** thought process

démarcher [demarʃe] *vt* to canvass for

démarcheur, -euse [demarʃœr, -øz] *nm,f* door-to-door salesman, *f* saleswoman

démarque [demark] *nf Com* markdown; **la d. inconnue** shrinkage

démarquer [demarke] **1** *vt* (*marchandises*) to mark down
2 se démarquer *vpr Sport* to lose one's marker; *Fig* **se d. de qn** (*se distinguer*) to distinguish oneself from sb

démarrage [demaraʒ] *nm* (*d'un moteur*) starting; (*d'une entreprise*) start-up; (*d'un projet, d'une campagne publicitaire*) start; **au d.** (*d'un véhicule*) when moving off; **faire un d.** (*coureur*) to put on a spurt; *Ordinat* **d. à chaud/froid** warm/cold start; **d. en côte** hill start

démarrer [demare] **1** *vi* (**a**) *(véhicule)* to move off; *(moteur)* to start; *(conducteur)* to drive off (**b**) *(commencer)* to start; **bien/mal d.** to get off to a good/bad start (**c**) *(commencer à réussir)* to take off

2 *vt* to start; *Ordinat* to boot (up), to start up

démarreur [demarœr] *nm Aut* starter (motor)

démasquer [demaske] *vt aussi Fig* to unmask

démâter [demate] **1** *vt* to dismast

2 *vi* to lose its mast

démêlant [demelɑ̃] *adj m & nm* (**produit**) **d.** conditioner, detangler

démêlé [demele] *nm* disagreement (**avec** with); **avoir des démêlés avec la justice** to be in trouble with the law

démêler [demele] **1** *vt (fil, laine, cheveux)* to untangle, to detangle; *(mystère)* to unravel; **d. le vrai du faux** to disentangle the truth from the lies

2 se démêler *vpr* **se d. de** to extricate oneself from

démembrement [demɑ̃brəmɑ̃] *nm (d'un empire)* breaking up; *(d'une propriété agricole)* division

démembrer [demɑ̃bre] *vt (empire)* to break up; *(propriété agricole)* to divide (up)

déménagement [demenaʒmɑ̃] *nm* move; **c'est pour quand le d.?** when are you/we/*etc.* moving?

déménager [45] [demenaʒe] **1** *vi* (**a**) *(personne, entreprise)* to move; **où déménage-t-il?** where's he moving to?; **d. à la cloche de bois** to blow town at night; *Fam* **allez, déménagez!** beat it! (**b**) *Fam Fig (musique)* to be mind-blowing; *(cocktail)* to pack a punch

2 *vt (meubles)* to move

déménageur [demenaʒœr] *nm* furniture mover; **avoir des épaules de d.** to have strong broad shoulders

démence [demɑ̃s] *nf* insanity; *Méd* dementia; *Fam* **c'est de la d.!** it's madness!

démener [46] [demne] **se démener** *vpr* (**a**) *(s'agiter)* to thrash about; **se d. comme un beau diable** *(pour se libérer)* to struggle like a madman (**b**) *(se dépenser)* to exert oneself (**c**) *(faire des efforts)* **se d. pour faire qch** to go to great lengths to do sth

dément, -e [demɑ̃, -ɑ̃t] **1** *adj (fou)* insane; *Fam (formidable)* fantastic; *Fam* **c'est d.!** it's unreal!

2 *nm,f* lunatic; *Méd* demented person

démenti [demɑ̃ti] *nm* denial; *Journ* disclaimer; **opposer un d. formel à qch** to issue a firm denial of sth

démentiel, -elle [demɑ̃sjɛl] *adj (idée, projet)* insane; *Fam (incroyable)* crazy

démentir [64a] [demɑ̃tir] **1** *vt* to deny; *(être en contradiction avec)* to belie

2 se démentir *vpr (cesser)* **leur honnêteté ne s'est jamais démentie** they've always been unfailing in their honesty

démerder [demɛrde] **se démerder** *vpr très Fam* to get by, to manage; **démerde-toi tout seul!** sort it out yourself!; **elle est assez grande pour se d. seule** she's old enough to take care of herself; **elle se démerde pas mal en cuisine/tennis** she's not a bad cook/tennis player; **se d. pour faire qch** to manage to do sth

démériter [demerite] *vi* to be at fault; **je ne vois pas en quoi il a démérité** I don't see how he is at fault

démesure [deməzyr] *nf* excess

démesuré, -e [deməzyre] *adj (en taille)* enormous; *(orgueil, ambition)* excessive

démesurément [deməzyremɑ̃] *adv* enormously

démettre¹ [47] [demɛtr] **1** *vt* **il m'a démis l'épaule** he dislocated my shoulder

2 se démettre *vpr* **se d. l'épaule/le genou** to dislocate one's shoulder/knee

démettre² [demɛtr] **1** *vt* **d. qn de ses fonctions** to remove sb from his/her post

2 se démettre *vpr* **se d. de ses fonctions** to resign from one's post

demeurant [dəmœrɑ̃] **au demeurant** *adv (malgré tout)* for all that; *(d'ailleurs)* after all

demeure [dəmœr] *nf* (**a**) *(château)* mansion; *Litt (résidence)* (place of) residence; *Euph* **dernière d.** last resting place (**b**) **mettre qn en d. de faire qch** to instruct sb to do sth; *Jur* to give sb notice to do sth (**c**) **à d.** permanently

demeuré, -e [dəmœre] **1** *adj Vieilli* mentally retarded; *Fam Péj* halfwitted

2 *nm,f Vieilli* mentally retarded person; *Fam Péj* halfwit

demeurer [dəmœre] *vi* (**a**) *(aux être) (rester)* to remain; **d. convaincu que...** to remain convinced that...; **d. fidèle à qn** to remain faithful to sb; **demeurons-en là** let's leave it at that; **il n'en demeure pas moins que...** the fact remains that... (**b**) *Sout (aux avoir) (habiter)* to reside

demi, -e [dəmi] **1** *adj* (**a**) *(après un nom)* **deux heures et demie** *(durée)* two and a half hours; *(moment)* half past two; **un litre/kilo et d.** a liter/kilo and a half; **il gagne trois fois et demie ce que je gagne** he earns three and a half times as much as I do (**b**) *(avant un nom ou un adjectif)* half; **une d.-cuillère de sucre** half a teaspoon of sugar

2 *nm* (**a**) *(moitié)* half (**b**) *(bière)* **un d.** a beer (**c**) *Sport (au football)* midfielder; **d. droite** halfback

3 *nf* **demie** *(heure)* **il est la demie** it's half past; **à la demie** at half past

4 *adv* half; **d. plein** half full; **à d.** half; **à d. mort** half dead; **faire les choses à d.** to do things by halves; **croire qn à d.** to half believe sb; **ouvrir qch à d.** to half open sth

demiard [dəmjar] *nm Can* half pint

demi-cercle (*pl* **demi-cercles**) [dəmisɛrkl] *nm* semicircle, half circle; **en d.** in a semicircle

demi-dieu (*pl* **demi-dieux**) [dəmidjø] *nm* demigod

demi-douzaine (*pl* **demi-douzaines**) [dəmiduzɛn] *nf* half-dozen; **une d. d'œufs/de stylos** half a dozen eggs/pens

demi-droite (*pl* **demi-droites**) [dəmidrwat] *nf Math* half-line

demi-écrémé, -e (*mpl* **demi-écrémés**, *fpl* **demi-écrémées**) [dəmiekreme] *adj (lait)* semi-skim

demi-finale (*pl* **demi-finales**) [dəmifinal] *nf* semifinal

demi-fond [dəmifɔ̃] *nm inv Sport* (**course de**) **d.** middle-distance race

demi-frère (*pl* **demi-frères**) [dəmifrɛr] *nm* half-brother

demi-gros [dəmigro] *nm inv* (**commerce de**) **d.** cash and carry

demi-heure (*pl* **demi-heures**) [dəmijœr] *nf* **une d.** half an hour, a half-hour; **toutes les demi-heures** every half-hour

demi-jour (*pl* **demi-jours**) [dəmiʒur] *nm* half-light

demi-journée (*pl* **demi-journées**) [dəmiʒurne] *nf* half-day

démilitariser [demilitarize] *vt* to demilitarize

demi-litre (*pl* **demi-litres**) [dəmilitr] *nm* half-liter; **un d. de vin** half a liter of wine

demi-lune (*pl* **demi-lunes**) [dəmilyn] *nf* half-moon

demi-mesure (*pl* **demi-mesures**) [dəmiməzyr] *nf (compromis)* half-measure

demi-mort, -e (*mpl* **demi-morts**, *fpl* **demi-mortes**) [dəmimɔr, -mɔrt] *adj* half-dead

demi-mot [dəmimo] **à demi-mot** *adv* **comprendre à d.** to take the hint; **nous nous comprenons à d.** we don't have to spell everything out to each other

déminage [deminaʒ] *nm* mine clearance; *(en mer)* minesweeping

déminer [demine] *vt* to clear of mines

démineur [deminœr] *nm (personne)* bomb-disposal expert; *(navire)* minesweeper

demi-pause (*pl* **demi-pauses**) [dəmipoz] *nf Mus* half-note rest

demi-pension [dəmipɑ̃sjɔ̃] *nf (à l'hôtel)* breakfast and one meal; **sept jours en d.** seven days breakfast and one meal; *Scol* **être en d.** to have school lunches

demi-pensionnaire (*pl* **demi-pensionnaires**) [dəmi-pɑ̃sjɔnɛr] *nmf (écolier)* student who has school lunches

demi-portion (*pl* **demi-portions**) [dəmipɔrsjɔ̃] *nf Fam Péj* runt

demi-queue (*pl* **demi-queues**) [dəmikø] *adj & nm* **(piano) d.** baby grand (piano)

démis, -e [demi, -iz] *adj (membre)* dislocated

demi-saison (*pl* **demi-saisons**) [dəmisɛzɔ̃] *nf* spring or autumn; **vêtements de d.** spring or autumn clothes

demi-sel [dəmisɛl] *adj inv (beurre)* slightly salted; **fromage d.** slightly salted cream cheese

demi-sœur (*pl* **demi-sœurs**) [dəmisœr] *nf* half-sister

demi-sommeil (*pl* **demi-sommeils**) [dəmisɔmɛj] *nm* half-sleep; **être dans un d.** to be half-asleep

demi-soupir (*pl* **demi-soupirs**) [dəmisupir] *nm Mus* eighth-note rest

démission [demisjɔ̃] *nf* resignation; *Fig* renunciation; **donner sa d.** to hand in one's resignation

démissionnaire [demisjɔnɛr] *adj* resigning

démissionner [demisjɔne] *vi* to resign (**de** from); *Fig* to give up

demi-tarif [dəmitarif] **1** *nm* (*pl* **demi-tarifs**) half-price
   2 *adj inv* **billet d.** *(de transports)* half-fare (ticket); *(de spectacle)* half-price ticket

demi-teinte (*pl* **demi-teintes**) [dəmitɛ̃t] *nf* halftone; *Fig* **être tout en demi-teintes** to be subtle in character

demi-ton (*pl* **demi-tons**) [dəmitɔ̃] *nm Mus* half step

demi-tour (*pl* **demi-tours**) [dəmitur] *nm* half-turn; *(en voiture)* U-turn; *Mil* about-turn; **faire d.** to turn back; **faire un d.** *(en voiture)* to do a U-turn; *Mil* **d. droite!** right about-turn!

démiurge [demjyrʒ] *nm* demiurge

demi-volée (*pl* **demi-volées**) [dəmivɔle] *nf (au tennis, au football)* half-volley

démobilisation [demɔbilizasjɔ̃] *nf* (**a**) *(de troupes)* demobilization (**b**) *Fig (désintérêt)* apathy

démobiliser [demɔbilize] *vt* (**a**) *(troupes)* to demobilize (**b**) *Fig (désintéresser)* to demotivate

démocrate [demɔkrat] **1** *adj* democratic
   2 *nmf* democrat

démocrate-chrétien, -enne (*mpl* **démocrates-chrétiens**, *fpl* **démocrates-chrétiennes**) [demɔkrat-kretjɛ̃, -ɛn] *adj & nm,f Pol* Christian Democrat

démocratie [demɔkrasi] *nf* democracy

démocratique [demɔkratik] *adj* democratic

démocratiquement [demɔkratikmɑ̃] *adv* democratically

démocratisation [demɔkratizasjɔ̃] *nf* democratization

démocratiser [demɔkratize] **1** *vt* to democratize
   2 se démocratiser *vpr* to become (more) democratic

démodé, -e [demɔde] *adj* old-fashioned

démoder [demɔde] **se démoder** *vpr* to go out of fashion

démographie [demɔgrafi] *nf* demography

démographique [demɔgrafik] *adj* demographic

demoiselle [dəmwazɛl] *nf* (**a**) *(jeune fille)* young lady; **d. de compagnie** lady's companion; **d. d'honneur** *(d'une souveraine)* lady-in-waiting; *(d'une mariée)* bridesmaid (**b**) *Vieilli (célibataire)* maiden lady; **c'est une vieille d.** she's never married (**c**) *(insecte)* dragonfly

démolir [demɔlir] *vt* (**a**) *(abattre)* to demolish, to pull down; *(mettre en pièces)* to demolish, to wreck; **d. une porte à coups de hache** to smash in a door with an ax; **l'alcool lui a démoli le foie** alcohol has ruined his/her liver (**b**) *Fig (théorie, adversaire)* to demolish; *(autorité)* to undermine; *(auteur, cinéaste, roman, film)* to pan (**c**) *Fam (battre)* to beat up; **d. le portrait**

à qn to smash sb's face in; **se faire d. (le portrait)** to get beaten up

démolition [demɔlisjɔ̃] *nf* demolition; **chantier de d.** demolition site; **entreprise de d.** demolition contractors; **en d.** being demolished

démon [demɔ̃] *nm aussi Fig* demon, devil; **le d.** the Devil; **le d. de midi** the mid-life crisis; *Can* **être en d.** to be furious

démoniaque [demɔnjak] *adj* demonic; *Fig (pervers)* fiendish

démonstratif, -ive [demɔ̃stratif, -iv] **1** *adj (affectueux) & Gram* demonstrative
   2 *nm Gram* demonstrative

démonstration [demɔ̃strasjɔ̃] *nf* (**a**) *Math* demonstration; **d. par l'absurde** reductio ad absurdum; **faire la d. de qch** to demonstrate sth (**b**) *(d'appareil)* demonstration; **être en d.** to be a display model (**c**) *(manifestation)* show; **d. de force** show of force; **faire de grandes démonstrations d'amitié** to make a great show of friendship

démontable [demɔ̃tabl] *adj* that can be dismantled

démontage [demɔ̃taʒ] *nm* dismantling

démonté, -e [demɔ̃te] *adj (mer)* raging

démonter [demɔ̃te] **1** *vt* (**a**) *(machine, meuble, tente)* to dismantle; *(pneu)* to remove (**b**) *Fam (déconcerter)* to throw; **se laisser d.** to get thrown (**c**) *Can (décourager)* to discourage
   2 se démonter *vpr* (**a**) *(machine, meuble)* to come apart (**b**) *Fam* **elle ne s'est pas démontée pour si peu** she wasn't so easily thrown

démontrable [demɔ̃trabl] *adj* demonstrable

démontrer [demɔ̃tre] *vt* to demonstrate; *Fam* **d. qch par A plus B** to prove sth conclusively

démoralisant, -e [demɔralizɑ̃, -ɑ̃t] *adj* demoralizing

démoralisation [demɔralizasjɔ̃] *nf* demoralization

démoraliser [demɔralize] **1** *vt* to demoralize
   2 se démoraliser *vpr* to become demoralized

démordre [demɔrdr] **démordre de** *vt ind* **ne pas d. de qch** to stick to sth; **elle n'en démord pas** she's sticking to her guns

démotiver [demɔtive] *vt* to demotivate; **se laisser d. par qch** to be put off by sth

démoulage [demulaʒ] *nm (d'un moulage)* removal from the mold; *(d'un gâteau)* turning out

démouler [demule] *vt (moulage)* to remove from the mold; *(gâteau)* to turn out

démuni, -e [demyni] *adj (pauvre)* destitute, penniless

démunir [demynir] **1** *vt* **d. qn de qch** to deprive sb of sth
   2 se démunir *vpr* **se d. de qch** to part with sth

démystification [demistifikasjɔ̃] *nf* demystification

démystifier [66] [demistifje] *vt* to demystify

dénatalité [denatalite] *nf* fall in the birth rate

dénationaliser [denasjɔnalize] *vt* to denationalize

dénaturé, -e [denatyre] *adj* (**a**) *(parents, goût, mœurs)* unnatural (**b**) *Chim* denatured

dénaturer [denatyre] *vt (faits, propos)* to distort; *Chim* to denature

dénégation [denegasjɔ̃] *nf* denial

déneiger [45] [deneʒe] *vt* to clear the snow from

déneigeuse [denɛʒøz] *nf Can* snowblower

déni [deni] *nm Jur* **d. de justice** denial of justice

déniaiser [denjeze] *vt Fam* **d. qn** *(dépuceler)* to take away sb's innocence; *(dégourdir)* to teach sb a thing or two

dénicher [deniʃe] *vt Fam (objet)* to unearth; *(personne)* to track down

denier [dənje] *nm* (**a**) *(monnaie française)* denier; *Fig* **deniers** funds; **le d. du culte** contribution to parish costs (**b**) *(de bas)* **bas de 30 deniers** 30-denier stockings

dénier [66] [denje] *vt* (**a**) *(nier) (faute, responsabilité)* to deny (**b**) *(refuser)* **d. à qn le droit de faire qch** to deny sb the right to do sth

dénigrement [denigrəmɑ̃] *nm* denigration; **une campagne de d.** a smear campaign

dénigrer [denigre] *vt* to denigrate

dénivelé [denivle] *nm* difference in level

dénivellation [denivɛlasjɔ̃] *nf* difference in level

dénombrable [denɔ̃brabl] *adj* countable

dénombrer [denɔ̃bre] *vt* to count

dénominateur [denɔminatœr] *nm Math* denominator; **le plus petit d. commun** the lowest common denominator

dénomination [denɔminasjɔ̃] *nf* designation

dénommé, -e [denɔme] *adj* **un d. Charles** someone by the name of Charles

dénoncer [16] [denɔ̃se] **1** *vt* **(a)** *(trahir) (malfaiteur)* to denounce (**à** to); *(élève)* to tattle on (**à** to) **(b)** *(protester contre) (abus)* to denounce **(c)** *(annuler) (traité, contrat)* to terminate
2 se dénoncer *vpr (malfaiteur)* to give oneself up (**à** to); *(élève)* to own up (**à** to)

dénonciation [denɔ̃sjasjɔ̃] *nf* denunciation

dénoter [denɔte] *vt* to denote, to indicate

dénouement [denumɑ̃] *nm (d'un livre)* ending; *(d'une pièce)* dénouement; *(d'une affaire)* outcome

dénouer [denwe] **1** *vt (nœud)* to untie, to undo; *(cheveux)* to undo, to let down; *Fig (intrigue)* to unravel
2 se dénouer *vpr (nœud)* to come undone; *(cheveux)* to come down

dénoyauter [denwajote] *vt* to pit

denrée [dɑ̃re] *nf* foodstuff; **denrées alimentaires** foodstuffs; **denrées de consommation courante** staple foods; **denrées périssables** perishable goods

dense [dɑ̃s] *adj* dense

densité [dɑ̃site] *nf* **(a)** *(de population) & Phys* density **(b)** *Ordinat* **à double d.** double-density

dent [dɑ̃] *nf* **(a)** *(d'homme, d'animal)* tooth; **faire ses dents** *(enfant)* to be teething; **se faire les dents sur qch** *(chat, enfant)* to cut one's teeth on sth; **manger du bout des dents** to pick at one's food; **mordre à belles dents dans qch** to take a good bite out of sth; **parler entre ses dents** to mumble, to mutter; *Fig* **se casser les dents sur qch** to take a spill over sth; *aussi Fig* **serrer les dents** to grit one's teeth; *Fig* **avoir les dents longues** to have great ambitions; *Fig* **avoir la d. dure** to have a sharp tongue; *Fig* **il n'a pas desserré les dents de la soirée** he hasn't opened his mouth all evening; *Fam* **être sur les dents** *(sur le qui-vive)* to be on the alert; *(surmené)* to be overworked; *Fam* **avoir une d. contre qn** to have a grudge against sb; *Fam* **avoir la d.** to be starving; **d. de lait/de sagesse** baby/wisdom tooth
(b) *(de peigne, de scie)* tooth; *(de roue)* cog; *(de fourchette)* prong; *(de timbre)* perforation; **en dents de scie** serrated; *Fig (évolution, progrès)* uneven

dentaire [dɑ̃tɛr] *adj* dental

denté, -e [dɑ̃te] *adj Tech* toothed; *(feuille)* jagged

dentelé, -e [dɑ̃tle] *adj (rivage, feuille)* jagged

dentelle [dɑ̃tɛl] *nf* lace; **robe de** *ou* **en d.** lace dress; **des crêpes d.** very thin pancakes; *Fam* **ne pas faire dans la d.** *(en paroles)* not to beat around the bush; *(en actions)* not to mess around

dentellière [dɑ̃təljɛr] *nf (personne)* lacemaker

dentelure [dɑ̃tlyr] *nf (d'un rivage, d'une feuille)* jagged outline; **dentelures** *(d'un timbre)* perforations

dentier [dɑ̃tje] *nm* (set of) false teeth, dentures

dentifrice [dɑ̃tifris] **1** *nm* toothpaste
2 *adj* **pâte d.** toothpaste

dentiste [dɑ̃tist] *nmf* dentist

dentition [dɑ̃tisjɔ̃] *nf* **(a)** *(croissance)* dentition **(b)** *(denture)* set of teeth

denture [dɑ̃tyr] *nf* set of teeth

dénudé, -e [denyde] *adj (campagne, arbre, fil)* bare

dénuder [denyde] **1** *vt (colline, arbre, fil)* to strip; **cette robe dénude le dos** this dress leaves the back bare
2 se dénuder *vpr* **(a)** *(colline)* to grow bare; *(arbre)* to lose its leaves **(b)** *(se déshabiller)* to strip (naked)

dénué, -e [denye] *adj* **d. de** *(intelligence, intérêt)* devoid of; **d. de tout fondement** totally without foundation

dénuement [denymɑ̃] *nm* destitution; **être dans le d.** to be destitute

déodorant [deodorɑ̃] *nm* deodorant

déodoriser [deodorize] *vt* to deodorize

déontologie [deɔ̃tɔlɔʒi] *nf* professional ethics

dépannage [depanaʒ] *nm (d'une machine)* (emergency) repairs; *(remorquage)* towing; *Ordinat* trouble-shooting; **service de d.** tow-truck service

dépanner [depane] *vt (machine)* to repair; *Fam (personne)* to help out (**de** with)

dépanneur [depanœr] *nm* **(a)** *(de voitures)* tow-truck mechanic; *(de téléviseurs)* (television) repairman **(b)** *Can (magasin)* convenience store

dépanneuse [depanøz] *nf (véhicule)* wrecker

dépareillé, -e [depareje] *adj (gant)* odd; *(service de table)* incomplete

déparer [depare] *vt* to spoil, to mar; **ce tableau ne dépare pas dans le salon** this painting looks pretty good in the living room

départ [depar] *nm* **(a)** *(d'une personne, d'un véhicule, d'un bateau)* departure; **les grands départs** the great vacation exodus; **être sur le d.** to be on the point of leaving; **excursions au d. de Nice** trips departing from Nice; **je regrette votre d.** I'm sorry you're leaving; **d. volontaire** *(d'employé)* voluntary departure **(b)** *(d'une course)* start; **ligne de d.** starting line; **faux d.** false start; **donner le d. (d'une course)** to give the starting signal (for a race); *aussi Fig* **prendre un bon/mauvais d.** to get off to a good/bad start **(c)** *(début)* start, beginning; **salaire de d.** starting salary; **au d.** at first, to start with

départager [45] [departaʒe] *vt* to decide between

département [departəmɑ̃] *nm* **(a)** *(de la France)* department *(division of local government)* **(b)** *(dans un ministère)* department; **le d. d'anglais** *(d'une faculté)* the English department

---

Département

A "département" is the chief administrative division of France. There are 95 "départements" in metropolitan France and 4 overseas, and each is administered by a "conseil général" and a "préfet". The number of the "département" corresponds to the first two figures in a zip code and the last two figures on a car license plate.

---

départemental, -e, -aux, -ales [departəmɑ̃tal, -o] **1** *adj* departmental
2 *nf* **départementale** secondary road

départir [64a] [departir] **se départir** *vpr Litt* **il ne s'est jamais départi de son calme/sa bonne humeur** his calm/his good humor never deserted him

dépassé, -e [depase] *adj* **(a)** *(démodé) (vêtement, technique)* old-fashioned **(b)** *(perdu)* overwhelmed; **être d. par les événements** to be overtaken by events

dépassement [depasmɑ̃] *nm* **(a)** *(en voiture)* passing, overtaking **(b)** *Fin* **il y a un d. de crédit de plusieurs millions** the budget has been exceeded by several million

dépasser [depase] **1** *vt* **(a)** *(aller plus loin que)* to go past **(b)** *(doubler)* to pass, to overtake **(c)** *(excéder) (limite de vitesse, temps imparti, poids)* to exceed; **d. la date limite de vente** *(produit)* to be past its pull date; **d. dix minutes** to last longer than ten minutes; **ne pas d. la dose prescrite** *(sur notice)* do not exceed the stated dose; **cela dépasse l'entendement** it's beyond belief (**d**) *(surpasser)* to outstrip; **d. qn d'une tête** to stand a head taller than sb; **d. qn en beauté** to be more beautiful than sb; **d. les espérances de qn** to exceed sb's expectations (**e**) *(exagérer)* **d. les bornes** to overstep the mark; **cela me dépasse** it's beyond me

2 *vi* (**a**) *(en voiture)* to pass, to overtake (**b**) *(se voir)* to stick out (**de** of); *(jupon)* to show

3 se dépasser *vpr* to surpass oneself

dépassionner [depasjɔne] *vt (débat)* to take the heat out of

dépatouiller [depatuje] **se dépatouiller** *vpr Fam* to cope, to manage; **se d. d'une situation** to get out of *or* to wriggle one's way out of a situation

dépaysé, -e [depeize] *adj* out of one's element

dépaysement [depeizmɑ̃] *nm (positif)* change of scene; *(négatif)* disorientation

dépayser [depeize] *vt (positivement)* to be a change of scene for; *(négativement)* to disorient

dépecer [16/46] [depəse] *vt (sujet: boucher)* to cut up; *(sujet: animal)* to tear up

dépêche [depɛʃ] *nf* dispatch; **d. d'agence** agency news item

dépêcher [depeʃe] **1** *vt (messager)* to dispatch

2 se dépêcher *vpr* to hurry; **dépêchez-vous!** hurry up!; **se d. de faire qch** to hurry to do sth; **dépêche-toi de finir ton travail** hurry up and finish your work

dépeindre [54] [depɛ̃dr] *vt* to depict

dépenaillé, -e [depənaje] *adj* ragged

dépénalisation [depenalizasjɔ̃] *nf* decriminalization

dépénaliser [depenalize] *vt* to decriminalize

dépendance [depɑ̃dɑ̃s] *nf* (**a**) *(asservissement)* dependence (**à** on); **être sous la d. de qn** to be under sb's domination (**b**) *(bâtiment)* outbuilding

dépendant, -e [depɑ̃dɑ̃, -ɑ̃t] *adj* dependent (**de** on)

dépendre [depɑ̃dr] *vi* to depend (**de** on); **cela ne dépend pas de nous** it's not up to us; *Fam* **ça dépend (des fois)** it depends

dépens [depɑ̃] *nmpl* (**a**) **aux d. de** at the expense of; **apprendre qch à ses d.** to learn sth to one's cost (**b**) *Jur* **être condamné aux d.** to be ordered to pay costs

dépense [depɑ̃s] *nf* (**a**) *(frais)* expenditure, expense; **dépenses** spending; **les dépenses du ménage** household expenses; **faire des dépenses** to spend money; **pousser (les gens) à la d.** to encourage people to spend; **il ne regarde pas à la d.** he spares no expense (**b**) **d. physique** physical exertion

dépenser [depɑ̃se] **1** *vt (de l'argent)* to spend; *Fig* **d. toute son énergie (à faire qch)** to use up all one's energy (in doing sth)

2 *vi* to spend (money); **d. sans compter** to spend lavishly

3 se dépenser *vpr* to burn up energy

dépensier, -ère [depɑ̃sje, -ɛr] *adj* extravagant

déperdition [depɛrdisjɔ̃] *nf (de chaleur, d'énergie)* loss

dépérir [deperir] *vi (personne)* to waste away; *(plante)* to wither; *(arbre)* to decay

dépêtrer [depetre] *Fam* **1** *vt* **d. qn de qch** to free sb from sth

2 se dépêtrer *vpr (se dégager)* to free oneself (**de** from); *Fig* **se d. de qch** to get oneself out of sth; *Fig* **se d. de qn** to get rid of sb

dépeuplement [depœpləmɑ̃] *nm (d'un pays)* depopulation

dépeupler [depœple] **1** *vt (pays)* to depopulate

2 se dépeupler *vpr (pays)* to become depopulated

déphasé, -e [defaze] *adj* (**a**) *Élec* out of phase (**b**) *Fam (désorienté)* disoriented

dépiauter [depjote] *vt Fam (animal)* to skin; *Fig* **d. un texte** to pull a text to pieces

dépilatoire [depilatwar] *adj* **crème d.** hair-removing cream

dépistage [depistaʒ] *nm (d'une maladie)* screening, testing; **d. du sida** Aids screening *or* testing

dépister [depiste] *vt (gibier, criminel)* to track down; *(maladie)* to detect

dépit [depi] *nm* (**a**) *(ressentiment)* spite; **par d.** out of spite (**b**) **en d. de** in spite of, despite; **en d. du bon sens** contrary to common sense

dépité, -e [depite] *adj* annoyed

déplacé, -e [deplase] *adj* (**a**) *(dérangé)* out of place; **avoir une vertèbre déplacée** to have a slipped disk (**b**) *(inconvenant) (observation)* uncalled-for

déplacement [deplasmɑ̃] *nm* (**a**) *(réarrangement)* moving; *(mutation)* transfer; **d. de vertèbre** slipped disk; *Ordinat* **d. du curseur** cursor movement; *Ordinat* **d. entre fichiers** movement between files (**b**) *(voyage)* trip; **déplacements** travel; **être en d.** to be on a (business) trip; *Fig* **valoir le d.** to be worth the trip

déplacer [16] [deplase] **1** *vt (objet)* to move; *(fonctionnaire, service)* to transfer; *Fig* **d. le problème** *(volontairement)* to avoid the issue; *(involontairement)* to miss the point

2 se déplacer *vpr* (**a**) *(changer de place)* to move around (**b**) *(voyager)* to travel (**c**) **se d. une vertèbre** to slip a disk

déplafonner [deplafɔne] *vt (prix, crédit)* to remove the ceiling on

déplaire [55a] [deplɛr] **1** *vi* **d. à qn** *(irriter)* to displease sb; **cet homme/cette maison me déplaît** I don't like that man/that house; **cela ne me déplairait pas** I wouldn't mind it; *Ironique* **ne vous/leur en déplaise** whether you/they like it or not

2 se déplaire *vpr* **il se déplaît à Paris** he doesn't like it in Paris; **elle ne se déplaît pas à Paris** she quite likes it in Paris

déplaisant, -e [deplɛzɑ̃, -ɑ̃t] *adj* unpleasant

déplaisir [deplezir] *nm* displeasure, annoyance; **à son grand d.** to his/her great annoyance

dépliant [deplijɑ̃] *nm* leaflet; *(d'un livre)* fold-out page

déplier [66] [deplije] **1** *vt (journal, lettre, mouchoir)* to unfold; *(canapé)* to open out; **d. les jambes** to stretch one's legs

2 se déplier *vpr* to unfold, to open out

déplisser [deplise] **1** *vt* to take the creases out of

2 se déplisser *vpr* to lose its creases

déploiement [deplwamɑ̃] *nm (d'ailes)* spreading; *(de troupes)* deployment; *Fig (de force)* display

déplorable [deplɔrabl] *adj* deplorable

déplorer [deplɔre] *vt* to deplore; **nous devrons travailler plus, (et) je le déplore, mais...** we'll have to do more work, I'm sorry to say, but...; **d. la mort de qn** to mourn sb's death; **d. la perte de qch** to lament the loss of sth

déployer [32] [deplwaje] **1** *vt (journal, carte)* to unfold, to open out; *(voiles, ailes)* to spread; *(troupes, police)* to deploy; *Fig (étaler)* to display

2 se déployer *vpr (voile)* to unfurl; *(troupes, police)* to deploy

déplumé, -e [deplyme] *adj* featherless; *Fam (chauve)* bald

déplumer [deplyme] **se déplumer** *vpr (oiseau)* to molt; *Fam (personne)* to go bald

dépoitraillé, -e [depwatraje] *adj Fam* with one's shirt open

dépoli, -e [depɔli] *adj (verre)* frosted

dépolitiser [depɔlitize] *vt* to depoliticize

dépolluer [depɔlɥe] *vt* to clean up

déportation [depɔrtasjɔ̃] *nf (en camp de concentration)* internment

déporté, -e [depɔrte] *nm,f (de camp de concentration)* internee

déporter [depɔrte] **1** *vt* **d. qn** *(en camp de concentration)* to send sb to a concentration camp

2 se déporter *vpr* **se d. vers la droite/gauche** to veer off to the right/left

déposer [depoze] **1** *vt* (**a**) *(mettre à terre)* to put down; *aussi Fig* **d. les armes** to lay down one's arms (**b**) *(laisser) (personne)* to drop (off); **d. qch chez qn** to drop sth off at sb's house; **d. une**

gerbe sur une tombe to lay a wreath on a grave; **d. un bai-ser sur le front de qn** to plant a kiss on sb's forehead; **d. la clé à la réception** to leave the key at the reception desk; **d. une caution** to leave a deposit; **d. de l'argent (à la banque)** to deposit money (at the bank); *Jur* **d. une plainte (contre qn)** to lodge a complaint (against sb); *Pol* **d. un projet de loi** to introduce a bill (**c**) *(marque, brevet)* to register; **marque dé-posée** registered trademark (**d**) *(monarque)* to depose

2 *vi Jur* **d. (en justice)** to give evidence (**contre** against)

3 se déposer *vpr (substance)* to settle

dépositaire [depozitɛr] *nmf* (**a**) *(de papiers)* depositary; *Fig (d'un secret)* guardian (**b**) *Com (de produits)* agent

déposition [depozisjɔ̃] *nf* (**a**) *Jur* statement *(made by witness)*; **faire/recueillir une d.** to make/to take a statement (**b**) *(d'un monarque)* deposing

déposséder [34] [depɔsede] *vt* to dispossess, to deprive (**de** of)

dépôt [depo] *nm* (**a**) *(action)* depositing; *(somme)* deposit; **faire un d.** *(à la banque)* to make a deposit; **mettre qch en d.** to put sth into storage; *Fin* **d. d'espèces** cash deposit; *Jur* **d. légal** registration of copyright; *Fin* **d. à vue** cash deposit (**b**) *(entre-pôt)* depot; *(de trains)* engine shed; **d. de munitions** muni-tions depot; **d. d'ordures** garbage dump (**c**) *(prison)* prison (**d**) *(substance)* deposit; *(limon)* silt; *(de bouilloire)* fur

dépoter [depɔte] *vt (plantes)* to repot

dépotoir [depɔtwar] *nm (dépôt d'ordures)* dump; *Fam (cham-bre)* dump; *(classe)* dumping ground

dépôt-vente *(pl* **dépôts-ventes)** [depovɑ̃t] *nm* ≃ consign-ment store

dépouille [depuj] *nf* (**a**) *(d'animal)* skin, hide; **d. (mortelle)** (mortal) remains (**b**) **dépouilles** *(trésor de guerre)* spoils, loot

dépouillé, -e [depuje] *adj (style)* bald; *(arbre)* bare

dépouillement [depujmɑ̃] *nm* (**a**) *(examen)* **d. du scrutin** counting of the votes; **d. du courrier** sorting through the mail (**b**) *(pauvreté)* poverty; *(sobriété)* austerity

dépouiller [depuje] **1** *vt* (**a**) *(priver)* to deprive (**de** of); **d. qn de ses vêtements** to strip sb; **se faire d.** *(dans une affaire)* to lose all one's money (**b**) *(examiner) (courrier)* to sort through; **d. le scrutin** to count the votes (**c**) *(animal)* to skin

2 se dépouiller *vpr* **se d. de qch** to rid oneself of sth; **les arbres se dépouillent de leurs feuilles** the trees are shed-ding their leaves

dépourvu, -e [depurvy] *adj* (**a**) **d. de qch** devoid of sth (**b**) **être pris au d.** to be caught off (one's) guard

dépoussiérer [34] [depusjere] *vt* to dust; *Fig (institution)* to dust off

dépravation [depravasjɔ̃] *nf* depravity

dépravé, -e [deprave] **1** *adj* depraved

2 *nm,f* degenerate

dépraver [deprave] *vt* to deprave

dépréciation [depresjasjɔ̃] *nf* depreciation

déprécier [66] [depresje] **1** *vt* to undervalue

2 se déprécier *vpr (valeurs, marchandises)* to depreciate

déprédation [depredasjɔ̃] *nf* depredation

dépressif, -ive [depresif, -iv] *adj* depressive

dépression [depresjɔ̃] *nf* (**a**) *(creux)* depression; **d. (atmos-phérique)** low, trough (**b**) *Psy* depression; **faire de la d.** to be suffering from depression; **faire une d.** to be depressed; **d. nerveuse** nervous breakdown

dépressurisation [depresyrizasjɔ̃] *nf* depressurization

dépressuriser [depresyrize] *vt (avion)* to depressurize

déprimant, -e [deprimɑ̃, -ɑ̃t] *adj* depressing

déprime [deprim] *nf Fam* depression; **avoir un (petit) coup de d.** to be feeling (a bit) low

déprimé, -e [deprime] *adj Psy* depressed

déprimer [deprime] **1** *vt (démoraliser)* to depress

2 *vi Fam* to be feeling low

déprogrammer [deprɔgrame] *vt (émission)* to cancel; *Ordi-nat* to remove from a program

dépuceler [9] [depysle] *vt Fam* to deflower

depuis [dəpɥi] **1** *prép* (**a**) *(indiquant le point de départ)* **d. hier/ ce matin/1995** since yesterday/this morning/1995; **d. l'âge de cinq ans** from the age of five; **d. leur rencontre** since they met; **d. ce temps-là** since then; **d. quand êtes-vous ici?** how long have you been here? (**b**) *(durée)* for; **je suis ici d. trois jours** I've been here for three days; **d. combien de temps êtes-vous mariés?** how long have you been married (for)?; **il l'aime d. toujours** he has always loved her; **d. long-temps** for a long time; **d. la nuit des temps** since the dawn of time (**c**) *(lieu)* from; **il ne m'a pas parlé d. Rouen** he hasn't spoken to me since (we left) Rouen

2 *adv* since (then)

3 *conj* **d. que** since; **d. que le monde est monde** since the world began

député, -e [depyte] *nm,f Pol* deputy, ≃ representative (**de** for); **d. (du Parlement) européen** Member of the European Parliament, MEP

déraciné, -e [derasine] **1** *adj* uprooted

2 *nm,f* person who has been uprooted

déraciner [derasine] *vt (arbre, personne)* to uproot

déraillement [derajmɑ̃] *nm* derailment

dérailler [deraje] *vi* (**a**) *(train, tram)* to leave the rails; **faire d. un train** to derail a train (**b**) *Fam (personne)* to talk drivel

dérailleur [derajœr] *nm (de bicyclette)* derailleur (gears)

déraison [derɛzɔ̃] *nf Litt* folly

déraisonnable [derɛzɔnabl] *adj* foolish

déraisonner [derɛzɔne] *vi Litt* to talk nonsense

dérangé, -e [derɑ̃ʒe] *adj (fou)* deranged

dérangeant, -e [derɑ̃ʒɑ̃, -ɑ̃t] *adj (film, personnage)* disturb-ing

dérangement [derɑ̃ʒmɑ̃] *nm* (**a**) *(gêne)* trouble; **je ne veux pas vous causer de d.** I don't want to put you to any trouble; **excusez-moi pour le d.** I'm sorry to trouble you (**b**) *(panne)* **la ligne est en d.** the line is out of order

déranger [45] [derɑ̃ʒe] **1** *vt* (**a**) *(papiers, livres)* to disturb; *(pièce)* to mess up (**b**) *(gêner) (personne)* to disturb; **ne pas d.** *(sur panneau)* do not disturb; **cela vous dérange si j'ouvre la fenêtre?** would you mind if I opened the window?; **si cela ne vous dérange pas** if that's all right by you; *Ironique* **je ne te dérange pas trop?** am I in your way?; *Fam* **et alors, ça te dérange?** do you have a problem with that? (**c**) *(perturber)* to upset; **avoir le cerveau dérangé** to be deranged

2 *vi (choquer)* to be disturbing

3 se déranger *vpr* **merci de vous être dérangé** thank you for your trouble; **ne vous dérangez pas pour moi** please don't go to any trouble on my account

dérapage [derapaʒ] *nm (en voiture)* skid; *(à skis)* sideslip; *Fig* mistake; *Fig* **le d. des prix** spiraling prices; **le d. de l'écono-mie** the downward spiral of the economy

déraper [derape] *vi (voiture)* to skid; *(à skis)* to sideslip; *Fig (prix)* to be rising uncontrollably; *(situation)* to go wrong

dératé, -e [derate] *nm,f Fam* **courir comme un d.** to run flat out

dératiser [deratize] *vt* **d. qch** to clear sth of rats

derechef [dərəʃɛf] *adv Litt* once more

déréglé, -e [deregle] *adj* (**a**) *(mécanisme)* not working prop-erly (**b**) *(estomac)* upset

dérèglement [dereglemɑ̃] *nm (d'un mécanisme)* malfunction-ing; **d. hormonal** hormone disorder

dérégler [34] [deregle] **1** *vt (mécanisme)* to cause to malfunc-tion

2 se dérégler *vpr (mécanisme)* to go wrong; **elle s'est déréglé le système digestif** she's ruined her digestive sys-tem

déridage [deridaʒ] *nm Méd* facelift

dérider [deride] **1** *vt* to cheer up

2 se dérider *vpr* to cheer up

dérision [derizjɔ̃] *nf* derision; **tourner qch en d.** to deride sth

dérisoire [derizwar] *adj (salaire, somme)* derisory; *(prix)* rock-bottom

dérivatif [derivatif] *nm* distraction (**à** from)

dérivation [derivasjɔ̃] *nf* (**a**) *(route, cours d'eau)* diversion; *Élec* **monté en d.** shunt connected (**b**) *Math* derivation

dérive [deriv] *nf Naut & Aviat* drift; **à la d., en d.** adrift; **aller à la d.** to drift, to go adrift; *Fig* to go downhill; **la d. des continents** continental drift

dérivé, -e [derive] **1** *adj* (**a**) *(sens, fonction)* derived; **produit d.** *Chim* by-product; *Fin* derivative (**b**) *Élec* **courant d.** shunt current

2 *nm* (**a**) *Chim* derivative (**b**) *(produit)* by-product

3 *nf Math* **dérivée** derivative

dériver¹ [derive] **1** *vt* (**a**) *(cours d'eau)* to divert; *Élec (courant)* to shunt (**b**) *Math (fonction)* to derive

2 dériver de *vt ind (mot)* to be derived from

dériver² [derive] *vi Naut & Aviat* to drift

dériveur [derivœr] *nm Naut* sailing dinghy *(with centerboard)*

dermatite [dermatit] *nf Méd* dermatitis

dermato [dermato] *nmf Fam* dermatologist

dermatologie [dermatɔlɔʒi] *nf* dermatology

dermatologique [dermatɔlɔʒik] *adj* dermatological

dermatologiste [dermatɔlɔʒist], **dermatologue** [dermatɔlɔg] *nmf* dermatologist

derme [derm] *nm* dermis

dernier, -ère [dernje, -er] **1** *adj* (**a**) *(ultime)* last; *(marquant la fin)* final; **au d. moment** at the last moment

(**b**) *(passé)* last; *(le plus récent)* latest; **au cours des dernières années** over the past *or* last few years

(**c**) *(dans l'espace)* last; **le d. rang** the back *or* last row; **la dernière marche de l'escalier** *(en haut)* the top step; *(en bas)* the bottom step; **au d. étage** on the top floor

(**d**) *Litt (extrême)* utmost; **de la dernière importance** of the utmost importance; **c'est du d. chic** it's the height of elegance

(**e**) *(le pire)* worst; **de d. ordre** very inferior; **être reçu d. au concours** to come last in the competition; **c'était la dernière chose à faire** that's the last thing you/he/*etc.* should have done

2 *nm,f* (**a**) *(dans un classement)* last; **les six derniers** the last six; **arriver dans les derniers** to be one of the last to finish; **il est arrivé le d.** *ou* **bon d.** he came in last; **c'est le d. de sa classe** he's bottom of his class; *Fam* **c'est le d. de mes soucis** that's the least of my worries

(**b**) *(dans une chronologie) (l'ultime)* last; *(le plus récent)* latest; **le d. en date** the most recent; **ce d. répondit...** the latter answered...; **c'est toujours le d. à sortir** he's always last out; **comment va la petite dernière?** how's the little one?

(**c**) *Péj* **on la traite comme la dernière des dernières** they treat her like the lowest of the low; **c'est vraiment le d. des menteurs** he's the world's biggest liar

3 *nf* **dernière** (**a**) *(spectacle)* last night

(**b**) *(nouveauté)* **tu as entendu la dernière de ton frère?** have you heard your brother's latest?

4 *adv* **en d.** last (of all); **il sort toujours en d.** he's always last out

dernièrement [dernjermã] *adv* lately, recently

dernier-né, dernière-née *(mpl* **derniers-nés,** *fpl* **dernières-nées)** [dernjene, dernjerne] *nm,f* youngest (child)

dérobade [derɔbad] *nf* (**a**) *(esquive)* evasion (**b**) *(d'un cheval)* swerve

dérobé, -e [derɔbe] *adj* (**a**) *(escalier, porte)* hidden, secret (**b**) *(volé)* stolen

dérobée [derɔbe] **à la dérobée** *adv* secretly, on the sly; **regarder qn à la d.** to steal a glance at sb

dérober [derɔbe] **1** *vt* (**a**) *(voler)* to steal (**à** from) (**b**) *(cacher)* to hide (**à** from)

2 se dérober *vpr* (**a**) *(s'échapper)* to slip away (**à** from); **se d. à la curiosité de qn** to avoid sb's prying eyes (**b**) *(éviter de répondre)* to be evasive (**c**) *(manquer) (sol, jambes)* to give way (**sous** beneath) (**d**) *(cheval)* to swerve

dérogation [derɔgasjɔ̃] *nf* exemption (**à** from); *Jur* waiver; *(à une loi)* derogation (**à** of)

déroger [45] [derɔʒe] *vi* **d. à l'usage/à la loi** to depart from custom/the law

dérouillée [deruje] *nf très Fam* thrashing, hammering; **prendre une d.** to get thrashed *or* hammered

dérouiller [deruje] **1** *vi très Fam* (**a**) *(être battu)* to get a hammering (**b**) *(souffrir)* to have a hard time of it

2 se dérouiller *vpr Fam* **se d. les jambes** to stretch one's legs

déroulement [derulmã] *nm (d'événement)* unfolding; **pendant tout le d. de la cérémonie** throughout the ceremony

dérouler [derule] **1** *vt (rouleau)* to unroll; *(store)* to let down; *(câble)* to unwind; *Ordinat* **d. un menu** to pull down a menu

2 se dérouler *vpr* (**a**) *(rouleau)* to unroll; *(store)* to come down; *(câble)* to unwind (**b**) *Fig (événement)* to unfold; **la manifestation s'est déroulée dans le calme** the demonstration passed off peacefully

déroutant, -e [derutã, -ãt] *adj* disconcerting

déroute [derut] *nf aussi Fig* rout; **l'ennemi fut mis en d.** the enemy was routed

dérouter [derute] *vt* (**a**) *(navire, avion)* to detour, to reroute (**b**) *(égarer) (poursuivants)* to throw off the scent (**c**) *Fig (étonner)* to throw

derrière [derjer] **1** *prép* behind; **les uns d. les autres** one behind the other; **sortir de d. un buisson** to come out from behind a bush; *aussi Fig* **les autres sont loin d. elle** the others are way behind her; *Fig* **il faut toujours être d. elle** you always have to be at her back; *Fig* **c'est lui qui est d. tout ça** he's the one behind it all

2 *adv* behind; **aller** *ou* **monter d.** *(en voiture)* to sit in the back

3 *nm* (**a**) *(de bâtiment)* back, rear; **le mur de d.** the back wall (**b**) *(de personne)* behind, backside; *(d'animal)* hindquarters; **recevoir des coups de pied dans le** *ou* **au d.** to get kicked in the behind

des [de] *voir* **de, un**

dès [dɛ] *prép (à partir de)* from; **d. 1840** as far back as 1840; **d. le matin** first thing in the morning; **d. leur arrivée** as soon as they arrive/arrived; **d. maintenant, d. à présent** from now on; **d. que tu seras là** as soon as you're here; **d. lors** *(dans le temps)* from then on; *(par conséquent)* consequently; **d. lors que...** since...

désabusé, -e [dezabyze] *adj* disillusioned

désaccord [dezakɔr] *nm* disagreement; **être en d. avec qn (sur qch)** to disagree with sb (about sth)

désaccordé, -e [dezakɔrde] *adj* out of tune

désaccoutumer [dezakutyme] **se désaccoutumer** *vpr* **se d.** to get out of the habit (**de** of)

désaffecté, -e [dezafɛkte] *adj* disused

désaffection [dezafɛksjɔ̃] *nf* disaffection (**à l'égard de** with)

désagréable [dezagreabl] *adj* unpleasant

désagrégation [dezagregasjɔ̃] *nf (désintégration)* disintegration

désagréger [59] [dezagreʒe] **1** *vt (désintégrer)* to cause to disintegrate

2 se désagréger *vpr* to disintegrate

désagrément [dezagremã] *nm* (**a**) *(gêne)* trouble; **causer du d. à qn** to inconvenience sb (**b**) *(souci, aspect négatif)* problem

désaltérant, -e [dezalterɑ̃, -ɑ̃t] *adj* thirst-quenching

désaltérer [34] [dezaltere] **1** *vt* **d. qn** to quench sb's thirst; **c'est une boisson qui désaltère** it's a thirst-quenching drink

  2 se désaltérer *vpr* to quench one's thirst

désambiguïser [dezɑ̃biɡɥize] *vt (situation)* to clarify; *(mot)* to disambiguate

désamorçage [dezamɔrsaʒ] *nm* **(a)** *(d'une bombe, d'un conflit)* defusing **(b)** *(d'une pompe)* draining

désamorcer [16] [dezamɔrse] *vt* **(a)** *(bombe, conflit, querelle)* to defuse **(b)** *(pompe)* to drain

désappointer [dezapwɛ̃te] *vt* Litt to disappoint

désapprobateur, -trice [dezaprɔbatœr, -tris] *adj* disapproving

désapprobation [dezaprɔbasjɔ̃] *nf* disapproval

désapprouver [dezapruve] *vt* to disapprove of

désarçonner [dezarsɔne] *vt* **(a)** *(jeter bas)* to unseat, to throw **(b)** Fig *(déconcerter)* to throw

désargenté, -e [dezarʒɑ̃te] *adj* Fam *(personne)* broke

désarmant, -e [dezarmɑ̃, -ɑ̃t] *adj* disarming

désarmé, -e [dezarme] *adj (touché)* disarmed; *(sans défense)* defenseless, helpless

désarmement [dezarməmɑ̃] *nm* **(a)** *(d'un pays, d'une région)* disarmament; **d. multilatéral** multilateral disarmament **(b)** *(de soldats)* disarming

désarmer [dezarme] **1** *vt* **(a)** *(malfaiteur)* to disarm **(b)** Fig *(toucher)* to disarm **(c)** *(navire)* to lay up

  2 *vi* **(a)** *(pays, région)* to disarm **(b)** *(cesser)* **sa colère ne désarme pas** he/she is still angry

désarroi [dezarwa] *nm* confusion; **jeter qn dans le d.** to throw sb into confusion; **il est en plein d.** *ou* **dans un grand d.** he's in a state of total confusion

désarticuler [dezartikyle] **1** *vt* to dislocate

  2 se désarticuler *vpr* to contort oneself; **se d. l'épaule** to dislocate one's shoulder

désastre [dezastr] *nm* disaster

désastreux, -euse [dezastrø, -øz] *adj* disastrous

désavantage [dezavɑ̃taʒ] *nm* disadvantage; **avoir un d. par rapport à qn** to be at a disadvantage compared with sb; **voir qn à son d.** to see sb in an unfavorable light

désavantager [45] [dezavɑ̃taʒe] *vt* to put at a disadvantage, to disadvantage; **être désavantagé par rapport à qn** to be at a disadvantage compared with sb

désavantageux, -euse [dezavɑ̃taʒø, -øz] *adj* disadvantageous

désaveu [dezavø] *nm* **(a)** *(reniement)* disowning **(b)** *(condamnation)* disapproval

désavouer [dezavwe] *vt* **(a)** *(renier)* to disown **(b)** *(condamner)* to disapprove of **(c)** Jur *(enfant)* to disown

désaxé, -e [dezakse] **1** *adj (psychiquement)* unbalanced, unhinged

  2 *nm,f* lunatic

desceller [desele] *vt* **(a)** *(pierre)* to loosen **(b)** *(acte, document)* to unseal

descendance [desɑ̃dɑ̃s] *nf* **(a)** *(filiation)* descent **(b)** *(postérité)* descendants

descendant, -e [desɑ̃dɑ̃, -ɑ̃t] **1** *adj (mouvement)* downward

  2 *nm,f* descendant

descendre [desɑ̃dr] **1** *vi (aux être)* **(a)** *(en s'approchant)* to come down; *(en s'éloignant)* to go down; **d. de qch** to come down from sth; **faire d. qn de qch** to get sb down from sth; **aider qn à d.** to help sb down; **d. à 40 m de profondeur** ≃ to go down to a depth of 130 feet; **d. en dessous des dix secondes** to get below ten seconds; **d. à Marseille/dans le Midi** to go down to Marseilles/to the South; Fig **d. dans la rue** to take to the streets

  (b) *(d'un escalier)* *(en s'approchant)* to come downstairs; *(en*

s'éloignant) to go downstairs; **d. à la cave** to go down to the cellar

  (c) *(d'un véhicule)* **d. d'un train/d'une voiture** to get off a train/out of a car; **d. de cheval/de vélo/de moto** to dismount; **tout le monde descend!** *(au terminus)* everybody out!

  (d) *(baisser)* *(marée)* to go out; **faire d. la fièvre** to reduce fever

  (e) *(tomber)* *(brouillard)* to come down

  (f) *(s'étendre)* to go down; *(route, rue)* to go downhill; **d. jusqu'à la taille/jusqu'aux chevilles** to come down to the waist/to the ankles; **ce chemin descend au village** this path goes down to the village

  (g) *(loger)* **d. chez qn** to stay with sb; **d. à l'hôtel** to stay at a hotel

  (h) *(être issu)* **d. de** to be descended from

  2 *vt (aux avoir)* **(a)** *(dévaler)* **d. un escalier/la rue/la rivière** *(en s'éloignant)* to go down a staircase/the street/the river; *(en s'approchant)* to come down a staircase/the street/the river

  (b) *(porter vers le bas)* *(en s'éloignant)* to take down; *(en s'approchant)* to bring down; **d. la poubelle** to take the trash down; **peux-tu me d. mon pull?** can you bring me down my sweater?

  (c) *(abaisser)* *(store, étagère)* to lower

  (d) Fam *(abattre)* *(avion, personne)* to shoot down

  (e) Fam *(consommer)* *(repas, boisson)* to put away; **qu'est-ce qu'il descend!** he's really putting it away!

descente [desɑ̃t] *nf* **(a)** *(action de descendre)* descent; **d. en rappel** rappelling **(b)** *(sortie)* **accueillir qn à sa d. du train** to meet sb off the train **(c)** *(incursion)* raid; **d. de police** police raid **(d)** *(route en pente)* slope; **ralentir dans la d.** to slow down when going downhill **(e)** *(en ski)* *(course)* downhill (race); **faire la d.** to do downhill (skiing) **(f)** **d. de lit** bedside rug **(g)** *(tuyau)* downspout **(h)** Fam **il a une bonne d.** he can really put it away

descriptible [dɛskriptibl] *adj* describable

descriptif, -ive [dɛskriptif, -iv] **1** *adj* descriptive

  2 *nm* description

description [dɛskripsjɔ̃] *nf* description; **faire la d. de** to give a description of; **d. de poste** job description

désembourber [dezɑ̃burbe] *vt* to pull out of the mud

désembuage [dezɑ̃bɥaʒ] *nm* defrosting

désemparé, -e [dezɑ̃pare] *adj (personne)* at a loss

désemparer [dezɑ̃pare] *vi* **sans d.** without stopping

désemplir [dezɑ̃plir] *vi* **ne pas d.** to be always full

désenchanté, -e [dezɑ̃ʃɑ̃te] *adj (personne)* disillusioned; *(sourire)* wistful

désenchantement [dezɑ̃ʃɑ̃tmɑ̃] *nm* disillusion

désenchanter [dezɑ̃ʃɑ̃te] *vt* to disillusion

désenclaver [dezɑ̃klave] *vt (région)* to open up

désencombrer [dezɑ̃kɔ̃bre] *vt (passage)* to clear (**de** of)

désendettement [dezɑ̃dɛtmɑ̃] *nm* debt clearing

désenfler [dezɑ̃fle] *vi* to go down, to become less swollen

désengagement [dezɑ̃ɡaʒmɑ̃] *nm* disengagement

désengager [45] [dezɑ̃ɡaʒe] **1** *vt (d'une obligation)* to free (**de** from); Mil *(d'un conflit)* to withdraw

  2 se désengager *vpr (d'une obligation)* to free oneself (**de** from); Mil *(d'un conflit)* to withdraw

désensabler [dezɑ̃sable] *vt* **(a)** *(chenal, port)* to clear of sand **(b)** *(bateau)* to get off the sand; *(voiture)* to dig out of the sand

désensibiliser [dezɑ̃sibilize] *vt aussi Fig* to desensitize

désépaissir [dezepɛsir] *vt* **(a)** *(sauce)* to thin down **(b)** *(cheveux)* to thin out

déséquilibre [dezekilibr] *nm* imbalance; **être en d.** to be unsteady

déséquilibré, -e [dezekilibre] **1** *adj* unbalanced

  2 *nm,f* unbalanced person

déséquilibrer [dezekilibre] *vt* (**a**) *(objet, personne)* to throw off balance (**b**) *Psy* to unbalance

désert, -e [dezɛr, -ɛrt] **1** *adj* *(lieu)* deserted; *(pays, région)* uninhabited

2 *nm* desert; **d. culturel** cultural desert *or* wasteland; **le d. de Gobi** the Gobi Desert; **d. de sable** sandy desert

déserter [dezɛrte] **1** *vt* (**a**) *(lieu, fonction)* to desert; *Mil* **d. son poste** to desert one's post (**b**) *Fig (cause)* to desert, to abandon
2 *vi (soldat)* to desert

déserteur [dezɛrtœr] *nm* deserter

désertification [dezɛrtifikasjɔ̃] *nf* (**a**) *(transformation en désert)* desertification (**b**) *(dépeuplement)* depopulation

désertion [dezɛrsjɔ̃] *nf* desertion

désertique [dezɛrtik] *adj* desert

désespérant, -e [dezɛspeɾɑ̃, -ɑ̃t] *adj (situation, personne)* hopeless; **être d'une lenteur/bêtise désespérante** to be incredibly slow/stupid

désespéré, -e [dezɛspere] **1** *adj* (**a**) *(qui ne laisse aucun espoir)* desperate; *(inconsolable)* in despair (**b**) *(exprimant le désespoir)* desperate (**c**) *(extrême) (mesure, solution)* desperate
2 *nm,f* desperate person

désespérément [dezɛsperemɑ̃] *adv* desperately

désespérer [34] [dezɛspere] **1** *vt (personne)* to drive to despair
2 *vi* to despair
3 désespérer de *vt ind* to despair of; **d. de faire qch** to despair of doing sth; **il ne désespère pas d'y arriver** he hasn't given up hope of getting there
4 se désespérer *vpr* to despair

désespoir [dezɛspwar] *nm* despair; **être au d.** to be in despair; **être au d. de faire qch** to be extremely sorry to do sth; **faire** *ou* **être le d. de qn** *(personne)* to be the despair of sb; **réduire qn au d.** to drive sb to despair

déshabillé [dezabije] *nm* negligée

déshabiller [dezabije] **1** *vt (personne)* to undress; **d. qn du regard** to undress sb with one's eyes
2 se déshabiller *vpr* (**a**) *(pour être nu)* to undress, to take off one's clothes (**b**) *(ôter son manteau)* to take off one's coat

déshabituer [dezabitɥe] **1** *vt* **d. qn de qch/de faire qch** to get sb out of the habit of sth/of doing sth
2 se déshabituer *vpr* **se d. de qch/de faire qch** to get out of the habit of sth/of doing sth

désherbage [dezɛrbaʒ] *nm* weeding

désherbant [dezɛrbɑ̃] *nm* weedkiller

désherber [dezɛrbe] *vt* to weed

déshérité, -e [dezerite] **1** *adj (démuni)* deprived
2 *nm,f* **les déshérités** the underprivileged

déshériter [dezerite] *vt* to disinherit

déshonneur [dezɔnœr] *nm* dishonor

déshonorant, -e [dezɔnɔrɑ̃, -ɑ̃t] *adj* dishonorable

déshonorer [dezɔnɔre] **1** *vt* to disgrace; **se croire/se sentir déshonoré de faire qch** to think/to feel it beneath oneself to do sth
2 se déshonorer *vpr* to disgrace oneself

déshumaniser [dezymanize] *vt* to dehumanize

déshydratation [dezidratasjɔ̃] *nf* dehydration

déshydraté, -e [dezidrate] *adj* dehydrated

déshydrater [dezidrate] **1** *vt* to dehydrate
2 se déshydrater *vpr* to become dehydrated

desiderata [deziderata] *nmpl* desiderata

design [dizajn] **1** *nm* design; **d. industriel** industrial design
2 *adj inv* designer; **un intérieur d.** a designer interior

désignation [deziɲasjɔ̃] *nf* (**a**) *(appellation)* designation (**b**) *(choix)* appointment

désigner [deziɲe] *vt* (**a**) *(montrer)* to point out; **d. qn/qch du doigt** to point to sb/sth (**b**) *(dénommer)* to refer to (**c**) *(choisir)* to designate, to appoint (**d**) **il est tout désigné pour le faire** he's just the man for the job

désillusion [dezilyzjɔ̃] *nf* disillusion

désillusionner [dezilyzjɔne] *vt* to disillusion

désincrustant, -e [dezɛ̃krystɑ̃, -ɑ̃t] **1** *adj* (**a**) *Tech (substance)* scaling (**b**) *(masque, savon)* cleansing
2 *nm* (**a**) *Tech* scale preventive (**b**) *(savon)* cleanser

désindustrialisation [dezɛ̃dystrijalizasjɔ̃] *nf* deindustrialization

désinence [dezinɑ̃s] *nf* *Gram* ending

désinfectant, -e [dezɛ̃fɛktɑ̃, -ɑ̃t] *adj & nm* disinfectant

désinfecter [dezɛ̃fɛkte] *vt* to disinfect

désinfection [dezɛ̃fɛksjɔ̃] *nf* disinfection

désinflation [dezɛ̃flasjɔ̃] *nf* *Écon* disinflation

désinformation [dezɛ̃fɔrmasjɔ̃] *nf* disinformation

désinformer [dezɛ̃fɔrme] *vt* to disinform

désinscrire [30] [dezɛ̃skrir] **se désinscrire** *vpr* *Ordinat* to unsubscribe

désintégration [dezɛ̃tegrasjɔ̃] *nf* (**a**) *(des roches)* weathering (**b**) *(d'un groupe, de la famille)* break-up (**c**) *Phys (de matière)* disintegration

désintégrer [34] [dezɛ̃tegre] **1** *vt* (**a**) *(roches)* to weather (**b**) *(groupe, famille)* to break up (**c**) *Phys (matière)* to disintegrate; *(atome)* to split
2 se désintégrer *vpr* (**a**) *(roches)* to weather (**b**) *(groupe, famille)* to break up (**c**) *Phys (matière)* to disintegrate

désintéressé, -e [dezɛ̃terese] *adj* disinterested

désintéresser [dezɛ̃terese] **se désintéresser** *vpr* **se d. de qn/qch** *(ne pas s'y intéresser)* to have no interest in sb/sth; *(s'en détacher)* to lose interest in sb/sth

désintérêt [dezɛ̃terɛ] *nm* disinterest

désintoxication [dezɛ̃tɔksikasjɔ̃] *nf* *Méd* detoxification

désintoxiquer [dezɛ̃tɔksike] **1** *vt (alcoolique)* to treat for alcoholism; *(drogué)* to treat for drug addiction
2 se désintoxiquer *vpr* (**a**) *(alcoolique)* to come off alcohol; *(drogué)* to come off drugs (**b**) *Fig (se remettre en forme)* to clean out one's system; *(perdre une habitude)* to get out of the habit

désinvolte [dezɛ̃vɔlt] *adj* (**a**) *(négligeant)* casual, offhand (**b**) *(à l'aise) (manière)* unselfconscious; *(mouvements)* easy

désinvolture [dezɛ̃vɔltyr] *nf* (**a**) *(excès de liberté)* casualness; **avec d.** casually (**b**) *(naturel) (de manières)* unselfconsciousness; *(de mouvement)* ease

désir [dezir] *nm* (**a**) *(souhait)* desire; **selon le d. de qn** in accordance with sb's wishes; **prendre ses désirs pour des réalités** to indulge in wishful thinking; **tes désirs sont des ordres** your wish is my command (**b**) **d. (sexuel)** (sexual) desire

désirable [dezirabl] *adj* desirable

désirer [dezire] *vt* (**a**) *(souhaiter)* to wish; **d. faire qch** to wish to do sth; **je désire qu'il vienne** I want him to come; **cela laisse à d.** it leaves a lot to be desired; **elle se fait d.** *(elle n'arrive pas)* she's keeping us waiting; **que désirez-vous?**, *Fam* **vous désirez?** *(dans un magasin)* how may I help you?; *(qu'est-ce que je vous sers?)* what would you like? (**b**) *(sexuellement)* to desire

désireux, -euse [dezirø, -øz] *adj* **être d. de faire qch** to be anxious to do sth

désistement [dezistəmɑ̃] *nm* withdrawal

désister [deziste] **se désister** *vpr* to withdraw

désobéir [dezɔbeir] *vi* to disobey; **d. à qn/qch** to disobey sb/sth

désobéissance [dezɔbeisɑ̃s] *nf* disobedience (**à** to); **d. civile** civil disobedience

désobéissant, -e [dezɔbeisɑ̃, -ɑ̃t] *adj* disobedient (**à** to)

désobligeant, -e [dezɔbliʒɑ̃, -ɑ̃t] *adj* disagreeable

désodorisant, -e [dezɔdɔrizɑ̃, -ɑ̃t] *adj & nm* deodorant

désodoriser [dezɔdɔrize] *vt* to deodorize

désœuvré, -e [dezœvre] *adj* idle

désœuvrement [dezœvrəmã] *nm* idleness; **par d.** for something to do

désolant, -e [dezɔlɑ̃, -ãt] *adj* (**a**) *(affligeant)* distressing (**b**) *(contrariant)* annoying

désolé, -e [dezole] *adj* (**a**) *(navré)* sorry; **je suis d. de vous déranger** I'm sorry to disturb you; **d., je n'ai pas le temps** sorry, I don't have the time (**b**) *(affligé)* upset (**c**) *(région)* desolate

désoler [dezole] **1** *vt* (**a**) *(navrer)* to upset (**b**) *(affliger)* to distress
   2 se désoler *vpr* to be upset

désolidariser [desɔlidarize] **se désolidariser** *vpr* **se d. de** to dissociate oneself from

désopilant, -e [dezopilã, -ãt] *adj* hilarious

désordonné, -e [dezɔrdɔne] *adj* (**a**) *(chambre, bureau, personne)* untidy (**b**) *(désorganisé) (personne, article, pensées)* disorganized; *(mouvements)* uncoordinated (**c**) *(vie)* disorderly

désordre [dezɔrdr] *nm* (**a**) *(manque d'ordre)* untidiness, mess; **en d.** untidy; **mettre qch en d.** to make a mess of sth (**b**) *(manque d'organisation)* disorder (**c**) *(trouble)* commotion; **mettre le d. dans une réunion** to disrupt a meeting (**d**) *(agitation)* **désordres** disturbances (**e**) *Méd* disorder

désorganisation [dezɔrganizasjɔ̃] *nf* disorganization

désorganisé, -e [dezɔrganize] *adj (personne)* disorganized

désorganiser [dezɔrganize] *vt* to disrupt

désorienté, -e [dezɔrjãte] *adj* (**a**) *(égaré)* disoriented (**b**) *(déconcerté)* bewildered

désorienter [dezɔrjãte] *vt (déconcerter)* to bewilder

désormais [dezɔrmɛ] *adv* from now on, in the future

désosser [dezose] **1** *vt (viande, poisson)* to bone
   2 se désosser *vpr* to contort oneself

despote [dɛspɔt] *nm aussi Fig* despot

despotique [dɛspɔtik] *adj* despotic

desquamation [dɛskwamasjɔ̃] *nf (de la peau)* flaking, peeling

desquels, desquelles [dekɛl] *voir* **lequel**

DESS [deəsɛs] *nm (abrév* **diplôme d'études supérieures spécialisées**) = postgraduate diploma

dessaisir [desezir] **1** *vt* (**a**) *(déposséder)* **d. qn de qch** to confiscate sth from sb (**b**) **d. un juge d'une affaire** to withdraw a judge from a case
   2 se dessaisir *vpr* **se d. de qch** to relinquish sth, to part with sth

dessaler [desale] **1** *vt* (**a**) *(viande, poisson)* to remove the salt from *(by soaking)*; *(eau de mer)* to desalinate (**b**) *Fam* **d. qn** to teach sb a thing or two
   2 *vi* (**a**) *(voilier)* to capsize (**b**) **mettre qch à d.** *(viande, poisson)* to soak sth to remove the salt
   3 se dessaler *vpr Fam* to learn a thing or two

dessaouler [desule] = **dessoûler**

dessèchement [desɛʃmã] *nm (de la peau)* drying up; *(de la végétation)* withering

dessécher [34] [deseʃe] **1** *vt (déshydrater) (peau)* to dry up; *(végétation)* to wither
   2 se dessécher *vpr (peau)* to dry up; *(végétation)* to wither

dessein [desɛ̃] *nm* intention, purpose; **à d.** intentionally; **dans ce d.** with this intention; **dans le d. de faire qch** with the intention of doing sth

desseller [desele] *vt (cheval)* to unsaddle

desserrer [desere] **1** *vt* (**a**) *(relâcher) (vis, ceinture, nœud)* to loosen; *(frein à main)* to release (**b**) *(décrisper) (poing)* to unclench; *(étreinte)* to relax; *Fig* **il n'a pas desserré les dents** he didn't open his mouth
   2 se desserrer *vpr* (**a**) *(vis, ceinture, nœud)* to come loose (**b**) *(étreinte)* to relax

dessert [desɛr] *nm* dessert; **qu'est-ce qu'il y a comme** *ou* **au d.?** what's for dessert?

desserte [desɛrt] *nf (meuble)* sideboard

desservir¹ [63] [desɛrvir] *vt* (**a**) *(passer par) (ville, localité)* to serve; **ce train dessert les gares de…** *(annonce)* this train stops at…; **ville bien desservie** town with good public transportation (**b**) *(conduire à) (pièce)* to lead to

desservir² [desɛrvir] *vt* (**a**) *(débarrasser) (table)* to clear; **vous pouvez d.** you may clear the table (**b**) *(nuire à)* **d. qn** to do sb a disservice

dessiller [desije] *vt Fig & Litt* **d. les yeux de qn** to open sb's eyes

dessin [desɛ̃] *nm* (**a**) *(technique, art)* drawing; **faire du d.** to draw; **d. industriel** industrial drawing (**b**) *(représentation)* drawing; **faire un d.** to do a drawing; *Fam Fig* **tu veux que je te fasse un d.?** do you want me to spell it out for you?; *Cin* **d. animé** cartoon; **d. humoristique** cartoon (**c**) *(motif) (sur tissu)* design, pattern; **un tissu à dessins géométriques** a fabric with geometric patterns *or* a geometric design (**d**) *(contour) (de la bouche, du visage)* outline

dessinateur, -trice [desinatœr, -tris] *nm,f* (**a**) *(artiste)* drawer; **d. de bandes dessinées** cartoonist; **d. humoristique** cartoonist (**b**) *(concepteur)* designer (**c**) *Tech* **d. industriel** draftsman

dessiner [desine] **1** *vt* (**a**) *(faire un dessin de)* to draw; **d. à l'encre/à la craie** to draw in ink/chalk (**b**) *(concevoir)* to design (**c**) *Fig (tracer) (lignes)* to outline; **vêtement qui dessine la taille** garment that shows off the waist; **visage bien dessiné** finely chiseled face
   2 se dessiner *vpr* (**a**) *(apparaître)* to stand out; **se d. à l'horizon** to stand out on the horizon; **un sourire se dessine sur ses lèvres** a smile flickers over her lips (**b**) *Fig (prendre forme) (changement, résultat)* to become apparent; *(projet)* to take shape

dessoûler [desule] *vt & vi Fam* to sober up

dessous [dəsu] **1** *adv* (**a**) *(sous)* underneath (**b**) **en d.** underneath; **l'appartement d'en d.** the downstairs apartment, the apartment downstairs; **en d. de** below; **tu es très en d. de la vérité** you're not even close; *Fam* **être en d. de tout** to be worse than useless (**c**) **prendre/porter qch par (en) d.** to take hold of/to carry sth from underneath; *Fig* **regarder qn par en d.** to look at sb furtively
   2 *nm (partie inférieure) (d'une assiette, d'une table)* underside; *(du pied)* bottom; **les gens du d.** the people below; **avoir le d.** to get the worst of it
   3 *nmpl* (**a**) *(partie cachée) (d'une affaire)* hidden side (**b**) *(sous-vêtements)* underwear

dessous-de-plat [dəsudpla] *nm inv* table mat

dessous-de-table [dəsudtabl] *nm inv* bribe; **verser un d. à qn** to bribe sb

dessous-de-verre [dəsudvɛr] *nm inv* coaster; *(en carton)* beer mat

dessus [dəsy] **1** *adv* on (it/them); **il a marché d.** he trod on it; **mais il n'y a pas l'adresse d.** but the address isn't on it
   2 *nm* (**a**) *(d'une table, du pied)* top; *(d'une assiette)* upper side; **l'étage du d.** the top floor (**b**) *Fig* **avoir le d.** to have the upper hand; **reprendre le d.** *(se remettre)* to get over it

dessus-de-lit [dəsydli] *nm inv* bedspread

déstabiliser [destabilize] *vt* to destabilize

destin [dɛstɛ̃] *nm* fate, destiny

destinataire [dɛstinatɛr] *nmf (d'une lettre)* addressee; *(de marchandises)* consignee; *(d'un mandat postal)* payee

destination [dɛstinasjɔ̃] *nf* destination; **trains/vols à d. de Paris** trains/flights to Paris; **arriver à d.** to reach one's destination

destinée [dɛstine] *nf* (**a**) *(vie)* destiny (**b**) *Litt* **être promis à de grandes** *ou* **hautes destinées** to be destined for great things (**c**) *(fatalité)* fate, destiny

destiner [dɛstine] **1** *vt* (**a**) *(réserver)* **d. qch à qn** *(bien, somme*

d'argent, emploi) to intend sth for sb (**b**) *(adresser)* **être destiné à qn** *(remarque, paquet)* to be meant for sb (**c**) *(assigner)* **d. une somme d'argent à qch** to allot *or* to assign a sum of money to sth; **cet argent est destiné à la recherche contre le sida** this money is going toward Aids research (**d**) *(concevoir pour)* **destiné à qch** (intended) for sth; **cette salle est destinée aux répétitions** this room is for rehearsing in (**e**) *(vouer)* **d. qn à qch** to destine sb for sth; *Litt* **le sort les destinait à se rencontrer** they were destined to meet
 2 se destiner *vpr* **se d. à qch** to intend to take up sth

destituer [dɛstitɥe] *vt (renvoyer) (officier)* to discharge; *(fonctionnaire)* to remove from office; *(souverain)* to depose

destitution [dɛstitysjɔ̃] *nf (d'un officier)* discharge; *(d'un fonctionnaire)* removal from office; *(d'un souverain)* deposition

déstressant, -e [destresɑ̃, -ɑ̃t] *Fam adj* destressing, relaxing

déstresser [destrese] *Fam* **1** *vi* to destress
 2 se déstresser *vpr* to destress (oneself)

destructeur, -trice [dɛstryktœr, -tris] *adj* destructive

destruction [dɛstryksjɔ̃] *nf* destruction

désuet, -ète [dezɥɛ, -ɛt, desɥɛ, -ɛt] *adj* (**a**) *(dépassé)* obsolete (**b**) *(démodé)* old-fashioned

désuétude [dezɥetyd, desɥetyd] *nf* disuse; **tomber en d.** *(mot, expression, pratique)* to become obsolete

désuni, -e [dezyni] *adj (famille, amis, amants)* divided

désunir [dezynir] *vt (personnes, famille)* to divide

désynchronisé, -e [desɛ̃krɔnize] *adj* out of synch

détachable [detaʃabl] *adj* detachable

détachant, -e [detaʃɑ̃, -ɑ̃t] **1** *adj* stain-removing
 2 *nm* stain remover

détaché, -e [detaʃe] *adj* (**a**) *(ton, air, manière)* detached (**b**) *(fonctionnaire)* on a temporary assignment

détachement [detaʃmɑ̃] *nm* (**a**) *(indifférence)* detachment (**de** from) (**b**) *(d'un fonctionnaire)* temporary assignment; **être en d.** to be on a temporary assignment (**c**) *(troupes)* detachment

détacher[1] [detaʃe] **1** *vt* (**a**) *(défaire) (étiquette, page perforée)* to detach; *(ceinture, liens)* to undo; *(rideau)* to take down; *(wagon)* to uncouple; **d. ses yeux de qch** to take one's eyes off sth (**b**) *(libérer) (prisonnier, animal)* to untie (**c**) *(déléguer) (fonctionnaire)* to send on a temporary assignment; *(militaire)* to detach (**d**) *Fig* **d. qn de qch** to turn sb away from sth (**e**) *(faire sonner)* **d. les syllabes d'un mot** to pronounce each syllable of a word separately; *Mus* **d. les notes** to detach the notes
 2 se détacher *vpr* (**a**) *(étiquette, bouton, page)* to come off; *(ceinture)* to come undone; *(écorce)* to peel off (**b**) *(se libérer) (animal)* to get loose (**c**) *Fig* **se d. de qn** *(en devenant adulte)* to break away from sb; *(par manque d'intérêt)* to grow apart from sb; **se d. de qch** to turn one's back on sth (**d**) *(se séparer) (groupe de coureurs)* to break away (**de** from) (**e**) *(ressortir)* to stand out (**sur** against)

détacher[2] [detaʃe] *vt (nettoyer)* to remove the stains from

détail [detaj] *nm* (**a**) *(élément)* detail (**b**) *(énumération) (d'un compte, d'un inventaire)* items; *(d'une facture)* breakdown; **elle m'a fait le d. de sa soirée** she gave me a detailed account of her party; *Fam Fig* **il n'a pas fait de d.!** he was a bit heavy-handed!; *Fam Fig* **il n'a pas fait dans le d.** he didn't go into detail; **en d.** in detail; **se perdre dans les détails** to get bogged down in detail (**c**) *Com* retail; **vendre/acheter au d.** to sell/to buy retail

détaillant, -e [detajɑ̃, -ɑ̃t] *nm,f Com* retailer

détaillé, -e [detaje] *adj (récit, description)* detailed; *(facture)* itemized

détaler [detale] *vi Fam (personne)* to take off; **faire d. qn** to send sb packing

détartrage [detartraʒ] *nm* (**a**) *(de dents)* scaling; **se faire faire un d.** to have one's teeth scaled (**b**) *(de bouilloire, de cafetière, de chaudière)* descaling

détartrer [detartre] *vt* (**a**) *(dents)* to scale (**b**) *(bouilloire, cafetière, chaudière)* to descale

détaxe [detaks] *nf* tax refund

détaxer [detakse] *vt* to exempt from tax; **marchandises détaxées** duty-free goods

détectable [detɛktabl] *adj* detectable

détecter [detɛkte] *vt* to detect

détecteur, -trice [detɛktœr, -tris] **1** *adj* detecting
 2 *nm* detector; **d. de faux billets** forged-banknote detector; **d. de fumée** smoke detector; **d. de mensonges** lie detector; **d. de mines** mine detector; *Ordinat* **d. de virus** virus detector

détection [detɛksjɔ̃] *nf* detection; *Ordinat* **d. d'erreurs** error detection; *Ordinat* **d. virale** virus detection

détective [detɛktiv] *nm* detective; **d. privé** private detective, private eye

déteindre [54] [detɛ̃dr] *vi (tissu)* to run (**sur** over); **d. au lavage** to run in the wash; *Fig* **cela a déteint sur eux** it's rubbed off on them

dételer [9] [detle] **1** *vt (chevaux)* to unharness; *(bœufs)* to unyoke
 2 *vi Fam* to stop working; **sans d.** non-stop

détendre [detɑ̃dr] **1** *vt* (**a**) *(relâcher) (corde)* to slacken; *(arc)* to unbend; *(ressort)* to release (**b**) *(décontracter) (personne)* to relax; **le yoga, ça détend** yoga is relaxing (**c**) **d. l'atmosphère** to make the atmosphere less tense
 2 se détendre *vpr* (**a**) *(corde)* to slacken; *(arc)* to unbend; *(ressort)* to lose its tension (**b**) *(se relaxer) (personne, visage)* to relax (**c**) *(atmosphère, situation)* to become less tense

détendu, -e [detɑ̃dy] *adj (personne, conversation)* relaxed

détenir [70] [detnir] *vt* (**a**) *(avoir en sa possession) (passeport, titres, pouvoir, record du monde)* to hold; *(secret, preuve)* to have (**b**) *(garder prisonnier)* to hold

détente [detɑ̃t] *nf* (**a**) *(relaxation)* relaxation (**b**) *Pol* détente (**c**) *(d'une arme)* trigger (**d**) *(d'un athlète)* spring; **avoir de la d.** to jump well (**e**) *(d'un gaz)* expansion (**f**) **être dur** *ou* **long à la d.** to be slow on the uptake

détenteur, -trice [detɑ̃tœr, -tris] *nm,f (d'argent, de titres, de record)* holder; *(d'arme)* possessor

détention [detɑ̃sjɔ̃] *nf* (**a**) *(de titres)* holding; *(d'armes)* possession (**b**) *(incarcération)* detention; **d. provisoire** detention pending trial

détenu, -e [detny] *nm,f* prisoner

détergent, -e [detɛrʒɑ̃, -ɑ̃t] *adj & nm* detergent

détérioration [deterjɔrasjɔ̃] *nf* deterioration

détériorer [deterjɔre] **1** *vt* to damage
 2 se détériorer *vpr* to deteriorate

déterminant, -e [detɛrminɑ̃, -ɑ̃t] **1** *adj* decisive
 2 *nm* (**a**) *Ling* determiner (**b**) *Math* determinant

détermination [detɛrminasjɔ̃] *nf* (**a**) *(fermeté)* determination (**b**) *(d'une date, d'un lieu, d'un prix)* determination, fixing; *(du sang, d'une bactérie)* typing

déterminé, -e [detɛrmine] *adj* (**a**) *(résolu)* determined; **être d. à faire qch** to be determined to do sth (**b**) *(défini)* specific

déterminer [detɛrmine] **1** *vt* (**a**) *(définir)* to determine, to fix; *(sang, bactérie)* to type (**b**) *(décider)* **d. qn à faire qch** to induce sb to do sth (**c**) *(causer) (changement)* to cause; *(action, décision)* to determine (**d**) *Gram* to determine
 2 se déterminer *vpr* **se d. à faire qch** to make up one's mind to do sth

déterré, -e [detere] *nm,f Fam* **avoir une mine de d.** to look like death warmed over

déterrer [detere] *vt aussi Fig* to dig up

détestable [detɛstabl] *adj* foul

détester [detɛste] **1** *vt* to detest, to hate; **je déteste être dérangé** I hate being disturbed; **ne pas d. faire qch** to quite like doing sth

2 se détester *vpr (soi-même)* to hate oneself; *(l'un l'autre)* to hate each other

détonant, -e [detɔnɑ̃, -ɑ̃t] **1** *adj aussi Fig* explosive
2 *nm* explosive

détonateur [detɔnatœr] *nm* detonator; *Fig* **servir de d. à qch** to spark sth off

détonation [detɔnasjɔ̃] *nf (bruit)* explosion; *(bruit d'arme à feu)* bang

détoner [detɔne] *vi (explosif)* to detonate; **faire d. qch** to detonate sth

détonner [detɔne] *vi* **(a)** *(chanteur)* to sing out of tune; *(instrumentiste)* to play out of tune **(b)** *(trancher) (couleurs)* to clash; **il détonne dans ce milieu** he's out of place in that environment

détordre [detɔrdr] *vt (fil)* to untwist

détour [detur] *nm* **(a)** *(parcours)* detour; **faire un d. (par)** to make a detour (via); **valoir le d.** *(site)* to be worth the trip **(b)** *Fig (biais)* roundabout means; **user de détours pour faire qch** to do sth in a roundabout way; **sans d.** without beating around the bush **(c)** *(tracé) (d'une route, d'une rivière)* bend; **faire un d.** to bend; *Fig* **au d. de la conversation** in the course of the conversation

détourné, -e [deturne] *adj aussi Fig (indirect)* roundabout, indirect

détournement [deturnəmɑ̃] *nm* **(a)** **d. d'avion** hijacking **(b)** *(d'un cours d'eau)* deviation **(c)** **d. de fonds** embezzlement

détourner [deturne] **1** *vt* **(a)** *(circulation, rivière)* to deviate; *(avion)* to hijack **(b)** *(éloigner)* **d. qn de** *(ami, famille)* to take sb away from; *(préoccupation, engagement)* to divert sb from; **d. qn du droit chemin** to lead sb astray; **d. l'attention de qn** to divert or to distract sb's attention; **d. la conversation** to change the subject; **d. les soupçons** to avert suspicion **(c)** *(voler) (fonds)* to embezzle (**à** from) **(d)** *(tourner)* **d. la tête** to turn one's head away; **d. les yeux** *ou* **le regard** to look away
2 se détourner *vpr aussi Fig* to turn away (**de** from)

détracteur, -trice [detraktœr, -tris] *nm,f* detractor

détraqué, -e [detrake] **1** *adj (appareil)* out of order; *(estomac)* upset; *(temps)* unsettled; *Fam (personne) (psychologiquement)* unhinged
2 *nm,f Fam* maniac

détraquer [detrake] **1** *vt (appareil)* to put out of order; *(santé)* to ruin; *(estomac)* to upset
2 se détraquer *vpr (appareil, santé)* to break down; *(temps)* to become unsettled; **se d. l'estomac** to upset one's stomach

détrempé, -e [detrɑ̃pe] *adj (terre, sol)* sodden, waterlogged

détresse [detrɛs] *nf* **(a)** *(angoisse)* distress **(b)** *(dénuement)* financial difficulties; **les familles dans la d.** families in dire need *or* straits **(c)** *(perdition)* **en d.** *(navire)* in distress; *(voiture, avion)* in difficulties **(d)** *Méd* **d. respiratoire** respiratory distress

détriment [detrimɑ̃] *nm* **au d. de** to the detriment of; **je l'ai appris à mon d.** I found it out to my cost

détritus [detritys] *nm* garbage

détroit [detrwa] *nm* strait; **le d. de Béring** the Bering Strait; **le d. de Gibraltar** the Strait of Gibraltar

détromper [detrɔ̃pe] **1** *vt* **d. qn** to set sb right (**sur** about)
2 se détromper *vpr* to realize that one was wrong; **détrompez-vous!** think again!

détrôner [detrone] *vt* **(a)** *(monarque)* to dethrone **(b)** *(théorie, méthode, produit)* to supersede

détrousser [detruse] *vt Hum* **d. qn** to relieve sb of his/her valuables

détruire [18] [detrɥir] **1** *vt* **(a)** *(démolir) (édifice, empire, avion)* to destroy **(b)** *(anéantir) (espoir, mariage, santé)* to ruin, to wreck **(c)** *(tuer)* to kill
2 se détruire *vpr (se faire du mal)* to ruin one's health

dette [dɛt] *nf aussi Fig* debt; **avoir des dettes** to be in debt; **être couvert** *ou* **criblé de dettes** to be crippled with debt; **d. extérieure** foreign debt; **la d. publique** *ou* **de l'État** the National Debt; **payer sa d. à la société** to pay one's debt to society

DEUG [dœg] *nm (abrév* **diplôme d'études universitaires générales)** = degree gained after a two-year course

> **DEUG**
> In French universities, students take the "DEUG" or the "DEUST" ("diplôme d'études universitaires scientifiques et techniques") after two years of courses. They may then take further courses leading to the "licence" (the equivalent of a bachelor's degree). Most students who obtain the "DEUG" choose to do this, while the majority of students who obtain the "DEUST" leave university and go straight into employment.

deuil [dœj] *nm* **(a)** *(décès)* bereavement; **il y a eu un d. dans leur famille** there has been a death in their family **(b)** *(tristesse)* mourning; **être en d.** to be in mourning; **journée de d. national** day of national mourning **(c)** *(tenue)* **porter le d. (de qn)** to be in mourning (for sb); **prendre/quitter le d.** to go into/to come out of mourning; *Fam Fig* **avoir les ongles en d.** to have dirty fingernails **(d)** **faire son d. de qch** to give sth up as lost

DEUST [dœst] *nm (abrév* **diplôme d'études universitaires scientifiques et techniques)** = degree gained after a two-year course *(see box at* **DEUG)**

Deutsche Mark [dɔjtʃmark, døtʃmark] *nm Anciennement* Deutschmark

deux [dø] **1** *adj inv* **(a)** *(chiffre)* two; **d. fois** twice; **des d. côtés du fleuve** on either side *or* on both sides of the river; **tous (les) d.** both; **tous les d. jours** every other day, every two days; **nous/vous/eux d.** the two of us/you/them; **vivre à d.** to live together; **les ordinateurs et moi, ça fait d.** I know absolutely nothing about computers **(b)** *(peu de)* **c'est à d. pas d'ici** it's only a short distance away, it's two minutes away; **je reviens dans d. minutes** I'll be back in a minute; **tu peux venir? – d. secondes!** can you come here? – just a minute!
2 *nm inv* two; **casser qch en d.** to break sth in two; **marcher par d.** to walk in pairs *or* twos; *(dans une procession)* to march two abreast; *Fam* **en moins de d.** in next to no time; *voir aussi* **trois**

deuxième [døzjɛm] *adj & nmf* second; *voir aussi* **cinquième**

deuxièmement [døzjɛmmɑ̃] *adv* secondly

deux-mâts [døma] *nm* two-master

deux-pièces [døpjɛs] *nm* **(a)** *(maillot de bain)* two-piece (bathing suit) **(b)** *(tailleur)* two-piece **(c)** *(appartement)* two-room apartment

deux-points [døpwɛ̃] *nm* colon

deux-roues [døru] *nm* two-wheeled vehicle

deux-temps [døtɑ̃] *nm (moteur)* two-stroke (engine)

deuzio [døzjo] *adv Fam* second

dévaler [devale] **1** *vt (escalier, pente)* to hurtle down
2 *vi (personne, pierres)* to hurtle down; *(eau, lave, boue)* to rush down

dévaliser [devalize] *vt* **(a)** *(cambrioler) (banque)* to rob; *(maison)* to burglarize; *Fig (commerçant)* to clean out **(b)** *(vider) (réfrigérateur, placard)* to raid

dévalorisation [devalɔrizasjɔ̃] *nf* **(a)** *(action) (de la monnaie)* devaluation; *(de marchandises)* marking down; *(résultat) (de la monnaie)* depreciation; *(de marchandises)* mark-down **(b)** *Fig (d'une personne, d'une politique)* discrediting; *(d'un diplôme, d'une profession)* devaluation

dévaloriser [devalɔrize] **1** *vt* **(a)** *(monnaie)* to devalue **(b)** *(personne, politique)* to discredit; *(qualification, diplôme)* to devalue

2 se dévaloriser *vpr* (**a**) *(monnaie)* to depreciate (**b**) *(personne)* to put oneself down

dévaluation [devalyasjɔ̃] *nf Fin* devaluation

dévaluer [devalɥe] **1** *vt (monnaie)* to devalue
2 se dévaluer *vpr* to fall in value

devancer [16] [dəvɑ̃se] *vt* (**a**) *(être devant) (concurrent)* to be/get ahead of; **d. son époque** to be ahead of one's time (**b**) *(arriver avant)* to arrive before (**c**) *(prévoir) (personne, critiques)* to forestall; *(demande)* to anticipate (**d**) *(faire avant) Mil* **d. l'appel** to enlist before call-up; *Fin* **d. une échéance** to settle an account early

devant [dəvɑ̃] **1** *prép* (**a**) *(en face de, en avant de)* in front of; **assis d. moi** sitting in front of me; **marcher droit d. soi** to walk straight on; **regardez d. vous!** look where you're going!; **passer d. qn/qch** *(dans la rue)* to go past sb/sth; **passer d. qn** *(dans une file d'attente)* to go in front of sb; **avoir du temps/de l'argent d. soi** to have time/money to spare; **tu as la vie d. toi** you've got your whole life ahead of you; **d. derrière** back to front (**b**) *(face à)* **d. le danger** in the face of danger; **égaux d. la loi** equal in the eyes of the law; **que faire d. tant d'injustice?** what can one do faced with so much injustice?
2 *adv* (**a**) *(en face)* in front; **je cherchais la gare et j'étais juste d.** I was looking for the station when I was standing right in front of it; **où est Martin? – je crois qu'il est d.** where's Martin? – he's up ahead, I think (**b**) *(en avant) (dans les premiers rangs)* at the front; *(en voiture)* in the front; **aller d.** to go in front; **marcher/courir d.** to walk/to run on ahead; **passez d.!** you go ahead of me!
3 *nm* front; *Fig* **prendre les devants** to make the first move

devanture [dəvɑ̃tyr] *nf (vitrine)* window; *(façade)* front

dévastateur, -trice [devastatœr, -tris] *adj* devastating

dévastation [devastasjɔ̃] *nf* devastation

dévaster [devaste] *vt* to devastate

déveine [devɛn] *nf Fam* bad luck; **être dans la d.** to be down on one's luck

développement [devlɔpmɑ̃] *nm* development; *(de pellicule)* developing; *(en cyclisme)* gear ratio; **en plein d.** *(entreprise, pays)* growing fast; **développements** *(d'une affaire)* developments; *Fig* **se lancer dans de grands développements** to go into detailed explanation

développer [devlɔpe] **1** *vt* to develop
2 se développer *vpr* to develop; *(s'étendre)* to spread

devenir[1] [dəvnir] *nm Litt* (**a**) *(évolution)* evolution; **être en perpétuel d.** to be constantly evolving (**b**) *(futur)* future

devenir[2] [70] [dəvnir] *(aux être) vi* to become; **il devint général** he became a general; **il était devenu (un) homme** he had grown into a man; **ça devient difficile** it's getting difficult; **d. vieux** to get *or* to grow old; **d. fou** to go mad; **c'est à d. fou!** it's enough to drive you mad!; **d. tout rouge** to go all red; **que devient-il?** how is he doing?; **qu'est-il devenu?** what's become of him?

dévergondé, -e [devɛrgɔ̃de] **1** *adj* shameless
2 *nm,f* shameless person

dévergonder [devɛrgɔ̃de] **se dévergonder** *vpr* to get into bad ways

déversement [devɛrsəmɑ̃] *nm (écoulement)* discharge; *(action)* pouring

déverser [devɛrse] **1** *vt* (**a**) *(eau)* to pour; *(sable, gravier, déchets)* to dump; *Fig (touristes, voyageurs)* to disgorge (**b**) **d. sa colère sur qn** to vent one's anger on sb; **d. des insultes sur qn** to shower sb with abuse
2 se déverser *vpr (rivière)* to empty (**dans** into)

dévestiture [devɛstityr] *nf Suisse* access; **(chemin de) d.** access road

dévêtir [71] [devetir] **1** *vt* to undress
2 se dévêtir *vpr* to undress

devez *voir* **devoir**[2]

déviation [devjasjɔ̃] *nf* (**a**) *(itinéraire modifié)* detour (**b**) *(modification)* deviation (**par rapport à** from)

dévier [66] [devje] **1** *vt* (**a**) *(circulation)* to detour (**b**) *(balle, coup)* to deflect
2 *vi (véhicule, missile)* to veer (**vers** towards); *(balle)* to deflect (**vers** towards); **d. de sa route** *(véhicule, missile)* to veer off course; *Fig* **d. de son sujet** to digress

devin [dəvɛ̃] *nm* soothsayer; *Fam* **je ne suis pas d.!** I'm not a mind-reader!

deviner [dəvine] *vt (énigme, secret)* to guess; *(futur)* to predict; *(pensée)* to read; **devine qui j'ai vu** guess who I saw; **je ne pouvais pas d.!** how was I supposed to know?

devinette [dəvinɛt] *nf* riddle; **jouer aux devinettes** to play at riddles; *Fig* to speak in riddles; **poser une d. à qn** to ask sb a riddle

devis [dəvi] *nm* estimate, quote; **faire faire un d. pour qch** to get an estimate *or* a quote for sth

dévisager [45] [devizaʒe] *vt* to stare at

devise [dəviz] *nf* (**a**) *(d'une personne)* motto (**b**) *(monnaie)* currency; **devises étrangères** foreign currency; **d. forte** hard currency

deviser [dəvize] *vi Litt* to converse

dévisser [devise] **1** *vt* to unscrew
2 *vi (alpiniste)* to fall
3 se dévisser *vpr* to unscrew; *(par accident)* to come unscrewed; *Fig* **se d. la tête** *ou* **le cou** to screw one's head around

de visu [devizy] *adv* with one's own eyes

dévitaliser [devitalize] *vt (dent)* to remove the nerve from

dévoiler [devwale] **1** *vt (visage, statue, plaque)* to unveil; *Fig (nom, secret, complot)* to disclose
2 se dévoiler *vpr (secret, complot)* to come to light

devoir[1] [dəvwar] *nm* (**a**) *(obligation)* duty; **faire qch par d.** to do sth out of a sense of duty; **un homme/une femme de d.** a man/a woman with a sense of duty; **faire** *ou* **remplir son d. (envers)** to do one's duty (by); **il est de mon d. de vous le dire** it is my duty to tell you (**b**) *(exercices) (en classe)* test; **devoirs** *(à la maison)* homework; **faire ses devoirs** to do one's homework; **devoirs de vacances** vacation homework (**c**) *Sout* **rendre les derniers devoirs à qn** to pay one's last respects to sb

devoir[2] [26] [dəvwar] **1** *vt (être redevable de)* **d. qch à qn** to owe sb sth, to owe sth to sb; **il me doit cent euros** he owes me a hundred euros; **je lui dois bien cela** it's the least I can do for him/her, I owe him/her that at least
2 *v aux* (**a**) *(indique l'obligation)* **d. faire qch** to have to do sth; **vous devez être là à trois heures** you must *or* you have to be there by three o'clock; **elle a cru d. refuser** she thought it advisable to refuse; **les commandes doivent être adressées à...** orders should be sent to...; **vous devriez rester** you should stay, you ought to stay; **il aurait dû m'avertir** he should have warned me, he ought to have warned me
(**b**) *(indique la nécessité)* **tu dois absolument lui en parler** you really must talk to him/her about it; **finalement, j'ai dû céder** I had to give way in the end; **il ne devait plus les revoir** *(il ne les reverrait plus)* he was (destined) never to see them again; **cela devait arriver!** it was bound to *or* it had to happen!
(**c**) *(indique l'intention)* **je devais partir lundi, mais...** I was meant to leave on Monday, but...; **le train doit arriver à midi** the train is due (to arrive) at noon
(**d**) *(indique la supposition)* **vous devez avoir faim** you must be hungry; **il ne doit pas avoir plus de 40 ans** he can't be more than 40; **il a dû me prendre pour un autre** he must have mistaken me for someone else; **la pollution devrait s'accroître d'ici la fin du siècle** pollution is expected to increase by the end of the century

3 se devoir *vpr* **je me dois à ma famille/mon travail** I must devote myself to my family/my work; **je me dois de le faire** it's my duty to do it; **comme il se doit** as is (only) right and proper

dévolu, -e [devɔly] **1** *adj (somme, responsabilités)* assigned (**à** to)

2 *nm* **jeter son d. sur** to set one's heart on

devons *voir* **devoir²**

dévorant, -e [devɔrɑ̃, -ɑ̃t] *adj (jalousie, passion)* consuming; *(envie)* overwhelming; *(curiosité)* burning; **avoir une faim dévorante** to be ravenous

dévorer [devɔre] *vt* (**a**) *(proie, nourriture, livre)* to devour; **être dévoré par les moustiques** to be eaten alive by mosquitoes; **d. qn des yeux** *ou* **du regard** to devour sb with one's eyes (**b**) *Fig (détruire)* **l'ambition/la jalousie la dévore** she is consumed by ambition/jealousy; **dévoré de remords** consumed with remorse (**c**) *Fig (fortune, kilomètres)* to eat up

dévot, -e [devo, -ɔt] **1** *adj* devout

2 *nm,f* devout person

dévotion [devɔsjɔ̃] *nf* (**a**) *(ferveur)* devoutness (**b**) *(adoration)* devotion; **avoir une d. pour** to be devoted to (**c**) **dévotions** *(prières)* devotions

dévoué, -e [devwe] *adj* devoted (**à** to)

dévouement [devumɑ̃] *nm* (**a**) *(abnégation)* devotion to duty (**b**) *(amour)* devotion (**à** to); **avec d.** devotedly

dévouer [devwe] **se dévouer** *vpr (se sacrifier)* to volunteer (**pour faire qch** to do sth); *(se consacrer)* to devote oneself (**à** to); **il faut que quelqu'un se dévoue** somebody has to do it; *Hum* **vous voulez que je finisse la tarte? bon, je me dévoue!** you want me to finish the pie? oh well, if I must!

dévoyé, -e [devwaje] *adj & nm,f* delinquent

dévoyer [32] [devwaje] **se dévoyer** *vpr Litt* to go astray

devra *etc. voir* **devoir²**

dextérité [dɛksterite] *nf* dexterity, skill; **avec d.** skillfully

dézipper [dezipe] *vt Ordinat* to unzip

DGSE [deʒɛəsə] *nf (abrév* **direction générale de la sécurité extérieure**) = French military intelligence service, ≃ CIA

diabète [djabɛt] *nm* diabetes; **avoir du d.** to have diabetes

diabétique [djabetik] *adj & nmf* diabetic

diable [djɑbl] *nm* (**a**) *(démon)* devil; **le d.** the Devil; **un petit d.** *(enfant)* a little devil; **avoir une faim de tous les diables** to be absolutely starving; **un bruit de tous les diables** a hell of a racket; *Fig* **avoir le d. au corps** to be possessed; *Can Fam* **être au d.** to be fed up; *Fig* **tirer le d. par la queue** to live from hand to mouth; **au d. l'avarice!** to hell with the expense!; **allez au d.!** go to hell!; **au d. (vauvert)** miles away!; **que le d. l'emporte!** he can go to hell!; **ce serait bien le d. si…** it would be surprising if… (**b**) *(marque la surprise, l'agacement)* **d.!** goodness me!; **où d. est-elle allée?** where the heck has she gone?; **que d.!** for goodness sake! (**c**) *(chariot)* (two-wheeled) cart (**d**) *(jouet)* jack-in-the-box

diablement [djɑbləmɑ̃] *adv Fam* damn, damned

diablesse [djɑblɛs] *nf (démon, méchante femme)* she-devil; *Vieilli (jeune fille)* devil

diablotin [djɑblɔtɛ̃] *nm* imp

diabolique [djabɔlik] *adj* diabolical

diaboliser [djabɔlize] *vt* to demonize

diabolo [djabɔlo] *nm (boisson)* **d. menthe/fraise** mint/strawberry syrup and lemonade

diadème [djadɛm] *nm* tiara

diagnostic [djagnɔstik] *nm* diagnosis; **faire un d.** to make a diagnosis; **ce médecin a un d. très sûr** this doctor makes very reliable diagnoses; *Ordinat* **d. d'autotest** self-test diagnosis

diagnostiquer [djagnɔstike] *vt* to diagnose

diagonal, -e, -aux, -ales [djagɔnal, -o] **1** *adj* diagonal

2 *nf* **diagonale** diagonal; **en diagonale** diagonally; *Fig* **lire qch en diagonale** to skim through sth

diagonalement [djagɔnalmɑ̃] *adv* diagonally

diagramme [djagram] *nm* diagram

dialecte [djalɛkt] *nm* (**a**) *(variante régionale)* dialect (**b**) *Suisse* Swiss German

dialectique [djalɛktik] **1** *adj* dialectical

2 *nf* dialectics *(singulier)*

dialogue [djalɔg] *nm* dialogue; *(conversation)* conversation; **c'est un d. de sourds** it's a dialogue of the deaf; *Ordinat* **mode de d.** interactive mode

dialoguer [djalɔge] *vi* to communicate; *(avec un ordinateur)* to interact

dialyse [djaliz] *nf Méd* dialysis

diamant [djamɑ̃] *nm* diamond

diamantaire [djamɑ̃tɛr] *nm (tailleur)* diamond cutter; *(vendeur)* diamond merchant

diamétralement [djametralmɑ̃] *adv* **d. opposés** diametrically opposed

diamètre [djamɛtr] *nm* diameter

diapason [djapazɔ̃] *nm Mus* (**a**) *(note)* pitch; *Fig* **se mettre au d.** to fall in with the others (**b**) *(appareil)* tuning fork

diaphane [djafan] *adj* diaphanous

diaphragme [djafragm] *nm* (**a**) *Anat* diaphragm (**b**) *(contraceptif)* diaphragm

diapo [djapo] *nf Fam* slide

diaporama [djaporama] *nm* slide show

diapositive [djapozitiv] *nf* slide

diarrhée [djare] *nf* diarrhea; **avoir la d.** to have diarrhea

diaspora [djaspɔra] *nf* diaspora

diatonique [djatɔnik] *adj* diatonic

diatribe [djatrib] *nf* diatribe (**contre** against)

dichotomie [dikɔtɔmi] *nf* dichotomy

dico [diko] *nm Fam* dictionary

Dictaphone® [diktafɔn] *nm* Dictaphone®

dictateur [diktatœr] *nm* dictator

dictatorial, -e, -aux, -ales [diktatɔrjal, -o] *adj* dictatorial

dictature [diktatyr] *nf* dictatorship

dictée [dikte] *nf* dictation; **écrire qch sous la d. de qn** to write sth at sb's dictation; **d. musicale** musical dictation

dicter [dikte] *vt* to dictate

diction [diksjɔ̃] *nf* diction

dictionnaire [diksjɔnɛr] *nm* dictionary; **d. électronique** electronic dictionary; **d. de langue** language dictionary

dicton [diktɔ̃] *nm* saying

didacticiel [didaktisjɛl] *nm Ordinat* tutorial

didactique [didaktik] **1** *adj* (**a**) *(ouvrage, voyage)* educational (**b**) *(terme, langage)* technical

2 *nf* didactics *(singulier)*

dièse [djɛz] **1** *nm Mus* sharp; *Tél* hash (sign)

2 *adj Mus* sharp; **fa d.** F sharp

diesel [djezɛl] **1** *adj* **moteur d.** diesel engine

2 *nm (carburant)* diesel

3 *nf (voiture)* diesel

diète [djɛt] *nf (régime) (partiel)* diet; *(total)* fast; **être à la d.** *(partielle)* to be on a diet; *(totale)* to be fasting

diététicien, -enne [djetetisjɛ̃, -ɛn] *nm,f* dietitian

diététique [djetetik] **1** *adj (menu, repas)* diet; *(magasin, restaurant)* health food

2 *nf* dietetics *(singulier)*

dieu, -x [djø] **1** *nm* (**a**) *(divinité)* god; *Fam* **comme un d.** *(chanter, jouer)* like a god (**b**) *(dans la religion chrétienne)* **D.** God; **le bon D.** God; **D. merci!, D. soit loué!** thank God!; **D. sait si j'ai travaillé** God knows I've worked hard enough; **D. seul le sait** God only knows

2 *exclam* **mon D.!** (good) God!; **D. qu'elle est petite!** God, she's small!; *Fam* **c'est pas D. possible!** it's just not possible!; *Fam* **bon D.!** for God's sake!; *très Fam* **nom de D.!** Christ almighty!

diffamation [difamasjɔ̃] *nf* (*paroles*) slander; (*écrits*) libel; **procès en d.** slander/libel trial

diffamatoire [difamatwar] *adj* (*paroles*) slanderous; (*écrits*) libelous

différé, -e [difere] **1** *adj Ordinat* **traitement d.** off-line processing

2 *nm* **en d.** (*émission*) pre-recorded

différemment [diferamã] *adv* differently

différence [diferãs] *nf* difference (**entre** between); **d. d'âge/de prix** age/price difference; **faire la d. (entre)** to make a distinction (between); **cela ne fait aucune** *ou* **pas de d.** it makes no difference; **à la d. de** unlike

différenciation [diferãsjasjɔ̃] *nf* differentiation

différencier [66] [diferãsje] **1** *vt* to differentiate (**de** *ou* **d'avec** from)

2 se différencier *vpr* (**a**) (*être différent*) to differ (**de/par** from/in) (**b**) (*chercher à être différent*) to differentiate oneself (**de** from)

différend [diferã] *nm* difference of opinion, disagreement (**entre** between); *Jur* dispute; **avoir un d. avec qn** to have a disagreement with sb

différent, -e [diferã, -ãt] *adj* different (**de** from); **différents cas** (*plusieurs*) various cases

différentiel, -elle [diferãsjɛl] **1** *adj & nm* differential

2 *nf* **différentielle** *Math* differential

différer [34] [difere] **1** *vt* (*jugement, paiement*) to defer; (*décision, départ*) to postpone

2 *vi* (*être différent*) to differ (**par** in)

difficile [difisil] **1** *adj* difficult; (*exigeant*) fussy; **le plus d. est fait** the most difficult part is over; **il est d. de le joindre** it's difficult to contact him; **il m'est d. d'accepter** it's difficult for me to accept; **être d. à vivre** to be difficult to get along with; **être d. sur qch** to be particular about sth

2 *nmf* **faire le d.** to be fussy

difficilement [difisilmã] *adv* with difficulty, not easily; **on peut d. le lui dire** you can hardly tell him/her that

difficulté [difikylte] *nf* difficulty; **être en d.** to be in difficulty *or* trouble; **faire des difficultés** to create difficulties; **avoir de la d. à faire qch** to have difficulty (in) doing sth; **avoir des difficultés en anglais** to have difficulties with English

difforme [difɔrm] *adj* deformed, misshapen

difformité [difɔrmite] *nf* deformity

diffus, -e [dify, -yz] *adj* (*lumière*) diffuse; (*impression, souvenir*) vague; (*douleur*) dull

diffuser [difyze] *vt* (**a**) (*lumière, chaleur*) to diffuse; (*livres*) to distribute; (*idée, nouvelle*) to spread (**b**) (*émission*) to broadcast

diffuseur [difyzœr] *nm* (*de lumière, de chaleur*) diffuser; **d. de parfum** room freshener

diffusion [difyzjɔ̃] *nf* (**a**) (*de lumière, de chaleur*) diffusion; (*de livres*) distribution; (*d'une idée, d'une nouvelle*) spreading (**b**) (*d'une émission*) broadcasting; **d. audionumérique** digital audio broadcasting, DAB; **d. hertzienne, d. terrestre** terrestrial broadcasting

digérer [34] [diʒere] *vt* (**a**) (*aliment*) to digest; **je ne digère pas le lait** I can't digest milk (**b**) (*assimiler intellectuellement*) to digest; *Fam* (*accepter*) to stomach, to take; **des vérités dures à d.** unpalatable truths

digeste [diʒɛst] *adj aussi Fig* easily digestible

digestif, -ive [diʒɛstif, -iv] **1** *adj* digestive

2 *nm* after-dinner liqueur

digestion [diʒɛstjɔ̃] *nf* digestion; **avoir une d. difficile** to have problems with one's digestion

Digicode® [diʒikɔd] *nm* door code (*for entry to a building*)

digital¹, -e¹, -aux¹, -ales¹ [diʒital, -o] *adj* (*numérique*) digital

digital², -e², -aux², -ales² [diʒital, -o] **1** *adj voir* **empreinte**

2 *nf* **digitale** *Bot* digitalis

digne [diɲ] *adj* (**a**) (*méritant*) **d. de** worthy of; **d. d'éloges** praiseworthy; **d. de foi** reliable; **être d. de faire qch** to be fit to do sth (**b**) (*approprié*) **d. de** worthy of; **peu d. de qn** unworthy of sb; **d. de ce nom** worthy of the name; *Hum* **tu es bien le d. fils de ton père** you're your father's son all right (**c**) (*grave*) dignified

dignement [diɲəmã] *adv* (**a**) (*avec dignité*) with dignity (**b**) (*de façon appropriée*) fittingly; **être d. récompensé** to be justly rewarded

dignitaire [diɲitɛr] *nm* dignitary

dignité [diɲite] *nf* dignity

digression [digrɛsjɔ̃] *nf* digression; **faire une d.** to digress

digue [dig] *nf* (**a**) (*dans un port*) dike; (*contre l'érosion*) sea wall (**b**) *Can* (*de billes de bois*) logjam

dilapider [dilapide] *vt* (*fortune*) to squander; (*fonds publics*) to embezzle

dilatation [dilatasjɔ̃] *nf* (**a**) (*des pupilles*) dilation; (*de l'estomac*) distension (**b**) (*d'un gaz*) expansion

dilater [dilate] **1** *vt* (**a**) (*pupilles*) to dilate; (*estomac*) to distend (**b**) (*gaz*) to expand

2 se dilater *vpr* (**a**) (*pupilles*) to dilate; (*estomac*) to distend (**b**) (*gaz*) to expand

dilemme [dilɛm] *nm* dilemma

dilettante [diletãt] *nmf* dilettante; **faire qch en d.** to dabble in sth

diligence [diliʒãs] *nf* (**a**) (*véhicule*) (stage)coach (**b**) *Litt* (*soin*) diligence

diligent, -e [diliʒã, -ãt] *adj Litt* (*zélé*) diligent

diluant [dilɥã] *nm* thinner

diluer [dilɥe] *vt* (*boisson*) to dilute; (*peinture*) to thin down; *Fig* (*discours, dissertation*) to pad out

dilution [dilysjɔ̃] *nf* (*de peinture*) thinning down; (*d'une boisson*) dilution

diluvien, -enne [dilyvjɛ̃, -ɛn] *adj* (*pluies*) torrential

dimanche [dimãʃ] *nm* Sunday; **le d. des Rameaux/de Pâques** Palm/Easter Sunday; *Fig* **conducteur du d.** Sunday driver; *voir aussi* **samedi**

dîme [dim] *nf Hist* tithe

dimension [dimãsjɔ̃] *nf* (**a**) (*grandeur*) dimension, size; **à deux/trois dimensions** two-/three-dimensional; **prendre les dimensions de qch** (*objet*) to take the measurements of sth (**b**) (*importance*) magnitude (**c**) (*aspect*) dimension

diminué, -e [diminɥe] *adj* **être d.** to have gone downhill

diminuer [diminɥe] **1** *vt* (**a**) (*réduire*) to reduce, to decrease (**b**) (*affaiblir*) to weaken (**c**) (*dénigrer*) (*personne*) to belittle; (*action*) to undermine

2 *vi* to decrease; (*fièvre*) to drop

3 se diminuer *vpr* to belittle oneself

diminutif, -ive [diminytif, -iv] *adj & nm* diminutive

diminution [diminysjɔ̃] *nf* reduction, decrease; **être en d.** (*effectifs*) to be dwindling; (*naissances, ventes*) to be falling

dinar [dinar] *nm* dinar

dinde [dɛ̃d] *nf* (**a**) (*volaille, viande*) turkey (**b**) *Fam* (*femme sotte*) silly goose

dindon [dɛ̃dɔ̃] *nm* turkey (cock); *Fig* **être le d. de la farce** to be made a fool of

dindonneau, -x [dɛ̃dɔno] *nm* poult, young turkey

dîner [dine] **1** *nm* (**a**) (*repas du soir*) dinner; (*soirée*) dinner party; **il y a des pâtes pour le** *ou* **au** *ou* **à d.** it's pasta for dinner (**b**) (*repas de midi*) lunch

2 *vi* (**a**) (*le soir*) to have dinner, to dine; **il dîna d'une tranche de jambon** he had a slice of ham for dinner (**b**) (*à midi*) to have lunch

dînette [dinɛt] *nf (service)* doll's tea set; **jouer à la d.** to have a dolls' tea party

dingo [dɛ̃go] **1** *Fam adj* crazy
2 *nm (chien sauvage d'Australie)* dingo
3 *nmf Fam* nutcase

dingue [dɛ̃g] *Fam* **1** *adj* **(a)** *(fou)* crazy; **être d. de qn/qch** to be crazy about sb/sth **(b)** *(incroyable)* incredible
2 *nmf (fou)* nutcase; **être un(e) d. de moto/cinéma** to be a motorcycle/movie nut

dinguer [dɛ̃ge] *vi Fam* **aller d. contre qch** to go crashing into sth; **envoyer d. qn** *(éconduire)* to send sb packing; **envoyer d. qch** to send sth flying

dinosaure [dinozor] *nm aussi Fig* dinosaur

diocèse [djosɛz] *nm Rel* diocese

diode [djod] *nf Élec* diode; **d. électroluminescente** light-emitting diode

dioxyde [dioksid] *nm Chim* dioxide; **d. de carbone** carbon dioxide

diphtérie [difteri] *nf Méd* diphtheria; **avoir la d.** to have diphtheria

diphtongue [diftɔ̃g] *nf Ling* diphthong

diplomate [diplomat] **1** *adj* diplomatic
2 *nm Culin* = dessert made of sponge cake pieces covered with custard and fruit, ≃ trifle
3 *nmf* diplomat

diplomatie [diplomasi] *nf* **(a)** *(habileté)* diplomacy; **user de d.** to be diplomatic **(b)** *(service)* diplomatic service

diplomatique [diplomatik] *adj* diplomatic

diplomatiquement [diplomatikmɑ̃] *adv* diplomatically

diplôme [diplom] *nm* diploma; *Univ* degree; **avoir des diplômes** to have qualifications

diplômé, -e [diplome] **1** *adj* qualified; *Univ* graduate; **un ingénieur d. de l'École polytechnique** an engineering graduate of the École Polytechnique
2 *nm,f* holder of a diploma; *Univ* graduate

dire¹ [dir] *nm* **au d. de qn** according to sb; **selon ses dires** according to him/her

dire² [27a] [dir] **1** *vt* **(a)** *(exprimer)* to say; **comment dit-on "soleil" en anglais?** how do you say "soleil" in English?; **il ne savait plus quoi d.** he didn't know what to say; **je sais ce que je dis!** I know what I'm talking about!; **laisse-les d., ils sont stupides!** let them talk, they're stupid!; **elle a dit qu'elle arriverait en retard** she said she would be late; **comment dirais-je?** how shall I put it?; **comme on dit** as the saying goes; **cela dit...** having said that...; **il est un peu lent, pour ne pas d. complètement idiot** he's a bit slow, or to put it bluntly he's a complete idiot; **qui dit mieux?** *(à une vente aux enchères)* any other bids?; **c'est vite dit** it's easier said than done

(b) *(communiquer)* **d. qch à qn** to tell sb sth; **d. à qn que...** to tell sb (that)...; **je t'ai déjà dit que oui!** I've already said yes!; **je vous l'avais bien dit!** I told you so!; *Fam* **c'est elle, je te dis** it's her, I tell you; **je lui ai fait d. de venir** I sent for him; **elle ne se le fit pas d. deux fois** she didn't wait to be told twice

(c) *(ordonner)* **d. à qn de faire qch** to tell sb to do sth; **faites ce qu'on vous dit** do as you're told; **taisez-vous, j'ai dit!** be quiet, I said!

(d) *(prétendre)* to say; **à ce qu'elle dit** according to her; **on le dit mort** he is said to have died

(e) *(langage enfantin) (rapporter)* to tell; **je vais le d. à ma mère** I'm going to tell my mom

(f) *(décider)* **disons à quatre heures** let's say four o'clock; **il est dit que je resterai célibataire** I'm destined to stay single

(g) *(penser)* **alors, qu'est-ce que tu en dis?** well, what do you think?; **qu'est-ce que tu dirais d'aller au cinéma?** how about going to the movies?; **on dirait qu'il pleut** it looks as if it's raining; **on dirait du Mozart** it sounds like Mozart; **on dirait du gin** *(au goût)* it tastes like gin; **on aurait dit qu'elle était hypnotisée** it looked as if she was hypnotized; **et d. que...!** and to think (that)...!

(h) *(objecter)* to say; **j'ai eu une augmentation importante, je n'ai rien à d.** I got a decent raise, I can't complain; **vous avez beau d.,...** you can say what you like, but...; **ce n'est pas pour d., mais...** I don't want to be rude, but...

(i) *(indiquer) (sujet: statistiques)* to show; **que dit le baromètre?** what does the barometer say?; **qu'est-ce qui vous dit qu'il viendra?** what makes you think he'll come?; **ce nom ne me dit rien** the name doesn't ring a bell; **quelque chose me dit que...** something tells me (that)...

(j) *(plaire)* **ça te dit de partir en vacances avec nous?** how would you like to come on vacation with us?; **ça ne me dit trop rien de manger chinois** I don't really feel like Chinese food; **ça ne me dit rien qui vaille** I don't like the look of it

(k) *(prière, messe)* to say; *(poésie)* to recite

(l) *(signifier)* **qui dit bordeaux dit bon vin** Bordeaux is synonymous with good wine

(m) *(locutions)* **c'est (tout) d.** need I say more?; **c'est d. s'il t'aime** that shows how much he loves you; **c'est beaucoup d.** that's saying (quite) a lot; **c'est peu d.** that's putting it mildly; **il n'y a pas à d.,...** there are no two ways about it,...; **pour ainsi d.** so to speak, as it were; **pour tout (vous) d.,...** to be honest (with you),...; **quelques jours, je ne dis pas, mais un mois!** a few days, that's fair enough, but a whole month!; *Fam* **je te dis pas la tête qu'il a faite!** you should have seen his face!; *Fam* **je ne te dis que ça** say no more, enough said; **c'est moi qui vous le dis** let me tell you, believe me; *Fam* **à qui le dites-vous!** tell me about it!; **vous m'en direz tant!** you don't say!; *Fam* **je ne te le fais pas d.!** tell me something I don't know!; *Fam* **tu l'as dit (, bouffi)!** you can say that again!; **cela va sans d.** that goes without saying; **dis donc!** *(au fait)* hey!; *(marque la surprise)* gosh!; *(marque l'indignation)* do you mind!; **tu me le donnes, dis?** give it to me, will you?

2 se dire *vpr* **(a)** *(l'un à l'autre)* **on se dit bonjour** we say hello

(b) *(penser)* **se d. que...** to think that...; **dis-toi bien que ça aurait pu être plus grave** it could have been worse, you know; **je me disais bien que je l'avais déjà vu quelque part** I knew I'd seen him somewhere before

(c) *(être exprimé)* **comment ça se dit en anglais?** how do you say that in English?; **ça se dit en français?** can you say that in French?

(d) *(se prétendre)* **elle se dit irlandaise** she says she's Irish

direct, -e [dirɛkt] **1** *adj* direct
2 *nm* **(a)** *(à la radio, à la télévision)* live broadcasting; **en d. de l'Opéra de Paris** live from the Paris Opera House **(b)** *(en boxe)* jab; **d. du droit/du gauche** straight right/left **(c)** *(train)* non-stop train **(pour** to)
3 *adv Fam* straight

directement [dirɛktəmɑ̃] *adv* **(a)** *(sans détour)* straight **(b)** *(sans intermédiaire)* directly

directeur, -trice [dirɛktœr, -tris] **1** *nm,f* **(a)** *(d'un magasin, d'un service)* manager; **d. artistique** *(d'un film)* artistic director; *(à la télévision)* production designer; *(d'un journal)* art editor; **d. commercial** sales director; **d. général** *(d'une entreprise)* chief executive officer; **d. de la rédaction** editorial director; **d. des ressources humaines** *ou* **du personnel** human resources manager **(b)** *(d'une école)* principal **(c)** *(d'une prison)* warden **(d)** *Univ* **d. de thèse** thesis supervisor
2 *adj (équipe, instances)* management; *(idée)* main; *(principe, force)* guiding

direction [dirɛksjɔ̃] *nf* **(a)** *(d'une entreprise, d'un théâtre)* management; *(d'une école)* running; *(d'un parti, d'un pays)* leadership; **sous la d. de qn** under the supervision of sb; *(orchestre)* conducted by sb (**b**) *(ensemble des cadres)* management; **d. commerciale** sales management; **d. générale** general management; **d. des ressources humaines** *ou* **du personnel** *(service)* personnel department (**c**) *(orientation)* direction; **toutes/autres directions** *(sur panneau)* all/other directions; **quelle d. ont-ils prise?** which way did they go?; **le train en d. de Strasbourg** the train to Strasbourg, the Strasbourg train (**d**) *(d'un véhicule)* steering; **d. assistée** power steering

directive [dirɛktiv] *nf* directive

directoire [dirɛktwar] *nm* (**a**) *Com (d'une société anonyme)* board of directors (**b**) *Hist* **le D.** the (French) Directory

dirham [diram] *nm* dirham

dirigeable [diriʒabl] *adj & nm* (**ballon**) **d.** dirigible, airship

dirigeant, -e [diriʒɑ̃, ɑ̃t] **1** *adj voir* **classe**
2 *nm,f (d'un parti, d'un pays)* leader; *(d'une entreprise)* manager; **d. syndical** union leader

diriger [45] [diriʒe] **1** *vt* (**a**) *(entreprise, équipe, projet)* to manage, to run; *(pays, parti)* to lead; *(séance)* to conduct; *(travaux)* to supervise; *(acteurs)* to direct; *(orchestre)* to conduct (**b**) *(arme, télescope, lumière)* to point (**sur** at) (**c**) *(pas)* to direct (**vers** towards); *(regard)* to turn (**vers** to); *(attention)* to turn (**sur** to); *(conversation)* to steer (**sur** onto) (**d**) *(orienter professionnellement)* to steer (**sur** *ou* **vers** towards)
2 se diriger *vpr* (**a**) *(aller)* **se d. vers** *(endroit)* to head for; *(personne)* to go up to; *(carrière, secteur)* to go into (**b**) *(s'orienter)* to find one's way around

dirigisme [diriʒism] *nm* state control

dirlo [dirlo] *nm Fam* principal

disais *etc. voir* **dire**²

discernement [disɛrnəmɑ̃] *nm (jugement)* discernment; **sans d.** rashly

discerner [disɛrne] *vt* (**a**) *(percevoir)* to make out (**b**) *(différencier)* **d. qch de** to distinguish sth from (**c**) *(deviner)* to discern

disciple [disipl] *nmf* disciple

disciplinaire [disipliner] *adj* disciplinary

discipline [disiplin] *nf (ordre, matière)* discipline

discipliné, -e [disipline] *adj* disciplined

discipliner [disipline] **1** *vt (enfant)* to control
2 se discipliner *vpr* to discipline oneself

disc-jockey (*pl* disc-jockeys) [diskʒɔkɛ] *nm* disk jockey

discographie [diskɔɡrafi] *nf* discography

discontinu, -e [diskɔ̃tiny] *adj* intermittent; *(ligne)* broken

discontinuer [diskɔ̃tinɥe] **sans discontinuer** *adv* without stopping

disconvenir [70] [diskɔ̃vnir] *vi Litt* **ne pas d. de qch** not to deny sth

discordant, -e [diskɔrdɑ̃, -ɑ̃t] *adj* (**a**) *(son, bruit)* discordant (**b**) *(couleurs)* clashing; *(opinions)* conflicting

discorde [diskɔrd] *nf* discord; **semer la d.** to make trouble

discothèque [diskɔtɛk] *nf* (**a**) *(boîte de nuit)* club, disco (**b**) *(organisme)* record library; *(collection)* record collection

discount [diskunt] *nm (rabais)* discount

discourir [22] [diskurir] *vi* **d. sur qch** to discourse on sth; *Péj* to air one's opinions on sth

discours [diskur] *nm* (**a**) *(allocution)* speech; **prononcer** *ou* **faire un d.** to make a speech; **d. de clôture/d'ouverture** closing/opening speech (**b**) *Gram* speech; **d. indirect/direct** reported *or* indirect/direct speech (**c**) *(paroles)* talk; **il m'a tenu un grand d. sur la tolérance** he gave me a great long speech about tolerance; **tous ces beaux d. ne nous avancent à rien** all this talking isn't getting us anywhere

discrédit [diskredi] *nm* discredit; **jeter le d. sur qn** to bring discredit on sb

discréditer [diskredite] **1** *vt* to discredit
2 se discréditer *vpr (personne)* to discredit oneself; **se d. auprès de** *ou* **aux yeux de qn** to discredit oneself with sb

discret, -ète [diskrɛ, -ɛt] *adj* (**a**) *(plein de retenue)* discreet; **tu sauras rester d.?** you'll keep it to yourself, won't you? (**b**) *(sobre) (personne)* unassuming; *(vêtements)* simple; *(maquillage)* natural (**c**) *(endroit)* quiet

discrètement [diskrɛtmɑ̃] *adv* (**a**) *(avec retenue)* discreetly; **il lui a parlé d.** he had a quiet word with her (**b**) *(sobrement) (habillé)* simply; **être d. maquillée** to be wearing natural make-up

discrétion [diskresjɔ̃] *nf* (**a**) *(retenue)* discretion; **manquer de d.** to be tactless (**b**) *(sobriété)* simplicity; **avec d.** *(s'habiller)* simply; *(se maquiller)* discreetly (**c**) **champagne à d.** unlimited champagne

discrimination [diskriminasjɔ̃] *nf* discrimination; **d. raciale/sexuelle** racial/sexual discrimination; **sans d. d'âge ni de sexe** regardless of age or sex

discriminatoire [diskriminatwar] *adj* discriminatory

disculper [diskylpe] **1** *vt* to exonerate (**de** from)
2 se disculper *vpr* to exonerate oneself (**de** from)

discussion [diskysjɔ̃] *nf* discussion; **avoir une d.** (**sur** *ou* **à propos de**) to have a discussion (about); **pas de d., au travail!** don't argue, get to work!

discutable [diskytabl] *adj* questionable

discutailler [diskytaje] *vi Fam Péj* to quibble

discuté, -e [diskyte] *adj (question)* disputed; *(livre, sujet)* much discussed

discuter [diskyte] **1** *vt (examiner)* to discuss; *(contester)* to question; *Fam* **d. le coup, d. le bout de gras** to have a chat
2 *vi* (**a**) *(parler)* to discuss; **d. avec qn sur** *ou* **de qch** to discuss sth with sb (**b**) *(protester)* to argue; **suis-moi sans d.** follow me and don't argue
3 se discuter *vpr* **ça se discute** that's debatable

dise *etc. voir* **dire**²

disette [dizɛt] *nf* food shortage

diseuse [dizøz] *nf* **d. de bonne aventure** fortune teller

disgrâce [disgrɑs] *nf* **tomber en d.** to fall into disfavor

disgracieux, -euse [disgrasjø, -øz] *adj (personne)* ungainly; *(visage, moue)* ugly

disjoindre [43] [disʒwɛ̃dr] **1** *vt* to separate
2 se disjoindre *vpr* to come apart

disjoint, -e [disʒwɛ̃, -ɛt] *adj (pièces)* separated

disjoncter [disʒɔ̃kte] **1** *vt (circuit électrique)* to break
2 *vi (circuit électrique)* to short-circuit; *Fam Fig* to crack up

disjoncteur [disʒɔ̃ktœr] *nm* circuit breaker

dislocation [dislɔkasjɔ̃] *nf (d'une articulation)* dislocation

disloquer [dislɔke] **1** *vt* (**a**) *(épaule, genou)* to dislocate (**b**) *(empire, État)* to break up
2 se disloquer *vpr (empire, État)* to break up; **se d. l'épaule** to dislocate one's shoulder

disneylandisation [disnɛlɑ̃dizasjɔ̃] *nf (d'un lieu, de l'histoire, de la culture)* Disneyfication

disneylandiser [3] [disnɛlɑ̃dize] *vt (lieu, histoire, culture)* to Disneyfy

disparaître [20] [disparɛtr] *vi* (**a**) *(devenir invisible)* to disappear, to vanish; **d. dans la foule** to disappear into the crowd; *Fam* **d. de la circulation** to drop out of circulation; *Fam* **disparais!** clear off! (**b**) *(mourir)* to die (**c**) *(douleur, sentiment)* to disappear; *(maladie, tradition)* to die out; **faire d. qch** to get rid of sth

disparate [disparat] *adj (éléments)* disparate; *(couleurs, objets, mobilier)* ill-matched

disparité [disparite] *nf (d'éléments)* disparity; *(de couleurs, d'objets, de mobilier)* mismatch; *(des salaires, des revenus)* inequality

disparition [disparisjɔ̃] *nf* (**a**) *(absence)* disappearance (**b**) *(décès)* death

disparu, -e [dispary] **1** *adj (personne)* missing; **être porté d.** to be reported missing
2 *nm,f (mort)* dead person; *(absent)* missing person

dispensaire [dispɑ̃sɛr] *nm* community health center

dispense [dispɑ̃s] *nf* (**a**) *(d'une obligation)* exemption (**b**) *(certificat)* certificate of exemption

dispenser [dispɑ̃se] **1** *vt* (**a**) **d. qn de qch/de faire qch** to exempt sb from sth/from doing sth; **se faire d. de qch** to be excused *or* let off sth; *Euph* **je vous dispense de vos commentaires** you can keep your remarks to yourself (**b**) *(soins, charité, faveurs)* to dispense

2 se dispenser *vpr* **se d. de qch/de faire qch** to get out of sth/of doing sth; **tu pourrais te d. de ce genre de commentaire!** you can keep that sort of remark to yourself!

dispersé, -e [dispɛrse] *adj (épars)* scattered

disperser [dispɛrse] **1** *vt (foule, famille, feuilles)* to scatter

2 se disperser *vpr (nuages, foule, famille)* to scatter, to disperse; *Fig (intellectuellement)* to spread oneself too thinly

dispersion [dispɛrsjɔ̃] *nf* (**a**) *(de manifestants, de nuages, d'une armée)* scattering, dispersal; *Fig (inattention)* lack of focus (**b**) *Suisse (peinture)* emulsion (paint)

disponibilité [disponibilite] *nf* (**a**) *(d'une personne, de places, d'un capital)* availability; **d. d'esprit** receptiveness (**b**) *(d'un fonctionnaire)* leave of absence; **être en d.** to be on leave of absence (**c**) *Fin* **disponibilités** available funds

disponible [disponibl] *adj* (**a**) *(personne, place, capital)* available; **êtes-vous d. ce soir?** are you free tonight? (**b**) *(fonctionnaire)* on leave of absence

dispos, -e [dispo, -oz] *adj (personne)* fit and well

disposé, -e [dispoze] *adj (personne)* **être bien/mal d.** to be in a good/bad mood; **être bien d. envers qn** to be well disposed toward sb; **être d. à faire qch** to feel disposed *or* willing to do sth

disposer [dispoze] **1** *vt* (**a**) *(objets, fleurs)* to arrange; *(table)* to set (**b**) **d. qn à (faire) qch** to dispose *or* to incline sb to (do) sth

2 *vi* (**a**) *Sout* **vous pouvez d.** you may go (**b**) *(décider)* *Prov* **l'homme propose, Dieu dispose** man proposes, God disposes

3 disposer de *vt ind* to have at one's disposal; **les renseignements dont je dispose** the information at my disposal; **le droit des peuples à d. d'eux-mêmes** the right of people to self-determination

4 se disposer *vpr* **se d. à faire qch** to get ready to do sth

dispositif [dispozitif] *nm* (**a**) *(appareil)* device (**b**) *(ensemble de moyens)* system; **d. policier** police presence (**c**) *Ordinat* **d. d'alimentation** power unit; *(pour papier)* sheet feed; **d. d'alimentation papier** *(d'une imprimante)* sheet feed, paper feed

disposition [dispozisjɔ̃] *nf* (**a**) *(arrangement)* arrangement (**b**) *(disponibilité)* **à la d. de qn** at sb's disposal; **mettre qch à la d. de qn** to put sth at sb's disposal; **je suis** *ou* **je me tiens à votre d.** I am at your service (**c**) *(tendance)* tendency (**à** to) (**d**) *(intentions)* **être dans de bonnes/mauvaises dispositions** to be in a good/bad mood; **être dans de bonnes dispositions à l'égard de qn** to be favorably disposed toward sb (**e**) *(dons)* **avoir des dispositions pour qch** to have an aptitude for sth (**f**) **dispositions** *(préparatifs)* arrangements; **prendre des dispositions pour faire qch** to make arrangements to do sth; **prendre ses dispositions** to make arrangements (**g**) *Jur* **dispositions** *(d'une loi)* clauses

disproportion [disproporsjɔ̃] *nf* disproportion (**entre** between)

disproportionné, -e [disproporsjone] *adj* disproportionate (**par rapport à** to)

dispute [dispyt] *nf* quarrel, argument

disputé, -e [dispyte] *adj (question)* controversial; *(match)* hard-fought; **ce poste sera très d.** there will be a lot of competition for this post

disputer [dispyte] **1** *vt* (**a**) *(match)* to play; *(combat)* to fight (**b**) *(se battre pour)* **d. qch à qn** to fight with sb over sth (**c**) *Fam (réprimander)* to tell off; **se faire d.** to get told off

2 se disputer *vpr* (**a**) *(se quereller)* to quarrel, to argue (**pour/avec** over/with) (**b**) *(avoir lieu)* **le match se disputera à Wimbledon** the match will be played at Wimbledon (**c**) *(se battre pour)* **se d. qch** to fight over sth

disquaire [diskɛr] *nmf* record dealer

disqualification [diskalifikasjɔ̃] *nf* disqualification

disqualifier [66] [diskalifje] *vt (sportif)* to disqualify

disque [disk] *nm* (**a**) *(enregistrement)* record; **mettre un d.** to play a record; **d. audionumérique** compact disk; **d. compact** compact disk, CD; **d. compact vidéo** video compact disk; **d. laser** laser disk; **d. vidéo numérique** digital video disk (**b**) *Ordinat* disk; **d. amovible** removable disk; **d. dur** hard disk; **d. fixe** fixed disk (**c**) *(cartilage)* disk (**d**) *(objet rond)* disk; **d. de stationnement** parking permit (**e**) *(en sport)* discus (**f**) *Tech* disk; **d. d'embrayage** clutch plate

disquette [diskɛt] *nf Ordinat* diskette, floppy (disk); **sur d.** on diskette, on floppy; **d. de démonstration,** *Fam* **d. démo** demo disk; **d. haute densité** high-density disk; **d. optique** optical disk, floptical disk

dissection [disɛksjɔ̃] *nf aussi Fig* dissection

dissemblable [disɑ̃blabl] *adj* dissimilar

dissémination [diseminasjɔ̃] *nf (de graines, de peuple)* scattering; *(de germes)* spreading

disséminer [disemine] **1** *vt (graines, peuple)* to scatter; *(germes)* to spread; **sa famille est disséminée dans le monde** his/her family is scattered all over the world

2 se disséminer *vpr* to be scattered

dissension [disɑ̃sjɔ̃] *nf* dissension

disséquer [34] [diseke] *vt aussi Fig* to dissect

dissertation [disɛrtasjɔ̃] *nf* essay; **faire une d.** to write an essay

disserter [disɛrte] *vi (parler)* **d. sur qch** to discourse on sth, *Péj* to hold forth on sth; *(écrire)* to write about sth

dissidence [disidɑ̃s] *nf* dissidence; **la d.** *(les opposants)* the dissidents

dissident, -e [disidɑ̃, -ɑ̃t] **1** *adj (en politique)* dissident; *(en religion)* dissenting

2 *nm,f (en politique)* dissident; *(en religion)* dissenter

dissimulateur, -trice [disimylatœr, -tris] **1** *adj* dissembling

2 *nm,f* dissembler

dissimulation [disimylasjɔ̃] *nf* (**a**) *(hypocrisie)* dissembling, deceit; **agir avec d.** to act in an underhand way (**b**) *(des sentiments, de la vérité)* concealment

dissimuler [disimyle] **1** *vt* to cover up, to conceal; *(sujet: rideau)* to screen off; **d. qch à qn** to conceal sth from sb; **avec un plaisir non dissimulé** with unconcealed delight

2 se dissimuler *vpr* to be hidden

dissipation [disipasjɔ̃] *nf* (**a**) *(de craintes, de soupçons)* dispelling; *(d'un malentendu)* clearing up; **après d. des brouillards matinaux** after the morning fog has cleared (**b**) *(à l'école)* unruly behavior (**c**) *Litt (débauche)* dissipation

dissipé, -e [disipe] *adj* (**a**) *(élève)* unruly (**b**) *Litt (débauché)* dissipated

dissiper [disipe] **1** *vt* (**a**) *(nuages)* to disperse; *(brouillard)* to clear; *(malentendu)* to clear up; *(craintes, soupçons)* to dispel (**b**) *(distraire)* to lead astray

2 se dissiper *vpr* (**a**) *(nuages)* to disperse; *(brouillard)* to clear; *(craintes, soupçons)* to vanish (**b**) *(se laisser distraire)* to be unruly

dissociable [disosjabl] *adj* separable

dissocier [66] [disosje] **1** *vt* to separate

2 se dissocier *vpr* **se d. de qch** to dissociate oneself from sth

dissolu, -e [disoly] *adj Litt* dissolute

dissolution [disolysjɔ̃] *nf* (**a**) *(d'un parlement, d'un mariage)* dissolution; *(d'une association)* breaking up (**b**) *(dans un liquide)* dissolving

dissolvais *etc. voir* **dissoudre**

dissolvant, -e [disɔlvɑ̃, -ɑ̃t] *adj & nm* (**produit**) **d.** solvent; *(pour ongles)* nail-polish remover

dissonant, -e [disɔnɑ̃, -ɑ̃t] *adj (sons)* dissonant; *Fig* clashing

dissoudre [3a] [disudr] **1** *vt* (**a**) *(substance)* to dissolve (**b**) *(parlement, mariage)* to dissolve; *(association)* to break up

2 se dissoudre *vpr (substance)* to dissolve; *(association)* to break up

dissuader [disɥade] *vt* **d. qn de faire qch** to dissuade sb from doing sth

dissuasif, -ive [disɥazif, -iv] *adj* deterrent; *(prix)* prohibitive; **avoir un effet d.** to be a deterrent

dissuasion [disɥazjɔ̃] *nf* dissuasion; *Mil* **force de d.** deterrent

dissymétrie [disimetri] *nf* asymmetry

distance [distɑ̃s] *nf* distance; **suivre qn à d.** to follow sb at a distance; **à quelle d. sommes-nous de la ville?** how far are we from the town?; **à une courte d. (de)** a short distance away (from); **à d.** *(déclencher)* by remote control; *(rester, observer)* at a distance; *aussi Fig* **tenir qn à d.** to keep sb at a distance; **conserver** *ou* **garder ses distances, se tenir à d.** to hold oneself aloof, to keep oneself to oneself; **prendre ses distances, prendre de la d.** to stand back; *Sport & Fig* **tenir la d.** to go the distance

distancer [16] [distɑ̃se] *vt aussi Fig* to outstrip, to outdistance; **se laisser d.** to fall *or* to lag behind; **d. qn de deux points/ de dix mètres** to go two points/ten yards ahead of sb

distant, -e [distɑ̃, -ɑ̃t] *adj* (**a**) *(éloigné)* distant; **nos deux maisons sont distantes d'un kilomètre** ≃ our two houses are half a mile apart (**b**) *Fig (froid)* distant, standoffish (**avec** with)

distendre [distɑ̃dr] **1** *vt (corde, élastique, vêtement)* to stretch; *(muscle)* to strain

2 se distendre *vpr (corde, élastique, vêtement)* to stretch; *(muscle)* to slacken

distillation [distilasjɔ̃] *nf* distillation

distiller [distile] *vt* (**a**) *(alcool, pétrole)* to distill; **eau distillée** distilled water (**b**) *(poison)* to distill; *Fig (colère, ennui)* to exude

distillerie [distilri] *nf (lieu)* distillery; *(procédé)* distilling

distinct, -e [distɛ̃, -ɛ̃kt] *adj* (**a**) *(séparé)* distinct, separate (**de** from) (**b**) *(clair) (silhouette, voix)* distinct, clear

distinctement [distɛ̃ktəmɑ̃] *adv* distinctly, clearly

distinctif, -ive [distɛ̃ktif, -iv] *adj* distinctive

distinction [distɛ̃ksjɔ̃] *nf* (**a**) *(différence)* distinction; **faire une d. entre deux choses** to make a distinction between two things; **sans d.** without distinction, indiscriminately; **sans d. de race ou de couleur** regardless of race or color (**b**) *(élégance)* distinction; **avoir de la d.** to be distinguished

distingué, -e [distɛ̃ge] *adj* distinguished

distinguer [distɛ̃ge] **1** *vt* (**a**) *(différencier)* to distinguish (**de** from); **il a appris à d. les champignons** he has learned how to tell the various kinds of mushroom apart; **on peut à peine les d. l'un de l'autre** you can hardly tell them apart (**b**) *(discerner) (objet, silhouette)* to make out; *(personne)* to pick out; **d. une nuance d'amertume dans la voix de qn** to detect a trace of bitterness in sb's voice

2 se distinguer *vpr* (**a**) *(s'illustrer)* to distinguish oneself (**par** by); **on ne peut vraiment pas dire qu'il se distingue par son intelligence** he hardly stands out as being very intelligent (**b**) *(se différencier)* **se d. de qn/qch (par)** to be distinguishable from sb/sth (by) (**c**) *(être perçu)* **au loin se distinguait la côte** the coastline could be made out in the distance

distinguo [distɛ̃go] *nm* distinction; **faire un d. entre** to make a distinction between

distordre [distɔrdr] *vt* to distort

distorsion [distɔrsjɔ̃] *nf* distortion; *(entre deux facteurs, deux salaires)* imbalance

distraction [distraksjɔ̃] *nf* (**a**) *(inattention)* absent-mindedness; **par d.** inadvertently, absent-mindedly (**b**) *(loisir)* activity; **ça manque de distractions, ici** there's nothing to do here

distraire [28] [distrɛr] **1** *vt* (**a**) *(détourner)* to distract (**de** from) (**b**) *(divertir)* to entertain, to amuse

2 se distraire *vpr (s'occuper)* to amuse oneself; *(se détendre)* to enjoy oneself

distrait, -e [distrɛ, -ɛt] *adj* (**a**) *(étourdi)* absent-minded; **d'un air d.** absent-mindedly (**b**) *(inattentif)* inattentive; **d'une oreille distraite** with only half an ear

distraitement [distrɛtmɑ̃] *adv* absent-mindedly

distrayais *etc. voir* **distraire**

distrayant, -e [distrɛjɑ̃, -ɑ̃t] *adj* entertaining

distribuer [distribɥe] *vt* (**a**) *(donner) (prix, bonbons, provisions, vivres)* to distribute (**à** to); *(dividendes)* to pay (**à** to); *(cartes)* to deal (**à** to); *(courrier)* to deliver (**à** to); *(eau, gaz, électricité)* to supply (**à** to); *(sourires, compliments)* to bestow (**à** on); **d. des coups** to lash out with one's fists (**b**) *(répartir) (tâches)* to assign; **d. les rôles** to cast a play/movie (**c**) *(commercialiser)* to distribute

distributeur, -trice [distribɥtœr, -tris] **1** *nm,f Com* distributor; **d. agréé** authorized distributor

2 *nm (appareil)* (vending) machine; **d. (automatique) de billets** ATM; **d. (automatique) de boissons/de cigarettes** drinks/cigarette machine

distribution [distribysjɔ̃] *nf* (**a**) *(remise)* distribution; *(de lettres, de marchandises)* delivery; **la d. des prix** *(à l'école)* prize-giving day (**b**) *(répartition) (de tâches)* assignment; *(d'une maison, d'un appartement)* layout; *(d'un film, d'une pièce) (action)* casting; *(acteurs)* cast (**c**) *Com* distribution; **grande d.** large-scale distribution (**d**) *(approvisionnement)* supply; **d. des eaux** water supply

district [distrikt] *nm* district

dit, -e [di, dit] **1** *pp voir* **dire²**

2 *adj* (**a**) *(décidé)* **à l'heure dite** at the agreed time (**b**) *(appelé)* known as

dithyrambique [ditirɑ̃bik] *adj* eulogistic

diurétique [djyretik] *adj & nm* diuretic

diurne [djyrn] *adj* diurnal

diva [diva] *nf* diva

divagations [divagasjɔ̃] *nfpl* raving

divaguer [divage] *vi* to rave

divan [divɑ̃] *nm* divan, couch

divergence [divɛrʒɑ̃s] *nf (de lignes, de rayons)* divergence; *(d'opinions)* difference

divergent, -e [divɛrʒɑ̃, -ɑ̃t] *adj (lignes)* divergent; *(opinions)* differing

diverger [45] [divɛrʒe] *vi (opinions, lignes, rayons)* to diverge (**de** from)

divers, -e [divɛr, -ɛrs] *adj* (**a**) *(différents)* varied; **d.** *(rubrique)* miscellaneous (**b**) *(plusieurs)* various; **diverses solutions sont possibles** there are various possible solutions

diversement [divɛrsəmɑ̃] *adv* in various ways

diversification [divɛrsifikasjɔ̃] *nf* diversification

diversifier [66] [divɛrsifje] **1** *vt (économie, cultures, activités)* to diversify; *(intérêts, couleurs)* to vary

2 se diversifier *vpr (entreprise, activités)* to diversify

diversion [divɛrsjɔ̃] *nf* diversion; **faire d.** to create a diversion

diversité [divɛrsite] *nf (variété)* variety, diversity

divertir [divɛrtir] **1** *vt (amuser)* to entertain, to amuse

2 se divertir *vpr* to enjoy oneself; **se d. de qch** to laugh at sth

divertissant, -e [divɛrtisɑ̃, -ɑ̃t] *adj* amusing, entertaining

divertissement [divɛrtismɑ̃] *nm* (**a**) *(amusement)* entertainment, amusement (**b**) *Mus* divertimento

dividende [dividɑ̃d] *nm Math & Fin* dividend

divin, -e [divɛ̃, -in] *adj aussi Fig* divine; **le d. Enfant** the Holy Child

divinement [divinmɑ̃] *adv* divinely

divinité [divinite] *nf* (**a**) *(nature de Dieu)* divinity (**b**) *(dieu)* deity

diviser [divize] **1** *vt* (**a**) *(partager)* to divide (**en/entre** into/ among); **d. 15 par 3** to divide 15 by 3 (**b**) *(opposer)* to divide; **l'opinion est divisée au sujet de cette affaire** opinion on the matter is divided; **d. pour mieux régner** divide and rule
2 se diviser *vpr* to divide (**en** into); **l'examen se divise en trois parties** the examination is divided into three parts; **le chemin se divise en deux** the road divides *or* forks

diviseur [divizœr] *nm Math* divisor; **plus grand commun d.** highest common factor

divisible [divizibl] *adj* divisible

division [divizjɔ̃] *nf* (**a**) *(séparation) & Math* division (**en** into); **faire une d.** to do a division; *Biol* **d. cellulaire** cell division; **d. du travail** division of labor (**b**) *(partie)* part, section; *Mil* division; **d. blindée** armored division (**c**) *(désaccord)* division

divisionnaire [divizjɔnɛr] **1** *adj* divisional
2 *nm* (**a**) *(commissaire)* ≃ police chief (**b**) *Mil* major general

divorce [divɔrs] *nm* divorce; *Fig (désaccord)* gulf; **demander le d.** to ask for a divorce; **obtenir le d.** to get a divorce

divorcé, -e [divɔrse] **1** *adj* divorced
2 *nm,f* divorcé, *f* divorcée

divorcer [16] [divɔrse] *vi* to get divorced, to get a divorce; **d. d'avec** *ou* **de qn** to divorce sb

divulgation [divylgasjɔ̃] *nf* disclosure (**de** of)

divulguer [divylge] *vt* to divulge, to disclose

dix [dis] *adj & nm inv* ten; *voir aussi* **trois**

dix-huit [dizɥit] *adj & nm inv* eighteen; *voir aussi* **trois**

dix-huitième [dizɥitjɛm] *nmf, nm & adj* eighteenth; *voir aussi* **cinquième**

dixième [dizjɛm] *nmf, nm & adj* tenth; *voir aussi* **cinquième**

dixit [diksit] **d. Paul** so Paul says

dix-neuf [diznœf] *adj & nm inv* nineteen; *voir aussi* **trois**

dix-neuvième [diznœvjɛm] *nmf, nm & adj* nineteenth; *voir aussi* **cinquième**

dix-sept [dis(s)ɛt] *adj & nm inv* seventeen; *voir aussi* **trois**

dix-septième [dis(s)ɛtjɛm] *nmf, nm & adj* seventeenth; *voir aussi* **cinquième**

dizaine [dizɛn] *nf* **une d. (de)** about ten, ten or so; *Math* **la colonne des dizaines** the tens column

djeune [dʒœn] *Fam Ironique* **1** *adj* young and hip
2 *nmf* hip young person

Djibouti [dʒibuti] *n* Djibouti

do [do] *nm inv (note)* C; *(chantée)* doh

doberman [dɔbɛrman] *nm* doberman

docile [dɔsil] *adj (enfant, animal)* docile

docilement [dɔsilmɑ̃] *adv* docilely

docilité [dɔsilite] *nf* docility

dock [dɔk] *nm* (**a**) *(bassin)* dock (**b**) *(entrepôt)* warehouse

docker [dɔkɛr] *nm* stevedore, longshoreman

docte [dɔkt] *adj Litt* learned

docteur [dɔktœr] *nm* (**a**) *(médecin)* doctor (**b**) *Univ* **être d. ès lettres/ès sciences** ≃ to have a PhD in arts/science; **être d. en droit** ≃ to have an LLD

doctoral, -e, -aux, -ales [dɔktɔral, -o] *adj Péj (air, ton)* pompous

doctorat [dɔktɔra] *nm Univ* doctorate; **d. d'État** = highest postgraduate research degree; **d. de 3e cycle** ≃ PhD

doctoresse [dɔktɔrɛs] *nf Vieilli* lady doctor

doctrine [dɔktrin] *nf* doctrine

docudrame [dɔkydram] *nm TV* docudrama

document [dɔkymɑ̃] *nm* document

documentaire [dɔkymɑ̃tɛr] *adj & nm* documentary

documentaliste [dɔkymɑ̃talist] *nmf (d'archives)* archivist; *(dans les écoles)* librarian

documentation [dɔkymɑ̃tasjɔ̃] *nf (action)* research; *(documents)* documentation (**sur** on)

documenté, -e [dɔkymɑ̃te] *adj (personne)* well-informed; *(étude, thèse)* documented

documenter [dɔkymɑ̃te] **se documenter** *vpr* to gather information *or* material (**sur** on)

dodeliner [dɔdəline] *vi* **il dodelinait de la tête** his head kept nodding

dodo [dodo] *nm (langage enfantin)* **faire d.** to sleep; **aller au d.** to go to beddy-byes

dodu, -e [dɔdy] *adj* plump, chubby

doge [dɔʒ] *nm Hist* doge

dogmatique [dɔgmatik] *adj* dogmatic

dogmatisme [dɔgmatism] *nm* dogmatism

dogme [dɔgm] *nm* dogma

dogue [dɔg] *nm* mastiff

doigt [dwa] *nm* (**a**) *(de la main)* finger; **d. de pied** toe; **le petit d.** the little finger; **lever le d.** *(en classe)* to put one's hand up; **porter une bague au d.** to wear a ring on one's finger; **faire signe à qn du d.** to beckon to sb; **être comme les (deux) doigts de la main** to be very close; **on peut les compter sur les doigts de la main** you can count them on the fingers of one hand; *Fig* **se faire taper sur les doigts** to get a rap over the knuckles; **filer** *ou* **glisser entre les doigts de qn** to slip through sb's fingers; **vous avez mis le d. dessus** you've put your finger on it; **obéir à qn au d. et à l'œil** to obey sb blindly; **savoir qch sur le bout des doigts** to have sth at one's fingertips; **mon petit d. me l'a dit** a little bird told me; **avoir des doigts de fée** to have nimble fingers; *Fig* **ne pas lever** *ou* **bouger le petit d.** not to lift a finger; *Fam* **tu te mets le d. dans l'œil (jusqu'au coude)** you couldn't be more wrong (if you tried); *Fam* **faire qch les doigts dans le nez** to do sth standing on one's head; *Fam* **gagner les doigts dans le nez** to win hands down; *Fam* **faire un d. d'honneur à qn** to give *or* to flip sb the bird
(**b**) *(petite quantité) (d'alcool)* drop; **être à deux doigts de qch/de faire qch** to be within a hair's breadth of sth/of doing sth

doigté [dwate] *nm* (**a**) *Mus (d'un morceau de musique)* fingering (**b**) *Fig (adresse)* dexterity; *(tact)* tact

dois, doive, *etc. voir* **devoir**²

doléances [dɔleɑ̃s] *nfpl* complaints; **présenter ses doléances** to air one's grievances

dollar [dɔlar] *nm* dollar

dolmen [dɔlmɛn] *nm* dolmen

DOM [dɔm] *nm Anciennement (abrév* **département d'outre-mer**) = French overseas department

domaine [dɔmɛn] *nm* (**a**) *(propriété)* estate, property; **être du d. public** to be in the public domain; **d. skiable** skiing area (**b**) *(matière)* field, domain; **c'est du d. du possible** it's within the realms of possibility (**c**) *Ordinat* domain

domanial, -e, -aux, -ales [dɔmanjal, -o] *adj* state-owned

dôme [dom] *nm Archit & Géog* dome

domestication [dɔmɛstikasjɔ̃] *nf* domestication

domestique [dɔmɛstik] **1** *adj (vie, soucis, querelle)* domestic; *(tâches, déchets)* household; **accidents domestiques** accidents in the home
2 *nmf* servant

domestiquer [dɔmɛstike] *vt (animal)* to domesticate; *(éléments)* to harness

domicile [dɔmisil] *nm* (place of) residence, home; **sans d. fixe** homeless; *Admin* of no fixed abode; **un(e) sans d. fixe** a homeless person; **travailler à d.** to work from home; **livrer à d.** to do home deliveries; *Jur* **d. conjugal** marital home

domicilié, -e [dɔmisilje] *adj* **d. à** resident at

dominant, -e [dɔminɑ̃, -ɑ̃t] **1** *adj (opinion)* prevailing; *(couleur, trait, idée)* dominant; *Biol* **caractère d.** dominant characteristic

2 *nf* **dominante** *(ce qui domine)* chief characteristic; **une tenue pâle, avec une dominante de rose** a pale, mainly pink outfit

dominateur, -trice [dɔminatœr, -tris] *adj (personne, ton, attitude)* domineering

domination [dɔminasjɔ̃] *nf* domination (**sur** over); **être sous la d. de qn** to be dominated by sb

dominer [dɔmine] **1** *vt* **(a)** *(assujettir) (personne)* to dominate; *(empire)* to rule over **(b)** *(surpasser) (adversaire, concurrent)* to surpass **(c)** *(prédominer dans)* to be the dominant feature of **(d)** *(maîtriser) (timidité, passions, larmes, sujet)* to master; *(paresse, envie)* to overcome; *(match)* to dominate; **d. la situation** to keep the situation under control **(e)** *(surplomber)* to dominate; **de leur terrasse, on domine la mer** their balcony overlooks the sea

2 *vi* **(a)** *(l'emporter)* to be dominant **(b)** *(prédominer)* to predominate

3 se dominer *vpr* to control oneself

dominicain, -e [dɔminikɛ̃, -ɛn] **1** *adj* Dominican

2 *nm,f* **(a)** *Rel* Dominican **(b)** *(de la République Dominicaine)* **D., Dominicaine** Dominican

dominical, -e, -aux, -ales [dɔminikal, -o] *adj* Sunday; **repos d.** day of rest; **ouverture dominicale des magasins** Sunday opening

Dominique [dɔminik] *nf* **la D.** Dominica

domino [dɔmino] *nm (plaquette)* domino; **jouer aux dominos** to play dominoes

dommage [dɔmaʒ] *nm* **(a)** *(préjudice)* harm; **causer un d. à qn** to do sb harm; **d. corporel** physical injury; **dommages et intérêts, dommages-intérêts** damages; **d. matériel** material damage **(b)** **dommages** *(dégâts matériels)* damage; *Mil* **dommages collatéraux** collateral damage **(c)** **(quel) d.!** what a pity!, what a shame!; **c'est (bien) d. qu'elle ne soit pas venue** it's a (real) pity that she didn't come **(d)** *Can* **beau d!** of course!, you bet!

dommageable [dɔmaʒabl] *adj* detrimental (**à** to)

dompter [dɔ̃(p)te] *vt (fauve, fleuve, nature)* to tame; *(sentiments, passions, personne)* to subdue

dompteur, -euse [dɔ̃(p)tœr, -øz] *nm,f* tamer

DOM-TOM [dɔmtɔm] *nmpl Anciennement (abrév* **départements et territoires d'outre-mer***)* = French overseas departments and territories

DON [deɔɛn] *nm Ordinat (abrév* **disque optique numérique***)* CD

don [dɔ̃] *nm* **(a)** *(cadeau)* gift; *(à un musée, une œuvre)* donation; **faire d. à qn de qch** to make a gift of sth to sb; **d. du sang/de sperme** blood/sperm donation; *Fig* **d. du ciel** godsend; **le d. de soi** self-sacrifice **(b)** *(aptitude)* gift, talent; *aussi Ironique* **avoir le d. de faire qch** to have a knack for doing sth

donateur, -trice [dɔnatœr, -tris] *nm,f* donor

donation [dɔnasjɔ̃] *nf* donation; *Jur* **d. entre vifs** donation inter vivos

donc [dɔk] *conj* **(a)** *(marque la conséquence)* so **(b)** *(emphatique)* **tu le savais d. depuis le début?** so you knew from the start?; **que voulez-vous d.?** whatever do you want?; **mais taisez-vous d.!** do be quiet!; **allons d.!** come on! **(c)** *(après interruption ou digression)* **je disais d. que…** I was saying, then, that…

dondon [dɔdɔ̃] *nf Fam Péj* **grosse d.** great lump of a woman/girl

donf [dɔf] **à donf** *adv Fam (vite)* like sixty; *(très fort)* at full blast; *(beaucoup)* really, like crazy; **je la kiffe à d., cette nana** I'm totally crazy about that girl

donjon [dɔʒɔ̃] *nm* keep

don Juan (*pl* **dons Juans**) [dɔʒɥɑ̃] *nm* Don Juan

donne [dɔn] *nf (aux cartes)* deal

donné, -e [dɔne] *adj* **(a)** *(offert)* given; *Fam* **c'est d.** it's dirt cheap; *Fam* **ce n'est pas d.** it doesn't come cheap **(b)** *(défini)* given; **à un moment d.** *(dans le passé)* at one point; *(dans le futur)* at some point; **étant d. la situation** given the situation; **étant d. que…** seeing that…

donnée [dɔne] *nf* **(a)** *(élément)* piece of information; **avoir toutes les données du problème** to have all the data or information on the problem **(b)** *Ordinat* **données** data; **données numériques** digital data

donner [dɔne] **1** *vt* **(a)** *(offrir, distribuer)* to give; **d. qch à qn** to give sth to sb, to give sb sth; **d. à boire à qn** to give sb something to drink; **d. à manger à** *(animal)* to feed; **c'est à qui de d.?** *(aux cartes)* whose deal is it?

(b) *(faire don de) (temps, vie)* to give; *(corps, organe)* to donate; **d. son sang** to give blood

(c) *(céder)* to give; *Fam (dénoncer)* to give away, to squeal on (**à** to); **en d. à qn pour son argent** to give sb their money's worth

(d) *(payer)* **je lui donne 15 euros de l'heure** I pay him/her 15 euros an hour; **je vous en donne dix euros** I'll give you ten euros for it

(e) *(confier)* **d. qch à garder à qn** to give sb sth to look after; **d. un vêtement à nettoyer** to hand in a garment to be dry-cleaned

(f) *(avis, ordre, conseil)* to give; **d. l'heure à qn** to tell sb the time; **tu lui donneras le bonjour de ma part** say hello to him/her for me; **d. des** *ou* **de ses nouvelles à qn** to keep in touch with sb

(g) *(chance, délai, occasion)* to give; **je vous donne une semaine, pas plus** I'll give you a week and no more

(h) *(causer)* **d. de l'appétit à qn** to give sb an appetite; **d. des boutons à qn** to give sb pimples; **d. mal à la tête à qn** to give sb a headache; **d. faim/sommeil/chaud à qn** to make sb hungry/sleepy/hot; **d. du souci à qn** to cause sb worry; **toute cette histoire m'a donné à réfléchir** the whole business made me think again

(i) *(produire) (récoltes)* to yield; *(fruits)* to bear; **les blés vont d. cette année** there will be a good crop of wheat this year; **ça n'a rien donné** nothing came of it; **qu'est-ce que ça donne?** *(comment ça se présente?)* how does it look?

(j) *(administrer)* to give; **d. un baiser/une gifle à qn** to give sb a kiss/a slap in the face; **tu peux d. un coup de balai dans la cuisine?** can you give the kitchen a sweep?

(k) *(bal, dîner, conférence)* to give; *(pièce de théâtre)* to put on, to perform; **qu'est-ce qu'on donne au cinéma?** what's showing at the movies?

(l) *(attribuer)* **je lui donne vingt ans** I'd say he's/she's twenty; **les médecins lui donnent deux jours (à vivre)** the doctors give him/her two days (to live)

(m) *(maladie)* to give

2 *vi (cogner)* **d. de la tête contre qch** to hit one's head against sth; *Fig* **je ne savais pas où d. de la tête** I didn't know where to start

3 *v impersonnel* **le spectacle le plus épouvantable qu'il m'ait été donné de voir** the most horrifying sight I've ever been unfortunate enough to witness; **il n'est pas donné à tout le monde d'être écrivain** not everyone can be a writer

4 donner dans *vt ind* **(a)** *(tomber)* **d. dans le piège** *ou* **le panneau** to fall into the trap

(b) *(avoir un penchant pour)* to have a tendency for

5 donner sur *vt ind (sujet: fenêtre)* to look onto; *(sujet: porte)* to lead into

6 se donner *vpr* **(a)** *(faire don de soi)* to give of oneself; **se d. à qch** to devote oneself to sth; **se d. en spectacle** to make an exhibition of oneself (**b**) *(à soi-même)* **se d. un coup de peigne/brosse** to run a comb through one's hair/to give one's hair a quick brush; **se d. un coup de marteau sur le pouce** to hit one's thumb with a hammer; **se d. le temps de réfléchir** to give oneself time to think; **se d. pour tâche de faire qch** to set oneself the task of doing sth

(**c**) *Litt (sexuellement)* to give oneself (**à** to)

(**d**) *(l'un l'autre)* **se d. des coups** to exchange blows; **se d. des baisers** to kiss (each other)

donneur, -euse [dɔnœr, -øz] *nm,f* (**a**) *(d'organe)* donor; **d. de sang** blood donor (**b**) *(aux cartes)* dealer

dont [dɔ̃] *pron relatif* (**a**) *(introduit le complément du verbe)* **la famille d. je descends** the family I'm descended from; **la façon d. il me regardait** the way (in which) he looked at me; **le livre d. j'ai besoin** the book (that) I need; **un film d. on parle beaucoup** a movie that is being talked about a lot; **l'homme d. elle se moque** the man she's making fun of

(**b**) *(introduit le complément du nom)* **la dame d. je connais le fils** the woman whose son I know; **la maison d. on voit le toit** the house whose roof can be seen; **un film d. voici le résumé** a movie of which this is a summary; **quelques-uns étaient là, d. votre frère** there were a few people there, including your brother

(**c**) *(introduit le complément de l'adjectif)* **la femme d. il est amoureux** the woman he is in love with; **le groupe d'enfants d. vous êtes responsable** the group of children you are responsible for; **le souvenir d. elle est si honteuse** the memory she is so ashamed of

dopage [dɔpaʒ] *nm* doping; *(de sportif)* drug-taking

doper [dɔpe] **1** *vt (droguer)* to dope

2 se doper *vpr* to take drugs

dorade [dɔrad] *nf* sea bream

doré, -e [dɔre] **1** *adj* (**a**) *(recouvert d'or)* gilded, gilt; **d. sur tranche** gilt-edged (**b**) *(couleur d'or)* (blé, lumière, peau, cheveux) golden; (gâteau passé au jaune d'œuf) glazed; (viande, pommes de terre, gâteau cuit) browned

2 *nm Can (poisson)* wall-eyed pike, yellow pike

dorénavant [dɔrenavɑ̃] *adv* from now on

dorer [dɔre] **1** *vt* (**a**) *(recouvrir d'or)* to gild; *Fig* **d. la pilule à qn** to sweeten the pill for sb (**b**) *(donner une couleur dorée à)* (peau) to turn golden; (gâteau) to glaze; (viande, pommes de terre) to brown

2 *vi (plat, gâteau)* to brown

3 se dorer *vpr* **se d. au soleil** to sunbathe; *Fig* **se d. la pilule** to catch some rays

dorloter [dɔrlɔte] *vt* to pamper, to coddle

dormant, -e [dɔrmɑ̃, -ɑ̃t] **1** *adj* **eaux dormantes** stagnant water

2 *nm Can Rail* tie

dormeur, -euse [dɔrmœr, -øz] *nm,f (personne endormie)* sleeper; **être un gros d.** to need a lot of sleep

dormir [29] [dɔrmir] *vi* (**a**) *(sommeiller)* to sleep; **elle dort** she's sleeping, she's asleep; **d. profondément** to be fast asleep; **je n'ai pas dormi de la nuit** I didn't sleep a wink (all night); **le café m'empêche de d.** coffee keeps me awake; *Fam* **ce n'est pas ça qui va m'empêcher de d.** I won't lose any sleep over it; **d. à poings fermés, d. comme un loir** to sleep like a log; **ne d. que d'un œil** to sleep with one eye open; **vous pouvez d. tranquille** *ou* **sur vos deux oreilles** you can rest easy; **avoir envie de d.** to be *or* to feel sleepy; **d. debout** to be asleep on one's feet (**b**) *Fig (ville, forêt)* to be sleeping; *(capitaux)* to lie idle

dorsal, -e, -aux, -ales [dɔrsal, -o] *adj* dorsal

dortoir [dɔrtwar] *nm* dormitory

dorure [dɔryr] *nf* (**a**) *(couche d'or)* gilding (**b**) *(ornement)* gilt

doryphore [dɔrifɔr] *nm* Colorado beetle

DOS [dɔs] *nm Ordinat* DOS

dos [do] *nm* (**a**) *(d'une personne, d'un animal)* back; **sur le d.** on one's back; **je n'ai rien à me mettre sur le d.** I've got nothing to wear; **à d. d'âne** on a donkey; **je ne l'ai vu que de d.** I only saw him from the back; **d. à d.** back to back; **faire le gros d.** *(chat)* to arch its back; **faire qch derrière** *ou* **dans le d. de qn** to do sth behind sb's back; *Fam* **je l'ai tout le temps sur le d.** she's always on my back; **s'enrichir sur le d. de qn** to get rich off sb; **avoir bon d.** *(personne)* to have a broad back; **elle a bon d., la grève des postes, dis plutôt que tu n'as pas écrit** why don't you admit you haven't written instead of blaming it on the mail strike?; *Fam* **en avoir plein le d.** to be sick of it, to be fed up with it; **se mettre qn à d.** to get sb's back up; **tourner le d. à qn** *(debout)* to stand with one's back to sb; *(assis)* to sit with one's back to sb; *(volontairement)* to turn one's back on sb; **dès qu'il a le d. tourné** as soon as his back is turned

(**b**) *(d'une chaise, d'une page, d'un chèque, de la main)* back; *(d'un livre)* spine; **voir au d.** (please) turn over, PTO

(**c**) **d. (crawlé)** backstroke

dosage [dozaʒ] *nm (d'ingrédients)* proportioning; *(de médicaments)* dosage

dos-d'âne [dodɑn] *nm inv* bump; **pont en d.** humpbacked bridge

dose [doz] *nf (d'un élément dans un mélange)* proportion; *(de médicament)* dose; *Fig* **à petites doses** in small doses; *Fam* **il faut une sacrée d. de culot pour faire cela** it takes a hell of a nerve to do that; **forcer la d.** to overdo it; *Fam* **avoir sa d. (de qch)** to have had more than enough (of sth)

doser [doze] *vt (médicament, ingrédient)* to measure out

doseur [dozœr] *nm* measure

dossard [dosar] *nm* number *(worn by competitor)*

dossier [dosje] *nm* (**a**) *(d'un siège)* back (**b**) *(documents)* file, dossier; *(d'un prisonnier, d'un malade, d'un élève)* record; *(chemise)* folder, file; *Ordinat (répertoire)* folder; *(fichier)* file; **constituer un d. sur qn/qch** to build up a file on sb/sth; *Ordinat* **d. système** system folder (**c**) *Fig (sujet)* question

dot [dɔt] *nf* dowry

dotation [dɔtasjɔ̃] *nf (fonds) (d'hôpital, de collège)* endowment; *(versés à un chef d'État)* emolument

doter [dɔte] *vt (équiper)* to equip (**de** with); **elle est dotée d'une intelligence remarquable** she is endowed with great intelligence

douairière [dwɛrjɛr] *adj & nf* dowager

douane [dwan] *nf* customs; **passer à la d.** to go through customs; **droits de d.** customs duty

douanier, -ère [dwanje, -ɛr] **1** *adj* customs; **union douanière** customs union; **barrières douanières** tariff barriers

2 *nm* customs officer

doublage [dublaʒ] *nm* (**a**) *(d'un vêtement)* lining (**b**) *(d'un film, d'une voix)* dubbing; *(par une doublure)* doubling

double [dubl] **1** *adj* (**a**) *(quantité, lit, chambre)* double; **en d. exemplaire** in duplicate; **fermer une porte à d. tour** to double-lock a door; **avoir la d. nationalité** to have dual nationality; *Mus* **d. croche** sixteenth note; *Ordinat* **d. densité** double density; **d. mètre** 2-meter rule; **d. vitrage** double glazing (**b**) *(ambigu)* **mener une d. vie** to lead a double life; **mot à d. sens** ambiguous word

2 *adv* double

3 *nm* (**a**) **le d. (de)** *(quantité, prix)* twice as much (as); *(nombre)* twice as many (as); **10 est le d. de 5** 10 is 2 times 5; **mettre qch en d.** to fold sth in two *or* half (**b**) *(exemplaire)* duplicate, copy; *(d'une clef)* duplicate; *Ordinat* backup; **avoir qch en d.** to have two of sth; **faire qch en d.** *(lettre, devoir)* to make two copies of sth (**c**) *(personne)* double (**d**) *(au tennis)* **d. messieurs/dames/mixte** men's/women's/mixed doubles

doublé, -e [duble] **1** *adj* (**a**) *(veste, gants)* lined (**de** with) (**b**) *(film)* dubbed

2 *nm (victoires)* double

double-clic [dubləklik] (*pl* **doubles-clics**) *nm Ordinat* double-click; **faire un d.** to double-click (**sur** on)

double-cliquer [3] [dubləklike] *vi Ordinat* to double-click (**sur** on)

doublement [dubləmɑ̃] **1** *adv* doubly
2 *nm (d'un nombre, d'une somme, d'une lettre)* doubling

doubler [duble] **1** *vt* (**a**) *(multiplier par deux)* to double (**b**) *(plier)* to fold in two *or* in half (**c**) *(vêtement)* to line (**d**) *(film, voix)* to dub; *(sujet: acteur)* to dub the voice of; *(sujet: cascadeur)* to stand in for (**e**) *(passer) (véhicule)* to pass, to overtake (**f**) *Fam (trahir)* to double-cross
2 *vi* (**a**) *(population, salaire)* to double; **d. de valeur** to double in value (**b**) *(véhicule)* to pass, to overtake
3 se doubler *vpr* **se doubler de** to be coupled with

doublure [dublyr] *nf* (**a**) *(d'un vêtement, d'un sac)* lining (**b**) *(au théâtre)* understudy; *(au cinéma)* stand-in

douce [dus] *voir* **doux**

douceâtre [dusɑtr] *adj (saveur)* sickly sweet; *(ton)* smarmy

doucement [dusmɑ̃] *adv (délicatement)* gently; *(bas)* softly; **allez-y d.!** gently does it!; *Fam* **(allez-y) d. avec le vin!** go easy on the wine!

doucereux, -euse [dusrø, -øz] *adj (personne, voix, ton)* smarmy

douceur [dusœr] *nf* (**a**) *(d'un son, d'une matière)* softness; *(d'un climat)* mildness; *(du miel, d'un parfum)* sweetness (**b**) *(de caractère)* gentleness; *(d'un sourire)* sweetness; **traiter qn avec d.** to treat sb gently; **en d.** gently; **la voiture a démarré en d.** the car started smoothly (**c**) **douceurs** *(sucreries)* candy

douche [duʃ] *nf* shower; **prendre une d.** to take a shower; *Fig* **avec lui, c'est la d. écossaise** you never know where you are with him; *Fig* **d. froide** terrible disappointment

doucher [duʃe] **1** *vt (pour laver)* **d. qn** to give sb a shower
2 se doucher *vpr* to take a shower

doudoune [dudun] *nf (anorak)* padded jacket

doué, -e [dwe] *adj* gifted, talented; **être d. pour** to have a gift for

douille [duj] *nf (d'une ampoule)* lamp socket; *(d'une cartouche)* case

douillet, -ette [dujɛ, -ɛt] *adj* (**a**) *(lit)* cozy (**b**) *(délicat)* **ne sois pas si d.!** don't be such a baby!

douillettement [dujɛtmɑ̃] *adv (confortablement)* cosily

douleur [dulœr] *nf (physique)* pain; *(diffuse)* ache; *(morale)* sorrow, grief; **nous avons la d. de vous faire part de...** we regret to inform you of...; *Fam* **j'ai compris ma d.** my worst fears came true

douloureux, -euse [dulurø, -øz] *adj* (**a**) *(coup, maladie, opération)* painful; *(au contact)* sore, tender; **mon dos est d.** my back is sore *or* aching (**b**) *(perte, événement)* sad; *(séparation, circonstances)* painful

doute [dut] *nm* (**a**) *(incertitude)* doubt; **être dans le d. (au sujet de qch)** to be doubtful (about sth); **mettre qch en d.** to question sth, to cast doubt on sth; **mettre en d. la parole de qn** to doubt sb's word; **il n'y a pas de** *ou* **aucun d.** there's no doubt about it; **sans d.** no doubt, probably; **sans aucun d.** without (any) doubt (**b**) *(soupçon)* doubt; **avoir des doutes sur** *ou* **au sujet de qn/qch** to have doubts about sb/sth

douter [dute] **1** *vi* to doubt; **d. de qn/qch** to doubt sb/sth; **elle ne doute de rien** she's very sure of herself; **j'en doute** I doubt it
2 *vt* **je doute qu'il soit assez fort** I doubt whether he's strong enough; **je n'ai jamais douté que tu viendrais** I never doubted that you'd come
3 se douter *vpr* **se d. de qch** to suspect sth; **je m'en doutais (bien)** I thought as much; *Fam* **on s'en serait douté!** I might have known!

douteux, -euse [dutø, -øz] *adj* (**a**) *(incertain)* doubtful (**b**) *(suspect)* dubious; **vêtements d.** *ou* **d'une propreté dou-**teuse dubious clothes; **d'un goût d.** *(plaisanteries, vêtements)* in dubious taste

douve [duv] *nf (d'un château)* moat

Douvres [duvr] *n* Dover

doux, douce [du, dus] **1** *adj* (**a**) *(au toucher)* soft; *(au goût)* mild (**b**) *(couleur, son, lumière)* soft; *(climat, hiver, tabac)* mild; *(vin, cidre)* sweet; *(pente)* gentle; **les médecines douces** alternative medicine (**c**) *(nature, regard, voix)* gentle; **faire les yeux d. à qn** to make sheep's eyes at sb; **d. comme un agneau** as gentle as a lamb
2 *adv Fam* **filer d.** to toe the line
3 *nf* **douce** *Fam* **en d.** on the quiet

douzaine [duzɛn] *nf* **une d. (de)** *(environ)* around a dozen, a dozen *or* so; **trois douzaines d'œufs** three dozen eggs

douze [duz] *adj & nm inv* twelve; *voir aussi* **trois**

douzième [duzjɛm] *nmf, nm & adj* twelfth; *voir aussi* **cinquième**

doyen, -enne [dwajɛ̃, -ɛn] *nm,f* (**a**) *(personne la plus âgée)* most senior member (**b**) *(d'une faculté)* dean

drachme [drakm] *nf* drachma

draconien, -enne [drakɔnjɛ̃, -ɛn] *adj (règlement)* draconian; *(régime)* very strict

dragage [dragaʒ] *nm (nettoyage)* dredging

dragée [draʒe] *nf (confiserie)* sugared almond; *(médicament)* sugar-coated pill

dragon [dragɔ̃] *nm* (**a**) *(animal mythologique, femme acariâtre)* dragon (**b**) *(soldat)* dragoon

drague [drag] *nf* (**a**) *(en travaux publics)* dredge (**b**) *Fam (flirt)* **ce mec-là, c'est un pro de la d.** that guy's a real pro at hitting on women; **c'est un lieu de d. idéal** it's an ideal place for hitting on people

draguer [drage] **1** *vt* (**a**) *(nettoyer)* to dredge (**b**) *Fam (hommes, femmes)* to hit on
2 *vi Fam* to cruise

dragueur, -euse [dragœr, -øz] **1** *nm (bateau)* dredger; **d. de mines** minesweeper
2 *nm,f Fam* **c'est un d.** he's always chasing women; **c'est une dragueuse** she's always chasing men

drain [drɛ̃] *nm* (**a**) *(conduit)* drain (**b**) *Méd* drainage tube

drainage [drɛnaʒ] *nm (d'un champ, d'une plaie)* draining

drainer [drene] *vt (sol, abcès)* to drain

dramatique [dramatik] **1** *adj* (**a**) *(de théâtre)* dramatic; **auteur d.** playwright (**b**) *(grave)* tragic
2 *nf* TV drama

dramatiser [dramatize] *vt* to dramatize

dramaturge [dramatyrʒ] *nm* dramatist, playwright

drame [dram] *nm* (**a**) *(genre littéraire, pièce)* drama (**b**) *Fig* tragedy; **faire un d. de qch** to make a drama out of sth

drap [dra] *nm* (**a**) *(linge)* **d. (de lit)** sheet; **d. de dessous/dessus** bottom/top sheet; *Fig* **être dans de beaux draps** to be in a real mess; **d. de bain** bath sheet; **d. de plage** beach towel (**b**) *(tissu)* cloth (**c**) *Belg (serviette)* towel

drapeau, -x [drapo] *nm* flag; *Fig* **être sous les drapeaux** to serve in the armed forces; **d. blanc** white flag; **d. tricolore** tricolor

draper [drape] **1** *vt (étoffe)* to drape
2 se draper *vpr* **se d. dans** to drape oneself in; *Fig* **se d. dans sa dignité** to stand on one's dignity

draperie [drapri] *nf (tenture)* drapery

drap-housse (*pl* **draps-housses**) [draus] *nm* fitted sheet

drapier, -ère [drapje, -ɛr] **1** *nm,f (marchand)* draper; *(fabricant)* cloth manufacturer
2 *adj* cloth

drastique [drastik] *adj* drastic

drave [drav] *nf Can (de rondins)* drive

draver [drave] *vt Can (rondins)* to float, to drive

draveur [dravœr] *nm Can* driver, raftsman

Dresde [drɛzd] *n* Dresden

dressage [drɛsaʒ] *nm (d'un animal)* training; *(d'un cheval)* breaking in

dresser [drese] **1** *vt* **(a)** *(élever)* to put up, to erect; **d. la tête** to raise *or* to lift one's head; *(pour regarder)* to look up; **d. les oreilles** to prick up *or* to cock its ears; *Fig* **d. l'oreille** to prick up one's ears **(b)** *(plan, rapport, liste)* to prepare, to draw up **(c)** *(animal)* to train (**à faire qch** to do sth); *(cheval)* to break in; *Fam* **ça va le d.!** that'll put him in his place! **(d)** *(exciter)* **d. qn contre qn** to set sb against sb

2 se dresser *vpr* **(a)** *(se lever)* to stand up, to rise **(b)** *(monument)* to stand; *(montagne)* to rise up; *Fig* **les obstacles qui se dressent sur notre chemin** the obstacles that stand in our way

dresseur, -euse [drɛsœr, -øz] *nm,f (d'animaux)* trainer

DRH [deɛraʃ] **1** *nf (abrév* **direction des ressources humaines)** human resources department

2 *nm,f (abrév* **directeur, -trice des ressources humaines)** human resources manager

dribble [dribl] *nm* dribble

dribbler [drible] *Sport* **1** *vi* to dribble

2 *vt (joueur)* to dribble around

drille [drij] *nm Fam* **c'est un joyeux d.** he's always good for a laugh

drogue [drɔg] *nf* **(a)** *(stupéfiant)* drug; **d. dure/douce** hard/soft drug **(b)** *Vieilli (médicament)* medicine

drogué, -e [drɔge] *nm,f* drug addict

droguer [drɔge] **1** *vt* **(a)** *(victime)* to drug; *(cheval)* to dope **(b)** *(malade)* to dose with drugs

2 se droguer *vpr* to take drugs; **se d. à qch** to be on sth

droguerie [drɔgri] *nf* hardware store

droguiste [drɔgist] *nmf* hardware dealer

droit¹, -e¹ [drwa, drwat] **1** *adj* **(a)** *(rectiligne, vertical)* straight; **se tenir d.** *(debout)* to stand (up) straight; *(assis)* to sit (up) straight; **d. comme un i** *ou* **un piquet** poker-straight **(b)** *(honnête)* upright

2 *nf* **droite** straight line

3 *adv* **écrire/marcher d.** to write/walk straight; **aller d. devant soi** to go straight ahead; **aller d. au but** to get to the point; **aller d. à la catastrophe** to be heading straight for disaster; **c'est tout d.** it's straight ahead

droit², -e² [drwa, drwat] **1** *adj (main, jambe, gant)* right; **du côté d.** on the right-hand side

2 *nf* **droite (a)** *(côté)* right; **tourner à droite** to turn (to the) right; **rouler à droite** to drive on the right; **le placard de droite** the right-hand cupboard, the cupboard on the right; **à ma droite, le château** to *or* on my right is the castle; *Fig* **courir à droite et à gauche** to run around all over the place **(b)** *Pol* **la droite** the right (wing); **de droite** *(candidat, journal)* right-wing; **voter à droite** to vote for the right

droit³ [drwa] *nm* **(a)** *(prérogative)* right; **avoir d. à qch** to have a right to sth; **avoir le d. de faire qch** to have the right to do sth; **donner d. à qch à qn** *(carte, abonnement)* to entitle sb to sth; **être dans son (bon) d.** to be within one's rights; **avoir des droits sur qn/qch** to have rights over sb/sth; **tous droits (de reproduction) réservés** *(sur livre)* all rights reserved; **de quel d. me critiques-tu?** what gives you the right to criticize me?; **droits acquis** vested interests; **d. d'aînesse** birthright; **d. d'asile** right of asylum; **avoir un d. de regard sur qch** to have the right to know about sth; **d. de réponse** right of reply; **d. de visite** *(d'un parent)* visiting rights; **d. de vote** right to vote; **les droits de l'homme** human rights

(b) *(en argent)* fee; *(imposition)* duty; *(taxe)* tax; **droits d'auteur** royalties; **droits de douane** (customs) duty; **d. d'entrée** admission fee; **droits d'inscription** registration fee; **droits de succession** inheritance *or* estate tax; **d. de timbre** stamp duty

(c) *Jur* law; **faire son d.** to study law; **d. administratif** administrative law; **d. des affaires** business law; **d. canon** canon law; **d. civil** civil law; **d. commercial** commercial law; **d. commun** common law; **d. communautaire** (European) Community law; **d. constitutionnel** constitutional law; **d. international** international law; **d. pénal** criminal law; **d. privé** private law; **d. public** public law; **d. du travail** labor laws

droitier, -ère [drwatje, -ɛr] **1** *adj* right-handed

2 *nm,f* right-handed person

droiture [drwatyr] *nf* rectitude

drôle [drol] *adj* **(a)** *(amusant)* funny **(b)** *(étrange)* funny; **c'est un d. de type** he's a weird *or* funny kind of guy; **faire une d. de tête** to pull a face; *Fam* **ça me fait tout d. de te voir ici** it feels really funny seeing you here **(c)** *Fam (en intensif)* **il faut un d. de courage pour faire ça** you need a hell of a lot of courage to do that; **j'ai eu une d. de grippe!** I had a bad case of flu

drôlement [drolmɑ̃] *adv* funnily; *Fam (très)* awfully; *Fam* **les prix ont d. augmenté** prices have gone up an awful lot; *Fam* **elle est d. bien** *(remarquable)* she's a terrific person; *(belle)* she's really hot

drôlerie [drolri] *nf* funniness

DROM [drom] *nm (abrév* **Département et Région d'outre-mer)** = French overseas department and region

dromadaire [drɔmadɛr] *nm* dromedary

dru, -e [dry] **1** *adj (herbe, blé, cheveux, barbe)* thick; *(pluie)* heavy

2 *adv* **pousser d.** to grow thickly; **tomber d.** *(pluie)* to fall heavily

druide [druid] *nm* druid

DST [deɛste] *nf (abrév* **Direction de la surveillance du territoire)** = French Secret Service

DTP [detepe] *nm (abrév* **diphtérie, tétanos, polio)** diphtheria, tetanus and polio vaccination

du [dy] *voir* **de**

dû, due *(mpl* **dus,** *fpl* **dues)** [dy] **1** *pp voir* **devoir²**

2 *adj* **(a)** *(que l'on doit)* due, owed; **en port dû** postage due **(b)** *(causé)* **être dû à qch** to be due to sth **(c)** **en bonne et due forme** in due form

3 *nm* due

dualisme [dɥalism] *nm* dualism

dualité [dɥalite] *nf* duality

dubitatif, -ive [dybitatif, -iv] *adj* doubtful

Dublin [dyblɛ̃] *n* Dublin

dublinois, -e [dyblinwa, -az] **1** *adj* of Dublin

2 *nm,f* **D., Dublinoise** Dubliner

duc [dyk] *nm* duke

ducal, -e, -aux, -ales [dykal, -o] *adj* ducal

duché [dyʃe] *nm* duchy

duchesse [dyʃɛs] *nf (femme)* duchess

due *voir* **dû**

duel [dɥɛl] *nm* duel; **se battre en d.** to fight a duel

dulcinée [dylsine] *nf Litt ou Hum* ladylove

dûment [dymɑ̃] *adv* duly

dumping [dœmpiŋ] *nm* dumping; **faire du d.** to dump

dune [dyn] *nf* dune

Dunkerque [dœ̃kɛrk] *n* Dunkirk

duo [dɥo] *nm (chanson)* duet; *(de comiques, de musiciens)* duo

duodénum [dɥɔdenɔm] *nm* duodenum

dupe [dyp] **1** *nf* dupe

2 *adj* **être d. (de)** to be taken in (by)

duper [dype] *vt* to dupe, to fool

duperie [dypri] *nf* deception

duplex [dyplɛks] *nm* **(a)** **(émission en) d.** link-up **(b)** *(appartement)* duplex

duplicata [dyplikata] *nm* duplicate

duplication [dyplikasjɔ̃] *nf* (**a**) *Biol* doubling (**b**) *Ordinat* **d. de logiciel** software copying

duplicité [dyplisite] *nf* duplicity

duquel [dykɛl] *voir* **lequel**

dur, -e [dyr] **1** *adj* (**a**) *(rigide)* hard; *(viande)* tough; *(pain)* stale (**b**) *(difficile, pénible) (travail, hiver)* hard; *(scène, film)* distressing (**c**) *(sévère, cruel)* harsh (**avec** with) (**d**) *Fam* **être d. de la feuille** to be hard of hearing

  2 *nm,f Fam (personne)* tough type; *Pol* hardliner; **un d. à cuire** a hard-boiled type; **jouer les durs** to act tough

  3 *nm* **bâtiment en d.** permanent building

  4 *nf Fam* **élever qn à la dure** to bring sb up the hard way

  5 *adv (travailler)* hard

durable [dyrabl] *adj* lasting

durablement [dyrabləmɑ̃] *adv* for a long time

duraille [dyraj] *adj Fam* hard

durant [dyrɑ̃] *prép* **d. le mois de mai** during May; **d. plusieurs années** for several years; **d. toute sa vie, sa vie d.** throughout his/her life; **parler des heures d.** to talk for hours on end

durcir [dyrsir] **1** *vt aussi Fig* to harden

  2 *vi* to harden

  3 se durcir *vpr aussi Fig* to harden

durcissement [dyrsismɑ̃] *nm aussi Fig* hardening

durée [dyre] *nf (d'un règne, d'une guerre, d'un séjour)* duration, length; *(d'une note)* length, value; **de courte d.** *(bonheur, soulagement)* short-lived; **d. de connexion** *(sur Internet)* on-line time; **d. de projection** *(d'un film)* running time; **d. de validité** *(d'un billet)* period of validity; **d. de vie** *(de personne)* lifespan; *(d'une pile)* life; *(d'une machine)* useful life; **d. de vol** flight time

durement [dyrmɑ̃] *adv (répondre, parler)* harshly; **d. éprouvé** sorely tried

durer [dyre] *vi* to last; **voilà trois ans que cela dure** it's been going on for three years; **ça ne peut pas d.** this can't go on; *Hum* **faire d. le plaisir** to prolong the agony

dureté [dyrte] *nf* (**a**) *(rigidité)* hardness; *(d'une viande)* toughness (**b**) *(d'un hiver)* severity (**c**) *(cruauté) (d'une personne)* harshness; **parler avec d.** to speak harshly

durillon [dyrijɔ̃] *nm (de la main)* callus; *(du pied)* corn

Durit® [dyrit] *nf* hose (connection)

DUT [deyte] *nm (abrév* **diplôme universitaire de technologie**) = post-baccalauréat technical qualification awarded after two years

duvet [dyvɛ] *nm* (**a**) *(poil)* down (**b**) *(sac de couchage)* sleeping bag (**c**) *Belg & Suisse* duvet, comforter

duveteux, -euse [dyvtø, -øz] *adj* downy

DVD [devede] *nm inv (abrév* **Digital Versatile Disc, Digital Video Disc**) DVD

DVD-ROM [devederɔm] *nm inv (abbr* **Digital Versatile Disc read-only memory, Digital Video Disc read-only memory**) DVD-ROM

dynamique [dinamik] **1** *adj* dynamic

  2 *nf* (**a**) *(science)* dynamics *(singulier)* (**b**) *(progrès)* dynamic

dynamiser [dinamize] *vt* to energize

dynamisme [dinamism] *nm* dynamism

dynamite [dinamit] *nf aussi Fig* dynamite

dynamiter [dinamite] *vt* to dynamite

dynamo [dinamo] *nf* dynamo

dynastie [dinasti] *nf* dynasty

dysenterie [disɑ̃tri] *nf* dysentery

dysfonctionnement [disfɔksjɔnmɑ̃] *nm* dysfunction

dyslexie [dislɛksi] *nf* dyslexia

dyslexique [dislɛksik] *adj* dyslexic

E

E¹, e [ə] *nm inv* E, e

E² (*abrév* **Est**) E

EAO [əao] *nm inv* (*abrév* **enseignement assisté par ordinateur**) CAL

eau, -x [o] *nf* (**a**) (*liquide*) water; **laver qch à grande e.** to wash sth down; **prendre l'e.** to let in water; **avoir l'e. courante** to have running water; *Fig* **mettre de l'e. dans son vin** to tone it down a bit; *Fig* **apporter de l'e. au moulin de qn** to strengthen sb's case; *Fig* **dans ces eaux-là** or thereabouts; *Can* **s'en aller à l'e.** to be going bankrupt; *Fam* **s'en aller en e. de boudin** to go down the tubes; *Fam* **il y a de l'e. dans le gaz** there's trouble brewing; **e. bénite** holy water; **e. de Cologne** eau de Cologne; **e. douce** fresh water; **e. de Javel** bleach; **j'en ai l'e. à la bouche!** my mouth's watering!; **elle a perdu les eaux** her waters have broken; **e. lourde** heavy water; **e. de mer** *ou* **salée** salt water; **e. minérale** mineral water; **e. oxygénée** hydrogen peroxide; **e. de pluie** rainwater; **e. du robinet** tap water; *Fig* **roman/film à l'e. de rose** sentimental novel/movie; **e. de Seltz** club soda; **e. de source** spring water; **eaux thermales** hot springs; *Vieilli* **prendre les eaux** to take the waters; **e. de toilette** toilet water; *aussi Fig* **e. de vaisselle** dishwater

(**b**) (*étendue*) water; **au bord de l'e.** by the water's edge; **tomber à l'e.** to fall into the water; *Fig* to fall through; *Fig* **se jeter à l'e.** to take the plunge; **les eaux territoriales françaises** French waters

(**c**) (*sécrétion*) **être tout en e.** to be dripping with perspiration; **j'en ai l'e. à la bouche!** my mouth's watering!; **elle a perdu les eaux** her waters have broken

(**d**) (*d'une pierre précieuse*) **un diamant de la plus belle e.** a diamond of the first water

eau-de-vie (*pl* **eaux-de-vie**) [odvi] *nf* brandy

eau-forte (*pl* **eaux-fortes**) [ofɔrt] *nf* (*estampe*) etching

ébahi, -e [ebai] *adj* astounded

ébats [eba] *nmpl* frolicking; **é. amoureux** lovemaking

ébattre [11] [ebatr] **s'ébattre** *vpr* to frolic

ébauche [eboʃ] *nf* (*dessin*) rough sketch; (*d'un roman*) outline; (*d'une lettre*) draft; *Fig* **l'é. d'un sourire** the ghost of a smile

ébaucher [eboʃe] *vt* (*tableau, roman*) to rough out; (*lettre*) to draft; *Fig* **é. un sourire** to give a faint smile; *Fig* **é. un geste** to make a movement

ébène [eben] *nf* ebony; (**d'un noir**) **d'é.**, (**noir**) **é.** jet black

ébéniste [ebenist] *nmf* cabinet maker

éberlué, -e [eberlɥe] *adj* flabbergasted

éblouir [ebluir] *vt aussi Fig* to dazzle

éblouissant, -e [ebluisɑ̃, -ɑ̃t] *adj aussi Fig* dazzling; **d'une beauté éblouissante** dazzlingly beautiful

éblouissement [ebluismɑ̃] *nm* dazzle, glare; (*malaise*) fit of dizziness; *Fig* **ce fut un é.** it was dazzling

éborgner [ebɔrɲe] **1** *vt* **é. qn** to put sb's eye out

2 s'éborgner *vpr* to put one's eye out

éboueur [ebwœr] *nm* garbage collector

ébouillanter [ebujɑ̃te] **1** *vt* to scald

2 s'ébouillanter *vpr* to scald oneself

éboulement [ebulmɑ̃] *nm* (**a**) (*écroulement*) collapse; (*de mine*) cave-in; **deux personnes sont mortes dans l'é. de la falaise** two people were killed when the cliff collapsed (**b**) (*gravats*) mass of fallen rocks

ébouler [ebule] **s'ébouler** *vpr* (*falaise, remblai*) to collapse; (*tunnel*) to cave in

éboulis [ebuli] *nm* mass of fallen rocks

ébouriffé, -e [eburife] *adj* (*cheveux, personne*) disheveled

ébouriffer [eburife] *vt* (*cheveux*) to ruffle; **é. qn** to ruffle sb's hair

ébranler [ebrɑ̃le] **1** *vt aussi Fig* to shake

2 s'ébranler *vpr* to move off

Èbre [ɛbr] *nm* **l'È.** the Ebro

ébrécher [34] [ebreʃe] *vt* (*verre, porcelaine*) to chip; (*lame*) to nick

ébriété [ebriete] *nf* **en état d'é.** in a state of inebriation

ébrouer [ebrue] **s'ébrouer** *vpr* (**a**) (*cheval*) to snort (**b**) (*chien*) to shake itself

ébruiter [ebrɥite] **1** *vt* (*secret*) to give away; (*nouvelle*) to spread

2 s'ébruiter *vpr* (*nouvelle*) to spread

EBS [əbeɛs] *nf* (*abrév* **encéphalite bovine spongiforme**) BSE

ébullition [ebylisjɔ̃] *nf* boiling; **arriver à é.** to come to the boil; **amener qch à é.** to bring sth to the boil; *Fig* **en é.** in turmoil

écaille [ekaj] *nf* (*de poisson*) scale; (*de tortue, d'huître*) shell; (*de peinture*) flake; **peigne en é.** tortoiseshell comb; **des lunettes d'é.** *ou* **en é.** horn-rimmed glasses

écailler [ekaje] **1** *vt* (**a**) (*poisson*) to scale (**b**) (*huître*) to open

2 s'écailler *vpr* (*émail, vernis à ongles*) to chip (off); (*peinture*) to peel (off)

écarlate [ekarlat] *adj* scarlet; *Fig* **devenir é.** to go bright red

écarquiller [ekarkije] *vt* **é. les yeux** to open one's eyes wide

écart [ekar] *nm* (**a**) (*entre deux chiffres*) difference (**entre** between); (*en distance, en temps, dans un classement*) gap (**entre** between); **ils ont trois ans d'é.** there's a three-year gap between them; **é. de niveau** (*dans une classe*) difference in ability; **é. de salaires** wage differential; **faire le grand é.** to do the splits (**c**) (*déviation*) **faire un é.** (*personne*) to jump aside; (*cheval*) to shy; (*voiture*) to swerve; *Fig* **écarts de conduite** misbehavior; *Fig* **écarts de langage** bad language (**d**) **mettre qn à l'é.** to keep sb out of things; **tenir qn à l'é. de qch** to keep sb out of sth; **se tenir à l'é.** to keep out of things; **un terrain à l'é. de la ville** a piece of land away from the town

écarté, -e [ekarte] *adj* (**a**) (*loin l'un de l'autre*) (*bras, pieds*) apart; (*yeux*) widely spaced; **avoir les dents écartées** to be gap-toothed (**b**) *Can* (*personne*) lost

écarteler [39] [ekartəle] *vt* to quarter; *Fig* **être écartelé** (**entre**) to be torn (between)

écartement [ekartəmɑ̃] *nm* (*distance*) space, gap

écarter [ekarte] **1** *vt* (**a**) (*séparer*) (*doigts, bras, jambes*) to spread; (*rideaux*) to draw (back); (*personnes, objets*) to move apart (**b**) (*repousser*) (*objet, branches*) to move aside; (*danger,* *soupçons)* to avert; **é. qn/qch de** to move sb/sth away from; **é. qn de son chemin** to push sb out of one's way (**c**) *(exclure) (candidat, proposition)* to turn down

2 s'écarter *vpr* (**a**) *(se séparer) (personnes)* to move apart; *(foule)* to part; *(routes)* to diverge (**b**) *(s'éloigner) (piéton)* to move away (**de** from); *(voiture)* to swerve (**de** from); *Fig* **s'é. du sujet** to wander from the subject (**c**) *Can (s'égarer)* to get lost

ecchymose [ekimoz] *nf* bruise

ecclésiastique [eklezjastik] **1** *adj* ecclesiastical
2 *nm* clergyman

écervelé, -e [esɛrvəle] **1** *adj* scatterbrained
2 *nm,f* scatterbrain

ECG [əseʒe] *nm Méd (abrév* **électrocardiogramme**) ECG

échafaud [eʃafo] *nm* scaffold; *Fig* **monter à l'é.** to go to the scaffold

échafaudage [eʃafodaʒ] *nm* scaffolding; **des échafaudages** scaffolding

échafauder [eʃafode] *vt (empiler)* to pile up; *Fig (système, argumentation)* to put together, to construct

échalas [eʃala] *nm Fam* **grand é.** beanpole

échalote [eʃalɔt] *nf* shallot

échancré, -e [eʃɑ̃kre] *adj* (**a**) *(vêtement)* low-cut (**b**) *(littoral)* jagged, indented

échancrer [eʃɑ̃kre] *vt* to cut out the neckline of

échancrure [eʃɑ̃kryr] *nf (décolleté)* low neckline

échange [eʃɑ̃ʒ] *nm* (**a**) *(d'objets, de prisonniers, d'idées)* exchange; **voulez-vous (me) faire l'é.?** could you exchange it/them (for me)?; **recevoir/donner qch en é. (de qch)** to receive/give sth in exchange (for sth); **de violents échanges** *(physiques)* violent clashes; *(verbaux)* violent exchanges; **échanges culturels** cultural exchanges (**b**) **échanges commerciaux** trade; **échanges internationaux** international trade (**c**) *(au tennis)* rally; **faire des échanges** to rally (**d**) *Ordinat* **é. de données** data exchange; **é. de données informatisé** electronic data interchange

échanger [45] [eʃɑ̃ʒe] *vt (objets, articles)* to exchange, to swap (**contre** for); *Fig (coups, idées)* to exchange; *(injures)* to trade

échangeur [eʃɑ̃ʒœr] *nm* interchange

échantillon [eʃɑ̃tijɔ̃] *nm* sample; **prélever un é. de qch** to take a sample of sth; **é. gratuit** free sample

échantillonnage [eʃɑ̃tijɔnaʒ] *nm* (**a**) *(action)* sampling (**b**) *(échantillons)* selection of samples

échantillonner [eʃɑ̃tijɔne] *vt (pour sondage)* to sample

échappatoire [eʃapatwar] *nf* way out

échappée [eʃape] *nf* (**a**) *(de coureurs)* breakaway; **être dans l'é.** to be part of the breakaway group (**b**) *(espace libre)* **une é. sur la mer** a sea view

échappement [eʃapmɑ̃] *nm* (**a**) *(de voiture)* exhaust; **des gaz d'é.** exhaust fumes (**b**) *Ordinat* escape

échapper [eʃape] **1 échapper à** *vt ind* **é. à qn** *(sujet: personne)* to get away from sb; **é. à qch** *(punition, mort)* to escape sth; *(corvée)* to get out of sth; **son nom m'échappe** her name escapes me; **je n'aurais pas dû le dire mais ça m'a échappé** I shouldn't have said it but it just slipped out; **rien ne lui échappe** he doesn't miss a thing; **la victoire nous a échappé** victory eluded us; **le vase m'a échappé des mains** the vase slipped out of my hands

2 *vi* **laisser é.** *(personne, animal)* to let escape; *(objet)* to drop; *(de l'air)* to let out; *(de la vapeur)* to let off; *(larme)* to let fall; *(secret, soupir, cri)* to let out; *(détail)* to overlook

3 *vt* **il l'a échappé belle** he had a narrow escape

4 s'échapper *vpr* (**a**) *(s'évader)* to escape (**de** from) (**b**) *(sortir) (eau, gaz)* to escape (**de** from); **un cri s'échappa de ses lèvres** she let out a cry

écharde [eʃard] *nf* splinter

écharpe [eʃarp] *nf* scarf; **l'é. tricolore** the tricolor sash; **avoir le bras en é.** to have one's arm in a sling

écharper [eʃarpe] *vt Fam* **se faire é.** to get torn to pieces

échasse [eʃas] *nf* (**a**) *(bâton)* stilt; **être monté sur des échasses** to be on stilts (**b**) *(oiseau)* stilt

échassier [eʃasje] *nm* wader

échaudé, -e [eʃode] *adj Fig* **être é.** to get one's fingers burnt

échauffement [eʃofmɑ̃] *nm* (**a**) *(d'un moteur)* overheating (**b**) *(excitation)* overexcitement (**c**) *(d'athlète)* warm-up

échauffer [eʃofe] **1** *vt* (**a**) *(moteur)* to overheat (**b**) *(exciter)* **é. les esprits** to get people worked up; **les esprits sont échauffés** feelings are running high; *Fam* **é. les oreilles à qn** to get on sb's nerves (**c**) *(athlète)* to warm up

2 s'échauffer *vpr* (**a**) *(moteur)* to get overheated (**b**) *(athlète)* to warm up (**c**) *(s'énerver) (personne)* to get worked up

échauffourée [eʃofure] *nf* brawl; *Mil* skirmish

échéance [eʃeɑ̃s] *nf (de dette, de facture)* date of payment; **à courte/longue é.** *(prêt)* short-/long-term; **venir à é.** to fall due; **faire face à ses échéances** to meet one's financial obligations; *Fig* **une é. électorale** an election

échéancier [eʃeɑ̃sje] *nm* (**a**) *(livre)* tickler (**b**) *(calendrier)* schedule

échéant [eʃeɑ̃] *adj m voir* **cas**

échec [eʃɛk] *nm* (**a**) *(défaite)* failure; *(revers)* setback; **subir é.** *(défaite)* to fail; *(revers)* to suffer a setback; *Can* **mettre en é.** *(au hockey)* to check; **faire é. à qch** to foil sth; **faire é. à qn** to frustrate sb; **l'é. scolaire** doing badly at school (**b**) *(jeu)* **échecs** chess; **é.!** check!; **é. et mat!** checkmate!

échelle [eʃɛl] *nf* (**a**) *(pour grimper)* ladder; **l'é. des pompiers** the fireman's ladder; *Fig* **l'é. sociale** the social ladder; *Fig* **é. des salaires** salary scale; **é. des valeurs** scale of values; **faire la courte é. à qn** to give sb a boost; **5 sur l'é. de Richter** 5 on the Richter scale (**b**) *(d'une carte)* scale; **l'é. est de 1/10 000** the scale is 1:10,000; *Fig* **sur une grande é.** on a large scale; **à l'é. nationale** on a national scale; *Ordinat* **intégration à grande/petite é.** large-/small-scale integration (**c**) *(dans un collant)* run; **faire une é. à son collant** to get a run in one's pantihose

échelon [eʃlɔ̃] *nm* (**a**) *(d'une échelle)* rung (**b**) *(d'une hiérarchie)* grade; **gravir tous les échelons** to climb to the top of the ladder (**c**) *(niveau)* level; **à l'é. national** on a national level; **à tous les échelons** at every level

échelonnement [eʃlɔnmɑ̃] *nm* (**a**) *(de paiements)* spreading; *(de vacances)* staggering (**b**) *(d'objets)* spacing

échelonner [eʃlɔne] **1** *vt* (**a**) *(paiements)* to spread; *(vacances)* to stagger (**b**) *(objets)* to space out

2 s'échelonner *vpr* (**a**) **les paiements s'échelonnent sur deux ans** the payments are spread over two years (**b**) *(objets)* to be spaced out

écheveau, -x [eʃvo] *nm (de fil)* skein; *Fig* **démêler l'é. d'une affaire compliquée** to untangle a complicated business

échevelé, -e [eʃəvle] *adj (personne)* disheveled; *Fig (course)* mad

échevin [eʃəvɛ̃] *nm Belg* deputy mayor

échinacée [eʃinase] *nf Bot & Méd* echinacea

échine [eʃin] *nf* (**a**) *(colonne vertébrale)* spine, backbone (**b**) *(de porc)* loin

échiné, -e [eʃine] *adj Can* exhausted

échiner [eʃine] **s'échiner** *vpr* **s'é. à faire qch** to wear oneself out doing sth

échiquier [eʃikje] *nm (d'échecs)* chessboard; *Fig* **l'é. politique** the political scene

écho [eko] *nm* (**a**) *(bruit)* echo; **il y a de l'é.** there's an echo; *Fig* **trouver un é.** to get a response; *Fig* **se faire l'é. de qch** to echo sth; *Fig* **j'en ai eu de très bons échos** I've had some very good feedback (**b**) **les échos** *(de journal)* gossip column

échographe [ekograf] *nf Méd* (ultrasound) scanner

échographie [ekografi] *nf* (ultrasound) scan; **passer une é.** to undergo a scan

échoir [14] [eʃwar] **1** vi (dette) to fall due; (investissement) to mature
2 échoir à vt ind to fall to
échoppe [eʃɔp] nf shop
échotier, -ère [ekɔtje, -ɛr] nm,f gossip columnist
échouer [eʃwe] **1** vi (a) (navire) to run aground; (baleine) to get beached; **navire échoué** stranded ship; Fam **é. dans un bar** to wind up in a bar (b) (rater) (projet, personne) to fail; **é. à un examen** to fail an exam; **faire é.** (projet) to wreck; (complot) to foil
2 vt (navire) to beach
3 s'échouer vpr (navire) to run aground; (baleine) to get beached
éclabousser [eklabuse] **1** vt to splash, to spatter (**avec** with); Fig **le scandale a éclaboussé certains de ses collègues** the scandal tarnished the reputation of some of his colleagues
2 s'éclabousser vpr to splash oneself
éclaboussure [eklabusyr] nf splash
éclair [eklɛr] **1** nm (a) (lumière) flash; (pendant un orage) flash of lightning; **éclairs** lightning; **être rapide comme l'é.** to be as quick as a flash; Fig **en un é.** in a flash (b) Fig (de lucidité, de génie) flash; **lancer des éclairs** (yeux) to flash (c) (gâteau) éclair
2 adj inv (visite, attaque) lightning
éclairage [eklɛraʒ] nm lighting; (par projecteurs) floodlighting
éclairagiste [eklɛraʒist] nmf (de cinéma, de théâtre) lighting technician
éclaircie [eklɛrsi] nf sunny spell
éclaircir [eklɛrsir] **1** vt (a) (rendre plus clair) (couleur, cheveux) to lighten; (teint) to clear (b) (rendre moins épais) (sauce) to thin (c) Fig (élucider) (mystère) to clear up
2 s'éclaircir vpr (a) (temps, ciel) to clear; (visage) to brighten up (b) (se dissiper) (brouillard) to clear; Fig (mystère) to be cleared up (c) (cheveux) to thin (d) **s'é. la voix** to clear one's throat
éclaircissement [eklɛrsismɑ̃] nm (a) (explication) explanation; **demander des éclaircissements (à qn) sur qch** to ask (sb) for an explanation of sth (b) (de cheveux) lightening
éclairé, -e [eklere] adj lit, Fig enlightened
éclairer [eklere] **1** vt (a) (pièce, vitrine) to light; **e. qn** to give sb some light; **éclairé au néon** neon-lit; Fig **é. qch d'un jour nouveau** to shed or to throw new light on sth; Fig **un sourire éclairait son visage** a smile lit up her face (b) Fig (informer) to enlighten; Fam **é. la lanterne de qn (sur qch)** to put sb in the picture (about sth)
2 vi **cette lampe éclaire mal** this lamp doesn't give much light
3 s'éclairer vpr (a) (personne) **s'é. au pétrole/gaz** to use oil lamps/gaslight; **s'é. à la bougie** to use candles for lighting (b) (devenir lumineux) (bâtiment, visage) to light up (c) Fig **tout s'éclaire!** everything's becoming clear!
éclaireur, -euse [eklɛrœr, -øz] **1** nm Mil scout; aussi Fig **partir en é.** to go off for a scout around
2 nm,f (boy) scout, f (girl) guide
éclat [ekla] nm (a) (fragment) (de bois, de verre) splinter; (de pierre) chip; **é. d'obus** piece of shrapnel; **des éclats d'obus** shrapnel; **des éclats de verre** (bris) broken glass; (projeté) flying glass; **voler en éclats** to shatter (b) (son) **é. de rire** burst of laughter; **partir d'un grand é. de rire** to burst out laughing; **rire aux éclats** to roar with laughter; **des éclats de voix** loud voices (c) Fig (scandale) scandal; **faire un é.** to create a scandal (d) (du soleil) glare; (d'un diamant) flash; (de couleurs) brilliance; **l'é. de ses yeux** the sparkle in his/her eyes; Fig **l'é. de la jeunesse** the bloom of youth (e) (d'une cérémonie, d'une époque) splendor; **action ou coup d'é.** brilliant feat
éclatant, -e [eklatɑ̃, -ɑ̃t] adj (a) (lumière, couleur, succès) brilliant; (teint) glowing; (preuve) striking; **être é. de santé** to be

glowing with health; **être dans une forme éclatante** to be in top form (b) (son, rire) loud
éclate [eklat] nf Fam **c'est l'é.** it's a laugh or hoot
éclaté, -e [eklate] adj (vision) fragmented
éclatement [eklatmɑ̃] nm (d'un obus, d'un pneu) bursting; (d'un verre) shattering; Fig (d'un groupe) break-up
éclater [eklate] **1** vi (a) (exploser) (obus, pneu, ballon) to burst; (verre) to shatter; Fig (groupe) to break up; **faire é. qch** to burst/shatter sth; **faire é. un pétard** to set off a firework (b) Fig **é. de rire** to burst out laughing; **é. en sanglots** to burst into tears; **é. en applaudissements** to burst into applause (c) (se déclencher) (guerre, incendie) to break out; (orage, scandale) to break
2 vt Fam **é. la tête à qn** to smash sb's head in
3 s'éclater vpr Fam to have a really good time
éclectique [eklɛktik] adj eclectic
éclipse [eklips] nf (de soleil, de lune) eclipse
éclipser [eklipse] **1** vt aussi Fig to eclipse
2 s'éclipser vpr Fam (s'esquiver) to slip away
éclopé, -e [eklɔpe] **1** adj lame
2 nm,f lame person
éclore [15] [eklɔr] vi (a) (œuf, poussin) to hatch (b) (fleur) to open (c) Fig (talent) to be born, to appear
éclosion [eklozjɔ̃] nf (a) (d'œuf, de poussin) hatching (b) (de fleurs) opening (c) Fig (d'un talent) birth
écluse [eklyz] nf lock; **(porte d')é.** lock or sluice gate
éclusier, -ère [eklyzje, -ɛr] nm,f lock keeper
écœurant, -e [ekœrɑ̃, -ɑ̃t] adj (a) (nourriture) nauseating; Fig (révoltant) disgusting (b) Fam (décourageant) sickening
écœurement [ekœrmɑ̃] nm (a) (nausée) nausea; Fig (indignation) disgust; **manger qch jusqu'à l'é.** to eat sth until one feels sick (b) Fam (découragement) discouragement
écœurer [ekœre] vt (a) **é. qn** (donner la nausée à) to make sb feel sick; Fig (indigner) to disgust sb (b) Fam (décourager) to sicken
écoguerrier, -ère [ekɔgɛrje, -ɛr] nm,f ecowarrior
écolabel [ekolabɛl] nm ecolabel
école [ekɔl] nf (a) (établissement, enseignement) school; **être à l'é.** to be at school; **aller à l'é.** to go to school; **reprendre l'é.** to go back to school; **faire l'é. buissonnière** to play hook(e)y; Fig **être à bonne é.** to be in good hands; Fam **je n'ai pas é. aujourd'hui** I don't have any classes today; **les grandes écoles** = university-level colleges specializing in professional training; **É. des beaux-arts** = art school in Paris; **é. de commerce** business school; **é. de conduite** driving school; **é. confessionnelle** faith-based school; **é. de danse** dancing school; **é. de dessin** art school; **é. hôtelière** hotel school; **é. libre** independent or private school; **é. maternelle**, Suisse **é. enfantine** nursery school; **é. militaire** military academy; **é. de musique** music school; **É. nationale d'administration** = university-level college preparing students for senior posts in law and economics; Anciennement **é. normale** teachers college; **É. normale supérieure** = university-level college preparing students for senior posts in teaching; **é. primaire** (bâtiment) primary school; (enseignement) primary education; **é. privée** private school; **é. publique** public school; Can & Suisse **é. secondaire** high school (b) (de pensée, d'art) school; **faire é.** to win a following

---

> ### Grandes écoles
> These are highly selective establishments which exist in parallel to the universities. Admission is usually only possible after two years of intensive preparatory studies ("écoles préparatoires") and a competitive examination (**concours** – see box at this entry). Graduates from these institutions typically go on to work in senior and executive posts in the civil service or the private sector. The "grandes écoles" include HEC (management),

Polytechnique, Centrale, the École des Mines and the École des Ponts et Chaussées (engineering), the ENA (senior civil service) and the École normale supérieure (humanities or science). Having been to a "grande école" is comparable in prestige to having a degree from Harvard or Yale in the US.

écolier, -ère [ekɔlje, -ɛr] *nm,f* schoolchild, schoolboy, *f* schoolgirl *(at primary school)*

écolo [ekɔlo] *adj & nmf Fam* green

écologie [ekɔlɔʒi] *nf* ecology

écologique [ekɔlɔʒik] *adj* ecological; *(produit)* eco-friendly, environmentally-friendly; *(politique, parti)* green

écologiste [ekɔlɔʒist] *adj & nmf* environmentalist

écomusée [ekɔmyze] *nm* living museum *(showing man in his natural and social environment)*

éconduire [18] [ekɔ̃dɥir] *vt Litt* (**a**) *(congédier)* to dismiss (**b**) *(refuser) (prétendant)* to reject

économat [ekɔnɔma] *nm* (**a**) *(fonction)* bursarship (**b**) *(bureau)* bursar's office

économe [ekɔnɔm] **1** *adj* economical, thrifty
2 *nmf (de collège)* bursar
3 *nm* (**couteau**) é. potato peeler

économie [ekɔnɔmi] *nf* (**a**) *(système)* economy; **é. dirigée** planned economy; **é. libérale** open-market economy; **é. de marché** market economy; **é. mondiale** global economy (**b**) *(gain)* saving; *(vertu)* economy, thrift; **avoir le sens de l'é.** to be thrifty; **faire une é. de temps/de 20%** to save time/ 20%; **faire l'é. d'un coup de fil** to save oneself a phone call (**c**) *(discipline)* economics *(singulier)*; **il enseigne l'é.** he teaches economics; **économies** savings; **faire des économies** to save money; **faire des économies de chauffage** to save money on heating; **faire des économies d'énergie** to save energy; **prendre sur ses économies** to dip into one's savings; **il n'y a pas de petites économies** every little bit helps

économique [ekɔnɔmik] *adj* (**a**) *(relatif à l'économie)* economic (**b**) *(avantageux)* economical

économiser [ekɔnɔmize] *vt (argent, temps, énergie)* to save; *(électricité, nourriture)* to economize on, to save on; **é. ses forces** to conserve one's strength; **é. sa salive** to save one's breath; **é. pour ses vacances** to save up for one's vacation

économiseur [ekɔnɔmizœr] *nm Ordinat* **é. d'écran** screen saver

économiste [ekɔnɔmist] *nmf* economist

écoper [ekɔpe] **1** *vt (barque)* to bale (out); **nous avons dû é.** we had to bale out
2 écoper de *vt ind Fam (être puni)* **é. d'une amende/de cinq ans de prison** to get a fine/five years in prison; **c'est encore moi qui vais é.** I'm going to get the blame again

écoproduit [ekɔprɔdɥi] *nm* eco-friendly *or* environmentally-friendly product

écorce [ekɔrs] *nf* (**a**) *(d'arbre)* bark; *(d'orange)* peel (**b**) **l'é. terrestre** the earth's crust

écorché, -e [ekɔrʃe] **1** *nm* anatomical model
2 *nm,f Fig* **é. (vif)** tortured soul

écorcher [ekɔrʃe] **1** *vt* (**a**) *(animal)* to skin; *(criminel)* to flay (**b**) *(érafler)* to graze; *Fig (nom)* to mispronounce; *Fig* **é. les oreilles à qn** to grate on sb's ears
2 s'écorcher *vpr* to graze oneself; **s'é. le genou** to graze one's knee

écorchure [ekɔrʃyr] *nf* graze

écorecharge [ekɔrəʃarʒ] *nf* eco-refill

écorner [ekɔrne] *vt (meuble)* to damage the corner(s) of; *(livre)* to dog-ear

écossais, -e [ekɔsɛ, -ɛz] **1** *adj (coutume, lande, personne)* Scottish; *(whisky)* Scotch; **une jupe écossaise** a tartan skirt
2 *nm,f* **É., Écossaise** Scot
3 *nm (tissu)* tartan

Écosse [ekɔs] *nf* **l'É.** Scotland

écosser [ekɔse] *vt* to shell

écosystème [ekɔsistɛm] *nm* ecosystem

écot [eko] *nm* **payer son é.** to pay one's share

écotaxe [ekotaks] *nf* ecotax

écotourisme [ekoturism] *nm* ecotourism

écoulement [ekulmã] *nm* (**a**) *(de liquide)* flow (**b**) *(de blessure)* discharge (**c**) *(de marchandises)* sale; *(de faux billets)* circulation (**d**) *(du temps)* passage

écouler [ekule] **1** *vt (marchandises)* to dispose of; *(faux billets)* to circulate
2 s'écouler *vpr* (**a**) *(liquide)* to flow out, to run out (**de** of) (**b**) *(marchandises)* to sell (**c**) *(temps)* to pass

écourter [ekurte] *vt (robe, texte)* to shorten; *(visite, discours)* to cut short

écoute [ekut] *nf* (**a**) *(d'une radio)* **être à l'é. (de)** to be listening in (to); **rester à l'é.** to stay tuned; **heure de grande é.** *Rad* peak listening time; *TV* peak viewing time, prime time; **indice d'é.** ratings; **écoutes téléphoniques** telephone tapping; **elle est sur é.** her phone's been tapped (**b**) **être à l'é. des autres** to be willing to lend a sympathetic ear

écouter [ekute] **1** *vt* (**a**) *(entendre)* to listen to; **é. qn jusqu'au bout** to hear sb out; **savoir é.** to be a good listener; **é. aux portes** to listen at doors; **faire é. qch à qn** to play sb sth; **écoute, ça suffit maintenant!** listen *or* look here, that's quite enough now! (**b**) *(suivre) (personne)* to listen to; **é. sa conscience** to listen to one's conscience
2 s'écouter *vpr* **il s'écoute trop** he coddles himself; **si je m'écoutais** if I did what I wanted; **s'é. parler** to like the sound of one's own voice

écouteur [ekutœr] *nm (du téléphone)* earpiece; **écouteurs** *(casque)* headphones

écoutille [ekutij] *nf Naut* hatchway

écouvillon [ekuvijɔ̃] *nm (pour bouteille, biberon)* bottle brush

écrabouiller [ekrabuje] *vt Fam* to squash, to crush; **se faire é. par une voiture** to get flattened by a car

écran [ekrã] *nm* (**a**) *(de télévision, de cinéma)* screen; **porter une pièce à l'é.** to adapt a play for the screen; **prochainement sur vos écrans** coming soon to a movie theater near you; **le grand/petit é.** the big/small screen; **é. panoramique** wide screen; **é. plat** flat screen (**b**) *Ordinat* screen, display; **à l'é.** on screen; **é. d'accueil** logo screen; **é. d'aide** help screen; **é. couleur** color screen *or* display; **é. à cristaux liquides** liquid crystal screen; **é. à fenêtres** split screen; **é. monochrome** monochrome screen; **é. rétro-éclairé** back-lit screen; **é. tactile** touch-sensitive screen; **é. de visualisation** VDU (**c**) *(pour protéger)* screen; **on ne peut pas voir le lac car les arbres font é.** you can't see the lake because it's screened by the trees; **é. de fumée** smoke screen; **é. solaire** sunscreen; **é. total** sun block

écrasant, -e [ekrazã, -ãt] *adj (poids, défaite, responsabilité)* crushing; *(majorité, victoire)* overwhelming

écrasé, -e [ekraze] *adj (nez)* flat; *Fig* **é. de travail** snowed under with work

écraser [ekraze] **1** *vt* (**a**) *(fruit, ail, membre)* to crush; *(insecte)* to squash; *(cigarette)* to stub out; *(piéton, chien)* to run over; **se faire é.** *(par une voiture)* to get run over; *Fam* **é. l'accélérateur** *ou* **le champignon** to step on the gas (**b**) *(vaincre) (adversaire, troupes)* to crush; **se faire é.** to be crushed (**c**) *Fam* **en é.** to sleep like a log (**d**) *très Fam* **écrase!** shut it!
2 s'écraser *vpr* (**a**) *(avion)* to crash (**b**) *Fam (ne rien dire)* to keep quiet

écrémage [ekremaʒ] *nm (sélection)* creaming off

écrémer [34] [ekreme] *vt (lait)* to skim; *Fig (sélectionner)* to cream off the best of

écrevisse [ekrəvis] *nf* crayfish

écrier [66] [ekrije] **s'écrier** *vpr* to cry out, to exclaim

écrin [ekrɛ̃] *nm* (jewel) case

écrire [30] [ekrir] **1** *vt (lettre, livre, chanson)* to write; *(noter)* to write down; **é. à qn** to write to sb; **é. un mot à qn** to drop sb a line; **je leur ai écrit de venir** I've written asking them to come; **il écrit bien** his handwriting is good; *(écrivain)* he writes well; **ce stylo écrit très bien** this pen writes very well

2 s'écrire *vpr* **(a)** *(s'orthographier)* to be spelled; **comment ça s'écrit?** how do you spell it? **(b)** *(correspondre)* to write to each other

écrit [ekri] *nm* **(a) mettre qch par é.** to put sth down in writing **(b)** *(texte)* (written) document; **écrits** *(œuvre)* writings **(c)** *(examen)* written examination

écriteau, -x [ekrito] *nm* notice

écritoire [ekritwar] *nf* writing case

écriture [ekrityr] *nf* **(a)** *(système, caractères)* writing; *Ordinat* write; *Tél* **é. prédictive** predictive text input **(b)** *(façon d'écrire)* (hand)writing; **elle a une belle é.** she has good handwriting **(c)** *(littérature)* writing; *TV & Cin* **é. de scénarios** scriptwriting **(d) écritures** *(comptabilité)* accounts; **tenir les écritures** to keep the accounts **(e)** *Rel* **l'É. sainte, les saintes Écritures** the Scriptures

écrivain [ekrivɛ̃] *nm* writer; **é. public** (public) letter writer

écrivais *etc. voir* **écrire**

écrou [ekru] *nm (de boulon)* nut

écrouer [ekrue] *vt Jur* to imprison

écroulé, -e [ekrule] *adj Fam* **é. (de rire)** doubled up with laughter

écroulement [ekrulmã] *nm* collapse

écrouler [ekrule] **s'écrouler** *vpr (bâtiment, prix, empire)* to collapse; *(espoirs)* to crumble away; **s'é. sur une chaise** to flop onto a chair; **s'é. de fatigue** to collapse with exhaustion

écru, -e [ekry] *adj (beige)* ecru; *(naturel)* unbleached

ecsta [ɛksta] *nf Fam* E, X

ecstasy [ɛkstazi] *nf* ecstasy

ECU, ÉCU [eky] *nm (abrév* **European Currency Unit***)* ECU

écu [eky] *nm* **(a)** *Hist* crown **(b)** *(bouclier)* shield

écueil [ekœj] *nm (rocher)* reef; *Fig (danger)* pitfall

écuelle [ekɥɛl] *nf* bowl

éculé, -e [ekyle] *adj (chaussure)* down-at-heel; *Fig (plaisanterie, argument)* hackneyed

écume [ekym] *nf (bave, sur la mer)* foam; *(sur la soupe, la confiture)* scum; **avoir l'é. à la bouche** to be foaming at the mouth; **é. (de mer)** *(magnésite)* meerschaum

écumer [ekyme] **1** *vt* **(a)** *(soupe, confiture)* to skim **(b)** *(piller)* to plunder; *Fig (parcourir)* to scour; **é. les mers** *(pirates)* to scour the seas

2 *vi* **é. (de rage)** to foam (with rage)

écumoire [ekymwar] *nf* skimmer; *Fig* **troué comme une é.** riddled with holes

écureuil [ekyrœj] *nm* squirrel; **é. roux/gris** red/gray squirrel

écurie [ekyri] *nf* stable; **é. (de courses)** *(de chevaux, de voitures)* (racing) stable

écusson [ekysõ] *nm* **(a)** *(armoiries)* escutcheon **(b)** *(de tissu)* badge

écuyer, -ère [ekɥije, -ɛr] **1** *nm Hist (gentilhomme)* squire

2 *nm,f* rider; **é. de cirque** circus rider

eczéma [egzema] *nm* eczema; **avoir ou faire de l'é.** to have eczema

édam [edam] *nm* Edam

edelweiss [edɛlvɛs] *nm* edelweiss

Éden [edɛn] *nm* **l'É.** Eden; *Fig* **un é.** a paradise

édenté, -e [edãte] *adj* toothless

EDF [ədeɛf] *nf (abrév* **Électricité de France***)* French electricity company

EDI [ədei] *nm Ordinat (abrév* **échange de données informatisé***)* EDI

édifiant, -e [edifjã, -ãt] *adj* edifying

édification [edifikasjõ] *nf* **(a)** *(d'un monument)* erection; *Fig (d'un empire, d'une fortune)* building up **(b)** *(instruction morale)* edification

édifice [edifis] *nm* building; *Fig* **apporter sa pierre à l'é.** to make a contribution; *Fig* **l'é. social** the social fabric

édifier [66] [edifje] *vt* **(a)** *(monument)* to erect; *Fig (empire, fortune)* to build up **(b)** *(instruire)* to edify

Édimbourg [edɛbur] *n* Edinburgh

édimbourgeois, -e [edɛburʒwa, -az] **1** *adj* of Edinburgh

2 *nm,f* **É., Édimbourgeoise** person from Edinburgh

édit [edi] *nm Hist* edict

éditer [edite] *vt* **(a)** *(publier)* to publish **(b)** *(commenter) (texte)* to edit **(c)** *Ordinat* to edit; **pouvant être édité** editable

éditeur, -trice [editœr, -tris] **1** *nm,f* **(a)** *(d'une maison d'édition)* publisher **(b)** *(commentateur)* editor

2 *nm Ordinat (de programme)* editor; **é. d'icônes** icon editor; **é. de logiciel** software company; **é. de texte** text editor

édition [edisjõ] *nf* **(a)** *(activité)* publishing **(b)** *(texte, exemplaire)* edition; *Hum* **où est le sucre? – dans le placard, troisième é.!** where's the sugar? – for the third time, it's in the cupboard!; **é. originale** first edition **(c)** *(d'un journal)* edition; **dernière é.** final edition; **é. spéciale** special edition **(d)** *Ordinat* editing; **é. de liens** linking; **é. pleine page** full-page editing; **é. électronique** electronic publishing

édito [edito] *nm Fam* editorial

éditorial, -e, -aux, -ales [editorjal, -o] **1** *adj* editorial

2 *nm* editorial

éditorialiste [editorjalist] *nmf* editorial writer

édredon [edradõ] *nm* comforter

éducateur, -trice [edykatœr, -tris] *nm,f* teacher; **é. spécialisé** special-needs teacher

éducatif, -ive [edykatif, -iv] *adj* educational

éducation [edykasjõ] *nf* **(a)** *(enseignement)* education; *(par les parents)* upbringing; **faire l'é. de qn** to educate sb; **é. manuelle et technique** handicraft classes; **l'É. nationale** the Department of Education; **é. physique** physical training *or* education; **é. religieuse** religious instruction; **é. sexuelle** sex education **(b)** *(savoir-vivre)* good manners; **avoir de l'é.** to have good manners; **manquer d'é.** to have no manners **(c)** *Fig (des réflexes, du goût)* training

édulcorant, -e [edylkorã, -ãt] **1** *adj* sweetening

2 *nm* sweetener; **é. de synthèse** artificial sweetener

édulcorer [edylkore] *vt (discours, compte rendu)* to water down; *(roman pornographique)* to tone down

éduquer [edyke] *vt* **(a)** *(donner un enseignement à) (enfant, peuple)* to educate; *(élever)* to bring up; **mal éduqué** ill-mannered **(b)** *Fig (réflexes, goût)* to train

EEE [əəə] *nm Pol (abrév* **Espace économique européen***)* EEA

EEG [əəʒə] *nm (abrév* **électroencéphalogramme***)* EEG

effaçable [efasabl] *adj* erasable

effacé, -e [efase] *adj* **(a)** *(personne, manières)* self-effacing **(b)** *(menton)* receding

effacement [efasmã] *nm* **(a)** *(d'un mot, d'un message, d'une bande)* erasing; *Ordinat* deletion; *(d'une tache)* removal; *(par le temps) (d'une inscription)* wearing away; *(des souvenirs)* fading **(b)** *(d'une personne)* self-effacement

effacer [16] [efase] **1** *vt* **(a)** *(mot, enregistrement, bande)* to erase; *(tableau)* to clean; *Ordinat (données)* to erase, to delete; *(écran)* to clear; *(tache, traces)* to remove; *(sujet: temps) (inscription)* to wear away **(b)** *Fig* **e. qch de sa mémoire** to erase sth from one's memory; **on efface tout et on recommence** we'll wipe the slate clean and make a fresh start

2 s'effacer *vpr* **(a)** *(disparaître) (inscription)* to wear away; *Fig (sentiment, souvenir)* to fade (away) **(b)** *(s'écarter)* to move aside; *Fig (se faire discret)* to keep in the background

effaceur [efasœr] *nm* **e. (d'encre)** ink eraser
effarant, -e [efarã, -ãt] *adj* astounding
effaré, -e [efare] *adj* astounded
effarement [efarmã] *nm* astonishment
effarer [efare] *vt* to astound
effaroucher [efaruʃe] **1** *vt* (a) *(effrayer)* to scare; *(faire reculer)* to scare away (b) *(choquer)* to shock
  2 s'effaroucher *vpr* (a) *(s'effrayer)* to take fright (**de** at) (b) *(s'offusquer)* to be shocked (**de** by)
effectif, -ive [efɛktif, -iv] **1** *adj (réel)* effective
  2 *nm (employés)* staff; *(d'un club, d'un bataillon)* strength; *(d'une classe)* size
effectivement [efɛktivmã] *adv* (a) *(en effet)* actually; **c'est pratique, hein? – e.!** it's practical, huh? – yes, it is! (b) *(réellement, de manière effective)* actually
effectuer [efɛktɥe] **1** *vt (mouvement, opération)* to perform; *(paiement, parcours, calcul, réservation)* to make; *(démarches)* to take; *(commande)* to place
  2 s'effectuer *vpr (mouvement, opération)* to be performed; *(paiement, parcours)* to be made
efféminé, -e [efemine] *adj* effeminate
effervescence [efɛrvesãs] *nf* excitement; **être en e.** *(ville, bureau)* to be buzzing with excitement
effervescent, -e [efɛrvesã, -ãt] *adj (médicament)* effervescent
effet [efɛ] *nm* (a) *(résultat, conséquence)* effect (**sur** on); **avoir pour e. de faire qch** to have the effect of doing sth; **faire e.** to take effect; **à cet e.** with that in mind; **rester** *ou* **demeurer sans e.** to have no effect; **sous l'e. de l'alcool/la drogue** under the influence of alcohol/drugs; **les feuilles sont tombées sous l'e. de la chaleur** the heat caused the leaves to drop off; **e. pervers** undesired effect; *Méd* side effect; **e. de serre** greenhouse effect; **e. secondaire** side effect; *Ordinat* **e. de transition** melt
  (b) *(impression)* impression; **quel e. ça te fait qu'elle revienne?** how do you feel about her coming back?; **ne faire aucun e. à qn** to make no impression on sb; **elle me fait l'e. d'une fille plutôt équilibrée** she strikes me as being a fairly well-balanced girl; **il me fait de l'e.** he does something for me; **faire un drôle d'e. à qn** to give sb a funny feeling; **faire bon/mauvais e. (à qn)** to make a good/bad impression (on sb)
  (c) *(but recherché)* **manquer son e.** *(plaisanterie)* to fall flat; **faire des effets de voix** to make striking use of one's voice; *Cin* **effets spéciaux** special effects; **e. de style** stylistic effect
  (d) *(application)* **prendre e.** to take effect
  (e) *(au tennis)* spin; **donner de l'e. à une balle** to put spin on a ball
  (f) *Fin* bill; **e. de commerce** bill of exchange
  (g) **effets (personnels)** *(affaires)* belongings
  (h) **en e., je m'en souviens** yes, I do remember; **en e., c'est ce que je me suis dit** that's just what I thought; **mais c'est monstrueux! – en e.!** it's abominable! – isn't it!; **j'ai dû partir, en e. j'étais pressé** I had to leave because I was in a hurry
effeuiller [efœje] *vt (fleur)* to pull the petals off; *(sujet: vent) (arbre)* to blow the leaves off; *Fig* **e. la marguerite** to play "he/she loves me, he/she loves me not"
efficace [efikas] *adj (méthode, remède)* effective; *(personne)* efficient
efficacement [efikasmã] *adv (avec succès)* effectively; *(de façon productive)* efficiently
efficacité [efikasite] *nf (d'une méthode, d'un remède)* effectiveness; *(d'une personne)* efficiency
effigie [efiʒi] *nf* effigy; **à l'e. de qn** bearing the image of sb
effilé, -e [efile] *adj (frange)* ragged; *(doigts)* tapering; *(outil, lame)* tapered; *(amandes)* slivered
effilocher [efiloʃe] **s'effilocher** *vpr* to fray

efflanqué, -e [eflãke] *adj* skinny
effleurement [eflœrmã] *nm* light touch
effleurer [eflœre] *vt (frôler)* to touch lightly; *(accidentellement)* to brush (against); *(surface de l'eau)* to skim; *Fig (sujet)* to touch on; **cette idée ne m'a jamais effleuré** the idea never crossed my mind
effluent [eflyã] *nm* **e. urbain** *(sewage)* effluent; **effluents radioactifs** radioactive waste
effluve [eflyv] *nm* emanation
effondré, -e [efɔdre] *adj (peiné)* grief-stricken; *(déçu)* shattered
effondrement [efɔdrəmã] *nm (d'un bâtiment, d'un mur, d'un toit)* collapse; *Fig (d'un plan)* falling through; *(d'un empire, des prix)* collapse; *(d'une personne)* dejection
effondrer [efɔdre] **s'effondrer** *vpr (bâtiment, mur, toit)* to collapse; *Fig (plan)* to fall through; *(empire, prix)* to collapse; *(personne)* to go to pieces; **s'e. dans un fauteuil** to sink *or* slump into an armchair
efforcer [16] [eforse] **s'efforcer** *vpr* **s'e. de faire qch** to do one's best to do sth
effort [efor] *nm* (a) *(physique, intellectuel)* effort; **allons, encore un (petit) e.** come on, try again; **son médecin lui a interdit tout e.** her doctor has forbidden any exertion; **sans e.** effortlessly; **faire un e. (pour faire qch)** to make an effort (to do sth); **faire des efforts** to make an effort; **faire l'e. de faire qch** to make the effort to do sth; **après l'e., le réconfort** I/you/*etc.* deserve this; **il est partisan du moindre e.** he doesn't believe in exerting himself (b) *Tech* strain, stress
effraction [efraksjɔ] *nf Jur* breaking and entering; **entrer par e.** to break in
effraie [efrɛ] *nf (oiseau)* barn owl
effranger [45] [efrãʒe] **1** *vt* to fray
  2 s'effranger *vpr* to fray
effrayant, -e [efrɛjã, -ãt] *adj* frightening; *(chaleur, appétit)* tremendous
effrayer [53] [efreje] **1** *vt (faire peur à)* to frighten, to scare; *(inquiéter)* to alarm
  2 s'effrayer *vpr* to be frightened (**de** at); **elle s'effraie pour un rien** the least little thing frightens her
effréné, -e [efrene] *adj (passion, luxe)* unbridled; *(galop, course)* frantic
effritement [efritmã] *nm (d'un mur, d'un revêtement)* crumbling; *(de la roche)* weathering; *Fig (de l'autorité, d'une majorité, de fonds)* erosion
effriter [efrite] **1** *vt (pain, fromage)* to crumble; *(roche)* to weather
  2 s'effriter *vpr (mur, revêtement)* to crumble; *(roche)* to weather; *Fig (autorité, majorité, fonds)* to be eroded
effroi [efrwa] *nm Litt* terror, dread
effronté, -e [efrɔte] *adj (personne, manières)* impudent; *(mensonge, menteur)* brazen
effrontément [efrɔtemã] *adv* impudently; *(mentir)* brazenly
effronterie [efrɔtri] *nf (d'une personne, de manières)* impudence; *(d'un mensonge)* brazenness
effroyable [efrwajabl] *adj* dreadful
effroyablement [efrwajabləmã] *adv* dreadfully
effusion [efyzjɔ] *nf* (a) **e. de sang** bloodshed (b) *(exubérance)* effusiveness; **avec e.** effusively
égailler [egaje] **s'égailler** *vpr* to disperse
égal, -e, -aux, -ales [egal, -o] **1** *adj* (a) *(équivalent)* equal (**à** to); **la partie n'est pas égale** they/we/you are not evenly matched; **ils sont de force/d'intelligence égale** they are equally strong/intelligent; **à prix é., tu peux trouver mieux** for the same price, you can find something better (b) *(constant) (respiration, son)* even; *(allure, pouls)* steady; *(sol)* level; *(climat)* equable; **être d'humeur égale** to be even-tempered; **rester é. à soi-même** to be still one's old self (c)

cela m'est é. it's all the same to me; *(cela ne m'intéresse pas)* I don't care

   2 *nm,f* equal; **être l'é. de qn** to be sb's equal; **traiter qn d'é. à é.** to treat sb as an equal; **sans é.** unequaled

également [egalmɑ̃] *adv (aussi)* as well, too

égaler [egale] *vt (personne, score, record)* to equal; **2 et 2 égalent 4** 2 and 2 equal 4

égalisation [egalizasjɔ̃] *nf* **(a)** *(équilibrage)* equalization; *Sport* **(but/point d')é.** equalizer **(b)** *(d'une surface)* leveling

égaliser [egalize] **1** *vt* **(a)** *(salaires, pression)* to equalize; *(cheveux)* to trim **(b)** *(sol)* to level

   2 *vi Sport* to even, to equalize

égalitaire [egalitɛr] *adj* egalitarian

égalité [egalite] *nf* **(a)** *(entre des quantités, des personnes)* equality; *(au tennis)* deuce; **être à é.** *(équipes)* to be tied; **é. des chances** equal opportunities; **é. des salaires** equal pay **(b)** *(constance) (de la respiration, d'un son)* evenness; *(de l'allure, du pouls)* steadiness; *(du sol)* levelness; *(du climat)* equability; **é. d'humeur** even-temperedness

égard [egar] *nm* **(a)** *(respect)* consideration; **par é. pour qn** out of consideration for sb; **égards** *(attentions)* consideration **(b)** *(aspect)* **à cet é.,...** in this respect,...; **je n'ai pas d'opinion à cet é.** I have no opinion on that score; **à certains/tous les égards** in some/all respects **(c)** *(locutions)* **à l'é. de qn** toward sb; **eu é. à** considering

égaré, -e [egare] *adj* **(a)** *(personne, animal)* lost **(b)** *(hagard) (air, regard)* distraught

égarement [egarmɑ̃] *nm* **(a)** *(folie)* distraction **(b)** **égarements** *(dérèglements de conduite)* wild behavior

égarer [egare] **1** *vt (objet)* to mislay; *(personne) (volontairement)* to mislead; *(soupçons)* to avert

   2 s'égarer *vpr* **(a)** *(se perdre) (personne, lettre)* to get lost **(b)** *(sortir du sujet)* to wander from the point

égayer [53] [egeje] **1** *vt (personne)* to cheer up; *(conversation)* to liven up; *(pièce, vêtement)* to brighten up

   2 s'égayer *vpr (s'animer)* to cheer up

Égée [eʒe] *n voir* **mer**

égérie [eʒeri] *nf* muse

égide [eʒid] *nf* **sous l'é. de** under the aegis of

églantier [eglɑ̃tje] *nm* wild rose (bush)

églantine [eglɑ̃tin] *nf* wild rose

églefin [egləfɛ̃] *nm* haddock

église [egliz] *nf* **(a)** *(bâtiment)* church; **aller à l'é.** *(à la messe)* to go to church; **se marier à l'é.** to get married in church, to have a church wedding **(b)** **l'É.** the Church; **l'É. catholique** the Catholic Church; **l'É. anglicane** the Church of England, the Anglican Church

ego [ego] *nm inv* ego

égocentrique [egosɑ̃trik] **1** *adj* self-centered, egocentric

   2 *nmf* self-centered person

égoïsme [egoism] *nm* selfishness, egoism

égoïste [egoist] **1** *adj* selfish, egoistic

   2 *nmf* selfish person, egoist

égorger [45] [egorʒe] *vt* to cut the throat of

égosiller [egozije] **s'égosiller** *vpr (en parlant)* to shout oneself hoarse; *(en chantant)* to sing at the top of one's voice

égout [egu] *nm* sewer

égoutier [egutje] *nm* sewer worker

égoutter [egute] **1** *vt* to drain

   2 *vi* **laisser é. qch** to leave sth to drain

   3 s'égoutter *vpr* to drain

égouttoir [egutwar] *nm* **(a)** *(dans l'évier)* draining board; *(mobile)* drainer **(b)** *(passoire)* colander

égratigner [egratiɲe] **1** *vt* to scratch; *Fig* to have a dig at

   2 s'égratigner *vpr* to scratch oneself; **s'é. la joue** to scratch one's cheek

égratignure [egratiɲyr] *nf* scratch; *Fig* dig

égrener [46] [egrəne] *vt* **(a)** *(maïs, pois)* to shell; *(grappe)* to pick the grapes off **(b)** *Fig* **é. son chapelet** to tell one's beads

égrillard, -e [egrijar, -ard] *adj* bawdy

Égypte [eʒipt] *nf* **l'É.** Egypt

égyptien, -enne [eʒipsjɛ̃, -ɛn] **1** *adj* Egyptian

   2 *nm,f* **É., Égyptienne** Egyptian

eh [e] *exclam* hey!; **eh bien** well; **eh oui!** that's right!

éhonté, -e [eɔ̃te] *adj* shameless

éjaculation [eʒakylasjɔ̃] *nf* ejaculation; **é. précoce** premature ejaculation

éjaculer [eʒakyle] *vi* to ejaculate

éjectable [eʒɛktabl] *adj* **siège é.** ejector seat

éjecter [eʒɛkte] *vt (cartouche, pilote)* to eject; *Fam (expulser)* to throw out (**de** of)

éjection [eʒɛksjɔ̃] *nf (d'une cartouche, du pilote)* ejection; *Fam (expulsion)* throwing out

élaboration [elabɔrasjɔ̃] *nf (d'un plan, d'une idée)* development; *(d'une constitution, d'une loi)* drawing up

élaboré, -e [elabɔre] *adj (technique, machine)* sophisticated; *(plan)* elaborate

élaborer [elabɔre] *vt (plan, idée)* to develop; *(constitution, loi)* to draw up

élagage [elagaʒ] *nm aussi Fig* pruning

élaguer [elage] *vt aussi Fig* to prune

élan¹ [elɑ̃] *nm* **(a)** *(course)* run-up; *(vitesse)* momentum; *Fig (impulsion)* boost; **prendre de l'é.** *ou* **son é.** to take a run-up; **saut sans/avec é.** standing/running jump; *Fig* **d'un seul é.** all in one go; *Fig* **emporté par son é.** carried away **(b)** *(transport) (d'enthousiasme)* burst; *(de tendresse, de passion)* surge **(c)** *(ferveur)* fervor

élan² [elɑ̃] *nm (cerf)* moose

élancé, -e [elɑ̃se] *adj* slim, slender

élancement [elɑ̃smɑ̃] *nm (douleur)* shooting pain

élancer [16] [elɑ̃se] **1** *vi* **la jambe m'élance** I've got shooting pains in my leg

   2 s'élancer *vpr (se précipiter)* to rush forward; *Sport* to take a run-up

élargir [elarʒir] **1** *vt* **(a)** *(route, rue)* to widen; *(vêtement)* to let out; *(trou)* to enlarge **(b)** *Fig (groupe, gamme de produits)* to expand; *(connaissances, débat)* to broaden **(c)** *Jur (prisonnier)* to release

   2 *vi Fam (personne)* to get bigger

   3 s'élargir *vpr* **(a)** *(route, rue)* to widen; *(chaussures, vêtement)* to stretch; *(trou)* to enlarge **(b)** *Fig (groupe, gamme de produits)* to expand; *(connaissances, débat)* to broaden

élargissement [elarʒismɑ̃] *nm* **(a)** *(d'une route, d'une rue)* widening; *(d'un trou)* enlargement **(b)** *Fig (d'un groupe, d'une gamme de produits)* expansion; *(des connaissances, d'un débat)* broadening **(c)** *Jur (d'un prisonnier)* release

élastique [elastik] **1** *adj (corps, matière)* elastic; *Fig (démarche)* springy; *(règlement, principes)* flexible; *(conscience)* accommodating

   2 *nm* **(a)** *(pour la couture)* elastic **(b)** *(de bureau)* rubber band **(c)** *(jeu)* **jouer à l'é.** to play elastics

électeur, -trice [elɛktœr, -tris] *nm,f* voter, elector; **mes électeurs** the people who voted for me

élection [elɛksjɔ̃] *nf* **(a)** *(d'un candidat)* election; **élections législatives** legislative elections *(held every five years)*; **élections municipales** = elections held every six years to elect members of the "Conseil municipal"; **é. présidentielle, élections présidentielles** presidential election(s) **(b)** *(choix)* **mon pays d'é.** my adopted country

---

Élections

All French citizens of eighteen or over are entitled to vote in elections, which take place on a Sunday. Polling places are often set up in local schools. Voters collect leaflets (each corresponding to the different political parties or candidates), go to a booth and put their chosen leaflet into the envelope provided, which is then placed in the ballot box ("l'urne") supervised by an "assesseur", who then utters the words "a voté!". The French electoral system is based on a type of proportional representation, rather than a first-past-the-post system. As from 2002 presidential elections take place every five years. General elections are also held every five years.

électoral, -e, -aux, -ales [elɛktɔral, -o] *adj (campagne, comité, promesses)* election

électorat [elɛktɔra] *nm* voters, electorate; **l'é. communiste/féminin** communist/female voters

électricien, -enne [elɛktrisjɛ̃, -ɛn] *nm,f* electrician

électricité [elɛktrisite] *nf* electricity; *(installation)* wiring; *Fig* **il y a de l'é. dans l'air** the atmosphere is electric; **é. statique** static (electricity)

électrifier [66] [elɛktrifje] *vt (chemin de fer)* to electrify; *(village)* to bring electricity to

électrique [elɛktrik] *adj aussi Fig* electric

électrisant, -e [elɛktrizɑ̃, -ɑ̃t] *adj (exaltant)* electrifying

électriser [elɛktrize] *vt aussi Fig* to electrify

électroaimant [elɛktrɔɛmɑ̃] *nm* electromagnet

électrocardiogramme [elɛktrokardjɔgram] *nm* electrocardiogram

électrochoc [elɛktrɔʃɔk] *nm* electric shock; **traitement par électrochocs** electric-shock treatment; **faire des électrochocs à qn** to give sb electric-shock treatment

électrocuter [elɛktrɔkyte] **1** *vt* to electrocute; **se faire é.** to be electrocuted

2 s'électrocuter *vpr* to electrocute oneself

électrocution [elɛktrokysjɔ̃] *nf* electrocution

électrode [elɛktrɔd] *nf* electrode

électroencéphalogramme [elɛktrɔɑ̃sefalɔgram] *nm* electroencephalogram

électrogène [elɛktrɔʒɛn] *adj* **groupe é.** generating unit

électrolyse [elɛktrɔliz] *nf* electrolysis

électroménager [elɛktrɔmenaʒe] **1** *adj m* **appareils électroménagers** household appliances

2 *nm* household appliances

électron [elɛktrɔ̃] *nm* electron; **é. libre** free electron; *Fig* maverick

électronicien, -enne [elɛktrɔnisjɛ̃, -ɛn] *nm,f* electronics engineer

électronique [elɛktrɔnik] **1** *adj (composant, jeu)* electronic; *(microscope, télescope)* electron; *(industrie)* electronics

2 *nf* electronics *(singulier)*

électrophone [elɛktrɔfɔn] *nm* record player

élégamment [elegamɑ̃] *adv (vêtu, maquillée)* elegantly, smartly

élégance [elegɑ̃s] *nf (d'une personne, d'un restaurant, d'un style)* elegance, smartness; *(d'un geste, d'un comportement)* courtesy; *(d'une méthode, d'une solution)* neatness; **habillé avec é.** elegantly *or* smartly dressed; **savoir perdre avec é.** to be a good loser

élégant, -e [elegɑ̃, -ɑ̃t] *adj (vêtements, restaurant, style)* elegant, smart; *(geste, comportement)* courteous; *(méthode, solution)* neat; **un procédé peu é.** callous behavior

élégie [eleʒi] *nf* elegy

élément [elemɑ̃] *nm* **(a)** *(partie) (d'une structure, d'un problème)* element; *(meuble)* unit; *Ordinat* **é. de menu** menu item **(b)** *(personne)* element; **j'ai de bons éléments dans ma classe** I have some good students in my class **(c)** *(naturel)* element; **les quatre éléments** the four elements; *Fig* **être dans son é.** to be in one's element **(d)** *Chim* element **(e)** *(d'une batterie, d'un accumulateur)* cell

élémentaire [elemɑ̃tɛr] *adj* **(a)** *(de base) (connaissance, cours,*

problème) elementary; *(minimal) (habitation)* basic; **c'est é.!** *(évident)* it's elementary! **(b)** *Chim & Phys* elementary

éléphant [elefɑ̃] *nm* elephant; **é. mâle/femelle** bull/cow elephant; **é. de mer** sea elephant; **é. d'Afrique/d'Asie** African/Indian elephant

éléphanteau, -x [elefɑ̃to] *nm* baby elephant

élevage [elvaʒ] *nm* **(a)** *(production)* breeding; *(d'abeilles, de volaille)* keeping; **faire de l'é.** *(de bétail)* to breed cattle; **é. intensif/en batterie** intensive/factory farming **(b)** *(ferme)* farm; **é. de poulets/de visons** poultry/mink farm

élévateur, -trice [elevatœr, -tris] **1** *adj* **chariot é.** fork-lift truck

2 *nm (appareil)* elevator

élévation [elevasjɔ̃] *nf* **(a)** *(action d'élever) (du niveau d'eau, de la voix, des prix, de la température)* raising; *(d'une statue)* erection; *Rel (de l'hostie)* elevation **(b)** *(dans l'air)* rising (up) **(c)** *(augmentation)* rise **(de** in) **(d)** *Litt (des sentiments)* nobility **(e)** *Archit (projection)* elevation **(f)** *(relief)* rise

élevé, -e [elve] *adj* **(a)** *(haut, important)* high; *(rythme, pouls)* rapid; *Fig (style, esprit)* elevated **(b)** *(éduqué)* **bien/mal é.** well-/ill-mannered; **c'est très mal é. de parler la bouche pleine** it's very bad manners to speak with your mouth full

élève [elɛv] *nmf* student, pupil; **é. infirmière** student nurse; *Mil* **é. officier** cadet

élever¹ [46] [elve] *vt* **(a)** *(éduquer)* to bring up, to raise; **bébé élevé au sein/au biberon** breast-/bottle-fed baby **(b)** *(faire l'élevage de)* to breed; *(abeilles, volaille)* to keep

élever² [elve] **1** *vt* **(a)** *(faire monter) (niveau d'eau, voix, prix, température)* to raise; **é. un nombre au carré/au cube** to square/cube a number; **é. un nombre à la puissance quatre** to raise a number to the power of four **(b)** *(dresser) (monument, statue)* to erect; *(bras, poing, yeux)* to raise; *Fig (objection)* to raise **(c)** *(rehausser) (plafond, plancher)* to raise; **é. qch de 20 cm** ≃ to raise sth by 8 inches **(d)** *(promouvoir)* to promote **(au rang de** to) **(e)** *(édifier) (esprit)* to improve; **é. le débat** to raise the tone of the debate

2 s'élever *vpr* **(a)** *(avec mouvement)* to rise (up); *(cri)* to go up **(b)** *(se dresser) (bâtiment, montagnes)* to stand **(c)** *(monter) (température, prix)* to rise **(d)** *(protester)* **s'é. contre** to rise up against **(e)** **s'é. à** *(atteindre)* to amount to

éleveur, -euse [elvœr, -øz] *nm,f (de bovins)* cattle farmer; **é. de chevaux/chiens** horse/dog breeder; **é. de moutons/poulets** sheep/poultry farmer

elfe [ɛlf] *nm* elf

éligibilité [eliʒibilite] *nf* eligibility

éligible [eliʒibl] *adj* eligible

élimé, -e [elime] *adj* worn, threadbare

élimination [eliminasjɔ̃] *nf* elimination; **procéder par é.** to use a process of elimination

éliminatoire [eliminatwar] *adj* **5 est une note é.** 5 counts as a fail; **il a eu une note é.** he didn't get a passing grade; **(épreuve) é.** qualifying heat

éliminer [elimine] *vt (candidat, suspect, toxines)* to eliminate **(de** from); *Sport (pour faute, dopage)* to disqualify; *(possibilité, théorie)* to rule out; **faites de l'exercice pour é.** do some exercise to clean out your system

élire [44] [elir] *vt* **(a)** *(candidat, représentant)* to elect **(b)** **é. domicile** to take up residence

élision [elizjɔ̃] *nf Ling* elision

élite [elit] *nf* elite; **d'é.** *(personnel)* top; *(régiment)* crack

élitisme [elitism] *nm* elitism

élitiste [elitist] *adj & nmf* elitist

élixir [eliksir] *nm* elixir; **é. d'amour** elixir of love

elle [ɛl] *pron personnel* **(a)** *(sujet) (personne)* she; *(chose, animal)* it; **ton amie viendra-t-e.?** is your friend coming?; **e., e. n'aurait pas levé le petit doigt** SHE wouldn't have raised a finger; **la France, e., a exprimé clairement sa position**

France, for its part, has clearly expressed its position; **si j'étais e., je me méfierais** if I were her, I'd be careful **(b)** *(objet direct) (personne)* her; *(chose)* it; **et e., tu l'oublies?** and what about her, have you forgotten her? **(c)** *(avec préposition) (personne)* her; *(réfléchi)* herself; *(chose, animal)* it; **dis-le-lui, à e.** tell HER; **ce n'est pas à moi, c'est à e.** it's not mine, it's hers; **elle possède une entreprise à e.** she has her own company; *Fam* **une relation à e.** a relation of her; **e. ne pense qu'à e.** she only thinks about herself **(d)** *(dans les comparaisons)* her; **il boit plus qu'e.** he drinks more than she does *or* than her

elle-même [ɛlmɛm] *pron personnel (personne)* herself; *(chose, animal)* itself

elles [ɛl] *pron personnel* **(a)** *(sujet)* they; **nos chambres sont-e. prêtes?** are our rooms ready?; **e., e. seraient déjà parties** THEY would have left by now; **mes filles, e., ont fait des études** my daughters, for their part, have been to college; **si j'étais e., je me méfierais** if I were them, I'd be careful **(b)** *(objet direct)* them; **et e., tu les oublies?** and what about them, have you forgotten them? **(c)** *(avec préposition)* them; *(réfléchi)* themselves; **dis-le-leur, à e.** tell THEM; **cette voiture est à e.** this car is theirs; **e. ont un appartement à e.** they have their own apartment; *Fam* **un parent à e.** a relative of theirs; **e. ne pensent qu'à e.** they only think about themselves **(d)** *(dans les comparaisons)* them; **je mange plus qu'e.** I eat more than they do *or* than them

elles-mêmes [ɛlmɛm] *pron personnel* themselves

ellipse [elips] *nf* **(a)** *Gram* ellipsis **(b)** *(courbe)* ellipse

elliptique [eliptik] *adj* elliptical

élocution [elɔkysjɔ̃] *nf* **(a)** *(diction)* diction **(b)** *Belg Scol (exposé)* talk, presentation

éloge [elɔʒ] *nm* **(a)** *(louange)* praise; **faire l'é. de qn/qch** to praise sb/sth; **digne d'éloges** praiseworthy **(b)** *(discours)* eulogy; **é. funèbre** funeral oration

élogieux, -euse [elɔʒjø, -øz] *adj (discours, article)* complimentary; **parler de qn/qch en termes é.** to speak very highly of sb/sth

éloigné, -e [elwaɲe] *adj (dans l'espace, dans le temps)* distant, remote; *(parent)* distant; **ils sont éloignés d'un kilomètre** ≃ they're half a mile apart; **être é. de qch** to be a long way (away) from sth; **se tenir é. de** to keep away from

éloignement [elwaɲəmɑ̃] *nm* **(a)** *(séparation)* separation; **l'é. est difficile à vivre** being apart is difficult **(b)** *(distance) (dans l'espace, dans le temps)* distance, remoteness

éloigner [elwaɲe] **1** *vt* **(a)** *(dans l'espace) (personne, objet)* to move away (**de** from); *(moustiques)* to keep away; **ce trajet nous éloigne du centre-ville** this route takes us away from the center of town **(b)** *(distraire, détourner) (crainte, pensée)* to dismiss; *(soupçons)* to avert; *(personne) (de son travail, d'une autre personne)* to keep away (**de** from) **2 s'éloigner** *vpr* **(a)** *(s'écarter)* to move away (**de** from); *(partir)* to go away (**de** from); *(orage)* to pass **(b)** *(se distraire, se détourner)* **s'é. de** *(vérité, sujet)* to wander from; *(famille, amis)* to distance oneself from; *(dans un couple)* to grow away from

élongation [elɔ̃gasjɔ̃] *nf* pulled muscle; **se faire une é.** to pull a muscle

éloquence [elɔkɑ̃s] *nf (expressivité)* eloquence

éloquent, -e [elɔkɑ̃, -ɑ̃t] *adj aussi Fig* eloquent; **ces chiffres sont éloquents** these figures speak for themselves

élu, -e [ely] **1** *adj (à un poste)* elected; *Rel* chosen **2** *nm,f* **(a)** *Rel* **les élus** the chosen ones **(b)** *(responsable)* elected representative **(c)** *Hum* **qui est l'heureuse élue?** who's the lucky lady?; **l'é. de son cœur** her beloved

élucider [elyside] *vt* to elucidate

élucubrations [elykybrasjɔ̃] *nfpl Péj* flights of fancy

éluder [elyde] *vt* to evade

Élysée [elize] *nm* **(le palais de) l'É.** the Élysée Palace *(residence of the President of the French Republic)*

> ### Élysée
> This eighteenth-century palace near the Champs-Élysées in Paris is the official residence of the French President. The name is often used to refer to the presidency itself.

émacié, -e [emasje] *adj* emaciated

émail, -aux [emaj, -o] *nm* enamel; *(sur porcelaine)* glaze; **en é.** *(ustensile de cuisine)* enamel

e-mail [imɛl] *(pl* **e-mails)** *nm Ordinat* e-mail; **envoyer un e. à qn** to e-mail sb

émaillé, -e [emaje] *adj* **(a)** *(métal, ustensile de cuisine)* enameled **(b)** *(porcelaine)* glazed **(c)** *Fig* **é. de** *(plein de)* studded with

émanation [emanasjɔ̃] *nf* **émanations** emanations; **émanations toxiques** toxic fumes; *Fig* **être l'é. de qch** to emanate from sth

émancipation [emɑ̃sipasjɔ̃] *nf* emancipation; *Fig (de l'esprit, de la pensée)* liberation

émancipé, -e [emɑ̃sipe] *adj* emancipated

émanciper [emɑ̃sipe] **1** *vt* to emancipate **2 s'émanciper** *vpr* to become emancipated

émaner [emane] **émaner de** *vt ind aussi Fig* to emanate from

émarger [45] [emarʒe] **1** *vi* to draw one's salary **2** *vt (apposer ses initiales sur)* to initial; *(signer)* to sign

émasculation [emaskylasjɔ̃] *nf* emasculation

émasculer [emaskyle] *vt* to emasculate

emballage [ɑ̃balaʒ] *nm* **(a)** *(action)* packing; *(dans du papier)* wrapping; **e. sous vide** vacuum-packing **(b)** *(contenant)* packaging; *(papier)* wrapping

emballé, -e [ɑ̃bale] *adj Fam (enthousiaste)* very excited, enthusiastic (**par** about)

emballer [ɑ̃bale] **1** *vt* **(a)** *(empaqueter)* to pack; *(dans du papier)* to wrap; *(pour la vente)* to package **(b)** *(moteur)* to race **(c)** *Fam (enthousiasmer)* to grab **(d)** *Fam (séduire)* to pick up **2 s'emballer** *vpr* **(a)** *(moteur)* to race; *(cheval)* to bolt **(b)** *Fam (s'enthousiasmer)* to get carried away **(c)** *(cours, monnaie)* to spiral out of control

embarcadère [ɑ̃barkadɛr] *nm* landing stage

embarcation [ɑ̃barkasjɔ̃] *nf* (small) boat

embardée [ɑ̃barde] *nf (d'une voiture)* swerve; *(d'un bateau)* yaw; **faire une e.** *(voiture)* to swerve; *(bateau)* to yaw

embargo [ɑ̃bargo] *nm* embargo; **mettre l'e. sur** to put an embargo on; **lever l'e. sur** to lift the embargo on

embarquement [ɑ̃barkəmɑ̃] *nm (de passagers)* boarding; *(de marchandises)* loading; **e. immédiat porte 5** *(annonce)* now boarding at gate 5

embarquer [ɑ̃barke] **1** *vt* **(a)** *(passagers)* to take on board; *(marchandises)* to load **(b)** *Fam (emporter)* to take (with one) **(c)** *Fam (entraîner) (en week-end, au cinéma)* to take off; *(arrêter)* to catch; **se laisser e. dans** *(affaire, discussion)* to get caught up in **2** *vi (sur un bateau) (monter)* to go on board, to board; *(pour une destination)* to embark **3 s'embarquer** *vpr* **(a)** *(sur un bateau) (monter)* to go on board, to board; *(pour une destination)* to embark **(b)** *Fam Fig* **s'e. dans** *(entreprise, discussion)* to embark on

embarras [ɑ̃bara] *nm* **(a)** *(situation difficile)* **mettre qn dans l'e.** to put sb in an awkward situation; **tirer qn d'e.** to get sb out of an awkward situation; **n'avoir que l'e. du choix** to be spoiled for choice **(b)** *(difficulté financière)* **être dans l'e.** to be in financial difficulties **(c)** *(gêne)* embarrassment **(d)** *(obstacle)* **être un e. pour qn** to be a bother to sb **(e)** *Méd* **e. gastrique** upset stomach

embarrassant, -e [ɑ̃barasɑ̃, -ɑ̃t] *adj* **(a)** *(qui gêne) (question, situation)* embarrassing **(b)** *(qui encombre)* cumbersome

embarrassé, -e [ãbarase] *adj* (**a**) *(gêné)* embarrassed; **je suis très e. de devoir le leur dire** I'm very embarrassed about having to tell them (**b**) *(encombré) (table, pièce)* cluttered (**de** with); **avoir les mains embarrassées** to have one's hands full

embarrasser [ãbarase] **1** *vt* (**a**) *(gêner)* to embarrass (**b**) *(encombrer) (table, pièce)* to clutter up (**de** with); **e. qn** *(vêtement, achats)* to hamper sb; *(empêcher le passage de)* to be in sb's way

2 s'embarrasser *vpr (s'encombrer)* **s'e. de** to burden oneself with; *Fig* **elle ne s'embarrasse pas de douceur** she doesn't worry about being gentle

embauche [ãboʃ] *nf* (**a**) *(action)* taking on, hiring (**b**) *(emploi)* employment

embaucher [ãboʃe] *vt* (**a**) *(engager)* to take on, to hire; **l'entreprise embauche en ce moment** the company is currently recruiting (people) (**b**) *Fam (pour corvée)* to recruit (**pour faire** to do)

embaumer [ãbome] *vt* (**a**) *(corps)* to embalm (**b**) *(répandre une odeur de)* to be fragrant with; **son parfum embaumait la pièce** the scent of her perfume filled the room; **le chèvrefeuille embaumait** there was a fragrant smell of honeysuckle

embaumeur [ãbomœr] *nm (de corps)* embalmer

embellie [ãbeli] *nf (éclaircie)* bright spell; *Naut* calm spell, lull; *Fig (de l'économie, d'une situation, etc.)* improvement; **courte e.** bright interval

embellir [ãbelir] **1** *vt (pièce, parc, personne)* to make more attractive; *Fig (histoire, vérité)* to embellish

2 *vi* to grow more attractive

embellissement [ãbelismã] *nm (d'un lieu)* improvement; *(d'un récit)* embellishment

emberlificoter [ãberlifikɔte] *Fam* **1** *vt* (**a**) *(fil)* to tangle up (**b**) *(duper)* to take in

2 s'emberlificoter *vpr* **s'e. dans** *(vêtements, mensonges)* to get tangled up in

embêtant, -e [ãbɛtã, -ãt] *adj Fam* annoying

embêtement [ãbɛtmã] *nm Fam* problem; **faire des embêtements à qn** to make trouble for sb

embêter [ãbete] *Fam* **1** *vt (contrarier, agacer)* to annoy; *(ennuyer)* to bore

2 s'embêter *vpr (s'ennuyer)* to be bored; *Ironique* **tu ne t'embêtes pas!** you don't do badly for yourself!; **s'e. à faire qch** *(prendre la peine de le faire)* to bother doing sth

emblée [ãble] **d'emblée** *adv* right away, straight away

emblématique [ãblematik] *adj* emblematic; *Fig* symbolic

emblème [ãblɛm] *nm aussi Fig* emblem

embobiner [ãbɔbine] *vt Fam (duper)* to take in

emboîter [ãbwate] **1** *vt (assembler)* to fit together; **e. qch dans qch** to fit sth into sth; **e. le pas à qn** to follow close on sb's heels; *Fig* to follow sb's lead

2 s'emboîter *vpr* to fit together

embolie [ãbɔli] *nf* embolism; **e. gazeuse/pulmonaire** air/pulmonary embolism; **e. cérébrale** clot on the brain, *Spéc* cerebral embolism

embonpoint [ãbɔ̃pwɛ̃] *nm* stoutness; **avoir/prendre de l'e.** to be/to get stout

embouché, -e [ãbuʃe] *adj Fam* **mal e.** *(grossier)* foulmouthed; *(de mauvaise humeur)* in a foul mood

embouchure [ãbuʃyr] *nf* (**a**) *(d'un instrument à vent)* mouthpiece (**b**) *(d'un cours d'eau)* mouth

embourber [ãburbe] **s'embourber** *vpr* (**a**) *(véhicule)* to get stuck in the mud (**b**) *Fig & Péj* to get bogged down

embourgeoisement [ãburʒwazmã] *nm (d'une personne)* attainment of middle-class respectability; *(d'un quartier)* gentrification

embourgeoiser [ãburʒwaze] **s'embourgeoiser** *vpr*

(personne) to become middle-class; *(quartier)* to become gentrified

embout [ãbu] *nm (d'un parapluie, d'une canne)* tip; *(d'un tuyau)* nozzle

embouteillage [ãbuteja3] *nm* traffic jam

embouteiller [ãbuteje] *vt (route)* to clog up

emboutir [ãbutir] *vt* (**a**) *(véhicule)* to crash into (**b**) *(métal)* to stamp

embranchement [ãbrãʃmã] *nm* (**a**) *(croisement)* junction; *(bifurcation) (d'une route)* fork (**b**) *(voie secondaire) (de route)* side road; *(de chemin de fer)* branch line (**c**) *Bot & Zool* sub-kingdom

embraser [ãbraze] *Litt* **1** *vt* (**a**) *(incendier)* to set ablaze (**b**) *(éclairer)* to set aglow (**c**) *Fig (exalter) (foule)* to inflame

2 s'embraser *vpr* (**a**) *(prendre feu)* to blaze up (**b**) *(rougeoyer)* to glow

embrassade [ãbrasad] *nf* embrace, hug

embrasser [ãbrase] **1** *vt* (**a**) *(donner un baiser à)* to kiss (**b**) *(étreindre)* to embrace, to hug; **qui trop embrasse mal étreint** one shouldn't spread oneself too thinly (**c**) *(adopter) (religion, doctrine, cause)* to embrace; *(carrière)* to take up (**d**) *(englober) (sujets, questions)* to embrace, to take in; **e. qch du regard** to take sth in at a glance

2 s'embrasser *vpr* to kiss (each other)

embrasure [ãbrazyr] *nf Constr* aperture; **se tenir dans l'e. de la porte** to stand in the doorway

embrayage [ãbrɛja3] *nm* (**a**) *(mécanisme)* clutch (**b**) *(action)* engaging the clutch

embrayer [53] [ãbreje] *vi* (**a**) *Aut* to engage the clutch (**b**) *Fam (commencer)* to get going (**sur** on)

embrigadement [ãbrigadmã] *nm* dragooning (**dans** into)

embrigader [ãbrigade] *vt* to dragoon (**dans** into)

embringuer [ãbrɛ̃ge] *Fam* **1** *vt* **e. qn dans qch** to get sb mixed up in sth

2 s'embringuer *vpr* **s'e. dans qch** to get mixed up in sth

embrocher [ãbrɔʃe] *vt* (**a**) *Culin (viande)* to put on a spit (**b**) *Fam (transpercer)* **e. qn** to skewer sb

embrouillamini [ãbrujamini] *nm Fam* muddle

embrouillé, -e [ãbruje] *adj* (**a**) *(fils)* tangled (**b**) *Fig (idées, raisonnement, esprit)* muddled; *(affaire)* complicated

embrouiller [ãbruje] **1** *vt* (**a**) *(fils)* to tangle (up) (**b**) *Fig (personne, situation, idées)* to muddle (up)

2 s'embrouiller *vpr (personne, idées)* to get muddled (up)

embroussaillé, -e [ãbrusaje] *adj (allée, jardin)* overgrown; *(cheveux)* messed up

embrumé, -e [ãbryme] *adj (horizon)* hazy; *(esprit)* fuddled

embruns [ãbrœ̃] *nmpl* spray

embryologie [ãbrijɔlɔ3i] *nf* embryology

embryon [ãbrijɔ̃] *nm* embryo

embryonnaire [ãbrijɔnɛr] *adj* embryonic

embûches [ãbyʃ] *nfpl* traps; **semé d'e.** full of pitfalls

embuer [ãbɥe] *vt (miroir, vitre)* to mist up; **yeux embués de larmes** eyes misted over with tears

embuscade [ãbyskad] *nf* ambush; **tendre une e. à qn** to set an ambush for sb; **tomber dans une e.** to be ambushed

embusquer [ãbyske] **s'embusquer** *vpr* (**a**) *(se mettre en embuscade)* to lie in ambush (**b**) *(se faire affecter loin du front)* to get a cushy posting

éméché, -e [emeʃe] *adj Fam* tipsy

émeraude [emrod] **1** *nf (pierre)* emerald

2 *nm & adj inv* emerald green

émergence [emɛrʒãs] *nf (apparition)* emergence

émerger [45] [emɛrʒe] *vi* (**a**) *(apparaître)* to emerge (**de** from) (**b**) *Fam (se lever)* to surface

émeri [emri] *nm* emery; **papier** *ou* **toile é.** emery paper

émérite [emerit] *adj* (**a**) *(expert)* highly skilled (**b**) *(professeur)* emeritus

émerveillement [emɛrvɛjmɑ̃] *nm* wonder

émerveiller [emɛrveje] **1** *vt (enchanter)* to fill with wonder; **être émerveillé par** to marvel at
2 s'émerveiller *vpr* **s'é. de** *ou* **devant** *(s'enchanter de)* to marvel at

émetteur, -trice [emɛtœr, -tris] **1** *adj* (a) *Fin (banque, organisme)* issuing (b) *Rad* **poste é.** transmitter; **station émettrice** transmitting station
2 *nm* transmitter

émettre [47] [emɛtr] **1** *vt* (a) *(cri, rot, soupir)* to give; *(son, lumière)* to give out, to emit; *(fumée, chaleur)* to give off, to emit (b) *Fig (opinion, objection, idée)* to voice (c) *Rad & TV* to transmit, to broadcast (d) *(billets de banque, actions, timbres-poste)* to issue
2 *vi Rad & TV* to transmit, to broadcast

émeu [emø] *nm* emu

émeus, émeut *voir* **émouvoir**

émeute [emøt] *nf* riot

émeutier, -ère [emøtje, -ɛr] *nm,f* rioter

émeuve *etc. voir* **émouvoir**

émietter [emjete] **1** *vt* (a) *(pain)* to crumble (b) *Fig (domaine, empire)* to break up
2 s'émietter *vpr (pain, roche)* to crumble

émigrant, -e [emigrɑ̃, -ɑ̃t] *nm,f* emigrant

émigration [emigrasjɔ̃] *nf* emigration

émigré, -e [emigre] **1** *nm,f* emigrant; *Hist* émigré
2 *adj (travailleur, population)* migrant

émigrer [emigre] *vi* to emigrate

émincer [16] [emɛ̃se] *vt (viande, légumes)* to slice thinly

éminemment [eminamɑ̃] *adv* eminently

éminence [eminɑ̃s] *nf* (a) *(de relief)* hill (b) *Rel* **É.** Eminence; *Fig* **l'é. grise** the éminence grise

éminent, -e [eminɑ̃, -ɑ̃t] *adj (personne)* eminent; **il nous a rendu d'éminents services** he rendered us outstanding service

émir [emir] *nm* emir

émirat [emira] *nm* emirate; **les Émirats arabes unis** the United Arab Emirates

émissaire [emisɛr] *nm (envoyé)* emissary

émission [emisjɔ̃] *nf* (a) *(de son, de substance)* emission (b) *Rad & TV (action)* transmission, broadcasting; *(ce qui est diffusé)* program (c) *(de billets de banque, d'actions, de timbres-poste)* issue

emmagasiner [ɑ̃magazine] *vt (marchandises)* to store; *(électricité, chaleur, connaissances)* to store up

emmailloter [ɑ̃majɔte] *vt (nourrisson)* to swaddle

emmancher [ɑ̃mɑ̃ʃe] **1** *vt* (a) *(outil)* to fit a handle on (b) *(tuyaux)* to fit together; *(pièce)* to fit (**dans** into)
2 s'emmancher *vpr (pièces)* to fit together; *Fam Fig* **bien/mal s'e.** to get off to a good/bad start

emmanchure [ɑ̃mɑ̃ʃyr] *nf* armhole

emmêler [ɑ̃mɛle] **1** *vt (fils, cheveux)* to tangle
2 s'emmêler *vpr (fils, cheveux)* to get tangled; *Fam* **s'e. les pédales** *ou* **les pinceaux** to get all muddled up

emménager [45] [ɑ̃menaʒe] *vi* to move in

emmener [46] [ɑ̃mne] *vt* (a) *(prendre avec soi) (personne)* to take; *(prisonnier)* to take away; *Fam (objet)* to take; **e. qn en voiture** to give sb a ride (b) *(entraîner) (équipier, peloton, sprint)* to lead

emmenthal [emɛ̃tal] *nm* Emmenthal

emmerdant, -e [ɑ̃mɛrdɑ̃, -ɑ̃t] *adj très Fam* (a) *(contrariant, agaçant)* damn annoying (b) *(ennuyeux)* boring as hell

emmerdement [ɑ̃mɛrdəmɑ̃] *nm très Fam* damned nuisance; **avoir des emmerdements** to have a hell of a lot of trouble

emmerder [ɑ̃mɛrde] **1** *vt très Fam* **e. qn** *(contrarier, agacer)* to get on sb's nerves; *(ennuyer)* to bore sb stiff; **je l'emmerde!** to hell with him/her!
2 s'emmerder *vpr très Fam (s'ennuyer)* to be bored stiff; **s'e. à faire qch** *(prendre la peine de le faire)* to bother doing sth;

Ironique **tu ne t'emmerdes pas!** you're not doing badly for yourself!; *(tu as du culot)* you've got a damn nerve!

emmerdeur, -euse [ɑ̃mɛrdœr, -øz] *nm,f très Fam* pain in the ass

emmitoufler [ɑ̃mitufle] **1** *vt* to wrap up (**dans** in)
2 s'emmitoufler *vpr* to wrap oneself up (**dans** in)

emmurer [ɑ̃myre] *vt* to wall up

émoi [emwa] *nm (trouble)* emotion; *(plaisir)* excitement; **être (tout) en é.** *(troublé)* to be in a flutter

émollient, -e [emɔljɑ̃, -ɑ̃t] *adj & nm* emollient

émoluments [emɔlymɑ̃] *nmpl* remuneration

émonder [emɔ̃de] *vt (arbre, texte)* to prune

émoticon [emɔtikɔ̃] *nm Ordinat* smiley, emoticon

émotif, -ive [emɔtif, -iv] **1** *adj* emotional
2 *nm,f* emotional person

émotion [emɔsjɔ̃] *nf* emotion; *(frayeur)* fright; **donner des émotions à qn** to give sb a real fright

émotivité [emotivite] *nf* **être d'une grande é.** to be highly emotional

émoulu, -e [emuly] *adj* **frais é. de l'université** fresh out of college

émoussé, -e [emuse] *adj (pointe, lame)* blunt; *Fig (sentiment, intérêt)* blunted

émoustiller [emustije] *vt* to arouse

émouvant, -e [emuvɑ̃, -ɑ̃t] *adj* moving

émouvoir [31a] [emuvwar] **1** *vt (toucher)* to move, to touch; *(troubler)* to upset
2 s'émouvoir *vpr (être touché)* to be moved *or* touched; **s'é. de qch** *(s'en inquiéter)* to be concerned about sth

empailler [ɑ̃paje] *vt* (a) *(animal)* to stuff (b) **e. une chaise** to bottom a chair with straw

empaler [ɑ̃pale] **1** *vt* to impale
2 s'empaler *vpr* to impale oneself

empaqueter [42] [ɑ̃pakte] *vt* to pack

emparer [ɑ̃pare] **s'emparer** *vpr* **s'e. de** *(lieu, personne, objet)* to seize; *(sujet: sentiment, doute)* to take hold of

empâter [ɑ̃pɑte] **1** *vt* to bloat
2 s'empâter *vpr* to become bloated

empattement [ɑ̃patmɑ̃] *nm* (a) *(d'une voiture)* wheelbase (b) *Typ* serif

empêché, -e [ɑ̃peʃe] *adj (retenu)* held up, detained

empêchement [ɑ̃pɛʃmɑ̃] *nm* hitch; **il a eu un e.** something came up

empêcher [ɑ̃peʃe] **1** *vt (action, événement)* to prevent, to stop; *(mouvement, passage)* to obstruct; **e. qn de faire qch** to prevent *or* stop sb (from) doing sth; *Fam* **ça ne m'empêchera pas de dormir** I won't lose any sleep over it; **il n'y a rien qui t'en empêche** there's nothing stopping you; **cela n'empêche que..., il n'empêche que...,** all the same,...; *Fam* **(il) n'empêche** all the same
2 s'empêcher *vpr* **je ne peux pas m'en e.** I can't help it; **je ne pouvais pas m'e. de rire** I couldn't help laughing

empêcheur, -euse [ɑ̃pɛʃœr, -øz] *nm,f Fam* **e. de tourner en rond** spoilsport

empennage [ɑ̃penaʒ] *nm (de flèche)* feathering, feathers; *(d'avion)* tail section

empereur [ɑ̃prœr] *nm* emperor

empesé, -e [ɑ̃pəze] *adj* (a) *(col, chemise)* starched (b) *Fig (personne, air, style)* stiff

empester [ɑ̃pɛste] **1** *vt (frigo, pièce)* to stink up; **e. l'alcool/le parfum/le fromage** to stink of alcohol/perfume/cheese
2 *vi* to stink

empêtrer [ɑ̃petre] **s'empêtrer** *vpr* to get entangled; **s'e. les pieds dans qch** to get one's feet caught in sth; *Fig* **s'e. dans** *(explications, mensonges)* to get tangled up in; *Fig* **s'e. dans une affaire** to get mixed up in a business; **s'e. de qn** to land oneself with sb

emphase [ãfɑz] *nf* pomposity; **avec e.** pompously

emphatique [ãfatik] *adj* pompous

emphysème [ãfizɛm] *nm* emphysema

empiècement [ãpjɛsmã] *nm (d'un vêtement)* yoke

empiétement [ãpjɛtmã] *nm* encroachment (**sur** on)

empiéter [34] [ãpjete] *vi* **e. sur** *(terrain, horaire, vie privée)* to encroach on

empiffrer [ãpifre] **s'empiffrer** *vpr Fam* to stuff oneself (**de** with)

empiler [ãpile] **1** *vt (livres, bois, boîtes)* to stack, to pile (up)
2 s'empiler *vpr* **(a)** *(livres, dossiers)* to pile up **(b)** *(passagers)* **s'e. dans** to cram into

empire [ãpir] *nm* **(a)** *Hist & Fig* empire; **un e. commercial** a business empire; **pas pour un e.!** not for all the tea in China!; **le premier E., l'E.** the First Empire; **le second E.** the Second Empire; **style/meubles E.** Empire style/furniture; **L'E. du milieu** the Middle Kingdom, the Celestial Empire **(b)** *Litt (influence)* influence; **avoir de l'e. sur qn** to have influence over sb; **faire qch sous l'e. de la boisson/ de la colère** to do sth under the influence of drink/in a fit of anger

empirer [ãpire] *vi* to worsen, to get worse

empirique [ãpirik] *adj* empirical

emplacement [ãplasmã] *nm* **(a)** *(endroit)* site, location; *(sur un marché, dans un parking)* space **(b)** *Ordinat* slot; **e. pour carte d'extension** expansion slot; **e. (pour) périphériques** extension slot

emplafonner [ãplafone] *vt Fam* to crash into

emplâtre [ãplɑtr] *nm* **(a)** *(pansement)* plaster **(b)** *Fam (personne)* drip

emplette [ãplɛt] *nf* purchase; **faire ses emplettes** to go shopping; **faire l'e. de qch** to purchase sth

emplir [ãplir] **1** *vt* to fill (**de** with)
2 s'emplir *vpr* to fill (up) (**de** with)

emploi [ãplwa] *nm* **(a)** *(utilisation)* use; **prêt à l'e.** ready to use; **e. du temps** schedule; **faire double e.** to be redundant; **e. saisonnier** seasonal job **(b)** *(situation)* job; *(embauche)* employment; **être sans e.** to be out of work, to be unemployed; **la crise/situation de l'e.** the employment crisis/situation; *Fig* **il a le physique** *ou* **la tête** *ou Fam* **la gueule de l'e.** he looks the part

emploi-jeunes [ãplwaʒœn] *nm inv* = job, usually in the public sector or in education, created for a young person as part of a program to combat unemployment

employabilité [ãplwajabilite] *nf* employability

employable [ãplwajabl] *adj (personne)* employable; *(objet)* usable

employé, -e [ãplwaje] *nm,f* employee; **e. de banque** bank clerk; **e. de bureau** office worker; **e. de maison** domestic employee

employer [32] [ãplwaje] **1** *vt* **(a)** *(utiliser) (outil, mot, technique, force)* to use; **e. les grands moyens** to take drastic measures; **e. son temps à faire qch** to spend one's time doing sth **(b)** *(faire travailler) (personne)* to employ; **elle l'emploie comme secrétaire** she employs her as a secretary
2 s'employer *vpr* **(a)** *(personne)* **s'e. à faire qch** to work on doing sth; **je m'y emploie** I'm working on it **(b)** *(être utilisé)* to be used

employeur, -euse [ãplwajœr, -øz] *nm,f* employer

empocher [ãpɔʃe] *vt* to pocket

empoignade [ãpwaɲad] *nf Fam* dust-up

empoigne [ãpwaɲ] *nf voir* **foire**

empoigner [ãpwaɲe] **1** *vt* to grab (hold of)
2 s'empoigner *vpr* to have a dust-up

empoisonnant, -e [ãpwazɔnã, -ãt] *adj Fam* irritating

empoisonnement [ãpwazɔnmã] *nm* **(a)** *(par une substance nocive)* poisoning **(b)** *Fam (ennui)* problem

empoisonner [ãpwazone] **1** *vt* **(a)** *(avec une substance nocive) (personne, nourriture, lieu)* to poison; *Fig* **empoisonné** *(paroles)* poisonous **(b)** *(empester) (lieu)* to stink up **(c)** *Fam (irriter)* **e. qn** to get on sb's nerves **(d)** *(altérer) (existence, relations)* to poison; **e. la vie de qn** to make sb's life a misery
2 s'empoisonner *vpr* to poison oneself; **s'e. l'existence** to make one's life a misery

emporté, -e [ãporte] *adj* quick-tempered

emportement [ãpɔrtəmã] *nm* anger

emporte-pièce [ãpɔrtəpjɛs] **1** *nm inv Tech* punch; *Culin* cookie cutter
2 à l'emporte-pièce *adj (jugement, style)* incisive

emporter [ãpɔrte] **1** *vt* **(a)** *(prendre avec soi)* to take; **plats à e.** *ou Suisse* **à l'e.** takeout meals **(b)** *(transporter)* to take away **(c)** *(entraîner) (sujet: courant)* to sweep away; *(sujet: vent)* to blow off; **il a eu une jambe emportée par un obus** a shell took one of his legs off; **e. qn** *(maladie)* to carry sb off; **e. la bouche** *ou Fam* **la gueule** *(moutarde, plat épicé)* to take the roof of your mouth off; *Fig* **se laisser e. par la colère/son imagination** to let one's anger/one's imagination get the better of one **(d)** *(conquérir) (position)* to take **(e)** **l'e.** *(gagner)* to win; *(prédominer)* to prevail; **l'e. sur qn** to beat sb; **l'e. sur qch** to prevail over sth
2 s'emporter *vpr* to lose one's temper (**contre qn** with sb)

empoté, -e [ãpɔte] *Fam* **1** *adj* clumsy
2 *nm,f* clumsy idiot

empourprer [ãpurpre] **1** *vt* to tinge with crimson
2 s'empourprer *vpr* to turn crimson

empoussiéré, -e [ãpusjere] *adj* dusty

empreinte [ãprɛ̃t] *nf* **(a)** *(trace) (de pas)* footprint; *(d'animal)* track; **e. digitale** fingerprint; **e. génétique** genetic fingerprint **(b)** *Fig (de l'éducation, du milieu)* stamp, mark

empressé, -e [ãprese] **1** *adj (prévenant)* attentive
2 *nm,f Péj* **faire l'e. auprès de qn** to dance attendance on sb

empressement [ãprɛsmã] *nm* **(a)** *(prévenance)* attentiveness **(b)** *(hâte)* eagerness (**à faire qch** to do sth); **il montre peu d'e. à faire les travaux** he doesn't seem very eager to do the work; **avec e.** eagerly; **mettre beaucoup d'e. à faire qch** to hasten to do sth

empresser [ãprese] **s'empresser** *vpr* **(a)** *(se dépêcher)* **s'e. de faire qch** to hasten to do sth **(b)** *(être prévenant)* **s'e. auprès de qn** to be attentive to sb

emprise [ãpriz] *nf* hold (**sur** over); **avoir de l'e. sur qn** to have a hold over sb; **sous l'e. de la colère** in a fit of anger

emprisonnement [ãprizɔnmã] *nm* imprisonment; **peine d'e.** prison sentence

emprisonner [ãprizone] *vt* to imprison

emprunt [ãprœ̃] *nm* **(a)** *(action)* borrowing **(b)** *(somme)* loan; **faire un e.** *(auprès d'une banque)* to take out a loan; **e. d'État** government loan; **lancer un e.** to issue a bond **(c)** *Ling* borrowing

emprunté, -e [ãprœ̃te] **1** *pp voir* **emprunter**
2 *adj* self-conscious, awkward

emprunter [ãprœ̃te] *vt* **(a)** *(objet, argent)* to borrow (**à** from) **(b)** *(route, chemin)* to take

emprunteur, -euse [ãprœ̃tœr, -øz] *nm,f* borrower

empuantir [ãpɥãtir] *vt (lieu)* to stink up

ému, -e [emy] **1** *pp voir* **émouvoir**
2 *adj (touché)* moved, touched; *(intimidé)* nervous; **voix émue** voice filled with emotion; **garder un souvenir é. de qch** to have fond memories of sth

émulation [emylasjɔ̃] *nf aussi Ordinat* emulation

émule [emyl] *nmf* emulator; **j'ai fait des émules** people followed my example

émuler [emyle] *vt Ordinat* to emulate

émulsifiant [emylsifjã] *nm* emulsifier

émulsion [emylsjɔ̃] *nf* emulsion

en¹ [ã] *prép* (**a**) *(indique la date ou la durée)* in; **en 1800** in 1800; **en hiver/été** in winter/summer; **en une minute/trois jours** in a minute/three days

(**b**) *(indique la destination)* to; **aller en Allemagne** to go to Germany; **partir en vacances** to go on vacation

(**c**) *(indique le lieu)* in; **vivre en France** to live in France; **en altitude** at altitude; **se promener en forêt** to walk in the forest; **en pleine mer** out at sea; **il y a quelque chose en lui qui me déplaît** there's something about him I don't like

(**d**) *(indique le moyen)* by; **en voiture/avion/train** by car/plane/train

(**e**) *(décrit un état)* in; **écrit en français** written in French; **en ruines** ruined; **être en colère/en larmes** to be angry/crying; **être en transe/en danger** to be in a trance/in danger; **être en arrêt maladie** to be on sick leave; **en trois parties** in three parts; **montre en or/en argent** gold/silver watch; **disponible en rouge/38** available in red/in size 38; **être bon en physique** to be good at physics; **payer en euros** to pay in euros; **la même chose en mieux/en moins bien** the same thing but better/but not as good

(**f**) *(indique une transformation, une progression)* into; **traduire qch en français** to translate sth into French; **transformer une chambre en bureau** to convert a bedroom into an office; **casser qch en deux** to break sth in two *or* in half; **peindre qch en rouge** to paint sth red; **réduire qch en poudre** to reduce sth to a powder; **se mettre en colère** to get angry; **aller de ville en ville** to go from town to town; **de jour en jour** by the day; **changer en bien/mal** to change for the better/for the worse

(**g**) *(en tant que)* as; **parler à qn en ami** to speak to sb as a friend; **parler en connaisseur** to speak as an expert; **agir en traître** to be disloyal

(**h**) *(avec un participe présent)* **entrer en criant** to come in shouting; **il s'est coupé en se rasant** he cut himself shaving; **c'est impoli de lire en mangeant** it's rude to read while you're eating; **traverser en courant** to run across; **répondre en maugréant** to grumble in reply; **dire qch en plaisantant** to say sth as a joke; **elle s'est cassé la jambe en tombant** she fell and broke her leg; **c'est en s'entraînant qu'il s'améliorera** he'll only get better if he practices

en² [ã] *pron* (**a**) *(avec les adjectifs construits avec de)* **il en est bien capable** he's quite capable of it; **et ta voiture? – j'en suis très content** how's your car? – I'm very pleased with it

(**b**) *(avec les verbes construits avec de)* **qu'en penses-tu?** what do you think of it?; **je ne m'en souviens plus** I can't remember; **on en reparlera** we'll talk about it later; **j'espère en tirer 200 euros** I hope to get 200 euros for it

(**c**) *(remplace le complément du nom)* **nous en avons la possibilité** we can do it; **elle en a mangé un morceau** she ate a piece of it; **j'en ai acheté un kilo** ≃ I bought two pounds

(**d**) *(remplace le nom)* **il y en a plusieurs** there are several of them; **elle en a cassé deux** she broke two of them; **est-ce que tu en veux?** do you want some?; **je n'en ai jamais vu** I've never seen one/any; **est-ce de l'or? – non, ce n'en est pas** is it gold? – no, it's not

(**e**) *(indique la cause)* **il en a perdu la raison** it made him lose his mind; **j'en suis tout retourné** I'm really upset about it

(**f**) *Fam (pour insister)* **il en a fait une histoire!** he made a real song and dance about it; **des balayeurs, il en faut** someone has to sweep the streets

(**g**) *(indique la provenance)* from there; **justement, j'en viens** I've just come from there

ENA [ena] *nf (abrév* **École nationale d'administration***)* = university-level college preparing students for senior posts in law and economics

enamouré, -e [ãnamure], **énamouré, -e** [enamure] *adj Vieilli ou Hum* amorous

enamourer [ãnamure], **énamourer** [enamure] **s'enamourer** *vpr* **s'e. de** to become enamored of

énarque [enark] *nmf* = graduate of the ENA

encabaner [ãkabane] **s'encabaner** *vpr Can* to shut oneself away

encadré [ãkadre] *nm (dans un texte)* box; *Ordinat* **e. graphique** graphics box; *Ordinat* **e. texte** text box

encadrement [ãkadrəmã] *nm* (**a**) *(cadre)* frame; **dans l'e. de la porte** in the doorway (**b**) *(fonction) (de personnel)* management; *(d'élèves, d'enfants)* supervision; *(personnes qui encadrent) (du personnel)* management; *Mil* officers (**c**) *Écon* **e. du crédit** credit squeeze

encadrer [ãkadre] *vt* (**a**) *(tableau, photo)* to frame (**b**) *(entourer) (mots, paragraphe)* to circle; **encadré par deux gendarmes** flanked by two policemen (**c**) *(guider) (personnel, équipe)* to manage; *(enfants, handicapés)* to supervise; *Mil (soldats)* to officer (**d**) *Fam (supporter)* **je ne peux pas l'e.** I can't stand him/her

encadreur, -euse [ãkadrœr, -øz] *nm,f* picture framer

encaissé, -e [ãkese] *adj (vallée)* deep; *(rivière)* with steep sides; *(route)* cut into the hillside

encaissement [ãkɛsmã] *nm* (**a**) *(d'un chèque)* cashing; *(d'argent)* collection (**b**) *(d'une vallée)* depth

encaisser [ãkese] *vt* (**a**) *(chèque)* to cash; *(argent)* to collect (**b**) *Fam (supporter) (coups, critiques)* to take; **je ne peux pas l'e.** I can't stand him/her; **il sait e.** he can take it; **qu'est-ce qu'il a encaissé!** he took a lot of punishment!

encanailler [ãkanaje] **s'encanailler** *vpr* to slum it

encart [ãkar] *nm (feuille)* insert; **e. publicitaire** advertising insert

en-cas [ãka] *nm inv* snack

encastrable [ãkastrabl] *adj (machine à laver, cuisinière)* that can be built in

encastré, -e [ãkastre] *adj* built-in

encastrer [ãkastre] **1** *vt* to build in

2 s'encastrer *vpr (éléments)* to fit together; *(machine à laver, cuisinière)* to fit (**dans** into); **la voiture s'est encastrée sous un camion** the car embedded itself under a truck

encaustique [ãkɔstik] *nf* wax, polish

enceinte¹ [ãsɛ̃t] *nf* (**a**) *(mur)* (surrounding) wall; *(palissade)* fence (**b**) *(espace)* enclosure; *(d'église, de couvent)* precinct(s); **dans l'e. du parc** within the park (**c**) *(baffle)* **e. (acoustique)** speaker

enceinte² [ãsɛ̃t] *adj f* pregnant; **e. de cinq mois** five months pregnant; **être e. de jumeaux** to be expecting twins; **elle est e. de Marc** she's pregnant by Marc

encens [ãsã] *nm* incense

encenser [ãsãse] *vt* **e. qn** to praise sb to the skies

encensoir [ãsãswar] *nm* censer

encéphalite [ãsefalit] *nf* encephalitis; **e. bovine spongiforme** bovine spongiform encephalopathy

encéphalogramme [ãsefalɔgram] *nm* encephalogram

encercler [ãsɛrkle] *vt* (**a**) *(ennemi, lieu)* to encircle, to surround (**b**) *(mot)* to circle, to ring

enchaînement [ãʃɛnmã] *nm* (**a**) *(série) (d'événements, de circonstances)* series, chain (**b**) *(liaison) (d'idées, de séquences)* linking (**c**) *(en danse)* sequence (of steps); *(en ballet)* enchaînement (**d**) *Ordinat* concatenation

enchaîner [ãʃene] **1** *vt* (**a**) *(animal, prisonnier)* to chain up; *Fig (peuple)* to enslave; *(presse)* to curb; **e. qn à** to chain sb (up) to (**b**) *(lier) (épisodes, séquences)* to link (up)

2 *vi* to move on; **e. sur un sujet** to move on to a subject

3 s'enchaîner *vpr* (**a**) *(personne)* **s'e. à** to chain oneself (up) to (**b**) *(séquences, épisodes)* to be linked together; **les événements se sont enchaînés rapidement** events happened very quickly

enchanté, -e [ãʃãte] *adj* (**a**) *(ravi)* delighted (**de** with); **e.**

(de faire votre connaissance)! pleased to meet you! **(b)** *(magique)* enchanted

enchantement [ãʃãtmã] *nm* **(a)** *(sortilège)* (magic) spell; **comme par e.** as if by magic **(b)** *(ravissement, merveille)* delight

enchanter [ãʃãte] *vt* **(a)** *(ravir)* to delight; **cette idée ne l'enchante pas** he's/she's not keen on the idea **(b)** *(ensorceler)* to bewitch

enchanteur, -eresse [ãʃãtœr, -trɛs] **1** *adj (sourire)* bewitching; *(spectacle, endroit)* enchanting, delightful

2 *nm* **(a)** *(sorcier)* sorcerer **(b)** *Fig (charmeur)* charmer

3 *nf* **enchanteresse** sorceress

enchâsser [ãʃase] *vt* **(a)** *(bijou)* to set **(b)** *(relique)* to enshrine

enchère [ãʃɛr] *nf* bid; **les enchères** the bidding; **vente aux enchères** auction; **faire monter les enchères** to up the bidding; *Fig* to raise the stakes; **vendre qch aux enchères** to sell sth at auction

enchérir [ãʃerir] *vi* to make a higher bid; **e. sur qn** to outbid sb; *Fig* to go one better than sb

enchevêtré, -e [ãʃəvetre] *adj (branchages, fils, explications)* tangled

enchevêtrement [ãʃəvɛtrəmã] *nm (de fils, branchages)* tangle

enchevêtrer [ãʃəvetre] **1** *vt (fils, branchages)* to tangle (up)

2 s'enchevêtrer *vpr (fils)* to get tangled (up)

enclave [ãklav] *nf* enclave

enclenchement [ãklãʃmã] *nm (d'une vitesse, d'un mécanisme)* engaging

enclencher [ãklãʃe] **1** *vt (vitesse, mécanisme)* to engage; *Fig (processus)* to get under way

2 s'enclencher *vpr (vitesse, mécanisme)* to engage; *Fig (processus)* to get under way

enclin, -e [ãklɛ̃, -in] *adj* **être e. à faire qch** to be inclined to do sth; **être e. à la paresse/la méfiance** to be inclined to be lazy/distrustful; **il est peu e. à partager ses secrets** he is reluctant to share his secrets; **peu e. au bavardage** not very talkative

enclos [ãklo] *nm (espace)* enclosure; *(pour chevaux)* paddock

enclume [ãklym] *nf* anvil; *Fig* **être entre le l'e. et marteau** to be between the devil and the deep blue sea

encoche [ãkɔʃ] *nf* notch; *Ordinat* **e. de protection contre l'écriture** write-protect notch

encodage [ãkɔdaʒ] *nm Ling & Ordinat* encoding

encoder [ãkɔde] *vt Ling & Ordinat* to encode

encoignure [ãkwaɲyr] *nf* **(a)** *(d'une pièce)* corner **(b)** *(meuble)* corner cupboard

encoller [ãkɔle] *vt (papier peint)* to paste

encolure [ãkɔlyr] *nf* **(a)** *(d'animal)* neck; **gagner d'une e.** to win by a neck **(b)** *(tour de cou)* collar size **(c)** *(d'un vêtement)* neck

encombrant, -e [ãkɔ̃brã, -ãt] *adj (meuble, valise, paquet)* cumbersome, bulky; *Fig (personne, témoin)* undesirable

encombre [ãkɔ̃br] *nm* **sans e.** without mishap

encombrement [ãkɔ̃brəmã] *nm* **(a)** *(état) (d'une pièce)* clutter; *(de lignes téléphoniques)* jamming; *(embouteillage)* traffic jam **(b)** *(volume) (d'un objet)* (overall) dimensions **(c)** *Ordinat* **faible e. sur le disque dur** low use of hard disk space

encombrer [ãkɔ̃bre] **1** *vt (pièce)* to clutter (up); *(passage, route)* to block; *(lignes téléphoniques)* to jam; **tu m'encombres, sors d'ici!** you're getting in my hair, get out!

2 s'encombrer *vpr* **s'e. de** *(colis, équipement)* to load oneself down with; *Fig (obligations, personne)* to saddle oneself with; **elle ne s'encombre pas de scrupules** she is quite unscrupulous

encontre [ãkɔ̃tr] **à l'encontre de** *prép* **aller à l'e. de** to go against

encorbellement [ãkɔrbɛlmã] *nm* corbeled structure; *(d'un étage supérieur)* overhang

encorder [ãkɔrde] **s'encorder** *vpr* to rope up

encore [ãkɔr] *adv* **(a)** *(toujours)* still; **pas e.** not yet; **elle n'est pas e. arrivée** she hasn't arrived yet; **je n'avais e. jamais vu ça** I'd never seen that before; **qu'il m'appelle par mon prénom, passe e., mais...** his calling me by my first name is one thing, but...; **e. heureux que les enfants n'aient pas été là!** it's just as well the children weren't there!

(b) *(davantage)* more; **en voulez-vous e.?** would you like some more?; **e. une tasse de café** another cup of coffee; **e. trois mois** three more months, another three months; **e. plus/moins** even more/less; **e. plus froid** even colder; **c'est e. pire/mieux** it's even worse/better; **mais e.?** and apart from that?

(c) *(de nouveau)* again; **il a e. cassé un verre** he's broken another glass; **qu'est-ce qu'il a e. fait?** what's he done this time?; **quoi e.?** now what?; **et puis quoi e.?** is that all?; **e. une fois** once more, once again; **e. vous!** you again!

(d) *(restrictif)* **si e....** if only...; **il vous en donnera dix euros, e.!** he'll give you ten euros for it, if that!; **e. ça, ce n'est même pas sûr** even then, it's not certain; **e. faudrait-il qu'elle accepte/qu'il le sache!** she has to agree/he has to know about it first!

(e) *(seulement)* only; **hier e. elle me disait que...** only yesterday she was telling me that...

(f) **e. que** although, even though

encorner [ãkɔrne] *vt* to gore

encoubler [ãkuble] **s'encoubler** *vpr Suisse* to trip over

encourageant, -e [ãkuraʒã, -ãt] *adj* encouraging

encouragement [ãkuraʒmã] *nm* encouragement; **des encouragements** encouragement

encourager [45] [ãkuraʒe] *vt* **(a)** *(personne)* to encourage; *(athlète, équipe)* to cheer on; **e. qn à faire qch** to encourage sb to do sth **(b)** *(promouvoir) (arts)* to encourage

encourir [22] [ãkurir] *vt* to incur

encrasser [ãkrase] **1** *vt (vêtements, mains)* to dirty; *Aut (bougie)* to soot up; *(moteur)* to clog

2 s'encrasser *vpr* to get dirty; *Aut (bougie)* to soot up; *(moteur)* to get clogged

encre [ãkr] *nf* ink; *Fig* **nuit d'e.** inky black night; **e. de Chine** Indian ink; **e. sympathique** invisible ink

encrier [ãkrije] *nm* inkpot; *(de pupitre)* inkwell

encroûter [ãkrute] **s'encroûter** *vpr Fam (personne)* to get into a rut

encrypter [3] [ãkripte] *vt Ordinat (données)* to encrypt

enculé, -e [ãkyle] *nm,f Vulg* asshole

enculer [ãkyle] *vt Vulg* to bugger; **va te faire e.!** fuck off!; *Fig* **e. les mouches** to nitpick

encyclique [ãsiklik] *nf Rel* encyclical

encyclopédie [ãsiklɔpedi] *nf* encyclopedia

encyclopédique [ãsiklɔpedik] *adj* encyclopedic

endémie [ãdemi] *nf* endemic disease

endémique [ãdemik] *adj* endemic

endetté, -e [ãdɛte] *adj* in debt; **très e.** heavily in debt

endettement [ãdɛtmã] *nm* debt

endetter [ãdɛte] **1** *vt* **e. qn** to get sb into debt

2 s'endetter *vpr* to get into debt

endeuiller [ãdœje] *vt (famille, nation)* to plunge into mourning; *(événement)* to cast a gloom over

endiablé, -e [ãdjable] *adj (personne, musique, rythme)* wild

endiguer [ãdige] *vt* **(a)** *(cours d'eau)* to dike (up) **(b)** *Fig (révolte, inflation, chômage)* to contain

endimanché, -e [ãdimãʃe] *adj* in one's Sunday best

endive [ãdiv] *nf* endive

endocrine [ãdɔkrin] *adj (glande)* endocrine

endoctrinement [ãdɔktrinmã] *nm* indoctrination

endoctriner [ãdɔktrine] *vt* to indoctrinate

endogène [ãdɔʒɛn] *adj Biol & Géol* endogenous

endolori, -e [ãdɔlɔri] *adj* painful

endommager [45] [ɑ̃dɔmaʒe] *vt* (**a**) *(abîmer)* to damage (**b**) *Ordinat* to corrupt

endormi, -e [ɑ̃dɔrmi] **1** *adj* (**a**) *(qui dort) (personne)* sleeping; *(voix, village)* sleepy; **être e.** *(personne)* to be asleep *or* sleeping; **avoir l'air e.** to look sleepy (**b**) *(inerte, lent) (personne)* sluggish (**c**) *Fig (passion, intérêt)* dormant
2 *nm,f (personne inerte, lente)* slowpoke

endormir [29] [ɑ̃dɔrmir] **1** *vt* **a. e. qn** *(bébé)* to send sb to sleep; *(anesthésier)* to put sb to sleep; *(ennuyer)* to send sb to sleep (**b**) *(apaiser) (douleur)* to deaden; **e. les soupçons** to allay suspicion (**c**) *(mettre en confiance) (électeurs, public)* to lull into a false sense of security
2 s'endormir *vpr* to fall asleep, to go to sleep

endossable [ɑ̃dosabl] *adj (chèque)* endorsable

endossement [ɑ̃dosmɑ̃] *nm (d'un chèque)* endorsement

endosser [ɑ̃dose] *vt* (**a**) *(vêtement)* to put on (**b**) *(responsabilité)* to assume (**c**) *(chèque)* to endorse

endroit [ɑ̃drwa] *nm* (**a**) *(lieu)* place, spot; **à quel e.?** where?; **c'est à cet e. que...** this is where...; **par endroits** here and there, in places (**b**) *(d'un vêtement)* right side; **à l'e.** the right way around (**c**) *Litt* **à l'e. de** *(personne)* toward; *(événement, objet)* with regard to

enduire [18] [ɑ̃dɥir] **1** *vt* to coat, to cover (**de** with)
2 s'enduire *vpr* **s'e. de** to cover oneself with

enduit [ɑ̃dɥi] *nm* coating; *(pour boucher)* filler

endurance [ɑ̃dyrɑ̃s] *nf* (**a**) *(physique)* stamina (**b**) *Sport* **épreuve/course d'e.** endurance test/race

endurant, -e [ɑ̃dyrɑ̃, -ɑ̃t] *adj* tough

endurci, -e [ɑ̃dyrsi] *adj* (**a**) *(dur) (personne)* hard (**b**) *(invétéré) (criminel)* hardened; *(célibataire)* confirmed

endurcir [ɑ̃dyrsir] **1** *vt* (**a**) *(moralement)* to harden (**b**) *(physiquement)* to toughen (up)
2 s'endurcir *vpr* (**a**) *(moralement)* to become hard (**b**) *(physiquement)* to toughen up

endurer [ɑ̃dyre] *vt* to endure, to bear

enduro [ɑ̃dyro] *nm Sport* enduro

énergétique [enɛrʒetik] *adj* (**a**) *(nourriture)* energy-giving (**b**) *(ressources, besoins)* energy

énergie [enɛrʒi] *nf* (**a**) *(dynamisme)* energy; **mettre toute son é. à qch/à faire qch** to devote all one's energy to sth/to doing sth; **avec é.** *(nier)* strongly; *(refuser, répondre)* forcefully; **sans é.** *(enfant)* listless; *(jouer)* listlessly (**b**) *(force)* energy, power; **é. hydroélectrique** hydroelectric power; **é. nucléaire** *ou* **atomique** nuclear power; **é. solaire** solar power *or* energy

énergique [enɛrʒik] *adj* (**a**) *(personne)* energetic, dynamic; *(geste)* brisk; *(visage)* strong (**b**) *(mesures)* strong; *(remède)* powerful

énergiquement [enɛrʒikmɑ̃] *adv (nier)* strongly; *(refuser)* forcefully; **serrer é. la main à qn** to shake sb's hand warmly

énergumène [enɛrɡymɛn] *nmf* eccentric

énervant, -e [enɛrvɑ̃, -ɑ̃t] *adj* irritating

énervé, -e [enɛrve] *adj (agacé)* irritated; *(excité)* edgy, agitated

énervement [enɛrvəmɑ̃] *nm (agacement)* irritation; *(excitation)* agitation

énerver [enɛrve] **1** *vt* **é. qn** *(agacer)* to get on sb's nerves, to irritate sb; *(exciter)* to make sb nervous
2 s'énerver *vpr* to get worked up

enfance [ɑ̃fɑ̃s] *nf (jeunesse)* childhood; *(de garçon)* boyhood; *(de fille)* girlhood; **la petite e.** early childhood; *Fam* **c'est l'e. de l'art** it's child's play

enfant [ɑ̃fɑ̃] *nmf* child; **faire l'e.** to act like a child; **je l'ai connu e.** I knew him when he was a child; **il lui a fait un e.** she had a child by him; **viens ici, mon e.** come here, my child; *Fam* **salut, les enfants!** hi, guys!; *Fam* **il n'y a plus d'enfants!** honestly, kids nowadays!; **e. en bas âge** infant; **e. bleu** blue baby; *Rel* **e. de chœur** altar boy; *Fig* **ce n'est pas**

un e. de chœur he's no angel; **e. terrible** enfant terrible; **e. trouvé** foundling; **e.unique** only child

enfantement [ɑ̃fɑ̃tmɑ̃] *nm Litt* childbirth

enfanter [ɑ̃fɑ̃te] *vt Litt* to give birth to

enfantillages [ɑ̃fɑ̃tijaʒ] *nmpl* childish behavior; **faire des e.** to be childish

enfantin, -e [ɑ̃fɑ̃tɛ̃, -in] *adj (voix)* child's; *(littérature)* children's; *(très facile)* childishly simple; *Péj (remarque, conduite)* childish

enfarger [45] [ɑ̃farʒe] *vi Can* to trip

enfariné, -e [ɑ̃farine] *adj (visage, cheveux)* covered with flour; *Fam* **arriver la gueule enfarinée** to arrive blithely ignorant of the facts

enfer [ɑ̃fɛr] *nm aussi Fig* **l'e.** hell; **aller à un train d'e.** to go like a bat out of hell; *Fig* **elle a vécu un véritable e.** she's been through sheer hell; *Fam* **c'est l'e. pour se garer ici** it's hell trying to park here; *Fam* **une soirée d'e.** one hell of a party; **l'e. est pavé de bonnes intentions** the road to hell is paved with good intentions

enfermement [ɑ̃fɛrməmɑ̃] *nm* imprisonment

enfermer [ɑ̃fɛrme] **1** *vt (personne, chose)* to shut up; **e. qn/qch à clef** to lock sb/sth up; **je suis enfermé toute la journée** I'm cooped up all day; *Fam* **elle est bonne à e.** she should be locked up
2 s'enfermer *vpr* to shut oneself up; **s'e. à clef** to lock oneself in; *Fig* **s'e. dans le silence** to retreat into silence

enferrer [ɑ̃fere] **s'enferrer** *vpr Fig* to get tangled up (**dans** in)

enfiévré, -e [ɑ̃fjevre] *adj (front, imagination)* fevered

enfiévrer [34] [ɑ̃fjevre] **1** *vt (personne, imagination)* to excite
2 s'enfiévrer *vpr* to get excited

enfilade [ɑ̃filad] *nf (de portes, de pièces)* series; **être en e.** to be adjoining

enfiler [ɑ̃file] **1** *vt* (**a**) *(aiguille, perles)* to thread (**b**) *(vêtements)* to slip on
2 s'enfiler *vpr* (**a**) *(gants, bottes)* to go on (**b**) *Fam (boisson, nourriture)* to put away

enfin [ɑ̃fɛ̃] *adv* (**a**) *(en dernier lieu)* finally, lastly (**b**) *(à la fin)* at last, finally (**c**) *(de résignation)* **e., n'en parlons plus!** look, let's forget about it!; **e., ce qui est fait est fait!** what's done is done! (**d**) *(d'exaspération)* **e. quoi, tu n'as plus dix ans!** for God's sake, you're not ten any more!; **mais e., je te l'avais dit!** but I told you, for God's sake! (**e**) *(d'hésitation, pour résumer)* well; **e., je ne dis pas non, mais...** well, I'm not saying no, but...; **elle n'est pas mal, e. pour son âge** she's not bad, for her age that is; **e. (bref), c'était la panique!** in short, it was panic!

enflammé, -e [ɑ̃flame] *adj* (**a**) *(brindille, torche, allumette)* burning (**b**) *(joues) (de froid)* glowing; *(de fièvre, de gêne)* burning (**c**) *Fig (discours)* fiery, passionate

enflammer [ɑ̃flame] **1** *vt* (**a**) *(mettre le feu à)* to set light to; *(allumette)* to strike (**b**) *Fig (imagination)* to stir; **la colère enflammait son regard** her eyes were blazing with anger
2 s'enflammer *vpr* (**a**) *(prendre feu)* to catch fire (**b**) *Fig (imagination)* to be stirred

enflé, -e [ɑ̃fle] *adj (rivière, membre)* swollen

enfler [ɑ̃fle] **1** *vt* (**a**) *(rivière, membre)* to swell; **e. les joues** to puff out one's cheeks (**b**) *Fig (exagérer) (histoire, succès)* to exaggerate
2 *vi (membre)* to swell (up)

enflure [ɑ̃flyr] *nf* (**a**) *(d'un membre)* swelling (**b**) *très Fam (imbécile)* jerk

enfoiré, -e [ɑ̃fware] *nm,f Vulg* son of a bitch, bastard

enfoncé, -e [ɑ̃fɔ̃se] *adj (yeux)* deep-set

enfoncement [ɑ̃fɔ̃smɑ̃] *nm (dans le sol)* dip; *(dans un mur)* recess

enfoncer [16] [ɑ̃fɔ̃se] **1** *vt* (**a**) *(clou)* to bang in; *(pieu)* to drive in; *(aiguille)* to stick in, to push in; **e. un couteau dans qch** to stick a knife into sth; **e. la main dans sa poche** to thrust one's hand into one's pocket; **e. son chapeau sur sa tête** to jam one's hat on one's head (**b**) *(porte)* to break down (**c**) *Fam (personne)* to humiliate

2 s'enfoncer *vpr (clou, couteau)* to go in; *(bateau)* to sink; **s'e. dans son fauteuil** to sink into one's armchair; **s'e. dans un bois** to go into the depths of a wood; *Fam* **enfonce-toi ça dans le crâne!** can't you get that into your thick head?

enfouir [ɑ̃fwir] **1** *vt* to bury (**dans/sous** in/under)

2 s'enfouir *vpr* to bury oneself

enfourcher [ɑ̃furʃe] *vt (cheval, vélo)* to get on, to mount

enfourner [ɑ̃furne] *vt (pain)* to put in the oven; *(poteries, briques)* to put in the kiln; *Fam (manger)* to stuff down

enfreindre [54] [ɑ̃frɛ̃dr] *vt* to infringe, to break

enfuir [38] [ɑ̃fɥir] **s'enfuir** *vpr* to run away (**de** from); *(d'une prison)* to escape (**de** from)

enfumé, -e [ɑ̃fyme] *adj (pièce, atmosphère)* smoky

enfumer [ɑ̃fyme] *vt* (**a**) *(pièce)* to fill with smoke (**b**) *(personne, abeilles)* to smoke out

enfuyais *etc. voir* **enfuir**

engagé, -e [ɑ̃gaʒe] **1** *adj (littérature, écrivain)* committed

2 *nm (soldat)* **e. (volontaire)** enlisted man

engageant, -e [ɑ̃gaʒɑ̃, -ɑ̃t] *adj (manière, sourire)* engaging

engagement [ɑ̃gaʒmɑ̃] *nm* (**a**) *(promesse)* undertaking, commitment; **prendre un e.** to enter into an undertaking; **prendre l'e. de faire qch** to undertake to do sth; **tenir ses engagements** to honor one's commitments; **sans e. (de votre part)** without obligation (on your part) (**b**) *(à une cause)* commitment (**c**) *(coup d'envoi) (au football)* kickoff; *(au hockey)* bully; *(au basket)* tip-off (**d**) *(commencement)* start; *(de poursuites)* institution (**e**) *(d'un employé)* appointment; *(d'un soldat)* enlistment

engager [45] [ɑ̃gaʒe] **1** *vt* (**a**) *(lier)* to commit; **e. sa parole** to give one's word; **cela ne vous engage à rien** it doesn't commit you to anything; **cela n'engage que moi** that's just my opinion (**b**) *(mettre en gage)* to pawn (**c**) *(embaucher) (employé)* to appoint; *(soldat)* to enlist (**d**) *(commencer) (conversation, négociations)* to begin, to start; *(poursuites)* to institute; **e. la partie** to start the match; **la partie est maintenant bien engagée** the match is now well under way (**e**) *(introduire) (clef)* to insert (**dans** in) (**f**) *(inciter)* **e. qn à faire qch** to urge sb to do sth

2 s'engager *vpr* (**a**) *(promettre)* **s'e. à faire qch** to promise to do sth, to undertake to do sth (**b**) *(prendre position)* to commit oneself (**c**) *(se lancer)* **s'e. dans une aventure** to get involved in an adventure (**d**) *(soldat)* to enlist, to join up (**e**) *(pénétrer)* **s'e. dans une rue** to turn into a street; **s'e. dans une forêt** to enter a forest (**f**) *(commencer) (négociations, conversation)* to begin

engeance [ɑ̃ʒɑ̃s] *nf Fam* crew, bunch

engelure [ɑ̃ʒlyr] *nf* chilblain

engendrer [ɑ̃ʒɑ̃dre] *vt* to father; *Fig (maladie, pauvreté)* to cause

engin [ɑ̃ʒɛ̃] *nm (machine)* machine; *(outil)* device; *Fam (objet)* thing; **e. blindé** armored vehicle; **e. de mort** deadly weapon; **e. spatial** spacecraft

englober [ɑ̃glɔbe] *vt* to include (**dans** in)

engloutir [ɑ̃glutir] *vt* (**a**) *(avaler) (boisson)* to gulp down; *(nourriture)* to wolf down (**b**) *(submerger) (bateau, village)* to submerge; *Fig (fortune)* to swallow up

engoncé, -e [ɑ̃gɔ̃se] *adj* **il avait l'air e. dans son manteau** his coat looked too tight for him

engorgement [ɑ̃gɔrʒəmɑ̃] *nm (blocage)* blocking; *(d'un marché)* glutting; *Méd (d'un organe)* congestion

engorger [45] [ɑ̃gɔrʒe] **1** *vt (bloquer)* to block, to clog; *(marché)* to glut

2 s'engorger *vpr (tuyau)* to be blocked *or* clogged; *Méd (organe)* to become engorged *or* congested

engouement [ɑ̃gumɑ̃] *nm* craze (**pour** for)

engouffrer [ɑ̃gufre] **1** *vt (nourriture)* to devour

2 s'engouffrer *vpr* **s'e. dans** to rush in to; **le vent s'engouffra par la porte** the wind rushed in through the door

engourdi, -e [ɑ̃gurdi] *adj* numb (**par** with)

engourdir [ɑ̃gurdir] **1** *vt* (**a**) *(membre)* to numb (**b**) *(douleur)* to dull

2 s'engourdir *vpr* to go numb, to go to sleep

engourdissement [ɑ̃gurdismɑ̃] *nm* numbness

engrais [ɑ̃grɛ] *nm* fertilizer

engraisser [ɑ̃grese] **1** *vt (animaux, personne)* to fatten up

2 *vi Fam* to get fatter

engranger [45] [ɑ̃grɑ̃ʒe] *vt (céréales)* to bring in; *Fig* to build up

engrenage [ɑ̃grənaʒ] *nm* (**a**) *(roues dentées)* gears (**b**) *Fig (d'événements)* chain; **l'e. de la violence** the cycle of violence; **être pris dans un e.** to get caught up in a system; **mettre le doigt dans l'e.** to get caught up in it

engrosser [ɑ̃grose] *vt très Fam (femme)* to knock up; **se faire e. (par)** to get knocked up (by)

engueulade [ɑ̃gœlad] *nf Fam (réprimande)* bawling out; *(querelle)* row

engueuler [ɑ̃gœle] *Fam* **1** *vt* **e. qn** to bawl sb out; **se faire e.** to get bawled out; **e. qn comme du poisson pourri** to call sb every name under the sun

2 s'engueuler *vpr* to have a row

enguirlander [ɑ̃girlɑ̃de] *vt* (**a**) *Fam* **e. qn** to bawl sb out; **se faire e.** to get bawled out (**b**) *(décorer)* to garland (**de** with)

enhardir [ɑ̃ardir] **1** *vt* to embolden

2 s'enhardir *vpr* to become bolder; **s'e. à faire qch** to pluck up the courage to do sth

énième [enjɛm] *adj* **après une é. tentative** after countless attempts; **pour la é. fois** for the umpteenth time

énigmatique [enigmatik] *adj* enigmatic

énigme [enigm] *nf (mystère)* enigma, mystery; *(devinette)* riddle

enivrant, -e [ɑ̃nivrɑ̃, -ɑ̃t] *adj (parfum)* heady; *(vitesse)* exhilarating

enivrement [ɑ̃nivrəmɑ̃] *nm* (**a**) *(par l'alcool)* intoxication (**b**) *Fig* exhilaration

enivrer [ɑ̃nivre] **1** *vt* (**a**) *(soûler)* to intoxicate, to make drunk (**b**) *Fig (exalter)* to exhilarate; **enivré par le succès** intoxicated with success

2 s'enivrer *vpr (se soûler)* to become intoxicated (**de** with), to get drunk (**de** on)

enjambée [ɑ̃ʒɑ̃be] *nf* stride; **marcher à grandes enjambées** to stride along

enjambement [ɑ̃ʒɑ̃bmɑ̃] *nm* enjambment

enjamber [ɑ̃ʒɑ̃be] *vt (obstacle)* to step over; *(sujet: pont) (rivière)* to span

enjeu, -x [ɑ̃ʒø] *nm (au jeu)* stake; *Fig (d'une guerre)* stakes; **quel est l'e. de cette élection?** what's at stake in this election?

enjoignais *etc. voir* **enjoindre**

enjoindre [43] [ɑ̃ʒwɛ̃dr] *vt Litt* **e. à qn de faire qch** to enjoin sb to do sth

enjôler [ɑ̃ʒole] *vt* to cajole

enjôleur, -euse [ɑ̃ʒolœr, -øz] **1** *adj* cajoling

2 *nm,f* charmer

enjoliver [ɑ̃ʒolive] *vt* to embellish

enjoliveur [ɑ̃ʒolivœr] *nm* hubcap

enjoué, -e [ɑ̃ʒwe] *adj* playful

enjouement [ɑ̃ʒumɑ̃] *nm* playfulness

enlacement [ɑ̃lasmɑ̃] *nm* (**a**) *(de rubans, de branches)* intertwining (**b**) *(étreinte)* embrace

enlacer [16] [ɑ̃lase] **1** *vt* (**a**) *(rubans, branches)* to intertwine (**b**) *(étreindre)* to embrace

2 s'enlacer *vpr (s'étreindre)* to embrace

enlaidir [ɑ̃ledir] **1** *vt (personne)* to make ugly, to disfigure; *(paysage, ville)* to disfigure
2 s'enlaidir *vpr* to make oneself look ugly
enlevé, -e [ɑ̃lve] *adj (style, rythme)* lively
enlèvement [ɑ̃lɛvmɑ̃] *nm* **(a)** *(de meubles, d'une tache)* removal, removing; *(de bagages)* collection; **e. des ordures** garbage collection **(b)** *(kidnapping)* kidnapping, abduction
enlever [46] [ɑ̃lve] **1** *vt* **(a)** *(vêtements, couvercle)* to remove, to take off; *(meubles)* to remove, to take away; *(tapis)* to take up; *(rideaux)* to take down; *(papier peint, étiquette, tache)* to remove; **e. qch à qn** to take sth away from sb; **elle me l'a enlevé des mains** she took it from me; **e. à qn la garde d'un enfant** to remove a child from sb's care; **e. à qn le goût de qch** to take away sb's taste for sth **(b)** *(kidnapper)* to kidnap, to abduct **(c)** *(remporter) (prix)* to carry off; *(victoire, contrat)* to win
2 s'enlever *vpr (couvercle, peinture)* to come off; *(tache)* to come out
enlisement [ɑ̃lizmɑ̃] *nm* sinking
enliser [ɑ̃lize] **1** *vt* **e. une voiture** to get a car stuck
2 s'enliser *vpr (personne, voiture)* to get stuck; *Fig* **s'e. dans ses explications** to get bogged down in explanations
enluminure [ɑ̃lyminyr] *nf* illumination
enneigé, -e [ɑ̃neʒe] *adj (montagne, champ, route)* snow-covered; *(village)* snowbound
enneigement [ɑ̃nɛʒmɑ̃] *nm* snow cover
ennemi, -e [ɛnmi] **1** *nm, f* enemy; **se faire un e. de qn** to make an enemy of sb; **passer à l'e.** to defect; *Prov* **le mieux est l'e. du bien** it's better to leave well alone; **e. public numéro un** public enemy number one
2 *adj* **en pays e.** in enemy country
ennui [ɑ̃nɥi] *nm* **(a)** *(souci)* worry; *(problème)* problem; **avoir des ennuis** *(soucis)* to be worried; *(problèmes)* to have problems; **avoir des ennuis de santé** to have health problems; **avoir des ennuis avec la police** to be in trouble with the police; **attirer des ennuis à qn** to get sb into trouble; **faire des ennuis à qn** to bother sb **(b)** *(lassitude)* boredom; **il est d'un e.!** his conversation is so boring!
ennuyé, -e [ɑ̃nɥije] *adj* **(a)** *(contrarié)* annoyed (**de** about) **(b)** *(las)* bored
ennuyer [32] [ɑ̃nɥije] **1** *vt* **(a)** *(contrarier)* to bother; **cela vous ennuierait-il d'attendre?** would you mind waiting? **(b)** *(agacer)* to annoy, to irritate **(c)** *(lasser)* to bore (**avec** with)
2 s'ennuyer *vpr* to be bored; **qu'est-ce qu'on s'ennuie ici!** it's so boring here!; **s'e. à cent sous de l'heure** to be bored to death
ennuyeux, -euse [ɑ̃nɥijø, -øz] *adj* **(a)** *(contrariant)* annoying, irritating; **comme c'est e.!** it's so annoying! **(b)** *(lassant)* boring
énoncé [enɔ̃se] *nm* **(a)** *(des faits)* statement; *(d'une sentence)* pronouncement **(b)** *(d'une question)* wording
énoncer [16] [enɔ̃se] *vt (opinion, conditions)* to state
énonciation [enɔ̃sjasjɔ̃] *nf (de faits)* statement
enorgueillir [ɑ̃nɔrgœjir] **1** *vt* to make proud
2 s'enorgueillir *vpr* **s'e. de qch/de faire qch** to pride oneself on sth/on doing sth
énorme [enɔrm] *adj* enormous, huge
énormément [enɔrmemɑ̃] *adv (lire, travailler, pleurer)* an awful lot; **je le regrette é.** I'm extremely sorry; **s'amuser é.** to have a great time; **il n'a pas é. d'argent** he hasn't got a huge amount of money
énormité [enɔrmite] *nf* **(a)** *(d'une demande, d'un crime)* enormity, outrageousness **(b)** *(d'une personne, d'une somme)* huge size **(c)** *(erreur)* glaring mistake; *(propos choquants)* outrageous remark
enquérir [7] [ɑ̃kerir] **s'enquérir** *vpr* to inquire (**de** about)

enquête [ɑ̃kɛt] *nf* **(a)** *(recherches)* inquiry; *(de journalistes, de policiers)* investigation (**sur** into); *Fam* **faire sa petite e.** to do a bit of investigating **(b)** *(sondage)* survey
enquêter [ɑ̃kete] *vi* **(a)** *(faire des recherches)* to hold an inquiry; *(police, journaliste)* to investigate; **e. sur qch** to investigate sth **(b)** *(faire un sondage)* to conduct a survey (**sur/auprès de** into/among)
enquêteur, -trice [ɑ̃kɛtœr, -tris] *nm, f* **(a)** *(policier)* investigator **(b)** *(sondeur)* researcher
enquiers, enquiert *voir* **enquérir**
enquiquinant, -e [ɑ̃kikinɑ̃, -ɑ̃t] *adj Fam (agaçant)* irritating, annoying
enquiquiner [ɑ̃kikine] *vt Fam (agacer)* to irritate, to annoy
enquiquineur, -euse [ɑ̃kikinœr, -øz] *nm, f Fam* nuisance, pain
enquis, -e *voir* **enquérir**
enraciné, -e [ɑ̃rasine] *adj (habitude, haine)* deep-rooted, deep-seated
enraciner [ɑ̃rasine] **s'enraciner** *vpr aussi Fig* to take root
enragé, -e [ɑ̃raʒe] **1** *adj (animal)* rabid
2 *nm, f Fam* fanatic
enrager [45] [ɑ̃raʒe] *vi* to be furious; **e. de devoir faire qch** to be really angry at having to do sth; **faire e. qn** *(taquiner)* to tease sb
enrayer [53] [ɑ̃reje] **1** *vt (machine)* to jam; *Fig (épidémie)* to check; *(inflation)* to curb
2 s'enrayer *vpr (machine)* to jam
enrégimenter [ɑ̃reʒimɑ̃te] *vt Péj (dans une organisation)* to enroll
enregistrement [ɑ̃rəʒistrəmɑ̃] *nm* **(a)** *(d'une naissance, d'un acte)* registration; *(de bagages)* check-in **(b)** *(disque)* recording; **e. vidéo** video recording; **e. sur bande/cassette** tape/cassette recording **(c)** *Ordinat (de données)* logging, recording; **e. de transactions** transaction logging
enregistrer [ɑ̃rəʒistre] **1** *vt* **(a)** *(naissance, acte)* to register; *(bagages)* to check in; **les meilleures ventes jamais enregistrées** the best sales ever recorded **(b)** *(disque, émission)* to record, to tape; *(données)* to store; *Ordinat* **programme enregistré** stored program **(c)** *Fam (mémoriser)* to note, to register
2 s'enregistrer *vpr (personne)* to record oneself
enregistreur, -euse [ɑ̃rəʒistrœr, -øz] **1** *adj (appareil)* recording
2 *nm* recorder, recording device; *Belg* tape recorder
enrhumé, -e [ɑ̃ryme] *adj* **être e.** to have a cold
enrhumer [ɑ̃ryme] **s'enrhumer** *vpr* to catch a cold
enrichi, -e [ɑ̃riʃi] *adj* **(a)** *(personne)* wealthy **(b)** *(céréales)* enriched (**en** with)
enrichir [ɑ̃riʃir] **1** *vt (personne, pays)* to make richer; *Fig (collection)* to enhance (**de** with); *(esprit)* to enrich, to improve
2 s'enrichir *vpr* **(a)** *(personne, pays)* to get richer; *Fig (collection)* to be enhanced (**de** by) **(b)** **s'e. l'esprit** to improve one's mind
enrichissant, -e [ɑ̃riʃisɑ̃, -ɑ̃t] *adj (expérience)* rewarding
enrichissement [ɑ̃riʃismɑ̃] *nm* **(a)** *(en argent)* acquiring of wealth **(b)** *(de l'esprit, d'une collection)* enrichment
enrober [ɑ̃rɔbe] *vt* **(a)** *(bonbon)* to coat (**de** with) **(b)** *Hum* **il est un peu enrobé** he's a bit chubby
enrôlement [ɑ̃rolmɑ̃] *nm* enrollment; *(d'un soldat)* enlistment
enrôler [ɑ̃role] **1** *vt* to enroll, to recruit; *(soldat)* to enlist
2 s'enrôler *vpr* to enroll; *(soldat)* to enlist
enroué, -e [ɑ̃rwe] *adj* hoarse, husky; **avoir la voix enrouée** to have a husky voice
enrouer [ɑ̃rwe] **1** *vt (voix, personne)* to make hoarse
2 s'enrouer *vpr* to get hoarse
enrouler [ɑ̃rule] **1** *vt* **(a)** *(rouler) (carte, tapis)* to roll up; *(câble, ruban)* to wind **(b)** *(envelopper)* to wrap up (**dans** in)

2 s'enrouler *vpr* (a) *(serpent)* to coil up; *(fil)* to wind (b) **s'e. dans une couverture** to wrap oneself up in a blanket

ENS [ɛns] *nf (abrév* **École normale supérieure** *) =* university-level college preparing students for senior posts in teaching

ENSA [ɛnsa] *nf (abrév* **École nationale supérieure d'agronomie** *) =* one of five competitive-entry agricultural engineering schools

ensablement [ɑ̃sabləmɑ̃] *nm* (a) *(d'un port)* silting up (b) *(dépôt) (dû à l'eau)* sandbank; *(dû au vent)* sand dune

ensabler [ɑ̃sable] **1** *vt (port)* to silt up
2 s'ensabler *vpr* (a) *(véhicule)* to get stuck in the sand (b) *(port)* to silt up

ensanglanter [ɑ̃sɑ̃glɑ̃te] *vt* to cover with blood; **des mains ensanglantées** bloodstained *or* bloody hands; **un festival ensanglanté par un attentat** a festival marred by an attempted murder

enseignant, -e [ɑ̃sɛɲɑ̃, -ɑ̃t] **1** *nm,f* teacher
2 *adj* **le corps e.** the teaching profession

enseigne [ɑ̃sɛɲ] **1** *nf* (a) *(panonceau)* sign; **e. lumineuse** illuminated sign; *Fig* **nous sommes tous logés à la même e.** we're all in the same boat (b) *Litt* **à telle e. que…** so much so that…
2 *nm* **e. (de vaisseau)** ensign

enseignement [ɑ̃sɛɲmɑ̃] *nm* (a) *(profession)* teaching; **être dans l'e.** to be a teacher (b) *(formation)* education; *Fig* **tirer un e. de qch** to learn a lesson from sth; **e. assisté par ordinateur** computer-aided learning; **e. par correspondance** distance learning; **e. primaire/secondaire** primary/secondary education; **e. professionnel/technique** vocational/technical education; **e. supérieur** higher education

enseigner [ɑ̃sɛɲe] **1** *vt* to teach; **e. qch à qn** to teach sb sth
2 *vi* to be a teacher, to teach

ensemble [ɑ̃sɑ̃bl] **1** *adv* together; **aller bien e.** *(personnes)* to be well matched; *(couleurs)* to go together; **ils sont partis tous e.** they left en masse; *Hum* **ne répondez pas tous e.** don't all answer at once
2 *nm* (a) *(totalité)* **l'e. des personnes présentes** all the people present; **l'e. de sa fortune** his whole fortune; **dans l'e.** on the whole (b) *(unité)* unity; **avec un parfait e.** *(répondre)* as one; *(danser)* in unison (c) *(groupe) (de gens)* group; *(d'objets, de faits)* set; *(de services)* package (d) *(tenue)* outfit; **e. pantalon** pantsuit (e) *(immeubles)* block; **grand e.** housing development (f) *Math* set

ensemblier [ɑ̃sɑ̃blije] *nm* interior designer; *(pour la télévision)* set designer

ensemencer [16] [ɑ̃səmɑ̃se] *vt* (a) *(champ)* to sow (b) *Biol* to culture

ensevelir [ɑ̃səvlir] *vt Litt* to bury

ensoleillé, -e [ɑ̃səleje] *adj* sunny

ensoleillement [ɑ̃səlɛjmɑ̃] *nm* **en raison de l'e. d'une pièce** because the room gets a lot of sun; **cinq heures d'e. par jour** five hours of sunshine a day; **jouir d'un e. exceptionnel** to get a lot of sun

ensommeillé, -e [ɑ̃səmeje] *adj* sleepy

ensorceler [9] [ɑ̃sɔrsəle] *vt* to cast *or* to put a spell on; *Fig* to bewitch, to captivate

ensorcellement [ɑ̃sɔrsɛlmɑ̃] *nm (action)* bewitching; *(état)* bewitchment; *Fig (charme)* charm

ensuite [ɑ̃sɥit] *adv (plus tard)* later; *(puis)* then, next; **et e., qu'est-ce qu'on fait?** what do you do next?; *Fam* **d'abord, c'est très cher, et e. ça ne te va pas du tout** for one thing it's very expensive, and for another it doesn't suit you at all

ensuivre [65] [ɑ̃sɥivr] **s'ensuivre** *vpr* **jusqu'à ce que mort s'ensuive** until dead; **il s'ensuit que…** it follows that…; **et tout ce qui s'ensuit** and all that goes with it

entacher [ɑ̃taʃe] *vt (réputation)* to sully

entaille [ɑ̃taj] *nf* (a) *(dans du bois)* notch; *(longue)* groove (b) *(blessure)* gash; **se faire une e. au doigt** to cut one's finger open

entailler [ɑ̃taje] *vt (blesser)* to gash

entame [ɑ̃tam] *nf* (a) *(de pain, de jambon)* first slice (b) *(aux cartes)* lead

entamer [ɑ̃tame] *vt* (a) *(blesser)* to cut into; *Fig (conviction, détermination)* to undermine (b) *(commencer) (pain, jambon)* to start on; *(bouteille, pot de confiture)* to open; *(travail, recherches, conversation, négociations)* to start; *(démarches)* to initiate; *(poursuites)* to institute (c) *(aux cartes)* **e. à trèfle** to open clubs

entartrer [ɑ̃tartre] **1** *vt (chaudière)* to scale
2 s'entartrer *vpr (chaudière)* to scale; *(dents)* to scale up

entassement [ɑ̃tasmɑ̃] *nm* (a) *(de pierres) (action)* piling up; *(tas)* pile (b) *(de passagers, du bétail)* crowding together

entasser [ɑ̃tase] **1** *vt* (a) *(pierres, livres, vêtements)* to pile up (b) *(passagers, bétail)* to crowd together
2 s'entasser *vpr* (a) *(objets)* to pile up (b) *(personnes)* to crowd together

entendement [ɑ̃tɑ̃dmɑ̃] *nm* **dépasser l'e.** to be beyond comprehension

entendeur [ɑ̃tɑ̃dœr] *nm* **à bon e., salut!** mark my words!

entendre [ɑ̃tɑ̃dr] **1** *vt* (a) *(ouïr)* to hear; **je n'entends rien (de ce que tu dis)** I can't hear a thing (you're saying); **je l'entends rire** I can hear him/her laughing; **e. dire que…** to hear that…; **e. qn dire qch** to hear sb say sth; **e. parler de** *(connaître l'existence de)* to hear of; *(être au courant de)* to hear about; **elle ne veut pas en e. parler!** she doesn't want to hear another word about it!; **il va m'e.!** I'll give him a talking-to!; **elle répétait à qui voulait l'e. que…** she'd tell anyone who'd listen that…; *Fam* **ce qu'il ne faut pas e.!** I've heard it all now!
(b) *(écouter) (témoin, suppliant)* to hear; **e. qn en confession** to hear sb's confession; **à vous e., il a eu tort** from what you say, he was in the wrong; **il n'a rien voulu e.** he wouldn't listen; **que Dieu vous entende** may God answer your prayers
(c) *(comprendre)* to understand; **laisser e. qch** to imply sth; **elle m'a laissé e. que…** she gave me to understand that…; **ce n'est pas ainsi qu'il l'entend** he doesn't see it like that
(d) *(vouloir dire)* to mean; **qu'entendez-vous par là?** what do you mean by that?
(e) *(vouloir)* **e. faire qch** to intend *or* to mean to do sth; **faites comme vous l'entendez** do as you think best; **il ne l'entendait pas ainsi** he wouldn't hear of it
2 *vi* to hear; **e. mal** to be hard of hearing; **j'ai mal entendu!** *(je n'ai pas entendu)* I didn't hear you properly!; *(je suis choqué)* I don't think I heard you right!; **tu entends?** *(menace)* got it?
3 s'entendre *vpr* (a) *(sympathiser)* to get on (**avec** with)
(b) *(se mettre d'accord)* to agree; **entendons-nous bien!** let's be clear about this!
(c) *(être entendu)* to be heard; **on ne s'entend plus ici** you can't hear yourself think in here
(d) *(être compris)* to be understood
(e) **s'e. aux affaires** to have a good head for business; **il s'y entend** he knows what he's talking about

entendu, -e [ɑ̃tɑ̃dy] *adj* (a) *(complice) (sourire)* knowing; **d'un air e.** knowingly (b) *(décidé)* **(c'est) e.!** fine!, all right! (c) **bien e.** of course

entente [ɑ̃tɑ̃t] *nf* (a) *(accord)* agreement, understanding (**entre** between) (b) *(harmonie)* **bonne e.** harmony

entériner [ɑ̃terine] *vt* to ratify

entérite [ɑ̃terit] *nf Méd* enteritis

enterrement [ɑ̃tɛrmɑ̃] *nm* (a) *(mise en terre)* burial (b) *(cérémonie)* funeral; *Fam* **faire une tête d'e.** to look miserable (c) *(cortège)* funeral procession

enterrer [ɑ̃tere] **1** *vt* (a) *(trésor, corps)* to bury; *Hum* **il nous enterrera tous** he'll outlive us all (b) *Fig (projet)* to scrap; *(affaire)* to bury; **e. sa vie de garçon** to have a stag party
2 s'enterrer *vpr Fig* to hide oneself away

entêtant, -e [ɑ̃tɛtɑ̃, -ɑ̃t] *adj (parfum, musique)* heady

en-tête *(pl* **en-têtes)** [ɑ̃tɛt] *nm* heading, letterhead; *Ordinat* header

entêté, -e [ɑ̃tete] **1** *adj* obstinate, stubborn
2 *nm,f* obstinate *or* stubborn person

entêtement [ɑ̃tɛtmɑ̃] *nm* obstinacy, stubbornness; **e. à faire qch** persistence in doing sth

entêter [ɑ̃tete] **s'entêter** *vpr* to persist; **s'e. à faire qch** to persist in doing sth

enthousiasmant, -e [ɑ̃tuzjasmɑ̃, -ɑ̃t] *adj* exciting

enthousiasme [ɑ̃tuzjasm] *nm* enthusiasm (**pour** for); **avec e.** enthusiastically; **sans e.** unenthusiastically

enthousiasmer [ɑ̃tuzjasme] **1** *vt (personne)* to fill with enthusiasm
2 s'enthousiasmer *vpr* to get enthusiastic (**pour** about)

enthousiaste [ɑ̃tuzjast] **1** *adj* enthusiastic
2 *nmf* enthusiast

enticher [ɑ̃tiʃe] **s'enticher** *vpr* **s'e. de qn/qch** to become infatuated with sb/sth

entier, -ère [ɑ̃tje, -ɛr] **1** *adj* (**a**) *(complet)* whole, entire; **la France entière** the whole of France; **il a mangé le gâteau tout e.** he ate the entire cake; **des heures entières** for hours on end; **le mystère reste e.** the mystery remains unsolved (**b**) *(responsabilité)* full; *(confiance)* complete; **jouir d'une entière liberté** to have absolute freedom; **donner entière satisfaction à qn** *(produit)* to give sb complete satisfaction (**c**) *(sans compromis) (personne)* uncompromising (**d**) *Math (nombre)* whole
2 *nm* (**a**) **j'ai écouté le disque en e.** I listened to the whole record; **elle a lu le livre en e.** she read the whole book; **le pays dans son e.** the entire country (**b**) *Math (nombre)* integer, whole number

entièrement [ɑ̃tjɛrmɑ̃] *adv* entirely; **je ne l'ai pas lu e.** I didn't read all of it

entité [ɑ̃tite] *nf* entity

entonner [ɑ̃tɔne] *vt* to start singing

entonnoir [ɑ̃tɔnwar] *nm* funnel

entorse [ɑ̃tɔrs] *nf* sprain, wrench; **se faire une e. au poignet** to sprain one's wrist; *Fig* **faire une e. au règlement** to stretch the rules; **faire une e. a son régime** to break one's diet

entortiller [ɑ̃tɔrtije] **1** *vt (envelopper)* to wrap (**dans** in); *(enrouler)* to wind (**autour de** around)
2 s'entortiller *vpr* (**a**) *(serpent, lierre)* to coil (**autour de** around) (**b**) *(s'empêtrer)* to get tangled up (**dans** in) (**c**) *(s'enrouler)* to wrap oneself up (**dans** in)

entour [ɑ̃tur] *nm* **à l'e. de** around

entourage [ɑ̃turaʒ] *nm (amis)* circle (of friends); *(de ministre, de souverain)* entourage; **dans son e. proche** among those close to him/her

entourer [ɑ̃ture] **1** *vt* (**a**) *(border, enceindre)* to surround (**de** with) (**b**) *(être autour de)* to surround; **les gens qui vous entourent** the people around you; **le monde qui nous entoure** the world around us; **entouré de mystère** shrouded in mystery; **un rang de perles entourait son cou** she had a string of pearls around her neck (**c**) *(soutenir) (personne)* to rally around; **elle est très entourée** she has a lot of people she can turn to for support
2 s'entourer *vpr* **s'e. d'amis/de belles choses** to surround oneself with friends/with beautiful things

entourloupe [ɑ̃turlup], **entourloupette** [ɑ̃turlupɛt] *nf Fam* dirty trick; **faire une e. à qn** to play a dirty trick on sb

entournure [ɑ̃turnyr] *nf Fam* **être gêné aux entournures** *(mal à l'aise)* to feel awkward; *(financièrement)* to feel the pinch

entracte [ɑ̃trakt] *nm* intermission

entraide [ɑ̃trɛd] *nf* mutual aid

entraider [ɑ̃trede] **s'entraider** *vpr* to help one another

entrailles [ɑ̃traj] *nfpl* entrails

entrain [ɑ̃trɛ̃] *nm* get-up-and-go; **être plein d'e.** to be full of life; **travailler avec e.** to beaver away; **faire qch sans e.** to do sth half-heartedly

entraînant, -e [ɑ̃trɛnɑ̃, -ɑ̃t] *adj (air, rythme)* lively

entraînement [ɑ̃trɛnmɑ̃] *nm* (**a**) *(en sport)* training; **un e.** a training session; **à l'e.** in training; **avoir de l'e.** to be well trained; **manquer d'e.** to be out of practice (**b**) *Tech* drive

entraîner [ɑ̃trene] **1** *vt* (**a**) *(sujet: rivière)* to carry away; *(sujet: locomotive)* to pull; **e. qn quelque part** to lead sb off somewhere; **il l'a entraîné dans sa chute** he dragged him down with him (**b**) *(exercer une influence sur)* to influence; **e. qn à faire qch** to lead sb to do sth; **e. qn dans un piège** to lure sb into a trap; **se laisser e.** to allow oneself to be led astray (**c**) *(causer) (dépense, modification)* to entail, to lead to; **e. un retard** to result in a delay (**d**) *(athlète, équipe)* to coach, to train; *(cheval)* to train; **e. qn à faire qch** to train sb to do sth (**e**) *Tech* to drive
2 s'entraîner *vpr (athlète)* to train; **s'e. à faire qch** to practice doing sth

entraîneur [ɑ̃trɛnœr] *nm (d'un athlète, d'une équipe)* coach; *(d'un cheval)* trainer

entraîneuse [ɑ̃trɛnøz] *nf* (**a**) *(de boîte de nuit)* hostess (**b**) *(d'un athlète, d'une équipe)* coach; *(d'un cheval)* trainer

entrapercevoir [60] [ɑ̃trapɛrsəvwar] *vt* to catch a fleeting glimpse of

entrave [ɑ̃trav] *nf (obstacle)* hindrance, impediment (**à** to)

entraver [ɑ̃trave] *vt* (**a**) *(mouvement, processus)* to hinder, to impede (**b**) *Fam* **j'y entrave que dalle** it beats me

entre [ɑ̃tr] *prép* (**a**) *(au milieu de)* between; *Fig* **e. les deux** *(ni l'un ni l'autre)* in between; **être e. la vie et la mort** to hover between life and death; **être e. deux âges** to be middle-aged; *Fig* **faire qch e. deux portes** to do sth in passing
(**b**) *(parmi)* among(st); **hésiter e. plusieurs solutions** to hesitate between several solutions; **plusieurs d'e. nous** several of us; **être dangereux e. tous** to be extremely dangerous; **e. autres** among others
(**c**) *(rapport réciproque) (deux personnes)* between; *(plus de deux personnes)* among(st); **se marier e. cousins** to intermarry with cousins; **ils se battent e. eux** they fight with each other; **qu'y a-t-il e. eux exactement?** what exactly is going on between them?; **soit dit e. nous** between you and me; *Fam* **il faut que je te parle e. quat'z'yeux** I've got to talk to you in private
(**d**) *(dans)* **tenir qch e. ses mains** to hold sth in one's hands; **e. ces murs** within these walls
(**e**) *(à travers)* through; **se faufiler e. les arbres** to thread one's way through the trees

entrebâillement [ɑ̃trəbajmɑ̃] *nm* **par l'e. de la porte** through the half-open door

entrebâiller [ɑ̃trəbaje] *vt (porte, fenêtre)* to half-open; **la porte était entrebâillée** the door was ajar

entrechat [ɑ̃trəʃa] *nm (pas de danse)* entrechat

entrechoquer [ɑ̃trəʃɔke] **1** *vt* to knock together; **e. des verres** to chink glasses
2 s'entrechoquer *vpr* to knock against one another; *(verres)* to chink

entrecôte [ɑ̃trəkot] *nf* rib steak; **e. à la bordelaise** rib steak in a shallots and red wine sauce

entrecoupé, -e [ɑ̃trəkupe] *adj (voix)* broken

entrecouper [ɑ̃trəkupe] *vt* to interrupt (**de** with)

entrecroiser [ɑ̃trəkrwaze] **1** *vt (ligne)* to intersect; *(fils)* to interlace
2 s'entrecroiser *vpr (lignes, routes)* to intersect; *(fils)* to interlace

entre-déchirer [ɑ̃trədeʃire] **s'entre-déchirer** *vpr* to tear each other to pieces

entre-deux [ɑ̃trədø] *nm inv* (**a**) *(intervalle)* intervening period (**b**) *Sport* jump ball

entre-deux-guerres [ɑ̃trədøgɛr] *nm inv* **l'e.** the inter-war period

entre-dévorer [ɑ̃trədevɔre] **s'entre-dévorer** *vpr* to devour one another *or* each other

entrée [ɑ̃tre] *nf* (**a**) *(action)* entry, entrance; *(de marchandises)* import; **faire son e.** to make one's entrance; **l'e. de la Suède dans la UE** Sweden's entry into the EU; **avant mon e. à l'université** before I went to college; **e. en scène** entrance (on to the stage); **e. en fonction** assumption of one's duties; **e. en matière** introduction; **e. en vigueur** coming into force; *Fig* **à l'e. de l'hiver** at the beginning of winter; *Fig* **d'e. (de jeu)** from the outset

(**b**) *(accès)* admission, admittance (**dans** *ou* **de** to); **avoir ses entrées dans un lieu** to have contacts in a place; **e. à l'hôpital** admission into the hospital; **e. interdite** *(sur panneau)* no admittance, no entry; **e. libre** *(dans un musée)* admission free; *(dans une boutique)* browsers welcome

(**c**) *(voie d'accès)* way in, entrance (**de** to); *(vestibule)* entrance hall; **e. des artistes** stage door; **e. principale** main entrance; **e. de service** service entrance

(**d**) *(hors-d'œuvre)* starter

(**e**) **faire 1000 entrées** *(film)* to sell 1,000 tickets

(**f**) *(dans un dictionnaire)* entry

(**g**) *Ordinat (processus)* input, entry; *(information)* entry; *(touche)* enter (key); **données d'e.** input (data); **e. (par le) clavier** keyboard input; **e. de gamme** entry level; **e. de papier** paper input; **e./sortie** input/output; **e./sortie parallèles** parallel input/output

entrefaites [ɑ̃trəfɛt] *nfpl* **sur ces e.** at that moment

entrefilet [ɑ̃trəfilɛ] *nm* short (news) item

entrejambe [ɑ̃trəʒɑ̃b] *nm* crotch

entrelacer [16] [ɑ̃trəlase] **1** *vt (rubans, branches)* to intertwine; *Ordinat* **écran entrelacé** interlaced screen

  2 s'entrelacer *vpr* to intertwine

entrelacs [ɑ̃trəla] *nm* interlaced design, tracery

entrelarder [ɑ̃trəlarde] *vt Culin (viande)* to lard; *Fig* **e. un discours de citations** to lace a speech with quotations

entremêler [ɑ̃trəmele] **1** *vt* to interweave (**de** with)

  2 s'entremêler *vpr* to be interwoven

entremets [ɑ̃trəmɛ] *nm* dessert

entremetteur, -euse [ɑ̃trəmɛtœr, -øz] *nm,f* go-between

entremise [ɑ̃trəmiz] *nf* intervention; **par l'e. de qn** through sb

entrepont [ɑ̃trəpɔ̃] *nm* 'tween decks; *(pour voyageurs)* steerage

entreposer [ɑ̃trəpoze] *vt* to store; *(marchandises)* to warehouse

entrepôt [ɑ̃trəpo] *nm* warehouse

entreprenant, -e [ɑ̃trəprənɑ̃, -ɑ̃t] *adj* enterprising; *(auprès des femmes)* forward

entreprendre [58] [ɑ̃trəprɑ̃dr] *vt* (**a**) *(commencer)* to undertake; **e. des démarches** to take steps; **e. de faire qch** to undertake to do sth (**b**) *(entretenir)* **e. qn sur qch** to engage sb in conversation about sth

entrepreneur, -euse [ɑ̃trəprənœr, -øz] *nm,f* (**a**) *(dans le bâtiment)* contractor (**b**) *(patron)* entrepreneur (**c**) **e. de pompes funèbres** mortician

entrepreneuriat [ɑ̃trəprənœrja] *nm* entrepreneurship

entrepris, -e[1] *voir* **entreprendre**

entreprise[2] [ɑ̃trəpriz] *nf* (**a**) *(action, initiative)* enterprise, undertaking; **la libre e.** free enterprise (**b**) *(firme)* company, firm; **e. privée** private company; **e. publique** public corporation

entrer [ɑ̃tre] **1** *vi (aux être)* (**a**) *(aller)* to go in, to enter; *(venir)* to come in, to enter; **e. dans qch** to go/come into sth, to enter sth; **e. dans une voiture/un ascenseur** to get into a car/an elevator; **e. par la fenêtre** to get in *or* to enter through the window; **e. en courant** to run in; **e. sans payer** to get in without paying; **e. en gare** to come into the station; **e. au port** to come into harbor; **laisser e. qn/qch** to let sb/sth in; **empêcher qn d'e.** to keep sb out; **faire e. qn** to let sb in; *(sujet: secrétaire, majordome)* to show sb in; **faire e. qch dans une pièce** to get sth into a room; *Théât* **Hamlet entre en scène** enter Hamlet; **entrez!** come/go in!

(**b**) *(pénétrer) (eau, air)* to go/come in; **le clou entra dans le mur** the nail went into the wall; **la clef n'entre pas dans la serrure** the key won't go in the lock

(**c**) *(heurter)* **e. dans qch** to run into sth, to run into sth; *Fam* **e. dans le décor** to go off the road

(**d**) *(faire tenir)* **faire e. qch dans qch** to insert sth in sth; **on n'y entrera jamais à vingt** we'll never get twenty people in; **il n'entre pas dans le carton** it won't go in the box

(**e**) *(devenir membre)* **e. dans l'armée** to go into the army; **e. en religion** to take (holy) orders; **e. aux PTT/chez Renault** to start working for the Post Office/for Renault; **e. au service de qn** to enter sb's service; **e. dans l'Union européenne** to join the European Union

(**f**) *(être admis)* **e. à l'université** to go to college; **e. à l'hôpital** to be admitted to the hospital; **e. en maternelle** to start nursery school

(**g**) *(faire partie de)* **e. dans une catégorie** to fall into a category; **e. dans la légende** to become a legend; **e. dans l'histoire** to go down in history; **e. en ligne de compte** to be taken into account; **e. dans les projets de qn** to be part of sb's plans; **e. dans la vie de qn** to come into sb's life; **e. dans la composition de qch** to go into the making of sth; **cela n'entre pas dans mes idées** I don't go along with that

(**h**) *(commencer)* **e. dans une colère terrible** to get extremely angry; **e. en campagne** *Mil* to take the field; *Pol* to go on the campaign trail; **e. en guerre** to enter the war; **e. en fonction** to take up one's duties; **e. en vigueur** to come into force *or* effect; **e. dans la vie active** to start one's working life; **e. dans une ère nouvelle** to enter a new era; **e. dans les détails** to go into detail; **on entre dans l'hiver** winter is just beginning

(**i**) *Ordinat* to log in *or* on

  2 *vt (aux avoir)* (**a**) *(introduire)* **e. des marchandises en fraude** to smuggle in goods

(**b**) *(enfoncer)* **e. ses ongles dans le cou de qn** to sink one's nails into sb's neck

(**c**) *Ordinat (données)* to enter, to input; *(au clavier)* to key in

  3 *v impersonnel* **il n'entre pas dans mes projets de le faire** it's not part of my plans to do it

entresol [ɑ̃trəsɔl] *nm* mezzanine (floor)

entre-temps [ɑ̃trətɑ̃] *adv* meanwhile, in the meantime

entretenir [70] [ɑ̃trətənir] **1** *vt* (**a**) *(soigner) (maison, jardin, routes, machine)* to maintain; **une moquette facile à e.** a carpet which is easy to look after; **e. sa forme** to keep in shape (**b**) *(payer pour) (famille, maîtresse)* to maintain, to support (**c**) *(maintenir)* **e. une correspondance avec qn** to keep up a correspondence with sb; **e. de bonnes relations avec qn** to remain on good terms with sb; **cela entretient leur amitié** that keeps their friendship going *or* alive (**d**) *(parler à)* **e. qn de qch** to converse with sb about sth

  2 s'entretenir *vpr* **s'e. avec qn (de qch)** to converse with sb (about sth)

entretenu, -e [ɑ̃trətəny] *adj* (**a**) **bien/mal e.** *(maison, jardin)* well-kept/badly kept (**b**) **une femme entretenue** a kept woman

entretien [ɑ̃trətjɛ̃] *nm* (**a**) *(soins) (d'une maison, d'un jardin, des routes, d'une machine)* maintenance; **facile/difficile d'e., d'e. facile/difficile** easy/difficult to maintain; **produits d'e.** (household) cleaning materials (**b**) *(subsistance) (d'une famille,* *d'une armée)* support, maintenance (**c**) *(conversation)* conversation; *(audience)* interview; **entretiens** *(négociations)* discussions, talks

entre-tuer [ɑ̃trətɥe] **s'entre-tuer** *vpr* to kill each other

entreverrai *etc. voir* **entrevoir**

entrevoir [73a] [ɑ̃trəvwar] *vt (rapidement)* to catch sight of, to catch a glimpse of; *(indistinctement)* to make out; **e. des difficultés** to foresee difficulties

entrevoyons *etc. voir* **entrevoir**

entrevu, -e[1] *voir* **entrevoir**

entrevue[2] [ɑ̃trəvy] *nf (rendez-vous)* interview; *(réunion)* meeting

entrouvert, -e [ɑ̃truvɛr, -ɛrt] *adj* half-open

entrouvrir [52] [ɑ̃truvrir] **1** *vt* to half-open

2 s'entrouvrir *vpr* to half-open

entuber [ɑ̃tybe] *vt Fam (duper)* to con; **se faire e.** to be conned

énumération [enymerasjɔ̃] *nf* listing

énumérer [34] [enymere] *vt* to list

envahir [ɑ̃vair] *vt (pays)* to invade; *(marché)* to flood; **un jardin envahi par les mauvaises herbes** a garden overgrown with weeds; *Fig* **un doute m'a envahi** I was overcome with doubt; *Fam* **e. qn** *(sujet: personne)* to intrude on sb

envahissant, -e [ɑ̃vaisɑ̃, -ɑ̃t] *adj (plantes)* invasive; *(odeur)* overwhelming; *Fam (personne)* intrusive

envahisseur [ɑ̃vaisœr] *nm* invader

enveloppant, -e [ɑ̃vlɔpɑ̃, -ɑ̃t] *adj* (**a**) *(couvrant)* **regard e.** look that takes/took everything in (**b**) *Fig (séduisant) (manières)* captivating

enveloppe [ɑ̃vlɔp] *nf* (**a**) *(de lettre)* envelope; **e. à fenêtre** window envelope; **envoyer qch sous e.** to send sth under cover; *Fig* **e. budgétaire** budget; *Fig* **l'e. de la recherche** the research budget (**b**) *(de paquet)* wrapping (**c**) *(de graines)* husk (**d**) *Fig (apparence)* **sous une e. de rudesse** beneath a rough exterior

enveloppé, -e [ɑ̃vlɔpe] *adj Fam* (**bien**) **e.** *(personne)* well-upholstered

envelopper [ɑ̃vlɔpe] **1** *vt* (**a**) *(marchandises, bébé)* to wrap (up); **enveloppé dans des bandages** swathed in bandages (**b**) *(entourer)* **e. qch du regard** to take sth in with one's gaze; **la nuit nous enveloppa** darkness closed in on us; **enveloppé de mystère/brume** shrouded in mystery/mist

2 s'envelopper *vpr* **s'e. dans une couverture** to wrap oneself up in a blanket

envenimer [ɑ̃vnime] **1** *vt (plaie)* to infect; *Fig (querelle, discussion)* to embitter

2 s'envenimer *vpr (plaie)* to get infected; *Fig (querelle, discussion)* to get acrimonious

envergure [ɑ̃vɛrgyr] *nf* (**a**) *(d'un oiseau, d'un avion)* wingspan (**b**) *Fig (ampleur)* scope; **de grande e., d'e.** *(réforme)* far-reaching; *(opération)* large-scale (**c**) *(de personne)* caliber; **manquer d'e.** to be of a low caliber

enverrai *etc. voir* **envoyer**

envers[1] [ɑ̃vɛr] *nm (d'un document, d'une assiette)* back; *(d'une médaille, d'une pièce)* reverse; **à l'e.** *(l'extérieur à l'intérieur)* inside out; *(de haut en bas)* the wrong way up, upside down; *(devant derrière)* the wrong way around, back to front; *Fig* **l'e. du décor** the other side of the picture; *Fam* **c'est le monde à l'e.!** what's the world coming to!

envers[2] [ɑ̃vɛr] *prép* toward; **e. et contre tous** in the face of all opposition

envi [ɑ̃vi] **à l'envi** *adv* **faire qch à l'e.** to vie with one another in doing sth

enviable [ɑ̃vjabl] *adj* enviable

envie [ɑ̃vi] *nf* (**a**) *(désir)* desire; *(caprice)* craving (**de** for); **avoir (très) e. qch/de faire qch** to (really) want sth/to do sth; **avoir e. de dormir** to feel sleepy; **avoir envie de rire/**

pleurer to feel like laughing/crying; **être pris d'une terrible e. de rire** to have a terrible urge to laugh; **donner à qn l'e. de faire qch** to make sb want to do sth; **il a e. que je le fasse** he wants me to do it; **je vais lui ôter l'e. de s'amuser** I'll stop his/her messing around; **ce gâteau me fait e.** that cake is tempting; **avoir e. de qn** *(sexuellement)* to want or to desire sb; **faire e. à qn** *(sujet: personne)* to tempt sb; *Fam* **ça lui a pris comme une e. de pisser** he just got a sudden urge (**b**) *(jalousie)* envy; **regarder qch avec e.** to look enviously at sth (**c**) *(au doigt)* hangnail; *(sur la peau)* birthmark

envier [66] [ɑ̃vje] *vt* to envy; **e. qch à qn** to envy sb sth; **n'avoir rien à e. à personne** to have no cause to be envious of anyone

envieux, -euse [ɑ̃vjø, -øz] **1** *adj* envious (**de** of) **2** *nm,f* envious person; **faire des e.** to make people envious

environ [ɑ̃virɔ̃] **1** *adv (à peu près)* about, around

2 environs *nmpl (alentours)* surrounding area; **aux** *ou* **dans les environs de Paris** in the vicinity of Paris; **aux environs de cinq heures** round about five o'clock

environnant, -e [ɑ̃vironɑ̃, -ɑ̃t] *adj* surrounding

environnement [ɑ̃vironmɑ̃] *nm* (**a**) *(milieu)* environment (**b**) *Ordinat* environment; **e. partagé** shared environment

environner [ɑ̃virone] **1** *vt* to surround; **environné de qch** surrounded by sth

2 s'environner *vpr* **s'e. de** to surround oneself with

envisageable [ɑ̃vizaʒabl] *adj* conceivable

envisager [45] [ɑ̃vizaʒe] *vt (considérer) (question, situation, solution)* to consider; *(projeter) (conséquence, événement)* to envisage; **e. l'avenir** to foresee the future; **e. de faire qch** to consider doing sth

envoi [ɑ̃vwa] *nm* (**a**) *(action)* sending; **e. recommandé** registered delivery (**b**) *(colis)* package; *(lettre)* letter; *(marchandises)* consignment (**de** of)

envol [ɑ̃vɔl] *nm (d'avion)* take-off; *(d'oiseau)* taking off

envolée [ɑ̃vole] *nf* flight; *Fig* **e. lyrique** flight of fancy; *Fig* **l'e. du dollar** the soaring price of the dollar

envoler [ɑ̃vole] **s'envoler** *vpr* (**a**) *(oiseau)* to fly away; *(avion)* to take off; **je m'envole dans une heure** my plane leaves in an hour; *Fig* **s'e. dans les sondages** to shoot up in the opinion polls (**b**) *(emporté par le vent) (chapeau)* to blow off; *(papiers)* to blow away (**c**) *Fam (disparaître) (personne, sac)* to vanish

envoûtant, -e [ɑ̃vutɑ̃, -ɑ̃t] *adj (fascinant)* bewitching

envoûtement [ɑ̃vutmɑ̃] *nm aussi Fig* bewitchment

envoûter [ɑ̃vute] *vt aussi Fig* to bewitch

envoyé, -e [ɑ̃vwaje] *nm,f (messager)* messenger; *(d'un gouvernement)* envoy; **e. spécial** *(journaliste)* special correspondent

envoyer [33] [ɑ̃vwaje] **1** *vt* to send; *(lancer)* to throw; **e. qch par courrier** to mail sth; **e. qch à qn** to send sb sth; *(lancer)* to throw sth to sb; **e. un baiser à qn** to blow sb a kiss; **e. chercher qn** to send for sb; **e. qn faire qch** to send sb to do sth; *Fam* **e. promener** *ou* **balader** *ou* **paître qn, e. qn sur les roses** to send sb packing; *Fam* **je vais tout e. promener** I'm going to give it all up; *Fig* **e. des fleurs à qn** to pat sb on the back

2 s'envoyer *vpr* (**a**) *(l'un l'autre)* **ils s'envoient des cartes postales** they send postcards to each other; *Fig* **s'e. des fleurs** *(mutuellement)* to sing one another's praises, to pat one another on the back; *(à soi-même)* to pat oneself on the back (**b**) *Fam* **s'e. un verre de vin** to knock back a glass of wine; *très Fam* **s'e. qn** to do it with sb; *très Fam* **s'e. en l'air** to do it

envoyeur, -euse [ɑ̃vwajœr, -øz] *nm,f* sender; **retour à l'e.** return to sender

enzyme [ɑ̃zim] *nf* enzyme; **lessive aux enzymes** biological washing powder

éolien, -enne [eɔljɛ̃, -ɛn] **1** *adj* **énergie éolienne** wind energy; **moteur é.** wind-powered engine

2 *nf* **éolienne** wind turbine

épagneul, -e [epaɲœl] *nm,f* spaniel; **é. breton** Brittany spaniel

épais, -aisse [epɛ, -ɛs] **1** *adj* thick; **é. de trois mètres** ≃ ten feet thick; *Fam* **elle n'est pas bien épaisse** she hasn't got much on her

2 *adv* (**a**) *(pousser)* thick(ly) (**b**) *Fam (beaucoup)* **il n'y en a pas é.** there's not much of it

3 *nm* **au plus é. de la forêt** in the depths of the forest

épaisseur [epɛsœr] *nf* thickness; *Fig (d'une personne)* depth; **avoir trois mètres d'é.** ≃ to be ten feet thick

épaissir [epesir] **1** *vt (sauce, peinture)* to thicken; *(ombre, mystère)* to deepen

2 *vi (sauce)* to thicken; *(personne)* to fill out

3 s'épaissir *vpr (cheveux, brouillard, sauce)* to thicken; *(personne)* to fill out; *(ombre, mystère)* to deepen

épaississant [epesisɑ̃] *nm (substance)* thickener

épaississement [epesismɑ̃] *nm (du brouillard, d'une sauce)* thickening

épanchement [epɑ̃ʃmɑ̃] *nm* (**a**) **é. de synovie** water on the knee (**b**) *Fig (de sentiments)* outpouring

épancher [epɑ̃ʃe] **1** *vt* **é. sa bile** to vent one's spleen; **é. son cœur** to pour out one's heart

2 s'épancher *vpr (personne)* to pour out one's heart

épandage [epɑ̃daʒ] *nm Agr* manure spreading, manuring

épandre [epɑ̃dr] **1** *vt Agr* to spread

2 s'épandre *vpr Litt* to spread (**sur** over)

épanoui, -e [epanwi] *adj (fleur)* in full bloom; *(visage, sourire)* beaming; *(personne)* well-adjusted

épanouir [epanwir] **1** *vt (fleur, pétales)* to open out

2 s'épanouir *vpr* (**a**) *(fleur)* to bloom (**b**) *(visage)* to light up (**c**) *(personne)* to blossom

épanouissant, -e [epanwisɑ̃, -ɑ̃t] *adj (travail, vie)* fulfilling

épanouissement [epanwismɑ̃] *nm* (**a**) *(action) (d'une fleur)* blooming; *(d'un visage)* lighting up; *(d'une personne)* blossoming (**b**) *(plénitude)* full bloom

épargnant, -e [eparɲɑ̃, -ɑ̃t] *nm,f* saver; **les petits épargnants** small investors

épargne [eparɲ] *nf* (**a**) *(action, vertu)* saving (**b**) *(sommes)* savings (**c**) *(épargnants)* **l'é. privée** private investors

épargner [eparɲe] **1** *vt* (**a**) *(argent, provisions)* to save (**b**) *(énergie, temps)* to save; **é. à qn la peine de faire qch** to save sb the trouble of doing sth; **épargne-moi les détails!** spare me the details! (**c**) *(prisonnier)* to spare

2 *vi* to save (**sur** on)

3 s'épargner *vpr* **s'é. la peine de faire qch** to save oneself the trouble of doing sth

éparpiller [eparpije] **1** *vt (objets, foule)* to scatter

2 s'éparpiller *vpr (objets, foule)* to scatter; *Fig (personne)* to take on too much

épars, -e [epar, -ars] *adj (maisons)* scattered; *(végétation, population, informations)* sparse; *(cheveux)* thin

épatant, -e [epatɑ̃, -ɑ̃t] *adj Fam* splendid

épaté, -e [epate] *adj Fam* dumbfounded

épater [epate] *vt Fam* to astound

épaule [epol] *nf* shoulder; **être large d'épaules** to be broad-shouldered; *Culin* **é. d'agneau** shoulder of lamb

épauler [epole] **1** *vt* (**a**) *(fusil)* to raise to one's shoulder (**b**) *(aider)* **é. qn** to back sb up

2 *vi* to take aim

épaulette [epolɛt] *nf* (**a**) *(rembourrage)* shoulder pad (**b**) *(bretelle)* shoulder strap

épave [epav] *nf aussi Fig* wreck

épée [epe] *nf* sword; *Sport* épée; **coup d'é.** swordthrust; *Fig* **un coup d'é. dans l'eau** a wasted effort; *Fig* **une é. de Damoclès** a Sword of Damocles

épeler [9] [eple] *vt & vi* to spell

éperdu, -e [eperdy] *adj (regard)* distraught; *(amour)* passionate

éperdument [eperdymɑ̃] *adv (aimer)* madly; **é. amoureux** head over heels in love, madly in love; *Fam* **je m'en fiche é.** I couldn't care less

éperlan [eperlɑ̃] *nm* smelt

éperon [eprɔ̃] *nm* spur

éperonner [eprɔne] *vt* to spur on

épervier [epervje] *nm* sparrowhawk

épeurant, -e [epœrɑ̃, -ɑ̃t] *adj Can* scary

éphèbe [efɛb] *nm* Adonis

éphémère [efemɛr] **1** *adj* short-lived, ephemeral

2 *nm* mayfly

épi [epi] *nm* (**a**) *(de grain)* ear; *(de fleur)* spike; **é. de maïs** corn-cob (**b**) *(de cheveux)* tuft of hair

épice [epis] *nf* spice; **quatre épices** allspice

épicé, -e [epise] *adj* spicy

épicéa [episea] *nm* spruce

épicentre [episɑ̃tr] *nm* epicenter

épicer [16] [epise] *vt* to spice

épicerie [episri] *nf* (**a**) *(magasin)* grocer's (shop); **é. fine** delicatessen (**b**) *(produits)* groceries (**c**) *Can Fig* **liste d'é.** *(de griefs)* shopping list

épicier, -ère [episje, -ɛr] *nm,f* grocer; *Péj* **d'é.** *(mentalité)* small-town, parochial

épicurien, -enne [epikyrjɛ̃, -ɛn] **1** *adj* epicurean; *Phil* Epicurean

2 *nm,f* epicure; *Phil* Epicurean

épidémie [epidemi] *nf* epidemic

épidémique [epidemik] *adj* epidemic

épiderme [epidɛrm] *nm* skin, *Spéc* epidermis

épidermique [epidɛrmik] *adj* epidermal; *Fig* **une réaction é.** a kneejerk reaction

épier [66] [epje] *vt (espionner) (personne, activités)* to spy on; *(observer) (signe, occasion)* to watch out for

épilation [epilasjɔ̃] *nf (des jambes)* removal of unwanted hair; *(des sourcils)* plucking; **se faire faire une é. maillot** to have one's bikini line done; **é. maillot brésilienne** Brazilian wax

épilatoire [epilatwar] *adj (crème)* hair-removing

épilepsie [epilɛpsi] *nf* epilepsy; **crise d'é.** epileptic fit

épileptique [epilɛptik] *adj & nmf* epileptic

épiler [epile] **1** *vt (jambes)* to remove the unwanted hair from; *(sourcils)* to pluck

2 s'épiler *vpr* **s'é. les jambes** to remove the unwanted hair from one's legs; **s'é. les sourcils** to pluck one's eyebrows; **s'é. les jambes à la cire** to wax one's legs

épilogue [epilɔg] *nm* epilogue

épiloguer [epilɔge] *vi* to hold forth (**sur** about)

épinard [epinar] *nm (plante)* spinach; **épinards** spinach; **épinards en branches** leaf spinach

épine [epin] *nf (piquant)* thorn; *(d'un animal)* spine, prickle; *Fig* **tirer une é. du pied à qn** *(tirer d'embarras)* to get sb out of a mess; *(soulager)* to relieve sb's mind; **é. dorsale** backbone

épinette [epinɛt] *nf* (**a**) *Can Bot* spruce (**b**) *(instrument)* spinet

épineux, -euse [epinø, -øz] *adj (arbuste, problème)* thorny; *(poisson)* spiny

épingle [epɛ̃gl] *nf* pin; **attacher qch avec des épingles** *(cheveux)* to pin sth up; *(tissu, feuilles)* to pin sth together; *Fig* **tirer son é. du jeu** to extricate oneself; *Fig* **être tiré à quatre épingles** to be dressed up to the nines; *Fig* **chercher une é. dans une botte de foin** to look for a needle in a haystack; *Fig* **monter qch en é.** to make too much of sth; **é. à chapeau** hatpin; **é. à cheveux** hairpin; **virage en é. à cheveux** hairpin turn; **é. à linge** clothespin; **é. de** *ou* **à nourrice, é. de sûreté** safety pin

épingler [epɛ̃gle] vt (a) (attacher) to pin (**à/sur** to/on) (b) Fam (arrêter) to nab; **se faire é.** to get nabbed

épinoche [epinɔʃ] nf stickleback

Épiphanie [epifani] nf Rel **l'É.** Epiphany

épique [epik] adj epic

épiscopal, -e, -aux, -ales [episkɔpal, -o] adj episcopal

épiscopat [episkɔpa] nm (fonction, évêques) episcopate

épisode [epizɔd] nm aussi Fig episode

épisodique [epizɔdik] adj (intermittent) occasional; (accessoire) minor

épisodiquement [epizɔdikmɑ̃] adv occasionally

épistémologie [epistemɔlɔʒi] nf epistemology

épistolaire [epistɔlɛr] adj epistolary; **être en relation é. avec qn** to correspond with sb

épitaphe [epitaf] nf epitaph

épithélium [epiteljɔm] nm epithelium

épithète [epitɛt] nf epithet; Gram attribute

épître [epitr] nf epistle

éploré, -e [eplɔre] adj tearful

épluchage [eplyʃaʒ] nm peeling; Fig detailed examination

épluche-légumes [eplyʃlegym] nm inv (potato) peeler

éplucher [eplyʃe] vt (peler) to peel; Fig (texte, journal) to go through in detail

épluchette [eplyʃɛt] nf Can **é. de blé d'Inde** corn-husking party

éplucheur [eplyʃœr] nm (potato) peeler

épluchure [eplyʃyr] nf (pelure) peeling

éponge [epɔ̃ʒ] **1** nf sponge; **donner un coup d'é. à qch** to wipe sth with a sponge; **d'un coup d'é.** with a sponge; **jeter l'é.** (à la boxe) & Fig to throw in the towel; Fig **passer l'é.** to forget all about it
2 adj inv tissu é. terry cloth; **serviette é.** terry towel

éponger [45] [epɔ̃ʒe] **1** vt (a) (liquide) to mop up (b) (surface) to sponge (down); (le front de quelqu'un) to mop (c) Fig (déficit) to mop up
2 s'éponger vpr s'é. le front to mop one's brow

épopée [epɔpe] nf aussi Fig epic

époque [epɔk] nf (a) (historique) era, age; Géol period; **la Belle É.** ≃ the early 20th Century; **quelle é. (nous vivons)!** what times we live in!; **être de son é.** to be in tune with the times; **meubles d'é.** period furniture (b) (moment précis) time; **à l'é.** at the time

---

La Belle Époque

This refers to the period of apparent stability and prosperity from the closing years of the 19th century to the beginning of the First World War, which found its expression in café and theater society, fashion, art and architecture. Its chief surviving monument is the area on the south side of the Champs-Élysées containing the "Petit Palais" and the "Grand Palais", erected at the time of the World's Fair of 1900.

épouiller [epuje] vt to delouse

époumoner [epumone] **s'époumoner** vpr (en criant) to shout oneself hoarse; (en chantant) to sing oneself hoarse

épouse [epuz] nf wife

épouser [epuze] vt to marry; Fig (cause) to espouse; Fig **é. la forme de qch** to take on the exact shape of sth

épousseter [42] [epuste] vt to dust

époustouflant, -e [epustuflɑ̃, -ɑ̃t] adj Fam astounding

époustoufler [epustufle] vt Fam to astound

épouvantable [epuvɑ̃tabl] adj dreadful, appalling

épouvantail [epuvɑ̃taj] nm (de jardin) scarecrow; Péj (personne laide) fright; (personne terrifiante) boogie man

épouvante [epuvɑ̃t] nf terror

épouvanté, -e [epuvɑ̃te] adj terror-stricken

épouvanter [epuvɑ̃te] vt to terrify

époux [epu] nm husband; **les é.** the married couple; **les é. Thomas** Mr and Mrs Thomas

éprendre [58] [eprɑ̃dr] **s'éprendre** vpr **s'é. de qn** to fall in love with sb

épreuve [eprœv] nf (a) (essai) test; **mettre qn/qch à l'é.** to put sb/sth to the test; **à l'é. du feu** fireproof; **à l'é. des balles** bulletproof; **un courage à toute é.** unfailing courage; **être mis à rude é.** (personne, patience) to be severely tested; **les bateaux furent mis à rude é. par la tempête** the boats took a battering from the storm; Fig **é. de force** trial of strength (b) (examen) (écrit) (examination) paper; (oral) test (c) (d'athlétisme) event; **é. contre la montre** time trial; **é. éliminatoire** heat (d) (adversité) trial, ordeal; **dans l'é.** in adversity (e) Typ proof (f) Phot print

épris, -e [epri, -iz] adj **é. de qn** in love with sb; **é. de qch** passionate about sth

éprouvant, -e [epruvɑ̃, -ɑ̃t] adj trying

éprouvé, -e [epruve] adj (a) (testé) (remède) proven, well-tried; (matériaux) tested (b) (famille) sorely tried; (région) hard-hit

éprouver [epruve] vt (a) (essayer) (méthode, personne, courage) to test (b) (ressentir) (sensation, sentiment, douleur) to feel (c) (subir) (perte) to suffer; (difficultés) to meet with

éprouvette [epruvɛt] **1** nf test tube
2 adj bébé é. test-tube baby

EPS [əpeɛs] nf (abrév **éducation physique et sportive**) Phys Ed

épuisant, -e [epɥizɑ̃, -ɑ̃t] adj exhausting

épuisé, -e [epɥize] adj (a) (très fatigué) exhausted (b) (sol) exhausted (c) (livre, édition) out of print; (marchandises) sold out

épuisement [epɥizmɑ̃] nm (a) (fatigue) exhaustion; **danser jusqu'à l'é.** to dance till one drops (b) (d'un sol, d'un stock, de ressources) exhaustion; **jusqu'à. é. des stocks** while stocks last

épuiser [epɥize] **1** vt (a) (fatiguer) to exhaust (b) (sol, stock, ressources, sujet) to exhaust
2 s'épuiser vpr (a) (se fatiguer) to exhaust oneself, to wear oneself out; **s'é. à faire qch** to wear oneself out doing sth (b) (source) to dry up; (stock, ressources) to run out

épuisette [epɥizɛt] nf landing net

épuration [epyrasjɔ̃] nf (de l'eau, du gaz) purification; (du pétrole, d'un minerai) refining; Fig (d'une langue) refining; Pol purge

épurer [epyre] vt (eau, gaz) to purify; (pétrole, minerai) to refine; Fig (langue) to refine; Pol (parti) to purge

équarrir [ekarir] vt (a) (bois, pierre) to square (b) (animal) to quarter

équarrissage [ekarisaʒ] nm (a) (du bois, de la pierre) squaring (b) (d'animaux) quartering

Équateur [ekwatœr] nm **l'É.** Ecuador

équateur [ekwatœr] nm equator; **sous l'é.** at the equator

équation [ekwasjɔ̃] nf equation; **é. du premier/deuxième degré** simple/quadratic equation

équatorial, -e, -aux, -ales [ekwatɔrjal, -o] adj equatorial

équatorien, -enne [ekwatɔrjɛ̃, -ɛn] **1** adj Ecuadorian
2 nm,f **É., Équatorienne** Ecuadorian

équerre [ekɛr] nf **é. (à dessin)** set square; **en é., à l'é.** at right angles; **d'é.** square, straight

équestre [ekɛstr] adj (statue, sports) equestrian; (exercices) horseback riding

équidés [ekɥide, ekide] nmpl horse family, Spéc Equidae

équidistant, -e [ekɥidistɑ̃, -ɑ̃t] adj equidistant (**de** from)

équilatéral, -e, -aux, -ales [ekɥilateral, -o] adj equilateral

équilibrage [ekilibraʒ] nm balancing

équilibre [ekilibr] nm (a) (d'un corps, d'un objet) balance; **mettre qch en é.** to balance sth; **perdre l'é.** to lose one's balance;

faire perdre l'é. à qn to throw sb off balance; **faire de l'é. sur qch** to balance on sth; **être en é. instable** to be precariously balanced (**b**) *(mental)* (mental) balance, equilibrium (**c**) **budget en é.** balanced budget; **é. budgétaire** balanced budget (**d**) *(d'un ensemble)* balance

équilibré, -e [ekilibre] *adj (chargement, alimentation)* balanced; *(personne)* well-balanced; *(vie)* stable

équilibrer [ekilibre] **1** *vt (charge, composition)* to balance; *(bateau, avion)* to trim; **é. un budget** to balance a budget

  2 s'équilibrer *vpr (l'un l'autre)* to balance each other out

équilibriste [ekilibrist] *nmf (funambule)* tightrope walker

équinoxe [ekinɔks] *nm* equinox

équipage [ekipaʒ] *nm* (**a**) *(d'un navire, d'un avion)* crew; **les hommes d'é.** the crew; **les membres de l'é.** the crew (**b**) *(voiture et chevaux)* equipage

équipe [ekip] *nf* (**a**) *Sport* team; **une é. de football** a soccer team (**b**) *(de chercheurs, de médecins)* team; *(d'ouvriers)* gang; *(à l'usine)* shift; *Mil* working party; **travailler en é.** to work as a team; **faire é. avec qn** to team up with sb; **é. dirigeante** management team; **é. de jour/nuit** day/night shift; **é. de secours** rescue team

équipée [ekipe] *nf (frasque)* escapade; *(promenade, voyage)* jaunt

équipement [ekipmã] *nm* (**a**) *(action)* *(d'un atelier, d'une cuisine)* equipping, fitting out (**de** with) (**b**) *(matériel)* equipment; *(de soldat)* kit (**c**) *(installations)* facilities; **équipements collectifs** public facilities; *Ordinat* **é. informatique** computer equipment

équiper [ekipe] **1** *vt (atelier, cuisine)* to equip, to fit out (**de** with); *(sportif, armée)* to equip (**de** with); **appartement avec cuisine équipée** apartment with cooking facilities

  2 s'équiper *vpr* to equip oneself (**de** with)

équipier, -ère [ekipje, -ɛr] *nm,f* team member

équitable [ekitabl] *adj* fair

équitablement [ekitabləmã] *adv* fairly

équitation [ekitasjɔ̃] *nf* horseback riding; **faire de l'é.** to go horseback riding

équivalence [ekivalɑ̃s] *nf* equivalence; *Univ* **avoir/obtenir une é.** to have/get an equivalent diploma

équivalent, -e [ekivalɑ̃, -ɑ̃t] **1** *adj* equivalent (**à** to)

  2 *nm* equivalent; **sans é.** without equal

équivaloir [69a] [ekivalwar] *vi* **é. à qch** *(valoir)* to be equivalent to sth; *(revenir à)* to amount to sth

équivaut *voir* **équivaloir**

équivoque [ekivɔk] **1** *adj* (**a**) *(ambigu)* *(terme, attitude)* equivocal, ambiguous (**b**) *(douteux)* *(conduite, passé)* dubious

  2 *nf* ambiguity; **sans é.** *(réponse, situation)* unequivocal; *(répondre)* unequivocally

érable [erabl] *nm (arbre, bois)* maple; **sirop d'é.** maple syrup

érablière [erablijɛr] *nf Can* maple grove

éradication [eradikasjɔ̃] *nf* eradication

éradiquer [eradike] *vt* to eradicate

érafler [erafle] **1** *vt (genou)* to graze; *(cuir)* to scuff; *(bois, meuble)* to scratch

  2 s'érafler *vpr* **s'é. le coude** to graze one's elbow

éraflure [eraflyr] *nf (au genou)* graze; *(sur cuir)* scuff mark; *(sur bois, sur meuble)* scratch

éraillé, -e [eraje] *adj* (**a**) *(voix)* hoarse (**b**) *(surface)* scratched

ère [ɛr] *nf* era; **en l'an 1150 de notre è.** in the year 1150 AD; **avant notre è.** BC

érection [erɛksjɔ̃] *nf* (**a**) *(construction)* erection (**b**) *(gonflement)* erection; **être en é.** *(personne)* to have an erection; *(organe)* to be erect

éreintant, -e [erɛ̃tɑ̃, -ɑ̃t] *adj Fam* exhausting

éreinté, -e [erɛ̃te] *adj Fam* exhausted

éreinter [erɛ̃te] **1** *vt* (**a**) *(fatiguer)* *(personne, animal)* to exhaust, to wear out (**b**) *(critiquer)* *(livre, auteur)* to tear to pieces

  2 s'éreinter *vpr* **s'é. à faire qch** to wear oneself out doing sth

érémiste [eremist] = **RMiste**

Erevan [erevan] *n* Yerevan

ergot [ɛrgo] *nm* (**a**) *(d'un coq)* spur (**b**) *(d'un chien)* dewclaw (**c**) *Tech* pin

ergoter [ɛrgɔte] *vi* to quibble (**sur** about)

Érié [erje] *n voir* **lac**

ériger [45] [eriʒe] **1** *vt* (**a**) *(dresser)* *(statue, temple, mât)* to erect (**b**) *(créer)* *(tribunal)* to establish, to set up (**c**) *Fig* **é. qn en qch** to set sb up as sth; **é. qch en qch** to elevate sth to the status of sth

  2 s'ériger *vpr* **s'é. en qch** to set oneself up as sth

ermitage [ɛrmitaʒ] *nm* hermitage

ermite [ɛrmit] *nm* hermit; **vivre en e.** to live the life of a recluse

érogène [erɔʒɛn] *adj* erogenous

érosion [erozjɔ̃] *nf* erosion

érotique [erɔtik] *adj* erotic

érotisme [erɔtism] *nm* eroticism

errance [erɑ̃s] *nf Litt* roving, wandering

errant, -e [ɛrɑ̃, -ɑ̃t] *adj (vie)* roving, wandering; **chevalier e.** knight-errant; **chien e.** stray dog

errata [ɛrata] *nmpl voir* **erratum**

erratique [ɛratik] *adj* erratic

erratum [ɛratɔm] *(pl* **errata** [ɛrata]*) nm* erratum

errements [ɛrmɑ̃] *nmpl* bad ways; **retomber dans ses e. passés** to fall back into one's bad old ways

errer [ɛre] *vi (marcher)* to wander; **e. par les rues** to roam the streets; **e. comme une âme en peine** to wander around like a lost soul

erreur [ɛrœr] *nf* (**a**) *(faute)* mistake, error; **faire** *ou* **commettre une e.** to make a mistake; **faire e.** to be mistaken; **être dans l'e.** to be mistaken; **induire qn en e.** to mislead sb; **par e.** by mistake; **sauf e. de ma part** if I'm not mistaken; **il y a e. sur la personne** you've/they've/*etc.* got the wrong person; **il n'y a pas d'e. (possible)** there's no doubt about it; **l'e. est humaine** to err is human; **e. de calcul** miscalculation; **e. de jeunesse** youthful indiscretion; **e. judiciaire** miscarriage of justice; **e. de jugement** error of judgment (**b**) *Ordinat* error; **message d'e.** error message; **correction des erreurs** error correction; **e. d'analyse (syntaxique)** parse error; **e. disque** disk error; **e. d'échantillonnage** sampling error; **e. d'écriture** write error; **e. de lecture** read error; **e. de logiciel** software *or* system error; **e. de programmation** programming error; **e. de saisie** keying error

erroné, -e [ɛrɔne] *adj* erroneous

ersatz [ɛrzats] *nm inv* ersatz, substitute

éructer [erykte] **1** *vi* to belch

  2 *vt Fig* **é. des injures** to hurl abuse

érudit, -e [erydi, -it] **1** *adj* erudite, scholarly

  2 *nm,f* scholar

érudition [erydisjɔ̃] *nf* erudition, scholarship

éruption [erypsjɔ̃] *nf* (**a**) *(d'un volcan)* eruption; **entrer en é.** to erupt (**b**) *(de boutons)* rash

érythème [eritɛm] *nm Méd* rash; **é. fessier** diaper rash; **é. solaire** sunburn

Érythrée [eritre] *nf* l'É. Eritrea

érythréen, -enne [eritreɛ̃, -ɛn] **1** *adj* Eritrean

  2 *nm,f* É., Érythréenne Eritrean

E/S *Ordinat (abrév* **entrée/sortie***)* I/O

es *voir* **être**²

ès [ɛs] *prép* **docteur ès lettres/sciences** ≃ PhD; **licencié ès lettres** ≃ BA; **licencié ès sciences** ≃ BS, BSc

ESB [əɛsbe] *nf (abrév* **encéphalite spongiforme bovine***)* BSE

esbroufe [ɛzbruf] *nf Fam* bluffing; **faire de l'e.** to bluff

escabeau, -x [ɛskabo] *nm* (**a**) *(tabouret)* stool (**b**) *(marche-pied)* stepladder

escadre [ɛskadr] *nf Naut* squadron; *Aviat* **e. aérienne** wing; **chef d'e.** *Naut* squadron commander; *Aviat* wing commander

escadrille [ɛskadrij] *nf* (**a**) *Naut* flotilla (**b**) *Aviat (unité)* flight

escadron [ɛskadrɔ̃] *nm* (**a**) *Mil* squadron; **chef d'e.** major (**b**) *Aviat* squadron (**c**) *Fig (groupe) (de personnes)* troop, band

escalade [ɛskalad] *nf* (**a**) *(d'un mur, d'une falaise)* climbing, scaling; *Sport* climbing; **faire de l'e.** to go climbing (**b**) *Fig (d'une guerre, des prix, de la violence)* escalation

escalader [ɛskalade] *vt* to climb, to scale

escalator® [ɛskalatɔr] *nm* escalator

escale [ɛskal] *nf* (**a**) *(arrêt)* lay over; **faire e.** *(en bateau)* to put into port; *(en avion)* to touch down; **faire e. à Athènes** *(en bateau)* to put in at Athens; *(en avion)* to lay over at Athens; **vol sans e.** nonstop flight; **e. technique** refueling stop (**b**) *(lieu) (pour bateau)* port of call; *(pour avion)* layover

escalier [ɛskalje] *nm (marches)* stairs; *(cage)* staircase; **dans l'e., dans les escaliers** on the stairs; **monter en e.** *(en ski)* to sidestep; **e. en colimaçon** spiral staircase; **e. mécanique, e. roulant,** *Can* **e. mobile** escalator; **e. de secours** fire escape; **e. de service** backstairs

escalope [ɛskalɔp] *nf* escalope

escamotable [ɛskamɔtabl] *adj (antenne, train d'atterrissage, phares)* retractable; *(meuble)* foldaway

escamotage [ɛskamɔtaʒ] *nm* (**a**) *(par un illusionniste)* vanishing (**b**) *(d'un train d'atterrissage)* retraction (**c**) *Fig (d'un problème)* dodging

escamoter [ɛskamɔte] *vt* (**a**) **e. qch** *(sujet: illusionniste)* to make sth vanish (**b**) *(voler)* to sneak off with (**c**) *(train d'atterrissage)* to retract (**d**) *Fig (problème)* to dodge

escampette [ɛskɑ̃pɛt] *nf Fam* **prendre la poudre d'e.** to make off

escapade [ɛskapad] *nf* jaunt; **faire une e.** to go on a jaunt

escarbille [ɛskarbij] *nf* cinder

escargot [ɛskargo] *nm* snail; **aller à une allure d'e.** *ou* **à la vitesse d'un e.** to go at a snail's pace; **marcher comme un e.** to walk at a snail's pace; *Fig* **opération e.** = slowing down of traffic by protesting truck drivers

escarmouche [ɛskarmuʃ] *nf* skirmish

escarpé, -e [ɛskarpe] *adj (route, montagne)* steep

escarpement [ɛskarpəmɑ̃] *nm (versant)* steep slope; *Géog* escarpment

escarpin [ɛskarpɛ̃] *nm* pump *(shoe)*

escarpolette [ɛskarpɔlɛt] *nf Vieilli (balançoire)* swing

escarre [ɛskar] *nf Méd* scab; *(due aux draps)* bedsore

escient [ɛsjɑ̃] *nm* **à bon e.** wisely; **à mauvais e.** unwisely

esclaffer [ɛsklafe] **s'esclaffer** *vpr* to burst out laughing, to roar with laughter

esclandre [ɛsklɑ̃dr] *nm (scandale, tapage)* scene; **faire** *ou* **causer un e.** to make a scene

esclavage [ɛsklavaʒ] *nm* slavery; **réduire qn en e.** to enslave sb

esclavagisme [ɛsklavaʒism] *nm* slavery; *(doctrine)* pro-slavery

esclave [ɛsklav] **1** *nmf* slave; **être vendu comme e.** to be sold into slavery; *Fig* **être l'e. de qn/qch** to be a slave to sb/sth **2** *adj Fig* **être e. de ses habitudes** to be a slave to one's habits

escogriffe [ɛskɔgrif] *nm* **(grand) e.** beanpole

escompte [ɛskɔ̃t] *nm* discount; *Fin* **taux d'e.** (bank) discount rate

escompter [ɛskɔ̃te] *vt (espérer)* to expect, to anticipate (**que** that); **e. faire qch** to expect to do sth

escorte [ɛskɔrt] *nf* escort; **sous (bonne) e.** under escort

escorter [ɛskɔrte] *vt* to escort

escouade [ɛskwad] *nf Mil* squad

escrime [ɛskrim] *nf Sport* fencing; **faire de l'e.** to fence

escrimer [ɛskrime] **s'escrimer** *vpr* to fight; **s'e. à faire qch** to struggle to do sth

escrimeur, -euse [ɛskrimœr, -øz] *nm,f* fencer

escroc [ɛskro] *nm* crook, swindler

escroquer [ɛskrɔke] *vt (personne)* to swindle, to cheat; **e. qch à qn,** **e. qn de qch** to swindle *or* to cheat sb out of sth

escroquerie [ɛskrɔkri] *nf (action)* swindling; *(résultat)* swindle; *(délit)* fraud; *Fam* **mais c'est de l'e.!** that's a rip-off!

escudo [ɛskydo] *nm* escudo

eskimo [ɛskimo] = **esquimau**

ésotérique [ezɔterik] *adj* esoteric

espace [ɛspas] *nm* (**a**) *(étendue, distance)* space; **laisser de l'e.** to leave space; **e. blanc** space; **E. économique européen** European economic area; **e. publicitaire** advertising space; **e. de rangement** storage space; **e. vital** living space; **espaces verts** parks, green spaces (**b**) *(durée)* **en l'e. d'une semaine** within a week (**c**) *(atmosphère)* space; **e. aérien** airspace (**d**) *Math* space; **e. à trois/quatre dimensions** three-/four-dimensional space (**e**) *Ordinat* **e. disque** disk space; **e. mémoire** memory space; **e. de stockage** storage space

espacement [ɛspasmɑ̃] *nm (action)* spacing out; *(résultat)* spacing; *(distance)* space; *Ordinat* **e. arrière** backspace

espacer [16] [ɛspase] **1** *vt (objets, paiements, visites)* to space out
2 s'espacer *vpr* (**a**) *(visites, lettres)* to become less frequent (**b**) *(personnes)* **espacez-vous** space yourselves out

espace-temps *(pl* **espaces-temps)** [ɛspastɑ̃] *nm Math & Phys* space-time (continuum)

espadon [ɛspadɔ̃] *nm* swordfish

espadrille [ɛspadrij] *nf* espadrille

Espagne [ɛspaɲ] *nf* **l'E.** Spain

espagnol, -e [ɛspaɲɔl] **1** *adj* Spanish
2 *nm (langue)* Spanish
3 *nm,f* **E., Espagnole** Spaniard; **les Espagnols** the Spanish

espagnolette [ɛspaɲɔlɛt] *nf* window fastener *(long vertical bar with pivoting central catch)*

espalier [ɛspalje] *nm* (**a**) *(mur)* espalier wall (**b**) *(de gymnase)* wall bars

espèce [ɛspɛs] *nf* (**a**) *(sorte)* kind, sort; **les gens de son e.** people like her, people of her kind; **de la pire e.** of the worst sort; **cela n'a aucune e. d'importance** that's of no importance whatsoever; *Fam* **cette e. d'idiot** that stupid idiot; *Fam* **e. d'idiot!** you idiot! (**b**) *Jur* **cas d'e.** specific case; **la loi applicable en l'e.** the law applicable to the case in point (**c**) **espèces** *(argent)* cash; **payer en espèces** to pay in cash; **espèces sonnantes et trébuchantes** hard cash (**d**) *Bot & Zool* species; **l'e. humaine** the human race, mankind

espérance [ɛsperɑ̃s] *nf* hope; **dans l'e. de faire qch** in the hope of doing sth; **dans l'e. que...** in the hope that...; **au-delà de nos espérances** beyond our expectations; **répondre aux espérances de qn** to live up to sb's expectations; **e. de vie** life expectancy

espérer [34] [ɛspere] **1** *vt* to hope for; **e. faire qch** to hope to do sth; **e. que** to hope that; **je ne vous espérais plus** I'd given you up
2 *vi* **j'espère bien** I hope so; **espérons!** let's hope so!

espiègle [ɛspjɛgl] *adj* mischievous

espion, -onne [ɛspjɔ̃, -ɔn] *nm,f* spy

espionnage [ɛspjɔnaʒ] *nm* espionage, spying; **faire de l'e.** to spy; **l'e. industriel** industrial espionage

espionner [ɛspjɔne] **1** *vt* to spy on
2 *vi* to spy

esplanade [ɛsplanad] *nf* esplanade

espoir [ɛspwar] *nm* (**a**) *(espérance)* hope; **avoir l'e. de faire**

qch to have hopes of doing sth; **avoir bon e.** to be full of hope; **reprendre e.** to become hopeful again; **nourrir l'e. de faire qch** to live in hope of doing sth; **dans l'e. de faire qch** in the hope of doing sth; **dans l'e. de vous voir bientôt** hoping to see you soon; **tous les espoirs sont permis** things look hopeful; **c'est sans e.** it's hopeless; *Ironique* **l'e. fait vivre** hope springs eternal **(b)** *(personne)* hope; **un e. du tennis français** one of the most promising French tennis players

esprit [ɛspri] *nm* **(a)** *(intellectuel)* mind; **avoir l'e. large/ étroit** to be broad-/narrow-minded; **avoir l'e. tranquille** to be easy in one's mind; **avoir l'e. mal tourné** to have a dirty mind; **avoir l'e. d'analyse/scientifique** to have an analytical/a scientific (turn of) mind; **perdre l'e.** to go out of one's mind; **reprendre ses esprits** to regain consciousness; **elle avait l'e. ailleurs** her thoughts were elsewhere; **elle n'a pas l'e. à ce qu'elle fait** her mind isn't on what she's doing; **je n'ai pas l'e. à plaisanter** I'm not in the mood for joking; **une pareille idée ne me serait jamais venue à l'e.** such an idea would never have crossed my mind; **qu'avez-vous à l'e.?** what are you thinking about?

(b) *(attitude mentale)* spirit; **avoir mauvais e.** to be the malicious type; **faire du mauvais e.** to be malicious; **e. de caste** class-consciousness; **e. de clocher** parochialism; **e. de compétition** competitive spirit; **e. de corps** esprit de corps; **e. d'entreprise** enterprise spirit; **e. d'équipe** team spirit; **e. de famille** family feeling

(c) *(humour)* wit; **avoir de l'e.** to be witty; **mots** *ou* **traits d'e.** witticisms; **faire de l'e.** to display one's wit

(d) *(personne)* **un e. fort** a freethinker; *Prov* **les grands esprits se rencontrent** great minds think alike

(e) *(sens)* spirit; **l'e. de la loi** the spirit of the law

(f) *(fantôme)* spirit; **e., es-tu là?** *(dans une séance de spiritisme)* is there anybody there?; **e. frappeur** poltergeist

(g) *Chim* (volatile) spirit

esquif [ɛskif] *nm* skiff; **un frêle e.** a frail barque

esquimau, -aude, -x, -audes [ɛskimo, -od] **1** *adj* Eskimo, Inuit

2 *nm (glace)* **E.**® ≃ ice-cream bar

3 *nm, f* **E., Esquimaude** Eskimo, Inuit

esquinté, -e [ɛskɛ̃te] *adj Fam (abîmé)* wrecked

esquinter [ɛskɛ̃te] *Fam* **1** *vt (abîmer)* to wreck; *(blesser)* to hurt

2 s'esquinter *vpr (s'abîmer)* **s'e. la jambe** to hurt one's leg; **s'e. la santé/les yeux (à faire qch)** to ruin one's health/eyes (doing sth)

esquisse [ɛskis] *nf (dessin)* sketch; *Fig (d'un projet, d'un roman)* outline; *(d'un sourire)* suggestion

esquisser [ɛskise] **1** *vt (dessiner)* to sketch; *Fig (plan, roman)* to outline; *Fig* **e. un sourire** to give a faint smile

2 s'esquisser *vpr (idée, projet)* to take shape

esquiver [ɛskive] **1** *vt aussi Fig* to dodge, to evade

2 s'esquiver *vpr* to slip away

essai [ɛse] *nm* **(a)** *(tentative)* try; **faire un e.** to have a try **(b)** *(test) (d'un produit, d'une voiture)* test, trial; **à l'e.** on a trial basis; *Ordinat* **e. approfondi** beta test; **e. nucléaire** nuclear test; *Ordinat* **e. de performance** benchmark **(c)** *(ouvrage)* essay **(d)** *(au rugby)* try

essaim [ɛsɛ̃] *nm aussi Fig* swarm

essaimer [eseme] *vi (abeilles)* to swarm; *Fig (population, famille)* to spread; *(entreprise)* to expand

essayage [ɛsɛjaʒ] *nm* fitting

essayer [53] [eseje] **1** *vt* **(a)** *(pour la première fois) (gadget, restaurant)* to try (out); *(voiture)* to test-drive; *(vin, plat)* to try, to taste; *(vêtement, chaussures)* to try on **(b)** *(tester) (machine, produit)* to test **(c)** *(tenter)* **e. de faire qch** to try to do sth

2 s'essayer *vpr* **s'e. à qch/à faire qch** to try one's hand at sth/at doing sth

ESSEC [ɛsɛk] *nf (abrév* **École supérieure des sciences économiques et commerciales**) = university-level business school

essence [esɑ̃s] *nf* **(a)** *(combustible)* gas(oline); **e. ordinaire** regular gas; **e. sans plomb** unleaded (gas) **(b)** *(extrait) (de plantes, de café)* essence; **e. de térébenthine** spirits of turpentine **(c)** *(caractère fondamental)* essence; **par e.** essentially **(d)** *(espèce)* species

essentiel, -elle [esɑ̃sjɛl] **1** *adj* **(a)** *(nécessaire)* essential, necessary (**à**/**pour** for) **(b)** *(principal) (condition, caractère)* essential; *(raison)* basic, main

2 *nm* **l'e.** *(le plus important)* the main thing; *(le minimum)* the essentials; **l'e. de** *(la majeure partie de)* the majority of

essentiellement [esɑ̃sjɛlmɑ̃] *adv* **(a)** *(principalement)* essentially, mainly **(b)** *(par nature)* essentially

esseulé, -e [esœle] *adj* isolated

essieu, -x [esjø] *nm* axle

essor [esɔr] *nm* **(a)** *(d'un oiseau)* flight; **prendre son e.** to fly off **(b)** *Fig (d'une industrie, d'une économie)* (rapid) growth; **en plein e.** booming; **prendre son e.** to take off

essorage [esɔraʒ] *nm (à la machine)* spin-drying; *(à la main)* wringing

essorer [esɔre] *vt (vêtements) (à la machine)* to spin-dry; *(à la main)* to wring out; *(salade)* to spin

essoreuse [esɔrøz] *nf (à tambour)* spin-drier

essoufflé, -e [esufle] *adj* out of breath

essoufflement [esufləmɑ̃] *nm* breathlessness; *Fig (de l'économie, d'une activité)* running out of steam

essouffler [esufle] **1** *vt* to make out of breath

2 s'essouffler *vpr* to get out of breath; *Fig (économie, activité)* to run out of steam

essuie [esɥi] *nm Belg (essuie-mains)* hand towel; *(torchon)* cloth, tea towel; *(serviette de bain)* bath towel

essuie-glace (*pl* **essuie-glaces**) [esɥiglas] *nm* windshield wiper

essuie-mains [esɥimɛ̃] *nm inv* hand towel

essuie-tout [esɥitu] *nm inv* paper towels

essuyer [32] [esɥije] **1** *vt* **(a)** *(surface)* to wipe; *(liquide)* to wipe up; *(larmes)* to wipe away; **e. la vaisselle** to dry the dishes **(b)** *(subir) (défaite, perte, insultes)* to suffer; *(refus)* to meet with; *(tempête)* to run into

2 s'essuyer *vpr* to wipe oneself; *(après un bain)* to dry oneself; **s'e. la bouche/les yeux** to wipe one's mouth/eyes

est¹ [ɛ] *voir* **être²**

est² [ɛst] **1** *nm* east; **un vent d'e.** an easterly wind; **le vent d'e.** the east wind; **à l'e.** in the east; **à l'e. de** (to the) east of; *Géog & Pol* **l'E.** the East

2 *adj inv (côte, face, régions)* eastern

estafilade [ɛstafilad] *nf* gash

estaminet [ɛstamine] *nm Belg (small)* café

estampe [ɛstɑ̃p] *nf* print

estampille [ɛstɑ̃pij] *nf (sur un document)* stamp; *(sur un produit)* mark

est-ce que [ɛskə] *adv interrogatif* **e. je peux entrer?** can I come in?; **est-ce qu'il est là?** is he here?; **e. tu la connais?** do you know her?; **est-ce qu'il connaissait la réponse?** did he know the answer?

esthète [ɛstɛt] *nmf* esthete

esthéticien, -enne [ɛstetisjɛ̃, -ɛn] *nm, f* beautician

esthétique [ɛstetik] **1** *adj* esthetic; *(beau)* esthetically pleasing

2 *nf (beauté)* esthetic quality

estimable [ɛstimabl] *adj* **(a)** *(digne de respect)* estimable **(b)** *(assez bon)* fairly good

estimation [ɛstimasjɔ̃] *nf* **(a)** *(détermination) (d'un prix, d'une distance, d'un poids)* estimation; *(de marchandises, d'une œuvre d'art)* valuation; *(de dommages, de besoins)* assessment **(b)** *(valeur, quantité estimée)* estimate

estime [ɛstim] *nf* (**a**) *(respect)* esteem, regard; **avoir de l'e. pour qn/qch** to esteem sb/sth; **baisser/remonter dans l'e. de qn** to go down/up in sb's estimation; **avoir un succès d'e.** to be a critical (though not a popular) success (**b**) *Naut* **à l'e.** by dead reckoning

estimer [ɛstime] **1** *vt* (**a**) *(déterminer)* *(prix, distance, poids)* to estimate; *(marchandises, œuvre d'art)* to value; *(dommages, besoins)* to assess (**b**) *(considérer)* to consider, to think (**que** that); **il n'a pas estimé nécessaire de me prévenir** he didn't consider it necessary to warn me (**c**) *(respecter)* *(personne)* to have a high opinion of; **e. qn à sa juste valeur** to value sb
2 s'estimer *vpr* **s'e. satisfait/heureux** to consider oneself satisfied/lucky

estival, -e, -aux, -ales [ɛstival, -o] *adj* summer

estivant, -e [ɛstivã, -ãt] *nm,f* vacationer

estocade [ɛstɔkad] *nf aussi Fig* deathblow; **donner l'e. à** to deal the deathblow to

estomac [ɛstɔma] *nm* (**a**) *(ventre)* stomach; **avoir l'e. vide** to have an empty stomach; **avoir l'e. dans les talons** to be starving (**b**) *Fam Fig (courage)* guts

estomaquer [ɛstɔmake] *vt Fam* to flabbergast

estomper [ɛstɔpe] **1** *vt Art (dessin)* to shade off; *Fig (paysage, contour, souvenir)* to blur
2 s'estomper *vpr (paysage, contour, souvenir)* to become blurred; *(peine)* to ease; *(rides)* to be smoothed out

Estonie [ɛstɔni] *nf* **l'E.** Estonia

estonien, -enne [ɛstɔnjɛ̃, -ɛn] **1** *adj* Estonian
2 *nm (langue)* Estonian
3 *nm,f* **E., Estonienne** Estonian

estourbir [ɛsturbir] *vt Fam* (**a**) *(tuer)* to bump off (**b**) *(étonner)* to astound

estrade [ɛstrad] *nf* platform

estragon [ɛstragɔ̃] *nm* tarragon

estropié, -e [ɛstrɔpje] **1** *adj* crippled
2 *nm,f* cripple

estropier [66] [ɛstrɔpje] *vt* (**a**) *(personne)* to cripple, to maim (**b**) *Fig (morceau de musique, langue étrangère)* to murder; *(mot, nom)* to mispronounce; *(texte)* to mutilate

estuaire [ɛstɥɛr] *nm* estuary

estudiantin, -e [ɛstydjãtɛ̃, -in] *adj* student

esturgeon [ɛstyrʒɔ̃] *nm* sturgeon

et [e] **1** *conj* (**a**) *(exprime l'addition, la simultanéité)* and; **et son frère et sa sœur** both his/her brother and his/her sister; **et d'un, il pleut, et de deux, je n'ai pas envie d'y aller** in the first place it's raining, and in the second place I don't want to go; **j'aime le café, et vous?** I like coffee, do you?; **et moi, alors?** what about me? (**b**) *(dans les nombres, les heures)* **vingt/trente et un** twenty-/thirty-one; **une livre et demie** a pound and a half; **il est quatre heures et demie/et quart** it's half/a quarter past four
2 *nm (symbole)* **et commercial** ampersand

ETA [ətea] *nf (abrév* **Euskadi ta Askatasuna**) ETA

étable [etabl] *nf* cowshed

établi¹ [etabli] *nm* workbench

établi², -e [etabli] *adj* established; **considérer qch comme une chose établie** to take sth for granted

établir [etablir] **1** *vt* (**a**) *(paix, relations, principe)* to establish; *(agence)* to set up; *(camp)* to pitch; *(prix)* to fix; *(devis, liste)* to draw up; *(record)* to set (**b**) *(démontrer)* to establish, to prove (**c**) *(autorité, réputation)* to establish (**sur** on)
2 s'établir *vpr* (**a**) *(dans une ville, un pays)* to settle (**b**) *(pour exercer un métier)* to set up in business (**c**) *(s'instaurer)* to become established

établissement [etablismã] *nm* (**a**) *(de la paix, de relations, d'un principe)* establishment; *(d'une agence)* setting up; *(d'un camp)* pitching; *(d'un prix)* fixing; *(d'un devis, d'une liste)* drawing up (**b**) *(démonstration)* establishment (**c**) *(installation)* *(d'une*

personne) settlement (**d**) *(institution)* establishment, institution; *(école)* school; **é. bancaire** bank; **é. de crédit** credit institution; **é. financier** financial institution; **é. hospitalier** hospital; **é. scolaire** school (**e**) *(entreprise)* business, firm; **les établissements Martin** Martin & Co

étage [etaʒ] *nm* (**a**) *(d'un bâtiment)* floor, story; **à deux étages** two-storied; **au troisième é.** on the fourth floor; **à l'é.** upstairs (**b**) *(d'un terrain)* level; *(d'un gâteau)* tier (**c**) *(d'une fusée)* stage

étager [45] [etaʒe] **s'étager** *vpr* to rise in tiers

étagère [etaʒɛr] *nf (meuble)* (set of) shelves; *(planche)* shelf

étai [etɛ] *nm Constr* prop

étain [etɛ̃] *nm* (**a**) *(métal)* tin (**b**) *(matériau pour vaisselle)* pewter; **un é.** a piece of pewter

étais, était *voir* **être²**

étal *(pl* **étals)** [etal] *nm* (**a**) *(au marché)* stall (**b**) *(de boucher)* butcher's block

étalage [etalaʒ] *nm* (**a**) *(vitrine)* window display (**b**) *Fig (ostentation)* display; **faire é. de son savoir/sa richesse** to show off one's knowledge/wealth

étalagiste [etalaʒist] *nmf* window dresser

étalement [etalmã] *nm (dans le temps)* staggering (**sur** over)

étaler [etale] **1** *vt* (**a**) *(étendre)* *(journal, papiers)* to spread out; *(nappe, beurre)* to spread; *(peinture, pommade)* to apply (**sur** to); *(cartes)* to lay down (**b**) *Fig (montrer)* *(richesse, connaissances)* to show off; *(vie privée)* to make a display of; **é. une affaire au grand jour** to make a matter public (**c**) *(dans le temps)* to stagger (**sur** over)
2 s'étaler *vpr* (**a**) *(village, parc)* to spread out (**b**) *(dans le temps)* to be spread (**sur** over) (**c**) *(se vautrer)* to sprawl (**d**) *Fam (tomber)* to fall flat on the ground; **s'é. de tout son long** to fall flat on one's face

étalon¹ [etalɔ̃] *nm (cheval)* stallion

étalon² [etalɔ̃] *nm (de mesure, monétaire)* standard; *Fig (modèle)* yardstick; *Écon* **l'é.-or** the gold standard

étamine [etamin] *nf Bot* stamen

étanche [etãʃ] *adj (bateau, récipient)* watertight; *(montre, bottes)* waterproof

étanchéité [etãʃeite] *nf (d'un bateau, d'un récipient)* watertightness; *(d'une montre, de bottes)* waterproofness

étancher [etãʃe] *vt* (**a**) *(liquide)* to stop the flow of; *(sang)* to staunch; *(larmes)* to dry (**b**) *(soif)* to quench

étang [etã] *nm* pond, pool

étant *voir* **être²**

étape [etap] *nf* (**a**) *(lieu)* stopover; **faire é.** to stop; *Fig* **brûler les étapes** *(dans la hiérarchie)* to shoot to the top; *(dans une tâche)* to cut corners (**b**) *(distance)* stage (**c**) *Fig (phase)* stage, step; **par étapes** in stages

état [eta] *nm* (**a**) *(façon d'être)* state, condition; *Phys* state; **l'é. des routes** road conditions; **à l'é. solide/naturel** in its solid/natural state; **à l'é. neuf** as good as new; **à l'é. pur** *(substance)* unalloyed; *Fig (bêtise, incompétence)* sheer, downright; **dans l'é. actuel des choses** as things stand; **être dans un triste é.** to be in a bad way; **être dans tous ses états** to be in a state; **en bon/mauvais é.** in good/bad condition; **remettre qch en é.** to repair sth; *(moteur)* to overhaul sth; **laisser les choses en l'é.** to leave things as they are; **être en é. de marche** to be in working order; *(voiture)* to be roadworthy; **être/se sentir en é. de faire qch** to be/feel up to doing sth; **é. d'alerte** state of alert; **faire qch sans états d'âme** *(sans scrupules)* to have no qualms about doing sth; **é. de choses** state of affairs; **é. d'esprit** state of mind; **c'est un é. de fait** it's an undeniable fact; **l'é. de guerre a été déclaré** a state of war has been declared; **é. de santé** state of health; **être dans un é. second** to be spaced out; **é. de siège** martial law; **é. d'urgence** state of emergency
(**b**) *Vieilli ou Hum (profession)* **épicier de son é.** grocer by trade

(**c**) *(autorité centrale)* **l'É.** the State; **É. membre** member state (**d**) *(inventaire) (des dépenses, des ventes)* statement; **faire é. de qch** to mention sth; **é. civil** *(d'une personne)* marital status; (**bureau de l')é. civil** *(à la mairie)* marriage clerk's office; **é. des lieux** inventory of fixtures *(in rented premises)*; **dresser** *ou* **faire un é. des lieux** to draw up an inventory of fixtures; *Fig* to take stock of the situation; **états de service** service record

(**e**) *Hist* **les États généraux** the States General

(**f**) *Ordinat* **é. d'attente** wait state; **en é. de veille** in standby mode

étatique [etatik] *adj* state

étatiser [etatize] *vt* to bring under state control

état-major (*pl* **états-majors**) [etamaʒɔr] *nm* (**a**) *Mil (officiers)* (general) staff; *(lieu)* headquarters (**b**) *(d'une firme)* management; *(d'un parti politique)* leadership

États-Unis [etazyni] *nmpl* **les É. (d'Amérique)** the United States (of America)

étau, -x [eto] *nm* (**a**) *Tech* vice (**b**) *Fig (restrictions)* stranglehold; **l'é. se resserre** the net is closing in

étayer [53] [eteje] *vt* (**a**) *(mur, plafond)* to shore up (**b**) *Fig (argumentation, théorie)* to support

etc. [ɛtsetera] *adv* etc.

et cætera, et cetera [ɛtsetera] *adv* et cetera

été¹ [ete] *nm* summer; **en é.** in (the) summer; **un jour d'é.** a summer's day; **é. indien** *ou Can* **des Indiens** Indian summer

été² [ete] *voir* **être²**

éteindre [54] [etɛ̃dr] **1** *vt (incendie, bougie, cigarette)* to put out, to extinguish; *(gaz)* to turn off; *(télévision, radio, radiateur)* to switch off, to turn off; *(lumière)* to turn off *or* out; **éteins dans le salon, s'il te plaît** can you turn out the light in the living room, please?

2 s'éteindre *vpr* (**a**) *(incendie, cigarette, lampe)* to go out (**b**) *(passion)* to fade; *(son, rires, voix)* to die away (**c**) *(disparaître)* *(personne)* to pass away; *(race)* to die out

éteint, -e [etɛ̃, -ɛ̃t] *adj* (**a**) **être é.** *(incendie, cigarette)* to be out; *(lampe, électricité, radio)* to be off (**b**) *(race, famille, volcan)* extinct (**c**) *(terne) (couleur)* dull; *(regard)* blank; *(voix)* faint; *(personne)* subdued

étendard [etɑ̃dar] *nm* (**a**) *(drapeau)* standard (**b**) *Fig (symbole)* **lever l'é. de la révolte** to raise the standard of revolt; **se ranger sous l'é. de qn** to join sb's camp

étendoir [etɑ̃dwar] *nm (à linge)* clothesline

étendre [etɑ̃dr] **1** *vt* (**a**) *(déployer) (carte, nappe)* to spread out; *(linge)* to hang up; *(beurre, pommade, ailes)* to spread; *(pâte)* to roll out; **é. les bras** to open one's arms wide; *Fam* **se faire é.** *(être assommé)* to be knocked out; *(à un examen)* to fail (**b**) *(coucher)* to lay down (**c**) *(influence, pouvoir, connaissances)* to extend (**à** to) (**d**) *(diluer)* to dilute (**e**) *Ordinat (mémoire)* to upgrade

2 s'étendre *vpr* (**a**) *(s'allonger)* to lie down (**b**) *(aller)* to stretch (**c**) *(incendie, épidémie, grève)* to spread; *(pouvoir, influence, connaissances)* to grow (**d**) *(s'attarder)* **s'é. sur un sujet** to dwell on a subject

étendu, -e [etɑ̃dy] **1** *adj* (**a**) *(large, important) (plaine, connaissances)* extensive; *(pouvoirs)* far-reaching (**b**) *(bras, jambes)* outstretched (**c**) *(personne)* lying (**d**) *(dilué)* diluted (**de** with)

2 *nf* **étendue** *(d'un champ, d'une région)* area; *(d'une grève, d'une épidémie, d'un problème)* scale, extent; *(d'eau, de sable, de terre)* expanse; *(des connaissances, du vocabulaire, des pouvoirs)* range

éternel, -elle [etɛrnɛl] **1** *adj* eternal; *(discussion, bavardages)* never-ending; **tu es un é. mécontent** you're never satisfied

2 *nm* (**a**) **l'É.** *(Dieu)* the Lord; *Hum* **c'est un grand fumeur/ paresseux devant l'É.** he's an incurable smoker/incurably lazy (**b**) **l'é. féminin** the archetypal female

éternellement [etɛrnɛlmɑ̃] *adv* for ever; *(reconnaissant)* eternally; **elle est é. mécontente** she's never satisfied

éterniser [etɛrnize] **s'éterniser** *vpr (durer)* to drag on (for ever); *(chez quelqu'un)* to outstay one's welcome

éternité [etɛrnite] *nf* eternity; **il y a une é.** *ou* **des éternités que je ne vous ai vu** I haven't seen you for ages

éternuement [etɛrnymɑ̃] *nm* sneeze

éternuer [etɛrnɥe] *vi* to sneeze

êtes *voir* **être²**

éther [etɛr] *nm* ether

éthéré, -e [etere] *adj* ethereal

Éthiopie [etjɔpi] *nf* **l'É.** Ethiopia

éthiopien, -enne [etjɔpjɛ̃, -ɛn] **1** *adj* Ethiopian **2** *nm,f* **É., Éthiopienne** Ethiopian

éthique [etik] **1** *adj* ethical **2** *nf* ethics *(singulier)*

ethnie [ɛtni] *nf* ethnic group

ethnique [ɛtnik] *adj* ethnic

ethnologie [ɛtnɔlɔʒi] *nf* ethnology

ethnologique [ɛtnɔlɔʒik] *adj* ethnological

ethnologue [ɛtnɔlɔg] *nmf* ethnologist

éthylique [etilik] *adj* **alcool é.** ethyl alcohol; **coma é.** alcohol-induced coma

éthylisme [etilism] *nm Méd* alcoholism

étiez *voir* **être²**

étincelant, -e [etɛ̃slɑ̃, -ɑ̃t] *adj* sparkling; *(étoile)* twinkling

étinceler [9] [etɛ̃sle] *vi (diamant, métal, lac)* to sparkle; *(étoile)* to twinkle; *(yeux) (de joie)* to sparkle (**de** with); *(de colère)* to glint (**de** with)

étincelle [etɛ̃sɛl] *nf aussi Fig* spark; **lancer des étincelles** to throw out sparks; *(diamant, yeux)* to sparkle; *Fig* **ça va faire des étincelles** sparks will fly; **avoir une é. de génie** to have a stroke of genius

étioler [etjɔle] **s'étioler** *vpr (plante)* to wilt; *(personne)* to grow sickly; *(esprit, mémoire)* to deteriorate

étions *voir* **être²**

étiqueter [42] [etikte] *vt aussi Fig* to label (**comme** as)

étiquette [etikɛt] *nf* (**a**) *(sur une valise, un produit)* label (**b**) *Fig (d'une personne)* label; **coller une é. à qn** to label sb; **é. politique** political affiliation (**c**) *(protocole)* **l'é.** etiquette

étirement [etirmɑ̃] *nm (des membres, du corps)* stretching; **faire des étirements** to do stretching exercises

étirer [etire] **1** *vt* to stretch **2 s'étirer** *vpr (personne, tissu, vêtement)* to stretch; *(journée, réunion)* to drag on (for ever)

étoffe [etɔf] *nf* material, fabric; *Fig* **avoir l'é. d'un chef d'État** to have the makings of a statesman; **avoir l'é. d'un héros** to be the stuff heroes are made of

étoffer [etɔfe] **1** *vt (discours, livre, personnage)* to flesh out **2 s'étoffer** *vpr (personne)* to fill out

étoile [etwal] *nf* (**a**) *(astre)* star; **un ciel sans étoiles** a starless sky; **coucher** *ou* **dormir à la belle é.** to sleep out (in the open); **né sous une bonne/mauvaise é.** born under a lucky/an unlucky star; **l'é. du berger** *(vue le matin)* the morning star; *(vue le soir)* the evening star; **é. filante** shooting star; **l'é. Polaire** the polestar (**b**) *(ornement, objet)* star; *(astérisque)* asterisk; **hôtel trois étoiles** three-star hotel; **é. de David** Star of David (**c**) *(vedette)* star (**d**) **é. de mer** starfish (**e**) *Ordinat* **connecté en é.** in a star configuration

étoilé, -e [etwale] *adj* (**a**) *(ciel, nuit)* starry (**b**) *(pare-brise)* starred

étonnamment [etɔnamɑ̃] *adv* surprisingly

étonnant, -e [etɔnɑ̃, -ɑ̃t] *adj* surprising; **ce n'est pas é. qu'il soit malade** it's not surprising that he's sick; **chose étonnante, elle est arrivée à l'heure** amazingly enough, she arrived on time

étonné, -e [etone] *adj* surprised (**de** at)

étonnement [etɔnmɑ̃] *nm* surprise; **à mon grand é.** to my amazement

étonner [etɔne] **1** *vt* to surprise; **elle n'est pas venue? ça m'étonne** she didn't come? I'm surprised; *Fam* **alors ça, ça m'étonnerait!** that'll be the day!; **ça m'étonne de toi** I'm surprised at you; *Fam* **tu m'étonnes!** you don't say!; **tu m'étonneras toujours!** you never cease to amaze me!

2 s'étonner *vpr* to be surprised (**de** at); **je ne m'étonne plus de rien** nothing surprises me any more

étouffant, -e [etufɑ̃, -ɑ̃t] *adj* (*air, chaleur, atmosphère*) stifling; (*temps*) oppressive

étouffe-chrétien [etufkretjɛ̃] *Fam* **1** *adj inv* heavy on the stomach

2 *nm inv* **c'est de l'é., cette tarte** this pie is very heavy on the stomach

étouffée [etufe] **à l'étouffée 1** *adj* braised

2 *adv* **cuire qch à l'é.** to braise sth

étouffement [etufmɑ̃] *nm* (*asphyxie*) suffocation

étouffer [etufe] **1** *vt* (**a**) (*personne*) to suffocate; *Euph* **ce ne sont pas les scrupules qui l'étouffent** she's not exactly overscrupulous (**b**) *Fig* (*cri, bâillement, rire*) to stifle; (*son*) to muffle; (*feu*) to smother; (*révolte*) to suppress; (*scandale, affaire*) to hush up

2 *vi* to suffocate; **é. de rire/colère** to choke with laughter/anger; **on étouffe ici** it's stuffy in here

3 s'étouffer *vpr* to suffocate; (*en mangeant*) to choke (**avec** on)

étourderie [eturdəri] *nf* (**a**) (*caractère*) absent-mindedness (**b**) (*faute*) careless mistake

étourdi, -e [eturdi] **1** *adj* (*distrait*) scatterbrained

2 *nm,f* scatterbrain

étourdir [eturdir] *vt* (*assommer*) to stun, to daze; *Fig* (*sujet: vin, éloges*) to make dizzy

étourdissant, -e [eturdisɑ̃, -ɑ̃t] *adj* (*bruit*) deafening; (*nouvelles, succès*) staggering; (*beauté*) stunning

étourdissement [eturdismɑ̃] *nm* **avoir un é.** to feel dizzy

étourneau, -x [eturno] *nm* starling

étrange [etrɑ̃ʒ] *adj* strange, odd; **chose é., il est revenu** strangely enough, he came back

étrangement [etrɑ̃ʒmɑ̃] *adv* strangely, oddly; **ressembler é. à qch** to look suspiciously like sth

étranger, -ère [etrɑ̃ʒe, -ɛr] *adj* (**a**) (*d'un autre pays*) foreign (**b**) (*inconnu*) strange, unfamiliar (**à** to) (**c**) (*extérieur*) **des éléments étrangers** outsiders; **elle est étrangère à cette société/au projet** she isn't involved with this company/the plan

2 *nm,f* (**a**) (*d'un autre pays*) foreigner (**b**) (*d'un autre groupe*) stranger, outsider

3 *nm* **l'é.** (*pays étrangers*) foreign countries; **aller/vivre à l'é.** to go/live abroad

étrangeté [etrɑ̃ʒte] *nf* strangeness, oddness

étranglé, -e [etrɑ̃gle] *adj* (*passage, vallée*) narrow; (*voix*) choked; *Méd* (*hernie*) strangulated

étranglement [etrɑ̃gləmɑ̃] *nm* (**a**) (*d'une personne*) strangling, strangulation; **mourir par é.** to be strangled (**b**) (*partie resserrée*) (*d'une rivière*) narrow part; (*d'une route*) bottleneck

étrangler [etrɑ̃gle] **1** *vt* (**a**) (*personne*) to strangle; *Fig* (*ruiner*) to cripple (**b**) (*resserrer*) (*taille, tube*) to constrict

2 s'étrangler *vpr* (*en mangeant*) to choke (**avec** on); **s'é. de colère/rire** to choke with anger/laughter (**b**) (*voix*) to choke; **les mots s'étranglèrent dans sa gorge** the words stuck in her throat

étrave [etrav] *nf Naut* stem

être¹ [ɛtr] *nm* (*personne, âme*) being; **un ê. cher** a loved one; **c'est un ê. méprisable** he's a despicable creature; **ê. humain** human being; **ê. vivant** living creature

être² [ɛtr] [2] **1** *vi* (**a**) (*indique la nature*) to be; **ê. professeur/informaticien** to be a teacher/computer expert; **ceci est un reptile** this is a reptile

(**b**) (*indique l'état*) to be; **ê. bien/mal** (*en bonne/mauvaise santé*) to be well/sick; **le temps est à l'orage** there's a storm brewing; **il serait mieux avec les cheveux courts** he would look better with short hair

(**c**) (*indique le lieu*) to be; **elle est chez elle** she's at home; **Rabat est au Maroc** Rabat is in Morocco; **j'en suis au chapitre IV** I'm on chapter IV; **où en es-tu dans ton travail?** how far have you gotten with your work?; **je ne sais plus où j'en suis** I don't know what I'm doing any more; **j'en suis à me demander si…** I'm beginning to wonder whether…

(**d**) (*indique le moment*) **nous sommes mercredi/le 16** it's Wednesday/the 16th today

(**e**) (*indique l'appartenance*) **ê. à qn** to belong to sb; *Fig* **je suis à vous** I'm all yours; **elle est de la famille** she's one of the family

(**f**) (*indique la provenance*) to be; **je suis de Lyon/du sud** I'm from Lyons/from the South; **l'enfant n'est pas de lui** it's not his child; **ce tableau est de Cézanne** this picture is by Cézanne

(**g**) (*indique l'obligation*) **ceci est à lire pour demain** this has to be read for tomorrow; **ce film est à voir absolument** this movie is a must-see

(**h**) (*aller*) to go; **as-tu déjà été à Baltimore?** have you ever been to Baltimore?; *Fam* **ça a été** it went OK

(**i**) (*exister*) to be; **la plus belle voiture qui soit** the most beautiful car in the world; *Litt* **elle n'est plus** she is no longer with us

(**j**) (*locutions*) **ê. tout le temps à se plaindre/à médire** to be always complaining/criticizing; **ne serait-ce que** if only

2 *v aux* (**a**) (*avec des verbes à l'actif*) to have/to be; **je suis sorti hier soir** I went out last night; **es-tu déjà allé en Chine?** have you ever been to China?; **elle est née en 1967** she was born in 1967; **j'étais parti très tôt** I had left very early; **il serait parti plus tôt s'il avait pu** he would have left earlier if he could; **ils se sont aimés** they loved each other; **nous nous étions trompés** we had made a mistake

(**b**) (*avec des verbes au passif*) to be; **nous y sommes/étions toujours bien reçus** we are/were always warmly welcomed there

3 *v impersonnel* to be; **il est cinq heures** it's five (o'clock); **il est difficile de juger** it's hard to tell; **il m'est impossible de vous répondre** it's impossible for me to give you an answer

étreindre [54] [etrɛ̃dr] *vt* to embrace; (*sujet: peur, douleur*) to grip

étreinte [etrɛ̃t] *nf* (*embrassade*) embrace; (*sexuelle*) coupling

étrenner [etrene] *vt* (*objet*) to use for the first time, to christen; (*vêtement*) to wear for the first time

étrennes [etrɛn] *nfpl* New Year's gift; (*pour facteur, éboueur*) ≃ Christmas bonus

étrier [etrije] *nm* (**a**) (*en équitation*) stirrup; **vider les étriers** to be thrown; *Fig* **mettre le pied à l'é. à qn** to give sb a helping hand (**b**) (*sur table d'examen*) stirrup

étriller [etrije] *vt* (**a**) (*cheval*) to curry (**b**) *Fig* (*critiquer*) to pan

étriper [etripe] **1** *vt* (*poisson, volaille*) to gut; *Fam Fig* **je vais l'é.!** I'll murder him!

2 s'étriper *vpr Fam* (*se battre*) to tear each other apart

étriqué, -e [etrike] *adj* (**a**) (*vêtement*) tight (**b**) *Fig* (*esprit, vie*) narrow

étroit, -e [etrwa, -at] *adj* (**a**) (*peu large*) narrow; *Fig* **avoir l'esprit é.** to be narrow-minded (**b**) (*serré*) tight; *Fig* (*liens, collaboration, surveillance*) close (**c**) (*logement, pièce*) poky; **être à l'é.** to be cramped

étroitement [etrwatmɑ̃] *adv* (*nouer, tenir*) tightly; *Fig* (*unir, collaborer, surveiller*) closely

étroitesse [etrwatɛs] *nf* narrowness; (*d'un logement, d'une pièce*) pokiness; *Fig* **é. d'esprit** narrow-mindedness

étron [etrɔ̃] *nm* piece of excrement

étrusque [etrysk] **1** *adj* Etruscan

  2 *nmf* É. Etruscan

étude [etyd] *nf* (**a**) *(examen)* study, survey; **mettre qch à l'é.** to study *or* to investigate sth; **é. de cas** case study; **é. de faisabilité** feasibility study; **faire une é. de marché** to do market research (**b**) **études** *(éducation)* studies; **j'ai arrêté mes études à seize ans** I left school at sixteen; **faire des études (de français/de droit)** to study French/law; **elle a fait ses études à Stanford** she studied at Stanford (**c**) *Scol (heure)* study period; *(salle)* study hall (**d**) *(morceau de musique, peinture)* study (**e**) *(bureau)* office

étudiant, -e [etydjɑ̃, -ɑ̃t] **1** *nm,f* student; **é. en médecine/en droit** medical/law student; **é. de première/seconde année** first-/second-year student, freshman/sophomore

  2 *adj (vie, mouvement)* student

étudié, -e [etydje] *adj* (**a**) *(recherché) (tenue, style)* carefully chosen (**b**) *Péj (affecté)* studied (**c**) *Com* **prix très étudiés** very reasonable prices

étudier [66] [etydje] **1** *vt* to study; *(leçon)* to prepare

  2 *vi* to study

  3 s'étudier *vpr (l'un l'autre)* to study each other

étui [etɥi] *nm* case; *(de revolver)* holster; **é. à lunettes** glasses case

étuve [etyv] *nf* (**a**) *(aux thermes)* steam room; *Fig* oven (**b**) *(pour sécher)* drying oven; *(pour stériliser)* sterilizer

étuvée [etyve] **à l'étuvée 1** *adj* braised

  2 *adv* **cuire qch à l'é.** to braise sth

étymologie [etimɔlɔʒi] *nf* etymology

EU [øy] *nmpl (abrév* **États-Unis)** USA

eu, -e *pp voir* **avoir**[1]

eucalyptus [økaliptys] *nm* eucalyptus

eucharistie [økaristi] *nf Rel* **l'e.** the Eucharist

euh [ø] *exclam* er!

eunuque [ønyk] *nm* eunuch

euphémisme [øfemism] *nm* euphemism

euphorie [øfɔri] *nf* euphoria

euphorique [øfɔrik] *adj* euphoric

euphorisant, -e [øfɔrizɑ̃, -ɑ̃t] **1** *adj (effet, atmosphère)* exhilarating; *(médicament)* antidepressant; *(drogue)* that produces a feeling of euphoria

  2 *nm* antidepressant; *(drogue)* drug that produces a feeling of euphoria

Euphrate [øfrat] *nm* **l'E.** the Euphrates

eurasien, -enne [ørazjɛ̃, -ɛn] **1** *adj* Eurasian

  2 *nm,f* **E., Eurasienne** Eurasian

eurêka [øreka] *exclam* eureka!

euro [øro] *nm (monnaie)* euro

euro- [øro] *préf* Euro-

Eurocorps [ørokɔr] *nm Mil* Eurocorps

eurocrate [ørokrat] *nmf* Eurocrat

eurodéputé, -e [ørodepyte] *nm,f* Euro MP

eurodevise [ørodəviz] *nf* Eurocurrency

eurodollar [ørodɔlar] *nm* Eurodollar

Europe [ørɔp] *nf* **l'E.** Europe; **l'E. centrale** central Europe; **l'E. de l'Est/de l'Ouest** Eastern/Western Europe; **l'E. du Nord** Northern Europe; **l'E. occidentale** Western Europe; **l'E. sociale** social Europe *(a united Europe committed to a progressive social and welfare policy)*; **l'E. verte** European agriculture

européen, -enne [ørɔpeɛ̃, -ɛn] **1** *adj* European

  2 *nm,f* **E., Européenne** European

eurosceptique [ørosɛptik] *nmf Pol* Euroskeptic

Eurovision [ørovizjɔ̃] *nf* Eurovision

eut *voir* **avoir**[1]

euthanasie [øtanazi] *nf* euthanasia

eux [ø] *pron personnel* (**a**) *(sujet)* they; **ils apprécient mon tra-**vail, e.! THEY like my work!; **les enfants, e.,** se sont amusés the children, for their part, enjoyed themselves; **si j'étais e., je me méfierais** if I were them, I'd be careful

  (**b**) *(objet direct)* them; **et e., tu les oublies?** and what about them, have you forgotten them?

  (**c**) *(avec préposition)* them; *(réfléchi)* themselves; **dis-le-leur, à e.** tell THEM; **ils ne pensent qu'à e.** they only think of themselves; **les deux maisons sont à e.** both houses are theirs; **ils ont leurs méthodes à e.** they have their own methods; *Fam* **un copain à e.** a friend of theirs

  (**d**) *(dans les comparaisons)* them; **je dépense plus qu'e.** I spend more than they do *or* than them

eux-mêmes [ømɛm] *pron personnel* themselves

évacuation [evakɥasjɔ̃] *nf* (**a**) *(de matières du corps)* discharge; *(des eaux de pluie, des eaux usées)* drainage (**b**) *(de personnes, d'un lieu)* evacuation

évacuer [evakɥe] *vt* (**a**) *(matières du corps)* to discharge; *(eaux de pluie, eaux usées)* to drain off (**b**) *(personnes, lieu)* to evacuate; **faire é. une salle** to evacuate a hall (**c**) *Fig (problème)* to solve

évadé, -e [evade] *nm,f* escaped prisoner

évader [evade] **s'évader** *vpr aussi Fig* to escape (**de** from)

évaluation [evalɥasjɔ̃] *nf (d'une propriété, d'un bien)* valuation; *(de dommages)* assessment; *(d'un poids, d'un nombre, des risques)* estimation

évaluer [evalɥe] *vt (propriété, bien)* to value; *(dommages)* to assess; *(poids, nombre, risques)* to estimate

évangéliser [evɑ̃ʒelize] *vt* to evangelize

évangéliste [evɑ̃ʒelist] *nm (prédicateur)* evangelist; *(de la Bible)* Evangelist

évangile [evɑ̃ʒil] *nm Rel* **l'É.** the Gospel; **l'É. selon saint Marc** the Gospel according to St Mark; *Fig* **prendre qch pour parole d'é.** to take sth as gospel (truth)

évanoui, -e [evanwi] *adj* unconscious; **tomber é.** to fall down in a faint

évanouir [evanwir] **s'évanouir** *vpr* (**a**) *(perdre conscience)* to faint (**b**) *(disparaître)* to fade (away)

évanouissement [evanwismɑ̃] *nm (syncope)* fainting fit

évaporation [evaporasjɔ̃] *nf* evaporation

évaporé, -e [evapore] *Péj* **1** *adj* scatterbrained

  2 *nm,f* airhead

évaporer [evapore] **s'évaporer** *vpr* (**a**) *(liquide)* to evaporate (**b**) *Fig (disparaître)* to vanish (into thin air)

évasé, -e [evaze] *adj (récipient)* wide-mouthed; *(jupe)* flared

évaser [evaze] *vt* to widen; *(jupe)* to be flared

évasif, -ive [evazif, -iv] *adj* evasive

évasion [evazjɔ̃] *nf* (**a**) *(fuite)* escape (**de** from); **é. de capitaux** flight of capital; **é. fiscale** tax evasion (**b**) *Fig (distraction)* escapism; **avoir besoin d'é.** to need to escape

Ève [ɛv] *npr* Eve; *Fam* **je ne le connais ni d'È. ni d'Adam** I don't know him from Adam

évêché [eveʃe] *nm (diocèse)* bishopric; *(palais)* bishop's palace

éveil [evɛj] *nm* awakening; **être en é.** to be alert

éveillé, -e [eveje] *adj* (**a**) *(non endormi)* awake (**b**) *(vif)* alert

éveiller [eveje] **1** *vt* (**a**) *(curiosité, soupçons, jalousie)* to arouse; *(intelligence, imagination)* to stimulate (**b**) *Litt (personne)* to wake

  2 s'éveiller *vpr* (**a**) *Litt (personne)* to awake (**b**) *Fig (curiosité, soupçons, jalousie)* to be aroused; *(intelligence, imagination)* to develop

événement [evɛnmɑ̃] *nm* event; **attendre la suite des événements** to wait and see what happens; **créer l'é.** to make big news; *Hum* **quand il fait la vaisselle, c'est (tout) un é.** it's a major event when he does the dishes

éventail [evɑ̃taj] *nm* (**a**) *(pour se rafraîchir)* fan; **en é.** fan-shaped (**b**) *(choix)* range

éventaire [evɑ̃tɛr] *nm* (**a**) *(étal)* stall (**b**) *(d'un marchand ambulant)* tray

éventé, -e [evɑ̃te] *adj (vin, parfum)* stale; *(bière)* flat

éventer [evɑ̃te] **1** *vt* (**a**) *(avec un éventail)* to fan (**b**) *(secret, complot)* to discover

2 s'éventer *vpr* (**a**) *(avec un éventail)* to fan oneself (**b**) *(vin, parfum)* to go stale; *(bière)* to go flat

éventrer [evɑ̃tre] *vt (personne, animal)* to disembowel; *(colis, matelas)* to rip open; *(fût, boîte)* to break open

éventualité [evɑ̃tɥalite] *nf* (**a**) *(circonstance)* eventuality; **parer à toute é.** to be prepared for all eventualities; **dans l'é. de** in the event of (**b**) *(possibilité)* possibility

éventuel, -elle [evɑ̃tɥɛl] *adj* possible

éventuellement [evɑ̃tɥɛlmɑ̃] *adv* possibly; **j'aurais é. besoin de votre concours** I may need your help

évêque [evɛk] *nm* bishop

Everest [evɛrɛst] *nm* **l'E., le mont E.** (Mount) Everest

évertuer [evɛrtɥe] **s'évertuer** *vpr* **s'é. à faire qch** to endeavor to do sth

éviction [eviksjɔ̃] *nf (d'un rival, d'une tête de parti)* ousting; *(d'un locataire)* eviction

évidemment [evidamɑ̃] *adv* of course, obviously

évidence [evidɑ̃s] *nf* (**a**) *(d'un fait, de la vérité)* obviousness; **c'est une é.!** obviously!; **nier l'é.** to deny the obvious; **se rendre à l'é.** to face facts; **de toute é., à l'é.** obviously (**b**) **en é.** *(visible)* in a prominent position; **mettre qch en é.** *(phénomène)* to highlight sth; **se mettre en é.** to try to get oneself noticed

évident, -e [evidɑ̃, -ɑ̃t] *adj* obvious; **tu crois qu'on va réussir? – c'est é.!** do you think we'll succeed? – of course (we will)!; **elle va se rendre compte, c'est é.** she's bound to notice; *Fam* **c'est pas é.!** *(pas facile)* it's not easy!

évider [evide] *vt* to hollow out

évier [evje] *nm* sink

évincer [16] [evɛ̃se] *vt (rival)* to oust (**de** from)

éviter [evite] **1** *vt* (**a**) *(s'écarter de)* to avoid; **é. de faire qch** to avoid doing sth; **il faut é. qu'il le voie** he mustn't be allowed to see it; **évite que ça se sache** don't let it get out (**b**) *(épargner)* **é. qch à qn** to save *or* to spare sb sth; **ça m'évitera d'avoir à le faire** it will save me having to do it

2 s'éviter *vpr* (**a**) **s'é. qch** to avoid sth (**b**) *(se fuir mutuellement)* to avoid each other

évocateur, -trice [evɔkatœr, -tris] *adj* evocative (**de** of)

évocation [evɔkasjɔ̃] *nf* evocation; **le pouvoir d'é. d'un lieu/mot** the evocative power of a place/word

évolué, -e [evɔlɥe] *adj (société)* advanced; *(personne)* broadminded; *Ordinat (langage)* high-level

évoluer [evɔlɥe] *vi* (**a**) *(se déplacer)* to move around; *Fig* **é. dans le milieu des artistes** to move in artistic circles (**b**) *(se développer)* to develop (**c**) *Ordinat* **faire é.** to upgrade

évolutif, -ive [evɔlytif, -iv] *adj* progressive; *Ordinat* upgradeable

évolution [evɔlysjɔ̃] *nf* (**a**) *(développement)* development (**b**) *Biol* evolution (**c**) **évolutions** *(déplacements)* movements

évoquer [evɔke] *vt* (**a**) *(se remémorer) (passé)* to recall, to evoke (**b**) *(faire penser à)* to be reminiscent of; **son nom ne m'évoque rien** his/her name means nothing to me (**c**) *(aborder)* to touch on, to mention (**d**) *(par la magie)* to call up, to invoke

ex [ɛks] *nmf Fam* ex

ex- [ɛks] *préf* ex-; **ex-femme/-ministre** ex-wife/minister

exacerbation [ɛgzasɛrbasjɔ̃] *nf* exacerbation

exacerber [ɛgzasɛrbe] **1** *vt* to exacerbate

2 s'exacerber *vpr* to become acute

exact, -e [ɛgzakt] *adj* (**a**) *(quantité, poids, nombre)* exact, precise; *(rapport, description)* exact, accurate; *(mot, réponse, heure, date)* right, correct; **c'est é. (vrai)** it's quite true; **il s'appelle bien Martin? – e.!** his name's Martin? – that's right! (**b**) *(ponctuel)* punctual, on time

exactement [ɛgzaktəmɑ̃] *adv* exactly

exactions [ɛgzaksjɔ̃] *nfpl* atrocities

exactitude [ɛgzaktityd] *nf* (**a**) *(précision, fidélité)* exactness; *(justesse)* correctness; **avec. e.** accurately (**b**) *(ponctualité)* punctuality; *Prov* **l'e. est la politesse des rois** punctuality is the politeness of kings

ex æquo [ɛgzeko] **1** *adj inv* **être e.** to tie, to be equally placed (**avec** with)

2 *nmf inv* **il y a deux e.** there's a two-way tie; **départager les e.** to break the tie

3 *adv* **être troisième e.** to tie for third place

exagération [ɛgzaʒerasjɔ̃] *nf* exaggeration

exagéré, -e [ɛgzaʒere] *adj (récit, geste)* exaggerated; *(prix, salaire, pessimisme)* excessive; **il n'est pas e. de dire que...** it's no exaggeration to say that...

exagérément [ɛgzaʒeremɑ̃] *adv* excessively

exagérer [34] [ɛgzaʒere] **1** *vt* to exaggerate; **il ne faut rien e., n'exagérons rien** let's not exaggerate

2 *vi (amplifier)* to exaggerate; *(abuser)* to go too far

exaltant, -e [ɛgzaltɑ̃, -ɑ̃t] *adj* stirring

exaltation [ɛgzaltasjɔ̃] *nf (excitation)* intense excitement

exalté, -e [ɛgzalte] **1** *adj (discours, sentiment)* impassioned; *(personne)* fanatical

2 *nm,f* fanatic

exalter [ɛgzalte] *vt* (**a**) *(exciter) (imagination)* to stir; *(ressentiment, orgueil)* to intensify (**b**) *(louer) (personne)* to exalt

exam [ɛgzam] *nm Fam* exam

examen [ɛgzamɛ̃] *nm* (**a**) *(d'un document, de faits)* examination; *(d'une machine)* checking; *(d'un local)* inspection; *(d'une demande)* consideration; **e. de conscience** soul-searching (**b**) **e. (médical)** physical (examination); **e. de la vue** eye test (**c**) *Scol & Univ* exam, examination; **e. blanc** practice test; **e. d'entrée** entrance exam; **e. de passage** final exam

examinateur, -trice [ɛgzaminatœr, -tris] *nm,f* examiner

examiner [ɛgzamine] **1** *vt* (**a**) *(étudier) (document, faits)* to examine; *(machine)* to check; *(local)* to inspect; *(demande)* to consider (**b**) *(observer)* to examine; *(horizon)* to scan; **e. qn de la tête aux pieds** to look sb up and down (**c**) *(patient)* to examine; **se faire e. par un médecin** to be examined by a doctor

2 s'examiner *vpr* (**a**) *(dans une glace)* to examine oneself (**b**) *(l'un l'autre)* to examine each other

exaspérant, -e [ɛgzasperɑ̃, -ɑ̃t] *adj* exasperating

exaspération [ɛgzasperasjɔ̃] *nf* exasperation

exaspérer [34] [ɛgzaspere] *vt* (**a**) *(personne)* to exasperate (**b**) *Litt (douleur, sentiment)* to aggravate

exaucement [ɛgzosmɑ̃] *nm* granting

exaucer [16] [ɛgzose] *vt* (**a**) *(souhait)* to grant (**b**) **e. qn** to grant sb's wish

excavateur [ɛkskavatœr] *nm* excavator, (mechanical) digger

excavation [ɛkskavasjɔ̃] *nf* (**a**) *(trou)* excavation; *(creusée par une bombe)* crater (**b**) *(action)* excavation

excavatrice [ɛkskavatris] *nf* = **excavateur**

excédant, -e [ɛkseda, -ɑ̃t] *adj* exasperating

excédent [ɛksedɑ̃] *nm* surplus; **budget en e.** surplus budget; **e. de poids** excess weight; **e. de bagages** excess baggage; **être en e.** to show a surplus

excédentaire [ɛksedɑ̃tɛr] *adj (production, poids)* excess; *(budget)* surplus; **balance commerciale e.** trade surplus

excéder [34] [ɛksede] *vt* (**a**) *(quantité, somme, limite)* to exceed; *(forces, compétences)* to be beyond; **e. ses pouvoirs** to exceed one's powers (**b**) *(irriter)* to exasperate

excellence [ɛksɛlɑ̃s] *nf* excellence; *Scol* **prix d'e.** class prize *(for overall performance)*; **par e.** par excellence; **Son/Votre E.** *(titre)* His/Her/Your Excellency

excellent, -e [ɛksɛlɑ̃, -ɑ̃t] *adj* excellent (**en** at)

exceller [ɛksele] *vi* to excel (**en** at)

excentré, -e [ɛksɑ̃tre] *adj* (**a**) *(quartier)* outlying (**b**) *Tech* off-center

excentricité [ɛksɑ̃trisite] *nf (de caractère, acte bizarre)* eccentricity

excentrique [ɛksɑ̃trik] **1** *adj (bizarre)* eccentric
2 *nmf (personne)* eccentric

excepté, -e [ɛksɛpte] **1** *prép* except, apart from
2 *adj* **les femmes exceptées** except for *or* apart from the women

excepter [ɛksɛpte] *vt* to except (**de** from); **sans e. les enfants** not forgetting the children

exception [ɛksɛpsjɔ̃] *nf* exception (**à** to); **c'est l'e. qui confirme la règle** it's the exception that proves the rule; **à quelques exceptions près** with a few exceptions; **un être d'e.** an exceptional person

exceptionnel, -elle [ɛksɛpsjɔnɛl] *adj* exceptional; **ne rien avoir d'e.** to be nothing special

exceptionnellement [ɛksɛpsjɔnɛlmɑ̃] *adv* exceptionally

excès [ɛksɛ] *nm* (**a**) *(excédent)* excess; **pécher par e. de zèle** to be overzealous; **avec e.** excessively, to excess; **sans e.** in moderation; **(jusqu')à l'e.** to excess, excessively; **tomber dans l'e. inverse** to go to the other extreme; **e. de vitesse** speeding; **faire un e. de vitesse** to speed (**b**) *(abus)* excess; **faire des e.** to overindulge

excessif, -ive [ɛksɛsif, -iv] *adj* excessive; **il est e.** he does things to excess

excessivement [ɛksɛsivmɑ̃] *adv (avec excès)* excessively; *Fam (extrêmement)* extremely, really

excision [ɛksizjɔ̃] *nf* excision

excitant, -e [ɛksitɑ̃, -ɑ̃t] **1** *adj (fascinant, provocant)* exciting; *(tonique)* stimulating
2 *nm* stimulant

excitation [ɛksitasjɔ̃] *nf* (**a**) *(incitation)* incitement (**à** to) (**b**) *(état)* excitement (**c**) *Méd* excitation

excité, -e [ɛksite] **1** *adj* excited
2 *nm,f (personne)* hothead

exciter [ɛksite] **1** *vt* (**a**) *(attiser) (curiosité, jalousie, pitié)* to arouse (**b**) *(encourager)* to urge on; **e. qn à la révolte** to incite sb to revolt (**c**) *(énerver)* to excite (**d**) *(nerf, muscle)* to excite
2 **s'exciter** *vpr* to get excited

exclamation [ɛksklamasjɔ̃] *nf* exclamation

exclamer [ɛksklame] **s'exclamer** *vpr* **s'e. de joie/douleur** to cry out with joy/pain; **"jamais!" s'exclama-t-il** "never!" he exclaimed

exclu, -e [ɛkskly] **1** *adj* (**a**) *(non compris)* **TVA exclue** excluding VAT (**b**) *(impensable)* out of the question; **il est e. qu'elle vienne avec nous** there's no question of her coming with us
2 *nm,f* outcast

exclure [17a] [ɛksklyr] *vt* (**a**) *(expulser)* **e. qn de qch** *(parti, école)* to expel sb from sth; *(fonction publique)* to remove sb from sth; *(salle, réunion)* to eject sb from sth (**b**) *(mettre à l'écart)* **e. qn de qch** to exclude sb from sth (**c**) *(ne pas considérer) (hypothèse, solution)* to rule out; **cela n'exclut pas que vous puissiez enseigner** that doesn't rule out the possibility of your teaching

exclusif, -ive [ɛksklyzif, -iv] *adj* exclusive; *(but, mission)* sole; **être e. dans ses amitiés** to be selective in one's choice of friends

exclusion [ɛksklyzjɔ̃] *nf* (**a**) *(d'un parti, d'une école)* expulsion; *(d'une fonction publique)* removal; *(d'une salle, d'une réunion)* ejection (**de** from) (**b**) **à l'e. de** with the exception of

exclusivement [ɛksklyzivmɑ̃] *adv* exclusively

exclusivité [ɛksklyzivite] *nf* (**a**) *(droit)* exclusive rights (**de** to); **en e.** exclusively; **film en première e.** recent release; *Fig* **ne pas avoir l'e. de l'intelligence** not to have a monopoly on intelligence (**b**) *(information)* exclusive, scoop

excommunier [66] [ɛkskɔmynje] *vt* to excommunicate

excréments [ɛkskremɑ̃] *nmpl* excrement

excrétion [ɛkskresjɔ̃] *nf* (**a**) *(action)* excretion (**b**) **excrétions** *(déchets)* excreta

excroissance [ɛkskrwasɑ̃s] *nf* excrescence

excursion [ɛkskyrsjɔ̃] *nf (en car, en voiture)* excursion, trip; *(d'une journée)* day trip; *(de plusieurs jours)* tour; **faire une e., partir en e.** to go on a trip/a tour

excursionniste [ɛkskyrsjɔnist] *nmf* excursionist; *(d'une journée)* day-tripper

excusable [ɛkskyzabl] *adj* excusable, forgivable

excuse [ɛkskyz] *nf* (**a**) *(raison)* excuse; **trouver des excuses à qn** to find excuses for sb; **ce n'est pas une e.!** that's no excuse! (**b**) **excuses** *(regrets)* apology; **faire** *ou* **présenter ses excuses à qn** to make one's apologies to sb

excuser [ɛkskyze] **1** *vt* (**a**) *(justifier) (personne, action)* to excuse; **e. qn auprès de qn** to apologize for sb to sb (**b**) *(pardonner) (personne, erreur, colère)* to excuse; **excusez-moi** *(j'ai fait une faute)* I'm sorry; *(pour attirer l'attention)* excuse me; **excuse-moi de te déranger** I'm sorry to disturb you; **excuse-moi de ne pas t'avoir téléphoné** I'm sorry I didn't call you; *Sout* **je vous prie de m'e.** I do beg your pardon; **tu es tout excusé** there's no need to apologize; *Hum* **excusez du peu!** if you please! (**c**) *(dispenser)* to excuse; **se faire e.** to ask to be excused
2 **s'excuser** *vpr* to apologize; **s'e. auprès de qn** to apologize to sb; **s'e. de qch/de faire qch** to apologize for sth/for doing sth; **je m'excuse!** I'm sorry!

exécrable [ɛgzekrabl] *adj* atrocious

exécrer [34] [ɛgzekre] *vt Litt* to loathe

exécutable [ɛgzekytabl] *adj* (**a**) *(réalisable)* possible, feasible (**b**) *Ordinat* executable

exécutant, -e [ɛgzekytɑ̃, -ɑ̃t] *nm,f* (**a**) *(employé)* subordinate; **ce n'est qu'un simple e.** he just carries out orders (**b**) *(musicien)* performer

exécuter [ɛgzekyte] **1** *vt* (**a**) *(effectuer) (travail, ordres)* to carry out; *(danse, morceau de musique)* to perform; *(peinture)* to execute (**b**) *Ordinat (programme)* to run; *(commande)* to execute (**c**) *(mettre à mort)* to execute; *Fam (battre)* to slaughter; *Fam (critiquer)* to savage
2 **s'exécuter** *vpr* to comply

exécuteur, -trice [ɛgzekytœr, -tris] *nm,f Jur* **e. testamentaire** executor; **exécutrice testamentaire** executrix

exécutif, -ive [ɛgzekytif, -iv] **1** *adj (pouvoir)* executive
2 *nm* **l'e.** the executive

exécution [ɛgzekysjɔ̃] *nf* (**a**) *(d'un travail, d'ordres)* carrying out; *(d'une danse, d'un morceau de musique)* performance; *(d'une peinture)* execution; **mettre qch à e.** to carry sth out (**b**) *Ordinat* execution (**c**) *(mise à mort)* execution

exécutoire [ɛgzekytwar] *adj* (**a**) **jugement e.** enforceable decision (**b**) **formule e.** executory formula

exégèse [ɛgzeʒɛz] *nf* exegesis; **faire l'e. de** to write a critical interpretation of

exemplaire¹ [ɛgzɑ̃plɛr] *adj* (**a**) *(comportement, courage)* exemplary (**b**) *(punition)* exemplary

exemplaire² [ɛgzɑ̃plɛr] *nm (livre, gravure)* copy; **en deux/trois exemplaires** in duplicate/triplicate; **photocopier qch en vingt exemplaires** to make twenty photocopies of sth; **le livre a été tiré à 10 000 exemplaires** 10,000 copies of the book were printed

exemple [ɛgzɑ̃pl] *nm* (**a**) *(modèle)* example (**pour** for); **donner l'e. (à qn)** to set (sb) an example; **suivre l'e. de qn** to follow sb's example; **prendre qn en e.** to model oneself on sb; **citer qn/qch en e.** to quote sb/sth as an example; **faire un e.** *(en punissant)* to set an example (**b**) *(cas, mot, phrase)* example; **être l'e. même de la bêtise** to be stupidity itself (**c**) **par e.** for example, for instance; *Fam* **ah ça par e.!** *(stupeur)* oh no!

exempt, -e [ɛgzɑ̃, -ɑ̃t] *adj* **e. de** *(service militaire)* exempt from; *(danger, problème)* free from; **e. de droits de douane** duty-free; **sa remarque n'était pas exempte d'une certaine amertume** her remark wasn't without a trace of bitterness

exempter [ɛgzãte] *vt (dispenser)* to exempt (**de** from)

exemption [ɛgzãpsjõ] *nf* exemption (**de** from)

exercé, -e [ɛgzɛrse] *adj (œil, oreille)* trained; *(main)* practiced

exercer [16] [ɛgzɛrse] **1** *vt* (**a**) *(entraîner) (corps, esprit, mémoire)* to train; **e. qn à qch/à faire qch** to train sb in sth/to do sth (**b**) *(user de) (autorité, talent, droit)* to exercise; **e. une influence sur qn** to exert an influence on sb; **e. une pression sur qn/qch** to exert pressure on sb/sth; **e. un contrôle sur qch** to exercise control over sth (**c**) *(profession)* to practice; **e. ses fonctions** to carry out one's duties; **e. le métier de journaliste** to work as a journalist
2 *vi (médecin, juriste)* to practice
3 s'exercer *vpr* (**a**) *(s'entraîner)* to practice; **s'e. à qch/à faire qch** to practice sth/doing sth (**b**) *(se manifester) (autorité, pouvoir)* to make itself felt

exercice [ɛgzɛrsis] *nm* (**a**) *(entraînement sportif ou scolaire)* exercise; **faire des exercices** to do (some) exercises; **prendre de l'e.** to (take) exercise (**b**) *Mil* drill; **être à l'e.** to be on parade (**c**) *(du pouvoir, d'un droit)* exercise (**d**) *(d'une profession)* practice; **dans l'e. de ses fonctions** in the exercise of one's duties; **être en e.** *(avocat, médecin)* to be in practice; *(président)* to be in office; **le président en e.** the incumbent president (**e**) **l'e. du culte** public worship (**f**) *(en comptabilité)* fiscal year

exergue [ɛgzɛrg] *nm (de médaille)* inscription; *(d'un texte)* epigraph; **en e.** *(citation)* as an epigraph

exfoliant, -e [ɛksfɔljã, -ãt] **1** *adj* exfoliating
2 *nm* exfoliant

exfolier [66] [ɛksfɔlje] **1** *vt (arbre, peau)* to exfoliate
2 s'exfolier *vpr* to exfoliate

exhaler [ɛgzale] **1** *vt (odeur)* to give off; *Fig (joie, colère)* to give vent to; *Fig* **cette maison exhale la tristesse** sadness pervades this house
2 s'exhaler *vpr (odeur)* to be given off

exhausser [ɛgzose] *vt (mur, édifice)* to heighten; **e. une maison d'un étage** to add a story to a house

exhaustif, -ive [ɛgzostif, -iv] *adj* exhaustive

exhiber [ɛgzibe] **1** *vt* (**a**) *(documents, passeport)* to produce (**b**) *Péj (savoir, richesses)* to show off, to flaunt
2 s'exhiber *vpr* to flaunt oneself

exhibition [ɛgzibisjõ] *nf Péj (de savoir, de richesses)* flaunting

exhibitionniste [ɛgzibisjɔnist] *nmf* exhibitionist

exhortation [ɛgzɔrtasjõ] *nf* exhortation (**à** to)

exhorter [ɛgzɔrte] *vt* **e. qn à qch/à faire qch** to exhort sb to sth/to do sth

exhumation [ɛgzymasjõ] *nf (d'un corps)* exhumation; *(d'un trésor, de vestiges)* excavation

exhumer [ɛgzyme] *vt (corps)* to exhume; *(trésor, vestiges)* to excavate

exigeant, -e [ɛgziʒã, -ãt] *adj (personne, travail)* exacting

exigence [ɛgziʒãs] *nf* (**a**) *(caractère)* exacting nature (**b**) *(condition)* requirement, demand; **satisfaire aux exigences de qch** to meet the requirements of sth (**c**) **exigences** *(salaire)* expected salary; **quelles sont vos exigences?** what salary do you expect?

exiger [45] [ɛgziʒe] *vt* (**a**) *(demander en insistant)* to demand (**de** from); **e. que qch soit fait** to demand that sth be done (**b**) *(nécessiter) (soin, action)* to require

exigible [ɛgziʒibl] *adj (dette, impôt)* payable

exigu, -uë [ɛgzigy] *adj* cramped, tiny

exiguïté [ɛgziɡɥite] *nf* crampedness

exil [ɛgzil] *nm* exile; **envoyer qn en e.** to send sb into exile; **être en e.** to be in exile

exilé, -e [ɛgzile] *nm,f* exile

exiler [ɛgzile] **1** *vt* to exile (**de** from)
2 s'exiler *vpr* to go into exile; *Fig* **s'e. de la ville** to cut oneself off from the town

existant, -e [ɛgzistã, -ãt] *adj* existing

existence [ɛgzistãs] *nf* (**a**) *Phil (être)* existence (**b**) *(vie)* life; **mener une e. tranquille** to lead a quiet life; **dans l'e.** in life (**c**) *(présence)* existence (**de** of) (**d**) *(durée) (d'une institution)* life

existentialisme [ɛgzistãsjalism] *nm Phil* existentialism

existentiel, -elle [ɛgzistãsjɛl] *adj* existential

exister [ɛgziste] **1** *vi* to exist; **rien n'existe pour lui que l'art** art is all that matters to him; **et l'amitié, cela existe, non?** there's such a thing as friendship, isn't there?
2 *v impersonnel* **il existe** there is/are

exode [ɛgzɔd] *nm* exodus; **e. rural** rural depopulation

exogène [ɛgzɔʒɛn] *adj Biol & Géol* exogenous

exonération [ɛgzɔnerasjõ] *nf* exemption; **e. fiscale** tax exemption

exonérer [34] [ɛgzɔnere] *vt (personne)* to exempt; *(marchandises)* to exempt from tax; **être exonéré d'impôts** to be exempt from tax

exorbitant, -e [ɛgzɔrbitã, -ãt] *adj (prix, demande)* exorbitant

exorbité, -e [ɛgzɔrbite] *adj (yeux)* protruding; *Fig* **ils regardaient, les yeux exorbités** they watched with bulging eyes

exorciser [ɛgzɔrsize] *vt aussi Fig* to exorcize

exorcisme [ɛgzɔrsism] *nm* exorcism

exorciste [ɛgzɔrsist] *nmf* exorcist

exotique [ɛgzɔtik] *adj* exotic; **poisson e.** tropical fish

expansé, -e [ɛkspãse] *adj (polystyrène)* expanded

expansif, -ive [ɛkspãsif, -iv] *adj (exubérant)* expansive

expansion [ɛkspãsjõ] *nf* (**a**) *(de gaz, de l'univers)* expansion; **l'univers en e.** the expanding universe (**b**) *(développement) (d'une ville, d'une industrie)* expansion; **taux d'e.** growth rate; **être en pleine e.** *(économie, entreprise)* to be booming

expansionnisme [ɛkspãsjɔnism] *nm* expansionism

expatriation [ɛkspatrijasjõ] *nf* expatriation

expatrié, -e [ɛkspatrije] *adj & nm,f* expatriate

expatrier [66] [ɛkspatrije] **1** *vt (personne)* to expatriate
2 s'expatrier *vpr* to leave one's country, to emigrate

expectative [ɛkspɛktativ] *nf* **être dans l'e.** to be waiting to see what happens

expectorant, -e [ɛkspɛktɔrã, -ãt] *adj & nm* expectorant

expectorer [ɛkspɛktɔre] *vt* to expectorate

expédient [ɛkspedjã] *nm* expedient; **vivre d'expédients** to live by one's wits

expédier [66] [ɛkspedje] *vt* (**a**) *(envoyer)* to send, to dispatch; **e. qch par bateau/par avion/par le train** to send sth by sea/air/rail (**b**) *(se débarrasser de)* to dispose of; **elle les a expédiés en colonie de vacances** she packed them off to camp (**c**) *(faire rapidement) (tâche)* to deal promptly with; *(devoirs, dissertation)* to dash off; **e. les affaires courantes** to deal with the day-to-day matters

expéditeur, -trice [ɛkspeditœr, -tris] **1** *nm,f* sender
2 *adj (bureau, gare)* dispatching

expéditif, -ive [ɛkspeditif, -iv] *adj* hasty

expédition [ɛkspedisjõ] *nf* (**a**) *(envoi)* dispatch, sending (**b**) *(marchandises)* consignment (**c**) *(voyage, opération militaire) & Fig* expedition; **partir en e.** to go on an expedition

expéditionnaire [ɛkspedisjɔnɛr] *adj Mil* expeditionary

expérience [ɛksperjãs] *nf* (**a**) *(pratique)* experience; **avoir de l'e.** to have experience; **avoir l'e. de qch** to have experience of sth; **savoir qch par e.** to know sth from experience; **faire l'e. de qch** to experience sth; **tenter l'e.** to give it a try (**b**) *(test scientifique)* experiment; **e. en laboratoire** laboratory experiment; **faire une e. (sur)** to carry out an experiment (on)

expérimental, -e, -aux, -ales [ɛksperimãtal, -o] *adj* experimental

expérimentalement [εksperimãtalmã] *adv* experimentally

expérimentation [εksperimãtasjɔ̃] *nf* experimentation; **e. sur l'homme** human experiments

expérimenté, -e [εksperimãte] *adj* experienced

expérimenter [εksperimãte] *vt (remède, vaccin)* to test, to try out (**sur** on)

expert, -e [εkspεr, -εrt] **1** *adj* expert, skilled (**en/dans** in); **être e. en la matière** to be an expert on the subject **2** *nm* expert; *(d'assurance)* adjuster

expert-comptable (*pl* **experts-comptables**) [εkspεrkɔ̃tabl] *nm* ≃ certified public accountant, CPA

expertise [εkspεrtiz] *nf* **(a)** *(évaluation) (d'une œuvre d'art)* valuation; *(de dommages)* assessment **(b)** *(rapport)* expert's report (**de** on) **(c)** *(compétence)* expertise

expertiser [εkspεrtize] *vt (œuvre d'art)* to value; *(dommages)* to assess

expiation [εkspjasjɔ̃] *nf* expiation (**de** of)

expiatoire [εkspjatwar] *adj* expiatory

expier [66] [εkspje] *vt* to atone for, to expiate

expiration [εkspirasjɔ̃] *nf* **(a)** *(respiration)* breathing out **(b)** *(d'un contrat, d'un bail)* expiration; **venir** *ou* **arriver à e.** to expire

expirer [εkspire] **1** *vi (Litt (mourir)* to expire **(b)** *(contrat, bail)* to expire **(c)** *(respirer)* to breathe out **2** *vt* to breathe out

explicatif, -ive [εksplikatif, -iv] *adj* explanatory; **notice explicative** directions for use

explication [εksplikasjɔ̃] *nf* explanation; **donner une e. à qch** to give an explanation for sth; **exiger des explications** to demand an explanation; **avoir une e. avec qn** *(discuter)* to talk things over with sb; *(se disputer)* to have it out with sb; **e. de textes** critical *or* textual analysis

explicite [εksplisit] *adj* explicit

explicitement [εksplisitmã] *adv* explicitly

expliquer [εksplike] **1** *vt* to explain; *(texte)* to analyze **2** **s'expliquer** *vpr (communiquer ses idées, se justifier)* to explain oneself; **je m'explique** let me explain **(b)** *(comprendre)* **je ne m'explique pas pourquoi il...** I can't understand why he... **(c)** *(être explicable)* **cela s'explique facilement** that's easily explained; **tout s'explique!** there's a reason for everything! **(d)** *(se parler)* to talk things over; **s'e. avec qn** *(discuter)* to talk things over with sb; *(se disputer)* to have it out with sb

exploit [εksplwa] *nm* feat

exploitant, -e [εksplwatã, -ãt] *nm,f* **(a)** **e. (agricole)** farmer; **petits exploitants** small farmers **(b)** *Cin* exhibitor

exploitation [εksplwatasjɔ̃] *nf* **(a)** *(d'une mine, d'une forêt)* working; *(d'une ligne de chemin de fer, d'une ferme)* running; *(d'une terre)* farming; *(des ressources naturelles, d'un brevet)* & *Fig Péj* exploitation; *Ordinat* **système d'e.** operating system; *Fig* **c'est de l'e.!** it's exploitation!; **l'e. de l'homme par l'homme** man's exploitation of man **(b)** *(entreprise)* concern; **e. agricole** farm; **e. minière** mine

exploiter [εksplwate] *vt* **(a)** *(mine, forêt)* to work; *(ressources naturelles, brevet)* to exploit; *(ligne de chemin de fer, ferme)* to run; *(terre)* to farm; *Fig (situation, talent, idée)* to exploit **(b)** *Péj (abuser de) (personne)* to exploit

exploiteur, -euse [εksplwatœr, -øz] *nm,f Péj* exploiter

explorateur, -trice [εksplɔratœr, -tris] *nm,f (personne)* explorer

exploration [εksplɔrasjɔ̃] *nf* exploration; **partir en e.** to go off exploring

exploratoire [εksplɔratwar] *adj* exploratory

explorer [εksplɔre] *vt* to explore

exploser [εksploze] *vi* **(a)** *(bombe, avion, chaudière)* to explode; **faire e. une bombe** to explode a bomb **(b)** *Fig (se mettre en colère)* to explode

explosif, -ive [εksplozif, -iv] **1** *adj aussi Fig* explosive **2** *nm* explosive

explosion [εksplozjɔ̃] *nf aussi Fig* explosion; **une e. de joie** an outburst of joy; **e. démographique** population explosion

exponentiel, -elle [εkspɔnãsjεl] **1** *adj* exponential **2** *nf* **exponentielle** exponential

export [εkspɔr] *nm* export; *Ordinat* **e. de données** data export

exportateur, -trice [εkspɔrtatœr, -tris] **1** *adj* exporting; **pays e. de vin** wine-exporting country **2** *nm,f* exporter

exportation [εkspɔrtasjɔ̃] *nf (action)* export(ation); *(produit)* export; *Ordinat (d'un fichier)* exporting; *Ordinat (données exportées)* exported data

exporter [εkspɔrte] *vt aussi Ordinat* to export (**vers** to)

exposant, -e [εkspozã, -ãt] **1** *nm,f (artiste, firme)* exhibitor **2** *nm* **(a)** *Math* exponent **(b)** *Typ (chiffre, lettre)* superscript; **3 en e.** superscript 3

exposé [εkspoze] *nm (de faits, d'une situation)* account; *Scol & Univ* talk; **après un bref e. de la situation** after outlining the situation; **faire un e.** to give a talk

exposer [εkspoze] **1** *vt* **(a)** *(montrer) (marchandises)* to display; *(œuvres d'art)* to exhibit **(b)** *(expliquer) (raisons, projet)* to set out; *(griefs, point de vue)* to air; **je leur ai exposé ma situation** I explained my situation to them **(c)** *(présenter)* **e. qch à la lumière/au soleil** to expose sth to the light/to the sun; **e. un film** to expose a film; **e. qn à la critique/au danger** to expose sb to criticism/to danger; **exposé au nord** facing north **2** **s'exposer** *vpr* **s'e. au danger** to put oneself in danger; **s'e. à la critique/à des poursuites** to lay oneself open to criticism/to prosecution; **ne t'expose pas trop longtemps** don't stay in the sun too long

exposition [εkspozisjɔ̃] *nf* **(a)** *(action) (de marchandises, de fleurs)* display; *(d'œuvres d'art)* exhibition **(b)** *(de musée)* exhibition **(c)** *(salon, foire)* exhibition, show; **l'E. universelle** the World's Fair **(d)** *(de faits, de raisons)* exposition **(e)** *(au froid, au danger, au soleil)* exposure (**à** to); *(d'une maison)* aspect; *Phot* exposure; **durée d'e.** exposure time

exprès¹, -esse [εksprεs] *adj (explicite)* express

exprès² [εksprεs] *adj inv* **lettre/paquet e.** special-delivery letter/package; **en e.** by special delivery

exprès³ [εksprε] *adv (à dessein)* on purpose, deliberately; *(spécialement)* specially; **je l'ai allumé sans le faire e.** I turned it on without meaning to; **c'est fait e.** it's deliberate; **on dirait un fait e.** you'd think it was done on purpose; **comme (par) un fait e., il pleuvait** and wouldn't you know it, it was raining

express [εksprεs] **1** *adj (train)* express **2** *nm* **(a)** *(train)* express **(b)** *(café)* espresso

expressément [εksprεsemã] *adv* **(a)** *(catégoriquement)* expressly **(b)** *(spécialement)* specially

expressif, -ive [εksprεsif, -iv] *adj* expressive

expression [εksprεsjɔ̃] *nf* **(a)** *(d'un sentiment, d'une opinion)* expression; *(du visage)* expression, look; **l'e. de son visage** the expression *or* look on her face; **sans e.** expressionless; **e. corporelle** self-expression through movement **(b)** *(locution)* expression **(c)** *Math* expression; *Fig* **réduit à sa plus simple e.** reduced to its simplest form; *Ordinat* **e. logique** logical expression

expressionnisme [εksprεsjɔnism] *nm* expressionism

expressionniste [εksprεsjɔnist] *adj & nmf* expressionist

exprimable [εksprimabl] *adj* expressible

exprimer [εksprime] **1** *vt* **(a)** *(sentiment, opinion)* & *Math* to express **(b)** *(jus)* to squeeze (**de** from) **2** **s'exprimer** *vpr (en parlant, en agissant)* to express oneself; **s'e. par gestes** to use sign language; **si je peux m'e. ainsi** if I can put it like that; **le président ne s'est pas en-**

core exprimé sur ce sujet the president has yet to voice an opinion on the matter

expropriation [ɛksprɔprijasjɔ̃] *nf* expropriation

exproprier [66] [ɛksprɔprije] *vt* to expropriate

expulser [ɛkspylse] *vt (étranger)* to deport, to expel (**de** from); *(locataire)* to evict (**de** from); *(élève, membre de parti)* to expel (**de** from); *(joueur)* to send off

expulsion [ɛkspylsjɔ̃] *nf (d'un étranger)* deportation (**de** from); *(d'un locataire)* eviction (**de** from); *(d'un élève, d'un membre de parti)* expulsion (**de** from); *(d'un joueur)* sending off

expurger [45] [ɛkspyrʒe] *vt* to expurgate

exquis, -e [ɛkski, -iz] *adj* exquisite; *(personne, sourire, temps)* delightful

exsangue [ɛksɑ̃g, ɛgzɑ̃g] *adj (patient, visage)* anemic; *Fig (pays, région)* bled white

extase [ɛkstaz] *nf* (a) *Rel & Psy* ecstasy (b) *(admiration)* rapture, ecstasy; **être en e. devant qn/qch** to be in raptures over sb/sth

extasier [66] [ɛkstazje] **s'extasier** *vpr (s'exclamer)* to go into raptures (**sur/devant** about/over); *(être en extase)* to be in raptures (**sur/devant** about/over)

extatique [ɛkstatik] *adj* ecstatic

extenseur [ɛkstɑ̃sœr] **1** *adj m (muscle)* extensor
     2 *nm (appareil)* chest expander

extensible [ɛkstɑ̃sibl] *adj* (a) *(métal)* tensile; *(vêtement, tissu)* stretch (b) *Ordinat* upgradeable

extensif, -ive [ɛkstɑ̃sif, -iv] *adj* **culture extensive** extensive farming

extension [ɛkstɑ̃sjɔ̃] *nf* (a) *(d'un muscle, d'un ressort)* stretching; **être en e.** *(ressort)* to be released; *(gymnaste)* to be fully stretched (b) *Fig (d'un territoire, d'une firme)* expansion; *(d'un contrat)* extension; *(d'une maladie, d'une langue)* spread; **prendre de l'e.** *(entreprise)* to expand; *(maladie, incendie)* to spread (c) **par e.** by extension (d) *Ordinat* expansion; **e. mémoire** memory upgrade

exténuer [ɛkstenɥe] **1** *vt* to exhaust
     2 s'exténuer *vpr* **s'e. à faire qch** to exhaust oneself doing sth

extérieur, -e [ɛksterjœr] **1** *adj* (a) *(surface, partie)* outer, external; *(escalier, éclairage, intérêts)* outside; *(signe, fragilité)* outward; *(facteur, cause)* external; **le monde e.** the outside world; **sans aide extérieure** without outside help (b) *(étranger) (commerce, politique)* foreign, external
     2 *nm* (a) *(d'un bâtiment, d'une boîte)* outside, exterior; **vu de l'e.** seen from the outside; **à l'e.** *(d'un bâtiment)* outside; *(d'une boîte)* on the outside; **à l'e. de la gare/ville** outside the station/town; *Fig* **juger de l'e.** to judge by appearances; **match à l'e.** away match; **jouer à l'e.** to play away (b) **l'e.** *(pays étrangers)* foreign countries; **à l'e.** abroad; **de l'e.** from abroad (c) *Cin* location shot; **tourner en e.** to film on location (d) *Belg Sport (joueur)* winger

extérieurement [ɛksterjœrmɑ̃] *adv* (a) *(dehors)* on the outside, externally (b) *(en apparence)* outwardly

extérioriser [ɛksterjɔrize] **1** *vt (sentiment)* to express; *Psy* to externalize
     2 s'extérioriser *vpr (sentiment)* to express itself; *(personne)* to express oneself

exterminateur, -trice [ɛkstɛrminatœr, -tris] **1** *adj (rage)* destructive
     2 *nm,f* exterminator

extermination [ɛkstɛrminasjɔ̃] *nf* extermination

exterminer [ɛkstɛrmine] *vt* to exterminate

externaliser [ɛkstɛrnalize] *vt Écon* to outsource

externat [ɛkstɛrna] *nm* (a) *(école)* day school (b) *(élèves)* day pupils (c) *(à l'hôpital)* externship

externe [ɛkstɛrn] **1** *adj (surface, partie)* external, outer; *(cause)* external; *Ordinat* **dispositif e.** external device; **à**

usage e. *(médicament)* for external use only (b) **élève e.** day pupil
     2 *nmf* (a) *(élève)* day pupil (b) *(étudiant en médecine)* **e. (des hôpitaux)** extern

extincteur [ɛkstɛ̃ktœr] *nm* fire extinguisher

extinction [ɛkstɛ̃ksjɔ̃] *nf* (a) **e. des feux** lights out (b) *(d'une espèce)* extinction; **espèce en voie d'e.** endangered species (c) **e. de voix** loss of voice; **avoir une e. de voix** to have lost one's voice

extirper [ɛkstirpe] **1** *vt (plante)* to root up; *Fig (vices)* to eradicate, to root out; **e. qn de son lit** to drag sb out of bed; **je n'ai pas pu lui e. le moindre renseignement** I couldn't get a single piece of information out of him/her
     2 s'extirper *vpr* **s'e. de qch** to extricate oneself from sth; **s'e. de son lit** to drag oneself out of bed

extorquer [ɛkstɔrke] *vt (argent, promesse)* to extort (**à** from)

extorsion [ɛkstɔrsjɔ̃] *nf* extortion; **e. de fonds** extortion of funds

extra [ɛkstra] **1** *adj inv* (a) *(de qualité supérieure)* top-quality (b) *Fam (remarquable)* great, neat
     2 *nm inv* (a) *(gâterie)* special treat; **s'offrir un e.** to treat oneself (b) *(serviteur)* extra hand; **faire des e. chez qn** to do occasional work for sb

extra- [ɛkstra] *préf* extra-

extraconjugal, -e, -aux, -ales [ɛkstrakɔ̃ʒygal, -o] *adj* extramarital

extracteur [ɛkstraktœr] *nm* extractor

extraction [ɛkstraksjɔ̃] *nf aussi Math* extraction; *(d'une balle)* removal; *Fig* **de haute/basse e.** of noble/humble extraction

extrader [ɛkstrade] *vt* to extradite

extradition [ɛkstradisjɔ̃] *nf* extradition

extrafin, -e [ɛkstrafɛ̃, -in] *adj* (a) *(petit pois)* extra-fine (b) *(de qualité supérieure)* top-quality

extrafort, -e [ɛkstrafɔr, -ɔrt] **1** *adj* extra-strong
     2 *nm* bias tape

extraire [28] [ɛkstrɛr] **1** *vt aussi Math* to extract (**de** from); *(balle)* to remove (**de** from); *(épingle, clou)* to pull out (**de** of); *(personne)* to free (**de** from); **cette citation est extraite de...** this quotation is taken from...
     2 s'extraire *vpr* **s'e. de qch** to extricate oneself from sth

extrait [ɛkstrɛ] *nm* (a) *(essence)* extract (b) *(de texte, de film)* extract; *(d'un acte)* abstract; **e. de casier judiciaire** = documentary evidence showing whether one has a criminal record; **e. de naissance** birth certificate

extralucide [ɛkstralysid] *adj & nmf* **(voyante) e.** clairvoyant

Extranet [ɛkstranɛt] *nm Ordinat* Extranet

extraordinaire [ɛkstraɔrdinɛr] *adj* (a) *(spécial) (mesures, messager, mission)* special (b) *(étonnant, remarquable)* extraordinary; *Fam (excellent)* fantastic; **cela n'a rien d'e.** that's nothing out of the ordinary; **si par e.** if by some remote chance

extraordinairement [ɛkstraɔrdinɛrmɑ̃] *adv* extraordinarily

extraplat, -e [ɛkstrapla, -at] *adj (montre, calculette)* slimline

extrapoler [ɛkstrapɔle] *vi* to extrapolate

extrascolaire [ɛkstraskɔlɛr] *adj (activités)* extracurricular

extraterrestre [ɛkstratɛrɛstr] *adj & nmf* extraterrestrial

extra-utérin, -e [ɛkstrayterɛ̃, -in] *adj voir* **grossesse**

extravagance [ɛkstravagɑ̃s] *nf* (a) *(d'un comportement, de vêtements)* extravagance; *(d'une personne)* eccentricity; **des idées d'une telle e.** such extravagant ideas (b) *(action, remarque)* piece of nonsense

extravagant, -e [ɛkstravagɑ̃, -ɑ̃t] *adj (idée, comportement, vêtements)* extravagant; *(personne)* eccentric

extraverti, -e [ɛkstravɛrti] *adj & nm,f* extrovert

extrême [ɛkstrɛm] **1** *adj* (a) *(point, limite)* furthest; *(jeunesse, vieillesse, froid, plaisir)* extreme; **en cas d'e. urgence** if it's extremely urgent; **d'une maigreur e.** extremely thin; *Pol* **e. droite/gauche** far *or* extreme right/left (**b**) *(excessif)* extreme

2 *nm* extreme; **passer d'un e. à l'autre** to go from one extreme to the other; **prudent à l'e.** cautious in the extreme

extrêmement [ɛkstrɛmmã] *adv* extremely

extrême-onction (*pl* **extrêmes-onctions**) [ɛkstrɛmõksjõ] *nf Rel* extreme unction

Extrême-Orient [ɛkstrɛmɔrjã] *nm* **l'E.** the Far East

extrémisme [ɛkstremism] *nm* extremism

extrémité [ɛkstremite] *nf* (**a**) *(bout) (d'une jambe, d'une corde)* end; *(d'un doigt)* tip; *(d'une aiguille, d'une épée)* point; **les extrémités** *(pieds et mains)* the extremities (**b**) *(acte désespéré)* se

livrer à une e. to do something desperate (**c**) *(situation désespérée)* extremity; **être à la dernière e.** to be on the brink of death

exubérance [ɛgzyberãs] *nf (d'une personne)* exuberance; *(d'une végétation)* lushness; **avec e.** exuberantly

exubérant, -e [ɛgzyberã, -ãt] *adj (personne, joie)* exuberant; *(végétation)* lush

exultation [ɛgzyltasjõ] *nf* exultation

exulter [ɛgzylte] *vi* to exult, to rejoice

exutoire [ɛgzytwar] *nm* outlet (**à** for)

ex-voto [ɛksvɔto] *nm inv Rel* votive offering

e-zine, ezine [izin] *nm Ordinat* e-zine, ezine

F

F¹, f [ɛf] *nm inv* F, f; **un F2/F3** *(appartement)* a two-/three-roomed apartment

F² (**a**) *(abrév* **franc(s)**) F, fr (**b**) *(abrév* **Fahrenheit**) F

fa [fa] *nm inv (note de musique)* F; *(chantée)* fa

fable [fɑbl] *nf* (**a**) *(récit)* fable (**b**) *(invention)* story

fabricant, -e [fabrikɑ̃, -ɑ̃t] *nm,f* manufacturer

fabrication [fabrikasjɔ̃] *nf (industrielle)* manufacture; *(manuelle)* making; **f. artisanale** production by craftsmen; **bombe de f. artisanale** home-made bomb; **f. assistée par ordinateur** computer-aided manufacture; **de f. française** French-made

fabrique [fabrik] *nf* factory

fabriquer [fabrike] *vt* (**a**) *(industriellement)* to manufacture; *(manuellement)* to make; *Fam* **qu'est-ce qu'elle fabrique?** what's she up to? (**b**) *(inventer)* to make up, to fabricate

fabulation [fabylasjɔ̃] *nf* fantasizing

fabuleusement [fabyløzmɑ̃] *adv* fabulously

fabuleux, -euse [fabylø, -øz] *adj* fabulous

fac [fak] *nf Fam* college; **à la f.** at college; **être en f. d'allemand** to be studying German at college

façade [fasad] *nf aussi Fig* façade

face [fas] *nf* (**a**) *(visage)* face; *Fig* **perdre/sauver la f.** to lose/save face (**b**) *(côté) (d'un disque)* side; *(d'une pièce de monnaie)* head (side); **changer un disque de f.** to turn a record over (**c**) *Fig (aspect)* side; **changer la f. des choses** to change the face of things (**d**) *(locutions)* **f. à** *(dans l'espace)* facing; *(difficultés, situation)* faced with; *(adversaire)* confronted with; **f. à f. (avec)** face to face (with); **faire f. à** *(lieu, personne)* to face, to be opposite; *(responsabilités, dépenses)* to meet; *(situation, difficultés)* to face up to; *(attaquer)* from the front; **en f.** opposite; *(de l'autre côté de la rue)* across the road; **regarder qn en f.** to look sb in the face; **dire qch en f. à qn** to tell sb sth to his/her face; **la maison (d')en f.** the house across the road; **en f. de** opposite, facing; **l'un en f. de l'autre** opposite *or* facing each other

face-à-face [fasafas] *nm inv (public)* face-to-face debate; *(privé)* one-on-one meeting

facétie [fasesi] *nf Litt* joke

facétieux, -euse [fasesjø, -øz] *adj Litt (personne)* mischievous

facette [fasɛt] *nf aussi Fig* facet; **à facettes** facetted; *(personnalité)* multi-faceted

fâché, -e [fɑʃe] *adj* (**a**) *(en colère)* angry (**contre** with *or* at) (**b**) *(brouillé)* on bad terms (**avec** with); *Fam* **elle est fâchée avec les maths** she's hopeless at math (**c**) *(contrarié)* sorry; **je ne suis pas f. que ça soit terminé** I'm not sorry that it's finished

fâcher [fɑʃe] **1** *vt (mettre en colère)* to make angry, to anger

2 se fâcher *vpr* (**a**) *(se mettre en colère)* to get angry (**contre** with) (**b**) *(se brouiller)* to fall out (**avec** with)

fâcheux, -euse [fɑʃø, -øz] *adj* unfortunate

facho [faʃo] *adj & nmf Fam* fascist

faciès [fasjɛs] *nm* features

facile [fasil] **1** *adj* (**a**) *(simple)* easy; **être f. à faire** to be easy to do; **c'est f. à dire** that's easily said; **f. d'emploi** easy to use (**b**) *(agréable)* easy-going; **être f. à vivre** to be easy to get along with (**c**) *Péj (superficiel)* facile (**d**) *Péj (femme, fille)* easy

2 *adv Fam (au moins)* easily

facilement [fasilmɑ̃] *adv* easily

facilité [fasilite] *nf* (**a**) *(simplicité)* easiness; **choisir la f.** to take the easy way out (**b**) *(aisance)* ease; **avoir des facilités pour qch** to have a talent for sth (**c**) **facilités de paiement** payment facilities

faciliter [fasilite] *vt* to make easier; **f. qch à qn** to make sth easier for sb; **tu ne me facilites pas la tâche!** you're not making things easy for me!

façon [fasɔ̃] *nf* (**a**) *(manière)* way, manner; **faire qch à sa f.** to do sth (in) one's own way; **de cette f.** (in) this way; **de f. à faire qch** so as to do sth; **de f. à ce qu'il t'entende** so that he hears you; **de telle f. que** in such a way that; **d'une** *ou* **de f. générale** generally speaking; **d'une f. ou d'une autre** one way or another; **de toute f.** anyway, in any case; *Sout* **vous ne me dérangez en aucune f.** you're not disturbing me in the least; **c'est une f. de parler** in a manner of speaking; **je ne tolère pas ces façons de parler!** I won't tolerate that sort of language!; *Can* **avoir de la f.** *(avoir des manières agréables)* to have pleasant manners; *(être beau parleur)* to speak well

(**b**) *(imitation)* **f. cuir** imitation leather

(**c**) *(fabrication)* making; *(facture)* craftsmanship, workmanship; *(main-d'œuvre)* labor

(**d**) **façons** *(comportement)* manners, behavior; **en voilà des façons!** what a way to behave!; **faire des façons** *(minauder)* to put on airs; **faire des façons pour accepter qch** to make a fuss about accepting sth; **sans façons** *(personne, repas)* unpretentious; **non merci, sans façons!** no thanks, really!

façonner [fasɔne] *vt* (**a**) *(travailler)* to shape (**b**) *(fabriquer)* to make (**c**) *Fig (personne, caractère)* to mold

fac-similé *(pl* fac-similés) [faksimile] *nm* facsimile

facteur¹, -trice [faktœr, -tris] **1** *nm,f (employé des Postes)* mailman, *f* mailwoman

2 *nm (de pianos, de clavecins)* maker; *(d'orgues)* builder

facteur² [faktœr] *nm* (**a**) *(élément)* factor; **le f. temps** the time factor (**b**) *Math* factor

factice [faktis] *adj* (**a**) *(faux)* imitation (**b**) *Fig (sourire)* forced; *(gaieté)* false

faction [faksjɔ̃] *nf* (**a**) *(groupe)* faction (**b**) *Mil* guard duty; **être de** *ou* **en f.** to be on guard duty

factotum [faktɔtɔm] *nm* factotum

factuel, -elle [faktɥɛl] *adj* factual

facturation [faktyrasjɔ̃] *nf* invoicing, billing

facture¹ [faktyr] *nf* (**a**) *(style) (d'une œuvre)* construction; *(d'un artiste)* style (**b**) *(de pianos, de clavecins)* making; *(d'orgues)* building

facture² [faktyr] *nf (document)* invoice, bill; **faire** *ou* **dresser une f.** to make out an invoice; **f. d'électricité/de gaz** electricity/gas bill; **f. détaillée** itemized invoice

facturer [faktyre] *vt* to invoice

facturette [faktyrɛt] *nf* credit card sales slip

facultatif, -ive [fakyltatif, -iv] *adj* optional

faculté [fakylte] *nf* (**a**) *(de médecine, de droit)* faculty (**b**) *(pouvoir)* capacity (**de** for) (**c**) **facultés mentales** faculties; **ne plus avoir toutes ses facultés** to no longer have all one's faculties

fada [fada] *Fam* **1** *adj* crazy
  2 *nmf* nutcase

fadaise [fadɛz] *nf* silly remark; **dire des fadaises** to talk nonsense

fadasse [fadas] *adj Fam* insipid

fade [fad] *adj* insipid

fadeur [fadœr] *nf* insipidness

fagot [fago] *nm* bundle of firewood; *Fig* **de derrière les fagots** *(bouteille de vin)* for special occasions; *(compliment, idée)* remarkable

fagoté, -e [fagɔte] *adj Péj* **mal/bizarrement f.** badly/oddly dressed

faiblard, -e [fɛblar, -ard] *adj Fam* a bit weak

faible [fɛbl] **1** *adj* (**a**) *(physiquement, moralement)* weak (**b**) *(raisonnement, plaisanterie)* weak; **être f. en qch** *(élève)* to be weak in sth (**c**) *(voix, odeur, lumière)* faint; *(vent)* light; **et le terme est f.!** and that's putting it mildly! (**d**) *(quantité)* small; *(prix, revenu)* low; *(avantage, chance, espoir)* slight; *(vitesse)* low; **à une f. hauteur/profondeur** not very high up/deep down
  2 *nmf* weakling; **les faibles d'esprit** the feeble-minded
  3 *nm* **avoir un f. pour qn/qch** to have a soft spot for sb/a weakness for sth

faiblement [fɛbləmã] *adv* *(résister, protester)* weakly, feebly; *(éclairer)* faintly

faiblesse [fɛblɛs] *nf* (**a**) *(physique, morale)* weakness; **avoir la f. de faire qch** to be weak enough to do sth; **donner des signes de f.** *(appareil)* to be showing signs of wear and tear; *(personne)* to be looking weak (**b**) *(médiocrité)* weakness (**en** at) (**c**) *(malaise)* **avoir une f.** to feel faint

faiblir [fɛblir] *vi* (**a**) *(devenir faible)* *(personne, monnaie)* to weaken; *(lumière)* to grow weaker; *(vent)* to drop (**b**) *(niveau scolaire)* to decrease; *(élève)* to get weaker

faïence [fajãs] *nf* (**a**) *(matière)* earthenware (**b**) *(objet)* piece of earthenware; **faïences** earthenware

faïencerie [fajãsri] *nf* (**a**) *(articles)* earthenware (**b**) *(fabrique)* pottery (works) (**c**) *(commerce)* pottery (trade)

faille [faj] *nf* (**a**) *(dans un raisonnement)* flaw; *(dans une amitié)* rift; **sans f.** *(raisonnement)* flawless; *(fidélité)* unwavering (**b**) *Géol* fault

faillir [35] [fajir] **1** *vi* **j'ai failli tomber** I nearly *or* almost fell; **j'ai bien failli me noyer** I very nearly drowned
  2 faillir à *vt ind Litt (réputation)* not to live up to; *(devoir)* to fail in

faillite [fajit] *nf* (**a**) *(d'entreprise)* bankruptcy; **être en f.** to be bankrupt; **faire f.** to go bankrupt (**b**) *(échec)* failure

faim [fɛ̃] *nf* hunger; **avoir f.** to be hungry; *Fig* **avoir f. de qch** to hunger for sth; *Fam* **avoir une grosse/petite f.** to be very hungry/a bit hungry; **avoir une f. de loup** to be ravenous; **rester sur sa f.** to remain hungry; *Fig* to be left unsatisfied

fainéant, -e [fɛneã, -ãt] **1** *adj* lazy, idle
  2 *nm,f* idler

fainéanter [fɛneãte] *vi* to idle about

fainéantise [fɛneãtiz] *nf* laziness, idleness

faire [36] [fɛr] **1** *vt* (**a**) *(fabriquer, produire)* to make; *(tache, trace)* to leave; **f. du bruit** to make some noise; **f. de la fumée** to give off smoke; **f. une erreur** to make a mistake; **f. de la betterave/du colza** to grow beets/rape; *Fam* **des femmes comme ça, on n'en fait plus** they don't make women like that any more; **f. un enfant à qn** to get sb pregnant; **f. des compliments à qn** to compliment sb; **je ferai de lui un**

homme/un avocat I'll make a man/a lawyer of him; **qu'est-ce que je vais f. de lui?** what am I going to do with him?; **qu'est-ce que tu vas f. de ce vieux bidon?** what are you going to do with that old can?; **qu'est-ce que j'ai fait de mes lunettes?** what have I done with my glasses?

(**b**) *(effectuer)* *(changements, effort, grimace, mouvement)* to make; **f. le ménage/la vaisselle** to do the housework/the dishes; **f. un pas en avant** to step forward; **faire demi-tour** to turn around; **f. une école de commerce** to study at a business school; **f. une licence** to study for a degree; **c'est moi qui fais tout ici** I have to do everything around here; **voilà une bonne chose de faite** that's one thing out of the way; **ce qui est fait est fait** what's done is done; **c'est bien fait pour elle** it serves her right

(**c**) *(occasionner)* **f. de la peine à qn** to hurt sb; **qu'est-ce que tu lui as fait?** what have you done to her? *Fam* **f. des ennuis à qn** to make trouble for sb; **ça m'a fait quelque chose/un choc** it upset/shocked me; **ça a fait du scandale** it caused a scandal; **ça ne fait rien** it doesn't matter; **qu'est-ce que ça peut faire?** what difference does it make?; **ça fait mauvais effet** it gives a bad impression; **le médicament n'a pas fait effet** the medicine didn't take effect

(**d**) *(changer)* **on ne peut rien y f.** nothing can be done about it; *Fam* **rien à f.!** no way!

(**e**) *(subir)* to have; **f. une dépression** to have depression; *Fam* **f. une pneumonie/une grippe** to have pneumonia/the flu; *Fam* **il m'a encore fait une grippe!** he's gone and got the flu again!

(**f**) *(pratiquer)* **f. du tennis/football** to play tennis/soccer; **f. de la voile** to sail; **f. du violon/piano** to play the violin/the piano; **f. du russe/de l'espagnol** to do Russian/Spanish

(**g**) *(constituer)* to make; **il ferait un excellent mari/pompier** he would make an excellent husband/firefighter; **f. l'affaire** to do the trick; **c'est cela qui fait ton charme** that's what gives you your charm; **cette chambre fait aussi bureau** this bedroom also serves as an office

(**h**) *(s'occuper à)* to do; **qu'est-ce qu'il fait dans la vie?** what line of work is he in?; **qu'est-ce que tu fais demain?** what are you doing tomorrow?; **f. des études** to study; **qu'est-ce que tu fais ici?** what are you doing here?

(**i**) *(parcourir)* to do; **f. 100 kilomètres par jour** ≃ to do 60 miles a day; **il a fait toute la ville pour la retrouver** he searched the whole town for her; **f. du cent à l'heure** ≃ to do 60 mph

(**j**) *(indique une mesure, une quantité)* to be; **la table fait un mètre de long** ≃ the table is three feet long; **2 et 2 font 4** 2 and 2 are *or* make 4; **combien ça fait en dollars?** how much is that in dollars?; **le bébé fait cinq kilos** ≃ the baby weighs eleven pounds

(**k**) *(agir comme)* **f. l'imbécile** to play the fool; **f. l'innocent** to play the innocent; **f. l'important** to act important; **il fait celui qui n'a pas entendu** he pretends he hasn't heard

(**l**) *(sembler)* to look; **il fait jeune/anglais** he looks young/English

(**m**) *(dire)* to say; **"à bientôt!", fit-elle** "see you soon!", she said; **ça a fait plouf** it went splash

(**n**) *(suivi d'un infinitif)* **f. voir qch à qn** to show sb sth; **f. traverser qn** to help sb across; **f. faire qch à qn** to make sb do sth; **elle m'a fait ranger ma chambre** she made me tidy my room; **f. réparer qch** to get *or* to have sth repaired; **f. construire une maison** to have a house built; **elle ne fait que se plaindre** she's always complaining; **je ne fais que répéter ses paroles** I'm just repeating what she said

(**o**) *(pour remplacer un verbe)* **il devait arroser les plantes mais il ne l'a pas fait** he was meant to water the plants but he didn't; **mais faites donc!** please do!

2 *vi* (**a**) *(agir)* to do; **f. vite** to be quick; **fais comme tu voudras** do as you like; **f. pour le mieux** to do one's best; **f.**

comme chez soi to make oneself at home; **comment f.?** how can I/we do it?; *Fam* **il faut f. avec** it'll have to do

(**b**) *Fam (faire ses besoins)* to go to the bathroom

3 *v impersonnel* (**a**) *(indique un état)* to be; **il fait froid/chaud** it's cold/hot; **il fait beau** it's fine; **il fait 20 degrés** it's 20 degrees; **il fait jour/nuit** it's light/night

(**b**) *(indique la distance, la durée)* **ça fait un mois qu'il est parti** he's been gone for a month; **ça fait une heure que je t'attends** I've been waiting for you for an hour; **ça fait 80 kilomètres que nous roulons** ≃ we've been driving for 50 miles

4 se faire *vpr* (**a**) *(avoir lieu)* **finalement ça ne s'est jamais fait** nothing happened in the end; **comment se fait-il que...?** how is it that...?

(**b**) *(être pratiqué)* to be done; **ça se fait beaucoup cette année** it's the in thing this year

(**c**) *(être acceptable)* **ça se fait** it's the done thing; **ça ne se fait pas** it's not the done thing

(**d**) *(être fabriqué)* to be made

(**e**) *(se confectionner)* **se f. un lit** to make a bed for oneself; **se f. une bibliothèque** to build up a library; **se f. un œuf sur le plat** to make oneself a fried egg; **se f. les ongles** to do one's nails

(**f**) *(fromage, vin)* to mature; *(chaussures)* to wear in

(**g**) *(provoquer)* **se f. mal** to hurt oneself; **se f. une entorse au poignet** to sprain one's wrist; **se f. du souci** to worry; **se f. une opinion** to form an opinion; **se f. des amis/des ennemis** to make friends/enemies; *Fam* **s'en f.** to worry; **elle ne s'en fait pas celle-là!** *(elle a du culot)* she has a nerve!; *(elle a beaucoup d'argent)* she doesn't have a care in the world!

(**h**) *(s'ériger en)* **se f. le défenseur des opprimés** to become established as a defender of the oppressed

(**i**) *(devenir)* **se f. vieux** to get old; **se f. beau** to do oneself up; **se f. moine** to become a monk; **il se fait tard** it's getting late

(**j**) *(avec un infinitif)* **se f. insulter** to be insulted; **se f. couper les cheveux** to have one's hair cut; **se f. prêter qch** to borrow sth; **se f. refaire le nez** to have a nose job

(**k**) *(s'habituer)* **se f. à qch** to get used to sth

(**l**) *(l'un l'autre)* **se f. des cadeaux** to give each other presents; **se f. des reproches** to blame each other

(**m**) *Fam* **il faut se le f. celui-là!** what a pain in the neck!

faire-part [fɛrpar] *nm inv* announcement

faire-valoir [fɛrvalwar] *nm inv (personne)* foil

fair-play [fɛrplɛ] **1** *adj inv* **être f.** to play fair

2 *nm* sportsmanship, fair play

fais *voir* **faire**

faisabilité [fəzabilite] *nf* feasibility

faisable [fəzabl] *adj* feasible

faisan [fəzɑ̃] *nm* pheasant

faisandé, -e [fəzɑ̃de] *adj (gibier)* high

faisane [fəzan] *adj f & nf* **(poule) f.** hen pheasant

faisceau, -x [fɛso] *nm* (**a**) *(rayons)* beam; **f. hertzien** electromagnetic wave; **f. lumineux** beam of light (**b**) *Fig (de preuves)* body

faiseur, -euse [fəzœr, -øz] **1** *nm,f* maker; **f. d'embarras** fussbudget; **f. de miracles** miracle worker

2 *nf* **faiseuse d'anges** backstreet abortionist

faisons *voir* **faire**

faisselle [fɛsɛl] *nf (fromage)* = type of soft white cheese; *(récipient)* cheese drainer

fait¹, -e [fɛ, fɛt] **1** *pp voir* **faire**

2 *adj* (**a**) *(fabriqué)* **tout f.** *(idée, expression)* fixed (**b**) *(adapté)* **être f. pour qn/qch** to be made for sb/sth; **ils sont faits l'un pour l'autre** they're made for each other; **être f. pour faire qch** *(personne)* to be cut out to do sth (**c**) *(bâti)* *Litt ou Hum* **être bien f. de sa personne** to be good-looking (**d**) *(maquillé)* **avoir les ongles/les yeux faits** to be wearing nail polish/eye make-up (**e**) *(fromage)* ripe

fait² [fɛ] *nm* (**a**) *(acte)* act; **les faits et gestes de qn** sb's every move; **prendre qn sur le f.** to catch sb in the act *or* red-handed; **prendre f. et cause pour qn** to stand up for sb

(**b**) *(réalité)* fact; **le f. d'habiter en ville** living in town; **mettre qn devant le f. accompli** to present sb with a fait accompli; **c'est un f. acquis** it's an established fact

(**c**) *(point précis)* **aller droit au f.** to get straight to the point; **en venir au f.** to come to the point

(**d**) *(événement)* event; **un f. nouveau s'est produit** there was a new development; **un f. divers** a news item; **faits divers** *(rubrique)* ≃ news in brief

(**e**) *(locutions)* **au f.** *(à propos)* by the way; **être au f. de qch** to know *or* to be informed about sth; **en f., de f.** in fact, as a matter of fact; **de ce f.** for that reason; **expert en f. de vins** expert as regards wine *or* when it comes to wine

faîte [fɛt] *nm* (**a**) *(d'un toit)* ridge; *(d'un arbre, d'une maison)* top; *(d'une montagne)* summit (**b**) *Fig* **le f. de la gloire** the height of glory

faites *voir* **faire**

faîtier, -ère [fɛtje, -ɛr] *adj Suisse (organisation, association)* umbrella

faitout *nm*, **fait-tout** *nm inv* [fɛtu] stewpot

fakir [fakir] *nm* fakir

falaise [falɛz] *nf* cliff

fallacieux, -euse [falasjø, -øz] *adj (prétexte)* false; *(argument, raisonnement)* specious; *(apparence)* misleading

falloir [37] [falwar] **1** *v impersonnel* (**a**) *(être nécessaire)* **faut-il tout cela?** is all that necessary?; **je l'ai fait parce qu'il le fallait** I did it because I had to; **il lui faut un nouveau pardessus** he needs a new coat; **il me faudrait un kilo de pommes** ≃ I need two pounds of apples; **je lui ai tout donné, qu'est-ce qu'il lui faut de plus!** I've given him/her everything, what more does he/her want!; **il m'a fallu trois jours pour le faire** it took me three days to do it; **il faut partir** I/we/you/*etc.* must go *or* have to go; **il lui faut se dépêcher** she has to hurry; **il fallait le dire!** why didn't you say so?; **je vous en prie, il ne fallait pas!** you shouldn't have!; **il faudrait qu'elle reste** she ought to stay; **il ne faudrait pas que je vous mette en retard** I'd better not make you late; **il faut toujours que tu fasses des histoires!** why do you always have to cause such a fuss!; **il a fallu qu'elle raconte à tout le quartier!** she had to go and tell the whole neighborhood!

(**b**) *(locutions) Fam* **il faut ce qu'il faut!** you might as well do things in style!; **il faut voir** *(il faut attendre)* we'll have to wait and see; *(il faut réfléchir)* I/we will have to think about it; *Fam* **elle lui a répondu, faut voir comment!** you wouldn't believe the way she answered him!

2 s'en falloir *vpr* **il s'en est fallu de peu** *ou* **peu s'en est fallu qu'elle ne meure** she very nearly died; **50 dollars** *ou* **peu s'en faut** the best part of $50; **loin** *ou* **tant s'en faut** far from it

fallu *voir* **falloir**

falot¹ [falo] *nm (lanterne)* lantern

falot², -e [falo, -ɔt] *adj* dreary, drab

falsification [falsifikasjɔ̃] *nf (de documents, de comptes)* falsification; *(d'une signature)* forging

falsifier [66] [falsifje] *vt (document, comptes)* to falsify; *(signature)* to forge

falzar [falzar] *nm Fam* pants

famé, -e [fame] *adj* **mal f.** disreputable

famélique [famelik] *adj* half-starved

fameusement [famøzmɑ̃] *adv Fam (très)* incredibly

fameux, -euse [famø, -øz] *adj* (**a**) *(célèbre)* famous (**pour** for); **c'est donc ça, ton f. régime!** so this is your famous diet! (**b**) *Fam (excellent)* brilliant; **pas f.** not much good

familial, -e, -aux, -ales [familjal, -o] **1** *adj (vie, atmosphère)* family; *(entreprise, hôtel)* family-run; *(paquet, format)* family-size

   2 *nf* **familiale** *(auto)* station wagon

familiariser [familjarize] **1** *vt* **f. qn avec qch** to familiarize sb with sth, to get sb used to sth

   2 se familiariser *vpr* **se f. avec qch** *(en le pratiquant)* to familiarize oneself with sth; *(en s'y habituant)* to get used to sth; *(lieu)* to get to know sth

familiarité [familjarite] *nf* **(a)** *(désinvolture)* informality **(b)** **familiarités** *(libertés)* familiarities

familier, -ère [familje, -ɛr] **1** *adj* **(a)** *(désinvolte)* informal (**avec** with) **(b)** *(langage, expression)* colloquial **(c)** *(connu)* familiar (**à** to)

   2 *nm,f (client)* regular visitor (**de** to)

familièrement [familjɛrmɑ̃] *adv* familiarly; **parler f. à qn** to be familiar with sb

famille [famij] *nf* **(a)** *(proches)* family; **de bonne f.** from a good family; **en f.** with one's family; **c'est de f.** it runs in the family; *Fam* **un repas des familles** a cozy little meal; **f. monoparentale** one-parent family; **f. nombreuse**, *Suisse* **grande f.** large family **(b)** *(d'animaux, de langues, de plantes)* family; **f. littéraire/politique** literary/political circle

famine [famin] *nf* famine; **crier f.** to be starving

fan [fan], **fana** [fana] *nmf Fam* fan

fanal, -aux [fanal, -o] *nm (lanterne)* lantern

fanatique [fanatik] **1** *adj* fanatical (**de** about)

   2 *nmf* fanatic; **f. de basket** basketball fanatic

fanatiser [fanatize] *vt* to make fanatical

fanatisme [fanatism] *nm* fanaticism

faner [fane] **1** *vi (fleur)* to wither; *Fig (beauté, teint)* to fade

   2 se faner *vpr (fleur)* to wither; *Fig (beauté, teint)* to fade

fanes [fan] *nfpl (de carottes, de radis)* tops

fanfare [fɑ̃far] *nf (orchestre)* brass band; **réveil en f.** brutal awakening

fanfaron, -onne [fɑ̃farɔ̃, -ɔn] **1** *adj* boastful

   2 *nm,f* braggart; **faire le f.** to brag, to boast

fanfaronnades [fɑ̃farɔnad] *nfpl* bragging, boasting

fanfaronner [fɑ̃farɔne] *vi* to brag, to boast

fanfreluches [fɑ̃frəlyʃ] *nfpl Péj* frills

fange [fɑ̃ʒ] *nf Litt* mire; **élevé dans la f.** brought up in the gutter

fanion [fanjɔ̃] *nm (d'un club)* pennant; *(balise)* flag; **fanions** *(guirlandes)* bunting

fanon [fanɔ̃] *nm (de baleine)* whalebone

fantaisie [fɑ̃tezi] **1** *adj inv* **collants f.** patterned pantihose; **kirsch f.** kirsch-flavored liqueur

   2 *nf* **(a)** *(envie)* whim; **faire qch à sa f.** to do sth as the fancy takes one **(b)** *(créativité)* imagination **(c)** *(œuvre musicale)* fantasia

fantaisiste [fɑ̃tezist] **1** *adj (personne)* eccentric; *(interprétation)* fanciful; *(horaires, mode de vie)* unorthodox

   2 *nmf (comédien)* variety artist

fantasmagorique [fɑ̃tasmagɔrik] *adj* phantasmagorical

fantasme [fɑ̃tasm] *nm* fantasy

fantasmer [fɑ̃tasme] *vi* to fantasize (**sur** about)

fantasque [fɑ̃task] *adj* whimsical

fantassin [fɑ̃tasɛ̃] *nm* foot soldier, infantryman

fantastique [fɑ̃tastik] **1** *adj* **(a)** *(littérature, conte, film)* fantasy **(b)** *Fam (excellent)* fantastic **(c)** *(créature)* fantastic

   2 *nm* **le f.** the fantastic; *(littérature)* fantasy literature

fantoche [fɑ̃tɔʃ] **1** *nm* puppet

   2 *adj* **gouvernement f.** puppet government

fantomatique [fɑ̃tɔmatik] *adj* ghostly

fantôme [fɑ̃tom] **1** *nm* ghost, phantom

   2 *adj (ville, train)* ghost

fanzine [fɑ̃zin] *nm* fanzine

FAO [ɛfao] *nf* **(a)** *(abrév* **fabrication assistée par ordinateur)** CAM **(b)** *(abrév* **Food and Agricultural Organization)** FAO

faon [fɑ̃] *nm* fawn

FAQ [ɛfaky] *Ordinat (abrév* **frequently asked questions, foire aux questions)** FAQ

far [far] *nm* **f. breton** = custard flan with prunes

faramineux, -euse [faraminø, -øz] *adj Fam* phenomenal

farandole [farɑ̃dɔl] *nf* farandole

farce [fars] *nf* **(a)** *(tour)* (practical) joke, prank; **faire une f. à qn** to play a (practical) joke on sb; **magasin de farces et attrapes** novelty store; *Can Fam* **c'est pas des farces!** it's true!, no kidding! **(b)** *(préparation culinaire)* stuffing **(c)** *(pièce de théâtre)* farce

farceur, -euse [farsœr, -øz] **1** *adj* mischievous

   2 *nm,f* (practical) joker, prankster

farcir [farsir] **1** *vt* **(a)** *(volaille, légume)* to stuff **(b)** *Fam (remplir)* to cram (**de** with)

   2 se farcir *vpr Fam* **se f. qch** *(corvée)* to get landed with sth; **se f. qn/qch** *(supporter)* to put up with sb/sth

fard [far] *nm* make-up; *Fam* **piquer un f.** to go red; **f. à joues** blush; **f. à paupières** eye shadow

fardeau, -x [fardo] *nm* load; *Fig* burden

farder [farde] **1** *vt (maquiller)* to make up

   2 se farder *vpr* to put on one's make-up; **se f. les yeux** to put eye shadow on

farfadet [farfadɛ] *nm* goblin

farfelu, -e [farfəly] *Fam* **1** *adj (personne, idée)* weird

   2 *nm,f* weirdo

farfouiller [farfuje] *vi Fam* to rummage (**dans** through)

farine [farin] *nf* flour; **f. de blé** wheat flour; **f. de maïs** cornstarch

farineux, -euse [farinø, -øz] **1** *adj* **(a)** *Péj (pommes de terre, banane)* floury **(b)** *(contenant de la fécule)* starchy

   2 *nmpl* starchy food

farniente [farnjɛ̃te] *nm* idleness

farouche [faruʃ] *adj* **(a)** *(animal)* timid; *(personne)* shy **(b)** *(haine, air, regard)* fierce

farouchement [faruʃmɑ̃] *adv* fiercely

fart [fart] *nm* (ski) wax

fascicule [fasikyl] *nm (d'une publication)* installment; *(brochure)* brochure

fascinant, -e [fasinɑ̃, -ɑ̃t] *adj* fascinating

fascination [fasinasjɔ̃] *nf* fascination; **exercer une f. sur qn** to fascinate sb

fasciner [fasine] *vt* **(a)** *(impressionner)* to fascinate **(b)** *(charmer)* to captivate

fascisme [faʃism] *nm* fascism

fasciste [faʃist] *adj & nmf* fascist

fashion [faʃœn] *adj Fam* trendy, cool

fasse *etc. voir* **faire**

faste¹ [fast] *nm* splendor

faste² [fast] *adj (jour)* lucky; *(période)* good

fast-food *(pl* **fast-foods)** [fastfud] *nm* fast-food restaurant

fastidieux, -euse [fastidjø, -øz] *adj* tedious

fastoche [fastɔʃ] *adj Fam* dead easy

fastueux, -euse [fastɥø, -øz] *adj* sumptuous

fat [fa(t)] *nm* conceited person

fatal, -e, -als, -ales [fatal] *adj* **(a)** *(mortel)* fatal; *Fig* fatal (**à** for); **le choc lui a été f.** the shock killed him; *Ordinat* **erreur fatale** fatal error **(b)** *(inévitable)* inevitable

fatalement [fatalmɑ̃] *adv* inevitably

fatalisme [fatalism] *nm* fatalism

fataliste [fatalist] **1** *adj* fatalistic

   2 *nmf* fatalist

fatalité [fatalite] *nf* **(a)** *(malédiction)* bad luck **(b)** *(inévitabilité)* inevitability

fatidique [fatidik] *adj* fateful

fatigant, -e [fatigã, -ãt] *adj* (a) *(épuisant)* tiring; **c'est f. pour le cœur/les yeux** it's a strain on the heart/the eyes (b) *(ennuyeux)* tiresome

fatigue [fatig] *nf* tiredness; **tomber** *ou* **être mort de f.** to be dead tired; **f. nerveuse** nervous exhaustion; **f. oculaire** eye-strain

fatigué, -e [fatige] *adj* (a) *(las)* tired; **f. par sa promenade** tired from one's walk; **f. par le voyage** travel-worn; **f. de qn/qch** tired of sb/sth; **f. de faire qch** tired *or* weary of doing sth (b) *(estomac, foie)* upset; *(cœur)* strained

fatiguer [fatige] **1** *vt* (a) *(personne)* to tire (out); *(yeux, cœur)* to strain; *(estomac, foie)* to upset; *Ironique* **si ça ne te fatigue pas trop** if it's not too much of an effort (b) *(ennuyer)* to wear out (c) *Fam* **f. la salade** to toss the salad
2 *vi* *(personne)* to get tired; *(moteur, voiture)* to labor
3 se fatiguer *vpr* (a) *(s'épuiser)* to get tired; **se f. à faire qch** to tire oneself out doing sth; **se f. les yeux/le cœur** to strain one's eyes/heart; *Ironique* **tu ne t'es pas fatigué** you didn't exactly strain yourself; **ne te fatigue pas, je m'en charge** don't bother, I'll see to it (b) *(se lasser)* **se f. de qn/qch** to get tired of sb/sth

fatras [fatra] *nm* jumble, muddle

fatwa [fatwa] *nf Rel* fatwa; **prononcer une f. contre qn** to declare *or* to issue a fatwa against sb

faubourg [fobur] *nm* suburb

fauche [foʃ] *nf Fam* thieving; **il y a de la f.** there are thieves about

fauché, -e [foʃe] *adj Fam* **f. (comme les blés)** (flat) broke

faucher [foʃe] *vt* (a) *(herbe, champ)* to mow; *(blé)* to reap (b) *(piéton)* to mow down; **se faire f. par une voiture** to be mown down by a car (c) *Fam (voler)* to swipe; **se faire f. qch** to get sth swiped

faucheur, -euse [foʃœr, -øz] **1** *nm,f (de blé)* reaper; *(d'herbe)* mower
2 *nm (insecte)* daddy-longlegs
3 *nf* **faucheuse** *(machine) (pour le blé)* reaper; *(pour l'herbe)* mower; **la Faucheuse** *(la Mort)* the Grim Reaper

faucheux [foʃø] *nm* daddy-longlegs

faucille [fosij] *nf* sickle; **la f. et le marteau** the hammer and sickle

faucon [fokõ] *nm* falcon, hawk; **f. pèlerin** peregrine falcon

faudra *etc. voir* **falloir**

faufiler [fofile] **1** *vt* to tack, to baste
2 se faufiler *vpr (à travers la foule)* to work one's way (**à travers** through); **il s'était faufilé parmi les invités** he had slipped in with the guests

faune [fon] *nf (animaux)* fauna, animal life; *Fig & Péj* **la f. des boîtes de nuit** the nightclub set; **elle fréquente une f. bizarre** she mixes with a weird crowd

faussaire [foser] *nmf* forger

fausse [fos] *adj voir* **faux**[1]

faussement [fosmã] *adv* (a) *(injustement)* wrongly, falsely (b) *(de façon hypocrite)* deceptively

fausser [fose] **1** *vt* (a) *(clef, axe)* to buckle, to bend (b) *(réalité, résultat)* to distort (c) **f. compagnie à qn** to give sb the slip
2 se fausser *vpr* (a) *(voix)* to become strained (b) *(clef, axe)* to buckle, to bend

fausset [fose] *nm Mus* falsetto; **voix de f.** falsetto voice

fausseté [foste] *nf* (a) *(d'une information, d'un raisonnement)* falseness (b) *(hypocrisie)* duplicity

faut *voir* **falloir**

faute [fot] *nf* (a) *(erreur)* mistake, error; *(au football)* foul; *(au tennis)* fault; **faire une f.** to make a mistake *or* an error; **être en f.** to be at fault; **prendre qn en f.** to catch sb out; **c'est de ma f.!** it's my fault!; **f. d'étourderie** *ou* **d'inattention** care-

less mistake; **f. de français** grammatical mistake; **f. de frappe** typing mistake; **f. d'orthographe** spelling mistake; **f. professionnelle** professional misconduct (b) *(manque)* **sans f.** without fail; **f. de temps** for lack of time; **f. de mieux** for lack *or* want of anything better; **f. de quoi** failing which, otherwise; **ce n'est pas f. d'avoir essayé** it's not for want of trying

fauteuil [fotœj] *nm* (a) *(siège)* armchair, easy chair; **f. à bascule** rocking chair; **f. d'orchestre** seat in the orchestra; **f. pivotant** swivel chair; **f. roulant** wheelchair (b) *Fig (à l'Académie française)* seat

fauteur [fotœr] *nm* **f. de troubles** troublemaker

fautif, -ive [fotif, -iv] **1** *adj* (a) *(coupable)* at fault, in the wrong (b) *(incorrect)* faulty
2 *nm,f (coupable)* person at fault *or* in the wrong

fauve [fov] **1** *adj* (a) *(roux)* fawn (b) *(odeur)* musky (c) *(en peinture)* Fauvist
2 *nm* (a) *(grand félin)* big cat; **sentir le f.** to smell of sweat (b) *(couleur)* fawn (c) *(en peinture)* Fauvist

fauvette [fovɛt] *nf* warbler

fauvisme [fovism] *nm* Fauvism

faux[1]**, fausse** [fo, fos] **1** *adj* (a) *(incorrect)* wrong; **c'est un f. problème** that's not the real problem; *Fam* **t'as tout f.** you're completely wrong; **f. ami** false friend; **faire une fausse couche** to have a miscarriage; **faire une fausse note** to hit a wrong note; **faire fausse route** to take the wrong road; *Fig* to be on the wrong track; **faire un f. sens** *(en traduisant)* to give an inaccurate translation; *(en français)* to give an inaccurate definition (b) *(mensonger)* false, untrue; *Fam* **c'est un f. jeton** *ou* **cul** he's two-faced; **f. témoignage** perjury (c) *(injustifié) (alerte, espoirs)* false (d) *(postiche)* false (e) *(billet, pièce, document)* forged; *(tableau, bijoux)* fake; *(plafond)* false (f) *Péj (hypocrite)* false
2 *adv (chanter, sonner)* out of tune, off key; *Fig* **sonner f.** not to ring true
3 *nm* (a) *(tableau, sculpture)* fake (b) *(document)* forgery; **f. en écriture** forgery

faux[2] [fo] *nf* scythe

faux-cul [foky] *très Fam* **1** *adj* **il est f.** he's a two-faced bastard
2 *nmf* two-faced bastard, *f* two-faced bitch

faux-filet *(pl* **faux-filets)** [fofilɛ] *nm* sirloin

faux-fuyant *(pl* **faux-fuyants)** [fofɥijã] *nm (prétexte)* subterfuge

faux-monnayeur *(pl* **faux-monnayeurs)** [fomɔnɛjœr] *nm* forger, counterfeiter

faux-semblant *(pl* **faux-semblants)** [fosãblã] *nm* pretense, sham

faveur [favœr] *nf* (a) *(considération)* favor; **avoir la f. de qn** to be in favor with sb; **de f.** *(marques)* of favor; *(régime, traitement)* special (b) *(privilège)* favor; **faire une f. à qn** to do sb a favor (c) **être en f. de qch** *(être favorable à)* to be in favor of sth; **en ma/sa f.** *(à mon/son avantage)* in my/her favor, to my/her advantage (d) *(ruban)* favor

favorable [favɔrabl] *adj* favorable (**à** to)

favorablement [favɔrabləmã] *adv* favorably

favori, -ite [favɔri, -it] *adj & nm,f* favorite

favoris [favɔri] *nmpl* sideburns

favorisé, -e [favɔrize] *adj (milieu, famille)* fortunate

favoriser [favɔrize] *vt* (a) *(avantager) (personne)* to favor (b) *(encourager) (croissance, emploi)* to encourage, to promote

favoritisme [favɔritism] *nm* favoritism

fax [faks] *nm (appareil)* fax (machine); *(message)* fax; **envoyer qch par f.** to send sth by fax; **f. modem** fax modem

faxer [fakse] *vt* to fax

fayot [fajo] *nm Fam* (a) *(haricot sec)* bean (b) *(élève)* brown-nose(r)

fayotage [fajotaʒ] *nm Fam* brown-nosing

fayoter [fajote] *vi Fam* to brown-nose

fébrile [febril] *adj aussi Fig* feverish

fébrilement [febrilmɑ̃] *adv* feverishly

fébrilité [febrilite] *nf* feverishness

fécond, -e [fekɔ̃, -ɔ̃d] *adj (femme, femelle, terre, imagination)* fertile; *(écrivain)* prolific; *Fig* **f. en qch** *(période, moment)* full of sth

fécondation [fekɔ̃dasjɔ̃] *nf (d'une femme, d'une femelle)* impregnation; *(d'un œuf, d'un ovule)* fertilization; **f. artificielle** artificial insemination; **f. in vitro** in vitro fertilization

féconder [fekɔ̃de] *vt (femme, femelle)* to impregnate; *(œuf, ovule)* to fertilize

fécondité [fekɔ̃dite] *nf* **(a)** *(d'une femme, d'une femelle)* fertility **(b)** *(d'un écrivain)* productiveness

fécule [fekyl] *nf* starch

féculent, -e [fekylɑ̃, -ɑ̃t] **1** *adj* starchy
2 *nm* starchy food

FED [ɛføde] *nm (abrév* **Fonds européen de développement**) EDF

FEDER [fedɛr] *nm (abrév* **Fonds européen de développement régional**) ERDF

fédéral, -e, -aux, -ales [federal, -o] *adj* federal

fédéralisme [federalism] *nm* federalism

fédéraliste [federalist] *adj & nmf* federalist

fédérateur, -trice [federatœr, -tris] *adj* federal

fédération [federasjɔ̃] *nf* federation

fédéré, -e [federe] *adj* federate

fée [fe] *nf* fairy; *Hum* **f. du logis** wonderful housewife; *Suisse* **f. verte** absinthe

feed-back [fidbak] *nm inv* feedback

féerie [feri, feeri] *nf (spectacle magnifique)* enchanting display

féerique [ferik, feerik] *adj (personnage, monde)* fairy; *(vision)* enchanting

feignais *etc. voir* **feindre**

feignant, -e [fɛɲɑ̃, -ɑ̃t] *Fam* **1** *adj* bone idle
2 *nm,f* idler

feindre [54] [fɛ̃dr] *vt (maladie, sentiment)* to feign; **inutile de f.** it's no use pretending; **f. de faire qch** to pretend to do sth

feint, -e [fɛ̃, fɛ̃t] *adj (maladie, joie)* feigned

feinte [fɛ̃t] *nf* **(a)** *(ruse)* ruse **(b)** *(au football)* dummy; *(en boxe)* feint

feinter [fɛ̃te] **1** *vt Fam (duper)* to take in
2 *vi (au football)* to dummy; *(en boxe)* to feint

fêlé, -e [fele] *adj* **(a)** *(verre, voix)* cracked **(b)** *Fam (fou)* cracked, nuts

fêler [fele] *vt* to crack

félicitations [felisitasjɔ̃] *nfpl* congratulations (**pour** on)

féliciter [felisite] **1** *vt* to congratulate (**de/pour** on); **f. qn d'avoir fait qch** to congratulate sb on having done sth
2 se féliciter *vpr* **se f. de qch/d'avoir fait qch** to congratulate oneself on sth/on having done sth

félin, -e [felɛ̃, -in] *adj & nm* feline

fêlure [felyr] *nf aussi Fig* crack

femelle [fəmɛl] *adj & nf* female

féminin, -e [feminɛ̃, -in] **1** *adj (personne, charme, visage)* feminine; *(hormone, population, sexe)* female; *(équipe, magazine, mode)* women's
2 *nm* feminine; **au f.** in the feminine

féminiser [feminize] **1** *vt* **(a)** *(ouvrir aux femmes)* to increase the number of women in **(b)** *(rendre efféminé)* to make effeminate
2 se féminiser *vpr* **(a)** *(profession, institution, carrière)* to attract more women **(b)** *(homme)* to become effeminate

féminisme [feminism] *nm* feminism

féministe [feminist] *adj & nmf* feminist

féminité [feminite] *nf* femininity

femme [fam] *nf* **(a)** *(adulte de sexe féminin)* woman; **des femmes, de la f.** *(libération, émancipation, droits)* women's; **la f. de ma vie** the love of my life; **elle est très f.** she's very feminine; *Fam* **une bonne f.** a woman; **f. d'affaires** businesswoman; **f. de chambre** *(dans un hôtel)* (chamber)maid; **f. fatale** femme fatale; **f. au foyer** housewife, homemaker; **f. de ménage,** *Belg* **f. d'ouvrage** cleaning lady; **f. du monde** society woman; **f. de tête** forceful woman **(b)** *(épouse)* wife

femmelette [famlɛt] *nf Péj (homme)* weakling

fémur [femyr] *nm* thighbone, *Spéc* femur

FEN [fɛn] *nf (abrév* **Fédération de l'Éducation Nationale**) = largest French teachers' union

fenaison [fənɛzɔ̃] *nf* haymaking

fendant, -e [fɑ̃dɑ̃, -ɑ̃t] *adj Fam* hilarious

fendiller [fɑ̃dije] **1** *vt (bois, vernis)* to crack; *(peau, lèvres)* to chap
2 se fendiller *vpr (bois, vernis)* to crack; *(peau, lèvres)* to chap

fendre [fɑ̃dr] **1** *vt* **(a)** *(bois)* to split; *(pierre, sol)* to crack; **f. le cœur à qn** to break sb's heart **(b)** *(traverser) (flots, mer)* to plow through; *(air)* to cut through
2 se fendre *vpr* **(a)** *(bois)* to split; *(pierre, sol)* to crack **(b)** *Fam* **se f. de qch** *(d'une somme)* to fork out sth; *(d'un cadeau)* to fork out on sth; **tu ne t'es pas fendu** *(ce n'était pas cher)* it didn't break the bank; *(tu ne t'es pas fatigué)* you didn't strain yourself **(c)** *Fam* **se f. la pipe** *ou* **la pêche** *ou* **la poire** to split one's sides (laughing)

fendu, -e [fɑ̃dy] *adj (jupe)* slit

fenêtre [fənɛtr] *nf* **(a)** *(ouverture)* window; **f. à guillotine** sash window **(b)** *Ordinat* window; **f. d'aide** help window; **f. déroulante** pull-down window

fennec [fenɛk] *nm* fennec

fenouil [fənuj] *nm* fennel

fente [fɑ̃t] *nf* **(a)** *(dans le bois)* split; *(dans le sol, dans un mur)* crack **(b)** *(d'une tirelire, d'une boîte aux lettres)* slot

féodal, -e, -aux, -ales [feɔdal, -o] *adj* feudal

féodalité [feɔdalite] *nf* feudalism

fer [fɛr] *nm* **(a)** *(métal)* iron; *Fig* **de f.** *(discipline, volonté)* iron; *(santé)* cast-iron; **croire qch dur comme f.** to believe very firmly in sth; **f. forgé** wrought iron **(b)** *(objet en fer)* **f. à cheval** horseshoe; *Fam* **les quatre fers en l'air** flat on one's back; *Fig* **f. de lance** spearhead **(c)** *(outil)* **f. à repasser** iron; **donner un coup de f. à qch** to iron sth; **marquer qch au f. rouge** to brand sth; **f. à souder** soldering iron **(d)** **fers** *(chaînes)* irons

ferai *etc. voir* **faire**

fer-blanc *(pl* **fers-blancs)** [fɛrblɑ̃] *nm* tin(plate); **en f.** tin

ferblanterie [fɛrblɑ̃tri] *nf* **(a)** *(commerce)* tinplate trade **(b)** *(articles)* tinware

férié, -e [ferje] *adj* **lundi prochain est f.** next Monday is a (public) holiday

férir [ferir] *vt* **sans coup f.** without any difficulty

ferme¹ [fɛrm] **1** *adj* **(a)** *(dur)* firm **(b)** *Jur* **trois ans de prison f., trois ans fermes** three years' imprisonment
2 *adv (travailler)* hard; *(discuter)* keenly; **s'ennuyer f.** to be bored stiff

ferme² [fɛrm] *nf* farm; **produits de la f.** farm produce

fermé, -e [fɛrme] *adj* **(a)** *(porte, récipient, boutique)* closed, shut; *(route)* closed **(b)** *(expression, visage)* impassive; **être f. à qch** *(ne pas être sensible à)* to have no appreciation of sth **(c)** *(société, club, milieu)* exclusive, select

fermement [fɛrməmɑ̃] *adv* firmly

ferment [fɛrmɑ̃] *nm aussi Fig* ferment

fermentation [fɛrmɑ̃tasjɔ̃] *nf* fermentation

fermenter [fɛrmɑ̃te] *vi* to ferment

fermer [fɛrme] **1** *vt* **(a)** *(porte, boîte, livre)* to close, to shut; *(maison)* to shut up; *(rideaux)* to close, to draw; *(vêtement)* to fasten, to do up; *(parenthèse)* to close; *(enveloppe)* to seal; **f. sa porte à**

qn to close one's door to sb; **f. les yeux/la bouche** to close one's eyes/one's mouth; *Fig* **f. les yeux sur qch** to turn a blind eye to sth; *Fam* **je n'ai pas fermé l'œil** I didn't sleep a wink; *Fam* **f. sa gueule, la f.** to shut up, to shut one's mouth (**b**) *(frontière, pays)* to close off (**c**) *(robinet, eau, électricité)* to turn off (**d**) *(compte bancaire)* to close (**e**) *(entreprise) (temporairement)* to close, to shut; *(définitivement)* to close down; **f. boutique** to shut up shop (**f**) *Ordinat (fichier, fenêtre)* to close; *(commande)* to end

2 *vi* (**a**) *(porte, boîte)* to close, to shut; **f. bien/mal** to close/not to close properly (**b**) *(entreprise, magasin) (temporairement)* to close, to shut; *(définitivement)* to close down

3 se fermer *vpr* (**a**) *(porte, boîte, yeux)* to close, to shut; *(vêtement)* to fasten, to do up (**b**) *(visage)* to freeze; *(personne)* to clam up

fermeté [fɛrməte] *nf* firmness; **avec f.** firmly

fermeture [fɛrmətyr] *nf* (**a**) *(d'une porte)* closing, shutting; *(d'une route, d'une frontière, d'un débat)* closing (**b**) *(cessation d'activité)* closing; **heure de f.** closing time (**c**) *(d'un compte bancaire)* closing (**d**) **f. Éclair®** *ou* **à glissière** zipper (**e**) *Ordinat (d'un fichier, d'une fenêtre)* closing; *(d'une commande)* ending

fermier, -ère [fɛrmje, -ɛr] **1** *adj (poulet)* free-range; *(beurre)* dairy

2 *nm,f* farmer

3 *nf* **fermière** *(épouse)* farmer's wife

fermoir [fɛrmwar] *nm (de collier, de sac)* clasp; *Can (fermeture à glissière)* zipper

féroce [ferɔs] *adj (animal, personne, critique)* ferocious; *(joie, moquerie)* savage; *(appétit)* ravenous

férocement [ferɔsmã] *adv* ferociously

férocité [ferɔsite] *nf* ferocity

Féroé [ferɔe] *nfpl* **les (îles) F.** the Faroe Islands, the Faroes

ferraille [fɛraj] *nf* (**a**) *(débris de fer)* scrap (iron); **mettre qch à la f.** to put sth on the scrap heap (**b**) *Fam (petite monnaie)* small change

ferré, -e [fɛre] *adj* (**a**) *(chaussure)* hobnailed; *(canne)* metal-tipped (**b**) *(calé)* **être f. en qch** to be well up on sth

ferrer [fɛre] *vt* (**a**) *(cheval)* to shoe (**b**) *(poisson)* to strike

ferreux, -euse [fɛrø, -øz] *adj* ferrous

ferronnerie [fɛrɔnri] *nf* (**a**) *(objets)* **f. (d'art)** (decorative) ironwork (**b**) *(travail)* ironwork (**c**) *(atelier)* ironworks *(singulier)*

ferronnier, -ère [fɛrɔnje, -ɛr] *nm,f* **f. (d'art)** worker in wrought iron

ferroviaire [fɛrɔvjɛr] *adj (réseau, trafic, ligne)* railroad; *(transports)* rail

ferrugineux, -euse [fɛryʒinø, -øz] *adj* ferruginous

ferrure [fɛryr] *nf* (**a**) *(garniture)* fitting (**b**) *(d'un cheval)* shoeing

ferry [fɛri] *nm* ferry

ferry-boat *(pl* **ferry-boats)** [fɛribot] *nm* ferry

fertile [fɛrtil] *adj aussi Fig* fertile; *Fig* **f. en qch** *(période)* full of sth

fertilisation [fɛrtilizasjɔ̃] *nf* fertilization

fertiliser [fɛrtilize] *vt* to fertilize

fertilité [fɛrtilite] *nf* fertility

féru, -e [fery] *adj* **f. de qch** passionately interested in sth

férule [feryl] *nf Litt* **être sous la f. de qn** to be under sb's sway

fervent, -e [fɛrvã, -ãt] **1** *adj* fervent; *(catholique)* devout

2 *nm,f* devotee **(de** of)

ferveur [fɛrvœr] *nf* fervor; **avec f.** fervently

fesse [fɛs] *nf* buttock; **fesses** butt

fessée [fese] *nf* spanking; **donner une f. à qn** to give sb a spanking

fessier, -ère [fesje, -ɛr] **1** *adj (muscle)* buttock, *Spéc* gluteal

2 *nm (muscle)* gluteal muscle

festif, -ive [fɛstif, -iv] *adj* festive

festin [fɛstɛ̃] *nm* feast, banquet

festival, -als [fɛstival] *nm* festival; **le f. d'Avignon** = theater

festival held in Avignon; **le f. de Cannes** the Cannes film festival

festivités [fɛstivite] *nfpl* festivities

feston [fɛstɔ̃] *nm* (**a**) *(en broderie)* scallop; **à festons** scalloped (**b**) *(guirlande) & Archit* festoon

festoyer [32] [fɛstwaje] *vi* to feast

feta [feta] *nf* feta cheese

fêtard, -e [fɛtar, -ard] *nm,f Fam* party animal

fête [fɛt] *nf* (**a**) *(célébration publique)* fête, fair; *(événement culturel)* festival; **f. foraine** amusement park; **la f. des Mères/Pères** Mother's/Father's Day; **la f. de la Musique** = annual music festival held on June 21; **la f. des Rois** Twelfth Night (**b**) *(soirée)* party; **organiser** *ou* **faire une f.** to have a party (**c**) *(manifestation de joie)* **en f.** in a festive mood; **avoir le cœur en f.** to be in raptures; *Fam* **faire la f.** to party; **être de la f.** to be one of the party; **faire f. à qn** to make a fuss of sb (**d**) *(du saint dont on porte le nom)* saint's day; *Ironique* **ça va être ta f.!** you're in for it!; *Fam* **faire sa f. à qn** to give sb a good hiding (**e**) *(jour chômé)* holiday; **les fêtes (de fin d'année)** the Christmas and New Year holidays; **f. légale** legal holiday; **f. nationale** national holiday; **la f. du Travail** Labor Day

---

Fête de la musique

This annual event takes place throughout France on June 21, the summer solstice. Both amateur and professional musicians take to the streets and there are many impromptu live performances, with bars and restaurants as well as museums and hospitals serving as free venues for jazz, classical, rock and many other styles of music. The festival was originally launched in 1982 by the minister of culture, Jack Lang, following the election of François Mitterrand's socialist government. Such has been its success and popularity in France that the event has now spread to many other European countries.

Fête-Dieu *(pl* **Fêtes-Dieu)** [fɛtdjø] *nf* **la F.** Corpus Christi

fêter [fɛte] **1** *vt* (**a**) *(anniversaire, événement)* to celebrate (**b**) *(personne)* to fête

2 se fêter *vpr* **ça se fête!** this calls for a celebration!

fétiche [fetiʃ] **1** *adj* lucky

2 *nm (objet de culte)* fetish; *(mascotte)* mascot

fétichisme [fetiʃism] *nm* fetishism

fétichiste [fetiʃist] **1** *adj* fetishistic

2 *nmf* fetishist

fétide [fetid] *adj* fetid

fétu [fety] *nm* **f. (de paille)** wisp of straw

feu¹, -x [fø] *nm* (**a**) *(élément, flammes, incendie)* fire; **mettre (le) f. à qch** to set fire to sth; **prendre f.** to catch fire; **allumer** *ou* **faire un f.** to make a fire; **au f.!** fire!; **en f.** *(lieu)* on fire; *Fig (joues, visage)* burning; **mettre une ville à f. et à sang** to ransack a town; **être tout f. tout flamme** to be burning with enthusiasm; **faire f. de tout bois** to use every available means; **ne pas faire long f.** not to last long; **dans le f. de l'action** in the heat of the action; *Fig* **sous le f. des projecteurs** in the limelight; *Vulg* **avoir le f. au cul** *(être pressé)* to be in a mad rush; *(sexuellement)* to be horny as hell; **f. d'artifice** *(spectacle)* fireworks display; **f. de Bengale** Bengal light; **f. de camp** campfire; **f. de cheminée** fire in the hearth; **f. follet** will-o'-the-wisp; **f. de forêt** forest fire; **f. de joie** bonfire; *Fig* **f. de paille** flash in the pan; *Can* **f. sauvage** cold sore (**b**) *(pour allumer une cigarette)* **avez-vous du f.?** do you have a light?

(**c**) *(brûleur)* burner; **à f. doux** *ou* **à petit f.** over a low heat; **à f. vif** over a high heat

(**d**) *(sur la chaussée)* **f. rouge/vert** red/green light; **feux de signalisation** *ou* **tricolores** traffic lights; *Fig* **donner le f. vert à qn** to give sb the green light

(**e**) *(phare)* **feux de brouillard** *ou* **antibrouillard** fog lights; **feux de croisement** low beams; **feux de détresse** hazard (warning) lights; **feux de position** sidelights; **feux de stationnement** parking lights

(**f**) *(tirs)* **faire f.** to fire, to shoot; **ouvrir le f.** to open fire; *Fig* **être pris entre deux feux** to be caught in the crossfire

2 *adj inv* **noir et f.** black-and-tan

feu², **-e** [fø] *adj* **f. M. Perrin** the late Mr Perrin; **f. mon mari** my late husband

feuillage [fœjaʒ] *nm* leaves, foliage

feuille [fœj] *nf* (**a**) *(de plante, d'arbre)* leaf; **f. morte** dead leaf; **f. de vigne** fig leaf (**b**) *(de papier)* sheet; **f. volante** loose sheet (**c**) *(journal)* paper; *Péj* **f. de chou** rag (**d**) *(document)* **f. d'impôt** tax return; **f. de maladie** = form given by doctor to patient for claiming reimbursement from Social Security; **f. de paie** *ou* **paye** pay stub; **f. de soins** medical expenses claim form (**e**) *Ordinat* **f. de calcul** spreadsheet

feuillet [fœjɛ] *nm* leaf

feuilleté, **-e** [fœjte] **1** *adj* (**a**) *(pâte)* flaky (**b**) *(verre)* laminated

2 *nm* **f. au jambon/au fromage** ham/cheese knish

feuilleter [42] [fœjte] *vt* (**a**) *(livre)* to leaf through (**b**) *Ordinat* **f. en arrière** to page up; **f. en avant** to page down

feuilleton [fœjtɔ̃] *nm* serial; **f. télévisé** television serial

feuillu, **-e** [fœjy] **1** *adj* (**a**) *(ayant beaucoup de feuilles)* leafy (**b**) *Bot* broad-leaved

2 *nm Bot* broad-leaved tree

feutre [føtr] *nm* (**a**) *(matière)* felt (**b**) *(chapeau)* felt hat (**c**) *(stylo)* felt-tip (pen)

feutré, **-e** [føtre] *adj* (**a**) *(garni de feutre)* felt(-covered) (**b**) *(assourdi)* muffled; **à pas feutrés** stealthily (**c**) *(vêtement)* matted

feutrer [føtre] **1** *vt* (**a**) *(garnir de feutre)* to cover with felt (**b**) *(assourdir)* to muffle (**c**) *(vêtement)* to mat

2 *vi (vêtement)* to felt

3 se feutrer *vpr (vêtement)* to felt

feutrine [føtrin] *nf* felt

fève [fɛv] *nf* (**a**) *(plante, graine)* broad bean (**b**) *(dans la galette des Rois)* charm (**c**) *Can (haricot)* bean

février [fevrije] *nm* February; *voir aussi* **janvier**

FF *nm Anciennement (abrév* **franc(s) français***)* FF

FFI [ɛfɛfi] *nfpl Hist (abrév* **Forces françaises de l'intérieur***)* = French Resistance forces in France during World War Two

FFL [ɛfɛfɛl] *nfpl Hist (abrév* **Forces françaises libres***)* Free French Army

fiabilité [fjabilite] *nf* reliability

fiable [fjabl] *adj* reliable

fiacre [fjakr] *nm* hackney carriage

fiançailles [fjɑ̃saj] *nfpl* engagement

fiancé, **-e** [fjɑ̃se] *nm,f* fiancé, *f* fiancée

fiancer [16] [fjɑ̃se] **se fiancer** *vpr* to get engaged (**avec** to); **être fiancés** to be engaged

fiasco [fjasko] *nm* fiasco

fibre [fibr] *nf* fiber; *Fig* **avoir la f. maternelle** to be the maternal type; **f. optique** fiber optics *(singulier)*; **f. de verre** fiberglass

fibreux, **-euse** [fibrø, -øz] *adj (tissu)* fibrous; *(viande)* stringy

fibrome [fibrom] *nm* fibroma

fibroscopie [fibrɔskɔpi] *nf Méd* fiber-optic endoscopy

ficelé, **-e** [fisəle] *adj Fam* (**a**) *(construit)* **bien/mal f.** *(scénario)* well/poorly put together (**b**) *(habillé)* got up

ficeler [9] [fisəle] *vt* (**a**) *(attacher)* to tie up; **ficelé comme un saucisson** trussed up like a chicken (**b**) *Fam (construire)* to put together

ficelle [fisɛl] *nf* (**a**) *(cordelette)* string; *Fig* **les ficelles du métier** the tricks of the trade (**b**) *(pain)* small baguette *or* French loaf

fiche¹ [fiʃ] *nf* (**a**) *(formulaire)* form; **f. d'état civil** = administrative record of birth details and marital status; **f. de paie** pay stub; **f. signalétique** personal details card (**b**) *(carte)* (index) card; **mettre qch sur fiches** to card-index sth; **f. cartonnée** index card; **f. cuisine** *(dans un magazine)* recipe card (**c**) *(prise)* plug; *(broche)* pin (**d**) *Ordinat* **f. d'état** report form

fiche² [fiʃ] = **ficher³**

ficher¹ [fiʃe] *vt (mettre sur fiches) (informations)* to file; *(personne)* to put on file

ficher² [fiʃe] **1** *vt (enfoncer)* **f. qch dans qch** to stick sth into sth

2 se ficher *vpr (balle, clou)* **se f. dans qch** to go into sth

ficher³ [fiʃe] *Fam* **1** *vt* (**a**) *(mettre)* to stick; **f. qn par terre** to send sb sprawling; **f. qch par terre** *(exprès)* to chuck sth on the floor; *(accidentellement)* to knock sth over; *Fig* to mess sth up; **f. qn à la porte** to kick sb out; **f. une gifle à qn** to give sb a slap in the face (**b**) *(faire)* to do; **qu'est-ce que tu fiches?** what are you up to? (**c**) **f. le camp** to clear off

2 se ficher *vpr* (**a**) *(se mettre)* **se f. un coup** to wallop oneself; **se f. par terre** to go sprawling; **se f. dedans** to screw up (**b**) *(se moquer)* **se f. de qn** to poke fun at sb; **se f. du monde** to thumb one's nose; **se f. de qch** not to give a damn about sth; **je m'en fiche** I don't give a damn

fichier [fiʃje] *nm* (**a**) *(ensemble de fiches)* (card-index) file (**b**) *(boîte)* card-index box; *(meuble)* card-index cabinet (**c**) *Ordinat* file; **f. joint** *(de courrier électronique)* attachment

fichu¹, **-e** [fiʃy] *adj Fam* (**a**) *(insupportable)* damn; *(caractère)* rotten (**b**) *(abîmé)* **être f.** to have had it; **c'est f. maintenant!** *(c'est raté)* we can forget it!; **c'est f. pour dimanche** we can forget Sunday (**c**) **être bien/mal f.** *(bien/mal bâti)* to have/not to have a nice body; *(bien/mal conçu)* to be well/badly designed; **être mal f.** *(malade)* to be under the weather (**d**) *(capable)* **être f. de faire qch** to be capable of doing sth

fichu² [fiʃy] *nm* headscarf

fictif, **-ive** [fiktif, -iv] *adj* fictitious

fiction [fiksjɔ̃] *nf* fiction; **œuvre de f.** work of fiction; **la réalité dépasse la f.** truth is stranger than fiction

ficus [fikys] *nm* ficus

fidèle [fidɛl] **1** *adj* (**a**) *(ami, époux)* faithful; *(lecteur, auditeur, client)* regular; **être f. à qn** to be faithful to sb; **être f. à qch** to be loyal *or* true to sth; *Fig* **être f. au poste** to be always there (**b**) *(copie, traduction, récit)* faithful (**à** to); *(mémoire, souvenir)* reliable

2 *nmf* (**a**) *(croyant)* believer; **les fidèles** the faithful; *(à l'église)* the congregation (**b**) *(partisan)* loyal supporter (**de** of) (**c**) *(d'un programme télévisé)* regular viewer (**de** of); *(d'un programme radio)* regular listener (**de** to)

fidèlement [fidɛlmɑ̃] *adv* faithfully

fidélisation [fidelizasjɔ̃] *nf* **f. de la clientèle** building of customer loyalty

fidéliser [fidelize] *vt* to win the loyalty of; **f. la clientèle** to create customer loyalty

fidélité [fidelite] *nf* (**a**) *(d'un époux, d'un ami)* faithfulness (**à** to); *(d'un client, à un principe)* loyalty (**à** to) (**b**) *(d'une traduction, d'une reproduction)* faithfulness

Fidji [fidʒi] *nfpl* **les îles F.** Fiji

fiduciaire [fidysjɛr] *adj Fin* **monnaie f.** paper money

fief [fjɛf] *nm* fief; *Fig* **un f. du parti socialiste** a safe Socialist seat

fieffé, **-e** [fjefe] *adj* inveterate

fiel [fjɛl] *nm aussi Fig* gall

fier¹, **fière** [fjɛr] **1** *adj* (**a**) *(satisfait)* proud (**de** of); **être f. de faire qch** to be proud to do sth; **f. comme un paon** proud as a peacock (**b**) *(hautain, noble)* proud

2 *nm,f Péj* **faire le f.** to put on airs

fier² [66] [fje] **se fier** *vpr* **se f. à qn/qch** *(avoir confiance en)* to trust sb/sth; *(compter sur)* to rely on sb/sth

fièrement [fjɛrmɑ̃] *adv* proudly

fierté [fjɛrte] *nf* (**a**) *(satisfaction)* pride; **avec f.** proudly; **tirer**

f. de qch to take pride in sth (**b**) *(amour-propre)* pride

fiesta [fjɛsta] *nf Fam* wild party

fièvre [fjɛvr] *nf* (**a**) *(élévation de la température)* fever; **avoir de la f.** to have a fever *or* a temperature; **elle a 40 de f.** = she has a temperature of 104 degrees; **avoir une f. de cheval** to have a raging fever (**b**) *(excitation)* frenzy; **dans la f. de la campagne électorale** in the heat *or* excitement of the election campaign

fiévreusement [fjevrøzmɑ̃] *adv* feverishly

fiévreux, -euse [fjevrø, -øz] *adj aussi Fig* feverish

fifre [fifr] *nm (instrument)* fife; *(joueur)* fife player

figé, -e [fiʒe] *adj* (**a**) *(locution)* set (**b**) *(sourire)* fixed (**c**) *(sauce)* congealed

figer [45] [fiʒe] **1** *vt* (**a**) *(immobiliser)* to paralyze; **figé sur place** rooted to the spot (**b**) *(solidifier)* to congeal
2 se figer *vpr (huile, sauce)* to congeal; *(regard, traits, sourire)* to freeze

fignoler [fiɲɔle] *vt Fam* to put the finishing touches to; **il ne reste plus qu'à f.** it's just a matter now of adding the finishing touches

figue [fig] *nf* fig; **f. de Barbarie** prickly pear

figuier [figje] *nm* fig tree; **f. de Barbarie** prickly pear (tree)

figurant, -e [figyrɑ̃, -ɑ̃t] *nm,f (dans une pièce de théâtre)* walk-on; *(dans un film)* extra

figuratif, -ive [figyratif, -iv] *adj* figurative

figuration [figyrasjɔ̃] *nf* **faire de la f.** to play bit parts

figure [figyr] *nf* (**a**) *(visage)* face; **faire bonne f.** to make a good impression; **faire f. d'intellectuel/de patriarche** to be seen as an intellectual/a patriarchal figure (**b**) *(représentation)* figure; *aussi Fig* **f. de proue** figurehead (**c**) *(personnage)* figure (**d**) *(en danse, en patinage artistique)* figure; **figures imposées** compulsory figures; **figures libres** freestyle (**e**) *Ling* **f. de rhétorique** figure of speech; **f. de style** stylistic device

figuré, -e [figyre] **1** *adj (sens)* figurative
2 *nm* **au f.** in the figurative sense

figurer [figyre] **1** *vt* to represent
2 *vi* (**a**) *(apparaître)* to appear (**sur/dans** on/in) (**b**) *(faire partie)* to figure (**parmi** among)
3 se figurer *vpr* **se f. que** to imagine that; **il se figure qu'il va gagner de l'argent** he thinks *or* believes that he's going to make money; **je suis à sec, figure-toi** believe it or not, I'm broke

figurine [figyrin] *nf* figurine

fil [fil] *nm* (**a**) *(brin, de toile d'araignée)* thread; **de f. en aiguille** little by little, bit by bit; *Fig* **ne tenir qu'à un f.** to hang by a thread; **f. conducteur** unifying thread; **f. à coudre** (sewing) thread; **f. dentaire** dental floss; **f. d'Écosse** lisle thread; **f. à plomb** plumb line; *Fig* **f. rouge** recurring theme
(**b**) *(métallique, électrique)* wire; *Fig* **donner du f. à retordre à qn** to give sb trouble; **f. de fer** wire; **f. de fer barbelé** barbwire
(**c**) *Fam (téléphone)* **au bout du f.** on the line; **coup de f.** call; **donner** *ou* **passer un coup de f. à qn** to give sb a call, to call sb (up)
(**d**) *(cours)* **au f. de l'eau** with the current; **au f. des jours/semaines** with the passing days/weeks; **perdre/reprendre le f. de qch** to lose/to pick up the thread of sth
(**e**) *Tél & Ordinat* **sans f.** *(téléphone)* cordless; *(Internet, téléphonie)* wireless
(**f**) *(tissu)* linen
(**g**) *(tranchant)* edge

filaire [filɛr] *adj Tél (téléphone)* corded, plug-in

filament [filamɑ̃] *nm* (**a**) *(d'une ampoule électrique)* filament (**b**) *(de viande)* fiber (**c**) *Biol* filament

filandreux, -euse [filɑ̃drø, -øz] *adj (viande, légumes)* stringy

filant, -e [filɑ̃, -ɑ̃t] *adj voir* **étoile**

filasse [filas] **1** *nf* tow
2 *adj inv* tow-colored

filature [filatyr] *nf* (**a**) *(fabrique)* (spinning) mill (**b**) *(surveillance)* shadowing; **prendre qn en f.** to shadow sb

file [fil] *nf* (**a**) *(queue)* line; **en f. indienne** in single file; **trois jours à la f.** three days in a row; **f. (d'attente)** line (**b**) *(sur la route)* lane; **se garer en double f.** to double-park (**c**) *Ordinat* **f. d'attente** print queue

filé, -e [file] *adj* (**a**) *(bas, collant)* with a run (**b**) *(verre)* spun (**c**) *(métaphore)* extended

filer [file] **1** *vt* (**a**) *(coton, verre)* to spin (**b**) *(développer) (image, métaphore)* to draw *or* to spin out (**c**) *Fam (donner)* **f. qch à qn** to give sb sth (**d**) *(surveiller) (suspect)* to shadow, to tail (**e**) *(bas, collant)* to put a run in (**f**) **f. le parfait amour** to live love's dream
2 *vi* (**a**) *(passer vite) (temps)* to fly; *(véhicule)* to speed along; **f. entre les mains** *ou* **les doigts à qn** *(argent)* to run through sb's fingers like water; *(personne)* to slip through sb's fingers (**b**) *Fam (partir)* **il faut que je file** I must dash; **allez, file!** off you go! (**c**) *(bas, collant)* to run

filet¹ [filɛ] *nm* (**a**) *(de lumière)* thin streak; *(d'air)* thin stream; *(d'eau)* trickle (**b**) *(petite quantité)* dash (**c**) *(d'une vis)* thread (**d**) *(de viande, de poisson)* fillet; **f. mignon** filet mignon *(small fillet steak)*

filet² [filɛ] *nm* (**a**) *(en mailles)* net; **f. à bagages** luggage rack; **f. à papillons** butterfly net; **f. de pêche** fishing net; **f. à provisions** string bag (**b**) *(au cirque)* (safety) net; **travailler sans f.** *(trapéziste)* to work without a net; *Fig* to take risks (**c**) *(au tennis)* net

filial, -e, -aux, -ales [filjal, -o] **1** *adj* filial
2 *nf* **filiale** subsidiary (company)

filiation [filjasjɔ̃] *nf* (**a**) *(lien de parenté)* filiation (**b**) *Fig (relation)* relationship (**avec** to)

filière [filjɛr] *nf* (**a**) *(voie obligée)* channels (**b**) *(domaine d'études)* field of study; **suivre une f. scientifique/commerciale** to study scientific/business subjects (**c**) *(organisation clandestine)* network

filiforme [filifɔrm] *adj* spindly

filigrane [filigran] *nm (dessin)* watermark; *Fig* **en f.** implicit

filin [filɛ̃] *nm* rope

fille [fij] *nf* (**a**) *(descendante)* daughter (**b**) *(enfant)* girl; **petite f.** little girl (**c**) *(femme)* **salut les filles!** hi, girls!; **f. de joie** prostitute; **jeune f.** girl; **vieille f.** old maid

fillette [fijɛt] *nf* little girl

filleul, -e [fijœl] *nm,f* godson, *f* goddaughter

film [film] *nm* (**a**) *(œuvre)* movie, film; **f. d'action** action movie; **f. d'animation** animated movie; **f. d'aventures** adventure movie; **f. d'épouvante** *ou* **d'horreur** horror movie; **f. policier** detective movie (**b**) *(déroulement)* **revoir le f. de sa vie** to see one's life flashing before one's eyes (**c**) *(emballage)* film; **f. alimentaire** Saran wrap®, plastic wrap (**d**) *(fine pellicule)* film

filmer [filme] *vt* to film

filmographie [filmɔgrafi] *nf* filmography

filon [filɔ̃] *nm* (**a**) *(de minéraux)* vein, seam (**b**) *Fam* **trouver le f.** to strike it rich

filou [filu] *nm (escroc)* rogue; *(enfant)* rascal

fils [fis] *nm* son; **f. de famille** young man of good social standing; *Péj* **f. à papa** daddy's boy

filtrage [filtraʒ] *nm* (**a**) *(contrôle)* screening (**b**) *(d'un liquide)* filtering

filtrant, -e [filtrɑ̃, -ɑ̃t] *adj (pouvoir)* filtering; *(verres, papier)* filter

filtre [filtr] **1** *adj (cigarette, café, papier)* filter
2 *nm* filter; **f. à air** air filter; **f. à café** coffee filter; *Phot* **f. coloré** color filter; *Ordinat* **f. écran** screen filter; **f. solaire** sunscreen

filtrer [filtre] **1** *vt* (**a**) *(liquide, son, lumière)* to filter (**b**) *(informations, visiteurs)* to screen

2 *vi (liquide)* to filter (**à travers** through); *(nouvelle)* to leak out; **laisser f. qch** to let sth filter through; *Fig* to leak sth

fin¹ [fɛ̃] *nf* (**a**) *(conclusion)* end; **"f."** *(au cinéma)* "the end"; **f. juillet** at the end of July; **à la f.** in the end; *Fam* **tu m'ennuies à la f.!** you're really annoying me!; **en f. de qch, à la f. de qch** at the end of sth; **chômeur en f. de droits** = unemployed person about to lose entitlement to compensation; **mettre f. à qch** to put an end to sth; **prendre f.** to come to an end; **toucher** *ou* **tirer à sa f.** to draw to a close; **avoir des fins de mois difficiles** to be always short of money at the end of the month; **f. de série** discontinued line; **f. de semaine** end of the week, *Can* weekend

(**b**) *(mort)* end, death

(**c**) *(but)* end, aim; **arriver** *ou* **parvenir à ses fins** to achieve one's ends; **à cette f.** to this end; **à toutes fins utiles** just in case

(**d**) *Ordinat* **f. de ligne** line end; **f. de page** pagebreak; **f. de session** logoff

fin², **fine** [fɛ̃, fin] **1** *adj* (**a**) *(papier, tranche, taille)* thin; *(cheveux, sable, pointe)* fine; **une petite pluie fine** drizzle (**b**) *(traits)* fine (**c**) *(de première qualité)* fine (**d**) **fines herbes** mixed herbs (**e**) **un f. connaisseur** a connoisseur (**f**) *(vue, odorat)* keen; **avoir l'ouïe fine** to have keen hearing (**g**) *(subtil)* subtle (**h**) *Can (gentil)* kind, sweet(-natured) (**i**) **le f. mot de l'histoire** the truth of the matter

2 *nm* **le f. du f.** the ultimate

3 *adv* (**a**) **f. prêt** all ready (**b**) *(finement)* finely

final, -e, -als *ou* **-aux, -ales** [final, -o] *adj* final

finale [final] **1** *nf* (**a**) *(compétition sportive)* final; **aller/être en f.** to reach/to be in the finals (**b**) *(de mot)* final syllable

2 *nm (d'un morceau de musique)* finale

finalement [finalmã] *adv* in the end, finally

finaliser [finalize] *vt* to finalize

finaliste [finalist] *adj & nmf* finalist

finalité [finalite] *nf* (**a**) *(objectif)* aim (**b**) *(en biologie)* finality

finance [finãs] *nf* (**a**) *(profession)* finance; **la haute f.** high finance (**b**) *(argent)* **moyennant f.** for a fee; **finances** finances

financement [finãsmã] *nm* financing

financer [16] [finãse] *vt* to finance

financier, -ère [finãsje, -εr] **1** *adj* financial

2 *nm* (**a**) *Fin* financier (**b**) *(gâteau)* = rectangular sponge finger made with almonds

financièrement [finãsjεrmã] *adv* financially

finasser [finase] *vi Fam* to resort to trickery

finaud, -e [fino, -od] **1** *adj* crafty

2 *nm,f* crafty devil

fine [fin] *nf* liqueur brandy

finement [finmã] *adv* (**a**) *(adroitement)* cleverly (**b**) *(délicatement)* finely

finesse [fines] *nf* (**a**) *(minceur)* fineness; *(de la taille)* slenderness, slimness (**b**) *(d'un visage)* fineness; *(d'un travail fait à la main)* delicacy (**c**) *(subtilité)* subtlety

fini, -e [fini] **1** *adj* (**a**) *(usé, à bout)* finished (**b**) *Péj (imbécile, escroc)* absolute (**c**) *(espace, temps, nombre)* finite

2 *nm (d'un objet manufacturé)* finish

finir [finir] **1** *vt* to finish; *(vie)* to end; **f. son assiette** to finish what's on one's plate

2 *vi* to end, to finish; **f. bien/mal** to end well/badly; *(film, roman)* to have a happy/sad ending; **mal f.** *(personne)* to come to a bad end; **f. de faire qch** to finish doing sth; **f. par faire qch** to end up doing sth; **en f. avec qn/qch** to have done with sb/sth; **à n'en plus f.** endless; **pour f.** *(en résumé)* to cut a long story short; *(finalement)* in the end

finish [finiʃ] *nm inv* finish

finition [finisjõ] *nf* finishing touch; **travail de f.** finishing touches; **les finitions de cette robe sont mal faites** this dress is badly finished

finlandais, -e [fɛ̃lãdε, -εz] **1** *adj* Finnish

2 *nm,f* **F., Finlandaise** Finn

Finlande [fɛ̃lãd] *nf* **la F.** Finland

finnois, -e [finwa, -az] **1** *adj* Finnish

2 *nm (langue)* Finnish

fiole [fjɔl] *nf (flacon)* phial

fioriture [fjɔrityr] *nf (dessin)* flourish

fioul [fjul] *nm* fuel oil

firmament [firmamã] *nm Litt* firmament

firme [firm] *nf* firm, company

FIS [fis] *nm (abrév* **Front islamique du salut)** **le F.** the Islamic Salvation Front

fisc [fisk] *nm* ≃ Internal Revenue Service

fiscal, -e, -aux, -ales [fiskal, -o] *adj* tax

fiscaliser [fiskalize] *vt* to tax

fiscalité [fiskalite] *nf* tax system

fissure [fisyr] *nf aussi Fig* crack

fissurer [fisyre] **1** *vt* to crack; *Fig* to split

2 se fissurer *vpr* to crack; *Fig* to split

fiston [fistõ] *nm Fam* son, lad

FIV [εfive] *nf (abrév* **fécondation in vitro)** IVF

fivete [fivεt] *nf (abrév* **fécondation in vitro et transfert embryonnaire)** GIFT

fixateur, -trice [fiksatœr, -tris] *Phot* **1** *adj* fixing

2 *nm* fixer

fixatif [fiksatif] *nm* fixative

fixation [fiksasjõ] *nf* (**a**) *(action)* fixing (**b**) *(de skis)* (ski) binding (**c**) *(obsession)* fixation; **faire une f. sur qn/qch** to become fixated on sb/sth

fixe [fiks] **1** *adj* (**a**) *(immobile)* (étagère, planche, regard) fixed (**b**) *(arrêté)* (prix, frais) fixed

2 *nm* (**a**) *(salaire)* fixed salary (**b**) *Tél (poste fixe)* fixed phone, landline phone (**c**) *Fam (de drogue)* fix *(of drug)*

fixement [fiksəmã] *adv* fixedly; **regarder f. qn/qch** to stare at sb/sth

fixer [fikse] **1** *vt* (**a**) *(immobiliser)* to fix; **f. son attention/son regard sur qch** to focus one's attention/one's gaze on sth; **f. qn (du regard)** to stare at sb (**b**) *(déterminer)* (date, heure, rendez-vous) to fix; *(prix, salaire)* to fix, to set (**à** at); **f. son choix sur qch** to decide on sth (**c**) *(informer)* **maintenant, tu es fixé** now you know

2 se fixer *vpr* (**a**) *(s'installer)* to settle down (**b**) **son choix s'est fixé sur celui-ci** she decided on this one (**c**) **se f. un objectif** to set oneself a target

fixité [fiksite] *nf (du regard)* fixedness

fjord [fjɔrd] *nm* fjord

flacon [flakõ] *nm (small)* bottle

flagada [flagada] *adj inv Fam* pooped

flageller [flaʒele] *vt* to flog, to whip

flageoler [flaʒɔle] *vi (jambes)* to shake, to tremble

flageolet [flaʒɔlε] *nm (haricot)* flageolet (bean)

flagornerie [flagɔrnəri] *nf* fawning, toadying

flagrant, -e [flagrã, -ãt] *adj* flagrant, blatant; **en f. délit** red-handed; **être pris en f. délit d'adultère** to be caught in flagrante

flair [flεr] *nm* sense of smell; **avoir du f.** to have a good sense of smell; *Fig* to have good intuition

flairer [flere] *vt aussi Fig* to smell

flamand, -e [flamã, -ãd] **1** *adj* Flemish

2 *nm (langue)* Flemish

3 *nm,f* **F., Flamande** Fleming

flamant [flamã] *nm* **f. rose** flamingo

flambant [flãbã] *adv* (**a**) *(locution)* **f. neuf** brand new (**b**) *Can Fam (complètement)* totally; **f. nu** stark naked

flambeau, -x [flɑ̃bo] *nm (torche)* torch; *Fig* **passer le f. à qn** to pass the torch on to sb

flambée [flɑ̃be] *nf* (a) *(feu)* blaze (b) *(de violence)* flare-up; *(des prix)* upsurge

flamber [flɑ̃be] 1 *vi* (a) *(brûler)* to blaze (b) *Fam (parier)* to gamble for big money
  2 *vt* (a) *(volaille)* to singe (b) *(crêpes)* to flambé

flambeur, -euse [flɑ̃bœr, -øz] *nm,f Fam* big-time gambler

flamboyant, -e [flɑ̃bwajɑ̃, -ɑ̃t] *adj* (a) *(regard)* blazing; **d'un rouge f.** flaming red (b) *Archit* flamboyant

flamboyer [32] [flɑ̃bwaje] *vi* to blaze

flamme [flam] *nf* (a) *(feu)* flame; **en flammes** on fire, ablaze; *Fig* **descendre qn/qch en flammes** to shoot sb/sth down in flames (b) *Fig (enthousiasme)* fire (c) *Litt (amour)* passion

flammèche [flamɛʃ] *nf* spark

flan [flɑ̃] *nm (dessert)* baked custard

flanc [flɑ̃] *nm* side; *(d'une armée)* flank; **être sur le f.** *(malade)* to be laid up; *(épuisé)* to be worn out; *Fam* **tirer au f.** to shirk

flancher [flɑ̃ʃe] *vi Fam* to give in

Flandre [flɑ̃dr] *nf* **la F., les Flandres** Flanders

flanelle [flanɛl] *nf* flannel

flâner [flɑne, flane] *vi* (a) *(se promener)* to stroll, to saunter (b) *(perdre son temps)* to hang around

flânerie [flɑnri, flanri] *nf (promenade)* stroll

flâneur, -euse [flɑnœr, flanœr, -øz] *nm,f (promeneur)* stroller

flanquer¹ [flɑ̃ke] *vt* (a) *(être à coté de)* to flank (b) *(accompagner)* **flanqué de** flanked by

flanquer² [flɑ̃ke] *Fam* 1 *vt* (a) *(jeter)* to chuck; **f. qn à la porte** *ou* **dehors** to kick sb out; *(licencier)* to fire sb; **f. qch par terre** to fling sth on the ground; *Fig* to mess sth up (b) **f. qch à qn** *(coup de pied, gifle)* to give sb sth; **f. la trouille** *ou* **les jetons à qn** to scare the living daylights out of sb
  2 **se flanquer** *vpr* **se f. par terre** to go sprawling

flapi, -e [flapi] *adj Fam* dead beat

flaque [flak] *nf (d'huile, de sang)* pool; **f. (d'eau)** puddle

flash [flaʃ] *nm* (a) *(sur un appareil photo)* flash (b) *(à la radio, à la télévision)* flash; **f. d'information** newsflash; **f. publicitaire** commercial

flash-back [flaʃbak] *nm inv* flashback

flasher [flaʃe] *vi Fam* **f. sur qn/qch** to fall for sb/sth in a big way

flasque¹ [flask] *adj (chair)* flabby

flasque² [flask] *nf* flask

flatter [flate] 1 *vt* (a) *(complimenter)* to flatter (b) *(avantager)* to flatter (c) *(caresser) (animal)* to stroke
  2 **se flatter** *vpr* to flatter oneself; **se f. de faire qch** to pride oneself on doing sth; **je ne m'en flatterais pas** it's not something I'd be proud of

flatterie [flatri] *nf* flattery

flatteur, -euse [flatœr, -øz] 1 *adj (remarque, portrait, couleur)* flattering; *(personne)* full of flattery
  2 *nm,f* flatterer

flatulence [flatylɑ̃s] *nf* flatulence

FLE [flə] *nm (abrév* **français langue étrangère)** French as a foreign language

fléau, -x [fleo] *nm* (a) *(calamité)* scourge; *Fig (chose pénible)* pain (b) *(à céréales)* flail (c) *(d'une balance à plateaux)* beam

fléchage [fleʃaʒ] *nm* signposting

flèche [flɛʃ] *nf* (a) *(projectile, signe)* arrow; **partir comme une f.** to shoot off; **monter en f.** *(avion, prix)* to shoot up (b) *(attaque verbale)* jibe (c) *(d'une église)* spire (d) *Ordinat* **f. de défilement** scroll arrow; **flèches verticales** up and down arrow keys

flécher [34] [fleʃe] *vt (route, direction)* to arrow; **itinéraire fléché** signposted route

fléchette [fleʃɛt] *nf* dart; **jouer aux fléchettes** to play darts

fléchir [fleʃir] 1 *vt* (a) *(bras, jambe, genou)* to bend (b) *(faire céder)* to sway
  2 *vi* (a) *(ployer) (branche)* to bend; *(jambes)* to give way; *(poutre)* to sag (b) *(faiblir)* to weaken (c) *(baisser) (prix, devises)* to fall

fléchissement [fleʃismɑ̃] *nm* (a) *(du genou)* bending; *(d'une poutre)* sagging (b) *(de prix, de devises, de résultats)* drop (**de** in)

flegmatique [flɛgmatik] *adj* phlegmatic

flegme [flɛgm] *nm* phlegm

flemmard, -e [flɛmar, -ard] *Fam* 1 *adj* lazy
  2 *nm,f* lazybones

flemmarder [flemarde] *vi Fam* to laze about

flemmardise [flemardiz] *nf Fam* laziness

flemme [flɛm] *nf Fam* laziness; **j'ai la f. (de le faire)** I can't be bothered (to do it)

flétan [fletɑ̃] *nm* halibut

flétri, -e [fletri] *adj* withered

flétrir [fletrir] 1 *vt (peau, plantes)* to wither
  2 **se flétrir** *vpr (visage, plantes)* to wither

fleur [flœr] *nf* (a) *(plante)* flower; **à fleurs** *(tissu)* floral; **en fleurs** *(arbre)* in flower; **être f. bleue** to be a romantic; *Fam* **faire une f. à qn** to do sb a favor; **fleurs des champs** wild flowers (b) *Can (farine)* flour (c) *(locutions)* **dans la f. de l'âge** in the prime of life; **la fine f. de qch** the cream of sth; **à f. d'eau** just above the surface of the water; **avoir les nerfs à f. de peau** to be all on edge

fleurdelisé [flœrdəlize] *nm Can (drapeau du Québec)* flag of Quebec

fleurer [flœre] 1 *vt Litt* to smell of
  2 *vi* **f. bon** to smell nice

fleuret [flœrɛ] *nm (épée)* foil

fleurette [flœrɛt] *nf Vieilli* **conter f. à qn** to whisper sweet nothings to sb

fleuri, -e [flœri] *adj* (a) *(couvert de fleurs) (arbre)* in flower (b) *(orné de fleurs) (tissu, robe)* floral; *(vaisselle)* flower-patterned (c) *(style)* flowery (d) *(teint)* florid

fleurir [flœrir] 1 *vi* (a) *(plantes)* to flower (b) *(art, commerce)* to flourish
  2 *vt (table)* to decorate with flowers; *(tombe)* to lay flowers on

fleuriste [flœrist] *nmf (commerçant)* florist

fleuron [flœrɔ̃] *nm (d'une collection)* jewel

fleuve [flœv] *nm* river; **le f. Jaune** the Yellow River

flexibilité [flɛksibilite] *nf aussi Fig* flexibility

flexible [flɛksibl] 1 *adj aussi Fig* flexible
  2 *nm (tuyau)* hose(pipe)

flexion [flɛksjɔ̃] *nf (fléchissement)* bending; **être en f.** *(muscle, membre)* to be flexed

flibustier [flibystje] *nm* buccaneer

flic [flik] *nm Fam* cop

flingue [flɛ̃g] *nm Fam* shooter, piece

flinguer [flɛ̃ge] *Fam* 1 *vt* (a) *(tuer)* to gun down (b) *(critiquer sévèrement)* to shoot down, to savage
  2 **se flinguer** *vpr* to blow one's brains out

flippant, -e [flipɑ̃, -ɑ̃t] *adj Fam (déprimant)* grim; *(effrayant)* creepy

flipper¹ [flipœr] *nm (appareil)* pinball machine; *(jeu)* pinball; **jouer au f.** to play pinball

flipper² [flipe] *vi Fam* (a) *(déprimer)* to feel down (b) *(paniquer)* to flip, to freak out; **ça me fait f.** that freaks me out

flirt [flœrt] *nm* (a) *(amourette)* flirtation (b) *(personne)* boyfriend, *f* girlfriend

flirter [flœrte] *vi aussi Fig* to flirt (**avec** with)

FLN [ɛfɛlɛn] *nm (abrév* **Front de libération nationale)** National Liberation Front *(in Algeria)*

FLNC [ɛfɛlɛnse] *nm (abrév* **Front de libération nationale de la Corse)** Corsican Liberation Front

FLNKS [ɛfɛlɛnkaɛs] *nm (abrév* **Front de libératio natio-**

nale kanak et socialiste) Kanak National Liberation Front (*in New Caledonia*)

flocon [flɔkɔ̃] *nm* flake; **flocons d'avoine** oat flakes; **f. de neige** snowflake

floconneux, -euse [flɔkɔnø, -øz] *adj* fluffy

flonflons [flɔ̃flɔ̃] *nmpl* oompah-pah

flop [flɔp] *nm Fam* flop; **faire un f.** to flop

flopée [flɔpe] *nf Fam* **une f.** *ou* **des flopées de qch** loads of sth, tons of sth

floraison [flɔrɛzɔ̃] *nf* flowering

floral, -e, -aux, -ales [flɔral, -o] *adj* floral

floralies [flɔrali] *nfpl* flower show

flore [flɔr] *nf* flora; **f. intestinale** intestinal flora

Floride [flɔrid] *nf* **la F.** Florida

florilège [flɔrilɛʒ] *nm* anthology

florin [flɔrɛ̃] *nm* florin

florissant, -e [flɔrisɑ̃, -ɑ̃t] *adj (affaire)* flourishing; *(santé)* blooming

flot [flo] *nm* (a) *(marée)* flood (tide) (b) *(quantité importante)* stream (**de** of) (c) *Litt* **les flots** *(la mer)* the waves (d) *(locutions)* **couler à flots** to flow freely; **être à f.** *(bateau)* to be afloat; *Fig (personne)* to have one's head above water; **remettre à f.** *(personne, entreprise)* to get back on an even keel

flottaison [flɔtɛzɔ̃] *nf* floating

flotte [flɔt] *nf* (a) *(bateaux)* fleet (b) *Fam (pluie)* rain; *(eau)* water

flottement [flɔtmɑ̃] *nm* (a) *(d'un drapeau)* fluttering (b) *(d'une devise)* floating; *(du taux de change)* fluctuation (c) *(hésitation)* wavering

flotter [flɔte] **1** *vi* (a) *(embarcation)* to float; *Fig* **il flotte dans sa veste** his jacket is far too big for him (b) *(drapeau)* to flutter; **f. au** *ou* **dans le vent** *(cheveux)* to stream in the wind

   2 *v impersonnel Fam* **il flotte** it's raining

flotteur [flɔtœr] *nm* float

flottille [flɔtij] *nf (de bateaux)* flotilla

flou, -e [flu] **1** *adj* (a) *(contour, photographie)* blurred, fuzzy (b) *(idée, réponse)* vague

   2 *nm (d'un contour, d'une photographie)* fuzziness; *(d'une idée, d'une réponse)* vagueness; **f. artistique** *(en photographie)* soft-focus effect; *Fig* deliberate vagueness

flouer [flue] *vt Fam* to swindle

flouse, flouze [fluz] *nm Fam (argent)* bread

fluctuant, -e [flyktɥɑ̃, -ɑ̃t] *adj* fluctuating

fluctuation [flyktɥasjɔ̃] *nf* fluctuation

fluctuer [flyktɥe] *vi* to fluctuate

fluet, -ette [flyɛ, -ɛt] *adj* thin

fluide [flɥid] **1** *adj (liquide)* fluid; *(circulation)* flowing freely; *(style, pensée)* flowing

   2 *nm* (a) *(substance)* fluid (b) *(pouvoir surnaturel)* occult power

fluidifier [66] [flɥidifje] *vt (sang)* to thin

fluidité [flɥidite] *nf (d'un corps)* fluidity; *(de la circulation)* free flow

fluo [flyo] *adj inv Fam* fluorescent

fluor [flyɔr] *nm* fluorine; **dentifrice au f.** fluoride toothpaste

fluorescent, -e [flyɔresɑ̃, -ɑ̃t] *adj* fluorescent

flûte [flyt] **1** *nf* (a) *(instrument)* flute; **f. à bec** recorder; **f. de Pan** panpipes; **f. traversière** concert flute (b) *(pain)* small baguette *or* French loaf (c) *(verre)* **f. à champagne** champagne flute

   2 *exclam Fam* damn!

flûtiste [flytist] *nmf* flutist

fluvial, -e, -aux, -ales [flyvjal, -o] *adj* river; *(alluvions)* fluvial

flux [fly] *nm* (a) *(de paroles)* flow (b) *(marée montante)* flow; **le f. et le reflux** the ebb and flow; **f. migratoire** flow of migrants (c) *(électrique, magnétique)* flux

fluxion [flyksjɔ̃] *nf* inflammation; **f. de poitrine** pneumonia

FM [ɛfɛm] *nf (abrév* **frequency modulation**) FM

FME [ɛfɛmə] *nm (abrév* **Fonds monétaire européen**) EMF

FMI [ɛfɛmi] *nm (abrév* **Fonds monétaire international**) IMF

FN [ɛfɛn] *nm (abrév* **Front national**) = French political party of the extreme right

FNSEA [ɛfɛnɛsəa] *nf (abrév* **Fédération nationale des syndicats d'exploitants agricoles**) = French farmers' union

FO [ɛfo] *nf (abrév* **Force ouvrière**) = French labor union

foc [fɔk] *nm* jib

focal, -e, -aux, -ales [fɔkal, -o] *adj* focal

focaliser [fɔkalize] **1** *vt* to focus (**sur** on)

   2 se focaliser *vpr* to focus (**sur** on)

fœtal, -e, -aux, -ales [fetal, -o] *adj* fetal

fœtus [fetys] *nm* fetus

fofolle [fɔfɔl] *adj voir* **foufou**

foi [fwa] *nf* (a) *(confiance)* faith, trust; **avoir f. en qn/qch** to have faith in sb/sth; **les candidatures devront nous parvenir le 1er mars dernier délai, le cachet de la poste faisant f.** ≃ applications should be postmarked no later than March 1st (b) *(croyance religieuse)* faith; **avoir/perdre la f.** to have/to lose faith (c) *(locutions)* **bonne f.** sincerity; **mauvaise f.** insincerity; **être de bonne/mauvaise f.** to be sincere/insincere; **ma f., oui!** yes, indeed!

foie [fwa] *nm* liver; *très Fam* **avoir les foies** to be scared shitless; **f. gras** foie gras; **f. de veau/volaille** calf's/chicken liver

foin [fwɛ̃] *nm (fourrage)* hay; **faire les foins** to make hay; *Fam* **faire du f.** *(causer un scandale)* to kick up a fuss; *(faire du bruit)* to make a din; *Can Fam* **avoir du f.** to be loaded

foire [fwar] *nf* (a) *(fête foraine)* amusement park; *Fam* **faire la f.** to live it up; *Fam* **c'est la f., ici** this place is a madhouse; **f. d'empoigne** free-for-all (b) *(salon international, professionnel)* (trade) fair

foirer [fware] *vi très Fam* to be a screw-up; **il a tout fait f.** he screwed everything up

foireux, -euse [fwarø, -øz] *adj très Fam (projet, affaire)* hopeless

fois [fwa] *nf* time; **une f.** once; **il était une f. un roi** once upon a time there was a king; **deux f.** twice; **deux f. par jour/mois** twice a day/month; **ça coûte trois f. rien** it costs next to nothing; **3 f. 4 fait 12** 3 times 4 is 12; **trois f. plus grand** three times as big; **neuf f. sur dix** nine times out of ten; **combien de f.?** how many times?, how often?; **toutes les f.** *ou* **chaque f. que** every time (that), whenever; **encore une f.** once more, once again; **une (bonne) f. pour toutes** once and for all; **une f. que** once, as soon as; **pour cette f.** this once; **pour une f.** for once; **pour une f. que j'étais à l'heure, personne n'était là** the one time I was on time and no one was there; **à la f. utile et pas cher** both useful and inexpensive; **une chose à la f.** one thing at a time; **l'autre f.** *(il y a peu)* the other day; *Fam* **des f.** *(parfois)* sometimes; *Fam* **des f. qu'il viendrait** in case he comes; *Fam* **non, mais des f.!** really now!

foison [fwazɔ̃] *nf* **à f.** in abundance

foisonnement [fwazɔnmɑ̃] *nm (abondance)* abundance

foisonner [fwazɔne] *vi* to abound (**de** *ou* **en** in); **f. d'idées** *(personne)* to have plenty of ideas

fol [fɔl] *voir* **fou**

folâtre [fɔlɑtr] *adj (personne)* playful

folâtrer [fɔlɑtre] *vi (personne)* to romp, to frolic

foldingue [fɔldɛ̃g] *adj Fam* nutty

folichon, -onne [fɔliʃɔ̃, -ɔn] *adj Fam* **ce n'est pas f.** it's not much fun

folie [fɔli] *nf* madness; **aimer qn à la f.** to be madly in love with sb; **aimer qch à la f.** to adore sth; **faire des folies** *(faire* *des achats extravagants)* to go mad; **c'est de la f.!** it's madness!; **c'est de la f. douce** it's sheer madness; **la f. des grandeurs** delusions of grandeur

folio [fɔljo] *nm* folio

folk [fɔlk] *adj & nm* folk

folklo [fɔlklo] *adj inv Fam (personne)* eccentric; *(endroit, soirée)* bizarre

folklore [fɔlklɔr] *nm* folklore

folklorique [fɔlklɔrik] *adj* **(a)** *(costume)* traditional; *(danse)* folk **(b)** *Fam (personne)* eccentric; *(endroit, soirée)* bizarre

folle [fɔl] *adj voir* **fou**

follement [fɔlmɑ̃] *adv* madly

follet [fɔlɛ] *adj m voir* **feu¹**

fomenter [fɔmɑ̃te] *vt* to foment

foncé, -e [fɔ̃se] *adj* dark

foncer [16] [fɔ̃se] **1** *vt* to darken
    2 *vi* **(a)** *(s'assombrir)* to darken **(b)** *(se hâter)* to get a move on; **f. sur qn/qch** *(se précipiter sur)* to swoop on sb/sth **(c)** *Fam (s'y mettre)* to put one's shoulder to the wheel

fonceur, -euse [fɔ̃sœr, -øz] *Fam* **1** *adj* go-getting
    2 *nm,f* go-getter

foncier, -ère [fɔ̃sje, -ɛr] *adj* **(a)** *(impôt, crédit)* land **(b)** *(fondamental)* fundamental, basic

foncièrement [fɔ̃sjɛrmɑ̃] *adv* fundamentally, basically

fonction [fɔ̃ksjɔ̃] *nf* **(a)** *(poste)* office; **entrer en fonctions, prendre ses fonctions** to take up one's duties; **être en f.** to be in office; **de f.** *(voiture, appartement)* company; **la f. publique** the civil service **(b)** *(rôle)* function; **faire f. de qch** to act as sth **(c)** *Ordinat* **f. de comptage de mots** word-count facility; **f. d'éditeur de texte** text-editing feature; **f. multimédia** multimedia facility; **f. recherche et remplacement** search-and-replace function; **f. de sauvegarde** save function **(d)** **en f. de** according to

fonctionnaire [fɔ̃ksjɔnɛr] *nmf* ≃ civil servant; **haut f.** ≃ senior civil servant

> ### Fonctionnaire
> This term covers a broader range of public service employees than the term "civil servant", from high-ranking members of the state administration to public-sector teachers and post office workers. "Fonctionnaires", of whom there are more than four and a half million in France, are normally recruited through competitive state examinations and enjoy greater job security and other privileges to which private-sector employees are not automatically entitled.

fonctionnariat [fɔ̃ksjɔnarja] *nm* employment by the state

fonctionnel, -elle [fɔ̃ksjɔnɛl] *adj* functional

fonctionnement [fɔ̃ksjɔnmɑ̃] *nm (d'une machine)* working, functioning; **en état de f.** in (good) working order; *Ordinat* **f. en réseau** networking

fonctionner [fɔ̃ksjɔne] *vi (machine, mécanisme)* to work, to function; *Ordinat* to run; **faire f. qch** to operate sth

fond [fɔ̃] *nm* **(a)** *(d'un récipient, de la mer, de l'océan)* bottom; *(d'un espace clos, de la gorge)* back; **être assis au f. de la classe** to be sitting at the back of the class; **c'est au f. du couloir/de la salle** it's at the (far) end of the hall/room; **la pièce du f.** the room at the end, the far room; **au fin f. de** in the depths of sth; **il n'en reste qu'un f.** there's only a drop left; **du f. du cœur** from the bottom of one's heart; **tu connais le f. de ma pensée** you know what my feelings really are; **à f.** *(à bloc)* all the way; *(complètement)* thoroughly; *(totalement)* totally; **à f. de train** at full tilt; *Fam* **à f. la caisse** *(très vite)* hell for leather; **au f., dans le f.** when it comes down to it; **de f. en comble** from top to bottom; **f. d'artichaut** artichoke heart; **f. de bouteille** *(contenu)* dregs; **f. de teint** foundation (cream) **(b)** *(substance essentielle)* **le f. du problème** the heart of the

problem; **avoir un bon/mauvais f.** to be basically a good/bad person; **le f. et la forme** form and content **(c)** *(arrière-plan)* background; **f. sonore** background music; **il y avait du jazz en f. sonore** there was jazz playing in the background

fondamental, -e, -aux, -ales [fɔ̃damɑ̃tal, -o] *adj* basic, fundamental

fondamentalement [fɔ̃damɑ̃talmɑ̃] *adv* fundamentally, basically

fondamentalisme [fɔ̃damɑ̃talism] *nm* fundamentalism

fondamentaliste [fɔ̃damɑ̃talist] *nmf* fundamentalist

fondant, -e [fɔ̃dɑ̃, -ɑ̃t] **1** *adj* **(a)** *(neige)* melting **(b)** *(poire)* that melts in the mouth; *(viande)* very tender
    2 *nm (bonbon)* fondant

fondateur, -trice [fɔ̃datœr, -tris] **1** *adj (mythe)* underlying; **membre f.** charter member
    2 *nm,f* founder

fondation [fɔ̃dasjɔ̃] *nf* **(a)** *(d'une ville, d'un hôpital)* founding **(b)** *(établissement)* foundation **(c)** **fondations** *(d'une construction)* foundations

fondé, -e [fɔ̃de] **1** *adj (reproches, doutes)* well-founded, justified; **être f. à faire qch** to have good reason to do sth
    2 *nm,f* **f. de pouvoir** agent *(holding power of attorney)*; *(mandant)* proxy

fondement [fɔ̃dmɑ̃] *nm* foundation

fonder [fɔ̃de] **1** *vt* **(a)** *(créer) (ville, hôpital)* to found; *(société, journal)* to start, to set up; **f. un foyer** to start a family **(b)** *(baser)* **f. qch sur qch** to base sth on sth; **f. de grands espoirs sur qn** to pin one's hopes on sb
    2 se fonder *vpr* **se f. sur qch** *(sujet: remarque, théorie)* to be based on sth; **sur quoi se fonde-t-il pour le nier?** what are his grounds for denying it?; **pour son livre, elle s'est fondée sur plusieurs articles** she based her book on several articles

fonderie [fɔ̃dri] *nf (usine)* foundry

fondre [fɔ̃dr] **1** *vt* **(a)** *(rendre liquide) (métal)* to melt down; *(sucre, sel)* to dissolve; *(neige, cire)* to melt **(b)** *(fabriquer) (cloche, arme)* to cast **(c)** *(combiner) (couleurs)* to blend; *(sociétés)* to merge
    2 *vi* **(a)** *(se liquéfier)* to melt; *(sucre)* to dissolve; **faire f. qch** to melt sth; *(sucre)* to dissolve sth; **f. dans la bouche** to melt in the mouth; **f. en larmes** to dissolve into tears; *Fig* **je fonds** my heart melts **(b)** *Fig (diminuer)* to melt away **(c)** *Fam (maigrir)* to lose weight
    3 fondre sur *vt ind* to swoop on
    4 se fondre *vpr* **se f. dans** to merge into

fonds [fɔ̃] **1** *nm* **(a)** *(capital)* funds; *(organisme)* fund; **prêter son argent à f. perdu** to lend one's money without security; **f. commun de placement** mutual fund; **F. européen de développement** European Development Fund; **F. européen de développement régional** European Regional Development Fund; **F. monétaire européen** European Monetary Fund; **F. monétaire international** International Monetary Fund; **f. de pension** pension fund **f. de roulement** working capital **(b)** *(d'un musée, d'une bibliothèque)* collection; *(ressources)* resource **(c)** **f. de commerce** business
    2 *nmpl (ressources financières)* funds; **être en f.** to be in funds; **f. publics** government funds; *(valeurs)* government securities

fondu, -e [fɔ̃dy] **1** *adj Fam (fou)* around the bend, out to lunch
    2 *nm,f Fam* **un f. d'informatique/de skateboard** a computer/skateboard freak
    3 *nm* **(a)** *(de couleurs)* blending **(b)** *Cin* fade-out; **f. enchaîné** dissolve

fondue [fɔ̃dy] *nf* **f. (savoyarde)** (cheese) fondue; **f. bourguignonne** fondue bourguignonne, = fondue consisting of cubes of raw beef cooked in hot oil

fongicide [fɔ̃ʒisid] **1** *adj* fungicidal
    2 *nm* fungicide

font *voir* **faire**

fontaine [fɔ̃tɛn] *nf (source naturelle)* spring; *(construction publique)* fountain

fonte [fɔ̃t] *nf* (**a**) *(de métaux)* melting down; **la f. des neiges** the thaw (**b**) *(alliage)* cast iron; **poêle en f.** cast-iron stove (**c**) *Typ* font

fonts [fɔ̃] *nmpl* **f. baptismaux** font

foot [fut] *nm Fam* soccer

football [futbol] *nm* soccer

footballeur, -euse [futbolœr, -øz] *nm,f* soccer player

footing [futiŋ] *nm* jogging; **faire du f.** to go jogging

for [fɔr] *nm* **dans** *ou* **en son f. intérieur** in one's heart of hearts, deep (down) inside

forage [fɔraʒ] *nm* drilling, boring

forain, -e [fɔrɛ̃, -ɛn] **1** *adj voir* **fête, marchand**
   2 *nm* amusement park stallkeeper

forçat [fɔrsa] *nm (prisonnier)* convict; **travailler comme un f.** to work like a slave

force [fɔrs] *nf* (**a**) *(vigueur)* strength; **ne pas se sentir/ne pas être de f. à faire qch** not to feel/not to be up to doing sth; **de f. égale, de même f.** equally matched; **dans la f. de l'âge** in the prime of life; **être à bout de forces** to have no strength left; **c'est au-dessus de ses forces** it's too much for him; **de toutes ses forces** *(pousser, frapper)* with all one's might; *(vouloir)* with all one's heart; **f. de caractère** strength of character; **c'est une f. de la nature** *(personne)* she's a force to be reckoned with; **les forces vives du pays** the country's resources
   (**b**) *(violence)* force; **faire qch de** *ou* **par la f.** to do sth by force; **par la f. des choses** through force of circumstance
   (**c**) *(puissance)* **f. centrifuge/centripète** centrifugal/centripetal force; *aussi Fig* **f. d'inertie** inertia; **f. motrice** motive power; *Fig* driving force
   (**d**) *(organisation)* **les forces armées** the armed forces; **les forces aériennes** the airforce; **f. de dissuasion** deterrent; **f. de frappe** strike force; **les forces de police** *ou* **de l'ordre** the police (force)
   (**e**) *(locutions)* **à f.** in the end; **à f. de volonté** through sheer willpower; **à f. d'insister, tu vas finir par m'agacer** if you keep going on about it, I'm going to get annoyed; **en f.** in force

forcé, -e [fɔrse] *adj* forced; *Fam* **c'est f.!** it's inevitable!

forcément [fɔrsemɑ̃] *adv* inevitably; **elle sera f. déçue** she's bound to be disappointed; **pas f.** not necessarily

forcené, -e [fɔrsəne] **1** *adj (partisan, individualisme)* fanatical; *(haine, lutte)* frenzied
   2 *nm,f* maniac

forceps [fɔrsɛps] *nm* forceps

forcer [16] [fɔrse] **1** *vt* (**a**) *(obliger)* to force; **f. qn à faire qch** to force sb to do sth; **f. la main à qn** to force sb's hand; **f. le respect/l'admiration** to command respect/admiration (**b**) *(faire céder) (porte)* to force (open) (**c**) *(voix)* to strain; *Fig* **f. la dose** to overdo it
   2 *vi (appuyer, tirer)* to force it; *(se surmener)* to overdo it; *Fam* **f. sur qch** to overdo sth
   3 se forcer *vpr (s'obliger)* to force oneself (**à faire qch** to do sth)

forcing [fɔrsiŋ] *nm Sport* sustained pressure; **faire le f.** to put the pressure on; *Fam Fig* **faire du f.** to put on a lot of pressure

forcir [fɔrsir] *vi* (**a**) *(vent, tempête)* to get stronger (**b**) *(personne)* to get bigger

forer [fɔre] *vt* to drill, to bore

forestier, -ère [fɔrɛstje, -ɛr] **1** *adj (zone, chemin)* forest; **exploitation forestière** *(activité)* forestry
   2 *nm* forest ranger

forêt [fɔrɛ] *nf* forest; **f.-noire** *(gâteau)* Black Forest cake; **f. vierge** virgin forest

foreuse [fɔrøz] *nf* drill

forfait¹ [fɔrfɛ] *nm (crime)* heinous crime

forfait² [fɔrfɛ] *nm* (**a**) *(contrat)* fixed-price contract; **travailler au f.** to work for a flat fee (**b**) **être au f.** *(fiscalement)* to pay an estimated amount of tax (**c**) *(prix global)* package deal; **f. week-end** weekend package (**d**) *(de ski)* pass

forfait³ [fɔrfɛ] *nm voir* **déclarer**

forfaitaire [fɔrfɛtɛr] *adj (indemnités)* basic; *(prix)* all-inclusive

forfanterie [fɔrfɑ̃tri] *nf* bragging

forge [fɔrʒ] *nf* forge

forger [45] [fɔrʒe] **1** *vt* (**a**) *(métal)* to forge; *Fig (caractère)* to form; *Prov* **c'est en forgeant qu'on devient forgeron** practice makes perfect (**b**) *(inventer) (histoire, excuse)* to make up
   2 se forger *vpr* **se f. une réputation** to carve out a reputation for oneself

forgeron [fɔrʒərɔ̃] *nm* (black)smith

formaliser [fɔrmalize] **1** *vt* to formalize
   2 se formaliser *vpr* to take offense (**de** at)

formalisme [fɔrmalism] *nm* formalism

formalité [fɔrmalite] *nf* formality; **les formalités d'usage** the usual formalities

format [fɔrma] *nm* format; *Ordinat* **f. d'écran** screen format; *Ordinat* **f. de fichier** file format; *Ordinat* **f. d'impression** print format; **f. de papier** paper format; **f. de poche** pocket format

formatage [fɔrmataʒ] *nm Ordinat* formatting

formater [fɔrmate] *vt Ordinat* to format

formateur, -trice [fɔrmatœr, -tris] **1** *adj* formative
   2 *nm,f* trainer

formation [fɔrmasjɔ̃] *nf* (**a**) *(de roches, d'un mot)* formation; *(du caractère)* forming (**b**) *(éducation)* training; **f. continue** *ou* **permanente** continuing education; **f. professionnelle** vocational training; **être en f.** to be undergoing training (**c**) *(groupe)* group

forme [fɔrm] *nf* (**a**) *(configuration)* shape, form; **formes** *(d'une femme)* curves; **en f. de qch** in the shape of sth; **en f. de L** L-shaped; **sous f. de qch** in the form of sth; **sous toutes ses formes** in all its forms; **sans f.** shapeless; **prendre f.** to take shape (**b**) *(manière)* form; **en bonne et due f.** in due form; **sans autre f. de procès** without further ado (**c**) *(convention)* **de pure f.** purely formal; **pour la f.** as a matter of form; **dans les formes** in the accepted way; **respecter les formes** to observe the proprieties (**d**) *(bonne santé physique)* form; **être en (pleine) f.** to be in (top) form

formel, -elle [fɔrmɛl] *adj* (**a**) *(personne)* positive; *(ordre)* express; *(démenti, refus)* flat; *(interdiction)* strict (**b**) *(apparent)* formal (**c**) *(soutenu)* formal

formellement [fɔrmɛlmɑ̃] *adv* (**a**) *(interdire)* strictly; *(affirmer)* categorically; *(identifier)* positively (**b**) *(du point de vue de la forme)* formally

former [fɔrme] **1** *vt* (**a**) *(créer) (gouvernement, projet)* to form (**b**) *(constituer)* to form; **ils forment une bonne équipe/un beau couple** they make a good team/a lovely couple (**c**) *(tracer) (lettre)* to form (**d**) *(entraîner)* to train (**e**) *(développer) (caractère)* to form; *(esprit, goût, jugement)* to develop
   2 se former *vpr* (**a**) *(apparaître)* to form; *(association, liens)* to be formed (**b**) *(mûrir) (goût)* to develop (**c**) *(apprendre son métier)* to train oneself

Formica® [fɔrmika] *nm* Formica®; **en F.** Formica®

formidable [fɔrmidabl] *adj* (**a**) *(fantastique)* great, fantastic (**b**) *(gigantesque)* tremendous

formol [fɔrmɔl] *nm* formalin

formulaire [fɔrmylɛr] *nm* form; **remplir un f.** to fill out a form; *Ordinat* **f. de saisie** input form

formulation [fɔrmylasjɔ̃] *nf* formulation, wording

formule [fɔrmyl] *nf* (**a**) *(expression)* expression, phrase; **selon la f. consacrée** as the expression goes; **f. magique** magic formula; **f. de politesse** polite phrase; *(au début d'une lettre)* standard opening; *(à la fin d'une lettre)* standard ending (**b**) *(so-*

lution) method; **nouvelle f.** *(menu, abonnement)* new-style **(c)** *(en mathématique, en chimie)* formula **(d)** *(automobile)* **f. 1/2** Formula 1/2

formuler [fɔrmyle] *vt* to formulate

forniquer [fɔrnike] *vi* to fornicate

FORPRONU [fɔrprɔny] *nf (abrév* **Force de protection des Nations unies***)* la **F.** UNPROFOR

forsythia [fɔrsisja] *nm* forsythia

fort, -e [fɔr, fɔrt] **1** *adj* **(a)** *(vigoureux)* strong; **f. comme un Turc** *ou* **un bœuf** as strong as an ox; **c'est une forte tête** she's very strong-minded; **c'est plus f. que moi!** I can't help it!; *Fam* **c'est un peu f.!** that's a bit much!; *Fam* **le plus f., c'est que...** the best of it is,...; *Fam* **trop f.!** cool!, awesome! **(b)** *(doué)* **être f. en qch** to be good at sth **(c)** *(boisson, odeur, vent, lumière, accent)* strong; *(mer)* heavy; *(voix)* loud **(d)** *(robuste) (personne)* large **(e)** *(considérable) (somme d'argent)* large; *(pente)* steep; **il y a de fortes chances (pour) que ça réussisse** there's a good chance it will work

2 *adv* **(a)** *(parler, crier, chanter)* loud, loudly; *(frapper, tirer)* hard; *(sentir)* strong; *Fam* **y aller f.** to overdo it; *Fam* **faire (très) f.** to do (really) brilliantly **(b)** *(très)* very **(c)** *(beaucoup)* very much; **avoir f. à faire (avec qn/qch)** to have one's work cut out (with sb/sth)

3 *nm* **(a)** *(spécialité)* strong point **(b)** *(citadelle)* fort **(c)** **au plus f. de qch** *(hiver)* in the depths of sth; *(été, épidémie, tempête)* at the height of sth

fortement [fɔrtəmɑ̃] *adv* **(a)** *(avec force) (tirer, pousser)* hard **(b)** *(intensément) (désirer, souhaiter, influencer)* strongly; *(impressionner, irriter)* greatly; *(insister)* firmly **(c)** *(très) (épicé)* highly; *(conseillé)* strongly

forteresse [fɔrtərɛs] *nf* fortress

fortifiant, -e [fɔrtifjɑ̃, -ɑ̃t] **1** *adj (nourriture, boisson)* fortifying **2** *nm* tonic

fortification [fɔrtifikasjɔ̃] *nf* fortification

fortifier [66] [fɔrtifje] *vt (ville, mur)* to fortify; *(muscles, corps, sentiment)* to strengthen

fortuit, -e [fɔrtɥi, -it] *adj* chance, fortuitous

fortune [fɔrtyn] *nf* **(a)** *(richesse)* fortune; **faire f.** to make one's fortune **(b)** *(hasard)* fortune, chance; **de f.** *(moyens, installation)* makeshift; **faire contre mauvaise f. bon cœur** to make the best of it

fortuné, -e [fɔrtyne] *adj (riche)* wealthy

forum [fɔrɔm] *nm* forum; *Ordinat* **f. de discussion** newsgroup

fosse [fos] *nf* **(a)** *(creux)* pit; **f. d'aisances** cesspool; **f. aux lions** lions' den; **f. d'orchestre** orchestra pit; **f. septique** septic tank **(b)** *(tombe)* grave; **f. commune** mass grave

fossé [fose] *nm (le long de la route)* ditch; *(autour d'un château)* moat; *Fig (entre personnes)* gulf

fossette [fosɛt] *nf* dimple

fossile [fosil] **1** *adj* fossil **2** *nm Fam aussi Fig* fossil

fossoyeur [foswajœr] *nm* gravedigger; *Fig* destroyer

fou, folle [fu, fɔl]

fol is used before masculine singular nouns beginning with a vowel or h mute.

1 *adj* **(a)** *(dément)* mad, insane; **f. de joie** beside oneself with joy; **f. à lier** raving mad; **être f. (amoureux) de qn/qch** to be mad about sb/sth **(b)** *(énorme)* tremendous; *(prix)* exorbitant **(c)** *(incroyable)* incredible **(d)** *(train)* runaway; *(boussole, aiguille)* crazy; **f. rire** uncontrollable giggling; **avoir un** *ou* **le f. rire** to have the giggles

2 *nm,f* madman, *f* madwoman; *Fam* **comme un f.** like mad; **entrer/sortir comme un f.** to storm in/out; **faire le f.** to play *or* to act the fool; **un f. furieux** a maniac; **un f. du volant** a reckless driver; *Prov* **plus on est de fous, plus on rit** the more the merrier

3 *nm* **(a)** *(aux échecs)* bishop **(b)** *(bouffon)* jester **(c)** **f. de Bassan** gannet

foudre [fudr] **1** *nf* lightning; *Litt* **s'attirer les foudres de qn** to bring down sb's wrath on one **2** *nm* **(a)** *(tonneau)* tun **(b)** **un f. de guerre** a great warrior; *Fig* **ce n'est pas un f. de guerre** he's no rocket scientist

foudroyant, -e [fudrwajɑ̃, -ɑ̃t] *adj (maladie)* violent; *(crise cardiaque)* massive; *(révélation, nouvelle)* devastating; *(succès)* stunning; *(vitesse, progrès)* lightning; *(regard)* withering

foudroyer [32] [fudrwaje] *vt* to strike; **être foudroyé** to be struck by lightning; **f. qn du regard** to give sb a withering look

fouet [fwɛ] *nm (pour punir)* whip; *(de cuisine)* whisk; **de plein f.** head-on

fouetter [fwete] **1** *vt* **(a)** *(punir)* to whip; *Fam* **il n'y a pas de quoi f. un chat** it's nothing to make a fuss about; *Fam* **avoir d'autres chats à f.** to have other fish to fry **(b)** *(cingler)* to lash (against) **(c)** *(battre) (œufs)* to beat, to whisk; *(crème)* to whip **2** *vi Fam (puer)* to stink

foufou, fofolle [fufu, fɔfɔl] *adj Fam* screwy

fougasse [fugas] *nf* = type of flat bread often made with olives, herbs, bacon, etc.

fougère [fuʒɛr] *nf* fern

fougue [fug] *nf* fire, spirit

fougueusement [fugøzmɑ̃] *adv (s'élancer)* impetuously; *(s'embrasser)* passionately

fougueux, -euse [fugø, -øz] *adj (personne, tempérament)* fiery, ardent; *(cheval)* spirited

fouille [fuj] *nf* **(a)** *(d'une maison, d'une personne)* search; **faire une f.** to make a search; **f. corporelle** *(rapide)* frisking; *(approfondie)* body search **(b)** **fouilles** *(archéologiques)* excavations, dig **(c)** *Fam (poche)* pocket

fouillé, -e [fuje] *adj (approfondi)* detailed

fouiller [fuje] **1** *vt* **(a)** *(maison, personne)* to search **(b)** *(problème)* to go thoroughly into **2** *vi* to search **(dans** in)

fouillis [fuji] *nm* jumble, muddle

fouine [fwin] *nf* stone marten

fouiner [fwine] *vi* to nose about **(dans** in)

foulard [fular] *nm* scarf; **le F. islamique** the Muslim headscarf

---

Le Foulard islamique

The principle of secularism has long been a cornerstone of the French education system, but it was traditionally up to school principals to decide whether girls should be allowed to wear the Muslim headscarf at school. With growing numbers of girls being suspended from school for insisting on wearing the headscarf, the government passed a law in 2004 prohibiting the display of **any** obvious religious signs at school (as well as in state jobs that involved contact with the public). This controversial measure was introduced to safegurd the principle of secularism and to keep issues of ethnicity and religion from being a divisive factor among children.

---

foule [ful] *nf (de gens)* crowd; **il ne supporte pas la f.** he can't stand crowds; *Fig* **une f. de qch** lots of sth

foulée [fule] *nf (d'un coureur)* stride; *Fig* **dans la f., j'ai vérifié les comptes** while I was at it, I checked the accounts

fouler [fule] **1** *vt (sol)* to tread; *(raisins)* to press; *Fig* **f. qch aux pieds** to trample sth underfoot **2** **se fouler** *vpr* **(a)** **se f. la cheville** to sprain one's ankle **(b)** *Fam (se fatiguer)* to strain oneself

foulure [fulyr] *nf* sprain; **se faire une f. à la cheville** to sprain one's ankle

four [fur] *nm* (**a**) *(de cuisine)* oven; **f. à gaz/électrique/à micro-ondes** gas/electric/microwave oven; **cuit au f.** *(pain)* baked; *(viande)* roasted; **il fait noir comme dans un f.** it's pitch black; **on ne peut être à la fois au f. et au moulin** you can't be in two places at once (**b**) **petits fours** *(gâteaux)* petits fours (**c**) *(industriel)* kiln; *Hist* **les fours crématoires** the gas ovens (**d**) *Fam (fiasco)* flop; **faire un f.** to flop

fourbe [furb] **1** *adj* deceitful
  2 *nmf* cheat

fourbi [furbi] *nm Fam* (**a**) *(désordre)* mess (**b**) *(truc)* thingamajig, thingumajig, whatsit

fourbu, -e [furby] *adj* exhausted

fourche [furʃ] *nf* (**a**) *(outil)* fork (**b**) *(de bicyclette, sur une route)* fork; *(des cheveux)* split end; **faire une f.** to fork (**c**) *Belg Scol* break, gap *(in one's schedule)*

fourcher [furʃe] *vi* **sa langue a fourché** she made a slip of the tongue

fourchette [furʃɛt] *nf* (**a**) *(ustensile)* fork; *Fam* **avoir un joli *ou* bon coup de f.** to have a hearty appetite (**b**) *(écart)* bracket; **f. de prix** price bracket

fourchu, -e [furʃy] *adj (tronc, route)* forked; **aux pieds fourchus** cloven-hoofed; **avoir les cheveux fourchus** to have split ends

fourgon [furgɔ̃] *nm* (**a**) *(véhicule)* van; **f. cellulaire** patrol wagon; **f. funèbre *ou* funéraire** hearse (**b**) *(d'un train)* **f. à bétail** cattle truck

fourgonnette [furgɔnɛt] *nf* small van

fourguer [furge] *vt Fam* **f. qch à qn** to unload sth onto sb

fourmi [furmi] *nf* ant; *Fig (personne travailleuse)* busy bee; **avoir des fourmis (dans les jambes)** to have pins and needles (in one's legs); **travail de f.** painstaking work

fourmilière [furmiljɛr] *nf* anthill; *Fig* hive of activity

fourmillement [furmijmɑ̃] *nm* (**a**) *(sensation)* pins and needles (**b**) *(agitation)* swarming

fourmiller [furmije] **1** *vi* to swarm, to teem
  2 fourmiller de *vt ind* to swarm with, to teem with

fournaise [furnɛz] *nf* (**a**) *(endroit surchauffé)* **c'est une vraie f. ici!** this place is like a furnace! (**b**) *Litt (feu)* blaze (**c**) *Can (poêle à bois)* (wood-burning) stove; *(poêle au charbon)* (coal-burning) stove; *(chaudière de chauffage central)* (central heating) furnace

fourneau, -x [furno] *nm* (**a**) *(de cuisine)* stove; **être aux fourneaux** to be cooking (**b**) *(de verrier, de fondeur)* furnace (**c**) *(d'une pipe)* bowl

fournée [furne] *nf aussi Fig* batch

fourni, -e [furni] *adj* (**a**) *(magasin)* **bien/mal f.** well/poorly stocked (**b**) *(barbe, sourcils)* bushy; **peu f.** sparse

fournil [furni] *nm* bakery

fournir [furnir] **1** *vt* (**a**) *(approvisionner)* to supply (**en** with) (**b**) *(procurer)* **f. qch à qn** to provide sb with sth (**c**) *(présenter) (preuve, alibi)* to provide; *(documents)* to provide; **pièces à f.** required documents (**d**) *(effort)* to make
  2 se fournir *vpr* **se f. en qch** to get supplies of sth; **se f. chez qn** to get one's supplies from sb

fournisseur, -euse [furnisœr, -øz] *nm,f* supplier; *Ordinat* **f. d'accès** access provider

fournitures [furnityr] *nfpl* **f. de bureau** office supplies; **f. scolaires** school supplies

fourrage [furaʒ] *nm* fodder

fourrager¹ [45] [furaʒe] *vi Fam (fouiller)* to rummage (**dans** in)

fourrager², -ère [furaʒe, -ɛr] *adj (plante)* fodder

fourre [fur] *nf Suisse (d'un oreiller)* pillowcase; *(pour un édredon)* quilt cover; *(d'un disque)* sleeve; *(d'un livre)* jacket

fourreau, -x [furo] *nm* (**a**) *(d'épée)* sheath, scabbard; *(de para-*

pluie) cover (**b**) **(robe) f.** sheath dress; **jupe f.** pencil skirt

fourrer [fure] **1** *vt* (**a**) *(gâteau, bonbon)* to fill (**à** with); **bonbon fourré** soft-centered candy (**b**) *Fam (mettre)* to stick
  2 se fourrer *vpr Fam* **où est-il allé se f.?** where's he hiding?; **ne pas savoir où se f.** not to know where to put oneself; **se f. dans une sale affaire** to get involved in a shady business

fourre-tout [furtu] **1** *adj inv (placard)* junk; **un texte/une loi f.** a ragbag of a text/a law
  2 *nm inv* (**a**) *(pièce)* junk room; *(placard)* junk cupboard (**b**) *(sac)* carryall, tote

fourreur [furœr] *nm* furrier

fourrière [furjɛr] *nf* pound; **mettre en f. *ou* à la f.** *(voiture)* to impound; *(chien)* to put in the pound

fourrure [furyr] *nf* fur; **de *ou* en f.** fur

fourvoyer [32] [furvwaje] *Litt* **se fourvoyer** *vpr* to lose one's way; *Fig* to go astray

foutage [futaʒ] *nm très Fam* **c'est du f. de gueule** you/they/ etc. gotta be kidding!

foutaise [futɛz] *nf très Fam* bullshit

foutoir [futwar] *nm très Fam* dump

foutre [futr] *très Fam* **1** *vt* (**a**) *(mettre)* to stick; **f. qch par terre** to chuck sth on the ground; **f. qn à la porte** to kick sb out; **f. qch en l'air** *(le faire échouer)* to screw sth up (**b**) *(faire)* to do; **ne rien f.** not to do a damn thing; **je n'en ai rien à f.!** I don't give a damn!; **qu'est-ce que ça peut f.?** what the hell does it matter? (**c**) *(donner) (correction, gifle)* to give; **f. la trouille à qn** to scare the shit out of sb (**d**) *(locutions)* **f. le camp** to get the hell out; **fous(-moi) le camp!** get the hell out of here!; **je t'en foutrais, du champagne!** champagne, as if!; *Vulg* **va te faire f.!** fuck off!
  2 se foutre *vpr* (**a**) *(se mettre)* **se f. un coup** to bang oneself; **se f. par terre** to go sprawling; **se f. dedans** to screw up (**b**) **se f. de (la gueule de) qn** *(se moquer de)* to take sb for an asshole; **se f. du monde** to have a hell of a nerve (**c**) **se f. de qn/qch** *(être indifférent à)* not to give a damn about sb/sth; **je m'en fous** I don't give a damn

foutu, -e [futy] *adj Fam* (**a**) *(maudit)* damn (**b**) *(en mauvais état, perdu)* **être f.** to have had it; **c'est f.!** forget it! (**c**) **être bien/ mal f.** *(bien/mal bâti)* to have/not to have a nice body; *(bien/ mal conçu)* to be well/badly designed; **être mal f.** *(malade)* to be under the weather (**d**) *(capable)* **être f. de faire qch** to be quite likely to do sth; **elle n'est même pas foutue d'être à l'heure** she can't even be bothered to turn up on time

fox [fɔks] *(pl* fox), **fox-terrier** *(pl* fox-terriers) [fɔkstɛrje] *nm* fox terrier

foyer [fwaje] *nm* (**a**) *(domicile)* home; **le f. conjugal** the marital home (**b**) *(famille)* family (**c**) *(résidence) (d'étudiants)* residence; *(de travailleurs, de délinquants)* home (**d**) *(de chaleur, d'infection)* source; *(d'incendie, de conflits)* seat (**e**) *(âtre)* hearth (**f**) *(de lunettes)* focus

fracas [fraka] *nm* crash

fracassant, -e [frakasɑ̃, -ɑ̃t] *adj (bruit)* deafening; *(nouvelle, révélation)* shattering; *(succès)* resounding

fracasser [frakase] **1** *vt* to smash
  2 se fracasser *vpr* to smash

fraction [fraksjɔ̃] *nf* (**a**) *(partie)* part, fraction; **pendant une f. de seconde** for a fraction of a second (**b**) *Math* fraction

fractionnement [fraksjɔnmɑ̃] *nm* splitting up

fractionner [fraksjɔne] **1** *vt* to split up (**en** into)
  2 se fractionner *vpr* to split up (**en** into)

fracture [fraktyr] *nf* fracture; **f. du crâne** fractured skull; *Fig* **la f. sociale** the gap between the haves and the have-nots in society

fracturer [fraktyre] **1** *vt* (**a**) *(serrure, porte)* to break open (**b**) *(os)* to fracture
  2 se fracturer *vpr* **se f. le tibia** to fracture one's tibia

fragile [fraʒil] *adj (matériau, objet)* fragile; *(santé, estomac, équilibre)* delicate; *(personne) (physiquement)* frail; *(mentalement)* sensitive; *(bonheur)* precarious; *(hypothèse)* shaky

fragiliser [fraʒilize] *vt* to weaken

fragilité [fraʒilite] *nf (d'un matériau, d'un objet)* fragility; *(d'une personne) (physique)* frailty; *(mentale)* sensitivity; *(du bonheur)* precariousness; *(d'une hypothèse)* shakiness; *(de la santé, de l'estomac, d'un équilibre)* delicacy

fragment [fragmɑ̃] *nm (d'un objet, de conversation)* fragment; *(d'un livre)* extract; *(de vérité)* shred

fragmentaire [fragmɑ̃tɛr] *adj* fragmentary

fragmenter [fragmɑ̃te] *vt* to fragment

fraîche [frɛʃ] *adj voir* **frais**[1]

fraîchement [frɛʃmɑ̃] *adv* (**a**) *(recevoir, accueillir)* coolly (**b**) *(récemment)* newly

fraîcheur [frɛʃœr] *nf (de la température, d'un accueil)* coolness; *(d'aliments, du teint)* freshness

fraîchir [frɛʃir] *vi (temps)* to freshen

frais[1], **fraîche** [frɛ, frɛʃ] **1** *adj* (**a**) *(vent, air, accueil)* cool (**b**) *(aliments, fleurs, teint)* fresh; **f. et dispos** hale and hearty (**c**) *(souvenir, nouvelles)* recent; *(encre, peinture)* wet

2 *adv* **servir/boire f.** *(sur étiquette)* serve/drink chilled; **f. émoulu de** fresh out of

3 *nm* **prendre le f.** to get a breath of fresh air; **mettre/conserver qch au f.** to put/keep sth in a cool place; **il fait f.** it's cool; *Can Fam Péj* **faire le f.** to show off

4 *nf* **à la fraîche** in the cool part of the day; *Can* **prendre la f.** *(sortir prendre l'air)* to go for a stroll; *(prendre froid)* to catch a chill

frais[2] [frɛ] *nmpl* expenses, costs; **faire de gros f.** to go to great expense; **tous f. payés** all expenses paid; **rentrer dans ses f.** to cover one's expenses; *Fig* **faire les f. de qch** *(être victime de)* to pay the price for sth; **faire les f. de la conversation** to keep the conversation going; **faire qch à ses f.** to do sth at one's own expense; **aux f. de la société** at the company's expense; **aux f. de la princesse** at the firm's/government's/*etc.* expense; **à grands/peu de f.** at great/little cost; **se mettre en f.** to go to great expense; **en être pour ses f.** to have been wasting one's time; **f. de déplacement** traveling expenses; **f. généraux** overhead; **f. d'inscription** membership fee; **f. de port** postage and packing; **f. de scolarité** school fees; *Can Tél* **appeler qn à f. virés** to call sb collect; **faux f.** incidental expenses

fraise[1] [frɛz] *nf (fruit)* strawberry; **glace à la f.** strawberry(-flavored) ice-cream; **f. des bois** wild strawberry

fraise[2] [frɛz] *nf (de dentiste)* drill

fraise[3] [frɛz] *nf (collerette)* ruff

fraisier [frezje] *nm* (**a**) *(plante)* strawberry plant (**b**) *(gâteau)* strawberry cream cake

framboise [frɑ̃bwaz] *nf* raspberry

framboisier [frɑ̃bwazje] *nm* raspberry bush

franc[1] [frɑ̃] *nm* franc; *Anciennement* **f. français/belge** French/Belgian franc; **f. suisse** Swiss franc; **f. CFA** CFA franc; **ancien/nouveau f.** old/new franc; **f. symbolique** nominal sum

franc[2], **franche** [frɑ̃, frɑ̃ʃ] **1** *adj* (**a**) *(sincère)* frank (**b**) *(zone, ville, port)* free (**c**) *(net) (couleur)* pure; *(rupture)* clean

2 *adv (parler)* frankly

français, -e [frɑ̃sɛ, -ɛz] **1** *adj* French

2 *nm (langue)* French; **parler f.** to speak French; *(correctement)* to speak properly; *Fam* **tu ne comprends pas le f.?** don't you understand plain English?

3 *nm,f* **F.** Frenchman; **Française** Frenchwoman; **les F.** the French

France [frɑ̃s] *nf* **la F.** France; *TV* **F. 2/3** = second/third French state-owned TV channel; **F. Télécom** = state-owned telecommunications company

Francfort [frɑ̃kfɔr] *n* Frankfurt

franche [frɑ̃ʃ] *adj voir* **franc**[2]

franchement [frɑ̃ʃmɑ̃] *adv* (**a**) *(sincèrement)* frankly (**b**) *(tout à fait, vraiment)* really (**c**) *(carrément)* **y aller f.** to get right down to it

franchir [frɑ̃ʃir] *vt (obstacle, difficulté)* to get over; *(porte)* to go through; *(fossé)* to jump (over); *(ligne d'arrivée, rivière, frontière)* to cross; *Fig (cap, seuil, niveau)* to pass

franchise [frɑ̃ʃiz] *nf* (**a**) *(sincérité)* frankness; **en toute f.** quite frankly (**b**) *(exonération)* exemption; **f. postale** ≃ postage paid (**c**) *(d'assurance)* deductible (**d**) *Com* franchise

franchouillard, -e [frɑ̃ʃujar, -ard] *adj Fam* typically French

francilien, -enne [frɑ̃siljɛ̃, -ɛn] **1** *adj* of the Île-de-France

2 *nm,f* **F., Francilienne** person from the Île-de-France

franciscain, -e [frɑ̃siskɛ̃, -ɛn] *adj & nm,f* Franciscan

franciser [frɑ̃size] *vt* to gallicize

franc-maçon, -onne *(pl* **francs-maçons, franc-maçonnes**) [frɑ̃masɔ̃, -ɔn] *nm,f* freemason

franc-maçonnerie [frɑ̃masɔnri] *nf* freemasonry

franco [frɑ̃ko] *adv* (**a**) *Fam (franchement)* **y aller f.** to get right down to it (**b**) *Com* **f. (de port)** postage paid; **f. à bord** free on board

francophile [frɑ̃kɔfil] *adj & nmf* Francophile

francophobe [frɑ̃kɔfɔb] *adj & nmf* Francophobe

francophone [frɑ̃kɔfɔn] **1** *adj* French-speaking

2 *nmf* French speaker

francophonie [frɑ̃kɔfɔni] *nf* French-speaking world

franc-parler [frɑ̃parle] *nm* outspokenness; **avoir son f.** to speak one's mind

franc-tireur *(pl* **francs-tireurs**) [frɑ̃tirœr] *nm (combattant)* irregular (soldier); *Fig* maverick

frange [frɑ̃ʒ] *nf* (**a**) *(des cheveux)* bangs (**b**) *(de tissu)* fringe (**c**) *Fig (minorité)* fringe

frangin, -e [frɑ̃ʒɛ̃, -in] *nm,f Fam* bro, brother, *f* sis, sister

frangipane [frɑ̃ʒipan] *nf* = almond-flavored custard

franglais [frɑ̃glɛ] *nm* Franglais

franquette [frɑ̃kɛt] *nf* **à la bonne f.** without ceremony

frappant, -e [frapɑ̃, -ɑ̃t] *adj* striking

frappe [frap] *nf* (**a**) *(sur un clavier d'ordinateur)* keying; *(sur une machine à écrire)* typing; *Ordinat* **f. en continu** type-ahead; *Ordinat* **f. au kilomètre** continuous input (**b**) *(de monnaie)* minting (**c**) *(au base-ball)* hit; *(au football)* kick; *(en boxe)* punch (**d**) *Fam (voyou)* hoodlum, punk (**e**) *Mil* strike; **frappe aérienne** airstrike

frappé, -e [frape] *adj* (**a**) *(champagne)* chilled; *(café)* iced (**b**) *Fam (fou)* crazy

frapper [frape] **1** *vt* (**a**) *(donner un ou des coups à)* to hit, to strike; *Fig (faire une forte impression sur)* to strike (**b**) *(monnaie)* to mint (**c**) *(champagne)* to put on ice (**d**) *Can (entrer en collision avec)* to hit

2 *vi* (**a**) *(donner un coup)* to strike, to hit; **f. du poing sur la table** to bang (on) the table; **f. des mains** *ou* **dans ses mains** to clap (one's hands); **f. à la porte** to knock on *or* at the door; *Fig* **tu frappes à la bonne/mauvaise porte** you've come to the right/wrong place; **entrez sans f.** *(sur écriteau)* go straight in (**b**) *Fam (agir)* to strike

3 **se frapper** *vpr* (**a**) *Fam (se faire du souci)* to get oneself worked up (**b**) *Can (entrer en collision)* to collide

frasques [frask] *nfpl* carryings-on

fraternel, -elle [fratɛrnɛl] *adj* fraternal, brotherly

fraterniser [fratɛrnize] *vi* to fraternize

fraternité [fratɛrnite] *nf* fraternity, brotherhood

fratricide [fratrisid] **1** *adj* fratricidal

2 *nmf (personne)* fratricide

3 *nm (crime)* fratricide

fraude [frod] *nf* fraud; **passer qch en f.** to smuggle sth in; **f. électorale** electoral fraud; **f. fiscale** tax evasion

frauder [frode] **1** *vt (douane)* to defraud; **f. le fisc** to evade tax **2** *vi* to cheat (**sur** on)

fraudeur, -euse [frodœr, -øz] *nm,f* defrauder

frauduleux, -euse [frodylø, -øz] *adj* fraudulent

frayer [53] [freje] **1** *vi (poisson)* to spawn; *Fig* **f. avec qn** to mix with sb
   2 se frayer *vpr* **se f. un chemin** to clear a way (for oneself)

frayeur [frejœr] *nf* fright; **faire une f. à qn** to give sb a fright

fredaines [frədɛn] *nfpl* pranks, escapades

fredonner [frədɔne] *vt & vi* to hum

free-lance [frilãs] **1** *adj inv* freelance
   2 *nm (travail)* freelance work; **travailler en f.** to work freelance
   3 *nmf (pl* **free-lances**) freelance, freelancer

freezer [frizœr] *nm* freezer compartment

frégate [fregat] *nf* (a) *(oiseau)* frigate bird (b) *(navire)* frigate

frein [frɛ̃] *nm* (a) *(de voiture)* brake; **donner un coup de f.** to put on the brakes; *Fig* **mettre un f. à qch** to curb sth; **freins à disque** disk brakes; **f. à main** parking brake; **f. moteur** engine brake (b) *(mors)* bit

freinage [frɛnaʒ] *nm* braking

freiner [frene] **1** *vt* (a) *(véhicule, processus)* to slow down; *(chute)* to break; *(inflation, production)* to curb (b) *(personne)* to restrain
   2 *vi* to brake
   3 se freiner *vpr* to restrain oneself

frelaté, -e [frəlate] *adj (vin)* adulterated

frelater [frəlate] *vt* to adulterate

frêle [frɛl] *adj* frail

frelon [frəlɔ̃] *nm* hornet

freluquet [frəlykɛ] *nm Fam* whippersnapper

frémir [fremir] *vi* (a) *(personne)* to tremble (**de** with) (b) *(eau chaude)* to simmer; *(feuillage)* to rustle

frémissant, -e [fremisã, -ãt] *adj (eau)* simmering; *(voix)* trembling; *(feuillage)* rustling

frémissement [fremismã] *nm* (a) *(de peur)* shudder; *(de plaisir, de joie)* thrill; *(de colère, d'impatience)* quiver (b) *(de l'eau)* simmering; *(des feuilles)* rustle

french cancan *(pl* **french cancans**) [frɛnʃkãkã] *nm* cancan

frêne [frɛn] *nm* ash

frénésie [frenezi] *nf* frenzy

frénétique [frenetik] *adj* frenzied

frénétiquement [frenetikmã] *adv* frenziedly

fréquemment [frekamã] *adv* frequently

fréquence [frekãs] *nf* frequency; **basse/haute f.** low/high frequency

fréquent, -e [frekã, -ãt] *adj* frequent

fréquentable [frekãtabl] *adj* **des gens peu fréquentables** people you wouldn't want to associate with

fréquentation [frekãtasjɔ̃] *nf* (a) *(d'un lieu)* frequenting; **la f. de qn** seeing sb regularly (b) **fréquentations** *(relations)* company; **avoir de mauvaises fréquentations** to keep bad company

fréquenté, -e [frekãte] *adj* **très f.** very busy; **bien/mal f.** of good/ill repute

fréquenter [frekãte] **1** *vt* (a) *(lieu)* to frequent (b) *(personne) (voir régulièrement)* to see regularly; *(sortir avec)* to date
   2 se fréquenter *vpr (se voir régulièrement)* to see each other regularly; *(sortir ensemble)* to date, to be dating

frère [frɛr] **1** *adj (pays, peuple)* fellow
   2 *nm* brother; **faux f.** false friend; **frères d'armes** brothers-in-arms

frérot [frero] *nm Fam* kid brother

fresque [frɛsk] *nf* fresco

fret [frɛ, frɛt] *nm* freight

frétillant, -e [fretijã, -ãt] *adj (poisson)* wriggling; *(personne) (de joie)* quivering (**de** with)

frétiller [fretije] *vi (poisson, personne)* to wriggle; **f. de joie** to quiver with joy

fretin [frətɛ̃] *nm aussi Fig* **menu f.** small fry

freudien, -enne [frødjɛ̃, -ɛn] *adj* Freudian

freux [frø] *nm* rook

FRF *Anciennement (abrév* **franc(s) français**) FF

friable [frijabl] *adj* crumbly

friand, -e [frijã, -ãd] **1** *adj* **être f. de qch** to be fond of sth
   2 *nm (salé)* = small savory tartlet; *(sucré)* = small almond cake

friandise [frijãdiz] *nf* tidbit, delicacy

fric [frik] *nm Fam* dough

fricassée [frikase] *nf (ragoût)* fricassee; *Belg* fried egg and bacon

friche [friʃ] *nf* fallow land; **en f.** fallow; **f. industrielle** industrial wasteland

frichti [friʃti] *nm Fam* grub

fricot [friko] *nm Fam* grub; **faire le f.** to do the cooking

fricoter [frikɔte] *Fam* **1** *vt* (a) *(manigancer)* to cook up (b) *(plat)* to cook
   2 *vi (avoir des activités suspectes)* to be involved in some shady business

friction [friksjɔ̃] *nf* (a) *(massage)* rubdown; *(du cuir chevelu)* scalp massage (b) *(heurt)* friction

frictionner [friksjone] **1** *vt (partie du corps)* to rub; *(personne)* to rub down
   2 se frictionner *vpr* to rub oneself

Frigidaire® [friʒidɛr] *nm* refrigerator

frigide [friʒid] *adj* frigid

frigidité [friʒidite] *nf* frigidity

frigo [frigo] *nm Fam* fridge

frigorifié, -e [frigɔrifje] *adj Fam (personne)* frozen stiff

frigorifier [66] [frigɔrifje] *vt (aliment)* to refrigerate

frigorifique [frigɔrifik] *adj voir* **camion**

frileux, -euse [frilø, -øz] *adj (personne)* sensitive to the cold; *(attitude, réponse)* timid

frime [frim] *nf Fam* show

frimer [frime] *vi Fam* to show off

frimeur, -euse [frimœr, -øz] *nm,f Fam* show-off

frimousse [frimus] *nf* (a) *Fam* cute little face (b) *Ordinat (smiley)* smiley

fringale [frɛ̃gal] *nf Fam (faim)* hunger; *Fig (envie)* craving (**de** for); **avoir la f.** to be starving

fringant, -e [frɛ̃gã, -ãt] *adj (personne)* dashing

fringuer [frɛ̃ge] *Fam* **1** *vt* to dress
   2 se fringuer *vpr (se vêtir)* to get dressed; *(choisir ses vêtements)* to dress; **il se fringue super bien** he dresses really well, he's a really snappy dresser

fringues [frɛ̃g] *nfpl Fam* gear

fripé, -e [fripe] *adj* crumpled

friper [fripe] **1** *vt* to crumple
   2 se friper *vpr* to get crumpled

friperie [fripri] *nf* second-hand clothes store

fripes [frip] *nfpl* second-hand clothes

fripier, -ère [fripje, -ɛr] *nm,f* second-hand clothes dealer

fripon, -onne [fripɔ̃, -ɔn] *Fam* **1** *adj* mischievous
   2 *nm,f* rascal

fripouille [fripuj] *nf Fam* rogue

friqué, -e [frike] *adj Fam* loaded

frire [19a] [frir] **1** *vt* to fry
   2 *vi* to fry; **faire f. qch** to fry sth

Frisbee® [frizbi] *nm* Frisbee®

frise [friz] *nf* frieze

frisé, -e [frize] **1** *adj (cheveux)* curly; *(personne)* curly-haired
2 *nf* **frisée** *(salade)* curly endive

friser [frize] **1** *vt* **(a)** *(cheveux)* to curl **(b)** *(approcher)* **f. la catastrophe** to come within an inch of disaster; **elle doit f. la quarantaine** she must be close to forty; **cela frise le ridicule** it's verging on the ridiculous
2 *vi (cheveux)* to curl; *(personne)* to have curly hair

frisette [frizɛt] *nf (de cheveux)* small curl

frisotter [frizɔte] **1** *vt (cheveux)* to frizz
2 *vi* to be frizzy

frisquet, -ette [friskɛ, -ɛt] *adj Fam* chilly; **il fait f.** it's chilly

frisson [frisɔ̃] *nm (de froid, de peur)* shiver; *(de plaisir)* thrill; **avoir des frissons** to shiver; **donner des frissons** *ou* **le f. à qn** *(de peur)* to give sb the shivers

frissonner [frisɔne] *vi* **(a)** *(personne) (de froid, de peur)* to shiver **(b)** *Litt (feuillage)* to quiver; *(eau)* to ripple

frit, -e [fri, frit] **1** *adj* fried
2 *nf* **frite** **(a)** *(de pomme de terre)* (French) fry **(b)** *Fam* **avoir la frite** to be in form

friteuse [fritøz] *nf* deep frier; **f. électrique** electric frier

friture [frityr] *nf* **(a)** *(mode de cuisson)* frying **(b)** *(corps gras)* frying fat **(c)** *(aliments)* fried food; **f. (de poissons)** fried fish **(d)** *Rad & Tél* crackling **(e)** *Belg (friterie)* French-fry vendor

frivole [frivɔl] *adj* frivolous

frivolité [frivɔlite] *nf* frivolity

froc [frɔk] *nm* **(a)** *Fam (pantalon)* pants **(b)** *(habit religieux)* habit

froid, -e [frwa, frwad] **1** *adj aussi Fig* cold
2 *adv* **boire/manger qch f.** to drink/to eat sth cold
3 *nm* cold; **les grands froids** the coldest part of the winter; **il fait f.** it's cold; *Fam* **il fait un f. de canard** it's freezing (cold); *Fig* **ça fait f. dans le dos** it sends a shiver down your spine; **avoir f.** to be cold; **j'ai f. aux mains** my hands are cold, I've got cold hands; *Fig* **ne pas avoir f. aux yeux** to have plenty of nerve; **à f.** *(répondre)* off the top of one's head; *(humour)* deadpan; **être en f. (avec qn)** to be on bad terms (with sb); **prendre f.** to catch cold

froidement [frwadmɑ̃] *adv (accueillir, recevoir)* coldly; *(abattre)* cold-bloodedly; *(répondre)* coolly

froideur [frwadœr] *nf* coldness; **avec f.** coldly

froissement [frwasmɑ̃] *nm* **(a)** *(bruit)* rustle **(b)** *(de muscle)* straining

froisser [frwase] **1** *vt* **(a)** *(tissu, papier)* to crumple, to crease **(b)** *Fig (sentiment, personne)* to offend
2 **se froisser** *vpr* **(a)** *(tissu)* to crease, to crumple **(b)** **se f. un muscle** to strain a muscle **(c)** *Fig (personne)* to take offense (**de** at)

frôlement [frolmɑ̃] *nm (contact)* brushing (**contre** against); *(son)* rustle

frôler [frole] **1** *vt* **(a)** *(effleurer)* to brush (against), to touch lightly **(b)** *Fig (la mort, la catastrophe)* to come close to; *(le ridicule)* to border on
2 **se frôler** *vpr* to brush (against) each other

fromage [frɔmaʒ] *nm* **(a)** *(produit laitier)* cheese; *Fam Fig* **faire tout un f. de qch** to make a great fuss about sth; **f. blanc** fromage frais; **f. de brebis** sheep's *or* ewe's milk cheese; **f. de chèvre** goat's cheese; **f. frais** soft cheese; **f. à pâte molle/dure** soft/hard cheese; **f. à tartiner** cheese spread **(b)** **f. de tête** headcheese

fromager, -ère [frɔmaʒe, -ɛr] **1** *adj* cheese
2 *nm,f (commerçant)* cheese seller; *(fabricant)* cheesemaker

fromagerie [frɔmaʒri] *nf (lieu de fabrication)* cheese dairy; *(magasin)* cheese shop

froment [frɔmɑ̃] *nm* wheat

fronce [frɔ̃s] *nf* gather

froncement [frɔ̃smɑ̃] *nm* **f. de(s) sourcils** frown

froncer [16] [frɔ̃se] *vt* **(a)** *(nez, front)* to wrinkle; **f. les sourcils** to frown **(b)** *(tissu)* to gather

fronde [frɔ̃d] *nf* **(a)** *(arme)* sling; *(jouet)* slingshot **(b)** *(révolte)* rebellion

frondeur, -euse [frɔ̃dœr, -øz] **1** *adj* rebellious
2 *nm,f* rebel

front [frɔ̃] *nm* **(a)** *(partie du visage)* forehead **(b)** *(avant)* front; **faire f.** to face up to things; **faire f. à qn/qch** to face up to sb/ sth; **de f.** *(marcher, avancer)* side by side; *(heurter, aborder un problème)* head-on; **mener plusieurs choses de f.** to have several things going at once; **f. de mer** seafront **(c)** *(audace)* **avoir le f. de faire qch** to have the nerve to do sth **(d)** *Mil & Météo* front

frontal, -e, -aux, -ales [frɔ̃tal, -o] *adj* **(a)** *(attaque, choc)* head-on; **machine à laver à chargement f.** front-loading washing machine **(b)** *Ordinat* front-end; **ordinateur f.** front end **(c)** *(os)* frontal

frontalier, -ère [frɔ̃talje, -ɛr] **1** *adj (région)* border, frontier
2 *nm,f (habitant)* person living near the border; *(travailleur)* cross-border commuter

frontière [frɔ̃tjɛr] **1** *adj (ville, poste)* border, frontier
2 *nf (entre pays)* border, frontier; *Fig (des langues)* boundary; *(de la connaissance)* frontier

frontispice [frɔ̃tispis] *nm* frontispiece

fronton [frɔ̃tɔ̃] *nm* **(a)** *(sur monument)* pediment **(b)** *(de pelote basque)* fronton

frottement [frɔtmɑ̃] *nm* **(a)** *(d'une chose contre une autre)* rubbing; *Tech* friction **(b)** *(heurt)* friction

frotter [frɔte] **1** *vt* to rub; *(allumette)* to strike; *(parquet)* to scrub; *Belg Fam* **f. la manche à qn** to soft-soap sb
2 *vi* to rub (**contre** against)
3 **se frotter** *vpr* to rub oneself; *aussi Fig* **se f. les mains** to rub one's hands; *Fig* **se f. à qn/qch** to be in contact with sb/ sth; *Fig* **se f. à qn** *(l'attaquer)* to cross swords with sb

frottis [frɔti] *nm Méd* smear; **f. vaginal** cervical smear

froufrou [frufru] *nm* **(a)** *(bruit)* rustling **(b)** **froufrous** *(vêtements)* frills; **robe à froufrous** frilly dress

froufrouter [frufrute] *vi* to rustle

froussard, -e [frusar, -ard] *adj & nm,f Fam* chicken

frousse [frus] *nf Fam* fear; **avoir la f.** to be scared; **flanquer la f. à qn** to scare the living daylights out of sb

fructifier [66] [fryktifje] *vi (arbres, idée)* to bear fruit; *(terre)* to be productive; *(placements, capital)* to yield a profit; **faire f. qch** *(idée, projet)* to bring sth to fruition

fructose [fryktoz] *nm* fructose

fructueux, -euse [fryktɥø, -øz] *adj* fruitful, profitable

frugal, -e, -aux, -ales [frygal, -o] *adj* frugal

frugalité [frygalite] *nf* frugality

fruit [frɥi] *nm aussi Fig* fruit; **des fruits** (some) fruit; **un f.** some fruit, a piece of fruit; **fruits confits** candied fruit; *Fig* **le f. défendu** the forbidden fruit; **fruits de mer** seafood; **f. de la passion** passion fruit; **fruits rouges** red berries and currants; **fruits secs** dried fruit; *Suisse* **petits fruits** fruits of the forest; *Fig* **porter ses fruits** *(d'une action, d'un investissement)* to bear fruit

fruité, -e [frɥite] *adj* fruity

fruitier, -ère [frɥitje, -ɛr] **1** *adj voir* **arbre**
2 *nm,f* fruit seller

frusques [frysk] *nfpl Fam* gear

fruste [fryst] *adj (style, personne)* rough, unsophisticated

frustrant, -e [frystrɑ̃, -ɑ̃t] *adj* frustrating

frustration [frystrasjɔ̃] *nf* frustration

frustré, -e [frystre] **1** *adj* frustrated
2 *nm,f* frustrated person

frustrer [frystre] *vt* **(a)** *(décevoir)* to frustrate **(b)** *(priver)* **f. qn de qch** to deprive sb of sth

FTP [ɛftepe] *nmpl (abrév* **Francs-tireurs et partisans***)* =

French Communist resistance group in the Second World War

fuchsia [fyʃja] **1** *adj inv* **(rose) f.** fuchsia
2 *nm (fleur, couleur)* fuchsia

fuel [fjul] *nm* fuel oil

fugace [fygas] *adj* fleeting

fugitif, -ive [fyʒitif, -iv] **1** *adj (fugace)* fleeting
2 *nm,f* fugitive, runaway

fugue [fyg] *nf* **(a)** *(composition musicale)* fugue **(b)** *(d'un enfant)* **faire une f.** to run away

fuguer [fyge] *vi* to run away

fugueur, -euse [fygœr, -øz] **1** *adj* who runs away a lot
2 *nm,f* runaway

fui *voir* **fuir**

fuir [38] [fчir] **1** *vt (pays)* to flee; *(personne)* to run away from; *(guerre)* to escape; *(responsabilités)* to shirk
2 *vi* **(a)** *(s'échapper)* to run away, to flee (**devant** from); **f. de son pays** to flee one's country **(b)** *(robinet, gaz, eau)* to leak **(c)** *(s'écouler rapidement)* to fly by

fuis, fuit *voir* **fuir**

fuite [fчit] *nf* **(a)** *(escapade)* flight (**devant** from); *Fig (devant des difficultés, des problèmes)* avoidance (**devant** of); **prendre la f.** to take flight; **être en f.** to be on the run; **mettre qn en f.** to put sb to flight; **la f. des capitaux** the flight of capital; **la f. des cerveaux** the brain drain **(b)** *(de liquide, de gaz, d'informations)* leak

fulgurant, -e [fylgyrã, -ãt] *adj* **(a)** *(attaque, changement, rapidité)* lightning; *(succès)* spectacular **(b)** *(douleur)* searing

fulminer [fylmine] *vi* to fulminate (**contre** against)

fumant, -e [fymã, -ãt] *adj* **(a)** *(âtre, cendres)* smoking; *(potage)* steaming **(b)** *Fam (remarquable)* **faire un coup f.** to pull off a masterstroke

fumé, -e [fyme] *adj* **(a)** *(poisson, viande)* smoked **(b)** *(verres)* tinted

fume-cigare [fymsigar] *nm inv* cigar holder

fumée [fyme] *nf (de feu, de cigarette)* smoke; *(d'un liquide chaud)* steam; *Prov* **il n'y a pas de f. sans feu** there's no smoke without fire

fumer [fyme] **1** *vt* **(a)** *(poisson, viande)* to smoke **(b)** *(tabac, cigarette)* to smoke; **f. la pipe** to smoke a pipe
2 *vi* **(a)** *(feu, moteur)* to smoke; *(liquide, plat)* to steam **(b)** *(fumeur)* to smoke; **f. comme un pompier** *ou* **un sapeur** to smoke like a chimney

fumet [fymɛ] *nm (d'un mets)* aroma

fumeur, -euse [fymœr, -øz] *nm,f* smoker; **fumeurs** *(sur panneau)* smoking

fumeux, -euse [fymø, -øz] *adj (idées, explications, projets)* hazy

fumier [fymje] *nm* **(a)** *(engrais)* manure, dung **(b)** *très Fam (injure)* bastard

fumigation [fymigasjɔ̃] *nf* fumigation; *Méd* inhalation; **faire des fumigations de désinfectant** to fumigate with disinfectant

fumiste [fymist] **1** *nmf Fam (sur qui on ne peut compter)* clown
2 *nm (technicien)* heating engineer
3 *adj Fam* unreliable

fumisterie [fymistəri] *nf* **(a)** *(métier)* heating engineering **(b)** *Fam (farce)* con

fumoir [fymwar] *nm* smoking room

funambule [fynãbyl] *nmf* tightrope walker

funèbre [fynɛbr] *adj* **(a)** *(cérémonie, marche)* funeral; **hymne** *ou* **chant f.** dirge **(b)** *(lugubre)* funereal

funérailles [fyneraj] *nfpl* funeral; **f. nationales** state funeral

funéraire [fynerɛr] *adj (dépenses, urne)* funeral; **pierre f.** tombstone, gravestone

funeste [fynɛst] *adj* **(a)** *(erreur, conséquence, influence)* disastrous **(b)** *Litt (accident)* fatal

funiculaire [fynikylɛr] *nm* funicular

fur [fyr] *nm* **au f. et à mesure** as one goes along, bit by bit; **au f. et à mesure de leurs recherches** as they progressed with their research

furax [fyraks] *adj inv Fam* livid

furet [fyrɛ] *nm* ferret

fureter [6] [fyrte] *vi (chercher)* to ferret about

fureur [fyrœr] *nf* **(a)** *(colère)* fury, rage **(b)** *(passion)* passion; **faire f.** to be all the rage

furibard, -e [fyribar, -ard] *adj Fam* livid

furibond, -e [fyribɔ̃, -ɔ̃d] *adj* furious

furie [fyri] *nf* **(a)** *(rage)* fury; **en f.** infuriated; **la f. du jeu** a passion for gambling **(b)** *Fig (femme)* shrew; **comme une f.** like a wild thing

furieux, -euse [fyrjø, -øz] **1** *adj* **(a)** *(en colère)* furious (**contre** with); *Fig (tempête)* raging; *(combat)* violent **(b)** *Fam (intense) (envie)* overwhelming, tremendous

furoncle [fyrɔ̃kl] *nm* boil

furtif, -ive [fyrtif, -iv] *adj* furtive, stealthy

furtivement [fyrtivmã] *adv* furtively, stealthily; **entrer f.** to sneak in

fusain [fyzɛ̃] *nm (crayon, dessin)* charcoal

fuseau, -x [fyzo] *nm* **(a)** *(pantalon)* ski pants **(b)** *(pour filer la laine)* spindle; *(pour faire de la dentelle)* bobbin **(c)** **f. horaire** time zone

fusée [fyze] *nf* **(a)** *(projectile)* rocket; **il est parti comme une f.** he shot off like a rocket; **f. éclairante** flare **(b)** *(d'axe)* spindle; *Aut* stub axle

fuselage [fyzlaʒ] *nm (d'un avion)* fuselage

fuselé, -e [fyzle] *adj (colonne, doigts)* tapering; *(voiture)* streamlined

fuser [fyze] *vi* **des rires/cris fusèrent de toutes parts** laughter was/cries were suddenly heard from all sides

fusible [fyzibl] *nm* fuze

fusil [fyzi] *nm* **(a)** *(arme)* gun, rifle; **f. à air comprimé** air gun; **f. d'assaut** assault rifle; **f. de chasse** shotgun; **f. à lunette** rifle with telescopic sight; *Fig* **changer son f. d'épaule** to change tack; **coup de f.** gunshot; *Fam* **c'est le coup de f. dans ce restaurant** the prices in this restaurant are extortionate; *Can* **partir/entrer en coup de f.** to storm in/out **(b)** *(personne)* shot **(c)** *(pour aiguiser)* steel

fusilier [fyzilje] *nm* fusilier; **f. marin** marine

fusillade [fyzijad] *nf (tir)* gunfire

fusiller [fyzije] *vt* **(a)** *(par un peloton d'exécution)* to shoot; *Fig* **f. qn du regard** to look daggers at sb **(b)** *Fam (abîmer)* to wreck

fusil-mitrailleur *(pl* **fusils-mitrailleurs)** [fyzimitrajœr] *nm* light machine-gun

fusion [fyzjɔ̃] *nf* **(a)** *(par la chaleur)* melting, *Spéc* fusion; *(en métallurgie)* smelting; **point de f.** melting point; **métal/roche en f.** molten metal/rock; **f. froide, f. à froid.** cold fusion **(b)** *(de sociétés)* merger; *Ordinat* **f. de fichiers** file merge

fusionner [fyzjone] *vi & vt aussi Ordinat* to merge

fustiger [45] [fystiʒe] *vt (critiquer)* to castigate

fût [fy] *nm* **(a)** *(tonneau)* cask, barrel **(b)** *(d'arbre)* bole **(c)** *(de colonne)* shaft **(d)** *(de fusil)* stock

futaie [fytɛ] *nf* forest *(producing timber from full-grown trees)*

futal, -als [fytal] *nm,* **fute** [fyt] *nm Fam* pants

futé, -e [fyte] **1** *adj* crafty; **il n'est pas très f.** he's not very bright; *aussi Ironique* **ça, c'est f.!** that was clever!
2 *nm,f* sharp customer

futile [fytil] *adj (argument, occupation, prétexte)* trivial, trifling; *(personne)* frivolous

futilement [fytilmã] *adv* frivolously

futilité [fytilite] *nf* triviality

futon [fytɔ̃] *nm* futon

futur, -e [fytyr] **1** *adj* future; **un f. artiste** a budding artist; **mon f. emploi/appartement** my next job/apartment; **mon f. mari** my husband-to-be

2 *nm,f Hum* **mon f./ma future** my intended

3 *nm* (**a**) *(avenir)* future (**b**) *Gram* future (tense); **au f.** in the future (tense); **f. antérieur** future perfect

futurisme [fytyrism] *nm* futurism

futuriste [fytyrist] **1** *adj* futuristic

2 *nmf* futurist

fuyant, -e [fɥijɑ̃, -ɑ̃t] *adj* (**a**) *(ligne, menton)* receding; **lignes fuyantes** perspective lines (**b**) *(personne, attitude)* evasive; *(yeux)* shifty

fuyard, -e [fɥijar, -ard] *nm,f* fugitive, runaway

fuyez *etc. voir* **fuir**

G

G¹, **g** [ʒe] *nm inv* G, g; **le G8** the G8

G² [ʒe] *nm Belg Fam* (*abrév* **GSM**) mobile (phone)

g. (**a**) (*abrév* **gauche**) L (**b**) (*abrév* **gramme(s)**) g

gabardine [gabardin] *nf* gabardine

gabarit [gabari] *nm* (**a**) (*dimension*) size (**b**) *Fam* (*corpulence*) **un grand/petit g.** a huge/tiny man, *f* woman (**c**) (*valeur*) caliber (**d**) (*instrument*) gauge (**e**) *Ordinat* template

Gabon [gabɔ̃] *nm* **le G.** Gabon

gabonais, -e [gabɔnɛ, -ɛz] **1** *adj* Gabonese

    2 *nm,f* **G., Gabonaise** Gabonese

gâcher [gɑʃe] *vt* (**a**) (*gaspiller*) to waste (**b**) (*gâter*) (*plaisir, soirée*) to spoil (**c**) (*mélanger*) (*mortier, plâtre*) to mix

gâchette [gɑʃɛt, gaʃɛt] *nf* trigger; *Fam* **avoir la g. facile** to be trigger-happy; **appuyer sur la g.** to pull the trigger

gâchis [gɑʃi] *nm* waste

gadelle [gadɛl] *nf Can Bot* currant; **g. rouge** redcurrant

gadget [gadʒɛt] *nm* gadget

gadoue [gadu] *nf* mud

gaélique [gaelik] *adj & nm* Gaelic

gaffe [gaf] *nf* (**a**) *Fam* (*maladresse*) blunder; **faire une g.** to put one's foot in one's mouth (**b**) (*perche*) boathook (**c**) *Fam* **faire g.** to be careful

gaffer [gafe] **1** *vt* (*objet flottant*) to hook; (*poisson*) to gaff

    2 *vi Fam* to put one's foot in mouth

gaffeur, -euse [gafœr, -øz] *nm,f Fam* blunderer

gag [gag] *nm* gag

gaga [gaga] *adj Fam* gaga

gage [gaʒ] *nm* (**a**) (*chez le prêteur sur gages*) pledge; *Fig* (*garantie*) guarantee; **laisser qch en g.** to leave sth as security; **mettre qch en g.** to pawn sth (**b**) (*preuve*) token; **en g. de notre amitié** as a token of our friendship (**c**) (*dans un jeu*) forfeit (**d**) *Vieilli* (*salaire*) **gages** wages

gager [45] [gaʒe] *vt Litt* **g. que...** to wager that...

gageure [gaʒyr] *nf* (**a**) (*action difficile*) challenge (**b**) *Litt* (*pari*) wager

gagnant, -e [gaɲɑ̃, -ɑ̃t] **1** *adj* winning

    2 *nm,f* winner; **partir g.** to have a strong probability of winning

gagne-pain [gaɲpɛ̃] *nm inv* livelihood

gagne-petit [gaɲpəti] *nmf inv* low wage earner

gagner [gaɲe] **1** *vt* (**a**) (*remporter*) (*course, prix, guerre*) to win; **rien n'est encore gagné!** it's not in the bag yet!

    (**b**) (*comme rémunération*) to earn; **g. sa vie** to earn one's living

    (**c**) (*obtenir*) to gain; **g. du temps** (*aller plus vite*) to save time; (*temporiser*) to gain time; **g. de l'espace** to save space; **chercher à g. du temps** to play for time; **c'est toujours ça de gagné** that's something, anyway; **tu as tout à g.** you've got everything to gain; **et moi, qu'est-ce que j'y gagne?** and what do I get out of it?

    (**d**) (*se concilier*) **g. qn à une cause** to win sb over to a cause; **g. la confiance/l'estime de qn** to win *or* to gain sb's confidence/respect

    (**e**) (*atteindre*) (*ville, sortie, porte*) to reach, to get to; (*sujet: maladie, infection*) to spread to; (*sujet: sentiment, sommeil*) to overcome; **le rire gagna l'assemblée tout entière** laughter spread through the whole audience

    (**f**) (*s'étendre à*) (*sujet: feu, épidémie*) to spread to; **g. du terrain** to gain ground

    (**g**) (*battre*) **g. qn de vitesse** to outstrip sb

    2 *vi* (**a**) (*être vainqueur*) to win; **g. haut la main** to win hands down

    (**b**) (*profiter*) **g. à qch/à faire qch** to benefit from sth/from doing sth; **g. à être connu** to improve with acquaintance; **j'ai gagné au change** I got the best of the deal

    (**c**) (*croître*) to increase; **g. en intensité/en vigueur** to increase in intensity/in strength

gagneur, -euse [gaɲœr, -øz] *nm,f* winner

gai, -e [gɛ] *adj* (**a**) (*personne, voix, décor, musique*) cheerful; **g. comme un pinson** happy as a lark; *Fam* **être un peu g.** (*ivre*) to be tipsy; *Ironique* **ça va être g.!** that'll be fun! (**b**) *Belg* (*agréable*) nice, pleasant (**c**) (*homosexuel*) = **gay**

gaiement [gɛmɑ̃] *adv* cheerfully; *Ironique* **allons-y g.!** let's do it!

gaieté [gete] *nf* cheerfulness, gaiety; **je ne le fais pas de g. de cœur** I don't enjoy doing it

gaillard, -e [gajar, -ard] **1** *adj* (**a**) (*vigoureux*) (*personne*) strong; (*vieillard*) sprightly (**b**) (*jovial*) (*humeur*) merry; (*grivois*) (*histoire, commentaire*) bawdy

    2 *nm* (**a**) (*homme*) hearty type; **un grand et solide g.** a great strapping man; **toi mon g., tu ne perds rien pour attendre!** just you wait, buster! (**b**) *Naut* **g. d'avant** forecastle; **g. d'arrière** poop

gaîment [gɛmɑ̃] = **gaiement**

gain [gɛ̃] *nm* (**a**) (*succès*) winning; **avoir** *ou* **obtenir g. de cause** to win one's case; **donner g. de cause à qn** to decide in favor of sb (**b**) (*profit*) gain, profit; **l'appât du g.** the lure of money (**c**) (*économie*) **ça fait un sacré g. de temps/de place** that saves an awful lot of time/space (**d**) **gains** (*au jeu*) winnings; (*à la Bourse*) profit (**e**) *Suisse* **par g. de paix** as a conciliatory gesture

gaine [gɛn] *nf* (**a**) (*étui*) sheath (**b**) *Anat & Bot* sheath (**c**) (*sous-vêtement*) girdle

gainer [gene] *vt* to sheathe (**de** in)

Gal. *Mil* (*abrév* **Général**) Gen.

gala [gala] *nm* gala; **en habit** *ou* **tenue de g.** in gala dress; *Fig* in one's best clothes

galamment [galamɑ̃] *adv* gallantly

galant, -e [galɑ̃, -ɑ̃t] **1** *adj* (*homme*) gallant; **rendez-vous g.** romantic rendezvous

    2 *nm Vieilli & Litt* gallant

galanterie [galɑ̃tri] *nf* gallantry; **dire des galanteries à qn** to pay sb compliments

Galapagos [galapagos] *nfpl* **les (îles) G.** the Galapagos (Islands)

galaxie [galaksi] *nf* galaxy

galbe [galb] *nm* curve

galbé, -e [galbe] *adj* shapely

gale [gal] *nf* (**a**) *Méd* scabies; *Fig* **je n'ai pas la g.!** I haven't got the plague! (**b**) *(de chien, de chat)* mange (**c**) *Bot* scab

galère [galɛr] *nf* (**a**) *(navire)* galley (**b**) *Fam (situation pénible)* hassle; **je me suis mis dans une g. pas possible** I got myself into a terrible mess; **être dans la même g.** to be in the same boat

galérer [34] [galere] *vi Fam* to have a hard time

galerie [galri] *nf* (**a**) *(passage, salle)* gallery; *Can (véranda)* porch; **g. d'art/de portraits** art/portrait gallery; **g. marchande** (shopping) mall (**b**) *(dans une mine)* gallery; *(de taupe)* tunnel (**c**) *(de voiture)* roof rack (**d**) *(de théâtre)* balcony; *Fig* **c'est pour (épater) la g.** it's just showing off

galérien [galerjɛ̃] *nm* galley slave

galet [galɛ] *nm* (**a**) *(caillou)* pebble; **plage de galets** shingle beach (**b**) *Tech* roller

galette [galɛt] *nf* (**a**) *(crêpe de blé noir)* buckwheat pancake; **g. des Rois** Twelfth Night cake (**b**) *(biscuit rond sablé)* butter cookie (**c**) *Belg (gaufrette)* wafer (**d**) *Fam (argent)* dough

galeux, -euse [galø, -øz] *adj (chien)* mangy; *(mur)* peeling

Galice [galis] *nf* **la G.** Galicia

galicien, -enne [galisjɛ̃, -ɛn] **1** *adj* Galician
2 *nm,f* **G., Galicienne** Galician

Galilée¹ [galile] *nf (région)* **la G.** Galilee

Galilée² [galile] *npr* Galileo

galimatias [galimatja] *nm* gibberish

galion [galjɔ̃] *nm* galleon

galipette [galipɛt] *nf Fam* somersault; **faire des galipettes** to do somersaults; *(ébats amoureux)* to have a romp *or* a bit of hanky-panky

galipote [galipɔt] *nf Can* **courir la g.** to chase women

Galles [gal] *voir* **pays**

gallicisme [galisism] *nm* Gallicism

gallois, -e [galwa, -az] **1** *adj* Welsh
2 *nm (langue)* Welsh
3 *nm,f* **G.** Welshman; **Galloise** Welshwoman; **les G.** the Welsh

gallon [galɔ̃] *nm* gallon

gallo-romain, -e *(mpl* **gallo-romains,** *fpl* **gallo-romaines)** [galorɔmɛ̃, -ɛn] *adj* Gallo-Roman

galoche [galɔʃ] *nf* clog *(with leather upper)*

galon [galɔ̃] *nm* (**a**) *(en couture)* braid (**b**) *(de militaire)* stripe; *Fam* **prendre du g.** to get promoted (**c**) *Can* **g. (à mesurer)** measuring tape

galop [galo] *nm* gallop; **au g.** at a gallop; *Fig* **allez, au travail et au g.!** come on, to work, and be quick about it!; **g. d'essai** trial run

galopade [galɔpad] *nf* (**a**) *(de cheval)* gallop (**b**) *(de personnes)* stampede

galopant, -e [galɔpɑ̃, -ɑ̃t] *adj (inflation)* galloping; *Vieilli Méd* **phtisie galopante** galloping consumption

galoper [galɔpe] *vi (cheval)* to gallop; *(enfant)* to charge

galopin [galɔpɛ̃] *nm Fam* urchin; **espèce de petit g.!** you little rascal!

galure [galyr] *nm,* **galurin** [galyrɛ̃] *nm Fam* hat

galvaniser [galvanize] *vt* to galvanize

galvauder [galvode] **1** *vt (nom, réputation)* to bring into disrepute; *(talents, dons)* to prostitute; *(mot)* to overuse
2 se galvauder *vpr* to damage one's reputation

gambade [gɑ̃bad] *nf* leap

gambader [gɑ̃bade] *vi* to leap *or* to frisk about

gambas [gɑ̃bas] *nfpl* large prawns

gamberger [45] [gɑ̃bɛrʒe] *vi Fam* to think hard

gambette [gɑ̃bɛt] *nf Fam (jambe)* leg

Gambie [gɑ̃bi] *nf* **la G.** the Gambia

gamelle [gamɛl] *nf (de soldat)* mess kit; *(d'ouvrier)* lunch pail;

(d'animal) bowl; *Hum (assiette)* plate; *Fam aussi Fig* **(se) ramasser** *ou* **(se) prendre une g.** to take a spill

gamète [gamɛt] *nm* gamete

gamin, -e [gamɛ̃, -in] **1** *nm,f (enfant)* kid; **une gamine de dix ans** a girl of ten
2 *adj* (**a**) *(jeune)* **elle était encore toute gamine** she was still just a child (**b**) *(puéril)* childish

gaminerie [gaminri] *nf (acte)* childish prank; *(comportement)* childishness

gamme [gam] *nf* (**a**) *(de couleurs, de prix, d'articles)* line, range; **produit bas/haut de g.** bottom-of-the-line/top-of-the-line product (**b**) *Mus* scale

gammée [game] *adj f voir* **croix**

ganache [ganaʃ] *nf* (**a**) *Fam (imbécile)* **vieille g.** old fool (**b**) *(d'un cheval)* lower jaw

Gand [gɑ̃] *n* Ghent

gang [gɑ̃g] *nm* gang

Gange [gɑ̃ʒ] *nm* **le G.** the Ganges

ganglion [gɑ̃glijɔ̃] *nm* ganglion; **j'ai des ganglions** I've got swollen glands

gangrène [gɑ̃grɛn] *nf* (**a**) *Méd* gangrene (**b**) *Fig* canker

gangrener [46] [gɑ̃grəne] **1** *vt* (**a**) *Méd* to turn gangrenous (**b**) *Fig* to corrupt
2 se gangrener *vpr* (**a**) *Méd* to go gangrenous (**b**) *Fig* to become corrupt

gangster [gɑ̃gstɛr] *nm* gangster

gangstérisme [gɑ̃gsterism] *nm* gangsterism

gangue [gɑ̃g] *nf (de minerai)* gangue; *(couche) (de boue, de glace)* layer; *Fig (carcan)* straitjacket

gant [gɑ̃] *nm* glove; **g. de base-ball** baseball mitt; **g. de boxe** boxing glove; **gants de caoutchouc** rubber gloves; **g. de toilette** ≃ washcloth; *Fig* **cela vous va comme un g.** it fits you like a glove; **prendre** *ou* **mettre des gants avec qn** to handle sb with kid gloves; **jeter le g. à qn** to throw down the gauntlet to sb; **relever le g.** to take up the gauntlet

ganté, -e [gɑ̃te] *adj (personne)* wearing gloves; *(main)* gloved

gantelet [gɑ̃tlɛ] *nm* gauntlet

garage [garaʒ] *nm (pour se garer, pour les réparations)* garage; **g. de** *ou* **à bicyclettes** bicycle shed; **g. d'autobus** bus depot; *Can* **vente de g.** garage sale

garagiste [garaʒist] *nmf (propriétaire)* garage owner; *(mécanicien)* garage mechanic

garant, -e [garɑ̃, -ɑ̃t] *nm,f* guarantor; **se porter g. de qn** *(à la banque)* to stand guarantor for sb; **se porter g. de qch** to vouch for sth

garantie [garɑ̃ti] *nf* (**a**) *(précaution)* guarantee, safeguard (**contre** against) (**b**) *(de produit)* guarantee, warranty; **être sous g.** to be under guarantee (**c**) *(certitude)* guarantee

garantir [garɑ̃tir] *vt* (**a**) *(promettre)* to guarantee; **g. à qn que** to give sb a guarantee that; **je te le garantis** I can vouch for it (**b**) *Fin (émission d'actions)* to underwrite; *(emprunt)* to secure (**c**) *(protéger)* to protect (**de** from)

garce [gars] *nf Fam* bitch

garçon [garsɔ̃] *nm* (**a**) *(enfant mâle, fils)* boy; *(jeune homme)* young man; **un mauvais g.** a bad sort; **vieux g.** confirmed bachelor; **g. manqué** tomboy (**b**) *(serveur)* waiter; **g. d'ascenseur** elevator operator; **g. de café** waiter; **g. d'honneur** best man

garçonne [garsɔn] *nf* **être coiffée à la g.** to have an urchin cut

garçonnet [garsɔnɛ] *nm* little boy

garçonnière [garsɔnjɛr] *nf* bachelor apartment

garde¹ [gard] *nf* (**a**) *(protection)* care; *Jur* **g. des enfants** *(après un divorce)* custody of the children (**b**) *(surveillance)* guarding; **être de g.** to be on duty; **monter la g.** to mount guard; **médecin de g.** doctor on call; **pharmacie de g.** emergency drug store (**c**) *(méfiance)* **mettre qn en g. contre qn/qch** to warn sb against sb/sth; **être** *ou* **se tenir sur ses gardes** to be on one's guard; **prendre g. à qn/qch** to watch out for sb/sth; **prendre g. que... (ne)** + *subjunctive* to be careful that...; **prendre g. de ne pas faire qch** to be careful not to do sth (**d**) *(groupe de soldats)* **la g.** the guard; **g. d'honneur** guard of honor; **la G. républicaine** the Republican Guard *(of Paris)* (**e**) *Jur* **g. à vue** police custody; **il a été mis/est resté en g. à vue** he was put/was held in police custody (**f**) *(en boxe, en escrime)* guard; **se mettre en g.** to take one's guard; **en g.!** on guard! (**g**) *Aut* **g. au sol** ground clearance (**h**) *(d'une épée)* hilt

garde² [gard] **1** *nm* (**a**) *(soldat) (sentinelle)* guard; *(dans une garde)* guardsman; **g. mobile** = member of the security police (**b**) *(dans un domaine particulier)* **g. champêtre** rural policeman; **g. du corps** bodyguard; **g. forestier** forest ranger (**c**) **le g. des Sceaux** the (French) Minister of Justice

2 *nmf* **g. de nuit** *(pour un malade)* night nurse *(privately employed)*; **g. d'enfants** babysitter

garde-à-vous [gardavu] *nm inv Mil* (position of) attention; **se mettre/être au g.** to stand to attention; **g.!** attention!

garde-barrière *(pl* **gardes-barrière(s))** [gardəbarjɛr] *nmf* grade-crossing gatekeeper

garde-boue [gardəbu] *nm inv* mudguard

garde-chasse *(pl* **gardes-chasse(s))** [gardəʃas] *nm* gamekeeper

garde-chiourme *(pl* **gardes-chiourme(s))** [gardəʃjurm] *nm (personne autoritaire et brutale)* martinet

garde-côte *(pl* **garde-côtes)** [gardəkot] *nm (bateau)* coastguard vessel

garde-feu [gardəfø] *nm inv* (**a**) *(grille)* fireguard (**b**) *Can (personne)* forest warden

garde-fou *(pl* **garde-fous)** [gardəfu] *nm (mur)* parapet; *(rambarde)* railing; *Fig* safeguard

garde-malade *(pl* **gardes-malade(s))** [gardəmalad] *nmf* nurse

garde-manger [gardəmɑ̃ʒe] *nm inv* pantry

garde-meuble *(pl* **garde-meubles)** [gardəmœbl] *nm* furniture warehouse; **mettre une table au g.** to put a table into storage

gardénia [gardenja] *nm* gardenia

garder [garde] **1** *vt* (**a**) *(conserver)* to keep; **g. qn à dîner** to get sb to stay for dinner; **g. la chambre** to keep to *or* to stay in one's room; **devoir g. le lit** to be confined to bed; **g. la tête froide** to keep a cool head (**b**) *(surveiller) (maison, sac, enfants)* to look after, to mind; *Jur* **g. qn à vue** to hold sb in custody (**c**) *(protéger)* to protect (**de** from); **que Dieu nous garde!** God protect us!

2 se garder *vpr* (**a**) *(se méfier)* **se g. de qn/qch** to beware of sb/sth (**b**) *(s'abstenir)* **se g. de faire qch** to be careful not to do sth (**c**) *Fam (conserver)* **tes réflexions, tu peux te les g.!** you can keep your thoughts to yourself! (**d**) *(se conserver) (denrées)* to keep

garderie [gardəri] *nf* daycare center; *(dans un magasin, une université)* babysitting service; *(le soir, après l'école)* babysitting service

garde-robe *(pl* **garde-robes)** [gardərob] *nf (armoire, vêtements)* wardrobe

gardien, -enne [gardjɛ̃, -ɛn] **1** *nm,f (concierge)* janitor; *(d'immeuble d'appartements)* superintendent; *(de musée, de parking)* attendant; *Fig (de libertés, traditions)* guardian; **g. de but** goalkeeper; **g. de nuit** night watchman; **g. de la paix** policeman; **g. de prison** prison guard

2 gardienne *nf* (**a**) *(personne)* **gardienne d'enfants** daycare worker (**b**) *Belg (école)* nursery school, kindergarten

gardiennage [gardjɛnaʒ] *nm (d'un bâtiment)* caretaking; *(de locaux)* guarding; **société de g.** security firm

gardon [gardɔ̃] *nm* roach; *Fig* **frais comme un g.** fresh as a daisy

gare¹ [gar] *nf* station; **g. maritime** harbor station; **g. de marchandises** freight station; **g. routière** bus station; **g. de triage** switchyard

gare² [gar] *exclam* (**a**) *(menace)* **g. à toi si on l'apprend** woe betide you if anyone finds out; *Fam* **si je te reprends à voler du gâteau, g. à tes fesses!** if I catch you stealing cake again, you've had it! (**b**) *(attention)* **g. aux orties!** mind the nettles!; **sans crier g.** without warning

garer [gare] **1** *vt (voiture)* to park

2 se garer *vpr* (**a**) *(automobiliste)* to park (**b**) **se g. de qn/qch** to steer clear of sb/sth; *Fam* **garez-vous!** get out of the way!

gargariser [gargarize] **se gargariser** *vpr* to gargle; *Fam Péj* **se g. de qch** to revel in sth

gargarisme [gargarism] *nm (produit)* mouthwash; *(action)* gargling; **faire des gargarismes** to gargle

gargote [gargɔt] *nf Péj* cheap restaurant

gargouillement [gargujmɑ̃] *nm* gurgling; *(d'estomac)* rumbling

gargouiller [garguje] *vi* (**a**) *(eau)* to gurgle (**b**) *(estomac)* to rumble

gargouillis [garguji] = **gargouillement**

garnement [garnəmɑ̃] *nm* scamp, rascal

garni, -e [garni] *adj* (**a**) **bien g.** *(bourse)* well-lined (**b**) *(plat, viande)* with vegetables

garnir [garnir] *vt* (**a**) *(munir)* to fit out (**de** with); *(commode, tiroir)* to line; *(siège) (rembourrer)* to stuff; *(couvrir)* to cover (**b**) *(embellir) (robe, chapeau)* to trim (**de** with) (**c**) *Culin (plat)* to garnish (**d**) *(remplir)* to fill (**de** with); *(cave)* to stock (**de** with)

garnison [garnizɔ̃] *nf* garrison; **ville de g.** garrison town; **être en g. à** to be garrisoned at

garniture [garnityr] *nf* (**a**) *(ornement) (d'un chapeau, d'une robe)* trimming; **g. de lit** bedding; **g. de cheminée** mantelpiece ornaments (**b**) *(d'un plat)* garnish; *(légumes)* vegetables; *(d'un vol-au-vent)* filling (**c**) *Aut* **g. d'embrayage** clutch lining; **g. de frein** brake lining; *(de disque de frein)* brake pad

Garonne [garɔn] *nf* **la G.** the Garonne

garrigue [garig] *nf* scrubland *(typical of southern France)*

garrocher [garɔʃe] *vt Can Fam* to throw

garrot¹ [garo] *nm* (**a**) *Méd* tourniquet (**b**) *(supplice)* garrote

garrot² [garo] *nm (de quadrupède)* withers; **mesurer 1,20 m au g.** to be 12 hands high

garrotter [garɔte] *vt (prisonnier)* to tie up; *Fig (opposants)* to muzzle

gars [gɑ] *nm Fam (jeune homme)* lad; *(homme)* guy

Gascogne [gaskɔɲ] *nf* **la G.** Gascony

gas-oil, gasoil [gazɔjl, gazwal] *nm* diesel oil

gaspillage [gaspijaʒ] *nm (d'argent, de nourriture, de temps)* wasting; **c'est du g.** it's a waste; **quel g.!** what a waste!

gaspiller [gaspije] *vt* to waste

gastéropode [gasterɔpɔd] *nm Zool* gastropod

gastrique [gastrik] *adj* gastric; **embarras g.** upset stomach

gastrite [gastrit] *nf Méd* gastritis

gastro-entérite *(pl* **gastro-entérites)** [gastroɑ̃terit] *nf Méd* gastroenteritis

gastro-entérologue *(pl* **gastro-entérologues)** [gastroɑ̃terɔlɔg] *nmf Méd* gastroenterologist

gastro-intestinal, -e, -aux, -ales [gastroɛ̃testinal, -o] *adj Méd* gastrointestinal

gastronome [gastrɔnɔm] *nmf* gastronome, gourmet

gastronomie [gastrɔnɔmi] *nf* gastronomy

gastronomique [gastrɔnɔmik] *adj* gastronomic

gastropode [gastrɔpɔd] *nm Zool* gastropod

gâté, -e [gɑte] *adj* (**a**) *(pourri) (fruit, dents)* bad (**b**) *Fig (enfant)* spoiled

gâteau, -x [gɑto] *nm* cake; *Suisse (tarte)* pie; **faire un g.** to make *or* to bake a cake; *Fam* **c'est du g.** it's a piece of cake; *Fam* **ce n'est pas du g.** it's no easy thing; *Fam* **se partager le g.** to share out the pie; **g. d'anniversaire** birthday cake; **g. de riz** rice pudding; **g. sec** cookie

gâter [gɑte] **1** *vt* (a) *(gâcher)* to spoil (b) *(choyer) (personne)* to spoil; **on n'est pas gâtés!** just our luck!

2 se gâter *vpr (affaires, temps)* to take a turn for the worse; *(aliment)* to go bad

gâterie [gɑtri] *nf (petit cadeau, friandise)* treat

gâteux, -euse [gɑtø, -øz] *Fam* **1** *nm,f* old dodderer

2 *adj (sénile)* senile; **avec leurs petits-enfants, ils sont complètement g.** they're totally gaga over their grandchildren

gâtisme [gɑtism] *nm* senility

GATT [gat] *nm Écon (abrév* **General Agreement on Tariffs and Trade)** **le G.** GATT

gauche [goʃ] **1** *adj* (a) *(par opposition à droite)* left (b) *(maladroit) (personne, attitude, démarche, style)* awkward, clumsy (c) *Tech (déformé)* warped

2 *nf* (a) *(côté)* left; **à ma g.** on my left; **le tiroir de g.** the left-hand drawer; **à g. (de)** on the left (of); **tournez à g.** turn left; **conduire à g.** to drive on the left; *Fam* **mettre de l'argent à g.** to put some money away (b) *Pol* **la g.** the left; **politique/ gouvernement de g.** left-wing politics/government; **voter à g.** to vote for the left; *Fam* **la g. caviar** champagne socialism; **la g. plurielle** = the rainbow coalition of socialists, communists and environmentalists in the government of Lionel Jospin *(elected in 1997)*

3 *nm (en boxe)* left; **un crochet du g.** a left hook; **un direct du g.** a straight left

gaucher, -ère [goʃe, -ɛr] **1** *adj* left-handed

2 *nm,f* left-hander

gauchisant, -e [goʃizɑ̃, -ɑ̃t] *adj* leftish, with a left-leaning bias

gauchisme [goʃism] *nm* leftism

gauchiste [goʃist] *adj & nmf* leftist

gaufre [gofr] *nf* waffle

gaufrette [gofrɛt] *nf* wafer (biscuit)

gaufrier [gofrije] *nm* waffle iron

Gaule [gol] *nf* **la G.** Gaul

gaule [gol] *nf* pole; *(pour pêcher)* fishing rod

gauler [gole] *vt* (a) *(arbre fruitier, noyer)* to beat; *(fruits, noix)* to bring down *(using a pole)* (b) *Fam (attraper)* to nab; **se faire g.** to get nabbed

gaullisme [golism] *nm* Gaullism

> **Gaullisme**
>
> The political ideology inspired by the ideas of General de Gaulle includes nationalism, independence from foreign powers, and a strong executive. Gaullists are strongly committed to the defense of France's prestige on the international scene.

gaulliste [golist] *adj & nmf* Gaullist

gaulois, -e [golwa, -az] **1** *adj* Gallic; **esprit g.** bawdy humor

2 *nmp* **les G.** the Gauls

3 *nf* **Gauloise**® *(popular brand of cigarette)*

gauloiserie [golwazri] *nf (plaisanterie)* bawdy joke; *(caractère)* bawdiness

gausser [gose] **se gausser** *vpr Litt* **se g. de qn** to mock sb; **vous vous gaussez!** you jest!

gaver [gave] **1** *vt (engraisser) (volaille)* to force-feed; *(personne) (de nourriture)* to stuff (**de** with); *Fig* **g. qn de qch** to force-feed sb sth

2 se gaver *vpr Fam* to stuff oneself (**de** with); *Fig* **se g. de romans policiers/jeux vidéo** to read detective novels/play video games till they're coming out of one's ears

gay [gɛ] *adj & nmf (homosexuel)* gay; **il/elle est g.** he's/she's gay

gaz [gaz] *nm* gas; *Fam* **il y a de l'eau dans le g.** things aren't going too well; *Fam* **mettre les g.** to step on the gas; *Aviat* to open up the throttle; **avoir des g.** to have wind; **g. carbonique** carbon dioxide; **g. de combat** poison gas; **g. d'échappement** exhaust fumes; **g. à effet de serre** greenhouse gas; **g. hilarant** laughing gas; **g. lacrymogène** tear gas; **g. naturel** natural gas; **g. de ville** gas mains; **avoir le g. de ville** to be connected to the gas main

Gaza [gaza] *n* **la bande de G.** the Gaza Strip

gaze [gaz] *nf* gauze

gazé, -e [gaze] **1** *adj* gassed

2 *nm,f (poison)* gas victim

gazéifier [66] [gazeifje] *vt* to gasify; *(boissons)* to carbonate

gazelle [gazɛl] *nf* gazelle; **avoir des yeux de g.** to be doe-eyed

gazer [gaze] **1** *vt (asphyxier)* to gas

2 *vi Fam* **ça gaze!** everything's OK!; **ça gaze?** how's it going?

gazette [gazɛt] *nf (journal)* newspaper

gazeux, -euse [gazø, -øz] *adj* (a) *(eau, boisson)* fizzy, carbonated (b) *Chim* gaseous

gazinière [gazinjɛr] *nf* gas stove

gazoduc [gazɔdyk] *nm* gas pipeline

gazole [gazɔl] *nm* diesel oil

gazomètre [gazɔmɛtr] *nm* gasometer

gazon [gazɔ̃] *nm* (a) *(herbe)* grass, turf (b) *(surface)* lawn

gazonner [gazɔne] *vt* to turf

gazouillement [gazujmɑ̃] *nm (des oiseaux)* twittering, chirping; *(d'un bébé)* gurgling; *(d'un ruisseau)* babbling

gazouiller [gazuje] *vi (oiseau)* to twitter, to chirp; *(bébé)* to gurgle; *(eau)* to babble

gazouillis [gazuji] = **gazouillement**

GDF [ʒedeɛf] *nm (abrév* **Gaz de France)** = French gas company

geai [ʒɛ] *nm* jay

géant, -e [ʒeɑ̃, -ɑ̃t] **1** *adj* (a) *(arbre, écran)* giant, gigantic; *(paquet)* giant(-size) (b) *Fam (formidable)* **c'est g.!** it's fantastic!

2 *nm,f* giant; *Fig* **les géants de la littérature classique** the giants *or* great names of classical literature; *Fig* **avancer** *ou* **aller à pas de g.** to make great strides

geignard, -e [ʒɛɲar, -ard] *Fam* **1** *adj* whining

2 *nm,f* whiner

geindre [54] [ʒɛ̃dr] *vi* (a) *(gémir)* to moan, to groan (**de** with) (b) *Fam (se plaindre constamment)* to whine

gel [ʒɛl] *nm* (a) *(verglas)* frost; *Fig* **g. des négociations** suspension of negotiations; **g. des prix/salaires** price/wage freeze (b) *(produit cosmétique)* gel; **g. coiffant** hair gel; **g. douche** shower gel

gélatine [ʒelatin] *nf* gelatine

gélatineux, -euse [ʒelatinø, -øz] *adj* gelatinous

gelé, -e [ʒəle] *adj* (a) *(lac, rivière)* frozen; *(plante)* frost-nipped (b) *Méd (orteil, doigt)* frostbitten (c) *(très froid)* frozen; **j'ai les pieds gelés/les mains gelées** my feet/hands are frozen (d) *(bloqué) (fonds)* frozen; *(négociations)* suspended

gelée [ʒəle] *nf* (a) *(gel)* frost; **g. blanche** hoarfrost (b) *Culin (confiture)* jelly; *(dessert)* Jell-O®; **gelée de framboises** raspberry jelly; **g. royale** royal jelly

geler [39] [ʒəle] **1** *vt* (a) *(lac, rivière, liquide)* to freeze; **fleurs/ salades gelées par le froid** flowers/lettuces nipped by the frost (b) *Fin (bloquer) (crédits, capital)* to freeze

2 *vi (lac, rivière)* to freeze (over); **on gèle dans cette salle** it's freezing in this room

3 *v impersonnel* **il gèle** it's freezing; **il gèle à pierre fendre** it's freezing hard; **il a gelé blanc cette nuit** there was a frost last night

4 se geler *vpr Fam* to freeze

gélifiant [ʒelifjɑ̃] *nm* gelling agent

gélule [ʒelyl] *nf* capsule

gelure [ʒəlyr] *nf* frostbite

Gémeaux [ʒemo] *nmpl Astron & Astrol* Gemini; **être G.** to be (a) Gemini

gémir [ʒemir] *vi (personne)* to groan, to moan (**de** with); *(vent)* to moan

gémissant, -e [ʒemisɑ̃, -ɑ̃t] *adj (personne)* groaning; *(voix)* wailing

gémissement [ʒemismɑ̃] *nm (d'une personne)* groan, moan; *(de vent)* moaning

gemme [ʒɛm] *nf* (a) *(pierre)* gem(stone) (b) *(résine)* pine resin

gênant, -e [ʒɛnɑ̃, -ɑ̃t] *adj* (a) *(témoin, situation, silence)* awkward; *(bruit, lumière)* irritating (b) *(encombrant) (objet)* cumbersome

gencive [ʒɑ̃siv] *nf* gum

gendarme [ʒɑ̃darm] *nm* gendarme, policeman; **jouer aux gendarmes et aux voleurs** to play cops and robbers; *Fam* **faire la g.** to lay down the law; **g. couché** speed bump; **g. mobile** = member of the flying squad

gendarmerie [ʒɑ̃darməri] *nf* (a) *(corps) (en France)* gendarmerie, police force; **g. mobile** = flying squad; **g. nationale** national police force; **la G. royale du Canada** the Royal Canadian Mounted Police (b) *(lieu)* gendarmes' headquarters

gendre [ʒɑ̃dr] *nm* son-in-law

gène [ʒɛn] *nm* gene

gêne [ʒɛn] *nf* (a) *(confusion)* embarrassment; **ressentir de la g.** to feel embarrassed; **où (il) y a de la g., (il n')y a pas de plaisir** we don't need to stand on ceremony (b) *(dérangement)* inconvenience (c) *(difficulté physique)* discomfort; **g. respiratoire** difficulty in breathing (d) *(manque d'argent)* **être dans la g.** to be in financial difficulties

gêné, -e [ʒene] *adj* (a) *(embarrassé)* embarrassed; *Fam* **il n'est pas g., lui!** he has a nerve! (b) *(serré)* **être g. dans un vêtement** to be uncomfortable in a garment (c) *(qui manque d'argent)* in financial difficulties

généalogie [ʒenealɔʒi] *nf* genealogy

généalogique [ʒenealɔʒik] *adj* genealogical; **arbre g.** family tree

gêner [ʒene] **1** *vt* (a) *(perturber) (sujet: bruit, fumée, chaleur)* to bother; *(opérations, déroulement)* to hamper; **g. la circulation** to hold up the traffic; **g. le passage** to be in the way; **pousse-toi, tu me gênes!** move over, you're in my way!; **ça te gêne si je fume?** do you mind if I smoke?; **cela ne te gênerait pas de me prêter ta voiture?** would you mind lending me your car?; **ce qui me gêne, c'est que…** what bothers me is that…; **sa présence me gêne** I feel awkward in his/her presence (b) *(être source d'inconfort)* **cette ceinture/ce col me gêne** this belt/this collar is uncomfortable (c) *(embarrasser)* to embarrass; **ça me gênerait de le rencontrer** I'd feel uncomfortable meeting him; *Fam* **et alors, ça te gêne?** what's it to you?

2 se gêner *vpr* (a) **je ne me suis pas gêné pour le lui dire** I didn't hesitate to tell him/her so; **elle aurait tort de se g.** she shouldn't feel bad about it; *aussi Ironique* **ne vous gênez pas pour moi!** don't mind me! (b) *(dans un lieu)* to be in each other's way (c) *Suisse (être intimidé)* to be shy

général, -e, -aux, -ales [ʒeneral, -o] **1** *adj* general; **assemblée/amnistie générale** general assembly/amnesty; **l'intérêt g.** the general interest; **à la surprise générale** to everyone's surprise; **à la demande générale** by popular request; **d'une façon générale** generally speaking; **en g.** *(globalement)* in general; *(habituellement)* as a rule, generally

2 *nm* (a) *Mil* general (b) *(ce qui est universel)* **passer du g. au particulier** to go from the general to the particular

3 *nf* **générale** (a) *Théât* dress rehearsal (b) *(femme de général)* general's wife

généralement [ʒeneralmɑ̃] *adv* generally

généralisation [ʒeneralizasjɔ̃] *nf* generalization

généraliser [ʒeneralize] **1** *vt* to generalize; *Méd* **un cancer généralisé** a generalized cancer

2 *vi* to generalize

3 se généraliser *vpr (utilisation, usage, phénomène)* to become widespread; *(conflit, grève)* to spread

généraliste [ʒeneralist] *adj & nmf* **(médecin) g.** general practitioner, GP

généralité [ʒeneralite] *nf* (a) *(notion générale)* generality; **s'en tenir à des généralités** to confine oneself to generalities (b) *(majorité)* **la g. de** the majority of

générateur, -trice [ʒeneratœr, -tris] **1** *adj (machine)* generating; *(organe)* generative; **être g. de** to generate

2 *nm* generator; *Ordinat* **g. de caractères** character generator; **g. d'effets numériques** digital-effects generator; **g. d'effets spéciaux** (special-)effects generator; **g. graphique** graphics generator

3 *nf* **génératrice** generator

génération [ʒenerasjɔ̃] *nf* (a) *(classe d'âge, degrés de filiation)* generation (b) *(action de produire)* generation; *Biol* **g. spontanée** spontaneous generation

générer [34] [ʒenere] *vt* to generate

généreusement [ʒenerøzmɑ̃] *adv* generously

généreux, -euse [ʒenerø, -øz] *adj* generous; **une terre généreuse** a fertile soil; **elle a des formes généreuses** she has generous curves

générique [ʒenerik] **1** *adj* generic

2 *nm Cin & TV* credits; **g. de fin** closing credits

générosité [ʒenerozite] *nf* generosity; **avec g.** generously

Gênes [ʒɛn] *n* Genoa

genèse [ʒənɛz] *nf* genesis; **la G.** Genesis

genêt [ʒənɛ] *nm* broom

généticien, -enne [ʒenetisjɛ̃, -ɛn] *nm,f* geneticist

génétique [ʒenetik] **1** *adj* genetic

2 *nf* genetics *(singulier)*

génétiquement [ʒenetikmɑ̃] *adv* genetically; **g. modifié** genetically modified

gêneur, -euse [ʒenœr, -øz] *nm,f* nuisance

Genève [ʒənɛv] *n* Geneva

genevois, -e [ʒənvwa, -az] **1** *adj* Genevan

2 *nm,f* **G., Genevoise** Genevan

genévrier [ʒənevrije] *nm* juniper

génial, -e, -aux, -ales [ʒenjal, -o] *adj* (a) *(invention, œuvre, artiste)* brilliant (b) *Fam (extraordinaire)* fantastic, great

génialement [ʒenjalmɑ̃] *adv* brilliantly

génie[1] [ʒeni] *nm* (a) *(qualité, personne)* genius; **avoir du g.** to be a genius; **une idée/invention de g.** a brilliant idea/invention; **un trait de g.** a stroke of genius; **avoir le g. de qch/pour faire qch** to have a genius for sth/for doing sth (b) *(être mythique)* genie; **son bon/mauvais g.** his good/evil genius

génie[2] [ʒeni] *nm Mil* **le (corps du) g.** ≃ the Engineers; **g. civil** civil engineering; *(corps)* civil engineers; **g. génétique** genetic engineering

genièvre [ʒənjɛvr] *nm (fruit)* juniper berry; *(arbre)* juniper (tree)

génique [ʒenik] *adj Méd* **thérapie g.** gene therapy

génisse [ʒenis] *nf* heifer

génital, -e, -aux, -ales [ʒenital, -o] *adj (glandes, hormones)* genital

géniteur, -trice [ʒenitœr, -tris] *nm,f Hum* parent

génocide [ʒenɔsid] *nm* genocide

génoise [ʒenwaz] *nf (gâteau)* sponge cake

génome [ʒenom] *nm Biol* genome

génothérapie [ʒenɔterapi] *nf Biol* genotherapy, gene therapy

génotype [ʒenotip] nm Biol genotype

genou, -x [ʒənu] nm knee; **enfoncé jusqu'aux genoux dans la boue** knee-deep in mud; **avoir les genoux en dedans** to be knock-kneed; **être à genoux** to be kneeling (down), to be on one's knees; **se mettre à genoux** to kneel (down); Fig **être à genoux devant qn** to worship sb; Fig **demander qch à genoux** to ask for sth on bended knee; Fig **être sur les genoux** to be on one's last legs; **tenir un enfant sur ses genoux** to hold a child on one's knee or one's lap

genouillère [ʒənujɛr] nf (protection du genou) kneepad; Méd knee bandage

genre [ʒɑr] nm (a) (sorte) kind, sort; **en tout g., en tous genres** of all kinds; **très bon dans son g.** very good in its own way; **c'est ce qu'on fait de mieux dans le g.** it's the best of its kind; **c'est tout à fait son g. d'arriver en retard** it's just like him/her to be late; **ce n'est pas le g. (de femme) à se plaindre** she's not the sort (of woman) to complain; **tu vois le g.** you know the sort; **un vin blanc g. sauternes** a white wine similar to Sauternes (b) (artistique, littéraire) genre; **le g. comique** comedy (c) (race) **le g. humain** the human race (d) (goût) **ça fait bon/mauvais g.** it's in good/bad taste (e) Gram gender

gens [ʒɑ̃] nmpl (individus) people; **les g. du pays** ou **du coin** the local people; **jeunes g.** (garçons et filles) young people; (jeunes hommes) young men; **g. de lettres** men and women of letters; **g. du voyage** traveling people

gent [ʒɑ̃] nf Vieilli ou Hum **la g. féminine/masculine** the fair/male sex

gentiane [ʒɑ̃sjan] nf (plante) gentian

gentil, -ille [ʒɑ̃ti, -ij] adj (a) (aimable) kind, nice (**avec** to); (sage) good; **sois g., ferme la fenêtre** do me a favor and close the window (b) (considérable) **une gentille somme** a nice little sum

gentilhomme [ʒɑ̃tijom] (pl **gentilshommes** [ʒɑ̃tizom]) nm gentleman

gentillesse [ʒɑ̃tijɛs] nf (bonté) kindness; **auriez-vous la g. de…?** would you be so kind as to…?; **elle a eu la g. de venir elle-même** she was kind enough to come herself; **dire des gentillesses à qn** to say kind things to sb

gentillet, -ette [ʒɑ̃tijɛ, -ɛt] adj Péj (roman, film) pleasant enough

gentiment [ʒɑ̃timɑ̃] adv (aimablement) kindly; (sagement) nicely

génuflexion [ʒenyflɛksjɔ̃] nf genuflexion; **faire une g.** to genuflect

géo [ʒeo] nf Fam Scol geog

géographe [ʒeograf] nmf geographer

géographie [ʒeografi] nf geography; **g. humaine/physique** human/physical geography

géographique [ʒeografik] adj geographic(al)

geôle [ʒol] nf Litt jail

geôlier, -ère [ʒolje, -ɛr] nm,f Litt jailer

géologie [ʒeoloʒi] nf geology

géologique [ʒeoloʒik] adj geological

géologue [ʒeolog] nmf geologist

géomètre [ʒeomɛtr] nm (**arpenteur**) **g.** (land) surveyor

géométrie [ʒeometri] nf geometry; **g. dans l'espace** solid geometry; **à g. variable** (avion) swing-wing; Fig that varies according to circumstances

géométrique [ʒeometrik] adj geometric(al)

géophysicien, -enne [ʒeofizisjɛ̃, -ɛn] nm,f geophysicist

géophysique [ʒeofizik] **1** adj geophysical
2 nf geophysics (singulier)

géopolitique [ʒeopolitik] **1** adj geopolitical
2 nf geopolitics (singulier)

Géorgie [ʒeorʒi] nf **la G.** (aux États-Unis, dans le Caucase) Georgia

géorgien, -enne [ʒeorʒjɛ̃, -ɛn] **1** adj Georgian
2 nm,f **G., Géorgienne** Georgian

géostationnaire [ʒeostasjonɛr] adj voir **satellite**

géothermie [ʒeotɛrmi] nf geothermics (singulier)

géothermique [ʒeotɛrmik] adj geothermal

gérance [ʒerɑ̃s] nf management; **prendre un commerce en g.** to take over the management of a business

géranium [ʒeranjom] nm geranium

gérant, -e [ʒerɑ̃, -ɑ̃t] nm,f manager

gerbe [ʒɛrb] nf (de blé) sheaf; (d'étincelles) shower; (d'eau) spray; **g. (de fleurs)** spray of flowers

gerber [ʒɛrbe] vi Vulg (vomir) to puke, to barf; Fig **ça me fait g.** it makes me want to throw up or to puke

gercé, -e [ʒɛrse] adj chapped

gercer [16] [ʒɛrse] **1** vt & vi to chap
2 se gercer vpr to chap

gerçure [ʒɛrsyr] nf **avoir des gerçures (aux mains/lèvres)** to have chapped hands/lips

gérer [34] [ʒere] vt to manage

gériatrie [ʒerjatri] nf Méd geriatrics (singulier)

gériatrique [ʒerjatrik] adj Méd geriatric

germain, -e [ʒɛrmɛ̃, -ɛn] adj voir **cousin[1]**

germanique [ʒɛrmanik] adj (a) Hist (relatif aux Germains) Germanic (b) (allemand) German (c) (langue) Germanic

germanophone [ʒɛrmanofon] **1** adj German-speaking
2 nmf German speaker

germe [ʒɛrm] nm (embryon, virus) germ; (de pomme de terre) eye; Fig **les germes de** (origine) the seeds of; **germes de soja** bean sprouts

germer [ʒɛrme] vi (plante, idée) to germinate; (pommes de terre) to sprout

germination [ʒɛrminasjɔ̃] nf Biol germination

gérondif [ʒerɔ̃dif] nm Gram gerund; (cas latin) gerundive

gérontologie [ʒerɔ̃tɔlɔʒi] nf Méd gerontology

gérontologue [ʒerɔ̃tɔlɔg] nmf Méd gerontologist

gésier [ʒezje] nm gizzard

gésir [40] [ʒezir] vi Litt to lie; **ci-gît…** (sur une tombe) here lies…

gestation [ʒɛstasjɔ̃] nf Biol gestation; Fig **en g.** in preparation

geste [ʒɛst] nm (a) (mouvement) gesture; **faire un g.** to make a gesture; **pas un g. ou je tire!** one move and I'll shoot!; **il lui montra la porte d'un g.** he motioned her toward the door; **d'un g. de la main** with a wave of the hand; **écarter qn d'un g.** to wave sb aside; **joindre le g. à la parole** to suit the action to the word (b) (action) gesture; **un beau g.** a nice gesture; **faire un g.** to make a gesture

gesticuler [ʒɛstikyle] vi to gesticulate

gestion [ʒɛstjɔ̃] nf management; **g. de bases de données** database management; Ordinat **g. des couleurs** color management; **g. d'entreprise** business management; Ordinat **g. de fichiers** file management; Ordinat **g. de mémoire** memory management; **g. sonore** sound handling, sound management; **g. des stocks** stock control

gestionnaire [ʒɛstjɔnɛr] **1** nmf (dirigeant) administrator
2 nm Ordinat manager, driver; **g. de fichiers** file manager; **g. de périphérique** device driver; **g. de projets** project management package; **g. de réseau** network manager

gestuel, -elle [ʒɛstɥɛl] **1** adj gestural
2 nf **gestuelle** body language

geyser [ʒezɛr] nm geyser

Ghana [gana] nm **le G.** Ghana

ghanéen, -enne [ganeɛ̃, -ɛn] **1** adj Ghanaian
2 nm,f **G., Ghanéenne** Ghanaian

ghetto [geto] nm ghetto

GIA [ʒeia] nm (abrév **Groupes islamiques armés**) GIA

gibecière [ʒibsjɛr] nf (de chasseur) game bag

gibelotte [ʒiblɔt] *nf Culin* g. **(de lapin)** fricassee of rabbit cooked in white wine

gibet [ʒibɛ] *nm* gibbet, gallows *(singulier)*

gibier [ʒibje] *nm* game; *aussi Fig* **gros g.** big game; **g. à plumes** game birds; **g. à poil** game animals; *Fig* **g. de potence** gallows bird

giboulée [ʒibule] *nf* sudden shower; **giboulées de mars** ≃ April showers

Gibraltar [ʒibraltar] *n* Gibraltar

giclée [ʒikle] *nf* (a) *(d'eau, de sang)* spurt (b) *Suisse (petite quantité)* spot, smidgen (c) *Suisse (averse)* (rain) shower

gicler [ʒikle] *vi* (a) *(eau, sang)* to spurt out; *(boue)* to splash up (b) *Suisse (pleuvoir)* to rain

gicleur [ʒiklœr] *nm Aut* jet

GIE [ʒeiə] *nm (abrév* **groupement d'intérêt économique**) economic interest group

gifle [ʒifl] *nf aussi Fig* slap in the face; **donner une g. à qn** to give sb a slap in the face

gifler [ʒifle] *vt (sujet: personne)* to slap in the face; *(sujet: vent)* to lash

gigahertz [ʒigaɛrts] *nm Phys* gigahertz

gigantesque [ʒigɑ̃tɛsk] *adj* gigantic

gigaoctet [ʒigaɔktɛ] *nm Ordinat* gigabyte

GIGN [ʒeiʒeɛn] *nm (abrév* **Groupe d'intervention de la gendarmerie nationale**) = special task force of the gendarmerie

gigogne [ʒigɔɲ] *adj* **tables gigognes** nest of tables; **lits gigognes** beds that fit one underneath the other; **poupées gigognes** nest of (Russian) dolls

gigolo [ʒigɔlo] *nm Fam* gigolo

gigot [ʒigo] *nm (d'agneau, de mouton)* leg

gigoter [ʒigɔte] *vi* to wriggle, to fidget

gigue¹ [ʒig] *nf (danse)* jig

gigue² [ʒig] *nf Fam* **une grande g.** *(fille)* a beanpole (of a girl)

gilet [ʒilɛ] *nm (sans manches)* vest; *(veste en laine)* cardigan; **g. pare-balles** bulletproof jacket; **g. de sauvetage** life jacket

gin [dʒin] *nm* gin; **g. tonic** gin and tonic

gingembre [ʒɛ̃ʒɑ̃br] *nm* ginger

gingivite [ʒɛ̃ʒivit] *nf Méd* gingivitis

ginseng [ʒɛsɑ̃, ʒinsɑ̃g] *nm* ginseng

girafe [ʒiraf] *nf* giraffe; *Fig (personne)* beanpole

giratoire [ʒiratwar] **1** *adj (mouvement)* gyratory
 2 *nm Suisse (rond-point)* traffic circle

girls band [gœrlzbɑ̃d] *n* girl band

girofle [ʒirɔfl] *nm voir* **clou**

giroflée [ʒirɔfle] *nf* stock

girolle [ʒirɔl] *nf* chanterelle (mushroom)

giron [ʒirɔ̃] *nm (partie du corps)* lap; *Fig* bosom

gironde [ʒirɔ̃d] *adj f Fam* curvy; *Péj* on the plump side

girondin, -e [ʒirɔ̃dɛ̃, -in] **1** *adj* of the Gironde
 2 *nm,f* **G., Girondine** person from the Gironde

girouette [ʒirwɛt] *nf aussi Fig* weathercock

gisais *etc. voir* **gésir**

gisement [ʒizmɑ̃] *nm (de minerai)* deposit; **g. de pétrole** oilfield

gît *voir* **gésir**

gitan, -e [ʒitɑ̃, -an] **1** *adj* gypsy
 2 *nm,f* gypsy
 3 *nf* **Gitane**® Gitane® *(popular brand of cigarette)*

gîte¹ [ʒit] *nm* (a) *(logement)* lodging; **offrir le g. et le couvert à qn** to offer sb board and lodging (b) *(en montagne, à la campagne)* **g. d'étape** = transit accommodations for hikers, cyclists, etc; **g. rural** gîte, = independent vacation cottage or apartment (c) *(du lièvre)* form (d) *Culin* shank

gîte² [ʒit] *nf Naut* list; **donner de la g.** to list

gîter [ʒite] *vi Naut* to list

givre [ʒivr] *nm* frost

givré, -e [ʒivre] *adj* (a) *(couvert de givre)* covered with frost (b) *Fam (fou)* crazy

glabre [glabr] *adj (rasé)* clean-shaven; *(imberbe) (personne)* smooth-chinned; *(visage)* hairless

glaçage [glasaʒ] *nm (d'un gâteau)* icing

glaçant, -e [glasɑ̃, -ɑ̃t] *adj (manières, accueil)* frosty

glace [glas] *nf* (a) *(eau à l'état solide)* ice; **glaces** *(du pôle)* ice fields; *(en mer)* ice floes; **le navire est pris dans les glaces** the ship is icebound; *Fig* **rester de g.** to remain impassive; *Fig* **rompre la g.** to break the ice; **g. pilée** crushed ice (b) *(de voiture)* window (c) *(miroir)* mirror; **g. sans tain** two-way mirror (d) *(crème congelée)* ice-cream; **g. à la vanille/à la fraise** vanilla/strawberry ice-cream; **g. à l'italienne** soft ice-cream; **de la g. à l'eau** sherbet; **une g. à l'eau** a Popsicle

glacé, -e [glase] *adj* (a) *(rivière, lac)* frozen (b) *(très froid) (pièce, eau, personne)* freezing (cold); *(avec des glaçons) (café)* iced; **j'ai les pieds glacés** my feet are freezing (c) *Fig (accueil, politesse, regard)* frosty (d) *(brillant) (papier, épreuve)* glossy (e) *Culin (fruits)* glacé

glacer [16] [glase] **1** *vt* (a) *(refroidir, intimider)* to chill; *Fig* **g. vous g. le sang** spine-chilling (b) *(gâteau)* to ice
 2 se glacer *vpr (sang)* to run cold

glaciaire [glasjɛr] *adj Géol (vallée)* glacial; **période g.** Ice Age

glacial, -e, -als *ou* **-aux, -ales** [glasjal, -o] *adj (température, froid, air, vent)* freezing, icy; *Fig (ton, accueil, sourire)* frosty; *(personne)* cold

glacier¹ [glasje] *nm (étendue de glace)* glacier

glacier² [glasje] *nm (vendeur)* ice-cream seller; *(fabricant)* ice-cream maker

glacière [glasjɛr] *nf (de pique-nique)* cooler; **cette chambre est une vraie g.!** this room's like an icebox!

glaciériste [glasjerist] *nm* glacier climber

glaçon [glasɔ̃] *nm (pour rafraîchir une boisson)* ice cube; *(pendant)* icicle; *Fig (personne)* cold fish; **glaçons** *(sur une rivière)* drift ice; **avec ou sans glaçons?** with or without ice?; **un whisky avec des glaçons** a whiskey on the rocks; **j'ai les pieds comme des glaçons** my feet are like blocks of ice

gladiateur [gladjatœr] *nm* gladiator

glaïeul [glajœl] *nm* gladiolus; **des glaïeuls** gladioli

glaire [glɛr] *nf (crachat)* phlegm; **g. cervicale** cervical mucus

glaise [glɛz] *nf* **(terre) g.** clay

glaive [glɛv] *nm (épée)* broadsword; *Fig (symbole)* sword

gland [glɑ̃] *nm* (a) *(de chêne)* acorn (b) *(de passementerie)* tassel (c) *Anat* glans (d) *très Fam (personne)* jerk

glande [glɑ̃d] *nf (organe)* gland; *très Fam* **foutre les glandes à qn** *(énerver)* to piss sb off; *(attrister)* to upset sb; **glandes lacrymales** tear glands; **glandes sudoripares** sweat glands

glander [glɑ̃de] *vi très Fam (ne rien faire)* to loaf around; *(attendre)* to hang around; **mais qu'est-ce qu'il glande?** *(que fait-il?)* what the hell's he up to?; **j'en ai rien à g.** I don't give a shit

glandeur, -euse [glɑ̃dœr, -øz] *nm,f très Fam* loafer, layabout

glandouiller [glɑ̃duje] *vi très Fam (ne rien faire)* to loaf around; *(attendre)* to hang around

glandulaire [glɑ̃dylɛr], **glanduleux, -euse** [glɑ̃dylø, -øz] *adj* glandular

glaner [glane] *vt aussi Fig* to glean

glapir [glapir] *vi (chien)* to yap; *(renard)* to bark; *(personne, radio)* to shriek

glapissements [glapismɑ̃] *nmpl (d'un chien)* yapping; *(d'un renard)* barking; *(d'une personne, de la radio)* shrieking

glas [gla] *nm* knell; **sonner le g.** to toll the knell; *Fig* **sonner le g. de qch** to sound the death knell for sth

glaucome [glokom] *nm Méd* glaucoma

glauque [glok] *adj* (a) *(eau)* murky; *(ambiance, personne)* creepy (b) *Fam (lugubre) (pièce)* dreary; *(film, plaisanteries)* tasteless, in bad taste

glissade [glisad] *nf* sliding; *(de patineur)* gliding; *(pas de danse)* glissade; **faire une g./des glissades** to slide

glissant, -e [glisɑ̃, -ɑ̃t] *adj* slippery; *Fig* **être sur un terrain g.** to be on dangerous ground

glisse [glis] *nf* **sports de g.** = sports involving sliding motion, e.g. skiing, surfing, snowboarding

glissement [glismɑ̃] *nm (action)* sliding; *(variation électorale)* swing (**à** to); **g. de sens** shift in meaning; **g. de terrain** landslide; *(moins important)* landslip

glisser¹ [glise] **1** *vi* (**a**) *(par accident)* to slip; *(roue)* to skid; **le couteau lui a glissé des mains** the knife slipped out of her hands; *Aviat* **g. sur l'aile** to sideslip (**b**) *(volontairement)* to slide; **se laisser g. le long d'une corde** to slide down a rope; *Ordinat* **faire g.** *(pointeur)* to drag (**c**) *(avancer régulièrement)* to glide; *Fig (dans le sommeil, vers le désespoir)* to slip (**d**) **g. sur** *(sujet)* to skip over (**e**) *(avoir une surface glissante)* to be slippery

2 *vt (introduire)* to slip; **g. un mot à l'oreille de qn** to drop a word in sb's ear

3 se glisser *vpr* to slip (**dans** into)

glisser² [glise] *nm Ordinat* **g. d'icônes** icon drag

glissière [glisjɛr] *nf* (**a**) *Tech* runner, slide; **à g.** sliding (**b**) **g. de sécurité** crash barrier (**c**) *Ind (pour le charbon)* chute

global, -e, -aux, -ales [glɔbal, -o] *adj (somme)* total; *(paiement)* lump; *(vision)* overall; *Scol* **méthode globale** word-recognition method

globalement [glɔbalmɑ̃] *adv* overall

globalité [glɔbalite] *nf* **prendre un problème dans sa g.** to tackle a problem as a whole

globe [glɔb] *nm* (**a**) *(sphère)* globe; **g. oculaire** eyeball (**b**) *(terre)* globe; **faire le tour du g.** to go around the world; **g. terrestre** *(terre)* earth; *(mappemonde)* globe (**c**) *(en verre) (d'une pendule)* glass dome

globe-trotter *(pl* **globe-trotters)** [glɔbtrɔtœr] *nmf* globe-trotter

globulaire [glɔbylɛr] *adj Méd* **numération g.** blood count

globule [glɔbyl] *nm (du sang)* corpuscle; **globules blancs/rouges** white/red corpuscles

globuleux, -euse [glɔbylø, -øz] *adj (yeux)* protruding

gloire [glwar] *nf* (**a**) *(renom)* glory; **tirer g. de qch** to glory in sth (**b**) *(personne célèbre)* celebrity; **il est la g. de notre école** he is the pride of our school (**c**) *(manifestation de respect)* **rendre g. à** to glorify; **g. à...!** glory to...!; **à la g. de qn** in praise of sb

glorieux, -euse [glɔrjø, -øz] *adj* glorious; **être promis à un avenir g.** to have a glorious future ahead of one; *Fam* **ce n'est pas très g.** *(pas très bon)* it's not exactly brilliant

glorifier [66] [glɔrifje] **1** *vt* to glorify

2 se glorifier *vpr* **se g. de (faire) qch** to glory in (doing) sth

gloriole [glɔrjɔl] *nf Fam* **faire qch par g.** to do sth in order to show off

glose [gloz] *nf (explication)* gloss

gloser [gloze] **gloser sur** *vt ind (discourir sur)* to ramble on about

gloss [glɔs] *nm (pour les lèvres)* lipgloss

glossaire [glɔsɛr] *nm (ouvrage)* glossary

glotte [glɔt] *nf Anat* glottis

glouglou [gluglu] *nm* (**a**) *(bruit d'un liquide)* gurgle; **faire g.** to gurgle (**b**) *(cri de la dinde)* gobble

gloussements [glusmɑ̃] *nmpl (d'une poule)* clucking; *(d'une dinde)* gobbling; *(d'une personne)* chuckling

glousser [gluse] *vi (poule)* to cluck; *(dinde)* to gobble; *(personne)* to chuckle

glouton, -onne [glutɔ̃, -ɔn] **1** *adj* greedy, gluttonous

2 *nm,f* glutton

3 *nm (animal)* wolverine

gloutonnement [glutɔnmɑ̃] *adv* greedily

gloutonnerie [glutɔnri] *nf* gluttony, greed

glu [gly] *nf (colle)* glue

gluant, -e [glyɑ̃, -ɑ̃t] *adj* slimy

glucide [glysid] *nm* carbohydrate

glucose [glykoz] *nm* glucose

gluten [glytɛn] *nm* gluten

glycémie [glisemi] *nf Méd* glycemia

glycérine [gliserin] *nf* glycerine

glycine [glisin] *nf (plante)* wisteria

gnangnan [ɲɑ̃ɲɑ̃] *adj inv Fam Péj (personne)* wishy-washy; *(livre, film)* soppy, slushy

gnognot(t)e [ɲɔɲɔt] *nf Fam (mauvaise qualité)* **c'est de la g.** it's a load of garbage; **c'est pas de la g., cette voiture** that car's quite something

gnole, gnôle [ɲol] *nf Fam* hooch

gnome [gnom] *nm* gnome; *Fig & Péj (homme)* midget

gnon [ɲɔ̃] *nm Fam (coup de poing)* thump; **se prendre un g.** to get thumped

GO 1 *Rad (abrév* **grandes ondes)** LW

2 [ʒeo] *nm (abrév* **gentil organisateur)** activity organizer *(at Club Méditerranée vacation villages)*

Go *nm Ordinat (abrév* **gigaoctet(s))** GB

go [go] **tout de go** *adv* straight away

goal [gol] *nm* goalkeeper

gobelet [gɔblɛ] *nm (en argent, en étain)* tumbler; **g. en plastique/carton** plastic/paper cup

gober [gɔbe] *vt (nourriture)* to gulp down; *Fig (croire)* to swallow

goberger [45] [gɔbɛrʒe] **se goberger** *vpr Fam* to have a good time

Gobi [gɔbi] *n voir* **désert**

godasse [gɔdas] *nf Fam* shoe

godelureau, -x [gɔdlyro] *nm Péj & Vieilli* popinjay

godet [gɔdɛ] *nm* (**a**) *(récipient)* pot; *Fam* **boire un g.** to have a drink (**b**) *(d'une noria)* scoop; *(d'un excavateur, d'une roue à eau)* bucket (**c**) *(d'une jupe)* **à godets** flared

godiche [gɔdiʃ] *Fam* **1** *adj* clumsy

2 *nf* clumsy oaf

godille [gɔdij] *nf* (**a**) *Naut* scull; **avancer à la g.** to scull (**b**) *(en ski)* wedeln; **faire de la g.** to wedeln

godiller [gɔdije] *vi* (**a**) *Naut* to scull (**b**) *(en ski)* to wedeln

godillot [gɔdijo] *nm* (**a**) *Mil* boot; *Fam (gros soulier)* clodhopper (**b**) *Fam Pol* party-liner

goéland [gɔelɑ̃] *nm* gull

goélette [gɔelɛt] *nf (navire)* schooner

goémon [gɔemɔ̃] *nm* wrack

gogo¹ [gogo] **à gogo** *adv Fam* galore

gogo² [gogo] *nm Fam* sucker, mug

goguenard, -e [gɔgnar, -ard] *adj* mocking

goguette [gɔgɛt] *nf Fam* **être en g.** *(faire la noce)* to be out for a good time

goinfre [gwɛ̃fr] *Fam* **1** *nmf* pig

2 *adj* piggish

goinfrer [gwɛ̃fre] **se goinfrer** *vpr Fam* to pig out (**de** on)

goinfrerie [gwɛ̃frəri] *nf* piggishness

goitre [gwatr] *nm Méd* goiter

golden [gɔldɛn] *nf* Golden Delicious (apple)

golf [gɔlf] *nm* golf; **(terrain de) g.** golf course; **g. miniature** miniature golf

golfe [gɔlf] *nm* gulf, bay; **le G.** the Gulf; **le g. Persique** the Persian Gulf; **les États** *ou* **les pays du G.** the Gulf States; **le g. du Bengale** the Bay of Bengal; **le g. de Gascogne** the Bay of Biscay; **le g. du Mexique** the Gulf of Mexico

golfeur, -euse [gɔlfœr, -øz] *nm,f* golfer

Gomina® [gɔmina] *nf* brilliantine

gominé, -e [gɔmine] *adj (cheveux)* plastered-down

gommage [gɔmaʒ] *nm* (**a**) *(pour effacer)* rubbing out, erasing (**b**) *(nettoyage de la peau)* face scrub; **se faire un g.** to give oneself a face scrub

gomme [gɔm] *nf* (**a**) *(pour effacer)* eraser (**b**) *(substance)* gum; **g. à mâcher** chewing gum (**c**) *Fam (locutions)* **mettre (toute) la g.** to get a move on; *(en voiture)* to step on it; **à la g.** useless

gommé, -e [gɔme] *adj (papier, enveloppe)* gummed

gommer [gɔme] *vt (effacer)* to rub out, to erase; *Fig (souvenir)* to erase

gond [gɔ̃] *nm (de porte)* hinge; **sortir de ses gonds** *(porte)* to come off its hinges; *Fig* to fly off the handle

gondole [gɔ̃dɔl] *nf (barque, présentoir)* gondola

gondoler [gɔ̃dɔle] **1** *vi (bois, disque)* to warp; *(papier)* to crinkle

2 se gondoler *vpr* (**a**) *(bois, disque)* to warp; *(papier)* to crinkle (**b**) *Fam (rire)* to kill oneself laughing

gondolier [gɔ̃dɔlje] *nm* gondolier

gonflable [gɔ̃flabl] *adj* inflatable

gonflage [gɔ̃flaʒ] *nm* **g. (des pneus)** tire pressure

gonflant, -e [gɔ̃flɑ̃, -ɑ̃t] *adj* (**a**) *(coiffure)* bouffant (**b**) *très Fam (énervant)* maddening

gonflé, -e [gɔ̃fle] *adj* (**a**) *(boursouflé)* swollen (**b**) *Fam* **être g.** *(personne)* to have a lot of nerve; **c'est g., ce qu'il a fait là** what he did took some nerve; **g. à bloc** *(sûr de soi)* raring to go

gonflement [gɔ̃fləmɑ̃] *nm (d'une partie du corps)* swelling

gonfler [gɔ̃fle] **1** *vt* (**a**) *(pneu, ballon, matelas pneumatique)* to blow up, to inflate; *(ses joues)* to puff out; *(sujet: vent) (voiles)* to fill (**b**) *(faire augmenter de volume)* to swell (**c**) *Fig (grossir) (résultats, conséquences)* to exaggerate; *Fam (moteur)* to soup up (**d**) *très Fam (énerver)* **g. qn** to get on sb's nerves

2 *vi* to swell; *(gâteau, pâte)* to rise

3 se gonfler *vpr (voiles, poumons)* to fill; *Fig* **se g. de joie** *(cœur)* to fill with joy

gonflette [gɔ̃flɛt] *nf Fam Péj* pumping iron; **faire de la g.** to pump iron

gong [gɔ̃g] *nm* (**a**) *(percussion)* gong (**b**) *(en boxe)* bell; *Fig* **sauvé par le g.** saved by the bell

gonzesse [gɔ̃zɛs] *nf très Fam* broad

goret [gɔrɛ] *nm* piglet; *Fam (enfant malpropre)* little pig

gorge [gɔrʒ] *nf* (**a**) *(gosier, cou)* throat; **avoir mal à la g.** to have a sore throat; **avoir la g. serrée** to have a lump in one's throat; *Fig* **cela m'est resté en travers de la g.** it stuck in my throat; **trancher la g. à qn** to cut sb's throat; *Fig* **être pris à la g.** to be in a stranglehold; **faire des gorges chaudes de qch** to laugh sth to scorn; **rire à g. déployée** to roar with laughter (**b**) *Litt (poitrine)* bosom (**c**) *(vallée)* gorge (**d**) *(d'une poulie)* groove

gorgé, -e [gɔrʒe] *adj* **une éponge gorgée d'eau** a sponge full of water; **sol g. d'eau** waterlogged earth

gorgée [gɔrʒe] *nf* mouthful; **boire qch à petites gorgées** to sip sth; **avaler qch d'une g.** to swallow sth in one gulp

gorger [45] [gɔrʒe] **se gorger** *vpr* to gorge oneself (**de** on *or* with); **se g. d'eau** *(sol)* to get waterlogged

gorgonzola [gɔrgɔ̃zɔla] *nm* Gorgonzola

gorille [gɔrij] *nm (animal)* gorilla; *Fam (garde du corps)* gorilla

gosier [gozje] *nm* throat; *Fam* **avoir le g. sec** to be parched

gosse [gɔs] *nmf* (**a**) *Fam (enfant)* kid; **g. de riches** rich kid (**b**) *Fam* **être beau g.** to be good-looking (**c**) *Can Fam* **gosses** balls

gosser [gose] *vt Can Fam* to whittle

gotha [gɔta] *nm* **le g. du show-business/de la finance** the show-business/financial elite

gothique [gɔtik] **1** *adj* Gothic; **écriture g.** Gothic script

2 *nm (style)* Gothic

gouache [gwaʃ] *nf* gouache

gouailleur, -euse [gwɑjœr, -øz] *adj (ton)* bantering

gouda [guda] *nm* Gouda

goudron [gudrɔ̃] *nm* tar; **goudrons** *(dans les cigarettes)* tar

goudronner [gudrɔne] *vt* to tar

gouffre [gufr] *nm* abyss; *Géol* sinkhole; *Fig* **être au bord du g.** to be on the edge of the abyss; *Fig* **un g. les sépare** there is a gulf between them; *Fig* **cette voiture est un g.** this car just swallows up money

gougère [guʒɛr] *nf Culin* gougère *(choux pastry with cheese)*

gouine [gwin] *nf très Fam* dike, = offensive term used to refer to a lesbian

goujat [guʒa] *nm* boor

goujon [guʒɔ̃] *nm (poisson)* gudgeon

goulache, goulasch [gulaʃ] *nm* goulash

goulafre [gulafr] *adj Belg* greedy

goulée [gule] *nf (de liquide)* gulp; *(d'air)* lungful

goulet [gulɛ] *nm (défilé)* gully; **g. d'étranglement** bottleneck

gouleyant, -e [gulɛjɑ̃, -ɑ̃t] *adj (vin)* easy-drinking

goulot [gulo] *nm (d'une bouteille)* neck; **boire au g.** to drink straight from the bottle

goulu, -e [guly] **1** *adj* greedy, gluttonous

2 *nm,f* glutton

goulûment [gulymɑ̃] *adv* greedily

goupille [gupij] *nf (d'une grenade)* pin

goupiller [gupije] *Fam* **1** *vt (arranger)* to fix (up)

2 se goupiller *vpr* **bien se g.** to work out well; **ça s'est mal goupillé** it didn't work out

goupillon [gupijɔ̃] *nm* (**a**) *(pour eau bénite)* sprinkler (**b**) *(pour biberons, bouteilles)* bottle brush

gourd, -e [gur, gurd] *adj* numb (with cold)

gourde [gurd] **1** *nf* (**a**) *(récipient)* flask (**b**) *Fam (femme niaise)* dope

2 *adj Fam* dopey

gourdin [gurdɛ̃] *nm* club, cudgel

gourer [gure] **se gourer** *vpr Fam* to goof; **se g. d'adresse/de jour** to get the wrong address/day

gourgane [gurgan] *nf Can* broad bean

gourmand, -e [gurmɑ̃, -ɑ̃d] **1** *adj (personne)* who likes his/her food; *(à l'excès)* greedy; *Fig (intéressé) (regard)* greedy; **cet enfant est très g.** *(de sucreries)* that child has a sweet tooth

2 *nm,f* person who likes his/her food; **quel g.!** he certainly likes his food!

gourmandise [gurmɑ̃diz] *nf* (**a**) *(d'une personne)* love of food; *Fig* **avec g.** greedily (**b**) **gourmandises** *(sucreries)* delicacies

gourmet [gurmɛ] *nm* gourmet; **un fin g.** a great gourmet

gourmette [gurmɛt] *nf (bracelet)* chain (bracelet)

gourou [guru] *nm aussi Fig* guru

gousse [gus] *nf (de haricot, de petit pois)* pod; **g. d'ail** clove of garlic; **g. de vanille** vanilla pod

gousset [gusɛ] *nm (poche)* fob (pocket)

goût [gu] *nm* (**a**) *(saveur)* taste; **avoir un g. de banane/d'alcool** to taste of banana/alcohol; **manquer de g., ne pas avoir de g.** to be tasteless

(**b**) *(sens)* taste

(**c**) *(préférence, convenance)* taste; **avoir des goûts de luxe** to have expensive tastes; **trouver qn/qch à son g.** to find sb/sth to one's taste; **avoir du g. pour** *ou* **le g. de qch** to have a taste for sth; **elle n'a plus (de) g. à rien** she doesn't want to do anything any more; **faire qch par g.** to do sth because one likes to; **prendre g. à qch** to acquire a taste for sth; **chacun ses goûts** each to his own; **des goûts et des couleurs on ne discute pas, tous les goûts sont dans la nature** there's no accounting for taste

(**d**) *(discernement, jugement)* taste; **s'habiller avec g.** to have good dress sense; **de bon g.** tasteful; **d'un g. douteux** in doubtful taste; **de mauvais g.** in bad taste

(**e**) *(style)* **quelque chose dans ce g.-là** something of that sort

goûter¹ [gute] *nm* (afternoon) tea; *(pour enfants)* (afternoon) snack; **l'heure du g.** teatime

goûter² [gute] **1** *vt* (**a**) *(essayer) (nourriture, boisson)* to taste, to try (**b**) *(apprécier)* to enjoy, to appreciate (**c**) *Belg & Can (avoir un goût de)* to taste of; **ce fruit goûte le pourri** this fruit tastes rotten

    2 *vi (à quatre heures)* to have tea; *(pour enfants)* to have a snack or an afternoon snack

    3 goûter à *vt ind (aliment)* to taste, to try; *Fig* to have a taste of

goûteur, -euse [gutœr, -øz] *nm,f* taster

goutte [gut] **1** *nf* (**a**) *(de liquide)* drop; **couler g. à g.** to drip; **il suait à grosses gouttes** the sweat was pouring off him; **gouttes** *(pour les yeux, les oreilles)* drops; *Fig* **c'est la g. d'eau qui fait déborder le vase** it's the straw that breaks/broke the camel's back; *Fam* **avoir la g. au nez** to have a runny nose; **se ressembler comme deux gouttes d'eau** to be as like as two peas in a pod (**b**) *(petite quantité)* drop; **encore une g. de café?** a drop more coffee?; *Fam* **boire la g.** to have a nip (**c**) *Méd (maladie)* gout; **avoir la g.** to have gout

    2 *adv Vieilli* **je n'y vois/entends g.** I can't see/understand anything

goutte-à-goutte [gutagut] *nm inv Méd* drip; **on lui a mis un g.** he/she was put on a drip

gouttelette [gutlɛt] *nf* droplet

goutter [gute] *vi* to drip

gouttière [gutjɛr] *nf* (**a**) *(le long du toit)* gutter (**b**) *(le long du mur)* drainpipe

gouvernail [guvɛrnaj] *nm Naut* rudder; **tenir le g.** to be at the helm

gouvernant, -e [guvɛrnã, -ãt] **1** *adj (classe, parti)* governing, ruling

    2 *nm* **les gouvernants** those in power

gouvernante [guvɛrnãt] *nf (d'enfants)* governess; *(d'une personne, d'un hôtel)* housekeeper

gouverne [guvɛrn] *nf* (**a**) *Aviat* **gouvernes** control surfaces (**b**) **pour votre g.** for your guidance

gouvernement [guvɛrnəmã] *nm* government; **sous le g. Giscard** during Giscard's term of office

gouvernemental, -e, -aux, -ales [guvɛrnəmãtal, -o] *adj* government; *(parti)* governing

gouverner [guvɛrne] **1** *vt* (**a**) *(diriger) (pays)* to govern, to rule; **un parti qui gouverne depuis des années** a party which has been in power for years (**b**) *(bateau)* to steer

    2 se gouverner *vpr* **le droit des peuples à se g. eux-mêmes** the right of peoples to self-government

gouverneur [guvɛrnœr] *nm* governor; *Can* **G. Général** governor-general; *Can* **Lieutenant-G.** lieutenant-governor

goyave [gɔjav] *nf* guava

GR [ʒeɛr] *nm (abrév* **(sentier de) grande randonnée**) = long-distance hiking path

grabat [graba] *nm* pallet

grabataire [grabatɛr] **1** *adj* bedridden

    2 *nmf* bedridden invalid

grabuge [grabyʒ] *nm Fam* rumpus; **il va y avoir du g.** there'll be a rumpus

grâce [gras] *nf* (**a**) *(charme)* grace; **avec g.** gracefully (**b**) **g. à qn/qch** *(avec l'aide de)* thanks to sb/sth (**c**) *Litt (bienveillance, faveur)* favor; **faites-moi la g. d'oublier cette histoire** do me the favor of forgetting this matter; **trouver g. aux yeux de qn** to find favor in sb's eyes; **de g.!** for pity's sake! (**d**) *(volonté)* **de bonne g.** willingly, readily; **de mauvaise g.** unwillingly, grudgingly (**e**) *(acquittement)* pardon; **demander** *ou* **crier g.** to beg for mercy; **faire g. à qn de qch** *(dette, tâche)* to let sb off sth; **je vous fais g. des détails** I'll spare you the details; **g. présidentielle** presidential pardon (**f**) *(remerciements)* **rendre g. à** to give thanks to (**g**) *Rel* grace

gracier [66] [grasje] *vt* to pardon

gracieusement [grasjøzmã] *adv* (**a**) *(avec grâce)* gracefully (**b**) *(aimablement)* graciously (**c**) *(gratuitement)* free of charge

gracieux, -euse [grasjø, -øz] *adj* (**a**) *(qui a du charme)* graceful (**b**) *(aimable)* gracious (**c**) *(gratuit)* **à titre g.** free of charge

gracile [grasil] *adj* slender

gradation [gradasjɔ̃] *nf* gradation

grade [grad] *nm* (**a**) *(dans l'armée, dans l'administration)* rank; **monter en g.** to be promoted; *Fam* **en prendre pour son g.** to be hauled over the coals (**b**) *Belg Scol & Univ (mention)* distinction

gradé, -e [grade] *nm,f Mil* non-commissioned officer, NCO

gradin [gradɛ̃] *nm (d'amphithéâtre, de stade)* row of seats; **les gradins** *(d'un stade)* the bleachers

graduation [graduasjɔ̃] *nf* graduation

gradué, -e [gradɥe] *adj* (**a**) *(qui porte une graduation)* graduated (**b**) *(progressif) (exercices, problèmes)* graded

graduel, -elle [gradɥɛl] *adj* gradual

graduellement [gradɥɛlmã] *adv* gradually

graduer [gradɥe] *vt* (**a**) *(diviser en degrés)* to graduate (**b**) *(augmenter)* to increase gradually

graffiti [grafiti] *nm* piece of graffiti; **des graffitis** graffiti

graillé, -e [graje] *adj Can (pour faire quelque chose)* well-equipped; *Fam (bien monté)* well-hung

grailler [graje] *vi très Fam (manger)* to eat

graillon [grajɔ̃] *nm* **sentir le g.** to smell of burnt fat

grain¹ [grɛ̃] *nm* (**a**) *(graine, fruit, céréales)* grain; **g. de café** coffee bean; **g. de poivre** peppercorn; **g. de raisin** grape (**b**) *(de sable, de poudre)* grain; *(de poussière)* speck; *(de chapelet)* bead; *Fig* **un g. de qch** *(un peu de)* a hint of sth; **pas un g. de bon sens/de vérité** not a grain of common sense/of truth; *Fam* **il a un g.** he has a screw loose; **mettre son g. de sel** to stick one's oar in; **g. de beauté** mole (**c**) *(d'un tissu, d'une photographie)* grain; *(de la peau)* rough side

grain² [grɛ̃] *nm Naut* squall; *Fig* **veiller au g.** to keep a weather eye open

graine [grɛn] *nf* seed; **monter en g.** to run to seed; *Fig (personne)* to shoot up; **regarde un peu ce qu'a fait ton cousin et prends-en de la g.!** just look at what your cousin's done and take a leaf out of his book!; **c'est de la mauvaise g.** he's bad news; **g. de voyou/voleur** little hooligan/thief

graissage [grɛsaʒ] *nm (d'une machine, d'un engrenage)* greasing

graisse [grɛs] *nf (d'animal, de personne)* fat; *(lubrifiant)* grease; **graisses animales/végétales** animal/vegetable fat

graisser [grese] *vt (machine, engrenage)* to grease; *(bottes)* to oil; **g. la patte à qn** to grease sb's palm

graisseux, -euse [grɛsø, -øz] *adj* (**a**) *(taché de graisse)* greasy (**b**) *(tumeur, tissu)* fatty

grammaire [gramɛr] *nf* (**a**) *(science, règles)* grammar; **faute/règle de g.** grammatical error/rule (**b**) *(livre)* grammar (book)

grammairien, -enne [gramɛrjɛ̃, -ɛn] *nm,f* grammarian

grammatical, -e, -aux, -ales [gramatikal, -o] *adj* grammatical

gramme [gram] *nm* gram; *aussi Fig* **pas un g. de** not an ounce of

grand, -e [grã, grãd] **1** *adj* (**a**) *(en taille)* big, large; *(en hauteur)* tall; *(en longueur)* long; *Phot* **g. angle** wide-angle lens

    (**b**) *(principal)* chief, main; **grandes lignes** *(de train)* main lines

    (**c**) *(adulte, plus âgé)* big; **tu es g. maintenant** you're a big boy now

    (**d**) *(en quantité, en intensité) (bruit)* loud; *(coup)* heavy; *(froid)* severe; *(différence, catastrophe)* big; **le g. amour** true love; **un acteur sans g. talent** a rather untalented actor; **il fait g. jour** it's broad daylight; **c'est un g. buveur** he's a big drinker; **les grands blessés** the seriously wounded (**e**) *(puissant, prestigieux)* great; **une grande dame de la littérature** a great literary lady

(**f**) *(dans un titre, un grade)* grand; **g. prêtre** high priest; **g. reporter** chief reporter

2 *adv* **ouvrir g. la bouche/la fenêtre** to open one's mouth/the window wide; **g. ouvert** wide open

3 *nm,f* **les grands** *(enfants)* the older ones; **grands et petits** old and young, grown-ups and children; **les grands de ce monde** those in high places; **les grands du pétrole** the oil giants; **mon g.** buddy, pal; **ma grande** dear

grand-chose [grɑ̃ʃoz] **1** *pron indéfini* **pas g.** not much; **ce ne sont que quelques fleurs, ce n'est pas g.** it's just a few flowers, nothing much

2 *nmf inv Fam (personne)* **un pas g.** a loser

grand-duc *(pl* **grands-ducs**) [grɑ̃dyk] *nm (noble)* grand duke; *Fam* **faire la tournée des grands-ducs** to go out on the town

grand-duché *(pl* **grands-duchés**) [grɑ̃dyʃe] *nm* grand duchy

Grande-Bretagne [grɑ̃dbrətaɲ] *nf* **la G.** Great Britain

grande-duchesse *(pl* **grandes-duchesses**) [grɑ̃ddyʃɛs] *nf* grand duchess

grandement [grɑ̃dmɑ̃] *adv (beaucoup)* greatly; **se tromper g.** to be greatly mistaken; **avoir g. le temps** to have ample time; **avoir g. de quoi vivre** to have plenty to live on

grandeur [grɑ̃dœr] *nf* (**a**) *(taille)* size; *(d'un arbre)* height, size; **g. nature** life-size (**b**) *(importance)* importance (**c**) *Math* magnitude (**d**) *(gloire)* greatness, grandeur; **g. et décadence d'un empire** rise and fall of an empire (**e**) *(des sentiments)* nobility; **g. d'âme** magnanimity (**f**) *Can* **à la g. de** throughout

grand-guignol [grɑ̃giɲol] *nm Péj* **c'est du g.** it's all blood and thunder

grandiloquence [grɑ̃dilokɑ̃s] *nf* grandiloquence

grandiloquent, -e [grɑ̃dilokɑ̃, -ɑ̃t] *adj* grandiloquent

grandiose [grɑ̃djoz] *adj* imposing

grandir [grɑ̃dir] **1** *vi (en taille)* to grow; *(en âge)* to grow up; *(en importance)* to increase, to grow

2 *vt* **g. qn** *(sujet: talons)* to make sb look taller; *Fig (sujet: expérience, épreuve)* to improve sb's standing

3 se grandir *vpr (en taille)* to make oneself taller

grandissant, -e [grɑ̃disɑ̃, -ɑ̃t] *adj* growing

grand-maman *(pl* **grand-mamans** *ou* **grands-mamans**) [grɑ̃mamɑ̃] *Suisse & Can (en langage enfantin)* granny, grandma

grand-mère *(pl* **grand-mères** *ou* **grands-mères**) [grɑ̃mɛr] *nf* grandmother; *Fam (vieille femme)* old granny

grand-oncle [grɑ̃tɔ̃kl] *(pl* **grands-oncles** [grɑ̃zɔ̃kl]) *nm* great-uncle

grand-papa *(pl* **grands-papas**) [grɑ̃papa] *Suisse & Can (en langage enfantin)* grandpa, grandad

grand-peine [grɑ̃pɛn] **à grand-peine** *adv* with great difficulty

grand-père *(pl* **grands-pères**) [grɑ̃pɛr] *nm* grandfather; *Fam (vieil homme)* granddad

grand-route *(pl* **grand-routes**) [grɑ̃rut] *nf* main road

grand-rue *(pl* **grand-rues**) [grɑ̃ry] *nf* high street, main street

grands-parents [grɑ̃parɑ̃] *nmpl* grandparents

grand-tante *(pl* **grand-tantes** *ou* **grands-tantes**) [grɑ̃tɑ̃t] *nf* great-aunt

grand-voile *(pl* **grand-voiles** *ou* **grands-voiles**) [grɑ̃vwal] *nf* mainsail

grange [grɑ̃ʒ] *nf* barn

granit(e) [granit] *nm* granite

granule [granyl] *nm* granule

granulé [granyle] *nm* granule

granuleux, -euse [granylø, -øz] *adj* granular

graphe [graf] *nm* graph

graphie [grafi] *nf Ling* written form

graphique [grafik] **1** *adj* graphic

2 *nm* diagram; *(sur un axe)* graph; *Ordinat* graphic; *Ordinat* **g. de gestion** management chart; **g. à** *ou* **en barres** bar chart

graphisme [grafism] *nm* (**a**) *(écriture)* handwriting (**b**) *Art (style)* style of drawing

graphiste [grafist] *nmf* graphic designer

graphite [grafit] *nm* graphite

graphologie [grafolɔʒi] *nf* graphology

graphologue [grafolɔg] *nmf* graphologist

grappe [grap] *nf (de raisin)* bunch; *(de fleurs, de gens)* cluster; *Vulg* **lâche-moi la g.!** fuck off!

grappiller [grapije] *vt (renseignements)* to glean; *(argent)* to make on the side

grappin [grapɛ̃] *nm Naut* grappling hook or iron; *Fam Fig* **mettre le g. sur qn/qch** to get one's hands on sb/sth

gras, grasse [grɑ, grɑs] **1** *adj* (**a**) *(nourriture, tissu)* fatty (**b**) *(gros)* *(personne, animal)* fat; *(poulet)* plump (**c**) *(graisseux)* *(chiffon, cheveux, peau)* greasy (**d**) *(épais)* *(terre)* heavy, clayey; *(crayon)* soft lead; *(toux)* loose; *(rire)* throaty (**e**) *Typ* bold; **caractères g.** bold type (**f**) *Fig (bénéfices, récompense)* handsome; **faire la grasse matinée** to sleep late (**g**) *(graveleux)* *(histoire)* dirty, smutty

2 *adv* **manger g.** to eat fatty food

3 *nm* (**a**) *(de la jambe, du bras)* fleshy part (**b**) *(du jambon, de la viande)* fat (**c**) *Typ* bold; **en g.** in bold

gras-double *(pl* **gras-doubles**) [grɑdubl] *nm* tripe

grassement [grɑsmɑ̃] *adv (récompenser, payer)* handsomely

grasseyer [graseje] *vi* = to pronounce one's r's at the back of the throat

grassouillet, -ette [grasujɛ, -ɛt] *adj* plump, chubby

gratifiant, -e [gratifjɑ̃, -ɑ̃t] *adj* rewarding, gratifying

gratification [gratifikasjɔ̃] *nf* (**a**) *(prime)* bonus (**b**) *(satisfaction)* gratification

gratifier [66] [gratifje] *vt* (**a**) **g. qn de qch** *(récompense)* to present sb with sth; *Ironique (sourire)* to bestow sth on sb (**b**) *(valoriser)* to gratify

gratin [gratɛ̃] *nm* (**a**) *(plat)* gratin *(baked dish with a topping of grated cheese and sometimes breadcrumbs)*; **au g.** au gratin; **chou-fleur au g.** cauliflower cheese; **g. dauphinois** = sliced potatoes baked with cream and browned on top (**b**) *Fam Fig* **le g.** *(le beau monde)* the upper crust

gratiné, -e [gratine] **1** *adj* (**a**) *(au gratin)* au gratin *(topped with grated cheese and sometimes breadcrumbs)* (**b**) *Fam Fig (addition)* huge; *(examen, problème)* tough

2 *nf* **gratinée** *Culin* onion soup au gratin

gratiner [gratine] **1** *vt* to brown

2 *vi* **faire g. qch** to brown sth

gratis [gratis] **1** *adv* free (of charge)

2 *adj* free

gratitude [gratityd] *nf* gratitude

gratos [gratos] *adj Fam* free (of charge)

gratouiller [gratuje] *vt Fam (démanger)* **ça (me) gratouille** it makes me itch

gratte [grat] *nf Can* snowplough

gratte-ciel [gratsjɛl] *nm inv* skyscraper

gratte-papier [gratpapje] *nm inv Péj* pen pusher

gratter [grate] **1** *vt (avec les ongles)* to scratch; *(avec un objet)* to scrape; *(effacer)* *(mot, inscription)* to scratch out; *(tache)* to scrape off; *Fam* **ça me gratte** it makes me itch; **pull qui gratte** scratchy sweater; *Fig* **g. les fonds de tiroir** to scrape around for money

2 *vi* **g. à la porte** to tap lightly at the door

3 se gratter *vpr* to scratch oneself; **se g. jusqu'au sang** to scratch oneself raw; **se g. la tête/l'oreille** to scratch one's head/ear; *très Fam* **tu peux toujours te g.!** you can take a running jump!

gratteux, -euse [gratø, -øz] *Can* **1** *adj* stingy, mean **2** *nm,f* miser

grattoir [gratwar] *nm* scraper; *(de boîte d'allumettes)* striking surface

grattouiller [gratuje] = **gratouiller**

gratuit, -e [gratɥi, -it] *adj* (a) *(billet, entrée, échantillon)* free; **à titre g.** free of charge (b) *(acte, violence)* gratuitous

gratuité [gratɥite] *nf* (a) *(fait de ne pas payer)* **la g. de l'enseignement/des soins hospitaliers** free education/hospital care (b) *(d'un acte, de la violence)* gratuitousness

gratuitement [gratɥitmã] *adv* (a) *(sans payer)* free (of charge) (b) *(sans motif)* gratuitously

gravats [gravɑ] *nmpl* rubble

grave [grav] **1** *adj* (a) *(sérieux, dramatique)* serious; **ce n'est pas g.** *(ça n'a pas d'importance)* it doesn't matter; **un accident qui a fait deux blessés graves** an accident in which two people were seriously injured (b) *(solennel) (visage, ton, expression)* grave, solemn (c) *(note, voix)* low, deep (d) *Fam (dérangé)* off one's rocker **2** *nm* **le g., les graves** *(notes)* the low notes; **les graves** *(sur une chaîne stéréo)* the bass **3** *adv Fam* in a bad way; **il me prend la tête g.** he really bugs me

graveleux, -euse [gravlø, -øz] *adj* (a) *(histoire, chanson)* smutty, dirty (b) *(terre)* gravelly

gravement [gravmã] *adv* (a) *(malade, blessé)* seriously (b) *(avec dignité)* gravely, solemnly

graver [grave] *vt (matériau, motif)* to engrave; *(sur bois)* to carve; *(disque)* to make; *Fig* **rester gravé dans la mémoire de qn** to be engraved in sb's memory

graveur, -euse [gravœr, -øz] **1** *nm,f* engraver; **g. sur bois** woodcarver **2** *nm Ordinat (de CD-ROM)* writer, burner

gravier [gravje] *nm* gravel

gravillon [gravijɔ̃] *nm (caillou)* piece of gravel; **du g., des gravillons** gravel; **gravillons** *(sur panneau)* loose gravel

gravir [gravir] *vt* to climb; *Fig* **g. les échelons** to climb the ladder

gravissime [gravisim] *adj* extremely serious

gravitation [gravitasjɔ̃] *nf* gravitation

gravité [gravite] *nf* (a) *Phys* gravity (b) *(solennité)* gravity (c) *(importance)* seriousness; **sans g.** *(blessure, problème)* minor

graviter [gravite] *vi* **g. autour de qch** to orbit sth; *Fig* **g. autour de qn** to hover around sb

gravure [gravyr] *nf* (a) *(action)* engraving; **g. sur bois** woodcarving (b) *(ouvrage)* engraving; **g. sur bois** woodcut; *Fig* **c'est une vraie g. de mode** she dresses like a fashion model

gré [gre] *nm* (a) *(goût)* **à mon/son g.** for my/his/her liking (b) *(volonté)* **contre son g.** against one's will; **de son propre g., de son plein g.** of one's own free will; **de bon g.** willingly, gladly; **bon g. mal g.** whether we/you/*etc.* like it or not; **faites-le venir de g. ou de force** make him come whether he wants to or not; **au g. des flots** at the mercy of the waves; **au g. des événements/des circonstances** *(agir, changer d'avis)* according to how events turn out/to the circumstances (c) *Sout (gratitude)* **nous vous saurions g. de bien vouloir…** we would be grateful if you would kindly…

grec, grecque [grɛk] **1** *adj* Greek **2** *nm (langue)* Greek; **g. ancien/moderne** ancient/modern Greek **3** *nm,f* **G., Grecque** Greek **4** *nf* **grecque** (a) *Culin* **à la grecque** *(légumes)* = marinated in olive oil, lemon juice and herbs and served cold (b) *(motif)* Greek key pattern

Grèce [grɛs] *nf* **la G.** Greece

gredin, -e [grədɛ̃, -in] *nm,f Fam Vieilli* rascal

gréement [gremã] *nm* (a) *Naut* rigging (b) *Can (ustensiles)* gear, equipment

greffe¹ [grɛf] *nf* (a) *(de peau, de tissu)* graft; *(d'organe)* transplant; **g. du cœur/du rein** heart/kidney transplant (b) *Bot (action)* grafting; *(bouture)* graft

greffe² [grɛf] *nm Jur* clerk of the court's office

greffé, -e [grefe] *nm,f Méd* **g. cardiaque** *ou* **du cœur** heart-transplant patient

greffer [grefe] *vt (peau, tissu, bouture)* to graft; *(organe)* to transplant

greffier, -ère [grefje, -ɛr] *nm Jur* clerk (of the court)

greffon [grɛfɔ̃] *nm (de tissu, de peau)* graft; *(d'organe)* transplant; *(bouture)* graft

grégaire [gregɛr] *adj* gregarious; **l'instinct g.** the herd instinct

grège [grɛʒ] *adj (beige)* whitish-beige

grégorien, -enne [gregɔrjɛ̃, -ɛn] *adj* Gregorian

grêle¹ [grɛl] *adj (jambes, mains)* skinny; *(tige, silhouette)* slender; *(voix, son)* shrill

grêle² [grɛl] *nf aussi Fig* hail

grêlé, -e [grele] *adj (peau)* pockmarked

grêler [grele] *v impersonnel* to hail

grêlon [grɛlɔ̃] *nm* hailstone

grelot [grəlo] *nm* (small) bell

grelotter [grəlɔte] *vi* to shiver (**de** with)

Grenade [grənad] *nf (aux Antilles)* **la G.** Grenada

grenade [grənad] *nf* (a) *(projectile)* grenade; **g. lacrymogène** tear-gas grenade (b) *(fruit)* pomegranate

grenadine [grənadin] *nf* grenadine

grenaille [grənɑj] *nf* (a) *(plombs)* shot (b) *Belg (revêtement)* grit, fine gravel; **grenailles errantes** *(sur panneau)* loose gravel

grenat [grəna] **1** *nm* garnet **2** *adj inv* dark red

grenier [grənje] *nm* (a) *(sous les combles)* attic (b) *(pour grain, fourrage)* granary; **g. à blé** wheat loft; **g. à foin** hayloft

grenouille [grənuj] *nf (animal)* frog; *Fig & Péj* **g. de bénitier** Bible thumper

grenouillère [grənujɛr] *nf (pour bébé)* sleepsuit

grès [grɛ] *nm* (a) *(pierre)* sandstone (b) *(céramique)* stoneware; **cruche en g.** stoneware jug

grésil [grezil, grezi] *nm* fine hail

grésillement [grezijmã] *nm (du feu, d'une radio)* crackling; *(de l'huile)* sizzling

grésiller [grezije] *vi (feu, radio)* to crackle; *(huile)* to sizzle

gressin [gresɛ̃] *nm* bread stick

grève¹ [grɛv] *nf (arrêt du travail)* strike; **se mettre en g.** to go on strike, to strike; **être en g., faire g.** to be on strike; **g. des Postes** postal strike; **g. de la faim** hunger strike; **g. générale** general strike; **g. sauvage** wildcat strike; **g. sur le tas** sit-down strike; **g. tournante** staggered strike; **g. du zèle** work-to-rule, slowdown

grève² [grɛv] *nf (le long de la mer)* shore; *(d'un fleuve)* bank

grever [46] [grəve] *vt (pouvoir d'achat)* to restrict; *(budget)* to put a strain on

gréviste [grevist] *nmf* striker; **g. de la faim** hunger striker

gribouillage [gribujaʒ] *nm (écriture)* scribble, scrawl; *(dessin)* doodle

gribouille [gribuj] *nm Can (dispute)* quarrel, fight

gribouiller [gribuje] *vt & vi (écrire)* to scrawl, to scribble; *(dessiner)* to doodle

gribouillis [gribuji] *nm* = **gribouillage**

grief [grijɛf] *nm* grievance, ground for complaint; **faire** *ou* **tenir g. à qn de qch** to hold sth against sb

grièvement [grijɛvmã] *adv* seriously, badly

griffe [grif] *nf* (a) *(d'animal)* claw; **faire ses griffes** *(chat)* to sharpen its claws; *Fig* **montrer les griffes** to show one's claws; **arracher qn des griffes de qn** to snatch sb out of sb's clutches (**b**) *(sur un bijou)* claw (**c**) *(sur vêtements)* label; *Fig (style)* stamp (**d**) *Belg (rayure)* scratch

griffé, -e [grife] *adj (vêtement)* designer

griffer [grife] *vt* to scratch

griffon [grifɔ̃] *nm* (**a**) *(chien)* griffon (**b**) *(créature mythique)* griffin

griffonner [grifɔne] *vt & vi (écrire)* to scrawl, to scribble; *(dessiner)* to sketch quickly

griffure [grifyr] *nf* scratch

grignoter [griɲɔte] **1** *vt* to nibble; *Fig (libertés)* to erode; *(capital, économies)* to eat into
 2 *vi* to nibble

gril [gril] *nm (de cuisine)* broiler, grill; **faire cuire qch sur le g.** to broil *or* to grill sth; *Fig* **être sur le g.** to be on tenterhooks

grillade [grijad] *nf (viande)* piece of grilled meat; *(poisson)* piece of grilled fish; **faire des grillades** to have a barbecue

grillage [grijaʒ] *nm (de fenêtre, de porte)* wire mesh; *(clôture)* wire netting

grillagé, -e [grijaʒe] *adj (fenêtre)* covered with wire mesh; *(jardin)* surrounded with wire netting

grille [grij] *nf* (**a**) *(à l'entrée d'un parc, d'un jardin)* gate; *(clôture basse)* railings (**b**) *(d'une cage, d'une fenêtre)* screen, netting; *Aut* **g. de radiateur** radiator grille (**c**) *(d'un évier, d'un égout)* grating, grate (**d**) *(tableau) (de mots croisés)* grid; **une g. de Loto** a Loto card; *Rad & TV* **g. des programmes** program schedule; **g. des salaires** salary scale

grille-pain [grijpɛ̃] *nm inv* toaster

griller [grije] **1** *vt* (**a**) *(rôtir) (viande)* to broil; *(pain)* to toast; *(café, marrons)* to roast (**b**) *(brûler)* to scorch, to burn; *(ampoule, fusible)* to blow; *Fam (cigarette)* to smoke (**c**) *Fam (dépasser)* **g. un concurrent** to leave a competitor standing; **g. un feu rouge** to jump the lights (**d**) *Fam (discréditer)* **il est grillé** his game's up
 2 *vi* (**a**) *(viande)* to broil; *(pain)* to toast; *(marrons)* to roast; *Fig* **g. d'impatience** to be burning with impatience (**b**) *(ampoule, fusible)* to blow
 3 se griller *vpr* **se g. au soleil** to roast in the sun; *Fam* **se g. auprès de qn** to spoil one's record with sb

grillon [grijɔ̃] *nm* cricket

grimaçant, -e [grimasɑ̃, -ɑ̃t] *adj* grimacing

grimace [grimas] *nf* grimace; **faire une g. (à qn)** to make *or* to pull a face (at sb); **faire la g.** to make *or* to pull a face; **faire une g. de douleur** to wince with pain

grimacer [16] [grimase] *vi* to make *or* to pull a face; **g. de douleur** to wince with pain

grimer [grime] **1** *vt* to make up
 2 se grimer *vpr* to put one's make-up on

grimpant, -e [grɛ̃pɑ̃, -ɑ̃t] *adj (plante)* climbing

grimpe [grɛ̃p] *nf Fam* rock climbing; **faire de la g.** to go rock climbing

grimpée [grɛ̃pe] *nf* (stiff) climb

grimper [grɛ̃pe] **1** *vi aussi Fig* to climb; **g. aux arbres** to climb trees; *Fam* **ça grimpe** it's steep
 2 *vt (montagne, escalier)* to climb; *Fig* **g. les échelons** to climb the ladder

grimpeur, -euse [grɛ̃pœr, -øz] *nm,f* climber

grinçant, -e [grɛ̃sɑ̃, -ɑ̃t] *adj (qui grince)* creaking; *Fig (caustique)* caustic

grincement [grɛ̃smɑ̃] *nm (d'une porte, de roues)* creaking; **grincements de dents** grinding of teeth; *Fig* gnashing of teeth

grincer [16] [grɛ̃se] *vi (porte, roues)* to creak; **g. des dents** to grind one's teeth

grincheux, -euse [grɛ̃ʃø, -øz] **1** *adj* grumpy
 2 *nm,f* grouch

gringalet [grɛ̃galɛ] **1** *nm* weakling
 2 *adj m* puny

griotte [grijɔt] *nf* morello (cherry)

grippal, -e, -aux, -ales [gripal, -o] *adj* **soulage les états grippaux** *(sur médicament)* relieves flu symptoms

grippe [grip] *nf* (**a**) *(maladie)* flu; **avoir la g.** to have the flu; **g. intestinale** intestinal flu (**b**) **prendre qn/qch en g.** to take a dislike to sb/sth

grippé, -e [gripe] *adj* (**a**) *(malade)* **être g.** to have the flu (**b**) *(moteur, mécanisme)* seized-up

grippe-sou *(pl* **grippe-sous** *ou* **grippe-sou)** [gripsu] *nm* skinflint, miser

gris, -e [gri, griz] **1** *adj* (**a**) *(couleur, temps)* gray; **il fait g. ce matin** it's a gray *or* dull morning; **g. ardoise** slate gray; **g. perle** pearl gray (**b**) *(ivre)* tipsy
 2 *nm* (**a**) *(couleur)* gray; *Ordinat* **tons de g.** shades of gray; **s'habiller en g.** to wear gray (**b**) *(tabac)* shag

grisaille [grizaj] *nf (caractère morne)* dreariness

grisant, -e [grizɑ̃, -ɑ̃t] *adj (succès, atmosphère)* intoxicating; *(aventure, soirée)* exhilarating

grisâtre [grizɑtr] *adj* grayish

grisé [grize] *nm Ordinat* gray tone

griser [grize] **1** *vt* (**a**) *(enivrer)* to make tipsy; *Fig* to intoxicate (**b**) *Ordinat* to shade
 2 se griser *vpr* **se g. de qch** *(air pur)* to get drunk on sth; *(paroles)* to get carried away by sth

grisonnant, -e [grizɔnɑ̃, -ɑ̃t] *adj (cheveux, personne)* graying; **avoir les tempes grisonnantes** to be graying at the temples

grisonner [grizɔne] *vi (cheveux, personne)* to go gray

grisou [grizu] *nm* firedamp; **coup de g.** firedamp explosion

grive [griv] *nf* thrush

grivois, -e [grivwa, -az] *adj* bawdy

grivoiserie [grivwazri] *nf (plaisanterie)* bawdy joke; *(histoire)* bawdy story; *(acte)* rude gesture

grizzli, grizzly [grizli] *nm* grizzly (bear)

Groenland [grɔɛnlɑ̃d] *nm* **le G.** Greenland

grog [grɔg] *nm* hot toddy

groggy [grɔgi] *adj inv Fam* groggy

grogne [grɔɲ] *nf Fam* discontent

grognement [grɔɲmɑ̃] *nm (d'un cochon)* grunt; *(d'un chien, d'un ours, d'une personne)* growl; **pousser des grognements** to grunt/to growl

grogner [grɔɲe] *vi* (**a**) *(gronder) (cochon)* to grunt; *(chien, personne)* to growl (**b**) *(protester)* to grumble

grognon [grɔɲɔ̃] *adj* grumpy

groin [grwɛ̃] *nm* snout

grol(l)e [grɔl] *nf très Fam* shoe

grommeler [9] [grɔmle] *vt & vi* to mutter

grommellements [grɔmɛlmɑ̃] *nmpl* muttering

grondement [grɔ̃dmɑ̃] *nm* (**a**) *(d'un chien)* growl (**b**) *(du tonnerre)* rumble; *(d'un torrent, des vagues, d'un moteur)* roar; *(des canons)* booming

gronder [grɔ̃de] **1** *vi* (**a**) *(chien)* to growl (**b**) *(tonnerre)* to rumble; *(torrent, vagues, moteur)* to roar; *(canons)* to boom; **la révolte/le mécontentement gronde** there are rumblings of rebellion/discontent
 2 *vt (réprimander)* to scold, to tell off; **se faire g.** to get told off

groom [grum] *nm* bellhop

gros, grosse [gro, gros] **1** *adj* (**a**) *(corpulent)* big, fat (**b**) *(important, abondant)* big; *(rhume)* bad; *(dépenses, averse, mer)* heavy; *(somme)* large; *(faute)* serious; **g. buveur/mangeur** big drinker/eater; **avoir un g. chagrin** to be very upset; **la plus grosse partie de qch** the majority of sth; **un mensonge g. comme une maison** a whopper of a lie; *très Fam* **g. lard** big fat slob; *Fam* **g. nigaud** *ou* **bêta!** you big numskull!; *Fam* **g. bonnet, grosse légume** big shot, bigwig (**c**) *(épais) (morceau, caractères)* big, large; *(toile)* coarse; *(pull, chaussettes, corde)* thick; *(chaussures)* strong, stout

(**d**) *(peu subtil) (voix)* gruff; *(rire)* coarse; **c'est un peu g.!** that's a bit much!; **g. mot** curse word

(**e**) *Mus* **grosse caisse** bass drum

2 *adv (beaucoup) (gagner, rapporter, risquer)* a lot; **je donnerais g. pour savoir qui a fait ça** I'd give a lot to know who did that

3 *nm,f* fat man, *f* fat woman

4 *nm* (**a**) *(partie la plus importante)* bulk; **le g. de** the majority of; **le plus g. est fait** the bulk of the work has been done (**b**) *Com* wholesale *(trade)*; **faire du g.** to sell wholesale; **de g.** *(commerce, boucher)* wholesale (**c**) **en g.** *(en grosses lettres)* in big *or* large letters; *(approximativement)* roughly; *Com* wholesale

groseille [grozεj] *nf* **g. (rouge)** redcurrant; **g. à maquereau** gooseberry

groseillier [grozeje] *nm* redcurrant bush; **g. à maquereau** gooseberry bush

grosse [gros] *voir* **gros**

grossesse [grosεs] *nf* pregnancy; **g. extra-utérine** ectopic pregnancy; **g. nerveuse** phantom pregnancy; **g. à risque** high-risk pregnancy

grosseur [grosœr] *nf* (**a**) *(taille, volume)* size; **de la g. d'un œuf** the size of an egg (**b**) *Méd* lump

grossier, -ère [grosje, -εr] *adj* (**a**) *(impoli) (personne)* rude (**envers** to); *(langage, plaisanterie)* crude; **un g. personnage** an uncouth individual (**b**) *(peu raffiné) (nourriture, tissu)* coarse, rough; *(dessin)* crude, rough; *(goûts, traits du visage)* coarse; *(ruse)* crude (**c**) *(important) (erreur)* gross

grossièrement [grosjεrmɑ̃] *adv* (**a**) *(de façon impolie)* rudely (**b**) *(sans raffinement)* crudely (**c**) *(approximativement)* roughly

grossièreté [grosjεrte] *nf* (**a**) *(incorrection)* coarseness (**b**) *(parole grossière)* coarse remark; *(obscénité)* dirty joke; **dire des grossièretés** to swear; **il aime raconter des grossièretés** he likes telling dirty jokes (**c**) *(caractère rudimentaire) (d'un dessin)* crudeness; *(d'un tissu, des goûts)* coarseness

grossir [grosir] **1** *vi (personne, animal)* to put on weight, to get fatter; *(mer)* to get rough; *(rivière)* to swell; **g. de quatre kilos** *(personne)* ≃ to put on nine pounds

2 *vt (sujet: loupe, microscope)* to magnify; *Fig (exagérer)* to exaggerate; **g. qn** *(sujet: vêtement)* to make sb look fat; **g. les rangs de qch** to swell the ranks of sth

grossissant, -e [grosisɑ̃, -ɑ̃t] *adj* **miroir g.** distorting mirror

grossissement [grosismɑ̃] *nm* (**a**) *(augmentation de taille)* increase in size (**b**) *(pouvoir grossissant)* magnification

grossiste [grosist] *nmf* wholesaler

grosso modo [grosomodo] *adv* roughly; **g. c'est une comédie** broadly speaking it's a comedy

grotesque [grotεsk] *adj* ludicrous, ridiculous

grotte [grot] *nf* cave; **g. artificielle** grotto

grouillant, -e [grujɑ̃, -ɑ̃t] *adj* swarming (**de** with)

grouiller [gruje] **1** *vi (se presser)* to swarm around; **g. de** to swarm with

2 se grouiller *vpr Fam* to get a move on

groupe [grup] *nm* (**a**) *(de gens, de choses)* group; *(de musiciens)* group, band; **en g.** in a group; **se mettre par groupes de trois** to get into *or* form groups of three; *Pol* **le G. des 8** the Group of Eight; **g. d'âge** age group; *Ordinat* **g. de discussion** discussion group; *Scol* **g. de niveau** track; *Pol* **g. de pression** pressure group (**b**) *(industriel, de presse)* group; *(hospitalier, scolaire)* complex (**c**) *Gram* **g. verbal/nominal** verbal/nominal group (**d**) *Mil* **g. de combat** unit (**e**) *Méd* **g. sanguin** blood group (**f**) *Élec* **g. électrogène** generator

groupement [grupmɑ̃] *nm (association)* group; **g. d'achat** purchasing co-operative; **g. de consommateurs** consumer group

grouper [grupe] **1** *vt* to group (together); *(moyens, ressources)* to pool

2 se grouper *vpr (dans une association)* to form a group; *(dans un lieu)* to gather; **rester groupés** to keep together

groupie [grupi] *nf Fam* groupie

groupuscule [grupyskyl] *nm* small group

gruau [gryo] *nm* (**a**) **g. (d'avoine)** groats; **(farine de) g.** (fine) wheat flour (**b**) *Can Culin* oatmeal, porridge

grue [gry] *nf* (**a**) *(oiseau)* crane; **faire le pied de g.** to hang around (**b**) *(machine)* crane; *TV & Cin* cherry picker (**c**) *très Fam Vieilli (prostituée)* hooker

gruger [45] [gryʒe] *vt (rouler)* to swindle

grumeau, -x [grymo] *nm (dans une sauce, une pâte)* lump

grumeleux, -euse [grymlø, -øz] *adj (sauce, pâte)* lumpy

gruyère [gryjεr] *nm* Gruyère (cheese)

GSM [ʒeεsεm] *nm Tél (abrév* **global system for mobile communications**) (**a**) *(système)* GSM; **réseau G.** GSM network (**b**) *Belg (téléphone portable)* cellphone

Guadeloupe [gwadlup] *nf* **la G.** Guadeloupe

guadeloupéen, -enne [gwadlupeɛ̃, -εn] **1** *adj* of Guadeloupe

2 *nm,f* **G., Guadeloupéenne** person from Guadeloupe

Guatemala [gwatemala] *nm* **le G.** Guatemala

guatémaltèque [gwatemaltεk] **1** *adj* Guatemalan

2 *nmf* **G.** Guatemalan

gué [ge] *nm* ford; **passer une rivière à g.** to ford a river

guéguerre [gegεr] *nf Fam* squabble

guenilles [gənij] *nfpl* (old) rags; **en g.** in rags

guenon [gənɔ̃] *nf* female monkey

guépard [gepar] *nm* cheetah

guêpe [gεp] *nf* wasp; *Fam* **pas folle, la g.!** she's nobody's fool!

guêpier [gepje] *nm* wasps' nest; *Fig (situation)* sticky situation; **se fourrer dans un g.** to get oneself into a sticky situation

guêpière [gεpjεr] *nf* basque

guère [gεr] *adv* **ne... g.** *(pas beaucoup)* not much; *(pas longtemps)* hardly, scarcely; **il n'a g. d'argent/d'amis** he hasn't got much money/many friends; **il n'y a g. qu'elle qui soit au courant** she's about the only one who knows what's going on; **il ne mange g. que du pain** he eats hardly anything but bread; **il n'y a g. plus de six ans** just over six years ago; **et celui-là, comment le trouvez-vous? – g. mieux!** and what do you think of that one? – not much better!

guéri, -e [geri] *adj aussi Fig* cured (**de** of)

guéridon [geridɔ̃] *nm* pedestal table

guérilla [gerija] *nf* guerrilla warfare

guérillero [gerijero] *nm* guerrilla

guérir [gerir] **1** *vt (personne, maladie)* to cure; *Fig* **g. qn de qch** *(timidité, habitude)* to cure sb of sth

2 *vi (personne)* to get better, to recover; *(blessure)* to heal

3 se guérir *vpr (soi-même)* to cure oneself; *Fig* **se g. de qch** *(timidité, habitude)* to cure oneself of sth

guérison [gerizɔ̃] *nf (rétablissement)* recovery

guérissable [gerisabl] *adj* curable

guérisseur, -euse [gerisœr, -øz] **1** *nm,f* healer

2 *nm (d'une tribu)* medicine man

guérite [gerit] *nf Mil* sentry box

guerre [gεr] *nf* (**a**) *(conflit)* war; *(technique)* warfare; **en temps de g.** in wartime; **être en g. (contre)** to be at war (with); **faire la g.** *(soldat)* to fight; **la drôle de g.** the phony war; **la Grande G.** the Great War; **la Première/la Seconde G. mondiale** the First/Second World War, World War One/Two; **la g. de 14** the 1914–18 War; **la g. de 70** the Franco-Prussian War; **la g. d'Algérie** the Algerian War of Independence; **la g. de Cent Ans** the Hundred Years' War; **g. civile** civil war; **la g. de Corée** the Korean War; **g. éclair** blitzkrieg; **la g. d'Espagne** the Spanish Civil War; **la g. froide** the cold war; **la g. du Golfe** the Gulf War; **la g. d'Indochine** the first Indo-Chinese War *(1946-1954)*; **g. sainte** holy war; **la g. de Sécession** the American Civil War; **la g. du Viêt Nam** the Vietnam War (**b**) *(locutions)* **elle fait la g. à son fils pour qu'il ne fume pas** she's fighting a running battle with her son about smoking; **faire la g. à qch** to wage war on sth; **partir en g. contre qch** to declare war on sth; **il est en g. ouverte contre sa hiérarchie** there's open war between him and his superiors; **à la g. comme à la g.** we'll/you'll/ *etc.* have to do the best we/you/*etc.* can; **c'est de bonne g.** that's fair enough; **de g. lasse** for the sake of peace and quiet

guerrier, -ère [gɛrje, -ɛr] **1** *adj* warlike; *(chant)* war
    2 *nm,f* warrior

guerroyer [32] [gɛrwaje] *vi Litt* to wage war (**contre** on)

guet [gɛ] *nm* **poste de g.** lookout post; **faire le g.** to be on the lookout

guet-apens (*pl* **guets-apens**) [gɛtapɑ̃] *nm (piège)* ambush; *Fig* trap; **tomber dans un g.** to be ambushed; *Fig* to fall into a trap

guêtre [gɛtr] *nf* gaiter; *Belg Fig* **il a la police à ses guêtres** the police are on his tail *or* hot on his heels

guetter [gete] *vt (occasion)* to watch out for; *(proie)* to lie in wait for; **il guette le facteur** he's on the lookout for the mailman; **la dépression le guette** he's on the verge of a nervous breakdown

gueulante [gœlɑ̃t] *nf très Fam* **pousser une g.** to kick up a stink

gueulard, -e [gœlar, -ard] *très Fam* **1** *adj (personne)* loud-mouthed; *(bébé)* screaming; *(couleur)* garish
    2 *nm,f (personne)* loudmouth; *(bébé)* screaming kid

gueule [gœl] *nf* (**a**) *(d'un animal)* mouth; *Fig* **se jeter dans la g. du loup** to put one's head in the lion's mouth (**b**) *très Fam (bouche)* mouth; **ça emporte** *ou* **arrache la g.** it takes the roof of your mouth off; **une grande g.** *(personne)* a loudmouth; **(ferme) ta g.!** shut your mouth!, shut up!; **avoir la g. de bois** to have a hangover (**c**) *très Fam (visage)* mug, face; **avoir une sale g.** *(mine patibulaire)* to look shady; *(mauvaise mine)* to look rotten; **faire la g.** to sulk; **faire la g. à qn** to be in a huff with sb; **faire une g. d'enterrement** to look really bummed out; **se foutre de** *ou* **se payer la g. de qn** to take sb for an asshole; **(s')en prendre plein la g.** to get a heap of abuse (**d**) *Fam (allure)* **avoir une drôle de g.** to look odd; **ce tableau a de la g.** that's some picture

gueuler [gœle] *très Fam* **1** *vi* to yell, to bawl; *(radio, télévision)* to blare; *(protester)* to kick up a fuss; **si je suis en retard, ça va g. à la maison** if I'm late, I'll get bawled out when I get home
    2 *vt* to bawl out, to yell out

gueuleton [gœltɔ̃] *nm Fam* blowout; **faire un g.** to have a blowout

gueux, gueuse¹ [gø, gøz] *nm,f Vieilli (mendiant)* beggar

gueuze, gueuse² [gøz] *nf* = type of strong double-fermented Belgian beer

gugusse [gygys] *nm Fam* clown; **faire le g.** to fool around

gui [gi] *nm* mistletoe

guibol(l)e [gibɔl] *nf Fam (jambe)* leg

guichet [giʃɛ] *nm* (**a**) *(de gare, de poste, de banque)* window; *(de théâtre)* box office; **on joue à guichets fermés** the performance is sold out; **g. automatique** *(de banque)* ATM (**b**) *(de porte de prison)* hatch; *(de confessionnal)* grille

guichetier, -ère [giʃtje, -ɛr] *nm,f (de gare)* ticket clerk; *(de poste, de banque)* teller

guide [gid] **1** *nm* (**a**) *(personne)* guide; **g. de haute montagne** mountain guide; **g.-interprète** bilingual tour guide (**b**) *(manuel)* guide (book); **g. de conversation** phrase book; **g. gastronomique** restaurant guide; **g. touristique** tourist guide

(**c**) *Belg (indicateur de chemin de fer)* train timetable; *(annuaire)* telephone directory
    2 *nf (scout)* Girl Scout

guider [gide] *vt* to guide; **se laisser g. par son intuition** to be guided by one's intuition

guidon [gidɔ̃] *nm* handlebars

guigne¹ [giɲ] *nf (cerise)* sweet cherry; *Fam* **se soucier de qn/ qch comme d'une g.** not to give a damn about sb/sth

guigne² [giɲ] *nf Fam (malchance)* bad luck; **avoir la g.** to be out of luck

guigner [giɲe] *vt Fam (avoir des vues sur)* to have one's eye on

guignol [giɲɔl] *nm* (**a**) **G.** *(personnage)* ≃ Punch (**b**) *Péj (personne)* clown, joker; **faire le g.** to clown around (**c**) *(spectacle)* ≃ Punch-and-Judy show

Guillaume [gijom] *npr* **G. le Conquérant** William the Conqueror

guillemets [gijmɛ] *nmpl* quotation marks; **entre g.** in quotation marks

guilleret, -ette [gijrɛ, -ɛt] *adj* jaunty, lively

guillotine [gijɔtin] *nf* guillotine

guillotiner [gijɔtine] *vt* to guillotine

guimauve [gimov] *nf (confiserie)* marshmallow; *Fig & Péj* **c'est de la g.** it's pure schmaltz

guimbarde [gɛ̃bard] *nf* (**a**) *Fam (vieille voiture)* jalopy (**b**) *(instrument de musique)* Jew's harp

guindé, -e [gɛ̃de] *adj (personne, air)* stiff; *(atmosphère)* strained; *(style)* stilted; *(réception)* posh

Guinée [gine] *nf* **la G.** Guinea; **la G. équatoriale** Equatorial Guinea

Guinée-Bissau [ginebiso] *nf* **la G.** Guinea-Bissau

guinéen, -enne [gineɛ̃, -ɛn] **1** *adj* Guinean
    2 *nm,f* **G., Guinéenne** Guinean

guingois [gɛ̃gwa] **de guingois** *adv* askew, lopsided

guinguette [gɛ̃gɛt] *nf* riverside café

guirlande [girlɑ̃d] *nf (de fleurs)* garland; **g. lumineuse** string of lights; **g. de Noël** piece of tinsel; **g. de papier** paper chain

guise [giz] *nf* **faire qch à sa g.** to do sth as one likes; **n'en faire qu'à sa g.** to do just as one likes; **en g. de** by way of

guitare [gitar] *nf* guitar; **g. basse** bass guitar; **g. électrique** electric guitar; **g. sèche** acoustic guitar

guitariste [gitarist] *nmf* guitarist

gus [gys] *nm Fam* guy

gustatif, -ive [gystatif, -iv] *adj* **papilles gustatives** taste buds

guttural, -e, -aux, -ales [gytyral, -o] *adj* guttural

Guyana [gɥijana] *nm* **le G.** Guyana

guyanais, -e [gɥijanɛ, -ɛz] **1** *adj* Guianese
    2 *nm,f* **G., Guyanaise** Guianese

Guyane [gɥijan] *nf* **la G.** Guiana; **la G. française** French Guiana

gym [ʒim] *nf Fam* gym

gymkhana [ʒimkana] *nm* rally

gymnase [ʒimnɑz] *nm* (**a**) *(salle)* gymnasium (**b**) *Suisse (lycée)* ≃ high school

gymnaste [ʒimnast] *nmf* gymnast

gymnastique [ʒimnastik] *nf* gymnastics; *Fig* **il faut faire toute une g. pour sortir de cette auto** you have to be a contortionist to get out of this car; **g. respiratoire** breathing exercises; **g. rythmique** eurhythmics *(singulier)*

gynécologie [ʒinekɔlɔʒi] *nf* gynecology

gynécologique [ʒinekɔlɔʒik] *adj* gynecological

gynécologue [ʒinekɔlɔg] *nmf* gynecologist

gypse [ʒips] *nm* gypsum

gyrophare [ʒirofar] *nm* rotating light

H

H, h [aʃ] *nm inv* H, h; **h. aspiré** aspirate h; **h muet** mute h

*ha [ɑ] *exclam* ah!; **ha, ha!** *(rire)* ha-ha!

habile [abil] *adj* (**a**) *(personne)* skillful; *(manœuvre, film, roman)* clever; **être h. de ses mains** to be good with one's hands; **être h. en affaires** to be a good businessman/business-woman (**b**) *Jur* **h. à faire qch** able to do sth

habilement [abilmɑ̃] *adv* skillfully

habileté [abilte] *nf* skill

habiliter [abilite] *vt Jur* **h. qn à faire qch** to enable sb to do sth; **être habilité à faire qch** to be authorized to do sth

habillage [abijaʒ] *nm* (**a**) *(d'une personne)* dressing (**b**) **h. intérieur** *(d'une voiture)* trim (**c**) *TV & Rad* station identification

habillé, -e [abije] *adj* (**a**) *(vêtu)* dressed; **h. en femme/cos-monaute** dressed (up) as a woman/an astronaut; **s'endor-mir tout h.** to go to sleep with one's clothes on (**b**) *(élégant) (personne, tenue)* smart; **soirée habillée** formal occasion

habillement [abijmɑ̃] *nm* (**a**) *(vêtements)* clothes (**b**) *(industrie)* clothing industry

habiller [abije] **1** *vt* (**a**) *(vêtir)* to dress; **h. qn en soldat/cow-boy** to dress sb up as a soldier/cowboy (**b**) *(fournir en vête-ments)* to clothe (**c**) *(garnir)* to cover (**d**) *(aller à)* **un rien t'ha-bille** you look good in anything

  2 s'habiller *vpr* (**a**) *(se vêtir)* to get dressed, to dress; **elle s'habille n'importe comment** she wears any old thing; **comment vous habillez-vous pour la soirée?** what are you wearing to the party?; **s'h. en femme/an astronaute** to dress up as a woman/spaceman (**b**) *(se fournir)* **elle s'ha-bille chez Dior** she buys her clothes from Dior (**c**) *(élégam-ment)* to dress up

habilleur, -euse [abijœr, -øz] *nm,f* dresser

habit [abi] **1** *nm* (**a**) *(vêtement)* **habits** clothes; **habits du di-manche** Sunday best (**b**) *(tenue)* **h. (de soirée)** evening dress, tails; **l'h. vert** = the green coat worn by a member of the Aca-démie française (**c**) *(religieux)* habit; *Prov* **l'h. ne fait pas le moine** appearances can be deceptive

  2 *nm ou nf Can* suit; **h. de neige** snowsuit

habitable [abitabl] *adj* (in)habitable

habitacle [abitakl] *nm (d'un avion)* cockpit; *(d'une voiture)* pas-senger compartment

habitant, -e [abitɑ̃, -ɑ̃t] **1** *nm,f* (**a**) *(d'une ville)* inhabitant, resident; *(d'une maison)* occupant; **loger chez l'h.** *(en voyage)* to stay with local people (**b**) *Can (fermier)* small-scale farmer

  2 *adj Can (nourriture, objets)* rustic; *Péj* **il est un peu h.** he's a bit of a hillbilly

habitat [abita] *nm (d'un animal, d'une plante)* habitat; *(de per-sonnes) (mode de peuplement)* settlement; *(conditions de loge-ment)* housing conditions

habitation [abitasjɔ̃] *nf* (**a**) *(fait de résider)* living; **locaux à usage d'h.** premises for residential use (**b**) *(lieu)* dwelling; **h. à loyer modéré** ≃ public-housing unit

habiter [abite] **1** *vt (maison, lieu)* to live in; *Fig (âme, personne)* to possess; **la région n'est pas habitée** the area is uninhabited

  2 *vi* to live (**à/en** in)

habitude [abityd] *nf* (**a**) *(comportement répété)* habit; **avoir l'h. ou avoir pour h. de faire qch** to be in the habit of doing sth; **ça ne la gênera pas, elle a l'h.** that won't bother her, she's used to it; **avoir l'h. de qch** to be used to sth; **prendre l'h. de faire qch** to get into the habit of doing sth; **faire qch par h.** to do sth out of habit; **ce n'est pas dans mes habitudes** I don't make a habit of it; **d'h.** usually; **meilleur/plus tôt que d'h.** better/earlier than usual; **comme d'h.** as usual (**b**) **habi-tudes** *(coutumes)* customs

habitué, -e [abitye] *nm,f (d'une maison)* regular visitor; *(d'un restaurant, d'un magasin)* regular (customer)

habituel, -elle [abityɛl] *adj* usual, customary

habituellement [abityɛlmɑ̃] *adv* usually

habituer [abitye] **1** *vt* **h. qn à qch/à faire qch** to get sb used to sth/to doing sth; **être habitué à qn/à qch/à faire qch** to be used *or* accustomed to sb/to sth/to doing sth

  2 s'habituer *vpr* **s'h. à qn/à qch/à faire qch** to get used *or* accustomed to sb/to sth/to doing sth; **tu finiras par t'h.** you'll get used to it in the end

*hâbleur, -euse [ɑblœr, -øz] *adj* boastful

*hache [aʃ] *nf* ax; *Fig* **enterrer la h. de guerre** to bury the hatchet

*haché, -e [aʃe] **1** *adj* (**a**) *(viande)* ground; *(légumes, herbes)* chopped (**b**) *(style, phrases)* jerky

  2 *nm* ground meat

*hacher [aʃe] *vt* to chop (up); *(viande) (dans un hachoir)* to grind; **h. menu qch** to chop sth (up) finely; *Fig* **h. qn menu (comme chair à pâté)** to make mincemeat of sb; *Fig* **se faire h.** *(se faire battre)* to be massacred

*hachette [aʃɛt] *nf* hatchet

*hachis [aʃi] *nm* **h. d'herbes** chopped herbs; **h. Parmentier** ≃ shepherd's pie; **h. de viande** ground meat

*hachisch [aʃiʃ] *nm* hashish

*hachoir [aʃwar] *nm* (**a**) *(couteau)* chopper (**b**) *(machine)* grin-der

*hachurer [aʃyre] *vt* to hatch

*hachures [aʃyr] *nfpl* hatching

*hagard, -e [agar, -ard] *adj (visage)* haggard; *(expression, re-gard, yeux)* wild

*haie [ɛ] *nf* (**a**) *(clôture)* hedge; **h. vive** quickset hedge (**b**) *(en athlétisme)* hurdle; *(en équitation)* fence; **400 mètres haies** 400-meter hurdles (**c**) *(d'arbres, de pieux, de curieux)* line, row; **h. d'honneur** guard of honor; **faire une h. d'honneur** to form a guard of honor

*haillons [ɑjɔ̃] *nmpl (vêtements)* rags; **en h.** in rags (and tat-ters)

*haine [ɛn] *nf* hate, hatred; **sa h. de/pour** his hatred of/for; *très Fam* **avoir la h.** *(être révolté)* to be full of rage; *(être furieux)* to be hopping mad

*haineux, -euse [ɛnø, -øz] *adj* full of hatred

*haïr [41] [air] **1** *vt* to hate

  2 se haïr *vpr (soi-même)* to hate oneself; *(l'un l'autre)* to hate each other

---

The symbol * indicates that the initial **h** is aspirate and that hence there is no liaison, e.g. **les haricots** [leariko] and not [lezariko], or contraction in spelling, e.g. **la haine** and not **l'haine**.

*__hais__ *voir* __haïr__

*__haïssable__ [aisabl] *adj* hateful

*__hait__ *voir* __haïr__

__Haïti__ [aiti] *n* Haiti

__haïtien, -enne__ [aisjɛ̃, -ɛn] __1__ *adj* Haitian
  __2__ *nm,f* __H., Haïtienne__ Haitian

*__halage__ [alaʒ] *nm* towing; __chemin de h.__ towpath

*__hâle__ [ɑl] *nm* (sun)tan

*__hâlé, -e__ [ɑle] *adj* (sun)tanned

__haleine__ [alɛn] *nf* breath; __avoir mauvaise h.__ to have bad breath; __courir à perdre h.__ to run until one is out of breath; __reprendre h.__ to get one's breath (back); __tenir qn en h.__ to keep sb in suspense; __hors d'h.__ out of breath, breathless; __travail de longue h.__ long job

*__haler__ [ale] *vt* to tow

*__haletant, -e__ [alatɑ̃, -ɑ̃t] *adj (coureur, malade, voix)* panting, gasping; *Fig (suspense)* unbearable; __respiration haletante__ panting, gasping

*__halètement__ [alɛtmɑ̃] *nm (d'un coureur, d'un malade)* panting, gasping

*__haleter__ [6] [alte] *vi (coureur, malade)* to pant, to gasp

*__hall__ [ol] *nm (d'une maison)* entrance hall; *(d'un hôtel)* foyer, lobby; *(d'un aéroport)* lounge; __h. d'accueil__ reception hall; __h. d'entrée__ entrance hall; __h. de gare__ station concourse; *Péj* __littérature/roman de h. de gare__ trashy literature/novel

*__halle__ [al] *nf* __(a)__ *(marché)* (covered) market; __h. au poisson__ fish market __(b)__ *Suisse (bâtiment)* hall; __h. de fête__ community center

---

Les Halles

"Les Halles" refers to the central Paris wholesale food markets, dating from the Second Empire. Once a tourist attraction and also a source of traffic congestion, they were moved to the outskirts, mainly to Rungis, near Orly, in the 1960s. After much delay and controversy, the site (infamously known as the "trou des Halles") was redeveloped in the late 1970s with a Metro station and a modern shopping mall, the "Forum des Halles".

---

*__hallebarde__ [albard] *nf* halberd; *Fam* __il pleut__ *ou* __tombe des hallebardes__ it's raining cats and dogs

__hallucinant, -e__ [alysinɑ̃, -ɑ̃t] *adj (extraordinaire)* striking; *(incroyable)* incredible

__hallucination__ [alysinasjɔ̃] *nf* hallucination; __avoir des hallucinations__ *(malade, ivrogne)* to have hallucinations; *Fig (se tromper)* to see things

__halluciner__ [alysine] *vi (avoir des hallucinations)* to hallucinate; *Fam Fig* __j'hallucine!__ I don't believe it!

__hallucinogène__ [alysinɔʒɛn] __1__ *adj* hallucinogenic
  __2__ *nm* hallucinogen

*__halo__ [alo] *nm aussi Fig* halo

__halogène__ [alɔʒɛn] *nm Chim* halogen; __(lampe à) h.__ halogen lamp

*__halte__ [alt] *nf* __(a)__ *(arrêt)* stop; __faire h.__ to stop; __h.(-là)!__ stop!; *Fig* __h.-là, je ne suis pas d'accord!__ hold on, I don't agree!; __h. à l'armement!__ stop the arms build-up! __(b)__ *(lieu)* stopping place; *Rail* halt; *Can (point de vue)* viewing point, scenic overlook; *(aire de repos routière)* rest area

*__halte-garderie__ *(pl* __haltes-garderies)__ [altəgardəri] *nf* crèche

__haltère__ [altɛr] *nm* dumbbell; __faire des haltères__ to do weightlifting

__haltérophile__ [alterɔfil] *nmf* weightlifter

__haltérophilie__ [alterɔfili] *nf* weightlifting

*__hamac__ [amak] *nm* hammock

*__Hambourg__ [ɑ̃bur] *n* Hamburg

*__hamburger__ [ɑ̃burgœr] *nm* burger

*__hameau, -x__ [amo] *nm* hamlet

__hameçon__ [amsɔ̃] *nm* (fish-)hook; *Fig* __mordre à l'h.__ to swallow the bait

*__hammam__ [amam] *nm* Turkish baths

*__hampe__ [ɑ̃p] *nf (d'un drapeau)* pole

*__hamster__ [amstɛr] *nm* hamster

*__hanche__ [ɑ̃ʃ] *nf* hip

*__hand__ [ɑ̃d] *nm Fam* handball

*__handball__ [ɑ̃dbal] *nm* handball

*__handballeur, -euse__ [ɑ̃dbalœr, -øz] *nm,f* handball player

*__handicap__ [ɑ̃dikap] *nm (physique, mental)* disability; *Sport & Fig* handicap; *Fig* __partir avec un h.__ to start at a disadvantage

*__handicapé, -e__ [ɑ̃dikape] __1__ *adj* disabled
  __2__ *nm,f* disabled person; __les handicapés__ the disabled; __h. mental__ mentally handicapped person; __h. moteur__ person with motor impairment

*__handicaper__ [ɑ̃dikape] *vt (physiquement, mentalement)* to disable; *Fig* to handicap

*__hangar__ [ɑ̃gar] *nm* shed; *(pour les trains, les bus)* depot; *(pour les avions)* hangar; __h. à bateaux__ boathouse

*__hanneton__ [antɔ̃] *nm* cockchafer; *Fam* __pas piqué des hannetons__ *(difficile)* tough; *(bon, beau)* incredible

__Hanoi__ [anɔj] *n* Hanoi

*__Hanovre__ [anɔvr] *n* Hanover

*__hanté, -e__ [ɑ̃te] *adj* haunted

*__hanter__ [ɑ̃te] *vt (sujet: fantôme, pensée)* to haunt; *Fig (bars, musées)* to hang around

*__hantise__ [ɑ̃tiz] *nf* obsession; __avoir la h. de qch__ to really dread sth

*__happer__ [ape] *vt (dans sa gueule, son bec)* to snap up; *(sujet: véhicule)* to hit

*__hara-kiri__ [arakiri] *nm* hara-kiri; __(se) faire h.__ to commit hara-kiri

*__harangue__ [arɑ̃g] *nf* harangue

*__haranguer__ [arɑ̃ge] *vt* to harangue

*__haras__ [ara] *nm* stud farm

*__harassant, -e__ [arasɑ̃, -ɑ̃t] *adj* exhausting

*__harassé, -e__ [arase] *adj* exhausted

*__harasser__ [arase] *vt* to exhaust

*__harcèlement__ [arsɛlmɑ̃] *nm* harassment; __h. sexuel__ sexual harassment

*__harceler__ [39] [arsəle] *vt (importuner)* to harass; *(insister auprès de)* to pester; __h. qn de questions__ to pester sb with questions; __être harcelé de remords/regrets__ to be plagued by remorse/regrets

*__harceleur, -euse__ [arsəlœr, -øz] *nm,f* pest; __h. téléphonique__ phone pest

*__harde__ [ard] *nf (de cerfs)* herd

*__hardes__ [ard] *nfpl (haillons)* rags

*__hardi, -e__ [ardi] *adj (audacieux, original)* bold; *(osé)* brazen

*__hardiesse__ [ardjɛs] *nf (audace, originalité)* boldness; *(caractère osé)* brazenness

*__hardiment__ [ardimɑ̃] *adv (avec audace)* boldly

*__hard-rock__ [ardrɔk] *nm inv* hard rock

*__harem__ [arɛm] *nm* harem

*__hareng__ [arɑ̃] *nm* herring; __h. saur__ smoked herring

*__harfang__ [arfɑ̃] *nm Can* snowy owl

*__hargne__ [arɲ] *nf* bad temper; __avec h.__ bad-temperedly

*__hargneux, -euse__ [arɲø, -øz] *adj (personne)* bad-tempered; __d'un ton h.__ bad-temperedly

*__haricot__ [ariko] *nm* __(a)__ *(légume)* bean; __haricots en grains__ dried beans; *Fam* __c'est la fin des haricots__ we've/they've/*etc.* had it now; *Fam* __courir sur le h. à qn__ to get on sb's nerves; __h. beurre__ butter bean; __h. blanc__ haricot bean; __h. rouge__ red kidney bean; __h. vert__ green bean __(b)__ *Culin* __h. de mouton__ mutton stew

*__harissa__ [arisa] *nf Culin* harissa *(hot pepper purée)*

*harki [arki] *nm* harki (*Algerian soldier who fought on the French side during the Franco-Algerian War*)

harmonica [armɔnika] *nm* harmonica, mouth organ

harmonie [armɔni] *nf* (**a**) (*accord*) *&* *Mus* harmony; **être en h. avec qch** to be in harmony with sth; **vivre en h.** to live in harmony (**b**) (*fanfare*) brass band

harmonieux, -euse [armɔnjø, -øz] *adj* harmonious

harmonique [armɔnik] *adj Mus* harmonic

harmonisation [armɔnizasjɔ̃] *nf* harmonization

harmoniser [armɔnize] **1** *vt* to harmonize (**avec** with)
2 s'harmoniser *vpr* to go well together

harmonium [armɔnjɔm] *nm* harmonium

*harnachement [arnaʃmɑ̃] *nm* (**a**) (*action*) harnessing (**b**) (*harnais*) harness; *Fig* (*vêtements*) get-up

*harnacher [arnaʃe] *vt* (*cheval*) to harness; *Fig* **il fallait voir comment elle était harnachée** you should have seen the get-up she was wearing

*harnais [arnɛ] *nm* (**a**) (*de cheval*) harness (**b**) **h. de sécurité** (*d'alpiniste, d'élagueur*) safety harness

*haro [aro] *nm* **crier h. sur** to rail against; **crier h. sur le baudet** to scream for blood

*harpe [arp] *nf* harp

*harpie [arpi] *nf aussi Fig* harpy

*harpiste [arpist] *nmf* harpist

*harpon [arpɔ̃] *nm* harpoon; **pêche au h.** harpoon fishing

*harponner [arpɔne] *vt* (**a**) (*poisson*) to harpoon (**b**) *Fam* (*sujet: police*) to nab; (*sujet: importun*) to corner

*hasard [azar] *nm* (**a**) (*sort*) chance, luck; **le h. a voulu que je sois à l'étranger** as it happened I was abroad; **coup de h.** stroke of luck; **par un heureux h.** by a happy coincidence; **ne rien laisser au h.** to leave nothing to chance; **le h. fait bien les choses!** what a stroke of luck!; **au h.** (*choisir, répondre*) at random; (*marcher*) aimlessly; **au h. de ses voyages/lectures** in the course of his/her travels/reading; **à tout h.** (*par précaution*) just in case; (*pour voir*) on the off chance; **par h.** by accident, by chance; **si par h. vous le voyez** if you (should) happen to see him; **comme par h.** as if by chance (**b**) **hasards** (*dangers*) hazards

*hasarder [azarde] **1** *vt* (*opinion, remarque*) to venture
2 se hasarder *vpr* (*dans l'obscurité, dans la jungle*) to venture; **se h. à faire qch** to risk doing sth

*hasardeux, -euse [azardø, -øz] *adj* risky, hazardous

*hasch [aʃ] *nm Fam* hash, pot

*haschisch [aʃiʃ] *nm* hashish

*hâte [ɑt] *nf* haste; **avoir h. de faire qch** (*avoir envie*) to be eager to do sth; **à la h.** hastily; **en h.** in a hurry, hurriedly

*hâter [ɑte] **1** *vt* (*accélérer*) to hasten; (*avancer*) to bring forward
2 se hâter *vpr* to hurry; **se h. de faire qch** to hurry to do sth

*hâtif, -ive [ɑtif, -iv] *adj* (*trop rapide*) hasty

*hâtivement [ɑtivmɑ̃] *adv* hastily

*hauban [obɑ̃] *nm* (**a**) *Naut* shroud (**b**) (*d'un pont*) stay

*hausse [os] *nf* rise, increase (**de** in); **être en h.** to be rising; **être à la h.** (*marché*) to be rising, to be bullish; **jouer à la h.** (*en Bourse*) to speculate on a rising *or* bull market

*haussement [osmɑ̃] *nm* **h. d'épaules** shrug; **avec un h. de sourcils** with raised eyebrows

*hausser [ose] **1** *vt* to raise; **h. la voix/les sourcils** to raise one's voice/eyebrows; **h. les épaules** to shrug (one's shoulders)
2 se hausser *vpr* to raise oneself (up); **se h. sur la pointe des pieds** to stand on tiptoe

*haussier [osje] *adj m voir* **marché**

*haut, -e [o, ot] **1** *adj* (**a**) (*dans l'espace, en quantité, en intensité*) high; **une femme de haute taille** a tall woman; **un mur h. de trois mètres** ≃ a ten-foot-high wall
(**b**) (*dans une hiérarchie*) high; **la haute couture** high fash-

ion; **les hauts salaires** the highly paid; **un athlète de h. niveau** a top-ranking athlete; **une montre de haute précision** a high-precision timepiece; **de hauts faits** daring deeds
(**c**) (*note*) high
(**d**) (*dans le temps*) early; **le h. Moyen Âge** the early Middle Ages
(**e**) **h. en couleur** (*récit, personnage*) colorful
2 *adv* (**a**) (*dans l'espace*) high; **comme il est dit plus h.** as mentioned above; **h. les mains!** hands up!; **gagner h. la main** to win hands down; **h. les cœurs!** cheer up!
(**b**) (*dans une hiérarchie*) highly
(**c**) (*dans la gamme*) high
(**d**) (*fort*) **dire qch tout h.** to say sth out loud; **dire tout h. ce que tout le monde pense tout bas** to say what everyone is thinking (but is too afraid to say)
(**e**) **en h.** at the top; (*à l'étage supérieur*) upstairs; **les gens d'en h.** the people above *or* upstairs; **en h. de** at the top of
3 *nm* (**a**) (*hauteur*) **le mur fait trois mètres de h.** ≃ the wall is ten feet high
(**b**) (*partie supérieure*) top; *Can* (*d'un immeuble*) top floor; **l'étagère du h.** the top shelf; **regarder qn de h. en bas** to look sb up and down; **connaître des hauts et des bas** to have one's ups and downs
(**c**) (*corsage*) top
4 *nf Fam* **haute** upper crust

*hautain, -e [otɛ̃, -ɛn] *adj* haughty

*hautbois [obwa] *nm* oboe

*haut-commissaire (*pl* hauts-commissaires) [okɔmisɛr] *nm* high commissioner

*haut-commissariat (*pl* hauts-commissariats) [okɔmisarja] *nm* high commission

*haut-de-chausses (*pl* hauts-de-chausses) [odəʃos] *nm* breeches

*haut-de-forme (*pl* hauts-de-forme) [odəfɔrm] *nm* top hat

*haute-contre (*pl* hautes-contre) [otkɔ̃tr] *nm* counter tenor

*haute-fidélité [otfidelite] *nf* hi-fi; **chaîne h.** hi-fi (system)

*hautement [otmɑ̃] *adv* (*très*) highly

*hauteur [otœr] *nf* (**a**) (*dimension*) height (**b**) (*altitude*) altitude; **prendre de la h.** to climb, to gain height; **à la h. de qch** (*dans l'espace*) level with sth; **à la h. du Mans** near Le Mans; *Fig* **être** *ou* **se montrer à la h. de qch** to be equal to *or* up to sth; **être à la h.** to be up to it; **à h. des yeux** at eye level; **l'eau nous arrivait à h. des épaules** the water came up to our shoulders; **contribuer à h. de 2 millions** to contribute 2 million (**c**) (*colline*) hill; **hauteurs** heights; **il y a de la neige sur les hauteurs** there's snow on the higher slopes (**d**) (*d'une note de musique*) pitch

*haut-fond (*pl* hauts-fonds) [ofɔ̃] *nm* shallow

*haut-fourneau (*pl* hauts-fourneaux) [ofurno] *nm* blast furnace

*haut-le-cœur [olakœr] *nm inv* **avoir un h.** to retch; **cette vision me donna un h.** the sight of it made me nauseous

*haut-parleur (*pl* haut-parleurs) [oparlœr] *nm* (loud)speaker

*Havane [avan] **1** *voir* **La Havane**
2 *nm* **h.** Havana (cigar)

*hâve [ɑv] *adj* (*visage*) gaunt; (*joues*) sunken

*havre [avr] *nm Litt* haven

Hawaii [awai] *n* Hawaii

hawaiien, -enne [awajɛ̃, -ɛn] **1** *adj* Hawaiian
2 *nm,f* **H., Hawaiienne** Hawaiian

*Haye [ɛ] *voir* **La Haye**

*hayon [ajɔ̃] *nm* (*d'une voiture*) hatchback

HCR [aʃseɛr] *nm* (*abrév* **Haut-Commissariat des Nations unies pour les réfugiés**) UNHCR

*hé [e] *exclam (pour interpeller)* hey!

hebdo [ɛbdo] *nm Fam* weekly; **h. télé** TV magazine program

hebdomadaire [ɛbdɔmadɛr] *adj & nm* weekly

hébergement [ebɛrʒəmɑ̃] *nm (d'un ami)* putting up; *(d'un sans-abri, d'un réfugié)* taking in; *(d'un fugitif)* harboring

héberger [45] [ebɛrʒe] *vt* **(a)** *(ami)* to put up; *(sans-abri, réfugié)* to take in; *(fugitif)* to harbor **(b)** *Ordinat (site Web)* to host

hébergeur [ebɛrʒœr] *nm Ordinat (de site Web)* host

hébété, -e [ebete] *adj* dazed

hébreu, -x [ebrø] **1** *adj m* Hebrew

2 *nm (langue)* Hebrew; *Fam* **c'est de l'h. pour moi** it's all Greek to me

3 *nmpl* **les Hébreux** the Hebrews

Hébrides [ebrid] *nfpl* **les H.** the Hebrides

HEC [aʃəse] *nf (abrév* **Hautes études commerciales**) = prestigious business school in Paris

hécatombe [ekatɔ̃b] *nf (tuerie)* slaughter, massacre; *Fig* **ç'a été une h. cette année à l'examen!** the exam results were disastrous this year!

hectare [ɛktar] *nm* hectare

hectogramme [ɛktɔgram] *nm* hectogram

hectolitre [ɛktɔlitr] *nm* hectoliter

hectomètre [ɛktɔmɛtr] *nm* hectometer

hédonisme [edɔnism] *nm* hedonism

hédoniste [edɔnist] **1** *adj* hedonistic

2 *nmf* hedonist

hégémonie [eʒemɔni] *nf* hegemony

*hein [ɛ̃] *exclam Fam* **(a)** *(pour faire répéter)* huh?, what? **(b)** *(pour insister)* **il fait beau aujourd'hui, h.?** it's a nice day, huh?; **ce n'est pas très bon, h.?** it's not very good, is it?; **ne refais jamais ça, h.!** don't ever do that again, OK?; **h. qu'il fait bien la cuisine!** he does cook well, doesn't he?

*hélas [elɑs] *exclam* unfortunately

*héler [34] [ele] *vt* to hail

hélice [elis] *nf* **(a)** *(d'un hélicoptère, d'un bateau)* propeller **(b)** *Math & Biol* helix

hélico [eliko] *nm Fam* chopper

hélicoïdal, -e, -aux, -ales [elikɔidal, -o] *adj* helical

hélicoptère [elikɔptɛr] *nm* helicopter

héliomarin, -e [eljɔmarɛ̃, -in] *adj Méd* **cure héliomarine** = course of treatment based on sun and sea air; **centre h.** = seaside convalescent home where heliotherapy is used

héliothérapie [eljɔterapi] *nf Méd* heliotherapy

héliport [elipɔr] *nm* heliport, helipad

héliporté, -e [elipɔrte] *adj (matériel)* transported by helicopter; *(troupes)* airborne

héliski [eliski] *nm* heliskiing

hélium [eljɔm] *nm* helium

*Helsinki [ɛlsinki] *n* Helsinki

helvétique [ɛlvetik] *adj* Swiss

hématie [emasi] *nf Biol* red blood corpuscle

hématologie [ematɔlɔʒi] *nf Méd* hematology

hématome [ematom] *nm* bruise, *Spéc* hematoma; **se faire un h.** to bruise oneself

hémicycle [emisikl] *nm* **l'h.** *(de l'Assemblée nationale)* the chamber

hémiplégie [emipleʒi] *nf Méd* hemiplegia

hémiplégique [emipleʒik] *adj & nmf Méd* hemiplegic

hémisphère [emisfɛr] *nm* hemisphere; **l'h. Nord/Sud** the Northern/Southern hemisphere

hémisphérique [emisferik] *adj* hemispheric(al)

hémistiche [emistiʃ] *nm* hemistich

hémoglobine [emɔglɔbin] *nf* hemoglobin; *Fig (dans un film)* blood and gore

hémophile [emɔfil] *Méd* **1** *adj* hemophilic

2 *nm* hemophiliac

hémophilie [emɔfili] *nf Méd* hemophilia

hémorragie [emɔraʒi] *nf* hemorrhage, bleeding; *Fig (des capitaux)* drain; **h. interne** internal bleeding

hémorroïdes [emɔrɔid] *nfpl* hemorrhoids, piles

*henné [ene] *nm* henna; **se faire un h.** to henna one's hair

*hennir [enir] *vi* to neigh, to whinny; *Fig (personne)* to bray

*hennissement [enismɑ̃] *nm* neigh, whinny; *Fig (d'une personne)* braying; **hennissements** neighing, whinnying; *Fig* braying

*hep [ɛp] *exclam* hey!

hépatique [epatik] *adj Méd* hepatic

hépatite [epatit] *nf* hepatitis; **h. A/B/C** hepatitis A/B/C

heptathlon [ɛptatlɔ̃] *nm* heptathlon

héraldique [eraldik] **1** *adj* heraldic

2 *nf* heraldry

herbage [ɛrbaʒ] *nm* pasture

herbe [ɛrb] *nf* **(a)** *(de gazon)* grass; *Fig* **couper l'h. sous le pied à qn** to cut the ground from under sb's feet; **en h.** *(céréale)* green; *Fig (débutant)* budding **(b)** *(plante)* herb; **fines herbes** mixed herbs; **omelette/fromage aux fines herbes** omelet/cheese with herbs; **mauvaise h.** weed; **herbes folles** wild grass; *Can* **h. à la puce** poison ivy **(c)** *Fam (drogue)* grass

herbeux, -euse [ɛrbø, -øz] *adj* grassy

herbicide [ɛrbisid] *adj & nm* **(produit) h.** weedkiller

herbier [ɛrbje] *nm (collection)* herbarium

herbivore [ɛrbivɔr] *Zool* **1** *adj* herbivorous

2 *nm* herbivore

herboriser [ɛrbɔrize] *vi* to collect plants

herboriste [ɛrbɔrist] *nmf* herbalist

herboristerie [ɛrbɔristəri] *nf (boutique)* herbalist's (store); *(commerce)* herb trade

herbu, -e [ɛrby] *adj* grassy

herculéen, -enne [ɛrkyleɛ̃, -ɛn] *adj* Herculean

*here [ɛr] *nm* **pauvre h.** poor creature

héréditaire [ereditɛr] *adj (maladie, titre)* hereditary; **c'est h.!** it runs in the family!

hérédité [eredite] *nf Biol* heredity; **avoir une lourde h.** to come from a family with a history of mental/physical illness

hérésie [erezi] *nf* heresy; *Fig* **c'est une h.** *ou* **de l'h.!** that's sacrilege!

hérétique [eretik] **1** *adj* heretical

2 *nmf* heretic

*hérissé, -e [erise] *adj* **(a)** *(cheveux)* spiky; *(moustache)* bristly **(b)** *(garni)* **h. de** bristling with

*hérisser [erise] **1** *vt* **(a)** *(ses plumes)* to ruffle up; **h. ses poils** to bristle **(b)** *Fig (mettre en colère)* **h. qn** to get sb's back up

2 **se hérisser** *vpr (animal)* to bristle; *(poils, cheveux)* to stand on end; *Fig (personne)* to bristle

*hérisson [erisɔ̃] *nm* hedgehog

héritage [eritaʒ] *nm* inheritance; *Fig (spirituel, intellectuel)* heritage; **faire un h.** to come into an inheritance

hériter [erite] **1** *vt* to inherit (**de** from)

2 **hériter de** *vt ind (fortune, objet, qualité)* to inherit; **h. de qn** to receive an inheritance from sb; *Fig* **h. de qn/qch** *(se retrouver avec)* to be landed with sb/sth

héritier, -ère [eritje, -ɛr] *nm,f* heir, *f* heiress (**de** to)

hermaphrodite [ɛrmafrɔdit] *nm & adj* hermaphrodite

hermétique [ɛrmetik] *adj* **(a)** *(récipient)* hermetically sealed; *(joint)* **(à l'air)** airtight; *(à l'eau)* watertight **(b)** *Fig (abscons)* abstruse; *(visage)* impenetrable; **être h. à qch** to be impervious to sth

hermétiquement [ɛrmetikmɑ̃] *adv* hermetically

hermine [ɛrmin] *nf (animal)* stoat; *(fourrure)* ermine

*hernie [ɛrni] *nf* hernia; **h. discale** slipped disk

héroïne¹ [erɔin] *nf (personnage)* heroine

héroïne² [erɔin] *nf (drogue)* heroin

héroïnomane [erɔinɔman] *nmf* heroin addict
héroïque [erɔik] *adj* heroic
héroïquement [erɔikmɑ̃] *adv* heroically
héroïsme [erɔism] *nm* heroism
*****héron** [erɔ̃] *nm* heron; **h. cendré** gray heron
*****héros** [ero] *nm* hero; **mourir en h.** to die a hero's death
herpès [ɛrpɛs] *nm Méd* herpes; *(buccal)* cold sore
*****herse** [ɛrs] *nf* (**a**) *(pour labourer)* harrow (**b**) *(de forteresse)* portcullis
hertz [ɛrts] *nm* hertz
hertzien, -enne [ɛrtsjɛ̃, -ɛn] *adj* Hertzian; *Rad* **réseau h.** radio relay system; *TV* **diffusion hertzienne** terrestrial broadcasting
hésitant, -e [ezitɑ̃, -ɑ̃t] *adj* hesitant
hésitation [ezitasjɔ̃] *nf* hesitation; **avoir une h.** to hesitate; **avec h.** hesitatingly; **sans h.** without hesitation
hésiter [ezite] *vi* to hesitate (**sur/entre** over/between); **je ne sais pas, j'hésite** I don't know, I can't make up my mind; **h. à faire qch** to hesitate to do sth
hétéro [etero] *adj & nmf Fam* straight, hetero
hétéroclite [eterɔklit] *adj* motley
hétérogène [eterɔʒɛn] *adj* mixed
hétérogénéité [eterɔʒeneite] *nf* heterogeneity
hétérosexualité [eterɔsɛksɥalite] *nf* heterosexuality
hétérosexuel, -elle [eterɔsɛksɥɛl] *adj & nm,f* heterosexual
*****hêtre** [ɛtr] *nm* beech
*****heu** [ø] *exclam* er
heure [œr] *nf* (**a**) *(soixante minutes)* hour; **cinq euros l'h.** *ou* **de l'h.** five euros an hour; *Scol* **h. de cours** period; **heures supplémentaires** overtime; **faire des heures supplémentaires** to do overtime
    (**b**) *(de la journée)* time; **à h. fixe** at regular intervals; **à toute h.** at any time; **à toute h. du jour ou de la nuit** at any hour of the day or night; **quelle h. est-il?** what time is it?, what's the time?; **quelle h. avez-vous?** can you tell me the time?; **il est deux heures** it's two o'clock; **cinq heures moins dix** ten to five; **trois heures vingt** twenty past three; **vingt heures quarante** eight forty p.m.; **à quelle h....?** what time...?; **ils devraient être arrivés à l'h. qu'il est** they ought to have arrived by now; **être à l'h.** *(personne)* to be on time; *(montre)* to be right; **mettre sa montre à l'h.** to set one's watch; **à la bonne h.!** marvelous!; **de bonne h.** early; **heures d'affluence** peak hours; **heures de bureau** office hours; **h. d'été** daylight-saving time; **heures d'ouverture** opening hours; **heures de pointe** rush hour
    (**c**) *(moment précis)* time; **l'h. du dîner/déjeuner** dinner/lunch time; **il est** *ou* **c'est l'h. (de faire qch)** it's time (to do sth); **son h. est venue** his time has come; **avoir son h. de gloire** to have one's moment of glory; **l'h. H** zero hour
    (**d**) *(moment présent)* **l'h. est grave** these are difficult times; **à l'h. actuelle** currently; **pour l'h.** for the present, for the time being; *Litt* **sur l'h.** at once
heureusement [œrøzmɑ̃] *adv* (**a**) *(par bonheur)* fortunately, luckily; **h. que j'étais là** it's a good thing I was there (**b**) *(avec succès)* successfully
heureux, -euse [œrø, -øz] **1** *adj* (**a**) *(satisfait)* happy (**de qch** with sth); **être h. en ménage** to be happily married; **vivre h.** to live happily; **être h. de faire qch** to be happy to do sth; **h. anniversaire!** happy birthday! (**b**) *(favorable) (dénouement)* successful; *(juste) (formule, style)* apt; *(choix)* happy (**c**) *(favorisé)* lucky; **par un h. concours de circonstances** by a lucky *or* fortunate coincidence; **h. au jeu/en amour** lucky at cards/in love; **s'estimer h. (de faire qch)** to consider oneself lucky (to do sth) (**d**) *(situation)* **c'est h. que vous soyez libre** it's a good thing you're free; *Fam* **encore h. (qu'il ait gardé le ticket de caisse)!** it's just as well (he held on to the receipt)!

    2 *nm,f* **si tu le lui donnes, tu vas faire un h.** if you give it to him, you'll make him a happy man; **faire des h.** to make some people happy
*****heurt** [œr] *nm (choc)* collision; *Fig (conflit)* clash; **sans heurts** smoothly, without a hitch
*****heurter** [œrte] **1** *vt* (**a**) *(cogner)* to hit; *(entrer en collision avec)* to collide with (**b**) *(choquer)* to offend
    2 *vi* (**a**) **h. contre qch** to hit sth (**b**) *Suisse* to knock; **h. à la porte** to knock at the door
    3 se heurter *vpr* (**a**) *(se cogner)* to collide (**à** *ou* **contre** with); *Fig* **se h. à qch** to meet with sth (**b**) *(couleurs, intérêts, personnes)* to clash
*****heurtoir** [œrtwar] *nm* (door) knocker
hévéa [evea] *nm* rubber tree
hexagonal, -e, -aux, -ales [ɛgzagɔnal, -o] *adj* hexagonal; *Fig* French
hexagone [ɛgzagɔn] *nm* hexagon; *Fig* **l'H.** France
hiatus [jatys] *nm* (**a**) *Ling & Anat* hiatus (**b**) *(décalage)* gap
hibernation [ibɛrnasjɔ̃] *nf* hibernation; *Méd* **h. artificielle** induced hypothermia
hiberner [ibɛrne] *vi* to hibernate
*****hibou, -x** [ibu] *nm* owl
*****hic** [ik] *nm inv Fam* **voilà le h.!** that's the snag!; **le h., c'est que…** the snag is…
*****hideusement** [idøzmɑ̃] *adv* hideously
*****hideux, -euse** [idø, -øz] *adj* hideous
hier [jɛr] *adv* yesterday; **h. matin/soir** yesterday morning/evening; **je m'en souviens comme si c'était h.** I remember it as if it were yesterday; **le journal d'h.** yesterday's paper; **cela ne date pas d'h.** that's nothing new; **je ne suis pas né d'h.** I wasn't born yesterday
*****hiérarchie** [jerarʃi] *nf* hierarchy
*****hiérarchique** [jerarʃik] *adj* hierarchical; **c'est mon supérieur h.** he's immediately above me in rank; **par la voie h.** through the official channels
*****hiérarchisé, -e** [jerarʃize] *adj* hierarchical
*****hiéroglyphe** [jerɔglif] *nm* hieroglyph
*****hi-fi** [ifi] *adj inv & nf inv* hi-fi
*****hi-han** [iɑ̃] *exclam* hee-haw!
hilarant, -e [ilarɑ̃, -ɑ̃t] *adj* hilarious
hilare [ilar] *adj* grinning
hilarité [ilarite] *nf* hilarity, mirth; **provoquer l'h. générale** to be the source of much hilarity
Himalaya [imalaja] *nm* **l'H.** the Himalayas
*****hindi** [indi] *nm* Hindi
hindou, -e [ɛ̃du] **1** *adj* Hindu
    2 *nm,f* **H., Hindoue** Hindu
hindouisme [ɛ̃duism] *nm* Hinduism
hip-hop [ipɔp] *nm inv (musique)* hip-hop
*****hippie** [ipi] *adj & nmf* hippy
hippique [ipik] *adj* **concours h.** horse show; **sport h.** equestrian sports
hippisme [ipism] *nm* horseback riding; *(courses)* horse racing
hippocampe [ipɔkɑ̃p] *nm* sea horse
hippodrome [ipɔdrom] *nm* racetrack *(for horses)*
hippopotame [ipɔpɔtam] *nm* hippopotamus
*****hippy** [ipi] = **hippie**
hirondelle [irɔ̃dɛl] *nf* swallow; *Prov* **une h. ne fait pas le printemps** one swallow doesn't make a summer; **h. de mer** tern
hirsute [irsyt] *adj (personne)* hairy; *(barbe)* shaggy; *(cheveux)* unkempt
hispanique [ispanik] *adj* Hispanic
hispano-américain, -e (*mpl* **hispano-américains**, *fpl* **hispano-américaines**) [ispanɔamerikɛ̃, -ɛn] **1** *adj* Spanish-American, Hispanic

2 *nm,f* **H., Hispano-Américaine** Spanish-American, Hispanic

hispanophone [ispanɔfɔn] **1** *adj* Spanish-speaking
2 *nmf* Spanish speaker

*****hisser** [ise] **1** *vt* to hoist (up); **ho! hisse!** heave-ho!
2 se hisser *vpr* to heave oneself up; **se h. sur la pointe des pieds** to stand on tiptoe; *Fig* **se h. jusqu'au pouvoir** to rise to power

histogramme [istɔgram] *nm* bar chart, histogram
histoire [istwar] *nf* **(a)** *(discipline)* history; **l'h. de France** French history; **h. de l'art** history of art; **sachez, pour la petite h., que...** let me tell you in passing that...; *Fig* **c'est de l'h. ancienne** that's all ancient history
(b) *(récit)* story; *Fam (mensonge)* fib, story; **raconter des histoires** *(mentir)* to tell fibs; **c'est toujours la même h.** it's always the same old story; **c'est une autre h.** it's quite a different matter; **une h. drôle** a joke, a funny story; **il m'est arrivé une drôle d'h.** a funny thing happened to me; **elle l'a dit, h. de dire quelque chose** she said it just for the sake of saying something; **c'est toute une h.** *(à raconter)* it's a long story; **c'est une h. de fous!** it's crazy!
(c) *(problème)* fuss; **c'est toute une h. pour lui faire prendre son bain** it's a really big deal getting him/her to take a bath; *Fam* **en voilà une h.!** what a fuss!, what a song and dance!; **faire des histoires** to make a fuss; **s'attirer des histoires** to get oneself into trouble; **faire des histoires à qn** to make trouble for sb; **au lit, et pas d'histoires!** off to bed now, and no fuss!

histologie [istɔlɔʒi] *nf* histology
historien, -enne [istɔrjɛ̃, -ɛn] *nm,f* historian
historique [istɔrik] **1** *adj (qui concerne l'histoire)* historical; *(important)* historic
2 *nm* historical account; *Ordinat (de document)* log; **faire l'h. des événements** to give a chronological account of events
historiquement [istɔrikmã] *adv* historically
*****hit-parade** *(pl* **hit-parades)** [itparad] *nm* charts
HIV [aʃive] *nm* HIV
hiver [ivɛr] *nm* winter; **en h.** in winter; **une soirée d'h.** a winter's night; **h. nucléaire** nuclear winter
hivernal, -e, -aux, -ales [ivɛrnal, -o] *adj* winter; *(temps)* wintry
hiverner [ivɛrne] *vi* to overwinter
*****HLM** [aʃɛlɛm] *nm ou nf (abrév* **habitation à loyer modéré)** ≃ low-rent apartment building
*****hochement** [ɔʃmã] *nm* **h. de tête** *(négatif)* shake of the head; *(affirmatif)* nod
*****hocher** [ɔʃe] *vt* **h. la tête** *(pour dire non)* to shake one's head; *(pour dire oui)* to nod
*****hochet** [ɔʃɛ] *nm* (child's) rattle
*****hockey** [ɔkɛ] *nm* **(a)** *(sport)* field hockey; **h. sur gazon** field hockey; **h. sur glace** (ice) hockey **(b)** *Can (crosse)* (ice-)hockey stick
*****holà** [ɔla] **1** *exclam (pour appeler)* stop!, hold on!; **h., on se calme, hein!** hey, cool it, OK?
2 *nm* **mettre le h. à qch** to put a stop to sth
*****holding** [ɔldiŋ] *nm* holding company
*****hold-up** [ɔldœp] *nm inv Fam* hold-up
*****hollandais, -e** [ɔlɑ̃dɛ, -ɛz] **1** *adj* Dutch
2 *nm (langue)* Dutch
3 *nm,f* **H.** Dutchman; **Hollandaise** Dutchwoman; **les H.** the Dutch
*****Hollande** [ɔlɑ̃d] *nf* **la H.** Holland
holocauste [ɔlɔkost] *nm* holocaust
hologramme [ɔlɔgram] *nm* hologram
holographie [ɔlɔgrafi] *nf* holography
*****homard** [ɔmar] *nm* lobster
homélie [ɔmeli] *nf* homily

homéopathe [ɔmeɔpat] *nmf* homeopath
homéopathie [ɔmeɔpati] *nf* homeopathy
homéopathique [ɔmeɔpatik] *adj* homeopathic; *Fig* **à dose h.** in small doses
Homère [ɔmɛr] *npr* Homer
homicide [ɔmisid] **1** *adj* homicidal
2 *nm* homicide; **h. involontaire** *ou* **par imprudence** manslaughter *(through negligence)*
hommage [ɔmaʒ] *nm* homage; **rendre h. à qn** to pay homage to sb; **hommages** respects; **mes hommages!** how do you do!
hommasse [ɔmas] *adj Péj* mannish
homme [ɔm] *nm* **(a)** *(adulte)* man; **rayon hommes** men's department; **parler à qn d'h. à h.** to have a man-to-man talk with sb; **il n'est pas h. à laisser passer cela** he's not the sort of man to let something like that happen; **comme un seul h.** in unison; *Fam* **mon h.** my man; **jeune h.** young man; **h. d'affaires** businessman; **h. de barre** helmsman; **h. de confiance** right-hand man; **h. d'église** man of the church; **h. d'équipage** crewman; **h. d'État** statesman; **h. à femmes** ladies' man; *Suisse* **h. du feu** fire fighter; **c'est l'h. fort du parti** he's the kingpin of the party; **h. de loi** lawyer; **h. de main** henchman; **h. du monde** gentleman; **h. de paille** figurehead; **h. de peine** laborer; **h. politique** politician; **h. à tout faire** handyman; **h. de troupe** private **(b)** *(genre humain)* **l'h.** man, mankind; **de mémoire d'h.** within living memory; **les premiers hommes** early man
homme-grenouille *(pl* **hommes-grenouilles)** [ɔmgrənuj] *nm* frogman
homme-orchestre *(pl* **hommes-orchestres)** [ɔmɔrkɛstr] *nm* one-man band
homme-sandwich *(pl* **hommes-sandwichs)** [ɔmsɑ̃dwitʃ] *nm* sandwich man
homo [ɔmo] *adj & nmf* gay
homogène [ɔmɔʒɛn] *adj* homogeneous
homogénéisation [ɔmɔʒeneizasjɔ̃] *nf* homogenization
homogénéiser [ɔmɔʒeneize] *vt* to homogenize
homogénéité [ɔmɔʒeneite] *nf* homogeneity
homologue [ɔmɔlɔg] *nmf* counterpart, opposite number
homologuer [ɔmɔlɔge] *vt (accord, décision, record)* to ratify; *(testament)* to prove
homonyme [ɔmɔnim] **1** *nm (mot)* homonym
2 *nmf (personne)* namesake
homophobe [ɔmɔfɔb] **1** *adj* homophobic
2 *nmf* homophobe
homophobie [ɔmɔfɔbi] *nf* homophobia
homosexualité [ɔmɔsɛksɥalite] *nf* homosexuality
homosexuel, -elle [ɔmɔsɛksɥɛl] *adj & nm,f* homosexual
*****Honduras** [ɔ̃dyras] *nm* **le H.** Honduras
*****hondurien, -enne** [ɔ̃dyrjɛ̃, -ɛn] **1** *adj* Honduran
2 *nm,f* **H., Hondurienne** Honduran
*****Hongrie** [ɔ̃gri] *nf* **la H.** Hungary
*****hongrois, -e** [ɔ̃grwa, -az] **1** *adj* Hungarian
2 *nm (langue)* Hungarian
3 *nm,f* **H., Hongroise** Hungarian
honnête [ɔnɛt] *adj* **(a)** *(intègre) (personne, conduite)* honest; **peu h.** dishonest; **être h. avec soi-même** to be honest with oneself **(b)** *(décent) (vie, gens)* decent; *(intentions)* honorable **(c)** *(acceptable) (prix, note, résultat)* fair; **un repas/film h. sans plus** an OK meal/movie, but nothing to write home about
honnêtement [ɔnɛtmã] *adv* **(a)** *(avec intégrité) (agir, se comporter)* honestly **(b)** *(franchement)* to be honest; **h., qu'est-ce que tu en penses?** be honest, what do you think? **(c)** *(raisonnablement)* decently
honnêteté [ɔnɛte] *nf* **(a)** *(intégrité)* honesty **(b)** *(décence)* decency

honneur [ɔnœr] *nm* honor; **mettre un point d'h. à faire qch** to make it a point of honor to do sth; **déclarer/jurer sur l'h. que…** to state/swear on one's honor that…; **sauver l'h.** to save one's honor; **en tout bien tout h.** with no ulterior motive; **en l'h. de qn** in sb's honor; **à qui ai-je l'h.?** to whom have I the honor (of speaking)?; *Fam* **en quel h. devrais-je t'aider?** give me one good reason why I should help you!; **à vous l'h.** after you; **être à l'h.** to have pride of place; **c'est tout à ton h.** it's to your credit; **faire h. à qn/qch** to be a credit to sb/sth; **faire h. à un repas** to do justice to a meal; **rechercher les honneurs** to court fame

*****honnir** [ɔnir] *vt* to disgrace

honorable [ɔnɔrabl] *adj* **(a)** *(profession, personne, intentions)* honorable **(b)** *(performance, résultat)* creditable, respectable

honorablement [ɔnɔrabləmɑ̃] *adv* **(a)** *(de façon respectable)* honorably **(b)** *(correctement)* **il s'en est h. tiré** he did quite creditably; **gagner h. sa vie** to earn a good living

honoraire [ɔnɔrɛr] **1** *adj (fonction, membre)* honorary
2 *nmpl* **honoraires** fee, fees

honorer [ɔnɔre] **1** *vt* **(a)** *(rendre hommage à)* to honor; **h. qn de sa confiance** to put one's trust in sb **(b)** *(acquitter) (facture, dette, engagements)* to honor **(c)** *(valoir de l'estime à) (personne, chose)* to be a credit to **(d)** *Hum (sexuellement)* to service
2 s'honorer *vpr* **s'h. de qch/d'avoir fait qch** to pride oneself on sth/on having done sth

honorifique [ɔnɔrifik] *adj* honorary

*****honoris causa** [ɔnɔriskoza] *adj* honoris causa; **docteur h.** doctor honoris causa, honorary doctor

*****honte** [ɔ̃t] *nf* **(a)** *(sentiment)* shame; **à ma grande h.** to my shame; **sans h.** shamelessly; **avoir h. (de)** to be ashamed (of); **avoir h. pour qn** to feel embarrassed for sb; **faire h. à qn** to make sb ashamed **(b)** *(chose scandaleuse)* disgrace; **c'est une h.!** it's a disgrace!

*****honteux, -euse** [ɔ̃tø, øz] *adj* **(a)** *(personne, air)* ashamed **(b)** *(conduite, acte)* shameful, disgraceful; **c'est h.!** it's a disgrace!

*****hop** [ɔp] *exclam* **allez h., saute!** go on, jump!; **allez h., tout le monde dehors!** come on, everybody out!; **h.-là!** oops(-a-daisy)!

hôpital, -aux [ɔpital, -o] *nm* hospital; *Prov* **c'est l'h. qui se moque de la charité** it's the pot calling the kettle black; **h. de campagne** field hospital; **h. de jour** day hospital; **h. militaire** military hospital; **h. psychiatrique** psychiatric hospital

*****hoquet** [ɔkɛ] *nm* hiccup; **avoir le h.** to have the hiccups

*****hoqueter** [42] [ɔkəte] *vi* to hiccup

horaire [ɔrɛr] **1** *adj* hourly
2 *nm* **(a)** *(des services de transport)* timetable, schedule; **être en retard sur l'h.** to be running late **(b)** *(emploi du temps)* schedule; **h. variable** *ou* **flexible** flexible hours, flextime; **horaires de travail** working hours

*****horde** [ɔrd] *nf* horde

horizon [ɔrizɔ̃] *nm aussi Fig* horizon; **ouvrir de nouveaux horizons à qn** to open up new horizons *or* prospects to sb; **à l'h.** on the horizon; **à l'h. 2020** in the year 2020; **h. intellectuel** intellectual horizons

horizontal, -e, -aux, -ales [ɔrizɔ̃tal, -o] **1** *adj* horizontal
2 *nf* **horizontale** horizontal line; **à l'horizontale** horizontal

horizontalement [ɔrizɔ̃talmɑ̃] *adv* horizontally; *(dans les mots croisés)* across

horloge [ɔrlɔʒ] *nf* clock; **réglé comme une h.** as regular as clockwork; **h. biologique** biological clock; **l'h. parlante** the speaking clock; *Ordinat* **h. du système** system clock; *Ordinat* **h. en temps réel** real-time clock

horloger, -ère [ɔrlɔʒe, -ɛr] **1** *adj* **l'industrie horlogère** the watchmaking industry
2 *nm,f* watchmaker

horloger-bijoutier *(pl* **horlogers-bijoutiers)** [ɔrlɔʒebi-ʒutje] *nm* jeweler and watchmaker

horlogerie [ɔrlɔʒri] *nf (industrie)* watchmaking; *(magasin)* watchmaker's (store); **l'h.** *(ouvrages)* clocks and watches

*****hormis** [ɔrmi] *prép Litt* except, save

hormonal, -e, -aux, -ales [ɔrmɔnal, -o] *adj* hormonal

hormone [ɔrmɔn] *nf* hormone

hormonothérapie [ɔrmɔnoterapi] *nf* hormone therapy

horodateur [ɔrɔdatœr] *nm* time and date stamping machine; *(de stationnement)* pay-and-display machine

horoscope [ɔrɔskɔp] *nm* horoscope

horreur [ɔrœr] *nf* **(a)** *(effroi)* horror **(b)** *(répugnance)* disgust; **avoir h. de qch** to hate sth; **avoir h. de faire qch** to hate doing sth; **avoir qn/qch en h.** to loathe sb/sth; **faire h. à qn** to disgust sb; *Fam* **c'est l'h.** it sucks **(c)** *(caractère horrible)* horror; **quelle h.!** how horrible!, how awful! **(d)** *(chose ou personne exécrable)* **être une h.** to be a nightmare **(e)** **horreurs** *(atrocités)* horrors; *(calomnies)* horrible things

horrible [ɔribl] *adj* **(a)** *(effrayant)* horrible **(b)** *(très laid)* hideous

horriblement [ɔribləmɑ̃] *adv (brûlé, défiguré)* horribly; *(cher, froid)* terribly

horrifiant, -e [ɔrifjɑ̃, -ɑ̃t] *adj* horrifying

horrifier [66] [ɔrifje] *vt* to horrify

horripilant, -e [ɔripilɑ̃, -ɑ̃t] *adj* exasperating

horripiler [ɔripile] *vt* to exasperate

*****hors** [ɔr] *prép* **(a)** *(dehors)* **h. de** outside; **h. d'ici!** get out (of here)!; **ça l'a mise h. d'elle** that infuriated her; **être h. de soi** to be beside oneself **(b)** *Litt (sauf)* except, save **(c)** *(en conjonction avec un nom)* **h. antenne** off-air; **h. d'atteinte** out of reach; **h. de combat** out of action; **h. jeu** offside; **mettre qn/qch h. la loi** to outlaw sb/sth; **h. pair** unrivaled; **h. piste** off piste; **h. de prix** extortionate; **h. de question** out of the question; **h. saison** off-season; **numéro h. série** special issue; **h. service** out of order; **h. sujet** not relevant; **h. taxe** net of tax; *(exempt de taxe)* tax-free; **boutique h. taxe** duty-free shop; **h. d'usage** *(vêtement)* worn out; *(machine)* beyond repair

*****hors-bord** [ɔrbɔr] *nm inv* speedboat; **moteur h.** outboard motor

*****hors-d'œuvre** [ɔrdœvr] *nm inv* **(a)** *(plat)* hors d'œuvre, appetizer **(b)** *Fig* starter, taster

*****hors-jeu** [ɔrʒø] *nm inv* offside

*****hors-la-loi** [ɔrlalwa] *nm inv* outlaw

*****hors-piste** [ɔrpist] *nm inv (en ski)* off-piste skiing; **faire du h.** to ski off piste

hortensia [ɔrtɑ̃sja] *nm* hydrangea

horticole [ɔrtikɔl] *adj* horticultural; **exposition h.** flower show

horticulteur [ɔrtikyltœr] *nm* nurseryman

horticulture [ɔrtikyltyr] *nf* horticulture

hospice [ɔspis] *nm* **(a)** *(asile)* home **(b)** *(monastère)* hospice

hospitalier[1], -ère[1] [ɔspitalje, -ɛr] *adj (accueillant)* hospitable

hospitalier[2], -ère[2] [ɔspitalje, -ɛr] *adj (relatif aux hôpitaux)* hospital; **en milieu h.** in a hospital environment; **personnel h.** hospital staff

hospitalisation [ɔspitalizasjɔ̃] *nf* hospitalization; **h. à domicile** home care

hospitaliser [ɔspitalize] *vt* to hospitalize; **faire h. qn** to have sb hospitalized

hospitalité [ɔspitalite] *nf* hospitality

hospitalo-universitaire [ɔspitaloyniversitɛr] *adj* **centre h.** teaching hospital

hostie [ɔsti] *nf Rel* host

hostile [ɔstil] *adj* hostile (**à** towards)

hostilité [ɔstilite] *nf* hostility (**contre** *ou* **envers** towards); **hostilités** hostilities; **reprendre les hostilités** to reopen *or* to resume hostilities

hosto [ɔsto] *nm Fam* hospital

The symbol * indicates that the initial **h** is aspirate and that hence there is no liaison, e.g. **les haricots** [leariko] and not [lezariko], or contraction in spelling, e.g. **la haine** and not **l'haine**.

hôte [ot] *nm* (**a**) *(personne qui invite)* host (**b**) *(invité)* guest, visitor; **h. payant** paying guest (**c**) *Biol* host

hôtel [otɛl] *nm* (**a**) *(pour l'hébergement)* hotel; **h. de passe** = hotel used as a brothel (**b**) *(bâtiment)* **h. des impôts** tax office; **l'h. de la Monnaie** ≃ the Royal Mint; **h. (particulier)** mansion, town house; **h. des ventes** salesroom; **h. de ville** city hall

hôtelier, -ère [otəlje, -ɛr] **1** *adj* **l'industrie hôtelière** the hotel industry
2 *nm,f* hotel keeper, hotelier

hôtellerie [otɛlri] *nf* (**a**) *(hôtel)* inn (**b**) *(secteur)* **l'h.** the hotel industry

hôtel-restaurant *(pl* **hôtels-restaurants**) [otɛlrɛstɔrɑ̃] *nm* hotel and restaurant

hôtesse [otɛs] *nf* (**a**) *(personne qui reçoit)* hostess (**b**) *(dans un avion)* hostess, stewardess; **h. d'accueil** receptionist; **h. de l'air** stewardess, flight attendant

****hotte** [ɔt] *nf* (**a**) *(panier)* basket; **la h. du Père Noël** Santa Claus's sack (**b**) *(pour la ventilation)* hood; **h. aspirante** extractor hood

****hou** [u] *exclam* boo!; **h.! la vilaine!** tut-tut, you naughty girl!

****houblon** [ublɔ̃] *nm* hops

****houe** [u] *nf* hoe

****houille** [uj] *nf* coal; **h. blanche** hydroelectric power

****houiller, -ère** [uje, -ɛr] **1** *adj (terrain)* rich in coal; **bassin h.** coalfield; **production houillère** coal output
2 *nf* **houillère** coalmine, colliery

****houle** [ul] *nf* swell

****houlette** [ulɛt] *nf* (**a**) *(de berger)* crook; *Fig* **sous la h. de** under the leadership of (**b**) *(petite bêche)* trowel

****houleux, -euse** [ulø, -øz] *adj (mer)* choppy; *Fig (réunion)* stormy

houmous [umus] *nm Culin* houmous, hummus

****houppette** [upɛt] *nf (de plumes)* small tufts; *(de cheveux)* quiff; *(à poudre)* powder puff

****hourra** [ura] **1** *exclam* hurray!; **hip, hip, hip, h.!** hip, hip, hurray!
2 *nm* hurray; **pousser des hourras** to cheer

houspiller [uspije] *vt* to tell off

****housse** [us] *nf* cover; *(contre la poussière)* dust sheet; *(pour canapé)* slipcover; *(dans une voiture)* seat cover

****houx** [u] *nm* holly

hovercraft [ɔvɛrkraft] *nm* hovercraft

****HS** [aʃɛs] *adj Fam (abrév* **hors service**) *(personne)* bushed, beat

HT (**a**) *(abrév* **haute tension**) HT (**b**) *(abrév* **hors taxe**) exclusive of tax

****HTML** [aʃteɛmɛl] *nm Ordinat (abrév* **Hyper Text Markup Language**) HTML

****hublot** [yblo] *nm (de bateau)* porthole; *(dans un avion, une machine à laver)* window

****huche** [yʃ] *nf* chest; **h. à pain** bread bin

****hue** [y, hy] *exclam (à un cheval)* giddy up!; **tirer à h. et à dia** to pull in opposite directions

****huées** [ɥe] *nfpl* booing; **quitter la scène sous les h.** to be booed off the stage

****huer** [ɥe] **1** *vt* to boo
2 *vi (hibou, chouette)* to hoot

huile [ɥil] *nf* (**a**) *(liquide)* oil; *Fig* **jeter de l'h. sur le feu** to add fuel to the fire; **une mer d'h.** a glassy sea; **h. d'amandes douces** almond oil; **h. d'arachide** groundnut oil; *Can* **h. de chauffage** heating oil; *Fig* **h. de coude** elbow grease; **h. essentielle** essential oil; **h. de foie de morue** cod-liver oil; **h. de moteur** engine oil; **h. d'olive** olive oil; **h. de ricin** castor oil; **h. solaire** suntan oil; **h. de tournesol** sunflower oil; **h. végétale** vegetable oil; **h. de vidange** sump oil (**b**) *(peinture)* oil painting (**c**) *Fam (personne importante)* big shot

huiler [ɥile] *vt* to oil; *Fig* **une mécanique bien huilée** a well-oiled machine

huileux, -euse [ɥilø, -øz] *adj* oily

huis [ɥi] *nm* **à h. clos** behind closed doors; *Jur* in camera

huissier [ɥisje] *nm* (**a**) *Jur* bailiff (**b**) *(portier)* usher

****huit** [ɥit] *adj & nm inv* eight; **h. jours** a week; **aujourd'hui/demain en h.** a week from today/tomorrow; **donner ses h. jours à qn** to give sb a week's notice; *voir aussi* **trois**

****huitaine** [ɥitɛn] *nf* (**a**) *(environ huit)* (about) eight (**b**) *(semaine)* week; **sous h.** within a week; **dans une h. de jours** in a week or so

****huitante** [ɥitɑ̃t] *adj inv Suisse* eighty

****huitième** [ɥitjɛm] *adj, nm & nmf* eighth; *voir aussi* **cinquième**

huître [ɥitr] *nf* oyster; **h. perlière** pearl oyster

****hulotte** [ylɔt] *nf* tawny owl

****hululement** [ylylmɑ̃] *nm* hoot; **des hululements** hooting

****hululer** [ylyle] *vi* to hoot

****hum** [œm] *exclam* hm!

humain, -e [ymɛ̃, -ɛn] **1** *adj* (**a**) *(relatif à l'homme)* human; **c'est h.** it's only human; **des pertes humaines énormes** a huge loss of life (**b**) *(compatissant)* humane
2 *nm* human (being)

humainement [ymɛnmɑ̃] *adv* (**a**) *(relatif à l'homme)* in human terms; **h. possible** humanly possible (**b**) *(avec bonté)* humanely

humaniser [ymanize] *vt* to make more human

humanisme [ymanism] *nm* humanism

humaniste [ymanist] *adj & nmf* humanist

humanitaire [ymanitɛr] **1** *adj* humanitarian; **organisation h.** relief *or* aid organization
2 *nmf (personne)* humanitarian (aid) worker

humanité [ymanite] *nf* (**a**) *(genre humain)* humanity, mankind (**b**) *(bonté)* humanity; **avec h.** humanely

humanoïde [ymanɔid] *nm* humanoid

humble [œ̃bl] *adj* humble; **à mon h. avis** in my humble opinion

humblement [œ̃bləmɑ̃] *adv* humbly

humecter [ymɛkte] *vt* to moisten

****humer** [yme] *vt (air)* to breathe in; *(parfum)* to smell

humérus [ymerys] *nm* humerus

humeur [ymœr] *nf* (**a**) *(disposition)* mood; **être de bonne/mauvaise h.** to be in a good/bad mood; **mettre qn de bonne/mauvaise h.** to put sb in a good/bad mood; **être d'une h. massacrante** to be in a foul mood; **plein de bonne h.** good-humored; **être/ne pas être d'h. à faire qch** to be/not be in the mood to do sth (**b**) *(caractère)* temper, temperament; **d'h. égale** even-tempered; **d'humeur inégale** *ou* **changeante** temperamental (**c**) *Litt (mauvaise humeur)* bad mood; **geste d'h.** ill-tempered gesture; **avec h.** irritably (**d**) *Anat* **h. aqueuse** aqueous humor; **h. vitrée** vitreous humor

humide [ymid] *adj (maison, linge)* damp, wet; *(climat)* humid; **les yeux humides (de larmes)** eyes moist with tears

humidificateur [ymidifikatœr] *nm* humidifier

humidifier [66] [ymidifje] *vt* to dampen; *(air)* to humidify

humidité [ymidite] *nf (d'une maison)* dampness; *(du climat, d'une région)* humidity; **il faut beaucoup d'h. à cette plante** this plant needs a lot of moisture; **craint l'h.** *(sur un paquet)* store in a dry place

humiliant, -e [ymiljɑ̃, -ɑ̃t] *adj* humiliating

humiliation [ymiljasjɔ̃] *nf* humiliation

humilier [66] [ymilje] **1** *vt* to humiliate
2 **s'humilier** *vpr* to humiliate oneself

humilité [ymilite] *nf* humility

humoriste [ymɔrist] *nmf* humorist

The symbol * indicates that the initial **h** is aspirate and that hence there is no liaison, e.g. **les haricots** [leariko] and not [lezariko], or contraction in spelling, e.g. **la haine** and not **l'haine**.

humoristique [ymɔristik] *adj* humorous; **dessin h.** cartoon

humour [ymur] *nm* humor; **avoir (le sens) de l'h.** to have a (good) sense of humor; **h. noir** black humor

*****huppe**[1] [yp] *nf (oiseau)* hoopoe

*****huppe**[2] [yp] *nf (d'un oiseau)* crest

*****huppé, -e** [ype] *adj* **(a)** *Fam (gens, endroit, quartier)* smart **(b)** *(oiseau)* crested

*****hurlement** [yrləmɑ̃] *nm (d'un loup, d'un chien)* howl; *(d'une personne)* scream; *(du vent)* roaring; *(d'une sirène)* wail

*****hurler** [yrle] **1** *vi (loup, chien)* to howl; *(personne)* to howl, to scream; *(vent, tempête)* to roar; *(sirène)* to wail; *(radio)* to blare; **j'ai dû h. pour qu'il m'entende** I had to shout for him to hear me; **h. de douleur/rage** to howl with pain/rage; **c'est à h. de rire** it's a scream; **h. à la lune** to bay at the moon; **il faut h. avec les loups** if you can't beat them, join them
  2 *vt (insultes, instructions)* to yell

hurluberlu [yrlybɛrly] *nm* oddball

*****Huron** [yrɔ̃] *n voir* **lac**

*****husky** *(pl* **huskies)** [œski] *nm* husky

*****hussard** [ysar] *nm* hussar

*****hussarde** [ysard] **à la h.** *adv* roughly

*****hutte** [yt] *nf* hut

hybride [ibrid] *adj & nm* hybrid

hydratant, -e [idratɑ̃, -ɑ̃t] *adj* moisturizing

hydratation [idratasjɔ̃] *nf (de la peau)* moisturizing

hydrate [idrat] *nm* hydrate; **h. de carbone** carbohydrate

hydrater [idrate] **1** *vt (peau)* to moisturize; *(organisme)* to hydrate
  2 s'hydrater *vpr* to take in water

hydraulique [idrolik] **1** *adj* hydraulic
  2 *nf (science)* hydraulics *(singulier)*

hydravion [idravjɔ̃] *nm* seaplane

hydre [idr] *nf* hydra

hydrocarbure [idrokarbyr] *nm* hydrocarbon

hydrocution [idrokysjɔ̃] *nf* = loss of consciousness caused by immersion in cold water

hydroélectricité [idroelɛktrisite] *nf* hydroelectricity

hydroélectrique [idroelɛktrik] *adj* hydroelectric

hydrogène [idroʒɛn] *nm* hydrogen

hydroglisseur [idroglisœr] *nm* jetfoil

hydrographie [idrografi] *nf* hydrography

hydrolyse [idroliz] *nf* hydrolysis

hydromel [idromɛl] *nm* mead

hydrophile [idrofil] *adj (coton)* absorbent

hydrothérapie [idroterapi] *nf* hydrotherapy

hydroxyde [idroksid] *nm* hydroxide

hyène [jɛn] *nf* hyena

Hygiaphone® [iʒjafɔn] *nm (au guichet)* grille; **parlez dans l'H.** speak into the grille

hygiène [iʒjɛn] *nf* hygiene; **par mesure d'h.** for hygiene reasons; **h. alimentaire** diet; **h. corporelle** personal hygiene; **h. mentale** mental health; **avoir une bonne h. de vie** to live healthily

hygiénique [iʒjenik] *adj* **(a)** *(propre)* hygienic; **peu h.** unhygienic **(b)** *(bon pour la santé)* healthy; **une promenade h.** a bracing walk

hymne [imn] *nm* hymn; **h. national** national anthem

hyper [ipɛr] *nm Fam (abrév* **hypermarché)** hypermarket, superstore

hyper- [ipɛr] *préf Fam* very, really

hyperactif, -ive [ipɛraktif, -iv] *adj* hyperactive

hyperbole [ipɛrbɔl] *nf* **(a)** *(figure de style)* hyperbole **(b)** *Math* hyperbola

hyperbolique [ipɛrbɔlik] *adj* hyperbolic

hyperglycémie [ipɛrglisemi] *nf* hyperglycemia

hyperlien [ipɛrljɛ̃] *nm Ordinat* hyperlink

hypermarché [ipɛrmarʃe] *nm* hypermarket, superstore

hypermétrope [ipɛrmetrɔp] *adj* farsighted

hypernerveux, -euse [ipɛrnɛrvø, -øz] **1** *adj* highly-strung
  2 *nm,f* highly-strung person

hyperréaliste [ipɛrealist] *adj* hyperrealistic

hypersensibilité [ipɛrsɑ̃sibilite] *nf* hypersensitivity

hypersensible [ipɛrsɑ̃sibl] *adj* hypersensitive

hypertendu, -e [ipɛrtɑ̃dy] *adj* **être h.** to have high blood pressure

hypertension [ipɛrtɑ̃sjɔ̃] *nf* high blood pressure, *Spéc* hypertension

hypertexte [ipɛrtɛkst] *nm Ordinat* hypertext

hypertrophie [ipɛrtrɔfi] *nf* enlargement, *Spéc* hypertrophy

hypertrophié, -e [ipɛrtrɔfje] *adj* enlarged, *Spéc* hypertrophied

hypnose [ipnoz] *nf* hypnosis; **sous h.** under hypnosis; **être en état d'h.** to be under hypnosis

hypnotique [ipnɔtik] *adj* hypnotic

hypnotiser [ipnɔtize] *vt* to hypnotize

hypnotisme [ipnɔtism] *nm* hypnotism

hypoallergénique [ipɔalɛrʒenik] *adj* hypoallergenic

hypocalorique [ipɔkalɔrik] *adj (régime, aliment)* low-calorie

hypocondriaque [ipɔkɔ̃drijak] *adj & nmf* hypochondriac

hypocrisie [ipɔkrizi] *nf* hypocrisy

hypocrite [ipɔkrit] **1** *adj* hypocritical
  2 *nmf* hypocrite

hypocritement [ipɔkritmɑ̃] *adv* hypocritically

hypodermique [ipɔdɛrmik] *adj* hypodermic

hypoglycémie [ipɔglisemi] *nf* hypoglycemia

hypokhâgne [ipɔkaɲ] *nf* = first-year humanities class preparing students for the entrance examination for the "École normale supérieure"

hypophyse [ipɔfiz] *nf* pituitary gland

hypotendu, -e [ipɔtɑ̃dy] *adj* **être h.** to have low blood pressure

hypotension [ipɔtɑ̃sjɔ̃] *nf* low blood pressure, *Spéc* hypotension

hypoténuse [ipɔtenyz] *nf* hypotenuse

hypothalamus [ipɔtalamys] *nm* hypothalamus

hypothécaire [ipɔtekɛr] *adj* **contrat h.** mortgage deed; **prêt h.** mortgage (loan)

hypothèque [ipɔtɛk] *nf* mortgage

hypothéquer [34] [ipɔteke] *vt (propriété)* to mortgage; *Fig* **h. son avenir** to sign away one's future

hypothermie [ipɔtɛrmi] *nf* hypothermia

hypothèse [ipɔtɛz] *nf* hypothesis; **dans l'h. où nous échouerions** should we fail; **ils ont écarté l'h. du suicide** they have ruled out the possibility of suicide

hypothétique [ipɔtetik] *adj* hypothetical

hystérectomie [isterɛktɔmi] *nf* hysterectomy

hystérie [isteri] *nf* hysteria; **h. collective** mass hysteria

hystérique [isterik] **1** *adj* hysterical
  2 *nmf* hysterical person

I

I, i [i] *nm inv* I, i

ibère [ibɛr] **1** *adj* Iberian

2 *nmf* **I.** Iberian

ibérique [iberik] *adj* Iberian

ibis [ibis] *nm* ibis

iceberg [ajsbɛrg, isbɛrg] *nm* iceberg; *Fig* **la partie cachée de l'i.** the hidden aspects of the problem; *Fig* **la partie visible de l'i.** the tip of the iceberg

ichtyologie [iktjɔlɔʒi] *nf* ichthyology

ici [isi] *adv* **(a)** *(dans l'espace)* here; **i. et là** here and there; **i. même** on this very spot; **les gens d'i.** the people from around here, the locals; **c'est i.** this is the place; **i. que ça s'est passé** this is where it happened; *Fig* **je reprends i. ses propres paroles** and here I'm using his/her own words; **i. Thomas** *(au téléphone)* this is Thomas **(b)** *(dans le temps)* **jusqu'i.** until now, up to now; **d'i. lundi/demain** by Monday/tomorrow; **d'i. là** by that time, by then; **d'i. peu** before long; **d'i. à ce que vous ayez fini, je serai parti** by the time you've finished, I'll have gone; **d'i. à ce qu'il la quitte, il n'y a pas loin** he will have left her before long

icône [ikon] *nf Rel & Ordinat* icon; *Ordinat* **i. de la corbeille** wastebasket *or* trash icon

iconoclaste [ikɔnɔklast] **1** *adj* iconoclastic

2 *nmf* iconoclast

iconographie [ikɔnɔgrafi] *nf* **(a)** *(dans un domaine particulier)* iconography **(b)** *(dans l'édition)* illustrations, art work

iconographique [ikɔnɔgrafik] *adj* iconographic

idéal, -e, -als *ou* **-aux, -ales** [ideal, -o] **1** *adj* ideal

2 *nm* ideal; **l'i.** the ideal thing; **dans l'i.** ideally; **l'i. serait que tu y ailles tout seul** it would be best if you went alone

idéalement [idealmɑ̃] *adv* ideally

idéalisation [idealizasjɔ̃] *nf* idealization

idéaliser [idealize] *vt* to idealize

idéalisme [idealism] *nm* idealism

idéaliste [idealist] **1** *adj* idealistic

2 *nmf* idealist

idée [ide] *nf* **(a)** *(inspiration)* idea; **i. de génie, i. lumineuse** brilliant idea; **avoir la bonne i. de faire qch** to have the bright idea of doing sth; **avoir une i. derrière la tête** to be up to something; **donner des idées à qn** to put ideas into sb's head; **quelle drôle d'i.!, en voilà une i.!** the very idea!; **se faire des idées** to imagine things; **i. fixe** obsession; **idées noires** black thoughts; **i. reçue** generally accepted idea **(b)** *(notion)* idea; **pour vous donner une i.** to give you an idea; **as-tu une i. du prix que ça coûte?** do you have any idea how much it costs?; **je n'en ai pas la moindre i.** I don't have the faintest idea; *Fam* **on n'a pas i. de faire des choses pareilles!** whoever heard of such a thing! **(c)** *(opinion)* view, opinion; **avoir une haute i. de qn/qch** to have a high opinion of sb/sth; **se faire une i. de qn/qch** to get an idea of sb/sth; **avoir sa petite i. sur qch** to have one's pet theory about sth; **avoir les idées larges** to be broad-minded; **fais à ton i.** do as you like; **changer d'i.** to change one's mind

(d) *(esprit)* **ça ne m'est jamais venu à l'i.** it's never occurred to me; **je ne peux pas lui ôter cela de l'i.** I can't get him/her to change his/her mind about it; **se mettre dans l'i. que/de faire qch** to get it into one's head that/to do sth; **cela m'était sorti de l'i.** it had slipped my mind

idem [idɛm] *adv* ditto

identifiant [idɑ̃tifjɑ̃] *nm Ordinat* identifier; **i. biométrique** biometric identifier

identification [idɑ̃tifikasjɔ̃] *nf* identification (**avec** *ou* **à** with); *Tél* **i. d'appel** caller identification, *Fam* caller ID; *Ordinat* **i. de l'utilisateur** user identification

identifier [66] [idɑ̃tifje] **1** *vt* to identify

2 s'identifier *vpr* **s'i. à** *ou* **avec** to identify with

identique [idɑ̃tik] *adj* identical (**à** to)

identitaire [idɑ̃titɛr] *adj* **les revendications identitaires des minorités ethniques** ethnic minorities' demands for recognition; **obsession i.** obsession with issues of identity

identité [idɑ̃tite] *nf* identity; **papiers** *ou* **pièces d'i.** identity papers

idéogramme [ideɔgram] *nm* ideogram

idéologie [ideɔlɔʒi] *nf* ideology

idéologique [ideɔlɔʒik] *adj* ideological

idiomatique [idjɔmatik] *adj* idiomatic; **expression i.** idiom

idiome [idjom] *nm* idiom

idiot, -e [idjo, -ɔt] **1** *adj* *(stupide)* idiotic, stupid; *(regrettable)* stupid, silly; **ce système n'est pas i.** this system is pretty smart

2 *nm,f* idiot; *Fam* **l'i. du village** the village idiot; **faire l'i.** *(faire des bêtises)* to act the fool; *(feindre de ne pas comprendre)* to act dumb

idiotie [idjɔsi] *nf* *(chose, parole idiote)* stupid thing; *(caractère stupide)* stupidity; **ne dites pas d'idioties!** don't talk garbage!

idolâtrer [idɔlɑtre] *vt* to idolize

idolâtrie [idɔlɑtri] *nf* idolatry

idole [idɔl] *nf* idol; **i. des jeunes** teen idol

idylle [idil] *nf* **(a)** *(aventure)* romance **(b)** *(poème)* idyll

idyllique [idilik] *adj* idyllic

IEP [iəpe] *nm* *(abrév* **Institut d'études politiques**) = higher-education establishment for political science students

if [if] *nm* yew

IFOP [ifɔp] *nm* *(abrév* **Institut français d'opinion publique**) = French market-research institute

IGF [iʒeɛf] *nm inv Anciennement* *(abrév* **impôt sur les grandes fortunes**) wealth tax

igloo, iglou [iglu] *nm* igloo

IGN [iʒeɛn] *nm* *(abrév* **Institut géographique national**) ≃ United States Geological Survey

---

IGN

Created in 1940, this state agency is responsible for the official map of France and for keeping a geographical database. It is organized into regional offices and sponsors a school which trains 200 students a year.

ignare [iɲar] **1** *adj* ignorant
2 *nmf* ignoramus
ignifuge [iɲnify3] **1** *adj* fireproof
2 *nm* fireproofing material
ignifugé, -e [iɲnify3e] *adj* fireproofed
ignoble [iɲɔbl] *adj* (**a**) *(personne, conduite)* vile (**b**) *(habitation, quartier)* filthy; *(nourriture)* disgusting
ignominie [iɲɔmini] *nf* (**a**) *(caractère)* ignominy; **se couvrir d'i.** to bring shame upon oneself (**b**) *(action)* shameful thing; **c'est une i.!** it's a disgrace!
ignorance [iɲɔrɑ̃s] *nf* ignorance; **être/tenir qn dans l'i.** to be/to keep sb in the dark
ignorant, -e [iɲɔrɑ̃, -ɑ̃t] **1** *adj* ignorant (**de** of)
2 *nm,f* ignoramus; **faire l'i.** to pretend one doesn't know
ignoré, -e [iɲɔre] *adj* unknown; *(négligé)* ignored; **vivre i.** to live in obscurity
ignorer [iɲɔre] **1** *vt* (**a**) *(ne pas savoir)* not to know (about); **j'ignorais qu'il était malade** I was unaware that he was sick; **il ignore tout de cela** he knows nothing about it; **ne rien i. de qch** to know all about sth; **personne n'ignore que…** everybody knows that…; **i. la peur/la jalousie** to feel no fear/jealousy (**b**) *(mépriser)* (personne, conseil, interdiction) to ignore
2 s'ignorer *vpr* (**a**) *(se mépriser l'un l'autre)* to ignore each other (**b**) *(se méconnaître)* **c'est un artiste qui s'ignore** he's an artist but he doesn't know it
iguane [igwan] *nm* iguana
il [il] *pron personnel* (**a**) *(personne)* he; *(chose, animal)* it; **ton père est-il toujours à l'hôpital?** is your father still in the hospital? (**b**) *(impersonnel)* it; **il est six heures** it's six o'clock; **il pleut** it's raining; **il existe de nombreuses possibilités** there are many possibilities
île [il] *nf* island; **dans une î.** on an island; **î. déserte** desert island; **les îles Anglo-Normandes** the Channel Islands; *Culin* **î. flottante** floating island *(beaten egg whites served on custard)*; **les îles Salomon** the Solomon Islands; **les îles de la Société** the Society Islands; **les îles Sous-le-Vent** the Leeward Islands
Île-de-France [ildəfrɑ̃s] *nf* **l'Î.** = administrative region including Paris
iliaque [iljak] *adj Anat* iliac; **os i.** ilium
illégal, -e, -aux, -ales [ilegal, -o] *adj* illegal
illégalement [ilegalmɑ̃] *adv* illegally
illégalité [ilegalite] *nf* illegality; **vivre dans l'i.** to live outside the law; **être dans l'i.** to break the law
illégitime [ilezitim] *adj (enfant)* illegitimate; *(union)* unlawful; *(demande)* unwarranted
illettré, -e [iletre] *adj & nm,f* illiterate
illettrisme [iletrism] *nm* illiteracy
illicite [ilisit] *adj* illicit, unlawful
illico [iliko] *adv Fam* **i. (presto)** pronto
illimité, -e [ilimite] *adj (pouvoirs, moyens, crédit)* unlimited; *(confiance)* boundless
illisible [ilizibl] *adj* (**a**) *(indéchiffrable)* illegible; *Ordinat (fichier, disquette)* unreadable (**b**) *(incompréhensible)* unreadable
illogique [ilɔʒik] *adj* illogical
illumination [ilyminasjɔ̃] *nf* (**a**) *(action d'illuminer)* illumination; *(par projecteurs)* floodlighting (**b**) *(lumière)* **illuminations** illuminations (**c**) *(inspiration)* flash of inspiration
illuminé, -e [ilymine] **1** *adj (éclairé)* lit up, illuminated; *(par projecteurs)* floodlit
2 *nm,f Péj* fanatic
illuminer [ilymine] **1** *vt (éclairer)* to light up, to illuminate; *(par projecteurs)* to floodlight; *Fig (visage, yeux)* to light up
2 s'illuminer *vpr aussi Fig* to light up (**de** with)
illusion [ilyzjɔ̃] *nf* illusion; **se faire des illusions** to delude oneself; **je ne me fais aucune i. sur ses intentions** I have

no illusions about his/her intentions; **perdre ses illusions** to become disillusioned; **enlever** *ou* **faire perdre ses illusions à qn** to disillusion sb; **faire i.** to take people in; **i. d'optique** optical illusion
illusionner [ilyzjɔne] **s'illusionner** *vpr* to delude oneself (**sur** about)
illusionniste [ilyzjɔnist] *nmf* conjurer
illusoire [ilyzwar] *adj* illusory
illustrateur, -trice [ilystratœr, -tris] *nm,f* illustrator
illustration [ilystrasjɔ̃] *nf* illustration
illustre [ilystr] *adj* illustrious; *Hum* **un i. inconnu** a famous person no one has ever heard of
illustré, -e [ilystre] **1** *adj* illustrated
2 *nm Vieilli (pour enfants)* comic
illustrer [ilystre] **1** *vt (livre, récit)* to illustrate (**de** with)
2 s'illustrer *vpr* to distinguish oneself (**par** by)
îlot [ilo] *nm (île)* small island; *(groupe d'immeubles)* block; *Fig* **î. de verdure** island of greenery
îlotage [ilotaʒ] *nm* community policing, crime watch
ils [il] *pron personnel* they; **les magasins sont-i. ouverts le dimanche?** are the stores open on Sunday?
image [imaʒ] *nf* (**a**) *(dans un miroir)* reflection, image; *(à la télévision)* picture; **vingt-quatre images par seconde** twenty-four frames a second; **être à l'i.** to be on camera; **nous n'avons plus d'i.** the picture's gone; **i. d'archives** library picture; *Cin & TV* stock shot; *Ordinat* **i. bitmap** bitmap image; **images de synthèse** computer-generated images; *Ordinat* **i. vectorielle** outline image (**b**) *Fig* image; **soigner son i.** to cultivate one's image; **donner une bonne/mauvaise i. de** to present a good/bad image of; **i. de marque** *(d'un produit)* brand image; *(d'un homme politique, d'une entreprise)* public image (**c**) *(dessin)* picture; *(récompense scolaire)* ≃ gold star
imagé, -e [imaʒe] *adj* vivid
imagerie [imaʒri] *nf* imagery; *Méd* **i. médicale** medical imaging; *Méd* **i. par résonance magnétique** magnetic resonance imaging
imaginable [imaʒinabl] *adj* imaginable
imaginaire [imaʒinɛr] **1** *adj (personnage, pays, animal)* imaginary
2 *nm* **l'i.** the imagination
imaginatif, -ive [imaʒinatif, -iv] *adj* imaginative
imagination [imaʒinasjɔ̃] *nf* imagination; **avoir de l'i.** to be imaginative
imaginer [imaʒine] **1** *vt* (**a**) *(inventer)* to devise (**b**) *(se figurer)* to imagine; **tu l'imagines avec des enfants!** just imagine him/her with children!; **j'imagine qu'elle viendra vers neuf heures** she'll come about nine o'clock, I should imagine
2 s'imaginer *vpr* (**a**) *(croire)* **s'i. que** to think that; **il s'imagine tout savoir** he thinks he knows it all (**b**) *(se figurer)* to imagine; *(soi-même)* to picture oneself; **tu t'imagines la tête qu'elle va faire** you can imagine how she'll take it; **je me l'imaginais bien plus grand** I imagined him much taller
imam [imam] *nm* imam
imbattable [ɛ̃batabl] *adj* unbeatable
imbécile [ɛ̃besil] **1** *adj* idiotic, stupid
2 *nmf* idiot, fool; **c'est un i. heureux** he's living in blissful ignorance; **faire l'i.** *(faire des bêtises)* to play *or* to act the fool; *(feindre de ne pas comprendre)* to act stupid
imbécillité [ɛ̃besilite] *nf* (**a**) *(caractère stupide)* idiocy, stupidity (**b**) *(parole, chose stupide)* idiotic thing; **dire des imbécillités** to talk nonsense
imberbe [ɛ̃bɛrb] *adj* beardless
imbiber [ɛ̃bibe] **1** *vt* **i. qch de qch** to soak sth in sth; **imbibé d'eau** *(coton, éponge)* saturated (with water); *(terrain)* waterlogged
2 s'imbiber *vpr* **s'i. de qch** to become soaked with sth

imbrication [ɛ̃brikasjɔ̃] *nf* overlapping; *Fig (ensemble complexe)* web; *Ordinat* embedding; *(de commandes)* nesting

imbriquer [ɛ̃brike] **1** *vt* to overlap; *Ordinat* to embed; *(commandes)* to nest

2 s'imbriquer *vpr (s'emboîter)* to overlap; *Fig (problèmes, situations)* to be interwoven

imbroglio [ɛ̃brɔljo] *nm* imbroglio

imbu, -e [ɛ̃by] *adj* **i. de sa personne** *ou* **de soi-même** full of oneself

imbuvable [ɛ̃byvabl] *adj* undrinkable; *Fig (personne)* insufferable

imitateur, -trice [imitatœr, -tris] *nm,f (amateur)* mimic; *(professionnel)* impersonator, impressionist

imitation [imitasjɔ̃] *nf* **(a)** *(d'une personne)* impersonation, impression; *(d'un produit, d'un style)* imitation; *(d'une signature, d'un billet)* forgery **(b)** *(copie)* imitation; *(contrefaçon)* knockoff; **bijoux en i. argent** imitation silver jewelry

imiter [imite] *vt (personne) (singer)* to imitate; *(faire une imitation de)* to impersonate; *(produit, style)* to imitate, to knock off; *(signature)* to forge; *(billet, pièce de monnaie)* to counterfeit; **il leva son verre et tout le monde l'imita** he raised his glass and everyone did the same

immaculé, -e [imakyle] *adj (draps, linge, réputation)* spotless; **d'un blanc i.** spotlessly white; *Rel* **l'Immaculée Conception** the Immaculate Conception

immangeable [ɛ̃mɑ̃ʒabl] *adj* inedible

immanquablement [ɛ̃mɑ̃kabləmɑ̃] *adv* inevitably

immatériel, -elle [imaterjɛl] *adj Phil* immaterial; *Fin (actif)* intangible; *Litt (pâleur, minceur)* ethereal

immatriculation [imatrikylasjɔ̃] *nf* registration (**à** with); **(numéro d')i.** license number

---

Immatriculation

The last two numbers on French license plates refer to the **département** *(see box at this entry)* where the vehicle was registered. Vehicles from the Val-de-Marne, for example, bear the number 94.

---

immatriculer [imatrikyle] *vt* to register (**à** with); **la voiture est immatriculée en Dordogne** the car has a Dordogne license plate

immature [imatyr] *adj* immature

immaturité [imatyrite] *nf* immaturity

immédiat, -e [imedja, -at] **1** *adj* immediate; *(contact)* direct; *(mort)* instantaneous

2 *nm* **dans l'i.** for the time being

immédiatement [imedjatmɑ̃] *adv* immediately

immémorial, -e, -aux, -ales [imemɔrjal, -o] *adj Litt* age-old; **en des temps immémoriaux** in ancient times

immense [imɑ̃s] *adj* immense

immensément [imɑ̃semɑ̃] *adv* immensely

immensité [imɑ̃site] *nf* immensity

immerger [45] [imɛrʒe] *vt* to immerse (**dans** in)

immérité, -e [imerite] *adj* unmerited, undeserved

immersion [imɛrsjɔ̃] *nf* immersion (**dans** in)

immettable [ɛ̃mɛtabl] *adj* unwearable

immeuble [imœbl] **1** *nm (bâtiment)* building; *(d'appartements)* apartment building

2 *adj voir* **bien**

immigrant, -e [imigrɑ̃, -ɑ̃t] *adj & nm,f* immigrant

immigration [imigrasjɔ̃] *nf* immigration

immigré, -e [imigre] *adj & nm,f* immigrant

immigrer [imigre] *vi* to immigrate

imminence [iminɑ̃s] *nf* imminence

imminent, -e [iminɑ̃, -ɑ̃t] *adj* imminent

immiscer [16] [imise] **s'immiscer** *vpr* to interfere (**dans** in)

immobile [imɔbil] *adj* motionless, still; *Fig (figé)* unchanging

immobilier, -ère [imɔbilje, -ɛr] **1** *adj* real-estate

2 *nm* **l'i.** real estate

immobilisation [imɔbilizasjɔ̃] *nf* **(a)** *(fait de ne plus bouger)* immobilization **(b)** *Fin* **immobilisations** fixed assets

immobiliser [imɔbilize] **1** *vt* **(a)** *(blessé)* to immobilize; *(train)* to bring to a standstill; *(véhicule) (avec un sabot)* to clamp **(b)** *(capital)* to tie up

2 s'immobiliser *vpr* to come to a stop

immobilisme [imɔbilism] *nm* opposition to change

immobilité [imɔbilite] *nf* stillness; *(d'un visage)* immobility

immodéré, -e [imɔdere] *adj* immoderate

immodérément [imɔderemɑ̃] *adv* immoderately

immoler [imɔle] *Litt* **1** *vt aussi Fig* to sacrifice (**à** to)

2 s'immoler *vpr* to sacrifice oneself; **s'i. par le feu** to die by setting fire to oneself

immonde [imɔ̃d] *adj (sale)* foul; *(ignoble, laid)* vile

immondices [imɔ̃dis] *nfpl* refuse

immoral, -e, -aux, -ales [imɔral, -o] *adj* immoral

immoralité [imɔralite] *nf* immorality

immortaliser [imɔrtalize] *vt* to immortalize

immortalité [imɔrtalite] *nf* immortality

immortel, -elle [imɔrtɛl] **1** *adj (dieu, être)* immortal; *(amour)* everlasting

2 *nm,f (membre de l'Académie française)* member of the Académie Française

3 *nf* **immortelle** *(plante)* everlasting flower

immuable [imɥabl] *adj (vérité)* unchanging, immutable; *(opinion, sourire)* fixed

immunisation [imynizasjɔ̃] *nf* immunization (**contre** against)

immuniser [imynize] *vt* to immunize (**contre** against)

immunitaire [imynitɛr] *adj (système, réactions, défenses)* immune

immunité [imynite] *nf* immunity; **i. parlementaire/diplomatique** parliamentary/diplomatic immunity

immunodéficitaire [imynɔdefisitɛr] *adj Méd* immunodeficient

immunodépresseur [imynɔdepresœr] *Méd* **1** *adj m* immunosuppressive

2 *nm* immunosuppressant

immunologie [imynɔlɔʒi] *nf* immunology

immunologique [imynɔlɔʒik] *adj* immunological

immunosuppresseur [imynɔsypresœr] *Méd* **1** *adj m* immunosuppressive

2 *nm* immunosuppressant

impact [ɛ̃pakt] *nm* impact; **avoir un i. sur qch** to have an impact on sth

impair, -e [ɛ̃pɛr] **1** *adj (nombre, jours)* odd; *(côté d'une rue)* odd-numbered

2 *nm* **(a)** *(à la roulette)* odd numbers **(b)** *(maladresse)* blunder; **faire** *ou* **commettre un i.** to make a blunder

impalpable [ɛ̃palpabl] *adj* impalpable

imparable [ɛ̃parabl] *adj (coup)* unstoppable; *Fig (argument, logique)* irrefutable

impardonnable [ɛ̃pardɔnabl] *adj* unforgivable; **j'ai encore pris votre parapluie, je suis i.** I've taken your umbrella again, how unforgivable of me!

imparfait, -e [ɛ̃parfɛ, -ɛt] **1** *adj* **(a)** *(qui a des défauts)* imperfect **(b)** *(inachevé)* unfinished

2 *nm Gram* imperfect (tense); **à l'i.** in the imperfect (tense)

impartial, -e, -aux, -ales [ɛ̃parsjal, -o] *adj* impartial, unbiased

impartialité [ɛ̃parsjalite] *nf* impartiality

impartir [ɛ̃partir] *vt Litt* **i. qch à qn** *(droit)* to grant sth to sb;

(tâche) to assign sth to sb; **dans le délai imparti** within the time allowed; **le temps qui vous est imparti** the time allotted to you

impasse [ɛ̃pas] *nf* (a) *(cul-de-sac)* dead end, cul-de-sac; *Fig* impasse, deadlock; *Fig* **être dans une i.** to be deadlocked; *Fig* **sortir de l'i.** to break the deadlock (b) **faire une i.** *(en révisant)* = to miss out part of a subject when reviewing

impassibilité [ɛ̃pasibilite] *nf* impassiveness

impassible [ɛ̃pasibl] *adj* impassive

impatiemment [ɛ̃pasjamɑ̃] *adv* impatiently

impatience [ɛ̃pasjɑ̃s] *nf* impatience; **avec i.** impatiently

impatient, -e [ɛ̃pasjɑ̃, -ɑ̃t] **1** *adj* impatient; **d'un air i.** impatiently; **être i. de faire qch** to be impatient to do sth
2 *nf* **impatiente** *(plante)* Busy Lizzie

impatienter [ɛ̃pasjɑ̃te] **1** *vt* to annoy, to irritate
2 s'impatienter *vpr* to get impatient (**de/contre** at/with)

impavide [ɛ̃pavid] *adj Litt* impassive

impayable [ɛ̃pɛjabl] *adj Fam (histoire, personne)* priceless

impayé, -e [ɛ̃peje] **1** *adj* unpaid
2 *nm* outstanding payment

impec [ɛ̃pɛk] *adj Fam* spotless; **i.!** *(parfait)* great!

impeccable [ɛ̃pɛkabl] *adj* impeccable; **d'une propreté i.** impeccably clean; *Fam* **i.!** *(parfait)* great!

impeccablement [ɛ̃pɛkabləmɑ̃] *adv* impeccably

impénétrable [ɛ̃penetrabl] *adj* (a) *(forêt, citadelle)* impenetrable (b) *(visage, caractère, air)* inscrutable; *(mystère, texte)* impenetrable; **les voies du Seigneur sont impénétrables** the Lord works in mysterious ways

impénitent, -e [ɛ̃penitɑ̃, -ɑ̃t] *adj* unrepentant

impensable [ɛ̃pɑ̃sabl] *adj* unthinkable; **il est i. que vous ne soyez pas remplacé** it's unthinkable that they're not going to replace you

imper [ɛ̃pɛr] *nm Fam* raincoat

impératif, -ive [ɛ̃peratif, -iv] **1** *adj* (a) *(ton, geste)* imperious (b) *(nécessité, besoin)* imperative; **il est i. de connaître l'anglais** it is imperative to know English
2 *nm* (a) *(exigence)* requirement; **savoir nager est un i.** it is essential to be able to swim; **les impératifs de la mode** the dictates of fashion (b) *Gram* imperative (mood); **à l'i.** in the imperative (mood)

impérativement [ɛ̃perativmɑ̃] *adv* **il faut i. que je la voie** it is imperative that I see her

impératrice [ɛ̃peratris] *nf* empress

imperceptible [ɛ̃pɛrsɛptibl] *adj* imperceptible (**à** to)

imperceptiblement [ɛ̃pɛrsɛptibləmɑ̃] *adv* imperceptibly

imperdable [ɛ̃pɛrdabl] *adj* **le match/le procès est i.** the match/the case can't be lost

imperfectible [ɛ̃pɛrfɛktibl] *adj* imperfectible

imperfection [ɛ̃pɛrfɛksjɔ̃] *nf* imperfection

impérial, -e, -aux, -ales [ɛ̃perjal, -o] **1** *adj aussi Fig* imperial
2 *nf* **impériale** *(d'un bus)* top deck

impérialisme [ɛ̃perjalism] *nm* imperialism

impérialiste [ɛ̃perjalist] *adj & nmf* imperialist

impérieux, -euse [ɛ̃perjø, -øz] *adj* (a) *(autoritaire)* imperious (b) *(nécessité, désir, besoin)* urgent, pressing

impérissable [ɛ̃perisabl] *adj (œuvre, souvenir)* enduring; **ça ne m'a pas laissé un souvenir i.** it didn't make a lasting impression on me

imperméabilisant, -e [ɛ̃pɛrmeabilizɑ̃, -ɑ̃t] **1** *adj* waterproofing
2 *nm* waterproofing agent

imperméabiliser [ɛ̃pɛrmeabilize] *vt* to waterproof

imperméable [ɛ̃pɛrmeabl] **1** *adj* impermeable; *(à l'eau)* waterproof; *Fig* **être i. à qch** to be impervious to sth
2 *nm* raincoat

impersonnel, -elle [ɛ̃pɛrsɔnɛl] *adj* impersonal

impertinemment [ɛ̃pɛrtinamɑ̃] *adv* impertinently

impertinence [ɛ̃pɛrtinɑ̃s] *nf* impertinence; **avec i.** impertinently

impertinent, -e [ɛ̃pɛrtinɑ̃, -ɑ̃t] **1** *adj* impertinent
2 *nm,f* impertinent person; **un petit i.** an impertinent little boy

imperturbable [ɛ̃pɛrtyrbabl] *adj (personne)* imperturbable; *(optimisme)* unshakeable

imperturbablement [ɛ̃pɛrtyrbabləmɑ̃] *adv* imperturbably

impétigo [ɛ̃petigo] *nm* impetigo

impétueusement [ɛ̃petɥøzmɑ̃] *adv* impetuously

impétueux, -euse [ɛ̃petɥø, -øz] *adj* (a) *(personne)* impetuous; *(tempérament)* fiery (b) *Litt (torrent)* raging

impétuosité [ɛ̃petɥozite] *nf (fougue)* impetuosity

impie [ɛ̃pi] *Litt* **1** *adj* impious
2 *nmf* impious person

impitoyable [ɛ̃pitwajabl] *adj* merciless

impitoyablement [ɛ̃pitwajabləmɑ̃] *adv* mercilessly

implacable [ɛ̃plakabl] *adj (personne, vengeance, logique)* implacable; *(avancée)* relentless

implant [ɛ̃plɑ̃] *nm* implant; **i. mammaire** breast implant; **implants (capillaires)** hair graft

implantation [ɛ̃plɑ̃tasjɔ̃] *nf* (a) *(installation)* establishment (b) *(des cheveux)* line; *(des dents)* arch

implanter [ɛ̃plɑ̃te] **1** *vt* (a) *(installer)* to establish (b) *(chirurgicalement)* to implant
2 s'implanter *vpr* to become established

implication [ɛ̃plikasjɔ̃] *nf* (a) *(engagement)* involvement (b) **implications** *(conséquences)* implications

implicite [ɛ̃plisit] *adj* implicit

implicitement [ɛ̃plisitmɑ̃] *adv* implicitly

impliquer [ɛ̃plike] **1** *vt* (a) *(compromettre)* to implicate (**dans** in) (b) *(supposer)* to imply; **i. que** to imply that
2 s'impliquer *vpr* to get involved (**dans** in)

implorer [ɛ̃plɔre] *vt* to implore, to beseech; **i. le pardon de qn** to beg sb's forgiveness; **i. qn de faire qch** to implore *or* to beseech sb to do sth

imploser [ɛ̃plɔze] *vi* to implode

implosion [ɛ̃plɔzjɔ̃] *nf* implosion

impoli, -e [ɛ̃pɔli] *adj* impolite, rude

impoliment [ɛ̃pɔlimɑ̃] *adv* impolitely, rudely

impolitesse [ɛ̃pɔlitɛs] *nf* (a) *(d'une personne, d'une remarque)* impoliteness, rudeness (b) *(acte)* impolite act; *(remarque)* rude remark

impondérable [ɛ̃pɔ̃derabl] *adj & nm* imponderable

impopulaire [ɛ̃pɔpylɛr] *adj* unpopular

import [ɛ̃pɔr] *nm* (a) *Com* import; *Ordinat* **i. de données** data import (b) *Belg (montant)* amount; **une facture d'un i. de 2000 euros** a bill for 2000 euros

importable [ɛ̃pɔrtabl] *adj (vêtement)* unwearable

importance [ɛ̃pɔrtɑ̃s] *nf* (a) *(d'un événement, d'un acte, d'une personne)* importance; **avoir de l'i. (pour)** to be important (to); **sans i.** unimportant; **cela n'a aucune i.** it's of no importance; **c'est d'une i. capitale** it's extremely important; **de la première** *ou* **de la plus haute i.** extremely important; **attacher** *ou* **donner de l'i. à qch** to attach importance to sth; **et alors, quelle i.?** well, so what? (b) *(d'une ville, d'une somme, d'un projet)* size; *(de dégâts, d'une catastrophe)* extent; **prendre de l'i.** *(société)* to expand; *(mouvement, parti)* to gain ground

important, -e [ɛ̃pɔrtɑ̃, -ɑ̃t] **1** *adj* (a) *(événement, acte, personne)* important (**pour** to); **il est i. que vous le sachiez** it's important for you to know; **peu i.** unimportant; **se donner des airs importants** to give oneself airs (b) *(ville, projet)* large; *(somme d'argent, dégâts, retard)* considerable; *(chiffre)* high
2 *nm,f Péj* **faire l'i.** to act important

3 *nm* l'i., c'est que tu sois satisfait the important thing is that you're satisfied

importateur, -trice [ɛ̃pɔrtatœr, -tris] **1** *nm,f* importer

2 *adj* importing; **les pays importateurs de pétrole** oil-importing countries

importation [ɛ̃pɔrtasjɔ̃] *nf* **(a)** *(de marchandises)* importing; **articles** *ou* **produits d'i.** imports; **licence d'i.** import license **(b)** *(produit)* import

importer¹ [ɛ̃pɔrte] *vt* **(a)** *(marchandises)* to import **(b)** *Ordinat* to download

importer² [ɛ̃pɔrte] **1** *vi* *(compter)* to matter (**à** to); **ce qui importe, c'est que tu viennes** the important thing is that you come

2 *v impersonnel* **(a)** *(être important)* **il importe que vous y soyez** it's important that you be there; **peu importe** it doesn't matter; **peu m'importe** I don't mind; **qu'importe?** what does it matter? **(b)** **faire qch n'importe où/quand/ comment** to do sth anywhere/any time/anyhow; *Fam* **n'importe comment, c'est trop tard** anyway, it's too late; **n'importe** never mind; **n'importe quel gamin** any child; **n'importe qui** anyone, anybody; **n'importe qui d'autre** anyone else; **n'importe quoi** anything; *Péj* **dire/écrire n'importe quoi** to talk/write nonsense; *Fam* **n'importe quoi!** nonsense!

import-export [ɛ̃pɔrɛkspɔr] *nm* import-export business

importun, -e [ɛ̃pɔrtœ̃, -yn] **1** *adj* *(personne, visiteur, question)* importunate; *(arrivée, remarque)* ill-timed

2 *nm,f* *(personne)* nuisance

importuner [ɛ̃pɔrtyne] *vt Sout* to bother

imposable [ɛ̃pozabl] *adj* taxable

imposant, -e [ɛ̃pozɑ̃, -ɑ̃t] *adj* imposing

imposé, -e [ɛ̃poze] *adj* *(taxé)* taxed; **être i. à la source** to be taxed at source

imposer [ɛ̃poze] **1** *vt* **(a)** *(une condition)* to impose (**à** on); **i. une tâche à qn** to set sb a task; **i. le respect** to command respect; **i. sa loi** to lay down the law; **i. le silence à qn** to make sb be quiet; **i. sa présence à qn** to impose on sb **(b)** *(soumettre à l'impôt)* to tax

2 *vi* **en i.** to be impressive; **en i. à qn** to impress sb

3 **s'imposer** *vpr* **(a)** *(faire reconnaître sa valeur)* to assert oneself; *(gagner)* to win **(b)** *(déranger)* **je ne voulais pas m'i.** I didn't want to impose **(c)** *(être nécessaire)* to be essential; **prendre les mesures qui s'imposent** to take the necessary steps **(d)** *(se contraindre)* **s'i. un sacrifice** to force oneself to make a sacrifice; **s'i. de faire qch** to make it a rule to do sth

imposition [ɛ̃pozisjɔ̃] *nf* *(taxation)* taxation

impossibilité [ɛ̃pɔsibilite] *nf* impossibility; **être** *ou* **se trouver dans l'i. de faire qch** to find it impossible to do sth

impossible [ɛ̃pɔsibl] **1** *adj* impossible; **i. à lire** impossible to read; **il est i. qu'il revienne avant lundi** he can't possibly be back before Monday; **il m'est i. de le faire** it's impossible for me to do it; **i. n'est pas français** there's no such word as can't; **rendre la vie i. à qn** to make life impossible for sb; **tu es i.!** you're impossible!

2 *nm* **tenter/demander l'i.** to attempt/to ask the impossible; **faire l'i. pour faire qch** to do everything possible to do sth

imposteur [ɛ̃pɔstœr] *nm* impostor

imposture [ɛ̃pɔstyr] *nf* deception

impôt [ɛ̃po] *nm* tax; **payer 1000 euros d'impôts** to pay 1,000 euros in tax; *Fam* **les impôts m'ont envoyé une lettre** the IRS has sent me a letter; **i. direct/indirect** direct/indirect tax; **i. foncier** property tax; *Anciennement* **i. sur les grandes fortunes** wealth tax; **impôts locaux** local taxes; **i. sur le revenu** income tax; **i. sur les sociétés** corporate tax; **i. de solidarité sur la fortune** wealth tax

---

Impôts locaux

These are taxes levied to finance local, departmental or regional government. The best-known are the "taxe d'habitation" (paid by rent-paying tenants), the "taxe foncière" (paid by homeowners) and the "taxe professionnelle" (paid by the self-employed). The rate of each tax is decided at local level.

---

impotence [ɛ̃pɔtɑ̃s] *nf* *(infirmité)* disability; *(due à la vieillesse)* infirmity

impotent, -e [ɛ̃pɔtɑ̃, -ɑ̃t] **1** *adj* *(infirme)* disabled; *(à cause de la vieillesse)* infirm

2 *nm,f* *(infirme)* disabled person; *(vieillard)* infirm person

impraticable [ɛ̃pratikabl] *adj* **(a)** *(où l'on ne peut pas passer)* impassable **(b)** *(terrain de sport)* unfit for play **(c)** *(irréalisable)* impracticable

imprécation [ɛ̃prekasjɔ̃] *nf Litt* imprecation

imprécis, -e [ɛ̃presi, -iz] *adj* imprecise

imprécision [ɛ̃presizjɔ̃] *nf* imprecision

imprégner [34] [ɛ̃preɲe] **1** *vt* **(a)** *(sujet: eau, odeur)* to impregnate **(b)** *Fig (influencer)* **être imprégné de qch** to be full of sth

2 **s'imprégner** *vpr* **(a)** *(s'imbiber)* to become impregnated (**de** with); **s'i. d'eau** to become soaked with water **(b)** *Fig* **s'i. d'un auteur** to immerse oneself in an author

imprenable [ɛ̃prənabl] *adj* **(a)** *(forteresse, ville)* impregnable **(b)** *(vue)* unobstructed

imprésario [ɛ̃presarjo] *nm* manager

imprescriptible [ɛ̃preskriptibl] *adj Jur* imperscriptible

impression [ɛ̃presjɔ̃] *nf* **(a)** *(sensation)* impression; **donner à qn l'i. que** to give sb the impression that; **faire bonne/mauvaise/forte i. (à qn)** to make a good/bad/strong impression (on sb); **ça m'a fait une drôle d'i.** it gave me a funny feeling; **j'ai l'i. de l'avoir déjà vue** I've a feeling that I've seen her before; **j'ai l'i. qu'elle est timide** I have the impression that she's shy **(b)** *(action d'imprimer)* printing; *(copie)* printout; *Ordinat* **i. écran** screen dump; **i. laser** laser printing; *(copie)* laser printout **(c)** *(motif)* **tissu à impressions florales** material with a floral pattern

impressionnable [ɛ̃presjɔnabl] *adj* *(personne)* impressionable

impressionnant, -e [ɛ̃presjɔnɑ̃, -ɑ̃t] *adj* *(imposant)* impressive; *(bouleversant)* upsetting

impressionner [ɛ̃presjɔne] *vt* **(a)** *(frapper)* to impress; *(bouleverser)* to upset; **se laisser i.** to let oneself be overawed **(b)** *Phot (pellicule)* to expose

impressionnisme [ɛ̃presjɔnism] *nm* impressionism

impressionniste [ɛ̃presjɔnist] *adj & nmf* impressionist

imprévisible [ɛ̃previzibl] *adj* *(temps, réaction, personne)* unpredictable; *(événement)* unforeseeable

imprévoyance [ɛ̃prevwajɑ̃s] *nf* lack of foresight

imprévoyant, -e [ɛ̃prevwajɑ̃, -ɑ̃t] *adj* lacking in foresight

imprévu, -e [ɛ̃prevy] **1** *adj* unexpected, unforeseen

2 *nm* **(a)** *(surprise)* **aimer l'i.** to like the unexpected; **un voyage plein d'i.** a journey full of surprises **(b)** *(incident)* unexpected *or* unforeseen event; **sauf i., à moins d'un i.** unless something unexpected happens

imprimable [ɛ̃primabl] *adj* printable

imprimante [ɛ̃primɑ̃t] *nf* printer; **i. à aiguilles** 24-pin printer; **i. à bulles (d'encre)** bubble-jet printer; **i. feuille à feuille** sheet-fed printer; **i. graphique** graphics printer; **i. à jet d'encre** ink-jet printer; **i. (à) laser** laser printer

imprimé, -e [ɛ̃prime] **1** *adj* printed

2 *nm* **(a)** *(formulaire)* form; **imprimés** *(journaux, prospectus)* printed matter **(b)** *(un tissu)* print; **un i. à fleurs/à motifs géométriques** a floral/geometric print

imprimer [ɛ̃prime] *vt* **(a)** *(livre)* to print; *Ordinat* to print (out); *Ordinat* **i. un écran** to do a print screen **(b)** *(motif, empreinte, tissu)* to print **(c)** *(mouvement)* to impart (**à** to)

imprimerie [ɛ̃primri] *nf* (**a**) *(technique)* printing (**b**) *(atelier, usine)* printing works; **l'I. nationale** = French government printing office

imprimeur [ɛ̃primœr] *nm* printer

improbable [ɛ̃prɔbabl] *adj* improbable, unlikely

improductif, -ive [ɛ̃prɔdyktif, -iv] *adj* unproductive

impromptu, -e [ɛ̃prɔ̃pty] *adj & nm* impromptu

imprononçable [ɛ̃prɔnɔ̃sabl] *adj* unpronounceable

impropre [ɛ̃prɔpr] *adj* (**a**) *(incorrect)* incorrect (**b**) *(inadapté)* **i. à qch** unfit for sth; **i. à la consommation** unfit for human consumption

improprement [ɛ̃prɔprəmɑ̃] *adv* incorrectly

improvisation [ɛ̃prɔvizasjɔ̃] *nf* improvisation; **faire une i.** to improvise

improvisé, -e [ɛ̃prɔvize] *adj* improvised

improviser [ɛ̃prɔvize] **1** *vt & vi* to improvise
2 s'improviser *vpr* **un départ en vacances, ça ne s'improvise pas** going on vacation isn't something you can do just like that

improviste [ɛ̃prɔvist] **à l'improviste** *adv* unexpectedly

imprudemment [ɛ̃prydamɑ̃] *adv (parler, agir)* rashly; *(conduire)* recklessly

imprudence [ɛ̃prydɑ̃s] *nf* (**a**) *(d'un acte, d'une personne)* rashness (**b**) *(acte)* **commettre une i.** to act rashly

imprudent, -e [ɛ̃prydɑ̃, -ɑ̃t] **1** *adj* rash; *(conducteur)* reckless
2 *nm,f* rash person

impubliable [ɛ̃pyblijabl] *adj* unpublishable

impudence [ɛ̃pydɑ̃s] *nf* impudence

impudent, -e [ɛ̃pydɑ̃, -ɑ̃t] *adj* impudent

impudeur [ɛ̃pydœr] *nf* shamelessness

impudique [ɛ̃pydik] *adj* shameless

impuissance [ɛ̃pɥisɑ̃s] *nf* (**a**) *(incapacité)* powerlessness (**à faire qch** to do sth) (**b**) *(sexuelle)* impotence

impuissant, -e [ɛ̃pɥisɑ̃, -ɑ̃t] **1** *adj* (**a**) *(désarmé)* powerless (**b**) *(sexuellement)* impotent
2 *nm* impotent man

impulsif, -ive [ɛ̃pylsif, -iv] **1** *adj* impulsive
2 *nm,f* impulsive person

impulsion [ɛ̃pylsjɔ̃] *nf* (**a**) *Tech* impulse (**b**) *Fig (élan)* impulse; **faire qch sous l'i. de la colère** to do sth in a fit of anger (**c**) *(essor)* impetus

impulsivité [ɛ̃pylsivite] *nf* impulsiveness

impunément [ɛ̃pynemɑ̃] *adv* with impunity

impuni, -e [ɛ̃pyni] *adj* unpunished

impunité [ɛ̃pynite] *nf* impunity; **agir en toute i.** to act with impunity

impur, -e [ɛ̃pyr] *adj* impure

imputable [ɛ̃pytabl] *adj* (**a**) *(erreur)* attributable (**à** to) (**b**) *Fin* chargeable (**sur** to)

imputer [ɛ̃pyte] *vt* (**a**) *(crime, erreur)* **i. qch à qn** to attribute sth to sb (**b**) *Fin* **i. des frais sur un compte** to charge expenses to an account

inabordable [inabɔrdabl] *adj (endroit)* inaccessible; *(prix, marchandises)* unaffordable; *(personne)* unapproachable

inacceptable [inaksɛptabl] *adj* unacceptable

inaccessible [inaksesibl] *adj* (**a**) *(lieu)* inaccessible; *(objectif)* unattainable (**b**) *(personne)* unapproachable (**c**) *(insensible)* **i. à la pitié** incapable of pity; **i. à la flatterie** impervious to flattery

inachevé, -e [inaʃəve] *adj* unfinished

inactif, -ive [inaktif, -iv] **1** *adj* (**a**) *(personne)* inactive; *Écon* **la population inactive** the non-working population (**b**) *(remède)* ineffective
2 *nm,f* **un i.** a person without paid employment; **les inactifs** the non-working population

inaction [inaksjɔ̃] *nf* inaction

inactivité [inaktivite] *nf* inactivity

inadapté, -e [inadapte] **1** *adj (personne) (socialement)* maladjusted; *(physiquement, mentalement)* handicapped; *(matériel)* unsuitable (**à** for)
2 *nm,f (socialement)* maladjusted person; *(physiquement, mentalement)* handicapped person; **les inadaptés** the maladjusted/handicapped

inadéquation [inadekwasjɔ̃] *nf* inadequacy

inadmissible [inadmisibl] *adj* inadmissible

inadvertance [inadvɛrtɑ̃s] **par inadvertance** *adv* inadvertently

inaliénable [inaljenabl] *adj Jur (droit)* inalienable

inaltérable [inalterabl] *adj* (**a**) *(métal, revêtement)* stable (**b**) *Fig (constant)* unwavering

inamical, -e, -aux, -ales [inamikal, -o] *adj* unfriendly

inamovible [inamɔvibl] *adj* (**a**) *(four, autoradio)* built-in (**b**) *(juge, magistrat)* permanent

inanimé, -e [inanime] *adj* (**a**) *(mort)* lifeless; *(inconscient)* unconscious; **tomber i.** to fall unconscious (**b**) *(objet)* inanimate

inanité [inanite] *nf (d'un effort)* futility; *(d'une conversation)* inanity

inanition [inanisjɔ̃] *nf* starvation; **mourir d'i.** to die of starvation

inaperçu, -e [inapɛrsy] *adj* **passer i.** to go unnoticed

inapplicable [inaplikabl] *adj (réforme, loi)* unenforceable; *(théorie)* inapplicable

inappréciable [inapresjabl] *adj (précieux)* invaluable

inapte [inapt] *adj (pour raisons médicales)* unfit; *(intellectuellement)* unsuited; **être i. à qch/à faire qch** *(pour raisons médicales)* to be unfit for sth/to do sth; *(intellectuellement)* to be unsuited for sth/to do sth; **être i. (au service)** *(appelé)* to be unfit (for service)

inaptitude [inaptityd] *nf (intellectuelle)* inaptitude; *(médicale, militaire)* unfitness (**à** for)

inarticulé, -e [inartikyle] *adj (son, cris)* inarticulate

inassouvi, -e [inasuvi] *adj (faim, désir, vengeance)* unsatisfied; *(soif)* unquenched

inattaquable [inatakabl] *adj* unassailable

inattendu, -e [inatɑ̃dy] *adj* unexpected

inattentif, -ive [inatɑ̃tif, -iv] *adj (distrait)* inattentive; **i. à qch** *(indifférent)* heedless of sth

inattention [inatɑ̃sjɔ̃] *nf* lack of attention; **un moment d'i.** a lapse of concentration

inaudible [inodibl] *adj* inaudible

inaugural, -e, -aux, -ales [inogyral, -o] *adj (discours, séance)* inaugural

inauguration [inogyrasjɔ̃] *nf (d'un bâtiment, d'une route)* (official) opening, inauguration; *(d'une statue, d'un monument)* unveiling

inaugurer [inogyre] *vt (bâtiment, route)* to officially open, to inaugurate; *(statue, monument)* to unveil; *Fig (politique, méthode)* to implement; *(époque)* to usher in

inavouable [inavwabl] *adj* shameful

inavoué, -e [inavwe] *adj* unconfessed

INC [iɛnse] *nm (abrév* **Institut national de la consommation***)* = national institute for consumer advice

inca [ɛ̃ka] **1** *adj* Inca
2 *nmf* **I.** Inca

incalculable [ɛ̃kalkylabl] *adj* incalculable; **un nombre i. de fois** countless times

incandescence [ɛ̃kɑ̃desɑ̃s] *nf* incandescence

incandescent, -e [ɛ̃kɑ̃desɑ̃, -ɑ̃t] *adj* incandescent

incantation [ɛ̃kɑ̃tasjɔ̃] *nf* incantation

incantatoire [ɛ̃kɑ̃tatwar] *adj* incantatory

incapable [ɛ̃kapabl] **1** *adj* (**a**) *(incompétent)* incapable, incompetent; *Jur* incompetent (**b**) **être i. de faire qch** to be

incapable of doing sth; **i. de lâcheté** incapable of cowardice
  2 *nmf* (**a**) *(incompétent)* incompetent; **espèce d'i.!** you use-less idiot! (**b**) *Jur* incompetent person

incapacité [ɛ̃kapasite] *nf* (**a**) *(impossibilité)* **i. à faire qch** inability to do sth; **être dans l'i. de faire qch** to be unable to do sth (**b**) *(incompétence)* incompetence (**c**) *(invalidité)* disability; **i. de travail** unfitness for work (**d**) *Jur* incompetence

incarcération [ɛ̃karserasjɔ̃] *nf* incarceration

incarcérer [34] [ɛ̃karsere] *vt* to incarcerate

incarnation [ɛ̃karnasjɔ̃] *nf aussi Fig* incarnation

incarné, -e [ɛ̃karne] *adj* (**a**) *Rel & Fig* incarnate (**b**) *(ongle)* ingrowing

incarner [ɛ̃karne] **1** *vt* (**a**) *(représenter)* to embody (**b**) *Théât & Cin* **i. (le rôle de) qn** to play (the part of) sb
  2 s'incarner *vpr* (**a**) *Rel* to become incarnate (**b**) *(ongle)* to become ingrown

incartade [ɛ̃kartad] *nf* indiscretion

incassable [ɛ̃kasabl] *adj* unbreakable

incendiaire [ɛ̃sɑ̃djɛr] **1** *adj (bombe)* incendiary; *Fig (discours)* inflammatory
  2 *nmf (personne)* arsonist

incendie [ɛ̃sɑ̃di] *nm* fire; **i. de forêt** forest fire; **un i. criminel** arson

incendier [66] [ɛ̃sɑ̃dje] *vt* (**a**) *(mettre le feu à)* to set on fire (**b**) *Fam (accabler de reproches)* **i. qn** to haul sb over the coals; **se faire i.** to get hauled over the coals

incertain, -e [ɛ̃sɛrtɛ̃, -ɛn] *adj (fait, donnée, résultat)* uncertain; *(temps)* unsettled; *(mémoire)* unreliable; *(personne)* indecisive; *(démarche, pas)* unsteady; *(couleur)* vague

incertitude [ɛ̃sɛrtityd] *nf* uncertainty; **être dans l'i. (quant à)** to be uncertain (about)

incessamment [ɛ̃sesamɑ̃] *adv* very soon; **il doit arriver i.** he'll be here any minute now; *Hum* **i. sous peu** very soon

incessant, -e [ɛ̃sesɑ̃, -ɑ̃t] *adj* incessant, constant

incessible [ɛ̃sesibl] *adj (pension, titre de propriété)* non-transferable; *(droit)* inalienable

inceste [ɛ̃sɛst] *nm* incest

incestueux, -euse [ɛ̃sɛstɥø, -øz] *adj* incestuous; **enfant i.** child of an incestuous relationship

inchangé, -e [ɛ̃ʃɑ̃ʒe] *adj* unchanged

incidemment [ɛ̃sidamɑ̃] *adv* in passing

incidence [ɛ̃sidɑ̃s] *nf* (**a**) *(répercussion)* impact (**sur** on) (**b**) *Méd & Phys* incidence

incident, -e [ɛ̃sidɑ̃, -ɑ̃t] **1** *nm* (**a**) *(événement sans conséquence)* hitch; **se dérouler sans i.** to pass off without incident; **i. de parcours** minor setback; **i. technique** technical hitch (**b**) *(événement plus grave)* incident; **i. diplomatique** diplomatic incident
  2 *adj (question, remarque)* incidental

incinérateur [ɛ̃sineratœr] *nm* incinerator

incinération [ɛ̃sinerasjɔ̃] *nf (de déchets)* incineration; *(d'une personne)* cremation

incinérer [34] [ɛ̃sinere] *vt (déchets)* to incinerate; *(personne)* to cremate

inciser [ɛ̃size] *vt (peau)* to make an incision in; *(abcès)* to lance

incisif, -ive [ɛ̃sizif, -iv] **1** *adj (remarque, personne, style)* incisive
  2 *nf* **incisive** incisor

incision [ɛ̃sizjɔ̃] *nf* incision; **pratiquer une i. dans** to make an incision in

incitation [ɛ̃sitasjɔ̃] *nf (à la violence, l'émeute)* incitement; *(encouragement)* incentive; **i. fiscale** tax incentive; **i. à l'achat** incentive to buy; **i. de mineurs à la débauche** corruption of minors

inciter [ɛ̃site] *vt* **i. qn à faire qch** to encourage sb to do sth; **i. qn à la prudence/la clémence** *(sujet: événement)* to incline sb to be cautious/merciful

inclassable [ɛ̃klasabl] *adj* unclassifiable; **un film/peintre i.** a movie/painter that cannot be pigeonholed

inclinable [ɛ̃klinabl] *adj (siège, dossier)* reclining

inclinaison [ɛ̃klinɛzɔ̃] *nf (d'un toit)* slope; *(d'une pente)* incline; *(de la tête, d'un chapeau)* tilt

inclination [ɛ̃klinasjɔ̃] *nf* (**a**) **i. de la tête** *(pour saluer)* nod (**b**) *(tendance)* inclination (**pour** for)

incliné, -e [ɛ̃kline] *adj (mât, toit)* sloping; *(table à dessin, dossier)* tilted

incliner [ɛ̃kline] **1** *vt* (**a**) *(pencher)* to tilt; **i. la tête** *(en avant)* to bow one's head; *(en signe de salut)* to nod; *(sur le côté)* to tilt one's head to one side (**b**) *(pousser)* **i. qn à faire qch** to incline sb to do sth; **i. qn à la prudence/la clémence** to incline sb to be cautious/merciful
  2 *vi* **j'incline à penser qu'elle a tort** I'm inclined to think she's wrong
  3 s'incliner *vpr* (**a**) *(terrain)* to slant, to slope; *(bateau)* to heel or keel over; *(avion)* to bank (**b**) *(se pencher)* *(en avant)* to lean forward; *(sur le côté)* to lean to one side; *(pour saluer)* to bow; *Fig* **s'i. devant qch** (**c**) *(se soumettre)* to give in (**devant** to) (**d**) *(être battu)* to lose (**devant** to)

inclure [17b] [ɛ̃klyr] *vt* (**a**) *(dans un courrier)* to enclose (**dans** with) (**b**) *(englober, insérer)* & *Math* to include

inclus, -e [ɛ̃kly, -yz] *adj* (**a**) *(compris)* **jusqu'à la page cinq incluse** up to and including page five; **jusqu'au mardi i.** through Tuesday, up to and including Tuesday; **du 7 au 18 i.** the 7th through the 18th, from the 7th to the 18th inclusive; **ils seront trente-cinq, professeurs i.** there will be thirty-five of them, including the teachers (**b**) *(dent)* impacted

inclusion [ɛ̃klyzjɔ̃] *nf* (**a**) *(dans un courrier)* enclosure (**dans** with) (**b**) *(insertion)* insertion (**c**) *(objet décoratif)* = flower, shell, etc. set into plastic and used as a paperweight, an ornament, jewelry, etc. (**d**) *(d'une dent)* impacting (**e**) *Ordinat (de fichier)* insertion

incognito [ɛ̃kɔɲito] **1** *adv* incognito
  2 *nm* **garder l'i.** to remain incognito

incohérence [ɛ̃kɔerɑ̃s] *nf (d'une personne, dans un film, une histoire)* inconsistency; *(d'un discours, d'idées)* incoherence

incohérent, -e [ɛ̃kɔerɑ̃, -ɑ̃t] *adj (personne, histoire, attitude)* inconsistent; *(idées, argumentation, discours)* incoherent; **tenir des propos incohérents** to talk incoherently

incollable [ɛ̃kɔlabl] *adj* (**a**) *(riz)* non-stick (**b**) *Fam (personne)* **elle est i. sur la question/en histoire** there's nothing she doesn't know about the subject/about history

incolore [ɛ̃kɔlor] *adj* colorless

incomber [ɛ̃kɔ̃be] **incomber à** *vt ind (responsabilité)* to lie with; *(devoirs)* to fall to; **il m'incombe/il lui incombe de...** it falls to me/to him to...

incombustible [ɛ̃kɔ̃bystibl] *adj* incombustible

incommensurable [ɛ̃kɔmɑ̃syrabl] *adj (richesse)* immeasurable; *(espace)* boundless; *Hum* **être d'une bêtise i.** to be incredibly stupid

incommodant, -e [ɛ̃kɔmɔdɑ̃, -ɑ̃t] *adj* discomforting

incommode [ɛ̃kɔmɔd] *adj (horaire, arrangement)* inconvenient; *(situation)* awkward

incommoder [ɛ̃kɔmɔde] *vt* to bother

incomparable [ɛ̃kɔ̃parabl] *adj (sans pareil)* beyond compare, matchless

incomparablement [ɛ̃kɔ̃parabləmɑ̃] *adv* incomparably

incompatibilité [ɛ̃kɔ̃patibilite] *nf* incompatibility; **i. d'humeur** ou **de caractère** mutual incompatibility

incompatible [ɛ̃kɔ̃patibl] *adj* incompatible (**avec** with)

incompétence [ɛ̃kɔ̃petɑ̃s] *nf* incompetence

incompétent, -e [ɛ̃kɔ̃petɑ̃, -ɑ̃t] *adj* incompetent

incomplet, -ète [ɛ̃kɔ̃plɛ, -ɛt] *adj* incomplete

incompréhensible [ɛ̃kɔ̃preɑ̃sibl] *adj* incomprehensible

incompréhension [ɛ̃kɔ̃preɑ̃sjɔ̃] *nf* incomprehension

incompressible [ɛ̃kɔ̃prɛsibl] *adj* (**a**) *(matériau)* incompressible (**b**) *Jur (peine)* to be served in full (**c**) *(dépenses)* which cannot be reduced

incompris, -e [ɛ̃kɔ̃pri, -iz] **1** *adj* misunderstood
2 *nm,f* **être un i.** to be misunderstood

inconcevable [ɛ̃kɔ̃səvabl] *adj* inconceivable

inconciliable [ɛ̃kɔ̃siljabl] *adj (théorie)* irreconcilable (**avec** with); *(mode de vie, activité)* incompatible (**avec** with)

inconditionnel, -elle [ɛ̃kɔ̃disjɔnɛl] **1** *adj (soutien, retrait)* unconditional; *(obéissance)* unquestioning, unconditional; *(supporter)* staunch
2 *nm,f* fan; **c'est un i. de la pêche/du hard rock** he's totally crazy about fishing/hard rock

inconfort [ɛ̃kɔ̃fɔr] *nm (matériel)* discomfort; *(moral)* awkwardness

inconfortable [ɛ̃kɔ̃fɔrtabl] *adj aussi Fig* uncomfortable

incongru, -e [ɛ̃kɔ̃gry] *adj* inappropriate; *(bruit)* rude

incongruité [ɛ̃kɔ̃grɥite] *nf* (**a**) *(manque d'à-propos)* inappropriateness (**b**) *(remarque déplacée)* inappropriate remark

inconnu, -e [ɛ̃kɔny] **1** *adj (auteur, civilisation, destination)* unknown (**de** to); *(lieu, visage)* strange; **il m'est i.** I've never heard of him/it; **né de père i.** *(sur document administratif)* father unknown; **i. à cette adresse** not known at this address; *Fam* **Durand? i. au bataillon!** Durand? never heard of him!
2 *nm,f (étranger)* stranger; *(personne non célèbre)* unknown
3 *nm* **la peur de l'i.** the fear of the unknown
4 *nf* **inconnue** *Math & Fig* unknown (quantity)

inconsciemment [ɛ̃kɔ̃sjamã] *adv* (**a**) *(sans réfléchir)* without thinking (**b**) *(dans l'inconscient)* subconsciously

inconscience [ɛ̃kɔ̃sjãs] *nf* (**a**) *(perte de connaissance)* unconsciousness; **sombrer** *ou* **tomber dans l'i.** to lose consciousness (**b**) *(manque de jugement)* recklessness; **c'est de l'i.!** it's sheer madness!

inconscient, -e [ɛ̃kɔ̃sjã, -ãt] **1** *adj* (**a**) *(évanoui)* unconscious (**b**) *(acte)* unconscious; **i. du danger** oblivious to the danger (**c**) *(irréfléchi) (personne)* reckless
2 *nm* **l'i.** the unconscious, the subconscious; **l'i. collectif** the collective unconscious

inconséquence [ɛ̃kɔ̃sekãs] *nf (caractère)* recklessness; *(acte)* reckless act

inconséquent, -e [ɛ̃kɔ̃sekã, -ãt] *adj* (**a**) *(irréfléchi)* reckless (**b**) *(illogique)* inconsistent

inconsidéré, -e [ɛ̃kɔ̃sidere] *adj (acte, remarque)* ill-considered; *(dépenses)* reckless

inconsistance [ɛ̃kɔ̃sistãs] *nf* (**a**) *(d'une pâte, d'une soupe)* thinness (**b**) *(d'une personne, d'une conduite)* inconsistency (**c**) *(d'une intrigue, d'un film, d'un roman)* thinness

inconsistant, -e [ɛ̃kɔ̃sistã, -ãt] *adj* (**a**) *(pâte, crème, soupe)* thin (**b**) *(conduite, personne)* inconsistent (**c**) *(intrigue, film, roman)* thin

inconsolable [ɛ̃kɔ̃sɔlabl] *adj* inconsolable

inconstance [ɛ̃kɔ̃stãs] *nf (instabilité)* changeableness; *(infidélité)* fickleness

inconstant, -e [ɛ̃kɔ̃stã, -ãt] *adj (instable)* changeable; *(infidèle)* fickle

inconstitutionnel, -elle [ɛ̃kɔ̃stitysjɔnɛl] *adj* unconstitutional

incontestable [ɛ̃kɔ̃tɛstabl] *adj* indisputable

incontestablement [ɛ̃kɔ̃tɛstabləmã] *adv* indisputably

incontesté, -e [ɛ̃kɔ̃tɛste] *adj* undisputed

incontinence [ɛ̃kɔ̃tinãs] *nf Méd* incontinence; **i. verbale** verbal diarrhea

incontinent, -e [ɛ̃kɔ̃tinã, -ãt] *adj Méd* incontinent

incontournable [ɛ̃kɔ̃turnabl] *adj (film, artiste)* that cannot be ignored; **son argument était i.** there was no getting away from her argument

incontrôlable [ɛ̃kɔ̃trolabl] *adj* (**a**) *(incendie, bâillements)* uncontrollable; **des éléments incontrôlables** rowdy elements (**b**) *(affirmation)* unverifiable

incontrôlé, -e [ɛ̃kɔ̃trole] *adj (éléments, bande)* uncontrolled

inconvenance [ɛ̃kɔ̃vnãs] *nf (indécence)* impropriety; **dire/ commettre une i.** to say/to do something improper

inconvenant, -e [ɛ̃kɔ̃vnã, -ãt] *adj (propos, remarque, acte)* improper

inconvénient [ɛ̃kɔ̃venjã] *nm* drawback, disadvantage; **je n'y vois pas d'i.** I have no objection

inconvertible [ɛ̃kɔ̃vɛrtibl] *adj (monnaie)* non-convertible

incorporation [ɛ̃kɔrpɔrasjɔ̃] *nf* (**a**) *(mélange)* blending, mixing (**de qch dans qch** of sth into sth) (**b**) *Mil* conscription

incorporé, -e [ɛ̃kɔrpɔre] *adj (flash, micro)* built-in

incorporer [ɛ̃kɔrpɔre] **1** *vt* (**a**) *(mélanger)* **i. qch à qch** to blend *or* to mix sth into sth (**b**) *(insérer)* to insert (**à** in) (**c**) *(troupes)* to draft
2 s'incorporer *vpr* **s'i. dans un groupe** to join a group

incorrect, -e [ɛ̃kɔrɛkt] *adj* (**a**) *(erroné)* incorrect, wrong (**b**) *(personne)* impolite; *(attitude)* improper (**c**) *(tenue) (déplacée)* unsuitable; *(indécente)* improper

incorrectement [ɛ̃kɔrɛktəmã] *adv* (**a**) *(en faisant des erreurs)* incorrectly, wrongly (**b**) *(impoliment)* impolitely (**c**) *(habillé) (de façon déplacée)* unsuitably; *(de façon indécente)* improperly

incorrection [ɛ̃kɔrɛksjɔ̃] *nf* (**a**) *(impolitesse)* impoliteness (**b**) *(action)* impolite action; *(propos)* impolite remark (**c**) *(grammaticale)* mistake

incorrigible [ɛ̃kɔriʒibl] *adj* incorrigible

incorruptible [ɛ̃kɔryptibl] **1** *adj* incorruptible
2 *nmf* incorruptible person

incrédule [ɛ̃kredyl] *adj (sceptique)* incredulous; **d'un air i.** with a look of disbelief

incrédulité [ɛ̃kredylite] *nf* incredulity

increvable [ɛ̃krəvabl] *adj* (**a**) *(pneu)* puncture-proof (**b**) *Fam (personne)* tireless; *(voiture, moteur)* indestructible

incriminer [ɛ̃krimine] *vt (personne)* to accuse; *(sujet: événement)* to condemn; *(comportement, décision)* to condemn

incrochetable [ɛ̃krɔʃtabl] *adj (serrure)* unpickable

incroyable [ɛ̃krwajabl] *adj* incredible; **c'est i., ça!** I don't believe it!; **d'une bêtise i.** incredibly stupid

incroyablement [ɛ̃krwajabləmã] *adv* incredibly

incroyance [ɛ̃krwajãs] *nf* unbelief

incroyant, -e [ɛ̃krwajã, -ãt] **1** *adj* unbelieving
2 *nm,f* unbeliever

incrustation [ɛ̃krystasjɔ̃] *nf* (**a**) *(ornement)* inlay (**b**) *(dépôt calcaire)* scale (**c**) *TV (image)* inset

incruste [ɛ̃kryst] *nf Fam* **si on l'invite, il va encore taper l'i.** if we invite him, we'll never get rid of him; **elle a tapé l'i. à ma soirée** she gatecrashed my party

incruster [ɛ̃kryste] **1** *vt* (**a**) *(bois, métal)* to inlay (**de** with) (**b**) *(entartrer)* to scale
2 s'incruster *vpr* (**a**) *(adhérer)* to become encrusted (**b**) *(chaudière, bouilloire)* to scale (**c**) *Fam (s'imposer)* **quand on l'invite, il s'incruste** once you invite him you can't get rid of him

incubateur [ɛ̃kybatœr] *nm* incubator

incubation [ɛ̃kybasjɔ̃] *nf* incubation; **période d'i.** incubation period

incuber [ɛ̃kybe] *vt* to incubate, to hatch

inculpation [ɛ̃kylpasjɔ̃] *nf* indictment; **sous l'i. d'assassinat** charged with murder

inculpé, -e [ɛ̃kylpe] *nm,f* **l'i.** the accused

inculper [ɛ̃kylpe] *vt* to indict, to charge (**de** with)

inculquer [ɛ̃kylke] *vt* to instill (**à qn** in sb)

inculte [ɛ̃kylt] *adj (terre, personne)* uncultivated

incultivable [ɛ̃kyltivabl] *adj* untillable

inculture [ɛ̃kyltyr] *nf* lack of culture

incurable [ɛ̃kyrabl] **1** *adj* incurable; **d'une paresse i.** incurably lazy

2 *nmf* person with an incurable disease

incurie [ɛ̃kyri] *nf Sout* negligence

incursion [ɛ̃kyrsjɔ̃] *nf* (**a**) *(invasion)* raid, incursion (**b**) *Fig (entrée soudaine)* intrusion; **faire une i. dans une pièce/une réunion** to burst into a room/a meeting

incurvé, -e [ɛ̃kyrve] *adj* bent, curved

indatable [ɛ̃databl] *adj* that cannot be dated

Inde [ɛ̃d] *nf* **l'I.** India

indé [ɛ̃de] *adj Fam* (*abbr* **indépendant**) indie; **le rock i.** indie (rock)

indéboulonnable [ɛ̃debulɔnabl] *adj* **il est i.!** they'll never be able to fire him!

indécence [ɛ̃desɑ̃s] *nf* indecency

indécent, -e [ɛ̃desɑ̃, -ɑ̃t] *adj* indecent

indéchiffrable [ɛ̃deʃifrabl] *adj* (**a**) *(illisible)* indecipherable (**b**) *(incompréhensible)* impenetrable

indéchirable [ɛ̃deʃirabl] *adj* tearproof

indécis, -e [ɛ̃desi, -iz] **1** *adj* (**a**) *(personne) (de caractère)* indecisive; *(ponctuellement)* undecided; **je suis encore indécise** I haven't made my mind up yet (**b**) *(peu net) (victoire, bataille)* inconclusive; *(contour)* vague

2 *nm,f* indecisive person; *Pol* **les i.** the floating voters

indécision [ɛ̃desizjɔ̃] *nf* (*de caractère*) indecisiveness; *(ponctuelle)* indecision

indécrottable [ɛ̃dekrɔtabl] *adj Fam (incorrigible)* hopeless; **être d'une bêtise i.** to be hopelessly stupid

indéfendable [ɛ̃defɑ̃dabl] *adj* indefensible

indéfini, -e [ɛ̃defini] *adj* (**a**) *(illimité)* indefinite (**b**) *(imprécis) (tristesse, malaise)* vague, undefined (**c**) *Gram (pronom, article)* indefinite

indéfiniment [ɛ̃definimɑ̃] *adv* indefinitely

indéfinissable [ɛ̃definisabl] *adj* indefinable

indéformable [ɛ̃defɔrmabl] *adj* that keeps its shape

indélébile [ɛ̃delebil] *adj* indelible

indélicat, -e [ɛ̃delika, -at] *adj* (**a**) *(sans tact)* tactless, insensitive (**b**) *(malhonnête)* dishonest

indélicatesse [ɛ̃delikatɛs] *nf* (**a**) *(manque de tact)* tactlessness (**b**) *(malhonnêteté)* dishonesty; *(acte malhonnête)* dishonest act; **commettre une i.** to behave dishonestly

indemne [ɛ̃dɛmn] *adj* (**a**) *(physiquement)* unhurt, unharmed; **elle est sortie i. de la collision** she was unhurt in the collision (**b**) *(moralement)* unscathed; **il est sorti i. du scandale** he emerged unscathed from the scandal

indemnisation [ɛ̃dɛmnizasjɔ̃] *nf* compensation

indemniser [ɛ̃dɛmnize] *vt* to compensate (**de** for)

indemnité [ɛ̃dɛmnite] *nf* (**a**) *(pour perte encourue)* compensation; *(pour délai, non-livraison)* penalty (**b**) *(allocation)* allowance; **i. journalière** daily *or* living allowance; **i. de licenciement** severance pay; **i. parlementaire** = salary paid to member of French parliament; **i. de transport** travel allowance

indémodable [ɛ̃demɔdabl] *adj* perennially fashionable

indémontrable [ɛ̃demɔ̃trabl] *adj* unprovable

indéniable [ɛ̃denjabl] *adj* undeniable

indéniablement [ɛ̃denjabləmɑ̃] *adv* undeniably

indépendamment [ɛ̃depɑ̃damɑ̃] *adv* independently; **i. de** apart from

indépendance [ɛ̃depɑ̃dɑ̃s] *nf* independence; **accéder à l'i.** to gain independence

indépendant, -e [ɛ̃depɑ̃dɑ̃, -ɑ̃t] **1** *adj* (**a**) *(personne, pays, vie)* independent (**de** of); *(travailleur)* self-employed, freelance; *(appartement)* self-contained; **i. de ma volonté** beyond my control (**b**) *Gram* **proposition indépendante** main clause

2 *nm,f (travailleur)* self-employed person, freelancer; **travailler en i.** to work on a freelance basis

indépendantisme [ɛ̃depɑ̃dɑ̃tism] *nm* independence movement

indépendantiste [ɛ̃depɑ̃dɑ̃tist] *nmf Pol (partisan de l'indépendance)* supporter of independence; *(activiste)* freedom fighter

indéracinable [ɛ̃derasinabl] *adj (préjugés)* deep-rooted

indescriptible [ɛ̃dɛskriptibl] *adj* indescribable

indésirable [ɛ̃dezirabl] *adj & nmf* undesirable

indestructible [ɛ̃dɛstryktibl] *adj* indestructible

indétectable [ɛ̃detɛktabl] *adj* undetectable

indéterminé, -e [ɛ̃detɛrmine] *adj* (**a**) *(date, heure)* unspecified; *(raison)* unknown (**b**) *(personne)* undecided

index [ɛ̃dɛks] *nm* (**a**) *(doigt)* forefinger, index finger (**b**) *(de livre)* index; *Fig* **mettre qn/qch à l'i.** to blacklist sb/sth (**c**) *Ordinat* index (**d**) *Méd* **i. glycémique** glycemic index

indexation [ɛ̃dɛksasjɔ̃] *nf Écon* indexation (**sur** to); *Ordinat* indexing

indexer [ɛ̃dɛkse] *vt* (**a**) *Écon* to index (**sur** to) (**b**) *aussi Ordinat (ajouter un index à)* to index

indic [ɛ̃dik] *nm Fam* stool piegon

indicateur, -trice [ɛ̃dikatœr, -tris] **1** *adj voir* **panneau, poteau**

2 *nm* (**a**) *(livre)* **i. des rues de Paris** Paris street finder; **i. des chemins de fer** train timetable (**b**) *(instrument)* indicator, gauge; *Aviat* **i. d'altitude** altimeter; **i. de niveau de carburant** fuel gauge (**c**) *(informateur)* informer (**d**) *Écon* indicator

indicatif, -ive [ɛ̃dikatif, -iv] **1** *adj* indicative (**de** of); **à titre i.** as a guide

2 *nm* (**a**) *Gram* indicative (mood); **à l'i.** in the indicative (**b**) *Tél* area code (**c**) *TV & Rad* theme song *or* tune

indication [ɛ̃dikasjɔ̃] *nf* (**a**) *(action)* indication (**b**) *(renseignement)* (piece of) information (**c**) *(directive)* instruction, direction; **sauf i. contraire** unless otherwise specified; *Théât* **indications scéniques** stage directions (**d**) *(sur notice pharmaceutique)* **indications:...** suitable for...

indice [ɛ̃dis] *nm* (**a**) *(signe)* sign, indication (**de** of); *(dans une enquête)* clue (**de** to) (**b**) *(chiffre indicateur) & Math* index; *Typ* subscript; *Méd* **i. de masse corporelle** body mass index; *Aut* **i. d'octane** octane rating; **i. des prix** price index; **i. de protection** *(d'une crème solaire)* protection factor

indicible [ɛ̃disibl] *adj Litt* indescribable

indien, -enne [ɛ̃djɛ̃, -ɛn] **1** *adj* Indian

2 *nm,f* **I., Indienne** *(d'Inde)* Indian; **I. (d'Amérique)** American Indian, Native American

indifféremment [ɛ̃diferamɑ̃] *adv (sans distinction)* equally

indifférence [ɛ̃diferɑ̃s] *nf* indifference

indifférencié, -e [ɛ̃diferɑ̃sje] *adj* undifferentiated

indifférent, -e [ɛ̃diferɑ̃, -ɑ̃t] *adj* (**a**) *(peu ou pas intéressé)* indifferent (**à** to); **laisser qn i.** to leave sb cold; **il m'est i.** I'm indifferent to him (**b**) *(sans importance)* irrelevant; **cela m'est i.** it makes no difference to me; **parler de choses indifférentes** to chat about nothing in particular

indifférer [34] [ɛ̃difere] *vt* **cela m'indiffère** it's all the same to me

indigence [ɛ̃diʒɑ̃s] *nf (matérielle)* destitution; *(intellectuelle)* poverty

indigène [ɛ̃diʒɛn] **1** *adj* native; *Bot & Zool* native, indigenous (**de** to)

2 *nmf* (**a**) *(autochtone) & Bot & Zool* native (**b**) *Suisse (citoyen)* citizen

indigent, -e [ɛ̃diʒɑ̃, -ɑ̃t] **1** *adj (person)* destitute; *(idée, imagination)* poor

2 *nm,f* pauper; **les indigents** the poor

indigeste [ɛ̃diʒɛst] *adj aussi Fig* indigestible

indigestion [ɛ̃diʒɛstjɔ̃] *nf* **avoir une i.** to have a stomach upset; **faire une i. de chocolat** to make oneself sick from eating chocolate; *Fig* **j'en ai une i.** I'm fed up with it

indignation [ɛ̃diɲasjɔ̃] *nf* indignation

indigne [ɛ̃diɲ] *adj (personne)* unworthy (**de** of); *(action, conduite)* shameful

indigner [ɛ̃diɲe] **1** *vt* to outrage

2 s'indigner *vpr* to be indignant (**de** at)

indignité [ɛ̃diɲite] *nf* (**a**) *(d'une personne)* unworthiness; *(d'une action)* shamefulness (**b**) *(action)* shameful act

indigo [ɛ̃digo] *nm & adj inv* indigo

indiqué, -e [ɛ̃dike] *adj (recommandé)* advisable; **il est tout à fait i. pour ce poste** he's the right person for the job

indiquer [ɛ̃dike] *vt* (**a**) *(montrer) (sujet: personne)* to point out; **i. qch du doigt** to point to *or* at sth; **i. le chemin à qn** to show sb the way, to direct sb (**b**) *(marquer) (sujet: panneau, étiquette, carte)* to show, to indicate; *(sujet: compteur)* to show, to read (**c**) *(donner) (date, adresse)* to give; **à l'heure indiquée** at the appointed time; **pourriez-vous m'i. le prix de ce vase?** could you tell me how much this vase costs? (**d**) *(recommander)* to recommend; **elle m'a indiqué un excellent dentiste/hôtel** she recommended an excellent dentist/hotel to me (**e**) *(dénoter)* to point to, to indicate

indirect, -e [ɛ̃dirɛkt] *adj aussi Gram* indirect

indirectement [ɛ̃dirɛktəmɑ̃] *adv* indirectly

indiscipline [ɛ̃disiplin] *nf* indiscipline

indiscipliné, -e [ɛ̃disipline] *adj* undisciplined; *(cheveux)* unmanageable

indiscret, -ète [ɛ̃diskrɛ, -ɛt] **1** *adj* (**a**) *(qui parle trop)* indiscreet (**b**) *(curieux)* inquisitive; **à l'abri des regards indiscrets** safe from prying eyes

2 *nm,f* (**a**) *(qui parle trop)* indiscreet person (**b**) *(curieux)* inquisitive person

indiscrétion [ɛ̃diskresjɔ̃] *nf* (**a**) *(manque de discrétion)* indiscretion (**b**) *(curiosité)* inquisitiveness; **sans i., combien l'avez-vous payé?** if you don't mind me asking, how much did you pay for it? (**c**) *(remarque)* indiscreet remark; **commettre une i.** to say something one shouldn't

indiscutable [ɛ̃diskytabl] *adj* indisputable

indiscutablement [ɛ̃diskytabləmɑ̃] *adv* indisputably

indispensable [ɛ̃dispɑ̃sabl] **1** *adj* indispensable, essential (**à qch** for sth); **i. à qn** indispensable to sb; **il est i. que tu y ailles** it is essential that you go

2 *nm* **l'i.** the essentials

indisponibilité [ɛ̃dispɔnibilite] *nf* unavailability

indisponible [ɛ̃dispɔnibl] *adj* unavailable

indisposé, -e [ɛ̃dispoze] *adj* indisposed, unwell; *Euph* **elle est indisposée** it's her time of the month

indisposer [ɛ̃dispoze] *vt* (**a**) *(rendre malade)* **i. qn** *(odeur, climat)* to make sb feel ill; *(nourriture)* to disagree with sb (**b**) *(contrarier)* to annoy

indisposition [ɛ̃dispozisjɔ̃] *nf* indisposition, slight illness

indissociable [ɛ̃disɔsjabl] *adj* indissociable (**de** from)

indissoluble [ɛ̃disɔlybl] *adj* indissoluble

indistinct, -e [ɛ̃distɛ̃, -ɛ̃kt] *adj* indistinct

indistinctement [ɛ̃distɛ̃ktəmɑ̃] *adv* (**a**) *(voir, parler)* indistinctly (**b**) *(indifféremment)* equally

individu [ɛ̃dividy] *nm* (**a**) *(être humain)* individual (**b**) *Péj (homme)* individual, character; **un drôle d'i.** a strange individual *or* character

individualiser [ɛ̃dividɥalize] *vt* (**a**) *(différencier)* to make individual (**b**) *(adapter)* to adapt to individual circumstances

individualisme [ɛ̃dividɥalism] *nm* individualism

individualiste [ɛ̃dividɥalist] **1** *adj* individualistic

2 *nmf* individualist

individualité [ɛ̃dividɥalite] *nf* individuality

individuel, -elle [ɛ̃dividɥɛl] *adj* individual; *(liberté, responsabilité)* personal; *(maison)* single-family; *(chambre)* single

individuellement [ɛ̃dividɥɛlmɑ̃] *adv* individually

indivisible [ɛ̃divizibl] *adj* indivisible

Indochine [ɛ̃dɔʃin] *nf* **l'I.** Indochina

indocile [ɛ̃dɔsil] *adj* disobedient

indo-européen, -enne *(mpl* **indo-européens**, *fpl* **indo-européennes)** [ɛ̃dɔørɔpeɛ̃, -ɛn] **1** *adj* Indo-European

2 *nm (langue)* Indo-European

3 *nm,f* **I., Indo-Européenne** Indo-European

indolence [ɛ̃dɔlɑ̃s] *nf* laziness

indolent, -e [ɛ̃dɔlɑ̃, -ɑ̃t] *adj* lazy

indolore [ɛ̃dɔlɔr] *adj* painless

indomptable [ɛ̃dɔ̃tabl] *adj* (**a**) *(animal)* untamable (**b**) *Fig (orgueil, caractère)* indomitable; *(passion)* uncontrollable

indompté, -e [ɛ̃dɔ̃te] *adj* (**a**) *(animal)* untamed (**b**) *Fig (passion, orgueil)* uncontrolled

Indonésie [ɛ̃dɔnezi] *nf* **l'I.** Indonesia

indonésien, -enne [ɛ̃dɔnezjɛ̃, -ɛn] **1** *adj* Indonesian

2 *nm,f* **I., Indonésienne** Indonesian

indu, -e [ɛ̃dy] *adj* **à une heure indue** at an ungodly hour; **il rentre à des heures indues** he comes home at all hours of the night

indubitable [ɛ̃dybitabl] *adj* indisputable, indubitable; **c'est i.** there's no doubt about it

indubitablement [ɛ̃dybitabləmɑ̃] *adv* undoubtedly

induire [18] [ɛ̃dɥir] *vt* (**a**) *(entraîner)* **i. qn à faire qch** to induce sb to do sth; **i. qn en erreur** to mislead sb (**b**) *(conclure)* to infer (**de** from)

indulgence [ɛ̃dylʒɑ̃s] *nf* (**a**) *(bienveillance)* indulgence, leniency; **faire preuve d'i. envers qn** to be indulgent toward sb; **rires sans i.** merciless laughter; **faire de qn un portrait sans i.** to describe sb warts and all (**b**) *Rel* indulgence

indulgent, -e [ɛ̃dylʒɑ̃, -ɑ̃t] *adj* indulgent

indûment [ɛ̃dymɑ̃] *adv* unduly

industrialisation [ɛ̃dystrijalizasjɔ̃] *nf* industrialization

industrialiser [ɛ̃dystrijalize] **1** *vt* to industrialize

2 s'industrialiser *vpr* to become industrialized

industrie [ɛ̃dystri] *nf* industry; **travailler dans l'i.** to work in industry; **l'i. alimentaire** the food industry; **l'i. automobile** the car industry; **l'i. lourde** heavy industry; **l'i. pharmaceutique** the pharmaceutical industry

industriel, -elle [ɛ̃dystrijɛl] **1** *adj* industrial; *Fam* **des magazines en quantité industrielle** vast quantities of magazines

2 *nm* manufacturer, industrialist

industriellement [ɛ̃dystrijɛlmɑ̃] *adv* industrially

industrieux, -euse [ɛ̃dystrijø, -øz] *adj Litt (habile)* skillful, ingenious; *(travailleur)* industrious

inébranlable [inebrɑ̃labl] *adj (mur, rocher)* immovable; *Fig* unshakeable

inédit, -e [inedi, -it] **1** *adj* (**a**) *(livre)* previously unpublished; *(disque)* previously unreleased (**b**) *(spectacle, projet, idée)* new, original

2 *nm (texte)* previously unpublished work; *(disque)* previously unreleased record

ineffable [inefabl] *adj* ineffable, unutterable

ineffaçable [inefasabl] *adj aussi Fig* indelible

inefficace [inefikas] *adj (personne)* inefficient; *(remède, méthode, loi)* ineffective

inefficacité [inefikasite] *nf (de personne)* inefficiency; *(d'un remède, d'une méthode, d'une loi)* ineffectiveness

inégal, -e, -aux, -ales [inegal, -o] *adj* (**a**) *(non égal) (parts, partage, force, lutte)* unequal (**b**) *(irrégulier) (sol)* uneven; *(pouls)* irregular; *Fig (travail, écrivain, style, qualité)* inconsistent; *(humeur)* changeable

inégalable [inegalabl] *adj* incomparable, matchless

inégalé, -e [inegale] *adj (qualité, personne)* unequaled; *(record)* unbeaten

inégalement [inegalmã] *adv* (**a**) *(injustement)* unequally (**b**) *(irrégulièrement)* unevenly

inégalitaire [inegalitɛr] *adj* unequal

inégalité [inegalite] *nf* (**a**) *(injustice)* inequality (**entre** between) (**b**) *(différence)* disparity (**de** in) (**c**) *(du sol)* unevenness; *Fig* **i. d'humeur** moodiness

inélégant, -e [inelegã, -ãt] *adj Litt (mal habillé)* inelegant; *(discourtois)* discourteous

inéligible [ineliʒibl] *adj* ineligible

inéluctable [inelyktabl] *adj* inescapable

inemployable [inãplwajabl] *adj* unusable

inemployé, -e [inãplwaje] *adj (objet, machine, talent)* unused; *(ressources)* untapped; *(forces)* unchannelled

inénarrable [inenarabl] *adj* comical

inepte [inɛpt] *adj (remarque, réponse, histoire)* inane; *(personne)* inept

ineptie [inɛpsi] *nf* (**a**) *(d'un comportement, d'un film)* inanity (**b**) *(action)* stupid thing; *(remarque)* stupid comment; **dire des inepties** to talk nonsense

inépuisable [inepɥizabl] *adj (réserves, sujet, curiosité)* inexhaustible; *(imagination)* limitless; **sur ce sujet-là, elle est i.** you can never get her off the subject

inerte [inɛrt] *adj* (**a**) *(masse, corps, matière)* inert (**b**) *(personne)* *(inanimé)* lifeless; *(passif)* apathetic

inertie [inɛrsi] *nf* (**a**) *Phys* inertia (**b**) *(manque de réaction)* apathy

inespéré, -e [inɛspere] *adj* unexpected, unhoped-for

inesthétique [inɛstetik] *adj* unesthetic

inestimable [inɛstimabl] *adj (dégâts, coût, richesse)* incalculable; *(aide, chance)* invaluable; *(œuvre d'art)* priceless; **d'une valeur i.** priceless

inévitable [inevitabl] *adj* inevitable, unavoidable

inévitablement [inevitabləmã] *adv* inevitably, unavoidably

inexact, -e [inɛgzakt] *adj* (**a**) *(incorrect)* *(réponse, description, détail)* inaccurate; *(somme, calcul)* wrong, incorrect (**b**) *(manquant de ponctualité)* unpunctual

inexactitude [inɛgzaktityd] *nf* (**a**) *(caractère erroné, erreur)* inaccuracy (**b**) *(manque de ponctualité)* unpunctuality

inexcusable [inɛkskyzabl] *adj* inexcusable, unforgivable

inexhaustible [inɛgzostibl] *adj Litt* inexhaustible

inexistant, -e [inɛgzistã, -ãt] *adj* non-existent; *Hum* **il est totalement i.** he's a total nonentity

inexistence [inɛgzistãs] *nf* non-existence

inexorable [inɛgzɔrabl] *adj (destin)* inexorable; *(juge)* pitiless; *(volonté)* inflexible

inexorablement [inɛgzɔrabləmã] *adv* inexorably

inexpérience [inɛksperjãs] *nf* inexperience

inexpérimenté, -e [inɛksperimãte] *adj* inexperienced

inexplicable [inɛksplikabl] *adj* inexplicable

inexpliqué, -e [inɛksplike] *adj* unexplained

inexploité, -e [inɛksplwate] *adj (mine)* unworked; *(terre)* undeveloped; *(ressources)* untapped

inexploré, -e [inɛksplɔre] *adj* unexplored

inexpressif, -ive [inɛkspresif, -iv] *adj* inexpressive, expressionless

inexprimable [inɛksprimabl] *adj* inexpressible

inexprimé, -e [inɛksprime] *adj* unexpressed

in extenso [inɛkstɛ̃so] *adv* in full

in extremis [inɛkstremis] *adv* at the last minute

inextricable [inɛkstrikabl] *adj* inextricable

inextricablement [inɛkstrikabləmã] *adv* inextricably

infaillibilité [ɛ̃fajibilite] *nf* infallibility

infaillible [ɛ̃fajibl] *adj* infallible

infailliblement [ɛ̃fajibləmã] *adv* infallibly

infaisable [ɛ̃fəzabl] *adj* not feasible, impossible

infamant, -e [ɛ̃famã, -ãt] *adj* (**a**) *(déclaration, accusation)* defamatory, slanderous (**b**) *Jur (peine)* involving loss of civil rights

infâme [ɛ̃fam] *adj (mensonge, personne)* despicable; *(acte, crime)* unspeakable; *(taudis)* squalid; *(odeur, nourriture)* revolting

infamie [ɛ̃fami] *nf* (**a**) *(caractère infâme)* infamy (**b**) *(action)* unspeakable act; *(remarque)* slanderous remark

infant, -e [ɛ̃fã, -ãt] *nm,f* infante, *f* infanta

infanterie [ɛ̃fãtri] *nf* infantry; **i. de marine** marine corps, marines

infanticide [ɛ̃fãtisid] **1** *adj* infanticidal
  2 *nmf (personne)* child-killer, infanticide
  3 *nm (crime)* infanticide

infantile [ɛ̃fãtil] *adj* (**a**) *(maladie)* childhood (**b**) *Péj (comportement, personne)* childish, infantile

infantiliser [ɛfãtilize] *vt Péj* **la télévision infantilise les gens** television reduces people to the level of children

infarctus [ɛ̃farktys] *nm* heart attack; **i. du myocarde** myocardial infarction, coronary thrombosis

infatigable [ɛ̃fatigabl] *adj* tireless

infatué, -e [ɛ̃fatɥe] *adj Litt* conceited; **i. de soi-même** full of oneself

infécond, -e [ɛ̃fekɔ̃, -ɔ̃d] *adj* infertile

infect, -e [ɛ̃fɛkt] *adj* foul

infecter [ɛ̃fɛkte] **1** *vt* (**a**) *(plaie, blessure)* to infect (**b**) *(atmosphère, eau, sol)* to contaminate
  2 s'infecter *vpr* to become infected

infectieux, -euse [ɛ̃fɛksjø, -øz] *adj* infectious

infection [ɛ̃fɛksjɔ̃] *nf* (**a**) *Méd & Ordinat* infection (**b**) *(puanteur)* stench, stink; **quelle i. dans cette pièce!** this room stinks!

inférieur, -e [ɛ̃ferjœr] **1** *adj* (**a**) *(qui est en bas)* *(étagère, niveau)* bottom; *(étages, lèvre, paupière, membres, mâchoire)* lower; **partie inférieure** bottom (part); **allez voir à l'étage i.** go and look on the floor below (**b**) *(dans une hiérarchie)* *(qualité, marchandises, intelligence)* inferior; **d'un rang i.** of a lower rank; **être rétrogradé à l'échelon i.** to be demoted to the grade below (**c**) *(dans une comparaison)* **i. à** *(qualité)* inferior to; *(quantité)* less than; **i. ou égal à** less than or equal to; **note inférieure à douze** grade below twelve (out of twenty); **i. en nombre** fewer in number; **i. à la moyenne** below average
  2 *nm,f* inferior

infériorité [ɛ̃ferjɔrite] *nf* inferiority

infernal, -e, -aux, -ales [ɛ̃fɛrnal, -o] *adj* (**a**) *(de l'enfer)* infernal; *Fig (cruauté, méchanceté)* diabolical (**b**) *Fam (insupportable) (chaleur, bruit)* infernal; **à une vitesse infernale** at breakneck speed; **des cadences infernales** an impossible rate of work; **cet enfant est i.** this child's a little devil

infertile [ɛ̃fɛrtil] *adj* infertile

infertilité [ɛ̃fɛrtilite] *nf* infertility

infester [ɛ̃fɛste] *vt (sujet: vermine)* to infest; *Fig (sujet: personnes)* to overrun; **infesté de** infested/overrun with

infidèle [ɛ̃fidɛl] **1** *adj* (**a**) *(déloyal)* unfaithful (**à** to) (**b**) *(inexact) (traduction, rapport)* inaccurate (**c**) *Rel* infidel
  2 *nmf Rel* infidel

infidélité [ɛ̃fidelite] *nf* (**a**) *(déloyauté)* unfaithfulness (**à** to); **faire des infidélités à** to be unfaithful to (**b**) *(manque d'exactitude) (dans une traduction, un compte rendu)* inaccuracy

infiltration [ɛ̃filtrasjɔ̃] *nf* (**a**) *(d'un liquide)* infiltration; **il y a des infiltrations dans le plafond** there are some leaks in the ceiling (**b**) *(d'espions)* infiltration (**c**) *(piqûre)* **faire des infiltrations à qn** to give sb injections

infiltrer [ɛ̃filtre] **1** *vt (noyauter) (parti, pays)* to infiltrate
  2 s'infiltrer *vpr* (**a**) *(fluide)* to infiltrate; **s'i. dans** to seep into (**b**) *(espion)* **s'i. dans** to infiltrate

infime [ɛ̃fim] *adj* tiny

infini, -e [ɛ̃fini] **1** *adj* infinite; **ça prend un temps i.** it takes forever *or* an eternity

2 *nm* **l'i.** infinity; **à l'i.** *(s'étendre, se refléter)* to infinity; *(discutailler)* ad infinitum

infiniment [ɛ̃finimɑ̃] *adv (énormément)* infinitely; **i. petit** infinitesimal; **i. reconnaissant** extremely grateful; **je regrette i.** I'm extremely sorry

infinité [ɛ̃finite] *nf* infinity; **une i. de** an infinite number of

infinitésimal, -e, -aux, -ales [ɛ̃finitezimal, -o] *adj* infinitesimal

infinitif, -ive [ɛ̃finitif, -iv] **1** *adj* infinitive
2 *nm* infinitive; **à l'i.** in the infinitive

infirmation [ɛ̃firmasjɔ̃] *nf Jur* invalidation

infirme [ɛ̃firm] **1** *adj* disabled
2 *nmf* disabled person; **les infirmes** the disabled

infirmer [ɛ̃firme] *vt* to invalidate

infirmerie [ɛ̃firməri] *nf (d'une prison, d'une caserne)* infirmary; *(à l'école, dans un bateau)* sick bay

infirmier [ɛ̃firmje] *nm* (male) nurse

infirmière [ɛ̃firmjɛr] *nf* nurse; **i. de jour/nuit** day/night nurse

infirmité [ɛ̃firmite] *nf* disability

inflammable [ɛ̃flamabl] *adj* inflammable, flammable

inflammation [ɛ̃flamasjɔ̃] *nf Méd* inflammation; **j'ai une i. au genou** my knee is inflamed

inflation [ɛ̃flasjɔ̃] *nf* inflation

inflationniste [ɛ̃flasjɔnist] *adj* inflationary

infléchir [ɛ̃fleʃir] **1** *vt* **(a)** *(rayon)* to bend **(b)** *(politique)* to change the direction of; **i. le cours des événements** to change the course of events
2 s'infléchir *vpr* **(a)** *(dévier) (route, ligne)* to bend **(b)** *(changer) (politique)* to change direction

inflexibilité [ɛ̃flɛksibilite] *nf* inflexibility

inflexible [ɛ̃flɛksibl] *adj* inflexible

inflexion [ɛ̃flɛksjɔ̃] *nf* **(a)** *(mouvement)* **i. du corps** bend of the body; *(pour saluer)* bow; **i. de (la) tête** tilt of the head; *(pour saluer, acquiescer)* nod **(b)** *(de la voix)* inflection **(c)** *(de courbe, rayon)* inflection

infliger [45] [ɛ̃fliʒe] *vt* **i. qch à qn** *(correction, punition)* to inflict sth on sb; *(peine, amende)* to impose sth on sb

influençable [ɛ̃flyɑ̃sabl] *adj* easily influenced

influence [ɛ̃flyɑ̃s] *nf* influence **(sur** on); **trafic d'i.** corruption (involving a public official)

influencer [16] [ɛ̃flyɑ̃se] *vt* to influence; **il ne faut pas te laisser i.** you mustn't let yourself be influenced; **il se laisse facilement i.** he's easily influenced

influent, -e [ɛ̃flyɑ̃, -ɑ̃t] *adj* influential

influer [ɛ̃flye] *vi* **i. sur** to influence

influx [ɛ̃fly] *nm* **i. nerveux** nerve impulse

info [ɛ̃fo] *nf Fam (nouvelle)* news item; **les infos** the news *(singulier)*

Infographie® [ɛ̃fɔgrafi] *nf* computer graphics

informateur, -trice [ɛ̃fɔrmatœr, -tris] *nm,f* informant; *(de police)* informer

informaticien, -enne [ɛ̃fɔrmatisjɛ̃, -ɛn] **1** *nm,f* computer scientist
2 *adj* **ingénieur i.** computer engineer

information [ɛ̃fɔrmasjɔ̃] *nf* **(a)** *(renseignement)* (piece of) information; **informations** information; **pour votre i.** for your information; **à titre d'i.** for information; **assurer l'i. du public en matière de santé** to insure that the public is kept informed about health matters; **le droit à l'i.** freedom of information **(b)** *(nouvelle)* news item; **une i. de dernière minute** some late news; **les informations** the news *(singulier)* **(c)** *(médias)* **l'i.** the media **(d)** *Ordinat* data, information; **traitement de l'i.** data processing; **théorie de l'i.** information theory **(e)** *Jur (enquête)* inquiry; *(instruction préparatoire)* preliminary investigation; **ouvrir une i.** to begin legal proceedings

informatique [ɛ̃fɔrmatik] *nf (traitement de l'information)* data processing; *(science)* computer science, computing; **travailler dans l'i.** to work in computers; **société/magazine/cours d'i.** computer company/magazine/course

informatisation [ɛ̃fɔrmatizasjɔ̃] *nf* computerization

informatiser [ɛ̃fɔrmatize] **1** *vt* to computerize
2 s'informatiser *vpr* to become computerized; **depuis que je me suis informatisé** since I got a computer

informe [ɛ̃fɔrm] *adj (masse, objet, vêtement)* shapeless; *(monstre, être)* misshapen

informé, -e [ɛ̃fɔrme] **1** *adj* informed; **bien i.** well-informed; **mal i.** ill-informed; **dans les milieux informés** in informed circles
2 *nm Jur* inquiry; **jusqu'à plus ample i.** until we have further information

informel, -elle [ɛ̃fɔrmɛl] *adj* informal

informer [ɛ̃fɔrme] **1** *vt* to inform **(de** of); **i. qn que...** to inform sb that...; **nous informons les voyageurs que...** we would like to inform passengers that...
2 s'informer *vpr (se renseigner)* to inquire, to ask **(de/au sujet de** about); *(se tenir au courant)* to keep oneself informed

inforoute [ɛ̃fɔrut] *nf Can Ordinat* information superhighway, infohighway

infortune [ɛ̃fɔrtyn] *nf* misfortune; **compagnons d'i.** companions in adversity

infortuné, -e [ɛ̃fɔrtyne] **1** *adj* unfortunate
2 *nm,f* unfortunate wretch

infoutu, -e [ɛ̃futy] *adj Fam* **être i. de faire qch** to be downright incapable of doing sth

infraction [ɛ̃fraksjɔ̃] *nf (à un règlement, à la loi)* infringement **(à** of); *(délit)* offense; **être en i.** to be committing an offense

infranchissable [ɛ̃frɑ̃ʃisabl] *adj (rivière, col, gouffre)* impassable; *(obstacle, difficulté)* insurmountable

infrarouge [ɛ̃fraruʒ] *adj & nm* infrared

infrastructure [ɛ̃frastryktyr] *nf* **(a)** *Constr* substructure **(b)** *(d'équipements)* infrastructure; **i. routière/touristique** road/tourist infrastructure

infructueux, -euse [ɛ̃fryktɥø, -øz] *adj* fruitless

infumable [ɛ̃fymabl] *adj* unsmokable

infuse [ɛ̃fyz] *adj f voir* science

infuser [ɛ̃fyze] **1** *vi (thé)* to brew; *(tisane)* to infuse; **faire i. qch** to brew sth
2 *vt* **(a)** *(faire pénétrer)* to instill **(dans** into) **(b)** *(herbes)* to infuse; *(thé)* to brew

infusion [ɛ̃fyzjɔ̃] *nf* **(a)** *(boisson)* herb tea; **une i. de camomille** some camomile tea **(b)** *(processus)* infusion; *(de thé)* brewing

ingénier [66] [ɛ̃ʒenje] **s'ingénier** *vpr* **s'i. à faire qch** to strive to do sth; **il s'ingénie à me contredire** he goes out of his way to contradict me

ingénierie [ɛ̃ʒeniri] *nf* engineering

ingénieur [ɛ̃ʒenjœr] *nm* engineer; **i. agronome** agricultural engineer; **i. électronicien** electronics engineer; **i. des mines** mining engineer; **i. des ponts et chaussées** civil engineer; **i. du son** sound engineer; **i. des travaux publics** civil engineer

ingénieur-conseil (*pl* **ingénieurs-conseils**) [ɛ̃ʒenjœrkɔ̃sɛj] *nm* consultant engineer

ingénieusement [ɛ̃ʒenjøzmɑ̃] *adv* ingeniously

ingénieux, -euse [ɛ̃ʒenjø, -øz] *adj* ingenious

ingéniosité [ɛ̃ʒenjozite] *nf* ingenuity

ingénu, -e [ɛ̃ʒeny] **1** *adj* ingenuous
2 *nm,f* ingenuous person

ingénuité [ɛ̃ʒenɥite] *nf* ingenuousness

ingérence [ɛ̃ʒerɑ̃s] *nf* interference **(dans** in)

ingérer [34] [ɛ̃ʒere] *vt* to ingest

ingestion [ɛ̃ʒɛstjɔ̃] *nf* ingestion

ingrat, -e [ɛ̃gra, -at] **1** *adj (personne)* ungrateful (**envers** to); *(sol, terre)* barren; *(tâche)* thankless; *(travail, sujet)* unrewarding; *(physique, visage)* unattractive

2 *nm,f* ungrateful person

ingratitude [ɛ̃gratityd] *nf* ingratitude

ingrédient [ɛ̃gredjã] *nm* ingredient

inguérissable [ɛ̃gerisabl] *adj* incurable

ingurgiter [ɛ̃gyrʒite] *vt (aliment, boisson)* to gulp down; *Fam Fig (connaissances)* to cram into one's head

inhabitable [inabitabl] *adj* uninhabitable

inhabité, -e [inabite] *adj* uninhabited

inhabituel, -elle [inabityɛl] *adj* unusual

inhalation [inalasjɔ̃] *nf* (**a**) *(respiration)* breathing in, inhalation (**b**) *Méd* (steam) inhalation; **le mieux pour les rhumes, c'est de faire des inhalations** inhaling steam is the best thing for a cold

inhaler [inale] *vt* to inhale

inhérent, -e [inerã, -ãt] *adj* inherent (**à** in)

inhiber [inibe] *vt* to inhibit

inhibition [inibisjɔ̃] *nf* inhibition

inhospitalier, -ère [inɔspitalje, -ɛr] *adj* inhospitable

inhumain, -e [inymɛ̃, -ɛn] *adj* inhuman

inhumanité [inymanite] *nf* inhumanity

inhumation [inymasjɔ̃] *nf* burial

inhumer [inyme] *vt* to bury

inimaginable [inimaʒinabl] *adj* unimaginable

inimitable [inimitabl] *adj* inimitable

inimitié [inimitje] *nf* enmity

ininflammable [inɛ̃flamabl] *adj* non-flammable

inintelligent, -e [inɛ̃teliʒã, -ãt] *adj* unintelligent

inintelligible [inɛ̃teliʒibl] *adj* unintelligible

inintéressant, -e [inɛ̃teresã, -ãt] *adj* uninteresting

ininterrompu, -e [inɛ̃terɔ̃py] *adj* continuous

inique [inik] *adj* iniquitous

iniquité [inikite] *nf* iniquity

initial, -e, -aux, -ales [inisjal, -o] **1** *adj* initial

2 *nf* **initiale** initial

initialement [inisjalmã] *adv* initially

initialisation [inisjalizasjɔ̃] *nf Ordinat* initialization

initialiser [inisjalize] *vt Ordinat (disque)* to initialize; *(ordinateur)* to boot (up)

initiateur, -trice [inisjatœr, -tris] **1** *nm,f (d'un projet, d'une réforme)* initiator

2 *adj* initiatory

initiation [inisjasjɔ̃] *nf* (**a**) *(formation)* introduction (**à** to) (**b**) *(rituels)* initiation (**à** into)

initiatique [inisjatik] *adj* initiatory

initiative [inisjativ] *nf* initiative; **à l'i. de qn** on sb's initiative; **prendre l'i. de faire qch** to take the initiative in doing sth; **faire qch de sa propre i.** to do sth on one's own initiative; **il n'a aucune i.** he has no initiative

initié, -e [inisje] *nm,f* initiate

initier [66] [inisje] **1** *vt* (**a**) *(former)* to introduce (**à** to) (**b**) *(rituellement)* to initiate (**à** to)

2 s'initier *vpr* **s'i. à qch** to start learning sth

injectable [ɛ̃ʒɛktabl] *adj* injectable

injecté, -e [ɛ̃ʒɛkte] *adj* **yeux injectés de sang** bloodshot eyes

injecter [ɛ̃ʒɛkte] *vt (substance, capitaux)* to inject (**dans** into)

injection [ɛ̃ʒɛksjɔ̃] *nf (de substance, de capital)* injection; **moteur à i.** fuel-injection engine

injonction [ɛ̃ʒɔ̃ksjɔ̃] *nf* injunction; **i. de payer** order to pay; **recevoir l'i. de faire qch** to get the order to do sth

injure [ɛ̃ʒyr] *nf* insult; **injures** abuse, insults; **faire i. à qn** to insult sb

injurier [66] [ɛ̃ʒyrje] *vt* to insult, to abuse

injurieux, -euse [ɛ̃ʒyrjø, -øz] *adj* insulting, abusive

injuste [ɛ̃ʒyst] *adj* unfair (**envers** *ou* **avec** to *or* towards)

injustement [ɛ̃ʒystəmã] *adv* unjustly, unfairly

injustice [ɛ̃ʒystis] *nf* (**a**) *(iniquité)* injustice, unfairness (**envers** towards); **i. sociale** social injustice (**b**) *(acte, parole)* injustice

injustifiable [ɛ̃ʒystifjabl] *adj* unjustifiable

injustifié, -e [ɛ̃ʒystifje] *adj* unjustified

inlassable [ɛ̃lɑsabl] *adj* untiring

inlassablement [ɛ̃lɑsabləmã] *adv* untiringly; *(répéter)* ceaselessly

inné, -e [ine] *adj* innate, inborn

innocemment [inɔsamã] *adv* innocently

innocence [inɔsãs] *nf* innocence; **en toute i.** in all innocence

innocent, -e [inɔsã, -ãt] **1** *adj* innocent (**de** of)

2 *nm,f (non coupable)* innocent person; *(idiot)* simpleton; **ne fais pas l'i.!** don't act the innocent!; *Prov* **aux innocents les mains pleines** the meek shall inherit the earth

innocenter [inɔsãte] *vt* to clear (**de** of)

innocuité [inɔkɥite] *nf* harmlessness

innombrable [inɔ̃brabl] *adj* innumerable, countless; *(foule)* huge

innommable [inɔmabl] *adj Péj (conduite, actes)* unspeakable; *(nourriture, odeur)* vile

innovateur, -trice [inɔvatœr, -tris] **1** *adj* innovative

2 *nm,f* innovator

innovation [inɔvasjɔ̃] *nf* innovation

innover [inɔve] *vi* to innovate

inoccupé, -e [inɔkype] *adj* unoccupied

inoculation [inɔkylasjɔ̃] *nf Méd* inoculation

inoculer [inɔkyle] *vt* (**a**) **i. un virus/un vaccin à qn** to inoculate sb with a virus/a vaccine; **i. une maladie à qn** to infect sb with a disease; *Fig* **elle nous a inoculé sa gaieté** she infected us with her cheerfulness (**b**) **i. qn (contre une maladie)** to inoculate sb (against a disease)

inodore [inɔdɔr] *adj* odorless

inoffensif, -ive [inɔfãsif, -iv] *adj* harmless

inondation [inɔ̃dasjɔ̃] *nf* flood; *(action)* flooding

inondé, -e [inɔ̃de] *adj (lieu)* flooded; **populations inondées** flood victims; **visage i. de larmes** face streaming with tears; **i. de lumière** flooded with light

inonder [inɔ̃de] *vt (lieu)* to flood; *Fig (marché)* to flood, to inundate (**de** with); **être inondé de réclamations** to be inundated with complaints

inopérable [inɔperabl] *adj* inoperable

inopérant, -e [inɔperã, -ãt] *adj* ineffective

inopiné, -e [inɔpine] *adj* unexpected

inopportun, -e [inɔpɔrtœ̃, -yn] *adj* inopportune

inoubliable [inublijabl] *adj* unforgettable

inouï, -e [inwi] *adj* (**a**) *(ahurissant)* incredible; **il leur est arrivé une histoire inouïe** something incredible happened to them; **c'est/vous êtes i.!** it's/you're incredible! (**b**) *(nouveau)* unheard-of

Inox® [inɔks] *nm* stainless steel

inoxydable [inɔksidabl] *adj (métal)* rustproof; **acier i.** stainless steel

inqualifiable [ɛ̃kalifjabl] *adj* unspeakable

inquiet, -ète [ɛ̃kjɛ, -ɛt] **1** *adj (anxieux) (personne, air, voix)* worried, anxious (**au sujet de** about); *(attente)* anxious

2 *nm,f* worrier

inquiétant, -e [ɛ̃kjetã, -ãt] *adj* (**a**) *(alarmant)* worrying (**b**) *(qui effraie) (air, sourire)* frightening

inquiéter [34] [ɛ̃kjete] **1** *vt* to worry; **être inquiété par la police** to be bothered by the police

2 s'inquiéter *vpr* (**a**) *(se faire du souci)* to worry; **il n'y a**

pas de quoi s'i. there's nothing to worry about; **s'i. pour qn** to be worried about sb; **ne t'inquiète pas pour elle!** don't (you) worry about her! (**b**) **s'i. de** *(se faire du souci pour)* to bother about; *(s'informer de)* to inquire about; **sans s'i. de rien** without a care in the world

inquiétude [ɛkjetyd] *nf* anxiety, worry; **sujet d'i.** cause for anxiety; **éprouver quelques inquiétudes** to feel a little worried; **soyez sans i.** rest easy

inquisiteur, -trice [ɛkizitœr, -tris] **1** *adj (regard)* inquisitive
   2 *nm* inquisitor; **le Grand I.** the Inquisitor General

inquisition [ɛkizisjɔ̃] *nf* inquisition; **l'I.** the Inquisition

inratable [ɛratabl] *adj* unmissable

insaisissable [ɛsezizabl] *adj* (**a**) *(personne)* elusive (**b**) *(son, différence, nuance)* imperceptible

insalubre [ɛsalybr] *adj (climat, habitation, pays)* insalubrious; *(occupation)* unhealthy

insanité [ɛsanite] *nf (de raisonnement, de propos)* insanity; **des insanités** complete nonsense

insatiable [ɛsasjabl] *adj* insatiable

insatisfait, -e [ɛsatisfɛ, -ɛt] **1** *adj (personne)* dissatisfied; *(désir)* unsatisfied
   2 *nm,f* **c'est un éternel i.** he's never satisfied

inscription [ɛskripsjɔ̃] *nf* (**a**) *(action) (dans un journal, un registre)* entering; *(immatriculation)* registration (**b**) *(sur une tombe, un mur)* inscription; *(dans un livre de comptes)* entry

inscrire [30] [ɛskrir] **1** *vt* (**a**) *(renseignements, date)* to write down; *(dans un journal, dans un registre)* to enter (**b**) *(pour participer)* **i. qn à un club/une activité** to enroll sb in a club/for an activity; **i. un enfant dans une école** to enroll a child at a school (**c**) *(dans la pierre)* to inscribe
   2 s'inscrire *vpr (à l'université)* to register (**à** at); *(à un tournoi, à un concours)* to enter (**à** for); *(à une activité)* to enroll (**à** for); *(dans une école)* to enroll (**dans** at); **s'i. dans un club/à un parti** to join a club/party; **s'i. sur les listes électorales** to register to vote; **s'i. en faux contre qch** to deny sth; **s'i. dans le cadre de** to come within the framework of

inscrit, -e [ɛskri, -it] **1** *adj (électeur, candidat)* registered
   2 *nm,f (à l'université)* registered student; *(à un concours)* registered entrant; *(électeur)* registered voter

insécable [ɛsekabl] *adj* indivisible

insecte [ɛsɛkt] *nm* insect

insecticide [ɛsɛktisid] **1** *adj* insecticidal
   2 *nm* insecticide

insectivore [ɛsɛktivɔr] **1** *adj* insectivorous
   2 *nm* insectivore

insécurité [ɛsekyrite] *nf* insecurity

INSEE [inse] *nm (abrév* **Institut national de la statistique et des études économiques***)* = French national institute of statistics and information about the economy

insémination [ɛseminasjɔ̃] *nf* insemination; **i. artificielle** artificial insemination

inséminer [ɛsemine] *vt* to inseminate

insensé, -e [ɛsɑ̃se] **1** *adj (projet, idée)* crazy; *(action, espoir, dépenses)* wild; **c'est i.!** it's crazy!
   2 *nm,f* madman, *f* madwoman

insensibilité [ɛsɑ̃sibilite] *nf* insensitivity (**à** to)

insensible [ɛsɑ̃sibl] *adj (à la douleur, au froid)* insensitive (**à** to); **i. à la critique** impervious to criticism; **elle demeura i. à leurs larmes** she remained unmoved by their tears

insensiblement [ɛsɑ̃sibləmɑ̃] *adv* imperceptibly

inséparable [ɛseparabl] *adj* inseparable

insérer [34] [ɛsere] **1** *vt* to insert (**dans** in); **i. une annonce dans un journal** to put an advertisement in a paper
   2 s'insérer *vpr* (**a**) *(s'attacher)* to be attached (**sur** to) (**b**) *(s'intégrer)* **s'i. dans** *(réformes, politique)* to fit into

insertion [ɛsɛrsjɔ̃] *nf* insertion; **i. sociale** (social) integration; **i. professionnelle** integration into the job market; *Or-*

dinat **mode d'i.** insert mode; *Ordinat* **i. de ligne** line insert; **i. publicitaire** advertisement

insidieusement [ɛsidjøzmɑ̃] *adv* insidiously

insidieux, -euse [ɛsidjø, -øz] *adj* insidious

insigne¹ [ɛsiɲ] *nm* badge; **insignes de la royauté** insignia of royalty

insigne² [ɛsiɲ] *adj* (**a**) *Sout (remarquable)* signal (**b**) *Hum (indiscrétion, maladresse)* remarkable

insignifiant, -e [ɛsiɲifjɑ̃, -ɑ̃t] *adj* insignificant

insinuation [ɛsinɥasjɔ̃] *nf* insinuation

insinuer [ɛsinɥe] **1** *vt* to insinuate; **que voulez-vous i.?** what are you insinuating?
   2 s'insinuer *vpr* **s'i. dans** *(froid, odeur)* to creep into; *(personne)* to worm one's way into; **le doute/l'idée qui s'insinue dans mon esprit** the doubt/the idea that is creeping into my mind; **s'i. dans les bonnes grâces de qn** to insinuate oneself into sb's favor

insipide [ɛsipid] *adj* insipid

insistance [ɛsistɑ̃s] *nf* insistence; **avec i.** insistently

insistant, -e [ɛsistɑ̃, -ɑ̃t] *adj* insistent

insister [ɛsiste] *vi* (**a**) *(persévérer)* to insist; **elle a beaucoup insisté** she was very insistent; **i. pour faire qch** to insist on doing sth; **elle a essayé la planche à voile mais elle n'a pas insisté** she tried windsurfing but soon gave it up; **j'ai dit non, n'insistez pas!** *ou* **inutile d'i.!** I said no, and that's final!; **ça ne répond pas – insiste encore un peu** there's no answer – keep trying for a bit (**b**) *(mettre l'accent sur)* **i. sur qch** to stress sth; **nous insistons particulièrement sur la ponctualité** we lay particular stress on punctuality

insolation [ɛsɔlasjɔ̃] *nf* (**a**) *Méd* sunstroke; **attraper une i.** to get sunstroke (**b**) *(ensoleillement)* sunshine

insolence [ɛsɔlɑ̃s] *nf* (**a**) *(impertinence)* insolence (**b**) *(remarque, action)* impertinence

insolent, -e [ɛsɔlɑ̃, -ɑ̃t] **1** *adj* (**a**) *(impertinent)* insolent (**envers** *ou* **avec** to) (**b**) *(dans la victoire)* haughty (**c**) *(succès)* outrageous; *(luxe)* unashamed
   2 *nm,f* insolent person

insolite [ɛsɔlit] **1** *adj* unusual, strange
   2 *nm* **l'i.** the unusual

insoluble [ɛsɔlybl] *adj* insoluble

insolvable [ɛsɔlvabl] *adj* insolvent

insomniaque [ɛsɔmnjak] *adj & nmf* insomniac

insomnie [ɛsɔmni] *nf* insomnia; **avoir des insomnies** to have insomnia; **j'ai eu une i. la nuit dernière** I couldn't sleep last night

insondable [ɛsɔ̃dabl] *adj (océan, gouffre, mystère)* unfathomable; *(bêtise)* immense

insonorisation [ɛsɔnɔrizasjɔ̃] *nf* soundproofing

insonoriser [ɛsɔnɔrize] *vt* to soundproof

insouciance [ɛsusjɑ̃s] *nf* carefree attitude; **vivre dans l'i.** to live a carefree life

insouciant, -e [ɛsusjɑ̃, -ɑ̃t] *adj* carefree; **i. de son avenir** unconcerned about his future

insoumis, -e [ɛsumi, -iz] **1** *adj* (**a**) *(peuple, tribus)* unsubdued (**b**) *(personne)* rebellious (**c**) *Mil (réfractaire au service militaire)* draft-dodging; *(déserteur)* absent without leave
   2 *nm* *Mil (réfractaire au service militaire)* draft dodger; *(déserteur)* soldier who is absent without leave

insoupçonnable [ɛsupsɔnabl] *adj (personne)* beyond suspicion

insoupçonné, -e [ɛsupsɔne] *adj* unsuspected (**de** by)

insoutenable [ɛsutnabl] *adj* (**a**) *(spectacle, odeur)* unbearable (**b**) *(opinion, position)* untenable

inspecter [ɛspɛkte] *vt* to inspect

inspecteur, -trice [ɛspɛktœr, -tris] *nm,f* inspector; **i. d'Académie** school inspector; **i. du désarmement** weapons inspector; **i. de police** police inspector; **i. du travail**

labor inspector; *Hum* **i. des travaux finis** idler *(who arrives after the work has been done)*

inspection [ɛ̃spɛksjɔ̃] *nf* **(a)** *(examen)* inspection; **faire l'i. de** to inspect **(b)** *(service)* inspectorate; **i. académique** accreditation agency; **i. du travail** Occupational Safety and Health Administration

inspiration [ɛ̃spirasjɔ̃] *nf* **(a)** *(créatrice)* inspiration; **avoir de l'i.** to be inspired; **un poème d'i. romantique** a poem in the romantic style **(b)** *(idée)* inspiration **(c)** *(d'air)* breathing in, inhaling

inspiré, -e [ɛ̃spire] *adj (style, poète, artiste, air)* inspired (**de** by); **être bien/mal i. de faire qch** to do the right/wrong thing in doing sth

inspirer [ɛ̃spire] **1** *vt* **(a)** *(donner de l'inspiration à)* to inspire; **ça m'a inspiré une chanson** it inspired me to write a song; *Hum* **ça ne m'inspire pas** it doesn't exactly inspire me **(b)** *(susciter)* **i. confiance à qn** to inspire confidence in sb; **ça m'inspire la plus grande inquiétude** it gives me great cause for concern **(c)** *(air)* to breathe in, to inhale
2 *vi* to breathe in
3 s'inspirer *vpr* **s'i. de** to be inspired by; **une toile inspirée de Renoir** a painting inspired by Renoir

instabilité [ɛ̃stabilite] *nf* instability; *(du temps)* changeability

instable [ɛ̃stabl] *adj* unstable; *(temps)* changeable

installateur, -trice [ɛ̃stalatœr, -tris] *nm,f* installer, fitter

installation [ɛ̃stalasjɔ̃] *nf* **(a)** *(fait d'installer)* *(d'une machine, du chauffage, d'un ascenseur)* installation; *(d'une cuisine)* fitting out; *(de rideaux)* putting up **(b)** *(emménagement)* move; **prévoir son i. dans une région** to plan to settle in an area **(c)** *(d'un ecclésiastique, d'un magistrat)* installation **(d)** *Ordinat* **programme d'i.** installation program; **i. en réseau** network installation **(e)** *(équipements)* **installations** *(d'une maison, d'un atelier)* installations; **l'i. électrique** the wiring; **installations sanitaires** plumbing; **installations touristiques** tourist facilities

installer [ɛ̃stale] **1** *vt* **(a)** *(mettre en place)* *(machine, chauffage, ascenseur)* to install, to put in; *(cuisine)* to fit out; *(rideaux)* to put up **(b)** *(placer)* **i. qn dans un fauteuil/devant la télévision** to settle sb down in an armchair/in front of the television; **je les ai installés dans la chambre bleue** I've put them in the blue room **(c)** *(aménager)* **les nouveaux bureaux sont très bien installés** the new offices are very well appointed; **il a installé son bureau au grenier** he set up his office in the attic **(d)** *(dans une fonction)* *(ecclésiastique, magistrat)* to install
2 s'installer *vpr (supermarché, cirque)* to be set up; *(personne) (dans un fauteuil)* to settle down; *(dans un bureau)* to install oneself; **confortablement installé dans un fauteuil** comfortably installed in an armchair; **s'i. à la campagne** to settle in the country; **des bourgeois bien installés** comfortably-off middle-class people; **s'i. comme médecin** to set up as a doctor; **un climat d'insécurité s'est installé dans le pays** a climate of insecurity has taken hold of the country

instamment [ɛ̃stamɑ̃] *adv* earnestly

instance [ɛ̃stɑ̃s] *nf* **(a)** *Litt (insistance)* plea, entreaty; **demander à qn de faire qch avec i.** to plead with sb to do sth **(b)** *Jur* proceedings; **en seconde i.** on appeal **(c)** *(autorité)* authority; **les instances internationales** the international authorities; **l'i. compétente** the relevant authority **(d)** *(cours)* **être en i. de divorce** to be waiting for a divorce; **courrier en i.** mail waiting to go out; **être en i.** *(affaire)* to be pending

instant [ɛ̃stɑ̃] *nm* moment, instant; **à chaque** *ou* **tout i.** all the time; **pendant un i.** for a moment; **un i.!** one moment!; **sans perdre un i.** without wasting a second; **d'un i. à l'autre** at any moment; **à l'i.** (just) a moment ago; **à l'i. même où** at the very moment that; **j'en reviens à l'i.** I just came back from there; **pour l'i.** for the moment; **dans un i.** in a moment; **en un i.** in no time at all

instantané, -e [ɛ̃stɑ̃tane] **1** *adj (mort, riposte)* instantaneous; *(café, soupe)* instant
2 *nm (photo)* snapshot

instantanément [ɛ̃stɑ̃tanemɑ̃] *adv* instantaneously

instar [ɛ̃star] **à l'instar de** *prép* following the example of; **à l'i. de ses parents, il sera enseignant** like his parents, he's going to be a teacher

instauration [ɛ̃stɔrasjɔ̃] *nf* establishment

instaurer [ɛ̃store] **1** *vt* to establish
2 s'instaurer *vpr* to be established

instigateur, -trice [ɛ̃stigatœr, -tris] *nm,f* instigator

instigation [ɛ̃stigasjɔ̃] *nf* instigation; **à l'i. de qn** at sb's instigation

instinct [ɛ̃stɛ̃] *nm* instinct; **faire qch d'i.** to do sth by instinct

instinctif, -ive [ɛ̃stɛ̃ktif, -iv] *adj* instinctive

instinctivement [ɛ̃stɛ̃ktivmɑ̃] *adv* instinctively

instit [ɛ̃stit] *nmf Fam* (primary-school) teacher

instituer [ɛ̃stitɥe] *vt* to establish

institut [ɛ̃stity] *nm* institute; **i. de beauté** beauty salon; **i. médico-légal** institute of forensic medicine

instituteur, -trice [ɛ̃stitytœr, -tris] *nm,f* (primary-school) teacher

institution [ɛ̃stitysjɔ̃] *nf* **(a)** *(création)* establishment **(b)** *(école)* private school **(c)** *(coutume)* institution **(d)** *Pol* **institutions** institutions

institutionnaliser [ɛ̃stitysjɔnalize] *vt* to institutionalize

institutionnel, -elle [ɛ̃stitysjɔnɛl] *adj* institutional

instructeur [ɛ̃stryktœr] **1** *nm* instructor
2 *adj m Jur* **juge i.** examining magistrate

instructif, -ive [ɛ̃stryktif, -iv] *adj* instructive

instruction [ɛ̃stryksjɔ̃] *nf* **(a)** *(éducation)* education; *Mil* training; **avoir de l'i.** to be well educated; **sans i.** uneducated; **i. civique** civics *(singulier)*; **i. musicale** musical training; **i. religieuse** religious instruction **(b)** *Ordinat* instruction **(c)** *(circulaire)* memo **(d)** *Jur (d'une affaire)* preliminary investigation **(e)** **instructions** *(directives)* instructions

instruire [18] [ɛ̃strɥir] **1** *vt* **(a)** *(enseigner à)* to teach, to educate; **i. par le jeu** to teach through play **(b)** *(soldats)* to train **(c)** *(informer)* **i. qn de qch** to inform sb of sth **(d)** *Jur (affaire)* to investigate
2 s'instruire *vpr* to educate oneself; **s'i. de** to find out about

instruit, -e [ɛ̃strɥi, -it] *adj* educated

instrument [ɛ̃strymɑ̃] *nm* **(a)** *(outil)* instrument; **i. de mesure/de précision** measuring/precision instrument; *Fig* **il n'a été qu'un i.** he was merely a tool **(b)** **i. (de musique)** (musical) instrument; **i. à vent/cordes** wind/string instrument

instrumental, -e, -aux, -ales [ɛ̃strymɑ̃tal, -o] *adj* instrumental

instrumentiste [ɛ̃strymɑ̃tist] *nmf* instrumentalist

insu [ɛ̃sy] **à l'insu de** *prép* without the knowledge of; **à leur i.** without their knowing; **je l'ai fait à mon i.** I did it without realizing

insubmersible [ɛ̃sybmɛrsibl] *adj* unsinkable

insubordination [ɛ̃sybɔrdinasjɔ̃] *nf* insubordination

insuccès [ɛ̃syksɛ] *nm* failure

insuffisamment [ɛ̃syfizamɑ̃] *adv* insufficiently, inadequately

insuffisance [ɛ̃syfizɑ̃s] *nf* **(a)** *(manque)* insufficiency; *(de personnel, de réserves)* shortage; *(de moyens)* inadequacy **(b)** *Méd (d'un organe)* insufficiency; **i. cardiaque** cardiac insufficiency; **i. respiratoire** respiratory failure *or* insufficiency **(c)** **insuffisances** *(faiblesses)* shortcomings

insuffisant, -e [ɛ̃syfizɑ̃, -ɑ̃t] *adj (quantité)* insufficient; *(moyens, mesures)* inadequate; **tes résultats sont insuffisants** your results are not good enough

insuffler [ɛ̃syfle] *vt Méd* to insufflate (**dans** into); **ce succès a insufflé un nouvel élan à l'entreprise** this success breathed new life into the company

insulaire [ɛ̃sylɛr] **1** *adj* island; *Péj (mentalité)* insular
  2 *nmf* islander

insuline [ɛ̃sylin] *nf* insulin

insulte [ɛ̃sylt] *nf* insult; **il nous a fait l'i. de refuser** he insulted us by refusing

insulter [ɛ̃sylte] *vt* to insult

insupportable [ɛ̃syportabl] *adj* unbearable

insurgé, -e [ɛ̃syrʒe] *adj & nm,f* insurgent

insurger [45] [ɛ̃syrʒe] **s'insurger** *vpr* to rise up (**contre** against)

insurmontable [ɛ̃syrmɔ̃tabl] *adj (difficulté, obstacle)* insurmountable; *(aversion, dégoût)* unconquerable

insurrection [ɛ̃syrɛksjɔ̃] *nf* uprising, rebellion; **en état d'i.** in a state of rebellion

insurrectionnel, -elle [ɛ̃syrɛksjɔnɛl] *adj* insurrectionary

intact, -e [ɛ̃takt] *adj* intact

intangible [ɛ̃tɑ̃ʒibl] *adj (loi, institution)* sacred

intarissable [ɛ̃tarisabl] *adj* inexhaustible

intégral, -e, -aux, -ales [ɛ̃tegral, -o] **1** *adj* (a) *(paiement, remboursement)* full; *(texte)* unabridged; *Fam* **un fumiste/crétin/menteur i.** a complete clown/idiot/liar (b) *Math* **calcul i.** integral calculus
  2 *nf* **intégrale** (a) *Math* integral (b) *(totalité)* **l'intégrale des symphonies de Beethoven/des œuvres de Shakespeare** the complete Beethoven symphonies/works of Shakespeare

intégralement [ɛ̃tegralmɑ̃] *adv (citer, rembourser)* fully, in full

intégralité [ɛ̃tegralite] *nf* **l'i.** the whole (**de** of); **dans son i.** in its entirety

intégrante [ɛ̃tegrɑ̃t] *adj f* **une partie i. de** an integral part of; **faire partie i. de** to be an integral part of

intégration [ɛ̃tegrasjɔ̃] *nf (au sein d'un groupe) & Math* integration; *(dans une grande école)* admission; *Écon* **i. horizontale/verticale** horizontal/vertical integration

intègre [ɛ̃tɛgr] *adj* upright, honest

intégrer [34] [ɛ̃tegre] **1** *vt (incorporer)* to integrate (**à/dans** into)
  2 s'intégrer *vpr* to become integrated (**à/dans** into); **cette sculpture s'intègre bien au paysage** this sculpture blends in well with the countryside

intégrisme [ɛ̃tegrism] *nm* fundamentalism

intégriste [ɛ̃tegrist] *adj & nmf* fundamentalist

intégrité [ɛ̃tegrite] *nf* integrity; *Ordinat* **i. des données** data integrity

intellect [ɛ̃telɛkt] *nm* intellect

intellectuel, -elle [ɛ̃telɛktɥɛl] **1** *adj* intellectual; *(fatigue)* mental; *(travail)* non-manual
  2 *nm,f* intellectual

intelligemment [ɛ̃teliʒamɑ̃] *adv* intelligently

intelligence [ɛ̃teliʒɑ̃s] *nf* (a) *(intellect)* intelligence; **avoir l'i. de faire qch** to have the intelligence to do sth; **i. artificielle** artificial intelligence (b) *(compréhension)* understanding (c) *(entente)* **vivre en bonne/mauvaise i. avec qn** to be on good/bad terms with sb (d) *(connivence)* **un regard/sourire d'i.** a knowing look/smile; **faire des signes d'i. à qn** to signal to sb

intelligent, -e [ɛ̃teliʒɑ̃, -ɑ̃t] *adj* intelligent, clever; *Ordinat* smart, intelligent

intelligentsia [ɛ̃telidʒɛnsja] *nf* **l'i.** the intelligentsia

intelligible [ɛ̃teliʒibl] *adj (compréhensible)* intelligible; *(clair)* clear; **à haute et i. voix** in a loud, clear voice

intello [ɛ̃telo] *nmf Fam souvent Péj* intellectual, highbrow

intempéries [ɛ̃tɑ̃peri] *nfpl* bad weather; **exposé aux i.** exposed to the elements

intempestif, -ive [ɛ̃tɑ̃pɛstif, -iv] *adj* untimely, ill-timed

intemporel, -elle [ɛ̃tɑ̃pɔrɛl] *adj (hors du temps)* timeless

intenable [ɛ̃tənabl] *adj (chaleur, situation)* intolerable, unbearable; *(position)* untenable; *Fam (enfant)* uncontrollable

intendance [ɛ̃tɑ̃dɑ̃s] *nf* (a) *Scol* bursary; *(bureau)* bursar's office (b) *Mil* commissariat (c) *(d'un domaine)* stewardship (d) *Fig (questions matérielles)* practical matters

intendant [ɛ̃tɑ̃dɑ̃] *nm* (a) *Scol* bursar (b) *Mil* quartermaster (c) *(d'un domaine)* steward

intendante [ɛ̃tɑ̃dɑ̃t] *nf* (a) *Scol* (woman) bursar (b) *(d'une maison)* housekeeper

intense [ɛ̃tɑ̃s] *adj* intense

intensément [ɛ̃tɑ̃semɑ̃] *adv* intensely

intensif, -ive [ɛ̃tɑ̃sif, -iv] *adj* intensive

intensification [ɛ̃tɑ̃sifikasjɔ̃] *nf* intensification

intensifier [66] [ɛ̃tɑ̃sifje] **1** *vt* to intensify
  2 s'intensifier *vpr* to intensify

intensité [ɛ̃tɑ̃site] *nf* intensity

intenter [ɛ̃tɑ̃te] *vt Jur* **i. une action contre qn** to bring an action against sb; **i. un procès à** *ou* **contre qn** to institute proceedings against sb

intention [ɛ̃tɑ̃sjɔ̃] *nf (projet)* intention; *Jur* intent; **avoir l'i. de faire qch** to intend to do sth; **dans l'i. de faire qch** with a view to *or* with the intention of doing sth; **elle a de bonnes intentions** she means well; **c'est l'i. qui compte** it's the thought that counts; **à l'i. de...** *(pour)* for...; *(en l'honneur de)* in honor of...; *(sur une lettre)* for the attention of...

intentionné, -e [ɛ̃tɑ̃sjɔne] *adj* **bien/mal i.** well-/ill-intentioned; **bien/mal i. envers qn** well-/ill-disposed toward sb

intentionnel, -elle [ɛ̃tɑ̃sjɔnɛl] *adj* intentional, deliberate

intentionnellement [ɛ̃tɑ̃sjɔnɛlmɑ̃] *adv* intentionally, deliberately

interactif, -ive [ɛ̃tɛraktif, -iv] *adj Ordinat* interactive

interaction [ɛ̃tɛraksjɔ̃] *nf* interaction

interallié, -e [ɛ̃tɛralje] *adj* allied

interbancaire [ɛ̃tɛrbɑ̃kɛr] *adj* interbank

intercalaire [ɛ̃tɛrkalɛr] **1** *adj (jour)* intercalary; **feuillet i.** insert
  2 *nm (feuillet)* insert; *(dans un classeur)* divider

intercaler [ɛ̃tɛrkale] **1** *vt (dans un texte, un film)* to insert, to include; *(dans un programme, entre deux événements)* to slot in
  2 s'intercaler *vpr* to come in between

intercéder [34] [ɛ̃tɛrsede] *vi* to intercede (**en faveur de/ auprès de** on behalf of/with)

intercepter [ɛ̃tɛrsɛpte] *vt (lettre, avion, ballon, personne)* to intercept; *(bruit, lumière)* to shut out

interchangeable [ɛ̃tɛrʃɑ̃ʒabl] *adj* interchangeable

interclasse [ɛ̃tɛrklas] *nm* = short recess between classes

intercontinental, -e, -aux, -ales [ɛ̃tɛrkɔ̃tinɑ̃tal, -o] *adj* intercontinental

intercours [ɛ̃tɛrkur] *nm Belg Scol* = short recess between classes

interdépartemental, -e, -aux, -ales [ɛ̃tɛrdepartəmɑ̃tal, -o] *adj* = shared by several French departments

interdépendant, -e [ɛ̃tɛrdepɑ̃dɑ̃, -ɑ̃t] *adj* interdependent

interdiction [ɛ̃tɛrdiksjɔ̃] *nf* (a) *(défense)* ban, banning; **i. de fumer/stationner** *(sur panneau)* no smoking/parking (b) *(suspension)* banning; **i. de séjour** = order banning former prisoner from certain areas

interdire [27b] [ɛ̃tɛrdir] **1** *vt* (a) *(défendre) (stationnement, port d'armes)* to ban; **i. qch à qn** to forbid sb sth; **le centre-ville est interdit aux camions** trucks are not allowed in the city center; **i. à qn de faire qch** *(personne)* to forbid sb to do sth; *(règlement)* to prohibit sb from doing sth; **il nous est interdit de révéler...** we are not allowed to reveal... (b) *(empêcher)* to prevent, to stop (**de faire qch** from doing sth)

2 s'interdire *vpr* **s'i. l'alcool** to abstain from drinking; **il s'interdit d'y penser** he doesn't let himself think about it

interdit, -e [ɛ̃tɛrdi, -it] **1** *adj* (**a**) *(défendu)* forbidden; **il est i. de fumer** smoking is not allowed; **i. au public** *(sur un écriteau)* no unauthorized entry; **un film i. aux moins de 18 ans** ≃ a movie with an NC-17 rating; **i. de séjour** = banned from living in certain areas; **être i. de chéquier** to have (had) one's checkbook facilities withdrawn; *Ordinat* **i. d'écriture** *(disquette)* write-protected (**b**) *(déconcerté)* disconcerted, taken aback

2 *nm,f Jur* **i. de séjour** = former prisoner banned from certain areas

3 *nm (social)* taboo; *(religieux)* interdict; **frapper qn/qch d'i.** to impose a ban on sb/sth

intéressant, -e [ɛ̃tɛresɑ̃, -ɑ̃t] **1** *adj* (**a**) *(attirant)* interesting (**b**) *(avantageux)* worthwhile; *(prix)* attractive; *(lucratif)* profitable

2 *nm,f Fam* **faire l'i.** to show off

intéressé, -e [ɛ̃terese] **1** *adj* (**a**) *(concerné)* **les parties intéressées** the interested parties, the persons concerned (**b**) *(égoïste)* *(personne)* self-seeking; *(sentiment)* self-interested; *(conseil)* biased; **agir dans un but i.** to have an ax to grind

2 *nm,f* **l'i.** the person concerned

intéresser [ɛ̃terese] **1** *vt* (**a**) *(captiver)* to interest; **l'art m'intéresse beaucoup** I'm very interested in art; **est-ce que ça t'intéresse d'aller au cinéma?** would you like to go to the movies? (**b**) *Ind & Com* **i. les employés (aux bénéfices)** to operate a profit-sharing scheme; **être intéressé dans une affaire** to have a financial interest in a business (**c**) *(concerner)* to concern, to affect

2 s'intéresser *vpr* **s'i. à qn/qch** to take an interest in sb/sth, to be interested in sb/sth

intérêt [ɛ̃terɛ] *nm* (**a**) *(avantage)* interest; **c'est dans mon i. de le faire** it's in my interest to do it; **elle a tout i. à se taire** she'd be well-advised to remain silent; **on a i. à réserver si on veut avoir des places** we'd better make a reservation if we want seats; *Fam* **tu n'as pas i. à recommencer!** you'd better not do it again!; **agir dans/contre l'i. de qn** to act in/against sb's interest(s); **agir par i. personnel** to act out of self-interest; **faire un mariage d'i.** to marry for money; **l'i. des vacances en groupe, c'est de faire des rencontres** the advantage of group vacations is that you meet people; *Fam* **tu viens à la réunion du syndicat? – y a i.!** are you coming to the union meeting? – you bet (I am)! (**b**) *(attrait)* interest; **sans i.** uninteresting (**c**) *(curiosité)* interest (**pour** in); **éprouver de l'i. pour qch** to be interested or to take an interest in sth (**d**) *Fin* interest; **i. fixe** fixed interest; **i. variable** variable-rate interest

interface [ɛ̃tɛrfas] *nf Ordinat* interface; **i. graphique** graphic interface; **i. d'imprimante** printer interface; **i. numérique** digital interface; **i. parallèle** parallel interface; **i. utilisateur** user interface; **i. vidéo numérique** digital video interface

interférence [ɛ̃tɛrferɑ̃s] *nf (d'ondes)* interference; *Fig (d'événements)* combination

interférer [34] [ɛ̃tɛrfere] *vi aussi Fig* to interfere

intergouvernemental, -e, -aux, -ales [ɛ̃tɛrguvɛrnəmɑ̃tal, -o] *adj* intergovernmental

intérieur, -e [ɛ̃terjœr] **1** *adj* (**a**) *(dans l'espace) (escalier)* interior, inside; *(cour)* inner; *(poche)* inside; *(partie)* inside, internal; *(mer)* inland (**b**) *(national)* domestic (**c**) *(vie, sentiments, force)* inner

2 *nm* (**a**) *(dedans)* inside, interior; **à l'i.** inside; **à l'i. de la gare** inside the station; **fermé de l'i.** locked from the inside; **tourné en i.** *(film)* shot indoors (**b**) *(d'un pays)* interior; **dans l'i. du pays** inland (**c**) *(maison)* home; **femme d'i.** housewife, homemaker

intérieurement [ɛ̃terjœrmɑ̃] *adv* inwardly

intérim [ɛ̃terim] *nm (travail intérimaire)* temporary work, temping; **faire de l'i.** to temp; **par i.,** *Belg* **ad i.** acting; **assurer l'i. (de qn)** to stand in (for sb)

intérimaire [ɛ̃terimɛr] **1** *adj (fonction, employé)* temporary; *(directeur, ministre)* acting; *(cabinet, gouvernement)* caretaker

2 *nmf (travailleur)* temporary worker; *(secrétaire)* temp

intérioriser [ɛ̃terjɔrize] *vt* to internalize

interjection [ɛ̃tɛrʒɛksjɔ̃] *nf* interjection

interligne [ɛ̃tɛrliɲ] *nm* line spacing; **dans l'i.** in the space between the lines; **simple/double i.** single/double spacing

interlocuteur, -trice [ɛ̃tɛrlɔkytœr, -tris] *nm,f* (**a**) *(dans une conversation)* speaker; **mon i.** the person I was/am speaking to (**b**) *(dans une négociation)* discussion partner

interloqué, -e [ɛ̃tɛrlɔke] *adj* taken aback

interlude [ɛ̃tɛrlyd] *nm* interlude

intermède [ɛ̃tɛrmɛd] *nm aussi Fig* interlude

intermédiaire [ɛ̃tɛrmedjɛr] **1** *adj* intermediate; **i. entre** halfway between; **trouver une solution i.** to find a compromise solution; **pointure i.** in-between size

2 *nmf (personne)* intermediary, go-between; *Com* middleman; **sans i.** directly

3 *nm* **par l'i. de** through; **sans l'i. de** without

interminable [ɛ̃tɛrminabl] *adj* interminable

interministériel, -elle [ɛ̃tɛrministerjɛl] *adj* interministerial

intermittence [ɛ̃tɛrmitɑ̃s] *nf* **par i.** intermittently, on and off

intermittent, -e [ɛ̃tɛrmitɑ̃, -ɑ̃t] **1** *adj (lumière, bruit, tir)* intermittent, sporadic; *(travail)* casual

2 *nm,f* casual worker

internat [ɛ̃tɛrna] *nm* (**a**) *Scol (système)* boarding; *(pensionnat)* boarding school (**b**) *Méd (concours)* entrance examination for an internship; *(formation)* internship

international, -e, -aux, -ales [ɛ̃tɛrnasjɔnal, -o] **1** *adj & nm,f* international

2 *nf* **l'Internationale** *(groupement)* the International; *(chant)* the Internationale

internationalisation [ɛ̃tɛrnasjɔnalizasjɔ̃] *nf* internationalization

internationaliser [ɛ̃tɛrnasjɔnalize] **1** *vt* to internationalize

2 s'internationaliser *vpr* to become international

internaute [ɛ̃tɛrnot] *nmf* Internet user

interne [ɛ̃tɛrn] **1** *adj (structure, paroi, hémorragie)* internal; *(côté)* inner; *(de l'entreprise)* in-house

2 *nmf (élève)* boarder; **i. (des hôpitaux)** intern

internement [ɛ̃tɛrnəmɑ̃] *nm (emprisonnement)* internment; *(hospitalisation)* confinement

interner [ɛ̃tɛrne] *vt (emprisonner)* to intern; *(hospitaliser)* to commit

Internet [ɛ̃tɛrnɛt] *nm* **l'I.** the Internet; **sur I.** on the Internet

interparlementaire [ɛ̃tɛrparləmɑ̃tɛr] *adj (réunion)* interparliamentary; *(commission)* joint

interpellation [ɛ̃tɛrpɛlasjɔ̃] *nf (appel)* calling out; *(au Parlement)* question; **la police a procédé à plusieurs interpellations** the police took several people in for questioning

interpeller [ɛ̃tɛrpəle] **1** *vt* (**a**) *(appeler)* to call (out) to; *(sujet: police)* to take in for questioning; *(ministre)* to question; *(à une réunion, un spectacle)* to heckle; *(sujet: sentinelle)* to challenge (**b**) *(toucher)* **ce roman m'a interpellé** I can really relate to this novel

2 s'interpeller *vpr (s'appeler)* to call (out) to each other; *(s'insulter)* to shout insults at each other

Interphone® [ɛ̃tɛrfɔn] *nm (de bureau, d'immeuble)* intercom; **à l'I.** on the intercom

interplanétaire [ɛ̃tɛrplanetɛr] *adj* interplanetary

interpolation [ɛ̃tɛrpɔlasjɔ̃] *nf* interpolation

interpoler [ɛ̃tɛrpɔle] *vt* to interpolate

interposé, -e [ɛ̃tɛrpoze] *adj* **par personne interposée** through an intermediary

interposer [ɛ̃tɛrpoze] **1** *vt* to interpose (**entre** between)
2 s'interposer *vpr (intervenir)* to intervene

interprétariat [ɛ̃tɛrpretarja] *nm* interpreting

interprétation [ɛ̃tɛrpretasjɔ̃] *nf* (**a**) *(d'un texte, d'un rêve, d'un rôle)* interpretation (**b**) *(traduction)* interpreting

interprète [ɛ̃tɛrprɛt] *nmf (dans une autre langue)* interpreter; *(d'un rôle, d'une œuvre musicale)* performer; *(porte-parole)* spokesman, *f* spokeswoman; **i. de conférence** conference interpreter

interpréter [34] [ɛ̃tɛrprete] *vt* (**a**) *(rôle, œuvre musicale)* to perform, to interpret (**b**) *(texte, paroles, geste, rêve)* to interpret; **mal i. les paroles de qn** to misinterpret sb's words

interro [ɛ̃tero] *nf Fam Scol (abrév* **interrogation***)* test

interrogateur, -trice [ɛ̃terɔgatœr, -tris] **1** *adj* questioning
2 *nm,f (examinateur)* (oral) examiner

interrogatif, -ive [ɛ̃terɔgatif, -iv] **1** *adj* (**a**) *(air, ton)* inquiring, questioning (**b**) *(pronom, phrase)* interrogative
2 *nm* interrogative
3 *nf* **interrogative** interrogative (clause)

interrogation [ɛ̃terɔgasjɔ̃] *nf* (**a**) *(question)* question; **i. directe/indirecte** direct/indirect question (**b**) *Scol* test; **i. écrite/orale** written/oral test (**c**) *(d'un prisonnier, d'un suspect)* questioning, interrogation (**d**) *Ordinat (d'une base de données) (question)* inquiry, query; *(activité)* interrogation; **i. à distance** remote interrogation

interrogatoire [ɛ̃terɔgatwar] *nm* questioning

interroger [45] [ɛ̃terɔʒe] **1** *vt* (**a**) *(personne)* to question; *(candidat, élève)* to test; **i. qn du regard** to look at sb questioningly (**b**) *Ordinat (base de données)* to query, to interrogate
2 s'interroger *vpr* to ask oneself, to wonder (**sur** about)

interrompre [ɛ̃terɔ̃pr] **1** *vt* to interrupt; *(trafic)* to hold up; *(grossesse)* to terminate
2 s'interrompre *vpr* to break off

interrupteur [ɛ̃teryptœr] *nm* switch; **i. à bascule** toggle switch; *Ordinat* **i. DIP** *ou* **à plusieurs positions** DIP switch

interruption [ɛ̃terypsjɔ̃] *nf (arrêt)* interruption; *(de négociations)* breaking off; **sans i.** non-stop, continuously; *Ordinat* **fonction d'i.** interrupt function; **i. volontaire de grossesse** termination (of pregnancy)

intersection [ɛ̃tersɛksjɔ̃] *nf* intersection, junction; **à l'i. des deux routes** where the two roads intersect *or* meet

intersidéral, -e, -aux, -ales [ɛ̃tersideral, -o] *adj* interstellar

interstice [ɛ̃tɛrstis] *nm* chink, crack

intersyndical, -e, -aux, -ales [ɛ̃tersɛ̃dikal, -o] **1** *adj* interunion
2 *nf* **intersyndicale** *(association)* interunion group

intertitre [ɛ̃tɛrtitr] *nm Journ* subheading; *Cin* subtitle

interurbain, -e [ɛ̃teryrbɛ̃, -ɛn] **1** *adj* interurban; *Vieilli Tél* **appel i.** long-distance call
2 *nm Vieilli Tél* long-distance service

intervalle [ɛ̃terval] *nm* (**a**) *(dans le temps, en musique)* interval; **un i. d'une heure** a one-hour interval; **à deux mois d'i.** two months apart; **par intervalles** at intervals, now and then; **dans l'i.** in the meantime, meanwhile (**b**) *(dans l'espace)* gap, space; **à un mètre d'i.** ≃ a yard apart (**c**) *Math* interval

intervenant, -e [ɛ̃tervɔnɑ̃, -ɑ̃t] *nm,f (dans une conférence, un débat)* speaker, contributor

intervenir [70] [ɛ̃tervɔnir] *vi* (**a**) *(agir, prendre la parole)* to intervene (**dans** in); **i. pour faire qch** to intervene *or* to step in to do sth; **i. en faveur de qn** to intervene on sb's behalf; **i. auprès de qn** to intercede with sb; **faire i. qn** to bring sb in (**b**) *(arriver) (événement, changement)* to occur; *(accord)* to be reached (**c**) *(jouer un rôle)* to play a part (**dans** in)

intervention [ɛ̃tervɑ̃sjɔ̃] *nf* (**a**) *(intercession, ingérence)* intervention (**en faveur de/auprès de** on behalf of/with) (**b**) *(prise de parole)* intervention; *(discours)* speech (**c**) *(opération)* **i. (chirurgicale)** operation

interventionniste [ɛ̃tervɑ̃sjɔnist] *adj & nmf* interventionist

interversion [ɛ̃terversjɔ̃] *nf* inversion, reversal

intervertir [ɛ̃tervertir] *vt (l'ordre de qch)* to invert, to reverse; *(objets, éléments)* to switch (around); *(rôles)* to reverse

intervienne *voir* **intervenir**

interview [ɛ̃tervju] *nm ou nf* interview

interviewer [ɛ̃tervjuve] *vt* to interview

intestin¹, -e [ɛ̃tɛstɛ̃, -in] *adj Litt* internal

intestin² [ɛ̃tɛstɛ̃, -in] *nm* intestine; **intestins** intestines, bowels; **gros i.** large intestine; **i. grêle** small intestine

intestinal, -e, -aux, -ales [ɛ̃tɛstinal, -o] *adj* intestinal

intime [ɛ̃tim] **1** *adj* intimate; *(hygiène, toilette)* personal; **être i. avec qn** to be close to sb; **avoir l'i. conviction que...** to be thoroughly convinced that...
2 *nmf* close friend; **pour les intimes** to my/her/*etc.* friends

intimement [ɛ̃timmɑ̃] *adv* intimately; **i. liés** *(amis)* very close; *(phénomènes)* closely linked; **être i. persuadé que...** to be thoroughly convinced that...

intimer [ɛ̃time] *vt* (**a**) *(ordonner)* **i. à qn l'ordre de faire qch** to order sb to do sth (**b**) *Jur* to summon before the Court of Appeal

intimidant, -e [ɛ̃timidɑ̃, -ɑ̃t] *adj* intimidating

intimidation [ɛ̃timidasjɔ̃] *nf* intimidation

intimider [ɛ̃timide] *vt* to intimidate; **ne te laisse pas i. par eux!** don't let them intimidate you!

intimité [ɛ̃timite] *nf (vie privée)* privacy; *(familiarité)* intimacy, closeness; **dans l'i.** in private; **le mariage a eu lieu dans la plus stricte i.** only close family and friends attended the wedding

intitulé [ɛ̃tityle] *nm (de livre)* title; *(de chapitre)* heading, title

intituler [ɛ̃tityle] **1** *vt (livre, chanson)* to give a title to; **un livre intitulé...** a book entitled *or* called...
2 s'intituler *vpr (livre, chanson)* to be entitled, to be called; *(personne)* to call oneself

intolérable [ɛ̃tɔlerabl] *adj* intolerable

intolérance [ɛ̃tɔlerɑ̃s] *nf* intolerance; *Méd* **i. à qch** intolerance to sth

intolérant, -e [ɛ̃tɔlerɑ̃, -ɑ̃t] *adj* intolerant

intonation [ɛ̃tɔnasjɔ̃] *nf* intonation

intouchable [ɛ̃tuʃabl] *adj & nmf* untouchable

intox [ɛ̃tɔks] *nf Fam* brainwashing

intoxication [ɛ̃tɔksikasjɔ̃] *nf (empoisonnement)* poisoning; *Fig* brainwashing; **i. alimentaire** food poisoning

intoxiquer [ɛ̃tɔksike] **1** *vt (empoisonner)* to poison; *Fig* to brainwash
2 s'intoxiquer *vpr* to poison oneself

intradermique [ɛ̃tradermik] *Méd* **1** *adj* intradermal
2 *nf* intradermal injection

intraduisible [ɛ̃tradɥizibl] *adj* untranslatable

intraitable [ɛ̃trɛtabl] *adj* uncompromising, inflexible (**sur** about)

intra-muros [ɛ̃tramyros] **1** *adj inv* **Londres/Paris i.** inner London/Paris
2 *adv* within the city

intramusculaire [ɛ̃tramyskylɛr] **1** *adj* intramuscular
2 *nf* intramuscular injection

Intranet [ɛ̃tranɛt] *nm Ordinat* Intranet

intransigeance [ɛ̃trɑ̃ziʒɑ̃s] *nf* intransigence

intransigeant, -e [ɛ̃trɑ̃ziʒɑ̃, -ɑ̃t] *adj (personne)* intransigent, uncompromising (**envers/sur** with/about); *(morale)* uncompromising

intransitif, -ive [ɛ̃trɑ̃zitif, -iv] *adj & nm Gram* intransitive

intransmissible [ɛ̃trãsmisibl] *adj* (**a**) *Biol* intransmissible (**b**) *Jur* untransferable

intransportable [ɛ̃trãspɔrtabl] *adj (objet)* untransportable; *(blessé)* unfit to travel

intraveineux, -euse [ɛ̃travɛnø, -øz] **1** *adj* intravenous
    2 *nf* **intraveineuse** intravenous injection

intrépide [ɛ̃trepid] *adj* intrepid, fearless

intrépidité [ɛ̃trepidite] *nf* fearlessness

intrigant, -e [ɛ̃trigã, -ãt] **1** *adj* scheming, plotting
    2 *nm,f* schemer

intrigue [ɛ̃trig] *nf (machination)* intrigue; *(liaison amoureuse)* (love) affair; *(d'un roman, d'un film)* plot

intriguer [ɛ̃trige] **1** *vt* to intrigue
    2 *vi* to scheme, to intrigue

intrinsèque [ɛ̃trɛ̃sɛk] *adj* intrinsic

intrinsèquement [ɛ̃trɛ̃sɛkmã] *adv* intrinsically

intro [ɛ̃tro] *nf Fam* intro; *(musicale)* theme song *or* tune

introductif, -ive [ɛ̃trodyktif, -iv] *adj* (**a**) *(discours, exposé)* introductory, opening (**b**) *Jur* introductory

introduction [ɛ̃trodyksjɔ̃] *nf* introduction; *(insertion)* insertion, introduction (**dans** into); **i. en Bourse** listing on the stock market

introduire [18] [ɛ̃trodyir] **1** *vt (dans une serrure, dans un trou)* to insert (**dans** into); *(marchandises)* to bring in; *(coutume, réforme, mesures, mode)* to introduce; *(étranger, visiteur)* to show in; **i. qn auprès de qn** *(faire entrer)* to show sb in to see sb; *(présenter)* to introduce sb to sb; **i. en Bourse** to list on the stock market; **i. sur le marché** to launch onto the market
    2 s'introduire *vpr* **s'i. dans une maison** to get into a house; **l'eau s'introduit partout** there's water coming in everywhere

intronisation [ɛ̃tronizasjɔ̃] *nf* enthronement; *Fig* establishment

introniser [ɛ̃tronize] *vt* to enthrone; *Fig* to establish

introspection [ɛ̃trospɛksjɔ̃] *nf* introspection

introuvable [ɛ̃truvabl] *adj (produit, denrées)* unobtainable; *(personne)* nowhere to be found

introversion [ɛ̃trovɛrsjɔ̃] *nf* introversion

introverti, -e [ɛ̃troverti] **1** *adj* introverted
    2 *nm,f* introvert

intrus, -e [ɛ̃try, -yz] *nm,f aussi Ordinat* intruder

intrusion [ɛ̃tryzjɔ̃] *nf* intrusion (**dans** into)

intuitif, -ive [ɛ̃tuitif, -iv] **1** *adj* intuitive
    2 *nm,f* **c'est un i.** he's the intuitive type

intuition [ɛ̃tuisjɔ̃] *nf* intuition; **avoir l'i. de qch/que** to sense sth/that

intuitivement [ɛ̃tuitivmã] *adv* intuitively

inuit [inuit] **1** *adj inv* Inuit
    2 *nmf inv* **les I.** the Inuit *or* Inuits

inusable [inyzabl] *adj aussi Fig* hard-wearing

inusité, -e [inyzite] *adj (mot)* uncommon

inutile [inytil] *adj (qui ne sert à rien)* useless; *(effort)* vain, pointless; *(précautions, démarche, bagages)* unnecessary; **c'est i.!** *(ça ne sert à rien)* it's pointless!; *(ce n'est pas nécessaire)* you/he/etc. needn't bother!; **i. de dire que…** needless to say,…; **c'est i. d'attendre** there's no point in waiting; **i. d'insister, je ne viens pas** there's no point insisting, I'm not coming

inutilement [inytilmã] *adv* needlessly, unnecessarily

inutilisable [inytilizabl] *adj* unusable

inutilisé, -e [inytilize] *adj* unused

inutilité [inytilite] *nf (d'un objet)* uselessness; *(d'un effort, d'un argument)* pointlessness

invaincu, -e [ɛ̃vɛ̃ky] *adj* undefeated

invalidant, -e [ɛ̃validã, -ãt] *adj* disabling

invalidation [ɛ̃validasjɔ̃] *nf Jur* invalidation

invalide [ɛ̃valid] **1** *adj* disabled

2 *nmf* disabled person, invalid; **i. de guerre** disabled ex-serviceman/ex-servicewoman

invalider [ɛ̃valide] *vt Jur* to invalidate

invalidité [ɛ̃validite] *nf* disability

invariable [ɛ̃varjabl] *adj* invariable

invariablement [ɛ̃varjabləmã] *adv* invariably

invasion [ɛ̃vazjɔ̃] *nf aussi Fig* invasion

invective [ɛ̃vɛktiv] *nf* invective; **invectives** abuse

invectiver [ɛ̃vɛktive] **1** *vt* to hurl abuse at
    2 s'invectiver *vpr* to hurl abuse at each other

invendable [ɛ̃vãdabl] *adj* unsellable

invendu, -e [ɛ̃vãdy] **1** *adj* unsold
    2 *nm* **invendus** unsold goods; *(journaux, livres)* unsold copies; *(revendus moins cher)* remainders

inventaire [ɛ̃vãtɛr] *nm* (**a**) *(liste)* inventory (**b**) *(de marchandises)* inventory; **faire** *ou* **dresser l'i. (des stocks)** to inventory; **fermé pour cause d'i.** *(sur un écriteau)* closed for inventory (**c**) *Fig (de peintures, de richesses artistiques)* survey

inventer [ɛ̃vãte] **1** *vt (machine)* to invent; *(concept, moyen)* to think up; *(histoire, excuse)* to make up; *(expression)* to coin; **qu'est-ce qu'il va encore i.?** what's he going to come out with next?; *Fam* **il n'a pas inventé la poudre** *ou* **le fil à couper le beurre** he'll never set the world alight
    2 s'inventer *vpr* **ça ne s'invente pas** you couldn't make that up if you wanted to; **s'i. un passé** to invent a past for oneself

inventeur, -trice [ɛ̃vãtœr, -tris] *nm,f* (**a**) *(d'une machine, d'un procédé)* inventor (**b**) *Jur (d'un trésor)* finder

inventif, -ive [ɛ̃vãtif, -iv] *adj* inventive

invention [ɛ̃vãsjɔ̃] *nf* (**a**) *(action)* invention; *(faculté)* inventiveness (**b**) *(chose découverte, mensonge)* invention (**c**) *Jur (d'un trésor)* finding

inventorier [66] [ɛ̃vãtɔrje] *vt* to inventory, to make an inventory of

invérifiable [ɛ̃verifjabl] *adj* unverifiable

inverse [ɛ̃vɛrs] **1** *adj aussi Math* inverse; **en sens i. (de)** in the opposite direction (to); **dans l'ordre i.** in reverse order; **dans le sens i. des aiguilles d'une montre** counterclockwise
    2 *nm* **l'i.** the opposite, the reverse; **faire l'i. (de)** to do the opposite (of); **à l'i. de** contrary to

inversement [ɛ̃vɛrsəmã] *adv* **et i.** and vice versa; **i., on peut dire que…** conversely, one can say that…; **i. proportionnel (à)** inversely proportional (to)

inverser [ɛ̃vɛrse] *vt (ordre, tendance)* to reverse; *(deux mots)* to invert

inversion [ɛ̃vɛrsjɔ̃] *nf (d'ordre, de mots)* inversion; *Ordinat* **i. vidéo** reverse video

invertébré, -e [ɛ̃vɛrtebre] *adj & nm* invertebrate

inverti, -e [ɛ̃vɛrti] **1** *adj (sucre)* invert
    2 *nm,f Vieilli (homosexuel)* homosexual, invert

investigateur, -trice [ɛ̃vɛstigatœr, -tris] **1** *adj (regard)* searching
    2 *nm,f* investigator

investigation [ɛ̃vɛstigasjɔ̃] *nf* investigation

investir [ɛ̃vɛstir] **1** *vt* (**a**) *(argent, temps, énergie)* to invest (**dans** in) (**b**) *(ville, édifice)* to besiege (**c**) *(charger)* **i. qn d'une mission** to entrust sb with a mission
    2 *vi* to invest (**dans** in)
    3 s'investir *vpr* **s'i. dans qch** to put a lot into sth

investissement [ɛ̃vɛstismã] *nm* investment; **i. à court/long terme** short-/long-term investment

investisseur [ɛ̃vɛstisœr] *nm* investor; **les investisseurs institutionnels** institutional investors

investiture [ɛ̃vɛstityr] *nf (d'un candidat)* nomination; *(d'un gouvernement)* voting in; *(d'un évêque)* investiture

invétéré, -e [ɛ̃vetere] *adj* inveterate

invincible [ɛ̃vɛ̃sibl] *adj (armée, adversaire)* invincible; *(peur)* unconquerable

inviolabilité [ɛ̃vjɔlabilite] *nf Jur* inviolability; *(d'un parlementaire)* immunity; **i. diplomatique** diplomatic immunity

inviolable [ɛ̃vjɔlabl] *adj (coffre)* burglarproof; *(droit, asile)* inviolable; *(parlementaire)* immune

invisibilité [ɛ̃vizibilite] *nf* invisibility

invisible [ɛ̃vizibl] *adj* invisible

invit' [ɛ̃vit] *nf Fam* invitation

invitation [ɛ̃vitasjɔ̃] *nf* invitation; **venir à** *ou* **sur l'i. de qn** to come at sb's invitation; **sur i.** by invitation

invite [ɛ̃vit] *nf* (a) *(invitation)* invitation (b) *Ordinat* prompt; **i. du DOS** DOS prompt; **i. du système** system prompt

invité, -e [ɛ̃vite] *nm,f* guest

inviter [ɛ̃vite] **1** *vt* (a) *(convier)* to invite; **i. qn à dîner** to invite *or* to ask sb to dinner (b) **i. qn à faire qch** *(inciter)* to urge sb to do sth; *(prier)* to request sb to do sth; **je vous invite à me suivre** would you be so kind as to follow me
2 *vi (payer)* **ce soir, c'est moi qui invite!** it's on me tonight!
3 s'inviter *vpr* to invite oneself

in vitro [invitro] *adj inv & adv* in vitro

invivable [ɛ̃vivabl] *adj* unbearable

in vivo [invivo] *adj inv & adv* in vivo

invocation [ɛ̃vɔkasjɔ̃] *nf* invocation

involontaire [ɛ̃vɔlɔ̃tɛr] *adj (mouvement, geste)* involuntary; *(erreur, réaction)* unintentional; *(témoin)* unwilling

involontairement [ɛ̃vɔlɔ̃tɛrmɑ̃] *adv* involuntarily, unintentionally

invoquer [ɛ̃vɔke] *vt* (a) *(raison, argument)* to put forward; *(prétexte, excuse)* to plead; *(loi, texte)* to refer to (b) *(Dieu, divinité, esprit)* to invoke; **i. l'aide de qn** to call upon sb's help

invraisemblable [ɛ̃vrɛsɑ̃blabl] *adj* (a) *(hypothèse)* unlikely (b) *(excuses, alibi)* implausible (c) *(extraordinaire)* incredible

invraisemblance [ɛ̃vrɛsɑ̃blɑ̃s] *nf (improbabilité)* unlikelihood; *(d'un récit, d'une excuse)* implausibility; **des invraisemblances** implausibilities

invulnérabilité [ɛ̃vylnerabilite] *nf* invulnerability

invulnérable [ɛ̃vylnerabl] *adj* invulnerable

iode [jɔd] *nm* iodine

iodé, -e [jɔde] *adj (eau, air)* iodized

ion [jɔ̃] *nm* ion

iota [jɔta] *nm inv* iota; **ça n'a pas changé d'un i.** it hasn't changed one iota; **ne pas bouger d'un i.** not to budge an inch

ipso facto [ipsofakto] *adv* ipso facto

Ipsos [ipsos] *nm* = French market research institute

ira, irai, *etc. voir* **aller[1]**

Irak [irak] *nm* l'**I.** Iraq

irakien, -enne [irakjɛ̃, -ɛn] **1** *adj* Iraqi
2 *nm,f* **I., Irakienne** Iraqi

Iran [irɑ̃] *nm* l'**I.** Iran

iranien, -enne [iranjɛ̃, -ɛn] **1** *adj* Iranian
2 *nm (langue)* Iranian
3 *nm,f* **I., Iranienne** Iranian

Iraq [irak] = **Irak**

iraquien, -enne [irakjɛ̃, -ɛn] = **irakien**

irascible [irasibl] *adj Litt* irascible

iriez *etc. voir* **aller[1]**

iris [iris] *nm* (a) *(de l'œil)* iris (b) *(fleur)* iris

irisé, -e [irize] *adj* iridescent

irlandais, -e [irlɑ̃dɛ, -ɛz] **1** *adj* Irish
2 *nm (langue)* Irish
3 *nm,f* **I.** Irishman; **Irlandaise** Irishwoman; **I. du Nord** person from Northern Ireland; **les I.** the Irish

Irlande [irlɑ̃d] *nf* l'**I.** Ireland, Eire; **l'I. du Nord** Northern Ireland, Ulster

IRM [iɛrɛm] *nf Méd (abrév* **imagerie par résonance magnétique***)* MRI

ironie [irɔni] *nf* irony; **l'i. du sort a voulu que...** as fate would have it,...

ironique [irɔnik] *adj* ironic(al)

ironiquement [irɔnikmɑ̃] *adv* ironically

ironiser [irɔnize] *vi* to be ironical (**sur** about)

irradiation [iradjasjɔ̃] *nf Phys & Méd* irradiation

irradier [66] [iradje] **1** *vi (rayons)* to radiate; *(douleur)* to spread
2 *vt* to irradiate

irraisonné, -e [irɛzɔne] *adj* irrational

irrationnel, -elle [irasjɔnɛl] *adj* irrational

irrattrapable [iratrapabl] *adj (retard)* that cannot be made up; *(erreur)* irredeemable

irréalisable [irealizabl] *adj (rêve)* unrealizable; *(projet)* impracticable

irréaliste [irealist] *adj* unrealistic

irréalité [irealite] *nf* unreality

irrecevable [irəsəvabl] *adj (inacceptable)* unacceptable; *Jur (preuve, demande)* inadmissible

irrécupérable [irekyperabl] *adj (argent)* irrecoverable; *(personne)* irredeemable; *(appareil, voiture)* beyond repair

irrécusable [irekyzabl] *adj* (a) *(indéniable) (preuve, signe)* indisputable (b) *Jur (témoignage, juge)* unimpeachable

irréductible [iredyktibl] **1** *adj* (a) *(volonté, optimisme)* indomitable, invincible; *(attachement, fidélité)* unshakeable; *(opposition, ennemi)* implacable (b) *(fracture, fraction)* irreducible
2 *nmf* die-hard

irréel, -elle [ireɛl] **1** *adj* unreal
2 *nm* **l'i.** the unreal; *Gram* **l'i. du présent/passé** the hypothetical present/past

irréfléchi, -e [irefleʃi] *adj* rash

irréfutable [irefytabl] *adj* irrefutable

irrégularité [iregylarite] *nf* (a) *(du sol, d'un terrain)* unevenness; *(du pouls, de traits, d'horaires)* irregularity (b) *(acte)* irregularity

irrégulier, -ère [iregylje, -ɛr] *adj* (a) *(sol, terrain)* uneven; *(rythme, respiration, traits, verbe)* irregular; *(résultats, athlète)* inconsistent (b) *(malhonnête) (procédure, situation)* irregular; **être en situation irrégulière** *(étranger)* not to have one's residence papers in order; *(voyageur)* not to hold a valid ticket

irrégulièrement [iregyljɛrmɑ̃] *adv* irregularly

irréligieux, -euse [irelɪʒjø, -øz] *adj* irreligious

irrémédiable [iremedjabl] *adj (préjudice, perte, problème)* irreparable; *(désastre)* irreversible

irrémissible [iremisibl] *adj Litt* (a) *(impardonnable)* unpardonable (b) *(irrémédiable)* irreversible

irremplaçable [irɑ̃plasabl] *adj* irreplaceable

irréparable [ireparabl] **1** *adj (tort, perte, erreur)* irreparable; *(affront)* unpardonable; *(vêtement, voiture, télévision)* beyond repair
2 *nm* **commettre l'i.** to go beyond the point of no return

irrépressible [irepresibl] *adj* irrepressible

irréprochable [ireprɔʃabl] *adj (personne, conduite)* irreproachable; *(tenue, travail)* impeccable; **d'une propreté i.** impeccably clean

irrésistible [irezistibl] *adj (personne, charme)* irresistible; *(envie, besoin)* compelling

irrésolu, -e [irezɔly] *adj* (a) *(personne)* indecisive; *(pas)* uncertain (b) *(problème)* unresolved

irrespect [irɛspɛ] *nm* disrespect (**envers** towards)

irrespectueux, -euse [irɛspɛktɥø, -øz] *adj* disrespectful (**envers** towards)

irrespirable [irɛspirabl] *adj (air)* unbreathable; *Fig (atmosphère)* unbearable

irresponsable [irɛspɔ̃sabl] **1** *adj* irresponsible
2 *nmf* irresponsible person

irrévérence [ireverãs] *nf* irreverence
irrévérencieux, -euse [ireverãsjø, -øz] *adj* irreverent
irréversible [irevɛrsibl] *adj* irreversible
irrévocabilité [irevɔkabilite] *nf* irrevocability
irrévocable [irevɔkabl] *adj* irrevocable
irrévocablement [irevɔkabləmã] *adv* irrevocably
irrigation [irigasjɔ̃] *nf* irrigation; **l'i. du cerveau** the blood supply to the brain
irriguer [irige] *vt* to irrigate; **le cerveau n'est plus irrigué** the brain is no longer being supplied with blood
irritable [iritabl] *adj* irritable
irritant, -e [iritã, -ãt] *adj* (a) *(personne, comportement)* irritating (b) *(substance)* irritant (**pour** to)
irritation [iritasjɔ̃] *nf aussi Méd* irritation
irrité, -e [irite] *adj* (a) *(énervé)* irritated (**contre** with) (b) *(enflammé)* irritated, inflamed
irriter [irite] **1** *vt (énerver, enflammer)* to irritate
   2 s'irriter *vpr* (a) *(s'énerver)* **s'i. contre qn/de qch** to get irritated with sb/at sth (b) *(s'enflammer)* to become irritated *or* inflamed
irruption [irypsjɔ̃] *nf* (a) *(entrée)* irruption; **faire i. dans** to burst into (b) *(invasion)* invasion (c) *(émergence)* upsurge
ISF [iɛsɛf] *nm inv (abrév* **impôt de solidarité sur la fortune)** wealth tax
islam [islam] *nm* **l'i.** Islam
islamique [islamik] *adj* Islamic
islamiste [islamist] *nmf* Islamic fundamentalist
islamophobe [islamɔfɔb] **1** *adj* Islamophobic
   2 *nmf* Islamophobe
islamophobie [islamɔfɔbi] *nf* Islamophobia
islandais, -e [islãdɛ, -ɛz] **1** *adj* Icelandic
   2 *nm (langue)* Icelandic
   3 *nm, f* **I., Islandaise** Icelander
Islande [islãd] *nf* **l'I.** Iceland
isobare [izɔbar] **1** *adj* isobaric
   2 *nf* isobar
isocèle [izɔsɛl] *adj* isosceles
isolant, -e [izɔlã, -ãt] **1** *adj (contre le froid, en électricité)* insulating; *(contre le bruit)* soundproofing
   2 *nm (contre le froid, en électricité)* insulating material; *(contre le bruit)* soundproofing (material)
isolation [izɔlasjɔ̃] *nf (électrique)* insulation; **i. acoustique** *ou* **phonique** soundproofing; **i. thermique** (thermal) insulation
isolationniste [izɔlasjɔnist] *adj & nmf* isolationist
isolé, -e [izɔle] *adj* (a) *(personne, cas, endroit, maison)* isolated (b) *(protégé) (en électricité, du froid)* insulated; *(du bruit)* soundproofed
isolement [izɔlmã] *nm* (a) *(d'une personne, d'une maison)* isolation (b) *(isolation)* insulation
isolément [izɔlemã] *adv (agir)* in isolation; *(interroger des gens)* individually

isoler [izɔle] **1** *vt* (a) *(séparer)* to isolate (**de** from) (b) *(protéger) (du froid, d'un courant électrique)* to insulate; *(du bruit)* to soundproof
   2 s'isoler *vpr* to isolate oneself
isoloir [izɔlwar] *nm* polling booth
isotherme [izɔtɛrm] **1** *adj* maintained at a constant temperature; **boîte/sac i.** cool box/bag; **bouteille i.** thermos (bottle)
   2 *nf* isotherm
Israël [israɛl] *n* Israel
israélien, -enne [israeljɛ̃, -ɛn] **1** *adj* Israeli
   2 *nm, f* **I., Israélienne** Israeli
israélite [israelit] **1** *adj* Jewish
   2 *nmf* Jew
issu, -e [isy] *adj* **être i. de** *(être originaire de)* to come from; *(résulter de)* to stem from
issue [isy] *nf* (a) *(sortie)* exit; *Fig (solution)* way out; **i. de secours** emergency exit (b) *(fin)* outcome; **à l'i. de** at the end of
Istanbul [istãbul] *n* Istanbul
isthme [ism] *nm* isthmus
Italie [itali] *nf* **l'I.** Italy
italien, -enne [italjɛ̃, -ɛn] **1** *adj* Italian
   2 *nm (langue)* Italian
   3 *nm, f* **I., Italienne** Italian
   4 *nf* **italienne** *Ordinat* **imprimer à l'italienne** to print landscape
italique [italik] **1** *adj* italic
   2 *nm* **en italique(s)** in italics
Ithaque [itak] *nf* Ithaca
itinéraire [itinerɛr] *nm* route, itinerary; **i. bis** = alternative route recommended when roads are highly congested, especially at peak vacation times; **i. touristique** tourist route
itinérance [itinerãs] *nf Tél* roaming
itinérant, -e [itinerã, -ãt] *adj (comédiens, exposition)* traveling; *(ambassadeur)* roving
itou [itu] *adv Fam Vieilli* likewise, too; **et moi i.!** me too!
IUFM [iyɛfɛm] *nm (abrév* **Institut universitaire de formation des maîtres)** ≃ teachers college
IUT [iyte] *nm (abrév* **Institut universitaire de technologie)** = vocational higher-education college
IVG [iveʒe] *nf (abrév* **interruption volontaire de grossesse)** termination (of pregnancy)
ivoire [ivwar] *nm* ivory
ivoirien, -enne [ivwarjɛ̃, -ɛn] **1** *adj* of the Ivory Coast
   2 *nm, f* **I., Ivoirienne** person from the Ivory Coast
ivre [ivr] *adj* drunk; **i. mort** blind drunk; **i. de joie** beside oneself with joy
ivresse [ivrɛs] *nf (ébriété)* drunkenness; *(extase)* exhilaration; **conduite en état d'i.** drunk-driving
ivrogne [ivrɔɲ] *nmf* drunkard
ivrognerie [ivrɔɲri] *nf* drunkenness
ixième [iksjɛm] *adj* umpteenth, nth; **pour la i. fois** for the umpteenth time

J

J, j [ʒi] *nm inv* J, j

j' [ʒ] *voir* **je**

jabot [ʒabo] *nm* (**a**) *(d'oiseau)* crop (**b**) *(de chemise)* frill, ruffle

jacassements [ʒakasmã] *nmpl* *(d'une pie, d'une personne)* chattering

jacasser [ʒakase] *vi (pie, personne)* to chatter

jachère [ʒaʃɛr] *nf* leaving land fallow; **laisser en j.** *(champ)* to leave fallow; *Fig (talent)* to leave undeveloped

jacinthe [ʒasɛ̃t] *nf* hyacinth

jacquard [ʒakar] *adj (pull)* argyle

jacquet [ʒakɛ] *nm* backgammon

jacter [ʒakte] *vi Fam* to gab

Jacuzzi® [ʒakuzi] *nm* Jacuzzi®

jade [ʒad] *nm* (**a**) *(pierre)* jade; **un collier en j.** a jade necklace (**b**) *(objet)* jade object

jadis [ʒadis] *Litt* **1** *adv* in times past, formerly
2 *adj* **au temps j.** in the olden days

jaguar [ʒagwar] *nm* jaguar

jaillir [ʒajir] *vi* (**a**) *(source, liquide)* to gush out; *(étincelles, flammes, foule)* to shoot out; *(lumière)* to flash (**b**) *(rires, cris)* to burst out

jais [ʒɛ] *nm* jet; **(d'un noir) de j.** jet-black

Jakarta [dʒakarta] *n* Jakarta

jalon [ʒalɔ̃] *nm* marker; *Fig (référence)* milestone, landmark; *Fig* **poser des jalons** to pave the way, to prepare the ground

jalonner [ʒalɔne] *vt (marquer) (parcelle, piste d'atterrissage)* to mark out; *(ponctuer) (route, côte)* to line (**de** with); *Fig* to punctuate

jalousement [ʒaluzmã] *adv* jealously

jalouser [ʒaluze] *vt* to be jealous of

jalousie [ʒaluzi] *nf* (**a**) *(sentiment)* jealousy; **éprouver de la j. envers qn** to feel jealous of sb; **être malade de j.** to be green with envy (**b**) *(store)* Venetian blind

jaloux, -ouse [ʒalu, -uz] **1** *adj* jealous (**de** of); **j. comme un tigre** wild with jealousy
2 *nmf* **c'est un j.** he's a jealous man; **faire des j.** to make people jealous

jamaïcain, -e, jamaïquain, -e [ʒamaikɛ̃, -ɛn] **1** *adj* Jamaican
2 *nmf* **J., Jamaïcaine** *ou* **Jamaïquaine** Jamaican

Jamaïque [ʒamaik] *nf* **la J.** Jamaica

jamais [ʒamɛ] *adv* (**a**) *(positif)* ever; **plus que j.** more than ever; **à (tout) j.** for good, for ever; **si j. elle revenait** if she ever came back; **le film le plus drôle que j'aie j. vu** the funniest movie I've ever seen (**b**) *(négatif)* never; **je ne l'ai j. vu** I've never seen him; **il a passé toute sa vie sans j. boire un verre d'alcool** he's gone his whole life without ever touching a drop of alcohol; **j. plus** never again; **j., au grand j., je ne le dirai** I'll never ever tell; **elle n'a j. que dix minutes de retard** she's only ten minutes late; *Fam* **j. de la vie!** not on your life!; *Prov* **j. deux sans trois** things come in threes

jambe [ʒãb] *nf* leg; **jambes nues** bare-legged; **traîner la j.** *(de*

fatigue) to drag one's feet; *(en boitant)* to drag one foot behind one; **à toutes jambes** as fast as one can; **prendre ses jambes à son cou** to take to one's heels; **être dans les jambes de qn** to be in sb's hair; **traiter qn par-dessous** *ou* **par-dessus la j.** to treat sb in an offhand manner; *Fam* **ça me fait une belle j.!** a lot of good that does me!; *Fam* **tenir la j. à qn** to bend sb's ear; **j. de bois** wooden leg

jambière [ʒãbjɛr] *nf* (**a**) *(de sport)* (shin) pad (**b**) *(pour tenir chaud)* legwarmer

jambon [ʒãbɔ̃] *nm* ham; **j. blanc** boiled ham; **j. cru** raw ham; **j. fumé** smoked ham; **j. de Parme** Parma ham; **j. d'York** boiled ham on the bone

jambonneau, -x [ʒãbɔno] *nm* knuckle of ham

jante [ʒãt] *nf* rim

janvier [ʒãvje] *nm* January; **en j., au mois de j.** in January; **nous sommes le 7 j.** it's January 7th; **j'y vais le 7 j.** I'm going on January 7th

Japon [ʒapɔ̃] *nm* **le J.** Japan

japonais, -e [ʒapɔnɛ, -ɛz] **1** *adj* Japanese
2 *nm (langue)* Japanese
3 *nm,f* **J., Japonaise** Japanese; **les J.** the Japanese

jappement [ʒapmã] *nm* yap, yelp; **jappements** yapping, yelping

japper [ʒape] *vi* to yap, to yelp

jaquette [ʒakɛt] *nf* (**a**) *(d'homme)* morning coat; *(de femme)* jacket; *Can (chemise de nuit)* nightdress (**b**) *(de livre)* (dust) jacket, (dust) cover

jardin [ʒardɛ̃] *nm (public)* garden; *(privé)* yard; *Fig* **c'est mon j. secret** I keep it very much to myself; **j. botanique** botanical garden(s); **j. de derrière** backyard; **j. d'enfants** kindergarten; **j. potager** vegetable garden; **j. public** park; **j. zoologique** zoo

jardinage [ʒardinaʒ] *nm* gardening

jardiner [ʒardine] *vi* to do some gardening

jardinet [ʒardinɛ] *nm* small garden

jardinier, -ère [ʒardinje, -ɛr] **1** *nm,f* gardener
2 *nf* **jardinière** (**a**) *(pour balcon)* window box; *(intérieure)* jardinière (**b**) *Culin* **jardinière (de légumes)** mixed vegetables

jargon [ʒargɔ̃] *nm* (**a**) *(argot, de métier)* jargon (**b**) *(langage incompréhensible)* gibberish

jarre [ʒar] *nf* (**a**) *(vase)* (earthenware) jar (**b**) *Can (bocal)* preserving jar

jarret [ʒarɛ] *nm* (**a**) *(de personne)* back of the knee; *(de cheval)* hock (**b**) *(pièce de viande) (de veau)* knuckle; *(de bœuf)* shin

jarretelle [ʒartɛl] *nf* garter

jarretière [ʒartjɛr] *nf* garter

jars [ʒar] *nm* (**a**) *Zool* gander (**b**) *Can* **faire le j.** to show off

jaser [ʒaze] *vi* (**a**) *(médire)* to gossip; **cela va faire j.** that'll set tongues wagging (**b**) *Can (bavarder)* to chatter (**de** about)

jasmin [ʒasmɛ̃] *nm* jasmine

jatte [ʒat] *nf* (**a**) *(petite)* bowl; *(grande)* basin (**b**) *Belg (récipient)* coffee cup; *(contenu)* cup of coffee

jauge [ʒoʒ] nf (**a**) *(instrument de mesure)* gauge; **j. d'essence** gas gauge; **j. de niveau d'huile** oil-level indicator; *(manuelle)* dipstick (**b**) *(de navire)* tonnage

jauger [45] [ʒoʒe] **1** vt (**a**) *(mesurer) (tonneau, réservoir)* to measure the capacity of; *(navire)* to measure the tonnage of (**b**) *Fig (personne, situation)* to size up

2 vi **j. 300 tonneaux** to have a tonnage of 300 tons

jaunâtre [ʒonɑtr] adj yellowish

jaune [ʒon] **1** adj *(couleur, objet); (teint)* sallow; **j. canari** canary yellow; **j. citron** lemon yellow; **j. moutarde** mustard yellow; **j. d'or** golden yellow; **j. paille** straw-colored

2 nm (**a**) *(couleur)* yellow (**b**) **j. d'œuf** (egg) yolk

3 nmf Péj (**a**) *(non gréviste)* scab, strikebreaker (**b**) Can *(lâche)* yellowbelly

4 adv **rire j.** to give a forced laugh

jauni, -e [ʒoni] adj yellowed

jaunir [ʒonir] vt & vi to turn yellow

jaunisse [ʒonis] nf jaundice; Fam Fig **en faire une j.** to get into a state about it

Java® [ʒava] nm Ordinat Java®

java [ʒava] nf Fam *(fête)* **faire la j.** to live it up

Javel [ʒavεl] n voir **eau**

javelot [ʒavlo] nm javelin

jazz [dʒaz] nm jazz

J.-C. *(abrév* **Jésus-Christ)** JC; **av. J.-C.** BC; **ap. J.-C.** AD

je [ʒə]

j' is used before a word beginning with a vowel or h mute.

pron personnel **I**

jean [dʒin] nm *(pantalon)* jeans; *(tissu)* denim; **un j.** (a pair of) jeans; **veste en j.** denim jacket

Jeanne [ʒan] npr **J. d'Arc** Joan of Arc

Jeep® [dʒip] nf Jeep®

Jéhovah [ʒeɔva] npr Jehovah

je-m'en-foutisme [ʒmɑ̃futism] nm très Fam couldn't-care-less attitude

je-m'en-foutiste *(pl* **je-m'en-foutistes)** [ʒmɑ̃futist] nmf très Fam couldn't-care-less type

je-ne-sais-quoi [ʒənsεkwa] nm inv **un j.** a certain something

jérémiades [ʒeremjad] nfpl whining

jerrican(e), jerrycan [dʒerikan, ʒerikan] nm jerry can

Jérusalem [ʒeryzalεm] n Jerusalem

jésuite [ʒezɥit] **1** adj Jesuit; Fig & Péj jesuitical

2 nm Jesuit

Jésus(-Christ) [ʒezy(kri)] npr Jesus (Christ)

jet¹ [ʒε] nm (**a**) *(lancer) (de pierre)* throwing; Fig **faire qch d'un seul j.** to do sth in one go (**b**) *(de liquide, de vapeur)* jet; **premier j.** *(d'un roman)* first draft; **j. d'eau** *(fontaine)* fountain

jet² [dʒεt] nm *(avion)* jet

jetable [ʒətablə] adj disposable

jeté, -e¹ [ʒəte] **1** nm (**a**) *(en danse)* jeté (**b**) **j. de lit** bedspread

2 adj très Fam crazy

jetée² [ʒəte] nf jetty, pier

jeter [42] [ʒəte] **1** vt (**a**) *(lancer)* to throw; *(plus fort)* to fling, to hurl; *(filets)* to cast; **j. qch à qn** to throw sb sth, to throw sth to sb; **j. qn à terre** to throw sb to the ground; **j. qch à terre** ou **par terre** to throw sth on the ground; **j. qn en prison** to throw sb in jail; **j. les bras autour de qn** to throw one's arms around sb; **j. quelques idées sur le papier** to jot down a few ideas; **j. le trouble dans l'esprit de qn** to trouble sb; **ça a jeté un froid** it cast a chill

(**b**) *(se défaire de)* to throw away or out; **j. son argent par les fenêtres** to throw one's money down the drain; Fam **se faire j. (de)** to get thrown out (of)

(**c**) *(émettre) (cri)* to utter; **j. un regard à qn** to glance at sb; **j.**

un coup d'œil (sur qch) to have a quick glance (at sth)

(**d**) *(établir)* **j. les fondements de qch** to lay the foundations for sth

(**e**) *Fam* **ça (en) jette!** it's really something!

2 se jeter vpr (**a**) *(fleuve, rivière)* **se j. dans** to flow into

(**b**) *(personne)* to throw oneself; **se j. dans le vide** *(suicidaire)* to jump; **se j. sur qn** to throw oneself at sb; Fig to pounce on sb; **se j. sur** *(nourriture)* to pounce on; *(occasion)* to jump at; **se j. à l'eau** to plunge into the water; Fig to take the plunge; **se j. par la fenêtre** to throw oneself out of the window; **se j. aux pieds de qn** to throw oneself at sb's feet; Fig **se j. à la tête de qn** *(le draguer)* to throw oneself at sb

jeton [ʒətɔ̃] nm (**a**) *(au jeu)* chip; *(pour téléphone, machine)* token; **j. de présence** *(objet)* token *(issued as voucher for attendance at meeting); (honoraires)* director's fees (**b**) Fam **avoir les jetons** to have the jitters

jeu, -x [ʒø] nm (**a**) *(amusement)* play; **faire qch par j.** to do sth for fun; Fig **entrer en j.** to come into play; Fig **c'est un j. d'enfant** it's child's play; **j. de mots** play on words, pun; **j. de rôles** role-play

(**b**) *(activité)* game; **mettre la balle en j.** to bring the ball into play; Fig **jouer le j.** to play the game; Fig **jouer franc j. (avec qn)** to play fair (with sb); Fig **se prendre au j.** to get caught up in it; Fig **faire le j. de qn** to play into sb's hands; **on aurait beau j. de répondre** it would be quite easy to answer; **j. d'adresse** game of skill; **j. de cartes** card game; **j. électronique** computer game; **le j. de l'oie** = board game similar to snakes and ladders; **les jeux Olympiques** the Olympic Games, the Olympics; **jeux de société** *(charades, devinettes)* parlor games; *(petits chevaux, jeu de l'oie)* board games; **j. télévisé** (television) game show; *(avec questions)* (television) quiz show; **j. vidéo** video game

(**c**) *(au casino)* **le j.** gambling; **se ruiner au j.** to bankrupt oneself gambling; **mettre qch en j.** *(argent, voiture, carrière)* to stake sth; Fig **être en j.** to be at stake; **les jeux sont faits** *(à la roulette)* les jeux sont faits; **faites vos jeux!** place your bets!; **jeux de hasard** games of chance

(**d**) *(cartes en main)* hand; **avoir du j.** to have a good hand; **cacher son j.** to hide one's hand; Fig to keep one's cards close to one's chest; Fig **sortir le grand j.** to pull out all the stops

(**e**) *(au tennis)* game; **j., set et match** game, set and match; **j. Federer** game (to) Federer; **j. blanc** love game

(**f**) *(d'un acteur)* acting; *(d'un musicien)* playing; **j. de jambes** *(d'un boxeur, d'un tennisman)* footwork

(**g**) *(d'outils, de clefs)* set; **j. de boules/quilles** set of bowls/skittles; **j. de cartes** deck of cards; **j. d'échecs** chess set

(**h**) **il y a du j.** *(ça bouge)* there's a bit of play or of a gap; **la vis a** ou **prend du j.** the screw is loose

(**i**) *(mécanisme)* **le j. de l'offre et de la demande** the system of supply and demand

jeu-concours *(pl* **jeux-concours)** [ʒøkɔ̃kur] nm competition

jeudi [ʒødi] nm Thursday; **le j. saint** Maundy Thursday; Fam **la semaine des quatre jeudis,** Can **dans la semaine des trois jeudis** when pigs fly; voir aussi **samedi**

jeun [ʒœ̃] **à jeun 1** adj **être à j.** *(sans avoir mangé ni bu)* not to have eaten or drunk anything; *(pas ivre)* to be sober

2 adv **prendre qch à j.** to take sth on an empty stomach

jeune [ʒœn] **1** adj *(personne, vin, pays)* young; *(apparence, allure)* youthful; *(coiffure, vêtement)* that makes one look young; **être j. d'esprit** to have a youthful outlook; **faire plus j. que son âge** to look younger than one's age; **elle n'est plus toute j.** she's not as young as she was

2 nmf **un j.** a youngster; **une j.** a girl; Fam **un petit j.** a young guy; **les jeunes** young people

3 adv **s'habiller j.** to dress in a youthful style; **ça fait j.** it makes you/her/etc. look young

jeûne [ʒøn] *nm* (a) *(période)* fast; **rompre le j.** to break one's fast (b) *(pratique)* fasting

jeûner [ʒøne] *vi* to fast

jeunesse [ʒœnɛs] *nf* (a) *(période)* youth (b) *(d'apparence, d'esprit)* youthfulness (c) *(jeunes gens)* young people

jeunot, -otte [ʒœno, -ɔt] *Fam* **1** *adj* youngish
2 *nm,f Péj* youngster

JF (a) *(abrév* **jeune fille)** girl (b) *(abrév* **jeune femme)** young woman

JH *(abrév* **jeune homme)** young man

jingle [dʒiŋgəl] *nm* jingle

JO [ʒio] **1** *nm (abrév* **Journal officiel)** = French government publication, ≃ Federal Register
2 *nmpl (abrév* **jeux Olympiques)** Olympic Games

joaillerie [ʒɔajri] *nf* (a) *(magasin)* jewelry store (b) *(bijoux)* jewelry

joaillier, -ère [ʒɔaje, -ɛr] *nm,f* jeweler

job [dʒɔb] *nm Fam* job

jockey [ʒɔkɛ] *nm* jockey

Joconde [ʒɔkɔ̃d] *nf* **la J.** the Mona Lisa

joggeur, -euse [dʒɔgœr, -øz] *nm,f* jogger

jogging [dʒɔgiŋ] *nm* (a) *(vêtement)* sweat suit (b) *(activité)* jogging; *(course)* run; **faire du j.** to go jogging, to jog

Johannesburg [ʒɔanɛsbur] *n* Johannesburg

joie [ʒwa] *nf* joy, delight; **avec j.** *(volontiers)* with pleasure, gladly; *Fam* **c'est pas la j.!** it's no fun!; **faire la j. de qn** to make sb happy; **se faire une j. de faire qch** *(envisager)* to look forward to doing sth; *(faire avec plaisir)* to be delighted to do sth; **faire une fausse j. à qn** to falsely raise sb's hopes; **j. de vivre** joie de vivre

joignable [ʒwaɲabl] *adj* contactable

joignais *etc. voir* **joindre**

joindre [43] [ʒwɛ̃dr] **1** *vt* (a) *(réunir)* to join; **j. les mains** to put one's hands together; *Fam Fig* **j. les deux bouts** to make ends meet (b) *(ajouter)* to add (**à** to); *(dans une lettre, un colis)* to enclose (**à** with); **j. le geste à la parole** to suit the action to the word; **j. l'utile à l'agréable** to combine business with pleasure (c) *(contacter)* to contact
2 se joindre *vpr* **se j. à qn** to join sb; **se j. à qch** to join in sth

joint, -e [ʒwɛ̃, -ɛ̃t] **1** *pp de* **joindre**
2 *adj* **sauter à pieds joints** to jump from a standing position; **les mains jointes** with hands together; **pièces jointes** *(dans une lettre)* enclosures
3 *nm* (a) *(d'étanchéité)* seal; *(articulation)* joint; **j. de culasse** cylinder head gasket; **j. de dilatation** expansion joint (b) *Fam (à fumer)* joint

jointure [ʒwɛ̃tyr] *nf (articulation)* joint

jojo [ʒoʒo] *Fam* **1** *nm voir* **affreux**
2 *adj inv* **ne pas être j.** *(physiquement)* not to look very nice; *(moralement)* not to be very nice

jojoba [ʒoʒoba] *nm* jojoba

joker [ʒɔkɛr] *nm (aux cartes)* joker; *Ordinat* wild card

joli, -e [ʒɔli] **1** *adj* (a) *(personne, ville, voix)* pretty, attractive; **il est j. garçon** he's good-looking; **j. comme un cœur** pretty as a picture; **faire le j. cœur** to flirt (b) *(situation, somme)* nice; **c'est bien j. tout ça mais…** that's all well and good but…; *Fam* **c'est pas j. j.** *(laid)* it's not a pretty sight; *(blâmable)* that's not very nice
2 *nm Ironique* **c'est du j.!** marvelous!

joliment [ʒɔlimã] *adv* (a) *(bien)* nicely; **c'est j. dit** that's nicely put; *Ironique* **te voilà j. arrangé!** you're in a real mess now! (b) *Fam (extrêmement)* really; **elle s'est j. fait engueuler** she got a good telling-off

jonc [ʒɔ̃] *nm (plante)* rush

joncher [ʒɔ̃ʃe] *vt* to strew (**de** with)

jonction [ʒɔ̃ksjɔ̃] *nf* junction

jongler [ʒɔ̃gle] *vi* (a) *(avec des balles)* & *Fig* to juggle (**avec** with) (b) *Can (rêvasser)* to daydream

jonglerie [ʒɔ̃glɔri] *nf aussi Fig* juggling

jongleur, -euse [ʒɔ̃glœr, -øz] *nm,f* juggler

jonquille [ʒɔ̃kij] *nf* daffodil

Jordanie [ʒɔrdani] *nf* **la J.** Jordan

jordanien, -enne [ʒɔrdanjɛ̃, -ɛn] **1** *adj* Jordanian
2 *nm,f* **J., Jordanienne** Jordanian

jos-connaissant [djokɔnɛsã] *nm Can Fam Péj* know-all

jouable [ʒwabl] *adj* playable

joual, -e [ʒwal] *Can* **1** *nm* joual *(French-Canadian dialect)*
2 *adj* **langue jouale** joual

joue [ʒu] *nf (de personne, d'animal)* cheek; **j. contre j.** cheek to cheek; **mettre qn en j.** to take aim at sb; **tenir qn en j.** to keep sb in one's sights; **en j.!** take aim!

jouer [ʒwe] **1** *vt* (a) *(parier)* to stake (**sur** on); *(cheval)* to back, to bet on
(b) *(participer à)* **j. la finale** to play in the final
(c) *(carte)* to play; *(pion, pièce)* to move
(d) *(rôle)* to act, to play; **j. la surprise** to pretend to be surprised; **j. les héros** to play the hero; *Hum* **j. la fille de l'air** to vanish into thin air
(e) *(air)* to play; **j. du Bach** to play (some) Bach
2 *vi* (a) *(s'amuser)* to play; *Fig* **j. sur les mots** to play with words; *Fig* **j. avec les sentiments de qn** to play with sb's feelings; *Fig* **j. avec son avenir** to risk one's future; *Fig* **j. avec le feu** to play with fire; **c'est à qui de j.?** whose turn is it?; *(aux échecs, aux dames)* whose move is it?; *Fig* **maintenant à vous de j.** now it's your turn
(b) *(acteur)* to act; *(troupe)* to perform; **il joue très mal** he's a very bad actor
(c) *(parier)* to gamble; **j. en Bourse** to speculate on the stock market
(d) *(fonctionner)* **j. en faveur/défaveur de qn** to work in sb's favor/against sb; **faire j. un ressort** to release a spring; *Fig* **faire j. ses relations pour obtenir qch** to pull a few strings to get sth
(e) *(bois)* to warp; *(pièce)* to work loose
(f) *Suisse (convenir)* to be alright; **avec un peu de chance ça pouvait j.** with a bit of luck it could work out
3 jouer à *vt ind* (a) *(pratiquer)* to play; **j. au tennis/aux cartes** to play tennis/cards; **j. au docteur** to play (at) doctors and nurses; **j. à la marchande** to play at stores; *Fig* **j. au plus fin** to try to outwit each other
(b) *(parier sur)* **j. aux courses** to bet on horses
4 jouer de *vt ind* **j. du piano/de la harpe** to play the piano/the harp; *Fig* **j. des coudes** to elbow one's way through
5 se jouer *vpr* (a) *(match)* to be played
(b) *(se décider)* **son sort est en train de se j.** his fate is hanging in the balance
(c) **se j. de qn** to trifle with sb; **se j. des lois** to make a mockery of the law; **se j. des difficultés** to make light of difficulties
(d) *(pièce de théâtre, film)* to be on *or* showing

jouet [ʒwɛ] *nm* toy; *Fig* **être le j. des dieux** to be the plaything of the gods

joueur, -euse [ʒwœr, -øz] **1** *nm,f* (a) *(d'un jeu, d'un sport, d'un instrument de musique)* player; **j. de tennis/cartes** tennis/card player; **être beau/mauvais j.** to be a good/bad loser (b) *(au casino)* gambler
2 *adj (enfant, chien)* playful

joufflu, -e [ʒufly] *adj (bébé, angelot)* chubby-cheeked; *(visage)* chubby

joug [ʒu] *nm aussi Fig* yoke

jouir [ʒwir] *vi* (a) *(profiter)* **j. de qch** to enjoy sth (b) *(sexuellement)* to come (c) *(être en possession)* **j. d'une bonne réputation** to have a good reputation; **j. d'une bonne santé** to enjoy good health

jouissance [ʒwisãs] *nf* (**a**) *(plaisir)* enjoyment; *(sexuel)* orgasm (**b**) *Jur (usage)* use

jouisseur, -euse [ʒwisœr, -øz] *nm,f* sensualist

jouissif, -ive [ʒwisif, -iv] *adj très Fam* orgasmic

joujou, -x [ʒuʒu] *nm (langage enfantin)* toy; **faire j.** to play

joule [ʒul] *nm* joule

jour [ʒur] *nm* (**a**) *(clarté)* daylight; **au petit j.** at daybreak; **en plein j.** in broad daylight; *Fig* **au grand j.** publicly; **travailler le** *ou* **de j.** to work days; **j. et nuit** day and night; *Fig* **elle et son mari, c'est le j. et la nuit** she and her husband are like night and day; **elle est belle comme le j.** she's a real beauty; **il fait j.** it's light

(**b**) *(journée)* day; **huit jours** a week; **quinze jours** two weeks; **un j. ou l'autre** one day; **de j. en j.** day by day; **du j. au lendemain** overnight; **nous l'attendons d'un j. à l'autre** we're expecting him/her any day (now); **un de ces jours** one of these days; **un beau j., elle décida de…** one day, she decided to…; **vivre au j. le j.** *(sans faire de projets)* to live from day to day; *(financièrement)* to live from hand to mouth; **mettre qch à j.** to update sth, to bring sth up to date; **tenir qch à j.** to keep sth up to date; **décidément, ce n'est pas mon j.!** it just isn't my day today!; **il y a les jours avec et les jours sans** there are good days and bad days; **le j. de l'an** New Year's Day; **j. de congé** day off; **j. férié** public holiday; **le jour J** D-day; **le j. de Noël** Christmas Day; **j. ouvrable** working day; **j. de repos** day off

(**c**) *(date)* day; **quel j. sommes-nous?** what's the date (today)?; **le j. de mes vingt ans** my twentieth birthday; **il y a six ans j. pour j.** six years ago to the day; **à ce j., nous n'avons toujours pas reçu votre lettre** to date we still have not received your letter

(**d**) *(époque)* **passer des jours heureux** to have a good time; **de nos jours** these days, nowadays; **les beaux jours** the fine days of summer; **pour mes vieux jours** for my old age

(**e**) *(vie)* **donner le j. à un enfant** to give birth to a child; **mettre fin à ses jours** to put an end to one's life; **ses jours ne sont plus en danger** we no longer fear for her life; **il vit le j. à Paris** he was born in Paris; **jusqu'à mon dernier j.** to my dying day

(**f**) *(éclairage)* light; *Fig* **voir qch sous un j. nouveau/sous son vrai j.** to see sth in a new light/in its true light; *Fig* **présenter qch sous un j. favorable** to present sth in a favorable light

(**g**) *(ouverture)* gap

Jourdain [ʒurdɛ̃] *nm* **le J.** the River Jordan

journal, -aux [ʒurnal, -o] *nm* (**a**) *(publication)* paper, newspaper; **j. (télévisé)** (television) news (**b**) *(récit d'événements, d'expériences)* journal; *Ordinat* log; **tenir un j.** to keep a journal; **j. de bord** log (book); **j. intime** journal; **J. officiel** = French government publication, ≃ Federal Register

---

Journal officiel
This bulletin prints information about new laws and summaries of parliamentary debates, and informs the public of any important government business. When new companies are established, they are obliged by law to publish an announcement in the "Journal officiel".

---

journalier, -ère [ʒurnalje, -ɛr] **1** *adj* daily
  2 *nm,f (ouvrier agricole)* day laborer

journalisme [ʒurnalism] *nm* journalism; **j. d'investigation** investigative journalism

journaliste [ʒurnalist] *nmf* journalist; **elle est j. au Monde** she's a journalist at Le Monde; **j. sportif** sports journalist

journalistique [ʒurnalistik] *adj* journalistic

journée [ʒurne] *nf* (**a**) *(par opposition à nuit)* day(time); **pendant la j.** in the daytime, during the day; **dans la j.** in the course of the day; **toute la j.** all day (**b**) *(unité de temps)* day; **j. de travail** *(jour non chômé)* working day; *(quantité de travail)* day's work; **faire la j. continue** *(personne)* to work through lunch; **j. portes ouvertes** open house

journellement [ʒurnɛlmã] *adv* daily

joute [ʒut] *nf (combat médiéval)* joust; *Fig* **joutes oratoires** verbal jousting

jouvence [ʒuvãs] *nf Litt* **cela a été un bain** *ou* **une cure de j.** it has rejuvenated me

jouvenceau, -x [ʒuvãso] *nm Hum* stripling

jouvencelle [ʒuvãsɛl] *nf Hum* maiden

jouxter [ʒukste] *vt* to adjoin

jovial, -e, -als *ou* **-aux, -ales** [ʒɔvjal, -o] *adj* jovial, jolly

jovialité [ʒɔvjalite] *nf* joviality, jolliness

joyau, -x [ʒwajo] *nm aussi Fig* jewel

joyeusement [ʒwajøzmã] *adv* joyfully

joyeux, -euse [ʒwajø, -øz] *adj* joyful; **j. anniversaire!** happy birthday!; **j. Noël!** Merry Christmas!

JT [ʒite] *nm (abrév* **journal télévisé**) TV news

jubilation [ʒybilasjɔ̃] *nf* jubilation

jubilé [ʒybile] *nm* jubilee

jubiler [ʒybile] *vi* to be jubilant; *(méchamment)* to gloat

jucher [ʒyʃe] **1** *vt* to perch (**sur** on)
  2 se jucher *vpr* to perch (**sur** on)

judaïque [ʒydaik] *adj* Jewish; *(loi)* Judaic

judaïsme [ʒydaism] *nm* Judaism

judas [ʒyda] *nm (ouverture)* spyhole, peephole

judéo-chrétien, -enne *(mpl* **judéo-chrétiens**, *fpl* **judéo-chrétiennes**) [ʒydeɔkretjɛ̃, -ɛn] *adj* Judeo-Christian

judiciaire [ʒydisjɛr] *adj (pouvoir, enquête, acte)* judicial; *(aide, autorité)* legal

judicieusement [ʒydisjøzmã] *adv* judiciously

judicieux, -euse [ʒydisjø, -øz] *adj* judicious; **peu j.** injudicious

judo [ʒydo] *nm* judo

judoka [ʒydɔka] *nmf Sport* judoka

juge [ʒyʒ] *nm* judge; **Monsieur le J.** Your Honor; **les juges** the bench; **je vous laisse j.** I'll let you be the judge; *Fig* **être à la fois j. et partie** to sit in judgment on oneself; **j. d'instruction** examining magistrate; **j. de ligne** line judge; **j. de touche** *(au football)* linesman

jugé [ʒyʒe] **au jugé** *adv (tirer)* blind; *(calculer)* roughly

jugement [ʒyʒmã] *nm* (**a**) *Jur (d'une affaire)* trial; **passer en j.** to stand trial (**b**) *Jur (décision)* decision; *(dans des affaires criminelles)* sentence (**c**) *(opinion)* judgment; **porter un j. sur qch** to pass judgment on sth; **j. de valeur** value judgment (**d**) *(discernement)* judgment

jugeote [ʒyʒɔt] *nf Fam* common sense

juger¹ [45] [ʒyʒe] **1** *vt* (**a**) *(affaire, prévenu)* to try; *(demande, litige)* to adjudicate (**b**) *(évaluer, condamner)* to judge (**sur** by); **à toi de j.** it's for you to judge (**c**) *(croire)* **j. que** to consider that; **on le jugeait fou** people thought he was crazy; **j. superflu de faire qch** to consider it superfluous to do sth
  2 juger de *vt ind* to judge; **jugez de ma surprise!** imagine my surprise!; **à en j. par…** judging by…

juger² = **jugé**

jugulaire [ʒygylɛr] *nf* (**a**) *(veine)* jugular (vein) (**b**) *(de casque)* chin strap

juguler [ʒygyle] *vt (rébellion)* to quell; *(inflation, épidémie)* to check

juif, -ive [ʒɥif, -iv] **1** *adj* Jewish
  2 *nm,f* **J., Juive** Jew

juillet [ʒɥijɛ] *nm* July; **le 14 j.** Bastille Day *(day of national celebration in France)*; *voir aussi* **janvier**

La fête du 14 juillet
The celebrations to mark the anniversary of the storming of the Bastille begin on July 13 with outdoor public dances ("les bals du 14 juillet") and firework displays, and continue on the 14th with a military parade in the morning. Firework displays are also held in the evening of "Bastille Day".

juin [ʒɥɛ̃] nm June; voir aussi **janvier**

juke-box [dʒykbɔks, ʒykbɔks] nm inv jukebox

Jules [ʒyl] npr **J. César** Julius Caesar

jules [ʒyl] nm Fam **mon/son j.** (mari, petit ami) my/her man or guy

julienne [ʒyljɛn] nf **j. de légumes** julienne of vegetables (cut into thin strips)

jumbo [dʒœmbo], **jumbo-jet** (pl **jumbo-jets**) [dʒœmbodʒɛt] nm jumbo (jet)

jumeau, -elle, -x, -elles [ʒymo, -ɛl] **1** adj (frère, sœur) twin **2** nm,f twin; (sosie) double; **vrais/faux jumeaux** identical/fraternal twins

jumelage [ʒymlaʒ] nm (de villes) making sister cities

jumelé, -e [ʒymle] adj (maisons) two-family; **villes jumelées** sister cities

jumeler [ʒymle] vt (villes) to make sister cities

jumelles [ʒymɛl] nfpl **(paire de) j.** (pair of) binoculars; **j. de théâtre** opera glasses

jument [ʒymɑ̃] nf mare

jungle [ʒɔ̃gl, ʒœ̃gl] nf aussi Fig jungle

junior [ʒynjɔr] **1** adj (mode, taille) junior **2** nmf Sport junior (19 to 20 years old)

junte [ʒœ̃t] nf junta

jupe [ʒyp] nf skirt; Fam **être dans les** ou **pendu aux jupes de sa mère** to be tied to one's mother's apron strings; **j. droite** straight skirt; **j. plissée** pleated skirt

jupe-culotte (pl **jupes-culottes**) [ʒypkylɔt] nf culottes

jupette [ʒypɛt] nf skirt

Jupiter [ʒypiter] npr (dieu, planète) Jupiter

jupon [ʒypɔ̃] nm petticoat, slip

Jura [ʒyra] nm **le J.** the Jura (Mountains)

jurassique [ʒyrasik] Géol **1** adj Jurassic **2** nm **le J.** the Jurassic period

juré, -e [ʒyre] **1** adj **ennemi j.** sworn enemy **2** nm,f juror; **les jurés** the jury

jurer [ʒyre] **1** vt to swear; **je le jure** I swear; **je te jure que c'est vrai!** I swear it's true!; **j. qch sur la tête de qn** to swear sth on sb's grave; **j'aurais juré qu'il était là** I could have sworn that it was there; **j. de faire qch** to swear to do sth; **ne j. que par** to swear by; Prov **il ne faut j. de rien** you never can tell **2** vi (a) (dire des gros mots) to swear (b) (couleurs, vêtements) to clash (**avec** with) **3 se jurer** vpr (a) (l'un à l'autre) **se j. fidélité** to swear to be faithful to each other (b) (à soi-même) **se j. que** to swear (to oneself) that; **se j. de faire qch** to swear to do sth

juridiction [ʒyridiksjɔ̃] nf (compétence) jurisdiction; (tribunaux) courts

juridique [ʒyridik] adj legal

jurisprudence [ʒyrisprydɑ̃s] nf case law; **faire j.** to set a (legal) precedent

juriste [ʒyrist] nmf legal expert; **j. d'entreprise** company lawyer

juron [ʒyrɔ̃] nm swearword

jury [ʒyri] nm (a) (d'un tribunal) jury (b) (pour l'attribution d'un prix) (panel of) judges; (d'examen) board of examiners

jus [ʒy] nm (a) (de fruits, de légumes) juice; (de viande) juices; **j. d'orange/de fruit** orange/fruit juice; Can Fam **j. de bras** elbow grease; Fam Hum **j. de chaussettes** (café) dishwater (b) Fam (courant électrique) juice; **prendre le j.** to get an electric shock

jusant [ʒyzɑ̃] nm ebb tide

jusque [ʒysk, ʒyskə] prép (a) **jusqu'à** (délimite un espace) as far as; (délimite une mesure) up to; **jusqu'ici** as far as here; **j.-là** as far as there; Fam **s'en mettre j.-là** to stuff oneself; **jusqu'où?** how far?; **avoir de l'eau jusqu'à la taille** to have water up to one's waist; **compter jusqu'à dix** to count (up) to ten; **jusqu'au bout (de la rue)** to the end (of the street); **j. dans les campagnes** right into the countryside; Fig **aller jusqu'au bout d'un raisonnement** to follow an argument through; **aller jusqu'à faire qch** to go so far as to do sth (b) (indique le temps) until, till; **jusqu'ici, jusqu'à maintenant, jusqu'à présent** until now, up to now; **j.-là, jusqu'alors** until then, up to then; **jusqu'à ce que** + subjunctive until, till; **jusqu'à (l'âge de) quinze ans** up to the age of fifteen; **jusqu'à nouvel ordre** until further notice; **jusqu'au jour** ou **moment où…** until the time when…; **si nous remontons jusqu'en** ou **jusqu'à 1800** if we go right back to 1800 (c) (également) **jusqu'à** even

justaucorps [ʒystokɔr] nm (de sport) leotard

juste [ʒyst] **1** adj (a) (équitable) fair (**avec** ou **envers** to); **à j. titre** rightly (b) (exact) (calcul, réponse) right, correct; (raisonnement) sound; (note) right; **arriver à l'heure j.** to arrive right on time; **avez-vous l'heure j.?** do you have the right time? (c) (trop petit) (chaussures, vêtement) tight; **une bouteille pour six, c'est un peu j.** one bottle won't go very far between six people (d) Fam (financièrement) **je suis un peu j. en ce moment** money's a bit tight at the moment **2** adv (a) (avec exactitude) (viser, parler) accurately; (chanter) in tune; Fam **tomber j.** to guess right; **tout j.!** that's right! (b) (précisément) just; **à dix heures j.** on the stroke of ten; **j. au coin/en face/à côté** just or right on the corner/opposite/next door; **arriver j. à temps** to arrive just in time; **ça fait dix euros tout j.** that's ten euros exactly (c) (à peine) just; **c'est tout j. s'il sait lire** he can barely read; **avoir j. le temps (de faire qch)** to have just enough time (to do sth); **ils ont tout j. fini de manger** they've only just finished eating (d) (trop peu) **calculer trop j. (pour)** not to allow enough (for) (e) **au j.** (exactement) exactly

justement [ʒystəmɑ̃] adv (a) (précisément) exactly; **j'allais j. t'appeler** I was just about to call you (b) (avec justesse) rightly (c) (avec justice) justly

justesse [ʒystɛs] nf (a) (précision) (d'une expression, d'une remarque) aptness (b) **de j.** (only) just; **j'ai eu mon train de j.** I (only) just caught my train

justice [ʒystis] nf (a) (équité) justice; **faire** ou **rendre j. à qn** to do justice to sb; **se faire j.** (se venger) to take the law into one's own hands; (se tuer) to take one's own life (b) Jur **la j.** the law; **aller en j.** to go to court; **passer en j.** to stand trial, to appear in court

justicier, -ère [ʒystisje, -ɛr] nm,f righter of wrongs

justifiable [ʒystifjabl] adj justifiable

justificatif, -ive [ʒystifikatif, -iv] **1** adj justificatory; **pièces justificatives** (d'un dossier) supporting documents **2** nm written proof

justification [ʒystifikasjɔ̃] nf (a) (explication) justification (**de** for or of) (b) (preuve) proof (c) Typ & Ordinat justification

justifié, -e [ʒystifje] adj (a) (légitime) justified; **peu j.** unjustified (b) Typ & Ordinat justified; **j. à droite/à gauche** right-/left-justified

justifier [66] [ʒystifje] **1** vt (a) (légitimer, démontrer) to justify (b) Typ & Ordinat to justify; **j. à droite/gauche** to right-/left-justify **2 se justifier** vpr to justify oneself

jute [ʒyt] nm jute; **(toile de) j.** burlap

juter [ʒyte] vi to be juicy

juteux, -euse [ʒytø, -øz] *adj aussi Fam Fig* juicy
juvénile [ʒyvenil] *adj* youthful

juxtaposer [ʒykstapoze] *vt* to juxtapose
juxtaposition [ʒykstapozisjɔ̃] *nf* juxtaposition

K

K, k¹ [ka] *nm inv* K, k

k² (*abrév* **kilo(s)**) k

K7 [kaset] *nf* (*abrév* **cassette**) tape, cassette

Kaboul [kabul] *n* Kabul

kaki¹ [kaki] *adj inv & nm inv* (*couleur*) khaki

kaki² [kaki] *nm* (*arbre, fruit*) persimmon

kaléidoscope [kaleidɔskɔp] *nm aussi Fig* kaleidoscope

kamikaze [kamikaz] *nm* kamikaze; *Fig* **être k.** to have a death wish

kanak, -e [kanak] = **canaque**

kangourou [kãguru] *nm* kangaroo

kapok [kapɔk] *nm* kapok

karaoké [karaɔke] *nm* karaoke

karaté [karate] *nm* karate

karatéka [karateka] *nmf* karate expert

karma [karma] *nm* karma

kart [kart] *nm* (go-)kart

karting [kartiŋ] *nm* karting, go-kart racing; **faire du k.** to go karting

kasher [kaʃɛr] *adj inv Rel* kosher

Katmandou [katmãdu] *n* Katmandu

kayak [kajak] *nm* (a) (*embarcation de sport*) canoe, kayak; **faire du k.** to go canoeing (b) (*esquimau*) kayak

kayakiste [kajakist] *nmf* canoeist

kazakh, -e [kazak] 1 *adj* Kazakh
   2 *nm,f* **K., Kazakhe** Kazakh

Kazakhstan [kazakstã] *nm* **le K.** Kazakhstan

keffieh [kefje] *nm* kaffiyeh

kendo [kɛndo] *nm* kendo

Kenya [kenja] *nm* **le K.** Kenya

kenyan, -e [kenjã, -an] 1 *adj* Kenyan
   2 *nm,f* **K., Kenyane** Kenyan

képi [kepi] *nm* kepi

kératine [keratin] *nf* keratin

kermesse [kɛrmɛs] *nf* (a) (*dans les Flandres*) village fair (b) (*fête de bienfaisance*) (charity) fête

kern [kɛrn] *nm Belg Pol* inner cabinet

kérosène [kerozɛn] *nm* kerosene

ketchup [kɛtʃœp] *nm* (tomato) ketchup

keuf [kœf] *nm très Fam* cop

kg (*abrév* **kilogramme(s)**) kg

KGB [kɑgebe] *nm* **le K.** the KGB

khâgne [kɑɲ] *nf* = second-year humanities class preparing students for the entrance examination for the "École normale supérieure"

khâgneux, -euse [kɑɲø, -øz] *nm,f* = student in the "khâgne"

Khartoum [kartum] *n* Khartoum

khmer, -ère [kmɛr] 1 *adj* Khmer
   2 *nm,f* **K., Khmère** Khmer; **les Khmers rouges** the Khmer Rouge

khôl [kol] *nm* kohl

kibboutz [kibuts] *nm inv* kibbutz

kidnapper [kidnape] *vt* to kidnap

kidnappeur, -euse [kidnapœr, -øz] *nm,f* kidnapper

kidnapping [kidnapiŋ] *nm* kidnapping

kif-kif [kifkif] *adj inv Fam* **c'est k. (bourricot)** it's six of one and half a dozen of the other

kiki [kiki] *nm Fam* (a) (*cou*) **serrer le k. à qn** to wring sb's neck (b) (*langage enfantin*) (*pénis*) willy (c) **c'est parti mon k.!** here we go!

kilo [kilo] *nm* kilo

kilobaud [kilɔbo] *nm Ordinat* kilobaud

kilocalorie [kilɔkalɔri] *nf* kilocalorie

kilogramme [kilɔgram] *nm* kilogram

kilohertz [kilɔɛrts] *nm* kilohertz

kilojoule [kilɔʒul] *nm* kilojoule

kilométrage [kilɔmetraʒ] *nm* (*distance*) ≃ mileage; **k. illimité** (*de voiture de location*) unlimited mileage

kilomètre [kilɔmɛtr] *nm* kilometer; **80 kilomètres à l'heure, 80 kilomètres-heure** ≃ 50 miles per *or* an hour; **taper du texte au k.** to type text straight in (*and leave the formatting etc. until later*); **k. zéro** = point near Notre-Dame from which distances from Paris are measured

kilométrique [kilɔmetrik] *adj voir* **borne**

kilo-octet (*pl* **kilo-octets**) [kilɔɔktɛ] *nm Ordinat* kilobyte

kilovolt [kilɔvɔlt] *nm* kilovolt

kilowatt [kilɔwat] *nm* kilowatt

kilowattheure [kilɔwatœr] *nm Phys* kilowatt-hour

kilt [kilt] *nm* kilt

kimono [kimɔno] *nm* kimono

kiné [kine] *Fam* 1 *nmf* (*médecin*) physio
   2 *nf* (*discipline*) physio

kinésiste [kinezist] *nmf Belg* physiotherapist, physical therapist

kinésithérapeute [keneziterapøt] *nmf* physiotherapy, physical therapist

kinésithérapie [kineziterapi] *nf* physiotherapy, physical therapy

Kinshasa [kinʃasa] *n* Kinshasa

kiosque [kjɔsk] *nm* (*pavillon*) pavilion; (*point de vente*) kiosk; **k. à journaux** newspaper kiosk, newsstand; **k. à musique** bandstand

kippa [kipa] *nf* kippa

kir [kir] *nm* kir (*white wine with blackcurrant liqueur*); **k. royal** kir royal (*champagne with blackcurrant liqueur*)

kirghiz, -e [kirgiz] 1 *adj* Kirg(h)iz
   2 *nm* (*langue*) Kirg(h)iz
   3 *nm,f* **K., Kirghize** Kirg(h)iz

Kirghizistan [kirgizistã] *nm* **le K.** Kirg(h)izia, Kirg(h)izstan

kirsch [kirʃ] *nm* kirsch

kit [kit] *nm* (self-assembly) kit; **en k.** in kit form; *Ordinat* **k. d'extension** *ou* **d'évolution** upgrade kit

kitch [kitʃ] = **kitsch**

kitchenette [kitʃənɛt] *nf* kitchenette

kitsch [kitʃ] *adj inv & nm inv* kitsch

kiwi [kiwi] *nm* (**a**) *(fruit)* kiwi fruit (**b**) *(oiseau)* kiwi

Klaxon® [klaksɔn] *nm* horn; **donner un coup de K.** to blow one's horn, to honk

klaxonner [klaksɔne] **1** *vi* to blow one's horn, to honk
2 *vt* to blow one's horn at, to honk at

klebs [klɛps] = **clebs**

Kleenex® [klinɛks] *nm inv* tissue, Kleenex®

kleptomane [klɛptɔman] *adj & nmf* kleptomaniac

kleptomanie [klɛptɔmani] *nf* kleptomania

klondike [klɔndajk] *nm Can Fam* plum job, high-paying job

km *(abrév* **kilomètre(s))** km

km/h *(abrév* **kilomètres à l'heure, kilomètres-heure)** kph

Ko *nm (abrév* **kilo-octet(s))** K, KB

K-O [kao] **1** *nm inv* knockout
2 *adj inv* (**a**) *(assommé)* knocked out; **mettre qn K-O** to knock sb out (**b**) *Fam (fatigué)* pooped

koala [kɔala] *nm* koala (bear)

kop [kɔp] *nm Belg Sport (club de supporters)* fan club; *(groupement de supporters)* fans

kopeck [kɔpɛk] *nm* kopeck; *Fam* **ça ne vaut pas un k.** it's not worth a bean

koter [kɔte] *vi Belg Fam* to rent a room

kouglof [kuglɔf] *nm* kugelhopf

Koweït [kɔwɛjt, kɔwɛt] *nm* **le K.** Kuwait

koweïtien, -enne [kɔwɛjtjɛ̃, kɔwɛtjɛ̃, -ɛn] **1** *adj* Kuwaiti
2 *nm,f* **K., Koweïtienne** Kuwaiti

krach [krak] *nm* **k. (boursier)** (stock-market) crash

kraft [kraft] *nm voir* **papier**

Kremlin [krɛmlɛ̃] *nm* **le K.** the Kremlin

kumquat [kɔmkwat, kumkwat] *nm (fruit)* kumquat

kung-fu [kuŋfu] *nm inv* kung fu

kurde [kyrd] **1** *adj* Kurdish
2 *nm (langue)* Kurdish
3 *nmf* **K.** Kurd

Kurdistan [kyrdistɑ̃] *nm* **le K.** Kurdistan

kW *(abrév* **kilowatt(s))** kW

K-way® [kawɛ] *nm inv* windbreaker

kWh *(abrév* **kilowattheure(s))** kWh

kyrielle [kirjɛl] *nf (de mots, de fautes)* string; *(d'insultes)* stream; *(d'enfants)* crowd; **elle a toute une k. d'amis** she has a ton of friends

kyste [kist] *nm* cyst

L

L, l¹ [ɛl] *nm inv* L, l

l² *(abrév* **litre(s))** l

l' [l] **1** *art défini voir* **le¹**
  2 *pron personnel voir* **la²**, **le²**

la¹ [la] *art défini voir* **le¹**

la² [la]

l' is used before a word beginning with a vowel or h mute.

pron personnel (femme, fille) her; *(chose, idée)* it; *(animal)* it, her;
je la connais bien I know her well; **il te la rendra demain**
he'll give it back to you tomorrow; **et ta cousine, tu l'as**
vue? have you seen your cousin?; **la voilà** here she/it is

la³ [la] *nm inv (note)* A; *(chantée)* la

là [la] **1** *adv* **(a)** *(là-bas)* there; *(ici)* here; **il est là** *(présent)* he's in;
(près d'ici) he's here; *(là-bas)* he's there; **est-ce que Paul est là?**
(au téléphone) is Paul there?; **je suis là pour ça** that's what I'm
here for; **à quelques mètres de là** a few yards away; **de là à**
Paris, il n'y a que quelques kilomètres it's only a few
miles (away) from Paris; **là en bas/haut** down/up there;
qui va là? who goes there?
  (b) *(à ce point)* **restons-en là** let's leave it at that; **la question**
n'est pas là that's not the point; **c'est bien là le problème**
that's the problem; **je sais bien qu'il est bizarre mais de**
là à dire qu'il est fou... I know he's strange, but to say he's
crazy...; **je ne vois là aucune raison de s'inquiéter** I can't
see any cause for concern; **de là sa réaction** hence his/her
reaction
  (c) *(avec un relatif)* **c'est là que j'habite** that's where I live;
c'est là que j'ai compris that's when I understood
  (d) **ce vin-là** that wine; **ces vins-là** those wines
  2 *exclam* **oh là là!** oh my gosh!; **alors là, je n'aurais jamais**
cru! I'd never have expected that!

là-bas [laba] *adv* over there; *(dans cette région, dans ce pays)*
there

label [labɛl] *nm* **(a)** *Com* quality label **(b)** *Ordinat* **l. de volume**
volume label

labeur [labœr] *nm Litt* labor

labo [labo] *nm Fam* lab; **l. photo** darkroom

laborantin, -e [labɔrɑ̃tɛ̃, -in] *nm,f* laboratory assistant

laboratoire [labɔratwar] *nm* laboratory; **l. d'analyses**
(médicales) medical laboratory

laborieusement [labɔrjøzmɑ̃] *adv* laboriously

laborieux, -euse [labɔrjø, -øz] *adj (difficile)* laborious; *Péj*
(style) labored; *Fam* **il n'a pas encore fini? c'est l.!** hasn't he
finished yet? he's making a big deal out of it!

labour [labur] *nm* **(a)** *(labourage)* plowing **(b)** **labours**
(champs) plowed land

labourage [labura ʒ] *nm* plowing

labourer [labure] *vt* **(a)** *(terre)* to plow **(b)** *Fig (griffer)* to claw;
visage labouré de rides face furrowed with wrinkles

laboureur [laburœr] *nm* plowman

labrador [labradɔr] *nm* labrador

labyrinthe [labirɛ̃t] *nm* maze, labyrinth

lac [lak] *nm* lake; **les Grands Lacs** the Great Lakes; **le l. Baï-**
kal Lake Baikal; **le l. Érié** Lake Erie; **le l. Huron** Lake Huron;
le l. Léman *ou* **de Genève** Lake Geneva; **le l. Michigan**
Lake Michigan; **le l. Ontario** Lake Ontario; **le l. Supérieur**
Lake Superior

lacer [16] [lase] **1** *vt (chaussures)* to tie (up); *(corset)* to lace up
  2 se lacer *vpr (chaussures)* to tie (up); *(corset)* to lace up

lacérer [34] [lasere] *vt (déchirer)* to tear to shreds; *(blesser)* to
lacerate

lacet [lasɛ] *nm* **(a)** *(de chaussure, de corset)* lace; **faire ses lacets**
to tie one's laces **(b)** *(tournant)* sharp bend; **faire des lacets** to
twist and turn **(c)** *(collet)* snare

lâche [laʃ] **1** *adj* **(a)** *(ressort, nœud)* loose; *(vêtement)* loose-fitting; *(discipline)* lax **(b)** *Péj (personne, acte, attitude)* cowardly
  2 *nmf* coward

lâchement [laʃmɑ̃] *adv (sans courage)* in a cowardly way

lâcher [laʃe] **1** *vt* **(a)** *(desserrer) (corde, ceinture)* to loosen
  (b) *(ne plus tenir)* to let go of; *(laisser tomber)* to drop; *Fam Fig*
(cesser d'importuner) to leave alone; **l. prise** to let go; *Fam* **il ne**
m'a pas lâché d'une semelle he stuck to me like a leech; *Fam*
lâche-moi les baskets *ou* **la grappe!** get off my back!; *Can*
Fam **l. son fou** to let one's hair down
  (c) *Fam (abandonner) (associé)* to walk out on; *(ami)* to let
down; *(amant)* to dump; *(emploi)* to chuck; **la voiture nous**
a lâchés the car died on us
  (d) *(distancer) (poursuivant)* to shake off; *(dans une course)* to
leave behind
  (e) *(libérer)* to release; **l. un chien sur qn** to set a dog on sb
  (f) *(laisser échapper) (juron, cri, pet)* to let out; *(sottise, plaisant-*
erie) to come out with; *Fam* **l. le morceau** to spill the beans
  2 *vi (corde, câble)* to break; *(mécanisme, pièce)* to go; *(moteur)* to
die; *(freins)* to fail; *Fig* **ses nerfs ont lâché** he/she broke down
  3 *nm (de colombes, de ballons)* release

lâcheté [laʃte] *nf* cowardice

lâcheur, -euse [laʃœr, -øz] *nm,f Fam* unreliable person

lacis [lasi] *nm (de nerfs, de fils)* network; *(de ruelles)* maze

laconique [lakɔnik] *adj* laconic

laconiquement [lakɔnikmɑ̃] *adv* laconically

lacrymal, -e, -aux, -ales [lakrimal, -o] *adj* tear, *Spéc* la-
chrymal

lacrymogène [lakrimɔʒɛn] *adj voir* **gaz, grenade**

lacté, -e [lakte] *adj (produit)* which contains milk; *(régime)* milk

lactique [laktik] *adj Chim* lactic

lactose [laktoz] *nm Chim* lactose

lacune [lakyn] *nf (dans une liste, ses connaissances, ses souvenirs)*
gap; **avoir des lacunes en qch** to have a patchy knowledge
of sth

lacustre [lakystr] *adj* lakeside

lad [lad] *nm* stable boy

là-dedans [ladədɑ̃] *adv* inside, in there; **il y a l. quelque**
chose que je ne comprends pas there's something here I
don't understand; **elle n'a rien à voir l.!** she has nothing to
do with it!; *Fam* **il y en a l.!** he/she has a lot going on upstairs!

là-dessous [latsu] *adv* underneath, under there; *Fig* **il y a quelque chose l.** there's something behind it

là-dessus [latsy] *adv* on there; *(sur ces mots)* with that; **tout le monde est d'accord l.** everybody agrees about it; **c'est l. que tu dois te concentrer** that's what you have to concentrate on

lagon [lagɔ̃] *nm* lagoon

lagopède [lagɔpɛd] *nm* **l. d'Écosse** grouse

lagune [lagyn] *nf* lagoon

là-haut [lao] *adv* up there; *(à un étage supérieur)* upstairs

La Havane [laavan] *n* Havana

La Haye [laɛ] *n* The Hague

laïc [laik] = **laïque**

laïciser [laisize] *vt* to secularize

laïcité [laisite] *nf (des écoles)* secularity; *Pol* secularism

laid, -e [lɛ, lɛd] *adj* **(a)** *(personne, visage, bâtiment)* ugly; **l. comme un pou** *ou* **à faire peur** as ugly as sin **(b)** *(langage enfantin) (méprisable)* mean, not nice

laideron [lɛdrɔ̃] *nm Péj (fille)* ugly girl; *(femme)* ugly woman

laideur [lɛdœr] *nf* **(a)** *(d'une personne, d'un visage, d'un bâtiment)* ugliness **(b)** *(bassesse)* meanness

laie [lɛ] *nf (animal)* wild sow

lainage [lɛnaʒ] *nm* **(a)** *(étoffe)* woolen fabric **(b)** *(vêtement en laine)* woolen garment; **lainages** woolens

laine [lɛn] *nf* **(a)** *(tissu)* wool; **en l.** woolen; **l. d'agneau** lambswool; **l. vierge** new wool; **(en) pure l.** pure wool **(b)** *(vêtement)* **(petite) l.** sweater **(c)** **l. de verre** glass wool

laineux, -euse [lɛnø, -øz] *adj (tissu)* fleecy; *(mouton, cheveux)* woolly

lainier, -ère [lɛnje, -ɛr] *adj* wool

laïque [laik] **1** *adj (État)* secular; *(école, enseignement)* non-religious

2 *nmf* layman, *f* laywoman

laisse [lɛs] *nf (pour chien)* leash; **tenir un chien en l.** to keep a dog on a leash

laissé-pour-compte, laissée-pour-compte *(mpl* **laissés-pour-compte,** *fpl* **laissées-pour-compte)** [lesepurkɔ̃t] *nm,f* reject

laisser [lese] **1** *vt* **(a)** *(permettre à)* **l. qn faire qch** to let sb do sth; **laissez-le faire!** leave him alone!; **le toit laissait passer la pluie** the roof let the rain in; **l. sécher la peinture** to let the paint dry; *Fig* **laissez-moi rire!** don't make me laugh!; *aussi Fig* **l. tomber qn/qch** to drop sb/sth; *Fam* **l. courir** to leave things alone; **l. dire** to let people talk; **laisse faire!** never mind!

(b) *(quitter) (mari, femme)* to leave; **l. qn tout seul** to leave sb all on their own; **bon, je vous laisse!** well, I'll be off!; **il a laissé une veuve et trois enfants** he left a widow and three children

(c) *(ne pas prendre)* to leave; **l. qch à qn** *(le lui réserver)* to leave sth for sb

(d) *(maintenir)* **l. qch ouvert/fermé** to leave sth open/closed

(e) *(oublier)* to leave

(f) *(traces, impression, souvenir)* to leave

(g) *(ne pas s'occuper de) (personne)* to leave; **laisse, je m'en occupe** don't bother about that, I'll see to it

(h) *(donner)* **l. qch à qn** *(en héritage)* to leave sb sth; *(pour qu'il s'en occupe)* to leave sth to sb; **l. le choix à qn** to give sb a choice; **cela nous laisse le temps de…** that leaves us time to…; **ils ont laissé les enfants à la grand-mère** they left the children with their grandmother; **je vous le laisse pour 50 euros** I'll let you have it for 50 euros

(i) *(perdre) (fortune, vie, membre)* to lose

(j) *Sout* **cela n'a pas laissé de le surprendre** it could not fail to surprise him

2 se laisser *vpr* **se l. décourager/embrasser** to let oneself be discouraged/kissed; **ne te laisse pas faire!** don't let her walk all over you!; **se l. aller** to let oneself go; **se l. aller au découragement** to let oneself get discouraged; **ce vin se laisse boire** this wine is very drinkable; **je me suis laissé dire que…** I hear that…; **se l. vivre** to take life as it comes

laisser-aller [leseale] *nm inv (relâchement)* carelessness; **il y a du l. dans cette maison!** things are a bit sloppy in this house!

laissez-passer [lesepase] *nm inv* pass

lait [lɛ] *nm* **(a)** *(aliment)* milk; **petit l.** whey; *Fig* **boire du petit l.** to lap it up; **l. de brebis/de chèvre/de vache** sheep's/goat's/cow's milk; *Belg* **l. battu** buttermilk; **l. caillé** curd; **l. condensé** condensed milk; **l. cru** unpasteurized milk; **l. demi-écrémé** semi-skim milk; **l. écrémé** skim milk; **l. entier** whole milk; **l. longue conservation** long-life milk; **l. maternel** mother's milk, breast milk; **l. maternisé** baby formula milk; **l. en poudre** powdered milk; **l. de soja** soya milk **(b)** *(cosmétique)* **l. après-soleil** after-sun (lotion); **l. bronzant** suntan lotion; **l. démaquillant** *ou* **de toilette** cleansing lotion

laitage [lɛtaʒ] *nm* dairy product

laitance [lɛtɑ̃s] *nf (de poisson)* milt; *Culin* soft roe

laiterie [lɛtri] *nf* dairy

laiteux, -euse [lɛtø, -øz] *adj (teint)* creamy; *(couleur, lumière)* milky

laitier¹, -ère [letje, -ɛr] **1** *adj* dairy

2 *nm,f (livreur)* milkman, *f* milkwoman

3 *nf* **laitière** *(vache)* dairy cow

laitier² [letje] *nm Ind* slag

laiton [lɛtɔ̃] *nm* brass

laitue [lɛty] *nf* lettuce

laïus [lajys] *nm (discours)* speech

lama¹ [lama] *nm Rel* lama; **le Grand l.** the Dalai Lama

lama² [lama] *nm (animal)* llama

lambda [lãbda] *adj inv (moyen)* average

lambeau, -x [lãbo] *nm (de tissu, de papier, de viande)* scrap; **vêtements en lambeaux** clothes in tatters; **tomber en lambeaux** to fall to pieces

lambin, -e [lãbɛ̃, -in] *Fam* **1** *adj* slow

2 *nm,f* slowpoke

lambiner [lãbine] *vi Fam* to dawdle

lambris [lãbri] *nm (en bois)* paneling; *(en marbre, en stuc)* lining

lambrissé, -e [lãbrise] *adj (de bois)* paneled; *(de marbre, de stuc)* lined

lambswool [lãbswul] *nm* lambswool; **en l.** lambswool

lame [lam] *nf* **(a)** *(d'épée, de couteau)* blade; *(épée)* sword; *Fig* **une fine l.** a fine swordsman; **visage en l. de couteau** hatchet face; **l. de rasoir** razor blade **(b)** *(bande) (de métal, de verre, de parquet)* strip; *(de store)* slat **(c)** *(vague)* wave; **l. de fond** groundswell

lamé, -e [lame] **1** *adj* lamé; **l. or** gold lamé

2 *nm* lamé; **en l.** lamé

La Mecque [lamɛk] *n* Mecca

lamelle [lamɛl] *nf* **(a)** *(de métal, de verre)* thin strip; *Culin* **couper en (fines) lamelles** to cut into (wafer-)thin slices **(b)** *(microscope)* cover glass

lamentable [lamãtabl] *adj* appalling, awful; *(personne)* hopeless, pathetic

lamentablement [lamãtabləmã] *adv (échouer)* miserably

lamentations [lamãtasjɔ̃] *nfpl* **(a)** *(cris, pleurs)* wailing **(b)** *Péj (plaintes)* moaning, complaining

lamenter [lamãte] **se lamenter** *vpr* to moan; **se l. sur qch** to bemoan sth

laminage [laminaʒ] *nm (du métal)* rolling; **l. à chaud/à froid** hot-/cold-rolling

laminer [lamine] *vt* **(a)** *(métal)* to roll **(b)** *Fig (revenus)* to erode; *(parti politique)* to annihilate

laminoir [laminwar] *nm Ind* rolling mill

lampadaire [lɑ̃padɛr] *nm* (**a**) *(d'intérieur)* floor lamp (**b**) *(réverbère)* lamppost

lampe [lɑ̃p] *nf* (**a**) *(appareil d'éclairage)* lamp; **l. à alcool** spirit lamp; **l. de bureau** desk lamp; **l. de chevet** bedside lamp; **l. à pétrole** oil lamp; **l. de poche** flashlight (**b**) *Fam* **s'en mettre plein la l.** to have a good blowout

lampée [lɑ̃pe] *nf Fam* gulp

lampe-tempête (*pl* **lampes-tempête**) [lɑ̃ptɑ̃pɛt] *nf* hurricane lamp

lampion [lɑ̃pjɔ̃] *nm* paper lantern

lampiste [lɑ̃pist] *nm* *(subalterne)* underling

lamproie [lɑ̃prwa] *nf* lamprey

lance [lɑ̃s] *nf* (**a**) *(pique)* spear (**b**) *(tuyau)* **l. d'incendie** fire hose

lancée [lɑ̃se] *nf* **continuer sur sa l.** to keep going; **j'ai fait les exercices 5 et 6, et sur ma l. j'ai aussi fait le 7** I did exercises 5 and 6, and while I was at it I did 7 as well

lance-flammes [lɑ̃sflam] *nm inv* flamethrower

lancement [lɑ̃smɑ̃] *nm* (**a**) *(d'une fusée, d'un projet, d'un produit)* launch(ing) (**b**) *Ordinat (d'impression)* start; *(de programme)* running

lance-missiles [lɑ̃smisil] *nm inv* missile launcher

lance-pierre (*pl* **lance-pierres**) [lɑ̃spjɛr] *nm* slingshot; *Fam Fig* **manger avec un l.** to wolf one's food down; *Fam Fig* **être payé avec un l.** to be paid peanuts

lancer [16] [lɑ̃se] **1** *vt* (**a**) *(projeter)* to throw (**à** to); *(flèche)* to shoot; *(fusée)* to launch; *(bombe)* to drop; *(étincelles)* to shoot out; *Fig (idée, proposition)* to throw out; *(remarque)* to come out with; *(plaisanterie)* to crack; *(juron)* to let out; **l. un coup d'œil à qn** to dart *or* to shoot a glance at sb; **l. le poids** to put the shot

(**b**) *(envoyer) (signaux de détresse, SOS)* to send out

(**c**) *(projet, produit, artiste)* to launch; *(mode)* to start; *Fin* **l. un emprunt** to issue a bond

(**d**) *(faire démarrer) (moteur)* to start (up); **être lancé** *(dans une course, dans un travail)* to have got going; **l. qn sur un sujet** to start sb (off) on a subject

(**e**) *Ordinat (impression)* to start; *(programme)* to run, to start (up)

2 *nm* (**a**) **(pêche au) l.** rod-and-reel fishing

(**b**) *Sport* **l. du javelot/du disque/du marteau** throwing the javelin/the discus/the hammer; **l. du poids** putting the shot; **l. franc** *(au basket)* free throw

3 se lancer *vpr* (**a**) *(se jeter)* **se l. dans le vide** to throw oneself off; **se l. en avant** to rush forward; **se l. à la poursuite de qn** to rush off in pursuit of sb

(**b**) *(s'engager)* **se l. dans** *(affaire, discussion, aventure)* to embark on; *(dépenses)* to get involved in; *(domaine)* to launch out into

(**c**) *(se faire connaître)* to make a name for oneself

lance-roquettes [lɑ̃srɔkɛt] *nm inv* rocket launcher

lance-torpilles [lɑ̃storpij] *nm inv* torpedo tube

lanceur, -euse [lɑ̃sœr, -øz] *nm,f (au base-ball)* pitcher; **l. de javelot/disque/marteau** javelin/discus/hammer thrower; **l. de poids** shot putter

lancinant, -e [lɑ̃sinɑ̃, -ɑ̃t] *adj (douleur)* shooting; *(souvenir, air, musique)* haunting; *(regret)* nagging

landau [lɑ̃do] *nm (voiture d'enfant)* baby carriage

lande [lɑ̃d] *nf* moor, heath

langage [lɑ̃gaʒ] *nm* (**a**) *(langue, vocabulaire)* language; *Fig* **changer de l.** to change one's tune; **l. chiffré** cipher, code (**b**) *Ordinat* language; **l. de description de page** page-description language; **l. d'imprimante par pages** page-printer language; **l. d'interrogation** query language; **l. machine** machine language; **l. naturel** natural language; **l. à objets** object-oriented language; **l. de programmation** program-

ming language; **l. utilisateur** user language

lange [lɑ̃ʒ] *nm (couche)* diaper; *Vieilli* **langes** swaddling clothes

langer [45] [lɑ̃ʒe] *vt (mettre une couche à)* to put a diaper on; *Vieilli* to wrap in swaddling clothes

langoureusement [lɑ̃gurøzmɑ̃] *adv* languorously

langoureux, -euse [lɑ̃gurø, -øz] *adj* languorous

langouste [lɑ̃gust] *nf* crayfish

langoustine [lɑ̃gustin] *nf* langoustine, Dublin Bay prawn

langue [lɑ̃g] *nf* (**a**) *(organe)* tongue; **tirer la l. à qn** to stick one's tongue out at sb; *Fig* **j'ai tiré la l.** *(peiné)* it was hard going; **avoir la l. bien pendue** to have the gift of the gab; **ne pas avoir la l. dans sa poche** never to be at a loss for words; **donner sa l. au chat** to give up; **tu as avalé** *ou* **perdu ta l.?** has the cat got your tongue?; *Culin* **l. de bœuf** ox tongue (**b**) *(langage, style, jargon)* language; **peuples/pays de l. anglaise** English-speaking people/countries; **parler la l. de bois** to come out with clichés; **l. étrangère** foreign language; **l. maternelle** native language, mother tongue; **l. morte** dead language; **l. d'oc** = medieval French dialect spoken in Southern France; **l. d'oïl** = medieval French dialect spoken in Northern France; **langues vivantes** *(matière)* modern languages (**c**) *(personne)* **une mauvaise l.** a backbiter; **une l. de vipère** a spiteful gossip (**d**) *(bande)* **l. de terre** strip of land

langue-de-chat (*pl* **langues-de-chat**) [lɑ̃gdəʃa] *nf* = light finger cookie

languedocien, -enne [lɑ̃gdɔsjɛ̃, -ɛn] **1** *adj* of the Languedoc

2 *nm,f* **L., Languedocienne** person from the Languedoc

languette [lɑ̃gɛt] *nf (de bois, de métal, de chaussure)* tongue

langueur [lɑ̃gœr] *nf* (**a**) *(apathie)* listlessness (**b**) *(mélancolie, rêverie)* languor

languir [lɑ̃gir] *vi* (**a**) *Litt ou Hum (dépérir)* to languish (**b**) *(attendre avec impatience)* **ne nous faites pas l.** don't keep us in suspense; *Litt* **l. de faire qch** to long to do sth (**c**) *(conversation)* to be flagging

lanière [lanjɛr] *nf (de sac, de sandale)* strap; *(de fouet)* lash; **découper qch en lanières** to cut sth into strips

lanoline [lanɔlin] *nf* lanolin

La Nouvelle-Orléans [lanuvɛlɔrleɑ̃] *n* New Orleans

lanterne [lɑ̃tɛrn] *nf* (**a**) *(lampe)* lantern; *Fig* **éclairer la l. de qn** to enlighten sb; **l. chinoise** Chinese lantern (**b**) *(de véhicule)* parking light

lanterner [lɑ̃tɛrne] *vi Fam* to dawdle; **faire l. qn** to keep sb hanging around

Laos [laos] *nm* **le L.** Laos

laotien, -enne [laosjɛ̃, -ɛn] **1** *adj* Laotian

2 *nm,f* **L., Laotienne** Laotian

lapalissade [lapalisad] *nf* statement of the obvious

laper [lape] *vt* to lap up

lapidaire [lapidɛr] *adj (style, formule)* concise, succinct

lapidation [lapidasjɔ̃] *nf* stoning

lapider [lapide] *vt (mettre à mort)* to stone (to death); *Fig (critiquer)* to lambast(e)

lapin [lapɛ̃] *nm* rabbit; **manteau en (peau de) l.** rabbitskin coat; **poser un l. à qn** to stand sb up; **mon petit l.** sweetheart; **l. de garenne** wild rabbit; *Fam* **un chaud l.** a horny devil; *Can Fam* **en criant l.** in a flash

lapine [lapin] *nf* doe (rabbit)

lapis [lapis], **lapis-lazuli** [lapislazyli] *nm inv* lapis lazuli

lapon, -one *ou* **-onne** [lapɔ̃, -ɔn] **1** *adj* Lapp

2 *nm,f* **L., Lapone** *ou* **Laponne** Lapp, Laplander

Laponie [lapɔni] *nf* **la L.** Lapland

laps [laps] *nm* **un l. de temps** a period of time; **un l. de temps de trois heures** a period of three hours

lapsus [lapsys] *nm (oral)* slip of the tongue; *(écrit)* slip of the pen; **faire un l.** to make a slip (of the tongue/pen); **un l. révélateur** a Freudian slip

laquais [lakɛ] *nm* footman; *Fig & Péj* lackey

laque [lak] **1** *nf* (**a**) *(vernis)* lacquer (**b**) *(pour les cheveux)* hair spray (**c**) *(peinture)* gloss (paint)
2 *nm (objet)* piece of lacquerwork; **des laques** lacquerware, lacquerwork

laquelle [lakɛl] *voir* **lequel**

laquer [lake] *vt* (**a**) *(vernir)* to lacquer (**b**) *(cheveux)* to lacquer (**c**) *(peindre)* to paint with gloss

larbin [larbɛ̃] *nm Fam* flunkey

larcin [larsɛ̃] *nm (vol)* petty theft

lard [lar] *nm* (**a**) *(du porc) (viande)* bacon; *(gras)* fat; *Fig* **se demander si c'est du l. ou du cochon** to wonder what to make of it; **l. fumé** smoked bacon; **l. maigre** bacon (**b**) *Fam (graisse)* **faire du l.** to sit around and get fat; **rentrer dans le l. à qn** to lay into sb

larder [larde] *vt Culin* to lard; *Fig* **l. qn de coups de couteau** to hack at sb with a knife; **l. un texte de citations** to pepper a text with quotations

lardon [lardɔ̃] *nm* (**a**) *Culin* piece of chopped bacon (**b**) *très Fam (enfant)* kid

large [larʒ] **1** *adj* (**a**) *(route, porte, chaussures)* wide; *(vêtement)* loose-fitting; *(visage, nez, geste)* broad; **l. d'épaules** broad-shouldered; **l. de deux mètres** ≃ six feet wide; **terme employé dans son sens l.** term used in its broad sense; **avoir l'esprit l., être l. d'esprit** to be broad-minded (**b**) *(considérable)* large; *(ressources)* ample; **dans une l. mesure** to a large extent (**c**) *(généreux)* generous
2 *nm* (**a**) *(espace)* **être au l.** to have plenty of room (**b**) *(haute mer)* open sea; **au l. de** off; **prendre le l.** to take to the open sea; *Fig (s'enfuir)* to beat it (**c**) *(largeur)* **faire trois mètres de l.** ≃ to be ten feet wide
3 *adv* **compter l.** to allow for more

largement [larʒəmɑ̃] *adv* (**a**) *(répandu, critiqué)* widely (**b**) *(abondamment) (récompenser, payer, servir)* generously; *(dépasser)* by a long way; **avoir l. de quoi vivre** to have easily enough to live on; **avoir l. le temps** to have plenty of time; **c'est l. suffisant, ça suffit l.** it's more than enough

largesse [larʒɛs] *nf* (**a**) *(générosité)* generosity (**envers** towards) (**b**) **largesses** *(dons)* generous gifts

largeur [larʒœr] *nf* (**a**) *(dimension)* width, breadth; *(de voie ferrée)* gauge; **en l., dans la l.** widthwise; **les policiers barraient la rue sur toute sa l.** the policemen blocked off the whole width of the street; *Rad* **l. de bande** bandwidth; *Ordinat* **l. de papier** paper width (**b**) *Fig* **l. d'esprit** *ou* **de vues** broadmindedness

largué, -e [large] *adj Fam (qui ne comprend plus)* lost

larguer [large] *vt* (**a**) *(amarres)* to cast off; *(cordage)* to loose; *(voile)* to unfurl (**b**) *(par avion) (parachutiste, vivres, bombe)* to drop (**c**) *Fam (abandonner)* to dump, to drop; **il a tout largué pour partir vivre aux Caraïbes** he dropped everything and went to live in the Caribbean

larme [larm] *nf* (**a**) *(pleur)* tear; **larmes de joie** tears of joy; **avoir facilement la l. à l'œil** to be easily moved to tears; **avoir les larmes aux yeux** to have tears in one's eyes; **en larmes** in tears; **larmes de crocodile** crocodile tears (**b**) *(petite quantité)* drop

larmoyant, -e [larmwajɑ̃, -ɑ̃t] *adj* (**a**) *(pleurnicheur) (voix, ton)* tearful (**b**) *Péj (histoire, film, sentimentalité)* slushy

larmoyer [32] [larmwaje] *vi* (**a**) *(yeux)* to water (**b**) *Péj (personne)* to snivel

larron [larɔ̃] *nm* **s'entendre comme larrons en foire** to be as thick as thieves

larve [larv] *nf* (**a**) *(de batracien, de poisson)* larva; *(d'insecte)* grub (**b**) *Fam (personne apathique)* wimp

larvé, -e [larve] *adj (guerre, conflit)* latent

laryngite [larɛ̃ʒit] *nf Méd* laryngitis

laryngologie [larɛ̃gɔlɔʒi] *nf Méd* laryngology

laryngologiste [larɛ̃gɔlɔʒist], **laryngologue** [larɛ̃gɔlɔg] *nmf Méd* throat specialist, *Spéc* laryngologist

larynx [larɛ̃ks] *nm Anat* larynx

las, lasse [lɑ, lɑs] *adj Litt* weary; **être l. de qch/de faire qch** to be weary of sth/of doing sth

lasagnes [lazaɲ] *nfpl* lasagne

lascar [laskar] *nm Fam* rascal

lascif, -ive [lasif, -iv] *adj* lascivious

lascivement [lasivmɑ̃] *adv* lasciviously

laser [lazɛr] *nm* laser

lassant, -e [lɑsɑ̃, -ɑ̃t] *adj* tiresome

lasser [lɑse] **1** *vt* to tire
2 se lasser *vpr* **se l. (de qch/de faire qch)** to get tired (of sth/of doing sth)

lassitude [lɑsityd] *nf* weariness

lasso [laso] *nm* lasso; **prendre un animal au l.** to lasso an animal

latent, -e [latɑ̃, -ɑ̃t] *adj* latent; **à l'état l.** latent

latéral, -e, -aux, -ales [lateral, -o] *adj (entrée, rue, vent, choc)* side

latéralement [lateralmɑ̃] *adv (se déplacer)* sideways; *(être situé)* at the side

latex [latɛks] *nm* latex

latin, -e [latɛ̃, -in] **1** *adj* Latin; *(langue)* Romance
2 *nm* Latin; **l. de cuisine** dog Latin; *Fig* **j'y perds mon l.** I can't make head or tail of it

latiniste [latinist] *nmf (spécialiste)* Latinist; *(étudiant)* Latin student

latino [latino] *nmf Fam* Latino

latino-américain, -e (*mpl* **latino-américains,** *fpl* **latino-américaines**) [latinoamerikɛ̃, -ɛn] **1** *adj* Latin-American
2 *nm, f* **L., Latino-Américaine** Latin-American

latitude [latityd] *nf* (**a**) *Géog* latitude; **à 30° de l. nord** at latitude 30° north; **sous ces latitudes** in these latitudes (**b**) *(liberté)* latitude, scope; **avoir/donner à qn toute l. pour agir** to have/to give sb total freedom of action

latrines [latrin] *nfpl* latrines

latte [lat] *nf* lath; *Fam* **donner un coup de l. à qn** to give sb a kick

lattis [lati] *nm* lathing

laudanum [lodanɔm] *nm* laudanum

lauréat, -e [lɔrea, -at] **1** *adj* (prize)winning
2 *nm, f* (prize)winner

laurier [lɔrje] *nm* (**a**) *(plante)* laurel; *Culin* bay leaves (**b**) *Fig (gloire)* **lauriers** laurels; **se reposer** *ou* **s'endormir sur ses lauriers** to rest on one's laurels; **être couvert de lauriers** to be covered with glory

laurier-rose (*pl* **lauriers-roses**) [lɔrjeroz] *nm* oleander

lavable [lavabl] *adj* washable; **l. en machine/à la main** machine-/hand-washable

lavabo [lavabo] *nm* (**a**) *(cuvette)* washbowl (**b**) **lavabos** *(toilettes)* restrooms

lavage [lavaʒ] *nm* washing; **l. de cerveau** brainwashing; **faire subir un l. de cerveau à qn** to brainwash sb; **faire un l. d'estomac à qn** to pump sb's stomach (out)

lavande [lavɑ̃d] **1** *nf (fleur)* lavender; **(eau de) l.** lavender water
2 *adj inv* **(bleu) l.** lavender blue

lavandière [lavɑ̃djɛr] *nf* (**a**) *(blanchisseuse)* washerwoman (**b**) *(oiseau)* wagtail

lave [lav] *nf* lava

lave-autos [lavoto] *nm inv Can* carwash

lave-glace (*pl* **lave-glaces**) [lavglas] *nm* windshield washer

lave-linge [lavlɛ̃ʒ] *nm inv* washing machine

lave-mains [lavmɛ̃] *nm inv* small washbowl

lavement [lavmɑ̃] *nm* enema

laver [lave] **1** *vt* (**a**) *(nettoyer)* to wash; *(plaie)* to bathe; **l. qch à l'eau froide** to wash sth in cold water; **il faut l. son linge sale en famille** one shouldn't wash one's dirty linen in public (**b**) *(disculper)* **l. qn d'une accusation/de tout soupçon** to clear sb of an accusation/of all suspicion (**c**) *(venger)* **l'affront a été lavé dans le sang** the insult was paid for in blood

2 se laver *vpr* (**a**) *(se nettoyer)* to wash (oneself), to wash up; **se l. les dents** to clean *or* to brush one's teeth; **se l. les cheveux/les mains** to wash one's hair/one's hands; *Fig* **je m'en lave les mains** I wash my hands of it (**b**) *(pouvoir être lavé)* **se l. à la main/à la machine** to be hand-/machine-washable

laverie [lavri] *nf* **l. automatique** Laundromat®

lavette [lavɛt] *nf* (**a**) *(de vaisselle)* dishcloth (**b**) *Belg & Suisse (gant de toilette)* washcloth (**c**) *Fam Fig (homme)* drip

laveur, -euse [lavœr, -øz] *nm,f* washer; **l. de vitres** window cleaner

lave-vaisselle [lavvɛsɛl] *nm inv* dishwasher

lave-vitre (*pl* **lave-vitres**) [lavvitr] *nm* windshield washer

lavis [lavi] *nm* (**a**) *(procédé)* washing (**b**) *(dessin)* wash drawing

lavoir [lavwar] *nm* (**a**) *(établissement)* **l. (public)** (public) washhouse (**b**) *(bassin)* washtub (**c**) *Belg (blanchisserie)* **l. (automatique)** self-service laundry

lavomatic [lavomatik] *nm* Laundromat®

laxatif, -ive [laksatif, -iv] *adj & nm* laxative

laxisme [laksism] *nm* laxness

laxiste [laksist] **1** *adj* lax

2 *nmf* lax person

layette [lɛjɛt] *nf* baby clothes

le¹, la, les [lə, la, le]

> **l'** is used instead of **le** or **la** before a word beginning with a vowel or h mute.

article défini (**a**) *(pour définir les noms)* the; **le soleil** the sun; **la lune** the moon; **l'étoile** the star; **les planètes** the planets; **le pull que je me suis acheté** the sweater I bought myself; **le Paris de 1900** Paris in 1900, the Paris of 1900; **oh, la jolie robe!** what a lovely dress!; **debout, les enfants!** get up, children!

(**b**) *(avec des notions ou des généralités)* **le français** French; **la biologie** biology; **l'amour** love; **l'homme et la femme** man and woman; **the chien est l'ami de l'homme** a dog is a man's best friend; **aider les pauvres** to help the poor; **fumer la pipe** to smoke a pipe

(**c**) *(avec les noms de lieux)* **la France** France; **les États-Unis** the United States; **le mont Blanc** Mont Blanc; **les Alpes** the Alps; **la Seine** the Seine

(**d**) *(avec les noms de personnes)* **la reine d'Angleterre** the Queen of England; **le roi Henri IV** King Henry IV; **le Docteur Goron** Doctor Goron

(**e**) *(avec les parties du corps)* **avoir les yeux verts** to have green eyes; **avoir mal à la gorge** to have a sore throat; **hausser les épaules** to shrug one's shoulders; **se laver les mains** to wash one's hands

(**f**) *(avec un adjectif)* **je préfère le rouge** I prefer the red one

(**g**) *(distributif)* **huit euros le mètre** eight euros a meter; **20 euros de l'heure** 20 euros an hour

(**h**) *(dans un complément de temps)* **le dimanche, il ne travaille pas** he doesn't work on Sundays; **il va à l'école le matin** he goes to school in the mornings; **il y fait vraiment froid l'hiver** it's really cold there in the winter; **je n'ai rien mangé de la journée** I haven't eaten all day; **Paris, le 9 novembre 1997** *(dans une lettre)* Paris, November 9, 1997; **je suis arrivé le 10** I arrived on the 10th

le² [lə]

> **l'** is used before a word beginning with a vowel or h mute.

pron personnel (**a**) *(homme, garçon)* him; *(chose, idée)* it; *(animal)* it, him; **elle l'admire** she admires him; **je te le rendrai**

demain I'll give it back to you tomorrow; **et lui, tu le connais?** do you know him?; **le voici** here it/he is (**b**) *(remplace une proposition)* **elle me l'a dit** she told me; **il me l'a confirmé** he confirmed it (**c**) *(remplace un adjectif, un nom)* **est-ce qu'elle est disponible? – oui, je crois qu'elle l'est** is she available? – yes, I think she is; **jaloux, il l'est sans aucun doute** he's undoubtedly jealous; **son frère est médecin, il voudrait l'être aussi** his brother is a doctor and he'd like to be one too

leader [lidœr] *nm* leader

leasing [lizin] *nm* leasing; **acheter une auto en l.** to buy a car on a leasing basis

Le Caire [ləkɛr] *n* Cairo

Le Cap [ləkap] *n* Cape Town

lèche [lɛʃ] *nf très Fam* bootlicking; **faire de la l.** to be a bootlicker

lèche-bottes [lɛʃbɔt] *Fam* **1** *adj inv* **elle est l.** she's a bootlicker

2 *nmf inv* bootlicker

lèche-cul [lɛʃky] *nm inv Vulg* brown-nose

lécher [34] [leʃe] **1** *vt* (**a**) *(avec la langue)* to lick; *Fam* **l. les bottes à qn** to lick sb's boots (**b**) *(fignoler) (travail, style)* to polish (**c**) *(effleurer) (sujet: vagues)* to lap against; *(sujet: flammes)* to lick

2 se lécher *vpr* **se l. les doigts** to lick one's fingers

lèche-vitrines [lɛʃvitrin] *nm Fam* window-shopping; **faire du l.** to go window-shopping

leçon [ləsɔ̃] *nf* (**a**) *(cours, contenu)* lesson; **leçons de chant** singing lessons; **l. de choses** general science *(in elementary school)*; **l. particulière** private lesson; **le bricolage en dix leçons** home improvement in ten easy lessons (**b**) *(conseil)* **faire la l. à qn** to give sb a lecture; **donner une l. à qn** to teach sb a lesson; **je n'ai pas de l. à recevoir de toi** I don't need your advice; **que cela te serve de l.!** let that be a lesson to you!

lecteur, -trice [lɛktœr, -tris] **1** *nm,f* (**a**) *(personne qui lit)* reader (**b**) *(dans l'édition)* (publisher's) reader (**c**) *Univ* foreign-language assistant

2 *nm* (**a**) *(dispositif)* **l. de cassettes** cassette player; **l. de CD** CD player; **l. de DVD** DVD player; **l. optique** optical reader (**b**) *Ordinat* **l. (de disquettes)** (disk) drive, floppy (disk) drive; **l. de bandes** tape drive; **l. de CD-ROM** *ou* **de disque optique** CD-ROM drive; **l. de disque dur** hard disk drive; **l. MP3** MP3 player; **l. Zip®** Zip® drive

lecteur-encodeur (*pl* **lecteurs-encodeurs**) [lɛktœr-ɑ̃kɔdœr] *nm Ordinat* reader-encoder

lectorat [lɛktɔra] *nm* (**a**) *Univ* assistantship (**b**) *(lecteurs)* readership

lecture [lɛktyr] *nf* (**a**) *(action de lire)* reading; **faire la l. à qn** to read aloud to sb; *Pol* **en deuxième l.** at the second reading (**b**) *(ce qu'on lit)* reading; **elle m'a apporté de la l.** she brought me something to read; **avoir de mauvaises lectures** to read the wrong things; **livre de l.** reading book (**c**) *(interprétation)* reading (**d**) *Ordinat* read(ing); **l. optique** optical reading; **l. au scanneur** scan; **en l. seule** in read-only mode; **l. sur disque** reading to disk

ledit, ladite [lədi, ladit] *(mpl* **lesdits** [ledi]*, fpl* **lesdites** [ledit]*) adj* the aforementioned

légal, -e, -aux, -ales [legal, -o] *adj* legal

légalement [legalmɑ̃] *adv* legally

légalisation [legalizasjɔ̃] *nf* legalization; *(de signature)* authentication

légaliser [legalize] *vt (rendre légal)* to legalize; *(authentifier)* to authenticate

légalité [legalite] *nf* (**a**) *(de mesure, décision)* legality (**b**) *(situation légale)* **la l.** the law; **agir en toute l.** to act within the law

légataire [legatɛr] *nmf* legatee; **l. universel** sole legatee

légendaire [leʒɑ̃dɛr] *adj* legendary

légende [leʒɑ̃d] *nf* (a) *(histoire, fable)* legend; *Fig (mensonge)* fairy tale; **entrer dans la l.** to become a legend; **de l.** *(personnage, pays)* fairytale (b) *(d'un dessin, d'une photo)* caption; *(d'une carte)* key

léger, -ère [leʒe, -ɛr] **1** *adj* (a) *(de peu de poids)* light; **l. comme une plume** as light as a feather; **avoir le cœur l.** to be light-hearted (b) *(blessure, amélioration, nuance)* slight; *(brise, vin, parfum)* light; *(tabac)* mild; *(thé, café)* weak; **il y a eu quelques blessés légers** some people were slightly injured (c) *(insuffisant) (preuves, arguments)* lightweight; *Fam* **ses résultats sont un peu légers** his grades are a little on the low side (d) *(désinvolte) (personne)* thoughtless; *(en amour)* fickle; **femme légère** *ou* **de mœurs légères** loose woman

2 *nf* **à la légère** *(agir, parler)* thoughtlessly; **prendre qch à la légère** to make light of sth

3 *adv* **je vais manger l.** I'll have a light meal; **s'habiller l.** to wear light clothes

légèrement [leʒɛrmɑ̃] *adv* (a) *(habillé)* lightly (b) *(un peu)* slightly; **ça sent l. le moisi** there's a slight smell of mildew; **pourrais-tu l. baisser le volume?** could you turn the volume down a little *or* slightly? (c) *(avec désinvolture) (agir)* thoughtlessly

légèreté [leʒɛrte] *nf* (a) *(d'un objet, d'un danseur, d'une démarche)* lightness (b) *(faiblesse) (d'une blessure, d'une nuance)* slightness; *(d'un vin)* lightness (c) *(désinvolture)* thoughtlessness; **avec l.** *(agir, parler)* thoughtlessly (d) *(en amour)* fickleness; *(des mœurs)* looseness

légiférer [34] [leʒifere] *vi* to legislate (**sur** on)

légion [leʒjɔ̃] *nf* legion; *Fig (multitude)* huge number; **ils sont l.** they are legion; **la L. (étrangère)** the Foreign Legion; **la L. d'honneur** the Legion of Honor

> **Légion d'honneur**
>
> Intended to reward not only acts of military bravery but also outstanding civilian achievements, the Legion of Honor is the highest distinction that can be conferred by the French state. It can be awarded regardless of the nationality of its recipients. It is divided into five ranks ("chevalier", "officier", "commandeur", "grand officier" and "grand-croix"). The order of the Legion of Honor is currently made up of one-third civilians and two-thirds soldiers. Among the most recent recipients of this award are the 22 players of the victorious French soccer team in the 1998 World Cup.

légionnaire [leʒjɔnɛr] *nm* (a) *Hist* legionary (b) *(à la Légion étrangère)* legionnaire

législateur, -trice [leʒislatœr, -tris] *Jur* **1** *nm,f* legislator

2 *nm (corps législatif)* legislature

3 *adj* legislative

législatif, -ive [leʒislatif, -iv] **1** *adj* legislative; **le pouvoir l.** the legislature

2 *nm* **le l.** legislative power

3 *nfpl* **les législatives** the legislative elections

législation [leʒislasjɔ̃] *nf* legislation

législature [leʒislatyr] *nf* (a) *(durée)* term of office (b) *(corps)* legislature

légiste [leʒist] *nm* jurist

légitime [leʒitim] *adj* (a) *(légal) (pouvoir, enfant)* legitimate; *(action)* lawful; *(propriétaire)* legal; *(héritier)* rightful (b) *(juste) (récompense, motif, désir)* legitimate (c) *(justifié) (colère, action)* justified; **l. défense** self-defense; **elle était en état de l. défense** she was acting in self-defense

légitimement [leʒitimmɑ̃] *adv* legitimately; *Jur* lawfully

légitimer [leʒitime] *vt* (a) *(enfant, union)* to legitimize (b) *(action, demande)* to justify (c) *(titre, pouvoir)* to recognize

légitimité [leʒitimite] *nf* legitimacy

legs [lɛ, lɛg] *nm* (a) *Jur* legacy, bequest; **faire un l. à qn** to leave sb a legacy (b) *Fig (héritage)* legacy

léguer [34] [lege] *vt* (a) *Jur* to bequeath (**à** to) (b) *(tradition, qualité)* to pass on (**à** to)

légume [legym] **1** *nm* (a) *(aliment)* vegetable; **légumes verts** green vegetables; **légumes secs** pulses (b) *Fam Fig (personne végétative)* vegetable

2 *nf Fam* **grosse l.** big shot

leitmotiv [lajtmɔtif, lɛtmɔtif] *nm* leitmotiv

Léman [lemɑ̃] *nm* **le lac L.** Lake Geneva

lendemain [lɑ̃dmɛ̃] *nm* (a) *(jour suivant)* **le l.** the next day; **le l. matin/soir** the next morning/evening; **le l. de la bataille** the day after the battle (b) *(avenir)* **penser au l.** to think of the future; **des lendemains prometteurs** a promising future; **sans l.** *(succès, aventures)* short-lived (c) *(période qui suit)* **au l. de la guerre/de ce scandale** soon after the war/this scandal

lent, -e [lɑ̃, lɑ̃t] *adj* slow; **être l. à comprendre** to be slow to understand; **avoir l'esprit l.** to be slow-witted

lente [lɑ̃t] *nf* nit

lentement [lɑ̃tmɑ̃] *adv* slowly; **l. mais sûrement** slowly but surely

lenteur [lɑ̃tœr] *nf* slowness; **avec l.** slowly; **les lenteurs de la justice** the slowness of the law

lentille [lɑ̃tij] *nf* (a) *(plante)* lentil; **l. d'eau** duckweed (b) *(en optique)* lens; **lentilles de contact** contact lenses

léopard [leɔpar] *nm* *(animal)* leopard; *(fourrure)* leopard skin

LEP [ɛlape, lɛp] *nm* *Anciennement (abrév* **lycée d'enseignement professionnel)** vocational high school

lèpre [lɛpr] *nf* leprosy

lépreux, -euse [leprø, -øz] **1** *adj* leprous

2 *nm,f* leper

lequel, laquelle [ləkɛl, lakɛl] *(mpl* **lesquels** [lekɛl], *fpl* **lesquelles** [lekɛl])

> **lequel** and **lesquel(le)s** contract with **à** to form **auquel** and **auxquel(le)s**, and with **de** to form **duquel** and **desquel(le)s**.

1 *pron relatif (personne)* who; *(après une préposition)* whom; *(chose)* which; **il était avec sa sœur, laquelle m'a reconnu** he was with his sister, who recognized me; **l'actrice à laquelle je pense** the actress (that) I'm thinking of *or* of whom I'm thinking; **le stylo avec l. j'écris** the pen I'm writing with *or* with which I'm writing

2 *adj relatif* **j'ai vu son adversaire, l. adversaire est impressionnant** I've seen his/her opponent, he's impressive; **auquel cas** in which case

3 *pron interrogatif* which (one)

les [le] **1** *art défini voir* **le**[1]

2 *pron personnel* them; **l. voilà** here they are

lesbien, -enne [lɛsbjɛ̃, ɛn] **1** *adj* lesbian

2 *nf* **lesbienne** lesbian

lèse-majesté [lɛzmaʒɛste] *nf inv* **crime de l.** high treason, crime of lese-majesty

léser [34] [leze] *vt* (a) *(désavantager) (personne)* to wrong; *(intérêts)* to harm; **la partie lésée** the injured party (b) *Méd* to injure

lésiner [lezine] *vi* to skimp (**sur** on); **ne pas l. sur les moyens** not to spare any expense

lésion [lezjɔ̃] *nf* lesion

lesquels, lesquelles [lekɛl] *voir* **lequel**

lessivable [lesivabl] *adj* washable

lessivage [lesivaʒ] *nm* washing

lessive [lesiv] *nf* (a) *(produit) (en poudre)* washing powder; *(liquide)* liquid detergent (b) *(action de laver)* **faire la l.** to do the laundry; **j'ai fait trois lessives ce matin** I've done the laundry three times this morning (c) *(linge propre)* laundry

lessivé, -e [lesive] *adj Fam* washed out

lessiver [lesive] *vt* (**a**) *(nettoyer)* to wash (**b**) *Fam (fatiguer)* to wear out

lessiveuse [lesivøz] *nf* (**a**) *Anciennement* boiler *(for clothes)* (**b**) *Belg (machine à laver)* washing machine

lest [lɛst] *nm (de bateau, ballon)* ballast; **lâcher du l.** to discharge ballast; *Fig (faire des concessions)* to make concessions

leste [lɛst] *adj* (**a**) *(agile)* nimble (**b**) *(grivois)* risqué, raunchy

lestement [lɛstəmã] *adv (avec agilité)* nimbly

lester [lɛste] *vt* (**a**) *(bateau, ballon)* to ballast (**b**) *Fam (poche, portefeuille)* to stuff

letchi [lɛtʃi] *nm* lychee

léthargie [letarʒi] *nf* lethargy

léthargique [letarʒik] *adj* lethargic

letton, -onne *ou* **-one** [lɛtɔ̃, -ɔn] **1** *adj* Latvian
2 *nm (langue)* Latvian
3 *nm,f* **L., Letonne** *ou* **Letone** Latvian

Lettonie [lɛtɔni] *nf* **la L.** Latvia

lettre [lɛtr] *nf* (**a**) *(de l'alphabet)* letter; **l. majuscule/minuscule** upper-case/lower-case letter; **écrire qch en toutes lettres** to write sth out in full; **au pied de la l.** literally; **à la l.** *(suivre, exécuter)* to the letter; **il fut surréaliste avant la l.** he was a surrealist before the word had been invented; **rester l. morte** to remain a dead letter; **gagner ses lettres de noblesse** to prove one's/its worth
(**b**) *(missive)* letter; **l. d'accompagnement** cover letter *(sent with other documents)*; **l. de change** bill of exchange; **l. de motivation** cover letter *(sent with job application)*; **l. ouverte (à)** open letter (to); **l. recommandée** registered letter; *Fam* **c'est passé comme une l. à la poste** it went off without a hitch; *Fam* **la nouvelle est passée comme une l. à la poste** the news was received without any fuss
(**c**) **lettres** *(littérature)* literature; *(à l'université)* humanities; **homme/femme de lettres** man/woman of letters; **avoir des lettres** to be well-read; **faculté de lettres** humanities department; **lettres classiques** classics; **lettres modernes** *(à l'université)* French

lettré, -e [letre] **1** *adj* (**a**) *(cultivé)* well-read (**b**) *Belg (sachant lire et écrire)* **il est l.** he can read and write
2 *nm,f* (**a**) *(personne cultivée)* well-read person (**b**) *Belg (personne sachant lire et écrire)* = person who can read and write

leu [lø] *nm* **à la queue l. l.** in single file

leucémie [løsemi] *nf* leukemia; **avoir une l.** to have leukemia

leucocyte [løkɔsit] *nm* leucocyte

leur¹, leurs [lœr] **1** *adj possessif* their; **l. chien** *(il y a un chien)* their dog; *(chacun a son chien)* their dogs; **leurs enfants** their children; **l. père et l. mère** their mother and father; **un de leurs amis** one of their friends, a friend of theirs; *Fam* **ils ont eu l. vendredi** they got Friday off (work)
2 *pron possessif* **le l., la l., les leurs** theirs; *(en insistant)* their own; **ils te prêtent le l.** you can borrow theirs; **ils n'en ont pas besoin, ils ont le l.** they don't need it, they've got their own
3 *nm* **il faut qu'ils y mettent du l.** they have to do their share
4 *nmpl* **les leurs** *(leur famille)* their family; **nous serons des leurs ce soir** we'll be joining them tonight

leur² [lœr] *pron personnel* to them; **donne-l. ta carte de visite** give them your business card; **je le l. ai montré** I showed it to them

leurre [lœr] *nm* (**a**) *(à la chasse)* decoy (**b**) *(illusion)* illusion

leurrer [lœre] **1** *vt (tromper)* to delude
2 **se leurrer** *vpr* to delude oneself (**sur** about)

levage [ləvaʒ] *nm* lifting; **appareil de l.** lifting apparatus

levain [ləvɛ̃] *nm* leaven; **pain au/sans l.** leavened/unleavened bread

levant [ləvã] **1** *adj m* **soleil l.** rising sun; **au soleil l.** at sunrise
2 *nm* (**a**) *Litt* **le l.** the east (**b**) **le L.** the Levant (**c**) *Belg Fam* **bien/mal l.** in a good/bad mood

levé, -e [ləve] **1** *adj* (**a**) *(en l'air) (main, poing)* raised (**b**) *(personne, soleil)* up
2 *nm (de terrain)* survey

levée [ləve] *nf* (**a**) *(d'une interdiction, de sanctions)* lifting; *(d'une séance)* close; *(d'un siège)* raising; *(de scellés)* breaking (**b**) *(de troupes)* levying (**c**) *(de lettres)* collection (**d**) *(aux cartes)* trick; **faire une l.** to take a trick (**e**) *(remblai)* levee (**f**) **l. de boucliers** general outcry; **l. du corps** taking the body from the house *(for the funeral)*; **l. d'écrou** release from prison

lever¹ [46] [ləve] **1** *vt* (**a**) *(objet)* to lift, to raise; **l. son verre (à qn/qch)** to raise one's glass (to sb/sth)
(**b**) *(bras, main, jambe)* to raise, to lift; **l. la tête** to look up; **l. les yeux au ciel** to raise one's eyes to heaven; **l. les bras au ciel** to throw up one's hands; **l. la main sur qn** to raise one's hand to sb; **l. le doigt** to put one's hand up; **il n'a pas levé le petit doigt** he didn't lift a finger; *Fam* **l. le pied** *(ralentir)* to slow down
(**c**) *(faire cesser) (embargo, peine, interdiction)* to lift; *(difficulté, doute, ambiguïté)* to remove; *(séance)* to close
(**d**) *(débusquer) (perdrix)* to flush; *très Fam (femme)* to pull; **l. un lièvre** to start a hare; *Fig* to open a can of worms
(**e**) *(faire sortir du lit) (enfant, malade)* to get up
(**f**) *(collecter) (courrier, impôts)* to collect
(**g**) *(enrôler) (troupes, armée)* to raise, to levy
(**h**) *(plan)* to draw
2 *vi* (**a**) *(blé, grain)* to shoot
(**b**) *(pâte)* to rise
3 **se lever** *vpr* (**a**) *(se mettre debout)* to stand up, to get up; **se l. de sa chaise** to get up from one's chair; **se l. de table** to leave the table
(**b**) *(quitter le lit)* to get up; *Fam* **se l. du pied gauche** to get out of bed on the wrong side
(**c**) *(apparaître) (soleil, lune)* to rise; *(vent)* to get up; *(jour)* to break
(**d**) *(s'éclaircir) (brouillard, brume)* to lift, to clear
(**e**) *(monter) (rideau de théâtre)* to go up, to rise

lever² [ləve] *nm* (**a**) *(du lit)* getting up; **demain, l. six heures trente** tomorrow, get out of bed at six thirty; **au l., buvez un jus d'orange** first thing in the morning, have a drink of orange juice (**b**) *(apparition)* **le l. du jour** daybreak; **le l. du soleil** sunrise (**c**) **l. de rideau** *(début du spectacle)* curtain up; *(première partie)* curtain raiser (**d**) *(de terrain)* survey

lève-tard [lɛvtar] *nmf inv Fam* late riser

lève-tôt [lɛvto] *nmf inv Fam* early riser

lève-vitre *(pl* **lève-vitres)** [lɛvvitr] *nm (manuel)* window winder; *(automatique)* window control

levier [ləvje] *nm aussi Fig* lever; **faire l.** to act as a lever; **l. de commande** control lever; *Fig* **être aux leviers de commande** to be in control; **l. (de changement) de vitesse** stick shift

lévitation [levitasjɔ̃] *nf* levitation; **être en l.** to be levitating

lèvre [lɛvr] *nf* (**a**) *(de la bouche)* lip; **un cigare aux lèvres** with a cigar in his/her mouth; **le sourire aux lèvres** with a smile on her lips; **manger du bout des lèvres** to pick at one's food; **rire du bout des lèvres** to force a laugh; **accepter du bout des lèvres** to accept grudgingly; *Fig* **nous étions tous suspendus à ses lèvres** we were all hanging on her every word (**b**) *(de la vulve)* **lèvres** labia; **les grandes/petites lèvres** the labia majora/minora (**c**) *(bord) (de plaie)* lip; *(de cratère)* rim

levrette [ləvrɛt] *nf* greyhound bitch

lévrier [levrije] *nm* greyhound; **l. afghan** Afghan hound

levure [ləvyr] *nf* yeast; **l. de boulanger** fresh *or* baker's yeast; **l. chimique** baking powder

lexical, -e, -aux, -ales [lɛksikal, -o] *adj* lexical

lexicographe [lɛksikɔgraf] *nmf* lexicographer

lexicographie [lɛksikɔgrafi] *nf* lexicography

lexique [lɛksik] *nm* (**a**) *(dictionnaire)* lexicon; *(glossaire)* glossary (**b**) *(mots d'un auteur)* vocabulary

lézard [lezar] *nm (animal)* lizard; *(cuir)* lizard skin

lézarde [lezard] *nf* crack

lézarder [lezarde] **1** *vt* to crack

    2 *vi Fam* to lounge in the sun

    3 se lézarder *vpr* to crack

liaison [ljɛzɔ̃] *nf* **(a)** *(dans les transports)* **l. aérienne/maritime/ferroviaire/routière** air/sea/rail/road link; **toutes les liaisons Paris-Téhéran sont suspendues** all services between Paris and Teheran have been suspended **(b)** *Tél* link; **l. radio/téléphonique** radio/telephone link; **l. par satellite** satellite link; **établir une l. radio** to establish radio contact; *Ordinat* **l. par modem** modem link; *Ordinat* **l. spécialisée** dedicated line **(c)** *(entre des personnes)* contact; **assurer la l. entre deux personnes/services** to liaise between two people/departments; **être en l. avec qn** to be in contact with sb; **travailler en l. (étroite) avec qn** to work (closely) with sb **(d)** *(relation amoureuse)* (love) affair **(e)** *(enchaînement logique)* connection **(f)** *Ling* liaison *(sounding of final consonant before initial vowel sound)*; **faire la l.** to make the liaison

liane [ljan] *nf* creeper

liant, -e [ljɑ̃, -ɑ̃t] **1** *adj* sociable

    2 *nm Tech* binder

liasse [ljas] *nf (de lettres, de papiers)* bundle; *(de billets)* wad

Liban [libɑ̃] *nm* **le L.** (the) Lebanon

libanais, -e [libanɛ, -ez] **1** *adj* Lebanese

    2 *nm,f* **L., Libanaise** Lebanese; **les L.** the Lebanese

libations [libasjɔ̃] *nfpl* libations; **faire des l.** *(boire)* to drink copious amounts (of alcohol)

libellé [libele] *nm* wording

libeller [libele] *vt (document, acte, contrat)* to word; **l. un chèque à l'ordre de** to make out a check to

libellule [libelyl] *nf* dragonfly

libéral, -e, -aux, -ales [liberal, -o] **1** *adj* **(a)** *Pol & (aux idées larges)* liberal **(b)** *Écon* free-market

    2 *nm,f Pol* Liberal

libéralisation [liberalizasjɔ̃] *nf* **(a)** *(d'un régime, des mœurs)* liberalization **(b)** *Écon* deregulation

libéraliser [liberalize] **1** *vt* **(a)** *(régime, mœurs)* to liberalize **(b)** *Écon* to deregulate

    2 se libéraliser *vpr (régime)* to become more liberal; *(mœurs)* to become freer

libéralisme [liberalism] *nm* **(a)** *Pol* liberalism **(b)** *Écon* free-market economics

libéralité [liberalite] *nf* **(a)** *(générosité)* generosity **(b)** *(cadeau)* generous gift; **vivre des libéralités de ses amis** to live off the generosity of one's friends

libérateur, -trice [liberatœr, -tris] **1** *adj* liberating

    2 *nm,f* liberator

libération [liberasjɔ̃] *nf* **(a)** *(mise en liberté) (d'un prisonnier)* release; *(d'un soldat)* discharge; **l. conditionnelle** (release on) parole **(b)** *(affranchissement)* liberation **(c)** *(fin de l'Occupation)* **la L.** the Liberation *(of France from the Germans in 1944-45)* **(d)** *(d'énergie, d'une substance)* release

libéré, -e [libere] **1** *adj* liberated; **jeune homme l. des obligations militaires** young man who has carried out his national service duties

    2 *nm,f* released prisoner

libérer [34] [libere] **1** *vt* **(a)** *(rendre sa liberté à) (otage, prisonnier)* to free, to release; *(pays, peuple)* to liberate **(b)** *(laisser partir) (élèves, étudiants)* to let go; *(soldat)* to discharge **(c)** *(soulager)* **l. qn d'un souci** *ou* **d'un poids** to take a weight off sb's mind **(d)** *(rendre disponible) (appartement, chambre d'hôtel)* to vacate **(e)** *(débloquer) (prix)* to free; *(cran de sûreté)* to release; *(instincts, passions)* to unleash; **l. le passage** to clear the way **(f)** *(décharger)* **l. qn de qch** *(dette)* to free sb from sth; *(engagement)* to release sb from sth **(g)** *(émettre) (substance, énergie)* to release

    2 se libérer *vpr* **(a)** *(s'affranchir)* to free oneself *(de* from) **(b)** *(se rendre disponible)* **je tâcherai de me l. ce jour-là** I'll try and be free that day; **je n'ai pas pu me l. plus tôt** I couldn't get away any earlier; **il y a un poste qui vient de se l.** a job vacancy has just come up

Liberia [liberja] *nm* **le L.** Liberia

libérien, -enne [liberjɛ̃, -ɛn] **1** *adj* Liberian

    2 *nm,f* **L., Libérienne** Liberian

libertaire [libɛrter] *adj & nmf* libertarian

liberté [libɛrte] *nf* **(a)** *(condition)* freedom, liberty; **en l.** *(fugitif)* at large; *(animal)* in the wild; **rendre sa l. à qn/un animal** to let sb/an animal go; **reprendre sa l.** to regain one's freedom; **mettre qn en l.** to set sb free; **(mise en) l. provisoire** *ou* **sous caution** (release on) bail; **l. conditionnelle** parole; **l. surveillée** probation; **mettre qn en l. provisoire/conditionnelle/surveillée** to release sb on bail/parole/probation **(b)** *(droit de l'individu)* freedom, liberty; **l., égalité, fraternité** liberty, equality, fraternity; **l. d'expression** freedom of expression *or* speech; **l. d'opinion** freedom of opinion; **l. de la presse** freedom of the press **(c)** *(absence de contrainte)* freedom; **l. d'entreprise** free enterprise; **avoir toute l. d'action** to have complete freedom of action; **avoir toute l. pour faire qch** to have complete freedom to do sth; **en toute l.** *(s'exprimer, agir)* freely; **prendre la l. de faire qch** to take the liberty of doing sth **(d)** *(familiarités)* **prendre** *ou* **se permettre des libertés avec** to take liberties with

libertin, -e [libɛrtɛ̃, -in] **1** *adj (personne)* dissolute; *(livre, propos)* licentious

    2 *nm,f* libertine

libertinage [libɛrtinaʒ] *nm* licentiousness

libidineux, -euse [libidinø, -øz] *adj* lustful

libido [libido] *nf* libido

libraire [librɛr] *nmf* bookseller

librairie [librɛri] *nf (magasin)* bookstore; *(activité)* bookselling

librairie-papeterie *(pl* **librairies-papeteries)** [librɛripapetri] *nf* bookstore and stationer's

libre [libr] *adj* **(a)** *(non soumis) (personne, pays)* free; **être l. de faire qch** to be free to do sth; **l. à vous de le faire** you're quite at liberty to do it; **donner l. cours à son enthousiasme/son imagination** to give one's enthusiasm/imagination free rein; **l. de** *(souci, contrainte, préjugé)* free from; **l. arbitre** free will; **l. pensée** free thinking; **l. penseur** free thinker **(b)** *(disponible) (personne, siège)* free; *(appartement, chambre)* available; *(toilettes)* vacant; **je n'ai pas eu une minute de l. aujourd'hui** I haven't had a spare minute today; **être l. comme l'air** to be as free as a bird; **avoir les mains libres** to have one's hands free; *Fig* to have a free hand; **l. de suite** *(dans une annonce)* available immediately; **la ligne n'est pas l.** the line's busy **(c)** *(non bloqué) (route)* clear; *Fig* **la voie est l.** the coast is clear **(d)** *(privé)* **enseignement/école l.** independent Catholic education/school; **radio l.** independent radio **(e)** *(non réglementé) (prix)* free; *(honoraires)* unrestricted; **la l. entreprise** free enterprise; **il pratique les honoraires libres** there are no restrictions on his fees

libre-échange [librefãʒ] *nm* free trade

librement [libromã] *adv* freely

libre-service *(pl* **libres-services)** [libroservis] *nm* **(a)** *(principe)* self-service; **station-service en l.** self-service gas station **(b)** *(magasin)* self-service store; *(restaurant)* self-service restaurant

Libreville [librovil] *n* Libreville

Libye [libi] *nf* **la L.** Libya

libyen, -enne [libjɛ̃, -ɛn] **1** *adj* Libyan

    2 *nm,f* **L., Libyenne** Libyan

lice [lis] *nf* **entrer en l.** to enter the fray

licence [lisɑ̃s] *nf* (**a**) *Univ* (bachelor's) degree; **l. ès** *ou* **de lettres/ès** *ou* **de sciences/en droit** arts/science/law degree; **faire une l.** to study for a degree (**b**) *(dans le commerce)* license (**c**) *Sport* permit *(giving right of entry into competition)* (**d**) *(liberté)* license; **l. poétique** poetic license (**e**) *(dérèglement)* licentiousness

licencié, -e [lisɑ̃sje] *nm,f* (**a**) *Univ* **l. ès lettres/ès** *ou* **en sciences/en droit** arts/science/law graduate (**b**) *Sport* permit holder

licenciement [lisɑ̃simɑ̃] *nm (pour raisons économiques)* layoff; *(pour faute professionnelle)* dismissal; **l. collectif** mass layoffs; **l. abusif** unfair dismissal

licencier [66] [lisɑ̃sje] *vt (pour raisons économiques)* to lay off; *(pour faute professionnelle)* to dismiss; **se faire l.** to be laid off

lichen [likɛn] *nm* lichen

lichette [liʃɛt] *nf Fam (de pain, fromage)* tiny bit

licol [likɔl] *nm* halter

licorne [likɔrn] *nf* unicorn

licou [liku] *nm* halter

LICRA [likra] *nf (abrév* **Ligue internationale contre le racisme et l'antisémitisme**) = anti-racist movement

lie [li] *nf* dregs; *Litt* **boire la coupe** *ou* **le calice jusqu'à la l.** to drink one's cup of sorrow to the dregs; *Fig* **la l. de la société** the dregs of society

lié, -e [lje] *adj* (**a**) *(attaché)* bound; **avoir les mains liées** to have one's hands tied; *Fig* **j'ai les mains liées** my hands are tied; *Fig* **être pieds et poings liés** to be bound hand and foot (**b**) *(en relation étroite)* **être (très) l. avec qn** to be (great) friends with sb

liège [ljɛʒ] *nm* cork; **bouchon de l.** cork

liégeois, -e [ljeʒwa, -az] **1** *adj* (**a**) *(de Liège)* of Liège (**b**) *Culin* **café/chocolat l.** coffee/chocolate ice cream topped with whipped cream
2 *nm,f* **L., Liégeoise** person from Liège

lien [ljɛ̃] *nm* (**a**) *(attache)* bond; *aussi Fig* **se libérer de ses liens** to free oneself from one's bonds (**b**) *(relation)* link, connection; **l. de parenté** *ou* **de famille** family relationship; **il y a un l. de parenté entre ces deux familles** the two families are related; **les liens du mariage** the bonds of marriage; **l. d'amitié** bond of friendship; **l. social** social *or* civic bond; **la crise du l. social** the breakdown of a sense of community in society (**c**) *Ordinat* **l. hypertexte** hypertext link

lier [66] [lje] **1** *vt* (**a**) *(attacher)* to tie up; *(sujet: contrat, serment)* to be binding on (**b**) *(unir) (personnes)* to bind together (**c**) *(établir un rapport entre) (événements, paragraphes)* to connect, to link; **tout est lié** everything's connected (**d**) *Culin (sauce)* to thicken (**e**) **l. amitié/conversation avec qn** to strike up a friendship/conversation with sb
2 se lier *vpr* **se l. (d'amitié) avec qn** to strike up a friendship with sb

lierre [ljɛr] *nm* ivy

liesse [ljɛs] *nf* jubilation; **en l.** jubilant

lieu¹, -x [ljø] *nm* (**a**) *(endroit)* place; **en l. sûr** in a safe place; **un l. de passage** a busy place; **les lieux** *(local)* the premises; *(d'un accident, d'un crime)* the scene; **quitter les lieux** to vacate the premises; **un haut l. de** a mecca for; **en haut l.** in high places; **l. de naissance** place of birth; **l. de perdition** den of vice; **l. public** public place; **l. de rendez-vous** meeting place; **l. saint** holy place
(**b**) *(pour indiquer un ordre)* **en premier l.** in the first place; **en dernier l.** last(ly)
(**c**) **l. commun** commonplace
(**d**) *(locutions)* **avoir l.** to take place; **il y a l. de supposer que…** there is reason to suppose that…; **il n'y a pas l. de s'inquiéter** there's no need to worry; **s'il y a l.** if necessary; **donner l. à qch** to give rise to sth; **tenir l. de qch** to take the

place of sth; **au l. de** instead of; **au l. de te plaindre** instead of complaining; **au l. de cela** instead

lieu² (*pl* **lieus**) [ljø] *nm (poisson)* **l. jaune** pollack; **l. noir** coalfish

lieu-dit (*pl* **lieux-dits**) [ljødi] *nm* locality

lieue [ljø] *nf* league; *Naut* **l. marine** league; **j'étais à cent** *ou* **mille lieues de penser que…** I never thought for a single moment that…

lieutenant [ljøtnɑ̃] *nm (dans l'armée de terre)* lieutenant; *(dans l'armée de l'air)* first lieutenant; *(dans la marine marchande)* mate

lieutenant-colonel (*pl* **lieutenants-colonels**) [ljøtnɑ̃kɔlɔnɛl] *nm (dans l'armée de terre)* lieutenant-colonel; *(dans l'armée de l'air)* lieutenant-colonel

lièvre [ljɛvr] *nm* hare; **courir deux lièvres à la fois** to try to do two things at once

lifter [lifte] *vt* (**a**) *(balle)* to put topspin on (**b**) *(faire un lifting à)* to perform a face-lift on; *Fig (rénover)* to give a face-lift to, to face-lift

liftier, -ère [liftje, -ɛr] *nm,f* elevator operator

lifting [liftiŋ] *nm* facelift; **se faire faire un l.** to have a facelift

ligament [ligamɑ̃] *nm* ligament

ligature [ligatyr] *nf Méd* ligature

ligaturer [ligatyre] *vt Méd* to ligature

ligne [liɲ] *nf* (**a**) *(trait)* line; **l. droite** straight line; **avancer en l. droite** to advance in a straight line; **lire les lignes de la main à qn** to read sb's palm; **l. d'arrivée** finish line; **l. blanche** *(sur la route)* white line; **l. continue** *(sur la route)* solid line; **l. de démarcation** demarcation line; **l. de départ** starting line; **l. discontinue** *(sur la route)* broken line; **l. de flottaison** waterline; **l. d'horizon** horizon; **l. jaune** *(sur la route)* yellow line; **l. de mire** line of sight; *Fig* **avoir qn dans sa l. de mire** to have sb in one's sights; **l. de touche** touchline
(**b**) *(d'écriture)* line; **lire entre les lignes** to read between the lines; **aller à la l.** to begin a new paragraph; **à la l.** *(en dictant)* new paragraph; *Fig* **entrer en l. de compte** to be taken into consideration
(**c**) *(contour, silhouette) (de voiture, d'objet)* line; *(de personne)* figure; **avoir la l.** to have a good figure
(**d**) *(rangée)* line; **se mettre en l.** to line up; *Mil & Fig* **en première l.** in the front line; *Mil* **les lignes ennemies** the enemy lines; *Fig* **sur toute la l.** completely
(**e**) *(orientation)* **l. d'action/de conduite** line of action/conduct; **la l. du parti** the party line; **l. directrice** guideline
(**f**) *(dans les transports)* **l. de chemin de fer** railroad line; **grandes lignes** main lines; **l. maritime/aérienne** shipping/air route; **l. d'autobus** bus service; *(parcours)* bus route; **lignes de banlieue** suburban lines; **l. de métro** subway line
(**g**) *Élec* **l. électrique** power line; **l. à haute tension** high-tension line
(**h**) *Tél* **l. (téléphonique)** (telephone) line; **rappelez plus tard, elle est en l.** call back later, her line's busy; **vous êtes en l.** please go ahead; **l. extérieure** outside line
(**i**) *(fil)* line; *(de pêche)* (fishing) line
(**j**) *(de produits)* line, range
(**k**) *(filiation)* **descendre en l. directe** *ou* **en droite l. de…** to be directly descended from…
(**l**) *Ordinat* line; **en l.** on line; **hors l.** off line; **changer de l.** to do a line feed; **l. d'état** status line
(**m**) *Belg (raie des cheveux)* part

lignée [liɲe] *nf* descendants; *Fig* **dans la l. de** in the tradition of

lignite [liɲit] *nm* lignite

ligoter [ligɔte] *vt* to tie up (**à** to)

ligue [lig] *nf* league

liguer [lige] **1** *vt* **être ligués contre** to be lined up against
2 se liguer *vpr (États)* to form a league (**avec/contre**

with/against); *(personnes)* to gang up (**avec/contre** with/against)

lilas [lila] *nm & adj inv* lilac

lilliputien, -enne [lilipysjɛ̃, -ɛn] *adj (minuscule)* Lilliputian

Lima [lima] *n* Lima

limace [limas] *nf* slug; *Fam (personne lente)* slowpoke

limaille [limaj] *nf* filings

limande [limɑ̃d] *nf* dab; **l.-sole** lemon sole

lime [lim] *nf (outil)* file; **l. à ongles** nail file

limer [lime] **1** *vt* to file; *(barreaux de cellule)* to file through

   2 se limer *vpr* **se l. les ongles** to file one's nails

limier [limje] *nm (chien)* bloodhound; *Fig* sleuth; **un fin l.** a supersleuth

limitatif, -ive [limitatif, -iv] *adj* restrictive

limitation [limitasjɔ̃] *nf* limitation; **l. des naissances** birth control; **l. de vitesse** speed limit

limite [limit] **1** *nf* (**a**) *(frontière)* boundary (**b**) *(maximum)* limit; **ma patience a des limites!** there are limits to my patience!; **mettre une l./des limites à qch** to set a limit/limits to sth; **c'est à la l. de la vulgarité/du supportable** it's bordering on vulgarity/the unacceptable; **dans la l. des stocks disponibles** while stocks last; **à la l., on pourrait changer d'hôtel** if it came to it, we could change hotels; **sans limites** unbounded, limitless

   2 *adj* **cas l.** borderline case; **vitesse l.** maximum speed; *Fam* **je ne lui ai pas mis une claque, mais c'était l.** I didn't slap him, but it was touch and go; *Fam* **je suis un peu l. financièrement** I'm a little short of money

limité, -e [limite] *adj (réduit)* limited; *Fam Péj (obtus)* thick

limiter [limite] **1** *vt* (**a**) *(délimiter) (pays, territoire)* to bound (**b**) *(restreindre)* to limit, to restrict (**à** to); *Fam* **l. les dégâts** to limit the damage

   2 se limiter *vpr (personne)* to limit oneself; **se l. à qch/à faire qch** *(personne)* to limit *or* restrict oneself to sth/to doing sth; **son œuvre se limite à quelques essais** his/her works amount to no more than a few essays

limitrophe [limitrɔf] *adj* neighboring; **être l. de** *(pays)* to border on; *(région)* to adjoin

limogeage [limɔʒaʒ] *nm* dismissal

limoger [45] [limɔʒe] *vt* to dismiss; **se faire l.** to be dismissed

limon [limɔ̃] *nm (alluvions)* silt

limonade [limɔnad] *nf (boisson gazeuse)* lemon soda

limousine [limuzin] *nf* limousine

limpide [lɛ̃pid] *adj (eau, diamant, regard)* limpid; *(explication)* lucid

limpidité [lɛ̃pidite] *nf (de l'eau, d'un diamant, d'un regard)* limpidity; *(d'une explication)* lucidity

lin [lɛ̃] *nm* (**a**) *(tissu)* linen (**b**) *(plante)* flax

linceul [lɛ̃sœl] *nm* shroud

linéaire [lineɛr] **1** *adj* (**a**) *(récit) & Math* linear (**b**) *(dessin)* line

   2 *nm (dans un magasin)* shelf space

linge [lɛ̃ʒ] *nm* (**a**) *(draps, serviettes, nappes)* linen; **l. de maison** household linen; **l. de table** table linen (**b**) *(lessive)* laundry (**c**) *(dessous)* **l. (de corps)** underwear; *Fam Fig* **du beau l.** top-drawer people (**d**) *(morceau de tissu)* cloth (**e**) *Suisse (serviette)* towel

lingerie [lɛ̃ʒri] *nf* (**a**) *(dessous)* underwear, lingerie (**b**) *(pièce)* linen room

lingot [lɛ̃go] *nm (de métal)* ingot; **l. (d'or)** gold bar *or* ingot

linguiste [lɛ̃gɥist] *nmf* linguist

linguistique [lɛ̃gɥistik] **1** *adj* linguistic

   2 *nf* linguistics *(singulier)*

lino [lino] *nm Fam* lino

linoléum [linɔleɔm] *nm* linoleum

linotte [linɔt] *nf voir* **tête**

linteau, -x [lɛ̃to] *nm Constr* lintel

lion [ljɔ̃] *nm* (**a**) *(animal)* lion; **tourner comme un l. en cage** to prowl around (**b**) *Astron & Astrol* **le L.** Leo; **être L.** to be (a) Leo

lionceau, -x [ljɔ̃so] *nm* lion cub

lionne [ljɔn] *nf* lioness

lipide [lipid] *nm* lipid

liposome [lipozom] *nm Chim* liposome

liposuccion [liposysjɔ̃] *nf* liposuction

liquéfaction [likefaksjɔ̃] *nf* liquefaction

liquéfier [66] [likefje] **1** *vt* to liquefy

   2 se liquéfier *vpr* to liquefy

liquette [likɛt] *nf* grandad shirt

liqueur [likœr] *nf* (**a**) *(spiritueux)* liqueur (**b**) *Can* **l. (douce)** soft drink

liquidation [likidasjɔ̃] *nf* (**a**) *Jur* liquidation; **être en l.** to have gone into liquidation; **l. judiciaire** official receivership (**b**) *(d'une dette, en Bourse)* settlement (**c**) *Com (de stocks)* selling off; **l. totale** *(sur une vitrine)* stock clearance (**d**) *Fam (meurtre)* liquidation

liquide [likid] **1** *adj (non solide)* liquid; *(trop fluide)* thin

   2 *nm* (**a**) *(substance)* liquid, fluid; **l. correcteur** correction fluid; **l. de frein** brake fluid; **l. vaisselle** dishwashing liquid (**b**) *(espèces)* cash; **payer en l.** to pay cash

liquider [likide] *vt* (**a**) *Jur (affaire)* to liquidate (**b**) *Fin (dette)* to settle (**c**) *Fam (tuer)* to liquidate (**d**) *Fam (travail, restes, bouteille)* to polish off (**e**) *(stocks)* to sell off; **on liquide** *(sur une vitrine)* stock clearance

liquidités [likidite] *nfpl Fin* liquid assets

liquoreux, -euse [likɔrø, -øz] *adj (vin)* syrupy

lire¹ [44] [lir] **1** *vt* (**a**) *(déchiffrer, interpréter)* to read; **l. qch à qn** to read sth to sb; **lu et approuvé** read and approved; **l. dans les pensées de qn** to read sb's thoughts (**b**) *Fig (deviner) (sur un visage, dans un regard)* to read

   2 se lire *vpr (se deviner)* to show

lire² [lir] *nf (monnaie)* lira

lis [lis] *nm* lily; **l. blanc** white lily

lisais *etc. voir* **lire¹**

Lisbonne [lizbɔn] *n* Lisbon

lise *etc. voir* **lire¹**

liseré [lizre], **liséré** [lizere] *nm* border, edging

liseron [lizrɔ̃] *nm* bindweed, convolvulus

lisibilité [lizibilite] *nf (d'une écriture)* legibility; *(d'un roman, d'un fichier informatique)* readability

lisible [lizibl] *adj (écriture)* legible; *(roman, fichier informatique)* readable

lisiblement [liziblǝmɑ̃] *adv* legibly

lisière [lizjɛr] *nf (d'un champ, d'une forêt)* edge

lisiez *etc. voir* **lire¹**

lissage [lisaʒ] *nm Ordinat* **l. de courbes/des caractères** curve/character smoothing

lisse [lis] *adj (surface, peau, eau)* smooth; *(pneu)* bald; *(cheveux)* sleek

lisser [lise] *vt (cheveux)* to smooth down; *(vêtement)* to smooth out; *(sujet: oiseau) (plumes)* to preen

liste [list] *nf* list; **l. d'attente** waiting list; *Ordinat* **l. de diffusion** distribution *or* discussion *or* mailing list; **l. électorale** electoral roll; *Ordinat* **l. de fichiers à imprimer** print list, print queue; **l. de mariage** wedding list; **l. noire** blacklist; **être sur (la) l. rouge** *(du téléphone)* to be unlisted

listing [listiŋ] *nm Ordinat* listing, printout

lit [li] *nm* (**a**) *(meuble)* bed; **être au l.** to be in bed; **aller au l.** to go to bed; **mettre qn au lit** to put sb to bed; **au l., les enfants!** bedtime, children!; **faire son l.** to make one's bed; **faire l. à part** to sleep in separate beds; **enfant d'un premier l.** child from a first marriage; **l. à baldaquin** four-poster (bed); **l. de camp** cot; **l. conjugal** marital bed; **grand l.** double bed; **l. d'enfant** crib; **lits jumeaux** twin beds; **être sur**

son l. de mort to be on one's death bed; l. **une place/deux places** single/double bed; **lits superposés** bunk beds (**b**) *(couche) (d'argile, de pierres)* bed, layer; *Culin* bed (**c**) *(de rivière)* bed; **sortir de son l.** to burst its banks

litanie [litani] *nf aussi Fig* litany

litchi [litʃi] *nm* lychee

literie [litri] *nf* bedding

lithium [litjɔm] *nm Chim* lithium; **piles au l.** lithium batteries

lithographie [litɔgrafi] *nf* (**a**) *(technique)* lithography (**b**) *(œuvre)* lithograph

litière [litjɛr] *nf* (**a**) *(pour cheval, pour chat)* litter (**b**) *(palanquin)* litter

litige [litiʒ] *nm (conflit)* dispute; *(procès)* lawsuit

litigieux, -euse [litiʒjø, -øz] *adj (question, cas)* contentious

litote [litɔt] *nf* understatement

litre [litr] *nm* liter

litron [litrɔ̃] *nm Fam* bottle of wine

littéraire [literɛr] **1** *adj* literary
2 *nmf* (**a**) *(doué pour la littérature)* literary person (**b**) *(étudiant)* student of literature

littéral, -e, -aux, -ales [literal, -o] *adj (traduction, sens)* literal

littéralement [literalmɑ̃] *adv* literally

littérature [literatyr] *nf (œuvres, documentation)* literature; *(métier)* writing

littoral, -e, -aux, -ales [litɔral, -o] **1** *adj* coastal
2 *nm* coast(line)

Lituanie [litɥani] *nf* **la L.** Lithuania

lituanien, -enne [litɥanjɛ̃, -ɛn] **1** *adj* Lithuanian
2 *nm (langue)* Lithuanian
3 *nm,f* **L., Lituanienne** Lithuanian

liturgie [lityrʒi] *nf* liturgy

liturgique [lityrʒik] *adj* liturgical

livide [livid] *adj (pâle)* pallid

living [liviŋ], **living-room** *(pl* **living-rooms**) [liviŋrum] *nm Vieilli* living room

livraison [livrɛzɔ̃] *nf* (**a**) *(de marchandises)* delivery; **payable à la l.** payable on delivery; **faire la l. de pain/journaux** to deliver the bread/the newspapers; **prendre l. de qch** to take delivery of sth; **l. à domicile** home delivery (**b**) *(d'ouvrage publié en fascicules)* part

livre¹ [livr] *nm* (**a**) *(ouvrage, partie d'un ouvrage)* book; **l. d'histoire/d'anglais** history/English book; **l. de chevet** bedside book; **l. de classe** *ou* **scolaire** schoolbook; **l. de cuisine** *ou* **de recettes** cookbook; **l. pour enfants** children's book; **l. d'images** picture book; **l. de poche** paperback; **l. de prières** prayer book (**b**) *(édition)* **l'industrie du l., le l.** the book trade (**c**) *(registre)* **l. de bord** *Naut* log(book); *Scol* (teacher's) record book; **l. de comptes** account book; **l. d'or** *(public)* register; *(privé)* guest book; **grand l.** ledger

livre² [livr] *nf* (**a**) *(unité de poids)* half kilo, ≃ pound; *Can* pound (**b**) *(monnaie britannique)* **l. (sterling)** pound (sterling)

livre-cassette *(pl* **livres-cassettes**) [livrəkasɛt] *nm* audio book

livrée [livre] *nf (de domestique)* livery

livrer [livre] **1** *vt* (**a**) *(marchandises)* to deliver; **nous livrons à domicile** we deliver; **vous serez livré dès demain** you'll receive delivery tomorrow (**b**) *(abandonner)* **l. un village au pillage/un pays à l'anarchie** to abandon a village to pillage/a country to anarchy; **livré à soi-même** left to oneself (**c**) *(remettre)* **l. qn à qn** *(coupable, complice)* to hand sb over to sb; **l. un secret à qn** to reveal a secret to sb (**d**) *(locutions)* **l. bataille** to join battle; **l. passage à qn** to let sb pass
2 se livrer *vpr* (**a**) *(se rendre)* to give oneself up (**à to**) (**b**) *(se confier)* to open up; **se l. à qn** to confide in sb (**c**) *(s'abandonner)* **se l. à qch** *(vice, spéculations)* to indulge in sth; *(désespoir)* to give way to sth (**d**) *(s'occuper)* **se l. à qch** *(occupations, re-*

cherches) to be engaged in sth; *(étude, lecture)* to devote oneself to sth

livret [livrɛ] *nm* (**a**) *(petit livre)* booklet; **l. (de caisse) d'épargne** bankbook, passbook; **l. de famille** family record book *(for registration of births and deaths)*; **l. militaire** service record; **l. scolaire** report card (**b**) *Mus (d'opéra)* libretto (**c**) *Suisse* multiplication table

livreur, -euse [livrœr, -øz] *nm,f* delivery man, *f* delivery woman

lob [lɔb] *nm* lob; **faire un l.** to hit a lob

lobe [lɔb] *nm Anat & Bot* lobe

lober [lɔbe] *vt & vi* to lob

lobotomie [lɔbɔtɔmi] *nf Méd* lobotomy

local, -e, -aux, -ales [lɔkal, -o] **1** *adj aussi Méd* local; *(averses)* scattered
2 *nm* (**a**) *(lieu) (de société, d'organisation)* premises; *(sans usage précis)* place; **locaux commerciaux** business premises (**b**) *Can Tél* extension

localement [lɔkalmɑ̃] *adv* locally

localisation [lɔkalizasjɔ̃] *nf* (**a**) *(repérage)* location; *(d'un appel téléphonique)* tracing (**b**) *Ordinat* **l. de logiciel** software localization

localisé, -e [lɔkalize] *adj (circonscrit)* localized

localiser [lɔkalize] *vt (repérer) (bruit, gène, personne)* to locate; *(appel téléphonique)* to trace

localité [lɔkalite] *nf (ville)* town; *(village)* village

locataire [lɔkatɛr] *nmf* tenant; *(chez le propriétaire)* lodger

locatif, -ive [lɔkatif, -iv] *adj voir* **charge**

location [lɔkasjɔ̃] *nf* (**a**) *(de voiture, d'équipement, de costume) (par le locataire)* renting; *(par le propriétaire)* renting out; **prendre qch en l.** to rent sth; **donner qch en l.** to rent sth out; **l. de voitures** car rental (**b**) *(de logement) (par le locataire)* renting; *(par le propriétaire)* renting out (**c**) *(appartement, maison)* rented accommodations (**d**) *(de places de spectacle)* booking

location-vente *(pl* **locations-ventes**) [lɔkasjɔ̃vɑ̃t] *nf* installment plan; **acheter qch en l.** to buy sth on the installment plan

loche [lɔʃ] *nf (poisson)* loach

locomoteur, -trice [lɔkɔmɔtœr, -tris] *adj* locomotor

locomotion [lɔkɔmɔsjɔ̃] *nf* locomotion; **moyen de l.** means of transportation

locomotive [lɔkɔmɔtiv] *nf* (**a**) *(de train)* locomotive, engine; **l. à vapeur** steam engine (**b**) *Fig (leader)* pacemaker; *(entreprise, secteur)* powerhouse

locuteur, -trice [lɔkytœr, -tris] *nm,f Ling* speaker

locution [lɔkysjɔ̃] *nf* expression, phrase

loft [lɔft] *nm* converted loft

logarithme [lɔgaritm] *nm* logarithm

loge [lɔʒ] *nf* (**a**) *(d'artiste)* dressing room (**b**) *(sièges)* box; *Fig* **être aux premières loges** to have a ringside seat (**c**) *(maçonnique, de concierge)* lodge (**d**) *Belg* **l. foraine** stall

logement [lɔʒmɑ̃] *nm* (**a**) *(habitation)* accommodations; *(maison)* house; *(appartement)* apartment; **l. de fonction** accommodations that go with the job; **logements sociaux** ≃ low-rent housing (**b**) *(action)* housing; **la crise du l.** the housing shortage

loger [45] [lɔʒe] **1** *vi (en permanence)* to live; *(temporairement)* to stay; **l. chez l'habitant** *(en vacances)* to stay in a private house
2 *vt* (**a**) *(héberger)* to put up; **être logé et nourri** to have board and lodging (**b**) *(contenir) (sujet: hôtel, maison)* to accommodate (**c**) *(placer)* to put
3 se loger *vpr* (**a**) *(en permanence)* **se l.** *(trouver à)* se l. *(en permanence)* to find somewhere to live; *(temporairement)* to find accommodations (**b**) *(se placer)* to lodge itself

logeur, -euse [lɔʒœr, -øz] *nm,f* landlord, *f* landlady *(of furnished apartments)*

loggia [lɔdʒja] *nf Archit* loggia

logiciel [lɔʒisjɛl] *nm Ordinat* software; **un l.** a (software) package; **l. d'application** application software; **l. bureautique** business software (package); **l. de communication** communications package, comms package, communications software; **l. de compression de données** data compression software; **l. de comptabilité** accounts package, accounts software; **l. de décompression** decompression software, decompressor; **l. de dessin** art package, drawing program; **l. espion** spyware; **l. d'exploitation** operating system software; **l. grapheur** graphics package, graphics software; **l. de jeu** games software; **l. de mise en page** desktop-publishing package; **l. de navigation** browser; **l. public** freeware; **l. de reconnaissance de caractères** OCR software, character-recognition software; **l. de reconnaissance vocale** voice-recognition software; **l. de réseau** network software; **l. de SGBD** DBMS software; **l. de télémaintenance** remote-access software; **logiciels de traitement de texte** word-processing software, word-processing software packages

logique [lɔʒik] **1** *adj* logical
2 *nf* logic; **en toute l.,...** logically,...; *Ordinat* **l. câblée** wired logic; **l. floue** fuzzy logic

logiquement [lɔʒikmɑ̃] *adv* **(a)** *(avec cohérence)* logically **(b)** *(normalement)* **l., il devrait bientôt être là** if all goes well, he should soon be here

logis [lɔʒi] *nm Litt (maison)* dwelling, abode

logistique [lɔʒistik] **1** *adj* logistic
2 *nf* logistics *(singulier)*

logo [logo] *nm* logo

logopède [logopɛd] *nmf Belg & Suisse* speech therapist

logotisé, -e [logotize] *adj Mktg* branded

loi [lwa] *nf* law; **nul n'est censé ignorer la l.** ignorance of the law is no excuse; **faire la** *ou* **sa l.** to lay down the law; *Pol* **l. de finances** appropriation bill; **la l. de la jungle** the law of the jungle; **l. martiale** martial law; **la l. de l'offre et de la demande** the law of supply and demand; **la l. du plus fort** the law of the strongest; **la l. du talion** an eye for an eye

loi-cadre *(pl* **lois-cadres)** [lwakadr] *nf* outline law

loin [lwɛ̃] **1** *adv* **(a)** *(dans l'espace)* far (**de** from); **la poste est l.** the post office is a long way away; **c'est encore l., le théâtre/Annecy?** is it far to the theater/Annecy?; **il y a l. d'ici à Paris** it's a long way to Paris; **plus l.** further (on); **voir plus l.** *(dans un texte)* see below; **de l.** *(reconnaître, admirer)* from a distance; *Prov* **l. des yeux, l. du cœur** out of sight, out of mind **(b)** *(dans le temps)* far away (**de** from); **comme c'est l., tout ça!** that all happened such a long time ago!; **ce jour est encore l.** that day is still a long way off; **d'aussi l.** *ou* **du plus l. qu'elle se souvienne** for as long as she can remember **(c)** *Fig* **de là à l'accuser de mensonge il n'y a pas l.** it's practically calling him/her a liar; **aller l.** *(réussir)* to go far; **aller trop l.** *(exagérer)* to go too far; **nous étions l. de penser que...** we never thought for a moment than...; **elle est l. d'être bête** she's far from stupid; **je ne suis pas fâché, l. de là!** I'm not mad, far from it!; **l. de moi l'idée d'insinuer que...** far be it from me to insinuate that...; **l. de moi cette idée!** I wouldn't dream of it!, perish the thought!; **pas l. de** *(presque)* not far off; **de l.** *(de beaucoup)* by far; **de l. en l.** *(temps en temps)* every now and then **(d)** *Suisse (absent)* **il est l.** he's not here
2 *nm* **au l.** in the distance

lointain, -e [lwɛ̃tɛ̃, -ɛn] **1** *adj (dans l'espace, dans le temps)* distant; *(ressemblance)* vague; *(air, regard)* faraway; **dans un avenir l.** in the distant future
2 *nm* **dans le l., au l.** in the distance

loir [lwar] *nm* dormouse

Loire [lwar] *nf* **la L.** the Loire

loisir [lwazir] *nm* **(a)** *(temps libre)* leisure; **activités de l.** leisure *or* spare-time activities; **avoir des loisirs** to have some spare time **(b)** *(activité)* pastime; **les loisirs** lei-

sure *or* spare-time activities (**c**) *Sout (possibilité, temps nécessaire)* **avoir le l. de faire qch** to have time to do sth; **donner** *ou* **laisser à qn le l. de faire qch** to give sb the opportunity to do sth; *Litt* **à l.** at one's leisure

lolo [lolo] *nm Fam* **(a)** *(langage enfantin) (lait)* milk **(b)** *(sein)* boob, tit

lombaire [lɔ̃bɛr] *Anat* **1** *adj* lumbar
2 *nf* lumbar vertebra

lombalgie [lɔ̃balʒi] *nf Méd* lumbago

lombric [lɔ̃brik] *nm* earthworm

Lomé [lɔme] *n* Lomé

londonien, -enne [lɔ̃dɔnjɛ̃, -ɛn] **1** *adj* London
2 *nm,f* **L., Londonienne** Londoner

Londres [lɔ̃dr] *n* London

long, longue [lɔ̃, lɔ̃g] **1** *adj* **(a)** *(dans l'espace)* long; *(personne)* tall; **l. de six mètres** ≃ 20 feet long **(b)** *(dans le temps)* long; **dix jours, c'est l.** ten days is a long time; **ce ne sera pas l.** it won't take long; **pendant de longues années** for many years; **longue durée** *(pile)* long-life; *(cassette)* extended play; **de longue durée** *(chômage, chômeur)* long-term **(c)** *(lent)* slow; **être l. à faire qch** to be slow to do sth
2 *nm* **(a)** *(dans l'espace)* **faire trois mètres de l.** ≃ to be ten feet long; **(tout) le l. de** *(all)* along; **de tout son l.** *(être étendu)* at full length; *(tomber)* flat on one's face; **de l. en large** up and down, to and fro; **en l.** *(couper, fendre)* lengthwise; *Fam* **expliquer qch en l. et en large** *ou* **en l., en large et en travers** to explain sth in great detail **(b)** *(dans le temps)* **tout au l. de** throughout
3 *adv* **(a)** *(beaucoup)* **en dire l.** *(être révélateur)* to speak volumes; **en savoir l. (sur)** to know a lot (about) **(b)** **s'habiller l.** to wear long clothes

long-courrier *(pl* **long-courriers)** [lɔ̃kurje] **1** *adj (navire)* ocean-going; *(avion)* long-haul
2 *nm (navire)* ocean-going ship; *(avion)* long-haul aircraft

longe¹ [lɔ̃ʒ] *nf (pour guider)* leading rein; *(pour attacher)* tether

longe² [lɔ̃ʒ] *nf Culin (de veau, de porc)* loin

longer [45] [lɔ̃ʒe] *vt* **(a)** *(sujet: personne, voiture) (route, rivière)* to go along; *(mur, côte)* to hug **(b)** *(sujet: sentier, canal, voie ferrée)* to run alongside

longévité [lɔ̃ʒevite] *nf (longue vie)* longevity; *(espérance de vie)* life expectancy

longiligne [lɔ̃ʒiliɲ] *adj* willowy

longitude [lɔ̃ʒityd] *nf Géog* longitude; **à 10° de l. ouest** at longitude 10° west

longitudinal, -e, -aux, -ales [lɔ̃ʒitydinal, -o] *adj* longitudinal, lengthwise

longtemps [lɔ̃tɑ̃] *adv* **(a)** *(attendre, rester)* (for) a long time; **ça ne durera pas l.** it won't last (for) long; *Fig* **tu peux attendre l.** you'll have a long wait **(b)** *(avec une préposition, avec "il y a")* **avant l.** before long; **pas avant l.** not for a long time; **cela existe depuis l.** it has existed for a long time; **pendant l.** for a long time; **je n'en ai pas pour l.** I won't be long; **il n'en a plus pour l.** *(il va bientôt mourir)* he doesn't have much longer to live; **il y a l.** a long time ago; **il y a l. qu'il est mort** he's been dead for a long time; **il y a l. que je ne l'ai pas vue** it's a long time since I saw her; **l. avant/après** long before/after

longue [lɔ̃g] **1** *adj voir* **long**
2 *nf* **à la l.** in the end

longuement [lɔ̃gmɑ̃] *adv (attendre, réfléchir, s'attarder)* for a long time; *(parler, expliquer)* at length; **il a l. insisté pour que je vienne** he kept on insisting I should come

longuet, -ette [lɔ̃gɛ, -ɛt] *adj Fam* longish

longueur [lɔ̃gœr] *nf* **(a)** *(dimension, durée)* & *Sport* length; **jardin de 100 mètres de l.** *ou* **d'une l. de dix mètres** ≃ garden 30 feet long; **en l., dans le sens de la l.** *(couper, fendre)* lengthwise; **avoir une l. d'avance sur** *Sport* to be one length ahead of; *Fig* to have a clear lead over; **à l. de journée/de**

semaine/d'année all day/week/year long (**b**) *Péj (développement trop long)* **longueurs** drawn-out passages; **il y a des longueurs dans le film** the movie is a little tedious in parts (**c**) *Rad* **l. d'ondes** wavelength; *Fig* **être sur la même l. d'ondes** to be on the same wavelength

longue-vue (*pl* **longues-vues**) [lɔ̃gvy] *nf* telescope

look [luk] *nm Fam* (**a**) **le l. des années 80** the 80s look; **avoir un l. d'enfer** to look incredible

looké, -e [luke] *adj Fam* **être l. punk/grunge** to have a punky/grungy look *or* image

looping [lupiŋ] *nm Aviat* loop; **faire un l./des loopings** to loop the loop

lopin [lɔpɛ̃] *nm* **l. de terre** patch *or* plot of land

loquace [lɔkas] *adj* talkative

loque [lɔk] *nf* (**a**) *(vêtement)* rag; **être en loques** to be in rags; **tomber en loques** to fall to pieces (**b**) *Belg (serpillière)* mop (**c**) *Fig (personne)* wreck

loquet [lɔkɛ] *nm* latch

lorgner [lɔrɲe] *vt* (**a**) *(regarder indiscrètement)* to eye; *(avec concupiscence)* to eye up (**b**) *(convoiter)* to have one's eye on

lorgnette [lɔrɲɛt] *nf* opera glasses; *Fig* **regarder *ou* voir les choses par le petit bout de la l.** to take a narrow-minded view of things

lorgnon [lɔrɲɔ̃] *nm (avec tige)* lorgnette; *(avec ressort)* pince-nez

lorrain, -e [lɔrɛ̃, -ɛn] **1** *adj* of Lorraine
2 *nm,f* **L., Lorraine** person from Lorraine

lors [lɔr] *adv* **l. de** *(pendant)* during; *(au moment de)* at the time of; *Litt* **depuis l.** from that time

lorsque [lɔrsk] *conj* when

losange [lɔzɑ̃ʒ] *nm (forme)* diamond; *(en géométrie)* rhombus

Los Angeles [lɔsɑ̃dʒələs] *n* Los Angeles

lot [lo] *nm* (**a**) *(dans une loterie)* prize; **gros l.** jackpot; *Fam Fig* **tirer le gros l.** to hit the jackpot; **l. de consolation** consolation prize (**b**) *Com (de marchandises)* batch; *(de serviettes, de casseroles)* set; *(de chaussettes, de savonnettes)* pack; *Fig* **dans le l., il y en aura bien un de bon** *(choses, personnes)* at least one out of this lot should be some use; **se détacher *ou* être au-dessus du l.** to stand out from the crowd (**c**) *(de terrain)* plot (**d**) *Litt (sort)* lot (**e**) *Ordinat* **traitement par lots** batch processing

loterie [lɔtri] *nf* lottery; **gagner à la l.** to win at the lottery; **l. nationale** national lottery

loti, -e [lɔti] *adj* **être bien/mal l.** to be well/badly off

lotion [losjɔ̃] *nf* lotion; **l. après-rasage** aftershave (lotion); **l. capillaire** hair lotion; **l. tonique** toner

lotissement [lɔtismɑ̃] *nm (ensemble résidentiel)* residential development

loto [lɔto] *nm* (**a**) *(jeu de hasard)* lotto (**b**) *(jeu national)* national lottery; **jouer au l.** to play the lottery

---

Loto

"Loto" is a popular game of chance with large cash prizes. Printed grids ("bulletins") are available at tobacco stores or special kiosks. Players mark six numbers on the grid and pay a fee. The twice-weekly prize draw is broadcast on television. "Loto Sportif" is a version of "Loto" in which players bet on the soccer results.

---

lotte [lɔt] *nf (de rivière)* burbot; *(de mer)* monkfish

lotus [lɔtys] *nm* lotus; **fleur de l.** lotus; **position du l.** lotus position

louable [lwabl] *adj (admirable)* praiseworthy, laudable

louage [lwaʒ] *nm* **contrat de l.** rental agreement; **voiture de l.** rental car

louange [lwɑ̃ʒ] *nf* praise; **digne de louange(s)** praiseworthy; **chanter les louanges de qn** to sing sb's praises

loubard [lubar] *nm Fam* hooligan

louche¹ [luʃ] *adj* shady

louche² [luʃ] *nf* ladle

loucher [luʃe] *vi (volontairement)* to squint; *(être atteint de strabisme)* to have a squint; **l. de l'œil gauche** to have a squint in one's left eye; *Fig* **l. sur qch** *(regarder)* to eye sth; *(convoiter)* to have one's eye on sth

louer¹ [lwe] *vt* (**a**) *(donner en location) (logement)* to rent out (**à** to); *(équipement, véhicule, costume)* to rent out (**à** to); **maison à l.** house for rent (**b**) *(prendre en location) (logement)* to rent (**à** from); *(équipement, véhicule, costume)* to rent (**à** from); *(place de spectacle)* to book

louer² [lwe] **1** *vt (exalter)* to praise; **l. qn de *ou* pour qch** to praise sb for sth; **louons le Seigneur!** praise the Lord!
2 se louer *vpr* **se l. de** to be very satisfied with sth; **je n'ai qu'à me l. de lui/de ses services** I have nothing but praise for him/for his work; **se l. d'avoir fait qch** to congratulate oneself on having done sth

loufdingue [lufdɛ̃g], **loufoque** [lufɔk] *adj Fam* crazy

louis [lwi] *nm* **l. (d'or)** louis(-d'or)

Louisiane [lwizjan] *nf* **la L.** Louisiana

loukoum [lukum] *nm* piece of Turkish delight; **des loukoums** Turkish delight

loup [lu] *nm* (**a**) *(mammifère)* wolf; *Fig* **il est connu comme le l. blanc** everybody knows him; **quand on parle du l. on en voit la queue** talk of the devil; *Fig* **jeune l.** young go-getter; *(en politique)* Young Turk; *Fam* **mon petit l., mon gros l.** darling, pet (**b**) *(poisson)* bass (**c**) *(demi-masque)* eye mask (**d**) **(vieux) l. de mer** *(marin)* sea dog

loupe [lup] *nf (instrument d'optique)* magnifying glass; **regarder qch à la l.** to look at sth through a magnifying glass; *Fig* to put sth under the microscope

louper [lupe] *Fam* **1** *vt* (**a**) *(ne pas réussir) (travail, plat)* to screw up, to botch; *(examen)* to flunk; **l. son entrée** *(au théâtre)* to fluff one's entrance; **loupé!** missed!; **la soirée est loupée** the party's a flop (**b**) *(ne pas prendre) (son tour, occasion, train)* to miss; **il n'en loupe pas une!** *(en actions)* it's one stupid thing after another!; *(en paroles)* he's always opening his big mouth!; **je ne vais pas le l.!** I won't let him get away with it!
2 *vi* **je lui ai dit qu'il attraperait froid et ça n'a pas loupé** I told him he'd catch cold and sure enough he did
3 se louper *vpr* (**a**) *(ne pas se rencontrer)* to miss each other (**b**) *(manquer son suicide)* to bungle it; *Ironique* **il ne s'est pas loupé!** he made a nice job of it!

loup-garou (*pl* **loups-garous**) [lugaru] *nm* werewolf; *(pour faire peur aux enfants)* boogieman

loupiote [lupjɔt] *nf Fam (lampe)* small light

loup-marin (*pl* **loups-marins**) [lumarɛ̃] *nm Can* seal

lourd, -e [lur, lurd] **1** *adj* (**a**) *(pesant)* heavy; **j'ai la tête lourde** my head feels heavy; **avoir l'estomac l.** to feel bloated; **yeux lourds de fatigue** eyes heavy with tiredness (**b**) *(à l'aspect pesant) (personne)* heavily built; *(tentures)* heavy (**c**) *(peu subtil) (personne, plaisanterie)* unsubtle; *(mouvement, style)* heavy (**d**) *(perte, dépenses, responsabilité)* heavy (**e**) *(temps)* close; *(parfum)* heavy (**f**) *(plein)* **l. de conséquences** fraught with consequences; **l. de menaces** ominous
2 *adv* **peser l.** to weigh a lot, to be heavy; *Fam* **pas l.** not much

lourdaud, -e [lurdo, -od] **1** *adj* oafish
2 *nm,f* oaf

lourdement [lurdəmɑ̃] *adv* heavily; **se tromper l.** to be greatly mistaken; **insister l.** to keep on insisting

lourder [lurde] *vt Fam* **l.** to give sb the boot; **se faire l. (par qn)** to get the boot (from sb)

lourdeur [lurdœr] *nf (poids, manque de subtilité)* heaviness; *(de la bureaucratie)* unwieldiness; *(d'une responsabilité, d'une tâche)* weight; *(du temps)* closeness; **l. d'esprit** slow-wittedness; **j'ai des lourdeurs d'estomac** I feel bloated

lourdingue [lurdɛ̃g] *adj Fam (style)* heavy; *(personne, plaisanterie)* unsubtle

loustic [lustik] *nm Fam* **un drôle de l.** *(louche)* a shady character

loutre [lutr] *nf* otter; *(fourrure)* otter skin

louve [luv] *nf* she-wolf

louveteau, -x [luvto] *nm* **(a)** *(animal)* wolf cub **(b)** *(jeune scout)* Cub Scout

louvoyer [32] [luvwaje] *vi Naut* to tack; *Fig* to hedge

Louvre [luvr] *nm* **le (palais du) L.** the Louvre

> **Louvre**
> This former royal palace became a museum in 1791–1793. It houses one of the richest art collections in the world. The museum was extended in 1989, with the construction of the glass "pyramide du Louvre" in the main courtyard, and again in 1993 when the Richelieu wing, formerly occupied by the ministry of finance, was inaugurated.

lover [lɔve] **se lover** *vpr (serpent)* to coil up; *(personne)* to curl up

low-cost [lokɔst] *nm ou nf* low-cost airline

loyal, -e, -aux, -ales [lwajal, -o] **1** *adj* **(a)** *(honnête)* fair **(b)** *(fidèle) (serviteur, ami)* loyal; **après vingt-cinq ans de bons et loyaux services** after twenty-five years of good and faithful service
   2 *nf* **loyale** *Fam* **se battre à la loyale** to fight cleanly

loyalement [lwajalmã] *adv* **(a)** *(honnêtement)* fairly **(b)** *(fidèlement)* loyally

loyaliste [lwajalist] *adj & nmf Pol* loyalist

loyauté [lwajote] *nf* **(a)** *(honnêteté)* fairness **(b)** *(fidélité)* loyalty (**envers** qn)

loyer [lwaje] *nm* rent; **j'ai trois loyers de retard** I'm three months behind with the rent; *Can* **être à l.** to be in rented accommodations

LP [ɛlpe] *nm (abrév* **lycée professionnel**) vocational secondary school

LSD [ɛlɛsde] *nm* LSD

lu, -e *voir* **lire**[1]

lubie [lybi] *nf* whim, fad

lubrifiant, -e [lybrifjã, -ãt] **1** *adj* lubricating
   2 *nm* lubricant

lubrifier [66] [lybrifje] *vt* to lubricate

lubrique [lybrik] *adj* lustful, lecherous

lucarne [lykarn] *nf* **(a)** *(dans un toit)* skylight; *(en saillie)* dormer (window) **(b)** *(au football)* top corner

lucide [lysid] *adj* lucid

lucidement [lysidmã] *adv* lucidly

lucidité [lysidite] *nf* lucidity

Lucifer [lysifɛr] *npr* Lucifer

luciole [lysjɔl] *nf* firefly

lucratif, -ive [lykratif, -iv] *adj* lucrative; **à but l.** profit-making; **sans but l.** non-profit

lucre [lykr] *nm Litt* lucre

ludique [lydik] *adj* play(ful)

ludothèque [lydɔtɛk] *nf* = toy and game library

luette [lɥɛt] *nf* **(a)** *Anat* uvula **(b)** *Can Fam (locution)* **se mouiller** *ou* **se rincer la l.** *(prendre un verre)* to wet one's whistle; *(se soûler)* to get plastered

lueur [lɥœr] *nf* **(a)** *(lumière faible)* glow; **à la l. d'une bougie/ des étoiles** by candlelight/starlight; **à la l. des derniers événements** in the light of recent events **(b)** *Fig (de lucidité, de colère)* flash; *(d'intelligence, d'espoir)* glimmer

luge [lyʒ] *nf* toboggan, sled; **faire de la l.** to go tobogganing *or* sledding

luger [45] [lyʒe] *vi* **(a)** *(descendre en luge)* to toboggan, to sled **(b)** *Suisse (déraper)* to skid

lugubre [lygybr] *adj* gloomy; *(son, cri)* mournful

lui [lɥi] *pron personnel* **(a)** *(sujet) (personne)* he; *(chose, animal)* it; **l., il aurait fait un effort** HE would have made an effort; **mon frère, l., n'est pas venu** as for my brother, he didn't come; **si j'étais l., je me méfierais** if I were him I'd be careful
   (b) *(objet direct) (personne)* him; *(chose, animal)* it; **et l., tu le connais?** and what about him, do you know him?
   (c) *(objet indirect) (homme)* to him; *(femme)* to her; *(chose, animal)* to it; **donnez-le-l.** give it to him/her/it; **je l. ai serré la main** I shook his/her hand; **il l. jeta une pierre** he threw a stone at him/her/it
   (d) *(avec préposition) (personne)* him; *(chose, animal)* it; **elle pense encore à l.** she still thinks about him; **dis-le-lui, à l.** tell HIM; **ce livre est à l.** this book is his
   (e) *(réfléchi) (personne)* himself; *(chose, animal)* itself; **il ne pense qu'à l.** he thinks only of himself; **il a un appartement à l.** he has his own apartment; **un ami à l.** a friend of his
   (f) *(dans les comparaisons)* him; **elle gagne plus que l.** she earns more than him *or* than he does

lui-même [lɥimɛm] *pron personnel (personne)* himself; *(chose, animal)* itself

luire [18] [lɥir] *vi (métal, astre, yeux)* to shine; *(surface de l'eau, trottoir mouillé)* to glisten; *(flamme, braises)* to glow

luisais *etc. voir* **luire**

luisant, -e [lɥizã, -ãt] **1** *adj (étoile, métal, yeux)* shining; *(surface, pelage, peau)* shiny; *(braise)* glowing; **front l. de sueur** forehead glistening with sweat
   2 *nm* sheen

lumbago [lɔ̃bago] *nm* lumbago

lumière [lymjɛr] *nf* **(a)** *(clarté)* light; **à la l. de la lune** by moonlight; **il y a de la l. chez lui** there's a light on/there are lights on at his place; *Fig* **j'ai besoin de tes lumières** I need the benefit of your knowledge; **l. d'ambiance** subdued lighting **(b)** *(locutions)* **à la l. de son exposé,...** in the light of his/ her account,...; **faire (toute) la l. sur qch** to get (right) to the bottom of sth; **mettre qch en l.** to bring sth out; *Fam* **ce n'est pas une l.** she's not very bright

lumignon [lyminɔ̃] *nm* small light

luminaire [lyminɛr] *nm* **magasin de luminaires** lighting store

luminescent, -e [lyminɛsã, -ãt] *adj* luminescent

lumineux, -euse [lyminø, -øz] *adj* **(a)** *(corps, cadran)* luminous; *(pièce, ciel)* bright **(b)** *(radieux) (regard)* radiant; *(teint)* glowing **(c)** *(explication, propos)* lucid; *(idée)* brilliant

luminosité [lyminozite] *nf* **(a)** *(du ciel)* brightness; *(d'un regard, du teint)* radiance; *Phot* **la l.** the amount of light available **(b)** *(d'un écran)* brightness

lump [lœmp] *nm* **œufs de l.** lumpfish roe

lunaire [lynɛr] *adj* lunar; *Fig* **un visage l.** a moon face

lunatique [lynatik] *adj* moody, temperamental

lunch (*pl* **lunchs** *ou* **lunches**) [lœ̃ntʃ] *nm* buffet lunch

lundi [lœ̃di] *nm* Monday; **le l. de Pâques/de la Pentecôte** Easter/Whit Monday; *voir aussi* **samedi**

lune [lyn] *nf* **(a)** *(astre)* moon; *Fig* **je ne te demande pas la l.** I'm not asking for the moon; **être dans la l.** to be miles away; **la nouvelle/pleine l.** the new/full moon; **l. de miel** honeymoon **(b)** *Fam (derrière)* behind

luné, -e [lyne] *adj Fam* **être bien/mal l.** to be in a good/bad mood

lunette [lynɛt] *nf* **(a)** *(pour la vue)* **lunettes** (eye)glasses; **lunettes noires** dark glasses; **lunettes de soleil**, *Belg* **lunettes solaires** sunglasses; **lunettes de vue** corrective glasses **(b)** *(instrument d'optique)* telescope **(c)** *(siège des W.-C.)* seat **(d)** *(de voiture)* **l. arrière** rear window

lupin [lypɛ̃] *nm* lupin

lurette [lyrɛt] *nf* **il y a belle l.** ages ago; **il y a belle l. que je ne l'ai pas vu** I haven't seen him for ages

luron [lyrɔ̃] *nm* **c'est un gai** *ou* **joyeux l.** he's a lively fellow

lusophone [lyzɔfɔn] **1** *adj* Portuguese-speaking **2** *nmf* Portuguese speaker

lustre[1] [lystr] *nm* (**a**) *(lampe)* chandelier (**b**) *(brillant)* luster (**c**) *(prestige)* luster

lustre[2] [lystr] *nm* **ça dure depuis des lustres** it's been going on for ages

lustrer [lystre] *vt (glace, meuble, voiture)* to polish; **lustré par l'usure** shiny with wear

lustrine [lystrin] *nf* cotton luster

luth [lyt] *nm* lute

luthier [lytje] *nm* stringed-instrument maker

lutin [lytɛ̃] *nm* imp, elf

lutrin [lytrɛ̃] *nm* (**a**) *(à la messe)* lectern; *(pour soutenir un livre, des feuilles)* reading stand (**b**) *Belg, Can & Suisse (pupitre à musique)* music stand

lutte [lyt] *nf* (**a**) *(combat)* fight, struggle; *(antagonisme)* conflict; *(contre une maladie, contre la pollution)* fight; **entrer/être en l. contre qn** to enter into/to be in conflict with sb; **gagner de haute l.** to win after a hard struggle; **l. armée** armed struggle; **la l. des classes** the class struggle (**b**) *Sport* wrestling; **faire de la l.** to wrestle

lutter [lyte] *vi* (**a**) *(se battre)* to struggle, to fight; **l. contre** *(adversaire, oppresseur)* to fight against; *(maladie, incendie, tentation)* to fight; *(sommeil)* to fight off (**b**) *(rivaliser)* **l. de vitesse avec qn** to race sb (**c**) *Sport* to wrestle (**avec** *ou* **contre** with)

lutteur, -euse [lytœr, -øz] *nm,f Sport* wrestler

luxation [lyksasjɔ̃] *nf Méd* dislocation

luxe [lyks] *nm* (**a**) *(abondance, richesse)* luxury; *(d'une maison, de l'ameublement)* luxuriousness (**b**) *(qualité)* **de l.** *(produits)* luxury; *(voiture, édition)* de luxe; **boutique de l.** luxury goods store (**c**) *(bien superflu)* luxury; *Fig* **s'offrir** *ou* **se payer le l. de faire qch** to give oneself the luxury of doing sth; **je vais faire nettoyer ce vieil imperméable, ce ne sera pas du l.** I'm going to have this old raincoat cleaned, and none too

soon (**d**) *(profusion)* **un l. de précautions/de détails** a wealth of precautions/details

Luxembourg [lyksãbur] **1** *n (ville)* Luxembourg **2** *nm* **le L.** Luxembourg

luxembourgeois, -e [lyksãburʒwa, -az] **1** *adj* of Luxembourg **2** *nm,f* **L., Luxembourgeoise** Luxembourger

luxer [lykse] **se luxer** *vpr* **se l. l'épaule/le poignet** to dislocate one's shoulder/one's wrist

luxueux, -euse [lyksɥø, -øz] *adj* luxurious

luxure [lyksyr] *nf Litt* lust

luxuriant, -e [lyksyrjã, -ãt] *adj (végétation, forêt, chevelure)* luxuriant; *(imagination)* fertile

luzerne [lyzɛrn] *nf* alfalfa

lycée [lise] *nm* ≃ high school *(for pupils aged fifteen to eighteen);* **l. professionnel** vocational secondary school; **l. technique** technical school

lycéen, -enne [liseɛ̃, -ɛn] *nm,f* ≃ high-school student

Lycra® [likra] *nm* Lycra®

lymphatique [lɛ̃fatik] *adj* (**a**) *Biol* lymphatic (**b**) *(personne)* lethargic

lymphe [lɛ̃f] *nf* lymph

lymphocyte [lɛ̃fɔsit] *nm Biol* lymphocyte

lyncher [lɛ̃ʃe] *vt* to lynch

lynx [lɛ̃ks] *nm* lynx; *Fig* **avoir des yeux de l.** to have eyes like a hawk

Lyon [ljɔ̃] *n* Lyons

lyonnais, -e [ljɔnɛ, -ɛz] **1** *adj* of Lyons **2** *nm,f* **L., Lyonnaise** person from Lyons

lyophilisé, -e [ljɔfilize] *adj* freeze-dried

lyre [lir] *nf* lyre

lyrique [lirik] *adj* (**a**) *(poème, poète)* lyric (**b**) *(passionné)* lyrical

lyrisme [lirism] *nm* lyricism; **parler de qch avec l.** to wax lyrical about sth

lys [lis] = **lis**

M

M, m¹ [ɛm] *nm inv* M, m

m² (**a**) M. (*abrév* **Monsieur**) Mr. (**b**) (*abrév* **mètre(s)**) m; **1 m 50** 1.5 m, ≃ 5 ft (**c**) *Gram* (*abrév* **masculin**) m

m' [m] *voir* **me**

ma [ma] *voir* **mon**

MA [ɛma] *nm* (*abrév* **maître auxiliaire**) substitute teacher

maboule, -e [mabul] *Fam* **1** *adj* (*fou*) crazy
2 *nm,f* nutcase

mac [mak] *nm très Fam* (*maquereau*) pimp

macabre [makabr] *adj* (*découverte, histoire*) macabre, gruesome; (*humour*) macabre

macadam [makadam] *nm* (**a**) (*revêtement*) macadam; **m. goudronné** tarmac(adam) (**b**) (*route*) road

macaque [makak] *nm* (**a**) (*singe*) macaque; **m. rhésus** rhesus monkey (**b**) *Fam* (*personne laide*) pig

macareux [makarø] *nm* puffin

macaron [makarɔ̃] *nm* (**a**) *Culin* macaroon (**b**) (*badge*) badge; (*décoration*) rosette; (*autocollant*) sticker; *Journ* **m. de presse** press badge

macaroni [makarɔni] *nm* (**a**) (*pâte*) piece of macaroni; **des macaronis** macaroni (**b**) (*Italien*) wop, = racist term used to refer to an Italian

MacDo [makdo] *nm Fam* McDonalds®

Macédoine [masedwan] *nf* **la M.** Macedonia

macédoine [masedwan] *nf* **m. de fruits** fruit salad; **m. de légumes** mixed vegetables

macédonien, -enne [masedɔnjɛ̃, -ɛn] **1** *adj* Macedonian
2 *nm,f* **M., Macédonienne** Macedonian

macération [maserasjɔ̃] *nf* steeping

macérer [34] [masere] **1** *vt* to steep
2 *vi* to steep; **faire m. qch** to steep sth; *Fig* **laisser m. qn** to leave sb to stew

mâche [maʃ] *nf* corn salad

mâcher [maʃe] *vt* (*nourriture*) to chew; **ne pas m. ses mots** not to mince one's words

machette [maʃɛt] *nf* machete

machiavélique [makjavelik] *adj* Machiavellian

machin [maʃɛ̃] *nm Fam* (**a**) (*objet*) thingy, thingumajig, thingumabob (**b**) (*personne*) what's-his-name, *f* what's-her-name; **monsieur M.** Mr. What's-his-name; **madame M.** Mrs. What's-her-name

machinal, -e, -aux, -ales [maʃinal, -o] *adj* (*action, geste, travail*) mechanical; (*réaction*) automatic

machinalement [maʃinalmã] *adv* (*agir*) mechanically; (*réagir, répondre*) automatically

machination [maʃinasjɔ̃] *nf* conspiracy

machine [maʃin] *nf* (**a**) (*appareil*) machine; **m. à café** coffee machine; **m. à calculer** calculator; (*plus grande*) calculating machine; **m. à coudre** sewing machine; **m. à écrire** typewriter; **écrire qch à la m.** to type sth; **m. à laver**, *Belg* **m. à lessiver** washing machine; **m. à sous** slot machine, one-armed bandit; **m. à tricoter** knitting machine (**b**) (*dans un bateau*) **stopper les machines** to stop engines; **faire m. arrière** to reverse engines; *Fig* to backtrack (**c**) (*locomotive*) engine; *Fam* (*moto*) machine (**d**) (*organisation*) machinery

machine-outil (*pl* **machines-outils**) [maʃinuti] *nf* machine tool

machiner [maʃine] *vt* to plot

machinisme [maʃinism] *nm* mechanization

machiniste [maʃinist] *nmf* (**a**) (*dans un théâtre*) sceneshifter, stagehand; (*au cinéma, à la télévision*) grip (**b**) (*conducteur d'autobus*) driver

machisme [matʃism, maʃism] *nm* machismo

macho [matʃo] *adj & nm Fam* macho

mâchoire [maʃwar] *nf* (**a**) (*d'une personne, d'un animal*) jaw (**b**) (*d'une poulie*) flange (**c**) **mâchoires** (*d'un étau, d'une tenaille*) jaws; (*de frein*) shoes

mâchonner [maʃɔne] *vt* (**a**) (*mâcher*) to chew (**b**) (*marmonner*) to mutter

mâchouiller [maʃuje] *vt Fam* to chew away at

maçon [masɔ̃] *nm* (**a**) (*d'ouvrage en briques*) bricklayer; (*d'ouvrage en pierre*) (stone)mason (**b**) (*franc-maçon*) mason

maçonnerie [masɔnri] *nf* (**a**) (*de briques*) brickwork; (*de pierres*) masonry, stonework (**b**) (*franc-maçonnerie*) masonry

maçonnique [masɔnik] *adj* masonic

macramé [makrame] *nm* macramé

macrobiotique [makrɔbjɔtik] **1** *adj* macrobiotic
2 *nf* macrobiotics (*singulier*)

macro-commande (*pl* **macro-commandes**) [makrɔkɔmãd] *nf Ordinat* macro(-command)

macroéconomie [makroekɔnɔmi] *nf* macro-economics (*singulier*)

macrolangage [makrolãgaʒ] *nm Ordinat* macro-language

maculer [makyle] *vt* to stain (**de** with)

Madagascar [madagaskar] *n* Madagascar

madame [madam] (*pl* **mesdames** [medam]) *nf* (**a**) (*titre*) Mrs.; **M. Martin** Mrs. Martin; **M. le Ministre** the Minister (**b**) (*en apostrophe*) madam; (*à l'école*) Miss; **M. le Ministre** Madam Minister; **au revoir, m.** goodbye; **M.,** (*dans une lettre*) Dear Madam,; *Fam* **et en plus, M. exige des excuses!** and so Her Ladyship wants an apology as well, does she?; **par ici, mesdames** this way, ladies; **mesdames, messieurs** ladies and gentlemen

madeleine [madlɛn] *nf* (*gâteau*) madeleine

mademoiselle [madmwazɛl] (*pl* **mesdemoiselles** [medmwazɛl]) *nf* (**a**) (*suivi d'un nom*) Miss; **M. Martin** Miss Martin; **Mesdemoiselles Martin et Durand** the Misses Martin and Durand (**b**) (*en apostrophe*) (*à l'école*) Miss; **merci m.** thank you; *Fam* **et en plus, M. se plaint!** so, Her Ladyship is complaining as well, is she?; **mesdemoiselles, un peu de silence je vous prie!** (*dans une classe*) let's have some quiet, girls, please! (**c**) (*dans une lettre*) **M.** Dear Madam (**d**) (*utilisé seul*) **M. se plaint que...** (*dans un magasin*) this young lady is complaining that...

Madère [madɛr] *n* Madeira

madère [madɛr] *nm* Madeira (wine)
madone [madɔn] *nf* Madonna
madras [madrɑs] *nm (tissu)* madras (cotton)
Madrid [madrid] *n* Madrid
madrier [madrije] *nm* beam
madrilène [madrilɛn] **1** *adj* of Madrid
2 *nmf* **M.** person from Madrid
maestria [maɛstrija] *nf* mastery
maf(f)ia [mafja] *nf* Mafia; **la M.** the Mafia
maf(f)ieux, -euse [mafjø, -øz] **1** *adj* Mafia
2 *nm,f* Mafioso
maf(f)ioso [mafjozo] (*pl* **maf(f)iosi** [mafjozi]) *nm* Mafioso
maganer [magane] *vt Can (chose)* to spoil, to waste; *(personne)* to manhandle
magasin [magazɛ̃] *nm* **(a)** *(boutique)* store; **avoir qch en m.** to have sth in stock; **courir** *ou* **faire les magasins** to go shopping; **grand m.** department store; *Can* **m. général** general store **(b)** *(entrepôt)* warehouse **(c)** *(d'un appareil photo, d'une arme)* magazine
magasinage [magazinaʒ] *nm* **(a)** *(mise en dépôt)* warehousing **(b)** *(droits)* warehouse charges **(c)** *Can* **faire du m.** to go shopping
magasiner [magazine] *vi Can* to go shopping
magasinier [magazinje] *nm* warehouseman
magazine [magazin] *nm* **(a)** *(journal)* magazine **(b)** *(émission à la radio ou à la télévision)* magazine program
mage [maʒ] *nm* magus
Maghreb [magrɛb] *nm* **le M.** the Maghreb
maghrébin, -e [magrebɛ̃, -in] **1** *adj* of the Maghreb
2 *nm,f* **M., Maghrébine** person from the Maghreb

> ### Maghrébin
> This term usually refers to people from Algeria, Morocco and Tunisia, although it can also refer to Libyans and Mauritanians. It has a particular resonance in contemporary France, where immigrants from these countries constitute the largest ethnic minority.

magicien, -enne [maʒisjɛ̃, -ɛn] *nm,f* magician
magie [maʒi] *nf* magic; **m. blanche/noire** white/black magic
magique [maʒik] *adj* **(a)** *(surnaturel)* magic **(b)** *(extraordinaire)* magical
magiquement [maʒikmɑ̃] *adv* magically
magistère [maʒistɛr] *nm* **(a)** *(diplôme)* = post-graduate vocational qualification **(b)** *(autorité)* authority
magistral, -e, -aux, -ales [maʒistral, -o] *adj* **(a)** *(admirable) (interprétation, démonstration)* masterly; *(réussite)* brilliant **(b)** *(énorme) (correction, dispute)* proper; *(erreur)* colossal **(c)** *(docte) (ton)* magisterial
magistralement [maʒistralmɑ̃] *adv* authoritatively
magistrat [maʒistra] *nm (qui rend la justice)* judge; *(qui applique la loi)* prosecuting attorney
magistrature [maʒistratyr] *nf* **la m.** the judicial authorities; **la m. assise** the Bench *or* judges; **la m. debout** the body of prosecuting attorneys
magma [magma] *nm* **(a)** *Géol* magma **(b)** *(ensemble confus)* jumble
magnanime [maɲanim] *adj* magnanimous
magnanimité [maɲanimite] *nf* magnanimity
magnat [magna] *nm* magnate, tycoon; **m. de la presse** press baron
magner [maɲe] **se magner** *vpr Fam* to get a move on
magnésium [maɲezjɔm] *nm* magnesium
magnétique [maɲetik] *adj* magnetic
magnétiser [maɲetize] *vt* **(a)** *(matériau, corps)* to magnetize **(b)** *(personne, foule)* to hypnotize

magnétisme [maɲetism] *nm (d'un matériau, de la terre, d'une personne)* magnetism
magnéto [maɲeto] *nm Fam* tape recorder
magnétophone [maɲetɔfɔn] *nm* tape recorder
magnétoscope [maɲetɔskɔp] *nm* video(recorder),VCR
magnificence [maɲifisɑ̃s] *nf* magnificence
magnifier [66] [maɲifje] *vt* to magnify, to glorify
magnifique [maɲifik] *adj* magnificent
magnifiquement [maɲifikmɑ̃] *adv* magnificently
magnitude [maɲityd] *nf* magnitude
magnolia [maɲɔlja] *nm* magnolia (tree)
magnum [magnɔm] *nm* magnum
magot [mago] *nm Fam* hoard
magouille [maguj] *nf Fam* scheming; **faire des magouilles** to scheme
magouiller [maguje] *vt & vi Fam* to scheme
magouilleur, -euse [magujœr, -øz] *nm,f Fam* schemer
magret [magrɛ] *nm (de canard)* fil(l)et
Mahomet [maɔmɛ] *npr* Mohammed
mai [mɛ] *nm* May; **le premier m.** *(fête)* May Day; **le huit m.** *(fête)* VE day; *voir aussi* **janvier**

> ### Mai 68
> The events of May 1968 came about when student protests, coupled with widespread discontent among workers, culminated in a general strike and rioting. De Gaulle's government survived the crisis, but the issues raised made the events a turning point in French social history.

maigre [mɛgr] **1** *adj* **(a)** *(très mince) (personne, partie du corps)* thin **(b)** *(sans gras) (viande)* lean; *(fromage, yaourt)* low-fat **(c)** *(peu abondant) (filet d'eau)* thin; *(repas, salaire)* meager; *(végétation, barbe)* sparse **(d)** *(peu conséquent) (conclusions, explication)* thin; *(succès)* very limited
2 *nm (de viande)* lean part
3 *nmf* thin person
4 *adv* **faire m.** not to eat meat
maigrelet, -ette [mɛgrəlɛ, -ɛt] *adj* skinny
maigreur [mɛgrœr] *nf (d'une personne)* thinness
maigrichon, -onne [megriʃɔ̃, -ɔn] *adj* skinny
maigrir [mɛgrir] *vi* to get thinner
mailing [mɛliŋ] *nm* mass mailing
maillage [majaʒ] *nm* networking
maille [maj] *nf* **(a)** *(de tricot)* stitch; **m. à l'endroit/à l'envers** plain/purl stitch **(b)** *(de filet)* mesh; *Fig* **passer entre les mailles du filet** to slip through the net **(c)** *(tissu)* knitted fabric **(d)** *(de chaîne)* link **(e)** **avoir m. à partir avec qn** to have a set-to with sb
maillet [majɛ] *nm* mallet
maillon [majɔ̃] *nm* link
maillot [majo] *nm (de footballeur, de coureur cycliste)* shirt, jersey; **m. de bain** *(pour femmes)* bathing costume; *(pour hommes)* (swimming) trunks; **m. de corps** undershirt; **m. jaune** yellow jersey *(in the Tour de France)*
main [mɛ̃] **1** *nf* hand; **avoir qch en m.** *(situation)* to have sth in hand; *(voiture)* to have the feel of sth; **avoir la m. heureuse** to be lucky; **avoir la m. leste** to be quick to raise one's hand; **avoir la m. lourde** *(être brutal)* to be heavy-handed; **il a eu la m. lourde avec le sel** he was a bit heavy-handed with the salt; **donner la m. à qn** to hold sb's hand; **faire m. basse sur qch** to get one's hands on sth; **mettre la m. sur qch** *(trouver ce que l'on cherchait)* to lay one's hands on sth; **mettre la m. à la pâte** *ou* **à l'ouvrage** to lend a hand; **mettre la dernière m. à qch** to put the finishing touches to sth; **en mettre sa m. au feu** *ou* **à couper** to stake one's life on it; **ne pas y aller de m. morte** *(en frappant, en insultant)* not to pull one's

punches; *(forcer une description, une action)* to overdo it; **prendre qn par la m.** to take sb's hand; *Fig* **se prendre par la m.** to take oneself in hand; **prendre qn/qch en m.** to take sb/sth in hand; **prendre qn la m. dans le sac** to catch sb red-handed; **perdre la m.** to lose one's touch; **à la m.** *(faire, fabriquer)* by hand; *(tenir, avoir)* in one's hand; **écrit à la m.** handwritten; **fait à la m.** *(pull, poterie)* handmade; **à deux mains** in both hands; **à quatre mains** *(morceau)* for four hands; *(jouer)* four-handed; **à m. armée** *(vol, attaque)* armed; **à main(s) nue(s)** with bare hands; **à pleines mains** by the handful; **de m. en m.** from hand to hand; **de la m. à la m.** cash in hand; **de m. de maître** with a master's hand; **de première m.** first-hand; **de seconde m.** second-hand; *Tél* **mains libres** hands-free; **en mains propres** in person; **haut les mains!, les mains en l'air!** hands up!; **les mains vides** empty-handed; *Fig* **les mains dans les poches** unprepared; **sous la m.** handy; **m. courante** handrail

  2 *adv* **tricoté/fait/cousu m.** hand-knitted/-made/-sewn

main-d'œuvre [mɛ̃dœvr] *nf* labor

main-forte [mɛ̃fɔrt] *voir* **prêter**

mainmise [mɛ̃miz] *nf* seizure (**sur** of)

maint, -e [mɛ̃, mɛ̃t] *adj indéfini Litt* many a; **maintes et maintes fois, en maintes et maintes occasions** time and (time) again

maintenance [mɛ̃tnɑ̃s] *nf* maintenance

maintenant [mɛ̃tnɑ̃] *adv* now

maintenir [70] [mɛ̃tnir] **1** *vt* **(a)** *(soutenir)* to hold in position **(b)** *(empêcher d'avancer) (foule)* to hold back; **m. qn à distance** to keep sb at a distance **(c)** *(conserver) (tradition, paix)* to maintain, to keep; *(décision)* to abide by; **m. qn en vie** to keep sb alive **(d)** *(affirmer)* to maintain (**que** that)

  2 se maintenir *vpr* to hold up

maintien [mɛ̃tjɛ̃] *nm* **(a)** *(conservation)* maintenance; *(de la loi)* upholding; **m. de l'ordre** maintenance of law and order **(b)** *(allure, posture)* bearing

maintiendrai *etc. voir* **maintenir**

maire [mɛr] *nm* mayor

Maire

In France, the mayor has obligations not only to the community but also to national government. He or she is responsible for promulgating national law as well as supervising the local police and officiating at civic occasions. Mayors are elected by the "conseil municipal" (and thus indirectly by the town's residents).

---

mairie [mɛri] *nf (lieu, administration)* city hall

Mairie

Also called the "hôtel de ville", this is the center of municipal government. The "mairie" serves as a vital information source for town residents. People go there to enquire about taxes, to get married in a civil ceremony, to enrol in certain community-sponsored classes, etc.

---

mais [mɛ] **1** *conj* **(a)** *(marque l'opposition ou la transition)* but; **non seulement..., m. aussi** *ou* **encore...** not only... but also...; **m. qu'est-ce qui t'arrive?** whatever's the matter with you?; **m. j'y pense, je ne l'ai pas encore appelée!** I've just remembered, I haven't called her yet! **(b)** *(emphatique)* **m. oui!** of course!; **m. non!** of course not!; **m. enfin** well really; **elle ne fait rien, m. vraiment rien** she does nothing all day, and I mean nothing; **j'ai faim, m. faim!** I'm so hungry!

  2 *nm* **il y a un m.** there's a but

maïs [mais] *nm* corn

maison [mɛzɔ̃] **1** *nf* **(a)** *(habitation)* house; **m. de campagne** *(résidence secondaire)* house in the country; **m. individuelle** single-family house; **m. de poupée** doll house **(b)** *(foyer)*

---

home; **à la m.** at home; **toute la m. dort** the whole house is asleep **(c)** *(entreprise)* company; **m. de couture** fashion house; **m. d'édition** publishing house; **m. mère** parent company **(d)** *(lignée)* house **(e)** *(institution)* **m. d'arrêt** prison; **m. close** *ou* **de passe** brothel; **m. de correction** *ou* **de redressement** reformatory; **m. de la culture** arts center; **m. des jeunes et de la culture** = youth club and arts center; **m. de repos** rest *or* convalescent home; **m. de retraite** retirement home

  2 *adj inv* **(a)** *(artisanal)* homemade **(b)** *(au sein de l'entreprise)* in-house **(c)** *Fam (en intensif)* almighty

Maison-Blanche [mɛzɔ̃blɑ̃ʃ] *nf* **la M.** the White House

maisonnée [mɛzɔne] *nf* household

maisonnette [mɛzɔnɛt] *nf* small house

maître [mɛtr] **1** *nm* **(a)** *(de situation, de chien)* master; **m. de maison** host; **en m.** authoritatively; **être m. de son destin** to be master of one's own destiny; **être m. de soi** to have self-control; **il n'était plus m. de ses actes** he didn't know what he was doing

  (b) *(dans des fonctions)* **m. (d'école)** (elementary-school) teacher; **m. assistant** assistant professor; **m. auxiliaire** substitute teacher; **m. de conférences** associate professor; **m. d'hôtel** *(dans une maison)* butler; *(dans un restaurant)* head waiter; **m. nageur** swimming instructor; **m. d'œuvre** project manager

  (c) *(titre octroyé à un peintre, à un musicien)* maestro; **les grands maîtres** the great masters; **être passé m. dans l'art de qch/de faire qch** to be a past master at sth/at doing sth **(d)** *(titre donné à un avocat)* = form of address for lawyer **(e)** **m. chanteur** blackmailer

  2 *adj* **m. mot** key word

maîtresse [mɛtrɛs] **1** *nf* mistress; **être m. de son destin** to be mistress of one's own destiny; **être m. de soi** to have self-control; **m. (d'école)** (elementary-school) teacher; **m. de maison** hostess

  2 *adj* main, principal; **m. femme** capable woman

maîtrise [metriz] *nf* **(a)** *(diplôme universitaire)* ≃ master's degree (**de** in) **(b)** *(contrôle) (de ses passions)* mastery; **m. de soi** self-control **(c)** *(connaissance)* mastery **(d)** *(école de chant)* choir school

maîtriser [metrize] **1** *vt* **(a)** *(soumettre) (agresseur)* to overpower; *(élèves, animal)* to control; *(flammes, opposition)* to subdue; *(incendie, épidémie)* to control **(b)** *(contrôler) (passion)* to control; *(peur)* to overcome **(c)** *(connaître parfaitement) (sujet, langue)* to master; **il ne maîtrise pas la langue** he hasn't mastered the language **(d)** *(rester maître de) (véhicule)* to have under control

  2 se maîtriser *vpr* to control oneself

Maïzena® [maizena] *nf* cornstarch

majesté [maʒɛste] *nf* **(a)** *(noblesse)* majesty **(b)** **Sa M. (le Roi)** His Majesty (the King); **Sa M. (la Reine)** Her Majesty (the Queen) **(c)** *Art* **la Vierge en m.** the Virgin in majesty

majestueux, -euse [maʒɛstɥø, -øz] *adj* majestic

majeur, -e [maʒœr] **1** *adj* **(a)** *(principal)* major **(b)** *(personne)* of age **(c)** *Mus (mode, intervalle)* major

  2 *nm (doigt)* middle finger

major [maʒɔr] *nm* **(a)** *(d'une promotion)* top student **(b)** *Mil (officier)* regimental adjutant *(with administrative duties)*; *Belg, Can & Suisse* ≃ major

majoration [maʒɔrasjɔ̃] *nf (d'une facture)* surcharge (**de** on); *(d'un prix)* increase (**de** in)

majordome [maʒɔrdɔm] *nm* butler

majorer [maʒɔre] *vt (facture)* to put a surcharge on; *(prix)* to increase

majorette [maʒɔrɛt] *nf (drum)* majorette

majoritaire [maʒɔritɛr] *adj* majority; **être m.** to be in the majority

majorité [maʒɔrite] *nf* **(a)** *(supériorité en nombre)* majority; **en**

m. for the most part; **avoir la m.** to be in the majority (**b**) *(dans des élections)* majority; **m. relative/absolue** relative/absolute majority (**c**) *(parti politique)* majority party (**d**) **m. civile** majority, coming of age

Majorque [maʒɔrk] *n* Majorca

majorquin, -e [maʒɔrkɛ̃, -in] **1** *adj* Majorcan
2 *nm,f* **M., Majorquine** Majorcan

majuscule [maʒyskyl] **1** *adj (lettre)* upper-case, capital
2 *nf* upper-case *or* capital letter

mal¹, maux [mal, mo] *nm* (**a**) *(douleur)* pain, ache; **avoir m. à l'estomac/à la tête/au dos** to have a stomachache/a headache/a backache; **avoir m. à la gorge** to have a sore throat; **j'ai m. au bras** my arm hurts, I have a sore arm; **avoir m. aux dents** to have a toothache; **avoir des maux d'estomac/de tête** to get stomachaches/headaches; **avoir m. au cœur** to be nauseous; **où avez-vous m.?** where does it hurt?; **faire m. à qn** to hurt sb; **mon genou/œil me fait m.** my knee/eye hurts; **se faire m.** to hurt oneself; *Fam* **attraper du m.** to catch cold; **ça fait m. au cœur de voir ça!** it's sickening to see things like that!; *Fam* **ça me ferait m.!** I'm not having it!; **être en m. de qch** to crave sth; **être en m. d'enfants** to be broody; **m. de cœur** nausea; **m. de dents** toothache; **m. de gorge** sore throat; **m. de mer** seasickness; **avoir le m. de mer** to be seasick; **m. du pays** homesickness; **avoir le m. du pays** to be homesick; *Litt* **m. du siècle** world-weariness; **m. de tête** headache; **m. des transports** travel sickness; *Prov* **aux grands maux les grands remèdes** desperate situations call for desperate remedies

(**b**) *(préjudice)* harm; **faire du m. à qn** to harm sb; **ça n'a jamais fait de m. à personne!** it never did anyone any harm!; **vouloir du m. à qn** to mean to harm sb; **cela fera plus de m. que de bien** it will do more harm than good; **le m. est fait** the damage has been done; **un m. nécessaire** a necessary evil; **il n'y a pas de m. à cela** there's no harm in that; *Fam* **il n'y a pas de m.** there's no harm done; **dire du m. de qn** to speak ill of sb; **ne pas penser à m.** to mean well

(**c**) *(contraire du bien)* wrong; **le bien et le m.** right and wrong, good and evil; **voir le m. partout** to always see the bad side

(**d**) *(difficulté)* **avoir du m. à faire qch** to have difficulty *or* trouble doing sth; *Fam* **avoir un m. de chien à faire qch** to have a hell of a time doing sth; **non sans m.** not without difficulty; **se donner du m. pour faire qch** to take pains to do sth; **donner du m. à qn** to give sb trouble

mal² [mal] **1** *adv* (**a**) *(médiocrement)* badly; *(incorrectement)* wrongly; **elle chante m.** she's a bad singer; **la porte est m. fermée** the door isn't closed properly; **il travaille m. à l'école** he's a poor student; **cette lampe éclaire m.** this lamp doesn't give much light; **m. comprendre** to misunderstand; **m. interpréter** to misinterpret; **m. choisir** to make the wrong choice; **ça va m. finir** it'll end in tears; **on y mange m.** the food's not very good there; **on dort m. dans ce canapé-lit** this sofa bed isn't very comfortable; **je ne pensais pas m. faire** I didn't think I was doing anything wrong; **aller de m. en pis** to go from bad to worse; **on voit m. d'ici** you can't see very well from here; *Fam* **se mettre m. avec qn** to fall out with sb; *Fam* **être m. avec qn** to be on bad terms with sb; **vous ne feriez pas m. de...** you would be wise to...

(**b**) *(en mauvaise santé)* **se sentir m.** to feel ill; **se trouver m.** to faint; **aller m.** to be ill *or* sick; **être au plus m.** to be at death's door; **être m. en point** to be in a bad way

(**c**) *(une certaine quantité)* **pas m. de** quite a lot of; **il y en a pas m.** there is/are quite a lot; **cela m'a pris pas m. de temps** it took me quite a while

2 *adj inv (contraire à la morale)* bad; **c'est très m. de faire ça** it's very naughty to do that; **c'est pas m.** it's not bad, it's quite good; **elle n'est pas m.** she's not bad; **on n'est pas m. ici** we've found a nice place here

malabar [malabar] *nm Fam* hulk

malade [malad] **1** *adj* (**a**) *(souffrant)* ill, sick; *(nauséeux)* nauseous; **tomber m.** to fall *or* to be taken ill; **je suis m. en bateau/voiture/avion** I suffer from seasickness/carsickness/airsickness; **être m. du cœur/du foie** to have heart/liver trouble; **être m. d'inquiétude/de jalousie** to be sick with worry/jealousy (**b**) *(qui fonctionne mal) (organe, dent)* bad; *Fig (industrie)* ailing (**c**) *(dérangé intellectuellement)* mad

2 *nmf* sick person; *(dans un hôpital)* patient; **un m. mental** a mentally ill person; *(dans un hôpital)* a mental patient; **un m. imaginaire** a hypochondriac

maladie [maladi] *nf* illness, disease; *Fig* **en faire une m.** to make a song and dance about it; **la m. d'Alzheimer** Alzheimer's disease; **m. bleue** cyanosis; **la m. de Parkinson** Parkinson's disease; **m. sexuellement transmissible** sexually transmitted disease; **m. de la vache folle** mad cow disease

maladif, -ive [maladif, -iv] *adj* (**a**) *(personne, teint)* sickly (**b**) *(curiosité, pensées)* morbid (**c**) *(susceptibilité, jalousie)* pathological

maladresse [maladrɛs] *nf* (**a**) *(manque d'habileté physique)* clumsiness, awkwardness; (**b**) *(manque de tact)* tactlessness; *(bévue)* blunder

maladroit, -e [maladrwa, -at] **1** *adj* (**a**) *(inhabile)* clumsy, awkward (**b**) *(manquant de tact)* tactless
2 *nm,f* (**a**) *(personne inhabile)* clumsy *or* awkward person (**b**) *(personne sans tact)* tactless person

maladroitement [maladrwatmɑ̃] *adv* (**a**) *(de façon gauche)* clumsily (**b**) *(sans tact)* tactlessly

malais, -e¹ [malɛ, -ɛz] **1** *adj* Malaysian
2 *nm (langue)* Malay
3 *nm,f* **M., Malaise** Malaysian

malaise¹ [malɛz] *nm* (**a**) *(trouble physique)* feeling of sickness; *(étourdissement)* dizzy spell; **avoir un m.** to feel faint (**b**) *(inconfort moral)* uneasiness (**c**) *(état de crise)* unrest

malaisé, -e [malɛze] *adj* difficult

Malaisie [malɛzi] *nf* **la M.** Malaysia

malaria [malarja] *nf* malaria; **avoir la m.** to have malaria

malavisé, -e [malavize] *adj Litt* unwise (**de faire qch** to do sth)

Malawi [malawi] *nm* **le M.** Malawi

malaxer [malakse] *vt* to knead

malchance [malʃɑ̃s] *nf* bad luck; **par m.** as bad luck would have it

malchanceux, -euse [malʃɑ̃sø, -øz] **1** *adj* unlucky
2 *nm,f* unlucky person

malcommode [malkɔmɔd] *adj* (**a**) *(appareil)* impractical; *(vêtement)* unsuitable (**b**) *Can (personne) (indiscipliné)* unruly; *(hargneux)* cantankerous

Maldives [maldiv] *nfpl* **les (îles) M.** the Maldives

maldonne [maldɔn] *nf* misdeal; *Fig* **il y a m.** something's gone wrong somewhere

mâle [mɑl] **1** *adj* (**a**) *(du sexe masculin)* male (**b**) *(viril) (courage, assurance)* manly; *(style)* virile (**c**) **prise m.** plug
2 *nm* male

malédiction [malediksjɔ̃] *nf* curse

maléfice [malefis] *nm* evil spell

maléfique [malefik] *adj* evil

malencontreusement [malɑ̃kɔ̃trøzmɑ̃] *adv* unfortunately

malencontreux, -euse [malɑ̃kɔ̃trø, -øz] *adj* unfortunate

malentendant, -e [malɑ̃tɑ̃dɑ̃, -ɑ̃t] **1** *adj* hard of hearing
2 *nm,f* person who is hard of hearing

malentendu [malɑ̃tɑ̃dy] *nm* misunderstanding

mal-en-train [malɑ̃trɛ̃] *adj Can* unwell; **avoir l'air m.** to look sickly *or* out-of-sorts

malfaçon [malfasɔ̃] *nf* defect

malfaisant, -e [malfəzɑ̃, -ɑ̃t] *adj* harmful

malfaiteur [malfɛtœr] *nm* criminal

malfamé, -e [malfame] *adj* disreputable

malformation [malfɔrmasjɔ̃] *nf* malformation

malfrat [malfra] *nm Fam* crook

malgache [malgaʃ] **1** *adj* Madagascan
 2 *nm (langue)* Malagasy
 3 *nmf* **M.** Madagascan

malgré [malgre] *prép (en dépit de)* in spite of, despite; **m. tout** *(en dépit de tout)* in spite of *or* despite everything; *(pourtant)* all the same

malhabile [malabil] *adj* clumsy, awkward

malheur [malœr] **1** *nm* **(a)** *(drame, catastrophe)* misfortune; **le m., c'est que…** the unfortunate thing is that…; **faire un m.** to be a big hit; **un m. n'arrive jamais seul** it never rains but it pours **(b)** *(chagrin, infortune)* misfortune; **faire le m. de qn** to cause sb a lot of unhappiness **(c)** *(malchance)* bad luck; **par m.** unfortunately; **porter m. à qn** to bring sb bad luck; **avoir le m. de faire qch** to make the big mistake of doing sth
 2 *exclam* hell!

malheureusement [malørøzmɑ̃] *adv* unfortunately; **m. pour toi, il ne reste plus de petites tailles** you're out of luck, there are no small sizes left

malheureux, -euse [malørø, -øz] **1** *adj* **(a)** *(triste)* unhappy, miserable **(b)** *(malchanceux) (personne)* unlucky; *(candidat, tentative)* unsuccessful; *(amour)* unrequited; **m. au jeu/en amour** unlucky at gambling/in love **(c)** *(regrettable)* unfortunate **(d)** *(négligeable)* miserable, wretched
 2 *nm,f* **(a)** *(personne infortunée)* poor wretch **(b)** *(indigent)* poor *or* needy person; **les m.** the poor, the needy

malhonnête [malɔnɛt] *adj* **(a)** *(personne, pratique)* dishonest **(b)** *(indécent) (proposition)* indecent

malhonnêteté [malɔnɛtte] *nf* dishonesty

Mali [mali] *nm* **le M.** Mali

malice [malis] *nf* **(a)** *(espièglerie)* mischief **(b)** *(méchanceté)* malice; **sans m.** without malice

malicieusement [malisjøzmɑ̃] *adv* mischievously

malicieux, -euse [malisjø, -øz] *adj (espiègle)* mischievous

malien, -enne [maljɛ̃, -ɛn] **1** *adj* Malian
 2 *nm,f* **M., Malienne** Malian

malignité [maliɲite] *nf* **(a)** *(méchanceté)* malice **(b)** *(d'une tumeur)* malignancy

malin, -igne [malɛ̃, -iɲ] **1** *adj* **(a)** *(rusé) (personne)* crafty; *(regard)* knowing; *Ironique* **c'est m.!** that's smart! **(b)** *(méchant) (plaisir)* perverse, malicious; **prendre un m. plaisir à faire qch** to take a perverse *or* malicious pleasure in doing sth **(c)** *(tumeur)* malignant
 2 *nm,f* crafty person; **faire le m.** to show off

malingre [malɛ̃gr] *adj* puny

malintentionné, -e [malɛ̃tɑ̃sjɔne] *adj* ill-intentioned

malle [mal] *nf* **(a)** *(valise)* trunk; *Fam* **se faire la m.** to clear off **(b)** *(de voiture)* trunk **(c)** *Can* **mettre une lettre à la m.** to mail a letter

malléable [maleabl] *adj* malleable

mallette [malɛt] *nf (porte-documents)* briefcase

malmener [46] [malmәne] *vt* **(a)** *(brutaliser) (personne)* to manhandle, to treat roughly; *(verbalement)* to attack; *(matériel, véhicule)* to mistreat **(b)** *(dominer)* **m. qn** to give sb a hard time

malnutrition [malnytrisjɔ̃] *nf* malnutrition

malodorant, -e [malɔdɔrɑ̃, -ɑ̃t] *adj* foul-smelling, smelly

malotru, -e [malɔtry] *nm,f* lout

Malouines [malwin] *nfpl* **les (îles) M.** the Falkland Islands, the Falklands

malpoli, -e [malpɔli] *Fam* **1** *adj* rude
 2 *nm,f* rude person

malpropre [malprɔpr] *adj* **(a)** *(sale) (mains)* dirty; *(apparence, travail)* slovenly **(b)** *(inconvenant)* smutty **(c)** *(malhonnête)* despicable

malsain, -e [malsɛ̃, -ɛn] *adj* **(a)** *(dangereux pour la santé)* unhealthy **(b)** *(pernicieux)* unhealthy; *(personne)* unwholesome

malséant, -e [malseɑ̃, -ɑ̃t] *adj Litt* unseemly

malt [malt] *nm* malt

maltais, -e [maltɛ, -ɛz] **1** *adj* Maltese
 2 *nm (langue)* Maltese
 3 *nm,f* **M., Maltaise** Maltese; **les M.** the Maltese

Malte [malt] *n* Malta

maltraitance [maltrɛtɑ̃s] *nf* ill-treatment

maltraitant, -e [maltrɛtɑ̃, -ɑ̃t] *adj* abusive

maltraiter [maltrɛte] *vt* **(a)** *(brutaliser)* to ill-treat **(b)** *(verbalement)* to attack

malus [malys] *nm* partial loss of no-claims bonus *(due to insurance claim)*

malveillance [malvɛjɑ̃s] *nf* spite

malveillant, -e [malvɛjɑ̃, -ɑ̃t] *adj* spiteful

malvenu, -e [malvәny] *adj* out of place, inappropriate

malversation [malvɛrsasjɔ̃] *nf* embezzlement

maman [mamɑ̃] *nf* mom; *(langage enfantin)* mommy

mamelle [mamɛl] *nf (de vache)* udder; *(de chienne, de truie)* teat

mamelon [mamlɔ̃] *nm* **(a)** *(du sein)* nipple **(b)** *(colline)* hillock

mamie [mami] *nf* grandma, gran(ny)

mammaire [mamɛr] *adj* mammary

mammifère [mamifɛr] **1** *adj* mammalian
 2 *nm* mammal

mammographie [mamɔgrafi] *nf* mammography

mammouth [mamut] *nm* mammoth

mamours [mamur] *nmpl Fam* kissing and cuddling; **faire des m. à qn** to kiss and cuddle sb

manager¹ [manadʒɛr] *nm* manager

manager² [45] [manadʒe] *vt* to manage

manant [manɑ̃] *nm* **(a)** *Hist (villageois)* villager; *(paysan)* peasant **(b)** *Litt (mufle)* lout

Manche [mɑ̃ʃ] *nf* **la M.** the (English) Channel

manche¹ [mɑ̃ʃ] *nf* **(a)** *(de vêtement)* sleeve; **en manches de chemise** in one's shirtsleeves; **manches longues/courtes** long/short sleeves; **manches ballon/raglan** puff/raglan sleeves **(b)** *(de jeu, de compétition)* round; *(au tennis)* set **(c)** *Fam* **faire la m.** to beg

manche² [mɑ̃ʃ] *nm* **(a)** *(d'outil)* handle; **m. à balai** broomstick; *(d'avion)* joystick **(b)** *(de guitare)* neck **(c)** *Fam* **s'y prendre comme un m.** to make a total mess of things

manchette [mɑ̃ʃɛt] *nf* **(a)** *(extrémité de la manche)* cuff **(b)** *(de journal)* headline **(c)** *(au catch)* forearm smash; *(au volley-ball)* dig

manchon [mɑ̃ʃɔ̃] *nm* **(a)** *(vêtement)* muff **(b)** *Tech* sleeve

manchot¹, -e [mɑ̃ʃo, -ɔt] **1** *adj (privé d'un bras)* one-armed; *Fam* **il n'est pas m.** *(adroit)* he's good with his hands; *(il peut le faire lui-même)* he has hands, doesn't he?
 2 *nm,f* one-armed person

manchot² [mɑ̃ʃo] *nm (oiseau)* penguin

mandale [mɑ̃dal] *nf très Fam* clout, slap

mandarin [mɑ̃darɛ̃] *nm* **(a)** *(de Chine)* mandarin **(b)** *Fig & Péj (personnage influent)* mandarin **(c)** *(langue)* Mandarin (Chinese)

mandarine [mɑ̃darin] *nf (fruit)* mandarin (orange)

mandat [mɑ̃da] *nm* **(a)** *(mission) (de député)* mandate; *(de président)* term of office **(b)** *(ordre)* warrant; **m. d'amener** = summons; **m. d'arrêt** arrest warrant; **m. de dépôt** committal order; **m. de perquisition** search warrant **(c)** *(mode de paiement)* order; **m. postal** money order **(d)** *(autorité)* mandate **(e)** *(procuration)* power of attorney

mandataire [mɑ̃datɛr] *nmf (d'électeurs)* representative; *(dans une réunion)* proxy

mandat-carte *(pl* **mandats-cartes***)* [mɑ̃dakart] *nm* money order *(in postcard form)*

mandater [mɑ̃date] *vt* (**a**) *(représentant)* to commission; *(membre parlementaire)* to give a mandate to (**b**) *(frais)* to pay by order

mandat-lettre (*pl* **mandats-lettres**) [mɑ̃dalɛtr] *nm* money order *(in letter-card form)*

mandibule [mɑ̃dibyl] *nf* mandible

mandoline [mɑ̃dɔlin] *nf* mandolin

mandrin [mɑ̃drɛ̃] *nm (pour percer)* punch; *(pour élargir un trou)* drift

manège [manɛʒ] *nm* (**a**) *(attraction foraine)* carousel, merry-go-round (**b**) *(en équitation)* riding school (**c**) *(manigances)* game

manette [manɛt] *nf* lever; **m. de jeux** joystick; *Fam* **à fond les manettes** at full speed

manga [mɑ̃ga] *nm* manga

manganèse [mɑ̃ganɛz] *nm* manganese

mangeable [mɑ̃ʒabl] *adj* (**a**) *(comestible)* edible (**b**) *(médiocre)* eatable

mangeoire [mɑ̃ʒwar] *nf* manger

manger [45] [mɑ̃ʒe] **1** *vt* (**a**) *(aliments)* to eat; **m. qn/qch des yeux** to look at sb/sth longingly; **m. ses mots** to mumble; **ça ne mange pas de pain** it doesn't cost anything; **je ne mange pas de ce pain-là** I don't go in for that sort of thing (**b**) *(attaquer)* to eat away (**c**) *(consommer)* to get through (**d**) *(dépenser)* to get through

2 *vi* to eat; **donner à m. à qn** to give sb something to eat; **m. comme quatre** *ou* **comme un ogre** to eat like a horse; **m. comme un oiseau** to eat like a sparrow; **m. à sa faim** to eat one's fill

3 se manger *vpr* to be eaten

mange-tout [mɑ̃ʒtu] *nm inv (pois)* snow pea; *(haricot)* string bean

mangeur, -euse [mɑ̃ʒœr, -øz] *nm,f* **gros m.** big eater; **tigre/requin m. d'hommes** man-eating tiger/shark; *Can Fam Péj* **m. de balustrades** sanctimonious man, *f* woman

mangue [mɑ̃g] *nf* mango

maniable [manjabl] *adj (outil)* handy; *(véhicule)* easy to handle

maniaque [manjak] **1** *adj* (**a**) *(pointilleux)* fussy (**b**) *(fou)* manic

2 *nmf* (**a**) *(pointilleux)* fussbudget; **être un m. de qch** to be fanatical about *or* obsessed with sth (**b**) *(fou)* maniac

manichéen, -enne [manikeɛ̃, -ɛn] *adj* Manichean

manichéisme [manikeism] *nm* Manicheism

manie [mani] *nf* (**a**) *(habitude)* odd habit (**b**) *(idée fixe)* mania, obsession; *Méd* mania

maniement [manimɑ̃] *nm* handling

manier [66] [manje] *vt* (**a**) *(manipuler) (objet)* to handle (**b**) *(utiliser) (véhicule)* to handle; *(outil, ironie)* to use

manière [manjɛr] *nf* (**a**) *(façon)* way, manner; **faire qch à sa m.** to do sth one's (own) way; **de m. à faire qch** so as to do sth; **de m. que** + *subjunctive* so that, in such a way that; **d'une** *ou* **de m. générale** generally speaking; **en aucune m.** under no circumstances; **de toute m.** in any case; **d'une certaine m.** in a manner of speaking, in a sense; **c'est sa m. d'être** that's the way he is; **la m. forte** strong-arm tactics (**b**) *(conduite)* **manières** manners; **faire des manières** *(agir de façon pompeuse)* to put on airs and graces; *(se faire prier)* to make a fuss (**c**) *(d'une œuvre)* **à la m. de** in the style of

maniéré, -e [manjere] *adj* affected

maniérisme [manjerism] *nm* mannerism

manif [manif] *nf Fam* demo, demonstration

manifestant, -e [manifɛstɑ̃, -ɑ̃t] *nm,f* demonstrator

manifestation [manifɛstasjɔ̃] *nf* (**a**) *(de sentiments)* display (**b**) *(rassemblement politique)* demonstration (**c**) *(événement organisé)* event

manifeste[1] [manifɛst] *adj* obvious, manifest

manifeste[2] [manifɛst] *nm* manifesto

manifestement [manifɛstəmɑ̃] *adv* obviously, manifestly

manifester [manifɛste] **1** *vt (exprimer)* to show

2 *vi* to demonstrate

3 se manifester *vpr* (**a**) *(personne)* to make oneself known (**b**) *(maladie)* to show *or* to manifest itself (**par** in)

manigancer [16] [manigɑ̃se] *vt* to scheme

manigances [manigɑ̃s] *nfpl* scheming

Manille [manij] *n* Manila

manioc [manjɔk] *nm* manioc, cassava

manipulateur, -trice [manipylatœr, -tris] **1** *nm,f* (**a**) *(de machines)* operator; **m. de laboratoire** laboratory technician; **m. radio(graphe)** X-ray technician (**b**) *Péj (de personnes)* manipulator

2 *nm (appareil de transmission)* (sending) key

manipulation [manipylasjɔ̃] *nf* (**a**) *(d'appareils, de produits)* handling; **m. génétique** genetic engineering (**b**) **manipulations** *(en science)* experiments, practical work (**c**) *Péj (de personnes)* manipulation (**d**) *Ordinat* **m. de colonnes** column handling

manipuler [manipyle] *vt* (**a**) *(appareils, produits)* to handle (**b**) *Péj (personnes)* to manipulate (**c**) *(statistiques)* to massage

manivelle [manivɛl] *nf* crank

manne [man] *nf (dans la Bible)* manna; *Fig (don inespéré)* godsend

mannequin [mankɛ̃] *nm* (**a**) *(personne)* model (**b**) *(de magasin, de couturier)* dummy

mannequinat [mankina] *nm* modeling

manœuvre[1] [manœvr] *nf* (**a**) *(conduite, direction) (de machines)* operation; *(de véhicules)* maneuvering; **faire une m.** to (do a) maneuver; **faire une fausse m.** *(en voiture)* to maneuver badly; *Fig* to get it wrong (**b**) *(intrigue)* maneuver; **manœuvres** maneuvering (**c**) *Mil (dans une bataille)* maneuver; **être en manœuvres** to be on maneuvers (**d**) *(d'un bateau)* maneuver

manœuvre[2] [manœvr] *nm (ouvrier)* unskilled worker

manœuvrer [manœvre] **1** *vt* (**a**) *(faire fonctionner) (machine)* to operate; *(véhicule)* to maneuver (**b**) *(influencer)* to influence

2 *vi aussi Fig* to maneuver

manoir [manwar] *nm* manor house

manomètre [manɔmɛtr] *nm* pressure gauge, manometer

manquant, -e [mɑ̃kɑ̃, -ɑ̃t] *adj* missing

manque [mɑ̃k] **1** *nm* (**a**) *(insuffisance)* lack; **par m. de** through lack of; **m. de chance!** bad luck!; **m. à gagner** loss of earnings (**b**) *(lacune)* gap (**c**) *(d'un drogué)* withdrawal symptoms; **être en (état de) m.** to have withdrawal symptoms

2 *nf Fam* **à la m.** useless, pathetic

manqué, -e [mɑ̃ke] **1** *adj* (**a**) *(occasion, rendez-vous)* missed (**b**) *(tentative, expérience)* unsuccessful (**c**) *(personne)* **c'est un poète/un médecin m.** he should have been a poet/doctor

2 *nm (gâteau)* = sponge cake with almond-flavored or fruit-flavored frosting

manquement [mɑ̃kmɑ̃] *nm* breach (**à** of)

manquer [mɑ̃ke] **1** *vt* (**a**) *(cible, train, occasion)* to miss (**b**) *(échouer à)* to fail

2 *vi* (**a**) *(faire défaut)* to be lacking; **le temps/la place me manque** I don't have enough time/space; **il/elle me manque** I miss him/her (**b**) *(échouer)* to fail; **ça n'a pas manqué, il est arrivé en retard** sure enough, he was late (**c**) *(être absent)* to be missing (**à** from)

3 *v impersonnel* **il ne manque personne** there's no one missing; **il manque quelques pages** there are a few pages missing; **il manque un bouton à ta veste** there's a button missing from your jacket; **il me manque dix euros** I'm ten euros short; **il ne manquait plus que cela!** that's all I/he/ *etc.* needed!

4 manquer à *vt ind (devoir, honneur)* to fail in; *(parole, promesses)* to break

5 manquer de *vt ind* (**a**) *(argent, main-d'œuvre)* to be short of, to lack; *(temps)* to be short of; *(courage, bon sens, charme)* to lack; **ne m. de rien** to have all that one needs; **m. de respect à qn** to show a lack of respect toward sb; **on manque d'air ici** there isn't enough air in here (**b**) *(faillir)* **m. (de) faire qch** to almost do sth (**c**) *(à la forme négative)* **ne pas m. de faire qch** to be sure to do sth; **je n'y manquerai pas** I certainly will

6 se manquer *vpr* to miss each other *(by not being in the same place at the same time)*

mansarde [mɑ̃sard] *nf* attic

mansardé, -e [mɑ̃sarde] *adj (chambre)* attic

mante [mɑ̃t] *nf* mantis; **m. religieuse** praying mantis

manteau, -x [mɑ̃to] *nm* coat; **m. de fourrure** fur coat; *Fig* **sous le m.** secretly

mantille [mɑ̃tij] *nf* mantilla

manucure [manykyr] **1** *nmf (personne)* manicurist

2 *nf (soin)* manicure; **se faire faire une m.** to have a manicure

manuel¹, -elle [manɥɛl] **1** *adj (travail, activité)* manual; **être m.** *(personne)* to be good with one's hands

2 *nm,f* (**a**) *(travailleur)* manual worker (**b**) *(personne adroite de ses mains)* **c'est un m.** he's good with his hands

manuel² [manɥɛl] *nm (d'utilisation, d'entretien)* manual, handbook; *(scolaire)* textbook

manuellement [manɥɛlmɑ̃] *adv* manually

manufacture [manyfaktyr] *nf (usine)* factory

manufacturer [manyfaktyre] *vt* to manufacture

manu militari [manymilitari] *adv* by force

manuscrit, -e [manyskri, -it] **1** *adj* handwritten

2 *nm* manuscript

manutention [manytɑ̃sjɔ̃] *nf* handling

manutentionnaire [manytɑ̃sjɔnɛr] *nmf* warehouseman, *f* warehousewoman

maous, -ousse [maus] *adj Fam* enormous

mappemonde [mapmɔ̃d] *nf* (**a**) *(carte)* map of the world *(in two hemispheres)* (**b**) *(globe)* globe

maquereau¹, -x [makro] *nm (poisson)* mackerel

maquereau², -x [makro] *nm très Fam (souteneur)* pimp

maquerelle [makrɛl] *nf très Fam* madam

maquette [makɛt] *nf* (**a**) *(de livre)* dummy (**b**) *(d'une construction architecturale)* (scale) model; *(de mise en page)* paste-up (**c**) *(jouet)* model; **m. d'avion/de bateau** model plane/boat

maquettiste [maketist] *nmf* (**a**) *(dans une entreprise)* model maker (**b**) *(graphiste)* graphic designer

maquignon [makiɲɔ̃] *nm* (**a**) *(marchand de chevaux)* horse dealer (**b**) *Fig (entremetteur malhonnête)* crooked dealer

maquillage [makijaʒ] *nm* (**a**) *(de visage) (action)* making up; *(produits)* make-up (**b**) *(de documents)* forging; *(de photos)* faking; *(de comptes)* falsification

maquiller [makije] **1** *vt* (**a**) *(personne, visage)* to make up (**b**) *(documents)* to forge; *(photos)* to fake; *(comptes)* to falsify; **m. un meurtre en suicide** to make a murder look like a suicide

2 se maquiller *vpr* to put one's make-up on

maquilleur, -euse [makijœr, -øz] *nm,f* make-up artist

maquis [maki] *nm* (**a**) *(végétation)* maquis (**b**) *Fig (d'une procédure, de l'administration)* jungle (**c**) *Hist* maquis *(Resistance movement in World War II)*; *Fig* **prendre le m.** to take to the hills

maquisard [makizar] *nm Hist* member of the maquis, Resistance fighter *(in World War II)*

marabout [marabu] *nm* (**a**) *(sorcier)* witchdoctor (**b**) *(oiseau)* marabou (**c**) *Can (personne acariâtre)* bad-tempered person

maracas [marakas] *nfpl* maracas

maraîcher, -ère [marɛʃe, -ɛr] **1** *adj* **culture maraîchère** truck farming; **produits maraîchers** truck

2 *nm,f* truck farmer

marais [marɛ] *nm* marsh

marasme [marasm] *nm* (**a**) *(ralentissement)* stagnation (**b**) *(découragement)* depression

marathon [maratɔ̃] *nm* marathon

marathonien, -enne [maratɔnjɛ̃, -ɛn] *nm,f* marathon runner

marâtre [marɑtr] *nf* (**a**) *(belle-mère)* stepmother (**b**) *(mère cruelle)* cruel mother

maraude [marod] *nf* (**a**) *(vol)* pilfering (**b**) **un taxi en m.** a cruising taxi

marauder [marode] *vi* (**a**) *(voler)* to pilfer (**b**) *(taxi)* to cruise for fares (**c**) *(rôdeur)* to prowl around

maraudeur, -euse [marodœr, -øz] *nm,f* pilferer

marbre [marbr] *nm* (**a**) *(roche)* marble; **en** *ou* **de m.** marble; *Fig* **rester de m.** to remain impassive (**b**) *(statue)* marble (statue) (**c**) *(de presse)* bed

marbré, -e [marbre] *adj* (**a**) *(surface, couverture de livre)* marbled; *(pierre)* veined (**b**) *(peau)* blotchy (**c**) **gâteau m.** marble cake

marbrier [marbrije] *nm* monumental mason

marbrière [marbrijɛr] *nf* marble quarry

marbrure [marbryr] *nf* (**a**) *(sur un livre)* marbling (**b**) *(sur la peau)* mottling

marc [mar] *nm* (**a**) *(de raisins, d'olives)* marc (**b**) *(eau-de-vie)* marc (brandy) (**c**) *(de café)* grounds

marcassin [markasɛ̃] *nm* young wild boar

marchand, -e [marʃɑ̃, -ɑ̃d] **1** *adj (prix)* trade

2 *nm,f (dans un magasin)* storekeeper; *(de vin)* merchant; *(de meubles, de chevaux)* dealer; **m. ambulant** street vendor; **m. forain** traveling stallkeeper; **m. de glaces** ice-cream seller; **m. de journaux** newsdealer; **m. de légumes** greengrocer; **m. de tableaux** art dealer; **m. de tapis** carpet dealer

marchandage [marʃɑ̃daʒ] *nm* haggling

marchander [marʃɑ̃de] **1** *vt* to haggle over

2 *vi* to haggle

marchandisage [marʃɑ̃dizaʒ] *nm* merchandizing

marchandise [marʃɑ̃diz] *nf* commodity; **marchandises** goods, merchandise

marche [marʃ] *nf* (**a**) *(d'escalier)* step, stair

(**b**) *(action de marcher)* walking; *(promenade)* walk; *(allure)* pace; **faire de la m.** to go walking; **faire une m.** to go for a walk; **à deux heures de m.** two hours' walk away; **m. à pied** walking

(**c**) *(défilé, manifestation)* march; **ouvrir la m.** to lead the way; **fermer la m.** to bring up the rear

(**d**) *(morceau de musique)* march; **m. funèbre** funeral march

(**e**) *(déplacement)* **être en m.** *(véhicule)* to be moving; *(mouvement, progrès)* to be on the march; **se mettre en m.** *(véhicule)* to move off; *(personne)* to set off *or* out; **dans le sens de la m.** *(en voyage)* facing forward; **dans le sens contraire de la m.** facing backward; **m. avant/arrière** *(vitesse)* forward/reverse gear; **faire m. arrière** *(véhicule)* to reverse; *Fig* to backtrack

(**f**) *(fonctionnement)* running, working; **mettre qch en m.** to start sth; **se mettre en m.** to start

(**g**) *(des événements, de l'histoire)* course; *(du temps)* march; **m. à suivre** procedure

marché [marʃe] *nm* (**a**) *(accord)* deal, bargain; *(plus officiel)* contract; **m. conclu!** it's a deal!; **par-dessus le m.** into the bargain; **bon m.** cheap (**b**) *(lieu public de vente)* market; **faire son m.** to go shopping; **m. aux puces** flea market (**c**) *(débouché économique)* market; **M. commun** Common Market; **m. immobilier** property market; **m. noir** black market; **M. unique (européen)** Single (European) Market; **m. du travail** labour market (**d**) *Fin* market; **m. des changes** foreign exchange market; **m. haussier/baissier** bull/bear market; **m. à terme** futures market

marchepied [marʃəpje] *nm* (**a**) *(de train)* step (**b**) *(escabeau)* steps (**c**) *Fig* stepping-stone

marcher [marʃe] *vi* (**a**) *(se déplacer à pied)* to walk; *(mettre le pied)* to step (**dans/sur** in/on); *aussi Fig* **m. sur les pieds de qn** to tread on sb's toes; *Fig* **m. droit** to keep on the straight and narrow (**b**) *(fonctionner) (machine)* to work, to run; *(plans)* to work; **faire m. qch** to work *or* to operate sth; **comment ça marche?** how does it work?; *Fig* **les affaires marchent (bien)** business is doing well; **ça marche!** *(d'accord)* sure! (**c**) *(avancer)* to march (**vers/sur** towards/on) (**d**) *Fam (croire sans réserve)* to fall for it; **faire m. qn** to pull sb's leg (**e**) *Fam (accepter)* to go along with it

marchette [marʃɛt] *nf Can (chariot d'enfant)* go-kart; *(support de marche)* walking frame

marcheur, -euse [marʃœr, -øz] *nm,f* walker

mardi [mardi] *nm* Tuesday; **M. gras** Shrove Tuesday; *voir aussi* **samedi**

> ### Mardi gras
> This is a very popular festival, falling on the eve of Ash Wednesday, at the end of the carnival. On this day, "crêpes" are prepared and eaten, and children dress up at school.

mare [mar] *nf* (**a**) *(étendue d'eau)* pond (**b**) *(grande quantité)* pool

marécage [marekaʒ] *nm* marsh, bog

marécageux, -euse [marekaʒø, -øz] *adj* (**a**) *(terrain)* marshy, boggy (**b**) *(plante)* marsh

maréchal, -aux [mareʃal, -o] *nm* **m. (de France)** *(officier général)* field marshal; *(d'un roi)* marshal; **m. des logis** sergeant

maréchal-ferrant [mareʃalfɛrɑ̃] *(pl* **maréchaux-ferrants** [mareʃoferɑ̃]*) nm* blacksmith

marée [mare] *nf* (**a**) *(de la mer)* tide; **à m. haute/basse** at high/low tide; **à la m. montante/descendante** when the tide comes in/goes out; **m. noire** oil slick (**b**) *Fig (de personnes)* surging mass (**c**) *(fruits de la pêche)* fresh seafood

marelle [marɛl] *nf* hopscotch

marémoteur, -trice [maremɔtœr, -tris] *adj (énergie)* tidal; **usine marémotrice** tidal power station

mareyeur, -euse [marɛjœr, -øz] *nm,f* fish wholesaler

margarine [margarin] *nf* margarine

marge [marʒ] *nf* (**a**) *(de page)* margin; **en m. de** on the fringes of; **vivre en m. (de la société)** to live on the fringes of society (**b**) *(liberté d'action)* leeway; **avoir de la m.** to have some leeway; *(temps)* to have time to spare; **m. d'erreur** margin of error; **m. de négociation/manœuvre** room for negotiation/maneuver; **m. de sécurité** safety margin (**c**) *(commerciale)* **m. (bénéficiaire)** profit margin

marger [45] [marʒe] *vt (page)* to feed in; *Ordinat* to set the margins for

marginal, -e, -aux, -ales [marʒinal, -o] **1** *adj* (**a**) *(personne, mode de vie)* on the fringes of society (**b**) *(secondaire) (occupations, importance)* marginal
2 *nm,f* dropout

marginalisation [marʒinalizasjɔ̃] *nf* marginalization

marginaliser [marʒinalize] **1** *vt* to marginalize
2 se marginaliser *vpr* to become marginalized

marguerite [margərit] *nf (fleur)* daisy

mari [mari] *nm* husband

mariage [marjaʒ] *nm* (**a**) *(cérémonie)* wedding; *(union)* marriage; **m. d'amour** love match; **m. blanc** marriage in name only *(primarily in order to acquire nationality)*; **m. civil/religieux** civil/church wedding; *Can* **m. obligé** shotgun wedding; **m. de raison** marriage of convenience (**b**) *(de choses)* combination, marriage; *(de couleurs)* blend(ing)

> ### Mariage
> In France, a civil ceremony (which takes place at the **mairie** - *see box at this entry*) is required of all couples wishing to marry, though some choose to have a church wedding as well. The traditional wedding involves a long and sumptuous meal at which the wedding cake, a "pièce montée", is served.

Marianne [marjan] *nf* = young woman symbolizing the French Republic

marié, -e [marje] **1** *adj* married; **non m.** unmarried, single
2 *nm,f* groom, *f* bride; **les mariés** the bride and groom; **les jeunes mariés** the newlyweds

marie-jeanne [mariʒan] *nf inv Fam (cannabis)* Mary Jane, pot

marier [66] [marje] **1** *vt* (**a**) *(sujet: prêtre)* to marry; *(sujet: père)* to marry off (**b**) *(qualités)* to combine; *(sociétés)* to merge; *(couleurs)* to blend; *(styles)* to harmonize
2 se marier *vpr* (**a**) *(personnes)* to get married, to marry; **se m. avec qn** to marry sb (**b**) *(couleurs)* to blend (**avec** with); *(styles)* to go together (**avec** with)

marieur, -euse [marjœr, -øz] *nm,f Fam* matchmaker

marihuana [marirwana], **marijuana** [mariʒyana] *nf* marijuana

marin, -e [marɛ̃, -in] **1** *adj* (**a**) *(air, brise)* sea; *(plante, animal)* marine (**b**) *(carte)* sea; *(mille)* nautical
2 *nm* seaman, sailor; **m. pêcheur** (deep-sea) fisherman; **m. d'eau douce** landlubber

marina [marina] *nf* marina

marinade [marinad] *nf (mélange aromatique)* marinade; **m. de poissons/de gibier** marinated fish/game

marine [marin] **1** *nf* (**a**) *(flotte)* navy; **la m. de guerre** the navy; **la m. marchande** the merchant marine; **la M. nationale** the French navy (**b**) *(navigation)* seamanship (**c**) *(tableau)* seascape
2 *adj inv* navy (blue)
3 *nm (fusilier)* marine

mariner [marine] **1** *vt* to marinate
2 *vi* (**a**) *(aliment)* to marinate; **faire m. qch** to marinate sth; **harengs marinés** pickled herrings (**b**) *Fam Fig (personne)* to hang around; **faire** *ou* **laisser m. qn** *(dans un lieu)* to keep sb hanging around; *(dans une situation)* to leave sb to stew

maringouin [marɛ̃gwɛ̃] *nm Can* mosquito

marinier [marinje] *nm* bargeman

marinière [marinjɛr] *nf* blouse

mariole [marjɔl] *nm Fam* wise guy; **faire le m.** to act the wise guy

marionnette [marjɔnɛt] *nf* puppet

marionnettiste [marjɔnetist] *nmf* puppeteer

marital, -e, -aux, -ales [marital, -o] *adj* marital

maritalement [maritalmɑ̃] *adv* **vivre m.** to cohabit

maritime [maritim] *adj* (**a**) *(navigation, plante, trafic)* maritime; *(ville)* seaside (**b**) *Can* **les Maritimes** the Maritimes

marivaudage [marivodaʒ] *nm Litt* light-hearted banter

marjolaine [marʒɔlɛn] *nf* marjoram

mark [mark] *nm Anciennement* (German) mark

marketing [marketiŋ] *nm* marketing

marmaille [marmaj] *nf Fam* brood, kids

marmelade [marməlad] *nf* compote; **m. (d'oranges)** (orange) marmalade; *Fig* **en m.** reduced to a pulp

marmite [marmit] *nf* (cooking) pot; *Fig* **faire bouillir la m.** to bring home the bacon

marmonner [marmɔne] *vt & vi* to mumble, to mutter

marmot [marmo] *nm Fam* kid

marmotte [marmɔt] *nf* marmot

marmotter [marmɔte] *vt* to mumble, to mutter

marner [marne] *vi Fam* to slog

Maroc [marɔk] *nm* **le M.** Morocco

marocain, -e [marɔkɛ̃, -ɛn] **1** *adj* Moroccan
2 *nm,f* **M., Marocaine** Moroccan

maronite [marɔnit] *adj & nmf* Maronite

maroquin [marɔkɛ̃] *nm* morocco (leather)

maroquinerie [marɔkinri] *nf* (a) *(fabrication)* leather tanning (b) *(magasin)* leather-goods store (c) *(articles)* leather goods

maroquinier [marɔkinje] *nm* (a) *(fabricant)* leather worker (b) *(commerçant)* leather-goods dealer

marotte [marɔt] *nf (idée fixe)* craze

marquant, -e [markɑ̃, -ɑ̃t] *adj (incident, personne, journée)* remarkable; *(épisode)* significant

marque [mark] *nf* (a) *(signe, trace)* mark (b) *(de produits, d'appareils)* brand; *(de voiture)* make; **de m.** *(produits)* branded; *(vêtements)* designer; **m. déposée** registered trademark (c) *(preuve) (d'amitié)* token; *(de confiance)* sign (d) *(cachet)* stamp; **porter la m. du génie** to bear the stamp of genius (e) *Ordinat* marker; **m. d'insertion** insertion marker (f) **de m.** *(important)* distinguished, prominent (g) **marques** *(repères)* marks; **à vos marques! prêts? partez!** on your marks! get set! go!

marqué, -e [marke] *adj* (a) *(visage)* lined; **il est très m.** his face is very lined (b) *(différence, penchant)* marked

marque-page *(pl* **marque-pages)** [markpaʒ] *nm* bookmark

marquer [marke] **1** *vt* (a) *(faire un signe sur)* to mark (b) *(écrire)* to write (c) *(délimiter)* to mark (d) *Sport (adversaire)* to mark; *(but, essai)* to score (e) *(indiquer)* to show (f) *(accentuer)* to mark; **m. le pas** to mark time; *Fig* **m. le coup** to mark the occasion (g) *(impressionner)* to make an impression on (h) *Ordinat* to mark

2 *vi (laisser une trace)* to leave a mark

marqueterie [markətri] *nf* marquetry

marqueur [markœr] *nm* (a) *(stylo)* (felt-tip) marker (b) *(biologique, génétique)* marker

marquis [marki] *nm* marquis

marquise [markiz] *nf* (a) *(auvent)* canopy (b) *(canapé)* (two-seater) sofa (c) *(personne)* marchioness

Marquises [markiz] *nfpl* **les (îles) M.** the Marquesas Islands

marraine [marɛn] *nf* (a) *(d'un enfant)* godmother (b) *(d'un bateau)* = woman who launches a new boat

Marrakech [marakɛʃ] *n* Marrakesh

marrant, -e [marɑ̃, -ɑ̃t] *adj Fam* funny

marre [mar] *adv Fam* **en avoir m. (de qn/qch)** to be fed up (with sb/sth); **en avoir m. de faire qch** to be fed up with doing sth

marrer [mare] **se marrer** *vpr Fam* to have a good laugh

marron¹ [marɔ̃] **1** *adj inv (couleur)* brown

2 *nm* (a) *(fruit)* chestnut; **marrons chauds** roast chestnuts; **marrons glacés** marrons glacés; **m. d'Inde** horse chestnut (b) *(couleur)* brown (c) *Fam (coup de poing)* thump; **flanquer un m. à qn** to whack sb

marron², -onne [marɔ̃, -ɔn] *adj (médecin, homme de loi)* quack

marronnier [marɔnje] *nm* horse chestnut (tree)

Mars [mars] *npr (dieu, planète)* Mars

mars [mars] *nm* March; *voir aussi* **janvier**

marseillais, -e [marsɛjɛ, -ɛz] **1** *adj* of Marseilles

2 *nm,f* **M., Marseillaise** person from Marseilles

3 *nf* **la Marseillaise** the Marseillaise

Marseille [marsɛj] *n* Marseilles

marsouin [marswɛ̃] *nm* (a) *Zool* porpoise (b) *Can Fam (malin)* rascal

marsupial, -e, -aux, -ales [marsypjal, -o] *adj & nm* marsupial

marteau, -x [marto] **1** *adj Fam* crazy

2 *nm* (a) *(outil)* hammer; **m. piqueur** pneumatic drill; *Fig* **être entre le m. et l'enclume** to be between the devil and the deep blue sea (b) *(de porte)* (door) knocker (c) *(de piano)* hammer

martel [martɛl] *nm* **se mettre m. en tête** to worry oneself sick

martèlement [martɛlmɑ̃] *nm* hammering

marteler [39] [martəle] *vt* (a) *(métal, pieu)* to hammer; **m. la table à coups de poing** to hammer on the table (b) *(mot, phrase)* to hammer out

martial, -e, -aux, -ales [marsjal, -o] *adj* martial

martien, -enne [marsjɛ̃, -ɛn] *adj & nm,f* Martian

martinet¹ [martinɛ] *nm (fouet)* strap

martinet² [martinɛ] *nm (oiseau)* swift

martingale [martɛ̃gal] *nf (sur un vêtement)* half belt

martiniquais, -e [martinikɛ, -ɛz] **1** *adj* Martinican

2 *nm,f* **M., Martiniquaise** Martinican

Martinique [martinik] *nf* **la M.** Martinique

martin-pêcheur *(pl* **martins-pêcheurs)** [martɛ̃pɛʃœr] *nm* kingfisher

martyr, -e [martir] **1** *adj (enfant)* battered; *(peuple)* martyred

2 *nm,f* martyr

martyre [martir] *nm* martyrdom

martyriser [martirize] *vt (maltraiter)* to batter; *(harceler)* to bully

marxisme [marksism] *nm* Marxism

marxisme-léninisme [marksismleninism] *nm* Marxism-Leninism

marxiste [marksist] *adj & nmf* Marxist

marxiste-léniniste [marksistleninist] *(pl* **marxistes-léninistes)** *adj & nmf* Marxist-Leninist

mas [ma, mas] *nm (en Provence) (ferme)* farm; *(maison)* farmhouse

mascara [maskara] *nm* mascara

mascarade [maskarad] *nf* masquerade; *Fig* sham

mascotte [maskɔt] *nf* mascot

masculin, -e [maskylɛ̃, -in] **1** *adj* (a) *(sexe, mode, métier)* male; *(trait de caractère, femme)* masculine (b) *(nom, genre)* masculine

2 *nm* masculine; **au m.** in the masculine

masculinité [maskylinite] *nf* masculinity

maskinongé [maskinɔ̃ʒe] *nm Can* muskellunge

maso [mazo] *Fam* **1** *adj* masochistic

2 *nmf* masochist

masochisme [mazoʃism] *nm* masochism

masochiste [mazoʃist] **1** *adj* masochistic

2 *nmf* masochist

masquage [maskaʒ] *nm Ordinat* masking

masque [mask] *nm* (a) *(déguisement)* mask; **m. à gaz/oxygène** gas/oxygen mask; **m. de plongée** diving mask (b) *(apparence)* façade; **lever le m.** to remove one's mask (c) *(soin cosmétique)* **m. (de beauté)** face mask *or* pack (d) *Ordinat* mask; **m. d'entrée, m. de saisie** input mask

masqué, -e [maske] *adj (personne)* masked

masquer [maske] *vt* to mask

massacrante [masakrɑ̃t] *adj f voir* **humeur**

massacre [masakr] *nm* (a) *(tuerie)* massacre (b) *Fig (travail mal fait)* mess; **faire un m.** *(travailler mal)* to make a complete mess; *(remporter un grand succès)* to be a runaway success

massacrer [masakre] *vt* (a) *(tuer, exterminer)* to massacre (b) *Fam (abîmer) (travail)* to make a mess of; *(mal interpréter) (morceau de musique, texte)* to murder

massage [masaʒ] *nm* massage; **faire un m. à qn** to give sb a massage

masse¹ [mas] *nf* (a) *(volume)* mass; **m. d'air** air mass; **taillé/sculpté dans la m.** carved/sculpted from the block; **tomber comme une m.** to fall in a heap (b) *(grande quantité)* mass; **de m.** *(culture, communication)* mass; **en m.** en masse; **une m. de** masses of; *Fam* **pas des masses** not much; *(nombre)* not many; **m. monétaire** money supply; **m. salariale** payroll (c) **les masses** *(le peuple)* the masses; **les masses labo-**

rieuses the toiling masses (**d**) *Phys* mass (**e**) *Élec* ground; **mettre qch à la m.** to ground sth; *Fam Fig* **être à la m.** to be off one's head

masse² [mas] *nf (marteau)* sledgehammer

massepain [maspɛ̃] *nm* marzipan

masser¹ [mase] **1** *vt (rassembler)* to assemble; *(troupes)* to mass **2 se masser** *vpr* to assemble

masser² [mase] **1** *vt (faire un massage à)* to massage; **se faire m.** to have a massage **2 se masser** *vpr* to massage oneself; **se m. les pieds** to massage one's feet

masseur, -euse [masœr, -øz] *nm,f* masseur, *f* masseuse

massicot [masiko] *nm* guillotine

massif, -ive [masif, -iv] **1** *adj* (**a**) *(formes, meuble, porte)* massive; *(personne)* heavily built (**b**) *(argent, or, bois)* solid (**c**) *(dose)* massive **2** *nm* (**a**) *(de plantes, d'arbres)* clump; **m. de fleurs** flower bed (**b**) *(ensemble de montagnes)* massif; **le M. central** the Massif Central *(mountains in central France)*

massivement [masivmɑ̃] *adv (répondre, voter)* en masse

mass media, mass-média(s) [masmedja] *nmpl* mass media

massue [masy] **1** *adj inv (argument)* sledgehammer **2** *nf* club

mastectomie [mastɛktɔmi] *nf* mastectomy

mastic [mastik] *nm (pour fenêtres)* putty; *(pour bois)* mastic

mastication [mastikasjɔ̃] *nf* chewing

mastiquer¹ [mastike] *vt (mâcher)* to chew

mastiquer² [mastike] *vt (fissures)* to fill (in); *(vitre)* to put putty around

mastoc [mastɔk] *adj inv Fam (personne)* hulking; *(construction)* clumsy

mastodonte [mastɔdɔ̃t] *nm* (**a**) *Fam (personne)* colossus; *(objet)* hulking great thing (**b**) *(animal)* mastodon

masturbation [mastyrbasjɔ̃] *nf* masturbation

masturber [mastyrbe] **1** *vt* to masturbate **2 se masturber** *vpr* to masturbate

m'as-tu-vu [matyvy] *nmf inv Fam* show-off

masure [mazyr] *nf* hovel

mat¹, -e [mat] *adj (métal, couleur)* matte; *(teint)* darkish; *(son)* dull

mat² [mat] **1** *adj inv (aux échecs)* checkmated **2** *nm* checkmate

mat' [mat] *nm Fam* **deux/trois heures du m.** two/three a.m. *or* in the morning

mât [mɑ] *nm* (**a**) *(d'un voilier)* mast (**b**) *(poteau)* pole; **m. de cocagne** greasy pole

matador [matadɔr] *nm* matador

match *(pl* **matchs** *ou* **matches)** [matʃ] *nm* game; **m. aller/retour** first/return leg; **un m. amical** an exhibition game; **m. nul** draw, tie; **faire m. nul** to draw, to tie

matelas [matla] *nm* mattress; **m. pneumatique** air mattress

matelassé, -e [matlase] *adj (tissu, blouson)* quilted; *(enveloppe)* padded

matelot [matlo] *nm* sailor

mater¹ [mate] *vt (se rendre maître de) (personne)* to bring to heel; *(rébellion)* to quash

mater² [mate] *vt Fam (regarder)* to ogle

matérialisation [materjalizasjɔ̃] *nf* materialization

matérialiser [materjalize] **se matérialiser** *vpr* to materialize

matérialisme [materjalism] *nm* materialism

matérialiste [materjalist] **1** *adj* materialistic **2** *nmf* materialist

matériau, -x [materjo] *nm* (**a**) *(substance)* material (**b**) **matériaux** *(de construction)* material(s); *(documents)* material

matériel¹, -elle [materjɛl] *adj (confort, besoins, dégâts)* material; *(organisation, problème)* practical

matériel² [materjɛl] *nm* (**a**) *(pour une activité, un sport)* equipment; **m. agricole** farm equipment; **m. de bureau** office equipment; **m. pédagogique** teaching material (**b**) *(d'une entreprise)* plant; **m. d'exploitation** working plant (**c**) *Ordinat* **m. (informatique)** (computer) hardware

matériellement [materjɛlmɑ̃] *adv* (**a**) *(sur le plan matériel)* materially (**b**) **c'est m. impossible** it's physically impossible

maternel, -elle [matɛrnɛl] *adj* (**a**) *(personne, attitude, gestes)* maternal (**b**) *(langue)* native

maternelle [matɛrnɛl] *nf* preschool, nursery (school)

> **Maternelle**
> Preschool education for children from two to six years old is provided by the state and is available to all families in France. Although it is not compulsory, a vast majority of children attend preschool and are thus well-prepared for entry into elementary school.

materner [matɛrne] *vt* to mother

maternisé, -e [matɛrnize] *adj* **lait m.** baby-formula milk

maternité [matɛrnite] *nf* (**a**) *(fait d'être mère)* motherhood (**b**) *(hôpital)* maternity hospital (**c**) *(tableau)* Madonna and Child

mathématicien, -enne [matematisjɛ̃, -ɛn] *nm,f* mathematician

mathématique [matematik] **1** *adj* (**a**) *(science)* mathematical (**b**) *(esprit)* logical; *(rigueur)* mathematical (**c**) *Fig (inévitable)* inevitable **2** *nfpl* **les mathématiques** mathematics *(singulier)*

mathématiquement [matematikmɑ̃] *adv* mathematically

matheux, -euse [matø, -øz] *nm,f Fam* mathematician

maths [mat] *nfpl Fam* math; **M. Sup/Spé** = first/second year of classes preparing students for entrance to science-oriented "grandes écoles"

matière [matjɛr] *nf* (**a**) *(substance)* material; **matières grasses** fat; **m. grise** gray matter; *Fam* **faire fonctionner sa m. grise** to exercise one's gray matter; **m. plastique** plastic; **matières premières** raw materials (**b**) *(sujet) (scolaire)* subject; *(pour en faire un film, un livre, une étude)* material; **il n'y a pas m. à rire** it's no laughing matter; **donner m. à qch** to give cause for sth; **en m. de** as regards (**c**) *(d'un corps physique)* matter

Matignon [matiɲɔ̃] *n* **(l'hôtel) M.** = French Prime Minister's offices

> **Matignon**
> The name of the Prime Minister's offices is often used to refer to the Prime Minister and his or her administrative staff, for example "L'Élysée et Matignon ont fini par se mettre d'accord".

matin [matɛ̃] *nm* morning; **ce m., *Can* à m.** this morning; **quatre heures du m.** four o'clock in the morning, 4 a.m.; **le jeudi 2 au m.** on the morning of Thursday the 2nd; **faire qch le m.** to do sth in the morning; **être du m.** to be a morning person; **tous les lundis m.** every Monday morning; **de grand** *ou* **bon m.** early in the morning, in the early morning; **au petit m.** in the small *or* early hours; **du m. au soir** from morning till night

matinal, -e, -aux, -ales [matinal, -o] *adj* (**a**) *(heure)* early; *(excursion, activité)* morning (**b**) *(personne)* **être m.** to be an early riser

mâtiné, -e [mɑtine] *adj* crossbred; **m. de** crossed with; *Fig* mixed with

matinée [matine] *nf* (**a**) *(matin)* morning; **dans la m.** in (the course of) the morning; **en fin de m.** toward the end of the morning (**b**) *(au théâtre, cinéma)* matinee

maton, -onne [matɔ̃, -ɔn] *nm,f Fam* hack, screw *(prison guard)*

matos [matos] *nm Fam* gear, stuff

matou [matu] *nm* tom, tomcat

matraquage [matrakaʒ] *nm* **(a)** *(avec une matraque)* bludgeoning **(b)** *(insistance)* **m. publicitaire** hype

matraque [matrak] *nf* bludgeon; *(d'agent de police)* nightstick

matraquer [matrake] *vt* **(a)** *(frapper)* to club **(b)** *Fig (harceler)* to bombard **(c)** *Fam (faire payer très cher)* to rip off, to fleece

matriarcal, -e, -aux, -ales [matrijarkal, -o] *adj* matriarchal

matrice [matris] *nf* **(a)** *(moule)* matrix, die; *(de disque)* matrix **(b)** *Math* matrix **(c)** *Ordinat* **m. d'aiguilles** dot matrix

matricide [matrisid] *nm* matricide

matriciel, -elle [matrisjɛl] *Ordinat* **1** *adj* **imprimante matricielle** dot-matrix printer
  2 *nf* **matricelle** dot matrix

matricule [matrikyl] **1** *nm (numéro)* number
  2 *nf (registre)* register

matrimonial, -e, -aux, -ales [matrimɔnjal, -o] *adj* matrimonial

matrone [matrɔn] *nf* **(a)** *Péj (femme corpulente)* stout woman **(b)** *Can (gardienne de prison)* prison guard

mature [matyr] *adj* mature

mâture [mɑtyr] *nf* masts

maturité [matyrite] *nf* **(a)** *(de personne)* maturity; *(de fruit)* ripeness; **manquer de m.** to be immature; **arriver** *ou* **venir à m.** *(fromage, vin)* to mature; *(fruit)* to ripen **(b)** *Suisse (baccalauréat)* school-leaving diploma *(from a 'gymnase', granting admission to a university)*

maudire [modir] *vt* to curse

maudit, -e [modi, -it] *adj* **(a)** *(damné)* cursed **(b)** *(avant le nom) (insupportable)* damn(ed)

maugréer [24] [mogree] *vi* to grumble (**contre** about *or* at)

maure [mɔr] **1** *adj* Moorish
  2 *nm* M. Moor

mauresque [mɔrɛsk] **1** *adj* Moorish
  2 *nf* M. Moorish woman

Maurice [mɔris] *n* **l'île M.** Mauritius

mauricien, -enne [mɔrisjɛ̃, -ɛn] **1** *adj* Mauritian
  2 *nm,f* **M., Mauricienne** Mauritian

Mauritanie [mɔritani] *nf* **la M.** Mauritania

mauritanien, -enne [mɔritanjɛ̃, -ɛn] **1** *adj* Mauritanian
  2 *nm,f* **M., Mauritanienne** Mauritanian

mausolée [mozɔle] *nm* mausoleum

maussade [mosad] *adj* **(a)** *(de mauvaise humeur)* sullen **(b)** *(temps, paysage)* gloomy

mauvais, -e [mɔvɛ, -ɛz] **1** *adj* **(a)** *(défectueux) (santé, vue, excuse)* poor **(b)** *(incompétent) (élève, professeur, mère)* bad (**en** at) **(c)** *(nuisible)* bad (**pour** for) **(d)** *(inapproprié) (clef, numéro, moment)* wrong **(e)** *(méchant) (personne)* bad, nasty; *(chien)* vicious **(f)** *(mer)* rough **(g)** *Fam* **la trouver** *ou* **l'avoir mauvaise** to be bummed *or* pissed
  2 *adv* **(a)** **sentir m.** to smell (bad) **(b)** **il fait m.** the weather's bad

mauve [mov] **1** *adj* mauve
  2 *nm (couleur)* mauve

mauviette [movjɛt] *nf Fam* wimp

max [maks] *nm Fam* **un m. de gens** *(le plus possible)* as many people as possible; *(énormément)* loads of people

max. *(abrév* **maximum***)* max.

maxi [maksi] *adv Fam* max, tops; **on sera vingt m.** there'll be twenty of us max *or* tops

maxillaire [maksilɛr] *nm* jawbone, *Spéc* maxilla

maxima [maksima] *voir* **maximum**

maximal, -e, -aux, -ales [maksimal, -o] *adj* maximum

maxime [maksim] *nf* maxim

maximiser [maksimize] *vt* to maximize

maximum [maksimɔm] *(pl* **maximums** *ou* **maxima** [maksima]) **1** *adj* maximum
  2 *nm* maximum; **faire le m. (pour faire qch)** to do one's very best (to do sth); **au m.** at the most; *Fam* **un m.** *(beaucoup)* loads; *Fam* **un m. de gens** *(le plus possible)* as many people as possible; *(énormément)* loads of people

maya [maja] **1** *adj* Maya, Mayan
  2 *nm (langue)* Mayan
  3 *nmf* **M.** Maya, Mayan

mayonnaise [majɔnɛz] *nf* mayonnaise

mazout [mazut] *nm (fuel)* oil

mazouté, -e [mazute] *adj (plage)* oil-polluted; *(oiseau)* covered in oil

Mbps *Ordinat (abrév* **mégabits par seconde***)* mbps

MDR *Ordinat & Tél (abrév écrite* **mort de rire***)* LOL

me [mə]

> **m'** is used before a word beginning with a vowel or h mute.

pron personnel **(a)** *(objet direct)* me; **il est venu me chercher** he came to pick me up; **me voici** here I am **(b)** *(objet indirect)* to me; **il m'a écrit** he wrote to me; **elle m'a serré la main** she shook my hand; **ils m'ont lancé des cailloux** they threw stones at me **(c)** *(dans les réfléchis)* myself; **je vais me doucher** I'm going to take a shower **(d)** *(dans les pronominaux)* **je me suis trompé** I made a mistake

mea culpa [meakylpa] *nm inv* **faire son m.** to own up

méandre [meɑ̃dr] *nm* **(a)** *(de rivière)* meander; *(de route)* bend; *Fig* **méandres** *(d'un raisonnement)* intricacies

mec [mɛk] *nm Fam (homme quelconque)* guy; **mon/son m.** *(amoureux)* my/her man *or* guy

mécanicien, -enne [mekanisjɛ̃, -ɛn] *nm,f* **(a)** *(garage* or *motor)* mechanic **(b)** *(conducteur de train)* engineer

mécanique [mekanik] **1** *adj* mechanical
  2 *nf* **(a)** *(science du mouvement)* mechanics *(singulier)* **(b)** *(des moteurs, des machines)* mechanical engineering **(c)** *(mécanisme)* mechanism

mécaniquement [mekanikmɑ̃] *adv* mechanically

mécanisation [mekanizasjɔ̃] *nf* mechanization

mécanisme [mekanism] *nm* **(a)** *(d'une machine, d'une montre, d'un moteur)* mechanism **(b)** *(de la pensée, de la parole)* mechanics

mécénat [mesena] *nm* sponsorship; **m. d'entreprise** corporate sponsorship

mécène [mesɛn] *nm* sponsor

méchamment [meʃamɑ̃] *adv* **(a)** *(avec méchanceté)* nastily **(b)** *Fam (en intensif)* **être m. déçu/embêté** to be terribly disappointed/annoyed

méchanceté [meʃɑ̃ste] *nf* **(a)** *(d'une personne, d'une remarque)* nastiness; *(d'un enfant)* naughtiness **(b)** *(action)* nasty action; *(parole)* nasty remark

méchant, -e [meʃɑ̃, -ɑ̃t] **1** *adj* **(a)** *(personne, remarque)* nasty; *(enfant)* naughty; *(animal)* vicious; **attention chien m.** *(sur panneau)* beware of the dog **(b)** *(désagréable) (affaire)* unpleasant; *(blessure, grippe)* nasty; *(humeur)* foul
  2 *nm,f Fam* baddie, baddy

mèche¹ [mɛʃ] *nf* **(a)** *(de bougie, de lampe)* wick; *(de charge explosive)* fuse **(b)** *(de perceuse)* bit **(c)** *(de cheveux)* strand; *(boucle)* lock; **se faire des mèches** to get highlights (in one's hair)

mèche² [mɛʃ] *nf* **être de m. avec qn** to be in cahoots with sb

méchoui [meʃwi] *nm* spit-roasted lamb

méconduite [mekɔ̃dɥit] *nf Belg* misbehavior

méconnaissable [mekɔnɛsabl] *adj* unrecognizable

méconnaître [20] [mekɔnɛtr] *vt* **(a)** *(faits)* to fail to take account of **(b)** *(talent, artiste)* to fail to recognize

méconnu, -e [mekɔny] *adj (talent, artiste)* unrecognized

mécontent, -e [mekɔ̃tɑ̃, -ɑ̃t] **1** *adj (insatisfait)* displeased (**de** with); *(contrarié)* annoyed
2 *nm,f* grumbler, grouch; *(électeur)* malcontent

mécontentement [mekɔ̃tɑ̃tmɑ̃] *nm (insatisfaction)* displeasure; *(contrariété)* annoyance

mécontenter [mekɔ̃tɑ̃te] *vt (ne pas satisfaire)* to displease; *(contrarier)* to annoy

Mecque [mɛk] *n voir* **La Mecque**

médaille [medaj] *nf* (**a**) *(prix, décoration)* medal; **la m. d'or/ d'argent/de bronze** the gold/silver/bronze medal (**b**) *(bijou) (avec le nom)* pendant *(with name engraved on it)*; *(à l'effigie d'un saint)* medal (**c**) *(de chat, de chien)* identity tag

médaillé, -e [medaje] **1** *adj (sportif)* holding a medal; *(soldat)* decorated
2 *nm,f (sportif)* medalist; *(soldat)* medal-holder

médaillon [medajɔ̃] *nm* (**a**) *(bijou)* locket (**b**) *(de poisson, de viande)* medallion

médecin [medsɛ̃] *nm* doctor; **m. généraliste** general practitioner, family practitioner; **m. légiste** medical examiner; **m. traitant** consulting physician; **m. du travail** = doctor who carries out the annual medical examination, required by law, of a company's employees

médecine [medsin] *nf* medicine; **exercer la m.** to practice medicine; **m. douce** *ou* **parallèle** alternative medicine; **m. générale** general medicine; **m. du travail** occupational medicine

média [medja] *nm* medium; **les médias** the media

médian, -e [medjɑ̃, -an] **1** *adj* median
2 *nf* **médiane** median

médiateur, -trice [medjatœr, -tris] **1** *adj* mediating
2 *nm,f* mediator
3 *nm* **le M. (de la République)** ≃ the Ombudsman

médiathèque [medjatɛk] *nf* media library

médiation [medjasjɔ̃] *nf* mediation

médiatique [medjatik] *adj (événement, campagne)* media; **il est très m.** *(il passe bien a la télé)* he comes over well on television

médiatisation [medjatizasjɔ̃] *nf* media coverage

médiatiser [medjatize] *vt* to give media coverage to

médiator [medjatɔr] *nm Mus* plectrum

médiatrice [medjatris] *nf* median

médical, -e, -aux, -ales [medikal, -o] *adj* medical

médicalisé, -e [medikalize] *adj* **logement m.** nursing home

médicaliser [medikalize] *vt* (**a**) *(région, pays, population)* to make medical care available to (**b**) *(grossesse)* to treat as a medical matter

médicament [medikamɑ̃] *nm* medicine; **m. de confort** = medication prescribed to relieve pain and symptoms rather than as a cure for the illness

médicinal, -e, -aux, -ales [medisinal, -o] *adj* medicinal

médico-légal, -e *(mpl* **médico-légaux**, *fpl* **médico-légales)** [medikolegal, -o] *adj* forensic

médico-social, -e *(mpl* **médico-sociaux**, *fpl* **médico-sociales)** [medikosɔsjal, -o] *adj* **centre m.** community health center

médiéval, -e, -aux, -ales [medjeval, -o] *adj* medieval

médiocre [medjɔkr] *adj* mediocre

médiocrement [medjɔkrəmɑ̃] *adv* indifferently

médiocrité [medjɔkrite] *nf* mediocrity

médire [27b] [medir] **médire de** *vt ind* to speak ill of

médisance [medizɑ̃s] *nf* (**a**) *(action)* scandalmongering, gossiping (**b**) *(propos)* piece of scandal *or* gossip; **médisances** scandal, gossip

médisant, -e [medizɑ̃, -ɑ̃t] *adj (paroles)* slanderous; *(personne)* scandalmongering

méditation [meditasjɔ̃] *nf* meditation

méditer [medite] **1** *vt* (**a**) *(considérer par une profonde réflexion)* to contemplate (**b**) *(préparer)* to mull over
2 *vi* to meditate
3 méditer sur *vt ind* to meditate on

Méditerranée [mediterane] *nf* **la (mer) M.** the Mediterranean (Sea)

méditerranéen, -enne [mediteraneɛ̃, -ɛn] **1** *adj* Mediterranean
2 *nm,f* **M., Méditerranéenne** person from a Mediterranean country

médium [medjɔm] *nmf (voyant)* medium

médius [medjys] *nm* middle finger

méduse [medyz] *nf* jellyfish

méduser [medyze] *vt* to dumbfound

meeting [mitiŋ] *nm* meeting; **m. aérien** air show

méfait [mefɛ] *nm* misdemeanor; **les méfaits du tabac** the damage caused by smoking

méfiance [mefjɑ̃s] *nf (manque de confiance)* distrust; *(suspicion)* mistrust, suspicion; **m.!** be careful!

méfiant, -e [mefjɑ̃, -ɑ̃t] *adj (n'ayant pas confiance)* distrustful; *(suspicieux)* suspicious (**à l'égard de** *ou* **avec** of)

méfier [66] [mefje] **se méfier** *vpr* to be careful; **se m. de qn** not to trust sb; **se m. de qch** *(faire attention à)* to watch out for sth; *(douter de)* to be wary of sth

méga¹ [mega] *nm Ordinat* megabyte, meg

méga² [mega] *adj inv Fam* mega

mégabit [megabit] *nm Ordinat* megabit

mégalo [megalɔ] *adj & nmf Fam* megalomaniac

mégalomane [megalɔman] *adj & nmf* megalomaniac

mégalomanie [megalɔmani] *nf* megalomania

mégalopole [megalɔpɔl] *nf* megalopolis

mégaoctet *(pl* **mégaoctets)** [megaɔktɛ] *nm Ordinat* megabyte

mégaphone [megafɔn] *nm* bullhorn

mégarde [megard] **par mégarde** *adv* inadvertently, accidentally

mégère [meʒɛr] *nf (femme)* shrew

mégot [mego] *nm* cigarette butt

mégoter [megɔte] *vi Fam* to skimp (**sur** on)

meilleur, -e [mɛjœr] **1** *adj* (**a**) *(comparatif de* **bon**) better (**que** than) (**b**) *(superlatif de* **bon**) **le m. élève** *(de la classe)* the best student; *(parmi deux élèves)* the better student
2 *nm,f (personne)* **le m.** *(de tous)* the best; *(des deux)* the better; *Fam* **alors ça, c'est la meilleure!** that's just great!
3 *nm (ce qu'il y a de mieux)* **le m.** the best; **pour le m. et pour le pire** for better and for worse
4 *adv* **il fait m.** it's warmer

méjuger [45] [meʒyʒe] **1** *vt Litt (mal juger)* to misjudge; *(sous-estimer)* to underestimate
2 **méjuger de** *vt ind (mal juger)* to misjudge; *(sous-estimer)* to underestimate

mél [mel] *nm (courrier électronique)* e-mail; *(adresse électronique)* e-mail address

mélancolie [melɑ̃kɔli] *nf* melancholy

mélancolique [melɑ̃kɔlik] *adj* melancholy

Mélanésie [melanezi] *nf* **la M.** Melanesia

mélanésien, -enne [melanezjɛ̃, -ɛn] **1** *adj* Melanesian
2 *nm (langue)* Melanesian
3 *nm,f* **M., Mélanésienne** Melanesian

mélange [melɑ̃ʒ] *nm* (**a**) *(action)* mixing (**b**) *(résultat)* mixture; **je ne fais jamais de mélanges** I never mix my drinks

mélanger [45] [melɑ̃ʒe] **1** *vt* (**a**) *(mettre ensemble)* to mix (**b**) *(confondre, déranger)* to mix up; **je mélange tout en français** I get everything in French mixed up (**c**) *(cartes)* to shuffle
2 **se mélanger** *vpr* (**a**) *(s'incorporer)* to mix (**b**) *(se confondre)* to get mixed up (**c**) *Fam* **se m. les pédales** *ou* **les pinceaux** to get into a muddle *or* a mix-up

mélangeur [melãʒœr] *nm* (**robinet**) **m.** mixing faucet

mélanome [melanom] *nm Méd* melanoma

mêlant [mɛlã] *adj m Can* **c'est pas m.** there's no doubt about it

mélasse [melas] *nf* molasses (*singulier*); *Fam* **être dans la m.** to be in a mess

Melba [mɛlba] *adj inv* **pêche M.** peach Melba

mêlé, -e [mele] *adj* (**a**) (*mélangé*) mixed (**de** with) (**b**) *Can* (*embrouillé*) mixed-up; (*désorienté*) disoriented; **être m. dans ses papiers** to be confused

mêlée [mele] *nf* (**a**) (*conflit*) fray, mêlée (**b**) (*au rugby*) scrum, scrummage

mêler [mele] **1** *vt* (**a**) (*mettre ensemble*) to mix (**à** *ou* **avec** with) (**b**) (*impliquer*) **m. qn à qch** (*affaire, conversation*) to involve sb in sth

2 se mêler *vpr* (**a**) (*substances*) to combine (**b**) (*se joindre*) **se m. à qch** (*foule*) to mingle with sth; (*cortège*) to join sth; (*conversation*) to join in sth (**c**) (*s'occuper*) **se m. de qch** to get involved in sth; **mêle-toi de tes affaires!** mind your own business!

mélèze [melɛz] *nm* larch (tree)

méli-mélo (*pl* **mélis-mélos**) [melimelo] *nm Fam* jumble

mélo [melo] *Fam* **1** *adj* (*qui tient du mélodrame*) melodramatic; (*qui donne dans la sensiblerie*) sentimental

2 *nm* melodrama

mélodie [melɔdi] *nf* (**a**) (*composition musicale*) melody, tune (**b**) (*de vers, d'une langue*) melodiousness, tunefulness

mélodieusement [melɔdjøzmã] *adv* melodiously, tunefully

mélodieux, -euse [melɔdjø, -øz] *adj* melodious, tuneful

mélodique [melɔdik] *adj* melodic

mélodiste [melɔdist] *nmf* melody writer

mélodramatique [melɔdramatik] *adj* melodramatic

mélodrame [melɔdram] *nm* melodrama

mélomane [melɔman] **1** *adj* music-loving

2 *nmf* music lover

melon [məlõ] *nm* (**a**) (*fruit*) melon (**b**) (*chapeau*) derby (hat)

membrane [mãbran] *nf* membrane

membre [mãbr] **1** *adj* (*État, pays*) member

2 *nm* (**a**) (*partie du corps*) limb; **m. supérieur/inférieur** upper/lower limb; **m. viril** male member (**b**) (*d'une association, d'un groupe*) member

mémé [meme] *nf* (*grand-mère*) grandma, granny; *Fam* (*vieille femme*) old granny

même [mɛm] **1** *adj indéfini* (**a**) (*avant le nom*) (*identique*) same; **j'ai la m. voiture que toi** I have the same car as you (do)

(**b**) (*après le nom, pour insister*) **je l'ai fait le jour m.** I did it that (very) same day; **c'est cela m.** that's it exactly; **c'est la gentillesse m.** she's kindness itself *or* personified

2 *pron indéfini* **le/la m.** the same (one); **j'ai les mêmes que lui** I have the same (ones) as him; **cela revient au m.** it comes *or* amounts to the same thing

3 *adv* (**a**) (*pour insister*) even; **il n'est m. pas beau** he's not even good-looking; **m. moi, je le sais!** even I know that!; **m. si je l'avais, je ne te le donnerais pas** even if I had it, I wouldn't give it to you; **elle habite ici m.** she lives in this very place; **aujourd'hui m.** this very day; **je pense m. qu'il sera d'accord** I think he'll actually agree

(**b**) **être à m. de faire qch** to be able *or* in a position to do sth; **dormir à m. le sol** to sleep on the bare ground; **porter un pull-over à m. la peau** to wear a sweater next to one's bare skin; **de m.** likewise; **Joyeux Noël – vous de m.** Merry Christmas – same to you; **il en est de m. des autres** the same goes for the others; **faire de m.** to follow suit; **de m. que qn** just like sb; **de m. que qch** just like sth; (*aussi bien que qch*) as well as sth; **tout de m.**, *Fam* **quand m.** all the same; *Fam* **enfin, quand m.!** honestly!; *Fam* **m. que je te l'avais déjà dit!** but I already TOLD you!

mémento [memẽto] *nm* (**a**) (*pour réviser*) review notes; **m. de chimie** chemistry review notes (**b**) (*carnet*) notebook

mémère [memɛr] *nf Fam Péj* old granny; **une grosse m.** a fat old bag

mémo [memo] *nm* memo

mémoire¹ [memwar] *nf* (**a**) (*faculté*) memory; **avoir de la m.** to have a good memory; **avoir la m. des noms/dates** to have a good memory for names/dates; **avoir la m. courte** to have a short memory; **se rafraîchir la m.** to refresh one's memory; **à la m. de qn** (*monument*) in memory of sb; **de m.** (*citer*) from memory; **de m. d'homme** within living memory; **pour m.** for the record; **si j'ai bonne m.** if I remember correctly; **avoir une m. d'éléphant** to have a memory like an elephant; **la m. collective** collective memory

(**b**) *Ordinat* memory; **mettre un dossier en m.** to write a file to memory; **carte d'extension de m.** memory expansion card; **m. cache** cache memory; **m. centrale** main memory; **m. à disque** disk memory, RAM disk; **m. étendue** extended memory; **m. expansée** expanded memory; **m. haute** high memory; **m. de masse** mass storage; **m. morte** read-only memory; **m. non effaçable** non-erasable memory; **m. paginée** expanded memory; **m. permanente** permanent memory; **m. tampon** buffer (store *or* memory); **m. vidéo** video memory; **m. vive** random-access memory, RAM; **m. vive dynamique** DRAM, dynamic random-access memory; **m. vive statique** static RAM, static random-access memory

mémoire² [memwar] *nm* (**a**) (*thèse*) thesis, dissertation (**b**) (*rapport*) report (**c**) **Mémoires** (*chronique*) memoirs

mémorable [memɔrabl] *adj* memorable

mémorandum [memɔrãdɔm] *nm* (**a**) (*note*) memorandum (**b**) (*carnet*) notebook

mémorial, -aux [memɔrjal, -o] *nm* (*monument*) memorial

mémoriser [memɔrize] *vt* to memorize

menaçant, -e [mənasã, -ãt] *adj* threatening, menacing

menace [mənas] *nf* threat (**de** of); **menaces de mort** death threats

menacer [16] [mənase] **1** *vt* to threaten (**de** with); **m. qn du poing** to shake one's fist at sb; **m. de faire qch** to threaten to do sth

2 *vi* (*tempête, orage, révolution*) to be brewing; **la pluie menace** it's threatening to rain

ménage [menaʒ] *nm* (**a**) (*nettoyage*) **faire le m.** (*à la maison*) to do the housework; *Fig* to have a shake-up; **faire des ménages** to go out cleaning (**b**) (*couple*) couple; **se mettre en m.** to move in together; **se mettre en m. avec qn** to move in with sb; **faire bon/mauvais m. (avec qn)** to get along well/badly (with sb); **m. à trois** ménage à trois (**c**) *Écon* household

ménagement [menaʒmã] *nm* care, caution; (*tact*) consideration; **sans m.** (*annoncer*) bluntly

ménager¹, -ère [menaʒe, -ɛr] **1** *adj* (**a**) (*de la maison*) (*équipement, appareils*) household (**b**) *Can* (*économe*) thrifty, careful (with money)

2 *nf* **ménagère** (*femme*) housewife, homemaker

ménager² [45] [menaʒe] **1** *vt* (**a**) (*utiliser avec parcimonie*) (*argent*) to use sparingly; (*forces*) to conserve, to save; (*santé*) to take care of; **ne pas m. sa peine** to put in a lot of effort (**b**) (*traiter avec soin*) to treat carefully; *Fig* **m. la chèvre et le chou** to keep everyone happy (**c**) (*arranger*) (*entrevue, réunion*) to arrange, to organize; (*sortie*) to provide; (*réconciliation*) to bring about

2 se ménager *vpr* (**a**) (*prendre soin de soi*) to take care of oneself, to look after oneself (**b**) (*se réserver*) to set aside

ménagerie [menaʒri] *nf* menagerie

mendiant, -e [mãdjã, -ãt] **1** *adj* (*moine, ordre*) mendicant

2 *nm,f* beggar

mendicité [mãdisite] *nf* begging

mendier [66] [mɑ̃dje] **1** *vt* to beg for
  2 *vi* to beg
mener [46] [məne] **1** *vt* (**a**) *(accompagner)* to take (**à** to) (**b**) *(cortège, course)* to lead; **m. qch à bien** to bring sth to a successful conclusion; *Fig* **m. la danse** to call the tune (**c**) *(vie)* to lead; **m. la vie dure à qn** to give sb a hard time (**d**) *(débat, enquête)* to lead (**e**) *(contrôler) (personne)* **m. qn à la baguette** to have sb under one's thumb; **m. qn par le bout du nez** to lead sb by the nose
  2 *vi* (**a**) *(dans un match, une compétition)* to lead; **m. par deux buts à un** to lead by two goals to one (**b**) **m. à un lieu** to lead to a place; *Fig* **cela ne mène à rien** this is getting us nowhere (**c**) *Fam* **elle n'en menait pas large** her heart was in her mouth
meneur, -euse [mənœr, -øz] **1** *nm,f (de parti politique)* leader; *(agitateur)* ringleader; **m. d'hommes** born leader; **m. de jeu** quizmaster; *Sport* playmaker
  2 *nf* **meneuse de revue** principal chorus girl; *Can* **meneuse de claques** cheerleader
menhir [menir] *nm* menhir
méninges [menɛ̃ʒ] *nfpl Fam* brains
méningite [menɛ̃ʒit] *nf* meningitis; **avoir une m.** to have meningitis
ménisque [menisk] *nm* meniscus
ménopause [menɔpoz] *nf* menopause
menotte [mənɔt] *nf* (**a**) *Fam (petite main)* little hand (**b**) **menottes** *(bracelets métalliques)* handcuffs; **mettre** *ou* **passer les menottes à qn** to handcuff sb, to put handcuffs on sb
mensonge [mɑ̃sɔ̃ʒ] *nm* (**a**) *(propos)* lie; **petit m., pieux m.** white lie (**b**) *(acte)* lying
mensonger, -ère [mɑ̃sɔ̃ʒe, -ɛr] *adj (propos)* untrue; *(publicité)* misleading
menstruation [mɑ̃stryasjɔ̃] *nf* menstruation
menstruel, -elle [mɑ̃stryɛl] *adj* menstrual
mensualiser [mɑ̃sɥalize] *vt* to pay monthly; **être mensualisé** *(pour les impôts)* = to pay one's income tax in advance monthly installments, the amount paid being an estimation based on previous years
mensualité [mɑ̃sɥalite] *nf* monthly payment
mensuel, -elle [mɑ̃sɥɛl] **1** *adj* monthly
  2 *nm (publication)* monthly (magazine)
mensuellement [mɑ̃sɥɛlmɑ̃] *adv* monthly, every month
mensuration [mɑ̃syrasjɔ̃] *nf* (**a**) *(action)* measurement, measuring (**b**) **mensurations** *(dimensions)* measurements; *Hum* vital statistics
mental, -e, -aux, -ales [mɑ̃tal, -o] **1** *adj* mental
  2 *nm* mental attitude
mentalement [mɑ̃talmɑ̃] *adv* mentally
mentalité [mɑ̃talite] *nf* mentality; **les mentalités ont changé** (people's) attitudes have changed; *Ironique* **jolie m.!** what an attitude!
menteur, -euse [mɑ̃tœr, -øz] **1** *adj (personne)* untruthful, lying
  2 *nm,f* liar
menthe [mɑ̃t] *nf (plante)* mint; **dentifrice à la m.** mint *or* mint-flavored toothpaste; **m. à l'eau** mint cordial
menthol [mɑ̃tɔl] *nm* menthol
mentholé, -e [mɑ̃tɔle] *adj* menthol, mentholated
mention [mɑ̃sjɔ̃] *nf* (**a**) *(fait de citer)* mention; **faire m. de qn/qch** to mention sb/sth (**b**) **rayer la m. inutile** *(sur formulaire)* delete where applicable (**c**) *(à un examen)* **m. passable** ≃ C; **m. assez bien** ≃ B; **m. bien/très bien** ≃ A
mentionner [mɑ̃sjɔne] *vt* to mention
mentir [64b] [mɑ̃tir] *vi* to lie (**à** to); **sans m.** honestly
menton [mɑ̃tɔ̃] *nm* chin; **m. en galoche** protruding chin; **m. fuyant** receding chin; **double m.** double chin

mentor [mɑ̃tɔr] *nm* mentor
menu¹, -e [məny] **1** *adj* (**a**) *(détail, monnaie)* small *(b)* *(taille)* slim; *(personne)* petite
  2 *adv* small, fine
menu² [məny] *nm* (**a**) *(au restaurant)* set menu, fixed-price menu (**b**) *Ordinat* menu; **contrôlé par m.** menu-driven; **m. d'aide** help menu; **m. déroulant** pull-down menu; **m. fichier** file menu; **m. local** pop-up menu; **m. primaire/secondaire/principal** primary/secondary/main menu
menuet [mənɥɛ] *nm* minuet
menuiserie [mənɥizri] *nf* (**a**) *(atelier)* (carpenter's) workshop (**b**) *(travail du bois, résultat)* carpentry, woodwork
menuisier [mənɥizje] *nm* carpenter
méprendre [58] [meprɑ̃dr] **se méprendre** *vpr* to be mistaken (**sur** about); **elle te ressemble à s'y m.** she looks exactly like you
mépris¹, -e *voir* **méprendre**
mépris² [mepri] *nm* contempt, scorn; **avec m.** scornfully, contemptuously; **avoir du m. pour qn** to despise sb; **au m. de qch** regardless of sth
méprisable [meprizabl] *adj* contemptible, despicable
méprisant, -e [meprizɑ̃, -ɑ̃t] *adj* scornful, contemptuous
méprise [mepriz] *nf* mistake
mépriser [meprize] *vt* (**a**) *(dédaigner) (personne, argent)* to despise (**b**) *(ignorer) (conseil, offre, danger)* to disregard
mer [mɛr] *nf* (**a**) *(étendue d'eau)* sea; **en haute** *ou* **pleine m.** (out) at sea; **au bord de la m.** at *or* by the seaside; **aller à la m.** to go to the seaside; **prendre la m.** to set sail, to put (out) to sea; *Fam* **ce n'est pas la m. à boire** it's no big deal; **une m. d'huile** a sea as calm as a millpond; **la m. Adriatique** the Adriatic Sea; **la m. d'Aral** the Aral Sea; **la m. Caspienne** the Caspian Sea; **la m. de Chine** the China Sea; **la m. de Corail** the Coral Sea; **la m. Égée** the Aegean Sea; **la m. d'Irlande** the Irish Sea; **la m. Morte** the Dead Sea; **la m. Noire** the Black Sea; **la m. du Nord** the North Sea; **la m. Rouge** the Red Sea; **la m. des Sargasses** the Sargasso Sea (**b**) *(marée)* tide
mercantile [mɛrkɑ̃til] *adj* mercenary
mercatique [mɛrkatik] *nf* marketing
mercenaire [mɛrsənɛr] *adj & nm* mercenary
mercerie [mɛrsəri] *nf* (**a**) *(magasin)* notions store (**b**) *(articles)* notions
merchandising [mɛrʃɑ̃dajziŋ] *nm* merchandising
merci [mɛrsi] **1** *exclam* thank you, thanks (**de** *ou* **pour** for); **(non) m.** no thank you, no thanks; **dire m. (à qn)** to say thank you *or* thanks (to sb); **m. bien, m. beaucoup** thank you *or* thanks very much
  2 *nm* thank you
  3 *nf* **être à la m. de qn/qch** to be at the mercy of sb/sth; **sans m.** merciless
mercier, -ère [mɛrsje, -ɛr] *nm,f* notions dealer
mercredi [mɛrkrədi] *nm* Wednesday; **le m. des Cendres** Ash Wednesday; *voir aussi* **samedi**
Mercure [mɛrkyr] *npr (dieu, planète)* Mercury
mercure [mɛrkyr] *nm* mercury
Mercurochrome® [mɛrkyrɔkrom] *nm* Mercurochrome®
merde [mɛrd] *Vulg* **1** *nf* shit; *Fig* **être dans la m.** to be in the shit; **ne pas se prendre pour de la m.** to think one is God's gift (to mankind); **c'est de la m.** *(c'est de la mauvaise qualité)* it's shit; **de m.** *(voiture, idée)* shitty
  2 *exclam* shit!; *Fig* **dire m. à qn** *(l'envoyer au diable)* to tell sb to fuck off; **je te dis m.!** *(bonne chance)* break a leg!; **m. alors!** oh shit!
merder [mɛrde] *vi très Fam (ne pas fonctionner) (projet)* to go down the tubes; **ça merde entre eux** things between them are really screwed up; **j'ai merdé à l'examen** I really screwed up in the exam

merdeux, -euse [mɛrdø, -øz] *très Fam* **1** *adj* **se sentir m.** to feel shitty

2 *nm,f (enfant)* **un petit m.** a little shit

merdier [mɛrdje] *nm Vulg* **être dans le m.** to be in the shit

merdique [mɛrdik] *adj très Fam* shitty

mère [mɛr] **1** *adj voir* **maison**

2 *nf* (**a**) *(parent)* mother; **elle est m. de trois enfants** she is the mother of three children; **m. célibataire** single mother; **être m. de famille** to be a wife and mother; **m. nourricière** foster mother; **m. patrie** mother country, motherland; **m. porteuse** surrogate mother; **m. poule** mother hen (**b**) *Fam (femme)* **la m. Martin** old Mrs. Martin

merguez [mɛrgɛz] *nf* merguez *(spicy North African sausage)*

méridien, -enne [meridjɛ̃, -ɛn] **1** *adj (ligne)* meridian, meridional

2 *nm Géog* meridian

3 *nf* **méridienne** *(canapé)* day bed

méridional, -e, -aux, -ales [meridjɔnal, -o] **1** *adj (du Sud)* southern; *(du sud de la France)* from the South of France

2 *nm,f (du Sud)* southerner; *(du sud de la France)* person from the South of France

meringue [mərɛ̃g] *nf* meringue

mérinos [merinos] *nm* (**a**) *Zool* merino (**b**) *Tex* **(laine *f*) m.** merino wool

merisier [mərizje] *nm (arbre)* wild cherry (tree); *(bois)* cherry(wood)

méritant, -e [meritɑ̃, -ɑ̃t] *adj* deserving

mérite [merit] *nm* merit; *(honneur)* credit; **avoir du m. (à faire qch)** to deserve credit (for doing sth); **au moins, son livre a le m. de la clarté** at least her book has the merit of being clearly written; **tout le m. lui revient** he deserves all the credit

mériter [merite] *vt* (**a**) *(après une action)* to deserve; **m. d'être puni/récompensé** to deserve to be punished/rewarded; **elle mérite qu'on le lui dise** she deserves to be told (**b**) *(demander)* to be worth; **m. réflexion** to be worth thinking about; **ce livre mérite d'être lu** this book is worth reading

méritoire [meritwar] *adj* commendable, praiseworthy

merlan [mɛrlɑ̃] *nm* (**a**) *(poisson)* whiting (**b**) *très Fam (coiffeur)* hairdresser

merle [mɛrl] *nm* blackbird

merlu [mɛrly] *nm* hake

mérou [meru] *nm* grouper

mérovingien, -enne [merɔvɛ̃ʒjɛ̃, -ɛn] **1** *adj* Merovingian

2 *nmpl* **les Mérovingiens** the Merovingians

merveille [mɛrvɛj] *nf* (**a**) *(chose remarquable)* marvel, wonder; **à m.** wonderfully (well); **se porter à m.** to be in the best of health; *Fig* **faire des merveilles** to work wonders; **les Sept Merveilles du monde** the Seven Wonders of the World (**b**) *(gâteau)* = sweet fritter

merveilleusement [mɛrvɛjøzmɑ̃] *adv* marvelously, wonderfully

merveilleux, -euse [mɛrvɛjø, -øz] **1** *adj* marvelous, wonderful

2 *nm* **le m.** the supernatural

mes [me] *voir* **mon**

mésalliance [mezaljɑ̃s] *nf* unsuitable marriage; **faire une m.** to marry beneath oneself

mésallier [66] [mezalje] **se mésallier** *vpr* to marry beneath oneself

mésange [mezɑ̃ʒ] *nf* tit; **m. bleue** blue tit; **m. charbonnière** coal tit

mésaventure [mezavɑ̃tyr] *nf* misadventure

mesdames [medam] *nfpl voir* **madame**

mesdemoiselles [medmwazɛl] *nfpl voir* **mademoiselle**

mésentente [mezɑ̃tɑ̃t] *nf* disagreement

mésestimer [mezɛstime] *vt* to underestimate

mésothérapie [mezoterapi] *nf* = treatment consisting of injecting minute quantities of medication into the affected area

mesquin, -e [mɛskɛ̃, -in] *adj* mean, petty

mesquinement [mɛskinmɑ̃] *adv* meanly

mesquinerie [mɛskinri] *nf* (**a**) *(d'un caractère, d'un procédé)* meanness, pettiness (**b**) *(action)* mean or petty thing (to do)

mess [mɛs] *nm* mess

message [mesaʒ] *nm* message; *Ordinat* **m. d'accueil** welcome message; *Ordinat* **m. d'alerte** warning message, alert box; *Ordinat* **m. électronique** e-mail; **envoyer un m. électronique à qn** to e-mail sb; *Ordinat* **m. d'erreur** error message; *Ordinat* **m. d'invite** *(du système)* prompt; **m. publicitaire** commercial; **m. texte** text message; **m. vocal** voicemail (message)

messager, -ère [mesaʒe, -ɛr] *nm,f* messenger

messagerie [mesaʒri] *nf* (**a**) *(service de transports)* courier company; **messageries aériennes** air-freight company (**b**) *(service télématique)* **m. électronique** electronic mail service, e-mail; **m. instantanée** instant messaging (service); **m. vocale** voice mail (service) (**c**) *(entreprise de routage)* **m. de presse** newspaper distribution service

messe [mɛs] *nf (office religieux, composition musicale)* mass; **aller à la m.** to go to mass; *Fig* **faire des messes basses** to whisper; **m. de minuit** midnight mass

messeigneurs [mesɛɲœr] *nmpl voir* **monseigneur**

Messie [mesi] *nm* **le M.** the Messiah

messieurs [mesjø] *nmpl voir* **monsieur**

mesurable [məzyrabl] *adj* measurable

mesure [məzyr] *nf* (**a**) *(dimension)* measurement; *(action)* measurement, measuring; **prendre les mesures de qn/qch** to measure sb/sth; *Fig* **prendre la m. de qn/qch** to size sb/sth up; **sur m.** *(costume)* made to measure; *(rôle, emploi)* ideal; **donner toute sa m.** to show what one is capable of; **être à la m. de qn/qch** to measure up to sb/sth; **être sans commune m. avec qch** to be out of proportion to sth; **elle a trouvé quelqu'un/un homme à sa m.** she met her match (**b**) *(moyen)* measure; **prendre des mesures** to take measures; **m. de sécurité** safety measure or precaution; **par m. d'économie** as a way to save money (**c**) *(quantité, unité)* measure; **sans commune m.** unrivaled (**d**) *(modération)* moderation; **sans m.** *(ambition, jalousie)* limitless (**e**) *Mus (temps)* time; *(division)* bar; **m. à quatre temps** four-four time; **battre la m.** to beat time; **en m.** in time (**f**) *(locutions)* **à m. que** as; **(au fur et) à m.** as one goes along; **dans une certaine m.** to some or a certain extent; **dans une large m.** to a large extent; **dans la m. où** in so far as; **dans la m. du possible** as far as is possible; **être en m. de faire qch** to be in a position to do sth

mesuré, -e [məzyre] *adj (pas)* measured; *(langage, personne)* restrained

mesurer [məzyre] **1** *vt* (**a**) *(dimensions, taille)* to measure; *(tissu)* to measure off (**b**) *(déterminer)* to assess (**c**) *(limiter)* to limit; **m. l'argent à qn** to ration out money to sb (**d**) **m. ses paroles** to moderate one's language

2 *vi* to measure; **m. 1,5 mètres** *(personne)* ≃ to be 5 feet tall; *(tour, colonne)* ≃ to be 5 feet high

3 se mesurer *vpr* **se m. avec** *ou* **à qn** to pit oneself against sb

met *voir* **mettre**

métabolique [metabɔlik] *adj* metabolic

métabolisme [metabɔlism] *nm* metabolism

métairie [metɛri] *nf* small farm *(worked by sharecropper)*

métal, -aux [metal, -o] *nm* metal

métallique [metalik] *adj* metallic

métallisé, -e [metalize] *adj (peinture, couleur)* metallic

métallo [metalo] *nm Fam* metalworker

métallurgie [metalyrʒi] *nf* (**a**) *(industrie)* metallurgical industry (**b**) *(procédé)* metallurgy

métallurgique [metalyrʒik] *adj* metallurgical

métallurgiste [metalyrʒist] *nm* (**a**) *(ouvrier)* metalworker (**b**) *(chef d'entreprise)* metallurgist

métamorphose [metamɔrfoz] *nf aussi Fig* metamorphosis

métamorphoser [metamɔrfoze] **1** *vt* to transform (**en** into)

    2 se métamorphoser *vpr Biol* to metamorphose; *Fig* to be transformed (**en** into)

métaphore [metafɔr] *nf* metaphor

métaphorique [metafɔrik] *adj* metaphorical

métaphoriquement [metafɔrikmɑ̃] *adv* metaphorically

métaphysique [metafizik] **1** *adj* metaphysical

    2 *nf* metaphysics *(singulier)*

métastase [metastɑz] *nf* metastasis

métayer, -ère [metɛje, -ɛr] *nm,f* sharecropper

météo [meteo] *Fam* **1** *adj* weather

    2 *nf (bulletin)* weather forecast; *(organisme)* weather bureau

météore [meteɔr] *nm* meteor

météorite [meteɔrit] *nf* meteorite

météorologie [meteɔrɔlɔʒi] *nf* meteorology

météorologique [meteɔrɔlɔʒik] *adj (bulletin, prévisions)* weather

météorologiste [meteɔrɔlɔʒist], **météorologue** [meteɔrɔlɔg] *nmf* meteorologist

métèque [metɛk] *nm* = racist term used to refer to any dark-skinned foreigner living in France, especially one from the Mediterranean

méthadone [metadɔn] *nf* methadone

méthane [metan] *nm* methane

méthanol [metanɔl] *nm* methanol

méthode [metɔd] *nf* (**a**) *(démarche)* method; **m. pour faire qch** method of doing sth (**b**) *(ordre)* method; **avec m.** methodically (**c**) *(livre)* **m. d'anglais** English primer; **m. de piano** piano tutor

méthodique [metɔdik] *adj* methodical

méthodiquement [metɔdikmɑ̃] *adv* methodically

méthodiste [metɔdist] *adj & nmf* Methodist

méthodologie [metɔdɔlɔʒi] *nf* methodology

méthodologique [metɔdɔlɔʒik] *adj* methodological

méthylène [metilɛn] *nm* methylene

méticuleusement [metikyløzmɑ̃] *adv* meticulously

méticuleux, -euse [metikylø, -øz] *adj* meticulous

méticulosité [metikylozite] *nf* meticulousness

métier [metje] *nm* (**a**) *(manuel, commercial)* trade; *(intellectuel)* profession; **exercer un m.** to have a job; **j'exerce le m. de journaliste** I'm a journalist by profession; **quel m. veux-tu faire plus tard?** what do you want to be when you grow up?; **il n'est pas** *ou* **il n'y a pas de sot m.** a job's a job; **être du m.** to be in the business; **connaître son m.** to know what one is doing; **parler m.** to talk shop (**b**) *(savoir-faire, expérience)* experience; **avoir du m.** to have experience; **elle a plusieurs années de m.** she has several years' experience (**c**) *(machine)* **m. à tisser** loom

métis, -isse [metis] **1** *adj (personne)* half-caste

    2 *nm,f (personne)* half-caste

métissage [metisaʒ] *nm* crossbreeding

métisser [metise] *vt* to cross(breed); **une population très métissée** a highly intermixed population; **musique métissée** crossover *or* fusion music

métrage [metraʒ] *nm* (**a**) *(action)* measuring (**b**) *(coupon de tissu)* length (**c**) *(longueur d'un film)* footage, length; **long/moyen/court m.** feature/medium-length/short movie

mètre¹ [mɛtr] *nm* (**a**) *(unité de longueur)* meter; **m. carré/cube** square/cubic meter (**b**) *(pour mesurer)* tape measure; *(en bois, en métal)* rule; **m. à ruban** tape measure

mètre² [mɛtr] *nm (en poésie)* meter

métreur [metrœr] *nm* materials appraiser

métrique¹ [metrik] *adj (système)* metric

métrique² [metrik] **1** *adj (en poésie)* metrical

    2 *nf* metrics *(singulier)*

métro [metro] *nm* subway; **le premier/dernier m.** the first/last (subway) train; **m. aerien** elevated *or* overhead railroad

métronome [metrɔnɔm] *nm* metronome

métropole [metrɔpɔl] *nf* (**a**) *(grande ville)* metropolis (**b**) *(pays)* mother country

métropolitain, -e [metrɔpɔlitɛ̃, -ɛn] **1** *adj (non insulaire)* metropolitan

    2 *nm Vieilli (métro)* subway

métrosexuel, -elle [metrɔsɛksyɛl] **1** *adj* metrosexual

    2 *nm* metrosexual

mets¹ [mɛ] *voir* **mettre**

mets² [mɛ] *nm* dish

mettable [mɛtabl] *adj* wearable

mette *etc. voir* **mettre**

metteur [mɛtœr] *nm* **m. en scène** director

mettre [47] [mɛtr] **1** *vt* (**a**) *(placer)* to put; **m. qch sur/dans qch** to put sth on/in sth; **m. qn à mal** *(verbalement)* to berate sb; *(physiquement)* to beat sb up

    (**b**) *(vêtement, chaussures, lunettes, pansement)* to put on

    (**c**) *(moquette)* to lay; *(papier peint, étagères)* to put up

    (**d**) *(allumer)* to put on, to switch on; **m. qch en marche** to turn sth on; **m. qch plus fort** to turn sth up; **m. de la musique** to put some music on; **m. le réveil (à cinq heures)** to set the alarm (for five o'clock); **faire m. le téléphone** to have the phone put in

    (**e**) **elle y a mis beaucoup d'argent** she's spent a lot of money on it

    (**f**) **elle a mis du temps/deux ans à le faire** it took her a while/two years to do it; **combien de temps met-on pour y aller?** how long does it take to get there?

    (**g**) **ça va prendre, mettons, trois mois** it will take, (let's) say, three months; **mettons que je n'ai rien dit** pretend I didn't say anything

    (**h**) *(écrire)* to put

    (**i**) *Fam* **qu'est-ce qu'on leur a mis!** we really thrashed them!; **m. les bouts** *ou* **les voiles** to get moving; *Vulg* **va te faire m.!** go fuck yourself!

    2 *vi* **m. bas** to give birth

    3 se mettre *vpr* (**a**) *(se placer)* **mets-toi là!** *(va là-bas)* stand there!; *(assieds-toi là-bas)* sit there!; **se m. au soleil** *(s'asseoir)* to sit in the sun; *(s'allonger)* to lie in the sun; **se m. au lit** to get into bed; **se m. sur le dos/ventre** to lie on one's back/stomach; *(en se tournant)* to turn (over) onto one's back/stomach; *Belg* **mettez-vous!** take a seat!, sit down!; *Fig* **se m. en avant** to push oneself forward; *Fig* **je ne savais plus où me m.** I didn't know where to put myself

    (**b**) *(maquillage, vêtement)* to put on; **je n'ai plus rien à me m.** I have nothing to wear

    (**c**) *(commencer)* **se m. à qch** *(activité)* to take sth up; **se m. au travail** to get (down) to work; **se m. à faire qch** to begin *or* to start doing sth; **le temps s'est mis à la pluie** it turned rainy; *Fam* **si tu t'y mets aussi!** don't YOU start!

    (**d**) **il a fallu se m. à trois pour la déplacer** it took three of us to move it

    (**e**) *Fam* **qu'est-ce qu'ils se sont mis!** they really laid into each other!

meuble [mœbl] **1** *adj* (**a**) *(sol, terre, roche)* soft (**b**) *(biens)* movable

    2 *nm* piece of furniture; **meubles** furniture; **être dans ses meubles** to have a place of one's own; *Fam* **faire partie des meubles** to be part of the furniture

meublé, -e [mœble] **1** *adj* furnished; **non m.** unfurnished

    2 *nm (chambre)* furnished room; *(appartement)* furnished apartment

meubler [mœble] **1** *vt* (**a**) *(pièce, maison)* to furnish (**de** with) (**b**) *(remplir)* to fill (**de** with); **m. la conversation** to make conversation
   2 se meubler *vpr* to furnish one's home

meuf [mœf] *nf très Fam (femme)* chick

meuglement [møgləmɑ̃] *nm* moo; **des meuglements** mooing

meugler [møgle] *vi* to moo

meule [møl] *nf* (**a**) *(d'herbe, de céréales)* stack; **m. de foin** haystack (**b**) *(de moulin)* millstone (**c**) *(de fromage)* round

meunier, -ère [mønje, -ɛr] **1** *adj* (**a**) *(industrie)* flour-milling (**b**) **(à la) meunière** *(poisson)* = coated with flour and fried in butter
   2 *nm,f* miller, *f* miller's wife

meurs, meurt *voir* **mourir**

meurtre [mœrtr] *nm* murder

meurtri, -e [mœrtri] *adj* bruised

meurtrier, -ère [mœrtrije, -ɛr] **1** *adj (guerre, attentat, colère)* murderous; *(arme, épidémie)* deadly
   2 *nm,f* murderer
   3 *nf* **meurtrière** *Archit* loophole

meurtrir [mœrtrir] *vt* to bruise

meurtrissure [mœrtrisyr] *nf* bruise

meute [møt] *nf aussi Fig* pack

MEV [mɛv] *nf Ordinat (abrév* **mémoire vive)** RAM

mexicain, -e [mɛksikɛ̃, -ɛn] **1** *adj* Mexican
   2 *nm,f* **M., Mexicaine** Mexican

Mexico [mɛksiko] *n* Mexico City

Mexique [mɛksik] *nm* **le M.** Mexico

mézigue [mezig] *pron personnel Fam* yours truly

mezzanine [mɛdzanin] *nf* (**a**) *(entre deux étages)* mezzanine (floor) (**b**) *(au théâtre)* mezzanine

mezzo-soprano *(pl* **mezzo-sopranos)** [mɛdzo-sɔprano]
   1 *nm (voix)* mezzo-soprano
   2 *nf (cantatrice)* mezzo-soprano

MF [ɛmɛf] *nf Rad (abrév* **modulation de fréquence)** FM

mg *(abrév* **milligramme(s))** mg

Mgr *Rel (abrév* **Monseigneur)** Mgr

mi [mi] *nm inv (note)* E; *(chantée)* mi

mi- [mi] *adv* **la mi-avril** mid-April; **à mi-hauteur** *(en montant)* halfway up; *(en descendant)* halfway down; **elle avait de l'eau jusqu'à mi-jambe** the water was halfway up her legs; **mi-amusé, mi-intrigué** half-amused, half-puzzled; **mi-figue, mi-raisin** *(sourire)* half-hearted; *(plaisanterie)* half-serious

miam-miam [mjammjam] *exclam* yum yum!

miaou [mjau] *exclam* meow!

miasme [mjasm] *nm* miasma

miaulement [mjolmɑ̃] *nm* meowing

miauler [mjole] *vi* to meow

mi-bas [miba] *nm inv (en laine)* knee sock; *(en voile)* popsock

mica [mika] *nm* mica

mi-carême *(pl* **mi-carêmes)** [mikarɛm] *nf* = third Thursday in Lent

miche [miʃ] *nf* (**a**) *(pain)* round loaf (**b**) *Fam* **miches** *(fesses)* butt

Michel-Ange [mikɛlɑ̃ʒ] *npr* Michelangelo

micheline [miʃlin] *nf* railcar

mi-chemin [miʃmɛ̃] **à mi-chemin** *adv* halfway

Michigan [miʃigɑ̃] *n voir* **lac**

mi-clos, -e *(mpl* **mi-clos,** *fpl* **mi-closes)** [miklo, mikloz] *adj* half-closed

micmac [mikmak] *nm Fam* (**a**) *(complications)* muddle (**b**) *Can (désordre)* mess

mi-côte [mikot] **à mi-côte** *adv* halfway up the hill

mi-course [mikurs] **à mi-course** *adv* at the halfway mark

micro [mikro] **1** *nm* (**a**) *(microphone)* mike (**b**) *Ordinat* micro(computer)
   2 *nf Ordinat* microcomputing

microbe [mikrɔb] *nm* (**a**) *(germe)* microbe, germ (**b**) *Fam (personne chétive)* little squirt

microbien, -enne [mikrɔbjɛ̃, -ɛn] *adj* microbial

microbiologie [mikrɔbjɔlɔʒi] *nf* microbiology

microchirurgie [mikroʃiryrʒi] *nf* microsurgery

microcircuit [mikrosirkɥi] *nm Ordinat* microcircuit; **micro-circuits** microcircuitry

microclimat [mikroklima] *nm* microclimate

microcosme [mikrokɔsm] *nm* microcosm

microéconomie [mikroekɔnɔmi] *nf* microeconomics *(singulier)*

microéconomique [mikroekɔnɔmik] *adj* microeconomic

microédition [mikroedisjɔ̃] *nf Ordinat* desktop publishing, DTP

microfiche [mikrofiʃ] *nf* microfiche

microfilm [mikrofilm] *nm* microfilm

micro-informatique [mikroɛ̃fɔrmatik] *nf Ordinat* microcomputing

micron [mikrɔ̃] *nm* micron

Micronésie [mikrɔnezi] *nf* **la M.** Micronesia

micro-ondes [mikroɔ̃d] *nm inv* microwave

micro-ordinateur *(pl* **micro-ordinateurs)** [mikroɔrdinatœr] *nm Ordinat* microcomputer

micro-organisme *(pl* **micro-organismes)** [mikroɔrganism] *nm* micro-organism

microphone [mikrofɔn] *nm* microphone

micropilule [mikropilyl] *nf* mini pill

microprocesseur [mikroprɔsɛsœr] *nm Ordinat* microprocessor

microscope [mikroskɔp] *nm* microscope; **au m.** under a microscope; **m. électronique** electron microscope

microscopique [mikroskɔpik] *adj* microscopic

microsillon [mikrosijɔ̃] *nm (de disque)* groove

micro-trottoir [mikrotrɔtwar] *(pl* **micros-trottoirs)** *nm* street interview

midi [midi] *nm* (**a**) *(heure)* twelve o'clock, midday; **m. et demie** half past twelve; **entre m. et deux** at lunchtime (**b**) *(moment du déjeuner)* lunchtime (**c**) *(partie sud)* south; **le M. (de la France)** the South of France

midinette [midinɛt] *nf* silly young girl

mi-distance [midistɑ̃s] **à mi-distance** *adv* halfway (**de** in)

mie [mi] *nf (de pain)* soft part, crumb

miel [mjɛl] *nm* honey

mielleusement [mjɛløzmɑ̃] *adv (parler)* in honeyed tones

mielleux, -euse [mjɛlø, -øz] *adj (discours, sourire)* sugary; *(personne)* smooth

mien, mienne [mjɛ̃, mjɛn] **1** *pron possessif* **le m., la mienne, les miens, les miennes** mine; *(en insistant)* my own; **je te prête le m.** you can borrow mine; **je n'en ai pas besoin, j'ai le m.** I don't need it, I have my own
   2 *nm* **j'y ai mis du m.** I did my share
   3 *nmpl* **les miens** *(ma famille)* my family

miette [mjɛt] *nf (de pain, de gâteau)* crumb; *Fig* **en miettes** in pieces; **mettre qch en miettes** *(briser)* to smash sth to pieces; **ne pas perdre une m. de qch** *(conversation)* not to miss a word of sth; **après le partage, elle n'a eu que des miettes** she had to make do with what little was left over after the inheritance was shared out

mieux [mjø] **1** *adv* (**a**) *(comparatif)* better; **m. que** better than; **il vaut m. les surveiller** it's best to watch them; **vous feriez m. de m'écouter** you'd do better to listen to me; **elle va m.** she's (feeling) better; **c'est on ne peut m.** it couldn't be better;

j'espérais m. de votre part I expected better of you; **plus on se voit et m. on s'apprécie** the more we see each other, the more we like each other; **de m. en m.** better and better; **faire qch à qui m. m.** to try to outdo each other in doing sth (**b**) *(superlatif)* **c'est elle qui s'exprime le m.** she expresses herself (the) best; **le plus tôt sera le m.** the sooner the better; **le m. serait de…** the best thing would be to…; **ils s'entendent le m. du monde** they get along extremely well; **être au m. avec qn** to be on the best of terms with sb; **un service des m. organisés** an extremely well-organized department

2 *adj* better; *(plus beau)* better-looking; **si tu n'as rien de m. à faire** if you have nothing better to do; **c'est le m. (de tous)** *(le plus beau)* he's the best-looking (of all)

3 *nm* **espérer m.** to hope for better things; **il y a un m.** *ou* **du m.** there's been a change for the better; **faire** *ou* **agir pour le m.** to act for the best; **faire de son m.** to do one's best; **fais du m. que tu peux** do the best you can

mièvre [mjɛvr] *adj* insipid

mièvrerie [mjɛvrəri] *nf* insipidness

mignon, -onne [miɲɔ̃, -ɔn] **1** *adj* (**a**) *(joli, charmant)* cute (**b**) *(gentil)* nice

    2 *nm (favori)* minion

    3 *nm,f* **mon m.** darling

migraine [migrɛn] *nf (douleur violente)* migraine; *(mal de tête)* headache; **avoir des migraines** to get migraines/headaches

migraineux, -euse [migrɛnø, -øz] *nm,f* migraine sufferer

migrant, -e [migrã, -ãt] *adj & nm,f* migrant

migrateur, -trice [migratœr, -tris] *adj (animaux)* migratory

migration [migrasjɔ̃] *nf* migration

migratoire [migratwar] *adj* migratory

migrer [migre] *vi aussi Ordinat* to migrate (**vers** to)

mijaurée [miʒɔre] *nf (jeune fille)* affected girl; **faire la** *ou* **sa m.** to give oneself airs

mijoter [miʒɔte] **1** *vt* (**a**) *(faire cuire)* to simmer; *(préparer avec soin)* to cook up (**b**) *(tramer)* to cook up

    2 *vi* to simmer; **faire m.** to simmer

mikado [mikado] *nm (jeu)* jackstraws, spillikins

mil¹ [mil] *adj inv* **l'an m.** the year one thousand

mil² [mij, mil] *nm (céréale)* millet

Milan [milã] *n* Milan

mildiou [mildju] *nm (des céréales)* mildew; *(de la vigne)* brown rot

mile [majl] *nm* mile

milice [milis] *nf* militia

milicien, -enne [milisjɛ̃, -ɛn] *nm,f* militiaman, *f* militiawoman

milieu, -x [miljø] *nm* (**a**) *(centre)* middle; **au m. de** in the middle of; **en plein** *ou* **au beau m. de qch** right in the middle of sth; **la table du m.** the middle table (**b**) *(environnement)* environment; *(social)* background; *Phys* medium; **le m. familial** the home environment; **dans les milieux autorisés** in official circles (**c**) *(position intermédiaire)* middle course; **le juste m.** the happy medium (**d**) *(pègre)* **le m.** the underworld

militaire [militɛr] **1** *adj* military; *(port)* naval

    2 *nm* serviceman; **m. de carrière** professional soldier

militant, -e [militã, -ãt] *adj & nm,f* militant

militantisme [militãtism] *nm* militancy

militarisation [militarizasjɔ̃] *nf* militarization

militariser [militarize] *vt* to militarize

militariste [militarist] **1** *adj* militaristic

    2 *nmf* militarist

militer [milite] *vi* to campaign (**pour** *ou* **en faveur de/contre** for/against)

milk-shake *(pl* **milk-shakes)** [milkʃɛk] *nm* milkshake

mille¹ [mil] **1** *adj inv* (**a**) *(cardinal)* a *or* one thousand; **deux m.** two thousand; **l'an m.** the year one thousand (**b**) *Fig (nombreux) (exemples, occasions)* countless; **je vous l'ai dit m. fois**

I've told you a thousand times; **vous avez m. fois raison** you're absolutely right; **c'est m. fois trop grand** it's far too big

    2 *nm inv* (**a**) *(nombre)* a *or* one thousand; **plusieurs centaines de m.** several hundred thousand; **cinq pour m.** five per thousand (**b**) *(locutions)* **mettre (en plein) dans le m.** to hit the bull's-eye; **gagner des m. et des cents** to make a mint; *voir aussi* **trois**

mille² [mil] *nm* **m. (marin** *ou* **nautique)** nautical mile

mille-feuille *(pl* **mille-feuilles)** [milfœj] *nm (pâtisserie)* ≃ napoleon

millénaire [milenɛr] **1** *adj* thousand-year-old

    2 *nm* millennium

mille-pattes [milpat] *nm inv* centipede, millipede

millepertuis [milpɛrtɥi] *nm* St John's wort

millésime [milezim] *nm (de vin, de voiture)* vintage, year; *(sur pièce de monnaie)* date

millésimé, -e [milezime] *adj (vin)* vintage; *(pièce de monnaie)* dated

millet [mijɛ] *nm* millet

milliard [miljar] *nm* billion

milliardaire [miljardɛr] **1** *adj* billionaire; **être m.** to be a billionaire; **être plusieurs fois m.** to be worth billions

    2 *nmf* billionaire

millibar [milibar] *nm* millibar

millième [miljɛm] *nmf, nm & adj* thousandth; *voir aussi* **cinquième**

millier [milje] *nm* thousand; **un m. de personnes** a thousand people; **des milliers de personnes** thousands of people; **par milliers** in thousands

milligramme [miligram] *nm* milligram

millilitre [mililitr] *nm* milliliter

millimètre [milimɛtr] *nm* millimeter

millimétré, -e [milimetre], **millimétrique** [milimetrik] *adj voir* **papier**

million [miljɔ̃] *nm* million; **un m. d'euros** a million euros; **quatre millions d'hommes** four million men; **par millions** in millions

millionnaire [miljɔnɛr] **1** *adj* millionaire; **être m.** to be a millionaire

    2 *nmf* millionaire

millivolt [milivɔlt] *nm* millivolt

mime [mim] **1** *nm (art)* mime

    2 *nmf (artiste)* mime (artist)

mimer [mime] *vt* (**a**) *(exprimer)* to mime (**b**) *(imiter)* to mimic

mimétisme [mimetism] *nm* mimicry

mimi [mimi] *nm* **1** *nm (langage enfantin)* kiss; **faire un m. à qn** to give sb a kiss

    2 *adj inv (mignon)* cute

mimique [mimik] *nf* expression

mimolette [mimɔlɛt] *nf* = type of Dutch hard cheese

mimosa [mimoza] *nm* mimosa

min *(abrév* **minute(s))** min.

min. *(abrév* **minimum)** min.

minable [minabl] **1** *adj* (**a**) *(mesquin, pauvre)* shabby (**b**) *(incompétent, insuffisant)* pathetic

    2 *nmf* failure, loser

minaret [minarɛ] *nm* minaret

minauder [minode] *vi* to simper

minauderie [minodri] *nf* simpering; **faire des minauderies** to simper

mince [mɛ̃s] **1** *adj* (**a**) *(fin) (tranche, mur)* thin; *(taille, personne)* slim (**b**) *(insuffisant)* slight; **c'est un peu m., comme excuse!** it's a rather lame excuse!

    2 *exclam Fam* **m. (alors)!** *(surprise)* gee (whiz)!; *(déception)* darn it!

minceur [mɛ̃sœr] *nf* (**a**) *(d'une tranche, d'un tissu)* thinness; *(de la taille, d'une personne)* slimness (**b**) *(insuffisance)* slightness

mincir [mɛ̃sir] *vi* to get slimmer

mine[1] [min] *nf* (**a**) *(gisement)* mine; *Fig* **une m. de renseignements** a mine of information; **m. de charbon** coalmine; *aussi Fig* **m. d'or** goldmine (**b**) *(de crayon)* lead (**c**) *(explosif)* mine (**d**) **les Mines** = government department responsible for supervising all construction projects involving tunneling; **École des Mines**, *Fam* **les Mines** = university-level institute for geological engineers

mine[2] [min] *nf* (**a**) *(expression)* look; **avoir bonne/mauvaise m.** to look well/ill; **avoir une m. de papier mâché** *ou* **de déterré** to look like death warmed over; **faire** *ou* **avoir triste m.** to look down in the dumps; **faire grise m.** not to look pleased; **faire m. de faire qch** to make as if to do sth (**b**) *(allure)* appearance; **juger les gens sur la m.** to judge people by appearances; *Fam* **ne pas payer de m.** not to be much to look at; *Fam* **m. de rien, il n'est pas bête** you wouldn't think it to look at him, but he's not stupid (**c**) *Péj* **mines** *(simagrées)* faces; **faire des mines** to make faces

miner[1] [mine] *vt* (**a**) *(creuser)* to eat away (**b**) *(ruiner moralement)* to wear down

miner[2] [mine] *vt* *(poser des explosifs dans)* to mine

minerai [minrɛ] *nm* ore; **m. de fer** iron ore

minéral, -e, -aux, -ales [mineral, -o] *adj & nm* mineral

minéralogique [mineralɔʒik] *adj* (**a**) **plaque m.** license plate (**b**) *Géol* mineralogical

minerve [minɛrv] *nf* neck brace

minestrone [minɛstrɔn] *nm* minestrone

minet, -ette [minɛ, -ɛt] *nm,f Fam* (**a**) *(chat)* pussy cat, kitty (**b**) *(personne coquette)* hip young person

mineur[1] [minœr] *nm (ouvrier)* miner; **m. de fond** pit worker

mineur[2], **-e** [minœr] **1** *adj* (**a**) *(secondaire)* minor (**b**) *(qui n'a pas la majorité légale)* underage (**c**) *Mus* minor
2 *nm,f* minor

mini [mini] *Fam* **1** *adj inv (jupe, robe)* mini
2 *nm* (**a**) *(mode)* **le m.** miniskirts (**b**) *(mini-ordinateur)* mini

miniature [minjatyr] **1** *nf* miniature; **en m.** in miniature
2 *adj* miniature

miniaturiser [minjatyrize] *vt* to miniaturize

minibus [minibys] *nm* minibus

minichaîne [miniʃɛn] *nf* mini-hifi

MiniDisc® [minidisk] *nm* MiniDisc®

mini-écouteur [miniekutør] *(pl* **mini-écouteurs**) *nm* earbud, in-ear headphone

minier, -ère [minje, -ɛr] *adj* mining

minigolf [minigɔlf] *nm* miniature golf

minijupe [miniʒyp] *nf* miniskirt

minima [minima] *voir* **minimum**

minimal, -e, -aux, -ales [minimal, -o] *adj* minimum; *(art)* minimal

minimaliste [minimalist] *adj & nmf* minimalist

minime [minim] **1** *adj* minimal
2 *nmf Sport* junior *(13 to 15 years old)*

mini-message [minimesaʒ] *nm* text message

minimex [minimɛks] *nm Belg (abrév* **minimum de moyens d'existence)** ≃ welfare

minimiser [minimize] *vt* to minimize

minimum [minimɔm] *(pl* **minimums** *ou* **minima** [minima]) **1** *adj* minimum
2 *nm* minimum; **avec un m. d'efforts** with a minimum of effort; **en un m. de temps** in as short a time as possible; **réduire qch au m.** to minimize sth; **faire le m. (pour faire qch)** to do the bare minimum (to do sth); **c'est vraiment le m. que tu puisses faire pour elle** it's the very least you can do for her; **au m.** at the very least; **le m. vital** a minimum to live on; **le strict m.** the absolute minimum; **m. vieillesse** basic state pension

mini-ordinateur *(pl* **mini-ordinateurs**) [miniɔrdinatœr] *nm* minicomputer

minipilule [minipilyl] *nf* mini pill

mini-slip [minislip] *(pl* **mini-slips**) *nm* tanga

ministère [ministɛr] *nm* (**a**) *(département)* government department; **m. des Affaires étrangères** ≃ State Department; **m. de la Défense (nationale)** ≃ Department of Defense; **m. de l'Éducation nationale** ≃ Department of Education (**b**) *(gouvernement)* government (**c**) *Jur* **le m. public** ≃ the District Attorney's office (**d**) *Rel* ministry

ministériel, -elle [ministerjɛl] *adj (arrêté, décret, entourage)* departmental; *(crise, remaniement)* cabinet

ministre [ministr] *nm* (**a**) *(homme d'État)* secretary; **m. des Affaires étrangères** ≃ Secretary of State; **m. de la Défense (nationale)** ≃ Secretary of Defence; **m. de l'Éducation nationale** ≃ Secretary of Education; **m. d'État** ≃ secretary of state; *Jur* **m. de la Justice** ≃ Attorney General; **Premier m.** Prime Minister; *Can (d'une province)* Premier (**b**) *(pasteur)* minister; **m. du culte** minister

Minitel® [minitɛl] *nm* = consumer information network accessible via home computer terminal; **le M. rose** = dating and erotic entertainment service available on Minitel®

Minitel®

The domestic viewdata service run by France Télécom has become a familiar part of French life. The basic monitor and keyboard are given free of charge, and the subscriber is charged for the services used on his or her ordinary telephone bill. The subscriber dials a four-figure number (typically 3615); a code word then gives access to the particular service required. Some Minitel® services are purely informative (the weather, road conditions, news, etc.); others are interactive (enabling users to carry out bank transactions, book tickets for travel, register for and obtain the results of nationwide examinations, for example). Minitel® also serves as an electronic telephone directory. Nowadays the services offered by Minitel® are increasingly available on the Internet.

---

minitéliste [minitelist] *nmf* Minitel® user

minois [minwa] *nm* pretty face

minorer [minɔre] *vt* (**a**) *(minimiser)* to downplay (**b**) *(faire baisser)* to reduce

minoritaire [minɔritɛr] *adj* minority; **être m.** to be in the minority

minorité [minɔrite] *nf* (**a**) *(de choses, de personnes)* minority; **être en m.** to be in the minority; **m. ethnique** ethnic minority (**b**) *(avant la majorité légale)* minority

Minorque [minɔrk] *n* Minorca

minorquin, -e [minɔrkɛ̃, -in] **1** *adj* Minorcan
2 *nm,f* **M., Minorquine** Minorcan

minoterie [minɔtri] *nf (moulin)* flour mill; *(activité)* flour-milling

minou [minu] *nm* (**a**) *Fam (chat)* pussy cat (**b**) *Can (boule de poussière)* piece of fluff, dust ball

Minsk [minsk] *n* Minsk

minuit [minɥi] *nm* midnight, twelve o'clock

minuscule [minyskyl] **1** *adj* (**a**) *(très petit)* tiny, minute (**b**) *(lettre)* lower-case, small
2 *nf* lower-case *or* small letter

minute [minyt] **1** *nf* (**a**) *(unité de temps)* minute; **une m. de silence** a minute's silence; **de dernière m.** last-minute; **faire qch à la m.** to do sth this very minute; **d'une m. à l'autre** any minute (**b**) *(court moment)* minute, moment; **la m. de vérité** the moment of truth; **m.!** hold on a minute! (**c**) *(de contrat)* minute; *(d'acte notarié, de jugement)* record
2 *adj (sur panneau)* **nettoyage m.** dry-cleaning while you wait; **talons m.** while-U-wait shoe repair shop

minuter [minyte] *vt* to time

minuterie [minytri] *nf (pour l'éclairage)* time switch; *(d'un four)* timer

minuteur [minytœr] *nm* timer

minutie [minysi] *nf* meticulousness; **avec m.** meticulously

minutieusement [minysjøzmã] *adv* meticulously

minutieux, -euse [minysjø, -øz] *adj* meticulous

mioche [mjɔʃ] *nmf Fam* kid

MIPS [mips] *nm Ordinat (abrév* **million d'instructions par seconde)** MIPS

mirabelle [mirabɛl] *nf* mirabelle plum

miracle [mirakl] **1** *nm* miracle; **faire un m.** to perform a miracle; *Fig* **faire des miracles** to work miracles; **par m.** by a miracle, miraculously

2 *adj inv* miracle

miraculé, -e [mirakyle] **1** *adj (malade)* miraculously cured; *(rescapé)* miraculously saved

2 *nm,f (malade)* miraculously cured person; *(rescapé)* miraculous survivor

miraculeusement [mirakyløzmã] *adv* miraculously

miraculeux, -euse [mirakylø, -øz] *adj* miraculous

mirador [miradɔr] *nm* watchtower

mirage [miraʒ] *nm* mirage

mire [mir] *nf* test pattern

mirer [mire] **se mirer** *vpr Litt* **(a)** *(se regarder)* to gaze at oneself **(b)** *(se refléter)* to be reflected

mirettes [mirɛt] *nfpl Fam* eyes

mirifique [mirifik] *adj* wonderful

miro [miro] *adj Fam* nearsighted

mirobolant, -e [mirɔbɔlã, -ãt] *adj* fabulous

miroir [mirwar] *nm* mirror; *Fig* **m. aux alouettes** lure; **m. de courtoisie** vanity mirror; **m. grossissant** magnifying mirror; **m. de poche** pocket mirror

miroiter [mirwate] *vi* to shimmer; *Fig* **faire m. qch à qn** to lure sb with the prospect of sth

miroton [mirɔtɔ̃] *nm* = beef boiled in sauce with onions

mis, -e *pp voir* **mettre**

misanthrope [mizɑ̃trɔp] **1** *adj* misanthropic

2 *nmf* misanthropist, misanthrope

mise [miz] *nf* **(a)** *(placement)* putting; **m. en accusation** committal (for trial); **m. en application** implementation; **m. en demeure** formal demand; **m. en disponibilité** leave of absence; *Can* layoff; **m. en examen** indictment; **m. à feu** *(d'une fusée)* launch; **m. de fonds** investment; **m. en garde** warning; **m. à jour** updating; **m. en liberté provisoire** release on bail; **m. à mort** killing; **m. en page(s)** page make-up; **m. à pied** suspension; *Can* layoff; **m. en place** putting into place; **m. en plis** set *(hairstyle)*; **m. au point** *(d'un objectif)* focusing; *(d'une technique)* perfecting; *(d'un moteur)* tuning; *(d'un document, d'un rapport)* finalization; *Fig* **faire une m. au point** to make things clear; **m. en route** start-up; **m. en scène** *(d'une pièce de théâtre, d'un film)* direction; **m. en service** *(d'une machine)* commissioning; **m. en vigueur** implementation

(b) *(habillement)* attire

(c) *(au jeu)* stake; *(à une vente aux enchères)* bid; *Fig* **sauver la m. à qn** to get sb out of a tight spot

(d) **être de m.** to be appropriate

(e) *Ordinat* **m. en attente des fichiers à imprimer** printer spooling; **m. en forme** formatting; **m. en mémoire** saving; **m. à niveau** upgrade; **m. en relation** *(avec un service)* log-on; **m. en réseau** networking; **m. sous tension** power-up

(f) *Suisse (vente)* auction (sale)

miser [mize] *vt* to stake (**sur** on); **m. sur qn/qch** *(parier)* to bet on sb/sth; *(compter sur)* to count on sb/sth; **m. sur tous les tableaux** to hedge one's bets

misérabilisme [mizerabilism] *nm* sordid realism

misérabiliste [mizerabilist] *adj* sordidly realistic

misérable [mizerabl] **1** *adj* **(a)** *(indigent) (personne)* poor; *(condition, existence)* wretched **(b)** *(pitoyable, insignifiant)* miserable

2 *nmf* **(a)** *(personne indigente)* poor wretch **(b)** *(coquin, fripouille)* scoundrel

misérablement [mizerabləmã] *adv* **(a)** *(pauvrement)* wretchedly **(b)** *(pitoyablement)* miserably

misère [mizɛr] *nf* **(a)** *(indigence)* extreme poverty; **être dans la m.** to be poverty-stricken; **être dans une m. noire** to be destitute; **salaire de m.** starvation wage **(b)** *(ennui)* trouble; **faire des misères à qn** to give sb trouble **(c)** *(vétille)* **payer qch une m.** to pay next to nothing for sth

miséreux, -euse [mizerø, -øz] *adj* poverty-stricken

miséricorde [mizerikɔrd] **1** *nf* mercy

2 *exclam Vieilli* mercy!

miséricordieux, -euse [mizerikɔrdjø, -øz] *adj* merciful (**envers** to)

misogyne [mizɔʒin] **1** *adj* misogynous

2 *nmf* misogynist

misogynie [mizɔʒini] *nf* misogyny

miss *(pl* **miss** *ou* **misses)** [mis] *nf (reine de beauté)* beauty queen; **M. Monde/France** Miss World/France

missel [misɛl] *nm* missal

missile [misil] *nm* missile; **m. guidé** smart missile

mission [misjɔ̃] *nf* **(a)** *(tâche)* mission; *(d'un employé)* task; **partir en m.** *(cadre)* to go away on business; *(diplomate)* to go off on a mission **(b)** *(groupe)* delegation; **m. scientifique** scientific expedition **(c)** *Rel (vocation, organisation)* mission; *(bâtiment)* mission (station)

missionnaire [misjɔnɛr] *adj & nmf* missionary

Mississippi [misisipi] *nm (fleuve)* **le M.** the Mississippi

missive [misiv] *nf Litt* missive

mistral [mistral] *nm* mistral

mitaine [mitɛn] *nf* fingerless glove; *Can & Suisse (moufle)* mitten

mite [mit] *nf* moth; **rongé aux mites** moth-eaten

mité, -e [mite] *adj* moth-eaten

mi-temps [mitã] **1** *nf inv (moitié)* half; *(pause)* half-time

2 *nm inv* part-time job; **travailler** *ou* **être à m.** to work part-time

miteux, -euse [mitø, -øz] *adj* shabby

mitigé, -e [mitiʒe] *adj (enthousiasme, accueil)* lukewarm; *(sentiments, impressions)* mixed

mitigeur [mitiʒœr] *nm* mixing faucet

mitonner [mitɔne] **1** *vt* **(a)** *(cuire à feu doux)* to simmer **(b)** *Fig (projet)* to concoct

2 *vi* to simmer

mitoyen, -enne [mitwajɛ̃, -ɛn] *adj (mur)* party; **maisons mitoyennes** *(deux)* two-family houses; *(rangée)* row houses

mitrailler [mitraje] *vt* to machine-gun; *Fig* **m. qn de questions** to bombard sb with questions

mitraillette [mitrajɛt] *nf* submachine gun

mitrailleuse [mitrajøz] *nf* machine gun

mitre [mitr] *nf* **(a)** *(d'évêque)* miter **(b)** *(de cheminée)* cowl

mi-voix [mivwa] **à mi-voix** *adv* in a low voice

mixage [miksaʒ] *nm* mixing

mixer¹ [mikse] *vt* **(a)** *(film)* to mix **(b)** *(ingrédients) (mélanger)* to mix; *(réduire à l'état liquide)* to blend

mixer², mixeur [miksœr] *nm (pour mélanger)* mixer; *(pour réduire à l'état liquide)* blender

mixité [miksite] *nf* coeducation

mixte [mikst] *adj (a) (des deux sexes)* mixed; **double m.** *(au tennis)* mixed doubles **(b)** *(combiné) (commission)* joint; *(mariage)* mixed; *(cuisinière)* gas-and-electric

mixture [mikstyr] *nf (a) (pharmaceutique)* mixture **(b)** *Fig* concoction

MJC [ɛmʒise] *nf* (*abrév* **maison des jeunes et de la culture**) community center

ml (*abrév* **millilitre(s)**) ml

MLF [ɛmɛlɛf] *nm* (*abrév* **Mouvement de libération des femmes**) ≃ Women's Liberation Movement

Mlle (*abrév* **Mademoiselle**) Miss

Mlles (*abrév* **Mesdemoiselles**) M. Armand et Duchêne Miss Armand and Miss Duchêne

MM (*abrév* **Messieurs**) Messrs.

mm (*abrév* **millimètre(s)**) mm

Mme (*abrév* **Madame**) Mrs.

Mmes (*abrév* **Mesdames**) M. Binoche et Huppert Mrs. Binoche and Mrs. Huppert

MMS [ɛmɛmɛs] *nm* *Tél* (*abrév* **multimedia message service**) MMS

Mo *nm* *Ordinat* (*abrév* **méga-octet(s)**) Mb

mobile [mɔbil] **1** *adj* (**a**) (*cloison*) movable; (*feuillets*) loose; (*cible*) moving (**b**) (*expression, regard*) shifting; (*visage*) lively (**c**) (*personne âgée, main d'œuvre, population*) mobile
     2 *nm* (**a**) (*motif*) motive (**de** for) (**b**) (*objet décoratif*) mobile (**c**) (*objet en mouvement*) moving body (**d**) (*téléphone*) cell(phone)

mobile home [mɔbilom] (*pl* **mobile homes**) *nm* camper, RV

mobilier, -ère [mɔbilje, -ɛr] **1** *adj Jur* movable
     2 *nm* furniture

mobilisation [mɔbilizasjɔ̃] *nf* mobilization; **m. générale** general mobilization

mobiliser [mɔbilize] **1** *vt* to mobilize; *Fig* (*énergie, courage*) to summon up
     2 se mobiliser *vpr* to mobilize (**contre/en faveur de** against/in support of)

mobilité [mɔbilite] *nf* mobility

Mobylette® [mɔbilɛt] *nf* moped

mocassin [mɔkasɛ̃] *nm* moccasin

moche [mɔʃ] *adj Fam* (**a**) (*laid*) ugly (**b**) (*moralement*) rotten

modal, -e, -aux, -ales [mɔdal, -o] *adj* modal

modalité [mɔdalite] *nf* (**a**) (*manière*) mode; **modalités de paiement** conditions of payment (**b**) (*d'un acte juridique*) clause

mode¹ [mɔd] **1** *adj inv* **c'est très m.** it's very fashionable
     2 *nf* (**a**) (*vestimentaire, de consommation*) fashion; **à la m.** fashionable; **revenir à la m.** to come back into fashion (**b**) (*manière*) **à la m. de Lyon/Provence** Lyons/Provence style

mode² [mɔd] *nm* (**a**) (*manière*) **m. de** means of; **m. de cuisson** cooking instructions; **m. d'emploi** instructions; **m. de paiement** means of payment; **m. de transport** mode of transport; **m. de vie** way of life (**b**) *Gram* mood (**c**) *Mus* mode (**d**) *Ordinat* mode; **m. paysage/portrait** landscape/portrait mode

modèle [mɔdɛl] **1** *adj* (*parfait*) model; (*appartement, maison*) show
     2 *nm* (**a**) (*exemple*) model; **prendre qn pour m.** to take sb as one's model; **m. de lettre** standard letter (**b**) (*personne*) **m. de générosité/fidélité** model of generosity/fidelity; **m. de vertu** paragon of virtue (**c**) (*exemplaire*) (*de voiture, d'appareil*) model; (*de robe*) style; (*de tricot*) pattern; **vous n'auriez pas un plus grand m.?** do you have it in a larger size?; **m. déposé** registered design (**d**) (*d'un peintre, d'un sculpteur*) model (**e**) (*maquette*) **m. réduit** scale model

modeler [39] [mɔdle] **1** *vt* (*argile, pot*) to model; *Fig* (*relief, caractère, destinée*) to shape; **m. sa personnalité sur celle de qn** to model oneself on sb
     2 se modeler *vpr* **se m. sur qn** to model oneself on sb

modélisme [mɔdelism] *nm* model-making

modem [mɔdɛm] *nm* *Ordinat* modem; **carte m.** modem card; **m. fax** fax modem

modem-câble [mɔdɛmkabl] *nm* *Ordinat* cable modem

modérateur, -trice [mɔderatœr, -tris] **1** *adj* moderating
     2 *nm* (**a**) (*personne*) moderator (**b**) (*de moteur*) regulator

modération [mɔderasjɔ̃] *nf* (**a**) (*retenue*) moderation; **avec m.** in moderation; **à consommer avec m.** (*dans les publicités*) drink in moderation (*health warning on all products advertising alcoholic drinks*) (**b**) (*réduction*) reduction

modéré, -e [mɔdere] *adj & nm,f* moderate

modérément [mɔderemɑ̃] *adv* moderately; *Euph* **j'ai m. apprécié sa remarque** I didn't much appreciate her remark

modérer [34] [mɔdere] **1** *vt* (**a**) (*passions, désirs, envies*) to moderate, to restrain; *Hum* **modère tes ardeurs!** control yourself!; **je te prie de m. ton langage!** please watch your language! (**b**) (*prix, vitesse*) to reduce
     2 se modérer *vpr* (*personne*) to calm down

moderne [mɔdɛrn] **1** *adj* modern
     2 *nm* **le m.** the modern style

modernisation [mɔdɛrnizasjɔ̃] *nf* modernization

moderniser [mɔdɛrnize] **1** *vt* to modernize
     2 se moderniser *vpr* to modernize

modernisme [mɔdɛrnism] *nm* modernism

moderniste [mɔdɛrnist] *adj & nmf* modernist

modernité [mɔdɛrnite] *nf* modernity

modeste [mɔdɛst] **1** *adj* modest
     2 *nmf* **faire le m.** to be modest

modestement [mɔdɛstəmɑ̃] *adv* modestly; **être m. logé** to live in modest surroundings

modestie [mɔdɛsti] *nf* modesty; **fausse m.** false modesty

modeux, -euse [mɔdø, -øz] *nm,f* *Fam* fashionista

modicité [mɔdisite] *nf* lowness

modifiable [mɔdifjabl] *adj* modifiable

modification [mɔdifikasjɔ̃] *nf* alteration, modification; **apporter** *ou* **faire une m. à qch** to make an alteration to sth

modifier [66] [mɔdifje] **1** *vt* to alter, to modify; *Gram* to modify
     2 se modifier *vpr* to alter

modique [mɔdik] *adj* modest

modiste [mɔdist] *nmf* milliner

modulable [mɔdylabl] *adj* (*horaires*) flexible; (*éclairage, chauffage*) adjustable

modulaire [mɔdylɛr] *adj* modular

modulation [mɔdylasjɔ̃] *nf* (**a**) (*des sons, de la voix*) modulation (**b**) (*adaptation*) adjustment (**en fonction de** in relation to) (**c**) *Rad* modulation; **m. de fréquence** frequency modulation

module [mɔdyl] *nm* (**a**) (*élément d'un tout*) unit; **m. (d'enseignement)** module (**b**) (*d'un vaisseau spatial*) module; **m. lunaire/de commande** lunar/command module (**c**) *Ordinat* **m. d'extension** plug-in

moduler [mɔdyle] **1** *vt* (**a**) (*sons, amplitude, voix*) to modulate (**b**) (*adapter*) to adjust (**en fonction de** in relation to)
     2 *vi* to modulate

modus vivendi [mɔdysvivɛ̃di] *nm inv* modus vivendi

moelle [mwal] *nf* marrow; *Fig* **jusqu'à la m.** to the core; **m. épinière** spinal cord; **m. osseuse** bone marrow

moelleusement [mwaløzmɑ̃] *adv* snugly

moelleux, -euse [mwalø, -øz] *adj* (**a**) (*au toucher*) soft (**b**) (*fromage, vin*) smooth; (*gâteau*) moist

moellon [mwalɔ̃] *nm* quarry stone

mœurs [mœr, mœrs] *nfpl* (**a**) (*coutumes*) customs; **entrer** *ou* **passer dans les m.** to become part of everyday life (**b**) (*d'animaux*) habits (**c**) (*sens moral*) morals; **bonnes m.** morality; **contraire aux bonnes m.** contrary to accepted standards of behavior; **femme de m. légères** *ou* **faciles** woman of easy virtue

mohair [mɔɛr] *nm* mohair; **un pull en m.** a mohair sweater

moi [mwa] **1** *pron personnel* (**a**) (*sujet*) I; **qui vient avec nous? – m.** who's coming with us? – I am *or* me; **m., quand je serai**

grand... when I grow up,...; **m., je n'aurais pas fait comme ça** I wouldn't have done it like that (**b**) *(objet direct)* me; **et m., tu m'oublies?** and what about me, have you forgotten me? (**c**) *(avec préposition)* me; **fais-m. voir, à m.** show ME; **ce livre est à m.** this book is mine; **j'ai mes petits secrets à m.** I have my own little secrets; *Fam* **un ami à m.** a friend of mine; **à m.!** help!; **je ne le fais pas que pour m.** I'm not doing it just for myself (**d**) *(dans les comparaisons)* me; **elle boit plus que m.** she drinks more than me *or* than I do
2 *nm* ego, self

moignon [mwaɲɔ̃] *nm* stump

moi-même [mwamɛm] *pron personnel* myself

moindre [mwɛ̃dr] *adj* (**a**) *(comparatif)* lesser; *(prix)* lower; *(quantité)* smaller; *(vitesse)* slower; **c'est un m. mal** it's not as bad as it might have been (**b**) *(superlatif)* **le/la m.** the least; **pas la m. chance/idée** not the slightest chance/idea; **au m. reproche** at the slightest reproach; **dans les moindres détails** in the smallest detail; **c'est la m. des choses** it's the least I/he/*etc.* can do; **on a fait venir un expert, et non des moindres** we called in an expert, and not just any old one

moine [mwan] *nm* monk

moineau, -x [mwano] *nm* sparrow

moins [mwɛ̃] **1** *adv* (**a**) *(comparatif)* less; **je gagne m. que vous** I earn less than you (do); **elle est m. intelligente que sa sœur** she's not as intelligent as her sister; **il n'est pas m. nerveux que toi** he's no less nervous than you (are); **m. de** *(argent, patience)* less; *(hommes, occasions)* fewer; *(un nombre)* less than; **elle a m. de vingt ans** she's under twenty; **m. tu feras d'exercice, plus tu grossiras** the less exercise you do, the fatter you'll get; **de m. en m.** less and less; **celui-ci coûte dix euros de m. que l'autre** this one costs ten euros less than the other one; **il y a eu 20% de visiteurs de m.** *ou* **en m.** there have been 20% fewer visitors; **il n'en est pas m. vrai que...** the fact remains that...
(**b**) *(superlatif)* **le m.** the least; **c'est celui qui me plaît le m.** that's the one I like (the) least; **les élèves les m. appliqués** the least industrious pupils; **pas le m. du monde** not in the least *or* slightest
(**c**) *(locutions)* **à m. d'un imprévu/d'un miracle** barring unforeseen circumstances/a miracle; **à m. de partir tout de suite** unless I/you/*etc.* leave at once; **à m. que...** + *subjunctive* unless...; **au m.** at least; *Fam* **tu as fait ton travail, au m.?** you've done your work, I hope?; **du m.** at least; **c'est pour le m. surprenant** it's surprising, to say the least; *Fam* **un m. que rien** a nobody
2 *prép (dans les calculs, les températures)* minus; **une heure m. cinq** five (minutes) to *or* of one; **il est m. vingt** it's twenty to *or* of; *Fam* **il était m. une** it was a close shave *or* call
3 *nm (signe)* minus (sign)

moins-value (*pl* **moins-values**) [mwɛ̃valy] *nf Fin* depreciation; *(après une vente)* capital loss

moire [mwar] *nf* moire

moiré, -e [mware] *adj* (**a**) *(tissu)* watered, moiré (**b**) *(aux reflets changeants)* shimmering

mois [mwa] *nm* (**a**) *(période)* month; **au m. d'août** in August; **un m. de vacances/salaire** a month's vacation/wages (**b**) *(paie mensuelle)* monthly salary; **treizième m.** extra month's salary *(paid as an annual bonus)*

Moïse [mɔiz] *npr* Moses

moisi, -e [mwazi] **1** *adj (aliment)* moldy; *(mur, livre)* mildewed
2 *nm (sur un aliment)* mold; *(sur un mur, un tissu)* mildew

moisir [mwazir] *vi* (**a**) *(aliment)* to go moldy; *(mur, livre)* to become mildewed (**b**) *(personne) (stagner)* to molder away; *(attendre longtemps)* to hang around; **m. en prison** to rot in jail

moisissure [mwazisyr] *nf* mold

moisson [mwasɔ̃] *nf* (**a**) *(récolte, époque)* harvest; **faire la m.** *ou* **les moissons** to harvest (**b**) *Fig (de documents, d'idées)* wealth

moissonner [mwasɔne] *vt* (**a**) *(céréales)* to harvest; *(champ)* to reap (**b**) *Fig (informations, idées)* to collect, to gather

moissonneur, -euse [mwasɔnœr, -øz] **1** *nm,f* harvester
2 *nf* **moissonneuse** *(machine)* harvester, reaper

moissonneuse-batteuse (*pl* **moissonneuses-batteuses**) [mwasɔnøzbatœz] *nf* combine harvester

moite [mwat] *adj (mains, front)* sticky, clammy; *(atmosphère, air)* muggy

moiteur [mwatœr] *nf (des mains, du front)* stickiness, clamminess; *(d'atmosphère, d'air)* mugginess

moitié [mwatje] *nf* (**a**) *(d'un tout)* half; **la m. des livres/de la journée** half (of) the books/the day; **m. anglais, m. canadien** half-English, half-Canadian; **c'est m. moins cher** it's half the price; *Fam* **m.-m.** fifty-fifty; **faire m.-m.** to split; **à m. plein/vide** half-full/-empty; **à m. mort** half-dead; **vendre qch à m. prix** to sell sth (at) half-price; **ne pas faire les choses à m.** not to do things by halves (**b**) *Fam (époux, épouse)* **ma m.** my other *or* better half

mojito [mɔito] *nm (cocktail)* mojito

moka [mɔka] *nm* (**a**) *(café)* mocha (**b**) *(gâteau)* coffee cake

molaire [mɔlɛr] *nf* molar

moldave [mɔldav] **1** *adj* Moldavian
2 *nmf* **M.** Moldavian

Moldavie [mɔldavi] *nf* **la M.** Moldavia

mole [mɔl] *nf Phys* mole

moléculaire [mɔlekylɛr] *adj* molecular

molécule [mɔlekyl] *nf* molecule

moleskine [mɔlɛskin] *nf* imitation leather

molester [mɔlɛste] *vt* to manhandle

molette [mɔlɛt] *nf* (**a**) *(de briquet, de clé)* wheel; *(de jumelles)* focus wheel (**b**) *(pour couper le verre)* cutting wheel

Molières [mɔljɛr] *nmpl* **les M.** *(cérémonie)* = French theater awards ceremony

mollard [mɔlar] *nm très Fam* gob of spit

mollasson, -onne [mɔlasɔ̃, -ɔn] *Fam* **1** *adj (personne)* lethargic
2 *nm,f* slob

molle [mɔl] *voir* **mou**[1]

mollement [mɔlmɑ̃] *adv* (**a**) *(avec abandon)* languidly; *(avec lenteur)* gently (**b**) *(sans énergie)* feebly

mollesse [mɔlɛs] *nf* (**a**) *(d'un coussin, d'un matelas)* softness; *(de tissus, de muscles)* flabbiness (**b**) *(d'une personne)* lethargy; *(d'un gouvernement)* laxness; *(du style)* limpness

mollet[1] [mɔlɛ] *adj m (œuf)* soft-boiled

mollet[2] [mɔlɛ] *nm* calf; **avoir des mollets de coq** to have spindly legs

molleton [mɔltɔ̃] *nm* (**a**) *(tissu) (en coton)* flannelette; *(en laine)* flannel (**b**) *(sous-nappe)* table felt

molletonné, -e [mɔltɔne] *adj* fleece-lined

mollir [mɔlir] *vi* (**a**) *(faiblir) (vent)* to die down; *(courage, enthousiasme)* to flag; **sentir ses jambes m.** to feel one's legs give way (**b**) *(devenir moins ferme) (matière)* to soften; *(sol)* to give way (**sous** beneath)

mollo [mɔlo] *adv Fam* **y aller m.** to take it easy

mollusque [mɔlysk] *nm* (**a**) *(animal)* mollusk (**b**) *Fam (personne)* slob

molosse [mɔlɔs] *nm* big dog

môme [mom] *nmf Fam (enfant)* kid

moment [mɔmɑ̃] *nm* (**a**) *(point précis dans le temps)* moment; **arriver au bon m.** to arrive at just the right time; **le m. venu** *(dans le passé)* when the time came; *(dans l'avenir)* when the time comes; **c'est le m. ou jamais** it's now or never; **c'est le m. ou jamais de le faire** now's the time to do it; **au m. de qch** at the time of sth; **au m. où j'allais me coucher, le téléphone a sonné** just as I was going to bed, the phone rang; **à quel m. de sa vie?** at what point in his/her life?; **à un m. donné** at one point; **dans ces moments-là** at times like that;

d'un m. à l'autre (at) any moment; **en ce m.** at the moment, just now; **jusqu'au m. où…** until…; **par moments** at times, now and again; **pour le m.** for the moment, for the time being; **sur le m.** at the time; **à tout m., à tous moments** *(sans cesse)* constantly; *(n'importe quand)* (at) any moment; **à ce m.-là** then; *(dans ces conditions)* in that case

(**b**) *(durée)* moment; **un m.!** just a moment!; **je suis à vous dans un m.** I'll be with you in a moment; **passer un bon m.** to have a good time; **ce n'est qu'un mauvais m. à passer** it'll soon be over with; **j'en ai pour un m.** I'll be a while; **ne pas avoir un m. à soi** not to have a moment to oneself; **dans un m. de bonté** in a moment of kindness

(**c**) *(temps présent)* **du m.** *(disque, star)* of the moment

(**d**) *(locutions)* **du m. que…** seeing that…

momentané, -e [mɔmɑ̃tane] *adj (bref)* brief; *(temporaire)* temporary

momentanément [mɔmɑ̃tanemɑ̃] *adv (brièvement)* briefly; *(temporairement)* temporarily

momie [mɔmi] *nf* mummy

momifier [66] [mɔmifje] **1** *vt* to mummify

2 se momifier *vpr* to become fossilized

mon, ma, mes [mɔ̃, ma, me]

> **ma** becomes **mon** before a word beginning with a vowel or mute h.

adj possessif (**a**) *(marquant la possession)* my; **m. chien** my dog; **ma voiture** my car; **m. ami/amie** my friend; **mes enfants** my children; **mon père et ma mère** my father and mother; **un de mes amis** one of my friends, a friend of mine; *Fam* **j'ai eu m. vendredi** I got Friday off (work) (**b**) *(en s'adressant à quelqu'un)* **non, m. général** no, General

monacal, -e, -aux, -ales [mɔnakal, -o] *adj* monastic

Monaco [mɔnako] *n* Monaco

monarchie [mɔnarʃi] *nf* monarchy

monarchique [mɔnarʃik] *adj* monarchical

monarchiste [mɔnarʃist] *adj & nmf* monarchist

monarque [mɔnark] *nm* monarch

monastère [mɔnastɛr] *nm (d'hommes)* monastery; *(de femmes)* convent

monastique [mɔnastik] *adj* monastic

monceau, -x [mɔ̃so] *nm* heap, pile

mondain, -e [mɔ̃dɛ̃, -ɛn] **1** *adj* (**a**) *(soirée, journaliste)* society (**b**) *Péj (personne)* **être très m.** to be a great socialite

2 *nm,f* socialite

3 *nf Fam Vieilli* **la mondaine** ≃ the vice squad

mondanités [mɔ̃danite] *nfpl* (**a**) *(événements)* society life (**b**) *(politesses)* social niceties; *(conversations superficielles)* social chitchat

monde [mɔ̃d] *nm* (**a**) *(univers, humanité)* world; **l'autre m.** the next world; **dans le m. entier** *(connu, en vente)* worldwide, all over the world; **personne au m.** no one in the world; **pour rien au m.** not for anything in the world; **mettre un enfant au m.** to bring a child into the world; **venir au m.** to come into the world; *Litt* **il n'est plus de ce m.** he is no longer of this world; **les meilleurs amis du m.** the best friends in the world; **en ce bas m.** here on earth; *Fam* **c'est (quand même) un m.!** that beats it all!; *Fam* **se faire un m. de qch** to get worked up about sth; **comme le m. est petit!** it's a small world!; **c'est le m. à l'envers** the world's gone crazy

(**b**) *(milieu)* world; **être du même m.** to belong to the same crowd; **le (beau) m.** (fashionable) society

(**c**) *(gens)* people; **tout le m.** everyone, everybody; **il y a du m.** *(beaucoup de gens)* there are a lot of people; **peu de m., pas grand m.** not many people; **avoir du m. à dîner** to have people to dinner; **comment va tout votre petit m.?** how are all the family?; *Can* **le grand m.** the grown-ups, the adults

(**d**) *(vie séculière)* world

mondial, -e, -aux, -ales [mɔ̃djal, -o] *adj* world, global; **guerre mondiale** world war

mondialement [mɔ̃djalmɑ̃] *adv* throughout the world

mondialisation [mɔ̃djalizasjɔ̃] *nf* globalization

mondialiser [mɔ̃djalize] **1** *vt* to globalize

2 se mondialiser *vpr* to become globalized

monégasque [mɔnegask] **1** *adj* Monegasque

2 *nmf* **M.** Monegasque

monétaire [mɔnetɛr] *adj (unité, système, questions)* monetary; *(marché)* money

monétarisme [mɔnetarism] *nm* monetarism

monétariste [mɔnetarist] *adj & nmf* monetarist

Monétique® [mɔnetik] *nf* electronic banking, e-banking

mongol, -e [mɔ̃gɔl] **1** *adj* Mongolian

2 *nm (langue)* Mongolian

3 *nm,f* **M., Mongole** Mongolian

Mongolie [mɔ̃gɔli] *nf* **la M.** Mongolia

mongolien, -enne [mɔ̃gɔljɛ̃, -ɛn] **1** *adj* **être m.** to have Down's syndrome

2 *nm,f (bébé)* Down's syndrome baby; *(personne)* person with Down's syndrome

mongolisme [mɔ̃gɔlism] *nm* Down's syndrome

moniteur, -trice [mɔnitœr, -tris] **1** *nm,f (d'activités sportives, d'auto-école)* instructor (**b**) *(dans une colonie de vacances)* (camp) counselor

2 *nm aussi Ordinat* monitor; **m. cardiaque** heart monitor

monitoring [mɔnitɔriŋ] *nm* monitoring

monnaie [mɔnɛ] *nf* (**a**) *(argent)* money; *(d'un pays)* currency; **m. électronique** electronic money, e-cash; **m. légale** legal tender; *UE* **m. unique** single currency; **fausse m.** counterfeit money; **c'est m. courante dans ce milieu** it's common in these circles; *Fam* **payer qn en m. de singe** to fob sb off (**b**) *(pièces)* change; **avoir la m. de 20 euros** to have change for 20 euros; **faire (de) la m.** to get some change; **faire la m. de 20 euros** to get change for 20 euros; **petite** *ou* **menue m.** small change

monnayable [mɔnejabl] *adj* convertible into cash; *Fig* **être m.** *(expérience, information)* to be worth money

monnayer [53] [mɔneje] **1** *vt* (**a**) *(terrains, biens)* to convert into cash (**b**) *(expérience, information)* to cash in on

2 se monnayer *vpr* **ici tout se monnaye** money can buy you anything here

monnayeur [mɔnejœr] *nm (appareil)* change machine

monochrome [mɔnokrom] *adj* monochrome

monocle [mɔnɔkl] *nm* monocle

monocoque [mɔnokɔk] *nm* monohull

monocorde [mɔnokɔrd] *adj* monotonous

monoculture [mɔnokyltyr] *nf* monoculture

monogame [mɔnɔgam] *adj* monogamous

monogamie [mɔnɔgami] *nf* monogamy

monogramme [mɔnɔgram] *nm* monogram

monoï [mɔnɔj] *nm inv* scented coconut oil

monokini [mɔnokini] *nm* monokini; **faire du m.** to go topless

monolingue [mɔnolɛ̃g] *adj* monolingual

monolithe [mɔnolit] *nm* monolith

monolithique [mɔnolitik] *adj aussi Fig* monolithic

monologue [mɔnolɔg] *nm* monologue; **m. intérieur** interior monologue

monologuer [mɔnolɔge] *vi* (**a**) *(monopoliser la parole)* to carry on a monologue (**b**) *(au théâtre)* to soliloquize

monôme [mɔnom] *nm Math* monomial

mononucléose [mɔnonykleoz] *nf* **m. (infectieuse)** mononucleosis

monoparental, -e, -aux, -ales [mɔnoparɑ̃tal, -o] *adj (famille)* single-parent, one-parent

monoparentalité [mɔnɔparɑ̃talite] *nf* single parenthood

monoplace [mɔnɔplas] *adj & nm* single-seater

monopole [mɔnɔpɔl] *nm* monopoly; **avoir le m. de qch** to have a monopoly on sth; **m. d'État** state monopoly

monopoliser [mɔnɔpɔlize] *vt* to monopolize

monoposte [mɔnɔpɔst] *nm Ordinat* stand-alone

monoski [mɔnɔski] *nm* monoski; **faire du m.** to monoski; **m. nautique** wakeboarding

monospace [mɔnɔspas] *nm* minivan, people carrier

monosyllabe [mɔnɔsilab] **1** *adj* monosyllabic
     2 *nm* monosyllable

monosyllabique [mɔnɔsilabik] *adj* monosyllabic

mono-tâche [mɔnɔtaʃ] *adj inv Ordinat* single-tasking

monothéisme [mɔnɔteism] *nm* monotheism

monotone [mɔnɔtɔn] *adj* monotonous

monotonie [mɔnɔtɔni] *nf* monotony

monoxyde [mɔnɔksid] *nm* **m. de carbone** carbon monoxide

monseigneur [mɔ̃sɛɲœr] (*pl* **messeigneurs** [mesɛɲœr]) *nm* (**a**) (*titre*) (*d'un prince*) His Royal Highness; (*d'un cardinal*) His Eminence; (*d'un évêque*) His Lordship (**b**) (*en s'adressant au prince*) Your Royal Highness; (*au cardinal*) Your Eminence; (*à l'évêque*) Your Lordship

monsieur [məsjø] (*pl* **messieurs** [mesjø]) *nm* (**a**) (*titre*) **M. Robert Marceau** Mr. Robert Marceau; **M. le Ministre** the Minister; *Fam* **m. je-sais-tout** Mr. Know-all; **m. météo** the weatherman; **m. tout-le-monde** the man in the street (**b**) (*en apostrophe*) sir; **M. le Ministre** Minister; **au revoir, m.** goodbye; **M.,...** (*dans une lettre*) Dear Sir,...; *Fam* **et en plus, M. exige des excuses!** His Lordship wants an apology as well, does he?; **que prendront ces messieurs?** what can I get for you, gentlemen?; **bonsoir, messieurs-dames!** good evening, everybody! (**c**) (*homme quelconque*) gentleman

monstre [mɔ̃str] **1** *adj Fam* huge; **j'ai un boulot m.** I've got a ton of work to do
     2 *nm* monster; **m. d'ingratitude/d'égoïsme** ungrateful/ selfish monster; **petit m.!** you little monster!; **m. sacré** giant

monstrueusement [mɔ̃stryøzmɑ̃] *adv* monstrously

monstrueux, -euse [mɔ̃stryø, -øz] *adj* (**a**) (*malformé*) monstrous (**b**) (*énorme*) huge; **être d'un égoïsme m.** to be extremely selfish (**c**) (*scandaleux*) monstrous

monstruosité [mɔ̃stryozite] *nf* monstrosity

mont [mɔ̃] *nm* mountain; *Fig* **être toujours par monts et par vaux** to be always on the move; **le m. Blanc** Mont Blanc

montage [mɔ̃taʒ] *nm* (**a**) (*pose*) (*de bijou*) mounting; (*d'appareils*) assembling (**b**) (*d'un film*) editing; (*image truquée*) montage; **m. vidéo** video(tape) editing (**c**) *Écon* **m. financier** financial arrangement (**d**) (*d'installation électrique*) wiring (up)

montagnard, -e [mɔ̃taɲar, -ard] **1** *adj* mountain
     2 *nm,f* mountain dweller

montagne [mɔ̃taɲ] *nf* (**a**) (*élévation*) mountain; (*région*) mountains; **à la m.** in the mountains; *Fig* **se faire une m. de qch** to make a great song and dance about sth; **en haute m.** high in the mountains (**b**) **faire de la m.** (*alpinisme*) to go mountain climbing; (*randonnée*) to go hill walking (**c**) *Fig* (*grande quantité*) **une m. de** a mountain of (**d**) **montagnes russes** (*attraction foraine*) rollercoaster

montagneux, -euse [mɔ̃taɲø, -øz] *adj* mountainous

montant [mɔ̃tɑ̃] *nm* (**a**) (*somme*) amount; **versement d'un m. de 500 euros** payment of 500 euros; **montants compensatoires** subsidies (**b**) (*d'échelle*) upright; (*de lit*) post; (*de fenêtre, de porte*) jamb

mont-de-piété (*pl* **monts-de-piété**) [mɔ̃dpjete] *nm* pawnshop

monté, -e [mɔ̃te] *adj* (*équipé*) **être bien m. (en qch)** to be well stocked (with sth); *Fam Fig* **être bien m.** to be well hung

monte-charge (*pl* **monte-charges**) [mɔ̃tʃarʒ] *nm* service elevator

montée [mɔ̃te] *nf* (**a**) (*côte*) slope, hill (**b**) (*d'une côte*) climb; (*d'un avion*) ascent; **la m. des eaux** the rise in the water level (**c**) (*des prix*) rise (**de** in) (**d**) (*apparition*) (*du nationalisme, du fascisme*) rise, growth

monte-plats [mɔ̃tpla] *nm inv* dumb waiter

monter [mɔ̃te] **1** *vt* (*aux avoir*) (**a**) (*colline, escalier*) (*en s'éloignant*) to go up, to climb (up); (*en s'approchant*) to come up, to climb (up); **m. la rue en courant** to run up the street
     (**b**) (*porter en haut*) (*en s'éloignant*) to take up; (*en s'approchant*) to bring up
     (**c**) (*son, chauffage*) to turn up
     (**d**) (*assembler*) (*meuble*) to assemble; (*tente*) to put up; (*bijou, photo*) to mount
     (**e**) (*pièce de théâtre*) to put on, to stage
     (**f**) (*film*) to edit
     (**g**) (*créer*) (*entreprise, magasin*) to set up; (*complot*) to hatch; **m. un coup** to plan a job
     (**h**) (*trousseau*) to put together
     (**i**) (*cheval*) to ride
     (**j**) (*locutions*) **m. la garde** to mount guard; **m. (la tête à) qn contre qn** to set sb against sb
     2 *vi* (*aux être*) (**a**) (*aller vers le haut*) to go up; (*venir vers le haut*) to come up; (*oiseau*) to fly up; (*avion*) to climb; **m. se coucher** to go (up) to bed; **faire m. qn** to show sb up; **m. sur qch** to climb onto sth; **m. à qch** to climb (up) sth; **m. à Paris** (*y déménager*) to move up to Paris; (*en visite*) to go up to Paris; **m. à la tête à qn** (*sang*) to rush to sb's head; *Fig* to go to sb's head; **les larmes lui sont montées aux yeux** his eyes filled with tears
     (**b**) (*prendre place*) **m. dans qch** (*voiture, barque*) to get in sth; (*train, autobus, avion*) to get on sth; **m. sur qch** to get on sth; **m. à bord** to go on board; **m. à bicyclette** to ride a bicycle; **m. à cheval** to ride, to go horseback riding; **m. en voiture** to get into a car
     (**c**) (*route*) to climb
     (**d**) (*prix, baromètre, marée*) to rise; **m. en flèche** (*prix*) to soar; **faire m. les prix** to raise prices; **m. à** (*s'élever à*) to amount to, to come to
     3 se monter *vpr* (**a**) (*s'élever*) **se m. à** to come to, to amount to
     (**b**) (*s'équiper*) **se m. en qch** to provide oneself with sth
     (**c**) *Fam* **se m. la tête** (*s'exalter*) to get carried away with oneself

monteur, -euse [mɔ̃tœr, -øz] *nm,f Cin* editor

Montevideo [mɔ̃tevideo] *n* Montevideo

montgolfière [mɔ̃gɔlfjɛr] *nf* hot-air balloon

monticule [mɔ̃tikyl] *nm* hillock, mound

montre [mɔ̃tr] *nf* (**a**) (*instrument*) watch; **à ma m. il est midi** by my watch it's twelve o'clock; **m. en main** exactly; **m. de plongée** diver's watch; **m. à quartz** quartz watch (**b**) (*preuve*) **faire m. de qch** to show sth

Montréal [mɔ̃real] *n* Montreal

montréalais, -e [mɔ̃reale, -ɛz] **1** *adj* of Montreal
     2 *nm,f* **M., Montréalaise** Montrealer

montre-bracelet (*pl* **montres-bracelets**) [mɔ̃trəbraslɛ] *nf* wristwatch

montrer [mɔ̃tre] **1** *vt* (**a**) (*révéler*) to show (**à** to); **tu devrais m. ça au médecin** you should let the doctor take a look at it; **m. le chemin à qn** to show sb the way; **m. les dents** to show or to bare one's teeth (**b**) (*désigner*) to point out; **m. qn/ qch du doigt** to point at sb/sth; *Fig* to point the finger at sb/ sth (**c**) (*faire preuve de*) to show
     2 se montrer *vpr* (**a**) (*se présenter*) (*personne*) to show oneself (**b**) (*s'avérer*) **se m. gentil/courageux** to be kind/courageous

montreur, -euse [mɔ̃trœr, -øz] *nm,f* **m. d'ours** bear tamer

monture [mɔ̃tyr] *nf* (**a**) (*de lunettes*) frame; (*de bijou*) setting (**b**) (*cheval*) mount

monument [mɔnymã] *nm* (**a**) *(statue)* monument; **m. funéraire** monument *(over a tomb)*; **m. aux morts** war memorial (**b**) *(édifice public)* monument; **m. classé** landmark (**c**) *Fig (livre, film)* masterpiece

monumental, -e, -aux, -ales [mɔnymãtal, -o] *adj* monumental

moquer [mɔke] **se moquer** *vpr* (**a**) *(rire)* **se m. de qn/qch** to make fun of sb/sth; *Fig* **il se moque du monde** who does he think he is? (**b**) *(ignorer)* **se m. de qch** not to care about sth; *Fam* **se m. de qch comme de l'an quarante** *ou* **comme de sa première chemise** not to give two hoots about sth

moquerie [mɔkri] *nf* mockery

moquette [mɔkɛt] *nf* wall-to-wall carpet; **poser de la m.** to lay wall-to-wall carpet

moqueur, -euse [mɔkœr, -øz] **1** *adj (remarque, rires)* mocking; *(personne)* given to mockery
    2 *nm* **les moqueurs** mocking people

moraine [mɔrɛn] *nf* moraine

moral, -e, -aux, -ales [mɔral, -o] **1** *adj* moral
    2 *nm* morale; **avoir le m.** to be in good spirits; **avoir le m. au beau fixe** to be in fine spirits; **avoir un m. d'acier** to be very resilient; *Fam* **avoir le m. à zéro** to feel really down; **remonter le m. à qn** to cheer sb up

morale [mɔral] *nf* (**a**) *(bien)* morals; **contraire à la m.** immoral (**b**) *(règles)* morality; **faire une leçon de m. à qn, faire la m. à qn** to lecture sb (**c**) *(d'une histoire)* moral

moralement [mɔralmã] *adv* morally

moralisateur, -trice [mɔralizatœr, -tris] **1** *adj (discours, personne)* moralizing
    2 *nm,f* moralizer

moraliste [mɔralist] **1** *adj* moralistic
    2 *nmf* moralist

moralité [mɔralite] *nf* (**a**) *(conduite, attitude)* morality; **être d'une m. irréprochable** to have impeccable moral standards (**b**) *(d'une histoire)* moral; **m.: quand on veut, on peut** the moral of the story is, you can do anything if you put your mind to it

moratoire [mɔratwar] *nm Jur* moratorium

morbide [mɔrbid] *adj* morbid

morbidité [mɔrbidite] *nf* morbidness

morceau, -x [mɔrso] *nm* (**a**) *(de nourriture)* piece, bit; *Fam* **le gros m.** *(le plus difficile)* the big one; *Fam* **manger un m.** to have a bite to eat; *Fam Fig* **lâcher** *ou* **cracher le m.** to spill the beans; **m. de choix** choice morsel; **bas morceaux** *(de viande)* cheap cuts (**b**) *(de savon, de tissu, de papier)* piece, bit; *(de sucre)* lump; *(de terre)* piece; **en morceaux** in pieces; **mettre qch en morceaux** to tear sth to pieces; **tomber en morceaux** to fall to pieces (**c**) *(de musique)* piece (**d**) *(extrait)* **m. d'anthologie** anthology piece; **m. de bravoure** purple passage; **morceaux choisis** selected passages *or* extracts

morceler [9] [mɔrsəle] *vt* to divide up

morcellement [mɔrsɛlmã] *nm* dividing up

mordant, -e [mɔrdã, -ãt] **1** *adj* (**a**) *(esprit, remarque, ton)* biting, caustic (**b**) *(froid)* biting
    2 *nm (causticité)* bite

mordicus [mɔrdikys] *adv Fam* stubbornly

mordiller [mɔrdije] *vt* to nibble

mordoré, -e [mɔrdɔre] *adj (couleur)* bronze

mordre [mɔrdr] **1** *vt* (**a**) *(sujet: personne, animal)* to bite; **m. qn au bras** to bite sb's arm, to bite sb on the arm; **se faire m. par un chien** to be bitten by a dog (**b**) *(entamer) (sujet: lime)* to bite into; *(sujet: acide)* to eat into
    2 *vi (personne, chien)* to bite; **m. dans une pomme** to bite into an apple; **ça mord?** *(poissons)* are the fish biting?
    3 mordre à *vt ind* (**a**) *(poisson)* & *Fig* **m. à l'appât** *ou* **à l'hameçon** to rise to the bait (**b**) *Fam (prendre goût à)* to take to
    4 mordre sur *vt ind (déborder)* **m. sur qch** to encroach

(up)on sth; **m. sur la ligne** *(sportif)* to have one's foot over the line
    5 se mordre *vpr* **se m. la langue** to bite one's tongue; *Fig* **se m. les doigts d'avoir fait qch** to kick oneself for doing sth; **vous vous en mordrez les doigts** you'll be sorry

mordu, -e [mɔrdy] *Fam* **1** *adj* (**a**) *(amoureux)* madly in love (**b**) *(passionné)* **être m. de qch** to be crazy about sth
    2 *nm,f* fanatic; **un m. de bridge/cinéma** a bridge/movie fanatic

morfal, -e, -als, -ales [mɔrfal] *nm,f Fam* greedy pig

morfler [mɔrfle] *vi Fam* (**a**) *(être abîmé)* to get smashed up; *(être blessé)* to get injured (**b**) *(être puni, pâtir)* to catch it

morfondre [mɔrfɔdr] **se morfondre** *vpr* (**a**) *(languir)* to mope (**b**) *Can (s'épuiser)* to wear oneself out

morgue[1] [mɔrg] *nf (arrogance)* haughtiness; **plein de m.** haughty

morgue[2] [mɔrg] *nf* morgue

moribond, -e [mɔribɔ̃, -ɔ̃d] **1** *adj* dying
    2 *nm,f* dying man, *f* dying woman

morille [mɔrij] *nf* morel

mormon, -e [mɔrmɔ̃, -ɔn] *adj & nm,f* Mormon

morne [mɔrn] *adj (personne, regard)* glum; *(silence)* gloomy; *(temps)* dismal, dreary

morose [mɔroz] *adj (personne, humeur)* morose; *(temps)* miserable

morosité [mɔrozite] *nf (d'une personne, de l'humeur)* moroseness; *(du temps)* miserable nature

morphine [mɔrfin] *nf* morphine

morphologie [mɔrfɔlɔʒi] *nf* morphology

morphologique [mɔrfɔlɔʒik] *adj* morphological

morpion [mɔrpjɔ̃] *nm* (**a**) *très Fam (pou)* crab (**b**) *Fam (enfant)* kid (**c**) *(jeu)* tic(k)-tac(k)-toe

mors [mɔr] *nm* bit; *Fig* **prendre le m. aux dents** to take the bit between one's teeth

morse[1] [mɔrs] *nm (animal)* walrus

morse[2] [mɔrs] *nm (code)* Morse (code)

morsure [mɔrsyr] *nf* bite

mort[1], **-e** [mɔr, mɔrt] **1** *pp voir* **mourir**
    2 *adj* (**a**) *(personne, feuille, langue)* dead; **plus m. que vif** more dead than alive; **m. de peur/d'inquiétude/de froid** frightened/worried/frozen to death; *Fam* **être m. de rire** to die laughing; *Fam* **être m. (de fatigue)** to be dead tired (**b**) *(hors d'usage) (pile)* dead; *Fam* **être m. (voiture, chaussures)** to have had it
    3 *nm,f* dead man, *f* dead woman; **les morts** the dead; *Rel* **le jour** *ou* **la fête des morts** All Souls' Day; **faire le m.** to pretend to be dead; *Fig* to lie low; **l'accident a fait trois morts** three people were killed in the accident
    4 *nf* death; **trouver la m. dans un accident** to die in an accident; **se donner la m.** to take one's own life; **mettre qn à m.** to put sb to death; **en vouloir à qn à m.** to have a huge grudge against sb; **la m. dans l'âme** with a heavy heart; *Fam* **c'est pas la m.!** it won't kill you/him/*etc.*!; *Méd* **m. subite du nourrisson** crib death

mort[2] [mɔr] *nm (aux cartes)* dummy

mortadelle [mɔrtadɛl] *nf* mortadella

mortaise [mɔrtɛz] *nf* mortise

mortalité [mɔrtalite] *nf* mortality, death rate; **m. infantile** infant mortality

mort-aux-rats [mɔrora] *nf inv* rat poison

mortel, -elle [mɔrtɛl] **1** *adj* (**a**) *(éphémère)* mortal (**b**) *(fatal) (maladie, accident)* fatal; *(dose)* lethal; *(champignon, poison)* deadly (**c**) *(péché, ennemi)* deadly; *(silence)* deathly; **d'une pâleur mortelle** deathly pale (**d**) *Fam (ennuyeux)* deadly boring (**e**) *Fam (excellent)* cool, awesome (**f**) *Fam (très mauvais)* hellish, gnarly
    2 *nm,f* mortal

mortellement [mɔrtɛlmã] *adv* (*blessé*) fatally; (*ennuyeux*) deadly

morte-saison (*pl* **mortes-saisons**) [mɔrtsɛzɔ̃] *nf* off-season; **à la m.** in the off-season

mortier [mɔrtje] *nm* mortar; **tirs de m.** mortar fire

mortifiant, -e [mɔrtifjã, -ãt] *adj* mortifying

mortification [mɔrtifikasjɔ̃] *nf* mortification

mortifié, -e [mɔrtifje] *adj* mortified

mortifier [66] [mɔrtifje] **1** *vt* to mortify

2 se mortifier *vpr* to mortify oneself

mort-né, -e (*mpl* **mort-nés**, *fpl* **mort-nées**) [mɔrne] **1** *adj aussi Fig* stillborn

2 *nm,f* stillborn child

mortuaire [mɔrtɥɛr] *adj* death

mort-vivant, morte-vivante (*mpl* **morts-vivants**, *fpl* **mortes-vivantes**) [mɔrvivã, -ãt] *nm,f* member of the living *or* walking dead; **les morts-vivants** the living *or* walking dead

morue [mɔry] *nf* (**a**) (*poisson*) cod (**b**) *très Fam* (*prostituée*) hooker

morve [mɔrv] *nf* snot

morveux, -euse [mɔrvø, -øz] **1** *adj* (*enfant*) runny-nosed; (*nez*) runny

2 *nm,f Fam Péj* (*gamin*) brat; (*jeune prétentieux*) upstart

mosaïque [mɔzaik] *nf* (**a**) (*en décoration*) mosaic (**b**) *Fig* (*de couleurs*) kaleidoscope; (*de populations*) medley

mosaïquer [mɔzaike] *vt TV* (*image*) to pixelize, to distort

Moscou [mɔsku] *n* Moscow

moscovite [mɔskɔvit] **1** *adj* Muscovite

2 *nmf* **M.** Muscovite

mosquée [mɔske] *nf* mosque

mot [mo] *nm* (**a**) (*parole*) word; **avoir son m. à dire** to have one's say; **avoir toujours le m. pour rire** to be always ready with a joke; **avoir des mots avec qn** to have words with sb; **avoir le dernier m.** to have the last word; **je n'ai pas dit mon dernier m.** I'm not finished yet; **dire un m.** *ou* **deux mots à qn** to have a word with sb; **se donner le m.** to pass the word around; **prendre qn au m.** to take sb at his/her word; **traduire m. à m., faire du m. à m.** to translate word for word; **répéter qch m. pour m.** to repeat sth word for word; **sans m. dire** without (saying) a word; **sur ces mots** and with these words; **en un m.** in a word; **au bas m.** at least; **à mots couverts** in veiled terms; **mots doux, mots d'amour** sweet nothings; **mots croisés** crossword; **faire des mots croisés** to do crosswords; **m. d'ordre** watchword, slogan; **m. de passe** password; **bon m.** witty remark; **gros m.** curse word; **dire des gros mots** to curse (**b**) (*message écrit*) note; **envoyer un m. à qn** to drop sb a line; **m. d'excuse** note (*explaining absence*) (**c**) *Ordinat* **m. de six bits** six-bit byte; **m. binaire** binary word

motard, -e [mɔtar, -ard] **1** *nm,f Fam* (*conducteur de moto*) biker

2 *nm* (*policier*) motorcycle policeman

mot-clef (*pl* **mots-clefs**) [mokle] *nm* keyword

motel [mɔtɛl] *nm* motel

moteur, -trice [mɔtœr, -tris] **1** *adj* (**a**) (*force, roue*) driving; **à deux/quatre roues motrices** two-/four-wheel drive (**b**) (*nerf, trouble*) motor

2 *nm* engine; (*électrique*) motor; *Fig* driving force; *Cin* **m.!** action!; **à m.** motor(-driven); **m. à deux/quatre temps** two-/four-stroke engine; **m. à explosion** internal-combustion engine; **m. à injection** fuel-injected engine; **m. à réaction** jet engine; *Ordinat* **m. de recherche** search engine

3 *nf Rail* **motrice** engine

motif [mɔtif] *nm* (**a**) (*raison*) reason (**de** for); **elle n'a aucun m. de mécontentement** she has no reason to be unhappy (**b**) (*dessin*) pattern, motif (**c**) (*dans un morceau de musique*) motif

motion [mɔsjɔ̃] *nf* motion; **m. de censure** motion of censure

motivant, -e [mɔtivã, -ãt] *adj* (*travail*) motivating; (*salaire, rémunération*) attractive

motivation [mɔtivasjɔ̃] *nf* motivation

motivé, -e [mɔtive] *adj* (**a**) (*personne*) motivated (**b**) (*action*) justified

motiver [mɔtive] *vt* (**a**) (*provoquer, stimuler*) to motivate (**b**) (*justifier*) to justify

moto [mɔto] *nf* motorcycle; **faire de la m.** to ride a motorcycle; **m. tout terrain** trail bike

motocross [mɔtokrɔs] *nm* motocross

motocrotte [mɔtokrɔt] *nf Fam* = motorized scooter with an attachment for cleaning up dog dirt in the street

motoculteur [mɔtokyltœr] *nm* motor cultivator

motocyclette [mɔtosiklɛt] *nf* motorcycle

motocycliste [mɔtosiklist] *nm* motorcyclist; *Mil* dispatch rider

motomarine [mɔtomarin] *nf Can* jet ski

motoneige [mɔtonɛʒ] *nf Can* snowmobile

motorisé, -e [mɔtorize] *adj* motorized; *Fam* **être m.** (*personne*) to have wheels

motrice [mɔtris] *voir* **moteur**

motricité [mɔtrisite] *nf* motor function

motte [mɔt] *nf* (**a**) (*de terre*) clod, clump (**b**) (*de beurre*) block

motus [mɔtys] *exclam* **m. (et bouche cousue)!** not a word!

mou¹, molle [mu, mɔl] **1** *adj* (**a**) (*matelas, substance*) soft; (*chair, ventre*) flabby; **j'ai les jambes molles** my legs are like Jell-O (**b**) (*personne, gouvernement*) spineless; (*protestation*) feeble; (*poignée de main*) limp

2 *nm,f Fam* wimp

3 *nm* (*d'un cordage, d'un câble*) slack

mou² [mu] *nm* (*abats*) lights, lungs

mouais [mwɛ] *exclam Fam* well, yeah!; **alors, t'as aimé le film? – m., j'ai vu pire** so, did you like the movie? – well, yeah, I've seen worse; **m., ce n'est pas mal** it's OK I guess

mouchard, -e [muʃar, -ard] *Fam* **1** *nm,f* (*informateur*) fink; (*à l'école*) tattletale

2 *nm* (*de camion*) tachograph

moucharder [muʃarde] *Fam* **1** *vt* (*personne*) to squeal on; (*élève*) to tattle on

2 *vi* (*élève*) to tattle on people

mouche [muʃ] *nf* (**a**) (*insecte*) fly; **prendre** *ou Suisse* **piquer la m.** to fly off the handle; **elle ne ferait pas de mal à une m.** she wouldn't hurt a fly; **quelle m. te pique?** what's got into you?; **m. tsé-tsé** tsetse fly; **fine m.** sharp customer (**b**) (*de cible*) bull's-eye; **faire m.** to hit the bull's-eye; *Fig* to hit home (**c**) (*accessoire cosmétique*) beauty spot

moucher [muʃe] *vt* (**a**) (*nez*) to blow; **m. un enfant** to blow a child's nose (**b**) *Fig* **m. qn** to put sb in his/her place (**c**) (*chandelle*) to snuff out

2 se moucher *vpr* to blow one's nose; *Fam* **ne pas se m. du coude** *ou* **du pied** to think one is the cat's whiskers

moucheron [muʃrɔ̃] *nm* midge

moucheté, -e [muʃte] *adj* (*cheval*) dappled; (*tissu*) speckled

mouchoir [muʃwar] *nm* handkerchief; **arriver dans un m.** to arrive neck and neck; **grand comme un m. de poche** no bigger than a pocket handkerchief; **m. en papier** tissue, Kleenex; **m. en tissu** handkerchief

moudre [48] [mudr] *vt* to grind

moue [mu] *nf* pout; **faire la m.** to pout

mouette [mwɛt] *nf* (sea)gull

moufle [mufl] *nf* mitten, mitt

mouflet, -ette [muflɛ, -ɛt] *nm,f Fam* kid

mouflon [muflɔ̃] *nm* moufflon

mouillage [mujaʒ] *nm* (**a**) (*de bateau*) (*manœuvre*) anchoring; (*emplacement*) anchorage; **être au m.** to be riding at anchor (**b**) (*du vin*) watering down

mouillé, -e [muje] *adj* **(a)** *(vêtement, personne, pieds)* wet; **tout m.** soaking wet **(b)** *(consonne)* palatalized

mouiller [muje] **1** *vt* **(a)** *(rendre humide)* to wet; **se faire m.** to get wet; *Fig* **m. sa chemise** to work up a sweat **(b)** *(vin, lait)* to water down **(c)** *(ancre)* to drop **(d)** *Fam (compromettre)* to involve **(e)** *Can Fam (fêter)* **il va falloir m. ça!** this calls for a celebration!

2 *vi (bateau)* to anchor

3 se mouiller *vpr* **(a)** *(personne)* to get wet; **se m. les pieds** to get one's feet wet **(b)** *Fam (prendre position)* to stick one's neck out

mouillette [mujɛt] *nf* finger *(of bread)*

mouise [mwiz] *nf très Fam* **être dans la m.** to be hard up

moulage [mulaʒ] *nm* **(a)** *(action)* casting **(b)** *(objet)* plaster cast

moule¹ [mul] *nm aussi Fig* mold; *Fig* **être coulé dans le même m.** to be cast in the same mold; **m. à gâteaux** cake pan; **m. à gaufres** waffle iron; **m. à tarte** pie dish

moule² [mul] *nf* mussel; **moules frites** mussels and French fries *(specialty of Belgium and the North of France)*; **moules marinières** moules marinières, = mussels in white wine; *Belg* **moules parquées** = mussels served raw

mouler [mule] *vt* **(a)** *(statue)* to mold **(b)** *(sujet: vêtement)* to be close-fitting

moulin [mulɛ̃] *nm* **(a)** *(bâtiment)* mill; **on y entre comme dans un m.** anyone can just walk in; **m. à eau** watermill; *Can* **m. à scie** sawmill; **m. à vent** windmill **(b)** *(appareil)* **m. à café** coffee grinder; **m. à légumes** vegetable mill *or* grinder; *Fig* **m. à paroles** chatterbox; **m. à poivre** pepper mill

mouliner [muline] *vt (aliment)* to pass through a food mill

moulinet [mulinɛ] *nm* **(a)** *(de canne à pêche)* reel **(b)** *(rotation)* **faire des moulinets (avec les bras)** to circle one's arms

Moulinette® [mulinɛt] *nf* food mill

moult [mult] *adv Hum ou Vieilli* many

moulu, -e [muly] **1** *pp voir* **moudre**

2 *adj* **(a)** *(café, poivre)* ground **(b)** *Fig* **être m. (de fatigue)** to be beat

moulure [mulyr] *nf* (ornamental) molding

moumoute [mumut] *nf Fam* **(a)** *(perruque)* rug, wig **(b)** *(veste)* sheepskin jacket

mourant, -e [murɑ̃, -ɑ̃t] **1** *adj* dying

2 *nm,f* dying man, *f* dying woman

mourir [49] [murir] *(aux être)* **1** *vi* **(a)** *(personne, animal, plante)* to die; **m. de sa belle mort** *ou* **de mort naturelle** to die a natural death; **m. de vieillesse** to die of old age; **m. assassiné** to be murdered; **m. d'inquiétude/de peur** to be worried/frightened to death; **m. de faim** to starve to death; *Fam (avoir très faim)* to be starving; **m. de soif/d'ennui** to die of thirst/boredom; **s'ennuyer à m.** to be bored to death; **aimer qn à en m.** to be desperately in love with sb; **à m. d'ennui** deadly boring; **à m. de rire** hilarious, hysterical; **m. d'envie de faire qch** to be dying to do sth; *Fig* **tu ne vas pas en m.!** it won't kill you! **(b)** *(coutume, industrie, civilisation)* to die out; *(feu, région)* to die

2 *v impersonnel* **il meurt des milliers d'enfants chaque jour** thousands of children die every day

3 se mourir *vpr Litt (personne)* to be dying

mouroir [murwar] *nm Fam Péj* old folks' home

mouron [murɔ̃] *nm Fam* **se faire du m.** to worry

mousquetaire [muskətɛr] *nm* musketeer

mousqueton [muskətɔ̃] *nm* **(a)** *(anneau)* snap clasp; *(d'alpiniste)* karabiner **(b)** *(arme)* carbine

moussaka [musaka] *nf* moussaka

moussant, -e [musɑ̃, ɑ̃t] *adj* **être peu m.** not to produce a lot of lather; **bain m.** bubble bath

mousse¹ [mus] *nf* **(a)** *(végétation)* moss **(b)** *(écume)* foam; *(sur un verre de bière)* head, froth; *(de savon)* lather; *Fam* **une m.** *(bière)* a beer; **m. à raser** shaving foam **(c)** *(plat, dessert)* mousse; **m. au chocolat/de saumon** chocolate/salmon mousse **(d)** *(matériau synthétique)* foam rubber

mousse² [mus] *nm* ship's boy

mousseline [muslin] *nf (tissu)* muslin; **m. de soie** chiffon

mousser [muse] *vi (bière)* to froth; *(savon, lessive)* to lather; *(vin, eau gazeuse)* to fizz; *Fam Fig* **se faire m.** to show off

mousseux, -euse [musø, -øz] **1** *adj* **(a)** *(vin, cidre)* sparkling **(b)** *(lait, bière)* frothy

2 *nm* sparkling wine

mousson [musɔ̃] *nf* monsoon

moussu, -e [musy] *adj* mossy

moustache [mustaʃ] *nf* **(a)** *(d'un homme)* mustache; **porter la m.** to have a mustache **(b)** *(de chat, de rongeur)* whiskers

moustachu, -e [mustaʃy] **1** *adj* with a mustache; **être m.** to have a mustache

2 *nm* man with a mustache

moustiquaire [mustikɛr] *nf* mosquito net

moustique [mustik] *nm* **(a)** *(insecte)* mosquito **(b)** *Fam (gamin)* kid, mite

moût [mu] *nm (de raisins)* must; *(de bière)* wort

moutard [mutar] *nm Fam* kid

moutarde [mutard] **1** *adj inv* **(jaune) m.** mustard (yellow)

2 *nf* mustard; *Fig* **la m. me monte au nez** I'm beginning to lose my temper; **m. forte/de Dijon** strong/Dijon mustard

moutardier [mutardje] *nm (pot)* mustard pot

mouton [mutɔ̃] *nm* **(a)** *(animal)* sheep; **(peau de) m.** sheepskin; **être frisé comme un m.** to have curly hair; *Fig* **revenons à nos moutons** let's get back to the subject; **compter les moutons** *(pour s'endormir)* to count sheep; *Fig* **m. à cinq pattes** rare bird **(b)** *(viande)* mutton **(c)** **moutons** *(écume)* whitecaps; *(poussière)* fluff **(d)** *Can* **m. noir** *(nuage)* rain cloud

moutonner [mutɔne] *vi (mer)* to be flecked with foam

moutonneux, -euse [mutɔnø, -øz] *adj* **(a)** *(mer)* foam-flecked **(b)** *(ciel)* dotted with fleecy clouds

mouture [mutyr] *nf* **(a)** *(action de moudre)* grinding **(b)** *(d'un ouvrage, d'un livre)* version

mouv' [muv] *nm Fam (abrév* **mouvement)** **c'est dans le m.** it's totally cool

mouvance [muvɑ̃s] *nf* **il faisait partie de la m. surréaliste** he moved in surrealist circles

mouvant, -e [muvɑ̃, ɑ̃t] *adj (terrain)* unstable; *(cible)* moving; *Fig (situation)* uncertain

mouvement [muvmɑ̃] *nm* **(a)** *(déplacement)* movement, motion; *(des marchandises, des capitaux)* movement; *(geste)* gesture; **faire un m.** to make a movement; **faire un faux m.** *(se faire mal)* to move the wrong way; **en m.** in motion; **ralentir le m.** to slow down; **suivre le m.** to go with the flow; **il y eut un m. de foule** a ripple ran through the crowd; **m. de tête** *(pour acquiescer)* nod; *(pour nier)* shake of the head **(b)** *(de gymnastique)* exercise **(c)** *(élan)* impulse; **m. d'humeur** outburst (of temper); **m. de colère** fit of rage **(d)** *(politique, artistique)* movement; **m. de grève** strike action; **mouvements sociaux** job action **(e)** *(d'un concerto, d'une symphonie)* movement

mouvementé, -e [muvmɑ̃te] *adj (discussion, débat)* animated, lively; *(journée, voyage, vie)* eventful

mouvoir [31b] [muvwar] **1** *vt Litt* **(a)** *(machine)* to drive; *(bateau)* to propel; **mû par la vapeur** steamdriven **(b)** *(pousser)* **mû par l'intérêt** prompted by self-interest

2 se mouvoir *vpr* to move

moyen¹, -enne [mwajɛ̃, -ɛn] *adj* **(a)** *(du milieu)* middle; **trouver un m. terme** to find a happy medium **(b)** *(coût, taille, vitesse)* average; **de taille moyenne** medium-sized; *(personne)* of average height **(c)** *(quelconque, médiocre)* average; **le Français m.** the average Frenchman

moyen² [mwajɛ̃] *nm* **(a)** *(façon, possibilité)* means, way; *aussi Hum* **trouver le m. de faire qch** to manage to do sth; **se**

donner les moyens de faire qch to provide oneself with the means to do sth; **faire qch par ses propres moyens** to do sth on one's own; **employer les grands moyens** to take extreme measures; **au m. de qch** by means of sth; **par tous les moyens** any way I/you/*etc.* can; **il n'y a pas m. de le lui faire comprendre** it's impossible to make him/her understand; **faire avec les moyens du bord** to make do with what one has; **moyens de communication/production/transport** means of communication/production/transportation (**b**) **avoir des moyens** *(capacité mentale)* to be bright; **perdre tous ses moyens** to go to pieces (**c**) **moyens** *(financiers)* means; **j'en ai/je n'en ai pas les moyens** I can/can't afford it

Moyen Âge [mwajɛnɑʒ] *nm* **le M.** the Middle Ages

moyenâgeux, -euse [mwajɛnɑʒø, -øz] *adj* medieval

moyen-courrier (*pl* **moyen-courriers**) [mwajɛ̃kurje] *nm* (**avion**) m. medium-haul aircraft

moyennant [mwajɛnɑ̃] *prép* (in return) for; **faire qch m. finance** to do sth in return for payment; **m. quoi** in return for which

moyenne [mwajɛn] **1** *adj voir* **moyen¹**
2 *nf* (**a**) *(niveau le plus courant)* average; **en m.** on average (**b**) *(à un examen)* passing grade; *(sur une période)* average (grade); **avoir 10 sur 20 de m.** to average 10 out of 20

moyennement [mwajɛnmɑ̃] *adv* moderately, fairly

Moyen-Orient [mwajɛnɔrjɑ̃] *nm* **le M.** the Middle East

moyeu [mwajø] *nm* hub

mozambicain, -e [mɔzɑ̃bikɛ̃, -ɛn] **1** *adj* Mozambican
2 *nm,f* **M., Mozambicaine** Mozambican

Mozambique [mɔzɑ̃bik] *nm* **le M.** Mozambique

mozzarella [mɔdzarɛla], **mozzarelle** [mɔdzarɛl] *nf* mozzarella

MP3 [ɛmpetrwa] *nm inv Ordinat* MP3

MRAP [mrap] *nm* (*abrév* **Mouvement contre le racisme, l'antisémitisme et pour la paix**) = French anti-racist pacifist movement

MRG [ɛmɛrʒe] *nm* (*abrév* **Mouvement des radicaux de gauche**) = French left-wing political party

MST¹ [ɛmɛste] *nf* (*abrév* **maladie sexuellement transmissible**) STD, STI

MST² [ɛmɛste] *nf* (*abrév* **maîtrise de sciences et techniques**) = master's degree in science and technology

mû [my] *voir* **mouvoir**

mucoviscidose [mykovisidoz] *nf* cystic fibrosis

mucus [mykys] *nm* mucus

mue [my] **1** *pp voir* **mouvoir**
2 *nf* (**a**) *(d'oiseaux, de mammifères)* molting; *(de reptiles)* sloughing (**b**) *(à la puberté)* breaking of the voice

muer [mɥe] **1** *vi* (**a**) *(mammifère)* to molt; *(serpent)* to slough (**b**) *(voix)* to break; **il commence à m.** his voice is breaking
2 se muer *vpr* **se m. en** to change into

muesli [mysli] *nm* muesli

muet, -ette [mɥɛ, -ɛt] **1** *adj* (**a**) *(personne)* dumb; *Fig (silencieux)* silent; **m. d'étonnement/de colère** speechless with astonishment/anger; **m. comme la tombe** as quiet as the grave; **il est resté m. comme une carpe** he didn't open his mouth (**b**) *(film, réprobation)* silent; *(rôle)* non-speaking (**c**) *Ling* silent
2 *nm,f* mute
3 *nm Cin* **le m.** silent movies

muezzin [mɥɛdzin] *nm* muezzin

mufle [myfl] *nm* (**a**) *Fam (homme)* lout (**b**) *(du bœuf, du bison)* muffle; *(du lion, du taureau)* muzzle

muge [myʒ] *nm* mullet

mugir [myʒir] *vi* (**a**) *(vache)* to moo; *(taureau)* to bellow (**b**) *(vent)* to howl

mugissement [myʒismɑ̃] *nm* (**a**) *(de vache)* moo; *(de taureau)* bellow; **des mugissements** *(de vache)* mooing; *(de taureau)* bellowing (**b**) *(du vent)* howling

muguet [mygɛ] *nm (plante)* lily of the valley

Muguet

On May Day in France, bunches of lily of the valley are sold in the streets and given as gifts. The flowers are supposed to bring good luck.

---

mulâtre [mylɑtr] *adj & nm* mulatto

mulâtresse [mylɑtrɛs] *nf* mulatto

mule¹ [myl] *nf (animal)* mule; *Fam (personne entêtée)* mule

mule² [myl] *nf (chaussure)* mule

mulet¹ [mylɛ] *nm (équidé)* mule

mulet² [mylɛ] *nm (poisson)* gray mullet

muletier, -ère [myltje, -ɛr] **1** *adj* **chemin** *ou* **sentier m.** mule track
2 *nm,f* mule driver

mulot [mylo] *nm* field mouse

multicarte [myltikart] *adj (représentant)* for several companies

multicolore [myltikɔlɔr] *adj* multicolored

multicoque [myltikɔk] *nm* multihull

multicritère [myltikritɛr] *nm Ordinat* multicriterion

multiculturel, -elle [myltikyltyrɛl] *adj* multicultural

multidisciplinaire [myltidisiplinɛr] *adj* multi-disciplinary

multi-écran (*pl* **multi-écrans**) [myltiekrɑ̃] *nm* split screen

multifonctions [myltifɔ̃ksjɔ̃] *adj* multi-functional

multiforme [myltifɔrm] *adj* multifaceted

multijoueur [myltiʒwœr] *adj* multiplayer

multilatéral, -e, -aux, -ales [myltilateral, -o] *adj* multilateral

multilingue [myltilɛ̃g] *adj* multilingual

multimédia [myltimedja] *adj & nm* multimedia

multimilliardaire [myltimiljardɛr] *adj & nmf* multimillionaire

multimillionnaire [myltimiljɔnɛr] *adj & nmf* multimillionaire

multinational, -e, -aux, -ales [myltinasjɔnal, -o] **1** *adj* multinational
2 *nf* **multinationale** multinational (company)

multiple [myltipl] **1** *adj* (**a**) *(nombreux)* many, numerous; **à usages multiples** multipurpose; **à de multiples reprises** repeatedly; *Ordinat* **à accès m.** multi-access (**b**) *(divers)* many, multiple
2 *nm Math* multiple; **le plus petit commun m.** the lowest common multiple

multiplex [myltiplɛks] *adj inv & nm inv* multiplex

multiplexe [myltiplɛks] *nm* multiplex (movie theater)

multiplicateur, -trice [myltiplikatœr, -tris] **1** *adj* multiplying
2 *nm* multiplier

multiplication [myltiplikasjɔ̃] *nf* (**a**) *(calcul)* multiplication (**b**) *(augmentation)* increase (**de** in)

multiplicité [myltiplisite] *nf* multiplicity

multiplier [66] [myltiplije] **1** *vt* (**a**) *(somme, chiffre)* to multiply (**par** by) (**b**) *(répéter)* **m. les mises en garde** to issue repeated warnings; **m. les erreurs** to make mistake after mistake
2 se multiplier *vpr* (**a**) *(augmenter)* to increase (**b**) *(se reproduire)* to multiply

multiposte [myltipɔst] *adj Ordinat* multi-station

multiprocesseur [myltiprɔsesœr] *nm Ordinat* multiprocessor

multiprogrammation [myltiprɔgramasjɔ̃] *nf Ordinat* multiprogramming

multipropriété [myltiprɔprijete] *nf* time-share; **acheter un appartement en m.** to buy a time-share apartment

multiracial, -e, -aux, -ales [myltirasjal, -o] *adj* multiracial

multirisque [myltirisk] *adj* comprehensive

multisalles [myltisal] *adj* **complexe m.** multiplex (movie theater)

multitâche [myltitɑʃ] *adj Ordinat* multitasking

multithérapie [myltiterapi] *nf Méd* combination therapy

multitraitement [myltitrɛtmã] *nm Ordinat* multiprocessing

multitude [myltityd] *nf* multitude (**de** of)

multi-utilisateurs [myltiytilizatœr] *adj inv Ordinat* multiuser

municipal, -e, -aux, -ales [mynisipal, -o] **1** *adj* municipal
   2 *nfpl* **les municipales** municipal *or* local (government) elections

> **Municipales**
>
> These are the elections where residents choose the city councils. Electors vote for a list of council members whose leader or "tête de liste" will become the mayor, a ceremonial and political post (*see box at* **maire**).

municipalité [mynisipalite] *nf* (**a**) *(commune)* municipality (**b**) *(maire et conseillers)* city council

munir [mynir] **1** *vt (personne)* to supply, to provide (**de** with); *(voiture, chambre)* to fit, to equip (**de** with)
   2 se munir *vpr* **se m. de qch** to take sth

munitions [mynisjɔ̃] *nfpl* ammunition, munitions

munster [mœ̃stɛr] *nm* Munster (cheese)

muqueuse [mykøz] *nf* mucous membrane

mur [myr] *nm* (**a**) *(construction)* wall; **l'ennemi est dans nos murs** the enemy is within the gates; **le m. de Berlin** the Berlin Wall; **le M. des lamentations** the Wailing *or* Western Wall; **m. porteur** load-bearing wall; **m. du son** sound barrier; **franchir le m. du son** to break the sound barrier; **m. de soutènement** retaining wall (**b**) *Fig (résistance)* brick wall

mûr, -e [myr] *adj* (**a**) *(fruit)* ripe; *Fig* **être m. pour qch** to be ripe for sth (**b**) *(personne, esprit)* mature (**c**) *(intense)* **après mûre réflexion** after careful consideration

muraille [myrɑj] *nf (d'une ville, d'un château)* wall; **la Grande M. de Chine** the Great Wall of China

mural, -e, -aux, -ales [myral, -o] *adj* wall

mûre [myr] *nf* mulberry; *(fruit de la ronce)* blackberry

mûrement [myrmã] *adv* **après avoir m. réfléchi** after careful consideration; **un projet m. réfléchi** a carefully thought-out plan

murène [myrɛn] *nf* moray (eel)

murer [myre] **1** *vt* (**a**) *(ville, jardin)* to wall in (**b**) *(porte, fenêtre, personne)* to wall up
   2 se murer *vpr* to shut oneself away; **se m. dans le silence/la solitude** to retreat into silence/solitude

muret [myrɛ] *nm (mur bas)* low wall; *(de pierres sèches)* dry-stone wall

murette [myrɛt] *nf* = **muret**

mûrier [myrje] *nm* (**a**) *(arbre)* mulberry tree (**b**) *(roncier)* blackberry bush

mûrir [myrir] *vi* (**a**) *(fruit)* to ripen (**b**) *(projet, sentiment)* to evolve, to develop (**c**) *(personne)* to mature

murmure [myrmyr] *nm* murmur

murmurer [myrmyre] *vt & vi* to murmur

musaraigne [myzarɛɲ] *nf* shrew

musarder [myzarde] *vi (flâner)* to wander around; *(fainéanter)* to lounge around

musc [mysk] *nm* musk

muscade [myskad] *nf* **m., noix (de) m.** nutmeg

muscat [myska] *nm* (**a**) *(raisin)* muscat grape (**b**) *(vin)* muscatel (wine)

muscle [myskl] *nm* muscle; **être tout en m.** to be all muscle

musclé, -e [myskle] *adj* (**a**) *(personne, bras, jambes)* muscular (**b**) *Fig (campagne électorale, discours)* punchy; *(intervention)* forceful; *(politique, mesure)* tough

muscler [myskle] **1** *vt* to develop the muscles of
   2 se muscler *vpr* to develop one's muscles

muscu [mysky] *Fam* = **musculation**

musculaire [myskylɛr] *adj (système, tissu, force)* muscular; *(fibre)* muscle

musculation [myskylasjɔ̃] *nf* body building; **faire de la m.** to do body building

musculature [myskylatyr] *nf* musculature

muse [myz] *nf* muse

museau, -x [myzo] *nm* (**a**) *(d'animal)* muzzle, snout (**b**) *Fam (visage)* face

musée [myze] *nm* museum; **m. (de peinture)** art gallery; **m. des horreurs** chamber of horrors

museler [9] [myzle] *vt aussi Fig* to muzzle

muselière [myzəljɛr] *nf* muzzle

musette [myzɛt] **1** *nf* (**a**) *(instrument de musique)* musette (**b**) *(sac)* bag; *(de soldat)* haversack; *(d'écolier)* satchel
   2 *nm Fam* **le m.** accordion music

muséum [myzeɔm] *nm* natural history museum

musical, -e, -aux, -ales [myzikal, -o] *adj* musical

musicalement [myzikalmã] *adv* musically

music-hall (*pl* **music-halls**) [myzikol] *nm (genre)* vaudeville; *(salle)* vaudeville theater; **un numéro de m.** a variety act

musicien, -enne [myzisjɛ̃, -ɛn] **1** *adj* musical
   2 *nm,f* musician

musicologie [myzikɔlɔʒi] *nf* musicology

musicologue [myzikɔlɔg] *nmf* musicologist

musique [myzik] *nf* (**a**) *(art, notation ou science)* music; **mettre qch en m.** to set sth to music; **faire de la m.** to make music; *Fig* **connaître la m.** to have heard it all before; *Can* **faire face à la m.** to face the music; **m. d'ambiance** *ou* **de fond** background music; **m. de chambre** chamber music; **m. classique** classical music; **m. folklorique** folk music; **m. religieuse** religious music; **m. sacrée** sacred music (**b**) *Belg, Suisse & Can* **m. à bouche** harmonica, mouth organ

musqué, -e [myske] *adj (odeur)* musky

must [mœst] *nm Fam* must; **c'est un m.** it's a must

mustang [mystãg] *nm* mustang

musulman, -e [myzylmã, -an] *adj & nm,f* Moslem, Muslim

mutant, -e [mytã, ãt] *adj & nm,f* mutant

mutation [mytasjɔ̃] *nf* (**a**) *(de personnel)* transfer (**b**) *(changement)* change, alteration

muter [myte] *vt* to transfer

mutilation [mytilasjɔ̃] *nf* mutilation

mutilé, -e [mytile] *nm,f* **mutilés de guerre** disabled ex-servicemen

mutiler [mytile] **1** *vt (personne)* to mutilate, to maim; *(partie du corps)* to badly injure; *(paysage)* to disfigure
   2 se mutiler *vpr* to mutilate oneself

mutin[1] [mytɛ̃] *nm* mutineer

mutin[2], -e [mytɛ̃, -in] *adj (espiègle)* mischievous

mutiner [mytine] **se mutiner** *vpr* to mutiny (**contre** against)

mutinerie [mytinri] *nf* mutiny

mutisme [mytism] *nm* silence; **observer un m. absolu** to maintain total silence

mutualité [mytɥalite] *nf* mutual insurance

mutuel, -elle [mytɥɛl] **1** *adj* mutual
   2 *nf* **mutuelle** mutual insurance company

Mutuelle

A "mutuelle" is a non-profit health insurance company which provides insurance complementary to that of the **Sécurité sociale** (*see box at this entry*). Often these companies are set up for a particular profession: there is a "mutuelle" for students, one for teachers, etc.

mutuellement [mytɥɛlmɑ̃] *adv* each other, one another
Myanmar [mjanmar] *nm* **le M.** Myanmar
mycose [mikoz] *nf* fungal infection, *Spéc* mycosis
mygale [migal] *nf* trapdoor spider
myocarde [mjɔkard] *nm* myocardium
myopathe [mjɔpat] *nmf* person with muscular dystrophy
myopathie [mjɔpati] *nf* muscular dystrophy
myope [mjɔp] **1** *adj* nearsighted, *Spéc* myopic; *Fig* **m. comme une taupe** as blind as a bat
  2 *nmf* nearsighted person
myopie [mjɔpi] *nf* nearsightedness, *Spéc* myopia
myosotis [mjɔzɔtis] *nm* forget-me-not
myriade [mirjad] *nf* myriad (**de** of)
myrrhe [mir] *nf* myrrh
myrtille [mirtij] *nf* blueberry
mystère [mistɛr] *nm* (**a**) *(énigme)* mystery; **faire des mys-**

tères to be mysterious; **faire m. de qch** to make a secret of sth; **il n'y a pas de m.** it's quite simple; *Fam* **m. et boule de gomme!** search me!, I don't have a clue! (**b**) *(pièce de théâtre)* mystery (play)
mystérieusement [misterjøzmɑ̃] *adv* mysteriously
mystérieux, -euse [misterjø, -øz] *adj* mysterious; *(secret)* secret
mysticisme [mistisism] *nm* mysticism
mystification [mistifikasjɔ̃] *nf* hoax
mystifier [66] [mistifje] *vt* to take in
mystique [mistik] **1** *adj* mystical
  2 *nmf* mystic
mythe [mit] *nm* myth; **elle fut un m. vivant** she was a legend in her own lifetime
mythique [mitik] *adj* mythical
mythologie [mitɔlɔʒi] *nf* mythology
mythologique [mitɔlɔʒik] *adj* mythological
mythomane [mitɔman] **1** *adj* **être m.** to be a pathological liar
  2 *nmf* pathological liar, *Spéc* mythomaniac
mythomanie [mitɔmani] *nf* mythomania
myxomatose [miksɔmatoz] *nf* myxomatosis

N

N¹, n [ɛn] *nm inv* N, n

N² [ɛn] **1** (*abrév* **Nord**) N

2 *nf* (*abrév* **route nationale**) = designation of major road, ≃ highway

nabot, -e [nabo, -ɔt] *nm,f Péj* midget

nacelle [nasɛl] *nf* (**a**) (*de montgolfière*) basket; (*de dirigeable*) gondola (**b**) (*de landau*) (*détachable*) bassinet; (*fixe*) carriage

nacre [nakr] *nf* mother-of-pearl; **un collier de** *ou* **en n.** a mother-of-pearl necklace

nacré, -e [nakre] *adj* pearly

nage [naʒ] *nf* (**a**) (*activité*) swimming; (*manière*) stroke; **traverser une rivière à la n.** to swim across a river; **le 100 mètres quatre nages** the 4 x 100 meters relay; **n. indienne** sidestroke; **n. libre** freestyle (**b**) **être en n.** to be bathed in perspiration

nageoire [naʒwar] *nf* (*de poisson*) fin; (*de dauphin, de cétacé*) flipper

nager [45] [naʒe] **1** *vi* to swim; **aller n.** to go for a swim; **n. vers la côte** to swim for the shore; *Fig* **n. entre deux eaux** to sit on the fence; *Fig* **n. dans son sang** to be bathed in blood; *Fig* **n. dans le bonheur** to be on cloud nine; *Fam* **il nage dans ses vêtements** his clothes are far too baggy on him; *Fam* **je nage complètement!** I'm totally at sea!

2 *vt* (**a**) (*la brasse, le crawl*) to do, to swim (**b**) (*disputer*) **n. le 100 mètres** to swim (in) the 100 meters

nageur, -euse [naʒœr, -øz] *nm,f* swimmer

naguère [nagɛr] *adv Litt* not long ago; (*autrefois*) formerly

naïf, -ïve [naif, -iv] **1** *adj* naive

2 *nm,f* (**a**) (*personne*) fool (**b**) (*peintre*) naive painter

nain, -e [nɛ̃, nɛn] **1** *adj* (*personne*) dwarf

2 *nm,f* dwarf; **n. de jardin** garden gnome

Nairobi [nerobi] *n* Nairobi

naissance [nɛsɑ̃s] *nf* (**a**) *aussi Fig* birth; **sourd/aveugle de n.** deaf/blind from birth, born deaf/blind; **français de n.** French by birth; **donner n. à un enfant** to give birth to a child; **donner n. à une rumeur** to give rise to a rumor; **il était blond à la n.** his hair was blond when he was born (**b**) (*d'ongle*) root; (*du cou*) base; **prendre n.** to originate; (*rivière*) to rise

naissant, -e [nɛsɑ̃, -ɑ̃t] *adj* (*jour*) dawning; (*beauté*) nascent; **une barbe naissante** stubble

naître [50a] [nɛtr] *vi* (*aux être*) (**a**) (*personne, animal*) to be born; **enfant à n.** unborn child; **il naît plus de filles que de garçons** more girls are born than boys; **elle est née en 1880** she was born in 1880; *Fam* **je ne suis pas né d'hier** I wasn't born yesterday (**b**) (*espoir*) to arise; (*projet, idée*) to originate (**de** in); **faire n.** (*espoir, doute, soupçons*) to give rise to; (*sourire*) to raise

naïvement [naivmɑ̃] *adv* naively

naïveté [naivte] *nf* naivety; **avoir la n. de croire qch** to be naive enough to believe sth

Namibie [namibi] *nf* **la N.** Namibia

namibien, -enne [namibjɛ̃, -ɛn] **1** *adj* Namibian

2 *nm,f* **N., Namibienne** Namibian

nana [nana] *nf Fam* girl, chick

nanisme [nanism] *nm* dwarfism

nano- [nano] *préf* nano-

nanti, -e [nɑ̃ti] **1** *adj* well-to-do

2 *nm,f* well-to-do person; **les nantis** the well-to-do

nantir [nɑ̃tir] *vt* **n. qn de qch** to provide sb with sth

napalm [napalm] *nm* napalm

naphtaline [naftalin] *nf* naphthalene; **boules de n.** mothballs; *Can Fig* **sortir qch de la n.** to take sth out of mothballs

Napoléon [napɔleɔ̃] *npr* Napoleon

nappage [napaʒ] *nm* coating

nappe [nap] *nf* (**a**) (*de table*) tablecloth; **mettre la n.** to put the tablecloth on; **ôter la n.** to take the tablecloth off (**b**) *Fig* **n. de brouillard** fog patch; **n. d'eau** expanse of water; **n. de pétrole** (*souterraine*) layer of oil; (*de marée noire*) oil slick; **n. phréatique** water table

napper [nape] *vt* to coat (**de** with)

napperon [naprɔ̃] *nm* mat

narcisse [narsis] *nm* (**a**) (*fleur*) narcissus (**b**) (*personne*) narcissist

narcissique [narsisik] *adj* narcissistic

narcissisme [narsisism] *nm* narcissism

narcodollars [narkodɔlar] *nmpl* drug money

narcotique [narkɔtik] *adj & nm* narcotic

narcotrafic [narkɔtrafik] *nm* drug trafficking

narcotrafiquant, -e [narkɔtrafikɑ̃, -ɑ̃t] *nm,f* drug trafficker

narguer [narge] *vt* to taunt

narine [narin] *nf* nostril

narquois, -e [narkwa, -az] *adj* taunting

narquoisement [narkwazmɑ̃] *adv* tauntingly

narrateur, -trice [naratœr, -tris] *nm,f* narrator

narratif, -ive [naratif, -iv] *adj* narrative

narration [narasjɔ̃] *nf* (**a**) (*genre*) narration (**b**) (*récit*) narrative

narrer [nare] *vt Litt* to narrate

narval, -als [narval] *nm* narwhal

nasal, -e, -aux, -ales [nazal, -o] *adj* nasal

nase [naz] **1** *adj* (**a**) *Fam* (*épuisé*) (*personne*) beat; (*machine, voiture*) kaput (**b**) (*stupide*) dumb (**c**) (*de mauvaise qualité*) crappy, lousy

2 *nmf* (*personne stupide*) idiot, jerk

naseau, -x [nazo] *nm* nostril

nasillard, -e [nazijar, -ard] *adj* nasal; (*vieux disque*) tinny

nasse [nas] *nf* pot

natal, -e, -als, -ales [natal] *adj* native; **sa maison natale** the house where he/she was born

nataliste [natalist] *adj* **politique n.** pro-birth policy

natalité [natalite] *nf* (**taux de**) **n.** birth rate

natation [natasjɔ̃] *nf* swimming; **faire de la n.** to swim; **n. synchronisée** synchronized swimming

natif, -ive [natif, -iv] **1** *adj* native; **être n. de** to be a native of

2 *nm,f* native

nation [nasjɔ̃] *nf* nation; **les Nations unies** the United Nations

national, -e, -aux, -ales [nasjɔnal, -o] **1** *adj* national
  2 *nmpl* **nationaux** nationals
  3 *nf* **nationale** *(route)* ≃ highway

nationalisation [nasjɔnalizasjɔ̃] *nf* nationalization

nationaliser [nasjɔnalize] *vt* to nationalize

nationalisme [nasjɔnalism] *nm* nationalism

nationaliste [nasjɔnalist] *adj & nmf* nationalist

nationalité [nasjɔnalite] *nf* nationality; **être de n. française** to be a French national

national-socialisme [nasjɔnalsɔsjalism] *nm* Hist National Socialism

nativité [nativite] *nf (Noël, peinture)* Nativity

natte [nat] *nf* **(a)** *(de cheveux)* braid **(b)** *(de paille)* mat

natter [nate] *vt (cheveux, paille)* to braid

naturalisation [natyralizasjɔ̃] *nf* naturalization

naturaliser [natyralize] *vt* to naturalize; **se faire n.** to become naturalized; **il s'est fait n. français** he was granted French citizenship

naturalisme [natyralism] *nm* naturalism

nature [natyr] **1** *nf* **(a)** *(univers)* nature; **contre n.** unnatural; **plus grand que n.** larger than life; **laisser faire la n.** to let nature take its course; *Fam* **elle n'est pas gâtée par la n.** nature hasn't been kind to her **(b)** *(campagne)* country; **en pleine n.** in the middle of the country; *Fig* **disparaître dans la n.** to vanish into thin air **(c)** *(caractère)* nature; **être timide de** *ou* **par n.** to be shy by nature; **être de n. à faire qch** to be likely to do sth; **chez elle, c'est une seconde n.** it's second nature to her; *Fam* **c'est une petite n.** he's a bit fragile **(d)** **payer en n.** to pay in kind **(e)** **n. morte** still life
  2 *adj inv* **(a)** *(omelette)* plain; *(yaourt)* natural; **thé n.** tea without milk **(b)** *Fam (personne)* natural

naturel, -elle [natyrɛl] **1** *adj* natural; *(besoin)* bodily; **mort naturelle** death from natural causes; **mais c'est tout n.** don't mention it
  2 *nm* **(a)** *(caractère)* nature; **être d'un n. peureux** to be timid by nature; *Prov* **chassez le n., il revient au galop** what's bred in the bone will come out in the flesh **(b)** *(simplicité)* naturalness; **avec (beaucoup de) n.** (very) naturally **(c)** **thon au n.** tuna in brine

naturellement [natyrɛlmɑ̃] *adv* naturally

naturisme [natyrism] *nm* naturism

naturiste [natyrist] *adj & nmf* naturist

naufrage [nofraʒ] *nm* (ship)wreck; *Fig (d'entreprise)* failure; **faire n.** *(bateau)* to be wrecked; *(marin)* to be shipwrecked; *Fig (entreprise)* to founder

naufragé, -e [nofraʒe] **1** *adj (bateau)* wrecked; *(marin)* shipwrecked
  2 *nm,f* shipwrecked person

nauséabond, -e [nozeabɔ̃, -ɔ̃d] *adj (odeur)* nauseating; *(personne, pièce)* foul-smelling; *Fig (thèses)* sickening

nausée [noze] *nf* **(a)** *(envie de vomir)* nausea, sickness; **avoir la n., avoir des nausées** to feel nauseous **(b)** *Fig* disgust; **ça me donne la n.** it makes me sick

nauséeux, -euse [nozeø, -øz] *adj* **se sentir n.** to feel sick *or* nauseous

nautique [notik] *adj* nautical

nautisme [notism] *nm* water sports

naval, -e, -als, -ales [naval] *adj* naval

navet [navɛ] *nm* turnip; *Fam* **c'est un n.** it's a load of trash; *(film)* it's a turkey

navette [navɛt] *nf* **(a)** *(véhicule)* shuttle; **faire la n. entre deux endroits/services** to shuttle back and forth between two places/departments; **n. gratuite** courtesy bus **(b)** *(fusée)* **n. (spatiale)** (space) shuttle

navetteur, -euse [navɛtœr, -øz] *nm,f Belg* commuter

navigable [navigabl] *adj* navigable

navigant, -e [navigɑ̃, -ɑ̃t] *adj voir* **personnel**

navigateur, -trice [navigatœr, -tris] **1** *nm,f (marin)* navigator; **n. solitaire** lone yachtsman
  2 *nm Ordinat* browser

navigation [navigasjɔ̃] *nf* navigation; **après un mois de n.** after a month at sea; *Ordinat* **n. sur l'Internet** Internet surfing, browsing the Web *or* the Internet

naviguer [navige] *vi* to sail **(vers** to); **n. sur l'Internet** to surf the Net, to browse the Web *or* the Internet

navire [navir] *nm* ship; **n.-école** training ship; **n. de guerre** warship

navrant, -e [navrɑ̃, -ɑ̃t] *adj* appalling; **un film n. de bêtise** an incredibly dumb movie

navré, -e [navre] *adj (personne, expression, ton)* distressed; **être n. (de qch)** to be terribly sorry (about sth)

navrer [navre] *vt* to appall

naze [naz] = **nase**

nazi, -e [nazi] *adj & nm,f Hist* Nazi

nazisme [nazism] *nm Hist* Nazism

NB *(abrév* **nota bene**) NB

NDLR *(abrév* **note de la rédaction**) Ed.

NdT *(abrév* **note du traducteur**) translator's note

ne [nə] *adv* **(a)** *voir* **aucun, guère, jamais, pas²**, **personne, plus, que⁴, rien** **(b)** *(utilisé seul)* **je n'ai que faire de vos conseils** I have no need of your advice; **elle est plus vigoureuse qu'elle n'y paraît** she's stronger than she looks; **qui ne connaît cette œuvre?** who doesn't know this work?

né, -e [ne] **1** *pp voir* **naître**
  2 *adj* born; **Mme Martin, née Dupond** Mrs. Martin, née Dupond; **né de parents anglais/inconnus** of English/unknown parentage; **être bien né** to be of noble birth; *Fig* **être né coiffé** to be born with a silver spoon in one's mouth; **c'est un conteur né** he's a born storyteller

néanmoins [neɑ̃mwɛ̃] *adv* nevertheless

néant [neɑ̃] *nm* **(a)** *(ce qui n'existe pas)* nothingness; **réduire qch à n.** to reduce sth to nothing **(b)** *(sur formulaire)* none

nébuleux, -euse [nebylø, -øz] **1** *adj aussi Fig* hazy
  2 *nf* **nébuleuse** *Astron* nebula

nécessaire [nesesɛr] **1** *adj* necessary (**à** for); **n. pour faire qch** necessary to do sth; **il est n. que vous y alliez** you must go; **elles n'ont pas jugé n. de me le dire** they didn't think it necessary to tell me
  2 *nm* **le n.** the necessities; **n'emportez que le strict n.** just take the basic essentials; **faire le n.** to do what's necessary; **n. à chaussures** shoe-cleaning kit; **n. de couture** sewing kit; **n. de toilette** toilet bag; **n. de voyage** overnight bag

nécessairement [nesesɛrmɑ̃] *adv* necessarily

nécessité [nesesite] *nf* necessity; **être dans la n. de faire qch** to have no choice but to do sth; **quelle n. y avait-il de le faire?** what need was there to do it?; **faire de n. vertu** to make a virtue out of necessity; **produits de première n.** basic essentials; *Prov* **n. fait loi** needs must

nécessiter [nesesite] *vt* to require, to necessitate

nécessiteux, -euse [nesesitø, -øz] **1** *adj* needy
  2 *nm,f* person in need; **les n.** the needy

nec plus ultra [nɛkplyzyltra] *nm inv* **le n.** the best there is

nécrologie [nekrɔlɔʒi] *nf (notice)* obituary; *(liste)* obituary column

nécrologique [nekrɔlɔʒik] *adj voir* **rubrique**

nécropole [nekrɔpɔl] *nf* necropolis

nécrose [nekroz] *nf* necrosis

nécroser [nekroze] **1** *vt* to necrose
  2 se nécroser *vpr* to necrose

nectar [nɛktar] *nm* nectar

nectarine [nɛktarin] *nf* nectarine

néerlandais, -e [neɛrlɑ̃dɛ, -ɛz] **1** *adj* Dutch
2 *nm (langue)* Dutch
3 *nm, f* **N.** Dutchman; **Néerlandaise** Dutchwoman; **les N.** the Dutch

nef [nɛf] *nf (d'église)* **n. (centrale)** nave; **n. latérale** aisle

néfaste [nefast] *adj* harmful

nèfle [nɛfl] *nf* medlar; *Fam* **des nèfles!** no way!

négatif, -ive [negatif, -iv] **1** *adj* negative
2 *nm* Phot negative
3 négative *nf* **dans la n.** if not; **répondre par la n.** to give a negative answer, to answer in the negative

négation [negasjɔ̃] *nf* **(a)** *(fait de nier)* negation **(b)** *Gram* negative

négationnisme [negasjɔnism] *nm* revisionism

négationniste [negasjɔnist] *adj & nmf* revisionist

négativement [negativmɑ̃] *adv (réagir)* negatively; *(répondre)* in the negative

négligé, -e [negliʒe] **1** *adj* **(a)** *(peu soigné)* slovenly **(b)** *(délaissé)* neglected
2 *nm (vêtement)* negligée, negligee

négligeable [negliʒabl] *adj* negligible; **un avantage non n.** a not inconsiderable advantage; **une quantité non n. de** a significant quantity of

négligemment [negliʒamɑ̃] *adv* **(a)** *(habillé)* carelessly **(b)** *(répondre, lire)* casually

négligence [negliʒɑ̃s] *nf* **(a)** *(manque de soin)* carelessness, negligence; *(abandon)* neglect; **avec n.** carelessly **(b)** *(acte négligent)* act of carelessness; *(oubli)* oversight; **par n.** through carelessness

négligent, -e [negliʒɑ̃, -ɑ̃t] *adj* careless, negligent

négliger [45] [negliʒe] **1** *vt* **(a)** *(délaisser)* to neglect **(b)** *(omettre)* to disregard; **n. de faire qch** to neglect to do sth
2 se négliger *vpr* to neglect oneself

négoce [negɔs] *nm* trade

négociable [negɔsjabl] *adj* negotiable

négociant, -e [negɔsjɑ̃, -ɑ̃t] *nm, f* merchant, dealer

négociation [negɔsjasjɔ̃] *nf* negotiation; **entamer des négociations sur qch** to enter into negotiations on sth; **être en n. avec qn** to be in negotiation with sb

négocier [66] [negɔsje] **1** *vt* **(a)** *(prêt, salaire, paix)* to negotiate; **prix à n.** price negotiable **(b)** *(virage)* to negotiate
2 *vi (discuter)* to negotiate (**avec** with)

nègre [nɛgr] **1** *nm* **(a)** *Injurieux* Negro **(b)** *Fig (écrivain)* ghost writer; **être le n. de qn** to ghost for sb
2 *adj* **(a)** **l'art n.** *Injurieux (personne)* Negro art **(b)** *Injurieux (personne)* Negro

négresse [negrɛs] *nf Injurieux* Negress

neige [nɛʒ] *nf* **(a)** *(flocons)* snow; *Can* **banc de n.** snow bank; **être bloqué par la n.** to be snowbound; **aller à la n.** to go on a skiing vacation; **fondre comme n. au soleil** to melt away; **être blanc comme n.** to be as white as snow; *Fig* to be as pure as the driven snow; **n. artificielle** *ou Can* **fabriquée** artificial snow; **n. carbonique** dry ice; **neiges éternelles** perpetual snow; **n. fondue** *(qui tombe)* sleet; *(par terre)* slush **(b)** *très Fam (cocaïne)* snow

neiger [45] [neʒe] *v impersonnel* to snow

neigeux, -euse [nɛʒø, -øz] *adj (temps, blanc)* snowy; *(pic, pente)* snow-covered

nem [nɛm] *nm* spring roll

néné [nene] *nm Fam* tit, boob

nénette [nenɛt] *nf Fam* **(a)** *(jeune fille)* chick **(b)** *(petite amie)* girl **(c)** *(tête)* **se casser la n.** to rack one's brains

nénuphar [nenyfar] *nm* water lily

néo- [neo] *préf* neo-

néo-calédonien, -enne *(mpl* **néo-calédoniens,** *fpl* **néo-calédoniennes)** [neokaledɔnjɛ̃, -ɛn] **1** *adj* New Caledonian
2 *nm, f* **N., Néo-Calédonienne** New Caledonian

néoclassique [neoklasik] *adj* neoclassical

néocolonialisme [neokɔlɔnjalism] *nm* neocolonialism

néolithique [neolitik] *Géol* **1** *adj* Neolithic
2 *nm* **le N.** the Neolithic period

néologisme [neɔlɔʒism] *nm* neologism

néon [neɔ̃] *nm (gaz)* neon; *(tube)* neon tube; *(enseigne)* neon sign

néonazi, -e [neonazi] *adj & nm, f* neo-Nazi

néonazisme [neonazism] *nm* neo-Nazism

néophyte [neɔfit] *nmf (nouvel adepte)* novice

néo-zélandais, -e *(mpl* **néo-zélandais,** *fpl* **néo-zélandaises)** [neozelɑ̃dɛ, -ɛz] **1** *adj* New Zealand
2 *nm, f* **N., Néo-Zélandaise** New Zealander

Népal [nepal] *nm* **le N.** Nepal

népalais, -e [nepalɛ, -ɛz] **1** *adj* Nepalese
2 *nm (langue)* Nepali
3 *nm, f* **N., Népalaise** Nepalese; **les N.** the Nepalese

néphrétique [nefretik] *adj voir* **colique**

népotisme [nepɔtism] *nm* nepotism

Neptune [nɛptyn] *npr (dieu, planète)* Neptune

nerf [nɛr] *nm* **(a)** *(optique, spinal)* nerve; **viande pleine de nerfs** meat full of gristle; **avoir les nerfs solides** to have strong nerves; **être malade des nerfs** to suffer from nerves; **être sur les nerfs** to live on one's nerves; **être à bout de nerfs** to be at the end of one's tether; **passer ses nerfs sur qn/qch** to take it out on sb/sth; *Fam* **avoir les nerfs en pelote** *ou* **en boule** to be all on edge; *Fam* **porter** *ou* **taper** *ou Can* **tomber sur les nerfs à qn** to get on sb's nerves; *Fam* **c'est un paquet** *ou* **une boule de nerfs** he's a bundle of nerves **(b)** *(force)* **un peu de n.!, du n.!** come on, go for it!

nerveusement [nɛrvøzmɑ̃] *adv* nervously

nerveux, -euse [nɛrvø, -øz] **1** *adj* **(a)** *(système, maladie)* nervous **(b)** *(émotif) (personne, rire, toux)* nervous **(c)** *(dynamique) (personne, style)* dynamic; **une conduite nerveuse** a jerky way of driving **(d)** *(corps, main)* sinewy; *(viande)* stringy
2 *nm, f* nervous person

nervosité [nɛrvozite] *nf (excitation)* nervousness; *(irritabilité)* irritability

nervure [nɛrvyr] *nf* **(a)** *(de feuille, d'aile d'insecte)* vein **(b)** *(de voûte)* rib

n'est-ce pas [nɛspɑ] *adv* **tu viendras, n.?** you'll come, won't you?; **tu l'as, n.?** you have it, don't you?; **n. qu'elle est mignonne?** she's cute, isn't she?; **le problème, n., c'est qu'il est déjà tard** the problem is that it's already late, don't you think?

Net [nɛt] *nm Ordinat* **le N.** the Net

net, nette [nɛt] **1** *adj* **(a)** *(propre)* clean; *Fig (conscience)* clear; **faire place nette** to clear everything out **(b)** *(précis) (contour)* sharp; *(différence, souvenir)* clear; *(écriture)* neat; *(cassure)* clean; **il fait plus froid, c'est très n.** it's noticeably colder **(c)** *(prix, salaire, profit)* net; **n. d'impôt** net of tax **(d)** *Fam* **il n'est pas n.** *(fou)* he's not all there; *(louche)* there's something fishy about him
2 *adv* **(a)** *(brutalement)* **refuser (tout) n.** to refuse point-blank; **s'arrêter n.** to stop dead; **se casser n.** to break clean off; **tué n.** killed outright **(b)** *Com* **100 euros n.** 100 euros net; **n. à payer** net payable

netiquette [nɛtikɛt] *nf Ordinat* netiquette

nettement [nɛtmɑ̃] *adv* **(a)** *(avec précision)* clearly **(b)** *(incontestablement)* distinctly **(c)** *(beaucoup)* much; **il va n. mieux** he's much better; **il est n. moins bon qu'elle** he's not nearly as good as her

netteté [nɛtte] *nf* **(a)** *(propreté)* cleanness **(b)** *(précision) (de cassure)* cleanness **(c)** *(clarté) (de vision, d'objet)* distinctness; *(d'image)* sharpness; *(de refus)* flatness

nettoiement [nɛtwamɑ̃] *nm* cleaning; **service du n.** sanitation service

nettoyage [nɛtwajaʒ] *nm* cleaning; **faire du n.** to do the cleaning; **faire le n. par le vide** to throw everything out;

grand **n. de printemps** spring cleaning; **n. à sec** dry-cleaning

nettoyant, -e [nɛtwajɑ̃, -ɑ̃t] **1** *adj* cleaning
2 *nm* cleaning product

nettoyer [32] [nɛtwaje] **1** *vt* (**a**) *(rendre propre)* to clean; **n. à sec** to dry-clean (**b**) *Fam (sujet: cambrioleur) (maison)* to clean out; **se faire n. au jeu** to be cleaned out gambling
2 se nettoyer *vpr* (**a**) **se n. les oreilles/les mains** to clean one's ears/hands (**b**) **le four se nettoie automatiquement** the oven is self-cleaning

neuf¹ [nœf] *adj & nm inv* nine; *voir aussi* **trois**

neuf², neuve [nœf, nœv] **1** *adj* new; **tout n.** brand new; **comme n.** as good as new; **quoi de n.?** what's new?
2 *nm* **habillé de n.** wearing new clothes; **acheter du n.** *(dans l'immobilier)* to buy new; **remettre qch à n.** to make sth as good as new; *(machine)* to recondition sth

neurasthénie [nørasteni] *nf* depression

neurasthénique [nørastenik] *adj & nmf* depressive

neurochirurgie [nøroʃiryrʒi] *nf* neurosurgery

neurochirurgien, -enne [nøroʃiryrʒjɛ̃, -ɛn] *nm,f* neurosurgeon

neuroleptique [nørolɛptik] *adj & nm* neuroleptic

neurologie [nørolɔʒi] *nf* neurology

neurologue [nørolɔg] *nmf* neurologist

neurone [nøron, nøron] *nm* neuron

neutraliser [nøtralize] **1** *vt* to neutralize
2 se neutraliser *vpr* to neutralize each other

neutralité [nøtralite] *nf* neutrality; **sortir de sa n.** to abandon one's neutral position

neutre [nøtr] **1** *adj* (**a**) *(ni masculin ni féminin)* neuter (**b**) *(impartial)* neutral (**c**) *(ton de voix, couleur)* neutral (**d**) *Chim & Él* neutral
2 *nm* (**a**) *Gram* neuter (**b**) *Can Aut* neutral; **se mettre sur le n.** to go into neutral

neutron [nøtrɔ̃] *nm* neutron

neuvième [nœvjɛm] *nmf, nm & adj* ninth; *voir aussi* **cinquième**

névé [neve] *nm* névé, firn

neveu, -x [nəvø] *nm* nephew; *Fam* **un peu, mon n.!** you bet!, sure thing!

névralgie [nevralʒi] *nf* neuralgia; **avoir des névralgies** to suffer from neuralgia

névralgique [nevralʒik] *adj* neuralgic

névrose [nevroz] *nf* neurosis; **n. obsessionnelle** obsessive-compulsive disorder; **n. post-traumatique** post-traumatic stress disorder

névrosé, -e [nevroze] *adj & nm,f* neurotic

New York [nujɔrk] *n* New York

new-yorkais, -e *(mpl* **new-yorkais,** *fpl* **new-yorkaises)** [njujɔrkɛ, -ɛz] **1** *adj* of New York
2 *nm,f* **N., New-Yorkaise** New Yorker

nez [ne] *nm* (**a**) *(organe)* nose; **n. en trompette** turned-up nose; **parler du n.** to speak through one's nose; **sentir qch à plein n.** to smell strongly of sth; **rire au n. de qn** to laugh in sb's face; **faire qch au n. et à la barbe de qn** to do sth right under sb's nose; **fermer** *ou* **claquer la porte au n. de qn** to shut the door in sb's face; **se trouver n. à n. avec qn** to find oneself face to face with sb; **avoir le n. dans son journal** to have one's nose in one's newspaper; **avoir le n. en l'air** to be looking up in the air; *Fig (rêvasser)* to have one's head in the clouds; *Fig* **mener qn par le bout du n.** to lead sb by the nose; *Fam* **fourrer** *ou* **mettre son n. dans les affaires de qn** to stick one's nose into sb's affairs; *Fam* **avoir un verre** *ou* **un coup dans le n.** to have had one too many; **je n'ai pas mis le n. dehors de toute la journée** I didn't set foot outside all day; **tu ne vois pas plus loin que le bout de ton n.** you can't see further than the end of your nose; *Fam* **elle nous**

a dans le n. she can't stand us; **ça lui pend au n.** she's got it coming to her; **ça se voit comme le n. au milieu de la figure** it's as plain as the nose on your face; **où est-il? – il est sous ton n.** *ou* **tu as le n. dessus** where is it? – it's under your nose
(**b**) *(odorat)* sense of smell; **avoir le n. fin** to have a good nose; *Fig* **avoir du n.** to be shrewd
(**c**) *(de bateau, d'avion)* nose
(**d**) *(parfumeur)* nose

ni [ni] *conj* **n... ni...** neither... nor...; **ni Pierre ni Paul ne sont venus** neither Pierre nor Paul came; **sans argent ni bagages** without money or luggage; **il est parti sans manger ni boire** he left without eating or drinking; **ni l'un ni l'autre** neither (of them); **ni plus ni moins** neither more nor less

niais, -e [njɛ, njɛz] **1** *adj* silly
2 *nm,f* fool

niaisage [njɛzaʒ] *nm Can* idleness

niaisement [njɛzmɑ̃] *adv* foolishly

niaiser [njɛze] *Can* **1** *vt* **n. qn** *(faire tourner en bourrique)* to drive sb crazy; *(se moquer de)* to laugh at sb; *(raconter des histoires à)* to pull sb's leg
2 *vi (ne rien faire)* to hang around doing nothing

niaiserie [njɛzri] *nf* (**a**) *(caractère stupide)* silliness (**b**) *(acte, remarque)* silly thing

niaiseux, -euse [njɛzø, -øz] *Can Fam* **1** *adj* silly
2 *nm,f* fool

Nicaragua [nikaragwa] *nm* **le N.** Nicaragua

nicaraguayen, -enne [nikaragwajɛ̃, -ɛn] **1** *adj* Nicaraguan
2 *nm,f* **N., Nicaraguayenne** Nicaraguan

niche [niʃ] *nf* (**a**) *(renfoncement)* niche, recess (**b**) *(de chien)* doghouse

nichée [niʃe] *nf (d'oisillons)* brood; *(de souris, de chiots)* litter

nicher [niʃe] **1** *vi (oiseau)* to nest (**dans** in)
2 *vt* **n. sa tête au creux de l'épaule de qn** to nestle one's head against sb's shoulder
3 se nicher *vpr* (**a**) *(oiseau)* to nest (**b**) *Fam (se cacher)* **où est-elle allée se n.?** where's she hiding (herself)?

nichon [niʃɔ̃] *nm Fam* boob, tit

nickel [nikɛl] **1** *nm* nickel
2 *adj inv Fam* (**a**) *(propre)* spotlessly clean (**b**) *(parfait)* perfect, just right; **ça s'est super bien passé, l'organisation et l'ambiance étaient n.!** it went really well, it was brilliantly organized and the atmosphere was perfect!

nicotine [nikɔtin] *nf* nicotine

nid [ni] *nm aussi Fig* nest; *Fig* **n. à poussière** dust trap; *Prov* **petit à petit, l'oiseau fait son n.** slow and steady wins the race

nid-de-poule *(pl* **nids-de-poule**) [nidpul] *nm* pothole

nièce [njɛs] *nf* niece

nier [66] [nje] **1** *vt* to deny; **je nie l'avoir vue** I deny having seen her; **on ne peut pas n. que...** there's no denying that...; **n. l'évidence** to deny the obvious
2 *vi (accusé)* to deny the charge

niet [njɛt] *exclam Fam* no way!, not a chance!

nigaud, -e [nigo, -od] *nm,f* numbskull; **gros n.!** you big numbskull!

Niger [niʒɛr] *nm* **le N.** *(pays)* Niger; *(fleuve)* the Niger

Nigeria [niʒerja] *nm* **le N.** Nigeria

nigérian, -e [niʒerjɑ̃, -an] **1** *adj* Nigerian
2 *nm,f* **N., Nigériane** Nigerian

nigérien, -enne [niʒerjɛ̃, -ɛn] **1** *adj* Nigerien
2 *nm,f* **N., Nigérienne** Nigerien

nihilisme [niilism] *nm* nihilism

nihiliste [niilist] **1** *adj* nihilistic
2 *nmf* nihilist

Nil [nil] *nm* **le N.** the Nile

n'importe [nɛ̃pɔrt] *voir* **importer²**

NIP [nip] *nm Can Fin (abrév* **numéro d'identification per-sonnelle**) ≃ PIN (number)

nipper [nipe] *Fam* **1** *vt* to dress; **bien nippé** all dressed up

2 se nipper *vpr* to dress

nippes [nip] *nfpl Fam (vêtements)* gear, togs

nippon, -onne *ou* **-one** [nipɔ̃, -ɔn] **1** *adj* Japanese

2 *nm,f* **N., Nipponne** *ou* **Nippone** Japanese; **les Nippons** the Japanese

nique [nik] *nf Fam* **faire la n. à qn** to thumb one's nose at sb

niquer [nike] *vt* **(a)** *très Fam (abîmer)* to bust **(b)** *Vulg (sexuellement)* to screw, to fuck **(c)** *très Fam (escroquer)* **se faire n.** to get screwed

nitrate [nitrat] *nm* nitrate

nitreux, -euse [nitrø, -øz] *adj* nitrous

nitrique [nitrik] *adj* nitric

nitroglycérine [nitrogliserin] *nf* nitroglycerine

niveau, -x [nivo] *nm* **(a)** *(hauteur, étage)* level; **n. de l'eau/de la mer** water/sea level; **au n. de la mer** at sea level; **au n. du carrefour, vous tournez à droite** when you come to the intersection, turn right; **au n. régional/local** at regional/local level; *Fam* **au n. sentimental** as far as one's love life is concerned; *aussi Fig* **se mettre au n. de qn** to put oneself on sb's level; **l'eau nous arrivait au n. de la taille** the water came up to our waists **(b)** *(degré)* level; *Scol* standard; **avoir le n. (requis), être au n.** to be up to standard; **ne pas avoir le n. pour passer un concours** not to be of a high enough standard to take a competitive examination; **elle a un très bon n. en physique** her physics is of a very high standard; **ils sont d'un n. social différent** they are from different social backgrounds; *Ordinat* **n. d'accès** *(dans un réseau)* access level; *Ordinat* **n. de gris** gray scale; **n. de langue** register; **n. de vie** standard of living

niveler [9] [nivle] *vt* **(a)** *(sol)* to level **(b)** *(fortunes)* to even out

nivellement [nivɛlmã] *nm (de terrain, des classes sociales)* leveling; **n. par le bas** leveling down

Nobel [nɔbɛl] *nm* **le N. de la paix** *(prix)* the Nobel peace prize; *(personne)* the winner of the Nobel peace prize

nobéliser [3] [nɔbelize] *vt (décerner un prix Nobel à)* to award the Nobel prize to

nobiliaire [nɔbiljɛr] *adj* **titre n.** title; **particule n.** nobiliary particle

noble [nɔbl] **1** *adj* noble; **le n. art** *(boxe)* the noble art

2 *nmf* nobleman, *f* noblewoman; **les nobles** the nobility

noblement [nɔbləmã] *adv* nobly

noblesse [nɔblɛs] *nf* nobility; **la haute et la petite n.** the nobility and the gentry; **n. oblige** noblesse oblige

noce [nɔs] *nf* **(a)** *(cérémonie du mariage)* wedding; *(ensemble des invités)* wedding party; **noces d'argent/d'or/de diamant** silver/golden/diamond wedding; **il l'a épousée en secondes noces** she's his second wife **(b)** *Fam* **faire la n.** to live it up **(c)** *Fam* **je n'étais pas à la n.** it was no picnic

noceur, -euse [nɔsœr, -øz] *nm,f Fam* party animal

nocif, -ive [nɔsif, -iv] *adj* harmful

nocivité [nɔsivite] *nf* harmfulness

noctambule [nɔktãbyl] *nmf* night owl

nocturne [nɔktyrn] **1** *adj (animal)* nocturnal; *(attaque, visite)* night; **évasion n.** escape by night

2 *nm (musique)* nocturne

3 *nf* **(a)** *(de magasin)* late-night opening **(b)** **match (disputé) en n.** evening game

nodal, -e, -aux, -ales [nɔdal, -o] *adj* nodal

nodule [nɔdyl] *nm Géol & Méd* nodule

Noé [noe] *n* Noah

Noël [nɔɛl] *nm* **(a)** *(fête)* Christmas; **à N.** at Christmas (time); **le jour de N.** Christmas Day; **arbre** *ou* **sapin de N.** Christmas tree; **joyeux N.!** Merry Christmas! **(b)** *(chanson)* **n.** (Christmas) carol **(c)** *(cadeau)* **(petit) n.** Christmas present

nœud [nø] *nm* **(a)** *(entrecroisement)* knot; **faire un n. (à qch)** to make *or* to tie a knot (in sth); **n. coulant** *(pour serrer)* slipknot; *(pour étrangler)* noose; **n. de vipères** nest of vipers **(b)** *(ornement)* bow; **n. de cravate** tie knot; **faire un n. de cravate** to knot a tie; **n. papillon,** *Fam* **n. pap** bow tie **(c)** *(de courbe) & Ordinat* node **(d)** *(sur bois)* knot **(e)** *Naut (vitesse)* knot; **filer** *ou* **faire 20 nœuds** to do *or* to make 20 knots **(f)** *Vulg (pénis)* cock, dick

noie *etc. voir* **noyer²**

noir, -e [nwar] **1** *adj* **(a)** *(couleur)* black; **la place était noire de monde** the square was swarming with people **(b)** *(très sombre)* dark; **il fait tout n.** it's pitch-black **(c)** *(sale)* black **(d)** *Fig (pensées, dessein, regard)* black; **être d'une humeur noire** to be in a black mood

2 *nm,f* **N.** Black (man); **Noire** Black (woman); **N. américain, Noire américaine** African-American

3 *nm* **(a)** *(couleur)* black; **en n. et blanc** *(film, photo)* black and white; **être en n.** to be dressed in black; **c'était écrit n. sur blanc** it was there in black and white **(b)** *(obscurité)* dark; **avoir peur du n.** to be afraid of the dark **(c)** *(salissure)* **avoir du n. sur le visage** to have a black mark on one's face **(d)** *(d'une cible)* bull's-eye **(e)** *(café)* **un (petit) n.** a (small) black coffee **(f)** *Fig* **voir tout en n.** to look on the dark side of everything **(g)** *Fam* **le travail au n.** moonlighting; **travailler au n.** to moonlight

4 *nf* **noire** *(note de musique)* quarter note

noirâtre [nwarɑtr] *adj* blackish

noirceur [nwarsœr] *nf* **(a)** *(couleur)* blackness; *Litt (d'un crime)* heinousness **(b)** *Can (obscurité)* dark, darkness; **dans la n.** in the dark *or* darkness; **avoir peur dans la n.** to be afraid of the dark

noircir [nwarsir] **1** *vt* to blacken; *Fig* **n. du papier** to write pages and pages; *Fig* **n. (la réputation de) qn** to blacken sb's reputation; *Fig* **n. le tableau** *ou* **la situation** to paint things blacker than they are

2 *vi* to turn *or* to go black

3 se noircir *vpr* **(a)** *(ciel)* to darken **(b)** **se n. le visage** to black one's face; *Théât* to black up

noise [nwaz] *nf* **chercher n.** *ou* **des noises à qn** to try to pick a quarrel with sb

noisetier [nwaztje] *nm (arbre)* hazel tree; *(bois)* hazel (wood)

noisette [nwazɛt] **1** *nf* **(a)** *(fruit)* hazelnut **(b)** *(petite quantité) (de beurre)* small knob; *(de gel)* small amount

2 *adj inv* **yeux n.** hazel eyes

noix [nwa] *nf* **(a)** *(fruit)* walnut; **n. de cajou** cashew nut; **n. de coco** coconut; **n. de pécan** pecan **(b)** *(petite quantité) (de beurre)* knob **(c)** **n. de veau** cushion of veal **(d)** *Fam* **à la n.** lousy

nom [nɔ̃] *nm* **(a)** *(de personne, de chose)* name; **un homme du n. de Pierre** a man by the name of Pierre; **n.... prénom...** *(sur formulaire)* surname... first name...; **vos n., prénoms et adresse** your full name and address; **porter le n. de sa mère** to be named for one's mother; **sous le n. de Leduc** under the name of Leduc; **se faire un n.** to make a name for oneself; **appeler les choses par leur n.** to call a spade a spade; **traiter qn de tous les noms** to call sb everything under the sun; **quelqu'un dont je tairai le n.** someone who shall remain nameless; **une impolitesse sans n.** unspeakable rudeness; **un grand n. de la musique** one of the great names in music; **faire une proposition au n. de qn** to make a proposal for sb *or* on behalf of sb; **au n. de la loi/de l'amitié** in the name of the law/of friendship; *Fam* **avoir un n. à coucher dehors** to have a totally unpronounceable name; **n. de baptême** Christian name; *Ordinat* **n. de champ** field name; *Ordinat* **n. de domaine** domain name; **n. d'emprunt** assumed name; **n. de famille** surname; *Ordinat* **n. de fichier** file name; **n. de jeune fille** maiden name; **n. à particule** aristocratic name *(with a nobiliary particle)*; **n.**

de plume nom de plume, pen name; *Fam* **n. à rallonges** *ou* **à tiroirs** long aristocratic name; **n. de scène** *ou* **de théâtre** stage name
  (b) *Gram* noun; **n. commun** common noun; **n. composé** compound (noun); **n. propre** proper noun
  (c) *Fam* **n. d'une pipe!, n. d'un chien!** hell!

nomade [nɔmad] **1** *adj* nomadic
  2 *nmf* nomad

nomadisme [nɔmadism] *nm* nomadism

nombre [nɔ̃br] *nm aussi Gram* number; **un grand/petit n. d'entre nous** many/a few of us; **le plus grand n.** the majority; **(bon) n. de** a good many; **supérieur en n.** superior in number(s); **nous sommes en n. suffisant** there are enough of us; **venir en n.** to come in large numbers; **ils sont au n. de huit** there are eight of them; **être au n.** *ou* **du n. de** to be among; **faire n.** to make up the numbers; *Phys* **n. atomique** atomic number; *Math* **n. décimal** decimal (number); *Math* **n. entier** whole number, integer; *Math* **n. premier** prime number

nombreux, -euse [nɔ̃brø, -øz] *adj* (*membres, objets*) numerous, many; (*famille, armée, groupe*) large; **nous sommes peu n.** there aren't many of us; **venir (très) n.** to come in (very) large numbers

nombril [nɔ̃bri, nɔ̃bril] *nm* navel; **une chemise ouverte jusqu'au n.** a shirt open to the waist; **il se prend pour le n. du monde** he thinks the whole world revolves around him; *Fig* **se regarder le n.** to contemplate one's navel; *Can* **ne pas avoir le n. sec** to be (still) wet behind the ears

nombrilisme [nɔ̃brilism] *nm* navel-gazing

nombriliste [nɔ̃brilist] *adj* self-absorbed

nomenclature [nɔmɑ̃klatyr] *nf* (*de termes techniques*) nomenclature; (*d'un dictionnaire*) word list

nominal, -e, -aux, -ales [nɔminal, -o] *adj* **(a)** (*prix, autorité*) *& Fin* nominal **(b)** (*par noms de famille*) **appel n.** roll call; **liste nominale** list of names **(c)** *Gram* noun

nominalement [nɔminalmɑ̃] *adv* **(a)** (*de nom seulement*) in name only **(b)** *Gram* (*employé*) as a noun

nominatif, -ive [nɔminatif, -iv] *adj* (*carte d'adhérent, billet*) nontransferable; *Fin* (*titre*) registered

nomination [nɔminasjɔ̃] *nf* **(a)** (*à un poste*) appointment (**à** to) **(b)** (*pour une remise de récompense*) nomination (**à** for)

nominativement [nɔminativmɑ̃] *adv* by name

nominé, -e [nɔmine] *adj* nominated (**à** for)

nommé, -e [nɔme] **1** *adj* (*personne, objet*) named
  2 *nm,f* **un n. Bertrand a appelé** someone called Bertrand rang

nommément [nɔmemɑ̃] *adv* **(a)** (*par son nom*) by name **(b)** (*spécialement*) especially, in particular

nommer [nɔme] **1** *vt* **(a)** (*donner un prénom à*) to name, to call **(b)** (*donner un nom à*) **on nomme aumôniers les prêtres attachés à un régiment** priests attached to a regiment are called chaplains **(c)** (*désigner*) to name; *Hum* **M. Boivin, pour ne pas le n.** without mentioning any names, Mr. Boivin **(d)** (*à un poste*) to appoint (**à** to); **être nommé à Lille** to be posted to Lille
  2 se nommer *vpr* **(a)** (*avoir pour nom*) to be called **(b)** (*s'identifier*) to give one's name

non [nɔ̃] **1** *adv* **(a)** (*en réponse, exprime la surprise, l'indignation*) no; **je pense que n.** I don't think so; **faire signe que n.** (*de la tête*) to shake one's head; **n. mais!** honestly! **(b)** (*n'est-ce pas?*) **c'est dégoûtant, n.?** it's disgusting, isn't it?; **il est pas mal, n.?** he's not bad-looking, is he? **(c)** (*pas*) not; **n. loin** not far; **qu'elle vienne ou n.** whether she comes or not; **elle veut déménager, lui n.** she wants to move but he doesn't; *Litt* **n. (pas) que je le craigne** not that I am afraid of him
  2 *nm inv* no

nonagénaire [nɔnaʒenɛr] *adj & nmf* nonagenarian

non-agression [nɔnagresjɔ̃] *nf voir* **pacte**

non-alcoolisé, -e [nɔnalkɔlize] *adj* non-alcoholic

non-aligné, -e [nɔnaliɲe] *adj Pol* non-aligned

nonante [nɔnɑ̃t] *adj & nm inv Belg & Suisse* ninety; *voir aussi* **trois**

non-assistance [nɔnasistɑ̃s] *nf Jur* **n. à personne en danger** = failure to assist a person in danger, for example at the scene of an accident

non-autorisé, -e [nɔnɔtɔrize] *adj Ordinat* (*nom de fichier*) illegal

non-belligérant, -e [nɔbeliʒerɑ̃, -ɑ̃t] *adj* non-belligerent

nonchalamment [nɔ̃ʃalamɑ̃] *adv* nonchalantly

nonchalance [nɔ̃ʃalɑ̃s] *nf* nonchalance; **avec n.** nonchalantly

nonchalant, -e [nɔ̃ʃalɑ̃, -ɑ̃t] *adj* nonchalant

non-conformisme [nɔ̃kɔ̃fɔrmism] *nm* non-conformism

non-conformiste [nɔ̃kɔ̃fɔrmist] *adj & nmf* non-conformist

non-conformité [nɔ̃kɔ̃fɔrmite] *nf* nonconformity

non-connecté, -e [nɔ̃kɔnɛkte] *adj Ordinat* off-line

non-dit [nɔ̃di] *nm* **le n.** what is unspoken; **un film riche en non-dits** a movie full of meaningful silences

non-formaté, -e [nɔ̃fɔrmate] *adj Ordinat* unformatted

non-fumeur, -euse [nɔ̃fymœr, -øz] **1** *adj* non-smoking
  2 *nm,f* non-smoker

non-ingérence [nɔnɛ̃ʒerɑ̃s] *nf* noninterference

non-initialisé, -e [nɔninisjalize] *adj Ordinat* uninitialized

non-initié, -e [nɔninisje] *nm,f* uninitiated person; **les non-initiés** the uninitiated

non-inscrit, -e [nɔnɛ̃skri, -it] *nm,f Pol* independent

non-intervention [nɔnɛ̃tɛrvɑ̃sjɔ̃] *nf* non-intervention

non-interventionniste [nɔnɛ̃tɛrvɑ̃sjɔnist] *adj* non-interventionist

non-lieu, -x [nɔ̃ljø] *nm Jur* **bénéficier d'un n.** to be discharged through lack of evidence

nonne [nɔn] *nf* nun

nono, -ote [nɔno, -ɔt] *nm,f Can Fam* idiot

non-paiement [nɔ̃pɛmɑ̃] *nm* non-payment

non-polluant, -e [nɔ̃pɔlɥɑ̃, -ɑ̃t] *adj* environmentally friendly

non-prolifération [nɔ̃prɔliferajɔ̃] *nf* nonproliferation

non-remboursable [nɔ̃rɑ̃bursabl] *adj* non-refundable

non-respect [nɔ̃rɛspɛ] *nm* (*d'une loi*) non-observance

non-retour [nɔ̃rətur] *nm* **point de n.** point of no return

non-salarié, -e [nɔ̃salarje] *nm,f* self-employed person

non-sens [nɔ̃sɑ̃s] *nm inv* **(a)** (*dans une traduction*) meaningless phrase **(b)** (*absurdité*) **un n.** a nonsense

non-stop [nɔnstɔp] *adj inv & adv Fam* non-stop

non-syndiqué, -e [nɔ̃sɛ̃dike] **1** *adj* non-union
  2 *nm,f* non-union worker

non-violence [nɔ̃vjɔlɑ̃s] *nf* non-violence

non-violent, -e [nɔ̃vjɔlɑ̃, -ɑ̃t] *adj* non-violent

non-voyant, -e (*mpl* **non-voyants**, *fpl* **non-voyantes**) [nɔ̃vwajɑ̃, -ɑ̃t] *nm,f* visually impaired person; **les non-voyants** the visually impaired

nord [nɔr] **1** *nm* north; **un vent du n.** a northerly *or* north wind; **le vent du n.** the north wind; **au n.** in the north; **n. de** (to the) north of; *Fig* **il ne perd pas le n.** he's keeping a cool head; **le grand N.** the Frozen North
  2 *adj inv* (*côte, face*) north; (*régions*) northern

nord-africain, -e (*mpl* **nord-africains**, *fpl* **nord-africaines**) [nɔrafrikɛ̃, -ɛn] **1** *adj* North African
  2 *nm,f* **N., Nord-Africaine** North African

nord-américain, -e (*mpl* **nord-américains**, *fpl* **nord-américaines**) [nɔramerikɛ̃, -ɛn] **1** *adj* North American
  2 *nm,f* **N., Nord-Américaine** North American

nord-coréen, -enne (*mpl* **nord-coréens**, *fpl* **nord-coréennes**) [nɔrkɔreɛ̃, -ɛn] **1** *adj* North Korean

     2 *nm,f* **N., Nord-Coréenne** North Korean

nord-est [nɔrɛst] *nm & adj inv* northeast

nordique [nɔrdik] **1** *adj* Nordic, Scandinavian

     2 *nmf* **N.** Scandinavian

nordiste [nɔrdist] *adj & nmf* Unionist

nord-nord-est [nɔrnɔrɛst] *nm & adj inv* north-northeast

nord-nord-ouest [nɔrnɔrwɛst] *nm & adj inv* north-north-west

nord-ouest [nɔrwɛst] *nm & adj inv* northwest

nord-vietnamien, -enne (*mpl* **nord-vietnamiens**, *fpl* **nord-vietnamiennes**) [nɔrvjɛtnamjɛ̃, -ɛn] **1** *adj* North Vietnamese

     2 *nm,f* **N., Nord-Vietnamienne** North Vietnamese

noria [nɔrja] *nf* noria

normal, -e, -aux, -ales [nɔrmal, -o] **1** *adj* (**a**) *(dans la norme, naturel)* normal; **c'est tout à fait n. que la jeunesse se rebelle** it's normal *or* it's only natural for young people to rebel; **ce n'est pas n.** (**que** + *subjunctive*) it's not right (that); **en temps n.** in normal circumstances (**b**) *(moyen) (poids, taille)* standard

     2 *nf* **normale** (**a**) **la normale** normal, the norm; **au-dessus/au-dessous de la normale** above/below average; **température au-dessous des normales saisonnières** temperature below the seasonal average (**b**) *Fam Univ* **Normale Sup'** = university-level college preparing students for senior posts in teaching

normalement [nɔrmalmɑ̃] *adv* normally

normalien, -enne [nɔrmaljɛ̃, -ɛn] *nm,f Univ* = student or former student of the "École normale supérieure"

normalisation [nɔrmalizasjɔ̃] *nf* (**a**) *(des relations diplomatiques)* normalization (**b**) *Ind* standardization

normaliser [nɔrmalize] *vt* (**a**) *(relations diplomatiques)* to normalize (**b**) *Ind* to standardize

normalité [nɔrmalite] *nf* normality

normand, -e [nɔrmɑ̃, -ɑ̃d] *aussi Hist* **1** *adj* Norman

     2 *nm,f* **N., Normande** Norman

Normandie [nɔrmɑ̃di] *nf* **la N.** Normandy

norme [nɔrm] *nf* (**a**) *(règle)* norm; **dans la n.** within the norm (**b**) *Ind & Com* standard

noroît [nɔrwa] *nm* northwester

Norvège [nɔrvɛʒ] *nf* **la N.** Norway

norvégien, -enne [nɔrveʒjɛ̃, -ɛn] **1** *adj* Norwegian

     2 *nm* *(langue)* Norwegian

     3 *nm,f* **N., Norvégienne** Norwegian

nos [no] *voir* **notre**

nostalgie [nɔstalʒi] *nf* nostalgia; *(mal du pays)* homesickness; **avoir la n. de qch** to feel nostalgic for sth; **avoir la n. du pays** to be homesick

nostalgique [nɔstalʒik] *adj* nostalgic

nota bene [nɔtabene] *nm inv* nota bene

notable [nɔtabl] *adj & nm* notable

notablement [nɔtabləmɑ̃] *adv* notably

notaire [nɔtɛr] *nm* notary (public)

notamment [nɔtamɑ̃] *adv* notably

notarié, -e [nɔtarje] *adj Jur* **acte n.** notarized deed

notation [nɔtasjɔ̃] *nf* (**a**) *(d'un travail scolaire)* grading (**b**) *(par des symboles)* notation; *Ordinat* **n. hexadécimale** hex *or* hexadecimal code

note [nɔt] *nf* (**a**) *(annotation, communication écrite)* note; **prendre des notes** to take (down) notes; **prendre bonne n. de qch** to take due note of sth; *Typ & Ordinat* **n. de** *ou* **en bas de page** footnote; **n. de service** memo (**b**) *(appréciation)* grade (**c**) *Mus* note (**d**) *(facture)* bill; *(dans un hôtel, un restaurant)* check; **n. de frais** expenses; **n. de téléphone** phone bill (**e**) *(nuance)* touch, note

notebook [nɔtbuk] *nm Ordinat* notebook

noter [nɔte] *vt* (**a**) *(mettre par écrit)* to note down, to make a note of (**b**) *(remarquer)* to note; **note bien que...** mind you,...; *Fig* **c'est noté, je note** got it (**c**) *(travail scolaire, élève)* to grade

notice [nɔtis] *nf* *(mode d'emploi)* instructions; *(d'un médicament)* directions

notification [nɔtifikasjɔ̃] *nf Jur* notification

notifier [66] [nɔtifje] *vt* **n. qch à qn** to notify sb of sth

notion [nosjɔ̃] *nf* (**a**) *(concept)* notion, concept; **perdre la n. du temps/de la réalité** to lose track of time/all sense of reality (**b**) **notions** *(connaissances sommaires)* basics; **avoir des notions de qch** to know the basics of sth

notoire [nɔtwar] *adj* *(fait)* well-known; *(criminel, mesquinerie)* notorious

notoriété [nɔtɔrjete] *nf* *(d'une personne)* fame; **il est de n. publique que...** it's common knowledge that...

notre, nos [nɔtr, no] *adj possessif* our; **n. chien** *(il y a un chien)* our dog; *(chacun a son chien)* our dogs; **nos enfants** our children; **n. père et n. mère** our mother and father; **un de nos amis** one of our friends, a friend of ours; *Fam* **nous avons n. vendredi** we have Friday off (work)

nôtre [notr] **1** *pron possessif* **le n., la n., les nôtres** ours; *(en insistant)* **our own**; **nous te prêtons le n.** you can borrow ours; **nous n'en avons pas besoin, nous avons le n.** we don't need it, we have our own; *Fam* **à la n.!** (here's) to us!

     2 *nm* **il faut y mettre du n.** we have to do our share

     3 *nmpl* **les nôtres** *(notre famille)* our family; **serez-vous des nôtres ce soir?** will you be joining us this evening?

nouba [nuba] *nf Fam* party; **faire la n.** to party

noué, -e [nwe] *adj* **avoir l'estomac n.** to have a knot in one's stomach; **avoir la gorge nouée** to have a lump in one's throat

nouer [nwe] **1** *vt* (**a**) *(ficelle, ruban, lacets)* to tie; *(cheveux)* to tie up; *(cravate)* to knot (**b**) *(relations)* to establish (**avec** with)

     2 se nouer *vpr* (**a**) *(amitié)* to be formed (**b**) *(intrigue)* to take shape

noueux, -euse [nwø, -øz] *adj* *(bois)* knotty; *(tronc d'arbre, mains, doigts)* gnarled

nougat [nuga] *nm* nougat

nougatine [nugatin] *nf* nougatine

nouille [nuj] **1** *nf* (**a**) *Culin* **nouilles** noodles; *(pâtes en général)* pasta (**b**) *Fam (personne) (molle)* drip; *(niaise)* dimwit

     2 *adj Fam (niais)* dumb, dopey

nounou [nunu] *nf* *(langage enfantin)* nanny

nounours [nunurs] *nm* *(langage enfantin)* teddy bear

nourri, -e [nuri] *adj* *(applaudissements)* prolonged; *(feu)* heavy

nourrice [nuris] *nf* (**a**) *(assistante maternelle)* **n. agréée** registered nurse *or* nursemaid (**b**) *Vieilli (qui allaite)* wet nurse

nourricier, -ère [nurisje, -ɛr] *adj Litt (terre)* nourishing

nourrir [nurir] **1** *vt* (**a**) *(personnes, animaux)* to feed (**de** with); **le lait nourrit** milk is nourishing (**b**) *(peau, visage, cuir)* to nourish; *(feu)* to feed (**c**) *Litt (entretenir) (idées de vengeance, illusion)* to harbor; *(espoir)* to cherish; *(projet)* to nurse

     2 se nourrir *vpr (manger)* to eat; **se n. de qch** to live on sth; *Fig & Litt* to feed on sth

nourrissant, -e [nurisɑ̃, -ɑ̃t] *adj* nourishing

nourrisson [nurisɔ̃] *nm* infant

nourriture [nurityr] *nf* food

nous [nu] **1** *pron personnel* (**a**) *(sujet)* we; **n. deux/tous** both/all of us; **n. autres Français** we French; **n., n. n'aurions pas fait comme ça** WE wouldn't have done it like that (**b**) *(objet direct)* us; **et n., tu n. oublies?** and what about us, have you forgotten us? (**c**) *(objet indirect)* to us; **lisez-le-n.** read it to us; **il n. a serré la main** he shook our hands; **les enfants n. ont jeté des pierres** the children threw stones at us (**d**) *(avec préposition)* us; **n. ne pensons pas qu'à n.** we're not just thinking of ourselves; **tu n. le montres, à n.?** can you show US?; **ce livre est à n.** this book is ours; **n. avons nos règles à n.** we have our own rules; *Fam* **un ami à n.** a friend of ours; **à n. deux** *(sur un ton menaçant)* I want a word with you; *Hum* I'm all yours

(e) *(dans les réfléchis)* ourselves; **n. n. sommes habillés** we got dressed

(f) *(dans les pronominaux)* **n. n. déciderons demain** we'll decide tomorrow

(g) *(réciproque)* each other

(h) *(dans les comparaisons)* us; **vous buvez plus que n.** you drink more than us *or* than we do

2 *nm* **le n. de majesté** the royal we

nous-mêmes [numɛm] *pron personnel* ourselves

nouveau, -elle, -x, -elles [nuvo, -ɛl] **1** *adj*

> **nouvel** is used before masculine singular nouns beginning with a vowel or h mute.

(a) *(récent, moderne, autre)* new; *(mode)* latest; **les nouveaux pères** modern fathers; *Fam* **tout n. tout beau** it's all new and exciting; **le nouvel an** the New Year; **nouvelle cuisine** nouvelle cuisine; *Péj* **n. riche** nouveau riche **(b)** *(avec une fonction adverbiale)* **les nouveaux arrivants** the newcomers; **les nouveaux élus** those newly elected; **n. pays industrialisé** newly industrialized country **(c)** **à n., de n.** again

2 *nm* **il y a du n.** there's been a new development; **rien de n. depuis la dernière fois** nothing new since last time

3 *nm,f (personne)* new person; *(à l'école)* new pupil

Nouveau-Brunswick [nuvobrœ̃zvik] *nm* **le N.** New Brunswick

Nouveau-Mexique [nuvomɛksik] *nm* **le N.** New Mexico

nouveau-né, -e *(mpl* **nouveau-nés,** *fpl* **nouveau-nées)** [nuvone] **1** *adj* newborn

2 *nm,f* newborn baby

nouveauté [nuvote] *nf* **(a)** *(caractère nouveau)* novelty **(b)** *(produit récent) (livre)* new publication; *(disque)* new release; *Fam* **ce n'est pas une n.!** that's nothing new!

nouvel [nuvɛl] *voir* **nouveau**

nouvelle [nuvɛl] *nf* **(a)** *(annonce d'un événement)* **une n.** a piece of news; **je viens d'apprendre la n.** I just heard the news; *Fam* **première n.!** that's news to me! **(b)** *(information)* **avoir des nouvelles de qn** *(directement)* to have heard from sb; *(indirectement)* to have had news about sb; *Fig* **vous aurez de mes nouvelles!** you'll be hearing from me!; **demander** *ou* **prendre des nouvelles de qn** to inquire *or* to ask about sb; **être sans nouvelles de qn** to have no news from sb; **aux dernières nouvelles,...** the last I/we/etc. heard,...; **les nouvelles vont vite!** (good) news travels fast!; **goûtez cela, vous m'en direz des nouvelles** try *or* taste this, you'll love it; **pas de nouvelles, bonnes nouvelles** no news is good news **(c)** *Journ* news item; **les nouvelles** the news **(d)** *(roman court)* short story

Nouvelle-Angleterre [nuvɛlɑ̃glətɛr] *nf* **la N.** New England

Nouvelle-Calédonie [nuvɛlkaledɔni] *nf* **la N.** New Caledonia

Nouvelle-Écosse [nuvɛlekɔs] *nf* **la N.** Nova Scotia

nouvellement [nuvɛlmɑ̃] *adv* newly, recently

Nouvelle-Orléans [nuvɛlɔrleɑ̃] *voir* **La Nouvelle-Orléans**

Nouvelles-Hébrides [nuvɛlzebrid] *nfpl* **les N.** the New Hebrides

Nouvelle-Zélande [nuvɛlzelɑ̃d] *nf* **la N.** New Zealand

novateur, -trice [nɔvatœr, -tris] **1** *adj* innovative

2 *nm,f* innovator

novembre [nɔvɑ̃br] *nm* November; **le onze n.** *(fête)* Veterans Day; *voir aussi* **janvier**

novice [nɔvis] *nmf aussi Rel* novice

noyade [nwajad] *nf* drowning

noyau, -x [nwajo] *nm* **(a)** *(de fruit)* pit **(b)** *(centre)* *(d'atome, de cellule)* nucleus; *(de la terre)* core **(c)** *(petit groupe)* small group; **le n. dur** the hard core **(d)** *Ordinat* node

noyauter [nwajote] *vt* to infiltrate

noyé, -e [nwaje] **1** *adj* **(a)** *(dans l'eau)* **mourir n.** to die by drowning; *Fig* **être n.** *(perdu)* to be out of one's depth **(b)** *(plein)* **yeux noyés de larmes** eyes brimming with tears **(c)** *(perdu)* **le village était n. dans la brume** the village was shrouded in mist; **les points essentiels sont noyés dans le détail** the essential points are buried in too many details

2 *nm,f* drowned person

noyer¹ [nwaje] *nm (arbre)* walnut (tree); *(bois)* walnut

noyer² [32] [nwaje] **1** *vt* **(a)** *(personne, animal)* to drown; *(terres, champs)* to swamp; *Fig* **n. une rébellion dans le sang** to brutally quash a rebellion; **n. son chagrin** *(dans l'alcool)* to drown one's sorrows (in drink); **n. le poisson** to confuse the issue deliberately **(b)** *(moteur)* to flood **(c)** *(diluer)* *(vin)* to drown

2 se noyer *vpr (accidentellement)* to drown; *(volontairement)* to drown oneself; *Fig* **se n. dans les détails** to get bogged down in details; **se n. dans un verre d'eau** to make a mountain out of a molehill

NPI [ɛnpei] *nm (abrév* **nouveau pays industrialisé)** NIC

nu, -e [ny] **1** *adj* **(a)** *(dévêtu)* *(personne)* naked; *(partie du corps)* bare; *Art* nude; **être tout nu** to be naked *or* in the nude; **se baigner tout nu** to go skinny-dipping; **nu comme un ver** stark naked; **aller pieds nus** to go barefoot; **se battre à mains nues** to fight with bare fists **(b)** *Fig (paysage, arbre, pièce)* bare; *(style)* plain

2 *nm Art* nude; **mettre qch à nu** *(surface)* to expose sth; *(fil électrique)* to strip sth

nuage [nɥaʒ] *nm* **(a)** *(dans le ciel)* cloud; **sans nuages** *(ciel)* cloudless; *Fig (vie, avenir)* uncloaded; *(bonheur)* perfect; *Fig* **être dans les nuages** to have one's head in the clouds; **n. radioactif** cloud of radioactive dust **(b)** *(de lait)* drop **(c)** *Can (foulard)* scarf

nuageux, -euse [nɥaʒø, -øz] *adj* cloudy

nuance [nɥɑ̃s] *nf* **(a)** *(de couleur)* shade **(b)** *(légère trace)* touch, hint **(c)** *(subtilité)* nuance; *(légère différence)* slight difference; **tout en nuances** full of nuances; **j'ai dit peut-être, pas oui, n.!** I said perhaps, not yes, there's a slight difference!; **être sans nuances** *(personne)* to see everything in black and white

nuancé, -e [nɥɑ̃se] *adj* full of nuances

nuancer [16] [nɥɑ̃se] *vt* to qualify

nucléaire [nykleɛr] **1** *adj* nuclear

2 *nm* **le n.** nuclear power

nucléon [nykleɔ̃] *nm Phys* nucleon

nudisme [nydism] *nm* nudism

nudiste [nydist] *nmf* nudist

nudité [nydite] *nf (d'une personne)* nudity, nakedness; *(d'un mur, d'un paysage)* bareness; *(d'un style)* plainness

nue [ny] *nf* **porter qn/qch aux nues** to praise sb/sth to the skies; **tomber des nues** to be taken aback

nuée [nɥe] *nf* **(a)** *(d'insectes, de criquets)* cloud, swarm; *(de personnes)* horde **(b)** *Litt (dans le ciel)* cloud

nui *voir* **nuire**

nuire [18] [nɥir] **1 nuire à** *vt ind* to harm; **nuit gravement à la santé** *(sur paquet de cigarettes)* tobacco seriously damages health; **mettre qn hors d'état de n.** *(en lieu sûr)* to put sb out of harm's way

2 se nuire *vpr* **se n. (à soi-même)** to do oneself harm

nuisais *etc. voir* **nuire**

nuisance [nɥizɑ̃s] *nf* nuisance; **nuisances acoustiques** noise pollution

nuise *voir* **nuire**

nuisette [nɥizɛt] *nf* baby-doll nightie

nuisible [nɥizibl] *adj* harmful (**à** to); **animaux nuisibles** vermin, pests

nuit [nɥi] *nf* night; **cette n.** *(ce soir)* tonight; *(passée)* last night; **bonne n.!** good night!; **le train/bateau de n.** the night train/boat; **voyager de n.** to travel by *or* at night; **il commence à faire n.** it's getting dark; **il fait n.** it's dark; **il fait n. noire** it's pitch-black; **à la n. tombante** at nightfall; *Fig* **perdu dans la n. des temps** lost in the mists of time; *Prov* **la n. porte conseil** it would be best to sleep on it; *Prov* **la n., tous les chats sont gris** all cats are gray in the dark; **passer une n. blanche** *(avoir une insomnie)* to have a sleepless night; *(volontairement)* to stay up all night; **n. de noces** wedding night

nuitée [nɥite] *nf* overnight stay

nul, nulle [nyl] **1** *adj* (**a**) *(inexistant) (différence, risques, écart)* nil (**b**) *(non valable) (bulletin de vote)* spoiled; *Jur* **n. et non avenu** null and void (**c**) *Fam (qui ne vaut rien) (réponse, personne)* useless; *(film, livre, chanson, blague)* lousy; **être n. en qch** to be lousy at sth; *Vulg* **c'est n. à chier!** it's a pile of crap!

2 *nm,f Fam* useless idiot

3 *adj indéfini Litt* no

4 *pron indéfini Litt* no-one, nobody

nullard, -e [nylar, -ard] *nm,f très Fam* useless jerk

nullement [nylmɑ̃] *adv* not at all

nulle part [nylpar] *adv* nowhere; **je ne les vois n.** I can't see them anywhere; **n. ailleurs** nowhere else

nullité [nylite] *nf (d'un contrat, d'un mariage)* nullity, invalidity

numéraire [nymerɛr] *nm* cash

numéral, -e, -aux, -ales [nymeral, -o] *adj & nm* numeral

numérateur [nymeratœr] *nm Math* numerator

numération [nymerasjɔ̃] *nf Math* numeration; *Méd* **n. globulaire** blood count

numérique [nymerik] *adj* (**a**) *(valeur, supériorité)* numerical (**b**) *Ordinat (ordinateur, donnée)* digital; **balance à affichage n.** digital scales

numérisation [nymerizasjɔ̃] *nf Ordinat* digitization

numériser [nymerize] *vt Ordinat* to digitize

numériseur [nymerizœr] *nm Ordinat* digitizer; **n. d'image** image digitizer

numéro [nymero] *nm* (**a**) *(chiffre)* number; *Fig* **tirer le bon n.** to strike (it) lucky; **n. azur** = special telephone number for which users are charged at local rate irrespective of distance; **n. de compte** account number; **n. de fax** fax number; **n. d'immatriculation** *(de véhicule)* license number; *Belg Vieilli & Suisse* **n. postal** zip code; **n. de téléphone** telephone number; **n. vert** toll-free number; **n. de vol** flight number (**b**) *(de périodique)* issue, number; **la suite au prochain n.** (to be) continued in the next issue; *Fig* watch this space; **n. spécial** special issue (**c**) *(spectacle)* act, number; *Fam Fig* **faire son petit n.** to do one's little act (**d**) *Fam (personne)* character

numérotation [nymerɔtasjɔ̃] *nf* (**a**) numbering (**b**) *Tél* dialing; **n. abrégée** speed dial

numéroter [nymerɔte] *vt* to number

numismate [nymismat] *nmf* numismatist

numismatique [nymismatik] **1** *adj* numismatic

2 *nf* numismatics *(singulier)*

nunuche [nynyʃ] *adj Fam* dumb

nu-pieds [nypje] **1** *nm inv* sandal

2 *adv* barefoot

nuptial, -e, -aux, -ales [nypsjal, -o] *adj (anneau, marche)* wedding; *(chambre, cortège)* bridal

nuque [nyk] *nf* nape, back of the neck

nurse [nœrs] *nf Vieilli* nanny

nu-tête [nytɛt] *adv* bareheaded

nutritif, -ive [nytritif, -iv] *adj* nutritious

nutrition [nytrisjɔ̃] *nf* nutrition

nutritionniste [nytrisjɔnist] *nmf* nutritionist

Nylon® [nilɔ̃] *nm* nylon

nymphe [nɛ̃f] *nf (déesse)* nymph

nymphette [nɛ̃fɛt] *nf* nymphet

nymphomane [nɛ̃fɔman] *adj & nf* nymphomaniac

nymphomanie [nɛ̃fɔmani] *nf* nymphomania

O

O¹, o [o] *nm inv* O, o

O² (*abrév* **ouest**) W

ô [o] *exclam Litt* O!

OAS [oaɛs] *nf* (*abrév* **Organisation de l'armée secrète**) OAS (*terrorist group opposed to Algerian independence*)

oasis [ɑazis] *nf* oasis; *Fig* haven

obédience [ɔbedjɑ̃s] *nf* **d'o. communiste/musulmane** of the Communist/Muslim persuasion

obéir [ɔbeir] *vi* (**a**) (*personne*) to obey; **o. à qn/qch** to obey sb/sth; **o. à une impulsion** to act on an impulse; **o. à qn au doigt et à l'œil** to be at sb's beck and call; **se faire o.** to command obedience (**b**) (*freins, mécanisme*) to respond (**à** to)

obéissance [ɔbeisɑ̃s] *nf* obedience (**à** to); **jurer o. à qn** to swear allegiance to sb

obéissant, -e [ɔbeisɑ̃, -ɑ̃t] *adj* obedient

obélisque [ɔbelisk] *nm* obelisk

obèse [ɔbɛz] **1** *adj* obese
2 *nmf* obese person

obésité [ɔbezite] *nf* obesity

objecter [ɔbʒɛkte] *vt* (**a**) (*rétorquer*) **n'avoir rien à o. à qch** to have no objection to sth; **o. que...** to object that... (**b**) (*invoquer*) **on lui objecta sa jeunesse** his/her youth was held against him/her

objecteur [ɔbʒɛktœr] *nm* **o. de conscience** conscientious objector

objectif, -ive [ɔbʒɛktif, -iv] **1** *adj* objective
2 *nm* (**a**) (*but, cible*) objective (**b**) (*d'un appareil photo*) lens; (*d'un microscope*) objective; *Fig* **devant l'o.** in front of the camera

objection [ɔbʒɛksjɔ̃] *nf aussi Jur* objection; **je ne vois pas d'o. à continuer le débat/à ce que vous partiez** I have no objection to our continuing the debate/to your leaving

objectivement [ɔbʒɛktivmɑ̃] *adv* objectively

objectivité [ɔbʒɛktivite] *nf* objectivity; **en toute o.** quite objectively

objet [ɔbʒɛ] *nm* (**a**) (*chose*) object; **(bureau des) objets trouvés** lost-and-found (office); **femme-o.** sex object; **o. d'art** objet d'art; **objets de valeur** valuables; **o. volant non identifié** unidentified flying object (**b**) *Gram* object; **o. direct/indirect** direct/indirect object (**c**) (*sujet*) (*d'une dispute, d'une conversation*) subject; **être** *ou* **faire l'o. de qch** to be the object of sth; *Hum* **l'o. de ses désirs** the object of his/her desires (**d**) (*but*) object, aim; **ma visite a pour o. de...** the object of my visit is to...; **sans o.** (*remarque, réclamation*) unjustified (**e**) *Ordinat* object

obligataire [ɔbligatɛr] *Fin* **1** *nmf* bondholder
2 *adj* (*emprunt, marché*) bond

obligation [ɔbligasjɔ̃] *nf* (**a**) (*contrainte*) obligation; **tu viens si tu veux, mais ce n'est pas une o.** you can come if you want, but you're not obliged to; **avoir l'o. de faire qch** to be under an obligation to do sth; **être** *ou* **se voir dans l'o. de faire qch** to be obliged to do sth; **sans o. d'achat** no purchase

necessary; **être dégagé des obligations militaires** to have done one's military service (**b**) *Fin* bond; **o. au porteur** bearer bond

obligatoire [ɔbligatwar] *adj* obligatory, compulsory; *Fam* (*inévitable*) inevitable

obligatoirement [ɔbligatwarmɑ̃] *adv* **vous devez o. montrer votre passeport** you are required to show your passport; **pas o.** not necessarily

obligé, -e [ɔbliʒe] *adj* (**a**) *Fam* (*inévitable*) inevitable (**b**) *Sout* (*reconnaissant*) **être o. à qn de qch** to be obliged to sb for sth

obligeance [ɔbliʒɑ̃s] *nf Sout* **avoir l'o. de faire qch** to be so kind as to do sth

obligeant, -e [ɔbliʒɑ̃, -ɑ̃t] *adj* obliging, kind

obliger [45] [ɔbliʒe] **1** *vt* (**a**) (*contraindre*) **o. qn à faire qch** to force sb to do sth; **son état de santé l'oblige au repos** the state of his/her health means he/she has to rest; **être obligé de faire qch** to be obliged to do sth; **ne te crois pas obligé de tout manger** don't feel you have to eat everything; **tu y es allé? – bien obligé!** did you go? – I had to! (**b**) *Sout* (*rendre service à*) **vous m'obligeriez en fermant la porte** I'd be obliged if you would close the door
2 **s'obliger** *vpr* **s'o. à faire qch** to force oneself to do sth

oblique [ɔblik] **1** *adj* (*ligne*) oblique; (*regard*) sidelong
2 *nf* oblique (line)

obliquement [ɔblikmɑ̃] *adv* obliquely

obliquer [ɔblike] *vi* **o. à gauche/à droite** to bear left/right

oblitérer [34] [ɔblitere] *vt* (**a**) (*timbre*) to cancel (**b**) *Litt* (*souvenirs, passé*) to obliterate

oblong, -ongue [ɔblɔ̃, -ɔ̃g] *adj* oblong

obnubiler [ɔbnybile] *vt* to obsess

obole [ɔbɔl] *nf* small contribution; **apporter** *ou* **verser son o. à qch** to make a small contribution to sth

obscène [ɔpsɛn] *adj* obscene

obscénité [ɔpsenite] *nf* obscenity; **dire des obscénités** to utter obscenities

obscur, -e [ɔpskyr] *adj* (**a**) (*sombre*) dark (**b**) (*difficile à comprendre*) obscure (**c**) (*pressentiment, impression*) vague (**d**) (*écrivain, peintre*) obscure

obscurantisme [ɔpskyrɑ̃tism] *nm* obscurantism

obscurcir [ɔpskyrsir] **1** *vt* (**a**) (*assombrir*) to darken (**b**) (*rendre confus*) (*faits, sens*) to obscure; (*jugement*) to cloud
2 **s'obscurcir** *vpr* (*pièce, ciel*) to darken, to grow dark; (*esprit, vue*) to grow dim

obscurément [ɔpskyremɑ̃] *adv* vaguely

obscurité [ɔpskyrite] *nf* (**a**) (*noirceur*) darkness; **dans l'o.** in the dark (**b**) (*anonymat*) obscurity

obsédant, -e [ɔpsedɑ̃, -ɑ̃t] *adj* (*souvenir, musique*) haunting; (*pensée*) obsessive

obsédé, -e [ɔpsede] *nm,f* fanatic; **o. (sexuel)** sex maniac; **un o. du cinéma/du ménage** a movie/cleaning fanatic

obséder [34] [ɔpsede] *vt* to obsess; **être obsédé par qch** to be obsessed by *or* with sth

obsèques [ɔpsɛk] *nfpl* funeral; **o. nationales** state funeral

obséquieux, -euse [ɔpsekjø, -øz] *adj* obsequious

observateur, -trice [ɔpsɛrvatœr, -tris] **1** *adj* observant
2 *nm,f* observer

observation [ɔpsɛrvasjɔ̃] *nf* (**a**) *(étude, surveillance)* observation; **être en o.** *(à l'hôpital)* to be under observation; **avoir l'esprit d'o.** to be very observant (**b**) *(remarque)* observation; *(critique)* remark (**c**) *(respect)* observance

observatoire [ɔpsɛrvatwar] *nm (astronomique, météorologique)* observatory; *Mil* observation post

observer [ɔpsɛrve] **1** *vt* (**a**) *(regarder)* to watch, to observe; **se sentir observé** to feel one is being watched (**b**) *(remarquer)* to notice; **faire o. qch à qn** to point sth out to sb; **faire o. à qn que...** to point out to sb that... (**c**) *(étudier)* to observe (**d**) *(respecter)* to observe; **o. une minute de silence** to observe a minute's silence
2 s'observer *vpr* (**a**) *(l'un l'autre)* to watch *or* to observe each other (**b**) *(phénomène, attitude)* to be seen

obsession [ɔpsesjɔ̃] *nf* obsession; **mais c'est une o.** *ou* **de l'o.!** you're/he's/*etc.*obsessed!

obsessionnel, -elle [ɔpsesjɔnɛl] *adj Psy* obsessional

obsidienne [ɔpsidjɛn] *nf* obsidian

obsolète [ɔpsɔlɛt] *adj* obsolete

obstacle [ɔpstakl] *nm aussi Fig* obstacle; *(aux courses)* fence, jump; **faire o. à qch** to stand in the way of sth

obstétricien, -enne [ɔpstetrisjɛ̃, -ɛn] *nm,f* obstetrician

obstétrique [ɔpstetrik] *nf* obstetrics *(singulier)*

obstination [ɔpstinasjɔ̃] *nf* obstinacy, stubbornness

obstiné, -e [ɔpstine] *adj (personne, caractère)* obstinate, stubborn; *(résistance, efforts)* dogged, determined; *(refus)* stubborn

obstinément [ɔpstinemɑ̃] *adv (travailler, avancer)* doggedly; *(refuser)* stubbornly

obstiner [ɔpstine] **s'obstiner** *vpr* to persist; **s'o. à faire qch** *(continuer)* to persist in doing sth; *(vouloir)* to be set on doing sth; **s'o. dans ses convictions** to cling stubbornly to one's convictions

obstruction [ɔpstryksjɔ̃] *nf* obstruction; **faire de l'o.** *Pol* to be obstructive; *Sport* to obstruct

obstructionnisme [ɔpstryksjɔnism] *nm Pol* obstructionism

obstruer [ɔpstrye] *vt* to obstruct

obtempérer [34] [ɔptɑ̃pere] **obtempérer à** *vt ind* to comply with; *Jur* **refus d'o.** obstruction

obtenir [70] [ɔptənir] *vt* to get, to obtain; **o. qch de qn** to get sth from sb; **faire o. qch à qn** to get sth for sb; **o. de faire qch** to get permission to do sth; **j'ai obtenu qu'elle revienne** I got her to come back

obtention [ɔptɑ̃sjɔ̃] *nf* obtaining; **depuis l'o. de son diplôme** since obtaining her diploma

obtenu, -e *voir* **obtenir**

obtiendrai *etc. voir* **obtenir**

obtienne *voir* **obtenir**

obturateur [ɔptyratœr] *nm Phot* shutter

obtus, -e [ɔpty, -yz] *adj (angle, personne)* obtuse

obus [ɔby] *nm* shell

OC *nfpl (abrév* **ondes courtes**) SW

oc [ɔk] *voir* **langue**

ocarina [ɔkarina] *nm* ocarina

occase [ɔkaz] *nf Fam* (**a**) *(affaire)* bargain (**b**) *(article de seconde main)* second-hand item; **d'o.** second-hand

occasion [ɔkazjɔ̃] *nf* (**a**) *(circonstance favorable)* opportunity, chance; **avoir l'o. de faire qch** to have the opportunity *or* chance to do sth; *Hum* **tu as encore perdu l'o. de te taire** why can't you keep your big mouth shut?; **c'est l'o. ou jamais** it's now or never; **c'est l'o. ou jamais d'essayer** now's the time to try; **venez boire un coup à l'o.** come for a drink when you get the chance; **à la première o.** at the first opportunity; *Prov* **l'o. fait le larron** opportunity makes the thief (**b**) *(moment)* occasion; **à plusieurs occasions** on several occa-

sions; **à l'o. de** *(pour fêter)* on the occasion of; **à l'o. d'une visite de routine** during a routine visit; **dans/pour les grandes occasions** on/for special occasions; **être l'o. de qch** to be the occasion of sth (**c**) *(affaire)* bargain (**d**) *(article de seconde main)* second-hand item; **le marché de l'o.** the second-hand market; **d'o.** second-hand

occasionnel, -elle [ɔkazjɔnɛl] *adj* occasional; *(rencontre)* chance; *(aide)* casual

occasionnellement [ɔkazjɔnɛlmɑ̃] *adv* occasionally

occasionner [ɔkazjɔne] *vt* to cause

occident [ɔksidɑ̃] *nm* west; *Pol* **l'O.** the West

occidental, -e, -aux, -ales [ɔksidɑ̃tal, -o] **1** *adj* western; **l'Europe occidentale** Western Europe
2 *nm,f* **O., Occidentale** Westerner

occidentaliser [ɔksidɑ̃talize] **1** *vt* to westernize
2 s'occidentaliser *vpr* to become westernized

occiput [ɔksipyt] *nm* back of the head

occire [ɔksir] *vt* to slay

occitan, -e [ɔksitɑ̃, -an] **1** *adj* of the langue d'oc
2 *nm (langue)* = language spoken in some parts of southern France

occlusion [ɔklyzjɔ̃] *nf* occlusion; **o. intestinale** intestinal obstruction

occulte [ɔkylt] *adj (surnaturel)* occult; *(secret)* secret; *(cause)* hidden; *(rôle)* clandestine

occulter [ɔkylte] *vt Astron* to occult; *(signal lumineux)* to block out; *Fig (informations, intentions)* to conceal

occupant, -e [ɔkypɑ̃, -ɑ̃t] **1** *adj (armée)* occupying
2 *nm,f (d'une maison)* occupier, occupant; *Mil* **l'o.** the occupying forces

occupation [ɔkypasjɔ̃] *nf* (**a**) *(d'un lieu)* & *Mil* occupation; *Hist* **l'O.** the Occupation; **grève avec o. des locaux** sit-down strike (**b**) *(activité)* occupation; **vaquer à ses occupations** to go about one's business

occupé, -e [ɔkype] *adj (personne)* busy; *(place)* taken; *(ligne téléphonique)* busy; *(toilettes)* occupied; **en territoire o.** in occupied territory

occuper [ɔkype] **1** *vt* (**a**) *(maison, lieu)* to occupy; *(place)* to take up, to occupy; **le magasin occupe le rez-de-chaussée** the store takes up *or* occupies the ground floor (**b**) *(par la force)* to occupy (**c**) *(temps)* to fill, to occupy (**d**) *(poste, fonction)* to have, to hold (**e**) **o. qn** *(employer)* to employ sb; *(donner une activité à)* to keep sb busy, to occupy sb
2 s'occuper *vpr* (**a**) *(avoir une activité)* to keep oneself busy *or* occupied, to occupy oneself; **s'o. en lisant** to spend one's time reading; **on a toujours de quoi s'o.** there's always something to keep you busy (**b**) **s'o. de** *(s'intéresser à)* to be interested in; *(se charger de)* to take care of; **s'o. de faire qch** to see about doing sth; **je m'en occuperai** I'll see to it; *Fam* **occupe-toi de ce qui te regarde** *ou* **de tes affaires** *ou* **de tes oignons!** mind your own business!; *Fam* **t'occupe (pas)!** keep your nose out!; *Ironique* **je vais m'o. de lui** I'll take care of him; **est-ce qu'on s'occupe de vous?** *(dans un magasin)* are you being attended to?

occurrence [ɔkyrɑ̃s] *nf* (**a**) *(circonstance)* **en l'o.** in this case (**b**) *Ling* occurrence

OCDE [osedeə] *nf (abrév* **Organisation de coopération et de développement économiques**) OECD

océan [ɔseɑ̃] *nm* ocean; **l'O.** *(l'Atlantique)* the Atlantic; **l'o. Atlantique/Pacifique/Indien** the Atlantic/Pacific/Indian Ocean; **l'o. (Glacial) Arctique** the Arctic Ocean; *Fig* **un o. de fleurs/couleurs** a sea of flowers/color

Océanie [ɔseani] *nf* **l'O.** Oceania

océanique [ɔseanik] *adj* oceanic

océanographie [ɔseanɔgrafi] *nf* oceanography

ocelot [ɔslo] *nm* ocelot

ocre [ɔkr] *nm & adj inv* ochre

octane [ɔktan] *nm* octane

octante [ɔktɑ̃t] *adj & nm inv Belg & Suisse* eighty; *voir aussi* **trois**

octave [ɔktav] *nf* octave

octet [ɔktɛ] *nm Ordinat* byte; **milliard d'octets** gigabyte

octobre [ɔktɔbr] *nm* October; *voir aussi* **janvier**

octogénaire [ɔktɔʒenɛr] *adj & nmf* octogenarian

octogonal, -e, -aux, -ales [ɔktɔgɔnal, -o] *adj* octagonal

octogone [ɔktɔgɔn] *nm* octagon

octroyer [32] [ɔktrwaje] **1** *vt* **o. qch à qn** to grant sb sth
  2 s'octroyer *vpr* **s'o. qch** to grant oneself sth

oculaire [ɔkylɛr] **1** *adj* **hygiène o.** eye care; **témoin o.** eyewitness
  2 *nm* eyepiece

oculiste [ɔkylist] *nmf* eye specialist

ode [ɔd] *nf* ode

odeur [ɔdœr] *nf* smell; **une o. de brûlé** a smell of burning; **sans o.** odorless; **bonne/mauvaise o.** pleasant/unpleasant smell; *Fig* **ne pas être en o. de sainteté auprès de qn** to be in sb's bad books

odieux, -euse [ɔdjø, -øz] *adj (comportement)* odious; *(crime)* heinous; **être o. avec qn** to be really mean to sb

odorant, -e [ɔdɔrɑ̃, -ɑ̃t] *adj (agréable)* sweet-smelling, fragrant; *(désagréable)* strong-smelling

odorat [ɔdɔra] *nm* (sense of) smell

odyssée [ɔdise] *nf* odyssey; **l'O.** the Odyssey

œcuménique [ekymenik, økymenik] *adj* ecumenical

œdème [edɛm, ødɛm] *nm* edema; **avoir un o. aux poumons** to have a pulmonary edema

œil [œj] (*pl* **yeux** [jø]) *nm* **(a)** *(organe)* eye; **avoir les yeux bleus** to have blue eyes; **o. de verre** glass eye; **un o. au beurre noir, un o. poché** a black eye; **j'ai le soleil dans les yeux** *ou* **dans l'o.** the sun's in my eyes; **visible à l'o.** visible to the naked eye; **voir qch de ses (propres) yeux** to see sth with one's own eyes; **je n'ai pas fermé l'o. de la nuit** I didn't sleep a wink all night; **faire qch les yeux fermés** to do sth with one's eyes closed; **ouvrir de grands yeux** to look surprised; **faire les gros yeux (à qn)** to glare (at sb); *Fam* **avoir de petits yeux** to look tired; **ouvrir des yeux ronds** to gape in amazement; *Fam* **entre quat'z'yeux** in private; **les yeux dans les yeux** gazing into each other's eyes; **o. pour o.(, dent pour dent)** an eye for an eye(, a tooth for a tooth); **je ne le fais pas pour ses beaux yeux** I'm not doing it just to please him; **tu as les yeux plus gros** *ou* **grands que le ventre** your eyes are bigger than your belly; **n'avoir plus que les** *ou* **ses yeux pour pleurer** to have nothing left but the clothes on one's back; *Fam* **mon o.!** my foot!; *Fam* **à l'o.** free; **faire les yeux doux à qn** to make eyes at sb; *Fam* **faire de l'o. à qn** to give sb the eye; **le mauvais o.** the evil eye; **sous mes/leurs yeux** right before my/their eyes; **avoir qch sous les yeux** to have sth in front of one; *Can Fam* **tomber dans l'o. à qn** to catch sb's eye
  (b) *(vue)* **yeux** (eye)sight, eyes; **avoir de bons/mauvais yeux** to have good/bad (eye)sight; **avoir des yeux de lynx** to be eagle-eyed
  (c) *(attention)* **avoir l'o. sur qch** to keep an eye on sth; **avoir qn à l'o.** to keep an eye on sb; **avoir l'o. à tout** to keep an eye on everything; *Fam* **ouvrir l'o. (et le bon)** to keep one's eyes open *or* peeled; **ne pas avoir les yeux en face des trous** to be half-asleep; *Fam* **ne pas avoir les yeux dans sa poche** to have sharp eyes; **fermer les yeux sur qch** to turn a blind eye to sth; **coup d'o.** glance; **au** *ou* **du premier coup d'o.** at a glance; **jeter un coup d'o. sur qch** to have a glance at sth; **avoir le coup d'o., avoir l'o.** to have a good eye; **ça vaut** *ou* **ça mérite le coup d'o.** it's worth a look
  (d) *(point de vue)* **voir qch d'un autre o.** to look at sth differently; **voir qch d'un bon/mauvais o.** to look favorably/un-

favorably on sth; **aux yeux de la loi** in the eyes of the law; **à mes yeux** in my eyes
  (e) *(dans la soupe)* speck of fat
  (f) *(d'un cyclone)* eye

œil-de-bœuf (*pl* **œils-de-bœuf**) [œjdəbœf] *nm* bull's-eye (window)

œillade [œjad] *nf* wink; **lancer une o. à qn** to wink at sb

œillère [œjɛr] *nf* blinder; *Fig* **avoir des œillères** to wear blinders

œillet [œjɛ] *nm* **(a)** *(fleur)* carnation **(b)** *(trou) (de vêtement, de chaussure)* eyelet **(c)** *(en papeterie)* reinforcement ring

œnologie [enɔlɔʒi, ønɔlɔʒi] *nf* enology

œnologue [enɔlɔg, ønɔlɔg] *nmf* enologist

œsophage [ezɔfaʒ, øzɔfaʒ] *nm* esophagus

œstrogène [ɛstrɔʒɛn, østrɔʒɛn] *adj & nm* estrogen

œuf [œf, *pl* ø] *nm* egg; **œufs** *(de poisson)* spawn, hard roe; *Fig* **mettre tous ses œufs dans le même panier** to put all one's eggs in one basket; *Fam Fig* **marcher sur des œufs** *(avancer)* to walk carefully; *(être prudent)* to be walking on eggshells; *Fam* **va te faire cuire un o.!** go jump in the lake!; **étouffer** *ou* **tuer qch dans l'o.** to nip sth in the bud; **œufs brouillés** scrambled eggs; **o. en chocolat** chocolate egg; **o. à la coque** boiled egg; **o. dur** hard-boiled egg; **o. mollet** soft-boiled egg; **œufs à la neige** floating islands *(beaten egg whites served on custard)*; **œufs en neige** beaten egg whites; **o. de Pâques** Easter egg; **o. au plat** *ou* **sur le plat** egg sunny-side up; **o. poché** poached egg; **o. à repriser** darning egg

œuvre [œvr] **1** *nf* **(a)** *(travail)* work; **être à l'o.** to be at work; **se mettre à l'o.** to get down to work; **mettre qch en o.** *(traité, loi, système)* to implement sth; **mettre tout en o.** to do everything possible; **les bonnes œuvres** charitable work **(b)** *(création)* work; *(ensemble de créations)* works; **o. d'art** work of art; **œuvres complètes/choisies** complete/selected works
  2 *nm Constr* **gros o.** shell; **à pied d'o.** on site; *Fig* ready to start work

œuvrer [œvre] *vi* to work (**pour** for)

offensant, -e [ɔfɑ̃sɑ̃, -ɑ̃t] *adj* offensive

offense [ɔfɑ̃s] *nf* **(a)** *(affront)* insult **(b)** *Rel* transgression

offenser [ɔfɑ̃se] **1** *vt* **(a)** *(insulter)* to offend; **sans vouloir vous o....** with all due respect... **(b)** *Litt (bon goût, délicatesse)* to offend against
  2 s'offenser *vpr* to take offense (**de** at)

offensif, -ive [ɔfɑ̃sif, -iv] *adj* offensive

offensive [ɔfɑ̃siv] *nf* offensive; **passer à l'o.** to go on the offensive; **o. de charme** charm offensive

offert, -e *voir* **offrir**

office [ɔfis] *nm* **(a)** *(charge)* office; **faire o. de secrétaire/témoin** to act as secretary/witness; **d'o.** without having any say in the matter; **être commis d'o.** to be appointed by the court **(b)** *(assistance)* **recourir aux bons offices de qn** to turn to sb for assistance **(c)** *Rel* service **(d)** *(pièce)* pantry **(e)** *(agence)* **o. du tourisme** tourist information center; *Suisse* **o. de poste** post office

officialiser [ɔfisjalize] *vt* to make official

officiel, -elle [ɔfisjɛl] *adj & nm* official

officiellement [ɔfisjɛlmɑ̃] *adv* officially

officier[1] [ɔfisje] *nm* officer; **o. de réserve** reserve officer

officier[2] [66] [ɔfisje] *vi* to officiate

officieusement [ɔfisjøzmɑ̃] *adv* unofficially; *(en confidence)* off-the-record

officieux, -euse [ɔfisjø, -øz] *adj* unofficial; *(confidentiel)* off-the-record

off-line [ɔflajn] *adj Ordinat* off-line

offrande [ɔfrɑ̃d] *nf* offering; **en o.** as an offering

offrant [ɔfrɑ̃] *nm* **vendre au plus o.** to sell to the highest bidder

offre [ɔfr] *nf* offer; *(dans un appel d'offres)* tender; *(dans une vente aux enchères)* bid; **o. d'emploi** job offer; **o. spéciale** special offer; **o. publique d'achat** takeover bid; **faire** *ou* **lancer une o. publique d'achat (sur)** to make a takeover bid (for); **l'o. et la demande** supply and demand

offrir [52] [ɔfrir] **1** *vt* (**a**) *(cadeau)* to give (**à** to); **c'est pour o.** it's a gift; **je t'offre un verre** I'll buy you a drink; **o. la main de sa fille à qn** to offer one's daughter's hand in marriage to sb (**b**) *(proposer)* to offer; **o. de faire qch** to offer to do sth; **combien t'en a-t-elle offert?** how much did she offer you for it? (**c**) *(présenter) (avantage, garantie)* to offer; **o. une résistance acharnée** to put up stiff resistance

2 s'offrir *vpr* (**a**) *(se proposer) (sexuellement)* to offer oneself; **s'o. pour faire qch** to offer to do sth; **s'o. aux regards** *(spectacle, vue)* to meet our/your/*etc.* eyes (**b**) *(se présenter) (occasion, possibilité)* to present itself (**c**) *(s'acheter)* **s'o. un bon cigare/ une semaine de vacances** to treat oneself to a good cigar/a week's vacation; **je ne peux pas m'o. de vacances** I can't afford a vacation

offset [ɔfsɛt] *nm inv* offset

offusquer [ɔfyske] **1** *vt* to offend

2 s'offusquer *vpr* to take offense (**de** at)

ogive [ɔʒiv] *nf* (**a**) *Archit* (diagonal) rib (**b**) *Mil (d'un obus)* head; *(d'une roquette)* nose cone; **o. nucléaire** nuclear warhead

OGM [ɔʒeɛm] *nm* (*abrév* **organisme génétiquement modifié**) genetically modified organism, GMO

ogre [ɔgr] *nm* ogre

ogresse [ɔgrɛs] *nf* ogress

oh [o] *exclam* oh!; *(pour interpeller)* hey!

ohé [ɔe] *exclam* hey!

ohm [om] *nm* ohm

oie [wa] *nf* goose; **o. sauvage** wild goose; *Fig* **une o. blanche** an innocent young thing

oignon [ɔɲ ɔ̃] *nm* (**a**) *(légume)* onion; **oignons blancs** *(pour les salades)* scallions; **petits oignons** *(au vinaigre)* pickling onions; *Fam Fig* **aux petits oignons** first-rate; *Fam* **mêle-toi de tes oignons** mind your own business; *Fam* **ce ne sont pas tes oignons** it's none of your business (**b**) *Bot* bulb (**c**) *Méd* bunion

oindre [43] [wɛ̃dr] *vt* (**a**) *(enduire)* to oil (**b**) *Rel* to anoint

oiseau, -x [wazo] *nm* bird; *Fam Fig* **c'est un drôle d'o.** he's an odd character; **o. de malheur, o. de mauvais augure** bird of ill omen; **o. marin** sea bird; **o. nocturne** nocturnal bird; *Fig* **o. de nuit** night owl; **o. de proie** bird of prey; **l'o. rare** the ideal person

oiseau-lyre *(pl* **oiseaux-lyres)** [wazolir] *nm* lyrebird

oiseau-mouche *(pl* **oiseaux-mouches)** [wazomuʃ] *nm* hummingbird

oiseleur [wazlœr] *nm* bird catcher

oiseux, -euse [wazø, -øz] *adj (conversation)* idle; *(débat)* pointless; *(explication)* unsatisfactory

oisif, -ive [wazif, -iv] **1** *adj* idle

2 *nm,f* person of leisure

oisillon [wazijɔ̃] *nm* fledgling

oisiveté [wazivte] *nf* idleness; *Prov* **l'o. est (la) mère de tous les vices** the Devil finds work for idle hands (to do)

OIT [oite] *nf* (*abrév* **Organisation internationale du travail**) ILO

okapi [ɔkapi] *nm* okapi

oléagineux, -euse [ɔleaʒinø, -øz] **1** *adj* oil-yielding

2 *nmpl* oil-yielding plants

oléoduc [ɔleɔdyk] *nm* pipeline

olé olé [ɔleɔle] *adj inv Fam (propos, spectacle)* risqué; *(gens)* wild

olfactif, -ive [ɔlfaktif, -iv] *adj* olfactory

olibrius [ɔlibrijys] *nm Fam* oddball

oligarchie [ɔligarʃi] *nf* oligarchy

oligarchique [ɔligarʃik] *adj* oligarchic

oligoélément [ɔligoelemɑ̃] *nm* trace element

olivâtre [ɔlivatr] *adj* olive-greenish; *(teint)* sallow

olive [ɔliv] **1** *nf* olive

2 *adj inv* olive (green)

oliveraie [ɔlivrɛ] *nf* olive grove

olivier [ɔlivje] *nm (arbre)* olive tree; *(bois)* olive (wood)

OLP [ɔɛlpe] *nf* (*abrév* **Organisation de libération de la Palestine**) PLO

olympiade [ɔlɛ̃pjad] *nf* Olympiad

olympique [ɔlɛ̃pik] *adj* Olympic

ombilical, -e, -aux, -ales [ɔ̃bilikal, -o] *adj* umbilical

omble [ɔ̃bl] *nm* **o.(-chevalier)** char

ombrage [ɔ̃braʒ] *nm* shade; **prendre o. de qch** to take umbrage at sth; **porter o. à qn** to give offense to sb

ombragé, -e [ɔ̃braʒe] *adj* shady

ombrageux, -euse [ɔ̃braʒø, -øz] *adj (personne)* touchy

ombre¹ [ɔ̃br] *nf* (**a**) *(forme)* shadow; **ombres chinoises** shadow play; *Fig* **jeter une o. sur qch** to cast a shadow over sth (**b**) *(zone sombre)* shade; **40 degrés à l'o.** 40 degrees in the shade; **faire de l'o. à qn** to be in sb's light; *Fig* to put sb in the shade; *Fig* **il y a une o. au tableau** there's a fly in the ointment (**c**) *(obscurité)* darkness; *Fig (anonymat)* obscurity; *Fig* **rester dans/sortir de l'o.** to remain in/emerge from obscurity; *Fig* **laisser qch dans l'o.** to keep sth dark; *Fig* **travailler dans l'o.** to work behind the scenes; *Fam* **mettre qn à l'o.** to put sb inside (**d**) *Litt (fantôme)* shade; *Fig* **n'être plus que l'o. de soi-même** to be a mere shadow of one's former self (**e**) *(trace)* hint; **vous n'avez pas l'o. d'une chance** you haven't the ghost of a chance; **il n'y a pas l'o. d'un doute** there isn't the shadow of a doubt; **pas l'o. d'un** not a single one (**f**) **o. à paupières** eye shadow

ombre² [ɔ̃br] *nm (poisson)* char

ombré [ɔ̃bre] *nm Ordinat* shading

ombrelle [ɔ̃brɛl] *nf* sunshade, parasol

OMC [ɔɛmse] *nf* (*abrév* **Organisation mondiale du commerce**) WTO

omelette [ɔmlɛt] *nf* omelet; *Fig* **on ne fait pas d'o. sans casser des œufs** you can't make an omelet without breaking eggs; **o. norvégienne** baked Alaska

omettre [47] [ɔmɛtr] *vt* to omit; **o. de faire qch** to omit to do sth

omis, -e *voir* **omettre**

omission [ɔmisjɔ̃] *nf (d'un mot, d'un détail)* omission; *(oubli)* oversight

omnibus [ɔmnibys] *nm* local train

omnipotence [ɔmnipɔtɑ̃s] *nf* omnipotence

omnipotent, -e [ɔmnipɔtɑ̃, -ɑ̃t] *adj* omnipotent

omniprésence [ɔmniprezɑ̃s] *nf* omnipresence

omniprésent, -e [ɔmniprezɑ̃, -ɑ̃t] *adj* omnipresent

omniscience [ɔmnisjɑ̃s] *nf* omniscience

omniscient, -e [ɔmnisjɑ̃, -ɑ̃t] *adj* omniscient

omnisports [ɔmnispɔr] *adj inv* **stade/centre o.** sports stadium/center

omnivore [ɔmnivɔr] **1** *adj* omnivorous

2 *nm* omnivore

omoplate [ɔmɔplat] *nf* shoulder blade

OMS [ɔɛmɛs] *nf* (*abrév* **Organisation mondiale de la santé**) WHO

on [ɔ̃] *pron indéfini* (**a**) *(indéterminé)* you, people, *Sout* one; *(quelqu'un)* somebody, someone; **on ne sait jamais** you never know; **on nous prend parfois pour deux sœurs** people sometimes take us for sisters; **on dit qu'il est malade, on le dit malade** they say he's sick; **on sonne** there's somebody at the door; **dans tous les pays où l'on parle français** in every country where French is spoken; **on m'a volé mon sac** my bag's been stolen, someone's stolen my bag (**b**) *Fam (nous)* we; **on ne s'est plus jamais quittés** we've been together ever since

onanisme [ɔnanism] *nm* onanism

once [ɔ̃s] *nf aussi Fig* ounce

oncle [ɔ̃kl] *nm* uncle; **o. d'Amérique** rich uncle

onctueux, -euse [ɔ̃ktɥø, -øz] *adj aussi Fig & Péj* smooth

onctuosité [ɔ̃ktɥozite] *nf* smoothness

onde [ɔ̃d] *nf* **(a)** *Phys* wave; *Rad* **grandes ondes** long wave; *Rad* **ondes courtes/moyennes** short/medium wave; **o. de choc** shock wave; **sur les ondes** on the radio; **passer sur les ondes** to be on the radio; **o. sonore** sound wave **(b)** *Litt (eau)* waters; **l'o. limpide du ruisseau** the clear waters of the stream

ondée [ɔ̃de] *nf* sudden downpour

on-dit [ɔdi] *nm inv* rumor, hearsay; **ce ne sont que des o.** it's only hearsay

ondoyant, -e [ɔ̃dwajɑ̃, -ɑ̃t] *adj Litt* undulating

ondoyer [32] [ɔ̃dwaje] *vi (blés)* to sway; *(drapeau)* to wave; *(surface de l'eau)* to ripple; *(flamme)* to flicker

ondulant, -e [ɔ̃dylɑ̃, -ɑ̃t] *adj (plaine)* rolling, undulating; *(vagues)* rippling; *(chevelure)* wavy; *(démarche)* swaying

ondulation [ɔ̃dylasjɔ̃] *nf (des vagues)* ripple; **les ondulations de la plaine** the rolling *or* undulating plain; **les ondulations de sa chevelure** her wavy hair

ondulé, -e [ɔ̃dyle] *adj (sol)* undulating; *(cheveux)* wavy; *(tôle, carton)* corrugated

onduler [ɔ̃dyle] *vi* to undulate; *(cheveux)* to be wavy; **o. des hanches** to sway one's hips

onduleur [ɔ̃dylœr] *nm Ordinat* uninterruptible power supply, UPS

onéreux, -euse [ɔnerø, -øz] *adj* costly

ONF [ɔɛnɛf] *nm (abrév* **Office national des forêts)** ≃ National Forestry Service

ONG [ɔɛnʒe] *nf (abrév* **organisation non gouvernementale)** NGO

ongle [ɔ̃gl] *nm* (finger)nail; *(des orteils)* (toe)nail; *(d'un animal)* claw; *(d'un oiseau de proie)* talon; **se faire les ongles** to do one's nails; **o. incarné** ingrowing nail; *Fig* **jusqu'au bout des ongles** to one's fingertips

onglée [ɔ̃gle] *nf* **j'ai l'o.** my fingers are numb with cold

onglet [ɔ̃glɛ] *nm* **(a)** *(d'un répertoire)* tab; *(d'un canif)* thumbnail groove; **dictionnaire à onglets** thumb-indexed dictionary **(b)** *Culin* flank of beef

onguent [ɔ̃gɑ̃] *nm Litt* ointment

onirique [ɔnirik] *adj* dreamlike

onomatopée [ɔnɔmatɔpe] *nf* onomatopoeia

ont *voir* **avoir¹**

Ontario [ɔ̃tarjo] *n voir* **lac**

ONU [ɔny, ɔɛny] *nf (abrév* **Organisation des Nations unies)** UN

onyx [ɔniks] *nm* onyx

onze [ɔ̃z] *adj & nm inv* eleven; *voir aussi* **trois**

onzième [ɔ̃zjɛm] *nmf, nm & adj* eleventh; *voir aussi* **cinquième**

OPA [opea] *nf (abrév* **offre publique d'achat)** takeover bid; **lancer une O. (sur)** to make a takeover bid (for)

opacité [ɔpasite] *nf* opacity

opale [ɔpal] *nf* opal

opaque [ɔpak] *adj aussi Fig* opaque

OPEP [ɔpɛp] *nf (abrév* **Organisation des pays exportateurs de pétrole)** OPEC

opéra [ɔpera] *nm* **(a)** *(genre, œuvre)* opera **(b)** *(lieu)* opera house; **aller à l'o.** to go to the opera; **l'O. (de Paris)** the Paris Opera House; **o. bouffe** comic opera

opérable [ɔperabl] *adj* operable

opérateur, -trice [ɔperatœr, -tris] **1** *nm,f (personne)* operator; *Cin* cameraman; **o. de saisie** keyboarder
    2 *nm* **(a)** *Math* operator **(b)** *Ordinat* **o. logique** logical operator

opération [ɔperasjɔ̃] *nf* **(a)** **o. (chirurgicale)** operation; **o. à cœur ouvert** open-heart surgery **(b)** *Math* operation; **faire des opérations** to do some calculations **(c)** *(transaction)* deal, transaction; **o. financière** financial transaction **(d)** *(action)* operation; **o. de police** police operation

opérationnel, -elle [ɔperasjɔnɛl] *adj* operational

opératoire [ɔperatwar] *adj (procédure)* operating

opérer [34] [ɔpere] **1** *vt* **(a)** *(réforme, restructuration)* to carry out; *(changement, distinction)* to make **(b)** *(patient)* to operate on; **se faire o.** to have an operation; **se faire o. des amygdales** to have one's tonsils (taken) out; **se faire o. du cœur/ de la hanche** to have a heart/hip operation; **se faire o. d'une tumeur** to have an operation to remove a tumor
    2 *vi* **(a)** *(être efficace)* to work **(b)** *(procéder)* to operate
    3 s'opérer *vpr (changement, transformation)* to take place

opérette [ɔperɛt] *nf* operetta

ophtalmo [ɔftalmo] *nmf Fam* ophthalmologist

ophtalmologie [ɔftalmɔlɔʒi] *nf Méd* ophthalmology

ophtalmologiste [ɔftalmɔlɔʒist], **ophtalmologue** [ɔftalmɔlɔg] *nmf Méd* ophthalmologist

opiner [ɔpine] *vi* **o. du chef** *ou* **du bonnet** to nod in agreement

opiniâtre [ɔpinjɑtr] *adj* stubborn

opinion [ɔpinjɔ̃] *nf* opinion (**de/sur** of/about); **se faire une o. sur qch** to make up one's mind about sth, to form an opinion about sth; **changer d'o.** to change one's mind; **les sans o.** *(dans un sondage)* the don't knows; **avoir une bonne/ mauvaise o. de qn/qch** to have a good/bad opinion of sb/ sth; **o. publique** public opinion

opiomane [ɔpjɔman] *nmf* opium addict

opium [ɔpjɔm] *nm* opium

opossum [ɔpɔsɔm] *nm* opossum

opportun, -e [ɔpɔrtœ̃, -yn] *adj (arrivée)* timely, opportune; *(moment, jour)* right

opportunément [ɔpɔrtynemɑ̃] *adv* opportunely

opportunisme [ɔpɔrtynism] *nm* opportunism

opportuniste [ɔpɔrtynist] *adj & nmf* opportunist

opportunité [ɔpɔrtynite] *nf (d'une arrivée)* timeliness; *(d'un projet, d'une décision)* advisability

opposant, -e [ɔpozɑ̃, -ɑ̃t] **1** *adj* opposing
    2 *nm,f* opponent (**à** of)

opposé, -e [ɔpoze] **1** *adj* **(a)** *(en contradiction) (armées, caractères, équipe)* opposing; *(intérêts)* conflicting **(b)** *(dans l'espace) (côtés, rivage, direction)* opposite **(c)** *(contre)* **être o. à qch** to be opposed to sth
    2 *nm (contraire)* **l'o.** the opposite; **à l'o.** *(côté)* on the opposite side; *(direction)* in the opposite direction; *Fig* on the other hand; **à l'o. de** *(côté)* on the opposite side to; *(contrairement à)* unlike; **à l'o. de sa mère, elle n'aimait pas la peinture** unlike her mother, she didn't like painting; **son deuxième film est à l'o. du premier** this second movie is the complete opposite of the first

opposer [ɔpoze] **1** *vt* **(a)** *(mettre en conflit) (armées, pays)* to bring into conflict (with each other); *(équipes)* to pit against each other; **o. à** *(armée, pays)* to bring into conflict with; *(équipe)* to pit against **(b)** *(objecter) (argument)* to put forward (**à** against); **o. une résistance vigoureuse** to put up stiff resistance **(c)** *(mettre en contraste) (théories, styles, conceptions)* to contrast
    2 s'opposer *vpr* **(a)** *(théories, styles, conceptions)* to contrast; *(équipes, adversaires)* to confront each other **(b)** **s'o. à qch** to be opposed to sth; **je m'oppose à ce qu'elle revienne** I'm against *or* opposed to her coming back

opposition [ɔpozisjɔ̃] *nf* **(a)** *(résistance)* opposition; *Pol* **l'o.** the Opposition; **faire o. à un chèque** to stop a check **(b)** *(contraste)* contrast; **tout cela est en o. totale avec ce que je pense** all that is the complete opposite of what I think; **par o. à qch** as opposed to sth

oppressant, -e [ɔprɛsɑ̃, -ɑ̃t] *adj* oppressive

oppresser [ɔprese] *vt* (**a**) *(sujet: situation, atmosphère)* to oppress (**b**) *Litt (peuple, nation)* to oppress

oppresseur [ɔprɛsœr] **1** *nm* oppressor
  2 *adj* oppressive

oppression [ɔprɛsjɔ̃] *nf* (**a**) *(asservissement)* oppression (**b**) *Méd* tightness of the chest

opprimé, -e [ɔprime] **1** *adj* oppressed
  2 *nm,f* **les opprimés** the oppressed

opprimer [ɔprime] *vt (peuple, nation)* to oppress

opprobre [ɔprɔbr] *nm Litt* opprobrium; **jeter l'o. sur qn** to cast opprobrium on sb

opter [ɔpte] *vi* **o. pour qch** to opt for sth; **o. entre deux choses** to choose between two things

opticien, -enne [ɔptisjɛ̃, -ɛn] *nm,f* optician

optimal, -e, -aux, -ales [ɔptimal, -o] *adj* optimum, optimal

optimiser [ɔptimize] *vt* to optimize

optimisme [ɔptimism] *nm* optimism; **avec o.** optimistically

optimiste [ɔptimist] **1** *adj* optimistic
  2 *nmf* optimist

option [ɔpsjɔ̃] *nf* (**a**) *(choix)* option (**b**) *(chose facultative)* optional extra; *Scol (matière)* option; **le flash est en o.** the flash is an optional extra; *Scol* **matières à o.** optional subjects (**c**) *(d'achat)* **prendre une o. sur qch** to take (out) an option on sth (**d**) *Ordinat* **o. d'impression** print option; **o. de menu** menu option

optionnel, -elle [ɔpsjɔnɛl] *adj* optional

optique [ɔptik] **1** *adj (nerf)* optic; *(verre)* optical
  2 *nf* (**a**) *(science)* optics *(singulier)*; **instruments d'o.** optical instruments (**b**) *(perspective)* perspective; **dans cette o.** from this perspective (**c**) *(d'un projecteur)* optical system

opulence [ɔpylɑ̃s] *nf* (**a**) *(richesse)* opulence (**b**) *(des formes)* fullness

opulent, -e [ɔpylɑ̃, -ɑ̃t] *adj (pays, personne)* opulent; *(pâturage)* abundant; *(poitrine)* full

opuscule [ɔpyskyl] *nm* opuscule

or¹ [ɔr] *nm* (**a**) *(métal)* gold; **montre/dent en or** gold watch/tooth; *Fam* **j'ai une femme en or** my wife is worth her weight in gold; **pour tout l'or du monde** for all the money in the world; *Fig* **c'est de l'or en barre** it's a safe investment; **le silence est d'or** silence is golden; **or fin** fine gold; **or massif** solid gold; **or noir** black gold; **or pur** pure gold; **l'or vert** agricultural earnings (**b**) *(couleur)* gold; **cheveux d'or** golden hair

or² [ɔr] *conj (pour introduire une précision)* now; *(pour introduire une opposition)* well

oracle [ɔrakl] *nm* oracle

orage [ɔraʒ] *nm* (thunder)storm; *aussi Fig* **il y a de l'o. dans l'air** there's a storm brewing

orageux, -euse [ɔraʒø, -øz] *adj aussi Fig* stormy

oraison [ɔrɛzɔ̃] *nf* prayer; **o. funèbre** funeral oration

oral, -e, -aux, -ales [ɔral, -o] **1** *adj* oral; **par voie orale** orally
  2 *nm (examen)* oral; **il n'est pas très bon à l'o.** his oral work isn't very good

oralement [ɔralmɑ̃] *adv* orally

orange [ɔrɑ̃ʒ] **1** *nf* orange; **o. givrée** = orange sorbet served inside the skin of a whole orange; **o. pressée** = freshly-squeezed orange juice served with water and sugar; **o. sanguine** blood orange
  2 *nm (couleur)* orange; **passer à l'o.** *(automobiliste)* to go through (the lights) on orange
  3 *adj inv* orange

orangé, -e [ɔrɑ̃ʒe] *adj* orange-colored

orangeade [ɔrɑ̃ʒad] *nf* orangeade

oranger [ɔrɑ̃ʒe] *nm* orange tree

orangeraie [ɔrɑ̃ʒrɛ] *nf* orange grove

orangerie [ɔrɑ̃ʒri] *nf* orangery

orang-outan (*pl* **orangs-outans**), **orang-outang** (*pl* **orangs-outangs**) [ɔrɑ̃utɑ̃] *nm* orang-utan

orateur, -trice [ɔratœr, -tris] *nm,f (personne éloquente)* orator; *(personne qui prend la parole)* speaker

oratoire¹ [ɔratwar] *adj* oratorical

oratoire² [ɔratwar] *nm (chapelle)* oratory

oratorio [ɔratɔrjo] *nm* oratorio

orbite [ɔrbit] *nf* (**a**) *Astron & Fig* orbit; **être en** *ou* **sur o.** to be in orbit; **mettre** *ou* **placer un satellite en** *ou* **sur o.** to put a satellite into orbit (**b**) *(de l'œil)* socket

Orcades [ɔrkad] *nfpl* **les (îles) O.** the Orkneys, the Orkney Islands

orchestral, -e, -aux, -ales [ɔrkɛstral, -o] *adj* orchestral

orchestration [ɔrkɛstrasjɔ̃] *nf aussi Fig* orchestration

orchestre [ɔrkɛstr] *nm* (**a**) *(de musiciens)* orchestra; **o. de chambre** chamber orchestra; **o. de jazz** jazz band (**b**) *(partie de la salle)* orchestra

orchestrer [ɔrkɛstre] *vt aussi Fig* to orchestrate

orchidée [ɔrkide] *nf* orchid

ordi [ɔrdi] *nm Fam* computer

ordinaire [ɔrdinɛr] **1** *adj* (**a**) *(habituel)* ordinary, usual; **peu** *ou* **pas o.** unusual (**b**) *(commun)* ordinary
  2 *nm* (**a**) *(habitude)* **d'o.** usually; **comme à l'o.** as usual; **moins/plus que d'o.** less/more than usual (**b**) *(moyenne)* **ça sort de l'o.** it's out of the ordinary (**c**) *(régime habituel)* standard fare; *Mil* (company) mess (**d**) *(essence)* regular

ordinal, -e, -aux, -ales [ɔrdinal, -o] *adj* ordinal

ordinariat [ɔrdinarja] *nm Belg Univ* tenured professorship

ordinateur [ɔrdinatœr] *nm* computer; **o. autonome** stand-alone (computer); **o. bloc-notes** notebook (computer); **o. de bureau** desktop (computer); **o. central** mainframe (computer); **o. domestique** home computer; **o. individuel** personal computer; **o. de poche** palmtop (computer); **o. portable** laptop (computer)

ordination [ɔrdinasjɔ̃] *nf* ordination

ordonnance [ɔrdɔnɑ̃s] *nf* (**a**) *(document)* prescription; **délivré seulement sur o.** available on prescription only (**b**) *(disposition)* arrangement (**c**) *Jur* order, ruling (**d**) *Mil* orderly

ordonné, -e [ɔrdɔne] **1** *adj* (**a**) *(vie)* orderly (**b**) *(personne, armoire, bureau)* tidy
  2 *nf* **ordonnée** *Math* ordinate; **axe des ordonnées** Y-axis

ordonner [ɔrdɔne] *vt* (**a**) *(mettre de l'ordre dans)* to organize (**b**) *(commander)* to order; **o. à qn de faire qch** to order sb to do sth (**c**) *Rel* to ordain

ordre [ɔrdr] *nm* (**a**) *(organisation)* order; **par o. alphabétique/chronologique** in alphabetical/chronological order; **procéder par o.** to do things in order; **par o. d'apparition à l'écran** in order of appearance; *Fig* **c'est dans l'o. des choses** it's in the nature of things
  (**b**) *(de pièce, de personne)* tidiness; **en o.** *(bureau, maison)* neat, tidy; *(comptes)* in order; **mettre de l'o.** to tidy up
  (**c**) *(discipline)* order; **maintenir/rétablir l'o.** to maintain/to restore order; **tout est rentré dans l'o.** everything has returned to normal; **l'o. établi** the established order; **l'o. public** law and order; **troubler l'o. public** to cause a breach of the peace
  (**d**) *(catégorie)* order; **de premier/second/troisième o.** first-/second-/third-rate; **renseignements/idées d'o. général** general information/ideas; **d'o. privé/pratique** of a private/practical nature; **du même o.** of the same order; **de l'o. de** in the order of
  (**e**) *(communauté)* order; **o. religieux** religious order; **entrer dans les ordres** to take holy orders; **l'o. des médecins** ≃ the American Medical Association

(**f**) *(commandement)* order; **donner l'o. à qn de faire qch** to give sb the order to do sth; **je ne suis pas à tes ordres!** I don't take orders from you!; **à vos ordres, mon général!** yes, sir!; **sur l'o. de qn** on the order of sb; **jusqu'à nouvel o.** until further order

(**g**) *Fin* order; **à l'o. de...** payable to (the order of)...

(**h**) **o. du jour** *(d'un comité)* agenda; *Mil* order of the day

ordure [ɔrdyr] *nf* (**a**) *(saleté)* dirt, filth (**b**) **ordures** *(déchets)* garbage; **ordures ménagères** household garbage; **jeter** *ou* **mettre qch aux ordures** to throw sth in the trash (**c**) *Fam (personne méprisable)* bastard

ordurier, -ère [ɔrdyrje, -ɛr] *adj* filthy

orée [ɔre] *nf* **à l'o. de la forêt/du bois** on the edge of the forest/wood

oreille [ɔrɛj] *nf* (**a**) *(d'une personne, d'un animal)* ear; **o. externe/interne** outer/inner ear; **avoir les oreilles décollées** to have sticking-out ears; *Fam* **avoir les oreilles en feuilles de chou** to have big cauliflower ears; **il partit l'o. basse** he went off with his tail between his legs; **tirer les oreilles à qn** to pull sb's ears; *Fig* to give sb a telling off; **n'écouter que d'une o., écouter d'une o. distraite** to listen with half an ear; **dire qch à l'o. de qn** to whisper sth in sb's ear; **dresser** *ou* **tendre l'o.** to prick up one's ears; **je n'en crois pas mes oreilles** I can't believe my ears; **les oreilles ont dû lui siffler** his ears must have been burning; **faire la sourde o.** to turn a deaf ear; **ce n'est pas tombé dans l'o. d'un sourd** it didn't fall on deaf ears; *Fig* **elle ne l'entend pas de cette o.** she won't hear of it; **être dur d'o.** to be hard of hearing; **avoir de l'o.** to have a good ear (**b**) *(d'un fauteuil)* wing; *(d'un plat, d'un vase)* handle; *(d'une casquette)* ear flap; **écrou à oreilles** wing nut

oreiller [ɔreje] *nm* pillow; **sur l'o.** in bed; **confidences sur l'o.** pillow talk

oreillette [ɔrɛjɛt] *nf* (**a**) *(du cœur)* auricle (**b**) *(d'une casquette)* ear flap

oreillons [ɔrɛjɔ̃] *nmpl* mumps; **avoir les o.** to have the mumps

Orénoque [ɔrenɔk] *nm* **l'O.** the Orinoco

ores [ɔr] **d'ores et déjà** *adv* already

orfèvre [ɔrfɛvr] *nm (d'or)* goldsmith; *(d'argent)* silversmith; *Fig* **être o. en la matière** to be an expert in the matter

orfèvrerie [ɔrfɛvrəri] *nf (travail de l'or)* goldsmith's trade; *(travail de l'argent)* silversmith's trade; *(objets)* plate

organe [ɔrgan] *nm* (**a**) *Anat* organ; **organes génitaux** genitals (**b**) *(d'une machine)* part; **organes de transmission** transmission system (**c**) *Fig (instrument)* organ; **o. de publicité** advertising agency; **l'o. officiel du parti** the official organ of the party (**d**) *Hum (voix)* voice

organigramme [ɔrganigram] *nm* organization chart; *Ordinat* (data) flow chart

organique [ɔrganik] *adj* organic

organisateur, -trice [ɔrganizatœr, -tris] **1** *adj* organizing **2** *nm,f* organizer; **o. d'événements** event organizer; **o. de conférences/de congrès** conference organizer; **o. de mariages** wedding planner; **o. de voyages** tour operator

organisation [ɔrganizasjɔ̃] *nf* (**a**) *(action, résultat)* organization (**b**) *(groupement)* organization; **o. à but non lucratif** non-profit organization; **o. politique/syndicale** political/labor-union organization; **O. mondiale du commerce** World Trade Organization; **O. mondiale de la santé** World Health Organization; **O. des Nations unies** United Nations Organization; **O. du Traité de l'Atlantique Nord** North Atlantic Treaty Organization

organisé, -e [ɔrganize] *adj* organized

organiser [ɔrganize] **1** *vt* to organize **2 s'organiser** *vpr* to get organized

organisme [ɔrganism] *nm* (**a**) *Biol & Zool* organism; *Anat*

system (**b**) *(organisation)* organization, body; **o. de crédit** credit institution; **o. international** international organization

organiste [ɔrganist] *nmf* organist

orgasme [ɔrgasm] *nm* orgasm

orge [ɔrʒ] *nf* barley

orgeat [ɔrʒa] *nm* **sirop d'o.** barley water

orgelet [ɔrʒəlɛ] *nm* sty *(on eye)*

orgie [ɔrʒi] *nf* orgy

orgue [ɔrg] **1** *nm* organ; **o. de Barbarie** barrel organ **2** *nfpl Mus* **orgues** organ; **les grandes orgues de la cathédrale** the great organ of the cathedral

orgueil [ɔrgœj] *nm* pride

orgueilleux, -euse [ɔrgœjø, -øz] *Péj* **1** *adj* proud **2** *nm,f* proud person

orient [ɔrjɑ̃] *nm* east; **l'O.** the East, the Orient; **en O.** in the East

orientable [ɔrjɑ̃tabl] *adj (grue)* swiveling; *(lampe, antenne)* adjustable

oriental, -e, -aux, -ales [ɔrjɑ̃tal, -o] **1** *adj (région, côte)* eastern; *(langue)* oriental **2** *nm,f* **O., Orientale** Oriental

orientateur, -trice [ɔrjɑ̃tatœr, -tris] = **orienteur**

orientation [ɔrjɑ̃tasjɔ̃] *nf* (**a**) *(détermination de position)* orientation; **avoir le sens de l'o.** to have a good sense of direction (**b**) *Scol* career counseling; **choisir une o.** to choose a course of study (**c**) *(d'une grue, d'une antenne)* positioning (**d**) *(d'une maison)* aspect (**e**) *(d'une politique, de recherches)* direction

orienté, -e [ɔrjɑ̃te] *adj (a)* *(disposé)* **maison/pièce orientée au sud** house/room facing south (**b**) *(peu objectif)* biased (**c**) *Ordinat* **o. ligne** line-orientated; **o. objet** object-orientated

orienter [ɔrjɑ̃te] **1** *vt (a)* *(bâtiment)* to orient; *(canon, fusil, télescope)* to point (**vers** *ou* **sur** at) (**b**) *(voyageur)* to direct, to guide; *Scol* **on l'a bien/mal orientée** she was given good/bad career counseling; **o. la conversation sur** to steer the conversation to; **o. ses recherches vers** to direct one's research toward **2 s'orienter** *vpr (a)* *(trouver sa route)* to get one's bearings (**b**) *Fig* **s'o. vers** *(sujet: étudiant)* to specialize in; *(sujet: recherches)* to be directed toward

orienteur, -euse [ɔrjɑ̃tœr, -øz] *nm,f Scol* career counselor

orifice [ɔrifis] *nm* opening; *(du corps)* orifice; *Tech* port

oriflamme [ɔriflam] *nf* (**a**) *Hist* oriflamme (**b**) *(bannière)* banner

origan [ɔrigɑ̃] *nm* oregano

originaire [ɔriʒinɛr] *adj* **être o. de** *(sujet: personne)* to be a native of; *(sujet: coutume, plat)* to originate from

original, -e, -aux, -ales [ɔriʒinal, -o] **1** *adj* (**a**) *(premier, nouveau)* original (**b**) *(excentrique)* eccentric **2** *nm,f (excentrique)* eccentric **3** *nm (œuvre, document)* original; *(d'un fichier, d'une disquette)* master copy

originalité [ɔriʒinalite] *nf* (**a**) *(nouveauté)* originality (**b**) *(excentricité)* eccentricity (**c**) *(trait original)* original feature

origine [ɔriʒin] *nf* origin; **des origines à nos jours** from the earliest times to the present day; **à l'o.** originally; **être à l'o. de qch** to be at the origin of sth; **être d'o. modeste** to be of humble origin; **être d'o. anglaise, être anglais d'o.** to be of English origin

originel, -elle [ɔriʒinɛl] *adj* original

orignal, -aux [ɔriɲal, -o] *nm* moose

oripeaux [ɔripo] *nmpl* rags, tatters

ORL [ɔɛrɛl] *nmf Méd (abrév* **oto-rhino-laryngologiste)** ENT specialist

orme [ɔrm] *nm* elm

ormeau, -x [ɔrmo] *nm* (**a**) *(arbre)* young elm (**b**) *(mollusque)* abalone

ornement [ɔrnəmã] *nm aussi Mus* ornament

ornemental, -e, -aux, -ales [ɔrnəmãtal, -o] *adj* ornamental

orner [ɔrne] *vt* to decorate (**de** with); *(vêtement)* to trim (**de** with)

ornière [ɔrnjɛr] *nf* rut; *Fig* **sortir de l'o.** to get out of trouble

ornithologie [ɔrnitɔlɔʒi] *nf* ornithology

ornithologiste [ɔrnitɔlɔʒist], **ornithologue** [ɔrnitɔlɔg] *nmf* ornithologist

oronge [ɔrɔ̃ʒ] *nf* agaric

orphelin, -e [ɔrfəlɛ̃, -in] **1** *adj* orphan(ed); **o. de père** fatherless; **o. de mère** motherless

     2 *nm,f* orphan

orphelinat [ɔrfəlina] *nm* orphanage

orque [ɔrk] *nf* killer whale

Orsay [ɔrsɛ] *n voir* **quai**

ORSEC [ɔrsɛk] *(abrév* **organisation des secours**) **le plan O.** = disaster contingency plan

---

Le plan ORSEC

This scheme is set in motion whenever there is a major disaster in France, such as flooding or forest fires. Under the provisions of the scheme, the "préfet", or chief of police, is empowered to mobilize both public and private resources to deal with a civil emergency.

---

orteil [ɔrtɛj] *nm* toe; **gros/petit o.** big/little toe

orthodontiste [ɔrtodɔ̃tist] *nmf* orthodontist

orthodoxe [ɔrtodɔks] **1** *adj aussi Rel* orthodox; **peu o.** unorthodox

     2 *nmf Rel (de stricte obédience)* person of orthodox beliefs; *(de l'Église orthodoxe)* member of the Orthodox Church

orthodoxie [ɔrtodɔksi] *nf* orthodoxy

orthogonal, -e, -aux, -ales [ɔrtɔgɔnal, -o] *adj* orthogonal

orthographe [ɔrtɔgraf] *nf* spelling; **avoir une bonne o.** to be good at spelling

orthographier [66] [ɔrtɔgrafje] *vt* to spell; **mal o. un mot** to misspell a word

orthographique [ɔrtɔgrafik] *adj* orthographic

orthopédie [ɔrtɔpedi] *nf* orthopedics *(singulier)*

orthopédique [ɔrtɔpedik] *adj* orthopedic

orthopédiste [ɔrtɔpedist] *nmf* **(a)** *(médecin)* orthopedist **(b)** *(fabricant)* maker of orthopedic apparatus

orthophonie [ɔrtɔfɔni] *nf* speech therapy

orthophoniste [ɔrtɔfɔnist] *nmf* speech therapist

ortie [ɔrti] *nf* nettle

ortolan [ɔrtɔlã] *nm* ortolan (bunting)

OS [ɔɛs] *nm (abrév* **ouvrier spécialisé**) semi-skilled worker

os [ɔs, *pl* o] *nm* bone; *Fam Fig (obstacle)* snag; **mouillé** *ou* **trempé jusqu'aux os** soaked to the skin; *Fam* **tomber sur un os** to hit a snag; *très Fam* **je l'ai dans l'os** I've had it; **os à moelle**, *Belg* **os à la moelle** marrowbone

oscar [ɔskar] *nm Cin (récompense)* Oscar; **les oscars** *(cérémonie)* Oscar night, the Oscars

oscarisé, -e [ɔskarize] *adj Cin* Oscar-winning; **l'acteur o. pour "Gladiator"** the actor who won an Oscar for "Gladiator"

oscariser [3] [ɔskarize] *vt Cin* to award an Oscar to

oscillateur [ɔsilatœr] *nm Phys* oscillator

oscillation [ɔsilasjɔ̃] *nf* **(a)** *(d'un pendule)* swing; *(d'une aiguille)* flickering; *(d'un bateau)* rocking; *Phys* oscillation **(b)** *Fig (du marché, de l'opinion)* fluctuation

osciller [ɔsile] *vi* **(a)** *(pendule)* to swing; *(aiguille)* to flicker; *(bateau)* to rock; *Phys* to oscillate **(b)** *(hésiter)* **o. entre** to waver between

osé, -e [oze] *adj* daring

oseille [ozɛj] *nf* **(a)** *(plante)* sorrel **(b)** *Fam (argent)* dough, bucks

oser [oze] *vt* **o. faire qch** to dare (to) do sth; **j'ose croire que...** I dare say that...; **si j'ose dire** if I may say so; **comment osez-vous!** how dare you!

osier [ozje] *nm* **(a)** *(arbre)* osier **(b)** *(en vannerie)* wicker

Oslo [ɔslo] *n* Oslo

osmose [ɔsmoz] *nf aussi Fig* osmosis

ossature [ɔsatyr] *nf* **(a)** *(d'un homme, d'un animal)* frame **(b)** *Fig (d'un bâtiment, d'un texte)* framework

osselets [ɔslɛ] *nmpl* **jouer aux o.** to play at knucklebones

ossements [ɔsmã] *nmpl* bones

osseux, -euse [ɔsø, -øz] *adj (visage, main)* bony; *(tissu, greffe)* bone

ossuaire [ɔsɥɛr] *nm* ossuary

ostensible [ɔstãsibl] *adj* open

ostensiblement [ɔstãsibləmã] *adv* openly

ostensoir [ɔstãswar] *nm Rel* monstrance

ostentation [ɔstãtasjɔ̃] *nf* ostentation; **sans o.** unostentatiously

ostéopathe [ɔsteɔpat] *nmf* osteopath

ostéopathie [ɔsteɔpati] *nf* osteopathy

ostéoporose [ɔsteɔpɔroz] *nf Méd* osteoporosis

ostracisme [ɔstrasism] *nm* ostracism

ostréiculteur, -trice [ɔstreikyltœr, -tris] *nm,f* oyster farmer

ostréiculture [ɔstreikyltyr] *nf* oyster farming

otage [ɔtaʒ] *nm* hostage; **prendre qn en o.** to take sb hostage

otalgie [ɔtalʒi] *nf Méd* earache, *Spéc* otalgia

OTAN [ɔtã] *nf (abrév* **Organisation du traité de l'Atlantique Nord**) **l'O.** NATO

otarie [ɔtari] *nf* sea lion

OTASE [ɔtaz] *nf (abrév* **Organisation du traité de l'Asie du Sud-Est**) **l'O.** SEATO

ôter [ote] **1** *vt* **(a)** *(enlever)* to take away, to remove; *(vêtement)* to take off; *(tache)* to remove; *(assiettes)* to clear away; **ô. qch à qn** to take sth away from sb; *(illusions)* to rid sb of sth; **cela lui a ôté l'appétit** it's made him/her lose his/her appetite; **je vais t'ô. l'envie de recommencer!** I'll teach you not to start that again!; **tu ne m'ôteras pas de l'idée que...** I'm quite convinced that... **(b)** *Math* **10 ôté de 30 égale 20** 10 from 30 leaves 20

     2 s'ôter *vpr* **ôtez-vous de là!** move out of the way!; **s'ô. une idée de la tête** to get an idea out of one's head

otite [ɔtit] *nf Méd* ear infection, *Spéc* otitis

oto-rhino *(pl* **oto-rhinos**) [ɔtorino] *nmf Fam* ENT specialist

oto-rhino-laryngologiste *(pl* **oto-rhino-laryngologistes**) [ɔtorinɔlarɛ̃gɔlɔʒist] *nmf* ear, nose and throat specialist

Ottawa [ɔtawa] *n* Ottawa

ou [u] *conj* or; **ou... ou (bien)...** either... or (else)...

où [u] **1** *adv* **(a)** *(interrogatif, relatif)* where; **d'où vient ce mot?** where does this word come from?; **par où est-il passé?** which way did he go?; **je ne sais pas où aller** I don't know where to go **(b)** *(indéfini)* **où que vous soyez** wherever you may be **(c)** *(exprime la conséquence)* **d'où sa tristesse** hence his/her sadness

     2 *pron relatif* **(a)** *(dans l'espace)* where; **là où** where; **partout où** wherever **(b)** *(dans le temps)* when **(c)** *(dans lequel, auquel)* **dans l'état où elle est** in the state she's in; **au prix où est le champagne** with champagne the price it is

OUA [oya] *nf (abrév* **Organisation de l'unité africaine**) **l'O.** the OAU

ouache [waʃ] *nf Can* bear's den

ouah [wa] *exclam* **(a)** *(aboiement)* woof! **(b)** *(exprime l'admiration)* wow!

ouailles [wɑj] *nfpl Litt ou Hum* flock

ouais [wɛ] *exclam Fam* yeah!

ouananiche [wananiʃ] *nf Can* freshwater salmon

ouaouaron [wawarɔ̃] *nm Can* bullfrog

ouate [wat] *nf* (a) *(pour soins)* absorbent cotton (b) *(pour rembourrage)* padding

ouatine [watin] *nf* quilting (material)

ouatiné, -e [watine] *adj* quilted

oubli [ubli] *nm* (a) *(trou de mémoire)* oversight; *(lacune)* omission (b) *(général)* oblivion; **tomber dans l'o.** to sink into oblivion (c) *(acte d'oublier)* forgetting

oublier [66] [ublije] **1** *vt* to forget; *(omettre)* to leave out; **o. de faire qch** to forget to do sth; *Hum* **il a oublié d'être bête** he's not lacking in brains
  2 s'oublier *vpr* (a) *(se relâcher)* to forget oneself; *Euph (chien)* to have an accident, to make a mess (b) *(sortir de la mémoire)* to be forgotten; **c'est comme le vélo, ça ne s'oublie pas** it's like riding a bike, once you learn you never forget

oubliettes [ublijɛt] *nfpl* dungeon; *Fig* **mettre qch aux o.** to shelve sth

ouèbe [wɛb] *nm Ordinat* **l'o.** the Web

ouest [wɛst] **1** *nm* west; **un vent d'o.** a westerly wind; **le vent d'o.** the west wind; **à l'o.** in the west; **à l'o. de** (to the) west of; *Géog & Pol* **l'O.** the West
  2 *adj inv (côte, face)* west; *(régions)* western

ouf [uf] *exclam* phew!, whew!; *Fam* **elle n'a pas eu le temps de dire o.** she didn't even have time to catch her breath

Ouganda [ugɑ̃da] *nm* **l'O.** Uganda

ougandais, -e [ugɑ̃dɛ, -ɛz] **1** *adj* Ugandan
  2 *nm,f* **O., Ougandaise** Ugandan

oui [wi] **1** *adv* yes; **répondre par o. ou par non** to answer yes or no; **je crois que o.** I think so; **faire signe que o.** to nod (one's head); **ah, o.?** really?; *Fam* **tu viens, o.?** are you coming?; *Fam* **tu viens, o. ou non?** are you coming or not?
  2 *nm inv Pol* aye; *Fam* **se quereller/pleurer pour un o., pour un non** to quarrel/to cry over the slightest thing

ouï-dire [widir] *nm* rumor, hearsay; **par o.** by hearsay

ouïe [wi] *nf* (a) *(sens)* hearing; **avoir l'o. fine** to have sharp ears; *Hum* **être tout o.** to be all ears (b) *(de poisson)* **ouïes** gills (c) *Mus* **ouïes** sound holes

ouille [uj] *exclam* ouch!, ow!

ouïr [51] [uir] *vt* (a) *Littéraire ou Hum* to hear; **j'ai ouï dire que tu avais déménagé** I heard that you had moved; **j'ai souvent ouï dire que...** I have often heard it said that... (b) *Jur* **o. des témoins** to hear witnesses

ouistiti [wistiti] *nm* marmoset; *Fam Fig* **un drôle de o.** an odd character

ouragan [uragɑ̃] *nm* hurricane; *Fig (de protestations)* storm; **entrer comme un o. dans une pièce** to burst into a room

Oural [ural] *nm* **l'O.** *(montagnes)* the Urals

ourler [urle] *vt* (a) *(faire un ourlet à)* to hem (b) *(border)* to edge (**de** with)

ourlet [urlɛ] *nm* (a) *(d'un vêtement)* hem; **faire un o. à** to put a hem on (b) *(de l'oreille)* rim

ours [urs] *nm aussi Fig* bear; *Prov* **il ne faut pas vendre la peau de l'o. avant de l'avoir tué** don't count your chickens before they hatch; **o. blanc** polar bear; **o. brun** brown bear; *Fig* **o. mal léché** boor; **o. en peluche** teddy bear; **o. polaire** polar bear

ourse [urs] *nf* she-bear; *Astron* **la Grande O.** the Great Bear; **la Petite O.** the Little Bear

oursin [ursɛ̃] *nm* sea urchin

ourson [ursɔ̃] *nm* bear cub

oust(e) [ust] *exclam (pour presser)* move it!; *(pour chasser)* scram!

outarde [utard] *nf Can* Canada goose

outer [3] [awte] *vt Fam (révéler l'homosexualité de)* to out

outil [uti] *nm aussi Fig* tool; **outils pédagogiques** teaching aids; **o. de production** production tool; **o. de travail** tool

outillage [utijaʒ] *nm* (a) *(ensemble d'outils)* (set of) tools (b) *(industriel, agricole)* equipment

outiller [utije] **1** *vt* to equip
  2 s'outiller *vpr (bricoleur)* to equip oneself; *(usine)* to equip itself

outrage [utraʒ] *nm (au bon goût, au bon sens)* insult (**à** to); *Euph & Litt* **faire subir les derniers outrages à une femme** to violate a woman; *Jur* **o. aux bonnes mœurs** affront to public decency; **o. à magistrat** contempt of court; **o. à la pudeur** public indecency

outrageant, -e [utraʒɑ̃, -ɑ̃t] *adj (proposition, refus)* insulting; *(plaisanterie, propos)* offensive; *(accusation)* outrageous

outrageusement [utraʒøzmɑ̃] *adv (excessivement)* outrageously

outrance [utrɑ̃s] *nf (d'une tenue, d'une attitude, de propos)* extravagance; **à o.** excessively

outre¹ [utr] *nf* wine skin

outre² [utr] **1** *prép* (a) *(en plus de)* besides (b) **o. mesure** unduly
  2 *adv* **en o.** besides; **passer o.** *(malgré une interdiction)* to carry on regardless; **passer o. à qch** to disregard sth
  3 *conj* **o. (le fait) que...** apart from the fact that...

outré, -e [utre] *adj* (a) *(indigné)* outraged (**de** *ou* **par** by) (b) *(excessif)* overdone

outre-Atlantique [utratlɑ̃tik] *adv* across the Atlantic

outrecuidance [utrəkɥidɑ̃s] *nf Litt* (a) *(insolence)* impertinence; **avoir l'o. de faire qch** to have the impertinence to do sth (b) *(orgueil)* presumptuousness

outrecuidant, -e [utrəkɥidɑ̃, -ɑ̃t] *adj* (a) *(insolent)* impertinent (b) *(orgueilleux)* presumptuous

outre-Manche [utrəmɑ̃ʃ] *adv* across the Channel

outre-mer [utrəmɛr] *adv* overseas; **la France d'o.** France's overseas territories and departments

outrepasser [utrəpase] *vt* to exceed, to go beyond

outre-Rhin [utrərɛ̃] *adv* across the Rhine

outre-tombe [utrətɔ̃b] **d'outre-tombe** *adj (voix)* sepulchral

ouvert, -e [uvɛr, -ɛrt] **1** *pp voir* **ouvrir**
  2 *adj* (a) *(porte, yeux, plaie, vêtement, magasin)* open; **grand o.** wide open; **être o. à qn** *(lieu, concours)* to be open to sb (b) *(gaz, robinet)* on (c) *Fig (franc, sans préjugés)* open; **avoir l'esprit o.** to be open-minded; **être o. à toute proposition** to be open to suggestions

ouvertement [uvɛrtəmɑ̃] *adv* openly

ouverture [uvɛrtyr] *nf* (a) *(d'une porte, d'une séance, d'un compte)* opening; *(des hostilités)* outbreak; **l'o. de la chasse/ de la pêche** the start of the hunting season/fishing season; **à l'o.** *(de la Bourse)* at the start of trading; *Fig* **o. d'esprit** open-mindedness; *Ordinat* **o. de session** log-on (b) *(orifice)* opening (c) **ouvertures** *(avances)* overtures; **faire des ouvertures à qn** to make overtures to sb (d) *Mus* overture (e) *Phot* aperture (f) *Pol* **politique d'o.** policy of conciliation (g) *(aux échecs, aux cartes)* opening

ouvrable [uvrabl] *adj voir* **jour**

ouvrage [uvraʒ] **1** *nm* (a) *(travail)* work; **se mettre à l'o.** to get down to work (b) *Constr* work; **ouvrages d'art** civil engineering works (c) *(livre)* work; **o. de référence** reference work (d) *(résultat d'un travail)* piece of work; *(tricot, broderie)* work
  2 *nf Fam* **c'est de la belle o.** that's a nice piece of work

ouvragé, -e [uvraʒe] *adj* elaborate

ouvrant, -e [uvrɑ̃, -ɑ̃t] *adj voir* **toit**

ouvre-boîtes [uvrəbwat] *nm inv* can opener

ouvre-bouteilles [uvrəbutɛj] *nm inv* bottle opener

ouvreur, -euse [uvrœr, -øz] *nm,f* usher, *f* usherette

ouvrier, -ère [uvrije, -ɛr] **1** *adj (quartier, tradition)* working-class; *(agitation)* **agitation ouvrière** social unrest

2 *nm,f* worker; **une famille d'ouvriers** a working-class family; **o. agricole** farm worker; **o. qualifié** skilled worker; **o. spécialisé** semi-skilled worker

3 *nm (dans les travaux publics, le bâtiment)* workman

4 *nf* **ouvrière** *(abeille, fourmi)* worker

ouvrir [52] [uvrir] **1** *vt* (**a**) *(porte, boîte, bouteille, rideaux)* to open; *(verrou)* to draw; *(avec une clef)* to unlock; *(robinet, gaz)* to turn on; *(électricité)* to switch on; **o. à qn** to let sb in; **ouvre, c'est moi** open the door, it's me (**b**) *Méd (abcès)* to lance; *(pour opérer)* to open up (**c**) *(lancer) (boutique, compte, débat)* to open; **o. la marche** to lead the way; *Ordinat* **o. une session** to log in, to log on (**d**) *Fig* **cela ouvre l'appétit** it whets the appetite; **o. son cœur à qn** to open one's heart to sb; **o. l'esprit à qn** to broaden sb's mind; **o. qch à qn** *(domaine, profession, perspectives)* to open up sth to sb

2 *vi (magasin, porte)* to open

3 s'ouvrir *vpr* (**a**) *(porte, yeux, séance, fleur)* to open; *Fig* **s'o. à qn** *(perspectives, domaine)* to open up for sb (**b**) *(se couper)* **s'o. la main/le menton** to cut open one's hand/chin; **s'o. les veines** to slash one's wrists (**c**) *(s'épancher)* to open up; **s'o. à qn de qch** to open one's heart to sb about sth, to confide in sb about sth

ouzbek [uzbɛk] **1** *adj* Uzbek

2 *nmf* **O.** Uzbek

Ouzbékistan [uzbekistɑ̃] *nm* **l'O.** Uzbekistan

ovaire [ɔvɛr] *nm* ovary

ovale [ɔval] *adj & nm* oval

ovariectomie [ɔvarjɛktɔmi] *nf Méd* ovariectomy

ovarien, -enne [ɔvarjɛ̃, -ɛn] *adj* ovarian

ovation [ɔvasjɔ̃] *nf* ovation; **faire une o. à qn** to give sb an ovation

ovationner [ɔvasjɔne] *vt* **o. qn** to give sb an ovation

overbooké, -e [ɔvœrbuke] *adj Fam (personne)* booked-up, busy; **je peux pas te voir cette semaine, je suis complètement o.** I can't see you this week, I've got a really hectic schedule

overdose [ɔvœrdoz] *nf aussi Fig* overdose; **faire une o. (de qch)** *(drogue)* to take an overdose (of sth); *Fig* to overdose (on sth)

ovin, -e [ɔvɛ̃, -in] *Zool* **1** *adj* ovine

2 *nm* sheep

ovni [ɔvni] *nm (abrév* **objet volant non identifié)** UFO

ovulation [ɔvylasjɔ̃] *nf* ovulation

ovule [ɔvyl] *nm* ovum

ovuler [ɔvyle] *vi* to ovulate

oxhydrique [ɔksidrik] *adj* oxyhydrogen

oxydant, -e [ɔksidɑ̃, -ɑ̃t] **1** *adj* oxidizing

2 *nm* oxidizer

oxydation [ɔksidasjɔ̃] *nf* oxidization

oxyde [ɔksid] *nm Chim* oxide; **o. de carbone** carbon monoxide

oxyder [ɔkside] **1** *vt* to oxidize

2 s'oxyder *vpr* to oxidize

oxygéné, -e [ɔksiʒene] *adj Chim* oxygenated; *(cheveux)* peroxide blonde, bleached

oxygène [ɔksiʒɛn] *nm* oxygen; *Fig* **j'ai besoin d'o.** I need some fresh air

oxygéner [34] [ɔksiʒene] **1** *vt* (**a**) *Chim (liquide, tissu vivant)* to oxygenate; *(élément, produit chimique)* to oxidize (**b**) *(cheveux)* to bleach, to peroxide

2 s'oxygéner *vpr (respirer)* to get some fresh air

oyat [ɔja] *nm* marram grass

ozone [ɔzon] *nm* ozone

P

P, p [pe] *nm inv* P, p

PAC [pak] *nf* (*abrév* **politique agricole commune**) CAP

PACA [paka] *nf* (*abrév* **Provence-Alpes-Côte d'Azur**) = region of southeastern France

pacage [pakaʒ] *nm* (*champ*) pasture

pacemaker [pɛsmɛkœr] *nm* pacemaker

pacha [paʃa] *nm* pasha; *Fig* **mener une vie de p.** to live like a lord

pachyderme [paʃidɛrm] *nm* pachyderm; *Fig* (*personne*) lumbering oaf

pacification [pasifikasjɔ̃] *nf* pacification

pacifier [66] [pasifje] *vt* to pacify

pacifique [pasifik] **1** *adj* (*sans violence, calme*) peaceful; (*qui aime la paix*) peace-loving
    2 *nm* **le P.** (*océan*) the Pacific; **le P. sud** the South Pacific

pacifisme [pasifism] *nm* pacifism

pacifiste [pasifist] *adj & nmf* pacifist

pack [pak] *nm* (*lot*) *& Sport* pack; **vendu en p.** sold in packs

pacotille [pakɔtij] *nf* junk; **de p.** (*marchandise*) shoddy; *Fig* third-rate; **des bijoux de p.** cheap trinkets

PACS [paks] *nm inv* (*abrév* **Pacte civil de solidarité**) civil solidarity pact (*bill introduced in the French parliament in 1998 allowing unmarried heterosexual or homosexual couples to legally formalize their relationship*)

PACS

The "Pacte civil de solidarité", more commonly known by its acronym "PACS", is a contract which offers legal recognition to adult cohabiting couples, including homosexuals. The law allows same-sex or heterosexual couples to register their union formally in a county court. Controversial when first proposed, the "PACS" became law in 1999, after more than 120 hours of parliamentary debate.

---

pacsé, -e [pakse] *nm,f* = person who has signed a "PACS" contract

pacser [3] [pakse] *Fam* **1** *vi* = to sign a "PACS" contract, to enter into a civil solidarity pact
    2 se pacser *vpr* = to sign a "PACS" contract, to enter into a civil solidarity pact

pacson [paksɔ̃] *nm Fam* (*argent*) packet

pacte [pakt] *nm* pact; **p. de non-agression** non-aggression pact; **le p. de Varsovie** the Warsaw Pact

pactiser [paktize] *vi* **p. avec l'ennemi** to make a pact with the enemy

pactole [paktɔl] *nm Fam* (*au loto*) jackpot; **un joli p.** a nice little sum

paddock [padɔk] *nm* paddock; *Fam* (*lit*) bed

paella [paɛla] *nf* paella

PAF [paf] *nm* (*abrév* **paysage audiovisuel français**) = French broadcasting

paf [paf] **1** *exclam* (*chute*) bang!; (*claque*) slap!; (*coup de poing*) wham!
    2 *adj inv Fam* (**a**) (*saoul*) plastered (**b**) *Belg* **être/rester p.** to be flabbergasted

pagaie [pagɛ] *nf* paddle

pagaïe, pagaille [pagaj] *nf Fam* (**a**) (*désordre*) mess; **en p.** in a mess; **arrête de mettre la p. dans mes affaires** stop messing up my things (**b**) (*confusion*) chaos; **semer la p.** to cause chaos (**c**) **des cadeaux/des jouets en p.** loads of presents/toys

pagayer [53] [pageje] *vi* to paddle

page¹ [paʒ] *nf* (**a**) (*d'un livre, d'un cahier, sur l'Internet*) page; *Fig* (*extrait*) passage; (*de l'histoire, d'une vie*) chapter; **en première p. (des journaux)** on the front page (of the newspapers); *Typ* **mettre qch en page(s)** to make sth up; **perdre la p.** to lose one's place; *Fig* **tourner la p.** to make a fresh start; *Ordinat* **p. d'accueil** home page; **p. centrale** (*d'un magazine*) center pages; **p. de garde** (*dans un livre*) flyleaf; *Ordinat* splash page; **les pages jaunes** (*de l'annuaire*) the Yellow Pages®; *Ordinat* **p. perso, p. personnelle** personal home page; *Ordinat* **p. précédente** page up; *Rad & TV* **p. de publicité** commercial break; *Ordinat* **p. suivante** page down (**b**) **être à la p.** (*à la mode*) to be up to date

page² [paʒ] *nm* page(boy)

pager, pageur [paʒœr] *nm Ordinat* pager

pagination [paʒinasjɔ̃] *nf* pagination

paginer [paʒine] *vt* to paginate

pagne [paɲ] *nm* loincloth; (*en paille*) grass skirt

pagode [pagɔd] *nf* pagoda

paie [pɛ] **1** *voir* **payer 2** *nf* (**a**) (*salaire*) pay, wages (**b**) *Fam* **ça fait une p.** it's ages ago; **ça fait une p. que je ne l'ai pas vue** I haven't seen her for ages

paiement [pɛmɑ̃] *nm* payment; *aussi Fig* **en p. de qch** as payment for sth; **p. à la commande** cash with order; **p. à la livraison** cash on delivery; *Ordinat* **p. sécurisé** secure (electronic) transaction

païen, -enne [pajɛ̃, -ɛn] *adj & nm,f* pagan, heathen

paiera *etc. voir* **payer**

paillard, -e [pajar, -ard] *adj* bawdy

paillasse [pajas] *nf* (**a**) (*matelas*) straw mattress (**b**) (*de l'évier*) draining board; (*de laboratoire*) bench

paillasson [pajasɔ̃] *nm aussi Fig* doormat

paille [paj] **1** *nf* (**a**) (*de céréales*) straw; *Fig* **être sur la p.** to be down and out; **tirer à la courte p.** to draw lots; **p. de fer** steel wool (**b**) (*pour boire*) straw; **boire avec une p.** to drink through a straw
    2 *adj inv* (*jaune*) straw-colored

paillé, -e [paje] *adj* (*chaise*) straw-bottomed

pailleté, -e [pajte] *adj* sequined

paillette [pajɛt] *nf* (**a**) (*sur vêtement*) sequin; **paillettes** (*pour se maquiller*) glitter; **à paillettes** sequined (**b**) (*d'or*) speck; (*de savon*) flake

paillote [pajɔt] *nf* straw hut

pain [pɛ̃] *nm* (**a**) *(aliment)* bread; *(miche)* loaf; *Fig* **avoir du p. sur la planche** to have a lot on one's plate; **gagner son p.** to earn one's living; **je ne mange pas de ce p.-là** I'm having nothing to do with that; **ça ne mange pas de p.** it won't cost you/him/*etc.* anything; **ôter le p. de la bouche à qn** to take the bread out of sb's mouth; **petit p.** (bread) roll; *Fig* **partir** *ou* **se vendre comme des petits pains** to sell like hot cakes; **p. azyme** unleavened bread; **p. bénit** consecrated bread; **p. bis** brown bread; **p. de campagne** farmhouse bread; **p. au chocolat** chocolate-filled pastry; **p. complet** wholewheat bread; **p. d'épices** ≃ gingerbread; **p. grillé** toast; *Can* **p. d'habitant** *ou* **de famille** *ou* **du pays** homemade bread; **p. au lait** sweet roll; **p. de mie** sliced white bread; **p. perdu** French toast; **p. aux raisins** raisin bread; **p. de seigle** rye bread; **p. au** *ou* **de son** bran bread; **p. de sucre** sugarloaf (**b**) *(de savon)* bar (**c**) *Fam (coup de poing)* punch

paintball [pɛjntbol] *nm* paintball; **faire du p.** to go paintballing

pair, -e [pɛr] **1** *adj (nombre, jours)* even
2 *nm* (**a**) *(égal)* **être jugé par ses pairs** to be judged by one's peers; **aller de p. avec qch** to go hand in hand with sth (**b**) *(noble)* peer (**c**) **jeune fille au p.** au pair; **être** *ou* **travailler au p.** to work as an au pair (**d**) *(au jeu)* even numbers

paire [pɛr] *nf* pair; *(de gibier à plumes, de pistolets)* brace; **il a reçu une p. de claques** he got his face slapped; *Fam Fig* **ça, c'est une autre p. de manches** that's a different kettle of fish

paisible [pɛzibl] *adj* peaceful; *(personne)* quiet

paisiblement [pɛzibləmɑ̃] *adv* peacefully

paître [50b] [pɛtr] **1** *vt (herbe)* to crop; *(feuilles)* to feed on
2 *vi* to feed; *(manger de l'herbe)* to graze; *(manger des feuilles)* to browse; *Fam Fig* **envoyer p. qn** to send sb packing

paix [pɛ] *nf* (**a**) *(entre États)* peace; **faire la p. (avec qn)** to make peace (with sb); *Fig* to make it up (with sb); **vivre en p. avec sa conscience** to have a clear conscience (**b**) *Rel* **p. à son âme** may his/her soul rest in peace; **allez en p.** go in peace (**c**) *(tranquillité)* peace; **avoir la p.** to have some peace (and quiet); **faire qch en p.** to do sth in peace (and quiet); **laisser qn en p.** to leave sb in peace; *Fam* **fiche-moi** *ou* **fous-moi la p.!** get off my back!; *Fam* **la p.!** quiet!

Pakistan [pakistɑ̃] *nm* **le P.** Pakistan

pakistanais, -e [pakistanɛ, -ɛz] **1** *adj* Pakistani
2 *nm,f* **P., Pakistanaise** Pakistani

Pal [pal] *adj inv TV (abrév* **phase alternation line***)* PAL

palabrer [3] [palabre] *vi Péj* to talk endlessly

palabres [palabr] *nfpl* endless discussion

palace [palas] *nm* luxury hotel

palais¹ [palɛ] *nm* (**a**) *(d'un roi, d'un noble)* palace; **le p. Bourbon** = home of the French parliament; **p. des congrès** conference center; **le p. de l'Élysée** the Élysée (Palace) *(official residence of the French President)*; **le p. Garnier** = the Paris Opera House; **le p. du Luxembourg** = home of the French Senate; **p. des sports** sports center (**b**) *(tribunal)* **le P. (de justice)** the law courts

palais² [palɛ] *nm (partie de la bouche, goût)* palate; **avoir le p. fin** to have a refined palate

palan [palɑ̃] *nm* hoist

pale [pal] *nf* blade

pâle [pal] *adj* (**a**) pale; **p. comme un linge** as white as a sheet; **p. comme la mort** deathly pale; *Fam Mil* **se faire porter p.** to report sick (**b**) *Fig (sourire)* faint; *(style)* colorless; **une p. imitation de qch** a pale imitation of sth

palefrenier [palfrənje] *nm* groom

paléolithique [paleɔlitik] *Géol* **1** *adj* Paleolithic
2 *nm* **le P.** the Paleolithic period

paléontologie [paleɔ̃tɔlɔʒi] *nf* paleontology

paléontologiste [paleɔ̃tɔlɔʒist], **paléontologue** [paleɔ̃tɔlɔg] *nmf* paleontologist

Palerme [palɛrm] *n* Palermo

Palestine [palɛstin] *nf* **la P.** Palestine

palestinien, -enne [palɛstinjɛ̃, -ɛn] **1** *adj* Palestinian
2 *nm,f* **P., Palestinienne** Palestinian

palet [palɛ] *nm* (**a**) *(pour hockey)* puck (**b**) *(gâteau sec)* = round butter cookie

paletot [palto] *nm* (short) overcoat; *Fam Fig* **tomber sur le p. à qn** *(l'attaquer)* to jump on sb; *(pour lui parler)* to buttonhole sb; *Belg Fig* **vieux paletots** old guard

palette [palɛt] *nf* (**a**) *(de peintre)* palette; *Fig (éventail)* range; *Ordinat* **p. graphique** graphics palette; *Ordinat* **p. d'outils** tool palette (**b**) *(pour la manutention)* pallet (**c**) *Culin (de mouton, de porc)* shoulder

palétuvier [paletyvje] *nm* mangrove

pâleur [palœr] *nf (d'une personne)* pallor; *(d'une couleur, de la lumière)* paleness; *(du style)* colorlessness; **d'une p. mortelle** deathly pale

pâlichon, -onne [paliʃɔ̃, -ɔn] *adj Fam* a bit pale

palier [palje] *nm* (**a**) *(d'escalier)* landing (**b**) *(dans une évolution)* plateau; **par paliers** in stages

palindrome [palɛ̃drom] *nm Ling* palindrome

pâlir [palir] *vi (personne)* to turn or to go pale; *(lumière, couleur, souvenir)* to fade; **p. de rage** to turn white with anger; *Fig* **faire p. qn de jalousie** to make sb green with envy

palissade [palisad] *nf* fence

palliatif, -ive [paljatif, -iv] **1** *adj* palliative
2 *nm Méd* palliative; *Fig* stopgap measure

pallier [66] [palje] **1** *vt (manque)* to compensate for; *(erreur, problème)* to lessen the impact of
2 pallier à *vt ind (manque)* to compensate for; *(erreur, problème)* to lessen the impact of

palmarès [palmarɛs] *nm (à un concours)* list of prize-winners; *(d'une compétition sportive)* list of winners; **le p. (de la chanson)** the charts; **être** *ou* **figurer au p.** *(d'un concours, d'une compétition)* to be among the (prize-)winners; *(de la chanson)* to be in the charts; **avoir** *ou* **compter cinquante victoires à son p.** to have fifty wins to one's credit

palme [palm] *nf* (**a**) *(de palmier)* palm (branch) (**b**) *(récompense)* **les palmes académiques** = decoration awarded to teachers; **la P. d'or** *(du festival de Cannes)* the Palme d'or (**c**) *(pour nager)* flipper

palmé, -e [palme] *adj* (**a**) *(feuille)* palmate (**b**) *(pattes)* webbed

palmeraie [palmərɛ] *nf* palm grove

palmier [palmje] *nm* (**a**) *(arbre)* palm (tree); **p. dattier** date palm (**b**) *(gâteau sec)* = sweet heart-shaped pastry

palmipède [palmipɛd] *nm Zool* web-footed bird, *Spéc* palmiped

palombe [palɔ̃b] *nf* wood pigeon

pâlot, -otte [palo, -ɔt] *adj Fam* a bit pale

palourde [palurd] *nf* clam

palpable [palpabl] *adj* palpable

palpation [palpasjɔ̃] *nf Méd* palpation

palper [palpe] *vt* (**a**) *(objet)* to feel (with one's hands); *Méd* to palpate (**b**) *Fam (somme)* to be paid, to get

palpitant, -e [palpitɑ̃, -ɑ̃t] **1** *adj* (**a**) *(cœur, pouls)* fluttering; *(plus fort)* throbbing; *(personne) (d'émotion)* quivering (**b**) *(passionnant)* thrilling
2 *nm Fam (cœur)* heart, ticker

palpitations [palpitasjɔ̃] *nfpl* palpitations

palpiter [palpite] *vi (cœur, pouls)* to flutter; *(plus fort)* to throb

paludisme [palydism] *nm* malaria

pâmer [pame] **se pâmer** *vpr Vieilli* to swoon; *Fig & Hum* **se p. d'aise** to be blissfully happy; *Fig & Hum* **se p. (devant)** to swoon (over)

pamphlet [pɑ̃flɛ] *nm* satirical tract

pamplemousse [pɑ̃pləmus] *nm* grapefruit

pan¹ [pɑ̃] *nm* (**a**) *(de chemise, de manteau)* tail; *(de jupe)* panel (**b**) *(morceau)* section, piece; *Fig (d'une époque)* part; **p. de mur** section of wall

pan² [pɑ̃] *exclam (coup de feu)* bang!; *(gifle)* whack!; **et p., la voilà qui entre!** and lo and behold, in she walks!

panacée [panase] *nf* panacea

panachage [panaʃaʒ] *nm* mixing; *(de liste électorale)* = voting for candidates from more than one list

panache [panaʃ] *nm* (**a**) *(plume)* plume (**b**) *(brio, éclat)* panache

panaché, -e [panaʃe] **1** *adj* multicolored; **p. de blanc** streaked with white, with white streaks; **un demi p.** a shandy
2 *nm (boisson)* shandy

panacher [panaʃe] *vt* to mix

panade [panad] *nf Fam* **être dans la p.** *(avoir des ennuis)* to be in a fix; *(manquer d'argent)* to be hard up

panafricain, -e [panafrikɛ̃, -ɛn] *adj* Pan-African

panais [panɛ] *nm* parsnip

Panama [panama] *nm* **le P.** Panama

panama [panama] *nm (chapeau)* panama hat

Paname [panam] *n Fam* Paris

panaméen, -enne [panameɛ̃, -ɛn] **1** *adj* Panamanian
2 *nm,f* **P., Panaméenne** Panamanian

panaméricain, -e [panamerikɛ̃, -ɛn] *adj* Pan-American

panard [panar] *nm Fam* (**a**) *(pied)* foot (**b**) *(plaisir intense)* **quel p.!** great!, terrific!; **ce n'est pas le p.** it's not exactly a load of laughs *or* a barrel of fun

panaris [panari] *nm* whitlow

pan-bagnat *(pl* **pans-bagnats)** [pɑ̃baɲa] *nm* = large bread roll filled with salade niçoise

pancarte [pɑ̃kart] *nf (affiche)* sign, notice; *(pour manifestation)* placard

pancréas [pɑ̃kreas] *nm* pancreas

panda [pɑ̃da] *nm* panda

pané, -e [pane] *adj* coated with breadcrumbs, breaded

panégyrique [panezirik] *nm* eulogy; **faire le p. de qn** to eulogize sb

panel [panɛl] *nm (groupe)* panel; *(échantillon)* sample (group)

paneuropéen, -enne [panørɔpeɛ̃, -ɛn] *adj* Pan-European

panier [panje] *nm* (**a**) *(corbeille)* basket; **mettre** *ou* **jeter qch au p.** to throw sth in the wastepaper basket; *Fig* **le dessus du p.** the pick of the bunch; *Fig* **c'est un p. de crabes** they're always at each other's throats; *Fam* **mettre la main au p. à qn** to goose sb; **p. à linge** linen basket; *Fam* **p. percé** *(personne dépensière)* spendthrift; *Can (personne indiscrète)* blabbermouth; **p. à provisions** shopping basket; **p. à salade** salad shaker; *Fam (convoi cellulaire)* paddy wagon (**b**) *(au basket-ball)* basket (**c**) *(pour diapositives)* slide magazine (**d**) *(de robe)* hoop

panier-repas *(pl* **paniers-repas)** [panjerɔpa] *nm* packed lunch

panique [panik] **1** *nf* panic; **être pris de p.** to panic; **ne pas céder à la p.** not to panic; **il y a eu un début de p.** people started to panic; **il y a eu un mouvement de p.** people panicked
2 *adj* **peur p.** panic

paniqué, -e [panike] *adj Fam* in a panic

paniquer [panike] *vt & vi Fam* to panic

panislamisme [panislamism] *nm* Pan-Islamism

panne [pan] *nf* breakdown; *Ordinat* failure, crash; **être en p.** *(machine)* to be out of order; *(automobiliste)* to have broken down; **tomber en p.** to break down; **tomber en p. d'essence, tomber en p. sèche** to run out of gas; *Fam* **il m'a fait le coup de la p.** he tried to pull the old "car won't start" trick on me; **p. (de courant** *ou* **d'électricité)** power failure *or* cut; **p. de moteur** engine failure; **p. de secteur** power failure

panneau, -x [pano] *nm* (**a**) *(pour afficher)* board; **p. d'affichage** bulletin board; **p. publicitaire** billboard (**b**) *(sur la route)* **p. (de signalisation routière), p. indicateur** road

sign (**c**) *(élément plan)* panel (**d**) *Fig* **tomber** *ou* **donner dans le p.** to fall into the trap

panonceau, -x [panɔso] *nm* (**a**) *(de notaire)* plaque (**b**) *(pancarte)* sign

panoplie [panɔpli] *nf* (**a**) *(habit)* costume, outfit; **une p. de Zorro/d'infirmière** a Zorro/nurse's costume (**b**) *(assortiment)* set

panorama [panɔrama] *nm* panorama; *Fig* overview

panoramique [panɔramik] *adj (vue)* panoramic; *(restaurant)* with panoramic views; *(écran)* wide

panouille [panuj] *nf Fam* (**a**) *(personne stupide)* idiot, jerk (**b**) *(petit rôle)* bit-part

panse [pɑ̃s] *nf* (**a**) *(de ruminant)* rumen (**b**) *Fam (ventre)* belly; **s'en mettre plein la p.** to stuff oneself

pansement [pɑ̃smɑ̃] *nm* dressing; **p. (adhésif)** Band-Aid®; **faire un p. (à qn)** to put a dressing on (sb); **refaire un p. à qn** to change sb's dressing

panser [pɑ̃se] *vt* (**a**) *(blessure)* to dress; *(membre)* to bandage; **p. qn** to dress sb's wounds; *Fig* **p. ses blessures** to lick one's wounds (**b**) *(cheval)* to groom

pantagruélique [pɑ̃tagryelik] *adj* gigantic

pantalon [pɑ̃talɔ̃] *nm* pants; **un p.** a pair of pants; **p. de golf** plus-fours; **p. à pattes d'éléphant** flares; **p. à pinces** pleated pants; **p. de pyjama** pajama bottoms; **p. de treillis** khakis

pantalonnade [pɑ̃talɔnad] *nf (spectacle)* burlesque farce

pantelant, -e [pɑ̃tlɑ̃, -ɑ̃t] *adj Litt (à bout de souffle)* panting

panthère [pɑ̃tɛr] *nf* leopard; **p. noire** panther

pantin [pɑ̃tɛ̃] *nm (jouet)* jumping jack; *Péj (fantoche)* puppet

pantois, -e [pɑ̃twa, -az] *adj* speechless; **en rester p.** to be speechless

pantomime [pɑ̃tɔmim] *nf (art)* mime; *(spectacle)* mime show

pantouflard, -e [pɑ̃tuflar, -ard] *adj & nm,f Fam* stay-at-home

pantoufle [pɑ̃tufl] *nf* slipper

pantoufler [pɑ̃tufle] *vi Fam* to join the private sector

PAO [peao] *nf Ordinat (abrév* **publication assistée par ordinateur)** DTP

paon [pɑ̃] *nm* peacock

papa [papa] *nm* dad; *(langage enfantin)* daddy; **p. gâteau** indulgent father; **p. poule** doting father; *Fam Péj* **de p.** old-fashioned; **jouer au papa et à la maman** to play mommies and daddies

papal, -e, -aux, -ales [papal, -o] *adj* papal

paparazzi [paparadzi] *nmpl* paparazzi

papauté [papote] *nf* papacy

papaye [papaj] *nf* papaya, pawpaw

papayer [papaje] *nm* papaya (tree), pawpaw (tree)

pape [pap] *nm* pope; *Fam* **sérieux comme un p.** deadly serious

papelard [paplar] *nm Fam* piece of paper

paperasse [papras] *nf Péj* papers, paperwork

paperasserie [paprasri] *nf Péj* (**a**) *(documents)* papers; **faire de la p.** to do paperwork (**b**) *(d'un système bureaucratique)* red tape

papeterie [papɛtri] *nf (usine)* paper mill; *(magasin)* stationery store; *(articles)* stationery

papetier, -ère [papətje, -ɛr] *nm,f* (**a**) *(industriel)* paper manufacturer (**b**) *(commerçant)* stationer

papi [papi] *nm* grandpa, granddad

papier [papje] *nm* (**a**) *(pour écrire)* paper; **un p.** a piece of paper; *Fam* **être dans les petits papiers de qn** to be in sb's good books; *Fam* **p. alu** aluminum foil; **p. avion** airmail paper; *Ordinat* **p. à bandes perforées** perforated paper; **p. de bonbon** candy wrapper; **p. cadeau** gift wrap, wrapping paper; *Ordinat* **p. continu** continuous paper *or* stationery; *Ordinat* **p. continu plié en accordéon** fanfold paper; **p. crépon** crêpe paper; *très Fam* **p. cul** toilet paper; **p. à dessin** drawing paper; **p. d'emballage** brown paper; **p. à en-tête** letterhead paper; **p. glacé** glazed paper; **papiers gras** litter; **p. hygiénique** toilet paper; **p. journal** newspaper; **p. kraft** brown paper; **p. à lettres** writing paper; *Ordinat* **p. listing** listing paper; **p. mâché** papier-mâché; **p. machine** typing paper; **p. millimétré** *ou* **millimétrique** graph paper; **p. à musique** music paper; *Fig* **être réglé comme du p. à musique** *(événement)* to be as regular as clockwork; **elle est réglée comme du p. à musique** you can set your watch by her; **p. peint** wallpaper; **p. recyclé** recycled paper; **p. de soie** tissue paper; **p. toilette** toilet paper; **p. de verre** sandpaper; **passer qch au p. de verre** to sandpaper sth

(**b**) **papiers** *(documents officiels)* papers; **papiers (d'identité)** *(identity)* papers; *(d'un automobiliste)* driver's license

(**c**) *Fam (article de journal)* article

papilles [papij] *nfpl* **p. gustatives** taste buds

papillon [papijɔ̃] *nm* (**a**) *(insecte)* butterfly; **p. de nuit** moth; *Fam* **minute p.!** hold on a minute! (**b**) *(écrou)* wing nut (**c**) *(sur document)* flag (**d**) *Fam (contravention)* (parking) ticket (**e**) *(nage)* butterfly

papillonner [papijɔne] *vi* (**a**) *(paupières)* to flutter (**b**) *(d'une personne à une autre)* to flit about

papillote [papijɔt] *nf* (**a**) *(en papier alu)* **cailles en papillotes** quails en papillotes *(cooked in aluminum foil)* (**b**) *(de gigot)* frill (**c**) *(bigoudi)* curlpaper; *Fam* **tu peux en faire des papillotes** you can chuck it away

papilloter [papijɔte] *vi (yeux)* to blink; *(lumière)* to flicker

papoter [papɔte] *vi Fam* to chat

papou, -e [papu] **1** *adj* Papuan
   2 *nm,f* **P., Papoue** Papuan

Papouasie-Nouvelle-Guinée [papwazinuvɛlgine] *nf* **la P.** Papua New Guinea

papouille [papuj] *nf Fam* **faire des papouilles à qn** to tickle sb

paprika [paprika] *nm* paprika

papy-boom [papibum] *nm Hum (augmentation de la proportion du troisième âge dans la population)* grandpa boom, elderly boom

papyrus [papirys] *nm* papyrus

paqson [paksɔ̃] = **pacson**

Pâque [pɑk] *nf* **P., la P. juive** Passover

paquebot [pakbo] *nm* liner

pâquerette [pakrɛt] *nf* daisy

pâques [pɑk] **1** *nfpl* **joyeuses p.!** Happy Easter!
   2 *nm* **P.** Easter; *Fam* **à P. ou à la Trinité!** never in a month of Sundays!

Pâques
In France, Easter is traditionally symbolized not only by eggs but also by bells; according to legend, church bells fly to Rome at Easter. At this time of the year, people give each other chocolate eggs, bells, fish or hens.

---

paquet [pakɛ] *nm* (**a**) *(sac)* packet; *(de sucre)* bag; *(de cigarettes)* pack; *(postal)* package (**b**) *Fam (grande quantité)* **un p. de** a pile *or* stack of; **toucher un joli p.** to make a bundle; **mettre le p.** to pull out all the stops; *Fam* **c'est un p. de nerfs** she's a bundle of nerves; **p.-cadeau** gift-wrapped package; **je vous fais un p.-cadeau?** would you like it gift-wrapped? (**c**) **p. de mer** big wave (**d**) *Ordinat* packet

paquetage [paktaʒ] *nm* (soldier's) pack; **faire son p.** to get one's kit ready

par [par] *prép* (**a**) *(à travers)* through; **p. la porte/le trou de la serrure** through the door/the keyhole; **regarder p. la fenêtre** *(de l'intérieur)* to look out (of) the window; *(de l'extérieur)* to look through the window; **passer p. Calais** to go via Calais; **p. ici/là** this/that way; **p. où est-il passé?** which way did he go?

(**b**) *(position)* **p. ici** over here; **p. là** over there; **p. 30 mètres de fond** ≃ at a depth of 100 feet; **p. endroits** in places

(**c**) *(pendant)* **p. une belle journée d'automne** on a beautiful autumn day; **p. cette chaleur** in this heat; **p. le passé** in the past; *Litt* **p. deux fois** twice

(**d**) *(introduit le complément d'agent)* by; **c'est p. eux que je l'ai appris** I found out from them; **faire faire qch p. qn** to have sth done by sb

(**e**) *(indique la cause)* out of; **faire qch p. amitié/pitié** to do sth out of friendship/pity; **p. hasard/erreur** by chance/mistake; **p. malheur** unfortunately, as bad luck would have it; **p. pitié!** for pity's sake!

(**f**) *(au moyen de)* with, by; **retenu p. une corde** held by a rope; **fermé p. un cadenas** padlocked; **p. train/avion/voiture/bateau** by train/plane/car/boat; **conduire/prendre qn p. la main** to lead/take sb by the hand; **tenir qn p. la taille** to hold sb around the waist; **pendu p. les pieds** hanging by the feet; **envoyer qch p. la poste** to send sth by mail; **répondre p. oui ou p. non** to answer yes or no; **se terminer p. un divorce/une dispute** to end in divorce/an argument; **p. tous les moyens** by every possible means; **il est monté p. l'escalier** he took the stairs up; **obtenir qch p. la force** to obtain sth by force; **appeler qn p. son nom** to call sb by his/her name

(**g**) *(selon)* according to; **p. ordre de grandeur** according to size

(**h**) *(distributif)* per, a; **deux p. deux** two by two; **p. groupes de six** in groups of six; **deux jours p. semaine** two days a week; **20 000 euros p. an** 20,000 euros a year; **un siège p. personne** one seat per person

(**i**) **de p.** *(à cause de)* due to; **de p. le monde** the world over

para [para] *nm Fam* para

parabole [parabɔl] *nf* (**a**) *(allégorie)* parable (**b**) *(courbe)* parabola (**c**) *(antenne)* (satellite *or* parabolic) dish

parabolique [parabɔlik] *adj* parabolic

paracétamol [parasetamɔl] *nm* paracetamol

parachever [46] [paraʃəve] *vt* to complete, to finish off

parachutage [paraʃytaʒ] *nm* parachuting

parachute [paraʃyt] *nm* parachute; **faire du p.** to go parachuting; **p. ascensionnel** parascending

parachuter [paraʃyte] *vt (vivres, soldats)* to parachute in; *Fam (nommer)* to draft in

parachutisme [paraʃytism] *nm* parachuting; **faire du p.** to go parachuting

parachutiste [paraʃytist] *nmf* (**a**) *(sportif)* parachutist (**b**) *(soldat)* paratrooper

parade¹ [parad] *nf* (**a**) *(exhibition)* show, ostentation; **faire p. de qch** to show sth off (**b**) *(défilé)* parade

parade² [parad] *nf* (**a**) *(en escrime, boxe)* parry (**b**) *(réplique)* riposte; *Fig* **je n'ai pas encore trouvé la p.** I haven't come up with a way of handling him/it/*etc.* yet

parader [parade] *vi* to show off

paradis [paradi] *nm* heaven; *Fig* paradise; **le p. terrestre** the Garden of Eden; *Fig* heaven on earth; **aller au p.** to go to heaven; **un p. fiscal** a tax haven; **le p.** *(d'un théâtre)* the peanut gallery; *Fam* **il ne l'emportera pas au p.** he won't get away with it, he'll be sorry

paradisiaque [paradizjak] *adj* heavenly

paradoxal, -e, -aux, -ales [paradɔksal, -o] *adj* paradoxical

paradoxalement [paradɔksalmã] *adv* paradoxically

paradoxe [paradɔks] *nm* paradox

parafe [paraf] = **paraphe**

parafer [parafe] = **parapher**

paraffine [parafin] *nf* kerosene

parafiscalité [parafiskalite] *nf* = taxes paid to the state and used for administration purposes

parages [paraʒ] *nmpl* (**a**) *Naut* waters (**b**) *(alentours)* **dans les p. de…** in the vicinity of…; *Fam* **est-ce qu'elle est dans les p.?** is she around?

paragraphe [paragraf] *nm* (**a**) paragraph (**b**) *Typ* paragraph (sign)

Paraguay [paragwɛ] *nm* **le P.** Paraguay

paraguayen, -enne [paragwɛjɛ̃, -ɛn] **1** *adj* Paraguayan
2 *nm,f* **P., Paraguayenne** Paraguayan

paraître [20] [parɛtr] **1** *vi* (**a**) *(apparaître)* to appear; *(étoile, lune)* to appear, to come out; **laisser p. sa déception** to let one's disappointment show; **un faible sourire parut sur ses lèvres** he smiled weakly; **elle ne pense qu'à p.** all she thinks about is showing off (**b**) *(livre)* to come out, to be published (**c**) *(sembler)* to seem, to appear; **cette décision me paraît bizarre** it seems like a strange decision to me; **elle paraissait furieuse** *(à la voir)* she looked furious; *(à l'entendre)* she sounded furious
2 *v impersonnel* (**a**) *(sembler)* **il me paraît utile de…** I think it would be useful to…; **demain, il n'y paraîtra plus** there'll be no trace of it tomorrow; **sans qu'il y paraisse** without it being apparent (**b**) **il paraît que…** *(on dit)* it seems *or* appears that…; **il paraît qu'elle s'en va, elle s'en va, paraît-il** it seems *or* appears that she's leaving, apparently she's leaving; **il paraît que ça fait maigrir** apparently it helps you lose weight; **il paraît que oui** so it would appear, apparently (so); **il paraît que non** it would appear not, apparently not; **à ce qu'il paraît** apparently
3 *nm* **le p.** appearance

parallèle [paralɛl] **1** *adj* parallel (**à** to *or* with); *(police, marché)* unofficial; **mener une vie p.** to lead a secret life; *Ordinat* **imprimante/interface p.** parallel printer/interface
2 *nf* parallel (line)
3 *nm* parallel; **mettre qch en p. avec qch, établir un p. entre qch et qch** to draw a parallel between sth and sth

parallèlement [paralɛlmɑ̃] *adv* parallel (**à** to *or* with); *(simultanément)* at the same time (**à** as)

parallélépipède [paralelepipɛd] *nm* parallelepiped

parallélisme [paralelism] *nm* parallelism; **p. (des roues)** (wheel) alignment

parallélogramme [paralelɔgram] *nm* parallelogram

paralysant, -e [paralizɑ̃, -ɑ̃t] *adj* paralyzing

paralysé, -e [paralize] *adj aussi Fig* paralyzed

paralyser [paralize] *vt aussi Fig* to paralyze; **le froid lui paralyse les mains** his hands are numb with the cold

paralysie [paralizi] *nf aussi Fig* paralysis; **p. générale** creeping paralysis

paralytique [paralitik] *adj & nmf* paralytic

paramédical, -e, -aux, -ales [paramedikal, -o] **1** *adj* paramedical
2 *nm* **les emplois du p.** paramedical jobs

paramétrable [parametrabl] *adj Ordinat* configurable; **p. par l'utilisateur** user-definable

paramétrage [parametraʒ] *nm Ordinat* configuration

paramètre [parametr] *nm Math & Fig* parameter; *Ordinat* parameter, setting; *(du DOS)* switch; **paramètres** settings

paramétrer [34] [parametre] *vt Ordinat* to configure

paramilitaire [paramilitɛr] *adj* paramilitary

parano [parano] *Fam* **1** *adj* paranoid
2 *nf* **faire de la p.** to be paranoid

paranoïa [paranɔja] *nf* paranoia

paranoïaque [paranɔjak] *adj & nmf* paranoiac

paranormal, -e, -aux, -ales [paranɔrmal, -o] *adj* paranormal

parapente [parapɑ̃t] *nm (activité)* paragliding; *(parachute)* paraglider; **faire du p.** to go paragliding

parapet [parapɛ] *nm* parapet

paraphe [paraf] *nm* initials

parapher [parafe] *vt* to initial

paraphrase [parafraz] *nf* paraphrase

paraphraser [parafraze] *vt* to paraphrase

paraplégie [parapleʒi] *nf* paraplegia

paraplégique [parapleʒik] *adj & nmf* paraplegic

parapluie [paraplɥi] *nm* umbrella

parapsychologie [parapsikɔlɔʒi] *nf* parapsychology

parascolaire [paraskɔlɛr] *adj* extra-curricular

parasite [parazit] **1** *nm aussi Fig* parasite; **parasites** *(à la radio)* interference
2 *adj (insecte, plante)* parasitic

parasol [parasɔl] *nm* parasol, sunshade; *(de plage)* beach umbrella

parastatal, -e, -aux, -ales [parastatal, -o] *adj Belg* semipublic

paratonnerre [paratɔnɛr] *nm* lightning conductor

paravent [paravɑ̃] *nm aussi Fig* screen; *Fig* **servir de p. à qch** to be a screen for sth

parbleu [parblø] *exclam Vieilli* good Lord!; *(évidemment)* good Lord, yes!

parc [park] *nm* (**a**) *(jardin)* park; *(d'un château)* grounds; **p. aquatique** water park; **p. naturel** nature reserve; **p. zoologique** zoo (**b**) *(enclos) (pour enfant)* playpen; **p. d'attractions** amusement park; **p. des expositions** exhibition center; **p. à huîtres** oyster bed; **p. de stationnement** parking lot; **p. à thème** theme park (**c**) *(ensemble)* **le p. automobile français** the number of cars in France

parcelle [parsɛl] *nf* small piece; **p. de terrain** plot; *Fig* **pas la moindre p. d'intelligence** not an ounce *or* shred of intelligence

parce que [parskə] *conj* because; **ce n'est pas parce qu'il fait froid qu'on doit rester à la maison** just because it's cold doesn't mean we have to stay home; **pourquoi ne viens-tu pas? – p.** why aren't you coming? – (just) because

parchemin [parʃəmɛ̃] *nm* parchment

parcimonie [parsimɔni] *nf* thrift; **avec p.** sparingly

parcimonieux, -euse [parsimɔnjø, -øz] *adj* thrifty

parcmètre [parkmɛtr] *nm* (parking) meter

parcourir [22] [parkurir] *vt* (**a**) *(lieu)* to walk around; *(pays)* to travel through; *(rues)* to walk through; *(mer)* to sail; **p. un lieu à la recherche de qn** to scour a place for sb; **p. la terre entière pour retrouver qn** to travel the world to find sb; **p. une distance de plusieurs kilomètres** to cover a distance of several miles; **il reste huit kilomètres à p.** ≃ there are five miles to go; *Fig* **un frisson me parcourut l'échine** *ou* **le dos** a shiver ran down my spine; *Fig* **un murmure a parcouru la foule** a murmur ran through the crowd (**b**) *(regarder) (texte, journal)* to skim through; *Ordinat* to scroll through; **p. qch des yeux** *ou* **du regard** to glance at sth

parcours [parkur] *nm (de défilé, de bus)* route; *(circuit automobile)* circuit; *(d'équitation, de golf, d'un fleuve)* course; *(évolution personnelle)* career, path; **p. du combattant** *Mil* assault course; *Fig* obstacle course; **faire un p. sans faute** *(cheval)* to have a clear round; *Fig (dans une carrière)* to have a copybook career; **refaire le p. pour retrouver qch** to retrace one's steps to find sth; **elle fait plusieurs fois le p. dans la journée** she does the journey several times a day

par-delà [pardəla] *prép & adv* beyond

par-derrière [pardɛrjɛr] **1** *prép* behind
2 *adv (attaquer)* from behind; *(se boutonner)* at the back; **passer p.** to go in the back door; *Fig* **dire des choses de qn p.** to talk about sb behind his/her back

par-dessous [pardəsu] **1** *prép* under, underneath
2 *adv* underneath

pardessus [pardəsy] *nm* overcoat

par-dessus [pardəsy] **1** *prép* over; **p. tout** above all
2 *adv* over; **j'ai mis un T-shirt avec une chemise p.** I wore a T-shirt with a shirt on top *or* over it

par-devant [pardəvã] **1** *prép Jur* **acte signé p. notaire** deed signed in the presence of a lawyer

2 *adv (attaquer)* from the front; *(se boutonner)* at the front

pardi [pardi] *exclam Fam* of course!

pardon [pardõ] *nm* **(a)** *(grâce)* forgiveness; **accorder son p. à qn** to forgive sb; **demander p. à qn** to apologize to sb; **(je vous demande) p.!** *(pour passer)* excuse me!; *(pour s'excuser)* (I'm) sorry!; **(je vous demande) p.?** *(je n'ai pas entendu)* pardon?; *(je suis indigné)* I beg your pardon!; *Fam* **elle est intelligente, mais sa fille, p.!** she's pretty smart but you should see her daughter! **(b)** *Rel* **le Grand P.** the Day of Atonement, Yom Kippur

pardonnable [pardɔnabl] *adj* forgivable, excusable

pardonner [pardɔne] **1** *vt* to forgive; **p. qch à qn** to forgive sb sth; **elle m'a pardonné d'avoir oublié** she forgave me for forgetting; **pour me/te/***etc.* **faire p.** to make it up; **tu es tout pardonné** I'll let you off

2 *vi* **(a)** *(oublier une faute)* to forgive **(b)** **ça ne pardonne pas** it's fatal

3 se pardonner *vpr* **je ne me le pardonnerai jamais** I'll never forgive myself

paré, -e [pare] *adj* **(a)** *(prêt)* prepared (**contre** for) **(b)** *(revêtu)* adorned (**de** with)

pare-avalanches [paravalãʃ] *nm inv* avalanche barrier

pare-balles [parbal] *adj inv* bulletproof

pare-boue [parbu] *nm inv* mudflap

pare-brise [parbriz] *nm inv* windshield

pare-chocs [parʃɔk] *nm inv* bumper

pare-feu [parfø] *nm inv* **(a)** *(dans la forêt)* firebreak **(b)** *(de cheminée)* fireguard **(c)** *Ordinat* firewall

pareil, -eille [parɛj] **1** *adj* **(a)** *(identique)* the same; **elles sont presque pareilles** they're almost the same; **ce n'est pas p.** it's not the same (thing); *Litt* **à nul autre p.** unparalleled; **p. que** *ou* **à** the same as, just like; *Fam* **si ça ne te plaît pas, c'est p.** if you don't like it, too bad **(b)** *(tel)* such; **en p. cas** in such cases; **dans des moments pareils** at times like these; **mais je n'ai jamais dit une chose pareille!** but I never said any such thing!

2 *nm,f* **elle n'a pas sa pareille** she's second to none; **sans p.** unparalleled; **mes pareils** my equals

3 *nf* **rendre la pareille à qn** *(se venger de quelqu'un)* to get one's own back on sb, to pay sb back; *(rendre un service à quelqu'un)* to repay sb

4 *nm Fam* **c'est du p. au même** it's six of one and half a dozen of the other

5 *adv Fam* the same; **faire p.** to do the same (thing)

pareillement [parɛjmã] *adv* **(a)** *(de la même manière)* in a similar manner, in the same way **(b)** *(aussi)* likewise

parement [parmã] *nm (de manche, de col)* facing

parent, -e [parã, -ãt] **1** *adj* related

2 *nm,f (tante, oncle, cousin)* relative, relation

3 *nmpl* **parents** *(père et mère)* parents; **parents adoptifs** adoptive parents; **parents biologiques** biological parents

parental, -e, -aux, -ales [parãtal, -o] *adj* parental

parentalité [parãtalite] *nf* parenthood

parenté [parãte] *nf* relationship; **avoir un lien de p. avec qn** to be related to sb

parenthèse [parãtɛz] *nf* parenthesis; *Fig (dans un discours)* digression; **entre parenthèses** in parentheses; *Fig (à propos)* incidentally, by the way

paréo [pareo] *nm* sarong

parer[1] [pare] **1** *vt* **(a)** *aussi Fig (éviter)* to parry **(b)** *(protéger)* to protect (**contre** against)

2 parer à *vt ind (accident)* to prevent; *(problème)* to avoid; **p. au plus pressé** to attend to the most urgent things first

parer[2] [pare] *Litt* **1** *vt (vêtir)* to adorn (**de** with); *Fig* **p. qn de toutes les vertus** to endow sb with every virtue

2 se parer *vpr* **(a)** *(s'habiller avec élégance)* to get dressed up (**de** in) **(b)** *Can (se préparer)* to get ready

pare-soleil [parsɔlɛj] *nm inv (de voiture)* sun visor

paresse [parɛs] *nf* **(a)** *(indolence)* laziness; **d'une p. incroyable** incredibly lazy **(b)** *(lenteur)* **p. intellectuelle** intellectual laziness; **p. intestinale** sluggishness of the bowels

paresser [parɛse] *vi* to laze around

paresseux, -euse [parɛsø, -øz] **1** *adj* **(a)** *(nonchalant)* lazy **(b)** *(intestin)* sluggish

2 *nm,f* lazy person

3 *nm (animal)* sloth

parfaire [36] [parfɛr] *vt (travail)* to finish off, to complete; *(technique)* to perfect

parfait, -e [parfɛ, -ɛt] **1** *adj* **(a)** *(sans fautes)* perfect **(b)** *(complet) (bonheur)* perfect, complete; *(ressemblance)* exact; *Fam* **un p. imbécile** a total idiot

2 *nm (dessert)* parfait; **p. au chocolat** chocolate parfait

parfaitement [parfɛtmã] *adv* **(a)** *(sans fautes)* perfectly; **parler p. l'anglais** to speak perfect English **(b)** *(complètement)* completely, thoroughly; *(compréhensible, clair, heureux)* perfectly; **ça m'est p. égal** it makes absolutely no difference to me; **j'ai p. conscience de...** I'm perfectly aware of... **(c)** *(tout à fait)* **vous affirmez que vous l'avez vu? - p.!** you say you saw it? - I certainly did!

parfois [parfwa] *adv* sometimes

parfum [parfœ̃] *nm* **(a)** *(essences)* perfume **(b)** *(senteur) (d'une fleur)* fragrance, scent; *(d'un vin)* bouquet; *Fig* **un p. de scandale** a whiff of scandal **(c)** *(de glace, de yaourt)* flavor **(d)** *Fam* **être au p.** to be in the know; **mettre qn au p.** to fill sb in

parfumer [parfyme] **1** *vt* **(a)** *(embaumer)* to scent **(b)** *(gâteau, glace)* to flavor (**à** with) **(c)** *(mouchoir)* to scent; **je vous parfume?** *(à une cliente)* would you like to try some perfume?

2 se parfumer *vpr* to put perfume on

parfumerie [parfymri] *nf (magasin)* perfumery; *(rayon)* perfume counter; *(produits)* perfumes; *(industrie)* perfume industry

parfumeur, -euse [parfymœr, -øz] *nm,f* perfumer

pari [pari] *nm* bet; **faire un p. avec qn** to make a bet with sb; **p. mutuel** ≃ pari-mutuel

paria [parja] *nm Fig* pariah, (social) outcast

parier [66] [parje] **1** *vt* to bet; **il y a fort** *ou* **gros à p. que...** the odds are that...; **je te parie qu'elle viendra** I bet you she'll come; **je l'aurais parié** I thought as much

2 *vi* to bet; **p. avec qn/sur qch** to bet with sb/on sth; **je te dis qu'elle viendra - on parie?** she'll come, I tell you - want to bet?

parieur, -euse [parjœr, -øz] *nm,f* better

parigot, -e [parigo, -ɔt] *Fam* **1** *adj* Parisian

2 *nm,f* **P., Parigote** Parisian

Paris [pari] *n* Paris

parisien, -enne [parizjɛ̃, -ɛn] **1** *adj* Parisian

2 *nm,f* **P., Parisienne** Parisian

parité [parite] *nf aussi Ordinat* parity; **nous devons arriver à une p. hommes-femmes au parlement** we must ensure that there are an equal number of men and women in parliament

parjure [parʒyr] **1** *nm (action)* perjury

2 *nmf (personne)* perjurer

3 *adj* treacherous

parjurer [parʒyre] **se parjurer** *vpr* to perjure oneself

parka [parka] *nm ou nf* parka

parking [parkiŋ] *nm* parking lot; **p. couvert** underground parking lot; **p. payant** paying parking lot

parkour [parkur] *nm* free-running, parkour

parlant, -e [parlã, -ãt] *adj (geste)* eloquent, meaningful; *(description)* vivid

parlé, -e [parle] *adj* **le français p.** spoken French; **journal p.** news (program)

parlement [parləmã] *nm* le P. Parliament; le P. européen the European Parliament

parlementaire [parləmãtɛr] **1** *adj* parliamentary

2 *nmf* member of parliament, Congressman, *f* Congresswoman

parlementarisme [parləmãtarism] *nm* parliamentary government

parlementer [parləmãte] *vi* to negotiate (**avec** with)

parler¹ [parle] **1** *vi* (**a**) *(s'exprimer)* to speak, to talk; *(avouer)* to talk; **elle parle bien** *(oratrice)* she's a good speaker; **p. par signes** to use sign language; **parlez-vous sérieusement?** are you serious?; **les résultats/faits parlent d'eux-mêmes** the results/facts speak for themselves; **p. pour ne rien dire** to talk for the sake of talking; **c'est comme si je parlais à un mur** it's like talking to a brick wall; **p. de qn/qch (à qn)** to talk (to sb) about sb/sth; **p. de** *(sujet: livre, film)* to be about; **on m'a beaucoup parlé de vous** I've heard a lot about you; **n'en parlons plus** let's drop the subject; **faire p. de soi** to be talked about; **p. de faire qch** to talk about doing sth

(**b**) *(locutions)* **je sais de quoi je parle** I know what I'm talking about; *Fam* **tu peux p.!** YOU can talk!; *Fam* **parle pour toi!** speak for yourself!; *Fam* **tu parles!** you bet!; *Fam* **tu parles d'une occasion/d'un idiot!** talk about an opportunity/an idiot!; *Fam* **sa timidité? parlons-en!** his shyness? that's a good one *or* you must be joking!; *Fam* **ne m'en parlez pas!** tell me about it!; **sans p. de...** not to mention...; **trouver à qui p.** to get more than one bargains for

2 *vt* *(langue)* to speak; **p. (le) français** to speak French; **ici on parle anglais** *(dans un magasin)* English spoken; **p. chiffons/cuisine** to talk about clothes/cooking; **p. affaires/politique** to talk business/politics

3 se parler *vpr* (**a**) *(langue)* to be spoken

(**b**) *(l'un à l'autre)* to talk to each other

parler² [parle] *nm* speech; *(régional)* dialect; **il a un p. très rude** he has a very abrupt way of speaking

parleur, -euse [parlœr, -øz] *nm,f Péj* **beau p.** smooth talker

parloir [parlwar] *nm* (**a**) *(d'une prison)* visiting room (**b**) *Belg* *(salon)* parlor

parlot(t)e [parlɔt] *nf Fam* chat; **faire la p. (avec qn)** to chat (with sb), to have a chat (with sb)

Parme [parm] *n* Parma

parmesan [parməzɑ̃] *nm* Parmesan (cheese)

parmi [parmi] *prép* among; **choisir p. plusieurs possibilités** to choose from several possibilities; **nous espérons vous revoir p. nous** we hope to see you back with us

parodie [parɔdi] *nf* parody

parodier [66] [parɔdje] *vt* to parody

parodique [parɔdik] *adj* parodic

paroi [parwa] *nf* (**a**) *(d'une falaise, d'une montagne)* face (**b**) *(d'une pièce, d'une caverne)* wall; *(d'un tunnel, de l'estomac)* lining

paroisse [parwas] *nf* parish

paroissial, -e, -aux, -ales [parwasjal, -o] *adj* parish

paroissien, -enne [parwasjɛ̃, -ɛn] *nm,f* parishioner

parole [parɔl] *nf* (**a**) *(mot)* word; **paroles** *(de chanson)* lyrics, words; **histoire sans paroles** short silent movie; **une p. blessante** a hurtful remark; *Ironique* **de belles paroles** fine words; **ce ne sont que des paroles en l'air** they're just empty threats

(**b**) *Fig (engagement)* promise, word; **tenir p.** to keep one's promise *or* word; **manquer à sa p.** to break one's promise *or* word; **il n'a qu'une p.** he's a man of his word; **donner sa p. (d'honneur) à qn que...** to give sb one's word that...; **(ma) p. d'honneur!** I give you my word!; **je te crois sur p.** I'll take your word for it

(**c**) **la p.** *(faculté de parler)* speech; *(diction)* delivery; **adresser la p. à qn** to speak to sb; **couper la p. à qn** to interrupt sb;

prendre la p. to speak; **laisser la p. à qn** to let sb speak; **la p. est à M. Renant, M. Renant a la p.** Mr. Renant has the floor; **la p. est d'argent mais le silence est d'or** speech is silver, silence is golden

(**d**) **p.!** *(aux cartes)* pass!; *(au poker)* check!; *(au bridge)* no bid!

parolier, -ère [parɔlje, -ɛr] *nm,f* lyricist

paroxysme [parɔksism] *nm* **atteindre son p.** to reach its peak *or* climax; **être au p. de la joie** to be ecstatically happy

parpaing [parpɛ̃] *nm* cinder block

parquer [parke] *vt* *(bétail)* to pen in; *(prisonniers)* to confine

parquet [parkɛ] *nm* (**a**) *(sol)* wooden floor; *(avec des motifs)* parquet floor (**b**) *Jur* district attorney's office

parrain [parɛ̃] *nm* *(pour un baptême, d'une organisation criminelle)* godfather; *(d'un sportif, d'un membre d'un club)* sponsor

parrainer [parene] *vt* *(sportif, nouveau membre)* to sponsor

parricide [parisid] **1** *adj* parricidal

2 *nmf & nm* parricide

pars *voir* **partir**

parsemer [46] [parsəme] *vt* to scatter (**de** with)

part¹ [par] *voir* **partir**

part² [par] *nf* (**a**) *(partie d'un tout)* part; *(d'un marché, d'un héritage, de travail)* share; *(d'un gâteau, d'une pizza)* slice; **diviser qch en parts égales** to divide sth into equal parts; **ils viennent pour une bonne p. des environs de Lille** they mostly come from the Lille area; **à p. entière** fully-fledged; **pour ma p.** personally, as for me; **faire la p. du feu** to cut one's losses; **la p. du lion** the lion's share

(**b**) *(participation)* share, part; **prendre p. à qch** to take part in sth; *(joie, douleur)* to share sth; **faire p. de qch à qn** to inform sb of sth, to tell sb about sth; **faire la p. des choses** to get things in perspective

(**c**) *(côté)* **de p. et d'autre** on both sides; **de p. en p.** right through; **d'une p...., d'autre p....** on the one hand..., on the other hand...; **de toutes parts** on all sides

(**d**) **de la p. de qn** *(en provenance de)* from sb; *(à la place de)* on sb's behalf; **c'est de la p. de qui?** *(au téléphone)* who's calling?; **ce serait bien aimable de votre p.** that would be very kind of you; **cela m'étonne de sa p.** that surprises me, coming from him/her

(**e**) *(locutions)* **prendre qn à p.** to take sb aside; **à p. lui/quelques erreurs** apart from him/a few mistakes; **c'est un cas à p.** he's a special case; *Fam* **à p. que...** apart from the fact that...

partage [parta3] *nm* (**a**) *(action)* *(d'une fortune, d'un domaine)* dividing up; *(de tâches, de responsabilités)* sharing out; **faire le p. de qch** to divide sth up; **sans p.** *(amour)* total; *Ordinat* **p. d'imprimantes** printer sharing (**b**) *(lot)* **recevoir qch en p.** to be left sth *(in a will)*

partagé, -e [parta3e] *adj* (**a**) *(entre plusieurs personnes)* shared; *(amour)* mutual; *Ordinat* **travail en temps p.** time-sharing (**b**) *(indécis)* **être p.** to be torn; **les avis sont partagés** opinions are divided

partager [45] [parta3e] **1** *vt* (**a**) *(répartir)* to divide (up); **p. son temps entre** to divide one's time between; **p. qch en deux** to divide sth in two (**b**) *(avoir en commun)* to share (**avec** with); **p. l'avis de qn** to share sb's opinion; **p. la joie de qn** to share (in) sb's joy

2 *vi* to share

3 se partager *vpr* (**a**) *(se répartir)* **ils se le sont partagé** they shared it between them (**b**) *(partager son temps)* to divide one's time (**entre** between)

partageur, -euse [parta3œr, -øz] *adj* willing to share

partance [partɑ̃s] *nf* **en p.** about to depart; **en p. pour Bordeaux** for Bordeaux

partant¹ [partɑ̃] *conj Litt* consequently, therefore

partant², -e [partɑ̃, -ɑ̃t] **1** *adj Fam* **je suis p.!** count me in!

2 *nm,f* *(coureur, cheval)* starter

partenaire [partɛnɛr] *nmf* partner; **les partenaires sociaux** workers and management

partenariat [partɛnarja] *nm* partnership

parterre [partɛr] *nm* (**a**) *(de fleurs)* flower bed; *(plate-bande)* border (**b**) *(au théâtre)* orchestra (**c**) *Fam (sol)* floor

parti[1] [parti] *nm* (**a**) *(camp)* side; **prendre le p. de qn** to take sb's side; **prendre p. pour qn** to side with sb; **prendre p. contre qn** to take sides against sb (**b**) **p. (politique)** *(political)* party; **le P. (communiste)** the Communist Party (**c**) *(personne)* **un beau p.** a good match (**d**) *(choix)* **prendre le p. de faire qch** to make up one's mind to do sth; **en prendre son p.** to resign oneself to the fact (**e**) *(profit)* **tirer p. de qch** to make good use of sth (**f**) **p. pris** bias; **avoir un p. pris contre** to be biased against; **être de p. pris** to be biased; **être sans p. pris** to be unbiased

parti[2], **-e** [parti] *adj Fam (ivre)* plastered, gone; *(drogué)* high

partial, -e, -aux, -ales [parsjal, -o] *adj* biased

partialement [parsjalmɑ̃] *adv* in a biased way

partialité [parsjalite] *nf* bias (**envers/contre** in favor of/against)

participant, -e [partisipɑ̃, -ɑ̃t] **1** *adj* participating

2 *nm,f (personne présente)* participant (**à** in); *(sportif)* competitor

participation [partisipasjɔ̃] *nf* (**a**) *(collaboration, en classe)* participation (**à** in); *(argent)* contribution (**à** towards); *(nombre de votants)* turnout (**à** at); **avec la p. de Jean Martin (dans le rôle de…)** with Jean Martin (as…); **p. aux frais** contribution toward costs; **p. aux bénéfices** profit-sharing (**b**) *Fin* interest (**à** in)

participe [partisip] *nm Gram* participle; **p. présent/passé** present/past participle

participer [partisipe] **participer à** *vt ind* (**a**) *(assister à)* to take part in, to participate in; *(spectacle)* to appear in; **p. activement à qch** to take an active part in sth (**b**) *(financièrement)* to contribute to (**c**) **p. aux bénéfices** to share in the profits

particulariser [partikylarize] *vt* to particularize

particularisme [partikylarism] *nm* particularism

particularité [partikylarite] *nf* distinctive feature

particule [partikyl] *nf* particle; **p. élémentaire** elementary *or* fundamental particle

particulier, -ère [partikylje, -ɛr] **1** *adj* (**a**) *(propre)* characteristic (**à** of) (**b**) *(remarquable)* unusual, exceptional; *(soin, intérêt)* particular (**c**) *Péj (bizarre)* peculiar (**d**) *(privé) (maison, voiture)* private; *(salle de bain)* en suite (**e**) **en p.** *(spécialement)* in particular; *(en privé)* in private

2 *nm (individu)* private individual; **un simple p.** an ordinary person; **vente de p. à p.** private sale

particulièrement [partikyljɛrmɑ̃] *adv* particularly; **j'attire tout p. votre attention sur…** I would particularly like to draw your attention to…

partie [parti] *nf* (**a**) *(morceau)* part; **la plus grande p. de qch** the greatest part of sth; **en p.** partly, in part; **en grande** *ou* **majeure p.** for the most part; **être en p. remboursé** to be partially refunded; **faire p. de qch** to be part of sth; *Fam* **faire p. des meubles** to be part of the furniture; **les parties communes** the communal areas; *Fam* **les parties** the private parts; **les parties génitales** the genitals

(**b**) *(domaine)* field, subject; **je ne suis pas de la p.** that's not my field

(**c**) *(d'un chanteur, d'un instrument)* part

(**d**) *(fête)* party; **ce n'est pas une p. de plaisir!** it's not my idea of fun!; **p. de campagne** day in the country; **p. de chasse** shooting party; *Fam* **p. de jambes en l'air** roll in the hay; *Can* **p. de sucre** sugaring-off party

(**e**) *(jeu)* game; **faire une p. de cartes** to have a game of cards; *Fig* **ce n'est que p. remise** we'll do it another time, let's take a rain check

(**f**) *Jur* party; **la p. adverse** the other side; **être p. prenante** to be an interested party; **p. civile** plaintiff; **se constituer** *ou* **se porter p. civile** to institute proceedings *(in a civil case)*

(**g**) *(locutions)* **avoir affaire à forte p.** to have a tough opponent on one's hands; **prendre qn à p.** to take sb to task; **avoir p. liée avec qn** to be hand in glove with sb

partiel, -elle [parsjɛl] **1** *adj* partial; **élection partielle** by-election; **travailler à temps p.** to work part-time

2 *nm Univ* end-of-quarter exam

3 *nf* **partielle** by-election

partiellement [parsjɛlmɑ̃] *adv* partially

partir [64a] [partir] *vi (aux être)* (**a**) *(s'en aller)* to go, to leave; *(commencer un voyage)* to set off; *(sans destination particulière)* to go off; *(bateau, avion)* to leave; *(moteur)* to start; *(fusil, pétard)* to go off; *Euph (mourir)* to pass away; **p. en vacances** to go (away) on vacation; **p. en promenade** to go for a stroll; **p. faire ses courses** to go out shopping; **p. en courant** to run off; **p. de rien** to start from nothing; **p. d'un éclat de rire** to burst out laughing; **être bien/mal parti** to get off to a good/bad start; **faire p.** *(fusil)* to fire; *(feux d'artifice)* to let off; *(moteur)* to start; *Fam* **c'est parti!** here we go!

(**b**) *(disparaître) (douleur, bleu)* to go, to disappear; *(tache)* to come out; *(peinture, vernis)* to come off; **faire p. une tache** to get a stain out

(**c**) *(sortir)* **p. de** *(sujet: route, chemin)* to start from; **en partant du principe que…** assuming that…; **ça partait d'un bon sentiment** the thought was there; **et, partant de là,…** on that assumption,…

(**d**) **à p. du village** from the village; **à p. d'aujourd'hui** from today (onward); **à p. de maintenant** from now on; **à p. de 200 euros** from 200 euros (upward)

partisan, -e [partizɑ̃, -an] **1** *nm* (**a**) *(fidèle)* supporter (**b**) *(combattant)* partisan

2 *adj (esprit)* partisan; **querelles partisanes** sectarian quarrels; **être p. de qch/de faire qch** to be in favor of sth/of doing sth

partitif, -ive [partitif, -iv] *adj & nm Gram* partitive

partition [partisjɔ̃] *nf (musique)* score

partout [partu] *adv* (**a**) *(en tous lieux)* everywhere; **p. où je vais** everywhere I go; **un peu p.** all over the place; **j'ai mal p.** I'm aching all over (**b**) **trois buts p.** *(au football)* three all; **15/30 p.** *(au tennis)* 15/30 all; **40 p.** *(au tennis)* deuce

partouze [partuz] *nf Fam* orgy

paru, -e *voir* **paraître**

parure [paryr] *nf (ensemble)* set; **p. de lit** set of bed linen

parution [parysjɔ̃] *nf* appearance, publication

parvenir [70] [parvǝnir] **parvenir à** *vt ind (aux être)* (**a**) *(atteindre) (endroit, personne)* to reach; **p. à ses fins** to achieve one's ends; **faire p. qch à qn** to send sth to sb (**b**) *(réussir)* **p. à faire qch** to manage to do sth

parvenu, -e [parvǝny] *nm,f Péj* upstart

parvis[1] [parvi] *nm* square *(in front of a church or a public building)*

pas[1] [pɑ] *nm* (**a**) *(enjambée, de danse)* step; *(allure)* pace; **p. à p.** step by step; **à p. de loup** stealthily; **marcher à grands p.** to stride along; **marcher à petits p.** to toddle along; **marcher d'un p. hésitant** to walk hesitantly; **faire un faux p.** to trip; *Fig* to make a faux pas; **faire un p. (vers)** to take a step (toward); **faire un p. en avant/en arrière** to (take a) step forward/back; **faire les cent p.** to pace up and down; **faire le premier p.** to take the first step; **marcher au p.** *(soldat)* to march in step; **rouler au p.** *(en voiture)* to crawl along; **ils habitent à deux p. d'ici** they live a few yards away; **j'y vais de ce p.** I'll do it right away; **p. de deux** pas de deux; **p. de course** *ou* **gymnastique** jog trot

(**b**) *(trace)* footprint; **revenir** *ou* **retourner sur ses p.** to retrace one's steps

(**c**) *(seuil)* **p. de la porte** doorstep

(**d**) *(passage)* **le p. de Calais** the Straits of Dover

(e) *(de vis, d'hélice)* pitch

(f) *(locutions)* **prendre le p. sur qch** to take precedence over sth; **tirer qn d'un mauvais p.** to get sb out of a tight corner

pas² [pɑ] *adv* not; **je ne sais p.** I don't know; **je ne l'ai p. vue** I haven't seen her; **il est difficile de ne p. le lui dire** it's difficult not to tell him; **qu'elle vienne ou p.** whether she comes or not; **viendra? viendra p.?** will he/she come or won't he/she?; **p. mal** not bad; **une explication p. claire** an unclear explanation; **p. un n'a réagi** not one of them reacted; **p. de sucre/lecteurs** no sugar/readers; **p. du tout** not at all

pascal¹, -e, -als *ou* **-aux, -ales** [paskal, -o] *adj* Easter; *(agneau)* paschal

pascal², -als [paskal] *nm Phys* pascal

passable [pasabl] *adj* passable, fair

passablement [pasabləmɑ̃] *adv* fairly

passade [pasad] *nf* passing fancy

passage [pasaʒ] *nm* **(a)** *(d'une route, d'une rivière)* crossing; *(d'un lieu)* passing; **on sourit sur son p.** people smile as he goes by; **les soldats ont tout détruit sur leur p.** the soldiers destroyed everything in their path; **être de p. dans une ville** to be passing through a town; *Fig* **et au p., je te ferai remarquer que…** and incidentally, let me draw your attention to the fact that…; *Fam* **p. à tabac** beating up; *Ordinat* **p. automatique à la ligne suivante** wordwrap

(b) *(chemin)* passage; *(ruelle)* alley(way); *(galerie commerciale)* (shopping) arcade; **p. clouté** crosswalk; **p. à niveau** grade crossing; **p. pour piétons** crosswalk; *(souterrain)* underpass; **p. souterrain** underpass

(c) *(extrait)* passage

(d) *(changement)* change, transition; **le p. de l'autocratie à la démocratie** the changeover *or* transition from autocracy to democracy

(e) *(moment)* **p. nuageux/pluvieux** cloudy/rainy spell; *Fam* **avoir un p. à vide** to go through a rough period

(f) *Psy* **p. à l'acte** acting out

passager, -ère [pasaʒe, -ɛr] **1** *adj* momentary; **des pluies passagères** occasional showers; **ils ont eu une petite brouille passagère** they fell out for a while
2 *nm,f* passenger; **p. clandestin** stowaway

passant¹ [pasɑ̃] *nm (de ceinture)* loop

passant², -e [pasɑ̃, -ɑ̃t] **1** *adj (rue)* busy
2 *nm,f* passer-by

passation [pasasjɔ̃] *nf (d'un accord)* signing; **p. de pouvoirs** transfer of power

passe¹ [pas] *nf* **(a)** *(au football)* pass; **p. en avant/en retrait** forward/back pass **(b)** *(d'une prostituée)* trick; **hôtel de p.** = hotel used by prostitutes and their clients; **maison de p.** brothel **(c)** *(à la roulette)* passe (any number above 18) **(d)** *Fig* **être en p. de faire qch** to be on the way to doing sth; **être dans une mauvaise p.** to be going through a rough period

passe² [pas] *nm Fam (clef)* master key

passé, -e [pase] **1** *adj* **(a)** *(écoulé) (temps)* past; **la semaine passée** last week; **il est quatre heures passées** it's after four; **elle a quarante ans passés** she's over forty **(b)** *(terminé)* over; **penser à son enfance passée** to think about one's childhood **(c)** *(décoloré)* faded **(d)** **p. de mode** out of fashion
2 *nm* **(a)** *(période)* **le p.** the past; **par le p.** in the past; **tout ça, c'est du p.** that's all in the past **(b)** *Gram* past (tense); **p. antérieur** past anterior; **p. composé** perfect (tense); **p. simple** preterite, past historic; **au p.** in the past (tense)
3 *prép* after

passe-droit *(pl* **passe-droits)** [pasdrwa] *nm* privilege

passéiste [paseist] *Péj* **1** *adj* living in the past
2 *nmf* person who lives in the past

passe-montagne *(pl* **passe-montagnes)** [pasmɔtaɲ] *nm* balaclava (helmet)

passe-partout [paspartu] **1** *nm inv* master key
2 *adj inv* all-purpose

passe-plat *(pl* **passe-plats)** [paspla] *nm* serving hatch

passeport [paspɔr] *nm aussi Fig* passport; **p. biométrique** biometric passport

passer [pase] **1** *vi* (aux être) **(a)** *(se déplacer)* to go past; **p. devant qn/qch** to go past sb/sth; **laisser p. qn** to let sb past; *(dans une queue)* to let sb in; **je ne peux pas p.** I can't get by *or* past; **p. sur les détails** to skip the details; **elle nous a fait p. dans son bureau** she showed us into her office; **mais où est-il passé?** where's he gone to?; **dire qch en passant** to mention sth in passing; **soit dit en passant** incidentally

(b) *(évoluer)* **p. de qch à qch** to go from sth to sth; **p. dans la classe supérieure** to move up a class; **p. en première/seconde** *(en voiture)* to shift into first/second; **p. capitaine** to be promoted to captain

(c) *(traverser)* **p. par le village/Paris** to go through the village/Paris; **par où est-il passé?** which way did he go?; **laisser p. qch** *(lumière, air)* to let sth in

(d) *(apparaître)* **p. à la radio/télévision** to be on the radio/television; **p. au cinéma** to be showing at the movies

(e) *(aller)* **je suis passé chez elle/à la boucherie** I stopped by her house/the butcher's; **le facteur est déjà passé** the mailman already delivered; **je ne fais que p.** I'm not staying

(f) *(disparaître)* to go; **laisser p. qch** *(occasion)* to pass up sth; *(erreur)* to miss sth; **le plus dur est passé** the worst is over; **j'avais mal à la tête mais ça m'a passé** I had a headache but it's gone away; **il était amoureux d'elle mais ça lui a passé** he was in love with her but he's gotten over it

(g) *(année, temps)* to pass, to go by

(h) *(être considéré)* **p. pour un génie** to be considered a genius; **faire p. qn pour** to pass sb off as

(i) *(être adopté) (loi, proposition)* to be passed, to go through

(j) **passe!** *(dans un jeu)* pass!

(k) *Fam* **il a bien failli y p.** *(mourir)* he nearly didn't make it; **toute sa fortune y est passée** she spent her entire fortune on it

2 *vt* (aux avoir) **(a)** *(pont, rivière, frontière)* to go over; *(porte, douane)* to go through; **il a passé la soixantaine** he's in his sixties

(b) *(donner) (ballon, témoin)* to pass; **p. qch à qn** to pass *or* to give sth to sb; *Fam* **p. son rhume à qn** to give sb one's cold; **p. la parole à qn** to give the floor to sb; **pourriez-vous me la p.?** *(au téléphone)* could you let me speak to her?

(c) *(mettre) (vêtement)* to slip on; **p. un coup d'éponge sur qch** to sponge sth down; **p. la tête par la fenêtre** to stick one's head out of the window; **p. le doigt sur qch** to run one's finger over sth; **p. la seconde/troisième** *(en voiture)* to shift into second/third; *Fam* **qu'est-ce qu'il va nous p.!** he's going to make us wish we'd never been born!

(d) *(film)* to show; *(disque)* to play; *(vidéo)* to put on

(e) *(temps, vacances)* to spend; **p. son temps à faire qch** to spend one's time doing sth; **pour p. le temps** to pass the time

(f) *(pardonner)* **elle lui passe tout** she lets him/her get away with everything

(g) *(omettre)* to leave out, to skip; **p. son tour** to skip a turn; **j'en passe et des meilleures** and that's not the half of it

(h) *(examen)* to take; *(visite médicale)* to have; **la voiture doit passer un contrôle** the car must go (in) to be tested

(i) *(accord, contrat)* to enter into, to sign; *(commande)* to place (à with)

(j) *(liquide)* to strain; *(café)* to filter

3 se passer *vpr* **(a)** *(se produire)* to happen; **que se passe-t-il?, qu'est-ce qui se passe?** what's happening?; **ça s'est bien passé** it went well; **l'histoire se passe en 1900/en Normandie** the story takes place in 1900/in Normandy; *Fam* **ça ne se passera pas comme ça!** over my dead body!

(b) *(mettre)* **se p. la main dans les cheveux** to run one's fingers through one's hair; **se p. de l'eau sur la figure** to splash one's face with water; **se p. de la crème sur les mains** to put some cream on one's hands

4 se passer de *vt ind (se priver de)* to do without; **il ne peut pas se p. de télévision** he can't live without TV

passereau, -x [pasro] *nm* passerine

passerelle [pasrɛl] *nf* **(a)** *(au-dessus d'une rue, d'un ruisseau)* footbridge **(b)** *(de navire)* bridge; **p. de débarquement** *ou* **d'embarquement** *(de navire)* gangway; *(d'avion) (amovible)* steps **(c)** *Fig (intermédiaire)* link **(d)** *Ordinat* **p. (de connexion) (avec)** gateway (to)

passe-temps [pastã] *nm inv* pastime

passe-thé [paste] *nm inv* tea-strainer

passeur, -euse [pasœr, -øz] *nm,f* **(a)** *(de bac)* ferryman, *f* ferrywoman **(b)** *(d'immigrants clandestins)* smuggler; **il trouva un p. qui l'aida à gagner les États-Unis** he found someone to get him over the border into the United States

passible [pasibl] *adj* liable (**de** to)

passif, -ive [pasif, -iv] **1** *adj* passive
2 *nm* **(a)** *Gram* passive; **au p.** in the passive **(b)** *Fin* liabilities

passif-agressif, passive-agressive [pasifagrɛsif, -iv] *(mpl* **passifs-agressifs,** *fpl* **passives-agressives)** *adj Psy* passive-aggressive

passion [pasjɔ̃] *nf* **(a)** *(sentiment dévorant)* passion; **avoir une p. pour qn/qch** to have a passion for sb/sth; **avoir la p. de qch** to have a passion for sth; **vivre une p.** to have a passionate love affair; **avec p.** passionately **(b)** *Rel* **la P. selon saint Jean** the St John Passion

passionnant, -e [pasjɔnɑ̃, -ɑ̃t] *adj* fascinating

passionné, -e [pasjɔne] **1** *adj* passionate; **p. de qch** really into sth
2 *nm,f* enthusiast; **un p. de football** a soccer enthusiast

passionnel, -elle [pasjɔnɛl] *adj (relation)* passionate

passionnément [pasjɔnemɑ̃] *adv* passionately

passionner [pasjɔne] **1** *vt (sujet: livre, film)* to fascinate; **son métier la passionne** she finds her job fascinating
2 se passionner *vpr* **se p. pour qch** to have a passion for sth

passivement [pasivmɑ̃] *adv* passively

passivité [pasivite] *nf* passivity, passiveness

passoire [paswar] *nf (avec un grillage)* sieve; *(avec de petits trous)* colander; *Fam* **ce gardien de but est une vraie p.!** this goalkeeper is really lousy *or* lets everything in!

pastel [pastɛl] *nm & adj inv* pastel

pastèque [pastɛk] *nf* watermelon; *Fam* **j'ai la tête comme une p.** my head's throbbing

pasteur [pastœr] *nm* **(a)** *Litt (berger)* shepherd **(b)** *(religieux)* pastor, minister

pasteurisation [pastœrizasjɔ̃] *nf* pasteurization

pasteuriser [pastœrize] *vt* to pasteurize

pastiche [pastiʃ] *nm* pastiche

pastille [pastij] *nf (bonbon mou)* pastille; *(médicament)* lozenge, pastille; **p. contre la toux** cough drop *or* lozenge; **p. de menthe** mint; **p. verte** = green label on a low-emission vehicle indicating that it may be driven on days when restrictions are placed on traffic due to high levels of atmospheric pollution

pastis [pastis] *nm* **(a)** *(boisson)* pastis **(b)** *Fam* **être dans le p.** to be in a mess

pastoral, -e, -aux, -ales [pastɔral, -o] **1** *adj* pastoral
2 *nf* **pastorale** *(musique)* pastorale

patachon [pataʃɔ̃] *nm Fam* **mener une vie de p.** to lead a wild life

Patagonie [patagɔni] *nf* **la P.** Patagonia

patapouf [patapuf] **1** *exclam* flop!
2 *nm (langage enfantin)* **gros p.** fatty

pataquès [patakɛs] *nm (faute de langage)* malapropism

patate [patat] *nf Fam (pomme de terre)* spud; *Fig (imbécile)* clod;

Can **patates frites** (French) fries; *Fig* **en avoir gros sur la p.** to be down in the mouth

patati [patati] *exclam Fam* **et p. et patata** and so on and so forth

patatras [patatra] *exclam Fam* crash!

pataud, -e [pato, -od] *adj Fam* clumsy

Pataugas® [patogas] *nm* canvas walking boot

pataugeoire [patoʒwar] *nf* wading pool

patauger [45] [patoʒe] *vi (s'embourber)* to squelch (**dans** in); *(barboter)* to splash about (**dans** in); *Fam (s'embrouiller)* to flounder (**dans** in)

patch [patʃ] *nm Méd* patch; **p. anti-tabac** nicotine patch

pâte [pat] **1** *nf* **(a)** *(pour une tarte)* pastry; *(pour le pain)* dough; *(pour un gâteau)* mixture; **p. brisée** shortcrust pastry; **p. à choux** choux pastry; **p. à crêpes** pancake batter; **p. feuilletée** puff *or* flaky pastry; **p. à frire** batter; **p. à pain** bread dough; **p. sablée** rich shortcrust pastry; **p. à tarte** pastry; **p. à tartiner** chocolate spread **(b)** *(mixture)* **p. d'amandes** marzipan; **p. de fruits** fruit jelly; **p. à modeler** modeling clay; **p. à papier** pulp
2 *nfpl* **pâtes (alimentaires)** pasta; **pâtes fraîches** fresh pasta

pâté [pate] *nm* **(a)** *(terrine)* pâté; **p. de campagne** pâté de campagne *(coarse pâté made with pork); Can* **p. chinois** shepherd's pie; **p. en croûte** pâté in a pastry shell; **p. de foie** liver pâté **(b)** *Belg (gâteau)* cake **(c)** **p. (de sable)** sandpie **(d)** **p. de maisons** block of houses **(e)** *(tache d'encre)* blot; **faire un p. sur qch** to get a blot on sth

pâtée [pate] *nf* **(a)** *(de chat)* cat food; *(de chien)* dog food **(b)** *Fam (défaite)* **prendre la p.** to get thrashed; **mettre la p. à qn** to thrash sb

patelin¹ [patlɛ̃] *nm Fam* village

patelin², **-e** [patlɛ̃, -in] *adj Litt & Péj* unctuous

patent, -e [patɑ̃, -ɑ̃t] *adj* **(a)** *(évident)* patent **(b)** **lettres patentes** letters patent

patente [patɑ̃t] *nf (impôt)* tax *(paid by self-employed people)*

patenté, -e [patɑ̃te] *adj* licensed

patère [patɛr] *nf (coat)* peg

paternaliste [patɛrnalist] *adj* paternalistic

paternel, -elle [patɛrnɛl] **1** *adj* paternal; *(ton)* fatherly; **du côté p.** on the father's side; **ma grand-mère paternelle** my grandmother on my father's side
2 *nm Fam* **le p.** the old man

paternité [patɛrnite] *nf* paternity, fatherhood; **recherche de p.** establishment of paternity

pâteux, -euse [patø, -øz] *adj* **(a)** *(nourriture)* doughy; **avoir la langue pâteuse** to have a furry tongue **(b)** *(sauce)* thick

pathétique [patetik] *adj* pathetic, moving

pathogène [patoʒɛn] *adj* pathogenic

pathologique [patolɔʒik] *adj aussi Fam Fig* pathological

patibulaire [patibylɛr] *adj* **avoir une mine p.** to have a sinister look

patiemment [pasjamɑ̃] *adv* patiently

patience [pasjɑ̃s] *nf* **(a)** *(qualité)* patience; **avoir de la p. (avec qn)** to be patient (with sb); **avoir une p. d'ange** to have the patience of a saint; **prendre son mal en p.** to suffer in silence; **perdre p.** to lose patience; **p., j'ai presque fini!** hold on *or* just a minute, I'm almost done!; *Prov* **p. et longueur de temps font plus que force ni que rage** = all in good time **(b)** *(jeu de cartes)* solitaire

patient, -e [pasjɑ̃, -ɑ̃t] **1** *adj* patient
2 *nm,f (malade)* patient

patienter [pasjɑ̃te] *vi* to wait; **faire p. qn** to ask sb to wait

patin [patɛ̃] *nm* **(a)** *(de patineur)* skate; **patins à glace/à roulettes** ice/roller skates; **faire du p. à glace/à roulettes** to go ice-/roller-skating; *Can Fam Fig* **être vite sur ses patins** to be quick off the mark **(b)** *(pour parquet)* cloth pad **(c)** *Tech* shoe; **p.**

de frein brake shoe (**d**) *très Fam* **rouler un p. à qn** *(embrasser)* to make out with sb

patinage [patinaʒ] *nm (sport)* skating; **p. artistique** figure skating; **p. de vitesse** speed skating

patine [patin] *nf* patina

patiner¹ [patine] *vi* (**a**) *(faire du patinage)* to skate (**b**) *(glisser)* *(voiture)* to skid; *(embrayage)* to slip; **ça patine!** it's like a skating rink!

patiner² [patine] *vt* to give a patina to

patinette [patinɛt] *nf* scooter

patineur, -euse [patinœr, -øz] *nm,f* skater

patinoire [patinwar] *nf* skating *or* ice rink; **ce trottoir est une vraie p.** this pavement is like an ice rink

pâtir [patir] *vi* to suffer (**de** because of)

pâtisserie [patisri] *nf* (**a**) *(magasin)* bakery; **p.-confiserie** confectionery store (**b**) *(gâteau)* pastry, cake (**c**) *(confection)* pastry-making; **faire de la p.** to make cakes

pâtissier, -ère [patisje, -ɛr] **1** *nm,f (artisan)* pastry cook; *(commerçant)* baker

    2 *adj voir* **crème**

patois [patwa] *nm* patois

patraque [patrak] *adj Fam* out of sorts

patriarcal, -e, -aux, -ales [patriarkal, -o] *adj* patriarchal

patriarche [patriarʃ] *nm* patriarch

patrie [patri] *nf* homeland; **ma seconde p.** my second home; *Fig* **la p. des arts** the cradle of the arts

patrimoine [patrimwan] *nm* heritage; *(biens)* property; **p. culturel** cultural heritage; *Biol* **p. génétique** genotype

patriote [patrijɔt] **1** *adj* patriotic

    2 *nmf* patriot

patriotique [patrijɔtik] *adj* patriotic

patriotisme [patrijɔtism] *nm* patriotism

patron, -onne [patrɔ̃, -ɔn] **1** *nm,f* (**a**) *(dirigeant)* boss; *(propriétaire)* owner (**b**) *Rel* patron saint (**de** of)

    2 *nm* (**a**) *(médecin)* senior consultant (**b**) *(pour la couture)* pattern

patronage [patrɔnaʒ] *nm* (**a**) *(parrainage)* patronage; **placé sous le p. de…** sponsored by… (**b**) *(organisation)* youth club

patronal, -e, -aux, -ales [patrɔnal, -o] *adj* employers'

patronat [patrɔna] *nm* employers

patronnesse [patrɔnɛs] *adj f* **dame p.** lady bountiful

patronyme [patrɔnim] *nm* patronymic

patrouille [patruj] *nf* patrol

patrouiller [patruje] *vi* to patrol

patte [pat] *nf* (**a**) *(jambe)* leg; *(pied)* *(de chien, de chat)* paw; *(d'oiseau)* foot; **pattes de devant** forelegs; *(pied)* front paws; **pattes de derrière** hind legs; *(pied)* back paws; **court/haut sur pattes** short-/long-legged; **marcher/se mettre à quatre pattes** to walk/to get down on all fours; *Fig* **tirer dans les pattes à qn** to give sb a hard time; *Fig* **retomber sur ses pattes** to land on one's feet; *Fig* **montrer p. blanche** to show one's credentials; *Fam* **bas les pattes!** hands off!; *Fam* **pattes de mouche(s)** cramped handwriting (**b**) *(de cartable, de sac)* tab (**c**) *(de poche)* flap; *(d'épaule)* epaulet (**d**) *Suisse (torchon)* cloth (**e**) **pattes** *(favoris)* sideburns

patte-d'oie [*pl* **pattes-d'oie**] [patdwa] *nf* (**a**) *(carrefour)* intersection (**b**) *(ride)* crow's foot

pattemouille [patmuj] *nf* damp cloth *(for ironing clothes)*

pâturage [patyraʒ] *nm (endroit)* pasture; **pâturages** pasture land

paume [pom] *nf* palm

paumé, -e [pome] *Fam* **1** *adj* lost

    2 *nm,f* loser

paumer [pome] *Fam* **1** *vt* to lose

    2 se paumer *vpr* to get lost

paupérisation [poperizasjɔ̃] *nf* impoverishment

paupière [popjɛr] *nf* eyelid

paupiette [popjɛt] *nf* **p. de veau** paupiette of veal

pause [poz] *nf* (**a**) *(dans une activité)* break; *(en parlant)* pause; **faire une p.** to have a break; *(en parlant)* to pause; **p. de midi** lunch break; **p.-café** coffee break (**b**) *Mus* whole rest

pauvre [povr] **1** *adj* (**a**) *(personne, sol)* poor; **p. en vitamine C** with a low vitamin C content; **p. de moi!** poor old me! (**b**) *(misérable)* *(robe, meubles)* shabby; *(sourire)* weak; *(excuse)* poor (**c**) *Péj* sad, pathetic; *Fam* **p. mec!** you loser!

    2 *nmf* poor man, *f* poor woman; **les pauvres** the poor; *Fig* **p. d'esprit** half-wit

pauvrement [povrəmɑ̃] *adv* poorly

pauvresse [povrɛs] *nf (fille)* poor girl; *(femme)* poor woman

pauvreté [povrəte] *nf aussi Fig* poverty

pavane [pavan] *nf Mus* pavane

pavaner [pavane] **se pavaner** *vpr* to strut about

pavé [pave] *nm* (**a**) *(morceau de grès)* paving stone; *Fam Péj (livre)* massive tome; *Fig* **un p. dans la mare** a bombshell (**b**) *(revêtement)* paving; *Fig* **tenir le haut du p.** to be at the top; *Fig* **battre le p.** to hang around the streets; *Fig* **être sur le p.** to be on the street (**c**) *Ordinat* keypad; **p. numérique** numeric keypad

paver [pave] *vt* to pave *(with small stones)*; *Fig* **l'enfer est pavé de bonnes intentions** the road to hell is paved with good intentions

pavillon [pavijɔ̃] *nm* (**a**) *(petite maison)* individual house; **p. de chasse** hunting lodge (**b**) *(d'hôpital)* wing (**c**) *(partie évasée)* *(d'un Klaxon®, d'un haut-parleur)* horn; *(d'une trompette)* bell; *(d'un entonnoir)* mouth; **p. de l'oreille** external ear (**d**) *(drapeau)* flag

pavillonnaire [pavijɔnɛr] *adj* **banlieue p.** suburb *(consisting of single-family residences as opposed to high-rise apartment buildings)*

pavoiser [pavwaze] *vi Fam* to gloat

pavot [pavo] *nm* poppy

payable [pɛjabl] *adj* payable; **p. comptant** payable in cash; **p. à la livraison** payable on delivery; **p. à vue** payable at sight

payant, -e [pɛjɑ̃, -ɑ̃t] *adj (qui paie) (hôte, élève)* paying; *(où il faut payer)* with a charge for admission; **l'entrée est payante** there is a charge for admission; *Fig* **ça s'est avéré p.** it turned out to be worth it

paye [pɛj] = **paie**

payement [pɛjmɑ̃] = **paiement**

payer [53] [peje] **1** *vt* (**a**) *(somme, dette, loyer, personne)* to pay; *(objet, service)* to pay for; **faire p. qch** *(service)* to charge for sth; *(somme)* to charge sth; **se faire p.** to get *or* to be paid; **je le lui ai payé 100 euros** I paid him/her 100 euros for it; *Fam* **p. qch à qn** *(le lui offrir)* to buy sth for sb; *Fig* **p. les pots cassés** to do the dirty work; *(dépense)* to foot the bill (**b**) *Fig (expier)* to pay for; **il l'a payé de sa vie** he paid for it with his life; **tu me le paieras!** you'll pay for it!; *Fam* **je suis payé pour le savoir** I've learned it the hard way

    2 *vi* (**a**) *(verser de l'argent)* to pay; **p. en liquide/par carte (de crédit)/par chèque** to pay (in) cash/by credit card/by check; **p. de sa poche** to pay out of one's own pocket (**b**) *Fig* **p. de sa personne** to put oneself out; **il ne paie pas de mine, mais il est doué** he doesn't look it, but he's talented (**c**) *(rapporter)* to pay

    3 se payer *vpr Fam* **se p. qch** *(s'offrir)* to treat oneself to sth; *(être chargé de)* to be saddled with sth; **se p. du bon temps** to have a blast; **se p. un arbre** to crash into a tree; **je me suis payé un 2 à l'oral** I got a 2 in the oral; **se p. la tête de qn** to take sb for an idiot; **se p. le culot de faire qch** to have the nerve to do sth

payeur, -euse [pɛjœr, -øz] *nm,f* payer; **mauvais p.** bad debtor, defaulter

pays [pei] *nm* (**a**) *(nation)* country; **p. de cocagne** land of plenty; **p. en voie de développement** developing country;

les p. de l'Est Eastern European countries (**b**) *(région)* region; **voir du p.** to travel around; **revenir au p.** to go back home; **p. de chasse/pêche** hunting/fishing country (**c**) **le P. basque** the Basque country; **le p. de Galles** Wales

paysage [peizaʒ] *nm* (**a**) *(site)* landscape; *(vue)* scenery; *Fig (ensemble)* scene; **le p. audiovisuel français** French broadcasting (**b**) *(peinture)* landscape (painting) (**c**) *Ordinat* **mode p.** landscape mode

paysager, -ère [peizaʒe, -ɛr] *adj (jardin)* landscaped; *(bureau)* open-plan

paysagiste [peizaʒist] *nmf* (**a**) *(peintre)* landscape painter (**b**) **(jardinier) p.** landscape gardener

paysan, -anne [peizɑ̃, -an] **1** *adj* country; *Péj* peasant; **syndicat p.** farmers' union

2 *nm,f* farmer; *Péj* peasant

paysannerie [peizanri] *nf* **la p.** the peasantry

Pays-Bas [peiba] *nmpl* **les P.** the Netherlands

PC [pese] *nm* (**a**) *(abrév* **parti communiste***)* CP (**b**) *(abrév* **personal computer***)* PC

PCF [peseɛf] *nm (abrév* **parti communiste français***)* French Communist Party

PCV [peseve] *nm* **(appel en) P.** collect call; **appeler en P.** to call collect

P-DG [pedeʒe] *nm inv (abrév* **président-directeur général***)* CEO

péage [peaʒ] *nm* (**a**) *(droit)* toll; **pont à p.** toll bridge (**b**) *(installation)* tollbooth (**c**) **chaîne (de télévision) à p.** pay channel

peau, -x [po] *nf* (**a**) *(derme)* skin; **avoir la p. grasse** to have oily skin; **avoir la p. blanche/noire** to be white/black; **avoir une p. de pêche** to have velvety skin; *Fig* **faire p. neuve** *(personne)* to turn over a new leaf; *(entreprise, parti)* to get a new image; **entrer dans la p. d'un personnage** to get right inside a character; **n'avoir que la p. et les os** to be nothing but skin and bone; **diminuer comme une p. de chagrin** to dwindle away; *Fam* **être bien/mal dans sa p.** to feel/not to feel good about oneself; *Fam* **avoir qch dans la p.** to have sth in one's blood; *Fam* **avoir qn dans la p.** to be crazy about sb; *Fam* **tenir à sa p.** to value one's life; *Fam* **risquer sa p.** to risk one's neck; *Fam* **sauver sa p.** to save one's skin; *Fam* **avoir la p. de qn** to have sb's hide; *Fam* **prendre douze balles dans la p.** to be shot by a firing squad; *Fam* **p. de vache** *(homme)* bastard; *(femme)* bitch

(**b**) *(dépouille) (d'un animal)* skin; *(d'un animal à fourrure)* pelt

(**c**) *(cuir)* hide, leather; *(d'un tambour)* skin; **p. de chamois** chamois (leather); **p. de mouton** sheepskin; **p. de serpent** snakeskin

(**d**) *(de fruit, de légume)* skin; *(d'agrume, de pomme)* peel; **p. de banane** banana skin; **p. d'orange** orange peel; *Fig* orange-peel skin

(**e**) *(du lait)* skin

(**f**) *(des ongles)* hangnail

peaufiner [pofine] *vt* to polish *(with a chamois leather)*; *Fam Fig (fignoler)* to add the final touches to

Peau-Rouge *(pl* **Peaux-Rouges***)* [poruʒ] *nmf* Red Indian

peausserie [posri] *nf* (**a**) *(commerce)* skin trade (**b**) *(marchandise)* leatherwear

pécari [pekari] *nm* peccary

peccadille [pekadij] *nf* peccadillo

péché [peʃe] *nm* sin; **les sept péchés capitaux** the seven deadly sins; **p. de jeunesse** youthful indiscretion; **p. mignon** weakness; **le p. originel** original sin

pêche¹ [pɛʃ] **1** *nf* (**a**) *(fruit)* peach; **p. blanche** white peach; **p. jaune** yellow peach (**b**) *Fam (coup)* clout (**c**) *Fam (forme)* **avoir la p.** to be in form

2 *adj inv* peach(-colored)

pêche² [pɛʃ] *nf* (**a**) *(activité)* fishing; **aller à la p.** to go fishing; **p. à la ligne** angling; **p. à la mouche** fly fishing; *Can* **p. sous**

la glace ice fishing (**b**) *(produits pêchés)* catch; **faire une bonne p.** to get a good catch

pécher [34] [peʃe] *vi* to sin; **il pèche par excès de timidité** he's painfully shy; **cette enquête pèche sur un point** the inquiry fails on one point; **p. par omission** to sin by omission

pêcher¹ [peʃe] *nm* peach tree

pêcher² [peʃe] **1** *vt* (**a**) *(chercher à prendre)* to fish for; *(prendre)* to catch; **p. la baleine** to go whaling (**b**) *Fam (trouver)* **où avez-vous pêché cela?** where did you pick that up?

2 *vi* to fish; **p. à la ligne** to go angling; *Fig* **p. en eau trouble** to fish in troubled waters

pécheresse [peʃrɛs] *voir* **pécheur**

pêcherie [pɛʃri] *nf* fishery, fishing ground

pécheur, -eresse [peʃœr, peʃrɛs] *nm,f* sinner

pêcheur, -euse [pɛʃœr, -øz] *nm,f* fisherman, *f* fisherwoman; **p. à la ligne** angler; **p. de baleines** whaler; **p. de corail** coral fisher; **p. de perles** pearl diver

pécore [pekɔr] *nmf Fam Péj* country bumpkin, yokel

pectoral, -e, -aux, -ales [pɛktɔral, -o] **1** *adj* pectoral

2 *nm* pectoral muscle

pécule [pekyl] *nm* savings, nest egg

pécuniaire [pekynjɛr] *adj* financial

pédagogie [pedagɔʒi] *nf* (**a**) *(discipline)* pedagogy (**b**) *(qualité du pédagogue)* teaching skills

pédagogique [pedagɔʒik] *adj (voyage, sortie)* educational; *(méthode)* teaching

pédagogue [pedagɔg] **1** *adj* **elle est très p.** she's a very good teacher

2 *nmf* (**a**) *(spécialiste)* educationalist (**b**) *(personne qui sait enseigner)* teacher

pédale [pedal] *nf* (**a**) *(de vélo, de voiture, de piano)* pedal; **p. d'accélérateur** gas pedal; **p. d'embrayage** clutch pedal; **p. de frein** brake pedal; *Fam Fig* **mettre la p. douce** to go easy; *Fam Fig* **perdre les pédales** *(s'affoler)* to lose one's head (**b**) *Fam Péj (homosexuel)* queer, = offensive term used to refer to a male homosexual

pédaler [pedale] *vi* to pedal; *Fam* **p. dans la choucroute** *ou* **la semoule** to be all at sea

pédalier [pedalje] *nm* (**a**) *(de vélo)* chain transmission (**b**) *(clavier d'orgue)* pedal board

Pédalo® [pedalo] *nm* pedal boat; **faire du P.** to go out on a pedal boat

pédant, -e [pedɑ̃, -ɑ̃t] **1** *adj* pedantic

2 *nm,f* pedant

pédé [pede] *nm très Fam* queer, = offensive term used to refer to a male homosexual

pédéraste [pederast] *nm* (**a**) *(homosexuel)* homosexual (**b**) *(pédophile)* pederast

pédestre [pedɛstr] *adj (voyage)* on foot; **chemin p.** footpath; **randonnée p.** hike

pédiatre [pedjatr] *nmf* pediatrician

pédiatrie [pedjatri] *nf* paediatrics *(singulier)*

pédicure [pedikyr] *nmf* chiropodist

pedigree [pedigre] *nm* pedigree

pédomètre [pedɔmɛtr] *nm* pedometer

pédoncule [pedɔ̃kyl] *nm* peduncle

pédophile [pedɔfil] *nmf* pedophile, child molester

pédophilie [pedɔfili] *nf* pedophilia

pègre [pɛgr] *nf* underworld

peignais, peigne, *etc. voir* **peindre**

peigne [pɛɲ] *nm* (**a**) *(pour les cheveux)* comb; **se donner un coup de p.** to run a comb through one's hair; **p. fin** fine-tooth comb; *Fig* **passer qch au p. fin** to go through sth with a fine-tooth comb (**b**) *(pour la laine)* card

peigne-cul *(pl* **peigne-culs***)* [pɛɲ ky] *nm très Fam Péj* creep

peignée [pɛɲe] *nf Fam* thrashing; **flanquer une p. à qn** to give sb a thrashing

peigner [pɛɲe] **1** *vt* **(a)** *(cheveux)* to comb; **p. un enfant** to comb a child's hair; *Fam* **p. la girafe** to waste one's time **(b)** *(laine)* to card

2 se peigner *vpr* to comb one's hair

peignoir [pɛɲwar] *nm* **(a)** *(vêtement d'intérieur)* housecoat; *(robe de chambre)* dressing gown; **p. (de bain)** bathrobe **(b)** *(chez le coiffeur)* cape

peinard, -e [pɛnar, -ard] *adj Fam (poste)* cushy; *(personne)* nice and comfortable

peindre [54] [pɛ̃dr] **1** *vt* **(a)** *(avec de la peinture)* to paint; **p. qch en vert** to paint sth green **(b)** *(décrire)* to depict

2 *vi* to paint

3 se peindre *vpr* **l'émotion/la consternation se peignit sur son visage** emotion/dismay was written on his/her face

peine [pɛn] *nf* **(a)** *(sanction)* punishment; **p. capitale** capital punishment; **p. de mort** death penalty; **p. de prison** prison sentence; **défense d'entrer sous p. d'amende** *(sur panneau)* trespassers will be prosecuted; **pour la** *ou* **ta p., tu vas descendre la poubelle** just for that, you can take the garbage down

(b) *(chagrin)* sorrow, sadness; **avoir de la p.** to be upset; **faire de la p. à qn** to upset sb; **elle fait p. à voir** she's a pitiful sight; **p. de cœur** heartache

(c) *(effort)* trouble; **se donner de la p. pour faire qch** to go to a lot of trouble to do sth; **donnez-vous** *ou* **prenez la p. d'entrer** please come in; **c'est p. perdue** it's a waste of time; **elle n'est pas au bout de ses peines** her troubles aren't over yet; **en être pour sa p.** to have nothing to show for one's trouble; **ça vaut la p. d'essayer** it's worth a try; **ça ne vaut pas la p.** it's not worth it; **ce n'est pas la p. de débarrasser la table** there's no point (in) clearing the table; **est-ce que ça vaut la p. que je vienne?** do I need to come?; *Ironique* **c'était bien la p. de se donner tout ce mal!** it was really worth going to all that trouble!

(d) *(difficulté)* difficulty; **avoir de la p. à faire qch** to have difficulty doing sth; **j'ai (de la) p. à croire que...** I find it hard to believe that...; **elle serait bien en p. de t'expliquer comment ça marche** she'd be hard put to explain to you how it works; **cela n'a pas été sans p.** it was no easy matter

(e) **à p.** hardly, scarcely; **c'est à p. si je le connais** I hardly know him; **il est à p. trois heures** it's only just three o'clock; **à p. étions-nous sortis que...** we'd only just gone out when...; **j'arrive à p.** I've only just arrived; **à p. arrivée, elle alluma une cigarette** no sooner had she arrived than she lit a cigarette

peiner [pɛne] **1** *vt* to upset, to sadden; **d'un ton peiné** in a sad voice

2 *vi* to labor

peint, -e *voir* **peindre**

peintre [pɛ̃tr] *nm* **(a)** *(artisan, artiste)* painter; **p. en bâtiment** house painter **(b)** *Fig* portrayer

peinture [pɛ̃tyr] *nf* **(a)** *(art, action)* painting; **faire de la p.** to paint; **p. à l'eau** watercolor (painting); **p. à l'huile** oil painting; **p. sur soie** silk painting **(b)** *(tableau)* painting, picture; *Fig (description)* depiction; *Fig* **je ne peux pas la voir en p.** I can't stand the sight of him; **p. murale** mural **(c)** *(matière)* paint; **p. fraîche** *(sur écriteau)* wet paint **(d)** *(surface peinte)* paintwork; **il faudra refaire les peintures** the paintwork will have to be done

peinturer [pɛ̃tyre] *vt Can* to paint

peinturlurer [pɛ̃tyrlyre] *vt Fam* to daub with paint; **se p. le visage** to plaster make-up on one's face

péjoratif, -ive [peʒɔratif, -iv] *adj* pejorative

Pékin [pekɛ̃] *n* Peking, Beijing

pékinois, -e [pekinwa, -az] **1** *adj* of Peking, of Beijing

2 *nm,f* person from Peking *or* Beijing

3 *nm* **(a)** *(chien)* pekin(g)ese **(b)** *(langue)* Pekingese, Mandarin

PEL [peəɛl] *nm Fin (abrév* **plan d'épargne-logement**) = savings plan entitling savers to low mortgages, ≃ savings-and-loan association account

pelade [pəlad] *nf* alopecia

pelage [pəlaʒ] *nm* coat, fur

pelé, -e [pəle] **1** *adj (personne, fourrure)* bald; *Fig (paysage)* bare; *(tissu)* threadbare

2 *nm Fam* **il y avait trois pelés et un tondu** there was hardly a soul there

pêle-mêle [pɛlmɛl] **1** *adv* higgledy-piggledy

2 *nm inv (cadre)* multiple (photo) frame

peler [39] [pəle] **1** *vt* to peel

2 *vi (peau)* to peel; **j'ai le nez qui pèle** my nose is peeling; *Fam Fig* **je pèle (de froid)** I'm freezing (cold)

3 se peler *vpr Fam* **on se pèle (de froid)** it's freezing (cold)

pèlerin [pɛlrɛ̃] *nm* pilgrim

pèlerinage [pɛlrinaʒ] *nm* pilgrimage; **faire un p., aller en p.** to go on a pilgrimage

pèlerine [pɛlrin] *nf* cape

pélican [pelikɑ̃] *nm* pelican

pelisse [pəlis] *nf* pelisse

pelle [pɛl] *nf* shovel; *(d'enfant)* spade; *Fig* **à la p.** by the bucketful; *Fam* **ramasser** *ou* **se prendre une p.** to fall flat on one's face; **p. mécanique** mechanical shovel; **p. à ordures** dustpan; **p. à tarte** pie server

pelletée [pɛlte] *nf* shovelful

pelleteuse [pɛltøz] *nf* mechanical shovel

pellicule [pelikyl] *nf* **(a)** *(de glace, de peinture)* thin layer; *(sur un liquide)* film **(b)** *Cin & Phot* film **(c)** *(dans les cheveux)* **pellicules** dandruff; **avoir des pellicules** to have dandruff

pelote [pəlɔt] *nf* **(a)** *(de laine, de ficelle)* ball; *Can* **p. de neige** snowball; *Fig* **avoir les nerfs en p.** to be on edge **(b)** *(sport)* **p. (basque)** pelota **(c)** **p. (à épingles)** pincushion

peloter [pəlɔte] *vt Fam* to pet

peloton [pəlɔtɔ̃] *nm* **(a)** *(en cyclisme)* pack; *aussi Fig* **le p. de tête** the leaders **(b)** *Mil* platoon; **p. d'exécution** firing squad **(c)** *(petite pelote)* small ball

pelotonner [pəlɔtɔne] **se pelotonner** *vpr* to curl up; *(pour avoir chaud)* to snuggle up

pelouse [pəluz] *nf* lawn; **p. interdite** *(sur panneau)* keep off the grass

peluche [pəlyʃ] *nf* **(a)** *(tissu)* plush; **jouet en p.** soft toy, stuffed animal **(b)** *(jouet)* soft toy, stuffed animal **(c)** *(bout d'étoffe)* piece of fluff

pelucheux, -euse [pəlyʃø, -øz] *adj* fluffy

pelure [pəlyr] *nf* **(a)** *(peau) (de fruit)* peel; *(de légumes)* peelings; **p. d'oignon** onion skin **(b)** *Fam (vêtement)* coat

pelvis [pɛlvis] *nm* pelvis

pénal, -e, -aux, -ales [penal, -o] *adj* penal

pénaliser [penalize] *vt* to penalize

pénalité [penalite] *nf* penalty

penalty [penalti] *nm* penalty

pénates [penat] *nmpl Fam* **regagner ses p.** to return home

penaud, -e [pəno, -od] *adj* sheepish; **d'un air p.** sheepishly

penchant [pɑ̃ʃɑ̃] *nm (tendance)* propensity (**pour** for); *(préférence)* penchant (**pour** for)

penché, -e [pɑ̃ʃe] *adj* leaning; *(écriture)* sloping

pencher [pɑ̃ʃe] **1** *vt (récipient, meuble)* to tilt; **p. la tête en avant/en arrière** to lean forward/backward; **p. la tête à droite** to lean one's head to the right

2 *vi (s'écarter de la position verticale)* to lean over; *(bateau)* to list; **p. vers la droite** to lean to the right; *Fig* **p. pour qch** to incline toward sth

3 se pencher *vpr* to lean over; **se p. en avant/en arrière/sur le côté** to lean forward/backward/to the side; **se p. par la fenêtre** to lean out of the window; *Fig* **se p. sur un problème** to look into a problem

pendaison [pɑ̃dɛzɔ̃] *nf* hanging; **p. de crémaillère** house-warming (party)

pendant¹, -e [pɑ̃dɑ̃, -ɑ̃t] **1** *adj* (**a**) *(qui pend)* hanging; *(jambes)* dangling; **le chien avait la langue pendante** the dog's tongue was hanging out (**b**) *(en attente)* pending
2 *nm* (**a**) **p. (d'oreille)** drop earring (**b**) *(d'un tableau, d'un bibelot)* matching piece (**de** to); **se faire p.** to go together

pendant² [pɑ̃dɑ̃] **1** *prép* (**a**) *(au cours de)* during; **p. mon séjour** during my stay (**b**) *(pour une durée de)* **p. dix minutes/deux mois** for ten minutes/two months; **p. tout le trajet** throughout the journey, for the whole journey; **p. ce temps(-là)** in the meantime
2 *conj* **p. que** while; **p. que vous y êtes** while you're at it

pendentif [pɑ̃dɑ̃tif] *nm (bijou)* pendant

penderie [pɑ̃dri] *nf* closet

pendouiller [pɑ̃duje] *vi Fam* to dangle

pendre [pɑ̃dr] **1** *vt* (**a**) *(accrocher)* to hang (up) (**b**) *(mettre à mort)* to hang; **p. qn haut et court** to string sb up; *Fam Fig* **qu'il aille se faire p. ailleurs** let him go hang; *Fig* **je veux bien être pendu si…** I'll be hanged if…
2 *vi* to hang; *(cheveux)* to hang down; *(langue d'un animal)* to hang out; *(bras, jambes)* to dangle; **ton pan de chemise pend** your shirt's hanging out; *Fam* **ça lui pend au nez** he's/she's got it coming to him/her
3 se pendre *vpr* (**a**) *(se suicider)* to hang oneself (**b**) *(s'accrocher)* **se p. à qch** to hang from sth; **se p. au cou de qn** to throw one's arms around sb's neck

pendu, -e [pɑ̃dy] **1** *adj* (**a**) *(mort)* hanged (**b**) *(accroché)* hanging up; **p. à** hanging from; **p. aux jupes de sa mère** clinging to one's mother's skirts; *Fig* **avoir la langue bien pendue** to be a great talker; **elle est toujours pendue au téléphone** she's always on the phone
2 *nm,f* hanged man, *f* hanged woman; **le p.** *(jeu)* hangman

pendule [pɑ̃dyl] **1** *nf* clock; *Fig* **remettre les pendules à l'heure** to get things straight
2 *nm* pendulum

pendulette [pɑ̃dylɛt] *nf* small clock

pêne [pɛn] *nm* bolt

pénétrant, -e [penetrɑ̃, -ɑ̃t] *adj (vent, froid)* piercing; *(pluie)* soaking; *(odeur, regard, esprit)* penetrating

pénétration [penetrasjɔ̃] *nf* penetration

pénétré, -e [penetre] *adj (air, ton)* earnest; **p. d'un sentiment/d'une idée** imbued with a feeling/an idea; **il est p. de son importance** he's full of his own importance

pénétrer [34] [penetre] **1** *vi* to penetrate; **p. dans une maison** to get into a house
2 *vt* (**a**) *(sujet: balle)* to penetrate; *(sujet: liquide)* to soak into; *Fig (pensée, intentions)* to fathom; *(marché)* to penetrate (**b**) *(sexuellement)* to penetrate
3 se pénétrer *vpr* **se p. d'une idée** to become convinced of an idea

pénible [penibl] *adj* (**a**) *(tâche, voyage, vie)* hard; *(hiver, froid)* severe (**b**) *(spectacle, nouvelles)* painful (**c**) *Fam (personne)* **ce qu'il est p.!** he's such a pain!

péniblement [penibləmɑ̃] *adv* with difficulty; **avancer** *ou* **marcher p.** to struggle along

péniche [peniʃ] *nf* barge

pénicilline [penisilin] *nf* penicillin

péninsule [penɛ̃syl] *nf* peninsula; **la p. Ibérique** the Iberian Peninsula

pénis [penis] *nm* penis

pénitence [penitɑ̃s] *nf* (**a**) *Rel (repentir)* penitence; *(peine)* penance; **faire p.** to repent (**b**) *(punition)* punishment; **mettre un enfant en p.** to punish a child

pénitencier [penitɑ̃sje] *nm* prison, penitentiary

pénitent, -e [penitɑ̃, -ɑ̃t] *adj & nm,f* penitent

pénitentiaire [penitɑ̃sjɛr] *adj* prison

penne [pen] *nmpl (pâtes)* penne

Pennsylvanie [pɛnsilvani] *nf* **la P.** Pennsylvania

pénombre [penɔ̃br] *nf* half-light

pensable [pɑ̃sabl] *adj* **ce n'est pas p.** it's unthinkable

pensant, -e [pɑ̃sɑ̃, -ɑ̃t] *adj* thinking; **mal p.** unorthodox

pense-bête (*pl* pense-bêtes) [pɑ̃sbɛt] *nm* reminder

pensée¹ [pɑ̃se] *nf (fleur)* pansy

pensée² [pɑ̃se] *nf (idée)* thought; *(activité)* thinking; **perdu dans ses pensées** lost in thought; **deviner les pensées de qn** to guess what sb is thinking; **dire le fond de sa p.** to say what one really thinks; **à la p. des vacances,…** at the thought of the vacation,…; **la seule p. de ce repas me met l'eau à la bouche** just thinking about this meal makes my mouth water; **la p. marxiste/bouddhiste** Marxist/Buddhist thought *or* thinking; **je suis avec vous en p.** *ou* **par la p.** you're in my thoughts; **avoir une p. pour qn** to think of sb

penser [pɑ̃se] **1** *vi* (**a**) *(songer, réfléchir)* to think; **p. à qn/qch** to think of *or* about sb/sth; **pensez-vous!** what an idea!; **vous n'y pensez pas!** you're not serious!; **n'y pensons plus** let's forget (about) it; **ce n'est même pas la peine d'y p.** it's not even worth thinking about; **ah, j'y pense!** by the way!; **rien que d'y p., ça me donne des frissons** just thinking about it gives me the shivers; **elle l'a fait sans p. à mal** she didn't mean any harm by it (**b**) *(se souvenir)* **p. à faire qch** to remember to do sth; **fais-moi p. à vérifier que…** remind me to check that…; **elle me fait p. à ma sœur** she reminds me of my sister
2 *vt* (**a**) *(estimer)* to think; **c'est bien ce que je pensais** I thought as much; **je pense que oui/non** I think/don't think so; *Fam* **pensez si j'étais furieux** you can imagine how angry I was; **p. du bien/du mal de qn** to think a lot/not to think much of sb (**b**) **p. faire qch** *(espérer)* to hope to do sth; *(avoir l'intention)* to be thinking of doing sth (**c**) *(croire à)* to mean; **elle ne pense pas ce qu'elle dit** she doesn't mean what she says (**d**) *(concevoir)* **c'est bien/mal pensé** it's well/badly thought out

penseur, -euse [pɑ̃sœr, -øz] *nm,f* thinker

pensif, -ive [pɑ̃sif, -iv] *adj* pensive, thoughtful; **d'un air p.** thoughtfully

pension [pɑ̃sjɔ̃] *nf* (**a**) *(allocation)* pension; **p. alimentaire** alimony; **p. de retraite** (retirement) pension (**b**) *(pensionnat)* boarding school; **mettre un enfant en p.** to send a child to boarding school (**c**) *(hôtel)* **p. (de famille)** boarding house; **être en p. chez qn** to board with sb; **prendre qn en p.** to take sb in as a lodger; **p. complète** American plan (**d**) *Belg (cessation d'activité)* retirement; **l'âge de la p.** retirement age

pensionnaire [pɑ̃sjɔnɛr] *nmf (dans une pension de famille, à l'école)* boarder; *(dans une maison privée)* lodger; *Fam (d'une prison)* inmate

pensionnat [pɑ̃sjɔna] *nm* boarding school

pensionné, -e [pɑ̃sjɔne] *nm,f* pensioner

pensionner [pɑ̃sjɔne] **1** *vt* to pension
2 *vi Can (être en pension)* to be a boarder

pensivement [pɑ̃sivmɑ̃] *adv* thoughtfully, pensively

pensum [pɛ̃sɔm] *nm (travail ennuyeux)* chore

pentagone [pɛ̃tagɔn] *nm* (**a**) *(figure)* pentagon (**b**) **le P.** *(aux États-Unis)* the Pentagon

pente [pɑ̃t] *nf* slope; **en p.** sloping; *Fig* **être sur une mauvaise p.** to be going downhill; *Fig* **remonter la p.** to get back on one's feet

Pentecôte [pɑ̃tkot] *nf Rel* Pentecost; *(jours fériés)* Whitsun

pentu, -e [pɑ̃ty] *adj* sloping

pénultième [penyltjɛm] *adj & nf* penultimate

pénurie [penyri] *nf* shortage, scarcity

PEP [pɛp] *nm Fin* (*abrév* **plan d'épargne populaire**) = personal pension plan

pépé [pepe] *nm Fam* (*grand-père*) grandpa, gramps; (*vieux monsieur*) grandpa

pépée [pepe] *nf Fam* chick

pépère [pepɛr] *Fam* **1** *nm* (**a**) **c'est un gros p.** (*enfant*) he's a chubby little thing (**b**) (*grand-père*) grandad

   2 *adj* (*endroit*) quiet; (*travail*) cushy; **un petit coin p.** a nice quiet little spot; **être p.** (*dans une situation confortable*) to have it easy

pépie [pepi] *nf Fam* **avoir la p.** to be parched

pépiement [pepimɑ̃] *nm* cheeping, chirping

pépier [66] [pepje] *vi* to cheep, to chirp

pépin [pepɛ̃] *nm* (**a**) (*de fruit*) seed; **sans pépins** seedless (**b**) *Fam* (*ennui*) hitch; **avoir un p.** to have a problem (**c**) *Fam* (*parapluie*) umbrella

pépinière [pepinjɛr] *nf* (**a**) (*d'arbustes*) nursery (**b**) *Fig* training ground (**de** for)

pépite [pepit] *nf* (*d'or*) nugget; **pépites de chocolat** chocolate chips

peps [pɛps] *nm Fam* energy, get-up-and-go; **avoir du p.** to have plenty of get-up-and-go, to be full of life

péquenaud, -e [pekno, -od] *nm,f Fam* peasant, yokel

péquiste [pekist] *Can* **1** *adj* of the Parti Québécois

   2 *nmf* (*membre*) member of the Parti Québécois; (*partisan*) supporter of the Parti Québécois

percale [pɛrkal] *nf* percale

perçant, -e [pɛrsɑ̃, -ɑ̃t] *adj* (*regard, cri*) piercing; (*voix*) penetrating; (*vue*) sharp

percée [pɛrse] *nf* (**a**) (*ouverture*) opening (**b**) *Mil, Sport & Fig* breakthrough

percement [pɛrsəmɑ̃] *nm* (*d'un trou, d'un passage, d'un tunnel*) boring; (*d'une avenue*) opening; (*d'un canal*) cutting

perce-neige [pɛrsənɛʒ] *nm ou nf inv* snowdrop

perce-oreille (*pl* perce-oreilles) [pɛrsɔrɛj] *nm* earwig

percepteur [pɛrsɛptœr] *nm* (**a**) (*receveur des impôts*) tax collector (**b**) *Belg* (*receveur des postes*) postmaster, *f* postmistress

perceptible [pɛrsɛptibl] *adj* (**a**) (*que l'on peut percevoir*) perceptible (**b**) (*impôt*) collectable

perception [pɛrsɛpsjɔ̃] *nf* (**a**) (*par les sens*) perception (**b**) (*d'impôts, de droits, de loyer*) collection (**c**) (*bureau*) tax office

percer [16] [pɛrse] **1** *vt* (**a**) (*transpercer*) (*corps, surface, armure*) to pierce; (*abcès*) to lance; **le soleil perce les nuages** the sun's breaking through the clouds (**b**) (*découvrir*) (*complot, secret*) to uncover; (*mystère, énigme*) to solve; **p. qch à jour** to see through sth (**c**) (*trouer*) to make a hole in; (*trou*) to make; (*avec une perceuse*) to drill, to bore; (*tunnel*) to bore; (*avenue*) to open; (*canal, fenêtre*) to cut; (*tonneau*) to broach; (*coffre-fort*) to crack; **se faire p. les oreilles** to have one's ears pierced

   2 *vi* (**a**) (*apparaître*) (*soleil*) to break through; (*dents*) to come through (**b**) (*être révélé*) to get out; **rien n'a percé de leur entretien** nothing's gotten out about their meeting (**c**) (*devenir célèbre*) to make a name for oneself

perceuse [pɛrsøz] *nf* drill

percevable [pɛrsəvabl] *adj* (*impôt*) collectable

percevoir [60] [pɛrsəvwar] *vt* (**a**) (*par les sens, l'intellect*) to perceive; (*bruit*) to hear; **être bien/mal perçu** to be well/badly received (**b**) (*impôts, loyers*) to collect; (*intérêts, allocation, commission*) to receive

perchaude [pɛrʃod] *nf Can* yellow perch

perche¹ [pɛrʃ] *nf* (*tige*) pole; (*pour micro*) boom; *Fam Fig* **une grande p.** (*personne*) a beanpole; *Fig* **tendre la p. à qn** to throw sb a line

perche² [pɛrʃ] *nf* (*poisson*) perch

percher [pɛrʃe] *vi* (**a**) (*oiseaux*) to perch; (*poules*) to roost (**b**) *Fam* (*personne*) to live

   2 *vt Fam* (*mettre*) to perch

   3 se percher *vpr* to perch

percheron [pɛrʃərɔ̃] *nm* percheron

perchiste [pɛrʃist] *nmf* (**a**) *Sport* pole vaulter (**b**) (*au ski*) ski-lift attendant (**c**) *Cin & TV* boom operator

perchman [pɛrʃman] *nm Cin & TV* boom operator

perchoir [pɛrʃwar] *nm aussi Fig* perch; (*pour les volailles*) roost

perclus, -e [pɛrkly, -yz] *adj* **p. de rhumatismes** crippled with rheumatism

percolateur [pɛrkɔlatœr] *nm* percolator

perçu, -e *voir* **percevoir**

percussion [pɛrkysjɔ̃] *nf* percussion

percussionniste [pɛrkysjɔnist] *nmf* percussionist

percutant, -e [pɛrkytɑ̃, -ɑ̃t] *adj* forceful

percuter [pɛrkyte] **1** *vt* to crash into

   2 *vi* (**a**) **p. contre qch** to crash into sth (**b**) *Fam* (*comprendre*) to catch on

   3 se percuter *vpr* to crash into each other

percuteur [pɛrkytœr] *nm* firing pin

perdant, -e [pɛrdɑ̃, -ɑ̃t] **1** *adj* losing; **partir p.** to start out with low hopes

   2 *nm,f* loser; **être bon/mauvais p.** to be a good/bad loser

perdition [pɛrdisjɔ̃] *nf* (**a**) *Rel* perdition; **lieu de p.** den of iniquity (**b**) *Naut* **navire en p.** ship in distress; *Fig* **entreprise en p.** company in difficulties

perdre [pɛrdr] **1** *vt* (**a**) (*égarer*) to lose; (*habitude*) to get out of; (*occasion*) to miss; *aussi Fig* **p. qn/qch de vue** to lose sight of sb/sth; **p. de son assurance/sa souplesse** to lose some of one's confidence/suppleness; **il perd son pantalon** his pants keep slipping down; **tu ne perds rien pour attendre!** just you wait!; **p. son temps** to waste one's time; **il n'y a pas de temps à p.** there's no time to lose; **tu n'as rien perdu en ne venant pas** you didn't miss anything by not coming; **y p.** (*dans un échange*) to lose out; (*dans une vente*) to make a loss; **p. au change** to lose out on the deal (**b**) (*ruiner*) **ta générosité/ton ambition te perdra** your generosity/ambition will ruin you

   2 se perdre *vpr* (**a**) (*s'égarer*) to get lost; *Fig* **se p. de vue** to lose touch with each other; **se p. en conjectures/dans les détails** to get lost in conjecture/details; *Fam* **je m'y perds** I'm lost (**b**) (*être gâché*) (*nourriture, récolte*) to go to waste; **il y a des claques qui se perdent** you/they/*etc.* need a good slap (**c**) (*disparaître*) (*usage, tradition*) to die out

perdreau, -x [pɛrdro] *nm* young partridge

perdrix [pɛrdri] *nf* partridge; **p. des neiges** ptarmigan

perdu, -e [pɛrdy] *adj* (*égaré*) lost; (*vêtement, récolte*) ruined; (*endroit*) out-of-the-way; (*emballage*) non-returnable; **p. dans ses pensées** lost in thought; **il est p.** (*d'un malade*) there's no hope for him; **à mes moments perdus, à mes heures perdues** in my spare time; **un de p., dix de retrouvés** there are plenty more fish in the sea

perdurer [pɛrdyre] *vi Litt* to continue

père [pɛr] *nm* (**a**) (*géniteur*) father; **p. de famille** father; **de p. en fils** from father to son; *Prov* **tel p., tel fils** like father, like son; **nos pères** our forefathers, our ancestors; *Fig* **le p. du cubisme** the father of cubism; *Fam* **(mon) petit p.** old buddy; **le p. Paul** old Paul; **le p. Noël** Santa Claus; *aussi Fam Fig* **croire au p. Noël** to believe in Santa Claus (**b**) *Rel* father; **le (révérend) p. Martin** Father Martin; **mon p.** father

pérégrinations [peregrinasjɔ̃] *nfpl* peregrinations

péremption [perɑ̃psjɔ̃] *nf* **date de p.** expiration date

péremptoire [perɑ̃ptwar] *adj* peremptory

pérennité [perenite] *nf* permanence

péréquation [perekwasjɔ̃] *nf* equalization

perestroïka [pɛrɛstrɔika] *nf* perestroika

perfectif, -ive [pɛrfɛktif, -iv] *adj & nm* perfective

perfection [pɛrfɛksjɔ̃] *nf* perfection; **à la p.** to perfection

perfectionné, -e [pɛrfɛksjɔne] *adj* sophisticated

perfectionnement [pɛrfɛksjɔnmɑ̃] *nm* (**a**) *(action)* perfecting, improving; *(formation)* further training; **cours de p.** proficiency course (**b**) *(résultat)* improvement; **apporter des perfectionnements à qch** to improve sth

perfectionner [pɛrfɛksjɔne] **1** *vt* to perfect, to improve
    2 se perfectionner *vpr* to improve; **se p. en allemand** to improve one's German

perfectionnisme [pɛrfɛksjɔnism] *nm* perfectionism

perfectionniste [pɛrfɛksjɔnist] **1** *adj* **être p.** to be a perfectionist
    2 *nmf* perfectionist

perfide [pɛrfid] *adj* perfidious, treacherous

perfidie [pɛrfidi] *nf Litt* (**a**) *(déloyauté)* perfidiousness (**b**) *(action)* perfidy

perforation [pɛrfɔrasjɔ̃] *nf* (**a**) *(action)* perforation; *Ordinat* punching (**b**) *(trou) & Méd* perforation; *Ordinat* punch (hole)

perforatrice [pɛrfɔratris] *nf (pour papier)* (hole) punch

perforer [pɛrfɔre] *vt* (**a**) *(papier, organe)* to perforate; *(cuir)* to punch; *(sujet: missile)* to pierce (**b**) *Ordinat (carte, bande)* to punch; **bande perforée** punched tape; **carte perforée** punch card

perforeuse [pɛrfɔrøz] *nf* hole punch

performance [pɛrfɔrmɑ̃s] *nf (en sport)* performance; *Fig (exploit)* feat, achievement; **performances** *(d'une voiture, d'un ordinateur)* performance

performant, -e [pɛrfɔrmɑ̃, -ɑ̃t] *adj (machine)* high-performance; *(personne)* highly efficient

perfusion [pɛrfyzjɔ̃] *nf* drip; **être sous p.** to be on a drip

péricliter [periklite] *vi* to collapse

péridurale [peridyral] *nf* epidural; **accoucher sous p.** to give birth under an epidural

Périgord [perigɔr] *nm* **le P.** Périgord

périgourdin, -e [perigurdɛ̃, -in] **1** *adj* of Périgord
    2 *nm,f* **P., Périgourdine** person from Périgord

péril [peril] *nm* peril, danger; **au p. de sa vie** at the risk of one's life; **en p.** in peril; **mettre qch en p.** to imperil *or* to endanger sth; **à ses risques et périls** at one's own risk; **il n'y a pas p. en la demeure** it's not a matter of urgency

périlleux, -euse [perijø, -øz] *adj* perilous, dangerous

périmé, -e [perime] *adj (billet, passeport, coupon)* out of date; *(nourriture, article)* past its expiration date; *(idée, conception)* outdated

périmètre [perimɛtr] *nm* perimeter; **dans un p. de 50 km** ≃ within a 30-mile radius

périnée [perine] *nm* perineum

période [perjɔd] *nf* period; **p. bleue/blanche/rouge** *(de trains)* = off-peak/peak/high-peak periods of rail schedules during which ticket prices vary accordingly; **p. d'essai** trial period

périodique [perjɔdik] **1** *adj* (**a**) *(cyclique)* periodic (**b**) *(hygiénique)* **serviette p.** sanitary napkin
    2 *nm* periodical

périodiquement [perjɔdikmɑ̃] *adv* periodically

péripétie [peripesi] *nf Litt* event

périph [perif] *nm Fam* beltway

périphérie [periferi] *nf* periphery; *(banlieue)* outskirts; **à la p. des grandes villes** on the outskirts of cities

périphérique [periferik] **1** *adj aussi Ordinat* peripheral; **boulevard p.** beltway; **radio** *ou* **station p.** = private radio station broadcasting from outside national territory
    2 *nm* (**a**) *(route)* beltway (**b**) *Ordinat* peripheral; **p. d'impression** printer peripheral; **p. de sortie** output device

périphrase [perifraz] *nf* circumlocution, *Spéc* periphrasis

périple [peripl] *nm (voyage)* tour, journey; *(par mer)* voyage

périr [perir] *vi* to perish

périscolaire [periskɔlɛr] *adj* extracurricular

périscope [periskɔp] *nm* periscope

périssable [perisabl] *adj (denrées, produit)* perishable; *Fig (sentiment)* transient

péristyle [peristil] *nm* peristyle

péritonite [peritɔnit] *nf* peritonitis

perle [pɛrl] *nf* (**a**) *(naturelle)* pearl; *(de verre, de métal) & Fig (de sueur)* bead; **p. fine/de culture** real/cultured pearl; *Fig* **jeter des perles aux pourceaux** to cast pearls before swine; *Fam Fig* **enfiler des perles** to waste one's time on trivia (**b**) *(personne)* gem, treasure; **c'est la p. des sœurs** she's the best sister in the world; **ma bonne est une p. rare** my maid is a real gem (**c**) *Hum (erreur)* howler (**d**) *Can (prunelle)* pupil *(of the eye)*

perlé, -e [pɛrle] *adj (orné de perles)* set with pearls; *(de perles de verre)* beaded; **grève perlée** slowdown

perler [pɛrle] *vi (larmes, sueur)* to form in beads

perlimpinpin [pɛrlɛ̃pɛ̃pɛ̃] *nm* **poudre de p.** magic powder

perm [pɛrm] *nf Fam* (**a**) *Mil* leave; **en p.** on leave (**b**) *Scol* study hall; **avoir deux heures de p.** to have two hours' private study

permanence [pɛrmanɑ̃s] *nf* (**a**) *(continuité)* permanence; **en p.** permanently (**b**) **la p. est assurée le dimanche** there's someone on duty *or* on call on Sundays; **être de p.** to be on duty *or* on call (**c**) *Scol* study hall; **avoir deux heures de p.** to have two hours' private study

permanent, -e [pɛrmanɑ̃, -ɑ̃t] **1** *adj (commission)* standing; *(spectacle)* continuous; *(tribunal)* permanent; **cinéma p.** movie theater
    2 *nm,f Pol* official
    3 *nf* **permanente** perm; **se faire faire une p.** to have a perm, to have one's hair permed

perméable [pɛrmeabl] *adj* permeable (**à** to); *Fig* susceptible (**à** to)

permettre [47] [pɛrmɛtr] **1** *vt* (**a**) *(autoriser)* to allow, to permit; **p. à qn de faire qch** to allow *or* to permit sb to do sth; **p. qch à qn** to allow sb sth; **permettez-moi de...** allow me to...; **permettez!** excuse me!; **vous permettez?** may I?; **il se croit tout permis** he thinks he can do whatever he likes; *Fam* **il est égoïste comme ce n'est pas permis!** he's incredibly selfish! (**b**) *(rendre possible)* to allow; **p. à qn de faire qch** to allow sb to do sth; **mes moyens ne me le permettent pas** I can't afford it; **si le temps le permet** weather permitting; **si mon emploi du temps le permet** if my schedule allows it
    2 se permettre *vpr* **se p. qch** to allow oneself sth; **se p. de faire qch** to take the liberty of doing sth; **je me permets d'attirer votre attention sur...** may I draw your attention to...

permis, -e [pɛrmi, -iz] **1** *adj* allowed, permitted
    2 *nm* permit, license; **p. de chasse** hunting permit; **p. de conduire** driver's license; *(examen)* driving test; **p. de construire** building permit; **p. de séjour** residence permit; **p. de travail** work permit

permissif, -ive [pɛrmisif, -iv] *adj* permissive

permission [pɛrmisjɔ̃] *nf* (**a**) *(autorisation)* permission; **demander/donner la p. à qn de faire qch** to ask/give sb permission to do sth (**b**) *Mil (congé)* leave; *(certificat)* pass; **en p.** on leave

permissionnaire [pɛrmisjɔnɛr] *nmf* person on leave

permutation [pɛrmytasjɔ̃] *nf* (**a**) *(échange)* exchange of posts; *Mil* transfer (**b**) *(de lettres, de chiffres)* transposition; *Math* permutation

permuter [pɛrmyte] **1** *vt (lettres, chiffres)* to transpose; *Math* to permute
    2 *vi* to exchange posts

pernicieux, -euse [pɛrnisjø, -øz] *adj* pernicious

péroné [perɔne] *nm* fibula

péroraison [perɔrɛzɔ̃] *nf* peroration

pérorer [perɔre] *vi Péj* to hold forth

Pérou [peru] *nm* **le P.** Peru; *Fig* **ce n'est pas le P.** *(pas extraordinaire)* it's no great shakes; *(peu d'argent)* it's not a fortune

peroxyde [perɔksid] *nm* peroxide

perpendiculaire [pɛrpɑ̃dikylɛr] *adj & nf* perpendicular (**à** to)

perpète [pɛrpɛt] *nf Fam* (**a**) *(perpétuité)* **condamné à p.** sentenced to life; **prendre p.** to get life; **jusqu'à p.** for ever (**b**) *(distance)* **à p.** miles away

perpétrer [34] [pɛrpetre] *vt* to perpetrate

perpette [pɛrpɛt] = **perpète**

perpétuel, -elle [pɛrpetɥɛl] *adj* perpetual; *(secrétaire, membre)* permanent

perpétuellement [pɛrpetɥɛlmɑ̃] *adv* perpetually

perpétuer [pɛrpetɥe] **1** *vt* to perpetuate
2 se perpétuer *vpr* to be perpetuated

perpétuité [pɛrpetɥite] *nf* perpetuity; **à p.** *(concession)* in perpetuity; *(emprisonnement)* for life; **être condamné (à la réclusion) à p.** to be sentenced to life (imprisonment)

perplexe [pɛrplɛks] *adj* perplexed, puzzled; **laisser qn p.** to perplex *or* to puzzle sb

perplexité [pɛrplɛksite] *nf* perplexity

perquisition [pɛrkizisjɔ̃] *nf* search; **faire une p.** to make a search

perquisitionner [pɛrkizisjɔne] **1** *vi* to make a search
2 *vt* to search

perron [perɔ̃] *nm* steps *(leading to a building)*

perroquet [perɔkɛ] *nm* (**a**) *(oiseau)* parrot; **p. de mer** puffin (**b**) *(voile)* topgallant

perruche [peryʃ] *nf* budgerigar

perruque [peryk] *nf* wig

perruquier, -ère [perykje, -ɛr] *nm,f* wig maker

pers [pɛr] *adj m Litt* blue-green

persan, -e [pɛrsɑ̃, -an] **1** *adj* Persian
2 *nm (langue)* Persian
3 *nm,f* **P., Persane** Persian

perse [pɛrs] **1** *adj* Persian
2 *nm (langue)* Persian
3 *nmf* **P.** Persian
4 *nf* **la P.** Persia

persécuter [pɛrsekyte] *vt* to persecute

persécution [pɛrsekysjɔ̃] *nf* persecution; **manie** *ou* **délire de p.** persecution mania

persévérance [pɛrseverɑ̃s] *nf* perseverance

persévérant, -e [pɛrseverɑ̃, -ɑ̃t] *adj* persevering

persévérer [34] [pɛrsevere] *vi* to persevere (**dans** in)

persienne [pɛrsjɛn] *nf* shutter

persiflage [pɛrsifla3] *nm (propos)* taunts, scoffs

persifler [pɛrsifle] *vt* to mock, to ridicule

persil [pɛrsi] *nm* parsley

persillé, -e [pɛrsije] *adj (viande)* marbled; *(assaisonné de persil)* sprinkled with chopped parsley; *(fromage)* veined

Persique [pɛrsik] *adj voir* **golfe**

persistance [pɛrsistɑ̃s] *nf* persistence (**à faire qch** in doing sth); **avec p.** persistently; **p. dans le mensonge** persistent lying

persistant, -e [pɛrsistɑ̃, -ɑ̃t] *adj* persistent; **à feuillage p.** evergreen

persister [pɛrsiste] *vi* (**a**) *(persévérer)* to persist (**dans** in); **p. à faire qch** to persist in doing sth (**b**) *(continuer)* to persist; **il persiste un doute** a doubt still remains

perso [pɛrso] *adj Fam (abrév* **personnel***)* personal, private

personnage [pɛrsɔnaʒ] *nm* (**a**) *(de fiction)* character; *aussi Fig* **jouer un p.** to play a part *or* a role (**b**) *(individu)* character (**c**)

(image publique) image, persona (**d**) *(personnalité)* important person; **p. célèbre** celebrity; **p. officiel** VIP; **un grand p. de l'État** a state dignitary

personnalisation [pɛrsɔnalizasjɔ̃] *nf* personalization

personnalisé, -e [pɛrsɔnalize] *adj* personalized; *(voiture, crédit)* customized

personnaliser [pɛrsɔnalize] *vt* to personalize; *(voiture)* to customize

personnalité [pɛrsɔnalite] *nf* (**a**) *(caractère)* personality; **avoir de la p.** to have lots of personality; **manquer de p.** to have no personality (**b**) *(personnage important)* personality (**c**) *Jur* **p. juridique** legal personality

personne [pɛrsɔn] **1** *nf* (**a**) *(individu)* person; **deux personnes** two people; **les personnes intéressées** those interested; **les personnes âgées** the elderly, elderly people; **une grande p.** a grown-up; **une jeune p.** a young lady
(**b**) *(soi-même)* **en p.** in person, personally; **être bien de sa p.** to be good-looking; **être satisfait de sa petite p.** to be pleased with oneself
(**c**) *Jur* **p. morale** legal entity; **p. physique** natural person
(**d**) *Gram* person
2 *pron indéfini* (**a**) *(quiconque)* anyone, anybody; **elle le sait mieux que p.** she knows better than anyone
(**b**) *(aucune personne)* no-one, nobody; **p. n'est venu** no-one has come; **il n'y a p. de blessé** no-one has been injured; **p. d'autre** no-one else, nobody else; **je n'y suis pour p.** I'm not at home to anyone; **ne connaissez-vous p. qui puisse nous aider?** don't you know anyone who could help us?; *Fam* **dès qu'il s'agit de travailler, il n'y a plus p.** as soon as there's work to be done, there's no-one in sight

personnel, -elle [pɛrsɔnɛl] **1** *adj* (**a**) *(à soi)* personal (**b**) *(égoïste)* selfish; *(intérêt)* vested
2 *nm (d'une firme, d'une école)* staff; *(d'une usine)* workforce; *(dans l'armée)* personnel; **faire partie du p. de...** to be on the staff of...; **manquer de p.** to be understaffed; **un membre du p.** a member of staff; **p. de bureau** office *or* clerical staff; **p. navigant** flight personnel; **p. au sol** ground personnel

personnellement [pɛrsɔnɛlmɑ̃] *adv* personally

personnifier [66] [pɛrsɔnifje] *vt* to personify; **il est la bêtise personnifiée** he's stupidity personified

perspective [pɛrspɛktiv] *nf* (**a**) *(de dessin)* perspective (**b**) *(idée)* prospect; **à la p. de faire qch** at the prospect of doing sth; **en p.** in prospect; **des perspectives de reprise** outlook for recovery; **des perspectives d'avenir** future prospects (**c**) *(point de vue)* viewpoint, point of view

perspicace [pɛrspikas] *adj* shrewd

perspicacité [pɛrspikasite] *nf* shrewdness

persuader [pɛrsɥade] **1** *vt* **p. qn (de qch)** to persuade *or* to convince sb (of sth); **p. qn de faire qch** to persuade sb to do sth; **être persuadé de qch/que...** to be convinced of sth/that...
2 se persuader *vpr* **se p. de qch/que...** to convince oneself of sth/that...

persuasif, -ive [pɛrsɥazif, -iv] *adj* persuasive

persuasion [pɛrsɥazjɔ̃] *nf* persuasion

perte [pɛrt] *nf* (**a**) *(d'un objet, d'une personne, d'un procès)* loss; **de lourdes pertes en hommes et en matériel** heavy losses of men and equipment; **à p. de vue** as far as the eye can see; **vendre qch à p.** to sell sth at a loss; *aussi Fig* **passer qch par pertes et profits** to write sth off; **p. sèche** dead loss; **ce n'est pas une grosse p.** it's no great loss (**b**) *(gaspillage)* **une p. de temps** a waste of time; **en pure p.** to no purpose (**c**) *(déperdition)* loss; **être en p. de vitesse** to be losing speed; *Fig* to be running out of steam; **pertes blanches** vaginal discharge; **p. de chaleur** heat loss; **p. de connaissance** loss of consciousness; *Ordinat* **p. de données irréparable**

irretrievable data loss (**d**) *(destruction)* ruin; **courir à sa p.** to be heading for disaster

pertinemment [pɛrtinamɑ̃] *adv* **savoir qch p.** to know sth for a fact

pertinence [pɛrtinɑ̃s] *nf* pertinence, relevance

pertinent, -e [pɛrtinɑ̃, -ɑ̃t] *adj* pertinent, relevant

perturbant, -e [pɛrtyrbɑ̃, -ɑ̃t] *adj* disturbing, upsetting

perturbateur, -trice [pɛrtyrbatœr, -tris] **1** *adj* disruptive **2** *nm,f* troublemaker

perturbation [pɛrtyrbasjɔ̃] *nf* disruption; **p. (atmosphérique)** (atmospheric) disturbance

perturber [pɛrtyrbe] *vt (services publics, circulation)* to disrupt; *(personne)* to perturb, to upset

péruvien, -enne [peryvjɛ̃, -ɛn] **1** *adj* Peruvian **2** *nm,f* **P., Péruvienne** Peruvian

pervenche [pɛrvɑ̃ʃ] *nf* (**a**) *(plante)* periwinkle; (**bleu**) **p.** periwinkle blue (**b**) *Fam (contractuelle)* meter maid

pervers, -e [pɛrvɛr, -ɛrs] **1** *adj* perverse **2** *nm,f* pervert

perversion [pɛrvɛrsjɔ̃] *nf* perversion

perversité [pɛrvɛrsite] *nf* perversity

pervertir [pɛrvɛrtir] **1** *vt* to pervert **2 se pervertir** *vpr* to become perverted

pesamment [pəzamɑ̃] *adv* heavily

pesant, -e [pəzɑ̃, -ɑ̃t] **1** *adj* heavy; *(sommeil)* deep; *(ambiance)* oppressive; **marcher à pas pesants** to walk heavily **2** *nm* **valoir son p. d'or** to be worth one's/its weight in gold

pesanteur [pəzɑ̃tœr] *nf* (**a**) *(attraction terrestre)* gravity (**b**) *(lourdeur)* heaviness

pesée [pəze] *nf* (**a**) *(pour connaître le poids)* weighing; *(de boxeur, de chevaux)* weigh-in (**b**) *(pression)* force

pèse-lettre (*pl* **pèse-lettres**) [pɛzlɛtr] *nm* letter scales

pèse-personne (*pl* **pèse-personnes**) [pɛzpɛrsɔn] *nm* scales

peser [46] [pəze] **1** *vt* to weigh; *Fig* **p. le pour et le contre** to weigh the pros and cons; *Fig* **p. ses mots** to weigh one's words; *Fig* **tout bien pesé** all things considered **2** *vi (être lourd)* to be heavy; **p. 55 kilos** ≃ to weigh 120 pounds; **p. sur qch** to press on sth; *Fig* **p. sur la conscience** to lie heavy on one's conscience; *Fig* **p. sur l'estomac** to lie heavy on the stomach; *Fig* **p. sur** *ou* **dans une décision** to carry weight in a decision; **la solitude me pèse** the solitude is getting me down **3 se peser** *vpr* to weigh oneself

peseta [pezeta] *nf Ancienment* peseta

peso [pezo] *nm* peso

pessimisme [pesimism] *nm* pessimism

pessimiste [pesimist] **1** *adj* pessimistic **2** *nmf* pessimist

peste [pɛst] *nf* (**a**) *(maladie)* plague; *Fig* **je me méfie de lui comme de la p.** I don't trust him as far as I could throw him; **la p. bubonique** the bubonic plague; *Hist* **la p. noire** the Black Death (**b**) *Fig & Péj (personne)* pest

pester [pɛste] *vi* **p. contre qn/qch** to curse sb/sth

pesticide [pɛstisid] **1** *adj* pesticidal **2** *nm* pesticide

pestiféré, -e [pɛstifere] **1** *adj* plague-stricken **2** *nm,f* plague victim; **traiter qn comme un p.** to treat sb like a pariah *or* a leper

pestilentiel, -elle [pɛstilɑ̃sjɛl] *adj* stinking

pet [pɛ] *nm Fam (gaz)* fart; **lâcher un p.** to fart; **ça ne vaut pas un p. (de lapin)** it's not worth a bean *or* a red cent; **il a toujours un p. de travers** there's always something the matter with him

pétale [petal] *nm* petal

pétanque [petɑ̃k] *nf* ≃ bowls *(played in the South of France)*

---

pétant, -e [petɑ̃, -ɑ̃t] *adj Fam* **à une heure pétante** at one o'clock sharp *or* on the dot

Pétaouchnock [petauʃnɔk] *n Fam* **ils l'ont envoyé à P.** they sent him to some place in the back of beyond *or* to Timbuktu

pétarade [petarad] *nf* (**a**) *(de feux d'artifice, d'armes à feu)* crackling (**b**) *(de véhicule)* backfiring

pétarader [petarade] *vi* (**a**) *(feux d'artifice, armes à feu)* to crackle (**b**) *(véhicule)* to backfire

pétard [petar] *nm* (**a**) *(feu d'artifice)* (fire)cracker (**b**) *Fam (pistolet)* shooter (**c**) *Fam (joint)* joint (**d**) *Fam (postérieur)* butt (**e**) *Fam* **être en p. (contre)** to be pissed (at)

pétasse [petas] *nf Vulg* slut

pétaudière [petodjɛr] *nf Fam* bedlam

pété, -e [pete] *adj Fam (ivre)* plastered

péter [34] [pete] *Fam* **1** *vi* (**a**) *(bois qui brûle)* to crackle; *(bouchon)* to pop; *(personne)* to fart; *Vulg* **il pète plus haut que son cul** he thinks he's God's gift to mankind (**b**) *(exploser)* to blow up; *Fig* **je veux que ça pète!** get your ass in gear! (**c**) *(casser)* to bust **2** *vt* (**a**) **p. le feu** *ou* **la forme** to be full of pep; **p. les plombs** to blow one's top (**b**) *(casser)* to bust **3 se péter** *vpr (se casser)* to bust; **se p. la gueule** to get wasted; *Can* **se p. les bretelles** to be full of oneself

pète-sec [pɛtsɛk] *adj inv Fam* curt

péteux, -euse [petø, -øz] *Fam Péj* **1** *adj (honteux)* sheepish **2** *nm,f* (**a**) *(lâche)* yellowbelly (**b**) *(prétentieux)* upstart

pétillant, -e [petijɑ̃, -ɑ̃t] *adj (vin, yeux)* sparkling; *(eau)* fizzy, carbonated

pétillement [petijmɑ̃] *nm (du vin, des yeux)* sparkling

pétiller [petije] *vi (vin, yeux)* to sparkle; **p. d'intelligence** *(yeux)* to sparkle with intelligence

petit, -e [pəti, -it] **1** *adj* (**a**) *(de taille réduite)* small, little; *(distance, séjour)* short; *(somme)* small; **tout p.** tiny; **un p. moment** a little while; *Fam* **une petite demi-heure** barely half an hour; *Fig* **se faire tout p.** to make oneself as inconspicuous as possible; **petites et moyennes entreprises** small and medium-sized businesses; *Can* **p. suisse** chipmunk (**b**) *(peu grave) (problème, erreur)* small; *(accident)* minor; *(rhume)* slight (**c**) *(jeune)* little, young; **mon p. frère** my little brother; **p. cousin** first cousin once removed; **un p. Anglais** an English boy (**d**) *(faible) (voix)* small; *(bruit)* little; **avoir une petite santé** to be delicate (**e**) *(de niveau inférieur) Scol* **les petites classes** the lower classes; **petite route** minor road; **p. commerçant/artisan** small storekeeper/craftsman (**f**) *(pour insister)* little; **p. crétin/con!** little idiot/bastard!; **mon p. ange** my little angel; **je fumerais bien une petite cigarette** I'd love a cigarette; *Fam* **p. nom** first name (**g**) *(mesquin)* petty **2** *nm,f* (**a**) *(enfant)* (little) boy, *f* (little) girl; **les petits** the little ones; *Fam* **mon p.** my dear; **pauvre p.!** poor little thing!

(b) *(en taille)* **les petits devant, les grands derrière** small people in front and the tall ones behind

3 *nm (d'un chien)* puppy; *(d'un chat)* kitten; **faire** *ou* **avoir des petits** to have puppies/kittens/*etc.*; *Fam* **faire des petits** *(argent)* to multiply

4 *adv (écrire)* small; **p. à p.** little by little

petit-beurre *(pl* **petits-beurre**) [pətibœr] *nm* butter cookie

petit-bourgeois, petite-bourgeoise *(mpl* **petits-bourgeois**, *fpl* **petites-bourgeoises**) [pətiburʒwa, pətiburʒwaz] *aussi Péj* **1** *adj* lower middle class

2 *nm,f* member of the lower middle class

petite-fille *(pl* **petites-filles**) [pətitfij] *nf* granddaughter

petitesse [pətitɛs] *nf (d'un objet)* smallness; *Péj (mesquinerie)* pettiness

petit-fils *(pl* **petits-fils**) [pətifis] *nm* grandson

pétition [petisjɔ̃] *nf* petition

petit-lait *(pl* **petits-laits**) [pətilɛ] *nm* whey; *Fam* **se boire comme du p.** to slip down easily; *Fig* **boire du p.** to lap it up

petit-nègre [pətinɛgr] *nm Fam (mauvais français)* pidgin French; **c'est du p.** *(mal écrit)* it's gibberish

petits-enfants [pətizɑ̃fɑ̃] *nmpl* grandchildren

petit-suisse *(pl* **petits-suisses**) [pətisɥis] *nm* = small dessert of thick fromage frais

pétoche [petɔʃ] *nf Fam* jitters; **avoir la p.** to have the jitters; **flanquer la p. à qn** to give sb the jitters

pétoire [petwar] *nf Fam (fusil)* popgun

pétri, -e [petri] *adj* **p. de qch** *(orgueil)* puffed up with sth; *(contradictions)* riddled with sth

pétrifier [66] [petrifje] *vt aussi Fig* to petrify

pétrin [petrɛ̃] *nm* kneading trough; *Fam* **être dans le p.** to be in a jam

pétrir [petrir] *vt (pâte à pain, argile)* to knead

pétrochimique [petroʃimik] *adj* petrochemical

pétrodollar [petrodɔlar] *nm Fin* petrodollar

pétrole [petrɔl] *nm* oil, petroleum

pétrolette [petrɔlɛt] *nf Fam* moped

pétrolier, -ère [petrɔlje, -ɛr] **1** *adj* **l'industrie pétrolière** the oil industry

2 *nm* (oil) tanker

pétrolifère [petrɔlifɛr] *adj* oil-bearing; **gisement p.** oilfield

pétulant, -e [petylɑ̃, -ɑ̃t] *adj* exuberant

pétunia [petynja] *nm* petunia

peu [pø] **1** *adv* **(a)** *(avec un verbe)* not much; **elle mange/parle p.** she doesn't eat/talk much

(b) *(avec un adjectif ou un adverbe)* not very; **il a agi p. honorablement** he didn't behave very honorably; **très/trop p.** very/too little

(c) *(avec un nom)* **p. de** *(temps, courage, vin)* little, not much; *(amis, lettres, illusions)* few, not many; **ne te fâche pas pour si p.** don't get mad over such a small thing; **c'est p. de chose** it's nothing; *Fam* **très p. pour moi!** not for me!

(d) *(un petit nombre)* few; **p. ont compris** few (people) understood

(e) *(indique la durée)* **sous p., avant p., d'ici p.** soon, shortly; **p. après** shortly afterward; **depuis p.** lately, recently; **c'est ouvert depuis p.** it hasn't been open long; **j'ai manqué le train de p.** I (only) just missed the train; **il y a p.** not very long ago, recently; **p. à p.** little by little, gradually

(f) **pour p. que** + *subjunctive* if by chance; **pour p. qu'il ait oublié la clé,...** if by chance he's forgotten the key,...

2 *nm* **(a)** *(petite quantité)* **le p. que je sais d'elle** the little I know about her; **le p. d'argent qu'il me reste** what little money I have left; **son p. d'instruction** what little education he has had

(b) **un p.** a little *or* a bit; **un peu grand/ennuyeux** a little *or* a bit big/boring; **un p. de temps/sucre** a bit of *or* a little time/sugar; **je le connais un p.** I know him slightly *or* a little;

un p. plus/moins a little *or* a bit more/less; **un tout petit p.** a tiny bit; **il est un p. artiste** he's something of an artist; **un p. plus et elle tombait** she very nearly fell; **pour un p. je l'aurais jeté dehors** I all but *or* I very nearly threw him out; **écoutez un p.** just listen; **viens un p. ici** come here a minute; *Fam* **tu ferais ça? - un p.!** you'd do that? - you bet!

(c) *(de temps)* **un p.** a bit, a little while; **restez encore un p.** stay a bit longer, stay a little (while) longer

peuchère [pøʃer] *exclam* heavens!

peuh [pø] *exclam* bah!

peuplade [pœplad] *nf* tribe

peuple [pœpl] *nm* **(a)** *(nation)* people; **le p. français** the French people **(b)** *(citoyens)* people; **les gens du p.** ordinary people **(c)** *Fam (foule)* crowd

peuplé, -e [pœple] *adj* inhabited (**de** by); **très/peu p.** densely/sparsely populated

peuplement [pœpləmɑ̃] *nm (d'une région)* populating

peupler [pœple] **1** *vt* **(a)** *(installer une population dans)* to populate **(b)** *(habiter)* to inhabit; *Fig* **peuplé de qch** full of sth

2 se peupler *vpr* to become populated

peuplier [pøplije] *nm* poplar

peur [pœr] *nf* fear; *(subite)* fright; **avoir p. (de)** to be afraid *or* frightened (of); *Fam* **avoir une p. bleue de qn/qch** to be scared *or* frightened to death of sb/sth; **faire p. à qn** to scare *or* to frighten sb; **par p. de qch** through fear of sth; **de p. de faire qch** for fear of doing sth; **de p. qu'il ne le fasse** for fear that he would do it; **j'ai bien p. qu'il (ne) soit en retard** I'm afraid he's going to be late

peureux, -euse [pœrø, -øz] **1** *adj* fearful

2 *nm,f* fearful person

peut *voir* **pouvoir**[2]

peut-être [pøtɛtr] *adv* perhaps, maybe; **p. que oui, p. que non** perhaps, perhaps not; **p. (bien) qu'elle viendra, p. viendra-t-elle** perhaps she'll come; **je ne suis p. pas riche, mais...** I may not be rich, but...; *Ironique* **tu le sais mieux que moi, p.?** you think you know better, do you?

peux *voir* **pouvoir**[2]

pèze [pɛz] *nm très Fam (argent)* dough

pH [peaʃ] *nm Chim* pH

phacochère [fakoʃer] *nm* warthog

phagocyter [fagosite] *vt Biol* to phagocytose; *Fig* to swallow up

phalange [falɑ̃ʒ] *nf (du doigt)* phalanx

phallique [falik] *adj* phallic

phallocrate [falokrat] *nm Péj* male chauvinist

phalloïde [faloid] *adj voir* **amanite**

phallus [falys] *nm* phallus

phantasme [fɑ̃tasm] = **fantasme**

pharamineux, -euse [faraminø, -øz] = **faramineux**

pharaon [faraɔ̃] *nm* Pharaoh

phare [far] **1** *nm* **(a)** *(pour navires)* lighthouse; *(pour avions)* beacon **(b)** *(de voiture)* headlight; **faire un appel de phares** to flash one's headlights; **se mettre en phares** to turn one's headlights on; **p. antibrouillard** foglight; **phares code** low beams

2 *adj* **film-p.** seminal movie; **épreuve-p.** star event

pharmaceutique [farmasøtik] *adj* pharmaceutical

pharmacie [farmasi] *nf* **(a)** *(science)* pharmacy **(b)** *(magasin)* drugstore **(c)** *(médicaments)* pharmaceuticals; **(armoire à) p.** medicine chest

pharmacien, -enne [farmasjɛ̃, -ɛn] *nm,f (vendeur)* druggist; *(chercheur)* pharmacist

pharmacologie [farmakolɔʒi] *nf* pharmacology

pharyngite [farɛ̃ʒit] *nf Méd* pharyngitis

pharynx [farɛ̃ks] *nm Anat* pharynx

phase [faz] *nf* phase; **cancer en p. terminale** terminal cancer; *Phys* **être en p.** to be in phase; *Fam* **être en p. (avec qn)** to be on the same wavelength (as sb)

phénicien, -enne [fenisjɛ̃, -ɛn] *Hist* **1** *adj* Phoenician
  2 *nm,f* **P., Phénicienne** Phoenician

phénix [feniks] *nm (animal mythologique)* phoenix; *Fig & Litt* paragon

phénoménal, -e, -aux, -ales [fenɔmenal, -o] *adj Fam* phenomenal

phénomène [fenɔmɛn] *nm* phenomenon; *Fam (personne)* character; **un p. de foire** a freak

Philadelphie [filadɛlfi] *n* Philadelphia

philanthrope [filɑ̃trɔp] *nmf* philanthropist

philanthropique [filɑ̃trɔpik] *adj* philanthropic

philatélie [filateli] *nf* philately, stamp collecting

philatéliste [filatelist] *nmf* philatelist, stamp collector

philharmonique [filarmɔnik] *adj* philharmonic

philippin, -e [filipɛ̃, -in] **1** *adj* Filipino
  2 *nm,f* **P., Philippine** Filipino

Philippines [filipin] *nfpl* **les P.** the Philippines

philosophale [filɔzɔfal] *adj f voir* **pierre**

philosophe [filɔzɔf] **1** *nmf* philosopher
  2 *adj* philosophical

philosopher [filɔzɔfe] *vi* to philosophize

philosophie [filɔzɔfi] *nf* philosophy; *Fig* **avec p.** philosophically

philosophique [filɔzɔfik] *adj* philosophical

philtre [filtr] *nm* philter; **p. d'amour** love potion

phlébite [flebit] *nf Méd* phlebitis

phlébologue [flebɔlɔg] *nmf Méd* vein specialist, *Spéc* phlebologist

Phnom Penh [pnɔmpɛn] *n* Phnom Penh

phobie [fɔbi] *nf* phobia; **avoir la p. de qch** to have a phobia about sth

phonème [fɔnɛm] *nm* phoneme

phonétique [fɔnetik] **1** *adj* phonetic
  2 *nf* phonetics *(singulier)*

phonographe [fɔnɔgraf] *nm Vieilli* phonograph

phoque [fɔk] *nm* **(a)** *(animal)* seal; *très Fam* **il est pédé comme un p.** he's a screaming queen **(b)** *(fourrure)* sealskin

phosphate [fɔsfat] *nm* phosphate; **sans phosphates** phosphate-free

phosphore [fɔsfɔr] *nm* phosphorus

phosphorescent, -e [fɔsfɔresɑ̃, -ɑ̃t] *adj* phosphorescent

photo [foto] **1** *nf* **(a)** *(cliché)* photo; **prendre qn/qch en p.** to take a photo of sb/sth; *Fam* **tu veux ma p.?** who are you staring at?; **p. d'identité** passport-sized photograph; **p. de mode** fashion photo; **p. souvenir** souvenir photo **(b)** *(activité)* **faire de la p.** *(en amateur)* to take photographs; *(en professionnel)* to be a photographer
  2 *adj inv voir* **appareil**

photocomposition [fotokɔpozisjɔ̃] *nf* photosetting

photocopie [fotokɔpi] *nf* photocopy

photocopier [66] [fotokɔpje] *vt* to photocopy

photocopieur [fotokɔpjœr] *nm, nf* photocopier

photocopieuse [fotokɔpjøz] *nf* photocopier

photoélectrique [fotoelɛktrik] *adj* photoelectric

photo-finish *(pl* **photos-finish)** [fotofiniʃ] *nf* photo finish; *(appareil)* photo-finish camera

photogénique [fotoʒenik] *adj* photogenic

photographe [fotograf] *nmf* **(a)** *(professionnel)* photographer; **p. de mode** fashion photographer; **p. de presse** press photographer **(b)** *(commerçant)* **chez le p.** at the photo store

photographie [fotografi] *nf* **(a)** *(technique)* photography; **faire de la p.** to take photographs **(b)** *(cliché)* photograph; **prendre une p. de** to take a photograph of; **p. aérienne** aerial photograph

photographier [66] [fotografje] *vt* to photograph; **se faire p.** to have one's photograph taken

photographique [fotografik] *adj* photographic

photogravure [fotogravyr] *nf* photogravure

Photomaton® [fotomatɔ̃] *nm* photo booth

photomontage [fotomɔ̃taʒ] *nm* photomontage

photon [fotɔ̃] *nm Phys* photon

photoreportage [fotorəpɔrtaʒ] *nm* photo report

photosensible [fotosɑ̃sibl] *adj* photosensitive

photostyle [fotostil] *nm Ordinat* light pen

photosynthèse [fotosɛ̃tez] *nf Biol* photosynthesis

phrase [fraz] *nf* sentence; *(musicale)* phrase; *Fig* **faire de grandes phrases** to use flowery language

phrasé [fraze] *nm Mus* phrasing

phraséologie [frazeolɔʒi] *nf* phraseology; *Péj* flowery language

phréatique [freatik] *adj voir* **nappe**

phrygien, -enne [friʒjɛ̃, -ɛn] *adj Hist* **bonnet p.** Phrygian cap *(red cloth cap worn during the French Revolution to symbolize the freedom of the people)*

phtisie [ftizi] *nf Vieilli* consumption

phylloxéra, phylloxera [filɔksera] *nm* phylloxera

physicien, -enne [fizisjɛ̃, -ɛn] *nm,f* physicist

physiologie [fizjolɔʒi] *nf* physiology

physiologique [fizjolɔʒik] *adj* physiological

physionomie [fizjɔnɔmi] *nf* **(a)** *(traits du visage)* features; **juger les gens à leur p.** to judge people by appearances **(b)** *(aspect)* face

physionomiste [fizjɔnɔmist] *adj* **être p.** to have a good memory for faces

physiothérapie [fizjoterapi] *nf* natural medicine

physique [fizik] **1** *adj* physical; *Fam* **je ne le supporte pas, c'est p.** I can't stand him, it's a gut feeling
  2 *nf (science)* physics *(singulier)*; **p. nucléaire** nuclear physics
  3 *nm (d'une personne)* physique; **avoir un p. avantageux** to have a good physique; **avoir le p. de l'emploi** to look the part

physiquement [fizikmɑ̃] *adv* physically

phytoplancton [fitoplɑ̃ktɔ̃] *nm* phytoplankton

phytothérapie [fitoterapi] *nf* herbal medicine

piaf [pjaf] *nm Fam* sparrow

piaffer [pjafe] *vi (cheval)* to paw the ground; *Fig* **p. d'impatience** to fidget impatiently

piaillement [pjajmɑ̃] *nm (d'un oiseau)* cheeping; *Fam (d'un enfant)* squealing

piailler [pjaje] *vi (oiseau)* to cheep; *Fam (enfant)* to squeal

pianiste [pjanist] *nmf* pianist

piano[1] [pjano] *nm* piano; **jouer** *ou* **faire du p.** to play the piano; **p. demi-queue** baby grand; **p. droit** upright piano; **p. à queue** grand piano

piano[2] [pjano] *adv Mus* piano; *Fig* gently

pianoter [pjanɔte] *vi Fam* **(a)** *(mal jouer)* to tinkle away **(b)** *(tapoter)* **p. sur qch** *(table)* to drum one's fingers on sth; *Fam (clavier)* to tap away at sth

piastre [pjastr] *nf* piaster; *Can Fam (dollar)* buck

piaule [pjol] *nf Fam* pad

piauler [pjole] *vi (poussins)* to cheep

PIB [peibe] *nm Écon (abrév* **produit intérieur brut)** GDP

pic [pik] *nm* **(a)** *(pioche)* pick(ax); **p. à glace** ice pick **(b)** *(sommet)* peak; **couler à p.** to sink like a stone; **tomber à p.** *(falaise)* to go straight down; *Fam* to come at just the right moment; **p. de pollution** pollution alert

picard, -e [pikar, -ard] **1** *adj* of Picardy
  2 *nm,f* **P., Picarde** person from Picardy

Picardie [pikardi] *nf* **la P.** Picardy

picaresque [pikarɛsk] *adj* picaresque

pichenette [piʃnɛt] *nf* flick

pichet [piʃɛ] *nm* pitcher

pickpocket [pikpɔkɛt] *nm* pickpocket

pick-up [pikœp] *nm inv* (**a**) *Vieilli (électrophone)* record player (**b**) *(véhicule)* pick-up (truck)

picoler [pikɔle] *vi Fam* to booze

picoleur, -euse [pikɔlœr, -øz] *nm,f Fam (buveur)* boozer

picorer [pikɔre] **1** *vt (sujet: oiseau)* to peck (at); *(sujet: personne)* to nibble

2 *vi (oiseau)* to pick about; *(personne)* to pick at one's food

picotement [pikɔtmã] *nm (dans la gorge, dans le nez)* tickling; *(dans les yeux)* stinging; *(sur la peau)* prickling; **picotements** *(dans les jambes, les doigs etc)* tingling

picoter [pikɔte] *vt* **j'ai la gorge qui (me) picote** I've got a tickle in my throat; **la fumée me picotait les yeux** the smoke made my eyes sting; **j'ai la peau qui (me) picote** my skin's prickling

Pictes [pikt] *nmpl* **les P.** the Picts

pictogramme [piktɔgram] *nm* pictogram

pictural, -e, -aux, -ales [piktyral, -o] *adj* pictorial

pic-vert *(pl* **pics-verts**) [pivɛr] = **pivert**

pie [pi] **1** *nf* magpie; *Fam (personne)* chatterbox; *Fam* **être bavard comme une p.** to be a real chatterbox

2 *adj inv (cheval)* piebald; *(vache)* black-and-white

pièce [pjɛs] *nf* (**a**) *(salle)* room

(**b**) *(élément)* piece; *(d'un mécanisme)* part; **un service complet de trente-six pièces** a complete thirty-six piece service; **coûter dix euros p.** to cost ten euros each; **travailler à la p.** to do piecework; *Fig* **être tout d'une p.** to be straightforward; *Fig* **une histoire fabriquée de toutes pièces** a completely made-up story; **mettre qch en pièces** to tear sth to pieces; **p. de bœuf** cut *or* piece of beef; **p. de collection** collector's item; **p. d'eau** ornamental lake; *(plus petite)* ornamental pond; **p. montée** = large tiered cake served at weddings, baptisms, etc.; **p. de musée** museum piece; **pièces de rechange, pièces détachées** spare parts, spares; **p. de résistance** main dish; *Fig* **pièce de résistance**

(**c**) *(argent)* **p. (de monnaie)** coin; **p. de deux euros** two-euro coin *or* piece

(**d**) **p. (de théâtre)** play

(**e**) *(raccord)* patch; **mettre une p. à qch** to put a patch on sth

(**f**) *(document)* document; **juger sur pièces** to judge on the evidence; **p. à conviction** exhibit *(in criminal case)*; **p. d'identité** proof of identity; **p. jointe** *(à une lettre)* enclosure

(**g**) *(aux échecs)* piece; *(aux dames)* checker

Pièce
Apartments in France are referred to in terms of the total number of rooms they have (excluding the kitchen and bathroom). "Un deux-pièces" is an apartment with a living room and one bedroom; "un cinq-pièces" is a five-room apartment.

piécette [pjesɛt] *nf* small coin

pied [pje] *nm* (**a**) *(d'une personne)* foot; **avoir les pieds plats** to have flat feet; **avoir un p. bot** to have a club foot; **se prendre les pieds dans qch** to get one's feet caught in sth; **avoir p.** to be within one's depth; **perdre p.** to get out of one's depth; **mettre p. à terre** *(de cheval, de vélo)* to dismount; **de p. en cap** from head to toe

(**b**) *(de cheval)* hoof; *Culin* **p. de porc** pig's trotter

(**c**) *(de vigne)* stock; *(de céleri, de salade)* head

(**d**) *(de chaise, de table)* leg; *(de verre)* stem; *(d'appareil photo, de lampadaire)* stand

(**e**) *(base)* foot

(**f**) **à p.** on foot; **j'y suis allé à p.** I walked there, I went there on foot; **faire cinq kilomètres à p.** ≃ to walk three miles; **tu en as pour dix minutes à p.** it'll take you ten minutes to walk (there)

(**g**) *(mesure)* foot; *Fig* **six pieds sous terre** six feet under

(**h**) *(locutions)* **mettre qch sur p.** to set sth up; **être sur p.** *(personne)* to be up and about; **être à p. d'œuvre** to be ready to get started on the job; **être sur un p. d'égalité avec qn** to be on an equal footing with sb; *Fig* **être sur le p. de guerre** to be ready for action; **avoir bon p. bon œil** to be hale and hearty; **avoir un p. dans la tombe** to have one foot in the grave; **avoir le p. marin** to be a good sailor; **mettre qn au p. du mur** to get sb with his/her back to the wall; **attendre qn de p. ferme** to be ready and waiting for sb; **se lever du p. gauche** to get out of bed on the wrong side; **faire qch au p. levé** to do sth at a moment's notice; **faire un p. de nez à qn** to thumb one's nose at sb; *Fam* **il chante/conduit comme un p.** he can't sing/drive to save his life; *Fam* **s'y prendre comme un p.** to botch sth; *Fam* **mettre les pieds dans le plat** to put one's foot in one's mouth; *Fam* **je ne remettrai jamais les pieds chez lui** I'll never set foot in his house again; *Fam* **faire des pieds et des mains pour obtenir qch** to move heaven and earth to get sth; *Fam* **faire du p. à qn** to play footsie with sb; *Fam* **ça lui fera les pieds!** that'll teach him/her a lesson!; *Fam* **prendre son p.** to get one's kicks; *Fam* **c'est le p.!** it's fantastic!

pied-à-terre [pjetatɛr] *nm inv* pied-à-terre

pied-bot *(pl* **pieds-bots**) [pjebo] *nm* club-footed person

pied-de-biche *(pl* **pieds-de-biche**) [pjedbiʃ] *nm (levier)* crowbar; *(pince)* nail puller

pied-de-poule *(pl* **pieds-de-poule**) [pjedpul] *adj inv & nm* hound's-tooth

piédestal, -aux [pjedɛstal, -o] *nm* pedestal; *Fig* **mettre** *ou* **placer qn sur un p.** to put *or* to set sb on a pedestal

pied-noir *(pl* **pieds-noirs**) [pjenwar] *nmf Fam* = French settler in North Africa

Pied noir
This is the name given to the French settlers who settled in North Africa (most notably in Algeria) during the period of French colonial expansion. Most of them resettled in France (mainly on the south coast) after the colonies regained their independence. The largest wave of these settlers to arrive in France was in 1962, following the Algerian war.

piège [pjɛʒ] *nm aussi Fig* trap; **tendre un p. (à)** to set a trap (for); **prendre un animal au p.** to catch an animal in a trap; **tomber dans un p.** to fall into a trap; *très Fam* **p. à cons** con

piéger [59] [pjeʒe] *vt* (**a**) *aussi Fig (attraper)* to trap; **se faire p.** to be trapped; **se laisser p.** to fall into a trap (**b**) *(placer une bombe dans)* to booby-trap; **colis piégé** package bomb; **lettre piégée** letter bomb; **voiture piégée** car bomb

Piémont [pjemõ] *nm* **le P.** Piedmont

piémontais, -e [pjemõtɛ, -ɛz] **1** *adj* Piedmontese

2 *nm (langue)* Piedmontese

3 *nm,f* **P., Piémontaise** Piedmontese

piercing [pirsiŋ] *nm* body piercing

pierraille [pjɛraj] *nf* loose stones

pierre [pjɛr] *nf* (**a**) *(matière, caillou)* stone; *(rocher)* rock; **mur de p.** stone wall; **maison en p.** stone(-built) house; **investir dans la p.** to invest in bricks and mortar; **poser la première p. de qch** to lay the foundation stone for sth; *Fig* **jeter la p. à qn** to reproach sb; *Fig* **faire d'une p. deux coups** to kill two birds with one stone; *Fig* **être malheureux comme les pierres** to be extremely unhappy; *Prov* **p. qui roule n'amasse pas mousse** a rolling stone gathers no moss; **p. d'achoppement** stumbling block; *aussi Fig* **p. angulaire** cornerstone; **p. à briquet** flint *(for lighter)*; **p. philosophale** philosopher's stone; **p. ponce** pumice stone; **p. de taille** dressed stone; **p. tombale** tombstone; *aussi Fig* **p. de touche** touchstone (**b**) *(en bijouterie)* stone; **p. précieuse** precious stone, gem; **p. fine** *ou* **semi-précieuse** semi-precious stone

pierreries [pjɛrəri] *nfpl* precious stones, gems

pierreux, -euse [pjɛrø, -øz] *adj (sol, route)* stony; *(lit de rivière)* gravelly

piétaille [pjetɑj] *nf Péj* rank and file

piété [pjete] *nf* **(a)** *(ferveur religieuse)* piety **(b)** *(affection)* **p. filiale** filial devotion

piétinement [pjetinmɑ̃] *nm (bruit)* stamping; *(marche sur place)* standing around; *Fig (stagnation)* lack of progress

piétiner [pjetine] **1** *vt* **p. qch** *(en trépignant)* to stamp on sth; *(en marchant)* to trample on sth; *(écraser)* to trample sth underfoot; **ils sont morts piétinés par la foule** they were trampled to death by the crowd

2 *vi* **(a)** **p. d'impatience** to stamp (one's feet) impatiently **(b)** *(faire du surplace)* to stand around; *Fig* to make no progress

piéton, -onne [pjetɔ̃, -ɔn] **1** *nm,f* pedestrian

2 *adj* **rue piétonne** pedestrian street; **zone piétonne** pedestrian area

piétonnier, -ère [pjetɔnje, -ɛr] *adj* pedestrian; **rue piétonnière** pedestrian street; **zone piétonnière** pedestrian area

piètre [pjɛtr] *adj Litt (compagnon)* wretched; *(excuse)* paltry; *(consolation)* small

pieu¹, -x [pjø] *nm (piquet)* stake

pieu², -x [pjø] *nm Fam (lit)* bed; **se mettre au p., aller au p.** to hit the sack *or* the hay

pieuter [pjøte] **se pieuter** *vpr Fam* to hit the sack *or* the hay

pieuvre [pjœvr] *nf* octopus

pieux, -euse [pjø, -øz] *adj* pious, devout

pif [pif] *nm Fam (nez)* schnozzle; *Fig* **faire qch au p.** to do sth by guesswork; **répondre au p.** to hazard a guess; **au p., je dirais...** at a rough guess, I'd say...

pif(f)er [pife] *vt* **je ne peux pas le p.** I can't stomach him

pifomètre [pifɔmɛtr] *nm Fam* **faire qch au p.** to do sth by guesswork; **répondre au p.** to hazard a guess; **au p., je dirais...** at a rough guess, I'd say...

pige [piʒ] *nf* **(a)** *(article)* freelance contribution; **faire des piges** to do freelance work **(b)** *Fam (année)* **elle a quarante-cinq piges** she's forty-five; **à soixante piges** at sixty

pigeon [piʒɔ̃] *nm* **(a)** *(oiseau)* pigeon; **p. d'argile** clay pigeon; **p. ramier** wood pigeon; **p. vole** ≃ Simon says; **p. voyageur** carrier pigeon, homing pigeon **(b)** *Fam Péj (personne)* sucker

pigeonnant, -e [piʒɔnɑ̃, -ɑ̃t] *adj Fam* **poitrine pigeonnante** high bust; **soutien-gorge p.** uplift bra

pigeonnier [piʒɔnje] *nm* dovecot

piger [45] [piʒe] *Fam* **1** *vt* to get; **ne rien p. à qch** *(maths, anglais)* not to have a clue about sth; **je n'ai rien pigé à ce qu'il a dit** I didn't understand a word of what he said

2 *vi* to get it

pigiste [piʒist] *nmf* freelance journalist

pigment [pigmɑ̃] *nm* pigment

pigmentation [pigmɑ̃tasjɔ̃] *nf* pigmentation

pignon¹ [piɲɔ̃] *nm (de mur)* gable; **avoir p. sur rue** to be of some standing

pignon² [piɲɔ̃] *nm (petite roue)* pinion

pignon³ [piɲɔ̃] *nm (graine)* pine nut

pilage [pilaʒ] *nm* crushing

pile¹ [pil] *nf* **(a)** *(tas)* pile; **en p.** in a pile **(b)** **p. (électrique)** battery; **marcher avec des piles** to run on batteries; **p. atomique** atomic pile

pile² [pil] **1** *nf (d'une pièce)* reverse; **p. ou face?** heads or tails?; **tirer à p. ou face** to flip a coin

2 *adv Fam* **s'arrêter p.** to stop dead; **tomber p.** to come at just the right time; **à six heures p.** at six sharp *or* on the dot; **nous étions p. dix à table** there were exactly ten of us at the table; **elle est arrivée p. le même jour que moi** she arrived on exactly the same day as I did

piler [pile] **1** *vt* **(a)** *(broyer)* to crush; *(amandes)* to grind **(b)** *Fam (battre)* to thrash

2 *vi Fam* to slam on the brakes

pileux, -euse [pilø, -øz] *adj* hair; **système p.** body hair

pilier [pilje] *nm* **(a)** *(colonne)* pillar **(b)** *Fig (défenseur)* pillar; *Fam Péj* **c'est un p. de bar** he's a regular barfly

pillage [pijaʒ] *nm* pillaging, looting; *(lors d'une émeute)* looting

pillard, -e [pijar, -ard] **1** *adj* pillaging, looting; *(lors d'une émeute)* looting

2 *nm,f* pillager; *(lors d'une émeute)* looter

piller [pije] *vt* to pillage, to loot; *(lors d'une émeute)* to loot

pilleur, -euse [pijœr, -øz] *nm,f* pillager; *(lors d'une émeute)* looter; **p. d'épaves** looter of wrecks

pilon [pilɔ̃] *nm* **(a)** *(de pharmacien)* pestle; *Fig* **mettre un livre au p.** to pulp a book **(b)** *(de poulet)* drumstick **(c)** *(jambe de bois)* wooden leg

pilonnage [pilɔnaʒ] *nm (bombardement)* bombardment

pilonner [pilɔne] *vt (bombarder)* to bombard

pilori [pilɔri] *nm* pillory; *aussi Fig* **mettre qn au p.** to pillory sb

pilosité [pilozite] *nf* hairiness

pilotage [pilɔtaʒ] *nm* **(a)** *(d'un navire, d'un avion)* piloting; **p. automatique** automatic piloting **(b)** *Ordinat* control

pilote [pilɔt] **1** *nm* **(a)** *(de navire, d'avion)* pilot; *(de voiture de course)* driver; *(de moto de course)* rider; *Fig* **servir de p. à qn** to show sb around; **p. automatique** automatic pilot, autopilot; **p. de chasse** fighter pilot; **p. d'essai** test pilot; **p. de ligne** airline pilot **(b)** *Ordinat* driver; **p. d'affichage** display driver; **p. d'imprimante** printer driver

2 *adj* **installation(-)p.** pilot plant; **université(-)p.** experimental university

piloter [pilɔte] *vt* **(a)** *(navire)* to pilot; *(avion)* to pilot, to fly; *(voiture)* to drive; *(moto)* to ride; *Fig (projet)* to be in charge of; *(touriste)* to show around **(b)** *Ordinat* to drive; **piloté par menu** menu-driven

pilotis [pilɔti] *nmpl* stilts

pilule [pilyl] *nf* pill, tablet; **la p.** *(contraceptif)* the pill; **prendre la p.** to be on the pill; **p. abortive** abortion pill; **p. du lendemain** morning-after pill

pimbêche [pɛ̃bɛʃ] **1** *nf (fille)* stuck-up girl; *(femme)* stuck-up woman

2 *adj* stuck-up

piment [pimɑ̃] *nm* **(a)** *(piquant)* chilli; **p. doux** (sweet) pepper **(b)** *Fig* spice

pimenter [pimɑ̃te] *vt aussi Fig* to spice up

pimpant, -e [pɛ̃pɑ̃, ɑ̃t] *adj* smart

pin [pɛ̃] *nm* pine; **p. maritime** maritime pine; **p. parasol** umbrella pine; **p. sylvestre** Scots pine

pinacle [pinakl] *nm* **être au p.** to be at the top; **porter qn au p.** to praise sb to the skies

pinailler [pinaje] *vi Fam* to nitpick (**sur** over)

pinailleur, -euse [pinajœr, -øz] *Fam* **1** *adj* nitpicking

2 *nm,f* nitpicker

pinard [pinar] *nm Fam* wine

pince [pɛ̃s] *nf* **(a)** *(outil)* pliers; *(de forgeron)* tongs; **p. à cheveux** barrette; **p. crocodile** crocodile clip; **p. à épiler** tweezers; **p. à linge** clothespin; **p. à sucre** sugar tongs; **p. à vélo** bicycle clip **(b)** *(des crustacés)* pincer, claw **(c)** *(sur un vêtement)* dart; **pantalon à pinces** pleated pants **(d)** *Fam* **serrer la p. à qn** to shake hands with sb **(e)** *Fam* **à pinces** on foot

pincé, -e [pɛ̃se] *adj (air)* stiff, starchy; *(sourire)* tight-lipped; *(lèvres)* pursed

pinceau, -x [pɛ̃so] *nm (brosse)* brush, paintbrush; **avoir un bon coup de p.** to be a good painter

pincée [pɛ̃se] *nf* pinch

pincement [pɛ̃smɑ̃] *nm* **(a)** **avoir un p. au cœur** *(être ému)* to feel a pang of sadness **(b)** *(fait de pincer)* pinching; *(des cordes d'un instrument)* plucking

pince-monseigneur (*pl* **pinces-monseigneur**) [pɛ̃smɔ̃sɛɲœr] *nf* jimmy

pince-nez [pɛ̃sne] *nm inv* pince-nez

pincer [16] [pɛ̃se] **1** vt (**a**) (serrer) to pinch, to nip; (lèvres) to purse; (cordes d'un instrument) to pluck (**b**) Fam (attraper) to catch; **se faire p.** to get caught (**c**) Fam **en p. pour qn** to be crazy about sb (**d**) Fam **ça pince** it's freezing

2 se pincer vpr **se p. le doigt** to catch one's finger; **se p. le nez** to hold one's nose

pince-sans-rire [pɛ̃ssɑ̃rir] **1** nmf inv person with a dry sense of humor

2 adj inv dry, deadpan

pincette [pɛ̃sɛt] nf (**a**) (petite pince) tweezers; **pincettes** (à feu) (fire) tongs; Fig **il n'est pas à prendre avec des pincettes** he's in a foul mood (**b**) Suisse (pince à linge) clothespin

pinçon [pɛ̃sɔ̃] nm pinch mark

pinède [pined] nf pine wood

pingouin [pɛ̃gwɛ̃] nm auk; (manchot) penguin

ping-pong [piŋpɔ̃g] nm table tennis, Ping-Pong®

pingre [pɛ̃gr] adj stingy

pingrerie [pɛ̃grəri] nf stinginess

pin's [pinz] nm inv badge

pinson [pɛ̃sɔ̃] nm chaffinch

pintade [pɛ̃tad] nf guinea fowl

pinte [pɛ̃t] nf pint; Can quart

pinter [pɛ̃te] Fam **1** vi to booze

2 se pinter vpr to get sozzled

pinteur, -euse [pɛ̃tœr, -øz] nm,f Belg & Suisse Fam boozer, alkie

pin-up [pinœp] nf inv pin-up

pioche [pjɔʃ] nf (**a**) (outil) pick, pickax (**b**) (aux cartes, aux dominos) stock, pile

piocher [pjɔʃe] **1** vt (creuser) to dig (with a pick)

2 vi (aux cartes, aux dominos) to pick up; Fig **p. dans qch** (tas) to plunge one's hand into sth; (économies, réserves) to dip into sth

piolet [pjɔlɛ] nm ice ax

pion¹ [pjɔ̃] nm (de jeu de société) piece; (aux échecs) pawn; (aux dames) checker; Fig **n'être qu'un p. (sur l'échiquier)** to be only a pawn in the game

pion², pionne [pjɔ̃, pjɔn] nm,f Fam (surveillant) supervisor (paid to supervise students outside class hours)

> **Pion**
>
> In French lycées, the "pions" (officially called "surveillants") are responsible for supervising students outside class hours; they are often college students who do the job to make a little extra money.

pioncer [16] [pjɔ̃se] vi Fam to sleep

pionnier, -ère [pjɔnje, -ɛr] nm,f aussi Fig pioneer

pipe [pip] nf (**a**) (de fumeur) pipe; Fam Fig **casser sa p.** to kick the bucket, to buy the farm (**b**) Vulg **faire** ou **tailler une p. à qn** to give sb a blowjob

pipeau, -x [pipo] nm Mus (reed) pipe; Fam **c'est du p.** it's all nonsense

pipelette [piplɛt] nf Fam gossip

pipeline, pipe-line (pl pipe-lines) [piplin, pajplajn] nm pipeline

piper [pipe] vt (**a**) (dés) to load; (cartes) to mark; Fig **les dés sont pipés** the dice are loaded (**b**) **ne pas p. (mot)** not to breathe a word

pipette [pipɛt] nf pipette; Suisse **ça ne vaut pas p.** it's not worth a bean or a red cent

pipi [pipi] nm Fam pee; **faire p.** to pee; **faire p. au lit** to wet the bed; Péj **c'est du p. de chat** (boisson) it's dishwater

pipole [pipɔl] nmf celebrity, Fam celeb; **c'est un bar fréquenté par les pipoles** the bar is a popular hang-out for celebs

piquant, -e [pikɑ̃, ɑ̃t] **1** adj (**a**) (au goût) spicy, hot; (moutarde) hot (**b**) (plante) prickly, thorny; (barbe) prickly; (vent) biting (**c**) Fig (détail, style, situation) piquant; (histoire) spicy; **une petite brune piquante** a striking little brunette

2 nm (**a**) (d'une plante) thorn; (d'un porc-épic, d'un hérisson) spine; (de barbelé) spike, barb (**b**) (d'un style, d'une situation) piquancy; (d'une histoire) spice; **avoir du p.** (femme) to be striking

pique¹ [pik] **1** nf (arme) pike; (d'un picador) lance

2 nm (carte) spade; (couleur) spades

pique² [pik] nf (méchanceté) spiteful remark; **envoyer** ou **lancer des piques à qn** to make cutting remarks to sb

piqué, -e [pike] **1** adj (**a**) (bois) wormeaten; (livre) foxed; (miroir) tarnished; (métal) pitted; Fam **une histoire/angine pas piquée des hannetons** ou **des vers** one heck of a story/sore throat (**b**) (vin) sour (**c**) Fam (fou) crazy (**d**) Mus (note) staccato

2 nm (**a**) Aviat **descente en p.** nose dive (**b**) (tissu) piqué

pique-assiette (pl pique-assiettes) [pikasjɛt] nmf Fam scrounger, sponger

pique-feu [pikfø] nm inv poker

pique-nique (pl pique-niques) [piknik] nm picnic; **faire un p.** to have a picnic

pique-niquer [piknike] vi to have a picnic, to picnic

piquer [pike] **1** vt (**a**) (avec une pointe) to prick; (sujet: guêpe) to sting; (sujet: puce, moustique) to bite; (cheval) to spur on; (bœuf) to goad; **la fumée me pique les yeux** the smoke is making my eyes sting; **ça me pique la gorge/le nez** it tickles my throat/nose

(**b**) Fam (faire une piqûre à) **p. qn** to give sb an injection; **p. un chien** to put a dog to sleep

(**c**) Fam (voler) to swipe (**à** from); **je me suis fait p. mon stylo** my pen got swiped

(**d**) (coudre) to stitch

(**e**) (enfoncer) to stick (**dans** into)

(**f**) Fam **p. un cent mètres** to sprint off; **p. une crise** to throw a fit; **p. une tête** to dive

(**g**) (vexer) **p. qn au vif** to cut sb to the quick

(**h**) (exciter) **p. la curiosité de qn** to arouse or to excite sb's curiosity

(**i**) (sujet: acide, vers) to eat into; (sujet: humidité) to spot, to mark

(**j**) Culin **p. qch d'ail** to stick garlic into sth

2 vi (**a**) Aviat **p. (du nez)** to nosedive; Fig **p. du nez** (s'assoupir) to nod off; (baisser les yeux) to look down

(**b**) (plat) to be spicy or hot; (vin) to be sour

(**c**) (guêpe) to sting; (puce, moustique) to bite; (plante) to be prickly; **tu piques!** (à un homme mal rasé) you're all bristly!

3 se piquer vpr (**a**) (se blesser) to prick oneself; **se p. le doigt** to prick one's finger

(**b**) (se faire une piqûre) to give oneself an injection; Fam (se droguer) to shoot up; **se p. à l'héroïne** to shoot heroin

(**c**) (se vexer) to take offense

(**d**) (vin) to (turn) sour

(**e**) (locutions) **se p. au jeu** to get into it; Litt **se p. de faire qch** to pride oneself on doing sth

piquet [pikɛ] nm (**a**) (pieu) stake, post; (de tente) peg (**b**) Vieilli Scol **mettre** ou **envoyer qn au p.** to send sb to stand in the corner (**c**) **p. de grève** picket

piquette [pikɛt] nf (**a**) Péj (vin) cheap wine (**b**) Fam (défaite) **prendre une** ou **la p.** to get a hammering

piqûre [pikyr] nf (**a**) (de guêpe) sting; (de puce, de moustique) bite; **p. d'épingle** pinprick (**b**) Méd injection, shot; **faire une p. à qn** to give sb an injection (**c**) **piqûres** (d'un tissu, du cuir) stitching (**d**) (de rouille, de moisi) spot, speck

piranha [pirana] nm piranha

piratage [pirataʒ] nm pirating; **p. informatique** hacking

pirate [pirat] **1** nm (**a**) (des mers) pirate; **p. de l'air** hijacker, skyjacker; **p. informatique** hacker (**b**) (escroc) crook

2 adj (radio, enregistrement) pirate

pirater [pirate] *vt (enregistrement, cassette)* to pirate; *Ordinat* to hack

piraterie [piratri] *nf* **(a)** *(sur les mers)* piracy **(b)** *Fig (escroquerie)* swindling

pire [pir] **1** *adj* **(a)** *(comparatif)* worse; **c'est de p. en p.** it's getting worse and worse; *Can Fam* **p. que p.** dire, as bad as it can get **(b)** *(superlatif)* worst

2 *nm* **le p., c'est que...** the worst thing about it is...; **craindre le/s'attendre au p.** to fear/to expect the worst; **au p....** if the worst comes to the worst...

pirogue [pirɔg] *nf* dugout (canoe)

pirouette [pirwɛt] *nf* **(a)** *(tour sur soi-même)* pirouette; *(saut périlleux)* somersault; **faire un p.** to pirouette **(b)** *Fig (dérobade)* flippant answer; **s'en tirer par une p.** to answer flippantly

pis¹ [pi] *nm (mamelle)* udder

pis² [pi] **1** *adv* **aller de mal en p.** to go from bad to worse

2 *adj Litt* worse

3 *nm* **(a)** *Litt (comparatif)* worse; **il y a p.** there is/are worse **(b)** *Litt (superlatif)* worst; **au p.** if the worst comes to the worst; **au p. aller** at the very worst **(c)** **dire p. que pendre de qn** to call sb every name under the sun

pis-aller [pizale] *nm inv* stopgap (solution)

pisciculture [pisikyltyr] *nf* fish farming

piscine [pisin] *nf* (swimming) pool; **p. couverte/en plein air** indoor/outdoor pool

Pise [piz] *n* Pisa

pisse [pis] *nf très Fam* piss

pisse-froid [pisfrwa] **1** *adj inv* **il est très p.** he's a bit of a cold fish

2 *nm inv Fam* cold fish

pissenlit [pisɑ̃li] *nm* dandelion; *Fam* **manger les pissenlits par la racine** to be pushing up the daisies

pisser [pise] **1** *vi* **(a)** *très Fam (uriner)* to piss; **c'est comme si je pissais dans un violon** it's like pissing in the wind; **laisse p.!** forget it!; **c'était à p. de rire** we pissed our pants (laughing) **(b)** *Fam (fuir)* to leak

2 *vt* **(a)** *très Fam* **p. du sang** to piss blood **(b)** *Fam* **son bras pissait le sang** blood was pouring from his/her arm

pisseux, -euse [pisø, -øz] *adj Fam (couleur)* washed out

pissotière [pisɔtjɛr] *nf Fam* (public) urinal

pistache [pistaʃ] **1** *nf (graine)* pistachio (nut); **glace à la p.** pistachio ice cream

2 *adj inv (couleur)* pistachio (green)

piste [pist] *nf* **(a)** *(trace)* track, trail; *(indices)* lead; **être sur la p. de qn** to be on sb's track; **suivre une fausse p.** to be on the wrong track **(b)** *Sport* track; *(de courses de chevaux)* racetrack; *(de course automobile)* racetrack; *(de ski)* run, piste; *(de cirque)* ring; **p. artificielle** *(de ski)* artificial *or* dry ski slope; **p. de danse** dance floor **(c)** *Aviat* runway; **p. d'atterrissage** landing strip; *(dans la brousse, dans la forêt)* airstrip **(d)** *(chemin)* track, trail; **p. cyclable** bicycle path **(e)** *(de magnétophone, de disque)* track; *Ordinat* **p. d'amorçage** boot track; *Ordinat* **p. magnétique** magnetic stripe

pister [piste] *vt (animal)* to track; *(personne)* to tail

pistil [pistil] *nm Bot* pistil

pistolet [pistɔlɛ] *nm* **(a)** *(arme à feu)* pistol, gun; **p. à air comprimé** air pistol; **p. à eau** water pistol **(b)** *(à peinture)* paint gun

pistolet-mitrailleur (*pl* **pistolets-mitrailleurs**) [pistɔlɛmitrajœr] *nm* submachine-gun

piston [pistɔ̃] *nm* **(a)** *Tech* piston **(b)** *Fam Fig (recommandation)* string-pulling; **il a eu la place par p.** someone pulled some strings to get him the job **(c)** *(d'instrument à vent)* valve

pistonner [pistɔne] *vt Fam* to pull strings for; **elle s'est fait p.** she got someone to pull strings for her

pistou [pistu] *nm (sauce)* pesto; *(soupe)* vegetable soup with pesto

pita [pita] *nf* pitta bread

pitance [pitɑ̃s] *nf Vieilli (nourriture)* sustenance

pit-bull (*pl* **pit-bulls**) [pitbul] *nm* pit bull (terrier)

piteux, -euse [pitø, -øz] *adj* **(a)** *(mauvais) (résultat)* poor, pitiful; **en p. état** in a sorry state **(b)** *(honteux)* shamefaced

pithiviers [pitivje] *nm Culin* = cake made of puff pastry containing rum and almond-flavored cream

pitié [pitje] *nf* **(a)** *(compassion)* pity; **avoir p. de qn** to pity sb; **il me faisait p.** I felt sorry for him; **faire p. (à voir)** to be a pitiful sight; **être sans p.** to be ruthless; **(par) p.!** *(pour demander grâce)* (have) mercy!; *(exprime l'agacement)* for pity's sake! **(b)** *(tristesse)* **quelle p.!** what a pity!

piton [pitɔ̃] *nm* **(a)** *Tech* eye bolt; *(d'alpiniste)* piton **(b)** *(sommet)* **p. (rocheux)** (rocky) peak

pitoyable [pitwajabl] *adj* **(a)** *(digne de pitié)* pitiful **(b)** *Péj (excuse, plaisanterie)* pathetic

pitre [pitr] *nm* clown; **faire le p.** to clown around

pitrerie [pitrəri] *nf* piece of clowning; **pitreries** clowning

pittoresque [pitɔrɛsk] *adj (lieu)* picturesque; *(description, style)* vivid

pivert [pivɛr] *nm* green woodpecker

pivoine [pivwan] *nf* peony

pivot [pivo] *nm* **(a)** *(axe)* pivot; *(de levier)* fulcrum; *(de compas, de boussole)* center pin; *(en dentisterie)* post **(b)** *Fig (d'un drame, d'une argumentation)* pivot **(c)** *(au basket)* pivot, post

pivotant, -e [pivɔtɑ̃, ɑ̃t] *adj (grue, lampe)* swiveling; *(présentoir)* revolving

pivoter [pivɔte] *vi* to pivot, to swivel (**sur** on); **faire p. qch** to swivel sth around

pixel [piksɛl] *nm Ordinat* pixel

pixélisé, -e [pikselize] *adj Ordinat* pixellated

pizza [pidza] *nf* pizza

pizzeria [pidzerja] *nf* pizzeria

PJ [peʒi] *nf Fam (abrév* **police judiciaire***)* ≃ FBI

placage [plakaʒ] *nm* **(a)** *(bois)* veneer; *(métal)* plating **(b)** *(au rugby)* tackle

placard [plakar] *nm* **(a)** *(armoire)* cupboard; *Fam Fig* **mettre qn au p.** to sideline sb; *Fam Fig* **mettre qch au p.** to put sth on ice, to shelve sth **(b)** *(affiche)* poster **(c)** *Fam (prison)* slammer, clink

placarder [plakarde] *vt (affiche)* to stick up, to put up; **p. un mur d'affiches** to cover a wall with posters

place [plas] *nf* **(a)** *(endroit, rôle)* place; **changer qch de p.** to move sth; *Fig* **se mettre à la p. de qn** to put oneself in sb's position; **mettre qch en p.** to put sth in place; **être en p.** *(objet)* to be in place; *(au pouvoir)* to be in office; **les gens en p.** people in high places; *Fig* **remettre qn à sa p.** to put sb in his/her place; **il ne tient pas en p.** he can't keep still; **à la p. de qn** *(au lieu de)* instead of sb; **à votre p....** if I were you...; **sur p.** on the spot; **faire p. nette** to clean up; **p. de parking** parking place *or* space

(b) *(espace)* room, space; **prendre beaucoup de p.** to take up a lot of room *or* space; **faire de la p. à qn** to make room for sb; *Fig* **faire p. à qn/qch** to make way for sb/sth

(c) *(siège)* seat; **(voiture à) deux/quatre places** two-/four-seater (car); **prendre p.** to take a seat; **p. assise** seat; **p. debout** *(billet)* standing ticket; **la p. du mort** the passenger seat

(d) *(poste)* job, post; *Suisse* **p. de travail** job

(e) *(lieu public)* square; **p. du marché** market place

(f) *(rang)* place

(g) *Mil* **p. forte** fortified town

(h) *Com & Fin* market; **sur la p. de Paris** on the Paris market; **p. financière** financial market

(i) *Belg (pièce d'habitation)* room

placé, -e [plase] *adj* **être bien/mal p. pour faire qch** to be well/badly placed to do sth

placebo [plasebo] *nm* placebo

placement [plasmã] *nm* (**a**) *(d'argent)* investment; **faire des placements** to invest (money) (**b**) *(à un emploi)* placement, placing

placenta [plasɛ̃ta] *nm* placenta

placer [16] [plase] **1** *vt* (**a**) *(mettre à sa place)* to place, to put; *(faire asseoir)* to seat (**b**) *(procurer un emploi à)* to find a job for, to place; **p. qn comme apprenti chez qn** to apprentice sb to sb (**c**) *(vendre)* to sell (**d**) *(dans la conversation)* to get in; *Fam* **avec elle, on ne peut pas en p. une!** you can't get a word in edgewise with her! (**e**) *(argent)* to invest

2 se placer *vpr* (**a**) *(debout)* to stand; *(assis)* to sit (**b**) **se p. sous la protection de qn** to place oneself under sb's protection; **il faut se p. dans son optique** you have to look at things from her point of view (**c**) *(trouver un emploi)* to find a job

placide [plasid] *adj* placid, calm

placoter [plakɔte] *vi Can Fam* to chat

plafond [plafɔ̃] *nm aussi Fig* ceiling; **être haut/bas de p.** to have a high/low ceiling; **prix/vitesse p.** maximum price/speed

plafonner [plafɔne] *vi (quantité, salaire)* to have reached a ceiling (**à** of)

plafonnier [plafɔnje] *nm* ceiling light

plage [plaʒ] *nf* (**a**) *(grève)* beach; **aller en vacances à la p.** to go on vacation to the seaside; **p. de sable/de galets** sandy/pebble beach (**b**) *(surface)* area (**c**) *(dans un emploi du temps, à la télé, à la radio)* slot; **p. horaire** time slot (**d**) *(d'un disque)* track (**e**) **p. arrière** *(d'une voiture)* back shelf

plagiaire [plaʒjɛr] *nmf* plagiarist

plagiat [plaʒja] *nm* plagiarism

plagier [66] [plaʒje] *vt* to plagiarize

plaid [plɛd] *nm* travel rug

plaider [plede] **1** *vt* to plead; **p. coupable/non coupable** to plead guilty/not guilty; **p. la cause de qn** *Jur* to plead sb's case; *Fig* to plead sb's cause

2 *vi (avocat)* to plead; **p. pour/contre qn** to defend/to prosecute sb; *Fig* **p. en faveur de qn/qch** to speak for sb/sth, to defend sb/sth

plaideur, -euse [plɛdœr, -øz] *nm,f* litigant

plaidoirie [plɛdwari] *nf Jur* speech for the defense

plaidoyer [plɛdwaje] *nm Jur* speech for the defense; *Fig* plea

plaie [plɛ] *nf* (**a**) *aussi Fig* wound (**b**) *(fléau)* affliction, scourge; *(personne, chose)* pest, nuisance

plaignant, -e [plɛɲɑ̃, -ɑ̃t] *nm,f Jur* plaintiff

plaindre [23] [plɛ̃dr] **1** *vt* to pity, to feel sorry for; **je vous plains de voyager dans ces conditions** I feel sorry for you having to travel in these conditions; **elle n'est pas à p.** she's got nothing to worry about

2 se plaindre *vpr* (**a**) *(protester)* to complain; **se p. de** to complain about; *(douleur)* to complain of (**b**) *(gémir)* to moan

plaine [plɛn] *nf* plain

plain-pied [plɛ̃pje] **de plain-pied** *adv (pièce)* on the same level (**avec** as); *(maison)* single-story

plainte [plɛ̃t] *nf* (**a**) *(protestation)* complaint (**b**) *(gémissement)* moan (**c**) *Jur* complaint; **porter p. contre qn (auprès de)** to lodge a complaint against sb (with); **p. contre X** complaint against person or persons unknown

plaintif, -ive [plɛ̃tif, -iv] *adj* plaintive

plaire [55a] [plɛr] **1** *vi* (**a**) *(être apprécié)* **cet homme me plaît** I like this man; **ce livre/film m'a plu** I liked *or* enjoyed the book/movie; **cette offre devrait lui p.** the offer should appeal to him; **ça plaît beaucoup** it's very popular; **je fais ce qui me plaît** I do whatever I want; **que cela te plaise ou non** whether you like it or not (**b**) *(se rendre agréable)* to please; **rien à faire, elle ne plaît pas** *(physiquement)* no matter what she does, no one finds her attractive

2 *v impersonnel* **s'il te/vous plaît** please; **s'il vous plaît!**

(dit par un client) excuse me!; *Belg (dit par un serveur)* there you go!; **et pas n'importe qui, s'il vous plaît** and not just anybody, if you please; **comme il vous plaira** just as you like

3 se plaire *vpr* (**a**) *(soi-même)* **elle se plaît dans cette robe** she likes herself in that dress (**b**) *(l'un l'autre)* to like each other (**c**) *(se trouver bien)* **je me plais beaucoup à Paris** I'm very happy in Paris; **se p. à faire qch** to enjoy *or* to like doing sth

plaisance [plɛzɑ̃s] *nf* **la (navigation de) p.** boating

plaisancier, -ère [plɛzɑ̃sje, -ɛr] *nm,f* (amateur) yachtsman, *f* yachtswoman

plaisant, -e [plɛzɑ̃, -ɑ̃t] **1** *adj* (**a**) *(agréable)* pleasant, agreeable (**b**) *(drôle)* funny, amusing

2 *nm* **mauvais p.** malicious joker

plaisanter [plɛzɑ̃te] **1** *vi* to joke; **dire qch en plaisantant** to say sth as a joke; **vous plaisantez!** you're joking!; **on ne plaisante pas avec la santé** you shouldn't take any chances with your health

2 *vt* to tease, to poke fun at (**sur** about)

plaisanterie [plɛzɑ̃tri] *nf (acte, propos)* joke; **elle ne comprend pas la p.** she can't take a joke; **par p.** for a joke; **tourner qch en p.** to make a joke out of sth; **les plaisanteries les plus courtes sont les meilleures** brevity is the soul of wit

plaisantin [plɛzɑ̃tɛ̃] *nm* joker

plaise *etc. voir* **plaire**

plaisir [plezir] *nm* (**a**) *(sensation agréable)* pleasure; **j'ai le p. de vous apprendre que…** I'm pleased to be able to tell you that…; **faire qch pour le p.** to do sth for fun; *Ironique* **je vous souhaite bien du p.!** best of luck!; **ça m'a fait p. de te revoir** I was pleased to see you again; **ça me ferait p. que tu viennes** I'd be pleased if you came; **fais-moi p., viens danser** do me a favor, come and dance; **si cela peut te faire p.** if it makes you happy; **il va se faire un p. de te téléphoner demain** he'll be only too pleased to call you tomorrow; **cela fait p. à voir** it's good to see; **prendre p. à qch/à faire qch** to enjoy sth/doing sth; **les plaisirs de la table** fine food and wine (**b**) *(distraction)* pleasure; **c'est son plus grand p.** it's his/her greatest pleasure

plan¹, -e [plɑ̃, plan] **1** *adj (terrain, surface)* flat; *Math* plane

2 *nm* (**a**) *Math* plane (**b**) *(surface)* **p. de cuisson** cooktop; **p. d'eau** lake; **p. incliné** inclined plane; **p. de travail** *(d'une cuisine)* worktop (**c**) *Cin, Phot et Fig* **au premier p.** in the foreground; **au second p.** in the background; **un artiste de premier p.** a leading artist; **sur le même p. (que)** on the same level (as); **sur le p. politique/économique** from a political/an economic point of view; **gros p.** close-up; **en gros p.** in close-up

plan² [plɑ̃, plan] *nm* (**a**) *(relevé)* plan; *(carte) (de ville)* map (**b**) *(projet)* plan; *Fam* **j'ai un bon p. pour les vacances** I've got a great idea for the vacation; **p. de carrière** career strategy; **p. d'occupation des sols** zoning ordinances (**c**) *(d'un roman, d'un devoir)* plan, framework (**d**) *Fin* **p. d'épargne** savings plan; **p. d'épargne en actions** investment trust; **p. d'épargne-logement** = savings plan entitling savers to low mortgages, ≃ savings-and-loan association account; **p. d'épargne-retraite** individual retirement account

plan³ [plɑ̃, plan] *nm Fam* **laisser qn en p.** to leave sb in the lurch; **tout laisser en p.** to drop everything

planant, -e [planɑ̃, ɑ̃t] *adj Fam* mind-blowing

planche [plɑ̃ʃ] *nf* (**a**) *(pièce de bois)* plank; *(plus large)* board; **faire la p.** *(flotter)* to float on one's back; *Fam* **c'est une vraie p. à pain** she's as flat as a pancake; **p. à découper** chopping board; **p. à dessin** drawing board; **p. à repasser** ironing board; **p. de salut** last hope (**b**) *Théât* **monter sur les planches** to go on the stage, to tread the boards (**c**) *(d'imprimerie, de gravure)* plate, block (**d**) *Sport* **p. (de surf)** surfboard; **p. (à voile)** windsurfer; *Can* **p. à neige** snowboard; **p. à rou-**

lettes skateboard; **faire de la p. à roulettes** to skateboard; **faire de la p. à voile** to go windsurfing

plancher¹ [plɑ̃ʃe] *nm* (**a**) *(sol)* floor; *Fam* **le p. des vaches** dry land, terra firma; *Fig* **mettre le pied au p.** to pull out the throttle (**b**) *Fig (minimum)* minimum; **prix p.** bottom price

plancher² [plɑ̃ʃe] **1** *vi Fam Scol* to have an exam
2 plancher sur *vt ind* **p. sur un problème** to work on a problem

plancton [plɑ̃ktɔ̃] *nm* plankton

plané [plane] *adj m voir* **vol¹**

planer [plane] *vi* (**a**) *(oiseau, planeur)* to glide; *(brume, fumée)* to hang; *Fig* **p. sur qn/qch** *(danger)* to hang over sb/sth (**b**) *Fam (se sentir bien)* to be floating on air, to be on a high; *(après s'être drogué)* to be high; *(rêver)* to dream

planétaire [planetɛr] *adj* (**a**) *Astron* planetary (**b**) *(expansion, action)* worldwide

planétarium [planetarjɔm] *nm* planetarium

planète [planɛt] *nf* planet

planeur [planœr] *nm (avion)* glider

planification [planifikasjɔ̃] *nf Écon* planning

planifier [66] [planifje] *vt* to plan

planisphère [planisfɛr] *nm* planisphere

planning [planiŋ] *nm* schedule; **p. familial** family planning; *(lieu)* family-planning clinic

planque [plɑ̃k] *nf Fam* (**a**) *(d'un gangster)* hideout; *(pour un butin)* hiding place (**b**) *(travail facile)* cushy job

planqué, -e [plɑ̃ke] *nm,f Fam* person with a cushy job; *Mil* draft dodger

planquer [plɑ̃ke] *Fam* **1** *vt* to hide
2 se planquer *vpr* to hide

plant [plɑ̃] *nm (d'arbre)* sapling; *(de plante)* seedling

plantaire [plɑ̃tɛr] *adj Anat* plantar

plantation [plɑ̃tasjɔ̃] *nf (exploitation agricole)* plantation

plante¹ [plɑ̃t] *nf* **p. du pied** sole (of the foot)

plante² [plɑ̃t] *nf (végétal)* plant; *Fam Fig* **une belle p.** *(femme)* a voluptuous woman; **p. d'appartement** house plant; **p. grasse** succulent (plant); **p. potagère** plant grown for food; **p. verte** house plant

planté, -e [plɑ̃te] *adj* (**a**) *(debout)* standing; *Fam* **rester p. (comme un piquet)** *(immobile)* to stand there doing nothing (**b**) **bien p.** *(robuste)* sturdy

planter [plɑ̃te] **1** *vt* (**a**) *(graines, fleurs, arbre)* to plant; **une colline plantée d'arbres** a hill planted with trees (**b**) *(clou)* to hammer in; *(tente)* to put up, to pitch; **p. un clou dans qch** to hammer a nail into sth; *Fig* **p. un baiser sur la joue à qn** to plant a kiss on sb's cheek (**c**) *Fam* **p. là qn** to dump sb; **il veut tout p. là** he wants to pack it all in (**d**) *Fam (tuer)* to knife to death
2 *vi Fam Ordinat* to go down, to crash
3 se planter *vpr* (**a**) *(se tenir immobile)* to stand (**b**) *Fam (se tromper)* to get it wrong (**c**) *Fam (tomber)* to take a spill (**d**) *Fam (en voiture)* to crash

planteur [plɑ̃tœr] *nm* (**a**) *(exploitant)* planter (**b**) *(cocktail)* planter's punch

plantigrade [plɑ̃tigrad] *nm Zool* plantigrade

planton [plɑ̃tɔ̃] *nm Mil* orderly

plantureux, -euse [plɑ̃tyrø, -øz] *adj (femme)* buxom; *(poitrine)* ample

plaquage [plakaʒ] = **placage (b)**

plaque [plak] *nf* (**a**) *(de métal)* plate, sheet; *(de marbre)* slab; *(de chocolat)* bar; *(de beurre)* pack; *(de verglas)* sheet; **p. chauffante** hotplate; **p. d'égout** manhole cover; *Fig* **p. tournante** hub, center (**b**) *(sur une porte)* nameplate; *(commémorative)* plaque; **p. d'immatriculation** *ou* **minéralogique** license plate; **p. de rue** street sign (**c**) *(sur la peau)* patch; **p. (dentaire)** (dental) plaque (**d**) *Fam* **être à côté de la p.** to be wide of the mark

plaqué, -e [plake] **1** *adj* **p. or/argent** gold-/silver-plated

2 *nm* (**a**) **p. or/argent** gold/silver plate; **montre en p. or** gold-plated watch (**b**) *(bois)* veneered wood

plaquer [plake] **1** *vt* (**a**) *(cheveux)* to plaster down; **p. qn contre un mur** to pin sb against a wall (**b**) *Fam (petit ami)* to dump; **tout p.** to chuck it all in (**c**) *(au rugby)* to tackle (**d**) *Mus (accord)* to play (**e**) *(bois)* to veneer; *(métal)* to plate
2 se plaquer *vpr* **se p. au sol** to lie flat on the ground; **se p. contre un mur** to flatten oneself against a wall

plaquette [plakɛt] *nf* (**a**) *(de métal)* (small) plate; *(portant une inscription)* (small) plaque; *Ordinat* circuit board; *Aut* **p. de frein** brake pad (**b**) *(de chocolat)* bar; *(de beurre)* pack (**c**) *(petit livre)* booklet (**d**) *Méd* **plaquettes** (blood) platelets

plasma [plasma] *nm Biol & Phys* plasma

plastic [plastik] *nm* plastic explosive

plasticage [plastikaʒ] *nm* bombing (**de** of)

plastifier [66] [plastifje] *vt* to laminate

plastiquage [plastikaʒ] = **plasticage**

plastique [plastik] **1** *adj & nm* plastic
2 *nf* (**a**) *(art)* art of modeling (**b**) *(du corps)* figure

plastiquer [plastike] *vt* to bomb

plastron [plastrɔ̃] *nm* (**a**) *(de chemise)* shirt front (**b**) *(d'escrimeur)* plastron

plat, -e [pla, plat] **1** *adj* (**a**) *(sans relief)* flat, level; *(chaussure)* flat; *(mer)* smooth; *(eau)* still; *Fam* **plate comme une limande** *(femme)* as flat as a pancake
(**b**) *Fig (ennuyeux)* flat, dull
(**c**) **à p.** *(pneu, batterie)* flat; *Fam* **être à p.** *(épuisé)* to be run down; **mettre qch à p.** to lay sth (down) flat; *Fig* **tomber à p.** *(proposition, plaisanterie)* to fall flat; **se mettre à p. ventre** to lie face down; *Fig* **se mettre à p. ventre devant qn** to grovel to sb
2 *nm* (**a**) *(assiette)* dish; *Fig* **mettre les petits plats dans les grands** to put on a great spread
(**b**) *(mets)* dish; *(partie du menu)* course; *Fam* **en faire tout un p.** to make a song and dance about it; **p. cuisiné** ready meal; **p. du jour** today's special, dish of the day; *Fam Fig* **p. de nouilles** meathead; **p. principal** *ou* **de résistance** main course
(**c**) *(de la main, d'une épée)* flat
(**d**) *(en cyclisme, en hippisme)* **sur le p.** on the flat
(**e**) **faire un p.** *(en plongeant)* to do a bellyflop
(**f**) *Fam* **faire du p. à qn** to hit on sb

platane [platan] *nm* plane tree

plateau, -x [plato] *nm* (**a**) *(plat)* tray; **p. à fromages** cheeseboard; **p. de fruits de mer** seafood platter (**b**) *(d'une balance)* pan; *(d'une platine, d'un four micro-ondes)* turntable (**c**) *Géog* plateau; **haut p.** high plateau (**d**) *TV & Cin* set (**e**) *(de vélo)* chain wheel

plateau-repas *(pl* **plateaux-repas)** [platorəpɑ] *nm* meal on a tray

plate-bande *(pl* **plates-bandes)** [platbɑ̃d] *nf* flower bed; *Fam* **marcher sur les plates-bandes de qn** to tread on sb's toes

plate-forme *(pl* **plates-formes)** [platfɔrm] *nf* (**a**) *(surface plane)* platform; **p. pétrolière** *ou* **de forage** oil rig (**b**) *Géog* **p. continentale** continental shelf (**c**) *Ordinat* platform

platement [platmɑ̃] *adv* (**a**) *(s'exprimer, écrire)* dully (**b**) *(s'excuser)* humbly

platine¹ [platin] *nf (tourne-disque)* turntable; **p. cassettes** cassette *or* tape deck; **p. laser** CD player

platine² [platin] **1** *nm* platinum
2 *adj inv* **cheveux (blonds) p.** platinum blond hair

platiné, -e [platine] *adj* (**a**) *(recouvert de platine)* platinum-plated (**b**) *(cheveux)* platinum blond; **une blonde platinée** a platinum blonde

platitude [platityd] *nf* (**a**) *(manque d'intérêt)* dullness (**b**) *(propos)* platitude; **débiter des platitudes** to talk in platitudes

Platon [platɔ̃] *npr* Plato

platonique [platɔnik] *adj (amour)* platonic

plâtras [platra] *nmpl* (plaster) rubble

plâtre [platr] *nm* plaster; *(sculpture)* plaster cast; *(pour jambe cassée)* plaster (cast); **avoir la jambe dans le p.** to have one's leg in plaster; *Fig* **essuyer les plâtres** to have to put up with the teething problems

plâtrer [platre] *vt* (**a**) *(mur, plafond)* to plaster; *(trou, fissure)* to plaster over (**b**) *(jambe, bras)* to put in plaster

plâtreux, -euse [platrø, -øz] *adj (fromage)* chalky

plâtrier [platrije] *nm* plasterer

plausible [plozibl] *adj* plausible

play-back [plɛbak] *nm inv* miming; **chanter en p.** to mime

play-boy (*pl* **play-boys**) [plɛbɔj] *nm* playboy

plèbe [plɛb] *nf* **la p.** the plebs

plébéien, -enne [plebejɛ̃, -ɛn] *adj & nm,f* plebeian

plébiscite [plebisit] *nm* plebiscite

plébisciter [plebisite] *vt* (**a**) *(élire)* **p. qn/qch** to vote for sb/sth by plebiscite (**b**) *Fig* to endorse

pléiade [plejad] *nf* **une p. de** a host of

plein, -e [plɛ̃, plɛn] **1** *adj* (**a**) *(rempli)* full (**de** of); **il a les doigts pleins d'encre** his fingers are covered with ink; **p. à craquer** full to bursting; **p. comme un œuf** chock-full (**b**) *(complet)* *(accord, pouvoirs)* full; **pleine lune** full moon; **pleine mer** high tide; **p. tarif** full price; *(de transports)* full fare; **travailler à p. temps** to work full-time (**c**) *(solide)* solid (**d**) *(en intensif)* **une pleine bouteille** a whole bottle; **p. sud** due south; **en p. (milieu du) désert/village** right in the middle of the desert/village; **en p. dans/devant/sur** right in/in front of/on; **en pleine figure/poitrine** right in the face/chest; **être en p. travail** to be hard at work; **en p. hiver** in the depths of winter; **en p. soleil** in the full heat of the sun (**e**) *(animal)* pregnant (**f**) *Fam (soûl)* plastered

2 *adv* **il avait des larmes p. les yeux** his eyes were full of tears; **elle avait de la colle p. les mains** her hands were covered with glue; **à p.** *(fonctionner)* at full capacity; *Fam* **gentil tout p.** really kind; *Fam* **p. de** *(beaucoup de)* lots *or* loads of

3 *nm* (**a**) *(d'essence)* **faire le p. (d'essence)** to fill up (with gas); **le p., s'il vous plaît** fill her up, please; *Fig* **faire le p. d'air pur/de soleil** to get a good dose of fresh air/of sunshine (**b**) *(trait)* downstroke (**c**) **battre son p.** to be in full swing

pleinement [plɛnmɑ̃] *adv* fully; **profiter p. de qch** to take full advantage of sth

plein-emploi [plɛnɑ̃plwa] *nm* full employment

plénier, -ère [plenje, -ɛr] *adj* plenary

plénipotentiaire [plenipɔtɑ̃sjɛr] *adj & nm* plenipotentiary

plénitude [plenityd] *nf* fullness

pléonasme [pleonasm] *nm* pleonasm

pléthore [pletɔr] *nf* plethora (**de** of)

pleurer [plœre] **1** *vi* (**a**) *(verser des larmes)* to cry, to weep (**sur/pour** over/for); **p. sur son sort** to bewail one's fate; **p. de joie** to weep for joy; **p. de rage** to cry with rage; **p. à chaudes larmes,** *Fam* **p. comme une madeleine** *ou* **comme un veau** to cry one's eyes out; **bête/triste à p.** terribly stupid/sad; **j'ai les yeux qui pleurent** my eyes are watering (**b**) *Fig & Péj (réclamer plaintivement)* to beg; **aller p. auprès de qn** to go begging to sb

2 *vt* (**a**) *(regretter)* *(personne disparue)* to mourn (for) (**b**) **p. toutes les larmes de son corps** to cry one's eyes out

pleurésie [plœrezi] *nf* pleurisy

pleureur [plœrœr] *adj m voir* **saule**

pleureuse [plœrøz] *nf* (hired) mourner

pleurnichard, -e [plœrniʃar, -ard] = **pleurnicheur**

pleurnicher [plœrniʃe] *vi Fam* to whine

pleurnicheur, -euse [plœrniʃœr, -øz] *Fam* **1** *nm,f* whiner **2** *adj* whining

pleurote [plœrɔt] *nm* oyster mushroom

pleurs [plœr] *nmpl* tears; **en p.** in tears

pleut *voir* **pleuvoir**

pleutre [pløtr] *adj & nm Litt* craven

pleuvoir [56] [pløvwar] **1** *v impersonnel* to rain; **il pleut** it's raining; **il pleut à verse** it's pouring (down); *Fam* **il pleut des cordes** it's coming down in buckets; *Fam* **il pleut comme vache qui pisse** it's raining cats and dogs; **des cadeaux comme s'il en pleuvait** gifts galore

2 *vi (obus, coups, insultes)* to rain down (**sur** on)

plèvre [plɛvr] *nf* pleura

Plexiglas® [plɛksiglas] *nm* Plexiglass®

plexus [plɛksys] *nm* plexus; **p. solaire** solar plexus

pli [pli] *nm* (**a**) *(de rideaux, de tissu, de papier)* fold; *(en couture)* pleat; **(faux) p.** crease; *Fig* **ça ne fait pas un p.** there's no doubt about it; *Fig* **prendre le p. (de faire qch)** to get into the habit (of doing sth); *Fig* **prendre un mauvais p.** to get into a bad habit (**b**) *(de la peau)* *(du ventre, du cou, du menton)* fold; *(de la bouche, des yeux)* wrinkle; *(du front)* line (**c**) *(enveloppe)* envelope; *(lettre)* letter; **sous p. séparé** under separate cover; **p. cacheté** sealed envelope; **envoyer qch sous p. cacheté** to send sth in a sealed envelope (**d**) *(aux cartes)* trick; **faire un p.** to take a trick (**e**) *Géol* fold

pliage [plijaʒ] *nm* folding

pliant, -e [plijɑ̃, -ɑ̃t] **1** *adj (chaise, table)* folding **2** *nm* folding stool

plie [pli] *nf* plaice

plier [66] [plije] **1** *vt* (**a**) *(draps, vêtements)* to fold; *(page)* to turn down; *(voile)* to furl; *(parapluie, pliant)* to fold up; *Fig* **p. bagage** to pack one's bags (**b**) *(courber)* *(branche, genou)* to bend; *Fam Fig* **être plié de rire/de douleur** to be doubled up with laughter/with pain; **être plié en deux** *ou* **en quatre** *(de rire)* to be doubled up *or* bent double; **être plié en deux** *(de douleur)* to be doubled up *or* bent double; **p. qn à la discipline/une règle** to impose discipline/a rule on sb

2 *vi* (**a**) *(se courber)* to bend (over); **p. sous le poids de qch** *(poutre, branches)* to bend under the weight of sth (**b**) *(se soumettre)* to submit, to yield; *(armée, troupes)* to give way

3 se plier *vpr* (**a**) *(pouvoir être plié)* *(parapluie, chaise)* to fold up (**b**) *(se soumettre)* **se p. à la discipline** to submit to discipline; **se p. aux lois** to obey the law; **se p. aux caprices/volontés de qn** to give in to sb's whims/wishes

plinthe [plɛ̃t] *nf* (**a**) *(de mur)* baseboard (**b**) *(de colonne)* plinth

plissé, -e [plise] **1** *adj* (**a**) *(visage, front)* wrinkled (**b**) **jupe plissée** pleated skirt **2** *nm* pleats

plissement [plismɑ̃] *nm* (**a**) *(des yeux)* screwing up (**b**) *Géol* fold

plisser [plise] **1** *vt* (**a**) *(front)* to wrinkle; *(lèvres)* to pucker; *(yeux)* to screw up (**b**) *(tissu, jupe)* to pleat

2 *vi (vêtement)* to crease

3 se plisser *vpr (étoffe)* to crease; *(bouche)* to pucker; *(yeux)* to wrinkle up; **son front se plissa** she frowned

pliure [plijyr] *nf (d'un tissu)* fold; *(de papier)* folding; *(du genou)* bend

plomb [plɔ̃] *nm* (**a**) *(métal)* lead; **ciel de p.** leaden sky; **soleil de p.** blazing sun; *Fig* **n'avoir pas de p. dans la tête** to be scatterbrained; **cela lui mettra un peu de p. dans la tête** *ou* **dans la cervelle** that'll knock some sense into him/her (**b**) *(de chasse)* shot; *Fam Fig* **avoir du p. dans l'aile** to be in a bad way (**c**) *Élec (fusible)* fuse; **faire sauter les plombs** to blow the fuses; *très Fam* **j'ai pété les plombs** I blew my top (**d**) *(pour la pêche)* sinker (**e**) *(sceau)* lead seal

plombage [plɔ̃baʒ] *nm* (**a**) *(fait de mettre des plombs)* weighting with lead (**b**) *(d'une dent)* filling

plombe [plɔ̃b] *nf Fam* hour

plombé, -e [plɔ̃be] *adj (toit)* lead(-covered); *Fig (teint)* livid; *(ciel)* leaden

plomber [plɔ̃be] **1** *vt* (a) *(couvrir de plomb)* to cover with lead (b) *(mettre des plombs à)* to weight with lead (c) *(dent)* to fill
2 se plomber *vpr (ciel)* to become leaden

plomberie [plɔ̃bri] *nf (installations, métier)* plumbing

plombier [plɔ̃bje] *nm* plumber

plonge [plɔ̃ʒ] *nf Fam* dishwashing, doing dishes; **faire la p.** to wash dishes

plongeant, -e [plɔ̃ʒɑ̃, -ɑ̃t] *adj (tir, décolleté)* plunging; **vue plongeante (sur)** bird's-eye view (of)

plongée [plɔ̃ʒe] *nf* (a) *(discipline)* diving; **faire de la p.** to dive; **p. sous-marine** skin *or* scuba diving (b) *(de sous-marin)* dive (c) *Cin & TV* high-angle shot; *(verticale)* bird's-eye view

plongeoir [plɔ̃ʒwar] *nm* diving board

plongeon [plɔ̃ʒɔ̃] *nm* (a) *(fait de plonger)* dive; **faire un p.** *(nageur, gardien de but)* to dive; *Fam Fig* **faire le p.** to hit the rocks (b) *(oiseau)* loon

plonger [45] [plɔ̃ʒe] **1** *vi* (a) *(nageur, sous-marin)* to dive (**dans** into) (b) *(avion, oiseau)* to dive (**sur** onto)
2 *vt aussi Fig* to plunge (**dans** into); **plongé dans ses pensées** lost *or* deep in thought; **la pièce fut plongée dans l'obscurité** the room was plunged into darkness
3 se plonger *vpr* **se p. dans l'étude** to immerse oneself in one's studies

plongeur, -euse [plɔ̃ʒœr, -øz] **1** *nm,f* (a) *(dans l'eau)* diver; **p. sous-marin** skin *or* scuba diver (b) *Fam (dans un restaurant)* dishwasher *(person)*
2 *nm (oiseau)* diver

plot [plo] *nm* (a) *Élec* contact (b) **p. de départ** starting block

plouc [pluk] *Péj* **1** *nm* hick, yokel
2 *adj Fam* uncool, lame; **ça fait p.!** that's so uncool!

plouf [pluf] *exclam* plop!; *(objet plus lourd)* splash!

ploutocratie [plutɔkrasi] *nf* plutocracy

ployer [32] [plwaje] **1** *vi (courber)* to bend; *(plancher, poutre)* to sag; *(sous un joug, un fardeau)* to bend
2 *vt* to bend

plu *voir* plaire, pleuvoir

pluie [plɥi] *nf* (a) *(précipitations)* rain; **pluies acides** acid rain; **p. battante** driving rain; **p. fine** drizzle; **temps de p.** rainy *or* wet weather; **sous la p.** in the rain; **parler de la p. et du beau temps** to talk of this and that; **il n'est pas tombé** *ou* **né de la dernière p.** he wasn't born yesterday; *Fam* **faire la p. et le beau temps** to rule the roost; *Prov* **après la p., le beau temps** ≃ it'll be alright in the end (b) *Fig (de coups, de projectiles)* hail, shower; *(d'injures, de compliments)* stream

plumage [plymaʒ] *nm* plumage

plumard [plymar] *nm Fam* bed

plume [plym] *nf* (a) *(d'oiseau)* feather; *Fam Fig* **il y a laissé des plumes** he didn't come out of it unscathed; *Fam Fig* **on lui a volé dans les plumes** they laid into him; **léger comme une p.** as light as a feather; *Hum* **perdre ses plumes** to go thin on top (b) *(de stylo)* nib; **p. (d'oie)** quill (pen); **écrire au fil de la p.** to write just what comes into one's head; **dessin à la p.** pen (and ink) drawing; **prendre la p.** to put pen to paper; **vivre de sa p.** to live by one's pen; **avoir la p. facile** to have a gift for writing

plumeau, -x [plymo] *nm* feather duster

plumer [plyme] *vt (volaille)* to pluck; *Fam (personne)* to fleece

plumier [plymje] *nm* pencil box

plupart [plypar] *nf* **la p.** most; **la p. des gens/des cas** most people/cases; **la p. d'entre eux** most of them; **la p. du temps** most of the time; *(en général)* in most cases; **pour la p.** for the most part, mostly

pluralisme [plyralism] *nm* pluralism

pluridisciplinaire [plyridisipliner] *adj* multi-disciplinary

pluriel, -elle [plyrjɛl] **1** *adj* plural
2 *nm* plural; **au p.** in the plural

plurilingue [plyrilɛ̃g] *adj* multilingual

plus 1 *adv* [ply] (a) *(comparatif)* more; **je gagne p. que vous** I earn more than you (do); **il est p. grand que moi** he's taller than I am *or* than me; **elle est p. jolie que belle** she is pretty rather than beautiful; **p. de** *(temps, hommes)* more; *(avec un nombre)* more than; **il a p. de vingt ans** he's over twenty; **p.... p....** the more... the more...; **p.... moins...** the more... the less...; **p. on va vers le sud, p. les jours allongent** the further south you go, the longer the days get; **de p. en p.** more and more; **de p. en p. froid** colder and colder; **celui-ci coûte dix euros de p. que l'autre** this one costs ten euros more than the other one; **cette année, il y a trois élèves de** *ou* **en p.** this year there are three more *or* extra pupils; **le vin est en p.** the wine is extra; **de p.** *(aussi)* furthermore; **en p.** *(aussi)* what's more; **en p. de** besides; **sans p. attendre** without further ado

(b) *(superlatif)* **le p.** the most; **la p. longue rue** *ou* **la rue la p. longue de la ville** the longest street in the town; **c'est tout ce qu'il y a de p. simple** nothing could be simpler; **une soirée des p. réussies** a most successful evening; **qui peut le p. peut le moins** you've/he's/*etc.* done more difficult things than that before

(c) *(indique la négation)* **ne... p.** no more, no longer; **je ne les vois p.** I don't see them any more, I no longer see them; **je ne le ferai p.** I won't do it again; **il n'y a p. rien** there's nothing left; **p. que dix minutes!** only ten minutes left!; **non p.** neither; **je ne suis jamais allé en Afrique – moi non p.** I've never been to Africa – neither have I, me neither

(d) *(locutions)* **p. ou moins** more or less; **ni p. ni moins** no more no less; **sans p.** but no more than that

2 *conj* [plys] *(dans les calculs, dans les températures)* plus
3 *nm* [plys] (a) *(signe)* plus (sign)
(b) *Fig (atout)* plus

plusieurs [plyzjœr] *adj indéfini & pron indéfini* several

plus-que-parfait *(pl* **plus-que-parfaits**) [plyskəparfɛ] *nm* pluperfect, past perfect

plus-value *(pl* **plus-values**) [plyvaly] *nf (bénéfice)* profit; *(augmentation de la valeur)* appreciation; *(excédent) (d'impôts)* surplus; **impôt sur les plus-values** capital-gains tax

Pluton [plytɔ̃] *npr (dieu, planète)* Pluto

plutonium [plytɔnjɔm] *nm* plutonium

plutôt [plyto] *adv* rather; *(à la place)* instead; **p. mourir!** I'd rather die!; **n'y va pas en voiture, prends p. le train** don't go by car, take the train instead; **p. que de faire qch** rather than doing sth

pluvial, -e, -aux, -ales [plyvjal, -o] *adj* pluvial; **eau pluviale** rainwater

pluvieux, -euse [plyvjø, -øz] *adj* rainy, wet

PME [peɛmə] *nf (abrév* **petite et moyenne entreprise**) small business

PMI [peɛmi] *nf (abrév* **petite et moyenne industrie**) small industrial firm

PMU [peɛmy] *nm (abrév* **Pari mutuel urbain**) = state-run betting system

PNB [peɛnbe] *nm (abrév* **produit national brut**) GNP

pneu [pnø] *nm* (a) *(de véhicule)* tire; **avoir un p. à plat/crevé** to have a flat/a puncture; **p. à clous, p. clouté** studded tire; *Can* **p. d'hiver** winter tire; **p. neige** snow tire; **p. pluie** wet-weather tire; *Can* **p. quatre-saisons** all-season tire (b) *(lettre)* express letter *(sent through a pneumatic dispatch system)*

pneumatique [pnømatik] **1** *adj (qui fonctionne à l'air)* pneumatic; *(gonflable)* inflatable
2 *nm* = pneu

pneumonie [pnømɔni] *nf* pneumonia

pneumothorax [pnømotɔraks] *nm* pneumothorax

poche [pɔʃ] nf (a) (de vêtement) pocket; **p. revolver** hip pocket; Fam **faire les poches à qn** to go through sb's pockets; **de p.** pocket; **en être de sa p., payer de sa p.** to pay out of one's own funds; Fig **connaître un endroit comme sa p.** to know a place like the back of one's hand; Fam Fig **se remplir les poches, s'en mettre plein les poches** to make a packet; **sans un sou en p.** without a penny in one's pocket; Fam **c'est dans la p.** it's in the bag (b) (sac) bag; **p. de glace** ice pack (c) (amas de substance) pocket; **p. de pétrole/gaz** pocket of oil/gas (d) (déformation) **poches sous les yeux** bags under the eyes; **son pantalon fait des poches aux genoux** his pants are baggy at the knees (e) (de kangourou) pouch (f) (zone) **p. de résistance/pauvreté** pocket of resistance/deprivation

pocher [pɔʃe] vt (a) (œuf, poisson) to poach (b) Fam **p. l'œil à qn** to give sb a black eye

pochette [pɔʃɛt] nf (a) (petit sac) (small) bag; (d'un disque) sleeve; (de photos) wallet; **p. d'allumettes** book of matches (b) (mouchoir) pocket handkerchief

pochette-surprise (pl **pochettes-surprises**) [pɔʃɛtsyrpriz] nf lucky bag; Fam **il a eu son permis dans une p.** it's a wonder he passed his driver's test

pochoir [pɔʃwar] nm stencil

podiatre [pɔdjatr] nmf Can podiatrist

podium [pɔdjɔm] nm podium; **monter sur le p.** to mount the podium

podomètre [pɔdɔmɛtr] nm pedometer

poêle¹ [pwal] nf frying pan; **passer qch à la p.** to fry sth

poêle² [pwal] nm (appareil de chauffage) stove; **p. à mazout** oil stove

poêlon [pwalɔ̃] nm casserole (dish)

poème [pɔɛm] nm poem; Fam **ta fille, c'est (tout) un p.!** your daughter's really something else!

poésie [pɔezi] nf (a) (art) poetry (b) (poème) poem

poète [pɔɛt] nm aussi Fig poet

poétesse [pɔetɛs] nf poetess

poétique [pɔetik] adj poetic

poétiquement [pɔetikmɑ̃] adv poetically

pogne [pɔɲ] nf Fam paw

pognon [pɔɲɔ̃] nm Fam dough

pogrom(e) [pɔgrɔm] nm pogrom

poids [pwa] nm (a) (masse) weight; **de tout son p.** with all one's weight; **perdre/prendre du p.** to lose/to gain weight; **vendre au p.** to sell by weight; Fam **il ne fait pas le p.** he's not up to scratch; **p. net/brut** net/gross weight; **p. léger** (en boxe) lightweight; **p. lourd** (camion) truck; (en boxe) heavyweight; **p. mouche** flyweight; **p. plume** (en boxe) featherweight; Fig lightweight (b) Fig (charge pénible) burden; Litt **le p. des ans** the weight of the years; **le p. des impôts** the burden of taxation (c) Fig (importance) weight; **donner du p. à qch** to give weight to sth; **avoir du p.** to carry weight; **faire deux poids deux mesures** to apply double standards (d) (sport) shot; **lancer le p.** to put the shot

poignant, -e [pwaɲɑ̃, -ɑ̃t] adj poignant

poignard [pwaɲar] nm dagger

poignarder [pwaɲarde] vt to stab; **se faire p.** to be stabbed

poigne [pwaɲ] nf grip; **avoir de la p.** to have a strong grip; Fig to be firm

poignée [pwaɲe] nf (a) (quantité, petit nombre) handful (b) (de porte, de sac) handle; (d'épée) hilt (c) **p. de main** handshake

poignet [pwaɲɛ] nm (a) (du bras) wrist; Fig **faire qch à la force du p.** to do sth by sheer hard work (b) (de chemise) cuff

poil [pwal] nm (a) (d'un animal, d'une personne, d'une plante) hair; (pelage) coat; (d'une brosse, d'un pinceau) bristle; **à p. long/ras** long-/short-haired; Fam **caresser qn dans le sens du p.** to rub sb the right way; Fam **tomber sur le p. à qn** to lay into sb; Fam **à p.** stark naked; Fam **se mettre à p.** to strip; Fam **avoir un p. dans la main** to be bone idle; Fam **re-**

prendre du p. de la bête to pick up again; Fam Fig **de tous poils** of all sorts; Fam **être de bon/mauvais p.** to be in a good/bad mood; Fam **au quart de p.** perfectly; Fam **à un p. près** very nearly; Fam **un p. plus haut/moins vite** a touch higher/slower; Fam **au p.** great; Fam **tomber au p.** to arrive at just the right moment (b) **p. à gratter** itching powder

poiler [pwale] **se poiler** vpr Fam to kill oneself laughing

poilu, -e [pwaly] **1** adj hairy
2 nm Fam poilu (French soldier in the 1914-1918 war)

poinçon [pwɛ̃sɔ̃] nm (de graveur) style; (de cordonnier) awl; (marque) hallmark

poinçonner [pwɛ̃sɔne] vt (perforer) to punch; (or, argent) to hallmark

poinçonneur, -euse [pwɛ̃sɔnœr, -øz] **1** nm,f (personne) ticket puncher
2 nf **poinçonneuse** punching machine

poindre [43] [pwɛ̃dr] vi (jour) to dawn, to break; (plantes, étoiles) to appear

poing [pwɛ̃] nm fist; **sabre/revolver au p.** sword/revolver in hand; **les poings sur les hanches** hands on hips, arms akimbo; **dormir à poings fermés** to sleep like a log

point¹ [pwɛ̃] nm (a) (endroit) point, spot; (en géométrie) point; **les quatre points cardinaux** the (four) points of the compass; Ordinat **p. de césure** breakpoint, hyphenation point; **p. chaud** (zone de conflits) hot spot, trouble spot; Ordinat (pour accès WiFi) hotspot; **p. de côté** (douleur) stitch; aussi Fig **p. de départ** starting point; **p. d'eau** (dans le désert) waterhole; **p. de mire** target; Fig focus; Aut **p. mort** neutral; Fig **être au p. mort** to be at a standstill; **p. noir** (comédon) blackhead; (embouteillage) troublespot; **p. de rencontre** meeting point; **p. de vente** (magasin) point of sale, sales outlet; **p. de vue** (panorama) viewpoint; (opinion) point of view; **du p. de vue international/économique** from an international/economic point of view

(b) (marque) dot; (en fin de ligne) period; Fig **mettre les points sur les i (à qn)** to make oneself perfectly clear (to sb); Typ & Ordinat **points par pouce** dots per inch; **deux points** colon; **p. d'exclamation** exclamation point; **p. final** period; Fam **un p., c'est tout!, p. final!** and that's that!; aussi Fig **p. d'interrogation** question mark; **points de suspension** suspension points; Ordinat **p. de tabulation** tab marker

(c) (aspect, question) point; **en tous points** in every way, in all respects; **p. faible/fort** weak/strong point

(d) (de couture, de tricot) stitch; **p. de croix** cross-stitch; **p. mousse** garter stitch

(e) (phase, degré) point, stage; **traiter un problème en trois points** to deal with a problem in three stages; **(cuit) à p.** done to a turn; (steak) medium-rare; **jusqu'à un certain p.** to a certain extent, up to a (certain) point; **au p. où j'en suis...** at the stage I've reached...; **à tel p. que..., au p. que...** to such an extent that..., so much so that...; **vous n'êtes pas malade à ce p.-là** you're not as ill as all that; **au plus haut p.** extremely

(f) (dans le temps) point; **être sur le p. de faire qch** to be about to do sth, to be on the point of doing sth; **arriver à p. nommé** to arrive just at the right moment

(g) (dans un score, dans un pourcentage) point; (dans une notation) grade; **bon p.** Scol ≃ gold star; Fig brownie point

(h) **mettre au p.** (objectif) to focus; (moteur) to tune; (technique) to perfect; (stratégie) to finalize; **être au p.** to be up to scratch

(i) Naut & Aviat **faire le p.** to take one's bearings; Fig to take stock; Fig **faire le p. sur qch** to take stock of sth

point² [pwɛ̃] adv Vieilli = **pas²**

pointage [pwɛ̃taʒ] nm (a) (contrôle) (de noms sur une liste) checking off; (de votes) counting; (au travail) (à l'arrivée) clocking in; (au départ) clocking out (b) (d'un télescope) pointing; (de fusil) aiming

pointe [pwɛ̃t] nf (**a**) (extrémité) (d'aiguille, de couteau) point; (de flèche) tip; (de balle) nose; (de chaussure) toe; (de sein) nipple; **p. d'asperge** asparagus tip; **en p.** pointed; **sur la p. des pieds** on tiptoe; **entrer sur la p. des pieds** to tiptoe in; **faire des pointes** (en danse) to go up on points

(**b**) (maximum) peak; **p. de vitesse** burst of speed; **faire une p. de vitesse** to put on a burst of speed; **vitesse de p.** top speed

(**c**) (summum) **être à la p. de la technique/de la recherche** to be at the cutting edge of technology/of research; **de p.** (secteur, industrie, technique) state-of-the-art

(**d**) (petite quantité) (d'accent, d'ironie) hint; (d'ail, de vanille) dash

(**e**) (raillerie) dig; **lancer des pointes à qn** to make digs at sb

(**f**) (clou) nail; (pour tapis) tack; (sur une chaussure de sport) spike; **chaussures à pointes** spiked shoes

pointer[1] [pwɛ̃te] **1** vt (**a**) (vérifier) (noms sur une liste) to check off; (votes) to count (**b**) (dresser) **p. les oreilles** to prick up its ears (**c**) (diriger) (télescope) to point (**sur** at); (fusil) to aim (**sur** at); (Ordinat (curseur) to position (**sur** on); **j'ai pointé le doigt vers lui** I pointed (my finger) at him

2 vi (**a**) (au travail) (à l'arrivée) to clock in; (à la sortie) to clock out; **p. à l'ANPE** ou **au chômage** to register as unemployed (**b**) (apparaître) (plante) to come up; (jour) to dawn (**c**) (se dresser) (clocher, tour, arbre) to rise (**d**) (au jeu de boules) to get one's ball nearest to the jack

3 se pointer vpr Fam to show up

pointer[2] [pwɛ̃tɛr] nm (chien) pointer

pointeur, -euse [pwɛ̃tœr, -øz] **1** nm,f (contrôleur) timekeeper; (en sport) scorer

2 nm Ordinat pointer

3 nf **pointeuse** (machine) timeclock

pointillé [pwɛ̃tije] nm (**a**) (trait) dotted line; (sur une feuille détachable) perforations; **découper suivant les pointillés** cut along the dotted line; **les frontières sont en p. sur la carte** the frontiers are drawn as dotted lines on the map (**b**) (technique de dessin) stippling

pointilleux, -euse [pwɛ̃tijø, -øz] adj particular, fussy (**sur** about)

pointu, -e [pwɛ̃ty] **1** adj (**a**) (en forme de pointe) pointed; (voix) shrill (**b**) Fig (susceptible) (ton de la voix, humeur) touchy (**c**) (accent) Parisian (**d**) Fig (spécialisé) specialized

2 adv **parler p.** to speak with a Parisian accent

pointure [pwɛ̃tyr] nf size; Fam Fig **une (grosse) p. du cinéma français** a big name in French cinema

point-virgule (pl **points-virgules**) [pwɛ̃virgyl] nm semicolon

poire [pwar] nf (**a**) (fruit) pear; Fig **couper la p. en deux** to meet each other halfway; (faire la moyenne entre deux quantités) to split the difference (**b**) (objet en forme de poire) (d'un appareil photo) bulb; (interrupteur) switch (**c**) Fam (tête) mug; **en pleine p.** right in the face (**d**) Fam (idiot) sucker; **et moi, bonne p., j'ai accepté** and like the sucker I am, I accepted

poireau, -x [pwaro] nm leek; Fam **faire le p.** to hang around

poireauter [pwarote] vi Fam to hang around

poirier [pwarje] nm (**a**) (arbre) pear tree; **faire le p.** to do a headstand, to stand on one's head (**b**) (bois) pear-tree wood

pois [pwa] nm (**a**) (plante) pea; **petit p.** (garden) pea; **p. cassés** split peas; **p. chiche** garbanzo (bean); **p. de senteur** sweet pea (**b**) (rond) (polka) dot; **à p.** polka-dot

poison [pwazɔ̃] **1** nm poison

2 nmf Fam (personne) pest

poisse [pwas] nf Fam bad luck

poisseux, -euse [pwasø, -øz] adj sticky

poisson [pwasɔ̃] nm (**a**) (animal) fish; **p. d'eau douce/de mer** freshwater/saltwater fish; Prov **petit p. deviendra grand** ≃ great oaks from little acorns grow; **p. d'argent**

silverfish; **p. d'avril** April fool; **p. rouge** goldfish; **p. volant** flying fish (**b**) Astron & Astrol **les Poissons** Pisces; **être Poissons** to be (a) Pisces

poisson-chat (pl **poissons-chats**) [pwasɔ̃ʃa] nm catfish

poissonnerie [pwasɔnri] nf fish store

poissonneux, -euse [pwasɔnø, -øz] adj full of fish

poissonnier, -ère [pwasɔnje, -ɛr] nm,f fish merchant

poitevin, -e [pwatvɛ̃, -in] adj (de Poitiers) of Poitiers; (du Poitou) of Poitou

poitrail [pwatraj] nm (d'animal) breast; Fam (poitrine) chest

poitrinaire [pwatrinɛr] adj & nmf Vieilli consumptive

poitrine [pwatrin] nf (**a**) (thorax) chest; (seins) bust; **serrer qn contre sa p.** to hold sb to one's breast; **ne pas avoir beaucoup de p.** to have a small bust (**b**) Culin (de veau) breast; (de bœuf) brisket; (de porc) belly

poivre [pwavr] nm pepper; **p. en grains** peppercorns; **p. et sel** (cheveux, barbe) pepper-and-salt

poivré, -e [pwavre] adj (**a**) (nourriture, odeur) peppery (**b**) Fig (histoire) spicy

poivrer [pwavre] **1** vt to put pepper on/in

2 se poivrer vpr Fam to get plastered

poivrier [pwavrije] nm (**a**) (plante) pepper plant (**b**) (petit pot) pepper pot; (moulin) pepper mill

poivron [pwavrɔ̃] nm bell pepper

poivrot, -e [pwavro, -ɔt] nm,f Fam drunk

poix [pwa] nf pitch

poker [pɔkɛr] nm poker

polaire [pɔlɛr] adj (faune, expédition) polar; (froid) Arctic; **laine p.** fleece, fleecy material

polar [pɔlar] nm Fam whodunnit

polarisation [pɔlarizasjɔ̃] nf (**a**) Phys polarization (**b**) Fig (focalisation) focusing

polariser [pɔlarize] **1** vt Phys to polarize; Fig (attention) to focus

2 se polariser vpr **se p. sur** to focus on

Polaroid® [pɔlarɔid] nm Polaroid® (camera)

pôle [pol] nm (**a**) Géog pole; **p. Nord/Sud** North/South Pole (**b**) Fig **p. d'intérêt** focus of interest; **p. d'attraction** center of attention

polémique [pɔlemik] **1** adj polemical

2 nf controversy; **une vive p. s'ensuivit** a heated debate ensued

polémiquer [pɔlemike] vi to debate

poli[1]**, -e** [pɔli] adj (lisse) polished

poli[2]**, -e** [pɔli] adj (courtois) polite (**avec** to)

police[1] [pɔlis] nf (**a**) (maintien de l'ordre) policing; **faire la p.** to keep order (**b**) (institution) **la p.** the police; **la p. est prévenue** the police have been called; **appeler p. secours** to call the police (in an emergency); **être de** ou **dans la p.** to be in the police; **p. de l'air et des frontières** airport and border police; **p. judiciaire** police investigation department; **p. mondaine** ou **des mœurs** vice squad; **p. montée** mounted police; **p. municipale** local police; **la p. nationale** the national police force; **p. secrète** secret police

police² [pɔlis] *nf* (**a**) *(d'assurance)* policy; **p. d'assurance** insurance policy (**b**) *Ordinat* **p. (de caractères)** font; **p. bitmap** *ou* **pixélisée** bitmap font; **p. de taille variable** scalable font; **p. vectorielle** outline font

polichinelle [pɔliʃinɛl] *nm* (**a**) *(marionnette)* Punch (**b**) *Fig & Péj* buffoon

policier, -ère [pɔlisje, -ɛr] **1** *adj (enquête, État, régime)* police; *(roman, film)* detective
  2 *nm* (**a**) *(personne)* policeman, police officer; **femme p.** policewoman, woman police officer (**b**) *(roman)* detective novel; *(film)* detective movie

policlinique [pɔliklinik] *nf* outpatients' clinic

poliment [pɔlimã] *adv* politely

polio [pɔljo] **1** *nf* polio; **avoir la p.** to have polio
  2 *nmf* polio victim

poliomyélite [pɔljɔmjelit] *nf* poliomyelitis

polir [pɔlir] *vt* to polish

polisson, -onne [pɔlisɔ̃, -ɔn] **1** *nm,f (enfant espiègle)* rascal
  2 *adj* (**a**) *(espiègle)* naughty (**b**) *(grivois)* saucy

politesse [pɔlitɛs] *nf* politeness; **par p.** out of politeness; **ce serait la moindre des politesses de le prévenir** it's only polite to warn him; **rendre la p. à qn** to return sb's favor

politicien, -enne [pɔlitisjɛ̃, -ɛn] **1** *nm,f* politician
  2 *adj Péj* **politique politicienne** politicking

politique [pɔlitik] **1** *adj* political
  2 *nf* (**a**) *(de gouvernement, d'entreprise)* policy; **p. intérieure/extérieure** domestic/foreign policy; **la p. du pire** = the policy of threatening disaster in order to achieve one's objectives; **la p. agricole commune** the Common Agricultural Policy (**b**) *(affaires publiques)* politics; **faire de la p.** *(en tant que politicien)* to be in politics; *(en tant que militant)* to be involved in politics
  3 *nm (personne)* politician

politiquement [pɔlitikmã] *adv* politically

politisation [pɔlitizasjɔ̃] *nf* politicization

politiser [pɔlitize] *vt* to politicize

politologue [pɔlitɔlɔg] *nmf* political scientist

polka [pɔlka] *nf* polka

pollen [pɔlɛn] *nm* pollen

polluant, -e [pɔlɥã, -ãt] **1** *adj* polluting; **produit p.** pollutant
  2 *nm* pollutant

pollué, -e [pɔlɥe] *adj* polluted

polluer [pɔlɥe] *vt* to pollute

pollueur, -euse [pɔlɥœr, -øz] **1** *nm,f* polluter
  2 *adj* polluting

pollution [pɔlysjɔ̃] *nf* pollution

polo [pɔlo] *nm* (**a**) *(sport)* polo (**b**) *(chemise)* polo shirt

polochon [pɔlɔʃɔ̃] *nm Fam* bolster; **bataille de polochons** pillow fight

Pologne [pɔlɔɲ] *nf* **la P.** Poland

polonais, -e [pɔlɔnɛ, -ɛz] **1** *adj* Polish
  2 *nm (langue)* Polish
  3 *nm,f* **P., Polonaise** Pole
  4 *nf* **polonaise** *(danse)* polonaise

poltron, -onne [pɔltrɔ̃, -ɔn] **1** *adj* cowardly
  2 *nm,f* coward

polyamide [pɔliamid] *nm* polyamide

polychrome [pɔlikrom] *adj* polychrome

polyclinique [pɔliklinik] *nf* polyclinic

polycopie [pɔlikɔpi] *nf (procédé)* duplication; *(document)* duplicate

polycopié, -e [pɔlikɔpje] **1** *adj* duplicated
  2 *nm* duplicate; *Scol & Univ* duplicated course material

polycopier [66] [pɔlikɔpje] *vt* to duplicate

polyculture [pɔlikyltyr] *nf* mixed farming

polyester [pɔliɛstɛr] *nm* polyester

polygame [pɔligam] **1** *adj* polygamous
  2 *nm* polygamist

polygamie [pɔligami] *nf* polygamy

polyglotte [pɔliglɔt] *adj & nmf* polyglot

polygone [pɔligon, pɔligɔn] *nm* (**a**) *(figure)* polygon (**b**) *Mil* **p. de tir** shooting range

polymère [pɔlimɛr] **1** *adj* polymeric
  2 *nm* polymer

Polynésie [pɔlinezi] *nf* **la P.** Polynesia; **la P. française** French Polynesia

polynésien, -enne [pɔlinezjɛ̃, -ɛn] **1** *adj* Polynesian
  2 *nm,f* **P., Polynésienne** Polynesian

polype [pɔlip] *nm* polyp

polyphonie [pɔlifɔni] *nf* polyphony

polysémique [pɔlisemik] *adj* polysemous

polystyrène [pɔlistirɛn] *nm* polystyrene

polytechnicien, -enne [pɔlitɛknisjɛ̃, -ɛn] *nm,f* graduate of the "École polytechnique"

Polytechnique [pɔlitɛknik] *nf* **(l'École) p., P.** = "grande école" specializing in technology

---

École polytechnique

Founded in 1794, this prestigious engineering college has close connections with the Department of Defense. Formerly situated in the heart of the 5th arrondissement, the college moved to Palaiseau, near Paris, in the 1970s. It is popularly known as "l'X". Students are effectively enlisted in the army and must repay their education through government service.

---

polythéisme [pɔliteism] *nm* polytheism

polyvalence [pɔlivalãs] *nf (en chimie)* polyvalency; *Fig (d'une personne)* versatility

polyvalent, -e [pɔlivalã, -ãt] **1** *adj* (**a**) *(en chimie)* polyvalent (**b**) *(salle)* multi-purpose; *(outil, personne)* versatile
  2 *nm* tax inspector

pomélo [pomelo] *nm* pomelo

pommade [pɔmad] *nf* ointment; *Fam* **passer de la p. à qn** to butter sb up

pomme [pɔm] *nf* (**a**) *(fruit)* apple; *Fam* **haut comme trois pommes** knee-high to a grasshopper; *Fam* **tomber dans les pommes** to pass out; *Fam* **être dans les pommes** to be out for the count; **p. d'Adam** Adam's apple; **p. de discorde** bone of contention; **p. de pin** pine cone; *(de sapin)* fir cone
  (**b**) *(partie arrondie)* *(de bois de lit, de canne)* knob; *(d'arrosoir)* rose; **p. de douche** shower head
  (**c**) *(pomme de terre)* **pommes allumettes** matchstick potatoes; **pommes chips** (potato) chips; **pommes dauphine** dauphine potatoes; **p. de terre** potato; **pommes (de terre) à l'eau** boiled potatoes; **pommes (de terre) frites** (French) fries; **pommes (de terre) sautées** sauté potatoes; **pommes vapeur** steamed potatoes
  (**d**) *Fam (personne)* **ma p.** yours truly; **ta p.** you; **sa p.** him/her
  (**e**) *Fam (idiot)* sucker; **être bonne p.** to be a sucker

pommeau, -x [pomo] *nm (d'un sabre, d'une selle)* pommel; *(d'une canne, d'un levier de vitesse)* knob

pommelé, -e [pɔmle] *adj* dappled; **gris p.** *(cheval)* dapple-gray; **ciel p.** mackerel sky

pommer [pome] *vi (chou, salade)* to form a heart

pommeraie [pɔmrɛ] *nf* apple orchard

pommette [pɔmɛt] *nf* cheekbone

pommier [pɔmje] *nm* apple tree; **p. sauvage** crab-apple tree

pompage [pɔ̃paʒ] *nm* pumping

pompe¹ [pɔ̃p] *nf (cérémonie)* pomp, ceremony; **en grande p.** with great (pomp and) ceremony

pompe² [pɔ̃p] nf (**a**) (machine) pump; **p. à essence** (distributeur) gas pump; (station-service) gas station; **p. à incendie** water pump (on a fire engine); **p. à vélo** bicycle pump; Fam **à toute p.** like lightning; Fam **faire des pompes** to do push-ups (**b**) Fam **pompes** (chaussures) shoes; Fig **il est à côté de ses pompes** he's not with it (**c**) **pompes funèbres** undertaker's, funeral home

pomper [pɔ̃pe] **1** vt (**a**) (puiser) (eau, air) to pump; (faire monter) to pump up; (évacuer) to pump out; Fam Fig **p. qn** (épuiser) to wear sb out; Fam **être pompé** to be pooped; Fam **tu me pompes l'air** you're getting on my nerves (**b**) Fam (boisson) to knock back (**c**) Fam Scol to copy, to crib (**sur** from)
2 vi (**a**) (faire marcher une pompe) to pump (**b**) Fam Scol to copy, to crib (**sur** from)

pompette [pɔ̃pɛt] adj Fam tipsy

pompeux, -euse [pɔ̃pø, -øz] adj Péj pompous

pompier¹ [pɔ̃pje] nm firefighter; **appeler les pompiers** to call the fire department

pompier², -ère [pɔ̃pje, -ɛr] adj Péj (style) pompous

pompiste [pɔ̃pist] nmf gas-station attendant

pom-pom girl [pɔmpɔmgœrl] nf cheerleader

pompon [pɔ̃pɔ̃] nm pompom, bobble; **bonnet à p.** bobble hat; Fam **c'est le p.!** that's the limit!

pomponner [pɔ̃pɔne] **se pomponner** vpr Fam to doll oneself up

ponce [pɔ̃s] adj voir **pierre**

poncer [16] [pɔ̃se] vt (**a**) (au papier de verre, avec une ponceuse) to sand (down) (**b**) (passer à la pierre ponce) to pumice

ponceuse [pɔ̃søz] nf sander

poncho [pɔ̃tʃo] nm poncho

poncif [pɔ̃sif] nm cliché, commonplace

ponction [pɔ̃ksjɔ̃] nf Méd puncture; (de poumon) tapping; **p. lombaire** lumbar puncture; Fig **faire des ponctions dans ses économies** to draw on one's savings; **p. fiscale** taxation

ponctualité [pɔ̃ktɥalite] nf punctuality

ponctuation [pɔ̃ktɥasjɔ̃] nf punctuation

ponctuel, -elle [pɔ̃ktɥɛl] adj (**a**) (à l'heure) punctual (**b**) (unique) one-of-a-kind; (isolé) selective

ponctuellement [pɔ̃ktɥɛlmɑ̃] adv (de façon limitée) on a one-of-a-kind basis

ponctuer [pɔ̃ktɥe] vt aussi Fig to punctuate (**de** with)

pondaison [pɔ̃dɛzɔ̃] nf egg-laying time

pondérale [pɔ̃deral] adj f voir **surcharge**

pondération [pɔ̃derasjɔ̃] nf (**a**) (modération) level-headedness (**b**) Écon weighting

pondéré, -e [pɔ̃dere] adj (**a**) (personne) level-headed (**b**) Écon weighted

pondeuse [pɔ̃døz] adj f & nf (**poule**) **p.** layer

pondre [pɔ̃dr] vt (**a**) (œuf) to lay (**b**) Fam (produire) to turn out

poney [pɔnɛ] nm pony

pont [pɔ̃] nm (**a**) (sur un cours d'eau) bridge; **les Ponts et Chaussées** ≃ the Highways Department; Fig **faire un p. d'or à qn** to offer sb a generous bonus (upon starting a job); **p. suspendu** suspension bridge (**b**) Fig (congés) long weekend; **le p. du premier mai** the May Day long weekend; **faire le p.** to make a long weekend of it (**c**) (d'un navire) deck; **sur le p.** on deck (**d**) (lien) **couper les ponts (avec qn)** to break off all relations (with sb); **p. aérien** airlift; Ordinat **p. routeur** routing node (**e**) Ind **p. roulant** traveling crane

pontage [pɔ̃taʒ] nm Méd bypass (operation)

ponte¹ [pɔ̃t] nf (action) (egg) laying; (œufs) eggs (laid)

ponte² [pɔ̃t] nm Fam (**grand**) **p.** (personnage important) big shot

pontife [pɔ̃tif] nm Rel pontiff; **le souverain p.** the Supreme Pontiff

pontifiant, -e [pɔ̃tifjɑ̃, -ɑ̃t] adj Péj pontificating

pontifical, -e, -aux, -ales [pɔ̃tifikal, -o] adj papal

pontifier [66] [pɔ̃tifje] vi to pontificate

pont-l'évêque [pɔ̃levɛk] nm inv Pont-l'Évêque (cheese)

pont-levis (pl **ponts-levis**) [pɔ̃ləvi] nm drawbridge

ponton [pɔ̃tɔ̃] nm pontoon

pop [pɔp] adj inv & nf pop

pop-corn [pɔpkɔrn] nm inv popcorn

pope [pɔp] nm Rel (Orthodox) priest

popeline [pɔplin] nf poplin

popote [pɔpɔt] **1** nf (**a**) Fam (cuisine) cooking; **faire la p.** to cook, do the cooking (**b**) Mil officers' mess
2 adj inv Fam stay-at-home

popotin [pɔpɔtɛ̃] nm Fam butt

populace [pɔpylas] nf rabble, mob

populaire [pɔpylɛr] adj (**a**) (du peuple, qui plaît) popular (**b**) (langue, expression) vernacular (**c**) (ouvrier) working-class; **les classes populaires** the working classes

populariser [pɔpylarize] vt to popularize

popularité [pɔpylarite] nf popularity

population [pɔpylasjɔ̃] nf population; **p. active** working population

populeux, -euse [pɔpylø, -øz] adj crowded

populisme [pɔpylism] nm populism

populo [pɔpylo] nm Fam (foule) crowd (of people)

pop-up [pɔpœp] n Ordinat (publicité) pop-up (ad)

porc [pɔr] nm (**a**) (animal) pig, hog; Fig (homme grossier ou sale) pig (**b**) (viande) pork (**c**) (cuir) pigskin

porcelaine [pɔrsəlɛn] nf (matière) porcelain, china; (objet) piece of porcelain; **une tasse de** ou **en p.** a porcelain or china cup

porcelet [pɔrsəlɛ] nm piglet

porc-épic (pl **porcs-épics**) [pɔrkepik] nm porcupine

porche [pɔrʃ] nm porch

porcherie [pɔrʃəri] nf aussi Fig pigpen

porcin, -e [pɔrsɛ̃, -in] **1** adj pig; Péj (visage, yeux) piggy
2 nmpl **porcins** pigs, hogs

pore [pɔr] nm pore; **elle sue la suffisance par tous les pores** she exudes or oozes self-importance

poreux, -euse [pɔrø, -øz] adj porous

porno [pɔrno] adj & nm Fam porn

pornographie [pɔrnɔgrafi] nf pornography

pornographique [pɔrnɔgrafik] adj pornographic

port¹ [pɔr] nm (**a**) (pour bateaux) harbor; (plus important) port; Fig **arriver à bon p.** to arrive safe and sound; **p. d'attache** home port; Fig home base; **p. de commerce** commercial port; **p. de pêche** fishing port; **p. de plaisance** marina (**b**) Ordinat port; **p. de communication** comms port, communications port; **p. d'entrée/sortie** input/output port; **p. d'E/S** I/O port; **p. d'extension** expansion port; **p. modem** modem port; **p. parallèle** parallel port; **p. série** serial port; **p. souris** mouse port

port² [pɔr] nm (**a**) (fait de transporter) carrying; **p. d'armes** carrying of firearms (**b**) (fait de revêtir) wearing; **le p. du casque est obligatoire** (sur panneau) safety helmets must be worn (**c**) (de marchandises) carriage; (de paquets, de lettres, de télégrammes) delivery; **p. et emballage** postage and packing; **p. franc** (de marchandises) carriage paid; **p. payé** (de magazine) postage paid (**d**) (allure) bearing; **elle a un p. de tête très gracieux** she holds her head very gracefully

portabilité [pɔrtabilite] nf Ordinat portability

portable [pɔrtabl] **1** adj (**a**) (ordinateur, machine à écrire) portable; (téléphone) cellular (**b**) (vêtement) wearable
2 nm (ordinateur) laptop, portable; (téléphone) cell(phone)

portage [pɔrtaʒ] nm Can portage

portager [45] [pɔrtaʒe] vi Can to portage

portail [pɔrtaj] nm aussi Ordinat portal

portant, -e [pɔrtã, -ãt] *adj* **être bien/mal p.** to be in good/poor health

portatif, -ive [pɔrtatif, -iv] *adj* portable

Port-au-Prince [pɔrɔprɛ̃s] *n* Port-au-Prince

porte [pɔrt] *nf* (**a**) *(de maison, de placard, de véhicule)* door; **à ma p.** on my doorstep; **de p. à p.** door to door; *Fig* **entre deux portes** briefly; **mettre qn à la p.** to throw sb out; *(d'un emploi)* to fire sb; **trouver p. close** to find nobody in; *Fam* **ce n'est pas la p. à côté** it's hardly just around the corner; **c'est la p. ouverte à...** it's leaving the door wide open to...; **(voiture) deux/quatre/cinq portes** two-/four-/five-door car; **p. cochère** carriage entrance; **p. de derrière** back door; **p. d'entrée**, *Belg* **p. de rue** front door; **p. tournante, p. à tambour** revolving door; **p. vitrée** glass door (**b**) *(d'une ville)* gate; **aux portes du désert** at the gateway to the desert; **p. (d'embarquement)** *(dans un aéroport)* (boarding) gate

porté, -e [pɔrte] *adj (enclin)* **être p. à faire qch** to be inclined to do sth; *Fam* **être p. sur la bouteille** to be fond of the bottle; *Fam* **être p. sur la chose** to have a one-track mind

porte-à-faux [pɔrtafo] **en porte-à-faux** *adv* overhanging; *Fig* **être en p.** to be awkwardly placed

porte-à-porte [pɔrtapɔrt] *nm* door-to-door selling; **faire du p.** *(pour vendre)* to sell from door to door; *(faire des enquêtes)* to go from door to door

porte-avions [pɔrtavjɔ̃] *nm inv* aircraft carrier

porte-bagages [pɔrtbaga3] *nm inv* (de bicyclette) carrier; *(de train)* luggage rack

porte-bébé *(pl* **porte-bébés)** [pɔrtbebe] *nm* baby carrier

porte-bonheur [pɔrtbɔnœr] *nm inv* (lucky) charm

porte-bouteilles [pɔrtbutɛj] *nm inv (pour stocker)* wine rack; *(pour porter)* bottle-carrier

porte-cartes [pɔrtəkart] *nm inv (portefeuille)* billfold *(with spaces for credit cards etc.)*

porte-cigarettes [pɔrtsigarɛt] *nm inv* cigarette case

porte-clefs, porte-clés [pɔrtəkle] *nm inv* key ring

porte-documents [pɔrtdɔkymã] *nm inv* briefcase

porte-drapeau *(pl* **porte-drapeaux** *ou* **porte-drapeau)** [pɔrtdrapo] *nm aussi Fig* standard bearer

portée [pɔrte] *nf* (**a**) *(petits)* litter; *(d'une truie)* farrow (**b**) *(amplitude) (d'un fusil, d'un émetteur, de la voix)* range; *Fig (d'un traité)* scope; **à p. de (la) main** within reach, to hand; **à p. de (la) voix** within earshot; **à la p. de toutes les bourses** within everyone's means; **c'est à ma p.** *(objet)* it's within my reach; *Fig (livre)* I can understand it; **hors de ma p.** *(objet)* beyond my reach; *Fig (livre)* beyond me; **hors de p.** out of reach (**c**) *Fig (impact) (de paroles, d'une décision)* significance (**d**) *Mus* stave

portefaix [pɔrtəfɛ] *nm* porter

porte-fenêtre *(pl* **portes-fenêtres)** [pɔrtfənɛtr] *nf* French window

portefeuille [pɔrtəfœj] *nm* (**a**) *(pour l'argent)* wallet, billfold; **faire un lit en p.** to make an apple-pie bed; **jupe p.** wrapover skirt (**b**) *Fin & Pol* portfolio; **p. d'actions/de titres** share/securities portfolio

porte-jarretelles [pɔrtʒartɛl] *nm inv* garter belt

porte-malheur [pɔrtmalœr] *nm inv* jinx

portemanteau, -x [pɔrtmãto] *nm (au mur)* coat rack; *(sur pied)* coat stand

portemine [pɔrtəmin] *nm* mechanical pencil

porte-monnaie [pɔrtmɔnɛ] *nm inv* purse; **p. électronique** electronic wallet

porte-parapluies [pɔrtparaplɥi] *nm inv* umbrella stand

porte-parole [pɔrtparɔl] *nm inv* spokesperson, spokesman, *f* spokeswoman

porte-plume [pɔrtəplym] *nm inv* penholder

porter [pɔrte] **1** *vt* (**a**) *(soutenir)* to carry; **mes jambes ne me portent plus** my legs won't carry me any further; **je ne le**

porte pas dans mon cœur he's not exactly my favorite person

(**b**) *(emporter)* to take; *(amener)* to bring

(**c**) *(vêtement, chapeau, lunettes)* to wear; *(signature, date)* to bear; *(prénom, nom)* to have; **p. une moustache/la barbe** to have a mustache/a beard; **p. les cheveux courts/longs** to wear one's hair short/long, to have short/long hair; **p. le nom de qn** to be named after sb; **p. le titre de...** *(livre, film)* to be entitled...

(**d**) *(produire) (fruits)* to bear

(**e**) *(diriger)* **p. un coup à qn** to strike sb; **p. la main à son front** to hold one's hand to one's forehead; **p. son attention sur qch** to turn one's attention to sth, to give sth one's attention; **p. une affaire devant les tribunaux** to bring a matter to court; **p. qch à la connaissance de qn** to bring sth to sb's attention

(**f**) *(inscrire)* to enter; **se faire p. malade** to report sick

(**g**) *(inciter)* **tout (me) porte à croire que...** everything leads me to believe that...

(**h**) *(à un niveau plus élevé)* **p. la température à 100°** to raise the temperature to 100°; **portez le liquide à ébullition** bring the liquid to the boil; **cela portera à 100 euros le prix du billet** that will bring the price of the ticket up to 100 euros

2 *vi* (**a**) *(cogner)* **p. sur/contre qch** to hit sth

(**b**) *(atteindre son objectif) (coup)* to strike home, to hit its target; *(voix)* to carry

3 porter sur *vt ind* (**a**) *(avoir pour sujet)* to be about

(**b**) *Fam* **p. sur les nerfs à qn** to get on sb's nerves

4 se porter *vpr* (**a**) *(physiquement)* **se p. bien** to be well; **je ne m'en porte pas plus mal** I'm none the worse for it; *Hum* **moins je le vois, mieux je me porte** the less I see of him, the better I feel

(**b**) *(devoir être porté)* to be worn; *(être à la mode)* to be fashionable

(**c**) *(se présenter comme)* **se p. acquéreur de qch** to offer to buy sth; **se p. candidat** to run as a candidate; **se p. caution** to stand surety

(**d**) *(aller)* **se p. au secours de qn** to go to sb's assistance

(**e**) **se p. sur** *(sujet: regard, choix)* to fall on

porte-savon *(pl* **porte-savons** *ou* **porte-savon)** [pɔrtsavɔ̃] *nm* soapdish

porte-serviettes [pɔrtsɛrvjɛt] *nm inv* towel rail

porteur, -euse [pɔrtœr, -øz] **1** *nm,f* (**a**) *(d'un message, de nouvelles)* bearer; **par p.** by messenger (**b**) *(de gare, d'aéroport)* porter; **p. d'eau** water carrier (**c**) *Méd* carrier; **p. sain** = carrier who doesn't have the symptoms of the disease (**d**) *(détenteur)* holder; *(d'un chèque)* bearer; **payable au p.** payable to bearer

2 *adj* (**a**) *Élec* **fréquence/onde porteuse** carrier frequency/wave (**b**) *(marché, créneau)* growth

porte-voix [pɔrtəvwa] *nm inv* megaphone; *(électrique)* bullhorn; **mettre ses mains en p.** to cup one's hands around one's mouth

portier [pɔrtje] *nm* doorkeeper; *(dans un hôtel)* doorman; **p. de nuit** night clerk

portière [pɔrtjɛr] *nf (d'une voiture, d'un train)* door

portillon [pɔrtijɔ̃] *nm* gate; *(d'un passage à niveau)* side gate; **p. (automatique)** *(de gare, de métro)* ticket barrier

portion [pɔrsjɔ̃] *nf* portion; **être réduit à la p. congrue** to get the smallest share

portique [pɔrtik] *nm* (**a**) *(colonnes)* portico (**b**) *(pour agrès)* (cross)beam

Porto [pɔrto] *n* Oporto

porto [pɔrto] *nm* port

portoricain, -e [pɔrtɔrikɛ̃, -ɛn] **1** *adj* Puerto Rican

2 *nm,f* **P., Portoricaine** Puerto Rican

Porto Rico [pɔrtoriko] *n* Puerto Rico

portrait [pɔrtrɛ] *nm* (**a**) *(peinture, dessin, photo)* portrait; **le p.** *(genre)* portrait painting, portraiture; **faire le p. de qn** to do a portrait of sb; *Fig* **c'est le p. vivant de son père, c'est tout le p. de son père** he's the spitting image of his father; *Fam* **il s'est fait abîmer** *ou* **arranger le p.** he got his face re-arranged; *Fam* **se faire tirer le p.** to have one's photo taken (**b**) *(description)* description; **faire le p. de qn/qch** to paint a picture of sb/sth (**c**) *Ordinat* **mode p.** portrait mode

portraitiste [pɔrtretist] *nmf* portrait painter, portraitist

portrait-robot (*pl* **portraits-robots**) [pɔrtrɛrɔbo] *nm* Identikit® picture; *Fig* profile

portuaire [pɔrtɥɛr] *adj* port, harbor

portugais, -e [pɔrtɥge, -ɛz] **1** *adj* Portuguese

2 *nm (langue)* Portuguese

3 *nm,f* **P., Portugaise** Portuguese

4 *nf* **portugaise** (**a**) *(huître)* Portuguese oyster (**b**) *Fam (oreille)* ear; **avoir les portugaises ensablées** to be as deaf as a post

Portugal [pɔrtɥgal] *nm* **le P.** Portugal

pose [poz] *nf* (**a**) *(de rideaux, de papier peint)* putting up, hang-ing; *(d'une vitre)* putting in; *(de moquette, de câbles)* laying; *(d'ap-pareils)* installation; *(d'une bombe)* planting; *Méd (d'un stérilet)* putting in; *(de ventouses)* application (**b**) *(pour photo, portrait)* pose; **prendre la p.** to pose; **garder la p.** to hold the pose; *Péj* **prendre des poses** to pose (**c**) *Phot* exposure; **pellicule de 24 poses** 24-exposure film

posé, -e [poze] *adj (réfléchi)* composed, calm

posément [pozemɑ̃] *adv* calmly

poser [poze] **1** *vt* (**a**) *(mettre)* to put down; **p. qch sur/sous qch** to put sth on/under sth; *Fig* **p. son regard sur qn/qch** to look at sb/sth

(**b**) *(formuler) (question)* to ask; *(hypothèse)* to put forward; *(principe)* to lay down; **p. une question à qn** to ask sb a ques-tion; **p. un problème à qn** to pose a problem for sb; **p. sa candidature** *(aux élections)* to run (as a candidate); *(à un poste)* to apply

(**c**) *(rideaux, papier peint)* to put up, to hang; *(vitre)* to put in; *(moquette, câble)* to lay; *(appareil)* to install; *(bombe)* to plant; *Méd* **p. qch à qn** *(stérilet)* to put sth in sb; *(ventouses)* to apply sth to sb

(**d**) *Math (opération, équation)* to set out; **je pose deux et je retiens un** put down two and carry one

(**e**) *Can (photographier)* to photograph, to take a photograph of

2 *vi (pour une photo, pour un tableau)* to pose; *Péj* **p. pour la galerie** to play to the gallery

3 se poser *vpr* (**a**) *(oiseau, avion)* to land; *Fig* **se p. sur** *(su-jet: regard)* to rest on

(**b**) *(question, problème)* to arise, to come up

(**c**) *(à soi-même)* **se p. des questions** to ask oneself ques-tions; *(avoir des doutes)* to have one's doubts

(**d**) *Fam* **comme bricoleur/cuisinier, il se pose un peu là!** some handyman/cook he is!; **comme enquiquineur, il se pose là!** he's a real pain in the neck!

(**e**) *(se prétendre)* **se p. en réformateur/redresseur de torts** to set oneself up as a reformer/a righter of wrongs

poseur, -euse [pozœr, -øz] *nm,f* (**a**) *(de câbles, de carrelage)* layer; **p. d'affiches** billsticker, billposter; **la police re-cherche les poseurs de bombes** the police are hunting the people who planted the bombs (**b**) *Péj (pédant)* show-off, po-seur

positif, -ive [pozitif, -iv] *adj* positive; **il est p.** *(à l'Alcotest, au contrôle antidopage)* his test result is positive

position [pozisjɔ̃] *nf* (**a**) *(emplacement)* position; **être en pre-mière/deuxième p.** *(dans une course)* to be in first/second place; *(sur une liste)* to be first/second; **arriver en pre-mière/deuxième p.** to come first/second (**b**) *(attitude, en danse)* position; **être/se mettre en p.** to be in/to get into po-sition; **en p. debout/assise** in a standing/sitting position (**c**) *(opinion)* position (**sur** on); **prendre p.** to take a stand; **rester**

sur ses positions to stand one's ground (**d**) *(situation)* posi-tion; **être en p. de faire qch** to be in a position to do sth; **p. sociale** social position

positionner [pozisjɔne] **1** *vt* to position

2 se positionner *vpr* to position oneself

positivement [pozitivmɑ̃] *adv* positively

positiver [3] [pozitive] *vi* to think positive

posologie [pozolɔʒi] *nf Méd* dosage

possédé, -e [posede] **1** *adj (du démon)* possessed

2 *nm,f* person possessed; **hurler comme un p.** to scream like one possessed

posséder [34] [posede] *vt* (**a**) *(biens matériels)* to possess, to own; *(talent, qualité)* to possess, to have (**b**) *(sujet)* to have a thorough knowledge of; *(langue, technique)* to have mastered (**c**) *(sujet: démon, passion)* to possess (**d**) *Fam (tromper)* to take in; **se faire p.** to be taken in (**e**) *Litt (femme)* to possess

possesseur [posesœr] *nm* owner; *(d'un titre)* holder

possessif, -ive [posesif, -iv] *adj & nm* possessive

possession [posesjɔ̃] *nf* (**a**) *(fait d'avoir)* ownership, posses-sion; *(d'un titre)* holding; **avoir qch en sa p.** to have sth in one's possession; **être en p. de qch** to be in possession of sth; **prendre p. de qch** to take possession of sth (**b**) *(bien, territoire)* possession (**c**) *(par le démon)* possession (**d**) *(maîtrise)* **être en p. de toutes ses facultés** to be in full possession of one's faculties; **être en pleine p. de ses moyens** to be at the peak of one's powers

possibilité [posibilite] *nf* (**a**) *(éventualité)* possibility (**b**) *(moyen, occasion)* opportunity, chance; **avoir la p. de faire qch** to have the opportunity *or* the chance of doing sth (**c**) **pos-sibilités** *(intellectuelles)* potential; *(financières)* means (**d**) *Ordi-nat* **possibilités d'extension** upgradeability

possible [posibl] **1** *adj* (**a**) *(faisable, vraisemblable)* possible; **il leur est p. de vous héberger** it's possible for them to put you up; **il est p. qu'il soit mort** it's possible that he's dead, he might be dead; **aussitôt que p., dès que p.** as soon as possible; *Fam* **pas p.!** I don't believe it!; **si p.** if possible (**b**) *(comme superlatif)* **elle nous en parle le moins/plus p.** she talks to us about it as little/much as possible; **le moins/plus souvent p.** as infrequently/frequently as possible; **le moins/plus de détails p.** as few/many details as possible; **la boîte la plus grande p.** the largest box possible; **tous les détails possibles (et imaginables)** every possible detail (**c**) *Fam (supportable)* **pas p.** *(personne, situation)* impossible; **ça n'est plus p.!** I've had enough!

2 *nm* **faire tout son p. (pour faire qch)** to do everything one possibly can (to do sth)

postal, -e, -aux, -ales [postal, -o] *adj (tarif, services, train)* mail

postdater [postdate] *vt* to postdate

post-doctorat [postdɔktɔra] *nm Univ* post-doctorate

post-doctoral, -e, -aux, -ales [postdɔktɔral] *adj Univ* post-doctorate

poste¹ [post] *nf* (**a**) *(service)* mail; **la P.** the mail service; **met-tre qch à la p.** to mail sth; **par la p.** by mail; **p. aérienne** airmail (**b**) *(lieu)* **(bureau de) p.** post office; **p. restante** gen-eral delivery

poste² [post] *nm* (**a**) *(fonction)* position, post; **p. à pourvoir** vacancy (**b**) *(appareil)* **p. (de radio/télévision)** radio/televi-sion (set); *Rad* **p. émetteur** *(équipement)* transmitter (**c**) *(local)* **p. (de police)** (police) station; **p. d'aiguillage** signal box; **p. d'essence** gas station; *Ordinat* **p. de travail** workstation (**d**) *(d'un soldat)* post; **être à son p.** to be at one's post; **p. de pilo-tage** cockpit (**e**) *(d'un standard)* extension (**f**) *(comptable)* entry, item

poster¹ [poste] **1** *vt (sentinelle, hommes, troupes)* to post, to sta-tion

2 se poster *vpr* to take up a position, to station oneself

poster² [pɔste] vt (courrier) to mail

poster³ [pɔstɛr] nm poster

postérieur, -e [pɔsterjœr] **1** adj (a) (dans le temps) later, subsequent; **p. à** after (b) (de derrière) (pattes) back, hind; Anat posterior

 2 nm Hum (derrière) posterior

postérieurement [pɔsterjœrmɑ̃] adv later, subsequently; **p. à** after

postérité [pɔsterite] nf posterity; **passer à la p.** (personne) to go down in history; (œuvre, mot) to be handed down to posterity

postface [pɔstfas] nf postscript

posthume [pɔstym] adj posthumous

postiche [pɔstiʃ] **1** adj false

 2 nm hairpiece

postier, -ère [pɔstje, -ɛr] nm,f postal worker

postillon [pɔstijɔ̃] nm (a) Hist (cocher) postilion (b) **postillons** (salive) shower of spit; **envoyer des postillons** to splutter

postillonner [pɔstijɔne] vi to splutter

postindustriel, -elle [pɔstɛ̃dystrijɛl] adj post-industrial

postmoderne [pɔstmɔdɛrn] adj post-modernist

postopératoire [pɔstɔperatwar] adj Méd post-operative

post-scriptum [pɔstskriptɔm] nm inv postscript

postsynchroniser [pɔstsɛ̃krɔnize] vt Cin to dub

postulant, -e [pɔstylɑ̃, -ɑ̃t] nm,f (à un emploi) applicant, candidate (**à** for)

postulat [pɔstyla] nm postulate

postuler [pɔstyle] vi **p. à** ou **pour un emploi** to apply for a job

posture [pɔstyr] nf (a) (attitude) posture (b) (situation) **être en fâcheuse p.** to be in an awkward situation

pot [po] nm (a) (récipient, contenu) pot; (en verre) jar; **p. à eau/à lait** water/milk pitcher; Fam **le p.** (pour enfant) the potty; **mettre en p.** (plante) to pot; Fam **quel p. de colle!** he sticks to you like glue!; **découvrir le p. aux roses** to find out what's been going on; **petit p.** (pour bébé) jar of baby food; **p. de chambre** chamber pot; **p. de fleurs** (récipient) flowerpot; (plante) pot of flowers; Fam **c'est un vrai p. de peinture!** (femme) she wears make-up an inch thick! (b) Fam (chance) **avoir du p.** to be lucky; **manque de p.,...** unfortunately,... (c) (tuyau) **p. (d'échappement)** exhaust pipe, tailpipe; **p. catalytique** catalytic converter (d) Fam (boisson) drink; **viens, je t'offre un p.** come on, I'll buy you a drink; **ils font un p. pour son départ à la retraite** they're having a little get-together for his/her retirement (e) Fam **plein p.** (à toute vitesse) like sixty

potable [pɔtabl] adj (a) (que l'on peut boire) drinkable; **eau p./non p.** drinking/non-drinking water (b) Fam (correct) passable

potache [pɔtaʃ] nm Fam schoolboy

potage [pɔtaʒ] nm soup; **p. aux légumes** vegetable soup

potager, -ère [pɔtaʒe, -ɛr] **1** adj voir **jardin, plante²**

 2 nm vegetable or kitchen garden

potasser [pɔtase] vt Fam (matière) to bone up on; (examen) to bone up for

potassium [pɔtasjɔm] nm Chim potassium

pot-au-feu [pɔtofø] nm inv = boiled beef with vegetables

pot-de-vin (pl **pots-de-vin**) [podvɛ̃] nm bribe

pote [pɔt] nm Fam buddy, pal

poteau, -x [pɔto] nm (a) (piquet) post; (de but) (goal)post; Fam **poteaux** (jambes) legs like tree trunks; **p. (d'exécution)** execution stake; Belg **p. d'éclairage** street lamp; **p. électrique** electricity pylon; **p. indicateur** signpost; **p. télégraphique** telegraph pole (b) Fam (ami) buddy, pal

potée [pɔte] nf = boiled beef or pork with vegetables

potelé, -e [pɔtle] adj chubby, plump

potence [pɔtɑ̃s] nf (a) (gibet) gallows (singulier) (b) (pièce de charpente) bracket

potentiel, -elle [pɔtɑ̃sjɛl] adj & nm potential

potentiellement [pɔtɑ̃sjɛlmɑ̃] adv potentially

poterie [pɔtri] nf (a) (art) pottery; **faire de la p.** to make pottery (b) (objet) piece of pottery; (objets) pottery

potiche [pɔtiʃ] nf (a) (vase) oriental vase (b) Fig figurehead

potier, -ère [pɔtje, -ɛr] nm,f potter

potin [pɔtɛ̃] nm Fam (a) **potins** (ragots) gossip (b) (bruit) row; **faire du p.** to kick up a fuss

potion [posjɔ̃] nf potion

potiron [pɔtirɔ̃] nm pumpkin

pot-pourri (pl **pots-pourris**) [popuri] nm (chanson) medley; (fleurs séchées) potpourri

pou, -x [pu] nm louse; Fam **chercher des poux dans la tête à qn** to try and pick a quarrel with sb

poubelle [pubɛl] nf (a) (récipient) garbage can; **jeter** ou **mettre qch à la p.** to throw sth out; **faire les poubelles** to scrounge in garbage cans (b) Ordinat trash (c) Fam (voiture) heap, jalopy

pouce [pus] nm (a) (doigt) thumb; (gros orteil) big toe; Fam **se tourner les pouces** to twiddle one's thumbs; Suisse **tenir les pouces à qn** to keep one's fingers crossed for sb; **p.!** (dans un jeu) truce!; Fig **manger sur le p.** to grab a bite to eat (b) (mesure) inch; **ne pas bouger d'un p.** not to move an inch (c) Can **faire du p.** (faire du stop) to hitch(hike)

Poucet [pusɛ] npr **le Petit P.** Tom Thumb

poudre [pudr] nf (a) (poussière) powder; **réduire qch en p.** to reduce sth to powder; Fig **jeter de la p. aux yeux à qn** to try and dazzle sb; **p. compacte/libre** (maquillage) pressed/loose powder; **p. à éternuer** sneezing powder; **p. à laver,** Belg **p. à lessiver** washing powder; **p. à récurer** scouring powder (b) (explosif) (gun)powder (c) Fam (héroïne) smack, skag; (cocaïne) coke

poudrer [pudre] **1** vt to powder; **une femme poudrée** a woman with a powdered face

 2 se poudrer vpr to powder one's face

poudrerie [pudrəri] nf (a) (fabrique de poudre) (gun)powder factory (b) Can (neige) drifting snow

poudreux, -euse [pudrø, -øz] **1** adj powdery; **neige poudreuse** powder snow

 2 nf **poudreuse** powder snow

poudrier [pudrije] nm (powder) compact

poudrière [pudrijɛr] nf (entrepôt) powder magazine; Fig powder keg

pouf [puf] **1** exclam (chute) thud!

 2 nm (a) (meuble) pouf (b) Belg **à p.** (à crédit) on the cuff; **taper à p.** (deviner) to make a wild guess

pouffer [pufe] vi **p. (de rire)** to burst out laughing

pouffiasse [pufjas] nf Vulg slut

pouilleux, -euse [pujø, -øz] **1** adj (personne) filthy; (quartier, maison) squalid

 2 nm,f bum, down-and-out

poulailler [pulaje] nm (a) (basse-cour) hen house (b) (au théâtre) **le p.** the peanut gallery

poulain [pulɛ̃] nm foal; Fig protégé

poulamon [pulamɔ̃] nm Can tomcod

poularde [pulard] nf fattened pullet

poule¹ [pul] nf (a) (animal) hen; Culin (boiling) fowl; Fig **la p. aux œufs d'or** the goose that lays the golden eggs; **quand les poules auront des dents** when pigs fly; **p. d'eau** moorhen; **p. faisane** hen pheasant; Péj **p. mouillée** wimp, wuss; **p. au pot** boiled chicken (b) (terme d'affection) **ma (petite) p.** darling (c) Fam Péj (femme légère) floozie; (maîtresse) mistress

poule² [pul] nf (compétition) tournament; (groupe) group

poulet [pulɛ] nm (a) (animal) chicken; **p. d'élevage** battery-farmed chicken; **p. fermier** free-range chicken; **p. de grain** corn-fed chicken; **p. rôti** roast chicken (b) (terme d'affection) **mon (petit) p.** darling (c) Fam (policier) cop

poulette [pulɛt] *nf* (a) *(jeune poule)* pullet (b) *(terme d'affection)* **ma p.** darling

pouliche [puliʃ] *nf* filly

poulie [puli] *nf* pulley

poulpe [pulp] *nm* octopus

pouls [pu] *nm* pulse; **tâter le p. à qn** to feel sb's pulse; **prendre le p. à qn** to take sb's pulse

poumon [pumɔ̃] *nm* lung; **p. d'acier** iron lung; **respirer à pleins poumons** to breathe deeply

poupe [pup] *nf Naut* stern, poop

poupée [pupe] *nf* (a) *(jouet)* doll; **jouer à la p.** to play with dolls; **p. mannequin** Barbie doll®; **poupées russes** Russian dolls (b) *Fam (jolie fille)* doll (c) *(pansement)* finger bandage

poupin, -e [pupɛ̃, -in] *adj (personne)* chubby-cheeked; **visage p.** baby face

poupon [pupɔ̃] *nm* (a) *(bébé)* tiny baby (b) *(jouet)* baby doll

pouponner [pupɔne] *vi* to play the doting mother/father

pour [pur] **1** *prép* (a) *(indique le but, la destination)* for; **tiens, c'est p. toi** here, it's for you; **livres p. enfants** children's books; **p. faire qch** (in order) to do sth; **p. ne pas être en retard** so as not to be late; **p. bien faire** to do things properly; **p. que** + *subjunctive* so that, in order that; **j'épargne p. quand je serai vieux** I'm saving for when I'm old; **p. affaires** on business; **je viens p. la machine à laver** I've come about the washing machine; **c'est p. cela qu'il est venu** that's why he came, that's the reason he came; **p. quoi faire?** what for?; **tout ça p. rien!** all that for nothing!; *Fam* **c'est fait p.** that's what it's there for

(b) *(indique la direction)* for; **partir p. l'Espagne** to leave for Spain; **le train p. Paris** the Paris train, the train to *or* for Paris

(c) *(dans le temps)* for; **j'en ai p. une heure** it'll take me an hour, I'll be an hour; **il sera ici p. midi** he'll be here by midday

(d) *(contre)* for; **il me l'a vendu p. trois fois rien** he sold it to me for next to nothing; **donnez-moi p. 30 euros d'essence** give me 30 euros' worth of gas

(e) *(en faveur de)* for, in favor of; **je suis p.** I'm (all) for it, I'm in favor of it

(f) *(à la place de)* for

(g) *(comme)* for; **j'avais p. ambition de…** my ambition was to…; **laisser qn p. mort** to leave sb for dead

(h) *(quant à, par rapport à)* for; **il est grand p. son âge** he's tall for his age; **p. ce qui est de…** as regards…, with regard to…; **p. moi, c'est absurde** in my opinion it's ridiculous, I think it's ridiculous

(i) *(indique le résultat)* **être trop faible p. marcher** to be too weak to walk; **cette situation n'était pas p. lui déplaire** the situation was rather to his/her liking

(j) *(à cause de)* for; **on l'apprécie p. sa gentillesse** people like her because she's so kind; **p. avoir désobéi** for having disobeyed, for disobeying

(k) *Litt (indique la concession)* **p. être célèbre, il n'en est pas moins modeste** although famous, he's nonetheless modest

(l) *(locutions)* **être p. beaucoup dans qch** to have a lot to do with sth; **je n'y suis p. rien!** it has nothing to do with me!; *Fam* **être p. faire qch** *(être sur le point de)* to be about to do sth; *Fam* **p. une surprise, c'est une surprise!** that's a real surprise!; **perdre p. perdre, autant que tu…** if you're going to lose anyway, you might as well…

2 *nm inv* **le p. et le contre** the pros and cons

pourboire [purbwar] *nm* tip; **cinq euros/dix pour cent de p.** a five euro/ten percent tip; **être payé au p.** to be paid in tips

pourceau, -x [purso] *nm Litt* swine

pourcentage [pursɑ̃taʒ] *nm* percentage; **être payé au p.** to be paid on a commission basis

pourchasser [purʃase] *vt* to pursue

pourfendre [purfɑ̃dr] *vt Hum (injustices, hypocrisie)* to combat

pourlécher [34] [purleʃe] **se pourlécher** *vpr* **se p. (les babines)** to lick one's lips

pourparlers [purparle] *nmpl* talks, negotiations; **entrer/être en p. (avec)** to enter into/be having talks (with); **p. de paix** peace talks *or* negotiations

pourpre [purpr] **1** *adj & nm* crimson

2 *nf (teinte naturelle)* purple (dye)

pourquoi [purkwa] **1** *adv & conj* why; **c'est p.…** that's why…; **p. pas?** why not?

2 *nm inv (raison)* **le p.** the reason for; **le p. et le comment** the whys and wherefores

pourrais etc. *voir* **pouvoir²**

pourri, -e [puri] **1** *adj* (a) *(bois, dent)* rotten; *(chair)* putrid; *(fruit, œufs)* bad (b) *Fam (corrompu)* corrupt (c) *Fam (déplaisant)* rotten (d) *Fam* **être p. de fric** to be filthy rich

2 *nm* (a) *(d'un fruit)* bad part; **sentir le p.** to smell rotten (b) *très Fam (personne)* bastard

pourriel [purjɛl] *nm Ordinat* spam e-mail; **pourriels** spam

pourrir [purir] **1** *vi (bois, dent)* to rot; *(corps)* to putrefy; *(aliments)* to go bad; *Fig* **p. en prison** to rot in jail

2 *vt* (a) *(gâter)* to rot (b) *Fam (enfant)* to spoil

pourriture [purityr] *nf* (a) *(décomposition)* rot (b) *Fam (corruption)* corruption (c) *très Fam (personne)* bastard

poursuite [pursɥit] *nf* (a) *(chasse)* pursuit; **se lancer à la p. de qn** to set off in pursuit of sb; **être à la p. de qch** *(bonheur, paix)* to be in pursuit of sth (b) *(continuation)* continuation (c) *Jur* **poursuites (judiciaires)** (legal) proceedings; *(en droit pénal)* prosecution; **engager des poursuites contre qn** to start proceedings against sb; *(en droit pénal)* to prosecute sb (d) *(course cycliste)* pursuit

poursuivant, -e [pursɥivɑ̃, -ɑ̃t] *nm,f* pursuer

poursuivre [65] [pursɥivr] **1** *vt* (a) *(pourchasser)* to pursue; *(sujet: idée, crainte)* to haunt; *(sujet: malchance)* to dog (b) *(idéal, rêve, but)* to pursue (c) *(harceler)* to pester (**de** with); *(sujet: créancier)* to hound; **p. qn de ses assiduités** to force one's attentions on sb (d) *Jur* **p. qn (en justice)** to bring proceedings against sb; *(en droit pénal)* to prosecute sb (e) *(continuer)* to continue, to go on with; **poursuivez** *(à quelqu'un qui parle)* go on

2 se poursuivre *vpr (continuer)* to continue, to go on

pourtant [purtɑ̃] *adv* yet; **tout avait p. bien commencé** yet it all started so well; **je ne peux p. pas l'empêcher de venir** still, I can't stop him/her from coming; **ça n'est p. pas compliqué!** it's not exactly complicated!

pourtour [purtur] *nm* circumference, perimeter

pourvoi [purvwa] *nm Jur* appeal; **p. en cassation** appeal to a higher court

pourvoir [73b] [purvwar] **1** *vt* **p. qn de qch** to provide sb with sth; **p. qch de qch** to equip *or* to fit sth with sth

2 pourvoir à *vt ind (besoins)* to provide for, to cater to

3 se pourvoir *vpr* (a) *(se munir)* **se p. de qch** to provide oneself with sth (b) *Jur* **se p. en cassation** to take one's case to the Court of Appeal

pourvoyeur, -euse [purvwajœr, -øz] *nm,f* supplier

pourvu¹ [purvy] **pourvu que** *conj* (a) *(condition)* **p. que tu y sois** provided (that) *or* so long as you're there (b) *(souhait)* **p. qu'il le fasse!** let's just hope he does it!

pourvu², -e *voir* **pourvoir**

pousse [pus] *nf* (a) *(des feuilles, des cheveux)* growth (b) *(bourgeon)* shoot; **p. de bambou** bamboo shoot; *Fig* **jeune p.** *(société)* start-up

poussé, -e [puse] *adj (en profondeur)* thorough

pousse-café [puskafe] *nm inv* (glass of) liqueur *(after coffee)*

poussée [puse] *nf* (a) *(pression)* pressure; *(d'un liquide)* upthrust; **la p. de la foule** the pushing and shoving of the crowd (b) *(croissance)* growth; *(de boutons, d'herpès)* eruption; **p. de fièvre** sudden rise in temperature; **p. démographique**

sudden population increase; **faire une p. de croissance** to shoot up (**c**) *Fig (des prix)* upsurge (**de** in)

pousse-pousse [puspus] *nm inv* rickshaw

pousser [puse] **1** *vt* (**a**) *(soumettre à une force)* to push; *(sujet: vent) (embarcation)* to drive; **p. qn du coude** to nudge sb with one's elbow; *Fam* **à la va comme je te pousse** slipshod; *Fam* **faut pas p. Mémé** *ou* **Mémère dans les orties!** don't push it *or* your luck!

(**b**) *(inciter)* **p. qn à faire qch** *(sujet: faim, jalousie)* to drive sb to do sth; *(sujet: personne)* to urge sb to do sth; **p. qn à qch** to drive sb to sth; **poussé par la curiosité** prompted by curiosity

(**c**) *(continuer)* **p. trop loin une plaisanterie** to take a joke too far; **il a poussé la générosité jusqu'à nous héberger** he was so generous that he even put us up

(**d**) *(émettre)* **p. un cri** to shout, to give a shout; **p. des cris** to shout; **p. un soupir** to sigh, to heave a sigh; **p. un gémissement** to groan; *Fam* **p. la chansonnette** to sing a song

2 *vi* (**a**) *(exercer une pression)* to push; *(aux toilettes)* to strain; *(en accouchant)* to push; *Fam* **faut pas p.!** don't push it *or* your luck!

(**b**) *(continuer)* **p. jusqu'au bois** to push on as far as the forest

(**c**) *(plante, cheveux, ongles)* to grow; *(bourgeon)* to sprout; *(dents)* to come through; *Fam (enfant)* to shoot up; **se laisser p. la barbe** to grow a beard

3 se pousser *vpr (pour faire de la place)* to move over *or* up

poussette [pusɛt] *nf (pour enfants)* stroller

poussière [pusjɛr] *nf* dust; **une p.** a speck of dust; *Fam* **faire la p.** *ou* **les poussières** to do the dusting, to dust; *Fig* **tomber en p.** to crumble to dust; *Fig* **mordre la p.** to bite the dust; *Fam* **dix euros et des poussières** ten-and-a bit euros

poussiéreux, -euse [pusjerø, -øz] *adj* dusty; *Fig* stuffy

poussif, -ive [pusif, -iv] *adj (moteur, personne)* wheezy

poussin, -e [pusɛ̃, -in] **1** *nm* chick; *Fam* **mon p.** sweetie

2 *nm,f Sport* junior *(9 years old)*

poutre [putr] *nf (en bois)* beam; *(en métal)* girder; **p. apparente** exposed beam; **p. maîtresse** main beam/girder

poutrelle [putrɛl] *nf* girder

pouvoir¹ [puvwar] *nm* (**a**) *(puissance)* power; **avoir du p. sur qn** to have power *or* influence over sb; **prendre le p.** to assume power; **être au p.** to be in power; **p. absolu** absolute power; **p. exécutif** executive power; **p. judiciaire** judicial power; **p. législatif** legislative power; **les pouvoirs publics** the authorities (**b**) *(attributions)* power; **il n'est pas en mon p. de…** it is not within my power to… (**c**) **p. d'achat** purchasing power

pouvoir² [57] [puvwar] **1** *vt* (**a**) *(être capable de)* can, to be able; **p. faire qch** can *or* to be able to do sth; **si je peux** if I can, if I'm able to; **je ne peux pas** I can't, I'm unable to; **comment a-t-il pu dire cela?** how could he say that?; **on n'y peut rien** it can't be helped, there's nothing that can be done about it; **on ne peut plus/moins aimable** extremely friendly/unfriendly; **il n'en peut plus** *(de fatigue)* he's exhausted; *(d'exaspération, d'impatience)* he can't take any more; **dès que je pourrai** as soon as I can; **où peut-il bien être?** where can he be?; **nous ne pouvons rien pour vous** we can't do anything for you

(**b**) *(avoir le droit, la permission de)* can, to be allowed; **vous pouvez partir** you can go; **puis-je entrer?** can I come in?; **si je puis m'exprimer ainsi** if I may use the phrase

(**c**) *(être possible)* **la porte a pu se fermer toute seule** the door might have *or* could have closed on its own; **tout le monde peut se tromper** anyone can make a mistake; **elle peut bien s'excuser, je ne lui pardonnerai pas** she can apologize all she likes, but I won't forgive her; *Fam* **qu'est-ce que ça peut te faire?** what's that got to do with you?

2 *v impersonnel* **cela se peut/se pourrait (bien)** it's quite possible; **il se peut qu'il vienne** he may *or* might come

PPCM [pepeseɛm] *nm Math (abrév* **plus petit commun multiple)** LCM

PQ [peky] *nm* (**a**) *Can Pol (abrév* **Parti Québécois)** PQ (**b**) *Fam (papier hygiénique)* toilet paper

pragmatique [pragmatik] *adj* pragmatic

pragois, -e [pragwa, -az] **1** *adj* of Prague

2 *nm,f* **P., Pragoise** person from Prague

Prague [prag] *n* Prague

praire [prɛr] *nf* clam

prairie [preri] *nf* meadow; *Géog* **la P.** the Prairies

praline [pralin] *nf* praline

praliné, -e [praline] *adj (chocolat)* praline-filled; *(glace)* praline-flavored

praticable [pratikabl] *adj* (**a**) *(route)* passable, negotiable; *(terrain)* playable (**b**) *(réalisable)* practicable

praticien, -enne [pratisjɛ̃, -ɛn] *nm,f (médecin)* (medical) practitioner

pratiquant, -e [pratikɑ̃, -ɑ̃t] **1** *adj* practicing; **je ne suis pas p.** I'm not religious

2 *nm,f* practicing Christian/Jew/Muslim/*etc.*

pratique [pratik] **1** *adj (méthode, personne)* practical; *(outil)* handy; *(date, heure, jour)* convenient; **avoir l'esprit p.** to have a practical turn of mind

2 *nf* (**a**) *(application)* practice; **mettre qch en p.** to put sth into practice; **dans la p.** in practice (**b**) *(expérience)* (practical) experience; **avoir une longue p. de qch** to have had a lot of (practical) experience of sth (**c**) *(d'un sport)* playing; **la p. du yoga** practicing *or* doing yoga (**d**) *(procédé, coutume)* practice

pratiquement [pratikmɑ̃] *adv* (**a**) *(concrètement)* in practice (**b**) *(presque)* practically

pratiquer [pratike] **1** *vt* (**a**) *(religion)* to practice; *(activité)* to take part in; *(langue)* to use; *(sport)* to play; **p. la natation** to swim; **p. le yoga** to practice *or* to do yoga; **les prix pratiqués ici** the prices being asked here (**b**) *(faire) (ouverture)* to make; *(opération chirurgicale)* to carry out

2 *vi* (**a**) *(médecin, avocat)* to practice (**b**) *(être religieux)* to practice one's religion; **il est catholique mais il ne pratique pas** he's a Catholic but he's not practicing

3 se pratiquer *vpr (sport)* to be played; *(coutume)* to be practiced

pré [pre] *nm* meadow

préadolescent, -e [preadɔlɛsɑ̃, -ɑ̃t] *nm,f* preadolescent

préalable [prealabl] **1** *adj* previous, prior (**à** to); *(accord)* prior; *(formalités)* preliminary

2 *nm (condition)* prerequisite, precondition; **au p.** first, beforehand

préalablement [prealabləmɑ̃] *adv* first, beforehand; **p. à…** prior to…

préambule [preɑ̃byl] *nm* preamble (**de** to); **sans p., elle annonça…** without any warning, she announced…

PréAO [preao] *nf Ordinat (abrév* **présentation assistée par ordinateur)** computer-assisted presentation

préau, -x [preo] *nm (de cour d'école)* covered area; *(salle)* hall

préavis [preavi] *nm* (advance) notice; **un p. de trois mois** three months' notice; **p. de grève** strike notice; **déposer un p. de grève** to give notice of strike action; **p. de licenciement** notice (of dismissal)

précaire [prekɛr] *adj (position)* precarious; *(santé)* delicate; **être en équilibre p.** to be precariously balanced; **il a un emploi p.** he has no job security

précambrien, -enne [prekɑ̃brijɛ̃, -ɛn] *Géol* **1** *adj* Precambrian

2 *nm* **le P.** the Precambrian period

précarité [prekarite] *nf* precariousness; **la p. de l'emploi** the lack of job security

précaution [prekosjɔ̃] *nf* (**a**) *(mesure)* precaution; **par (mesure de) p.** as a precaution; **prendre des** *ou* **ses précautions** to take precautions; *Prov* **deux précautions valent mieux qu'une** better safe than sorry **(b)** *(prudence)* caution, care; **pour plus de p.** to be on the safe side

précautionneux, -euse [prekosjɔnø, -øz] *adj* careful

précédemment [presedamɑ̃] *adv* previously, before

précédent, -e [presedɑ̃, -ɑ̃t] **1** *adj* previous

2 *nm* precedent; **sans p.** unprecedented, without precedent

précéder [34] [presede] **1** *vt* to precede; **je l'ai précédé de dix minutes** I got there ten minutes before he did

2 *vi* **la page qui précède** the preceding *or* previous page; **dans les jours qui précèdent** in the preceding days; **ce qui précède** the foregoing

précepte [presɛpt] *nm* precept

précepteur, -trice [preseptœr, -tris] *nm,f* (private) tutor

préchauffage [preʃofaʒ] *nm* preheating

préchauffer [preʃofe] *vt* to preheat

prêcher [preʃe] **1** *vt* **(a)** *(enseigner)* to preach **(à** to) **(b)** *(prôner)* to advocate; *Hum* **p. la bonne parole** to spread the good word

2 *vi* *(prononcer un sermon)* to preach; *Fig* **p. dans le désert** to be a voice crying in the wilderness; *Fig* **p. pour sa paroisse** to look after one's own interests

prêchi-prêcha [preʃipreʃa] *nm inv Fam Péj* preachifying

précieusement [presjøzmɑ̃] *adv* **garder** *ou* **conserver qch p.** to keep sth safe

précieux, -euse [presjø, -øz] *adj* **(a)** *(coûteux)* precious **(b)** *(conseil, temps)* valuable **(à** to) **(c)** *(style, personne)* precious, affected

préciosité [presjozite] *nf Litt* affectation, preciosity

précipice [presipis] *nm* chasm, abyss; *(d'une falaise, d'un ravin)* precipice; *Fig* abyss; *Fig* **être au bord du p.** to be on the edge of an abyss

précipitamment [presipitamɑ̃] *adv* hurriedly, hastily; **entrer/sortir p.** to rush *or* to dash in/out

précipitation [presipitasjɔ̃] *nf* **(a)** *(hâte)* haste; **dans ma p., j'ai oublié les clés** I was in such a hurry, I forgot the keys **(b)** *Chim* precipitation **(c)** **précipitations** *(pluies)* precipitation

précipité, -e [presipite] **1** *adj* hasty, hurried

2 *nm Chim* precipitate

précipiter [presipite] **1** *vt* **(a)** *(entraîner)* to throw down, to hurl down; *Fig* to plunge; **p. qn dans le vide** to hurl sb over the edge **(b)** *(hâter)* to speed up; *(événements)* to precipitate; *(la mort de quelqu'un)* to hasten; **il ne faut rien p.** we mustn't rush things **(c)** *Chim* to precipitate

2 *vi Chim* to precipitate

3 se précipiter *vpr* **(a)** *(se hâter)* to rush, to hurry **(b)** *(s'accélérer)* **les événements se sont précipités** things started happening quickly **(c)** *(se jeter)* to rush **(sur/vers** at/towards)

précis, -e [presi, -iz] **1** *adj* precise, exact; **à deux heures précises** at two o'clock precisely *or* exactly; **penser à quelque chose de p.** to have something specific in mind

2 *nm* précis, summary; *(livre)* handbook; **p. d'histoire de France** short history of France

précisément [presizemɑ̃] *adv* precisely, exactly

préciser [presize] **1** *vt* **(a)** *(déterminer) (date)* to specify **(b)** *(clarifier) (pensée)* to clarify; **je tiens à p. que…** I wish to make it clear that…; **pourriez-vous p.?** could you be more specific?

2 se préciser *vpr* to become clear(er); *(idée)* to take shape

précision [presizjɔ̃] *nf* **(a)** *(d'une information, d'une description)* accuracy; *(de mouvements)* preciseness, precision; **avec p.** precisely **(b)** *(détail)* **une p.** a precise detail; **donner** *ou* **apporter des précisions sur qch** to give precise details about sth; **demander des précisions sur qch** to ask for further information about sth

précoce [prekɔs] *adj (enfant)* precocious; *(fruit, été)* early; *(sénilité, calvitie)* premature

précocité [prekɔsite] *nf* precociousness; *(d'un fruit, d'une saison)* earliness

précolombien, -enne [prekɔlɔ̃bjɛ̃, -ɛn] *adj* pre-Columbian

préconçu, -e [prekɔ̃sy] *adj* preconceived

préconiser [prekɔnize] *vt* to advocate; *(remède)* to recommend

précuit, -e [prekɥi, -it] *adj* precooked

précurseur [prekyrsœr] **1** *nm* precursor, forerunner

2 *adj m* **signe p.** forewarning

prédateur [predatœr] *nm* predator

prédécesseur [predesesœr] *nm* predecessor

prédécoupé, -e [predekupe] *adj* precut

prédestination [predɛstinasjɔ̃] *nf* predestination

prédestiné, -e [predɛstine] *adj* predestined **(à qch/à faire qch** for sth/to do sth)

prédestiner [predɛstine] *vt* to predestine **(à qch/à faire qch** for sth/to do sth)

prédicat [predika] *nm Gram* predicate

prédicateur, -trice [predikatœr, -tris] *nm,f* preacher

prédiction [prediksjɔ̃] *nf* prediction

prédilection [predilɛksjɔ̃] *nf* predilection, partiality; **de p.** favorite; **avoir une p. pour qch** to be partial to sth, *Sout* to have a predilection for sth

prédire [27b] [predir] *vt* to predict; **p. qch à qn** to predict sth for sb; **elle m'a prédit que je voyagerais** she predicted that I would travel

prédisposer [predispoze] *vt* to predispose **(à** to)

prédisposition [predispozisjɔ̃] *nf* predisposition **(à** to)

prédominant, -e [predɔminɑ̃, -ɑ̃t] *adj* predominant

prédominer [predɔmine] *vi* to predominate

préélectoral, -e, -aux, -ales [preelɛktɔral, -o] *adj* pre-electoral, pre-election

préemballé, -e [preɑ̃bale] *adj* prepacked

prééminence [preeminɑ̃s] *nf* pre-eminence

prééminent, -e [preeminɑ̃, -ɑ̃t] *adj* pre-eminent

préempter [preɑ̃pte] *vt Jur* to pre-empt

préemption [preɑ̃psjɔ̃] *nf Jur* pre-emption

préenregistré, -e [preɑ̃rəʒistre] *adj* prerecorded

préétablir [preetablir] *vt* to pre-establish

préexistant, -e [preɛgzistɑ̃, -ɑ̃t] *adj* pre-existing

préexister [preɛgziste] *vi* to pre-exist; **p. à qch** to pre-exist sth

préfabrication [prefabrikasjɔ̃] *nf* prefabrication

préfabriqué, -e [prefabrike] **1** *adj* prefabricated

2 *nm* prefabricated material; **c'est du p.** it's prefabricated

préface [prefas] *nf* preface, foreword **(à** *ou* **de** to)

préfacer [16] [prefase] *vt* to preface

préfectoral, -e, -aux, -ales [prefɛktɔral, -o] *adj* = relating to a "préfecture" or "préfet"

préfecture [prefɛktyr] *nf* prefecture; *(ville)* = administrative center of a "département"; **la P. de police** police headquarters

---

Préfecture

This refers to the main administrative office of each **département** *(see box at this entry)*. The word has also come to refer to the town where the office is located. People go to the "préfecture" to obtain a driver's license or a "carte de séjour", for example.

---

préférable [preferabl] *adj* preferable **(à** to); **il serait p. de le revoir** *ou* **que nous le revoyions** it would be preferable to see him again

préféré, -e [prefere] *adj & nm,f* favorite

préférence [preferɑ̃s] *nf* preference; **de p.** preferably; **de p. à** in preference to

préférentiel, -elle [preferɑ̃sjɛl] *adj* preferential

préférer [34] [prefere] *vt* to prefer (**à** to); **je préférerais du thé** I'd prefer tea, I'd rather have tea; **je préférerais que vous veniez** I'd prefer it if you came, I'd rather you came; **p. faire qch** to prefer to do sth

préfet [prefɛ] *nm* (**a**) *(fonctionnaire)* prefect *(administrative head of a "département")*; **p. de police** = chief commissioner of police (**b**) *Belg Scol* principal

préfigurer [prefigyre] *vt* to prefigure, to foreshadow

préfixe [prefiks] *nm* prefix

pré-formaté, -e (*mpl* **pré-formatés**, *fpl* **pré-formatées**) [preformate] *adj Ordinat* pre-formatted

préhension [preɑ̃sjɔ̃] *nf* gripping

préhistoire [preistwar] *nf* prehistory

préhistorique [preistɔrik] *adj* prehistoric

pré-impression [preɛ̃presjɔ̃] *nf Typ* pre-press

préindustriel, -elle [preɛ̃dystrijɛl] *adj* pre-industrial

préinscription [preɛ̃skripsjɔ̃] *nf* pre-check-in

préjudice [preʒydis] *nm (à une cause)* prejudice, detriment; *(à une personne)* harm, wrong; *Jur* tort; **subir un p. matériel** to sustain damage; **subir un p. moral** to suffer mental distress; **porter p. à qn** to do sb harm; **au p. de qch** to the detriment of sth

préjugé [preʒyʒe] *nm* prejudice, bias (**contre** against); **avoir un p. contre qn/qch** to be prejudiced *or* biased against sb/sth; **n'avoir aucun p.** to be totally unprejudiced *or* unbiased

prélasser [prelase] **se prélasser** *vpr* to lounge

prélat [prela] *nm* prelate

prélavage [prelavaʒ] *nm* pre-wash

prélèvement [prelɛvmɑ̃] *nm* (**a**) *(en argent)* deduction (**sur** from); **faire un p. sur un compte** to debit an account; **p. automatique** direct debit; **prélèvements obligatoires** = tax and social security contributions (**b**) *(extraction) (d'un organe)* removal; *(de sécrétions)* taking a sample; *(d'un échantillon)* taking; **faire un p. de sang** *ou* **sanguin à qn** to take a blood sample from sb (**c**) *(partie prélevée) (de sécrétions)* swab; *(de sang)* sample

prélever [46] [prelve] *vt* (**a**) *(argent)* to deduct (**sur** from); *(impôt)* to levy (**b**) *(organe)* to remove; *(sécrétions, échantillon)* to take; **p. du sang à qn** to take a blood sample from sb

préliminaire [preliminɛr] **1** *adj* preliminary
2 *nmpl* **préliminaires** preliminaries

prélude [prelyd] *nm Mus & Fig* prelude (**de** *ou* **à** to)

prématuré, -e [prematyre] **1** *adj* premature; **être p. de six semaines** to be six weeks premature
2 *nm,f* premature baby

prématurément [prematyremɑ̃] *adv* prematurely

préméditation [premeditasjɔ̃] *nf* premeditation; **meurtre avec p.** premeditated murder

préméditer [premedite] *vt* to premeditate

prémenstruel, -elle [premɑ̃stryɛl] *adj* premenstrual

premier, -ère [prəmje, -ɛr] **1** *adj* (**a**) *(initial, dominant)* first; **les trois premières années** the first three years; **la première marche** the bottom step; **le p. rang** the front row; **prendre la première place** *(dans une course)* to take the lead; **le p. venu** the first person who comes along; **les premiers arrivés** the first to arrive; **je suis le p. concerné** I'm the one most affected; **en p.** in the first place, firstly (**b**) *(original)* primary, original
2 *nm,f* (**a**) *(dans un classement)* first; **arriver le p.** *ou* **en p.** to arrive first; **être le p. de sa classe** to be at the top of one's class; **être le p. à faire qch** to be (the) first to do sth; *voir aussi* **cinquième** (**b**) *(acteur)* **jeune p.** (young) romantic lead; *Fig* **avoir des airs de jeune p.** to look like a movie star
3 *nm (date)* **le p. janvier** January first; **le p. de l'an** New Year's Day
4 *nf* **première** (**a**) *(d'une pièce)* first *or* opening night; *(d'un film)* première (**b**) *(classe)* ≃ eleventh grade (**c**) *(de train,*

d'avion) first class; **voyager en première** to travel first-class (**d**) *(vitesse)* first (gear) (**e**) *(de chaussure)* insole (**f**) *Fam* **de première** *(de très bonne qualité)* first-rate, first-class

premièrement [prəmjɛrmɑ̃] *adv* first, in the first place

prémisse [premis] *nf* premise

prémix [premiks] *nm (boisson)* ready-mixed alcoholic drink

prémolaire [premɔlɛr] *nf* premolar

prémonition [premɔnisjɔ̃] *nf* premonition

prémonitoire [premɔnitwar] *adj* premonitory

prémunir [premynir] **se prémunir** *vpr* **se p. contre qch** to be on one's guard against sth

prenant, -e [prənɑ̃, -ɑ̃t] *adj (livre, spectacle)* fascinating; *(travail)* time-consuming

prénatal, -e, -als, -ales [prenatal] *adj* prenatal

prendre [58] [prɑ̃dr] **1** *vt* (**a**) *(saisir)* to take; **p. qch dans un tiroir** to take sth out of a drawer; **prends-le par la poignée** take hold of it by the handle; **c'est à p. ou à laisser** take it or leave it; *Fam* **il faut savoir le p.** you have to know how to handle him; *Fam* **c'est toujours ça de pris** that's something at least; *Fam* **qu'est-ce qu'on va p.!** we're in for it!
(**b**) *(enlever)* to take (away); **p. qch à qn** to take sth (away) from sb; **cela m'a pris du temps/deux heures** it took me a while/two hours; **p. 20 euros de l'heure** to take 20 euros an hour
(**c**) *(s'emparer de) (personne, gibier)* to catch; *(ville, région)* to take, to capture; **se laisser p.** to let oneself be *or* to get caught; *Fig* to let oneself be taken in
(**d**) *(aller chercher)* to collect, to pick up; **attends, je vais p. mon parapluie** hold on, I'll get my umbrella
(**e**) *(acheter)* to get; *(chambre, studio)* to take; **cette robe me plaît, je la prends** I like this dress, I'll take it
(**f**) *(bonne, assistant)* to take on; *(pensionnaire)* to take in; *(travail)* to take; **être pris** *(élève, candidat)* to be accepted; *(acteur)* to get the part
(**g**) *(repas, boisson)* to have; *(bain, douche, médicament)* to take
(**h**) *(moyen de transport)* to take
(**i**) *(apparence)* to take on, to assume; *(attitude)* to take; *(accent)* to pick up
(**j**) **p. l'eau** *(bateau)* to be leaking, to be letting in water
(**k**) *(personne)* **p. qn comme exemple** to take sb as an example; **p. qn/qch pour** to take sb/sth for
(**l**) *Fam (arriver)* **qu'est-ce qui lui prend?** what's come over him/her?; **ça te prend souvent?** do you get like that often?
2 *vi* (**a**) *(ciment, flan)* to set
(**b**) *(plante)* to take (root)
(**c**) *(feu)* to catch
(**d**) *(réussir) (vaccin)* to take effect; *(mode)* to catch on; *Fam* **avec moi, ça ne prend pas!** you can't fool me!
(**e**) *(tourner)* **p. à gauche/droite** to go left/right
(**f**) **p. sur soi** to restrain *or* to contain oneself
3 **se prendre** *vpr* (**a**) *(s'accrocher)* **se p. dans une porte/à un clou** to get caught in the door/on a nail
(**b**) *(se considérer)* **se p. pour un héros** to consider oneself a hero; **pour qui vous prenez-vous?** who do you think you are?
(**c**) *(locutions)* **s'en p. à qn/qch** to take it out on sb/sth; **ne t'en prends qu'à toi-même** you have only yourself to blame; **s'y p. bien avec qn** to know how to handle sb; **s'y p. mal avec qn** not to handle sb the right way; **vous vous y prenez mal** you're going about it the wrong way; **s'y p. à deux fois pour faire qch** to take two attempts to do sth

preneur, -euse [prənœr, -øz] *nm,f* (**a**) *(acheteur)* buyer, purchaser; **trouver p.** to find a buyer; **je suis p.!** I'm interested! (**b**) **p. d'otages** hostage taker; **p. de son** sound engineer

prenne *etc. voir* **prendre**

prénom [prenɔ̃] *nm* first *or* given name

prénommé, -e [prenɔme] *adj* **le p. Victor** the man/boy called Victor

prénommer [prenɔme] **1** *vt* to call, to name

2 se prénommer *vpr* **il se prénomme Adam** his first *or* given name is Adam

prénuptial, -e, -aux, -ales [prenypsjal, -o] *adj* premarital; **examen p.** premarital medical check-up

préoccupant, -e [preɔkypɑ̃, -ɑ̃t] *adj* worrying

préoccupation [preɔkypasjɔ̃] *nf* concern, preoccupation; **j'ai d'autres préoccupations** I have other things to worry about

préoccupé, -e [preɔkype] *adj* worried

préoccuper [preɔkype] **1** *vt* to worry; **être préoccupé par qch** to be worried about sth; **sa santé me préoccupe** I'm worried about his/her health

2 se préoccuper *vpr* **se p. de qn/qch** to concern oneself with sb/sth

prépa [prepa] *nf Fam Scol* preparatory class *(for the entrance exam to the "grandes écoles")*; **faire une p., être en p.** to be studying for the entrance exam to the "grandes écoles"

préparateur, -trice [preparatœr, -tris] *nm,f* laboratory assistant; **p. en pharmacie** pharmacist's assistant

préparatifs [preparatif] *nmpl* preparations (**de** for)

préparation [preparasjɔ̃] *nf* preparation (**à** for); **faire une p. militaire** = to take an officer training course in preparation for military service; **faire une p. aux grandes écoles** = to prepare for the entrance exam to the "grandes écoles"

préparatoire [preparatwar] *adj* preparatory

préparer [prepare] **1** *vt* (**a**) *(discours, repas, plat)* to prepare; *(réunion, soirée, vacances)* to make preparations for, to arrange; *(ordonnance)* to make up; **plats tout préparés** ready meals; *Fig* **je suis sûr qu'il nous prépare quelque chose** I'm sure he's up to something (**b**) *(personne)* **p. qn à qch** to prepare sb for sth; *(entraîner)* to train sb for sth (**c**) *(examen)* to prepare for, to study for

2 se préparer *vpr* (**a**) *(être imminent)* to be in the offing (**b**) *(s'apprêter)* to get ready; **se p. à qch/à faire qch** to prepare *or* to get ready for sth/to do sth (**c**) *(se faire)* **se p. qch** *(boisson, plat)* to make oneself sth; **tu te prépares bien des désillusions** you're in for a big disappointment

prépayé, -e [prepeje] *adj* prepaid

prépondérant, -e [prepɔ̃derɑ̃, -ɑ̃t] *adj* predominant

préposé, -e [prepoze] *nm,f* *(employé)* employee; *(dans un vestiaire)* attendant; **p. (des postes)** mailman, *f* mailwoman

préposer [prepoze] *vt* **p. qn à qch** to appoint sb to sth

préposition [prepozisjɔ̃] *nf Gram* preposition

prépuce [prepys] *nm Anat* foreskin

préraphaélite [prerafaelit] *adj & nm* Pre-Raphaelite

préretraite [preretret] *nf* early retirement; *(pension)* early retirement pension; **partir en p.** to take early retirement

prérogative [prerɔgativ] *nf* prerogative

près [prɛ] *adv* (**a**) *(dans l'espace)* near, close; *(dans le temps)* close; **de p.** closely; **voir qch de p.** to see sth close up; **à quelques détails p.** except for a few details; **la longueur, à cinq centimètres p.** ≃ the length, to within two inches; **à deux minutes p., je ratais le train** two minutes later and I would have missed the train; **je n'en suis pas à cinq euros p.** five euros more or less doesn't matter; **à peu de chose(s) p.** more or less (**b**) **p. de** *(dans l'espace)* near (to), close to; *(dans le temps)* close to; *(environ)* nearly, almost; **p. de là** nearby, close by; **p. de chez eux** near (to) *or* close to where they live; *Fam* **être p. de ses sous** to be tight-fisted; *Hum* **nous ne sommes pas p. de le revoir** we won't see him again in a hurry (**c**) **à peu p.** *(pas tout à fait)* nearly, almost; *(approximativement)* about, approximately; **il est à peu p. certain que…** it's pretty certain that…

présage [prezaʒ] *nm* omen, sign; **mauvais p.** bad omen

présager [45] [prezaʒe] *vt* (**a**) *(annoncer)* to presage; **cela ne présage rien de bon** it doesn't bode well (**b**) *(prévoir)* to predict; **ces gros nuages noirs laissent p. un orage** those big black clouds are a sure sign of a storm

pré-salé (*pl* **prés-salés**) [presale] *nm (mouton)* salt-meadow sheep; *(viande)* salt-meadow lamb

presbyte [presbit] *adj* farsighted

presbytère [presbiter] *nm* presbytery

presbytérien, -enne [presbiterjɛ̃, -ɛn] *adj & nm,f* Presbyterian

presbytie [presbisi] *nf* farsightedness

préscolaire [preskɔler] *adj* preschool

prescription [preskripsjɔ̃] *nf* (**a**) *Jur* **après cinquante ans, il y a p.** the statute of limitations expires after fifty years (**b**) *(ordonnance)* prescription (**c**) *(instruction)* rule, regulation

prescrire [30] [preskrir] *vt* *(médicament)* to prescribe; **à la date prescrite** on the date specified

préséance [preseɑ̃s] *nf* precedence, priority (**sur** over)

présélection [preselɛksjɔ̃] *nf* preselection; *(de candidats)* shortlisting

présélectionner [preselɛksjɔne] *vt* to preselect; *(candidats)* to shortlist

présence [prezɑ̃s] *nf* (**a**) *(dans un lieu)* presence; *(à l'école)* attendance; **il ignore votre p.** he doesn't know you're here; **avoir de la p.** *(acteur)* to have great presence; **les parties en p.** the parties present; **en p. de toute la famille** in front of the whole family; **en p. du virus** when the virus is present (**b**) **p. d'esprit** presence of mind

présent¹, -e [prezɑ̃, -ɑ̃t] **1** *adj* (**a**) *(physiquement)* present; **les personnes présentes** those present; **Jacques Martelin, ici p., vous le dira** Jacques Martelin, who is here with us, will tell you; **Tardieu? – p.!** Tardieu? – here! *or* present! (**b**) *(situation, moment)* present; **vivre dans l'instant p.** to live in the present

2 *nm* (**a**) *Gram* present (tense); **le p. du subjonctif/de l'indicatif** the present subjunctive/indicative; **au p.** in the present (**b**) *(moment présent)* present; **vivre dans le p.** to live in the present (**c**) **à p.** at present, (just) now; **jusqu'à p.** up to now, until now; **jusqu'à p., je n'ai pas reçu de nouvelles** I haven't received any news as yet; **dès à p.** from now on; **à p. que…** now that…

3 *nf* **par la présente** *(par cette lettre)* hereby

présent² [prezɑ̃] *nm Litt (cadeau)* present, gift; **faire p. de qch à qn** to present sth to sb

présentable [prezɑ̃tabl] *adj* presentable

présentateur, -trice [prezɑ̃tatœr, -tris] *nm,f* presenter; *(d'un spectacle télévisé)* host, emcee; **p. de journal télévisé** newscaster; **p. principal** anchor

présentation [prezɑ̃tasjɔ̃] *nf* (**a**) *(de faits, d'un billet)* presentation; **10% de réduction sur p. de la carte** 10% discount on presentation of this card (**b**) *(apparence)* *(d'une personne)* appearance; *(d'un document)* presentation, layout; **recherche hôtesses, excellente p.** *(petite annonce)* hostesses required, must have smart appearance; *Ordinat* **p. assistée par ordinateur** computer-aided presentation (**c**) *(dans un groupe)* introduction (**à** to); **faire les présentations** to make the introductions (**d**) *(d'un film)* showing, presentation; **p. de mode** fashion show

présenter [prezɑ̃te] **1** *vt* (**a**) *(montrer)* to show, to present; *(symptôme)* to present; *(facture)* to submit (**b**) *(par écrit)* to present; *(oralement)* *(arguments)* to present, to set out; *(spectacle)* to present, to host; **p. ses condoléances à qn** to offer sb one's condolences (**d**) *(projet de loi)* to bring in, to introduce; **p. sa candidature à un poste** to apply for a job (**e**) *(personne)* **p. qn à qn** to introduce sb to sb; **je vous présente Marie** this is Marie

2 *vi Fam* **bien/mal p.** to look/not to look good

3 se présenter *vpr* (**a**) *(occasion, cas)* to arise, to present itself; **ça se présente bien** things are looking promising (**b**)

(à un poste) to apply (**à** for); **se p. à un examen** to take an examination; **se p. aux élections** to be a candidate at the elections, to run for election (**c**) *(arriver)* to turn up; **présentez-vous au commissariat à huit heures** be at the police station at eight o'clock; **se p. chez qn** to call on sb (**d**) *(dire son nom)* to introduce oneself (**à** to) (**e**) **le bébé se présente par la tête/le siège** the baby is presenting normally/in a breech position

présentoir [prezãtwar] *nm* display unit

préservatif [prezɛrvatif] *nm* condom; **p. féminin** female condom

préservation [prezɛrvasjɔ̃] *nf* preservation, protection

préserver [prezɛrve] **1** *vt* to preserve, to protect (**de** from); **le ciel m'en préserve!** heaven forbid!

2 se préserver *vpr* to protect oneself (**de** from)

présidence [prezidãs] *nf* (**a**) *(d'un état)* presidency (**b**) *(d'un club)* chairmanship

président, -e [prezidã, -ãt] *nm,f* (**a**) *(d'un état)* president; **le p. de la République** the President of the Republic (**b**) *(d'une assemblée, d'un club)* chairman, *f* chairwoman; **P. du conseil d'administration** Chairman of the Board; **p.-directeur général** chief executive officer (**c**) *(magistrat)* presiding judge; **p. du jury** chairman of the jury

présidentiel, -elle [prezidãsjɛl] **1** *adj* presidential

2 *nfpl* **présidentielles** presidential elections

Présidentielles

In France, since 1873, the president has been traditionally elected for a renewable seven-year term ("le septennat"). However, as a result of a referendum held in September 2000, the French parliament ruled that the seven-year term of office was to be replaced in 2002 by a five-year term ("le quinquennat"). Candidates are usually nominated by the main political parties, but anyone who collects the requisite number of sponsors can run. If no candidate wins an outright majority in the first round of voting, a runoff between the two frontrunners is held two weeks later.

présider [prezide] **1** *vt* (**a**) *(conseil)* to preside over; *(réunion)* to chair (**b**) *(banquet)* to be the guest of honor at

2 présider à *vt ind Litt* **p. aux destinées de…** to preside over the destinies of…

présomption [prezɔ̃psjɔ̃] *nf* presumption; **p. d'innocence** presumption of innocence

présomptueux, -euse [prezɔ̃ptɥø, -øz] *adj* presumptuous

presque [prɛsk] *adv* (**a**) *(à peu près)* almost, nearly; **p. jamais/rien** scarcely *or* hardly ever/anything; **je ne dors p. pas** I hardly *or* barely get any sleep; **rien ou p.** scarcely anything (**b**) *(devant un nom)* **la p. totalité de son œuvre** nearly *or* almost all of his/her work

presqu'île [prɛskil] *nf* peninsula

pressant, -e [prɛsã, -ãt] *adj* *(besoin)* pressing, urgent; *(demande, vendeur)* insistent; *Fam Euph* **avoir un besoin p.** to be bursting *(to go to the bathroom)*

presse [prɛs] *nf* (**a**) *(ensemble des journaux)* press; **travailler dans la p.** to work in journalism; **je l'ai lu dans la p.** I read it in the papers; *Fig* **avoir bonne/mauvaise p. (auprès de)** to be well/badly thought of (by); **la p. écrite** the print media, the press; **la p. à scandale, la p. à sensation** the popular press (**b**) *Tech* press (**c**) *(pour imprimer)* (printing) press; **mettre qch sous p.** to send sth to press

pressé, -e [prɛse] *adj* (**a**) *(personne)* in a hurry *or* rush; **p. de faire qch** in a hurry to do sth; **être p. par le temps** to be pushed for time; **d'un pas p.** hurriedly; **on n'est pas p.** there's no rush (**b**) *(urgent)* urgent; **aller** *ou* **parer au plus p.** to deal with the most urgent thing(s) first

presse-agrumes [prɛsagrym] *nm inv* juice extractor, juicer

presse-ail [prɛsaj] *nm inv* garlic press

presse-citron [prɛssitrɔ̃] *nm inv* lemon squeezer

presse-fruits [prɛsfrɥi] *nm inv* juicer

pressentiment [prɛsãtimã] *nm* presentiment; *(d'un malheur)* foreboding; **j'ai le p. que…** I have a (funny) feeling that…

pressentir [64a] [prɛsãtir] *vt* (**a**) *(deviner)* to have a premonition of, to sense; *(malheur)* to have a foreboding of (**b**) **p. qn (pour qch)** to sound sb out (about sth)

presse-papiers [prɛspapje] *nm inv* paperweight; *Ordinat* clipboard

presse-purée [prɛspyre] *nm inv* potato masher

presser [prɛse] **1** *vt* (**a**) *(agrume, éponge)* to squeeze; *(raisin, pommes)* to press; **p. qn contre son cœur** to clasp sb in one's arms, to hug sb (**b**) *(sonnette, bouton)* to press, to push (**c**) *(harceler)* **p. qn de questions** to bombard sb with questions; **p. qn de faire qch** to urge sb to do sth (**d**) *(faire se hâter)* *(personne)* to hurry (up); *(travail, mouvement)* to speed up; **p. le pas** *ou* **l'allure** to speed up, to quicken one's pace

2 *vi* **le temps presse** there isn't much time (left); **rien ne presse** there's no hurry *or* rush; **allons, pressons!** come on, let's move it!

3 se presser *vpr* (**a**) *(se dépêcher)* to hurry (up); **se p. de faire qch** to hurry to do sth; **faire qch sans se p.** to take one's time doing sth (**b**) *(se serrer)* **se p. contre** to press (oneself) against; **se p. autour de** to crowd around

pressing [prɛsiŋ] *nm* dry cleaner's

pression [prɛsjɔ̃] *nf* (**a**) *Tech* pressure; **mettre qch sous p.** to pressurize sth; **sous p.** *(récipient)* pressurized; *Fig* **être sous p.** to be under pressure; *Méd* **p. artérielle** blood pressure; *Météo* **p. atmosphérique** atmospheric pressure; **zone de hautes/basses pressions** area of high/low pressure (**b**) *(action de presser)* pressure; **d'une simple p. du doigt** at the touch of a button (**c**) *Fig (influence)* pressure; **faire p. sur qn** to put pressure on sb, to pressure sb; **subir des pressions** to be under pressure; *Fam* **mettre la p. à qn** to pressure sb, to put pressure on sb (**d**) *(bouton)* snap fastener (**e**) **bière (à la) p.** draft beer; **une p., s'il vous plaît** ≃ a beer, please

pressoir [prɛswar] *nm* (**a**) *(instrument)* press (**b**) *(lieu)* press house, press room

pressurer [prɛsyre] *vt (exploiter)* to squeeze

pressurisation [prɛsyrizasjɔ̃] *nf* pressurization

prestance [prɛstãs] *nf* presence; **avoir de la p.** to have (great) presence

prestataire [prɛstatɛr] **1** *nmf* (**a**) *(bénéficiaire)* person receiving benefits (**b**) *(fournisseur)* **p. de service** service provider

2 *nm Ordinat* **p. d'accès** access provider

prestation [prɛstasjɔ̃] *nf* (**a**) *(allocation)* benefit; **prestations familiales** welfare; **prestations sociales** welfare (**b**) **prestations** *(services fournis)* services (**c**) *(fait de fournir)* provision; **p. de service** provision of a service (**d**) *(d'un comédien)* performance (**e**) **p. de serment** taking the oath

preste [prɛst] *adj* nimble

prestement [prɛstəmã] *adv* promptly

prestidigitateur, -trice [prɛstidiʒitatœr, -tris] *nm,f* conjurer, magician

prestidigitation [prɛstidiʒitasjɔ̃] *nf* conjuring, magic

prestige [prɛstiʒ] *nm* prestige; **de p.** *(voiture, hôtel)* luxury; *(réalisation)* prestige; **le p. de l'uniforme** the glamor of a uniform

prestigieux, -euse [prɛstiʒjø, -øz] *adj* prestigious

présumer [prezyme] **1** *vt (supposer)* to presume, to assume; **p. qn innocent** to presume sb (to be) innocent

2 présumer de *vt ind* **trop p. de soi** to be overconfident; **p. de ses forces** to overestimate one's strength

présupposer [presypoze] *vt* to presuppose

présure [prezyr] *nf* rennet

prêt¹, -e [prɛ, prɛt] *adj* ready; **être p. à tout** to be prepared to do anything; **être p. à faire qch** to be ready to do sth

prêt² [prɛ] *nm* (*action*) lending; (*somme*) loan; **p. bancaire** bank loan; **p. immobilier** home loan, ≃ mortgage

prêt-à-porter [prɛtapɔrte] *nm* (**a**) (*vêtements*) ready-to-wear clothes (**b**) (*secteur*) ready-to-wear (clothing business)

prétendant, -e [pretɑ̃dɑ̃, -ɑ̃t] **1** *nm,f* (*à un poste*) applicant, candidate (**à** for); (*à un bien, à un titre*) claimant (**à** to); (*au trône*) pretender (**à** to)
   2 *nm* (*d'une femme*) suitor

prétendre [pretɑ̃dr] **1** *vt* (*déclarer*) to maintain, to claim; **on prétend que…** people say that…, it is said that…; **à ce qu'il prétend** according to him; **il ne prétend pas être artiste** he doesn't claim or pretend to be an artist; **on le prétend fou** they say he's crazy
   2 prétendre à *vt ind* to lay claim to; **p. à la victoire** to aim to win
   3 se prétendre *vpr* to claim to be

prétendu, -e [pretɑ̃dy] *adj* (*coupable, voleur*) alleged; (*progrès, égalité, héros*) so-called

prétendument [pretɑ̃dymɑ̃] *adv* supposedly

prête-nom (*pl* **prête-noms**) [prɛtnɔ̃] *nm Fig* figurehead

prétentieux, -euse [pretɑ̃sjø, -øz] **1** *adj* pretentious
   2 *nm,f* pretentious person

prétention [pretɑ̃sjɔ̃] *nf* (**a**) (*vanité*) pretentiousness, pretension; **sans p.** (*repas, maison, personne*) unpretentious (**b**) (*revendication, ambition*) pretension, claim (**à** to); **avoir la p. de faire qch** to claim or to pretend to be able to do sth; **quelles sont vos prétentions?** (*salaire demandé*) what sort of salary are you looking for?

prêter [prɛte] **1** *vt* (**a**) (*temporairement*) to lend, to loan; **p. qch à qn** to lend sth to sb, to lend sb sth; **p. sur gages** to lend against security; *Prov* **on ne prête qu'aux riches** = people don't lend money to those who really need it; *Fig* people are judged according to their reputation (**b**) (*donner*) **p. son appui** *ou* **son concours à qn** to give sb one's support; **p. assistance** *ou* **secours à qn** to lend *or* to give assistance to sb; **p. main-forte à qn** to lend sb a hand; **p. l'oreille (à)** lend an ear (to); **p. attention à qch** to pay attention to sth; **p. serment** to take an oath; **p. le flanc à la critique** to lay oneself open to criticism (**c**) (*attribuer*) **p. qch à qn** (*propos, intentions*) to attribute *or* to ascribe sth to sb
   2 prêter à *vt ind* **p. à confusion** to give rise to confusion; **cela prête à rire** that's laughable
   3 se prêter *vpr* (**a**) (*consentir*) **se p. à** to lend oneself to (**b**) (*convenir*) **se p. à** to lend itself to; **la situation ne s'y prête pas** the situation isn't ideal

prétérit [preterit] *nm* preterite (tense); **au p.** in the preterite

prêteur, -euse [prɛtœr, -øz] **1** *nm,f* lender; **p. sur gages** pawnbroker
   2 *adj* ready *or* willing to lend things; **je ne suis pas p.** I don't like lending things

prétexte [pretɛkst] *nm* pretext, excuse; **pour toi, tout est p. à rire** you find cause for laughter in everything; **sous p. de faire qch** on the pretext of doing sth; **sous p. que…** on the pretext that…; **sous aucun p.** on no account, under no circumstances

prétexter [pretɛkste] *vt* to give as a pretext *or* an excuse; **il a prétexté qu'il était malade** he gave the excuse that he was ill; **p. la fatigue** to plead tiredness

Pretoria [pretɔrja] *n* Pretoria

prêtre [prɛtr] *nm* priest

prêtresse [prɛtrɛs] *nf* priestess

prêtrise [prɛtriz] *nf* priesthood

preuve [prœv] *nf* (**a**) (*pour démontrer*) piece of evidence; **il nous faut des preuves** we need proof *or* evidence; **faire la p. de qch** to prove sth; **avoir la p. que/de…** to have proof

that/of…; **faire p. d'intelligence/de courage** to show intelligence/courage; **faire ses preuves** (*personne*) to prove oneself, to show one's ability; (*technique*) to be tried and tested; **jusqu'à p. du contraire** until there's proof to the contrary; *Fam* **elle ne m'aime pas: la p., elle ne m'écrit jamais** I know she doesn't like me because she never writes to me; **j'en veux pour p.…** the proof of it is…; **p. d'achat** proof of purchase (**b**) *Jur* evidence (**c**) (*témoignage*) **une p. d'amour/ d'amitié** a token of love/friendship (**d**) *Math* **faire la p. d'une opération** to prove *or* to test the validity of a mathematical operation; **faire la p. par neuf** to cast out nines

prévaloir [69b] [prevalwar] **1** *vi* to prevail (**sur** over); **faire p. son opinion** to win acceptance for one's opinion
   2 se prévaloir *vpr* **se p. de qch** (*profiter de*) to take advantage of sth; (*s'enorgueillir*) to pride oneself on sth

prévenant, -e [prevnɑ̃, -ɑ̃t] *adj* (*personne*) kind (**envers** *ou* **avec** to), considerate (**envers** *ou* **avec** towards); (*geste*) thoughtful (**envers** *ou* **avec** towards)

prévenir [70] [prevnir] *vt* (**a**) (*informer*) to inform, to let know (**de** about *or* of); (*mettre en garde*) to warn; **tu es prévenu!** you've been warned!; **partir sans p.** to leave without telling anyone *or* without warning (**b**) (*empêcher*) (*maladie*) to prevent, to guard against; (*danger, accident*) to avert; *Prov* **mieux vaut p. que guérir** prevention is better than cure (**c**) (*devancer*) (*désir*) to anticipate; (*objection*) to forestall

préventif, -ive [prevɑ̃tif, -iv] *adj* preventive; *Jur* **détention préventive** custody; **être en détention préventive** to be remanded in custody

prévention [prevɑ̃sjɔ̃] *nf* (**a**) (*pour empêcher*) prevention; **p. routière** road safety (**b**) *Jur* custody; **mettre qn en p.** to remand sb in custody

prévenu, -e [prevny] *nm,f Jur* defendant, accused

prévisible [previzibl] *adj* foreseeable

prévision [previzjɔ̃] *nf* forecast; (*activité*) forecasting; **en p. de qch** in expectation *or* anticipation of sth; **prévisions budgétaires** budget projections *or* forecasts; **prévisions météorologiques** weather forecast

prévisionnel, -elle [previzjɔnɛl] *adj* (*coûts*) estimated; (*budget*) projected; (*analyse*) preliminary

prévoir [73c] [prevwar] *vt* (**a**) (*météo*) to forecast; (*réaction, difficultés, retards*) to expect, to anticipate; **on ne peut pas tout p.** you can't think of everything (**b**) (*programmer*) (*sortie, vacances*) to plan; **la réunion est prévue pour demain** the meeting is scheduled for tomorrow; **il faudra p. des vêtements de pluie** we'll have to take waterproof clothes; **qu'est-ce que tu as prévu pour le dessert?** what are you planning to have for dessert?; **comme prévu** as planned; **cela s'est passé comme prévu** it went according to plan; **plus tôt/tard que prévu** sooner/later than expected; **cela n'était pas prévu au programme** that wasn't on the agenda

prévoyance [prevwajɑ̃s] *nf* foresight, forethought

prévoyant, -e [prevwajɑ̃, -ɑ̃t] *adj* far-sighted

prie-Dieu [pridjø] *nm inv* prie-dieu, prayer stool

prier [66] [prije] **1** *vi* to pray (**pour** for)
   2 *vt* (**a**) (*dieu*) to pray to (**b**) (*supplier*) to beg; **il ne s'est pas fait p. pour venir** he didn't need much persuading to come; **allez, viens, arrête de te faire p.!** come on, stop being so difficult!; **sans se faire p.** without hesitation (**c**) (*demander à*) **p. qn de faire qch** to ask sb to do sth; **je te prie de te dépêcher!** please hurry up!; **taisez-vous, je vous prie!** please be quiet!; **je te prie de croire qu'elle a été surprise!** she was surprised, believe you me!; **je vous en prie!** (*faites-le*) please do!, of course!; (*taisez-vous*) stop it!; (*il n'y a pas de quoi*) you're welcome!

prière [prijɛr] *nf* (**a**) *Rel* prayer; **faire** *ou* **dire sa p.** to say one's prayers (**b**) (*demande*) request; **p. de ne pas fumer** (*sur écriteau*) no smoking; **p. de fermer la porte** (*sur écriteau*) please close the door

prieuré [prijœre] *nm* priory

primaire [primɛr] **1** *adj* (**a**) *(école, couleur, secteur, ère)* primary (**b**) *Péj (personne)* simple-minded; *(réaction, racisme)* narrow-minded

2 *nm* (**a**) *Scol* primary education; **être en p.** to be at primary or elementary school (**b**) *Géol* Primary era (**c**) *Écon* primary sector

primate [primat] *nm Zool* primate

primauté [primote] *nf* primacy

prime[1] [prim] *adj* (**a**) **de p. abord** at first sight; *Litt* **dès sa p. jeunesse** since her early youth (**b**) *Math* **B p.** B prime

prime[2] [prim] *nf (d'assurance)* premium; *(allocation)* grant; *(sur salaire)* bonus; **et vous aurez droit à un stylo en p.** and you will receive a free pen; *Fig* **en p.** into the bargain; **p. d'ancienneté** seniority bonus; **p. d'assurance** insurance premium; **p. de départ** severance pay, golden handshake; **p. de licenciement** severance pay; **p. de transport** transportation allowance

primer[1] [prime] **1** *vt (avoir la priorité sur)* to take precedence over

2 *vi* to come first; **p. sur** to take precedence over

primer[2] [prime] *vt (attribuer un prix à)* to award a prize to; **primé** *(taureau)* prize(winning); *(roman, film)* prizewinning, award-winning

primeur [primœr] *nf* (**a**) **primeurs** *(fruits et légumes)* (early) fruit and vegetables; **marchand de primeurs** fruit and vegetable retailer *(selling early produce)* (**b**) *(exclusivité)* **avoir la p. d'une nouvelle** to be the first to hear a piece of news

primevère [primvɛr] *nf* primrose

primitif, -ive [primitif, -iv] **1** *adj* primitive; *(originel)* original

2 *nm (artiste)* primitive

primo [primo] *adv* first(ly), in the first place

primordial, -e, -aux, -ales [primɔrdjal, -o] *adj* essential, primordial

prince [prɛ̃s] *nm* prince; **comme un p.** *(traité, élevé, habillé)* like a prince; **être** *ou* **se montrer bon p.** to be very decent; **le p. charmant** Prince Charming

prince-de-galles [prɛ̃sdəgal] *adj inv* Prince of Wales check

princesse [prɛ̃sɛs] *nf* princess

princier, -ère [prɛ̃sje, -ɛr] *adj* princely

principal, -e, -aux, -ales [prɛ̃sipal, -o] **1** *adj aussi Gram* main; *(question, raison, but)* main, principal; *(rôle, acteur)* leading

2 *nm* (**a**) *(ce qui compte le plus)* **le p.** the main thing, the most important thing (**b**) *(d'une école)* principal

principalement [prɛ̃sipalmã] *adv* mainly, principally

principauté [prɛ̃sipote] *nf* principality

principe [prɛ̃sip] *nm* principle; **un accord de p.** an agreement in principle; **partir du p. que...** to assume that...; **c'est une question de p.** it's a matter of principle; **avoir pour p. de...** to make it a matter of principle to...; **avoir des principes** to have (high) principles; **en p.** in principle, theoretically; **par p.** on principle

printanier, -ère [prɛ̃tanje, -ɛr] *adj* spring

printemps [prɛ̃tã] *nm* spring; **au p.** in (the) spring(time); **une journée de p.** a spring day; *Fig* **ses vingt-six p.** her twenty-six summers

prion [priɔ̃] *nm Biol* prion

prioritaire [prijɔritɛr] *adj* (that has) priority; **être p.** to have priority; *(en voiture)* to have the right of way

priorité [prijɔrite] *nf* (**a**) *(précédence)* priority; **donner la p. à qn/qch** to give sb/sth priority; **leur dossier sera traité en p.** their file will get priority treatment; **avoir la p. sur** to have priority over (**b**) *Aut* right of way, priority; **avoir la p.** to have the right of way; **accorder** *ou* **laisser la p. à une voiture** to yield to a car; **refuser la p.** to refuse to yield; **p. à droite** *(sur panneau)* = yield to vehicles coming from the right

pris, -e[1] [pri, priz] *pp voir* **prendre**

2 *adj* (**a**) *(siège)* occupied, taken; **avoir les mains prises** to have one's hands full (**b**) *(personne)* busy; **je suis déjà p. ce jour-là** I have a previous engagement that day (**c**) *(saisi)* **p. de peur** seized with fear; **p. de panique** panic-stricken; **p. de remords** racked with guilt (**d**) *(gelé)* frozen (over) (**e**) *(encombré)* **avoir le nez p.** to have a blocked nose; **avoir la gorge prise** to have a sore throat (**f**) **avoir la taille bien prise** to have a trim waist

prise[2] [priz] *nf (d'une ville, de prisonniers)* taking, capture; *(à la pêche)* catch; *(de drogue)* seizure

(**b**) *(de médicaments)* taking

(**c**) *Élec* **p. (de courant** *ou* **électrique)** *(femelle)* outlet; *(mâle)* plug; **p. multiple** adapter; *Ordinat* **p. péritel** scart connector; **p. de terre** ground (connection)

(**d**) *Cin, Phot & TV* **p. de son** sound recording; **p. de vue** *(cliché)* shot; *(de tournage)* take; *(action)* shooting

(**e**) *Tech* **en p.** in gear, engaged; *Fig* **en p. (directe) sur** *ou* **avec qch** in touch with sth

(**f**) *(de judo, de lutte)* hold; *(pour se retenir)* hold; *(plus ferme)* grasp, grip; *(pour le pied)* foothold; *Fig* **avoir p. sur qn** to have a hold on *or* over sb; **lâcher p.** to lose one's grip; *Fig* to give up; **donner p. aux reproches/critiques** to lay oneself open to reproach/criticism; **être aux prises avec des difficultés** to be grappling with difficulties; **être aux prises avec qn** to be at odds with sb

(**g**) *(locutions) Fam* **p. de bec** argument, squabble; **p. en charge** *(par un taxi) (d'un passager)* picking up; *(somme)* minimum charge; *(par la Sécurité sociale)* (guaranteed) reimbursement; **p. de conscience** awareness, realization; **p. de contact** initial contact *or* meeting; **p. de notes** note-taking; **p. d'otages** hostage-taking; **p. de position** stance; **p. de pouvoir** (political) takeover; **faire une p. de sang à qn** to take a blood sample from sb

priser[1] [prize] **1** *vt* **p. du tabac** to take snuff

2 *vi* to take snuff

priser[2] [prize] *vt Litt (estimer)* to prize, to value

prisme [prism] *nm* prism

prison [prizɔ̃] *nf* (**a**) *(lieu de détention)* prison, jail; **mettre qn en prison** to put sb in jail; **faire de la p.** to serve a prison sentence (**b**) *(peine)* imprisonment; **cinq ans de p.** five years' imprisonment

prisonnier, -ère [prizɔnje, -ɛr] **1** *nm,f* prisoner; **faire qn p.** to take sb prisoner; **p. de droit commun** common criminal; **p. de guerre** prisoner of war, POW; **p. d'opinion** prisoner of conscience; **p. politique** political prisoner

2 *adj* imprisoned, in prison; **ils sont encore prisonniers sous les décombres** they are still trapped in the rubble; **être p. de** to be a prisoner of; *Fig* to be a slave to

privation [privasjɔ̃] *nf* (**a**) *(action de priver)* deprivation (**b**) **privations** *(manque)* hardship, privation; **s'imposer des privations** to deprive oneself, to go without

privatisation [privatizasjɔ̃] *nf* privatization

privatiser [privatize] *vt* to privatize

privautés [privote] *nfpl* (undue) familiarity; **prendre** *ou* **se permettre des p. avec qn** to be over-familiar with sb

privé, -e [prive] **1** *adj* private; **à titre p.** in a private capacity

2 *nm* (**a**) *(secteur)* **le p.** the private sector; *Scol* the private-education system; **mes enfants sont dans le p.** my children go to a private school (**b**) *(intimité)* **dans le p.** privately; **connaître qn dans le p.** to know sb personally; **en p.** in private (**c**) *Fam (détective)* private eye

priver [prive] **1** *vt* **p. qn de qch** to deprive sb of sth; **p. qn de sorties** not to allow sb to go out; **être privé de dessert** to go without dessert; **privé d'eau/d'air/de sommeil** deprived of water/air/sleep; **ça ne le prive pas du tout de ne plus fumer** he doesn't find it a hardship not to smoke any more

2 se priver *vpr* to do *or* to go without; **se p. de** to do *or* to go without; *(plaisir)* to deprive oneself of, to deny oneself; **ne pas se p. de faire qch** not to hesitate to do sth

privilège [privilɛʒ] *nm* privilege

privilégié, -e [privileʒje] **1** *adj (personne, site)* privileged; *(conditions)* privileged, favorable; *(relations)* special

2 *nm,f* privileged person; **les privilégiés** the privileged

privilégier [66] [privileʒje] *vt (personne, groupe)* to privilege; *(facteur, aspect)* to prioritize

prix [pri] *nm* (**a**) *(coût)* à **tout p.** at all costs, at any price; **à aucun p.** not at any price, on no account; **se vendre à p. d'or** to fetch huge prices; **acheter qch à p. d'or** to pay a (small) fortune for sth; **payer qch au p. fort** to pay a high price for sth; **faire un p. à qn** to give sb a good deal; **je vous fais un p. d'ami** I'll offer you a special price; **y mettre le p.** to pay a high price; **la santé/le bonheur, ça n'a pas de p.** you can't put a price on health/happiness; **mettre à p. la tête de qn** to put a price on sb's head; **c'est mon dernier p.** that's my final offer; **votre p. sera le mien** name your price; **au p. coûtant** at cost price; **p. de revient** cost price; **p. de vente** selling price (**b**) *(importance)* **attacher beaucoup de p.** *ou* **un grand p. à qch** to set great store by sth (**c**) *(récompense)* prize; **p. de consolation** consolation prize; **le p. Goncourt** = prestigious French literary prize; **p. Nobel** *(récompense)* Nobel Prize; *(personne)* Nobel laureate; **le p. Nobel de la Paix** *(récompense)* the Nobel Peace Prize

pro [pro] *nmf Fam* pro

probabilité [prɔbabilite] *nf* probability, likelihood; **selon toute p.** in all probability *or* likelihood; *Math* **calcul des probabilités** theory of probability

probable [prɔbabl] *adj* probable, likely; **il est p. qu'elle viendra** she'll probably come; **peu p.** improbable, unlikely; **il est peu p. qu'elle vienne** she's not likely *or* she's unlikely to come

probablement [prɔbabləmɑ̃] *adv* probably

probant, -e [prɔbɑ̃, -ɑ̃t] *adj* convincing, conclusive

probité [prɔbite] *nf* probity, integrity

problématique [prɔblematik] **1** *adj* problematic(al)

2 *nf* set of problems

problème [prɔblɛm] *nm* problem; **c'est tout un p.!** it's such a problem!; **peau/cheveux à problèmes** problem skin/hair; **avoir des problèmes familiaux/d'argent** to have family/money problems

procédé [prɔsede] *nm* (**a**) *(façon de faire)* method; **échange de bons procédés** exchange of friendly services (**b**) *(technique)* process; **p. de fabrication** manufacturing process; *Péj* **ça sent le p.** it seems rather artificial

procéder [34] [prɔsede] **1** *vi* (**a**) *(agir)* to proceed, to act; **p. par ordre** to do things in order; **p. avec méthode** to proceed methodically; **p. par élimination** to follow a process of elimination (**b**) *Sout* **p. de** *(venir de)* to arise out of, to originate in

2 procéder à *vt ind (recherches, arrestation, vérification)* to carry out; *(élections)* to hold

procédure [prɔsedyr] *nf* (**a**) *(méthode)* procedure (**b**) *Jur* proceedings; **engager une p.** to take proceedings (**c**) *Ordinat* procedure; **p. de chargement** loading procedure

procédurier, -ère [prɔsedyrje, -ɛr] *adj* quibbling; *Jur* litigious

procès [prɔsɛ] *nm Jur* (legal) proceedings; *(civil)* lawsuit; *(criminel)* (criminal) trial; **engager un p.** to take legal action; **faire** *ou* **intenter un p. à qn** to take proceedings against sb; **être en p. avec qn** to be involved in legal proceedings with sb; **gagner/perdre son p.** to win/to lose one's case; **faire un p. d'intention à qn** to accuse sb on the basis of assumptions not facts; **faire le p. de qn/qch** *(critiquer)* to attack sb/sth; *Fig* **sans autre forme de p.** without (any) further ceremony, without further ado

processeur [prɔsesœr] *nm Ordinat* processor; **p. central** central processing unit, CPU; **p. de données** data processor

procession [prɔsesjɔ̃] *nf* procession

processus [prɔsesys] *nm* process

procès-verbal [prɔsɛvɛrbal] *(pl* **procès-verbaux** [prɔsɛvɛrbo]) *nm* (**a**) *Jur* police report *(about an offense)*; *(amende)* fine; *(contravention)* ticket (**b**) *(rapport)* (official) report; *(d'une réunion)* minutes; *(d'un témoignage)* record

prochain, -e [prɔʃɛ̃, -ɛn] **1** *adj* (**a**) *(qui suit)* next; **ce sera pour une prochaine fois** let's take a rain check; **à la prochaine (fois)!** see you (soon)!; *Fam* **je descends à la prochaine** I'm getting off at the next stop (**b**) *(imminent)* imminent; **dans un avenir p.** in the near *or* not too distant future; **un jour p.** one day soon

2 *nm (semblable)* **aimer son p.** to love one's neighbor

prochainement [prɔʃɛnmɑ̃] *adv* shortly, soon; **p. sur vos écrans** coming soon to a movie theater near you

proche [prɔʃ] **1** *adj* (**a**) *(dans l'espace)* near, close; **p. de qch** close to *or* near sth (**b**) *(dans l'avenir)* near, imminent; **dans un avenir p.** in the near *or* not too distant future; **la fin est p.** the end is nigh (**c**) *(récent)* recent (**d**) *(semblable, intime)* close (**de** to); **ils sont proches parents** they are closely related (**e**) **de p. en p.** gradually, step by step

2 *nm* close relative *or* relation

Proche-Orient [prɔʃɔrjɑ̃] *nm* **le P.** the Middle East

proclamation [prɔklamasjɔ̃] *nf* proclamation

proclamer [prɔklame] *vt* to proclaim; *(résultats de scrutin)* to declare

procréation [prɔkreasjɔ̃] *nf* procreation

procréer [24] [prɔkree] *vi* to procreate

procuration [prɔkyrasjɔ̃] *nf* proxy, power of attorney; **par p.** by proxy, *Spéc* per pro(curationem); *Fig* **vivre par p.** to live vicariously *or* by proxy

procurer [prɔkyre] **1** *vt* **p. qch à qn** *(sujet: personne)* to get sth for sb; *(sujet: chose)* to bring sb sth

2 se procurer *vpr* to get (hold of), to obtain

procureur [prɔkyrœr] *nm Jur* procurator, proxy; **p. général/de la République** ≃ district attorney

prodigalité [prɔdigalite] *nf* extravagance, prodigality

prodige [prɔdiʒ] **1** *nm* wonder, marvel; *(personne)* prodigy; **faire des prodiges** to work wonders; **tenir du p.** to be extraordinary, to be something of a miracle

2 *adj* **enfant p.** child prodigy

prodigieusement [prɔdiʒjøzmɑ̃] *adv* prodigiously

prodigieux, -euse [prɔdiʒjø, -øz] *adj* prodigious, extraordinary

prodigue [prɔdig] *adj (dépensier)* wasteful, spendthrift; *(généreux)* lavish, unsparing (**de** *in or* with)

prodiguer [prɔdige] *vt* **p. qch à qn** to lavish sth on sb; **p. des conseils à qn** to pour out advice to sb

producteur, -trice [prɔdyktœr, -tris] **1** *adj* **pays p. de blé/pétrole** wheat-growing/oil-producing country

2 *nm,f* producer

productif, -ive [prɔdyktif, -iv] *adj* productive

production [prɔdyksjɔ̃] *nf* (**a**) *Ind & Cin* production; *(d'électricité)* production, generation (**b**) *(produit)* product; *Cin* production; *(d'une usine)* output; **p. littéraire** literary output

productivité [prɔdyktivite] *nf* productivity

produire [18] [prɔdɥir] **1** *vt* (**a**) *(marchandise, émission, gaz)* to produce; *(chaleur, électricité, odeur)* to generate, to produce (**b**) *(résultat, effet)* to produce, to bring about; *(irritation, sensation)* to cause

2 se produire *vpr* (**a**) *(événement)* to happen (**b**) *(acteur)* to appear

produit [prɔdɥi] *nm* (**a**) *(marchandise)* product; **produits agricoles** agricultural *or* farm produce; **p. de beauté** beauty product, cosmetic; **p. chimique** chemical; **p. de consommation** consumer product; **p. d'entretien** (household) cleaning product; **p. fini** finished product; **p. intérieur brut** gross domestic product; **p. de luxe** luxury product; **p. manu-**

facturé manufactured product; **produits ménagers** (household) cleaning products; **p. national brut** gross national product **(b)** *(profit)* yield; **p. d'une vente** proceeds of a sale; **le p. de dix années de travail** the result of ten years' work; **vivre du p. de la terre** to live off the land **(c)** *Math (d'une multiplication)* product **(d)** *(création)* **c'est le p. de son imagination** it's the product of his/her imagination

proéminent, -e [prɔeminɑ̃, -ɑ̃t] *adj* prominent

prof [prɔf] *nmf Fam* teacher

profanateur, -trice [prɔfanatœr, -tris] *nm,f (de tombes)* desecrator

profanation [prɔfanasjɔ̃] *nf* desecration, violation

profane [prɔfan] **1** *adj* non-religious, secular; *Fig* **être p. en la matière** to know nothing about the subject
2 *nmf (non-initié)* layman, *f* laywoman

profaner [prɔfane] *vt (église)* to desecrate; *(tombe)* to desecrate, to violate; *(souvenir, mémoire)* to defile

proférer [34] [prɔfere] *vt* to utter

professer [prɔfese] *vt* to profess

professeur [prɔfesœr] *nm* teacher; *(à l'université)* professor; *Can Univ* **p. adjoint** ≃ assistant professor; *Can Univ* **p. agrégé** ≃ associate professor; **p. des écoles** primary-school teacher; **p. principal** homeroom teacher

profession [prɔfesjɔ̃] *nf* **(a)** *(métier)* profession, occupation; *(d'artisans)* trade; **de p.** *(musicien)* professional; *(menuisier)* by trade; **p. libérale** profession; **sans p.** *(dans un questionnaire)* not working; **je suis sans p.** I don't work **(b)** *(déclaration)* **faire p. de qch** to profess sth; **p. de foi** profession of faith

professionnalisation [prɔfesjɔnalizasjɔ̃] *nf* professionalization

professionnalisme [prɔfesjɔnalism] *nm* professionalism

professionnel, -elle [prɔfesjɔnɛl] **1** *adj (attitude, sportif)* professional; *(enseignement)* vocational; *(maladie)* occupational
2 *nm,f* professional

professionnellement [prɔfesjɔnɛlmɑ̃] *adv* professionally

professoral, -e, -aux, -ales [prɔfesɔral, -o] *adj* **(a)** *(de professeur)* professorial **(b)** *(pédant)* patronizing, lecturing

professorat [prɔfesɔra] *nm* teaching profession *(especially in higher education)*

profil [prɔfil] *nm aussi Fig* profile; **dessiner qn de p.** to draw sb in profile; **se mettre de p.** to turn one's face *(so it is in profile)*; *Fig* **adopter un p. bas** to adopt a low profile; **p. de poste** job description; **avoir le p. de l'emploi** to fit the job description

profilé, -e [prɔfile] **1** *adj (carrosserie)* streamlined
2 *nm* section

profiler [prɔfile] **se profiler** *vpr* to stand out (in profile), to be outlined (**sur** *ou* **contre** against); *(problèmes)* to emerge, to loom; *(solution)* to emerge; *(événement)* to be in the offing

profit [prɔfi] *nm* **(a)** *(avantage)* profit, benefit; **mettre qch à p.** to put sth to good use; **tirer p. de qch** to take advantage of sth; **ce manteau m'a fait du p.** this coat has served me well; **au p. des pauvres** in aid of the poor; **concert donné au p. des orphelins** benefit concert for orphans; **perdre des voix au p. de qn** to lose votes to sb **(b)** *(gain)* profit; **il n'y a pas de petits profits** every little bit helps

profitable [prɔfitabl] *adj* profitable

profiter [prɔfite] **1 profiter de** *vt ind* to take advantage of; **je profite d'un moment de calme pour vous dire que…** I'm using these few moments of peace and quiet to tell you that…; **p. de la vie/de sa jeunesse** to make the most of life/one's youth
2 profiter à *vt ind* to be of benefit to, to benefit; **ses vacances lui ont bien profité** his/her vacation has done him/her a lot of good
3 *vi Fam (enfant, plante)* to thrive

profiteur, -euse [prɔfitœr, -øz] *nm,f Péj* profiteer

profond, -e [prɔfɔ̃, -ɔ̃d] **1** *adj* **(a)** *(trou, lac, voix)* deep; *(décolleté)* plunging; *(forêt)* dense, thick; *(sommeil)* deep, sound **(b)** *(cause)* underlying **(c)** *(paroles)* profound; *(haine, silence, dégoût)* profound, deep; *(soupir)* heavy
2 *adv* deep
3 *nm* **au plus p. de mon cœur** in my heart of hearts, deep down; **au plus p. de la nuit** at dead of night

profondément [prɔfɔ̃demɑ̃] *adv (choqué, déçu, ému)* deeply, profoundly; *(aimer, mépriser)* deeply; *(dormir)* soundly; *(creuser)* deep; **p. endormi** sound *or* fast asleep; **j'en suis p. convaincu** I'm quite convinced of it

profondeur [prɔfɔ̃dœr] *nf* **(a)** *(de l'eau, d'un trou)* depth; **faire six mètres de p.** ≃ to be 20 feet deep; **en p.** *(étude, analyse)* in-depth; *Phot* **p. de champ** depth of field **(b)** *(d'un sentiment)* depth; *(d'un texte)* profoundness, profundity

profusion [prɔfyzjɔ̃] *nf* profusion, abundance; **à p.** in profusion

progéniture [prɔʒenityr] *nf* progeny, offspring

progiciel [prɔʒisjɛl] *nm Ordinat* software package; **p. de communication** comms package

prognathe [prɔgnat] *adj (visage)* undershot, underhung, *Spéc* prognathous

programmable [prɔgramabl] *adj* programmable

programmateur, -trice [prɔgramatœr, -tris] **1** *nm,f Rad & TV* program planner
2 *nm Tech* automatic control (device); *Ordinat* programmer

programmation [prɔgramasjɔ̃] *nf* **(a)** *TV & Rad* program planning **(b)** *Ordinat* programming

programme [prɔgram] *nm* **(a)** *(émissions, œuvres)* program; *(brochure) (de télévision)* TV guide; *(de cinéma)* movie guide; *(au concert, au théâtre)* program **(b)** *(d'activités)* program **(c)** *Scol* curriculum; *(d'un cours)* syllabus; **les auteurs au** *ou* **du p.** the books on the syllabus **(d)** *(d'un parti politique)* manifesto; **p. électoral** (election) platform; *Fig* **c'est tout un p.!** that'll be interesting! **(e)** *Ordinat* program; **p. d'amorçage** boot program; **p. d'arrière-plan** background program; **p. d'auto-test** self-test program; **p. de configuration** configuration program; **p. de conversion** conversion program; **p. détecteur de virus** virus-detection program; **p. éditeur de liens** link program, linker; **p. d'évaluation de performance** benchmark program; **p. de formatage** formatter

programmer [prɔgrame] *vt* **(a)** *Ordinat* to program **(b)** *TV & Rad* to schedule **(c)** *(vacances, changements)* to plan

programmeur, -euse [prɔgramœr, -øz] *nm,f Ordinat* programmer

progrès [prɔgrɛ] *nm* progress; **faire des p.** to make progress; **être en p.** to be making progress; *Fam* **il y a du** *ou* **un p.** there's been an improvement

progresser [prɔgrɛse] *vi* **(a)** *(avancer) (armée)* to advance, to progress; *(marcheur)* to make progress **(b)** *(épidémie, incendie)* to spread; *(chômage, délinquance)* to rise, to increase **(c)** *(faire des progrès)* to make progress

progressif, -ive [prɔgrɛsif, -iv] *adj* progressive; *(changement)* gradual

progression [prɔgrɛsjɔ̃] *nf* **(a)** *(avance) (d'une armée)* advance, progress; *(de marcheurs)* progress **(b)** *(d'un incendie, d'une épidémie)* spread; *(de la délinquance, du chômage)* rise, increase; **être en p.** *(secteur économique)* to be growing *or* expanding; *(maladie)* to be spreading; *(chômage, criminalité)* to be rising, to be on the increase

progressiste [prɔgrɛsist] *adj & nmf* progressive

progressivement [prɔgrɛsivmɑ̃] *adv* progressively

prohiber [prɔibe] *vt* to prohibit, to forbid

prohibitif, -ive [prɔibitif, -iv] *adj* prohibitive

prohibition [prɔibisjɔ̃] *nf* prohibition; *Hist* **la P.** Prohibition

proie [prwa] *nf* prey; **être la p. de qn** to fall prey *or* victim to sb; **être en p. à** *(remords, doute)* to be racked *or* tormented by; *(hallucinations)* to suffer from; **lâcher la p. pour l'ombre** to go chasing after rainbows

projecteur [pʀɔʒɛktœʀ] *nm* **(a)** *Cin & Phot* projector **(b)** *(dans un stade, sur un monument)* floodlight; *Théât* spotlight; *Fig* **sous les projecteurs de l'actualité** in the limelight

projectile [pʀɔʒɛktil] *nm* missile

projection [pʀɔʒɛksjɔ̃] *nf* **(a)** *(lancer)* projection; *(d'un liquide, de boue)* splashing; *(de graisse)* spattering; *(de cendres, de roches)* spewing out; **des projections de boue** splashes of mud **(b)** *Cin* projection; *(séance)* screening, showing; **p. de diapositives** slide show; **p. privée** private screening **(c)** *Math, Géom & (prévision)* projection

projectionniste [pʀɔʒɛksjɔnist] *nmf* projectionist

projet [pʀɔʒɛ] *nm* *(intention)* plan; *(étude)* project; **faire des projets** to make plans; **p. de loi** bill; **en p.** at the planning stage; **c'est resté à l'état de p.** it never got off the ground

projeter [42] [pʀɔʒte] **1** *vt* **(a)** *(lancer)* to project; *(graisse)* to spatter; *(liquide, boue)* to splash; *(cendres, roches)* to spew out; **être projeté au sol** to be hurled to the ground **(b)** *(prévoir)* to plan; **p. de faire qch** to plan to do sth **(c)** *(film)* to show, to screen **(d)** *(faire apparaître) (ombre)* to cast, to throw; *(image)* to project **(e)** *Psy* to project (**sur** onto)
    2 se projeter *vpr (ombre)* to be cast

prolétaire [pʀɔletɛʀ] *adj & nmf* proletarian

prolétariat [pʀɔletaʀja] *nm* proletariat

prolétarien, -enne [pʀɔletaʀjɛ̃, -ɛn] *adj* proletarian

prolifération [pʀɔlifeʀasjɔ̃] *nf* proliferation

proliférer [34] [pʀɔlifeʀe] *vi* to proliferate

prolifique [pʀɔlifik] *adj* prolific

prolixe [pʀɔliks] *adj* wordy, verbose

prolo [pʀɔlo] *Fam* **1** *adj* working-class
    2 *nmf* pleb, prole

prologue [pʀɔlɔg] *nm* prologue (**de** to)

prolongation [pʀɔlɔ̃gasjɔ̃] *nf* *(de discussions)* prolongation; *(d'un congé, d'un séjour)* extension; **jouer les prolongations** *(au football)* to play overtime

prolongé, -e [pʀɔlɔ̃ʒe] *adj* *(absence, séjour)* prolonged, lengthy; *(effort)* prolonged, sustained; *(week-end)* long; **pas d'utilisation prolongée sans avis médical** *(sur un médicament)* ≃ if symptoms persist, consult your doctor

prolongement [pʀɔlɔ̃ʒmɑ̃] *nm* **(a)** *(d'une rue)* continuation; *(d'un mur, d'une voie de chemin de fer)* extension; **être dans le p. de qch** *(meuble)* to be flush with sth; *(rue)* to be a continuation of sth **(b)** **prolongements** *(d'une action)* repercussions

prolonger [45] [pʀɔlɔ̃ʒe] **1** *vt (vie, débat, repas)* to prolong; *(séjour, absence)* to prolong, to extend; *(mur, route, voie ferrée)* to extend
    2 se prolonger *vpr (séjour, absence)* to be prolonged *or* extended; *(réunion)* to go on; *(rue)* to continue, to extend

promenade [pʀɔmnad] *nf* **(a)** *(marche)* walk; *(courte)* stroll; **faire une p.** to go for a walk/stroll; **faire une p. en voiture** to go for a drive; **faire une p. à bicyclette** to go for a bike ride; **faire une p. à cheval** to go horseback riding; **l'heure de la p.** *(d'un détenu)* exercise time **(b)** *(avenue)* promenade

promener [46] [pʀɔmne] **1** *vt* **(a)** *(personne, chien)* to take for a walk; *Fig* **p. qn de musée en musée** to take sb from museum to museum; *Fam* **cela te promènera un peu** it'll get you out a bit **(b)** *(passer)* **p. sa main/son regard sur qch** to run one's hand/one's eyes over sth
    2 se promener *vpr* **(a)** *(à pied)* to go for a walk; **aller se p.** to go for a walk; *Ordinat* **se p. dans** *(texte)* to scroll through **(b)** *(mains, regard)* **se p. sur** to wander over

promeneur, -euse [pʀɔmnœʀ, -øz] *nm,f* walker

promesse [pʀɔmɛs] *nf* promise; **faire une p. à qn** to make sb a promise; **tenir sa p.** to keep one's promise; **p. de Gascon** empty promise; **p. d'achat/de vente** agreement to buy/to sell

prometteur, -euse [pʀɔmɛtœʀ, -øz] *adj* promising

promettre [47] [pʀɔmɛtʀ] **1** *vt* **(a)** *(s'engager à)* to promise; **p. qch à qn** to promise sb sth; **je ne peux rien te p.** I can't promise (you) anything; **tu me le promets?** (do you) promise?; **je te promets de le faire** I promise you I'll do it; **je le ferai, c'est promis** I'll do it, I promise; **p. monts et merveilles à qn** to promise sb the earth *or* the moon **(b)** *(être prometteur)* **la soirée promet d'être amusante** it promises to be an amusing evening; *Fam* **ça ne promet rien de bon** it doesn't look good
    2 *vi (projet, enfant)* to be promising; *Fam Ironique* **ça promet!** that's promising!
    3 se promettre *vpr* **se p. qch** *(à soi-même)* to promise oneself sth; *(l'un l'autre)* to promise each other sth; **se p. de faire qch** *(à soi-même)* to resolve to do sth; **ils se sont promis de ne jamais se quitter** they promised each other they'd never part

promis, -e [pʀɔmi, -iz] **1** *adj* promised
    2 *nm,f Vieilli* betrothed

promiscuité [pʀɔmiskɥite] *nf* overcrowding; **vivre dans la p.** to live in crowded accommodations

promo [pʀɔmo] *nf Fam* promo; **en p.** on special offer

promontoire [pʀɔmɔ̃twaʀ] *nm* promontory, headland

promoteur, -trice [pʀɔmɔtœʀ, -tʀis] *nm,f* **(a)** **p. (immobilier)** real-estate developer **(b)** *(créateur)* originator (**de** of)

promotion [pʀɔmosjɔ̃] *nf* **(a)** *(avancement)* promotion; **p. à l'ancienneté** promotion by seniority; **p. interne** internal promotion; **p. sociale** upward mobility **(b)** *(d'une école)* class; **premier de sa p.** first in one's class **(c)** *(dans le commerce)* promotion; **faire la p. de qch** to promote sth; **la p. de la semaine** this week's special offer; **en p.** on special offer

promotionnel, -elle [pʀɔmosjɔnɛl] *adj (article)* promotional; *(tarif)* special; **vente promotionnelle** special offer

promouvoir [31a] [pʀɔmuvwaʀ] *vt aussi Fig* to promote; **être promu chef du personnel** to be promoted to personnel manager

prompt, -e [pʀɔ̃, pʀɔ̃t] *adj (réaction)* prompt; **p. à faire qch** quick to do sth; **p. à la riposte** quick with a riposte

promptement [pʀɔ̃tmɑ̃, pʀɔ̃ptəmɑ̃] *adv Litt* promptly

promptitude [pʀɔ̃tityd] *nf Litt (d'une réaction)* promptness

promu, -e *voir* **promouvoir**

promulgation [pʀɔmylgasjɔ̃] *nf* promulgation

promulguer [pʀɔmylge] *vt* to promulgate

prôner [pʀone] *vt* to advocate

pronom [pʀɔnɔ̃] *nm Gram* pronoun; **p. personnel/indéfini/interrogatif** personal/indefinite/interrogative pronoun

pronominal, -e, -aux, -ales [pʀɔnɔminal, -o] *adj Gram* pronominal

prononcé, -e [pʀɔnɔ̃se] **1** *adj* pronounced, strong
    2 *nm Jur* **le p. du jugement** the verdict

prononcer [16] [pʀɔnɔ̃se] **1** *vt* **(a)** *(articuler)* to pronounce; **mal p. un mot** to mispronounce a word **(b)** *(dire) (mot)* to utter; *(discours)* to deliver; *(sentence, divorce)* to pronounce
    2 se prononcer *vpr* **(a)** *(être articulé)* to be pronounced; **ça s'écrit comme ça se prononce** it's written as it's pronounced **(b)** *(s'exprimer)* to give one's opinion; *(juge)* to give a verdict; **se p. pour** *ou* **en faveur de qn/qch** to express one's support for sb/sth; **se p. contre qn/qch** to express one's opposition to sb/sth; **50 pour cent ne se prononcent pas** *(dans un sondage)* 50 per cent are undecided

prononciation [pʀɔnɔ̃sjasjɔ̃] *nf* pronunciation; **elle a une bonne/mauvaise p.** her pronunciation is good/bad

pronostic [pʀɔnɔstik] *nm* forecast; *(d'un médecin)* prognosis

propagande [pʀɔpagɑ̃d] *nf* propaganda; **faire de la p. pour qn/qch** to put out propaganda for sb/sth; *(pour une élection)* to campaign for sb/sth

propagation [pʀɔpagasjɔ̃] *nf* spreading

propager [45] [prɔpaʒe] **1** vt to spread
2 se propager vpr (**a**) (épidémie, nouvelle, idée) to spread (**b**) (lumière, son) to be propagated

propane [prɔpan] nm Chim propane

propension [prɔpɑ̃sjɔ̃] nf propensity (**à** for); **p. à faire qch** propensity to do sth

prophète [prɔfɛt] nm prophet; **p. de malheur** prophet of doom; Prov **nul n'est p. en son pays** no man is a prophet in his own country

prophétie [prɔfesi] nf prophecy

prophétique [prɔfetik] adj prophetic

prophylactique [prɔfilaktik] adj prophylactic

propice [prɔpis] adj **le moment p.** the right moment; **p. à qch** good for sth; **un endroit p. au repos** a restful spot; **un endroit p. aux rencontres** a good place to meet people

proportion [prɔpɔrsjɔ̃] nf proportion; **respecter les proportions** to get the proportions right; **en p. de qch** in proportion to sth; **hors de (toute) p. avec** out of (all) proportion to; **toutes proportions gardées** relatively speaking

proportionné, -e [prɔpɔrsjɔne] adj (**a**) (bâti) **bien-/mal p.** well-/badly-proportioned (**b**) (lié) **être p. à** to be proportionate to

proportionnel, -elle [prɔpɔrsjɔnɛl] **1** adj proportional (**à** to); **inversement p. à qch** inversely proportional to sth
2 nf **proportionnelle** Pol proportional representation; **être élu à la proportionelle** to be elected by proportional representation

proportionnellement [prɔpɔrsjɔnɛlmɑ̃] adv proportionally (**à** to)

propos [prɔpo] nm (**a**) (sujet) **à p. de qn/qch** about sb/sth; **à ce p.,...** speaking of which...; **à tout p.** constantly; **à p., avez-vous lu ce livre?** by the way, have you read this book?; **c'est à quel p.?** what's it about?; **arriver fort à p.** to arrive at just the right moment; **juger à p. de faire qch** to think it right to do sth; **hors de p.** (remarque) inappropriate (**b**) (intention) purpose, intention; **de p. délibéré** deliberately, on purpose (**c**) (parole) **des p.** talk, words; **tenir des p. étonnants** to say some surprising things

proposer [prɔpoze] **1** vt (suggérer) to suggest, to propose; (offrir) to offer; (amendement, loi) to introduce; **p. qch à qn** to suggest or to propose sth to sb; (argent, travail) to offer sb sth; **je vous en propose 1000 euros/un bon prix** I'll give you 1,000 euros/a good price for it; **voilà ce que je vous propose** this is what I suggest; **le cinéma Le César vous propose cette semaine...** Le César will be showing the following movies this week...; **je leur ai proposé de venir avec moi** I suggested (to them) that they should come with me; **elle m'a proposé de m'aider** she offered to help me; **je propose qu'on y aille demain** I suggest going tomorrow
2 se proposer vpr (**a**) (être volontaire) to offer one's services; **se p. pour faire qch** to offer to do sth (**b**) **se p. de faire qch** (en avoir l'intention) to propose to do sth

proposition [prɔpozisjɔ̃] nf (**a**) (suggestion) suggestion, proposal; (offre) offer; **faire une p. (à qn)** to make a suggestion or proposal (to sb); **faire des propositions à une femme** to proposition a woman; **sur la p. de qn** at sb's suggestion; **p. de loi** bill (**b**) Phil & Math proposition (**c**) Gram clause; **p. principale** main clause

propre [prɔpr] **1** adj (**a**) (impeccable) (personne, linge, maison) clean; (bébé) toilet-trained; (animal domestique) housebroken; (copie d'élève) neat; **n'utilise pas la serviette des autres, ce n'est pas p.!** don't use other people's towels, it's not hygienic!; **p. comme un sou neuf** spick and span; Fam **nous voilà propres!** now we're in a mess! (**b**) (à soi) own; **voir qch de ses propres yeux** to see sth with one's own eyes; **ce sont là ses propres paroles** those are his/her very words (**c**) (particulier) **être p. à qn/qch** to be characteristic of or peculiar to

sb/sth (**d**) (adapté) **être p. à qch** to be suitable for sth (**e**) (littéral) **au sens p.** in the literal sense, literally
2 nm (**a**) (caractéristique) characteristic feature (**b**) **appartenir en p. à qn** to be sb's sole property (**c**) (sens propre) **au p.** literally (**d**) **recopier qch au p.** to make a clean copy of sth (**e**) (propreté) **sentir le p.** to smell clean; Belg **faire du p.** to spring-clean (**f**) Fam **c'est du p.!** that's a fine way to behave!

propre-à-rien (pl **propres-à-rien**) [prɔprarjɛ̃] nmf good-for-nothing

proprement [prɔprəmɑ̃] adv (**a**) (avec propreté) cleanly; (vêtu) tidily; **manger p.** to eat without making a mess (**b**) (strictement) strictly; **c'est un problème p. urbain** it's strictly an inner-city problem; **à p. parler** strictly speaking; **voilà la bibliothèque p. dite** there's the actual library (**c**) Fam (vraiment) **c'est p. scandaleux!** it's an absolute disgrace!

propreté [prɔprəte] nf (hygiène) cleanliness; (des vêtements, de la vaisselle, d'une maison) cleanness; (d'un travail) neatness

propriétaire [prɔprijetɛr] nmf (**a**) (d'une voiture, d'une propriété, d'un hôtel) owner; **devenir** ou **se rendre p. de qch** to become the owner of sth; **être p.** to be a landowner; (de maison) to be a homeowner; **p. foncier** landowner (**b**) (d'une location) landlord, f landlady

propriété [prɔprijete] nf (**a**) (fait de posséder) ownership; **p. littéraire** copyright; **p. foncière** property ownership; Jur **p. intellectuelle** intellectual property (**b**) (chose ou terre possédée) property; **p. privée** private property (**c**) (caractéristique) property

proprio [prɔprijo] nmf Fam landlord, f landlady

propulser [prɔpylse] **1** vt to propel
2 se propulser vpr Fam **se p. en tête du peloton** to shoot to the front of the pack

propulsion [prɔpylsjɔ̃] nf propulsion; **sous-marin à p. nucléaire** nuclear-powered submarine

prorata [prɔrata] nm inv proportion; **au p. de qch** in proportion to sth

prorogation [prɔrɔgasjɔ̃] nf (de contrat, de bail) extension

proroger [45] [prɔrɔʒe] vt (contrat, bail) to extend; (échéance) to defer

prosaïque [prɔzaik] adj prosaic

proscrire [30] [prɔskrir] vt to ban, to proscribe

proscrit, -e [prɔskri, -it] **1** adj banned, proscribed
2 nm,f Litt (banni) exile

prose [proz] nf prose; **en p.** (écrire) in prose; (texte, poème) prose

prosélytisme [prɔzelitism] nm proselytism; **faire du p.** to proselytize

prosodie [prɔzɔdi] nf prosody

prospecter [prɔspɛkte] vt (**a**) (terrain) to prospect (**b**) (client) to canvass; (marché) to explore

prospecteur, -trice [prɔspɛktœr, -tris] nm,f (**a**) (de terrain) prospector (**b**) (de clients) canvasser

prospection [prɔspɛksjɔ̃] nf (**a**) (de terrain) prospecting; **faire de la p.** to prospect; **p. minière/pétrolière** mining/oil exploration (**b**) (de clients) canvassing; **faire de la p.** to explore the market; **p. téléphonique** telephone canvassing

prospectus [prɔspɛktys] nm (**a**) (brochure) leaflet (**b**) Fin prospectus

prospère [prɔspɛr] adj prosperous; (santé) glowing

prospérer [34] [prɔspere] vi to prosper

prospérité [prɔsperite] nf prosperity; **en période de p.** in times of prosperity

prostate [prɔstat] nf Anat prostate (gland)

prosterner [prɔstɛrne] **se prosterner** vpr (saluer) to prostrate oneself (**devant** before); Fig (s'abaisser) to grovel, to kowtow (**devant** to)

prostitué, -e [prɔstitɥe] nm,f (homme) male prostitute; (femme) prostitute

prostituer [prɔstitɥe] **1** *vt* to prostitute

2 se prostituer *vpr* to prostitute oneself

prostitution [prɔstitysjɔ̃] *nf* prostitution

prostré, -e [prɔstre] *adj* prostrate

protagoniste [prɔtagɔnist] *nmf* protagonist

protecteur, -trice [prɔtɛktœr, -tris] **1** *adj (qui protège)* protective (**avec** towards); *Péj (ton)* patronizing

2 *nm,f* **(a)** *(d'une personne)* protector; *(d'une prostituée)* pimp **(b)** *(des arts)* patron

protection [prɔtɛksjɔ̃] *nf* **(a)** *(défense)* protection (**contre** from *or* against); **de p.** *(écran, visière, vernis)* protective; **sous la p. de la police** under police protection; **p. de l'environnement** protection of the environment; **p. sociale** social welfare system; *Ordinat* **p. d'accès logique** logical access protection; **p. contre l'écriture** write-protection; **p. contre la copie** copy protection; **p. de fichiers** file protection; **p. par mot de passe** password protection **(b)** *(serviette hygiénique)* **p. (féminine)** sanitary napkin

protectionnisme [prɔtɛksjɔnism] *nm Écon* protectionism

protectionniste [prɔtɛksjɔnist] *adj & nmf* protectionist

protectorat [prɔtɛktɔra] *nm* protectorate

protégé, -e [prɔteʒe] **1** *adj* protected; *Ordinat* **p. contre la copie** copy-protected

2 *nm,f* protégé, *f* protégée

protège-cahier *(pl* **protège-cahiers)** [prɔteʒkaje] *nm* notebook cover

protège-dents [prɔteʒdɑ̃] *nm inv* gum shield

protéger [59] [prɔteʒe] **1** *vt* to protect (**contre/de** against/from); **ça protège bien** it gives good protection; **que Dieu vous protège!** God keep you!; *Ordinat* **p. contre l'écriture** *ou* **en écriture** to write-protect

2 se protéger *vpr* to protect oneself (**contre/de** against/from)

protège-slip *(pl* **protège-slips)** [prɔteʒslip] *nm* panty-liner

protéine [prɔtein] *nf* protein

protestant, -e [prɔtɛstɑ̃, -ɑ̃t] *adj & nm,f* Protestant

protestantisme [prɔtɛstɑ̃tism] *nm* Protestantism

protestataire [prɔtɛstatɛr] *nmf* protester

protestation [prɔtɛstasjɔ̃] *nf* **(a)** *(plainte)* protest; **émettre des protestations** to voice one's protest; **en signe de p.** as a protest **(b)** **des protestations d'amitié** protestations of friendship

protester [prɔtɛste] **1** *vi* to protest (**contre** against); **p. auprès de qn** to protest to sb

2 protester de *vt ind (innocence, bonne foi)* to protest

prothèse [prɔtɛz] *nf* prosthesis; **p. auditive** hearing aid; **p. dentaire** *(complète)* false teeth, dentures; *(partielle)* bridge

protocole [prɔtɔkɔl] *nm* **(a)** *(usages)* protocol **(b)** **p. d'accord** protocol of agreement; **le P. de Kyoto** the Kyoto Protocol **(c)** *Ordinat* protocol; **p. de téléchargement** download protocol; **p. de transmission** transmission protocol

proton [prɔtɔ̃] *nm* proton

prototype [prɔtɔtip] *nm* prototype

protozoaire [prɔtɔzɔɛr] *nm* protozoan; **les protozoaires** the Protozoa

protubérance [prɔtyberɑ̃s] *nf* protuberance

protubérant, -e [prɔtyberɑ̃, -ɑ̃t] *adj* protuberant

proue [pru] *nf* bows, prow

prouesse [prues] *nf* feat; **faire des prouesses pour obtenir qch** to work wonders to get sth

prouver [pruve] **1** *vt* **(a)** *(établir comme vrai)* to prove; **p. qch à qn** to prove sth to sb; **p. qch par A plus B** to prove sth in a logical fashion; **cela reste à p.** it is yet to be proved **(b)** *(être la preuve de)* to prove, to show (**que** that)

2 se prouver *vpr* **se p. qch** *(à soi-même)* to prove sth to oneself

provenance [prɔvnɑ̃s] *nf* origin; **marchandises de p.**

italienne goods of Italian origin; **en p. de Bordeaux** from Bordeaux

provençal, -e, -aux, -ales [prɔvɑ̃sal, -o] **1** *adj* Provençal

2 *nm (langue)* Provençal

3 *nm,f* **P., Provençale** person from Provence

Provence [prɔvɑ̃s] *nf* **la P.** Provence

provenir [70] [prɔvnir] *vi* **p. de** to come from; *(difficultés)* to arise from

proverbe [prɔvɛrb] *nm* proverb; **comme dit le p.** as the proverb goes

proverbial, -e, -aux, -ales [prɔvɛrbjal, -o] *adj* proverbial

providence [prɔvidɑ̃s] *nf* **(a)** *(sort)* providence; **cette auberge est la p. des marcheurs** this inn is a haven for walkers **(b)** **la P.** Providence

providentiel, -elle [prɔvidɑ̃sjɛl] *adj* providential

province [prɔvɛ̃s] **1** *nf* **(a)** *(région)* province; *Can* **les Provinces Maritimes** the Maritime Provinces **(b)** **la p.** the provinces; **de p.** provincial; **en p.** in the provinces; **arriver de sa p.** to be new in town

2 *adj inv Fam Péj* provincial

provincial, -e, -aux, -ales [prɔvɛ̃sjal, -o] *adj & nm,f* provincial

proviseur [prɔvizœr] *nm* **(a)** *(directeur)* principal **(b)** *Belg (adjoint)* vice principal

provision [prɔvizjɔ̃] *nf* **(a)** *(réserve)* stock, supply; **provisions** *(nourriture)* shopping; **faire des provisions** *ou* **faire p. de qch** to stock up on sth **(b)** *(de compte bancaire)* credit; *(acompte)* deposit

provisionnel, -elle [prɔvizjɔnɛl] *adj voir* **tiers**

provisoire [prɔvizwar] *adj* temporary; **à titre p.** temporarily

provisoirement [prɔvizwarmɑ̃] *adv* temporarily, provisionally

provocant, -e [prɔvɔkɑ̃, -ɑ̃t] *adj* provocative

provocateur, -trice [prɔvɔkatœr, -tris] **1** *adj* provocative; **agent p.** agent provocateur

2 *nm,f* troublemaker

provocation [prɔvɔkasjɔ̃] *nf* provocation; **il l'a dit par p.** he said it to be provocative

provoquer [prɔvɔke] *vt* **(a)** *(personne)* to provoke **(b)** *(réaction)* to provoke; *(incendie, mort, malaise)* to cause; *(jalousie, colère)* to arouse; **p. l'accouchement** to induce labor

proxénète [prɔksenɛt] *nmf* pimp

proxénétisme [prɔksenetism] *nm* pimping

proximité [prɔksimite] *nf* closeness, proximity; **à p.** close by; **à p. de qch** close to sth; **commerces de p.** local stores; **emplois de p.** = employment in the community *(as a way of reducing unemployment)*

Prozac® [prɔzak] *nm Pharm* Prozac®

prude [pryd] *Péj* **1** *adj* prudish

2 *nf* prude

prudemment [prydamɑ̃] *adv* carefully, cautiously

prudence [prydɑ̃s] *nf* care, caution; **par (mesure de) p.** as a precaution

prudent, -e [prydɑ̃, -ɑ̃t] *adj (personne)* careful, cautious; *(décision)* wise, sensible

prud'homme [prydɔm] *nm Jur* member of a labor relations board; **conseil des prud'hommes** labor relations board

prune [pryn] **1** *nf (fruit)* plum; *(liqueur)* plum brandy; *Fam* **pour des prunes** for nothing

2 *adj inv* plum-colored

pruneau, -x [pryno] *nm* **(a)** *(fruit)* prune **(b)** *Fam (balle)* slug

prunelle [prynɛl] *nf (pupille)* pupil; *Fig* **j'y tiens comme à la p. de mes yeux** it's the apple of my eye

prunier [prynje] *nm* plum tree; *Fam* **secouer qn comme un p.** to shake sb like a rag doll

prurit [pryrit] *nm Méd* pruritus

Prusse [prys] *nf voir* **bleu**

PS [peɛs] *nm* (**a**) (*abrév* **Parti socialiste**) Socialist Party (**b**) (*abrév* **post-scriptum**) PS

psalmodier [66] [psalmɔdje] **1** *vt* to chant; *Fig* to drone out **2** *vi* to chant; *Fig* to drone on

psaume [psom] *nm* psalm

pseudo [psødo] *nm Fam* pseudonym

pseudo- [psødo] *préf* pseudo-; **un p.-intellectuel** a pseudo-intellectual

pseudonyme [psødɔnim] *nm* (*pour un écrivain*) pen name, pseudonym; (*pour la scène*) stage name

psy [psi] *nmf Fam* (*médecin*) shrink

psychanalyse [psikanaliz] *nf* psychoanalysis; **faire une p.** to be in psychoanalysis

psychanalyser [psikanalize] *vt* to psychoanalyze; **se faire p.** to be psychoanalyzed

psychanalyste [psikanalist] *nmf* psychoanalyst

psyché [psiʃe] *nf* (*miroir*) cheval glass

psychédélique [psikedelik] *adj* psychedelic

psychiatre [psikjatr] *nmf* psychiatrist

psychiatrie [psikjatri] *nf* psychiatry

psychiatrique [psikjatrik] *adj* psychiatric

psychique [psiʃik] *adj* psychic

psychisme [psiʃism] *nm* psyche

psychodrame [psikodram] *nm* role-play, *Spéc* psychodrama

psychologie [psikɔlɔʒi] *nf* (**a**) (*étude, mentalité*) psychology; **comprendre la p. de qn** to understand the way sb's mind works (**b**) (*intuition*) perception; **faire preuve de p.** to be very perceptive; **tu manques de p.** you're not very perceptive

psychologique [psikɔlɔʒik] *adj* psychological

psychologiquement [psikɔlɔʒikmɑ̃] *adv* psychologically

psychologue [psikɔlɔg] **1** *nmf* psychologist; *Fig* **être fin p.** to be a good psychologist **2** *adj* **être p.** to be a good psychologist

psychopathe [psikɔpat] *nmf* psychopath

psychose [psikoz] *nf* psychosis; **p. maniaco-dépressive** manic depression; *Fig* **la p. de la maladie** an obsessive fear of illness

psychosomatique [psikosɔmatik] *adj* psychosomatic

psychothérapeute [psikoterapøt] *nmf* psychotherapist

psychothérapie [psikoterapi] *nf* psychotherapy; **p. de groupe** group therapy

psychotique [psikɔtik] *adj & nmf* psychotic

PTT [petete] *nfpl* (*abrév* **Postes, Télécommunications et Télédiffusion**) *Anciennement* ≃ Post Office and Telecommunications Service

pu *voir* **pouvoir²**

puant, -e [pɥɑ̃, -ɑ̃t] *adj* stinking; *Fig* cocky

puanteur [pɥɑ̃tœr] *nf* stink, stench

pub [pyb] *nf Fam* (**a**) (*secteur*) advertising (**b**) (*message*) ad

pubère [pybɛr] *adj* pubescent

puberté [pybɛrte] *nf* puberty

pubis [pybis] *nm Anat* pubis; (*os*) pubic bone

public, -ique [pyblik] **1** *adj* public **2** *nm* (*d'un spectacle*) audience; **en p.** in public; (*émission*) before a live audience; **le grand p.** the general public

publication [pyblikasjɔ̃] *nf* (**a**) (*d'un ouvrage, d'une nouvelle*) publication; **p. assistée par ordinateur** desktop publishing (**b**) (*ouvrage*) publication

publiciel [pyblisjɛl] *nm Can Ordinat* public-domain software

publiciste [pyblisist] *nmf Fam* advertising executive

publicitaire [pyblisitɛr] **1** *adj* advertising **2** *nmf* advertising executive

publicité [pyblisite] *nf* (**a**) (*secteur*) advertising; **être dans la p.** to be in advertising; **faire de la p. pour qch** to advertise sth; *Fig* **faire de la p. à qn** to be publicity for sb; **p. comparative** comparative advertising; **p. mensongère** misleading

advertising (**b**) (*message*) advertisement, ad; **une pleine page de p.** a full-page advertisement

publier [66] [pyblije] *vt* to publish; (*communiqué*) to issue

Publiphone® [pyblifɔn] *nm* card phone

publiquement [pyblikmɑ̃] *adv* publicly

puce [pys] *nf* (**a**) (*insecte*) flea; **le marché aux puces, les puces** the flea market; *Fig* **mettre la p. à l'oreille à qn** to make sb suspicious; *Fam* **secouer les puces à qn** to give sb a good telling off; *Fam* **être excité comme une p.** to be jumping up and down with excitement (**b**) *Ordinat* (micro)chip; **p. mémoire** memory chip; **p. de reconnaissance vocale** voice recognition chip (**c**) (*terme affectueux*) **ma p.** sweetie

puceau, -x [pyso] *nm & adj m Fam* virgin

pucelle [pysɛl] *nf & adj f* virgin; **la P. d'Orléans, Jeanne la P.** The Maid of Orléans, Joan of Arc

puceron [pysrɔ̃] *nm* aphid

pudeur [pydœr] *nf* modesty; **avec p.** modestly; **sans p.** boldly; **par p.** out of a sense of decency; **avoir la p. de faire qch** to have the decency to do sth

pudibond, -e [pydibɔ̃, -ɔ̃d] *adj* prudish

pudique [pydik] *adj* modest

puer [pɥe] **1** *vi* to stink; **il pue des pieds** his feet stink **2** *vt* to stink of; *Fig* **p. la méchanceté/l'hypocrisie** to be oozing spitefulness/hypocrisy

puéricultrice [pɥerikyltris] *nf* nursery nurse

puériculture [pɥerikyltyr] *nf* child care

puéril, -e [pɥeril] *adj* childish, puerile

pugilat [pyʒila] *nm* brawl

pugnace [pygnas] *adj Litt* pugnacious

puis¹ [pɥi] *adv* then; **et p.** (*ensuite*) and then; (*d'ailleurs*) and besides; **et p. c'est tout!** and that's all there is to it!; **et p. après?** (*et ensuite?*) then what?; *Fam (et alors?)* so what?

puis² *voir* **pouvoir²**

puisatier [pɥizatje] *nm* well digger

puiser [pɥize] *vt* (*eau, carte*) to draw (**à** from); *Fig* (*inspiration, idées*) to draw (**dans/chez** from); **p. dans ses réserves** to draw on one's reserves; **p. dans la caisse** to have one's hand in the till

puisque [pɥiskə] *conj* since, as; **p. c'est comme ça** if that's the way it is; **p. je te dis que je l'ai vu!** I'm telling you I saw him!; **tu en es bien sûr? – mais p. je te le dis!** are you really sure? – I said I was, didn't I?

puissamment [pɥisamɑ̃] *adv* powerfully

puissance [pɥisɑ̃s] *nf* power; **p. de feu** fire power; **les grandes puissances** the great powers; *Math* **élever un nombre à la p. trois/quatre** to raise a number to the third/fourth power; **dix (à la) p. quatre** ten to the power of four; **en p.** (*meurtrier*) potential

puissant, -e [pɥisɑ̃, -ɑ̃t] *adj* powerful

puisse *etc. voir* **pouvoir²**

puits [pɥi] *nm* (**a**) (*pour l'eau*) well; **p. de pétrole** oil well; *Fig* **c'est un p. de science** she's a fount of knowledge (**b**) (*de mine*) shaft, pit

pull [pyl] *nm Fam* sweater

pull-over (*pl* pull-overs) [pylɔvœr] *nm* sweater

pulluler [pylyle] *vi* (**a**) (*se reproduire*) to proliferate (**b**) (*exister en profusion*) to abound

pulmonaire [pylmɔnɛr] *adj* pulmonary

pulpe [pylp] *nf* (**a**) (*de fruit*) pulp; **yaourt à la p. de fruits** yoghurt with real fruit (**b**) (*des doigts, des orteils*) pad; (*des dents*) pulp

pulpeux, -euse [pylpø, -øz] *adj* fleshy; (*femme*) curvaceous

pulsar [pylsar] *nm Astron* pulsar

pulsation [pylsasjɔ̃] *nf* (*de cœur*) *& Mus* beat; **pulsations cardiaques** heartbeats

pulsion [pylsjɔ̃] *nf* impulse; **pulsions sexuelles** sexual urges; **p. de mort** death wish

pulvérisateur [pylverizatœr] *nm* spray

pulvérisation [pylverizasjɔ̃] *nf (de liquides)* spraying

pulvériser [pylverize] *vt* **(a)** *(réduire en poudre)* to pulverize; *Fam (voiture)* to smash up **(b)** *(vaporiser)* to spray **(c)** *Fam (record)* to smash

puma [pyma] *nm* puma

punaise [pynɛz] *nf* **(a)** *(insecte)* bug; *Fam* **oh p.!** darn it! **(b)** *(pour accrocher)* thumbtack

punaiser [pynɛze] *vt Fam* to pin up; **p. qch à qch** to pin sth to sth

punch¹ [pɔ̃ʃ] *nm (boisson)* punch

punch² [pœnʃ] *nm* punch; *Fig (de personne)* drive

punching-ball *(pl* **punching-balls)** [pœnʃiŋbol] *nm* punch-ball

punir [pynir] *vt (personne, crime)* to punish; **p. qn de mort** to punish sb with death; **p. qn d'un crime** to punish sb for a crime; **me voilà puni de ma gourmandise!** it serves me right for being greedy!

punitif, -ive [pynitif, -iv] *adj* punitive

punition [pynisjɔ̃] *nf* punishment; **p. corporelle** corporal punishment

punk [pœnk] *adj inv & nmf* punk

pupille¹ [pypij] *nmf (orphelin)* ward; **pupilles de la Nation** war orphans

pupille² [pypij] *nf (de l'œil)* pupil

pupitre [pypitr] *nm* **(a)** *(d'écolier)* desk; *(d'orateur)* lectern; *(de musicien)* music stand **(b)** *Ordinat* **p. (de commande)** console (desk); **p. de visualisation** visual display unit

pupitreur, -euse [pypitrœr, -øz] *nm,f Ordinat* console operator

pur, -e [pyr] *adj* **(a)** *(or, air)* pure; *(ciel)* clear; *(whisky, gin)* straight, neat; **pure laine** pure wool; **biscuits p. beurre** all-butter cookies **(b)** *(recherche, mathématiques, théorie)* pure; **un communiste p. et dur** a hard-line Communist; **la vérité pure et simple** the plain and simple truth; **du vol p. et simple** sheer robbery; **c'est de la folie pure** it's sheer madness **(c)** *(lignes)* clean; *(visage)* clean-cut

purée [pyre] **1** *nf* purée; **réduire qch en p.** to purée sth; *Fig* to smash sth to a pulp; **p. (de pommes de terre)** mashed potatoes; *Fam Fig* **p. de pois** pea souper
2 *exclam Fam (colère)* hell!; *(surprise)* wow!

purement [pyrmɑ̃] *adv* purely; **p. et simplement** purely and simply

pureté [pyrte] *nf* purity; *(du ciel)* clearness; *(de lignes)* cleanness

purgatoire [pyrgatwar] *nm* purgatory

purge [pyrʒ] *nf* **(a)** *(pour raisons médicales)* purge **(b)** *(à des fins politiques)* purge **(c)** *(de freins, de radiateur)* bleeding

purger [45] [pyrʒe] *vt* **(a)** *(patient)* to purge **(b)** *(freins, radiateur)* to bleed **(c)** *(peine)* to serve

purifiant, -e [pyrifjɑ̃, -ɑ̃t] *adj* purifying

purificateur, -trice [pyrifikatœr, -tris] *adj* purifying

purification [pyrifikasjɔ̃] *nf* purification; **p. ethnique** ethnic cleansing

purifier [66] [pyrifje] **1** *vt aussi Fig* to purify; *(sang, teint)* to cleanse
2 se purifier *vpr* to be purified

purin [pyrɛ̃] *nm* liquid manure

puriste [pyrist] *nmf* purist

puritain, -e [pyritɛ̃, -ɛn] **1** *nm,f* puritan; *Hist* Puritan
2 *adj* puritanical; *Hist* Puritan

puritanisme [pyritanism] *nm* puritanism; *Hist* Puritanism

pur-sang [pyrsɑ̃] *nm inv* thoroughbred

purulent, -e [pyrylɑ̃, -ɑ̃t] *adj* suppurating

pus [py] *nm* pus

pusillanime [pyzilanim] *adj Litt* pusillanimous

pustule [pystyl] *nf* pustule

putain [pytɛ̃] *Vulg* **1** *nf* **(a)** *(prostituée)* whore **(b)** **cette p. de machine/cravate** this fucking machine/tie
2 *exclam* fuck!

pute [pyt] *nf Vulg* whore; **fils de p.** son of a bitch

putois [pytwa] *nm* polecat; *Fam* **crier comme un p.** to scream blue murder

putréfaction [pytrefaksjɔ̃] *nf* putrefaction; **matière en p.** putrefying matter

putréfier [66] [pytrefje] **1** *vt* to putrefy
2 se putréfier *vpr* to putrefy

putrescent, -e [pytresɑ̃, -ɑ̃t] *adj* putrescent

putride [pytrid] *adj* putrid

putsch [putʃ] *nm* putsch

putschiste [putʃist] **1** *adj* putsch
2 *nmf* putschist

puzzle [pœzl] *nm* jigsaw (puzzle); *Fig* puzzle

P.-V. [peve] *nm Fam (abrév* **procès-verbal***)* (parking) ticket

PVC [pevese] *nm (abrév* **polychlorure de vinyle***)* PVC; **siège en P.** PVC seat

PVD [pevede] *nm (abrév* **pays en voie de développement***)* developing country

pygmée [pigme] *nmf* pygmy

pyjama [piʒama] *nm* pajamas; **un p.** a pair of pajamas

pylône [pilon] *nm* pylon; *(pour fils télégraphiques)* mast

pyramidal, -e, -aux, -ales [piramidal, -o] *adj* pyramid-shaped

pyramide [piramid] *nf* pyramid; **p. des âges** population pyramid; **structure en p.** pyramid-like structure

pyrénéen, -enne [pireneɛ̃, -ɛn] **1** *adj* Pyrenean
2 *nm (chien)* Pyrenean mountain dog
3 *nm,f* **P., Pyrénéenne** Pyrenean

Pyrénées [pirene] *nfpl* **les P.** the Pyrenees

Pyrex® [pirɛks] *nm* Pyrex®; **plat en P.** Pyrex® dish

pyrogravure [pirogravyr] *nf* poker work, pyrography; *(gravure)* pyrograph

pyrolyse [piroliz] *nf* pyrolysis; **four à p.** self-cleaning oven

pyromane [piroman] *nmf* arsonist; *Psy* pyromaniac

pyromanie [piromani] *nf* pyromania

pyrotechnique [piroteknik] *adj* pyrotechnic

python [pitɔ̃] *nm* python

Q

Q, q [ky] *nm inv* Q, q

Qatar [katar] *nm* **le Q.** Qatar

QCM [kyseɛm] *nm inv* (*abrév* **questionnaire à choix multiple**) multiple-choice questionnaire

QG [kyʒe] *nm inv* (*abrév* **quartier général**) HQ

QI [kyi] *nm inv* (*abrév* **quotient intellectuel**) IQ

quad [kwad] *nm* quad bike; **faire du q.** to go quad biking

quadra [kwadra] *nmf Fam* fortysomething

quadragénaire [kwadraʒenɛr] **1** *adj* **être q.** to be in one's forties
2 *nmf* person in his/her forties

quadrangulaire [kwadrɑ̃gylɛr] *adj* quadrangular

quadrature [kwadratyr] *nf* quadrature; **c'est la q. du cercle** it's like trying to square the circle

quadriceps [kwadrisɛps] *nm* quadriceps

quadrilatère [kwadrilatɛr, kadrilatɛr] *nm* quadrilateral

quadrillage [kadrijaʒ] *nm* (**a**) (*par la police*) tight surveillance (**b**) (*d'un tissu*) check pattern; (*sur une carte*) grid

quadrille [kadrij] *nm* quadrille

quadrillé, -e [kadrije] *adj* (*papier*) squared

quadriller [kadrije] *vt* (**a**) (*quartier, ville, région*) to put under tight surveillance (**b**) (*papier*) to mark into squares

quadrimoteur [kwadrimɔtœr, kadrimɔtœr] **1** *adj* four-engined
2 *nm* four-engined plane

quadriparti, -e [kwadriparti], **quadripartite** [kwadripartit] *adj* (*traité*) quadripartite; (*conférence, commission*) (*entre partis*) four-party; (*entre pays*) four-power

quadriphonie [kwadrifoni] *nf* quadraphony

quadrupède [kwadrypɛd, kadrypɛd] *adj & nm* quadruped

quadruple [kwadrypl, kadrypl] **1** *adj* quadruple, fourfold; *Mus* **q. croche** sixty-fourth note
2 *nm* **le q. (de)** (*quantité, prix*) four times as much (as); (*nombre*) four times as many (as); **douze est le q. de trois** twelve is four times three

quadrupler [kwadryple, kadryple] *vt & vi* to quadruple, to increase fourfold

quadruplés, -ées [kwadryple, kadryple] *nm,f pl* quadruplets

quai [kɛ] *nm* (**a**) (*de gare, de métro*) platform (**b**) (*d'un port*) quay; **se mettre à q.** to berth (**c**) (*d'une rivière, d'un fleuve*) embankment; **le Q. des Orfèvres** Police Headquarters (*in Paris*); **le Q. d'Orsay** the French Foreign Office

qualificatif, -ive [kalifikatif, -iv] *Gram* **1** *adj* (*adjectif*) qualifying
2 *nm* term

qualification [kalifikasjɔ̃] *nf* (**a**) (*formation*) qualification (**b**) (*d'une équipe, d'un sportif*) qualification (**c**) (*désignation*) description

qualifié, -e [kalifje] *adj* (**a**) (*compétent*) qualified (**pour faire qch** to do sth) (**b**) (*délit, vol*) aggravated

qualifier [66] [kalifje] **1** *vt* (**a**) (*appeler*) to describe (**de** as) (**b**)

(*autoriser*) **q. qn pour qch/pour faire qch** to qualify sb for sth/to do sth
2 se qualifier *vpr* (*sportif, équipe*) to qualify (**pour** for)

qualitatif, -ive [kalitatif, -iv] *adj* qualitative

qualité [kalite] *nf* (**a**) (*d'un produit*) quality; **de q.** quality; **de bonne/mauvaise q.** of good/poor quality; *Ordinat* **q. brouillon, q. liste rapide, q. listing** draft quality; *Ordinat* **q. courrier** (*near*) letter quality; **la q. de la vie** the quality of life (**b**) (*d'une personne*) quality; **elle n'a pas que des qualités** she isn't all good (**c**) (*occupation*) occupation; (*fonction*) capacity; **en q. de** in my/her/*etc.* capacity as

quand [kɑ̃] **1** *conj* (**a**) (*lorsque*) when; **je lui en parlerai q. je le verrai** I'll mention it to him when I see him; *Fam* **q. je pense que le voyage devait être annulé!** when I think that they were going to cancel the trip!; **q. bien même** even if (**b**) (*alors que*) when
2 *adv* when; **q. viendra-t-il?** when will he come?; **demande-lui q. il va partir** ask him when he's going to leave; **à q. le mariage?** when's the wedding?; **de q. est ce journal?** what's the date of this paper?; **pour q. est la réunion?** when is the meeting?

quant [kɑ̃] **quant à** *prép* as for

quant-à-soi [kɑ̃taswa] *nm inv* **rester sur** *ou* **se tenir sur son q.** to keep oneself to oneself

quantième [kɑ̃tjɛm] *nm* day of the month

quantifiable [kɑ̃tifjabl] *adj* quantifiable

quantifier [66] [kɑ̃tifje] *vt* to quantify

quantitatif, -ive [kɑ̃titatif, -iv] *adj* quantitative

quantitativement [kɑ̃titativmɑ̃] *adv* quantitatively

quantité [kɑ̃tite] *nf* quantity; **en grande/petite q.** in large/small quantities; **en q.** in abundance; **q. de gens/réponses** a great many people/replies

quarantaine [karɑ̃tɛn] *nf* (**a**) (*environ quarante*) **une q. (de)** about forty, forty or so (**b**) (*âge*) **avoir la q.** to be about forty; **approcher de la q.** to be pushing forty (**c**) (*isolement*) quarantine; **mettre qn en q.** to put sb in quarantine; *Fig* to send sb to Coventry

quarante [karɑ̃t] *adj & nm inv* forty; *Fam* **se ficher de qch comme de l'an q.** not to give two hoots about sth; *Can* **vieux comme l'an q.** ancient, as old as the hills; *voir aussi* **trois**

quarante-cinq tours [karɑ̃tsɛ̃tur] *nm inv* single, 45

quarantième [karɑ̃tjɛm] *nmf, nm & adj* fortieth; *voir aussi* **cinquième**

quart¹ [kar] *adj* **le q. monde** (*dans les pays riches*) the underclass

quart² [kar] *nm* (**a**) (*fraction*) quarter; **un q. de siècle/de beurre** a quarter (of a) century/kilo of butter; **un q. d'heure** a quarter of an hour; *Fam* **passer un mauvais q. d'heure** to have a bad time of it; **faire passer un mauvais q. d'heure à qn** to give sb a hard time; **deux heures et q.** (a) quarter past *or* after two; **deux heures moins le q.** (a) quarter to *or* of two; **il est moins le q.** it's (a) quarter to *or* of; **démarrer** *ou*

partir au q. de tour *(voiture)* to start the first time; *(personne)* to fly off the handle; **q. de cercle** quadrant; **q. de finale** quarter final; *Mus* **q. de soupir** sixteenth rest (b) *(bouteille, pichet)* quarter liter (c) *(veille sur un bateau)* watch; **être de q.** to be on watch

quart-arrière [kararjɛr] *nm Can* quarterback

quarte [kart] *nf Mus* fourth

quarté [karte] *nm* = system of betting on four horses in the same race

quartette [kwartɛt] *nm* jazz quartet

quartier [kartje] *nm* (a) *(d'une ville)* district, neighborhood; **les beaux quartiers** the fashionable neighborhoods; **les quartiers nord de la ville** the north side of the town; **de q., du q.** local (b) *(morceau)* *(d'une orange)* segment; *(d'une pomme)* piece (c) *(de la lune)* quarter (d) *(de viande)* quarter (e) *(en héraldique)* quarter; **avoir quatre quartiers de noblesse** to belong to the established nobility (f) *(locutions)* **avoir q. libre** to be off duty; **ne pas faire de q.** to give no quarter

quartz [kwarts] *nm* quartz; **horloge/montre à q.** quartz clock/watch

quasi [kazi] *adv* almost, nearly

quasi- [kazi] *préf* **la q.-totalité des membres** almost all the members

quasiment [kazimã] *adv* almost, nearly; **je n'ai q. rien senti** I hardly felt a thing

quaternaire [kwatɛrnɛr] *Géol* **1** *adj* Quaternary
   2 *nm* Quaternary era

quatorze [katɔrz] *adj & nm inv* fourteen; *voir aussi* **trois**

quatorzième [katɔrzjɛm] *nmf, nm & adj* fourteenth; *voir aussi* **cinquième**

quatrain [katrɛ̃] *nm* quatrain

quatre [katr] *adj & nm inv* four; **aux q. coins du monde** throughout the world; **monter l'escalier q. à q.** to rush up the stairs; *Fig* **se mettre en q. pour qn/pour faire qch** to bend over backward for sb/to do sth; *voir aussi* **trois**

quatre-quarts [katkar, katrəkar] *nm inv* ≃ pound cake

quatre-quatre [katkatr] *nm inv ou nf inv* four-wheel drive, SUV

quatre-saisons [katsɛzɔ̃, katrəsɛzɔ̃] *nfpl* **marchand des q.** fruit-and-vegetable seller *(with outdoor stall)*

quatre-vingt [katrəvɛ̃] *voir* **quatre-vingts**

quatre-vingt-dix [katrəvɛ̃dis] *adj & nm inv* ninety; *voir aussi* **trois**

quatre-vingt-dixième [katrəvɛ̃dizjɛm] *adj, nmf & nm* ninetieth; *voir aussi* **cinquième**

quatre-vingtième [katrəvɛ̃tjɛm] *adj, nmf & nm* eightieth; *voir aussi* **cinquième**

quatre-vingts [katrəvɛ̃] *adj & nm inv* eighty; **quatre-vingt-deux** eighty-two; **page quatre-vingt** page eighty; *voir aussi* **trois**

quatrième [katrijɛm] **1** *adj* fourth; **le q. âge** extreme old age; *Fam* **en q. vitesse** in a hurry, at breakneck speed
   2 *nmf* fourth
   3 *nf* (a) *(classe)* ≃ ninth grade (b) *(vitesse)* fourth (gear); *voir aussi* **cinquième**

quatrièmement [katrijɛmmã] *adv* fourthly

quatuor [kwatɥɔr] *nm* quartet; **q. à cordes** string quartet

que¹ [k(ə)] *pron relatif* (a) *(objet)* *(personne)* that, whom; *(chose)* that, which; **l'homme q. vous voyez** the man (that) you see; **la tarte q. j'ai fait cuire** the pie (that) I baked; **c'est le meilleur q. nous ayons** it is the best (that) we have (b) *(attribut)* **il mourut en brave soldat qu'il était** he died like the brave soldier he was (c) *(dans le temps)* **il y a trois mois q. j'habite Paris** I've been living in Paris for three months; **un jour q. j'étais de service** one day when I was on duty

que² [k(ə)] *pron interrogatif* what; **q. voulez-vous?** what do you want?; **il ne savait q. penser** he didn't know what to think

que³ [k(ə)] *adv exclamatif* **qu'elle est intelligente!** she's so intelligent!; **q. de monde!** what a lot of people!

que⁴ [k(ə)] *conj* (a) *(complétif)* that; **je pense qu'il a raison** I think (that) he's right; **je veux qu'il vienne** I want him to come; **c'est q. je ne le savais pas** I just didn't know
   (b) *(exprime le souhait)* **qu'elle entre!** let her come in!
   (c) *(exprime l'hypothèse)* **q. la machine chauffe, et il y aura un accident** let the machine get hot and there will be an accident; **qu'il essaie encore une fois!** just let him try again!
   (d) *(dans une alternative)* **q. tu le veuilles ou non** whether you like it or not
   (e) *(relie deux conditionnels)* **il me le dirait lui-même q. je ne le croirais pas** he could tell me himself and I still wouldn't believe it
   (f) *(afin que, pour que)* **approchez qu'on vous entende** come closer so (that) we can hear you
   (g) *(pour ne pas répéter une autre conjonction)* **quand tu iras mieux et q. tu voudras sortir** when you're better and you want to go out; **si ça te plaît et que tu veux l'acheter...** if you like it and you want to buy it...
   (h) *(dans les comparaisons)* **plus/moins grand q. moi** bigger/smaller than me; **aussi grand q. moi** as big as me
   (i) **ne... q.** only; **il n'a qu'une jambe** he only has one leg; **il ne me reste plus q. cinq euros** I've only got five euros left
   (j) *Fam* **ah! q. non!** surely not!; **il va au cercle – qu'il dit!** he's going to the club – so he says!

Québec [kebɛk] **1** *nm (province)* **le Q.** Quebec
   2 *n (ville)* Quebec

québécisme [kebesism] *nm* = word or expression peculiar to Quebec French

québécois, -e [kebekwa, -az] **1** *adj* of Quebec
   2 *nm (langue)* Quebec French
   3 *nm,f* **Q., Québécoise** Quebecker

quel, quelle [kɛl] **1** *adj interrogatif (personne)* which; *(chose)* which, what; **q. homme?** which man?; **quelle heure est-il?** what time is it?, what's the time?; **q. genre d'homme est-ce?** what sort of a man is he?; **si tu savais à q. point il y tient** if you knew how much he cares about it; **à q. film faites-vous référence?** which or what movie are you referring to?; **quelles sont ses raisons?** what are his/her reasons?; *Litt* **q. est cet homme?** who is this man?
   2 *adj exclamatif* **q. homme!** what a man!; **quelle surprise!** what a surprise!; **quelle bêtise de sa part!** how stupid of him!
   3 *adj relatif* **q. que soit le coupable** whoever the culprit may be; **q. que soit le résultat** whatever the result may be; **q. que soit l'endroit où...** no matter where...
   4 *pron interrogatif* which (one)

quelconque [kɛlkɔ̃k] **1** *adj indéfini* **donne-moi un livre q.** give me any book; **sous un prétexte q.** on some pretext or other
   2 *adj (insignifiant)* ordinary

quelle [kɛl] *voir* **quel**

quelque [kɛlk] **1** *adj indéfini* some; **quelques** some, a few; **il y a quelques jours** a few days ago; **et quelque(s)** or so; **cent et quelques mètres** a hundred yards plus; **q.... que +** *subjunctive* whatever; **sous q. prétexte que ce soit** on whatever pretext; **de q. côté que vous regardiez** whichever way you look
   2 *adv* some, about; **q. dix ans** some or about ten years; **les q. 1000 euros qu'il m'a prêtés** the 1,000 euros or so that he lent me

quelque chose [kɛlkəʃoz] *pron indéfini* something; **avez-vous q. à dire?** do you have anything or something to say?; **est-ce que je peux te dire q.?** can I tell you something?; **q. d'autre/de neuf** something else/new; **cela m'a fait q.** it touched me; **ça te ferait vraiment q. si je m'en allais?**

would it really matter to you if I went away?; *Fam* **ah, mais c'est q., ça!** that's a little too much!; *Fam* **un petit q.** *(cadeau)* a little something

quelquefois [kɛlkəfwa] *adv* sometimes

quelque part [kɛlkəpar] *adv* somewhere; *(dans les questions, les hypothèses)* anywhere; **q. où tu n'es jamais allé** somewhere you've never been before; *Fam* **je lui ai donné un coup de pied q.** I kicked him where it hurts

quelques-uns, quelques-unes [kɛlkəzœ̃, -yn] *pron indéfini* some, a few (**de** of)

quelqu'un [kɛlkœ̃] *pron indéfini* (**a**) *(une personne)* someone, somebody; *(dans les questions, les hypothèses)* anyone, anybody; **q. de trop** one too many; **q. d'important** someone important; **c'est q. de bien** he's a decent person (**b**) *(personne importante)* somebody

quémander [kemɑ̃de] *vt* to beg for (**à** from)

qu'en-dira-t-on [kɑ̃diratɔ̃] *nm* **le q.** gossip

quenelle [kənɛl] *nf Culin* quenelle

quenotte [kənɔt] *nf Fam* tooth

quenouille [kənuj] *nf (pour filer)* distaff; *Fig* **tomber en q.** to go to rack and ruin

quéquette [kekɛt] *nf Fam* willy, peter

querelle [kərɛl] *nf* quarrel; **chercher q. à qn** to try to pick a quarrel with sb; **q. de clocher** petty dispute

quereller [kərele] **se quereller** *vpr* to quarrel (**avec** with)

querelleur, -euse [kərɛlœr, -øz] *adj* quarrelsome

quérir [kerir] *vt Litt* **aller q. qn/qch** to go and fetch sb/sth

qu'est-ce que [kɛskə] **1** *pron interrogatif* what; **q. vous voulez?** what do you want?; **q. c'est que ça?** what's that?; *Fam* **q. tu avais besoin d'aller lui dire ça?** what did you have to go and tell him that for?

2 *pron exclamatif* **qu'est-ce qu'il fait beau!** what lovely weather!; **qu'est-ce qu'il fait chaud!** it's so hot!; **qu'est-ce qu'on a rigolé!** we had such a good laugh!; **q. tu as changé!** how you've changed!; **q. j'ai mangé!** I've eaten so much!

qu'est-ce qui [kɛski] *pron interrogatif* what

question [kɛstjɔ̃] *nf* (**a**) *(interrogation)* question (**sur** about); **q. de confiance** vote of confidence; **q. piège** trick question; **q. subsidiaire** tie-breaker (**b**) *(affaire)* question, matter; **le dossier en q.** the file in question; **remettre qch en q.** to call sth into question; **une q. d'argent/de temps/d'habitude** a question *or* matter of money/of time/of habit; **c'est une q. de vie ou de mort** it's a matter of life or death; **il est q. qu'ils déménagent** there's some talk of them moving; **il n'en est pas q.** it's out of the question; **là n'est pas la q.** that's not the point; *Fam* **pas q.!** no way!, no chance!; *Fam* **q. argent, ça va** moneywise *or* as far as money goes, things are OK

questionnaire [kɛstjɔnɛr] *nm* questionnaire; **q. à choix multiple** multiple-choice questionnaire

questionner [kɛstjɔne] *vt* to question (**sur** about)

quête [kɛt] *nf* (**a**) *(recherche)* quest, search (**de** for); **se mettre en q. de qn/qch** to go in search of sb/sth (**b**) *(collecte)* collection; **faire la q.** *(à l'église)* to take the collection

quêter [kete] **1** *vt* to seek

2 *vi* to collect money (**pour** for)

quêteux, -euse [kɛtø, -øz] *nm,f Can* beggar

quetsche [kwɛtʃ] *nf* (**a**) *(prune)* dark-red plum (**b**) *(eau-de-vie)* plum brandy

queue [kø] *nf* (**a**) *(d'animal)* tail; **n'avoir ni q. ni tête** to have neither rhyme nor reason; **une histoire sans q. ni tête** a shaggy-dog story; **faire une q. de poisson à qn** to cut (in) in front of sb; **finir en q. de poisson** *(pièce de théâtre, projet)* to end up in the air

(**b**) *(d'une casserole)* handle; *(d'une comète, d'un cerf-volant)* tail; *(d'un fruit, d'une fleur)* stalk; *(d'une note de musique)* stem

(**c**) *(d'une procession)* rear; **de q.** *(voiture, wagon)* rear; **être en**

q. de peloton to be at the back of the pack; **être en q. de classement** to be at the bottom of the standings

(**d**) *(file)* line; **à la q. leu leu** in single file; **faire la q.** to stand in line

(**e**) *(pour le billard)* cue

(**f**) *Vulg (pénis)* cock

queue-de-cheval *(pl* **queues-de-cheval)** [kødʃəval] *nf* ponytail

queue-de-pie *(pl* **queues-de-pie)** [kødpi] *nf Fam* tails

qui¹ [ki] *pron relatif* (**a**) *(personne)* who, that; *(animal, chose)* which, that; **vous q. êtes du pays, pourriez-vous me dire si…** you being from the country, could you tell me if…; **je le vois q. vient** I can see him coming

(**b**) *(ce qui)* **q. plus est** what's more; **voilà q. me plaît** that's what I like

(**c**) *(après une préposition)* who, whom; **voilà l'homme à q. je pensais** there's the man (who) I was thinking about; **il cherche quelqu'un avec q. jouer** he's looking for someone to play with; **c'est à q. finira le premier** everyone's trying to be the first to finish

(**d**) *(n'importe qui)* whoever; **emmenez q. vous voulez** take whoever you like with you; **q. que vous soyez** whoever you are; **je défie q. que ce soit de le prouver** I challenge anyone to prove it

qui² [ki] *pron interrogatif* who; *(complément d'objet ou après une préposition)* who, whom; **q. a dit cela?** who said that?; **savez-vous q. a dit cela?** do you know who said that?; **à q. est-ce?** whose is it?; **de q. parlez-vous?** who are you talking about?; **de q. êtes-vous le fils?** whose son are you?; **q. d'autre?** who else?; *Fam* **q. ça?** who's that?; *Fam* **il est là – q. donc?** he's here – who?

quiche [kiʃ] *nf* quiche; **q. lorraine** quiche lorraine

quiconque [kikɔ̃k] *pron indéfini (sujet)* whoever, anyone who; *(complément)* anyone, anybody; **q. désobéira sera puni** anyone who disobeys will be punished; **sans l'aide de q.** without anyone's help

quidam [kidam] *nm* guy

quiétude [kjetyd] *nf Litt* peace; **en toute q.** *(sans être dérangé)* without being disturbed; *(sans souci)* with an easy mind

quignon [kiɲɔ̃] *nm* hunk

quille¹ [kij] *nf* (**a**) **quilles** *(jeu)* skittles (**b**) *Fam* **la q.** *(fin du service militaire)* discharge (**c**) *Fam* **quilles** *(jambes)* legs

quille² [kij] *nf (d'un bateau)* keel

quilleur, -euse [kijœr, -øz] *nm,f Can* skittle player

quincaillerie [kɛ̃kajri] *nf* (**a**) *(magasin)* hardware store (**b**) *(ustensiles)* hardware (**c**) *Fam (bijoux voyants)* cheap jewelry

quincaillier, -ère [kɛ̃kaje, -ɛr] *nm,f* hardware dealer

quinconce [kɛ̃kɔ̃s] **en quinconce** *adv* in staggered rows

quinine [kinin] *nf* quinine

quinquagénaire [kɛ̃kaʒenɛr] **1** *adj* **être q.** to be in one's fifties

2 *nmf* person in his/her fifties

quinquennal, -e, -aux, -ales [kɛ̃kenal, -o] *adj (plan)* five-year; *(exposition, élection)* five-yearly

quinquennat [kɛ̃kena] *nm* five-year term

quintal, -aux [kɛ̃tal, -o] *nm* quintal (*= 100 kg*)

quinte [kɛ̃t] *nf* (**a**) *(accès)* **q. de toux** coughing fit (**b**) *Mus* fifth

quinté [kɛ̃te] *nm* = bet in which the bettor predicts the first five horses to finish a race

quintessence [kɛ̃tesɑ̃s] *nf* quintessence

quintet [kɛ̃tɛt] *nm* (jazz) quintet

quintette [kɛ̃tɛt, kɥɛtɛt] *nm* quintet; **q. à cordes** string quintet

quintuple [kɛ̃typl] **1** *adj* quintuple, fivefold

2 *nm* **le q. (de)** *(quantité, prix)* five times as much (as); *(nombre)* five times as many (as); **quinze est le q. de trois** fifteen is five times three

quintupler [kɛ̃typle] *vt & vi* to quintuple, to increase fivefold

quintuplés, -ées [kɛ̃typle] *nm,f pl* quintuplets

quinzaine [kɛ̃zɛn] *nf* (**a**) *(environ quinze)* **une q. (de)** about fifteen, fifteen or so (**b**) *(deux semaines)* two weeks; *Com* = sale lasting two weeks

quinze [kɛ̃z] **1** *adj inv* fifteen; **q. jours** two weeks

2 *nm inv* fifteen; **demain en q.** two weeks from tomorrow; *voir aussi* **trois**

quinzième [kɛ̃zjɛm] *nmf, nm & adj* fifteenth; *voir aussi* **cinquième**

quiproquo [kiprɔko] *nm* mix-up

quittance [kitɑ̃s] *nf* receipt; **q. de loyer** rent receipt

quitte [kit] *adj* (**a**) *(libéré)* **nous sommes quittes** we're quits (**b**) *(locutions)* **en être q. pour qch** to get off with sth; *Belg* **être q. de qch** to be deprived of sth; **q. ou double** double or nothing; **q. à faire qch** even if it means doing sth

quitter [kite] **1** *vt* (**a**) *(personne, lieu)* to leave; *(chambre d'hôtel)* to vacate; **q. la route** *(par accident)* to go off the road; *(délibérément)* to turn off the road; **un ami très cher vient de nous q.** we have just lost a very dear friend; *Ordinat* **q. le système** to quit (the system) (**b**) *(fonctions, poste)* to leave (**c**) *(vêtement)* to take off (**d**) *(au téléphone)* **ne quittez pas** hold the line (**e**) **ne pas q. qn/qch des yeux** to keep one's eye on sb/sth

2 se quitter *vpr* to part; **ils ne se quittent plus** they are inseparable

qui-vive [kiviv] *nm* **être** *ou* **se tenir sur le q.** to be on the alert

quoi¹ [kwa] *pron relatif* (**a**) what; **ce à q. je m'oppose** what I object to; **après q.** after which; **sur q.** whereupon; **avoir de q. vivre** to have enough to live on; **avez-vous de q. écrire?** do you have something to write with?; **il n'y a pas de q. être fier** that's nothing to be proud of; **il y a de q. se mettre en colère!** it's enough to make you really angry!; **je suis en colère – il y a de q.** I'm angry – you've every right to be; **il n'y a pas de q.** *(après des remerciements)* don't mention it, not at all (**b**) **q. que tu dises** whatever you say; **q. qu'il advienne** whatever happens; **q. qu'il en soit** be that as it may

quoi² [kwa] *pron interrogatif* what; **q. d'autre?** what else?; **q. de neuf?** what's new?; **q. de plus simple?** what could be simpler?; **je ne sais q. penser** I don't know what to think; **à q. pensez-vous?** what are you thinking about?; **de q. parlez-vous?** what are you talking about?; **à q. bon?** what's the use?; *Fam* **tu es sourd ou q.?** are you deaf or what?; *Fam* **q.? (pardon?)** what?

quoi³ [kwa] *exclam* what!; **et q. encore!** what next!; *Fam* **enfin, c'était nul, q.!** it was crap, basically!; **décide-toi, q.!** well, make up your mind!

quoique [kwak] *conj* (al)though; **q. je le sache déjà** (al)though I already know

quolibet [kɔlibɛ] *nm* gibe, jeer

quorum [kwɔrɔm] *nm* quorum; **atteindre le q.** to have a quorum

quota [kɔta] *nm* quota; *Can Fig* **avoir son q.** to be fed-up

quote-part (*pl* **quotes-parts**) [kɔtpar] *nf* share

quotidien, -enne [kɔtidjɛ̃, -ɛn] **1** *adj (de chaque jour) (promenade, repas, entraînement)* daily; *(préoccupations)* everyday; **leurs disputes étaient devenues presque quotidiennes** they'd got to the stage where they were arguing almost every day

2 *nm* (**a**) *(journal)* daily (paper); **grand q.** national daily (paper) (**b**) *(routine)* daily life; **au q.** on a day-to-day basis

quotidiennement [kɔtidjɛnmɑ̃] *adv* daily

quotient [kɔsjɑ̃] *nm* quotient; **q. intellectuel** intelligence quotient

R

R, r [ɛr] *nm inv* R, r

rab [rab] *nm Fam (nourriture)* extra; **faire du r.** *(au travail)* to put in a bit of overtime; **en r.** left over

rabâchage [rabaʃaʒ] *nm* tedious repetition

rabâcher [rabaʃe] **1** *vi* to say the same thing over and over again
2 *vt (conseils, recommandations)* to keep on repeating; *(leçon)* to repeat parrot-fashion

rabais [rabɛ] *nm* discount, reduction; **faire un r. à qn (sur qch)** to give sb a discount (on sth); *Fig* **au r.** *(travail)* badly paid

rabaisser [rabese] **1** *vt* **(a)** *(prétentions)* to moderate **(b)** *(personne, valeur, talents)* to belittle
2 se rabaisser *vpr* to belittle oneself

Rabat [raba] *n* Rabat

rabat [raba] *nm* **(a)** *(de sac à main, d'enveloppe)* flap **(b)** *(de costume officiel)* bands

rabat-joie [rabaʒwa] **1** *adj inv* **être r.** to be a killjoy
2 *nm inv* killjoy

rabattable [rabatabl] *adj (siège, dossier)* fold-down

rabatteur, -euse [rabatœr, -øz] *nm,f* **(a)** *(à la chasse)* beater **(b)** *Fig* tout

rabattre [11] [rabatr] **1** *vt* **(a)** *(col)* to turn down **(b)** *(couvercle)* to close; *(strapontin) (en se levant)* to fold up; *(pour s'asseoir)* to fold down **(c)** *(gibier, foule)* to drive **(vers** towards) **(d)** *(somme)* to deduct **(de** from) **(e)** *(prétentions)* to moderate
2 se rabattre *vpr* **(a)** *(strapontin)* to fold down **(b)** *(véhicule)* to pull back in **(c)** *(foule)* **se r. vers qch** to veer off toward sth **(d)** *(avoir recours)* **se r. sur qn/qch** to fall back on sb/sth

rabbin [rabɛ̃] *nm* rabbi; **grand r.** chief rabbi

rabibocher [rabiboʃe] *Fam* **1** *vt* to patch things up between
2 se rabibocher *vpr* to patch things up (**avec** with)

rabiot [rabjo] = **rab**

râble [rabl] *nm (de lièvre, lapin)* back; **r. de lièvre** *(plat)* saddle of hare

râblé, -e [rable] *adj* stocky

rabot [rabo] *nm* plane

raboter [rabote] *vt* to plane

raboteuse [rabotøz] *nf* planing machine

raboteux, -euse [rabotø, -øz] *adj* uneven

rabougri, -e [rabugri] *adj (plante, personne)* stunted

rabougrir [rabugrir] **se rabougrir** *vpr* to shrivel up

rabrouer [rabrue] *vt* to snub

racaille [rakaj] *nf (voyous)* scum; *Vieilli (populace)* rabble

raccommodage [rakɔmɔdaʒ] *nm (de vêtements)* mending; *(de bas, de chaussettes)* darning; **faire du r.** to do some mending/darning

raccommoder [rakɔmɔde] **1** *vt* **(a)** *(vêtement)* to mend; *(bas, chaussette)* to darn **(b)** *Fam (personnes)* to patch things up between
2 se raccommoder *vpr Fam* to patch things up (**avec** with)

raccompagner [rakɔ̃paɲe] *vt* to take back

raccord [rakɔr] *nm* **(a)** *(de papier peint)* join; *(de peinture)* touch-up **(b)** *(pièce d'assemblage)* connection **(c)** *Cin* continuity; *(plan)* link

raccordement [rakɔrdəmã] *nm* **(a)** *(lien)* link, connection **(b)** *Ordinat* link

raccorder [rakɔrde] **1** *vt* **(a)** *(relier) (canalisations, bâtiments, routes)* to link up, to connect (**à** to); *Ordinat* to connect **(b)** *(bande magnétique)* to splice
2 se raccorder *vpr* to link up; *Ordinat* **se r. à** to link up to

raccourci [rakursi] *nm* short cut; **en r.** *(en bref)* in brief; *(en miniature)* in miniature; *Ordinat* **r. clavier** keyboard shortcut

raccourcir [rakursir] **1** *vt* to shorten (**de** by)
2 *vi* to get shorter

raccrocher [rakroʃe] **1** *vt* to hang up again; **r. l'appareil** *ou* **le téléphone** to hang up
2 *vi* **(a)** *(au téléphone)* to hang up, to put the phone down; **r. au nez de qn** to hang up on sb, to put the phone down on sb **(b)** *Fam (sportif)* to retire
3 se raccrocher *vpr* **se r. à qch** to catch hold of sth; *Fig (espérance)* to cling to sth

race [ras] *nf* **(a)** *(ethnie)* race; **la r. blanche/noire** the white/black race; **la r. humaine** the human race **(b)** *(animale)* breed; **de r.** *(chien)* pedigree; *(cheval)* thoroughbred

racé, -e [rase] *adj (animal)* pure-bred; *(cheval, voiture)* thoroughbred; *(personne)* noble-looking

rachat [raʃa] *nm* **(a)** *(d'une voiture, d'un appartement)* repurchase, buying back **(b)** *(d'une société)* buy-out **(c)** *(d'un péché)* atonement

racheter [6] [raʃte] **1** *vt* **(a)** *(acheter davantage de)* to buy some more **(b)** *(remplacer)* to buy another (**à** for) **(c)** *(compagnie)* to buy out **(d)** *(après une vente)* to buy back (**à** from) **(e)** *(otage, prisonnier)* to pay a ransom for **(f)** *(faute, faiblesse)* to make up for; *(péché)* to atone for; *(honneur, réputation)* to retrieve
2 se racheter *vpr* to make amends, to redeem oneself

rachitique [raʃitik] *adj (malade)* suffering from rickets; *(très maigre)* scrawny

rachitisme [raʃitism] *nm* rickets *(singulier)*

racial, -e, -aux, -ales [rasjal, -o] *adj* racial

racine [rasin] *nf* root; **prendre r.** *(plante, personne)* to take root; **r. carrée/cubique** square/cube root

racisme [rasism] *nm* racism

raciste [rasist] *adj & nmf* racist

racket [rakɛt] *nm Fam* racket

racketter [rakɛte] *vt Fam (personne)* to extort money from; **se faire r.** to pay protection money

raclage [raklaʒ] *nm* scraping

raclée [rakle] *nf Fam* thrashing; **mettre une r. à qn** *(battre)* to give sb a good thrashing; *(vaincre)* to thrash sb; **prendre une r.** to get a thrashing

raclement [rakləmã] *nm* scraping (noise)

racler [rakle] **1** *vt* to scrape; *(peinture, boue)* to scrape off; *Fig* **r. les fonds de tiroirs** to scrape some money together; *Fam* **r.**

la gorge *ou* **le gosier** *(vin)* to be rough on the throat
  2 se racler *vpr* **se r. la gorge** to clear one's throat
raclette [raklɛt] *nf* (**a**) *(plat)* raclette *(Swiss dish consisting of potatoes covered in melted cheese)* (**b**) *(outil)* scraper
racloir [raklwar] *nm* scraper
racolage [rakɔlaʒ] *nm* *(d'une prostituée)* soliciting; *(d'un publicitaire)* touting for business; **faire du r.** *(prostituée)* to solicit; *(publicitaire)* to tout for business
racoler [rakɔle] **1** *vt* *(sujet: prostituée)* to solicit; *(sujet: commerçant)* to tout for
  2 *vi* *(prostituée)* to solicit; *(commerçant)* to tout for business
racoleur, -euse [rakɔlœr, -øz] **1** *adj* *(publicité, affiche)* eye-catching
  2 *nm,f* *(politicien)* = canvasser who attempts to recruit party members using unscrupulous means; *(commerçant)* tout
  3 *nf* **racoleuse** streetwalker
racontable [rakɔ̃tabl] *adj* relatable; **ce n'est pas r. devant les enfants** it's not something to be spoken about in front of the children
racontar [rakɔ̃tar] *nm* piece of gossip; **racontars** gossip
raconter [rakɔ̃te] **1** *vt* (**a**) *(histoire, mensonge)* to tell; *(événement)* to tell about; **r. qch à qn** *(histoire)* to tell sb sth; *(événement)* to tell sb about sth (**b**) *(dire)* to say; **qu'est-ce qu'il raconte?** what's he talking about?; **alors, qu'est-ce que tu racontes (de beau** *ou* **de neuf)?** so what's new?
  2 se raconter *vpr* (**a**) *(parler de soi)* to talk about oneself (**b**) *(être raconté)* to be talked about
racornir [rakɔrnir] **1** *vt* (**a**) *(durcir)* to harden (**b**) *(ratatiner)* to shrivel
  2 se racornir *vpr* (**a**) *(durcir)* to harden (**b**) *(se ratatiner)* to shrivel
radar [radar] *nm* radar; *Fam* **être** *ou* **avancer au r.** to be on automatic pilot
rade [rad] *nf* harbor; **en r. deToulon** off Toulon; *Fam* **laisser en r.** *(personne)* to leave in the lurch; *(projet)* to jettison; *Fam* **être en r.** *(personne)* to be stranded
radeau, -x [rado] *nm* raft; **r. pneumatique** inflatable raft; **r. de sauvetage** life raft
radial, -e, -aux, -ales [radjal, -o] *adj voir* **carcasse**
radiateur [radjatœr] *nm* radiator; **r. électrique** electric heater
radiation[1] [radjasjɔ̃] *nf* *(sur une liste)* striking off
radiation[2] [radjasjɔ̃] *nf* *(d'une onde)* radiation
radical, -e, -aux, -ales [radikal, -o] **1** *adj* radical; **c'est r. (contre)** *(médicament, méthode)* it works like magic (on)
  2 *nm* *(d'un mot)* stem
radicalement [radikalmɑ̃] *adv* radically
radicaliser [radikalize] **1** *vt* to radicalize
  2 se radicaliser *vpr* to become more radical
radier [66] [radje] *vt* to strike off (**de** from)
radiesthésiste [radjɛstezist] *nmf* diviner
radieux, -euse [radjø, -øz] *adj* *(soleil, personne)* radiant; *(temps)* glorious
radin, -e [radɛ̃, -in] *Fam* **1** *adj* stingy
  2 *nm,f* miser, tightwad
radiner [radine] **se radiner** *vpr Fam* to show up; **tu te radines?** are you coming or not?
radio [radjo] **1** *nf* (**a**) *(poste)* radio; *(station)* radio station; **à la r.** on the radio; **faire de la r.** to work in radio; **r. libre** independent radio station; **r. locale** local radio station (**b**) *(radiotéléphonie)* radio (**c**) *Méd* X-ray; **passer une r.** to have an X-ray
  2 *nm* *(opérateur)* radio operator
  3 *adj inv* radio
radioactif, -ive [radjoaktif, -iv] *adj* radioactive
radioactivité [radjoaktivite] *nf* radioactivity
radioamateur [radjoamatœr] *nm* radio ham
radiocassette [radjokasɛt] *nf* radio cassette player
radiodiffuser [radjodifyze] *vt* to broadcast

radiodiffusion [radjodifyzjɔ̃] *nf* broadcasting
radiographie [radjografi] *nf* (**a**) *(technique)* radiography (**b**) *(cliché)* X-ray
radiographier [66] [radjɔgrafje] *vt* to X-ray
radioguidé, -e [radjogide] *adj* radio-controlled; *(missile)* guided
radiologie [radjɔlɔʒi] *nf* radiology
radiologique [radjɔlɔʒik] *adj* radiological
radiologue [radjɔlɔg], **radiologiste** [radjɔlɔʒist] *nmf* *(médecin)* radiologist; *(technicien)* radiographer
radiophonique [radjofonik] *adj* *(de radio)* radio; *(bon pour la radio)* good for radio
radioreportage [radjorəpɔrtaʒ] *nm* *(activité)* radio reporting; *(émission)* radio report
radioreporter [radjorəpɔrtɛr] *nmf* radio reporter
radio-réveil (*pl* **radios-réveils**) [radjorevɛj] *nm* radio-alarm (clock)
radioscopie [radjoskɔpi] *nf* radioscopy
radioscopique [radjoskɔpik] *adj* *(examen)* X-ray
radio-taxi (*pl* **radio-taxis**) [radjotaksi] *nm* radio taxi
radiotélescope [radjotelɛskɔp] *nm* radio telescope
radiotélévisé, -e [radjotelevize] *adj* broadcast on both radio and television
radiothérapie [radjoterapi] *nf* radiotherapy
radis [radi] *nm* radish; *Fam* **ne plus avoir un r.** not to have a bean; **r. noir** black radish
radium [radjɔm] *nm* radium
radius [radjys] *nm* radius
radon [radɔ̃] *nm Chim* radon
radotage [radɔtaʒ] *nm* *(rabâchage)* going on and on; *(divagations)* rambling
radoter [radɔte] **1** *vi* *(rabâcher)* to go on and on; *(divaguer)* to ramble on
  2 *vt Fam* **qu'est-ce que tu radotes?** what are you rambling on about?
radoteur, -euse [radɔtœr, -øz] *nm,f* rambling old fool
radoub [radu] *nm* **bassin de r.** dry dock
radoucir [radusir] **1** *vt* (**a**) *(temps)* to make milder (**b**) *(personne)* to calm down; *(caractère)* to soften
  2 se radoucir *vpr* (**a**) *(temps)* to become milder (**b**) *(personne)* to calm down
radoucissement [radusismɑ̃] *nm* (**a**) *(de la température)* milder spell (**b**) *(d'une personne)* calming down
rafale [rafal] *nf* (**a**) *(de vent, de pluie)* gust; **par** *ou* **en rafales** in gusts (**b**) *(de coups de feu)* burst
raffermir [rafermir] **1** *vt* (**a**) *(peau, muscles)* to firm up (**b**) *(autorité, courage)* to strengthen
  2 se raffermir *vpr* (**a**) *(muscles, peau)* to firm up (**b**) *(gouvernement)* *(devenir plus intransigeant)* to take a stronger line; *(devenir plus fort)* to become stronger; *(autorité)* to strengthen
raffermissement [rafermismɑ̃] *nm* (**a**) *(des muscles, de la peau)* firming up (**b**) *(de l'autorité, du pouvoir)* strengthening
raffinage [rafinaʒ] *nm* refining
raffiné, -e [rafine] *adj* refined
raffinement [rafinmɑ̃] *nm* refinement
raffiner [rafine] **1** *vt* to refine
  2 raffiner sur *vt ind* to be overparticular about
raffinerie [rafinri] *nf* refinery; **r. de pétrole/sucre** oil/sugar refinery
raffoler [rafɔle] **raffoler de** *vt ind Fam* **r. de qch** to be mad about sth
raffut [rafy] *nm Fam* *(bruit)* din, racket; **faire du r.** *(bruit)* to make a din; *(scandale)* to set tongues wagging; *(pour protester)* to kick up a fuss
rafiot [rafjo] *nm Péj* old tub
rafistolage [rafistɔlaʒ] *nm Fam* patching up

rafistoler [rafistɔle] *vt Fam* to patch up

rafle [rafl] *nf* raid; **la police a fait une r. dans le club** the police raided the club

rafler [rafle] *vt Fam* to swipe

rafraîchir [rafreʃir] **1** *vt* (**a**) *(rendre frais) (aliment, boisson)* to chill; *(pièce)* to air; *(atmosphère)* to cool (**b**) *(raviver) (couleur, maquillage, peintures)* to freshen up; *(appartement)* to brighten up; *Fam* **r. la mémoire à qn** to refresh sb's memory
2 *vi* to cool down
3 se rafraîchir *vpr* (**a**) *(temps)* to turn cooler (**b**) *(se mouiller le visage)* to freshen up (**c**) *Fam (boire)* to have a cold drink

rafraîchissant, -e [rafreʃisɑ̃, -ɑ̃t] *adj* refreshing

rafraîchissement [rafreʃismɑ̃] *nm* (**a**) *(de la température, d'une boisson)* cooling (**b**) *(boisson)* cold drink; **rafraîchissements** refreshments (**c**) *Ordinat* refresh

rafting [raftiŋ] *nm* rafting

ragaillardir [ragajardir] *Fam* **1** *vt* to buck up
2 se ragaillardir *vpr* to buck up

rage [raʒ] *nf* (**a**) *(maladie)* rabies (**b**) *(colère)* rage; **faire r.** *(tempête)* to rage; **avoir la r. au cœur** to be seething with rage; **ivre** *ou* **fou de r.** furious; **mettre qn en r.** to enrage sb; **r. de dents** raging toothache (**c**) *(passion)* passion (**de qch** for sth); **avoir la r. du jeu** to have a passion for gambling

rageant, -e [raʒɑ̃, -ɑ̃t] *adj Fam* infuriating

rager [45] [raʒe] *vi Fam* to fume; **faire r. qn** to make sb mad

rageur, -euse [raʒœr, -øz] *adj (ton, voix)* furious

rageusement [raʒøzmɑ̃] *adv* furiously

raglan [raglɑ̃] *nm* raglan coat

ragot [rago] *nm Fam* piece of gossip; **ragots** gossip

ragoût [ragu] *nm* stew; **en r.** stewed

ragoûtant, -e [ragutɑ̃, -ɑ̃t] *adj* **peu** *ou* **pas r.** *(plat)* unappetizing; *(personne)* unsavory

rai [rɛ] *nm (de lumière)* ray

raï [raj] *nm inv* rai,= North African popular music influenced by rock music

raid [rɛd] *nm* raid; **r. aérien** air raid

raide [rɛd] **1** *adj* (**a**) *(membre, articulation)* stiff; *(cheveux)* straight; *(câble)* taut (**b**) *(escalier, pente)* steep (**c**) *(personne, démarche)* stiff; **r. comme un piquet** as stiff as a ramrod (**d**) *(caractère)* inflexible; *(manières)* stiff (**e**) *Fam (difficile à croire)* far-fetched (**f**) *Fam (osé)* risqué (**g**) *Fam (fort) (alcool)* rough
2 *adv* (**a**) *(de façon abrupte)* steeply (**b**) *(brutalement)* **tomber r.** to fall to the ground; **tomber r. mort** to drop dead

raideur [rɛdœr] *nf* (**a**) *(d'un membre, d'une articulation, d'un mouvement)* stiffness; **avoir une r. dans le cou/à l'épaule** to have a stiff neck/shoulder (**b**) *(d'une personne)* stiffness (**c**) *(de caractère)* inflexibility (**d**) *(d'une pente)* steepness

raidillon [rɛdijɔ̃] *nm (chemin)* steep path; *(partie de route)* steep rise

raidir [rɛdir] **1** *vt (bras, jambes)* to brace; *(corde, câble)* to tauten; *(tissu)* to stiffen
2 se raidir *vpr* (**a**) *(membres, articulations)* to stiffen; *(câble)* to tauten (**b**) *(personne)* to tense up

raidissement [rɛdismɑ̃] *nm* (**a**) *(d'une matière, des muscles)* stiffening; *(d'une corde)* tautening (**b**) *(montée de la tension)* **r. des rapports internationaux** increase of tension in international relations; **le r. des ouvriers face à la direction** the tougher line taken by the workers with the management

raie¹ [rɛ] *nf* (**a**) *(motif)* stripe (**b**) *(dans les cheveux)* part (**c**) *(des fesses)* cleft

raie² [rɛ] *nf (poisson)* skate

raifort [rɛfɔr] *nm* horseradish

rail [raj] *nm* (**a**) *(sur une voie de chemin de fer)* rail; *Fig* **remettre qn sur les rails** to get sb back on the rails (**b**) **le r.** *(les chemins de fer)* rail (**c**) **r. de sécurité** crash barrier (**d**) *(couloir) (aérien, maritime)* lane

railler [raje] *vt* to mock

raillerie [rajri] *nf* gibe

railleur, -euse [rajœr, -øz] **1** *adj* mocking
2 *nm,f* scoffer

rainette [rɛnɛt] *nf* (**a**) *(grenouille)* tree frog (**b**) *(pomme)* pippin

rainure [rɛnyr] *nf* groove

raisin [rɛzɛ̃] *nm* grapes; **raisins de Corinthe** currants; **raisins secs** raisins; **raisins de Smyrne** sultanas

raisinet [rɛzinɛ] *nm Suisse* redcurrant

raison [rɛzɔ̃] *nf* (**a**) *(motif)* reason (**de** for); **en r. de qch** because of sth; **être absent pour r. de santé** to be absent for health reasons; **à plus forte r.** all the more so; **r. de plus (pour faire qch)** all the more reason (to do sth); **la r. pour laquelle il est venu** the reason (why) he came; **la r. d'État** reasons of State; **r. d'être** raison d'être; **r. de vivre** reason for living
(**b**) *(entendement)* reason; **recouvrer la r.** to come to one's senses; **perdre la r.** to take leave of one's senses; **entendre r.** to listen to reason; **de r.** *(âge)* of reason; *(mariage)* of convenience
(**c**) *(satisfaction)* satisfaction; **avoir r. de qn/qch** to get the better of sb/sth
(**d**) *(proportion)* **à r. de** at the rate of
(**e**) *(désignation)* **r. sociale** company name
(**f**) *(locutions)* **avoir r. (de faire qch)** to be right (to do sth); **donner r. à qn** *(personne)* to admit that sb is right; *(événement)* to prove sb right; **se faire une r.** to accept the inevitable, to resign oneself; **comme de r.** as one might expect; **plus que de r.** more than is reasonable

raisonnable [rɛzɔnabl] *adj* reasonable

raisonnablement [rɛzɔnabləmɑ̃] *adv* (**a**) *(avec bon sens)* reasonably (**b**) *(modérément)* in moderation

raisonné, -e [rɛzɔne] *adj (argumentation, choix)* reasoned

raisonnement [rɛzɔnmɑ̃] *nm (argumentation)* argument; *(faculté)* reasoning; **tenir un r.** to use an argument; **r. par l'absurde** reductio ad absurdum

raisonner [rɛzɔne] **1** *vt (personne)* to reason with
2 *vi* (**a**) *(penser)* to reason (**sur** about); *Fam* **r. comme une pantoufle** to talk through one's hat (**b**) *(discuter)* to argue (**avec** with)
3 se raisonner *vpr (personne)* to see reason

raisonneur, -euse [rɛzɔnœr, -øz] **1** *adj* reasoning; *Péj* argumentative
2 *nm,f Péj* arguer

rajeunir [raʒœnir] **1** *vt* (**a**) **r. qn** *(faire paraître plus jeune)* to make sb look younger; *(faire se sentir plus jeune)* to make sb feel younger (**b**) *(donner un âge moins élevé à)* **r. qn** to underestimate how old sb is; **r. qn de trois ans** to take three years off sb's age (**c**) *(robe, veste)* to update (**d**) *(organisation, bureau)* to modernize; *(équipe)* to bring new blood into
2 *vi (physiquement)* to look younger; *(moralement)* to seem younger; **il a rajeuni de dix ans** he looks ten years younger; **ça ne nous rajeunit pas!** we're showing our age!
3 se rajeunir *vpr (se prétendre plus jeune)* to make oneself out to be younger than one is

rajeunissant, -e [raʒœnisɑ̃, -ɑ̃t] *adj* rejuvenating

rajeunissement [raʒœnismɑ̃] *nm* (**a**) *(après un traitement)* rejuvenation (**b**) *(de la population, d'un secteur professionnel)* decrease in age

rajout [raʒu] *nm* (**a**) addition (**b**) *(pour les cheveux)* **rajouts** extensions

rajouter [raʒute] *vt* to add; *Fam* **en r.** to exaggerate

rajuster [raʒyste] **1** *vt (vêtement)* to adjust, to straighten
2 se rajuster *vpr* to straighten one's clothes

râle [rɑl] *nm (bruit aux poumons)* rale; *(d'un agonisant)* death rattle

ralenti, -e [ralɑ̃ti] **1** *adj* slow
2 *nm* (**a**) *(régime du moteur)* idling speed; **au r.** *(vivre, fonctionner)*

at a slower pace; **tourner au r.** *(moteur, usine)* to turn over (**b**) *Cin* slow motion; **au r.** in slow motion

ralentir [ralɑ̃tir] *vt & vi* to slow down

ralentissement [ralɑ̃tismɑ̃] *nm* slowing down; *(embouteillage)* hold-up

ralentisseur [ralɑ̃tisœr] *nm (dos d'âne)* speed bump

râler [rɑle] *vi* (**a**) *Fam (protester)* to moan (**b**) *(mourant)* to give a death rattle

râleur, -euse [rɑlœr, -øz] *Fam* **1** *adj* bad-tempered, grumpy **2** *nm,f* moaner

ralliement [ralimɑ̃] *nm* rallying; **cri de r.** rallying cry

rallier [66] [ralje] **1** *vt* (**a**) *(regagner) (lieu)* to return to (**b**) *(gagner à sa cause)* to win over (**à** to) (**c**) *(réunir) (adhérents)* to rally; **r. tous les suffrages** to win general approval (**d**) *(regrouper) (troupes)* to rally

2 se rallier *vpr* **se r. à** *(avis)* to come around to; *(parti)* to join; *(cause)* to rally to

rallonge [ralɔ̃ʒ] *nf* (**a**) *(de table)* extension (**b**) *(électrique)* extension cord (**c**) *Fam (d'argent)* extra money; *(de temps)* extra time

rallonger [45] [ralɔ̃ʒe] **1** *vt (vêtement)* to lengthen; *(période, route)* to extend (**de** by)

2 *vi* to get longer

rallumer [ralyme] **1** *vt* (**a**) *(appareil électrique, lumière)* to switch on again (**b**) *(feu, cigarette)* to light again; *(querelle, colère, espoir)* to rekindle

2 se rallumer *vpr* (**a**) *(lumière, appareil électrique)* to come back on (**b**) *(feu, guerre, dispute)* to flare up again; *(espoir)* to rekindle

rallye [rali] *nm* (**a**) *(épreuve sportive)* (car) rally (**b**) *(soirée)* = dance attended by young people from rich families looking for a marriage partner

RAM [ram] *nf Ordinat* RAM

ramadan [ramadɑ̃] *nm* Ramadan; **faire le r.** to observe Ramadan

ramage [ramaʒ] *nm* (**a**) *(chant des oiseaux)* song (**b**) **ramages** *(motif)* leafy design

ramassage [ramasaʒ] *nm* (**a**) *(de fruits, de noix)* gathering (**b**) *(d'ordures, de vêtements, de vieux journaux)* collection; **car de r. scolaire** school bus

ramassé, -e [ramase] *adj* (**a**) *(trapu) (personne)* stocky (**b**) *(style)* compact

ramasse-miettes [ramasmjɛt] *nm inv* = small brush and pan for clearing crumbs off the table

ramasser [ramase] **1** *vt* (**a**) *(prendre par terre) (objet, personne)* to pick up; *(fruits, noix, coquillages)* to gather; *(champignons)* to pick; *(pommes de terre)* to dig up; *Fam* **se faire r. par la police** to get picked up by the police (**b**) *(copies, affaires, informations)* to collect; *(cartes)* to pick up; **r. ses forces** to gather one's strength (**c**) *(enfants, ouvriers, courrier)* to pick up, to collect (**d**) *Fam (gifle)* to get; *(procès-verbal)* to pick up; *(maladie)* to catch

2 se ramasser *vpr* (**a**) *(après une chute)* to pick oneself up (**b**) *(se pelotonner)* to curl up (**c**) *Fam (tomber)* to fall flat on one's face; *(échouer)* to screw up (**d**) *(gifle)* to get; *(P-V)* to pick up

ramassette [ramasɛt] *nf Belg* dustpan

ramasseur, -euse [ramasœr, -øz] *nm,f* (**a**) *(de champignons)* picker; *(de fruits)* gatherer (**b**) *(au tennis)* **r. de balles** ball boy, *f* ball girl

ramassis [ramasi] *nm Péj (de choses)* jumble; *(de gens)* bunch; *(d'idées)* hodgepodge; **un r. de mensonges** a tissue of lies

rambarde [rɑ̃bard] *nf* (guard)rail

ramdam [ramdam] *nm Fam* racket; **faire du r.** to make a heck of a racket

rame¹ [ram] *nf (pour plantes grimpantes)* stick

rame² [ram] *nf (aviron)* oar

rame³ [ram] *nf* (**a**) *(de papier)* ream (**b**) *(de wagons)* train; **r. (de métro)** (subway) train

rameau, -x [ramo] *nm* (**a**) *(d'arbre)* branch (**b**) **les Rameaux** Palm Sunday

ramener [46] [ramne] **1** *vt* (**a**) *(amener)* to bring back; *(raccompagner)* to take back; **r. qn en voiture** to give sb a lift back; **r. qn à la vie** to bring sb back to life; **r. qn à la raison** to bring sb back to his/her senses (**b**) *Fam (rapporter, revenir avec)* to bring back; **r. tout à soi** to bring everything back to oneself (**c**) *(remettre) (couverture, châle)* to pull up (**sur** over) (**d**) *(rétablir) (ordre, paix)* to restore (**e**) *(réduire)* **r. qch à qch** to reduce sth to sth (**f**) *Fam* **r. sa fraise, la r.** to show off

2 se ramener *vpr* (**a**) *(se réduire)* **se r. à** to boil down to (**b**) *Fam (arriver)* to show up

ramequin [ramkɛ̃] *nm* ramekin

ramer [rame] *vi* (**a**) *(pagayer)* to row (**b**) *Fam (peiner)* to sweat blood

rameur, -euse [ramœr, -øz] *nm,f* rower

ramier [ramje] *adj m voir* **pigeon**

ramification [ramifikasjɔ̃] *nf (d'une plante)* ramification; *(d'une famille, d'une science)* branch; **ramifications** *(d'une société, d'une affaire)* ramifications

ramifier [66] [ramifje] **se ramifier** *vpr* to branch out (**en** into)

ramolli, -e [ramɔli] *adj Fam (mentalement)* soft-headed

ramollir [ramɔlir] **1** *vt (substance)* to soften; *Fam* **r. qn** *(intellectuellement)* to make sb soft in the head

2 se ramollir *vpr (substance)* to soften; *Fam Fig (personne)* to become unfit

ramollissement [ramɔlismɑ̃] *nm* softening; **r. cérébral** softening of the brain

ramon [ramɔ̃] *nm Belg* broom

ramonage [ramɔnaʒ] *nm* chimney sweeping

ramoner [ramɔne] *vt (cheminée)* to sweep

ramoneur [ramɔnœr] *nm* (chimney) sweep

rampant, -e [rɑ̃pɑ̃, -ɑ̃t] *adj* (**a**) *(plante)* creeping; *(animal)* crawling; *Péj (personne, caractère)* groveling (**b**) **personnel r.** *(de l'aviation)* ground crew (**c**) *(inflation)* rampant

rampe [rɑ̃p] *nf* (**a**) *(d'escalier)* banister, handrail (**b**) *(plan incliné)* slope, incline; **r. d'accès** *(d'un pont)* access ramp; *(d'une autoroute)* ramp; **r. de lancement** launching ramp (**c**) *(rebord d'une scène de théâtre)* footlights

ramper [rɑ̃pe] *vi (animal, enfant, soldat)* to crawl; *Péj* **r. devant qn** to grovel to sb

ramure [ramyr] *nf* (**a**) *(d'un arbre)* branches (**b**) *(d'un cerf)* antlers

rancard [rɑ̃kar] *nm Fam (rendez-vous)* meeting; *(amoureux)* date

rancarder [rɑ̃karde] *très Fam* **1** *vt* **r. qn sur qch** to tip sb off about sth

2 se rancarder *vpr* to find out (**sur** about)

rancart [rɑ̃kar] *nm Fam* **mettre qch au r.** to chuck sth out; **mettre qn au r.** to throw sb on the scrap heap

rance [rɑ̃s] **1** *adj* rancid

2 *nm* **goût de r.** rancid taste

ranch [rɑ̃tʃ] *nm* ranch

rancir [rɑ̃sir] *vi* to go rancid

rancœur [rɑ̃kœr] *nf* resentment, rancor; **avoir de la r. pour** *ou* **contre qn** to feel resentment toward sb

rançon [rɑ̃sɔ̃] *nf* ransom; *Fig* **la r. de la gloire** the price of fame

rançonner [rɑ̃sɔne] *vt* **r. qn** to hold sb to ransom

rancune [rɑ̃kyn] *nf* spite; **garder r. à qn, avoir de la r. contre qn** to have a grudge against sb, to bear sb a grudge; **sans r.!** no hard feelings!

rancunier, -ère [rɑ̃kynje, -ɛr] **1** *adj* spiteful

2 *nm,f* spiteful person

randonnée [rɑ̃dɔne] *nf* (**a**) *(marche à pied)* **r. (pédestre)** hike; *(activité)* hiking, rambling; *(avec sac à dos)* backpacking;

(en montagne) hill-walking; **faire une r.** to go for a hike; **faire de la r.** to go hiking *or* rambling; *(avec sac à dos)* to go backpacking; *(en montagne)* to go hill-walking (**b**) *(en voiture)* drive; *(à vélo)* ride (**c**) *(excursion à ski)* ski-mountaineering

randonneur, -euse [rɑ̃dɔnœr, -øz] *nm,f (à pied)* hiker, rambler; *(avec sac à dos)* backpacker

rang [rɑ̃] *nm* (**a**) *(d'arbres, de sièges)* row; **se mettre en r. (par deux/trois)** to line up (in twos/threes); *Hum* **en r. d'oignons** in a neat row; **en rangs serrés** in serried ranks; *Fig* **se mettre sur les rangs** to put oneself in the running (**b**) *(position sociale)* station; *(de militaire)* rank; **de haut r.** highranking (**c**) *(classement)* rank; **par r. de taille** in order of size (**d**) *Can (chemin)* concession road

rangé, -e [rɑ̃ʒe] *adj* (**a**) *(maison, chambre)* neat (**b**) *(personne)* steady; *(vie)* settled

rangée [rɑ̃ʒe] *nf* row

rangement [rɑ̃ʒmɑ̃] *nm* (**a**) *(action)* tidying up; **faire du r.** to do some tidying up; **faire du r. dans ses affaires** to put away one's things (**b**) *(placard)* **rangements** storage space (**c**) *Ordinat* storage

ranger [45] [rɑ̃ʒe] **1** *vt* (**a**) *(pièce, maison)* to tidy (up) (**b**) *(affaires, vêtements)* to put away (**c**) *(mettre)* to put (**d**) *(classer)* to rank (**parmi** among); **r. par** *(ordre alphabétique, taille)* to arrange by (**e**) *(véhicule, vélo)* to park (**f**) *(soldats, élèves)* to line up (**g**) *Ordinat* **r. en mémoire** to store

2 se ranger *vpr* (**a**) *(se disposer)* to line up (**b**) *(s'écarter) (piéton)* to stand aside; *(véhicule)* to pull over (**c**) *(prendre position pour)* **se r. du côté de qn** to side with sb, to take sb's side; (**d**) *(se mettre)* **r. à l'opinion de qn** to come around to sb's opinion (**d**) *(se mettre)* to go (**e**) *Fam (s'assagir)* to settle down; **se r. des voitures** to settle down

ranimer [ranime] **1** *vt* (**a**) *(personne) (après un évanouissement)* to bring around; *(après un arrêt cardiaque)* to resuscitate (**b**) *(feu)* to rekindle (**c**) *(sentiment, souvenir, espoir)* to reawaken; *(débat)* to revive

2 se ranimer *vpr* (**a**) *(personne)* to come around (**b**) *(feu)* to flicker into life

rap [rap] *nm Mus* rap

rapace [rapas] **1** *nm* bird of prey

2 *adj* (**a**) *(oiseau)* predatory (**b**) *(personne)* grasping

rapacité [rapasite] *nf* rapaciousness

rapatrié, -e [rapatrije] **1** *adj* repatriated

2 *nm,f* repatriate

rapatriement [rapatrimɑ̃] *nm* repatriation

rapatrier [66] [rapatrije] *vt* to repatriate

râpe [rɑp] *nf* (**a**) *(de cuisine)* grater; **r. à fromage** cheese grater (**b**) *(lime)* rasp (**c**) *Suisse Fam Péj (avare)* miser

râpé, -e [rɑpe] **1** *adj* (**a**) *(fromage, carotte)* grated (**b**) *(vêtement)* threadbare (**c**) *Fam (raté)* **c'est r.!** we've had it!

2 *nm (fromage)* grated cheese

râper [rɑpe] *vt* (**a**) *(carotte, fromage)* to grate (**b**) *(racler)* **ce vin râpe la gorge** this wine's rough on the throat (**c**) *(limer)* to rasp

rapetasser [raptase] *vt Fam (vêtement)* to patch up

rapetisser [raptise] **1** *vt* (**a**) *(rendre plus petit)* to make smaller (**b**) *(dévaluer)* to belittle (**c**) *(faire paraître plus petit)* to make look smaller

2 *vi (vêtement, personne)* to shrink

râpeux, -euse [rɑpø, -øz] *adj (langue)* rough; *(vin)* harsh

raphia [rafja] *nm* raffia

rapiat, -e [rapja, -at] *Fam* **1** *adj (avare)* stingy

2 *nm,f* skinflint

rapide [rapid] **1** *adj* (**a**) *(coureur, voiture, itinéraire)* fast; *(pouls, progrès)* rapid; **r. comme l'éclair** as quick as lightning; **r. comme une flèche** as swift as an arrow (**b**) *(courant)* swiftflowing (**c**) *(prompt) (personne, esprit, intelligence)* quick (**d**) *(fait en peu de temps) (lecture, décision)* quick (**e**) *(pente)* steep

2 *nm* (**a**) *(train)* express (train) (**b**) *(dans un fleuve)* rapid

rapidement [rapidmɑ̃] *adv* quickly, rapidly

rapidité [rapidite] *nf* (**a**) *(d'actions, d'une décision, d'une réponse)* speed; **r. d'esprit** quickness of mind (**b**) *Ordinat* **r. d'impression** print speed; **r. de traitement** processing speed

rapiécer [16/34] [rapjese] *vt* to patch

rapine [rapin] *nf Litt* pillage

raplapla [raplapla] *adj inv Fam* (**a**) *(pneu, coussin)* flat as a pancake (**b**) *(personne)* pooped

rappel [rapɛl] *nm* (**a**) *(d'un événement, d'une promesse)* reminder; **r. de couleurs** repeat of colors; **r. à l'ordre** *(d'un membre d'une assemblée)* call to order; *(d'un employé)* warning; **le r. des titres (de l'actualité)** the headlines; **dernier r.** *(de facture)* final demand (**b**) *(d'un ambassadeur, de réservistes)* recall (**c**) *(d'un salaire)* back pay (**d**) *(de vaccin)* booster; **faire un r.** to have a booster (**e**) *(au théâtre)* curtain call; *(à un concert)* encore (**f**) *(en alpinisme)* rappelling; **faire une descente** *ou* **descendre en r., faire du r.** to rappel down (**g**) *Ordinat (de texte)* restore

rappeler [9] [rapəle, raple] **1** *vt* (**a**) *(appeler) (personne)* to call back; *(chien)* to call off

(**b**) *(au téléphone) (sujet: personne appelée)* to call back; *(sujet: personne qui appelle)* to call again; **r. dix fois** to call ten times (**c**) *(faire revenir) (personne)* to call back; *(ambassadeur)* to recall; **r. qn à l'ordre** *(membre d'une association)* to call sb to order; *(employé)* to warn sb (**d**) *(acteur, chanteur)* to call back (**e**) *(faire penser à)* **r. qn/qch à qn** to remind sb of sb/sth; **cela ne me rappelle rien** it doesn't ring a bell (**f**) *(remettre en mémoire)* **r. qch à qn** to remind sb of sth; **rappelez-moi votre nom** what was your name again?; **r. qn au bon souvenir de qn** to remember sb to sb

2 se rappeler *vpr* (**a**) **se r. qn/qch** *(se souvenir de)* to remember sb/sth; **rappelle-toi que...** don't forget that... (**b**) *Fam (au téléphone)* **on se rappelle la semaine prochaine** we'll talk again next week

rappeur, -euse [rapœr, -øz] *nm,f* rapper

rappliquer [raplike] *vi Fam* to show up

rapport [rapɔr] *nm* (**a**) *(relation)* **rapports** relations, relationship; **avoir de bons/mauvais rapports avec qn** to be on good/bad terms with sb; **entretenir des rapports amicaux avec qn** to stay on friendly terms with sb; **mettre qn en r. avec qn** to put sb in touch with sb; **être en r. avec qn** to be in touch with sb; **r. de forces** battle of wills

(**b**) *(lien)* connection, link (**avec** with); **avoir un r. avec qch** to have something to do with sth; **n'avoir aucun r. avec qch** to have nothing to do with sth; **faire le r.** to make the connection; **être sans r. avec qch** to be unconnected with sth; **en r. avec** *(lié à)* in keeping with; **par r. à qch** *(en comparaison)* compared with sth

(**c**) *(aspect)* **sous ce r.** in this respect; **bien sous tous rapports** nice in every respect

(**d**) *(proportion)* ratio, proportion; **en r. avec** in proportion to; **d'un bon r. qualité-prix** good value for money

(**e**) *(compte rendu)* report; **faire** *ou* **rédiger un r. sur qch** to draw up a report on sth; **r. annuel** annual report; **r. commercial** market report

(**f**) *(profit)* return, yield; **d'un bon r.** profitable; **d'un mauvais r.** unprofitable

(**g**) **rapports** *(relations sexuelles)* (sexual) intercourse; **avoir des rapports avec qn** to have sex with sb

rapporter [rapɔrte] **1** *vt* (**a**) *(apporter avec soi)* to bring back; **r. qch à qn** to bring sb sth back (**b**) *(rendre)* to bring back (**à** to); *(remporter)* to take back (**à** to) (**c**) *(ajouter) (poche, pièce)* to sew on (**d**) *(raconter)* to report; **on rapporte que...** it is reported that... (**e**) *(produire) (bénéfice, intérêt)* to yield; **r. de l'argent** to be profitable; **r. qch à qn** *(financièrement)* to bring sb in sth; *Fig (moralement)* to bring sb sth (**f**) *Péj (répéter)* to report (**à** to) (**g**) *(sujet: chien)* to retrieve; **rapporte!** fetch!

2 se rapporter *vpr* (**a**) **se r. à qch** *(concerner)* to relate to sth (**b**) *(se remettre)* **s'en r. à qn/qch** to rely on sb/sth

rapporteur, -euse [raportœr, -øz] **1** *adj Péj* sneaky

2 *nm,f Péj* telltale, tattletale

3 *nm* (**a**) *(d'une commission)* reporter (**b**) *(instrument)* protractor

rapproché, -e [raproʃe] *adj (dans l'espace, dans le temps)* close; *(yeux)* close-set; **des maisons très rapprochées** houses very close together; **des rendez-vous très rapprochés (dans le temps)** appointments very close to each other

rapprochement [raproʃmã] *nm* (**a**) *(rapport) (de faits, d'idées)* connection; **faire le r. (entre deux choses)** to make a connection (between two things) (**b**) *(de deux objets)* bringing together (**c**) *(réconciliation) (entre personnes)* reconciliation; *(entre pays)* rapprochement

rapprocher [raproʃe] **1** *vt* (**a**) *(mettre plus près) (deux ou plusieurs objets)* to move closer together; *(objet)* to move closer (**de** to); **ça te rapprochera (de chez toi)** that'll get you a bit closer (to home) (**b**) *(réunir)* to join (**c**) *(séances)* to group closer together (**d**) *(unir) (personnes)* to bring together (**e**) *(lier) (idées, textes)* to compare (**de** with)

2 se rapprocher *vpr* (**a**) *(aller plus près)* to get closer (**de** to); **se r. de la vérité** to get close to the truth (**b**) *(devenir proche)* to get closer (**de** to); *(après une brouille)* to become reconciled (**de** with) (**c**) **se r. de qn/qch** *(ressembler à)* to be similar to sb/sth

rapsodie [rapsodi] *nf* rhapsody

rapt [rapt] *nm* abduction

raquer [rake] *très Fam* **1** *vt* to fork out

2 *vi* to pay up, to cough up

raquette [rakɛt] *nf* (**a**) *(de tennis, de badminton, de squash)* racket (**b**) *(de ping-pong)* paddle (**c**) *(pour marcher dans la neige)* snowshoe

rare [rar] *adj* (**a**) *(peu commun, peu fréquent)* rare; **c'est r. qu'il pleuve ici** it rarely rains here; **cela n'a rien de r.** it's quite common (**b**) *(peu nombreux, peu abondant)* **être r.** to be scarce; **c'est une des rares personnes que je connaisse à s'y opposer** he's one of the few people I know who's against it (**c**) *(exceptionnel)* rare (**d**) *(clairsemé) (végétation)* sparse; **avoir le cheveu r.** to have thinning hair (**e**) **tu te fais r.** we've hardly seen you lately

raréfaction [rarefaksjõ] *nf* (**a**) *(d'une denrée, de l'argent)* growing scarcity (**b**) *(de l'air)* rarefaction

raréfier [66] [rarefje] **se raréfier** *vpr* (**a**) *(denrée, argent)* to become scarce (**b**) *(air)* to become rarefied

rarement [rarmã] *adv* rarely, seldom

rareté [rarte] *nf* (**a**) *(de denrées, de main-d'œuvre)* scarcity; *(de visites)* infrequency; *(d'un phénomène, d'un mot, d'une maladie)* rareness (**b**) *(objet rare)* rarity

RAS [ɛraɛs] *Fam (abrév* **rien à signaler***)* everything OK

ras, -e [rɑ, rɑz] **1** *adj* (**a**) *(cheveux)* close-cropped; *(barbe)* short; *(tapis)* short-pile (**b**) *(entier) (mesure)* full; **deux cuillerées rases** two level spoonfuls (**c**) *(locutions)* **à r. bord** to the brim; **en rase campagne** in the open country

2 *nm* (**a**) *(bord)* **à** *ou* **au r. de** level with; **voler au r. du sol/ de l'eau** to fly close to the ground/water; *Fam Fig* **au r. des pâquerettes** lowbrow (**b**) **r. du cou** *(pull-over)* crew-neck sweater

3 *adv* short; *Fam* **en avoir r. le bol (de qch)** to have had it up to here (with sb) *or* to be sick and tired (of sth)

rasade [razad] *nf* glassful

rasage [razaʒ] *nm* shaving

rasant, -e [razã, -ãt] *adj* (**a**) *Fam (personne, discours, film)* boring (**b**) *(lumière)* low-angled; *(tir)* grazing

rascasse [raskas] *nf* scorpion fish

rasé, -e [raze] *adj* shaven; **r. de près** close-shaven

rase-mottes [razmɔt] *nm inv Fam* **faire du** *ou* **voler en r.** to hedgehop

raser [raze] **1** *vt* (**a**) *(visage, personne)* to shave; *(moustache, barbe, cheveux)* to shave off (**b**) *(passer très près de) (sol, eau)* to skim; *(filet, trottoir)* to graze; **r. les murs** to hug the walls (**c**) *(détruire) (bâtiment, ville)* to raze to the ground (**d**) *Fam (ennuyer)* to bore

2 se raser *vpr* (**a**) *(se couper la barbe)* to shave, to have a shave; **se r. les jambes** to shave one's legs (**b**) *Fam (s'ennuyer)* to be bored

raseur, -euse [razœr, -øz] *nm,f Fam* bore

rasibus [razibys] *adv Fam* **la balle est passée r.** the bullet whizzed past really close

ras-le-bol [ralbɔl] *Fam* **1** *nm inv* discontent

2 *exclam* enough's enough!

rasoir [razwar] **1** *nm* razor; **r. électrique** electric razor *or* shaver

2 *adj inv Fam* boring

rassasier [66] [rasazje] **1** *vt (faim, curiosité)* to satisfy; **r. qn** to satisfy sb's hunger

2 se rassasier *vpr* **se r. de qch** to get one's fill of sth

rassemblement [rasãbləmã] *nm* (**a**) *(attroupement)* gathering (**b**) *(de documents, d'objets)* collecting, gathering (**c**) *(union politique)* union (**d**) *Mil* fall in, parade; **sonner le r.** to sound the assembly

rassembler [rasãble] **1** *vt* (**a**) *(personnes, choses, documents)* to gather (together) (**b**) *(courage, forces)* to muster, to summon up; **r. ses idées** to collect one's thoughts; **r. ses esprits** to collect oneself

2 se rassembler *vpr (manifestants)* to gather, to assemble; *(famille)* to get together

rasseoir [10a] [raswar] **se rasseoir** *vpr* to sit down again

rasséréner [34] [raserene] **1** *vt* **r. qn** to put sb's mind at rest

2 se rasséréner *vpr* to calm down

rassir [rasir] *vi* to go stale

rassis, -e [rasi, -iz] *adj* (**a**) *(pain)* stale (**b**) *Litt (personne, esprit)* calm

rassurant, -e [rasyrã, -ãt] *adj* reassuring

rassuré, -e [rasyre] *adj* at ease; **me voilà r.!** that's a relief!

rassurer [rasyre] **1** *vt* to reassure; **ah, tu me rassures!** well, that's a relief!

2 se rassurer *vpr* to reassure oneself; **rassurez-vous** rest assured

rasta [rasta] *adj inv & nmf* Rasta

rat [ra] **1** *nm* (**a**) *(animal)* rat; **r. d'égout** sewer rat; *Fam* **être fait comme un r.** to be caught like a rat in a trap; **petit r. (de l'Opéra)** ballet pupil (at the Opéra de Paris); **mon petit r.** darling; *Fam* **r. de bibliothèque** bookworm; **r. d'hôtel** hotel thief; *Can (sournois)* tricky customer

2 *adj* (**a**) *(avare)* stingy (**b**) *Can (sournois)* wily, sly

ratage [rataʒ] *nm Fam* botch-up

ratatiné, -e [ratatine] *adj* (**a**) *(fruit)* shriveled (**b**) *Fam (vieillard)* wizened (**c**) *Fam (véhicule)* smashed-up

ratatiner [ratatine] **1** *vt Fam* (**a**) *(voiture)* to smash up (**b**) *(équipe)* to thrash

2 se ratatiner *vpr* (**a**) *(fruit)* to shrivel up (**b**) *(vieillard)* to become wizened

ratatouille [ratatuj] *nf* ratatouille

rate[1] [rat] *nf (organe)* spleen

rate[2] [rat] *nf (animal)* female rat

raté, -e [rate] **1** *nm,f Fam* loser

2 *nm* misfiring; *Fig* hitch; **avoir des ratés** to misfire

râteau, -x [rɑto] *nm* (**a**) *(de jardin)* rake (**b**) *Suisse Fam Péj (avare)* miser, skinflint

râtelier [rɑtəlje] *nm* (**a**) *(pour le fourrage)* rack; *Fig* **manger à tous les râteliers** to have a finger in every pie (**b**) *(à outils, à armes)* rack (**c**) *Fam (dentier)* (set of) false teeth

rater [rate] **1** *vt* **(a)** *(examen)* to fail; *(vie, plat)* to make a mess of; **c'est raté** it hasn't worked; *Fig* **r. son coup** to make a mess of things **(b)** *(train, avion, personne, occasion)* to miss; **tu n'as pas raté grand-chose** you didn't miss much **(c)** *Fam (locutions)* **ne pas r. qn** to let sb have it; **elle n'en rate pas une** she's always putting her foot in her mouth

2 *vi* to fail; **faire r. qch** to ruin sth; **j'étais sûr qu'elle allait oublier, et ça n'a pas raté** I was sure she was going to forget, and sure enough she did

3 se rater *vpr Fam* **(a)** *(ne pas se rencontrer)* to miss each other **(b)** *(personne suicidaire)* to bungle one's suicide attempt

ratiboiser [ratibwaze] *vt Fam* **(a)** *(ruiner)* to clean out; **se faire r.** to be cleaned out **(b)** *(cheveux)* **se faire r.** to get scalped

ratier [ratje] *nm (chien)* ratter

ratière [ratjɛr] *nf* rat trap

ratification [ratifikasjɔ̃] *nf* ratification

ratifier [66] [ratifje] *vt (traité, acte)* to ratify; *(décision)* to confirm

ratio [rasjo] *nm* ratio

ration [rasjɔ̃] *nf (de pain, de nourriture)* ration; *Fig (de critiques, de difficultés)* share; **r. alimentaire** food ration

rationaliser [rasjɔnalize] *vt* to rationalize

rationnel, -elle [rasjɔnɛl] *adj* rational

rationnellement [rasjɔnɛlmɑ̃] *adv* rationally

rationnement [rasjɔnmɑ̃] *nm* rationing

rationner [rasjɔne] **1** *vt* to ration

2 se rationner *vpr* to ration oneself

ratissage [ratisaʒ] *nm* **(a)** *(allée, sol)* raking **(b)** *Fam (par la police)* combing

ratisser [ratise] **1** *vt* **(a)** *(allée, sol)* to rake; *(feuilles)* to rake up **(b)** *Fam (quartier)* to comb **(c)** *Fam (personne)* to clean out; **se faire r.** *(au jeu)* to be cleaned out

2 *vi* **r. large** to cast one's net wide

raton [ratɔ̃] *nm* **(a)** *(animal)* young rat; **r. laveur** raccoon **(b)** *Fam (Maghrébin)* = racist term used to refer to a North African Arab

ratonnade [ratɔnad] *nf* = racist attack on North African Arabs

ratoureux, -euse [raturø, -øz] *Can* **1** *adj* wily, devious

2 *nm,f* shady customer

RATP [ɛratpe] *nf (abrév* **Régie autonome des transports parisiens)** = Parisian transportation authority

rattachement [rataʃmɑ̃] *nm (d'une région)* uniting **(à** with)

rattacher [rataʃe] **1** *vt* **(a)** *(attacher de nouveau) (lacets, chien, objet)* to tie up again **(à** to); *(cheveux)* to put up again; **r. qch sur qch** to tie sth onto sth again **(b)** *(région)* to unite **(à** with) **(c)** **être rattaché à** *(faire partie de)* to be attached to **(d)** *(lier)* **c'était la seule chose qui nous rattachait l'un à l'autre** it was the only thing that bound us together; **c'est tout ce qui le rattache à la vie** it's the only thing keeping him alive

2 se rattacher *vpr* **se r. à qch** to be linked to sth

rattrapage [ratrapaʒ] *nm* **être admis au r.**, **être admis à passer les épreuves de r.** = to be allowed to take further oral exams to gain a passing grade in the baccalauréat; **cours de r.** remedial class

rattraper [ratrape] **1** *vt* **(a)** *(prisonnier, chien)* to recapture; **se faire r. par la police** to get caught by the police **(b)** *(objet ou personne qui tombe)* to catch **(c)** *(rejoindre) (personne, voiture)* to catch up with **(d)** *(regagner)* **r. le temps perdu** to make up for lost time; **r. son retard** to catch up; **avoir du sommeil à r.** to have to catch up on some sleep **(e)** *(rétablir) (erreur)* to correct; *(situation)* to salvage

2 se rattraper *vpr* **(a)** *(se retenir)* to catch oneself in time; **se r. à qch** to catch hold of sth **(b)** *(se reprendre)* to stop oneself **(c)** *(se faire pardonner)* to make up for it **(d)** *(compenser son retard)* to catch up

rature [ratyr] *nf* crossing-out, deletion; **faire une r.** to make a deletion

raturer [ratyre] *vt (mot)* to cross out, to delete; **les devoirs raturés ne seront pas corrigés** homework with too many crossings-out will not be marked

rauque [rok] *adj (cri)* raucous; *(voix) (enrouée)* hoarse; *(voilée)* husky

ravagé, -e [ravaʒe] *adj* **(a)** *(visage)* ravaged, haggard **(b)** *Fam (fou)* nuts

ravager [45] [ravaʒe] *vt* to ravage, to devastate

ravages [ravaʒ] *nmpl (du feu, de la tempête)* devastation; *(d'une guerre, d'une maladie)* ravages; **faire des r.** to wreak havoc; *Fig (mode)* to be all the rage; *(jeune femme)* to break hearts

ravageur, -euse [ravaʒœr, -øz] *adj* devastating

ravalement [ravalmɑ̃] *nm* cleaning

ravaler [ravale] **1** *vt* **(a)** *(façade)* to clean; **se faire r. la façade** to have a facelift **(b)** *(avaler de nouveau) (salive)* to swallow; *Fig* **faire r. ses paroles à qn** to make sb eat his/her words **(c)** *(cacher) (sanglot, larmes)* to choke back; *(colère, indignation, reproches)* to stifle **(d)** *(abaisser)* **r. qn à** to lower sb to

2 se ravaler *vpr* to lower oneself; *Fam* **se r. la façade** to put on the warpaint

ravaudage [ravodaʒ] *nm Vieilli (de vêtements)* mending, repairing

ravauder [ravode] *vt* **(a)** *Vieilli (vêtements)* to mend, to repair **(b)** *Can (errer)* to wander about; *(faire l'idiot)* to fool around **(c)** *Can (faire du bruit)* to make a racket

rave[1] [rav] *nf (radis)* radish; *(navet)* turnip

rave[2] [rɛv] *nf (soirée)* rave

ravi, -e [ravi] *adj* delighted **(de** with); **je suis r. de vous voir** I'm delighted to see you; **je suis r. que ça te plaise** I'm delighted you like it; **r. de vous connaître** pleased to meet you

ravier [ravje] *nm* hors d'oeuvres dish

ravigotant, -e [ravigɔtɑ̃, -ɑ̃t] *adj Fam* invigorating

ravigote [ravigɔt] *nf* = highly seasoned oil-and-vinegar dressing with herbs and capers

ravigoter [ravigɔte] *vt Fam* **r. qn** to put new life into sb

ravin [ravɛ̃] *nm* ravine

ravine [ravin] *nf* gully

raviné, -e [ravine] *adj (visage)* deeply lined

ravinement [ravinmɑ̃] *nm* gullying

raviner [ravine] *vt* to gully

ravioli [ravjɔli] *nm* piece of ravioli; **des raviolis** ravioli

ravir [ravir] *vt* **(a)** *(plaire)* to delight; **à r.** *(jouer, chanter)* delightfully; **belle à r.** ravishingly beautiful; **aller à r. à qn** to suit sb beautifully **(b)** *Litt* **r. qch à qn** to rob sb of sth

raviser [ravize] **se raviser** *vpr* to change one's mind

ravissant, -e [ravisɑ̃, -ɑ̃t] *adj* delightful

ravissement [ravismɑ̃] *nm* **(a)** *(enchantement)* rapture, ecstasy; **avec r.** *(écouter, contempler)* with great delight **(b)** *Litt (d'une femme)* ravishing

ravisseur, -euse [ravisœr, -øz] *nm,f* abductor

ravitaillement [ravitajmɑ̃] *nm (action)* supplying **(en** with); *(marchandises)* supplies; **r. (en carburant)** refueling

ravitailler [ravitaje] **1** *vt (personne, groupe)* to supply; *(véhicule)* to refuel

2 se ravitailler *vpr* to get in supplies; **se r. (en carburant)** to refuel

raviver [ravive] *vt* **(a)** *(feu)* to rekindle **(b)** *(couleur)* to brighten up **(c)** *(colère, souvenir, querelle)* to rekindle; *(douleur)* to revive

ravoir [ravwar] **1** *vt* **(a)** *(avoir de nouveau)* to have back **(b)** *Fam (nettoyer)* to get clean

2 se ravoir *vpr Belg (reprendre haleine)* to get one's breath back; *(retrouver ses esprits)* to come to one's senses

rayé, -e [rɛje] *adj* **(a)** *(tissu)* striped **(b)** *(disque, parquet, carrosserie de voiture)* scratched **(c)** *(canon de fusil)* rifled

rayer [53] [ʀɛje] *vt* (**a**) *(verre, carrosserie de voiture, disque)* to scratch (**b**) *(mention, mot)* to cross out; **r. qn du barreau** to disbar sb; **r. qn/le nom de qn d'une liste** to cross sb/sb's name off a list

rayon¹ [ʀɛjɔ̃] *nm* (**a**) *(faisceau) (de lumière)* ray, beam; **r. laser** laser beam; **r. de soleil** sunbeam; *Fig* **être le r. de soleil de qn** to be sb's ray of sunshine; **rayons X** X-rays (**b**) *(d'un cercle)* radius; **dans un r. de quatre kilomètres (autour de)** within a radius of two and a half miles (of); **r. d'action** range (**c**) *(de roue)* spoke

rayon² [ʀɛjɔ̃] *nm* (**a**) *(dans un magasin)* department; *Fig* **c'est mon r.** that's my department (**b**) *(d'une étagère)* shelf; *Fam Fig* **en connaître un r. (sur qch)** to know a thing or two (about sth) (**c**) **r. de miel** honeycomb

rayonnage [ʀɛjɔnaʒ] *nm* shelving, shelves

rayonnant, -e [ʀɛjɔnɑ̃, -ɑ̃t] *adj (chaleur, lumière)* radiant; *Fig (visage)* beaming; **r. de bonheur** radiant with happiness; **r. de santé** glowing with health

rayonne [ʀɛjɔn] *nf* rayon

rayonnement [ʀɛjɔnmɑ̃] *nm* (**a**) *(du soleil)* radiance (**b**) *(influence)* influence

rayonner [ʀɛjɔne] *vi* (**a**) *(soleil, visage)* to beam; **r. de joie** to beam with joy (**b**) *(voyager)* to travel around *(from a central base)* (**c**) *(se propager)* to spread its influence (**d**) *(avenues, douleur)* to radiate

rayure [ʀɛjyʀ] *nf* (**a**) *(motif)* stripe; **tissu à rayures** striped material (**b**) *(sur miroir, sur carrosserie)* scratch (**c**) *(d'un canon de fusil)* groove

raz de marée [ʀɑdmaʀe] *nm inv* tidal wave; *Fig* **r. électoral** landslide

razzia [ʀazja] *nf* raid; *Fam* **faire une r. sur qch** to raid sth

RD [ɛʀde] *nf* (*abrév* **route départementale**) secondary road

RDA [ɛʀdea] *nf Anciennement* (*abrév* **République démocratique allemande**) GDR

rdc (*abrév* **rez-de-chaussée**) first floor

RDS [ɛʀdeɛs] *nm* (*abrév* **Remboursement de la Dette Sociale**) = contribution paid by every taxpayer in France toward the social security deficit

ré [ʀe] *nm inv (note)* D; *(chantée)* re

réabonnement [ʀeabɔnmɑ̃] *nm* subscription renewal

réabonner [ʀeabɔne] **1 r. qn** to renew sb's subscription (**à** to)
     2 se réabonner *vpr* to renew one's subscription (**à** to)

réac [ʀeak] *adj & nmf Fam Péj* reactionary

réaccoutumer [ʀeakutyme] **1** *vt* to reaccustom (**à** to)
     2 se réaccoutumer *vpr* **se r. à qch** to become reaccustomed to sth

réacteur [ʀeaktœʀ] *nm* (**a**) *(moteur)* jet engine (**b**) **r. nucléaire** nuclear reactor

réaction [ʀeaksjɔ̃] *nf* (**a**) *(attitude)* reaction; **n'avoir aucune r.** not to react; **il eut une r. de peur/de colère** his reaction was one of fear/anger; **faire qch par r.** to do sth as a reaction; **en r. à qch** in reaction to sth; **rester sans r.** not to react; **r. en chaîne** chain reaction (**b**) *(d'un organe, du corps)* reaction; **r. cutanée** skin reaction

réactionnaire [ʀeaksjɔnɛʀ] *adj & nmf Péj* reactionary

réactiver [ʀeaktive] *vt (feu, négociations, sentiments)* to revive

réactualisation [ʀeaktɥalizasjɔ̃] *nf* updating

réactualiser [ʀeaktɥalize] *vt* to update

réadaptation [ʀeadaptasjɔ̃] *nf* rehabilitation

réadapter [ʀeadapte] **1** *vt* to rehabilitate
     2 se réadapter *vpr* to readjust

réaffirmer [ʀeafiʀme] *vt* to reaffirm

réagir [ʀeaʒiʀ] *vi* to react (**à/contre** to/against); **r. sur qch** to affect sth

réajuster [ʀeaʒyste] = **rajuster**

réalisable [ʀealizabl] *adj* (**a**) *(projet, proposition)* feasible; *(rêve)* attainable (**b**) *(avoirs)* realizable

réalisateur, -trice [ʀealizatœʀ, -tʀis] *nm,f (d'un film, d'un feuilleton)* director; *(d'une émission de radio ou de télévision)* producer

réalisation [ʀealizasjɔ̃] *nf* (**a**) *(d'un projet)* realization; *(d'un rêve)* fulfillment (**b**) *(d'un film, d'un feuilleton)* direction; *(d'une émission de radio ou de télévision)* production (**c**) *(d'une œuvre d'art)* creation

réaliser [ʀealize] **1** *vt* (**a**) *(comprendre)* to realize (**que** that) (**b**) *(ambition, projet)* to realize; *(rêve)* to fulfill (**c**) *(œuvre d'art)* to create (**d**) *(film, feuilleton)* to direct; *(émission de radio ou de télévision)* to produce (**e**) *(bénéfices)* to make; **r. un chiffre d'affaires de dix millions d'euros** to have sales figures of ten million euros
     2 se réaliser *vpr* (**a**) *(prédiction, rêve)* to come true (**b**) *(personne)* to fulfill oneself

réalisme [ʀealism] *nm* realism; **faire preuve de r.** to be realistic; **avec r.** realistically

réaliste [ʀealist] **1** *adj (personne, description, portrait)* realistic; *(écrivain, peintre)* realist
     2 *nmf* realist

réalité [ʀealite] *nf* reality; **c'est une r.** it's a reality; **en r.** in reality; *Ordinat* **r. virtuelle** virtual reality

réamorcer [16] [ʀeamɔʀse] *Ordinat* **1** *vt* to reboot
     2 se réamorcer *vpr* to reboot

réanimation [ʀeanimasjɔ̃] *nf* resuscitation; **service de r.** intensive-care unit; **en r.** in intensive care; **r. cardiorespiratoire** CPR

réanimer [ʀeanime] *vt* to resuscitate

réapparaître [20] [ʀeapaʀɛtʀ] *vi* to reappear; *(douleur)* to come back, to recur

réapparition [ʀeapaʀisjɔ̃] *nf* reappearance; *(d'une douleur)* recurrence

réapprovisionner [ʀeapʀɔvizjɔne] **1** *vt (magasin)* to restock (**en** with); *(personne)* to resupply (**en** with)
     2 se réapprovisionner *vpr* to stock up again (**en** with)

réargenter [ʀeaʀʒɑ̃te] *vt* to resilver

réarmement [ʀeaʀməmɑ̃] *nm* rearmament

réarmer [ʀeaʀme] **1** *vt* (**a**) *(région, pays)* to rearm (**b**) *(arme à feu)* to recock; *(appareil photo)* to reset
     2 *vi (pays, région)* to rearm

réassortir [ʀeasɔʀtiʀ] **1** *vt (magasin)* to restock
     2 se réassortir *vpr* to restock

rebaptiser [ʀəbatize] *vt (rue)* to rename

rébarbatif, -ive [ʀebaʀbatif, -iv] *adj* (**a**) *(sujet, tâche)* daunting; *(style)* off-putting (**b**) *(visage, mine)* forbidding

rebâtir [ʀəbatiʀ] *vt* to rebuild

rebattre [11] [ʀəbatʀ] *vt* **r. les oreilles à qn de qch** to go on to sb about sth

rebattu, -e [ʀəbaty] *adj (histoire, sujet)* hackneyed

rebelle [ʀəbɛl] **1** *adj* (**a**) *(personne, esprit)* rebellious; *(camp, armée, troupes)* rebel; **r. à toute discipline** unamenable to discipline (**b**) *(mèches, boucle)* unruly (**c**) *(fièvre)* stubborn; **r. aux antibiotiques** resistant to antibiotics
     2 *nmf* rebel

rebeller [ʀəbɛle] **se rebeller** *vpr* to rebel (**contre** against)

rébellion [ʀebɛljɔ̃] *nf* rebellion

rebelote [ʀəbəlɔt] *exclam Fam* not again!

rebiffer [ʀəbife] **se rebiffer** *vpr Fam* to hit back (**contre** at)

rebiquer [ʀəbike] *vi Fam (mèche)* to stick up

reblochon [ʀəblɔʃɔ̃] *nm* Reblochon *(type of cheese from Savoie)*

reboisement [ʀəbwazmɑ̃] *nm* reforestation

reboiser [ʀəbwaze] *vt* to reforest

rebond [ʀəbɔ̃] *nm (d'un ballon)* bounce

rebondi, -e [ʀəbɔ̃di] *adj (joues, personne)* chubby

rebondir [ʀəbɔ̃diʀ] *vi* (**a**) *(ballon)* to bounce; **r. contre** *ou* **sur qch** to bounce off sth (**b**) *Fig (affaire, crise)* to be revived; **faire**

r. la discussion to get the discussion going again (**c**) *Can (chèque)* to bounce

rebondissement [rəbɔ̃dismɑ̃] *nm* (**a**) *(d'un ballon)* bounce (**b**) *Fig (d'une affaire)* revival

rebord [rəbɔr] *nm (d'une table, d'un puits)* edge; *(de fenêtre)* sill

reboucher [rəbuʃe] *vt* (**a**) *(bouteille)* to recork; *(tube)* to put the top back on (**b**) *(trou)* to fill in again

rebours [rəbur] **à rebours** *adv* the wrong way; *Fig* the wrong way around

rebouteux, -euse [rəbutø, -øz] *nm,f Fam* bonesetter

reboutonner [rəbutɔne] **1** *vt* to button up again
  2 se reboutonner *vpr* to do oneself up again

rebrousse-poil [rəbruspwal] **à rebrousse-poil** *adv* the wrong way; **prendre qn à r.** to rub sb the wrong way

rebrousser [rəbruse] *vt* **r. chemin** to turn back

rebuffade [rəbyfad] *nf* rebuff; **essuyer une r.** to meet with a rebuff

rébus [rebys] *nm* rebus

rebut [rəby] *nm* (**article de**) **r.** reject; **mettre qch au r.** to throw sth out

rebutant, -e [rəbytɑ̃, -ɑ̃t] *adj (tâche, manières, personne) (décourageant)* off-putting; *(repoussant)* repulsive

rebuter [rəbyte] *vt* (**a**) *(décourager)* to put off (**b**) *(déplaire)* to disgust

récalcitrant, -e [rekalsitrɑ̃, -ɑ̃t] *adj & nm,f* recalcitrant

recaler [rəkale] *vt Fam* to fail; **être recalé, se faire r.** to fail

récapitulatif, -ive [rekapitylatif, -iv] **1** *adj* recapitulatory
  2 *nm* recapitulation

récapitulation [rekapitylasjɔ̃] *nf* recapitulation; **faire la r. de qch** to recapitulate sth

récapituler [rekapityle] *vt & vi* to recapitulate

recaser [rəkɑze] *Fam* **1** *vt* (**a**) *(retrouver un emploi à)* to find a new job for (**b**) *(retrouver un logement à)* to rehouse
  2 se recaser *vpr* (**a**) *(retrouver un emploi)* to find a new job (**b**) *(se remarier)* to get hitched again

recel [rəsɛl] *nm* receiving stolen goods; **r. de malfaiteur** harboring a (known) criminal

receler [39] [rəsəle] *vt* (**a**) *(biens volés)* to receive; *(criminel)* to harbor (**b**) *Litt (renfermer) (secret, trésor)* to conceal

receleur, -euse [rəsəlœr, -øz] *nm,f* receiver

récemment [resamɑ̃] *adv* recently

recensement [rəsɑ̃smɑ̃] *nm (d'objets)* inventory; *(de la population)* census

recenser [rəsɑ̃se] *vt (objets)* to make an inventory of; *(habitants)* to take a census of

récent, -e [resɑ̃, -ɑ̃t] *adj* recent

recentrer [rəsɑ̃tre] *vt* (**a**) *(parti politique)* to reorientate (**b**) *(balle)* to center again

récépissé [resepise] *nm* receipt

réceptacle [reseptakl] *nm* (**a**) *(d'objets)* receptacle; *(de personnes)* gathering place (**b**) *Ordinat* **r. pour extension** extension slot

récepteur, -trice [reseptœr, -tris] **1** *adj* receiving
  2 *nm* (**a**) *(de téléphone)* receiver (**b**) *Rad & TV* set, receiver (**c**) *Ordinat* **r. de données** data receiver

réceptif, -ive [reseptif, -iv] *adj* receptive (**à** to)

réception [resepsjɔ̃] *nf* (**a**) *(accueil)* reception; **faire une bonne/mauvaise r. à qn** to give sb a good/poor reception (**b**) *(d'une lettre, d'une commande, de biens)* receipt; **à payer à la r.** cash on delivery; **r. des travaux** acceptance of work (**c**) *(soirée)* reception (**d**) *(dans un hôtel)* reception desk, front desk (**e**) *(d'une radio)* reception (**f**) *(d'un gymnaste)* landing; *(d'un joueur de football)* control

réceptionner [resepsjɔne] **1** *vt (marchandises livrées)* to take delivery of (**b**) *(ballon)* to take
  2 se réceptionner *vpr* to land

réceptionniste [resepsjɔnist] *nmf* receptionist

récessif, -ive [resesif, -iv] *adj* recessive

récession [resesjɔ̃] *nf* recession

recette [rəsɛt] *nf* (**a**) *(pour plat) & Fig* recipe (**de** for) (**b**) *(bureau)* tax office (**c**) *(gain)* **recettes** takings; **recettes fiscales** tax revenue; **faire r.** to be a success

recevable [rəsəvabl] *adj (excuse, témoignage)* admissible

recevant, -e [rəsəvɑ̃, -ɑ̃t] *adj Can (personne)* hospitable, who likes entertaining

receveur, -euse [rəsəvœr, -øz] *nm,f* (**a**) *(fonctionnaire)* **r. des contributions** tax collector; **r. des Postes** postmaster, *f* postmistress (**b**) *(de bus)* (bus) conductor, *f* (bus) conductress

recevoir [60] [rəsəvwar] **1** *vt* (**a**) *(lettre, coup de téléphone, fleurs)* to receive, to get (**de** from); **r. la visite de qn** to have a visit from sb; **r. des nouvelles de qn** to hear from sb; **je n'ai de conseils à r. de personne!** I don't need advice from anybody!; **nous avons bien reçu votre lettre** we are in receipt of your letter
  (**b**) *(blâme, gifle, coup, balle)* to get; *Fam* **qu'est-ce que j'ai reçu!** I really got it!
  (**c**) *(amis, invités)* to receive, to welcome; **être mal/bien reçu** to get a poor/good reception; **r. qn à dîner** to have sb (over) to dinner; **aimer r.** to enjoy entertaining; **savoir r.** to be a good host/hostess; **ils reçoivent très peu** they don't do much entertaining
  (**d**) *(clients)* to see; **le docteur ne reçoit que sur rendez-vous** the doctor will see patients by appointment only
  (**e**) *(proposition, projet)* to receive
  (**f**) *(élève, candidat)* to admit; **être reçu à l'Académie française** to be admitted to the Académie française; **être reçu à un examen** to pass an exam
  (**g**) *(pluie, soleil, lumière)* to get; **r. des radiations** to be exposed to radiation, to receive a dose of radiation
  (**h**) *(chaîne)* to get; *(station de radio)* to pick up, to receive
  (**i**) *(communion, absolution)* to receive
  2 se recevoir *vpr (gymnaste)* to land

rechange [rəʃɑ̃ʒ] **de rechange** *adj* spare; *Fig* alternative

rechaper [rəʃape] *vt (pneu)* to retread; **pneu rechapé** retread

réchapper [reʃape] *vi* **r. de qch** to survive sth

recharge [rəʃarʒ] *nf* (**a**) *(de stylo, de briquet)* refill; **r. d'encre** ink refill (**b**) *(action) (d'une batterie)* recharging

rechargeable [rəʃarʒabl] *adj (briquet, vaporisateur)* refillable; *(pile)* rechargeable

recharger [45] [rəʃarʒe] **1** *vt* (**a**) *(batterie, pile)* to recharge; *Fam* **r. ses batteries** *ou* **ses accus** to recharge one's batteries (**b**) *(camion, arme, appareil photo)* to reload (**c**) *(stylo, briquet, vaporisateur)* to refill
  2 se recharger *vpr Ordinat* to reload

réchaud [reʃo] *nm* (portable) stove; **r. à gaz** gas burner

réchauffé, -e [reʃofe] **1** *adj* (**a**) *(plat)* reheated, warmed over (**b**) *(plaisanterie)* stale
  2 *nm* **c'est du r.** *(plaisanterie)* that's a stale joke; *(nouvelles, politique)* that's old hat

réchauffement [reʃofmɑ̃] *nm* warming up; **le r. de la planète** *ou* **de l'atmosphère** global warming

réchauffer [reʃofe] **1** *vt* (**a**) *(plat)* to reheat, to warm over (**b**) *(personne)* to warm up (**c**) *Fig* to rekindle; *(cœur)* to warm
  2 se réchauffer *vpr* (**a**) *(temps)* to get warmer (**b**) *(personne)* to get warm; **se r. les pieds/les mains** to warm one's feet/one's hands

rechausser [rəʃose] **se rechausser** *vpr* to put one's shoes on again

rêche [rɛʃ] *adj* rough

recherche [rəʃɛrʃ] *nf* (**a**) *(prospection, quête)* search (**de** for); *(de la célébrité, du pouvoir)* pursuit (**de** of); **être à la r. de** to be in search of (**b**) **recherches** *(par la police)* *(pour retrouver une personne disparue)* search, hunt; **faire des**

recherches to make inquiries (**c**) *(scientifique)* research (**sur** into); **faire de la r.** to do research; **faire des recherches sur qch** to do research into sth (**d**) *(raffinement)* elegance; **avec r.** elegantly; **sans r.** *(style)* straightforward (**e**) *Ordinat* find, search; **r. et remplacement** search and replace; **r. et remplacement global** global search and replace

recherché, -e [rəʃɛrʃe] *adj* (**a**) *(demandé) (objet)* sought-after (**b**) *(apprécié) (personne)* in demand (**c**) *(raffiné)* elegant; *(plat)* exquisite (**d**) *(criminel)* wanted

rechercher [rəʃɛrʃe] *vt* (**a**) *(chercher) (personne, objet, solution)* to look for, to search for; *(emploi)* to look for; *(sens, mot)* to look up; *(faveurs, honneurs)* to seek (**b**) *Ordinat* **r. qch** to search *or* to do a search for sth; **r. et remplacer** to search and replace; **r. vers le bas/haut** to search forward/backward

rechigner [rəʃiɲe] *vi* **r. à qch** to balk at sth; **r. à faire qch** to be reluctant to do sth; **faire qch en rechignant** to do sth with bad grace; **faire qch sans r.** to do sth without (making) a fuss

rechute [rəʃyt] *nf* relapse; **faire une r.** to have a relapse

rechuter [rəʃyte] *vi* to have a relapse

récidive [residiv] *nf* (**a**) *(d'un délinquant)* repeat offense (**b**) *(d'une maladie)* recurrence

récidiver [residive] *vi* (**a**) *(délinquant)* to commit another offense; *Fig* to do it again (**b**) *(maladie)* to recur

récidiviste [residivist] *nmf* repeat offender

récif [resif] *nm* reef; **r. de corail** *ou* **corallien** coral reef

récipient [resipjɑ̃] *nm* container

réciproque [resiprɔk] **1** *adj (sentiments)* mutual; *(bénéfices, accord, concessions)* reciprocal; **elle ne veut plus me voir, et c'est r.** she doesn't want to see me again, and the feeling's mutual
  2 *nf* **la r.** the reverse

réciproquement [resiprɔkmɑ̃] *adv* mutually; **et r.** and vice versa

récit [resi] *nm* story; **faire le r. de qch** to give an account of sth

récital, -als [resital] *nm* recital

récitant, -e [resitɑ̃, -ɑ̃t] *nm,f* narrator

récitation [resitasjɔ̃] *nf* recitation

réciter [resite] *vt* to recite

réclamation [reklamasjɔ̃] *nf* complaint; **faire une r.** to make *or* to lodge a complaint; **le service des réclamations, les réclamations** the complaints department

réclame [reklam] *nf* (**a**) *(publicité)* advertising; **faire de la r. pour qch** to advertise sth (**b**) *(annonce)* advertisement (**c**) *(promotion)* **en r.** on special offer

réclamer [reklame] **1** *vt* (**a**) *(demander)* to ask for; *(droit, allocation)* to claim; **la fillette réclame ses parents** the little girl is calling for her parents (**b**) *(exiger)* to demand; **r. des dommages et intérêts** to claim damages (**c**) *(nécessiter)* to require
  2 se réclamer *vpr* **se r. de qn** *(se recommander)* to mention sb's name; **se r. de qch** *(d'un parti, d'une idéologie)* to identify with sth

reclasser [rəklase] *vt* (**a**) *(fichiers)* to reclassify (**b**) *(chômeur)* to find a new job for (**c**) *(personnel, salaires)* to regrade

reclus, -e [rəkly, -yz] **1** *adj* cloistered
  2 *nm,f* recluse

réclusion [reklyzjɔ̃] *nf (peine)* imprisonment; **r. à perpétuité** life imprisonment

recoiffer [rəkwafe] **se recoiffer** *vpr* (**a**) *(arranger ses cheveux)* to redo one's hair (**b**) *(remettre son chapeau)* to put one's hat back on

recoin [rəkwɛ̃] *nm (d'un lieu)* nook; *(de la mémoire)* recess

reçois, reçoit, reçoive, *etc. voir* **recevoir**

recoller [rəkɔle] *vt (objet cassé)* to stick back together; *(timbre)* to stick back on; *(enveloppe)* to stick back down; *Fam* **r. les morceaux** to patch things up

récoltant, -e [rekɔltɑ̃, -ɑ̃t] **1** *adj* **apiculteur r.** honey producer; **viticulteur r.** = winegrower who harvests his own grapes
  2 *nm,f* **mis en bouteille chez le r.** estate-bottled

récolte [rekɔlt] *nf* (**a**) *(action)* harvesting; **faire la r.** to harvest the crops (**b**) *(résultat)* harvest (**c**) *(d'informations)* crop

récolter [rekɔlte] *vt (cultures)* to harvest; *Fig (renseignements, documents)* to collect; *Fam (ennuis, maladie)* to get

recommandable [rəkɔmɑ̃dabl] *adj (personne, lieu)* reputable; **peu r.** *(personne, lieu)* disreputable

recommandation [rəkɔmɑ̃dasjɔ̃] *nf (appui, conseil)* recommendation

recommandé, -e [rəkɔmɑ̃de] **1** *adj* (**a**) *(lettre)* registered (**b**) *(conseillé)* recommended; **ce n'est pas très r.** it's not very advisable
  2 *nm* **en r.** by registered mail

recommander [rəkɔmɑ̃de] **1** *vt* (**a**) *(lieu, produit, personne)* to recommend (**à** to) (**b**) *(conseiller)* to advise; **r. à qn de faire qch** to advise sb to do sth; **r. la prudence à qn** to advise sb to be cautious (**c**) *(lettre, paquet)* to register
  2 se recommander *vpr* (**a**) *(demander de l'aide)* **se r. à qn** to commend oneself to sb (**b**) **se r. de qn** *(pour un emploi)* to give sb's name as a reference (**c**) *Suisse (insister)* **se r. auprès de qn que...** to point out to sb that...

recommencement [rəkɔmɑ̃smɑ̃] *nm* renewal; **la vie est un éternel** *ou* **perpétuel r.** life is a constant succession of new beginnings

recommencer [16] [rəkɔmɑ̃se] **1** *vt* to start *or* to begin again
  2 *vi* to start *or* to begin again; **ne recommencez pas!** don't do it again!
  3 recommencer à *vt ind* **r. à faire qch** to start *or* to begin to do sth again

récompense [rekɔ̃pɑ̃s] *nf* reward; *(prix)* award; **1000 euros de r.** 1,000 euros reward; **en r. (de)** as a reward (for)

récompenser [rekɔ̃pɑ̃se] *vt* to reward (**de** for); **ce film a été récompensé à Cannes** this movie won an award at Cannes

recomposer [rəkɔ̃poze] *vt (numéro de téléphone)* to redial

recompter [rəkɔ̃te] *vt* to count again

réconciliation [rekɔ̃siljasjɔ̃] *nf* reconciliation

réconcilier [66] [rekɔ̃silje] **1** *vt* to reconcile (**avec** with); **r. qn avec la vie** to renew sb's appetite for life
  2 se réconcilier *vpr* to make it up (**avec** with)

reconductible [rəkɔ̃dyktibl] *adj (bail, contrat)* renewable

reconduction [rəkɔ̃dyksjɔ̃] *nf* (**a**) *(d'un bail, d'un contrat)* renewal; **r. tacite** *(d'un accord)* tacit renewal (**b**) *(d'un budget, d'une politique, d'une grève)* continuation

reconduire [18] [rəkɔ̃dɥir] *vt* (**a**) *(personne)* to take sb back; **r. qn (à la porte)** to show sb out; **r. qn à la frontière** to escort sb back to the border (**b**) *(bail, contrat)* to renew (**c**) *(budget, politique, grève)* to continue

réconfort [rekɔ̃fɔr] *nm* comfort

réconfortant, -e [rekɔ̃fɔrtɑ̃, -ɑ̃t] *adj* comforting

réconforter [rekɔ̃fɔrte] *vt* to comfort; **cela me réconforte de le savoir** I'm glad to hear it

reconnaissable [rəkɔnɛsabl] *adj* recognizable (**à** by *or* from); **r. entre tous** unmistakable

reconnaissance [rəkɔnɛsɑ̃s] *nf* (**a**) *(action de reconnaître)* recognition; **en r. de qch** in recognition of sth (**b**) *(d'un droit, d'un gouvernement)* recognition; **r. de dette** IOU (**c**) *(gratitude)* gratitude (**pour** for); **avec r.** gratefully (**d**) *Mil* reconnaissance; **partir en r.** to go off on reconnaissance; *Fam Fig* to go and reconnoiter (**e**) *Ordinat* **r. de l'écriture manuscrite** handwriting recognition; **r. optique des caractères** optical character recognition, OCR; **r. de la parole, r. vocale** speech recognition

reconnaissant, -e [rəkɔnɛsɑ̃, -ɑ̃t] *adj* grateful; **être r. à**

qn de qch to be grateful to sb for sth; **je vous serais r. de ne plus en parler** I'd be grateful if you didn't mention it again

reconnaître [20] [rəkɔnɛtr] **1** *vt* (**a**) *(identifier)* to recognize (**à** by *or* from); **je te reconnais bien là!** that's just like you! (**b**) *(admettre) (vérité, droit, gouvernement)* to recognize; *(enfant)* to acknowledge; **r. qn pour chef** to recognize sb as leader (**c**) *(avouer) (erreur, faute)* to acknowledge; **je reconnais que j'ai en tort** I admit I was wrong (**d**) *(accorder)* **je lui reconnais des qualités** I recognize his/her qualities (**e**) *(position, terrain)* to reconnoiter

2 se reconnaître *vpr* (**a**) *(soi-même)* to recognize oneself (**b**) *(l'un l'autre)* to recognize each other (**c**) *(s'avouer)* **se r. vaincu/coupable** to acknowledge defeat/one's guilt (**d**) *(se retrouver)* to find one's way around; **je ne me reconnais plus** I can't find my way around any more (**e**) *(être identifiable)* **le mâle se reconnaît à...** the male can be recognized by...

reconnu, -e [rəkɔny] *adj* recognized

reconquérir [7] [rəkɔ̃kerir] *vt (estime, amitié)* to win back; *(territoire)* to reconquer

reconquête [rəkɔ̃kɛt] *nf* reconquest

reconsidérer [34] [rəkɔ̃sidere] *vt* to reconsider

reconstituant, -e [rəkɔ̃stitɥɑ̃, -ɑ̃t] *adj & nm* tonic

reconstituer [rəkɔ̃stitɥe] *vt* (**a**) *(reformer) (armée, gouvernement)* to reconstitute; *(société, parti)* to revive; *(fortune, forces)* to build up again (**b**) *(rétablir) (objet archéologique, faits)* to piece together; *(bâtiment, quartier)* to restore (**c**) *(avec simulation) (crime)* to reconstruct

reconstitution [rəkɔ̃stitysjɔ̃] *nf (d'un crime, d'une bataille)* reconstruction; **r. historique** historical reconstruction

reconstruction [rəkɔ̃stryksjɔ̃] *nf* reconstruction, rebuilding

reconstruire [18] [rəkɔ̃strɥir] *vt* to reconstruct, to rebuild

reconversion [rəkɔ̃vɛrsjɔ̃] *nf* (**a**) *(d'une usine)* conversion; **r. économique** economic restructuring (**b**) *(d'une personne)* retraining

reconvertir [rəkɔ̃vɛrtir] **1** *vt* (**a**) *(entreprise)* to convert (**b**) *(personne)* to retrain

2 se reconvertir *vpr (entreprise)* to convert (**dans** to); *(personne)* to retrain; **se r. dans qch** to retrain for a new career in sth

recopier [66] [rəkɔpje] *vt* (**a**) *(faire un double de)* to recopy (**b**) *(mettre au propre)* to copy out

record [rəkɔr] **1** *adj inv (chiffre, vitesse)* record

2 *nm* record; **détenir le r. (de qch)** to hold the record (for sth); **battre le r. (de qch)** to break the record (for sth)

recordman [rəkɔrdman] *(pl* **recordmen** [rəkɔrdmɛn]*) nm* (men's) record holder

recordwoman [rəkɔrdwuman] *(pl* **recordwomen** [rəkɔrdwumɛn]*) nf* (women's) record holder

recoucher [rəkuʃe] **1** *vt (personne)* to put to bed again

2 se recoucher *vpr* to go back to bed

recoudre [21] [rəkudr] *vt (bouton)* to sew back on; *(déchirure, plaie)* to sew *or* to stitch up; *Fam (personne)* to stitch up

recoupement [rəkupmɑ̃] *nm* crosscheck; **faire le r.** to crosscheck; **par r.** by crosschecking

recouper [rəkupe] **1** *vt* (**a**) *(couper à nouveau) (vêtement)* to re-cut; **r. du pain** to cut some more bread; **r. une tranche de gâteau** to cut another slice of cake (**b**) *(faire coïncider)* to confirm; **r. des témoignages** to crosscheck testimony

2 se recouper *vpr (témoignages)* to tally

recourbé, -e [rəkurbe] *adj (bec)* curved; *(nez)* hooked

recourber [rəkurbe] **1** *vt* to bend

2 se recourber *vpr* to bend

recourir [22] [rəkurir] **1** *vt (épreuve sportive)* to run again

2 *vi (courir de nouveau)* to run again

3 recourir à *vt ind* (**a**) *(personne)* to turn to (**b**) *(moyen, violence)* to resort to

recours [rəkur] *nm* (**a**) *(personne, chose)* recourse; **en dernier r.** as a last resort; **avoir r. à qn** to turn to sb; **avoir r. à qch** to resort to sth (**b**) *Jur* **r. en cassation** appeal; *Can* **r. collectif** class action; **r. en grâce** petition for reprieve

recouvrement [rəkuvrəmɑ̃] *nm (de dettes, d'une facture)* recovery; *(de l'impôt)* collection

recouvrer [rəkuvre] *vt* (**a**) *(biens, argent, santé)* to recover; *(forces, liberté, vue)* to regain; *(courage, enthousiasme)* to get back (**b**) *(percevoir) (dettes)* to recover; *(impôts)* to collect

recouvrir [52] [rəkuvrir] *vt* (**a**) *(couvrir de nouveau) (cahier, toit)* to re-cover; *(enfant)* to cover up again (**b**) *(couvrir complètement)* to cover (**de** with) (**c**) *(tapisser)* to cover (**de** with) (**d**) *(inclure)* to cover

recracher [rəkraʃe] *vt* to spit out

récré [rekre] *nf Fam* recess

récréatif, -ive [rekreatif, -iv] *adj (activité)* entertaining; *(lecture)* light

récréation [rekreasjɔ̃] *nf* (**a**) *(à l'école)* recess (**b**) *(détente)* recreation

recréer [24] [rəkree] *vt* to re-create

récrier [66] [rekrije] **se récrier** *vpr (mécontents)* to protest (**contre** about)

récrimination [rekriminasjɔ̃] *nf* recrimination

récriminer [rekrimine] *vi* to make recriminations (**contre** against)

récrire [30] [rekrir] **= réécrire**

récriture [rekrityr] **= réécriture**

recroquevillé, -e [rəkrɔkvije] *adj* huddled up

recroqueviller [rəkrɔkvije] **se recroqueviller** *vpr (personne)* to huddle up; *(papier, feuille morte)* to shrivel up

recru, -e [rəkry] *adj Litt* **r. (de fatigue)** exhausted

recrudescence [rəkrydesɑ̃s] *nf* renewed outbreak

recrue [rəkry] *nf* recruit; **faire une nouvelle r.** to gain a new recruit

recrutement [rəkrytmɑ̃] *nm* recruitment

recruter [rəkryte] **1** *vt* to recruit; **r. par concours** to recruit by competition

2 se recruter *vpr* to be recruited (**parmi** from)

rectal, -e, -aux, -ales [rɛktal, -o] *adj* rectal

rectangle [rɛktɑ̃gl] *nm* rectangle

rectangulaire [rɛktɑ̃gylɛr] *adj* rectangular

recteur [rɛktœr] *nm (d'une académie)* commissioner of education

rectificatif, -ive [rɛktifikatif, -iv] **1** *adj (lettre)* of amendment; *(texte, facture)* amended

2 *nm* correction

rectification [rɛktifikasjɔ̃] *nf (d'un texte, d'un calcul, d'une erreur)* correction; *(d'un compte, d'une courbe)* adjustment; *(d'un alignement)* straightening; **faire** *ou* **apporter une r.** to make a correction

rectifier [66] [rɛktifje] *vt* (**a**) *(texte, calcul, erreur)* to correct; *(prix, compte, courbe)* to adjust; *(alignement)* to straighten; **r. le tir** to adjust the range; *Fig* to take a slightly different tack (**b**) *Fam (tuer)* to bump off

rectiligne [rɛktiliɲ] *adj (mouvement, figure)* rectilinear; *(avenue)* straight

rectitude [rɛktityd] *nf (d'un jugement, d'un raisonnement)* soundness

recto [rɛkto] *nm* front, *Spéc* recto; **r. verso** on both sides

rectorat [rɛktɔra] *nm* ≃ board of education

rectum [rɛktɔm] *nm* rectum

reçu¹, -e¹ *voir* **recevoir**

reçu², -e² [rəsy] **1** *nm* receipt

2 *nm,f (à un examen)* successful candidate

recueil [rəkœj] *nm (de poèmes, de chansons, de recettes)* collection; *(de lois)* body; **r. de morceaux choisis** anthology

recueillement [rəkœjmã] *nm* meditation; **avec r.** meditatively

recueilli, -e [rəkœji] *adj* meditative

recueillir [5] [rəkœjir] **1** *vt* (**a**) *(argent, renseignements)* to collect (**b**) *(votes)* to win; *Fig* **r. le fruit de qch** to reap the fruit of sth (**c**) *(personne, animal)* to take in (**d**) *(miel)* to gather (**e**) *Jur* **r. un héritage** to inherit

2 se recueillir *vpr* to meditate; **se r. pour prier** to gather one's thoughts before praying

recuire [18] [rəkɥir] *vt (plat)* to cook longer

recul [rəkyl] *nm* (**a**) *(mouvement) (d'un glacier, d'une armée)* retreat; *(d'un canon)* recoil; **avoir un mouvement de r.** to recoil (**b**) *(déclin)* decline (**c**) *(baisse)* decline (**de** in) (**d**) *(espace nécessaire)* room to move back (**e**) *Fig (distance)* **considérer qch avec du r.** to consider sth with detachment; **manquer de r.** to be too closely involved; **prendre du r.** to stand back from things

reculade [rəkylad] *nf (d'une armée)* retreat; *Fig & Péj* climbdown

reculé, -e [rəkyle] *adj (endroit, époque)* remote

reculer [rəkyle] **1** *vi* (**a**) *(aller en arrière) (personne)* to move back; *(automobiliste, voiture)* to reverse; *(troupes)* to retreat; *(glacier, eaux)* to recede; **faire r. la foule** to move the crowd back (**b**) *(régresser) (épidémie)* to lose ground; *(chômage)* to decline; *Fig* **faire r. la maladie** to bring the disease under control (**c**) *(renoncer)* to retreat (**devant** in the face of); **il ne recule devant rien** nothing daunts him; **faire r. qn** to put sb off; **il est trop tard pour r.** it's too late to pull out; **c'est r. pour mieux sauter** it's just putting off the inevitable

2 *vt* (**a**) *(meuble)* to move back; *(voiture)* to reverse (**b**) *(paiement, décision)* to postpone

reculons [rəkylõ] **à reculons** *adv* backward; *Fig (avec réticence)* unwillingly, under protest

récupérable [rekyperabl] *adj (déchets)* salvageable; **les heures supplémentaires sont récupérables** additional time off may be taken in exchange

récupération [rekyperasjõ] *nf* (**a**) *(d'une somme d'argent, d'un objet)* recovery; **la r. des heures supplémentaires** time off in exchange; **temps de r.** *(d'un sportif)* recovery time (**b**) *(de déchets)* salvage (**c**) *(d'un parti, d'une pensée)* exploitation

récupérer [34] [rekypere] *vt* (**a**) *(objet prêté ou perdu)* to get back, to recover; *Ordinat (fichier, données)* to retrieve (**b**) *(passer prendre) (personne, affaires, objet)* to collect; *(bagages)* to retrieve, to reclaim (**c**) *(retrouver) (forces)* to recover (**d**) *(recycler)* to salvage (**e**) *(détourner à son profit) (mouvement, idée)* to exploit (**f**) **r. des heures supplémentaires** to take time off in exchange

récurer [rekyre] *vt* to scour; **poudre/tampon à r.** scouring powder/pad

récurrent, -e [rekyrã, -ãt] *adj* recurring; *Ordinat* **processus r.** recursive process

récusable [rekyzabl] *adj (témoignage)* impugnable

récuser [rekyze] **1** *vt* to challenge

2 se récuser *vpr* to decline to give an opinion

recyclable [rəsiklabl] *adj* recyclable

recyclage [rəsiklaʒ] *nm* (**a**) *(de matériaux)* recycling (**b**) *(d'une personne)* retraining

recyclé, -e [rəsikle] *adj* recycled

recycler [rəsikle] **1** *vt* (**a**) *(matériaux)* to recycle (**b**) *(personne)* to retrain

2 se recycler *vpr (personne)* to retrain

rédacteur, -trice [redaktœr, -tris] *nm,f (d'un journal)* editor; *(d'un dictionnaire)* compiler; **r. en chef** editor in chief

rédaction [redaksjõ] *nf* (**a**) *(d'un texte)* writing; *(d'un dictionnaire)* compiling (**b**) *(poste)* editorship; *(personnel)* editorial staff; *(département)* editorial department; **(salle de) r.** editorial office (**c**) *Scol* essay, composition

rédactionnel, -elle [redaksjonɛl] *adj* editorial

reddition [rɛdisjõ] *nf* surrender

redécouvrir [52] [rədekuvrir] *vt (auteur, œuvre)* to rediscover

redéfinir [rədefinir] *vt Ordinat (touche)* to redefine

redemander [rədəmãde] *vt* (**a**) *(en reposant une question)* to ask again; **r. de l'aide à qn** to ask sb again for help (**b**) *(pour en avoir plus)* **r. du pain/des timbres** to ask for more bread/stamps; **r. un litre/un kilo de qch** ≃ to ask for another two pints/two pounds of sth; **des gens comme ça, on en redemande** there aren't enough people like that in the world; *Ironique* **il en redemande** he's still asking for it (**c**) *(pour récupérer)* **r. qch** to ask for sth back

redémarrer [rədemare] *vi (voiture)* to start again; *(économie, ventes)* to take off again; *Ordinat* to reboot; **faire r. une voiture** to start a car again

rédemption [redãpsjõ] *nf* redemption

redéploiement [rədeplwamã] *nm* redeployment

redescendre [rədesãdr, rədɛsãdr] **1** *vi (en s'approchant)* to come back down; *(en s'éloignant)* to go back down; **r. de voiture** to get back out of the car

2 *vt* (**a**) *(apporter)* to bring back down; *(emporter)* to take back down (**b**) *(escalier, rivière)* to go/to come back down

redevable [rədəvabl] *adj* **être r. de qch à qn** to be indebted to sb for sth; **je vous suis r. de 100 euros** I owe you 100 euros

redevance [rədəvãs] *nf (pour la télévision)* license fee

redevenir [70] [rədəvənir] *vi* to become again; **r. silencieux** to fall silent again; **r. normal** to get back to normal

rédhibitoire [redibitwar] *adj (prix)* prohibitive; *(conditions, salaire)* unacceptable

rediffuser [rədifyze] *vt (émission)* to rerun, to rebroadcast; *(film)* to show again

rediffusion [rədifyzjõ] *nf (d'une émission)* rerun, rebroadcasting; *(d'un film)* rerun

rédiger [45] [rediʒe] *vt (contrat)* to draw up; *(article, lettre)* to write; *(ordonnance)* to write out; **savoir r.** to write well; **être bien/mal rédigé** to be well/badly written

redingote [rədɛ̃gɔt] *nf* (**a**) *(manteau cintré)* tailored coat (**b**) *(manteau à basques)* frock coat

redire [27a] [rədir] **1** *vt* (**a**) *(répéter)* to say again, to repeat; **pourrais-tu lui r. que…?** could you tell him again that…?; **on ne le redira jamais assez** it can never be said often enough (**b**) *(révéler)* to repeat (**à** to)

2 redire à *vt ind* **avoir** *ou* **trouver à r. à qch** to find fault with sth; **il n'y a rien à r. à cela** there's nothing wrong with that

redite [rədit] *nf (useless)* repetition

redondance [rədõdãs] *nf aussi Ordinat* redundancy; **redondances** redundancy

redondant, -e [rədõdã, -ãt] *adj* redundant

redonner [rədɔne] *vt* (**a**) *(donner davantage de)* **redonne-lui de la soupe** give him/her some more soup (**b**) *(rendre)* to give back; **r. de l'appétit/du courage à qn** to restore sb's appetite/courage; **r. envie à qn de faire qch** to make sb want to do sth again; **r. des forces à qn** to give sb back his/her strength (**c**) *(donner de nouveau)* to give again

redorer [rədɔre] *vt* to regild; *Fig* **r. son blason** to restore one's reputation

redoublant, -e [rədublã, -ãt] *nm,f (élève)* pupil repeating a year

redoublé, -e [rəduble] *adj* **frapper à coups redoublés** to knock harder

redoublement [rədubləmã] *nm* (**a**) *(de douleur, de joie, de prudence)* increase (**b**) *(d'une syllabe)* reduplication (**c**) *Scol* repeating of a year; **le professeur principal décidera des redoublements** the principal will decide who will have to repeat the year

redoubler [rəduble] **1** *vt* (**a**) *(douleur, joie, prudence)* to increase; *(efforts)* to redouble (**b**) *Scol* **r. une classe** to repeat a year

2 *vi* (**a**) *Scol* to repeat a year (**b**) *(sentiment)* to intensify (**c**) *(orage)* to intensify, to become more severe; *(vent)* to grow stronger

3 redoubler de *vt ind* **r. de violence** *(orage, vent)* to become more and more severe; **r. d'efforts** to redouble one's efforts; **r. de prudence/d'attention/de douceur** to be twice as cautious/attentive/gentle

redoutable [rədutabl] *adj (adversaire, arme)* formidable; *(maladie)* dreadful

redouter [rədute] *vt* to dread; **r. de faire qch** to dread doing sth; **je redoute qu'il ne soit déjà trop tard** I'm afraid it's already too late

redoux [rədu] *nm* milder weather

redressement [rədrɛsmɑ̃] *nm* (**a**) *(économique, financier)* recovery (**b**) *(correction)* **r. fiscal** tax adjustment (**c**) *Jur* **r. judiciaire** receivership; **être mis en r. judiciaire** to go into receivership

redresser [rədrɛse] **1** *vt* (**a**) *(objet penché)* to put up straight; **r. la tête** to hold up one's head; *(la lever)* to raise one's head (**b**) *(rectifier) (erreur, situation)* to rectify; *(économie, entreprise)* to put back on its feet (**c**) *(bois courbé, tôle cabossée)* to straighten (out)

2 *vi (automobiliste)* to straighten up

3 se redresser *vpr* (**a**) *(personne)* to straighten up (**b**) *(économie, pays, ventes)* to recover

redresseur [rədrɛsœr] *nm* **r. de torts** righter of wrongs

réducteur, -trice [redyktœr, -tris] *adj (simpliste)* simplistic

réduction [redyksjɔ̃] *nf* (**a**) *(des prix, des dépenses, de la production)* reduction (**de** in); **la r. du temps de travail** = reduction of the working week in France from 39 to 35 hours, introduced by the government of Lionel Jospin in 1998 and phased in from 2000 onwards (**b**) *(rabais)* reduction; **faire une r. de 30 euros (à qn)** to give (sb) a reduction of 30 euros (**c**) *(reproduction)* small reproduction (**d**) *(d'une fracture)* setting

réduire [18] [reduir] **1** *vt* (**a**) *(diminuer)* to reduce (**de** by); *(texte)* to shorten, to cut; **réduit de moitié** half size (**b**) *(transformer)* **r. qch en qch** to reduce sth to sth (**c**) *(contraindre)* **r. qn à qch** *(misère, désespoir)* to reduce sb to sth; **en être réduit à faire qch** to be reduced to doing sth (**d**) *(fracture)* to set (**e**) *(photographie, dessin)* to reduce

2 *vi (sauce)* to reduce; **faire r. qch** to reduce sth

3 se réduire *vpr* (**a**) **se r. à** *(se ramener à)* to come down to (**b**) **se r. en** *(se transformer en)* to be reduced to

réduit [redui] *nm (pièce)* small room

rééchelonnement [reeʃəlɔnmɑ̃] *nm* rescheduling

rééchelonner [reeʃəlɔne] *vt* to reschedule

réécrire [30] [reekrir] *vt* to rewrite

réécriture [reekrityr] *nf* rewriting

rééditer [reedite] *vt* (**a**) *(ouvrage)* to reissue (**b**) *(fait)* to repeat

réédition [reedisjɔ̃] *nf* (**a**) *(d'un ouvrage)* reissue (**b**) *(d'un fait)* repeat

rééducation [reedykasjɔ̃] *nf* (**a**) *(d'une partie du corps)* re-education; *(d'un handicapé, d'un accidenté)* rehabilitation, *Fam* rehab; **faire de la r.** *(chez un kinésithérapeute)* to have physiotherapy (**b**) *(de délinquants)* rehabilitation

rééduquer [reedyke] *vt (handicapé, accidenté, délinquant)* to rehabilitate, *Fam* to rehab; *(partie du corps)* to re-educate

réel, -elle [reɛl] **1** *adj* real

2 *nm* (**a**) *(nombre)* real number (**b**) **le r.** *(la réalité)* reality

réélection [reelɛksjɔ̃] *nf* re-election

réélire [44] [reelir] *vt* to re-elect

réellement [reɛlmɑ̃] *adv* really

réembaucher [reɑ̃boʃe] *vt* to take on again

réenregistrable [reɑ̃rəʒistrabl] *adj* rerecordable

réenregistrer [reɑ̃rəʒistre] *vt* to rerecord

rééquilibrage [reekilibraʒ] *nm (de pneus)* balancing; *Fig* **le r. du budget** balancing the budget again

rééquilibrer [reekilibre] *vt (pneus)* to balance; *Fig (budget)* to balance again

réessayer [53] [reeseje] **1** *vt* to try again; *(vêtement)* to try on again

2 *vi* to try again

réévaluer [reevalue] *vt (monnaie)* to revalue; *(prix)* to reassess

réexamen [reɛgzamɛ̃] *nm* re-examination; *(d'une décision)* reconsideration

réexaminer [reɛgzamine] *vt* to re-examine; *(décision)* to reconsider

réexpédier [66] [reɛkspedje] *vt* (**a**) *(à une autre adresse)* to send on, to forward (**b**) *(à l'expéditeur)* to send back, to return

réexpédition [reɛkspedisjɔ̃] *nf* (**a**) *(à une autre adresse)* forwarding (**b**) *(à l'expéditeur)* return

refaire [36] [rəfɛr] **1** *vt* (**a**) *(faire à nouveau) (travail)* to do again, to redo; *(voyage)* to make again; **r. du riz** to cook some more rice; **r. ses lacets** to tie one's laces again; *Hum* **ton éducation est à r.** where were you brought up?; **et si c'était à r.?** and if you had to do it again?; **r. le monde** to put the world to rights; **r. sa vie** to make a new life for oneself (**b**) *(remettre en état) (pièce, appartement)* to do up; **r. la peinture de qch** to repaint sth; **r. la moquette de qch** to recarpet sth; **r. qch à neuf** *(moteur)* to recondition sth; *(appartement)* to renovate sth completely (**c**) *Fam (duper)* to take in; **je me suis fait r. de 100 euros** I was done out of 100 euros

2 se refaire *vpr* (**a**) *(se changer)* to change the way one is; **on ne se refait pas** you can't change the way you are (**b**) *(se rétablir)* **se r. une santé** to recover (**c**) *Fam (financièrement)* to recoup one's losses (**d**) *(s'habituer)* **se r. à qch** to get used to sth again

réfection [refɛksjɔ̃] *nf* repair

réfectoire [refɛktwar] *nm* refectory, dining hall

référence [referɑ̃s] *nf* (**a**) *(renvoi)* reference (**à** to); **faire r. à qch** to refer to sth; **en r. à** with reference to (**b**) *(sur une lettre, sur un document)* reference; **r. à rappeler** please quote reference (**c**) *(d'employeur)* **références** references

référencer [16] [referɑ̃se] *vt Ordinat* to reference

référendum [referɛ̃dɔm] *nm* referendum; **faire un r.** to hold a referendum

référer [34] [refere] **1 référer à** *vt ind* **en r. à qn** to refer the matter to sb

2 se référer *vpr* **se r. à qch** to refer to sth; **se r. à un auteur** to refer to an author

refermer [rəfɛrme] **1** *vt* to shut *or* to close again

2 se refermer *vpr (porte)* to close *or* to shut again; *(fleur, blessure)* to close up

refiler [rəfile] *vt Fam* **r. qch à qn** *(pour s'en débarrasser)* to palm sth off on sb; *(maladie)* to give sb sth

réfléchi, -e [refleʃi] *adj* (**a**) *(personne)* thoughtful (**b**) *(action, opinion)* considered; **c'est tout r.** I've made up my mind; **tout bien r.** all things considered (**c**) *(verbe, pronom)* reflexive

réfléchir [refleʃir] **1** *vt (image, lumière, son)* to reflect (**b**) **r. que** to realize that

2 *vi* to think (**à** *ou* **sur** about); **je réfléchis** I'm thinking; *(avant de décider)* I'm thinking about it; **sans r.** without thinking

3 se réfléchir *vpr* to be reflected

réfléchissant, -e [refleʃisɑ̃, -ɑ̃t] *adj* reflective

réflecteur, -trice [reflɛktœr, -tris] *adj* reflecting

reflet [rəflɛ] *nm* (**a**) *(dans un miroir, dans l'eau)* reflection; *(d'un tissu)* sheen; *(de la lune)* glint; **reflets** *(de cheveux)* highlights (**b**) *Fig (image)* reflection; **être le r. de qn** to be exactly like sb; **être le r. d'une époque** to symbolize an era

refléter [34] [rəflete] **1** *vt aussi Fig* to reflect

2 se refléter *vpr aussi Fig* to be reflected

refleurir [rəflœrir] **1** *vi* to flower again; *Fig* to flourish again

2 *vt (tombe)* to put fresh flowers on

réflexe [refleks] **1** *adj* reflex

2 *nm* reflex; **avoir de bons réflexes** to have good reflexes; **devenir un r.** to become automatic; **avoir le r. de faire qch** to do sth instinctively; **r. conditionné** conditioned reflex

réflexion [refleksjɔ̃] *nf* (**a**) *(d'une image, de la lumière, du son)* reflection (**b**) *(pensée)* reflection, thought; **r. faite, à la r.** on reflection, on second thoughts (**c**) *(remarque)* remark; **faire une r. à qn** to make a remark to sb

réflexologie [refleksɔlɔʒi] *nf* reflexology

réflexologiste [refleksɔlɔʒist] *nmf* reflexologist

refluer [rəflye] *vi* *(liquide)* to flow back; *(marée)* to ebb; *(foule)* to surge back

reflux [rəfly] *nm* *(de la marée)* ebb; *(d'une foule)* backward surge

refondre [rəfɔ̃dr] *vt* *(ouvrage)* to revise

refonte [rəfɔ̃t] *nf* *(d'un ouvrage)* revision

reformater [rəfɔrmate] *vt* Ordinat *(page, disque)* to reformat

réformateur, -trice [refɔrmatœr, -tris] **1** *adj* reforming

    2 *nm,f* reformer

réforme [refɔrm] *nf* reform; *Hist* **la R.** the Reformation

réformé, -e [refɔrme] **1** *adj* *(protestant)* Protestant

    2 *nm,f* *(recrue)* recruit rejected as unfit; *(soldat)* soldier discharged as unfit

reformer [rəfɔrme] **1** *vt* to re-form; **r. les rangs** to fall into line again

    2 se reformer *vpr* to re-form

réformer [refɔrme] *vt* (**a**) *(abus, loi)* to reform (**b**) *(recrue)* to reject as unfit; *(soldat)* to discharge as unfit

réformisme [refɔrmism] *nm* reformism

réformiste [refɔrmist] *adj & nmf* reformist

reformuler [rəfɔrmyle] *vt* to reformulate

refoulé, -e [rəfule] *adj* repressed

refouler [rəfule] **1** *vt* (**a**) *(faire reculer) (foule)* to drive *or* to force back; *(étranger)* to turn away (**b**) *(sentiments, colère, souvenir)* to repress; *(larmes)* to hold back

    2 *vi* **l'évier refoule** the water's coming up through the drain in the sink

réfractaire [refrakter] *adj* (**a**) *(rebelle)* insubordinate; **r. à** *(loi, conseils, proposition)* unwilling to accept (**b**) *(brique, argile)* fireproof (**c**) *(prêtre)* non-juring

réfraction [refraksjɔ̃] *nf* refraction

refrain [rəfrɛ̃] *nm* *(d'une chanson)* chorus, refrain; *Fam* **c'est toujours le même r.** it's always the same old story

refréner [rəfrene], **réfréner** [refrene] [34] *vt* to curb

réfrigérant, -e [refriʒerɑ̃, -ɑ̃t] *adj* (**a**) *(appareil, produit)* refrigerating (**b**) *Fam (accueil, personne)* frosty

réfrigérateur [refriʒeratœr] *nm* refrigerator

réfrigération [refriʒerasjɔ̃] *nf* refrigeration

réfrigéré, -e [refriʒere] *adj* (**a**) *(wagon)* refrigerated; **wagon/camion/bateau r.** reefer (**b**) *Fam (personne)* frozen

réfrigérer [34] [refriʒere] *vt* *(aliment, boisson)* to refrigerate

refroidir [rəfrwadir] **1** *vt* (**a**) *(eau)* to cool (down) (**b**) *Fig (amitié)* to cool; *(enthousiasme)* to dampen; *Fam* **sa réaction m'a refroidi** her reaction dampened my enthusiasm (**c**) *très Fam (tuer)* to bump off

    2 *vi* (**a**) *(devenir froid)* to get cold; *(devenir moins chaud)* to cool down; **laisser r. qch** *(volontairement)* to let sth cool down; *(par négligence)* to let sth get cold (**b**) *(temps)* to get colder

    3 se refroidir *vpr* (**a**) *(temps)* to get colder (**b**) *Fig (amitié, relations)* to cool (**c**) *(prendre froid)* to catch a chill

refroidissement [rəfrwadismɑ̃] *nm* (**a**) *(de la température)* drop in temperature; *(de l'eau)* cooling (**b**) *(indisposition)* chill (**c**) *Fig (dans une amitié, dans des relations)* cooling off

refuge [rəfyʒ] *nm* (**a**) *(lieu) & Fig* refuge; **trouver/chercher r. (auprès de qn)** to find/seek refuge (with sb) (**b**) *(en montagne)* (mountain) hut (**c**) *(sur la route)* traffic island

    2 *adj* **valeur r.** safe investment

réfugié, -e [refyʒje] *nm,f* refugee

réfugier [66] [refyʒje] **se réfugier** *vpr* to take refuge (**dans** in)

refus [rəfy] *nm* *(d'une invitation, d'une offre)* refusal; *(d'une proposition, d'un candidat, d'un manuscrit)* rejection; **essuyer un r.** to meet with a refusal; **opposer un r. à qn/qch** to turn sb/sth down; *Fam* **ce n'est pas de r.** I won't say no; **r. de priorité** *(infraction)* failure to yield

refuser [rəfyze] **1** *vt* (**a**) *(offre, invitation, demande)* to refuse, to turn down; *(proposition, marchandises, manuscrit)* to reject; **r. qch à qn** to refuse sb sth (**b**) *(clients, spectateurs)* to turn away (**c**) *(candidat)* **être refusé** to fail

    2 *vi* to refuse; **r. de faire qch** to refuse to do sth

    3 se refuser *vpr* (**a**) *(être rejeté)* **une offre pareille, ça ne se refuse pas** you can't refuse an offer like that (**b**) **se r. qch** *(se priver de)* to deny oneself sth; **ne rien se r.** not to stint oneself (**c**) *(résister)* **se r. à l'évidence** to shut one's eyes to the facts; **se r. à tout commentaire** to refuse to comment; **se r. à faire qch** to refuse to do sth

réfuter [refyte] *vt* to refute

regagner [rəgaɲe] *vt* (**a**) *(confiance, affection, estime)* to regain, to get back (**b**) *(argent perdu)* to win back; **r. le temps perdu** to make up for lost time (**c**) **r. du terrain** *(reprendre l'avantage)* to make up lost ground (**d**) *(endroit)* to get back to; **r. son foyer** to get back home

regain [rəgɛ̃] *nm* *(d'intérêt, d'activité)* renewal; **un r. d'espoir** renewed hope

régal, -als [regal] *nm* treat

régalade [regalad] *nf* **boire à la r.** to drink without letting the bottle touch one's lips

régaler [regale] **1** *vt* **r. qn** to give sb a delicious meal

    2 *vi* *Fam* **c'est moi qui régale** (it's) my treat

    3 se régaler *vpr* **je me régale** *(en mangeant)* I'm really enjoying it; *(je m'amuse)* I'm having a great time

regard [rəgar] *nm* (**a**) *(coup d'œil)* look; **porter son r. sur qn/qch** to look at sb/sth; **jeter** *ou* **lancer un r. à qn** to glance at sb; **jeter un r. à** *ou* **sur qch** to glance at sth; **lancer un r. furieux à qn** to glare at sb; **chercher qn/qch du r.** to look around for sb/sth; **interroger qn du r.** to give sb a questioning look; **soustraire qn/qch aux regards (de qn)** to keep sb/sth hidden (from sb); **attirer le r.** to attract attention; **sous les regards de la foule** while the crowd looked on; *Fig* **porter un nouveau r./un r. critique sur qch** to take a fresh look/a critical look at sth (**b**) *(expression)* look (**c**) *(ouverture) (d'une porte)* peephole; *(d'un égout)* manhole (**d**) *(locutions)* **au r. de la loi** in the eyes of the law; **en r.** *(en face)* opposite

regardant, -e [rəgardɑ̃, -ɑ̃t] *adj* (**a**) *Fam (avare)* careful with money (**b**) *(exigeant)* particular (**sur** about)

regarder [rəgarde] **1** *vt* (**a**) *(personne, objet)* to look at; *(émission, film)* to watch; **r. qn droit dans les yeux** to look sb in the eye; **r. qn fixement** to stare at sb; **r. qn faire qch** to watch sb do sth; **regarde où tu marches!** watch where you're going!; *Fam* **non, mais tu ne m'as pas regardé!** what do you take me for?

    (**b**) *(considérer)* to regard, to consider (**comme** as); **r. qch en face** to face up to sth; **r. les choses telles qu'elles sont** to see things as they are

    (**c**) *(concerner)* to concern; **cela ne regarde que moi** that's nobody's business but mine; **cela ne vous regarde pas** that's none of your business

    2 *vi* (**a**) *(observer)* to look; **r. autour de soi/en bas/en arrière** to look around/down/back; **r. par** *ou* **à la fenêtre** *(du dedans)* to look out of the window; *(du dehors)* to look in through the window

    (**b**) *(être orienté)* **r. sur** *ou* **vers** *(jardin, rue)* to look onto

    3 regarder à *vt ind* (**a**) *(apparence, détail)* to pay attention to; **r. à la dépense** to be careful with one's money; **y r. à**

deux fois avant de faire qch to think twice before doing sth; **y r. de près** to look at it closely

(**b**) *Belg (veiller sur)* to look after

4 se regarder *vpr* (**a**) *(soi-même)* to look at oneself; *Fam* **elle ne s'est pas regardée!** she can talk!

(**b**) *(l'un l'autre)* to look at each other; **se r. dans les yeux** to look into each other's eyes

(**c**) *(se faire face)* to face each other

regarnir [rəgarnir] *vt (garde-manger, étagères)* to restock

régate [regat] *nf* regatta

régence [reʒɑ̃s] **1** *adj inv* **style R.** Regency style

2 *nf* regency; *Hist* **la R.** the Regency

régénération [reʒenerasjɔ̃] *nf* (**a**) *(d'une cellule, de la peau)* regeneration (**b**) *Ordinat* **r. de l'écran** screen refresh

régénérer [34] [reʒenere] **1** *vt* to regenerate

2 se régénérer *vpr* to regenerate

régent, -e [reʒɑ̃, -ɑ̃t] *nm,f* (**a**) *(chef du gouvernement)* regent (**b**) *Belg Scol* (secondary) schoolteacher

régenter [reʒɑ̃te] *vt* **vouloir tout r.** to want to run the whole show

reggae [rege] **1** *adj inv* reggae

2 *nm* **le r.** reggae

régie [reʒi] *nf* (**a**) *(entreprise publique)* state-controlled company (**b**) *Cin & TV (organisation)* production management (**c**) *TV (lieu)* control room

regimber [rəʒɛ̃be] *vi (personne)* to balk (**contre** at); **il est inutile de r.** it's no use protesting

régime [reʒim] *nm* (**a**) **r. (alimentaire)** diet; **être au r.** to be on a diet; **faire** *ou* **suivre un r.** to diet; **se mettre au r.** to go on a diet; **r. amincissant** slimming diet; *Fam* **être au r. sec** to be on an alcohol-free diet; *Hum* to be on the wagon (**b**) *(forme de gouvernement)* government, regime (**c**) *(pénitentiaire, hospitalier)* system; *(de retraite)* scheme; **r. matrimonial** marriage settlement; **r. de Sécurité sociale** = division of social security system applying to some professional groups (**d**) *(d'un moteur)* speed; **r. de croisière** cruising speed; *Fig* **à ce r.** at this rate (**e**) *(d'une rivière, d'un fleuve)* rate of flow (**f**) *(de bananes, de dattes)* bunch

régiment [reʒimɑ̃] *nm (unité militaire)* regiment; *Fig (d'admirateurs, de créanciers)* host; *Fam* **il y en a pour un r.** there's enough for a whole army

région [reʒjɔ̃] *nf* area, region; **la r. parisienne** the Paris area *or* region; **la R.** = administrative area comprising several "départements"; **en r.** *(en province)* in the provinces

régional, -e, -aux, -ales [reʒjɔnal, -o] *adj* regional

régionalisme [reʒjɔnalism] *nm* regionalism

régionaliste [reʒjɔnalist] **1** *adj* regionalist

2 *nmf* regionalist; *(écrivain)* regional writer

régir [reʒir] *vt* (**a**) *(déterminer)* to govern (**b**) *(domaine)* to manage

régisseur [reʒisœr] *nm* (**a**) *(d'un domaine)* manager (**b**) *Cin & TV* assistant production manager; *Théât* stage manager

registre [rəʒistr] *nm* (**a**) *(livre)* register; *(de comptabilité)* account book; **r. du commerce** trade register; **r. de l'état civil** register of births, marriages and deaths (**b**) *(d'une voix, d'un instrument)* register (**c**) *Ordinat* register; **r. d'accès mémoire** memory access register (**d**) *(d'une œuvre)* style

réglable [reglabl] *adj* adjustable

réglage [reglaʒ] *nm* (**a**) *(d'un siège, d'un appareil)* adjustment; **r. automatique** automatic control (**b**) *(d'une radio, d'une télévision)* tuning; **r. du contraste** contrast control

règle [regl] *nf* (**a**) *(de conduite, de grammaire)* rule; *Fig* **la r. du jeu** the rules of the game; **en r.** *(passeport, papiers)* in order; **en r. générale** as a general rule; **dans** *ou* **selon les règles de l'art** according to the book; **r. d'or** golden rule; *Math* **r. de trois** rule of three (**b**) *(pour tracer des lignes)* ruler (**c**) *Ordinat (sur écran)* ruler line (**d**) **règles** *(menstruation)* period; **avoir ses règles** to have one's period

réglé, -e [regle] *adj* (**a**) *(papier)* ruled (**b**) *(organisé)* well-ordered (**c**) *(résolu)* **c'est r.** it's settled (**d**) *(jeune fille)* who has started her periods

règlement [regləmɑ̃] *nm* (**a**) *(résolution)* settlement; **en cours de r.** being settled; **r. à l'amiable** amicable settlement; **r. de comptes** settling of scores (**b**) *(paiement)* payment; **pour r. de tout compte** in full settlement (**c**) *(règle)* regulations; **r. intérieur** *(d'une école)* school rules; *(d'un bureau)* company rules; **c'est le r.** that's the rule

réglementaire [regləmɑ̃tɛr] *adj (tenue)* regulation; **faire qch dans le temps r.** to do sth in the time allowed

réglementation [regləmɑ̃tasjɔ̃] *nf* (**a**) *(action)* regulation (**b**) *(ensemble de lois)* regulations; **la r. du travail** labor legislation

réglementer [regləmɑ̃te] *vt* to regulate

régler [34] [regle] **1** *vt* (**a**) *(mécanisme, appareil, image)* to adjust; *(radio, moteur)* to tune (**b**) *(journée, emploi du temps)* to plan (**c**) **r. qch sur qch** *(conduite)* to model sth on sth; *(pas)* to adjust sth to sth (**d**) *(résoudre)* (question, dispute) to settle; **r. ses affaires** to put one's affairs in order; **r. qch à l'amiable** to settle sth out of court (**e**) *(payer)* (facture) to settle, to pay; *(employé, commerçant, loyer)* to pay; *(achats)* to pay for

2 *vi* to pay

3 se régler *vpr* (**a**) **se r. sur qn** to model oneself on sb (**b**) *(se conclure)* to be settled

réglette [reglɛt] *nf* small ruler; *Ordinat* **r. de clavier** key strip

réglisse [reglis] *nf* liquorice

réglo [reglo] *adj inv Fam* on the level

régnant, -e [reɲɑ̃, -ɑ̃t] *adj (prince, famille)* reigning; *(idéologie, opinion)* prevailing

règne [rɛɲ] *nm* (**a**) *(d'un souverain)* reign; *Fig (de l'argent, de la technologie)* rule (**b**) *(végétal, animal)* kingdom

régner [34] [reɲe] *vi* (**a**) *(souverain)* to reign, to rule (**sur** over); **r. en maître sur qch** to reign supreme over sth (**b**) *(exister)* (idée) to prevail; *(silence, atmosphère)* to reign; **faire r. la paix/l'ordre** to keep the peace/law and order; *Ironique* **la confiance règne!** there's confidence for you!

regonfler [rəgɔ̃fle] *vt (ballon, pneu)* to blow up again, to re-inflate

regorger [45] [rəgɔrʒe] *vi* **r. de qch** to be overflowing with sth; **r. de monde** to be packed with people

régresser [regrese] *vi* (**a**) *(criminalité, idéologie, production)* to decline (**b**) *(personne)* to regress

régression [regrɛsjɔ̃] *nf* (**a**) *(de la criminalité, d'une idéologie, de la production)* decline; **être en r.** to be on the decline (**b**) *(d'une personne)* regression; **être en r.** to be regressing

regret [rəgrɛ] *nm* regret (**de** for); **avoir des regrets** to have regrets; **à r.** with regret; **j'ai le r.** *ou* **je suis au r. de vous annoncer que...** I regret to tell you that...; **à mon (grand) r.** (much) to my regret

regrettable [rəgrɛtabl] *adj* regrettable

regretter [rəgrɛte] *vt* (**a**) *(avoir des remords sur)* to regret; **je ne regrette rien** I have no regrets; **il me ferait presque r. ma gentillesse** I'm almost sorry I was so kind to him; **r. de faire qch** to regret to do sth; **r. d'avoir fait qch** to regret having done sth; **r. que** + *subjunctive* to be sorry that; **il est à r. que...** it is to be regretted that...; **je regrette!** I'm sorry! (**b**) *(personne, endroit)* to miss; **r. sa jeunesse/son enfance** to wish one was young/a child again

regroupement [rəgrupmɑ̃] *nm* (**a**) *(action)* grouping; *(d'animaux, d'enfants)* roundup; *(de sociétés)* amalgamation; *Mil* regrouping; **le r. familial** = policy of authorizing the families of immigrant workers in possession of long-term work permits to join their relatives in France (**b**) *(groupe)* grouping

regrouper [rəgrupe] **1** *vt* (**a**) *(personnes, objets)* to gather together; *(animaux, enfants)* to round up (**b**) *(sociétés)* to amalgamate

2 se regrouper *vpr* (**a**) *(personnes)* to gather together (**b**) *(sociétés)* to amalgamate

régularisation [regylarizasjɔ̃] nf (**a**) (d'une situation) regularization; (d'un compte) adjustment (**b**) (d'un fleuve, d'un fonctionnement, de la circulation) regulation

régulariser [regylarize] vt (**a**) (situation) to regularize; (compte) to adjust; **ils ont régularisé la situation** (ils se sont mariés) they made it official (**b**) (fleuve, fonctionnement, circulation) to regulate

régularité [regylarite] nf (**a**) (exactitude) regularity (**b**) (constance) steadiness (**c**) (d'une décision, d'une situation) legality

régulateur, -trice [regylatœr, -tris] **1** adj regulating
2 nm regulator

régulation [regylasjɔ̃] nf control; **r. des naissances** birth control

régulier, -ère [regylje, -ɛr] **1** adj (**a**) (à intervalles fixes) regular (**b**) (constant) steady; (travail, résultats) consistent (**c**) (écriture, ligne, couche) even; (traits du visage) regular (**d**) (légal) (situation) legitimate; **être en situation régulière** to have one's papers in order (**e**) Gram regular (**f**) Fam (honnête) on the level (**g**) (clergé) regular
2 nf **régulière** Fam Hum (épouse) old lady; (maîtresse) bit on the side

régulièrement [regyljɛrmɑ̃] adv (**a**) (à intervalles fixes) regularly (**b**) (avec constance) steadily (**c**) (réparti, étalé) evenly (**d**) (selon la loi) legitimately

régurgiter [regyrʒite] vt (nourriture) to regurgitate

réhabilitation [reabilitasjɔ̃] nf (**a**) (de délinquant) rehabilitation (**b**) (de bâtiment, de quartier) renovation

réhabiliter [reabilite] **1** vt (**a**) (délinquant) to rehabilitate (**b**) (personne accusée) to clear (**c**) (bâtiment, quartier) to renovate
2 se réhabiliter vpr to rehabilitate oneself

réhabituer [reabitɥe] **1** vt **r. qn à qch/à faire qch** to get sb used to sth/to doing sth again
2 se réhabituer vpr se r. **à qch/à faire qch** to get used to sth/to doing sth again

rehausser [rəose] vt (**a**) (mur, bâtiment) to make higher (**b**) (couleur, teint) to set off; (détail) to accentuate

réimplanter [reɛ̃plɑ̃te] **1** vt to relocate
2 se réimplanter vpr to relocate

réimpression [reɛ̃presjɔ̃] nf reprinting; **en cours de r.** (ouvrage) being reprinted

réimprimer [reɛ̃prime] vt to reprint

rein [rɛ̃] nm (**a**) (organe) kidney; **r. artificiel** kidney or dialysis machine (**b**) **reins** (bas du dos) lower back; **la chute** ou **le creux des reins** the small of the back; **avoir mal aux reins** to have a pain in the small of one's back; Fig **avoir les reins solides** to be tough; (financièrement) to have money behind one

réincarnation [reɛ̃karnasjɔ̃] nf reincarnation

réincarner [reɛ̃karne] **se réincarner** vpr to be reincarnated (**en** as)

reine [rɛn] nf (**a**) (souveraine, épouse d'un roi) queen; **un port** ou **un maintien de r.** a queenly bearing; **la r. Victoria** Queen Victoria; **la r. mère** the Queen Mother (**b**) (femme) **r. de beauté** beauty queen; **la r. du bal** the belle of the ball (**c**) (abeille) queen (bee) (**d**) **la petite r.** (cyclisme) cycling

reine-claude (pl **reines-claudes**) [rɛnklod] nf greengage

reinette [rɛnɛt] nf pippin; **r. grise** russet

réinitialiser [reinisjalize] vt Ordinat to reset; (mémoire) to reinitialize

réinscription [reɛ̃skripsjɔ̃] nf reregistration

réinscrire [30] [reɛ̃skrir] **1** vt to reregister (**à** for)
2 se réinscrire vpr to reregister (**à** for)

réinsérer [34] [reɛ̃sere] **1** vt (**a**) (personne) to reintegrate (**dans** into) (**b**) Ordinat (bloc) to reinsert
2 se réinsérer vpr to reintegrate (**dans** into)

réinsertion [reɛ̃sɛrsjɔ̃] nf reintegration; **r. sociale** rehabilitation

réintégrer [34] [reɛ̃tegre] vt (**a**) (fonctionnaire) **r. qn (dans ses fonctions)** to reinstate sb (**b**) (lieu) **r. son domicile** to return to one's home

réintroduire [18] [reɛ̃trɔdɥir] vt to reintroduce

réitérer [34] [reitere] vt (demande, promesse, question) to repeat, to reiterate; (démarche) to repeat

rejaillir [rəʒajir] vi to spurt out; Fig **r. sur qn** (scandale) to reflect on sb

rejet [rəʒɛ] nm (**a**) (de produits chimiques) discharge (**b**) (d'une proposition, d'une personne, d'une greffe) rejection (**c**) (en poésie) enjambment

rejeter [42] [rəʒte] vt (**a**) (relancer) to throw back (**b**) (candidature, offre, greffe) to reject; (témoignage) to disallow; (réclamation, accusation) to dismiss; (projet de loi) to throw out (**c**) (personne) to reject (**d**) (repousser) **r. ses cheveux en arrière** to toss one's hair back; **r. la tête en arrière** to throw one's head back; **r. un mot en fin de phrase** to put a word at the end of a sentence (**e**) (déchets, gaz toxiques) to discharge; (nourriture) to regurgitate; (épaves) to cast up (**f**) (blâme, responsabilité) to shift (**sur** on)

rejeton [rəʒtɔ̃] nm Fam Hum (enfant) kid

rejoindre [43] [rəʒwɛ̃dr] **1** vt (**a**) (personne) (pour un rendez-vous) to meet; (rattraper) to catch up (with) (**b**) (aboutir sur) (rue, rivière) to join (up with) (**c**) (atteindre) (lieu) to reach; (régiment, poste) to return to (**d**) (concorder avec) to coincide with
2 se rejoindre vpr (**a**) (amis) to meet up (**b**) (rivières, routes, lignes) to join up (**c**) (propos, idées) to coincide

rejouer [rəʒwe] vt (match, point) to replay; (morceau de musique) to play again; (pièce de théâtre) to do again

réjoui, -e [reʒwi] adj joyful

réjouir [reʒwir] **1** vt (personne) to delight
2 se réjouir vpr to be delighted (**de** at); **se r. que** + subjunctive to be delighted that; **se r. de faire qch** to be delighted to be doing sth; Suisse **se r. de qch/de faire qch** to look forward to sth/to doing sth

réjouissance [reʒwisɑ̃s] nf rejoicing; **en signe de r.** to mark the occasion; **réjouissances** festivities

réjouissant, -e [reʒwisɑ̃, -ɑ̃t] adj delightful

relâche [rəlɑʃ] nf (**a**) (arrêt) **sans r.** without a break (**b**) (au théâtre) **il y a r. ce soir** there is no performance this evening; **faire r.** to be closed; **r.** (sur panneau) closed

relâché, -e [rəlɑʃe] adj (mœurs, conduite) lax

relâchement [rəlɑʃmɑ̃] nm (**a**) (des muscles) relaxing; (d'une corde) slackening (**b**) (d'une discipline) relaxation; (des mœurs) laxness; (des efforts) let-up; (de l'attention) wavering; **il y a du r. dans votre travail** you're letting your work slide

relâcher [rəlɑʃe] **1** vt (**a**) (muscles) to relax; (corde, étreinte) to loosen (**b**) (discipline) to relax; (efforts) to let up; **r. son attention** to let one's attention waver (**c**) (prisonnier) to release, to let go
2 se relâcher vpr (**a**) (muscles) to relax; (corde) to slacken; (étreinte) to loosen (**b**) (discipline, mœurs) to become lax; (élève, employé) to slack off; (attention) to waver

relais [rəlɛ] nm (**a**) (épreuve sportive) (**course de) r.** relay (race); **r. 4 x 100 mètres** 4 x 100-meter relay (**b**) (relève) **passer le r. à qn** to hand over to sb; **prendre le r. (de)** to take over (from) (**c**) (intermédiaire) intermediary (**d**) (auberge) post house; **r. gastronomique** gourmet restaurant (**e**) (dispositif émetteur) relay

relance [rəlɑ̃s] nf (**a**) (de l'économie, de la production) revival (**b**) (au jeu) raise

relancer [16] [rəlɑ̃se] vt (**a**) (lancer de nouveau) to throw again; (rendre) to throw back (**b**) (économie, ventes, production) to boost (**c**) (moteur) to restart; Ordinat (programme) to rerun; (logiciel) to restart (**d**) (client) to follow up

relater [rəlate] vt Litt (raconter) to relate

relatif, -ive [rəlatif, -iv] **1** *adj* relative; **r. à** relating to; **tout est r.** it's all relative

2 *nm (pronom)* relative pronoun

3 *nf* **relative** *(proposition)* relative clause

relation [rəlasjɔ̃] *nf* **(a)** *(rapports entre personnes)* relationship; **être en r. avec qn** to be in touch with sb; **mettre qn en r. (avec qn)** to put sb in touch (with sb); **avoir de bonnes/ mauvaises relations avec qn** to be on good/bad terms with sb; **r. (amoureuse)** (love) affair; **relations extérieures** foreign affairs; **relations publiques** public relations; **relations sexuelles** (sexual) intercourse **(b)** *(lien) (entre des phénomènes, des faits)* relationship, connection; **être sans r. avec qch** to bear no relation to sth; **en r. avec...** in relation to...; **r. de cause à effet** cause-and-effect relationship; **relations spatiales** spatial relations **(c)** *(connaissance)* acquaintance; **avoir des relations** to have contacts; **une r. de travail** a colleague **(d)** *(récit)* account

relationnel, -elle [rəlasjɔnɛl] *adj* relational; *Ordinat* **base de données relationnelles** relational database

relativement [rəlativmɑ̃] *adv* **(a)** *(assez)* relatively **(b)** **r. à** *(par rapport à)* compared to

relativiser [rəlativize] *vt* to put into perspective; **il faut r.** you have to put things into perspective

relativisme [rəlativism] *nm* relativism

relativité [rəlativite] *nf* relativity

relax [rəlaks] *adj Fam* laid-back

relaxant, -e [rəlaksɑ̃, -ɑ̃t] *adj* relaxing

relaxation [rəlaksasjɔ̃] *nf* relaxation; **faire de la r.** to do relaxation exercises

relaxer [rəlakse] **1** *vt* **(a)** *(détendre)* to relax **(b)** *(prisonnier)* to release

2 se relaxer *vpr* to relax

relayer [53] [rəleje] **1** *vt (personne)* to take over from

2 se relayer *vpr* **(a)** *(se remplacer)* to take turns; **se r. pour faire qch** to take turns doing sth; **on se relaie toutes les trois heures** we change over every three hours **(b)** *(coureurs)* to take over from each other

relecture [rəlɛktyr] *nf* **(a)** *(d'épreuves)* proofreading **(b)** *(d'un livre, d'un texte)* rereading

reléguer [34] [rəlege] *vt* to relegate (**à/en** to); *Fig* **r. qch au second plan** to push sth into the background

relent [rəlɑ̃] *nm* **(a)** *(odeur)* stench **(b)** *(de scandale)* whiff

relevable [rələvabl] *adj (dossier, appuie-tête)* adjustable; *(accoudoir)* folding

relevé, -e [rələve] **1** *adj* **(a)** *(style)* lofty **(b)** *(sauce, plat)* spicy, highly seasoned

2 *nm (d'un compteur)* reading; **r. de compte** bank statement; **r. d'identité bancaire** = document giving details of one's bank account

---

Relevé d'identité bancaire

An "RIB" is a small slip of paper with all of a person's bank details. Employers, utility companies and other financial institutions may ask for one to effect standing orders.

---

relève [rələv] *nf* relief; **assurer** *ou* **prendre la r. (de qn)** to take over (from sb)

relèvement [rələvmɑ̃] *nm* **(a)** *(d'une économie, d'un pays)* recovery **(b)** *(des salaires, des tarifs, d'un impôt)* raising

relever [46] [rələve] **1** *vt* **(a)** *(objet renversé)* to pick up; *(personne)* to help back up; **r. la tête** to look up; *Fig* to stand up for oneself

(b) *(économie, pays)* to revive

(c) *(col)* to turn up; *(manches, bas de pantalon)* to roll up, to turn up; *(voilette, jupe)* to lift (up); *(cheveux)* to put up

(d) *(augmenter)* to raise

(e) *(contradiction, erreur)* to pick out; *(traces, empreinte)* to find

(f) *(prêter attention à)* **r. l'allusion** to pick up on the hint; **je n'ai pas relevé** I let it go

(g) *(adresse, coordonnées)* to take down; *(compteur)* to read; *(copies)* to collect; **r. le gaz** to read the gas meter

(h) *(défi)* to accept

(i) *(sauce, plat)* to spice up

(j) *(remplacer) (troupes, sentinelle)* to relieve

(k) *(libérer)* **r. qn de ses fonctions** to relieve sb of his/her duties

2 relever de *vt ind* **(a)** *(dépendre de) (personne, autorité)* to be answerable to; **r. de l'article 7** to come under article 7; **cette affaire relève de la justice** this is a matter for the courts; **son cas relève de la folie** he's/she's well and truly insane

(b) *(se remettre de)* to be recovering from

3 se relever *vpr* **(a)** *(après une chute)* to get up

(b) *(accoudoir, siège)* to lift up

(c) *(se remettre)* **se r. de qch** to get over sth, to recover from sth

relief [rəljɛf] *nm* **(a)** *(d'un paysage, d'une médaille)* relief; **en r.** in relief; *Fig* **mettre qch en r.** *(idées, qualité)* to bring sth out; *(beauté)* to set sth off; *(avantage)* to highlight sth; **sans r.** *(paysage, style)* flat **(b)** *Litt* **reliefs** *(d'un repas)* remains; *Fig (de la gloire)* shreds **(c)** *Ordinat* highlight; **mettre qch en r.** to highlight sth

relier [66] [rəlje] **1** *vt* **(a)** *(mettre en contact)* to connect, to link (**à** to) **(b)** *(idées, faits)* to link together **(c)** *(livre)* to bind

2 se relier *vpr Ordinat* to link up

relieur, -euse [rəljœr, -øz] *nm,f* (book)binder

religieusement [rəliʒjøzmɑ̃] *adv* **(a)** *(selon la religion)* religiously; **se marier r.** to get married in church **(b)** *(avec révérence)* reverently **(c)** *(scrupuleusement)* religiously

religieux, -euse [rəliʒjø, -øz] **1** *adj* religious; *(mariage)* church; *Fig (silence)* respectful

2 *nm (moine)* monk

3 *nf* **religieuse (a)** *(sœur)* nun **(b)** *(gâteau)* cream puff

religion [rəliʒjɔ̃] *nf* religion; **entrer en r.** to join a religious order

reliquaire [rəlikɛr] *nm* reliquary

reliquat [rəlika] *nm (d'argent)* remainder; **r. de caisse** cash balance; **r. de compte** account balance

relique [rəlik] *nf* relic

relire [44] [rəlir] **1** *vt* **(a)** *(livre, auteur, notes)* to reread **(b)** *(épreuves)* to proofread

2 se relire *vpr* to read (over) what one has written

reliure [rəljyr] *nf* **(a)** *(activité, art)* bookbinding **(b)** *(couverture)* binding

reloger [45] [rələʒe] *vt* to rehouse

relooker [rəluke] *vt Fam* to revamp

reluire [18] [rəlɥir] *vi (parquet, meuble, métal)* to shine, to gleam; **faire r. qch** to polish sth (up)

reluisant, -e [rəlɥizɑ̃, -ɑ̃t] *adj* **(a)** *(parquet, meuble, métal)* shining, gleaming **(b)** *Fig* **ce qu'il a fait n'est pas très r.** what he did doesn't reflect very well on him

reluquer [rəlyke] *vt Fam* to ogle

remâcher [rəmɑʃe] *vt (colère, échec)* to brood over

remake [rimɛk] *nm* remake

remaniement [rəmanimɑ̃] *nm* **(a)** *(d'un texte)* revision **(b)** **r. ministériel** cabinet reshuffle

remanier [66] [rəmanje] *vt* **(a)** *(texte)* to revise **(b)** *(ministère)* to reshuffle

remariage [rəmarjaʒ] *nm* remarriage

remarier [66] [rəmarje] **se remarier** *vpr* to remarry; **se r. avec qn** to remarry sb

remarquable [rəmarkabl] *adj* remarkable (**par** for)

remarquablement [rəmarkabləmɑ̃] *adv* remarkably

remarque [rəmark] *nf* **(a)** *(orale)* remark; **faire une r.** to make a remark; **faire une r. à qn sur qch** to pass a remark to sb about sth **(b)** *(écrite)* comment

remarqué, -e [rəmarke] *adj (entrée, absence)* conspicuous; *(intervention)* that attracted attention

remarquer [rəmarke] **1** *vt* (**a**) *(observer)* to notice; **faire r. qch à qn** to point sth out to sb; **je vous ferai r. que...** I'd like to point out that...; **se faire r.** to attract attention; *Fam* **remarque, il n'est pas le seul** he's not the only one, mind you (**b**) *(dire)* to remark, to observe

2 se remarquer *vpr (tache, cicatrice)* to show

remballer [rãbale] *vt (marchandises)* to repack; *Fig (compliment)* to keep to oneself

rembarrer [rãbare] *vt Fam* to snub; **se faire r.** to be snubbed *or* rebuffed

remblai [rãblɛ] *nm* embankment

remblayer [53] [rãbleje] *vt (route, voie ferrée)* to bank (up)

rembobiner [rãbɔbine] **1** *vt* to rewind

2 se rembobiner *vpr* to rewind

rembourrage [rãburaʒ] *nm (action, matériau)* stuffing

rembourrer [rãbure] *vt* to stuff

remboursable [rãbursabl] *adj (emprunt)* repayable; *(frais)* refundable

remboursement [rãbursəmã] *nm (d'un emprunt)* repayment; *(de frais)* refund

rembourser [rãburse] *vt* (**a**) *(frais, achat)* to refund; *(emprunt, dettes)* to pay back; **ce médicament est remboursé à 70%** 70% of the cost of this medicine will be refunded (**b**) *(personne)* to pay back; **r. qn de qch** to reimburse sb for sth; **se faire r.** to get a refund; *Fam* **remboursez!** *(au théâtre)* give us our money back!

rembrunir [rãbrynir] **se rembrunir** *vpr (visage, personne)* to become sullen

remède [rəmɛd] *nm* remedy, cure (**contre** for); **r. de bonne femme** old wives' remedy; **r. de cheval** kill-or-cure remedy

remédier [66] [rəmedje] **remédier à** *vt ind (erreur, situation)* to remedy; *(inconvénient)* to make up for

remembrement [rəmãbrəmã] *nm (de terres)* grouping of land

remémorer [rəmemɔre] **se remémorer** *vpr* to remember

remerciement [rəmɛrsimã] *nm* **lettre de r.** thank-you letter; **remerciements** thanks; *(dans un discours)* acknowledgments

remercier [66] [rəmɛrsje] *vt* (**a**) *(dire merci à)* to thank (**de** *ou* **pour** for); **r. qn d'avoir fait qch** to thank sb for doing sth; **(non,) je vous remercie** no, thank you (**b**) *Euph (congédier)* to ask to leave

remettre [47] [rəmɛtr] **1** *vt* (**a**) **r. qch à qn** *(lettre, télégramme, colis)* to deliver sth to sb; *(rapport)* to submit sth to sb; *(démission)* to hand sth in to sb; *(rançon)* to hand sth over to sb; **r. qn à la justice** to turn sb over to the police; **r. son sort entre les mains de qn** to put one's fate in sb's hands

(**b**) *(retarder)* to postpone (**à** to *or* till); **r. qch à plus tard** to put sth off till later

(**c**) *(replacer)* to put back; **r. qch à sa place** *ou* **en place** to put sth back in its place; **r. qch en cause** *ou* **en question** to call sth into question; **r. qn en liberté** to set sb free

(**d**) *(reconnaître)* **je ne vous remets pas** I can't place you

(**e**) *(dans un état antérieur)* **r. une montre à l'heure** to set a watch to the right time; **r. qch à zéro** to reset sth to zero; **r. qch en marche** *(moteur, machine)* to restart sth; **r. qch en ordre** *(dossiers, maison)* to tidy sth (up)

(**f**) *(rétablir la santé de)* to make better

(**g**) *(manteau, chapeau)* to put back on

(**h**) *(chauffage, télévision)* to turn on again; *(disque, chanson)* to put on again

(**i**) *(ajouter) (sel, eau)* to add (**dans** to)

(**j**) *Fam (recommencer)* **on remet ça?** how about another (one)?; **tu ne vas pas r. ça!** you're not going to start that again, are you?; *Belg* **r. le couvert** to start again

(**k**) *Belg & Suisse (céder)* to sell

2 se remettre *vpr* (**a**) *(dans un endroit, dans un état)* **se r. debout** to get up again; **se r. au lit** to go back to bed; **se r. en cause** *ou* **en question** to question oneself; **le temps s'est remis au beau** the weather has brightened up again

(**b**) *(recommencer)* **se r. à qch/à faire qch** to start sth/doing sth again; **se r. au français/au tennis** to take up French/tennis again

(**c**) *(après une maladie, un choc)* to recover (**de** from); *Fig* **voyons, remettez-vous!** come on, pull yourself together!

(**d**) *(faire confiance)* **je m'en remets à vous** I'll leave it to you, it's up to you

(**e**) *(se placer)* **se r. entre les mains de qn** to place oneself in sb's hands

(**f**) *Fam (renouer)* **se r. ensemble** to get back together again

réminiscence [reminisãs] *nf (souvenir imprécis)* vague recollection

remise [rəmiz] *nf* (**a**) *(dans son lieu ou son état d'origine)* **r. en état** *(d'une maison)* restoration; **r. à neuf** *(d'une machine)* reconditioning; **r. en question** *ou* **cause** questioning (**b**) *(d'une lettre)* delivery (**à** to); *(d'une machine)* handing over (**à** to); **r. des prix** prize ceremony (**c**) *(réduction)* **r. de peine** reduction of sentence (**d**) *(rabais)* discount; **faire une r. à qn** to give sb a discount (**e**) *(appentis)* shed (**f**) *Ordinat* **r. à blanc** *(d'une disquette)* reformatting; **r. en forme** *(de texte)* reformatting

remiser [rəmize] *vt* to put away

rémission [remisjɔ̃] *nf* (**a**) *(d'un péché)* remission; *Fig* **sans r.** *(travailler)* unremittingly; *(punir)* mercilessly (**b**) *(d'une maladie)* remission; **être en r.** to be in remission

remix [rəmiks] *nm Mus* remix

remixage [rəmiksaʒ] *nm Mus* remixing

remixer [rəmikse] *vt Mus* to remix

remmener [46] [rãmne] *vt* to take back; **r. qn en voiture** to drive sb back

remodeler [39] [rəmɔdle] *vt* (**a**) *(refaçonner)* to remodel (**b**) *(réorganiser)* to restructure

remontant [rəmɔ̃tã] *nm* tonic

remontée [rəmɔ̃te] *nf* (**a**) *(d'une pente)* ascent (**b**) *(dans un classement sportif)* recovery (**c**) *(des eaux)* rising (**d**) *(pour skieurs)* **r. mécanique** ski lift

remonte-pente (*pl* **remonte-pentes**) [rəmɔ̃tpãt] *nm* ski tow

remonter [rəmɔ̃te] **1** *vt* (**a**) *(pente, escalier) (en s'éloignant)* to go up again, to climb back up; *(en s'approchant)* to come up again, to climb back up; **r. la rue** to go/come up the street; **r. la rivière** to go upstream (**b**) *(hausser) (étagère, poster)* to move up; *(pantalon, jupe)* to hitch up; *(manche, chaussettes)* to pull up; *(fermeture éclair)* to do up; *(vitre de voiture)* to roll up (**c**) *(porter en haut)* to take/bring up (**d**) *(horloge, montre)* to wind (up) (**e**) *(revigorer) (personne)* to cheer up (**f**) *(pièces d'une machine)* to reassemble

2 *vi* (**a**) *(dans l'espace) (personne)* to go/come back up; *(marée)* to flow; *(baromètre)* to rise again; *(route, ruelle)* to climb again; *(jupe)* to ride up; **r. en voiture** to get back in one's car; *Fig* **r. dans les sondages** to improve one's position in the polls (**b**) *(dans le temps)* to go back (**à** to); **ça remonte à loin** *(tradition)* it goes back a long way; *(épisode)* it was a long time ago (**c**) *(actions, monnaie, température)* to go up again, to rise again

3 se remonter *vpr (moralement)* to cheer up; *(physiquement)* to recover one's strength

remontoir [rəmɔ̃twar] *nm* winder

remontrance [rəmɔ̃trãs] *nf* remonstrance; **faire des remontrances à qn** to remonstrate with sb

remontrer [rəmɔ̃tre] **1** *vt* **en r. à qn** to show one knows better than sb

2 se remontrer *vpr* to show oneself again

remords [rəmɔr] *nm* remorse; **avoir du** *ou* **des r.** to feel remorse; **je n'ai aucun r.!** I'm not the least bit sorry!

remorque [rəmɔrk] *nf* (**a**) *(véhicule)* trailer (**b**) **prendre qch en r.** to take sth in tow; *Fig* **être à la r.** to lag behind

remorquer [rəmɔrke] *vt (voiture, bateau)* to tow; *(train)* to pull

remorqueur [rəmɔrkœr] *nm* tug(boat)

rémoulade [remulad] *nf Culin* (**sauce**) **r.** remoulade (sauce) *(mayonnaise sauce with mustard and herbs)*

rémouleur [remulœr] *nm* knife grinder

remous [rəmu] *nm (d'une rivière)* eddy; *(d'un bateau)* wash; *Fig (de la foule)* ripple; *Fig* **provoquer** *ou* **faire des r.** to cause a stir

rempailler [rɑ̃paje] *vt* to reseat

rempart [rɑ̃par] *nm* rampart; **remparts** walls; **faire un r. de son corps à qn** to shield sb with one's body

rempiler [rɑ̃pile] *vi Fam Hum* to sign up again

remplaçable [rɑ̃plasabl] *adj* replaceable

remplaçant, -e [rɑ̃plasɑ̃, -ɑ̃t] *nm,f (personne)* replacement; *(d'un médecin)* locum tenens; *(d'un enseignant)* substitute teacher

remplacement [rɑ̃plasmɑ̃] *nm* replacement; **en r. de qn/qch** in place of sb/sth; **faire des remplacements** *(professeur)* to work as a substitute teacher

remplacer [16] [rɑ̃plase] *vt* (**a**) *(être à la place de)* to take the place of, to replace; *(professionnellement)* to stand in for; **se faire r.** to get somebody to stand in *or* cover for one (**b**) *(substituer)* to replace (**par** with)

remplir [rɑ̃plir] **1** *vt* (**a**) *(récipient)* to fill (**de** with); *(espace, trou)* to fill (in); *Fig (journée, vie)* to take up; **r. qn de joie/colère** to fill sb with joy/anger (**b**) *(formulaire)* to fill in *or* out; *(chèque)* to write, to make out; *(page)* to fill (**c**) *(promesse, rôle, contrat)* to fulfill; *(devoirs, tâche)* to carry out
2 se remplir *vpr* to fill up (**de** with); *Fig* **se r. les poches** to line one's pockets

remplissage [rɑ̃plisaʒ] *nm* (**a**) *(d'un tonneau, d'un réservoir)* filling (up); *(d'un trou, d'un espace)* filling (in) (**b**) *Péj* **faire du r.** *(dans un texte)* to pad

remplumer [rɑ̃plyme] **se remplumer** *vpr Fam* (**a**) *(financièrement)* to be in funds again (**b**) *(grossir)* to put some weight back on

rempocher [rɑ̃pɔʃe] *vt* to put back in one's pocket

remporter [rɑ̃pɔrte] *vt* (**a**) *(reprendre)* to take back *or* away (**b**) *(gagner) (prix, victoire)* to win; *(succès)* to achieve; *Fig* **r. tous les suffrages** to meet with universal approval

rempoter [rɑ̃pɔte] *vt* to repot

remuant, -e [rəmɥɑ̃, -ɑ̃t] *adj* hyperactive

remue-ménage [rəmymenaʒ] *nm inv* commotion; **faire du r.** to cause a commotion *or* stir

remuer [rəmɥe] **1** *vt* (**a**) *(partie du corps)* to move around; *(lèvres)* to move; **r. la queue** *(chien)* to wag its tail; **r. les oreilles** *(chien)* to waggle its ears (**b**) *(mobilier, objets)* to move, to shift (**c**) *(sauce, café)* to stir; *(salade)* to toss; *(terre)* to turn over; *Fig (vieux souvenirs, passé)* to rake up; **r. ciel et terre pour faire qch** to move heaven and earth to do sth (**d**) *(émouvoir)* to move
2 *vi (personne)* to move; *(queue)* to wag; **arrête de r.!** don't fidget!, keep still!
3 se remuer *vpr* (**a**) *(bouger)* to move (**b**) *Fam (être actif)* to have plenty of get-up-and-go; **remue-toi un peu!** get up off your butt!

rémunérateur, -trice [remyneratœr, -tris] *adj (travail)* remunerative; *(placement)* interest-bearing

rémunération [remynerasjɔ̃] *nf* remuneration (**de** for); *(salaire)* pay

rémunérer [34] [remynere] *vt (personne)* to pay; *(travail, services)* to pay for; **travail bien/mal rémunéré** well-paid/badly-paid job

renâcler [rənɑkle] *vi (personne)* to balk (**à faire** at doing); **il a accepté en renâclant** he accepted grudgingly

renaissance [rənɛsɑ̃s] *nf* (**a**) *(d'une personne)* rebirth (**b**) *(des lettres, des arts)* renaissance; **la R.** the Renaissance

renaître [50a] [rənɛtr] *vi* (**a**) *(personne)* to be born again; **r. de ses cendres** to rise again from its ashes (**b**) *(industrie, arts, espoir)* to revive; *Litt (printemps, plantes)* to return; *(nature)* to reawaken; **faire r. la confiance** to restore confidence

rénal, -e, -aux, -ales [renal, -o] *adj* renal

renard [rənar] *nm* (**a**) *(animal)* fox; *Fig* **c'est un vieux r.** he's a sly old fox (**b**) *(fourrure)* fox (fur)

renardeau, -x [rənardo] *nm* fox cub

rencard, rencart [rɑ̃kar] = **rancard**

renchérir [rɑ̃ʃerir] *vi* (**a**) *(prix, loyers, marchandises)* to go up (**b**) *(dire ou faire plus)* to go one better (**sur** than)

rencontre [rɑ̃kɔ̃tr] *nf* (**a**) *(de personnes)* meeting; *(de routes, de cours d'eau)* junction; **faire la r. de qn** to meet sb; **faire de mauvaises rencontres** to meet the wrong kind of people; **aller à la r. de qn** to go to meet sb (**b**) *(d'athlétisme)* meet; *(match)* game, match

rencontrer [rɑ̃kɔ̃tre] **1** *vt* (**a**) *(personne)* to meet; **r. qn par hasard** to bump into *or* to run into sb (**b**) *(trouver)* to come across; *(opposition, difficulté)* to encounter, to come up against
2 se rencontrer *vpr* (**a**) *(gens, rivières)* to meet (**b**) *Hum (être d'accord)* **les grands esprits se rencontrent** great minds think alike

rendement [rɑ̃dmɑ̃] *nm* (**a**) *(d'une terre, d'un impôt)* yield; *(d'un investissement)* return, yield (**b**) *(de travailleurs, d'une usine, d'une machine)* output; *(d'un ordinateur)* throughput; **travailler à plein r.** *(usine)* to work at full capacity

rendez-vous [rɑ̃devu] *nm inv* (**a**) *(rencontre)* appointment; *(amoureux)* date; **avoir r. chez le médecin** to have an appointment with the doctor; **donner r. à qn** to arrange to meet sb; **prendre r. avec qn/chez le médecin** to make an appointment with sb/with the doctor (**b**) *(endroit)* meeting place

rendormir [29] [rɑ̃dɔrmir] **se rendormir** *vpr* to fall asleep again

rendre [rɑ̃dr] **1** *vt* (**a**) *(objet emprunté)* to give back, to return (**à** to); *(achat)* to take back (**à** to); *(copies, cadeau)* to give back (**à** to); *(otages)* to hand back (**à** to); **r. sa liberté à qn** to set sb free (**b**) *(rembourser)* to pay back
(**c**) *(en retour)* **je lui ai rendu son compliment/son invitation** I returned his/her compliment/his/her invitation; **r. la monnaie à qn** to give sb his/her change; *Fig* **r. à qn la monnaie de sa pièce** to get even with sb; **r. les armes** *(soldats)* to surrender; *Fig* to give up; *Fig* **elle l'aime, mais il ne le lui rend pas** she loves him, but the feeling isn't mutual
(**d**) *(vomir)* to bring up
(**e**) *(son)* to make; *(jus, eau)* to release
(**f**) *Jur (jugement, verdict)* to deliver; **r. la justice** to dispense justice
(**g**) *(sens, nuance)* to render, to express
(**h**) *(faire devenir)* to make; **r. qn triste** to make sb sad; **r. qn fou** to drive sb mad; **r. qn aveugle/sourd** to make sb go blind/deaf; *Fig* **l'amour l'a rendu aveugle** he was blinded by love
2 *vi* (**a**) *(terre)* to be productive; *(placement)* to yield (**b**) *(vomir)* to vomit
3 se rendre *vpr* (**a**) *(aller)* **se r. à** to go to; **se r. chez qn** to call on sb
(**b**) *(se soumettre)* to give oneself up
(**c**) *(devenir)* **se r. malade/utile** to make oneself ill/useful
(**d**) *(locutions)* **se r. compte de qch/que...** to realize sth/that...; *Fam* **tu te rends compte!** who'd have believed it!; **se r. à la raison** to see reason

rendu, -e [rɑ̃dy] *adj* (**a**) *(arrivé)* **être r.** to have arrived (**b**) *Vieilli (fatigué)* tired out

rêne [rɛn] *nf* rein; *Fig* **c'est lui qui tient les rênes** he's the one who's really in charge

renégat, -e [rənega, -at] *nm,f* renegade

renfermé, -e [rɑ̃fɛrme] **1** *adj (personne)* withdrawn
 2 nm odeur de r. musty smell; **sentir le r.** to smell musty
renfermer [rɑ̃fɛrme] **1** *vt (contenir)* to contain
 2 se renfermer *vpr* to withdraw into oneself
renflé, -e [rɑ̃fle] *adj* bulging
renflement [rɑ̃fləmɑ̃] *nm* bulge
renflouer [rɑ̃flue] *vt* (**a**) *(bateau échoué)* to refloat (**b**) *(entreprise, personne)* to bail out
renfoncement [rɑ̃fɔ̃smɑ̃] *nm* recess
renforcement [rɑ̃fɔrsəmɑ̃] *nm (d'une poutre, d'une armée, d'une équipe)* strengthening, reinforcement; *(de la sécurité)* tightening up
renforcer [16] [rɑ̃fɔrse] **1** *vt* (**a**) *(poutre, armée, équipe)* to strengthen, to reinforce; *(sécurité)* to tighten up (**b**) *(couleur, éclairage)* to intensify (**c**) *(crainte)* to heighten; *(impression, convictions)* to strengthen; **r. qn dans une opinion** to confirm sb in an opinion
 2 se renforcer *vpr (tendance, impression, convictions)* to grow
renfort [rɑ̃fɔr] *nm* **renforts** reinforcements; *Fig* **demander du r.** to ask for help; **à grand r. de qch** with the help of lots of sth
renfrogné, -e [rɑ̃frɔɲe] *adj* scowling
renfrogner [rɑ̃frɔɲe] **se renfrogner** *vpr* to scowl
rengager [45] [rɑ̃gaʒe] **1** *vt (personnel)* to take on again; *(combat)* to renew; *(conversation, partie, débat)* to pick up again
 2 se rengager *vpr Mil* to re-enlist
rengaine [rɑ̃gɛn] *nf* tune; *Fam Fig* **c'est toujours la même r.** it's (always) the same old story
rengainer [rɑ̃gɛne] *vt (épée)* to sheathe; *Fig (compliment)* to keep to oneself
rengorger [45] [rɑ̃gɔrʒe] **se rengorger** *vpr* to strut
reniement [rənimɑ̃] *nm (d'une foi)* denial; *(d'idées, d'une action)* repudiation
renier [66] [rənje] **1** *vt (fils, racines)* to disown; *(foi)* to deny; *(action, idées)* to repudiate
 2 se renier *vpr* to repudiate one's opinions
reniflement [rənifləmɑ̃] *nm* (**a**) *(action)* sniffing (**b**) *(bruit)* sniff
renifler [rənifle] **1** *vi* to sniff
 2 *vt (fleur)* to sniff (at); *(tabac à priser)* to sniff; *Fig (bonne affaire, embrouille)* to sniff out
renipper [rənipe] *Can1 vt (rénover) (maison, pièce)* to renovate, to do up
 2 se renipper *vpr* to smarten oneself up
renne [rɛn] *nm* reindeer
renom [rənɔ̃] *nm* renown; **de r.** famous, renowned; **de grand r.** extremely famous
renommé, -e [rənɔme] *adj* renowned, famous (**pour** for)
renommée [rənɔme] *nf* fame, renown; **un musicien de r. internationale** a world-famous musician, a musician of international repute *or* renown
renommer [rənɔme] *vt Ordinat (fichier)* to rename
renoncement [rənɔ̃smɑ̃] *nm* renunciation (**à** of)
renoncer [16] [rənɔ̃se] **renoncer à** *vt ind (droit, projet, activité)* to give up, to abandon; *(vacances, voyage)* to sacrifice, to forego; *(titre)* to renounce; **r. à faire qch** to give up doing sth; *(avant d'avoir commencé)* to give up the idea of doing sth; **je renonce!** I give up!
renonciation [rənɔ̃sjasjɔ̃] *nf* renunciation (**à** of)
renoncule [rənɔ̃kyl] *nf* buttercup
renouer [rənwe] **1** *vt* (**a**) *(ruban, lacet)* to tie (up) again; *(cravate)* to do up again (**b**) *(conversation, relations)* to resume; *(amitié)* to renew
 2 renouer avec *vt ind* **r. avec qn** to take up with sb again; **r. avec qch** *(tradition)* to revive sth; *(habitude)* to go back to sth
renouveau, -x [rənuvo] *nm* revival

renouvelable [rənuvlabl] *adj (contrat, énergie)* renewable; *(expérience)* repeatable
renouveler [9] [rənuvle] **1** *vt* (**a**) *(stock, équipement)* to renew, to replace; *(eau)* to change (**b**) *(passeport, abonnement, demande)* to renew; *(expérience)* to repeat (**c**) *(style)* to change
 2 se renouveler *vpr* (**a**) *(cellule)* to be renewed (**b**) *(se produire de nouveau)* to recur, to happen again (**c**) *(changer)* to change; **un artiste/auteur qui ne se renouvelle pas** an artist/author whose style never changes
renouvellement [rənuvɛlmɑ̃] *nm* (**a**) *(de stock, d'équipement)* replacement, renewal (**b**) *(d'un style)* change (**c**) *(d'un traité, d'un contrat)* renewal
rénovateur, -trice [renovatœr, -tris] **1** *adj* reforming
 2 *nm,f* reformer
rénovation [renovasjɔ̃] *nf* (**a**) *(d'un bâtiment, du mobilier)* renovation; **en (cours de) r.** undergoing renovation (**b**) *(d'une institution)* updating, reform
rénover [renove] *vt* (**a**) *(bâtiment, mobilier)* to renovate (**b**) *(institution)* to update, to reform
renseigné, -e [rɑ̃seɲe] *adj* **bien/mal r.** well-/ill-informed
renseignement [rɑ̃seɲəmɑ̃] *nm* (**a**) *(précision)* piece of information; **renseignements** information; **pour tout r....** for information...; **prendre des renseignements sur qn/qch** to make inquiries about sb/sth; **aller aux renseignements** to go and make inquiries (**b**) *Tél* **les renseignements (téléphoniques)** information; **appeler les renseignements** to call information (**c**) **les renseignements généraux** = secret intelligence branch of the French police, ≃ the FBI
renseigner [rɑ̃seɲe] **1** *vt* **r. qn (sur qch)** to give sb some information (about sth), to inform sb (about sth); **on vous a mal renseigné** you have been misinformed
 2 se renseigner *vpr* to make inquiries; *(sur un point précis)* to find out (**sur** about)
rentabiliser [rɑ̃tabilize] *vt* to make profitable
rentabilité [rɑ̃tabilite] *nf* profitability
rentable [rɑ̃tabl] *adj* profitable
rente [rɑ̃t] *nf* (**a**) *(revenu)* **rentes** private income (**b**) *(pension)* annuity, pension; **r. viagère** life annuity (**c**) *(emprunt d'État)* (government) loan
rentier, -ère [rɑ̃tje, -ɛr] *nm,f* person of private means
rentré, -e [rɑ̃tre] *adj* (**a**) *(yeux)* sunken (**b**) *(colère)* suppressed
rentre-dedans [rɑ̃trədədɑ̃] *nm inv Fam* **faire du r. à qn** to come on to sb
rentrée [rɑ̃tre] *nf* (**a**) *(retour)* return; **la r. (des classes)** the start of the new school year; **r. parlementaire** reopening of Parliament; **la r. sociale** the return to work (**b**) *(d'argent)* **attendre une r. d'argent** to expect some money

---

La rentrée

The time of the year when children go back to school – in September – has considerable cultural significance in France. Coming after the long summer vacation or "grandes vacances", it is the time when academic, political, social and business activity begins again in earnest.

---

rentrer [rɑ̃tre] **1** *vi (aux être)* (**a**) *(entrer de nouveau) (en s'éloignant)* to go in again; *(en s'approchant)* to come in again; *(entrer)* to go/come in, to enter; **rentre!** come in!
 (**b**) *(à la maison)* to go/come back home, to return home; **r. de vacances/de Paris** to come back from vacation/from Paris; **r. en France/à Paris** to return to France/to Paris; **r. dans son pays** to go back to one's own country; **r. tard/tôt** to come *or* to get home late/early; **en rentrant chez moi** on my way home; **en rentrant de l'école** on my/his/*etc.* way home from school
 (**c**) *(reprendre ses occupations) (école)* to re-open; *(élève, professeur)* to go back

(d) *(tenir) (objets)* to go in, to fit (in); **je ne rentre plus dans ce pantalon!** I can't get into these pants any more! **(e)** *(pénétrer)* to get in; **r. dans qch** to get into sth **(f)** *(être inclus)* **r. dans une catégorie** to fall into a category **(g)** *(argent)* to come in **(h)** *(recouvrer)* **r. dans ses frais** to recover one's expenses **(i)** **r. dans** *(sujet: voiture)* to crash into; *(sujet: piéton)* to bang into; *Fam Fig* **elle m'est rentrée dedans** *ou* **dans le chou** she laid into me **2** *vt (aux avoir)* **(a)** *(linge, troupeau) (en venant)* to bring in; *(en allant)* to take in **(b)** *(introduire, mettre)* to put in; **r. qch dans qch** to put sth into sth **(c)** *(train d'atterrissage)* to retract, to raise; **r. ses griffes** *(chat)* to retract its claws; *Fig* to draw in one's claws; **r. le ventre** to pull one's stomach in **(d)** *(colère, larmes)* to stifle

renversant, -e [rãversã, -ãt] *adj Fam* astounding

renverse [rãvers] **à la renverse** *adv* **partir** *ou* **tomber à la r.** to fall backward; *Fig* **j'ai failli tomber à la r.** you could have knocked me over with a feather

renversé, e [rãverse] *adj* **(a)** *(à l'envers) (image)* reversed **(b)** *(tombé)* overturned **(c)** *Fam (stupéfait)* staggered

renversement [rãversəmã] *nm* **(a)** *(d'une tendance, des rôles)* reversal; *(d'opinions)* (dramatic) shift; **r. de situation** reversal of the situation **(b)** *(d'un gouvernement)* overthrow

renverser [rãverse] **1** *vt* **(a)** *(tendance, rôles)* to reverse; *(ordre)* to invert; *Fig* **r. la vapeur** to do a U-turn; **r. la situation** to reverse the situation **(b)** *(pencher en arrière)* **r. la tête** to tilt one's head back **(c)** *(faire tomber)* to knock over; *(liquide)* to spill; **se faire r. par une voiture** to be knocked down by a car **(d)** *(gouvernement)* to overthrow **(e)** *Fam (stupéfier)* to stagger **2 se renverser** *vpr* **(a)** *(récipient)* to fall over; *(véhicule)* to overturn **(b)** *(personne)* **se r. en arrière** to lean back

renvoi [rãvwa] *nm* **(a)** *(de lettres, de marchandises, de colis)* return, sending back **(b)** *(d'employés)* dismissal; *(d'un élève)* expulsion, exclusion **(c)** *(ajournement)* postponement; *Jur* adjournment **(d)** *(dans un texte)* cross-reference **(e)** *Jur (devant une autre juridiction)* transfer **(devant** to) **(f)** *(éructation)* burp, belch; **avoir des renvois** to burp, to belch

renvoyer [33] [rãvwaje] **1** *vt* **(a)** *(au point de départ) (personne)* to send back; *(cadeau, lettre)* to send back, to return; *(ballon)* to throw back; *(balle de tennis)* to return **(b)** *(employé)* to dismiss; *(élève)* to expel, to exclude; *(visiteur)* to send away **(c)** *(son)* to echo; *(chaleur, lumière)* to reflect **(d)** *(ajourner)* *Jur* to adjourn **(e)** *(lecteur)* to refer **(à** to) *Ordinat* to cross-refer **(f)** *Jur (devant une autre juridiction)* to transfer **(devant** to) **(g)** *(envoyer de nouveau) (e-mail, SMS)* to resend **2** *vi Can* to vomit

réorganisation [reɔrganizasjɔ̃] *nf* reorganization

réorganiser [reɔrganize] **1** *vt* to reorganize **2 se réorganiser** *vpr* to get reorganized

réorienter [reɔrjãte] *vt* to reorient; *Univ* **r. un étudiant** to change a student's major

réouverture [reuvertyr] *nf* reopening

repaire [rəper] *nm (d'animaux)* den, lair; *(de malfrats)* haunt

repaître [50c] [rəpɛtr] *Litt* **1** *vt* **r. ses yeux de qch** to feast one's eyes on sth **2 se repaître** *vpr* **(a)** *(manger à satiété)* to eat one's fill **(b)** *Fig* **se r. de qch** to revel in sth

répandre [repãdr] **1** *vt* **(a)** *(renverser) (accidentellement)* to spill; *(volontairement)* to spread **(b)** *(émettre) (lumière)* to shed; *(odeur, chaleur)* to give off **(c)** *(larmes, sang)* to shed **(d)** *(rumeur, terreur, doctrine)* to spread **2 se répandre** *vpr* **(a)** *(liquide)* to spill **(b)** *(odeur, chaleur)* to spread **(c)** *(rumeur, opinion, pratique)* to become widespread **(d)** *(foule, touristes)* to spill **(dans** into) **(e)** **se r. en excuses** to apologize profusely

répandu, -e [repãdy] *adj (commun)* widespread

réparable [reparabl] *adj* **(a)** *(chaussure, machine)* repairable **(b)** *(erreur)* which can be set right; *(perte financière)* which can be made up

reparaître [20] [rəparɛtr] *vi* to reappear

réparateur, -trice [reparatœr, -tris] **1** *adj (sommeil)* refreshing **2** *nm,f* repairman, *f* repairwoman

réparation [reparasjɔ̃] *nf* **(a)** *(action)* repairing, fixing; *(résultat)* repair; **faire des réparations** to do repairs **(b)** *(dédommagement)* reparation; **demander r. (de qch)** to seek redress (for sth)

réparer [repare] *vt* **(a)** *(toit, appareil, chaussures)* to repair, to fix; *(déchirure, accroc)* to mend **(b)** *(faute)* to make amends for; *(erreur)* to fix, to rectify; *(dommage)* to make good

reparler [rəparle] *vi* to speak again; **r. à qn** to speak to sb again; **elle ne lui a pas reparlé depuis** she hasn't spoken to him since; **r. de qch** to speak about sth again; **on en reparlera** we'll talk about it later

repartie, répartie [reparti] *nf* retort; **avoir l'esprit de r., avoir de la r.** to be good at repartee

repartir [64a] [rəpartir] *vi (voyageur, train)* to set off again (**pour** to); *(machine)* to start (up) again; *Fam* **c'est reparti, ils ont encore mis la musique à fond!** they're at it again, they've turned their music on full blast!; *Fam* **c'est reparti comme en quarante!** here we go!

répartir [repartir] **1** *vt* **(a)** *(tâches, argent, vivres)* to divide (**entre** between); *(responsabilités)* to allocate (**entre** between); *(frais)* to share (**entre** between) **(b)** *(dans le temps)* to spread (out) (**sur** over) **(c)** *(classifier)* to divide (**en** into) **(d)** *(poids, charge)* to distribute **2 se répartir** *vpr* **(a)** *(se diviser)* to split up (**en** into) **(b)** *(se classer)* to be divided (**en** into) **(c)** **se r. qch** to divide sth up

répartition [repartisjɔ̃] *nf* **(a)** *(de la population, du poids)* distribution **(b)** *(des tâches, d'argent, de vivres)* distribution (**entre** between); *(des dépenses, des responsabilités)* allocation (**entre** to) **(c)** *(dans le temps)* spreading (**sur** over)

repas [rəpɑ] *nm* meal; **prendre un r.** to have a meal; **r. d'affaires** business lunch/dinner; **r. chaud/froid** hot/cold meal; **r. de noce** wedding meal

repassage [rəpasaʒ] *nm* ironing; **faire du r.** to do some ironing

repasser [rəpase] **1** *vi* **(a)** *(passer à nouveau) (aller)* to go by again, to pass by again; *(venir)* to come by again, to pass by again; *(retourner)* to go/come back; **r. chez qn** to drop in on sb again **(b)** *(film)* to be showing again **2** *vt* **(a)** *(vêtement)* to iron **(b)** *(montagne, frontière)* to go across again **(c)** *(cassette, disque)* to play again; *(film)* to show again **(d)** *(leçon)* to go over; **r. qch dans son esprit** to go over sth in one's mind **(e)** *(examen)* to retake **(f)** **r. qch à qn** *(donner à nouveau)* to give sb sth again **(g)** *(au téléphone)* **je vous le repasse** I'll put him back on (for you)

repêchage [rəpɛʃaʒ] *nm* **(a)** *(d'un véhicule, d'un noyé)* fishing out **(b)** *(d'un candidat)* **épreuve de r.** repeat exam; **être reçu au r.** to pass second time around

repêcher [rəpeʃe] *vt* **(a)** *(retirer de l'eau)* to fish out **(b)** *(candidat)* to let through

repeindre [54] [rəpɛ̃dr] *vt* to repaint

repenser [rəpãse] **1** *vt (concept)* to rethink **2 repenser à** *vt ind* to think again about; **quand j'y repense** when I think back

repenti, -e [rəpãti] *adj* repentant, penitent

repentir[1] [rəpãtir] *nm (remords)* regret

repentir[2] [64a] [rəpãtir] **se repentir** *vpr* to repent; **se r. de qch/d'avoir fait qch** to repent of sth/doing sth; *Fig* to regret sth/doing sth

repérage [rəperaʒ] *nm* **(a)** *Ordinat* marking, flagging **(b)** *(d'un lieu de tournage)* scouting for locations

répercussion [repɛrkysjɔ̃] *nf* (**a**) *(du son)* reverberation (**b**) *(conséquence)* repercussion (**sur** on)

répercuter [repɛrkyte] **1** *vt* (**a**) *(son, lumière)* to reflect (**b**) *(ordre, augmentation)* to pass (**sur** on to)

2 se répercuter *vpr* (**a**) *(son, lumière)* to be reflected (**b**) *(avoir des conséquences)* **se r. sur** to have repercussions on

repère [rəpɛr] *nm* (**a**) *(point de référence)* mark; *(pour s'orienter)* landmark; *aussi Fig* **point de r.** reference point (**b**) *(dans le temps)* reference point (**c**) *Ordinat* marker, flag

repérer [34] [repere] **1** *vt* (**a**) *(marquer) (terrain)* to mark out (**b**) *(trouver) (défaut, endroit)* to locate; *(lieu de tournage)* to scout for locations (**c**) *Fam (apercevoir)* to spot; **se faire r.** to attract attention

2 se repérer *vpr* to get one's bearings, to find one's way around

répertoire [repɛrtwar] *nm* (**a**) *(liste)* index, list (**b**) *(carnet)* notebook with alphabetical index; **r. à onglets** thumb index (**c**) *Ordinat* directory; **r. central** *ou* **principal** main directory; **r. racine** root directory (**d**) *(d'un théâtre, d'un artiste)* repertoire

répertorier [66] [repɛrtɔrje] *vt* to list

répéter [34] [repete] **1** *vt* (**a**) *(redire, refaire)* to repeat (**b**) *(pièce de théâtre, rôle)* to rehearse

2 *vi (acteur)* to rehearse

3 se répéter *vpr (personne)* to repeat oneself; *(événement)* to recur, to happen again; **l'histoire se répète** history repeats itself

répétitif, -ive [repetitif, -iv] *adj* repetitive

répétition [repetisjɔ̃] *nf* (**a**) *(d'un mot, d'une action, d'un événement)* repetition; **fusil à r.** repeating rifle; **avoir des rhumes à r.** to have one cold after another (**b**) *(d'une pièce de théâtre)* rehearsal; **r. générale** dress rehearsal (**c**) *Ordinat* **fonction de r.** repeat function

repeuplement [rəpœpləmɑ̃] *nm (d'un pays)* repopulation; *(d'un étang)* restocking; *(d'une forêt)* replanting

repeupler [rəpœple] **1** *vt (pays)* to repopulate; *(étang)* to restock; *(forêt)* to replant

2 se repeupler *vpr (pays)* to be repopulated; *(étang)* to be restocked; *(forêt)* to be replanted

repiquage [rəpikaʒ] *nm* (**a**) *(de plants)* pricking out, planting out (**b**) *(d'un disque, d'une cassette)* taping

repiquer [rəpike] **1** *vt* (**a**) *(plants)* to prick out, to plant out (**b**) *(disque, cassette)* to record (**c**) *Fam (reprendre)* to catch again

2 *vi Fam* **il y a repiqué** he's been at it again

répit [repi] *nm* respite, breathing space; **sans r.** *(travailler)* without a break, continuously

replacer [16] [rəplase] **1** *vt* (**a**) *(remettre à sa place)* to put back; **r. les évènements dans leur contexte** to put events into their context (**b**) *Can (reconnaître)* to recognize

2 se replacer *vpr (trouver un emploi)* to find (oneself) a new job

replanter [rəplɑ̃te] *vt* to replant

replâtrer [rəplɑtre] *vt* (**a**) *(mur)* to replaster (**b**) *Péj* to patch up

replet, -ète [rəplɛ, -ɛt] *adj (personne)* podgy; *(visage)* chubby

repli [rəpli] *nm* (**a**) *(d'une armée)* retreat, withdrawal (**b**) *(de la monnaie, des prix)* fall (**c**) *(d'un vêtement, de la peau, d'un terrain)* fold; *(d'une rivière)* bend

replier [66] [rəplije] **1** *vt* (**a**) *(objet)* to fold up; *(lame de couteau)* to fold away; *(jambes)* to tuck up; *(ailes)* to fold (**b**) *(troupes)* to withdraw

2 se replier *vpr* (**a**) *(objet)* to fold up; *Fig* **se r. sur soi-même** to withdraw into oneself (**b**) *(troupes)* to retreat, to withdraw

réplique [replik] *nf* (**a**) *(réponse)* retort, rejoinder; **sans r.** unanswerable (**b**) *(d'un acteur)* line(s); **donner la r. à qn** to play opposite sb (**c**) *(copie)* replica; *(sosie)* double

répliquer [replike] **1** *vt* **r. que** to reply that; **je lui ai répliqué que...** I replied that...

2 *vi* to reply; *(avec impertinence)* to answer back; **r. à qn** to answer sb back

replonger [45] [rəplɔ̃ʒe] **1** *vt aussi Fig* to plunge back (**dans** into)

2 *vi* (**a**) *(plonger à nouveau)* to dive in again; *Fig* **r. dans l'alcoolisme/la délinquance** to relapse into alcoholism/delinquency (**b**) *Fam (délinquant)* to reoffend

3 se replonger *vpr* **se r. dans qch** to immerse oneself in sth again

répondant [repɔ̃dɑ̃] *nm Fam* **avoir du r.** to have plenty of money stashed away

répondeur [repɔ̃dœr] *nm* **r. (automatique** *ou* **téléphonique)** (telephone) answering machine

répondre [repɔ̃dr] **1** *vt* to answer, to reply; **je n'ai rien répondu** I made no reply

2 répondre à *vt ind* (**a**) *(personne, lettre, question)* to answer, to reply to; *(salut)* to return; *(accusation)* to answer; **elle n'a pas encore répondu** she hasn't answered yet; **r. par un sourire** to answer with a smile; *Mil* **r. à l'appel** to answer the roll call

(**b**) *(téléphone, porte)* to answer; **laisse, je vais r.!** leave it, I'll get it!; **ça ne répond pas** there's no answer

(**c**) *(amour)* to return

(**d**) *(besoin, critères)* to meet; **ne pas r. à l'attente de qn** to fall short of sb's expectations

(**e**) **les freins ne répondent plus** the brakes aren't responding any more

3 répondre de *vt ind* to answer for; **j'en réponds** I guarantee it; **je ne réponds de rien** I'm promising nothing

4 se répondre *vpr (personnes)* to answer each other

réponse [repɔ̃s] *nf* (**a**) *(à une question, à une lettre)* answer, reply (**à** to); *(à une offre d'emploi)* reply (**à** to); *Fig (solution)* answer (**à** to); **avoir r. à tout** to have an answer for everything (**b**) *(réaction)* response (**c**) *Ordinat* answering; **r. automatique** unattended answering; **temps de r.** response time

report [rəpɔr] *nm* (**a**) *(de notes, de corrections)* transfer (**sur** to) (**b**) *(d'un rendez-vous)* postponement (**c**) *(en comptabilité)* carrying forward (**d**) *(dans une élection)* **r. de voix (sur)** transfer (to)

reportage [rəpɔrtaʒ] *nm* (**a**) *(article, émission)* report (**b**) *(activité)* reporting

reporter¹ [rəpɔrtɛr] *nm* reporter; **r.-cameraman** television news reporter; **r.-photographe** photojournalist

reporter² [rəpɔrte] **1** *vt* (**a**) *(objet)* to take back, to return (**b**) *(affection)* to transfer (**sur** to) (**c**) *(différer)* **r. qch à plus tard** to postpone sth *or* to put sth off until later (**d**) *(en comptabilité)* to carry forward (**e**) *(notes, corrections)* to transfer (**sur** to) (**f**) *(dans une élection)* **r. sa voix sur qn** to transfer one's vote to sb

2 se reporter *vpr* (**a**) *(se référer)* **se r. à** *(document)* to refer to (**b**) **se r. sur** *(sujet: colère, affection)* to be transferred to

repos [rəpo] *nm* (**a**) *(détente)* rest; **un mois de r.** a month's rest; **prendre du r.** to rest; **le r. éternel** eternal rest (**b**) *(tranquillité)* peace; **ce n'est pas de tout r.!** it's not exactly restful! (**c**) *Mil* **r.!** (stand) at ease!

reposant, -e [rəpozɑ̃, -ɑ̃t] *adj* restful, relaxing

reposé, -e [rəpoze] *adj* rested, refreshed

repose-pied [rəpozpje] *nm inv* footrest

reposer [rəpoze] **1** *vt* (**a**) *(remettre)* to put back (down), to replace (**b**) *(appuyer)* **r. sa tête contre** *ou* **sur qch** to lean one's head against *or* on sth (**c**) *(détendre) (jambes, esprit)* to rest; **ça le reposera** it'll be a rest for him; **une couleur qui repose les yeux** a color that is restful to the eyes (**d**) *(question)* to ask again; *(problème)* to bring up again; **r. une question à qn** to ask sb a question again (**e**) *Mil* **reposez armes!** order arms!

2 *vi* (**a**) *(s'appuyer)* **r. sur** to rest on; *Fig (être basé sur)* to be based on; *(dépendre de)* to depend on (**b**) *(liquide)* to settle; *(pâte à tarte)* to rest (**c**) *(personne décédée)* to lie; **qu'il repose en paix** may he rest in peace

3 se reposer *vpr* (**a**) *(se relaxer)* to rest; **se r. les yeux/les**

jambes to rest one's eyes/legs (**b**) *(question, problème)* to crop up again (**c**) **se r. sur qn/qch** *(s'en remettre à)* to rely on sb/sth

repose-tête [rəpoztɛt] *nm inv* headrest

repoussant, -e [rəpusɑ̃, -ɑ̃t] *adj* repulsive

repousser [rəpuse] **1** *vt* (**a**) *(écarter)* to push aside *or* away; *(en arrière)* to push back (**b**) *(ennemi, attaque, avances)* to repel; *(offre, idée)* to reject, to turn down; *(prétendant)* to rebuff (**c**) *(rendez-vous, réunion)* to postpone, to put off (**à** until)
2 *vi (arbre, plante)* to shoot up again; *(cheveux, herbe, feuilles)* to grow again

repoussoir [rəpuswar] *nm (femme)* ugly woman; **servir de r. à qn** to serve as a foil to sb

répréhensible [repreɑ̃sibl] *adj* reprehensible

reprendre [58] [rəprɑ̃dr] **1** *vt* (**a**) *(ville, territoire, fugitif)* to recapture (**à** from)
(**b**) *(se resservir de)* **r. du pain/vin** to take *or* to have some more bread/wine; **vous reprendrez bien un peu de thé?** would you like some more tea?
(**c**) *(rechercher) (personne)* to pick up (again)
(**d**) *(récupérer) (objet)* to take back; **r. sa place** *(s'asseoir)* to return to one's seat; *Com* **les articles en solde ne sont ni repris ni échangés** ≃ sale goods are not returnable
(**e**) *(surprendre)* **r. qn à faire qch** to catch sb doing sth again; **on ne m'y reprendra plus!** I won't be caught again!; **que je ne t'y reprenne plus!** don't let me catch you at it again!
(**f**) *(conversation, fonctions, lutte)* to resume, to take up again; *(négociations, relations)* to re-open, to take up again; **r. le travail** to return *or* to go back to work; **r. connaissance** to regain consciousness; **r. la parole** to speak again; **"oui, mais...", reprit-il** "yes, but...", he continued; *Fam* **ça le reprend!** he's off again!
(**g**) *(répéter)* to repeat; *(refrain)* to take up
(**h**) *(retoucher) (vêtement)* to alter
(**i**) *(corriger)* to correct
2 *vi* (**a**) *(recommencer) (cours)* to start again; *(pourparlers, hostilités)* to resume, to re-open
(**b**) *(prendre de la vigueur) (affaires)* to recover, to pick up; *(plante)* to pick up
3 se reprendre *vpr* (**a**) *(se ressaisir)* to pull oneself together
(**b**) *(se corriger)* to correct oneself
(**c**) *(recommencer)* **s'y r. à plusieurs fois pour faire qch** to make several attempts at doing sth

repreneur [rəprənœr] *nm* purchaser, buyer

représailles [rəprezaj] *nfpl* reprisals, retaliation; **user de r. contre** to take retaliatory measures *or* to retaliate against; **en r.** in retaliation, as a reprisal

représentant, -e [rəprezɑ̃tɑ̃, -ɑ̃t] *nm,f* representative; **r. de commerce** sales representative

représentatif, -ive [rəprezɑ̃tatif, -iv] *adj* representative (**de** of)

représentation [rəprezɑ̃tasjɔ̃] *nf* (**a**) *(de la réalité, d'un concept)* representation (**b**) *(spectacle)* performance (**c**) *(métier)* commercial traveling (**d**) *Pol* **r. proportionnelle** proportional representation

représentativité [rəprezɑ̃tativite] *nf* representativeness

représenter [rəprezɑ̃te] **1** *vt* (**a**) *(candidat, papiers)* to present again (**b**) *(figurer)* to represent, to depict; **r. qn sous les traits de** to depict sb as (**c**) *(être le porte-parole de)* to represent (**d**) *(constituer, équivaloir à)* to represent; **r. qch pour qn** to represent sth for sb
2 se représenter *vpr* (**a**) *(occasion)* to arise again (**b**) *(s'imaginer)* to imagine (**c**) **se r. à** *(examen)* to retake; *(poste)* to apply for again; **se r. aux élections** to run for election again

répressif, -ive [represif, -iv] *adj* repressive

répression [represjɔ̃] *nf* repression; *(d'une émeute, d'un abus)* suppression

réprimande [reprimɑ̃d] *nf* reprimand, rebuke; **faire des réprimandes à qn** to reprimand *or* to rebuke sb

réprimander [reprimɑ̃de] *vt* to reprimand, to rebuke

réprimer [reprime] *vt* (**a**) *(retenir)* to repress, to suppress (**b**) *(crime, révolte)* to suppress

repris [rəpri] *nm* **r. de justice** ex-convict

reprise [rəpriz] *nf* (**a**) *(d'un débat, des hostilités)* resumption; *(des négociations)* re-opening, resumption (**b**) *(des affaires)* recovery; **les grévistes ont voté la r. du travail** the strikers have voted to go back to work; **r. économique** economic recovery (**c**) *(d'une émission télévisée)* rerun (**d**) *(d'un moteur)* pick-up, acceleration (**e**) **à plusieurs/trois reprises** several/three times (**f**) *(raccommodage)* **faire une r. à qch** to mend sth (**g**) *(somme payée à un locataire)* = money paid for the furnishings *(paid to outgoing tenant)*; *(rachat d'un objet d'occasion)* trade-in

repriser [rəprize] *vt* to mend

réprobateur, -trice [reprobatœr, -tris] *adj* reproving

réprobation [reprobasjɔ̃] *nf* reproof

reproche [rəprɔʃ] *nm* (**a**) *(remontrance)* reproach; **faire des reproches à qn (sur qch)** to reproach sb (for sth); **sans r.** *(vie, personne)* beyond reproach, blameless (**b**) *(critique)* criticism

reprocher [rəprɔʃe] **1** *vt* **r. qch à qn** to blame *or* to reproach sb for sth; **r. à qn de faire qch** to blame *or* to reproach sb for doing sth; **je ne vous reproche rien** I'm not blaming you for anything; **qu'est-ce que vous reprochez à ce livre?** what do you have against the book?
2 se reprocher *vpr* **se r. qch** to blame *or* to reproach oneself for sth; **tu n'as rien à te r.** you have nothing to blame yourself for; **se r. d'avoir fait qch** to blame oneself for doing sth

reproducteur, -trice [rəprodyktœr, -tris] *adj* reproductive

reproduction [rəprodyksjɔ̃] *nf* (**a**) *(sexuelle)* reproduction (**b**) *(d'un document, d'une image, du son)* reproduction, reproducing; *(copie)* reproduction

reproduire [18] [rəprodɥir] **1** *vt* (**a**) *(son, image, document)* to reproduce; **nous reproduisons ici l'article du Monde** we reprint here the article from Le Monde (**b**) *(acte)* to repeat
2 se reproduire *vpr* (**a**) *(sexuellement)* to reproduce (**b**) *(événement)* to recur, to happen again

reprogrammable [rəprogramabl] *adj Ordinat (touche)* reprogrammable

reprogrammer [rəprograme] *vt Ordinat* to reprogram

réprouver [repruve] *vt* to condemn

reptation [rɛptasjɔ̃] *nf* crawling

reptile [rɛptil] *nm* reptile

repu, -e [rəpy] **1** *pp voir* **repaître**
2 *adj* pleasantly full

républicain, -e [repyblikɛ̃, -ɛn] *adj & nm,f* republican

république [repyblik] *nf* republic; **r. bananière** banana republic; **la R. centrafricaine** the Central African Republic; *Anciennement* **la R. démocratique allemande** the German Democratic Republic; **la R. démocratique du Congo** the Democratic Republic of Congo; **la R. dominicaine** the Dominican Republic; *Anciennement* **la R. fédérale d'Allemagne** the Federal Republic of Germany; **la R. Tchèque** the Czech Republic

répudiation [repydjasjɔ̃] *nf* repudiation

répudier [66] [repydje] *vt* to repudiate

répugnance [repynɑ̃s] *nf* (**a**) *(aversion)* repugnance, loathing (**pour** for); **avoir de la r. pour qn/qch** to loathe sb/sth (**b**) *(appréhension)* reluctance (**à faire qch** to do sth)

répugnant, -e [repynɑ̃, -ɑ̃t] *adj* repulsive

répugner [repyne] *vi* (**a**) *(appréhender)* **r. à faire qch** to be reluctant to do sth (**b**) *(être répugnant)* **r. à qn** to be repugnant to sb, to repel sb

répulsion [repylsjɔ̃] *nf* repulsion

réputation [repytasjɔ̃] *nf* reputation; **avoir (une) bonne/mauvaise r.** to have a good/bad reputation; **sa r. de chirurgien** his reputation as a surgeon; **connaître qn de r.** to know sb by reputation; **avoir la r. d'être franc** to have a reputation for being frank

réputé, -e [repyte] *adj* well-known, renowned (**pour** for); **être r. intelligent** to be reputed to be intelligent

requérir [7] [rəkerir] *vt* (**a**) *(solliciter)* *(faveur)* to ask for, to seek; *(présence, aide)* to request (**b**) *(nécessiter)* *(explication, soin, patience)* to require, to call for (**c**) *Jur (sentence)* to demand, to call for

requête [rəkɛt] *nf* (**a**) *(demande)* request; *Ordinat* query; **adresser une r. à qn** to make a request to sb (**b**) *Jur* petition

requiem [rekɥijɛm] *nm inv* requiem

requiers, requiert *voir* **requérir**

requin [rəkɛ̃] *nm* shark

requinquer [rəkɛ̃ke] *Fam* **1** *vt* to perk up

   2 se requinquer *vpr* to perk up

requis, -e [rəki, -iz] **1** *pp voir* **requérir**

   2 *adj* requisite, required; **les conditions requises** the requirements

réquisition [rekizisjɔ̃] *nf* (**a**) *(de vivres, de véhicules)* requisitioning, commandeering (**b**) *Jur (plaidoirie)* closing speech for the prosecution

réquisitionner [rekizisjɔne] *vt* to requisition, to commandeer

réquisitoire [rekizitwar] *nm Jur* closing speech for the prosecution; *Fig* indictment (**contre** of)

RER [ɛrəɛr] *nm (abrév* **Réseau express régional**) = express rail network serving Paris and its suburbs

RESA [reza] *nf (abrév* **réservation**) = TGV seat-reservation ticket

rescapé, -e [rɛskape] **1** *adj* surviving

   2 *nm,f* survivor

rescousse [rɛskus] *nf* **aller/venir à la r. de qn** to go/to come to sb's rescue; **appeler qn à la r.** to call on sb for help

réseau, -x [rezo] *nm* (**a**) *(de routes, de voies ferrées, de rivières)* network, system; **r. autoroutier** highway system; **r. ferroviaire** rail network (**b**) *Fig (de relations)* network, circle (**c**) *Ordinat* network; **mise en r.** networking; **r. de télématique** *ou* **de communication de données** datacomms network; **r. de données** data network; **r. local** local area network, LAN; **grand r.** wide area network, WAN; **r. numérique à intégration de services** integrated services digital network; **r. à valeur ajoutée** value-added network, VAN

réséda [rezeda] *nm* reseda

réservation [rezɛrvasjɔ̃] *nf* reservation, booking; **faire une r.** to make a reservation

réserve [rezɛrv] *nf* (**a**) *(restriction)* reservation; **émettre des réserves (sur qch)** to voice reservations (about sth); **sous r. de qch** subject to sth; **sans r.** *(éloges, admiration)* unqualified (**b**) *(discrétion)* reserve; **sortir de sa r.** to come out of one's shell (**c**) *(de vivres, d'équipement, d'argent)* reserve; **en r.** in reserve (**d**) *Mil* reserve (**e**) *(de chasse, de pêche)* reserve; *Can* **r. faunique** wildlife reserve; **r. indienne** (Native American) reservation; **r. naturelle** nature reserve (**f**) *(de magasin)* storeroom; *(de bibliothèque, de musée)* reserve collection

réservé, -e [rezɛrve] *adj* (**a**) *(chambre, siège)* reserved, booked (**b**) *(consacré)* **être r. à qn/qch** to be reserved for sb/sth (**c**) *(personne, attitude)* reserved

réserver [rezɛrve] **1** *vt* (**a**) *(chambre, place)* to reserve, to book; **vous avez réservé?** do you have a reservation? (**b**) *(mettre de côté)* to set aside, to put by (**à/pour** for); **r. le meilleur pour la fin** to save the best till last (**c**) *Fig* **r. son jugement** to reserve judgment; **r. une surprise à qn** to have a surprise in store for sb; **r. un bon accueil à qn** to welcome sb with open arms; **ce que le sort nous réserve** what fate has in store for us

   2 se réserver *vpr* (**a**) *(garder pour soi)* **se r. qch** to keep sth for oneself; **se r. le droit de faire qch** to reserve the right to do sth (**b**) **se r. pour qch** to save oneself for sth

réserviste [rezɛrvist] *nm Mil* reservist

réservoir [rezɛrvwar] *nm* (**a**) *(bassin)* reservoir (**b**) *(cuve)* tank; **r. d'essence** gas tank

résidence [rezidɑ̃s] *nf* (**a**) *(demeure)* residence; **r. principale** main residence; **r. secondaire** second home (**b**) *(habitations de standing)* luxury apartment building (**c**) *Jur* **en r. surveillée** under house arrest (**d**) *(séjour)* residence

résident, -e [rezidɑ̃, -ɑ̃t] **1** *adj* (**a**) *(personne)* resident (**b**) *Ordinat* **r. en mémoire** memory-resident

   2 *nm,f* (**a**) *(habitant)* resident (**b**) *(étranger)* foreign resident; **les résidents français aux États-Unis** French nationals resident in the United States (**c**) *Belg* **second r.** weekender, vacation resident

résidentiel, -elle [rezidɑ̃sjɛl] *adj* residential

résider [rezide] *vi* (**a**) *(personne)* to reside (**b**) *(consister)* to lie (**dans** in)

résidu [rezidy] *nm (reste)* residue; **résidus** *(déchets)* waste

résiduel, -elle [rezidɥɛl] *adj* residual

résignation [reziɲasjɔ̃] *nf* resignation

résigné, -e [reziɲe] *adj* resigned (**à** to)

résigner [reziɲe] **se résigner** *vpr* to resign oneself (**à** to); **se r. à faire qch** to resign oneself to doing sth

résiliable [reziljabl] *adj (contrat)* which may be terminated

résiliation [reziljasjɔ̃] *nf (d'un contrat)* termination

résilier [66] [rezilje] *vt (accord, contrat)* to terminate

résille [rezij] *nf* hairnet

résine [rezin] *nf* resin

résiné [rezine] *adj m & nm* **(vin) r.** retsina

résineux, -euse [rezinø, -øz] **1** *adj* (**a**) *(bois, odeur)* resinous (**b**) *(arbre, forêt)* coniferous

   2 *nm* conifer

résistance [rezistɑ̃s] *nf* (**a**) *(action)* resistance (**à** to); **n'offrir aucune r.** to put up *or* to offer no resistance; **opposer une r. à qn/qch** to resist sb/sth; **r. passive** passive resistance (**b**) *Hist* **la R.** the Resistance (**c**) *(endurance)* stamina (**d**) *Élec* resistance (**e**) *(conducteur)* *(d'un appareil)* element (**f**) *(d'un matériau)* resistance

résistant, -e [rezistɑ̃, -ɑ̃t] **1** *adj (matériau)* tough; *(plante)* hardy; **c'est quelqu'un de très r.** he has a lot of stamina

   2 *nm,f (combattant)* freedom fighter; *(pendant la Résistance)* member of the Resistance

résister [reziste] **résister à** *vt ind* (**a**) *(attaque, agresseur)* to resist (**b**) *(tentation, influence, personne)* to resist; **je n'ai pas pu r., je les ai achetées** I couldn't resist, I bought them (**c**) *(supporter)* *(douleur, pression, froid)* to withstand; *(mauvais traitement)* to stand up to; *(maladie, épidémie, fatigue)* to overcome (**d**) *(s'opposer à)* to stand up to

résolu, -e [rezɔly] **1** *pp voir* **résoudre**

   2 *adj (personne)* determined, resolute; **être r. à faire qch** to be determined to do sth

résolument [rezɔlymɑ̃] *adv* resolutely

résolution [rezɔlysjɔ̃] *nf* (**a**) *(décision)* resolution; **prendre la r. de faire qch** to make a resolution to do sth; **prendre des résolutions** to make resolutions (**b**) *(d'un problème)* solving (**c**) *(détermination)* determination, resolve (**d**) *(d'un écran)* resolution

résolvais *etc. voir* **résoudre**

résonance [rezɔnɑ̃s] *nf aussi Tech* resonance; *Fig (écho)* echo

résonner [rezɔne] *vi* (**a**) *(retentir)* to resound (**b**) *(faire un écho)* to echo

résorber [rezɔrbe] **1** *vt* (**a**) *(surplus, déficit)* to absorb; *(chômage)* to bring down; *(dettes)* to clear (**b**) *(sang, pus)* to resorb

   2 se résorber *vpr* (**a**) *(surplus, déficit)* to be absorbed; *(chômage)* to be brought down (**b**) *(sang, pus)* to be resorbed

résorption [rezɔrpsjɔ̃] *nf (d'un surplus, d'un déficit)* absorption; *(du chômage)* bringing down

résoudre [3b] [rezudr] **1** vt (**a**) *(difficulté, conflit, crise)* to resolve; *(équation, énigme, problème)* to solve (**b**) *(décider)* **r. de faire qch** to resolve to do sth (**c**) *(décomposer)* **r. qch en qch** to resolve sth into sth
  2 se résoudre vpr **se r. à faire qch** to resolve to do sth; **je ne peux pas me r. à la quitter** I can't bring myself to leave her

respect [rɛspɛ] nm respect (**pour** for); **élevé dans le r. des traditions** brought up to respect traditions; **avoir du r. pour qn** to have respect for sb; **manquer de r. envers qn** to show sb a lack of respect; **tenir qn en r.** to keep sb at a distance; **sauf le r. que je vous dois, sauf votre r.** with all due respect; **respects** *(hommages)* respects

respectabilité [rɛspɛktabilite] nf respectability

respectable [rɛspɛktabl] adj respectable

respecter [rɛspɛkte] **1** vt to respect; **faire r. la loi** to enforce the law; **se faire r.** to command respect; **r. la priorité** *(en voiture)* to give way
  2 se respecter vpr (**a**) *(soi-même)* to respect oneself; **comme tout homme qui se respecte** like any self-respecting man (**b**) *(l'un l'autre)* to respect each other

respectif, -ive [rɛspɛktif, -iv] adj respective

respectivement [rɛspɛktivmã] adv respectively

respectueusement [rɛspɛktɥøzmã] adv respectfully

respectueux, -euse [rɛspɛktɥø, -øz] adj respectful (**de/ envers** of/to)

respirable [rɛspirabl] adj breathable; Fig **l'atmosphère n'était plus r.** the atmosphere had become oppressive

respirateur [rɛspiratœr] nm respirator

respiration [rɛspirasjɔ̃] nf breathing; **reprendre sa r.** to pause for breath; **retenir sa r.** to hold one's breath; **r. artificielle** artificial respiration

respiratoire [rɛspiratwar] adj *(organe)* respiratory; *(appareil, exercice, problème)* breathing

respirer [rɛspire] **1** vi (**a**) *(personne, plante)* to breathe (**b**) Fig *(être soulagé)* **je respire!** I can breathe again! (**c**) Fig *(se reposer)* to have a break
  2 vt (**a**) *(inhaler)* to breathe (in) (**b**) *(exprimer)* **r. la santé** to be glowing with health; **il ne respire pas l'intelligence** he doesn't exactly radiate intelligence

resplendir [rɛsplãdir] vi (**a**) *(briller)* to shine (**b**) *(personne)* to be radiant; **r. de joie/santé** to radiate joy/health

resplendissant, -e [rɛsplãdisã, -ãt] adj *(personne, beauté)* radiant; **r. de joie/santé** radiant with joy/health; **il a une mine resplendissante** he looks wonderfully well

responsabiliser [rɛspɔ̃sabilize] vt **r. qn** to give sb a sense of responsibility

responsabilité [rɛspɔ̃sabilite] nf *(morale)* responsibility; *(légale)* liability (**de** for); **accepter une r.** to take on or to accept a responsibility; **avoir la r. de qn/qch** to be responsible for sb/sth; **décliner toute r.** to accept no liability; **avoir un poste à responsabilités** to have a responsible job; **r. civile** civil liability; **r. limitée** limited liability; **r. au tiers** third-party liability

responsable [rɛspɔ̃sabl] **1** adj (**a**) *(moralement)* responsible (**de** for); *(légalement)* liable (**de** for) (**b**) *(mûr)* responsible
  2 nmf (**a**) *(auteur, coupable)* person responsible (**de** for); **qui est le r. de cette plaisanterie?** who's (the person) responsible for this prank? (**b**) *(personne qui a la responsabilité)* person in charge (**c**) *(dirigeant élu)* official

resquiller [rɛskije] vi Fam *(au théâtre, au concert)* to sneak in without paying; *(dans un bus, dans le métro)* to dodge paying one's fare

resquilleur, -euse [rɛskijœr, -øz] nm,f Fam *(au théâtre, au cinéma)* = person who sneaks in without paying; *(dans un bus, dans le métro)* farebeater

ressac [rəsak] nm undertow

ressaisir [rəsezir] **se ressaisir** vpr to pull oneself together

ressasser [rəsase] vt (**a**) *(mentalement)* to brood over (**b**) *(répéter)* to keep coming out with

ressemblance [rəsãblãs] nf *(entre personnes)* resemblance, likeness; *(entre choses)* similarity

ressemblant, -e [rəsãblã, -ãt] adj *(portrait)* lifelike

ressembler [rəsãble] **1 ressembler à** vt ind (**a**) *(personne)* to resemble, to be like; **à quoi ressemble-t-elle?** what does she look like? (**b**) Fig *(chose)* **cela ne ressemble à rien** it doesn't look like anything; **cela ne lui ressemble pas** that's not like her
  2 se ressembler vpr to be alike, to resemble each other; **ils se ressemblent comme des frères** you'd take them for brothers; **se r. comme deux gouttes d'eau** to be as like as two peas in a pod; **les jours se suivent et ne se ressemblent pas** day follows day and you never know what to expect; Prov **qui se ressemble s'assemble** birds of a feather flock together

ressemeler [9] [rəsəmle] vt to resole

ressentiment [rəsãtimã] nm resentment (**de/contre** at/ against)

ressentir [64a] [rəsãtir] **1** vt to feel
  2 se ressentir vpr **se r. de qch** *(personne, pays)* to feel the effects of sth; *(travail)* to show the effects of sth

resserrement [rəsɛrmã] nm *(d'une amitié, de liens)* strengthening

resserrer [rəsere] **1** vt (**a**) *(nœud, ceinture, écrou)* to tighten (**b**) Fig *(amitié, liens)* to strengthen
  2 se resserrer vpr (**a**) *(vallée, route)* to narrow (**b**) *(nœud)* to tighten (**c**) Fig *(liens)* to strengthen

resservir [63] [rəsɛrvir] **1** vt *(plat)* to serve up again; **r. qn** to give sb another helping
  2 vi to be used again (**à** for)
  3 se resservir vpr **se r. de qch** *(plat)* to take another helping of sth; *(objet)* to use sth again

ressort [rəsɔr] nm (**a**) *(pièce)* spring (**b**) *(force morale)* resilience; **avoir du r.** to be resilient (**c**) *(motivation)* motive (**d**) **être du r. de qn** to be sb's responsibility (**e**) **en dernier r.** Jur without appeal; Fig as a last resort

ressortir¹ [64a] [rəsɔrtir] **1** vi *(aux être)* (**a**) *(personne) (en s'éloignant)* to go back out; *(en s'approchant)* to come back out (**b**) *(se détacher)* to stand out; **faire r.** *(couleur)* to bring out; *(regard, yeux, fait)* to highlight
  2 vt *(aux avoir)* (**a**) *(parapluie, vêtements)* to get out again (**b**) Fig *(histoire)* to trot out again
  3 v impersonnel *(aux être)* **il ressort de ceci que...** it emerges from this that...

ressortir² [rəsɔrtir] **ressortir à** vt ind (**a**) *(être de la compétence de)* to come under the jurisdiction of (**b**) Litt *(dépendre de)* to come within the province of

ressortissant, -e [rəsɔrtisã, -ãt] nm,f national

ressouder [rəsude] **1** vt to resolder; Fig to re-establish
  2 se ressouder vpr *(os, fracture)* to knit

ressource [rəsurs] nf (**a**) *(moyen)* possibility; **je n'ai d'autre r. que de...** the only course of action open to me is to...; **avoir de la r.** to be resourceful; **en dernière r.** as a last resort (**b**) **ressources** *(argent, moyens d'action)* resources; **être sans ressources** to have no means of support; **ressources humaines** human resources (**c**) *(d'une nation)* **ressources** resources

ressourcer [16] [rəsurse] **se ressourcer** vpr Fam to get back in touch with one's inner self

ressusciter [resysite] **1** vt (**a**) *(un mort)* to raise from the dead; Fig **ça ne va pas le r.** it won't bring him back (**b**) Fig *(querelle, mode)* to revive
  2 vi to rise from the dead; **j'ai l'impression de r.** I feel like a new person

restant, -e [rɛstɑ̃, -ɑ̃t] **1** *adj* remaining
2 *nm* remainder, rest
3 restants *nmpl Can (de nourriture)* leftovers

restaurant [rɛstɔrɑ̃] *nm* restaurant; **aller au r.** to eat out; **r. d'entreprise** staff cafeteria; **r. universitaire** university cafeteria

restaurateur, -trice [rɛstɔratœr, -tris] *nm,f* **(a)** *(de tableaux)* restorer **(b)** *(de restaurant)* restaurateur, restaurant owner

restauration [rɛstɔrasjɔ̃] *nf* **(a)** *(de tableaux, de bâtiments)* restoration **(b)** *(métier)* restaurant business; **r. rapide** fast food **(c)** *Hist* **la R.** the Restoration *(return to power of the Bourbon dynasty 1814-1830)* **(d)** *Ordinat* restore **(e)** *Suisse (restaurant)* restaurant

restaurer [rɛstɔre] **1** *vt* **(a)** *(rétablir, réparer)* to restore **(b)** *Ordinat* to restore **(c)** *Litt (faire manger)* **r. qn** to give sb something to eat
2 se restaurer *vpr* to have something to eat

reste [rɛst] *nm* **(a)** *(de travail, d'argent, de vin)* rest, remainder; **le r. du temps** the rest of the time; **le r. (des gens)** the rest; **il y avait un r. de beurre/lait** there was a bit of butter/milk left (over) **(b) restes** *(d'un repas)* leftovers **(c)** *(ossements)* **restes** remains **(d)** *(locutions)* **du** *ou* **au r.** besides; **pour le r.** as for the rest; **avoir qch de r.** to have sth to spare; **pour ne pas être en r.** *(pour ne pas avoir de dette)* so as not to be indebted; *(pour ne pas être surpassé)* so as not to be outdone; **partir sans demander son r.** to leave without further ado; *Fam* **avoir de beaux restes** to still have one's looks

rester [rɛste] *(aux être)* **1** *vi* **(a)** *(subsister)* to remain, to be left; **les cinq euros qui restent** the remaining five euros, the five euros left; **c'est tout ce qui me reste** that's all I have left; **le nom lui est resté** the name stayed with him
(b) *(demeurer)* to stay, to remain; **restez où vous êtes** stay where you are; **r. assis** to stay seated; **r. au lit** to stay in bed; **r. (à) dîner** to stay to dinner; **r. sur place** to stay put; *Fam* **j'y suis, j'y reste** here I am and here I stay; *Fam* **y r.** *(mourir)* to kick the bucket; **que cela reste entre nous** this is strictly between ourselves; **r. sur une impression** to be left with an impression; **cela m'est resté sur l'estomac** *(plat)* it's lying heavy on my stomach; *Fig* it still rankles with me; **en r. là** to stop there; **r. dans les mémoires** to live on in people's memories; **le plus dur reste à faire** the hardest part is still to be done
2 *v impersonnel* **il me reste cinq euros** I've got five euros left; **il ne me reste qu'à vous remercier** it only remains for me to thank you; **il reste beaucoup de choses à faire** there are still a lot of things to be done; **il reste que...** the fact remains that...; **il n'en reste pas moins que...** it is nevertheless the case that...; **(il) reste à savoir si c'est vrai** it remains to be seen whether it's true

restituer [rɛstitɥe] *vt* **(a)** *(reconstituer) (inscription, texte)* to restore; *(passé, ambiance)* to recreate **(b)** *(rendre) (objets volés)* to restore, to return; *(argent, prêt)* to repay, to pay back **(c)** *(son)* to reproduce

restitution [rɛstitysjɔ̃] *nf* **(a)** *(reconstitution) (d'un texte)* restoration; *(d'une ambiance, du passé)* recreation **(b)** *(d'objets volés)* return **(c)** *(d'argent, d'un prêt)* repayment **(c)** *(du son)* reproduction

Restoroute® [rɛstɔrut] *nm* highway eatery

restreindre [54] [rɛstrɛ̃dr] **1** *vt* to restrict (**à** to)
2 se restreindre *vpr* **(a)** *(réduire ses dépenses)* to cut down **(b)** *(domaine, recherche)* to become more restricted

restreint, -e [rɛstrɛ̃, -ɛ̃t] *adj* *(production, vocabulaire)* restricted (**à** to); *(espace, service)* limited

restrictif, -ive [rɛstriktif, -iv] *adj* restrictive

restriction [rɛstriksjɔ̃] *nf* **(a)** *(diminution)* restriction **(b)** *(réserve)* reservation; **faire des restrictions** to express some reservations; **sans r.** *(accord)* unconditional; *(approuver)*

unreservedly **(c)** *Ordinat* **r. d'accès** access restriction **(d)** **restrictions** *(mesures de rationnement)* restrictions

restructuration [rəstryktyrasjɔ̃] *nf* restructuring

restructurer [rəstryktyre] *vt* to restructure

résultant, -e [rezyltɑ̃, -ɑ̃t] **1** *adj* resulting
2 *nf* **résultante** consequence, result

résultat [rezylta] *nm* result; **sans r.** to no effect; *Fam* **r.: il a été licencié** the upshot was he was dismissed; **donner des résultats** to produce results; **résultats d'exercice** *ou* **d'exploitation** operating income

résulter [rezylte] **1** *vi* **r. de qch** to result from sth
2 *v impersonnel* **il en résulte que...** the result of this is that...

résumé [rezyme] *nm* **(a)** *(d'un texte)* summary, résumé; **faire le r. de qch** *(d'un texte)* to give a summary of sth; *(d'une histoire, d'une situation)* to sum sth up; **en r.** *(en bref)* in short **(b)** *(livre)* study guide

résumer [rezyme] **1** *vt (article, idées)* to summarize; *(situation, histoire)* to sum up
2 se résumer *vpr* **(a)** *(personne)* to sum up **(b)** *(se réduire)* **se r. à qch** to come down to sth

résurgence [rezyrʒɑ̃s] *nf* resurgence

resurgir [rəsyrʒir] *vi* to reappear suddenly

résurrection [rezyrɛksjɔ̃] *nf aussi Fig* resurrection

rétabli, -e [retabli] *adj (après une maladie)* recovered

rétablir [retablir] **1** *vt* **(a)** *(téléphone, eau, gaz)* to restore **(b)** *(guérir)* to restore to health **(c)** *(faits, vérité)* to re-establish **(d)** *(ordre, relations, réputation)* to restore **(e)** *(réhabiliter)* **r. qn (dans ses fonctions)** to reinstate sb; **r. qn dans ses droits** to restore sb's rights
2 se rétablir *vpr* **(a)** *(malade)* to recover **(b)** *(silence, calme)* to return; *(situation)* to return to normal

rétablissement [retablismɑ̃] *nm* **(a)** *(de l'ordre, de la paix, d'une dynastie)* restoration **(b)** *(des communications, des relations)* restoration **(c)** *(d'un employé)* reinstatement **(d)** *(d'un malade)* recovery

rétamé, -e [retame] *adj Fam (fatigué)* pooped

rétamer [retame] *vt* **(a)** *(casserole)* to retin **(b)** *(miroir)* to resilver **(c)** *Fam (au jeu)* to clean out; **se faire r.** *(se faire battre)* to get hammered

retaper [rətape] **1** *vt* **(a)** *Fam (vieille maison, voiture)* to do up **(b)** *Fam (lit)* to straighten **(c)** *Fam* **r. qn** to buck sb up
2 se retaper *vpr Fam (convalescent)* to get back on one's feet

retard [rətar] *nm* **(a)** *(dans le temps)* delay; *(d'une personne attendue)* lateness; **je vous prie d'excuser mon r.** please excuse me for being late; **être en r.** to be late; *(sur un programme)* to be behind; **sans r.** without delay; **avoir du r.** to be late; **avoir une heure de r.** to be an hour late; **prendre du r.** *(personne)* to fall behind; *(train)* to be running late; **r. de paiement** late payment **(b)** *(dans un développement)* backwardness; **pays en r. sur les autres** country lagging behind the others; **être en r. pour son âge** to be backward for one's age; **en r. sur son temps** behind the times; **r. mental** backwardness **(c)** *(d'un véhicule)* **r. à l'allumage** retarded ignition

retardataire [rətardatɛr] **1** *nmf* latecomer
2 *adj* **un élève r.** a pupil who arrives late

retardé, -e [rətarde] *adj* **(a)** *(départ, arrivée)* late **(b)** *(mentalement) (enfant)* backward

retardement [rətardəmɑ̃] *nm* **à r.** *(bombe)* time; *(longtemps après)* belatedly

retarder [rətarde] **1** *vt* **(a)** *(faire arriver en retard)* to delay; **r. qn dans ses études** to hold sb back in his/her studies **(b)** *(différer)* to delay; **r. qch d'une heure/d'une semaine** to put sth back an hour/a week **(c)** *(montre, horloge)* to put back (**de** by)
2 *vi* **(a)** *(horloge)* to be slow; **ma montre retarde/je retarde de dix minutes** my watch is/I'm ten minutes slow

(**b**) **r. sur son temps** *ou* **son époque** to be behind the times (**c**) *Fam (ne pas être au courant)* to be behind the times

retendre [rətɑ̃dr] *vt (cordes)* to retighten

retenir [70] [rətənir] **1** *vt* (**a**) *(faire rester) (personne)* to keep, to detain; **r. qn prisonnier/en otage** to keep *or* to hold sb prisoner/hostage; **je ne vous retiens pas** I won't hold you back; **r. qn à dîner** to have sb stay for dinner; **r. qn par le bras** to hold sb back by the arm; **r. l'attention de qn** *(candidature, proposition)* to catch sb's attention

(**b**) *(conserver) (eau, chaleur)* to retain

(**c**) *(retirer) (argent)* to withhold; *(cotisation, impôt)* to deduct (**sur** from); **retenu à la source** deducted at source

(**d**) *(se souvenir de) (leçon, nom)* to remember; **je le retiens, ton ami!** I won't forget your friend in a hurry!

(**e**) *(réserver) (place, chambre, table)* to reserve, to book

(**f**) *(accepter) (projet, suggestion)* to adopt; **votre candidature n'a pas été retenue** your application was unsuccessful

(**g**) *(contenir) (colère)* to contain; *(larmes)* to hold back; *(cri)* to stifle; *(respiration, souffle)* to hold

(**h**) *(garder en arrière) (personne, foule, chien)* to hold back, to restrain

(**i**) *(empêcher)* **r. qn de faire qch** to restrain sb from doing sth, to hold sb back from doing sth; **qu'est-ce qui te retient de le lui dire?** what's stopping you from telling her?; **qu'est-ce qui vous retient?** what's holding you back?

2 se retenir *vpr* (**a**) *(s'accrocher)* to hold on (**à** to)

(**b**) *(se contenir)* to restrain oneself; **se r. de faire qch** to stop oneself (from) doing sth

rétention [retɑ̃sjɔ̃] *nf* retention; **faire de la r. d'information** to withhold information

retentir [rətɑ̃tir] *vi* (**a**) *(Klaxon®, alarme)* to sound; *(tonnerre, canon)* to rumble; *(coup de feu, cri)* to ring out; **l'explosion retentit dans toute la ville** the explosion was heard right across the city (**b**) *(lieu)* **r. de** to resound *or* to echo with (**c**) *Fig* **r. sur** to have an impact on

retentissant, -e [rətɑ̃tisɑ̃, -ɑ̃t] *adj* (**a**) *(voix)* ringing (**b**) *(succès, échec)* resounding; *(scandale)* sensational

retentissement [rətɑ̃tismɑ̃] *nm (d'un événement)* impact; **avoir un r. sur qch** to have an impact on sth

retenue [rətəny] *nf* (**a**) *(d'une somme)* deduction; **r. sur salaire** wage deduction; *(mensuel)* salary deduction (**b**) *(dans un calcul)* carry over; **n'oublie pas la r.** don't forget to carry over (**c**) *Scol* detention (**d**) *(discrétion)* restraint (**e**) *(barrage)* dam

réticence [retisɑ̃s] *nf* hesitation, unwillingness; **sans r.** unhesitatingly

réticent, -e [retisɑ̃, -ɑ̃t] *adj (hésitant)* hesitant, unwilling

rétif, -ive [retif, -iv] *adj (cheval)* stubborn; *(personne)* recalcitrant

rétine [retin] *nf* retina

retiré, -e [rətire] *adj* (**a**) *(lieu, vie)* secluded; **vivre r. du monde** to lead a secluded life (**b**) **être r. des affaires** to be retired from business

retirer [rətire] **1** *vt* (**a**) *(faire sortir)* to take out; *(objet coincé)* to get out; *(bouchon, épine)* to pull out (**de** of); **r. un enfant d'une école** to remove a child from a school; **r. qch de la circulation** to withdraw sth from circulation; **r. qch du marché** to take sth off the market; **r. les mains de ses poches** to take one's hands out of one's pockets

(**b**) *(argent)* to withdraw (**de** from), to take out (**de** of); *(bagages, billet)* to collect (**de** from), to pick up (**de** from)

(**c**) *(obtenir)* **r. un profit de qch** to make a profit out of sth; **r. du plaisir de qch** to get pleasure from sth

(**d**) *(ôter) (gants, lunettes, vêtement)* to take off, to remove

(**e**) *(confisquer)* to take away (**à** from); **r. son permis de conduire à qn** to ban sb from driving

(**f**) *(ramener en arrière) (main)* to remove

(**g**) *(ne pas maintenir) (offre, plainte, candidature)* to withdraw; **je retire ce que j'ai dit** I take back what I said

2 se retirer *vpr* (**a**) *(s'en aller) (personne)* to withdraw; *(foule)* to move back; **vous pouvez vous r.** you may go

(**b**) *(eaux, mer)* to recede; *(marée)* to ebb

(**c**) **se r. d'une association/élection** to withdraw from a partnership/an election; **se r. des affaires** to retire from business

retombées [rətɔ̃be] *nfpl* (**a**) *(répercussions)* repercussions; **avoir des retombées sur qch** to have repercussions on sth (**b**) *(déchets)* **retombées radioactives** radioactive fallout

retomber [rətɔ̃be] *vi (aux être)* (**a**) *(tomber de nouveau)* to fall again; **r. dans son fauteuil** to fall back into one's armchair; **laisser r. ses bras** to drop one's arms (**b**) *(après un saut, après avoir été en l'air) (personne, ballon)* to land; **r. sur ses pattes** *(chat)* to land on its feet; *Fig* **r. sur ses pattes** to land on one's feet (**c**) *(retourner)* **r. dans l'oubli** to sink back into obscurity; **r. dans le désespoir/le chaos** to fall back into despair/chaos; **r. en enfance** to lapse into one's second childhood (**d**) *(redevenir)* **r. malade** to fall ill again (**e**) *(rencontrer)* **r. sur qch** to come across sth again; *Fam* **r. sur qn** to bump into sb again (**f**) *(se répercuter)* **r. sur qn** *(blâme, responsabilité)* to fall on sb; *Fam* **ça va me r. dessus** I'm going to take the rap for it (**g**) *(baisser) (enthousiasme, intérêt, attention)* to fall off (**h**) *(cheveux, rideaux)* to hang (down) (**sur** over)

rétorquer [retɔrke] *vt* to retort

retors, -e [rətɔr, -ɔrs] *adj (personne)* crafty, wily

rétorsion [retɔrsjɔ̃] *nf* retaliation

retouche [rətuʃ] *nf* (**a**) *(sur photo)* touching up; *TV, Cin & Ordinat* **r. d'image(s)** image editing *or* retouching (**b**) *(d'un texte, d'un vêtement)* alteration

retoucher [rətuʃe] *vt* (**a**) *(texte, vêtement)* to alter (**b**) *(photo)* to touch up

retour [rətur] **1** *nm* (**a**) *(d'une personne, d'une saison)* return (**à** to); **être de r. (de)** to be back (again) (from); **de r. chez moi** back home; **à mon r.** on my return; **en r. (de)** in return (for); **payer qn de r.** to repay sb in kind; **par r. (du courrier)** by the next mail; **par un juste r. des choses** as is/was only right and proper; *Fam* **être sur le r.** to be past one's prime; **r. à l'envoyeur** return to sender; **r. de manivelle** backlash; *Fig* **il y a eu un r. de manivelle** it backfired (**b**) *(trajet)* return journey (**c**) *(changement) (de fortune)* reversal; **r. d'âge** change of life (**d**) *Ordinat* **r. d'information** feedback; **r. ligne** line feed; **r. chariot obligatoire** hard carriage return (**e**) *(sur clavier)* return; **r. arrière** backspace; **r. de chariot** carriage return

2 *adj inv (match, touche)* return

retournement [rəturnəmɑ̃] *nm (de situation)* turnaround (**de** in), reversal (**de** of)

retourner [rəturne] **1** *vt (aux avoir)* (**a**) *(gant, vêtement)* to turn inside out; *(poche)* to turn out; *Fam* **r. sa veste** to change sides; *Fig* **r. le couteau dans la plaie** to twist the knife, to rub it in (**b**) *(terre, matelas, crêpe)* to turn (over); *(carte)* to turn over *or* up; *Fig (idée, projet)* to turn over (**c**) *Fam (bouleverser) (personne)* to shake (**d**) *(renverser) (situation)* to reverse (**e**) *(rendre) (livre, lettre, compliment)* to return (**à** to) (**f**) *Fig (utiliser)* **r. un argument contre qn** to turn an argument against sb

2 *vi (aux être)* to go back, to return (**à** to)

3 *v impersonnel Fam* **voilà de quoi il retourne** that's what it's all about

4 se retourner *vpr* (**a**) *(dormeur, voiture)* to turn over; **il doit se r. dans sa tombe** he must be turning in his grave (**b**) *Fig (s'organiser)* to get organized (**c**) *(tourner la tête)* to turn around; **partir sans se r.** to leave without looking back (**d**) **se r. contre qn** *(personne)* to turn against sb; *(action, ambition)* to backfire on sb (**e**) *(aller)* **s'en r. quelque part** to return somewhere

retracer [16] [rətrase] *vt (événement, vie)* to recount

rétractation [retraktasjɔ̃] *nf* retraction

rétracter[1] [retrakte] **1** *vt (griffes, antennes)* to retract

2 se rétracter *vpr (muscle)* to retract

rétracter² [retrakte] **1** *vt (paroles)* to retract, to withdraw
2 se rétracter *vpr (se dédire)* to retract

rétraction [retraksjɔ̃] *nf* retraction

retrait [rǝtrɛ] *nm* (a) *(d'un permis)* withdrawal; **r. du permis de conduire** driving ban (b) *(d'une candidature)* withdrawal (c) *(fait de récupérer)* **r. des bagages** baggage reclaim (d) *(d'argent)* withdrawal; **r. d'espèces** cash withdrawal (e) *(des eaux)* receding (f) *(en typographie)* indent; **mettre qch en r.** to indent sth (g) **en r.** *(étagère)* recessed; *(maison)* set back; *Fig* **être/rester en r.** *(personne)* to be/stay in the background

retraite [rǝtrɛt] *nf* (a) *(de la vie active)* retirement; **être à la r.** to be retired; **prendre sa r.** to retire; **être mis à la r.** to be retired; **r. anticipée** early retirement (b) *(pension)* (retirement) pension; **r. complémentaire** supplementary pension (c) *(procession)* **r. aux flambeaux** torchlight procession (d) *(refuge)* retreat; *(de voleurs)* hideout (e) *(expérience religieuse)* retreat; **faire une r.** to go into retreat (f) *Mil* retreat

retraité, -e [rǝtrɛte] **1** *adj* retired
2 *nm,f* retiree

retraitement [rǝtrɛtmɑ̃] *nm* reprocessing

retraiter [rǝtrɛte] *vt* to reprocess

retranchement [rǝtrɑ̃ʃmɑ̃] *nm* entrenchment; *Fig* **forcer qn dans ses (derniers) retranchements** to drive sb to the wall

retrancher [rǝtrɑ̃ʃe] **1** *vt* (a) *(soustraire)* *(chiffre)* to take away (**de** from); **r. qch sur une somme** to deduct sth from a sum of money (b) *(ôter)* *(passage, nom)* to remove (**de** from)
2 se retrancher *vpr (troupes)* to dig in; *Fig* **se r. dans le silence** to take refuge in silence; **se r. derrière qn/qch** to hide behind sb/sth

retransmettre [47] [rǝtrɑ̃smɛtr] *vt Rad & TV* to broadcast

retransmission [rǝtrɑ̃smisjɔ̃] *nf Rad & TV* broadcast

retravailler [rǝtravaje] **1** *vt (discours, texte, pas de danse)* to work on again
2 *vi* (a) *(reprendre le travail)* to go back to work (b) *(retrouver du travail)* to work again

rétréci, -e [retresi] *adj* (a) **un pull r.** a sweater that has shrunk (b) *(route)* narrow

rétrécir [retresir] **1** *vt (vêtement)* to take in
2 *vi (vêtement, tissu)* to shrink
3 se rétrécir *vpr (route)* to narrow

rétrécissement [retresismɑ̃] *nm* (a) *(action)* *(de route)* narrowing; *(de vêtement, de tissu)* shrinking (b) *(partie étroite)* *(de tuyau, de route)* narrowing

rétribuer [retribɥe] *vt (employé)* to pay; *(travail)* to pay for

rétribution [retribysjɔ̃] *nf* payment, remuneration

rétro [retro] **1** *adv* **s'habiller r.** to wear retro clothes; **meublé r.** furnished in retro style
2 *adj inv* retro
3 *nm* (a) *(style)* retro (b) *Fam (rétroviseur)* rear-view mirror

rétroactes [retroakt] *nmpl Belg* antecedents; **j'ignore tout des r. de cette affaire** I know nothing of the events which gave rise to this situation

rétroactif, -ive [retroaktif, -iv] *adj* retroactive; **avec effet r. au 1ᵉʳ janvier** backdated to January 1st

rétroactivement [retroaktivmɑ̃] *adv* retroactively, with retrospective or retroactive effect

rétroactivité [retroaktivite] *nf* retroactivity

rétrocéder [34] [retrosede] *vt (revendre)* to resell

rétrograde [retrograd] *adj (idée, mesure, politique)* reactionary

rétrograder [retrograde] **1** *vt (fonctionnaire)* to demote
2 *vi (conducteur)* to downshift; **r. de troisième en seconde** to downshift from third to second

rétroprojecteur [retroprɔʒɛktœr] *nm* overhead projector

rétrospectif, -ive [retrɔspɛktif, -iv] **1** *adj* retrospective
2 *nf* **rétrospective** retrospective; *Cin* retrospective; **une r. Roman Polanski** a Roman Polanski festival

rétrospectivement [retrɔspɛktivmɑ̃] *adv* retrospectively, in retrospect

retroussé, -e [rǝtruse] *adj (manches)* rolled-up; *(nez)* snub, turned-up

retrousser [rǝtruse] *vt* (a) *(manches, pantalon)* to roll up; *(babines)* to curl up (b) *(jupe)* to tuck up

retrouvailles [rǝtruvaj] *nfpl* reunion

retrouver [rǝtruve] **1** *vt* (a) *(personne disparue, objet perdu)* to find again; *(adresse, nom)* to find; **r. son chemin** to find one's way again; **nous avons retrouvé notre petite maison** here we are back in our little house again; **je ne retrouverai jamais une occasion pareille** I'll never have another opportunity like it
(b) *(recouvrer)* *(santé, forces, enthousiasme)* to recover; *(voix, appétit)* to get back; **r. la forme** to get fit again, to be back in form
(c) *(reconnaître)* **r. qch chez qn** to recognize sth in sb; **r. qn dans qch** to recognize sb in sth
(d) *(rencontrer)* *(thème, image, motif)* to come across (**dans** in)
(e) *(rejoindre)* *(amis, parents)* to meet, to see; *(lieu)* to get back to
2 se retrouver *vpr* (a) *(être)* to find oneself; **se r. à la rue/sans un sou** to find oneself homeless/penniless
(b) *(trouver son chemin)* to find one's way (**dans** around); *Fig* **je ne m'y retrouve plus!** I'm completely lost!
(c) *Fam (financièrement)* **s'y r.** to get one's money back
(d) *(se rencontrer)* to meet; *Fig* **on se retrouvera!** I'll get even with you!; **comme on se retrouve!** fancy meeting you!
(e) *(soi-même)* to find oneself again
(f) *(se reconnaître)* **se r. en qn** to recognize oneself in sb

rétroviseur [retrovizœr] *nm* rear-view mirror; **r. extérieur** side mirror

reuf [rœf] *nm Fam* brother, bro

reum [rœm] *nf Fam* old lady

réunification [reynifikasjɔ̃] *nf* reunification

réunifier [66] [reynifje] *vt* to reunify

Réunion [reynjɔ̃] *nf* **la R.** Réunion

réunion [reynjɔ̃] *nf* (a) *(de faits)* gathering (together); *(d'ensembles mathématiques, de pays)* union; *(d'entreprises)* merging (b) *(assemblée)* meeting; **être en r.** to be in a meeting; **r. de famille** family gathering

réunionnais, -e [reynjɔnɛ, -ɛz] **1** *adj* of Réunion
2 *nm,f* **R., Réunionnaise** person from Réunion

réunir [reynir] **1** *vt* (a) *(rassembler)* *(objets)* to put together; *(faits, documents)* to gather together; *(fonds)* to get together, to raise (b) *(amis, famille)* to get together; *(après une rupture, une séparation)* to reunite (c) *(qualités, avantages)* to have, to possess (d) **r. qch à qch** to join sth to sth
2 se réunir *vpr* (a) *(personnes)* to meet, to get together; **se r. autour de qn/qch** to gather around sb/sth (b) *(routes)* to meet (c) *(entreprises)* to merge; *(États)* to unite

reup [rœp] *nm Fam* dad, old man

reuss [rœs] *nf Fam* sister, sis

réussi, -e [reysi] *adj* successful; *Ironique* **c'est r.!** bravo!

réussir [reysir] **1** *vt* (a) *(bien faire)* to make a success of; *(au rugby)* *(essai)* to score; **son soufflé était très réussi** his/her soufflé was a great success (b) *(examen)* to pass
2 *vi* (a) *(démarche, projet)* to be successful (b) *(personne)* to do well, to be successful
3 réussir à *vt ind* (a) **r. à un examen** to pass an exam; **r. à faire qch** to manage to do sth (b) **r. à qn** *(climat, plat)* to agree with sb; **tout lui réussit** he's successful in everything he does; **les réunions de famille ne me réussissent pas** family gatherings aren't my scene or aren't for me

réussite [reysit] *nf* (a) *(succès)* success; **fêter sa r. à un examen** to celebrate passing an exam; **la r. sociale** social success (b) *(aux cartes)* solitaire; **faire une r.** to play solitaire

réutiliser [reytilize] *vt* to reuse

revaloir [69a] [rəvalwar] *vt* **je te revaudrai ça** *(je me vengerai)* I'll get you back for this!; *(je te rendrai service)* I'll do the same for you some time

revalorisation [rəvalɔrizasjɔ̃] *nf* **(a)** *(d'une monnaie)* revaluation; *(des salaires, des retraites)* increase **(b)** *(d'une image, d'une profession)* upgrading

revaloriser [rəvalɔrize] *vt* **(a)** *(monnaie)* to revalue; *(salaire, retraite)* to increase **(b)** *(image, profession)* to upgrade

revanchard, -e [rəvɑ̃ʃar, -ard] *adj & nm,f Péj* revanchist

revanche [rəvɑ̃ʃ] *nf* **(a)** *(vengeance)* revenge; **prendre sa r. (sur qn)** to get one's revenge (on sb) **(b)** *(d'un match, d'un jeu)* return game **(c)** *(locutions)* **en r.** on the other hand; **à charge de r.** on condition that I do the same for you

rêvasser [rɛvase] *vi* to daydream

rêve [rɛv] *nm* **(a)** *(de dormeur)* dream; **faire un r.** to (have a) dream; **faites de beaux rêves!** sweet dreams! **(b)** *(idéal)* dream; **de r.** *(voiture, maison)* dream; *(silhouette)* gorgeous

rêvé, -e [rɛve] *adj* perfect, ideal

revêche [rəvɛʃ] *adj* bad-tempered

réveil [revɛj] *nm* **(a)** *(d'une personne)* waking, awakening; **à mon r., au r.** on waking **(b)** *(d'un volcan)* renewed rumblings; *(de la nature, des nationalismes)* reawakening **(c)** *(pendule)* alarm (clock)

réveille-matin [revɛjmatɛ̃] *nm inv* alarm clock

réveiller [reveje] **1** *vt* **(a)** *(personne endormie)* to wake (up), to awaken; *Fig* **r. les consciences** to stir people's consciences **(b)** *(raviver) (douleur)* to revive

2 se réveiller *vpr* **(a)** *(personne endormie)* to wake (up), to awake; *(personne dans le coma)* to regain consciousness; *Fig (peuple)* to wake up **(b)** *(douleur)* to come back **(c)** *(nature)* to reawaken

réveillon [revɛjɔ̃] *nm (repas)* midnight supper; *(soirée)* midnight party *(after midnight mass on Christmas Eve or New Year's Eve)*

Réveillons

Christmas is traditionally a family celebration. In Catholic families, the miniature "crèche" is decorated and everyone goes to midnight mass on Christmas Eve, after which the long and copious Christmas dinner is served: this includes oysters and, for dessert, the traditional "bûche de Noël" or yule log. The presents under the Christmas tree are opened either on Christmas Eve or on Christmas Day morning. The "réveillon de la Saint-Sylvestre" on New Year's Eve is usually celebrated among friends, either at home or in a restaurant. Champagne is drunk at midnight and everybody embraces and wishes each other a happy New Year. New Year greeting cards can, in theory, be sent up until the end of January.

réveillonner [revɛjɔne] *vi* to see in Christmas/the New Year *(with a midnight supper and party)*

révélateur, -trice [revelatœr, -tris] **1** *adj (signe, attitude, remarque)* revealing

2 *nm* **(a)** *(indice)* sign **(b)** *Phot* developer

révélation [revelasjɔ̃] *nf* **(a)** *(action) (d'un secret, d'intentions)* revelation, disclosure; **faire des révélations** to disclose important information **(b)** *(découverte fondamentale)* revelation **(c)** *(personne)* discovery **(d)** *(divine)* revelation

révéler [34] [revele] **1** *vt* **(a)** *(dévoiler)* to reveal **(b)** *(témoigner de)* to show

2 se révéler *vpr* **(a)** *(personne)* to reveal oneself *or* one's character; *(talent, génie)* to be revealed, to reveal itself **(b)** **se r. intelligent/exact** to turn out to be intelligent/correct; **il s'est révélé un bon ami** he proved to be a good friend

revenant, -e [rəvnɑ̃, -ɑ̃t] *nm,f* **(a)** *(fantôme)* ghost **(b)** *Fam* **tiens, un r.!** hello, stranger!

revendeur, -euse [rəvɑ̃dœr, -øz] *nm,f* retailer; *(d'articles d'occasion)* secondhand dealer

revendicatif, -ive [rəvɑ̃dikatif, -iv] *adj (mouvement)* protest

revendication [rəvɑ̃dikasjɔ̃] *nf* demand, claim

revendiquer [rəvɑ̃dike] *vt* **(a)** *(demander)* to claim, to demand; *(droits)* to assert; *(territoire, succession)* to lay claim to; **r. le droit de faire qch** to claim the right to do sth **(b)** *(assumer) (responsabilité)* to claim; *(attentat)* to claim responsibility for

revendre [rəvɑ̃dr] *vt* **(a)** *(après achat)* to resell; *Fig* **avoir du temps/de l'énergie à r.** to have time/energy to spare **(b)** *(vendre de nouveau)* to sell again

revenez-y [rəvnezi] *nm inv Fam* **ce gâteau a un goût de r.** this cake brings you back for more

revenir [70] [rəvənir, rəvnir] *(aux être)* **1** *vi* **(a)** *(retourner, rentrer)* to come back, to return; **r. à Paris/en France** to come back to Paris/France; **r. de Paris** to come back from Paris; *Fig* **r. de loin** *(avoir failli mourir)* to have been at death's door; *(avoir eu de graves ennuis)* to have had a close shave; **je reviens tout de suite** I'll be back in a minute; **quand l'été reviendra** when it's summer again

(b) **r. dans qch** *(refrain, image)* to crop up in sth

(c) **ses propos me sont revenus** what he said got back to me

(d) **r. à la mémoire à qn** to come back to sb; **ça me revient maintenant!** it's come back to me!; **les forces me sont revenues** I got my strength back

(e) *Fam* **j'en suis revenu, de l'informatique!** I'm finished with computers!; **je n'en reviens pas!** I can't get over it!

(f) *Fam* **il a une tête qui ne me revient pas** I don't like the look(s) of him

(g) *Culin* **faire r. qch** to brown sth

(h) **r. cher** to work out expensive

2 revenir à *vt ind* **(a)** *(coûter)* **r. à 100 euros par personne** to work out at 100 euros each; **ça me revient à 200 euros par mois** it costs me 200 euros a month

(b) *(équivaloir à)* **cela revient à dire que...** that amounts to saying that...

3 revenir sur *vt ind* **(a)** *(sujet)* to get back to

(b) *(aveux)* to retract; *(promesse, décision)* to go back on

4 *v impersonnel* **il me revient encore 100 euros** I still have 100 euros owing to me; **il lui revient de le faire** it's up to him/her to do it

5 s'en revenir *vpr Litt* to return, to make one's way back

revente [rəvɑ̃t] *nf* resale

revenu [rəvəny, rəvny] *nm (d'une personne)* income; *(de l'État)* revenue

rêver [rɛve] **1** *vt* to dream of; **r. que...** to dream (that)...

2 *vi* **(a)** *(dormeur)* to dream; *Fig* **on croit r.!** we must be dreaming! **(b)** *(rêvasser)* to daydream

3 rêver à *vt ind* to dream of

4 rêver de *vt ind* **(a)** *(voir en rêve)* to dream of; *Fig* **j'en rêve la nuit** I dream about it at night **(b)** *(souhaiter)* to dream of; **r. de faire qch** to dream of doing sth

réverbération [revɛrberasjɔ̃] *nf (de la lumière, de la chaleur)* reflection; *(du son)* reverberation, echo

réverbère [revɛrber] *nm* street lamp

réverbérer [34] [revɛrbere] *vt (chaleur, lumière)* to reflect, to throw back; *(son)* to reverberate

reverdir [rəvɛrdir] *vi* to grow green again

révérence [reverɑ̃s] *nf* **(a)** *(salut) (d'une femme)* curtsey; **faire la r. à qn** to curtsey to sb; *Fig* **tirer sa r.** to leave **(b)** *(respect)* reverence (**envers** *ou* **pour** for)

révérend, -e [reverɑ̃, -ɑ̃d] **1** *adj* reverend

2 *nm* reverend

révérer [34] [revere] *vt* to revere

rêverie [rɛvri] *nf (activité, moment)* daydream, reverie

revers [rəvɛr] *nm* **(a)** *(de pièce)* reverse side, back; *(de la main)* back; **prendre l'ennemi à r.** *(par l'arrière)* to attack the enemy from the rear; *(par le côté)* to attack the enemy from the side; *Fig* **c'est le r. de la médaille** that's the other side of the coin (**b**) *(de veste)* lapel; *(de pantalon)* cuff (**c**) *(échec)* **r. de fortune** reversal of fortune, setback (**d**) *(au tennis)* backhand (stroke)

reverser [rəvɛrse] *vt* (**a**) *(somme)* to transfer (**à** *ou* **sur** to) (**b**) *(liquide)* to pour out again

réversible [revɛrsibl] *adj* reversible

revêtement [rəvɛtmɑ̃] *nm (enduit)* coating; *(de sol, d'un mur intérieur)* covering; *(d'un mur extérieur)* facing; *(pour canalisation, pour câble)* sheathing; *(de la chaussée)* surface (material)

revêtir [71] [rəvetir] *vt* (**a**) *(habiller)* **r. qn de qch** to dress sb in sth (**b**) *(endosser) (vêtement)* to don (**c**) *(enduire)* to coat; *(sol)* to cover; *(mur extérieur)* to face; *(chaussée)* to surface (**d**) *Fig (caractère, aspect, forme)* to assume, to take on (**e**) **pièce revêtue d'une signature** document bearing a signature

rêveur, -euse [rɛvœr, -øz] **1** *adj* dreamy; **laisser qn r.** to leave sb baffled
  2 *nm,f* dreamer

rêveusement [rɛvøzmɑ̃] *adv* dreamily

revient [rəvjɛ̃] *nm voir* **prix**

revigorant, -e [rəvigɔrɑ̃, -ɑ̃t] *adj (vent, bain)* invigorating; *(boisson)* reviving

revigorer [rəvigɔre] *vt (vent, bain)* to invigorate; *(boisson)* to revive

revirement [rəvirmɑ̃] *nm (de sentiments, d'opinion)* complete change, about-face

réviser [revize] *vt* (**a**) *(texte, loi)* to revise; *(contrat, procès, politique)* to review (**b**) *(leçon, programme)* to review (**c**) *(voiture, moteur)* to service (**d**) *Ordinat (texte, document)* to edit

révision [revizjɔ̃] *nf* (**a**) *(d'un texte, d'une loi)* revision; *(d'un contrat, d'un procès, d'une politique)* review; **r. des salaires** salary review (**b**) *(d'une leçon, d'un programme)* review; **faire des révisions** to review (**c**) *(d'une voiture, d'un moteur)* service (**d**) *Ordinat* edit

révisionnisme [revizjɔnism] *nm* revisionism

revisiter [rəvizite] *vt* (**a**) *(visiter à nouveau)* to revisit (**b**) *(voir sous un jour nouveau)* to reinterpret

revisser [rəvise] *vt* to screw back again

revitalisant, -e [rəvitalizɑ̃, -ɑ̃t] *adj* revitalizing

revitaliser [rəvitalize] *vt* to revitalize

revivre [72] [rəvivr] **1** *vt (passé, expérience)* to relive
  2 *vi* (**a**) *(recouvrer son énergie)* to come alive again; **se sentir r.** to feel alive again; **faire r. qn** to bring sb back to life (**b**) **r. dans qn/qch** to live on in sb/sth; **faire r. qch** *(coutume, tradition)* to revive sth; *(village)* to bring sth back to life

révocable [revɔkabl] *adj (fonctionnaire)* removable; *(testament)* revocable

révocation [revɔkasjɔ̃] *nf (d'un fonctionnaire)* removal; *(d'un testament)* revocation

revoici [rəvwasi] *prép Fam* **me r.!** here I am again!; **le r. au travail** he's back at work

revoilà [rəvwala] = **revoici**

revoir¹ [rəvwar] **au revoir 1** *exclam* goodbye
  2 *nm inv* goodbye

revoir² [73a] [rəvwar] **1** *vt* (**a**) *(rencontrer) (personne)* to see *or* to meet again (**b**) *(leçon)* to review; *(comptes, texte)* to go over again (**c**) *(se représenter mentalement)* to see again
  2 se revoir *vpr* (**a**) *(se rencontrer)* to see each other again, to meet again (**b**) *(soi-même)* to see oneself again

revoler [rəvɔle] *vi* (**a**) *(voler de nouveau)* to fly again (**b**) *Can (être projeté dans toutes les directions) (objets, personnes)* to fly in every direction; *(jaillir) (liquide, sang)* to splatter; **les fenêtres ont revolé en miettes** the windows were smashed to smithereens

révoltant, -e [revɔltɑ̃, -ɑ̃t] *adj* appalling, revolting

révolte [revɔlt] *nf* revolt; **en r. (contre)** in revolt (against)

révolté, -e [revɔlte] *adj* (**a**) *(indigné)* outraged, appalled (**de** by) (**b**) *(en révolte)* rebellious

révolter [revɔlte] **1** *vt* to outrage, to appall; **ça me révolte d'entendre ça!** I'm appalled to hear that!
  2 se révolter *vpr* to revolt, to rebel (**contre** *ou* **devant** against)

révolu, -e [revɔly] *adj (jours, époque)* past, bygone; **avoir quarante ans révolus** to be over forty years of age

révolution [revɔlysjɔ̃] *nf* revolution; **faire la r.** to cause a revolution; *Fig* **être en r.** to be up in arms; *Hist* **la R.** the French Revolution

révolutionnaire [revɔlysjɔnɛr] *adj & nmf* revolutionary

révolutionner [revɔlysjɔne] *vt* (**a**) *(transformer) (industrie, théorie)* to revolutionize (**b**) *Fam (mettre en émoi) (village)* to cause a stir in

revolver [revɔlvɛr] *nm* revolver

révoquer [revɔke] *vt* (**a**) *(fonctionnaire)* to remove from office (**b**) *(décret, contrat, testament)* to revoke

revue [rəvy] *nf* (**a**) *(examen)* review; **passer qch en r.** *(problèmes, possibilités)* to review sth; **r. de presse** *(de l'actualité)* review of the papers; *(sur un sujet particulier)* press review (**b**) *(magazine)* magazine; *(scientifique, littéraire)* review, journal (**c**) *(spectacle)* revue

révulsé, -e [revylse] *adj (yeux)* rolled (up); *(personne)* disgusted

révulser [revylse] **1** *vt (dégoûter)* to disgust
  2 se révulser *vpr (yeux)* to roll (up)

Reykjavik [rekjavik] *n* Reykjavik

rez-de-chaussée [redʃose] *nm inv* first floor; **au r.** on the first floor

rez-de-jardin [redʒardɛ̃] *nm inv* garden level

RF [ɛrɛf] *nf (abrév* **République française)** = written abbreviation seen on official documents, government buildings, etc.

RFA [ɛrɛfa] *nf Anciennement (abrév* **République fédérale d'Allemagne)** FRG

RG [ɛrʒe] *nmpl (abrév* **Renseignements généraux)** = secret intelligence branch of the French police, ≃ the FBI

rhabiller [rabije] **1** *vt (personne)* to dress sb again
  2 se rhabiller *vpr (mettre ses vêtements)* to get dressed again; *Fam* **il peut aller se r.** he might as well give up and go home

rhapsodie [rapsɔdi] *nf* rhapsody

Rhénanie [renani] *nf* **la R.** the Rhineland

Rhésus [rezys] *nm* Rhesus factor; **R. positif/négatif** Rhesus positive/negative

rhétorique [retɔrik] **1** *adj (effet)* rhetorical
  2 *nf* rhetoric

Rhin [rɛ̃] *nm* **le R.** the Rhine

rhinocéros [rinɔserɔs] *nm* rhinoceros

rhino-pharyngite *(pl* **rhino-pharyngites)** [rinofarɛ̃ʒit] *nf* inflammation of the nose and throat, *Spéc* rhinopharyngitis

Rhodes [rɔd] *n* Rhodes

rhododendron [rɔdɔdɛ̃drɔ̃] *nm* rhododendron

Rhône [ron] *nm* **le R.** the Rhone

rhubarbe [rybarb] *nf* rhubarb

rhum [rɔm] *nm* rum

rhumatisant, -e [rymatizɑ̃, -ɑ̃t] *adj & nm,f* rheumatic

rhumatismal, -e, -aux, -ales [rymatismal, -o] *adj* rheumatic

rhumatisme [rymatism] *nm* rheumatism; **avoir des rhumatismes** to have rheumatism; **r. articulaire** rheumatoid arthritis; **r. articulaire aigu** rheumatic fever

rhumatologie [rymatɔlɔʒi] *nf* rheumatology

rhumatologue [rymatɔlɔg] *nmf* rheumatologist

rhume [rym] *nm* cold; **attraper un r.** to catch a cold; **r. de cerveau** head cold; **r. des foins** hay fever

riant, -e [rijã, -ãt] *adj* (**a**) *(visage)* smiling, cheerful; *(yeux)* laughing, merry (**b**) *(paysage, campagne)* pleasant

RIB [rib] *nm (abrév* **relevé d'identité bancaire**) = document showing details of one's bank account *(see box at* **relevé***)*

ribambelle [ribãbɛl] *nf (de personnes)* string, crowd

ricanement [rikanmã] *nm* sneer, snigger

ricaner [rikane] *vi* to sneer, to snigger

richard, -e [riʃar, -ard] *nm,f Péj* moneybags

riche [riʃ] **1** *adj* (**a**) *(personne, pays)* rich, wealthy (**b**) *(cuisine, aliment)* rich (**c**) *(vocabulaire)* extensive; *(style)* elaborate; *(description)* detailed (**d**) *(luxueux) (demeure)* luxurious; *(étoffe)* rich; *(vêtement)* sumptuous (**e**) *Fam* **c'est une r. idée** that's a fabulous idea (**f**) **r. en qch** rich in sth; **la journée a été r. en événements** it's been an action-packed day (**g**) **r. de** *(espérances)* full of; **livre/expérience r. d'enseignements** very instructive book/experience

2 *nmf* rich person; **les riches** the rich

richement [riʃmã] *adv* richly

richesse [riʃɛs] *nf* (**a**) *(d'une personne, d'un pays)* wealth; **c'est le tableau qui fait la r. de notre musée** this painting is the prize item in our museum's collection; **richesses** *(biens)* riches, wealth; *Fam* **voilà toutes mes richesses** this is everything I've got (**b**) *(luxe) (d'une demeure)* luxuriousness; *(de vêtements)* sumptuousness (**c**) **richesses** *(ressources)* resources (**d**) *(du sol, d'un gisement)* richness; *(de la végétation)* lushness (**e**) *(de l'imagination)* vividness, liveliness; *(d'un style)* elaborateness; *(du vocabulaire)* richness; *(d'une description)* detailed nature

richissime [riʃisim] *adj Fam* extremely wealthy

ricin [risɛ̃] *nm voir* **huile**

ricocher [rikɔʃe] *vi (projectile)* to ricochet (**sur** off); *(sur l'eau)* to bounce (**sur** off)

ricochet [rikɔʃɛ] *nm (projectile)* ricochet; *(sur l'eau)* bounce; **faire des ricochets** *(pour s'amuser)* to skim pebbles; *Fig* **par r.** indirectly

ric-rac [rikrak] *adv Fam* (**a**) *(de justesse)* **réussir un examen r.** to scrape through an exam (**b**) **être r.** *(financièrement)* to be a bit strapped for cash

rictus [riktys] *nm* grimace

ride [rid] *nf* (**a**) *(sur le visage)* wrinkle, line; *Fam* **ne pas prendre une r.** not to age (**b**) *(sur l'eau)* ripple

ridé, -e [ride] *adj* wrinkled

rideau, -x [rido] *nm* (**a**) *(dans une pièce)* drape; **r. de fer** *(de boutique)* metal shutter; *Hist (en Europe)* Iron Curtain (**b**) *(de théâtre)* curtain (**c**) *(écran) (d'arbres)* screen, curtain; *(de feu, de fumée)* wall; *(de pluie)* curtain

rider [ride] **1** *vt* (**a**) *(front)* to wrinkle, to line; *(peau)* to wrinkle, to shrivel (**b**) *(eau, sable)* to ripple

2 se rider *vpr* (**a**) *(front, peau)* to become wrinkled *or* lined (**b**) *(eau)* to ripple

ridicule [ridikyl] **1** *adj* ridiculous, ludicrous; *(prix)* ridiculously low; **se rendre r.** to make a fool of oneself

2 *nm* (**a**) *(absurdité)* ridiculousness (**b**) *(dérision)* ridicule; **tourner qn/qch en r.** to ridicule sb/sth; **se couvrir de r.** to make a complete fool of oneself

ridiculement [ridikylmã] *adv* ridiculously, ludicrously

ridiculiser [ridikylize] **1** *vt* to ridicule, to make fun of

2 se ridiculiser *vpr* to make oneself look ridiculous, to make a fool of oneself

rien [rjɛ̃] **1** *pron indéfini* (**a**) *(avec* ne*)* nothing; **r. ne l'affecte** nothing affects him; **r. de ce que j'ai proposé ne leur a plu** they didn't like anything I suggested; **r. ne va plus!** *(au casino)* no more bets!; **ne... r.** nothing, not anything; **je n'ai r. à faire** I have nothing to do; **il n'a r. mangé du tout** he hasn't eaten a thing; **personne n'osa r. dire** nobody dared say anything; **il n'y a r. de nouveau** there's nothing new, there isn't anything new; **ce n'est r.** it's nothing; **comme si de r. n'était** as if nothing had happened; **elle ne ressemble en r. à sa sœur**

she's nothing like her sister; *Litt* **il n'en est r.** such is not the case; **il n'a r. d'un don Juan** he's no Casanova; *Fam* **r. de r.** nothing at all

(**b**) *(sans* ne*)* **qu'avez-vous fait? – r. /presque r.** what did you do? – nothing/hardly anything; **de r.** *(je vous en prie)* you're welcome, don't mention it; **pour r.** *(gratuitement)* for nothing; **pourquoi demandez-vous cela? – pour r.** why do you ask? – no reason; **un petit problème de r. du tout** a trivial little problem; **quinze à r.** *(au tennis)* fifteen love

(**c**) *(quelque chose)* anything; **y a-t-il r. de plus triste?** is there anything more depressing?; **sans r. faire** without doing anything; **sans nous gêner en r.** without troubling us at all *or* in the slightest

(**d**) *(locutions)* **r. que** just, only; **je frémis r. que d'y songer** just thinking about it makes me shudder; **r. que la vérité** nothing but the truth; **élever quatre enfants, ce n'est pas r.!** raising four children is quite an achievement!

2 *nm* (**a**) *(bagatelle)* **un r. l'habille** she looks good in anything; **s'énerver pour un r.** to get annoyed over nothing; **il court un kilomètre comme un r.** he can run a kilometer just like that

(**b**) **un r. long/bête** *(un peu)* a bit long/stupid; **un r. de...** *(un petit peu de)* a little...; **en un r. de temps** in no time at all

rieur, -euse [rijœr, -øz] *adj (air, visage)* cheerful, bright; *(yeux)* laughing, merry

Riga [riga] *n* Riga

rigide [riʒid] *adj* (**a**) *(matériau)* rigid; *(couverture de livre)* hard (**b**) *Fig (personne, règlement, système)* rigid, inflexible

rigidité [riʒidite] *nf (d'un matériau)* rigidity; *Fig (d'une personne, d'un règlement, d'un système)* rigidity, inflexibility; **r. cadavérique** rigor mortis

rigolade [rigɔlad] *nf Fam* (**a**) *(amusement)* fun (**b**) **c'était de la r.** *(c'était facile)* it was a walkover; **ça n'est pas de la r.** *(c'est sérieux)* it's no joke; **prendre qch à la r.** to treat sth as a joke

rigolard, -e [rigɔlar, -ard] *adj Fam (air)* grinning

rigole [rigɔl] *nf (petit fossé)* channel; *(filet d'eau)* rivulet

rigoler [rigɔle] *vi Fam* (**a**) *(rire)* to laugh (**b**) *(s'amuser)* to have a laugh (**c**) *(plaisanter)* to joke (**avec** about); *Fig* **il ne faut pas r. avec le fisc** you shouldn't play games with the IRS

rigolo, -ote [rigɔlo, -ɔt] *Fam* **1** *adj* funny

2 *nm,f (plaisantin)* scream, hoot; *Péj (fumiste)* clown

rigorisme [rigɔrism] *nm* strictness

rigoriste [rigɔrist] **1** *adj* strict, rigorous

2 *nmf* strict moralist

rigoureusement [rigurøzmã] *adv* (**a**) *(strictement) (interdit)* strictly; *(exact)* absolutely; *(contraire)* rigorously (**b**) *(scrupuleusement)* **suivre r. les consignes** to follow the instructions to the letter (**c**) *(sévèrement)* severely

rigoureux, -euse [rigurø, -øz] *adj* (**a**) *(dur) (punition, mesures, conditions)* severe, harsh; *(hiver)* hard; *(climat)* harsh (**b**) *(strict) (neutralité)* strict; *(analyse)* rigorous; **être r. dans qch** *(personne)* to be rigorous in sth

rigueur [rigœr] *nf* (**a**) *(dureté)* harshness, severity; *(de la loi)* rigor (**b**) *(austérité)* austerity (**c**) *(exactitude) (d'une analyse)* rigor; **manquer de r.** *(style, personne)* to be sloppy (**d**) *(locutions)* **à la r.** *(si nécessaire)* if need be; **être de r.** to be compulsory; **tenir r. à qn de qch** to hold sth against sb

rillettes [rijɛt] *nfpl* potted meat *(made from pork, rabbit, goose, etc.)*

rime [rim] *nf* rhyme; **sans r. ni raison** without rhyme or reason

rimer [rime] *vi* (**a**) *(mot)* to rhyme (**avec** with) (**b**) *Fig* **ne r. à rien** not to make any sense

Rimmel® [rimɛl] *nm* mascara

rinçage [rɛ̃saʒ] *nm* (**a**) *(action)* rinsing (**b**) *(pour les cheveux)* tint, rinse

rince-doigts [rɛ̃sdwa] *nm inv* finger bowl

rincée [ʀɛ̃se] *nf* (**a**) *Fam (averse)* downpour (**b**) *Fam (volée de coups)* walloping

rincer [16] [ʀɛ̃se] **1** *vt (vêtements, vaisselle, cheveux)* to rinse; *(verre, tasse)* to rinse (out)

2 se rincer *vpr (à l'eau douce)* to rinse oneself; **se r. la bouche** to rinse out one's mouth; *Fam* **se r. l'œil** to get an eyeful

ring [ʀiŋ] *nm* (**a**) *(de boxe)* ring; **le r.** *(la boxe)* boxing (**b**) *Belg (rocade)* ring road

ringard, -e [ʀɛ̃gaʀ, -aʀd] *Fam* **1** *adj* (**a**) *(démodé)* uncool, geeky (**b**) *(de mauvais goût)* tacky

2 *nm,f* geek, square

ringardise [ʀɛ̃gaʀdiz] *nf Fam* tackiness

ringardiser [3] [ʀɛ̃gaʀdize] *vt Fam* to make tacky

Rio de Janeiro [ʀijodədʒaneʀo] *n* Rio de Janeiro

ripaille [ʀipaj] *nf Fam* **faire r.** to have a blowout

riposte [ʀipɔst] *nf* (**a**) *(en boxe, en escrime)* riposte (**b**) *(réponse)* riposte, retort (**c**) *(représailles)* counterattack

riposter [ʀipɔste] **1** *vt* **il m'a riposté que...** he retorted that...

2 *vi* (**a**) *(en boxe, en escrime)* to riposte (**b**) *(user de représailles)* to counterattack

3 riposter à *vt ind (attaque, injures)* to counter

ripou (*pl* **ripoux** *ou* **ripous**) [ʀipu] *Fam* **1** *adj (policier)* crooked

2 *nm* crooked cop

riquiqui [ʀikiki] *adj inv (tout petit)* teeny-weeny; *(portion, cadeau)* stingy, mean; *(maillot de bain)* skimpy

rire¹ [ʀiʀ] *nm* laughter, laughing

rire² [61] [ʀiʀ] **1** *vi* (**a**) *(personne)* to laugh; **r. comme un bossu,** *Fam* **r. comme une baleine** to laugh oneself silly; **r. jaune** to give a forced laugh; **r. aux éclats** to roar with laughter; **r. aux larmes** to cry with laughter; **r. tout bas** to laugh to oneself (**b**) *(s'amuser)* to have fun, to have a laugh; **pour r.** for a joke; **vous voulez r.!** you're joking!; **laissez-moi r.!** don't make me laugh!

2 rire de *vt ind (se moquer de) (personne, remarques, situation)* to laugh at; *Litt* **je ris de leurs insultes** I'm impervious to their insults; **il vaut mieux en r.** you have to laugh

3 se rire *vpr Litt* **se r. de** *(se moquer de)* to laugh at; *(se jouer de)* to make light of

ris¹ [ʀi] *nm (sur une voile)* reef

ris² [ʀi] *nm* **r. de veau** calf's sweetbread

risée [ʀize] *nf* (**a**) *(moquerie)* mockery, derision; **s'exposer à la r. publique** to expose oneself to public scorn (**b**) **être la r. de** to be the laughing stock of

risette [ʀizɛt] *nf Fam* little smile; **fais des risettes à ton papa!** smile for daddy!, give daddy a smile!

risible [ʀizibl] *adj* laughable, ridiculous

risque [ʀisk] *nm* risk; **prendre un r./des risques** to take a risk/risks; **courir le r. de faire qch** to risk doing sth; **c'est un r. à courir** it's a risk I/we/*etc.* have to take; **avoir le goût du r.** to like taking risks; **les risques du métier** occupational hazards; **faire qch à ses risques et périls** to do sth at one's own risk; **au r. de sa vie** at the risk of his/her life; **au r. de faire qch** at the risk of doing sth

risqué, -e [ʀiske] *adj* (**a**) *(dangereux)* risky (**b**) *(osé)* risqué

risquer [ʀiske] **1** *vt* (**a**) *(mettre en danger) (vie, réputation)* to risk; **qu'est-ce que tu risques?** what have you got to lose?; **r. sa tête** to put one's head on the block; **r. le tout pour le tout** to go for broke (**b**) **r. un œil** to peep out; **r. une question** to venture a question

2 risquer de *vt ind* **il risque de se faire renvoyer** he's in danger of being fired; **ça risque de durer longtemps** that may well last for a long time; *Fam* **il risque de gagner** he stands a good chance of winning; *Fam* **il ne risque pas de te le dire** fat chance of him telling you

3 se risquer *vpr* to take risks/a risk; **se r. à faire qch** to venture to do sth; **je ne m'y risquerais pas** I wouldn't risk it

risque-tout [ʀiskətu] *nmf inv* daredevil

rissoler [ʀisɔle] *vt & vi* to brown

ristourne [ʀistuʀn] *nf* discount; **faire une r. à qn** to give sb a discount

rital, -e, -als, -ales [ʀital] *nm,f Fam (Italien)* wop, = racist term used to refer to an Italian

rite [ʀit] *nm* (**a**) *(religieux)* rite; **r. de passage** *ou* **initiatique** rite of passage (**b**) *Fig (cérémonie, habitude)* ritual

ritournelle [ʀituʀnɛl] *nf (phrase musicale)* ritornello; *Fam* **c'est toujours la même r.** it's always the same old story

rituel, -elle [ʀitɥɛl] **1** *adj* ritual

2 *nm* ritual; **r. d'initiation** initiation rites

rituellement [ʀitɥɛlmɑ̃] *adv* invariably

rivage [ʀivaʒ] *nm* shore

rival, -e, -aux, -ales [ʀival, -o] **1** *adj* rival

2 *nm,f* rival; **sans r.** unrivaled

rivaliser [ʀivalize] *vi* **r. avec qn** to compete with sb; **r. de qch avec qn** to try to outdo sb in sth

rivalité [ʀivalite] *nf* rivalry

rive [ʀiv] *nf* (**a**) *(de rivière)* bank; *(de lac, de mer)* shore (**b**) **la r. gauche/droite** *(à Paris)* the Left/Right Bank

---

Rive droite, rive gauche

The Right (north) Bank of the Seine is traditionally associated with business and trade, and has a reputation for being more conservative than the Left Bank. The Left (south) Bank includes districts traditionally favored by artists, students and intellectuals, and has a reputation for being Bohemian and unconventional.

---

river [ʀive] *vt* (**a**) *(fixer)* to rivet; *Fig* **être rivé à qch** to be glued to sth; **avoir les yeux rivés sur qn/qch** not to be able to take one's eyes off sb/sth (**b**) *(goupille, clou)* to clinch; *Fam* **r. son clou à qn** to shut sb up

riverain, -e [ʀivʀɛ̃, -ɛn] **1** *adj (propriété) (le long d'une rivière)* riverside, waterside; *(autour d'un lac)* lakeside, waterside

2 *nm,f* (**a**) *(près d'une rivière)* owner of a riverside property; *(près d'un lac)* owner of a lakeside property (**b**) *(d'une rue)* resident; **interdit sauf aux riverains** *(sur panneau)* ≃ no entry except for access

rivet [ʀivɛ] *nm* rivet

rivetage [ʀivtaʒ] *nm* riveting

riveter [42] [ʀivte] *vt* to rivet

riveteuse [ʀivtøz] *nf* riveting machine

rivière [ʀivjɛʀ] *nf* (**a**) *(cours d'eau)* river (**b**) *(de lave, de boue)* river (**c**) **r. de diamants** diamond necklace, *Spéc* diamond rivière

rixe [ʀiks] *nf* brawl

riz [ʀi] *nm* rice; **r. basmati** basmati rice; **r. cantonais** Cantonese rice; **r. créole** boiled rice; **r. au lait** rice pudding; **r. pilaf** pilaf *or* pilau rice

riziculture [ʀizikyltyʀ] *nf* rice growing

rizière [ʀizjɛʀ] *nf* rice field, paddy field

RMI [ɛʀɛmi] *nm (abrév* **revenu minimum d'insertion***)* ≃ welfare

RMiste [ɛʀɛmist] *nmf* ≃ person on welfare

RN [ɛʀɛn] *nf (abrév* **route nationale***)* = designation of major road, ≃ state highway

RNIS [ɛʀɛnis] *nm Ordinat (abrév* **réseau numérique à intégration de services***)* ISDN

robe [ʀɔb] *nf* (**a**) *(de femme)* dress; **r. de grossesse** maternity dress; **r. d'intérieur** housecoat; **r. de mariée** wedding dress; **r. du soir** evening gown (**b**) **r. de chambre** robe; **pommes de terre en r. de chambre** *ou* **des champs** baked potatoes (**c**) *(d'avocat, de juge)* robe, gown (**d**) *(habit religieux)* robe (**e**) *(pelage) (de cheval)* coat (**f**) *(du vin)* color

robinet [ʀɔbinɛ] *nm* faucet

robinetterie [rɔbinɛtri] *nf* plumbing

robineux [rɔbinø] *nm Can Fam* hobo

robot [rɔbo] *nm* robot; **r. ménager** food processor

robotique [rɔbɔtik] **1** *adj* robotic
2 *nf* robotics *(singulier)*

robotisation [rɔbɔtizasjɔ̃] *nf* automation, robotization

robotiser [rɔbɔtize] *vt* to automate, to robotize

robuste [rɔbyst] *adj (personne)* robust; *(bras, jambe)* sturdy; *(appétit)* healthy; *(plante)* hardy; **être d'une santé r.** to have a strong constitution

robustesse [rɔbystɛs] *nf (d'une personne)* robustness; *(d'une plante)* hardiness; *(d'un véhicule)* sturdiness

roc [rɔk] *nm* rock

rocade [rɔkad] *nf (route)* bypass

rocaille [rɔkaj] **1** *nf* **(a)** *(terrain)* stony ground **(b)** *(jardin)* rockery
2 *adj inv (style)* rocaille

rocailleux, -euse [rɔkajø, -øz] *adj* **(a)** *(pierreux)* stony, rocky **(b)** *Fig (voix)* harsh, rough

rocambolesque [rɔkãbɔlɛsk] *adj* fantastic, incredible

roche [rɔʃ] *nf* rock

rocher [rɔʃe] *nm* **(a)** *(masse de pierre)* rock; *(escarpé)* crag; **le R.** = Monaco; **le r. de Gibraltar** the Rock of Gibraltar **(b)** *(paroi)* rock face **(c)** **r. (au chocolat)** chocolate *(containing nuts)*

rocheux, -euse [rɔʃø, -øz] *adj (paysage, région)* rocky; **la paroi rocheuse** the rock face; **les (montagnes) Rocheuses** the Rocky Mountains

rock [rɔk] **1** *adj inv (concert, groupe, chanteur)* rock
2 *nm inv* **le r.** rock; **danser le r.** to jive

rocker [rɔkœr] *nm*, **rockeur, -euse** [rɔkœr, -øz] *nm,f (musicien)* rock musician; *(fan)* rock fan

rocking-chair (*pl* **rocking-chairs**) [rɔkiɲtʃɛr] *nm* rocking chair

rock'n roll [rɔkɛnrɔl] *nm* **le r.** rock and roll

rococo [rɔkoko] **1** *adj inv* **(a)** *(meuble, style)* rococo **(b)** *(démodé)* old-fashioned
2 *nm* rococo

rodage [rɔdaʒ] *nm (d'une voiture)* breaking in; **en r.** *(sur panneau)* breaking in

rodéo [rɔdeo] *nm (avec des chevaux)* rodeo; *(avec des voitures)* high-speed joyride; *Fig (bagarre)* free-for-all

roder [rɔde] *vt (moteur, voiture)* to break in; *Fig (entreprise, spectacle)* to get into its stride; *(équipe, structure)* to break in; **être rodé** *(entreprise, spectacle)* to be into its stride; *(employé)* to have got the hang of things

rôder [rode] *vi* to be on the prowl

rôdeur, -euse [rodœr, -øz] *nm,f* prowler

rogne [rɔɲ] *nf Fam* bad temper; **être en r. (contre)** to be mad (at); **mettre qn en r.** to make sb mad; **se mettre ou très Fam se ficher en r.** to get mad

rogner [rɔɲe] **1** *vt* **(a)** *(griffes, ongles)* to clip, to trim; *Fig (économies)* to eat away at; *Fig* **r. les ailes à qn** to clip sb's wings **(b)** *(retrancher)* **r. qch à qn** to gradually take sth away from sb **(c)** *Ordinat (image)* to crop
2 rogner sur *vt ind* **r. sur qch** to cut down on sth

rognon [rɔɲɔ̃] *nm Culin* kidney

rognures [rɔɲyr] *nfpl (de cuir, de métal)* trimmings, parings

rogue [rɔg] *adj* arrogant, haughty

roi [rwa] **1** *nm* **(a)** *(souverain)* king; **tirer les rois** = to celebrate Twelfth Night; **les Rois mages** the Three Wise Men; **le R.-Soleil** the Sun King *(Louis XIV)* **(b)** *Fig (le plus grand) (des animaux)* king; **c'est le r. des imbéciles** he's a prize idiot; *très Fam* **c'est le r. des cons** he's a complete asshole **(c)** *(aux cartes, aux échecs)* king
2 *adj inv* **bleu r.** royal blue

Tirer les rois

The French traditionally celebrate Epiphany with a round, almond-flavored pastry ("la galette des Rois") containing a small porcelain figurine ("la fève" – originally a dried bean). The pastry is shared out and the person who finds the "fève" is appointed "king" or "queen" and given a cardboard crown to wear. This tradition is called "tirer les Rois".

roitelet [rwatlɛ] *nm (oiseau)* wren

rôle [rol] *nm* **(a)** *(d'une pièce de théâtre)* part, role; *Fig* **avoir le beau r.** to have the easy job; **premier r.** leading role; **r.-titre** title role **(b)** *(fonction) (du médecin, d'un organe, d'une activité)* role, function **(dans** in**)**; **jouer un r. de premier plan** to play a key role; **jouer un r. secondaire** to play second fiddle

roller [rɔlœr] **1** *nm* rollerblading; **faire du r.** to go rollerblading
2 rollers *nmpl* rollerblades

rolleur, -euse [rɔlœr, -øz] **1** *nm,f (personne qui pratique le roller)* rollerblader
2 *nm* rollerblading; **faire du r.** to go rollerblading
3 rolleurs *nmpl* rollerblades

ROM [rɔm] *nf Ordinat* ROM

romain, -e¹ [rɔmɛ̃, -ɛn] **1** *adj* Roman
2 *nm (caractère d'imprimerie)* roman
3 *nm,f* **R., Romaine** Roman

romaine² [rɔmɛn] *nf (salade)* romaine (lettuce); *Fig* **être bon comme la r.** to be extremely kind

roman¹ [rɔmɑ̃] *nm* **(a)** *(en prose)* novel; **le nouveau r.** the anti-novel, the nouveau roman; **r. d'amour** love story, romance; *Fam* **r. à l'eau de rose** soppy love story, soppy romance; **r. noir** thriller; **r. policier** detective novel **(b)** *(poème)* romance **(c)** *Fig* **c'est du r.** *(c'est invraisemblable)* it's just a fairy tale; *Fig* **c'est tout un r.** *(c'est incroyable)* it's quite a tale

roman², -e [rɔmɑ̃, -an] **1** *adj* **(a)** *(langue)* Romance **(b)** *Archit* Romanesque
2 *nm* **(a)** *(langue)* Romance **(b)** *Archit* Romanesque style

romance [rɔmɑ̃s] *nf (chanson)* sentimental song *or* ballad

romancer [16] [rɔmɑ̃se] *vt (événement, histoire)* to romanticize; *(biographie)* to fictionalize

romanche [rɔmɑ̃ʃ] *adj & nm* Romansch

romancier, -ère [rɔmɑ̃sje, -ɛr] *nm,f* novelist

romand, -e [rɔmɑ̃, -ɑ̃d] **1** *adj (Suisse)* French-speaking
2 *nm,f* **R., Romande** French-speaking Swiss person

romanesque [rɔmanɛsk] *adj* **(a)** *(personne, aventure)* romantic **(b)** *(technique)* novelistic

roman-feuilleton (*pl* **romans-feuilletons**) [rɔmɑ̃fœjtɔ̃] *nm* serial

roman-fleuve (*pl* **romans-fleuves**) [rɔmɑ̃flœv] *nm* saga

romanichel, -elle [rɔmaniʃɛl] *nm,f (Tsigane)* gypsy

roman-photo (*pl* **romans-photos**) [rɔmɑ̃fɔto] *nm* photo-story

romantique [rɔmɑ̃tik] **1** *adj* **(a)** *(peinture, littérature, artiste)* Romantic **(b)** *(personne, idées, film)* romantic
2 *nmf* **(a)** *(artiste, auteur)* Romantic(ist) **(b)** *(personne)* romantic

romantisme [rɔmɑ̃tism] *nm* **(a)** *(courant artistique)* Romanticism **(b)** *(attitude, sensibilité)* romanticism

romarin [rɔmarɛ̃] *nm* rosemary

rombière [rɔ̃bjɛr] *nf Fam* old biddy

Rome [rɔm] *n* Rome

rompre [rɔ̃pr] **1** *vt* **(a)** *(casser)* to break; **r. ses digues** *(fleuve)* to burst its banks **(b)** *(négociations, fiançailles, relations)* to break off; *(contrat, charme, monotonie)* to break; *(équilibre)* to upset **(c)** *(locutions)* **applaudir à tout r.** to applaud wildly; **r. les rangs** to fall out
2 *vi* **(a)** *(casser)* to break **(b)** *(se séparer)* to split up (**avec** with); **r. avec sa famille** to break off relations with one's family **(c)** **r. avec la tradition** to break with tradition

3 se rompre *vpr (se casser)* to break; **son cœur battait à se r.** his heart was pounding; *Fig* **se r. le cou** to break one's neck

rompu, -e [rɔ̃py] *adj* (a) *(exténué)* **être r. (de fatigue)** to be worn out (b) *(expérimenté)* **r. à qch** used to sth

romsteck [rɔmstɛk] *nm* rump steak

ronce [rɔ̃s] *nf* (a) *(arbuste)* bramble (bush), blackberry bush (b) *(dans le bois)* **r. de noyer** burr walnut

ronchon, -onne [rɔ̃ʃɔ̃, -ɔn] *Fam* **1** *adj* grouchy, grumpy
2 *nm,f* grumbler, grouser

ronchonnement [rɔ̃ʃɔnmɑ̃] *nm Fam* grumbling, grousing

ronchonner [rɔ̃ʃɔne] *vi Fam* to grumble, to grouse

roncier [rɔ̃sje] *nm*, **roncière** [rɔ̃sjɛr] *nf* thick bramble bush

rond, -e [rɔ̃, rɔ̃d] **1** *adj* (a) *(balle, table, nappe)* round; *(ventre)* rounded; *(poitrine)* full; *(personne, joues, silhouette)* plump; **avoir le dos r.** to be round-shouldered (b) *(plein)* *(voix)* full (c) *(chiffre, compte)* round (d) **être r. en affaires** to be straightforward where business is concerned (e) *Fam (ivre)* plastered; **r. comme une queue de pelle** stewed to the gills
2 *adv* **tout r.** *(exactement)* exactly
3 *nm* (a) *(figure)* circle; **en r.** in a circle; *Fam* **faire des ronds de jambe** to bow and scrape; *Fam* **en rester comme deux ronds de flan** to be absolutely staggered; **r. de serviette** napkin ring (b) *Fam (sou)* **il n'a pas un r.** he's flat broke

rond-de-cuir *(pl* **ronds-de-cuir)** [rɔ̃dkɥir] *nm Fam Péj* pen or pencil pusher

ronde [rɔ̃d] *nf* (a) *(danse)* round (dance); *(chanson)* round, roundelay (b) *(de gardien, de vigile)* round(s); *(de policier)* beat; **faire une/sa r.** *(gardien, vigile)* to patrol; *(policier)* to be on the beat (c) *Mus (note)* whole note (d) **à la r.** *(autour)* around; **à huit kilomètres à la r.** ≃ within a radius of five miles

rondeau, -x [rɔ̃do] *nm* rondo

rondelet, -ette [rɔ̃dlɛ, -ɛt] *adj* (a) *(personne)* plump, chubby (b) *(somme)* tidy

rondelle [rɔ̃dɛl] *nf* (a) *(de citron, de saucisson)* slice; **couper qch en rondelles** to slice sth (b) *Can* **r. (de hockey)** puck (c) *(d'écrou)* washer

rondement [rɔ̃dmɑ̃] *adv* (a) *(avec entrain)* briskly, promptly; **mener qch r.** to make short work of sth (b) *(franchement)* bluntly, frankly

rondeur [rɔ̃dœr] *nf* (a) *(d'un corps)* roundness; *(des joues)* plumpness (b) **rondeurs** *(d'une femme)* curves (c) *(amabilité)* **avec r.** bluntly, frankly

rondin [rɔ̃dɛ̃] *nm* log

rondo [rɔ̃do] *nm* rondo

rondouillard, -e [rɔ̃dujar, -ard] *adj Fam (personne)* plump, chubby

rond-point *(pl* **ronds-points)** [rɔ̃pwɛ̃] *nm (sens giratoire)* traffic circle

ronéotyper [rɔneɔtipe] *vt* to xerox®

ronflant, -e [rɔ̃flɑ̃, -ɑ̃t] *adj Péj* high-flown, high-sounding

ronflement [rɔ̃fləmɑ̃] *nm* (a) *(d'une personne)* snoring (b) *(d'un moteur, d'une machine)* whirring, purring

ronfler [rɔ̃fle] *vi* (a) *(dormeur)* to snore (b) *(moteur)* to whir, to purr; *(poêle)* to purr

ronfleur, -euse [rɔ̃flœr, -øz] *nm,f (personne)* snorer

ronger [45] [rɔ̃ʒe] **1** *vt* (a) *(bois)* to gnaw (at), to nibble (at); *(os)* to gnaw (on); **rongé par les vers** worm-eaten (b) *(acide, rouille)* to eat away or into; *(falaise)* to erode (c) *(tourmenter)* **être rongé de chagrin** to be tormented with grief; **être rongé de remords/par la jalousie/par l'anxiété** to be eaten up with remorse/jealousy/anxiety; **être rongé par la maladie** to be wasted by illness (d) *Fig* **r. son frein** to champ at the bit
2 se ronger *vpr* **se r. les ongles** to bite one's nails

rongeur, -euse [rɔ̃ʒœr, -øz] **1** *adj (mammifère)* rodent-like
2 *nm* rodent

ronron [rɔ̃rɔ̃], **ronronnement** [rɔ̃rɔnmɑ̃] *nm* (a) *(d'un chat)* purr (b) *(d'un moteur)* purr, whirr; *(d'un avion, d'une voix)* drone; *(d'une machine)* whirr (c) *(routine)* humdrum routine

ronronner [rɔ̃rɔne] *vi* (a) *(chat)* to purr (b) *(moteur)* to purr, to whirr; *(avion)* to drone; *(machine)* to whirr

roquefort [rɔkfɔr] *nm* Roquefort

roquet [rɔkɛ] *nm Péj (chien)* yappy (little) dog

roquette¹ [rɔkɛt] *nf (salade)* arugula

roquette² [rɔkɛt] *nf (projectile)* rocket; **r. antichar** anti-tank rocket

rorqual, -als [rɔrkwal] *nm* rorqual, finback whale

rosace [rozas] *nf* (a) *(vitrail)* rose window (b) *(au plafond)* ceiling rose (c) *(de guitare)* rose

rosaire [rozɛr] *nm* rosary; **dire** *ou* **réciter son r.** to say the rosary

rosâtre [rozatr] *adj* pinkish

rosbif [rozbif] *nm* (a) *(viande) (rôtie)* roast beef; *(à rôtir)* roasting beef (b) *Fam (Britannique)* Brit, = pejorative or humorous term used to refer to a British person

rose [roz] **1** *adj* pink; *Fig* **tout n'est pas r.** it's not all rosy; **r. bonbon** candy pink; **r. thé** tea rose; **vieux r.** old rose
2 *nf* (a) *(fleur)* rose; **frais comme une r.** fresh as a daisy; *Fam* **ne pas sentir la r.** to be a bit smelly; **r. trémière** hollyhock (b) **r. des sables** desert rose; **r. des vents** compass card
3 *nm* pink; **voir la vie** *ou* **tout en r.** to see everything through rose-tinted glasses

rosé, -e [roze] **1** *adj* pinkish
2 *nm (vin)* rosé

roseau, -x [rozo] *nm* reed

rosée [roze] *nf* dew

roseraie [rozrɛ] *nf* rose garden

rosette [rozɛt] *nf* (a) *(nœud)* bow; *(ornement)* rosette (b) *(insigne)* rosette *(especially of the Legion of Honour)*

rosier [rozje] *nm* rose tree, rosebush

rosière [rozjɛr] *nf Vieilli* = village maiden awarded a wreath of roses for her virtuous conduct

rosir [rozir] **1** *vt* to turn pink
2 *vi* to go *or* to turn pink

rosse [rɔs] *Péj* **1** *adj Fam (personne, conduite, remarque)* rotten
2 *nf* (a) *(cheval)* hack (b) *Fam (homme)* swine; *(femme)* bitch

rossée [rɔse] *nf Fam* beating, walloping

rosser [rɔse] *vt Fam* **r. qn** to beat sb up, to give sb a good hiding; **se faire r.** to get a hiding

rossignol [rɔsiɲɔl] *nm* (a) *(oiseau)* nightingale (b) *Fam (objet)* white elephant

rot [ro] *nm Fam* belch, burp; *(de bébé)* burp; **faire un r.** *(adulte)* to belch, to burp; *(bébé)* to burp

rotatif, -ive [rɔtatif, -iv] **1** *adj (pompe, moteur)* rotary
2 *nf* **rotative** rotary press

rotation [rɔtasjɔ̃] *nf* rotation; *(du stock, de fonds)* turnover

roter [rɔte] *vi Fam* to belch, to burp

rôti, -e [roti] **1** *adj* roast
2 *nm (viande)* roast; **r. de porc** *(cuit)* roast pork; *(non cuit)* roast of pork

rotin¹ [rɔtɛ̃] *nm* rattan; **chaise en r.** cane *or* rattan chair

rotin² [rɔtɛ̃] *nm Fam Vieilli (sou)* **il n'a plus un r.** he's flat broke

rôtir [rotir] **1** *vt* *(viande)* to roast
2 *vi* (a) *(viande)* to roast (b) **r. au soleil** to bask in the sun
3 se rôtir *vpr* **se r. au soleil** to bask in the sun

rôtisserie [rotisri] *nf* (a) *(boutique du rôtisseur)* = store selling roast meat (b) *(restaurant)* grillroom, steakhouse

rôtissoire [rotiswar] *nf (rotating)* spit, rotisserie

rotonde [rɔtɔ̃d] *nf* rotunda

rotor [rɔtɔr] *nm* rotor

rotule [rɔtyl] *nf* kneecap; *Fam* **être sur les rotules** to be dead beat

roturier, -ère [rɔtyrje, -ɛr] **1** *adj* common
  2 *nm,f* commoner

rouage [rwaʒ] *nm* **(a)** *(d'un mécanisme)* works **(b)** *Fig (d'une administration, d'une organisation)* workings

roublard, -e [rublar, -ard] *Fam* **1** *adj (personne, air)* wily, cunning
  2 *nm,f* wily *or* cunning devil

roublardise [rublardiz] *nf Fam* **(a)** *(caractère)* cunning, wiliness **(b)** *(acte)* crafty *or* cunning trick

rouble [rubl] *nm* ruble

roucoulade [rukulad] *nf (d'oiseaux)* cooing; *Fam* **roucoulades** *(d'amoureux)* billing and cooing

roucoulement [rukulmɑ̃] *nm (d'un pigeon)* cooing; *Fig (d'amoureux)* billing and cooing

roucouler [rukule] **1** *vi (pigeon)* to coo; *Fig (amoureux)* to bill and coo
  2 *vt (mots doux, promesses)* to coo

roue [ru] *nf* **(a)** *(d'un véhicule)* wheel; **être la cinquième r. du carrosse** to be the fifth wheel; **faire la r.** *(oiseau)* to spread its tail; *Fig & Péj* to strut, to swagger; **un deux-roues** a two-wheeled vehicle; **r. libre** freewheel; **descendre en r. libre** to freewheel downhill; **r. de secours** spare wheel **(b)** *(figure de gymnastique)* cartwheel

roué, -e [rwe] *Litt* **1** *adj* cunning, sly
  2 *nm,f* cunning person

rouer [rwe] *vt* **r. qn de coups** to beat sb black and blue

rouerie [ruri] *nf (acte)* cunning *or* sly trick (**envers** played on)

rouet [rwɛ] *nm* spinning wheel

rouge [ruʒ] **1** *adj* **(a)** *(tissu, objet, joue, vin)* red; **r. cerise** cherry-red; **r. sang** blood-red **(b)** *(personne)* **r. de colère/d'émotion** red in the face with anger/emotion; **être r. de honte** to blush with shame; **être r. comme une écrevisse** to be as red as a lobster; **être r. comme une tomate** *ou* **une pivoine** to be as red as a beet **(c)** *(chauffé)* *(fer)* red-hot
  2 *adv* **se fâcher tout r.** to lose one's temper completely; **voir r.** to see red
  3 *nm* **(a)** *(couleur)* red; **peindre/teindre qch en r.** to paint/dye sth red; **le r. lui monte aux joues** he's/she's going red in the face **(b)** *(chaleur extrême)* **porter** *ou* **chauffer qch au r.** to heat sth until it is red-hot **(c)** *(cosmétique)* **r. à lèvres** lipstick; **se mettre du r.** to put some *or* one's lipstick on **(d)** *Fam* **passer au r.** *(signal d'arrêt)* to turn *or* to go red **(e)** *(vin)* red wine; *Fam* **gros r.** plonk **(f)** *Fam Fig* **être dans le r.** *(financièrement)* to be in the red
  4 *nmf (communiste)* Red

rougeâtre [ruʒatr] *adj* reddish

rougeaud, -e [ruʒo, -od] **1** *adj* red-faced
  2 *nm,f* red-faced person

rouge-gorge *(pl* **rouges-gorges**) [ruʒgɔrʒ] *nm* robin

rougeoiement [ruʒwamɑ̃] *nm* red glow

rougeole [ruʒɔl] *nf* measles *(singulier)*; **avoir la r.** to have measles

rougeoyant, -e [ruʒwajɑ̃, -ɑ̃t] *adj* glowing (red)

rougeoyer [32] [ruʒwaje] *vi* to turn red

rouget [ruʒɛ] *nm* red mullet

rougeur [ruʒœr] *nf* **(a)** *(due à la chaleur, à l'émotion)* flush; *(due à la honte, à la gêne)* blush **(b)** *(tache)* blotch **(c)** *(couleur)* redness

rougir [ruʒir] **1** *vt* **(a)** *(ciel, feuilles)* to turn red **(b)** *(visage)* to redden
  2 *vi* **(a)** *(ciel, feuilles)* to turn red **(b)** *(personne)* to turn red; *(de honte, de gêne)* to blush, to go red; *Fig (avoir honte)* to be ashamed; **r. jusqu'aux oreilles** to blush to the roots of one's hair; **r. de colère/d'émotion** to flush with anger/emotion

rougissant, -e [ruʒisɑ̃, -ɑ̃t] *adj (personne, visage)* blushing

rouille [ruj] **1** *adj inv* rust(-colored)
  2 *nf* **(a)** *(sur le fer)* rust **(b)** *(sauce)* = spicy sauce made with garlic and chillis, traditionally served with fish soup

rouillé, -e [ruje] *adj* **(a)** *(métal, clef)* rusty, rusted **(b)** *Fig (personne)* rusty

rouiller [ruje] **1** *vt (métal, clef)* to rust, to make rusty
  2 *vi (métal, clef)* to rust, to go rusty
  3 **se rouiller** *vpr* **(a)** *(métal, clef)* to rust, to get rusty **(b)** *Fig (personne) (physiquement)* to get stiff; *(intellectuellement) (langue, connaissances)* to get rusty

roulade [rulad] *nf* **(a)** *(en gymnastique)* **r. avant/arrière** forward/backward roll; **faire des roulades** to do rolls **(b)** *(vocalise)* roulade **(c)** *(charcuterie)* rolled and stuffed meat

roulage [rulaʒ] *nm Belg (circulation)* traffic; **accident de r.** traffic accident

roulant, -e [rulɑ̃, -ɑ̃t] *adj* **(a)** *(porte)* sliding; *(pont)* traveling **(b)** *(capital)* working **(c)** *Fam (drôle) (personne, blague, histoire)* comical

roulé, -e [rule] **1** *adj* **(a)** *(journal, carte, tapis)* rolled(-up); *(charcuterie)* rolled **(b)** *Fam (femme)* **être bien roulée** to be curvy
  2 *nm (gâteau)* jelly roll

rouleau, -x [rulo] *nm* **(a)** *(bande) (de papier, de Scotch®, de pellicule)* roll; *Fam* **être au bout du r.** to be at the end of one's tether **(b)** *(objet circulaire) (pour peindre)* roller; **r. compresseur** steamroller; **r. à pâtisserie,** *Can & Suisse* **r. à pâte** rolling pin; **r. de printemps** spring roll, egg roll **(c)** *(vague)* billow, roller **(d)** *(bigoudi)* roller **(e)** *(saut en hauteur)* **r. dorsal** Fosbury flop; **r. ventral** western roll

roulé-boulé *(pl* **roulés-boulés**) [rulebule] *nm* roll *(executed tucked up in a ball)*

roulement [rulmɑ̃] *nm* **(a)** *(d'une balle)* rolling **(b)** *(bruit)* **un r. de tonnerre** a roll *or* rumble of thunder; **des roulements de tambour** drum rolls **(c)** *(alternance)* rotation; **par r.** in rotation **(d)** *(pièce)* bearing; **r. à billes** ball bearing **(e)** *Fin (de fonds)* circulation; *(de capitaux)* turnover

rouler [rule] **1** *vt* **(a)** *(pierre, tonneau)* to roll (along) **(b)** *(tapis, papier, manches)* to roll up; *(cigarette)* to roll **(c)** *(yeux)* to roll **(d)** *(balancer)* **r. les épaules** to roll one's shoulders; **r. les hanches** to swing one's hips **(e)** *Fam (duper)* to swindle (**de** out of); **se faire r.** to be had **(f)** *(locutions)* **r. les r** to roll one's r's; *très Fam* **r. une pelle** *ou* **un palot** *ou* **un patin à qn** to make out with sb
  2 *vi* **(a)** *(balle)* to roll; **faire r. qch sur le sol** to roll sth along the ground **(b)** *(dégringoler) (personne)* to roll, to tumble **(c)** *(dans une voiture, dans un train)* to go, to travel; **on a beaucoup roulé** we drove for a long time; **ça roule bien ce matin** there are no traffic problems this morning; **à quelle vitesse rouliez-vous?** what speed were you doing? **(d)** *Fam* **ça roule** everything's fine **(e)** *Fig* **r. sur l'or** to be rolling in money **(f)** *(conversation)* **r. sur qch** to be about sth **(g)** *(tonnerre)* to roll, to rumble; *(tambour)* to roll **(h)** *(navire)* to roll
  3 **se rouler** *vpr* **(a)** *(sur soi-même)* **se r. par terre** to roll about on the floor; *(dehors)* to roll about on the ground **(b)** **se r. une cigarette** to roll a cigarette; *Fam* **se r. les pouces, se les r.** to twiddle one's thumbs

roulette [rulɛt] *nf* **(a)** *(de meuble)* castor; **à roulettes** *(meuble)* on castors; *Fam* **marcher** *ou* **aller comme sur des roulettes** to go like clockwork **(b)** *Fam (de dentiste)* drill **(c)** *(au jeu)* roulette; **r. russe** Russian roulette

rouli-roulant *(pl* **rouli-roulants**) [rulirulɑ̃] *nm Can* skateboard

roulis [ruli] *nm* roll

roulotte [rulɔt] *nf (de bohémiens)* caravan

roulure [rulyr] *nf très Fam* whore

roumain, -e [rumɛ̃, -ɛn] **1** *adj* Romanian
  2 *nm (langue)* Romanian
  3 *nm,f* **R., Roumaine** Romanian

Roumanie [rumani] *nf* **la R.** Romania

round [rawnd, rund] *nm* round

roupie [rupi] *nf* rupee

roupiller [rupije] *vi Fam* to sleep, to snooze

roupillon [rupijɔ̃] *nm Fam* snooze; **piquer un r.** to have a snooze

rouquin, -e [rukɛ̃, -in] *Fam* **1** *adj (personne)* red-haired
    2 *nm,f* redhead

rouspéter [34] [ruspete] *vi Fam* to moan and groan, to grumble (**contre** about)

rouspéteur, -euse [ruspetœr, -øz] *Fam* **1** *adj* grumpy
    2 *nm,f* moaner, grumbler

rousse [rus] *voir* **roux**

roussette [rusɛt] *nf* **(a)** *(poisson)* spotted dogfish **(b)** *(chauve-souris)* flying fox **(c)** *(grenouille)* common frog

rousseur [rusœr] *nf (couleur)* redness

roussi [rusi] *nm* **ça sent le r.** there's a smell of burning; *Fig* there's trouble brewing

roussir [rusir] **1** *vt* **(a)** *(rendre roux)* to turn brown **(b)** *(brûler)* to scorch, to singe
    2 *vi (feuilles, arbres)* to turn brown

rouste [rust] *nf Fam* thrashing, hammering; **flanquer une r. à qn** to give sb a thrashing *or* a hammering

routage [rutaʒ] *nm (d'imprimés)* sorting and mailing

routard, -e [rutar, -ard] *nm,f Fam* backpacker

route [rut] *nf* **(a)** *(voie)* road; **prendre la r. de Paris** to take the Paris road; **r. à double voie** *ou* **à deux voies** divided highway; **par la r.** by road; **r. départementale** secondary road; **r. nationale** main road, ≃ state highway **(b)** *(itinéraire)* route, way; **montrer la r. à qn** to show sb the way; **c'est sur ma r.** it's on my way; **r. des vins** wine trail **(c)** *(trajet)* **après trois heures de r.** after three hours on the road; **se mettre en r.** *(personne)* to set off; **en r.!** let's be off!; *Fam Hum* **en r., mauvaise troupe!** c'mon guys, let's get moving!; **bonne r.!** have a good trip! **(d)** *Fig (chemin)* path **(e)** *(marche)* **mettre qch en r.** *(moteur)* to start sth up; *(projet, travaux)* to get sth under way; **avoir qch en r.** to be working on sth; *Fam* **ils ont un bébé en r.** they've got a baby on the way

routeur [rutœr] *nm Ordinat* router

routier, -ère [rutje, -ɛr] **1** *adj* road
    2 *nm* **(a)** *(conducteur)* truck driver, trucker **(b)** *(restaurant)* truck stop

routine [rutin] *nf* **(a)** *(habitude)* routine; **s'enliser dans/sortir de la r.** to get into/out of a rut **(b)** *Ordinat* **r. d'édition/de logiciel** edit/software routine

routinier, -ère [rutinje, -ɛr] *adj (tâches, travail)* routine; **être r.** to be set in one's ways

rouvrir [52] [ruvrir] **1** *vt* to reopen
    2 se rouvrir *vpr* to reopen, to open again

roux, rousse [ru, rus] **1** *adj (feuilles)* russet, reddish-brown; *(cheveux)* red; *(personne)* red-haired; *(sucre)* brown
    2 *nm,f (personne)* red-haired person, redhead
    3 *nm* **(a)** *(couleur)* russet, reddish-brown **(b)** *(préparation culinaire)* roux

royal, -e, -aux, -ales [rwajal, -o] *adj* **(a)** *(palais, visite)* royal **(b)** *(cadeau)* magnificent; *(pourboire)* huge **(c)** *(indifférence)* utter; *Fam* **ficher une paix royale à qn** to leave sb in complete peace

royalement [rwajalmã] *adv* **(a)** *(payé)* royally **(b)** *Fam* **je m'en fiche** *ou* **moque r.** I couldn't care less

royalisme [rwajalism] *nm* royalism

royaliste [rwajalist] **1** *adj* royalist; *Fig* **être plus r. que le roi** to overdo it
    2 *nmf* royalist

royalties [rwajalti] *nfpl* royalties

royaume [rwajom] *nm* kingdom; *Fig* realm

Royaume-Uni [rwajomyni] *nm* **le R.** the United Kingdom

royauté [rwajote] *nf (monarchie)* monarchy; *(dignité)* kingship

RPR [ɛrpeɛr] *nm Pol (abrév* **Rassemblement pour la République**) = right-wing French political party

RSVP *(abrév* **répondez s'il vous plaît***)* RSVP

ruade [rɥad] *nf (d'un cheval)* lashing out, kick

Ruanda [rwãda] = **Rwanda**

ruandais, -e [rwãdɛ, -ɛz] = **rwandais**

ruban [rybã] *nm* ribbon; **r. adhésif** adhesive tape; **r. encreur** *(de machine à écrire)* typewriter ribbon; *Ordinat* **r. perforé** punchtape

rubéole [rybeɔl] *nf* German measles *(singulier)*, rubella

rubicond, -e [rybikɔ̃, -ɔ̃d] *adj (teint)* florid, rubicund

rubis [rybi] *nm* **(a)** *(pierre précieuse)* ruby; *Fig* **payer r. sur l'ongle** to pay cash on the nail **(b)** *(de montre, d'horloge)* jewel

rubrique [rybrik] *nf (article)* column; *(page)* page; *(cahier)* section; **r. nécrologique** obituary section

ruche [ryʃ] *nf* **(a)** *(abri)* beehive **(b)** *(essaim)* hive; *Fig (ville, école)* hive of activity

rucher [ryʃe] *nm* apiary

rude [ryd] *adj* **(a)** *(fruste)* rough, uncouth **(b)** *(sévère) (personne, voix)* harsh **(c)** *(peau, tissu)* rough **(d)** *(hiver, climat)* severe, harsh **(e)** *(tâche, métier)* tough

rudement [rydmã] *adv* **(a)** *(répondre)* harshly; **être r. éprouvé** to be severely tested **(b)** *(frapper, heurter)* hard **(c)** *Fam (très)* really

rudesse [rydɛs] *nf* harshness; **avec r.** harshly

rudimentaire [rydimãtɛr] *adj* rudimentary

rudiments [rydimã] *nmpl (d'une matière)* rudiments; **avoir des r. de chinois** to speak basic Chinese

rudoyer [32] [rydwaje] *vt* to treat harshly

rue [ry] *nf* street; **être/se retrouver à la r.** to be/find oneself out on the street; **mettre/jeter qn à la r.** to put/throw sb out on the street; **r. piétonnière** *ou* **piétonne** pedestrian zone; **r. principale** main street; **la grande r.** the main street

ruée [rɥe] *nf* rush; **la r. vers l'or** the gold rush

ruelle [rɥɛl] *nf* lane, alley(way)

ruer [rɥe] **1** *vi (cheval)* to kick; *Fig* **r. dans les brancards** to rebel
    2 se ruer *vpr* **se r. sur qn** to rush at sb; **se r. sur qch** to make a rush for sth; **les invités se sont rués sur le buffet** the guests made a dash for the buffet

rugby [rygbi] *nm* rugby; **r. à treize/quinze** Rugby League/ Union

rugbyman [rygbiman] *(pl* **rugbymen** [rygbimɛn]*)* *nm* rugby player

rugir [ryʒir] **1** *vi (fauve)* to roar **(b)** *(personne)* to roar (**de** with) **(c)** *(vent, tempête)* to howl
    2 *vt* to roar

rugissement [ryʒismã] *nm* **(a)** *(d'un fauve)* roar; **des rugissements** roaring **(b)** *(d'une personne)* roar; **pousser des rugissements de colère** to roar with anger **(c)** *(du vent, d'une tempête)* howling

rugosité [rygozite] *nf* roughness; **rugosités** rough patches

rugueux, -euse [rygø, -øz] *adj* rough

ruine [rɥin] *nf* **(a)** *(écroulement) (d'un édifice)* **en r.** in ruins, ruined; **tomber en ruine(s)** to go to ruin **(b)** **ruines** *(décombres)* ruins **(c)** *Fig (d'une personne, d'une société)* ruin, downfall; **aller** *ou* **courir à la r.** to be on the road to ruin **(d)** *(vieille maison)* ruin **(e)** *Fam* **c'est la r.!** *(c'est coûteux)* it's outrageously expensive!

ruiner [rɥine] **1** *vt* to ruin; *(espoirs)* to ruin, to dash
    2 se ruiner *vpr (perdre son argent)* to ruin *or* to bankrupt oneself; *(dépenser beaucoup d'argent)* to spend a fortune

ruineux, -euse [rɥinø, -øz] *adj* ruinously expensive; **ce n'est pas r.** it won't ruin you/us/etc.

ruisseau, -x [rɥiso] *nm* **(a)** *(cours d'eau)* brook, stream **(b)** *Fig (de sang, de lave)* stream; *(de larmes)* flood **(c)** *(caniveau)* gutter

ruisselant, -e [rɥislɑ̃, -ɑ̃t] *adj* dripping (**de** with)

ruisseler [9] [rɥisle] *vi* (**a**) *(liquide)* to stream, to run (**b**) *(surface)* to drip, to stream (**de** with); **le front ruisselant de sueur** with one's forehead dripping with sweat; **ses joues ruisselaient de larmes** tears were streaming down his/her cheeks

ruissellement [rɥisɛlmɑ̃] *nm* streaming, running

rumba [rumba] *nf* rumba

rumeur [rymœr] *nf* (**a**) *(bruit confus)* distant murmur; *(de la circulation, d'une ville)* hum; *(de voix)* murmur (**b**) *(nouvelle)* rumor

ruminant [ryminɑ̃] *nm* ruminant

rumination [ryminasjɔ̃] *nf* rumination, ruminating

ruminer [rymine] **1** *vt (herbe)* to chew; *Fig (idée, projet)* to mull over

 2 *vi* to ruminate, to chew the cud; *Fig* to brood

rumsteck [rɔmstɛk] *nm* rump steak

rupestre [rypɛstr] *adj* (**a**) **peinture r.** rock painting; *(dans une caverne)* cave painting (**b**) *(plante)* rock

rupin, -e [rypɛ̃, -in] *Fam* **1** *adj (riche) (personne)* loaded; *(quartier)* plush, smart

 2 *nm,f* **c'est un r.** he's loaded; **les rupins** the rich

rupture [ryptyr] *nf* (**a**) *(d'une corde, d'une poutre)* breaking; *(d'un barrage)* bursting; *(d'un tendon)* rupture (**b**) *(interruption)* *(de négociations)* breaking off (**de** of), breakdown (**de** in); **être en r. avec qn/qch** to be at odds with sb/sth; **en r. avec la tradition** in a break with tradition; **être en r. de stock** to be out of stock (**c**) *(annulation) (de fiançailles)* breaking off; *(de contrat)* breach (**d**) *(entre amoureux)* break-up; **être au bord de la r.** to be on the verge of breaking up

rural, -e, -aux, -ales [ryral, -o] **1** *adj (région, vie)* rural; *(chemin)* country

 2 *nm,f* country person

ruse [ryz] *nf* (**a**) *(procédé)* ruse, trick; **r. de guerre** stratagem (of war); *Fig* dodge (**b**) *(calcul)* **faire qch par la r.** to do sth by trickery

rusé, -e [ryze] *adj* cunning, crafty

ruser [ryze] *vi* to use trickery *or* cunning

russe [rys] **1** *adj* Russian

 2 *nm (langue)* Russian

 3 *nmf* **R.** Russian

Russie [rysi] *nf* **la R.** Russia

rustaud, -e [rysto, -od] **1** *adj* uncouth

 2 *nm,f* hick

Rustine® [rystin] *nf* repair patch *(for mending inner tube of bicycle)*

rustique [rystik] *adj* (**a**) *(manières, vie)* rustic; *(meuble)* rustic-style (**b**) *(plante)* hardy

rustre [rystr] **1** *adj* uncouth

 2 *nm* boor, lout

rut [ryt] *nm (de mâle)* rut(ting); *(de femelle)* heat; **en r.** *(mâle)* rutting; *(femelle)* in heat

rutabaga [rytabaga] *nm* rutabaga

rutilant, -e [rytilɑ̃, -ɑ̃t] *adj* gleaming

rutiler [rytile] *vi* to gleam

Rwanda [rwɑ̃da] *nm* **le R.** Rwanda

rwandais, -e [rwɑ̃dɛ, -ez] **1** *adj* Rwandan

 2 *nm,f* **R., Rwandaise** Rwandan

rythme [ritm] *nm* (**a**) *(succession)* rhythm; *(allure)* pace; **manquer de r.** *(film)* to be a bit slow; **au r. de** at the rate of; **r. cardiaque/respiratoire** heart/breathing rate; **les rythmes scolaires** the way in which the school year is organized (**b**) *(en musique)* rhythm; **en r.** in time; **marquer le r.** to beat time; **suivre le r.** to follow the beat; *Fig* to keep up; **avoir le sens du r.** to have a sense of rhythm; **avoir le r. dans la peau** to have rhythm in one's blood (**c**) *(d'une phrase)* rhythm

rythmé, -e [ritme] *adj* rhythmic(al)

rythmer [ritme] *vt* to give rhythm to

rythmique [ritmik] **1** *adj* rhythmic(al)

 2 *nf (en poésie)* rhythmics *(singulier)*

S

S¹, s [ɛs] *nm inv* S, s; **faire des s** to zigzag; **en S** (*crochet*) S-shaped; (*route*) zigzagging

S² (**a**) (*abrév* **sud**) S (**b**) (*abrév* **seconde(s)**) sec

s' [s] *voir* **se**

SA [ɛsa] *nf* (*abrév* **société anonyme**) Inc.

sa [sa] *voir* **son¹**

sabbat [saba] *nm* Sabbath

sabbatique [sabatik] *adj* (*repos, année, congé*) sabbatical; **prendre un an de congé s.** to take a year's sabbatical

sable [sabl] **1** *nm* sand; *Fam* **être sur le s.** (*sans travail*) to be out of work; (*sans argent*) to be down and out; *Fam* **mettre qn sur le s.** to ruin sb; **sables mouvants** quicksands
2 *adj inv* sand-colored

sablé, -e [sable] **1** *adj voir* **pâte**
2 *nm* shortbread cookie

sabler [sable] *vt* (**a**) (*chemin*) to sand; (*route*) to grit (**b**) (*bâtiment*) to sandblast (**c**) **s. le champagne** to crack open a bottle of champagne

sableuse [sabløz] *nf* sandblaster

sableux, -euse [sablø, -øz] *adj* sandy

sablier [sablije] *nm* hourglass

sablonneux, -euse [sablɔnø, -øz] *adj* sandy

sabord [sabɔr] *nm* = type of square porthole; *Fam Vieilli* **mille sabords!** shiver me timbers!

saborder [sabɔrde] **1** *vt* (*navire*) & *Fig* to scuttle
2 se saborder *vpr* to scuttle one's ship

sabot [sabo] *nm* (**a**) (*de cheval*) hoof; *Fam* **ça ne se trouve pas sous le s. d'un cheval** it doesn't grow on trees (**b**) (*chaussure*) clog; *Fam* **je te vois venir avec tes gros sabots** I can see what you're after (**c**) **s. de Denver** Denver boot

sabotage [sabɔtaʒ] *nm* sabotage; (*acte*) act of sabotage

saboter [sabɔte] *vt* (*voiture, entreprise, plan de paix*) to sabotage; (*travail*) to botch

saboteur, -euse [sabɔtœr, -øz] *nm,f* saboteur

sabre [sabr] *nm* saber; **s. au clair** with drawn sword

sabrer [sabre] *vt* (**a**) **une cicatrice lui sabrait la joue** there was the gash of a scar on his/her cheek (**b**) *Fam* (*raccourcir*) to slash (**c**) *Fam* (*critiquer*) to slam (**d**) *Fam* **se faire s.** (*étudiant*) to flunk; **il s'est fait s. par le prof** the teacher flunked him (**e**) **s. le champagne** to crack open a bottle of champagne

sac¹ [sak] *nm* (**a**) (*contenant, contenu*) bag (**de** of); (*grand et en toile*) sack (**de** of); **s. de sable** sandbag; *Fam* **un s. de nœuds** a hornet's nest; **partir s. au dos** to set off with one's backpack on one's back; *Fam* **vider son s.** to get it off one's chest; *Fam* **je les mets dans le même s.** they're as bad as each other; *Fam* **l'affaire est dans le s.** it's in the bag; **s. de couchage** sleeping bag; **s. à dos** rucksack, backpack; **s. à main** handbag; *Fam* **s. d'os** bag of bones; **s. à ouvrage** work bag; **s. poubelle** garbage bag; **s. à provisions** shopping bag; *Fam* **s. à vin** drunk; **s. de voyage** travel *or* overnight bag (**b**) *Anciennement très Fam* (*somme*) 10 francs

sac² [sak] *nm* (*pillage*) sacking; **mettre une ville à s.** to sack a town

saccade [sakad] *nf* jerk, jolt; **par saccades** in fits and starts

saccadé, -e [sakade] *adj* jerky

saccage [sakaʒ] *nm* havoc; **se livrer à un s. de** to wreak havoc in

saccager [45] [sakaʒe] *vt* (**a**) (*piller*) (*ville*) to sack; (*maison*) to ransack (**b**) (*dévaster*) (*ville, maison*) to wreak havoc in; **la récolte fut saccagée par l'orage** the crops were devastated by the storm

saccharose [sakaroz] *nm Chim* saccharose

sacerdoce [sasɛrdɔs] *nm* priesthood; *Fig* vocation

sacerdotal, -e, -aux, -ales [sasɛrdɔtal, -o] *adj* priestly

sachant, sache, *etc. voir* **savoir²**

sachet [saʃɛ] *nm* sachet; **s. de thé** teabag; **thé en sachets** teabags; **en s.-cuisson** boil-in-bag

sacoche [sakɔʃ] *nf* (**a**) (*de vélo*) saddlebag (**b**) (*besace*) bag (**c**) *Belg & Can* handbag, purse

sacquer [sake] *Fam* **1** *vt* (**a**) (*renvoyer*) to fire; **se faire s.** to be fired (**b**) (*noter sévèrement*) to give a bad grade to; **se faire s. par un prof** to get a bad grade from a teacher (**c**) (*supporter*) **je ne peux pas le s.** I can't stand him
2 *vi* (*professeur*) to be a tough grader

sacrant, -e [sakrɑ̃, -ɑ̃t] *adj Can Fam* (*fâcheux*) bothersome

sacre [sakr] *nm* (**a**) (*d'un roi*) coronation; (*d'un évêque*) consecration; *Fig* rite (**b**) *Can* (*juron*) curse word, expletive

sacré, -e [sakre] **1** *adj* (**a**) *Rel* & *Fig* sacred (**b**) *Fam* (*maudit*) damn; **s. Paul, qu'est-ce qu'on ferait sans lui?** good old Paul, what would we do without him?
2 *nm* **le s.** the sacred

sacrement [sakrəmɑ̃] *nm* sacrament; **le saint S.** the Blessed Sacrament; **recevoir les derniers sacrements** to receive the last rites

sacrément [sakremɑ̃] *adv Fam* damn

sacrer [sakre] **1** *vt* (*roi*) to crown; (*évêque*) to consecrate; **s. qn roi** to crown sb king; *Fig* **il a été sacré champion de France en 1995** he won the French championship in 1995
2 *vi Can* to swear

sacrifice [sakrifis] *nm* sacrifice; **offrir qn/qch en s.** to offer sb/sth up as a sacrifice; **faire le s. de sa vie** to sacrifice one's life; *Fig* **faire des sacrifices (pour)** to make sacrifices (for)

sacrifier [66] [sakrifje] **1** *vt aussi Fig* to sacrifice (**à** to); **sacrifié** (*prix*) rock-bottom; (*article*) at a rock-bottom price
2 *vi* **s. à la mode** to be a slave to fashion
3 se sacrifier *vpr* to sacrifice oneself (**pour** for); *Fam* **allez, je me sacrifie, je vais les chercher à la gare!** OK, I'll be the martyr and pick them up from the station!

sacrilège [sakrilɛʒ] **1** *adj* sacrilegious
2 *nmf* (*personne*) sacrilegious person
3 *nm* (*acte*) sacrilege

sacristie [sakristi] *nf* sacristy, vestry

sacro-saint, -e (*mpl* **sacro-saints,** *fpl* **sacro-saintes**) [sakrosɛ̃, -ɛ̃t] *adj aussi Ironique* sacrosanct

sadique [sadik] **1** *adj* sadistic
2 *nmf* sadist

sadisme [sadism] *nm* sadism
sadomaso [sadɔmazo] *adj inv Fam* S & M, SM
sadomasochisme [sadɔmazɔʃism] *nm* sadomasochism
sadomasochiste [sadɔmazɔʃist] **1** *adj* sadomasochistic
  2 *nmf* sadomasochist
safari [safari] *nm* safari; **en s.** on safari; **s.-photo** photographic safari
safran [safrɑ̃] **1** *nm (plante, épice)* saffron
  2 *adj inv* **(jaune) s.** saffron (yellow)
saga [saga] *nf aussi Fig* saga
sagace [sagas] *adj* shrewd, astute
sagacité [sagasite] *nf* shrewdness, astuteness; **avec s.** shrewdly, astutely
sage [saʒ] **1** *adj* (a) *(avisé) (personne, décision)* wise, sensible (b) *(calme) (enfant, animal)* good, well-behaved; **s. comme une image** as good as gold (c) *(chaste) (personne)* good; *(tenue, robe)* sober
  2 *nm* wise man; **un vieux s.** a wise old man
sage-femme (*pl* **sages-femmes**) [saʒfam] *nf* midwife
sagement [saʒmɑ̃] *adv* (a) *(raisonnablement)* wisely, sensibly (b) *(tranquillement)* quietly
sagesse [saʒɛs] *nf* (a) *(intelligence)* wisdom, good sense; **avoir la s. de faire qch** to be wise *or* sensible enough to do sth; **plein de s.** very sensible; *Fig* **la voix de la s.** the voice of reason (b) *(calme)* good behavior
Sagittaire [saʒitɛr] *nm Astron & Astrol* **le S.** Sagittarius; **être S.** to be (a) Sagittarius
sagouin [sagwɛ̃] *nm Fam (personne)* slob
Sahara [saara] *nm* **le S.** the Sahara (Desert)
saharienne [saarjɛn] *nf* safari jacket
Sahel [sael] *nm* **le S.** the Sahel
saignant, -e [sɛɲɑ̃, -ɑ̃t] *adj* (a) *(blessure)* bleeding (b) *(viande)* rare
saignée [seɲe] *nf* blood-letting; *Fig* drain; **faire une s. à qn** to bleed sb
saignement [sɛɲmɑ̃] *nm* bleeding; **s. de nez** nosebleed
saigner [seɲe] **1** *vi (personne, blessure)* to bleed; **je saigne du nez** my nose is bleeding, I have a nosebleed; *Fig & Litt* **mon cœur saigne** my heart bleeds; *Fam* **ça va s.** there's going to be trouble
  2 *vt (poulet, personne)* to bleed; *Fig* **s. qn à blanc** to bleed sb dry
  3 se saigner *vpr Fig* **se s. aux quatre veines** to bleed oneself dry
saillant, -e [sajɑ̃, -ɑ̃t] *adj (qui dépasse)* projecting; *(pommettes)* prominent; *(muscles)* bulging; *Fig (trait)* salient
saillie [saji] *nf* (a) *(partie en avant)* projection; **faire s.** to project, to jut out (b) *(par un mâle)* covering
saillir [67] [sajir] **1** *vt (femelle)* to cover
  2 *vi (s'avancer)* to project, to jut out (**sur** over)
sain, -e [sɛ̃, sɛn] *adj* healthy; *(fruit, gestion)* sound; *(lectures)* wholesome; **s. de corps et d'esprit** sound in body and mind; **s. et sauf** safe and sound
sainement [sɛnmɑ̃] *adv* (a) *(vivre)* healthily (b) *(juger)* sensibly
saint, -e [sɛ̃, sɛ̃t] **1** *adj (lieu)* holy; *(personne, vie)* saintly; **s. patron** patron saint; **s. Pierre** St Peter; **sainte Catherine** St Catherine; *Fam* **avoir une sainte horreur de qch** to have a holy horror of sth; *Fam* **ne rien faire de toute la sainte journée** to do nothing the whole damn day
  2 *nm,f aussi Fig* saint; **ne savoir plus à quel s. se vouer** not to know which way to turn; *Hum* **il vaut mieux s'adresser à Dieu qu'à ses saints** it's best to go right to the top
  3 *nm* **le S. des Saints** the Holy of Holies
saint-bernard [sɛ̃bɛrnar] *nm inv (chien)* St Bernard
Saint-Cyr [sɛ̃sir] *n* Saint-Cyr military academy
Sainte-Lucie [sɛ̃tlysi] *n* St. Lucia
sainte-nitouche (*pl* **saintes-nitouches**) [sɛ̃tnituʃ] *nf* little

hypocrite; **avec ses airs de s.** looking as if butter wouldn't melt in his/her mouth
Saint-Esprit [sɛ̃tɛspri] *nm* **le S.** the Holy Ghost *or* Spirit; *Hum* **par l'opération du S.** by magic
sainteté [sɛ̃tte] *nf (d'une personne)* saintliness; *(de la loi, d'un serment)* sanctity; *(d'un lieu)* holiness; **sa S. (le pape)** His Holiness (the Pope)
saint-frusquin [sɛ̃fryskɛ̃] *nm Fam* **tout le s.** the whole caboodle; **il s'est pointé avec tout son s.** he turned up with all his gear
saint-glinglin [sɛ̃glɛ̃glɛ̃] **à la saint-glinglin** *adv Fam* **on sera payés à la s.** we'll be paid when pigs fly; **repoussé à la s.** postponed till whenever
saint-honoré [sɛ̃tɔnɔre] *nm inv* Saint-Honoré *(choux pastry ring filled with confectioner's custard)*
Saint-Jean [sɛ̃ʒɑ̃] *nf* (a) **la S.** Midsummer Day (b) *Can* **la Saint-Jean-Baptiste** Saint-Jean-Baptiste Day *(July 24)*
Saint-Laurent [sɛ̃lɔrɑ̃] *nm* **le S.** the St. Lawrence (River); **la Voie maritime du S.** the St. Lawrence Seaway
Saint-Marin [sɛ̃marɛ̃] *n* San Marino
saint-nectaire [sɛ̃nɛktɛr] *nm inv* = type of firm cheese
Saint-Père [sɛ̃pɛr] *nm* **le S.** the Holy Father
Saint-Pétersbourg [sɛ̃petɛrsbur] *n* St. Petersburg
Saint-Pierre-et-Miquelon [sɛ̃pjɛremiklɔ̃] *n* St. Pierre and Miquelon
Saint-Siège [sɛ̃sjɛʒ] *nm* **le S.** the Holy See
Saint-Sylvestre [sɛ̃silvɛstr] *nf* **la S.** New Year's Eve
sais *voir* **savoir²**
saisie [sezi] *nf (de biens)* seizure; *Ordinat* **s. de données** data capture, keyboarding; *Ordinat* **s. automatique/manuelle** automatic/manual input
saisine [sezin] *nf Jur* referral to a court
saisir [sezir] **1** *vt* (a) *(attraper) (personne, objet)* to take hold of; *(brusquement)* to grab; **s. l'occasion (de faire qch)** to seize or to grasp the opportunity (to do sth); **j'ai été saisi par le froid** the cold really hit me (b) *(comprendre) (signification, nuance)* to grasp, to get; *(nom)* to catch, to get (c) *Ordinat (données)* to key (d) *Jur (biens)* to seize (e) *Jur* **s. un tribunal d'une affaire** to refer a matter to a court (f) *(viande)* to seal
  2 *vi (comprendre)* to get it
  3 se saisir *vpr* **se s. de qn/qch** to take hold of sb/sth; *(brusquement)* to grab sb/sth
saisissant, -e [sezisɑ̃, -ɑ̃t] *adj (froid)* biting; *(ressemblance)* striking; *(scène)* gripping
saisissement [sezismɑ̃] *nm* (a) *(sensation de froid)* sudden chill (b) *(émotion)* shock
saison [sɛzɔ̃] *nf* season; **en cette s.** at this time of year; **en toute s.** all (the) year round; **faire une bonne/mauvaise s.** *(équipe)* to have a good/bad season; **être de s.** *(fruits)* to be in season; **des fraises! mais ce n'est pas la s.!** strawberries! but it isn't the season for them!; **un temps de s.** seasonal weather; **la belle s.** the summer months; **la haute/basse s.** the high/low season; **la morte s.** the off season; **la s. touristique** the tourist season; **la s. des amours** the mating season; **la s. des pluies** the rainy season
saisonnier, -ère [sɛzɔnje, -ɛr] **1** *adj* seasonal
  2 *nm,f* seasonal worker
sait *voir* **savoir²**
saké [sake] *nm* sake
salade [salad] *nf* (a) *(plante)* lettuce (b) *(plat)* salad; **s. composée** mixed salad; **s. de fruits** fruit salad; **s. grecque** Greek salad; **s. mixte** mixed salad; **s. niçoise** salade niçoise; **s. de tomates/de riz** tomato/rice salad; **s. verte** green salad; **haricots verts en s.** green-bean salad (c) *Fam (désordre)* mess (d) *Fam* **vendre sa s.** to make a pitch (e) *Fam* **salades** *(mensonges)* tall stories, fibs
saladier [saladje] *nm* salad bowl

salaire [salɛr] nm (a) (mensuel) salary; (hebdomadaire, journalier) wages; Prov **toute peine mérite s.** the laborer is worthy of his hire; **s. de départ** starting salary; **s. minimum interprofessionnel de croissance** guaranteed minimum wage (b) (récompense) reward (**de** for); **le s. de la peur** the wages of fear

salaison [salɛzɔ̃] nf (action) salting; **des salaisons** salted meats

salamalecs [salamalɛk] nmpl Fam bowing and scraping

salamandre [salamɑ̃dr] nf salamander

salami [salami] nm salami

salant [salɑ̃] adj m voir **marais**

salarial, -e, -aux, -ales [salarjal, -o] adj wage; (mensuel) salary

salarié, -e [salarje] **1** adj (a) (travailleur) (payé mensuellement) salaried; (payé hebdomadairement) wage-earning (b) (travail) paid

2 nm,f (payé mensuellement) salaried employee; (payé hebdomadairement) wage-earner; **salariés** (d'une société) employees

salarier [66] [salarje] vt to put on one's salaried staff

salaud [salo] Vulg **1** nm bastard

2 adj **c'était vraiment s. de faire ça** that was a really shitty thing to do; **t'as vraiment été s.!** you were a real shit!

sale [sal] **1** adj (a) (peu soigné) dirty (b) Fam (grave) (maladie, situation) nasty; (affaire) dirty; **avoir une s. tête** ou **gueule** (antipathique) to look really nasty; (malade) to look awful; **faire un s. coup à qn** to play a dirty trick on sb; **s. bête** horrible beast; **s. boulot** rotten job; **faire le s. boulot** to do the dirty work; **s. gosse** little brat; **s. temps** filthy weather; **s. type** nasty character

2 nm Fam **mettre une chemise au s.** to put a dirty shirt in the wash

salé, -e [sale] **1** adj (a) (conservé au sel) salt; (additionné de sel) salted; (au goût) salty (b) Fig (histoire, plaisanterie) spicy (c) Fam (condamnation) stiff; (addition) steep

2 nm **le s.** savory food; **petit s.** salt pork

salement [salmɑ̃] adv (a) (manger, boire) in a disgusting manner (b) Fam (blessé, touché) really badly; **je suis s. emmerdé** I'm in real trouble

saler [sale] vt to salt

saleté [salte] nf (a) (manque de soin) dirtiness; (crasse) dirt; **faire des saletés** to make a mess (b) (objet) trash, junk; **manger des saletés** to eat junk food (c) (acte ou remarque obscène) obscenity (d) Fam (personne) bastard

salière [saljɛr] nf saltshaker

saligaud [saligo] nm Fam (ignoble individu) bastard

salin, -e [salɛ̃, -in] **1** adj saline

2 nm (marais salant) salt marsh

salir [salir] **1** vt to make dirty, to dirty; Fig **s. le nom/la mémoire de qn** to sully sb's name/memory

2 se salir vpr to get dirty; Fig **se s. les mains** to get one's hands dirty

salissant, -e [salisɑ̃, -ɑ̃t] adj (a) (travail) dirty, messy (b) (tissu, vêtement) easily soiled; (couleur) that shows the dirt

salissure [salisyr] nf dirty mark

salivaire [salivɛr] adj (glande) salivary

salive [saliv] nf saliva

saliver [salive] vi to salivate; Fig **s. devant qch** to drool at the sight of sth

salle [sal] nf (a) (pièce) room; **s. d'armes** (pour l'escrime) fencing hall; (pour les armes) armory; **s. d'attente** waiting room; **s. de bain(s)** bathroom; Ordinat **s. blanche** clean room; **s. des coffres** vaults; **s. commune** common room; **s. d'embarquement** (d'un aéroport) departure lounge; **s. d'exposition** showroom; (pour une foire) exhibition hall; **s. des fêtes** community hall; (d'un village) village hall; **s. de garde** (d'hôpital) staff room; (de caserne) guardroom; **s. de jeu** (dans une

maison) rumpus room; (dans un casino) gaming room; **s. des machines** (d'un navire) engine-room; **s. à manger** dining room; (meubles) dining-room suite; **s. d'opération** operating room; **s. des pas perdus** (dans une gare) concourse; **s. des professeurs** staff room; **s. de réunion** meeting room; **s. du trône** throneroom; **s. des urgences** emergency room; **s. des ventes** salesroom (b) (pour le cinéma, pour le théâtre) **s. (de spectacle)** auditorium; **toute la s. applaudit** the whole audience applauded; **les salles obscures** the movies

salmonelle [salmɔnɛl] nf salmonella

salmonellose [salmɔneloz] nf salmonella poisoning

Salomon [salɔmɔ̃] voir **île**

salon [salɔ̃] nm (a) (pièce) living room; (dans un bateau) lounge; (dans un train) saloon car; Can **s. de barbier** barbershop; **s. de coiffure** hairdresser's salon; **s. d'essayage** fitting room; **s. de thé** tea room (b) (meubles) suite (c) (exposition) exhibition; **le S. des Arts ménagers** ≃ the Home Crafts Show; **le S. de l'Automobile** ou **de l'Auto** the Automobile Show; **le S. du Livre** the Book Fair; **le S. nautique** the Boat Show (d) (littéraire) salon; **tenir s.** to hold a salon

salon-lavoir (pl **salons-lavoirs**) [salɔ̃lavwar] nm Belg & Suisse (lavomatique) laundromat

salopard [salɔpar] nm Vulg bastard

salope [salɔp] nf Vulg (femme méprisable) bitch; (homme méprisable) bastard

saloper [salɔpe] vt très Fam (a) (salir) to dirty, to mess up (b) (mal faire) to make an unholy mess of

saloperie [salɔpri] nf très Fam (a) (camelote) trash, junk (b) (coup bas) dirty trick (c) **dire des saloperies sur qn** to bitch about sb

salopette [salɔpɛt] nf overalls

salpêtre [salpɛtr] nm saltpeter

salsa [salsa] nf salsa

salsifis [salsifi] nm salsify

saltimbanque [saltɛ̃bɑ̃k] nm traveling acrobat

salto [salto] nm somersault

salubre [salybr] adj healthy

salubrité [salybrite] nf healthiness; **la s. publique** public health

saluer [salɥe] **1** vt (en arrivant) to greet; (en partant) to take one's leave of; (s'incliner devant) to bow to; (sujet: soldat) to salute; **s. qn d'une inclination de la tête** to nod to sb; **il est passé sans me s.** he walked past me without saying hello; **saluez-le de ma part** give him my regards; Rel **je vous salue, Marie** hail Mary

2 se saluer vpr (en arrivant) to greet each other; (en partant) to take leave of each other

salut [saly] **1** nm (a) (salutation) greeting; **faire un s. à qn** (en se découvrant) to raise one's hat to sb; (en inclinant la tête) to nod to sb (b) (de soldat) salute; **faire le s. militaire** to give a salute (c) (sauvegarde) rescue; Rel salvation

2 exclam Fam **s.!** (en arrivant) hi!; (en partant) bye!

salutaire [salytɛr] adj (décision, mesure) salutary; (remède) beneficial; **être s. à qn** to do sb good

salutation [salytasjɔ̃] nf greeting

Salvador [salvadɔr] nm **le S.** El Salvador

salvadorien, -enne [salvadɔrjɛ̃, -ɛn] **1** adj Salvadorean

2 nm,f **S., Salvadorienne** Salvadorean

salve [salv] nf salvo, volley

Samaritain [samaritɛ̃] nm **le bon S.** the good Samaritan

samba [sɑ̃mba] nf samba

samedi [samdi] nm Saturday; **le S. saint** Easter Saturday; **s. prochain/dernier** next/last Saturday; **s. matin** Saturday morning; **s. soir** Saturday night ou evening; **dans la nuit de s. à dimanche** on Saturday night; **s. 11 mai 1997** Saturday May 11, 1997; **nous sommes s. aujourd'hui** today's Saturday; **je commence s.** I'm starting on Saturday; **il vient le s./**

tous les samedis he comes on Saturdays/every Saturday; **un s. sur deux** every other Saturday; **s. en huit/quinze** a week/two weeks from Saturday; **passer tout son s. à faire qch** to spend one's entire Saturday doing sth; *Belg & Suisse* **faire le** *ou* **son s.** to do the weekly cleaning

Samoa [samɔa] *nfpl* **les S. occidentales** Western Samoa

samouraï [samuraj] *nm* samurai

samovar [samɔvar] *nm* samovar

sampler¹ [sãplœr] *nm Mus* sampler

sampler² [sãple] *vt Mus* to sample

SAMU [samy] *nm* (*abrév* **Service d'aide médicale d'urgence**) = ambulance service; **appeler le S.** to call an ambulance; **le S. social** = mobile medical and support service for homeless people

sanatorium [sanatɔrjɔm] *nm* sanatorium

sanctifier [66] [sãktifje] *vt* (**a**) (*rendre saint*) to sanctify (**b**) (*révérer*) **que Ton nom soit sanctifié** hallowed be Thy name

sanction [sãksjɔ̃] *nf* (*punition*) sanction; *Fig* (*désavantage*) price; **prendre une s. contre qn** to take action against sb; **s. pénale** penalty; **sanctions économiques** economic sanctions

sanctionner [sãksjɔne] *vt* (**a**) (*punir*) to punish (**b**) (*approuver*) to sanction; **sanctionné par l'usage** sanctioned by custom

sanctuaire [sãktɥer] *nm aussi Fig* sanctuary

sandale [sãdal] *nf* sandal

sandalette [sãdalɛt] *nf* (light) sandal

sandre [sãdr] *nm* pikeperch

sandwich (*pl* **sandwichs** *ou* **sandwiches**) [sãdwitʃ] *nm* sandwich; **s. au jambon** ham sandwich; **s. grec** gyro; *Fam* **pris en s. (entre)** sandwiched (between)

San Francisco [sãfrãsisko] *n* San Francisco

sang [sã] *nm* blood; **animaux à s. chaud/froid** warm-/cold-blooded animals; **être en s.** to be covered in blood; *Fig* **avoir le s. bleu** to have blue blood; *Fig* **avoir le s. chaud** to be hot-blooded; *Fig* **avoir qch dans le s.** to have sth in one's blood; *Fam* **avoir du s. de navet** to be spineless; *Fam* **se faire du mauvais s.** to get all worked up; *Fam* **se ronger les sangs, se faire un s. d'encre** to worry oneself sick; **le s. lui monta au visage** the blood rushed to his/her face; **mon s. n'a fait qu'un tour** (*de peur*) my heart missed a beat; (*de colère*) I saw red; *très Fam* **bon s. (de bonsoir)!, bon s. de bon Dieu!** for God's sake!

sang-froid [sãfrwa] *nm inv* composure, calm; **garder son s.** to keep calm, to keep one's head; **perdre son s.** to lose one's head, to lose one's composure; **tuer qn de s.** to kill sb in cold blood

sanglant, -e [sãglã, -ãt] *adj* bloody; *Fig* (*offensant*) scathing

sangle [sãgl] *nf* strap; (*de selle*) girth

sangler [sãgle] *vt* to put straps on; (*cheval*) to girth

sanglier [sãglije] *nm* (wild) boar

sanglot [sãglo] *nm* sob

sangloter [sãglɔte] *vi* to sob

sangria [sãgrija] *nf* sangria

sangsue [sãsy] *nf* (*animal, personne*) leech

sanguin, -e [sãgɛ̃, -in] *adj* (*tempérament*) fiery; (*teint, visage*) ruddy

sanguinaire [sãginɛr] *adj* (**a**) (*homme*) bloodthirsty (**b**) (*combat*) bloody

Sanisette® [sanizɛt] *nf* = paying automatic public toilet

sanitaire [sanitɛr] **1** *adj* (**a**) (*personnel*) medical; (*mesures*) health (**b**) (*installation*) sanitary
2 *nmpl* **les sanitaires** (*toilettes*) the toilet; (*salle de bains et W.-C.*) the bathroom

sans [sã] **1** *prép* (**a**) (*indique l'absence, la privation, l'exclusion*) without; **s. parler** without speaking; **non s. difficulté** not without difficulty (**b**) (*indique la condition*) but for; **s. vous, je**

ne l'aurais jamais fait but for you, I'd never have done it; **s. cela, s. quoi** otherwise; *Fam* **sois sage, s. ça tu seras puni!** be good or else you'll be punished!
2 *adv Fam* without it/them; **faire s.** to do without
3 *conj* **s. que nous le sachions** without our knowing

sans-abri [sãzabri] *nmf inv* homeless person; **les s.** the homeless

San Salvador [sãsalvadɔr] *n* San Salvador

sans-cœur [sãkœr] *nmf inv Fam* heartless person

sans-culotte (*pl* **sans-culottes**) [sãkylɔt] *nm Hist* sans-culotte (*person with extreme republican sympathies during the French Revolution*)

sans-emploi [sãzãplwa] *nmf inv* unemployed person; **les s.** the unemployed

sans-faute [sãfot] *nm inv* (*de compétition hippique*) clear round; **faire un s.** (*cheval*) to have a clear round; *Fig* (*personne*) not to put a foot wrong

sans-fil ® [sãfil] *nm inv* cordless telephone

sans-gêne [sãʒɛn] **1** *adj inv* ill-mannered
2 *nm* lack of manners

sans-le-sou [sãləsu] *nmf inv Fam* penniless person

sans-logis [sãlɔʒi] *nmf* homeless person; **les s.** the homeless

sans-papiers [sãpapje] *nmf* illegal immigrant

sans-patrie [sãpatri] *nmf inv* stateless person

santé [sãte] *nf* health; **être en bonne s.** to be in good health; **avoir une bonne/mauvaise s.** to be healthy/unhealthy; **être en parfaite s.** to be perfectly healthy; **avoir une petite s.** to be delicate; **c'est bon/mauvais pour la s.** it's good/bad for your health; **boire à la s. de qn** to drink sb's health; **(à votre) s.!** cheers!, good health!; *Suisse Fam* **s.!** (*quand on éternue*) bless you!; **la s. publique** public health

santiag [sãtjag] *nf Fam* cowboy boot

santon [sãtɔ̃] *nm* Christmas creche figure

São Tomé et Príncipe [saɔtɔmeeprɛ̃sip] *n* São Tomé e Príncipe

saoudien, -enne [saudjɛ̃, -ɛn] **1** *adj* Saudi (Arabian)
2 *nm,f* **S., Saoudienne** Saudi (Arabian)

saoul, saouler = **soûl, soûler**

sape [sap] *nf* (**a**) (*tranchée*) sap; *Fig* **travail de s.** undermining (**b**) *Fam* **sapes** (*vêtements*) gear

saper [sape] **1** *vt* (**a**) *aussi Fig* to undermine; **s. le moral à qn** to sap sb's morale (**b**) *Fam* (*habiller*) to dress; **être bien sapé** to be all dolled up
2 **se saper** *vpr Fam* to dress

sapeur-pompier (*pl* **sapeurs-pompiers**) [sapœrpɔ̃pje] *nm* fireman; **les sapeurs-pompiers** (*service*) the fire department

saphir [safir] *nm* sapphire

sapin [sapɛ̃] *nm* (**a**) (*arbre*) fir (tree) (**b**) *Fam* **ça sent le s.** that sounds as if you're heading for an early grave; **il sent le s.** he's done for (**c**) *Can* **se faire passer un s.** (*se faire avoir*) to be taken for a ride

sapristi [sapristi] *exclam Fam Vieilli ou Hum* good heavens!

saquer [sake] = **sacquer**

sarabande [sarabãd] *nf* (*danse, air*) saraband; *Fam* (*tapage*) racket

Sarajevo [sarajevo] *n* Sarajevo

sarbacane [sarbakan] *nf* blowpipe; (*jouet*) peashooter

sarcasme [sarkasm] *nm* sarcasm; (*remarque*) sarcastic remark

sarcastique [sarkastik] *adj* sarcastic

sarcler [sarkle] *vt* (*jardin*) to weed; (*sol*) to hoe; (*champ*) to clean

sarclette [sarklɛt] *nf* hoe

sarcloir [sarklwar] *nm* hoe

sarcome [sarkom] *nm Méd* sarcoma; **s. de Kaposi** Kaposi's sarcoma

sarcophage [sarkɔfaʒ] *nm* sarcophagus

Sardaigne [sardɛɲ] *nf* **la S.** Sardinia

sarde [sard] **1** *adj* Sardinian

   2 *nm (langue)* Sardinian

   3 *nmf* **S.** Sardinian

sardine [sardin] *nf* sardine; **sardines à l'huile/à la tomate** sardines in oil/in tomato sauce; *Fam* **serrés comme des sardines** packed together like sardines

sardonique [sardɔnik] *adj* sardonic

Sargasses [sargas] *voir* **mer**

SARL [ɛsaɛrɛl] *nf (abrév* **société à responsabilité limitée**) corporation

sarment [sarmɑ̃] *nm (tige)* bine; *(de vigne)* vine shoot

saroual, -als [sarwal], **sarouel** [sarwɛl] *nm* = baggy pants worn by North Africans

sarrasin, -e [sarazɛ̃, -in] **1** *adj Hist* Saracen

   2 *nm (plante)* buckwheat

   3 *nm,f Hist* **S., Sarrasine** Saracen

sarriette [sarjɛt] *nf* savory

sas [sɑs] *nm (pièce étanche)* airlock

Satan [satɑ̃] *npr* Satan

satané, -e [satane] *adj Fam* confounded

satanique [satanik] *adj* satanic; *Fig (cruauté, sourire)* fiendish, evil

satanisme [satanism] *nm* satanism; *Fig (méchanceté)* fiendishness, evil

sataniste [satanist] *adj & nmf* satanist

satellitaire [satelitɛr] *adj* satellite

satellite [satelit] **1** *nm* **(a)** *(corps céleste, engin)* satellite; **émission retransmise par s.** satellite broadcast; **télévision par s.** satellite television; **s.-espion** spy satellite; **s. géostationnaire** geostationary satellite; **s. de télécommunications** telecommunications satellite; **s. de télédiffusion** broadcast satellite **(b)** *Pol* satellite

   2 *adj* **pays s.** satellite state

satiété [sasjete] *nf* **manger/boire à s.** to eat/to drink one's fill

satin [satɛ̃] *nm* satin

satiné, -e [satine] **1** *adj (tissu)* satiny; *(papier)* glazed; *(peau)* satin-smooth; **peinture satinée** silk-finish paint

   2 *nm* satin finish; *(de la peau)* satin smoothness

satire [satir] *nf* satire; **faire la s. de qch** to satirize sth

satirique [satirik] *adj* satirical

satiriser [3] [satirize] *vt* to satirize

satiriste [satirist] *nmf* satirist

satisfaction [satisfaksjɔ̃] *nf* satisfaction; **à la s. générale** to everyone's satisfaction; **donner (entière) s. à qn** *(personne)* to give sb (complete) satisfaction; *(travail)* to fulfill sb (completely); **obtenir s.** to obtain satisfaction

satisfaire [36] [satisfɛr] **1** *vt* to satisfy

   2 satisfaire à *vt ind (demande, condition, besoins)* to satisfy; *(règlement, normes de sécurité)* to comply with; *(obligation)* to fulfill

   3 se satisfaire *vpr* **se s. de qch** to be satisfied with sth; **se s. de peu** to be content with very little; *Péj* to be easily satisfied

satisfaisant, -e [satisfəzɑ̃, -ɑ̃t] *adj (acceptable)* satisfactory; *(qui contente)* satisfying

satisfait, -e [satisfɛ, -ɛt] *adj* **(a)** *(heureux)* satisfied *(de* with); *Ironique* **vous voilà s.!** well, you asked for it!; **s. ou remboursé** *(dans une publicité)* satisfaction or your money back **(b)** *(suffisant)* satisfied

satisfecit [satisfesit] *nm inv Litt* **décerner un s. à qn** to congratulate sb on a job well done

saturation [satyrasjɔ̃] *nf aussi Fig* saturation; *(du réseau routier)* gridlock; *aussi Fig* **arriver à s.** to reach saturation point; *Ordinat (disquette)* to become full

saturer [satyre] **1** *vt* to saturate (*de* with); **les appels ont saturé le standard** the calls have jammed the switchboard

   2 *vi Fam* **je sature** I've had it up to here

Saturne [satyrn] *npr (dieu, planète)* Saturn

satyre [satir] *nm* **(a)** *(demi-dieu)* satyr **(b)** *Fam (obsédé sexuel)* sex maniac

sauce [sos] *nf* **(a)** *(accompagnement)* sauce; **s. aux champignons** mushroom sauce; **s. de soja** soy sauce; **s. tomate** tomato sauce; *Fam Fig* **allonger la s.** to pad it out; *Fam* **mettre qch à toutes les sauces** to use sth in every way imaginable; *Fam* **à quelle s. sera-t-il mangé?** what'll be in store for him? **(b)** *Fam (pluie)* **prendre la s.** to get soaked

saucée [sose] *nf Fam (pluie)* downpour; **recevoir une s.** to get soaked

saucer [16] [sose] *vt* **(a)** *(assiette)* to mop up the sauce from **(b)** *Fam* **se faire s.** to get soaked

saucier [sosje] *nm* sauce chef

saucière [sosjɛr] *nf* sauce boat

sauciflard [sosiflar] *nm Fam* (slicing) sausage

saucisse [sosis] *nf* sausage; **s. de Francfort** frankfurter; **s. sèche** = thin salami-type sausage; **s. de Strasbourg/Toulouse** = type of beef/pork sausage

saucisson [sosisɔ̃] *nm* (slicing) sausage; **s. à l'ail** garlic sausage; *Hum* **s. à pattes** sausage dog; **s. pur porc** 100% pork sausage; **s. sec** salami

saucissonné, -e [sosisɔne] *adj Fam* trussed up

saucissonner [sosisɔne] *vt Fam* **(a)** *(attacher)* to tie up **(b)** *(diviser)* **le film a été saucissonné** the movie was divided up into episodes; **un film saucissonné par des publicités** a movie with frequent commercial breaks

sauf¹, sauve [sof, sov] *adj (personne)* safe, unharmed; **avoir la vie sauve** to escape with one's life; **laisser la vie sauve à qn** to spare sb's life; **l'honneur est s.** honor is saved

sauf² [sof] *prép* except (for), apart from; **s. imprévu** unless anything unforeseen happens; **s. erreur de ma part** if I'm not mistaken; **s. votre respect** with all due respect; **s. s'il pleut** unless it rains; *Fam* **s. que…** except that…

sauf-conduit (*pl* **sauf-conduits**) [sofkɔ̃dɥi] *nm* safe conduct

sauge [soʒ] *nf* sage

saugrenu, -e [sogrəny] *adj* preposterous

saule [sol] *nm* willow; **s. pleureur** weeping willow

saumâtre [somɑtr] *adj (goût, eau)* brackish; *Fig* bitter

saumon [somɔ̃] **1** *nm* salmon; **s. fumé** smoked salmon, lox; **s. mariné** gravlax

   2 *adj inv* **(rose) s.** salmon-pink

saumoné, -e [somɔne] *adj voir* **truite**

saumure [somyr] *nf* brine

sauna [sona] *nm* sauna

saupoudrer [sopudre] *vt* to sprinkle (*de* with)

saupoudreuse [sopudrøz] *nf* dredger

saur [sɔr] *adj m voir* **hareng**

saurai, saurais, *etc. voir* **savoir²**

saurien [sɔrjɛ̃] *nm* saurian

saut [so] *nm (bond)* jump, leap; **faire un s.** to jump, to leap; *Fig* **faire un s. à Paris/chez le boulanger/en ville** to pop over to Paris/over to the bakery/into town; *Fig* **faire un s. de plusieurs années** to skip several years; **au s. du lit** first thing in the morning; **s. de l'ange** swan dive; **s. à l'élastique** bungee jumping; **s. en hauteur** high jump; **s. en longueur** broad jump; **s. en parachute** parachute jump; *(activité)* parachute jumping; **faire du s. en parachute** to go parachute jumping; **s. à la perche** pole vaulting; **s. périlleux** somersault; **s. en** *ou* **à skis** ski jump; *(activité)* ski jumping; **faire du s. à skis** to go ski jumping; *Ordinat* **s. de page** page break

saute [sot] *nf* **sautes de température** sudden changes in temperature; **sautes d'humeur** mood swings

sauté, -e [sote] **1** *adj* sautéed, sauté
2 *nm* **s. de lapin** sauté of rabbit

saute-mouton [sotmutɔ̃] *nm inv* leapfrog; **jouer à s.** to play leapfrog

sauter [sote] **1** *vt* **(a)** *(fossé, barrière)* to jump (over), to leap over; *Fig* **s. le pas** to take the plunge
(**b**) *(omettre) (page, ligne, repas)* to skip; *(maille)* to drop; **s. une classe** to skip a year
(**c**) *Vulg (coucher avec)* to screw; **se faire s. par qn** to screw sb
2 *vi* **(a)** *(bondir)* to jump, to leap; **s. sur un pied** to hop; **s. à pieds joints** to jump with one's feet together; **s. à la perche** to pole-vault; **s. à la corde** to jump rope; **s. en parachute** to do a parachute jump; **s. à la gorge de qn** to go for sb; *(chien)* to fly at sb's throat; **s. au cou de qn** to fling one's arms around sb's neck; **s. aux yeux** to be obvious; **s. au plafond** *(bouchon)* to hit the ceiling; *Fig (de surprise)* to jump out of one's skin; *(d'indignation)* to hit the roof; **s. de joie** to jump for joy; *aussi Fam Fig* **s. sur qn** to pounce on sb; **faire s. un enfant sur ses genoux** to bounce a child on one's knees; **s. sur l'occasion** to jump at the opportunity; *Fig* **s. du coq à l'âne** to jump from one subject to another; **nous allons s. directement à la page cinq** we're going to jump straight to page five; *Fam* **et que ça saute!** and make it snappy!
(**b**) *(exploser)* to blow up; *(bouton)* to come off; *(fusible)* to blow; *Fig (gouvernement)* to fall; **faire s.** *(rocher)* to blast; *(pont, mine)* to blow up; *(serrure)* to force; *Fig (gouvernement)* to bring down; *(personne)* to fire; *Fam* **faire s. la banque** to break the bank
(**c**) *Culin* **faire s.** to sauté

sauterelle [sotrɛl] *nf* grasshopper; *(nuisible)* locust

sauterie [sotri] *nf Vieilli ou Hum* hop

sauteur, -euse [sotœr, -øz] **1** *adj* jumping
2 *nm,f* jumper; **s. en hauteur** high jumper; **s. en longueur** broad jumper; **s. à la perche** pole vaulter

sautillement [sotijmɑ̃] *nm* hopping about

sautiller [sotije] *vi* to hop about; **s. d'un pied sur l'autre** to hop from one foot to the other; **avancer en sautillant** to hop along

sautoir [sotwar] *nm* **(a)** *(collier)* chain; **s. de perles** string of pearls (**b**) *(de stade)* jumping area

sauvage [sovaʒ] **1** *adj* **(a)** *(plante, animal)* wild; **redevenir s.** *(animal apprivoisé)* to go back to the wild; **à l'état s.** wild (**b**) *(peuple, tribu)* savage, primitive (**c**) *(violent) (personne, agression)* savage (**d**) *(peu sociable)* unsociable (**e**) *(non autorisé)* unauthorized; **immigration s.** illegal immigration
2 *nmf* **(a)** *Vieilli (indigène)* savage; *Fam Hum* **on n'est pas des sauvages!** we're not savages!; *Fam Hum* **bande de sauvages!** you bunch of savages! (**b**) *(brute)* savage (**c**) *(solitaire)* recluse

sauvagement [sovaʒmɑ̃] *adv* savagely

sauvageon, -onne [sovaʒɔ̃, -ɔn] *nm,f (enfant)* little savage

sauvagerie [sovaʒri] *nf* **(a)** *(cruauté)* savagery (**b**) *(insociabilité)* unsociability

sauvegarde [sovgard] *nf* **(a)** *(protection)* safeguard (**contre** against); **s. des ressources naturelles** conservation of natural resources (**b**) *Ordinat* saving, backup; **faire la s. d'un fichier** to save a file; **s. automatique** autosave, automatic backup; **s. externe** off-line backup; **s. en ligne** on-line backup; **copie de s.** backup (copy)

sauvegarder [sovgarde] *vt* **(a)** *(protéger)* to safeguard (**contre** against) (**b**) *Ordinat (fichier)* to save, to back up; **s. un fichier sur disque** to save a file to disk

sauver [sove] **1** *vt* **(a)** *(personne)* to save, to rescue (**de** from); *(âme)* to save; **s. la vie à qn** to save sb's life; **le malade est sauvé** the patient is out of danger (**b**) *(navire, marchandises)* to salvage; **s. les apparences** to keep up appearances; *Fam Fig* **s. les meubles** to salvage something from the wreckage
2 *vi* **sauve qui peut!** every man for himself!

3 se sauver *vpr* **(a)** *(s'échapper)* to escape (**de** from) (**b**) *(s'enfuir)* to run away; *Fam* **sauve-toi, tu vas être en retard** be off, you'll be late (**c**) *(lait)* to boil over

sauvetage [sovtaʒ] *nm* **(a)** *(d'un accidenté)* rescue (**b**) *(d'un navire, de marchandises)* salvage; *(d'une entreprise)* rescue

sauveteur [sovtœr] *nm* rescuer

sauvette [sovɛt] **à la sauvette** *adv (pour ne pas être vu)* on the sly; *(à la hâte)* in a hurry; **vendre à la s.** *(illégalement)* to peddle illegally on the streets; **marchand à la s.** illegal street vendor

sauveur [sovœr] *nm* savior

savamment [savamɑ̃] *adv* **(a)** *(avec érudition)* learnedly (**b**) *(habilement)* cleverly, skillfully

savane [savan] *nf* **(a)** *(dans les pays chauds)* savanna (**b**) *Can (marécage)* swamp

savant, -e [savɑ̃, -ɑ̃t] **1** *adj* **(a)** *(érudit)* learned (**b**) *(habile)* clever, skillful (**c**) *(animal)* performing
2 *nm (scientifique)* scientist; *(érudit)* scholar

savate [savat] *nf* **(a)** *Fam (pantoufle)* slipper; **traîner la s.** *(être pauvre)* to be down at heel (**b**) *Fam* **comme une s.** atrociously (**c**) *Sport* kick boxing

saveur [savœr] *nf* **(a)** *(d'un vin, d'un aliment)* flavor (**b**) *Fig (d'une remarque, d'un récit)* savor

Savoie [savwa] *nf* **la S.** Savoy

savoir¹ [savwar] *nm* knowledge, learning

savoir² [62] [savwar] **1** *vt* **(a)** *(avoir connaissance de)* to know; **s. qch par cœur** to know sth by heart; **je n'en sais rien** I don't know; **je n'en sais trop rien** I'm not very sure; **en s. trop** to know too much; **qu'est-ce j'en sais?** what do I know?; **va s.!** who knows?; **je ne veux pas le s.** I don't want to know; **il n'a rien voulu s.** he didn't want to know; **reste à s. si…** it remains to be seen whether…; **je crois s. qu'il est ici** I understand he's here; **faire s. qch à qn** to tell sb sth, to let sb know about sth; **je le sais par ma sœur** I heard about it from my sister; **à s.** that is (to say), namely; **pas que je sache** not that I know of; **à ce que je sache, pour autant que je sache** as far as I know; **on ne sait jamais** you never know
(**b**) *(être conscient de)* to know; **sans le s.** without realizing; **sachez que…** be advised that…, please note that…
(**c**) *(connaître)* **qui tu sais** you know who; **je ne le savais pas si jaloux** I didn't know he was so jealous
(**d**) *(être capable de)* **s. faire qch** to be able to do sth, to know how to do sth; **savez-vous nager/conduire?** can you swim/drive?; **je ne saurais vous le dire** I really couldn't tell you
(**e**) *Belg (pouvoir)* **je ne sais pas l'attraper** I can't reach it
2 se savoir *vpr* **(a)** *(se répandre)* **ça se saura vite** it'll soon get out
(**b**) *(avoir conscience d'être)* **il se savait perdu/surveillé** he knew he was doomed/being watched

savoir-faire [savwarfɛr] *nm* expertise, know-how

savoir-vivre [savwarvivr] *nm* good manners; **manquer de s.** to have no manners

savon [savɔ̃] *nm* soap; **s. à barbe** shaving soap; **s. de Marseille** household soap; *Fam* **passer un s. à qn** to give sb a telling-off

savonner [savɔne] **1** *vt (mains, vêtement)* to soap; *(en faisant mousser)* to lather
2 se savonner *vpr* to soap oneself; **se s. les mains** to soap one's hands

savonnette [savɔnɛt] *nf* bar of soap

savonneux, -euse [savɔnø, -øz] *adj* soapy

savourer [savure] *vt aussi Fig* to savor

savoureux, -euse [savurø, -øz] *adj (plat)* tasty; *(vin)* full-flavored; *Fig (récit, détails)* spicy

savoyard, -e [savwajar, -ard] **1** *adj* Savoyard
2 *nm,f* **S., Savoyarde** Savoyard

saxo [sakso] *nm Fam (instrument)* sax; *(musicien)* sax player

saxon, -onne [saksɔ̃, -ɔn] **1** *adj* Saxon
  2 *nm,f* **S., Saxonne** Saxon

saxophone [saksɔfɔn] *nm* saxophone

saxophoniste [saksɔfɔnist] *nmf* saxophonist

saynète [sɛnɛt] *nf (petite pièce)* sketch

sbire [sbir] *nm Péj* henchman

scabreux, -euse [skabrø, -øz] *adj* obscene

scalp [skalp] *nm (chevelure)* scalp

scalpel [skalpɛl] *nm* scalpel

scalper [skalpe] *vt* to scalp

scandale [skɑ̃dal] *nm* scandal; **faire s.** *(affaire)* to cause a scandal; **faire un s.** *(personne)* to make a scene; **au grand s. de** much to the indignation of; **c'est un s.!** it's a scandal!

scandaleux, -euse [skɑ̃dalø, -øz] *adj* scandalous, outrageous

scandaliser [skɑ̃dalize] **1** *vt* to scandalize, to shock
  2 se scandaliser *vpr* to be scandalized *or* shocked (**de** by); **elle ne se scandalise de rien** nothing shocks her

scander [skɑ̃de] *vt (slogan)* to chant; *(vers)* to scan

scandinave [skɑ̃dinav] **1** *adj* Scandinavian
  2 *nmf* **S.** Scandinavian

Scandinavie [skɑ̃dinavi] *nf* **la S.** Scandinavia

scanner[1] [skanɛr] *nm* scanner; **on lui a fait un s.** he/she was given a scan

scanner[2] [skane] *vt Ordinat* to scan

scanneur [skanœr] *nm Ordinat & TV* scanner; **s. à main** handheld scanner; **s. à plat** flatbed scanner

scaphandre [skafɑ̃dr] *nm* (**a**) *(de plongeur)* diving suit (**b**) *(d'astronaute)* space suit

scaphandrier [skafɑ̃drije] *nm* diver

scarabée [skarabe] *nm* beetle

scarlatine [skarlatin] *nf* scarlet fever; **avoir la s.** to have scarlet fever

scarole [skarɔl] *nf* endive

scatologique [skatɔlɔʒik] *adj* scatological

sceau, -x [so] *nm* seal; *Fig* **le s. du génie** the mark of genius; **sous le s. du secret** under the seal of secrecy

scélérat, -e [selera, -at] *Litt* **1** *adj* villainous
  2 *nm,f* villain

scellé, -e [sele] **1** *adj* sealed
  2 *nm* seal; **apposer/lever les scellés** to put on/to remove the seals

sceller [sele] *vt* (**a**) *(apposer un sceau sur)* & *Fig* to seal (**b**) *Constr* to embed

scénario [senarjo] *nm* script, screenplay; *Fig* scenario

scénariste [senarist] *nmf* scriptwriter

scène [sɛn] *nf* (**a**) *(plateau)* stage; **la s.** *(le métier d'acteur)* the stage; **mettre en s.** *(pièce de théâtre)* to stage; *(film)* to direct; **entrer en s.** *(acteur)* to come on; *Fig* to appear on the scene; **sortir de s.** to go off; **quitter la s.** to retire from the stage; *Fig* **la s. politique/internationale** the political/international scene; *Fig* **occuper le devant de la s.** to be in the limelight, to hold center stage (**b**) *(d'une pièce de théâtre, d'un film)* scene (**c**) *(action)* action; **la s. se passe au Moyen Âge** the action takes place in the Middle Ages (**d**) *(événement)* scene; **des scènes de panique** scenes of panic (**e**) *Fam (dispute)* scene; **il m'a fait une s.** he made a scene; **s. de ménage** domestic squabble (**f**) *(peinture)* **une s. de chasse** a hunting scene

scénique [senik] *adj* theatrical

scepticisme [sɛptisism] *nm* skepticism

sceptique [sɛptik] **1** *adj* skeptical
  2 *nmf* skeptic

sceptre [sɛptr] *nm* scepter

schéma [ʃema] *nm* (**a**) *(dessin)* diagram (**b**) *(résumé)* outline (**c**) *Ordinat* **s. de clavier** keyboard map

schématique [ʃematik] *adj* schematic; *Péj* oversimplified

schématiquement [ʃematikmɑ̃] *adv (à l'aide d'un schéma)* schematically; *(en gros)* in outline

schématiser [ʃematize] *vt* to schematize; *Péj* to oversimplify

schisme [ʃism] *nm* schism

schiste [ʃist] *nm* schist, shale

schizophrène [skizɔfrɛn] *adj & nmf* schizophrenic

schizophrénie [skizɔfreni] *nf* schizophrenia

schlinguer [ʃlɛ̃ge] *vi très Fam* to stink

schnaps [ʃnaps] *nm* schnapps

schnock, schnoque [ʃnɔk] *nm Fam* **un vieux s.** an old dodderer

schuss [ʃus] *nm* schuss; **descendre la piste en s.** *ou* **tout s.** to schuss down the slope

sciatique [sjatik] **1** *adj* sciatic
  2 *nf* sciatica

scie [si] *nf* (**a**) *(outil)* saw; **s. circulaire** circular saw; **s. mécanique** *ou* **à main** handsaw; **s. à métaux** hacksaw (**b**) **s. musicale** musical saw

sciemment [sjamɑ̃] *adv* knowingly

science [sjɑ̃s] *nf* (**a**) *(savoir)* science; *Fig* **je n'ai pas la s. infuse** I can't be expected to know everything (**b**) *(domaine spécifique)* science; **sciences économiques** economics; **sciences exactes** exact sciences; **sciences expérimentales** experimental science; **sciences humaines** ≃ social sciences; **sciences naturelles** natural science; **Sciences Po** = prestigious higher education establishment for students wishing to enter the Civil Service, the media, etc.

science-fiction [sjɑ̃sfiksjɔ̃] *nf* science fiction; *Fig & Hum* **c'est de la s.!** it's unreal!

scientifique [sjɑ̃tifik] **1** *adj* scientific
  2 *nmf* scientist

scientifiquement [sjɑ̃tifikmɑ̃] *adv* scientifically

scier [66] [sje] *vt* (**a**) *(bois, métal)* to saw; *(pour enlever) (branche)* to saw off (**b**) *Fam (étonner)* to dumbfound

scierie [siri] *nf* sawmill

scieur [sjœr] *nm* sawyer

scinder [sɛ̃de] **1** *vt* to split up (**en** into)
  2 se scinder *vpr* to split up (**en** into)

scintillement [sɛ̃tijmɑ̃] *nm (de bijou, de lumière, des yeux)* sparkling; *(d'étoile)* twinkling

scintiller [sɛ̃tije] *vi (bijou, lumière, yeux)* to sparkle; *(étoile)* to twinkle

scission [sisjɔ̃] *nf* split; **faire s.** to split away

sciure [sjyr] *nf* sawdust

sclérose [skleroz] *nf* sclerosis; *Fig* ossification; **s. en plaques** multiple sclerosis

scléroser [skleroze] **1** *vt Méd* to sclerose
  2 se scléroser *vpr Méd* to sclerose; *Fig* to become fossilized

scolaire [skɔlɛr] *adj* (**a**) *(résultats, réussite)* academic; *(réforme, organisation, vie)* school (**b**) *Péj (esprit, mentalité)* bookish

scolarisation [skɔlarizasjɔ̃] *nf* education

scolariser [skɔlarize] *vt* to send to school; **enfant scolarisé** child attending school

scolarité [skɔlarite] *nf* schooling; **prolonger la s.** to raise the age at which students can leave school

scoliose [skɔljoz] *nf* curvature of the spine

scoop [skup] *nm* scoop

scooter [skutɛr] *nm (motor)* scooter; **s. des mers** jet ski

scorbut [skɔrbyt] *nm* scurvy

score [skɔr] *nm* score; *(en politique)* result

scories [skɔri] *nfpl (dans l'industrie)* slag; *(d'éruption volcanique)* scoria

scorpion [skɔrpjɔ̃] *nm* (**a**) *(animal)* scorpion (**b**) *Astron & Astrol* **le S.** Scorpio; **être S.** to be (a) Scorpio

Scotch® [skɔtʃ] *nm (ruban adhésif)* scotch tape®

scotch [skɔtʃ] *nm (boisson)* scotch

scotché, -e [skɔtʃe] *adj* **(a)** *(collé)* scotchtaped; *Fam Fig* **être s. devant la télé** to be glued to the TV **(b)** *Fam (stupéfait)* **je suis resté s.** I was staggered

scotcher [skɔtʃe] *vt* **(a)** to scotch-tape **(b)** *Fam (stupéfaire)* to stagger, to flabbergast; **ça m'a vraiment scotché!** I was staggered!

scout [skut] *nm* Scout

scoutisme [skutism] *nm (activité)* scouting; *(mouvement)* scout movement

scratcher [skratʃe] *vt (DJ)* to scratch

scribe [skrib] *nm* **(a)** *Péj* pen *or* pencil pusher **(b)** *Hist* scribe

scribouillard, -e [skribujar, -ard] *nm,f Fam Péj* pen *or* pencil pusher

script [skript] *nm* **(a)** *(écriture)* printing; **écrire en s.** to print **(b)** *Cin* (movie) script

scripte [skript] *nmf Cin (homme)* continuity man; *(femme)* continuity girl

scrupule [skrypyl] *nm* scruple; **sans scrupules** *(personne)* unscrupulous; *(agir)* unscrupulously

scrupuleusement [skrypyløzmã] *adv* scrupulously

scrupuleux, -euse [skrypylø, -øz] *adj* scrupulous; **peu s.** unscrupulous

scrutateur, -trice [skrytatœr, -tris] **1** *adj Litt (esprit, regard)* searching

2 *nm,f (d'un scrutin)* teller

scruter [skryte] *vt* to scrutinize; *(horizon, paysage)* to scan

scrutin [skrytɛ̃] *nm* **(a)** *(élection)* poll; **s. secret** secret vote **(b)** *(vote)* ballot **(c)** *(système)* voting system; **s. majoritaire** election by majority vote; **s. proportionnel** voting by proportional representation; **s. uninominal** voting for a single candidate

sculpter [skylte] *vt* to sculpt; *(dans du bois)* to carve (**dans** out of)

sculpteur [skyltœr] *nm* sculptor; **s. sur bois** woodcarver

sculptural, -e, -aux, -ales [skyltyral, -o] *adj (art)* sculptural; *(silhouette, beauté)* statuesque

sculpture [skyltyr] *nf (œuvre, art)* sculpture; **s. sur bois** woodcarving; **faire de la s.** to sculpt

SDF [ɛsdeɛf] *nmf inv (abrév* **sans domicile fixe)** person of no fixed abode; *(sans abri)* homeless person; **les S.** *(sans abri)* the homeless

SDN [ɛsdeɛn] *nf (abrév* **Société des Nations)** **la S.** the League of Nations

se [sə]

---

s' is used before a word beginning with a vowel or h mute.

---

pron personnel **(a)** *(soi) (homme)* himself; *(femme)* herself; *(chose)* itself; *(indéfini)* oneself; *(pluriel)* themselves; **se flatter** to flatter oneself; **il se rase** he is shaving; *Fam* **on s'est blessés** we hurt ourselves

(b) *(à soi) (homme)* to himself; *(femme)* to herself; *(chose)* to itself; *(indéfini)* to oneself; *(pluriel)* to themselves; **elle s'est coupé le doigt** she has cut her finger; *Fam* **on va s'acheter une voiture** we're going to buy (ourselves) a car

(c) *(réciproque) (objet direct)* each other; *(objet indirect)* to each other; **se nuire (l'un à l'autre)** to hurt each other; **ils se sont quittés en bons termes** they parted on good terms

(d) *(passif)* **ça se mange froid** you eat it cold; **les couteaux se rangent dans ce tiroir** the knives go in this drawer

séance [seɑ̃s] *nf* **(a)** *(réunion)* session, meeting; **tenir s.** to be in session **(b)** *(de travail, d'entraînement)* session; **s. de photo** photo session; **s. de pose** sitting *(c) Cin & Th* perfor-mance; *Cin* **s. privée** private showing **(d)** *TV* **à la s.** *(film, programme)* pay-per-view **(e)** **s. tenante** straightaway, at once

séant, -e [seɑ̃, -ɑ̃t] **1** *adj Litt (convenable)* fitting

2 *nm Litt ou Hum* **se mettre sur son s.** to sit up

seau, -x [so] *nm* bucket; *(contenu)* bucket(ful); *Fam* **il pleut à seaux** it's pouring down; **s. à champagne** champagne bucket; **s. à charbon** coal scuttle; **s. à glace** ice bucket

sébacé, -e [sebase] *adj* sebaceous

sébum [sebɔm] *nm* sebum

sec, sèche [sɛk, sɛʃ] **1** *adj* **(a)** *(temps, saison, sol, peau, bois)* dry; *(morue, fruit)* dried; **à pied s.** without getting one's feet wet; **avoir la gorge sèche** *(avoir soif)* to be dry **(b)** *(vin, cidre)* dry **(c)** *(maigre) (personne)* lean; **être s. comme un coup de trique** to be wiry **(d)** *(austère) (personne)* hard; *(réponse, ton, voix)* sharp; **avoir le cœur s.** to be hard-hearted **(e)** *(non appuyé) (coup)* sharp **(f)** *(sans rien ajouter)* **boire qch s.** to drink sth neat

2 *adv* **(a)** *(beaucoup) (frapper, pleuvoir)* hard; *(boire)* heavily; **démarrer s.** to shoot off **(b)** *Fam* **aussi s.** right away

3 *nm* **(a)** **tenir au s.** *(sur une étiquette)* keep in a dry place **(b)** **être à s.** *(source, puits, rivière)* to be dry; *Fam (sans argent)* to be broke

sécable [sekabl] *adj* divisible

sécateur [sekatœr] *nm* pruning shears

sécession [sesesjɔ̃] *nf* secession; **faire s. (de)** to secede (from)

séchage [seʃaʒ] *nm* drying

sèche [sɛʃ] **1** *nf Fam* cig, smoke

2 *adj voir* **sec**

sèche-cheveux [sɛʃʃəvø] *nm inv* hairdryer

sèche-linge [sɛʃlɛ̃ʒ] *nm inv (appareil)* tumble dryer; *(armoire)* airing cupboard

sèche-mains [sɛʃmɛ̃] *nm inv* hand dryer

sèchement [sɛʃmã] *adv (parler, répondre)* curtly

sécher [34] [seʃe] **1** *vt* **(a)** to dry; *Fam* **s.** to skip a class

2 *vi* **(a)** *(vêtement, cheveux)* to dry; **mettre du linge à s.** to put clothes out to dry **(b)** *Fam (ne pouvoir répondre)* to be stumped

3 **se sécher** *vpr* to dry oneself; **se s. les cheveux/les mains** to dry one's hair/hands

sécheresse [seʃrɛs, seʃrɛs] *nf* **(a)** *(absence de pluie)* drought **(b)** *(de l'air, du sol, de la peau)* dryness **(c)** *(des manières, du ton)* curtness *(du cœur)* hardness; *(du style)* dryness

séchoir [seʃwar] *nm* **(a)** *(appareil)* dryer; **s. (à cheveux)** hairdryer **(b)** *(dispositif pliant)* **s. (à linge)** clotheshorse

second, -e [səgɔ̃, -ɔ̃d] **1** *adj* second; *(rôle)* supporting, minor

2 *nm* **(a)** *(assistant)* assistant; *Mil* second-in-command; *Naut* first mate; *(de duelliste)* second **(b)** *(étage)* third floor

3 *nm,f* second; **je préfère le s.** I prefer the second one; *voir aussi* **cinquième**

secondaire [səgɔ̃dɛr] **1** *adj* **(a)** *Scol* secondary; **établissement d'enseignement s.** secondary school, high school **(b)** *(pas essentiel)* secondary; *(personnage, rôle) Théât* minor; *Fig* secondary; **c'est s.** it's of secondary importance **(c)** *Écon & Géol* secondary

2 *nm Géol* secondary era; *Écon* secondary sector

seconde [səgɔ̃d] *nf* **(a)** *(unité de temps)* second; **(attendez) une s.!** just a second!; **pendant une fraction de s.** for a fraction of a second **(b)** *(vitesse)* second (gear) **(c)** *(dans les transports)* second class; **voyager en s.** to travel second-class **(d)** *(classe)* ≃ tenth grade **(e)** *Mus* second

seconder [səgɔ̃de] *vt* to assist

secouer [səkwe] **1** *vt* **(a)** *(arbre, tête, bouteille)* to shake; *(coussin, oreiller)* to plump up; *(vêtements, tapis)* to shake out; *(sujet: vent, vagues)* to buffet; **nous avons été secoués pendant la traversée** we were shaken about during the crossing; *Fam* **s. les puces à qn** *(réprimander)* to tell sb off **(b)** *(sujet: choc, maladie, nouvelles)* to shake (up) **(c)** *(se débarrasser de) (poussière, joug)* to shake off **(d)** *très Fam* **j'en ai rien à s.** I don't give a damn

2 *vi* **ça secoue** *(en avion, en train)* it's bumpy; *(en bateau)* it's rough

3 se secouer *vpr* (**a**) *(s'agiter)* to shake oneself (**b**) *(agir)* to snap out of it

secourable [səkurabl] *adj* helpful

secourir [22] [səkurir] *vt* to help, to assist

secourisme [səkurism] *nm* first aid

secouriste [səkurist] *nmf* first-aider

secours [səkur] *nm* (**a**) *(aide)* help; *(financier, matériel)* aid; *Mil (renforts)* relief; **appel au s.** call for help; **appeler au s.** to call out for help; **au s.!** help!; **premiers s.** first aid; **porter s. à qn** to give sb help; **demander du s.** to ask for help; **aller au s. de qn** to go to sb's assistance; **cela m'a été d'un grand s.** it's been a great help to me (**b**) **de s.** *(trousse, poste)* first-aid; *(sortie, éclairage)* emergency; *(roue)* spare; *Ordinat (copie, fichier)* back-up

secousse [səkus] *nf* jolt, jerk; **par secousses** *(avancer)* jerkily; **s. (tellurique)** (earth) tremor

secret¹, -ète [səkrɛ, -ɛt] *adj* (**a**) *(non divulgué)* secret (**b**) *(personne)* reticent

secret² [səkrɛ] *nm* (**a**) *(confidence, mystère)* secret; **garder un s.** to keep a secret; **mettre qn dans le s.** to let sb in on the secret; **être dans le s.** to be in on the secret; **ne pas avoir de secrets pour qn** *(discipline)* to hold no secrets for sb; **ce n'est un s. pour personne** it's no secret; **le s. du bonheur/ de la réussite** the secret of happiness/of success; **secrets d'alcôve** pillow talk; **s. d'État** state secret; **s. de fabrication** trade secret; **s. de Polichinelle** open secret; **emporter un s. dans la tombe** to take a secret to the grave (**b**) *(discrétion)* secrecy; **dans le plus grand s.** in the strictest secrecy; **en s.** *(en cachette)* in secret; **s. bancaire** banking secrecy; **s. professionnel** professional secrecy (**c**) **mettre qn au s.** *(l'enfermer)* to put sb in solitary confinement

secrétaire [səkretɛr] **1** *nmf* secretary; **s. d'ambassade** secretary; **s. de direction** personal assistant; **s. d'État** Secretary of State; **s. général** secretary general; *Com* company secretary; **s. médicale** medical secretary; **s. particulier** private secretary; **s. de rédaction** copy editor
  2 *nm (meuble)* writing desk

secrétariat [səkretarja] *nm* (**a**) *(fonction)* secretaryship (**b**) *(bureau)* secretary's office; *(d'un organisme international)* secretariat (**c**) *(métier)* secretarial work (**d**) *Pol* **s. d'État** ministry

secrètement [səkrɛtmɑ̃] *adv* secretly

sécréter [34] [sekrete] *vt* to secrete; *Fig (ennui)* to exude

sécrétion [sekresjɔ̃] *nf* secretion

sectaire [sɛktɛr] *adj & nmf* sectarian

sectarisme [sɛktarism] *nm* sectarianism

secte [sɛkt] *nf* sect

secteur [sɛktœr] *nm* (**a**) *(zone)* area, district; *Fam* **changer de s.** to move somewhere else (**b**) *Élec* mains; **branché sur le s.** plugged into the mains (**c**) *Écon* sector; **le s. privé/public** the private/public sector; **s. primaire/secondaire/tertiaire** primary/secondary/tertiary sector; *Fam* **ce n'est pas mon s.** that's not my line (**d**) *Math & Ordinat* sector; *Ordinat* **s. d'initialisation** boot sector

section [sɛksjɔ̃] *nf* (**a**) *(division)* *(d'un livre, d'un bâtiment, d'une autoroute)* section; *(d'une ligne d'autobus)* stage; *(d'un parti politique, d'un syndicat)* branch (**b**) *(de l'infanterie)* platoon; *(de l'artillerie)* section (**c**) *(coupe)* section; **ça fait cinq centimètres de s.** ≃ the diameter of the section is two inches (**d**) *Scol* = one of the groups into which "baccalauréat" students are divided, depending on their chosen area of specialization

sectionner [sɛksjɔne] *vt* (**a**) *(couper)* to sever (**b**) *(fractionner)* *(service, circonscription)* to divide into sections

sectoriel, -elle [sɛktɔrjɛl] *adj* sectorial

sécu [seky] *nf Fam (abrév* **Sécurité sociale)** welfare

séculaire [sekylɛr] *adj* (**a**) *(très ancien)* centuries-old (**b**) *(qui existe depuis un siècle)* a hundred years old (**c**) *(qui a lieu tous les cent ans)* centennial

séculier, -ère [sekylje, -ɛr] *adj* secular

secundo [səgɔ̃do] *adv* secondly

sécurisant, -e [sekyrizɑ̃, -ɑ̃t] *adj* reassuring

sécuriser [sekyrize] *vt* to reassure; *Fin* **s. un paiement** *(sur Internet)* to guarantee the security of a transaction

sécuritaire [sekyritɛr] *adj (politique, idéologie)* law-and-order; **mesures sécuritaires** drastic security measures

sécurité [sekyrite] *nf* (**a**) *(ordre, stabilité)* security; **être/se sentir en s.** to be/feel secure; **s. de l'emploi** job security; **s. nationale/internationale** national/international security (**b**) *(absence de danger)* safety; **s. routière** road safety; **S. routière** = French road-safety organization (**c**) *(dispositif)* safety catch; **porte munie d'une s.-enfants** door with a childproof lock (**d**) **S. sociale** welfare

> ### Sécurité sociale
> The "Sécu", as it is popularly known, was created in 1945 and provides services such as welfare, pensions and maternity payments. These services are paid for by obligatory insurance contributions ("cotisations") made by employers ("cotisations patronales") and employees ("cotisations salariales"). Many French people have complementary health insurance provided by a "mutuelle" which guarantees payment of all or part of the expenses not covered by the "Sécurité sociale".

sédatif, -ive [sedatif, -iv] *adj & nm* sedative

sédentaire [sedɑ̃tɛr] *adj* (**a**) *(vie, travail, travailleur)* sedentary; *(population)* settled (**b**) *(casanier)* stay-at-home

sédentariser [sedɑ̃tarize] **1** *vt (population)* to settle
  2 se sédentariser *vpr* to settle

sédiment [sedimɑ̃] *nm* sediment

sédimentaire [sedimɑ̃tɛr] *adj* sedimentary

sédimentation [sedimɑ̃tasjɔ̃] *nf* sedimentation

séditieux, -euse [sedisjø, -øz] **1** *adj* seditious
  2 *nm,f* insurgent

sédition [sedisjɔ̃] *nf* sedition

séducteur, -trice [sedyktœr, -tris] **1** *nm,f* seducer, *f* seductress
  2 *adj* seductive

séduction [sedyksjɔ̃] *nf* (**a**) *(physique)* seduction; *(par le charme)* charming (**b**) *(moyen de séduire)* attraction; **pouvoir de s.** power of attraction

séduire [18] [sedɥir] *vt* (**a**) *(charmer)* *(sujet: personne)* to charm; *(sujet: projet, proposition)* to appeal to (**b**) *(sexuellement)* to seduce

séduisant, -e [sedɥizɑ̃, -ɑ̃t] *adj* attractive

séfarade [sefarad] **1** *adj* Sephardic
  2 *nmf* Sephardic Jew

segment [sɛgmɑ̃] *nm* segment

segmenter [sɛgmɑ̃te] *vt aussi Ordinat* to segment

ségrégation [segregasjɔ̃] *nf* segregation

ségrégationniste [segregasjɔnist] *adj & nmf* segregationist

seiche [sɛʃ] *nf* cuttlefish; **os de s.** cuttlebone

seigle [sɛgl] *nm* rye

seigneur [sɛɲœr] *nm* (**a**) *Hist* lord; **à tout s. tout honneur** honor where honor is due; **en grand s.** in grand style (**b**) *Rel* **le S.** the Lord

seigneurial, -e, -aux, -ales [sɛɲœrjal, -o] *adj (droits, domaine)* seigniorial

sein [sɛ̃] *nm (de femme)* breast; *Litt (poitrine)* bosom; **serrer** *ou* **presser qn sur son s.** to press sb to one's bosom; **donner le s. à un enfant, nourrir un enfant au s.** to breast-feed a child; **au s. de** within

Seine [sɛn] *nf* **la S.** the Seine

séisme [seism] *nm* earthquake; *Fig & Litt* upheaval

seize [sɛz] *adj & nm inv* sixteen; *voir aussi* **trois**

seizième [sɛzjɛm] *nmf, nm & adj* sixteenth; *voir aussi* **cinquième**

Seizième

This term often refers to the upper-class social background, lifestyle, way of dressing, etc. associated with the sixteenth arrondissement in Paris: "elle est très seizième".

---

séjour [seʒur] *nm* (**a**) *(période)* stay; **s. linguistique** language-learning trip (**b**) *(pièce)* **(salle de) s.** living room (**c**) *Litt (lieu)* abode

séjourner [seʒurne] *vi* to stay

sel [sɛl] *nm* (**a**) *(substance)* salt; **gros s.** coarse salt; **s. fin** fine salt; **sels de bain** bath salts; **sels** *(à respirer)* (smelling) salts (**b**) *Fig (esprit)* piquancy

sélect, -e [selɛkt] *adj Fam (soirée, clientèle)* select

sélectif, -ive [selɛktif, -iv] *adj* selective; *Ordinat* **en mode s.** in veto mode

sélection [selɛksjɔ̃] *nf* selection

sélectionné, -e [selɛksjɔne] **1** *adj* selected
   2 *nm,f (sportif)* selected competitor; *(d'une équipe)* selected player

sélectionner [selɛksjɔne] *vt* to select; *Ordinat (texte)* to block, to select

sélectionneur, -euse [selɛksjɔnœr, -øz] *nm,f* selector

self [sɛlf] *nm Fam* self-service restaurant

self-service (*pl* **self-services**) [sɛlfsɛrvis] *nm (restaurant)* self-service restaurant; *(magasin)* self-service store

selle [sɛl] *nf* (**a**) *(de cheval, de bicyclette, de moto)* saddle; **se mettre en s.** to mount; **monter sans s.** to ride bareback (**b**) **selles** *(matières fécales)* stools; **aller à la s.** to have a bowel movement (**c**) *Culin* **s. de mouton/d'agneau** saddle of mutton/lamb

seller [sele] *vt* to saddle

sellette [sɛlɛt] *nf Fam* **mettre qn/être sur la s.** to put sb/to be in the hot seat

selon [sǝlɔ̃] *prép* (**a**) *(d'après)* according to; **s. moi** in my opinion (**b**) *(conformément à)* in accordance with; **s. toute vraisemblance** in all probability (**c**) *(en fonction de)* **varier s. les cas/les saisons** to vary from case to case/season to season; *Fam* **c'est s.** it all depends; **s. que...** depending on whether...

SEM [sɛm] *nf Écon (abrév* **société d'économie mixte***)* = company financed by state and private capital

semailles [sǝmaj] *nfpl* (**a**) *(action)* sowing; **(temps des) s.** sowing time (**b**) *(graines)* seeds

semaine [sǝmɛn] *nf* (**a**) *(sept jours)* week; **vivre à la petite s.** to live from day to day; **jour de s.** weekday; **en s.** during the week, on weekdays; **la s. de 35 heures** the 35-hour working week; **la s. sainte** Holy Week (**b**) *(salaire)* weekly pay; *(argent de poche)* weekly allowance (**c**) *Mil (tour de service)* week's duty; **être de s.** to be on duty for the week; **officier de s.** duty officer for the week

semainier [sǝmenje] *nm (agenda)* desk diary

sémantique [semɑ̃tik] **1** *adj* semantic
   2 *nf* semantics *(singulier)*

sémaphore [semafɔr] *nm Rail* semaphore signal; *Naut* signal station

semblable [sɑ̃blabl] **1** *adj* (**a**) *(pareil)* similar; **s. à qch** similar to sth, like sth; **je n'ai rien dit de s.** I said nothing of the sort (**b**) *(tel)* **de semblables projets/propos** such plans/remarks, plans/remarks like that
   2 *nm (être humain)* fellow man; **vous et vos semblables** you and your kind

semblant [sɑ̃blɑ̃] *nm* (**a**) *(apparence)* **un s. de** a semblance of (**b**) **faire s.** to pretend; **faire s. de faire qch** to pretend to do sth; **en faisant s. de rien** without making it obvious

sembler [sɑ̃ble] **1** *vi* to seem
   2 *v impersonnel* **il semble que...** it seems that...; **il me/leur**

---

semble que... it seems to me/them that...; **me semble-t-il** it seems to me; **il me semble avoir entendu son nom** I have a feeling I've heard his/her name; **il me semble idiot d'attendre encore plus longtemps** it seems stupid to me to wait any longer; **faites comme bon vous semble** *ou* **semblera** do as you think best; **il le fera si bon lui semble** he'll do it if he thinks fit

semé, -e [sǝme] *adj* **s. de** strewn with; *(fleurs)* dotted with; *(étoiles)* studded with; *(citations)* sprinkled with; **s. d'embûches** full of traps

semelle [sǝmɛl] *nf* sole; **s. (intérieure)** insole; **s. de caoutchouc/de cuir** rubber/leather sole; **ne pas avancer d'une s.** to make no progress whatsoever; **il ne reculera pas d'une s.** he won't give an inch; **ne pas quitter qn d'une s.** to be always at sb's heels; **c'est de la s.!** it's like shoe leather!

semence [sǝmɑ̃s] *nf (graine)* seed; *(sperme)* semen

semer [46] [sǝme] *vt* (**a**) *(graines)* to sow (**b**) *(discorde, confusion, panique, doute)* to sow, to spread; *Prov* **qui sème le vent récolte la tempête** he who sows the wind shall reap the whirlwind (**c**) *Fam (distancer)* to shake off (**d**) *Fam (perdre)* to lose

semestre [sǝmɛstr] *nm* half-year, six-month period; *Scol & Univ* semester

semestriel, -elle [sǝmɛstrijɛl] *adj* half-yearly, six-monthly

semi-automatique [sǝmiɔtɔmatik] *adj* semi-automatic

semi-liberté [sǝmilibɛrte] *nf Jur* partial release

sémillant, -e [semijɑ̃, -ɑ̃t] *adj (personne)* spirited; *(regard)* bright

séminaire [seminɛr] *nm* (**a**) *(colloque)* seminar (**b**) *Rel* seminary

séminariste [seminarist] *nm Rel* seminarist

sémiologie [semjɔlɔʒi] *nf* semiology

sémiotique [semjɔtik] **1** *adj* semiotic
   2 *nf* semiotics *(singulier)*

semi-précieux, -euse (*mpl* **semi-précieux**, *fpl* **semi-précieuses**) [sǝmipresjø, -øz] *adj* semi-precious

semi-remorque (*pl* **semi-remorques**) [sǝmirǝmɔrk] *nm* semitrailer

semis [sǝmi] *nm* (**a**) *(action)* sowing (**b**) *(terrain)* seedbed (**c**) *(jeune plante)* seedling

sémite [semit] **1** *adj* Semitic
   2 *nmf* **S.** Semite

sémitique [semitik] *adj* Semitic

semoir [sǝmwar] *nm* (**a**) *(sac)* seed bag (**b**) *(machine)* seeder

semonce [sǝmɔ̃s] *nf (remontrance)* reprimand; *aussi Fig* **coup de s.** warning shot

semoule [sǝmul] *nf* semolina

sempiternel, -elle [sɑ̃pitɛrnɛl] *adj* never-ending, endless

sénat [sena] *nm* senate

Sénat

The Sénat is the upper house of the French Parliament. Its members are elected for a nine-year mandate by the Deputies of the **Assemblée nationale** *(see box at this entry)* and certain other government officals. The President of the Senate may deputize for the President of the Republic in the case of incapacity or death. The powers of the Senate are almost as extensive as those of the "Assemblée nationale", although the latter is empowered to override the decisions of the Senate in cases where the two houses disagree.

---

sénateur [senatœr] *nm* senator

sénatorial, -e, -aux, -ales [senatɔrjal, -o] *adj* senatorial

Sénégal [senegal] *nm* **le S.** Senegal

sénégalais, -e [senegalɛ, -ɛz] **1** *adj* Senegalese
   2 *nm,f* **S., Sénégalaise** Senegalese; **les S.** the Senegalese

sénile [senil] *adj* senile

sénilité [senilite] *nf* senility

senior [senjɔr] *adj & nmf Sport* senior *(above the age of 20)*

sens¹ *voir* **sentir**

sens² [sɑ̃s] *nm* (**a**) *(de la perception)* sense; **les cinq s.** the five senses; **le sixième s.** the sixth sense

(**b**) **les s.** *(sensualité)* the senses; **plaisir des s.** sensual pleasure

(**c**) *(jugement)* sense; **avoir le s. de l'humour/du ridicule** to have a sense of humor/of the ridiculous; **avoir le s. des affaires/de l'orientation** to have good business sense/a good sense of direction; **s. commun** common sense; **s. moral** moral sense; **s. pratique** practical sense; **bon s.** common sense; **un homme de bon s.** a sensible man

(**d**) *(avis)* **à mon s.** to my mind

(**e**) *(signification) (d'un mot)* meaning, sense; **au s. propre/figuré** in the literal/figurative sense, literally/figuratively; **cela n'a aucun s.** it doesn't make (any) sense; **en ce s. que...** in the sense that...

(**f**) *(direction)* direction; **tenir qch dans le mauvais s.** to hold sth the wrong way around; **en s. inverse** in the opposite direction; **dans le s. des aiguilles d'une montre** clockwise; **dans le s. inverse des aiguilles d'une montre** counterclockwise; **dans le s. du courant** with the current; **dans le s. de la longueur** lengthwise, lengthways; **dans le s. de la largeur** widthwise, across; **s. dessus dessous** *(en désordre)* upside down; **s. devant derrière** back to front, the wrong way around; **dans les deux s.** both ways; *Fig* **ces mesures vont dans le bon s.** these measures are a step in the right direction; *Ordinat* **s. de déroulement** flow direction; **s. giratoire** traffic circle; **s. interdit** *(sur panneau)* no entry; **s. unique** *(sur panneau)* one way

sensas(s) [sɑ̃sas] *adj Fam* fantastic, great

sensation [sɑ̃sasjɔ̃] *nf* (**a**) *(perception physique)* sensation (**b**) *(impression)* feeling; **avoir la s. que...** to have a *or* the feeling that... (**c**) *(scandale)* **faire s.** to create a sensation

sensationnel, -elle [sɑ̃sasjɔnɛl] *adj* (**a**) *(à sensation)* sensational (**b**) *Fam (fantastique)* fantastic, great

sensé, -e [sɑ̃se] *adj* sensible

sensibilisation [sɑ̃sibilizasjɔ̃] *nf* (**a**) **s. de l'opinion (à qch)** increasing public awareness (of sth) (**b**) *Phot & Méd* sensitization

sensibiliser [sɑ̃sibilize] *vt* (**a**) *(rendre conscient)* **s. qn à qch** to increase sb's awareness of sth; **s. l'opinion (à qch)** to increase public awareness (of sth) (**b**) *Phot & Méd* to sensitize

sensibilité [sɑ̃sibilite] *nf* sensitivity; **avoir une s. à fleur de peau** to be hypersensitive

sensible [sɑ̃sibl] *adj* (**a**) *(émotif)* sensitive (**b**) *(réceptif)* **être s. à qch** to be sensitive to sth; *(influence)* to be susceptible to sth (**c**) *(douloureux)* sensitive (**d**) *(appréciable)* noticeable, appreciable; **de manière s.** noticeably (**e**) *(balance, thermomètre, plaque)* sensitive; **s. à la lumière** light-sensitive

sensiblement [sɑ̃sibləmɑ̃] *adv* (**a**) *(notablement)* noticeably, appreciably (**b**) *(à peu près)* roughly, more or less

sensiblerie [sɑ̃sibləri] *nf* sentimentality

sensoriel, -elle [sɑ̃sɔrjɛl] *adj* sensory

sensualité [sɑ̃sɥalite] *nf* sensuality

sensuel, -elle [sɑ̃sɥɛl] *adj* sensual

sent *voir* **sentir**

sentence [sɑ̃tɑ̃s] *nf* (**a**) *(jugement)* sentence (**b**) *(maxime)* maxim

sentencieux, -euse [sɑ̃tɑ̃sjø, -øz] *adj* sententious

senteur [sɑ̃tœr] *nf* scent; *(dans un parfum)* note

senti, -e [sɑ̃ti] *adj* **bien s.** appropriate

sentier [sɑ̃tje] *nm* path; *Fig* **sortir des sentiers battus** to go off the beaten track; **sur le s. de la guerre** on the warpath

sentiment [sɑ̃timɑ̃] *nm* feeling; **prendre qn par les sentiments** to appeal to sb's feelings; *Fam* **ça partait d'un bon s.** it was well meant; **en affaires, je ne fais pas de s.** I don't let

sentiment interfere with business; **avoir le s. que...** to have a *or* the feeling that...; **j'avais le s. de m'être trompé** I had the feeling I'd made a mistake

sentimental, -e, -aux, -ales [sɑ̃timɑ̃tal, -o] **1** *adj (personne, chanson, valeur)* sentimental; **vie sentimentale** love life

2 *nm,f* **c'est un(e) grand(e) sentimental(e)** he's/she's a great romantic

sentimentalisme [sɑ̃timɑ̃talism] *nm* sentimentalism; **faire du s.** to be sentimental

sentinelle [sɑ̃tinɛl] *nf* sentry

sentir [64a] [sɑ̃tir] **1** *vt* (**a**) *(douleur, sensation tactile)* to feel; *Fam Fig* **je ne sens plus mes jambes/mes pieds** *(de froid)* I can't feel my legs/my feet; *(de fatigue)* my legs/my feet are killing me

(**b**) *(être conscient de) (danger)* to sense; **s. que...** to have a *or* the feeling that...; **faire s. à qn que...** to make sb feel that...; **se faire s.** to make itself felt; *Fig* **on sent l'influence de Wagner** one can detect Wagner's influence; *Fam* **je l'ai sentie passer** *(claque, fracture)* I knew all about it

(**c**) *(parfum, fleur)* to smell; **faire s. qch à qn** to let sb smell sth

(**d**) *(avoir l'odeur de)* to smell of; **ça sent le brûlé** there's a smell of burning; **ça sent bon le pain frais** there's a delicious smell of fresh bread; *Fig & Péj* **ce livre sent l'effort** this book is very labored; **s. le soufre** to smack of heresy

(**e**) *Fam (supporter)* **je ne peux pas le s.** I can't stand him

(**f**) *Fam (être convaincu par)* **je ne le sens pas, ton projet** I'm not convinced by your plan; **je ne la sens pas pour le rôle** my feeling is that she's not right for the part

2 *vi* (**a**) *(avoir comme odeur)* **s. bon/mauvais** to smell good/bad; **s. fort** to have a strong smell

(**b**) *Fam (puer)* to smell; **s. des pieds** to have smelly feet

3 **se sentir** *vpr* (**a**) *(être perceptible)* **cela se sent** you can tell

(**b**) *(suivi d'un adjectif ou d'un infinitif)* **se s. revivre** to feel oneself coming alive again; **se s. bien/fatigué** to feel well/tired; *Fam* **tu ne te sens pas bien, non?** have you taken leave of your senses?; **se s. capable de faire qch** to feel capable of doing sth

(**c**) *(avoir)* **se s. le courage de faire qch** to feel up to doing sth

(**d**) *Fam (se contrôler)* **il ne se sent plus!** he's too big for his boots!

(**e**) *Fam (se supporter)* **ils ne peuvent pas se s.** they can't stand each other

seoir [10a] [swar] *Litt* **1** *vi* **s. à** to suit

2 *v impersonnel* **il lui sied mal de...** it ill becomes him to...

Séoul [seul] *n* Seoul

séparable [separabl] *adj* separable (**de** from)

séparation [separasjɔ̃] *nf* (**a**) *(de personnes, d'objets)* separation (**de** from); *Ordinat* **s. automatique des pages** automatic pagination (**b**) *(cloison)* partition, division (**c**) *Jur* **s. de biens** = marriage settlement under which husband and wife administer their separate properties

séparatisme [separatism] *nm* separatism

séparatiste [separatist] *adj & nmf* separatist

séparé, -e [separe] *adj* (**a**) *(notions, chambres)* separate (**b**) *(personnes)* separated (**de** from); **nous vivons séparés** we live apart

séparément [separemɑ̃] *adv* separately

séparer [separe] **1** *vt* (**a**) *(éloigner)* to separate (**de** from) (**b**) *(partager)* to divide (**en** into) (**c**) *(opposer)* to divide; **tout les sépare** they are poles apart

2 **se séparer** *vpr* (**a**) *(époux)* to separate (**de** from), to split up (**de** with) (**b**) *(foule, assemblée)* to break up (**c**) *(se défaire)* **se s. de qch** to part with sth; **se s. de qn** *(employé)* to let sb go (**d**) *(rivière, route)* to divide (**en** into); **c'est ici que nos chemins se séparent** this is where we go our separate ways

sept [sɛt] *adj & nm inv* seven; *voir aussi* **trois**

septante [sɛptɑ̃t] *adj inv Belg & Suisse* seventy; *voir aussi* **trois**

septembre [sɛptɑ̃br] *nm* September; *voir aussi* **janvier**

septennat [sɛptena] *nm* seven-year term

septentrional, -e, -aux, -ales [sɛptɑ̃trijɔnal, -o] *adj* northern

septicémie [sɛptisemi] *nf* blood poisoning, septicemia

septième [sɛtjɛm] *nmf, nm & adj* seventh; *voir aussi* **cinquième**

septique [sɛptik] *adj* septic

septuagénaire [sɛptɥaʒenɛr] *adj & nmf* septuagenarian

sépulcre [sepylkr] *nm* sepulcher

sépulture [sepyltyr] *nf Litt* (a) *(inhumation)* burial (b) *(lieu)* burial place

séquelles [sekɛl] *nfpl (d'une maladie, d'un accident)* after-effects; *(d'une guerre, d'une catastrophe)* aftermath

séquençage [sekɑ̃saʒ] *nm Biol* sequencing

séquence [sekɑ̃s] *nf* (a) *(d'objets, de mots)* sequence; *Ordinat* **s. de caractères** character string, sequence of characters (b) *(de film)* sequence (c) *(de cartes)* run

séquestre [sekɛstr] *nm (action)* sequestration; **mettre qch sous s.** to sequester sth

séquestrer [sekɛstre] *vt* (a) *(personne)* **s. qn** to keep sb locked up (b) *(biens)* to sequester

séquoia [sekɔja] *nm* sequoia

sera, serai, serais, *etc. voir* **être²**

sérail [seraj] *nm* seraglio; *Fig* inner circle

serbe [sɛrb] **1** *adj* Serb, Serbian
   2 *nmf* **S.** Serb, Serbian

Serbie [sɛrbi] *nf* **la S.** Serbia

serbo-croate *(pl* **serbo-croates)** [sɛrbɔkrɔat] **1** *adj* Serbo-Croat, Serbo-Croatian
   2 *nm (langue)* Serbo-Croat

Sercq [sɛrk] *n* Sark

serein, -e [sərɛ̃, -ɛn] *adj (personne, visage, esprit)* serene; *(ciel, nuit)* clear

sereinement [sərɛnmɑ̃] *adv* calmly

sérénade [serenad] *nf* (a) *Mus* serenade; **donner la s. à qn** to serenade sb (b) *Fam (tapage)* racket

sérénité [serenite] *nf* serenity; **avec s.** serenely

serf, serve [sɛrf, sɛrv] *nm,f Hist* serf

sergent [sɛrʒɑ̃] *nm* sergeant

sergent-chef *(pl* **sergents-chefs)** [sɛrʒɑ̃ʃɛf] *nm* staff sergeant

série [seri] *nf* (a) *(suite, collection)* series; *(d'échantillons)* range; *(de casseroles)* set; **des démissions en s.** a series of resignations (b) *Rad & TV* series (c) *Ind* **production en s.** mass production; **fabriquer qch en s.** to mass-produce sth; **voiture de s.** standard car; **s. limitée** limited run *(dans un classement)* group; *Sport* heat; **(film de) s. B** B movie (e) *(locutions)* **s. noire** *(suite de catastrophes)* series *or* catalog of disasters; **(roman de) s. noire** crime thriller

sérieusement [serjøzmɑ̃] *adv* seriously; **parlez-vous s.?** are you serious?

sérieux, -euse [serjø, -øz] **1** *adj* (a) *(personne, lecture)* serious; **d'un air s.** seriously; **ce n'est pas s.!** you're not serious!; *Fam* **s. comme un pape** as solemn as a judge (b) *(offre, acheteur)* serious, genuine; *(information, entreprise)* reliable; *(employé)* conscientious (c) *(important) (problèmes, ennuis)* serious; *(progrès)* good
   2 *nm* (a) *(application)* conscientiousness; **avec s.** conscientiously (b) *(gravité)* **garder son s.** to keep a straight face; **prendre qn/qch au s.** to take sb/sth seriously; **se prendre au s.** to take oneself seriously

sérigraphie [serigrafi] *nf* silk-screen printing

serin [sərɛ̃] *nm (oiseau)* canary

seriner [sərine] *vt Fam* **s. qch à qn** to go on and on to sb about sth; **s. à qn que...** to keep telling sb that...

seringue [sərɛ̃g] *nf* syringe

serment [sɛrmɑ̃] *nm* (a) *(parole solennelle)* oath; **prêter s.** to take an oath; **sous s.** under oath (b) *(promesse)* pledge; *(d'amoureux)* vow; **faire le s. de faire qch** to swear *or* to vow to do sth

sermon [sɛrmɔ̃] *nm* (a) *Rel* sermon (b) *Fam (remontrance)* lecture, sermon

sermonner [sɛrmɔne] *vt Fam* to lecture

séronégatif, -ive [serɔnegatif, -iv] **1** *adj* HIV negative
   2 *nm,f* person who is HIV negative

séropositif, -ive [serɔpozitif, -iv] **1** *adj* HIV positive
   2 *nm,f* person who is HIV positive

sérotonine [serɔtɔnin] *nf* serotonin

serpe [sɛrp] *nf* billhook

serpent [sɛrpɑ̃] *nm* (a) *(reptile)* snake; **s. à sonnette** rattlesnake (b) *Écon* **le s. monétaire européen** the European currency snake

serpenter [sɛrpɑ̃te] *vi* to wind

serpentin [sɛrpɑ̃tɛ̃] *nm (cotillon)* streamer

serpillière [sɛrpijɛr] *nf* floorcloth; **passer la s. dans la cuisine** to clean the kitchen floor

serpolet [sɛrpɔlɛ] *nm* wild thyme

serre [sɛr] *nf* (a) *(local)* greenhouse (b) **serres** *(d'oiseau de proie)* claws, talons

serré, -e [sere] **1** *adj* (a) *(chaussures, vêtement)* tight; *(personnes)* packed together; *(écriture)* cramped; *(rangs)* serried; *(dents)* clenched; *(lèvres)* pressed tightly together (b) *(emploi du temps, budget)* tight; *(surveillance, lutte, score)* close (c) *(café)* strong
   2 *adv* **écrire s.** to have cramped handwriting; *Fig* **jouer s.** to play a tight game

serre-livres [sɛrlivr] *nm inv* book end

serrement [sɛrmɑ̃] *nm* **avoir un s. de cœur** to feel a pang

serrer [sere] **1** *vt* (a) *(tenir)* to grip; **s. la main à qn** to shake hands with sb, to shake sb's hand; **s. qn dans ses bras** to hug sb; **s. qn/qch contre soi** to hold sb/sth tightly to one; *Fig* **s. le cœur à qn** to wring sb's heart (b) *(sujet: vêtement, chaussures)* to be too tight for (c) *(nœud, écrou, ceinture)* to tighten; *(joint)* to clamp; *(poings)* to clench; **s. les dents** to clench one's teeth; *Fig* to grit one's teeth; *Fam Fig* **s. les fesses** to be scared stiff (d) *(rapprocher)* to put close together; **s. les rangs** to close ranks (e) *(raser) (trottoir)* to hug; **s. qn de près** to follow sb closely; **évite de s. la voiture de devant** don't drive too close to the car in front (f) *Litt (ranger)* to put away
   2 *vi* **serrez à droite/gauche** *(sur panneau)* keep to the right/left
   3 se serrer *vpr* (a) *(se rapprocher)* to squeeze up; **se s. contre qn** to snuggle up to sb (b) *Fig* **ma gorge se serra** I had a lump in my throat (c) *(pour se saluer)* **se s. la main** to shake hands

serre-tête [sɛrtɛt] *nm inv* headband

serriculture [serikyltyr] *nf* hothouse growing

serrure [seryr] *nf* lock

serrurerie [seryrri] *nf (métier)* locksmith's trade; *(magasin)* locksmith's (store)

serrurier [seryrje] *nm* locksmith

sers, sert, *etc. voir* **servir**

sertir [sɛrtir] *vt (pierre précieuse)* to set

sérum [serɔm] *nm* serum; **s. physiologique** saline solution

servage [sɛrvaʒ] *nm* serfdom; *Fig* bondage

servante [sɛrvɑ̃t] *nf* (maid)servant

serve [sɛrv] *voir* **serf**

serveur, -euse [sɛrvœr, -øz] **1** *nm,f* (a) *(dans un bar)* bartender; *(dans un restaurant)* waiter, *f* waitress (b) *(au tennis)* server
   2 *nm Ordinat* server; **s. de fichiers** file server; **s. de réseau**

network server; **s. télématique** bulletin board (system); **s. Web** web server

serviable [sɛrvjabl] *adj* obliging, helpful

service [sɛrvis] *nm* (**a**) *(pour un client, pour un maître)* service; *Écon* **services** services; **faire le s.** *(à table)* to wait on; **être au s. de qn** to be in sb's service; **à votre s.** at your service; **s. compris/non compris** service included/not included; **premier/deuxième s.** *(au restaurant)* first/second sitting; **s. après-vente** *(dépannage)* after-sales service; *Ordinat* **s. en ligne** on-line service

(**b**) *Mil* **s. militaire** *ou* **national** military service; **faire son s.** to do one's military service; **bon pour le s.** fit for service

(**c**) *(au tennis)* service; **au s., Martin** Martin to serve

(**d**) *(travail)* duty; **être de s.** to be on duty; **prendre/quitter son s.** to go on/off duty; **reprendre du s.** to be employed for a supplementary period; *Fam* **le crétin de s.** the inevitable *or* obligatory idiot

(**e**) *(département)* department; **s. d'ordre** *(surveillance)* crowd control; *(personnes)* = police, security staff, etc. in charge of crowd control; **s. du personnel** personnel department; **s. public** public utility; **s. de renseignements** military intelligence department; *Ordinat* **s. télématique** bulletin board service

(**f**) *(d'une machine)* **en s.** in service; **mettre qch en s.** to bring sth into service; **hors s.** out of order

(**g**) *(de transports en commun)* service; **assurer le s. entre** to provide a service between

(**h**) *(aide)* favor; **rendre (un) s. à qn** *(personne)* to do sb a favor; *(objet)* to be of use to sb; **rendre un mauvais s. à qn** to do sb a bad turn

(**i**) *(de vaisselle)* set

Service militaire

Military service (for a period of ten months) used to be compulsory for French men aged between 18 and 26 unless they were declared unfit for service ("réformé"). As an alternative to military service, some chose to work overseas, often in developing countries, as part of a voluntary aid scheme known as "la coopération". However, following the "loi de programmation" 1997-2002, a reform was introduced in order to gradually abolish military service and move towards an exclusively professional army.

---

serviette [sɛrvjɛt] *nf* (**a**) *(en tissu)* **s. (de table)** napkin; **s. (de toilette)** towel; **s. de plage** beach towel (**b**) *(sac)* briefcase (**c**) **s. hygiénique** sanitary napkin

serviette-éponge *(pl* **serviettes-éponges)** [sɛrvjɛtepɔ̃ʒ] *nf* terry towel

servile [sɛrvil] *adj* servile; *(imitation, traduction)* slavish

servilement [sɛrvilmɑ̃] *adv* servilely; *(imiter, traduire)* slavishly

servir [63] [sɛrvir] **1** *vt* (**a**) *(client, convive, nourriture)* to serve; **tout le monde est servi?** *(à table)* has everybody been served?; **s. frais** *(sur étiquette)* serve chilled; **s. à boire à qn** to give sb a drink; *Ironique* **côté ennuis, je suis servi!** I've got more than my share of worries! (**b**) *(favoriser) (personne)* to serve; *(intérêts)* to further (**c**) *(au tennis)* to serve (**d**) *(aux cartes)* **à vous de s.** it's your deal

2 *vi (dans une administration)* to serve (**sous** under)

3 servir à *vt ind* (**a**) *(être utile à)* to be of use to; **ça peut toujours s.** it might still come in useful (**b**) *(être utilisé pour)* **s. à qch/à faire qch** to be used for sth/for doing sth; **ne s. à rien** to be useless; **ne pas s. à grand-chose** not to be much use; **à quoi ça sert?** *(objet)* what's that used for?; *(démarche)* what's the use of that?

4 servir de *vt ind (faire fonction de) (objet)* to serve as, to be used as; *(personne)* to act as; **ça me sert de porte-crayons** I use it as a pencil-holder

5 *v impersonnel Litt* **il ne sert à rien de pleurer** there's no point in crying

6 se servir *vpr* (**a**) *(prendre)* to help oneself; **je me suis déjà servie deux fois** I've already had two helpings; **se s. des pâtes/du poulet** to help oneself to pasta/to chicken (**b**) *(plat, vin)* to be served; **le champagne se sert frappé** champagne should be served chilled (**c**) **se s. de qn/qch** *(utiliser)* to use sb/sth (**d**) *(s'approvisionner)* **se s. chez...** to shop at...

serviteur [sɛrvitœr] *nm* servant

servitude [sɛrvityd] *nf* (**a**) *(asservissement)* servitude (**b**) *(contrainte)* constraint

ses [se] *voir* **son**[1]

sésame [sezam] *nm* (**a**) *(plante)* sesame (**b**) *Fig* **s., ouvre-toi!** open sesame!

session [sesjɔ̃] *nf* (**a**) *(d'une assemblée, d'un tribunal)* session, sitting (**b**) *(période d'examens)* (exam) session; **s. de rattrapage** repeat exams

SET® [ɛsœte] *nf Ordinat (abrév* **secure electronic transaction)** SET®

set [sɛt] *nm* (**a**) *(au tennis)* set (**b**) **s. de table** *(napperon)* table mat

setter [setɛr] *nm* setter; **s. irlandais** Irish setter

seuil [sœj] *nm* (**a**) *(entrée)* doorway, threshold; **sur le s.** in the doorway (**b**) *Fig* threshold; *Litt* **au s. de...** on the threshold of...; **s. de rentabilité** break-even point

seul, -e [sœl] **1** *adj* (**a**) *(unique)* only; **une seule personne** *(et pas plus)* a single person; *(parmi d'autres)* only one person; **comme un s. homme** as one man; **il suffit d'une seule fois** once is enough; **la seule pensée de sa venue** the mere thought of him/her coming (**b**) *(isolé)* alone; **se sentir s.** to feel lonesome *or* alone; **être s. au monde** to be alone in the world; **parler s. à s. à qn** to speak to sb in private; **faire qch tout s.** to do sth (by) oneself *or* on one's own; **parler tout s.** to talk to oneself; **cela va tout s.** it's plain sailing, it's straightforward; **ça descend tout s.** *(boisson)* it just slides down (**c**) *(seulement)* only, alone; **s. un miracle...** only a miracle...

2 *nm,f* **le s.** the only one; **un s.** *(personne, objet)* only one

seulement [sœlmɑ̃] *adv* only; **je te demande s. un peu de patience** I'm just asking you to be a bit patient; **non s. ... mais en plus...** not only... but also...; *Fam* **essaie s.!** just you try!

sève [sɛv] *nf* (**a**) *(d'une plante)* sap (**b**) *Fig (de la jeunesse)* vitality

sévère [sevɛr] *adj* severe; *(principe, règle)* strict; **être s. envers** *ou* **avec qn** to be hard on sb

sévèrement [sevɛrmɑ̃] *adv* severely; *(de façon stricte)* strictly

sévérité [severite] *nf* severity; *(d'une discipline, d'une éducation)* strictness

sévices [sevis] *nmpl* ill-treatment; **s. sexuels** sexual abuse

Séville [sevij] *n* Seville

sévir [sevir] *vi* (**a**) *(agir avec rigueur)* to act ruthlessly; **s. contre qn/qch** to deal ruthlessly with sb/sth (**b**) *(épidémie, guerre)* to rage; *(malfaiteurs)* to operate; **la crise qui sévit actuellement** the present crisis

sevrage [səvraʒ] *nm (d'un enfant)* weaning; *(d'un drogué, d'un alcoolique)* withdrawal

sevrer [səvre] *vt* (**a**) *(enfant)* to wean; *(drogué)* to get off drugs; *(alcoolique)* to get off drink (**b**) *Litt (priver)* **s. qn de qch** to deprive sb of sth

sexagénaire [sɛgzaʒenɛr, sɛksaʒenɛr] *nmf* person in his/her sixties

sex-appeal [sɛksapil] *nm Fam* sex appeal

sexe [sɛks] *nm* (**a**) *(genre)* sex; *Hum* **le beau s.** the fair sex; **le s. faible** the weaker sex; **le s. fort** the stronger sex (**b**) *(organes sexuels)* genitals (**c**) *(sexualité)* sex

sexisme [sɛksism] *nm* sexism

sexiste [sɛksist] *adj & nmf* sexist

sexologue [sɛksɔlɔg] *nmf* sexologist

sexothérapeute [sɛksoterapøt] *nmf* sex therapist

sex-shop (*pl* **sex-shops**) [sɛksʃɔp] *nm* sex shop

sextant [sɛkstã] *nm* sextant

sextuor [sɛkstɥɔr] *nm* sextet

sextuplé, -e [sɛkstyple] *nm,f* sextuplet

sexualité [sɛksɥalite] *nf* sexuality

sexué, -e [sɛksɥe] *adj (plante, animal)* sexed; *(reproduction)* sexual

sexuel, -elle [sɛksɥɛl] *adj (rapport)* sexual; *(vie, acte, organe)* sex

sexuellement [sɛksɥɛlmã] *adv* sexually

sexy [sɛksi] *adj inv Fam* sexy

seyant, -e [sejã, -ãt] *adj* becoming

Seychelles [seʃɛl] *nfpl* **les S.** the Seychelles

SF [ɛsɛf] *nf Fam (abrév* **science fiction**) sci-fi, SF

SFIO [ɛsɛfio] *nf (abrév* **Section française de l'Internationale ouvrière**) = French Socialist Party 1905–1969

shaker [ʃekœr] *nm* cocktail shaker

shakespearien, -enne [ʃɛkspirjɛ̃, -ɛn] *adj* Shakespearean

shampoing, shampooing [ʃãpwɛ̃] *nm* shampoo; **faire un s. à qn** to shampoo sb's hair, to give sb a shampoo

shampooiner, shampouiner [ʃãpwine] *vt* to shampoo

shampooineur, -euse, shampouineur, -euse [ʃãpwinœr, -øz] **1** *nm,f* shampooer

2 *nf* **shampouineuse (à moquettes)** *(machine)* carpet shampooer

shérif [ʃerif] *nm* sheriff

shetland [ʃɛtlãd] **1** *nfpl* **les (îles) S.** the Shetland Islands, the Shetlands

2 *nm* **(a)** *(laine)* Shetland wool; *(pull)* Shetland sweater **(b)** *(poney)* Shetland pony

shiatsu [ʃiatsu] *nm* shiatsu, shiatzu

shinto [ʃinto], **shintoïsme** [ʃintɔism] *nm* Shinto, Shintoism

shit [ʃit] *nm très Fam* hash

shoot [ʃut] *nm* shot

shooter [ʃute] **1** *vi (au football)* to shoot

2 se shooter *vpr Fam (se droguer)* to shoot up; **se s. à l'héroïne** to shoot (up) heroin

shopping [ʃɔpiŋ] *nm* shopping; **faire du s.** to go shopping

short [ʃɔrt] *nm* (pair of) shorts

show [ʃo] *nm* show

show-business [ʃobiznɛs] *nm* show business

si¹ [si] *adv* **(a)** *(tellement)* so; **un si bon dîner** such a good dinner; **il n'est pas si bête (que ça)** he's not that stupid; **il était si nerveux qu'il a tout oublié** he was so nervous (that) he forgot everything **(b)** *(indique la concession)* **si... que** + *subjunctive* however...; **si jeune qu'il soit** however young he may be; **si habile soit-il** however capable (he may be) **(c)** *(oui)* yes; **je crois que si** I think so; **mais si, je l'ai vue** I DID see her; **tu ne sais pas? – si,** you don't know? – yes, I do **(d) si bien que...** *(indique le résultat)* so that...

si² [si] **1** *conj* **(a)** *(exprime l'hypothèse, la condition)* if; **qui le fera si ce n'est moi?** who'll do it if I don't?; **un des plus grands, si ce n'est le plus grand** one of the biggest, if not the biggest; **si ce n'est que...** *(sauf que)* apart from the fact that...; **et si elle l'apprend?** and what if she finds out?; **si on faisait une partie de bridge?** what about a game of bridge?; **oui, si on veut** yes, if you like; **si seulement...** if only...; **si tant est que...** + *subjunctive* if... **(b)** *(combien)* how; **pensez si j'étais furieux!** imagine how angry I was! **(c)** *(dans les questions indirectes)* if, whether; *Fam* **si je connais Paris?** do I know Paris?; *Fam* **si c'est pas malheureux (de voir ça)!** isn't it just awful (to see that)!

2 *nm inv* **tes si et tes mais** your ifs and buts

si³ [si] *nm inv (note)* B; *(chantée)* ti

siamois, -e [sjamwa, -az] **1** *adj* **frères s.** Siamese twins; **sœurs siamoises** Siamese twins

2 *nm (chat)* Siamese (cat)

Sibérie [siberi] *nf* **la S.** Siberia

sibérien, -enne [siberjɛ̃, -ɛn] **1** *adj* Siberian

2 *nm,f* **S., Sibérienne** Siberian

sibyllin, -e [sibilɛ̃, -in] *adj (énigmatique)* cryptic, enigmatic

SICAV [sikav] *nf inv Fin (abrév* **société d'investissement à capital variable**) **(a)** *(organisme)* ≃ mutual fund **(b)** *(titre)* share in a mutual fund

Sicile [sisil] *nf* **la S.** Sicily

sicilien, -enne [sisiljɛ̃, -ɛn] **1** *adj* Sicilian

2 *nm (langue)* Sicilian

3 *nm,f* **S., Sicilienne** Sicilian

sida [sida] *nm (abrév* **syndrome immunodéficitaire acquis**) AIDS; **avoir le s.** to have AIDS

side-car (*pl* **side-cars**) [sajdkar, sidkar] *nm* sidecar

sidéen, -enne [sideɛ̃, -ɛn] **1** *adj* suffering from AIDS

2 *nm,f* AIDS sufferer

sidéral, -e, -aux, -ales [sideral, -o] *adj* sidereal

sidérant, -e [siderã, -ãt] *adj Fam* staggering

sidérer [34] [sidere] *vt Fam* to stagger

sidérurgie [sideryrʒi] *nf* **(a)** *(technique)* steel metallurgy **(b)** *(industrie)* steel industry

sidérurgique [sideryrʒik] *adj (industrie, usine)* steel

sidérurgiste [sideryrʒist] *nmf* steelworker

siècle [sjɛkl] *nm* **(a)** *(cent ans)* century; **au vingtième s.** in the twentieth century; **avoir un s.** to be a hundred years old; *Fam* **ça fait des siècles que j'attends** I've been waiting for ages **(b)** *(époque)* age; **le s. des Lumières** the Age of Enlightenment; **il est de son s.** he's a man of his times

sied *voir* **seoir**

siège [sjɛʒ] *nm* **(a)** *(meuble)* seat; **s. avant/arrière** front/back seat; **s. pliant** folding chair; **s. pour enfant** *(en voiture)* child seat **(b)** *(d'une société, d'un organisme)* headquarters; **avoir son s. à...** to be headquartered at...; **s. administratif** administrative headquarters; **s. social** head office **(c)** *(lieu d'origine)* seat **(d)** *Mil* siege; **faire le s. de** to lay siege to; **lever le s.** to raise the siege; *Fam (partir)* to make tracks **(e)** *Pol* seat **(f)** *Méd* **accouchement par le s.** breech delivery; **se présenter par le s.** to be in the breech position

siéger [59] [sjeʒe] *vi* **(a)** *(tribunal, assemblée)* to sit **(b)** *(se trouver)* **c'est là que siège le mal** that's the root of the matter

sien, sienne [sjɛ̃, sjɛn] **1** *pron possessif* **le sien, la sienne, les siens, les siennes** *(possesseur masculin)* his; *(possesseur féminin)* hers; *(en insistant)* his/her own; **il te prête le s.** you can borrow his; **elle n'en a pas besoin, elle a le s.** she doesn't need it, she has her own; **on doit acheter la sienne** you must buy your own; **chacun doit apporter le s.** everyone must bring their own; **chaque pays a le s.** each country has its own

2 *nm* **il faut qu'il y mette du s.** he should do his share

3 *nmpl* **les siens** *(sa famille)* his/her family

4 *nfpl Fam* **il a encore fait des siennes** he's been up to his old tricks again

Sierra Leone [sjeraleɔn] *nf* **la S.** Sierra Leone

sieste [sjɛst] *nf* siesta, nap; **faire la s.** to have a nap

sifflant, -e [siflã, -ãt] *adj (respiration, toux)* wheezing

sifflement [sifləmã] *nm (d'une personne, du vent)* whistling; *(d'un serpent, de la vapeur)* hissing; *(d'un asthmatique)* wheezing; **sifflements d'oreilles** ringing in the ears

siffler [sifle] **1** *vt* **(a)** *(air)* to whistle **(b)** *(chien, personne)* to whistle at **(c)** *(acteur, pièce)* to boo **(d)** *Fam (verre, bouteille)* to knock back

2 *vi* **(a)** *(personne, merle, bouilloire)* to whistle; *(serpent)* to hiss **(b)** *(avec un sifflet)* to blow one's whistle

sifflet [siflɛ] *nm* (**a**) *(instrument)* whistle; *Fam* **couper le s. à qn** to shut sb up (**b**) *(au théâtre)* **sifflets** booing, boos

siffleux [sifló] *nm Can* groundhog, woodchuck

siffloter [siflɔte] *vt & vi* to whistle to oneself

sigle [sigl] *nm (acronyme)* acronym; *(suite d'initiales)* abbreviation

signal, -aux [siɲal, -o] *nm* (**a**) *(signe)* signal; **faire un s.** to signal; **envoyer** *ou* **lancer un s.** to send a signal; **au s., levez-vous** when the signal is given, stand up; **s. lumineux** warning light (**b**) *(panneau)* sign (**c**) *(dispositif sonore)* **d'alarme** alarm (signal); **s. d'alerte** warning (signal); *Tél* **s. d'appel** call-waiting signal; **s. de détresse** distress signal; **s. sonore** warning sound (**d**) *Ordinat* **s. d'avertissement de réception** acknowledge; **s. horodateur** time and date signal; **s. d'invitation à transmettre** proceed-to-send signal

signalement [siɲalmã] *nm* description, particulars

signaler [siɲale] **1** *vt* (**a**) *(faire remarquer)* to point out (**à** to); **s. à qn que...** to point out to sb that... (**b**) *(rapporter)* to report (**à** to); **rien à s.** nothing to report (**c**) *(par un panneau)* to signpost (**d**) *Ordinat (marquer)* to flag up
  2 se signaler *vpr* to distinguish oneself (**par** by); **se s. à l'attention de qn** to catch sb's eye

signalétique [siɲaletik] *adj* **fiche s.** personal details card; **plaque s.** identification plate

signalisation [siɲalizasjɔ̃] *nf (signaux routiers)* signs and markings; *(signaux ferroviaires)* signals; *(de piste d'atterrissage)* lights and markings; **s. routière** road signs

signaliser [siɲalize] *vt (route)* to signpost and mark; *(voie ferrée)* to install signals on; *(piste d'atterrissage)* to install lights and markings on

signataire [siɲatɛr] *nmf* signatory

signature [siɲatyr] *nf* (**a**) *(griffe)* signature; **présenter qch à la s.** to present sth for signature; *Com & Ordinat* **s. électronique** e-signature; **s. numérique** digital signature (**b**) *(acte)* signing

signe [siɲ] *nm* (**a**) *(indice)* sign; **il n'a pas donné s. de vie** there's been no sign of him; **il n'y a aucun s. de vie dans la maison** there's no sign of life at the house; **en s. de désapprobation/solidarité** as a sign of disapproval/solidarity; **s. avant-coureur** forerunner; **donner des signes d'usure** to show signs of wear
  (**b**) *(symbole)* sign, symbol; **s. moins/plus/égale** minus/plus/equals sign; **signes de ponctuation** punctuation marks
  (**c**) *Astrol* **s. du zodiaque** sign of the zodiac; **être né sous le s. du Capricorne** to be born under the sign of Capricorn; *Fig* **le sommet a eu lieu sous le s. de la réconciliation** the summit was held in a spirit of reconciliation
  (**d**) *(trait distinctif)* mark; **signes particuliers** distinguishing marks
  (**e**) *(geste)* sign, gesture; **faire un s. à qn** to gesture to sb; **parler par signes** to use sign language; **faire s. à qn** *(de la main)* to signal to sb; *(le contacter)* to get in touch with sb; **faire s. à qn de faire qch** to signal to sb to do sth; **faire s. que oui** *(de la tête)* to nod (one's head); **faire s. que non** *(de la tête)* to shake one's head; *(du doigt)* to shake one's finger; **faire un s. de la main (à qn)** to wave (at sb); **faire s. de tête (à qn)** to nod (to sb)
  (**f**) *Rel* **s. de croix** sign of the cross; **faire le s. de croix** to make the sign of the cross

signer [siɲe] **1** *vt (contrat, lettre, tableau)* to sign; *Fam Fig* **ça c'est signé!** no prizes for guessing who did that!
  2 *vi* to sign; **s. de son nom** to sign one's name
  3 se signer *vpr* to cross oneself

signet [siɲɛ] *nm (de livre, de page Web)* bookmark; *Ordinat* **créer un s. sur une page** to bookmark a page

significatif, -ive [siɲifikatif, -iv] *adj* significant; **s. de qch** indicative of sth

signification [siɲifikasjɔ̃] *nf* (**a**) *(d'un mot, d'un symbole)* meaning, sense; *(d'un fait)* significance (**b**) *Jur (d'un jugement)* notification

signifier [66] [siɲifje] *vt* (**a**) *(vouloir dire)* to mean; **qu'est-ce que ça signifie?** *(indignation)* what's the meaning of this? (**b**) *(notifier) (intentions)* to make known (**à** to); **s. son congé à qn** *(sujet: propriétaire, employeur)* to give sb notice; **s. qch à qn** to inform *or* to notify sb of sth

signofil(e) [siɲofil] *nm Suisse Aut* turn signal

silence [silãs] *nm* (**a**) *(absence de bruit)* silence; **un s. de mort** a deadly silence; **rompre le s.** to break the silence; **garder le s. (sur)** to keep silent (about); **faire qch en s.** to do sth in silence; **passer qch sous s.** not to mention sth (**b**) *Mus* rest

silencieusement [silãsjøzmã] *adv* silently

silencieux, -euse [silãsjø, -øz] **1** *adj* silent; *(qui ne fait pas beaucoup de bruit)* quiet
  2 *nm (d'un véhicule)* muffler; *(d'une arme)* silencer

silex [silɛks] *nm* flint

silhouette [silwɛt] *nf* (**a**) *(du corps)* figure (**b**) *(d'un objet)* silhouette, outline

silice [silis] *nf* silica

silicium [silisjɔm] *nm Chim* silicon

silicone [silikɔn] *nf* silicone

sillage [sijaʒ] *nm (d'un navire)* wake; *Fig* **marcher dans le s. de qn** to follow in sb's wake

sillon [sijɔ̃] *nm* (**a**) *(d'un champ)* furrow (**b**) *(de disque)* groove

sillonner [sijɔne] *vt (parcourir)* to criss-cross

silo [silo] *nm* silo

simagrées [simagre] *nfpl* airs and graces; **faire des s.** to make a fuss

simiesque [simjɛsk] *adj* monkey-like, ape-like

similaire [similɛr] *adj* similar (**à** to)

similarité [similarite] *nf* similarity

simili [simili] *nm Fam (imitation)* imitation

similicuir [similikɥir] *nm* imitation leather

similitude [similityd] *nf* similarity

simple [sɛ̃pl] **1** *adj* (**a**) *(sans prétentions)* simple (**b**) *(facile)* simple, easy; **c'est s. comme bonjour** it's as easy as pie (**c**) *(crédule)* simple; **s. d'esprit** simple-minded (**d**) *(pur)* **c'est une s. question de temps** it's simply a matter of time (**e**) *(ordinaire)* ordinary; **s. soldat** private (soldier) (**f**) *(composé d'un élément) (nœud)* single; **cornet s.** *(de glace)* cone with one scoop; *Ordinat* **s. densité** single density
  2 *nm* (**a**) *(au tennis)* singles (match) (**b**) *(somme, quantité)* **varier du s. au double** to vary by twice as much (**c**) *(personne)* **un s. d'esprit** a simpleton

simplement [sɛ̃pləmã] *adv* simply; **le plus s. du monde** as if it was the most natural thing in the world; **prendre les choses s.** to take things as they come

simplet, -ette [sɛ̃plɛ, -ɛt] *adj (personne)* simple; *(idée, explication)* simplistic

simplicité [sɛ̃plisite] *nf* simplicity; **recevoir qn en toute s.** to entertain sb very simply; **d'une s. enfantine** childishly simple

simplificateur, -trice [sɛ̃plifikatœr, -tris] *adj* simplifying

simplification [sɛ̃plifikasjɔ̃] *nf* simplification

simplifier [66] [sɛ̃plifje] *vt aussi Math* to simplify; **ça me simplifiera l'existence** it'll make my life easier

simplissime [sɛ̃plisim] *adj Fam* easy as pie

simpliste [sɛ̃plist] *adj Péj* simplistic

simulacre [simylakr] *nm* (**a**) *(représentation)* reconstruction (**b**) *(parodie)* **s. de combat/négociations** sham fight/negotiations; **ce fut un s. de procès** the trial was a farce

simulateur, -trice [simylatœr, -tris] **1** *nm,f (d'un sentiment)* pretender; *(d'une maladie)* malingerer
  2 *nm Tech* simulator

simulation [simylasjɔ̃] *nf* (**a**) *(action)* feigning (**b**) *(d'un vol, d'un phénomène) & Ordinat* simulation

simulé, -e [simyle] *adj* (**a**) *(sentiment, maladie)* feigned; *(combat)* sham (**b**) *(vol, phénomène)* simulated

simuler [simyle] *vt* (**a**) *(sentiment, maladie, folie)* to feign (**b**) *(vol, phénomène)* to simulate

simultané, -e [simyltane] *adj* simultaneous

simultanéité [simyltaneite] *nf* simultaneousness, simultaneity

simultanément [simyltanemã] *adv* simultaneously

sincère [sɛ̃sɛr] *adj* sincere

sincèrement [sɛ̃sɛrmã] *adv* sincerely; **s., je trouve que...** frankly, I think...

sincérité [sɛ̃serite] *nf* sincerity; **en toute s.** in all sincerity

sinécure [sinekyr] *nf* sinecure; *Fam* **ce n'est pas une s.** it's not exactly a rest cure

sine die [sinedje] *adv* sine die

sine qua non [sinekwanɔn] *adj inv* **une condition s.** a prerequisite

Singapour [sɛ̃gapur] *n* Singapore

singapourien, -enne [sɛ̃gapurjɛ̃, -ɛn] **1** *adj* Singaporean **2** *nm,f* **S., Singapourienne** Singaporean

singe [sɛ̃ʒ] *nm* monkey; **grand s.** ape; **malin/adroit comme un s.** as crafty/clever as a monkey; **faire le s.** to clown around

singer [45] [sɛ̃ʒe] *vt (personne)* to ape, to mimic; *(sentiment)* to feign

singeries [sɛ̃ʒri] *nfpl (grimaces, gestes)* antics; **faire des singeries** to clown around

singulariser [sɛ̃gylarize] **1** *vt* **s. qn (de)** to set sb apart (from), to make sb stand out (from) **2 se singulariser** *vpr* to draw attention to oneself; **il se singularise par sa façon de parler** the way he speaks makes him stand out

singularité [sɛ̃gylarite] *nf* peculiarity

singulier, -ère [sɛ̃gylje, -ɛr] **1** *adj* (**a**) *Gram* singular (**b**) *(combat)* single (**c**) *(remarquable)* remarkable; *(étrange)* peculiar, odd **2** *nm Gram* singular; **au s.** in the singular

singulièrement [sɛ̃gyljɛrmã] *adv* (**a**) *(étrangement)* oddly (**b**) *(en particulier)* especially, particularly (**c**) *(beaucoup)* remarkably, extremely

sinistre [sinistr] **1** *adj* (**a**) *(effrayant)* sinister; *(à faire froid dans le dos)* spooky (**b**) *(déprimant) (paysage)* bleak; *(soirée, repas)* dismal, grim (**c**) **un s. imbécile** an awful idiot **2** *nm* (**a**) *(catastrophe)* disaster (**b**) *Jur (dommage)* damage

sinistré, -e [sinistre] **1** *adj (population)* stricken; *(bâtiment)* damaged; *(région, zone)* disaster **2** *nm,f* disaster victim

sinistrose [sinistroz] *nf Fam* pessimism, gloom

sinologue [sinɔlɔg] *nmf* sinologist

sinon [sinɔ̃] *conj* (**a**) *(autrement)* otherwise, or else (**b**) *(excepté)* except (**c**) *(si ce n'est)* if not

sinueux, -euse [sinɥø, -øz] *adj (ligne)* sinuous; *(chemin, courant)* winding, meandering; *Fig (raisonnement)* tortuous

sinuosité [sinɥozite] *nf (d'un chemin, d'une rivière)* bend; *Fig* **les sinuosités d'un raisonnement** the twists and turns of an argument

sinus¹ [sinys] *nm Anat* sinus

sinus² [sinys] *nm Math* sine

sinusite [sinyzit] *nf* sinusitis

sionisme [sjɔnism] *nm* Zionism

sioniste [sjɔnist] *adj & nmf* Zionist

sioux [sju] **1** *adj* Sioux **2** *nmf* **S.** Sioux

siphon [sifɔ̃] *nm* (**a**) *(tube)* siphon (**b**) *(bouteille)* (soda) siphon (**c**) *(d'un évier, d'une canalisation)* U-bend, trap

siphonné, -e [sifɔne] *adj Fam (fou)* cracked, crazy

siphonner [sifɔne] *vt* to siphon

sire [sir] *nm* **S.** *(à un souverain)* Sire; *Péj* **un triste s.** an unsavory character

sirène [sirɛn] *nf* (**a**) *(personnage fantastique)* mermaid, siren; *Fig (femme)* siren (**b**) *(dispositif sonore)* siren

sirop [siro] *nm* syrup; **s. de fraise/menthe** strawberry/mint cordial; **s. contre la toux** cough syrup

siroter [sirɔte] *vt Fam* to sip

sirupeux, -euse [sirypø, -øz] *adj* syrupy; *(musique)* slushy

sismique [sismik] *adj* seismic

sismographe [sismɔgraf] *nm* seismograph

sismologie [sismɔlɔʒi] *nf* seismology

sitar [sitar] *nm* sitar

sitcom [sitkɔm] *nm ou nf* sitcom

site [sit] *nm* (**a**) *(emplacement)* site (**b**) *(pittoresque)* beauty spot; **s. classé** conservation area; **s. historique/archéologique** historic/archaeological site; **s. touristique** place of interest, tourist attraction (**c**) *Ordinat* site; **s. Web** website

sitôt [sito] *adv* **elle le fera s. ses devoirs finis** she'll do it as soon as she's finished her homework; **s. dit, s. fait** no sooner said than done; **s. que** as soon as; **s. après** immediately after; **on ne le reverra pas de s.** we won't see him again in a hurry

situation [sitɥasjɔ̃] *nf* (**a**) *(d'une ville, d'un bâtiment)* position, location (**b**) *(circonstances)* situation; **être en s. de faire qch** to be in a position to do sth; **mettre qn en s.** to give sb experience of a real-life situation; **l'homme de la s.** the right man for the job; **s. de famille** marital status (**c**) *(emploi)* job, position (**d**) *Fin (de compte)* balance

situé, -e [sitɥe] *adj* situated

situer [sitɥe] **1** *vt* (**a**) *(placer)* to situate (**b**) *(trouver)* to locate (**c**) *(dans le temps)* to set; **je situe l'action au milieu du XIXᵉ siècle** I'd say the action takes place in the middle of the 19th century (**d**) *Fig (catégoriser)* to categorize **2 se situer** *vpr* (**a**) *(être)* to be; **se s. à droite** to be right-wing (**b**) *(avoir lieu)* to take place

six [sis] *adj & nm inv* six; *voir aussi* **trois**

sixième [sizjɛm] **1** *adj, nmf & nm* sixth; *voir aussi* **cinquième** **2** *nf Scol (enseignement secondaire)* ≃ sixth grade

sixièmement [sizjɛmmã] *adv* in the sixth place, sixthly

six-quatre-deux [siskatdø] **à la six-quatre-deux** *adv Fam* in a slapdash way

sixte [sikst] *nf Mus* sixth

Skaï® [skaj] *nm* imitation leather

skate [skɛt], **skateboard** [skɛtbɔrd] *nm* skateboard; **faire du s.** to skateboard

skateboardeur, -euse [skɛtbɔrdœr, -øz] *nm,f* skateboarder

skatepark [skɛtpark] *nm* skatepark

skateur, -euse [skatœr, -øz] *nm,f* skateboarder, skater

skeleton [skəlɛtɔn] *nm (luge, sport)* skeleton

sketch *(pl sketches)* [skɛtʃ] *nm* sketch

ski [ski] *nm* (**a**) *(matériel)* ski (**b**) *(activité)* skiing; **faire du s.** to ski; **s. alpin/de fond** downhill/cross-country skiing; **s. artistique** freestyle skiing; **s. nautique** water skiing

skiable [skjabl] *adj voir* **domaine**

skier [66] [skje] *vi* to ski

skieur, -euse [skjœr, -øz] *nm,f* skier

skin [skin], **skinhead** [skinɛd] *nm* skinhead

skipper [skipœr] *nm* skipper

skyscraper [skajskrɛpœr] *nm Mktg* skyscraper ad

slalom [slalɔm] *nm* slalom; *Fig* **faire du s. (entre)** to dodge in and out (between); **s. géant** giant slalom; **s. spécial** special slalom

slalomer [slalɔme] *vi* to slalom; *Fig* to dodge in and out (**entre** between)

slalomeur, -euse [slalɔmœr, -øz] *nm,f* slalom skier

slave [slav] **1** *adj* Slav, Slavonic
2 *nm (langue)* Slavonic
3 *nmf* S. Slav

slip [slip] *nm (d'homme)* briefs, underpants; *(de femme)* panties; **s. de bain** *(d'homme)* swimming trunks; *(de femme)* bikini bottom

slogan [slɔgɑ̃] *nm* slogan

slovaque [slɔvak] **1** *adj* Slovak
2 *nm (langue)* Slovak
3 *nmf* S. Slovak

Slovaquie [slɔvaki] *nf* la S. Slovakia

slovène [slɔvɛn] **1** *adj* Slovene
2 *nm (langue)* Slovene
3 *nmf* S. Slovene

Slovénie [slɔveni] *nf* la S. Slovenia

slow [slo] *nm* slow dance

smala(h) [smala] *nf Fam (famille)* tribe

smash [smaʃ] *nm* smash; **faire un s.** to smash the ball

smasher [smaʃe] **1** *vt* to smash
2 *vi* to smash the ball

SME [ɛsɛmə] *nm (abrév* **Système monétaire européen***)* EMS

SMIC [smik] *nm (abrév* **salaire minimum interprofessionnel de croissance***)* guaranteed minimum wage

smicard, -e [smikar, -ard] *nm,f Fam* minimum wage earner

smoking [smɔkiŋ] *nm* tuxedo

SMS [ɛsɛmɛs] *nm Tél (abrév* **short message service***)* *(service)* SMS; *(message)* text (message); **envoyer un SMS à qn** to text sb, to send sb a text

snack [snak], **snack-bar** *(pl* **snack-bars***)* [snakbar] *nm* snack bar

SNCF [ɛsɛnseɛf] *nf (abrév* **Société nationale des chemins de fer français***)* = French national railroad company

sniffer [snife] *vt Fam (drogue)* to sniff

snob [snɔb] **1** *adj* snobbish
2 *nmf* snob

snober [snɔbe] *vt* to snub

snobinard, -e [snɔbinar, -ard] *Fam Péj* **1** *adj* stuck-up
2 *nm,f* stuck-up type

snobisme [snɔbism] *nm* snobbery, snobbishness

sobre [sɔbr] *adj* **(a)** *(personne) (qui n'a pas bu)* sober; *(qui boit ou mange peu)* abstemious **(b)** *(repas, vie)* simple **(c)** *(style, lignes, discours)* sober

sobrement [sɔbrəmɑ̃] *adv (s'exprimer, s'habiller)* soberly

sobriété [sɔbrijete] *nf* **(a)** *(tempérance)* temperance, sobriety **(b)** *(d'un repas, d'une vie)* simplicity **(c)** *(d'un style, de lignes, d'un discours)* sobriety; **s'exprimer avec s.** to speak soberly

sobriquet [sɔbrikɛ] *nm* nickname

soccer [sɔkœr] *nm Can* soccer

sociabilité [sɔsjabilite] *nf* sociability

sociable [sɔsjabl] *adj* sociable

social, -e, -aux, -ales [sɔsjal, -o] **1** *adj (ordre, politique, réforme)* social
2 *nm* **le s.** social issues

social-démocrate, sociale-démocrate *(mpl* **sociaux-démocrates***, fpl* **sociales-démocrates***)* [sɔsjaldemɔkrat, sɔsjodemɔkrat] *adj & nmf* social democrat

social-démocratie *(pl* **social-démocraties***)* [sɔsjaldemɔkrasi] *nf* social democracy

socialement [sɔsjalmɑ̃] *adv* socially

socialisation [sɔsjalizasjɔ̃] *nf* socialization

socialiser [sɔsjalize] *vt* to socialize

socialisme [sɔsjalism] *nm* socialism

socialiste [sɔsjalist] *adj & nmf* socialist

sociétaire [sɔsjetɛr] *nmf* **(a)** *(membre)* member **(b)** *(actionnaire)* stockholder

société [sɔsjete] *nf* **(a)** *(communauté)* society; **en s.** in society; **s. de consommation** consumer society; **la haute s.** high society **(b)** *(association)* society, association; *(sportive)* club; *Hist* **la S. des Nations** the League of Nations; **la S. protectrice des animaux** ≃ the ASPCA **(c)** *(compagnie)* company, firm; **s. par actions** incorporated company; **s. anonyme** corporation; **s. en participation** joint venture; **s. à responsabilité limitée** corporation **(d)** *(présence)* company

socioculturel, -elle [sɔsjɔkyltyrɛl] *adj* sociocultural

socio-économique *(pl* **socio-économiques***)* [sɔsjɔekɔnɔmik] *adj* socioeconomic

sociolinguistique [sɔsjɔlɛ̃gɥistik] **1** *adj* sociolinguistic
2 *nf* sociolinguistics *(singulier)*

sociologie [sɔsjɔlɔʒi] *nf* sociology

sociologique [sɔsjɔlɔʒik] *adj* sociological

sociologiquement [sɔsjɔlɔʒikmɑ̃] *adv* sociologically

sociologue [sɔsjɔlɔg] *nmf* sociologist

socioprofessionnel, -elle [sɔsjɔprɔfɛsjɔnɛl] *adj* socioprofessional

socle [sɔkl] *nm (de statue, de colonne)* plinth, pedestal; *(de vase, de pendule, d'appareil)* base; *Ordinat* **s. orientable** *ou* **pivotant** *(d'un moniteur)* swivel base

socquette [sɔkɛt] *nf* bobby sock

Socrate [sɔkrat] *npr* Socrates

soda [sɔda] *nm* soda (pop)

sodium [sɔdjɔm] *nm* sodium

sodomie [sɔdɔmi] *nf* sodomy, buggery

sodomiser [sɔdɔmize] *vt* to sodomize, to bugger

sœur [sœr] *nf* **(a)** *(parente)* sister; *Fam* **et ta s.!** get lost!; **s. de lait** foster sister **(b)** *Rel* nun, sister

sœurette [sœrɛt] *nf Fam* kid sister

sofa [sɔfa] *nm* sofa, settee

Sofia [sɔfja] *n* Sofia

SOFRES [sɔfrɛs] *nf (abrév* **Société française d'enquêtes par sondage***)* = French opinion-poll company

software [sɔftwɛr] *nm Ordinat* software

soi [swa] *pron personnel* **(a)** *(personne indéfinie)* oneself; *(homme)* himself; *(femme)* herself; **chez s.** at home; **il faut regarder devant s.** you must keep looking in front of you; **revenir à soi** to regain consciousness **(b)** *(chose, concept)* **en s.** in itself, per se

soi-disant [swadizɑ̃] **1** *adv* supposedly
2 *adj inv* so-called

soie [swa] *nf* **(a)** *(étoffe)* silk; **s. grège/naturelle** raw/natural silk **(b)** *(de sanglier, de porc)* bristle

soierie [swari] *nf* **(a)** *(tissu)* silk **(b)** *(commerce)* silk trade

soif [swaf] *nf aussi Fig* thirst; **avoir s.** to be thirsty; **donner s. à qn** to make sb thirsty; **boire jusqu'à plus s.** to drink one's fill; *Fig* **s. de qch/de faire qch** thirst for sth/to do sth

soignant, -e [swaɲɑ̃, -ɑ̃t] *adj* **personnel s.** nursing staff; **équipe soignante** team of nursing staff

soigné, -e [swaɲe] *adj* **(a)** *(travail)* careful **(b)** *(style)* polished **(b)** *(personne, apparence)* neat, tidy; *(mains, ongles, jardin)* well-kept **(c)** *Fam (addition)* shockingly high

soigner [swaɲe] **1** *vt* **(a)** *(maladie)* to treat **(b)** *(malade) (sujet: médecin)* to treat; *(sujet: parent, infirmière)* to look after, to take care of; *Fam Fig* **il faut te faire s.!** you need your head examined! **(c)** *(apparence, invités, image)* to look after, to take care of; *(travail, présentation)* to take care over
2 se soigner *vpr* **(a)** *(personne) (médicalement)* to treat oneself; *(faire attention à soi)* to take care of oneself, to look after oneself **(b)** *(maladie)* **ça se soigne très bien** it's easily treated; *Fam Hum* **ça se soigne, tu sais!** they have a cure for that these days, you know!

soigneur [swaɲœr] *nm* trainer; *(en boxe)* second

soigneusement [swaɲøzmɑ̃] *adv* carefully

soigneux, -euse [swaɲø, -øz] *adj* **(a)** *(attentif)* careful (**de** with) **(b)** *(méticuleux)* tidy, neat

soi-même [swamɛm] *pron personnel* oneself; *Prov* **on n'est jamais si bien servi que par s.** if you want something done, do it yourself

soin [swɛ̃] *nm* (**a**) *(attention)* care; **avec s.** carefully, with care; **sans s.** *(travail, exécution)* careless; *(travailler, exécuter)* carelessly; **aux bons soins de** *(sur une lettre)* care of..., c/o...; **avoir** *ou* **prendre s. de qn/qch** to look after *or* to take care of sb/sth; **prendre s. de faire qch** to take care to do sth; **confier à qn le s. de faire qch** to entrust sb with the task of doing sth; **laisser à qn le s. de faire qch** to leave it to sb to do sth; **les soins du ménage** housekeeping (**b**) *(traitement)* **soins** care, attention; **soins de beauté** beauty care; **être aux petits soins pour** *ou* **avec qn** to wait on sb hand and foot (**c**) *(traitement médical)* **premiers soins, soins d'urgence** first aid; **soins à domicile** home care *or* nursing; **soins intensifs** intensive care; **soins médicaux** medical care, healthcare; **soins palliatifs** palliative care

soir [swar] *nm* evening; **ce s.** this evening, tonight; **à ce s.!** see you tonight!; **à dix heures du s.** at ten o'clock in the evening *or* at night; **le jeudi 2 au s.** on the evening of Thursday the 2nd; **tous les lundis s.** every Monday evening; **faire qch le s.** to do sth in the evening; **être du s.** to be a night owl

soirée [sware] *nf* (**a**) *(soir)* evening; **dans la s.** in (the course of) the evening; **en fin de s.** toward the end of the evening (**b**) *(fête)* party; **s. dansante** dance (**c**) *Théât & Cin* evening performance; **le film passe en s.** there is an evening performance of the movie

sois, soit¹, *etc. voir* **être²**

soit² **1** *adv* [swat] all right
    2 *conj* [swa] (**a**) *(supposons)* **s. un point P** given a point P (**b**) *(c'est-à-dire)* that is to say (**c**) **s... s...** either... or...; **s. l'un, s. l'autre** (either) one or the other

soixantaine [swasɑ̃tɛn] *nf* (**a**) *(environ soixante)* **une s. (de)** about sixty, sixty or so (**b**) *(âge)* **avoir la s.** to be around sixty; **approcher de la s.** to be pushing sixty

soixante [swasɑ̃t] *adj & nm inv* sixty; **s. et onze** seventy-one; *voir aussi* **trois**

soixante-dix [swasɑ̃tdis] *adj inv & nm* seventy; *voir aussi* **trois**

soixante-dixième [swasɑ̃tdizjɛm] *nmf, nm & adj* seventieth; *voir aussi* **cinquième**

soixante-huitard, -e (*mpl* **soixante-huitards**, *fpl* **soixante-huitardes**) [swasɑ̃tɥitar, -ard] *nm,f* = person involved in the events of May 1968

soixantième [swasɑ̃tjɛm] *nmf, nm & adj* sixtieth; *voir aussi* **cinquième**

soja [sɔʒa] *nm* soya

sol¹ [sɔl] *nm* (**a**) *(surface) (dehors)* ground; *(à l'intérieur)* floor; **au s.** at ground level (**b**) *(territoire)* soil (**c**) *(matière)* soil

sol² [sɔl] *nm inv (note)* G; *(chantée)* so

sol-air [sɔlɛr] *adj inv (missile)* ground-to-air

solaire [sɔlɛr] *adj (système, chauffage, four)* solar; *(lotion, crème)* sun

solarium [sɔlarjɔm] *nm* (**a**) *(établissement)* solarium (**b**) *(terrasse)* sun terrace

soldat [sɔlda] *nm* (**a**) *(personne)* soldier; **s. de deuxième classe** *ou* **de première classe** private first class; **s. Dubois!** private Dubois!; **le S. inconnu** the Unknown Soldier (**b**) *(jouet)* (toy) soldier; **s. de plomb** tin soldier

solde¹ [sɔld] *nf (rémunération)* pay; *Péj* **à la s. de qn** in sb's pay

solde² [sɔld] *nm* (**a**) *(de compte)* balance; **pour s. (de tout compte)** in (full *or* final) settlement (**b**) *(rabais)* **acheter qch en s.** to buy sth on sale; **vendre qch en s.** to sell sth off; **c'était en s.** it was on sale; **des soldes** *(articles)* sale goods; **faire les soldes** *(acheteur)* to do the sales; **faire des soldes** *(magasin)* to have a sale

solder [sɔlde] **1** *vt* (**a**) *(compte)* to close (**b**) *(article)* to sell off, to clear
    2 se solder *vpr* **se s. par qch** *Fin* to show sth; *Fig (résultat, échec)* to end in sth

soldeur, -euse [sɔldœr, -øz] *nm,f* discount trader

sole [sɔl] *nf (poisson)* sole

soleil [sɔlɛj] *nm* (**a**) *(astre)* sun; **s. de minuit** midnight sun (**b**) *(lumière, chaleur)* sun, sunshine; **il y a** *ou* **il fait du s.** the sun's shining, it's sunny; *Fig* **se faire une place au s.** to find a place in the sun; *Fig* **avoir des biens au s.** to own property

solennel, -elle [sɔlanɛl] *adj* (**a**) *(occasion, cérémonie)* formal; *(serment, déclaration)* solemn (**b**) *Péj* pompous

solennellement [sɔlanɛlmɑ̃] *adv (officiellement)* formally; *(gravement)* solemnly

solennité [sɔlanite] *nf* (**a**) *(d'une occasion, d'une cérémonie)* formality; *(d'un serment, d'une déclaration)* solemnity (**b**) *Péj* pomposity

Solex® [sɔlɛks] *nm* moped

solfège [sɔlfɛʒ] *nm* (**a**) *(théorie)* rudiments of music (**b**) *(recueil)* music primer

solfier [66] [sɔlfje] *vt* to sol-fa

solidaire [sɔlidɛr] *adj* (**a**) *(personne)* **être s. de qn** to stand by sb, to support sb; **se sentir s. de qn** to feel a sense of solidarity with sb (**b**) *(pièces)* interdependent; **roue s. d'une autre** wheel integral with another

solidairement [sɔlidɛrmɑ̃] *adv* jointly

solidariser [sɔlidarize] **se solidariser** *vpr* to show solidarity (**avec** with)

solidarité [sɔlidarite] *nf (entre personnes)* solidarity; **par s. avec qn** out of fellow-feeling for sb, in order to show solidarity with sb

solide [sɔlid] **1** *adj* (**a**) *(résistant) (mur, meuble)* solid; *(tissu)* strong; *(personne)* sturdy; **s. sur ses jambes** steady on one's feet; **être s. comme un chêne** *ou* **un roc** to be hale and hearty (**b**) *(amitié, relation, liens)* strong (**c**) *(éducation, argumentation)* sound; *Fig* **ça ne repose sur rien de s.** there's no sound basis for that (**d**) *(repas)* solid; *(appétit)* healthy (**e**) *(position, affaire)* sound, strong (**f**) *(non liquide)* solid
    2 *nm* (**a**) *(corps)* solid (**b**) *Fam* **c'est du s.!** *(meuble)* that's pretty solid!; *(vêtement)* it's indestructible!

solidement [sɔlidmɑ̃] *adv (construit)* solidly; *(attaché, implanté)* firmly

solidifier [66] [sɔlidifje] **1** *vt* to solidify
    2 se solidifier *vpr* to solidify

solidité [sɔlidite] *nf* (**a**) *(d'un objet)* solidity; *(d'un matériau)* strength; **être d'une s. à toute épreuve** to be able to stand up to anything (**b**) *(d'un jugement)* soundness (**c**) *(d'une amitié)* strength

soliloque [sɔlilɔk] *nm* soliloquy

soliste [sɔlist] *nmf* soloist

solitaire [sɔlitɛr] **1** *adj* (**a**) *(personne) (par choix)* solitary; *(involontairement)* lonely; **passer des vacances solitaires** to spend one's vacation alone (**b**) *(arbre, maison)* solitary, lone
    2 *nmf (personne)* loner; **en s.** *(vivre, travailler)* on one's own, alone; *(naviguer)* single-handed; *(course)* solo; *(navigation)* single-handed
    3 *nm* (**a**) *(jeu)* solitaire (**b**) *(diamant)* solitaire

solitairement [sɔlitɛrmɑ̃] *adv* on one's own, alone

solitude [sɔlityd] *nf* (**a**) *(retraite)* solitude; *(involontaire)* loneliness; **aimer la s.** to like being alone (**b**) *(d'un lieu)* loneliness

solive [sɔliv] *nf Constr* joist

sollicitation [sɔlisitasjɔ̃] *nf* request

solliciter [sɔlisite] *vt* (**a**) *(entretien, audience)* to request; *(emploi)* to apply for (**b**) *(personne)* **s. qn (pour faire qch)** to appeal to sb (to do sth); **être sollicité de toutes parts** to be very much in demand (**c**) *(attention, regards)* to attract; *(curiosité)* to arouse

sollicitude [sɔlisityd] *nf* solicitude, concern (**pour** for)

solo [sɔlo] **1** *adj inv* solo

2 *nm* solo; **jouer en s.** to play solo

sol-sol [sɔlsɔl] *adj inv (missile)* ground-to-ground

solstice [sɔlstis] *nm* solstice; **s. d'été/d'hiver** summer/winter solstice

soluble [sɔlybl] *adj* (a) *(produit)* soluble; *(café)* instant (b) *(problème)* solvable

solution [sɔlysjɔ̃] *nf* (a) *(de problème, de situation, d'équation)* solution, answer (**de** to); **s. de facilité** easy way out (b) *(liquide)* solution

solutionner [sɔlysjɔne] *vt Fam* to solve

solvabilité [sɔlvabilite] *nf* solvency

solvable [sɔlvabl] *adj* solvent

solvant [sɔlvɑ̃] *nm* solvent

somali, -e [sɔmali] **1** *adj* Somali

2 *nm (langue)* Somali

3 *nm,f* **S., Somalie** Somali

Somalie [sɔmali] *nf* **la S.** Somalia

somalien, -enne [sɔmaljɛ̃, -ɛn] **1** *adj* Somalian

2 *nm,f* **S., Somalienne** Somalian

somatique [sɔmatik] *adj* somatic

somatiser [sɔmatize] *vt* to react psychosomatically to

sombre [sɔ̃br] *adj* (a) *(couleur)* dark (b) *(forêt, pièce)* dark; *(ciel)* dull; **il fait s.** *(temps)* it's dull; *(dans une pièce)* it's dark (c) *(visage, pensées, caractère)* gloomy, somber (d) *(sinistre)* **une s. histoire de...** a sordid tale of... (e) *Fam* **un s. imbécile** a total idiot

sombrement [sɔ̃brəmɑ̃] *adv (tristement)* gloomily, somberly

sombrer [sɔ̃bre] *vi* (a) *(navire)* to sink; *(empire)* to founder; *(affaire)* to fail (b) *(personne)* **s. dans la déprime/la misère** to sink into depression/destitution

sombrero [sɔ̃brero] *nm* sombrero

sommaire [sɔmɛr] **1** *adj* (a) *(récit)* brief (b) *(rudimentaire) (examen)* hasty; *(connaissances, repas, étude)* basic; *(jugement, exécution)* summary; **faire une toilette s.** to wash up quickly

2 *nm (table des matières)* contents; **et au s. de l'émission de ce soir...** coming up in tonight's program...

sommairement [sɔmɛrmɑ̃] *adv* (a) *(expliquer, raconter)* briefly (b) *(de façon rudimentaire) (meublé)* basically; *(juger)* summarily

sommation [sɔmasjɔ̃] *nf* (a) *Jur (injonction)* demand (b) *Mil* warning

somme¹ [sɔm] *nf voir* **bête**

somme² [sɔm] *nf* (a) *(d'une addition)* sum, total; **faire la s. de** to add up (b) *(quantité) (d'objets)* number; *(de travail, d'efforts)* amount (c) *(argent)* **s. (d'argent)** sum (of money); **pour la s. de 500 euros** for 500 euros; **dépenser des sommes folles** to spend vast sums of money; **c'est une s.!** that's a lot of money! (d) *(locutions)* **en s.** *(tout compte fait)* on the whole; *(en bref)* in short; **s. toute** when all's said and done

somme³ [sɔm] *nm* nap, snooze; **faire un (petit) s.** to have or to take a nap or a snooze

sommeil [sɔmɛj] *nm* (a) *(repos)* sleep; **avoir s.** to be or to feel sleepy; **dormir d'un s. de plomb** to sleep like a log; **avoir le s. léger/profond** to be a light/heavy sleeper; **chercher le s.** to try to sleep; **tomber de s.** to be dead on one's feet; **je manque de s.** I haven't been getting enough sleep; **j'en perds le s.** I'm losing sleep over it; *Fig* **le s. éternel** eternal rest; **s. paradoxal** REM sleep (b) **en s.** *(projet)* (lying) dormant; *Fig* **laisser qch en s.** to put sth on hold

sommeiller [sɔmeje] *vi* (a) *(personne)* to doze (b) *Fig* to lie dormant

sommelier [sɔməlje] *nm* wine waiter; *Suisse* waiter

sommer [sɔme] *vt* **s. qn de faire qch** to charge sb to do sth

sommes *voir* **être²**

sommet [sɔmɛ] *nm* (a) *(de montagne)* top, summit; *(d'arbre, de toit)* top; *(de vague)* crest; *(de la tête)* crown (b) *Fig (de hiérarchie)*

top; *(du pouvoir, de la gloire)* height (c) *(rencontre politique)* summit; **conférence/rencontre au s.** summit conference/meeting (d) *(d'angle)* vertex

sommier [sɔmje] *nm* base; **s. à ressorts/lattes** box-spring/slatted base

sommité [sɔmite] *nf* leading figure or light

somnambule [sɔmnɑ̃byl] **1** *adj* **être s.** to be a sleepwalker, to walk in one's sleep

2 *nmf* sleepwalker

somnambulisme [sɔmnɑ̃bylism] *nm* sleepwalking

somnifère [sɔmnifɛr] *nm (substance)* sedative; *(cachet)* sleeping pill

somnolence [sɔmnɔlɑ̃s] *nf* sleepiness, drowsiness; **peut provoquer un état de s.** *(sur notice)* may cause drowsiness

somnolent, -e [sɔmnɔlɑ̃, -ɑ̃t] *adj* sleepy, drowsy

somnoler [sɔmnɔle] *vi* to doze

somptuaire [sɔ̃ptɥɛr] *adj* extravagant

somptueusement [sɔ̃ptɥøzmɑ̃] *adv* sumptuously

somptueux, -euse [sɔ̃ptɥø, -øz] *adj* sumptuous

somptuosité [sɔ̃ptɥozite] *nf* sumptuousness

son¹, sa, ses [sɔ̃, sa, se]

> **sa** becomes **son** before a word beginning with a vowel or mute h.

adj possessif (possesseur masculin) his; *(possesseur féminin)* her; *(d'animal, de chose, de pays)* its; *(possesseur indéfini)* one's; **un de ses amis** one of his/her friends, a friend of his/hers; **chacun a pris s. sac** everyone took their bag; **perdre s. temps** to waste one's time; *Fam* **elle a eu s. vendredi** she got Friday off

son² [sɔ̃] *nm (de voix, d'instrument)* & *Cin* sound; *Fig* **n'entendre qu'un s. de cloche** to hear only one side of the story; **(spectacle) s. et lumière** son et lumière; **s. 3D** surround sound

son³ [sɔ̃] *nm (de grains)* bran

sonal, -als [sɔnal] *nm Offic* jingle

sonar [sɔnar] *nm* sonar

sonate [sɔnat] *nf* sonata; **s. pour violon** violin sonata

sondage [sɔ̃daʒ] *nm* (a) *(de population)* poll, survey; **faire un s.** to carry out a poll or a survey; **s. d'opinion** opinion poll; **s. par téléphone** telephone poll or survey (b) *(de terrain)* boring, drilling

sonde [sɔ̃d] *nf* (a) *(de bateau)* sounding line (b) *(de pompe, de puits)* sounding rod (c) *Météo* & *Av* **s. aérienne** sounding balloon; **s. spatiale** space probe (d) *Méd (pour examiner)* probe; *(pour intervenir)* tube (e) *(de terrain)* borer, drill

sondé, -e [sɔ̃de] *nm,f* respondent

sonder [sɔ̃de] *vt* (a) *(fond)* to sound; *Fig (mystère)* to fathom (b) *Météo (atmosphère)* to probe (c) *(terrain)* to bore, to drill; *Fig* **s. le terrain** to see how the land lies (d) *(personne, opinion, intentions)* to sound out (e) *Méd (blessure)* to probe; *(patient)* to sound

sondeur, -euse [sɔ̃dœr, -øz] **1** *nm (appareil)* sounder

2 *nm,f (d'opinions)* pollster

songe [sɔ̃ʒ] *nm Litt* dream; **en s.** in a dream; **faire un s.** to have a dream

songer [45] [sɔ̃ʒe] **1 songer à** *vt ind* (a) *(penser à, se souvenir de)* to think about (b) *(envisager)* to consider; **il ne faut pas y s.** that's quite out of the question; **s. à faire qch** to think of doing sth

2 *vt* **s. que** to think that

songerie [sɔ̃ʒri] *nf Litt* reverie

songeur, -euse [sɔ̃ʒœr, -øz] *adj* (a) *(rêveur)* dreamy (b) *(pensif)* pensive, thoughtful

sonnant, -e [sɔnɑ̃, -ɑ̃t] *adj* **arriver à dix heures sonnantes** to arrive on the stroke of ten or at ten o'clock sharp

sonné, -e [sɔne] *adj* (a) *(accompli)* **avoir quarante ans bien sonnés** to be well over forty (b) *Fam (étourdi)* groggy (c) *Fam (fou)* crazy

sonner [sɔne] **1** vi (**a**) (horloge) to strike; (cloches, téléphone) to ring; (réveil) to go off; **faire s. son réveil (à six heures)** to set one's alarm (for six o'clock); **s. creux** (mur) to sound hollow; Fig to ring hollow; Fig **s. faux** not to ring true; Fig **s. bien/mal** to sound good/bad

(**b**) (heure) **six heures sonnèrent** the clock struck six; Fig **son heure** ou **sa dernière heure a sonné** his/her last hour has come

(**c**) (à la porte) **on a sonné** that was the bell, there's someone at the door; **s. chez qn** to ring sb's bell; **s. avant d'entrer** (sur panneau) ring before entering

(**d**) (jouer) **s. du clairon/de la trompette** to sound the bugle/the trumpet

2 vt (**a**) (cloche) to ring; Fam **s. les cloches à qn** to tell sb off; **se faire s. les cloches** to get a good telling-off

(**b**) (heure) to strike; (messe, repas) to ring the bell for

(**c**) (domestique, infirmière) to ring for; Fam **on ne t'a pas sonné!** nobody asked you!

(**d**) Fam (assommer) to knock out

(**e**) Belg (appeler) to telephone, to call

sonnerie [sɔnʀi] nf (**a**) (son) (de cloches, du téléphone) ringing; (de clairon, de trompette) call (**b**) (sonnette) bell (**c**) (de téléphone portable) ringtone; **télécharger des sonneries** to download ringtones; **s. polyphonique** polyphonic ringtone

sonnet [sɔnɛ] nm sonnet

sonnette [sɔnɛt] nf bell; **s. d'alarme** alarm bell; aussi Fig **tirer la s. d'alarme** to sound the alarm

sono [sɔno] nf Fam PA system

sonore [sɔnɔʀ] **1** adj (**a**) (effet) sound; (pollution) noise (**b**) (voix) ringing; (rire) resounding; (salle) echoing (**c**) Ling (consonne) voiced

2 nf Ling voiced consonant

sonorisation [sɔnɔʀizasjɔ̃] nf (**a**) (de film) addition of the soundtrack (**de** to) (**b**) (de salle) fitting of a PA system (**de** to) (**c**) (équipement) PA system, public-address system

sonoriser [sɔnɔʀize] vt (**a**) (film) to add the soundtrack to (**b**) (salle) to fit with a PA system

sonorité [sɔnɔʀite] nf tone

sont voir **être²**

Sopalin® [sɔpalɛ̃] nm paper towels

sophisme [sɔfism] nm sophism

sophistication [sɔfistikasjɔ̃] nf sophistication

sophistiqué, -e [sɔfistike] adj sophisticated

soporifique [sɔpɔʀifik] adj aussi Fig soporific

soprano [sɔpʀano] **1** adj (saxophone) soprano

2 nmf (personne) soprano

3 nm soprano (voice)

sorbet [sɔʀbɛ] nm sherbet

sorbetière [sɔʀbətjɛʀ] nf ice-cream maker

sorbier [sɔʀbje] nm sorb (tree), service (tree)

sorcellerie [sɔʀsɛlʀi] nf witchcraft, sorcery

sorcier [sɔʀsje] **1** adj Fam **ce n'est pas s.** it's simple enough

2 nm sorcerer, wizard

sorcière [sɔʀsjɛʀ] nf sorceress, witch; Fam Péj **vieille s.** old witch

sordide [sɔʀdid] adj (**a**) (pièce, quartier) squalid (**b**) (crime, détails, avarice) sordid

sorgho [sɔʀgo] nm sorghum

Sorlingues [sɔʀlɛ̃g] nfpl **les S.** the Scilly Isles

sornettes [sɔʀnɛt] nfpl twaddle, nonsense

sors, sort¹, etc. voir **sortir¹**

sort² [sɔʀ] nm (**a**) (condition) lot; Fam **faire un s. à qch** (bouteille, plat) to polish sth off (**b**) (destin) fate (**c**) (hasard) chance; **tirer au s.** to draw lots; **le s. en est jeté** the die is cast (**d**) (magique) spell; **jeter un s. à qn** to cast a spell on sb; **conjurer le mauvais s.** to ward off bad luck

sortable [sɔʀtabl] adj Fam **tu n'es pas s.!** I can't take you anywhere!

sortant, -e [sɔʀtɑ̃, -ɑ̃t] adj (numéro de loterie) winning; (élu) outgoing

sorte [sɔʀt] nf (**a**) (genre) sort, kind; **toutes sortes de choses/gens, des choses/gens de toutes sortes** all sorts or kinds of things/people; **un homme de la s.** a man of that kind; **une s. de...** a sort or kind of...; **je n'ai rien dit/fait de la s.** I said/did no such thing, I said/did nothing of the sort (**b**) (manière) **de la s.** in that way; **en quelque s.** as it were, in a way; **de s. que je puisse...** so that I can...; **de s. qu'il est arrivé en retard** with the result that he arrived late; **de s. à faire qch** so as to do sth; **faire en s. que** + subjunctive to see to it that; **fais en s. d'être à l'heure** see to it that you're on time

sortie [sɔʀti] nf (**a**) (fait de sortir d'un lieu) **c'était ma première s. depuis...** it was my first time out since...; **à sa s. de l'hôpital/de prison** when he/she came out of the hospital/prison; **à la s. de l'école/du travail** after school/work; **à la s. des bureaux** when the office workers go home

(**b**) (issue) exit, way out; **à la s. de la gare** at the station exit; **s. d'autoroute** freeway exit; **s. de secours** emergency exit

(**c**) (d'un livre, d'un journal) publication; (d'un film, d'un disque) release; (d'un modèle) launch; **à sa s. dans les salles parisiennes** when released in Parisian movie theaters

(**d**) (de liquide, d'air) outflow

(**e**) (dispositif) outlet

(**f**) (de marchandises) export

(**g**) (dépense) **sorties** outgoings

(**h**) (excursion) trip, outing; **priver qn de s.** to stop sb from going out; **s. en mer** short sea trip; **jour de s.** day out; **ce soir je suis de s.** I'm going out tonight; **désolé, mais elle est de s.** sorry, but she's out

(**i**) Mil sortie

(**j**) Fam (emportement) outburst

(**k**) Ordinat exit; (information) output; **s. d'imprimante** printer output; **dispositif de s.** output device; **signal de s.** output signal; **s. écran** screen output; **s. imprimante** printout; **s. imprimée** printed output; **s. parallèle** parallel output; **s. série** serial output

sortie-de-bain (pl **sorties-de-bain**) [sɔʀtidbɛ̃] nf bathrobe

sortilège [sɔʀtilɛʒ] nm spell

sortir¹ [64a] [sɔʀtiʀ] **1** vt (aux avoir) (**a**) (enfant, chien) to take out; (voiture) to get out; **s. qn de** (situation) to get sb out of

(**b**) (objet) to take out (**de** of); **et si tu sortais ton bon whisky?** how about breaking out your good whiskey?

(**c**) (mettre sur le marché) (livre, journal) to bring out, to publish; (film, disque) to bring out, to release

(**d**) Fam (dire) to come out with

(**e**) Fam (expulser) to throw out; (vaincre) to knock out

2 vi (aux être) (**a**) (aller) to go out (**de** of); (venir) to come out (**de** of); (partir) to leave; (s'extraire, finir de travailler) to get out (**de** of); **s. en courant/en boitant** to run/limp out; **est-ce que je peux s.?** (en classe) may I be excused?; **sortez (d'ici)!** get out (of here)!; **s. de table** to leave the table; **je sors d'une mauvaise grippe** I'm just getting over a bad case of the flu; **il est sorti discrédité de ce scandale** he came out of this scandal with his reputation in ruins; **cela ne doit pas s. d'ici** (secret) it mustn't go any further; Fam **d'où sors-tu?** (d'où viens-tu?) where did you spring from?; (tu n'es pas au courant) what planet have you been on?; **cela m'est sorti de la tête** it's gone right out of my head; **il ne sortira pas grand-chose de tout cela** nothing much will come of all this

(**b**) (pour s'amuser) to go out; **s. avec qn** to go out with sb, to date sb; Fig **il faut s. un peu!** (pour être au courant) what planet have you been on?

(**c**) (livre, journal) to come out, to be published; (film, disque) to come out, to be released (**d**) *(être issu)* **s. de** *(famille, milieu)* to come from; **elle sort d'Harvard** she went to Harvard

(**e**) *(numéro de loto, sujet d'examen)* to come up

(**f**) *(apparaître) (fleur)* to come out; *(dent)* to come through; **les yeux lui sortaient de la tête** his/her eyes were popping out of his/her head

(**g**) *Ordinat (d'un système)* to exit

3 se sortir *vpr* **se s. de** *(situation)* to get out of; **s'en s.** *(d'un travail)* to manage; *(d'une difficulté)* to get through it; *(malade)* to pull through

sortir² [sortir] *nm* **au s. du cinéma** on coming out of the movie theater; **au s. de l'école** after school; **au s. de l'hiver** at the end of winter

SOS [ɛsoɛs] *nm* SOS; **lancer un S. (à)** to send (out) an SOS (to); **S. Amitié** = hotline for people in need of emotional support; **S. femmes battues** = hotline for female victims of domestic violence; **S. médecins** = emergency medical service; **S.-Racisme** = anti-racist movement

sosie [sozi] *nm* lookalike, double; **c'est un s. de Brando** he's a Brando lookalike; **c'est le s. de mon frère** he's my brother's double

sot, sotte [so, sot] **1** *adj* stupid, foolish; **il n'y a pas de sot métier** there's no such thing as a worthless profession
2 *nm,f* fool

sottement [sotmɑ̃] *adv* stupidly, foolishly

sottise [sotiz] *nf* (**a**) *(stupidité)* stupidity, foolishness (**b**) *(action)* stupid act; **faire des sottises** to do stupid things; **faire une s.** to do something stupid (**c**) *(parole)* stupid remark; **dire des sottises** to say stupid things; **dire une s.** to say something stupid

sottisier [sotizje] *nm* collection of howlers

sou [su] *nm* (**a**) *(argent)* **être sans le s.** to be penniless; **il est toujours en train de compter ses sous** he's always counting every penny; **avoir des sous** to have money; **c'est une affaire de gros sous** there's big money involved; **être près de ses sous** to be a penny-pincher; *Fig* **n'avoir pas (pour) un s. de courage/bon sens** not to have an ounce of courage/common sense (**b**) *(pièce)* **un s. est un s.** every penny counts (**c**) *(ancienne monnaie)* sou (**d**) *Can (cent)* cent

soubassement [subasmɑ̃] *nm* (**a**) *(de construction)* base (**b**) *Can (sous-sol)* basement

soubresaut [subrəso] *nm* *(de véhicule)* jolt; *(de personne)* jerk

soubrette [subrɛt] *nf* *Théât* maid

souche [suʃ] *nf* (**a**) *(d'arbre)* stump; *Fam* **rester (planté) comme une s.** to be rooted to the spot; **dormir comme une s.** to sleep like a log (**b**) *(de famille)* founder; **faire s.** to found a line (**c**) *(de virus)* strain (**d**) *(de chèques, de tickets)* stub (**e**) *(de langue)* root

souci¹ [susi] *nm* (**a**) *(inquiétude)* worry, anxiety; **avoir des soucis** to have worries; **se faire du s. (pour)** to worry (about); **donner du s. à qn** to worry sb; **c'est le dernier** *ou* **le cadet de mes soucis** that's the least of my worries (**b**) *(soin)* concern (**de** for); **avoir le s. de plaire** to be anxious to please

souci² [susi] *nm* *(fleur)* marigold

soucier [66] [susje] **se soucier** *vpr* **se s. de** to worry about; **ne se s. de rien** not to worry about anything; *Fam* **se s. de qch comme de l'an quarante** *ou* **de sa première chemise** not to give a damn about sth

soucieux, -euse [susjø, -øz] *adj* (**a**) *(attentif)* anxious, concerned (**de** about); **être s. de faire qch** to be anxious to do sth; **peu s. de qch** unconcerned about sth (**b**) *(inquiet)* worried

soucoupe [sukup] *nf* saucer; **s. volante** flying saucer

soudain, -e [sudɛ̃, -ɛn] **1** *adv* suddenly, all of a sudden
2 *adj* sudden

soudainement [sudɛnmɑ̃] *adv* suddenly

soudaineté [sudɛnte] *nf* suddenness

Soudan [sudɑ̃] *nm* **le S.** the Sudan

soudanais, -e [sudanɛ, -ɛz] **1** *adj* Sudanese
2 *nm,f* **S., Soudanaise** Sudanese; **les S.** the Sudanese

soudard [sudar] *nm* *Fam* brutish soldier

soude [sud] *nf* soda; **s. caustique** caustic soda

souder [sude] **1** *vt* (**a**) *(par alliage)* to solder; *(par soudure autogène)* to weld (**b**) *(os fracturé)* to knit (**c**) *Fig (groupes, personnes)* to unite
2 se souder *vpr* (**a**) *(os)* to knit (together) (**b**) *Fig (groupe)* to unite

soudeur, -euse [sudœr, -øz] *nm,f* *(avec soudure par alliage)* solderer; *(avec soudure autogène)* welder

soudoyer [32] [sudwaje] *vt* to bribe

soudure [sudyr] *nf* (**a**) *(opération) (par alliage)* soldering; *(autogène)* welding (**b**) *(résultat) (par alliage)* soldered joint; *(autogène)* weld (**c**) *(d'os)* knitting (**d**) *Fig* **faire la s.** to make ends meet

soufflage [suflaʒ] *nm* *(du verre)* blowing

souffle [sufl] *nm* (**a**) *(d'air, de vent)* breath, puff (**b**) *(respiration)* breathing; **avoir du s.** to have stamina; **retenir son s.** to hold one's breath; **manquer de s.** to be short-winded; **avoir le s. court** to be short of breath; **à bout de s.** out of breath; **jusqu'à mon dernier s.** as long as I live and breathe, to my dying day; *Fig* **couper le s. à qn** to take sb's breath away (**c**) *(d'une explosion)* blast (**d**) *(d'hélices)* slipstream, wash (**e**) *Méd* murmur; **s. au cœur** heart murmur (**f**) *(force créatrice)* inspiration (**g**) *(impulsion)* **donner un nouveau s. à qch** to give sth a new lease of life

soufflé, -e [sufle] **1** *adj* (**a**) *Culin* soufflé (**b**) *Fam (ahuri)* flabbergasted, staggered
2 *nm* soufflé; **s. au fromage/au chocolat** cheese/chocolate soufflé

souffler [sufle] **1** *vt* (**a**) *(fumée, poussière)* to blow; *(bougie)* to blow out (**b**) *(dire)* to whisper (**à** to); **s. une réplique à un acteur** to prompt an actor; **quelqu'un a dû lui s. l'idée** someone must have given him/her the idea; **ne pas s. mot (de qch)** not to breathe a word (about sth); **on ne souffle pas!** no prompting! (**c**) *Fam (prendre)* to swipe (**à** from); **se faire s. qch** to have sth swiped (**d**) *(détruire)* to blast (**e**) *Fam (ahurir)* to stagger (**f**) *(verre)* to blow (**g**) *(aux dames)* to huff; **s. n'est pas jouer** huffing doesn't count as a turn
2 *vi* (**a**) *(expirer)* to blow; **s. dans ses doigts** to blow on one's fingers; **s. dans une trompette** to blow a trumpet; **inspirez! soufflez!** inhale! exhale! (**b**) *(se reposer)* **laisser s. qn** to give sb time to catch his/her breath (**c**) *(haleter)* to pant, to puff; *Fam* **s. comme un bœuf** to puff and pant (**d**) *(vent)* to blow; **le vent soufflait en rafales** there were gusts of wind; *Fig* **un vent de révolte soufflait sur le pays** there was a spirit of revolt in the country

soufflerie [sufləri] *nf* (**a**) *(d'orgue, de forge)* bellows (**b**) *(de climatiseur)* blower

soufflet [suflɛ] *nm* (**a**) *(de forge)* bellows (**b**) *Rail (couloir)* connecting vestibule (**c**) *(en couture)* gusset (**d**) *(d'orgue)* swell (**e**) *Litt (gifle)* slap (in the face)

souffleter [42] [suflɔte] *vt* *Litt* **s. qn** to slap sb's face

souffleur, -euse [suflœr, -øz] **1** *nm* **s. de verre** glass blower
2 *nm,f (au théâtre)* prompter
3 *nf* **souffleuse** *Can* snowblower

souffrance [sufrɑ̃s] *nf* (**a**) *(douleur)* suffering (**b**) **en s.** *(travail)* pending

souffrant, -e [sufrɑ̃, -ɑ̃t] *adj (indisposé)* unwell, sick

souffre-douleur [sufrədulœr] *nm inv* object of abuse

souffreteux, -euse [sufrətø, -øz] *adj* sickly

souffrir [52] [sufrir] **1** *vi* to suffer (**de** from); **faire s. qn** *(phy-*

siquement) to hurt sb; *(moralement)* to make sb suffer; **je souffre de la voir malade** it upsets me to see her ill

2 *vt* (**a**) *(physiquement)* **s. le martyre** to go through agony; **faire s. le martyre à qn** to put sb through agony (**b**) *(supporter)* **je ne peux pas la s.** I can't stand her; **je ne peux pas s. qu'on vienne me déranger** I can't stand being disturbed; **il ne souffre pas la contradiction** he can't stand being contradicted; *Litt* **souffrez que je fasse une critique** permit me to make a criticism (**c**) *Litt (admettre)* **situation qui ne souffre aucun retard** situation that admits of no delay

3 se souffrir *vpr* **ils ne peuvent pas se s.** they can't stand each other

soufre [sufr] *nm* sulfur

souhait [swɛ] *nm* wish; **faire un s.** to make a wish; **à s.** *(à merveille)* perfectly; **doré/ensoleillé à s.** beautifully golden/sunny; **à vos souhaits!** bless you!

souhaitable [swɛtabl] *adj* desirable; **il serait s. que tu lui parles** it is desirable that you should talk to him/her

souhaiter [swete] *vt* to wish for; **s. qch à qn** to wish sb sth; **s. faire qch** to hope to do sth; **s. à qn de faire qch** to hope that sb does sth; **s. que** + *subjunctive* to hope that; **je vous souhaite une bonne année/un joyeux anniversaire** best wishes for a Happy New Year/a happy birthday; *Ironique* **je te souhaite bien du plaisir!** have fun!

souiller [suje] *vt Litt* (**a**) *(vêtements)* to soil, to dirty (**de** with) (**b**) *(réputation, mémoire)* to tarnish

souillon [sujɔ̃] *nf Litt* slut, sloven

souillure [sujyr] *nf Litt* (**a**) *(sur un vêtement)* stain (**b**) *Fig (morale)* blot, blemish

souk [suk] *nm* (**a**) *(marché)* souk (**b**) *Fam (lieu en désordre)* shambles *(singulier)*

soul [sul] *adj inv & nf* soul

soûl, -e [su, sul] **1** *adj* drunk

2 *nm* **tout son s.** to one's heart's content

soulagement [sulaʒmɑ̃] *nm* relief (**pour** to)

soulager [45] [sulaʒe] **1** *vt (douleur)* to ease, to relieve; *(esprit, chagrin)* to soothe; *(personne)* to relieve; **ce médicament vous soulagera** this medicine will make you feel better; **donne-moi un de tes sacs, ça te soulagera** give me one of your bags, that will take some of the weight off you; *Fam* **s. qn de son portefeuille** to relieve sb of his/her wallet

2 se soulager *vpr* (**a**) *(en parlant)* to ease one's mind (**b**) *Fam (satisfaire un besoin naturel)* to relieve oneself

soûlant, -e [sulɑ̃, -ɑ̃t] *adj Fam* exhausting

soûlard, -e [sular, -ard], **soûlaud, -e** [sulo, -od] *nm,f Fam* drunkard

soûler [sule] *Fam* **1** *vt* (**a**) *(enivrer)* **s. qn** to make sb drunk; *Fig (sujet: parfum, succès, idées)* to go to sb's head (**b**) *(ennuyer)* **arrête, tu me soûles!** stop, you're giving me a headache!

2 se soûler *vpr* to get drunk; *Fig* **se s. de paroles** to like the sound of one's own voice

soulèvement [sulɛvmɑ̃] *nm* (**a**) *(de terrain)* rising (**b**) *(révolte)* uprising

soulever [46] [sulve] **1** *vt* (**a**) *(charge, personne, couvercle)* to lift (up); *(rideau)* to raise (**b**) *(agiter) (poussière)* to raise, to throw up; *Fig* **s. le cœur à qn** to make sb feel sick (**c**) *(doutes, question, objection)* to raise (**d**) *(population)* to rouse, to stir up (**e**) *(passion, enthousiasme, indignation)* to excite, to arouse; **s. un tollé** to raise an outcry

2 se soulever *vpr* (**a**) *(s'élever)* to rise (**b**) *(se lever) (personne)* to raise oneself, to lift oneself up (**c**) *(se révolter)* to rise up

soulier [sulje] *nm* shoe; *Fam Fig* **être dans ses petits souliers** to feel awkward

souligner [suliɲe] *vt* (**a**) *(mot, passage)* to underline (**b**) *(yeux, taille)* to emphasize (**c**) *Fig (mettre en valeur)* to emphasize

soûlon [sulɔ̃] *nm Suisse & Can Fam* drunk, drunkard

soumettre [47] [sumɛtr] **1** *vt* (**a**) *(population, pays, passions)* to subdue (**b**) *(rapport, demande, projet)* to submit (**à** to) (**c**) **s. qn à** *(examen)* to subject sb to; *(épreuve)* to put sb through; *(traitement)* to put sb on; **être soumis à des règles strictes** to be bound by strict rules; **s. les revenus à l'impôt** to make income liable to tax

2 se soumettre *vpr (obéir)* to submit; **se s. à** *(autorité)* to submit to; *(volonté)* to comply with; *(loi, décision)* to abide by

soumis, -e [sumi, -iz] *adj (docile)* submissive, obedient (**à** to)

soumission [sumisjɔ̃] *nf* (**a**) *(à une loi, à une autorité)* submission (**à** to) (**b**) *(docilité)* submissiveness, obedience (**à** to)

soupape [supap] *nf* valve; **s. de sécurité** safety valve

soupçon [supsɔ̃] *nm* (**a**) *(suspicion)* suspicion; **avoir des soupçons sur qn** to have (one's) suspicions about sb; **être au-dessus** *ou* **à l'abri de tout s.** to be above all suspicion; **éveiller les soupçons** to arouse suspicion; **de graves soupçons pèsent sur lui** grave suspicions hang over him (**b**) *(faible quantité) (de vinaigre, d'ail)* dash, hint; *(de fièvre, de fard, d'ironie)* touch; *(de vin)* drop

soupçonner [supsɔne] *vt* to suspect; **s. qn de qch/de faire qch** to suspect sb of sth/of doing sth; **je soupçonne qu'il le sait** I suspect that he knows

soupçonneux, -euse [supsɔnø, -øz] *adj* suspicious

soupe [sup] *nf* (**a**) *(plat)* soup; *Fam* **à la s.!** come and get it!; *Fam* **être s. au lait** to flare up easily (**b**) **s. populaire** soup kitchen

soupente [supɑ̃t] *nf (sous un toit)* loft; *(sous un escalier)* closet

souper¹ [supe] *nm* (**a**) *(dîner)* dinner (**b**) *(après le spectacle)* supper

souper² [supe] *vi* (**a**) *(dîner)* to have dinner (**b**) *(après le spectacle)* to have supper (**c**) *Fam Fig (être excédé)* **avoir soupé de qn/qch** to be fed up with sb/sth

soupeser [46] [supəze] *vt (objet)* to feel the weight of, to weigh in one's hand; *Fig (problème, argument)* to weigh

soupière [supjɛr] *nf* soup tureen

soupir [supir] *nm* (**a**) *(souffle)* sigh; **pousser un s.** to let out *or* to give a sigh; **rendre le dernier s.** to breathe one's last; **un gros s.** a heavy *or* deep sigh (**b**) *Mus* quarter rest

soupirail, -aux [supiraj, -o] *nm* cellar window

soupirant [supirɑ̃] *nm Hum* suitor, admirer

soupirer [supire] **1** *vt* to sigh

2 *vi* to sigh; **en soupirant** with a sigh

3 soupirer après *vt ind Litt* to long for, to yearn for

souple [supl] *adj* (**a**) *(branche)* flexible; *(corps, danseur)* supple; *(reliure)* limp; *(cuir)* soft, supple (**b**) *Fig (système, loi, personne)* flexible; *(esprit)* adaptable

souplesse [suplɛs] *nf* (**a**) *(de branche)* flexibility; *(de corps, de danseur)* suppleness; **en s.** *(démarrer)* smoothly (**b**) *Fig (de système, de loi, de personne)* flexibility

source [surs] *nf* (**a**) *(d'eau)* spring; **s. d'eau minérale** mineral spring; **s. thermale** hot spring (**b**) *(de rivière)* source; **prendre sa s.** to rise (**c**) *(de chaleur, d'énergie)* source (**d**) *Fig (du mal, de richesse, d'informations)* source; **tenir qch de bonne s.** to have sth on good authority *or* from a reliable source; **apprendre qch de s. sûre** to learn sth from a reliable source; **s. de revenus** source of revenue (**e**) *Ordinat* **s. de données** data source; **code s.** source code

sourcier [sursje] *nm* water diviner

sourcil [sursil] *nm* eyebrow

sourciller [sursije] *vi* **ne pas s.** not to bat an eyelid *or* turn a hair; **sans s.** without batting an eyelid, without turning a hair

sourcilleux, -euse [sursijø, -øz] *adj* fussy, finicky

sourd, -e [sur, surd] **1** *adj* (**a**) *(personne)* deaf; **devenir s.** to go deaf; *Fig* **rester s. à qch** to turn a deaf ear to sth, to be deaf to sth; **s. de naissance** deaf from birth; **s. d'une oreille** deaf in one ear; *Fam* **s. comme un pot** deaf as a post (**b**) *(douleur, bruit)* dull; *(voix)* hollow; *(désir, lutte)* secret; *(hostilité)* veiled; *(consonne)* voiceless

2 *nm,f (personne)* deaf person; **les sourds** the deaf, deaf people; **comme un s.** *(crier)* at the top of one's voice; *(frapper, taper)* wildly

3 *nf* **sourde** *Ling* voiceless consonant

sourdine [surdin] *nf* mute; *(d'un piano)* soft pedal; **en s.** *(violons)* muted; *(en secret)* on the quiet; *Fam Fig* **mets-la en s.!** can it!

sourdingue [surdɛ̃g] *Fam* **1** *adj* hard of hearing
2 *nmf* deaf person

sourd-muet, sourde-muette *(mpl* **sourds-muets,** *fpl* **sourdes-muettes)** [surmɥɛ, surdmɥɛt] **1** *adj* deaf-and-dumb
2 *nm,f* deaf mute

souriant, -e [surjã, -ãt] *adj* smiling

souriceau, -x [suriso] *nm* young mouse

souricière [surisjɛr] *nf* mousetrap; *Fig* trap

sourire [61] [surir] **1** *vi* (a) *(personne)* to smile (**à** at); *Ironique* **ça fait s.** it makes you laugh (b) *(être favorable)* **la chance lui sourit** fortune smiles on him/her; **tout lui sourit** everything goes right for him/her
2 *nm* smile; **le s. aux lèvres** with a smile on one's lips; **faire un s. à qn** to give sb a smile; **avoir le s.** to have a smile on one's face; **garder le s.** to keep smiling; **retrouver le s.** to be smiling again

souris [suri] *nf* (a) *(animal)* mouse; **s. blanche** white mouse (b) *Ordinat* mouse; **s. à trois boutons** three-button mouse; **s. à infrarouge** infrared mouse; **s. optique** optical mouse; **s. sans fil** cordless mouse; **s. tactile** touchpad mouse (c) *Fam (femme)* dame (d) *(de gigot)* knuckle end

sournois, -e [surnwa, -az] **1** *adj* underhand(ed)
2 *nm,f* underhand(ed) person

sournoisement [surnwazmã] *adv* underhandedly

sournoiserie [surnwazri] *nf* underhandedness

sous [su] *prép* (a) *(position)* under(neath); **s. terre** underground; **nager s. l'eau** to swim underwater; **lettre s. enveloppe** letter in an envelope; **s. la pluie** in the rain; **s. les tropiques** in the tropics; **s. les yeux de qn** before sb's eyes; **s. cet angle** from that angle; **chercher un mot s. la lettre S** to look up a word under the letter S (b) *(à l'époque de) (monarque, président)* under; **s. la IIIᵉ République** during the Third Republic (c) *(d'ici)* within; **s. huitaine** within a week; **s. peu** shortly, before long (d) *(locutions)* **connu s. le nom de...** known as...; **être s. antibiotiques** to be on antibiotics; **opérer s. anesthésie** to operate under anesthetic; **s. le poids de qch** under the weight of sth; **travailler s. les ordres de qn** to work under sb; **s. certaines conditions** on certain conditions; **s. peine de mort** on *or* under pain of death

sous-alimentation [suzalimãtasjɔ̃] *nf* malnutrition, undernourishment

sous-alimenté, -e *(mpl* **sous-alimentés,** *fpl* **sous-alimentées)** [suzalimãte] *adj* malnourished, undernourished

sous-bois [subwa] *nm inv* undergrowth

sous-chef *(pl* **sous-chefs)** [suʃɛf] *nm* second-in-command

sous-continent *(pl* **sous-continents)** [sukɔ̃tinã] *nm* subcontinent

sous-couche *(pl* **sous-couches)** [sukuʃ] *nf* undercoat

souscripteur, -trice [suskriptœr, -tris] *nm,f (d'un emprunt)* subscriber (**de** to); *(d'une police d'assurance)* policy holder

souscription [suskripsjɔ̃] *nf (à un emprunt)* subscription (**à** to); **la s. d'une police d'assurance** taking out an insurance policy

souscrire [30] [suskrir] **1** *vt (police d'assurance)* to take out
2 souscrire à *vt ind aussi Fig* to subscribe to

sous-culture *(pl* **sous-cultures)** [sukyltyr] *nf* subculture

sous-cutané, -e *(mpl* **sous-cutanés,** *fpl* **sous-cutanées)** [sukytane] *adj* subcutaneous

sous-développé, -e *(mpl* **sous-développés,** *fpl* **sous-développées)** [sudevlɔpe] *adj (pays)* underdeveloped

sous-développement [sudevlɔpmã] *nm* underdevelopment

sous-directeur, -trice *(mpl* **sous-directeurs,** *fpl* **sous-directrices)** [sudirɛktœr, -tris] *nm,f (dans une entreprise)* assistant manager

sous-division [sudivizjɔ̃] *nf* subdivision

sous-emploi [suzãplwa] *nm* underemployment

sous-employé, -e *(mpl* **sous-employés,** *fpl* **sous-employées)** [suzãplwaje] *adj* underemployed

sous-ensemble *(pl* **sous-ensembles)** [suzãsãbl] *nm* subset

sous-entendre [suzãtãdr] *vt* to imply

sous-entendu *(pl* **sous-entendus)** [suzãtãdy] *nm* insinuation

sous-équipé, -e *(mpl* **sous-équipés,** *fpl* **sous-équipées)** [suzekipe] *adj* underequipped

sous-estimer [suzɛstime] *vt* to underestimate

sous-évaluer [suzevalɥe] *vt* to undervalue

sous-exposer [suzɛkspoze] *vt* to underexpose

sous-fifre *(pl* **sous-fifres)** [sufifr] *nm Fam* underling

sous-homme *(pl* **sous-hommes)** [suzɔm] *nm* subhuman

sous-jacent, -e *(mpl* **sous-jacents,** *fpl* **sous-jacentes)** [suʒasã, -ãt] *adj* underlying

Sous-le-Vent [sulvã] *n* **les îles S.** the Leeward Islands

sous-lieutenant *(pl* **sous-lieutenants)** [suljøtnã] *nm* (a) *(dans l'armée de terre)* second lieutenant (b) *(dans la marine)* sub-lieutenant (c) *(dans l'armée de l'air)* second lieutenant

sous-locataire *(pl* **sous-locataires)** [sulɔkatɛr] *nmf* subtenant

sous-location *(pl* **sous-locations)** [sulɔkasjɔ̃] *nf* (a) *(par le locataire)* subletting (b) *(par le sous-locataire)* subrenting

sous-louer [sulwe] *vt* (a) *(sujet: locataire)* to sublet (b) *(sujet: sous-locataire)* to subrent

sous-main [sumɛ̃] *nm inv* desk blotter; *Fig* **en s.** secretly

sous-marin, -e *(mpl* **sous-marins,** *fpl* **sous-marines)** [sumarɛ̃, -in] **1** *adj* underwater
2 *nm* submarine; **s. nucléaire** nuclear(-powered) submarine

sous-marinier *(pl* **sous-mariniers)** [sumarinje] *nm* submariner

sous-multiple *(pl* **sous-multiples)** [sumyltipl] *nm Math* submultiple (**de** of)

sous-nappe *(pl* **sous-nappes)** [sunap] *nf* undercloth

sous-officier *(pl* **sous-officiers)** [suzɔfisje] *nm* non-commissioned officer

sous-payer [53] [supeje] *vt* to underpay

sous-peuplé, -e *(mpl* **sous-peuplés,** *fpl* **sous-peuplées)** [supœple] *adj* underpopulated

sous-plat *(pl* **sous-plats)** [supla] *nm Belg* table mat

sous-préfecture *(pl* **sous-préfectures)** [suprefɛktyr] *nf* subprefecture

sous-préfet *(pl* **sous-préfets)** [suprefɛ] *nm* subprefect

sous-production [suprɔdyksjɔ̃] *nf* underproduction

sous-produit *(pl* **sous-produits)** [suprɔdɥi] *nm* by-product; *Fig* poor imitation

sous-prolétaire *(pl* **sous-prolétaires)** [suprɔletɛr] *nmf* member of the underclass

sous-prolétariat *(pl* **sous-prolétariats)** [suprɔletarja] *nm* underclass

sous-pull *(pl* **sous-pulls)** [supyl] *nm* thin sweater

sous-répertoire *(pl* **sous-répertoires)** [superɛrtwar] *nm Ordinat* subdirectory

sous-secrétaire *(pl* **sous-secrétaires)** [susəkretɛr] *nmf* **s. d'État** Undersecretary of State

soussigné, -e [susiɲe] *adj & nm,f* undersigned; **je, s. Éric Blanc, donne mon autorisation à...** I, the undersigned Éric Blanc, hereby authorize...

sous-sol (*pl* **sous-sols**) [susɔl] *nm* (**a**) (*d'une maison*) basement (**b**) *Géol* subsoil

sous-tasse (*pl* **sous-tasses**) [sutas] *nf* saucer

sous-tendre [sutɑ̃dr] *vt* (*théorie*) to underlie

sous-titrage (*pl* **sous-titrages**) [sutitraʒ] *nm* *Cin* subtitling

sous-titre (*pl* **sous-titres**) [sutitr] *nm* (*de livre, de film*) subtitle

sous-titrer [sutitre] *vt* *Cin* to subtitle; **film sous-titré en anglais** movie with English subtitles

sous-total (*pl* **sous-totaux**) [sutɔtal, -o] *nm* subtotal

soustraction [sustraksjɔ̃] *nf* subtraction

soustraire [28] [sustrɛr] **1** *vt* (**a**) (*enlever*) **s. qch à qn** to take sth away *or* to remove sth from sb; **s. qn au danger/à l'influence de qn** to protect *or* to shield sb from danger/from sb's influence (**b**) (*chiffre, somme*) to subtract (**de** from)

2 se soustraire *vpr* **se s. à** (*influence, regard*) to avoid, to elude; (*obligation*) to shirk

sous-traitance [sutrɛtɑ̃s] *nf* subcontracting; **travaux effectués en s.** subcontracted work

sous-traitant, -e [sutrɛtɑ̃, -ɑ̃t] **1** *adj* subcontracting
2 *nm* subcontractor

sous-traiter [sutrete] *vt* to subcontract

sous-verre [suvɛr] *nm inv* (*cadre*) glass mount; (*photo, image*) = photograph *or* picture mounted under glass

sous-vêtement [suvɛtmɑ̃] *nm* undergarment; **sous-vêtements** underwear

soutane [sutan] *nf* cassock

soute [sut] *nf* (*de bateau*) store; (*d'avion*) hold; **s. à bagages** (*d'avion*) baggage hold

soutenable [sutnabl] *adj* (**a**) (*supportable*) bearable (**b**) (*défendable*) tenable

soutenance [sutnɑ̃s] *nf Univ* oral examination

soutènement [sutɛnmɑ̃] *nm voir* **mur**

souteneur [sutnœr] *nm* pimp

soutenir [70] [sutnir] **1** *vt* (**a**) (*maintenir*) to support, to hold up (**b**) (*aider*) to support (**c**) (*opinion, théorie*) to maintain, to uphold; **s. que...** to maintain that... (**d**) *Univ* (*thèse*) to defend (**e**) (*conversation, vitesse, rythme*) to keep up, to maintain (**f**) (*résister à*) (*regard*) to hold; **s. la comparaison** to bear comparison

2 se soutenir *vpr* (*personnes*) to support each other; **se s. moralement** to give each other moral support

soutenu, -e [sutny] *adj* (**a**) (*attention, effort, intérêt*) sustained; (*rythme*) steady (**b**) (*style, langage*) formal, elevated (**c**) (*couleur*) deep

souterrain, -e [sutɛrɛ̃, -ɛn] **1** *adj* (**a**) (*eau, explosion*) underground; (*économie*) black (**b**) *Fig* (*manœuvres*) secret
2 *nm* underground passage

soutien [sutjɛ̃] *nm* (**a**) (*aide*) support; **apporter son s. à qn/qch** to give sb/sth one's support (**b**) (*personne, groupe*) support; **s. de famille** breadwinner

soutien-gorge (*pl* **soutiens-gorge**) [sutjɛ̃gɔrʒ] *nm* bra; **s. à armatures/d'allaitement/de sport** underwired/nursing/sports bra

soutif [sutif] *nm Fam* bra

soutirer [sutire] *vt* (**a**) (*vin*) to rack, to decant (**b**) **s. qch à qn** (*argent, information*) to extract sth from sb

souvenance [suvnɑ̃s] *nf* **avoir s. de qch** to recollect sth

souvenir [70] [suvnir] **1** *nm* (**a**) (*réminiscence*) memory; **en s. de** in memory of; **en s. du passé** for old times' sake; **garder un bon/mauvais s. de qch** to have good/bad memories of sth; **souvenirs d'enfance** childhood memories (**b**) (*objet*) memento; (*touristique*) souvenir (**c**) (*dans une formule de politesse*) **mes meilleurs souvenirs à votre sœur** (my) kindest regards to your sister

2 *v impersonnel Litt* **il me souvient que...** I recall that...

3 se souvenir *vpr* **se s. de** to remember; **se s. que** to

remember that; **je ne me souviens de rien** I can't remember anything

souvent [suvɑ̃] *adv* often; **le plus s.** usually, more often than not; **plus s. qu'à son tour** far too often

souverain, -e [suvrɛ̃, -ɛn] **1** *adj* (*puissance, état, remède*) sovereign; (*bonheur, mépris*) supreme
2 *nm, f* sovereign

souverainement [suvrɛnmɑ̃] *adv* (*intelligent, doué*) supremely; (*agacer, déplaire*) intensely

souveraineté [suvrɛnte] *nf* sovereignty

soviétique [sɔvjetik] *Anciennement* **1** *adj* Soviet
2 *nmf* **S.** Soviet (citizen)

soyeux, -euse [swajø, -øz] **1** *adj* silky
2 *nm* silk merchant

soyez, soyons, *etc. voir* **être**[2]

SPA [ɛspea] *nf* (*abrév* **Société protectrice des animaux**) ≃ ASPCA

spa [spa] *nm* (**a**) (*bain à remous bouillonnant*) spa bath (**b**) (*centre d'hydrothérapie*) (health) spa

spacieusement [spasjøzmɑ̃] *adv* **être logé s.** to have spacious accommodations

spacieux, -euse [spasjø, -øz] *adj* spacious

spaghetti [spageti] *nm* piece of spaghetti; **des spaghettis** spaghetti

spammer [spame] *vt Ordinat* to spam

spammeur [spamœr] *nm Ordinat* spammer

spamming [spamiŋ] *nm Ordinat* spamming

sparadrap [sparadra] *nm* Band-Aid®

spartiate [sparsjat] **1** *adj* Spartan; *Fig* **à la s.** in a spartan way
2 *nfpl* **spartiates** Roman sandals

spasme [spasm] *nm* spasm

spasmodique [spasmɔdik] *adj* spasmodic

spasmophilie [spasmɔfili] *nf* spasmophilia

spatial, -e, -aux, -ales [spasjal, -o] *adj* (**a**) (*de l'espace*) spatial (**b**) (*de l'espace interplanétaire*) space

spatio-temporel, -elle (*mpl* **spatio-temporels**, *fpl* **spatio-temporelles**) [spasjotɑ̃pɔrɛl] *adj* spatio-temporal

spatule [spatyl] *nf* (**a**) (*de cuisinier, de peintre*) spatula (**b**) (*de ski*) tip (**c**) (*oiseau*) spoonbill

speaker, speakerine [spikœr, spikrin] *nm, f* announcer

spécial, -e, -aux, -ales [spesjal, -o] *adj* (**a**) (*particulier, extraordinaire*) special (**b**) (*bizarre*) peculiar, odd

spécialement [spesjalmɑ̃] *adv* (*particulièrement*) especially, particularly; (*exprès*) specially

spécialisation [spesjalizasjɔ̃] *nf* specialization

spécialisé, -e [spesjalize] *adj* (*travail, enseignement*) specialized; (*ouvrier*) semiskilled; (*école, hôpital*) special

spécialiser [spesjalize] **se spécialiser** *vpr* to specialize (**dans** *ou* **en** in)

spécialiste [spesjalist] *nmf* specialist (**de/en** in)

spécialité [spesjalite] *nf* specialty; **s. maison** specialty of the house

spécieux, -euse [spesjø, -øz] *adj Litt* specious

spécification [spesifikasjɔ̃] *nf* specification

spécificité [spesifisite] *nf* distinctiveness

spécifier [66] [spesifje] *vt* to specify

spécifique [spesifik] *adj* specific

spécifiquement [spesifikmɑ̃] *adv* specifically

spécimen [spesimɛn] *nm* (**a**) (*modèle*) specimen (**b**) (*livre, fascicule*) specimen copy

spectacle [spɛktakl] *nm* (**a**) (*représentation*) show; **le s.** (*industrie*) show business; **film à grand s.** epic (movie); **s. de variétés** variety show (**b**) (*vue*) sight; **se donner en s.** to make an exhibition *or* a spectacle of oneself

spectaculaire [spɛktakylɛr] *adj* spectacular

spectateur, -trice [spɛktatœr, -tris] *nm, f* (**a**) (*d'un événement* *sportif)* spectator; *(d'un spectacle)* member of the audience; **spectateurs** *(au spectacle)* audience **(b)** *(témoin)* witness

spectre [spεktr] *nm* **(a)** *(fantôme)* ghost, phantom; *Fig (de la guerre, de la misère)* specter **(b)** *Phys* spectrum

spéculateur, trice [spekylatœr, -tris] *nm,f* speculator

spéculation [spekylasjɔ̃] *nf* speculation; **s. à la baisse** bear operations; **s. à la hausse** bull operations

spéculer [spekyle] *vi* **(a)** *(intellectuellement)* to speculate (**sur** on *or* about) **(b)** *(à la Bourse)* to speculate (**sur** in); *Fig* **s. sur qch** to count *or* to bank on sth

spéculoos [spekylos] *nm Belg* = ginger biscuit

speech *(pl* **speeches)** [spitʃ] *nm Fam* speech; **faire un s.** to make a speech; **faire un s. à qn sur qch** to give sb a speech about sth

speed [spid] *Fam* **1** *adj (nerveux)* hyper
   2 *nm (amphétamines)* speed

speedé, -e [spide] *adj Fam (hyperactif)* hyped up, hyper

speeder [spide] *vi Fam* to get a move on

spéléologie [speleolɔʒi] *nf* **(a)** *(exploration)* spelunking **(b)** *(science)* speleology

spéléologue [speleolɔg] *nmf* **(a)** *(explorateur)* spelunker **(b)** *(spécialiste)* speleologist

spencer [spɛ̃sɛr] *nm* short jacket

spermatozoïde [spɛrmatozoid] *nm* spermatozoon

sperme [spɛrm] *nm* sperm, semen

sphère [sfɛr] *nf* **(a)** *(boule)* sphere **(b)** *(d'activité, d'influence)* sphere; **les hautes sphères de la politique** the higher realms of politics

sphérique [sferik] *adj* spherical

sphinx [sfɛ̃ks] *nm* **(a)** *(monstre fabuleux)* sphinx **(b)** *(insecte)* hawk *or* sphinx moth

spirale [spiral] *nf* spiral; **en s.** *(s'élever)* in a spiral; *(escalier, coquillage)* spiral

spiritisme [spiritism] *nm* spiritualism

spiritualité [spiritɥalite] *nf* spirituality

spirituel, -elle [spiritɥɛl] *adj* **(a)** *(pouvoir, vie)* spiritual **(b)** *(fin)* witty; *Ironique* **que c'est s.!** very witty!

spirituellement [spiritɥɛlmɑ̃] *adv* **(a)** *(moralement)* spiritually **(b)** *(finement)* wittily

spiritueux [spiritɥø] *nm* spirit

spleen [splin] *nm Litt* spleen, melancholy; **avoir le s.** to be melancholic

splendeur [splɑ̃dœr] *nf* splendor; **c'est une s.** it's splendid

splendide [splɑ̃did] *adj* splendid; *(soleil)* brilliant; *(œuvre d'art, personne)* magnificent

splendidement [splɑ̃didmɑ̃] *adv* splendidly

spolier [66] [spɔlje] *vt* to despoil (**de** of)

spongieux, -euse [spɔ̃ʒjø, -øz] *adj* spongy

sponsor [spɔnsɔr] *nm* sponsor

sponsoriser [spɔnsɔrize] *vt* to sponsor

spontané, -e [spɔ̃tane] *adj* spontaneous

spontanéité [spɔ̃taneite] *nf* spontaneity

spontanément [spɔ̃tanemɑ̃] *adv* spontaneously

sporadique [spɔradik] *adj* sporadic

spore [spɔr] *nf* spore

sport [spɔr] **1** *nm* **(a)** *(activité)* sport; **de s.** *(chaussures, terrain, voiture)* sports; **faire du s.** to do sports; **s. de combat** combat sport; **s. d'équipe/individuel** team/individual sport; **sports extrêmes** extreme sports; **sports d'hiver** winter sports; **aller aux sports d'hiver** to go skiing; **sports nautiques** water sports **(b)** *Fam (locutions)* **il va y avoir du s.!** there's going to be some fun!; **c'est du s.** it's a tough job
   2 *adj inv (vêtement)* casual

sportif, -ive [spɔrtif, -iv] **1** *adj* **(a)** *(résultats, journal, club)* sports **(b)** *(fair-play)* sporting **(c)** *(dynamique)* sporty
   2 *nm,f* sportsman, *f* sportswoman

sportivité [spɔrtivite] *nf* sportsmanship

spot [spɔt] *nm* **(a)** *(projecteur)* spot, spotlight **(b)** *(à la télé, à la radio)* **s. publicitaire** commercial

spoutnik [sputnik] *nm* sputnik

spray [sprɛ] *nm* spray, aerosol; **parfum en s.** spray-on perfume

sprint [sprint] *nm* *(accélération finale)* (final) sprint; *(course)* sprint; *Fam* **piquer un s.** to sprint

sprinter¹ [sprintœr] *nm* sprinter

sprinter² [sprinte] *vi* to sprint

squale [skwal] *nm* shark

square [skwar] *nm* public garden

squash [skwaʃ] *nm* squash

squat [skwat] *nm* squat

squatter¹ [skwatœr] *nm* squatter

squatter² [skwate], **squattériser** [skwaterize] *vt (bâtiment)* to squat in; *Fam Fig (monopoliser)* to take over, to hog

squatteur, -euse [skwatœr, -øz] *nm,f* squatter

squelette [skəlɛt] *nm* **(a)** *(d'être humain, d'animal)* skeleton; **c'est un vrai s.** he's/she's a bag of bones; **c'est un s. ambulant** he's/she's a walking skeleton **(b)** *Fig (de roman, de bâtiment)* skeleton, framework

squelettique [skəlɛtik] *adj* **(a)** *(personne, partie du corps)* skeleton-like **(b)** *(personnel, armée)* skeleton

SRAS [sras] *nm Méd (abrév* **syndrome respiratoire aigu sévère)** SARS

Sri Lanka [srilɑ̃ka] *nm* **le S.** Sri Lanka

sri lankais, -e [srilɑ̃kɛ, -ɛz] **1** *adj* Sri Lankan
   2 *nm,f* **S., Sri Lankaise** Sri Lankan

SRPJ [ɛsɛrpeʒi] *nm (abrév* **Service régional de la police judiciaire)** = regional crime unit

stabilisateur, -trice [stabilizatœr, -tris] **1** *adj* stabilizing
   2 *nm (de vélo)* stabilizer

stabilisation [stabilizasjɔ̃] *nf* stabilization

stabiliser [stabilize] **1** *vt* to stabilize
   2 se stabiliser *vpr* to stabilize; *(personne)* to settle down

stabilité [stabilite] *nf* stability

stable [stabl] *adj* stable

stade [stad] *nm* **(a)** *(sportif)* stadium **(b)** *(étape)* stage; **en être au s. embryonnaire** to be at an embryonic stage

stage [staʒ] *nm (professionnel)* training course; **être en s.** to be on a training course; **s. en entreprise** internship; **s. de formation** training course, internship; **faire un s. de tennis/ de voile** to have tennis/sailing lessons; *(vacances)* to go on a tennis/sailing vacation

stagiaire [staʒjɛr] *adj & nmf* trainee, intern

stagnant, -e [stagnɑ̃, -ɑ̃t] *adj* stagnant

stagnation [stagnasjɔ̃] *nf* stagnation

stagner [stagne] *vi* to stagnate

stalactite [stalaktit] *nf* stalactite

stalagmite [stalagmit] *nf* stalagmite

stalinien, -enne [stalinjɛ̃, -ɛn] *adj & nm,f* Stalinist

stalle [stal] *nf (dans une écurie, une église)* stall

stand [stɑ̃d] *nm* **(a)** *(d'exposition)* stand; *(de foire)* stall; **s. de tir** rifle range **(b)** *(de course automobile)* **s. (de ravitaillement)** pit

standard [stɑ̃dar] **1** *adj inv* standard
   2 *nm* **(a)** *(norme)* standard **(b)** **s. (téléphonique)** switchboard

standardisation [stɑ̃dardizasjɔ̃] *nf* standardization

standardiser [stɑ̃dardize] *vt* to standardize

standardiste [stɑ̃dardist] *nmf (switchboard)* operator

standing [stɑ̃diŋ] *nm (social)* standing; **de grand s.** *(appartement)* luxury; *(quartier)* select

staphylocoque [stafilokɔk] *nm* staphylococcus

star [star] *nf* star

starlette [starlɛt] *nf* starlet

starter [startɛr] *nm* (**a**) *(de voiture)* choke (**b**) *(dans une course)* starter

starting-block *(pl* **starting-blocks**) [startiŋblɔk] *nm* starting block

start-up [startœp] *(pl* **start-ups**) *nf* dot com (company)

station [stasjɔ̃] *nf* (**a**) *(de métro)* station; *(de train, de bus)* stop; **s. de taxis** taxi stand (**b**) *(ville, village)* **s. balnéaire** seaside resort; **s. de ski** ski resort; **s. de sports d'hiver** winter sports resort; **s. thermale** spa (town) (**c**) *(établissement)* station; **s. d'essence** gas station; **s. de lavage** car wash; **s. spatiale** space station (**d**) *(position)* **s. debout** standing position (**e**) **s. de radio** radio station (**f**) *Ordinat (d'un réseau)* station, node; **s. d'accueil** docking station; **s. individuelle** stand-alone workstation; **s. de travail** workstation

stationnaire [stasjɔnɛr] *adj (satellite)* stationary; *(baromètre)* steady; *(état d'un malade)* stable

stationnement [stasjɔnmɑ̃] *nm* (**a**) *(de voitures)* parking; **en s.** parked; **s. alterné semi-mensuel** = system in which parking is permitted on one side of the street only for alternating periods of two weeks; **s. interdit** *(sur panneau)* no parking; **s. gênant** *(sur panneau)* ≃ restricted parking (**b**) *Can (parking)* parking lot

stationner [stasjɔne] *vi* to park; **défense de s.** *(sur panneau)* no parking

station-service *(pl* **stations-service**) [stasjɔ̃sɛrvis] *nf* service station, gas station

statique [statik] **1** *adj* static
2 *nf* statics *(singulier)*

statisticien, -enne [statistisjɛ̃, -ɛn] *nm,f* statistician

statistique [statistik] **1** *adj* statistical
2 *nf* (**a**) *(donnée)* statistic (**b**) *(science)* statistics *(singulier)*

statistiquement [statistikmɑ̃] *adv* statistically

statuaire [statɥɛr] *adj & nf* statuary

statue [staty] *nf* statue

statuer [statɥe] **statuer sur** *vt ind* to give a ruling on

statuette [statɥɛt] *nf* statuette

statu quo [statykwo] *nm* status quo

stature [statyr] *nf* stature

statut [staty] *nm* (**a**) *(position)* status; **s. juridique** *ou* **légal** legal status; **s. social** social status (**b**) **statuts** *(d'une société, d'une association)* bylaws, statutes

statutaire [statytɛr] *adj* statutory

St *(abrév* **Saint**) St.

Ste *(abrév* **Sainte**) St.

Sté *(abrév* **Société**) Co.

steak [stɛk] *nm* steak; **s. frites** steak with fries; **un s. haché** a hamburger; **du s. haché** ground beef; **s. au poivre** pepper steak; **s. tartare** steak tartare *(raw minced beef served with a raw egg)*

stèle [stɛl] *nf* stele

stellaire [stelɛr] *adj* stellar

stencil [stɛnsil] *nm* stencil

sténo [steno] **1** *nf (abrév* **sténographie**) shorthand; **prendre qch en s.** to take sth down in shorthand
2 *nmf* *(abrév* **sténographe**) stenographer

sténodactylo [stenodaktilo] **1** *nf* shorthand typing
2 *nmf* shorthand typist

sténodactylographie [stenodaktilɔgrafi] *nf* shorthand typing

sténographe [stenɔgraf] *nmf* stenographer

sténographie [stenɔgrafi] *nf* shorthand

sténographier [66] [stenɔgrafje] *vt* to take down in shorthand

sténographique [stenɔgrafik] *adj* shorthand

stentor [stɑ̃tɔr] *nm voir* **voix**

steppe [stɛp] *nf* steppe

stéréo [stereo] **1** *adj inv* stereo
2 *nf* stereo; **en s.** in stereo

stéréophonie [stereɔfɔni] *nf* stereophony

stéréophonique [stereɔfɔnik] *adj* stereophonic

stéréotype [stereotip] *nm* stereotype

stéréotypé, -e [stereotipe] *adj* stereotyped

stérile [steril] *adj* (**a**) *(personne, animal)* sterile; *(mariage)* childless; *(terre)* barren (**b**) *(discussion, efforts)* futile (**c**) *(instrument, chambre)* sterile

stérilet [sterilɛ] *nm* coil, IUD

stérilisation [sterilizasjɔ̃] *nf* sterilization

stériliser [sterilize] *vt* to sterilize

stérilité [sterilite] *nf* (**a**) *(d'une personne, d'un animal)* sterility; *(de la terre)* barrenness (**b**) *(d'une discussion, d'efforts)* futility

sterling [stɛrliŋ] *adj inv voir* **livre²**

sterne [stɛrn] *nf* tern

sternum [stɛrnɔm] *nm* breastbone, *Spéc* sternum

stéthoscope [stetɔskɔp] *nm* stethoscope

steward [stjuwart, stiwart] *nm* steward

stick [stik] *nm (de colle, pour les lèvres)* stick; **déodorant en s.** stick deodorant

stigmate [stigmat] *nm* (**a**) *(trace)* mark (**b**) *Rel* **stigmates** stigmata

stigmatiser [stigmatize] *vt (dénoncer)* to condemn

stimulant, -e [stimylɑ̃, -ɑ̃t] **1** *adj* stimulating; *(résultats)* encouraging
2 *nm* (**a**) *(remède)* stimulant (**b**) *Fig* stimulus, incentive

stimulateur [stimylatœr] *nm* **s. cardiaque** pacemaker

stimulation [stimylasjɔ̃] *nf* stimulation

stimuler [stimyle] *vt* to stimulate

stipuler [stipyle] *vt* to stipulate

stock [stɔk] *nm* stock; **en s.** in stock

stockage [stɔkaʒ] *nm* (**a**) *(de marchandises)* stocking (**b**) *Ordinat* storage; **s. en mémoire tampon** buffering

stock-car *(pl* **stock-cars**) [stɔkkar] *nm (voiture)* stock car; *(sport)* stock-car racing

stocker [stɔke] *vt* (**a**) *(marchandises)* to stock (**b**) *Ordinat* to store

Stockholm [stɔkɔlm] *n* Stockholm

stoïcisme [stɔisism] *nm* (**a**) *(attitude)* stoicism (**b**) *(doctrine philosophique)* Stoicism

stoïque [stɔik] *adj* stoical

stoïquement [stɔikmɑ̃] *adv* stoically

stomatologie [stɔmatɔlɔʒi] *nf* stomatology

stop [stɔp] **1** *exclam* stop!; *(dans un télégramme)* stop; **savoir dire s.** to know when to say stop
2 *nm* (**a**) *(panneau)* stop sign (**b**) *(d'un véhicule)* brake light (**c**) *Fam (auto-stop)* hitching, hitchhiking; **faire du s.** to hitch, to hitchhike

stopper [stɔpe] *vt & vi (arrêter)* to stop

store [stɔr] *nm* (**a**) *(de fenêtre)* blind; **s. vénitien** Venetian blind (**b**) *(de magasin)* awning

strabisme [strabism] *nm* squint

stradivarius [stradivarjys] *nm* Stradivarius

strangulation [strɑ̃gylasjɔ̃] *nf* strangulation

strapontin [strapɔ̃tɛ̃] *nm (siège)* folding seat, tip-up seat

Strasbourg [strazbur] *n* Strasbourg

strasbourgeois, -e [strazburʒwa, -waz] **1** *adj* of Strasbourg
2 *nm,f* **S., Strasbourgeoise** person from Strasbourg

strass [stras] *nm* paste; **en s.** *(bijou)* paste

stratagème [strataʒɛm] *nm* stratagem

strate [strat] *nf* stratum

stratège [strateʒ] *nm* strategist

stratégie [strateʒi] *nf* strategy

stratégique [strateʒik] *adj* strategic

stratification [stratifikasjɔ̃] *nf* stratification

stratifié, -e [stratifje] *adj* (**a**) *(roche)* stratified (**b**) *(bois)* laminated

stratosphère [stratɔsfɛr] *nf* stratosphere

streptocoque [strɛptɔkɔk] *nm* streptococcus

stress [strɛs] *nm* stress

stressant, -e [strɛsɑ̃, -ɑ̃t] *adj* stressful

stresser [strɛse] **1** *vt* to put under stress; **être stressé** to be stressed
2 *vi Fam* to get stressed

Stretch® [strɛtʃ] *nm* stretch material; **une jupe en S.** a stretch skirt

strict, -e [strikt] *adj* (**a**) *(obligation, principes)* strict; **au sens s.** in the strict sense of the word; **le s. minimum** the bare minimum; **le s. nécessaire** the bare essentials; **c'est la stricte vérité** that's the absolute truth; **c'est son droit le plus s.** it's his/her absolute right (**b**) *(personne)* strict (**sur** about) (**c**) *(costume, coupe de cheveux)* severe

strictement [striktəmɑ̃] *adv* (**a**) *(rigoureusement)* strictly; **je ne comprends s. rien** I don't understand a single thing (**b**) *(habillé)* severely

stricto sensu [striktosɛ̃sy] *adv* strictly speaking

strident, -e [stridɑ̃, -ɑ̃t] *adj* strident, shrill

strie [stri] *nf* groove

strié, -e [strije] *adj* grooved

string [striŋ] *nm* thong, G-string

strip-tease *(pl* **strip-teases)** [striptiz] *nm* striptease

strip-teaseur, -euse *(mpl* **strip-teaseurs,** *fpl* **strip-teaseuses)** [striptizœr, øz] *nm,f (homme)* male stripper; *(femme)* stripper

stroboscope [strɔbɔskɔp] *nm* strobe, stroboscope

strophe [strɔf] *nf* stanza, verse

structural, -e, -aux, -ales [stryktyral, -o] *adj* structural

structuralement [stryktyralmɑ̃] *adv* structurally

structuralisme [stryktyralism] *nm* structuralism

structuraliste [stryktyralist] *adj & nmf* structuralist

structure [stryktyr] *nf* (**a**) *(disposition)* structure (**b**) *(organisation)* **s. d'accueil** reception facilities (**c**) *Ordinat* **s. en anneau** ring structure; **s. en arbre** tree structure; **s. de bloc** block structure

structuré, -e [stryktyre] *adj* (**a**) *(ensemble, langage)* structured (**b**) *Ordinat* **fichier non s.** flat file

structurel, -elle [stryktyrɛl] *adj* structural

structurer [stryktyre] *vt* to structure

strychnine [striknin] *nf* strychnine

stuc [styk] *nm* stucco

studieusement [stydjøzmɑ̃] *adv* studiously

studieux, -euse [stydjø, -øz] *adj (personne)* studious; *(vacances)* study

studio [stydjo] *nm* (**a**) *(pour travailler)* studio; **s. de cinéma** movie studio; **tourné en s.** filmed in the studio; **s. d'enregistrement** recording studio (**b**) *(logement)* studio apartment

stupéfaction [stypefaksjɔ̃] *nf* amazement, astonishment

stupéfait, -e [stypefɛ, -ɛt] *adj* amazed, astounded

stupéfiant, -e [stypefjɑ̃, -ɑ̃t] **1** *adj* amazing, astounding
2 *nm* drug, narcotic

stupéfier [66] [stypefje] *vt* to amaze, to astound

stupeur [stypœr] *nf* amazement, astonishment

stupide [stypid] *adj* stupid

stupidement [stypidmɑ̃] *adv* stupidly

stupidité [stypidite] *nf* (**a**) *(caractère)* stupidity (**b**) *(remarque)* stupid remark; **dire des stupidités** to say stupid things

style [stil] *nm* style; **de s.** *(meuble)* period; **s. Louis XIII/Régence** Louis XIII-/Regency-style; **avoir du s.** to have style, to be stylish; *Fam* **ça serait bien son s.!** that would be just his/her style!; **s. de vie** lifestyle; *Gram* **s. direct/indirect** direct/indirect speech

stylé, -e [stile] *adj (domestique)* trained

stylet [stilɛ] *nm* (**a**) *(poignard)* stiletto (**b**) *Ordinat* **s. lumineux** light pen

styliser [stilize] *vt* to stylize

stylisme [stilism] *nm* designing

styliste [stilist] *nmf* designer

stylistique [stilistik] **1** *adj* stylistic
2 *nf* stylistics *(singulier)*

stylo [stilo] *nm* pen; **s. à encre** *ou* **à plume** fountain pen; **s. (à) bille** ballpoint (pen); *Ordinat* **s. optique** light pen

stylo-feutre *(pl* **stylos-feutres)** [stiloføtr] *nm* felt-tip (pen)

su¹, -e *voir* **savoir**

su² [sy] *nm* **au vu et au su de tout le monde** quite openly

suave [sɥav] *adj* (**a**) *(parfum, mélodie)* sweet (**b**) *(ton, manières)* suave, smooth

suavité [sɥavite] *nf* (**a**) *(d'un parfum, d'une mélodie)* sweetness (**b**) *(des manières)* suavity

subalterne [sybaltɛrn] **1** *adj (officier, position)* subordinate, minor; *(employé)* junior
2 *nmf* subordinate

subconscient, -e [sybkɔ̃sjɑ̃, -ɑ̃t] *adj & nm* subconscious

subdiviser [sybdivize] **1** *vt* to subdivide (**en** into)
2 se subdiviser *vpr* to be subdivided (**en** into)

subdivision [sybdivizjɔ̃] *nf* subdivision

subir [sybir] *vt* (**a**) *(violence, conséquences)* to suffer; *(défaite, pertes)* to suffer, to sustain; *(influence)* to be under; **faire s. qch à qn** to subject sb to sth (**b**) *(examen, opération, changement)* to undergo (**c**) *Fam (personne)* to put up with

subit, -e [sybi, -it] *adj* sudden

subitement [sybitmɑ̃] *adv* suddenly, all of a sudden

subjectif, -ive [sybʒɛktif, -iv] *adj* subjective

subjectivement [sybʒɛktivmɑ̃] *adv* subjectively

subjectivité [sybʒɛktivite] *nf* subjectivity

subjonctif, -ive [sybʒɔ̃ktif, -iv] *Gram* **1** *adj* subjunctive
2 *nm* subjunctive; **au s.** in the subjunctive

subjuguer [sybʒyge] *vt (séduire)* to captivate

sublimation [syblimasjɔ̃] *nf* sublimation

sublime [syblim] **1** *adj* sublime
2 *nm* **le s.** the sublime

sublimement [syblimmɑ̃] *adv* sublimely

sublimer [syblime] *vt* to sublimate

subliminal, -e, -aux, -ales [sybliminal, -o] *adj* subliminal

submerger [45] [sybmɛrʒe] *vt* to submerge; **submergé de travail** snowed under with work

submersible [sybmɛrsibl] **1** *adj* submersible
2 *nm* submarine

subodorer [sybɔdɔre] *vt Fam (danger, complot)* to scent

subordination [sybɔrdinasjɔ̃] *nf* subordination

subordonné, -e [sybɔrdɔne] **1** *adj Gram (proposition)* subordinate
2 *nm,f (personne)* subordinate
3 *nf* **subordonnée** *Gram* subordinate clause

subordonner [sybɔrdɔne] *vt* (**a**) *(dans une hiérarchie)* **être subordonné à qn** to be subordinate to sb (**b**) *(faire passer après)* **s. qch à qch** to accord less importance to sth than to sth (**c**) *(faire dépendre)* **être subordonné à qch** to be dependent on sth

subornation [sybɔrnasjɔ̃] *nf Jur* subornation

suborner [sybɔrne] *vt* (**a**) *Jur (témoin)* to suborn, to bribe (**b**) *Litt (séduire)* to seduce

subrepticement [sybrɛptismɑ̃] *adv* surreptitiously

subséquent, -e [sypsekɑ̃, -ɑ̃t] *adj* subsequent

subside [sybzid] *nm* subsidy, grant

subsidiaire [sybzidjɛr] *adj* subsidiary

subsidier [66] [sybzidje] *vt Belg (subventionner)* to subsidize

subsistance [sybzistɑ̃s] *nf* subsistence; **pourvoir à la s. de sa famille** to keep *or* to support one's family

subsistant, -e [sybzistɑ̃, -ɑ̃t] *adj* remaining
subsister [sybziste] *vi* (**a**) *(chose)* to remain (**b**) *(personne)* to subsist
substance [sypstɑ̃s] *nf* substance; **en s.** in substance
substantiel, -elle [sypstɑ̃sjɛl] *adj* substantial
substantiellement [sypstɑ̃sjɛlmɑ̃] *adv* substantially
substantif, -ive [sypstɑ̃tif, -iv] *Gram* **1** *adj* substantive
  2 *nm* noun, substantive
substantiver [sypstɑ̃tive] *vt* to use as a noun *or* substantively
substituer [sypstitɥe] **1** *vt* **s. qn/qch à** to substitute sb/sth for
  2 se substituer *vpr* **se s. à** to substitute for, to take the place of
substitut [sypstity] *nm* (**a**) *Jur* deputy public prosecutor (**b**) *(remplacement)* substitute
substitution [sypstitysjɔ̃] *nf* substitution
substrat [sypstra] *nm Géol* substratum
subterfuge [syptɛrfyʒ] *nm* subterfuge; **user de subterfuges** to resort to subterfuge
subtil, -e [syptil] *adj* subtle
subtilement [syptilmɑ̃] *adv* subtly
subtiliser [syptilize] *vt* to make off with; **on lui a subtilisé son portefeuille** someone made off with his/her wallet
subtilité [syptilite] *nf* subtlety
subtropical, -e, -aux, -ales [syptrɔpikal, -o] *adj* subtropical
subvenir 70] [sybvənir] **subvenir à** *vt ind* to meet
subvention [sybvɑ̃sjɔ̃] *nf* subsidy, grant
subventionner [sybvɑ̃sjɔne] *vt* to subsidize
subversif, -ive [sybvɛrsif, -iv] *adj* subversive
subversion [sybvɛrsjɔ̃] *nf* subversion
suc [syk] *nm* (**a**) *(de fruit, de viande)* juice (**b**) *Fig & Litt* essence
succédané [syksedane] *nm* substitute (**de** for); **un s. de café** ersatz coffee
succéder [syksede] **1 succéder à** *vt ind* (**a**) *(personne)* to succeed, to take over from (**b**) *(phénomène)* **la résignation succéda à la colère** anger gave way to resignation
  2 se succéder *vpr* to follow one another
succès [syksɛ] *nm* (**a**) *(réussite)* success; **avoir du s.** *(œuvre, artiste)* to be successful; *(suggestion)* to be very well-received; **il a beaucoup de s. auprès des jeunes** he's very popular with young people; **avoir un s. fou (auprès de qn)** to be a big hit (with sb); **faire le s. de qn** to make sb's name; **avec s.** successfully; **sans s.** unsuccessfully; **à s.** successful (**b**) *(pièce, chanson)* hit, success
successeur [syksesœr] *nm* successor (**de** to)
successif, -ive [syksesif, -iv] *adj* successive
succession [syksesjɔ̃] *nf* (**a**) *(suite)* succession (**b**) *(remplacement)* succession (**à** to); **prendre la s. de qn** to succeed sb, to take over from sb (**c**) *Jur (par héritage)* succession; *(biens)* inheritance
successivement [syksesivmɑ̃] *adv* successively
succinct, -e [syksɛ̃, -ɛ̃t] *adj* succinct
succinctement [syksɛ̃tmɑ̃] *adv* succinctly
succion [sysjɔ̃, syksjɔ̃] *nf* suction
succomber [sykɔ̃be] *vi* to succumb (**à** to); **s. sous le nombre** to yield to greater numbers
succulent, -e [sykylɑ̃, -ɑ̃t] *adj (nourriture)* succulent
succursale [sykyrsal] *nf* branch
sucer [16] [syse] *vt* to suck
sucette [sysɛt] *nf* (**a**) *(confiserie)* lollipop (**b**) *(tétine)* pacifier
suçon [sysɔ̃] *nm Fam* hickey
suçoter [sysɔte] *vt* to suck (at)
sucre [sykr] *nm* (**a**) *(aliment, morceau)* sugar; *Fig* **être tout s. tout miel** to be all sweetness and light; **s. candi** candy sugar; **s. de canne** cane sugar; **s. cristallisé** granulated sugar; **s.**

glace confectioner's sugar; **s. en morceaux/en poudre** lump/finely granulated sugar; **s. roux** brown sugar; **s. semoule** finely granulated sugar (**b**) **s. d'orge** *(substance)* barley sugar; *(bâton)* stick of barley sugar
sucré, -e [sykre] *adj* (**a**) *(naturellement)* sweet; *(additionné de sucre)* sweetened (**b**) *Fig (paroles, sourire)* sugary
sucrer [sykre] **1** *vt* (**a**) *(boisson)* to sugar; *(mets)* to sweeten; *Fam Fig* **s. les fraises** *(trembler)* to shake; *(être gâteux)* to be an old dodderer (**b**) *Fam (supprimer) (passage, émission)* to cut; **on lui a sucré sa prime** he/she has been deprived of his/her bonus
  2 *vi (miel, aspartame)* to sweeten
  3 se sucrer *vpr Fam* (**a**) *(prendre du sucre)* to help oneself to sugar (**b**) *(s'enrichir)* to line one's pockets
sucrerie [sykrəri] *nf* (**a**) *(usine)* sugar refinery (**b**) *(friandise)* **sucreries** sweet things
Sucrette® [sykrɛt] *nf* (artificial) sweetener
sucrier, -ère [sykrije, -ɛr] **1** *adj* sugar
  2 *nm* (**a**) *(récipient)* sugar bowl; *(verseur)* sugar shaker (**b**) *(fabricant)* sugar manufacturer
sud [syd] **1** *nm* south; **le vent du s.** the south wind; **dans le S. de l'Angleterre** in the South of England; **au s.** in the south; **au s. de** (to the) south of; **vers le s.** south, southward
  2 *adj inv* southern
sud-africain, -e (*mpl* **sud-africains**, *fpl* **sud-africaines**) [sydafrikɛ̃, -ɛn] **1** *adj* South African
  2 *nm,f* **S., Sud-Africaine** South African
sud-américain, -e (*mpl* **sud-américains**, *fpl* **sud-américaines**) [sydamerikɛ̃, -ɛn] **1** *adj* South American
  2 *nm,f* **S., Sud-Américaine** South American
sud-coréen, -enne (*mpl* **sud-coréens**, *fpl* **sud-coréennes**) [sudkɔreɛ̃, -ɛn] **1** *adj* South Korean
  2 *nm,f* **S., Sud-Coréenne** South Korean
sud-est [sydɛst] **1** *nm* southeast; **le S. asiatique** Southeast Asia
  2 *adj inv* southeast
sudiste [sydist] *adj & nmf Hist* Confederate
sud-ouest [sydwɛst] *nm & adj inv* southwest
Suède [sɥɛd] *nf* **la S.** Sweden
suédine [sɥedin] *nf* suedette
suédois, -e [sɥedwa, -az] **1** *adj* Swedish
  2 *nm (langue)* Swedish
  2 *nm,f* **S., Suédoise** Swede
suée [sɥe] *nf Fam* sweat; **prendre une s.** to work up a sweat
suer [sɥe] **1** *vi* (**a**) *(personne)* to sweat; **s. à grosses gouttes** to be pouring with sweat; *Fam* **faire s. qn** *(embêter)* to bug sb; *Fam* **se faire s.** to be bored stiff (**b**) *(mur)* to ooze (**c**) *Fig (travailler)* to labor, to sweat
  2 *vt (ennui, hypocrisie)* to ooze; **s. sang et eau** to sweat blood and tears
sueur [sɥœr] *nf* sweat; **être en s.** to be sweating *or* in a sweat; **avoir des sueurs froides** to be in a cold sweat; **à la s. de son front** by the sweat of one's brow
suffire [19b] [syfir] **1** *vi* to be enough, to be sufficient (**à/pour** for); **ça suffit!** that's enough!, that'll do!
  2 *v impersonnel* **il suffit d'appuyer sur le bouton** you just have to press the button; **il suffit que je sorte deux minutes pour que le téléphone sonne** I only have to go out for two minutes for the phone to start ringing; **il a suffi de quelques mots pour le persuader** a few words were enough to persuade him
  3 se suffire *vpr* **se s. (à soi-même)** to be self-sufficient
suffisamment [syfizamɑ̃] *adv* sufficiently, enough; **s. de** sufficient, enough
suffisance [syfizɑ̃s] *nf (vanité)* self-importance
suffisant, -e [syfizɑ̃, -ɑ̃t] *adj* (**a**) *(satisfaisant)* sufficient, enough (**b**) *(vaniteux)* self-important, conceited

suffixe [syfiks] *nm Gram & Ordinat* suffix

suffocant, -e [syfɔkã, -ãt] *adj* (a) *(chaleur)* suffocating, stifling (b) *Fig (nouvelle, réponse)* staggering, astounding

suffocation [syfɔkasjɔ̃] *nf* suffocation

suffoquer [syfɔke] **1** *vt* (a) *(sujet: odeur, fumée, chaleur)* to suffocate (b) *Fig (sujet: nouvelles)* to stagger, to astound
2 *vi* to suffocate, to choke; *Fig* **s. de colère/d'indignation** to choke with anger/indignation

suffrage [syfraʒ] *nm (voix)* vote; *(système)* suffrage; **s. direct/indirect** direct/indirect suffrage; **s. universel** universal suffrage

suffragette [syfraʒɛt] *nf* suffragette

suggérer [34] [sygʒere] *vt* (a) *(proposer)* to suggest (**à** to); **s. de faire qch** to suggest doing sth; **s. à qn de faire qch** to suggest to sb that he/she should do sth (b) *(faire penser à)* to evoke

suggestif, -ive [sygʒɛstif, -iv] *adj* (a) *(ton, musique)* evocative (b) *(plaisanterie, geste)* suggestive

suggestion [sygʒɛstjɔ̃] *nf* suggestion

suicidaire [sɥisidɛr] **1** *adj* suicidal
2 *nmf* suicidal person

suicide [sɥisid] *nm* suicide

suicidé, -e [sɥiside] **1** *adj* who has committed suicide
2 *nm,f* suicide

suicider [sɥiside] **se suicider** *vpr* to commit suicide

suie [sɥi] *nf* soot

suif [sɥif] *nm* tallow

suintant, -e [sɥɛ̃tã, -ãt] *adj (rocher, mur)* oozing, dripping; *(plaie)* weeping

suintement [sɥɛ̃tmã] *nm (de rochers, de mur)* oozing, dripping; *(de plaie)* weeping

suinter [sɥɛ̃te] *vi* (a) *(rocher, mur)* to ooze, to drip; *(plaie)* to weep (b) *(liquide)* to ooze

suis *voir* **être²**, **suivre**

Suisse [sɥis] *nf* **la S.** Switzerland; **la S. alémanique/romande** German-/French-speaking Switzerland

suisse [sɥis] **1** *adj* Swiss
2 *nm* (a) *(employé d'église)* verger (b) *Can* chipmunk (c) *Fam Fig* **manger/boire qch en s.** to eat/to drink sth without sharing it
3 *nmf* **S.** Swiss (person); **les Suisses** the Swiss

Suissesse [sɥisɛs] *nf* Swiss (woman)

suit *voir* **suivre**

suite [sɥit] *nf* (a) *(reste)* rest (**de** of); **faire s. à qch** to follow (on) from sth; **s. à votre lettre du 10 mars** further to your letter of March 10; **donner s. à** *(demande, lettre)* to follow up; *(commande)* to deal with; *(décision)* to give effect to; **prendre la s. de** *(personne)* to take over from; *(affaires)* to take over; **à la s. (les uns des autres)** one after the other; **à la s. de cette discussion** following this discussion
(b) *(de roman, de film)* sequel; *(nouvel épisode)* continuation; **s. à la page 30** continued on page 30; **s. et fin** concluded; **la s. au prochain numéro** continued in the next issue
(c) *(cohérence)* coherence; **sans s.** *(paroles, pensées)* incoherent; *(parler)* incoherently; **avoir de la s. dans les idées** to be very single-minded
(d) *(escorte)* *(d'un président)* suite; *(d'un monarque)* retinue
(e) *(série)* series
(f) *Math* series
(g) *Mus* suite
(h) *(conséquence)* consequence; **suites** *(de maladie)* aftereffects; **mourir des suites d'une blessure** to die as the result of an injury; **par s.** consequently; **par s. de qch** as a result of sth
(i) *(appartement)* suite
(j) *(locutions)* **de s.** in a row; **et ainsi de s.** and so on; **tout de s.**, *Fam* **de s.** right away, immediately; **par la s.** afterward(s)

suivant¹ [sɥivã] **1** *prép* (a) *(direction)* along (b) *(selon)* according to (c) *(conformément à)* **s. son habitude** as is/was his/her habit
2 *conj* **s. que** according to whether

suivant², -e [sɥivã, -ãt] **1** *adj* (a) *(page, jour)* next, following; **voir page six et suivantes** see page six and following; **notre méthode est la suivante** our method is as follows (b) *(personne)* next
2 *nm,f* *(prochain)* **le s., la suivante** the next (one); **au s.!** next!
3 *nf* **suivante** *(personnage de théâtre)* attendant

suiveur [sɥivœr] *nm* (a) *(personne sans initiative)* follower (**de** of) (b) *(dans une course cycliste)* **les suiveurs** = officials and backup squads following a cycle race

suivi, -e [sɥivi] **1** *adj* (a) *(discours, raisonnement)* coherent (b) *(correspondance)* regular; *(travail, effort, qualité)* consistent (c) *(émission, feuilleton)* popular
2 *nm* *(d'un dossier)* follow-up; *(d'une procédure)* monitoring; **assurer le s. de qch** *(dossier)* to follow sth through; *(progrès, procédure)* to monitor

suivre [65] [sɥivr] **1** *vt* (a) *(aller derrière)* to follow; **nous sommes suivis** we're being followed; **partez, je vous suis** you go, I'll follow; **s. qn des yeux** *ou* **du regard** to follow sb with one's eyes
(b) *(se placer après)* to follow, to come after
(c) *(longer)* to go along, to follow
(d) *(accompagner)* to go with, to accompany
(e) *(ligne de conduite, conseil, intuition)* to follow; **s. son idée** to do things one's own way
(f) *(comprendre)* to follow; **là je ne la suis plus** she's lost me there
(g) *(faire attention à, observer)* *(propos, démonstration)* to follow; *(malade, élève)* to monitor the progress of; **suivez bien ce que je vais dire** pay attention to what I'm about to say; **c'est une affaire à s.** it's worth keeping an eye on
(h) *(mode, traitement, régime)* to follow; **s. le mouvement** to follow the crowd; **s. l'exemple de qn** to follow sb's example; **voici la marche à s.** this is what you have to do
(i) *(assister à)* *(série de concerts, de conférences)* to attend; *(cours)* to follow
2 *vi* (a) *(venir après)* to follow; **le reste du repas suit** the rest of the meal is coming; **les personnes dont les noms suivent** the following people; **faire s. une lettre** to forward a letter; **(prière de) faire s.** *(sur une enveloppe)* please forward; **faire s. ses bagages** to have one's luggage sent on; **à s.** *(à la fin d'un feuilleton)* to be continued
(b) *(comprendre)* to follow; *(faire attention)* to pay attention
(c) *(élève)* to keep up
(d) *Fig (progresser au même rythme)* *(salaire)* to keep up
3 **se suivre** *vpr* to follow each other

sujet¹, -ette [syʒɛ, -ɛt] **1** *adj* **être s. à qch** *(maladie)* to be subject *or* prone to sth; **être s. à caution** to be unconfirmed; **être s. à faire qch** to be apt *or* liable to do sth
2 *nm,f* *(d'un monarque)* subject

sujet² [syʒɛ] *nm* (a) *(cause)* cause (**de** for); **s. de querelle** *ou* **dispute** cause for dispute; **avoir s. de se plaindre** to have cause for complaint (b) *(thème)* subject, topic; **changer de s.** to change the subject; **au s. de qn/qch** about sb/sth; **elle ne m'a rien dit à ce s.** she said nothing to me about it; **à ce s., je voulais vous dire que...** talking of which, I meant to tell you (that)... (c) *Gram & Ling* subject (d) *(individu)* individual; *Scol* **brillant s.** brilliant pupil (e) *(d'une expérience)* subject

sujétion [syʒesjɔ̃] *nf Litt* (a) *(servitude)* subjection (**à** to) (b) *(contrainte)* constraint

sulfate [sylfat] *nm* sulfate

sulfater [sylfate] *vt Agr & Ind* to sulfate

sulfure [sylfyr] *nm* sulfide

sulfureux, -euse [sylfyrø, -øz] *adj* (a) *(substance)* sulfurous;

(eau, source) sulfur (**b**) *Fig (écrits, discours)* subversive; *(charme)* fiendish

sulfurique [sylfyrik] *adj* sulfuric

sulfurisé, -e [sylfyrize] *adj* **papier s.** wax paper

sulky [sylki] *nm* sulky

sultan [syltã] *nm* sultan

sultanat [syltana] *nm* sultanate

sultane [syltan] *nf (épouse d'un sultan)* sultana, sultaness

summum [sɔmɔm] *nm* **le s. de** the height of

sumo [symo] *nm* sumo (wrestling)

sunnite [synit] *adj & nmf* Sunni

sup [syp] *adj inv Fam* **faire des heures s.** to work overtime

super [sypɛr] **1** *adj inv & exclam Fam* great, terrific
2 *nm* premium gas; **s. sans plomb** premium unleaded

super- [sypɛr] *préf Fam* very, really

superbe [sypɛrb] **1** *adj* (**a**) *(lieu, temps, spectacle)* superb, magnificent (**b**) *(personne)* beautiful
2 *nf Litt* pride, haughtiness

superbement [sypɛrbəmã] *adv* superbly, magnificently

supercarburant [sypɛrkarbyrã] *nm* premium gasoline

supercherie [sypɛrʃəri] *nf* deception, hoax

supérette [sypɛrɛt] *nf* superette, mini-market

superfétatoire [sypɛrfetatwar] *adj Litt* superfluous

superficialité [sypɛrfisjalite] *nf* superficiality

superficie [sypɛrfisi] *nf* (**a**) *(étendue)* (surface) area (**b**) *(surface)* surface

superficiel, -elle [sypɛrfisjɛl] *adj* superficial

superficiellement [sypɛrfisjɛlmã] *adv* superficially

superflu, -e [sypɛrfly] **1** *adj* superfluous
2 *nm* **le s.** the superfluous

super-géant [sypɛrʒeã] *(pl* **super-géants**) *nm Sport* super giant slalom, super G

supergrand [sypɛrgrã] *nm* superpower

super-huit [sypɛrɥit] *adj inv & nm inv Cin* super-eight

supérieur, -e [syperjœr] **1** *adj* (**a**) *(plus haut)* upper; **on a dû évacuer les étages supérieurs** the upper floors had to be evacuated; **elle est à l'étage s.** she's on the floor above (**b**) *(plus grand)* superior (**à/en** to/in); **s. à la moyenne** above average (**c**) *(intelligence, esprit)* superior (**d**) *(dans une hiérarchie) (rang, grade)* higher; *(cadre)* senior; **passer dans la classe supérieure** to go up into the class above (**e**) *(manières, ton)* superior, condescending
2 *nm,f aussi Rel* superior

supérieurement [syperjœrmã] *adv* exceptionally

supériorité [syperjɔrite] *nf* superiority

superlatif, -ive [sypɛrlatif, -iv] *adj & nm* superlative

supermarché [sypɛrmarʃe] *nm* supermarket

supernova [sypɛrnɔva] *(pl* **supernovae**) [sypɛrnɔve]) *nf* supernova

superpétrolier [sypɛrpetrɔlje] *nm* supertanker

superposable [sypɛrpozabl] *adj (caisses)* stacking; *(images)* superimposable

superposé, -e [sypɛrpoze] *adj (images)* superimposed

superposer [sypɛrpoze] **1** *vt (caisses)* to stack; *(images)* to superimpose (**à** on); *Ordinat* **s. une écriture** to overwrite
2 se superposer *vpr (caisses, chaises)* to stack, to be stackable; *(images)* to be superimposed

superposition [sypɛrpozisjɔ̃] *nf (de caisses, de chaises)* stacking; *(d'images)* superimposition; *Ordinat* **mode de s. d'écriture** overwrite mode

superproduction [sypɛrprɔdyksjɔ̃] *nf* blockbuster, big-budget movie

superpuissance [sypɛrpɥisãs] *nf* superpower

supersonique [sypɛrsɔnik] *adj* supersonic

superstar [sypɛrstar] *nf* superstar

superstitieux, -euse [sypɛrstisjø, -øz] *adj* superstitious

superstition [sypɛrstisjɔ̃] *nf* superstition

supertanker [sypɛrtãkœr] *nm* supertanker

superviser [sypɛrvize] *vt* to supervise; *Ordinat* to control

superviseur [sypɛrvizœr] *nm* supervisor; *Ordinat* **s. d'alimentation** power supply controller

supervision [sypɛrvizjɔ̃] *nf* supervision

supplanter [syplãte] *vt* to supplant, to supersede

suppléance [sypleãs] *nf* substitute post

suppléant, -e [sypleã, -ãt] **1** *adj (fonctionnaire)* acting, temporary; *(juge)* surrogate
2 *nm,f* substitute, replacement (**de** for)

suppléer [24] [syplee] **1** *vt* (**a**) *(personne)* to stand in for, to replace; **se faire s.** to be replaced (**b**) *Litt (manque)* to supply, to make up (for)
2 suppléer à *vt ind* to make up for, to compensate for

supplément [syplemã] *nm* (**a**) *(surcroît)* **un s. de** *(information, travail)* additional, extra; **en s.** extra (**b**) *(de prix)* extra or additional charge; *(de billet de train)* supplement (**c**) *(livre, magazine)* supplement (**d**) *(de plat)* extra portion

supplémentaire [syplemãtɛr] *adj* additional, extra

suppliant, -e [syplijã, -ãt] *adj* imploring, pleading

supplication [syplikasjɔ̃] *nf* entreaty, plea

supplice [syplis] *nm* (**a**) *(torture)* torture (**b**) *(tourment, douleur)* torture, agony; **être au s.** to be in agony; **mettre qn au s.** to torture sb

supplicié, -e [syplisje] *nm,f* victim of torture

supplier [66] [syplije] *vt* **s. qn de faire qch** to implore or to beg sb to do sth; **je vous en supplie!** I beg you!

supplique [syplik] *nf* petition

support [sypɔr] *nm* (**a**) *(étai)* support (**b**) *(d'outils, de lampe)* stand (**c**) *Fig (de communication)* medium; **s. audiovisuel** audiovisual aid; **s. publicitaire** advertising medium; **s. visuel** visual aid (**d**) *Ordinat* **s. d'affichage** billboard; **s. de sortie** output medium; **s. de souris** mouse support; **s. de stockage** storage medium

supportable [sypɔrtabl] *adj* (**a**) *(douleur)* bearable; *(comportement)* tolerable (**b**) *(acceptable)* reasonable

supporter¹ [sypɔrtɛr] *nm* supporter

supporter² [sypɔrte] **1** *vt* (**a**) *(résister à) (sujet: matériau, plante)* to withstand; **je supporte bien la chaleur** I can take the heat; **il ne supporterait pas le voyage** the journey would kill him; **je ne supporte pas l'aspirine/l'alcool** I can't take aspirin/alcohol (**b**) *(tolérer) (personne, situation)* to put up with; **je ne la supporte pas** I can't stand her; **il ne supporte pas qu'on le contredise** he can't stand or bear being contradicted (**c**) *(assumer) (conséquence, coût)* to bear (**d**) *(soutenir) (plafond, structure)* to support
2 se supporter *vpr (l'un l'autre)* to put up with each other; **ils ne se supportent plus** they can't stand each other anymore

supposé, -e [sypoze] *adj (voleur)* alleged; *(auteur)* supposed

supposer [sypoze] *vt* (**a**) *(imaginer)* to suppose, to assume (**que** that); **à s. que...** + *subjunctive* suppose or supposing that...; **on suppose que...** it's thought that...; **être supposé faire qch** to be supposed to do sth (**b**) *(impliquer)* to imply (**que** that)

supposition [sypozisjɔ̃] *nf* supposition, assumption

suppositoire [sypozitwar] *nm* suppository

suppôt [sypo] *nm* henchman; **s. de Satan** fiend

suppression [sypresjɔ̃] *nf* (**a**) *(de loi, d'impôt)* abolition; *(de train)* cancellation; *(de crédits, d'emploi, de service)* axing (**b**) *(de mot, de phrase)* deletion (**c**) *Jur (de document)* suppression

supprimer [syprime] **1** *vt* (**a**) *(loi, impôt)* to abolish; *(autobus, train)* to cancel; *(financement, crédits)* to withdraw; *(emploi, service)* to ax; *(mot, phrase)* to delete (**b**) *Jur (document)* to suppress (**c**) *(sucre, sel)* to cut out (**de** from) (**d**) *(ôter)* **s. qch à qn** to take sth away from sb (**e**) *(tuer)* to do away with
2 se supprimer *vpr* to do away with oneself

suppurer [sypyre] *vi* to suppurate

supputation [sypytasjɔ̃] *nf* calculation

supputer [sypyte] *vt* to calculate

supranational, -e, -aux, -ales [sypranasjɔnal, -o] *adj* supranational

supranationalité [sypranasjɔnalite] *nf* supranationality

suprématie [sypremasi] *nf* supremacy

suprême [syprɛm] **1** *adj* (a) *(effort, bonheur)* supreme (b) *(dernier)* final, last

2 *nm Culin* **s. de volaille** chicken supreme

suprêmement [syprɛmmɑ̃] *adv* supremely

sur¹ [syr] *prép* (a) *(dessus)* on; *(avec mouvement)* on, onto; **s. la photo** in the picture; **regarder s. la carte** to look at the map; **la clef est s. la porte** the key's in the door; *aussi Fig* **les uns s. les autres** on top of each other

(b) *(au-dessus de)* over, above; **un pont s. une rivière** a bridge over *or* across a river

(c) *(vers)* toward; **fenêtre qui donne s. le jardin** window which looks onto the garden; **la police a tiré s. la foule** the police fired at the crowd; **s. la droite/gauche** on *or* to the right/left

(d) *(à propos de)* on, about; **savoir qch s. qn** to know sth about sb

(e) *(parmi)* out of; **7 s. 10** 7 out of 10; **une fois s. deux** every other time; **une femme s. deux** one in two women

(f) *(mesure)* by; **trois mètres s. deux** ≃ nine feet by six; **virages s. 4 kilomètres** *(sur un panneau)* ≃ bends for 2.5 miles

(g) *(avec)* **vivre s. ses économies** to live on *or* off one's savings; **s. des paroles de Prévert/une musique des Beatles** to words by Prévert/Beatles music; **ne me parle pas s. ce ton!** don't talk to me in that tone of voice!

sur², -e [syr] *adj (fruit)* sour

sur- [syr] *préf* over-

sûr, -e [syr] **1** *adj* (a) *(lieu)* safe; **peu s.** unsafe (b) *(digne de confiance) (personne, mémoire)* trustworthy, reliable; *(ami)* true; *(information, entreprise, goût)* reliable (c) *(certain)* sure, certain (**de** of); **je suis s. de te l'avoir dit** I'm sure I told you; **s. de soi** self-assured; **être s. et certain (de qch)** to be absolutely certain (of sth)

2 *nm* **le plus s. serait de...** the safest thing would be to...

surabondance [syrabɔ̃dɑ̃s] *nf* overabundance; **une s. de richesses/de détails** a wealth of riches/details

surabondant, -e [syrabɔ̃dɑ̃, -ɑ̃t] *adj* overabundant

surabonder [syrabɔ̃de] *vi* to be overabundant

suractivé, -e [syraktive] *adj* superactivated

surajouter [syraʒute] **1** *vt* to add (on)

2 se surajouter *vpr* to be added (on)

suralimentation [syralimɑ̃tasjɔ̃] *nf (de personne)* overfeeding; *(de malade)* feeding up

suralimenter [syralimɑ̃te] *vt (personne)* to overfeed; *(malade)* to feed up

suranné, -e [syrane] *adj* outdated, old-fashioned

surarmement [syrarməmɑ̃] *nm* excessive arms buildup

surbooker [syrbuke] *vt* to overbook

surbooking [syrbukiŋ] *nm* overbooking

surcapacité [syrkapasite] *nf* overcapacity

surcharge [syrʃarʒ] *nf* (a) *(poids) (de bagages)* excess weight; *(de véhicule)* excess load; **prendre des passagers en s.** to take on excess passengers; **rouler en s.** to drive an overloaded vehicle; *Méd* **s. pondérale** excess weight (b) *(action) (de véhicule)* overloading (c) *(d'accumulateur électrique)* overcharge (d) *Fig* **une s. de travail** excess work (e) *(à payer)* surcharge (f) *(correction)* correction

surcharger [45] [syrʃarʒe] *vt* (a) *(véhicule, cheval, estomac)* to overload; **s. qn de travail** to overload sb with work (b) *(accu-*

mulateur électrique) to overcharge (c) *(épreuves, texte)* to write over with corrections

surchauffe [syrʃof] *nf* overheating

surchauffer [syrʃofe] *vt & vi* to overheat

surchoix [syrʃwa] *adj inv* top-quality

surclasser [syrklase] *vt* to outclass

surconsommation [syrkɔ̃sɔmasjɔ̃] *nf* overconsumption

surcroît [syrkrwa] *nm* **un s. de travail/dépenses** extra work/expenditure; **par s., de s.** in addition, moreover

surdéveloppé, -e [syrdevlɔpe] *adj* overdeveloped

surdéveloppement [syrdevlɔpmɑ̃] *nm* overdevelopment

surdimensionné, -e [syrdimɑ̃sjɔne] *adj* oversize(d)

surdiplômé, -e [syrdiplome] *adj* overqualified

surdité [syrdite] *nf* deafness

surdose [syrdoz] *nf* overdose

surdoué, -e [syrdwe] **1** *adj* gifted

2 *nm,f* gifted child

sureau, -x [syro] *nm* elder (tree)

sureffectif [syrefɛktif] *nm* overstaffing; **en s.** surplus

surélevé, -e [syrelve] *adj* (a) *(voie ferrée)* elevated (b) *(arche, rez-de-chaussée)* raised

surélever [46] [syrelve] *vt* to heighten, to raise

sûrement [syrmɑ̃] *adv* (a) *(probablement)* probably (b) *(absolument)* **s.!** certainly!; **s. pas!** certainly not! (c) *(sans risque)* safely

suremploi [syrɑ̃plwa] *nm* overemployment

surenchère [syrɑ̃ʃɛr] *nf (dans une vente)* higher bid; *Fig* **faire de la s.** to try to outdo one's rivals

surenchérir [syrɑ̃ʃerir] *vi* to bid higher; **s. sur qn** to outbid sb; *Fig* to go one further than sb

surencombré, -e [syrɑ̃kɔ̃bre] *adj* congested (**de** with)

surendetté, -e [syrɑ̃dɛte] *adj* overindebted

surendettement [syrɑ̃dɛtmɑ̃] *nm* overindebtedness

surentraîner [syrɑ̃trɛne] *vt* to overtrain

suréquipement [syrekipmɑ̃] *nm* overequipment

suréquiper [syrekipe] *vt* to overequip

surestimer [syrɛstime] **1** *vt* (a) *(importance, capacité, personne)* to overestimate (b) *(œuvre d'art)* to overvalue

2 se surestimer *vpr* to overestimate oneself

sûreté [syrte] *nf* (a) *(absence de danger)* safety; **être en s.** to be safe; **mettre qch en s.** to put sth in a safe place; **pour plus de s.** to be on the safe side; **de s.** *(rasoir, épingle)* safety (b) *(du goût, du jugement)* soundness (c) *(d'un pays)* security; **la s. de l'État** national security

surévaluation [syrevalɥasjɔ̃] *nf* overvaluation

surévaluer [syrevalɥe] *vt (objet, antiquité)* to overvalue; *(efficacité, capacités)* to overestimate

surexcitation [syrɛksitasjɔ̃] *nf* overexcitement

surexciter [syrɛksite] *vt* to overexcite

surexploiter [syrɛksplwate] *vt* to overexploit

surexposer [syrɛkspoze] *vt* to overexpose

surexposition [syrɛkspozisjɔ̃] *nf* overexposure

surf [sœrf] *nm* surfing; **faire du s.** to go surfing, to surf

surface [syrfas] *nf* (a) *(partie extérieure)* surface; **en s.** on the surface; *Fig* superficially; **remonter à la s.** to rise to the surface, to surface; **faire s.** *(remonter, se réveiller)* to surface (b) *(étendue)* (surface) area; **grande s.** large supermarket; **s. de réparation** *(au football)* penalty area; **s. au sol** floor area; **s. utile** floor space; **s. de vente** sales area (c) *Ordinat* **s. d'affichage** display area; **s. d'enregistrement** read-write surface

surfait, -e [syrfɛ, -ɛt] *adj* overrated

surfer [sœrfe] *vi* to surf; **s. sur l'Internet** to surf the Net *or* the Internet

surfeur, -euse [sœrfœr, -øz] *nm,f* surfer

surfiler [syrfile] *vt (vêtement)* to overcast, to oversew

surfin, -e [syrfɛ̃, -in] *adj* superfine

surgé [syrʒe] *nmf Fam* head supervisor *(person in charge of school discipline)*

surgelé, -e [syrʒəle] **1** *adj* frozen
  2 *nmpl* **surgelés** frozen foods

surgeler [39] [syrʒəle] *vt* to freeze

surgénérateur [syrʒeneratœr] *nm* breeder reactor

surgir [syrʒir] *vi (personne)* to appear suddenly; *(difficulté)* to crop up

surhomme [syrɔm] *nm* superman

surhumain, -e [syrymɛ̃, -ɛn] *adj* superhuman

surimposer [syrɛ̃poze] *vt* to overtax

surimposition [syrɛ̃pozisjɔ̃] *nf* overtaxation

surimpression [syrɛ̃presjɔ̃] *nf* **(a)** *(d'images)* superimposition; **en s.** superimposed **(b)** *Ordinat* overprinting, overstrike

Surinam(e) [syrinam] *nm* **le S.** Surinam

surinfection [syrɛ̃fɛksjɔ̃] *nf* secondary infection

surinformation [syrɛ̃fɔrmasjɔ̃] *nf* information overload

surinformé, -e [syrɛ̃fɔrme] *adj* overinformed

surinvestissement [syrɛ̃vɛstismɑ̃] *nm Fin & Psy* overinvestment

sur-le-champ [syrləʃɑ̃] *adv* at once, immediately

surlendemain [syrlɑ̃dmɛ̃] *nm* **le s.** two days later; **le s. de leur départ** two days after they left

surligner [syrliɲe] *vt* to highlight

surligneur [syrliɲœr] *nm* highlighter (pen)

surlouer [syrlwe] *vt* to overbook

surmédiatisation [syrmedjatizasjɔ̃] *nf* excessive media coverage

surmédiatiser [syrmedjatize] *vt* to give excessive media coverage to

surmenage [syrmənaʒ] *nm* overwork; **s. intellectuel** mental strain

surmené, -e [syrməne] *adj* overworked

surmener [46] [syrməne] **1** *vt* to overwork
  2 se surmener *vpr* to overdo it

surmonter [syrmɔ̃te] **1** *vt* **(a)** *(être placé sur)* to surmount **(b)** *Fig (obstacle, difficulté)* to overcome
  2 se surmonter *vpr* to control oneself

surnager [45] [syrnaʒe] *vi* to float (on the surface)

surnaturel, -elle [syrnatyrɛl] **1** *adj* supernatural
  2 *nm* **le s.** the supernatural

surnom [syrnɔ̃] *nm* nickname

surnombre [syrnɔ̃br] *nm* **il y avait trois passagers en s.** there were three passengers too many; **les exemplaires/passagers en s.** the excess copies/passengers

surnommer [syrnɔme] *vt* to nickname

surpasser [syrpase] **1** *vt (rival)* to surpass, to outdo
  2 se surpasser *vpr* to surpass *or* to excel oneself

surpayer [53] [syrpeje] *vt (personne)* to overpay; *(activité)* to pay too much for

surpeuplé, -e [syrpœple] *adj (pays, région)* overpopulated; *(plage)* overcrowded

surpeuplement [syrpœpləmɑ̃] *nm (de pays, de région)* overpopulation; *(de plage)* overcrowding

surplace [syrplas] *nm* **faire du s.** *(cycliste)* to do a track stand; *Fig (automobiliste)* to crawl along; *(dans une carrière, dans des négociations)* to make no headway

surplomb [syrplɔ̃] *nm* overhang; **en s.** overhanging

surplomber [syrplɔ̃be] *vt* to overhang

surplus [syrply] *nm* surplus; **le s. de marchandises** the surplus goods, the goods that are left (over)

surpopulation [syrpɔpylasjɔ̃] *nf* overpopulation

surprenant, -e [syrprənɑ̃, -ɑ̃t] *adj* surprising; **et, chose surprenante...** and surprisingly...

surprendre [58] [syrprɑ̃dr] **1** *vt* **(a)** *(prendre par surprise)* to surprise; **s. qn en train de faire qch** to catch sb doing sth; **être surpris par la pluie** to be caught in the rain **(b)** *(découvrir)* *(conversation)* to overhear; *(regard)* to catch **(c)** *(étonner)* to surprise; **cela me surprendrait qu'il revienne** *ou* **s'il revenait** I'd be surprised if he came back
  2 se surprendre *vpr* **se s. à faire qch** to find oneself doing sth

surpris, -e [syrpri, -iz] *adj* surprised; **être s. de qch/de faire qch** to be surprised at sth/to do sth

surprise [syrpriz] *nf* surprise; **à sa grande s.** to his/her great surprise, much to his/her surprise; **à la s. générale** to everyone's surprise; **sans s.** *(expédition, voyage)* uneventful; **prendre qn par s.** to take sb by surprise

surprise-partie *(pl* **surprises-parties)** [syrprizparti] *nf Vieilli* party

surproduction [syrprɔdyksjɔ̃] *nf* overproduction

surqualifié, -e [syrkalifje] *adj* overqualified

surréalisme [syrrealism] *nm* surrealism

surréaliste [syrrealist] *adj & nmf* surrealist

sursaut [syrso] *nm* **(a)** *(mouvement)* start, jump; **en s.** with a start **(b)** *(regain)* *(d'énergie)* burst

sursauter [syrsote] *vi* to start, to jump; **faire s. qn** to make sb jump, to startle sb

surseoir [10b] [syrswar] **surseoir à** *vt ind (jugement)* to suspend; **s. à l'exécution d'un condamné** to reprieve a condemned man

sursis [syrsi] *nm* **(a)** *(d'exécution) & Fig* reprieve; **un an de prison avec s.** a one-year suspended sentence **(b)** *(de conscrit)* deferment of call-up

sursitaire [syrsitɛr] **1** *adj (conscrit)* provisionally exempted
  2 *nm* provisionally exempted conscript

surtaxe [syrtaks] *nf (de lettre)* surcharge

surtaxé, -e [syrtakse] *adj (numéro de téléphone)* premium-rate

surtout [syrtu] *adv* **(a)** *(particulièrement)* particularly, especially; *Fam* **s. que...** especially as... **(b)** *(avant tout)* above all; **s. pas!** certainly not!

surveillance [syrvejɑ̃s] *nf (de travail, d'élèves)* supervision; *(par la police, par un gardien)* surveillance, observation; *(de malade, de phénomène)* watch; **être sous s.** to be under surveillance; **s. médicale** medical supervision

surveillant, -e [syrvejɑ̃, -ɑ̃t] *nm,f* **(a)** *(d'une prison)* guard **(b)** *(d'un hôpital)* supervisor **(c)** *Scol (pendant les examens)* proctor; *(chargé de la discipline)* supervisor

surveiller [syrveje] **1** *vt* **(a)** *(contrôler)* *(travail, élèves)* to supervise; *(température, cuisson)* to keep a watch on; *(examen)* to supervise **(b)** *(prendre soin de)* to watch (over) **(c)** *(situation)* to keep an eye on; **s. son langage** to watch *or* to mind one's language; **s. sa ligne** to watch one's figure
  2 se surveiller *vpr* to keep a watch on oneself

survenir [70] [syrvənir] *vi (événements)* to occur; *(crise, difficulté)* to arise

survêt [syrvɛt] *nm Fam* = **survêtement**

survêtement [syrvɛtmɑ̃] *nm* tracksuit

survie [syrvi] *nf* survival

survivance [syrvivɑ̃s] *nf (vestige)* survival, relic

survivant, -e [syrvivɑ̃, -ɑ̃t] **1** *adj* surviving
  2 *nm,f* survivor

survivre [72] [syrvivr] **survivre à** *vt ind (personne)* to survive, to outlive; *(période, théorie)* to outlive; *(accident, maladie)* to survive

survol [syrvɔl] *nm* **(a)** **le s. d'un lieu** flying over a place **(b)** *Fig (de problème, de question)* cursory glance (**de** at)

survoler [syrvɔle] *vt* **(a)** *(lieu)* to fly over **(b)** *Fig (problème, question)* to skim over

survolté, -e [syrvɔlte] *adj Fam (personne)* overexcited; *(ambiance)* highly charged

sus [sys, sy] **1** *exclam* **s. à l'ennemi!** at them!

2 *adv* **en s.** in addition; **en s. de** in addition to, over and above

susceptibilité [syseptibilite] *nf* touchiness, sensitivity; **ménager la s. de qn** to tread carefully where sb is concerned

susceptible [syseptibl] *adj* (a) *(ombrageux)* touchy, sensitive (b) **s. de** *(interprétations, critiques)* open to; **être s. de faire qch** to be liable *or* likely to do sth

susciter [sysite] *vt* *(ennuis, problèmes)* to cause, to create; *(étonnement)* to cause; *(hostilité, intérêt)* to arouse; *(admiration, commentaires)* to attract

susdit, -e [sysdi, -it] *adj* aforesaid, above-mentioned

susmentionné, -e [sysmãsjɔne] *adj* above-mentioned, aforesaid

susnommé, -e [sysnɔme] *adj & nm,f* above-named

suspect, -e [syspɛ(kt), -ɛkt] **1** *adj* *(personne, action)* suspicious, suspect; *(idées, preuve, aliment)* suspect; **s. de qch** suspected of sth

2 *nm,f* suspect

suspecter [syspɛkte] *vt* *(personne)* to suspect (**de** of); *(sincérité)* to suspect, to question

suspendre [syspãdr] **1** *vt* (a) *(vêtements, tableau, hamac)* to hang (up); **s. qch au mur/au plafond** to hang sth on the wall/from the ceiling (b) *(interrompre)* to suspend; *(séance)* to adjourn (c) *(démettre de ses fonctions)* to suspend

2 se suspendre *vpr* to hang (**à** from)

suspendu, -e [syspãdy] *adj* (a) *(pendu)* hanging; **s. au mur/au plafond** hanging on the wall/from the ceiling; *Fig* **être s. aux lèvres de qn** to be hanging on sb's every word (b) *(interrompu)* suspended; *(séance)* adjourned

suspens [syspã] **en suspens** *adv* (a) *(en l'air)* suspended (b) *(en attente)* outstanding

suspense [syspɛns] *nm* suspense

suspension [syspãsjɔ̃] *nf* (a) *(de négociations, d'un travail)* suspension; *(d'une séance)* adjournment (b) *(retrait)* **s. du permis de conduire** driving ban (c) *(mise à pied)* suspension (d) *(de voiture)* suspension

suspicieux, -euse [syspisjø, -øz] *adj* suspicious

suspicion [syspisjɔ̃] *nf* suspicion

sustenter [systãte] **se sustenter** *vpr Hum* to take sustenance

susurrer [sysyre] *vt & vi* to whisper, to murmur

suture [sytyr] *nf* suture; **point de s.** stitch

suzerain, -e [syzrɛ̃, -ɛn] *nm,f* suzerain

svastika [svastika] *nm* swastika

svelte [svɛlt] *adj* slender

sveltesse [svɛltɛs] *nf* slenderness

SVP [ɛsvepe] *(abrév* **s'il vous plaît)** please

swahili, -e [swaili] **1** *adj* Swahili

2 *nm (langue)* Swahili

Swaziland [swazilãd] *nm* **le S.** Swaziland

sweat-shirt *(pl* **sweat-shirts)** [switʃœrt, swɛtʃœrt] *nm* sweatshirt

swing [swiŋ] *nm* swing

swinguer [swiŋge] *vi* to swing

sycomore [sikɔmɔr] *nm* sycamore (tree)

syllabe [silab] *nf* syllable

syllabique [silabik] *adj* syllabic

sylphide [silfid] *nf* sylph

sylvestre [silvɛstr] *adj* woodland, sylvan

sylviculture [silvikyltyr] *nf* forestry

symbiose [sɛ̃bjoz] *nf* symbiosis; *Fig* **en s. avec qn/qch** in harmony with sb/sth

symbole [sɛ̃bɔl] *nm* symbol

symbolique [sɛ̃bɔlik] **1** *adj* symbolic; *(paiement, geste)* token

2 *nf (système de symboles)* system of symbols

symboliquement [sɛ̃bɔlikmã] *adv* symbolically

symboliser [sɛ̃bɔlize] *vt* to symbolize

symbolisme [sɛ̃bɔlism] *nm* symbolism

symétrie [simetri] *nf* symmetry

symétrique [simetrik] *adj* symmetrical

symétriquement [simetrikmã] *adv* symmetrically

sympa [sɛ̃pa] *adj Fam* nice

sympathie [sɛ̃pati] *nf* (a) *(affinité)* liking; **avoir** *ou* **éprouver de la s. pour qn** to like sb; **inspirer la s.** to be likable (b) *(compassion, condoléances)* sympathy

sympathique [sɛ̃patik] *adj* (a) *(agréable)* nice (b) *Anat* sympathetic

sympathisant, -e [sɛ̃patizã, -ãt] *nm,f* sympathizer

sympathiser [sɛ̃patize] *vi* to get on well (**avec** with)

symphonie [sɛ̃fɔni] *nf* symphony

symphonique [sɛ̃fɔnik] *adj* *(forme, poème)* symphonic; *(orchestre)* symphony

symposium [sɛ̃pozjɔm] *nm* symposium

symptomatique [sɛ̃ptɔmatik] *adj* symptomatic (**de** of)

symptôme [sɛ̃ptom] *nm* symptom

synagogue [sinagɔg] *nf* synagogue

synchrone [sɛ̃kron] *adj* synchronous (**avec** with)

synchronisation [sɛ̃krɔnizasjɔ̃] *nf* synchronization

synchroniser [sɛ̃krɔnize] *vt* to synchronize (**avec** with)

synclinal, -e, -aux, -ales [sɛ̃klinal, -o] *adj* synclinal

syncope [sɛ̃kɔp] *nf* (a) *(perte de connaissance)* blackout; **tomber en s.** to black out; *Fam* **elle a failli avoir une s.** she nearly fainted (b) *Mus* syncopation

syncopé, -e [sɛ̃kɔpe] *adj Mus* syncopated

syndic [sɛ̃dik] *nm* **s. (de copropriété)** property manager

> ### Syndic
> A "syndic" is an administrative body which represents the interests of the owners of all the apartments in a building, collectively known as the "syndicat de copropriété". The role of the "syndic" is to ensure the upkeep of the building and to organize meetings during which a vote is taken on any repairs, improvements, etc., that are deemed necessary. The services of the "syndic" are paid for by the owners of the apartments.

syndical, -e, -aux, -ales [sɛ̃dikal, -o] *adj* (labor) union

syndicaliser [sɛ̃dikalize] = **syndiquer**

syndicalisme [sɛ̃dikalism] *nm* (a) *(mouvement)* labor unionism (b) *(activité)* **faire du s.** to be involved in labor union activities

syndicaliste [sɛ̃dikalist] **1** *adj* (labor) union

2 *nmf* (labor) union activist

syndicat [sɛ̃dika] *nm* (a) *(de travailleurs)* (labor) union (b) *(d'employeurs, de producteurs)* association; **s. patronal** employers' association (c) **s. d'initiative** tourist (information) office

syndiqué, -e [sɛ̃dike] **1** *adj* belonging to a (labor) union; **être s.** to belong to a (labor) union

2 *nm,f* (labor) union member

syndiquer [sɛ̃dike] **1** *vt* to unionize

2 se syndiquer *vpr* (a) *(se constituer en syndicat)* to form a (labor) union (b) *(adhérer à un syndicat)* to join a (labor) union

syndrome [sɛ̃drom] *nm Méd* syndrome; **s. prémenstruel** premenstrual syndrome

synergie [sinɛrʒi] *nf* synergy

synode [sinɔd] *nm* synod

synonyme [sinɔnim] **1** *adj* synonymous (**de** with)

2 *nm* synonym

synopsis [sinɔpsis] *nm Cin* synopsis

synovial, -e, -aux, -ales [sinɔvjal, -o] *adj* synovial

syntagme [sɛ̃tagm] *nm* phrase

syntaxe [sɛ̃taks] *nf Gram & Ordinat* syntax

syntaxique [sɛ̃taksik] *adj* (**a**) *Gram* syntactic (**b**) *Ordinat* syntax

synthèse [sɛ̃tɛz] *nf* (**a**) *(exposé)* summary; **faire la s. (de qch)** to summarize (sth) (**b**) *(opération chimique)* synthesis; **de s.** synthetic

synthétique [sɛ̃tetik] **1** *adj* (**a**) *(présentation)* all-encompassing; *(bilan)* summary (**b**) *(tissu, fibres)* synthetic, man-made **2** *nm* synthetic material

synthétiser [sɛ̃tetize] *vt* to synthesize

synthétiseur [sɛ̃tetizœr] *nm* synthesizer

syphilis [sifilis] *nf* syphilis

syphilitique [sifilitik] *adj & nmf* syphilitic

Syrie [siri] *nf* **la S.** Syria

syrien, -enne [sirjɛ̃, -ɛn] **1** *adj* Syrian **2** *nm,f* **S., Syrienne** Syrian

systématique [sistematik] *adj (automatique, méthodique)* systematic; **il est toujours en retard, c'est s.** he's consistently late

systématiquement [sistematikmɑ̃] *adv* systematically

systématiser [sistematize] *vt* to systematize

système [sistɛm] *nm* system; *Fam* **il me tape** *ou* **porte sur le s.** he gets on my nerves; **s. D** resourcefulness; *Ordinat* **s. d'exploitation** operating system; *Ordinat* **s. de gestion de bases de données** database management system; **s. nerveux** nervous system; **s. solaire** solar system

T

T, t [te] *nm inv* T, t; **en T** T-shaped; **disposer qch en T** to arrange sth in a T-shape

t' [t] *voir* **te, tu**

T9 [tenœf] *nm Tél* predictive text input

ta [ta] *voir* **ton**[1]

tabac[1] [taba] **1** *nm* (**a**) *(plante, produit)* tobacco; *Fam Fig* **du même t.** of the same ilk; **t. blond** Virginia tobacco; **t. brun** dark tobacco; **t. à chiquer** chewing tobacco; **t. à priser** snuff (**b**) *(boutique)* **(bureau de) t.** tobacco store *(which also sells stamps and lottery tickets)*
2 *adj inv* buff

tabac[2] [taba] *nm* **coup de t.** *(tempête)* squall; *Fam* **passer qn à t.** to beat sb up; *Fam* **faire un t.** to be a big hit

tabagie [tabaʒi] *nf* (**a**) *Fam* **c'est une vraie t. ici** you can't see a thing for the smoke in here (**b**) *Can (bureau de tabac)* tobacco store

tabagisme [tabaʒism] *nm* smoking

tabasser [tabase] *vt Fam* **t. qn** to beat sb up; **se faire t.** to be *or* to get beaten up

tabatière [tabatjɛr] *nf* (**a**) *(boîte)* snuffbox (**b**) *(lucarne)* skylight

tabelle [tabɛl] *nf Suisse* register, list

tabernacle [tabɛrnakl] *nm* tabernacle

tablar(d) [tablar] *nm Suisse* shelf

table [tabl] *nf* (**a**) *(meuble)* table; **mettre** *ou* **dresser la t.** to set the table; **être à t.** to be at the table; **se mettre** *ou* **passer à t.** to sit down at the table; *Fam Fig* **se mettre à t.** *(avouer)* to spill the beans; **à t.!** food's ready!; *Fig* **faire t. rase de qch** to make a clean sweep of sth; **t. basse** coffee table; **t. de billard** billiard table; **t. de chevet** bedside table; **t. de cuisson** cooktop; **t. à dessin** drawing board; **faire t. d'hôte** = to provide a meal where all paying guests eat at the same table; **t. de jeu** card table; **t. à langer** changing table; **t. des négociations** negotiating table; **s'asseoir à la t. des négociations** to sit down to negotiate; **t. de nuit** bedside table; **t. d'opération** operating table; **t. d'orientation** orientation *or* panoramic table; **t. à repasser** ironing board; **t. ronde** *(conférence)* round table; **t. roulante** trolley
(**b**) *(restaurant)* **les meilleures tables de Paris** the finest restaurants in Paris
(**c**) *(écrit)* table; **Tables de la Loi** Tables of the Law; **t. des matières** (table of) contents; **t. de multiplication** multiplication table
(**d**) *(console)* **mettre qn sur t. d'écoute** to tap sb's phone; **il est sur t. d'écoute** his phone is being tapped; **t. de mixage** mixing desk
(**e**) *(d'un instrument à cordes)* **t. d'harmonie** sounding board
(**f**) *Ordinat* **t. à digitaliser** digitizing pad; **t. des fichiers** file allocation table, FAT; **t. traçante** plotter

tableau, -x [tablo] *nm* (**a**) *(panneau, support)* board; **t. (noir)** (black)board; **t. d'affichage** bulletin board; **t. de bord** *(d'une voiture)* dashboard; *(d'un avion)* instrument panel; *Ordinat* control panel; *Ordinat* **t. interactif** interactive whiteboard (**b**)

(œuvre d'art) painting, picture; **t. de maître** old master (**c**) *Fig & Hum (scène)* scene; **faire un joli/charmant t.** to make a pretty/charming sight *or* scene; *Fig* **pour compléter le t. ...** to crown it all ... (**d**) *(au théâtre)* scene; **t. vivant** tableau (vivant) (**e**) *(liste)* list, table; *(graphique)* chart; **t. de chasse** *(de chasseur, d'aviateur)* bag; *Fig (conquêtes)* list of conquests (**f**) *Ordinat* **t. de connexions** plugboard (**g**) *(locutions)* **gagner sur les deux/sur tous les tableaux** to win on both/all counts

tablée [table] *nf (personnes à table)* table

tabler [table] **tabler sur** *vt ind* to count *or* to bank on

tablette [tablɛt] *nf* (**a**) *(d'une étagère)* shelf; *(dans un avion)* table; **t. arrière** *(d'une voiture)* back shelf (**b**) *(de chocolat)* bar; *(de chewing-gum)* stick (**c**) *Ordinat* **t. graphique** graphics tablet

tableur [tablœr] *nm Ordinat* spreadsheet; **t. de graphiques** graphics spreadsheet

tablier [tablije] *nm* (**a**) *(vêtement)* apron; *(d'écolier)* smock; *Fig* **rendre son t.** to hand in one's notice (**b**) *(de cheminée)* hood (**c**) *(de pont)* roadway

tabloïd(e) [tablɔid] *adj & nm* tabloid

tabou, -e [tabu] *adj & nm* taboo

taboulé [tabule] *nm Culin* tabbouleh

tabouret [taburɛ] *nm* stool; **t. de bar/de piano** bar/piano stool

tabulateur [tabylatœr] *nm* tab key, tabulator

tabulation [tabylasjɔ̃] *nf* tab

tac [tak] **du tac au tac** *adv* like a shot

tache [taʃ] *nf* (**a**) *(de boue, de sang, d'huile)* stain; *(de peinture, de couleur, de lumière)* splash; **tu as fait une t. à ta chemise** you have a stain on your shirt; *Fig* **faire t.** to stick out like a sore thumb; **t. d'encre** inkstain; *Fig* **faire t. d'huile** to spread (**b**) *(sur la peau, sur un fruit)* mark; **t. de rousseur** freckle; **t. de vin** strawberry mark (**c**) *Fig (atteinte)* blot, stain; **sans t.** *(réputation)* spotless

taché, -e [taʃe] *adj* stained; **t. d'encre/de sang** ink-/blood-stained

tâche [tɑʃ] *nf* task, job; **être à la t.** to be on piecework; *Ordinat* **t. d'arrière-plan** *ou* **de fond** background task *or* job

tacher [taʃe] **1** *vt* (**a**) *(vêtement)* to stain (**b**) *(réputation)* to sully, to tarnish
2 *vi* to stain
3 se tacher *vpr (personne)* to stain one's clothes; *(tissu, vêtement)* to stain

tâcher [taʃe] **1** *vt* **tâchez que cela ne se reproduise plus** make sure it doesn't happen again
2 tâcher de *vt ind* to try to

tâcheron [tɑʃrɔ̃] *nm Péj* drudge

tacheté, -e [taʃte] *adj* speckled (**de** with); **chat noir t. de blanc** black cat with white markings

tacheter [42] [taʃte] *vt* to spot, to speckle

tachycardie [takikardi] *nf* tachycardia

tachymètre [takimɛtr] *nm* tachometer; *Aut* speedometer

tacite [tasit] *adj* tacit

tacitement [tasitmɑ̃] *adv* tacitly

taciturne [tasityrn] *adj* taciturn

tacot [tako] *nm Fam Péj* jalopy

tact [takt] *nm* tact; **avoir du t.** to be tactful; **plein de t.** very tactful; **manquer de t.** to be tactless

tacticien, -enne [taktisjɛ̃, -ɛn] *nm,f* tactician

tactile [taktil] *adj* tactile

tactique [taktik] **1** *adj* tactical
   2 *nf* tactics *(pluriel)*

tadjik [tadʒik] **1** *adj* Tadjik
   2 *nmf* **T.** Tadjik

Tadjikistan [tadʒikistɑ̃] *nm* **le T.** Tadjikistan

taf [taf] *nm très Fam (travail)* work; *(emploi)* job; **j'ai du t.** *(travail)* I have work to do; *(emploi)* I have a job

taffe [taf] *nf très Fam (de cigarette)* drag

taffetas [tafta] *nm* taffeta

tag [tag] *nm* tag *(piece of graffiti)*

Tage [taʒ] *nm* **le T.** the Tagus

tagliatelle [taljatɛl] *nf* piece *or* strand of tagliatelle; **des tagliatelles** tagliatelle

taguer [tage] *vt* to cover in graffiti

tagueur, -euse [tagœr, -øz] *nm,f* tagger *(graffiti artist)*

Tahiti [taiti] *n* Tahiti

tahitien, -enne [taisjɛ̃, -ɛn] **1** *adj* Tahitian
   2 *nm (langue)* Tahitian
   3 *nm,f* **T., Tahitienne** Tahitian

tai chi [tajʃi] *nm* tai chi

taie [tɛ] *nf* **(a)** *(enveloppe)* **t. (d'oreiller)** pillowcase, pillow slip **(b)** *(sur l'œil)* leucoma

taïga [taiga] *nf* taiga

taillader [tajade] *vt* to slash, to gash

taille [taj] *nf* **(a)** *(dimensions)* size; **une pêche de la t. d'un melon** a peach the size of a melon; **quelle t. faites-vous?** what size are you?, what size do you take?; **la t. en dessus/dessous** the next size up/down; **t. unique** one size **(b)** *(hauteur)* height; **de petite t.** short; *Fig* **être de t. à faire qch** to be capable of doing sth; *Fig* **trouver un adversaire à sa t.** to meet one's match **(c)** *(importance)* **de t.** *(erreur, mensonge)* big **(d)** *(partie du corps, sur un vêtement)* waist; **avoir la t. fine** to have a slim waist; **avoir une t. de guêpe** to be wasp-waisted; **pantalon à t. basse** hiphuggers **(e)** *(action) (de pierre)* cutting; *(d'un arbre)* pruning; *(d'une haie)* trimming **(f)** *Ordinat* **t. de champ** field size; **t. de disque dur** hard disk size; **t. de mémoire** memory size **(g)** *Hist (impôt)* tallage

taillé, -e [taje] *adj* **être t. pour faire qch** to be cut out to do sth

taille-crayon *(pl* **taille-crayon** *ou* **taille-crayons)** [tajkrɛjɔ̃] *nm* pencil sharpener

tailler [taje] **1** *vt* **(a)** *(pierre, diamant)* to cut; *(arbre, vigne)* to prune; *(haie, barbe)* to trim; *(crayon)* to sharpen; **t. une armée en pièces** to cut an army to pieces **(b)** *(vêtement)* to cut out
   2 se tailler *vpr* **(a)** *(se couper)* **se t. la barbe** to trim one's beard **(b)** *(se faire)* **se t. un chemin à travers qch** to carve one's way through sth **(c)** *(s'attribuer)* **se t. un beau succès** to be very successful; **se t. un empire** to carve out an empire for oneself **(d)** *Fam (partir)* to beat it

tailleur [tajœr] *nm* **(a)** *(couturier)* tailor **(b)** *(ensemble pour femme)* suit **(c)** **s'asseoir en t.** to sit cross-legged

tailleur-pantalon *(pl* **tailleurs-pantalons)** [tajœrpɑ̃talɔ̃] *nm* pantsuit

taillis [taji] *nm* copse, coppice

tain [tɛ̃] *nm* silvering; **glace** *ou* **miroir sans t.** two-way mirror

taire [55b] [tɛr] **1** *vt (affaire, secret)* to say nothing about, not to mention; *(vérité)* to hide; **une personne dont je tairai le nom** a person who shall remain nameless
   2 se taire *vpr* **(a)** *(être silencieux)* to be quiet *or* silent; *(cesser de parler)* to stop talking, to fall silent; *(décider de ne rien dire)* to keep quiet *or* silent; **tais-toi!** be quiet!; **faire t. qn** to make sb

be quiet; *(adversaire, critique)* to silence; **tu as perdu une occasion de te t.** you should have kept your mouth shut **(b)** *(bruit)* to stop

taisais, taise, *etc. voir* **taire**

Taiwan [tajwan] *n* Taiwan

taiwanais, -e [tajwanɛ, -ɛz] **1** *adj* Taiwanese
   2 *nm,f* **T., Taiwanaise** Taiwanese

tajine [taʒin] *nm* tajine

talc [talk] *nm* talcum powder, talc

talé, -e [tale] *adj* bruised

talent [talɑ̃] *nm* **(a)** *(don)* talent; **son t. de pianiste** his talent as a pianist; **homme/musicien de t.** talented man/musician; **avoir du t.** to be talented **(b)** *(artiste)* **un jeune t.** a talented newcomer

talentueusement [talɑ̃tɥøzmɑ̃] *adv* with talent

talentueux, -euse [talɑ̃tɥø, -øz] *adj* talented

talion [taljɔ̃] *nm voir* **loi**

talisman [talismɑ̃] *nm* talisman

talkie-walkie *(pl* **talkies-walkies)** [tɔkiwɔki] *nm* walkie-talkie

Tallinn [talin] *n* Tallin

Talmud [talmyd] *nm* **le T.** the Talmud

taloche [talɔʃ] *nf Fam (gifle)* thump

talon [talɔ̃] *nm* **(a)** *(du pied, de chaussure, de bas)* heel; *Fig* **être sur les talons de qn** to be on sb's heels; **t. d'Achille** Achilles' heel; **talons aiguilles** stiletto heels; *(chaussures)* stilettos; **talons hauts** high heels; **talons plats** flat heels **(b)** *(de chèque)* stub **(c)** *(aux cartes)* stock

talonner [talɔne] **1** *vt* **(a)** *(suivre)* **t. qn** to follow on sb's heels **(b)** *(cheval)* to spur on
   2 *vi (au rugby)* to heel

talonnette [talɔnɛt] *nf (dans une chaussure)* heel pad

talonneur [talɔnœr] *nm (au rugby)* hooker

talquer [talke] *vt* to put talcum powder on

talus [taly] *nm* **(a)** *(terrain en pente)* slope **(b)** *(d'une voie ferrée, d'un canal)* embankment

tamanoir [tamanwar] *nm* great anteater

tamaris [tamaris] *nm* tamarisk

tambouille [tɑ̃buj] *nf Fam* **(a)** *(cuisine)* cooking; **faire la t.** to do the cooking **(b)** *(nourriture)* grub

tambour [tɑ̃bur] *nm* **(a)** *(instrument de musique)* drum; **sans t. ni trompette** quietly, without any fanfare; **faire qch t. battant** to do sth briskly **(b)** *(personne)* drummer **(c)** *(d'une machine à laver)* drum; **t. de frein** brake drum **(d)** *(à broder)* (embroidery) hoop, tambour

tambourin [tɑ̃burɛ̃] *nm (instrument plat)* tambourine; *(tambour)* tambourin

tambouriner [tɑ̃burine] **1** *vi* to drum
   2 *vt* to drum out

tamis [tami] *nm (pour la farine)* sieve; *(pour le sable)* sifter; **passer au t.** *(farine)* to sieve; *(sable)* to sift

Tamise [tamiz] *nf* **la T.** the Thames

tamisé, -e [tamize] *adj (lumière)* subdued

tamiser [tamize] *vt (farine)* to sieve; *(sable)* to sift

tamoul, -e [tamul] **1** *adj* Tamil
   2 *nm (langue)* Tamil
   3 *nm,f* **T., Tamoule** Tamil

tampon [tɑ̃pɔ̃] **1** *nm* **(a)** *(de coton)* pad; **t. hygiénique** *ou* **périodique** tampon **(b)** *(cachet, instrument)* stamp; *(de la poste)* postmark; **t. dateur** date stamp; **t. encreur** ink pad **(c)** *(pour nettoyer)* pad; **t. à récurer** scourer, scouring pad **(d)** *(bouchon)* plug, stopper **(e)** *(à l'extrémité des wagons)* & *Fig* buffer
   2 *adj inv* **État/zone t.** buffer state/zone

tamponner [tɑ̃pɔne] **1** *vt* **(a)** *(document)* to stamp; *(lettre)* to postmark **(b)** *(plaie)* to dab **(c)** *(heurter)* to crash into
   2 se tamponner *vpr* **(a)** *(se heurter)* to crash into each

other (**b**) *(s'essuyer)* **se t. le front** to mop one's brow; **se t. les yeux** to dab one's eyes; *très Fam* **s'en t. (le coquillard)** not to give a damn

tamponneuse [tɑ̃pɔnøz] *adj f voir* **auto**

tam-tam (*pl* **tam-tams**) [tamtam] *nm (tambour africain)* tom-tom

tancer [16] [tɑ̃se] *vt Litt* to berate, to scold

tanche [tɑ̃ʃ] *nf* tench

tandem [tɑ̃dɛm] *nm* (**a**) *(bicyclette)* tandem (**b**) *(groupe de deux personnes)* duo; **travailler en t.** to work in tandem

tandis [tɑ̃di, tɑ̃dis] **tandis que** *conj* (**a**) *(marque l'opposition)* while, whereas (**b**) *(marque la simultanéité)* while

tanga [tɑ̃ga] *nm* thong, tanga

tangage [tɑ̃gaʒ] *nm (d'un bateau)* pitching

tangent, -e [tɑ̃ʒɑ̃, -ɑ̃t] **1** *adj* Math tangential (**à** to); *Fig* **c'était t.** it was touch and go, it was a near thing

2 *nf* **tangente** *Math* tangent (**à** to); *Fam* **prendre la tangente** *(partir)* to slip away

tangible [tɑ̃ʒibl] *adj* tangible

tango [tɑ̃go] *nm (danse, musique)* tango; **danser le t.** to tango, to dance the tango

tanguer [tɑ̃ge] *vi (bateau)* to pitch; **tout tanguait autour de moi** everything was spinning around me

tanière [tanjɛr] *nf* (**a**) *(d'animal)* den, lair (**b**) *(retraite)* retreat

tanin [tanɛ̃] *nm* tannin

tank [tɑ̃k] *nm* tank

tanker [tɑ̃kœr] *nm* tanker

tannant, -e [tanɑ̃, -ɑ̃t] *adj Fam (ennuyeux)* annoying

tanné, -e [tane] *adj* (**a**) *(hâlé)* weather-beaten (**b**) *Can Fam* **être t.** *(en avoir assez)* to be fed up

tanner [tane] *vt* (**a**) *(peaux)* to tan (**b**) *Fam (harceler)* to pester

tannerie [tanri] *nf (établissement)* tannery; *(industrie)* tanning

tanneur [tanœr] *nm* tanner

tannin [tanɛ̃] = **tanin**

tant [tɑ̃] *adv* (**a**) *(tellement, à tel point)* so much; **t. de** *(quantité)* so much; *(nombre)* so many; **j'ai t. mangé que j'ai vomi** I ate so much I threw up; **pas t. que ça** *(quantité)* not that much; *(nombre)* not that many; **t. il est vrai que...** since it is the case that...

(**b**) *(dans des comparaisons)* **t. que** as much as; **t. pour vous que pour moi** for you as much as for me; **n'aimer rien t. que...** to like nothing more than...

(**c**) *(substitué à un chiffre, à une date)* **t. pour cent** so much per cent; **votre lettre du t.** your letter of such and such a date

(**d**) **t. que** *(aussi longtemps que)* as long as; *(pendant que)* while; **t. que vous y êtes** while you're at it

(**e**) *(locutions)* **t. bien que mal** somehow or other; **t. et si bien que** so much so that; **t. s'en faut** far from it; **s'il était un t. soit peu intelligent** if he was at all intelligent; **t. qu'à faire, autant en acheter deux** you/we/*etc.* might as well buy two; **en t. que** *(comme)* as; **t. mieux!** so much the better!; **t. mieux pour toi!** good for you!; **t. pis!** too bad!; **t. pis pour toi!** too bad (for you)!

tante [tɑ̃t] *nf* (**a**) *(parente)* aunt (**b**) *très Fam (homosexuel)* queer, = offensive term used to refer to a male homosexual

tantine [tɑ̃tin] *nf Fam* auntie, aunty

tantinet [tɑ̃tinɛ] *nm Fam* **un t.** a tiny bit

tantôt [tɑ̃to] *adv* (**a**) *(parfois)* **t. triste, t. gai** sometimes sad, sometimes happy (**b**) *(cet après-midi)* this afternoon

Tanzanie [tɑ̃zani] *nf* **la T.** Tanzania

tanzanien, -enne [tɑ̃zanjɛ̃, -ɛn] **1** *adj* Tanzanian

2 *nm,f* **T., Tanzanienne** Tanzanian

taoïsme [taoism] *nm* Taoism

taon [tɑ̃] *nm* gadfly, horsefly

tapage [tapaʒ] *nm* (**a**) *(bruit)* din, row; **faire du t.** to kick up a din *or* row; **t. nocturne** breach of the peace *(at night)* (**b**) *(publicité)* fuss; **faire du t. autour de qch** to make a fuss about sth

tapageur, -euse [tapaʒœr, -øz] *adj* (**a**) *(enfant)* rowdy (**b**) *(vêtements, couleur)* loud, flashy; *(publicité)* blatant (**c**) *(liaison)* scandalous

tapant, -e [tapɑ̃, -ɑ̃t] *adj* **à sept/dix heures t.** *ou* **tapantes** at seven/ten o'clock sharp

tape [tap] *nf (pour punir)* tap; *(affectueuse)* pat

tapé, -e [tape] *adj Fam (fou)* crazy

tape-à-l'œil [tapalœj] *Fam* **1** *adj inv* gaudy, flashy

2 *nm* **c'est du t.** it's just show

tapecul [tapky] *nm Fam (véhicule)* rattletrap

taper [tape] **1** *vt* (**a**) *(frapper)* to hit; *(affectueusement)* to pat; *(table)* to bang

(**b**) *(dactylographier)* **t. qch (à la machine)** to type sth

(**c**) *Ordinat* to key; **tapez entrée ou retour** select enter or return

(**d**) *Fam (emprunter de l'argent à)* to bum money off; **t. qn de dix euros** to bum ten euros off sb

2 *vi* (**a**) *(frapper)* to knock; *(avec le poing)* to bang; **t. à la porte** to knock on the door; **t. du pied** to stamp one's foot; **t. du poing sur qch** to bang on sth; **t. dans un ballon** to kick a ball around; *Fam* **t. dans l'œil à qn** to take sb's fancy; **t. sur qn** to hit sb; *Fig (critiquer)* to knock sb

(**b**) *(soleil)* to beat down; *Fam* **ça tape** it's scorching

(**c**) *(dactylographier)* **t. (à la machine)** to type; **t. au toucher** to touch-type

3 **se taper** *vpr* (**a**) *(se cogner)* **se t. la tête/le coude** to bang one's head/elbow; *Fig* **c'est à se t. la tête contre les murs** it's enough to drive you up the wall

(**b**) *Fam (repas, boisson)* to have; **je me taperais bien une bière** I could stand a beer

(**c**) *Fam (corvée)* to get stuck with; **on s'est tapé les embouteillages** we got stuck in the traffic jams

(**d**) *très Fam (coucher avec)* to screw

(**e**) *Fam (se moquer)* **ses histoires de fesses, je m'en tape!** I couldn't care less about his/her sex life!

tapette [tapɛt] *nf* (**a**) *(pour tapis)* carpet beater; *(contre les mouches)* fly swatter (**b**) *(piège)* **t. (à souris)** mousetrap (**c**) *(petite tape)* tap (**d**) *très Fam (homosexuel)* queer, = offensive term used to refer to a male homosexual

tapeur, -euse [tapœr, -øz] *nm,f Fam* scrounger, sponger

tapin [tapɛ̃] *nm très Fam* **faire le t.** to work the streets

tapinois [tapinwa] **en tapinois** *adv* stealthily

tapioca [tapjɔka] *nm* tapioca

tapir¹ [tapir] *nm* tapir

tapir² [tapir] **se tapir** *vpr (se blottir)* to crouch; *(se cacher)* to hide

tapis [tapi] *nm* (**a**) *(de sol)* carpet; *(de petite taille)* rug; *Fig* **mettre qch sur le t.** to bring sth up for discussion; **t. roulant** *(de marchandises, pour bagages)* conveyor belt; *(pour piétons)* moving walkway, travelator; **t. de salle de bain** bath mat; **t. de sol** earth mat; *Ordinat* **t. de souris** mouse pad; **t. de yoga** yoga mat (**b**) *(en boxe)* canvas; **aller au t.** to go down; **envoyer qn au t.** to floor sb

tapis-brosse (*pl* **tapis-brosses**) [tapibrɔs] *nm* doormat

tapisser [tapise] *vt* (**a**) *(pièce, appartement)* to paper, to wallpaper; *(fauteuil, canapé)* to upholster (**b**) *(couvrir)* **être tapissé de** *(sujet: mur)* to be covered with; *(sujet: sol)* to be carpeted with (**c**) *(paroi d'un organe)* to line

tapisserie [tapisri] *nf* (**a**) *(broderie)* tapestry work; **faire de la t.** to do tapestry work (**b**) *(tenture)* tapestry; *Fig* **faire t.** to be a wallflower (**c**) *(papier peint)* wallpaper

tapissier, -ère [tapisje, -ɛr] *nm,f* (**a**) *(tisseur)* tapestry maker (**b**) *(de meubles)* upholsterer (**c**) *(décorateur)* interior decorator

tapotement [tapɔtmɑ̃] *nm* tapping

tapoter [tapɔte] **1** *vt* to tap; *(joue, main)* to pat

2 *vi* **t. sur qch** to tap on sth

tapuscrit [tapyskri] *nm* typescript

taquet [takɛ] *nm* (**a**) *(de machine à écrire)* stop; *Ordinat* **t. de tabulation** tab stop (**b**) *(butée)* stop

taquin, -e [takɛ̃, -in] *adj* teasing

taquiner [takine] *vt (faire enrager)* to tease

taquinerie [takinri] *nf* **ce n'est qu'une t.** I'm/he's/she's/*etc.* only teasing; **j'en ai assez de ses taquineries** I've had enough of his/her teasing

tarabiscoté, -e [tarabiskɔte] *adj* overelaborate

tarabuster [tarabyste] *vt* (**a**) *(harceler)* to pester (**b**) *(préoccuper)* to bother

tarama [tarama] *nm* taramasalata

taratata [taratata] *exclam Fam* nonsense!

tarauder [tarode] *vt* (**a**) *(acier)* to tap (**b**) *(obséder)* to gnaw at

tard [tar] **1** *adv* late; **plus t.** later (on); **au plus t.** at the latest; **t. dans la nuit** late at night; **pas plus t. qu'hier** only yesterday

2 *nm* **sur le t.** late in life

tarder [tarde] **1** *vi* to delay; **pourquoi tarde-t-elle?** why is she taking so long?; **il ne devrait pas t.** he shouldn't be long; **tu vas recevoir une gifle, cela ne va pas t.** you're going to get slapped before long; **sans t.** without delay; **t. à faire qch** to take a long time to do sth

2 *v impersonnel* **il me tarde de partir/qu'elle parte** I can't wait to leave/for her to leave

tardif, -ive [tardif, -iv] *adj (regrets, excuse)* belated; *(heure, récolte)* late

tardivement [tardivmɑ̃] *adv (prendre des mesures, s'excuser)* belatedly; *(rentrer, arriver)* late; *(se marier)* late in life

tare [tar] *nf* (**a**) *(défaut)* defect; *Hum* **ça n'est pas une t.!** it's not a crime! (**b**) *(pour calculer le poids net)* tare

taré, -e [tare] *adj* (**a**) *(anormal)* retarded (**b**) *Fam (fou)* crazy

tarentule [tarɑ̃tyl] *nf* tarantula

targette [tarʒɛt] *nf* bolt

targuer [targe] **se targuer** *vpr* **se t. de qch/de faire qch** to pride oneself on sth/on doing sth

tarif [tarif] *nm* (**a**) *(tableau des prix)* price list (**b**) *(prix)* rate; *(d'un billet d'avion, de train)* fare; **quels sont vos tarifs?** how much do you charge? (**c**) *(pour passagers)* to pay full fare; *(pour marchandises)* to pay the full rate; **faire un t. réduit pour les étudiants** to offer a student discount; **t. douanier** customs rate; **tarifs postaux** postal rates

tarifaire [tarifɛr] *adj (lois)* tariff

tarifer [tarife] *vt* to price

tarification [tarifikasjɔ̃] *nf* pricing

tarin [tarɛ̃] *nm Fam (nez)* schnozz, snoot

tarir [tarir] **1** *vt (source, rivière)* to dry up; *(larmes)* to dry; *(créativité, inspiration)* to cause to dry up

2 *vi* (**a**) *(eau, source)* to dry up (**b**) *Fig (conversation, inspiration)* to dry up; **il ne tarit pas sur le sujet** he never stops talking *or* shuts up about it; **ne pas t. d'éloges sur qn/qch** to be full of praise for sb/sth

3 **se tarir** *vpr* to dry up

tarissement [tarismɑ̃] *nm* drying up

tarot [taro] *nm* tarot; **jouer aux tarots** to play tarot

tartan [tartɑ̃] *nm* tartan

tartare [tartar] **1** *adj (sauce)* tartar; *(steak)* tartare

2 *nm (steak)* steak tartare *(raw minced beef served with a raw egg)*

3 *nmf* **T.** Tartar

tarte [tart] **1** *nf* (**a**) *(salée ou sucrée)* (open) pie; *Fam* **ce n'est pas de la t.** it's no easy matter; **t. à la crème** *(au cinéma)* custard pie; *Fig* cliché; **t. aux pommes** apple pie; **t. Tatin** tarte Tatin *(caramelized apples covered in shortcrust pastry and turned out upside down)* (**b**) *Fam (gifle)* slap

2 *adj Fam* (**a**) *(ridicule)* stupid-looking, dorky (**b**) *(stupide)* thick

tartelette [tartəlɛt] *nf* tartlet

Tartempion [tartɑ̃pjɔ̃] *nm Fam* so-and-so

tartignole [tartiɲɔl] *adj Fam* ridiculous

tartine [tartin] *nf* (**a**) *(tranche de pain)* slice of bread and butter; **t. de confiture** slice of bread and jam; **faire des tartines** to butter (some) bread (**b**) *Fam (texte)* screed; **en mettre des tartines** to write reams

tartiner [tartine] *vt* (**a**) *(beurre, pain)* to spread (**b**) *Fam (enduire en grande quantité)* **t. qn/qch de qch** to cover sb/sth in sth (**c**) *Fam (texte)* to churn out

tartre [tartr] *nm* (**a**) *(des dents, du vin)* tartar (**b**) *(dans une chaudière, dans une bouilloire)* scale

tas [ta] *nm* (**a**) *(amas)* pile, heap; **mettre qch en t.** to pile sth up (**b**) *Fam (grand nombre)* **un t. de, des t. de** a ton of (**c**) *(locutions)* **apprendre qch sur le t.** to learn sth on the job; *Fam* **dans le t. il y en aura bien un qui t'ira** you'll find one to suit you out of all that lot; *Fam* **tirer dans le t.** to fire at random

Tasmanie [tasmani] *nf* **la T.** Tasmania

tasse [tas] *nf* cup; **t. à café/thé** coffee/tea cup; **t. de café/thé** cup of coffee/tea; *Fam Fig* **boire la t.** *(en nageant)* to get a mouthful of water

tassé, -e [tase] *adj* (**a**) *(serré)* crammed, squashed (**b**) *Fam* **bien t.** *(fort)* *(café)* strong; *(alcool)* stiff; *(dans un grand verre)* large; **il a 50 ans bien tassés** he's 50 if he's a day

tasseau, -x [taso] *nm* batten

tassement [tasmɑ̃] *nm* (**a**) *(de terre, de neige)* packing down; **t. de vertèbres** spinal compression (**b**) *(de fondations)* settling (**c**) *(déclin)* slowdown (**de** in)

tasser [tase] **1** *vt* (**a**) *(objets, personnes)* to cram, to pack (**dans** into) (**b**) *(terre, neige)* to pack down

2 **se tasser** *vpr* (**a**) *(fondations)* to settle (**b**) *(personne)* to shrink (**c**) **se t. dans qch** *(se serrer dans)* to squeeze into sth (**d**) *Fam* **ça se tassera** *(ça s'arrangera)* things will settle down

taste-vin [tastəvɛ̃] *nm inv (tasse)* wine taster (cup)

tata [tata] *nf Fam* auntie, aunty

tatami [tatami] *nm* tatami

tâter [tɑte] **1** *vt* (**a**) *(toucher)* to feel (**b**) *Fig* **t. le terrain** to see how the land lies

2 **tâter de** *vt ind (métier)* to try one's hand at; *(prison)* to have a taste of

3 **se tâter** *vpr (hésiter)* to be of two minds

tâte-vin [tɑtvɛ̃] = taste-vin

tatie [tati] *nf Fam* auntie, aunty

tatillon, -onne [tatijɔ̃, -ɔn] *adj* finicky

tâtonnements [tɑtɔnmɑ̃] *nmpl* (**a**) *(dans le noir)* groping (**b**) *Fig (essai)* trial and error; *(de la science, de la recherche)* tentative progress

tâtonner [tɑtɔne] *vi* (**a**) *(dans le noir)* to grope about (**b**) *Fig (chercher)* to proceed by trial and error

tâtons [tɑtɔ̃] **à tâtons** *adv* **entrer/sortir à t.** to feel one's way in/out

tatou [tatu] *nm* armadillo

tatouage [tatwaʒ] *nm (action)* tattooing; *(motif)* tattoo

tatouer [tatwe] *vt* to tattoo; **se faire t.** to get a tattoo

tatoueur [tatwœr] *nm* tattoo artist

taudis [todi] *nm* slum; *Fig* dump

taulard, -e [tolar, -ard] *nm,f Fam* jailbird

taule [tol] *nf Fam* can; **faire de la t.** to do time

taulier, -ère [tolje, -ɛr] *nm,f Fam (propriétaire)* (hotel) owner; *(gérant)* (hotel) manager

taupe [top] *nf* (**a**) *(animal)* mole (**b**) *Fam (espion)* mole (**c**) *Fam Péj* **vieille t.** old hag

taupinière [topinjɛr] *nf* molehill

taureau, -x [tɔro] *nm* (**a**) *(animal)* bull; *Fam* **prendre le t. par les cornes** to take the bull by the horns (**b**) *Astron & Astrol* **T.** Taurus; **être T.** to be (a) Taurus

tauromachie [tɔrɔmaʃi] *nf* bullfighting

tautologie [totɔlɔʒi] *nf* tautology
tautologique [totɔlɔʒik] *adj* tautological
taux [to] *nm* (**a**) *(montant) (des salaires, des impôts)* rate (**b**) *(pourcentage)* rate; *(d'alcool, de cholestérol)* level; **à t. fixe** fixed-rate; **t. de change** exchange rate; **t. de croissance** growth rate; **t. d'écoute** ratings; **t. d'épargne** savings rate; **t. d'inflation** rate of inflation; **t. d'intérêt** interest rate; **t. de pénétration** *(d'un marché)* penetration rate (**c**) *Ordinat* ratio, rate
tavelé, -e [tavle] *adj* marked
tavelure [tavlyr] *nf* mark
taverne [tavɛrn] *nf* (**a**) *(restaurant)* restaurant (**b**) *Can* beer parlor, tavern
tavernier, -ère [tavɛrnje, -ɛr] *nm,f* innkeeper
taxation [taksasjɔ̃] *nf* taxation
taxe [taks] *nf* tax; **toutes taxes comprises** inclusive of tax; **t. d'aéroport** airport tax; **t. d'apprentissage** = tax paid by businesses to fund training programs; **t. d'habitation** local tax; **t. professionnelle** = tax paid by companies and self-employed people; **t. sur la valeur ajoutée** value-added tax
taxer [takse] *vt* (**a**) *(imposer)* to tax (**b**) *(accuser)* **t. qn de négligence** to accuse sb of negligence (**c**) *Fam (soutirer)* **t. qch à qn** to cadge sth off sb
taxi [taksi] *nm* (**a**) *(voiture)* taxi, cab; **prendre un t.** to take a taxi (**b**) *Fam (chauffeur)* taxi driver
taxidermiste [taksidɛrmist] *nmf* taxidermist
taximètre [taksimɛtr] *nm* meter
Taxiphone® [taksifɔn] *nm* pay phone
Tbilissi [tbilisi] *n* Tbilisi
Tchad [tʃad] *nm* **le T.** Chad
tchadien, -enne [tʃadjɛ̃, -ɛn] **1** *adj* Chadian
 2 *nm,f* **T., Tchadienne** Chadian
tchador [tʃadɔr] *nm* chador
tchatche [tʃatʃ] *nf Fam* **avoir la t.** to have the gift of the gab
tchatcher [3] [tʃatʃe] *vi Fam* to chat
tchatcheur, -euse [tʃatʃœr, -øz] *nm,f Fam* smooth talker
tchatcher [3] [tʃate] *vi Ordinat* to chat online
tchécoslovaque [tʃekɔslɔvak] *Anciennement* **1** *adj* Czechoslovakian
 2 *nmf* **T.** Czechoslovak
Tchécoslovaquie [tʃekɔslɔvaki] *nf Anciennement* **la T.** Czechoslovakia
tchèque [tʃɛk] **1** *adj* Czech
 2 *nm (langue)* Czech
 3 *nmf* **T.** Czech
tchétchène [tʃetʃɛn] **1** *adj* Chechen
 2 *nmf* **T.** Chechen
Tchétchénie [tʃetʃeni] *nf* **la T.** Chechnya
tchin-tchin [tʃintʃin] *exclam Fam* cheers!
TD [tede] *nm Univ (abrév* **travaux dirigés***)* tutorial
te [tə]

---

t' is used before a word beginning with a vowel or h mute.

---

pron personnel (**a**) *(objet direct)* you; **te voilà** there you are (**b**) *(objet indirect)* to you; **j'ai vu qu'elle t'a serré la main** I saw her shake your hand; **ils t'ont lancé des cailloux?** did they throw stones at you? (**c**) *(dans les réfléchis)* yourself; **va te doucher** go take a shower (**d**) *(dans les pronominaux)* **tu t'es trompée** you made a mistake
té [te] *nm (règle)* T-square; **en té** T-shaped
technicien, -enne [tɛknisjɛ̃, -ɛn] *nm,f* technician
technicité [tɛknisite] *nf* technical nature
technico-commercial, -e, -aux, -ales [tɛknikokɔmɛrsjal, -jo] **1** *adj (service)* technical sales; **agent t.** sales engineer
 2 *nm,f* sales engineer
technicolor® [tɛknikɔlɔr] *nm* Technicolor®

technique [tɛknik] **1** *adj* technical
 2 *nf (d'un artiste, d'un spécialiste)* technique; **avec lui, j'ai ma t.** I have my own way of dealing with him; **t. de vente** sales technique
 3 *nm* **le t.** *(enseignement)* technical training
techniquement [tɛknikmɑ̃] *adv* technically
techno [tɛknɔ] *adj inv & nf* techno
technocrate [tɛknɔkrat] *nmf* technocrat
technocratie [tɛknɔkrasi] *nf* technocracy
technologie [tɛknɔlɔʒi] *nf* technology; **de haute t.** high-tech
technologique [tɛknɔlɔʒik] *adj* technological
teck [tɛk] *nm* teak
teckel [tekɛl] *nm* dachshund
tectonique [tɛktɔnik] **1** *adj* tectonic
 2 *nf* tectonics *(singulier)*; **t. des plaques** plate tectonics
Te Deum [tedeɔm] *nm inv* Te Deum
teenager [tinɛdʒœr] *nmf Fam* teenager, teen
tee-shirt *(pl* tee-shirts*)* [tiʃœrt] *nm* T-shirt, tee-shirt
Téflon® [teflɔ̃] *nm* Teflon®
tégument [tegymɑ̃] *nm* integument
Téhéran [teerɑ̃] *n* Tehran
teignais, teigne, *etc. voir* **teindre**
teigne [tɛɲ] *nf* (**a**) *(maladie)* ringworm (**b**) *Fam (homme)* rat; *(femme)* cow
teigneux, -euse [tɛɲø, -øz] *adj Fam (personne)* nasty
teindre [54] [tɛ̃dr] **1** *vt (vêtement, cheveux)* to dye; **t. qch en rouge** to dye sth red
 2 se teindre *vpr* (**a**) *(se colorer)* **se t. les cheveux (en blond)** to dye one's hair (blond) (**b**) *Litt* **se t. de** *(se mêler de)* to be tinged with
teint *voir* **teindre**
teint [tɛ̃] *nm* (**a**) *(du visage)* complexion; **t. de rose** rosy complexion (**b**) *(d'un tissu)* color; **tissu bon** *ou* **grand t.** colorfast material; *Fig* **bon t.** *(catholique, communiste)* staunch, dyed-in-the-wool
teinte [tɛ̃t] *nf* (**a**) *(couleur)* shade, tint (**b**) *Fig (nuance)* tinge
teinter [tɛ̃te] **1** *vt* (**a**) *(colorer)* to tint; *(bois, meuble)* to stain (**b**) *Fig (nuancer)* **teinté de** tinged with
 2 se teinter *vpr* **se t. de** to become tinged with
teinture [tɛ̃tyr] *nf* (**a**) *(produit)* dye (**b**) *(action)* dyeing (**c**) *(préparation pharmaceutique)* tincture; **t. d'iode** tincture of iodine
teinturerie [tɛ̃tyrri] *nf (pressing)* dry cleaner's
teinturier, -ère [tɛ̃tyrje, -ɛr] *nm,f* dry cleaner
tek [tɛk] = **teck**
tel, telle [tɛl] **1** *adj* (**a**) *(semblable)* such; **un t. homme** such a man; **une telle conduite** such behavior; **de telles choses** such things; **t. père, t. fils** like father like son; **rien de t. qu'un bon chocolat chaud** there's nothing like a nice cup of hot chocolate; **à t. ou t. endroit** in such and such a place; **il n'a rien dit de t.** he said nothing of the kind; **sa bonté est telle que...** he's/she's so kind that...
 (**b**) *(comme)* **t. que** such as, like; **voir les choses telles qu'elles sont** to see things as they are; **t. que je le connais, il ne sera pas d'accord** knowing him, he won't agree; *Litt* **t. une bête furieuse** like an enraged animal
 (**c**) *(locutions)* **à t. point que** to such an extent that; **de telle sorte que...** so that..., in such a way that...; **elle me l'a dit t. quel** *ou Fam* **t. que** she told me just like that
 2 *pron indéfini* **t. ou t. vous dira que...** some people will tell you that...
 3 *pron démonstratif* such; **t. est mon désir** such is my wish
 4 *nm,f* **un t., une telle** so-and-so
télé [tele] *nf Fam (appareil)* **la t.** TV; **travailler à la t.** to work in TV
téléachat [teleaʃa] *nm (à la télévision)* teleshopping; *(par Internet)* on-line shopping

télécabine [telekabin] *nf* cable car
Télécarte® [telekart] *nf* phone card
téléchargement [teleʃaʁʒəmɑ̃] *nm Ordinat* downloading
télécharger [17] [teleʃaʁʒe] *vt* to download; *(vers le serveur)* to upload
télécommande [telekɔmɑ̃d] *nf* remote control
télécommander [telekɔmɑ̃de] *vt* (a) *(appareil)* to operate by remote control (b) *Fig (complot, soulèvement)* to mastermind from a distance
télécommunications [telekɔmynikasjɔ̃] *nfpl* **les t.** telecommunications
téléconférence [telekɔ̃feʁɑ̃s] *nf* teleconference
télécopie [telekɔpi] *nf* fax
télécopieur [telekɔpjœʁ] *nm* fax (machine)
télédiffuser [teledifyze] *vt* to televise
télédiffusion [teledifyzjɔ̃] *nf* televising
tel écran-tel écrit [telekʁɑ̃telekʁi] *adj Ordinat* WYSIWYG
télé-enseignement [teleɑ̃sɛɲmɑ̃] *nm* distance learning
téléfilm [telefilm] *nm* movie made for television, TV movie
télégénique [teleʒenik] *adj* telegenic
télégramme [telegram] *nm* telegram
télégraphe [telegraf] *nm* telegraph
télégraphier [66] [telegrafje] *vt* to cable, to wire
télégraphique [telegrafik] *adj (fil, poteau)* telegraph; **en style t.** in telegraphic style
télégraphiste [telegrafist] *nmf* (a) *(technicien)* telegraphist (b) *(porteur)* telegraph messenger
téléguidage [telegidaʒ] *nm* remote control
téléguidé, -e [telegide] *adj* remote-controlled
téléguider [telegide] *vt* (a) *(voiture, missile)* to operate by remote control (b) *Fig (complot, soulèvement)* to mastermind from a distance
télématique [telematik] **1** *adj* telematic
2 *nf* telematics *(singulier)*
télémessage [telemesaʒ] *nm Tél* text message
télémessagerie [telemesaʒri] *nf* electronic messaging
téléobjectif [teleɔbʒɛktif] *nm* telephoto lens
télépaiement [telepɛmɑ̃] *nm* telepayment
télépathe [telepat] **1** *adj* telepathic
2 *nmf* telepathist
télépathie [telepati] *nf* telepathy
télépathique [telepatik] *adj* telepathic
téléphérique [teleferik] *nm* cable car
téléphone [telefɔn] *nm* (a) *(appareil, système)* phone, telephone; **avoir le t.** to have a phone; **être au t.** to be on the phone; **un coup de t.** a phone call; *Fam* **par le t. arabe** on the grapevine; **t. cellulaire** cellular phone, cellphone; **t. mobile** mobile (phone), cell(phone); **t. portatif** portable phone; **t. public** public phone; *Pol* **t. rouge** hot line; **t. sans fil** cordless phone; **t. de voiture** car phone (b) *(numéro)* phone number
téléphoner [telefɔne] **1** *vt* (a) *(nouvelle)* to phone, to telephone (à to) (b) *Fam* **c'était téléphoné** you could see it coming, it was telegraphed
2 *vi* to phone, to telephone; **t. à qn** to phone sb
3 se téléphoner *vpr* to phone each other
téléphonie [telefɔni] *nf* telephony; **t. sans fil** wireless telephony; **la t. mobile** the mobile phone sector
téléphonique [telefɔnik] *adj* telephone
téléphoniste [telefɔnist] *nmf* (telephone) operator
téléportation [teleportasjɔ̃] *nf* teleportation
téléporter [3] [teleporte] *vt* to teleport
télé-poubelle [telepubɛl] *nf Fam* trash television
téléprompteur [teleprɔ̃ptœʁ] *nm* Teleprompter®
téléprospecteur, -trice [teleprɔspɛktœʁ, -tris] *nm,f* telemarketer

téléprospection [teleprɔspɛksjɔ̃] *nf* telemarketing
télé-réalité, téléréalité [telerealite] *nf TV* reality television, reality TV
téléreportage [teler(ə)pɔrtaʒ] *nm (activité)* television reporting; *(document)* television report
téléroman [telerɔmɑ̃] *nm Can* television serial
télescopage [telɛskɔpaʒ] *nm (de trains)* telescoping; **télescopages en série** *(de véhicules)* pile-up
télescope [telɛskɔp] *nm* telescope
télescoper [telɛskɔpe] **1** *vt (véhicules, trains)* to crash into
2 se télescoper *vpr (véhicules, trains)* to concertina (b) *(souvenirs, images)* to intermingle
télescopique [telɛskɔpik] *adj* telescopic
téléscripteur [teleskriptœʁ] *nm* teleprinter, teletypewriter
télésiège [telesjɛʒ] *nm* chair lift
téléski [teleski] *nm* ski tow
téléspectateur, -trice [telespɛktatœʁ, -tris] *nm,f* (television) viewer
télésurveillance [telesyrvɛjɑ̃s] *nf* electronic surveillance
Télétexte® [teletɛkst] *nm* teletext
télétravail [teletravaj] *nm* teleworking
télétravailleur, -euse [teletravajœʁ, -øz] *nm,f* teleworker
télévente [televɑ̃t] *nf* = teleshopping
télé-vérité [televerite] *nf TV* reality television, reality TV
télévisé, -e [televize] *adj* televised
téléviseur [televizœʁ] *nm* television (set)
télévision [televizjɔ̃] *nf* (a) *(organisme, technique, émissions)* television; **à la t.** on television; **travailler à la t.** to work in television; **t. par câble** cable television; **t. en circuit fermé** closed-circuit television; **t. commerciale** commercial television; **t. haute définition** high-definition television; **t. numérique** digital television (b) *(poste)* television (set); **regarder la t.** to watch television; **t. en couleur, t. couleur** color television
télévisuel, -elle [televizɥɛl] *adj* television
télex [telɛks] *nm* telex
télexer [telɛkse] *vt* to telex
tellement [tɛlmɑ̃] *adv* (a) *(si)* so; **c'était t. intéressant que...** it was so interesting that...; **ce n'est pas t. beau** it's not all that beautiful (b) *(tant)* so much; **t. de** *(nombre)* so many; *(quantité)* so much; **elle a t. grandi** she's grown so much; **je n'ai pas t. aimé** I didn't like it that much; **je n'ai plus t. envie d'y aller** I'm no longer that eager to go; **il a t. crié que...** he shouted so much that...; *Fam* **je vais craquer t. il m'énerve** he annoys me so much I'm going to crack up
tellurique [telyrik] *adj (courants)* telluric; **secousse t.** earth tremor
téméraire [temerɛʁ] *adj* reckless
témérité [temerite] *nf* recklessness
témoignage [temwaɲaʒ] *nm* (a) *Jur* evidence, testimony; **porter t. (en faveur de/contre qn)** to give evidence (on behalf of/against sb); **faux t.** perjury (b) *(compte rendu)* report, account (c) *(démonstration)* **en t. d'amitié** as a token of friendship
témoigner [temwaɲe] **1** *vt* (a) *(attester)* **t. que** to testify that (b) *(sentiments, gratitude)* to show (à to)
2 *vi* to testify, to give evidence (**en faveur de/contre** on behalf of/against)
3 témoigner de *vt ind* (a) *(montrer)* to show (b) *(se porter garant de)* to testify to
témoin [temwɛ̃] **1** *nm* (a) *(d'un événement, d'un mariage)* witness; **être t. de qch** to witness sth, to be a witness to sth; **prendre qn à t.** to call sb to witness; **Dieu m'est t. que...** as God is my witness...; **t. à charge** witness for the prosecution; **t. oculaire** eyewitness (b) *(dans un duel)* second (c) *(preuve)* **t. les coups que j'ai reçus** witness the blows I received

(**d**) *(dans un relais)* baton (**e**) *Rel* **T. de Jéhovah** Jehovah's Witness (**f**) *Can Ordinat* cookie

2 *adj inv (animal, plante)* control; **appartement t.** model apartment

tempe [tɑ̃p] *nf* temple

tempérament [tɑ̃peramɑ̃] *nm* (**a**) *(caractère)* disposition; *Fam* **avoir du t.** *(avoir du caractère)* to have character (**b**) **acheter qch à t.** to buy sth on the installment plan

tempérance [tɑ̃perɑ̃s] *nf* moderation, temperance

température [tɑ̃peratyr] *nf* temperature; **avoir de la t.** to have a (high) temperature; *Fig* **prendre la t. de qch** to gauge the temperature of sth

tempéré, -e [tɑ̃pere] *adj (climat)* temperate

tempérer [34] [tɑ̃pere] *vt (enthousiasme, passion)* to moderate

tempête [tɑ̃pɛt] *nf* storm; *Fig* **une t. d'applaudissements** thunderous applause; *Fig* **une t. dans un verre d'eau** a tempest in a teapot; **t. de neige** snowstorm, blizzard; **t. de sable** sandstorm

tempêter [tɑ̃pete] *vi* to storm, to rage

tempétueux, -euse [tɑ̃petyø, -øz] *adj Litt* stormy

temple [tɑ̃pl] *nm aussi Fig* temple; *(protestant)* church

tempo [tɛ̃po, tɛmpo] *nm* tempo

temporaire [tɑ̃pɔrɛr] *adj* temporary

temporairement [tɑ̃pɔrɛrmɑ̃] *adv* temporarily

temporel, -elle [tɑ̃pɔrɛl] *adj* (**a**) *(qui concerne le temps)* temporal (**b**) *(terrestre)* temporal, worldly

temporellement [tɑ̃pɔrɛlmɑ̃] *adv* temporally

temporisateur, -trice [tɑ̃pɔrizatœr, -tris] *adj (stratégie)* delaying

temporiser [tɑ̃pɔrize] *vi* to play for time, to stall

temps [tɑ̃] *nm* (**a**) *(durée)* time; **avoir le t. de faire qch** to have (the) time to do sth; **avoir tout le t.** to have plenty of time; **prendre le t. de faire qch** to take the time to do sth; **prendre son t.** to take one's time; **ça prend du t.** it takes time; **ça a pris un certain t.** it took quite a while; **donner** *ou* **laisser le t. à qn de faire qch** to give sb the time to do sth; *Fig* **en deux t. trois mouvements** in a jiffy; **avec le t.** in *or* with time, with time; **combien de t. faut-il pour y aller?** how long does it take to get there?; *Prov* **le t., c'est de l'argent** time is money; *Ordinat* **base de t.** time base; *Ordinat* **t. d'adressage** address speed

(**b**) *(moment)* time; **en t. de crise** in a crisis; **en t. de guerre/paix** in wartime/peacetime; **de t. en t., de t. à autre** from time to time; **en même t. (que)** at the same time (as); **pendant ce t.** meanwhile, in the meantime; **il y a peu de t.** not long ago, a little while ago; **peu de t. après** shortly after; **d'ici quelque t.** soon, shortly; **tout le t.** all the time; **les premiers t.** at the beginning; **ces t.-ci** these days; **ces derniers t.** this last while; **il y est resté quelque t.** he stayed there for a while; **ça n'a qu'un t.** it won't last forever; **les t. forts de l'actualité** the main points of the news; **t. libre** free time; **t. mort** lull; *(au basket-ball)* time out

(**c**) *(époque)* time, days; **de mon t.** in my day *or* time; **du t. de ma jeunesse** in my younger days; **de tout t.** from time immemorial; **dans le t.** in the old days; **en ce t.-là** at that time, then; **par les t. qui courent** these days; **être de son t., vivre avec son t.** to move with the times; **être en avance sur son t.** to be ahead of one's time; **le bon vieux t.** the good old days; **les t. sont durs** times are hard

(**d**) *(heure)* **faire qch à t.** to do sth in time; **en t. voulu** *ou* **utile** in due course; **il est t. qu'elle descende** it's time she came down; **il n'est plus t.** it's too late; **le paquet est enfin arrivé mais il était t.!** the package finally arrived and it's about time too!

(**e**) *(occasion)* **il y a un t. pour tout** there's a time for everything; **chaque chose en son t.** all in good time

(**f**) *(météo)* weather; **par tous les t.** in all weathers; **quel t. fait-il?** what's the weather like?

(**g**) *Gram* tense

(**h**) *Mus* beat

(**i**) *(d'un athlète)* time

tenable [tənabl] *adj (situation)* bearable

tenace [tənas] *adj* (**a**) *(personne)* stubborn, tenacious (**b**) *(préjugé, volonté)* stubborn; *(odeur, douleur, souvenir)* lingering; *(habitude)* deep-rooted (**c**) *(colle)* strong

ténacité [tenasite] *nf* (**a**) *(d'une personne)* stubbornness, tenacity; **avec t.** stubbornly; *(travailler)* doggedly (**b**) *(d'un préjugé)* stubbornness; *(d'une odeur, d'une douleur, d'un souvenir)* lingering nature; *(d'une habitude)* deep-rootedness

tenailler [tənaje] *vt Litt* to torture; **tenaillé par la faim** ravenously hungry; **tenaillé par la douleur** gripped with pain

tenailles [tənaj] *nfpl* pincers

tenancier, -ère [tənɑ̃sje, -ɛr] *nm,f (d'un bar, d'une maison de jeu)* manager

tenant, -e [tənɑ̃, -ɑ̃t] **1** *adj voir* **séance**

2 *nm* (**a**) *(partisan)* champion, defender (**b**) **le t. du titre** the titleholder (**c**) *(locutions)* **d'un seul t.** in one piece; **les tenants et les aboutissants** *(d'une affaire)* the ins and outs

tendance [tɑ̃dɑ̃s] **1** *nf* (**a**) *(d'une personne)* tendency; **avoir t. à faire qch** to have a tendency to do sth; **avoir une t. à qch** to have a tendency to sth (**b**) *(de l'économie, du marché, d'une mode)* trend

2 *adj Fam (à la mode)* trendy

tendanceur [tɑ̃dɑ̃sœr] *nm Mktg* trendspotter

tendancieusement [tɑ̃dɑ̃sjøzmɑ̃] *adv* tendentiously

tendancieux, -euse [tɑ̃dɑ̃sjø, -øz] *adj* tendentious

tendeur [tɑ̃dœr] *nm (pour bagages)* elastic strap

tendinite [tɑ̃dinit] *nf* tendinitis

tendon [tɑ̃dɔ̃] *nm* tendon; **t. d'Achille** Achilles tendon

tendre¹ [tɑ̃dr] **1** *adj* (**a**) *(bois, pierre, métal)* soft; *(viande, légume)* tender (**b**) *(couleur)* delicate, soft (**c**) *(personne, geste, cœur)* tender; **ne pas être t. (pour** *ou* **avec qn)** to be hard (on sb) (**d**) **l'âge t.** early childhood; **depuis ma plus t. enfance** since my earliest childhood

2 *nmf (personne)* softhearted person

tendre² [tɑ̃dr] **1** *vt* (**a**) *(corde)* to tighten; *(toile)* to stretch; *(muscle)* to tense; *(arc)* to bend (**b**) *(voile, filet)* to spread; *(papier peint, tapisserie)* to hang; **une pièce tendue de velours rouge** a room whose walls are covered in red velvet (**c**) *(piège)* to set (**à** for) (**d**) *(main, bras, jambe)* to stretch out, to hold out (**à** to); **les bras tendus** with outstretched arms; *Fig* **t. la main à qn** *(l'aider)* to offer sb a hand; *Fig* **t. l'oreille** to prick up one's ears

2 *vi* **t. vers zéro** to tend toward zero

3 tendre à *vt ind* (**a**) *(avoir pour but) (idéal)* to aim for (**b**) *(avoir tendance à)* **t. à faire qch** to tend to do sth (**c**) **t. à sa fin** to come to an end

4 se tendre *vpr (cordage)* to become taut; *Fig (relations, situation)* to become strained

tendrement [tɑ̃drəmɑ̃] *adv* tenderly, lovingly

tendresse [tɑ̃drɛs] *nf* (**a**) *(affection)* tenderness, affection; **avoir de la t. pour qn** to feel affection for sb; **avec t.** tenderly, affectionately (**b**) **tendresses** *(démonstrations)* expressions of affection

tendron [tɑ̃drɔ̃] *nm* (**a**) *(de veau)* flank (**b**) *Fam (jeune fille)* slip of a girl

tendu, -e [tɑ̃dy] *adj* (**a**) *(corde, toile)* taut, tight (**b**) *(main)* outstretched (**c**) *(relations, visage)* strained; *(personne, atmosphère, situation)* tense

ténèbres [tenɛbr] *nfpl* **les t.** the darkness

ténébreux, -euse [tenebrø, -øz] **1** *adj Litt* (**a**) *(obscur) (forêt)* dark, gloomy (**b**) *(mystérieux) (affaire)* murky; *(style)* obscure (**c**) *(personne)* melancholic

2 *nm* **beau t.** tall dark handsome man

teneur [tənœr] *nf* (**a**) *(d'un document, d'un discours)* content; *(d'un contrat)* terms (**b**) *(quantité)* content; **t. en eau/or** water/gold content

tenir [70] [tənir] **1** *vt* (**a**) *(à la main, sur ses genoux)* to hold; **t. qn par le cou/les épaules** to have one's arm around sb's neck/shoulders; *Fig* **je tiens mon homme/la solution** I have my man/the answer; *Fam* **t. un bon rhume** to have an awful cold; *Fam* **qu'est-ce qu'il tient!** *(il est idiot)* what an idiot *or* jerk!; **tenez!** *(c'est pour vous)* here (you are)!; **tiens, voilà Paul!** oh, there's Paul!; *Prov* **un tiens vaut mieux que deux tu l'auras** ≃ a bird in the hand is worth two in the bush

(**b**) *(dans une position)* to hold; *(dans un état)* to keep; **t. sa droite** *(en voiture)* to keep to the right

(**c**) *(boutique, hôtel)* to run; *(caisse)* to be in charge of

(**d**) *(rôle)* to have

(**e**) *(parole, promesse)* to keep

(**f**) *(maîtriser)* *(enfants, cheval)* to control; **t. sa langue** to hold one's tongue

(**g**) *(résister à)* *Fam* **t. l'alcool** to hold one's drink; **t. la route** *(voiture)* to hold the road

(**h**) *(avoir)* **t. qch de qn** *(caractéristique)* to get sth from sb; **je tiens la nouvelle de ma mère** I got the news from my mother

(**i**) *(considérer)* **t. qn pour responsable** to hold sb responsible; **t. qch pour vrai** to consider sth to be true

2 *vi* (**a**) *(nœud, corde)* to hold; *(construction)* to stay up; *(autocollant, pansement)* to stay on; *(personne)* to last; *Fam* **il ne tient plus sur ses jambes** *ou* **debout** *(fatigué)* he's ready to drop, he's dead on his feet; *(ivre)* he can hardly stand; **t. debout** *(argument)* to stand up; **t. bon** *(personne)* to hold out; **je n'y tiens plus** I can't stand it any longer

(**b**) *(durer)* to last; **mon offre/le pari tient toujours** my offer/the bet still stands; **ça tient toujours pour dimanche?** are we still OK for Sunday?

(**c**) *(être contenu)* to fit; **on tient à dix autour de cette table** this table seats ten; **ma conclusion tiendra en trois mots** my conclusion can be summed up in three words

3 *v impersonnel* **il ne tient qu'à vous que cela se fasse** it depends entirely on you whether it gets done; **s'il ne tenait qu'à moi…** if it was just up to me…; **qu'à cela ne tienne** that's not a problem

4 tenir à *vt ind* (**a**) *(liberté, amitié)* to value; *(ami)* to care about; *(objet)* to be attached to; **t. à faire qch** to be anxious *or* eager to do sth; **je tiens à ce que tout soit rangé** I want everything to be tidy; **si vous y tenez** if you insist

(**b**) *(provenir de)* to be the result of, to be due to

5 tenir de *vt ind (ressembler à)* *(personne)* to take after; *Fam* **entre son oncle et son père, il a de qui t.!** it's not surprising when you consider his uncle and his father!; **cela tient du miracle** it's something of a miracle

6 se tenir *vpr* (**a**) *(rester)* *(debout)* to stand; *(assis)* to sit; **se t. debout** to be standing, to stand; **se t. tranquille** to keep quiet

(**b**) *(se comporter)* **bien se t.** to behave (oneself); *Fig* **il n'a qu'à bien se t.!** he'd better watch his step!; **se t. mal à table** to have no table manners

(**c**) *(s'accrocher)* to hold on (à to); **tenez-vous bien!** hold tight!; *Fig* **et alors, tiens-toi bien…!** and would you believe it…!; **se t. par la main** to hold hands; **ils se tenaient par la taille** they had their arms around each other's waist

(**d**) *(avoir lieu)* to be held, to take place

(**e**) *(être plausible)* to hang together

(**f**) **s'en t. à** *(généralités, sujet, budget)* to keep to; *(décision, consignes)* to abide by; **il ne s'en tint pas là** he didn't stop there; **je ne sais pas à quoi m'en t.** I don't know where I stand

(**g**) *(locutions)* **tiens-le-toi pour dit!** I'm telling you for the last time!

tennis [tenis] **1** *nm* (**a**) *(sport)* tennis; **t. de table** table tennis (**b**) *(court)* tennis court

2 *nm ou nf (chaussure)* tennis shoe

tennisman [tenisman] *(pl* **tennismen** [tenismɛn]) *nm* tennis player

ténor [tenɔr] **1** *adj (saxophone)* tenor

2 *nm* (**a**) *(voix, chanteur)* tenor (**b**) *Fig* **un t. de la politique** an influential figure in politics

tenseur [tɑ̃sœr] **1** *adj* **muscle t.** tensor

2 *nm* tensor

tension [tɑ̃sjɔ̃] *nf* (**a**) *(raideur, désaccord)* tension; **être sous t.** to be tense; **mettre qn sous t.** to put sb under stress; **t. nerveuse** nervous tension (**b**) **t. (artérielle)** blood pressure; **avoir de la t.** to have high blood pressure; **prendre la t. de qn** to take sb's blood pressure (**c**) *(électrique)* voltage, tension; **basse/haute t.** low/high voltage *or* tension

tentaculaire [tɑ̃takylɛr] *adj (ville)* sprawling; *(société, organisme)* octopus-like

tentacule [tɑ̃takyl] *nm* tentacle

tentant, -e [tɑ̃tɑ̃, -ɑ̃t] *adj* tempting

tentateur, -trice [tɑ̃tatœr, -tris] **1** *adj* tempting

2 *nm* tempter; *Rel* **le T.** the Tempter

3 *nf* **tentatrice** temptress

tentation [tɑ̃tasjɔ̃] *nf* temptation

tentative [tɑ̃tativ] *nf* attempt; **t. d'assassinat** attempted murder; **t. d'évasion** attempt to escape; **t. de suicide** suicide attempt

tente [tɑ̃t] *nf* (**a**) *(de camping)* tent; **coucher sous la t.** to sleep under canvas; **t. igloo** igloo tent (**b**) *Méd* **t. à oxygène** oxygen tent

tenter [tɑ̃te] *vt* (**a**) *(mettre à l'épreuve)* **t. sa chance** to try one's luck; *Fam* **t. le coup** to have a go; **t. le tout pour le tout** to go for broke (**b**) *(séduire)* to tempt; **être tenté de faire qch** to be tempted to do sth; **se laisser t.** to let oneself be tempted; **j'ai envie de me laisser t.** *(accepter)* I'm tempted to say yes; *(faire quelque chose)* I'm tempted to do it (**c**) *(essayer)* to try, to attempt; **t. de faire qch** to try *or* to attempt to do sth

tenture [tɑ̃tyr] *nf (tapisserie)* hanging

tenu, -e¹ [təny] *adj* (**a**) **bien/mal t.** *(maison, jardin)* well/poorly kept (**b**) *(contraint)* **être t. de faire qch** to be obliged to do sth; **être t. à qch** to be bound by sth (**c**) *(note)* held

ténu, -e [teny] *adj* (**a**) *(fil)* fine; *(nuance)* subtle; *(lien)* tenuous; *(espoir)* slender (**b**) *(voix)* thin

tenue² [təny] *nf* (**a**) *(habillement)* outfit; *(militaire)* dress; **en t. légère** *(en vêtements d'été)* in light clothing; *Fam* **en petite t.** scantily dressed; **t. de combat** battledress; **t. de soirée** evening dress (**b**) *(bonne conduite)* good behavior; **un peu de t.!** mind your manners!; **manquer de t.** to lack manners (**c**) *(maintien)* posture (**d**) *(niveau)* standard (**e**) *(d'une maison)* running (**f**) **t. de route** *(d'un véhicule)* road-holding

tequila [tekila] *nf* tequila

ter [tɛr] *adj* **5 t.** ≃ 5B

tercet [tɛrsɛ] *nm* tercet

térébenthine [terebɑ̃tin] *nf* turpentine

Tergal® [tɛrgal] *nm* Dacron®

tergiversations [tɛrʒiversasjɔ̃] *nfpl* equivocation

tergiverser [tɛrʒiverse] *vi* to equivocate

terme¹ [tɛrm] *nm* (**a**) *(fin)* end; **toucher à son t.** *(projet)* to be nearing completion; *(période)* to be drawing to a close; **mettre un t. à qch** to put an end to sth; **mener qch à bon t.** to bring sth to a successful conclusion (**b**) *(date limite)* time (limit); **à court/long t.** *(projet, prévisions)* short-/long-term; **à court/ long t. …** in the short/long term… (**c**) *(d'une femme enceinte)* **être à t.** to have reached term; **avant t.** *(accoucher)* prematurely; *(accouchement)* premature (**d**) *(loyer)* rent; *(date de paiement du loyer)* rent day

terme² [tɛrm] *nm* (**a**) *(mot)* term; **en d'autres termes** in other words (**b**) *(relations)* **être en bons/mauvais termes avec qn** to be on good/bad terms with sb (**c**) **termes** *(d'un contrat)* terms

terminaison [tɛrminɛzɔ̃] *nf* (**a**) *(d'un mot)* ending (**b**) *Anat* **t. nerveuse** nerve ending

terminal, -e, -aux, -ales [tɛrminal, -o] **1** *adj (de la fin)* final; *Méd (phase)* terminal; **être en phase terminale** *(malade)* to be terminally ill

2 *nm* (**a**) *(dans un aéroport)* terminal (**b**) *Ordinat* terminal, VDU

3 *nf Scol* **terminale** ≃ twelfth grade, senior year

terminer [tɛrmine] **1** *vt (discours, lettre, repas)* to end, to finish (**par** with); *(travail)* to finish, to complete; **en t. avec qch** to put an end to sth

2 se terminer *vpr (saison)* to come to a close; *(soirée, concert, vacances)* to end (**par** with); *(rue)* to end; **se t. en** *(mot)* to end in

terminologie [tɛrminɔlɔʒi] *nf* terminology

terminus [tɛrminys] *nm* terminus

termite [tɛrmit] *nm* termite

terne [tɛrn] *adj* dull

ternir [tɛrnir] **1** *vt (meuble)* to fade; *(miroir, métal, réputation)* to tarnish

2 se ternir *vpr (meuble)* to fade; *(miroir, métal, réputation)* to become tarnished

terrain [tɛrɛ̃] *nm* (**a**) *(parcelle)* piece *or* plot of land (**b**) *(espace au sol, relief)* ground; **tout t.** *(véhicule)* all-terrain (**c**) *(terre)* soil (**d**) *(destiné à une activité) (de football)* field; *(de golf)* course; **t. d'atterrissage** landing strip; **t. d'aviation** airfield; **t. à bâtir** development site; **t. de camping** campsite; *Fig* **t. d'entente** common ground; **t. de jeu** *(pour les sports)* sports field; *(pour les enfants)* playground; **t. de sport** sports ground; **t. vague** waste ground (**e**) *Méd* **présenter un t. favorable à qch** to be prone to sth (**f**) *(locutions)* **être sur son t.** to be on familiar ground; **sur le t.** *(apprendre)* in the field; **perdre/céder du t.** to lose/give ground; **préparer le t.** to pave the way

terrasse [tɛras] *nf* (**a**) *(d'un café, d'un restaurant)* sidewalk area; **en t.** outside; **prix des consommations en t.** price of drinks served outside (**b**) *(de maison, d'appartement)* terrace; **(toit en) t.** terrace (roof) (**c**) *(levée de terre)* terrace; **en terrasses** *(jardin)* terraced; *(culture)* terrace

terrassement [tɛrasmɑ̃] *nm* (**a**) *(action)* excavation (**b**) *(remblai)* earthwork

terrasser [tɛrase] *vt (sujet: adversaire)* to floor; *(sujet: émotion, fatigue, nouvelle)* to overwhelm; *(sujet: maladie)* to lay low

terrassier [tɛrasje] *nm* laborer

terre [tɛr] *nf* (**a**) *(monde)* world; *Fig* **t. à t.** down-to-earth; *Fig* **revenir sur t.** to come down to earth; *Fig* **avoir les pieds sur t.** to have one's feet on the ground

(**b**) *(planète)* **la T.** (the) Earth

(**c**) *(sol)* ground; *(étendue)* land; **à t.**, **par t.** on the ground; *Can Fam Fig* **être à t.** to be *or* to feel down; **tomber par t.** to fall down; **faire tomber qch par t.** to drop sth; **sous t.** underground; **basses terres** lowlands; **hautes terres** highlands

(**d**) *Élec* ground; **relier** *ou* **raccorder à la t.** to ground

(**e**) *(opposé à la mer)* land; **t. ferme** terra firma

(**f**) *(matière)* soil, earth; **cultiver la t.** to cultivate the soil; **t. battue** mud; *(de court de tennis)* clay; **t. de Sienne** sienna

(**g**) *(propriété)* **une t.** a piece of land; **terres** land

(**h**) *(territoire)* land, country; **terres australes** southern lands; **la t. Adélie** Adélie Land; **la T. de Feu** Tierra del Fuego; **la T. promise** the Promised Land; **la T. sainte** the Holy Land

(**i**) *(élément)* earth

(**j**) *(argile)* clay; **cruche de** *ou* **en t.** earthenware jug; **t. cuite** terracotta; **une t. cuite** a piece of terracotta

terreau, -x [tɛro] *nm* compost

Terre-Neuve [tɛrnœv] *n* Newfoundland

terre-neuve [tɛrnœv] *nm inv* Newfoundland (dog)

terre-plein [*pl* **terre-pleins**] [tɛrplɛ̃] *nm (plate-forme)* platform; **t. central** *(sur route)* median strip

terrer [tere] **se terrer** *vpr aussi Fig* to go to earth

terrestre [terestr] *adj* (**a**) *(plante)* ground; *(animal)* land; *(transports)* surface (**b**) *(magnétisme, attraction)* of the earth (**c**) *(matériel)* worldly

terreur [terœr] *nf* (**a**) *(effroi)* terror; **vivre dans la t.** to live in terror (**b**) *(emploi de la violence)* terror; *Fig (personne)* terror; **jouer les terreurs** to play the tough guy

terreux, -euse [terø, -øz] *adj* (**a**) *(odeur)* earthy (**b**) *(mains)* muddy (**c**) *(teint, ciel, couleur)* muddy

terrible [teribl] *adj* (**a**) *(affreux, remarquable)* terrible (**b**) *Fam (formidable)* terrific, great; **pas t.** nothing special

terriblement [teribləmɑ̃] *adv* terribly

terrien, -enne [terjɛ̃, -ɛn] **1** *adj* (**a**) *(qui possède des terres)* landowning; **propriétaire t.** landowner (**b**) *(famille, vertu)* rural (**c**) *(de la Terre)* Earth

2 *nm,f (habitant de la Terre)* earthling

terrier¹ [terje] *nm (d'un lapin)* burrow, hole; *(d'une taupe)* hole; *(d'un renard)* earth

terrier² [terje] *nm (chien)* terrier

terrifiant, -e [terifjɑ̃, -ɑ̃t] *adj* terrifying

terrifier [66] [terifje] *vt* to terrify

terril [teril] *nm* slag heap

terrine [terin] *nf* terrine

territoire [teritwar] *nm* (**a**) *(d'un État, d'un animal)* territory; **t. d'outre-mer** overseas territory; *Can* **Territoires du Nord-Ouest** Northwest Territories (**b**) *(de juge, d'évêque)* jurisdiction; *(de commune, d'arrondissement)* area

territorial, -e, -aux, -ales [teritɔrjal, -o] *adj* territorial

territorialité [teritɔrjalite] *nf* territoriality

terroir [terwar] *nm* soil; **du t.** *(produit, accent, expression)* local

terrorisant, -e [terɔrizɑ̃, -ɑ̃t] *adj* terrifying

terroriser [terɔrize] *vt (sujet: personne)* to terrorize; *(sujet: expérience, souvenir)* to terrify

terrorisme [terɔrism] *nm* terrorism

terroriste [terɔrist] *adj & nmf* terrorist

tertiaire [tɛrsjɛr] **1** *adj* tertiary

2 *nm* (**a**) *(secteur économique)* service sector (**b**) *Géol* Tertiary era

tertio [tɛrsjo] *adv* thirdly

tertre [tɛrtr] *nm* hillock, mound

tes [te] *voir* **ton¹**

tessiture [tesityr] *nf Mus* range

tesson [tesɔ̃] *nm* shard; **t. de bouteille** piece of broken bottle

test [test] **1** *adj inv* test; *(période)* trial

2 *nm* test; **t. de paternité** paternity test; **t. de grossesse** pregnancy test

Testament [tɛstamɑ̃] *nm* **l'Ancien/le Nouveau T.** the Old/the New Testament

testament [tɛstamɑ̃] *nm (dernières volontés)* will; *Fig* legacy; **ceci est mon t.** this is my last will and testament

testamentaire [tɛstamɑ̃tɛr] *adj voir* **exécuteur**

tester [tɛste] *vt (élève, produit)* to test

testicule [tɛstikyl] *nm* testicle

testostérone [tɛstɔsterɔn] *nf* testosterone

tétanie [tetani] *nf* spasms, *Spéc* tetany; **avoir une crise de t.** to go into spasms

tétanique [tetanik] **1** *adj* tetanic

2 *nmf* tetanus sufferer

tétaniser [tetanize] *vt (muscle)* to cause spasms in; *Fig* **tétanisé de peur** paralyzed with fear

tétanos [tetanos] *nm* tetanus

têtard [tɛtar] *nm* tadpole

tête [tɛt] *nf* **(a)** *(d'une personne, d'un animal)* head; **cent cinquante têtes de bétail** a hundred and fifty head of cattle; **j'ai la t. qui tourne** my head is spinning; **tenir t. à qn** to stand up to sb; *Fam* **j'en ai par-dessus la t.** I've had it up to here; *Fam* **avoir la t. près du bonnet** to have a short fuse; *Fam* **faire une grosse t.** *ou* **une t. au carré à qn** to smash sb's face in; *Fam* **tu es tombé sur la t. ou quoi?** are you out of your mind or what?; *Fig* **marcher la t. haute** to walk with one's head held high; **la t. la première** head first; *Fig* **foncer t. baissée** to jump in head first; **de la t. aux pieds** from head to foot; **la t. nue** bare-headed; *Fam* **50 euros par t. de pipe** 50 euros a head; **t. de mort** death's head

(b) *(visage)* face; **faire une drôle de t.** to look odd, to make an odd face; **avoir une drôle de t.** to look odd, to have an odd face; **faire la t.** to be in a huff

(c) *(personne)* **une t. rousse/blonde** a redhead/blonde; **nos chères têtes blondes** *(enfants)* our little ones; **t. brûlée** hothead; *Fam* **c'est une t. à claques** he/she has a face you just want to slap; *Fam* **t. de cochon** pig-headed person; *Fam* **c'est une t. de lard** *ou* **mule** he's/she's pig-headed; **t. de linotte** bird-brain; **t. de Turc** whipping boy; **forte t.** strong-minded person; *Fam* **grosse t.** highbrow; *Fam* **avoir la grosse t.** to have a big head, to be bigheaded

(d) *(esprit)* mind; *(cerveau)* brains; **des idées plein la t.** full of ideas; **avoir qch en t.** to have sth in mind; **ne pas avoir de t.** to be very forgetful; **avoir toute sa t.** to be all there; **perdre la t.** to lose it; **faire qch à t. reposée** to do sth at one's leisure; **où ai-je la t.!** what am I thinking of!; **être t. en l'air** to have one's head in the clouds; **ne rien avoir dans la t.** to be empty-headed; **avoir la t. dure** to be pig-headed; **mettre qch dans la t. de qn** to put sth in sb's head; **se mettre en t. de faire qch** to get it into one's head to do sth; **se mettre dans la t. que…** to get it into one's head that…; **n'en faire qu'à sa t.** to do exactly as one pleases; **avoir une idée derrière la t.** to have an ulterior motive; **de t.** *(calculer, additionner)* in one's head

(e) *(cheveux)* hair

(f) *(d'une liste)* top; *(de chapitre)* heading; **t. d'affiche** top of the bill

(g) *(d'ail)* head; *(d'un arbre)* top; *(du fémur)* head

(h) *(d'une procession, d'un cortège)* head; *(d'un train)* front; **le wagon de t.** the front car; **prendre la t.** *(dans une course, dans un jeu)* to take the lead; **prendre la t. d'une entreprise** to take over as the head of a company; **être à la t. de qch** *(entreprise, fortune)* to be at the head of sth; *(protestation, révolte)* to be the leader of sth; **arriver en t.** to come in first; **être en t.** to be in the lead; **t. de lit** headboard; **t. de pont** bridgehead; **t. de série** *(au tennis)* seed

(i) *(appareil)* **t. chercheuse** homing device; *Ordinat* **t. d'écriture** writing *or* write head; *Ordinat* **t. de lecture** read(ing) head; **t. à palpeur** sensor head

tête-à-queue [tɛtakø] *nm inv* spin; **faire un t.** to spin around

tête-à-tête [tɛtatɛt] *nm inv* *(rendez-vous)* tête-à-tête; **en t.** in private; **en t. avec** alone with

tête-bêche [tɛtbɛʃ] *adv (dormir)* head to foot

tête-de-nègre [tɛtdənɛgr] *adj inv & nm inv* dark brown

tétée [tete] *nf* feed; **donner la t. à un enfant** to feed a child

téter [34] [tete] *vt* **(a)** *(lait)* to suck; **t. sa mère** to feed **(b)** *(cigare, pipe, stylo)* to suck on

tétine [tetin] *nf* **(a)** *(d'un biberon)* nipple **(b)** *(sucette)* pacifier

téton [tetɔ̃] *nm* **(a)** *Fam (sein de femme)* tit, boob **(b)** *(d'une pièce détachée)* lug

tétraèdre [tetraɛdr] **1** *adj* tetrahedral
    2 *nm* tetrahedron

tétralogie [tetralɔʒi] *nf* tetralogy

tétraplégie [tetrapleʒi] *nf* quadriplegia

tétraplégique [tetrapleʒik] *adj & nmf* quadriplegic

tétras [tetra] *nm* grouse

têtu, -e [tety] **1** *adj* stubborn, obstinate; *Fam* **t. comme une mule** as stubborn as a mule
    2 *nm,f* stubborn *or* obstinate person

teuf [tœf] *nf Fam* party

teufer [3] [tœfe] *vi Fam* to party

teuf-teuf *(pl* **teufs-teufs**) [tœftœf] *Fam* **1** *nf (voiture)* jalopy
    2 *nm (bruit)* chug-chug

teuton, -onne [tøtɔ̃, -ɔn] **1** *adj* Teutonic
    2 *nm,f* **T., Teutonne** Teuton

texan, -e [tɛksɑ̃, -an] **1** *adj* Texan
    2 *nm,f* **T., Texane** Texan

texte [tɛkst] *nm* **(a)** *(d'un livre, d'un dépliant)* text; **t. publicitaire** advertising copy; **lire un auteur dans le t.** to read an author in the original; **textes choisis (de)** selected passages (from) **(b)** *(d'un opéra)* libretto; *(d'une chanson)* words; *(d'un acteur)* lines; *(d'une pièce de théâtre)* script

textile [tɛkstil] **1** *adj* textile
    2 *nm* **(a)** *(fibre)* textile **(b)** *(industrie)* **le t.** the textile industry, textiles

texto [tɛksto] *Fam* **1** *nm Tél* text message; **envoyer un t. à qn** to text sb, to send sb a text (message)
    2 *adv* word for word; **t.!** those were his/her/*etc.* very words!

textuel, -elle [tɛkstɥɛl] *adj* **(a)** *(analyse)* textual **(b)** *(traduction)* word-for-word, literal; *Fam* **t.!** those were his/her/*etc.* very words!

textuellement [tɛkstɥɛlmɑ̃] *adv* word for word, literally

texture [tɛkstyr] *nf (d'une substance, du sol)* texture

TF1 [teɛffœ̃] *nf (abrév* **Télévision Française 1**) = French commercial television channel

TGB [teʒebe] *nf (abrév* **très grande bibliothèque**) = the new French national library in the Tolbiac area of Paris

TGV [teʒeve] *nm (abrév* **train à grande vitesse**) high-speed train

thaï, thaïe [taj] **1** *adj* Thai
    2 *nm (langue)* Thai
    3 *nm,f* **T., Thaïe** Thai

thaïlandais, -e [tajlɑ̃dɛ, -ɛz] **1** *adj* Thai
    2 *nm,f* **T., Thaïlandaise** Thai

Thaïlande [tajlɑ̃d] *nf* **la T.** Thailand

thalassothérapie [talasoterapi] *nf* thalassotherapy, seawater therapy

thé [te] *nm* **(a)** *(boisson)* tea; **t. au citron** tea with lemon; **t. glacé** iced tea; **t. à la menthe** mint tea; **t. nature/au lait** tea without milk/with milk; **t. en sachets** tea bags **(b)** *(goûter)* tea; **t. dansant** tea dance

théâtral, -e, -aux, -ales [teatral, -o] *adj* **(a)** *(œuvre, production)* theatrical; *(effet)* dramatic; *(représentation)* stage **(b)** *Péj (artificiel)* melodramatic

théâtre [teatr] *nm* **(a)** *(édifice, salle)* theater; **t. de marionnettes** puppet theater; **t. de verdure** open-air theater **(b)** *(art, métier)* theater; **c'est un homme de t.** he works in theater; **faire du t.** *(professionnellement)* to be an actor/actress; *(en amateur)* to do some acting; **adapté pour le t.** adapted for the stage **(c)** *(œuvres) (d'un auteur)* plays; *(genre)* theater; **t. de boulevard** light comedies **(d)** *Fig (attitude artificielle)* **c'est du t.** it's an act **(e)** *(d'un crime, d'un accident)* scene

théière [tejɛr] *nf* teapot

théine [tein] *nf* theine

thématique [tematik] **1** *adj* thematic
    2 *nf* themes

thème [tɛm] *nm* **(a)** *(d'un discours, d'une œuvre, d'un morceau de musique)* theme **(b)** *(traduction)* prose **(c)** *(d'un verbe, d'un nom)* stem **(d)** *Astrol* **t. (astral)** birth chart

théocratie [teɔkrasi] *nf* theocracy

théocratique [teɔkratik] *adj* theocratic

théologie [teɔlɔʒi] *nf* theology

théologien, -enne [teɔlɔʒjɛ̃, -ɛn] *nm, f* theologian

théologique [teɔlɔʒik] *adj* theological

théorème [teɔrɛm] *nm* theorem

théoricien, -enne [teɔrisjɛ̃, -ɛn] *nm, f* theoretician, theorist

théorie [teɔri] *nf* theory; **en t.** in theory

théorique [teɔrik] *adj* theoretical

théoriquement [teɔrikmɑ̃] *adv* theoretically

thérapeute [terapøt] *nmf* therapist

thérapeutique [terapøtik] **1** *adj* therapeutic **2** *nf* (a) *(science)* therapeutics *(singulier)* (b) *(traitement)* therapy

thérapie [terapi] *nf* therapy; **t. de groupe** group therapy

thermal, -e, -aux, -ales [tɛrmal, -o] *adj* thermal

thermalisme [tɛrmalism] *nm* hydrotherapy

thermes [tɛrm] *nmpl* (a) *(établissement de soins)* thermal baths, spa (b) *(chez les Anciens)* thermae, public baths

thermique [tɛrmik] *adj* thermal

thermoélectrique [tɛrmoelɛktrik] *adj* thermoelectric

thermomètre [tɛrmomɛtr] *nm* thermometer; *Fig (de l'opinion, d'une tendance)* barometer; **t. médical** clinical thermometer

thermonucléaire [tɛrmonykleɛr] *adj* thermonuclear

Thermos® [tɛrmos] *nm ou nf* (**bouteille**) **T.** Thermos® (bottle)

thermostat [tɛrmosta] *nm* thermostat

thésard, -e [tezar, -ard] *nm, f* PhD student

thésaurisation [tezɔrizasjɔ̃] *nf* hoarding

thésauriser [tezɔrize] *vt & vi* to hoard

thesaurus [tezɔrys] *nm* thesaurus

thèse [tɛz] *nf* (a) *(proposition intellectuelle)* thesis; **roman/littérature à t.** novel/literature of ideas (b) *Univ* thesis *(submitted for doctorate)*

thon [tɔ̃] *nm* tuna; **t. blanc** longfin tuna; **t. au naturel/à l'huile** tuna in brine/in oil

thoracique [tɔrasik] *adj* thoracic

thorax [tɔraks] *nm* thorax

thriller [srilœr] *nm* thriller

thrombose [trɔ̃boz] *nf* thrombosis

thune [tyn] *nf* (a) *très Fam (argent)* cash, dough; **ne pas avoir une t.** to be flat broke (b) *Suisse* = Swiss five-franc coin

thuya [tyja] *nm* thuja

thym [tɛ̃] *nm* thyme

thyroïde [tirɔid] *adj & nf* thyroid

thyroïdien, -enne [tirɔidjɛ̃, -ɛn] *adj* thyroid

tiaffe [tjaf] *nf Suisse Fam* (a) *(chaleur)* heatwave (b) *(neige fondante)* slush

tiare [tjar] *nf* tiara

Tibet [tibɛ] *nm* **le T.** Tibet

tibétain, -e [tibetɛ̃, -ɛn] **1** *adj* Tibetan **2** *nm (langue)* Tibetan **3** *nm, f* **T., Tibétaine** Tibetan

tibia [tibja] *nm* shinbone, *Spéc* tibia

Tibre [tibr] *nm* **le T.** the Tiber

tic [tik] *nm* (a) *(convulsion involontaire)* tic, twitch; **t. nerveux** nervous tic *or* twitch (b) *(manie)* habit, mannerism; **t. de langage** verbal mannerism

ticket [tikɛ] *nm* ticket; *Fam Fig* **avoir un** *ou* **le t. avec qn** to have made a hit with sb; **t. de caisse** sales slip; **t. modérateur** = portion of the cost of treatment paid by the patient; **t. de quai** platform ticket; **t. de rationnement** ration coupon

ticket-repas *(pl* **tickets-repas***)* [tikɛrəpɑ] *nm* meal ticket

ticket-restaurant *(pl* **tickets-restaurant***)* [tikɛrɛstɔrɑ̃] *nm* meal ticket

tic-tac [tiktak] *nm inv (d'une horloge)* tick-tock, ticking

tie-break *(pl* **tie-breaks***)* [tajbrɛk] *nm* tie break

tiédasse [tjedas] *adj Péj* lukewarm, tepid

tiède [tjɛd] **1** *adv* **il fait t.** it's mild **2** *adj* (a) *(vent)* mild; *(bain, boisson)* tepid, lukewarm (b) *Péj (peu enthousiaste)* half-hearted **3** *nf Suisse* heatwave

tiédeur [tjedœr] *nf* (a) *(du vent)* mildness; *(de l'eau)* tepidness (b) *Péj (manque d'enthousiasme)* half-heartedness

tiédir [tjedir] **1** *vt (réchauffer)* to warm (up); *(refroidir)* to cool (down) **2** *vi* (a) *(devenir plus chaud)* to warm up; *(devenir moins chaud)* to cool down (b) *Fig (amitié, passion)* to cool off

tien, tienne [tjɛ̃, tjɛn] **1** *pron possessif* **le t., la tienne, les tiens, les tiennes** yours; *(en insistant)* your own; **tu me prêtes le t.?** can I borrow yours?; **tu n'en as pas besoin, tu as le t.** you don't need it, you have your own; *Fam* **à la tienne!** cheers! **2** *nm* **il faut que tu y mettes du t.** you should really do your share **3** *nmpl* **les tiens** *(ta famille)* your family **4** *nfpl Fam* **tu as encore fait des tiennes!** you've been up to your old tricks again!

tiendrais, tienne, tiens, *etc. voir* **tenir**

tierce [tjɛrs] **1** *adj voir* **tiers 2** *nf* (a) *Mus* third (b) *(aux cartes)* tierce

tiercé [tjɛrse] *nm* = forecast of the first three horses in a race; **jouer au t.** to bet on the horses; **le t. gagnant** the winning combination

tiers, tierce [tjɛr, tjɛrs] **1** *adj* third; **le t. état** the third estate; **une tierce personne** a third party **2** *nm* (a) *(fraction)* third; **t. payant** = system of direct payment for medical treatment by the insurer; **t. provisionnel** interim tax payment *(approximately one third of previous year's tax)* (b) *(personne)* third party

tiers-monde *(pl* **tiers-mondes***)* [tjɛrmɔ̃d] *nm* **le t.** the Third World

tifs [tif] *nmpl Fam* hair

TIG [tiʒ] *nm (abrév* **travail d'intérêt général***)* community service

tige [tiʒ] *nf* (a) *(d'une plante)* stem, stalk; **rosier sur t.** standard rose (b) *(d'une chaussure)* upper (c) *(en métal)* rod (d) *Fam (cigarette)* butt

tignasse [tiɲas] *nf Fam* mop (of hair)

Tigre [tigr] *nm* **le T.** the Tigris

tigre [tigr] *nm* tiger; **t. du Bengale** Bengal tiger

tigré, -e [tigre] *adj (rayé)* striped

tigresse [tigrɛs] *nf* tigress

tilde [tild] *nm* tilde

tilleul [tijœl] *nm* (a) *(arbre)* lime (tree) (b) *(infusion)* lime-blossom tea

tilt [tilt] *nm* **faire t.** *(au billard électrique)* to signal the end of the game; *Fig* **ça a fait t.** it clicked

timbale [tɛ̃bal] *nf* (a) *(gobelet)* (metal) drinking cup; *Fig* **décrocher la t.** to hit the jackpot (b) *(tambour)* kettledrum; **les timbales** *(dans un orchestre)* the timpani (c) *(moule, plat)* timbale

timbre [tɛ̃br] *nm* (a) *(vignette)* stamp; **t. de collection** collector's stamp; **t. fiscal** excise or tax stamp (b) *(instrument encreur, marque)* stamp; **t. dateur** date stamp (c) *(sonnette)* bell; **t. de bicyclette** bicycle bell (d) *(d'une voix, d'un instrument)* timbre, tone; **voix sans t.** toneless voice (e) *(pour traitement médical)* patch; **t. tuberculinique** TB patch

Timbre fiscal
These stamps are sold at most tobacco stores and are used to pay fees due for obtaining official documents, such as identity papers, vehicle documents and legal certificates.

timbré, -e [tɛ̃bre] *adj* (a) *(document, enveloppe)* stamped (b) *Fam (fou)* mad

timbre-poste (*pl* **timbres-poste**) [tɛ̃brəpɔst] *nm* (postage) stamp

timbrer [tɛ̃bre] **1** *vt* (**a**) *(lettre, paquet)* to put a stamp/stamps on (**b**) *(passeport, document)* to stamp

2 *vi Suisse (au chômage)* to register as unemployed

timide [timid] **1** *adj* (**a**) *(personne, sourire, voix)* shy (**b**) *(critique, protestation, tentative)* timid

2 *nmf* shy person; **c'est un grand t.** he's very shy

timidement [timidmɑ̃] *adv* (**a**) *(sourire, parler)* shyly (**b**) *(critiquer, protester)* timidly

timidité [timidite] *nf* (**a**) *(d'une personne)* shyness (**b**) *(d'une critique, d'une protestation)* timidity

timing [tajmiŋ] *nm* timing

timoré, -e [timɔre] *adj* timorous, fearful

tintamarre [tɛ̃tamar] *nm Fam* din, racket; **faire du t.** to make a din *or* racket

tintement [tɛ̃təmɑ̃] *nm (de clochettes)* tinkling; *(de pièces de monnaie)* jingling; **t. d'oreilles** ringing in the ears

tinter [tɛ̃te] *vi* (**a**) *(clochettes)* to tinkle; *(pièces de monnaie)* to jingle (**b**) *(oreilles)* to ring

tintin [tɛ̃tɛ̃] *exclam Fam* no way, José!; **faire t.** to go without

tintouin [tɛ̃twɛ̃] *nm Fam* (**a**) *(bruit)* din, racket (**b**) *(souci)* trouble

TIOP [tjɔp] *nm Banque (abrév* **taux interbancaire offert à Paris**) PIBOR

tipi [tipi] *nm* tepee

tique [tik] *nf* tick

tiquer [tike] *vi Fam (personne)* to wince; **il n'a pas tiqué** he didn't bat an eyelid

TIR [tir] *nm (abrév* **transports internationaux routiers**) TIR

tir [tir] *nm* (**a**) *(activité)* shooting; **t. à l'arc** archery; **faire du t. à l'arc** to do archery; **t. à la carabine** rifle shooting; **t. au pigeon** clay pigeon shooting (**b**) *(coup de feu)* shot (**c**) *(à la pétanque)* throw; **t. (au but)** *(au football)* shot (at goal) (**d**) *(stand)* rifle range; **t. (forain)** shooting gallery

tirade [tirad] *nf Théât* monologue; *Fig* tirade

tirage [tiraʒ] *nm* (**a**) *(impression)* printing (**b**) *(nombre d'exemplaires) (d'un journal)* circulation; *(d'un livre)* print run; **édition à t. limité** limited edition (**c**) *(d'une cheminée)* draft (**d**) *(de loterie)* draw (**de** for); **t. au sort** drawing lots; **procéder à un t. au sort** to draw lots

tiraillement [tirajmɑ̃] *nm* (**a**) *(crampe)* **tiraillements d'estomac** stomach cramps (**b**) *(conflit)* **tiraillements (entre)** conflict (between)

tirailler [tiraje] **1** *vt* (**a**) *(tirer sur)* to pull at, to tug at (**b**) *(écarteler)* **être tiraillé entre** to be torn between

2 *vi* (**a**) *(avec une arme)* to shoot wildly (**b**) *(peau)* **j'ai la peau qui tiraille** my skin feels tight

tirailleur [tirajœr] *nm (soldat éclaireur)* skirmisher

Tirana [tirana] *n* Tirana

tirant [tirɑ̃] *nm (de botte)* boot strap (**b**) **t. d'eau** draft *(volume of water)*

tire [tir] *nf* (**a**) *Fam (voiture)* car (**b**) *Can (confiserie)* molasses candy, taffy

tiré, -e [tire] **1** *adj* (**a**) *(traits)* drawn; **avoir les traits tirés** to look drawn (**b**) *(cheveux)* scraped back

2 *nf Fam* **tirée** *(trajet)* long haul

tire-au-flanc [tiroflɑ̃] *nm inv Fam* shirker

tire-bouchon (*pl* **tire-bouchons**) [tirbuʃɔ̃] *nm* corkscrew; **en t.** *(queue)* curly

tire-bouchonner [tirbuʃɔne] **1** *vt (mèche, fil)* to twist; **chaussettes tire-bouchonnées** socks bunched up around the ankles

2 *vi* to twist; *(pantalon)* to be crumpled; **mes chaussettes tire-bouchonnent** my socks are all bunched up around my ankles

tire-d'aile [tirdɛl] **à tire-d'aile** *adv* **s'envoler à t.** to fly swiftly away; *Fig* **partir** *ou* **s'éloigner à t.** to fly off

tire-fesses [tirfɛs] *nm inv Fam* T-bar

tire-jus [tirʒy] *nm inv très Fam* snot rag

tire-lait [tirlɛ] *nm inv* breast pump

tire-larigot [tirlarigo] **à tire-larigot** *adv Fam* to one's heart's content

tirelire [tirlir] *nf* piggy bank; *Fig* **casser sa t.** to break into one's piggy bank

tirer [tire] **1** *vt* (**a**) *(vers soi)* to pull; *(chaussettes)* to pull up; **t. qch vers le haut/bas** to pull sth up/down; **t. qn par la manche** to pull at sb's sleeve; **t. qn par le bras** to pull sb by the arm; **t. les cheveux à qn** to pull sb's hair

(**b**) *(rideaux)* to draw; *(store)* to pull down; *(verrou) (fermer)* to shoot; *(ouvrir)* to draw

(**c**) *(extraire)* **t. qch de qch** to pull sth out of sth; **t. de l'eau d'un puits** to draw water from a well; **une citation tirée d'un texte** a quotation taken from a text; **t. qn d'embarras** to get sb out of a tight spot; **t. qn de son lit** to drag sb out of bed; **t. son origine de qch** to have its origin in sth; **t. une conclusion de qch** to draw a conclusion from sth; **t. une leçon de qch** to learn a lesson from sth

(**d**) *(tendre) (tissu, fil)* to pull tight; *Fig* **t. les ficelles** to pull the strings

(**e**) *(carte)* to draw; **t. les cartes** *(cartomancienne)* to read the cards; **t. qch au sort** to draw lots for sth; **t. qn au sort** to draw lots to choose sb

(**f**) *(tracer) (trait)* to draw; *(plan)* to draw up

(**g**) *(imprimer)* to print; *Fam Hum* **se faire t. le portrait** to have one's photograph taken

(**h**) *(chèque)* to draw (**sur** on)

(**i**) *(coup de feu, balle)* to fire; *(flèche)* to shoot; *(feu d'artifice)* to let off; **t. un coup de revolver (sur)** to fire a gun (at)

(**j**) *(locutions) très Fam* **plus qu'un mois à t.!** just one more month to get through!; **je te tire mon chapeau!** I take my hat off to you!

2 *vi* (**a**) *(exercer une traction)* to pull; **t. sur qch** *(corde)* to pull on sth; *(pull, gilet)* to pull sth out of shape; *(par tic)* to pull at sth

(**b**) *(personne armée, arme)* to shoot; **t. à la carabine** to shoot with a rifle; **t. sur qn/qch** to shoot sb/sth; **t. dans le dos à qn** to shoot sb in the back

(**c**) *(peau)* to feel tight

(**d**) *(être imprimé)* **t. à 100 000 exemplaires** to have a circulation of 100,000

(**e**) *(cheminée)* to draw

(**f**) *(à la pétanque)* to throw; *(au football)* to shoot

(**g**) *(aspirer)* **t. sur une cigarette/pipe** to puff on a cigarette/pipe

(**h**) *(locutions)* **ça ne tire pas à conséquence** it's of no consequence; **t. à sa fin** *(période, journée)* to be drawing to a close; *(réserves, économies)* to be running out; *Fam* **t. au flanc** to shirk

3 **tirer sur** *vt ind (se rapprocher de) (couleur)* to verge on

4 **se tirer** *vpr* (**a**) *(se sortir)* **se t. de qch** to get out of sth; **s'en t.** *(d'une maladie, d'un accident)* to pull through; *(financièrement)* to make it; **s'en t. avec qch** to get away with sth

(**b**) *Fam (partir)* to make tracks

tiret [tirɛ] *nm* dash

tirette [tirɛt] *nf* (**a**) *(d'un bureau)* pull-out shelf; *(d'une table)* leaf (**b**) *(de distributeur)* pull handle (**c**) *Belg (fermeture Éclair®)* zipper

tireur, -euse [tirœr, -øz] **1** *nm,f* gunman; **t. d'élite** marksman, *f* markswoman; **c'est un bon t.** he's a good shot; **un t. embusqué** a sniper

2 *nf* **tireuse de cartes** fortune teller

tiroir [tirwar] *nm* drawer; *Fig* **à tiroirs** *(roman)* = containing individual episodes within the main storyline

tiroir-caisse (*pl* **tiroirs-caisses**) [tirwarkɛs] *nm* till, cash register

tisane [tizan] *nf* herbal tea

tison [tizɔ̃] *nm* (fire)brand

tisonner [tizɔne] *vt* to poke

tisonnier [tizɔnje] *nm* poker

tissage [tisaʒ] *nm* (**a**) *(activité)* weaving; **t. à la main/méca-nique** hand-loom/power-loom weaving (**b**) *(établissement in-dustriel)* cloth mill

tisser [tise] **1** *vt* (**a**) *(textile, liens, intrigue)* to weave (**b**) *(sujet: araignée)* to spin

2 se tisser *vpr (liens, intrigue)* to be woven

tisserand, -e [tisrã, -ãd] *nm,f* weaver

tissu [tisy] *nm* (**a**) *(étoffe)* material, cloth; *Fig (urbain, social)* fab-ric; **t. d'ameublement** furnishing fabric (**b**) *Fig (de men-songes, d'incohérences)* tissue (**c**) *Biol* tissue

tissu-éponge (*pl* **tissus-éponges**) [tisyepɔ̃ʒ] *nm* (terry) toweling

titan [titã] *nm* Titan; **travail de t.** Herculean task

titane [titan] *nm* titanium

titi [titi] *nm Fam* street urchin

titiller [titije] *vt* to titillate

titrage [titraʒ] *nm* (**a**) *(de film)* titling (**b**) *(d'un alcool)* determi-nation of the strength

titre [titr] *nm* (**a**) *(de livre, de chanson, de film)* title (**b**) *(de chapi-tre, de page)* heading; **les gros titres** the headlines; **faire les gros titres** to hit the headlines (**c**) *(chanson, morceau)* track; **un CD deux/trois titres, un deux/trois titres** two-track/three-track CD (**d**) *(d'une personne)* title; **en t.** *(titulaire)* permanent; *(attitré)* official (**e**) *(qualité de champion)* title (**f**) *(di-plôme)* qualification (**g**) *(certificat)* **t. de propriété** title deed; **t. de transport** ticket (**h**) *Fin* security (**i**) *(d'un alcool)* strength; *(de l'or, d'une monnaie)* fineness; *(d'un alliage)* grade (**j**) *(locutions)* **à ce t.** *(pour cette raison)* therefore; *(en cette qualité)* as such; **à quel t.?** *(de quel droit)* on what grounds?; **au même t. que** in the same way as; **à t. gratuit** free of charge; **à t. d'exemple** by way of example

titré, -e [titre] *adj (personne)* titled

titrer [titre] *vt* (**a**) *(livre, film)* to title (**b**) *(alcool)* to determine the strength of

tituber [titybe] *vi* to stagger (**de** with)

titulaire [titylɛr] **1** *adj* (**a**) *(dans l'administration)* with a perma-nent contract; *(professeur d'université)* with tenure (**b**) *(déten-teur)* **être t. de qch** to be the holder of sth

2 *nmf (détenteur)* holder

titularisation [titylarizasjɔ̃] *nf* granting of permanent con-tract; *(à l'université)* granting of tenure

titulariser [titylarize] *vt* to give a permanent contract to; *(pro-fesseur d'université)* to give tenure to

TNT [teɛnte] *nm (abrév* **trinitrotoluène**) TNT

toast [tost] *nm* (**a**) *(de pain)* piece *or* slice of toast; **t. beurré** piece *or* slice of buttered toast; **des toasts** toast (**b**) *(hommage)* toast; **porter un t. à qn** to drink a toast to sb

toboggan [tɔbɔgã] *nm* (**a**) *(de terrain de jeu)* slide; *(dans une piscine)* flume; **faire du t.** to play on the slide (**b**) *(pour march-andises)* chute (**c**) *(viaduc)* overpass (**d**) *Can (traîneau)* tobog-gan; **faire du t.** to go tobogganing

toc [tɔk] **1** *exclam* **t. t.!** knock knock!; *Fig* **et t.!** so there!

2 *adj inv Fam (faux)* fake; *(de mauvais goût)* tacky

3 *nm Fam* **bijoux en t.** fake jewelry; **c'est du t.** it's fake

toccata [tɔkata] *nf Mus* toccata

tocsin [tɔksɛ̃] *nm* alarm bell

toge [tɔʒ] *nf* (**a**) *(de magistrat, d'avocat)* gown (**b**) *(romaine)* toga

Togo [togo] *nm* **le T.** Togo

togolais, -e [tɔgɔlɛ, -ɛz] **1** *adj* Togolese

2 *nm,f* **T., Togolaise** Togolese

tohu-bohu [tɔybɔy] *nm (désordre)* confusion; *(bruit)* hubbub

toi [twa] *pron personnel* (**a**) *(sujet)* you; **t., ne m'énerve pas!**

don't annoy me!; **t., tu aurais certainement cédé** YOU would probably have given in

(**b**) *(objet direct)* you; **et t., il t'a salué?** and what about you, did he say hello to you?

(**c**) *(réfléchi)* yourself; **tais-t.!** be quiet!

(**d**) *(avec préposition)* you; **je ne te le prêterai pas, à t.** I won't lend it to YOU; **c'est à t., tout ça?** is that all yours?; **tu auras ta chambre à t.** you'll have your own room; *Fam* **une copine à t.** a friend of yours; **tu ne penses qu'à t.** you think only of yourself

(**e**) *(dans les comparaisons)* you; **je n'en sais pas plus que t.** I don't know any more about it than you (do)

toile [twal] *nf* (**a**) *(tissu)* cloth; **t. d'araignée** cobweb, spider's web; **t. cirée** oilcloth; **t. de fond** backdrop; *Fig* **en t. de fond** as a backdrop; **t. (de lin)** linen; **un pantalon en t.** linen pants; **t. à matelas** ticking; **t. de tente** canvas (**b**) *(tableau)* painting, canvas (**c**) *Fam (film)* **se faire une t.** to go to the mo-vies (**d**) *Ordinat* **la T.** the Web

toilettage [twalɛtaʒ] *nm* (**a**) *(d'un chien)* grooming (**b**) *(d'un texte)* tidying up

toilette [twalɛt] *nf* (**a**) *(action de se laver)* washing; **faire sa t.** to wash up (**b**) **toilettes** *(W.-C.)* restroom; *(publiques)* comfort station; **toilettes pour dames** ladies' room; **toilettes pour hommes** men's room (**c**) *(vêtements)* outfit; **porter bien la t.** to look good in formal clothes

toiletter [twalete] **1** *vt* (**a**) *(chien)* to groom (**b**) *(texte)* to tidy up

2 se toiletter *vpr Can* to dress up (smartly)

toi-même [twamɛm] *pron personnel* yourself; *Fam* **menteur! – t.!** liar! – liar yourself!

toise [twaz] *nf* height gauge

toiser [twaze] **1** *vt* to look up and down

2 se toiser *vpr* to look each other up and down

toison [twazɔ̃] *nf* (**a**) *(de mouton)* fleece; **la T. d'or** the Golden Fleece (**b**) *(chevelure)* mane (of hair)

toit [twa] *nm* roof; *Fig* **être sans t.** not to have a roof over one's head; **accueillir qn sous son t.** to take sb in; **t. de chaume** thatched roof; **t. ouvrant** sun roof

toiture [twatyr] *nf* roofing, roof

Tokyo [tɔkjo] *n* Tokyo

tôle¹ [tol] *nf* (**a**) *(matériau)* sheet metal; **t. ondulée** corrugated iron (**b**) *(feuille)* metal sheet

tôle² = **taule**

tolérable [tɔlerabl] *adj* tolerable; **votre comportement n'est pas t.** your behavior is intolerable

tolérance [tɔlerãs] *nf* tolerance; *(concession)* concession; *Pol* **t. zéro** zero tolerance

tolérant, -e [tɔlerã, -ãt] *adj* tolerant

tolérer [34] [tɔlere] **1** *vt* to tolerate; **je ne tolère pas qu'on me parle sur ce ton!** I won't tolerate being spoken to like that!

2 se tolérer *vpr* to tolerate each other

tôlier [tolje] = **taulier**

tollé [tɔle] *nm* outcry; **t. général** public outcry

TOM [tɔm] *nm (abrév* **territoire d'outre-mer**) overseas ter-ritory

tomahawk [tɔmaok] *nm* tomahawk

tomate [tɔmat] *nf* tomato

tombal, -e, -als *ou* **-aux, -ales** [tɔ̃bal, -o] *adj voir* **pierre**

tombant, -e [tɔ̃bã, -ãt] *adj (épaules)* sloping; *(oreilles)* floppy

tombe [tɔ̃b] *nf* (**a**) *(sépulture)* grave; *(avec un monument)* tomb; **emporter un secret dans la t.** to take a secret to the grave; **suivre qn dans la t.** to follow sb to the grave (**b**) *(pierre tom-bale)* gravestone, tombstone

tombeau, -x [tɔ̃bo] *nm* tomb; *Fig* **à t. ouvert** at breakneck speed

tombée [tɔ̃be] *nf* **la t. du jour** *ou* **de la nuit** nightfall

tomber [tɔ̃be] **1** *vi (aux être)* (**a**) *(personne, objet)* to fall (down); *(précipitations, feuilles)* to fall; **t. de qch** *(chaise, échelle)* to fall off sth; *(arbre)* to fall out of sth; **t. dans un piège** to fall into a trap; **faire t. qn/qch** to knock sb/sth over; **laisser t.** *(objet)* to drop; *Fam* **laisser t. qn** to let sb down; *Fam* **laisse t., c'est inutile** forget it, it's pointless; **t. à l'eau** *(personne, objet)* to fall in (the water); *(projet)* to fall through; *Fig* **il faut être tombé bien bas** you have to have sunk pretty low; **t. de haut** to come back to earth with a bump
(**b**) *(gouvernement, ville)* to fall
(**c**) *(nouvelle)* to come through
(**d**) *(mourir)* to fall; *Fam* **t. comme des mouches** to be dropping like flies
(**e**) *(vent, prix, fièvre)* to drop; *(conversation)* to flag; *(enthousiasme)* to wane
(**f**) *(nuit)* to fall
(**g**) *(devenir brusquement)* **t. amoureux de qn,** *Can* **t. en amour avec qn** to fall in love with sb; *Fam* **t. enceinte** to get pregnant
(**h**) *(date, événement)* to fall
(**i**) *(pendre)* *(draperie, vêtement)* to hang; **ses cheveux lui tombent jusqu'aux reins** her hair hangs right down her back
(**j**) *(locutions)* **t. bien** to come at just the right time; **t. mal** to come at the wrong time; **je suis bien/mal tombé** *(chanceux/malchanceux)* I was lucky/unlucky; **ça tombe sous le sens** it stands to reason; **t. sur qn** *(l'agresser)* to fall upon sb; *(le rencontrer par hasard)* to bump into sb; **t. sur qch** to come across sth; **il fallait que ça tombe sur moi!** it had to happen to me!
2 *vt Fam (aux avoir)* (**a**) *(séduire)* to pick up
(**b**) *(enlever)* **t. la veste** to take off one's jacket

tombereau, -x [tɔ̃bro] *nm* (**a**) *(charrette)* tipcart (**b**) *(contenu)* cartload

tombeur [tɔ̃bœr] *nm Fam* womanizer, ladykiller

tombola [tɔ̃bɔla] *nf* raffle

tome [tom] *nm (volume)* volume

tomme [tom] *nf =* cheese made in Savoie

ton¹, ta, tes [tɔ̃, ta, te]

> **ta** becomes **ton** before a word beginning with a vowel or mute h.

adj possessif your; **t. chien** your dog; **ta voiture** your car; **t. ami/amie** your friend; **tes enfants** your children; **t. père et ta mère** your mother and father; **un de tes amis** one of your friends, a friend of yours; *Fam* **tu as eu t. vendredi** you got Friday off

ton² [tɔ̃] *nm* (**a**) *(qualité de voix)* tone; **hausser/baisser le t.** to raise/lower one's voice; **sur le t. de la plaisanterie** in a joking tone of voice (**b**) *(goût)* **il est de bon t. de le faire** it's good form to do it (**c**) *(gamme)* key; *(intervalle musical)* tone; **donner le t.** to give the pitch; *Fig* to set the tone (**d**) *Ling* tone; **langue à tons** tonal language (**e**) *(teinte)* shade, tone; *Ordinat* **tons de gris** shades of gray

tonal, -e, -als, -ales [tonal] *adj Mus* tonal

tonalité [tonalite] *nf* (**a**) *(au téléphone)* dial tone (**b**) *(d'un morceau de musique)* key; *Fig (d'une œuvre)* tone

tondeuse [tɔ̃døz] *nf* (**a**) *(de jardin)* **t. (à gazon)** (lawn) mower (**b**) *(de coiffeur)* clippers

tondre [tɔ̃dr] *vt* (**a**) *(herbe)* to mow; *(mouton)* to shear; **se faire t.** *(très court)* to have one's hair cropped; *(complètement)* to have all one's hair shaved off (**b**) *Fam (dépouiller)* to fleece

toner [tonɛr] *nm* toner

tong [tɔ̃g] *nf* thong, flip-flop

Tonga [tɔ̃ga] *nfpl* **les (îles) T.** Tonga

tonicité [tonisite] *nf* (**a**) *(des muscles)* tone (**b**) *(de l'air, du climat)* bracing effect

tonifiant, -e [tonifjɑ̃, -ɑ̃t] *adj (air, marche)* bracing

tonifier [66] [tonifje] *vt (peau, muscles)* to tone up; *(esprit)* to stimulate

tonique [tonik] **1** *adj* (**a**) *(climat, vent)* bracing, invigorating (**b**) *(boisson, remède)* tonic (**c**) *(personne)* energetic, dynamic (**d**) *(accent)* tonic; *(syllabe)* accented
2 *nm* (**a**) *(remède)* tonic (**b**) *(lotion)* toner
3 *nf Mus* tonic, keynote

tonitruant, -e [tonitryɑ̃, -ɑ̃t] *adj (voix, bruit)* thundering

tonnage [tonaʒ] *nm* tonnage

tonnant, -e [tonɑ̃, -ɑ̃t] *adj (voix)* thundering

tonne [ton] *nf* metric ton, tonne; *Fam Fig* **des tonnes de qch** tons of sth; *Fam* **en faire des tonnes** to go overboard

tonneau, -x [tono] *nm* (**a**) *(récipient)* barrel, cask; *Fig* **du même t.** of the same type (**b**) *(en voiture)* roll; **faire un t.** to roll over

tonnelier [tonəlje] *nm* cooper

tonnelle [tonɛl] *nf (charmille)* arbor, bower

tonner [tone] **1** *vi* (**a**) *(canons)* to thunder (**b**) *(fulminer)* to thunder (**contre** against)
2 *v impersonnel* **il tonne** it's thundering

tonnerre [tonɛr] *nm* thunder; **un t. d'applaudissements** thunderous applause; *Fam Fig* **du t.** terrific

tonsure [tɔ̃syr] *nf* tonsure

tonte [tɔ̃t] *nf (des moutons)* shearing; *(du gazon)* mowing

tonton [tɔ̃tɔ̃] *nm Fam* uncle

tonus [tonys] *nm* (**a**) *Fig (dynamisme)* energy, dynamism (**b**) *(d'un muscle)* tone

top [top] **1** *nm* (**a**) *(signal sonore)* beep; **au quatrième t. il sera midi** at the fourth stroke it will be twelve o'clock (**b**) *Fam* **être au t. niveau** *(sportif)* to be at one's peak; **c'est le t.!** it's the real deal!
2 *adj Fam* great, awesome

topaze [topaz] *nf* topaz

toper [tope] *vi Fam* **tope(-là)!** it's a deal!

topinambour [topinɑ̃bur] *nm* Jerusalem artichoke

top modèle (*pl* **top modèles**) [topmodɛl] *nm* supermodel

topo [topo] *nm Fam (discours)* lecture; *(exposé)* rundown; *Fig* **c'est toujours le même t.** it's always the same old story

topographie [topografi] *nf* topography

topographique [topografik] *adj* topographical

toponymie [toponimi] *nf* toponymy

top secret [topsəkrɛ] *adj inv* top secret

toquade [tokad] *nf Fam (pour une personne)* crush (**pour** on); *(pour un lieu, pour un objet)* craze (**pour** for)

toque [tok] *nf (de fourrure)* fur hat; *(de jockey)* cap; *(de cuisinier)* hat

toqué, -e [toke] *Fam* **1** *adj* crazy (**de** about)
2 *nm,f* nutcase

toquer [toke] **se toquer** *vpr Fam* **se t. de qn** to go crazy over sb

Torah [tora] *nf* **la T.** the Torah

torche [torʃ] *nf* torch; **t. électrique** flashlight

torcher [torʃe] *Fam* **1** *vt* (**a**) *(fesses, enfant)* to wipe (**b**) *(travail)* to botch (**c**) *(bouteille)* to polish off
2 **se torcher** *vpr* to wipe one's backside

torchis [torʃi] *nm* cob (for building)

torchon [torʃɔ̃] *nm* (**a**) *(de cuisine)* dishtowel; *Fam* **le t. brûle** they're at each other's throats; *Fig* **il ne faut pas mélanger les torchons et les serviettes** they're in a different league (**b**) *Fam (texte peu soigné)* mess (**c**) *Fam (journal)* rag (**d**) *Belg (serpillère)* floorcloth

tordant, -e [tordɑ̃, -ɑ̃t] *adj Fam* hilarious

tord-boyaux [torbwajo] *nm Fam* rotgut

tordre [tordr] **1** *vt (barre de fer, métal)* to bend; *(fil de fer)* to twist; *(linge)* to wring; **t. le cou à qn** to wring sb's neck; **t. le bras à qn** to twist sb's arm

2 se tordre *vpr* **se t. les mains** to wring one's hands; **se t. la cheville** to twist one's ankle; **se t. de douleur** to writhe in pain; *Fam* **se t. (de rire)** to kill oneself (laughing)

tordu, -e [tɔrdy] **1** *adj* (**a**) *(objet)* twisted (**b**) *Fam (dérangé)* crazy, nuts; **avoir l'esprit t.** to have a warped mind

2 *nm,f Fam* maniac

toréador [tɔreadɔr] *nm* bullfighter, toreador

toréer [24] [tɔree] *vi* to fight *(in the bullring)*

torero [tɔrero] *nm* bullfighter

torgnole [tɔrɲɔl] *nf très Fam* clout

tornade [tɔrnad] *nf* tornado; **comme une t.** like a whirlwind

Toronto [tɔrɔ̃to] *n* Toronto

torpeur [tɔrpœr] *nf* torpor

torpillage [tɔrpijaʒ] *nm* torpedoing

torpille [tɔrpij] *nf* (**a**) *(engin militaire)* torpedo (**b**) *(poisson)* torpedo, electric ray

torpiller [tɔrpije] *vt aussi Fig* to torpedo

torpilleur [tɔrpijœr] *nm* torpedo boat

torréfaction [tɔrefaksjɔ̃] *nf* roasting

torréfier [66] [tɔrefje] *vt* to roast

torrent [tɔrɑ̃] *nm (cours d'eau)* torrent; *Fig (de larmes, de lumière)* flood; *(d'injures)* torrent; *(de questions)* barrage; **pleuvoir à torrents** to pour down

torrentiel, -elle [tɔrɑ̃sjɛl] *adj* torrential

torride [tɔrid] *adj* torrid

tors, -e[1] [tɔr, tɔrs] *adj* twisted

torsade [tɔrsad] *nf* (**a**) *(point de tricot)* cable; **pull à torsades** cable(-knit) sweater (**b**) *(de cheveux)* twist, coil

torsadé, -e [tɔrsade] *adj (pull)* cable(-knit)

torsader [tɔrsade] *vt* to twist

torse[2] [tɔrs] *nm* chest; **t. nu** stripped to the waist

torsion [tɔrsjɔ̃] *nf* twisting

tort [tɔr] *nm* (**a**) *(faute)* fault; **avoir tous les torts** to be entirely to blame; **c'est un t. de l'avoir fait** it was a mistake to do it; **avoir t. (de faire qch)** to be wrong (to do sth); **tu n'as pas t.** you're quite right; **donner t. à qn** *(personne)* to blame sb; *(résultat, preuve)* to prove sb wrong; **être en t.** *ou* **dans son t.** to be in the wrong (**b**) *(dommage)* wrong; **faire du t. à qn** to harm sb; *(désavantager)* to penalize sb (**c**) *(locutions)* **à t.** wrongly; **à t. ou à raison** rightly or wrongly; **à t. et à travers** *(dépenser)* recklessly; *(parler)* wildly

torticolis [tɔrtikɔli] *nm* stiff neck; **avoir le** *ou* **un t.** to have a stiff neck

tortilla [tɔrtija] *nf (chips)* corn chip

tortillard [tɔrtijar] *nm Fam* local train

tortiller [tɔrtije] **1** *vt (papier, ruban, cheveux)* to twist; *(moustache)* to twirl

2 *vi Fam* **il n'y a pas à t.** there are no two ways about it

3 se tortiller *vpr (personne)* to wriggle

tortillon [tɔrtijɔ̃] *nm (de papier)* twist

tortionnaire [tɔrsjɔnɛr] *nmf* torturer

tortue [tɔrty] *nf* (**a**) *(reptile)* tortoise; **t. d'eau douce** terrapin; **t. de mer** turtle (**b**) *Fig (personne lente)* slowpoke

tortueusement [tɔrtɥøzmɑ̃] *adv (hypocritement)* deviously

tortueux, -euse [tɔrtɥø, -øz] *adj* (**a**) *(sinueux)* winding, tortuous (**b**) *(attitude, esprit)* devious; *(langage)* tortuous

torture [tɔrtyr] *nf aussi Fig* torture; *Fig* **mettre qn à la t.** to torture sb

torturer [tɔrtyre] **1** *vt aussi Fig* to torture

2 se torturer *vpr* to torture oneself; **se t. l'esprit** to rack one's brains

torve [tɔrv] *adj* menacing

toscan, -e [tɔskɑ̃, -an] **1** *adj* Tuscan

2 *nm (langue)* Tuscan

3 *nm,f* **T., Toscane** Tuscan

Toscane [tɔskan] *nf* **la T.** Tuscany

tôt [to] *adv* (**a**) *(bientôt, vite)* soon, early; **nous n'étions pas plus t. rentrés que...** no sooner had we returned than...; **au plus t.** at the earliest; *Fam* **ce n'est pas trop t.!** and about time too!; **elle a eu t. fait de changer d'avis** she soon changed her mind; **t. ou tard** sooner or later (**b**) *(de bonne heure)* early

total, -e, -aux, -ales [tɔtal, -o] **1** *adj* total

2 *nm* total; **faire le t.** to work out the total; **au t.** in all, in total; *(tout compte fait)* all in all; *Fam* **t., ils se sont fâchés** the upshot was that they fell out

3 *nf* **totale** *Fam* **on a eu droit à la totale: verglas, embouteillages, barrages routiers** black ice, traffic jams, truck drivers' roadblocks, you name it, we had it

totalement [tɔtalmɑ̃] *adv* totally

totaliser [tɔtalize] *vt* (**a**) *(additionner)* to total, to add up (**b**) *(avoir au total)* to have a total of

totalitaire [tɔtalitɛr] *adj* totalitarian

totalitarisme [tɔtalitarism] *nm* totalitarianism

totalité [tɔtalite] *nf* **la t. de** all of; **payer qch en t.** to pay sth in full

totem [tɔtɛm] *nm (mât)* totem pole

touareg [twarɛg] **1** *adj* Tuareg

2 *nm (langue)* Tuareg

3 *nmf* **T.** Tuareg

toubib [tubib] *nm Fam* doc

toucan [tukɑ̃] *nm* toucan

touchant, -e [tuʃɑ̃, -ɑ̃t] *adj* touching

touche [tuʃ] *nf* (**a**) *(d'un piano, d'un clavier)* key; *Ordinat* **t. alt** alt (key) (**b**) *(tache de couleur)* touch; **mettre la t. finale à qch** to put the finishing touches to sth (**c**) *(style)* touch (**d**) *(en escrime)* hit; *(à la pêche)* bite; *Fam* **avoir une t. avec qn** to make a hit with sb; *Fam* **faire une t.** to make a hit (**e**) *(remise en jeu)* throw-in; *(par les avants au rugby)* line-out; **sortir en t.** to go into touch; *aussi Fig* **rester sur la t.** to stay on the sidelines (**f**) *Fam (allure)* look; **avoir une drôle de t.** to look weird (**g**) *(de violon)* fingerboard; *(de guitare)* fret

touche-à-tout [tuʃatu] *nmf inv Fam* (**a**) *(enfant)* **c'est un t.** he's into everything (**b**) *(qui a plusieurs occupations)* dabbler

toucher[1] [tuʃe] *nm* (**a**) *(sens)* **le t.** touch; **au t.** to the touch (**b**) *(d'un pianiste)* touch

toucher[2] [tuʃe] **1** *vt* (**a**) *(être en contact avec)* to touch; *(cible, adversaire)* to hit; **je touche du bois!** knock on wood!; *Fam* **pas touche!** hands off! (**b**) *(blesser)* to hit (**à** in) (**c**) *(émouvoir)* to touch, to move (**d**) *(concerner)* to concern, to affect (**e**) *(port)* to put in at; **t. le fond** *(navire)* to touch bottom; *Fig (moralement)* to hit rock bottom; **t. terre** *(bateau)* to reach dry land (**f**) *(argent, intérêt, paie)* to get; *(chèque)* to cash; **t. le tiercé** to win the tiercé (**g**) *(jouxter)* to adjoin (**h**) *(dire)* **t. un mot à qn (de qch)** to have a word with sb (about sth)

2 toucher à *vt ind* (**a**) *(prendre, modifier)* to touch; *Fig* **avec son air de ne pas y t.** looking as if butter wouldn't melt in his/her mouth (**b**) *(problème, question)* to touch on (**c**) *(approcher de)* **t. au but** to be nearing one's goal; **t. à sa fin** to be nearing its end (**d**) *(concerner)* to concern

3 se toucher *vpr (être en contact)* to touch; *(maisons)* to adjoin

touer [twe] *vt Can* to tow

touffe [tuf] *nf* tuft

touffu, -e [tufy] *adj* (**a**) *(bois, végétation)* dense; *(barbe, cheveux)* bushy (**b**) *Fig (livre)* dense

touiller [tuje] *vt Fam* to stir; *(salade)* to toss

toujours [tuʒur] *adv* (**a**) *(exprime la continuité, la répétition)* always; **t. plus nombreux** more and more numerous; **un ami de t.** a lifelong friend; **pour t.** for ever; **depuis t.** always (**b**) *(encore)* still; **cherchez le.** keep looking; **alors, il est rentré? – t. pas** so, is he back? – not yet (**c**) *(quoi qu'il en soit)* **t. est-il que...** the fact remains that...; **elle peut t. attendre!** she'll have a long wait!; **c'est t. ça (de pris)** at least it's something

toulousain, -e [tuluzɛ̃, -ɛn] **1** *adj* of Toulouse
2 *nm,f* **T., Toulousaine** person from Toulouse

Toulouse [tuluz] *n* Toulouse

toundra [tundra] *nf* tundra

toupet [tupɛ] *nm* (**a**) *Fam (audace)* cheek, nerve; **avoir du t., ne pas manquer de t.** to have a cheek *or* a nerve (**b**) *(de cheveux)* tuft of hair, quiff

toupie [tupi] *nf* (**a**) *(jouet)* (spinning) top (**b**) *Fam (femme)* **vieille t.** old bag

toupin [tupɛ̃] *nm Suisse* cow bell

tour¹ [tur] *nf* (**a**) *(construction)* tower; **t. de contrôle** control tower; **la T. Eiffel** the Eiffel Tower (**b**) *(immeuble)* high-rise (**c**) *(aux échecs)* rook, castle (**d**) *Ordinat* tower

tour² [tur] *nm* (**a**) *(circonférence)* circumference; **t. de cou/de taille** collar/waist size *or* measurement; **avoir 75 cm de t. de taille** ≃ to have a waist measurement of 30 inches; **perdre cinq cm de t. de taille** ≃ to lose two inches from around the waist; **t. de tête** hat size
  (**b**) *(mouvement circulaire)* **faire le t. (de qch)** to go around (sth); **faire faire à qn le t. du propriétaire** to show sb around *(a house)*; *Fig* **faire le t. de qch** *(situation, problème)* to review sth; *Fam* **faire le t. du cadran** to sleep for twelve hours; **faire un t. d'horizon** to review matters; **faire le t. du monde** to go around the world; **t. d'honneur** lap of honor; **t. de piste** lap
  (**c**) *(de potier)* wheel
  (**d**) *(tournure) (d'une situation)* turn; **prendre un certain t.** to take a certain turn; **t. d'esprit** turn of mind; **t. de phrase** turn of phrase
  (**e**) *(rotation)* turn; **donner un t. de clé** to turn the key; **à t. de bras** *(frapper)* with all one's might; *Fig (distribuer)* in huge quantities; **se faire un t. de reins** to strain one's back
  (**f**) *(promenade à pied)* stroll; *(à bicyclette, en voiture)* ride; **faire un t.** to go for a stroll/ride
  (**g**) *(alternance)* turn; **à qui le t.?** whose turn is it?; **chacun (à) son t.** each in turn; **t. à t.** in turn; **à t. de rôle** in turn
  (**h**) *Pol* **t. (de scrutin)** ballot
  (**i**) *(mauvais coup)* trick; **jouer un t. à qn** to play a trick on sb; **jouer un t. de cochon à qn** to play a dirty trick on sb; **cela te jouera des tours** you'll live to regret it
  (**j**) *(de prestidigitateur)* trick; **t. de force** feat; *Fam* **en un t. de main** in no time at all; **t. de passe-passe** trick *(using sleight of hand)*

Touraine [turɛn] *nf* **la T.** Touraine

tourbe [turb] *nf* peat

tourbeux, -euse [turbø, -øz] *adj* peaty

tourbillon [turbijɔ̃] *nm* (**a**) *(de vent)* whirlwind; *(de poussière, de fumée)* swirl; *(de neige)* flurry (**b**) *(d'eau)* whirlpool (**c**) *Fig (de la vie, d'activité)* whirl

tourbillonnant, -e [turbijɔnɑ̃, -ɑ̃t] *adj* whirling

tourbillonner [turbijɔne] *vi aussi Fig* to whirl

tourelle [turɛl] *nf* turret

tourisme [turism] *nm* tourism; **faire du t.** to do some touring *or* sightseeing; **t. écologique** ecotourism; **t. organisé** package tourism; **t. sexuel** sex tourism; **t. spatial** space tourism

touriste [turist] **1** *adj (classe)* tourist
2 *nmf* tourist; *Fig & Péj* **faire qch en t.** to play at doing sth; **t. sexuel** sex tourist

touristique [turistik] *adj* tourist; *(route)* scenic

tourment [turmɑ̃] *nm Litt* torment

tourmente [turmɑ̃t] *nf* (**a**) *Litt (tempête)* storm (**b**) *(agitation politique)* upheaval

tourmenté, -e [turmɑ̃te] *adj* (**a**) *(paysage)* wild (**b**) *(mer, vie, période)* turbulent (**c**) *(visage, personne, âme)* tortured

tourmenter [turmɑ̃te] **1** *vt* to torment
2 se tourmenter *vpr* to worry

tournage [turnaʒ] *nm (d'un film)* shooting, filming; **sur le t.** on shoot

tournant, -e [turnɑ̃, -ɑ̃t] **1** *adj* (**a**) *(fauteuil, siège)* swivel; *(pont)* swing (**b**) *(grève)* rotating
2 *nm* (**a**) *(de route, de rivière)* bend (**b**) *Fig (changement)* turning point (**de** in)

tourné, -e [turne] *adj* (**a**) *(formulé)* **bien/mal t.** well/badly phrased (**b**) *(disposé)* **avoir l'esprit mal t.** to have a dirty mind (**c**) *Belg* **être bien/mal t.** to be in a good/bad mood

tournebouler [turnəbule] *vt Fam* to upset

tournebroche [turnəbrɔʃ] *nm* spit

tourne-disque *(pl* **tourne-disques)** [turndisk] *nm* record player

tournedos [turnədo] *nm* tournedos, fillet steak

tournée [turne] *nf* (**a**) *(du facteur, d'un inspecteur)* round; **faire sa t.** to do one's rounds; **faire la t. de** *(magasins, musées)* to go around; **faire sa t. électorale** to go on one's election tour; **faire la t. des grands-ducs** to go out on the town (**b**) *(théâtrale, musicale)* tour; **en t.** on tour (**c**) *Fam (consommations)* round

tournemain [turnəmɛ̃] **en un tournemain** *adv Litt* in an instant

tourner [turne] **1** *vt* (**a**) *(clé, tête, yeux)* to turn; **t. et retourner qch entre ses mains** to turn sth over and over in one's hands; *Fig* **t. et retourner qch (dans tous les sens)** to go over and over an idea (in one's mind); **t. le dos à qn/qch** *(action)* to turn one's back on sb/sth; *(position)* to have one's back to sb/sth; **t. les talons** *(partir)* to turn on one's heel; **t. la tête à qn** *(succès, vin)* to go to sb's head; *(personne)* to turn sb's head
  (**b**) *(page)* to turn (over)
  (**c**) *(remuer)* to stir; *(salade)* to toss
  (**d**) *(film, documentaire, scène)* to shoot, to film
  (**e**) *(attention, pensées)* to turn (**vers** to)
  (**f**) *(changer)* **t. qn/qch en ridicule** to make fun of sb/sth
  (**g**) *(contourner) (coin de la rue)* to turn, to go around; *(obstacle, difficulté, loi)* to get around
  (**h**) *(confectionner) (pièce détachée)* to turn on a lathe; *(pot)* to throw; *Fig (phrase)* to turn; *(compliment)* to word
2 *vi* (**a**) *(clé, roue, aiguille, planète)* to turn; *(porte)* to swing; *(toupie)* to spin; **l'heure tourne** time passes; **t. de l'œil** to pass out
  (**b**) *(se déplacer en rond)* to go around; *aussi Fig* **t. en rond** to go around in circles; *Fam* **il y a quelque chose qui ne tourne pas rond** there's something not right somewhere; *Fam* **il ne tourne pas rond en ce moment** he's not quite himself at the moment; *Fig* **t. autour de qch** *(avoir pour centre)* to center on sth; *(par convoitise)* to hover around sth; *(valoir environ)* to be in the region of sth; *Fig* **t. autour du pot** to beat around the bush
  (**c**) *(entreprise, moteur)* to run
  (**d**) *(obliquer)* to turn; **tournez à gauche** turn left
  (**e**) *(changer) (vent)* to shift (**à** to); *(chance)* to turn
  (**f**) *(lait)* to turn, to go bad
  (**g**) *(avoir telle issue)* **t. court** to end abruptly; **bien/mal t.** *(personne)* to turn out well/badly; **ça va mal t.** it's going to end badly; **t. à l'aigre** to turn sour
  (**h**) *(dans un film)* to act
3 se tourner *vpr* to turn (**vers** towards); *Fig* **se t. vers qn/qch** to turn to sb/sth; *Fam* **se t. les pouces** to twiddle one's thumbs

tournesol [turnəsɔl] *nm* sunflower

tourneur, -euse [turnœr, -øz] *nm,f (ouvrier)* turner

tournevis [turnəvis] *nm* screwdriver; **t. cruciforme** Phillips® screwdriver

tournicoter [turnikɔte] *vi Fam* to wander around

tourniquet [turnikɛ] *nm* (**a**) *(barrière)* turnstile (**b**) *(porte à tambour)* revolving door (**c**) *(présentoir)* revolving stand (**d**) *(arroseur)* sprinkler

tournis [turni] *nm Fam* **avoir le t.** to feel dizzy; **donner le t. à qn** to make sb dizzy

tournoi [turnwa] *nm* tournament

tournoiement [turnwamɑ̃] *nm (des oiseaux)* wheeling; *(des feuilles mortes)* swirl

tournoyer [32] [turnwaje] *vi (oiseaux)* to wheel; *(des feuilles mortes)* to swirl (around); **faire t. qch** to twirl sth

tournure [turnyr] *nf* (a) *(des événements)* turn; **prendre une mauvaise t.** to take a turn for the worse (b) *(forme)* **prendre t.** to take shape; **t. d'esprit** turn of mind; **t. (de phrase)** turn of phrase

tournus [turnys] *nm Suisse* schedule

tour-opérateur (*pl* **tour-opérateurs**) [turɔperatœr] *nm* tour operator

tourte [turt] *nf* pie

tourteau, -x [turto] *nm (crustacé)* edible crab

tourtereau, -x [turtəro] *nm* young turtledove; *Fig* **tourtereaux** *(amoureux)* lovebirds

tourterelle [turtərɛl] *nf* turtledove

tourtière [turtjɛr] *nf* (a) *(pour tourte)* pie dish (b) *Can* = (ground) pork pie

tous [tu, tus] *voir* **tout**

Toussaint [tusɛ̃] *nf* **la T.** All Saints' Day

> **Toussaint**
>
> All Saints' Day (November 1st) is a public holiday in France. It is the traditional occasion for a visit to the cemetery to lay flowers (usually chrysanthemums) on the graves of family and loved ones.

tousser [tuse] *vi* to cough; *Fig (moteur)* to splutter

toussotement [tusɔtmɑ̃] *nm* slight cough

toussoter [tusɔte] *vi (avoir une toux)* to have a slight cough; *(pour attirer l'attention)* to give a slight cough

tout, toute (*pl* **tous, toutes**) [tu, tut]

When **tous** is a pronoun as in **3 (b)**, it is pronounced [tus].

1 *adj (entier)* **t. l'univers** the whole universe; **t. mon argent** all my money; **toute la journée** the whole day; **je ne l'ai pas vu de toute la journée** I haven't seen him all day; **le T.-Paris** anyone who's anyone in Paris

2 *adj indéfini* (a) *(n'importe quel)* any; **t. élève en retard sera puni** any pupil arriving late will be punished; **à t. moment** at any time; **t. autre que vous** anybody but you

(b) *(chaque)* every; **tous les élèves de la classe** every pupil *or* all the pupils in the class; **toutes nos chambres ont l'air conditionné** all our rooms have air-conditioning; **tous les deux jours** every second day, every other day; **ils se retournèrent t. deux** they both turned around

(c) *(emploi intensif)* **à la toute dernière minute** at the very last minute; **de toute beauté** magnificent; **donner toute satisfaction à qn** to give sb complete *or* full satisfaction; **pour toute réponse, il éclata en sanglots** his only answer was to burst into tears; **je suis t. à toi** I'm all yours

3 *pron indéfini* (a) *(au singulier)* everything; **elle a t. de son père** she's her father's daughter; **il a t. du fonctionnaire** he's the typical civil servant; **être t. pour qn** to mean everything to sb; **manger de t.** to eat everything *or* anything; **elle fera t. pour t'ennuyer** she'll do anything to annoy you; **t. ce qu'il y a d'intéressant dans ce film, c'est...** the only interesting thing in this movie is...; **ce sera t.?** *(dans un magasin)* will that be all *or* everything?; **elle est jolie/gentille comme t.** she's really pretty/nice; **tu n'y vas pas et c'est t.!** you're not going and that's that!; *Fam* **...et t. et t.!** ...and all that sort of stuff

(b) *(au pluriel)* all; **ils sont tous partis** they all left

4 *adv* (a) *(très)* very; **t. près** very close

(b) *(complètement)* **être t. en blanc** to be (dressed) all in white; **être t. en sueur** to be pouring with sweat; **t. autrement** quite differently; **être t. à qch** to be engrossed in sth; **t. enfant, il...** as a very young child, he...

(c) *(suivi d'un gérondif)* **t. en conduisant/écrivant** while driving/writing

(d) **t. ignorant/secrétaire que je suis** *ou* **sois...** I may be ignorant/just a secretary, but...

(e) *(expressions)* **t. à fait** *(complètement)* quite, completely; *(exactement)* exactly; **pas du t.** not at all; **t. à coup** suddenly, all of a sudden; **t. à l'heure** *(dans le futur)* in a little while, shortly; *(dans le passé)* a little while ago; **à t. à l'heure!** see you later!; **t. de suite** right away, immediately; **à t. de suite** see you in a minute

5 *nm* **le t.** *(l'ensemble)* the whole; **le t., c'est de se concentrer** the most important thing is to concentrate

tout-à-l'égout [tutalegu] *nm inv* mains drainage

toutefois [tutfwa] *adv* however

toute-puissance [tutpɥisɑ̃s] *nf* absolute power

tout-fou (*pl* **tout-fous**) [tufu] *adj m Fam* batty

toutou [tutu] *nm Fam* doggie

tout-petit (*pl* **tout-petits**) [tupəti] *nm* tot, toddler

tout-puissant, toute-puissante (*mpl* **tout-puissants**, *fpl* **toutes-puissantes**) [tupɥisɑ̃, -ɑ̃t] **1** *adj* all-powerful

2 *nm* **le T.** the Almighty

tout-terrain (*pl* **tout-terrains**) [tuterɛ̃] *adj (véhicule)* all-terrain, off-road; *(vélo)* mountain

tout-va [tuva] **à tout va 1** *adv* like crazy, right left and centre; **le gouvernement privatise à t.** the government are privatising things like crazy

2 *adj* galore; **le magasin proposait des réductions à t.** the store was offering discounts galore

tout-venant [tuvənɑ̃] *nm* **le t.** *(gens)* ordinary people; *(choses)* ordinary things

toux [tu] *nf* cough; **t. sèche/grasse** dry/loose cough

toxicité [tɔksisite] *nf* toxicity

toxico [tɔksiko] *nmf Fam* addict

toxicologie [tɔksikɔlɔʒi] *nf* toxicology

toxicomane [tɔksikɔman] **1** *adj* addicted to drugs

2 *nmf* drug addict

toxicomanie [tɔksikɔmani] *nf* drug addiction

toxine [tɔksin] *nf* toxin

toxique [tɔksik] *adj* toxic, poisonous; *(gaz)* poison

toxoplasmose [tɔksoplazmoz] *nf* toxoplasmosis

TP [tepe] *nmpl Scol & Univ* (*abrév* **travaux pratiques**) practical work

TPI [tepei] *nm* (*abrév* **Tribunal pénal international**) International Court of Justice

trac[1] [trak] *nm* nerves; *(au théâtre)* stage fright; **avoir le t.** to be nervous; *(acteur)* to have stage fright

trac[2] [trak] **tout à trac** *adv Vieilli* out of the blue

traçabilité [trasabilite] *nf* traceability

tracas [traka] *nm* worry, trouble

tracasser [trakase] **1** *vt* to worry, to bother

2 se tracasser *vpr* to worry (**pour** about)

tracasserie [trakasri] *nf* worry; **les tracasseries administratives** red tape

tracassier, -ère [trakasje, -ɛr] *adj* nitpicking

trace [tras] *nf* (a) *(d'animal, d'une personne, de pneus)* tracks; **être sur la t. de qn/qch** to be on the track of sb/sth; **disparaître sans laisser de t.** to disappear without trace; **perdre la t. de qn** to lose track of sb; *Fig* **marcher sur** *ou* **suivre les traces de qn** to follow in sb's footsteps; **t. directe** *(en ski)* direct descent (b) *(tache)* mark; **des traces de gras** grease marks; **des traces de doigts** finger marks; **des traces de pas** footprints; *Fig* **laisser des traces chez qn** *(traumatisme)* to leave its mark on sb; *aussi Fig* **effacer toute t. de qch** to cover up all traces of sth (c) *(petite quantité, vestige)* trace

tracé [trase] *nm* (**a**) *(plan)* layout; **faire le t. de qch** to plan the layout of sth (**b**) *(d'une côte)* line

tracer [16] [trase] **1** *vt* (**a**) *(ligne, plan)* to draw; *Math (courbe, graphique)* to plot; *(lettre)* to write; *Fig* **t. les grandes lignes de qch** to give the general outline of sth (**b**) *(route, chemin)* to mark out; *Fig* **son chemin est tout tracé** his/her path is all mapped out for him/her
2 *vi* (**a**) *Fam (aller vite)* to bomb along (**b**) *Suisse* **t. après qn** *(le poursuivre)* to chase sb

traceur [trasœr] *nm Ordinat* **t. (de courbes)** plotter; **t. à tambour** drum plotter

trachée-artère *(pl* **trachées-artères)** [traʃeartɛr] *nf* windpipe, *Spéc* trachea

trachéite [trakeit] *nf* throat infection

tract [trakt] *nm* leaflet

tractations [traktasjɔ̃] *nfpl* dealings, negotiations

tracter [trakte] *vt* to tow

tracteur [traktœr] *nm* tractor

traction [traksjɔ̃] *nf* (**a**) *(en gymnastique) (aux anneaux)* pull-up; *(à la barre fixe)* chin-up; *(au sol)* push-up (**b**) *(véhicule)* **t. avant/arrière** front-wheel/rear-wheel drive (**c**) *(action)* traction, pulling

tradition [tradisjɔ̃] *nf* tradition; **dans la plus pure t. française** in true French tradition

traditionalisme [tradisjɔnalism] *nm* traditionalism

traditionaliste [tradisjɔnalist] *adj & nmf* traditionalist

traditionnel, -elle [tradisjɔnɛl] *adj* (**a**) *(fondé sur la tradition)* traditional (**b**) *(habituel)* usual

traditionnellement [tradisjɔnɛlmɑ̃] *adv* traditionally

traducteur, -trice [tradyktœr, -tris] **1** *nm,f* translator
2 *nm Ordinat* translator

traduction [tradyksjɔ̃] *nf (action, texte)* translation (**de/en** from/into); **t. automatique/simultanée** machine/simultaneous translation; **t. assistée par ordinateur** computer-assisted translation

traduire [18] [tradɥir] **1** *vt* (**a**) *(texte, terme)* to translate (**de/en** from/into); *Fig (sentiment)* to express (**b**) **t. qn en justice** to bring sb before the courts
2 *vi* to translate (**de/en** from/into)
3 se traduire *vpr (terme)* to be translated; *Fig* **se t. par qch** *(se manifester par)* to be expressed by sth; *(avoir pour résultat)* to result in sth

traduisible [tradɥizibl] *adj* translatable

trafic [trafik] *nm* (**a**) *(de véhicules)* traffic; **t. aérien** air traffic (**b**) *(de marchandises)* traffic; **t. de drogue** drug trafficking

traficoter [trafikɔte] *Fam* **1** *vi* to be a small-time swindler
2 *vt* (**a**) *(vin)* to doctor; *(comptes)* to fiddle (**b**) *(manigancer)* **je me demande ce qu'il traficote** I wonder what he's up to

trafiquant, -e [trafikɑ̃, -ɑ̃t] *nm,f Péj* trafficker; **t. d'armes** arms dealer; **t. de drogue** drug trafficker

trafiquer [trafike] *vt Fam* (**a**) *(moteur)* to tinker with; *(freins, compteur)* to tamper with; *(vin)* to doctor; *(comptes)* to fiddle (**b**) *(manigancer)* **qu'est-ce qu'il trafique?** what's he up to?

tragédie [traʒedi] *nf* tragedy; *Fam Fig* **ce n'est pas une t.!** it's not the end of the world!

tragédien, -enne [traʒedjɛ̃, -ɛn] *nm,f* tragic actor, *f* tragic actress

tragi-comédie *(pl* **tragi-comédies)** [traʒikɔmedi] *nf* tragi-comedy

tragi-comique *(pl* **tragi-comiques)** [traʒikɔmik] *adj* tragi-comic

tragique [traʒik] **1** *adj* tragic
2 *nm* (**a**) *(d'un événement)* tragedy; *Fig* **prendre qch au t.** to make a big thing out of sth (**b**) *(genre)* **le t.** tragedy (**c**) *(auteur)* tragic author

trahir [trair] **1** *vt* (**a**) *(personne, pays)* to betray (**b**) *(secret)* to betray, to give away (**c**) *(gêne, ignorance)* to betray (**d**) *(sujet: jambes, forces)* to fail
2 se trahir *vpr* to give oneself away

trahison [traizɔ̃] *nf (d'une personne, d'un pays)* betrayal; *Jur* treason; **haute t.** high treason

train [trɛ̃] *nm* (**a**) *(moyen de transport, véhicule)* train; **voyager en t.** *ou* **par le t.** to travel by train; **être dans un t.** to be on a train; *Fig* **prendre le t. en marche** to jump *or* climb on the bandwagon; **t. autocouchette(s)** car-sleeper train; **t. de banlieue** commuter train; **t. corail** express train; **t. électrique** electric train; **t. express** express train; **t. à grande vitesse** high-speed train; **t. de marchandises** freight train (**b**) *(de réformes)* series (**c**) *(derrière) (de chien)* rump; *Fam (d'une personne)* backside, rear (**d**) *(allure)* pace; **au t. où vont les choses** at the rate things are going; **à ce t.-là** at this rate; **aller bon t.** to go at a good pace; **rouler à un t. d'enfer** to go hell for leather (**e**) **t. d'atterrissage** *(d'un avion)* landing gear, undercarriage (**f**) *Can Fam (vacarme)* noise, racket (**g**) *(locutions)* **en t.** *(projet, affaire)* under way; **mettre qch en t.** to get sth started; **être en t. de faire qch** to be doing sth; **mener grand t.** to live it up; **t. de vie** lifestyle

traînailler [trɛnaje] = **traînasser**

traînant, -e [trɛnɑ̃, -ɑ̃t] *adj* (**a**) *(robe)* trailing (**b**) *(voix)* drawling; *(démarche, pas)* dragging

traînard, -e [trɛnar, -ard] *nm,f (promeneur)* straggler; *(travailleur)* dawdler

traînasser [trɛnase] *vi Fam* (**a**) *(errer)* to hang around (**b**) *(être lent)* to dawdle

train-couchettes [trɛ̃kuʃɛt] *nm inv* sleeper (train)

traîne [trɛn] *nf* (**a**) *(d'une robe)* train (**b**) *(à la pêche)* dragnet (**c**) *Can* **t. sauvage** toboggan (**d**) *Fam* **être à la t.** to lag behind

traîneau, -x [trɛno] *nm (tiré par des chevaux)* sleigh; *(tiré par des chiens)* sled

traînée [trɛne] *nf* (**a**) *(trace)* trail; **se répandre comme une t. de poudre** to spread like wildfire (**b**) *Fam Péj (femme)* slut

traîne-misère [trɛnmizer] *nmf inv Fam* down-and-out

traîner [trɛne] **1** *vt* (**a**) *(tirer) (objet, corps)* to drag; *(wagon)* to pull (**b**) *Fig* **t. un rhume** to have a nagging cold (**c**) *Péj (vieilles affaires)* to drag around; **t. qn au théâtre** to drag sb along to the theater (**d**) *(locutions)* **t. les pieds** to drag one's feet; *Fam* **t. ses guêtres** *ou* **bottes** to hang around
2 *vi* (**a**) **t. par terre** *(jupe)* to trail on the ground (**b**) *(rester en arrière)* to lag behind (**c**) *(errer)* to hang around (**d**) *(virus)* to go around (**e**) *(affaires, livres, vêtements)* to lie around; **laisser t. qch** to leave sth lying around (**f**) *(être lent) (personne)* to dawdle; *(conversation, intrigue)* to drag; **t. en longueur** to drag on; **ça ne traîne pas avec vous!** you don't dawdle!
3 se traîner *vpr* (**a**) *(sur le sol)* to crawl; *Fig (être fatigué)* to feel like a wet rag; *(aller à contrecœur)* to drag oneself along (**b**) *(journée, soirée)* to drag on

training [trɛniŋ] *nm (survêtement)* tracksuit

train-train [trɛ̃trɛ̃] *nm Fam* routine; **le t. quotidien** the daily grind

traire [28] [trɛr] *vt* (**a**) *(vache, chèvre)* to milk (**b**) *(lait)* to draw

trait [trɛ] *nm* (**a**) *(ligne)* line; **d'un t. de plume** with a stroke of the pen; *Fig* **c'est sa sœur t. pour t.** she is the spitting image of her sister; *Fig* **tirer un t. sur qch** to put sth behind one; **t. d'union** hyphen; *Fig* link (**b**) *(du visage)* features; **des traits réguliers/fins** regular/fine features; **avoir les traits tirés** to look drawn (**c**) *(caractéristique)* feature, trait; **les grands traits de qch** the main features of sth; **t. de caractère** character trait (**d**) *Fig* **t. d'esprit** flash of wit; **t. de génie** stroke of genius (**e**) *(de lumière)* shaft (**f**) *(locutions)* **avoir t. à qch** to be connected with sth, to relate to sth; **boire qch à longs traits** to gulp sth down; **boire/lire qch d'un (seul) t.** to drink/to read sth in one go

traitable [trɛtabl] *adj (sujet)* manageable

traitant, -e [trɛtɑ̃, -ɑ̃t] *adj (shampoing, crème)* medicated

traite [trɛt] *nf* (a) *Fin* draft, bill; **t. bancaire** bank draft (b) *(des vaches)* milking (c) *(trafic)* **la t. des Blanches** the white slave trade; **la t. des Noirs** the slave trade (d) *(locutions)* **(tout) d'une t., d'une seule t.** in one go

traité [trete] *nm* (a) *(ouvrage)* treatise (**de** *ou* **sur** on) (b) *(accord)* treaty

traitement [trɛtmɑ̃] *nm* (a) *(de personne, de maladie)* treatment; **t. de choc** shock treatment; **t. de faveur** preferential treatment (b) *(de matières premières)* processing; *(de l'eau)* treatment (c) *(rémunération)* salary (d) *Ordinat* processing; **données en t., capacité** *ou* **débit de t.** throughput; **t. à distance** teleprocessing; **t. des données** data processing, DP; **t. électronique de l'information** electronic data processing, EDP; **t. d'images** image processing; **t. de l'information** *ou* **des informations** data processing, DP; **t. par lots** batch processing; **t. en temps réel** real time processing; **t. de texte** word processing, WP; *(logiciel)* word processor, word-processing software; **t. de texte à balises** word processing with embedded visible commands; **t. vectoriel** vector processing

traiter [trete] 1 *vt* (a) *(se conduire envers)* to treat; **t. qn en ami/frère** to treat sb like a friend/a brother (b) *(qualifier)* **t. qn de lâche/de menteur** to call sb a coward/a liar (c) *(patient, maladie)* to treat (d) *(matières premières, minerai)* to process; *(eau, bois, cultures)* to treat (e) *Ordinat (informations)* to process; **données non traitées** raw data (f) *(marché)* to negotiate; *(affaire)* to handle; **t. avec qn** to deal with sb (g) *(sujet, question, demande)* to deal with

2 **traiter de** *vt ind (sujet, problème)* to deal with

3 **se traiter** *vpr* (a) *(l'un l'autre)* **se t. d'imbéciles/lâches** to call each other idiots/cowards (b) *(être guéri)* **cette maladie se traite très bien maintenant** this disease responds very well to treatment now

traiteur [trɛtœr] *nm* caterer; **chez le t.** at the deli

traître, -esse [trɛtr, trɛtrɛs] 1 *adj (personne, virage)* treacherous; *(soleil, vin)* deceptively strong; **pas un t. mot** not a single word

2 *nm,f* traitor; **être t. à sa patrie** to be a traitor to one's country; **en t.** treacherously

traîtreusement [trɛtrøzmɑ̃] *adv* treacherously

traîtrise [trɛtriz] *nf* (a) *(caractère)* treachery (b) *(action)* act of treachery

trajectoire [traʒɛktwar] *nf* path, trajectory

trajet [traʒɛ] *nm* (a) *(voyage)* journey; **faire le t. en voiture** to do the journey by car; **deux heures de t.** a two-hour journey (b) *(distance)* distance (c) *(itinéraire)* route

tralala [tralala] *nm inv Fam* **faire des tralalas** to make a great fuss; **... et tout le t.** ... etcetera, etcetera

tram [tram] = **tramway**

trame [tram] *nf (d'un tissu)* weft; *Fig (d'un récit)* framework

tramer [trame] 1 *vt (complot)* to hatch; **t. quelque chose** to be plotting something

2 **se tramer** *vpr* **il se trame quelque chose** there's something afoot

tramontane [tramɔ̃tan] *nf* tramontana

trampoline [trɑ̃pɔlin] *nm* (a) *(appareil)* trampoline (b) *(sport)* trampolining; **faire du t.** to do trampolining

tramway [tramwɛ] *nm* streetcar

tranchant, -e [trɑ̃ʃɑ̃, -ɑ̃t] 1 *adj* (a) *(outil, épée, bord)* sharp (b) *Fig (ton, personne)* curt

2 *nm (d'une lame)* cutting edge; *(de la main)* edge; *Fig* **à double t.** double-edged

tranche [trɑ̃ʃ] *nf* (a) *(de pain, de melon, de viande)* slice; **t. napolitaine** Neapolitan ice cream (b) *(d'un livre)* edge; **doré sur t.** gilt-edged (c) *(partie)* installment; *(de revenus)*

group; *(d'imposition)* bracket; **t. d'âge** age bracket; **t. horaire** *(time)* slot; **t. de vie** slice of life (d) *Fam* **s'en payer une t.** to have the time of one's life

tranché, -e [trɑ̃ʃe] *(opinion)* clear-cut

tranchée [trɑ̃ʃe] *nf* trench

trancher [trɑ̃ʃe] 1 *vt* (a) *(cordage, câble)* to cut; *(gorge)* to slit, to cut; **t. la tête à qn** to cut off sb's head; **la machine lui a tranché le doigt** the machine severed his/her finger (b) *(question, différend)* to settle

2 *vi* (a) *(décider)* to decide; *Fig* **t. dans le vif** to take drastic action (b) *(couleurs)* to contrast (**sur** with)

tranquille [trɑ̃kil] *adj* (a) *(paisible)* quiet; *(mer)* calm; *(sommeil)* peaceful; **laisser qn t.** to leave sb alone (b) *(rassuré)* **se sentir t.** to feel at peace; **vous pouvez dormir t.** you can rest easy; **soyez t.** don't worry; **je ne suis pas t.** I'm feeling uneasy; **avoir l'esprit t.** to have peace of mind

tranquillement [trɑ̃kilmɑ̃] *adv (calmement)* calmly; *(doucement)* quietly; *(dormir)* peacefully; *(partir)* with one's mind at rest

tranquillisant, -e [trɑ̃kilizɑ̃, -ɑ̃t] 1 *adj* (a) *(nouvelles, paroles)* reassuring; *(effet)* soothing (b) *(médicament)* tranquillizing

2 *nm* tranquillizer

tranquilliser [trɑ̃kilize] 1 *vt* to reassure

2 **se tranquilliser** *vpr* to set one's mind at rest

tranquillité [trɑ̃kilite] *nf (calme)* quietness; *(de la mer)* calmness; *(du sommeil)* peacefulness; **avoir besoin de t.** to need peace and quiet; **en toute t.** *(sans être dérangé)* without being disturbed; *(sans souci)* with an easy mind; **t. d'esprit** peace of mind

tranquillos [trɑ̃kilos] *adv Fam (tranquillement)* **vas-y t., inutile de faire des excès de vitesse** take your time, there's no need to break the speed limit; **ils étaient en train de siroter mon whisky, t.** they were sipping away at my whisky, without a care in the world

transaction [trɑ̃zaksjɔ̃] *nf* (a) *(opération)* transaction (b) *Jur* compromise

transactionnel, -elle [trɑ̃zaksjɔnɛl] *adj* (a) *Jur (solution)* compromise (b) *Psy (analyse)* transactional

transalpin, -e [trɑ̃zalpɛ̃, -in] *adj* transalpine

transat [trɑ̃zat] 1 *nm Fam* deckchair

2 *nf* transatlantic race

transatlantique [trɑ̃zatlɑ̃tik] 1 *adj* transatlantic

2 *nm* (a) *(paquebot)* transatlantic liner (b) *(chaise longue)* deckchair

transbahuter [trɑ̃sbayte] *vt Fam* to schlep, to lug

transbordement [trɑ̃sbɔrdəmɑ̃] *nm* transfer; *Naut* transshipment

transcendant, -e [trɑ̃sɑ̃dɑ̃, -ɑ̃t] *adj* transcendent; *Fam* **ce n'est pas t.** it's nothing special

transcendantal, -e, -aux, -ales [trɑ̃sɑ̃dɑ̃tal, -o] *adj* transcendental

transcender [trɑ̃sɑ̃de] 1 *vt* to transcend

2 **se transcender** *vpr* to surpass oneself

transcontinental, -e, -aux, -ales [trɑ̃skɔ̃tinɑ̃tal,-o] *adj* transcontinental

transcription [trɑ̃skripsjɔ̃] *nf* (a) *(action)* transcription; *(dans un autre alphabet)* transliteration; **t. phonétique** phonetic transcription; **t. génétique** genetic transcription (b) *(texte)* transcript

transcrire [30] [trɑ̃skrir] *vt* to transcribe; *(dans un autre alphabet)* to transliterate

transcutané, -e [trɑ̃skytane] *adj* transcutaneous

transdermique [trɑ̃sdɛrmik] *adj* transdermal

transe [trɑ̃s] *nf* trance; **être en t.** to be in a trance; *Fig* to be beside oneself

transept [trɑ̃sɛpt] *nm* transept

transférer [34] [trɑ̃sfere] *vt* to transfer

transfert [trãsfɛr] nm transfer; Psy transference; Tél **t. d'appels** call transfer; Ordinat **t. de données** data transfer; Ordinat **t. électronique de fonds** electronic funds transfer, EFT

transfigurer [trãsfigyre] vt to transfigure

transformable [trãsfɔrmabl] adj convertible

transformateur [trãsfɔrmatœr] nm transformer

transformation [trãsfɔrmasjɔ̃] nf **(a)** (changement) transformation; (d'un local) conversion **(b)** (de matières premières) processing **(c)** (au rugby) conversion; **faire une t.** to convert

transformer [trãsfɔrme] **1** vt **(a)** (changer) to transform; (local, maison) to convert; **t. qn/qch en qch** to turn sb/sth into sth **(b)** (matières premières) to process **(c)** (au rugby) (essai) to convert

  2 se transformer vpr to change; **se t. en qch** to turn into sth

transfuge [trãsfyʒ] nmf defector

transfuser [trãsfyze] vt (sang) to transfuse; Fam **t. qn** to give sb a transfusion

transfusion [trãsfyzjɔ̃] nf **t. (sanguine)** (blood) transfusion; **faire une t. à qn** to give sb a transfusion

transgénique [trãsʒenik] adj transgenic

transgresser [trãsgrese] vt (règlement, loi) to infringe; (ordres) to disobey

transgression [trãsgrɛsjɔ̃] nf (du règlement, de la loi) infringement; (d'ordres) disobeying

transhumance [trãzymãs] nf = the moving of livestock to different pastures according to the season

transhumer [trãzyme] vt & vi = to move to different pastures according to the season

transi, -e [trãzi] adj **(a)** (paralysé) **t. (de peur)** paralyzed with fear; **t. (de froid)** chilled to the bone **(b)** Fam (amoureux) bashful

transiger [45] [trãziʒe] **1** vi to compromise (sur on); **t. avec sa conscience** to compromise one's principles

  2 vt Can (contrat) to negotiate

transistor [trãzistɔr] nm **(a)** Élec (dispositif) transistor **(b)** (poste de radio) transistor (radio)

transit [trãzit] nm **(a)** (de passagers, de marchandises) transit; **en t.** in transit; **circulation de t.** through traffic **(b)** (intestinal) transit; **facilite le t. intestinal** (sur paquet) keeps you regular

transiter [trãzite] **1** vt (marchandises) to forward

  2 vi (marchandises, voyageurs) to pass in transit (**par** through)

transitif, -ive [trãzitif, -iv] adj Gram transitive

transition [trãzisjɔ̃] nf transition; **assurer la t.** to insure a smooth transition; **sans t.** abruptly

transitivement [trãzitivmã] adv transitively

transitivité [trãzitivite] nf transitivity

transitoire [trãzitwar] adj transitional

translation [trãslasjɔ̃] nf Math translation

translucide [trãslysid] adj translucent

transmanche [trãzmãʃ] adj inv cross-Channel

transmetteur [trãsmɛtœr] nm Ordinat & Biol transmitter

transmettre [47] [trãsmɛtr] **1** vt **(a)** (lumière, chaleur, énergie) to transmit **(b)** (maladie, virus) to pass on, to transmit (**à** to) **(c)** (recette, don) to hand on (**à** to); (tradition, objet) to hand down (**à** to); (pouvoir) to hand over (**à** to) **(d)** (message, ordre, amitiés) to pass on (**à** to) **(e)** Rad & TV (information) to transmit; (émission) to broadcast **(f)** Jur (propriété, droit) to transfer; (actions) to assign; **t. ses pouvoirs à qn** to hand over to sb

  2 se transmettre vpr **(a)** (maladie, virus) to be passed on **(b)** (recette, don) to be handed on; (tradition, objet) to be handed down

transmissible [trãsmisibl] adj **(a)** (maladie) transmissible; **maladie sexuellement t.** sexually transmitted disease **(b)** (droit, fortune) transferable

transmission [trãsmisjɔ̃] nf **(a)** (de la chaleur, de la lumière, d'une maladie, d'un virus) transmission; (d'un message, d'un ordre) passing on; (d'une tradition) handing down; **t. de pensée** thought transference **(b)** Rad & TV (d'une image, d'un message) transmission; (d'une émission) broadcasting **(c)** Ordinat transmission; **t. de données** data transmission or transfer; **t. par modem** modem transmission; **t. de paquets** packet transmission **(d)** Jur (d'une propriété, d'un droit) transfer, transference; (d'actions) assignment **(e)** Mil **les transmissions** the signals

transocéanien, -enne [trãzɔseanjɛ̃, -ɛn], **transocéanique** [trãzɔseanik] adj transoceanic

transparaître [20] [trãsparɛtr] vi to show (through)

transparence [trãsparãs] nf **(a)** (d'un tissu, d'une allusion, d'un parti politique) transparency; **on peut le lire par t.** you can read it by holding it up to the light **(b)** Cin back projection

transparent, -e [trãsparã, -ãt] **1** adj aussi Fig transparent

  2 nm transparency

transpercer [16] [trãspɛrse] vt (sujet: lame, flèche, balle) to pierce; (sujet: froid, vent, pluie) to go right through

transpiration [trãspirasjɔ̃] nf **(a)** (sueur) sweat, perspiration **(b)** (action) sweating, perspiration

transpirer [trãspire] vi **(a)** (personne) to sweat, to perspire; **t. des pieds/des aisselles** to have sweaty feet/armpits; **t. à grosses gouttes** to drip with sweat **(b)** Fig (secret, nouvelles) to leak out **(c)** Fam **t. sur** (travailler à) to sweat over

transplant [trãsplã] nm Méd transplant

transplantation [trãsplãtasjɔ̃] nf **(a)** (d'arbres, de personnes) transplantation **(b)** (d'organes) transplant; **t. cardiaque/rénale** heart/kidney transplant

transplanté, -e [trãsplãte] adj (organe) transplanted; **malade t.** transplant patient

transplanter [trãsplãte] vt to transplant

transport [trãspɔr] nm **(a)** (de marchandises, de passagers) transport; **les transports** transportation; **les transports aériens** air transportation; **les transports en commun** public transportation; **t. fluvial** inland waterway transportation; **transports publics urbains** rapid transit **(b)** Jur (de biens, de droits) transfer **(c)** Litt (émotion) rapture; (de joie) transports; (de colère) outbursts

transportable [trãspɔrtabl] adj (marchandises) transportable; (blessé) able to be moved

transporter [trãspɔrte] vt **(a)** (passagers, troupes, marchandises) to transport, to carry; **t. qn à l'hôpital** to take sb to the hospital **(b)** (sujet: film, roman) to transport **(c)** Litt (ravir) to transport; **t. qn de joie** to make sb rapturous

transporteur [trãspɔrtœr] nm carrier; **t. routier** road hauler

transposer [trãspoze] vt **(a)** (mots, morceau de musique) to transpose **(b)** **t. un roman à l'écran/à la scène** to adapt a novel for the screen/for the stage

transposition [trãspozisjɔ̃] nf **(a)** (mot, morceau de musique) transposition **(b)** **t. à l'écran/à la scène** screen/stage adaptation

transsexuel, -elle [trãssɛksɥɛl] adj & nmf transsexual

Transsibérien [trãssiberjɛ̃] nm **le T.** the Trans-Siberian Railroad

transvaser [trãsvaze] vt to pour, to transfer; (vin) to decant

transversal, -e, -aux, -ales [trãsvɛrsal, -o] adj (vallée) transverse; (rue) cross; **coupe transversale** cross-section

transversalement [trãsvɛrsalmã] adv crosswise

trapèze [trapɛz] nm **(a)** (forme géométrique) trapezoid **(b)** (appareil de gymnastique) trapeze; **faire du t.** to perform on the trapeze

trapéziste [trapezist] nmf trapeze artist

trappage [trapaʒ] nm Can trapping

trappe [trap] nf **(a)** (dans le plancher) trap door; **passer à la t.** to be whisked away (without trace) **(b)** (piège) trap

trappeur [trapœr] *nm* trapper

trapu, -e [trapy] *adj* (**a**) *(homme, cheval)* thickset, stocky; *(bâtiment)* squat (**b**) *Fam (élève, professeur)* brainy (**c**) *Fam (problème)* tough

traquenard [traknar] *nm* trap

traquer [trake] *vt (gibier, criminel)* to hunt; *(vedette)* to hound

traumatisant, -e [tromatizã, -ãt] *adj* traumatic

traumatiser [tromatize] *vt* to traumatize

traumatisme [tromatism] *nm* traumatism, trauma; **t. crânien** severe head injury

travail, -aux [travaj, -o] *nm* (**a**) *(activité)* work; *(de l'imagination, de la mémoire)* workings; **se mettre au t.** to get (down) to work; **allons, au t.!** come on, let's get (down) to work!; **cesser le t.** to stop work; **à t. égal, salaire égal** equal pay for equal work

(**b**) *(emploi)* work, job; **chercher du t.** to look for work *or* a job; **être sans t.** not to have a job, to be out of work; **t. à mi-temps/à plein temps** part-time/full-time work; **t. de bureau** office work; **les travaux des champs** work in the fields; *Univ* **travaux dirigés** tutorial; **travaux forcés** hard labor; *Jur* **t. d'intérêt général** community service; **t. manuel** manual labor; *Scol* **travaux manuels** arts and crafts; **travaux ménagers** housework; **t. de nuit** night work; *Scol & Univ* **travaux pratiques** practical work

(**c**) *(tâche)* (piece of) work, job; **un t. bien/mal fait** a good/bad piece of work; **faire de petits travaux** to do odd jobs; **c'est du beau t.** it's a fine piece of work; *Fam & Ironique* **c'est du beau t.!** that was clever!

(**d**) *(lieu de travail)* work

(**e**) *Ordinat* job; **t. multitâche** multitasking; **t. en réseau** networking

(**f**) *(devoir)* work

(**g**) **travaux** *(réparations)* work; **le magasin est en travaux** there's work being done on the store; **attention travaux** *(sur panneau)* men working

(**h**) *(de l'accouchement)* labor

(**i**) *(façonnage)* **le t. du bois** woodwork; **le t. du fer** ironworking; **le t. de l'ivoire/de pierres précieuses** the shaping of ivory/precious stones

travaillant, -e [travajã, -ãt] *Can* **1** *adj* hardworking

2 *nm, f* hard worker

travaillé, -e [travaje] *adj* (**a**) *(fer, bois, pierre)* worked (**b**) *(style)* elaborate (**c**) *(tourmenté)* **être t. par qch** to be tormented by sth

travailler [travaje] **1** *vt* (**a**) *(matière, pâte)* to work (**b**) *(sujet, rôle, style)* to work on; *(texte, auteur)* to study; *(morceau de musique, technique)* to practice (**c**) *(inquiéter)* to torment

2 *vi* (**a**) *(personne)* to work; **t. à la pièce** to do piecework; **t. dans qch** to work in sth; **faire t. son argent** to make one's money work for one; **faire t. son imagination** to use one's imagination; *Fam* **t. du chapeau** to have a screw loose (**b**) *(s'entraîner) (sportif)* to train; *(musicien)* to practice (**c**) *(câble)* to strain; *(bois)* to warp; *(murs)* to crack; *(vin)* to ferment (**d**) *(agir)* **t. pour/contre qn** to be on sb's side/against sb

3 travailler à *vt ind (roman, documentaire)* to work on; **t. à la perte de qn** to try to ruin sb

travailleur, -euse [travajœr, -øz] **1** *adj* hard-working

2 *nm, f* worker; **t. manuel/intellectuel** manual/non-manual worker; **t. indépendant** self-employed worker, freelancer

travailliste [travajist] *Pol* **1** *nmf* member of the Labor Party

2 *adj (parti)* Labor

travée [trave] *nf* (**a**) *(de sièges)* row (**b**) *Archit* bay

traveller's check, traveller's cheque [travlœrʃɛk] *nm* traveler's check

travelling [travliŋ] *nm Cin (déplacement)* tracking; *(plan)* tracking shot; **faire un t.** to do a tracking shot; **t. avant/arrière** track in/out

travelo [travlo] *nm Fam* transvestite

travers [travɛr] *nm* (**a**) *(défaut)* failing (**b**) *(largeur)* breadth; *Culin* **t. de porc** spare ribs (**c**) *(locutions)* **à t. qch, au t. de qch** through sth; **à t. les siècles** down the centuries; **à t. le monde** throughout the world; **voir à t. qch** to see through sth; **passer au t. de qch** to go through sth; **marcher de t.** not to walk in a straight line; *Fig* **aller de t.** to go wrong; **être de t.** *(chapeau, tableau)* to be crooked; **prendre qch de t.** to take sth the wrong way; **regarder qn de t.** to look sideways at sb; **comprendre qch de t.** to misunderstand sth; **en t.** crosswise; **en t. de qch** across sth; **se mettre en t. de qch** to get in the way of sth

traverse [travɛrs] *nf (sur une voie ferrée)* tie

traversée [travɛrse] *nf (d'un cours d'eau)* crossing; *(d'une ville, d'une forêt)* going through; *Fig* **t. du désert** time in the wilderness

traverser [travɛrse] *vt* (**a**) *(rue, pont, cours d'eau)* to cross; *(ville, pays, forêt)* to go through; *Fig* **t. l'esprit à qn** *(idée, doute)* to cross sb's mind (**b**) *(tissu, mur)* to go (right) through (**c**) *(crise, période)* to go through; **t. les siècles** to come down through the ages

traversier, -ère [travɛrsje, -ɛr] **1** *adj voir* **flûte**

2 *nm Can (bac)* ferry

traversin [travɛrsɛ̃] *nm* bolster

travesti [travɛsti] *nm* transvestite

travestir [travɛstir] **1** *vt* (**a**) *(personne)* to to dress up (**en** as) (**b**) *(vérité, faits, pensée)* to distort

2 se travestir *vpr* (**a**) *(se déguiser)* to put on fancy dress (**b**) *(s'habiller en femme)* to dress up in drag

traviole [travjɔl] **de traviole** *adv Fam* **marcher de t.** to be staggering all over the place; **être de t.** to be lopsided

trayeuse [trɛjøz] *nf* milking machine

trébucher [trebyʃe] *vi* to trip, to stumble (**sur/contre** over/against); **faire t. qn** to trip sb up

trèfle [trɛfl] *nm* (**a**) *(plante)* clover; **t. à quatre feuilles** four-leaf clover (**b**) *(carte)* club; *(couleur)* clubs (**c**) *(emblème irlandais)* shamrock

tréfonds [trefɔ̃] *nm Litt* **au t. de son cœur** in one's heart of hearts; **au t. de son âme** in the depths of one's soul

treillage [trɛjaʒ] *nm (clôture)* trellis fencing

treille [trɛj] *nf* (**a**) *(tonnelle)* vine arbor (**b**) *(vigne)* climbing vine

treillis [trɛji] *nm* (**a**) *(treillage)* trellis; **t. métallique** wire mesh (**b**) *(tissu)* canvas (**c**) *(uniforme militaire)* combat uniform

treize [trɛz] **1** *adj inv* thirteen; **t. à la douzaine** a baker's dozen; *Fam* **en avoir t. à la douzaine** to have more than one knows what to do with

2 *nm inv* thirteen; *voir aussi* **trois**

treizième [trɛzjɛm] *adj, nmf & nm* thirteenth; *voir aussi* **cinquième**

trekking [trɛkiŋ] *nm* trek

tréma [trema] *nm* diaeresis; **e/i t.** e/i diaeresis

tremblant, -e [trãblã, -ãt] *adj* (**a**) *(genoux, main)* trembling, shaky; **être t. de peur** to be trembling *or* shaking with fear; **être t. de froid/fièvre** to be shivering with cold/fever (**b**) *(voix)* quavering

tremble [trãbl] *nm* aspen

tremblement [trãbləmã] *nm* (**a**) *(du corps, de la main)* trembling, shaking; *(de peur)* shudder; *(de fièvre)* shivering; **être pris de tremblements** to start to shake; **avec un t. dans la voix** with a tremor in his/her voice; *Fam* **et tout le t.** blah, blah, blah (**b**) *(de la voix)* quavering (**c**) **t. de terre** earthquake

trembler [trãble] *vi* (**a**) *(main, genoux)* to shake, to tremble; *(lèvres)* to tremble; **t. de colère/peur** to tremble *or* to shake with anger/fear; **t. de froid** to shiver with cold; **t. comme une feuille** to shake like a leaf; **t. de tout son corps** to be shaking all over (**b**) *(voix)* to quaver (**c**) *(terre, bâtiment)* to shake; *(feuilles)* to quiver; *(flamme)* to flicker; **faire t. les vitres** to make the windows shake *or* rattle; **faire t. un bâtiment** to rock *or* to shake a building (**d**) *(avoir peur)* to tremble; **t. de tout son corps** to tremble all over; **t. devant qn** to be terrified of sb; **t. pour qn** to tremble for sb

tremblotant, -e [trɑ̃blɔtɑ̃, -ɑ̃t] *adj (personne, corps)* trembling; *(voix)* tremulous; *(lumière)* flickering

tremblote [trɑ̃blɔt] *nf Fam* **avoir la t.** to be shaky; *(de peur)* to have the jitters; *(de froid)* to have the shivers

tremblotement [trɑ̃blɔtmɑ̃] *nm (des mains)* trembling, shaking; *(de la voix)* quavering; *(de la lumière)* flickering

trembloter [trɑ̃blɔte] *vi (personne, mains)* to tremble *or* to shake slightly; *(voix)* to quaver; *(lumière)* to flicker

trémière [tremjɛr] *adj f voir* **rose**

trémolo [tremɔlo] *nm* tremolo; *Fig* **avec des trémolos dans la voix** with a tremor in one's voice

trémousser [tremuse] **se trémousser** *vpr* to jig about; **se t. sur sa chaise** to wriggle about on one's chair

trempage [trɑ̃paʒ] *nm* soaking

trempe [trɑ̃p] **1** *nf* (**a**) *(force de caractère)* caliber; **une femme de sa t.** a woman of her caliber (**b**) *Fam (volée de coups)* hiding
2 *adj Can & Suisse (personne, vêtements)* soaked, drenched; *(chaussures, jardin)* waterlogged

trempé, -e [trɑ̃pe] *adj* (**a**) *(personne, vêtement)* soaked; **t. de sueur** *(personne)* dripping with sweat; *(vêtement)* saturated with sweat (**b**) *(acier, verre)* hardened; *Fig* **bien t.** *(caractère)* sturdy

tremper [trɑ̃pe] **1** *vt* (**a**) *(mouiller)* to soak; **se faire t. (par la pluie)** to get soaked (**b**) *(plonger)* to dip (**dans** in); **t. les lèvres** to take a small sip (**c**) *(acier)* to quench
2 *vi* (**a**) **faire t. qch, mettre qch à t.** *(linge)* to soak sth (**b**) *Fig (se compromettre)* **t. dans qch** to be mixed up in sth
3 se tremper *vpr (se baigner)* to have a quick dip; **se t. les pieds dans l'eau** to dip one's feet in the water

trempette [trɑ̃pɛt] *nf Fam* **faire t.** to have a quick dip

tremplin [trɑ̃plɛ̃] *nm (pour sauteur, pour plongeur) & Fig* springboard; *(pour skieur)* ski jump

trench-coat *(pl* **trench-coats**) [trɛnʃkot] *nm* trench coat

trentaine [trɑ̃tɛn] *nf* (**a**) *(nombre)* **une t. (de)** about thirty (**b**) *(âge)* **avoir la t.** to be about thirty; **approcher de la t.** to be pushing thirty

trente [trɑ̃t] **1** *adj inv* thirty; *(au tennis)* **t. à** thirty all
2 *nm inv* thirty; *Fig* **être sur son t. et un** to be dressed up to the nines; *voir aussi* **trois**

trente-six [trɑ̃tsis] **1** *adj inv* thirty-six; *Fam (beaucoup)* umpteen; *Fig* **voir t. chandelles** *(après un coup sur la tête)* to see stars; *Fam* **il n'y a pas t. solutions** there are no two ways about it
2 *nm inv* thirty-six; *Fig* **tous les t. du mois** once in a blue moon; *Can Fam* **être sur son t.** to be dressed up to the nines; *voir aussi* **trois**

trente-sixième [trɑ̃tsizjɛm] *adj Fam Fig* **être au t. dessous** to be really down in the dumps; *voir aussi* **cinquième**

trente-trois tours [trɑ̃ttrwatur] *nm inv* LP

trentième [trɑ̃tjɛm] *nmf, nn & adj* thirtieth; *voir aussi* **cinquième**

trépanation [trepanasjɔ̃] *nf* trepanning

trépaner [trepane] *vt* to trepan

trépas [trepɑ] *nm Litt* death; **passer de vie à t.** to depart this life

trépasser [trepase] *vi Litt* to depart this life

trépidant, -e [trepidɑ̃, -ɑ̃t] *adj (vie, activité)* hectic

trépidation [trepidasjɔ̃] *nf (d'une machine, d'un moteur)* vibration

trépied [trepje] *nm* (**a**) *(d'appareil photo)* tripod (**b**) *(tabouret)* three-legged stool

trépignement [trepiɲəmɑ̃] *nm* stamping (of feet)

trépigner [trepiɲe] *vi* to stamp (one's feet); **t. de colère/d'impatience** to jump up and down with rage/impatience

très [trɛ] *adv* very; **avoir t. faim/chaud/froid** to be very hungry/hot/cold; **avoir t. envie de faire qch** to really want to do sth; **t. estimé** highly respected; **t. aimé** much liked; **t. peu utilisé** very rarely used

trésor [trezɔr] *nm* (**a**) *(objets précieux)* treasure; *Fam* **mon t.** darling; *Fig* **des trésors de patience/générosité** boundless patience/generosity; **t. de guerre** war chest (**b**) *(dans une église)* relics and ornaments (**c**) **le T. (public)** ≃ the Treasury

trésorerie [trezɔrri] *nf* (**a**) *(bureau)* accounting department (**b**) *(ressources)* funds, finances

trésorier, -ère [trezɔrje, -ɛr] *nm,f* treasurer

tressaillement [tresajmɑ̃] *nm (de surprise, de peur)* jump, start; *(de plaisir)* quiver; *(de douleur)* wince

tressaillir [67] [tresajir] *vi (de surprise, de peur)* to jump, to start; *(de plaisir)* to quiver; *(de douleur)* to wince

tressautement [tresotmɑ̃] *nm (secousse)* jolt

tressauter [tresote] *vi (être secoué)* to jolt about

tresse [trɛs] *nf* (**a**) *(de cheveux)* braid; **se faire des tresses** to braid one's hair (**b**) *(de fil)* braid (**c**) *Suisse (pain)* plaited loaf

tresser [trese] *vt (cheveux)* to braid; *(paille, osier)* to plait; *(panier, guirlande)* to weave; *Fig* **t. des couronnes à qn** to sing sb's praises

tréteau, -x [treto] *nm* trestle

treuil [trœj] *nm* winch, windlass

trêve [trɛv] *nf* (**a**) *(amnistie)* truce (**b**) *Fig (pause, arrêt)* respite, rest; *Fam* **t. de plaisanteries!** joking apart; **sans t.** unremittingly; *Fam* **t. des confiseurs** = truce over Christmas and New Year between opposing political parties

Trèves [trɛv] *n* Trier

tri [tri] *nm* (**a**) *(d'objets, d'idées)* sorting out; *(de lettres)* sorting; *(de candidats)* selection; **faire le t. dans qch** to sort sth out; **il va falloir faire le t.** we'll have to sort through them; **faire du t. dans ses vêtements/papiers** to sort through one's clothes/papers; **t. postal** mail sorting (**b**) *Ordinat* sort; **effectuer un t.** to do a sort; **t. alphabétique** alphabetic sort

triage [trijaʒ] *nm* sorting out; *(de lettres)* sorting

trial [trijal] *nm* motorcycle trials

triangle [trijɑ̃gl] *nm* triangle; **t. des Bermudes** Bermuda Triangle; **le T. d'or** the Golden Triangle; **t. rectangle** right-angled triangle

triangulaire [trijɑ̃gylɛr] *adj* triangular

triathlon [triatlɔ̃] *nm* triathlon

tribal, -e, -aux, -ales [tribal, -o] *adj* tribal

tribord [tribɔr] *nm* starboard; **à t.** on the starboard side

tribu [triby] *nf* tribe

tribulations [tribylasjɔ̃] *nfpl* tribulations, troubles

tribun [tribœ̃] *nm* (**a**) *(magistrat romain)* tribune (**b**) *(orateur)* popular orator

tribunal, -aux [tribynal, -o] *nm (bâtiment)* courthouse; *(magistrats)* court; **porter une affaire devant les tribunaux** to take a case to court; **t. administratif** = court which deals with civil law; **t. de commerce** commercial court; **t. pour enfants** juvenile court; **t. de grande instance** ≃ circuit court; **t. d'instance** ≃ county court; **t. militaire** military tribunal

tribune [tribyn] *nf* (**a**) *(d'orateur)* rostrum, platform (**b**) *(débat)* forum; **t. libre** *(dans un journal)* opinion column (**c**) **les tribunes** *(dans un stade)* the stands; **t. d'honneur** grandstand; **t. de la presse** press gallery

tribut [triby] *nm* tribute; **le pays a payé un lourd t. à la guerre** the war cost the country dearly

tributaire [tribytɛr] *adj* (**a**) *(dépendant)* **être t. de** to be dependent on (**b**) *(cours d'eau)* tributary

tricentenaire [trisɑ̃tnɛr] **1** *adj* three-hundred-year-old
2 *nm* tercentenary, tricentennial

triceps [trisɛps] *nm* triceps

triche [triʃ] *nf Fam* cheating

tricher [triʃe] *vi* to cheat; **t. sur qch** to lie about sth; **t. aux cartes/à un examen** to cheat at cards/on a test

tricherie [triʃri] *nf* cheating

tricheur, -euse [triʃœr, -øz] *nm,f* cheat

trichloréthylène [triklɔretilɛn] *nm* trichlorethylene

tricolore [trikɔlɔr] **1** *adj* (**a**) *(à trois couleurs)* three-colored (**b**) *(de la France)* French
2 *nmpl* **les tricolores** the French team

tricorne [trikɔrn] *nm* three-cornered hat, tricorn

tricot [triko] *nm* (**a**) *(activité)* knitting; **faire du t.** to do some knitting (**b**) *(ouvrage)* knitting (**c**) *(chandail)* sweater; **t. de corps** undershirt (**d**) *(tissu)* knitted fabric

tricoter [trikɔte] **1** *vt* to knit; **tricoté (à la) main** hand-knitted
2 *vi* to knit; **t. à la main/à la machine** to hand-knit/machine-knit

tricycle [trisikl] *nm* tricycle; **faire du t.** to go tricycling

trident [tridã] *nm* (**a**) *(dans la mythologie)* trident (**b**) *(fourche)* three-pronged fork

tridimensionnel, -elle [tridimãsjɔnɛl] *adj* three-dimensional

triennal, -e, -aux, -ales [trienal, -o] *adj* *(élection, révision)* three-yearly, triennial; *(bail)* three-year

trier [66] [trije] *vt* (**a**) *(lettres)* to sort; *(vêtements, informations)* to sort *or* to go through; *(fruits, lentilles)* to pick over; **t. qn/qch sur le volet** to hand-pick sb/sth (**b**) *Ordinat* to sort; **t. par ordre alphabétique** to sort in alphabetical order

trifouiller [trifuje] *vi Fam* **qu'est-ce que tu trifouilles?** what are you up to?; **t. dans qch** to rummage around in sth

triglycéride [trigliserid] *nf* triglyceride

trigonométrie [trigɔnɔmetri] *nf* trigonometry

trigonométrique [trigɔnɔmetrik] *adj* trigonometric

trilatéral, -e, -aux, -ales [trilateral, -o] *adj* trilateral

trilingue [trilɛ̃g] *adj* trilingual

trille [trij] *nm* trill

trilogie [trilɔʒi] *nf* trilogy

trimaran [trimarã] *nm* trimaran

trimbal(l)er [trɛ̃bale] *Fam* **1** *vt* *(paquets)* to lug *or* to schlep around; *(enfants)* to trail around
2 se trimbal(l)er *vpr* to trail around; **elle se trimbal(l)e partout avec sa marmaille** she trails her kids around with her everywhere she goes

trimer [trime] *vi Fam* to slave away; **faire t. qn** to keep sb hard at it

trimestre [trimɛstr] *nm* quarter; *Scol & Univ* trimester

trimestriel, -elle [trimɛstrijɛl] *adj* quarterly

tringle [trɛ̃gl] *nf* rod; **t. à rideau** curtain rod

trinité [trinite] *nf* *(groupe de trois éléments)* trinity; *Rel* **la (sainte) T.** the (Holy) Trinity; **la T.** *(fête)* Trinity Sunday

Trinité-et-Tobago [triniteetɔbago] *n* Trinidad and Tobago

trinquer [trɛ̃ke] *vi* (**a**) *(porter un toast)* to clink glasses; **t. à qch** to drink to sth; **t. à la santé de qn** to drink a toast to sb (**b**) *Fam (souffrir)* to be the one who suffers

trio [trijo] *nm* (**a**) *(groupe de trois personnes)* threesome, trio (**b**) *(en musique)* trio

triolet [trijɔlɛ] *nm Mus* triplet

triomphal, -e, -aux, -ales [trijɔ̃fal, -o] *adj* triumphant

triomphalement [trijɔ̃falmã] *adv* triumphantly

triomphalisme [trijɔ̃falism] *nm* crowing; **sans faire de t. ...** while I don't want to crow...

triomphant, -e [trijɔ̃fã, -ãt] *adj* triumphant; **d'un ton t.** triumphantly

triomphe [trijɔ̃f] *nm* triumph (**sur** over); **faire un t. à qn** to give sb an ovation; **porter qn en t.** to carry sb on one's shoulders

triompher [trijɔ̃fe] **1** *vi* (**a**) *(gagner)* to triumph; *Fig (vérité)* to prevail (**b**) *(exulter)* to crow
2 triompher de *vt ind* to triumph over

trip [trip] *nm Fam (d'un drogué)* trip; **faire un t.** to trip; **être dans un t. écolo** to be on an environmental kick

triparti, -e [triparti], **tripartite** [tripartit] *adj* tripartite

tripatouillage [tripatujaʒ] *nm Fam (de textes, de comptes)* tampering with; *(de statistiques)* massaging

tripatouiller [tripatuje] *vt Fam* (**a**) *(textes, comptes)* to tamper with; *(statistiques)* to massage (**b**) *(cheveux)* to play *or* to fiddle with; *(bouton)* to pick at

tripe [trip] *nf* (**a**) **tripes** *(d'un animal)* entrails; *Fam (d'une personne)* guts; *Fam* **prendre qn aux tripes** to get sb right there (**b**) **tripes** *(plat)* tripe (**c**) *Fam Fig* **avoir la t. républicaine** to be a republican through and through

triperie [tripri] *nf (boutique)* tripe store

tripette [tripɛt] *nf Fam* **ça ne vaut pas t.** it's not worth a damn

triphasé, -e [trifɑze] *adj Élec* three-phase

triphtongue [triftɔ̃g] *nf* triphthong

tripier, -ère [tripje, -ɛr] *nm,f* tripe butcher

triple [tripl] **1** *adj* (**a**) *(à trois éléments)* triple; **en t. exemplaire** in triplicate; *Mus* **t. croche** thirty-second note (**b**) *(trois fois plus grand)* triple, treble (**c**) *(emploi intensif) Fam* **t. buse** prize idiot; **au t. galop** at breakneck speed
2 *nm* **le t. (de)** *(quantité, prix)* three times as much (as); *(nombre)* three times as many (as); **douze est le t. de quatre** twelve is three times four

triplé, -e [triple] **1** *nm,f* triplet
2 *nm (triple succès)* triple victory; *(pari)* = bet on the first three horses in a race

triplement [triplamã] *adv* trebly, triply

tripler [triple] **1** *vt (somme, quantité)* to treble, to triple; **t. une classe** to repeat a year twice
2 *vi* to treble, to triple

Tripoli [tripɔli] *n* Tripoli

triporteur [tripɔrtœr] *nm* delivery tricycle

tripot [tripo] *nm* gambling den

tripotée [tripɔte] *nf Fam* (**a**) *(défaite)* hammering (**b**) *(grand nombre)* **une t. de** loads of

tripoter [tripɔte] *vt Fam* (**a**) *(objet, appareil, cheveux)* to play with, to fiddle with; *(boutons, plaie)* to touch (**b**) *(personne)* to feel up, to grope

triptyque [triptik] *nm* triptych

trique [trik] *nf* cudgel; *Fam* **mener qn à la t.** to rule sb with a rod of iron

trisomie [trizɔmi] *nf Méd* **t. 21** Down's syndrome

trisomique [trizɔmik] *adj Méd* with Down's syndrome; **être t.** to have Down's syndrome

triste [trist] *adj* (**a**) *(malheureux)* sad (**b**) *(sinistre)* dreary, depressing; *Fam* **c'était pas t.!** *(soirée)* it was quite an evening!; *Fam* **il est pas t., son frère!** his brother's quite a character! (**c**) *(pénible)* sad; *(époque)* grim; **dans un t. état** in a sorry state; **c'est la t. réalité** that's the sad *or* harsh reality (**d**) *Péj* sad

tristement [tristamã] *adv* sadly; **t. célèbre** notorious

tristesse [tristɛs] *nf* (**a**) *(d'une personne, d'un événement)* sadness; **c'est avec t. que je vous annonce...** I am sorry to have to tell you... (**b**) *(aspect sinistre)* dreariness

tristounet, -ette [tristunɛ, -ɛt] *adj Fam* gloomy

trithérapie [triterapi] *nf Méd* triple (combination) therapy

triton [tritɔ̃] *nm* (**a**) *(amphibien)* newt (**b**) *(mollusque)* triton, trumpet shell (**c**) *(personnage mythologique)* Triton

triturer [trityre] **1** *vt* (**a**) *(broyer)* to grind (**b**) *Fam (tripoter)* to fiddle with
2 se triturer *vpr Fam* **se t. la cervelle** *ou* **les méninges** to rack one's brains

triumvirat [trijɔmvira] *nm* triumvirate

trivial, -e, -aux, -ales [trivjal, -o] *adj* (**a**) *(vulgaire)* vulgar, coarse (**b**) *(commun)* banal

trivialité [trivjalite] *nf* (**a**) *(vulgarité)* vulgarity, coarseness (**b**) *(expression)* vulgar *or* coarse expression (**c**) *(banalité)* banality

troc [trɔk] *nm* (**a**) *(échange)* exchange (**b**) *(système économique)* barter; **faire du t.** to barter

troène [trɔɛn] *nm* privet

troglodyte [trɔglɔdit] *nm (personne)* cave dweller, *Spéc* troglodyte

trogne [trɔɲ] *nf Fam* face, mug

trognon [trɔɲɔ̃] **1** *nm (de pomme)* core
  2 *adj inv Fam (mignon)* cute

Troie [trwa] *n* Troy

troïka [trɔika] *nf* troika

trois [trwa] **1** *adj inv* three; **le t. août** (on) August third; **à t. heures** at three o'clock; **page t.** page three; **Henri T.** Henry the Third; **nous étions t.** there were three of us; **les t. quarts du temps** most of the time; **couper/partager qch en t.** to cut/divide sth into three; **t. par t.** three by three; **(hôtel) t. étoiles** three-star hotel; **en t. dimensions** in 3-D
  2 *nm inv* three

trois-huit [trwaɥit] *nm inv* **faire les t.** = to work three alternating eight-hour shifts

troisième [trwazjɛm] **1** *adj, nmf & nm* third; **le t. âge** senior citizens
  2 *nf* (**a**) *Scol* ≃ eighth grade (**b**) *(vitesse)* third (gear); *voir aussi* **cinquième**

troisièmement [trwazjɛmmɑ̃] *adv* thirdly

trois-mâts [trwamɑ] *nm inv* three-master

trois-pièces [trwapjɛs] *nm inv* (**a**) *(appartement)* three-room apartment; **t. cuisine** three-and-a-half-room apartment (**b**) *(costume)* three-piece suit

trois-quarts [trwakar] *nm inv* (**a**) *(manteau)* three-quarter-length coat (**b**) *(au rugby)* three-quarter

trolley [trɔlɛ], **trolleybus** [trɔlɛbys] *nm* trolleybus

trombe [trɔ̃b] *nf* waterspout; **il pleut des trombes** it's pouring down; **sous les trombes d'eau** in the torrential rain; *Fam Fig* **passer/partir en t.** to tear past/off

trombine [trɔ̃bin] *nf Fam* face

trombone [trɔ̃bɔn] *nm* (**a**) *(agrafe)* paper clip (**b**) *(instrument)* trombone; **t. à coulisse/à pistons** slide/valve trombone (**c**) *(instrumentiste)* trombone player, trombonist

trompe [trɔ̃p] *nf* (**a**) *(d'éléphant)* trunk; *(d'insecte)* proboscis (**b**) *(instrument à vent)* horn (**c**) *Anat* **t. d'Eustache/de Fallope** Eustachian/Fallopian tube

trompe-l'œil [trɔ̃plœj] *nm inv (décor)* trompe l'œil; **en t. trompe l'œil**

tromper [trɔ̃pe] **1** *vt* (**a**) *(abuser)* to fool (**sur** about) (**b**) *(être infidèle à)* to be unfaithful to (**c**) *(vigilance, surveillance)* to elude, to escape (**d**) *Fig* **t. son ennui** to relieve the boredom; **t. sa faim** to stave off one's hunger
  2 se tromper *vpr (faire une erreur)* to make a mistake; *(avoir tort)* to be mistaken; **se t. dans les dates/proportions** to get the dates/the proportions wrong; **se t. de numéro** *(au téléphone)* to dial the wrong number; **se t. d'heure/de jour** to get the time/day wrong

tromperie [trɔ̃pri] *nf* deceit, deception

trompeter [42] [trɔ̃pəte] *vt (nouvelles)* to shout from the rooftops

trompette [trɔ̃pɛt] *nf* trumpet; *Fig* **avoir le nez en t.** to have a turned-up nose; **t. bouchée** muted trumpet

trompette-de-la-mort (*pl* **trompettes-de-la-mort**) [trɔ̃pɛtdəlamɔr] *nf Bot* horn of plenty

trompettiste [trɔ̃pɛtist] *nmf* trumpet player, trumpeter

trompeur, -euse [trɔ̃pœr, -øz] *adj* (**a**) *(volontairement)* deceitful (**b**) *(symptôme, apparences)* deceptive; *(publicité)* misleading

tronc [trɔ̃] *nm* (**a**) *(d'un arbre, d'un corps)* trunk; *Fig* **t. commun** core syllabus; *Fam* **se casser le t.** to strain oneself (**b**) *(dans une église)* poor box

tronche [trɔ̃ʃ] *nf Fam (tête)* nut; *(visage)* mug; **faire la t.** to sulk

tronçon [trɔ̃sɔ̃] *nm* piece; *(de route)* section

tronçonner [trɔ̃sɔne] *vt* to cut into sections

tronçonneuse [trɔ̃sɔnøz] *nf* chain saw

trône [tron] *nm aussi Fam Fig* throne

trôner [trone] *vi* (**a**) *Hum (personne)* to sit on one's throne (**b**) *(objet)* to have pride of place

tronquer [trɔ̃ke] *vt (mot, scène)* to shorten

trop [tro] *adv* (**a**) *(avec un adjectif ou un adverbe)* too; **ça va? – pas t. mal** how's it going? – not too bad; *Fam* **il est vraiment t.!** he's too much! (**b**) *(avec un verbe)* too much; **il n'y tient pas t.** he's not too bothered; **je ne sais pas t.** I'm not too sure; **ça te plaît? – pas t.** do you like it? – not much; **on ne saurait t. le répéter** it can't be repeated too often (**c**) *(quantité)* too much; *(nombre)* too many; **t. de** *(quantité)* too much; *(nombre)* too many; **nous sommes t.** there are too many of us; **il y a deux assiettes de** *ou* **en t.** there are two plates too many; **payer 50 euros de t.** *ou* **en t.** to pay 50 euros too much; **c'est une fois de t.** that's once too often; **se sentir de t.** to feel in the way; **t., c'est t.!** enough is enough!; **c'en est t.!** this really is too much!

trophée [trɔfe] *nm* trophy

tropical, -e, -aux, -ales [trɔpikal, -o] *adj* tropical

tropique [trɔpik] *nm* (**a**) *(parallèle)* tropic; **le T. du Cancer/du Capricorne** the tropic of Cancer/of Capricorn (**b**) **les tropiques** *(région)* the tropics; **sous les tropiques** in the tropics

trop-perçu (*pl* **trop-perçus**) [tropɛrsy] *nm* overpayment

trop-plein (*pl* **trop-pleins**) [troplɛ̃] *nm* (**a**) *(excédent)* overflow (**b**) *(dispositif d'évacuation)* overflow pipe

troquer [trɔke] *vt* **t. qch contre qch** to exchange sth for sth

troquet [trɔkɛ] *nm Fam* small café

trot [tro] *nm* trot; **aller au t.** to trot; *Fam Fig* **allez-y, et au t.!** go on, and be quick about it!; **t. attelé** harness race

trotskiste, trotskyste [trɔtskist] *adj & nmf* Trotskyist

trotte [trɔt] *nf Fam (distance)* **il y a une bonne t. d'ici à chez elle** it's a fair distance from here to her house

trotter [trɔte] *vi* (**a**) *(cheval)* to trot (**b**) *(personne)* to trot around (**c**) *Fig* **cet air me trotte dans la tête depuis hier** I haven't been able to get that tune out of my head since yesterday; **cette idée me trottait dans la tête** the idea was running through my head

trotteur [trɔtœr] *nm* (**a**) *(cheval)* trotter (**b**) *(chaussure)* flat shoe

trotteuse [trɔtøz] *nf (de montre)* second hand

trottiner [trɔtine] *vi (personne)* to trot around

trottinette [trɔtinɛt] *nf* scooter; **faire de la t.** to ride a scooter

trottoir [trɔtwar] *nm* sidewalk; *Fam* **faire le t.** to work the streets; **t. roulant** moving sidewalk

trou [tru] *nm* (**a**) *(ouverture)* hole; *(d'aiguille)* eye; *Fam Fig* **faire son t.** to find one's niche; **t. d'air** air pocket; **le t. dans la couche d'ozone** the hole in the ozone layer; *aussi Fig Vulg* **t. du cul** asshole; **t. noir** black hole; *Fig* **je suis tombé de l'échelle, et après c'est le t. noir** I fell off the ladder, and after that it's all a blank; **t. de serrure** keyhole; **t. de souris** mouse hole (**b**) *(dans un emploi du temps, dans ses connaissances)* gap; **j'ai un t. de cinq à sept** I'm free between five and seven; **avoir un t. (de mémoire)** to have a memory lapse (**c**) *(déficit)* hole, dent; *Fam* **le t. de la sécu** the Social Security deficit (**d**) *Fam Péj (lieu reculé)* hole; **il n'est jamais sorti de son t.** he has never been out of his own backyard (**e**) *Fam (prison)* clink, slammer (**f**) **faire le t. normand** = to drink a glass of Calvados between courses to aid digestion

troubadour [trubadur] *nm* troubadour

troublant, -e [trublɑ̃, -ɑ̃t] *adj* (**a**) *(déconcertant)* disconcerting (**b**) *(sensuel)* provocative

trouble¹ [trubl] **1** *adj* (**a**) *(liquide)* cloudy; *(lumière)* dim; *(image, photo)* blurred (**b**) *(comportement, affaire)* shady; *(période)* murky

2 *adv* **voir t.** to have blurred vision

trouble² [trubl] *nm* (**a**) *(désordre)* confusion, disorder; **semer** *ou* **jeter le t. dans l'esprit de qn** to confuse sb (**b**) *(émoi)* agitation (**c**) **troubles** *(révolte)* unrest (**d**) **troubles** *(maladie)* disorder; **troubles de la vision/respiratoires** eye/respiratory disorder; **troubles de la personnalité** personality disorder

trouble-fête [trubləfɛt] *nm inv* party-pooper, spoilsport; **jouer les t.** to be a party-pooper

troubler [truble] **1** *vt* (**a**) *(eau)* to make cloudy; *Fig (esprit)* to cloud; **t. la vue à qn** to blur sb's vision (**b**) *(sommeil, silence)* to disturb; *(bonheur)* to spoil; **t. l'ordre public** to disturb the peace (**c**) *(mettre en émoi)* to make flustered; *(rendre perplexe)* to confuse

2 se troubler *vpr* (**a**) *(liquide)* to get cloudy; *(vue)* to become blurred (**b**) *(se déconcerter)* to become flustered; **sans se t.** unperturbed

trouée [true] *nf (dans une haie, dans un mur)* gap, opening; **une t. de ciel bleu** a patch of blue sky

trouer [true] **1** *vt* to make a hole in

2 se trouer *vpr* **mes chaussures se sont trouées au bout d'une semaine** there was a hole in my shoes after a week

troufion [trufjɔ̃] *nm Fam* grunt

trouillard, -e [trujar, -ard] *Fam* **1** *adj* yellow-bellied, chicken **2** *nm,f* yellow-belly, chicken

trouille [truj] *nf Fam* fear; **avoir la t.** to be scared stiff

trouillomètre [trujɔmɛtr] *nm Fam* **avoir le t. à zéro** to be scared stiff

troupe [trup] *nf* (**a**) *(groupe)* troop, band; **t. de théâtre** company, troupe (**b**) *(de soldats)* troop; **troupes** *(armée)* troops, forces

troupeau, -x [trupo] *nm (de bétail, d'éléphants)* herd; *(de moutons)* flock; *(d'oies)* gaggle; *Péj (de gens)* herd

trousse [trus] *nf* (**a**) *(étui)* kit; **t. d'écolier** pencil case; **t. de secours** first-aid kit; **t. de toilette** toilet bag (**b**) *(locutions)* **être aux trousses de qn** to be hot on sb's heels; **avoir qn aux trousses** to have sb hot on one's heels

trousseau, -x [truso] *nm* (**a**) *(de clés)* bunch (**b**) *(de mariée)* trousseau (**c**) *(de pensionnaire)* clothes

trousser [truse] *vt* (**a**) *Culin (volaille)* to truss (**b**) **bien troussé** *(compliment)* well-turned (**c**) *Vieilli (retrousser)* to turn up

trouvaille [truvaj] *nf* (**a**) *(chose trouvée)* find (**b**) *(bonne idée)* brainwave

trouver [truve] **1** *vt* (**a**) *(en cherchant)* to find; *(procédé, vaccin)* to discover; **je ne trouve pas mes clefs** I can't find my keys; **aller t. qn** to go and see sb; **t. quelque chose à redire** to be sure to have something to say; **t. le sommeil** to get to sleep; **exemple bien trouvé** well-chosen example; **je me demande où il est allé t. ça** I wonder where he got that idea from; *Ironique* **tu as trouvé ça tout seul?** did you think of that all by yourself?

(**b**) *(par hasard)* to find, to come across; **t. porte close** to find nobody home; *Fig* **il va t. à qui parler!** he'll have me/him/ *etc.* to reckon with!; *Fig* **t. son maître** to meet one's match; **t. la mort** to meet one's death

(**c**) *(juger)* to find; *(penser)* to think; **je trouve ça idiot** I think it's stupid; **qu'est-ce qu'elle lui trouve?** what does she see in him?; **je trouve que...** I think (that)...; **t. le temps long** to feel that the time is dragging

2 se trouver *vpr* (**a**) *(dans une situation, dans un lieu)* to be;

où se trouve la gare? where's the station?; **se t. dans l'impossibilité de faire qch** to be unable to do sth

(**b**) *(être disponible)* **ça se trouve dans les supermarchés** you can find *or* get it in supermarkets

(**c**) *(se sentir)* to feel; **je me trouve bien ici** I like it here; **se t. beau/gros** to think one is good-looking/fat; **se t. mal** to feel faint

(**d**) *(arriver)* **il se trouve que...** as it happens...; *Fam* **si ça se trouve** maybe

trouvère [truvɛr] *nm* trouvère

truand [tryɑ̃] *nm Fam* crook

truander [tryɑ̃de] *Fam* **1** *vt* to rip off; **se faire t.** to get ripped off

2 *vi (à un examen)* to cheat (**à** in)

trublion [tryblijɔ̃] *nm* troublemaker

truc [tryk] *nm Fam* (**a**) *(chose)* thing; **j'ai un t. à faire/à te dire** I have something to do/to tell you (**b**) *(astuce)* trick; **connaître les trucs du métier** to know the tricks of the trade (**c**) *(personne)* **T.** what's-his-name, *f* what's-her-name (**d**) *(domaine)* **c'est vraiment son t.** he's really into it; **ce n'est pas son t.** it's not his/her thing

trucage [trykaʒ] *nm* (**a**) *(dans un film)* special effect (**b**) *(d'une photographie)* faking; *(d'un match, d'une élection)* rigging; *(de comptes)* fiddling

truchement [tryʃmɑ̃] *nm* **par le t. de...** through...

trucider [tryside] *vt Fam Hum* to bump off

trucmuche [trykmyʃ] *nm Fam* (**a**) *(chose)* thingy (**b**) **T.** *(personne)* what's-his-name, *f* what's-her-name

truculence [trykylɑ̃s] *nf (d'un récit, d'un style)* colorfulness; *(d'une personne)* flamboyance

truculent, -e [trykylɑ̃, -ɑ̃t] *adj (récit, style)* colorful; *(personne)* flamboyant

truelle [tryɛl] *nf* trowel

truffe [tryf] *nf* (**a**) *(champignon, au chocolat)* truffle (**b**) *(de chien)* nose

truffer [tryfe] *vt* (**a**) *(plat)* to garnish with truffles (**b**) *Fig (remplir)* **être truffé de** *(citations, balles)* to be peppered with; *(fautes)* to be riddled with

truie [trɥi] *nf* sow

truite [trɥit] *nf* trout; **t. arc-en-ciel/saumonée** rainbow/salmon trout

truquage [trykaʒ] = **trucage**

truquer [tryke] *vt* (**a**) *(photographie)* to fake; *(match, élection)* to rig; *(comptes)* to fiddle; *(dés)* to load (**b**) *(scène)* to use special effects in

trust [trœst] *nm* trust

truster [trœste] *vt aussi Fam* to monopolize

tsar [tsar, dzar] *nm* czar, tsar

tsé-tsé [tsetse] *nf inv voir* **mouche**

TSF [teɛsɛf] *nf (abrév* **télégraphie sans fil***)* *Vieilli (procédé)* wireless telegraphy; *(poste)* wireless

t-shirt *(pl* **t-shirts)** [tiʃœrt] = **tee-shirt**

tsigane [tsigan] = **tzigane**

TSVP *(abrév* **tournez s'il vous plaît***)* PTO

TTC [tetese] *(abrév* **toutes taxes comprises***)* inclusive of tax

tu¹, -e *voir* **taire**

tu² [ty] *pron personnel* you; **tu as raison** you're right; *Fam* **t'as déjà fini?** have you already finished?; **être à tu et à toi avec qn** to be on first-name terms with sb; **dire tu à qn** to address sb as "tu"

Tuamotu [twamotu] *nfpl* **les T.** the Tuamotu Archipelago

tuant, -e [tɥɑ̃, -ɑ̃t] *adj Fam* (**a**) *(fatigant)* exhausting (**b**) *(insupportable)* exasperating

tuba [tyba] *nm* (**a**) *(instrument de musique)* tuba (**b**) *(de plongée)* snorkel

tube [tyb] *nm* (**a**) *(tuyau)* tube; *Fam Fig* **à pleins tubes** at full blast; **t. digestif** digestive tract; **t. à essai** test tube (**b**) *Fam (chanson)* hit (**c**) *(emballage)* tube; **t. de rouge à lèvres** lipstick

tubercule [tybɛrkyl] *nm (plante)* tuber

tuberculeux, -euse [tybɛrkylø, -øz] **1** *adj* with tuberculosis; **être t.** to have tuberculosis

2 *nm,f* person with tuberculosis

tuberculose [tybɛrkyloz] *nf* tuberculosis; **avoir la t.** to have tuberculosis

tubéreuse [tyberøz] *nf* tuberose

tubulaire [tybylɛr] *adj* tubular

TUC [tyk] *nm (abrév* **travaux d'utilité collective**) = community work project for unemployed young people

tuer [tɥe] **1** *vt* (**a**) *(être vivant)* to kill; **t. qn d'un coup de revolver/de couteau** to shoot/stab sb to death; **c'est le chagrin qui l'a tué** he died of grief; *Fig* **t. le temps** to kill time (**b**) *Fam (épuiser)* **tous ces déplacements m'ont tué** all that traveling was a killer; **ces escaliers/ces enfants me tuent** these stairs/these children will be the death of me (**c**) *Fam (sidérer)* **ça me tue!** it kills me!

2 se tuer *vpr* (**a**) *(se suicider)* to kill oneself (**b**) *(dans un accident)* to die, to be killed (**c**) *(l'un l'autre)* to kill one another (**d**) *Fig* **se t. au travail** *ou* **à la tâche** to work oneself to death; **se t. à faire qch** to wear oneself out doing sth

tuerie [tyri] *nf* slaughter

tue-tête [tytɛt] **à tue-tête** *adv* at the top of one's voice

tueur, -euse [tɥœr, -øz] **1** *adj* killer

2 *nm,f* killer; **t. à gages** hired killer; **t. en série** serial killer

tuile [tɥil] *nf* (**a**) *(de toit)* tile (**b**) **t. aux amandes** = type of thin almond cookie (**c**) *Fam (problème)* **il m'arrive une t.** I'm in a jam

tulipe [tylip] *nf (fleur)* tulip

tulle [tyl] *nm* (**a**) *(tissu)* tulle (**b**) *Méd* **t. gras** = dressing used for burns

tuméfié, -e [tymefje] *adj* swollen

tuméfier [tymefje] *vt* to cause to swell

tumeur [tymœr] *nf* tumor; **t. au cerveau** brain tumor

tumoral, -e, -aux, -ales [tymɔral, -o] *adj* tumorous, tumoral

tumulte [tymylt] *nm (de la foule)* commotion; *(des passions)* turmoil

tumultueux, -euse [tymyltɥø, -øz] *adj (réunion)* noisy, tumultuous; *(vie, période)* tumultuous; *(relation)* stormy

tuner [tynœr, tynɛr] *nm* tuner

tungstène [tœkstɛn] *nm* tungsten

tunique [tynik] *nf* tunic

Tunis [tynis] *n* Tunis

Tunisie [tynizi] *nf* **la T.** Tunisia

tunisien, -enne [tynizjɛ̃, -ɛn] **1** *adj* Tunisian

2 *nm,f* **T., Tunisienne** Tunisian

tunisois, -e [tynizwa, -az] **1** *adj* of Tunis

2 *nm,f* **T., Tunisoise** person from Tunis

tunnel [tynɛl] *nm* tunnel; **le t. sous la Manche** the Channel Tunnel, *Fam* the Chunnel

tuque [tyk] *nf Can* bobble hat

turban [tyrbã] *nm* turban

turbin [tyrbɛ̃] *nm Fam (travail)* grind; **aller au t.** to go off to the daily grind

turbine [tyrbin] *nf* turbine

turbiner [tyrbine] *vi Fam (travailler)* to slog (away)

turbo [tyrbo] **1** *adj* turbocharged

2 *nm* turbo; *Fam* **mettre le t.** to move into high gear

turboréacteur [tyrboreaktœr] *nm* turbojet (engine)

turbot [tyrbo] *nm* turbot

turbulence [tyrbylãs] *nf* (**a**) **turbulences** *(dans l'atmosphère)* turbulence (**b**) *(d'un enfant)* boisterousness

turbulent, -e [tyrbylã, -ãt] *adj (enfant, classe)* boisterous

turc, turque [tyrk] **1** *adj* Turkish

2 *nm (langue)* Turkish

3 *nm,f* **T., Turque** Turk

turf [tœrf, tyrf] *nm (activité)* racing

turfiste [tœrfist, tyrfist] *nmf* racegoer

turkmène [tyrkmɛn] **1** *adj* Turkoman

2 *nm (langue)* Turkmen

3 *nmf* **T.** Turkoman

Turkménistan [tyrkmenistã] *nm* **le T.** Turkmenistan

turlupiner [tyrlypine] *vt Fam* to bother

turluter [tyrlyte] *vi Can Fam* to trill, to sing tra-la-la

turpitude [tyrpityd] *nf* (**a**) *(d'une conduite)* vileness, turpitude (**b**) *(action)* vile act

turque [tyrk] *voir* **turc**

Turquie [tyrki] *nf* **la T.** Turkey

turquoise [tyrkwaz] *nf, nm inv & adj inv* turquoise

tutelle [tytɛl] *nf* (**a**) *Jur* guardianship; *Pol* **territoires sous t.** trust territories (**b**) *(protection)* protection

tuteur, -trice [tytœr, -tris] **1** *nm,f* guardian; **t. légal** legal guardian

2 *nm (pour plante)* support

tutoiement [tytwamã] *nm* = use of the familiar "tu" instead of the more formal "vous"; **le t. est de rigueur** everybody calls each other "tu"

Tutoiement et vouvoiement

Traditionally, non-native French speakers waited until they were addressed using the informal "tu" form before using it themselves, except when speaking to young children. However, over the past twenty or thirty years people in France have become much more casual about using "tu" , and it is now commonly used among co-workers, while the "vous" form tends to be used when talking to people from an older generation or to hierarchical superiors (see *also entries* **tu** *and* **vous**).

---

tutoriel [tytɔrjɛl] *nm* tutorial

tutoyer [32] [tytwaje] **1** *vt* **t. qn** = to address sb as "tu"

2 se tutoyer *vpr* = to address each other as "tu"

tutti quanti [tutikwãti] *adv* **et t.** blah, blah, blah

tutu [tyty] *nm* tutu

tuyau, -x [tɥijo] *nm* (**a**) *(canalisation)* pipe; *(de cheminée)* flue; *(flexible)* tube; **t. d'arrosage** garden hose; **t. d'échappement** exhaust (pipe); **t. d'incendie** fire hose; **t. de poêle** stove pipe (**b**) *Fam (conseil)* tip; *(information)* tip-off

tuyauter [tɥijɔte] *vt Fam (conseiller)* to give a tip to (**sur** about); *(informer)* to tip off (**sur** about)

tuyauterie [tɥijɔtri] *nf* piping, pipes

TV [teve] *nf (abrév* **télévision**) TV

TVA [tevea] *nf (abrév* **taxe à la valeur ajoutée**) VAT

tweed [twid] *nm* tweed

twin-set (*pl* **twin-sets**) [twinsɛt] *nm* twinset

tympan [tɛ̃pã] *nm* (**a**) *Anat* eardrum (**b**) *Archit* tympanum

type [tip] **1** *adj* typical; **lettre t.** standard letter

2 *nm* (**a**) *(genre)* type (**b**) *(personnification)* **le t. même de** the classic example of (**c**) *(apparence)* **avoir le t. latin/nordique** to have Latin/Nordic looks (**d**) *Fam (homme)* guy, dude

typé, -e [tipe] *adj* **il est italien – oui, et il est très t.** he's Italian – yes, he looks typically Italian

typhoïde [tifɔid] **1** *adj (fièvre)* typhoid

2 *nf* typhoid (fever)

typhon [tifɔ̃] *nm* typhoon

typhus [tifys] *nm* typhus (fever)

typique [tipik] *adj* typical

typiquement [tipikmã] *adv* typically

typographe [tipɔɡraf] *nmf* typographer

typographie [tipɔgrafi] *nf* typography, letterpress printing
typographique [tipɔgrafik] *adj* typographic
tyran [tirã] *nm* tyrant
tyrannie [tirani] *nf* tyranny
tyrannique [tiranik] *adj* tyrannical

tyranniser [tiranize] *vt (population)* to tyrannize; *(famille, collègue)* to bully
tzar [tsar, dzar] = **tsar**
tzigane [tsigan, dzigan] **1** *adj* gypsy
2 *nmf* T. gypsy

U

U, u [y] *nm inv* U, u; **en U** U-shaped; **tables disposées en U** tables arranged in a horseshoe (shape)

ubac [ybak] *nm* = shady side of an Alpine mountain, *Spéc* ubac

ubiquité [ybikɥite] *nf* ubiquity; **avoir le don d'u.** to have the ability to be in several places at the same time

UDF [ydeɛf] *nf Pol* (*abrév* **Union pour la démocratie française**) = right-of-center French political party

UE *nf* (*abrév* **Union européenne**) EU

UEM [yɑɛm] *nf Écon* (*abrév* **Union économique et monétaire**) EMU

UEO [yəo] *nf* (*abrév* **Union de l'Europe occidentale**) WEU

ufologie [yfɔlɔʒi] *nf* ufology

UFR [yɛfɛr] *nf* (*abrév* **unité de formation et de recherche**) = department (*in university*)

UHF [yaʃɛf] *Rad* (*abrév* **ultra-haute fréquence**) UHF

UHT [yaʃte] (*abrév* **ultra-haute température**) UHT

Ukraine [ykrɛn] *nf* **l'U.** the Ukraine

ukrainien, -enne [ykrɛnjɛ̃, -jɛn] **1** *adj* Ukrainian

  2 *nm* (*langue*) Ukrainian

  3 *nm,f* **U., Ukrainienne** Ukrainian

ukulélé [jukulele] *nm* ukelele

ulcération [ylserasjɔ̃] *nf* ulceration

ulcère [ylsɛr] *nm* ulcer; **avoir un u. à l'estomac** to have a stomach ulcer

ulcéré, -e [ylsere] *adj* (**a**) *Méd* ulcerated (**b**) *Fig* (*en colère*) seething

ulcérer [34] [ylsere] **1** *vt* (**a**) *Méd* to ulcerate (**b**) *Fig* (*mettre en colère*) **u. qn** to make sb seethe

  2 s'ulcérer *vpr Méd* to ulcerate

ULM [yɛlɛm] *nm inv Aviat* (*abrév* **ultraléger motorisé**) microlight

ultérieur, -e [ylterjœr] *adj* later, subsequent (**à** to)

ultérieurement [ylterjœrmɑ̃] *adv* later (on), subsequently

ultimatum [yltimatɔm] *nm* ultimatum; **adresser un u. à qn** to give sb an ultimatum

ultime [yltim] *adj* last; (*préparatifs*) final

ultra- [yltra] *préf* ultra-

ultra-confidentiel, -elle [yltrakɔ̃fidɑ̃sjɛl] *adj* top-secret

ultra-conservateur, -trice [yltrakɔ̃sɛrvatœr] *adj Pol* ultra-conservative

ultramoderne [yltramɔdɛrn] *adj* high-tech

ultraportatif [yltrapɔrtatif] *nm* notebook computer

ultrarapide [yltrarapid] *adj* ultrafast

ultrasensible [yltrasɑ̃sibl] *adj* ultra-sensitive

ultrason [yltrasɔ̃] *nm Phys* ultrasound; **ultrasons** ultrasonic waves

ultraviolet, -ette [yltravjɔlɛ, -ɛt] *adj & nm* ultraviolet

ululer [ylyle] *vi* to ululate

Ulysse [ylis] *npr* Ulysses

UME [yɛmə] *nf* (*abrév* **union monétaire européenne**) EMU

un, une [œ̃, yn] **1** *adj* one; **il est une heure** it's one o'clock; **page un** page one; **un jour** one day; **un, deux, trois, partez!** one, two, three, go!

  2 *pron indéfini* one; **un de mes amis** one of my friends, a friend of mine; **un de ces jours** one of these days; **en voilà une qui sait ce qu'elle veut!** there's somebody who knows what she wants!; **il n'y en a pas un qui parle anglais** not one of them speaks English; *Fam* **être menteur/hypocrite comme pas un** to be a dreadful liar/hypocrite; **(l')un de nous, (l')un d'entre nous** one of us

  3 *art indéfini* (*pl* **des**) (**a**) (*en général*) a; (*devant une voyelle ou un h muet*) an; **un jour/une pomme/une heure** a day/an apple/an hour; **cela tombe un mardi** it falls on a Tuesday; **il y a des agrafes dans le tiroir** there are (some) staples in the drawer; **est-ce qu'il te reste des agrafes?** do you have any staples left?; **il y a des jours où…** there are days when…, some days…

  (**b**) (*intensif*) **il y a un de ces mondes en ville!** the town is so busy!; **il est d'une bêtise!** he's so stupid!; **il a fait une de ces têtes!** you should have seen his face!; **tu m'as fait une peur!** you gave me such a scare!

  4 *nm* (*chiffre*) one

  5 *nf* (**a**) (*première page*) **la une** (*d'un journal*) the front page; **faire la une** (*d'un magazine*) to appear on the front cover; (*d'un journal*) to appear on the front page

  (**b**) **il n'a fait ni une ni deux** he didn't hesitate for a moment

unanime [ynanim] *adj* unanimous

unanimité [ynanimite] *nf* unanimity; **à l'u.** unanimously; **faire l'u.** to be accepted unanimously

underground [œndœrgrawnd] *adj inv & nm inv* underground

une [yn] *voir* **un**

UNEF [ynɛf] *nf* (*abrév* **Union nationale des étudiants de France**) = French union of students

Unesco [ynɛsko] *nf* (*abrév* **United Nations Educational Scientific and Cultural Organization**) Unesco

Unetelle *voir* **Untel**

uni, -e [yni] *adj* (**a**) (*famille, couple*) close (**b**) (*sans irrégularité*) (*sol, surface*) smooth, level (**c**) (*couleur*) plain; (*tissu, vêtement*) plain

Unicef [ynisɛf] *nf* (*abrév* **United Nations International Children's Emergency Fund**) **l'U.** Unicef

unicellulaire [yniselylɛr] *adj* unicellular

unidimensionnel, -elle [ynidimɑ̃sjɔnɛl] *adj* one-dimensional

unidirectionnel, -elle [ynidirɛksjɔnɛl] *adj* unidirectional

unidose [ynidoz] *adj* single-dose sachet

unifamilial, -e, -aux, -ales [ynifamiljal, -o] *Belg & Can* **1** *adj* (*logement*) for a single family

  2 unifamiliale *nf* single-family house

unificateur, -trice [ynifikatœr, -tris] *adj* unifying

unification [ynifikasjɔ̃] *nf* unification

unifier [66] [ynifje] *vt* (**a**) (*parti politique, pays*) to unify (**b**) (*tarifs, poids et mesures*) to standardize

uniforme [yniform] **1** adj (opinions, expression) uniform; (vie) unchanging; (allure, surface) even; (mouvement) regular
2 nm uniform
uniformément [yniformemã] adv uniformly, evenly
uniformisation [yniformizasjɔ̃] nf standardization
uniformiser [yniformize] vt to standardize
uniformité [yniformite] nf (a) (monotonie) monotony (b) (de couleurs, de teintes) uniformity
unijambiste [yniʒɑ̃bist] **1** adj one-legged
2 nmf one-legged person
unilatéral, -e, -aux, -ales [ynilateral, -o] adj (décision, désarmement) unilateral; (contrat, accord) one-sided
unilingue [ynilɛ̃g] adj unilingual, monolingual
uninominal, -aux [yninominal, -o] adj m voir **scrutin**
union [ynjɔ̃] nf (a) (entre personnes) closeness, unity; **vivre en parfaite u. avec qn** to live in perfect harmony with sb (b) (association) (de partis, de consommateurs) union, association; **u. douanière/économique/monétaire** customs/economic/monetary union; **l'U. européenne** the European Union; Anciennement **l'U. soviétique** the Soviet Union (c) (mariage) marriage; **u. libre** cohabitation; **vivre en u. libre** to cohabit
unique [ynik] adj (a) (seul) only; (parti, prix) single; (occasion, cas) unique; **être u. en son genre** to be one of a kind; **u. au monde** unlike anything else in the world; **c'est son seul et u. défaut** it's his/her one and only fault (b) (incomparable) unique (c) Fam (très drôle) priceless
uniquement [ynikmã] adv just, only
unir [ynir] **1** vt (a) (relier) (personnes, territoires) to unite; (qualités) to combine (à with) (b) (réunir) **l'amitié qui nous unit** the friendship that unites us (c) (marier) to join in marriage (d) (sol, surface) to smooth, to level
2 s'unir vpr (a) (s'associer) to join together, to unite; **s'u. à qn** to join forces with sb (b) (se marier) to become joined in marriage
unisexe [yniseks] adj unisex
unisson [ynisɔ̃] nm unison; **à l'u.** in unison
unitaire [yniter] adj (système) unitary; (prix) unit
unité [ynite] nf (a) (pour mesurer) unit; **u. de longueur/de poids** unit of measurement/weight (b) (élément simple) unit; **dix euros l'u.** ten euros each; Com **prix à l'u.** unit price; **vendu à l'u.** sold singly; **chiffre des unités** units figure; **u. de production** production unit; Univ **u. de valeur** credit (c) (cohésion) (d'une nation, d'une association) unity; (du style) consistency (d) Ordinat unit; (de disque) drive; **u. de bande** tape unit; **u. centrale** central processing unit; **u. de disque/logique** disk/logical drive
univers [yniver] nm (a) (espace) universe (b) Fig (milieu) world
universaliser [yniversalize] vt to universalize
universalité [yniversalite] nf universality
universel, -elle [yniversel] adj universal; (savoir) all-embracing
universellement [yniverselmã] adv universally
universitaire [yniversiter] **1** adj (ville, études) university
2 nmf (a) (enseignant) academic (b) Belg & Suisse (étudiant) university student; (diplômé) graduate
université [yniversite] nf university, college; **aller à l'u.** to go to college; **u. d'été** summer school; Pol party conference (for young members); **u. du troisième âge** = classes for senior citizens
Untel, Unetelle [ɛ̃tɛl, yntɛl] nm,f what's-his-name, f what's-her-name; **M./Mme U.** Mr./Mrs. So-and-So
uppercut [ypɛrkyt] nm uppercut
uranium [yranjɔm] nm uranium; **u. appauvri/enrichi** depleted/enriched uranium
Uranus [yranys] npr (dieu, planète) Uranus
urbain, -e [yrbɛ̃, -ɛn] adj (a) (développement, milieu, transport) urban (b) Litt (poli) urbane
urbanisation [yrbanizasjɔ̃] nf urbanization

urbaniser [yrbanize] vt to urbanize
urbanisme [yrbanism] nm city planning, urban development
urbaniste [yrbanist] **1** adj urban
2 nmf city planner
urbanité [yrbanite] nf Litt urbanity
urbi et orbi [yrbiɛtɔrbi] adv urbi et orbi; Fig far and wide
urée [yre] nf urea
urètre [yrɛtr] nm urethra
urgence [yrʒɑ̃s] nf (a) (caractère pressé) urgency; **en cas d'u.** in an emergency; **d'u.** urgently; **être opéré d'u.** to have an emergency operation; **il y a u.** it's a matter of urgency (b) (à l'hôpital) emergency; **les urgences** (service) the emergency room
urgent, -e [yrʒɑ̃, -ɑ̃t] adj urgent; **il est u. de le faire** it must be done urgently
urgentiste [yrʒɑ̃tist] nmf Méd emergency doctor
urger [45] [yrʒe] vi Fam **ça urge** it's urgent
urinaire [yriner] adj urinary
urine [yrin] nf urine
uriner [yrine] vi to urinate
urinoir [yrinwar] nm (public) urinal
urique [yrik] adj (acide) uric
urne [yrn] nf (a) (pour voter) ballot box; **aller aux urnes** to go to the polls (b) (vase) urn
uro-génital, -e (mpl uro-génitaux, fpl uro-génitales) [yroʒenital, -o] adj urogenital
urologie [yrolɔʒi] nf urology
urologue [yrolɔg] nmf urologist
URSS [yɛrɛsɛs, yrs] nf Anciennement (abrév **Union des républiques socialistes soviétiques**) **l'U.** the USSR
URSSAF [yrsaf] nf (abrév **Union de recouvrement des cotisations de Sécurité sociale et d'Allocations familiales**) = organization which collects social security and welfare payments
urticaire [yrtiker] nf nettle rash, Spéc urticaria; **avoir une crise d'u.** to come out in nettle rash; Fam **donner de l'u. à qn** to set sb's teeth on edge
Uruguay [yrygwɛ] nm **l'U.** Uruguay
uruguayen, -enne [yrygwɛjɛ̃, -ɛn] **1** adj Uruguayan
2 nm,f **U., Uruguayenne** Uruguayan
us [ys] nmpl **les us et coutumes** the habits and customs
usage [yzaʒ] nm (a) (utilisation) use; **faire u. de qch** to use sth; **faire bon u. de qch** to put sth to good use; **avoir l'u. de qch** to have the use of sth; **à u. externe/interne** (médicament) for external/internal use; **à l'u. des écoles/des étudiants** for use in schools/by students; **à usages multiples** multi-purpose; **hors d'u.** out of order; Jur **u. de faux** use of forged documents (b) (d'un terme, d'une expression) usage; **entrer dans l'u.** (mot) to come into common use; **le bon u.** correct usage (c) (des vêtements) **faire de l'u.** to wear well; **ce manteau vous fera de l'u.** you'll get a lot of wear out of this coat (d) (coutume) custom, practice; **c'est l'u.** it's the done thing; **comme il est d'u. en France** as is customary in France; **il est d'u. de** it's customary to
usagé, -e [yzaʒe] adj (vêtement, livre) worn; (ticket) used
usager [yzaʒe] nm user
usant, -e [yzɑ̃, -ɑ̃t] adj Fam (a) (vie, travail) exhausting, wearing (b) (personne) tiresome
usé, -e [yze] adj (a) (vêtements) worn, worn-out; **u. jusqu'à la corde** threadbare (b) (eaux) waste (c) (sujet, plaisanterie) tired, stale (d) (épuisé) worn-out
user [yze] **1** vt (a) (consommer) (énergie, électricité) to use (b) (abîmer) (vêtements, chaussures) to wear out; Fig (résistance) to break down; **u. qch jusqu'à la corde** to wear sth until it's threadbare (c) (épuiser) (personne) to wear down
2 user de vt ind (patience, violence, ruse) to use; (droit) to exercise; **u. de douceur avec qn** to handle sb gently; **u. de son**

influence pour faire qch to use one's influence to do sth

3 s'user *vpr* (**a**) *(tissu, pneus, semelles)* to wear out; *(talons)* to wear down (**b**) *Fig (personne)* **s'u. à faire qch** to wear oneself out doing sth

usinage [yzinaʒ] *nm* machining

usine [yzin] *nf* factory, plant; **u. de fabrication** manufacturing plant; **u. à gaz** gasworks; **u. de montage** assembly plant; *Fig* overly complicated system

usiner [yzine] *vt (façonner)* to machine

usité, -e [yzite] *adj (mot)* in common use; **très u.** very common; **peu u.** little used

ustensile [ystɑ̃sil] *nm* implement, tool; **u. de cuisine** kitchen utensil

usuel, -elle [yzɥɛl] *adj* everyday; *(dénomination)* common

usufruit [yzyfrɥi] *nm Jur* usufruct

usuraire [yzyrɛr] *adj* usurious

usure¹ [yzyr] *nf (intérêt, délit)* usury

usure² [yzyr] *nf (de pneu)* wear; *(du sol, de roches)* wearing away; **résister à l'u.** to wear well; *Fam* **avoir qn à l'u.** to wear sb down; **guerre d'u.** war of attrition

usurier, -ère [yzyrje, -ɛr] *nm,f* usurer

usurpateur, -trice [yzyrpatœr, -tris] *nm,f* usurper

usurpation [yzyrpasjɔ̃] *nf (d'un titre, de droits, du pouvoir)* usurpation

usurper [yzyrpe] *vt (titre, droits)* to usurp (**sur** from)

ut [yt] *nm inv (note)* C

utérin, -e [yterɛ̃, -in] *adj* uterine

utérus [yterys] *nm* uterus, womb

utile [ytil] *adj* useful (**à** to); **en quoi puis-je vous être u.?** what can I do for you?; **vous nous avez été bien u.** you've been very helpful to us; **se rendre u.** to make oneself useful; **en temps u.** in due course

utilement [ytilmɑ̃] *adv* usefully; **il m'a u. renseigné** he gave me some useful information

utilisable [ytilizabl] *adj* usable; **facilement u.** easy to use

utilisateur, -trice [ytilizatœr, -tris] *nm,f* user; **u. final** end user

utilisation [ytilizasjɔ̃] *nf* use

utiliser [ytilize] *vt* (**a**) *(se servir de)* to use (**b**) *Péj (personne)* to use (**c**) *Ordinat* to run

utilitaire [ytilitɛr] **1** *adj* (**a**) utilitarian; *(véhicule)* commercial (**b**) *Ordinat* utility

2 *nm Ordinat* utility; **u. de conversion** conversion utility

utilitarisme [ytilitarism] *nm* utilitarianism

utilité [ytilite] *nf (fonction)* usefulness; **être d'une grande u. (à qn)** to be very useful (to sb)

utopie [ytɔpi] *nf* utopia

utopique [ytɔpik] *adj* utopian

utopiste [ytɔpist] *nmf* Utopian

UV¹ [yve] *nf inv Univ (abrév **unité de valeur**)* credit

UV² [yve] *nm inv (abrév **ultraviolet**)* UV; **faire des UV** to go to a tanning salon

V

V, v [ve] *nm inv* (**a**) *(lettre)* V, v; *Fam* **à la vitesse grand V** at top speed (**b**) *(abrév* **voir**) see

va *voir* **aller**[1]

vacance [vakɑ̃s] *nf* (**a**) *(d'un poste)* vacancy; **pendant la v. du pouvoir** while there is no one officially in power (**b**) **vacances** *(d'écoliers, de travailleurs)* vacation; **un jour de vacances** a day's holiday; **prendre des vacances** to take a vacation; **être en vacances** to be on vacation; **partir en vacances** to go away on vacation; *Fam* **faire des vacances à qn** to give sb a break; **vacances de neige** winter sports vacation; **vacances de Noël/Pâques** Christmas/Easter holidays; **vacances scolaires** school holidays; *Scol* **les grandes vacances** the summer vacation

vacancier, -ère [vakɑ̃sje, -ɛr] *nm,f* vacationer

vacant, -e [vakɑ̃, -ɑ̃t] *adj* vacant

vacarme [vakarm] *nm* uproar, din; **faire du v.** to make an uproar

vacataire [vakatɛr] *nmf* short-term worker

vacation [vakasjɔ̃] *nf* (**a**) *(de juge, d'expert)* sitting, session (**b**) *(rémunération)* fees

vaccin [vaksɛ̃] *nm* vaccine

vaccination [vaksinasjɔ̃] *nf* vaccination, inoculation

vacciner [vaksine] *vt* to vaccinate, to inoculate (**contre** against); **se faire v. (contre)** to get vaccinated (against); *Fam* **je suis vacciné!** I've learned my lesson!; *Fam* **je suis majeur et vacciné!** I'm old enough to look after myself now!

vachard, -e [vaʃar, -ard] *adj Fam (coup)* mean, dirty; *(question)* nasty

vache [vaʃ] **1** *nf* (**a**) *(animal)* cow; **v. à lait** dairy cow; *Fig* milch cow; **v. laitière** dairy cow; *Fam* **manger de la v. enragée** to have a hard time of it; *Fam* **parler français comme une v. espagnole** to speak lousy French; *Fam* **comme une v. qui regarde passer les trains** with a vacant look on one's face (**b**) *Fam (homme)* swine; *(femme)* cow (**c**) *(cuir)* cowhide (**d**) *Fam (interjection)* **la v., qu'est-ce qu'il fait froid!** God, it's so cold!

2 *adj Fam* rotten, nasty; **être v. avec qn** to be rotten to sb

vachement [vaʃmɑ̃] *adv Fam (très)* very, really; *(beaucoup)* a hell of a lot

vacher, -ère [vaʃe, -ɛr] *nm,f* cowherd, *f* cowgirl

vacherie [vaʃri] *nf Fam (action)* dirty trick; *(remarque)* nasty remark

vacherin [vaʃrɛ̃] *nm* (**a**) *(fromage)* = type of soft cheese (**b**) *(dessert)* = meringue with cream, ice cream and fruit

vachette [vaʃɛt] *nf* (**a**) *(petite vache)* small cow; *(jeune vache)* calf (**b**) *(cuir)* calfskin

vacillant, -e [vasijɑ̃, -ɑ̃t] *adj* (**a**) *(flamme)* flickering; *(démarche)* staggering (**b**) *(santé, mémoire)* failing

vacillation [vasijasjɔ̃] *nf*, **vacillement** [vasijmɑ̃] *nm (d'une flamme)* flickering

vaciller [vasije] *vi* (**a**) *(chanceler)* to be unsteady, to sway; **v. sur ses jambes** to stagger; **tout vacillait autour de moi** everything was swimming around me (**b**) *(flamme)* to flicker (**c**) *(mémoire, raison)* to fail

va-comme-je-te-pousse [vakɔmʃtəpus] **à la va-comme-je-te-pousse** *adv Fam* any old how

vacuité [vakɥite] *nf* vacuity

vadrouille [vadruj] *nf* (**a**) *Fam (balade)* ramble, saunter; **partir** *ou* **aller en v.** to roam about; **il est rarement à son bureau, il est toujours en v.** he's rarely at his desk, he's always wandering around somewhere (**b**) *Can* mop

vadrouiller [vadruje] *vi Fam* to roam about

va-et-vient [vaevjɛ̃] *nm inv* (**a**) *(mouvement)* backward and forward movement; **faire le v. (entre)** *(personne)* to go back and forth (between) (**b**) *(circulation) (de personnes)* comings and goings (**c**) *(dispositif électrique)* two-way wiring (system)

vagabond, -e [vagabɔ̃, -ɔ̃d] **1** *adj* (**a**) *(vie)* wandering, roving (**b**) *Fig (pensées)* wandering, roaming; **avoir l'humeur vagabonde** to be in a restless mood

2 *nm,f* vagrant, tramp

vagabondage [vagabɔ̃daʒ] *nm* vagrancy

vagabonder [vagabɔ̃de] *vi (personne)* to wander, to roam; *Fig (pensées, imagination)* to wander, to stray

vagin [vaʒɛ̃] *nm* vagina

vaginal, -e, -aux, -ales [vaʒinal, -o] *adj* vaginal

vagir [vaʒir] *vi (nouveau-né)* to cry

vagissement [vaʒismɑ̃] *nm (de nouveau-né)* cry, wail

vague[1] [vag] *nf* (**a**) *(d'eau)* wave; *Fig* **faire des vagues** to make waves; **arriver par vagues** to come in waves; *aussi Fig* **v. de fond** ground swell (**b**) *(ondulations) (de chevelure, de dunes)* wave (**c**) *(courant artistique)* **nouvelle v.** new wave (**d**) *(d'enthousiasme, de tendresse)* wave, surge; **v. de chaleur** heat wave; **v. de froid** cold spell (**e**) *(afflux) (d'immigrants)* influx

vague[2] [vag] **1** *adj* (**a**) *(impression, geste, souvenir)* vague; *(forme)* indistinct; **regarder qn d'un air v.** to look vacantly at sb; **rester v. sur qch** to be vague about sth (**b**) *(avant le nom)* **quelque v. écrivain** some writer or other

2 *nm* (**a**) *(imprécision)* vagueness; **rester dans le v.** to be vague; **avoir du v. à l'âme** to be melancholy (**b**) *(vide)* **regard perdu dans le v.** faraway look

vaguelette [vaglɛt] *nf* wavelet

vaguement [vagmɑ̃] *adv* vaguely

vahiné [vaine] *nf* Tahitian woman

vaillamment [vajamɑ̃] *adv* valiantly

vaillance [vajɑ̃s] *nf* valor, courage

vaillant, -e [vajɑ̃, -ɑ̃t] *adj* (**a**) *(courageux)* valiant, courageous; *(cœur)* stout (**b**) *(en forme)* **être v.** to be in good health

vaille, vailles *voir* **valoir**

vain, -e [vɛ̃, vɛn] *adj* (**a**) *(sans résultat) (démarche, entreprise)* futile; *(efforts)* vain; **en v.** in vain (**b**) *(vide de sens) (paroles, promesse)* empty; *(espoirs, regrets)* vain (**c**) *Litt (personne)* vain

vaincre [68] [vɛ̃kr] *vt* (**a**) *(adversaire)* to defeat; *(en sport)* to beat (**b**) *Fig (maladie, difficulté)* to overcome

vaincu, -e [vɛ̃ky] **1** *adj* beaten, defeated; **s'avouer v.** to admit defeat

2 *nm,f* defeated man, *f* defeated woman

vainement [vɛnmɑ̃] *adv* in vain

vainqueur [vɛ̃kœr] **1** *nm* (**a**) *(dans une compétition sportive)* winner (**b**) *(d'une bataille, d'une lutte)* victor

2 *adj m (personne)* conquering, victorious

vairon[1] [vɛrɔ̃] *adj* **avoir les yeux vairons** to have different-colored eyes

vairon[2] [vɛrɔ̃] *nm (poisson)* minnow

vais *voir* **aller**[1]

vaisseau, -x [vɛso] *nm* (**a**) **v. (sanguin)** blood vessel (**b**) **v. spatial** spaceship (**c**) *(d'une église)* nave (**d**) *Litt* ship, vessel; **v. de guerre** warship

vaisselier [vɛsəlje] *nm (meuble)* dresser

vaisselle [vɛsɛl] *nf* dishes, crockery; **faire** *ou* **laver la v.** to do the dishes

val [val] *nm* valley

valable [valabl] *adj* (**a**) *(ticket, raison, excuse)* valid; **ce qui est v. pour l'un est v. pour l'autre** what goes for one goes for the other (**b**) *(compétent) (interlocuteur)* authorized (**c**) *(de qualité) (roman)* good; *(idée)* valid

valdinguer [valdɛ̃ge] *vi Fam* **aller v. contre/sur qch** to go flying against/onto sth; **envoyer v. qch** to send sth flying

Valence [valɑ̃s] *n* (**a**) *(en Espagne)* Valencia (**b**) *(en France)* Valence

valériane [valerjan] *nf* valerian

valet [valɛ] *nm* (**a**) *(au jeu de cartes)* jack, knave (**b**) *(domestique)* **v. (de chambre)** valet; **v. de ferme** farmhand; **v. de pied** footman (**c**) *(meuble)* **v. de nuit** valet

valétudinaire [valetydinɛr] *adj & nmf* valetudinarian

valeur [valœr] *nf* (**a**) *(prix)* value, worth; **avoir de la v.** to be valuable; **de peu de v./de grande v.** of little/of great value; **d'une v. de 20 euros** worth 20 euros; **prendre de la v.** to increase in value; **v. d'achat** purchase value; **v. ajoutée** added value; **v. en Bourse** stock-market value; **v. marchande** market value; **valeurs mobilières** stocks and shares; **v. nominale** nominal value (**b**) *(qualité, mérite)* value; **de v.** *(livre, œuvre)* of considerable merit; **homme de v.** *(de mérite)* man of merit; **avoir v. légale** to be legally binding; **attacher de la v. à qch** to value sth; **mettre en v.** to show to advantage; *(teint, yeux)* to bring out; *(mot)* to emphasize; **se mettre en v.** to show oneself off to advantage; **prendre toute sa v.** *(terme, expression)* to take on its full meaning (**c**) *(titre)* security; **valeurs de tout repos** gilt-edged securities (**d**) *(d'une note)* time, length; *(d'une carte)* value (**e**) *(équivalent)* equivalent (**f**) *(morale)* **valeurs** values (**g**) *Litt (courage)* valor

valeureux, -euse [valørø, -øz] *adj Litt* gallant

validation [validasjɔ̃] *nf (d'un titre de transport)* validation; *(d'un document)* authentication

valide [valid] *adj* (**a**) *(contrat)* valid (**b**) *(personne) (en bonne santé)* fit; *(non blessé)* uninjured

valider [valide] *vt* (**a**) *(élection, mariage)* to validate; *(document)* to authenticate; **v. un titre de transport** *(dans une machine)* to stamp a ticket (**b**) *Ordinat (option)* to confirm; *(cellule, case)* to select

validité [validite] *nf (d'un contrat, d'un passeport)* validity

valise [valiz] *nf* (**a**) *(bagage)* suitcase; *aussi Fig* **faire ses valises** to pack one's bags (**b**) *(courrier)* **la v. diplomatique** the diplomatic pouch (**c**) *Fam (sous les yeux)* bag

vallée [vale] *nf* valley; *Litt* **une v. de larmes** a vale of tears

vallon [valɔ̃] *nm* small valley

vallonné, -e [valɔne] *adj (région)* undulating, hilly

vallonnement [valɔnmɑ̃] *nm* undulation

valoche [valɔʃ] *nf Fam* case, bag

valoir [69a] [valwar] **1** *vi* (**a**) *(avoir comme valeur)* to be worth; **v. cher** *(objet en vente)* to be expensive; *(objet précieux)* to be worth a lot; *Fig* **ne pas v. cher** *(personne)* not to be up to much; **ne rien v.** *(objet)* to be worthless; *(idée)* to be useless; **ce climat ne vous vaut rien** this climate doesn't suit you; **il ne vaut pas mieux que son frère** he's no better than his brother; **ça vaut mieux comme ça** it's better that way

(**b**) *(avoir un intérêt)* **et ça vaut pour tout le monde** and that goes for everyone; **faire v. qch** *(opinions, droits)* to assert sth

2 *vt* (**a**) *(équivaloir à)* to be equivalent to; **un euro vaut plus d'un dollar** one euro is worth over a dollar; **ça ne vaut pas ce qui m'est arrivé l'autre jour** that's nothing compared to what happened to me the other day; **rien ne vaut un bon petit déjeuner** there's nothing like a good breakfast

(**b**) *(rapporter)* **v. qch à qn** *(punition)* to earn sb sth; *(soucis, ennuis)* to bring sb sth; **qu'est-ce qui me vaut cet honneur?** to what do I owe this honor?

3 *v impersonnel* **il vaut/vaudrait mieux faire qch** it's/it would be better to do sth; **il vaut mieux que vous restiez** you'd better stay, it would be better if you stayed; *Prov* **mieux vaut tard que jamais** better late than never

4 **se valoir** *vpr* **tous les métiers se valent** one job is as good as another; **ils se valent** *(péjoratif)* they're as bad as each other; *(admiratif)* they're as good as each other

valorisant, -e [valɔrizɑ̃, -ɑ̃t] *adj* gratifying

valorisation [valɔrizasjɔ̃] *nf* (**a**) *(augmentation de la valeur)* increase in value (**b**) *(développement)* development

valoriser [valɔrize] *vt (bien, monnaie)* to increase the value of; *(région)* to develop; *(personne)* to boost the self-esteem of

valse [vals] *nf* (**a**) *(morceau de musique, air de danse)* waltz (**b**) **la v. des ministres** frequent cabinet reshuffles

valse-hésitation *(pl* **valses-hésitations***)* [valsezitasjɔ̃] *nf Fam* pussyfooting, shilly-shallying

valser [valse] *vi* to waltz; **faire v. qn** to waltz with sb; *Fig* **faire v. les millions** to spend money like water; *Fam* **envoyer v. qn/qch** to send sb/sth flying

valseur, -euse [valsœr, -øz] *nm,f* waltzer

valu, -e *voir* **valoir**

valve [valv] *nf* valve

vamp [vɑ̃p] *nf Fam* vamp

vampire [vɑ̃pir] *nm* (**a**) *(suceur de sang)* vampire (**b**) *Fig (parasite)* bloodsucker

vampiriser [vɑ̃pirize] *vt Fam* to dominate psychologically

van[1] [vɑ̃] *nm (fourgon à chevaux)* horse box

van[2] [van] *nm (camionnette)* van

Vancouver [vɑ̃kuvɛr] *n* Vancouver

vandale [vɑ̃dal] *nmf* vandal

vandaliser [vɑ̃dalize] *vt* to vandalize

vandalisme [vɑ̃dalism] *nm* vandalism

vanille [vanij] *nf* vanilla

vanillé, -e [vanije] *adj* vanilla-flavored

vanité [vanite] *nf* (**a**) *(suffisance)* vanity; **tirer v. de qch** to pride oneself on sth (**b**) *Litt (insignifiance)* futility, emptiness

vaniteux, -euse [vanitø, -øz] **1** *adj* vain

2 *nm,f* vain person

vanne[1] [van] *nf (de canalisation, d'écluse)* sluice gate, floodgate; **ouvrir/fermer les vannes** to open/close the floodgates

vanne[2] [van] *nf Fam (remarque blessante)* dig, jibe; **envoyer une v. à qn** to have a dig at sb

vanné, -e [vane] *adj Fam* **être v.** to be dead beat

vanneau, -x [vano] *nm (oiseau)* lapwing, peewit

vanner [vane] *vt* (**a**) *Fam (fatiguer)* to wear out, to exhaust (**b**) *(grain)* to winnow

vannerie [vanri] *nf* (**a**) *(activité)* basket making, basketry (**b**) *(objets)* basketwork, wickerwork

vannier [vanje] *nm* basket worker *or* maker

vantard, -e [vɑ̃tar, -ard] **1** *adj* bragging, boastful

2 *nm,f* braggart, boaster

vantardise [vɑ̃tardiz] *nf (caractère)* bragging, boastfulness; *(parole)* boast

vanter [vɑ̃te] **1** *vt* to praise, to speak highly of

2 **se vanter** *vpr* to boast, to brag (**de** about)

Vanuatu [vanwatu] *n* Vanuatu

va-nu-pieds [vanypje] *nmf inv* tramp, beggar

vapes [vap] *nfpl Fam* **être dans les v.** to be all woozy; **tomber dans les v.** to pass out

vapeur[1] [vapœr] *nf* (**a**) *(d'eau bouillante)* **v. (d'eau)** steam; **cuire qch à la v.** to steam sth; **à toute v.** full steam ahead; *Fig* at full speed (**b**) *(gaz)* **vapeurs** *(d'alcool, d'essence)* fumes (**c**) *Méd* **avoir des vapeurs** to have a fit of the vapors

vapeur[2] [vapœr] *nm (bateau)* steamer, steamship

vaporeux, -euse [vaporø, -øz] *adj* (**a**) *(atmosphère)* steamy (**b**) *(robe)* flimsy

vaporisateur [vaporizatœr] *nm (de parfum)* spray, atomizer; *(pour plantes)* spray

vaporiser [vaporize] **1** *vt* (**a**) *(pulvériser)* to spray (**b**) *(transformer en vapeur)* to vaporize
   2 se vaporiser *vpr* to vaporize

vaquer [vake] **1** *vi (parlement, tribunal)* to be on vacation
   2 vaquer à *vt ind* **v. à qch** to attend to sth; **v. à ses affaires** *ou* **occupations** to go about one's business

varappe [varap] *nf* rock climbing; **faire de la v.** to go rock climbing

varapper [varape] *vi* to go rock climbing

varappeur, -euse [varapœr, -øz] *nm,f* rock climber

vareuse [varøz] *nf* (**a**) *(de marin)* pea jacket (**b**) *(d'uniforme)* tunic (**c**) *(veste large)* loose-fitting jacket

variable [varjabl] **1** *adj* (**a**) *(temps, humeur)* changeable; *(vitesse)* varying (**b**) *(différent)* varied; **être v.** to vary
   2 *nf* variable; *Ordinat* **v. de mémoire** memory variable

variante [varjɑ̃t] *nf* variant, variation

variation [varjasjɔ̃] *nf* (**a**) *(écart)* change (**de** in); **les variations de la température** the variations in the temperature (**b**) *Mus* variation

varice [varis] *nf* varicose vein

varicelle [varisɛl] *nf* chickenpox, *Spéc* varicella; **avoir la v.** to have chickenpox

varié, -e [varje] *adj (alimentation, paysage, travail)* varied; *(vocabulaire)* wide

varier [66] [varje] **1** *vt (alimentation, occupations)* to vary; *Ironique* **pour v. les plaisirs** by way of a pleasant change
   2 *vi* to vary, to change; **les opinions varient sur ce point** opinions differ on this point; **il n'a jamais varié sur ce point** he's never changed his mind about it

variété [varjete] **1** *nf* variety
   2 *nfpl* **variétés** *TV* variety show; *(musique)* easy-listening; **chanteur de variétés** middle-of-the-road singer; **disque de v.** easy-listening record

variole [varjɔl] *nf* smallpox; **avoir la v.** to have smallpox

Varsovie [varsɔvi] *n* Warsaw

vas *voir* **aller**

vasculaire [vaskylɛr] *adj* vascular

vase[1] [vɑz] *nm* vase; *Fig* **vivre en v. clos** to live in isolation; **vases communicants** communicating vessels

vase[2] [vɑz] *nf* mud, silt

vasectomie [vazɛktɔmi] *nf* vasectomy

vaseline [vazlin] *nf* Vaseline®, petroleum jelly

vaseux, -euse [vazø, -øz] *adj* (**a**) *Fam (mal en point)* out of sorts (**b**) *(peu clair) (idée)* woolly; *(explication)* confused (**c**) *(plaisanterie)* unsavory (**d**) *(rivière)* muddy, silty

vasistas [vazistɑs] *nm* fanlight

vasoconstricteur, -trice [vazokɔ̃striktœr, -tris] *adj & nm* vasoconstrictor

vasodilatateur, -trice [vazodilatatœr, -tris] *adj & nm* vasodilator

vasomoteur, -trice [vazomɔtœr, -tris] *adj (nerf)* vasomotor

vasouillard, -e [vazujar, -ard] *adj Fam (idée)* confused, muddled; **se sentir v.** to feel a bit under the weather

vasouiller [vazuje] *vi Fam* to flounder

vassal, -e, -aux, -ales [vasal, -o] *nm,f* vassal

vaste [vast] *adj* (**a**) vast, immense (**b**) *Fam (plaisanterie)* big, great; **c'est une v. fumisterie** it's a complete farce

Vatican [vatikɑ̃] *nm* **le V.** the Vatican; **la cité du V.** Vatican City

va-tout [vatu] *nm inv* **jouer son v.** to stake one's all

Vauban [vobɑ̃] *voir* **barrière**

vaudeville [vodvil] *nm Théât* light farce; **tourner au v.** to become farcical

vaudou, -e [vodu] *adj & nm* voodoo

vaudrai, vaudras, *etc. voir* **valoir**

vau-l'eau [volo] **à vau-l'eau** *adv* **aller à v.** to fall through

vaurien, -enne [vorjɛ̃, -ɛn] *nm,f* (**a**) *(brigand)* good-for-nothing (**b**) *(enfant)* rascal

vaut *voir* **valoir**

vautour [votur] *nm* vulture

vautrer [votre] **se vautrer** *vpr* (**a**) *(cochon)* to wallow (**dans** in) (**b**) *(personne)* to sprawl (**dans** in); *Fig* **se v. dans la débauche** to wallow in vice

vauvert [vovɛr] *voir* **diable**

va-vite [vavit] **à la va-vite** *adv* in a rush

vaux *voir* **valoir**

VDQS [vedekyɛs] *nm (abrév* **vin délimité de qualité supérieure)** = label certifying a wine's origin

veau, -x [vo] *nm* (**a**) *(animal)* calf (**b**) *(viande)* veal (**c**) *(cuir)* calfskin (**d**) *Fam (personne lente)* lump (**e**) *Fam (voiture)* car with poor acceleration

vecteur [vɛktœr] *nm* (**a**) *Math* vector (**b**) *(d'information, de progrès)* vehicle

vectoriel, -elle [vɛktɔrjɛl] *adj* vectorial; *Ordinat* **police vectorielle** outline font

vécu, -e [veky] **1** *pp voir* **vivre**
   2 *adj (expérience)* real-life
   3 *nm* real-life experience

vedettariat [vədɛtarja] *nm* stardom

vedette [vədɛt] *nf* (**a**) *(acteur)* star; **v. de la chanson** singing star; **v. de cinéma** movie star; **avoir la v., être en v.** *(dans un spectacle)* to top the bill; *(dans un film)* to be the main star (**b**) *Fig (de la politique)* leading light (**c**) *(bateau à moteur) (de plaisancier)* launch; *(de police)* patrol boat

végétal, -e, -aux, -ales [veʒetal, -o] **1** *adj (huile)* vegetable
   2 *nm* vegetable, plant

végétalien, -enne [veʒetaljɛ̃, -ɛn] *adj & nm,f* vegan

végétarien, -enne [veʒetarjɛ̃, -ɛn] *adj & nm,f* vegetarian

végétatif, -ive [veʒetatif, -iv] *adj (appareil)* vegetative; *Fig & Péj (existence)* vegetable-like

végétation [veʒetasjɔ̃] *nf* (**a**) *(flore)* vegetation (**b**) *Méd* **végétations (adénoïdes)** adenoids

végéter [34] [veʒete] *vi Péj (personne)* to vegetate

véhémence [veemɑ̃s] *nf Litt* vehemence; **avec v.** vehemently

véhément, -e [veemɑ̃, -ɑ̃t] *adj Litt* vehement, violent

véhicule [veikyl] *nm* (**a**) *(moyen de transport)* vehicle; **v. utilitaire** commercial vehicle (**b**) *(support) (du son, de la lumière)* vehicle

véhiculer [veikyle] *vt* (**a**) *(transporter)* to transport, to convey (**b**) *(transmettre)* to convey

veille [vɛj] *nf* (**a**) *(jour qui précède)* **la v.** the previous day, the day before; **à la v. de la réunion** the day before the meeting; **la v. au soir** the previous evening, the evening before; **la v. de Noël** Christmas Eve; *Fig* **être à la v. de qch/de faire qch** to be on the verge of sth/of doing sth (**b**) *(éveil)* wakefulness; **entre la v. et le sommeil** between waking and sleeping; **après deux jours de v.** after staying up for two nights (**c**) *(garde)* (night) watch; **prendre la v.** to take one's turn on watch (**d**) *Ordinat* standby mode; **en v.** in standby mode

veillée [veje] *nf* (a) *(soirée)* evening; **v. au coin du feu** evening spent around the fire; **v. d'armes** knightly vigil (b) *(d'un mort)* watch, vigil; **v. funèbre** wake (c) *Can (fête)* party

veiller [veje] **1** *vt (malade)* to sit up with; **v. un mort** to keep vigil over a dead body

2 *vi* to stay up

3 veiller à *vt ind* **v. à qch** to see to sth; **v. aux intérêts de qn** to look after sb's interests; **v. à ce que qn fasse qch** to make sure *or* to see to it that sb does sth; *Fig* **v. au grain** to keep an eye open for trouble

4 veiller sur *vt ind* **v. sur qn** to take care of sb

5 se veiller *vpr Suisse Fam* to be careful

veilleur [vɛjœr] *nm* **v. de nuit** night watchman

veilleuse [vɛjøz] *nf* (a) *(lampe)* night light; *(sur une télévision, sur un magnétoscope)* standby; *Fig* **mettre qch en v.** *(projet, problème)* to put sth on the back burner; *Fam* **la mettre en v.** to pipe down (b) *(d'un chauffe-eau, d'un réchaud)* pilot light (c) **veilleuses** *(d'une automobile)* sidelights

veinard, -e [vɛnar, -ard] *Fam* **1** *adj* lucky

2 *nm,f* lucky devil

veine [vɛn] *nf* (a) *Anat* vein; **v. cave** vena cava (b) *Fam (chance)* luck; **avoir de la v.** to be lucky; *Fam* **avoir une v. de cocu** to have the luck of the devil (c) *(dans le marbre, le bois)* vein (d) *(filon) (de minerai)* vein; *(de charbon)* seam (e) *(inspiration)* vein; **en v. de plaisanterie** in humorous vein; **être en v. de générosité** to be in a generous mood

veiné, -e [vene] *adj (marbre, bois)* grained

veineux, -euse [vɛnø, -øz] *adj (système, circulation)* venous

veinule [venyl] *nf* venule

Velcro® [vɛlkro] *nm (tissu)* Velcro®; *(fermeture)* Velcro® fastening

vêler [vɛle] *vi* to calve

vélin [velɛ̃] *nm* vellum

véliplanchiste [veliplɑ̃ʃist] *nmf* windsurfer

velléitaire [veleiter] **1** *adj* indecisive

2 *nmf* indecisive person

velléités [veleite] *nfpl* vague desire; **avoir des v. de faire qch** to toy with the idea of doing sth

vélo [velo] *nm* bike; **aller au bureau en v.** to bike to the office, to go to the office on one's bike; **faire du v.** *(comme activité)* to go cycling; **est-ce que tu sais faire du v.?** can you ride a bike?; **v. d'appartement** exercise bike; **v. de course** racing cycle; **v. tout-terrain** mountain bike

vélocité [velosite] *nf* speed, swiftness

vélodrome [velodrom] *nm* velodrome

vélomoteur [velomotœr] *nm* moped

velours [vəlur] *nm* (a) *(tissu)* velvet; **veste/rideaux en v.** velvet jacket/curtains; **v. côtelé** *ou* **à côtes** corduroy (b) *Fig* **faire des yeux de v. à qn** to make eyes at sb

velouté, -e [vəlute] **1** *adj* velvety

2 *nm* (a) *(texture)* velvetiness (b) *(soupe)* cream soup; **v. d'asperges** cream of asparagus soup

velouteux, -euse [vəlutø, -øz] *adj* velvety

Velpeau® [vɛlpo] *voir* **bande¹**

velu, -e [vəly] *adj* hairy

Vélux® [velyks] *nm* = window built into a sloping roof

venaison [vɛnɛzɔ̃] *nf* venison

vénal, -e, -aux, -ales [venal, -o] *adj* (a) *Péj (intéressé)* venal, mercenary (b) *(valeur)* market

venant [vənɑ̃] *nm* **à tout v., à tous venants** to all comers, to all and sundry

vendable [vɑ̃dabl] *adj* salable, sellable; **facilement/difficilement v.** easy/difficult to sell

vendange [vɑ̃dɑʒ] *nf* (a) **vendanges** *(période)* grape-harvesting time (b) *(récolte)* grape harvest; **faire la v.** *ou* **les vendanges** to harvest *or* to pick the grapes (c) *(raisin récolté)* grapes (harvested); **une bonne v.** a good vintage

vendanger [45] [vɑ̃dɑʒe] **1** *vi* to harvest the grapes

2 *vt (vigne)* to pick the grapes from

vendangeur, -euse [vɑ̃dɑʒœr, -øz] *nm,f* grape picker

vendetta [vɑ̃deta] *nf* vendetta

vendeur, -euse [vɑ̃dœr, -øz] **1** *adj* **être v.** to be willing to sell

2 *nm,f (dans un magasin)* (sales)clerk; *(non professionnel)* seller; **v. ambulant** traveling salesman; **v. à domicile** door-to-door salesman; **v. de journaux** newspaper seller *or* vendor

vendre [vɑ̃dr] **1** *vt* (a) *(article, produit)* to sell; **v. qch 50 euros** to sell sth for 50 euros; **v. qch à qn** to sell sb sth, to sell sth to sb; **à v.** *(sur panneau)* for sale; *Fig* **v. son âme au diable** to sell one's soul to the devil (b) *(trahir) (personne)* to sell out; *(secret)* to sell; **v. la mèche** to spill the beans

2 se vendre *vpr* (a) *(produit, article)* to be sold; **cela se vend comme des petits pains** it's selling like hot cakes (b) *(soi-même)* to sell oneself

vendredi [vɑ̃drədi] *nm* Friday; **le v. saint** Good Friday; *voir aussi* **samedi**

vendu, -e [vɑ̃dy] **1** *adj (corrompu)* bribed

2 *nm,f* traitor

vénéneux, -euse [venenø, -øz] *adj* poisonous

vénérable [venerabl] *adj* venerable

vénération [venerasjɔ̃] *nf* veneration; **avoir de la v. pour qn** to hold sb in veneration

vénère [vener] *Fam* **1** *adj* pissed

2 *vt* **v. qn** to bug sb, to piss sb off

vénérer [34] [venere] *vt* to venerate

vénérien, -enne [venerjɛ̃, -ɛn] *adj* venereal

Venezuela [venezɥela] *nm* **le V.** Venezuela

vénézuélien, -enne [venezɥeljɛ̃, -ɛn] **1** *adj* Venezuelan

2 *nm,f* **V., Vénézuélienne** Venezuelan

vengeance [vɑ̃ʒɑs] *nf* revenge, vengeance; **la v. est un plat qui se mange froid** revenge is a dish best eaten cold

venger [45] [vɑ̃ʒe] **1** *vt* to avenge; **v. qn de qch** to avenge sb for sth

2 se venger *vpr* to get one's revenge; **se v. sur qn (de qch)** to get one's revenge on sb (for sth); *Fam* **pas la peine de te v. sur moi!** there's no point in taking it out on me!

vengeur, -eresse [vɑ̃ʒœr, -ʒrɛs] *Litt* **1** *adj* vengeful

2 *nm,f* avenger

véniel, -elle [venjɛl] *adj (péché)* venial

venimeux, -euse [vənimø, -øz] *adj aussi Fig* venomous

venin [vənɛ̃] *nm aussi Fig* venom

venir [70] [vənir] *(aux être)* **1** *vi* (a) *(arriver)* to come (**de** from); **il vient passer quelques jours** he's coming to spend a few days; **viens me voir** come and see me; **d'où venez-vous?** where do you come from?; **je viens!** I'm coming!; **v. vers qn** to come up to sb; **vous y viendrez!** you'll come around to it, you'll change your mind; **dans les mois/années qui viennent** in the coming months/years; **le moment est venu de nous en aller** it's time we left; **le jour viendra où...** the day will come when...; **ton tour viendra** your turn will come, you'll get your turn; **l'eau leur venait aux genoux** the water came up to their knees

(b) *(tirer son origine)* to come (**de** from); **la maison lui vient de sa mère** he/she inherited the house from his/her mother

(c) **en v. à qch/à faire qch** to come to sth/to do sth; **j'en suis venu à me demander si...** I began to wonder whether...; **où voulez-vous en v.?** what are you getting at?; **en v. aux mains** to come to blows

(d) **venir de faire qch** to have just done sth; **je viens de le lui dire** I've just told him/her; **je venais de terminer** I'd just finished

2 *v impersonnel* **s'il venait à pleuvoir** if it happened to rain; **il m'est venu une idée intéressante** an interesting idea occurred to me

3 s'en venir *vpr Litt* to come along

Venise [vəniz] *n* Venice

vénitien, -enne [venisjɛ̃, -ɛn] **1** *adj* Venetian

    2 *nm,f* **V.,Vénitienne** Venetian

vent [vɑ̃] *nm* (**a**) *(air)* wind; **les cheveux au v.** with one's hair streaming in the wind; **quel bon v. vous amène?** to what do I/we owe the pleasure?; *Fig* **avoir le v. en poupe** to have the wind in one's sails; *Fig* **avoir du v. dans les voiles** to be three sheets to the wind; **avoir v. de qch** to get wind of sth; **ce n'est que du v.** it's just hot air; *Fam* **être dans le v.** to be with it; **contre vents et marées** come hell or high water; *Ironique* **bon v.!** good riddance! (**b**) *(flatulence)* wind; **avoir des vents** to have wind

vente [vɑ̃t] *nf (transaction)* sale; *(activité)* selling; *Can (soldes)* sale; **en v.** for sale; **en v. libre** available over the counter; **mettre qch en v.** to put sth up for sale; **v. de charité** charity sale; **v. par correspondance** mail order (selling); **v. à crédit** credit selling; **v. au détail** retailing; **v. aux enchères** (sale by) auction; **v. en gros** wholesaling; **v. en ligne** e-tail, online selling; **v. à tempérament** installment plan

venter [vɑ̃te] *v impersonnel* **il vente** it's windy

venteux, -euse [vɑ̃tø, -øz] *adj* windy

ventilateur [vɑ̃tilatœr] *nm* (**a**) *(pour aérer)* fan (**b**) *Ordinat* **v. de refroidissement** cooling fan (**c**) *(d'une automobile)* blower

ventilation [vɑ̃tilasjɔ̃] *nf* (**a**) *(aération)* ventilation (**b**) *(des dépenses)* breakdown

ventiler [vɑ̃tile] *vt* (**a**) *(aérer)* to ventilate (**b**) *(dépenses)* to break down

ventouse [vɑ̃tuz] *nf* (**a**) *(pour fixer)* suction grip; *(pour déboucher)* plunger; **faire v.** to adhere by suction (**b**) *(en verre)* cupping glass; **poser des ventouses à qn** to cup sb

ventral, -e, -aux, -ales [vɑ̃tral, -o] *adj* ventral

ventre [vɑ̃tr] *nm* (**a**) *(estomac)* stomach; **avoir le v. plein/vide** to have a full/an empty stomach; **avoir du v.** to have a paunch; **v. à terre** at full speed, flat out; **avoir mal au v.** to have a stomachache; *Fig* **ça fait mal au v. de voir ça** it makes me sick to see that; *Fig* **ça me ferait mal au v.!** it would kill me!; **ne rien avoir dans le v.** to have no guts (**b**) *(utérus)* womb (**c**) *(d'une bouteille)* bulge

ventricule [vɑ̃trikyl] *nm* ventricle

ventriloque [vɑ̃trilɔk] *nmf* ventriloquist

ventru, -e [vɑ̃try] *adj* (**a**) *(gros)* potbellied (**b**) *(colonne)* bulbous

venu, -e [vəny] **1** *adj* **bien v.** appropriate; **mal v.** inappropriate

    2 *nm,f* **le premier v.** *(n'importe qui)* anybody; **un nouveau v.** a newcomer

    3 *nf* **venue** *(d'une personne, du printemps)* coming; **dès sa venue au monde** since he/she came into the world

Vénus [venys] *npr (déesse, planète)* Venus

vêpres [vɛpr] *nfpl* vespers

ver [vɛr] *nm* (**a**) *(dans la terre)* worm; *(dans un fruit)* grub; *Fig* **tirer les vers du nez à qn** to drag it out of sb; **v. luisant** glow-worm; **v. à soie** silkworm; **v. de terre** earthworm (**b**) *Méd* **v. solitaire** tapeworm; **avoir le v. solitaire** to have a tapeworm (**c**) *Ordinat* **v. informatique** worm

véracité [verasite] *nf* truthfulness

véranda [verɑ̃da] *nf* veranda(h)

verbal, -e, -aux, -ales [vɛrbal, -o] *adj* verbal

verbalement [vɛrbalmɑ̃] *adv* verbally

verbaliser [vɛrbalize] **1** *vt (exprimer)* to verbalize

    2 *vi (policier)* to record the details of an offense; *(contractuel)* to write a parking ticket

verbe [vɛrb] *nm Gram* verb; **v. à particule** *(en anglais)* phrasal verb

verbeux, -euse [vɛrbø, -øz] *adj* verbose

verbiage [vɛrbjaʒ] *nm* verbiage

verdâtre [vɛrdatr] *adj* greenish

verdeur [vɛrdœr] *nf* (**a**) *(d'un fruit, d'un vin)* tartness (**b**) *(du langage)* crudeness (**c**) *(vitalité)* vigor, vitality

verdict [vɛrdikt] *nm* verdict; **prononcer** *ou* **rendre un v.** to return a verdict

verdir [vɛrdir] **1** *vt* to turn green

    2 *vi* to turn green; *Fig* **v. de jalousie/de peur** to go *or* to turn green with envy/white with fear

verdoyant, -e [vɛrdwajɑ̃, -ɑ̃t] *adj* green

verdoyer [32] [vɛrdwaje] *vi Litt* to be green

verdure [vɛrdyr] *nf* (**a**) *(couleur)* greenness (**b**) *(végétation)* greenery (**c**) *(légumes verts)* greens

véreux, -euse [verø, -øz] *adj* (**a**) *(fruit)* wormy, maggoty (**b**) *Péj (affaires, financier)* shady, dubious

verge [vɛrʒ] *nf* (**a**) *(pénis)* penis (**b**) *(baguette)* cane (**c**) *Can (mesure)* yard

verger [vɛrʒe] *nm* orchard

vergetures [vɛrʒətyr] *nfpl* stretch marks

verglacé, -e [vɛrglase] *adj* icy

verglas [vɛrgla] *nm* glare ice, glaze

vergogne [vɛrgɔɲ] **sans vergogne 1** *adj* shameless

    2 *adv* shamelessly

véridique [veridik] *adj* truthful

vérifiable [verifjabl] *adj* verifiable

vérificateur, -trice [verifikatœr, -tris] **1** *nm,f (personne)* inspector, examiner; **v. de comptes** auditor

    2 *nm Ordinat* **v. orthographique** spellchecker

vérification [verifikasjɔ̃] *nf* (**a**) *(d'un travail, des votes)* checking; **v. de comptes** *ou* **d'écritures** audit(ing) of accounts (**b**) *Ordinat* **v. antivirale** antiviral check; **v. orthographique** spellcheck

vérifier [66] [verifje] **1** *vt* to check; *(comptes)* to audit; **il doit être là, je vais v.** he must be there, I'll check

    2 **se vérifier** *vpr* to prove correct

véritable [veritabl] *adj* (**a**) *(histoire, ami)* true; *(nom, or, cuir)* real (**b**) *(en intensif)* real

véritablement [veritabləmɑ̃] *adv* really

vérité [verite] *nf* (**a**) *(d'une déclaration)* truth; **dire la v.** to tell the truth; **c'est la v.** it's true, it's a fact; **à la v.** to tell the truth; **en v.** really, actually; **dire à qn ses quatre vérités** to tell sb a few home truths (**b**) *(d'un personnage, d'une description)* trueness to life (**c**) *(sincérité)* **un accent de v.** a ring of truth

verlan [vɛrlɑ̃] *nm* back slang

Verlan

This form of slang, mostly used among young French people and particularly in the disadvantaged areas of large cities, involves inverting the syllables of words and making any spelling changes necessary to facilitate pronunciation. The word "verlan" is itself the inverted form of "l'envers", meaning "the other way around". Some "verlan" terms are used or understood by the majority of French speakers, e.g. "laisse béton!" ("laisse tomber!" = "forget it!"), "ripou" ("pourri", used to refer to corrupt policemen), "meuf" ("femme") and "beur" ("arabe"). It is, however, an extremely generative form of slang and new words are constantly being invented.

---

vermeil, -eille [vɛrmɛj] **1** *adj* bright red

    2 *nm* silver gilt

vermicelle [vɛrmisɛl] *nm* vermicelli

vermifuge [vɛrmifyʒ] *nm* vermifuge

vermillon [vɛrmijɔ̃] *adj inv & nm* vermilion

vermine [vɛrmin] *nf* (**a**) *(insectes)* vermin; **couvert** *ou* **grouillant de v.** crawling with vermin (**b**) *Péj (racaille)* **la v.** vermin

vermisseau, -x [vɛrmiso] *nm* small worm; *Fig (personne)* worm

vermoulu, -e [vɛrmuly] *adj* worm-eaten

vermouth [vɛrmut] *nm* vermouth

vernaculaire [vɛrnakylɛr] *adj* **langue v.** vernacular

verni, -e [vɛrni] *adj* (a) *(meuble, bois, parquet)* varnished; *(chaussures)* patent (leather); *(ongles)* varnished, painted (b) *Fam (chanceux)* lucky

vernir [vɛrnir] *vt* to varnish

vernis [vɛrni] *nm* (a) *(pour le bois)* varnish; **v. à ongles** nail varnish *or* polish; **se mettre du v. à ongles** to varnish *or* paint one's nails (b) *Fig* **un v. de culture** a smattering of knowledge

vernissage [vɛrnisaʒ] *nm* (a) *(du bois)* varnishing (b) *(d'une exposition)* opening, private viewing

vérole [verɔl] *nf Vieilli* syphilis; **la petite v.** smallpox

verra, verrai, *etc. voir* **voir**

verrat [vera] *nm* breeding boar

verre [vɛr] *nm* (a) *(matière)* glass; **sous v.** under glass; **gravure sous v.** glass-mounted engraving; **v. blanc** glass; **v. dépoli/feuilleté** frosted/laminated glass (b) *(récipient)* glass; **v. à dents** tooth glass; **v. doseur** *ou* **gradué** ≃ measuring glass; **v. à eau** large wineglass; **v. à pied** stemmed glass; **v. à vin** wineglass; **v. à whisky** whiskey glass (c) *(contenu)* glass(ful) (d) *(boisson)* drink; **boire** *ou* **prendre un v.** to have a drink (e) *(de lunettes)* lens; **verres de contact** contact lenses; **v. à double foyer** bifocals; **verres teintés** *ou* **fumés** tinted lenses

verrée [vere] *nf Suisse (tournée)* round (of drinks); *(rencontre)* cocktail party

verrerie [vɛrri] *nf* (a) *(fabrication)* glassmaking (b) *(atelier)* glassworks (c) *(marchandise)* glassware

verrier [vɛrje] *nm (artisan)* glassmaker

verrière [vɛrjɛr] *nf* (a) *(toit)* glass roof; *(paroi)* glass wall (b) *(pièce)* conservatory

verroterie [vɛrɔtri] *nf* glass jewelry

verrou [vɛru] *nm* bolt; **mettre** *ou* **tirer le v.** to bolt the door; *Fig* **sous les verrous** behind bars, inside

verrouillage [vɛrujaʒ] *nm* (a) *(d'une porte)* bolting; *(à clé)* locking (b) *(d'un mécanisme)* locking; **v. central** central locking (c) *Ordinat* **v. des fichiers** file lock; **v. en lecture seule** read-only lock; **v. en majuscule(s)** caps lock

verrouiller [vɛruje] *vt* (a) *(porte)* to bolt; *(à clé)* to lock; *(prisonnier)* to lock up (b) *(quartier)* to close off, to seal off (c) *Ordinat (capitales)* to lock on; **verrouillé en majuscule(s)** *(clavier)* with caps lock on

verrue [vɛry] *nf* wart; **v. plantaire** verruca

vers[1] [vɛr] *nm (poétique)* line; **faire des v.** to write verse *or* poetry; **v. blancs** blank verse; **v. libres** free verse

vers[2] [vɛr] *prép* (a) *(dans la direction de)* toward (b) *(aux alentours de) (dans le temps)* about; *(dans l'espace)* near; **v. la fin** toward the end; *Fam* **v. les trois heures** about *or* around 3 o'clock

versant [vɛrsã] *nm* slope, side

versatile [vɛrsatil] *adj* changeable, fickle

versatilité [vɛrsatilite] *nf* changeability, fickleness

verse [vɛrs] **à verse** *adv* **il pleut à v.** it's pouring (down); **la pluie tombait à v.** the rain was coming down in torrents

versé, -e [vɛrse] *adj* **être v. dans qch** to be well-versed in sth

Verseau [vɛrso] *nm Astron & Astrol* **le V.** Aquarius; **être V.** to be (an) Aquarius *or* an Aquarian

versement [vɛrsəmã] *nm* payment

verser [vɛrse] **1** *vt* (a) *(liquide)* to pour (out) (**dans** into); **v. à boire à qn** to pour sb a drink, to pour a drink for sb (b) *(larmes, sang)* to shed (c) *(argent)* to pay; **v. de l'argent sur son compte** to deposit money into one's account (d) *Jur (document)* to add (**à** to)
2 *vi (véhicule)* to overturn
3 verser dans *vt ind* to lapse into

verset [vɛrsɛ] *nm* verse

verseur, -euse [vɛrsœr, -øz] **1** *adj voir* **bec**
2 *nf* **verseuse** pot *(for coffee machine)*

versification [vɛrsifikasjɔ̃] *nf* versification

version [vɛrsjɔ̃] *nf* (a) *(d'un événement, d'un texte)* version (b) *(traduction)* translation; **v. anglaise/espagnole** *(à l'école)* translation from English/Spanish (c) *Cin* **en v. originale** in the original language; **en v. française** dubbed *(into French)* (d) *Ordinat* **v. bêta** beta version

verso [vɛrso] *nm* back; **voir au v.** see over(leaf)

vert, -e [vɛr, vɛrt] **1** *adj* (a) *(couleur)* green; *Fig* **v. de peur** white with fear; *Fig* **v. de jalousie** green with envy; *Fig* **avoir la main verte** to have a green thumb (b) *(jeune) (bois)* green; *(fruit)* unripe; *(vin)* too young (c) *(écologique)* green (d) *(vieillard)* sprightly (e) *(histoire, propos)* spicy (f) *(réprimande)* sharp
2 *nm* (a) *(couleur)* green; **passer au v.** *(signal d'arrêt)* to go *or* to turn green; **v. amande** almond green; **v. bouteille** bottle green; **v. d'eau** sea green; **v. émeraude** emerald green; **v. olive** olive green; **v. pomme** apple green (b) *Fam* **se mettre au v.** to go to the country (c) *Pol* **les Verts** ≃ the Green Party
3 *nfpl* **vertes** *Fam* **en dire de vertes** to tell spicy stories; **il en a vu des vertes et des pas mûres** he's been through a lot

vert-de-gris [vɛrdəgri] **1** *nm inv* verdigris
2 *adj* gray-green

vertébral, -e, -aux, -ales [vɛrtebral, -o] *adj* vertebral

vertèbre [vɛrtɛbr] *nf* vertebra

vertébré, -e [vɛrtebre] *adj & nm* vertebrate

vertement [vɛrtəmã] *adv* sharply

vertical, -e, -aux, -ales [vɛrtikal, -o] **1** *adj* vertical; **en position verticale** *(objet)* in a vertical position, upright
2 *nf* **verticale** vertical; **à la verticale** vertically

verticalement [vɛrtikalmã] *adv* vertically; *(dans les mots croisés)* down

vertige [vɛrtiʒ] *nm* (a) *(au-dessus du vide)* vertigo; **avoir le v.** *(toujours)* to suffer from vertigo; *(ponctuellement)* to feel dizzy; **donner le v. à qn** *(vide)* to make sb dizzy; *Fig* to make sb's head spin (b) *(étourdissement)* dizziness, giddiness; **avoir des vertiges** to have dizzy spells

vertigineusement [vɛrtiʒinøzmã] *adv* **grimper v.** to rocket; **chuter v.** to plummet

vertigineux, -euse [vɛrtiʒinø, -øz] *adj (hauteur)* dizzy; *(vitesse)* breakneck; *(somme, hausse des prix)* staggering

vertu [vɛrty] *nf* (a) *(propriété)* property (b) *(qualité morale)* virtue (c) *Litt (chasteté)* virtue; **femme de petite v.** woman of easy virtue (d) **en v. de qch** *(principe, loi)* in accordance with sth; **en v. des pouvoirs qui me sont conférés** by virtue of the powers bestowed upon me; **en v. de quoi est-il intervenu?** what gave him the right to intervene?

vertueux, -euse [vɛrtɥø, -øz] *adj* virtuous; *(intention)* honorable

verve [vɛrv] *nf* verve; **être en v.** to be in top form

verveine [vɛrvɛn] *nf* (a) *(plante)* verbena (b) *(tisane)* verbena tea

vésicule [vezikyl] *nf* vesicle; **v. biliaire** gall bladder

vespasienne [vɛspazjɛn] *nf* street urinal

vespéral, -e, -aux, -ales [vɛsperal, -o] *adj Litt* evening

vessie [vesi] *nf* bladder; *Fig* **prendre des vessies pour des lanternes** to believe that the moon is made of green cheese; **il voudrait nous faire prendre des vessies pour des lanternes** he's trying to pull the wool over our eyes

veste [vɛst] *nf* jacket; **v. droite/croisée** single-/double-breasted jacket; *Fam Fig* **prendre une v.** *(échouer)* to come unstuck; *(être rejeté)* to get turned down

vestiaire [vɛstjɛr] *nm* (a) *(d'un théâtre)* checkroom; *(d'un stade)* locker room; *Fig* **laisser sa fierté au v.** to forget one's pride (b) **récupérer son v.** to collect one's things from the cloakroom

vestibule [vɛstibyl] *nm* (entrance) hall

vestiges [vɛstiʒ] *nmpl* (a) *(ruines)* remains (b) *(traces)* relics

vestimentaire [vɛstimãtɛr] *adj (dépenses)* clothing

veston [vɛstɔ̃] *nm* jacket

Vésuve [vezyv] *nm* **le V.** Vesuvius

vêtement [vɛtmã] *nm* garment, article of clothing; **vêtements** clothes, clothing; **vêtements de travail** work clothes

vétéran [veterã] *nm* veteran

vétérinaire [veterinɛr] **1** *adj* veterinary
  2 *nmf* veterinarian

vétille [vetij] *nf* trifle, triviality

vêtir [71] [vetir] *Litt vt (personne)* to clothe, to dress (**de** in)
  2 se vêtir *vpr* to dress (oneself) (**de** in)

vétiver [vetivɛr] *nm* vetiver

veto [veto] *nm* veto; **opposer son v. à qch** to veto sth; **droit de v.** right of veto

vêtu, -e [vety] *adj* dressed (**de** in)

vétuste [vetyst] *adj* dilapidated

vétusté [vetyste] *nf* dilapidation

veuf, veuve [vœf, vœv] **1** *adj* **être v.** to be a widower; **être veuve** to be a widow
  2 *nm,f* widower, *f* widow

veuille *etc. voir* **vouloir**[1]

veule [vøl] *adj Litt (personne)* spineless

veulerie [vølri] *nf Litt* spinelessness

veut *voir* **vouloir**[1]

veuvage [vœvaʒ] *nm (d'homme)* widowerhood; *(de femme)* widowhood

veux *voir* **vouloir**[1]

vexant, -e [vɛksã, -ãt] *adj* **(a)** *(blessant)* hurtful **(b)** *(contrariant)* annoying

vexation [vɛksasjɔ̃] *nf* humiliation

vexatoire [vɛksatwar] *adj* humiliating

vexer [vɛkse] **1** *vt* to hurt, to upset; *Fam* **être vexé comme un pou** to be extremely upset
  2 se vexer *vpr* to get upset (**de** at)

VF [veɛf] *nf (abrév* **version française**) **en VF** dubbed *(into French)*

via [vja] *prép* via

viabiliser [vjabilize] *vt* to service

viabilité[1] [vjabilite] *nf (d'un fœtus, d'un projet)* viability

viabilité[2] [vjabilite] *nf (d'un chemin)* practicability

viable [vjabl] *adj* viable

viaduc [vjadyk] *nm* viaduct

viager, -ère [vjaʒe, -ɛr] **1** *adj* life
  2 *nm* life annuity; **mettre qch en v.** to sell sth in return for a life annuity; **acheter une maison en v.** to buy a house so as to provide the seller with a life annuity

Viagra® [vjagra] *nm Pharm* Viagra®

viande [vjãd] *nf* meat; **v. blanche/rouge** white/red meat; **v. hachée** ground meat

viander [vjãde] **se viander** *vpr très Fam* to get smashed up

vibrant, -e [vibrã, -ãt] *adj (discours, hommage)* rousing, stirring

vibraphone [vibrafɔn] *nm* vibraphone

vibration [vibrasjɔ̃] *nf* vibration

vibrato [vibrato] *nm* vibrato

vibrer [vibre] *vi* **(a)** *(objet)* to vibrate **(b)** *(personne)* to be stirred; **sa voix vibrait de colère** his/her voice was shaking with anger; **faire v. qn** to stir sb

vibromasseur [vibromasœr] *nm* vibrator

vicaire [vikɛr] *nm (dans la religion catholique)* assistant priest; *(dans la religion anglicane)* curate

vice [vis] *nm* **(a)** *(défaut moral)* vice **(b)** *(défectuosité)* defect; **v. caché** hidden *or* latent defect; **v. de fabrication** manufacturing defect; *Jur* **v. de forme** legal flaw **(c)** *(débauche)* vice; *Fig* **mais c'est du v.!** it's an obsession!

vice-amiral [visamiral] *(pl* **vice-amiraux** [visamiro]) *nm* vice admiral

vice-consul *(pl* **vice-consuls**) [viskɔ̃syl] *nm* vice consul

vice-présidence *(mpl* **vice-présidences**) [visprezidãs] *nf (d'état, d'organisation)* vice-presidency; *(d'entreprise)* vice-chairmanship

vice-président, -e *(mpl* **vice-présidents**, *fpl* **vice-présidentes**) [visprezidã, -ãt] *nm,f (d'état, d'organisation)* vice-president; *(d'entreprise)* vice-chairman

vice versa [visvɛrsa] *adv* vice versa

vichy [viʃi] *nm (tissu)* gingham

vicié, -e [visje] *adj* **(a)** *(air)* polluted **(b)** *Jur* invalidated

vicieux, -euse [visjø, -øz] *adj* **(a)** *(pervers)* depraved **(b)** *(perfide)* underhand **(c)** *(chien)* vicious

vicissitudes [visisityd] *nfpl* vicissitudes

vicomte [vikɔ̃t] *nm* viscount

vicomtesse [vikɔ̃tɛs] *nf* viscountess

victime [viktim] *nf* victim; *(d'un accident)* casualty; **être v. d'un attentat/d'une agression** to be the victim of an assassination attempt/of an attack; **être la v. d'une illusion/d'un malentendu** to labor under an illusion/a misconception

victimisation [viktimizasjɔ̃] *nf* victimization

victimiser [viktimize] *vt* to victimize

victoire [viktwar] *nf* victory; *(en sport)* win, victory; **chanter** *ou* **crier v.** to claim victory

victorien, -enne [viktɔrjɛ̃, -ɛn] *adj* Victorian

victorieusement [viktɔrjøzmã] *adv* victoriously

victorieux, -euse [viktɔrjø, -øz] *adj* victorious; *(air, sourire)* triumphant

victuailles [viktɥaj] *nfpl* provisions

vidange [vidãʒ] *nf* **(a)** *(d'un moteur)* oil change; **faire la v.** to change the oil **(b)** *(d'une fosse septique)* draining, emptying **(c)** *Belg (verre consigné)* returnable empties **(d)** *Can* **vidanges** *(ordures ménagères)* refuse, garbage

vidanger [45] [vidãʒe] *vt* **(a)** *(huile)* to change; *(moteur)* to change the oil in **(b)** *(fosse septique)* to drain, to empty

vide [vid] **1** *adj* empty; *(regard)* blank; **v. de sens** devoid of meaning, meaningless
  2 *nm Phys* vacuum; *(espace)* empty space, gap; *Fig (dans un emploi du temps)* gap; **rouler à v.** *(bus)* to have no passengers; **emballé sous v.** vacuum-packed; **faire le v.** to create a vacuum; *Fig (se ressourcer)* to switch off; *Fig* **faire le v. dans son esprit** to clear one's mind; **regarder dans le v.** to stare into space; **c'est comme si je parlais dans le v.** it's like talking to a brick wall; **avoir peur du v.** to be afraid of *or* to have no head for heights; **il y a un v. juridique concernant cela** there's nothing in the law to cover that; **v. sanitaire** ventilation *or* crawl space

vidé, -e [vide] *adj Fam (épuisé)* dead beat

vidéo [video] **1** *adj inv* video
  2 *nf* video; *Ordinat* **v. inversée** reverse video

vidéocassette [videokasɛt] *nf* video cassette

vidéo-clip [videoklip] *nm* video

vidéoconférence [videokɔ̃ferãs] *nf* videoconference; *(concept)* videoconferencing

vidéodisque [videodisk] *nm* videodisk

vide-ordures [vidɔrdyr] *nm inv* garbage chute

vidéoprojecteur [videoprɔʒɛktœr] *nm* video projector

vidéoprojection [videoprɔʒɛksjɔ̃] *nf* video projection

vidéothèque [videotɛk] *nf* video library

vide-poches [vidpɔʃ] *nm inv* **(a)** *(de voiture) (dans le tableau de bord)* storage tray; *(dans la porte)* door pocket **(b)** *(de maison)* tidy

vide-pomme *(pl* **vide-pommes**) [vidpɔm] *nm* apple corer

vider [vide] **1** *vt* **(a)** *(enlever le contenu de)* to empty (**de** of); *Fam Fig* **v. son sac** to get it off one's chest; *Fig* **v. son cœur** to pour out one's feelings **(b)** *Fam (épuiser)* to wear out **(c)** *Fam (expulser)* to chuck out; **se faire v.** to be chucked out **(d)** **v. les lieux** to vacate the premises **(e)** *(poisson)* to gut; *(volaille)* to draw

(f) *Ordinat* **v. l'écran** to clear the screen; **v. la corbeille** to empty the wastebasket *or* the trash

2 se vider *vpr* to empty; **se v. de son sang** to bleed to death

videur, -euse [vidœr, -øz] *nm,f* bouncer

vie [vi] *nf* **(a)** *(d'êtres vivants)* life; **être en v.** to be alive; **être entre la v. et la mort** to be fighting for one's life; **donner la v. à un enfant** to give birth to a child; **avoir la v. dure** *(mauvaise herbe, parasite)* to be hard to kill off; *(superstitions, préjugés)* to die hard; **entre eux, c'est à la v., à la mort** they'd die for each other; **être plein de v.** to be full of life; **sans v.** lifeless **(b)** *(animation)* life; **donner de la v. à qch** to liven sth up **(c)** *(durée d'existence)* life, lifetime; **pour la v.** for life; **une (seule) fois dans la v.** once in a lifetime **(d)** *(biographie)* life story; *Fam* **raconter sa v. à qn** to tell sb one's life story **(e)** *(façon de vivre)* life; **c'est la v. de château!** this is the life!; **v. nocturne** nightlife; *Fam Vieilli* **faire la v.** to live it up **(f)** *(subsistance)* **la v. est très chère dans ces pays** the cost of living is very high in these countries

vieil [vjɛj] *voir* **vieux**

vieillard [vjɛjar] *nm* old man

vieille [vjɛj] **1** *adj f voir* **vieux**

2 *nf (poisson)* wrasse

vieillerie [vjɛjri] *nf (objet)* old thing

vieillesse [vjɛjɛs] *nf* old age

vieilli, -e [vjeji] *adj* **(a)** *(mot, style)* old-fashioned, dated **(b)** *(personne)* aged

vieillir [vjejir] **1** *vi* **(a)** *(personne)* to get old, to age **(b)** *(mot, film, chanson)* to be dated **(c)** *(fromage, vin)* to mature

2 *vt (personne) (par l'apparence)* to age; **v. qn (de deux ans)** to make sb out to be (two years) older than he/she is

3 **se vieillir** *vpr* **(a)** *(par l'apparence)* to make oneself look older **(b)** *(se dire plus âgé)* to pretend to be older than one is

vieillissant, -e [vjejisɑ̃, -ɑ̃t] *adj (personne)* aging; *(institution, style)* which is becoming outdated

vieillissement [vjejismɑ̃] *nm* **(a)** *(d'une personne, de la population)* aging; **retarder le v. de la peau** to delay the ageing process **(b)** *(d'un fromage, d'un vin)* maturing

vieillot, -otte [vjejo, -ɔt] *adj* old-fashioned

vielle [vjɛl] *nf* hurdy-gurdy

Vienne [vjɛn] *n* Vienna

vienne, viens, *etc. voir* **venir**

viennois, -e [vjɛnwa, -az] **1** *adj* Viennese; **un pain v.** a Vienna loaf

2 *nm,f* **V., Viennoise** Viennese

viennoiserie [vjɛnwazri] *nf (gâteaux)* = pastries made with sweetened dough (croissant, brioche, etc.); *(magasin)* = store selling pastries made with sweetened dough (croissant, brioche, etc.)

vierge [vjɛrʒ] **1** *adj* **(a)** *(personne)* **être v.** to be a virgin; **une fille v.** a virgin **(b)** *(sol, huile)* virgin **(c)** *(page, cassette)* blank; *(casier judiciaire)* clean **(d)** *Ordinat (ligne, espace)* blank; *(disquette)* blank, unformatted

2 *nf* **(a)** *(personne)* virgin; **la (Sainte) V.** the Blessed Virgin (Mary) **(b)** *Astron & Astrol* **la V.** Virgo; **être V.** to be (a) Virgo

Viêt Nam [vjɛtnam] *nm* **le V.** Vietnam

vietnamien, -enne [vjɛtnamjɛ̃, -ɛn] **1** *adj* Vietnamese

2 *nm (langue)* Vietnamese

3 *nm,f* **V., Vietnamienne** Vietnamese

vieux, vieille [vjø, vjɛj]

vieil is used before masculine singular nouns beginning with a vowel or h mute.

1 *adj* old; **plus/moins v. que qn** older/younger than sb; **v. comme le monde** as old as the hills; **être v. jeu** to be old-fashioned

2 *nm,f* **(a)** *(personne)* old man, f old woman; **les v.** old people,

the elderly; *Fam* **un v. de la vieille** an old-timer **(b)** *Fam* **il a pris un coup de v.** he's aged **(c)** *Fam (parent)* **mes v.** my folks; **mon v.** my old man; **ma vieille** my old lady **(d)** *Fam (ami)* **mon v.** old buddy; **ma vieille** old girl

vif, vive [vif, viv] **1** *adj* **(a)** *(plein de vie) (personne, discussion)* lively **(b)** *(brusque) (ton)* abrupt, sharp; **tu as été un peu trop v. avec elle** you were a bit curt with her **(c)** *(imagination)* vivid; *(intelligence)* sharp; *(mouvement)* quick; *Euph* **il n'est pas très v.** he's not too smart **(d)** *(vent, douleur)* sharp **(e)** *(couleur)* bright **(f)** *(satisfaction, intérêt)* great; *(félicitations)* warm **(g)** **dire qch à qn de vive voix** to tell sb sth personally

2 *nm* **(a)** *Jur* living person **(b)** *(à la pêche)* live bait **(c)** *(locutions)* **à v.** *(plaie)* open; **avoir les nerfs à v.** to be on edge; **entrer dans le v. du sujet** to get to the heart of the matter; **une photo prise sur le v.** a natural *or* unposed photo

vif-argent *(pl* **vifs-argents)** [vifarʒɑ̃] *nm* quicksilver; *Fig (personne)* live wire

vigie [viʒi] *nf* **(a)** *(matelot)* lookout; **être de v.** to be on the lookout **(b)** *(poste) (sur un bateau)* lookout post; *(sur un train)* observation box

vigilance [viʒilɑ̃s] *nf* vigilance

vigilant, -e [viʒilɑ̃, -ɑ̃t] *adj* vigilant

vigile [viʒil] *nm* (night) watchman

vigne [viɲ] *nf* **(a)** *(petit arbre)* vine **(b)** *(vignoble)* vineyard **(c)** **v. vierge** Virginia creeper

vigneron, -onne [viɲərɔ̃, -ɔn] *nm,f* wine grower

vignette [viɲɛt] *nf* **(a)** *(pharmaceutique)* label *(showing details of medication and which has to be attached to the "feuille de maladie" in order to qualify for reimbursement by the Social Security)* **(b)** **la v. (automobile)** the (road) tax disk **(c)** *(motif)* vignette

vignoble [viɲɔbl] *nm* vineyard; **le v. français/californien** the French/Californian vineyards

vigoureusement [vigurøzmɑ̃] *adv* vigorously

vigoureux, -euse [vigurø, -øz] *adj (personne, animal)* vigorous; *(plante, arbre)* sturdy; *(résistance)* strong

vigueur [vigœr] *nf* **(a)** *(d'une personne, d'un animal, d'un style)* vigor; *(d'une plante, d'un arbre)* sturdiness **(b)** **en v.** *(décret)* in force; **entrer en v.** to come into force

VIH [veiaʃ] *nm (abrév* **virus de l'immunodéficience humaine)** HIV

viking [vikiɲ] **1** *adj* Viking

2 *nmf* **V.** Viking

vil, -e [vil] *adj* **(a)** *Litt (personne, motif)* vile **(b)** *(bas)* **à v. prix** at a very low price

vilain, -e [vilɛ̃, -ɛn] **1** *adj* **(a)** *(laid)* ugly **(b)** *(déplaisant)* nasty **(c)** *(pas sage)* naughty

2 *nm,f* **oh, le v./la vilaine!** *(à un enfant)* you naughty boy/girl!

3 *nm* **(a)** *Fam* **il va y avoir du v.** there's going to be trouble **(b)** *Hist* villein

vilebrequin [vilbrəkɛ̃] *nm* **(a)** *(outil)* brace **(b)** *(dans un moteur)* crankshaft

vilenie [vileni] *nf Litt* **(a)** *(caractère)* vileness **(b)** *(action)* vile deed

villa [villa] *nf* villa

village [vilaʒ] *nm* village; **v. de pêcheurs** fishing village; **v. de vacances, v.-vacances** vacation village; **le v. mondial** *ou* **planétaire** the global village

villageois, -e [vilaʒwa, -az] *nm,f* villager

ville [vil] *nf* town; *(de grande taille)* city; **grande v.** city; **en v.** in (the) town; *(au centre ville)* downtown; **aller en v.** to go into town; **habiter à la v.** to live in a town *(as opposed to the country)*; **v. basse/haute** lower/upper part of town; **v. champignon** boom town; **v. d'eaux** spa (town); **v. nouvelle** new town; **v. planétaire** global village

ville-dortoir *(pl* **villes-dortoirs)** [vildɔrtwar] *nf* bedroom community

villégiature [vileʒjatyr] *nf* vacation; **lieu de v.** resort

Vilnius [vilnjys] *n* Vilnius

vin [vɛ̃] *nm* (**a**) *(boisson)* wine; **avoir le v. gai/triste** to be/not to be happy in one's cups; **grand v.** great wine; **v. d'appellation contrôlée** wine of guaranteed origin; **v. blanc/rouge/rosé** white/red/rosé wine; **v. cuit** fortified wine; **v. mousseux** sparkling wine; **v. de pays** regional wine; **v. de table** *ou* **ordinaire** table wine (**b**) **v. d'honneur** reception *(where wine is served)*

vinaigre [vinɛgr] *nm* vinegar; *Fam* **tourner au v.** to turn sour; **v. blanc** distilled vinegar; **v. à l'estragon** tarragon vinegar

vinaigrette [vinɛgrɛt] *nf* vinaigrette, French dressing

vinasse [vinas] *nf Fam* cheap wine

vindicatif, -ive [vɛ̃dikatif, -iv] *adj* vindictive

vindicte [vɛ̃dikt] *nf* **désigner qn à la v. publique** to expose sb to public condemnation

vineux, -euse [vinø, -øz] *adj* (**a**) *(goût, odeur)* winy (**b**) *(couleur)* wine(-colored)

vingt [vɛ̃] **1** *adj inv* twenty; **v.-quatre heures sur v.-quatre** round the clock, twenty-four hours a day
2 *nm inv* twenty; *voir aussi* **trois**

vingtaine [vɛ̃tɛn] *nf* **une v. (de)** about twenty, twenty or so

vingtième [vɛ̃tjɛm] *adj, nmf & nm* twentieth; *voir aussi* **cinquième**

vinicole [vinikɔl] *adj (région)* wine-growing

vintage [vintedʒ] **1** *adj inv (vêtements etc.)* vintage
2 *nm (mode)* vintage

vinyle [vinil] *nm* vinyl

viol [vjɔl] *nm* (**a**) *(crime sexuel)* rape; **v. collectif** gang-rape (**b**) *(d'un sanctuaire)* violation

violacé, -e [vjɔlase] *adj* purplish-blue

violation [vjɔlasjɔ̃] *nf* (**a**) *(de la loi, de règles)* violation (**b**) *(d'une sépulture)* desecration; **v. de domicile** illegal entry

viole [vjɔl] *nf* viol

violemment [vjɔlamɑ̃] *adv* violently

violence [vjɔlɑ̃s] *nf (physique)* violence; *(verbale)* fierceness; *(d'un sentiment)* intensity; **se faire v.** to force oneself

violent, -e [vjɔlɑ̃, -ɑ̃t] *adj (personne, douleur, quartier)* violent; *(vent, paroles)* fierce; *(odeur)* pungent; *(effort)* strenuous; **mort violente** violent death

violenter [vjɔlɑ̃te] *vt (femme)* to assault

violer [vjɔle] *vt* (**a**) *(personne)* to rape (**b**) *(trêve, loi)* to violate, to break; *(traité, confiance)* to break; *(secret)* to divulge (**c**) *(sépulture)* to desecrate

violet, -ette [vjɔlɛ, -ɛt] **1** *adj* purple
2 *nm (couleur)* purple
3 *nf* **violette** *(fleur)* violet

violeur [vjɔlœr] *nm* rapist

violon [vjɔlɔ̃] *nm* (**a**) *(instrument)* violin; *Fam* **accordez vos violons** make sure you get your stories straight; **v. d'Ingres** hobby (**b**) *(musicien)* violin (player); **premier v.** *(dans un orchestre)* first violin, concertmaster (**c**) *Fam (prison)* **le v.** the cells, the lockup

violoncelle [vjɔlɔ̃sɛl] *nm* cello

violoncelliste [vjɔlɔ̃sɛlist] *nmf* cellist

violoniste [vjɔlɔnist] *nmf* violinist, violin player

vipère [vipɛr] *nf* adder, viper; *Fig (personne)* viper

virage [viraʒ] *nm* (**a**) *(mouvement)* turn (**b**) *(d'une route)* bend; **la route fait des virages** there are bends in the road; **prendre un v.** to take a bend; **v. sans visibilité** blind corner (**c**) *Fig (changement)* change of direction

viral, -e, -aux, -ales [viral, -o] *adj* viral

virée [vire] *nf Fam (en voiture)* spin; *(dans les bars)* bar hop; **faire une v.** *(en voiture)* to go for a spin; *(dans les bars)* to barhop

virement [virmɑ̃] *nm* (**a**) *(de banque)* transfer; **v. automatique** automatic transfer; **v. bancaire/interbancaire** bank/interbank transfer; **v. postal** post-office transfer (**b**) *Naut* **v. de bord** tacking

virer [vire] **1** *vt* (**a**) *(somme)* to transfer (**sur** to) (**b**) *Fam (personne, objet)* to chuck out; **se faire v.** to get chucked out
2 *vi* (**a**) *(véhicule)* to turn; **v. de bord** *(voilier)* to tack (**b**) *(couleur)* to change; **le parfum a viré** the perfume smells off
3 **virer à** *vt ind* **v. à l'orange/au vert** to turn orange/green
4 se virer *vpr Fam* **vire-toi de là!** move your butt!

virevolte [virvɔlt] *nf* (**a**) *(d'un danseur)* spin (**b**) *(changement brusque)* U-turn, about-face

virevolter [virvɔlte] *vi (danseur)* to spin around

virginal, -e, -aux, -ales [virʒinal, -o] *adj* virginal

Virginie [virʒini] *nf* **la V.** Virginia; **la V.-occidentale** West Virginia

virginité [virʒinite] *nf* virginity

virgule [virgyl] *nf* (**a**) *(signe de ponctuation)* comma; *Fig* **ne pas changer une v. à qch** not to make a single alteration to sth (**b**) *(entre deux chiffres)* decimal point; **trois v. cinq** three point five; *Ordinat* **v. fixe** fixed point; *Ordinat* **v. flottante** floating point

viril, -e [viril] *adj* (**a**) *(propre à l'homme)* male; *(sexuellement)* virile (**b**) *(énergique) (action)* manly; *(allure, démarche)* masculine

virilité [virilite] *nf* virility

virologie [virɔlɔʒi] *nf* virology

virtualité [virtɥalite] *nf* potentiality

virtuel, -elle [virtɥɛl] *adj* potential; *(image)* virtual

virtuellement [virtɥɛlmɑ̃] *adv* virtually

virtuose [virtɥoz] *nmf* virtuoso

virtuosité [virtɥozite] *nf* virtuosity

virulence [virylɑ̃s] *nf* virulence

virulent, -e [virylɑ̃, -ɑ̃t] *adj* virulent

virus [virys] *nm Méd & Ordinat* virus

vis¹ *voir* **vivre, voir**

vis² [vis] *nf* screw; *Fig* **serrer la v. à qn** to crack down on sb

visa [viza] *nm* (**a**) *(pour passeport)* visa; **v. d'entrée/de sortie** entry/exit visa (**b**) *(d'un film)* **v. de censure** certificate; **v. d'exploitation** exploitation license

visage [vizaʒ] *nm* face; **elle a changé de v.** her face *or* expression changed; **à deux visages** two-faced; **à v. découvert** openly; **sous un autre** *ou* **nouveau v.** in a new light; **v. pâle** paleface

visagiste [vizaʒist] *nmf* facialist; **coiffeur-v.** hair stylist

vis-à-vis [vizavi] **1** *prép* **v. de** *(en face de)* opposite *or* facing; *(envers)* toward; *(en comparaison de)* compared with, next to
2 *nm* (**a**) *(personne)* person opposite; **mon v.** the person opposite me; **il n'y a pas de v.** there's nothing opposite (**b**) *(meuble)* vis-à-vis

viscéral, -e, -aux, -ales [viseral, -o] *adj Anat* visceral; *Fig (haine)* deep-seated; *(peur)* gut-wrenching; *(réaction)* gut

viscères [visɛr] *nmpl* viscera, internal organs

viscose [viskoz] *nf* viscose

viscosité [viskozite] *nf (de liquide)* viscosity; *(de surface)* stickiness

visée [vize] *nf* (**a**) *(action)* aiming (**b**) *Fig* **visées** *(intentions)* aims; **avoir des visées sur qn/qch** to have designs on sb/sth

viser¹ [vize] **1** *vt* (**a**) *(cible)* to aim at; *Fig (poste)* to set one's sights on (**b**) *Fig* **ces paroles te visent** these remarks are aimed at you; **qui visais-tu par cette remarque?** who was your remark aimed at?; **je me suis senti visé** I felt the remark was aimed at me (**c**) *très Fam (regarder)* **vise un peu la fille!** check out that girl!
2 *vi* to aim, to take aim; *Fig* **v. haut** to aim high; **v. juste** to aim straight; *Fig* to hit the bull's-eye
3 **viser à** *vt ind* **v. à qch** to aim at sth; **v. à faire qch** to aim to do sth

viser² [vize] *vt (passeport)* to visa; *(document)* to stamp

viseur [vizœr] *nm* *(d'un appareil photo)* viewfinder; *(d'une arme)* sight

visibilité [vizibilite] *nf* visibility

visible [vizibl] *adj* (**a**) *(signe, changement)* visible (**b**) *(clair)* obvious; **il est v. que...** it's obvious that... (**c**) *Fam* **je ne suis pas v.** I'm not receiving visitors

visiblement [vizibləmã] *adv* visibly

visière [vizjɛr] *nf* (**a**) *(d'une casquette)* peak (**b**) *(d'un casque)* visor (**c**) *(pour protéger les yeux)* eyeshade

visioconférence [visjokõferãs] *nf* videoconference; *(concept)* videoconferencing

vision [vizjõ] *nf* (**a**) *(sens)* sight (**b**) *(point de vue)* view (**c**) *(d'un créateur)* vision (**d**) *(hallucination)* vision; **avoir des visions** to have visions, to see things

visionnaire [vizjɔnɛr] *adj & nmf* visionary

visionner [vizjɔne] *vt (film)* to view

visionneuse [vizjɔnøz] *nf* viewer

visiophonie [vizjɔfɔni] *nf* video teleconferencing

visite [vizit] *nf* (**a**) *(à une personne, d'un lieu touristique)* visit; **faire une v.** *ou* **rendre v. à qn** to visit sb, to pay sb a visit; **recevoir la v. de qn** to have a visit from sb; **v. officielle** official visit (**b**) *Fam (personne)* visitor; **avoir de la v.** *(un visiteur)* to have a visitor; *(plusieurs visiteurs)* to have visitors (**c**) *(d'un médecin)* **visites (à domicile)** (house) calls (**d**) *(inspection)* *(d'un bâtiment, d'un navire)* inspection, examination (**e**) **v. médicale** physical (examination)

visiter [vizite] **1** *vt* (**a**) *(lieu touristique)* to visit; *(maison à vendre)* to view; **faire v. qch à qn** to show sb around sth (**b**) *(inspecter)* *(bâtiment)* to inspect, to examine (**c**) *(patient)* to visit; *(client)* to call on
  2 se visiter *vpr* to be open to visitors; **le musée se visite en deux heures** it takes two hours to go around the museum

visiteur, -euse [vizitœr, -øz] *nm,f* (**a**) *(touriste, invité)* visitor (**b**) *(représentant)* **v. médical** medical representative (**c**) **v. de prison** prison visitor

vison [vizõ] *nm* mink; *Fam (manteau)* mink coat

visqueux, -euse [viskø, -øz] *adj* (**a**) *(surface)* sticky (**b**) *(substance)* viscous (**c**) *Péj (personne, manière)* slimy

visser [vise] **1** *vt* (**a**) *(à quelque chose)* to screw on; *(ensemble)* to screw together; **être vissé à qch** be screwed to sth; **un chapeau vissé sur la tête** with a hat clamped on his/her head; *Fam* **être vissé sur sa chaise** to be glued to one's chair; *Fam* **être bien/mal vissé** to be in a good/foul mood (**b**) *(couvercle)* to screw on (**c**) *Fam (personne)* to crack down on, to put the screws on; **il a toujours vissé ses gosses** he has always kept a tight rein on his kids
  2 se visser *vpr (à quelque chose)* to screw on; *(ensemble)* to screw together

visualisation [vizyalizasjõ] *nf* visualization; *Ordinat* **console** *ou* **unité** *ou* **écran de v.** (visual) display unit; *Ordinat* **v. de la page à l'écran** page preview

visualiser [vizyalize] *vt* (**a**) *(imaginer)* to visualize (**b**) *(rendre visible)* to make visible; *Ordinat* to display

visuel, -elle [vizɥɛl] **1** *adj* visual
  2 *nm Ordinat* visual display unit, VDU

visuellement [vizɥɛlmã] *adv* visually

vit *voir* **vivre, voir**

vital, -e, -aux, -ales [vital, -o] *adj* vital; **carte Vitale** = smart card on which information about a patient is recorded, used when making payments to a doctor or pharmacist for purposes of reclaiming medical expenses

vitalité [vitalite] *nf* vitality

vitamine [vitamin] *nf* vitamin; **la v. E** vitamin E

vitaminé, -e [vitamine] *adj* with added vitamins, vitamin-enriched

vite [vit] *adv* (**a**) *(rapidement)* quickly, fast; **v.!** quick!, quickly!; **plus v.!** faster!; **ça ne va pas v.** it's slow work; *Fam* **et plus v.**

que cela! now then, get a move on!; **au plus v.** as quickly as possible; *Fig* **parler trop v.** to speak too soon; **c'est v. dit** it's easy to say; *Fam* **faire qch v. fait (bien fait)** to do sth in no time (**b**) *(sous peu)* soon; **avoir v. fait de faire qch** to be quick to do sth

vitesse [vitɛs] *nf* (**a**) *(rapidité)* speed; **prendre de la v.** to pick up *or* to gather speed; *Fam* **prendre qn de v.** to beat sb to it; **à quelle v. allait-il?** how fast was he going?, what speed was he going at?; **une Europe à deux vitesses** a two-speed Europe; **à toute v.** at top speed; **à une v. folle** *(rouler)* at breakneck speed; *Fam* **en v.** quickly; **v. de croisière** cruising speed; *Fig* **trouver sa v. de croisière** to get into the swing of things; **v. de frappe** keying speed (**b**) *(d'un moteur)* gear; **changer de v.** to shift gears; **passer en deuxième/troisième v.** to shift into second/third (gear); *Fam Fig* **en quatrième v.** at top speed (**c**) *Ordinat* **v. d'affichage** display speed; **v. de calcul** processing *or* computing speed; **v. d'écriture** write speed; **v. d'exécution** execution speed; **v. d'impression** print speed; **v. du processeur** processor speed; **v. de traitement** processing speed

viticole [vitikɔl] *adj (région)* wine-growing

viticulteur, -trice [vitikyltœr, -tris] *nm,f* wine grower

viticulture [vitikyltyr] *nf* wine growing

vitrage [vitraʒ] *nm (vitres)* windows

vitrail, -aux [vitraj, -o] *nm* stained-glass window

vitre [vitr] *nf* window (pane); *(plaque de verre)* pane (of glass); *(de voiture, de train)* window; **faire les vitres** to clean the windows

vitré, -e [vitre] *adj (porte)* glazed

vitrer [vitre] *vt* to glaze

vitreux, -euse [vitrø, -øz] *adj (yeux, regard)* glazed, glassy

vitrier [vitrije] *nm* glazier

vitrification [vitrifikasjõ] *nf* (**a**) *(du sable)* vitrification (**b**) *(du parquet)* varnishing, sealing

vitrifier [66] [vitrifje] *vt* (**a**) *(sable)* to vitrify (**b**) *(parquet)* to varnish, to seal

vitrine [vitrin] *nf* (**a**) *(de magasin)* (store) window; *Fig* showcase; **mettre qch en v.** to display *or* to put sth in the window (**b**) *(armoire)* display cabinet

vitriol [vitrijɔl] *nm* vitriol; *Fig* **au v.** vitriolic

vitupérer [34] [vitypere] **vitupérer contre** *vt ind* to protest about

vivable [vivabl] *adj Fam (maison)* livable in; *(situation)* tolerable; **il n'est pas v.** he's impossible to live with

vivace [vivas] *adj* (**a**) *(plante)* perennial (**b**) *(croyance, tradition, sentiment)* deep-rooted; *(souvenir)* vivid

vivacité [vivasite] *nf* (**a**) *(d'une personne, d'une discussion)* liveliness, vivacity; *(d'une imagination)* vividness; *(d'une intelligence)* sharpness; *(d'un mouvement)* quickness; **v. d'esprit** quick-wittedness (**b**) *(de couleur)* brightness (**c**) *(de paroles)* snappiness

vivant, -e [vivã, -ãt] **1** *adj* (**a**) *(en vie)* alive (**b**) *(être, organisme)* living (**c**) *(rue, conversation, enfant)* lively (**d**) *Fig (souvenir)* vivid; *Hum* **j'en suis la preuve vivante** I'm the living proof
  2 *nm* (**a**) **les vivants** the living (**b**) **de son v.** in one's lifetime; **du v. de qn** in sb's lifetime

vivats [viva] *nmpl* cheers

vive¹ [viv] *adj voir* **vif**

vive² [viv] *nf (poisson)* weever

vive³ [viv] *exclam* **v. le roi!** long live the King!; **v. la télévision!** God bless television!

vivement [vivmã] *adv* (**a**) *(rapidement)* quickly (**b**) *(en colère)* sharply (**c**) *(éclairé, coloré)* brightly (**d**) *(remercier)* warmly; *(regretter)* deeply; **s'intéresser v. à qch** to take a keen interest in sth; **être v. ému** to be deeply moved (**e**) *(marque l'impatience)* **v. les vacances!** I can't wait for the vacation!; **v. qu'il parte!** I'll be glad when he's gone!

viveur [vivœr] *nm* fast liver

vivier [vivje] *nm (à l'air libre)* fish pond; *(aquarium)* fish tank; *Fig* breeding ground (**de** for)

vivifiant, -e [vivifjɑ̃, -ɑ̃t] *adj (air, climat)* invigorating, bracing

vivifier [66] [vivifje] *vt* to invigorate

vivipare [vivipar] *adj* viviparous

vivisection [vivisɛksjɔ̃] *nf* vivisection

vivoter [vivɔte] *vi* (**a**) *(personne)* to struggle to get by (**b**) *(entreprise, usine)* to struggle along

vivre [72] [vivr] **1** *vi* (**a**) *(être en vie)* to live, to be alive; **v. vieux** to live to a ripe old age; *Prov* **qui vivra verra** time will tell (**b**) *(mener une certaine existence)* to live; **avoir beaucoup vécu** to have seen life; **être facile/difficile à v.** to be easy/difficult to live with *or* to get along with; **se laisser v.** to take life as it comes; **il fait bon v. ici** life is pleasant here; *Fam* **je vais t'apprendre à v.!** I'll teach you some manners! (**c**) *(économiquement)* to live; **travailler pour v.** to work for a living; **faire v. sa famille** to support one's family; **v. de qch** to live on sth; *Fig* **v. d'amour et d'eau fraîche** to live on fresh air

2 *vt* (**a**) **v. sa vie** to live one's own life (**b**) *(événements, guerre)* to live through; *(moments difficiles, expérience)* to go through

vivres [vivr] *nmpl* provisions, supplies; *Fig* **couper les v. à qn** to cut off sb's allowance

vivrier, -ère [vivrije, -ɛr] *adj* **cultures vivrières** food crops

vlan, v'lan [vlɑ̃] *exclam* bang!, wham!

vlimeux [vlimø] *nm Can Fam* (**a**) *(chanceux)* lucky devil (**b**) *(intrigant)* crafty devil

vMCJ [veɛmʒise] *Méd (abrév* **variant de la maladie de Creutzfeldt-Jakob**) vCJD

VO [veo] *nf (abrév* **version originale**) **en VO** in the original language

vocabulaire [vɔkabylɛr] *nm* (**a**) *(d'une science)* glossary; *(d'une langue)* vocabulary (**b**) *(d'une personne)* vocabulary

vocal, -e, -aux, -ales [vɔkal, -o] *adj* vocal

vocalise [vɔkaliz] *nf* voice exercise; **faire des vocalises** to do voice exercises

vocation [vɔkasjɔ̃] *nf* (**a**) *(d'une personne)* vocation, calling (**b**) *(d'un pays, d'une institution)* role, mission; **région à v. agricole/industrielle** agricultural/industrial region

vociférations [vɔsiferasjɔ̃] *nfpl* shouting

vociférer [34] [vɔsifere] **1** *vt* to shout (**contre** at)

2 *vi* to shout (**contre** about)

vodka [vɔdka] *nf* vodka

vœu, -x [vø] *nm* (**a**) *(souhait)* wish; **faire un v.** to make a wish; **faire le v. que** + *subjunctive* to pray that (**b**) *(promesse)* vow; **faire le v. de faire qch** to vow to do sth (**c**) *Rel* **faire v. de pauvreté/silence** to take a vow of poverty/silence; **prononcer ses vœux** to take one's vows (**d**) *(au moment d'une fête)* **tous mes/nos vœux, avec mes/nos meilleurs vœux** best wishes, with all good wishes; **tous mes vœux de bonheur** best wishes for your future happiness; **vœux de Bonne** *ou* **de Nouvelle Année** New Year's greetings

vogue [vɔg] *nf* fashion, vogue; **en v.** fashionable, in vogue

voguer [vɔge] *vi Litt* to sail

voici [vwasi] *prép* (**a**) *(pour présenter, pour montrer)* here is/are; **v. Paul** here's Paul; **v. mes neveux** *(en les présentant)* these are my nephews; *(ils arrivent)* here are my nephews; **nous v. à Paris/installés** here we are in Paris/all settled in; **la v. qui vient** here she comes; **la pendule que v.** this clock; **v. ce dont il s'agit** this is what it's all about; **v. ce qu'il m'a dit** this is what he told me; **v. pourquoi** this is why; **tu voulais des fruits, eh bien, en v.** you wanted some fruit, well here you are (**b**) *(il y a)* **v. trois ans** three years ago; **v. dix ans que je la connais** I've known her for ten years now

voie [vwa] *nf* (**a**) *(route)* road; **route à quatre voies** four-lane road; **les voies de communication** the road and rail links; **v. express** *ou* **rapide** expressway; **v. publique** public highway; **v. sans issue** dead end

(**b**) **par la v. des airs** by air; **par v. de terre/de mer** by land/sea

(**c**) *(pour train)* track; **v. ferrée** railroad line; *Fam* **mettre qn sur une v. de garage** to put sb on the sidelines

(**d**) *Ordinat* **v. d'accès** path; **v. d'entrée** input channel; **v. de transmission de données** data link

(**e**) *Fig (chemin)* way; **mettre qn sur la v.** to put sb on the right track; **être sur la bonne v.** to be on the right track; **par la v. diplomatique/hiérarchique** through diplomatic/official channels; **la v. est libre** the coast's clear

(**f**) **en v. d'achèvement** nearing completion; **en v. de construction** under construction; **un pays en v. de développement** a developing country; **être en v. de disparition** *(animal)* to be dying out; **être en v. de guérison** to be on the road to recovery

(**g**) *Jur* **v. de fait** assault and battery

(**h**) *Anat* passage, duct; **les voies digestives** the digestive tract; **par v. buccale** orally

(**i**) **v. d'eau** leak

(**j**) **la V. lactée** the Milky Way

voilà [vwala] *prép* (**a**) *(pour présenter, pour montrer)* there is/are; **v. Paul** there's Paul; **v. mes neveux** *(en les présentant)* these are my nephews; *(ils arrivent)* there are my nephews; **nous v. à Paris/installés** here we are in Paris/all settled in; **la v. qui vient** here she comes; **la pendule que v.** that clock; **v. ce que j'avais à dire** that's what I wanted to say; **v. ce qu'il m'a dit** that's what he told me; **tu voulais des fruits, eh bien, en v.** you wanted some fruit, well there you go; **v. pourquoi** that's why; **en v. assez** that's enough; **en v. une idée!** what an idea!; **v. tout** that's all; **nous v. bien!** what are we going to do now?; **et v.!** there you go! (**b**) *(il y a)* **v. trois ans** three years ago; **v. dix ans que je le connais** I've known him for ten years

voilage [vwalaʒ] *nm (tissu)* net; **voilages** *(rideaux)* net curtains

voile¹ [vwal] *nf (de bateau)* sail; *(activité)* sailing; **faire de la v.** to sail; **toutes voiles dehors** in full sail; *Fam* **marcher à v. et à vapeur** to be AC/DC

voile² [vwal] *nm* (**a**) *(de femme)* veil; **prendre le v.** *(religieuse)* to take the veil (**b**) *(devant les yeux)* film, mist; **un v. de fumée/de brouillard** a veil of smoke/fog; *Fam* **jeter un v. sur qch** to draw a veil over sth; *Méd* **avoir un v. au poumon** to have a shadow on one's lung (**c**) *Anat* **v. du palais** soft palate, velum

voilé, -e [vwale] *adj* (**a**) *(femme)* veiled (**b**) *(lumière) (par le brouillard)* hazy; *(par les nuages)* dim; *(photo)* fogged; **le ciel est v.** it's hazy (**c**) *(voix)* husky; **des yeux voilés de larmes** eyes blurred with tears (**d**) *(allusion)* veiled; **en termes voilés** in veiled terms (**e**) *(roue, tige)* buckled

voiler [vwale] **1** *vt* (**a**) *(femme)* to veil; *(statue)* to cover; *Fig (trouble, émotion)* to hide, to conceal (**b**) *(lumière)* to dim; *(ciel, soleil)* to cover; *(photo)* to fog (**c**) *(roue, tige)* to buckle

2 se voiler *vpr* (**a**) *(personne)* to wear a veil; *Fig* **se v. la face** to hide *or* to bury one's head in the sand (**b**) *(voix)* to become husky (**c**) *(ciel)* to cloud over; *(soleil)* to become hazy; *(yeux)* to mist over (**d**) *(roue, tige)* to buckle

voilette [vwalɛt] *nf (hat)* veil

voilier [vwalje] *nm (bateau à voiles)* sailboat; *(bateau de plaisance)* yacht; **faire du v.** to go yachting

voilure [vwalyr] *nf* (**a**) *(d'un bateau)* sails (**b**) *(d'un avion)* wings

voir [73a] [vwar] **1** *vt* (**a**) *(distinguer)* to see; **v. page 23/ci-après** see page 23/below; **je l'ai vu de mes propres yeux, je l'ai vu comme je te vois** I saw it with my own eyes; **je le vois qui arrive** I can see him coming; **je l'ai vu tomber/courir** I saw him fall/running; **faire v. qch à qn** to show sth to sb, to show sb sth; **faites v.!** let me see (it)!, let's have a look!; **laisser v. son ignorance/émotion** to show one's ignorance/emotion (**b**) *(rendre visite à, fréquenter)* to visit; **aller/venir v. qn** to go/to come and see sb

(**c**) *(comprendre, constater)* to see; **à ce que je vois** from what I can see; **voyez vous-même!** see for yourself!; **on voit bien que...** you can see (that)...; **on verra bien** we'll see; **c'est ce que nous verrons!** we'll see about that!; *Fam* **vu?** understood?, OK?

(**d**) *(considérer)* to see; **nous verrons demain** we'll see tomorrow

(**e**) *(imaginer, envisager)* to see; **je ne le vois pas marié** I can't imagine him married; **elle voit en lui un père/un ami** she sees him as a father figure/a friend; **sa façon de v. les choses** his way of looking at things; **se faire bien/mal v. de qn** to get into sb's good/bad books; **être bien/mal vu** to be well/badly thought of; **c'est plutôt mal vu dans ce milieu** it's rather frowned upon in these circles

(**f**) *Fam (pour renforcer)* **essayez v.** just try; *(menace)* just you try it; **voyons v.** let's see, let's have a look

(**g**) *(locutions)* *Fam* **on aura tout vu!** we've seen it all now!; *Fam* **c'est tout vu, tu n'y vas pas!** you're not going and that's that!; **il faut le v. pour le croire** you have to see it to believe it; **j'aimerais (bien) t'y v.!** I'd like to see you try!; *Fam* **en faire v. à qn** to give sb a hard time; **voyez-vous** *(pour insister)* you see; *Fam* **je ne peux pas le v.** I can't stand the sight of him; *Fam* **file, je t'ai assez vu!** off you go, I've had enough of you!; **il n'a rien à v. là-dedans** *ou* **à y v.** he's got nothing to do with it; **ça n'a rien à voir!** *(dans une discussion)* that's beside the point, that's got nothing to do with it!; **voyons!** *(indique la désapprobation)* come on!; *Fam* **va v. là-bas si j'y suis!** get lost!; *très Fam* **va te faire v.!** get the hell out!

2 *vi* to see; (**y**) **v. bien/mal** to have good/poor eyesight; **on n'y voit rien** you can't see a thing; *Fig* **v. grand** to think big

3 voir à *vt ind* **il va v. à nous loger** he'll see that we have somewhere to stay; *Fam* **il faudrait v. à vous dépêcher!** you'd better get a move on!

4 se voir *vpr* (**a**) *(objet, phénomène)* to be seen; **la cathédrale se voit de loin** you can see the cathedral from miles away; **cela ne se voit pas tous les jours** it's not something you see every day; **ça se voit que j'ai pleuré?** can you tell I've been crying?

(**b**) *(soi-même)* to see oneself; **elle ne se voit pas du tout avec des enfants** she just can't see herself with children

(**c**) *(avec un adjectif, un infinitif)* **se v. forcé de faire qch** to find oneself forced to do sth; **se v. refuser qch** to find oneself refused sth

(**d**) *(l'un l'autre)* *(se distinguer, se rencontrer)* to see each other

voire [vwar] *adv* indeed

voirie [vwari] *nf* = municipal department responsible for road maintenance and garbage collection

voisin, -e [vwazɛ̃, -in] **1** *adj* (**a**) *(personne, pays, ville)* neighboring; *(chambre)* next (**de** to); **les pays voisins de la France** the countries bordering on France; **deux maisons voisines** two houses next to each other (**b**) *(semblable)* similar (**de** to)

2 *nm,f* neighbor; **v. de palier** next-door neighbor; **mon v. de table** the person sitting next to me (at the table)

voisinage [vwazinaʒ] *nm* (**a**) *(proximité)* proximity, closeness (**b**) *(ensemble des voisins)* neighborhood (**c**) *(alentours)* vicinity; **dans le v.** in the vicinity (**d**) **entretenir des relations de bon v. avec qn** to be on neighborly terms with sb

voisiner [vwazine] *vi* **v. avec qch** to be side by side with sth

voiture [vwatyr] *nf* (**a**) *(automobile)* car; **en v.** by car; **v. de course** racing car; **v. de fonction** company car; **v. de location** rental car; **v. d'occasion** used car; **v. de sport** sports car; **v. de tourisme** private *or* touring car; **petite v.** *(jouet)* toy car (**b**) *(wagon)* car; **en v.!** all aboard!; **v. fumeurs** smoker; **v. non-fumeurs** non-smoker (**c**) *(carriole)* *(pour passagers)* carriage; *(pour marchandises)* cart; **v. à bras** barrow, handcart (**d**) **v. d'enfant** baby carriage

voix [vwa] *nf* (**a**) *(d'une personne)* voice; **à v. haute, à haute v.** aloud; **à v. basse** in a low voice; **élever la v.** to speak up; *(se mettre en colère)* to raise one's voice; **donner de la v.** *(chien)* to bay; *(personne)* to shout, to bawl; **donner de la v. contre qch** *(protester)* to protest vehemently against sth; **rester sans v.** to remain speechless; *Cin* **v. off** voice-over; **une v. de stentor** a booming voice (**b**) *Fig (de la raison)* voice; *(du sang)* call (**c**) *Mus (partie vocale)* voice; **chanter à trois v.** to sing in three parts; **être en v.** to be in good voice; **v. de basse/de ténor** bass/tenor voice; **v. de fausset** falsetto (voice); **v. de tête** head voice (**d**) *(d'électeur)* vote; **donner sa v. à qn** to vote for sb; **élu à la majorité des v.** elected by a majority; **mettre une question aux v.** to put a question to the vote (**e**) *Gram* voice; **à la v. active/passive** in the active/passive voice

vol[1] [vɔl] *nm* (**a**) *(d'un oiseau, d'un avion)* flight; **à trois heures de v. de Paris** three hours' flying time from Paris; **prendre son v.** to fly off; **en plein v.** mid-flight; **à v. d'oiseau** as the crow flies; **de haut v.** *(escroc)* big-time; *(discipline)* high-flying; **v. charter** charter flight; **v. habité** manned flight; **v. inaugural** inaugural flight; **v. intérieur** domestic flight; **v. de nuit** night flight; **v. plané** glide; *Fam Fig* **faire un v. plané** to go flying (**b**) *(nuée d'oiseaux)* flock, flight

vol[2] [vɔl] *nm (délit)* theft, stealing; *Fam* **c'est du v.!** it's a rip-off!, it's daylight robbery!; **v. avec effraction** breaking and entering; **v. à l'étalage** shoplifting; **v. à main armée** armed robbery; **v. à la portière** = act of theft whereby the thief opens the door of a vehicle waiting at traffic lights etc. and steals any available valuable items before the driver has time to react; **v. à la tire** pickpocketing

volage [vɔlaʒ] *adj* fickle, flighty

volaille [vɔlaj] *nf (oiseau)* fowl; **la v.** poultry

volant, -e [vɔlɑ̃, -ɑ̃t] **1** *adj (qui vole)* flying; **personnel v.** flight crew

2 *nm* (**a**) *(d'une automobile)* (steering) wheel; **prendre le v.** to take the wheel; **je te recommande la prudence au v.** take care when driving (**b**) *(de badminton)* shuttlecock (**c**) *(d'une robe)* flounce (**d**) *(de carnet)* tear-off portion

volatil, -e[1] [vɔlatil] *adj* volatile

volatile[2] [vɔlatil] *nm aussi Hum* winged creature

volatiliser [vɔlatilize] **se volatiliser** *vpr* to vanish into thin air

vol-au-vent [vɔlovɑ̃] *nm inv* vol-au-vent

volcan [vɔlkɑ̃] *nm* volcano; *Fig (personne)* spitfire; *Fig (situation)* volcano

volcanique [vɔlkanik] *adj (roche)* volcanic; *Fig (tempérament)* fiery

volcanologue [vɔlkanɔlɔg] *nmf* volcanologist

volée [vɔle] *nf* (**a**) *(d'oiseaux)* flock, flight; *Fig (d'enfants)* swarm (**b**) *(au football, au tennis)* volley; **attraper une balle à la v.** to catch a ball in midair (**c**) *(de flèches)* flight; *Fam (de coups)* shower; *Fam* **recevoir une v.** to get a good thrashing (**d**) **sonner à toute v.** to ring out

voler[1] [vɔle] *vi (oiseau, avion)* to fly; **faire v. un cerf-volant** to fly a kite; *Fig* **v. de ses propres ailes** to stand on one's own two feet, to fend for oneself; *Fig* **v. au secours de qn** to fly to sb's assistance

voler[2] [vɔle] *vt* (**a**) *(objet, argent)* to steal (**à** from); **se faire v. qch** to have sth stolen; *Fig* **il ne l'a pas volé** *(il le mérite)* he's earned it; *(c'est bien fait pour lui)* it serves him right; *Prov* **qui vole un œuf vole un bœuf** = there's no such thing as a petty thief (**b**) *(personne)* to rob; *(léser)* to swindle, to cheat

volet [vɔlɛ] *nm* (**a**) *(de fenêtre, de magasin)* shutter (**b**) *(d'un dépliant)* page; *(d'un formulaire)* section; *Fig (d'un plan)* stage

voleter [42] [vɔlte] *vi* to flutter

voleur, -euse [vɔlœr, -øz] **1** *nm,f* thief; **au v.!** stop thief!

2 *adj (personne)* thieving; **être v.** to be a thief

Volga [vɔlga] *nf* **la V.** the Volga

volière [vɔljɛr] *nf* aviary

volley [vɔlɛ] *nm Fam* volleyball

volley-ball [vɔlebol] *nm* volleyball; **v. de plage** beach volleyball

volleyeur, -euse [vɔlɛjœr, -øz] *nm,f* **(a)** *(joueur de volley-ball)* volleyball player **(b)** *(au tennis)* volleyer

volontaire [vɔlɔ̃tɛr] **1** *adj* **(a)** *(action, omission)* deliberate **(b)** *(enfant)* willful; *(menton, front)* determined
    2 *nmf* volunteer

volontairement [vɔlɔ̃tɛrmɑ̃] *adv* **(a)** *(spontanément)* voluntarily **(b)** *(délibérément)* deliberately

volontariat [vɔlɔ̃tarja] *nm* **(a)** *(travail bénévole)* voluntary work **(b)** *(dans l'armée)* = voluntary service in the armed forces

volontarisme [vɔlɔ̃tarism] *nm* voluntarism

volontariste [vɔlɔ̃tarist] *adj* voluntarist

volonté [vɔlɔ̃te] *nf* **(a)** *(faculté)* will; **la v. de vaincre/de puissance** the will to win/for power; **de sa propre v.** of one's own accord; **avec la meilleure v. du monde** with the best will in the world; **à v.** at will; **vin à v.** *(dans un restaurant)* unlimited wine **(b)** *(détermination)* willpower; **avoir de la v.** to have willpower **(c)** **bonne v.** willingness; **mauvaise v.** unwillingness; **mettre de la mauvaise v. à faire qch** to do sth with bad grace **(d)** *(souhait)* wish; **ses dernières volontés** his last wishes

volontiers [vɔlɔ̃tje] *adv* **(a)** *(avec plaisir)* willingly, gladly; **v.!** I'd be glad to! **(b)** **être v. pessimiste/bavard** to be naturally pessimistic/chatty

volt [vɔlt] *nm* volt

voltage [vɔltaʒ] *nm* voltage

volte-face [vɔltəfas] *nf inv* about-face; *Fig* U-turn; **faire v.** to turn around; *Fig* to do a U-turn

voltige [vɔltiʒ] *nf* **(a)** *(sur un cheval)* acrobatics on horseback; *(sur un trapèze)* acrobatics; **haute v.** flying trapeze acrobatics **(b)** *(acrobatie aérienne)* aerobatics

voltiger [45] [vɔltiʒe] *vi* **(a)** *(sur un cheval)* to perform on horseback; *(sur un trapèze)* to perform on the trapeze **(b)** *(feuilles)* to flutter

volubile [vɔlybil] *adj* voluble

volubilité [vɔlybilite] *nf* volubility

volume [vɔlym] *nm* **(a)** *(livre)* volume **(b)** *(d'un solide, d'un fluide, des ventes)* volume **(c)** *(du son, de la voix)* volume; **baisser/monter le v.** to turn the volume down/up; **v. sonore** noise level

volumineux, -euse [vɔlyminø, -øz] *adj* voluminous, bulky

volupté [vɔlypte] *nf* sensual pleasure

voluptueusement [vɔlyptɥøzmɑ̃] *adv* voluptuously

voluptueux, -euse [vɔlyptɥø, -øz] *adj* voluptuous

volute [vɔlyt] *nf* **(a)** *(de fumée)* curl, wreath **(b)** *Archit* helix

vomi [vɔmi] *nm* vomit

vomir [vɔmir] **1** *vt* **(a)** *(aliment)* to vomit, to bring up **(b)** *(fumée, flammes)* to vomit, to belch forth; *Fig (injures)* to spew out **(c)** *Fig (détester)* to loathe
    2 *vi* to be sick, to vomit; **avoir envie de v.** to feel nauseous

vomissement [vɔmismɑ̃] *nm (action)* vomiting; **avoir des vomissements** to vomit

vomitif, -ive [vɔmitif, -iv] *adj & nm* emetic

vont *voir* **aller**[1]

vorace [vɔras] *adj* voracious

voracement [vɔrasmɑ̃] *adv* voraciously

voracité [vɔrasite] *nf* voracity

vortex [vɔrtɛks] *nm* vortex

vos [vo] *voir* **votre**

Vosges [voʒ] *nfpl* **les V.** the Vosges

votant, -e [vɔtɑ̃, -ɑ̃t] *nm,f* voter

votation [vɔtasjɔ̃] *nf Suisse* vote

vote [vɔt] *nm* **(a)** *(pour une élection)* vote; *(action)* voting; **le v.**

des femmes women's vote; **v. à bulletin secret** secret ballot; **v. à main levée** vote by a show of hands; **v. par procuration** proxy vote; **v. de protestation** protest vote **(b)** *(d'une loi)* passing; **v. de confiance** vote of confidence

voter [vɔte] **1** *vi* to vote **(pour/contre** for/against); **v. à bulletin secret** to vote in a secret ballot; **v. à main levée** to vote by a show of hands; **v. par procuration** to vote by proxy
    2 *vt* **(a)** *(loi)* to pass **(b)** *(crédit)* to vote

votre, vos [vɔtr, vo] *adj possessif* your; **v. chien** your dog; **vos enfants** your children; **v. père et v. mère** *(à une personne)* your mother and father; *(à plusieurs personnes)* your mothers and fathers; **un de vos amis** one of your friends, a friend of yours; *Fam* **vous avez v. vendredi** you have Friday off

vôtre [votr] **1** *pron possessif* **le v., la v., les vôtres** yours; *(en insistant)* your own; **vous me prêtez le v.?** can I borrow yours?; **vous n'en avez pas besoin, vous avez le v.** you don't need it, you have your own; *Fam* **à la v.!** cheers!
    2 *nm* **il faut que vous y mettiez du v.** you should do your share
    3 *nmpl* **les vôtres** *(votre famille)* your family; **je serai des vôtres ce soir** I'll be joining you tonight

voudra, voudrai, *etc. voir* **vouloir**[1]

vouer [vwe] **1** *vt* **(a)** *(jurer)* to vow **(à** to) **(b)** *(consacrer)* to devote **(à** to) **(c)** **voué à l'échec** doomed to failure
    2 **se vouer** *vpr* **se v. à qch** to devote oneself to sth

vouloir[1] [74] [vulwar] **1** *vt* **(a)** *(désirer)* to want; **rentrons, voulez-vous?** let's go in, shall we?; **si vous (le) voulez** if you like; **faites comme vous (le) voudrez** do what you like, do as you please; **que veux-tu que je fasse?** what do you want me to do?; **le mauvais sort voulut que...** as bad luck would have it...; **v. faire qch** to want to do sth; **quand j'ai voulu l'embrasser** when I tried to kiss him; **faire qch sans le v.** to do sth unintentionally; **le moteur ne veut pas démarrer** the engine won't start; **j'aurais tant voulu la voir** I would really have liked to see her; **que lui voulez-vous?** what do you want from him/her?; *(pourquoi le cherchez-vous?)* what do you want him/her for?; **ne pas v. de qn/qch** not to want sb/sth; **je ne veux pas de ça chez moi** I won't have that in my house; **en v.** *(être accrocheur)* to be very determined; **en v. à qn (de qch/d'avoir fait qch)** to bear sb a grudge (for sth/for doing sth); **ils en veulent à mon argent** they're after my money
    (b) *(dans les formules de politesse)* **veuillez vous asseoir** please sit down; **voulez-vous faire moins de bruit!** will you please make less noise!
    (c) *(exiger)* **la coutume veut que...**+ *subjunctive* custom dictates that...; **le règlement veut que...** + *subjunctive* the rules state that...
    (d) *(locutions)* **je veux bien** *(volontiers)* with pleasure; *(j'admets)* granted, fair enough; **c'est comme ça, que veux-tu** that's the way it is, what can you do?; *Fam* **en veux-tu, en voilà** galore; **tu l'auras voulu!** if that's the way you want it!; **v. dire** to mean; *Fam* **je veux!** *(absolument)* absolutely!
    2 **se vouloir** *vpr* **(a)** *(vouloir être)* **elle se veut différente** she likes to think she's different; **il se voulait rassurant** he was trying to be reassuring
    (b) **s'en v. (de qch/de faire qch)** to be annoyed with oneself (about sth/for doing sth)

vouloir[2] [vulwar] *nm* will; **bon v.** goodwill; **mauvais v.** ill will

voulu, -e [vuly] **1** *pp voir* **vouloir**[1]
    2 *adj* **(a)** *(requis)* required **(b)** *(délibéré)* deliberate, intentional

vous [vu] *pron personnel* **(a)** *(sujet)* you; **v. deux/tous** both/all of you; **v. autres les intellectuels** you intellectuals; **v., v. auriez certainement refusé** YOU would probably have refused
    (b) *(objet direct)* you; **et v., on v. a servis?** and what about you, have you been served?

(**c**) *(objet indirect)* to you; **vous a-t-elle serré la main?** did she shake your hand?; **elle v. a jeté un regard furieux** she glared at you

(**d**) *(réfléchi) (singulier)* yourself; *(pluriel)* yourselves; **taisez-v.!** be quiet!

(**e**) *(réciproque)* each other

(**f**) *(avec préposition)* you; **v. ne pensez qu'à v.** you think only of yourself; **je v. le montre, à v.?** shall I show it to YOU?; **cet argent n'est pas à v.** this money isn't yours; **v. aurez une chambre à v.** you'll have your own room; *Fam* **une connaissance à v.** an acquaintance of yours

(**g**) *(dans les comparaisons)* you; **elle est aussi surprise que v.** she's as surprised as you (are)

(**h**) *(remplace "on")* you

vous-même [vumɛm] *pron personnel* yourself

vous-mêmes [vumɛm] *pron personnel* yourselves

voûte [vut] *nf* (**a**) *(arche)* arch; **la v. céleste** the vault *or* canopy of heaven; **v. d'ogive** vault (**b**) *Anat* **v. du palais** roof of the mouth; **v. plantaire** arch (of the foot)

voûté, -e [vute] *adj* bent; **avoir le dos v.** to have a stoop

voûter [vute] **se voûter** *vpr* to become bent, to begin to stoop

vouvoiement [vuvwamã] *nm* = use of the formal "vous" instead of the more familiar "tu"; **le v. est de rigueur** everybody calls each other "vous"; *see also* **tutoiement**

vouvoyer [32] [vuvwaje] **1** *vt* **v. qn** = to address sb as "vous"

2 se vouvoyer *vpr* = to address each other as "vous"

voyage [vwajaʒ] *nm* trip, journey; **être en v.** to be away; **partir en v.** to go on a trip; **bon v.!** have a good trip!; **v. d'affaires** business trip; **v. d'agrément** pleasure trip; **v. de noces** honeymoon; **v. organisé** package vacation *or* tour

voyager [45] [vwajaʒe] *vi* to travel

voyageur, -euse [vwajaʒœr, -øz] *nm,f* traveler; *(passager)* passenger; **v. de commerce** traveling salesman

voyagiste [vwajaʒist] *nmf* tour operator

voyais *etc. voir* **voir**

voyance [vwajãs] *nf* clairvoyance

voyant, -e [vwajã, -ãt] **1** *adj (de mauvais goût)* loud, garish

2 *nm,f (extralucide)* clairvoyant

3 *nm* **v. (lumineux)** warning light; **v. d'huile/d'essence** oil/fuel warning light

voyelle [vwajɛl] *nf* vowel

voyeur, -euse [vwajœr, -øz] *nm,f* voyeur, *f* voyeuse

voyeurisme [vwajœrism] *nm* voyeurism

voyez, voyons, *etc. voir* **voir**

voyou [vwaju] *nm* lout, hooligan

VPC [vepese] *nf (abrév* **vente par correspondance**) mail order (selling)

vrac [vrak] **en vrac** *adv* (**a**) *(sans emballage)* loose (**b**) *(en désordre)* higgledy-piggledy, in a jumble

vrai, -e [vrɛ] **1** *adj* (**a**) *(indéniable)* true; **c'est v.!** that's true!, that's right!; *Fam* **elle est gentille, pas v.?** she's nice, isn't she?; *Fam* **c'est pas v.!** you're joking! (**b**) *(véritable)* real; *(tableau, antiquité)* genuine; **il a été un v. père pour moi** he was like a father to me

2 *nm* **être dans le v.** to be right; **à v. dire, à dire v.** as a matter of fact, to tell the truth; *Fam* **pour de v.** for real

vraiment [vrɛmã] *adv* really

vraisemblable [vrɛsãblabl] *adj* probable, likely; *(crédible)* believable, credible; **il est v. qu'il sera là demain** he'll probably be there tomorrow

vraisemblablement [vrɛsãblabləmã] *adv* probably

vraisemblance [vrɛsãblãs] *nf* probability, likelihood; *(crédibilité)* credibility; **selon toute v.** in all probability

vrille [vrij] *nf* (**a**) *(de la vigne)* tendril (**b**) *(outil)* gimlet (**c**) *(en avion)* spin; **descendre en v.** to spin down

vrillé, -e [vrije] *adj (corde)* twisted

vriller [vrije] **1** *vt* to bore into

2 *vi* (**a**) *(avion)* to spin (**b**) *(corde)* to twist

vrombir [vrɔbir] *vi* to hum

vrombissement [vrɔbismã] *nm* hum, humming

VRP [veɛrpe] *nm (abrév* **voyageur représentant placier**) sales rep

VTT [vetete] *nm (abrév* **vélo tout terrain**) mountain bike

vu¹, -e¹ [vy] **1** *pp voir* **voir**

2 *adj* **faire qch ni vu ni connu** to do sth without being seen

vu² [vy] **1** *prép* in view of; **vu que** seeing that

2 *nm* **au vu et au su de tout le monde** openly

vue² [vy] *nf* (**a**) *(faculté de voir)* sight, eyesight; **perdre la v.** to lose one's sight; **avoir une bonne/mauvaise v.** to have good/bad eyesight

(**b**) *(regard)* **connaître qn de v.** to know sb by sight; **hors de v.** out of sight; **hors de ma v.!** (get) out of my sight!; **une personnalité en v.** a prominent personality; **mettre qch en v.** to display sth prominently; **à v. d'œil** before one's eyes, visibly; *Fam* **à v. de nez** at a rough guess; *Fam* **en mettre plein la v. à qn** to dazzle sb

(**c**) **seconde v.** second sight

(**d**) *(opinion)* view; **c'est une v. de l'esprit** that's a very theoretical point of view

(**e**) *(panorama)* view; **chambre avec v.** room with a view; *Fig* **v. d'ensemble** overall view

(**f**) *Can Fam* **les vues** the movies; **aller aux (petites) vues** to go to the movies

(**g**) *(locutions)* **à la v. de qn/qch** at the sight of sb/sth; **à première v.** at first sight; **à v.** *(tirer)* on sight; *(voler)* visually; **avoir qch en v.** to have sth in mind; **en v. de qch/de faire qch** with a view to sth/to doing sth; **avoir des vues sur qn/qch** to have designs on sb/sth

vulgaire [vylgɛr] *adj* (**a**) *(grossier)* vulgar (**b**) *(courant)* common (**c**) *(quelconque)* ordinary, common

vulgairement [vylgɛrmã] *adv* (**a**) *(grossièrement)* vulgarly (**b**) *(communément)* commonly

vulgarisation [vylgarizasjɔ] *nf* popularization

vulgariser [vylgarize] *vt* to popularize

vulgarité [vylgarite] *nf* vulgarity

vulnérabilité [vylnerabilite] *nf* vulnerability

vulnérable [vylnerabl] *adj* vulnerable

vulve [vylv] *nf* vulva

W

W, w [dubləve] *nm inv* W, w

wagon [vagɔ̃] *nm* (**a**) *(de passagers)* car; *(de marchandises)* car; **w. à bagages** baggage car; **w. à bestiaux** stock car; **w. frigorifique** refrigerated van; **w. de marchandises** freight car, boxcar (**b**) *(contenu)* carload (**de** of)

wagon-citerne (*pl* **wagons-citernes**) [vagɔ̃sitɛrn] *nm* tank car

wagon-lit (*pl* **wagons-lits**) [vagɔ̃li] *nm* sleeping car, sleeper

wagon-restaurant (*pl* **wagons-restaurants**) [vagɔ̃rɛstɔrɑ̃] *nm* dining car

Walkman® [wɔkman] *nm* Walkman®

Wallis-et-Futuna [walisefutuna] *n* Wallis and Futuna Islands

wallon, -onne [walɔ̃, -ɔn] **1** *adj* Walloon
2 *nm (langue)* Walloon
3 *nm,f* **W., Wallonne** Walloon

Wallonie [walɔni] *nf* **la W.** = the south and southeast regions of Belgium, where French and Walloon are spoken

WAP [wap] *nm Tél (abrév* **wireless application protocol**) WAP

wapiti [wapiti] *nm* wapiti, American elk

Washington [waʃintɔn, waʃiŋtɔn] *n* Washington

wassingue [wasɛ̃g] *nf* floorcloth

water-polo [watɛrpɔlo] *nm* water polo

watt [wat] *nm* watt

W.-C. [vese, dubləvese] *nmpl* toilet

Web [wɛb] *nm inv Ordinat* **le W.** the Web

webcam [wɛbkam] *nf Ordinat* webcam

webcast [wɛbkast] *nm Ordinat* webcast

weblog [wɛblɔg] *nm Ordinat* weblog

webmarketing [wɛbmarketiŋ] *nm* e-marketing

webmestre [wɛbmɛstr] *nm Ordinat* webmaster

week-end (*pl* **week-ends**) [wikɛnd] *nm* weekend; **partir en w.** to go away for the weekend

western [wɛstɛrn] *nm* western

whisky [wiski] *nm (écossais)* whiskey, whisky, scotch; *(irlandais, américain)* whiskey

white-spirit [wajtspirit] *nm* white spirit

WiFi [wifi] *adj & nm Ordinat (abrév* **wireless fidelity**) WiFi

WWW [dubləvedubləvedubləve] *nm Ordinat (abrév* **World Wide Web**) WWW

wysiwyg [wiziwig] *adj & nm Ordinat* WYSIWYG

X

X, x [iks] *nm inv* **(a)** *(lettre)* X, x **(b)** *(nombre ou personne inconnus)* X, x; **Monsieur X** Mr X; **x fois** umpteen times; **dans x années** in x number of years **(c)** *Fam Univ* **l'X** = the "École Polytechnique", a "grande école" specializing in technology **(d)** *Cin* **film classé X** adults-only movie **(e)** *Jur* **accoucher sous X** to give birth anonymously; **naître sous X** to be born to an unidentified mother **(f)** *Fam (ecstasy)* X, E

xénophobe [gsenɔfɔb] **1** *adj* xenophobic
  2 *nmf* xenophobe
xénophobie [gsenɔfɔbi] *nf* xenophobia
xérès [gzerɛs, kserɛs] *nm (vin)* sherry
xylophone [ksilɔfɔn, gzilɔfɔn] *nm* xylophone
xylophoniste [gzilɔfɔnist] *nmf* xylophone player

Y

Y, y¹ [igrɛk] *nm inv* Y, y

y² [i] **1** *adv* there; **n'y être pour personne** not to be in for anyone; **vous n'y êtes pas du tout** you're way off the mark; **pendant que tu y es, tu pourrais m'apporter…** while you're at it, you could bring me…

2 *pron* **j'y pense** I'm thinking about it; **il y croit** he believes in it/them; **elle s'y intéresse** she's interested in it/them; **elle y compte** she's counting on it; **je n'y suis pour rien** I have nothing to do with it

yacht [jɔt] *nm* yacht

yachting [jɔtiŋ] *nm* yachting; **faire du y.** to go yachting

yaourt [jaurt] *nm* yoghurt; **y. maigre** low-fat yoghurt; **y. nature/aux fruits** plain *or* natural/fruit yoghurt

yaourtière [jaurtjɛr] *nf* yoghurt maker

Yémen [jemɛn] *nm* **le Y.** Yemen

yéménite [jemenit] **1** *adj* Yemeni

2 *nmf* **Y.** Yemeni

yen [jɛn] *nm* yen

yeux [jø] *voir* œil

yé-yé [jeje] *adj inv* Vieilli (chanteur, groupe) 60s-style pop; (mode) 60s

yiddish [jidiʃ] *adj inv & nm* Yiddish

yoga [jɔga] *nm* yoga; **faire du y.** to do yoga

yoghourt [jogurt] = **yaourt**

yogi [jɔgi] *nm* yogi

yogourt [jogurt] = **yaourt**

Yom Kippour [jɔmkipur] *nm* Yom Kippur

yorkshire [jɔrkʃœr], **yorkshire-terrier** (*pl* **yorkshire-terriers**) [jɔrkʃœrtɛrje] *nm* Yorkshire terrier

yougoslave [jugɔslav] **1** *adj* Yugoslav, Yugoslavian

2 *nmf* **Y.** Yugoslav, Yugoslavian

Yougoslavie [jugɔslavi] *nf* **la Y.** Yugoslavia; **l'ex-Y.** the former Yugoslavia

youpala [jupala] *nm* baby bouncer

youpi [jupi] *exclam* yippee!

youyou [juju] *nm* dinghy

Yo-Yo® [jojo] *nm inv* yo-yo

yuan [juan] *nm* yuan

yucca [juka] *nm* yucca

Yukon [jukɔ̃] *nm* **le Y.** the Yukon

Z

Z, z [zɛd] *nm inv* Z, z

ZAC [zak] *nf (abrév* **zone d'aménagement concerté**) = zone developed by the state and subsequently sold to the public or private sectors

ZAD [zad] *nf (abrév* **zone d'aménagement différé**) = zone which the state has the priority to build on or sell

Zagreb [zagrɛb] *n* Zagreb

Zaïre [zair] *nm* **le Z.** Zaire

zaïrois, -e [zairwa, -az] **1** *adj* Zairean
  2 *nm,f* **Z., Zaïroise** Zairean

Zambie [zãbi] *nf* **la Z.** Zambia

zambien, -enne [zãbjɛ̃, -ɛn] **1** *adj* Zambian
  2 *nm,f* **Z., Zambienne** Zambian

Zanzibar [zãzibar] *n* Zanzibar

zapper [zape] **1** *vi* to channel-hop, to channel-surf
  2 *vt Fam* **(a)** *(supprimer)* to scrap, to scratch **(b)** *(oublier)* to forget; **excuse-moi, j'ai complètement zappé** I'm sorry, I completely forgot *or* it totally slipped my mind

zapping [zapiŋ] *nm* zapping, channel-hopping; **faire du z.** to zap, to channel-hop

zébré, -e [zebre] *adj* striped (**de** with)

zèbre [zɛbr] *nm* zebra; *Fam* **un drôle de z.** a strange character

zébrure [zebryr] *nf* streak; *(d'un zèbre, d'un tigre)* stripe; *Fig (cicatrice)* weal

zébu [zeby] *nm* zebu

zélateur, -trice [zelatœr, -tris] *nm,f* zealot

zélé, -e [zele] *adj* zealous

zèle [zɛl] *nm* zeal; **faire du z.** to be overzealous

zen [zɛn] **1** *adj inv* Zen; *Fam* **c'est très z. chez toi!** your place is very minimalist!; **après mon cours de yoga, je suis z.** after my yoga class I'm totally relaxed
  2 *nm* Zen

zénith [zenit] *nm* zenith; *aussi Fig* **être à son z.** to be at one's zenith

ZEP [zɛp] *nf (abrév* **zone d'éducation prioritaire**) = zone targeted for special help in education

zéphyr [zefir] *nm (vent)* zephyr

zéro [zero] **1** *nm* **(a)** *(chiffre)* zero **(b)** *(note)* zero **(c)** *Fam (personne)* loser **(d)** *(au football)* **trois à z.** three zero, three nothing; *(au tennis)* **trois sets à z.** three sets to love **(e)** *(dans une graduation)* zero; **repartir à z.** to go back to square one; *Fam* **avoir le moral à z.** to be feeling really down; *très Fam* **les avoir à z.** to be scared stiff
  2 *adj* **z. degré Celsius** zero degrees Celsius; **z. faute** no mistakes; **z. heure** twelve (midnight)

zeste [zɛst] *nm* zest, peel; **un z. de citron** a piece of lemon zest *or* peel

zeugma [zøgma], **zeugme** [zøgm] *nm Ling* zeugma

zézaiement [zezɛmã] *nm* lisp

zézayer [53] [zezeje] *vi* to lisp

ZI [zɛdi] *nf (abrév* **zone industrielle**) industrial park

zibeline [ziblin] *nf* sable

zieuter [zjøte] = **zyeuter**

zigoto [zigɔto] *nm Fam* **c'est un drôle de z.** he's an oddball; **faire le z.** to clown around

zigouiller [ziguje] *vt Fam* to do in; **se faire z.** to get done in

zigzag [zigzag] *nm* zigzag; **en z.** *(chemin)* zigzag; *(éclair)* forked; **faire des zigzags** *(route)* to zigzag; *(personne ivre)* to zigzag along; **marcher en z.** to walk in a zigzag

zigzaguer [zigzage] *vi (route)* to zigzag; *(personne ivre)* to zigzag along

Zimbabwe [zimbabwe] *nm* **le Z.** Zimbabwe

zimbabwéen, -enne [zimbabweɛ̃, -ɛn] **1** *adj* Zimbabwean
  2 *nm,f* **Z., Zimbabwéenne** Zimbabwean

zinc [zɛ̃g] *nm* **(a)** *(métal)* zinc **(b)** *Fam (comptoir)* counter, bar **(c)** *Fam (avion)* plane

zinzin [zɛ̃zɛ̃] *Fam* **1** *adj* off one's rocker
  2 *nm (truc)* thingumajig, thingamajig, whatsit

Zip® [zip] *nm* zipper

zippé, -e [zipe] *adj* with a zipper, zip-up

zipper [zipe] *vt Ordinat* to zip

zizanie [zizani] *nf* discord; **semer la z.** to sow discord

zizi [zizi] *nm (langage enfantin)* willy, peter

zizique [zizik] *nf Fam* music

zloty [zlɔti] *nm* zloty

zodiaque [zɔdjak] *nm* **le z.** the zodiac

zombie [zɔ̃bi] *nm Fam* zombie

zona [zona] *nm* shingles *(singulier)*; **avoir un z.** to have shingles

zonard, -e [zonar, -ard] *nm,f Fam (marginal)* dropout

zone [zon] *nf* **(a)** *(espace)* zone; **z. artisanale** small industrial park *(for craft-based businesses)*; **z. dangereuse** danger zone; *Météo* **z. de dépression, z. dépressionnaire** trough of low pressure; *UE* **z. euro** euro zone *or* area, Euroland; **zone d'exclusion aérienne** no-fly zone; **z. fumeurs/non-fumeurs** smoking/no-smoking area; *Météo* **z. de haute pression** area of high pressure; **zone industrielle** industrial park; **z. interdite** prohibited *or* restricted area; *Hist* **z. libre** unoccupied France; *Hist* **z. occupée** occupied France; **z. scientifique** science park; **z. tempérée** temperate zone; **z. verte** green belt **(b)** *Péj* **de seconde z.** second-rate **(c)** *Fam Péj* **la z.** *(bidonville)* the slums; *Fig* **c'est la z.!** it's a dump! **(d)** *Ordinat* **z. de dialogue** dialogue box; **z. d'état** status box; **z. tampon** *(en mémoire)* (memory) buffer; **z. de travail** work area

---

Zone

The Paris area is divided into fare zones for public transportation. Zones 1 and 2 cover metropolitan Paris and certain areas of the nearby suburbs. The remaining zones cover the outer suburbs: "j'habite en zone 3", "une carte orange quatre zones".
France is divided into three "zones" (A, B and C), the schools in the different zones taking their mid-semester and Easter vacations at different times to avoid swamping the public transportation system and tourist infrastructure.

zoner [zone] *vi très Fam* to hang around

zoo [zo, zoo] *nm* zoo

zoologie [zɔɔlɔʒi] *nf* zoology

zoologique [zɔɔlɔʒik] *adj* zoological; **jardin** *ou* **parc z.** zoo

zoologiste [zɔɔlɔʒist], **zoologue** [zɔɔlɔg] *nmf* zoologist

zoom [zum] *nm* (**a**) *(effet)* zoom (**b**) *(objectif)* zoom (lens)

zooplancton [zɔɔplãktɔ̃] *nm Zool* zooplankton

zou [zu] *exclam Fam* **(allez) z.!** scat!

zouave [zwav] *nm (soldat)* Zouave; *Fam (pitre)* fool; *Fam* **faire le z.** to play the fool

zoulou, -e [zulu] **1** *adj* Zulu
2 *nm,f* **Z., Zouloue** Zulu

Zoulouland [zuzulãd] *nm* **le Z.** Zululand, Kwazulu

zozoter [zɔzɔte] *vi Fam* to lisp

ZUP [zyp] *nf (abrév* **zone à urbaniser en priorité**) priority-development zone

Zurich [zyrik] *n* Zurich

zut [zyt] *exclam Fam* nuts!; **et puis z.!** what the heck!

zyeuter [zjøte] *vt Fam (regarder) (discrètement)* to have a look *or* a peek at; *(avec insistance)* to ogle

zygomatique [zigɔmatik] *adj* zygomatic

Supplement
Supplément

French Conjugation Tables

Conjugaisons françaises

Full listings of the conjugations of French regular **-er, -ir** and **-re** verbs are given on pages (4) and (5). On the following pages you will find a list of model irregular verbs. Numbers after verbs in the French-English side of the dictionary, eg [20], refer you to these tables where you will find their irregular forms.

The more common verbs such as **aller, avoir, être** and **faire** are shown in full for all persons and all tenses. In other cases, where complete forms have not been shown they follow the pattern indicated by the first person singular and/or plural.

As the perfect tense is always formed simply by **avoir** or **être** plus the past participle, this has not been shown apart from the verbs mentioned above. Similarly, the conditional tense can always be formed in the same way as the future tense but with the endings **-ais, -ais, -ait, -ions, -iez** and **-aient**. When not shown, the imperative has the same form as the present tense ("tu", "nous" and "vous" forms).

Toutes les formes des verbes réguliers en **-er, -ir** et **-re** sont données pages (4) et (5), suivies d'une liste de conjugaisons irrégulières types. Les nombres apparaissant après les verbes dans la partie français-anglais du dictionnaire, par exemple [20], renvoient à cette liste.

Toutes les personnes et tous les temps sont donnés systématiquement pour les verbes d'usage fréquent tels qu'**aller, avoir, être** et **faire**. Dans tous les autres cas, seules les formes particulières, c'est-à-dire celles qui ne suivent pas le modèle déterminé par la première personne du singulier et/ou du pluriel, sont indiquées.

Le passé composé étant toujours formé sur le modèle **avoir/être** + participe passé, il n'a pas été inclus dans nos listes, sauf pour les verbes mentionnés ci-dessus. De même, le conditionnel se construira à partir du futur.

INDICATIVE

Present	Imperfect	Perfect	Past Historic	Future
REGULAR -er verb aimer				
j'aime	j'aimais	j'ai aimé	j'aimai	j'aimerai
tu aimes	tu aimais	tu as aimé	tu aimas	tu aimeras
il aime	il aimait	il a aimé	il aima	il aimera
nous aimons	nous aimions	nous avons aimé	nous aimâmes	nous aimerons
vous aimez	vous aimiez	vous avez aimé	vous aimâtes	vous aimerez
ils aiment	ils aimaient	ils ont aimé	ils aimèrent	ils aimeront
REGULAR -ir verb choisir				
je choisis	je choisissais	j'ai choisi	je choisis	je choisirai
tu choisis	tu choisissais	tu as choisi	tu choisis	tu choisiras
il choisit	il choisissait	il a choisi	il choisit	il choisira
nous choisissons	nous choisissions	nous avons choisi	nous choisîmes	nous choisirons
vous choisissez	vous choisissiez	vous avez choisi	vous choisîtes	vous choisirez
ils choisissent	ils choisissaient	ils ont choisi	ils choisirent	ils choisiront
REGULAR -re verb attendre				
j'attends	j'attendais	j'ai attendu	j'attendis	j'attendrai
tu attends	tu attendais	tu as attendu	tu attendis	tu attendras
il attend	il attendait	il a attendu	il attendit	il attendra
nous attendons	nous attendions	nous avons attendu	nous attendîmes	nous attendrons
vous attendez	vous attendiez	vous avez attendu	vous attendîtes	vous attendrez
ils attendent	ils attendaient	ils ont attendu	ils attendirent	ils attendront

CONDITIONAL Present	SUBJUNCTIVE Present	Imperfect	IMPERATIVE	PARTICIPLE Present	Past
j'aimerais	j'aime	j'aimasse		aimant	aimé
tu aimerais	tu aimes	tu aimasses	aime		
il aimerait	il aime	il aimât			
nous aimerions	nous aimions	nous aimassions	aimons		
vous aimeriez	vous aimiez	vous aimassiez	aimez		
ils aimeraient	ils aiment	ils aimassent			
je choisirais	je choisisse	je choisisse		choisissant	choisi
tu choisirais	tu choisisses	tu choisisses	choisis		
il choisirait	il choisisse	il choisît			
nous choisirions	nous choisissions	nous choisissions	choisissons		
vous choisiriez	vous choisissiez	vous choisissiez	choisissez		
ils choisiraient	ils choisissent	ils choisissent			
j'attendrais	j'attende	j'attendisse		attendant	attendu
tu attendrais	tu attendes	tu attendisses	attends		
il attendrait	il attende	il attendît			
nous attendrions	nous attendions	nous attendissions	attendons		
vous attendriez	vous attendiez	vous attendissiez	attendez		
ils attendraient	ils attendent	ils attendissent			

INDICATIVE

Present	Imperfect	Perfect	Past Historic	Future
1. avoir				
j'ai	j'avais	j'ai eu	j'eus	j'aurai
tu as	tu avais	tu as eu	tu eus	tu auras
il a	il avait	il a eu	il eut	il aura
nous avons	nous avions	nous avons eu	nous eûmes	nous aurons
vous avez	vous aviez	vous avez eu	vous eûtes	vous aurez
ils ont	ils avaient	ils ont eu	ils eurent	ils auront
2. être				
je suis	j'étais	j'ai été	je fus	je serai
tu es	tu étais	tu as été	tu fus	tu seras
il est	il était	il a été	il fut	il sera
nous sommes	nous étions	nous avons été	nous fûmes	nous serons
vous êtes	vous étiez	vous avez été	vous fûtes	vous serez
ils sont	ils étaient	ils ont été	ils furent	ils seront

3a. absoudre

j'absous	j'absolvais		j'absolus	j'absoudrai
il absout				
nous absolvons				

3b. résoudre PAST PARTICIPLE résolu

4a. accroître

j'accrois	j'accroissais		j'accrus	j'accroîtrai
il accroît				
nous accroissons				

4b. croître *follows the above pattern except for the following*

je croîs			je crûs	

5. accueillir

j'accueille	j'accueillais		j'accueillis	j'accueillerai
nous accueillons				

6. acheter

j'achète	j'achetais		j'achetai	j'achèterai
nous achetons				
ils achètent				

7. acquérir

j'acquiers	j'acquérais		j'acquis	j'acquerrai
il acquiert				
nous acquérons				
ils acquièrent				

8. aller

je vais	j'allais	je suis allé	j'allai	j'irai
tu vas	tu allais	tu es allé	tu allas	tu iras
il va	il allait	il est allé	il alla	il ira
nous allons	nous allions	nous sommes allés	nous allâmes	nous irons
vous allez	vous alliez	vous êtes allés	vous allâtes	vous irez
ils vont	ils allaient	ils sont allés	ils allèrent	ils iront

| CONDITIONAL | SUBJUNCTIVE | | IMPERATIVE | PARTICIPLE | |
Present	Present	Imperfect		Present	Past
j'aurais	j'aie	j'eusse		ayant	eu
tu aurais	tu aies	tu eusses	aie		
il aurait	il ait	il eût			
nous aurions	nous ayons	nous eussions	ayons		
vous auriez	vous ayez	vous eussiez	ayez		
ils auraient	ils aient	ils eussent			
je serais	je sois	je fusse		étant	été
tu serais	tu sois	tu fusses	sois		
il serait	il soit	il fût			
nous serions	nous soyons	nous fussions	soyons		
vous seriez	vous soyez	vous fussiez	soyez		
ils seraient	ils soient	ils fussent			
	j'absolve	*not used*		absolvant	absous (oute)
	nous absolvions				
	j'accroisse	j'accrusse		accroissant	accru
	nous accroissions	nous accrussions			
		je crûsse			crû
	j'accueille	j'accueillisse		accueillant	accueilli
	nous accueillions	nous accueillissions	accueille accueillons accueillez		
	j'achète	j'achetasse		achetant	acheté
	nous achetions	nous achetassions			
	j'acquière	j'acquisse		acquérant	acquis
	nous acquérions	nous acquissions			
j'irais	j'aille	j'allasse		allant	allé
tu irais	tu ailles	tu allasses	va		
il irait	il aille	il allât			
nous irions	nous allions	nous allassions	allons		
vous iriez	vous alliez	vous allassiez	allez		
ils iraient	ils aillent	ils allassent			

INDICATIVE

Present	Imperfect	Perfect	Past Historic	Future
9. appeler				
j'appelle nous appelons ils appellent	j'appelais		j'appelai	j'appellerai
10a. s'asseoir				
je m'assieds/ assois il s'assied/assoit nous nous asseyons/ assoyons	je m'asseyais/ assoyais		je m'assis	je m'assiérai/assoirai
10b. surseoir *follows pattern of oi forms of* **s'asseoir**				
				je surseoirai
11. battre				
je bats il bat nous battons	je battais		je battis	je battrai
12. boire				
je bois il boit nous buvons ils boivent	je buvais		je bus	je boirai
13. bouillir				
je bous il bout nous bouillons	je bouillais		je bouillis	je bouillirai
14. choir				
je chois il chut ils choient			il chût	
15. clore				
je clos il clôt ils closent				je clorai
16. commencer				
je commence nous commençons vous commencez ils commencent	je commençais		je commençai	je commencerai
17a. conclure				
je conclus il conclut nous concluons	je concluais		je conclus	je conclurai
17b. inclure PAST PARTICIPLE inclus				

| CONDITIONAL | SUBJUNCTIVE | | IMPERATIVE | PARTICIPLE | |
Present	Present	Imperfect		Present	Past
	j'appelle	j'appelasse		appelant	appelé
	nous appelions	nous appelassions			
	je m'asseye/ assoie	je m'assisse		asseyant/ assoyant	assis
	nous nous asseyions/ assoyions	nous nous assissions			
je surseoirais					
	je batte	je battisse		battant	battu
	nous battions	nous battissions			
	je boive	je busse		buvant	bu
	nous buvions	nous bussions			
	je bouille	je bouillisse		bouillant	bouilli
	nous bouillions	nous bouillissions			
					chu
	je close				clos
	nous closions				
	je commence	je commençasse		commençant	commencé
	nous commencions	nous commençassions			
	je conclue	je conclusse		concluant	conclu
	nous concluions	nous conclussions			

INDICATIVE

Present	Imperfect	Perfect	Past Historic	Future
18. conduire				
je conduis il conduit nous conduisons	je conduisais		je conduisis	je conduirai
19a. confire				
je confis il confit nous confisons	je confisais		je confis	je confira
19b. suffire PAST PARTICIPLE suffi (invariable)				
20. connaître				
je connais il connaît nous connaissons	je connaissais		je connus	je connaîtrai
21. coudre				
je couds il coud nous cousons	je cousais		je cousis	je coudrai
22. courir				
je cours il court nous courons	je courais		je courus	je courrai
23. craindre				
je crains il craint nous craignons	je craignais		je craignis	je craindrai
24. créer				
je crée nous créons	je créais		je créai	je créerai
25. croire				
je crois il croit nous croyons ils croient	je croyais		je crus	je croirai
26. devoir				
je dois il doit nous devons ils doivent	je devais		je dus	je devrai
27a. dire				
je dis il dit nous disons vous dites	je disais		je dis	je dirai

CONDITIONAL Present	SUBJUNCTIVE Present	Imperfect	IMPERATIVE	PARTICIPLE Present	Past
	je conduise	je conduisisse		conduisant	conduit
	nous conduisions	nous conduisissions			
	je confise	je confisse		confisant	confit
	nous confisions	nous confissions			
	je connaisse	je connusse		connaissant	connu
	nous connaissions	nous connussions			
	je couse	je cousisse		cousant	cousu
	nous cousions	nous cousissions			
	je coure	je courusse		courant	couru
	nous courions	nous courussions			
	je craigne	je craignisse		craignant	craint
	nous craignions	nous craignissions			
	je crée	je créasse		créant	créé
	nous créions	nous créassions			
	je croie	je crusse		croyant	cru
	nous croyions	nous crussions			
	je doive	je dusse		devant	dû (due), dus (dues)
	nous devions	nous dussions			
	je dise	je disse		disant	dit
	nous disions	nous dissions			

INDICATIVE

Present	Imperfect	Perfect	Past Historic	Future

27b. contredire, interdire, etc. PRESENT vous contredisez, interdisez

28. distraire

Present	Imperfect	Perfect	Past Historic	Future
je distrais	je distrayais			je distrairai
il distrait				
nous distrayons				
ils distraient				

29. dormir

Present	Imperfect	Perfect	Past Historic	Future
je dors	je dormais		je dormis	je dormirai
il dort				
nous dormons				

30. écrire

Present	Imperfect	Perfect	Past Historic	Future
j'écris	j'écrivais		j'écrivis	j'écrirai
il écrit				
nous écrivons				

31a. émouvoir

Present	Imperfect	Perfect	Past Historic	Future
j'émeus	j'émouvais		j'émus	j'émouvrai
il émeut				
nous émouvons				
ils émeuvent				

31b. mouvoir PAST PARTICIPLE mû (mue), mus (mues)

32. employer

Present	Imperfect	Perfect	Past Historic	Future
j'emploie	j'employais		j'employai	j'emploierai
nous employons				
ils emploient				

33. envoyer

Present	Imperfect	Perfect	Past Historic	Future
j'envoie	j'envoyais		j'envoyai	j'enverrai
nous envoyons				
ils envoient				

34. espérer

Present	Imperfect	Perfect	Past Historic	Future
j'espère	j'espérais		j'espérai	j'espérerai
nous espérons				
ils espèrent				

35. faillir

Present	Imperfect	Perfect	Past Historic	Future
je faillis				je faillirai

36. faire

Present	Imperfect	Perfect	Past Historic	Future
je fais	je faisais	j'ai fait	je fis	je ferai
tu fais	tu faisais	tu as fait	tu fis	tu feras
il fait	il faisait	il a fait	il fit	il fera
nous faisons	nous faisions	nous avons fait	nous fîmes	nous ferons
vous faites	vous faisiez	vous avez fait	vous fîtes	vous ferez
ils font	ils faisaient	ils ont fait	ils firent	ils feront

37. falloir

Present	Imperfect	Perfect	Past Historic	Future
il faut	il fallait		il fallut	il faudra

CONDITIONAL Present	SUBJUNCTIVE Present	Imperfect	IMPERATIVE	PARTICIPLE Present	Past
	je distraie			distrayant	distrait
	nous distrayions				
	je dorme	je dormisse		dormant	dormi
	nous dormions	nous dormissions			
	j'écrive	j'écrivisse		écrivant	écrit
	nous écrivions	nous écrivissions			
	j'émeuve	j'émusse		émouvant	ému
	nous émouvions	nous émussions			
	j'emploie	j'employasse		employant	employé
	nous employions	nous employassions			
	j'envoie	j'envoyasse		envoyant	envoyé
	nous envoyions	nous envoyassions			
	j'espère	j'espérasse		espérant	espéré
	nous espérions	nous espérassions			
				faillant	failli
je ferais	je fasse	je fisse		faisant	fait
tu ferais	tu fasses	tu fisses	fais		
il ferait	il fasse	il fît			
nous ferions	nous fassions	nous fissions	faisons		
vous feriez	vous fassiez	vous fissiez	faites		
ils feraient	ils fassent	ils fissent			
	il faille	il fallût			fallu

INDICATIVE

Present	Imperfect	Perfect	Past Historic	Future
38. fuir				
je fuis	je fuyais		je fuis	je fuirai
il fuit				
nous fuyons				
ils fuient				
39. geler				
je gèle	je gelais		je gelai	je gèlerai
nous gelons	nous gelions			
ils gèlent				
40. gésir				
je gis	je gisais			
il gît				
nous gisons				
41. haïr				
je hais	je haïssais		je haïs	je haïrai
il hait				
nous haïssons				
42. jeter				
je jette	je jetais		je jetai	je jetterai
nous jetons				
ils jettent				
43. joindre				
je joins	je joignais		je joignis	je joindrai
nous joignons				
44. lire				
je lis	je lisais		je lus	je lirai
nous lisons				
45. manger				
je mange	je mangeais		je mangeai	je mangerai
nous mangeons				
46. mener				
je mène	je menais		je menai	je mènerai
nous menons				
ils mènent				
47. mettre				
je mets	je mettais		je mis	je mettrai
il met				
nous mettons				
48. moudre				
je mouds	je moulais		je moulus	je moudrai
il moud				
nous moulons				

CONDITIONAL Present	SUBJUNCTIVE Present	Imperfect	IMPERATIVE	PARTICIPLE Present	Past
	je fuie	je fuisse		fuyant	fui
	nous fuyions	nous fuissions			
	je gèle	je gelasse		gelant	gelé
		nous gelassions			
				gisant	
	je haïsse	je haïsse		haïssant	haï
	nous haïssions	nous haïssions			
	je jette	je jetasse		jetant	jeté
	nous jetions	nous jetassions			
	je joigne	je joignisse		joignant	joint
	nous joignions	nous joignissions			
	je lise	je lusse		lisant	lu
	nous lisions	nous lussions			
	je mange	je mangeasse		mangeant	mangé
	nous mangions	nous mangeassions			
	je mène	je menasse		menant	mené
	nous menions	nous menassions			
	je mette	je misse		mettant	mis
	nous mettions	nous missions			
	je moule	je moulusse		moulant	moulu
	nous moulions	nous moulussions			

INDICATIVE

Present	Imperfect	Perfect	Past Historic	Future
49. mourir				
je meurs il meurt nous mourons ils meurent	je mourais		je mourus	je mourrai
50a. naître				
je nais il naît nous naissons	je naissais		je naquis	je naîtrai
50b. paître no PAST HISTORIC; PAST PARTICIPLE pu (invariable; rare)				
50c. repaître as paître but PAST HISTORIC je repus				
51. ouïr				
j'ois il oit nous oyons ils oient	j'oyais		j'ouïs	j'ouïrai
52. ouvrir				
j'ouvre nous ouvrons	j'ouvrais		j'ouvris	j'ouvrirai
53. payer				
je paie/paye nous payons ils paient/payent	je payais		je payai	je paierai/payerai
54. peindre				
je peins il peint nous peignons	je peignais		je peignis	je peindrai
55a. plaire				
je plais il plaît	je plaisais nous plaisions		je plus	je plairai
55b. taire PRESENT il tait				
56. pleuvoir				
il pleut	il pleuvait		il plut	il pleuvra
57. pouvoir				
je peux/puis il peut nous pouvons	je pouvais		je pus	je pourrai

CONDITIONAL Present	SUBJUNCTIVE Present	Imperfect	IMPERATIVE	PARTICIPLE Present	Past
	je meure	je mourusse		mourant	mort
	nous mourions	nous mourussions			
	je naisse	je naquisse		naissant	né
	nous naissions	nous naquissions			
	j'oie	j'ouïsse		oyant	ouï
	nous oyions				
	j'ouvre			ouvrant	ouvert
	nous ouvrions		ouvre ouvrons ouvrez		
	je paie/paye nous payions	je payasse nous payassions		payant	payé
	je peigne	je peignisse		peignant	peint
	nous peignions	nous peignissions			
	je plaise nous plaisions	je plusse nous plussions		plaisant	plu
				pleuvant	plu
	il pleuve	il plût			
	je puisse	je pusse		pouvant	pu
	nous puissions	nous pussions			

INDICATIVE

Present	Imperfect	Perfect	Past Historic	Future
58. prendre				
je prends	je prenais		je pris	je prendrai
il prend				
nous prenons				
ils prennent				
59. protéger				
je protège	je protégeais		je protégeai	je protégerai
nous protégeons				
ils protègent				
60. recevoir				
je reçois	je recevais		je reçus	je recevrai
il reçoit				
nous recevons				
ils reçoivent				
61. rire				
je ris	je riais		je ris	je rirai
il rit				
nous rions				
62. savoir				
je sais	je savais		je sus	je saurai
il sait				
nous savons				
63. servir				
je sers	je servais		je servis	je servirai
il sert				
nous servons				
64a. sortir				
je sors	je sortais		je sortis	je sortirai
il sort				
nous sortons				
64b. mentir PAST PARTICIPLE is invariable				
65. suivre				
je suis	je suivais		je suivis	je suivrai
il suit				
nous suivons				
66. supplier				
je supplie	je suppliais		je suppliai	je supplierai
nous supplions				
67. tressaillir				
je tressaille	je tressaillais		je tressaillis	je tressaillirai
nous tressaillons				

CONDITIONAL	SUBJUNCTIVE		IMPERATIVE	PARTICIPLE	
Present	Present	Imperfect		Present	Past
	je prenne	je prisse		prenant	pris
	nous prenions	nous prissions			
	je protège	je protégeasse		protégeant	protégé
	nous protégions	nous protégeassions			
	je reçoive	je reçusse		recevant	reçu
	nous recevions	nous reçussions			
	je rie	je risse		riant	ri
	nous riions	nous rissions			
	je sache	je susse		sachant	su
	nous sachions	nous sussions	sache sachons sachez		
	je serve	je servisse		servant	servi
	nous servions	nous servissions			
	je sorte	je sortisse		sortant	sorti
	nous sortions	nous sortissions			
	je suive	je suivisse		suivant	suivi
	nous suivions	nous suivissions			
	je supplie	je suppliasse		suppliant	supplié
	nous suppliions	nous suppliassions			
	je tressaille	je tressaillisse		tressaillant	tressailli
	nous tressaillions	nous tressaillissions			

INDICATIVE

Present	Imperfect	Perfect	Past Historic	Future
68. vaincre				
je vaincs	je vainquais		je vainquis	je vaincrai
il vainc				
nous vainquons				
69a. valoir				
je vaux	je valais		je valus	je vaudrai
il vaut				
nous valons				
69b. prévaloir *follows the above pattern except for the following*				
70. venir				
je viens	je venais		je vins	je viendrai
il vient				
nous venons				
ils viennent				
71. vêtir				
je vêts	je vêtais		je vêtis	je vêtirai
il vêt				
nous vêtons				
72. vivre				
je vis	je vivais		je vécus	je vivrai
il vit				
nous vivons				
73a. voir				
je vois	je voyais		je vis	je verrai
il voit				
nous voyons				
ils voient				
73b. pourvoir *follows the above pattern except for the following*				
			je pourvus	je pourvoirai
73c. prévoir *follows the above pattern except for the following*				
			je prévus	je prévoirai
74. vouloir				
je veux	je voulais		je voulus	je voudrai
il veut				
nous voulons				
ils veulent				

| CONDITIONAL | SUBJUNCTIVE | | IMPERATIVE | PARTICIPLE | |
Present	Present	Imperfect		Present	Past
	je vainque	je vainquisse		vainquant	vaincu
	nous vainquions	nous vainquissions			
	je vaille	je valusse		valant	valunous
	nous valions	nous valussions			
	je prévale				
	je vienne	je vinsse		venant	venu
	nous venions	nous vinissions			
	je vête	je vêtisse		vêtant	vêtu
	nous vêtions	nous vêtissions			
	je vive	je vécusse		vivant	vécu
	nous vivions	nous vécussions			
	je voie	je visse		voyant	vu
	nous voyions	nous vissions			
je pourvoirais					
je prévoirais					
	je veuille	je voulusse	veuille	voulant	voulu
	nous voulions	nous voulussions	veuillons		
			veuillez		

Guide de communication en anglais

La correspondance

Ce guide a pour objectif de vous aider à rédiger un courrier en anglais : vous y trouverez des conseils sur la mise en page, les formules d'appel et de politesse, la rédaction de l'adresse ainsi que de nombreux modèles de lettres et suggestions de tournures à employer dans la correspondance privée ou commerciale, le courrier électronique et les documents transmis par télécopie.

Formules d'appel et formules de politesse

La formule de politesse varie en fonction de la formule d'appel utilisée.

■ formule d'appel	■ formule de politesse
Lorsqu'on ne connaît pas le nom de la personne à qui l'on s'adresse :	
Dear Sir **Dear Madam**	Respectfully yours
Lorsqu'on ne sait pas s'il s'agit d'un homme ou d'une femme : **Dear Sir or Madam** ou **Dear Sir/Madam**	
Lorsqu'on s'adresse à une société ou à un organisme sans préciser le nom du destinataire : **Dear Sirs** **Dear Gentlemen**	
Lorsqu'on connaît le nom de la personne à qui l'on s'adresse :	
Dear Mr. Jameson **Dear Mrs. Lucas** **Dear Miss Crookshaw** **Dear Ms. Greening**	Sincerely yours Sincerely
(L'abréviation Ms. est de plus en plus employée lorsqu'on s'adresse à une femme car elle permet de ne pas préciser s'il s'agit d'une femme mariée (Mrs.) ou non (Miss).) **Dear Dr. Illingworth**	Style moins soutenu : **With best wishes** **With kind regards** **Kindest regards**
Aux États-Unis, l'abréviation est généralement suivie d'un point : Mr., Mrs., Ms., Dr.	Plus rare : **Respectfully yours** **Respectfully**
Lorsqu'on s'adresse au rédacteur en chef d'un journal : **Sir**	
à un député : **Dear Mr./Mrs. Brown**	
à un représentant ou membre du Congrès : **Sir/Madam** **Dear Congressman/Congresswoman Fox**	

Lorsqu'on s'adresse à de la famille ou à des amis :

■ En début de lettre

Dear Bill
Dear Helen
Dear Tom and Barbara
Dear all
Dear Mom and Dad
Dear Uncle Ralph/Auntie Ann
My dear Alex
Dearest/My dearest Kate

■ En fin de lettre

With love
Love
Love from
Love and best wishes

Plus affectueux :
With all my/our love
Much love

Plus familier :
Lots of love

Plus soutenu :
Yours
Best wishes
Regards

Présentation d'une lettre dactylographiée

Les paragraphes sont alignés à gauche, sans retrait, et séparés par une ligne de blanc.

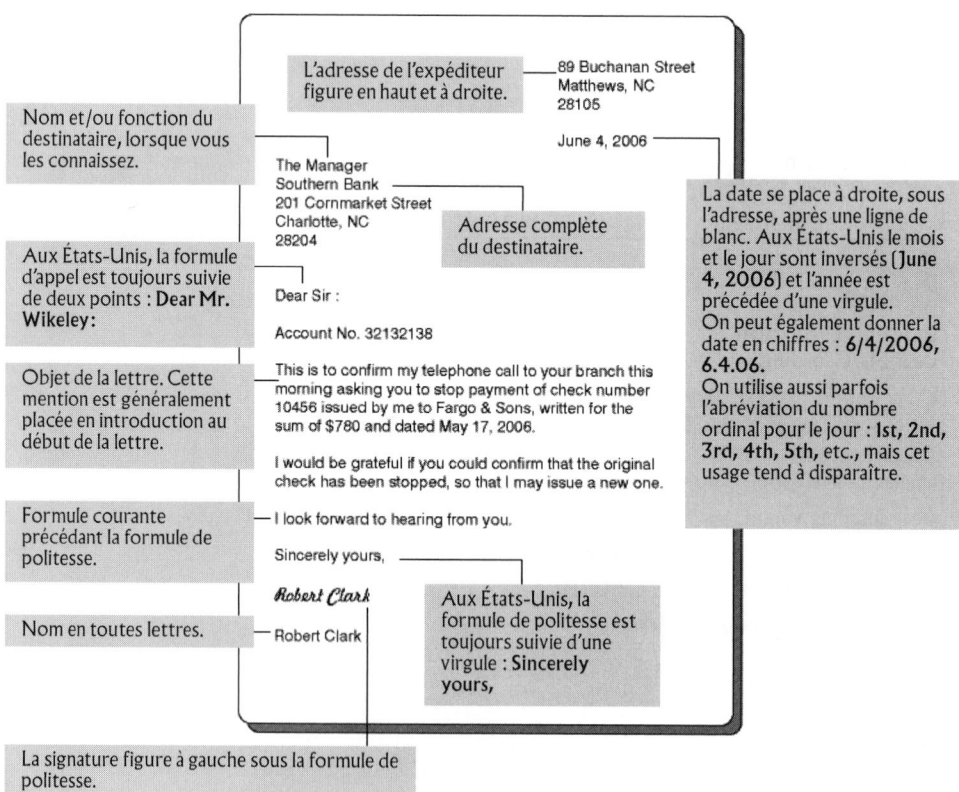

L'adresse de l'expéditeur figure en haut et à droite.

89 Buchanan Street
Matthews, NC
28105

June 4, 2006

Nom et/ou fonction du destinataire, lorsque vous les connaissez.

The Manager
Southern Bank
201 Cornmarket Street
Charlotte, NC
28204

Adresse complète du destinataire.

La date se place à droite, sous l'adresse, après une ligne de blanc. Aux États-Unis le mois et le jour sont inversés (June 4, 2006) et l'année est précédée d'une virgule.
On peut également donner la date en chiffres : 6/4/2006, 6.4.06.
On utilise aussi parfois l'abréviation du nombre ordinal pour le jour : 1st, 2nd, 3rd, 4th, 5th, etc., mais cet usage tend à disparaître.

Aux États-Unis, la formule d'appel est toujours suivie de deux points : Dear Mr. Wikeley:

Dear Sir :

Account No. 32132138

Objet de la lettre. Cette mention est généralement placée en introduction au début de la lettre.

This is to confirm my telephone call to your branch this morning asking you to stop payment of check number 10456 issued by me to Fargo & Sons, written for the sum of $780 and dated May 17, 2006.

I would be grateful if you could confirm that the original check has been stopped, so that I may issue a new one.

Formule courante précédant la formule de politesse.

I look forward to hearing from you.

Sincerely yours,

Nom en toutes lettres.

Robert Clark

Robert Clark

Aux États-Unis, la formule de politesse est toujours suivie d'une virgule : Sincerely yours,

La signature figure à gauche sous la formule de politesse.

Présentation d'une lettre manuscrite à un ami

Chaque paragraphe commence par un alinéa.

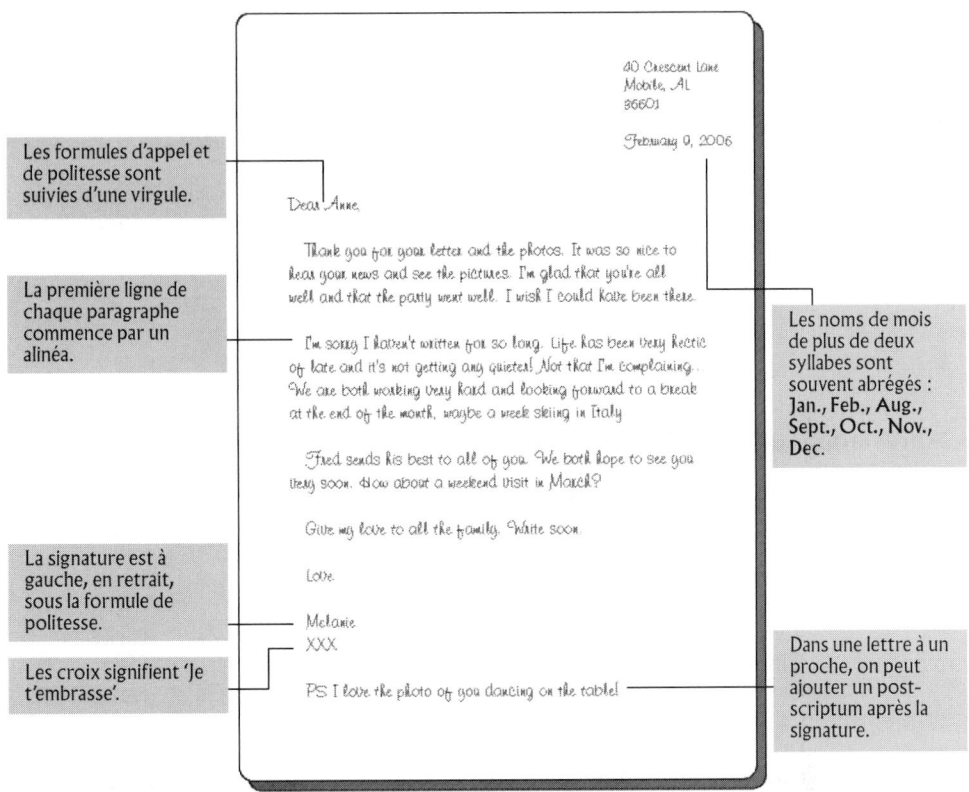

Les formules d'appel et de politesse sont suivies d'une virgule.

La première ligne de chaque paragraphe commence par un alinéa.

La signature est à gauche, en retrait, sous la formule de politesse.

Les croix signifient 'Je t'embrasse'.

Les noms de mois de plus de deux syllabes sont souvent abrégés : Jan., Feb., Aug., Sept., Oct., Nov., Dec.

Dans une lettre à un proche, on peut ajouter un post-scriptum après la signature.

Enveloppes et adresses

L'adresse doit être aussi précise que possible. Les sites Web des services postaux des différents pays peuvent être utiles pour trouver l'adresse complète d'un particulier, d'un organisme ou d'une entreprise, y compris le code postal précis.

États-Unis : www.usps.gov
Canada : www.canadapost.ca
Royaume-Uni : www.royalmail.com
Irlande : www.anpost.ie
Australie : www.auspost.com.au
Nouvelle-Zélande : www.nzpost.co.nz

Il est recommandé de n'inclure aucun signe de ponctuation et de rédiger l'adresse en majuscules (voir les modèles ci-dessous).

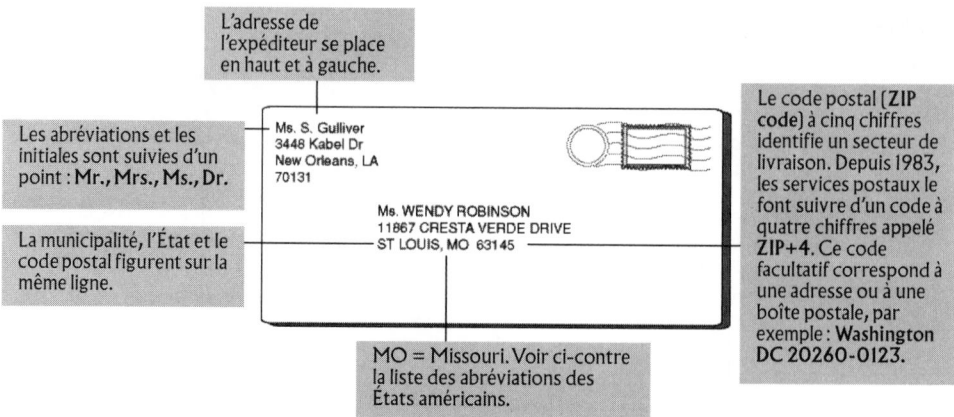

L'adresse de l'expéditeur se place en haut et à gauche.

Les abréviations et les initiales sont suivies d'un point : Mr., Mrs., Ms., Dr.

La municipalité, l'État et le code postal figurent sur la même ligne.

Le code postal (**ZIP code**) à cinq chiffres identifie un secteur de livraison. Depuis 1983, les services postaux le font suivre d'un code à quatre chiffres appelé **ZIP+4**. Ce code facultatif correspond à une adresse ou à une boîte postale, par exemple : **Washington DC 20260-0123.**

Ms. S. Gulliver
3448 Kabel Dr
New Orleans, LA
70131

Ms. WENDY ROBINSON
11867 CRESTA VERDE DRIVE
ST LOUIS, MO 63145

MO = Missouri. Voir ci-contre la liste des abréviations des États américains.

▪ Abréviations utilisées dans les adresses

Les abréviations suivantes s'emploient couramment dans les adresses. Elles peuvent figurer aussi bien dans l'en-tête de la lettre que sur l'enveloppe.

Apt	Apartment	**Ln**	Lane
Av ou **Ave**	Avenue	**Mtn**	Mountain
Blvd	Boulevard	**Pkwy**	Parkway
Cir	Circle	**Pl**	Place
Cres	Crescent	**Plz**	Plaza
Ct	Court	**Rdg**	Ridge
Dr	Drive	**Rd**	Road
Est	Estate	**Rm**	Room
Gdns	Gardens	**Rt**	Route
Grv	Grove	**Sq**	Square
Hts	Heights	**St**	Street
Jct	Junction	**Ter**	Terrace

▪ Abréviations des États américains

AL	Alabama		MT	Montana
AK	Alaska		NE	Nebraska
AZ	Arizona		NV	Nevada
AR	Arkansas		NH	New Hampshire
CA	California		NJ	New Jersey
CO	Colorado		NM	New Mexico
CT	Connecticut		NY	New York
DE	Delaware		NC	North Carolina
DC	District of Columbia		ND	North Dakota
FL	Florida		OH	Ohio
GA	Georgia		OK	Oklahoma
HI	Hawaii		OR	Oregon
ID	Idaho		PA	Pennsylvania
IL	Illinois		RI	Rhode Island
IN	Indiana		SC	South Carolina
IA	Iowa		SD	South Dakota
KS	Kansas		TN	Tennessee
KY	Kentucky		TX	Texas
LA	Louisiana		UT	Utah
ME	Maine		VT	Vermont
MD	Maryland		VA	Virginia
MA	Massachusetts		WA	Washington
MI	Michigan		WV	West Virginia
MN	Minnesota		WI	Wisconsin
MS	Mississippi		WY	Wyoming
MO	Missouri			

Modèles de lettres

Lettre à un ami

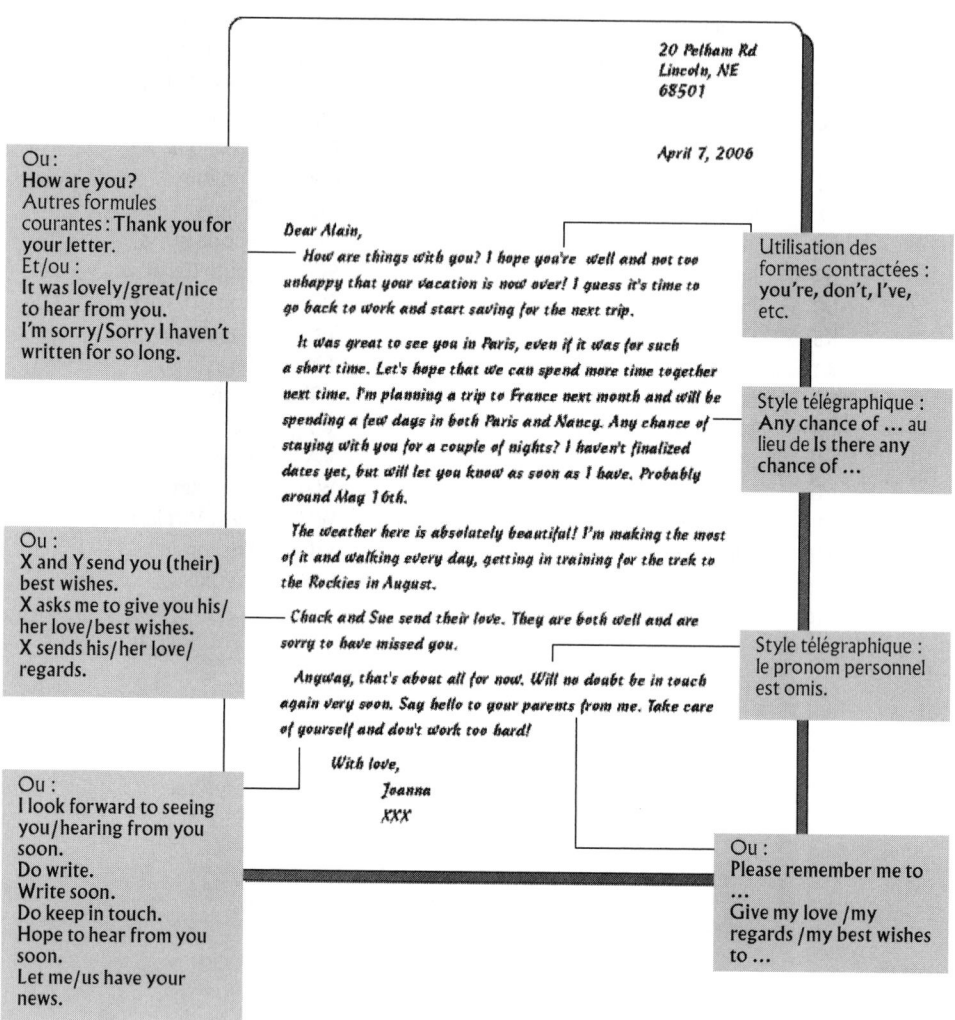

Ou :
How are you?
Autres formules courantes : Thank you for your letter.
Et/ou :
It was lovely/great/nice to hear from you.
I'm sorry/Sorry I haven't written for so long.

Ou :
X and Y send you (their) best wishes.
X asks me to give you his/her love/best wishes.
X sends his/her love/regards.

Ou :
I look forward to seeing you/hearing from you soon.
Do write.
Write soon.
Do keep in touch.
Hope to hear from you soon.
Let me/us have your news.

20 Pelham Rd
Lincoln, NE
68501

April 7, 2006

Dear Alain,

How are things with you? I hope you're well and not too unhappy that your vacation is now over! I guess it's time to go back to work and start saving for the next trip.

It was great to see you in Paris, even if it was for such a short time. Let's hope that we can spend more time together next time. I'm planning a trip to France next month and will be spending a few days in both Paris and Nancy. Any chance of staying with you for a couple of nights? I haven't finalized dates yet, but will let you know as soon as I have. Probably around May 16th.

The weather here is absolutely beautiful! I'm making the most of it and walking every day, getting in training for the trek to the Rockies in August.

Chuck and Sue send their love. They are both well and are sorry to have missed you.

Anyway, that's about all for now. Will no doubt be in touch again very soon. Say hello to your parents from me. Take care of yourself and don't work too hard!

With love,
Joanna
XXX

Utilisation des formes contractées : you're, don't, I've, etc.

Style télégraphique : Any chance of ... au lieu de Is there any chance of ...

Style télégraphique : le pronom personnel est omis.

Ou :
Please remember me to ...
Give my love /my regards /my best wishes to ...

Cartes de vœux

Dans les pays anglo-saxons, les cartes de vœux s'envoient au mois de décembre, avant Noël, et non en janvier comme en France.

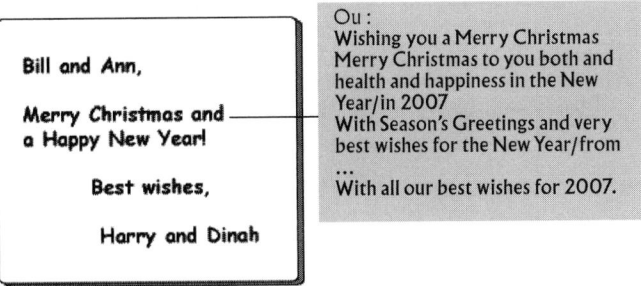

Bill and Ann,

Merry Christmas and a Happy New Year!

Best wishes,

Harry and Dinah

Ou :
Wishing you a Merry Christmas
Merry Christmas to you both and health and happiness in the New Year/in 2007
With Season's Greetings and very best wishes for the New Year/from
...
With all our best wishes for 2007.

- ## Pour souhaiter un anniversaire

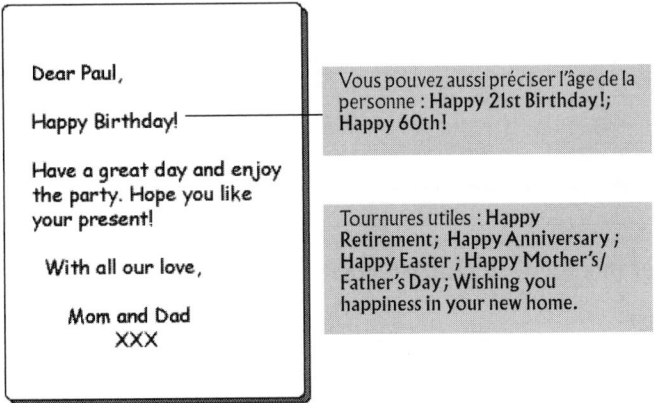

Dear Paul,

Happy Birthday!

Have a great day and enjoy the party. Hope you like your present!

With all our love,

Mom and Dad
XXX

Vous pouvez aussi préciser l'âge de la personne : Happy 21st Birthday!; Happy 60th!

Tournures utiles : Happy Retirement; Happy Anniversary ; Happy Easter ; Happy Mother's/Father's Day ; Wishing you happiness in your new home.

- ## Pour souhaiter bonne chance

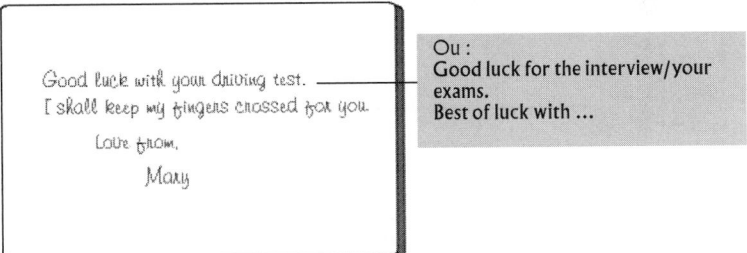

Good luck with your driving test.
I shall keep my fingers crossed for you.
Love from,
Mary

Ou :
Good luck for the interview/your exams.
Best of luck with ...

- ## Pour féliciter

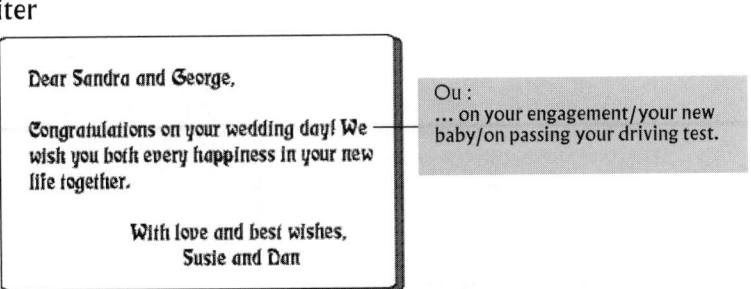

Dear Sandra and George,

Congratulations on your wedding day! We wish you both every happiness in your new life together.

With love and best wishes,
Susie and Dan

Ou :
... on your engagement/your new baby/on passing your driving test.

Invitations et réponses

- ## Carton d'invitation à un mariage

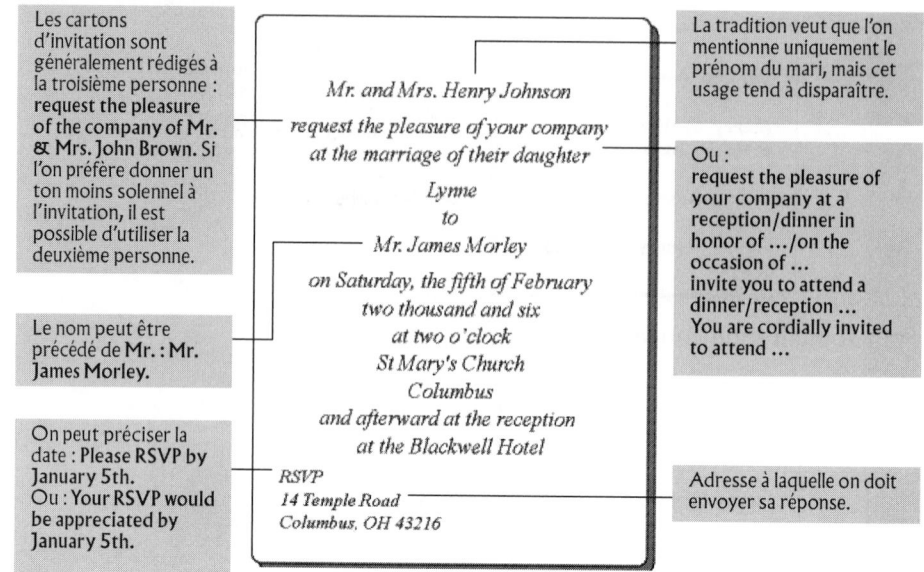

Les cartons d'invitation sont généralement rédigés à la troisième personne : **request the pleasure of the company of Mr. & Mrs. John Brown.** Si l'on préfère donner un ton moins solennel à l'invitation, il est possible d'utiliser la deuxième personne.

Le nom peut être précédé de **Mr. : Mr. James Morley.**

On peut préciser la date : **Please RSVP by January 5th.** Ou : **Your RSVP would be appreciated by January 5th.**

Mr. and Mrs. Henry Johnson
request the pleasure of your company
at the marriage of their daughter
Lynne
to
Mr. James Morley
on Saturday, the fifth of February
two thousand and six
at two o'clock
St Mary's Church
Columbus
and afterward at the reception
at the Blackwell Hotel
RSVP
14 Temple Road
Columbus, OH 43216

La tradition veut que l'on mentionne uniquement le prénom du mari, mais cet usage tend à disparaître.

Ou : **request the pleasure of your company at a reception/dinner in honor of .../on the occasion of ... invite you to attend a dinner/reception ... You are cordially invited to attend ...**

Adresse à laquelle on doit envoyer sa réponse.

- ## Pour accepter une invitation officielle

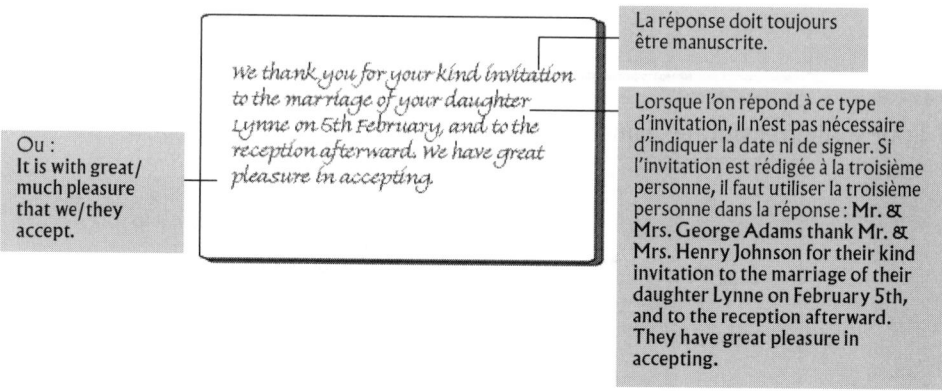

Ou : **It is with great/ much pleasure that we/they accept.**

We thank you for your kind invitation to the marriage of your daughter Lynne on 5th February, and to the reception afterward. We have great pleasure in accepting.

La réponse doit toujours être manuscrite.

Lorsque l'on répond à ce type d'invitation, il n'est pas nécessaire d'indiquer la date ni de signer. Si l'invitation est rédigée à la troisième personne, il faut utiliser la troisième personne dans la réponse : **Mr. & Mrs. George Adams thank Mr. & Mrs. Henry Johnson for their kind invitation to the marriage of their daughter Lynne on February 5th, and to the reception afterward. They have great pleasure in accepting.**

- ## Pour refuser une invitation officielle

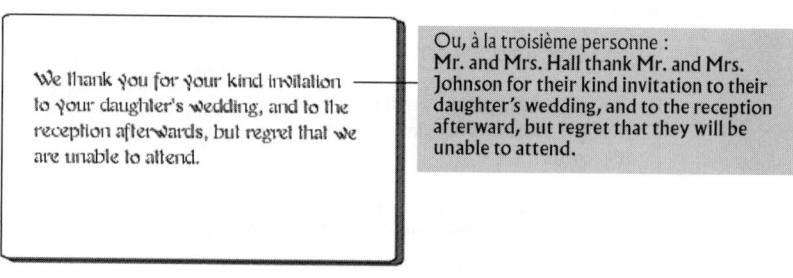

We thank you for your kind invitation to your daughter's wedding, and to the reception afterwards, but regret that we are unable to attend.

Ou, à la troisième personne : **Mr. and Mrs. Hall thank Mr. and Mrs. Johnson for their kind invitation to their daughter's wedding, and to the reception afterward, but regret that they will be unable to attend.**

- ## Carton d'invitation : soirée entre amis

James and Melissa

INVITE YOU TO

a house-warming party

ON: Friday September 13th
AT: 45 Rowan Crescent
FROM: 8pm onward

Please bring a bottle   RSVP

Ou :
We're giving a dinner party/
cocktail party/birthday party
next Friday and hope you will be
able to come.

We are celebrating our
engagement by holding a dinner
dance at the ... on ..., and would
be delighted if you could join us.

I'm having/planning a party —
come along, and bring a friend.

- ## Réponse à une invitation : soirée entre amis

46 Hatton Street
Baltimore, Md
21203

August 23, 2006

Dear James and Melissa,

Thank you so much for the invitation to your house-warming party. I'd love to come. It will be great to see you and, of course, your new home.

If you need any help with food, I'd be only too glad to bring something along, as well as a bottle, of course!

Thanks once again for the kind invitation. I look forward to seeing you.

Love,

Emily

Ou :
I'd love to come to your
party. It was good of
you to invite me.

Thank you for your
invitation to dinner/
for the weekend — I
look forward to it very
much.

Thank you so much for
your invitation, but I'm
afraid I/we won't be
able to come.

I was/We were
delighted to get your
invitation but
unfortunately I/we
can't come.

Remerciements

167 Ecclesall Road
Austin, Tx
78712

May 31st, 2006

Dear Ann and Ralph

Thank you so much for the beautiful crystal decanter and wine glasses you sent us as a wedding present. They will look wonderful on our dinner table and I intend to make good use of them.

I was so glad that you could come to the wedding. I hope you enjoyed it as much as we did. It was quite a hectic day really, but of course a wonderful one! Give my thanks to Tracey for the catering. Everyone said how delicious the food was.

We had a lovely honeymoon and are now busy settling in to our new home. You must come very soon for a meal to try out the glasses.

Many thanks once again!

With much love,

Katie

XXX

Ou :
bought us

Ou :
We were both delighted
you could come... ;
It was really nice to see
you at the wedding.

Ou :
I can't thank you
enough for...
Thank you very much
for ...

Ou :
Say thank you to ...

Réservations

Les réservations de billets ou de chambres d'hôtel se font de plus en plus par Internet et par courrier électronique. Pour toute réservation faite par téléphone, il est recommandé de confirmer par écrit.

▪ Lettre de réservation

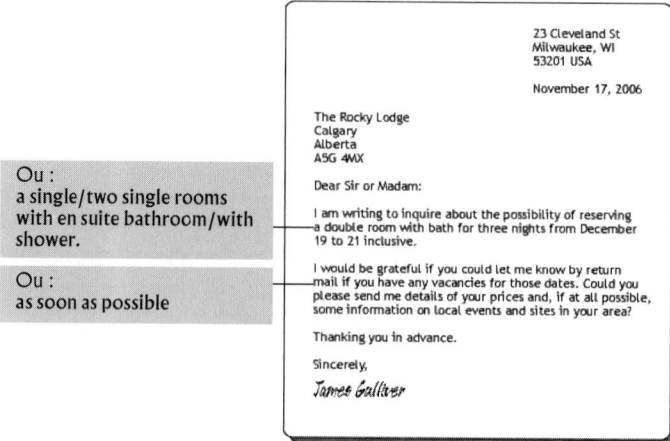

Ou :
a single/two single rooms with en suite bathroom/with shower.

Ou :
as soon as possible

23 Cleveland St
Milwaukee, WI
53201 USA

November 17, 2006

The Rocky Lodge
Calgary
Alberta
A5G 4MX

Dear Sir or Madam:

I am writing to inquire about the possibility of reserving a double room with bath for three nights from December 19 to 21 inclusive.

I would be grateful if you could let me know by return mail if you have any vacancies for those dates. Could you please send me details of your prices and, if at all possible, some information on local events and sites in your area?

Thanking you in advance.

Sincerely,

James Gulliver

▪ Pour confirmer une réservation

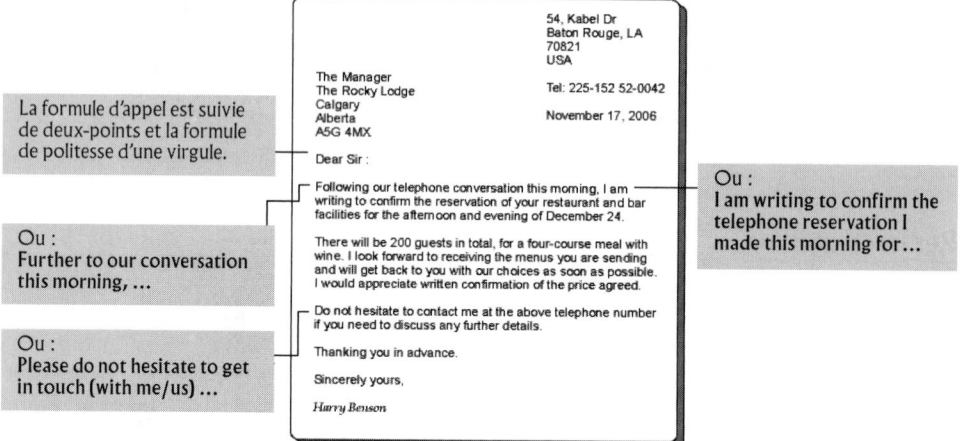

La formule d'appel est suivie de deux-points et la formule de politesse d'une virgule.

Ou :
Further to our conversation this morning, ...

Ou :
Please do not hesitate to get in touch (with me/us) ...

54, Kabel Dr
Baton Rouge, LA
70821
USA

The Manager
The Rocky Lodge
Calgary
Alberta
A5G 4MX

Tel: 225-152 52-0042

November 17, 2006

Dear Sir :

Following our telephone conversation this morning, I am writing to confirm the reservation of your restaurant and bar facilities for the afternoon and evening of December 24.

There will be 200 guests in total, for a four-course meal with wine. I look forward to receiving the menus you are sending and will get back to you with our choices as soon as possible. I would appreciate written confirmation of the price agreed.

Do not hesitate to contact me at the above telephone number if you need to discuss any further details.

Thanking you in advance.

Sincerely yours,

Harry Benson

Ou :
I am writing to confirm the telephone reservation I made this morning for...

▪ Pour annuler une réservation

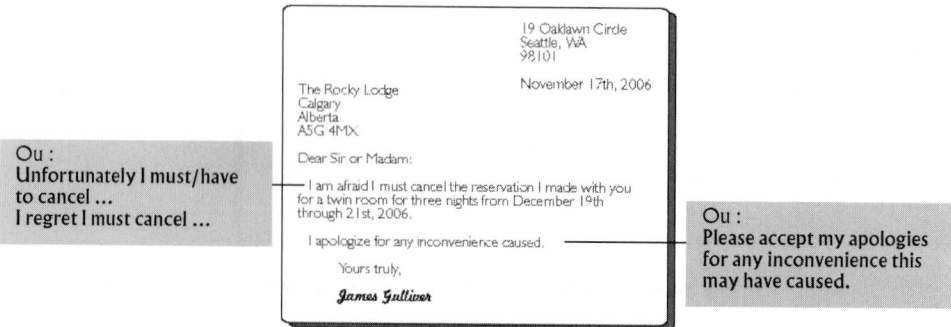

Ou :
Unfortunately I must/have to cancel ...
I regret I must cancel ...

19 Oaklawn Circle
Seattle, WA
98101

November 17th, 2006

The Rocky Lodge
Calgary
Alberta
A5G 4MX

Dear Sir or Madam:

I am afraid I must cancel the reservation I made with you for a twin room for three nights from December 19th through 21st, 2006.

I apologize for any inconvenience caused.

Yours truly,

James Gulliver

Ou :
Please accept my apologies for any inconvenience this may have caused.

Demande de renseignements

30501 Ocean Drive
Santa Barbara, CA
92677
USA

Tourist Information   February 27, 2006
Office12
Stadium Road
Cardiff
South Wales
CF35 5HH

Dear Sir or Madam:

I am planning a trip to South Wales in May this year and
would be grateful if you would send me information about
different types of accommodations available. Could you
recommend a reasonable hotel or bed and breakfast?

I would also appreciate information on car rentals and, if
possible, on events in the area in May.

Thanking you in advance for your help, I look forward to
hearing from you.

Sincerely,

Michael Douglas

Michael S. Douglas

Ou :
I am writing to ask
whether ...
I wish to know whether
...
Could you please send
me/advise me/let me
know ...
Would you kindly send
me/inform me ....

Ou :
Thanking you in
anticipation, ...
Thank you in advance
for your help, ...

Réclamations

Si vous ne connaissez
pas le nom du
destinataire, adressez
votre lettre au
**Customer Services
Manager.** Pour les
plus petites
entreprises ou les
entreprises familiales,
vous pouvez adresser
votre lettre au
directeur : **The
Manager.**

Ou :
I wish to complain
about...
I wish to complain
most strongly
about...

Ou :
The service I received
was extremely
unsatisfactory...
I am extremely
unhappy with the
service I received...

12 Reed Ave
Tuscaloosa, AL
35401

The Customer Services Manager
Goldenrod Bus Company
Montgomery, AL
36104

August 4th, 2006

Dear Sir or Madam

I am writing to complain about the inconvenience caused to me
last week by your company's inadequate performance.

I was traveling on the 9.30 bus from Montgomery to Mobile on
August 1. The bus was due to arrive in Mobile at midday. It did
not arrive until 5 o'clock in the afternoon, making me miss an
important meeting. Added to this inconvenience, there were no
announcements informing passengers of why this was happening.

I am more than disappointed with the service I received and feel
I am entitled to compensation that reflects adequately the
inconvenience suffered.

I look forward to receiving your response within the next 14 days.

Respectfully yours,

G. Roberts

Mr. G. Roberts

Ou :
I trust/hope that you will
see your way to offering
adequate compensation
for the inconvenience
suffered/caused.

Ou :
I look forward to
receiving a reasonable
offer of compensation.

Il est recommandé de
préciser le délai dans
lequel vous souhaitez
obtenir une réponse.

La correspondance commerciale

Pour prendre rendez-vous

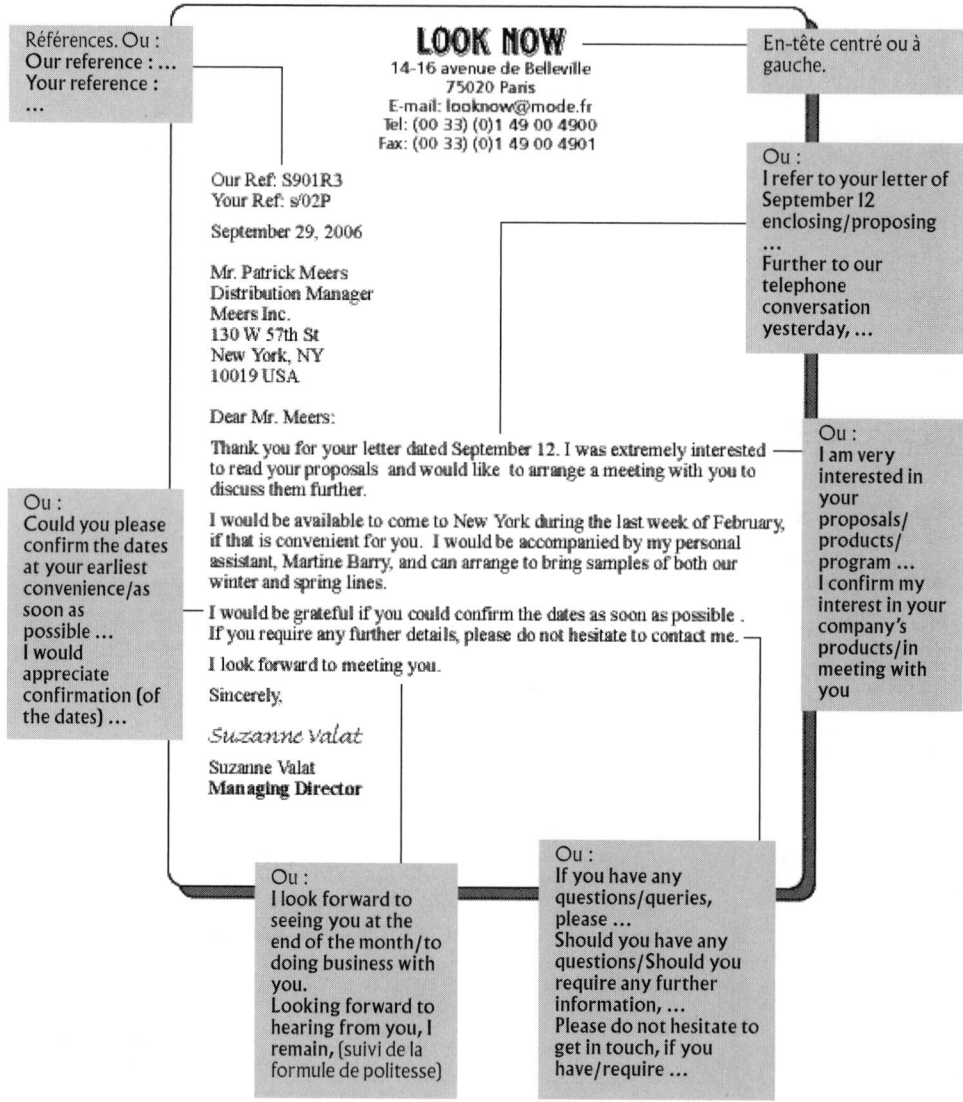

Références. Ou :
Our reference : ...
Your reference :
...

LOOK NOW
14-16 avenue de Belleville
75020 Paris
E-mail: looknow@mode.fr
Tel: (00 33) (0)1 49 00 4900
Fax: (00 33) (0)1 49 00 4901

En-tête centré ou à gauche.

Our Ref: S901R3
Your Ref: s/02P

September 29, 2006

Mr. Patrick Meers
Distribution Manager
Meers Inc.
130 W 57th St
New York, NY
10019 USA

Dear Mr. Meers:

Thank you for your letter dated September 12. I was extremely interested to read your proposals and would like to arrange a meeting with you to discuss them further.

I would be available to come to New York during the last week of February, if that is convenient for you. I would be accompanied by my personal assistant, Martine Barry, and can arrange to bring samples of both our winter and spring lines.

I would be grateful if you could confirm the dates as soon as possible. If you require any further details, please do not hesitate to contact me.

I look forward to meeting you.

Sincerely,

Suzanne Valat

Suzanne Valat
Managing Director

Ou :
I refer to your letter of September 12 enclosing/proposing
...
Further to our telephone conversation yesterday, ...

Ou :
I am very interested in your proposals/products/program ...
I confirm my interest in your company's products/in meeting with you

Ou :
Could you please confirm the dates at your earliest convenience/as soon as possible ...
I would appreciate confirmation (of the dates) ...

Ou :
I look forward to seeing you at the end of the month/to doing business with you.
Looking forward to hearing from you, I remain, (suivi de la formule de politesse)

Ou :
If you have any questions/queries, please ...
Should you have any questions/Should you require any further information, ...
Please do not hesitate to get in touch, if you have/require ...

Réponse à une demande de renseignements

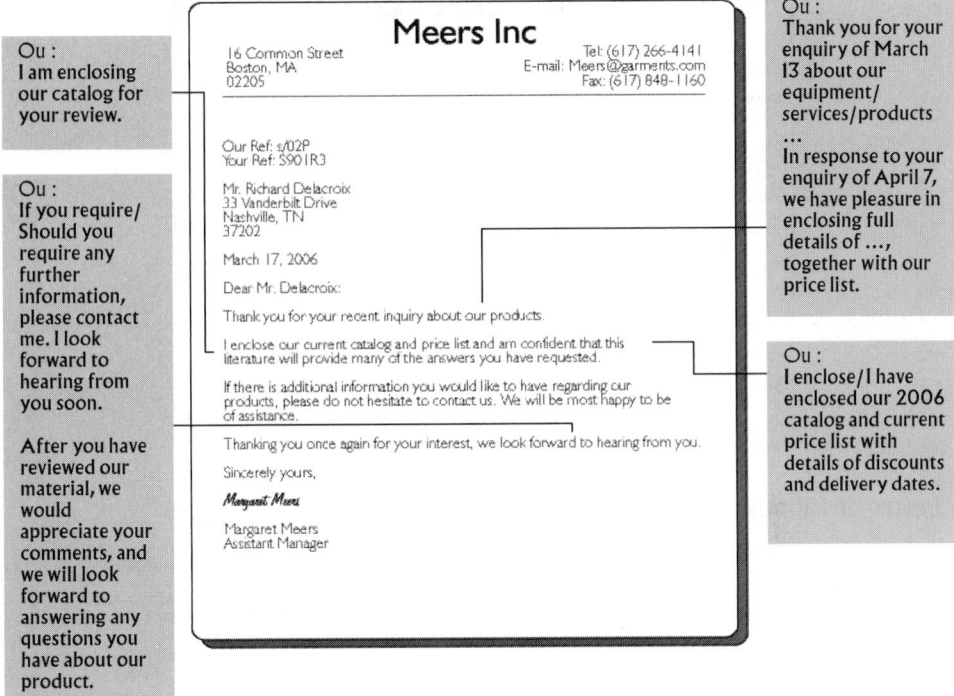

Ou :
I am enclosing our catalog for your review.

Ou :
If you require/ Should you require any further information, please contact me. I look forward to hearing from you soon.

After you have reviewed our material, we would appreciate your comments, and we will look forward to answering any questions you have about our product.

Meers Inc

16 Common Street
Boston, MA
02205

Tel: (617) 266-4141
E-mail: Meers@garments.com
Fax: (617) 848-1160

Our Ref: s/02P
Your Ref: S901R3

Mr. Richard Delacroix
33 Vanderbilt Drive
Nashville, TN
37202

March 17, 2006

Dear Mr. Delacroix:

Thank you for your recent inquiry about our products.

I enclose our current catalog and price list and am confident that this literature will provide many of the answers you have requested.

If there is additional information you would like to have regarding our products, please do not hesitate to contact us. We will be most happy to be of assistance.

Thanking you once again for your interest, we look forward to hearing from you.

Sincerely yours,

Margaret Meers

Margaret Meers
Assistant Manager

Ou :
Thank you for your enquiry of March 13 about our equipment/ services/products
...
In response to your enquiry of April 7, we have pleasure in enclosing full details of ..., together with our price list.

Ou :
I enclose/I have enclosed our 2006 catalog and current price list with details of discounts and delivery dates.

Commande

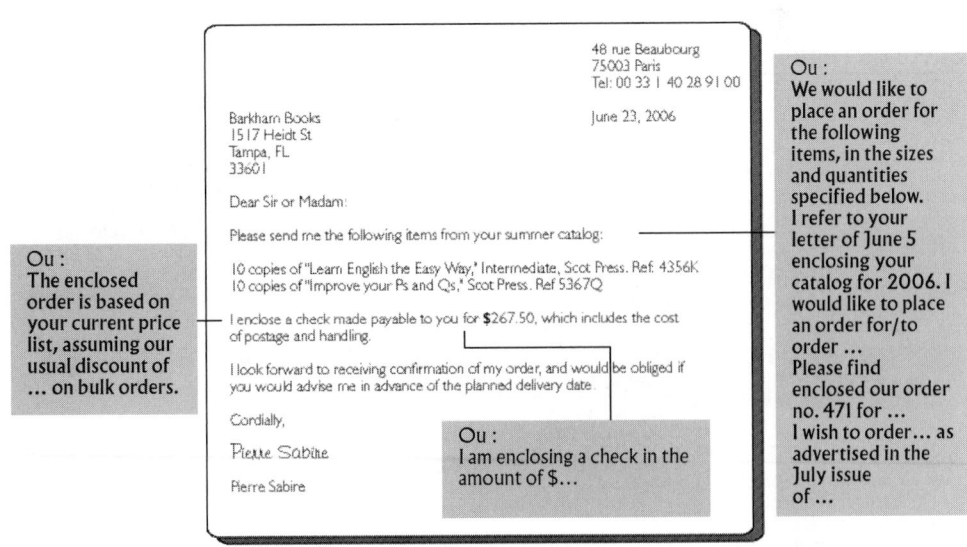

48 rue Beaubourg
75003 Paris
Tel: 00 33 1 40 28 91 00

Barkharn Books
1517 Heidt St
Tampa, FL
33601

June 23, 2006

Dear Sir or Madam:

Please send me the following items from your summer catalog:

10 copies of "Learn English the Easy Way," Intermediate, Scot Press. Ref. 4356K
10 copies of "Improve your Ps and Qs," Scot Press. Ref 5367Q

I enclose a check made payable to you for $267.50, which includes the cost of postage and handling.

I look forward to receiving confirmation of my order, and would be obliged if you would advise me in advance of the planned delivery date.

Cordially,

Pierre Sabire

Pierre Sabire

Ou :
The enclosed order is based on your current price list, assuming our usual discount of ... on bulk orders.

Ou :
I am enclosing a check in the amount of $...

Ou :
We would like to place an order for the following items, in the sizes and quantities specified below.
I refer to your letter of June 5 enclosing your catalog for 2006. I would like to place an order for/to order ...
Please find enclosed our order no. 471 for ...
I wish to order... as advertised in the July issue of ...

Facture

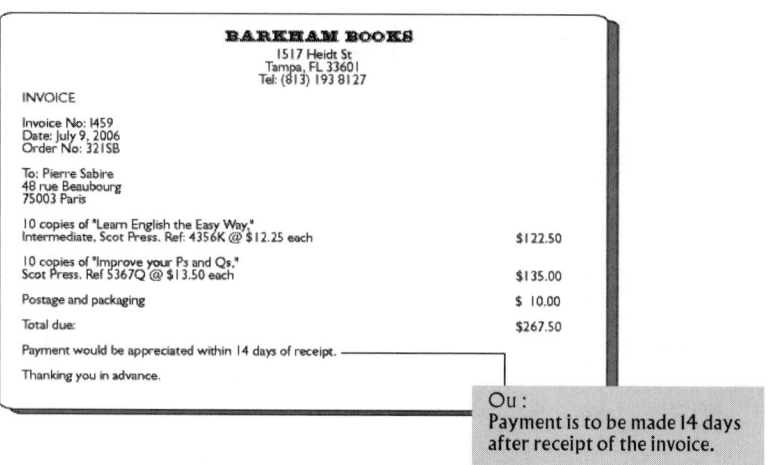

INVOICE

Invoice No: I459
Date: July 9, 2006
Order No: 321SB

To: Pierre Sabire
48 rue Beaubourg
75003 Paris

10 copies of "Learn English the Easy Way," Intermediate, Scot Press. Ref: 4356K @ $12.25 each	$122.50
10 copies of "Improve your Ps and Qs," Scot Press. Ref 5367Q @ $13.50 each	$135.00
Postage and packaging	$ 10.00
Total due:	$267.50

Payment would be appreciated within 14 days of receipt.

Thanking you in advance.

Ou :
Payment is to be made 14 days after receipt of the invoice.

■ Lettre de rappel

Our records indicate that payment on your account is overdue in the amount of $ ... If the amount has already been paid, please disregard this notice. If you have not yet mailed your payment, please use the enclosed envelope to send payment in full.

Thank you in advance for your anticipated cooperation in this matter.

■ Deuxième rappel

On July 12, 2006 we notified you of your overdue account for order no. ...

To date we still have not received payment for the above order.

Please give this matter your most urgent attention. Payment must be made within the next ten days.

Envoi du règlement

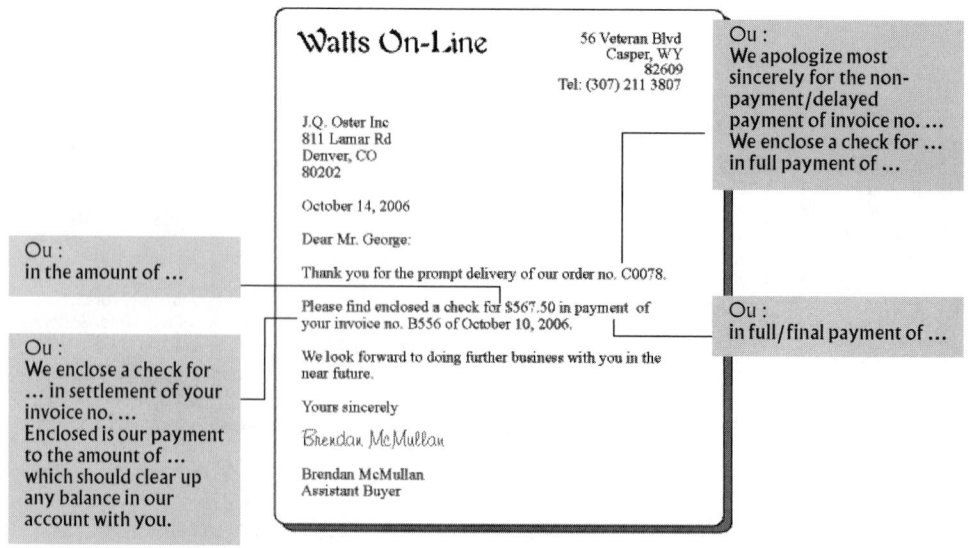

Watts On-Line

56 Veteran Blvd
Casper, WY
82609
Tel: (307) 211 3807

J.Q. Oster Inc
811 Lamar Rd
Denver, CO
80202

October 14, 2006

Dear Mr. George:

Thank you for the prompt delivery of our order no. C0078.

Please find enclosed a check for $567.50 in payment of your invoice no. B556 of October 10, 2006.

We look forward to doing further business with you in the near future.

Yours sincerely

Brendan McMullan

Brendan McMullan
Assistant Buyer

Ou :
We apologize most sincerely for the non-payment/delayed payment of invoice no. ...
We enclose a check for ... in full payment of ...

Ou :
in the amount of ...

Ou :
We enclose a check for ... in settlement of your invoice no. ...
Enclosed is our payment to the amount of ... which should clear up any balance in our account with you.

Ou :
in full/final payment of ...

Recherche d'emploi

Lettre de motivation

Dans les pays anglo-saxons, la lettre de candidature doit toujours être dactylographiée, sauf si l'annonce spécifie qu'il faut envoyer une lettre manuscrite.

- **Demande de stage**

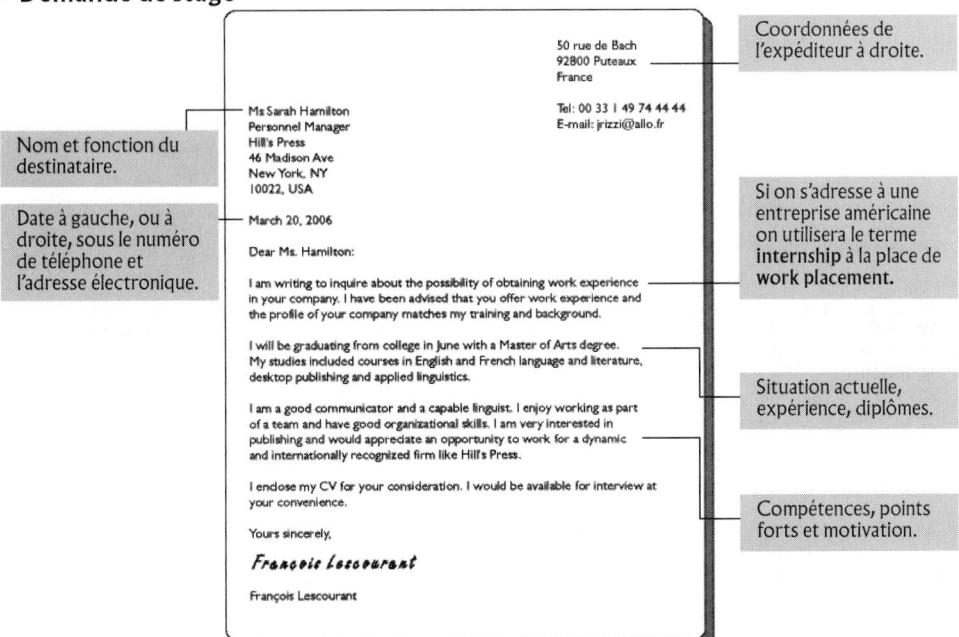

Coordonnées de l'expéditeur à droite.

Nom et fonction du destinataire.

Date à gauche, ou à droite, sous le numéro de téléphone et l'adresse électronique.

Si on s'adresse à une entreprise américaine on utilisera le terme **internship** à la place de **work placement.**

Situation actuelle, expérience, diplômes.

Compétences, points forts et motivation.

- **Candidature spontanée**

Si vous connaissez quelqu'un travaillant déjà dans l'entreprise, signalez-le.

Ou :
As you will note from the enclosed CV, I have majored in physics and have participated in significant research.

Ou :
at your convenience. I would like to learn more about ..., and I will contact your office early next week to arrange an appointment at your convenience.

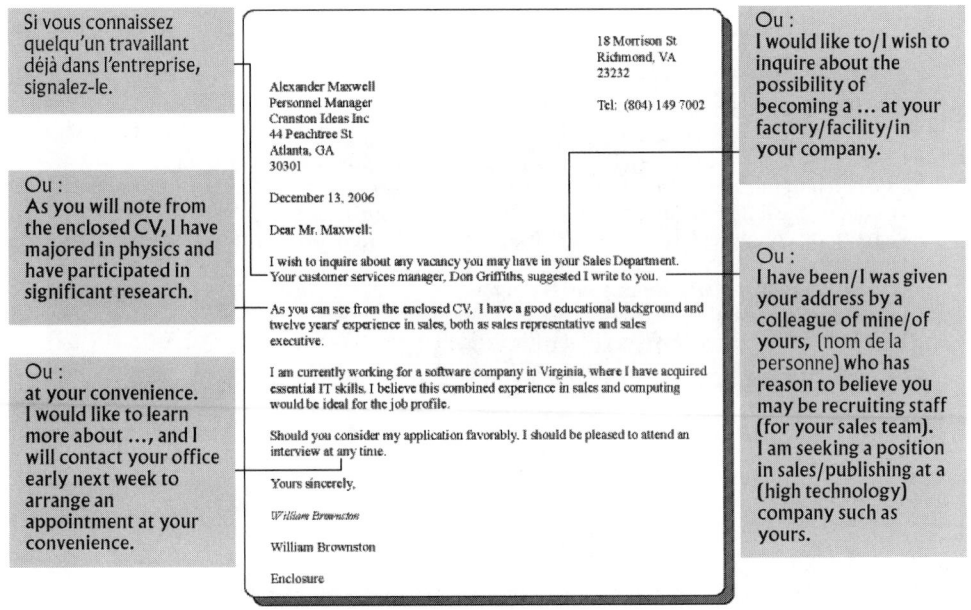

Ou :
I would like to/I wish to inquire about the possibility of becoming a ... at your factory/facility/in your company.

Ou :
I have been/I was given your address by a colleague of mine/of yours, (nom de la personne) who has reason to believe you may be recruiting staff (for your sales team). I am seeking a position in sales/publishing at a (high technology) company such as yours.

Réponse à une annonce

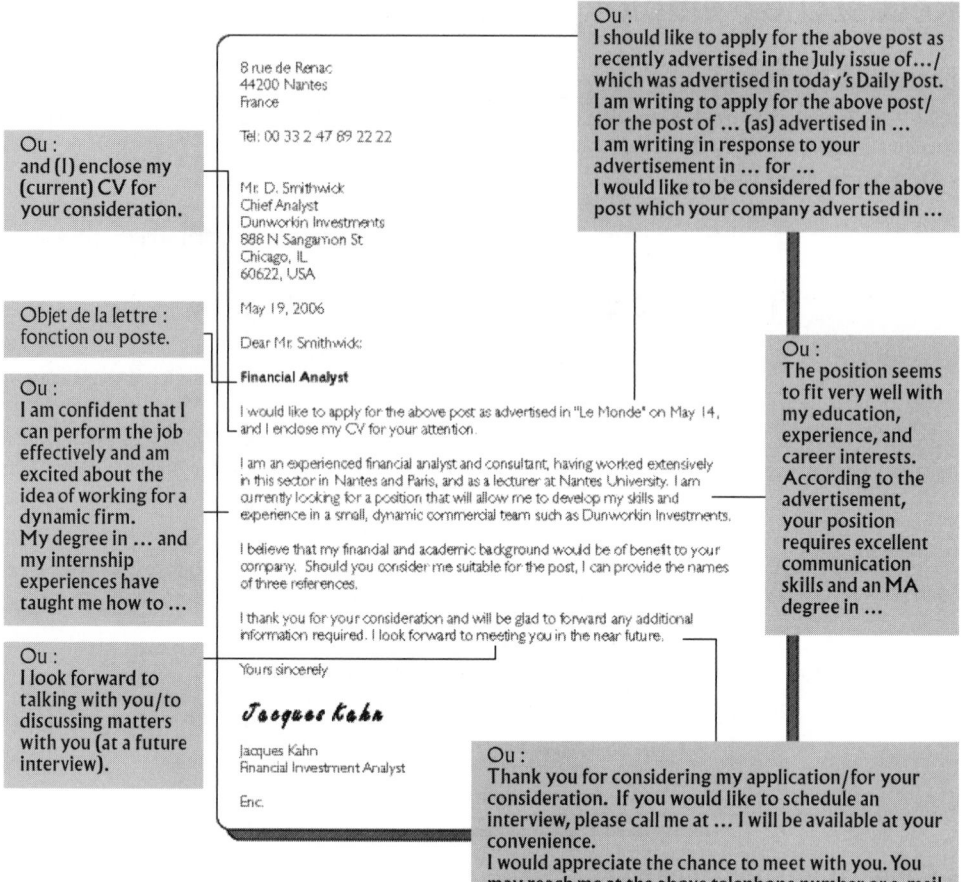

Ou :
I should like to apply for the above post as recently advertised in the July issue of.../ which was advertised in today's Daily Post.
I am writing to apply for the above post/ for the post of ... (as) advertised in ...
I am writing in response to your advertisement in ... for ...
I would like to be considered for the above post which your company advertised in ...

Ou :
and (I) enclose my (current) CV for your consideration.

8 rue de Renac
44200 Nantes
France

Tel: 00 33 2 47 89 22 22

Mr. D. Smithwick
Chief Analyst
Dunworkin Investments
888 N Sangamon St
Chicago, IL
60622, USA

May 19, 2006

Dear Mr. Smithwick:

Objet de la lettre : fonction ou poste.

Financial Analyst

I would like to apply for the above post as advertised in "Le Monde" on May 14, and I enclose my CV for your attention.

Ou :
I am confident that I can perform the job effectively and am excited about the idea of working for a dynamic firm.
My degree in ... and my internship experiences have taught me how to ...

I am an experienced financial analyst and consultant, having worked extensively in this sector in Nantes and Paris, and as a lecturer at Nantes University. I am currently looking for a position that will allow me to develop my skills and experience in a small, dynamic commercial team such as Dunworkin Investments.

I believe that my financial and academic background would be of benefit to your company. Should you consider me suitable for the post, I can provide the names of three references.

I thank you for your consideration and will be glad to forward any additional information required. I look forward to meeting you in the near future.

Ou :
I look forward to talking with you/to discussing matters with you (at a future interview).

Yours sincerely

Jacques Kahn

Jacques Kahn
Financial Investment Analyst

Enc.

Ou :
The position seems to fit very well with my education, experience, and career interests. According to the advertisement, your position requires excellent communication skills and an MA degree in ...

Ou :
Thank you for considering my application/for your consideration. If you would like to schedule an interview, please call me at ... I will be available at your convenience.
I would appreciate the chance to meet with you. You may reach me at the above telephone number or e-mail address.

Tournures utiles :

I know how to/I can operate a cash register/a computer/power equipment
I am computer literate/a good communicator/a good organizer
I am a capable linguist/can speak fluent English and German
I have good computer/IT/language/editing/communication/organizational skills
I can learn new tasks and enjoy/can accept a challenge
I enjoy working/can work with a variety of people
I work well in a team, and can also work under pressure
I perform well under stress/am good with difficult customers
I can handle multiple tasks simultaneously

Curriculum vitae

- **Diplômé américain ayant une première expérience**

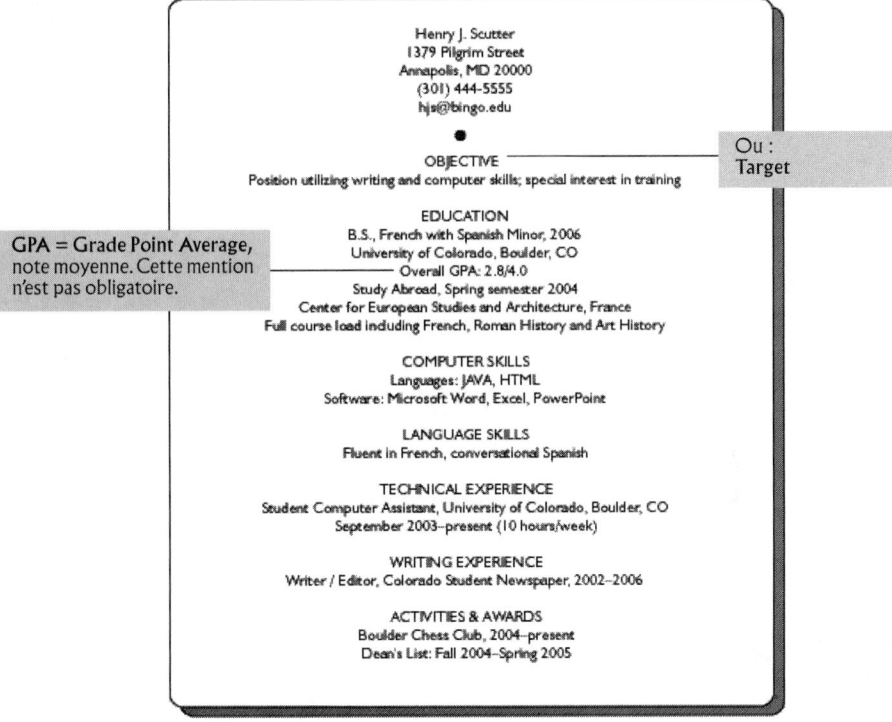

Ou :
Target

GPA = Grade Point Average, note moyenne. Cette mention n'est pas obligatoire.

- **Cadre américain**

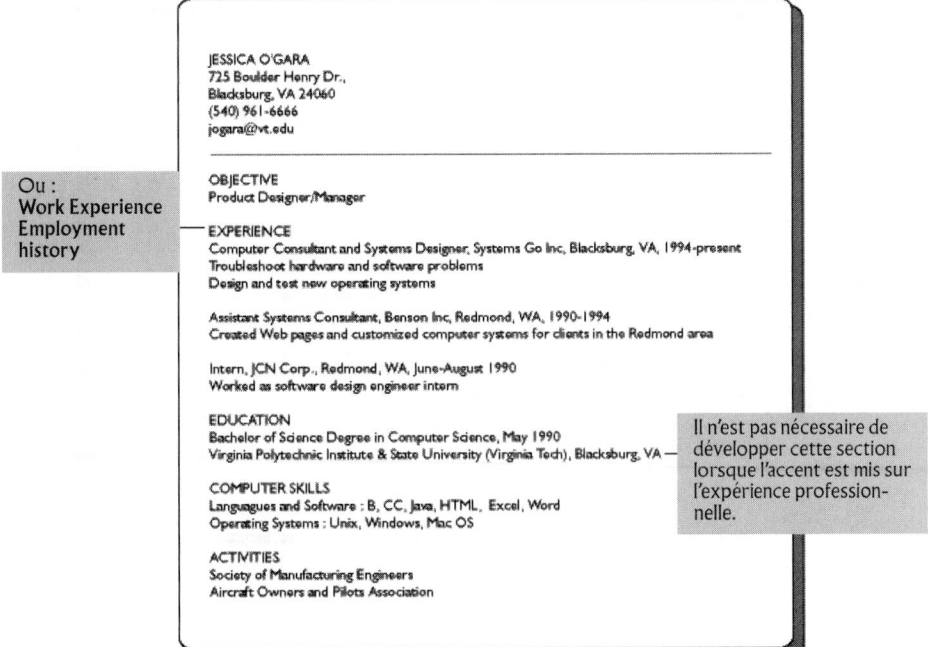

Ou :
Work Experience
Employment history

Il n'est pas nécessaire de développer cette section lorsque l'accent est mis sur l'expérience professionnelle.

▪ Diplômé français ayant une première expérience

Isabelle Murat
40, impasse de la Colline
75003 Paris
Tel: (00 33) (0)1 40 30 40 40
E-mail: imurat@ubet.fr

| *Nationality* | French |
| *Date of Birth* | 13/2/1980 |

Professional Experience

April/May 2006	Three-month placement at Cabinet Desmoulin, Paris
	Customer Services
Summer 2005	Organizer in school summer camp, Port-de-Bouc

Education

2004–2006	Ecole Technique Supérieure, Bordeaux
	Three-year diploma course in Civil Engineering
2003–2004	Baccalauréat S (equivalent high school) in: Maths, Physics, Chemistry,
	Biology, French, English, Geography, History

| *Languages* | French, English (fluent) |
| | German, Greek (basic) |

| *Interests* | Horseback-riding, mountaineering |
| | Opera singing |

Vous n'êtes pas obligé de préciser votre nationalité ou votre âge. Ces informations, tout comme la situation de famille, sont souvent omises.

▪ Cadre français

Laurent Marie
25, rue des Arquebusiers
76000 Rouen

Tel: 02 24 24 24 45 73
E-mail: mariel@battisto.com.fr

Human Resources Consultant

Work Experience

1997–present	Human Resources Consultant, Cabinet Battisto-Langlade, Rouen
	Advising companies on accounting, recruitment strategies
1993–1996	Personnel Manager, Conseil général, Le Havre
	Recruiting, planning of training programs, staff follow-up
1991–1992	Assistant to Personnel Manager, Société Pierre et Fils, Le Havre

Education

1989	Master of Business Administration, Boston University
1987–1988	DEA 'Langage et Médias' - Paris X
1986	Master's Degree in History - Paris IV
1982	Baccalauréat (equivalent high school), specializing in Math,
	Académie de Paris.

Other Experience

Year spent in Africa (1990–91) as part of a mission with the voluntary medical aid organization,
"Médecins sans frontières"
Member of a voluntary association promoting adult literacy

| *Languages* | Fluent English and Spanish |

| *Computer Skills* | Mac OS, Word, Excel |

La télécopie

Dans une entreprise

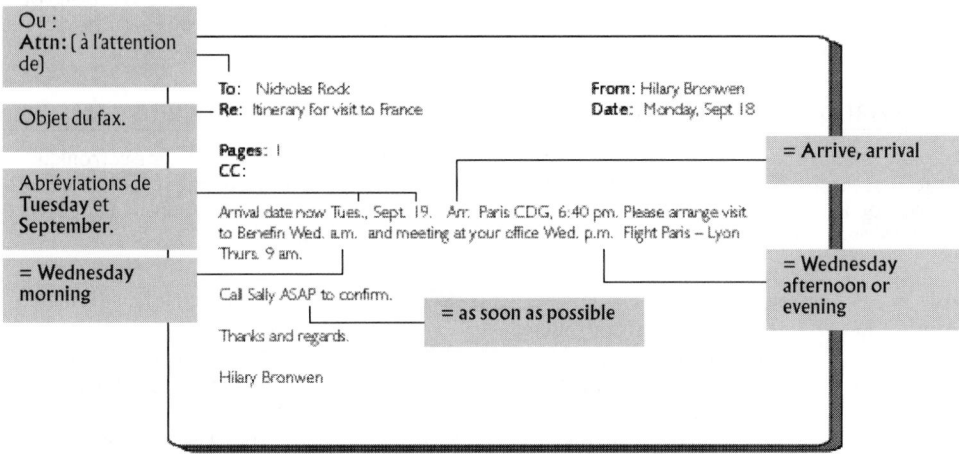

Ou :
Attn: (à l'attention de)

Objet du fax.

Abréviations de Tuesday et September.

= Wednesday morning

To: Nicholas Rock
Re: Itinerary for visit to France
From: Hilary Bronwen
Date: Monday, Sept 18

Pages: 1
CC:

= Arrive, arrival

Arrival date now Tues., Sept. 19. Arr. Paris CDG, 6:40 pm. Please arrange visit to Benefin Wed. a.m. and meeting at your office Wed. p.m. Flight Paris – Lyon Thurs. 9 am.

Call Sally ASAP to confirm.

= as soon as possible

= Wednesday afternoon or evening

Thanks and regards.

Hilary Bronwen

Pour confirmer une réservation

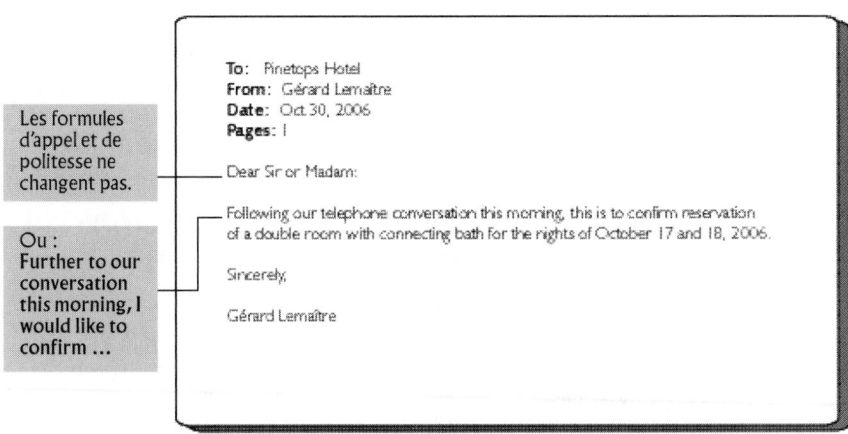

Les formules d'appel et de politesse ne changent pas.

Ou :
Further to our conversation this morning, I would like to confirm ...

To: Pinetops Hotel
From: Gérard Lemaître
Date: Oct 30, 2006
Pages: 1

Dear Sir or Madam:

Following our telephone conversation this morning, this is to confirm reservation of a double room with connecting bath for the nights of October 17 and 18, 2006.

Sincerely,

Gérard Lemaître

Le courrier électronique

Le courrier électronique étant un moyen de communication rapide, le style des messages est souvent familier et télégraphique et l'emploi des abréviations et des acronymes est très courant. Selon la netiquette, ou code de conduite sur le réseau, il est déconseillé d'écrire un message tout en majuscules car cela pourrait être interprété comme un signe de mauvaise humeur.

Les formules d'appel traditionnelles (**Dear...**) sont généralement omises. Si vous connaissez bien votre correspondant, vous pouvez commencer par une formule familière telle que **Hello** ou **Hi**, suivie du prénom de la personne.

Abréviations utilisées dans le courrier électronique et les forums

Les abréviations et acronymes qui suivent sont couramment employés dans le courrier électronique et les forums de discussion. Il est cependant conseillé de ne les utiliser que lorsque l'on est sûr que le destinataire connaît leur signification. Les abréviations suivies de la mention *Fam* appartiennent à un registre plus familier et doivent être réservées à une correspondance plus relâchée.

Adv	advice (conseil)	**ISTM** *Fam*	it seems to me (il me semble que)
AFAICT *Fam*	as far as I can tell (pour autant que je sache)	**ITRO** *Fam*	in the region of (environ)
AFAIK *Fam*	as far as I know (pour autant que je sache)	**LOL** *Fam*	laughing out loud (mort de rire)
AFK	away from keyboard (indique que l'on va quitter son poste)	**NRN** *Fam*	no reply necessasry (réponse facultative)
AIUI *Fam*	as I understand (si j'ai bien compris)	**NW!** *Fam*	no way! (sûrement pas!)
ASL *Fam*	age/sex/location (âge/sexe/ lieu de résidence)	**OMG!** *Fam*	oh my God! (mon Dieu!, j'y crois pas!)
B4 *Fam*	before (avant)	**OTOH** *Fam*	on the other hand (d'un autre côté)
BAK	back at keyboard (de retour devant l'écran)	**OTT** *Fam*	over the top (excessif)
BBL *Fam*	be back later (je reviens)	**PD**	public domain (domaine public)
BTW *Fam*	by the way (à propos)	**POV**	point of view (point de vue)
cld	could	**prhps**	perhaps (peut-être)
Doc	document	**ROFL** *Fam*	rolling on the floor laughing (mort de rire (à s'en rouler par terre))
EOF	end of file (fin de fichier)		
F2F *Fam*	face-to-face (en face, face à face)	**RTFM** *très Fam*	read the f***ing manual (regarde dans le manuel, nom de Dieu!)
FOC	free of charge (gratuit, gratuitement)		
Foll	following, to follow (suivant, à suivre)	**RUOK** *Fam*	are you OK? (ça va?)
		TIA *Fam*	thanks in advance (merci d'avance)
FYI	for your information (pour ton information)	**TNX** *Fam*	thanks (merci)
HTH *Fam*	hope this *or* that helps (j'espère que cela te sera utile)	**TTYL** *Fam*	talk to you later (à plus tard)
		TVM *Fam*	thanks very much (merci beaucoup)
IIRC *Fam*	if I recall correctly (si mes souvenirs sont bons)		
IMO, IMHO *Fam*	in my (humble) opinion (à mon (humble) avis)	**VR**	virtual reality (réalité virtuelle)
		WRT *Fam*	with regard to (en ce qui concerne)
IOW *Fam*	in other words (autrement dit)	**urgt**	**urgent**

Message interne

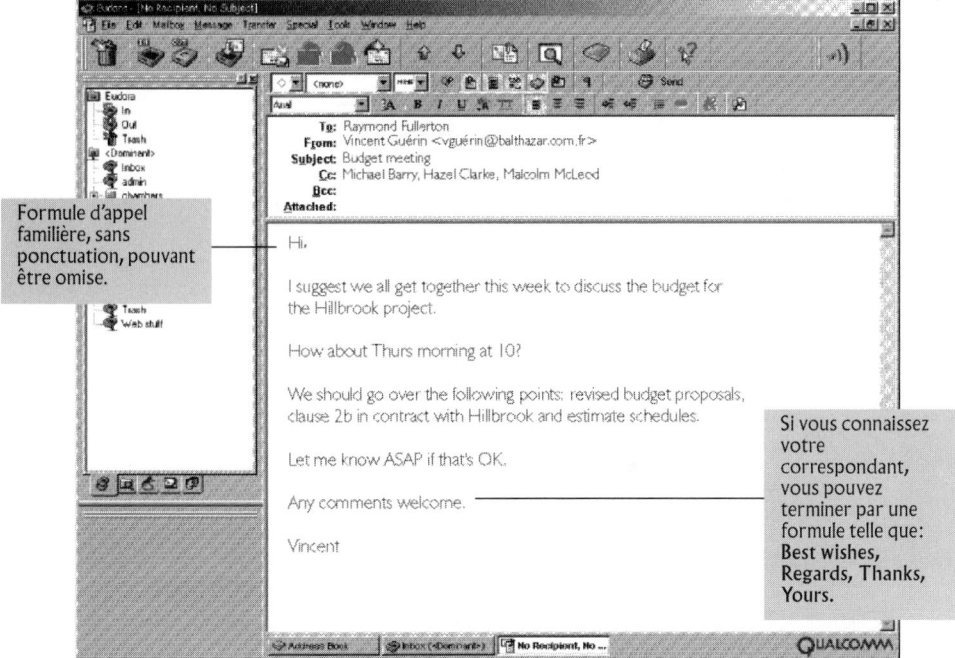

Formule d'appel familière, sans ponctuation, pouvant être omise.

Si vous connaissez votre correspondant, vous pouvez terminer par une formule telle que: Best wishes, Regards, Thanks, Yours.

Message d'une entreprise à une autre

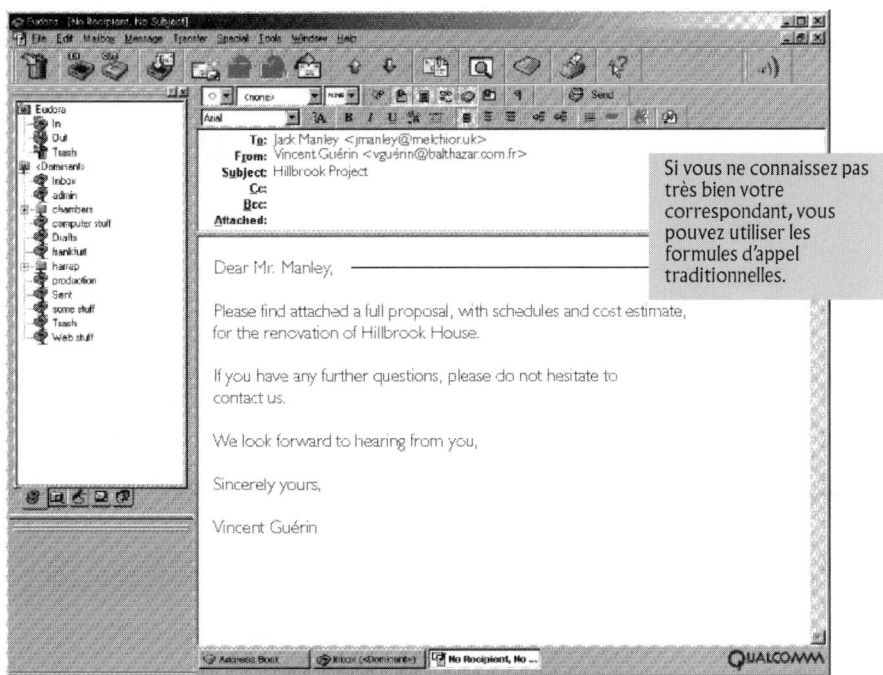

Si vous ne connaissez pas très bien votre correspondant, vous pouvez utiliser les formules d'appel traditionnelles.

Les petites annonces

Emploi

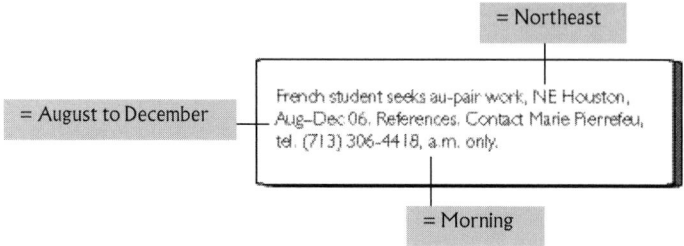

= Northeast

= August to December

French student seeks au-pair work, NE Houston, Aug–Dec 06. References. Contact Marie Pierrefeu, tel. (713) 306-4418, a.m. only.

= Morning

= Part time

= Including, inclusive of

= Male or Female

= Please

Sales Assistant
M/F, good presentation, French-speaking, at least 1 yr experience preferred. PT, incl. Sats. Sal. negotiable. Pls send CV to Personnel Manager, Stanhopes, 14 Lincoln Rd, Newport.

= Year

= Salary

= Saturdays

Vente

DRYER: Kenmore electric. Good condition, $95. Call 364-9999, between 6–8p.m.

= inch

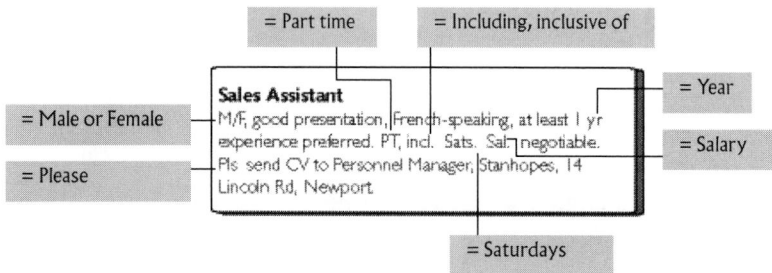

DVD PLAYER, VCR, and TV 14" screen. As new. $590 OBO. 530-7949 leave msg.

= or best offer

= Message

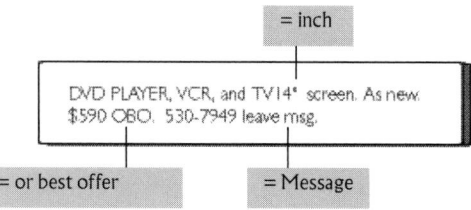

Olympus, super VHS camera, high resolution, digital effects, auto/manual focusing, etc., orig. $2500, asking $995. 4383 Powell St. 121-7409

= Original price, originally

Immobilier

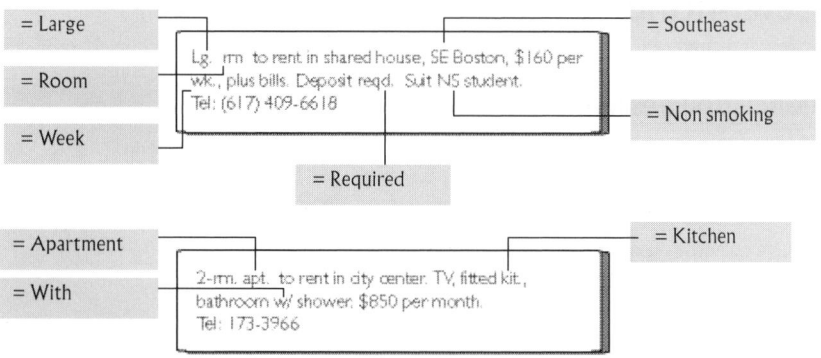

= Large

= Room

= Week

= Southeast

= Non smoking

= Required

Lg. rm to rent in shared house, SE Boston, $160 per wk., plus bills. Deposit reqd. Suit NS student.
Tel: (617) 409-6618

= Apartment

= With

= Kitchen

2-rm. apt. to rent in city center. TV, fitted kit., bathroom w/ shower. $850 per month.
Tel: 173-3966

Rencontres

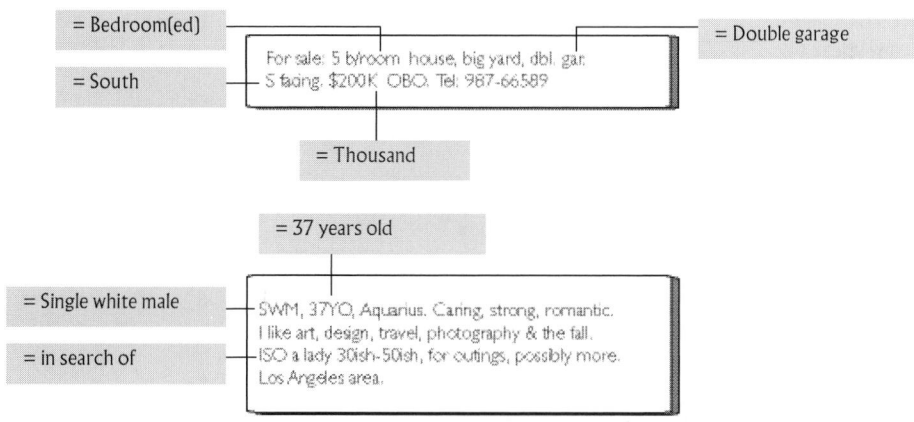

= Bedroom(ed)

= South

= Double garage

= Thousand

For sale: 5 b/room house, big yard, dbl. gar.
S facing. $200K OBO. Tel: 987-66589

= 37 years old

= Single white male

= in search of

SWM, 37YO, Aquarius. Caring, strong, romantic. I like art, design, travel, photography & the fall.
ISO a lady 30ish-50ish, for outings, possibly more. Los Angeles area.

Abréviations utilisées dans les petites annonces :

a/c, AC	air conditioning	ft.	foot, feet
adj.	adjoining	furn.	furnished
appt.	appointment	gar.	garage
apt.	apartment	hr.	hour
avail.	available	kit.	kitchen
bdrm., bedrm., BR	bedroom	mo.	month
bsmt.	basement	nr.	near
bldg.	building	OBO	or best offer
bus.	business	opt.	optional
c/a, cac	central air conditioning	osp.	off-street parking
cond.	condition	ref.	reference
del.	deliver; delivery	rm.	room
det.	detached	sal.	salary
DR, din.	dining room	sgl.	single
dble	double	unfurn.	unfurnished
ea.	each	vac.	vacancy
elec.	electric	wk.	week
exch.	exchange	WPM	words per minute
fr.	family room	yr.	year

Le téléphone

Prononciation des numéros de téléphone

20995   Two zero double nine five

Pour obtenir un renseignement

- Can I have directory assistance *or* information please?
- I'm trying to get through to a Las Vegas number.
- What is the (country) code for Canada?
- How do I get an outside line?

Pour demander un interlocuteur

Hello,
- could I speak to …?
- can I speak to …?
- I'd like to speak to …
- (could I have) extension 593 please?

Pour répondre à un appel

- Robert McQueen speaking, can I help you?
- Hello, this is …
- Yes, speaking (pour confirmer que l'on est bien la personne demandée)
- Hold on/hold please, I'll (just) get him/her.
- I'm sorry, he's/she's not here. Can I take a message?
- I'm afraid he's away on business/out of the office/off sick/on vacation.

Pour laisser un message

sur un répondeur :
- I'm returning your call.
- I'll be in Detroit next week, perhaps we can …
- I'd like to talk to you about …
- Could you call me back, so we can discuss …?

une autre personne :
- Could you ask him/her to call me on …?
- Could you tell him/her I won't be able to …?
- I'll call back later.
- I need to speak to him/her urgently.
- Please ask him/her to confirm. Thank you.

Pour demander une confirmation

- Could you spell that please?
- Could you speak a bit more slowly please?
- I'm sorry I didn't catch that. Could you repeat that please?
- Let me check, 11 a.m. Wednesday 10th. Yes, that's fine.

Pour conclure un appel

- Thank you, I look forward to seeing you on Wednesday. Goodbye.
- Thank you for your help.

Message de répondeur téléphonique

- We are unable to take your call at the moment/I am not here at the moment. Please leave a message after the tone.

French Communication Guide

Letters

When sending a letter or other written communication, particular attention should be paid to the grammar and spelling as these are sensitive topics. Spelling mistakes and grammatical errors in a letter are considered very bad form, even in private correspondence.

The style should be simple and clear. It is a good idea to keep sentences short and to use active rather than passive verbs. Each paragraph should deal with one idea only. The idea is presented in the first sentence of the paragraph and is then developed. A new idea is expressed in a new paragraph.

Layout

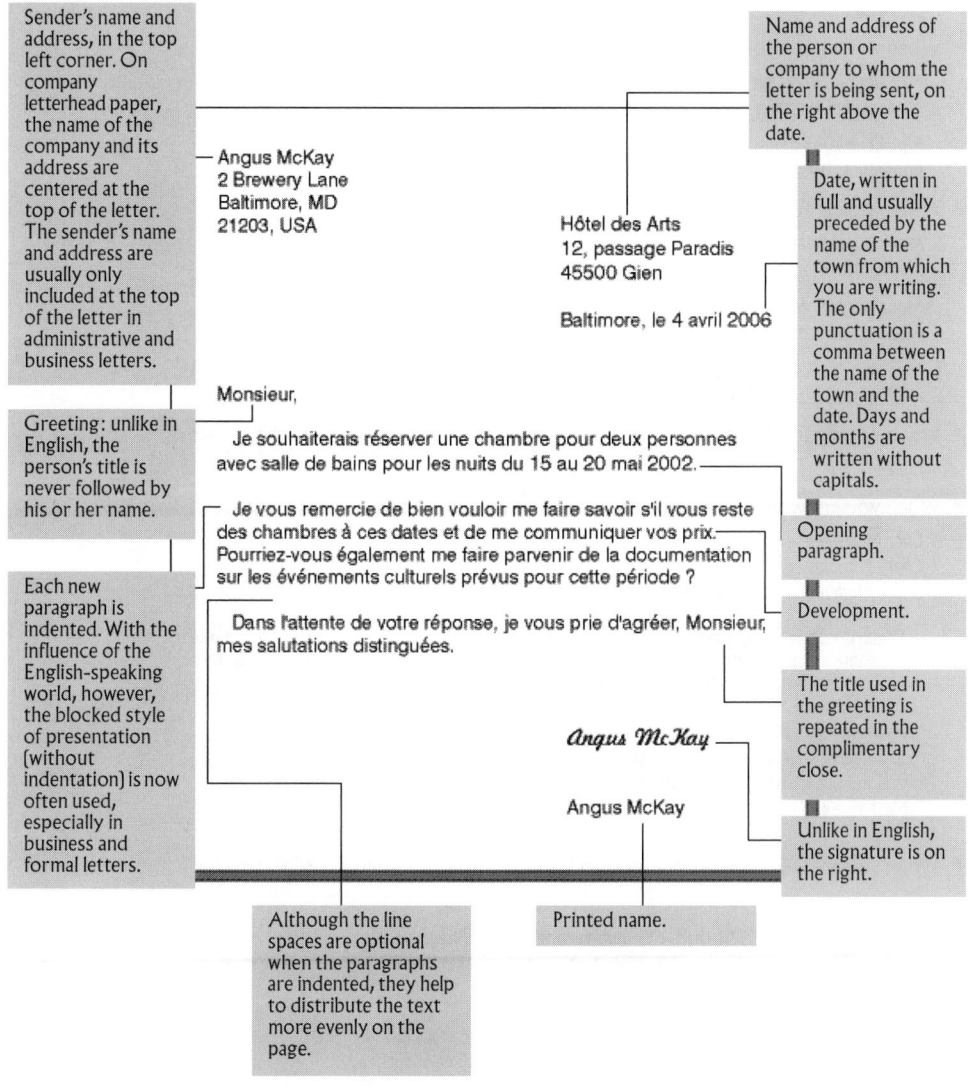

Sender's name and address, in the top left corner. On company letterhead paper, the name of the company and its address are centered at the top of the letter. The sender's name and address are usually only included at the top of the letter in administrative and business letters.

Greeting: unlike in English, the person's title is never followed by his or her name.

Each new paragraph is indented. With the influence of the English-speaking world, however, the blocked style of presentation (without indentation) is now often used, especially in business and formal letters.

Name and address of the person or company to whom the letter is being sent, on the right above the date.

Date, written in full and usually preceded by the name of the town from which you are writing. The only punctuation is a comma between the name of the town and the date. Days and months are written without capitals.

Opening paragraph.

Development.

The title used in the greeting is repeated in the complimentary close.

Unlike in English, the signature is on the right.

Although the line spaces are optional when the paragraphs are indented, they help to distribute the text more evenly on the page.

Printed name.

Angus McKay
2 Brewery Lane
Baltimore, MD
21203, USA

Hôtel des Arts
12, passage Paradis
45500 Gien

Baltimore, le 4 avril 2006

Monsieur,

Je souhaiterais réserver une chambre pour deux personnes avec salle de bains pour les nuits du 15 au 20 mai 2002.

Je vous remercie de bien vouloir me faire savoir s'il vous reste des chambres à ces dates et de me communiquer vos prix. Pourriez-vous également me faire parvenir de la documentation sur les événements culturels prévus pour cette période ?

Dans l'attente de votre réponse, je vous prie d'agréer, Monsieur, mes salutations distinguées.

Angus McKay

Angus McKay

Beginnings

The opening greetings and endings used in letters written in French follow certain well-established rules:

- If you do not know the person you are writing to, whether you know their name or not, or if you know them only slightly:

Monsieur
Madame

> The greetings *Monsieur* and *Madame* are equivalent to *Dear Sir* and *Dear Madam* in English.

Mademoiselle

> *Mademoiselle* is used for an unmarried young woman. If in doubt, use *Madame*.

- When you are unsure whether the recipient of the letter is male or female:

Madame, Monsieur

- When the letter is addressed to a company rather than to an individual:

Messieurs

- When writing to the head of a company or institution:

Monsieur le Directeur
Madame la Directrice

Monsieur le Président
Madame la Présidente

- When writing to a minister, to the Prime Minister or the President:

Monsieur le Ministre
Madame le Ministre

> The form *Madame la Ministre* is equally acceptable now.

Monsieur le Premier Ministre
Madame le Premier Ministre

Monsieur le Président de la République
Madame la Présidente de la République

- When writing to a lawyer:

Cher Maître

> This form is used irrespective of whether one is addressing a man or woman in this context.

- When you know the person you are writing to and want to sound less formal:

Cher Monsieur
Chère Madame
Chère Mademoiselle (for an unmarried young woman)

> These greetings are never followed by the name of the person. The equivalent of *Dear Mr. Allen* is *Monsieur* if you don't know him very well, or *Cher Monsieur* if you know him better and want to sound less formal. Always write the title in full and avoid abbreviations like M., Mme and Mlle.

> If you are writing to more than one person, you need to repeat *Cher* before each title: *Cher Monsieur, Chère Madame,....*

- When you are writing to a colleague you do not know or know only slightly:

Cher collègue
Chère collègue

Cher confrère
Chère consœur

> The titles *Cher confrère* and *Chère consœur* are used between professionals such as doctors and lawyers.

Cher ami
Chère amie

> The titles *Cher ami* and *Chère amie* are still slightly formal and are not used between friends but between colleagues or acquaintances.

- When you are writing to a relative, to a friend or to a colleague with whom you are on first name terms:

  Cher Olivier
  Chère Sandrine

- When writing to a relative or close friend, especially if they are younger than you, you can also use:

  Mon cher Olivier
  Ma chère Sandrine

Endings

The complimentary close should correspond in form and tone to the opening greeting. The title used at the beginning (Monsieur, Cher Monsieur, etc.) is always repeated in the ending of the letter:

- The most neutral endings are:

  Veuillez agréer, Monsieur (Madame), mes salutations distinguées.
  Veuillez recevoir, Monsieur (Madame), mes salutations distinguées.
  Veuillez agréer, Monsieur (Madame), l'expression de mes sentiments distingués.
  Je vous prie d'agréer, Monsieur le Directeur (Madame la Directrice), mes salutations distinguées.
  Je vous prie d'agréer, cher Maître, mes salutations distinguées. ———
  Je vous remercie d'avance et vous prie d'agréer, Monsieur (Madame), mes salutations distinguées.
  Dans l'attente d'une réponse de votre part, veuillez agréer, Messieurs, nos salutations distinguées.

  > This form is used when addressing a lawyer specifically.

- If you want to end on a more respectful note, such as when writing to a superior:

  Veuillez agréer, Monsieur (Madame), l'expression de ma considération distinguée.
  Je vous prie d'agréer, Monsieur (Madame), l'expression de mon profond respect.
  Veuillez agréer, je vous prie, Monsieur le Président (Madame la Présidente), l'expression de ma respectueuse considération.

- If you want to show your gratitude:

  Veuillez agréer, Monsieur (Madame), l'expression de ma profonde gratitude.
  Veuillez agréer, Monsieur (Madame), l'expression de ma respectueuse reconnaissance.
  Croyez, Monsieur (Madame), à toute ma reconnaissance.
  Croyez, Monsieur (Madame), à ma sincère gratitude.

- Although still formal, the following endings are more friendly:

  Veuillez agréer, cher Monsieur (chère Madame), l'expression de mes sentiments les plus cordiaux.
  Veuillez croire, cher Monsieur (chère Madame), à mon meilleur souvenir.
  Veuillez recevoir, cher ami (chère amie), mes plus cordiales salutations. ———
  Croyez, cher Olivier (chère Sandrine), à mon amical souvenir.

  > As noted above, the expression *cher ami*, although more friendly, is still formal and should not be used for a friend.

- Simplified and more informal endings are becoming more common. The following endings can be found more and more in everyday business letters, e-mails and faxes:

  Salutations distinguées.
  Cordialement. (more friendly)
  Bien à vous. (even more friendly)

- The following endings are used when writing to friends or relatives:

Polite:	Friendly:	Informal:
Amitiés.	*Je t'embrasse.*	*Grosses bises.*
Amicalement.	*À bientôt.*	*Bisous.*
Bien amicalement.	*Embrasse Pierre de ma part.*	
Bien affectueusement.		
Bien à toi.		

Addresses and zip codes

- You might often see "bis" and "ter" after the street number in a French address. For example:

  > 3 bis, rue des Lilas
  > 11 ter, avenue de Bernay

They indicate that there is more than one residence, whether in the form of a self-contained apartment or an annex to the main house or premises, at the address in question. "Bis" is used to indicate that there is a second residential (or business) unit, "ter" a third, the equivalent of 3b or 11c in English.

- The first two numbers of a French zip code correspond to the administrative code number of the relevant "département." All zip codes for Paris begin with 75. This system also applies to vehicle licence plates. For example:

  > 20, boulevard Arago
  > 75013 Paris

In the example above, the first two numbers indicate the city of Paris while the last two figures indicate that the address is located in the thirteenth "arrondissement" (district) of the city.

- The abbreviation "Cedex" is often found in French business addresses. For example:

  > Société Delacour
  > 77170 Fontainebleau Cedex

This is a special zip code ensuring rapid delivery of mail to businesses and certain institutions. In these cases, the first two figures, as in other zip codes, denote geographical location but the following three figures denote an individual code assigned to the company in question.

- In Belgium addresses are often written with the street number coming after the street name, and the zip code before the town. For an apartment or a house where there are more than three mailboxes it is usual to add the mailbox number (not the apartment number) after the street number. For example:

  > Monsieur Luc Dujardin
  > rue du Clocher 143, bte 12   The abbreviation for **boîte**.
  > 1040 Bruxelles

- Swiss addresses are also usually written with the street number appearing after the street name, and the zip code before the town. If writing from outside Switzerland one may include the abbreviation CH (for "Confederatio Helvetica" or the Swiss Confederation). For example:

  > Monsieur André Roux
  > Avenue du Peyrou 4
  > CH - 2000 Neuchâtel

- In Canada, it is usual to write the name of the town or municipality, followed by the abbreviation corresponding to the province in which it is located, followed by the zip code, all on the same line. For example:

  > Madame Chantal Lemoine
  > 3567 rue Drummond
  > Montréal (Québec) H3G 1M8

  The name of the province is usually given in parentheses after the name of the town or municipality. Alternatively an abbreviation can be used to designate the province: for example QC for **Québec**. If the abbreviated form is used then there is no need for brackets.

The websites of the various postal services in French-speaking countries are a useful source of information regarding addresses and zip codes in particular.

France: www.laposte.fr
Belgium: www.post.be
Luxembourg: www.pt.lu
Switzerland: www.poste.ch
Canada: www.canadapost.ca

Envelopes

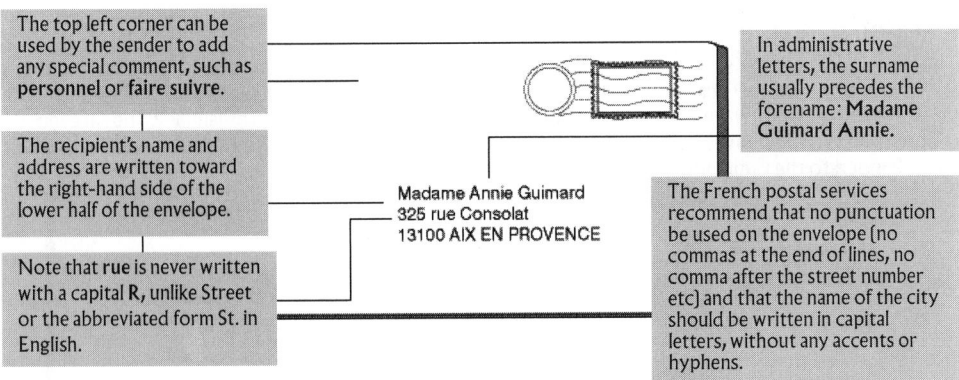

The top left corner can be used by the sender to add any special comment, such as **personnel** or **faire suivre**.

The recipient's name and address are written toward the right-hand side of the lower half of the envelope.

Note that **rue** is never written with a capital R, unlike Street or the abbreviated form St. in English.

In administrative letters, the surname usually precedes the forename: **Madame Guimard Annie**.

The French postal services recommend that no punctuation be used on the envelope (no commas at the end of lines, no comma after the street number etc) and that the name of the city should be written in capital letters, without any accents or hyphens.

Madame Annie Guimard
325 rue Consolat
13100 AIX EN PROVENCE

It is standard practice to write a return address on the back of the envelope at the top, in case the letter gets lost.

Model letters

Chatty letter to a friend/relative

When writing to friends and relatives, as in English, a more informal style is perfectly acceptable.

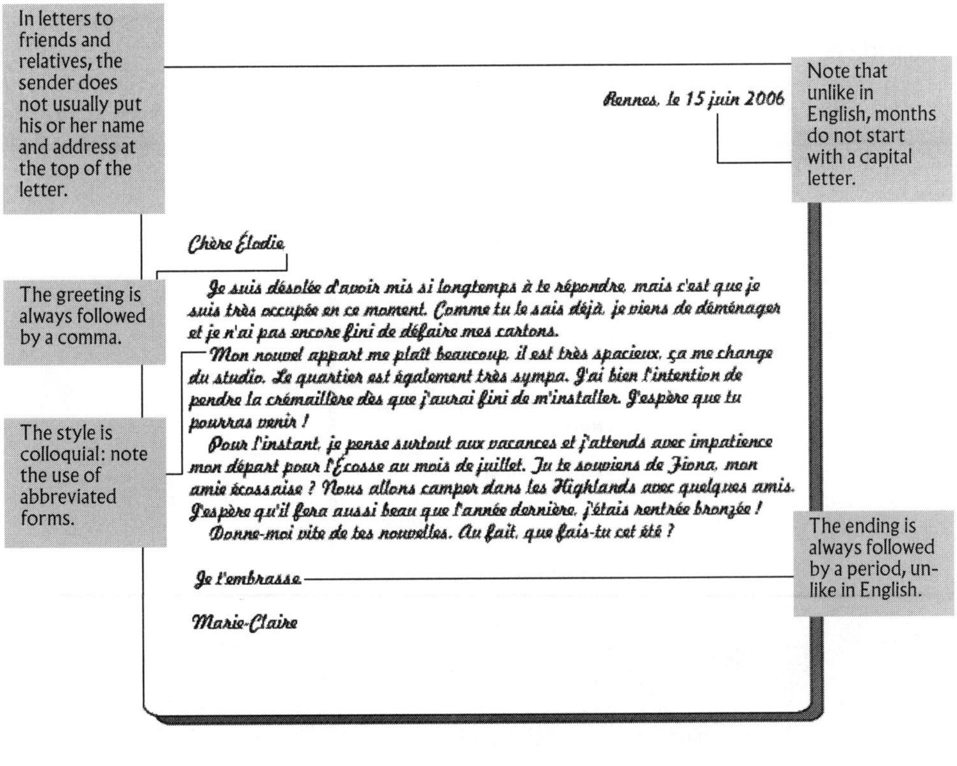

In letters to friends and relatives, the sender does not usually put his or her name and address at the top of the letter.

Note that unlike in English, months do not start with a capital letter.

The greeting is always followed by a comma.

The style is colloquial: note the use of abbreviated forms.

The ending is always followed by a period, unlike in English.

Rennes, le 15 juin 2006

Chère Élodie,

Je suis désolée d'avoir mis si longtemps à te répondre, mais c'est que je suis très occupée en ce moment. Comme tu le sais déjà, je viens de déménager et je n'ai pas encore fini de défaire mes cartons.

Mon nouvel appart me plaît beaucoup, il est très spacieux, ça me change du studio. Le quartier est également très sympa. J'ai bien l'intention de pendre la crémaillère dès que j'aurai fini de m'installer. J'espère que tu pourras venir !

Pour l'instant, je pense surtout aux vacances et j'attends avec impatience mon départ pour l'Écosse au mois de juillet. Tu te souviens de Fiona, mon amie écossaise ? Nous allons camper dans les Highlands avec quelques amis. J'espère qu'il fera aussi beau que l'année dernière, j'étais rentrée bronzée !

Donne-moi vite de tes nouvelles. Au fait, que fais-tu cet été ?

Je t'embrasse.

Marie-Claire

Greeting cards

▪ Season's greetings

The use of greeting cards is not as widespread in France as in English-speaking countries. Greeting cards are usually sent for New Year's rather than Christmas. You can send a New Year's card at any time from before Christmas until the end of January, although usually before the middle of January. They are mostly sent to friends and relatives who live far away and business acquaintances. They are always mailed and are never handed to the recipient.

> *Bonne et heureuse année 2007 à tous les trois.*
>
> *À très bientôt, j'espère.*
>
> *Laurence*

> *Cher Simon, chère Odile,*
> *Tous nos vœux de bonheur pour l'année 2007 !*
>
> *Bien à vous.*
>
> *Vincent et Sylvie*

> Chère Mathilde,
> Que cette nouvelle année t'apporte joie et bonheur et soit l'occasion de nous voir souvent !
> Irène

> Cher Jérôme, chère Nicole,
> Nous vous remercions de vos vœux et nous vous souhaitons à notre tour une nouvelle année pleine de joie et de bonheur.
>
> Affectueusement
>
> Pascale et Jean-Pierre

▪ Birthdays

Birthday cards are not as popular in France as in English-speaking countries. As with other types of greeting cards, they are mostly sent to friends and relatives who live far away rather than to people who one sees regularly. Birthday cards are not usually handed directly to the recipient and presents are not systematically accompanied by a card.

> *Cher Thomas,*
>
> *Bon anniversaire !*
> *Dommage que nous ne puissions pas célébrer ensemble tes 30 ans.*
> *Je penserai à toi dimanche en buvant un verre à ta santé !*
>
> *Je t'embrasse.*
>
> *Julie*

Useful phrases:

Joyeux anniversaire !
Pierre se joint à moi pour te souhaiter un très bon anniversaire.

■ Congratulations

Written congratulations are usually sent after the announcement of a birth, engagement, wedding or promotion.

> *Grenoble, le 2 juillet 2006*
>
> *Bravo ! Tes parents m'ont appris que tu as été reçu à tes examens. Quel soulagement, tu vas enfin pouvoir profiter de vacances bien méritées. Toutes mes félicitations et bon courage pour la suite de tes études !*
>
> *Je t'embrasse.*
>
> *Marie*

Useful phrases:

■ For an engagement/a wedding:
C'est avec grand plaisir que j'ai appris tes fiançailles avec Pierre.
Tous nos vœux de bonheur à tous les deux. (less formal)

■ For a birth:
C'est avec joie que nous avons appris la naissance de Matthieu.
Félicitations à tous les deux et tous nos vœux de bonheur pour votre bébé.

■ For a promotion/success:
C'est avec grand plaisir que j'ai appris votre promotion/nomination au poste de ...
Je vous adresse mes sincères félicitations, ainsi que celles de mes collègues. (formal)

Letter of complaint

For serious complaints, or if a first letter has been ignored, it is standard practice to send this type of letter by registered mail ("lettre recommandée avec accusé de réception").

Martine Fernet
Les Jardins du Bourg
74500 Thonon-les-Bains

Les Déménageurs Express
Service Clientèle
11 Haute Rue
74500 Thonon-les-Bains

Thonon-les-Bains, le 5 avril 2006

Monsieur,

Concise explanation of nature of complaint.

Une de vos équipes vient d'effectuer notre déménagement et je suis au regret de vous annoncer que le travail a été exécuté de façon déplorable puisque certains de nos meubles et objets personnels ont été endommagés.

En effet, nous nous sommes rendus compte au déballage qu'un miroir avait été rayé, qu'une commode Louis XV avait perdu un pied et que le piano présentait une grande rayure sur sa partie inférieure.

Development

Demand for action.

Très surprise par la négligence et le manque de professionnalisme de votre équipe, je me vois dans l'obligation de vous demander un dédommagement pour ces dégâts. Je tiens à vous rappeler que l'option que nous avions choisie nous garantissait un service haut de gamme, ce qui est loin d'avoir été le cas.

Dans l'attente d'une réponse de votre part, je vous prie d'agréer, Monsieur, mes salutations distinguées.

Martine Fernet

Martine Fernet

Useful phrases:

Je vous ai commandé le 20 décembre dernier une armoire que vous deviez me livrer dans les quinze jours. Or je n'ai toujours rien reçu trois semaines plus tard.
Je suis surpris de constater que ... / Je m'étonne de ...
Je suis vivement surpris de ... (stronger)
J'ai le regret de vous signaler que ...
Nous regrettons de devoir vous signaler une erreur dans ...
Nous vous demandons donc de bien vouloir ...
Je vous prie de bien vouloir faire le nécessaire/d'annuler ma commande et de me rembourser la somme de ...

Apologizing

Even if you have already apologized by telephone, in some situations, for example if you have missed a formal appointment, a letter of apology is expected.

Ann Thorne
10, rue des Acacias
75017 Paris

TECHNO-MEDIA
À l'attention de Madame Dubreuil
14, rue du Vieux Marché
78100 Saint-Germain-en-Laye

Paris, le 3 septembre 2006

Madame,

Je suis vraiment navrée de n'avoir pas pu me présenter à l'entretien que vous m'aviez fixé le lundi 3 septembre 2006, à 14 heures. En effet, ainsi que je vous l'ai expliqué lors de mon appel hier matin, aucun train ne circulait en direction de Saint-Germain-en-Laye, en raison d'une grève surprise du personnel de la SNCF.

Je ne peux que vous renouveler mes excuses pour ce fâcheux incident indépendant de ma volonté. Vous serait-il possible de me proposer un nouveau rendez-vous, au jour et à l'heure qui vous conviendraient ?

Je vous remercie à l'avance de votre compréhension et je vous prie d'agréer, Madame, l'expression de ma considération distinguée.

Ann Thorne

Ann Thorne

Apologize and recall briefly what happened.

Give the specific reason for the mishap.

End on a hopeful note: you hope the person you are apologizing to will excuse you.

Useful phrases:

Veuillez accepter toutes nos excuses pour ce malencontreux incident. (formal)
Nous tenons à vous présenter nos excuses pour ... (formal)
Je suis vraiment navré de ce malentendu.
J'espère que vous ne me tiendrez pas rigueur de cet oubli.
Excuse-moi de ne pas t'avoir prévenu plus tôt/de t'avoir fait faux bond hier soir. (informal)

Making a reservation

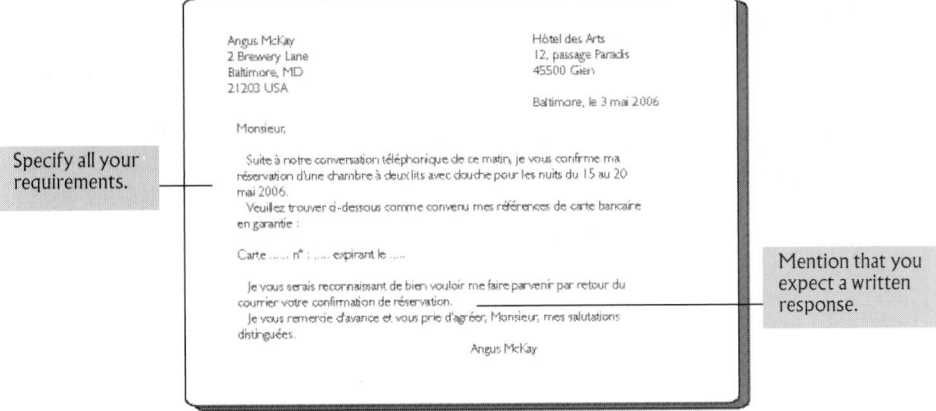

Specify all your requirements.

Mention that you expect a written response.

Angus McKay
2 Brewery Lane
Baltimore, MD
21203 USA

Hôtel des Arts
12, passage Paradis
45500 Gien

Baltimore, le 3 mai 2006

Monsieur,

Suite à notre conversation téléphonique de ce matin, je vous confirme ma réservation d'une chambre à deux lits avec douche pour les nuits du 15 au 20 mai 2006.
Veuillez trouver ci-dessous comme convenu mes références de carte bancaire en garantie :

Carte ..... n° : ..... expirant le .....

Je vous serais reconnaissant de bien vouloir me faire parvenir par retour du courrier votre confirmation de réservation.
Je vous remercie d'avance et vous prie d'agréer, Monsieur, mes salutations distinguées.

Angus McKay

Useful phrases:

Je vous confirme ma réservation de votre appartement ... pour la période du ...
Je vous remercie de bien vouloir me faire savoir s'il vous reste des chambres à ces dates et de me communiquer vos prix.
Veuillez trouver ci-joint comme convenu un chèque de ... euros à titre d'arrhes.

Letter of thanks to a friend/relative

Be specific: recall the circumstances.

Thank the person explicitly.

Crest, le 3 juin 2006

Chère Marion, cher Yves,

Ces trois jours passés chez vous ont été formidables. Votre maison est un havre de paix, vraiment agréable à vivre. Tout était parfait. Les balades que nous avons faites en montagne m'ont beaucoup plu et m'ont fait prendre conscience que je n'étais pas en grande forme : j'ai donc pris la décision de me remettre au sport !

Encore un grand merci pour ce charmant séjour.

Grosses bises à tous les deux, je file à la poste !

A très bientôt.

Paul

Useful phrases:

Merci pour ton cadeau si généreux/pour ton aide si précieuse.
Merci pour cette magnifique écharpe qui m'a fait très plaisir.
Nous tenons à vous remercier pour la belle lampe que vous nous avez offerte.

Invitations and replies

- ### Letter of invitation

> *Paris, le 25 mai 2006*
>
> *Cher Andrew,*
>
> *Que dirais-tu de venir passer quelques jours à la campagne ? Nous louons une maison en Normandie avec des amis du 7 au 15 juillet. Thomas nous a promis d'être des nôtres. Cela nous ferait très plaisir que tu te joignes à nous.*
>
> *Tu trouveras ci-joint un plan détaillé de la région.*
>
> *Donne-nous vite ta réponse !*
>
> *À bientôt.*
>
> *Pierre*

Useful phrases:

À l'occasion du week-end du 1er mai, nous invitons quelques amis dans notre maison de campagne.
Pour fêter l'anniversaire de Simon, nous organisons une soirée le ..., à partir de ...
Nous comptons sur votre présence.

- ### Invitation card

These are usually made by a printer, who can suggest standard formulas.

> *M. et Mme Tessier*
> *seront heureux de vous recevoir à*
> *l'occasion du baptême*
> *de leur fils*
>
> **Nicolas**
>
> *le samedi 16 juin*
> *à partir de 15 heures*
>
> *4, villa du Puits - 26500 Crest   R.S.V.P.*

Abbreviation of "Répondez s'il vous plaît".

Useful phrases:

Sophie Tessier recevra ses amis le ... à partir de ...
Jacques Tessier vous invite à venir assister à sa soutenance de thèse le ... à partir de ...
Nous organisons une soirée le ... à l'occasion de ... Nous serions très heureux si vous pouviez vous joindre à nous.

- # Wedding invitation

Monsieur et Madame Tessier Monsieur et Madame Legrand

ont le plaisir de vous faire part
du mariage de leurs enfants

Nathalie et Sylvain

et vous prient d'assister à la bénédiction nuptiale qui
leur sera donnée
le samedi 16 juin 2006 à 16 heures en l'église
Saint-Christophe à Crest
ainsi qu'au dîner organisé à partir de 20 heures
au restaurant Les Tilleuls de Crest.

Réponse souhaitée avant le 10 mai

4, villa du Puits   6, rue des Bains
26500 Crest   25000 Besançon

For traditional weddings, the invitation is made by the parents of the couple.

Useful phrases:

Monsieur et Madame X vous prient d'assister à la messe de mariage qui sera célébrée le ...
en l'église ...
Monsieur et Madame X recevront à l'hôtel Les Tilleuls à l'issue de la cérémonie religieuse.
Nathalie Tessier et Sylvain Legrand sont heureux de vous annoncer leur mariage qui sera célébré le ... à ... à la mairie de Crest.
Un vin d'honneur sera servi à l'issue de la cérémonie à la salle des fêtes de Crest.

- # Declining an invitation

Valence, le 15 juillet 2006

Chère Aude,

Je viens de recevoir ta lettre, et je suis
très touché que tu aies pensé à m'inviter
pour ton anniversaire, mais, malheureusement,
je dois partir à Londres dès la semaine
prochaine pour raisons professionnelles et je
ne pourrai pas me joindre à vous.
J'espère bien sûr que tes 30 ans seront
dignement célébrés, et dans la bonne
humeur ; je penserai à toi ce jour-là, en buvant
un verre à ta santé !
Comme cadeau d'anniversaire, je serai ravi de
t'accueillir à Londres. On met à ma disposition
un grand appartement et un week-end serait
suffisant pour te dépayser.
J'attends donc ta réponse et je te souhaite un
très bon anniversaire.

Je t'embrasse.

Simon

Useful phrases:

Je suis vraiment déçu de ne pouvoir accepter mais je ne pourrai pas me libérer car des obligations professionnelles me retiennent à Paris à cette date.

Nous regrettons de ne pouvoir nous libérer et nous espérons avoir très prochainement l'occasion de nous réunir.

Nous vous remercions de votre aimable invitation que nous avons le regret de ne pouvoir accepter, étant déjà retenus ce jour-là. (formal)

■ Accepting an invitation

Express your pleasure at being invited.

Thank the sender for the invitation.

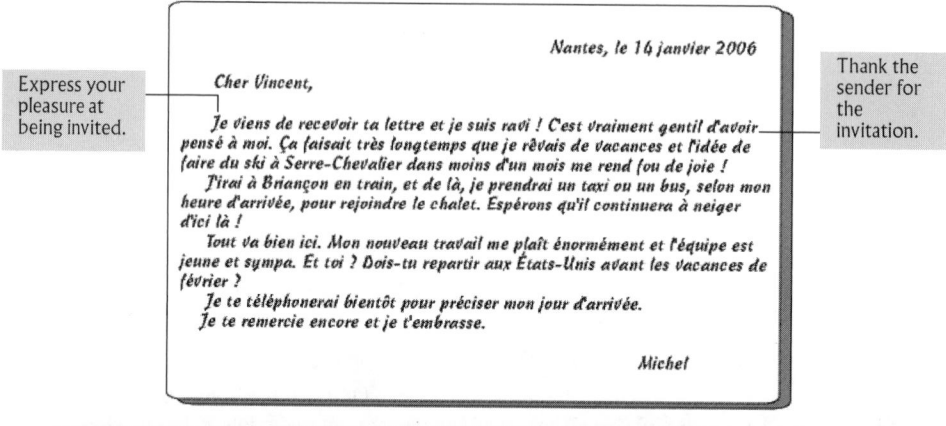

Nantes, le 14 janvier 2006

Cher Vincent,

Je viens de recevoir ta lettre et je suis ravi ! C'est vraiment gentil d'avoir pensé à moi. Ça faisait très longtemps que je rêvais de vacances et l'idée de faire du ski à Serre-Chevalier dans moins d'un mois me rend fou de joie !

J'irai à Briançon en train, et de là, je prendrai un taxi ou un bus, selon mon heure d'arrivée, pour rejoindre le chalet. Espérons qu'il continuera à neiger d'ici là !

Tout va bien ici. Mon nouveau travail me plaît énormément et l'équipe est jeune et sympa. Et toi ? Dois-tu repartir aux États-Unis avant les vacances de février ?

Je te téléphonerai bientôt pour préciser mon jour d'arrivée.

Je te remercie encore et je t'embrasse.

Michel

Useful phrases:

C'est avec grand plaisir que j'accepte votre invitation pour le .../que je me joindrais à vous le ...

Je me réjouis à l'idée de vous revoir.

Nous vous remercions de votre invitation au mariage de Sylvain, que nous acceptons avec joie/auquel nous viendrons avec grand plaisir.

Letter to authorities: official statement

This type of statement follows a set formula in French.

The adjective soussigné varies according to the gender: Je soussignée Madame X ..., Nous soussignés ...

The standard procedure is to give your name, occupation, date and place of birth, nationality and address.

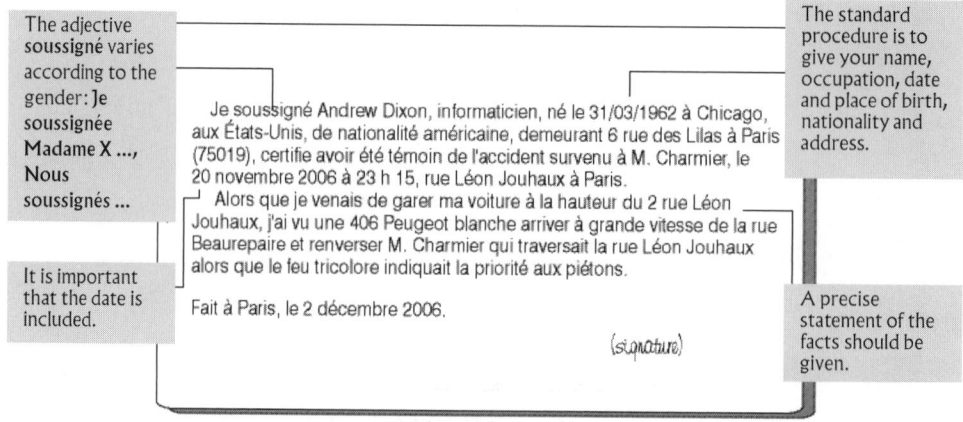

Je soussigné Andrew Dixon, informaticien, né le 31/03/1962 à Chicago, aux États-Unis, de nationalité américaine, demeurant 6 rue des Lilas à Paris (75019), certifie avoir été témoin de l'accident survenu à M. Charmier, le 20 novembre 2006 à 23 h 15, rue Léon Jouhaux à Paris.

Alors que je venais de garer ma voiture à la hauteur du 2 rue Léon Jouhaux, j'ai vu une 406 Peugeot blanche arriver à grande vitesse de la rue Beaurepaire et renverser M. Charmier qui traversait la rue Léon Jouhaux alors que le feu tricolore indiquait la priorité aux piétons.

Fait à Paris, le 2 décembre 2006.

(signature)

It is important that the date is included.

A precise statement of the facts should be given.

Asking for a brochure/information

Angus McKay
2 Brewery Lane
Baltimore, MD
21203 USA

Office du tourisme
11 place du Général de Gaulle
06600 Antibes

Baltimore, le 4 avril 2006

Madame, Monsieur,

Souhaitant passer mes vacances (du 1er au 16 juillet) dans la région d'Antibes, je vous serais reconnaissant de bien vouloir me faire parvenir une liste des hôtels et des chambresd'hôte, à Antibes même ou dans les environs.

Pourriez-vous également me faire parvenir de la documentation sur les événements culturels prévus pour cette période ?

Je vous remercie d'avance et je vous prie d'agréer, Madame, Monsieur, mes salutations distinguées.

Angus McKay

Angus McKay

Business correspondence

Business to business (general)

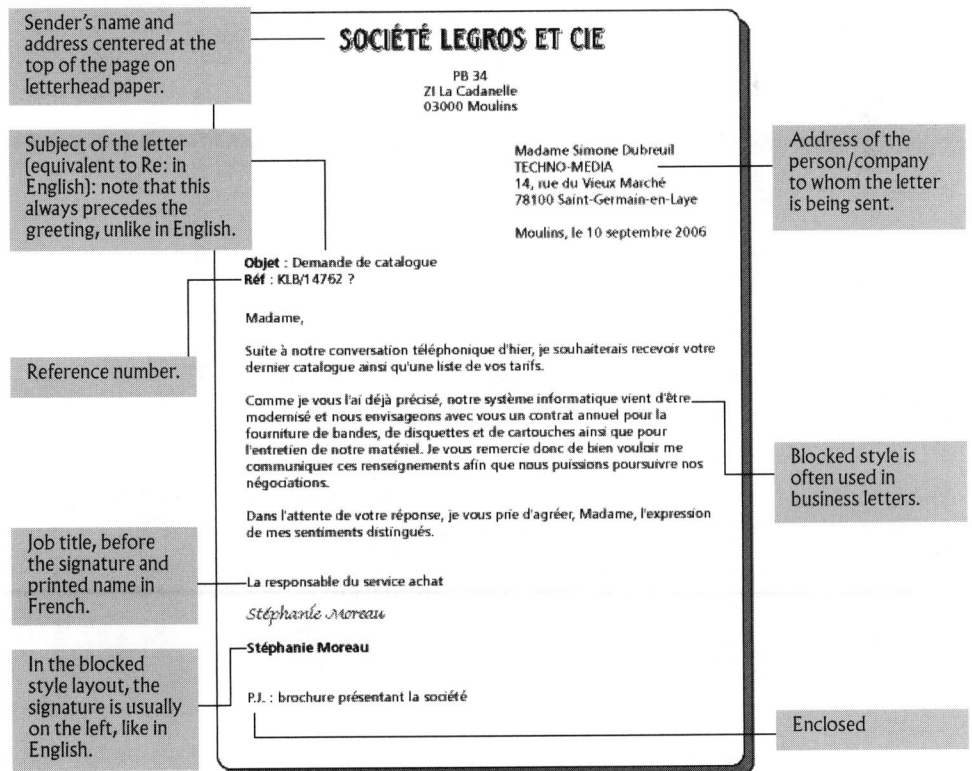

Sender's name and address centered at the top of the page on letterhead paper.

Subject of the letter (equivalent to Re: in English): note that this always precedes the greeting, unlike in English.

Reference number.

Job title, before the signature and printed name in French.

In the blocked style layout, the signature is usually on the left, like in English.

SOCIÉTÉ LEGROS ET CIE

PB 34
ZI La Cadanelle
03000 Moulins

Madame Simone Dubreuil
TECHNO-MEDIA
14, rue du Vieux Marché
78100 Saint-Germain-en-Laye

Moulins, le 10 septembre 2006

Objet : Demande de catalogue
Réf : KLB/14762 ?

Madame,

Suite à notre conversation téléphonique d'hier, je souhaiterais recevoir votre dernier catalogue ainsi qu'une liste de vos tarifs.

Comme je vous l'ai déjà précisé, notre système informatique vient d'être modernisé et nous envisageons avec vous un contrat annuel pour la fourniture de bandes, de disquettes et de cartouches ainsi que pour l'entretien de notre matériel. Je vous remercie donc de bien vouloir me communiquer ces renseignements afin que nous puissions poursuivre nos négociations.

Dans l'attente de votre réponse, je vous prie d'agréer, Madame, l'expression de mes sentiments distingués.

La responsable du service achat

Stéphanie Moreau

Stéphanie Moreau

P.J. : brochure présentant la société

Address of the person/company to whom the letter is being sent.

Blocked style is often used in business letters.

Enclosed

Useful phrases:

En réponse à votre lettre du ...,
Nous avons bien reçu votre lettre du ... et nous vous en remercions.
Nous sommes tout particulièrement intéressés par ...
Nous vous remercions de l'intérêt que vous portez à notre société et nous restons à votre disposition pour toutes informations complémentaires.

Placing an order

A letter placing an order needs to specify the items required, as well as the conditions of delivery and payment.

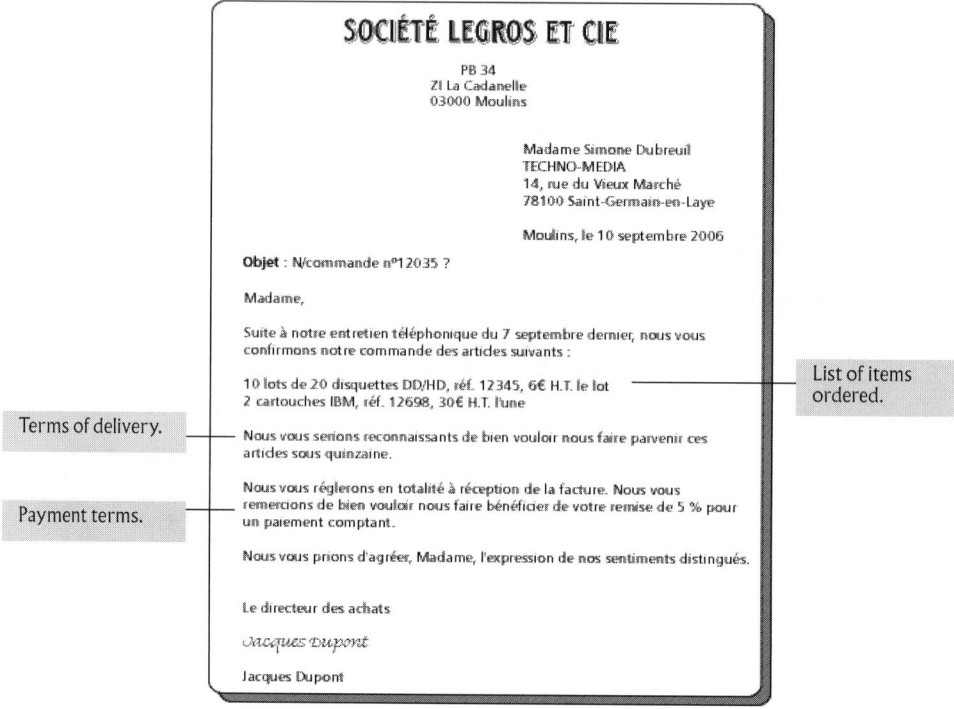

SOCIÉTÉ LEGROS ET CIE

PB 34
ZI La Cadanelle
03000 Moulins

Madame Simone Dubreuil
TECHNO-MEDIA
14, rue du Vieux Marché
78100 Saint-Germain-en-Laye

Moulins, le 10 septembre 2006

Objet : N/commande n°12035 ?

Madame,

Suite à notre entretien téléphonique du 7 septembre dernier, nous vous confirmons notre commande des articles suivants :

10 lots de 20 disquettes DD/HD, réf. 12345, 6€ H.T. le lot — *List of items ordered.*
2 cartouches IBM, réf. 12698, 30€ H.T. l'une

Terms of delivery. — Nous vous serions reconnaissants de bien vouloir nous faire parvenir ces articles sous quinzaine.

Payment terms. — Nous vous réglerons en totalité à réception de la facture. Nous vous remercions de bien vouloir nous faire bénéficier de votre remise de 5 % pour un paiement comptant.

Nous vous prions d'agréer, Madame, l'expression de nos sentiments distingués.

Le directeur des achats

Jacques Dupont

Jacques Dupont

Useful phrases:

Veuillez nous faire parvenir les articles suivants ...
Nous vous prions de bien vouloir nous expédier ...
Nous vous passons commande de ...
Veuillez trouver ci-joint notre bon de commande n° ...

Informing a customer

TECHNO-MEDIA
14, rue du Vieux Marché
78100 Saint-Germain-en-Laye
http:\\www.technomedia.fr

Saint-Germain-en-Laye, le 10 septembre 2006

Monsieur,

Nous avons le plaisir de vous informer que vous pouvez désormais consulter notre catalogue et passer vos commandes sur notre site Web.

Notre site est entièrement sécurisé. Si vous souhaitez bénéficier de nos services en ligne, il suffit de vous enregistrer en vous connectant à :

http:\\www.technomedia.fr

Dans l'espoir que ce nouveau service vous donnera entière satisfaction, nous vous prions d'agréer, Monsieur, nos meilleures salutations.

La responsable du site Web

Sylvie Legrand

Sylvie Legrand

Useful phrases:

Nous vous informons que ...
Nous tenons à vous signaler que ...
Nous restons à votre entière disposition pour tous renseignements complémentaires.
Veuillez noter notre nouvelle adresse à partir du ...

Dealing with a customer complaint

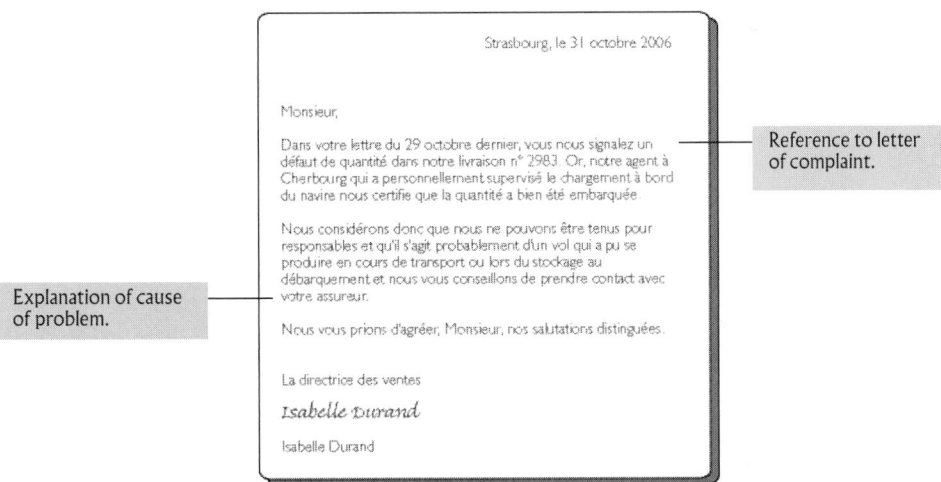

Strasbourg, le 31 octobre 2006

Monsieur,

Dans votre lettre du 29 octobre dernier, vous nous signalez un défaut de quantité dans notre livraison n° 2983. Or, notre agent à Cherbourg qui a personnellement supervisé le chargement à bord du navire nous certifie que la quantité a bien été embarquée.

Reference to letter of complaint.

Nous considérons donc que nous ne pouvons être tenus pour responsables et qu'il s'agit probablement d'un vol qui a pu se produire en cours de transport ou lors du stockage au débarquement et nous vous conseillons de prendre contact avec votre assureur.

Explanation of cause of problem.

Nous vous prions d'agréer, Monsieur, nos salutations distinguées.

La directrice des ventes

Isabelle Durand

Isabelle Durand

Useful phrases:

Nous vous prions de bien vouloir nous excuser pour cette regrettable erreur.
Veuillez accepter nos excuses pour le dérangement que nous avons pu vous causer.
Nous avons pris des mesures pour que cela ne se reproduise plus.

Invoice

Company name, registered office, telephone and fax numbers, telex number, e-mail address and company registration number.

Date of invoice.

Reference number of listed items.

Precise description of products or services.

Total including VAT.

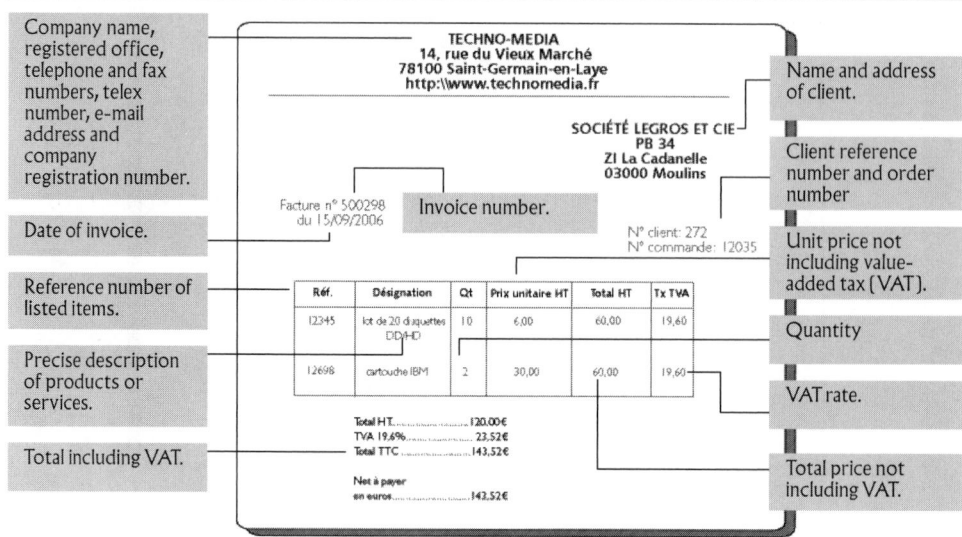

Name and address of client.

Client reference number and order number

Unit price not including value-added tax (VAT).

Quantity

VAT rate.

Total price not including VAT.

Reply to invoice

Briefly explain the mistake.

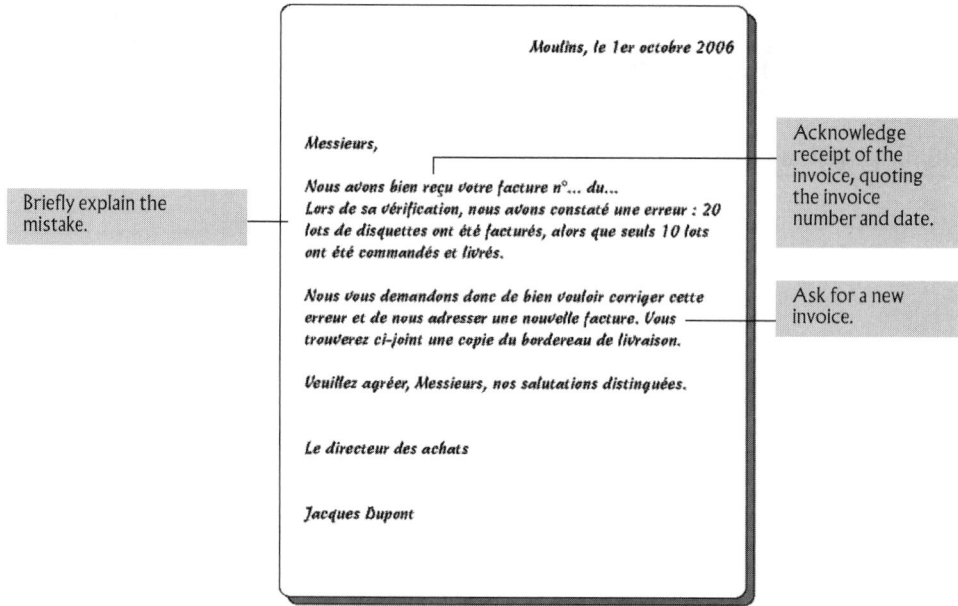

Acknowledge receipt of the invoice, quoting the invoice number and date.

Ask for a new invoice.

Useful phrases:

Nous accusons réception de votre facture n°...
Les prix ne sont pas ceux qui ont été convenus lors de la commande, à savoir : ...
En vérifiant la facture que vous venez de nous faire parvenir, nous constatons que le montant ne correspond pas à notre commande.
Nous avons décelé l'erreur suivante : ...

Employment

Cover letter

When applying for a job in France, it is customary to write the cover letter ("lettre de motivation") by hand. Apart from adding a more personal touch, it is not unusual for French companies to use the services of a graphologist who analyzes the applicants' handwriting. A letter of application is quite formal in its presentation. It should be concise, properly structured in paragraphs and have the standard opening and closing formulas. You should cover the following points:

- Emphasize what you consider important in your CV
- Add information about your objectives
- Explain why you are interested in the company
- Convince the reader that you are the right person for the job

Marielle Gondrand
Villa La Tourelle
37000 Tours

Centre culturel La Vague
3, place de la Mairie
37000 Tours

Tours, le 1er octobre 2006

Monsieur,

Votre annonce parue dans Les Nouvelles de Tours du 28 septembre 2006 pour un poste de secrétaire a retenu toute mon attention.

Introductory paragraph mentioning where you saw the vacancy advertised.

Je viens de terminer mon BTS de secrétariat et je suis à la recherche d'un emploi. Au cours de mes études, j'ai eu l'occasion de faire deux stages : l'un à la Banque Moreau et l'autre à la Maison des Jeunes de Tours. Par ailleurs, je m'occupe bénévolement du secrétariat d'une association à but non lucratif de mon quartier.

Outline of your current employment situation, qualifications and previous experience.

Why you are interested in the company.

Je suis très attirée par les métiers de la culture, et ceci, ainsi que le rayonnement de votre société au niveau régional, m'incite à vouloir rejoindre votre équipe.

Je me tiens à votre disposition pour un entretien éventuel.

Indicate that you are available for interview.

Standard complimentary close.

Je vous prie d'agréer, Monsieur, mes salutations distinguées.

Marielle Gondrand

Useful phrases:

En réponse à votre annonce parue dans Les Nouvelles de Tours du …, je me permets de vous adresser mon curriculum vitae pour le poste de secrétaire.
Je dispose de plusieurs années d'expérience dans différentes entreprises.
Au cours de mes cinq années d'expérience auprès de la société X, j'ai acquis une bonne maîtrise de …
En espérant que ma candidature retiendra votre attention, je vous prie d'agréer, Madame, Monsieur, l'expression de mes sentiments distingués.

Asking for work experience

Work experiences are very popular in France and are a compulsory part of many courses. It is therefore advisable to send your request well in advance.

This type of letter is always handwritten in French (see Cover letter on previous page).

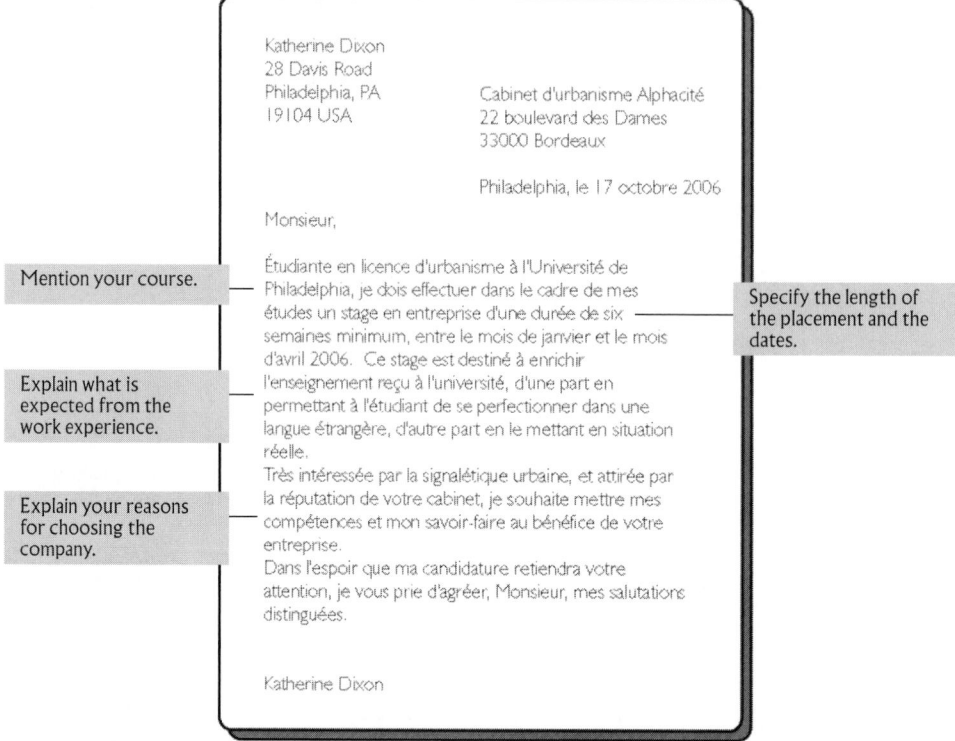

Mention your course.

Explain what is expected from the work experience.

Explain your reasons for choosing the company.

Specify the length of the placement and the dates.

Katherine Dixon
28 Davis Road
Philadelphia, PA
19104 USA

Cabinet d'urbanisme Alphacité
22 boulevard des Dames
33000 Bordeaux

Philadelphia, le 17 octobre 2006

Monsieur,

Étudiante en licence d'urbanisme à l'Université de Philadelphia, je dois effectuer dans le cadre de mes études un stage en entreprise d'une durée de six semaines minimum, entre le mois de janvier et le mois d'avril 2006. Ce stage est destiné à enrichir l'enseignement reçu à l'université, d'une part en permettant à l'étudiant de se perfectionner dans une langue étrangère, d'autre part en le mettant en situation réelle.

Très intéressée par la signalétique urbaine, et attirée par la réputation de votre cabinet, je souhaite mettre mes compétences et mon savoir-faire au bénéfice de votre entreprise.

Dans l'espoir que ma candidature retiendra votre attention, je vous prie d'agréer, Monsieur, mes salutations distinguées.

Katherine Dixon

Useful phrases:

Vous trouverez ci-joint mon curriculum vitae.
Je vous remercie de l'attention que vous porterez à ma demande et reste à votre disposition pour un entretien.
Je reste à votre disposition pour vous rencontrer et vous fournir tout autre renseignement.
En vous remerciant à l'avance de bien vouloir examiner ma demande, je vous prie d'agréer ...

Curriculum vitae

The presentation of a CV in French is in many ways similar to an American CV. The following differences should be respected.

- The title "Curriculum Vitae" should never be included in a French CV.
- Only mention hobbies if they add something personal to your profile or if they are particularly relevant to the job.
- Do not include references on your CV: references are not commonly used in France apart from certain jobs where personal recommendation would be expected, such as catering, cleaning, child care, etc.
- Even if you do not complete your degree, you can mention the fact that you studied for it by using the word "niveau", i.e. "niveau licence".

■ Experienced (French)

Laure Battisto
25, rue des Arquebusiers
76000 Rouen
Tél : 02 24 24 45 73   42 ans
Télécopie : 02 24 21 13 39   divorcée
E-mail : lbattisto@battisto.com.fr   un enfant (11 ans)

Consultante en Ressources humaines
14 ans d'expérience

Expérience professionnelle

1997 – 2006   Consultante en Ressources humaines, Cabinet Battisto-Langlade, Rouen : conseil auprès d'entreprises, audit, recrutement

1993 – 1996   Directrice des Ressources humaines, Conseil général, Le Havre : recrutement, planification des formations, suivi du personnel

1991 – 1992   Assistante du Directeur des Ressources humaines, Société Pierre et Fils, Le Havre

Formation

1989   Master of Business Administration, Boston University

1987 – 1988   DEA 'Langage et Médias' – Paris X

1986   Maîtrise d'Histoire – Paris IV

1982   Baccalauréat Mathématiques – Académie de Paris

Autres expériences

1990 – 1991   Voyage en Afrique dans le cadre d'une mission Médecins sans frontières

Langues
Bilingue anglais
Espagnol : lu, écrit, parlé

Divers
Bonne maîtrise du traitement de texte sur PC et sur Mac
Responsable d'une association bénévole luttant contre l'analphabétisme

■ Experienced (American)

John Farmer
18 rue de Turenne
75004 Paris
Tél: 01 42 22 37 89   Né le 17 juin 1962
E-mail: jfarmer@nxl.fr   Marié, 2 enfants (11 et 14 ans)
                                             Nationalité américaine

Directeur des ventes : 6 ans d'expérience
14 ans d'expérience dans la fonction commerciale
Connaissance approfondie du marché informatique

Depuis 1996   Softlux France, Paris
                     Directeur des ventes Europe
                     · Encadrement d'une équipe de 20 commerciaux
                     · Diversification et développement des marchés existants
                     · Augmentation du chiffre d'affaires (+ 53 %)

1988 – 1996   ICN Europe, Amsterdam
                     Directeur commercial
                     · Responsable de la politique commerciale et du marketing
                     · Recrutement et encadrement d'une équipe de 7 commerciaux
                     · Dépassement des objectifs fixés: 1994:118 %, 1993: 110%

1983 – 1987   Société ADB, Paris
                     Ingénieur commercial grands comptes
                     · Responsable du développement des ventes pour le secteur de la grande distribution sur la région parisienne
                     · Ouverture de nouveaux comptes

Formation
1988   MBA, Harvard Business School
1984   MS (équivalent de la maîtrise) en Économie et Gestion, Université de Boston
1980   High school diploma (équivalent du baccalauréat)

Langues
Anglais : langue maternelle
Français : bilingue

■ Recent graduate (French)

Isabelle Murat
30, impasse de la Colline
75004 Paris
Tél : 01 40 22 57 93

25 ans
Célibataire

Formation

septembre 04 – juin 2006	École Technique Supérieure, Bordeaux : Section Statistiques et Prévisions
septembre 04 – juin 05	Mathématiques spéciales (Lycée Louis Leduc, Paris)
septembre 03 – juin 04	Mathématiques supérieures (Lycée Louis Leduc, Paris)
juin 2003	Baccalauréat C (mention bien)

Expérience professionnelle

| avril – mai 2006 | Stage de 3 mois au Cabinet Desmoulin-Marketing et Communication, 44, rue des Francs-Bourgeois, 75004 Paris : relance et suivi de la clientèle |
| juillet – septembre 2003 | Animatrice dans un camp d'adolescents à Port-de-Bouc (13) |

Langues
Bilingue allemand
Anglais courant

Divers

juillet 2005	Séjour de deux mois en Allemagne, à Dortmund
juin 2003	Obtention du diplôme du BAFA (Brevet d'aptitude aux fonctions d'animateur)
juillet 97 – juin 98	Séjour d'un an à Munich

Loisirs
Course à pied, vélo, aérobic
Théâtre dans une troupe d'amateurs

■ Recent graduate (American)

Martha Jacobs
493 Huntington Avenue
Boston
MA 02575
États-Unis
Tél : (617) 267-1680
E-mail: mjacobs@totem.com

23 ans, célibataire
Nationalité américaine

Traductrice anglais/français/espagnol
Début de spécialisation en informatique

FORMATION

2004 – 2006	Diplôme de traducteur technique Université McGill, Montréal
2000 – 2004	BA (équivalent de la licence) en français et espagnol, mention très bien Université de Boston
1999	High school diploma (équivalent du baccalauréat)

EXPÉRIENCE PROFESSIONNELLE

2005 – 2006	Éditions Dulis, Montréal Travaux de traduction en free-lance
juin 2004 – septembre 2005	Société AX Networks, Boston Stage de 3 mois dans le service de traduction : adaptation de logiciels pour le marché européen
1999 – 2000	Lycée Dupuis, Grenoble Assistante de français

LANGUES
Anglais : langue maternelle
Français : bilingue (2 ans à Montréal, 1 an à Grenoble)
Espagnol : courant

CONNAISSANCES INFORMATIQUES
Word, Excel et Access (sur PC et Mac)

LOISIRS
Escrime, violoncelle

Faxes

Faxes, which are by definition a form of rapid communication, can generally be drafted in a more casual and concise way than letters. The endings are usually short and simplified.

Business

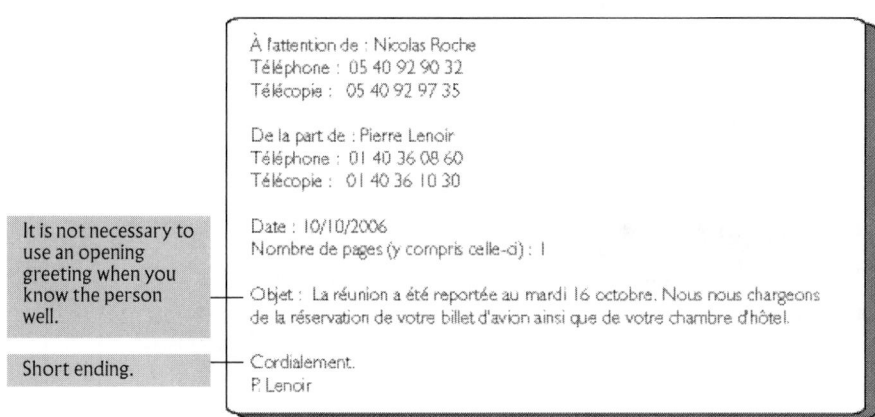

It is not necessary to use an opening greeting when you know the person well.

Short ending.

À l'attention de : Nicolas Roche
Téléphone : 05 40 92 90 32
Télécopie : 05 40 92 97 35

De la part de : Pierre Lenoir
Téléphone : 01 40 36 08 60
Télécopie : 01 40 36 10 30

Date : 10/10/2006
Nombre de pages (y compris celle-ci) : 1

Objet : La réunion a été reportée au mardi 16 octobre. Nous nous chargeons de la réservation de votre billet d'avion ainsi que de votre chambre d'hôtel.

Cordialement.
P. Lenoir

Booking a hotel room

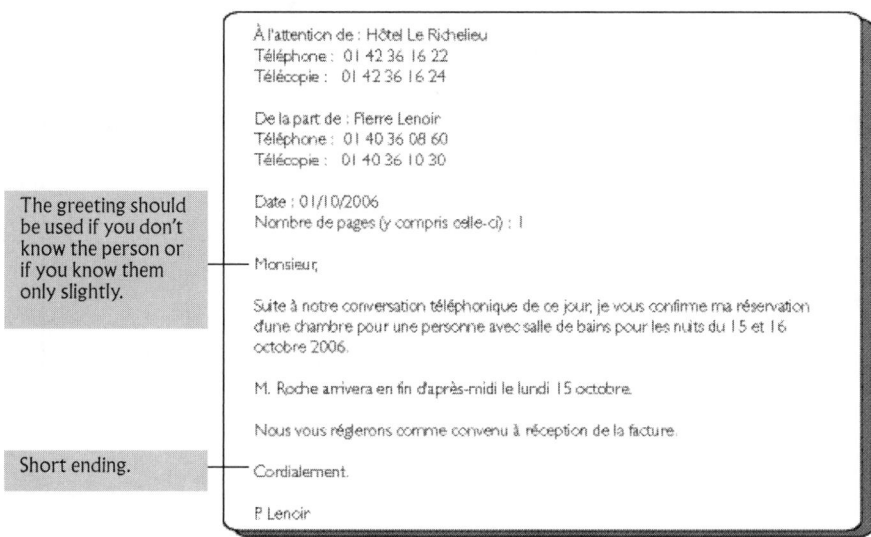

The greeting should be used if you don't know the person or if you know them only slightly.

Short ending.

À l'attention de : Hôtel Le Richelieu
Téléphone : 01 42 36 16 22
Télécopie : 01 42 36 16 24

De la part de : Pierre Lenoir
Téléphone : 01 40 36 08 60
Télécopie : 01 40 36 10 30

Date : 01/10/2006
Nombre de pages (y compris celle-ci) : 1

Monsieur,

Suite à notre conversation téléphonique de ce jour, je vous confirme ma réservation d'une chambre pour une personne avec salle de bains pour les nuits du 15 et 16 octobre 2006.

M. Roche arrivera en fin d'après-midi le lundi 15 octobre.

Nous vous réglerons comme convenu à réception de la facture.

Cordialement.

P. Lenoir

■ Alternative endings:

Salutations.
Salutations distinguées.
Bien à vous. (more friendly)

E-mail

Because of the nature of the medium, e-mails are not subject to the formal code of letter-writing that is prevalent in French.

E-mails in French are often written in slightly less telegraphic style than tends to be the case in English, this being mainly due to the fact that French contains fewer of the abbreviated forms that characterize so much of this type of communication in English. Endings are usually rather informal. Note that the symbol @ is pronounced "arrobas" or "arobase" in French.

Within a company

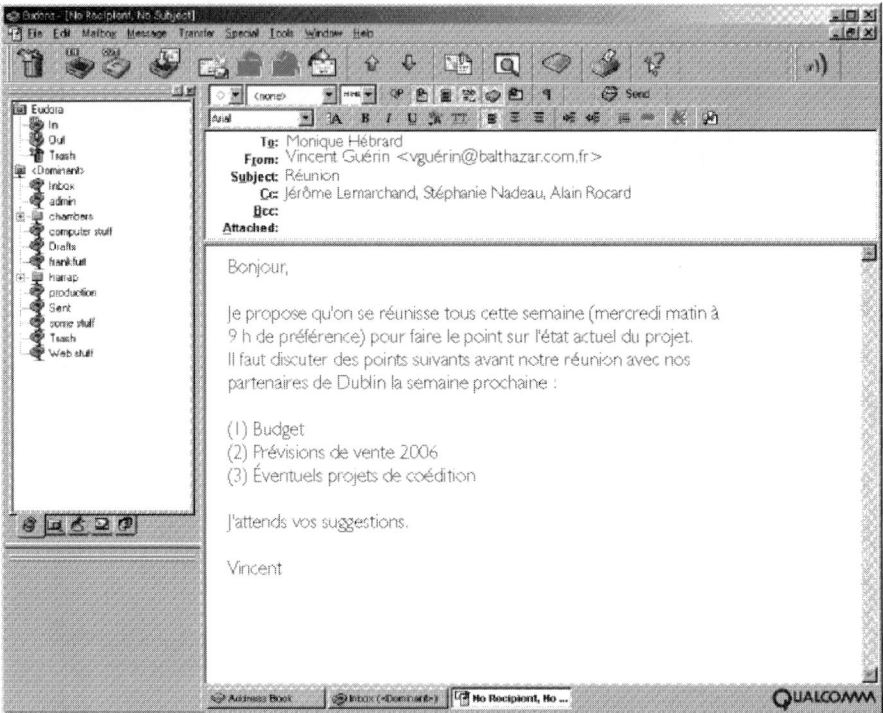

Business to business

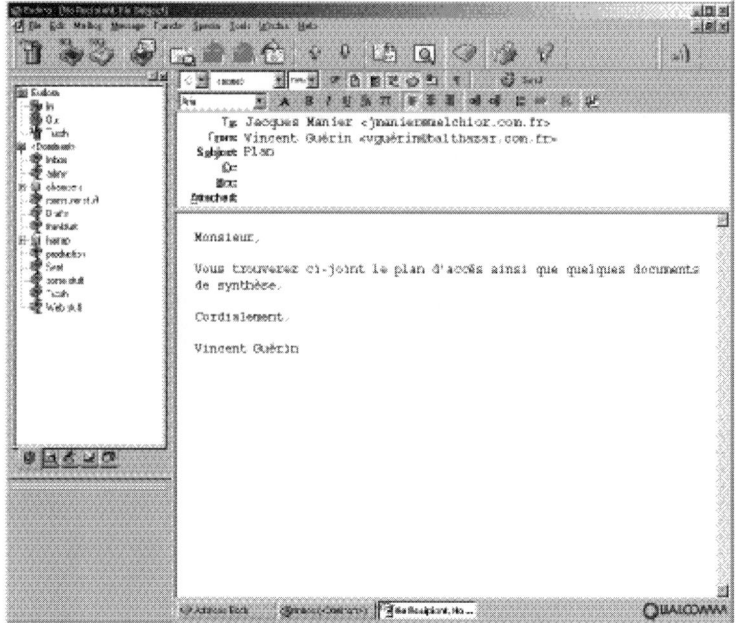

Abbreviations and acronyms

Below is a list of French abbreviations that are used in e-mail correspondence, in newsgroups and chat-rooms. These abbreviations should only be used when you are sure that the person to whom you are sending the message understands what they mean. Some are familiar in register (labelled *Fam*) and therefore should only be used in casual correspondence with friends or very close colleagues.

Note that because English is the main language of the Internet, English abbreviations are much more well established than French ones.

A+ *Fam*	à plus tard	**impr.**	impression/imprimer/imprimante
actu *Fam*	actualités		
alld	allemand	**info** *Fam*	information
alp *Fam*	à la prochaine	**K7** *Fam*	cassette
ama *Fam*	à mon avis	**ltr**	lettre
amha *Fam*	à mon humble avis	**m**	même
angl	anglais	**mdr** *Fam*	mort de rire
bcp *Fam*	beaucoup	**MMS** *Fam*	mes meilleurs souvenirs
BAL	boîte à lettres	**nvx**	nouveaux
B.D.	base de données	**p**	pour
cad	c'est-à-dire	**pb, pbm**	problème
dc	donc	**pr**	pour
doc.	documents	**quoi 2/9** *Fam*	quoi de neuf ?
doss	dossier	**RAS** *Fam*	rien à signaler
ds	dans	**stp**	s'il te plaît
envoy.	envoyer	**suiv.**	suivant
err	erreur	**svp**	s'il vous plaît
esp	espagnol	**svt**	souvent
ex.	exemple	**urgt**	urgent
fr	français	**we**	week-end

Advertisements

Job advertisement

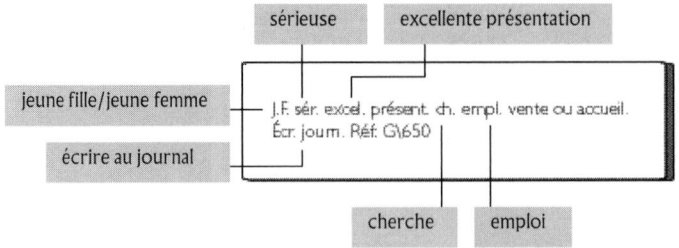

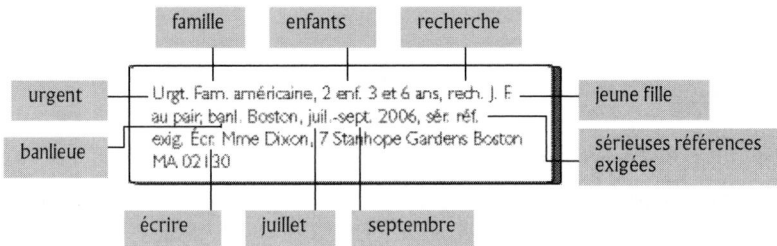

Offering goods for sale

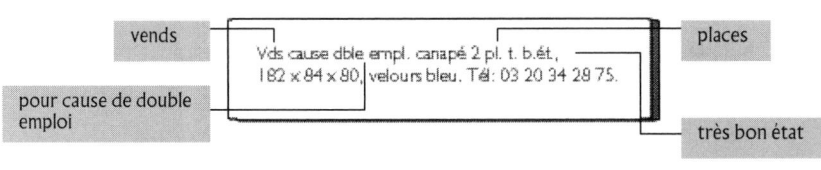

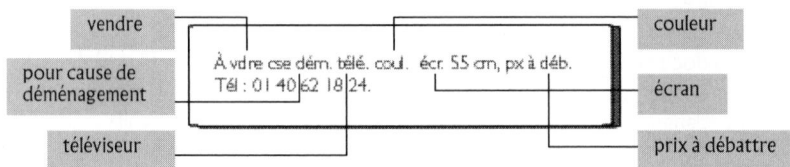

Accommodations to rent

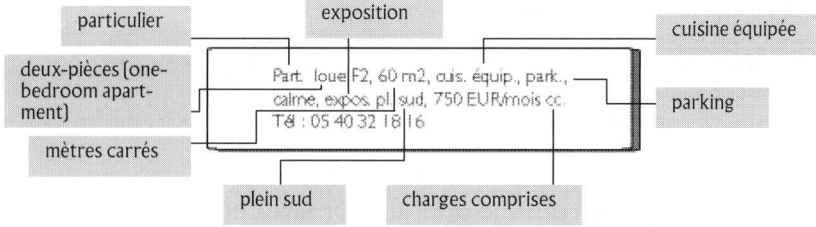

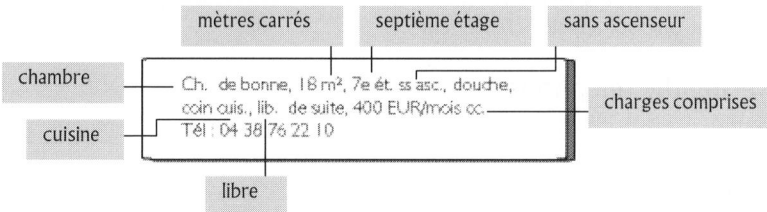

Personal advertisement

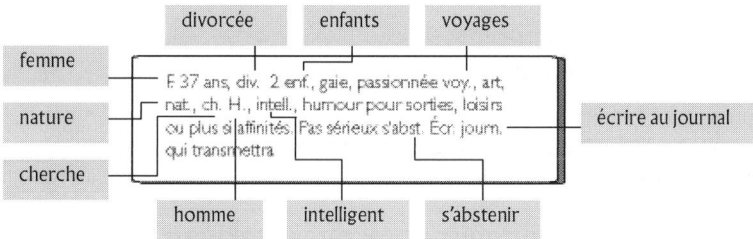

Common abbreviations:

à déb.	à débattre	park.	parking
appt.	appartement	pces.	pièces
balc.	balcon	px	prix
c.c.	charges comprises/chauffage central	rdc.	rez-de-chaussée
ch.	chambre/cherche	sdb.	salle de bains
compr.	comprenant	séj.	séjour
cuis.	cuisine	sér.	sérieux
env.	envoyer	tbe	très bon état
équip.	équipé	tt.conf.	tout confort
gar.	garage	se prés.	se présenter
gren.	grenier	Sté.	société

Telephone calls

Pronunciation of telephone numbers

When giving their phone numbers, French people say them two by two: 01 45 67 44 32: zéro un, quarante-cinq, soixante-sept, quarante-quatre, trente-deux.

This can be a little disconcerting for the English speaker and you may have to ask them to repeat giving one number at a time.

Asking for information from the operator or switchboard

- Est-ce que vous pouvez me passer les renseignements, s'il vous plaît ?
- J'essaie d'obtenir un numéro à Marseille.
- Quel est l'indicatif pour le Maroc, s'il vous plaît ?
- Comment fait-on pour appeler à l'extérieur ?

Answering the telephone

Informally:
- Allô ?

To which the caller replies:
- Allô, (c'est) Georges? *or* Salut, Georges, c'est Christophe, etc.

More formally:
- Allô, Hélène Chapsal à l'appareil (, je vous écoute).

In a company or institution:
- Éditions Paoli, bonjour.

Asking to speak to someone

- Je voudrais parler à Monsieur Dupont.
- Pouvez-vous me passer le service du/des ..., s'il vous plaît ?
- Pouvez-vous me passer le poste 321, s'il vous plaît ? (pronounced trois cent vingt-et-un)

Phrases used by a receptionist or secretary taking a call

- Qui dois-je annoncer ?
- C'est de la part de qui ?

When putting a caller through:
- Je vous le passe.
- Ne quittez pas, je vous le passe.

When the caller cannot be connected immediately:
- C'est occupé.
- Il est en communication, voulez-vous patienter ?

Asking the caller if he or she wishes to leave a message:
- Voulez-vous lui laisser un message ?

To which the caller may reply:
- Pouvez-vous lui demander de me rappeler ?

Recorded messages

If you are put through to an answering machine, the usual recorded message while waiting is:

Nous vous demandons de bien vouloir patienter quelques instants. Nous allons donner suite à votre appel.

If you have to leave a message, you will hear the following standard set of sentences:

Vous êtes bien en communication avec ... Nous ne pouvons répondre à votre appel. Veuillez nous laisser votre nom et numéro de téléphone après le signal sonore et nous vous rappellerons dès que possible. Merci.

English-French
Anglais-Français

A

A, a¹ [eɪ] *n* (**a**) *(letter)* A, a *m inv*; **to get from A to B** aller d'un point à un autre; **from A to Z** de A à Z; **A bomb** bombe *f* A; **A side** *(of record)* face *f* A; **A-Z** *(street guide)* index *m* des rues; **an A-Z of gardening** le jardinage de A à Z (**b**) *Sch (grade)* **to get an A** *(on a test)* avoir mention bien ou très bien; *(on homework, essay)* ≃ avoir entre 14 et 20 (**c**) *Mus* la *m inv*

a² [ə, *stressed* eɪ] *indefinite art* (**a**) *(in general)* un (une); **a man** un homme; **a woman** une femme; **an hour** une heure; **he's got a red nose** il a le nez rouge; **I don't have a car** je n'ai pas de voiture; **what a day!** quelle journée! (**b**) *(with professions, nationalities)* **he's an American/a father/a lawyer** il est américain/père/avocat (**c**) *(with prices, rates)* **50 cents a pound** 50 cents la livre; **three times a week** trois fois par semaine; **30 miles an hour** ≃ 50 kilomètres (à l')heure (**d**) *(a certain)* **a Mr. Watkins phoned** un certain M. Watkins a appelé

AA [eɪ'eɪ] *n (abbr* **Alcoholics Anonymous***)* AA *mpl*

AAA *n* [eɪeɪ'eɪ] *(abbr* **American Automobile Association***)* = club automobile américain

AB [eɪ'biː] *n (abbr* **Artium Baccalaureus***) (diploma)* ≃ licence *f* de lettres; *(graduate)* ≃ licencié(e) *m,f* ès lettres

abaci ['æbəsaɪ] *pl of* **abacus**

aback [ə'bæk] *adv* **taken a. (by)** déconcerté(e) (par)

abacus ['æbəkəs] *(pl* **abaci** ['æbəsaɪ] *or* **abacuses** ['æbəkəsɪz]*) n* boulier *m*

abandon [ə'bændən] **1** *n* **with a.** avec abandon; **to drive with reckless a.** conduire avec insouciance
2 *vt* abandonner; *(match)* interrompre; **to a. ship** abandonner le navire

abase [ə'beɪs] *vt* **to a. oneself** s'abaisser, s'humilier

abashed [ə'bæʃt] *adj* penaud(e); **to be** *or* **feel a. (at sth)** avoir honte (de qch)

abate [ə'beɪt] *vi (of storm, pain)* se calmer; *(of noise)* diminuer

abattoir ['æbətwɑː(r)] *n* abattoir *m*

abbess ['æbɪs] *n* abbesse *f*

abbey ['æbɪ] *(pl* **abbeys***) n* abbaye *f*

abbot ['æbət] *n* abbé *m*

abbreviate [ə'briːvɪeɪt] *vt* abréger

abbreviation [əbriːvɪ'eɪʃən] *n* abréviation *f*

ABC [eɪbiː'siː] *n* (**a**) *(alphabet)* alphabet *m*; **an ABC of gardening** un ABC du jardinage (**b**) *(abbr* **American Broadcasting Corporation***)* = chaîne de télévision américaine

abdicate ['æbdɪkeɪt] **1** *vt* **to a. the throne** abdiquer; **to a. responsibility** abdiquer devant ses responsabilités
2 *vi (of monarch)* abdiquer

abdication [æbdɪ'keɪʃən] *n (of throne)* abdication *f*; *(of responsibilities)* abandon *m*

abdomen ['æbdəmən] *n Anat & Zool* abdomen *m*

abdominal [æb'dɒmɪnəl] *adj Anat* abdominal(e)

abdominals [æb'dɒmɪnəlz] *npl (exercises)* abdominaux *mpl*

abduct [əb'dʌkt] *vt* enlever

abduction [əb'dʌkʃən] *n* enlèvement *m*

aberration [æbə'reɪʃən] *n* aberration *f*; **in a moment of a.** dans un moment de folie

abet [ə'bet] *(pt & pp* **abetted***) vt Law* **to aid and a. sb** être le complice de qn

abetting [ə'betɪŋ] *n Law* **aiding and a.** complicité *f*

abeyance [ə'beɪəns] *n* **in a.** *(of law, custom)* en désuétude

abhor [əb'hɔː(r)] *(pt & pp* **abhorred***) vt* détester, avoir horreur de

abhorrence [əb'hɒrəns] *n* horreur *f*

abhorrent [əb'hɒrənt] *adj* odieux(euse)

abide [ə'baɪd] *vt (tolerate)* **I can't a. him** je ne peux pas le supporter

▸**abide by** *vt insep (promise)* tenir; *(rule, decision)* se plier à, se soumettre à; **I a. by what I said** je maintiens ce que j'ai dit

abiding [ə'baɪdɪŋ] *adj (impression)* durable; **my a. memory of him is his generosity** je garde de lui le souvenir de quelqu'un de très généreux

ability [ə'bɪlɪtɪ] *(pl* **abilities***) n* (**a**) *(talent, skill)* capacités *fpl* (**in** en), compétence *f* (**in** en) (**b**) *(capability)* capacité *f* (**to** à); **to the best of one's a.** de son mieux

abject ['æbdʒekt] *adj (miserable)* malheureux(euse); *(contemptible)* abject(e); **to make an a. apology** s'excuser platement; **a. poverty** misère *f* noire

ablaze [ə'bleɪz] *adj* en feu, en flammes; **to set sth a.** embraser qch; *Fig* **her eyes were a. with anger** ses yeux brillaient de colère

able ['eɪbəl] *adj* (**a**) *(competent) (person, performance)* compétent(e) (**b**) **to be a. to do sth** *(be physically capable)* pouvoir faire qch; *(know how to)* savoir faire qch; **I won't be a. to come** je ne pourrai pas venir; **we waited all afternoon, but we weren't a. to see him** nous avons attendu tout l'après-midi mais nous n'avons pas réussi à le voir

able-bodied ['eɪbəl'bɒdɪd] *adj* robuste; *Naut* **a. seaman** matelot *m* de deuxième classe

ably ['eɪblɪ] *adj* de façon compétente; **a. assisted by** efficacement assisté par

abnormal [æb'nɔːməl] *adj* anormal(e)

abnormality [æbnɔː'mælɪtɪ] *(pl* **abnormalities***) n (irregularity)* anomalie *f*; *(physical)* malformation *f*

abnormally [æb'nɔːməlɪ] *adv* anormalement

aboard [ə'bɔːd] **1** *adv (on ship, airplane)* à bord; **to go a.** monter à bord
2 *prep (ship, airplane)* à bord de; *(bus, train)* dans

abode [ə'bəʊd] *n Lit* demeure *f*; *Law* **of no fixed a.** sans domicile fixe

abolish [ə'bɒlɪʃ] *vt* abolir; *(law)* abroger

abolition [æbə'lɪʃən] *n* abolition *f*; *(of law)* abrogation *f*

abominable [ə'bɒmɪnəbəl] *adj* abominable; **the a. snowman** l'abominable homme *m* des neiges

abomination [əbɒmɪ'neɪʃən] *n* abomination *f*

aborigine [æbə'rɪdʒɪnɪ] *n* aborigène *mf*

abort [ə'bɔːt] **1** *vt* (**a**) *Med (woman)* avorter; **the fetus was**

aborted la grossesse a été interrompue (**b**) *(project)* & *Comput* abandonner

2 *vi Med* avorter, faire une fausse couche

abortion [ə'bɔːʃən] *n* avortement *m*, IVG *f*; **to have an a.** se faire avorter

abortive [ə'bɔːtɪv] *adj (attempt, plan)* avorté(e)

abound [ə'baʊnd] *vi* abonder (**in** *or* **with** en)

about [ə'baʊt] **1** *prep* (**a**) *(regarding)* **a book a. France** un livre sur la France; **the good/bad thing a....** ce qu'il y a de bien/de mauvais dans...; **what's it a.?** de quoi s'agit-il?; **to talk a. sth** parler de qch; **to argue a. sth** se disputer au sujet de qch; **we must do something a. this problem** il faut faire quelque chose à ce sujet

(**b**) *(in various parts of)* **to walk a. the town** se promener dans la ville; **to look a. the room** parcourir la pièce du regard

2 *adv* (**a**) *(in different directions, places)* **to walk a.** se promener; **to run a.** courir à droite et à gauche; **to be lying a.** traîner

(**b**) *(in the general area)* **is Jack a.?** est-ce que Jack est dans les environs *ou* parages?; **there was nobody a.** il n'y avait personne

(**c**) *(approximately)* environ, à peu près; **a. thirty** environ trente, une trentaine; **a. ten years** environ dix ans, une dizaine d'années; **at a. one o'clock** vers une heure; **she's a. as tall as you** elle est grande à peu près comme toi; **I've just a. finished** j'ai pratiquement terminé; **a. time!** ce n'est pas trop tôt!

(**d**) *(on the point of)* **to be a. to do sth** aller faire qch, être sur le point de faire qch; **I'm not a. to...** *(have no intention of)* je n'ai pas l'intention de...

about-face [ə'baʊt'feɪs] *n (radical change)* volte-face *f inv*

above [ə'bʌv] **1** *prep* (**a**) *(physically)* au-dessus de; **the Seine a. Paris** la Seine en amont de Paris

(**b**) *(with numbers)* plus de; **the temperature didn't rise a. 50°F** ≃ la température n'a pas dépassé 10°C

(**c**) *(in rank)* **he is a. me** il est mon supérieur

(**d**) *(not subject to)* **to be a. suspicion** être au-dessus de tout soupçon; **her behavior is a. criticism** il n'y a rien à redire à son attitude

(**e**) *(superior to)* **he thinks he's a. all that** il se croit au-dessus de tout ça; **she's not a. telling lies** elle est capable de mentir

(**f**) **a. all** surtout; **they value friendship a. all else** ils font passer l'amitié avant tout le reste

2 *adv* (**a**) *(in general)* au-dessus; **the tenants (of the apartment) a.** les locataires du dessus; **from a.** *(from one's superiors)* d'en haut

(**b**) *(in book, document)* ci-dessus

aboveboard [ə'bʌvbɔːd] *adj (honest)* franc (franche), honnête

above-mentioned [əbʌv'menʃənd], **above-named** [əbʌv'neɪmd] *adj* susdit(e), susnommé(e)

abrasion [ə'breɪʒən] *n (on skin)* écorchure *f*

abrasive [ə'breɪsɪv] **1** *n (substance)* abrasif *m*

2 *adj (surface, substance)* abrasif(ive); *(person, manner)* caustique

abreast [ə'brest] *adv* de front; **to come a. of** arriver à la hauteur de; **to keep a. of** *(events, progress)* se tenir au courant de

abridged [ə'brɪdʒd] *adj* abrégé(e)

abroad [ə'brɔːd] *adv* à l'étranger; **our colleagues from a.** nos collègues étrangers; **to get a.** *(of news)* se répandre

abrupt [ə'brʌpt] *adj* (**a**) *(sudden)* brusque, soudain(e); **the train came to an a. halt** le train s'est brusquement *ou* soudainement arrêté (**b**) *(curt)* abrupt(e), brusque

abruptly [ə'brʌptlɪ] *adv* (**a**) *(suddenly)* brusquement, soudainement (**b**) *(curtly)* de façon abrupte, avec brusquerie

abscess ['æbses] *n* abcès *m*

abscond [əb'skɒnd] *vi Formal* s'enfuir, prendre la fuite

abseil ['æbseɪl] *vi* descendre en rappel; **to a. down sth** descendre qch en rappel

abseiling ['æbseɪlɪŋ] *n* rappel *m*, descente *f* en rappel; **to go a.** faire du rappel

absence ['æbsəns] *n* absence *f*; **in the a. of** *(person)* en l'absence de; *(thing)* faute de; *Law* **sentenced in one's a.** condamné(e) par contumace; *Prov* **a. makes the heart grow fonder** l'éloignement renforce l'affection

absent 1 *adj* ['æbsənt] *(pupil, expression)* absent(e); *Mil* **a. without leave** porté(e) manquant(e)

2 *vt* [æb'sent] **to a. oneself (from)** s'absenter (de)

absentee [æbsən'tiː] *n* absent(e) *m,f*; **a. landlord** propriétaire *m* absentéiste

absenteeism [æbsən'tiːɪzm] *n* absentéisme *m*

absent-minded [æbsənt'maɪndɪd] *adj* distrait(e)

absent-mindedness [æbsənt'maɪndɪnɪs] *n* distraction *f*

absolute ['æbsəluːt] *adj* (**a**) *(total)* absolu(e); **a. majority** majorité *f* absolue; **a. monarch** monarque *m* absolu (**b**) *(emphatic)* **he's an a. fool!** il est complètement idiot!; **a. garbage!** n'importe quoi!; **an a. disgrace/disaster** un véritable scandale/désastre

absolutely [æbsə'luːtlɪ] *adv* absolument; **you're a. right** vous avez absolument *ou* tout à fait raison; **do you support him? – a./a. not** vous le soutenez? – absolument/absolument pas

absolution [æbsə'luːʃən] *n Rel* absolution *f*

absolve [əb'zɒlv] *vt Rel* absoudre (**from** *or* **of** de); *(from duty)* dispenser (**from** *or* **of** de); **to be absolved from blame** être innocenté(e)

absorb [əb'zɔːb] *vt (liquid)* absorber; *(losses)* essuyer; **to be absorbed in sth** être absorbé(e) par qch

absorbent [əb'zɔːbənt] *adj* absorbant(e); **a. cotton** coton *m* hydrophile

absorbing [əb'zɔːbɪŋ] *adj (work)* absorbant(e); *(book, question)* passionnant(e)

abstain [əb'steɪn] *vi* s'abstenir (**from** de)

abstemious [əb'stiːmɪəs] *adj* sobre

abstention [əb'stenʃən] *n Pol* abstention *f*

abstinence ['æbstɪnəns] *n* abstinence *f*

abstract ['æbstrækt] **1** *n* (**a**) *(concept)* **the a.** l'abstrait *m* (**b**) *(of article)* résumé *m*

2 *adj* abstrait(e)

3 *vt* [æb'strækt] *Formal (remove)* extraire (**from** de)

abstraction [æb'strækʃən] *n* abstraction *f*

abstruse [əb'struːs] *adj* obscur(e)

absurd [əb'sɜːd] *adj* absurde

absurdity [əb'sɜːdɪtɪ] *(pl* **absurdities**) *n* absurdité *f*

abundance [ə'bʌndəns] *n* abondance *f*; **an a. of talent** un grand talent; **in a.** en abondance

abundant [ə'bʌndənt] *adj* abondant(e); **to be a. in sth** abonder en qch

abundantly [ə'bʌndəntlɪ] *adv* en abondance; **a. clear** tout à fait clair(e)

abuse 1 *n* [ə'bjuːs] (**a**) *(of power)* abus *m* (**b**) *(insults)* injures *fpl*, insultes *fpl*; **term of a.** injure *f*, insulte *f* (**c**) *(cruelty)* mauvais traitements *mpl*, maltraitance *f*; **(sexual) a.** sévices *mpl* sexuels

2 *vt* [ə'bjuːz] (**a**) *(misuse)* abuser de (**b**) *(insult)* injurier, insulter (**c**) *(ill-treat) (physically)* maltraiter; *(sexually)* faire subir des sévices sexuels à

abusive [ə'bjuːsɪv] *adj (person, language)* grossier(ère)

abysmal [ə'bɪzməl] *adj (ignorance)* sans bornes; *(performance, quality)* épouvantable

abyss [ə'bɪs] *n also Fig* abîme *m*, gouffre *m*

AC[1] ['eɪ'siː] *n Elec (abbr* **alternating current***)* courant *m* alternatif

AC[2] ['eɪ'siː] *n (abbr* **air-conditioning***)* climatisation *f*; *Fam* clim *f*

a/c *n (abbr* **account***)* compte *m*

academic [ækə'demɪk] **1** *n (university teacher)* universitaire *mf; (intellectual)* intellectuel(elle) *m,f*
  2 *adj* (**a**) *(of school)* scolaire; *(of university)* universitaire; **her a. achievements are impressive** elle a fait de brillantes études; **a. year** année *f* universitaire (**b**) *(intellectual)* intellectuel(elle) (**c**) *(theoretical)* théorique; **it's entirely a. whether he did it or not** qu'il l'ait fait ou non n'a aucune importance

academy [ə'kædəmɪ] *(pl* **academies**) *n* académie *f;* **a. of music** conservatoire *m* (de musique)

accede [æk'siːd] *vi Formal* (**a**) **to a. to** *(request, demand)* accéder à; *(agreement, changes)* accepter (**b**) *(of monarch)* **to a. to the throne** accéder au trône

accelerate [ək'seləreɪt] **1** *vt (progress)* accélérer; *(downfall)* précipiter
  2 *vi (of car, driver)* accélérer; *(of pace)* s'accélérer

acceleration [əkselə'reɪʃən] *n* accélération *f*

accelerator [ək'seləreɪtə(r)] *n* accélérateur *m*

accent ['æksənt] *n* accent *m;* **to put the a. on sth** *(emphasize)* mettre l'accent sur qch

accentuate [æk'sentʃʊeɪt] *vt* accentuer

accept [ək'sept] *vt* (**a**) *(gift, apology, defeat)* accepter; *(responsibility)* assumer (**for** de); *(concede)* admettre; **to a. (that)...** admettre que... (**b**) *(into a university)* admettre

acceptable [ək'septəbəl] *adj* acceptable; **to be a. to sb** *(suit)* convenir à qn

acceptance [ək'septəns] *n* (**a**) *(of invitation, apology, defeat)* acceptation *f;* **to find a.** être reconnu(e) (**b**) *(to a university)* admission *f;* **a. speech** = discours prononcé par le lauréat d'un prix

access ['ækses] **1** *n* accès *m* (**to** à); **to have a. to sth** avoir accès à qch; **to gain a. to** *(get inside)* s'introduire dans; *(reach)* accéder à; **a. ramp** bretelle *f* d'accès; **a. road** route *f* d'accès; *(of highway)* bretelle *f* d'accès; *Comput* **a. code** code *m* d'accès; *Comput* **a. provider** fournisseur *m* d'accès; *Comput* **a. time** temps *m* d'accès
  2 *vt Comput* accéder à

accessible [ək'sesəbəl] *adj (place, explanation)* accessible; *(person)* joignable

accession [ək'seʃən] *n (to power, throne)* accession *f; (library book)* acquisition *f*

accessory [ək'sesərɪ] *(pl* **accessories**) *n* (**a**) *(extra)* accessoire *m* (**b**) *Law* complice *mf* (**to** de)

accident ['æksɪdənt] *n* accident *m;* **by a.** par accident *ou* hasard; **to have an a.** avoir un accident; **a. insurance** assurance *f* accidents

accidental [æksɪ'dentəl] *adj* accidentel(elle); *Law* **a. death** mort *f* accidentelle

accidentally [æksɪ'dentəlɪ] *adv* accidentellement

accident-prone ['æksɪdəntprəʊn] *adj* prédisposé(e) aux accidents

acclaim [ə'kleɪm] **1** *n* louanges *fpl;* **to meet with great critical a.** être salué(e) par la critique
  2 *vt (person)* acclamer; *(performance, movie)* applaudir

acclamation [æklə'meɪʃən] *n (cheering)* acclamations *fpl*

acclimatize [ə'klaɪmətaɪz] **1** *vt (animal, plant)* acclimater; **to become acclimatized to** *(person)* s'habituer à, s'accoutumer à
  2 *vi* s'acclimater (**to** à)

accolade ['ækəleɪd] *n* honneur *m*

accommodate [ə'kɒmədeɪt] *vt* (**a**) *(provide room for)* loger (**b**) *(satisfy)* satisfaire

accommodating [ə'kɒmədeɪtɪŋ] *adj (helpful)* obligeant(e); *(easy to please)* accommodant(e)

accommodation [əkɒmə'deɪʃən] *n* (**a**) **accommodations** *(lodging)* logement *m; (in hotel)* chambre *f* (d'hôtel) (**b**) *Formal (agreement)* compromis *m*

accompaniment [ə'kʌmpənɪmənt] *n Mus* accompagnement *m; Culin* garniture *f*

accompany [ə'kʌmpənɪ] *(pt & pp* **accompanied**) *vt* accompagner; **to be accompanied by sth** s'accompagner de qch

accomplice [ə'kʌmplɪs] *n* complice *mf*

accomplish [ə'kʌmplɪʃ] *vt (task)* accomplir; *(aim)* atteindre

accomplished [ə'kʌmplɪʃt] *adj (musician, cook)* accompli(e); *(actor)* doué(e); *(performance)* très au point

accord [ə'kɔːd] **1** *n* accord *m;* **in a. with** en accord avec; **with one a.** d'un commun accord; **of one's own a.** de son plein gré
  2 *vt* accorder (**to** à)

▸**accord with** *vt insep* concorder avec

accordance [ə'kɔːdəns] *n* **in a. with** en accord avec; **his statement is not in a. with the facts** sa déclaration ne concorde pas avec les faits

according to [ə'kɔːdɪŋtuː] *prep* (**a**) *(depending on)* selon; **a. whether one is rich or poor** selon que l'on est riche ou pauvre; **a. which method you use** selon la méthode utilisée (**b**) *(in conformity with)* selon; **to go a. plan** se dérouler comme prévu (**c**) *(citing a source)* selon, d'après

accordingly [ə'kɔːdɪŋlɪ] *adv* (**a**) *(appropriately)* en conséquence (**b**) *(therefore)* par conséquent

accordion [ə'kɔːdɪən] *n* accordéon *m*

accost [ə'kɒst] *vt* accoster, aborder

account [ə'kaʊnt] *n* (**a**) *(at bank)* compte *m; Com* **accounts department** comptabilité *f*
  (**b**) *(reckoning)* **to keep (an) a. of sth** tenir un compte de qch; **to take sth into a., to take a. of sth** *(consider)* tenir compte de qch, prendre qch en compte; **taking everything into a.** *(after all)* au bout du compte; **to call sb to a.** demander des comptes à qn; **to be brought to a.** avoir des comptes à rendre
  (**c**) *(importance)* **of no a.** sans importance
  (**d**) *(on a. of* *(because of)* à cause de; **on no a., not on any a.** en aucun cas, surtout pas; **to set up in business on one's own a.** s'installer à son compte; **don't do it on my a.!** ne le faites surtout pas pour moi!
  (**e**) *(report)* description *f;* **to give an a. of sth** faire le récit de qch; *Fig* **to give a good a. of oneself** *(in fight, contest)* bien se défendre; **by all accounts** au dire de tous

▸**account for** *vt insep* (**a**) *(explain, justify)* expliquer; **five people have still not been accounted for** *(are still missing)* cinq personnes n'ont toujours pas été retrouvées; **there's no accounting for taste** chacun ses goûts (**b**) *(constitute)* constituer

accountability [əkaʊntə'bɪlɪtɪ] *n* responsabilité *f* (**to** envers)

accountable [ə'kaʊntəbəl] *adj* responsable (**to sb** envers qn; **for sth** de qch); *(for sum of money)* redevable (**for** de); **to hold sb a.** tenir qn pour responsable

accountancy [ə'kaʊntənsɪ] *n* comptabilité *f*

accountant [ə'kaʊntənt] *n* comptable *mf*

accounting [ə'kaʊntɪŋ] *n* comptabilité *f;* **a. period** période *f* comptable

accrue [ə'kruː] *vi Fin (of interest)* s'accumuler; **to a. to sb** *(of interest, benefits)* revenir à qn

accumulate [ə'kjuːmjʊleɪt] **1** *vt* accumuler
  2 *vi* s'accumuler

accumulation [əkjuːmjʊ'leɪʃən] *n* accumulation *f*

accuracy ['ækjʊrəsɪ] *n (of calculation, translation)* exactitude *f,* précision *f; (of firearm, shot)* précision *f; (of portrayal)* fidélité *f*

accurate ['ækjʊrət] *adj (calculation, translation)* exact(e), précis(e); *(firearm, shot)* précis(e); *(portrayal)* fidèle

accurately ['ækjʊrətlɪ] *adv (calculate, translate)* avec exactitude *ou* précision; *(aim)* avec précision; *(portray)* fidèlement

accusation [ækjʊ'zeɪʃən] *n* accusation *f;* **to make an a. (against sb)** porter *ou* lancer une accusation (contre qn)

accuse [ə'kjuːz] *vt* **to a. sb (of sth/of doing sth)** accuser qn (de qch/de faire qch)

accused [ə'kjuːzd] *(pl* **accused**) *n Law* **the a.** l'inculpé(e) *m,f*

accuser [əˈkjuːzə(r)] *n* accusateur(trice) *m,f*

accusing [əˈkjuːzɪŋ] *adj (look, tone)* accusateur(trice)

accustom [əˈkʌstəm] *vt* accoutumer, habituer; **to be accustomed to sth/to doing sth** être habitué à qch/à faire qch; **to get** *or* **to grow accustomed to sth/to doing sth** s'accoutumer *ou* s'habituer à qch/à faire qch

AC/DC [ˈeɪsiːˈdiːsiː] **1** *n Elec (abbr* **alternating current/direct current)** courant alternatif/courant continu

2 *adj Fam (bisexual)* **to be A.** marcher à voile et à vapeur

ace [eɪs] **1** *n* (**a**) *(in cards)* as *m*; **a. of spades** as de pique; *Fig* **to have an a. up one's sleeve** avoir un atout en réserve; **to come within an a. of doing sth** être à deux doigts de faire qch (**b**) *(tennis)* ace *m* (**c**) *Fam (expert)* as *m*; **flying a.** as de l'aviation

2 *adj Fam (very good)* super *inv*

acerbic [əˈsɜːbɪk] *adj* acerbe

acetate [ˈæsɪteɪt] *n Chem* acétate *m*

acetic acid [æˈsiːtɪkˈæsɪd] *n* acide *m* acétique

ache [eɪk] **1** *n* douleur *f*; **aches and pains** douleurs *fpl*

2 *vi (of person)* avoir mal; **my head aches** j'ai mal à la tête; **my leg aches** j'ai mal à la jambe, ma jambe me fait mal; *Fig* **to be aching to do sth** mourir d'envie de faire qch

achieve [əˈtʃiːv] *vt (aim)* atteindre, parvenir à; **to a. success** réussir; **to a. a lot** faire beaucoup de chemin

achievement [əˈtʃiːvmənt] *n (action)* réalisation *f*; *(thing achieved)* réussite *f*

Achilles' heel [əkɪliːzˈhiːl] *n* talon *m* d'Achille

acid [ˈæsɪd] **1** *n* (**a**) *(chemical)* acide *m* (**b**) *Fam (LSD)* acide *m*; **a. house** *(music)* acid house *m*

2 *adj* (**a**) *(chemical, taste)* acide; **a. rain** pluies *fpl* acides; *Fig* **a. test** test *m* décisif (**b**) *(tone, remark)* aigre

acidic [əˈsɪdɪk] *adj* acide; *(tone, remark)* aigre

acidity [əˈsɪdɪtɪ] *n (of chemical, taste)* acidité *f*; *(of tone, remark)* aigreur *f*

acknowledge [əkˈnɒlɪdʒ] *vt (mistake, debt, truth)* admettre, reconnaître; **to a. (receipt of) a letter** accuser réception d'une lettre; **this restaurant is acknowledged to be the best in the city** ce restaurant est considéré comme le meilleur de la ville; **she didn't a. me** *or* **my presence** elle m'a ignoré

acknowledg(e)ment [əkˈnɒlɪdʒmənt] *n (of mistake, debt, truth)* reconnaissance *f*; **in a. of** *(service, achievement)* en reconnaissance de; *(letter)* en réponse à; **acknowledgments** *(in book)* remerciements *mpl*; **a. slip** *(for letter)* accusé *m* de réception

ACLU [eɪsiːelˈjuː] *n (abbr* **American Civil Liberties Union)** = organisme américain qui milite pour les droits civiques

acne [ˈækni] *n* acné *f*

acolyte [ˈækəlaɪt] *n* disciple *mf*

acorn [ˈeɪkɔːn] *n* gland *m*

acoustic [əˈkuːstɪk] *adj* acoustique; **a. guitar** guitare *f* acoustique

acoustics [əˈkuːstɪks] *npl* acoustique *f*

acquaint [əˈkweɪnt] *vt* (**a**) *(with person)* **to be acquainted with sb** connaître qn; **to become** *or* **to get acquainted (with)** faire *ou* lier connaissance (avec) (**b**) *(with facts, situation)* **to be acquainted with sth** connaître qch; **to a. sb with sth** mettre qn au courant de qch; **to a. oneself with sth** se familiariser avec qch

acquaintance [əˈkweɪntəns] *n* (**a**) *(person)* connaissance *f* (**b**) *(familiarity) (with person, facts)* familiarité *f*; **to make sb's a.** faire la connaissance de qn

acquiesce [ækwɪˈes] *vi* consentir (**in/to** à)

acquiescence [ækwɪˈesəns] *n* consentement *m* (**in/to** à)

acquiescent [ækwɪˈesənt] *adj* consentant(e)

acquire [əˈkwaɪə(r)] *vt (knowledge, reputation, property)* acquérir; *(habit, accent, air)* prendre; **to a. a taste for sth** prendre

goût à qch; **it's an acquired taste** c'est quelque chose que l'on apprend à aimer

acquisition [ækwɪˈzɪʃən] *n* acquisition *f*

acquisitive [əˈkwɪzɪtɪv] *adj* matérialiste

acquit [əˈkwɪt] *(pt & pp* **acquitted)** *vt* (**a**) *Law* acquitter (**b**) **to a. oneself well/badly** s'en sortir *ou* s'en tirer bien/mal

acquittal [əˈkwɪtəl] *n Law* acquittement *m*

acre [ˈeɪkə(r)] *n* = 4047 m², ≃ demi-hectare *m*; **acres of forest** des hectares de forêt; *Fam* **acres of space** plein de place

acrid [ˈækrɪd] *adj* âcre

acrimonious [ækrɪˈməʊnɪəs] *adj (person, remark)* hargneux(-euse); *(discussion)* virulent(e)

acrimony [ˈækrɪmənɪ] *n* acrimonie *f*, hargne *f*

acrobat [ˈækrəbæt] *n* acrobate *mf*

acrobatic [ækrəˈbætɪk] *adj* acrobatique

acrobatics [ækrəˈbætɪks] **1** *n* acrobatie *f*

2 *npl Fig* **mental a.** gymnastique *f* intellectuelle

acronym [ˈækrənɪm] *n* sigle *m*

across [əˈkrɒs] **1** *prep* (**a**) *(from one side to the other of)* **to go a. sth** traverser qch; **to run a. the road** traverser la route en courant; **to swim a. a river** traverser une rivière à la nage; **the bridge a. the river** le pont sur la rivière; **she threw it a. the room** elle l'a lancé à l'autre bout de la pièce

(**b**) *(on the other side of)* de l'autre côté de; **she lives a. the road** elle habite en face; **the woman (from) a. the road** la femme d'en face

(**c**) *(throughout)* **a. the country** dans tout le pays; **a. the political spectrum** dans l'ensemble de la classe politique

2 *adv* (**a**) *(from one side to the other)* **to run/to swim a.** traverser en courant/à la nage; **go a. and see her** traverse et va la voir; **to get sth a. to sb** faire comprendre qch à qn; **I can't get the argument a. to them** je n'arrive pas à leur faire comprendre cet argument

(**b**) *(with distance)* **it's 10 inches/5 miles a.** ≃ ça fait 25,5 cm/8 km de large

(**c**) **a. from me/my house** en face de moi/de chez moi

(**d**) *(in crosswords)* horizontalement

across-the-board [əˈkrɒsðəˈbɔːd] *adj* général(e), systématique

acrylic [əˈkrɪlɪk] **1** *n (fabric)* acrylique *m*

2 *adj (paint, fiber)* acrylique; *(garment)* en acrylique

act [ækt] **1** *n* (**a**) *(thing done)* acte *m*; **to be in the a. of doing sth** être en train de faire qch; **to catch sb in the a. of doing sth** surprendre qn en train de faire qch; **to catch sb in the a.** prendre qn sur le fait *ou* en flagrant délit; *Fam* **to get in on the a.** *(get involved)* se mettre dans le coup; **a. of war** acte *m* de guerre; *Law* **a. of God** catastrophe *f* naturelle

(**b**) *(of play)* acte *m*; *(in cabaret, circus)* numéro *m*; *Fig* **to put on an a.** faire semblant; *Fig* **to get one's a. together** se secouer; *Fig* **to clean up one's a.** *(of organization)* faire le ménage; *(of student)* s'améliorer; *Fig* **it's all an a.** c'est du cinéma

(**c**) *Law* **a. (of Congress)** loi *f*

2 *vt* (**a**) *(character)* jouer (le rôle de), tenir le rôle de; *(play)* jouer; *Fig* **to a. the part** se conduire comme il convient

(**b**) *(behave like)* **to a. the fool** faire l'imbécile; *Fam* **a. your age!** arrête de faire l'enfant!

3 *vi* (**a**) *(take action)* agir; **to a. for sb** *(of lawyer)* représenter qn; **to a. as secretary/chairperson** remplir les fonctions de secrétaire/président; **a. as a warning** servir d'avertissement; **to a. as an incentive** être une motivation

(**b**) *(behave)* agir, se comporter; **to a. stupid** faire l'idiot

(**c**) *(of actor)* jouer; **I always wanted to a.** j'ai toujours voulu être acteur

▶**act on** *vt insep (advice, suggestion)* suivre; **she acted on the information we gave her** elle a suivi les indications que nous lui avons données

▶**act out** *vt sep (fantasy)* vivre; *(scene)* jouer

▸**act up** vi (of car, child, injury) faire des siennes

acting ['æktɪŋ] **1** n (performance) jeu m; (profession) métier m d'acteur
  2 adj (temporary) par intérim

action ['ækʃən] n (**a**) (individual act) acte m, action f; Prov **actions speak louder than words** les actes en disent plus long que les paroles (**b**) (activity) action f; **to take a.** prendre des mesures; **to go into a.** passer à l'action; **to be out of a.** (machine, car) être en panne; (person) être hors service; Fam **where's the a. around here?** où est-ce que ça bouge par ici?; Fam **we want a piece of the a.** nous voulons notre part du gâteau; Com **a. plan** objectifs mpl (**c**) Mil combats mpl; **to see a.** combattre; **missing in a.** porté(e) disparu(e) (**d**) (of movie, novel) action f (**e**) Law action f, procès m; **to take a. against sb** intenter un procès à qn

activate ['æktɪveɪt] vt déclencher

active ['æktɪv] adj (**a**) (person, mind, imagination) actif(ive); (interest, dislike) vif (vive); (volcano) en activité; **to be a. in doing sth** s'employer activement à faire qch; Mil **on a. duty** or **service** en service actif (**b**) Gram actif(ive)

actively ['æktɪvlɪ] adv activement; **to a. dislike sb** détester cordialement qn

activist ['æktɪvɪst] n Pol militant(e) m,f

activity [æk'tɪvɪtɪ] (pl **activities**) n activité f; (in street) animation f; **a. book** livre jeu m; **a. center** centre m aéré

actor ['æktə(r)] n acteur m

actress ['æktrɪs] n actrice f

actual ['æktʃʊəl] adj (**a**) (real) réel(elle); (example) concret(ète); **in a. fact** en fait (**b**) (specific) **I can't remember her a. words** je ne me rappelle pas ses paroles exactes; **although the garden is big, the a. house is small** le jardin est grand, mais la maison elle-même est petite

actually ['æktʃʊəlɪ] adv (**a**) (really) réellement, vraiment; **what a. happened?** qu'est-ce qui s'est passé au juste?; **what she a. means is...** en réalité, ce qu'elle veut dire c'est... (**b**) (in fact) en fait; **I'm not sure, a.** en fait, je ne suis pas sûr

actuary ['æktʃʊərɪ] (pl **actuaries**) n actuaire mf

acumen ['ækjʊmən] n flair m; **business a.** sens m des affaires

acupuncture ['ækjʊpʌŋktʃə(r)] n acupuncture f, acuponcture f

acupuncturist ['ækjʊpʌŋktʃərɪst] n acupuncteur(trice) m,f, acuponcteur(trice) m,f

acute [ə'kju:t] adj (**a**) (pain) aigu(ë); (remorse, embarrassment) vif (vive); (problem, shortage) grave (**b**) (eyesight) perçant(e) (**c**) (accent, angle) aigu(ë)

acutely [ə'kju:tlɪ] adv (painful, embarrassing) extrêmement; (aware) profondément

A.D. [eɪ'di:] adv (abbr **Anno Domini**) apr. J.-C.

ad [æd] n Fam (classified) petite annonce f; (on radio, TV) pub f

Adam ['ædəm] n Fam **I wouldn't know him from A.** je ne le connais ni d'Ève ni d'Adam; **A.'s apple** pomme f d'Adam

adamant ['ædəmənt] adj formel(elle), catégorique (**about** sur); **to be a. that...** soutenir que...

adapt [ə'dæpt] **1** vt adapter; **to a. oneself to sth** s'adapter à qch
  2 vi s'adapter

adaptable [ə'dæptəbəl] adj (instrument, tool) adaptable; (person) souple

adaptation [ædæp'teɪʃən] n (of book, play) adaptation f; (of machine, design) modification f

adapter, adaptor [ə'dæptə(r)] n (for foreign plugs) adaptateur m

ADC [eɪdi:'si:] n Mil (abbr **aide-de-camp**) aide m de camp

add [æd] vt ajouter (**to** à); (figures) additionner; **this book adds little to the debate** ce livre n'apporte pas grand-chose au débat

▸**add up 1** vt sep (figures) additionner

  2 vi (give correct total) être juste ou exact(e); (make sense) tenir debout

▸**add up to** vt insep (amount to) **it adds up to $126** ça fait 126 dollars au total ou en tout; **it all adds up to an enjoyable excursion** tout cela fera de cette excursion un moment bien agréable; **it doesn't a. up to much** ça ne fait pas grand-chose au bout du compte

adder ['ædə(r)] n (snake) vipère f

addict ['ædɪkt] n (**drug**) **a.** toxicomane mf; **heroin a.** héroïnomane mf; **to be a TV a.** être accro à la télé

addicted [ə'dɪktɪd] adj **to be a. to sth** (drugs) être dépendant(e) de qch; (TV program) être accro à qch

addiction [ə'dɪkʃən] n (to drugs) dépendance f (**to** à), accoutumance f (**to** à); (to chocolate, movies) passion f (**to** pour)

addictive [ə'dɪktɪv] adj (substance) qui crée une dépendance ou accoutumance; **soap operas are very a.** on devient vite accro aux feuilletons

Addis Ababa ['ædɪs'æbəbə] n Addis-Abeba

addition [ə'dɪʃən] n (action) addition f; (thing added) ajout m (**to** à); (person) nouveau venu (nouvelle venue) m,f; **she's the latest a. to the team** c'est la dernière arrivée dans l'équipe; **in a. (to)** en plus (de)

additional [ə'dɪʃənəl] adj supplémentaire

additive ['ædɪtɪv] n additif m

addled ['ædəld] adj (egg) pourri(e); (brain) confus(e)

add-on ['ædɒn] n Comput produit m supplémentaire ou complémentaire

address [ə'dres] **1** n (**a**) (of person, letter) adresse f; **a. book** carnet m d'adresses (**b**) (speech) discours m, allocution f
  2 vt (**a**) (letter, remarks, criticism) adresser (**to** à) (**b**) (speak to) (person, crowd) s'adresser à; **he addressed her as "Your Majesty"** il l'a appelée "Votre Majesté" (**c**) (question, problem) aborder; **to a. oneself to sth** (problem) aborder qch; (task) entreprendre qch

adenoids ['ædɪnɔɪdz] npl Anat végétations fpl

adept [ə'dept] adj habile (**at** à); **to be a. at doing sth** être habile à faire qch

adequate ['ædɪkwət] adj (enough) suffisant(e); (satisfactory) satisfaisant(e), adéquat(e); **you were given a. warning** on vous a prévenu suffisamment à l'avance

adequately ['ædɪkwɪtlɪ] adv (sufficiently) suffisamment; (suitably) convenablement

adhere [əd'hɪə(r)] vi (stick) adhérer (**to** à); **to a. to** (rule) observer; (belief) adhérer à; (plan) se conformer à

adherence [əd'hɪərəns] n (to rule) observation f (**to** de); (to belief, plan) adhésion f (**to** à)

adherent [əd'hɪərənt] n adhérent(e) m,f

adhesion [əd'hi:ʒən] n (**a**) (stickiness) adhérence f (**b**) (to belief, plan) adhésion f (**to** à)

adhesive [əd'hi:sɪv] **1** n adhésif m, colle f
  2 adj adhésif(ive), collant(e); **a. tape** ruban m adhésif

ad hoc ['æd'hɒk] adj (measure) ad hoc inv; (arrangement) temporaire; **a. committee** comité m spécial ou ad hoc; **on an a. basis** au coup par coup

ad infinitum ['ædɪnfɪ'naɪtəm] adv à l'infini; **and so on a.** et ainsi de suite à n'en plus finir

adjacent [ə'dʒeɪsənt] adj adjacent(e); (street) voisin(e); (room) contigu(ë); (community) riverain(e)

adjective ['ædʒɪktɪv] n adjectif m

adjoin [ə'dʒɔɪn] vt être contigu(ë) ou attenant(e) à

adjoining [ə'dʒɔɪnɪŋ] adj contigu(ë), attenant(e); **the a. room** la pièce voisine

adjourn [ə'dʒɜ:n] **1** vt (meeting, trial) ajourner, remettre à plus tard
  2 vi (of meeting, trial) être ajourné(e); **to a. to another room** passer dans une autre pièce

adjournment [ə'dʒɜ:nmənt] n ajournement m

adjudge [ə'dʒʌdʒ] *vt (prize, award)* adjuger; **to a. sb guilty/ the winner** déclarer qn coupable/vainqueur

adjudicate [ə'dʒuːdɪkeɪt] *vt* juger

adjudication [ədʒuːdɪ'keɪʃən] *n* jugement *m*, décision *f*

adjudicator [ə'dʒuːdɪkeɪtə(r)] *n (in dispute)* arbitre *m*; *(in competition)* juge *m*

adjunct ['ædʒʌŋkt] *n (thing)* accessoire *m*

adjust [ə'dʒʌst] **1** *vt (machine, mechanism)* régler, ajuster; *(pay, figures)* ajuster; *(clothes)* rajuster; **to a. oneself to sth** s'adapter à qch
2 *vi (of person)* s'adapter (**to** à)

adjustable [ə'dʒʌstəbəl] *adj* ajustable, réglable

adjustment [ə'dʒʌstmənt] *n (of machine, mechanism)* réglage *m*; *(to pay, figures)* réajustement *m*; **to make an a. to sth** régler qch; **a period of a.** une période d'adaptation

ad-lib ['æd'lɪb] **1** *adv* en improvisant, de manière improvisée
2 *vi (pt & pp **ad-libbed**)* improviser

adman ['ædmæn] *n Fam* publicitaire *m*

administer [əd'mɪnɪstə(r)] *vt* **(a)** *(estate, funds)* administrer, gérer; *(territory)* administrer **(b)** *(give) (punishment, medication)* administrer; *(blow)* donner

administration [ədmɪnɪ'streɪʃən] *n* **(a)** *(work)* administration *f* **(b)** *(government)* gouvernement *m*

administrative [əd'mɪnɪstrətɪv] *adj* administratif(ive)

administrator [əd'mɪnɪstreɪtə(r)] *n* administrateur(trice) *m,f*

admirable ['ædmərəbəl] *adj* admirable

admiral ['ædmərəl] *n* amiral *m*

admiration [ædmə'reɪʃən] *n* admiration *f* (**for** pour)

admire [əd'maɪə(r)] *vt* admirer

admirer [əd'maɪərə(r)] *n* admirateur(trice) *m,f*

admiring [əd'maɪərɪŋ] *adj (look, glance)* admiratif(ive)

admissible [əd'mɪsɪbəl] *adj (behavior, error)* admissible, acceptable; *Law* recevable

admission [əd'mɪʃən] *n* **(a)** *(entry) (to school, hospital)* admission *f*; *(to museum, exhibition)* entrée *f*; *(price)* (prix *m* d')entrée *f*; **no a.** *(sign)* entrée interdite **(b)** *(acknowledgment) (of guilt)* aveu *m*; *(of crime)* confession *f*; **by his own a.** de son propre aveu

admit [əd'mɪt] *(pt & pp **admitted**)* **1** *vt* **(a)** *(allow to enter)* laisser entrer; *(to the hospital, college)* admettre; **to be admitted to hospital** être admis(e) à l'hôpital; **children not admitted** *(sign)* les enfants ne sont pas admis; **a. one** *(on ticket)* entrée valable pour une personne **(b)** *(acknowledge) (fact, mistake, guilt)* admettre, reconnaître; *(crime)* avouer; **I must a. you're right** je dois reconnaître que vous avez raison; **to a. defeat** s'avouer vaincu(e)
2 *vi* **to a. to** *(mistake)* reconnaître; **I a. to being in a bad mood yesterday** je dois admettre que j'étais de mauvaise humeur hier

admittance [əd'mɪtəns] *n (entry)* accès *m*; **to gain a.** parvenir à entrer; **to refuse sb a.** refuser de laisser entrer qn; **no a.** *(sign)* entrée interdite

admittedly [əd'mɪtɪdlɪ] *adv* de l'aveu général; **a., it was dark when I saw him** je dois convenir qu'il faisait sombre quand je l'ai vu

admonish [əd'mɒnɪʃ] *vt (reprimand)* admonester, faire des remontrances à (**for** pour)

ad nauseam [æd'nɔːsɪæm] *adv* à n'en plus finir

ado [ə'duː] *n* **without more** *or* **further a.** sans plus de cérémonie *ou* de manières; **much a. about nothing** beaucoup de bruit pour rien

adobe [ə'dəʊbɪ] *n (clay)* adobe *m*; **an a. house** une maison d'adobe

adolescence [ædə'lesəns] *n* adolescence *f*

adolescent [ædə'lesənt] *n* adolescent(e) *m,f*

adopt [ə'dɒpt] *vt (child, custom, approach, measures)* adopter; *(career, candidate)* choisir; *(tone, attitude)* prendre

adopted [ə'dɒptɪd] *adj (child)* adopté(e); *(son, daughter)* adoptif(ive); **my a. country** mon pays d'adoption

adoption [ə'dɒpʃən] *n* adoption *f*

adorable [ə'dɔːrəbəl] *adj* adorable

adoration [ædə'reɪʃən] *n* adoration *f*

adore [ə'dɔː(r)] *vt* adorer

adorn [ə'dɔːn] *vt* orner, parer (**with** de)

adornment [ə'dɔːnmənt] *n (decorations)* ornements *mpl*, parure *f*

ADP [eɪdiː'piː] *n Comput (abbr **automatic data processing**)* traitement *m* automatique des données

adrenalin(e) [ə'drenəlɪn] *n* adrénaline *f*

Adriatic [eɪdrɪ'ætɪk] *n* **the A. (Sea)** la mer Adriatique, l'Adriatique *f*

adrift [ə'drɪft] *adv & adj* **to be a.** *(of boat)* aller à la dérive; **to go a.** *(of plan)* tomber à l'eau; **to come a.** *(come apart)* se défaire

adroit [ə'drɔɪt] *adj* habile (**at doing sth** à faire qch)

ADSL [eɪdiːɛs'ɛl] *n Comput (abbr **Asynchronous Digital Subscriber Line**)* ADSL *m*

adulation [ædjʊ'leɪʃən] *n* adulation *f*

adult [ə'dʌlt] **1** *n* adulte *mf*
2 *adj* adulte; *(movie)* pour adultes; **a. education** enseignement *m* pour adultes

adulterate [ə'dʌltəreɪt] *vt (food)* empoisonner; *(wine)* frelater; *(language)* corrompre

adulteration [ədʌltə'reɪʃən] *n (of food)* empoisonnement *m*; *(of wine)* frelatage *m*

adulterer [ə'dʌltərə(r)] *n* adultère *mf*

adulterous [ə'dʌltərəs] *adj* adultère

adultery [ə'dʌltərɪ] *n* adultère *m*; **to commit a.** commettre l'adultère

adulthood [ə'dʌlthʊd] *n* âge *m* adulte

advance [əd'vɑːns] **1** *n* **(a)** *(forward movement)* avance *f*; *(progress)* progrès *m*; **the a. or advances in medicine** le progrès *ou* les progrès en médecine; **to make advances to sb** faire des avances à qn; **in a.** *(book, apply, inform)* à l'avance; *(pay)* d'avance; **six weeks in a.** six semaines à l'avance; **thank you in a.** *(in letter)* merci d'avance, avec mes remerciements anticipés; **a. booking** réservation *f* à l'avance; **a. notice** *or* **warning** préavis *m* **(b)** *(loan)* avance *f*
2 *vt* **(a)** *(move forward)* faire avancer; *(chess piece)* avancer; *(science, knowledge)* faire progresser, faire avancer **(b)** *(idea, opinion)* avancer, mettre en avant **(c)** *(loan)* avancer
3 *vi (move forward)* s'avancer (**towards** vers); *(make progress)* avancer

advanced [əd'vɑːnst] *adj* avancé(e); **she's very a. for her age** elle est très en avance pour son âge

advantage [əd'vɑːntɪdʒ] *n* avantage *m* (**over** sur); **to take a. of** profiter de; **to turn a situation to one's a.** tourner une situation à son avantage; **it would be to your a. to...** il serait dans votre intérêt de...; **a. Williams** *(in tennis)* avantage Williams

advantageous [ædvən'teɪdʒəs] *adj* avantageux(euse) (**to** pour)

advent ['ædvənt] *n (arrival)* arrivée *f*; *Rel* **A.** l'Avent *m*

adventure [əd'ventʃə(r)] *n* aventure *f*; **a. story** récit *m* d'aventures; *(novel)* roman *m* d'aventure(s)

adventurer [əd'ventʃərə(r)] *n* aventurier(ère) *m,f*

adventurous [əd'ventʃərəs] *adj (person)* aventureux(euse); *(plan)* audacieux(euse)

adverb ['ædvɜːb] *n* adverbe *m*

adversary ['ædvəsərɪ] *(pl **adversaries**)* *n* adversaire *mf*

adverse ['ædvɜːs] *adj* défavorable

adversely ['ædvɜːslɪ] *adv* **to influence sb a.** exercer une influence défavorable sur qn; **a. affected** affecté(e)

adversity [əd'vɜːsɪtɪ] *n* adversité *f*; **in a.** dans l'adversité

advertise ['ædvətaɪz] **1** *vt* **(a)** *(product, service)* faire de la réclame *ou* de la publicité pour; *(job)* mettre une annonce pour; **advertised on TV** vu(e) à la télé **(b)** *(call attention to)* **he didn't want to a. his presence** il ne voulait pas se faire remarquer

2 *vi (for job)* mettre une annonce; *(to sell product)* faire de la publicité *ou* de la réclame; **to a. for sb** passer une annonce pour trouver qn

advertisement ['ædvətaɪzmənt] *n (for product, service)* publicité *f*, réclame *f*; *(for job, event)* annonce *f*; *Fig* **you're not a good a. for your school** vous ne faites pas honneur à votre école

advertiser ['ædvətaɪzə(r)] *n* annonceur(euse) *m,f*

advertising ['ædvətaɪzɪŋ] *n* publicité *f*; **a. agency** agence *f* de publicité; **a. campaign** campagne *f* de publicité

advice [əd'vaɪs] *n* conseil(s) *m(pl)* (**on** sur); **a piece of a.** un conseil; **that's good a.** c'est un bon conseil; **to give sb a.** donner des conseils à qn; **to ask sb's a.** demander conseil à qn; **to take sb's a.** suivre le conseil *ou* les conseils de qn; **advice column** *(in newspaper)* courrier *m* du cœur; **advice columnist** *(in newspaper)* = responsable de la rubrique courrier du cœur

advisable [əd'vaɪzəbəl] *adj* recommandé(e)

advise [əd'vaɪz] *vt* **(a)** *(give advice to)* conseiller; **to a. sb to do sth** conseiller à qn de faire qch; **to a. sb against doing sth** déconseiller à qn de faire qch; **I wouldn't a. it** je ne le conseillerais *ou* recommanderais pas **(b)** *(inform)* **to a. sb that...** aviser qn que...

adviser, advisor [əd'vaɪzə(r)] *n* conseiller(ère) *m,f*

advisory [əd'vaɪzərɪ] *adj* consultatif(ive); **in an a. capacity** en tant que conseiller

advocate 1 *n* ['ædvəkət] **(a)** *Law* avocat *m* **(b)** *(of cause, doctrine)* partisan(e) *m,f*

2 *vt* ['ædvəkeɪt] *(policy, plan)* préconiser, conseiller

AEC [eɪiː'siː] *n (abbr* **Atomic Energy Commission**) ≃ Commissariat *m* à l'énergie atomique, CEA *m*

Aegean [ɪ'dʒiːən] *n* **the A. (Sea)** la mer Égée

aegis = **egis**

aeon = **eon**

aerate ['eəreɪt] *vt (liquid, blood)* oxygéner

aerial ['eərɪəl] **1** *n (of radio, TV)* antenne *f*

2 *adj* aérien(enne)

aerobics [eə'rəʊbɪks] *n* aérobic *m*

aerodynamic [eərəʊdaɪ'næmɪk] *adj* aérodynamique

aerogram(me) ['eərəgræm] *n* aérogramme *m*

aeronautic [eərə'nɔːtɪk], **aeronautical** [eərə'nɔːtɪkəl] *adj* aéronautique

aerosol ['eərəsɒl] *n* aérosol *m*; **a. spray** atomiseur *m*

aerospace ['eərəʊspeɪs] *n* **a. science** aérospatiale *f*; **the a. industry** l'aérospatiale *f*

aesthetic = **esthetic**

aesthetics = **esthetics**

afar [ə'fɑː(r)] *adv Lit* **from a.** de loin

affable ['æfəbəl] *adj* affable, courtois(e)

affair [ə'feə(r)] *n* **(a)** *(matter, concern)* affaire *f*; **that's my a.!** c'est mes affaires!; **to put one's affairs in order** mettre de l'ordre dans ses affaires; **current affairs** les questions *fpl* d'actualité; **foreign affairs** les affaires étrangères; **affairs of state** les affaires de l'État; **in the present state of affairs** dans l'état actuel des choses **(b)** *(sexual)* liaison *f*; **to have an a. with sb** avoir une liaison avec qn **(c)** *(event)* affaire *f*; **the wedding was a quiet a.** le mariage fut célébré dans l'intimité; **what kind of a. was it?** c'était comment?

affect¹ [ə'fekt] *vt* **(a)** *(have effect on) (person, organ, health)* affecter; *(decision)* influencer; *(of issue, law)* concerner **(b)** *(move emotionally)* affecter, toucher; **to be deeply affected by sth** être très affecté(e) par qch

affect² [ə'fekt] *vt (indifference, interest)* affecter, feindre; **to a. an accent** prendre un accent

affectation [æfek'teɪʃən] *n* affectation *f*

affected [ə'fektɪd] *adj (unnatural)* affecté(e), maniéré(e)

affection [ə'fekʃən] *n* affection *f*

affectionate [ə'fekʃənət] *adj* affectueux(euse) (**towards** avec *ou* envers)

affidavit [æfɪ'deɪvɪt] *n* *Law* déclaration *f* par écrit et sous serment

affiliate 1 *n* [ə'fɪlɪət, ə'fɪlɪeɪt] *(person)* affilié(e) *m,f*

2 *vt* [ə'fɪlɪeɪt] affilier (**to** *or* **with** à); **affiliated company** filiale *f*

affiliation [əfɪlɪ'eɪʃən] *n* affiliation *f*

affinity [ə'fɪnɪtɪ] *(pl* **affinities**) *n* **(a)** *(liking, attraction)* affinité *f* (**for** *or* **with/between** avec/entre); **to have an a. with sb/sth** avoir des affinités avec qn/qch **(b)** *(relationship, connection)* lien *m* (**between/with** entre/avec)

affirm [ə'fɜːm] *vt* **(a)** *(state)* affirmer **(b)** *(confirm)* confirmer

affirmation [æfə'meɪʃən] *n* **(a)** *(statement)* affirmation *f*, assertion *f* **(b)** *(confirmation)* confirmation *f*

affirmative [ə'fɜːmətɪv] **1** *n* **to answer in the a.** répondre affirmativement *ou* par l'affirmative

2 *adj* affirmatif(ive); **a. action** mesures *fpl* d'embauche antidiscriminatoires *(en faveur des minorités)*, discrimination *f* positive

affix 1 *n* ['æfɪks] *Ling* affixe *m*

2 *vt* [ə'fɪks] attacher (**to** à); *(notice, poster)* fixer (**to** à)

afflict [ə'flɪkt] *vt* affliger; **afflicted with rheumatism** affligé(e) de rhumatismes

affliction [ə'flɪkʃən] *n (illness)* affection *f*; *(misfortune)* malheur *m*

affluent ['æfluənt] *adj* riche; **the a. society** la société d'abondance

afford [ə'fɔːd] *vt* **(a)** *(financially)* **to be able to a. sth** avoir les moyens d'acheter qch; **I can't a. it** mes moyens ne me le permettent pas; **we can't a. a new car** nous ne pouvons pas nous offrir une nouvelle voiture; **she can a. to eat out twice a week** elle peut se permettre d'aller au restaurant deux fois par semaine **(b)** *(non-financial use)* **I can't a. to wait** je ne peux pas attendre; **I can't a. not to** je n'ai pas le choix; **we can't a. another mistake** nous ne pouvons pas nous permettre une nouvelle erreur **(c)** *Formal (give)* offrir, procurer

affordable [ə'fɔːdəbəl] *adj (price, purchase)* abordable; *(house)* (d'un prix) abordable

affront [ə'frʌnt] **1** *n* affront *m*, offense *f*

2 *vt* offenser, faire (un) affront à; **to be/to feel affronted** être/se sentir offensé(e)

Afghan ['æfgæn] **1** *n* **(a)** *(person)* Afghan(e) *m,f* **(b)** *(dog)* lévrier *m* afghan

2 *adj* afghan(e); **A. hound** lévrier *m* afghan

Afghanistan [æf'gænɪstæn] *n* l'Afghanistan *m*

afield [ə'fiːld] *adv* **further a.** plus loin

AFL-CIO [eɪef'elsiːaɪ'əʊ] *n (abbr* **American Federation of Labor and Congress of Industrial Organizations**) = confédération syndicale américaine

afloat [ə'fləʊt] *adv & adj* à flot; **to stay a.** *(of boat, company)* se maintenir à flot

afoot [ə'fʊt] *adv* **there's something a.** il se prépare *ou* se trame quelque chose

aforementioned [ə'fɔːmenʃənd] *adj* susmentionné(e)

afraid [ə'freɪd] *adj* **(a)** *(scared)* **to be a. (of)** avoir peur (de); **that's (exactly) what I was a. of!** c'est bien ce que je craignais!; **I was a. there would be an accident** je craignais un accident **(b)** *(sorry)* **I'm a. so/not** je crains que oui/que non; **I'm a. she's out** je regrette, elle est sortie; **I'm a. I can't help you** j'ai bien peur de ne pouvoir vous aider

afresh [ə'freʃ] *adv* de nouveau, à nouveau; **to start a.** recommencer

Africa ['æfrɪkə] *n* l'Afrique *f*

African ['æfrɪkən] **1** *n* Africain(e) *m,f*
   2 *adj* africain(e)

African-American ['æfrɪkənə'merɪkən] **1** *n* Noir(e) *m,f* américain(e)
   2 *adj* noir(e) américain(e)

Afrikaans [æfrɪ'kɑːnz] *n* afrikaans *m*

aft [ɑːft] *adv Naut* à l'arrière

after ['ɑːftə(r)] **1** *prep* (**a**) *(with time)* après; **a. dinner** après dîner; **a. three days** au bout de trois jours; **the day a. the battle** le lendemain de la bataille; **it's a. five** il est cinq heures passées; **it's twenty a. six** il est six heures vingt; **a. all** *(all things considered)* après tout; *(despite everything)* finalement (**b**) *(with motion)* après; **to run a. sb** courir après qn; **close the door a. you** fermez la porte derrière vous; **a. you!** après vous! (**c**) *(in search of)* **to be a. sb/sth** chercher qn/qch; **the police are a. him** il est recherché par la police; **she's a. a raise** elle cherche une augmentation (de salaire) (**d**) *(expressing sequence)* après; **a. her, he is the best** après elle, c'est lui le meilleur (**e**) *(expressing repetition)* **day a. day** jour après jour; **year a. year** d'une année sur l'autre, tous les ans; **time a. time** cent fois; **it's one thing a. another** j'ai/nous avons/ *etc.*des problèmes à n'en plus finir (**f**) *(in honor of)* **to name sb/sth a. sb** donner le nom de qn à qn/qch
   2 *adv* après; **soon/long a.** peu/longtemps après; **the week a.** la semaine d'après; **the day a.** le lendemain
   3 *conj* (*when subject changes)* après que + *indicative or Fam subjunctive; (when subject stays the same)* après + *infinitive*; **I came a. he left** je suis arrivé après qu'il est *ou Fam* soit parti; **a. I saw him I went out** je suis sorti après l'avoir vu; **a. doing sth** après avoir fait qch

afterbirth ['ɑːftəbɜːθ] *n* placenta *m*

aftercare ['ɑːftəkeə(r)] *n (after operation)* soins *mpl* postopératoires; *(of convalescent, delinquent)* surveillance *f*

aftereffect ['ɑːftərəfekt] *n (of drug)* effet *m* secondaire; *Fig (of event)* répercussion *f*, contrecoup *m*

afterlife ['ɑːftəlaɪf] *n* vie *f* après la mort

aftermath ['ɑːftəmæθ] *n* suites *fpl*, conséquences *fpl*

afternoon [ɑːftə'nuːn] *n* après-midi *m inv or f inv*; **in the a.** (pendant) l'après-midi; **at two o'clock in the a.** à deux heures de l'après-midi; **good a.!** bonjour!

after-party ['ɑːftəpɑːtɪ] *n* after *m*

aftersales service ['ɑːftə'seɪlz'sɜːvɪs] *n Com* service *m* après-vente

aftershave ['ɑːftəʃeɪv] *n* **a. (lotion)** (lotion *f*) après-rasage *m*

aftersun ['ɑːftəsʌn] *n (cream)* crème *f* après-soleil; *(lotion)* lotion *f* après-soleil

aftertaste ['ɑːftəteɪst] *n also Fig* arrière-goût *m*

afterthought ['ɑːftəθɔːt] *n* réflexion *f* après coup; **as an a.** après coup

afterward ['ɑːftəwəd], **afterwards** ['ɑːftəwədz] *adv* après; **I regretted it a.** par la suite, je l'ai regretté

again [ə'gen] *adv* (**a**) *(in general)* de nouveau, encore; **to begin a.** recommencer; **he never came back a.** il n'est plus jamais revenu; **don't do it a.!** ne recommence pas!; **not you a.!** encore toi!; **once a.** encore une fois, une fois de plus; **a. and a.** à maintes reprises; **now and a.** de temps en temps, de temps à autre; **half as much a.** moitié plus; **I'd like half as much a.** je voudrais encore la moitié de ça; **what did you say a.?** qu'avez-vous dit déjà? (**b**) *(besides)* en outre; **(then) a.** *(on the other hand)* d'un autre côté; **a., I may have imagined it** cela dit, il se peut aussi que je l'aie imaginé

against [ə'genst] *prep* (**a**) *(in opposition to)* contre; **to be a. sb/sth** être contre qn/qch, être opposé(e) à qn/qch; **to have something/nothing a. sb/sth** avoir quelque chose/ne rien

avoir contre qn/qch; **a. the law** contraire à la loi, illégal(e) (**b**) *(as protection from)* contre; **to warn sb a. sb/sth** mettre qn en garde contre qn/qch (**c**) *(in contact with)* contre; **to lean a. sth** s'appuyer contre qch (**d**) *(in comparison with)* contre; **three deaths this year (as) a. thirty in 1990** trois morts cette année contre trente en 1990; **the pound rose/fell a. the dollar** la livre a augmenté/chuté par rapport au dollar

age [eɪdʒ] **1** *n* (**a**) *(of person)* âge *m*; **to be twenty years of a.** avoir vingt ans, être âgé(e) de vingt ans; **what a. is she?**, **what's her a.?** quel âge a-t-elle?; **he doesn't look his a.** il ne fait pas son âge; **people of all ages** des gens de tout âge; **a. group** tranche *f* d'âge; **a. of consent** = âge légal où l'on peut avoir des rapports sexuels; **a. limit** limite *f* d'âge (**b**) *(old)* **a.** vieillesse *f* (**c**) *(adulthood)* **to come of a.** atteindre sa majorité; **to be under a.** *Law* être mineur(e); *(not old enough to buy alcohol etc.)* ne pas avoir l'âge (**d**) *(era)* âge *m*, époque *f* (**e**) *Fam (long time)* **it's ages since I saw him** il y a une éternité que je ne l'ai pas vu; **I've been waiting (for) ages** ça fait une éternité que j'attends
   2 *vt & vi (continuous* **ageing** *or* **aging**) vieillir

aged *adj* (**a**) [eɪdʒd] *(of the age of)* **a. twenty** âgé(e) de vingt ans (**b**) ['eɪdʒɪd] *(old)* âgé(e), vieux (vieille)

ageing, aging ['eɪdʒɪŋ] **1** *n (of person, wine)* vieillissement *m*; **a. process** processus *m* de vieillissement
   2 *adj (becoming older)* vieillissant(e); *(old)* vieux (vieille)

ageism, agism ['eɪdʒɪzəm] *n* âgisme *m*

ageist, agist ['eɪdʒɪst] **1** *adj (action, policy)* qui relève de l'âgisme
   2 *n* = personne qui fait preuve d'âgisme

agency ['eɪdʒənsɪ] *(pl* **agencies**) *n* (**a**) *Com* agence *f*; **advertising/travel a.** agence de publicité/de voyages (**b**) **through the a. of** par l'entremise *ou* l'intermédiaire de

agenda [ə'dʒendə] *n (of meeting)* ordre *m* du jour; *Fig* programme *m*; **what's on today's a.?** *(for meeting)* quel est l'ordre du jour?; *(for activities)* qu'est-ce qu'il y a au programme pour aujourd'hui?; *Fig* **to set the a.** mener le jeu

agent ['eɪdʒənt] *n* (**a**) *(representative, spy)* agent *m* (**b**) *(instrument)* agent *m*; **to be the a. of sth** être l'instrument de qch

age-old ['eɪdʒəʊld] *adj* séculaire

aggravate ['ægrəveɪt] *vt* (**a**) *(worsen)* aggraver; **aggravated assault** coups *mpl* et blessures *fpl* (**b**) *Fam (annoy)* agacer, exaspérer

aggravating ['ægrəveɪtɪŋ] *adj* (**a**) *(worsening)* aggravant(e) (**b**) *Fam (annoying)* agaçant(e), exaspérant(e)

aggravation [ægrə'veɪʃən] *n* (**a**) *(worsening)* aggravation *f* (**b**) *Fam (annoyance)* embêtements *mpl*

aggregate ['ægrɪgət] **1** *n* total *m*, ensemble *m*
   2 *adj* collectif(ive)

aggression [ə'greʃən] *n* agressivité *f*; **an act of a.** une agression

aggressive [ə'gresɪv] *adj* agressif(ive)

aggressively [ə'gresɪvlɪ] *adv (violently)* d'une manière agressive; *(speak)* d'un ton agressif; *(vigorously)* énergiquement, avec dynamisme

aggressor [ə'gresə(r)] *n* agresseur *m*

aggrieved [ə'griːvd] *adj (expression, tone)* vexé(e); **to be** *or* **to feel a.** se sentir lésé(e)

aghast [ə'gɑːst] *adj* horrifié(e) (**at** par)

agile ['ædʒaɪl] *adj* agile

agility [ə'dʒɪlɪtɪ] *n* agilité *f*

aging = ageing

agism, agist = ageism, ageist

agitate ['ædʒɪteɪt] **1** *vt (liquid, person)* agiter
   2 *vi* **to a. for/against sth** mener une campagne en faveur de/contre qch

agitated ['ædʒɪteɪtɪd] *adj (person)* agité(e)

agitation [ædʒɪ'teɪʃən] *n* agitation *f*

agitator ['ædʒɪteɪtə(r)] *n Pol* agitateur(trice) *m,f*

aglow [ə'gləʊ] *adj (sky)* embrasé(e); **to be a. with** *(of person)* rayonner de

agnostic [æg'nɒstɪk] *n & adj* agnostique *mf*

ago [ə'gəʊ] *adv* **ten years a.** il y a dix ans; **long a.** il y a long-temps; **not long a.** il n'y a pas longtemps; **as long a. as 1840** déjà en 1840, dès 1840; **a short time a., a little while a.** il y a peu de temps, tout à l'heure; **how long a. was that?** c'était il y a combien de temps?

agog [ə'gɒg] *adj* en émoi; **he was a. to hear the latest news** il brûlait d'apprendre les dernières nouvelles

agonize ['ægənaɪz] *vi* se ronger les sangs, se tourmenter (**over** à propos de)

agonizing ['ægənaɪzɪŋ] *adj (pain, death)* atroce; *(silence, wait)* angoissant(e); *(decision, dilemma)* pénible, déchirant(e)

agony ['ægənɪ] *(pl* **agonies)** *n (physical pain)* douleur *f* atroce; *(mental pain)* angoisse *f*; **to be in a.** être au supplice *ou* au martyre; **it's a. walking in these shoes!** c'est un véritable supplice de marcher avec ces chaussures!

agoraphobia [ægərə'fəʊbɪə] *n* agoraphobie *f*

agrarian [ə'greərɪən] *adj* agraire

agree [ə'griː] **1** *vt* **(a)** *(reach agreement on) (price, time, conditions)* se mettre d'accord sur; **to a. to do sth** convenir de faire qch; **(are we) agreed?** (nous sommes) d'accord?

(b) *(concur)* **to a. (that)...** s'accorder à dire que...; **I a. that's expensive, but...** c'est cher, j'en conviens, mais...; **everyone agrees (that) he's the best** tout le monde s'accorde à dire qu'il est le meilleur

(c) *(consent)* **to a. to do sth** accepter de faire qch, consentir à faire qch; **we'll have to a. to differ on that** je crois qu'ici il va nous falloir accepter nos différences d'opinion; **it is generally agreed that...** il est généralement admis que...

2 *vi* **(a)** *(be of same opinion, concur)* être d'accord (**about/with** sur/avec); *(after discussion)* se mettre d'accord; **I quite** *or* **entirely a.** je suis entièrement d'accord; **I'm afraid I can't a.** j'ai bien peur de ne pas être du même avis; **I couldn't a. more!** ça c'est bien dit!; **I don't a. with all this violence on television** je n'approuve pas toute cette violence à la télévision

(b) *(match) (of statements, facts, opinions)* concorder, coïncider (**with** avec); *Gram* s'accorder (**with** avec)

(c) *(accept)* consentir (**to** à); **to a. to a condition/proposal** accepter une condition/une proposition

▶**agree on** *vt insep* être d'accord sur; *(after discussion)* se mettre d'accord sur

▶**agree with** *vt insep (of food)* réussir à

agreeable [ə'griːəbəl] *adj* **(a)** *(pleasant)* agréable; *(person)* aimable **(b)** *(acceptable)* **if that is a. to you** si cela vous convient

agreed [ə'griːd] *adj (price, time)* convenu(e)

agreement [ə'griːmənt] *n* **(a)** *(contract, assent) & Gram* accord *m* (**on** *or* **about** sur); **to come to an a.** tomber *ou* se mettre d'accord; **by mutual a.** d'un commun accord; **the proposal met with unanimous a.** la proposition a été reçue à l'unanimité; **to be in a. with sb** être d'accord avec qn; **to be in a. with a decision** approuver une décision **(b)** *(of facts, account)* **to be in a. with** concorder avec

agribusiness ['ægrɪbɪznɪs] *n (company)* agro-industrie *f*; *(sector)* agro-industries *fpl*

agricultural [ægrɪ'kʌltʃərəl] *adj* agricole; **a. college** = école supérieure d'agriculture et d'agronomie; **a. laborer** ouvrier *m* agricole

agriculture ['ægrɪkʌltʃə(r)] *n* agriculture *f*

agronomy [ə'grɒnəmɪ] *n* agronomie *f*

aground [ə'graʊnd] *adv* **to run a.** *(of ship)* s'échouer; *(of project, government)* échouer

ahead [ə'hed] *adv* **(a)** *(in space)* devant; **to go on a.** partir de-

vant; **the road a. was clear** devant nous/moi/*etc.*la route était libre; **a. of** devant **(b)** *(winning)* **to be a.** être en tête; **to get a.** *(in career)* avancer; **to get a. of sb** dépasser qn; *(in sports)* **France are two goals a.** la France a deux buts d'avance **(c)** *(in time)* **to plan a.** faire des projets; **in the years a.** dans les années à venir; **a. of** *(prior to)* avant; **a. of schedule** *(flight, train)* en avance sur l'horaire; *(project)* en avance sur les prévisions; **to be a. of one's time** être en avance sur son temps

ahoy [ə'hɔɪ] *exclam* **a. there!** oh(é)!; **ship a.!** ohé du bateau!

AI [eɪ'aɪ] *n* **(a)** *Comput (abbr* **artificial intelligence)** IA *f* **(b)** *Biol (abbr* **artificial insemination)** insémination *f* artificielle **(c)** *Pol (abbr* **Amnesty International)** Amnesty International *f*

aid [eɪd] **1** *n* **(a)** *(help, for disaster relief)* aide *f*, secours *m*; **with the a. of sb** avec l'aide de qn; **with the a. of sth** à l'aide de qch; **to go to sb's a.** aller *ou* se porter au secours de qn; **in a. of** *(fund-raising event)* au profit de; *Fam* **what's (all) this in a. of?** c'est en quel honneur?; **a. worker** *(voluntary)* volontaire *mf*; *(paid)* employé(e) *m,f* d'une organisation humanitaire **(b)** *(device)* outil *m*; **teaching aids** matériel *m* pédagogique, supports *mpl* pédagogiques

2 *vt* aider; *Law* **to a. and abet sb** être le complice de qn

aide [eɪd] *n* assistant(e) *m,f*, conseiller(ère) *m,f*

aide-de-camp ['eɪd'dəkɒn] *(pl* **aides-de-camp)** *n Mil* aide *m* de camp

aiding ['eɪdɪŋ] *n Law* **a. and abetting** complicité *f*

AIDS, Aids [eɪdz] *n* sida *m*; **A. clinic** = clinique spécialisée dans le traitement du sida; **A. sufferer** sidéen(enne) *m,f*, malade *mf* du sida; **A. virus** virus *m* du sida

ailing ['eɪlɪŋ] *adj (person)* souffrant(e); *(company, economy)* qui bat de l'aile

ailment ['eɪlmənt] *n* mal *m*

aim [eɪm] **1** *n* **(a)** *(at target)* **to take a. (at)** viser; **her a. was good** elle visait bien **(b)** *(goal)* but *m*, dessein *m*; **with the a. of doing sth** dans le but *ou* dessein de faire qch

2 *vt (stone)* lancer (**at** à); *(camera)* braquer (**at** sur); **to a. a gun at sb/sth** mettre qn/qch en joue; **to a. a blow at sb** chercher à frapper qn; **to be aimed at sb** *(of remarks, TV program)* être destiné(e) à qn

3 *vi* **to a. at** *(with gun)* viser; **to a. to do sth** *(intend)* avoir l'intention de faire qch

aimless ['eɪmlɪs] *adj (existence, remark)* sans but

ain't [eɪnt] *very Fam* **(a)** = **is not, am not, are not (b)** = **has not, have not**

air [eə(r)] **1** *n* **(a)** *(in general)* air *m*; **by a.** par avion; **to be on the a.** *(of person)* être à l'antenne; *(of program)* être diffusé(e); **to throw sth (up) in the a.** lancer qch en l'air; **our plans are up in the a.** *(undecided)* nos projets n'ont toujours pas de forme précise; **to be in the a.** *(of rumor)* circuler; *(of feeling, idea)* être dans l'air; **a. bag** Air Bag® *m*; **a. filter** filtre *m* à air; **the A. Force** l'Armée *f* de l'air; **a. freight** fret *m* aérien; **a. freshener** désodorisant *m*; **a. hostess** hôtesse *f* de l'air; **a. mattress** matelas *m* pneumatique; **a. rage** = comportement agressif de certains passagers d'avion; **a. raid** raid *m* aérien; **a. rifle** fusil *m* à air comprimé; **a. show** salon *m* de l'aéronautique; **a. steward** steward *m*; **a. stewardess** hôtesse *f* de l'air; **a. terminal** aérogare *f*; **a. traffic control** contrôle *m* aérien; **a. traffic controller** contrôleur *m* aérien, aiguilleur *m* du ciel **(b)** *(melody)* air *m* **(c)** *(look)* air *m*, apparence *f*; **he has a certain a. about him** c'est quelqu'un qui en impose; **to give oneself** *or* **to put on airs** se donner des airs

2 *vt* **(a)** *(room, clothing, bedding)* aérer **(b)** *(opinions, grievances)* exposer

airborne ['eəbɔːn] *adj (seeds, particles)* en suspension dans l'air; *(troops)* aéroporté(e); **once we are a.** une fois que nous aurons décollé

aircon ['eəkɒn] *n (abbr* **air conditioning)** clim *f*

air-conditioned [ˈeəkənˈdɪʃənd] *adj* climatisé(e), à air conditionné

air-conditioning [ˈeəkənˈdɪʃənɪŋ] *n* climatisation *f*

air-cooled [ˈeəkuːld] *adj* refroidi(e) par air

aircraft [ˈeəkrɑːft] (*pl* **aircraft**) *n* avion *m*; **a. carrier** porte-avions *m inv*

air-crew [ˈeəkruː] *n Aviat* équipage *m*

airfare [ˈeəfeə(r)] *n* prix *m* du billet (d'avion)

airfield [ˈeəfiːld] *n* champ *m ou* terrain *m* d'aviation

airing [ˈeərɪŋ] *n* **to give sth an a.** *(room, clothes, bedding)* aérer qch; *(opinions, grievances)* exposer

airless [ˈeəlɪs] *adj (room)* qui sent le renfermé; *(evening, atmosphere)* lourd(e)

airlift [ˈeəlɪft] **1** *n* pont *m* aérien
2 *vt (supplies, troops)* transporter par avion; *(refugees)* évacuer par avion

airline [ˈeəlaɪn] *n* ligne *f ou* compagnie *f* aérienne; **a. pilot** pilote *m* de ligne

airlock [ˈeəlɒk] *n* (**a**) *(in submarine, spacecraft)* sas *m* (**b**) *(in pipe)* poche *f* d'air

airmail [ˈeəmeɪl] **1** *n (service)* poste *f* aérienne; **a. letter** aérogramme *m*
2 *adv* **to send sth a.** envoyer qch par avion
3 *vt (letter)* envoyer par avion

airplane [ˈeəpleɪn] *n* avion *m*

airport [ˈeəpɔːt] *n* aéroport *m*

air-sea rescue [ˈeəsiːˈreskjuː] *n* sauvetage *m* aérien en mer

airship [ˈeəʃɪp] *n* dirigeable *m*

airsick [ˈeəsɪk] *adj* **to be a.** avoir le mal de l'air

airspace [ˈeəspeɪs] *n* espace *m* aérien

airstrip [ˈeəstrɪp] *n* piste *f* d'atterrissage

airtight [ˈeətaɪt] *adj* hermétique

airtime [ˈeətaɪm] *n* (**a**) *Rad & TV* temps *m* d'antenne (**b**) *Tel* communications *fpl*; **a. provider** fournisseur *m* de communications sans fil

airwaves [ˈeəweɪvz] *npl* ondes *fpl* (hertziennes)

airworthy [ˈeəwɜːðɪ] *adj (aircraft)* en état de voler

airy [ˈeərɪ] *adj* (**a**) *(room, house)* clair(e) et spacieux(euse) (**b**) *(person, attitude)* insouciant(e), désinvolte

airy-fairy [ˈeərɪˈfeərɪ] *adj Fam (idea, scheme)* farfelu(e)

aisle [aɪl] *n (in supermarket, movie theater)* allée *f*; *(in church) (at side)* bas-côté *m*; *(central)* allée; *(in plane, bus)* couloir *m*; *Fam* **she had them rolling in the aisles** *(of comedian)* elle a fait mourir le public de rire; **a. seat** *(in plane)* place *f* côté couloir

ajar [əˈdʒɑː(r)] *adv & adj* entrouvert(e)

aka [eɪkeɪˈeɪ] *adv (abbr* **also known as***)* alias

akin [əˈkɪn] *adv & adj* **to be a. to** être apparenté(e) à

alabaster [ˈæləbæstə(r)] *n* albâtre *m*

alacrity [əˈlækrɪtɪ] *n* empressement *m*

à la mode [ælæˈməʊd] *adj (with ice cream)* servi(e) avec de la crème glacée

alarm [əˈlɑːm] **1** *n* (**a**) *(signal, device)* alarme *f*; **to raise** *or* **to give the a.** donner l'alarme; **a. clock** réveil *m*, réveille-matin *m inv*; **a. signal** signal *m* d'alarme (**b**) *(fright, anxiety)* alarme *f*, frayeur *f*; **there's no cause for a.** il n'y a aucune raison de s'alarmer
2 *vt* effrayer, alarmer; **to be alarmed at sth** s'alarmer *ou* s'effrayer de qch

alarming [əˈlɑːmɪŋ] *adj* alarmant(e), inquiétant(e)

alarmist [əˈlɑːmɪst] *n & adj* alarmiste *mf*

alas [əˈlæs] *exclam* hélas!

Albania [ælˈbeɪnɪə] *n* l'Albanie *f*

Albanian [ælˈbeɪnɪən] **1** *n* (**a**) *(person)* Albanais(e) *m,f* (**b**) *(language)* albanais *m*
2 *adj* albanais(e)

albatross [ˈælbətrɒs] *n* albatros *m*

albeit [ɔːlˈbiːɪt] *conj* quoique, bien que

albino [ælˈbaɪnəʊ, ælˈbiːnəʊ] *(pl* **albinos***) n* albinos *mf*

album [ˈælbəm] *n (record, for photos, stamps)* album *m*

albumen [ˈælbjʊmɪn] *n* (**a**) *(in egg)* albumen *m* (**b**) *(in blood)* albumine *f*

alchemy [ˈælkəmɪ] *n* alchimie *f*

alcohol [ˈælkəhɒl] *n* alcool *m*

alcoholic [ælkəˈhɒlɪk] **1** *n (person)* alcoolique *mf*
2 *adj* alcoolique; *(drink)* alcoolisé(e)

alcoholism [ˈælkəhɒlɪzəm] *n* alcoolisme *m*

alcopop [ˈælkəʊpɒp] *n* alcopop *m*

alcove [ˈælkəʊv] *n (in wall)* niche *f*; *(larger)* renfoncement *m*

alder [ˈɔːldə(r)] *n* au(l)ne *m*

ale [eɪl] *n* = bière anglaise au malt

alert [əˈlɜːt] **1** *n* alerte *f*; **to be on the a.** être en état d'alerte, être sur le qui-vive
2 *adj (watchful)* éveillé(e); *(lively)* vif (vive); **to be a. to sth** *(aware of)* être conscient(e) de qch
3 *vt* alerter; **to a. sb to a danger** alerter *ou* avertir qn d'un danger

Aleutian Islands [ælˈuːʃənˈaɪləndz] *npl* **the A.** les îles *fpl* Aléoutiennes

Alexandria [ælɪgˈzɑːndrɪə] *n* Alexandrie

alfalfa [ælˈfælfə] *n Bot & Culin* luzerne *f*

alfresco [ælˈfreskəʊ] *adv & adj* en plein air

algae [ˈældʒiː] *npl* algues *fpl*

algebra [ˈældʒɪbrə] *n* algèbre *f*

Algeria [ælˈdʒɪərɪə] *n* l'Algérie *f*

Algerian [ælˈdʒɪərɪən] **1** *n* Algérien(enne) *m,f*
2 *adj* algérien(enne)

Algiers [ælˈdʒɪəz] *n* Alger

algorithm [ˈælgərɪðəm] *n Comput* algorithme *m*

alias [ˈeɪlɪəs] *(pl* **aliases***)* **1** *n* nom *m* d'emprunt, faux nom
2 *adv* alias

alibi [ˈælɪbaɪ] *n Law* alibi *m*

alien [ˈeɪlɪən] **1** *n* (**a**) *Formal (foreigner)* étranger(ère) *m,f* (**b**) *(from outer space)* extraterrestre *mf*
2 *adj* (**a**) *(strange)* étranger(ère); **violence is completely a. to his nature** il n'est pas du tout d'un naturel violent (**b**) *(from outer space)* extraterrestre

alienate [ˈeɪlɪəneɪt] *vt (supporters, readers)* s'aliéner; **they feel alienated from society** ils se sentent exclus *ou* mis à l'écart de la société

alight¹ [əˈlaɪt] *adj* (**a**) *(burning)* en flammes, en feu; **to set sth a.** mettre le feu à qch (**b**) *(illuminated)* éclairé(e), illuminé(e)

alight² [əˈlaɪt] *(pt & pp* **alighted** *or* **alit** [əˈlɪt]*) vi* (**a**) *Formal (from train, car)* descendre (**b**) *(of bird, eyes, glance)* se poser (**on** sur)

align [əˈlaɪn] *vt* aligner; **to a. oneself with sb** s'aligner sur qn

alignment [əˈlaɪnmənt] *n* alignement *m*; **out of a.** désaligné(e); **in a. (with)** aligné(e) (sur)

alike [əˈlaɪk] **1** *adj* semblable, pareil(eille); **to look a.** se ressembler
2 *adv (dress, think)* de la même façon; **old and young a.** les vieux comme les jeunes

alimentary canal [ælɪˈmentərɪkəˈnæl] *n Anat* tube *m* digestif

alimony [ˈælɪmənɪ] *n Law* pension *f* alimentaire

alit [əˈlɪt] *pt & pp of* **alight²**

alive [əˈlaɪv] *adj* (**a**) *(living)* **to be a.** être vivant(e); **to keep sb a.** maintenir qn en vie; **to keep a memory/custom a.** entretenir un souvenir/une tradition; **to stay a.** survivre; **to be a. and well** bien se porter; **the oldest woman a.** la doyenne du monde (**b**) *(aware)* **to be a. to sth** avoir parfaitement conscience de qch (**c**) *(full of vitality)* **I've never felt so a.** je ne me suis jamais senti aussi bien de ma vie; **to come a.** s'animer (**d**) *(teeming)* **to be a. with sth** grouiller de qch

alkali [ˈælkəlaɪ] *n* alcali *m*

alkaline [ˈælkəlaɪn] *adj* alcalin(e)

all [ɔːl] **1** *adj* (**a**) *(every one of)* tous (toutes); **a. men** tous les hommes; **a. the girls** toutes les filles; **a. the others** tous les autres; **a. four of them** tous les quatre; **at a. hours** à des heures impossibles

(**b**) *(the whole of)* tout(e); **a. the wine** tout le vin; **a. day** toute la journée; **a. her life** toute sa vie; **a. the time** tout le temps

(**c**) *(for emphasis)* **a. sorts of things** toutes sortes de choses; **what's a. that noise?** c'est quoi, tout ce bruit?; **in a. honesty** en toute honnêteté; **for a. his wealth...** il a beau être riche...; **it's not a. that easy** ce n'est pas si facile (que ça); **you, of a. people, should understand** si quelqu'un doit comprendre ça, c'est bien toi; **of a. the stupid things to say!** ce n'est vraiment pas malin de dire un truc pareil!

2 *pron* (**a**) *(everyone)* tous (toutes) *mpl, fpl*; **a. of us** nous tous; **a. of them say that..., they a. say that...** ils disent tous que...; **a. together** tous ensemble

(**b**) *(everything)* tout *m*; **that's a.** c'est tout; **he ate a. of it, he ate it a.** il a tout mangé; **I said was...** tout ce que j'ai dit, c'est...; **I did a. I could** j'ai fait tout ce que j'ai pu; **it was a. I could do not to laugh** j'ai bien failli rire; **best/worst of a., ...** le mieux/le pire, c'est que...; **I like this best of a.** c'est ce que je préfère; **most of a.** surtout; **when a. is said and done** au bout du compte; **it's a. the same to me** ça m'est égal; **thirty men in a.** trente hommes en tout *ou* au total; **a. in a.** dans l'ensemble; **it cost $260, a. in a.** ça a coûté 260 dollars tout compris; *Ironic* **it cost a. of $2** ça a coûté la coquette somme de 2 dollars

3 *adv* (**a**) *(entirely)* tout; **a. alone** tout(e) seul(e); **to be a. in black** être tout en noir; **to be a. for sth** être pour qch; **a. ears/smiles** tout ouïe/sourire; **I forgot a. about it** j'ai complètement oublié; **he's not a. bad** il n'a pas que de mauvais côtés; **a. over Spain/the world** dans toute l'Espagne/le monde entier; **a. over (the place)** partout; **a. too soon** trop tôt; **a. along** depuis le début; **a. but** *(almost)* presque, pratiquement; **it's/he's a. yours** il est à vous; *Fam* **a. in** *(exhausted)* crevé(e)

(**b**) **at a.** *(in the slightest)* du tout; **do you know her at a.?** tu la connais?; **if it's at a. possible** si c'était possible; **not at a.** pas du tout; *(when thanked)* je t'en prie

(**c**) *(with comparatives)* **a. the better/worse** d'autant mieux/plus mal; **a. the easier/faster** d'autant plus facile/rapide

(**d**) *(in games)* **two a.** deux partout; **four (games) a.** *(in tennis)* quatre jeux partout; **15 a.** *(in tennis)* 15 partout

4 *n* **to give one's a.** se donner à fond

Allah [ˈælə] *n* Allah

all-around [ˈɔːləˈraʊnd], **all-round** [ˈɔːlˈraʊnd] *adj (education, improvement)* général(e); **an a. athlete** un athlète complet

allay [əˈleɪ] *vt (doubts, suspicions)* dissiper; *(fear, pain)* soulager

all-clear [ˈɔːlˈklɪə(r)] *n (after air-raid)* (signal *m*) fin *f* d'alerte; *Fig (for project)* feu *m* vert

allegation [ælɪˈɡeɪʃən] *n* allégation *f*

allege [əˈledʒ] *vt* alléguer, prétendre; **it is alleged that...** on prétend que...

alleged [əˈledʒd] *adj (thief, culprit)* présumé(e)

allegedly [əˈledʒɪdlɪ] *adv* prétendument; **he a. stole $500** il aurait volé 500 dollars

allegiance [əˈliːdʒəns] *n (to party, cause)* fidélité *f*; *(to king)* allégeance *f*

allegory [ˈælɪɡərɪ] *(pl* **allegories***)* *n* allégorie *f*

all-embracing [ɔːlɪmˈbreɪsɪŋ] *adj (term, category)* large

allergenic [æləˈdʒenɪk] *adj Med* allergisant(e)

allergic [əˈlɜːdʒɪk] *adj* allergique (**to** à)

allergy [ˈælədʒɪ] *(pl* **allergies***)* *n* allergie *f* (**to** à)

alleviate [əˈliːvɪeɪt] *vt* soulager, calmer

alley [ˈælɪ] *(pl* **alleys***)* *n (street)* ruelle *f*; *Fig* **that's right up**

your a.! c'est tout à fait ton rayon!; **a. cat** chat *m* de gouttière

alleyway [ˈælɪweɪ] *n (street)* ruelle *f*

alliance [əˈlaɪəns] *n* alliance *f*; **to enter into an a. with sb** former une alliance avec qn

allied [ˈælaɪd] *adj (countries)* allié(e); *(issues, phenomena)* lié(e)

alligator [ˈælɪɡeɪtə(r)] *n* alligator *m*; **a. shoes/handbag** chaussures *fpl*/sac *m* en crocodile

all-important [ˈɔːlɪmˈpɔːtənt] *adj* essentiel(elle), capital(e)

all-inclusive [ˈɔːlɪn] *adj (price, vacation)* tout compris

alliteration [əlɪtəˈreɪʃən] *n* allitération *f*

all-night [ˈɔːlnaɪt] *adj (party, session)* qui dure toute la nuit

allocate [ˈæləkeɪt] *vt (resources, money)* affecter, attribuer (**to** à); *(duties)* assigner (**to** à); *(time)* prévoir (**to** pour)

allocation [æləˈkeɪʃən] *n (distribution)* affectation *f*; *(share)* part *f*

allot [əˈlɒt] *(pt & pp* **allotted***)* *vt (resources, money)* attribuer (**to** à); *(duties, job)* assigner (**to** à); **in the allotted time** dans le temps imparti

allotment [əˈlɒtmənt] *n (distribution of money)* affectation *f*; *(share)* part *f*

all-out [ˈɔːˈlaʊt] *adj (resistance, effort)* acharné(e); *(strike, war)* total(e)

allow [əˈlaʊ] *vt* (**a**) *(permit)* permettre; **to a. sb to do sth** permettre à qn de faire qch; **a. me!** *(offering help)* permettez(-moi)!; **smoking is not allowed** il est interdit de fumer; **I'm not allowed to do it** je n'ai pas l'autorisation de le faire; **to a. oneself to be deceived/persuaded** se laisser abuser/convaincre (**b**) *(allocate, grant)* accorder; *(time)* compter, prévoir

▶**allow for** *vt insep* tenir compte de; **add another hour to a. for delays** il faut prévoir une heure de plus au cas où il y aurait des retards

allowable [əˈlaʊəbəl] *adj (error, delay)* admissible

allowance [əˈlaʊəns] *n* (**a**) *(money given)* rente *f*, pension *f*; *(pocket money)* argent *m* de poche; **travel a.** indemnité *f* de transport (**b**) **to make a. for sth** tenir compte de qch; **I'm tired of making allowances for him** j'en ai assez de lui trouver des excuses

alloy [ˈælɔɪ] *n* alliage *m*

all-powerful [ˈɔːlˈpaʊəfʊl] *adj* tout-puissant (toute-puissante)

all-purpose [ˈɔːlˈpɜːpəs] *adj* universel(elle); **a. cleaner/adhesive** détachant *m*/colle *f* tous usages

all right [ɔːlˈraɪt] **1** *adj* **are you a.?** ça va?; **he was in a car crash but he's a.** il a eu un accident de voiture mais il n'a rien; **it's a.** *(acceptable)* ce n'est pas mal; *(not a problem)* ce n'est pas grave; **to be a. for money** avoir suffisamment d'argent; **to be a. at math/French** se débrouiller en maths/français

2 *adv (yes)* oui; **is it a. if I smoke?** ça ne vous dérange pas si je fume?; **a., let's get started** bon, commençons

all-round = **all-around**

allspice [ˈɔːlspaɪs] *n* poivre *m* de la Jamaïque

all-star [ˈɔːlstɑː(r)] *adj* **an a. cast** une distribution prestigieuse

all-time [ˈɔːltaɪm] *adj (record)* absolu(e); **unemployment has reached an a. high/low** le chômage n'a jamais été aussi élevé/bas

allude [əˈluːd] *vi* **to a. to** faire allusion à

allure [əˈlʊə(r)] *n* attrait *m*

allusion [əˈluːʒən] *n* allusion *f*; **to make an a. to sth** faire allusion à qch

ally 1 *n* [ˈælaɪ] *(pl* **allies***)* allié(e) *m,f*

2 *vt* [əˈlaɪ] *(pt & pp* **allied***)* **to a. oneself with** s'allier à *ou* avec

almanac [ˈɔːlmənæk] *n* almanach *m*

almighty [ɔːlˈmaɪtɪ] **1** *n* **the A.** le Tout-Puissant

2 *adj Fam (fuss, row)* terrible

almond ['ɑːmənd] *n* amande *f*; **a. tree** amandier *m*

almost ['ɔːlməʊst] *adv* presque; **it's a. six o'clock** il est presque six heures; **we're a. there** *(in journey)* nous sommes presque arrivés; *(in task)* nous avons presque fini; **she a. missed the bus** elle a failli rater l'autobus

alms [ɑːmz] *npl* aumône *f*

aloft [ə'lɒft] *adv* en l'air

alone [ə'ləʊn] *adv & adj* seul(e); **to leave sb a.** laisser qn tranquille; **to leave sth a.** ne pas toucher à qch; **I did it a.** je l'ai fait tout seul; **to go it a.** faire cavalier seul; **we are not a. in thinking that…** nous ne sommes pas les seuls à penser que…; **you a. can help me** vous seul pouvez m'aider; **I can't afford a bicycle, let a. a car!** je n'ai pas assez d'argent pour m'acheter une bicyclette, encore moins une voiture!

along [ə'lɒŋ] **1** *prep* le long de; **to walk a. the shore** marcher le long de la côte; **to sail a. the coast** longer la côte; **I was walking a. the street** je marchais dans la rue; *Fig* **somewhere a. the way** à un moment donné

2 *adv* **to move a.** avancer; **she'll be a. in ten minutes** elle sera là dans dix minutes; **to bring sth a.** apporter qch; **to bring sb a.** amener qn; **he knew all a.** il le savait depuis le début; **a. with** *(as well as)* ainsi que

alongside [ə'lɒŋ'saɪd] *prep (next to)* à côté de; *(along)* le long de; *Naut* **to come a. a ship/wharf** accoster un bateau/quai

aloof [ə'luːf] **1** *adj* distant(e)

2 *adv* **to remain a. (from sth)** rester à l'écart (de qch)

aloud [ə'laʊd] *adv* à haute voix; **I was thinking a.** je pensais tout haut

alpha ['ælfə] *n* alpha *m*; *Phys* **a. rays** rayons *mpl* alpha

alphabet ['ælfəbet] *n* alphabet *m*

alphabetical [ælfə'betɪkəl] *adj* alphabétique; **in a. order** dans l'ordre alphabétique

alphabetically [ælfə'betɪklɪ] *adv* alphabétiquement

alphasort ['ælfəsɔːt] *vt Comput* trier par order alphabétique

Alpine ['ælpaɪn] *adj* alpin(e); **an A. village** un village des Alpes

Alps [ælps] *npl* **the A.** les Alpes *fpl*

already [ɔːl'redɪ] *adv* déjà; **have you finished a.?** vous avez déjà fini?; *Fam* **enough, a.!** ça suffit comme ça!

alright = **all right**

Alsatian [æl'seɪʃən] **1** *n (person from Alsace)* Alsacien(enne) *m,f*

2 *adj* alsacien(enne)

also ['ɔːlsəʊ] *adv* aussi; **not only… but a.…** non seulement… mais en plus…

also-ran ['ɔːlsəʊræn] *n (in horse race)* cheval *m* non classé; *Fig (person)* perdant(e) *m,f*

altar ['ɔːltə(r)] *n* autel *m*; **a. boy** enfant *m* de chœur

alter ['ɔːltə(r)] **1** *vt* changer; *(garment)* faire des retouches à; **he altered his opinion later** il a changé d'avis plus tard; **that doesn't a. the fact that…** cela ne change rien au fait que…

2 *vi* changer

alteration [ɔːltə'reɪʃən] *n (to design, plan)* modification *f*, changement *m*; *(to schedule)* changement; *(to garment)* retouche *f*

altercation [ɔːltə'keɪʃən] *n* altercation *f*

alter ego ['æltə'riːgəʊ] *n* alter ego *m*

alternate 1 *adj* [ɔːl'tɜːnət] **(a)** *(by turns)* alterné(e); **on a. days** un jour sur deux **(b)** *(alternative)* alternatif(ive)

2 ['ɔːltəneɪt] *vt* employer tour à tour

3 ['ɔːltəneɪt] *vi* alterner (**with** avec)

alternately [ɔːl'tɜːnətlɪ] *adv* tour à tour, alternativement

alternating ['ɔːltəneɪtɪŋ] *adj* alterné(e); *Elec* **a. current** courant *m* alternatif

alternative [ɔːl'tɜːnətɪv] **1** *n (choice)* choix *m*, solution *f*; **there is no a.** il n'y a pas le choix; **she had no a. but to obey** elle n'a pu faire autrement que d'obéir

2 *adj* **(a)** *(plan, route)* de remplacement; **an a. proposal** une contre-proposition **(b)** *(music, comedy)* alternatif(ive); **a. energy** énergies *fpl* de substitution; **a. medicine** médecine *f* douce

alternatively [ɔːl'tɜːnətɪvlɪ] *adv* **(a)** *(on the other hand)* sinon; **you could travel by train or a. by bus** vous pourriez voyager en train ou bien en autobus **(b)** *(in a different way)* autrement

alternator ['ɔːltəneɪtə(r)] *n* alternateur *m*

although [ɔːl'ðəʊ] *conj* bien que + *subjunctive*; **a. it's late** bien qu'il soit tard

altitude ['æltɪtjuːd] *n* altitude *f*

alto ['æltəʊ] *(pl* **altos)** *n (male voice)* haute-contre *f*; *(female voice)* contralto *m*; **a. clef** clef *f* d'ut; **a. saxophone** saxophone *m* alto

altogether [ɔːltə'geðə(r)] **1** *adv* **(a)** *(entirely)* complètement; **I was not a. pleased** je n'étais pas ravi **(b)** *(in total)* **a. the bill came to $63** en tout l'addition s'élevait à 63 dollars

2 *n Fam* **in the a.** *(naked)* nu(e) comme un ver

altruism ['æltruɪzəm] *n* altruisme *m*

altruistic [æltrʊ'ɪstɪk] *adj* altruiste

aluminum [ə'luːmɪnəm] *n* aluminium *m*; **a. foil** papier *m* d'aluminium

alumna [ə'lʌmnə] *(pl* **alumni** [ə'lʌmnaɪ]) *n Sch* ancienne élève *f*; *Univ* ancienne étudiante *f*

alumni [ə'lʌmnaɪ] *pl of* **alumna** *or* **alumnus**

alumnus [ə'lʌmnəs] *(pl* **alumni** [ə'lʌmnaɪ]) *n Sch* ancien élève *m*; *Univ* ancien étudiant *m*

always ['ɔːlweɪz] *adv* toujours; **I can a. try** je peux toujours essayer

always-on ['ɔːlweɪz'ɒn] *adj Comput (Internet connection)* permanent

AM ['eɪ'em] *n Rad (abbr* **amplitude modulation)** AM

am [æm] *1st pers singular of* **be**

a.m. ['eɪ'em] *adv (abbr* **ante meridiem)** du matin; **five a.m.** cinq heures du matin

amalgam [ə'mælgəm] *n* amalgame *m*

amalgamate [ə'mælgəmeɪt] **1** *vt (metals, ideas)* amalgamer; *(companies)* fusionner

2 *vi (of companies)* fusionner

amass [ə'mæs] *vt* amasser, accumuler

amateur ['æmətə(r)] **1** *n* amateur *m*

2 *adj (painter, musician)* amateur; *Pej (work, performance)* d'amateur

amateurish [æmə'tɜːrɪʃ] *adj Pej* d'amateur

amaze [ə'meɪz] *vt* stupéfier; **I was amazed by his courage** son courage m'a stupéfié

amazement [ə'meɪzmənt] *n* stupéfaction *f*, stupeur *f*; **in a.** avec stupéfaction *ou* stupeur

amazing [ə'meɪzɪŋ] *adj* **(a)** *(surprising)* stupéfiant(e); **it's a. that no one helped her** il est incroyable que personne ne lui soit venu en aide **(b)** *(excellent)* formidable

Amazon ['æməzən] *n* **(a) the A.** *(river)* l'Amazone *f*; *(region)* l'Amazonie *f* **(b)** *(female warrior)* Amazone *f*

ambassador [æm'bæsədə(r)] *n* ambassadeur(drice) *m,f*

amber ['æmbə(r)] **1** *n (color, stone)* ambre *m*

2 *adj (jewelry)* d'ambre; *(color)* couleur d'ambre, ambré(e)

ambience, ambiance ['æmbɪəns] *n* ambiance *f*

ambiguity [æmbɪ'gjuːɪtɪ] *(pl* **ambiguities)** *n* ambiguïté *f*

ambiguous [æm'bɪgjʊəs] *adj* ambigu(ë)

ambition [æm'bɪʃən] *n* ambition *f*

ambitious [æm'bɪʃəs] *adj* ambitieux(euse)

ambivalent [æm'bɪvələnt] *adj* ambivalent(e)

amble ['æmbəl] *vi* marcher d'un pas tranquille

ambulance ['æmbjʊləns] *n* ambulance *f*; **a. man** ambulancier *m*; **a. woman** ambulancière *f*

ambush ['æmbʊʃ] **1** *n also Fig* embuscade *f*

2 *vt also Fig* tendre une embuscade à; **to be ambushed** tomber dans une embuscade

ameba = amoeba

amen ['eɪ'men] *exclam* amen!, ainsi soit-il!

amenable [ə'miːnəbəl] *adj* souple; **to prove a. to a suggestion** approuver une proposition

amend [ə'mend] *vt (text, law)* modifier, amender; *(error)* corriger

amendment [ə'mendmənt] *n (to law, proposal)* amendement *m*

amends [ə'mendz] *npl* **to make a. (for sth)** faire amende honorable (pour qch); **to make a. to sb for sth** dédommager qn de qch

amenities [ə'miːnɪtɪz] *npl (facilities)* équipements *mpl* collectifs

America [ə'merɪkə] *n* l'Amérique *f*

American [ə'merɪkən] **1** *n* Américain(e) *m,f*
    2 *adj* américain(e); **A. Indian** Indien(enne) *m,f* d'Amérique

amethyst ['æmɪθɪst] *n* améthyste *f*

amiable ['eɪmɪəbəl] *adj* aimable

amicable ['æmɪkəbəl] *adj* amical(e); **an a. agreement** un arrangement à l'amiable

amid [ə'mɪd], **amidst** [ə'mɪdst] *prep* au milieu de

amino acid [æ'miːnəʊ'æsɪd] *n* acide *m* aminé

amiss [ə'mɪs] *adv & adj* **there's something a.** il y a quelque chose qui ne va pas; **to take sth a.** prendre qch de travers, mal prendre qch; **a cup of coffee wouldn't go a.** une tasse de café serait bienvenue

ammeter ['æmiːtə(r)] *n Elec* ampèremètre *m*

ammonia [ə'məʊnɪə] *n* ammoniac *m*

ammunition [æmjʊ'nɪʃən] *n (for guns)* munitions *fpl*; *Fig (in debate, argument)* arguments *mpl*

amnesia [æm'niːzɪə] *n* amnésie *f*

amnesty ['æmnɪstɪ] *(pl* amnesties*)* n* amnistie *f*

amoeba, ameba [ə'miːbə] *(pl* amoebae, amebae [ə'miːbiː] *or* amoebas, amebas*)* n* amibe *f*

amok [ə'mɒk] *adv* **to run a.** être pris(e) de folie furieuse

among [ə'mʌŋ], **amongst** [ə'mʌŋst] *prep* parmi; **a. the crowd** au milieu de la foule; **we are a. friends** nous sommes entre amis; **they quarrel a. themselves** ils se disputent entre eux; **the money was divided a. them** l'argent a été divisé entre eux; **a. the best** parmi les meilleurs; **a. other things** entre autres choses

amoral [eɪ'mɒrəl] *adj* amoral(e)

amorphous [ə'mɔːfəs] *adj (mass, lump)* informe; *(ideas, beliefs)* confus(e)

amount [ə'maʊnt] *n (a) (sum of money)* somme *f (b) (quantity)* quantité *f*; **a large a. of time/effort** beaucoup de temps/d'énergie; **a certain a. of discomfort** un certain manque de confort; **in large amounts** en grande quantité; **in small amounts** en petites quantités

▸**amount to** *vt insep (a) (add up to)* s'élever à; **her debts a. to $700** ses dettes s'élèvent à 700 dollars *(b) (mean)* **it amounts to the same thing** cela revient au même; *Fig* **he'll never a. to much** il n'arrivera jamais à rien

amp [æmp] *n (a) Elec (unit)* ampère *m (b) Fam (amplifier)* ampli *m*

ampere ['æmpeə(r)] *n Elec* ampère *m*

ampersand ['æmpəsænd] *n* esperluette *f*

amphetamine [æm'fetəmɪn] *n* amphétamine *f*

amphibian [æm'fɪbɪən] **1** *n* amphibie *m*
    2 *adj* amphibie

amphibious [æm'fɪbɪəs] *adj* amphibie

amphitheater ['æmfɪθɪətə(r)] *n* amphithéâtre *m*

ample ['æmpəl] *adj (a) (large) (woman, bosom)* fort(e) *(b) (plentiful)* abondant(e); **to have a. time to do sth** avoir largement

le temps de faire qch; **to have a. opportunity to do sth** avoir tout loisir de faire qch; **this will be a.** ce sera largement suffisant

amplifier ['æmplɪfaɪə(r)] *n* amplificateur *m*

amplify ['æmplɪfaɪ] *(pt & pp* amplified*)* vt (essay, remarks)* développer; *(current, volume)* amplifier

amply ['æmplɪ] *adv* amplement, largement

amputate ['æmpjʊteɪt] *vt* amputer

amputation [æmpjʊ'teɪʃən] *n* amputation *f*

Amsterdam [æmstə'dæm] *n* Amsterdam

amuck [ə'mʌk] = amok

amulet ['æmjʊlet] *n* amulette *f*

amuse [ə'mjuːz] *vt (a) (make laugh)* amuser *(b) (occupy)* occuper; **to a. oneself by doing sth** se distraire en faisant qch; **to keep sb amused** distraire qn

amusement [ə'mjuːzmənt] *n (a) (enjoyment)* amusement *m*; **much to everyone's a.** au grand amusement de tous *(b) (pastime)* distraction *f*; **a. park** parc *m* d'attractions

amusing [ə'mjuːzɪŋ] *adj* amusant(e)

an [ən, *stressed* æn] *see* a²

anabolic steroid [ænə'bɒlɪk'steroɪd] *n* stéroïde *m* anabolisant

anachronism [ə'nækrənɪzəm] *n* anachronisme *m*; **to be an a.** faire figure d'anachronisme

anaconda [ænə'kɒndə] *n* anaconda *m*

anagram ['ænəgræm] *n* anagramme *f*

anal ['eɪnəl] *adj* anal(e)

analgesic [ænəl'dʒiːzɪk] **1** *n* analgésique *m*
    2 *adj* analgésique

analog ['ænəlɒg] *n* analogue *m*; **a. clock** horloge *f* à affichage analogique

analogous [ə'næləgəs] *adj* analogue (**to** à)

analogy [ə'nælədʒɪ] *(pl* analogies*)* n* analogie *f*

analysis [ə'næləsɪs] *(pl* analyses [ə'næləsiːz]*)* n* analyse *f*; *Psy* psychanalyse *f*; *Fig* **in the final a.** en fin de compte, au bout du compte

analyst ['ænəlɪst] *n* analyste *mf*; *Psy* (psych)analyste *mf*

analytic [ænə'lɪtɪk], **analytical** [ænə'lɪtɪkəl] *adj* analytique

analyze ['ænəlaɪz] *vt* analyser; *Psy* psychanalyser

anarchist ['ænəkɪst] *n* anarchiste *mf*

anarchy ['ænəkɪ] *n* anarchie *f*

anathema [ə'næθəmə] *n (a) Rel* anathème *m (b) (repellent)* **the very idea was a. to her** l'idée même lui faisait horreur

anatomical [ænə'tɒmɪkəl] *adj* anatomique

anatomy [ə'nætəmɪ] *n* anatomie *f*

ANC [eɪen'siː] *n (abbr* **African National Congress***)* ANC *m*

ancestor ['ænsestə(r)] *n* ancêtre *mf*

ancestral [æn'sestrəl] *adj* ancestral(e); **a. home** demeure *f* ancestrale

ancestry ['ænsestrɪ] *n (descent)* ascendance *f*

anchor ['æŋkə(r)] **1** *n (a) Naut* ancre *f*; *Fig* planche *f* de salut; **at a.** au mouillage; **to drop a.** jeter l'ancre; **to weigh a.** lever l'ancre *(b) (of radio, TV program)* présentateur(trice) *m,f* principal(e)
    2 *vt (a) Naut* ancrer *(b) (fix securely)* ancrer (**to** à) *(c) (radio, TV program)* présenter
    3 *vi Naut* jeter l'ancre

anchorman ['æŋkəmən] *n (of radio, TV program)* présentateur *m* principal

anchorperson ['æŋkəpɜːsən] *n (of radio, TV program)* présentateur(trice) *m,f* principal(e)

anchorwoman ['æŋkəwʊmən] *n (of radio, TV program)* présentatrice *f* principale

anchovy ['æntʃəʊvɪ] *(pl* anchovies*)* n* anchois *m*

ancient ['eɪnʃənt] **1** *adj* ancien(enne); *Fig (person, car)* très vieux (vieille); **a. history** histoire *f* ancienne; **A. Rome** la Rome antique

  2 *n* **the ancients** les anciens *mpl*

ancillary [æn'sılərı] *adj* auxiliaire

and [ænd, *unstressed* ənd, ən] *conj* (a) *(in general)* et; **she can read a. write** elle sait lire et écrire; **my mother a. father** mon père et ma mère; **chicken a. fries** du poulet-frites; **a vodka a. orange** une vodka orange; **do that again a. I'll hit you!** si tu recommences, je te frappe!; **wait a. see** tu verras bien; **nice a. warm** bien chaud(e)

  (b) *(to)* **go a. look for it** va le chercher; **come a. see me** viens me voir; **try a. help me** essaie de m'aider

  (c) *(in numbers)* **two hundred a. two** deux cent deux; **four a. a half** quatre et demi; **an hour a. twenty minutes** une heure vingt; **four a. five make nine** quatre et *ou* plus cinq font neuf

  (d) *(expressing repetition)* **hours a. hours** pendant des heures et des heures; **better a. better** de mieux en mieux; **smaller a. smaller** de plus en plus petit(e); **she talked a. talked** elle n'arrêtait pas de parler

  (e) **a. so on a. so forth** et ainsi de suite

Andalusia [ændə'luːsıə] *n* l'Andalousie *f*

Andes ['ændiːz] *npl* **the A.** les Andes *fpl*

Andorra [æn'dɔːrə] *n* l'Andorre *f*

Andorran [æn'dɔːrən] **1** *n* Andorran(e) *m,f*

  2 *adj* andorran(e)

androgynous [æn'drɒdʒınəs] *adj* androgyne

anecdotal [ænık'dəʊtəl] *adj* anecdotique

anecdote ['ænıkdəʊt] *n* anecdote *f*

anemia [ə'niːmıə] *n* anémie *f*

anemic [ə'niːmık] *adj* anémique *f*

anemone [ə'nemənı] *n (flower)* anémone *f*; **sea a.** anémone de mer

anesthetic [ænəs'θetık] *n (substance)* anesthésique *m*; *(process)* anesthésie *f*; **under a.** sous anesthésie; **local/general a.** anesthésie locale/générale

anesthetist [ə'niːsθətıst] *n* anesthésiste *mf*

anesthetize [ə'niːsθətaız] *vt* anesthésier

anew [ə'njuː] *adv* encore, de nouveau; **to start a.** recommencer

angel ['eındʒəl] *n* ange *m*; *Fam* **you're an a.!** tu es un ange!; *Culin* **a. food cake** ≃ gâteau *m* de Savoie

Angeleno [ændʒə'liːnəʊ] *(pl* **Angelenos)** *n* = personne née à *ou* habitant Los Angeles

angelic [æn'dʒelık] *adj* angélique

anger ['æŋgə(r)] **1** *n* colère *f*; **a fit of a.** un accès de colère; **to speak in a.** parler sous le coup de la colère

  2 *vt* mettre en colère

  3 *vi* **to be slow/quick to a.** ne pas se mettre facilement/se mettre facilement en colère

angina [æn'dʒaınə] *n* angine *f* de poitrine

angle ['æŋgəl] **1** *n* (a) *Math* angle *m*; **at an a. of...** formant un angle de...; **the car hit them at an a.** la voiture les a heurtés de biais; **the store stands at an a. to the street** le magasin fait l'angle (b) *(viewpoint)* point *m* de vue; **seen from this a.** vu sous cet angle

  2 *vi* (a) *(fish)* pêcher à la ligne (b) *Fam* **to a. for an invitation** chercher à se faire inviter

angler ['æŋglə(r)] *n (person)* pêcheur(euse) *m,f* à la ligne; **a. fish** baudroie *f*, lotte *f* de mer

Anglican ['æŋglıkən] *n & adj* anglican(e) *m,f*

angling ['æŋglıŋ] *n (fishing)* pêche *f* à la ligne

Anglo-American ['æŋgləʊə'merıkən] *adj* anglo-américain(e)

Anglo-Saxon ['æŋgləʊ'sæksən] **1** *n* (a) *(person)* Anglo-Saxon(onne) *m,f* (b) *(language)* anglo-saxon *m*

  2 *adj* anglo-saxon(onne)

Angola [æŋ'gəʊlə] *n* l'Angola *m*

Angolan [æŋ'gəʊlən] **1** *n* Angolais(e) *m,f*

  2 *adj* angolais(e)

angora [æŋ'gɔːrə] *n* angora *m*; **a. sweater** pull *m* en angora; **a. cat/rabbit** chat *m*/lapin *m* angora

angrily ['æŋgrılı] *adv* avec colère

angry ['æŋgrı] *adj (person)* en colère, fâché(e); *(voice, speech, letter)* furieux(euse); **to get a. (with)** se fâcher (contre), se mettre en colère (contre); **to make sb a.** mettre qn en colère

angst [æŋst] *n* angoisse *f*

anguish ['æŋgwıʃ] *n* angoisse *f*

anguished ['æŋgwıʃt] *adj (look, cry)* d'angoisse; *(person)* tourmenté(e)

angular ['æŋgjʊlə(r)] *adj* anguleux(euse)

animal ['ænıməl] *n* animal *m*; **the a. kingdom** le règne animal; **a. lover** = personne qui aime les animaux; **a. rights** les droits *mpl* des animaux; **he's an a.** *(uncivilized person)* c'est une brute

animate 1 *adj* ['ænımıt] animé(e)

  2 *vt* ['ænımeıt] animer

animated ['ænımeıtıd] *adj (expression, discussion)* animé(e); **to become a.** s'animer; **a. cartoon** dessin *m* animé

animation [ænı'meıʃən] *n* animation *f*

animator ['ænımeıtə(r)] *n Cin* animateur(trice) *m,f*

animism ['ænımızəm] *n* animisme *m*

animosity [ænı'mɒsıtı] *n* animosité *f*

aniseed ['ænısiːd] *n (flavor)* anis *m*; *(seed)* graine *f* d'anis

Ankara ['æŋkərə] *n* Ankara

ankle ['æŋkəl] *n* cheville *f*; **a. boots** chaussures *fpl* montantes; **a. socks** socquettes *fpl*

anklet ['æŋklət] *n (ankle bracelet)* bracelet *m* de cheville

annals ['ænəlz] *npl* annales *fpl*

annex 1 *vt* [æ'neks] annexer

  2 *n* ['æneks] *(of building, document)* annexe *f*

annexation [ænek'seıʃən] *n* annexion *f*

annihilate [ə'naıəleıt] *vt* anéantir

annihilation [ənaıə'leıʃən] *n* anéantissement *m*

anniversary [ænı'vɜːsərı] *(pl* **anniversaries)** *n* anniversaire *m*; **wedding a.** anniversaire de mariage

anno Domini ['ænəʊ'dɒmınaı] *adv* en l'an de grâce

annotate ['ænəteıt] *vt* annoter

announce [ə'naʊns] *vt* annoncer

announcement [ə'naʊnsmənt] *n (of news)* annonce *f*; *(formal statement)* avis *m*

announcer [ə'naʊnsə(r)] *n (on radio, TV program)* annonceur(euse) *m,f*, speaker (speakerine) *m,f*

annoy [ə'nɔı] *vt* agacer; **to get annoyed** se mettre en colère, se fâcher; **to be annoyed with sb** être en colère contre qn

annoyance [ə'nɔıəns] *n (feeling)* agacement *m*; *(annoying thing)* ennui *m*

annoying [ə'nɔıŋ] *adj* agaçant(e), ennuyeux(euse); **how a.!** comme c'est ennuyeux!

annual ['ænjʊəl] **1** *n* (a) *(plant)* plante *f* annuelle (b) *(book)* publication *f* annuelle; *(for children)* album *m* (publié une fois par an)

  2 *adj* annuel(elle)

annually ['ænjʊəlı] *adv (every year)* tous les ans; *(per year)* par an

annul [ə'nʌl] *(pt & pp* **annulled)** *vt Law (contract, marriage)* annuler

anode ['ænəʊd] *n* anode *f*

anodyne ['ænəʊdaın] *adj (bland)* anodin(e)

anoint [ə'nɔınt] *vt* oindre (**with** de); **to a. sb king** sacrer qn roi

anomalous [ə'nɒmələs] *adj* anormal(e)

anomaly [ə'nɒməlı] *(pl* **anomalies)** *n* anomalie *f*

anon[1] [ə'nɒn] *adv Lit (soon)* bientôt

anon² [əˈnɒn] *adj* (*abbr* **anonymous**) anonyme

anonymity [ænəˈnɪmɪtɪ] *n* anonymat *m*

anonymous [əˈnɒnɪməs] *adj* anonyme; **to remain a.** garder l'anonymat

anorak [ˈænəræk] *n* anorak *m*

anorexia [ænəˈreksɪə] *n* anorexie *f*; **a. nervosa** anorexie mentale

anorexic [ænəˈreksɪk] *adj* anorexique

another [əˈnʌðə(r)] *adj & pron* (**a**) (*additional*) un (une) autre *m,f*; **a. cup of tea** une autre tasse de thé; **in a. ten years** dans dix ans; **don't say a. word** plus un mot; **a. Picasso/Vietnam** un nouveau Picasso/Viêt Nam (**b**) (*different*) un (une) autre *m,f*; **that's quite a. matter** c'est une toute autre affaire; **a. time, perhaps** (*declining invitation*) une autre fois, peut-être; **what with one thing and a., I forgot** avec tout ce qui s'est passé, j'ai oublié; **one way or a.** d'une façon ou d'une autre (**c**) (*reciprocal*) **they saw one a.** ils se sont vus

answer [ˈɑːnsə(r)] **1** *n* (*to question, letter*) réponse *f*; (*to problem*) solution *f*; **I knocked but there was no a.** j'ai frappé mais personne n'a répondu; **there's no a.** (*on telephone*) ça ne répond pas; **he has an a. to everything** il a réponse à tout; *Formal* **in a. to your letter** en réponse à votre lettre
  2 *vt* répondre à; **"I'll do it tomorrow," he answered** "je le ferai demain", a-t-il répondu; **to a. the telephone** répondre au téléphone; **to a. the door** ouvrir (la porte)
  3 *vi* (*of person*) répondre

►**answer back** *vi* (*be impertinent*) répondre

►**answer for** *vt insep* répondre de; **he has a lot to a. for** il a beaucoup de comptes à rendre

►**answer to** *vt insep* (**a**) (*be accountable to*) **to a. to sb** être responsable devant qn; **she answers to no one** elle n'a de comptes à rendre à personne (**b**) (*correspond to*) (*description*) répondre à (**c**) **the dog answers to the name of Rover** le chien répond au nom de Rover

answerable [ˈɑːnsərəbəl] *adj* **to be a. to sb** être responsable devant qn; **he is a. to nobody** il n'a de comptes à rendre à personne

answering machine [ˈɑːnsərɪŋˈməʃiːn] *n* répondeur *m* (téléphonique)

ant [ænt] *n* fourmi *f*; **a. hill** fourmilière *f*

antagonism [ænˈtæɡənɪzəm] *n* antagonisme *m*

antagonist [ænˈtæɡənɪst] *n* antagoniste *mf*

antagonize [ænˈtæɡənaɪz] *vt* rendre hostile

Antarctica [ænˈtɑːktɪkə] *n* l'Antarctique *m*

ante [ˈæntɪ] *n Fam* **to up the a.** (*in gambling, conflict*) augmenter la mise

anteater [ˈæntiːtə(r)] *n* fourmilier *m*

antecedents [æntɪˈsiːdəns] *npl* antécédents *mpl*

antelope [ˈæntɪləʊp] *n* antilope *f*

antenatal [æntɪˈneɪtəl] *adj* prénatal(e)

antenna [ænˈtenə] *n* (**a**) (*pl* **antennae** [ænˈteniː]) (*of insect, snail*) antenne *f* (**b**) (*pl* **antennas**) (*of radio, TV*) antenne *f*

anterior [ænˈtɪərɪə(r)] *adj Formal & Anat* antérieur(e) (**to** à)

anteroom [ˈæntɪruːm] *n* antichambre *f*

anthem [ˈænθəm] *n* hymne *m*; **national a.** hymne national

anthology [ænˈθɒlədʒɪ] (*pl* **anthologies**) *n* anthologie *f*

anthracite [ˈænθrəsaɪt] *n* anthracite *m*

anthrax [ˈænθræks] *n* (*disease*) anthrax *m*

anthropologist [ænθrəˈpɒlədʒɪst] *n* anthropologue *mf*

anthropology [ænθrəˈpɒlədʒɪ] *n* anthropologie *f*

anti- [ˈæntɪ] *pref* anti-; **a.American** antiaméricain(e)

antiaircraft [ˈæntɪˈeəkrɑːft] *adj* (*gun, defenses*) antiaérien(enne)

antibiotic [æntɪbaɪˈɒtɪk] *n* antibiotique *m*

antibody [ˈæntɪbɒdɪ] (*pl* **antibodies**) *n Med* anticorps *m*

Antichrist [ˈæntɪkraɪst] *n* Antéchrist *m*

anticipate [ænˈtɪsɪpeɪt] *vt* (**a**) (*expect*) prévoir, s'attendre à; (*foresee*) anticiper; **we hadn't anticipated such stiff resistance** nous ne nous attendions pas à une telle résistance; **as anticipated, there was trouble** comme on s'y attendait, il y eut des problèmes (**b**) (*foreshadow*) préfigurer, annoncer

anticipation [æntɪsɪˈpeɪʃən] *n* (**a**) (*foresight*) prévoyance *f*; **in a. of trouble** en prévision de troubles; *Formal* **thanking you in a.** en vous remerciant d'avance, avec mes remerciements anticipés (**b**) (*eagerness*) impatience *f*

anticlimax [æntɪˈklaɪmæks] *n* déception *f*

antics [ˈæntɪks] *npl* bouffonneries *fpl*; **he's been up to his usual a.** il a encore fait des siennes

anticyclone [æntɪˈsaɪkləʊn] *n Met* anticyclone *m*

antidepressant [æntɪdɪˈpresənt] *n* antidépresseur *m*

antidote [ˈæntɪdəʊt] *n also Fig* antidote *m* (**to** contre)

antidumping [æntɪˈdʌmpɪŋ] *adj* (*laws, legislation*) antidumping *inv*

antiestablishment [æntɪˈstæblɪʃmənt] *adj Pol* anticonformiste

antifreeze [ˈæntɪfriːz] *n* antigel *m*

Antigua and Barbuda [ænˈtiːɡɑːnbɑːˈbjuːdə] *n* Antigua-et-Barbuda

antihistamine [æntɪˈhɪstəmɪn] *Med* **1** *n* antihistaminique *f*
  2 *adj* antihistaminique; **a. tablet** médicament *m* antihistaminique

antipathy [ænˈtɪpəθɪ] *n* antipathie *f* (**towards** pour)

antiperspirant [æntɪˈpɜːspɪrənt] *n* déodorant *m*

Antipodes [ænˈtɪpədiːz] *npl* **the A.** l'Australie *f* et la Nouvelle-Zélande

antiquarian [æntɪˈkweərɪən] **1** *n* (*dealer*) antiquaire *mf*; (*collector*) collectionneur(euse) *m,f* d'antiquités
  2 *adj* (*book*) ancien(enne); **a. bookstore** = librairie spécialisée dans les livres anciens

antiquated [ˈæntɪkweɪtɪd] *adj* (*building, installation*) vétuste; (*idea, method*) vieillot(otte)

antique [ænˈtiːk] **1** *n* antiquité *f*; **a. dealer** antiquaire *mf*; **a. store** magasin *m* d'antiquités
  2 *adj* ancien(enne); **an a. clock** une pendule ancienne *ou* d'époque; **a. furniture** meubles *mpl* anciens

antiquity [ænˈtɪkwɪtɪ] (*pl* **antiquities**) *n* (*historical period, ruin*) antiquité *f*

antiracist [æntɪˈreɪsɪst] *adj* antiraciste

anti-Semitic [æntɪsɪˈmɪtɪk] *adj* antisémite

antiseptic [æntɪˈseptɪk] **1** *n* antiseptique *m*
  2 *adj* (**a**) (*antibacterial*) antiseptique (**b**) *Fig* (*lacking character or warmth*) (*place*) aseptisé(e); (*person*) froid(e)

antisocial [æntɪˈsəʊʃəl] *adj* (**a**) (*disruptive*) asocial(e) (**b**) (*unsociable*) peu sociable

antithesis [ænˈtɪθɪsɪs] (*pl* **antitheses** [ænˈtɪθɪsiːz]) *n* (*opposite*) opposé *m*, antithèse *f*

antlers [ˈæntləz] *npl* bois *mpl*

antonym [ˈæntənɪm] *n* antonyme *m*

Antwerp [ˈæntwɜːp] *n* Anvers

anus [ˈeɪnəs] *n* anus *m*

anvil [ˈænvɪl] *n* enclume *f*

anxiety [æŋˈzaɪətɪ] (*pl* **anxieties**) *n* (**a**) (*worry, concern*) inquiétude *f*; (*stronger*) anxiété *f*; **my main a. is...** mon principal souci est...; **there is no cause for a.** il n'y a pas de quoi s'inquiéter; **to feel a.** être anxieux(euse) (**b**) (*eagerness*) désir *m*, souci *m*; **in her a. to help** dans son désir *ou* souci de se rendre utile

anxious [ˈæŋkʃəs] *adj* (**a**) (*worried*) inquiet(ète); (*stronger*) anxieux(euse); **to be a. for sb** être inquiet *ou* s'inquiéter pour qn; **to be a. about sth** être inquiet *ou* s'inquiéter pour qch (**b**) (*worrying*) (*moment*) d'angoisse; (*period*) angoissant(e) (**c**) **to be a. to do sth** (*impatient*) être impatient(e) de faire qch; (*eager*) tenir à faire qch

anxiously ['æŋkʃəslɪ] *adv* (**a**) *(worriedly)* avec inquiétude; *(stronger)* anxieusement (**b**) *(with impatience)* impatiemment, avec impatience

any ['enɪ] **1** *pron* (**a**) *(some)* **do you have a.?** en avez-vous?; **is/ are there a. left?** en reste-t-il?; **can a. of them speak English?** y en a-t-il parmi eux qui parlent anglais?

(**b**) *(in negatives)* **I don't have a.** je n'en ai pas; **there was nothing in a. of the boxes** il n'y avait rien dans aucune des boîtes; **few, if a., can read** aucun, ou presque aucun, ne sait lire

(**c**) *(no particular one)* n'importe lequel (laquelle) *m,f*; **a. of us** n'importe lequel d'entre nous

(**d**) *(every one)* tous ceux (toutes celles) *mpl, fpl*; **keep a. you find** garde tous ceux que tu trouveras

2 *adj* (**a**) *(some) (singular)* du (de la); *(plural)* des; **do you have a. milk/flour/apples?** avez-vous du lait/de la farine/ des pommes?

(**b**) *(in negatives)* **he doesn't have a. money** il n'a pas d'argent; **without a. doubt** sans aucun doute; **that won't do a. good** ça ne servira à rien

(**c**) *(no particular)* n'importe quel (quelle); **come a. day** venez n'importe quel jour; **a. minute now** d'une minute à l'autre

(**d**) *(every)* tout(e); **a. pupil who forgets his books will be punished** tout élève qui oubliera ses livres sera puni; **at a. rate, in a. case** en tout cas

3 *adv* (**a**) *(with comparative)* **I'm not a. better** je ne vais pas mieux; **does that make it a. easier?** est-ce que c'est plus facile comme ça?; **do you want a. more tea?** veux-tu encore du thé?; **I don't like her a. more than you do** je ne l'aime pas plus que toi

(**b**) *Fam* **that didn't help us a.** ça ne nous a été d'aucun secours

anybody ['enɪbɒdɪ] *pron* (**a**) *(indeterminate)* quelqu'un; **would a. like some more cake?** quelqu'un veut-il encore du gâteau?; **she'll know if a. does** si quelqu'un doit le savoir, c'est bien elle

(**b**) *(in negatives)* **not a.** ne... personne; **there isn't a. here** il n'y a personne ici; **there was hardly a.** il n'y avait presque personne

(**c**) *(no matter who)* n'importe qui; **a. will tell you so** n'importe qui *ou* tout le monde vous le dira; **bring along a. you like** amenez qui vous voudrez; **a. else** *or* **a. but her would have refused** tout autre qu'elle aurait refusé; **it's a.'s guess** Dieu seul le sait; **he's not just a.!** ce n'est pas n'importe qui!

(**d**) *(person with status)* **he'll never be a.** il ne fera jamais rien dans la vie

anyhow ['enɪhaʊ] *adv* (**a**) *(however)* de toute façon *ou* manière; **a., let's get back to what we were saying** bref, revenons à ce que nous disions; **I don't care, I'm going a.** ça m'est égal, j'y vais quand même (**b**) *Fam (carelessly)* n'importe comment

anymore ['enɪmɔː(r)] *adv* **they don't live here a.** ils n'habitent plus ici; **I won't do it a.** je ne le ferai plus (jamais)

anyone ['enɪwʌn] = **anybody**

anyplace ['enɪpleɪs] = **anywhere**

anything ['enɪθɪŋ] **1** *pron* (**a**) *(indeterminate)* quelque chose; **is there a. I can do?** est-ce que je peux faire quelque chose?; **do you have a. to write with?** as-tu de quoi écrire?; **will there be a. else?** *(in store)* et avec ceci?; **do you have a. smaller?** avez-vous quelque chose de plus petit?; *(money)* vous n'avez pas plus petit?; **if a. should happen to me** s'il m'arrivait quelque chose *ou* quoi que ce soit; **is (there) a. the matter?** il y a quelque chose qui ne va pas?

(**b**) *(in negatives)* **not a.** ne... rien; **he doesn't do a.** il ne fait rien; **hardly a.** presque rien

(**c**) *(no matter what)* n'importe quoi; **he eats a.** il mange de tout; **I love a. French** j'aime tout ce qui est français; **she would do a. for me** elle ferait n'importe quoi pour moi; **he was a. but friendly** il était tout sauf amical; **are you**

angry? – a. but tu es fâché? – non, loin de là

2 *adv* **is it a. like the other one?** est-ce qu'il ressemble un peu à l'autre ou pas du tout?; **she doesn't look a. like her sister** elle ne ressemble pas du tout à sa sœur; **the food wasn't a. like as bad as they said** la nourriture était loin d'être aussi mauvaise que ce qu'on m'avait dit; *Fam* **as funny/ strong as a.** drôle/fort(e) comme tout; *Fam* **to work like a.** travailler comme un fou (une folle); *Fam* **it's not that you're wrong or a.** ce n'est pas que tu aies tort

anytime ['enɪtaɪm] *adv* n'importe quand; **come over a.** venez quand vous voulez; **you're welcome a.** vous serez toujours le bienvenu

anyway ['enɪweɪ] = **anyhow (a)**

anywhere ['enɪweə(r)] *adv* (**a**) *(in questions)* quelque part; **did you go a. yesterday?** êtes-vous allé quelque part hier?; **can you see it a.?** tu le vois?

(**b**) *(in negatives)* **not a.** ne... nulle part; **I can't find it a.** je ne le trouve nulle part; **we're not getting a.** nous n'avançons pas; **he isn't a. near as smart as her** il est loin d'être aussi intelligent qu'elle

(**c**) *(no matter where)* n'importe où; **put it a.** mets-le n'importe où; **I'd know her a.** je la reconnaîtrais entre mille; **it's miles from a.** c'est loin de tout; **a. else** n'importe où

AO(C)B [eɪəʊ(siː)'biː] *(abbr* **any other (competent) business***)* divers

A-OK ['eɪəʊ'keɪ] *Fam* **1** *adj* génial(e), cool; **everything's A-OK** tout baigne; **he's A-OK** c'est un type bien

2 *adv* parfaitement; **it went A-OK** ça s'est passé vachement bien

aorta [eɪ'ɔːtə] *n* aorte *f*

apart [ə'pɑːt] *adv* (**a**) *(at a distance)* à l'écart (**from** de); **to stand a.** *(of person)* se tenir à l'écart; **the garage stands a. from the house** le garage est séparé de la maison

(**b**) *(separated)* **they are far a.** ils sont très éloignés l'un de l'autre; **the two towns are 10 miles a.** ≃ les deux villes sont à 16 kilomètres l'une de l'autre; **they're never a.** ils ne se séparent jamais; **with one's legs a.** les jambes écartées; **two years a.** à deux ans d'intervalle; **to live a.** vivre séparément; **it's difficult to tell them a.** il est difficile de les distinguer l'un de l'autre; **joking a.,...** blague à part,...

(**c**) *(to pieces)* **to take sth a.** *(machine)* démonter qch; **to come a.** *(of garment)* se découdre

(**d**) *(excepting)* **a. from** à part; **a. from the fact that...** indépendamment du fait que...

apartheid [ə'pɑːtaɪt] *n* apartheid *m*

apartment [ə'pɑːtmənt] *n* appartement *m*; **a. block, a. building** immeuble *m* d'habitation, *Can* bloc-appartement *m*

apathetic [æpə'θetɪk] *adj* qui manque d'enthousiasme; **to be a. about sth** être indifférent(e) à qch

apathy ['æpəθɪ] *n* manque *m* d'enthousiasme

ape [eɪp] **1** *n (animal)* grand singe *m*; *Fam* **to go a.** piquer une crise

2 *vt (imitate)* singer

aperitif [əperɪ'tiːf] *n* apéritif *m*

aperture ['æpətjʊə(r)] *n* ouverture *f*

apex ['eɪpeks] *n* sommet *m*

aphasia [ə'feɪzɪə] *n Med* aphasie *f*

aphid ['eɪfɪd] *n* puceron *m*

aphorism ['æfərɪzəm] *n* aphorisme *m*

aphrodisiac [æfrəʊ'dɪzɪæk] **1** *n* aphrodisiaque *m*

2 *adj* aphrodisiaque

apiece [ə'piːs] *adv* chacun(e); **they cost $3 a.** ils valent 3 dollars pièce *ou* chacun

aplenty [ə'plentɪ] *adv* en abondance

aplomb [ə'plɒm] *n* sang-froid *m*

apocalypse [ə'pɒkəlɪps] *n* apocalypse *f*

apocalyptic [əpɒkə'lɪptɪk] *adj* apocalyptique

apocryphal [əˈpɒkrɪfəl] *adj* apocryphe; **the story is a.** c'est une histoire inventée

apolitical [eɪpəˈlɪtɪkəl] *adj* apolitique

apologetic [əpɒləˈdʒetɪk] *adj (tone, smile)* désolé(e); **to be a. about sth** s'excuser de qch; **she was pretty a. about it** elle s'est répandue en excuses

apologize [əˈpɒlədʒaɪz] *vi* s'excuser; **to a. to sb for sth** s'excuser de qch auprès de qn, présenter ses excuses à qn pour qch; **she apologized for being late/for not telling him earlier** elle s'est excusée d'être en retard/de ne pas le lui avoir dit plus tôt

apology [əˈpɒlədʒɪ] *(pl* **apologies**) *n* excuses *fpl*; **to make/to offer an a.** faire/présenter des excuses; **I owe you an a.** je vous dois des excuses; *Pej* **an a. for a dinner** un semblant de dîner

apoplectic [æpəˈplektɪk] *adj Fig (angry)* furieux(euse); **to be a. with rage** s'étrangler de rage

apoplexy [ˈæpəpleksɪ] *n Med* apoplexie *f; Fig (anger)* rage *f*

apostle [əˈpɒsəl] *n* apôtre *m*

apostolic [æpɒsˈtɒlɪk], **apostolical** [æpɒsˈtɒlɪkəl] *adj* apostolique

apostrophe [əˈpɒstrəfɪ] *n* apostrophe *f*

app [æp] *n Fam Comput (abbr* **application**) application *f*

appall [əˈpɔːl] *vt (shock)* choquer, scandaliser; *(fill with horror)* horrifier; **to be appalled at** *or* **by sth** être choqué(e)/horrifié(e) par qch; **it appalls me to think that…** je suis horrifié(e) à la pensée que…

appalling [əˈpɔːlɪŋ] *adj (behavior)* scandaleux(euse); *(conditions, smell, weather, movie)* épouvantable

apparatus [æpəˈreɪtəs] *n (machine)* appareil *m; (set of machines, in laboratory)* équipement *m; (in gym)* agrès *mpl;* **a piece of a.** un appareil

apparel [əˈpærəl] *n (a) (clothes)* habillement *m,* vêtements *mpl; (industry)* confection *f* **(b)** *Formal or Literary (outfit, garb)* mise *f*

apparent [əˈpærənt] *adj (a) (obvious)* clair(e), évident(e); **it soon became a. that…** il est vite devenu évident que… **(b)** *(seeming)* apparent(e)

apparently [əˈpærəntlɪ] *adv* apparemment; **a. he's going to Venice** il paraît qu'il va à Venise

apparition [æpəˈrɪʃən] *n* apparition *f*

appeal [əˈpiːl] **1** *n (a) (call)* appel *m* (**for** à); **to make an a. for help** lancer un appel à l'aide; **charity a.** = appel aux dons lancé par une organisation caritative
(b) *Law* appel *m;* **on a.** en seconde instance; **A.** *or* **Appeals Court, Court of A.** *or* **Appeals** cour *f* d'appel
(c) *(attraction)* attrait *m;* **to have great a.** *(of idea)* être très attrayant(e); *(of person)* avoir beaucoup de charme; **their music has a wide a.** leur musique attire un public très varié
2 *vt Law* **to a. a decision** faire appel d'une décision
3 *vi (a) (make a plea)* **to a. (to sb) for help/money** demander de l'aide/de l'argent (à qn); **to a. to sb's generosity** faire appel à la générosité de qn
(b) **to a. to sb** *(attract)* attirer qn
(c) *Law* se pourvoir en appel; **to a. against a decision** faire appel d'une décision

appealing [əˈpiːlɪŋ] *adj (idea)* séduisant(e); *(person, manner)* sympathique

appear [əˈpɪə(r)] *vi (a) (come into view)* apparaître; *(of publication)* paraître; **where did you a. from?** d'où sors-tu?; **to a. from nowhere** sortir de nulle part; **to a. on TV** passer à la télé **(b)** *Law* comparaître **(c)** *(look, seem)* sembler; **to a. to be lost** avoir l'air d'être perdu(e); **there appears to be a mistake** il semble qu'il y ait une erreur; **so it would a.** c'est ce qu'on dirait

appearance [əˈpɪərəns] *n (a) (arrival)* apparition *f,* arrivée *f;* **to put in an a.** faire acte de présence **(b)** *(of actor)* **to make a television a.** passer à la télévision **(c)** *(of publication)* parution

f **(d)** *Law (in court)* comparution *f* **(e)** *(looks, demeanor)* apparence *f;* **it's wrong to judge by appearances** il ne faut pas se fier aux apparences; **appearances can be deceptive** les apparences peuvent être trompeuses; **to keep up appearances** sauver les apparences

appease [əˈpiːz] *vt (anger, person)* apaiser, calmer; *Pol* composer avec

appeasement [əˈpiːzmənt] *n (of person, anger)* apaisement *m; Pol* conciliation *f*

append [əˈpend] *vt (list, document)* joindre (**to** à); *(one's signature)* apposer (**to** à)

appendage [əˈpendɪdʒ] *n* appendice *m;* **she was tired of being treated as her husband's a.** elle en avait assez de n'être traitée que comme la femme de son mari

appendicitis [əpendɪˈsaɪtɪs] *n* appendicite *f*

appendix [əˈpendɪks] *(pl* **appendixes** *or* **appendices** [əˈpendɪsiːz]) *n (a) Anat* appendice *m;* **to have one's a. (taken) out** se faire opérer de l'appendicite **(b)** *(of book)* appendice *m*

appetite [ˈæpɪtaɪt] *n (a) (for food)* appétit *m;* **to have a good a.** avoir bon appétit; **to spoil sb's a.** couper l'appétit à qn; **to give sb an a.** donner faim à qn; *(of fresh air, walk)* creuser qn **(b)** *(enthusiasm) (for knowledge, travel)* soif *f* (**for** de); *(for music, movies)* goût *m* (**for** pour)

appetizer [ˈæpɪtaɪzə(r)] *n also Fig* amuse-gueule *m*

appetizing [ˈæpɪtaɪzɪŋ] *adj* appétissant(e)

applaud [əˈplɔːd] *vt & vi* applaudir

applause [əˈplɔːz] *n (clapping)* applaudissements *mpl; (approval)* approbation *f*

apple [ˈæpəl] *n* pomme *f;* **he was the a. of her eye** *(her favorite)* elle tenait à lui comme à la prunelle de ses yeux; **a. core** trognon *m* de pomme; **a. juice** jus *m* de pomme; **a. pie** *(without top crust)* tarte *f* aux pommes; *(with top crust)* tourte *f* aux pommes; **as American as a. pie** typiquement américain(e); **a. tart** tarte(lette) *f* aux pommes; **a. tree** pommier *m*

applecart [ˈæpəlkɑːt] *n* **to upset the a.** *(spoil plan)* tout chambouler

apple-pie [ˈæpəlpaɪ] *adj* **in a. order** parfaitement en ordre

applesauce [ˈæpəlsɔːs] *n Culin* compote *f* de pommes

appliance [əˈplaɪəns] *n* appareil *m;* **electrical/domestic a.** appareil électrique/ménager

applicable [əˈplɪkəbəl] *adj* applicable; **the rule is a. to everybody** la règle s'applique à tous; **delete where not a.** *(on form)* rayer les mentions inutiles

applicant [ˈæplɪkənt] *n (for job)* candidat(e) *m,f* (**for** à)

application [æplɪˈkeɪʃən] *n (a) (for job)* candidature *f* (**for** à); *(for passport, patent)* demande *f* (**for** de); **a. form** *(for job)* formulaire *m* de candidature; *(detailed)* dossier *m* de candidature; *(for grant, benefits)* formulaire *m* de demande **(b)** *(of rule, theory, paint)* application *f* **(c)** *(effort)* application *f,* assiduité *f*

applied [əˈplaɪd] *adj (math, physics)* appliqué(e)

apply [əˈplaɪ] *(pt & pp* **applied**) **1** *vt (a) (put on)* appliquer (**to** sur) **(b)** *(use) (system, theory)* appliquer (**to** à); **to a. one's mind to sth** concentrer ses efforts sur qch; **to a. oneself (to one's work)** s'appliquer
2 *vi (a)* **to a. to sb for sth** s'adresser à qn pour obtenir qch; **to a. for a job** poser sa candidature pour un poste; **to a. for a grant** faire une demande de bourse **(b)** *(of law, rule)* s'appliquer (**to** à)

appoint [əˈpɔɪnt] *vt (person)* nommer; *(committee)* constituer; **to a. sb to a post** nommer qn à un poste; **to a. sb (as) manager** nommer qn directeur(trice)

appointed [əˈpɔɪntɪd] *adj Formal (agreed) (place, hour)* convenu(e), dit(e)

appointment [əˈpɔɪntmənt] *n (a) (meeting, with doctor)* rendez-vous *m inv;* **to make an a. with sb** prendre rendez-vous avec qn; *(with dentist, doctor)* prendre rendez-vous chez qn **(b)**

(to job) nomination *f*; *(of committee)* constitution *f*; **to make an a.** pourvoir un poste

apportion [ə'pɔːʃən] *vt* répartir

appraisal [ə'preɪzəl] *n (of standards, personnel)* évaluation *f*

appraise [ə'preɪz] *vt (performance, situation)* évaluer; *(value)* estimer

appreciable [ə'priːʃɪəbəl] *adj (change, difference)* appréciable, sensible

appreciate [ə'priːʃɪeɪt] **1** *vt* (**a**) *(be grateful for) (help)* être reconnaissant(e) de; *(kindness)* être sensible à; **I a. your helping me** je vous suis reconnaissant de m'avoir aidé (**b**) *(grasp, understand)* être conscient(e) de; **he doesn't a. how lucky he is** il ne se rend pas compte de la chance qu'il a (**c**) *(acknowledge)* apprécier
   2 *vi (of goods, investment)* prendre de la valeur; *(of value)* augmenter

appreciation [əpriːʃɪ'eɪʃən] *n* (**a**) *(gratitude)* gratitude *f*, reconnaissance *f*; **in a. of** en reconnaissance de (**b**) *(understanding)* conscience *f*; **she has no a. of what is involved** elle ne se rend pas compte de ce que cela implique (**c**) *(review, assessment)* critique *f*; **a musical/wine a. society** une société d'amateurs de musique/de vin (**d**) *Fin* **a. of assets** plus-value *f* d'actif

appreciative [ə'priːʃɪətɪv] *adj* (**a**) *(grateful)* reconnaissant(e); **to be a. of sb's help/efforts** être reconnaissant à qn de son aide/des ses efforts (**b**) *(review)* élogieux(euse); *(response)* favorable; **the audience was very a.** le public a beaucoup aimé; **to be a. of sth** apprécier qch

apprehend [æprɪ'hend] *vt* (**a**) *Law (arrest)* appréhender (**b**) *Formal (understand)* comprendre

apprehension [æprɪ'henʃən] *n* (**a**) *(fear)* appréhension *f* (**b**) *Law (arrest)* arrestation *f*

apprehensive [æprɪ'hensɪv] *adj* inquiet(ète); **to be a. about sth/doing sth** appréhender qch/de faire qch

apprentice [ə'prentɪs] **1** *n* apprenti(e) *m,f*
   2 *vt* **to a. sb to sb** placer qn en apprentissage chez qn

apprenticeship [ə'prentɪʃɪp] *n also Fig* apprentissage *m*; **to serve one's a.** faire ses premières armes

approach [ə'prəʊtʃ] **1** *n* (**a**) *(coming) (of person, season)* approche *f*; **to make an a. to sb** *(proposal)* faire une proposition à qn (**b**) *(method)* approche *f* (**to** de); **let's try a different a.** essayons d'aborder le problème différemment (**c**) *(route of access)* voie *f* d'accès; **the approaches to a town** les abords *mpl* d'une ville
   2 *vt* (**a**) *(get nearer to)* approcher de; **I'm approaching forty-five** je vais sur mes quarante-cinq ans (**b**) *(go up to)* aborder; *(organization)* approcher; **to be easy/difficult to a.** être d'un abord facile/difficile (**c**) *(problem)* aborder
   3 *vi* approcher

approachable [ə'prəʊtʃəbəl] *adj (person)* d'un abord facile

approaching [ə'prəʊtʃɪŋ] *adj (vacation, season)* qui approche; *(car)* qui vient en sens inverse

appropriate[1] [ə'prəʊprɪət] *adj (suitable)* approprié(e) (**to** à); *(moment)* opportun(e)

appropriate[2] [ə'prəʊprɪeɪt] *vt* (**a**) *(take, steal)* s'approprier (**b**) *(set aside) (money, funds)* affecter (**to** à)

appropriately [ə'prəʊprɪətlɪ] *adv (suitably)* de manière appropriée; *(properly)* convenablement

appropriation [əprəʊprɪ'eɪʃən] *n (of funds)* affectation *f*

approval [ə'pruːvəl] *n* approbation *f*; **to meet with sb's a.** obtenir l'approbation de qn; *Com* **on a.** à l'essai

approve [ə'pruːv] *vt (action, proposal)* approuver; *(treaty)* ratifier

▸**approve of** *vt insep* approuver; **I don't a. of your friends** tes amis ne me plaisent pas; **she doesn't a. of them smoking** elle n'aime pas qu'ils fument

approving [ə'pruːvɪŋ] *adj* approbateur(trice)

approx. *(abbr* **approximately**) env.

approximate 1 *adj* [ə'prɒksɪmɪt] approximatif(ive)
   2 *vi* [ə'prɒksɪmeɪt] **to a. to sth** se rapprocher de qch

approximately [ə'prɒksɪmətlɪ] *adv* approximativement, environ

approximation [əprɒksɪ'meɪʃən] *n* approximation *f*

Apr. *(abbr* **April**) avr

APR [eɪpiː'ɑː(r)] *n Fin (abbr* **annual percentage rate**) TEG *m*

apricot ['eɪprɪkɒt] *n (fruit)* abricot *m*; **a. tree** abricotier *m*

April ['eɪprɪl] *n* avril *m*; **A. showers** ≃ giboulées *fpl* de mars; **A. Fools' Day** le premier avril; *see also* **May**

apron ['eɪprən] *n* (**a**) *(clothing)* tablier *m*; **he's still tied to his mother's a. strings** *(dependent on her)* il est toujours pendu aux jupes de sa mère (**b**) *Aviat* aire *f* de stationnement

apt [æpt] *adj* (**a**) *(word, description)* juste (**b**) *(likely)* **to be a. to do sth** avoir tendance à faire qch

aptitude ['æptɪtjuːd] *n* aptitude *f*, don *m*; **to have an a. for sth** avoir une aptitude *ou* un don pour qch; **a. test** test *m* d'aptitude

aptly ['æptlɪ] *adv (described)* justement; *(chosen)* bien

aquamarine [ækwəmə'riːn] **1** *n (gem)* aigue-marine *f*
   2 *adj (color)* bleu vert *inv*

aquarium [ə'kweərɪəm] *n* aquarium *m*

Aquarius [ə'kweərɪəs] *n* le Verseau; **to be (an) A.** être (du) Verseau

aquarobics [ækwə'rəʊbɪks] *n* aquagym *f*

aquatic [ə'kwætɪk] *adj* aquatique

aqueduct ['ækwɪdʌkt] *n* aqueduc *m*

aquiline ['ækwɪlaɪn] *adj* aquilin(e)

Arab ['ærəb] **1** *n* Arabe *mf*
   2 *adj* arabe

Arabia [ə'reɪbɪə] *n* l'Arabie *f*

Arabian [ə'reɪbɪən] *adj* arabe; **the A. Sea** la mer d'Oman

Arabic ['ærəbɪk] **1** *n (language)* arabe *m*
   2 *adj* arabe; **A. numerals** chiffres *mpl* arabes

arable ['ærəbəl] *adj* arable

arachnid [ə'ræknɪd] *n Zool* arachnide *m*

arbiter ['ɑːbɪtə(r)] *n (in dispute)* arbitre *m*; **the a. of taste** l'arbitre des élégances

arbitrary ['ɑːbɪtrərɪ] *adj* arbitraire

arbitrate ['ɑːbɪtreɪt] **1** *vt* arbitrer
   2 *vi* servir d'arbitre (**between** entre)

arbitration [ɑːbɪ'treɪʃən] *n* arbitrage *m*; **to go to a.** *(of parties)* avoir recours à l'arbitrage

arbitrator ['ɑːbɪtreɪtə(r)] *n* médiateur(trice) *m,f*

arc [ɑːk] *n* arc *m*; **a. lamp** lampe *f* à arc

arcade [ɑː'keɪd] *n* (**a**) *(for shopping)* galerie *f* marchande (**b**) *Archit* galerie *f* (**c**) *(for games)* galerie *f* de jeux

arch[1] [ɑːtʃ] **1** *n* (**a**) *Archit* arche *f* (**b**) *(of foot)* voûte *f* plantaire; **to have fallen arches** avoir les pieds plats
   2 *vt* **to a. one's back** *(inward)* se cambrer; *(outward)* se voûter

arch[2] [ɑːtʃ] *adj* **a. enemy** ennemi(e) *m,f* juré(e)

arch[3] [ɑːtʃ] *adj (mischievous)* espiègle

archaeological, archeological [ɑːkɪə'lɒdʒɪkəl] *adj* archéologique

archaeologist, archeologist [ɑːkɪ'ɒlədʒɪst] *n* archéologue *mf*

archaeology, archeology [ɑːkɪ'ɒlədʒɪ] *adj* archéologie *f*

archaic [ɑː'keɪɪk] *adj* archaïque

archangel ['ɑːkeɪndʒəl] *n* archange *m*

archbishop [ɑːtʃ'bɪʃəp] *n* archevêque *m*

archduke [ɑːtʃ'djuːk] *n* archiduc *m*

archeological, archeologist, *etc.* = **archaeological, archaeologist,** *etc.*

archer ['ɑːtʃə(r)] *n* archer *m*

archery ['ɑːtʃərɪ] *n* tir *m* à l'arc

archetypal [ɑːkɪ'taɪpəl], **archetypical** [ɑːkɪ'tɪpɪkəl] *adj* the a. **French village** l'archétype *m* du village français
archetype ['ɑːkɪtaɪp] *n* archétype *m*
archetypical [ɑːkɪ'tɪpɪkəl] = **archetypal**
Archimedes [ɑːkɪ'miːdɪz] *n* Archimède *m*
archipelago [ɑːkɪ'peləgəʊ] (*pl* **archipelagoes** or **archipelagos**) *n* archipel *m*
architect ['ɑːkɪtekt] *n* architecte *mf*; **he was the a. of his own downfall** il a été l'artisan de sa propre ruine
architecture ['ɑːkɪtektʃə(r)] *n* architecture *f*
archives ['ɑːkaɪvz] *npl* archives *fpl*
archway ['ɑːtʃweɪ] *n* arche *f*
arctic ['ɑːktɪk] **1** *n* the A. l'Arctique *m*; **the A. Circle** le cercle (polaire) arctique; **the A. Ocean** l'océan *m* Arctique
  2 *adj* (**a**) *(climate)* arctique (**b**) *Fam (very cold)* **a. weather** un froid polaire
ardent ['ɑːdənt] *adj (desire, love)* ardent(e); *(admirer, believer)* fervent(e)
ardor ['ɑːdə(r)] *n (of desire, love)* ardeur *f*; *(religious)* ferveur *f*
arduous ['ɑːdjʊəs] *adj* ardu(e), pénible
are [ɑː(r)] *plural and 2nd pers singular of* **be**
area ['eərɪə] *n* (**a**) *(surface)* superficie *f*, surface *f*; **the room is 26 square feet in a.** ≃ la pièce a une surface de 8 mètres carrés (**b**) *(region)* région *f*; *(of countryside, forest)* zone *f*; *(in building)* partie *f*; *(of town, city)* quartier *m*; *(of knowledge)* domaine *m*; **the Chicago a.** la région de Chicago; **an a. of agreement** un terrain d'entente; *Tel* **a. code** indicatif *m*; *Com* **a. manager** directeur(trice) *m,f* régional(e)
arena [ə'riːnə] *n* (**a**) *(Roman)* arène *f*; *(stadium)* stade *m* (**b**) *(area of activity) (economic, international)* scène *f*
aren't [ɑːnt] (**a**) = **are not** (**b**) **a. I?** = **am I not?**
Argentina [ɑːdʒən'tiːnə] *n* l'Argentine *f*
Argentine ['ɑːdʒəntaɪn] **1** *n (person)* Argentin(e) *m,f*
  2 *adj* argentin(e)
Argentinian [ɑːdʒən'tɪnɪən] **1** *n* Argentin(e) *m,f*
  2 *adj* argentin(e)
arguable ['ɑːgjʊəbəl] *adj* (**a**) *(questionable)* discutable; **it is a. whether it would have made any difference** on peut se demander si ça aurait changé quoi que ce soit (**b**) *(conceivable)* défendable; **it is a. that...** on pourrait soutenir que...
arguably ['ɑːgjʊəblɪ] *adv* **it's a. the city's best restaurant** on peut dire que c'est le meilleur restaurant de la ville
argue ['ɑːgjuː] **1** *vt (position)* défendre; **to a. the case for sth** plaider en faveur de qch; **to a. that...** soutenir que...
  2 *vi (quarrel)* se disputer (**about** à propos de); **to a. for sth** plaider en faveur de qch; **to a. against sb/sth** s'opposer à qn/qch; **don't a.!** ne discute pas!, pas de discussion!
argument ['ɑːgjʊmənt] *n* (**a**) *(quarrel)* dispute *f*; *(debate)* discussion *f*; **to have an a. about sth** *(quarrel)* se disputer à propos de qch; *(debate)* discuter de qch; **to get into an a.** se disputer; **and I don't want any arguments!** et pas de discussion! (**b**) *(reason)* **an a. for/against doing sth** une raison de faire/de ne pas faire qch (**c**) *(point)* argument *m* (**for/against** en faveur de/contre); **for a.'s sake** à titre d'exemple
argumentative [ɑːgjʊ'mentətɪv] *adj (person)* qui a l'esprit de contradiction; *(tone)* agressif(ive)
aria ['ɑːrɪə] *n* aria *f*
arid ['ærɪd] *adj* aride
Aries ['eəriːz] *n* le Bélier; **to be (an) A.** être (du) Bélier
arise [e'raɪz] (*pt* **arose** [ə'rəʊz], *pp* **arisen** [ə'rɪzən]) *vi (of problem, possibility)* surgir; *(of situation)* naître; *(of question)* se poser; *(of storm)* se lever; **if the need arises** si le besoin s'en fait sentir
aristocracy [ærɪs'tɒkrəsɪ] *n* aristocratie *f*
aristocrat ['ærɪstəkræt] *n* aristocrate *mf*
aristocratic [ærɪstə'krætɪk] *adj* aristocratique
Aristotle ['ærɪstɒtəl] *pr n* Aristote

arithmetic [ə'rɪθmətɪk] *n (calculations)* calculs *mpl*; *(subject)* calcul *m*, arithmétique *f*
arithmetical [ærɪθ'metɪkəl] *adj* arithmétique; **an a. error** une erreur de calcul
ark [ɑːk] *n* arche *f*
arm [ɑːm] **1** *n* (**a**) *(of person, chair, garment)* bras *m*; **to carry sb/sth in one's arms** porter qn/qch dans ses bras; **to take sb's a.** prendre qn par le bras; **a. in a.** bras dessus bras dessous; **to receive sb with open arms** *(warmly welcome)* recevoir qn à bras ouverts; *Fig* **to keep sb at a.'s length** tenir qn à distance (**b**) **arms** *(weapons)* armement *m*; **to bear arms** porter les armes; **arms race** course *f* aux armements (**c**) *(in heraldry)* **(coat of) arms** armoiries *fpl*
  2 *vt (person, country)* armer; **to a. oneself with the facts** s'armer de faits
armadillo [ɑːmə'dɪləʊ] (*pl* **armadillos**) *n* tatou *m*
Armageddon [ɑːmə'gedən] *n* l'Apocalypse *f*; *Fig* apocalypse *f*
armaments ['ɑːməmənts] *npl* armement *m*, armes *fpl*
armband ['ɑːmbænd] *n (at funeral, for swimming)* brassard *m*
armchair ['ɑːmtʃeə(r)] *n* fauteuil *m*; **an a. sportsman** un sportif en chambre
armed [ɑːmd] *adj* armé(e) (**with** de); **a. forces** forces *fpl* armées; **a. robbery** vol *m* à main armée
Armenia [ɑː'miːnɪə] *n* l'Arménie *f*
Armenian [ɑː'miːnɪən] **1** *n* Arménien(enne) *m,f*
  2 *adj* arménien(enne)
armhole ['ɑːmhəʊl] *n* emmanchure *f*
armistice ['ɑːmɪstɪs] *n* armistice *m*; **A. Day** l'Armistice
armor ['ɑːmə(r)] *n* (**a**) *(of knight)* armure *f*; **suit of a.** armure complète (**b**) *Mil (of tank)* blindage *m*; *(tanks)* blindés *mpl*
armored car ['ɑːməd'kɑː(r)] *n* voiture *f* blindée
armory ['ɑːmərɪ] (*pl* **armories**) *n (store)* arsenal *m*
armpit ['ɑːmpɪt] *n* aisselle *f*
army ['ɑːmɪ] (*pl* **armies**) *n* armée *f*; *(land forces)* armée de terre; **to be in the a.** être dans l'armée, être militaire
aroma [ə'rəʊmə] *n* arôme *m*
aromatic [ærəʊ'mætɪk] *adj* aromatique
arose [ə'rəʊz] *pt of* **arise**
around [ə'raʊnd] **1** *prep* (**a**) *(position)* autour de; **a. the table** autour de la table; **there were hills all a. the town** il y avait des collines tout autour de la ville; **there were posters all a. the walls** il y avait des posters partout sur les murs; **a. here** par ici
  (**b**) *(motion)* autour de; **to look a. a room** jeter un coup d'œil à une pièce; **to travel a. the world** faire le tour du monde; **to walk a. the town/the streets** se promener en ville/dans les rues
  2 *adv* (**a**) *(surrounding)* autour; **a garden with a fence a.** un jardin avec une clôture autour; **all a.** tout autour; **for miles a.** à des kilomètres à la ronde
  (**b**) *(in different directions)* **to walk a.** se promener; **there were books lying all a.** il y avait des livres qui traînaient partout
  (**c**) *(in the general area)* dans le coin; **is Jack a.?** est-ce que Jack est dans le coin?; **there was nobody a.** il n'y avait personne
  (**d**) *(approximately)* environ; **at a. one o'clock** vers une heure
arousal [ə'raʊzəl] *n (sexual)* excitation *f*; *(of interest, suspicion)* éveil *m*
arouse [ə'raʊz] *vt (sleeping person)* réveiller; *(emotion, desire, suspicion)* éveiller; *(enthusiasm, opposition)* soulever; *(sexually)* exciter
arraign [ə'reɪn] *vt Law* traduire en justice
arraignment [ə'reɪnmənt] *n Law* lecture *f* de l'acte d'accusation
arrange [ə'reɪndʒ] **1** *vt* (**a**) *(put in order)* arranger; *(classify)* ranger (**b**) *(organize) (wedding, meeting)* arranger; *(time, date)* fixer;

(accommodations) s'occuper de; *(outing)* organiser; *(one's affairs)* mettre en ordre; **to a. where to go/what to do** prévoir où aller/quoi faire; **it was arranged that...** il a été prévu que...; **an arranged marriage** un mariage arrangé

2 *vi* **to a. to do sth** s'arranger pour faire qch; *(with someone else)* convenir *ou* prévoir de faire qch; **they arranged for a taxi to meet me** ils se sont arrangés pour qu'un taxi vienne me chercher

arrangement [əˈreɪndʒmənt] *n* **(a)** *(of objects, furniture)* disposition *f* **(b)** *(plan)* arrangement *m*; **to make arrangements** prendre des dispositions, faire le nécessaire; **I've made all the arrangements** j'ai tout arrangé **(c)** *(agreement)* arrangement *m*; **the a. was that...** il avait été convenu que...; **viewing by a.** *(sign)* visites sur rendez-vous; **to come to an a. with sb** parvenir à un arrangement avec qn **(d)** *Mus* arrangement *m*

array [əˈreɪ] *n* *(collection)* collection *f*, éventail *m*

arrears [əˈrɪəz] *npl* arriéré *m*; **to be two months in a. with the rent** devoir deux mois de loyer; **to be in a. with one's work** avoir du travail en retard

arrest [əˈrest] **1** *n* arrestation *f*; **to be under a.** être en état d'arrestation; **to make an a.** procéder à une arrestation

2 *vt* *(capture, stop)* arrêter; *(attention)* attirer

arresting [əˈrestɪŋ] *adj (striking)* saisissant(e)

arrival [əˈraɪvəl] *n* arrivée *f*; **on a.** à l'arrivée; **a new a.** *(at work, in club)* un nouveau venu (une nouvelle venue); *(baby)* un nouveau-né (une nouveau-née)

arrive [əˈraɪv] *vi* **(a)** *(at place)* arriver; **to a. at** *(solution, decision)* arriver à, parvenir à **(b)** *Fam (attain success)* réussir, arriver

arrogance [ˈærəgəns] *n* arrogance *f*

arrogant [ˈærəgənt] *adj* arrogant(e)

arrow [ˈærəʊ] *n* flèche *f*

arrowhead [ˈærəʊhed] *n* pointe *f* de flèche

arrowroot [ˈærəʊruːt] *n Culin* arrow-root *m*

arsenal [ˈɑːsənəl] *n* arsenal *m*; *(of devices, arguments)* panoplie *f*

arsenic [ˈɑːsənɪk] *n* arsenic *m*

arson [ˈɑːsən] *n* incendie *m* criminel *ou* volontaire

arsonist [ˈɑːsənɪst] *n* incendiaire *mf*

art [ɑːt] *n* **(a)** *(in general)* art *m*; *(school subject)* arts *mpl* plastiques; *(college course)* beaux-arts *mpl*; **the arts in America** la création artistique aux États-Unis; **arts and crafts** artisanat *m*; **a. gallery** *(museum)* musée *m* d'art; *(store)* galerie *f* d'art; **a. school** école *f* des beaux-arts, beaux-arts *mpl* **(b)** *Univ* **arts** lettres *fpl* **(c)** *(technique)* art *m*; **there's an a. to making pastry** la pâtisserie, c'est tout un art; **the a. of war/conversation** l'art de la guerre/de la conversation

artefact [ˈɑːtɪfækt] = **artifact**

arteriosclerosis [ɑːˌtɪərɪəʊskləˈrəʊsɪs] *n Med* artériosclérose *f*

artery [ˈɑːtərɪ] *(pl* **arteries***) n* artère *f*

artful [ˈɑːtfʊl] *adj* **(a)** *(skillful) (person)* habile; *(solution, reply)* astucieux(euse) **(b)** *(cunning)* malin(igne)

arthritic [ɑːˈθrɪtɪk] *adj* arthritique

arthritis [ɑːˈθraɪtɪs] *n* arthrite *f*

arthropod [ˈɑːθrəpɒd] *n Zool* arthropode *m*

arthrosis [ɑːˈθrəʊsɪs] *n Med* arthrose *f*

artichoke [ˈɑːtɪtʃəʊk] *n* **(globe) a.** artichaut *m*

article [ˈɑːtɪkəl] **1** *n* article *m*; **a. of clothing** vêtement *m*; *Gram* **definite/indefinite a.** article défini/indéfini

2 *vt Law* mettre en apprentissage (**to** chez)

articulate¹ [ɑːˈtɪkjʊlət] *adj (person)* qui s'exprime avec facilité; *(account)* clair(e)

articulate² [ɑːˈtɪkjʊleɪt] *vt* **(a)** *(word)* articuler; **to a. one's words** articuler **(b)** *(idea, feeling)* exprimer

articulation [ɑːtɪkjʊˈleɪʃən] *n* articulation *f*

artifact [ˈɑːtɪfækt] *n (manufactured object)* objet *m*

artificial [ɑːtɪˈfɪʃəl] *adj* artificiel(elle); **a. insemination** insé-

mination *f* artificielle; *Comput* **a. intelligence** intelligence *f* artificielle; **a. respiration** respiration *f* artificielle; **a. sweetener** édulcorant *m* (de synthèse)

artificially [ɑːtɪˈfɪʃəlɪ] *adv* artificiellement

artillery [ɑːˈtɪlərɪ] *n* artillerie *f*

artisan [ɑːtɪˈzæn] *n* artisan *m*

artist [ˈɑːtɪst] *n* artiste *mf*

artistic [ɑːˈtɪstɪk] *adj* artistique; *(temperament, person)* artiste

artistry [ˈɑːtɪstrɪ] *n (of painting, game)* qualité *f* artistique; *(of painter, tennis player)* art *m*

artless [ˈɑːtlɪs] *adj (simple)* naturel(elle); *(clumsy)* maladroit(e)

artwork [ˈɑːtwɜːk] *n (in book, magazine)* illustrations *fpl*

arty [ˈɑːtɪ] *adj Fam (person)* prétentieux(euse) *(et passionné d'art)*

arugula [əˈruːgələ] *n Bot & Culin* roquette *f*

arum lily [ˈeərəmˈlɪlɪ] *n Bot* calla *f*

Aryan [ˈeərɪən] **1** *n* Aryen(enne) *m,f*

2 *adj* aryen(enne)

as [əz, *stressed* æz] **1** *adv* **(a)** *(with manner)* **as promised/planned** comme promis/prévu; **A as in Anne** A comme Anne

(b) *(in comparisons)* **as tall as me** aussi grand(e) que moi; **as white as a sheet** blanc (blanche) comme un linge; **twice as big as** deux fois plus grand que; **I came as fast as I could** je suis venu aussi vite que j'ai pu; **as much money/many people as** autant d'argent/de gens que; **as much/many as you want** autant que tu veux; **as soon as possible** dès que possible; **as recently as last week** pas plus tard que la semaine dernière

(c) **as if** comme si; **it isn't as if** *or* **though it's difficult** ce n'est pourtant pas compliqué; **she looked as if** *or* **though she was angry** elle avait l'air fâché; **it looks as if** *or* **though he's already left** on dirait qu'il est déjà parti

(d) **as well** aussi, également; **he has two cars as well as a motorcycle** il a une moto et aussi deux voitures

(e) **as for** quant à

2 *conj* **(a)** *(with time)* **he went out as I came in** il sortit au moment où j'entrais; **as the day went on** à mesure que la journée passait; **we'll see as we go along** nous verrons au fur et à mesure; **as you get older** en vieillissant, avec l'âge; **as always** comme toujours

(b) *(with manner)* comme; **as I was saying** comme je disais; **do as you're told** fais ce qu'on te dit; **as often happens,...** comme c'est souvent le cas,...; **it's hard/far enough as it is** c'est assez difficile/loin comme ça; **as it were** pour ainsi dire

(c) *(concessive)* **late as it was,...** bien qu'il fût tard,...; **try as she might,...** elle avait beau essayer,...; **strange as it may seem,...** aussi étrange que cela puisse paraître,...; **much as I like her,...** je l'aime bien, mais...

(d) *(because)* puisque, comme

(e) *(in addition)* **mother is well, as are the children** maman va bien, et les enfants aussi

3 *prep* comme; **to work as a team** travailler en équipe; **to regard sb as a friend** considérer qn comme un ami; **I meant it as a compliment** c'était un compliment; **she used it as a bandage** elle s'en est servi comme d'un bandage; **as a woman, I think that...** en tant que femme, je pense que...

ASAP [eɪeɪesˈpiː] *adv (abbr* **as soon as possible***)* dès que possible

asbestos [æsˈbestəs] *n* amiante *f*

asbestosis [æsbesˈtəʊsɪs] *n Med* asbestose *f*

ascend [əˈsend] **1** *vt (mountain)* gravir, faire l'ascension de; *(throne)* accéder à; *(stairs)* gravir

2 *vi* monter

ascendancy, ascendency [əˈsendənsɪ] *n* ascendant *m*

ascendant, ascendent [əˈsendənt] *n* **to be in the a.** prospérer

Ascension [əˈsenʃən] *n Rel* l'Ascension *f*

ascent [ə'sent] *n also Fig* ascension *f*

ascertain [æsə'teɪn] *vt* établir

ascetic [ə'setɪk] **1** *n* ascète *mf*
  2 *adj* ascétique

ASCII ['æskɪ] *n* (*abbr* **American Standard Code for Information Interchange**) ASCII *m*

ascribe [ə'skraɪb] *vt* attribuer (**to** à)

ASEAN ['æziæn] *n* (*abbr* **Association of Southeast Asian Nations**) ANASE *f*

aseptic [eɪ'septɪk] *adj* aseptique

asexual [eɪ'seksjʊəl] *adj* asexué(e)

ash¹ [æʃ] *n* (*tree*) frêne *m*

ash² [æʃ] *n* (*from fire, cigarette*) cendre *f*; *Rel* **A. Wednesday** mercredi *m* des Cendres

ashamed [ə'ʃeɪmd] *adj* honteux(euse); **to feel a.** avoir honte; **to be a. of** avoir honte de; **I am a. to say that...** j'avoue à ma grande honte que...; **there is nothing to be a. of** il n'y a pas de quoi avoir honte; **you ought to be a. of yourself!** tu devrais avoir honte!

ashcan ['æʃkæn] *n* poubelle *f*

ashen ['æʃən] *adj* blême

ashore [ə'ʃɔː(r)] *adv* (*on land*) à terre; **to go a.** débarquer

ashtray ['æʃtreɪ] *n* cendrier *m*

Asia ['eɪʒə] *n* l'Asie *f*; **A. Minor** l'Asie mineure

Asian ['eɪʒən] **1** *n* Asiatique *mf*
  2 *adj* (*from the Far East*) asiatique; (*from Indian subcontinent*) du sous-continent indien

Asian-American ['eɪʒənə'merɪkən] **1** *n* Américain(e) *m,f* d'origine asiatique
  2 *adj* américain(e) d'origine asiatique

Asiatic [eɪʒɪ'ætɪk] **1** *n* Asiatique *mf*
  2 *adj* asiatique

aside [ə'saɪd] **1** *adv* **to stand a.** s'écarter; **to take sb a.** prendre qn à part; **to put** *or* **to set sth a.** (*reserve*) mettre qch de côté; **politics a.,...** toute question de politique mise à part,...; **a. from** à part
  2 *n* aparté *m*

asinine ['æsɪnaɪn] *adj* stupide

ask [ɑːsk] **1** *vt* (**a**) (*inquire about*) demander; **to a. (sb) a question** poser une question (à qn); **to a. sb sth** demander qch à qn; **to a. sb the time** demander l'heure à qn; **to a. sb the way** demander son chemin à qn; **don't a. me!** je n'en ai pas la moindre idée!
  (**b**) (*request*) demander; **to a. sb for sth** demander qch à qn; **to a. to do sth** demander à faire qch; **to a. sb to do sth** demander à qn de faire qch; **to a. a favor of sb, to a. sb a favor** demander un service à qn; **if it isn't asking too much** si ce n'est pas trop demander; **to a. sb's permission to do sth** demander à qn la permission de faire qch
  (**c**) (*invite*) inviter; **to a. sb to lunch** inviter qn à déjeuner
  2 *vi* (**a**) (*inquire*) se renseigner (**about** sur)
  (**b**) (*request*) demander; **you only have to a.!** il n'y a qu'à demander!; **to a. for sth** demander qch; *Fam* **he was asking for it** il l'a cherché

▶**ask after** *vt insep* demander des nouvelles de

askance [ə'skæns] *adv* **to look a. at sb** regarder qn de travers

askew [ə'skjuː] *adv* de travers

asking ['ɑːskɪŋ] *n* **it's yours for the a.** il suffit de le demander pour l'obtenir; **a. price** prix *m* demandé

ASL [eɪes'el] *n* (*abbr* **American Sign Language**) = langage par signes d'origine américaine

asleep [ə'sliːp] *adj* **to be a.** dormir; **to fall a.** s'endormir; **to be fast** *or* **sound a.** dormir profondément

asocial [eɪ'səʊʃəl] *adj* asocial(e)

asparagus [ə'spærəgəs] *n* asperge *f*

aspect ['æspekt] *n* (**a**) (*of problem, subject*) aspect *m* (**b**) (*of building*) exposition *f*

asperity [æ'sperɪtɪ] *n* (*of character, voice*) rudesse *f*

aspersions [ə'spɜːʃənz] *npl* **to cast a. on sth** dénigrer qch; **to cast a. on sb's honor** porter atteinte à l'honneur de qn

asphalt ['æsfælt] *n* asphalte *m*

asphyxiate [æs'fɪksɪeɪt] *vt* asphyxier

asphyxiation [æsfɪksɪ'eɪʃən] *n* asphyxie *f*

aspic ['æspɪk] *n* *Culin* gelée *f*

aspirate ['æspərət] *adj* *Ling* aspiré(e)

aspiration [æspɪ'reɪʃən] *n* (*ambition*) aspiration *f*

aspire [ə'spaɪə(r)] *vi* **to a. to do sth** aspirer à faire qch

aspirin ['æsprɪn] *n* aspirine *f*

aspiring [ə'spaɪrɪŋ] *adj* **to be an a. actor/writer** aspirer à devenir acteur/écrivain

ass¹ [æs] *n* (**a**) (*animal*) âne *m* (**b**) *Fam* (*idiot*) imbécile *mf*; **to make an a. of oneself** se ridiculiser

ass² [æs] *n very Fam* (*behind*) cul *m*

assail [ə'seɪl] *vt* (**a**) (*attack*) attaquer (**b**) **to a. sb with questions** assaillir qn de questions; **assailed by doubts** en proie au doute

assailant [ə'seɪlənt] *n* agresseur *m*

assassin [ə'sæsɪn] *n* assassin *m*

assassinate [ə'sæsɪneɪt] *vt* assassiner

assassination [əsæsɪ'neɪʃən] *n* assassinat *m*

assault [ə'sɔːlt] **1** *n Mil* assaut *m* (**on** de); *Law* agression *f* (**on** contre); (*criticism*) attaque *f* (**on** contre); *Law* **a. and battery** coups *mpl* et blessures *fpl*; *Mil* **a. course** parcours *m* du combattant; **a. rifle** fusil *m* d'assaut
  2 *vt Law* agresser; **to be sexually assaulted** être victime d'une agression sexuelle

assemble [ə'sembəl] **1** *vt* (*people*) rassembler, réunir; (*facts, objects*) rassembler; (*machine, furniture*) assembler, monter
  2 *vi* (*of people*) se rassembler, se réunir

assembly [ə'semblɪ] *n* (*pl* **assemblies**) *n* (**a**) (*gathering*) & *Pol* assemblée *f* (**b**) (*of machine, furniture*) assemblage *m*, montage *m*; **a. instructions** instructions *fpl* de montage; *Ind* **a. line** chaîne *f* de montage

assent [ə'sent] **1** *n* assentiment *m*
  2 *vi* donner son assentiment (**to** à)

assert [ə'sɜːt] *vt* (*one's rights, point of view*) faire valoir; **to a. one's authority** asseoir son autorité; **to a. oneself** s'imposer; **to a. that...** affirmer que...

assertion [ə'sɜːʃən] *n* (*statement*) déclaration *f*; (*of right*) revendication *f*

assertive [ə'sɜːtɪv] *adj* assuré(e); **he's not a. enough** il ne s'affirme pas assez

assertiveness [ə'sɜːtɪvnɪs] *n* assurance *f*; **a. training** = cours pour adultes visant à améliorer la confiance en soi des participants

assess [ə'ses] *vt* (**a**) (*value, damage*) estimer; **to a. sb's income** (*for tax purposes*) évaluer les revenus de qn (**b**) (*situation, impact*) étudier, analyser; (*performance, ability, quality*) évaluer

assessment [ə'sesmənt] *n* (**a**) (*of value*) estimation *f*; (*for insurance or tax purposes*) évaluation *f* (**b**) (*of situation*) étude *f*, analyse *f*; (*of performance, ability, quality*) évaluation *f*

assessor [ə'sesə(r)] *n Fin* contrôleur *m*

asset ['æset] *n* (**a**) (*advantage*) atout *m*; **she is a great a. to the firm** c'est quelqu'un de très précieux pour l'entreprise (**b**) *Fin* **assets** actif *m*, avoir *m*; (*personal*) patrimoine *m*; **assets and liabilities** l'actif et le passif; *Fin* **a. stripper** = personne qui rachète une société pour profiter de la réalisation de l'actif; *Fin* **a. stripping** démembrement *m* (*suite au rachat d'une société*)

assiduous [ə'sɪdjʊəs] *adj* assidu(e)

assign [ə'saɪn] *vt* (*task*) assigner (**to** à); (*funds*) affecter (**to** à); (*importance*) attacher (**to** à); **to a. sb to do sth** charger qn de faire qch

assignation [æsɪg'neɪʃən] *n Formal or Hum* (*meeting*) rendez-vous *m inv*

assignment [ə'saɪnmənt] *n* (**a**) *(of funds)* affectation *f*; *(of tasks)* distribution *f* (**b**) *(task)* Sch devoir *m*; Journ reportage *m*; *(of soldier, politician)* mission *f*

assimilate [ə'sɪmɪleɪt] **1** *vt* assimiler
2 *vi (of immigrants)* s'assimiler, s'intégrer

assimilation [əsɪmɪ'leɪʃən] *n* assimilation *f*

assist [ə'sɪst] **1** *vt (person)* aider, assister; *(process, development)* faciliter; **to a. sb in doing** *or* **to do sth** aider qn à faire qch; Med **assisted conception** aide *f* médicale à la procréation
2 *vi* aider

assistance [ə'sɪstəns] *n* aide *f*, secours *m*; **to come to sb's a.** venir en aide à qn; **can I be of any a.?** puis-je être utile à quelque chose?

assistant [ə'sɪstənt] *n* assistant(e) *m,f*; (**sales**) **a.** vendeur(euse) *m,f*; **a. manager** sous-directeur(trice) *m,f*; Univ **a. professor** ≃ maître *m* assistant, Can ≃ professeur *m* adjoint

assizes [ə'saɪzɪz] *npl* Law assises *fpl*

associate 1 *n* [ə'səʊsɪət] *(in business)* associé(e) *m,f*; *(in crime)* complice *mf*
2 *adj* [ə'səʊsɪət] associé(e); Univ **a. professor** maître *m* de conférences, Can professeur *m* agrégé
3 *vt* [ə'səʊsɪeɪt] (**a**) *(mentally)* associer (**with** à) (**b**) **to be associated with** avoir des liens avec
4 *vi* [ə'səʊsɪeɪt] **to a. with sb** fréquenter qn

associated [ə'səʊsɪeɪtɪd] *adj* associé(e); **a. company** société *f* affiliée

association [əsəʊsɪ'eɪʃən] *n* association *f*; **the name has unfortunate associations for her** ce nom lui évoque des souvenirs désagréables; **in a. with** en association avec

assorted [ə'sɔːtɪd] *adj (colors, flavors)* variés(ées); *(cookies, candy)* assortis(ies)

assortment [ə'sɔːtmənt] *n* assortiment *m*

assuage [ə'sweɪdʒ] *vt* Lit apaiser

assume [ə'sjuːm] *vt* (**a**) *(suppose)* supposer; **I a. he'll come** je suppose qu'il viendra; **he was assumed to be rich** on le supposait riche; **let us a. that...** supposons *ou* mettons que... (**b**) *(power, control)* prendre; *(name)* adopter; **to a. responsibility for sth** devenir responsable de qch; **an assumed name** un nom d'emprunt (**c**) *(appearance, shape)* prendre

assumption [ə'sʌmpʃən] *n* (**a**) *(supposition)* supposition *f*; **to work on the a. that...** se fonder sur l'hypothèse que... (**b**) *(of power)* prise *f* (**c**) Rel **the A.** l'Assomption *f*

assurance [ə'ʃʊərəns] *n* (**a**) *(guarantee)* assurance *f*; **he gave me his a.** il me l'a assuré (**b**) *(confidence)* assurance *f*

assure [ə'ʃʊə(r)] *vt* assurer; **to a. sb of sth** assurer qn de qch

assured [ə'ʃʊəd] *adj (victory, success)* assuré(e), certain(e); *(person, performance)* plein(e) d'assurance

assuredly [ə'ʃʊərɪdlɪ] *adv* assurément

asterisk ['æstərɪsk] *n* astérisque *m*

asteroid ['æstərɔɪd] *n* astéroïde *m*

asthma ['æsmə] *n* asthme *m*

asthmatic [æs'mætɪk] *n & adj* asthmatique *mf*

astonish [ə'stɒnɪʃ] *vt* étonner; **to be astonished at** *or* **by sth** être étonné(e) par qch

astonishing [ə'stɒnɪʃɪŋ] *adj (amazing)* incroyable; *(performance)* extraordinaire; **I find it a. that...** je m'étonne que... + subjunctive

astonishment [ə'stɒnɪʃmənt] *n* étonnement *m*; **to my a.** à mon grand étonnement

astound [ə'staʊnd] *vt* stupéfier

astounding [ə'staʊndɪŋ] *adj* stupéfiant(e), incroyable

astral ['æstrəl] *adj* astral(e)

astray [ə'streɪ] *adv* **to go a.** *(become lost)* s'égarer; **to lead sb a.** *(morally)* détourner qn du droit chemin

astride [ə'straɪd] *prep* à cheval sur, à califourchon sur

astringent [ə'strɪndʒənt] **1** *n* Med astringent *m*
2 *adj* Med astringent(e); Fig *(person, voice)* caustique

astrologer [ə'strɒlədʒə(r)] *n* astrologue *mf*

astrological [æstrə'lɒdʒɪkəl] *adj* astrologique

astrology [ə'strɒlədʒɪ] *n* astrologie *f*

astronaut ['æstrənɔːt] *n* astronaute *mf*

astronomer [ə'strɒnəmə(r)] *n* astronome *mf*

astronomic [æstrə'nɒmɪk], **astronomical** [æstrə'nɒmɪkəl] *adj* astronomique

astronomy [ə'strɒnəmɪ] *n* astronomie *f*

astrophysics [æstrəʊ'fɪzɪks] *n* astrophysique *f*

Astroturf® ['æstrəʊtɜːf] *n* gazon *m* artificiel

astute [ə'stjuːt] *adj* astucieux(euse)

astutely [ə'stjuːtlɪ] *adv* astucieusement

asunder [ə'sʌndə(r)] *adv* Lit **to tear sth a.** mettre qch en pièces

asylum [ə'saɪləm] *n* asile *m*; (**mental**) **a.** asile d'aliénés

asymmetric [eɪsɪ'metrɪk], **asymmetrical** [eɪsɪ'metrɪkəl] *adj* asymétrique

asymmetry [eɪ'sɪmɪtrɪ] *n* asymétrie *f*

at [æt, *unstressed* ət] *prep* (**a**) *(with place)* à; **at the office** au bureau; **at college** à l'université; **at the station** à la gare; **at the top/bottom (of)** en haut/bas (de); **at John's (house)** chez John; **at home** chez soi, à la maison
(**b**) *(with time)* à; **at six o'clock** à six heures; **at night** la nuit; **at Christmas** à Noël; **at the beginning** au début; **at (the age of) twenty** à (l'âge de) vingt ans
(**c**) *(with price, speed)* à; **at 60 mph** ≃ à 95 km/h; **at 50 cents a pound** à 50 cents la livre
(**d**) *(with direction)* **to look at sb/sth** regarder qn/qch; **to shout at sb** crier après qn; **to throw sth at sb** jeter qch à qn
(**e**) *(with cause)* **to be angry at sb** être fâché(e) contre qn; **to be surprised at sth** être surpris(e) de *ou* par qch; **to be shocked at sth** être choqué(e) par qch
(**f**) *(with activity)* **to be at work/lunch** être en train de travailler/déjeuner; **while you're at it** tant que tu y es; **to be good/bad at sth** *(subject)* être bon (bonne)/mauvais(e) en qch; **to be good/bad at doing sth** être/ne pas être doué(e) pour faire qch
(**g**) Comput *(in e-mail addresses)* **at (sign)** arrobas *m*; **'gwilson at xmail, dot, com'** 'gwilson, arrobas, xmail, point, com'

atavistic [ætə'vɪstɪk] *adj* atavique

atchoo [æ'tʃuː] *exclam* atchoum!

ate [eɪt] *pt of* **eat**

atheism ['eɪθɪɪzəm] *n* athéisme *m*

atheist ['eɪθɪɪst] *n* athée *mf*

Athens ['æθənz] *n* Athènes *f*

athlete ['æθliːt] *n* athlète *mf*; **a.'s foot** mycose *f*

athletic [æθ'letɪk] *adj (fit)* athlétique

athletics [æθ'letɪks] *npl* sports *mpl*

Atlantic [ət'læntɪk] **1** *n* **the A.** l'Atlantique *m*
2 *adj (coast)* atlantique; *(island)* de l'Atlantique; **the A. Ocean** l'océan Atlantique

atlas ['ætləs] *n* atlas *m*

ATM [eɪtiː'em] *n* Fin *(abbr* **automated** *or* **automatic teller machine)** DAB *m*

atmosphere ['ætməsfɪə(r)] *n* atmosphère *f*; Fig atmosphère, ambiance *f*

atmospheric [ætməs'ferɪk] *adj (pressure)* atmosphérique; Fig *(music, lighting)* d'ambiance

atoll ['ætɒl] *n* Geog atoll *m*

atom ['ætəm] *n* atome *m*; **a. bomb** bombe *f* atomique

atomic [ə'tɒmɪk] *adj* atomique; **a. bomb** bombe *f* atomique; **a. energy** énergie *f* atomique; **a. warfare** guerre *f* atomique *ou* nucléaire

▶**atone for** [ə'təʊn] *vt insep (sin, crime)* expier; *(mistake)* racheter, réparer

atonement [ə'təʊnmənt] *n (for sin, crime)* expiation *f; (for mistake, behavior)* réparation *f*

atrocious [ə'trəʊʃəs] *adj (crime)* atroce; *(behavior)* ignoble; *(meal)* infect(e); *(decision, joke)* très mauvais(e); *(weather, conditions, journey)* épouvantable

atrocity [ə'trɒsɪtɪ] *(pl* **atrocities***) n* atrocité *f*

atrophy ['ætrəfɪ] *(pt & pp* **atrophied***) vi* s'atrophier

attach [ə'tætʃ] *vt (label, importance)* attacher (**to** à); *(blame, responsibility)* imputer (**to** à); *(document)* joindre (**to** à); *(employee)* détacher (**to** à); **to a. oneself to sb** ne pas lâcher qn d'une semelle; **to be attached to** *(like)* être attaché(e) à

attachment [ə'tætʃmənt] *n (***a***) (device)* accessoire *m* (**b**) *(fondness)* attachement *m*; **to form an a. to sb** s'attacher à qn (**c**) *Comput (of e-mail)* fichier *m* joint

attack [ə'tæk] **1** *n* attaque *f*; **to be** *or* **to come under a.** être attaqué(e); **to launch an a. on** attaquer; **an a. of nerves** une crise de nerfs; **to have an a. of doubt** être assailli(e) par le doute
2 *vt* attaquer; *(rights)* porter atteinte à; *(problem, task)* s'attaquer à; **to be attacked** se faire attaquer

attacker [ə'tækə(r)] *n (assailant)* agresseur *m*; *(in sports)* attaquant(e) *m,f*

attain [ə'teɪn] *vt (goal, ambition)* réaliser; *(rank, age)* atteindre

attainable [ə'teɪnəbəl] *adj (goal, ambition)* réalisable

attainment [ə'teɪnmənt] *n (of goal, ambition)* réalisation *f*

attempt [ə'tempt] **1** *n* tentative *f*; **to make an a. at doing sth** essayer *ou* tâcher de faire qch; **they made no a. to help** ils n'ont pas essayé d'aider; **to make an a. on sb's life** attenter à la vie de qn; **at the first a.** du premier coup
2 *vt* **to a. to do sth** essayer *ou* tenter de faire qch; **to a. a smile** essayer de sourire; *Law* **attempted murder** tentative *f* d'assassinat

attend [ə'tend] **1** *vt (meeting)* assister à; *(school)* aller à; *(of doctor)* suivre
2 *vi (be present)* être présent(e)

▸**attend to** *vt insep (matter, problem, customer)* s'occuper de

attendance [ə'tendəns] *n (presence)* présence *f*; **to be in a. on sb** s'occuper de qn; **there was a good/poor a.** il y avait beaucoup de/peu de monde; **a. list** *or* **roll** registre *m* des présences

attendant [ə'tendənt] *n (in museum, parking lot)* gardien(enne) *m,f*; *(in checkroom)* préposé(e) *m,f*; *(at gas station)* pompiste *mf*

attention [ə'tenʃən] *n (***a***) (in general)* attention *f*; **to pay a. to** *(listen to)* écouter attentivement; *(watch)* regarder attentivement; **to pay a. to detail** faire attention aux détails; **to give sb/sth one's full a.** consacrer toute son attention à qn/qch; **to attract** *or* **to catch sb's a.** attirer l'attention de qn; **to draw a. to oneself** se faire remarquer; **your a. please, ladies and gentlemen** mesdames et messieurs, votre attention s'il vous plaît; **for the a. of Mr. Harvey** *(in letter)* à l'attention de M. Harvey; *Med* **a. deficit disorder** troubles *mpl* de l'attention; **a. span** capacité *f* de concentration (**b**) *(repairs)* **the engine needs some a.** le moteur a besoin d'être réparé (**c**) *Mil* **a.!** garde-à-vous!; **to stand at** *or* **to a.** être au garde-à-vous

attentive [ə'tentɪv] *adj (paying attention)* attentif(ive); *(considerate)* attentionné(e) (**to** pour)

attentively [ə'tentɪvlɪ] *adv* attentivement

attest [ə'test] **1** *vt* attester
2 *vi* **to a. to** témoigner de

attic ['ætɪk] *n* grenier *m*

attire [ə'taɪə(r)] *n* tenue *f*

attitude ['ætɪtjuːd] *n (***a***) (behavior)* attitude *f* (**b**) *(opinion)* opinion *f*; **attitudes have changed** les mentalités ont changé; **what's your a. to abortion?** quelle est votre position sur l'avortement?; **to take the a. that...** considérer que...; *Com*

a. survey enquête *f* d'attitudes (**c**) *(pose)* pose *f*; **to strike an a.** prendre une pose affectée

attn. *Com (abbr* **attention** *or* **for the attention of***)* à l'attention de

attorney [ə'tɜːnɪ] *(pl* **attorneys***) n (lawyer)* avocat(e) *m,f*; **A. General** ≃ ministre *m* de la Justice

attract [ə'trækt] *vt* attirer; **I'm extremely attracted to her** elle me plaît énormément; **the thought of working for him doesn't a. me** la perspective de travailler pour lui ne m'attire guère

attraction [ə'trækʃən] *n (***a***) (power)* attirance *f*; **the prospect holds little a. for me** cette perspective ne m'attire guère (**b**) *(attractive aspect)* attrait *m*

attractive [ə'træktɪv] *adj (person, offer)* séduisant(e); *(prospect)* attrayant(e); **do you find her a.?** est-ce qu'elle te plaît?

attribute 1 ['ætrɪbjuːt] attribut *m*
2 *vt* [ə'trɪbjuːt] attribuer (**to** à)

attrition [ə'trɪʃən] *n* usure *f*; **war of a.** guerre *f* d'usure

attuned [ə'tjuːnd] *adj* **to be a. to sth** être accoutumé(e) à qch

atypical [eɪ'tɪpɪkəl] *adj* atypique

auburn ['ɔːbən] *adj (hair)* auburn *inv*

auction ['ɔːkʃən] **1** *n* vente *f* aux enchères; **to put sth up for a.** mettre qch aux enchères; **a. room** salle *f* des ventes
2 *vt* vendre aux enchères

▸**auction off** *vt sep* vendre aux enchères

auctioneer [ɔːkʃə'nɪə(r)] *n* commissaire-priseur *m*

audacious [ɔː'deɪʃəs] *adj* audacieux(euse)

audacity [ɔː'dæsɪtɪ] *n* audace *f*

audible ['ɔːdɪbəl] *adj* audible

audience ['ɔːdɪəns] *n (***a***) (spectators, listeners)* public *m*; **a. participation** participation *f* du public (**b**) *(meeting with monarch, Pope)* audience *f*; **to grant sb an a.** accorder une audience à qn

audio ['ɔːdɪəʊ] *adj* **a. cassette** cassette *f* audio; **a. equipment** équipement *m* sonore

audiovisual [ɔːdɪəʊ'vɪzjʊəl] *adj* audiovisuel(elle)

audit ['ɔːdɪt] *Fin* **1** *n* audit *m*
2 *vt* vérifier

audition [ɔː'dɪʃən] **1** *n* audition *f*
2 *vt & vi* auditionner

auditor ['ɔːdɪtə(r)] *n Fin* commissaire *m* aux comptes

auditorium [ɔːdɪ'tɔːrɪəm] *n (of theater, concert hall)* salle *f*; *(lecture hall)* amphithéâtre *m*

auditory ['ɔːdɪtərɪ] *adj* auditif(ive)

Aug. *(abbr* **August***)* août

augment [ɔːg'ment] *vt* augmenter, accroître

augur ['ɔːgə(r)] *vi* **to a. well/badly** être de bon/mauvais augure

August ['ɔːgəst] *n* août *m*; *see also* **May**

august [ɔː'gʌst] *adj Lit (distinguished)* auguste

aunt [ɑːnt] *n* tante *f*

auntie, aunty ['ɑːntɪ] *(pl* **aunties***) n Fam* tata *f*, tantine *f*

au pair [əʊ'peə(r)] *n (jeune fille f)* au pair *f*

aura ['ɔːrə] *n* aura *f*; *(of place)* atmosphère *f*

aural ['ɔːrəl] *adj* auditif(ive)

auspices ['ɔːspɪsɪz] *npl* **under the a. of** sous l'égide de

auspicious [ɔː'spɪʃəs] *adj* prometteur(euse)

Aussie ['ɒzɪ] *n Fam* Australien(enne) *m,f*

austere [ɒ'stɪə(r)] *adj* austère

austerity [ɒ'sterɪtɪ] *n* austérité *f*

Australasia [ɒstrə'leɪʒə] *n* l'Australasie *f*

Australasian [ɒstrə'leɪʒən] **1** *n* natif(ive) *m,f* de l'Australasie
2 *adj* d'Australasie

Australia [ɒ'streɪlɪə] *n* l'Australie *f*

Australian [ɒ'streɪlɪən] **1** *n* Australien(enne) *m,f*
2 *adj* australien(enne)

Austria ['ɒstrɪə] *n* l'Autriche *f*

Austrian ['ɒstrɪən] **1** n Autrichien(enne) m,f
2 adj autrichien(enne)

autarchy ['ɔːtɑːkɪ] n autocratie f

authentic [ɔː'θentɪk] adj authentique

authenticate [ɔː'θentɪkeɪt] vt authentifier

authenticity [ɔːθen'tɪsɪtɪ] n authenticité f

author ['ɔːθə(r)] n auteur m

authoritarian [ɔːθɒrɪ'teərɪən] adj autoritaire

authoritative [ɔː'θɒrɪtətɪv] adj (a) (voice, manner) autoritaire (b) (work, document) qui fait autorité

authority [ɔː'θɒrɪtɪ] (pl **authorities**) n (a) (power) autorité f; **the authorities** les autorités fpl; **I'd like to speak to someone in a.** je voudrais parler à un responsable (b) (authorization) autorisation f; **to give sb a. to do sth** autoriser qn à faire qch; **on one's own a.** de son propre chef (c) (expert) **to be an a. on sth** faire autorité en matière de qch; **to have sth on good a.** tenir qch de source sûre

authorization [ɔːθəraɪ'zeɪʃən] n autorisation f

authorize ['ɔːθəraɪz] vt autoriser; **to a. sb to do sth** autoriser qn à faire qch

autism ['ɔːtɪzəm] n autisme m

autistic [ɔː'tɪstɪk] adj autiste

auto ['ɔːtəʊ] (pl **autos**) n voiture f, auto(mobile) f

auto- [ɔːtəʊ] pref auto-

autobiographical [ɔːtəʊbaɪə'græfɪkəl] adj autobiographique

autobiography [ɔːtəʊbaɪ'ɒgrəfɪ] (pl **autobiographies**) n autobiographie f

autocrat ['ɔːtəkræt] n autocrate m

autocratic [ɔːtə'krætɪk] adj autocratique

autograph ['ɔːtəgrɑːf] **1** n autographe m; **a. album** album m d'autographes
2 vt signer, dédicacer

automat ['ɔːtəmæt] n = cafétéria équipée de distributeurs automatiques

automate ['ɔːtəmeɪt] vt automatiser

automated ['ɔːtəmeɪtɪd] adj automatisé(e); **a. teller machine** distributeur m automatique (de billets)

automatic [ɔːtə'mætɪk] **1** n (car) (voiture f) automatique f; (pistol) (pistolet m) automatique m; (washing machine) machine f à laver automatique
2 adj automatique; Comput **a. data processing** traitement m automatique des données; Aviat **a. pilot** pilote m automatique; Fig **to be on a. pilot** marcher au radar; **a. teller machine** distributeur m automatique (de billets)

automatically [ɔːtə'mætɪklɪ] adv automatiquement

automation [ɔːtə'meɪʃən] n automatisation f

automaton [ɔː'tɒmətən] n automate m

automobile [ɔːtəməʊ'biːl] n voiture f, auto(mobile) f

autonomous [ɔː'tɒnəməs] adj autonome

autonomy [ɔː'tɒnəmɪ] n autonomie f

autopsy ['ɔːtɒpsɪ] (pl **autopsies**) n autopsie f

autumn ['ɔːtəm] n automne m; **in (the) a.** en automne

autumnal [ɔː'tʌmnəl] adj automnal(e)

auxiliary [ɔːg'zɪlɪərɪ] **1** n (pl **auxiliaries**) (person) auxiliaire mf; Ling auxiliaire m
2 adj auxiliaire

avail [ə'veɪl] **1** n **of no a.** (not effective) inutile; **to no a.** (in vain) en vain
2 vt **to a. oneself of sth** profiter de qch

availability [əveɪlə'bɪlɪtɪ] n disponibilité f

available [ə'veɪləbəl] adj disponible; **tickets are still a.** il reste des tickets; **this model is a. in black and in green** ce modèle existe en noir et en vert

avalanche ['ævəlɑːntʃ] n also Fig avalanche f

avant-garde [ævɒn'gɑːd] adj d'avant-garde, avant-gardiste

avarice ['ævərɪs] n avarice f

Ave. (abbr **avenue**) av.

avenge [ə'vendʒ] vt venger; **to a. oneself on sb** se venger sur qn

avenue ['ævɪnjuː] n avenue f; Fig possibilité f

aver [ə'vɜː(r)] (pt & pp **averred**) vt Lit déclarer, affirmer

average ['ævərɪdʒ] **1** n moyenne f; **on a.** en moyenne; **above/below a.** supérieur(e)/inférieur(e) à la moyenne
2 adj moyen(enne)
3 vt atteindre la moyenne de; **to a. eight hours' work a day** travailler en moyenne huit heures par jour
▶**average out** vi **it'll a. out over a month** sur un mois ça s'équilibrera
▶**average out at** vt insep **my expenses a. out at $900 per month** mes dépenses s'élèvent en moyenne à 900 dollars par mois

averse [ə'vɜːs] adj opposé(e) (**to** à); **he is not a. to a glass of wine** il prend volontiers un verre de vin

aversion [ə'vɜːʃən] n aversion f; **to have an a. to sb/sth** avoir qn/qch en aversion

avert [ə'vɜːt] vt (a) (turn away) (eyes, thoughts) détourner (**from** de) (b) (prevent) (misfortune, accident) éviter, prévenir

aviary ['eɪvɪərɪ] (pl **aviaries**) n volière f

aviation [eɪvɪ'eɪʃən] n aviation f

avid ['ævɪd] adj avide (**for** de)

avidly ['ævɪdlɪ] adv avidement, avec avidité

avocado [ævə'kɑːdəʊ] (pl **avocados**) n avocat m

avoid [ə'vɔɪd] vt éviter; (question) esquiver; **to a. doing sth** éviter de faire qch; **to a. sb/sth like the plague** fuir qn/qch comme la peste

avoidable [ə'vɔɪdəbəl] adj évitable

avowed [ə'vaʊd] adj déclaré(e)

AWACS ['eɪwæks] n Mil (abbr **Airborne Warning and Control System**) AWACS m

await [ə'weɪt] vt attendre; Law **to be awaiting trial** être en instance de jugement

awake [ə'weɪk] **1** adj éveillé(e); **he lay a. for hours worrying** l'inquiétude l'a tenu éveillé pendant des heures; Fig **he was a. to the danger** il avait conscience du danger
2 vt (pt **awaked** or **awoke** [ə'wəʊk], pp **awaked** or **awoken** [ə'wəʊkən]) réveiller
3 vi s'éveiller, se réveiller; Fig **to a. to a danger** prendre conscience d'un danger

awaken [ə'weɪkən] (pt **awakened** [ə'weɪkənd], pp **awakened** or **awoken** [ə'wəʊkən]) **1** vt réveiller
2 vi s'éveiller, se réveiller

awakening [ə'weɪkənɪŋ] n réveil m

award [ə'wɔːd] **1** n (prize) prix m; Law dommages-intérêts mpl
2 vt (prize, contract) décerner; (damages) accorder; **to a. sb sth** décerner qch à qn

award-winning [ə'wɔːdwɪnɪŋ] adj (movie, book) primé(e); (writer, author) lauréat(e)

aware [ə'weə(r)] adj **to be a. of sth** avoir conscience de qch; **to be a. that...** savoir que...; **not that I am a. of** pas que je sache; **as far as I'm a.** autant que je sache; **to become a. of sth** se rendre compte de qch; **politically a.** politisé(e)

awareness [ə'weənɪs] n conscience f

awash [ə'wɒʃ] adj (flooded) inondé(e)

away [ə'weɪ] adv (a) (in space) **a long way a.** très loin; **far a.** dans le lointain, au loin; **it's 10 miles a.** ≃ c'est à 16 kilomètres (d'ici); **to keep a. from** ne pas s'approcher de; **to go a.** partir, s'en aller; **go a.!** va-t-en!; **to put sth a.** ranger qch; **to take sth a. from sb** retirer qch à qn; **to stand a. from sth** se tenir à l'écart de qch; **to turn a.** se détourner (b) (not at school, work) **to be a.** être absent(e) (c) (in time) **Christmas is only two weeks a.** nous ne sommes qu'à deux semaines de Noël; **right a.** tout de suite

awe [ɔ:] *n* crainte *f* mêlée de respect; **to be in a. of sb/sth** éprouver pour qn/qch une crainte mêlée de respect

awe-inspiring ['ɔ:ɪnspaɪərɪŋ] *adj* imposant(e)

awesome ['ɔ:səm] *adj* (**a**) *(incredible)* impressionnant(e) (**b**) *Fam (wonderful)* super *inv*

awful ['ɔ:fʊl] *adj* horrible, effroyable; **an a. lot of people** plein de monde; **it cost an a. lot** ça a coûté beaucoup d'argent

awfully ['ɔ:flɪ] *adv* (**a**) *(very badly)* terriblement mal (**b**) *(very)* très; **I'm a. sorry** je regrette infiniment *ou* énormément; **I'm a. glad** je suis rudement content

awhile [ə'waɪl] *adv* **wait a.** attendez un moment *ou* un peu

awkward ['ɔ:kwəd] *adj* (**a**) *(clumsy)* gauche, maladroit(e) (**b**) *(inconvenient) (situation)* embarrassant(e); *(silence)* gêné(e), embarrassé(e); *(location)* peu pratique; **to arrive at an a. moment** arriver au mauvais moment; *Fam* **he's an a. customer** il n'est pas commode

awl [ɔ:l] *n* alène *f*, poinçon *m*

awning ['ɔ:nɪŋ] *n (over window, storefront)* store *m*

awoke [ə'wəʊk] *pt of* **awake**

awoken [ə'wəʊkən] *pp of* **awake, awaken**

AWOL ['eɪwɒl] *adj (abbr* **absent without leave)** **to go A.** *Mil* s'absenter sans permission; *Fig* disparaître

awry [ə'raɪ] *adv* **to go a.** aller de travers

ax, axe [æks] **1** *n* hache *f*; *Fig* **to have an ax to grind** agir dans un but intéressé; *Fig* **to get the ax** *(person)* être viré; *(program, plan, etc.)* être annulé ou supprimé
2 *vt Fam (jobs)* supprimer; *(costs)* réduire

axes ['æksɪːz] *pl of* **axis**

axiom ['æksɪəm] *n* axiome *m*

axiomatic [æksɪə'mætɪk] *adj (evident)* évident(e)

axis ['æksɪs] *(pl* **axes** ['æksɪːz]) *n Math* axe *m*; *Hist* **the A. powers** les puissances *fpl* de l'Axe

axle ['æksəl] *n (of vehicle)* essieu *m*

azalea [ə'zeɪlɪə] *n* azalée *f*

Azerbaijan [æzəbaɪ'dʒɑːn] *n* l'Azerbaïdjan *m*

Azerbaijani [æzəbaɪ'dʒɑːnɪ], **Azeri** [ə'zeərɪ] **1** *n* Azerbaïdjanais(e) *m,f*, Azéri(e) *m,f*
2 *adj* azerbaïdjanais(e), azéri(e)

Azores [ə'zɔːz] *npl* **the A.** les Açores *fpl*

Aztec ['æztek] **1** *n* Aztèque *mf*
2 *adj* aztèque

azure ['æʒə(r)] **1** *n* azur *m*
2 *adj* d'azur, azuré(e)

B

B, b [biː] *n* (**a**) *(letter)* B, b *m inv*; **B-movie** (film *m* de) série *f* B (**b**) *Mus* si *m* (**c**) *Sch (grade)* **to get a B** *(on test)* avoir mention assez bien; *(on homework, essay)* ≃ avoir 12 ou 13 sur 20

b. *(abbr* **born**) né(e)

BA [biːˈeɪ] *n* (*abbr* **Bachelor of Arts**) **to have a BA in history** ≃ avoir une licence en histoire; **John Smith BA** ≃ John Smith, licencié ès lettres/en histoire/*etc.*

baa [bɑː] **1** *exclam* bêê!
2 *vi* (*pt & pp* **baaed** *or* **baa'd** [bɑːd]) bêler

babble [ˈbæbəl] **1** *vi* (**a**) *(of baby)* babiller; *(of adult)* bafouiller; **what are you babbling on about?** qu'est-ce que tu baragouines? (**b**) *(of water)* murmurer
2 *n* murmure *m*

babe [beɪb] *n* (**a**) *Lit (baby)* **b. (in arms)** bébé *m* (**b**) *Fam (woman)* belle nana *f* (**c**) *Fam (term of endearment)* chéri(e) *m,f*

baboon [bəˈbuːn] *n* babouin *m*

baby [ˈbeɪbɪ] **1** *n* (*pl* **babies**) (**a**) *(child)* bébé *m*; **b. brother** petit frère *m*; **b. sister** petite sœur *f*; **b. boom** baby-boom *m*; **b. carriage** landau *m*; **b. grand** *(piano)* demi-queue *m*; **b. talk** langage *m* enfantin (**b**) *(idioms)* **to throw the b. out with the bathwater** jeter le bébé avec l'eau du bain; **to leave sb holding the b.** refiler le bébé à qn
2 *vt* (*pt & pp* **babied**) materner

baby-faced [ˈbeɪbɪfeɪst] *adj* au visage poupin

babyhood [ˈbeɪbɪhʊd] *n* petite enfance *f*

babyish [ˈbeɪbɪʃ] *adj Pej* de bébé

babysit [ˈbeɪbɪsɪt] (*pt & pp* **babysat** [ˈbeɪbɪsæt]) *vi* faire du baby-sitting; **to b. for sb** garder l'enfant/les enfants de qn

babysitter [ˈbeɪbɪsɪtə(r)] *n* baby-sitter *mf*

bachelor [ˈbætʃələ(r)] *n* célibataire *m*; **b. pad** *or* **apartment** garçonnière *f*; **b. party** enterrement *m* de vie de garçon; **to have a b. party** enterrer sa vie de garçon; *Univ* **B. of Arts** *(degree)* ≃ licence *f* ès lettres/en histoire/*etc*; *(person)* ≃ licencié(e) *m,f* ès lettres/en histoire/*etc*; *Univ* **B. of Science** *(degree)* ≃ licence *f* ès sciences; *(person)* ≃ licencié(e) *m,f* ès sciences

bachelorette [bætʃələˈret] *n* célibataire *f*; **b. party** enterrement *m* de vie de jeune fille; **to have a b. party** enterrer sa vie de jeune fille

bacillus [bəˈsɪləs] (*pl* **bacilli** [bəˈsɪlaɪ]) *n Biol* bacille *m*

back [bæk] **1** *n* (**a**) *(of person, animal)* dos *m*; *also Fig* **to turn one's b. on sb** tourner le dos à qn; **to sit/to stand with one's b. to sb** tourner le dos à qn; **b. pain** mal *m* de dos; **to have b. problems** avoir des problèmes de dos; **b. slapping** *(self-congratulatory)* félicitations *fpl* excessives
(**b**) *(of hand, book)* dos *m*; *(of page)* dos, verso *m*; *(of chair)* dossier *m*; *(of car)* arrière *m*; *(of throat)* fond *m*; **at the b. (of), in b. (of)** *(behind)* derrière; *(at far end of)* au fond (de); **the dress fastens at the b.** cette robe s'attache dans le dos; **at the b. of the book** à la fin du livre; **the b. of the neck** la nuque; **he knows Manhattan like the b. of his hand** il connaît Manhattan comme sa poche; *Fam* **in the b. of beyond** au diable; **b. to front** devant derrière, à l'envers
(**c**) *(in sports)* arrière *mf*

(**d**) *(idioms)* **to do sth behind sb's b.** faire qch derrière le dos de qn; **I'll be glad to see the b. of him** je serai content d'en être débarrassé; **with one's b. to the wall** *(in desperate situation)* le dos au mur; **put your b. into it!** il faut t'y mettre!; **to break the b. of the work** faire le plus gros du travail; *Fam* **the boss was on my b. all day** j'ai eu le patron sur le dos toute la journée; *Fam* **get off my b.!** fiche-moi la paix!; *Fam* **to put** *or* **to get sb's b. up** braquer qn
2 *adj* (**a**) *(in space) (part, wheel)* arrière *inv*; *Fig* **to put sth on the b. burner** remettre qch à plus tard; **b. door** porte *f* de derrière; *Fig* **he got it through the b. door** il a magouillé pour l'avoir; **the b. page** la dernière page; **b. road** petite route *f*; **b. room** chambre *f* du fond; *Fig* **to take a b. seat** rester discret(ète)
(**b**) *(in time)* **b. number** *(of magazine, newspaper)* vieux numéro *m*; **b. pay** rappel *m* de salaire; **b. rent** arriéré(s) *m(pl)* de loyer
3 *adv* (**a**) *(in space)* en arrière; **to stand** *or* **to step b.** reculer; **to jump b.** faire un bond en arrière; **we passed it 5 miles b.** ≃ nous l'avons dépassé à 8 km d'ici
(**b**) *(in return, retaliation)* **to hit sb b.** rendre son coup à qn; **to call sb b.** rappeler qn; **if you kick me I'll kick you b.** si tu me donnes un coup de pied, je te le rendrai; **to get one's own b. (on sb)** prendre sa revanche (sur qn); **to get b. at sb** prendre sa revanche sur qn
(**c**) *(to original starting point)* **to come b.** revenir; **to go b.** retourner; **when will she be b.?** quand sera-t-elle de retour?; **b. in Georgia, the situation was getting serious** la situation s'aggravait en Géorgie; **(once) b. in New York he phoned the hospital** de retour à New York il a téléphoné à l'hôpital; **a few pages b.** quelques pages plus haut
(**d**) *(in time)* **a few years b.** il y a quelques années; **b. when...** à l'époque où...; **b. in 1982** en 1982; **as far b. as 1914** dès 1914
4 *vt* (**a**) *(support)* soutenir, appuyer; *(financially)* financer
(**b**) *(bet on)* parier *ou* miser sur
(**c**) *(move backward)* **to b. one's car into the garage** entrer au garage en marche arrière; **to b. one's car into a lamppost** rentrer dans un lampadaire en faisant marche arrière
5 *vi* *(move backward)* reculer; *(in car)* faire marche arrière

▶**back away** *vi* reculer (**from** devant)

▶**back down** *vi* *(in argument)* céder; *(in conflict)* faire marche arrière

▶**back off** *vi* reculer

▶**back on to** *vt insep* donner sur

▶**back out** *vi* (**a**) *(move backward)* sortir à reculons; *(in car)* sortir en marche arrière (**b**) *(from agreement)* se dédire

▶**back up 1** *vt sep* (**a**) *(support)* soutenir, appuyer; *(story, account)* étayer (**b**) *Comput (data, file)* sauvegarder
2 *vi* (**a**) *(move backward)* reculer; *(in car)* faire marche arrière (**b**) *Comput* sauvegarder

backache [ˈbækeɪk] *n* mal *m* au dos; **I have a b.** j'ai mal au dos

backbiting [ˈbækbaɪtɪŋ] *n Fam* médisance *f*

backbone ['bækbəʊn] n épine f dorsale, colonne f vertébrale; *Fig* **he's got no b.** il n'a rien dans le ventre

backbreaking ['bækbreɪkɪŋ] adj (work) éreintant(e)

backdate ['bækdeɪt] vt antidater

backdoor ['bækdɔːr] adj louche; **b. methods** méthodes fpl peu respectables

backdrop ['bækdrɒp] n *Theat* toile f de fond; *Fig* **against a b. of continuing violence** avec, comme toile de fond, un climat de violence permanente

backer ['bækə(r)] n (of political party) partisan m; (for project) commanditaire m

backfire [bæk'faɪə(r)] vi (of car) pétarader; *Fig* **the plan backfired on them** leur plan s'est retourné contre eux

backgammon ['bækgæmən] n backgammon m

background ['bækgraʊnd] n (a) (of scene) arrière-plan m, fond m; **in the b.** à l'arrière-plan, dans le fond; *Fig* **to stay in the b.** rester dans l'ombre; **b. music** (in restaurant) musique f d'ambiance; **she likes b. music when she's working** elle aime travailler avec un fond sonore; **b. noise** bruit m de fond (**b**) (social) origines fpl; (educational) formation f; (professional) expérience f; **from a disadvantaged b.** d'un milieu défavorisé; **we need someone with a b. in computers** il nous faut quelqu'un qui s'y connaisse en informatique; (**c**) (circumstances) contexte m; **against a b. of discord** dans un climat de mécontentement; **can you give me some b. information?** pouvez-vous me donner quelques renseignements?; **I need a bit more b.** il me faut plus de données; **b. reading** lectures fpl complémentaires

backhand ['bækhænd] n (in tennis) revers m

backhanded [bæk'hændɪd] adj (compliment) équivoque

backing ['bækɪŋ] n (support) soutien m; **financial b.** financement m

backlash ['bæklæʃ] n (reaction) contrecoup m (**against** à); (political) réaction f (**against** à)

backlit ['bæklɪt] adj *Comput* rétro-éclairé(e)

backlog ['bæklɒg] n retard m; **to have a b. of work** avoir du travail en retard

backpack ['bækpæk] **1** n sac m à dos
2 vi faire de la randonnée; **she backpacked around Europe** elle a fait toute l'Europe, sac à dos

backpacker ['bækpækə(r)] n routard(e) m,f

back-pedal ['bæk'pedəl] vi *Fig* faire marche arrière

backrest ['bækrest] n dossier m

back-seat ['bæksiːt] adj *Fam* **b. driver** = personne qui donne des conseils au conducteur; **I don't want any b. driving** je n'ai besoin des conseils de personne quand je conduis

backside [bæk'saɪd] n *Fam* derrière m, postérieur m

backslash ['bækslæʃ] n *Comput* barre f oblique inversée

backsliding ['bækslaɪdɪŋ] n *Fam* rechute f; **she was on the lookout for any signs of b.** elle nous surveillait pour voir si nous nous relâchions

backspace ['bækspeɪs] n *Comput* retour m en arrière

backstage [bæk'steɪdʒ] adv also *Fig* dans les coulisses

backstairs [bæk'steəz] **1** n escalier m de service
2 adj (secret) secret(ète); (unfair) déloyal(e)

backstitch ['bækstɪtʃ] n (in sewing) point m de piqûre

backstreet ['bækstriːt] n petite rue f; **b. abortion** avortement m clandestin

backstroke ['bækstrəʊk] n (in swimming) dos m crawlé

backtalk ['bæktɔːk] n *Fam* impertinence f

back-to-back [bæktə'bæk] **1** adj (victories, meetings) consécutifs(ives)
2 adv (**a**) (physically) dos à dos (**b**) (consecutively) de suite

backtrack ['bæktræk] vi (**a**) (retrace one's steps) revenir sur ses pas (**b**) (renege) faire marche arrière; **to b. on a promise/decision** revenir sur une promesse/une décision

backup ['bækʌp] n (support) soutien m, appui m; *Mil* renforts mpl; *Comput* **b. copy/file** copie f/fichier m de sauvegarde; **b. system** système m de sauvegarde; **b. team** (providing support) équipe f technique; (on standby) équipe f de remplacement

backward ['bækwəd] **1** adj (**a**) (direction) en arrière; **she left without a b. glance** elle est partie sans se retourner (**b**) (child) retardé(e), attardé(e); (country) en retard
2 adv en arrière; (walk) à reculons; (fall) à la renverse; (read) à l'envers; **to walk b. and forward** aller et venir; *Fig* **to know sth b.** connaître qch à fond

backwardness ['bækwədnɪs] n (of child) arriération f mentale; (of country) retard m

backwards ['bækwədz] adv = **backward**

backwash ['bækwɒʃ] n (of boat) remous m; *Fig* conséquences fpl néfastes

backwater ['bækwɔːtə(r)] n (**a**) (of river) bras m mort (**b**) (isolated place) trou m perdu

backyard [bæk'jɑːd] n jardin m de derrière

bacon ['beɪkən] n (**a**) (food) bacon m (**b**) (idioms) *Fam* **to save sb's b.** sauver la peau de qn; *Fam* **to bring home the b.** (earn wages) faire bouillir la marmite; (succeed) réussir

bacteria [bæk'tɪərɪə] npl bactéries fpl

bacterial [bæk'tɪərɪəl] adj bactérien(enne)

bacteriological [bæktɪərɪə'lɒdʒɪkəl] adj bactériologique

bacteriology [bæktɪərɪ'ɒlədʒɪ] n bactériologie f

bad [bæd] (comparative **worse** [wɜːs], superlative **worst** [wɜːst]) **1** adj (**a**) (of poor quality, unpleasant) mauvais(e); **it's not b.** (fair) ce n'est pas mal; (good) ce n'est pas mal du tout; **to be b. at math** être mauvais en maths; **to be b. at cooking** être mauvais(e) cuisinier(ère); **things are going from b. to worse** c'est de pire en pire ou de mal en pis; **it was a b. time to leave** ce n'était pas le moment de partir; **to have a b. time** passer un mauvais moment; **there's b. blood between them** il y a de la rancune entre eux; **to get into sb's b. books** se faire prendre en grippe par qn; **b. check** chèque m sans provision; *Fin* **b. debts** créances fpl douteuses; **in b. faith** de mauvaise foi; **b. feeling** animosité f; **to be a b. loser** être mauvais(e) perdant(e); **b. luck** malchance f; **b. manners** mauvaises manières fpl; **in a b. mood** de mauvaise humeur; *Fam* **she's b. news** elle ne t'/lui/etc. apportera que des ennuis
(**b**) (unfortunate) **it's (really) too b.!, that's too b.!** c'est vraiment dommage!; **to have a b. effect on sth** nuire à qch; **he'll come to a b. end** il finira mal
(**c**) (not healthy) **to have a b. back/heart** avoir le dos/cœur fragile; **smoking is b. for you** fumer est mauvais pour la santé; **to be in a b. way** aller mal
(**d**) (wicked) (person, behavior) méchant(e); **to use b. language** dire des gros mots
(**e**) (serious) (mistake, accident) grave; (pain) fort(e); **I've got a really b. headache** j'ai vraiment très mal à la tête; **to have a b. cold** avoir un gros rhume
(**f**) (rotten) mauvais(e); **to go b.** (of fruit) se gâter, pourrir; (of milk) tourner; *Fig* **a b. apple** une brebis galeuse
(**g**) (guilty) **to feel b. about sth** s'en vouloir de qch
2 adv *Fam* **she wants it b.** elle en meurt d'envie; **he was beaten b.** il s'est fait méchamment tabasser
3 n mauvais m; *Fam* **my b.!** c'est ma faute!

baddie, baddy ['bædɪ] (pl **baddies**) n *Fam* méchant(e) m,f

bade [bæd, beɪd] pt of **bid**

badge [bædʒ] n (of company, organization) badge m; (fashion accessory) pin's m; *Mil* insigne m

badger ['bædʒə(r)] **1** n (animal) blaireau m
2 vt harceler; **to b. sb into doing sth** harceler qn jusqu'à ce qu'il fasse qch

bad-looking [bæd'lʊkɪŋ] adj **not b.** pas mal

badly ['bædlɪ] adv (comparative **worse** [wɜːs], superlative **worst** [wɜːst]) (**a**) (not well) mal; **to do b.** (on test, in competition) avoir un mauvais résultat; **he didn't do b.** il ne s'en est pas mal tiré; **she took it very b.** elle a très mal pris la chose; **to be b. off for sth** *(lacking)* manquer de qch; **to be b. off for money** avoir des problèmes d'argent; **to get on b. (with sb)** ne pas s'entendre (avec qn) **(b)** *(seriously) (damaged, broken)* gravement; **to be b. beaten** *(physically)* être roué(e) de coups; *(in match, competition)* être battu(e) à plates coutures; **b. wounded** gravement *ou* grièvement blessé(e) **(c)** *(greatly)* **to want sth b.** avoir très envie de qch; **to be b. in need of sth** avoir grand besoin de qch

bad-mannered [bæd'mænəd] *adj* mal élevé(e)

badminton ['bædmɪntən] *n* badminton *m*

bad-mouth ['bædmaʊθ] *vt Fam* dire du mal de

badness ['bædnɪs] *n* **(a)** *(poor quality)* mauvaise qualité *f* **(b)** *(wickedness)* méchanceté *f*

bad-tempered [bæd'tempəd] *adj (person)* grincheux(euse); *(remark)* désagréable

baffle ['bæfəl] *vt* **(a)** *(confuse)* laisser perplexe; **to be baffled** être perplexe; **I'm baffled as to why she did it** je ne comprends vraiment pas pourquoi elle a fait cela **(b)** *(foil) (plot, attempt)* déjouer

baffling ['bæfəlɪŋ] *adj* déconcertant(e)

bag [bæg] **1** *n (of paper, plastic)* sac *m*; *(purse)* sac à main; **bags under the eyes** des poches sous les yeux; *Fam* **to be a b. of bones** être un sac d'os; *Fig* **it's in the b.** *(of deal, victory)* c'est dans la poche

2 *vt (pt & pp* **bagged)** **(a)** *(put in bag)* mettre en sac **(b)** *(in hunting)* abattre, tuer **(c)** *Fam (claim)* accaparer

bagel ['beɪgəl] *n* = petite couronne de pain, *Can* bagel *m*

baggage ['bægɪdʒ] *n* bagages *mpl*; *Fig* **to have a lot of (emotional) b.** avoir accumulé des échecs sentimentaux; *Aviat* **b. handler** bagagiste *mf*; *Aviat* **b. reclaim** retrait *m* des bagages; **b. room** consigne *f*

baggy ['bægɪ] *adj (garment) (by design)* large; *(out of shape)* déformé(e)

Baghdad [bæg'dæd] *n* Bagdad

bagpipes ['bægpaɪps] *npl* cornemuse *f*

bah [bɑː] *exclam* bah!

Bahamas [bə'hɑːməz] *npl* **the B.** les Bahamas *fpl*

Bahrain [bɑː'reɪn] *n* Bahreïn

Bahraini [bɑː'reɪnɪ] **1** *n* Bahreïni(e) *m,f*
2 *adj* bahreïni(e)

bail [beɪl] *n Law (guarantee)* caution *f*; **on b.** sous caution; **to grant sb b.** libérer qn sous caution; **to post b. for sb** se porter garant(e) de qn

▶**bail out** *vt sep* **to b. sb out** *Law* se porter garant(e) de qn; *Fig* tirer qn d'affaire; *Fig* **to b. a company out** renflouer une entreprise

bailiff ['beɪlɪf] *n Law* huissier *m*

bait [beɪt] **1** *n also Fig* appât *m*; *Fig* **to rise to the b.** mordre à l'hameçon; *Fig* **to swallow** *or* **to take the b.** mordre à l'hameçon

2 *vt* **(a)** *(torment)* harceler **(b)** *(attach bait to)* mettre l'appât à

baize [beɪz] *n* feutre *m*

bake [beɪk] **1** *vt (food)* (faire) cuire au four; *(clay)* cuire

2 *vi* **(a)** *(of food)* cuire **(b)** *Fam* **I'm baking** je crève de chaleur

baked [beɪkt] *adj* **b. beans** haricots *mpl* blancs à la tomate; **b. potato** pomme *f* de terre au four

baker ['beɪkə(r)] *n* boulanger(ère) *m,f*; **b.'s** *(store)* boulangerie *f*; **b.'s dozen** treize à la douzaine

bakery ['beɪkərɪ] *(pl* **bakeries)** *n* boulangerie *f*

baking ['beɪkɪŋ] **1** *n* **to do some b.** *(bread)* faire du pain; *(cakes, pies)* faire de la pâtisserie; **b. pan** *(for meat)* plat *m* à rôtir; *(for cake)* moule *m* à gâteau; **b. powder** levure *f* chimique; **b. sheet** *or* **tray** plaque *f* (du four); **b. soda** bicarbonate *m* de soude

2 *adj Fam* **it's b. (hot)** on crève de chaleur

balaclava [bælə'klɑːvə] *n* passe-montagne *m*

balance ['bæləns] **1** *n* **(a)** *(equilibrium)* équilibre *m*; **to keep/lose one's b.** garder/perdre son équilibre; *Fig* **to catch sb off b.** prendre qn au dépourvu; **the b. of power** l'équilibre des pouvoirs; **on b.** tout compte fait; **to strike a b.** trouver le juste milieu

(b) *(of bank account)* solde *m*; *(in accounting)* bilan *m*; *Econ* **b. of trade/payments** balance *f* commerciale/des paiements; **b. sheet** bilan

(c) *(for weighing)* balance *f*; *Fig* **to hang** *or* **to be in the b.** *(of decision, result)* être en jeu

2 *vt (object)* maintenir en équilibre; **he sought to b. the claims of the two parties** il a tenté de contenter les deux partis; **they b. each other well** *(of people)* ils sont complémentaires; *Fin* **to b. the books** arrêter les comptes

3 *vi* **(a)** *(physically)* tenir en équilibre

(b) **she couldn't get the accounts to b.** elle n'arrivait pas à équilibrer les comptes

balanced ['bælənst] *adj (account, reporting)* objectif(ive); *(judgment)* pondéré(e); **b. diet** alimentation *f* équilibrée

balancing act ['bælənsɪŋ'ækt] *n Fig* **to do a b.** faire des acrobaties

balcony ['bælkənɪ] *(pl* **balconies)** *n (in house, theater)* balcon *m*

bald [bɔːld] *adj* **(a)** *(person)* chauve; *(tire)* lisse; **to go b.** devenir chauve, perdre ses cheveux; *Fam* **as b. as a coot** chauve comme un œuf; **b. eagle** aigle *m* à tête blanche; **b. patch** tonsure *f* **(b)** *(plain)* **the b. truth** la vérité toute nue; **a b. statement of the facts** une simple exposition des faits

balderdash ['bɔːldədæʃ] *n Fam* bêtises *fpl*, balivernes *fpl*

balding ['bɔːldɪŋ] *adj* qui commence à perdre ses cheveux; **a b. man** un homme à la calvitie naissante

baldly ['bɔːldlɪ] *adv (reply)* sèchement

baldness ['bɔːldnɪs] *n* **(a)** *(of person)* calvitie *f* **(b)** *(of statement, demand)* sécheresse *f*

bale [beɪl] *n (of cloth, paper)* balle *f*; *(of hay)* botte *f*

▶**bale out** *vi (of pilot)* s'éjecter; *Fig (from difficult situation)* s'éclipser

Balearic [bælɪ'ærɪk] *n & adj* **the Balearics, the B. Islands** les (îles *fpl*) Baléares *fpl*

baleful ['beɪlfəl] *adj* sinistre, maléfique; **she gave me a b. look** elle m'a lancé un regard noir

Bali ['bɑːlɪ] *n* Bali

Balinese [bælɪ'niːz] *adj* balinais(e)

balk [bɔːlk] **1** *vt (runner, racehorse)* empêcher de passer

2 *vi* reculer **(at** devant)

Balkan ['bɔːlkən] **1** *n* **the Balkans** les Balkans *fpl*

2 *adj* balkanique

ball[1] [bɔːl] *n* **(a)** *(in game) (for soccer, football, basketball)* ballon *m*; *(for baseball, tennis, golf)* balle *f*; *(for pool)* bille *f*, boule *f*; *(of paper, of fire)* boule; *(of wool)* pelote *f*; **to roll sth (up) into a b.** mettre qch en boule; **b. bearing** *(ball)* bille; *(device)* roulement *m* à billes; **b. boy/girl** *(in tennis)* ramasseur(euse) *m,f* de balles; **b. cock** soupape *f* à flotteur; **b. game** *(in general)* jeu *m* de balle; *(baseball match)* match *m* de baseball; *Fig* **that's a whole new b. game** *(irrelevant)* ça n'a rien à voir; *(different situation)* c'est une autre paire de manches **(b)** *(of foot)* plante *f* **(c)** *Vulg* **balls** *(testicles)* couilles *fpl*; *(nonsense)* conneries *fpl*; *Fig* **to have a lot of balls** avoir des couilles **(d)** *(idioms)* **to be on the b.** *(alert)* avoir de la présence d'esprit; *(knowledgeable)* connaître son affaire; **to start the b. rolling** faire démarrer les choses; **the b. is in your court** la balle est dans votre camp; **to play b.** *(cooperate)* jouer le jeu

ball[2] [bɔːl] *n (party)* bal *m*; *Fam* **to have a b.** s'éclater; **b. gown** robe *f* de bal

ballad ['bæləd] *n* ballade *f*

ball-and-socket joint [bɔːlən'sɒkɪt'dʒɔɪnt] *n Anat* articulation *f* à emboîtement; *Tech* joint *m* à rotule

ballast ['bæləst] *n* (**a**) *Naut* lest *m* (**b**) *Rail* ballast *m*

ballerina [bælə'riːnə] *n* ballerine *f*; **prima b.** danseuse *f* étoile

ballet ['bæleɪ] *n* danse *f* classique; *(work)* ballet *m*; **b. dancer** danseur(euse) *m,f* classique; **b. shoe** chausson *m* de danse

ballistic [bə'lɪstɪk] *adj (missile)* balistique; *Fam Fig* **to go b.** piquer une crise

ballistics [bə'lɪstɪks] *npl* balistique *f*

balloon [bə'luːn] **1** *n* (**a**) *(for party, travel)* ballon *m*; *Fam Fig* **when the b. goes up** quand il va y avoir du grabuge (**b**) *(in cartoon)* bulle *f*
  2 *vi (swell)* gonfler

ballooning [bə'luːnɪŋ] *n* **to go b.** faire du ballon

balloonist [bə'luːnɪst] *n* aérostier *m*

ballot ['bælət] **1** *n (process)* tour *m* de scrutin; *(vote)* scrutin *m*, vote *m*; **to hold a b.** organiser des élections; **to put sth to a b.** soumettre qch à un vote; **b. box** urne *f*; **this matter should be decided at the b. box** c'est aux urnes que doit se décider cette question; **b. paper** bulletin *m* de vote; **b. rigging** fraude *f* électorale
  2 *vt* consulter

ballpark ['bɔːlpɑːk] **1** *n* terrain *m* de base-ball
  2 *adj* **a b. figure** une estimation

ballpoint ['bɔːlpɔɪnt] *n* **b. (pen)** stylo *m* (à) bille

ballroom ['bɔːlruːm] *n* salle *f* de bal; **b. dancing** danses *fpl* de salon

ballsy ['bɔːlzi] *adj very Fam* culotté(e)

ballyhoo [bælɪ'huː] *n Fam* battage *m* publicitaire

balm [bɑːm] *n* baume *m*

balmy ['bɑːmɪ] *adj (weather)* doux (douce)

baloney [bə'ləʊnɪ] *n* (**a**) *Fam (nonsense)* bêtises *fpl* (**b**) *(sausage)* = saucisse à base de bœuf, veau et porc, mangée froide

balsa ['bɔːlsə] *n* balsa *m*

balsam ['bɔːlsəm] *n* balsam *m*

balsamic vinegar [bɔːl'sæmɪk'vɪnɪgə(r)] *n Culin* vinaigre *m* balsamique

Baltic ['bɒltɪk] **1** *n* **the B.** la Baltique
  2 *adj (state)* balte; **the B. Sea** la mer Baltique

balustrade [bælə'streɪd] *n* balustrade *f*

bamboo [bæm'buː] *n* bambou *m*; **b. shoots** pousses *fpl* de bambou

bamboozle [bæm'buːzəl] *vt Fam* embobiner

ban [bæn] **1** *n* interdiction *f*; **to impose a b. on sth** interdire qch
  2 *vt (pt & pp banned)* interdire; **to b. sb from doing sth** interdire à qn de faire qch

banal [beɪnəl] *adj* banal(e)

banality [bə'nælɪtɪ] *(pl* **banalities***) n* banalité *f*

banana [bə'nɑːnə] *n* banane *f*; **b. tree** bananier *m*; *Fam* **to be/ go bananas** *(mad)* être/devenir cinglé(e); *Fam* **b. republic** république *f* bananière; *also Fig* **b. skin** peau *f* de banane; **b. split** banana split *m inv*

band¹ [bænd] *n* (**a**) *(of metal)* bande *f*, bague *f*; *(around hat)* ruban *m*; *(around cigar)* bague; *(of color)* bande, raie *f* (**b**) *Rad* bande *f* de fréquence (**c**) *(of ages, tax)* tranche *f*; *(of salaries)* catégorie *f*

band² [bænd] *n (of friends)* groupe *m*, cercle *m*; *(of robbers)* bande *f*; *(of musicians) (rock)* groupe *m*; *(jazz)* orchestre *m*, groupe
► **band together** *vi* se liguer (**against** contre)

bandage ['bændɪdʒ] **1** *n* bandage *m*; *(for support)* bande *f*
  2 *vt* bander; **to b. sb's arm** bander le bras à qn
► **bandage up** *vt sep* bander

Band-Aid® ['bændeɪd] *n* sparadrap *m*

bandit ['bændɪt] *n* bandit *m*

bandmaster ['bændmɑːstə(r)] *n* chef *m* de musique

bandsman ['bændzmən] *n* musicien *m*

bandstand ['bændstænd] *n* kiosque *m* à musique

b & w *n Phot & Cin (abbr* **black and white***)* noir et blanc *inv*

bandwagon ['bændwægən] *n Fam* **to jump on the b.** prendre le train en marche

bandwidth ['bændwɪθ] *n Comput* bande *f* passante; *Rad* largeur *f* de bande

bandy¹ ['bændɪ] *adj* **to have b. legs** avoir les jambes arquées

bandy² ['bændɪ] *(pt & pp* **bandied***) vt (words, insults)* échanger; **her name was being bandied about as a possible candidate** son nom est revenu plusieurs fois parmi ceux des candidats possibles

bandy-legged [bændɪ'leg(ɪ)d] *adj* aux jambes arquées

bane [beɪn] *n* plaie *f*; **he's the b. of my life** il m'empoisonne l'existence

bang [bæŋ] **1** *n* (**a**) *(noise)* claquement *m*; *(explosion)* détonation *f*; **the door shut with a b.** la porte s'est refermée en claquant (**b**) *(blow)* coup *m* violent; **to get a b. on the head** recevoir un coup sur la tête
  2 *adv* (**a**) *Fam* **b. went my hopes of a quiet weekend** pour le week-end tranquille, c'était loupé (**b**) *Fam (exactly)* **b. in the middle** en plein milieu; **b. on time** pile à l'heure
  3 *exclam (sound of gun)* pan!; *(explosion)* boum!
  4 *vt (hit)* frapper (violemment); **to b. one's head** se cogner la tête
  5 *vi (of door, window)* claquer, battre; **the door banged shut** la porte se ferma en claquant; **to b. on** *or* **on the door** frapper à la porte à coups violents; **to b. into sth** se cogner à qch
► **bang about, bang around** *vi (make noise)* faire du potin

Bangkok [bæŋ'kɒk] *n* Bangkok

Bangladesh [bæŋglə'deʃ] *n* le Bangladesh

Bangladeshi [bæŋglə'deʃɪ] **1** *n* Bangladeshi *mf*, Bangladais(e) *m,f*
  2 *adj* bangladeshi, bangladais(e)

bangle ['bæŋgəl] *n* bracelet *m*

bangs [bæŋz] *npl (in hair)* frange *f*

banish ['bænɪʃ] *vt (exile)* bannir (**from** de); *Fig (thought, fear)* chasser

banishment ['bænɪʃmənt] *n* bannissement *m*

banister ['bænɪstə(r)] *n* rampe *f* d'escalier

banjo ['bændʒəʊ] *(pl* **banjos** *or* **banjoes***) n* banjo *m*

bank¹ [bæŋk] **1** *n* (**a**) *(of river)* berge *f*, bord *m*; *(of earth)* talus *m* (**b**) *(of clouds, fog)* banc *m* (**c**) *(of lights, switches)* rangée *f*
  2 *vt* **the road is banked by trees** la route est bordée d'arbres
  3 *vi* (**a**) *(of clouds, snow)* s'amonceler (**b**) *(of plane)* virer

bank² [bæŋk] **1** *n* (**a**) *(financial institution)* banque *f*; **b. account** compte *m* en banque; **b. balance** solde *m*; **b. charges** frais *mpl* bancaires; **b. clerk** employé(e) *m,f* de banque; **b. draft** traite *f* bancaire; **b. loan** prêt *m* bancaire; *Fin* **b. rate** taux *m* de l'escompte; **b. statement** relevé *m* de banque; **b. teller** guichetier(ère) *m,f* (**b**) *(in gambling)* banque *f*; **to break the b.** faire sauter la banque; *Fig* **it won't break the b.** ça ne me/te/le/etc. ruinera pas (**c**) *(store)* **blood b.** banque *f* du sang; **data b.** banque de données
  2 *vt (funds)* mettre *ou* déposer à la banque
  3 *vi* **to b. with sb** avoir un compte chez qn; **who do you b. with?** à quelle banque êtes-vous?
► **bank on** *vt insep (outcome, success)* compter sur

bankbook ['bæŋkbʊk] *n* livret *m* ou carnet *m* de compte

banker ['bæŋkə(r)] *n Fin* banquier(ère) *m,f*

banking ['bæŋkɪŋ] *n (business)* opérations *fpl* bancaires; **she's in b.** elle travaille dans la banque

banknote ['bæŋknəʊt] *n* billet *m* de banque

bankroll ['bæŋkrəʊl] *vt (finance)* financer

bankrupt ['bæŋkrʌpt] **1** *n Fin* failli(e) *m,f*
  2 *adj* failli(e); **to be b.** être en faillite; **to go b.** faire faillite; *Fig* **to be morally b.** avoir perdu toute crédibilité
  3 *vt Law* mettre en faillite; *Fig (make poor)* ruiner

bankruptcy ['bæŋkrəptsɪ] *n Law* faillite *f*; *Fig (poverty)* ruine *f*

banner ['bænə(r)] *n* (a) *(flag)* bannière *f*; **the Star-Spangled B.** la bannière étoilée; **b. headline** manchette *f* (b) *Comput (for advertising on the Internet)* bandeau *m*, bannière *f* publicitaire

bannister ['bænɪstə(r)] = **banister**

banns [bænz] *npl* bans *mpl*

banquet ['bæŋkwɪt] *n* banquet *m*

bantam ['bæntəm] *n* = poulet de petite taille

bantamweight ['bæntəmweɪt] *n (in boxing)* poids *m* coq

banter ['bæntə(r)] **1** *n* taquineries *fpl*
2 *vi* plaisanter

baptism ['bæptɪzəm] *n* baptême *m*; *Fig* **a b. of fire** un baptême du feu

baptismal [bæp'tɪzməl] *adj (certificate)* de baptême; **b. font** fonts *mpl* baptismaux

Baptist ['bæptɪst] *n* baptiste *mf*

baptize [bæp'taɪz] *vt* baptiser

bar [bɑː(r)] **1** *n* (a) *(of metal)* barre *f*; *(of gold)* lingot *m*; *(of chocolate) (large)* tablette *f*; *(smaller)* barre; *(on window)* barreau *m*; **b. of soap** savonnette *f*, morceau *m* de savon; **to be behind bars** être derrière les barreaux; **b. chart** histogramme *m*; *Comput* **b. code** code-barres *m*
(b) *(obstacle)* obstacle *m*; **to be a b. to sth** faire obstacle à qch; **to impose a b. on sth** interdire qch
(c) *Law* **the B.** ≃ l'Ordre *m* des avocats, le barreau; **to be called to the B.** s'inscrire au barreau; **to study for the B.** faire son droit; **the prisoner at the b.** l'accusé(e) *m,f*
(d) *(pub, in hotel)* bar *m*; *(counter)* comptoir *m*, bar; **b. hop** virée *f* des bars
(e) *Mus* mesure *f*
2 *vt (pt & pp* **barred)** (a) *(door)* barrer; **to b. sb's way** barrer le passage à qn
(b) *(ban) (from club, restaurant)* exclure; **to b. sb from doing sth** interdire à qn de faire qch
3 *prep* sauf, à l'exception de; **the finest b. none** sans conteste le (la) meilleur(e)

barb [bɑːb] *n* (a) *(on hook, arrow)* barbillon *m* (b) *(remark)* pique *f*

Barbadian [bɑːˈbeɪdɪən] **1** *n* = personne née à ou habitant la Barbade
2 *adj* de la Barbade

Barbados [bɑːˈbeɪdɒs] *n* la Barbade

barbarian [bɑːˈbeərɪən] *n & adj* barbare *mf*

barbaric [bɑːˈbærɪk] *adj* barbare; *(manners, behavior)* de barbare

barbarism ['bɑːbərɪzəm] *n* barbarie *f*

barbarity [bɑːˈbærɪtɪ] *(pl* **barbarities)** *n (cruelty)* barbarie *f*; *(act)* atrocité *f*

barbarous ['bɑːbərəs] *adj* barbare

barbecue, barbeque ['bɑːbɪkjuː] **1** *n* barbecue *m*; **to have a b.** faire un barbecue; **b. sauce** sauce *f* barbecue
2 *vt* cuire au barbecue

barbed [bɑːbd] *adj* (a) *(hook)* barbelé(e); **b. wire** (fil *m* de fer) barbelé *m* (b) *(remark, comment)* acerbe

barbeque = **barbecue**

barber ['bɑːbə(r)] *n* coiffeur *m* pour hommes, *Can* barbier *m*; **to go to the b.'s** aller chez le coiffeur

barbershop ['bɑːbəʃɒp] *n* salon *m* de coiffure *(pour hommes)*; **b. quartet** = quatuor chantant en harmonie

barbiturate [bɑːˈbɪtjʊreɪt] *n* barbiturique *m*

barbwire [bɑːbˈwaɪə(r)] *n* (fil *m* de fer) barbelé *m*

bard [bɑːd] *n Lit (poet)* barde *m*; **the B.** Shakespeare

bare ['beə(r)] **1** *adj* (a) *(not covered)* nu(e); *(countryside)* nu, dénudé(e); **in one's b. feet** (les) pieds nus; **to lay sth b.** mettre qch à nu, exposer qch (b) *(empty) (room, cupboard)* vide; **to strip a house b.** tout enlever dans une maison (c) *(just sufficient)* **the b. minimum** le strict minimum; **the b. bones of**

the case les grandes lignes de l'affaire; **the b. necessities (of life)** le strict nécessaire; **a b. majority** une petite *ou* faible majorité
2 *vt* mettre à nu, découvrir; **to b. one's teeth** montrer les dents; **to b. one's heart** *or* **soul to sb** ouvrir son cœur à qn

bareback ['beəbæk] **1** *adj* **b. rider** cavalier(ère) *m,f* qui monte à cru
2 *adv* **to ride b.** monter à cru

barefaced ['beəfeɪst] *adj (impudence, lie, liar)* éhonté(e)

barefoot ['beəfʊt], **barefooted** ['beəfʊt(ɪd)] **1** *adj* (aux) pieds nus
2 *adv* nu-pieds, (les) pieds nus

bareheaded [beəˈhedɪd] **1** *adj* nu-tête *inv*, à la tête nue
2 *adv* nu-tête, (la) tête nue

bare-legged [beəˈleg(ɪ)d] **1** *adj* aux jambes nues
2 *adv* (les) jambes nues

barely ['beəlɪ] *adv* (a) *(scarcely)* à peine; **b. enough** tout juste assez (b) *(sparsely)* **b. furnished** avec très peu de meubles

barf [bɑːf] *vi Fam* vomir

bargain ['bɑːgɪn] **1** *n* (a) *(agreement)* marché *m*, affaire *f*; **to make** *or* **to strike a b. with sb** conclure un marché avec qn; **you haven't kept your side** *or* **part of the b.** vous n'avez pas tenu votre part du marché; **to drive a hard b.** ne pas faire de cadeaux; **into the b.** *(in addition)* par-dessus le marché, en plus (b) *(good buy)* affaire *f*, occasion *f*; **b. basement** rayon *m* des soldes, solderie *f*; **b. hunter** acheteur(euse) *m,f* à la recherche de bonnes affaires; **b. price** prix *m* exceptionnel
2 *vi* **to b. with sb** négocier avec qn

▸**bargain away** *vt sep (rights, privileges)* brader

▸**bargain for** *vt insep (reaction, question)* s'attendre à; **I didn't b. for that** je ne m'y attendais pas; **he got more than he bargained for** il ne s'attendait pas à cela

▸**bargain on** *vt insep* **I didn't b. on that** je ne m'y attendais pas

barge [bɑːdʒ] *n* péniche *f*

▸**barge in** *vi (enter)* faire irruption

barhop ['bɑːhɒp] *vi* faire les bars

baritone ['bærɪtəʊn] *n* baryton *m*

barium ['beərɪəm] *n Chem* baryum *m*

bark[1] [bɑːk] **1** *n (of tree)* écorce *f*
2 *vt* **to b. one's shins** s'écorcher les jambes

bark[2] [bɑːk] **1** *n (of dog)* aboiement *m*; *Fig* **his b. is worse than his bite** il n'est pas si méchant qu'il y paraît
2 *vt (order)* aboyer
3 *vi* aboyer **(at** après); *(of person)* crier **(at** sur); *Fam Fig* **you're barking up the wrong tree** tu fais fausse route

barkeep ['bɑːkiːp], **barkeeper** ['bɑːkiːpə(r)] *n* serveur *m*, barman *m*

barley ['bɑːlɪ] *n* orge *m*; **b. sugar** *(candy)* sucre *m* d'orge

barman ['bɑːmən] *n* serveur *m*, barman *m*

barn [bɑːn] *n* grange *f*; *(for cows)* étable *f*; *(for horses)* écurie *f*; **b. dance** bal *m* folklorique; **b. owl** effraie *f*

barnacle ['bɑːnəkəl] *n* bernacle *f*

barnstorming ['bɑːnstɔːmɪŋ] *adj (speech, performance)* plein(e) de brio

barnyard ['bɑːnjɑːd] *n* cour *f* de ferme

barometer [bəˈrɒmɪtə(r)] *n* baromètre *m*

baron ['bærən] *n* baron *m*; *Fig* **press/oil b.** magnat *m* de la presse/du pétrole

baroness ['bærənes] *n* baronne *f*

baronet ['bærənet] *n* baronet *m*

baroque [bəˈrɒk] **1** *n* baroque *m*
2 *adj* baroque

barracks ['bærəks] *npl* caserne *f*; **to be confined to b.** être consigné(e)

barracuda [bærəˈkjuːdə] *n* barracuda *m*

barrage ['bærɑːʒ] **1** *n* (a) *(dam)* barrage *m* (b) *Mil* tir *m* de barrage; *Fig (of questions, abuse)* flot *m*

2 *vt* **to b. sb with** *(questions)* assaillir qn de; *(criticism)* accabler qn de

barrel ['bærəl] *n* **(a)** *(container)* tonneau *m*, fût *m*; *(of oil)* baril *m*; *Fam* **to have sb over a b.** tenir qn à sa merci; *Fam* **the party wasn't exactly a b. of laughs** cette soirée, ça n'a pas été une partie de rigolade; **b. organ** orgue *m* de Barbarie **(b)** *(of gun)* canon *m*

barren ['bærən] *adj* *(woman, land, discussion)* stérile; *(landscape)* désolé(e)

barrenness ['bærənnıs] *n* *(of land, discussion)* stérilité *f*

barrette [bə'ret] *n* barrette *f*

barricade ['bærɪkeɪd] **1** *n* barricade *f*

2 *vt* barricader; **to b. oneself** se barricader

barrier ['bærɪə(r)] *n also Fig* barrière *f*; **the Great B. Reef** la Grande Barrière

barring ['bɑːrɪŋ] *prep* sauf; **b. accidents** sauf imprévu; **b. a miracle** à moins d'un miracle

barrow ['bærəʊ] *n* *(wheelbarrow)* brouette *f*

bartender ['bɑːtendə(r)] *n* serveur(euse) *m,f* *(de bar)*

barter ['bɑːtə(r)] **1** *n* troc *m*

2 *vt* troquer (**for** contre)

3 *vi* marchander

basalt ['bæsɔːlt] *n* basalte *m*

base [beɪs] **1** *n* **(a)** *(of cliff, column)* pied *m*; *(of lamp, statue)* socle *m*; *(of spine)* bas *m*; *(of pitcher)* cul *m*; *(of triangle, structure)* base *f*; *Fin* **b. rate** taux *m* de base **(b)** *(for expedition, campaign)* base *f*; *(for tourism)* point *m* de départ; **b. camp** camp *m* de base **(c)** *(in baseball)* base *f*; *Fig* **we didn't get past first b.** nous ne sommes pas arrivés à grand-chose; **to touch b. (with sb)** entrer en contact (avec qn)

2 *adj* **(a)** *Formal (motive, conduct)* bas (basse), vil(e) **(b)** **b. metals** métaux *mpl* vils

3 *vt* *(hopes, opinion)* fonder (**on** sur); **to be based on** *(of calculation, movie)* être basé(e) sur; **to be based in** *(of job, troops, company)* être basé à

baseball ['beɪsbɔːl] *n* base-ball *m*; **b. cap** casquette *f*; **b. mitt** gant *m* de base-ball

baseboard ['beɪsbɔːd] *n* plinthe *f*

Basel ['bɑːzəl] *n* Bâle

baseless ['beɪslɪs] *adj* sans fondement

baseline ['beɪslaɪn] *n* *(in tennis)* ligne *f* de fond

basement ['beɪsmənt] *n* sous-sol *m*; **b. apartment** = appartement en partie en sous-sol

bases ['beɪsiːz] *pl of* **basis**

bash [bæʃ] *Fam* **1** *n* **(a)** *(blow)* coup *m*; *(with fist)* coup de poing **(b)** *(party)* fête *f*

2 *vt* **to b. one's head** se cogner la tête

bashful ['bæʃfʊl] *adj* timide; *(modest)* modeste

bashfulness ['bæʃfʊlnɪs] *n* timidité *f*; *(modesty)* modestie *f*

BASIC ['beɪsɪk] *n* *Comput (abbr* **Beginners' All-purpose Symbolic Instruction Code**) basic *m*

basic ['beɪsɪk] **1** *n* **the basics** l'essentiel *m*; *(of language, science)* les rudiments *mpl*; **let's get down to basics** venons-en à l'essentiel; **to get back to basics** *(traditional values)* retrouver les vraies valeurs

2 *adj* *(principle, problem, vocabulary)* de base; *(accommodations, understanding)* rudimentaire; **I get the b. idea** je vois en gros de quoi il s'agit; **to be b. to sth** être essentiel(elle) à qch; **b. pay** salaire *m* de base

basically ['beɪsɪklɪ] *adv* **(a)** *(on the whole)* en gros; *(in fact)* en fait **(b)** *(fundamentally)* fondamentalement

basil ['bæzəl, 'beɪzəl] *n* basilic *m*

basilica [bə'zɪlɪkə] *n* basilique *f*

basin ['beɪsən] *n* **(a)** *(for cooking)* bol *m*; *(for washing hands)* lavabo *m*; *(plastic, for doing dishes)* bassine *f*, cuvette *f* **(b)** *Geog* bassin *m*

basis ['beɪsɪs] *(pl* **bases** ['beɪsiːz]*)* *n* *(for discussion)* base *f*; *(for* opinion, accusation*)* fondement *m*; **to be paid on a weekly/monthly b.** être payé à la semaine/au mois; **on an informal b.** à titre non officiel; **to have a b. in fact** être fondé(e); **on the b. of what you've told me** d'après ce que tu m'as dit

bask [bɑːsk] *vi* **to b. in the sun** se chauffer au soleil; **he basked in her approval** il se délectait à l'idée qu'il avait son approbation

basket ['bɑːskɪt] *n* *(of fruit, for washing)* corbeille *f*; *(for shopping, in basketball)* panier *m*; *Fam* **he's a real b. case** il est complètement cinglé

basketball ['bɑːskɪtbɔːl] *n* basket(-ball) *m*; **b. player** basketteur(euse) *m,f*

basketful ['bɑːskɪtfʊl] *n* (plein) panier *m*

Basle [bɑːl] *n* Bâle

basmati rice [bæs'mɑːtɪ'raɪs] *n* *Culin* riz *m* basmati

Basque [bɑːsk] **1** *n* **(a)** *(person)* Basque *mf* **(b)** *(language)* basque *m*

2 *adj* basque; **the B. Country** le Pays basque

bas-relief [bɑːrɪ'liːf] *n* bas-relief *m*

bass¹ [bæs] *n* *(seawater)* bar *m*; *(freshwater)* perche *f*

bass² [beɪs] **1** *n* *(voice, singer, guitar)* basse *f*; *(on amplifier)* basses *fpl*; *(doublebass)* contrebasse *f*

2 *adj* *(voice)* de basse; *(guitar, clarinet)* bas (basse); **b. clef** clef *f* de fa; **b. drum** grosse caisse *f*

basset ['bæsɪt] *n* **b. (hound)** basset *m*

bassinet [bæsɪ'net] *n* berceau *m*

bassist ['beɪsɪst] *n* bassiste *mf*

bassoon [bə'suːn] *n* basson *m*

bastard ['bɑːstəd] **1** *n* **(a)** *(illegitimate child)* bâtard(e) *m,f* **(b)** *Vulg (unpleasant man)* salaud *m*; **you lucky b.!** sacré veinard!

2 *adj* *(child)* bâtard(e)

baste [beɪst] *vt* *(meat)* arroser de son jus

bastion ['bæstɪən] *n also Fig* bastion *m*

bat¹ [bæt] *n* *(animal)* chauve-souris *f*; *Fam* **like a b. out of hell** comme un fou (une folle)

bat² [bæt] **1** *n* *(for baseball)* batte *f*; *(for table tennis)* raquette *f*

2 *vt* *(pt & pp* **batted**) **she didn't b. an eyelid** elle n'a pas sourcillé *ou* bronché

3 *vi* *(in baseball)* manier la batte

batch [bætʃ] *n* *(of bread)* fournée *f*; *(of people)* groupe *m*; *(of goods)* lot *m*; *Comput* **b. file** fichier *m* séquentiel; *Comput* **b. processing** traitement *m* par lots

bated ['beɪtɪd] *adj* **with b. breath** en retenant son souffle

bath [bɑːθ] *n* bain *m*; **to take a b.** prendre un bain; **to give sb a b.** baigner qn; **b. mat** tapis *m* de bain; **b. salts** sels *mpl* de bain; **b. towel** drap *m* de bain

bathe [beɪð] **1** *vt* *(wound)* laver; **bathed in tears/sweat** baigné(e) de larmes/de sueur

2 *vi* *(take a bath)* prendre un bain; *Old-fashioned (swim)* se baigner

bather ['beɪðə(r)] *n* baigneur(euse) *m,f*

bathing ['beɪðɪŋ] *n* **b. is prohibited** *(sign)* la baignade est interdite; **b. cap** bonnet *m* de bain; **b. suit** maillot *m* de bain; **b. trunks** slip *m* de bain

bathos ['beɪθɒs] *n* chute *f* du sublime au ridicule

bathrobe ['bɑːθrəʊb] *n* peignoir *m* de bain

bathroom ['bɑːθruːm] *n* salle *f* de bains; *(toilet)* toilettes *fpl*; **b. scales** pèse-personne *m*

bathtub ['bɑːθtʌb] *n* baignoire *f*, *Can* bain *m*

batik [bə'tiːk] *n* batik *m*

baton [bə'tɒn] *n* *(in relay race)* témoin *m*; *(of conductor)* baguette *f*

battalion [bə'tæljən] *n* bataillon *m*

▶**batten down** ['bætən] *vt insep* **to b. down the hatches** condamner les panneaux; *Fig* dresser ses batteries

batter¹ ['bætə(r)] *n* *(in baseball)* batteur *m*

batter² ['bætə(r)] *n* *(in cooking)* pâte *f* à frire

batter³ ['bætə(r)] *vt* *(beat)* cogner sur; *(person)* battre

battered ['bætəd] *adj* (a) **b. women** femmes *fpl* battues; **b. child** enfant *m* martyr (b) *(hat, saucepan, car)* cabossé(e); *(furniture, house)* délabré(e)

battering ram ['bætərɪŋræm] *n* bélier *m*

battery ['bætərɪ] *(pl* **batteries)** *n* (a) *(of radio, clock)* pile *f*; *(of car)* batterie *f*; **to be b. operated** *or* **powered** fonctionner sur piles; **b. charger** chargeur *m* de piles/batteries (b) *Mil* batterie *f*; *Fig (of criticism, complaints)* déluge *m* (c) **a b. of tests** une batterie de tests

battle ['bætəl] **1** *n* bataille *f*; *Fig* combat *m*, lutte *f*; **it was a b. of wits between them** ils ont joué au plus fin; **to do b. with sb** être en conflit avec qn; **that's half the b.** la partie est à moitié gagnée; **b. cry** cri *m* de guerre; **a b. royal** une violente empoignade

2 *vi* se battre, lutter

battleax, battleaxe ['bætəlæks] *n* hache *f* d'armes; *Fam Pej (woman)* virago *f*

battlefield ['bætəlfiːld], **battleground** ['bætəlgraʊnd] *n also Fig* champ *m* de bataille

battle-hardened ['bætəl'hɑːdənd] *adj* aguerri(e)

battlements ['bætəlmənts] *npl* remparts *mpl*

battle-scarred ['bætəl'skɑːd] *adj* marqué(e) par la guerre

battleship ['bætəlʃɪp] *n* cuirassé *m*

batty ['bætɪ] *adj Fam* dingue

bauble ['bɔːbəl] *n* *(on Christmas tree)* boule *f*; *(worthless thing)* babiole *f*

baud [bɔːd] *n Comput* baud *m*; **b. rate** débit *m* en bauds

bauxite ['bɔːksaɪt] *n* bauxite *f*

Bavaria [bə'veərɪə] *n* la Bavière

Bavarian [bə'veərɪən] **1** *n* Bavarois(e) *m,f*

2 *adj* bavarois(e)

bawdy ['bɔːdɪ] *adj* grivois(e), paillard(e)

bawl [bɔːl] **1** *vt* brailler

2 *vi* brailler; **to b. at sb** hurler après qn

▶**bawl out** *vt sep* (a) *(shout)* hurler (b) *(reprimand)* passer un savon à

bay¹ [beɪ] *n* *(shrub)* laurier *m*; **b. leaf** feuille *f* de laurier

bay² [beɪ] **1** *n* (a) *(on coastline)* baie *f*; **the B. of Bengal** le golfe du Bengale; **the B. of Biscay** le golfe de Gascogne (b) *Archit* travée *f*; *(recess)* renfoncement *m*, niche *f*; **b. window** bow-window *m* (c) **to keep** *or* **to hold sb at b.** tenir qn à distance; **to keep** *or* **to hold sth at b.** se préserver de qch

2 *vi (of dog, wolf)* hurler; **to b. for sb's blood** réclamer la tête de qn

bayonet ['beɪənɪt] **1** *n* baïonnette *f*

2 *vt* **to b. sb** passer qn à la baïonnette

bazaar [bə'zɑː(r)] *n* (a) *(in Middle East)* bazar *m* (b) *(for charity)* vente *f* de charité

bazooka [bə'zuːkə] *n* bazooka *m*

BBC [biːbiː'siː] *n* *(abbr* **British Broadcasting Corporation**) BBC *f*

BB gun [biːbiː'bɪʌn] *n* carabine *f* à air comprimé

BBQ [biːbiː'kjuː] *n Fam (abbr* **barbecue** *or* **barbeque)** barbecue *m*, barbeuk *m*

BC [biː'siː] *adv (abbr* **before Christ**) av. J.-C.

be [biː] **1** *vi (present* **I am, you/we/they are, he/she/it is**; *pt* **were** [wɜː(r)]; *1st and 3rd person singular* **was** [wɒz]; *pp* **been** [biːn]) (a) *(with state, condition)* être; **she's smart/pretty** elle est intelligente/jolie; **I'm a doctor/lawyer** je suis médecin/avocat; **they're Canadian/Spanish** ils sont canadiens/espagnols; **to be hungry/thirsty** avoir faim/soif; **to be cold/hot** *(of person)* avoir froid/chaud; *(of thing)* être froid(e)/chaud(e); **it's cold/hot** *(weather)* il fait froid/chaud; **to be 3 ft long/wide** ≃ faire 1 m de long/de large; **three and two are five** trois et deux font cinq

(b) *(with location)* être; **where is the station?** où est *ou* se trouve la gare?; **here I am** me voici; **there you are!** te voilà!; **where was I?** *(after digression)* où en étais-je?

(c) *(with time, date)* **it's six o'clock** il est six heures; **what day is it today?** quel jour sommes-nous?; **today's Friday/the tenth** c'est vendredi/le dix; **when is the concert?** quand a lieu le concert?; **it's been two weeks since I saw him** je l'ai vu il y a quinze jours

(d) *(with age)* **to be twenty (years old)** avoir vingt ans; **how old is he?** quel âge a-t-il?

(e) *(with cost)* coûter, valoir; **how much is it?** combien ça coûte?; **the tickets are $5 each** les billets valent 5 dollars

(f) *(with health)* aller; **how are you?** comment vas-tu?; **I'm fine** ça va; **he's better/worse** il va mieux/plus mal

(g) *(with imperatives)* **be good!** sois sage!; **don't be stupid!** ne sois pas ridicule!; **let's be reasonable!** soyons raisonnables!

(h) *(with question tags)* **she's beautiful, isn't she?** elle est belle, n'est-ce pas *ou* non?; **they're big, aren't they?** ils sont grands, n'est-ce pas *ou* non?; **he isn't English, is he?** il n'est pas anglais, si?

(i) *(as past participle of go)* **I've been to New York/to the museum** je suis allé à New York/au musée; **where have you been?** où étais-tu passé?

2 *v aux* (a) *(in continuous tenses)* **to be doing sth** faire qch; **I was reading when the phone rang** j'étais en train de lire quand le téléphone a sonné; **she is/was laughing** elle rit/riait; **I'm leaving tomorrow** je pars demain; **it's raining** il pleut; **I've been waiting for hours** ça fait des heures que j'attends

(b) *(with passives)* **he was killed** il a été tué; **he wasn't allowed to go** on ne l'a pas autorisé à y aller

(c) *(followed by infinitive)* **the house is to be sold** la maison doit être vendue; **there is to be an election** des élections sont prévues; **she was never to see them again** elle ne devait jamais les revoir; **you are not to mention this to anyone** tu ne dois en parler à personne

beach [biːtʃ] **1** *n* plage *f*; **b. ball** ballon *m* de plage; **b. hut** cabine *f* sur la plage; **b. towel** drap *m* de plage

2 *vt (boat, ship)* échouer

beachcomber ['biːtʃkəʊmə(r)] *n* = personne qui ramasse des objets échoués ou abandonnés sur la plage

beachhead ['biːtʃhed] *n* tête *f* de pont

beacon ['biːkən] *n* *(signal, buoy)* balise *f*; *(lighthouse)* phare *m*; *(bonfire)* feu *m* d'alarme; *Fig* **a b. of hope** une source d'espoir

bead [biːd] *n* perle *f*; **a string of beads** un collier

beady ['biːdɪ] *adj* **to have one's b. eyes on sb/sth** surveiller qn/qch de près

beady-eyed ['biːdɪ'aɪd] *adj Pej* aux yeux de fouine; *Fig* au regard perçant

beagle ['biːgəl] *n* beagle *m*

beak [biːk] *n* *(of bird)* bec *m*; *Fam (nose)* nez *m* crochu

beaker ['biːkə(r)] *n* gobelet *m*

be-all and end-all ['biːɔːl'nendɔːl] *n Fam* **winning isn't the b.** gagner n'est pas tout

beam [biːm] **1** *n* (a) *(in building, in gymnastics)* poutre *f* (b) *(of sun, moon)* rayon *m*; *(of flashlight, headlight)* faisceau *m* lumineux; *Phys* faisceau (c) *(idioms) Fam* **to be on b.** être sur la bonne voie; *Fam* **to be off b.** être à côté de la plaque; *Fam* **broad in the b.** *(of person)* large de hanches

2 *vt (program, information)* transmettre

3 *vi (shine) (of sun, moon)* briller; **to b. with pride/pleasure** rayonner de fierté/de plaisir

bean [biːn] *n* (a) *(vegetable)* haricot *m*; *(of coffee)* grain *m*; **b. curd** pâte *f* de soja (b) *(idioms) Fam* **to be full of beans** être plein(e) d'énergie; *Fam* **it isn't worth a b.** ça ne vaut pas un radis; **he doesn't know beans about it** il n'y connaît rien

beanbag ['bi:nbæg] n (for juggling) balle f lestée; (for sitting on) fauteuil m poire

beanie ['bi:nɪ] n **b. (hat)** bonnet m

beanpole ['bi:npəʊl] n (**a**) (stick) rame f (**b**) Fam (thin person) asperge f

beansprout ['bi:nspraʊt] n germe m de soja

beanstalk ['bi:nstɔ:k] n tige f de haricot

bear[1] [beə(r)] n (animal) ours m; (female) ourse f; **b. cub** ourson m; **to give sb a b. hug** serrer qn très fort dans ses bras; Fin **b. market** marché m à la baisse

bear[2] [beə(r)] (pt **bore** [bɔ:(r)], pp **borne** [bɔ:n]) **1** vt (**a**) (carry) porter; (weight, load) supporter; (bring) apporter; **to b. sth away** emporter qch; **to b. sth in mind** (remember) se souvenir de qch; (take into account) tenir compte de qch; **it bears no relation to...** cela n'a aucun rapport avec...; **to b. the responsibility for sth** assumer la responsabilité de qch (**b**) (endure) supporter; **I can't b. him** je ne peux pas le supporter; **I can't b. the pain** la douleur est insupportable; **I couldn't b. it any longer** je n'en pouvais plus; **he can't b. losing** il ne supporte pas de perdre; **it doesn't b. thinking about** l'idée même en est insupportable (**c**) (produce) (child) donner naissance à; Fin (interest) rapporter; **she bore him three children** elle lui a donné trois enfants; **to b. fruit** (of tree) porter des fruits; (of effort, plan) porter ses fruits

2 vi (move) **to b. (to the) right/left** tourner à droite/gauche

▸**bear down (up)on** vt insep foncer sur

▸**bear out** vt sep confirmer, corroborer

▸**bear up** vi tenir le coup; **b. up!** courage!

▸**bear with** vt insep supporter; **if you could b. with me** si vous voulez bien patienter

bearable ['beərəbəl] adj supportable

beard [bɪəd] n barbe f; **to have a b.** porter la barbe

bearded ['bɪədɪd] adj barbu(e)

bearer ['beərə(r)] n (of news, check) porteur(euse) m,f; (of passport) titulaire mf

bearing ['beərɪŋ] n (**a**) (comportment) port m (**b**) (in mechanism, engine) palier m (**c**) (orientation) **to take a (compass) b. (on sth)** relever la position (de qch) au compas; **to find** or **to get one's bearings** s'orienter; Fig s'y retrouver; **to lose one's bearings** être désorienté(e) (**d**) (relevance) rapport m (**on** avec)

beast [bi:st] n (**a**) (animal) bête f; **b. of burden** bête de somme (**b**) Fam (unpleasant person) peau f de vache; (cruel person) brute f

beastly ['bi:stlɪ] adj Fam (unpleasant) horrible

beat [bi:t] **1** n (of heart) battement m; (in bar, of music) temps m; (rhythm) rythme m

2 adj Fam (exhausted) crevé(e)

3 vt (pt **beat**, pp **beaten** ['bi:tən]) (**a**) (person, eggs) battre; **to b. a drum** battre du tambour; **to b. its wings** (of bird) battre des ailes; **to b. a path through the crowd** se frayer un chemin à travers la foule; Fam **b. it!** dégage! (**b**) (defeat) battre; **that will take some beating** c'est difficile de faire mieux; **I left early to b. the traffic** je suis parti tôt pour éviter les embouteillages; **he beat me to it** il a été plus rapide que moi; **you can't b. a good book** rien de tel qu'un bon livre; Prov **if you can't b. them, join them** il faut savoir hurler avec les loups; Fam **that beats everything!** ça c'est la meilleure!; Fam **it beats me why he did it** je ne pige vraiment pas pourquoi il a fait ça; Fam **it beats me!** ça me dépasse!

4 vi (**a**) (of heart) battre (**b**) **to b. around** or **about the bush** tourner autour du pot

▸**beat back** vt sep repousser

▸**beat down 1** vt sep (price) faire baisser; **I b. her down to $40** je lui ai fait baisser son prix à 40 dollars

2 vi (of rain) tomber à verse; (of sun) taper

▸**beat off** vt sep repousser

▸**beat out** vt sep (fire, flames) étouffer

▸**beat up** vt sep (assault) tabasser

beaten ['bi:tən] **1** adj **b. earth** terre f battue; Fig **off the b. track** à l'écart

2 pp of **beat**

beater ['bi:tə(r)] n (**a**) (in cookery) fouet m (**b**) (in hunting) rabatteur m

beatification [bi:ætɪfɪ'keɪʃən] n béatification f

beating ['bi:tɪŋ] n (punishment) correction f; (in fight) raclée f; (defeat) défaite f; **to give sb a b.** (as punishment) donner une correction à qn; (beat up) flanquer une raclée à qn

beat-up ['bi:tʌp] adj Fam (car) tout(e) déglingué(e)

beaut [bju:t] n Fam **what a b.!** quelle merveille!

beautician [bju:'tɪʃən] n esthéticien(enne) m,f

beautiful ['bju:tɪfʊl] adj (person, weather, music) (très) beau (belle); (smell, taste) très bon (bonne)

beautifully ['bju:tɪfʊlɪ] adv merveilleusement bien

beautify ['bju:tɪfaɪ] (pt & pp **beautified**) vt embellir

beauty ['bju:tɪ] (pl **beauties**) n (attribute, person) beauté f; (object) bijou m; **that's the b. of it** c'est ça qui est bien; **b. contest** concours m de beauté; **b. parlor** or **salon** institut m de beauté; **b. queen** reine f de beauté; **b. spot** (on face) grain m de beauté; (in country) site m remarquable

beaver ['bi:və(r)] n castor m

▸**beaver away** vi travailler d'arrache-pied (**at** à)

becalmed [bɪ'kɑ:md] adj encalminé(e)

became [bɪ'keɪm] pt of **become**

because [bɪ'kɒz] conj parce que; **why?** – (just) **b.** pourquoi? – parce que; **b. of** à cause de

beck [bek] n **to be at sb's b. and call** être aux ordres de qn

beckon ['bekən] **1** vt faire signe à; **to b. sb in** faire signe à qn d'entrer

2 vi (of prospect) être attirant(e); **to b. to sb** faire signe à qn; **fame beckons for him** la gloire l'attend

become [bɪ'kʌm] (pt **became** [bɪ'keɪm], pp **become**) **1** vt Formal (of behavior) être digne de; (of clothes, color) aller bien à

2 vi (**a**) (come to be) devenir; **to b. old** vieillir; **to b. thin** maigrir; **to b. known** (of truth) être révélé(e) (**b**) **what will b. of him?** que va-t-il devenir?; **I don't know what has become of her** je ne sais pas ce qu'elle est devenue

becoming [bɪ'kʌmɪŋ] adj (behavior) convenable; (clothes, color) seyant(e)

BEd [bi:'ed] n Univ (abbr **Bachelor of Education**) (qualification) = diplôme universitaire d'aptitude à l'enseignement; (person) = titulaire d'un BEd

bed [bed] **1** n (**a**) (for sleeping) lit m; **to be in b.** être au lit; **to go to b.** aller au lit; **to put a child to b.** coucher un enfant; **to go to b. with sb** coucher avec qn; Fam **to get out of b. on the wrong side** se lever du pied gauche; **b. and breakfast** (accommodations) chambre f avec petit déjeuner; **to stay in a b. and breakfast** ≃ prendre une chambre d'hôte (**b**) (of river) lit m (**c**) (of flowers) parterre m; (of vegetables) carré m (**d**) Culin lit m; **on a b. of rice** garni(e) de riz (**e**) Geol couche f

2 vt (pt & pp **bedded**) Fam Old-fashioned or Hum coucher avec

bedbug ['bedbʌg] n punaise f

bedclothes ['bedkləʊðz] npl draps mpl et couvertures fpl

bedding ['bedɪŋ] n draps mpl et couvertures fpl

bedevil [bɪ'devəl] vt **to be bedeviled by sth** (complaints) être assailli(e) de qch; (problems) (of person) être accablé(e) de qch; (of project) être sapé(e) par qch

bedfellow ['bedfeləʊ] n Fig **they make strange bedfellows** ils forment une drôle de paire

bedlam ['bedləm] n (chaos) bazar m

Bedouin ['bedʊɪn] **1** n Bédouin(e) m,f

2 adj bédouin(e)

bedpan ['bedpæn] *n* bassin *m*

bedpost ['bedpəʊst] *n* colonne *f* de lit

bedraggled [bɪ'drægəld] *adj (person, clothes)* débraillé(e); *(hair)* échevelé(e)

bedridden ['bedrɪdən] *adj* alité(e); *(permanently)* grabataire

bedrock ['bedrɒk] *n Geol* substrat *m* rocheux; *Fig (of beliefs, faith)* fondement *m*

bedroll ['bedrəʊl] *n* matériel *m* de couchage

bedroom ['bedruːm] *n* chambre *f* (à coucher); *Fig* **b. community** cité-dortoir *f*

bedside ['bedsaɪd] *n* chevet *m*; **b. lamp** lampe *f* de chevet; **to have a good b. manner** *(of doctor)* savoir s'y prendre avec les malades; **b. table** table *f* de nuit *ou* de chevet

bedsore ['bedsɔː(r)] *n* escarre *f*

bedspread ['bedspred] *n* dessus-de-lit *m inv*

bedsprings ['bedsprɪŋz] *npl* ressorts *mpl* de sommier

bedstead ['bedsted] *n* châlit *m*

bedtime ['bedtaɪm] *n* **b.!** c'est l'heure d'aller au lit!; **it's past my b.** je devrais déjà être couché; **b. story** histoire *f (pour endormir un enfant)*

bed-wetting ['bedwetɪŋ] *n* énurésie *f* nocturne

bee [biː] *n* abeille *f; Fam* **he's got a b. in his bonnet about it** c'est son idée fixe

beech [biːtʃ] *n* hêtre *m*

beechnut ['biːtʃnʌt] *n* faîne *f*

beef [biːf] **1** *n* (a) *(meat)* bœuf *m*; **b. stew** ragoût *m* de bœuf (b) *Fam (strength)* **to have plenty of b.** avoir du muscle; **give it some b.!** allez, du nerf! (c) *Fam (complaint)* **what's your b.?** c'est quoi ton problème?

2 *vi Fam (complain)* rouspéter (**about** contre)

▸**beef up** *vt sep Fam (text, resources)* étoffer

beefeater ['biːfiːtə(r)] *n (at the Tower of London)* = garde de la Tour de Londres

beefsteak ['biːfsteɪk] *n* bifteck *m*

beefy ['biːfɪ] *adj Fam (muscular)* costaud(e)

beehive ['biːhaɪv] *n* (a) *(for bees)* ruche *f* (b) *(hairstyle)* ≃ choucroute *f*

beekeeper ['biːkiːpə(r)] *n* apiculteur(trice) *m,f*

beeline ['biːlaɪn] *n Fam* **to make a b. for** foncer droit sur

been [biːn] *pp of* **be**

beep [biːp] **1** *n (of computer, alarm clock)* bip *m*

2 *vt (with pager)* biper

3 *vi (of computer, alarm clock)* faire bip

beeper ['biːpə(r)] *n (pager)* bip *m*

beer [bɪə(r)] *n* bière *f*; **b. garden** = jardin ou terrasse où les clients d'un pub peuvent consommer; **b. glass** verre *m* à bière

beery ['bɪərɪ] *adj (smell, taste)* de bière; *(breath)* qui sent la bière

beeswax ['biːzwæks] *n* cire *f* d'abeille

beet [biːt] *n (red vegetable)* betterave (rouge); *(white vegetable)* betterave *f* (potagère); *Fam* **to go b. red** devenir rouge comme une tomate

beetle ['biːtəl] *n* scarabée *m*

befall [bɪ'fɔːl] *(pt* **befell** [bɪ'fel], *pp* **befallen** [bɪ'fɔːlən]) *vt Lit* arriver à

befit [bɪ'fɪt] *(pt & pp* **befitted**) *vt Formal* convenir à

befitting [bɪ'fɪtɪŋ] *adj* convenable

before [bɪ'fɔː(r)] **1** *prep* (a) *(with time)* avant; **I got here b. you** je suis arrivé avant toi; **the day b. the battle** la veille de la bataille; **b. that,...** avant,...

(b) *(with place)* devant; **b. my very eyes** sous mes propres yeux

(c) *(in importance)* avant; **she puts her family b. everything else** pour elle, la famille passe avant tout le reste

2 *adv* (a) *(with time)* avant; **two days b.** deux jours avant; **the day b.** le jour précédent, la veille; **the year b.** l'année précédente; **I've seen her b.** je l'ai déjà vue; **I've told you b.** je te l'ai déjà dit

(b) *(in space)* **this page and the one b.** cette page et celle d'avant *ou* la précédente

3 *conj* **b. doing sth** avant de faire qch; **come and see me b. you leave** venez me voir avant de partir; **give it to her b. she cries** donne-le-lui avant qu'elle (ne) se mette à pleurer

beforehand [bɪ'fɔːhænd] *adv* à l'avance; **check b.** vérifiez au préalable

befriend [bɪ'frend] *vt* **to b. sb** se prendre d'amitié pour qn

befuddled [bɪ'fʌdəld] *adj (person)* perdu(e); *(mind)* embrouillé(e); **b. with drink** abruti(e) par l'alcool

beg [beg] *(pt & pp* **begged**) **1** *vt* **to b. sb to do sth** supplier qn de faire qch; **he begged a favor of me** il m'a supplié de lui rendre un service; **to b. sb's forgiveness** implorer le pardon de qn; **I b. your pardon** *(I apologize)* (je vous demande) pardon; *(what did you say?)* pardon?; **I b. to differ** je me permets d'être d'un autre avis; **this begs the question why** on peut se demander pourquoi

2 *vi (for money)* mendier; **I b. of you!** je vous en supplie!; **to b. for sth** *(money)* mendier qch; *(help)* implorer qch; **to b. for mercy** demander grâce

▸**beg off** *vi (from invitation)* se décommander

began [bɪ'gæn] *pt of* **begin**

beggar ['begə(r)] **1** *n* mendiant(e) *m,f; Prov* **beggars can't be choosers** nécessité fait loi

2 *vt* **to b. belief** être incroyable; **to b. description** être indescriptible

begin [bɪ'gɪn] *(pt* **began** [bɪ'gæn], *pp* **begun** [bɪ'gʌn]) **1** *vt* commencer; *(piece of work, new chapter)* commencer, entamer; **to b. to do sth, to b. doing sth** commencer à faire qch; **he began laughing** il s'est mis à rire; **I couldn't (even) b. to explain** je ne peux (vraiment) pas expliquer

2 *vi* commencer; **to b. by doing sth** commencer par faire qch; **to b. again** recommencer; **to b. with,...** pour commencer,...

beginner [bɪ'gɪnə(r)] *n* débutant(e) *m,f*

beginning [bɪ'gɪnɪŋ] *n* début *m*, commencement *m*; **in** *or* **at the b.** au début, au commencement; **at the b. of the year/month** au début de l'année/du mois; **I knew from the b. something was wrong** j'ai su dès le début que quelque chose n'allait pas; **to start from the b.** commencer au commencement; **from b. to end** *(read)* du début à la fin

begonia [bɪ'gəʊnɪə] *n* bégonia *m*

begrudge [bɪ'grʌdʒ] *vt* (a) *(resent)* **to b. doing sth** faire qch à contrecœur, rechigner à faire qch (b) *(envy)* **to b. sb sth** envier qch à qn

beguile [bɪ'gaɪl] *vt* (a) *(enchant)* envoûter (b) *(deceive)* enjôler; **to b. sb into doing sth** faire faire qch à qn en le séduisant

beguiling [bɪ'gaɪlɪŋ] *adj* enjôleur(euse)

begun [bɪ'gʌn] *pp of* **begin**

behalf [bɪ'hɑːf] *n* **in** *or* **on b. of sb, in** *or* **on sb's b.** *(act, speak, accept award)* au nom de qn; *(come, convey message)* de la part de qn; **don't worry on my b.** ne vous inquiétez pas pour moi

behave [bɪ'heɪv] *vi (of person)* se conduire, se comporter; *(be good)* bien se tenir; *(of car, machine)* marcher, fonctionner; **b. yourself!** tiens-toi bien!; *(to child)* sois sage!

behavior [bɪ'heɪvjə(r)] *n* comportement *m*, conduite *f*; **to be on one's best b.** se tenir particulièrement bien

behavioral [bɪ'heɪvjərəl] *adj* de comportement

behaviorism [bɪ'heɪvjərɪzəm] *n Psy* behaviorisme *m*

behead [bɪ'hed] *vt* décapiter

beheld [bɪ'held] *pt & pp of* **behold**

behest [bɪ'hest] *n* **at sb's b., at the b. of sb** sur ordre de qn

behind [bɪ'haɪnd] **1** *prep* derrière; **he hid b. it** il s'est caché derrière; **to be b. sb** *(support)* être avec qn; **to be b. schedule** avoir du retard; **to put sth b. one** *(forget)* ne plus penser à qch; **she's ten minutes b. them** elle a dix minutes de retard sur eux; **to be b. the times** *(old-fashioned)* retarder sur son temps;

the reasons b. sth les raisons de qch; **what's b. all this?** qu'est-ce que ça cache?

2 adv derrière; **from b.** (viewed) de derrière; (attacked) par-derrière; **to stay** or **to remain b.** (not leave) rester; **to be b. with one's work** avoir du travail en retard; **to be b. with the rent** être en retard pour payer le loyer; **they are only three points b.** (in contest) ils ne sont qu'à trois points

3 n Fam (buttocks) derrière m

behindhand [bɪ'haɪndhænd] adv en retard; **to be b. with the rent** être en retard pour payer le loyer; **to be b. with one's work** avoir du travail en retard

behind-the-scenes [bɪ'haɪndðə'siːnz] adj secret(ète); **a b. look at politics** un regard en coulisse sur la politique

behold [bɪ'həʊld] (pt & pp **beheld** [bɪ'held]) vt Lit voir; **a sight to b.** un spectacle

beholden [bɪ'həʊldən] adj Formal **to be b. to sb** être redeva-ble à qn

beholder [bɪ'həʊldə(r)] n Prov **beauty is in the eye of the b.** ce qu'on aime est toujours beau

beige [beɪʒ] **1** n beige m

2 adj beige

Beijing [beɪ'ʒɪŋ] n Pékin, Beijing

being ['biːɪŋ] n **(a)** (creature) être m **(b)** (existence) **to come into b.** naître; **to be in b.** exister

Beirut [beɪ'ruːt] n Beyrouth

Belarus [belə'ruːs] n la Biélorussie

belated [bɪ'leɪtɪd] adj tardif(ive); **wishing you a b. happy birthday** je te souhaite un bon anniversaire avec un peu de retard

belch [beltʃ] **1** n (burp) rot m; **to give a (loud) b.** roter (bruyamment)

2 vt **to b. smoke/flames** (of fire, chimney) cracher de la fu-mée/des flammes

3 vi (of person) roter

beleaguered [bɪ'liːgəd] adj (city, army) assiégé(e); (govern-ment) assailli(e) de toutes parts; (person) accablé(e)

Belfast [bel'faːst] n Belfast

belfry ['belfrɪ] (pl **belfries**) n beffroi m, clocher m

Belgian ['beldʒən] **1** n Belge mf

2 adj belge

Belgium ['beldʒəm] n la Belgique

Belgrade [bel'greɪd] n Belgrade

belie [bɪ'laɪ] vt (feelings, background) ne pas refléter

belief [bɪ'liːf] n **(a)** (conviction) conviction f; (religious) croyance f; **in the b. that...** étant convaincu(e) que...; **it is my b. that...** je suis convaincu(e) que... **(b)** (confidence) foi f (**in** en)

believable [bɪ'liːvəbəl] adj crédible, plausible

believe [bɪ'liːv] **1** vt croire; **I b. (that) I'm right** je crois que j'ai raison; **I b. him to be alive** je crois qu'il est vivant; **she is believed to be in hiding** on pense qu'elle se cache; **I don't b. a word of it** je n'en crois pas un mot; **I could scarcely b. my eyes** j'en croyais à peine mes yeux; **I don't b. it!** c'est pas vrai!

2 vi **(a)** **to b. in sth** (have faith in) croire à qch; **to b. in God** croire en Dieu; **to b. in sb** (have confidence in) avoir foi en qn; **to b. in oneself** avoir confiance en soi **(b)** **to believe in sth** (be in favor of) croire à qch; **I don't b. in making promises** je n'aime pas faire de promesses **(c)** (think, suppose) croire; **I b. not** je ne crois pas, je crois que non; **I b. so** je crois (que oui)

believer [bɪ'liːvə(r)] n **(a)** (religious person) croyant(e) m,f; **to be a b.** être croyant(e) **(b)** (supporter) **to be a b. in sth** croire à qch

belittle [bɪ'lɪtəl] vt rabaisser; **to b. oneself** se rabaisser

Belize [be'liːz] n le Belize

bell [bel] n (of church) cloche f; (handbell, on cat) clochette f; (on door, bicycle) sonnette f; **to ring the b.** (on door) sonner; Fig **bells and whistles** accessoires mpl; **b. jar** cloche f; **b. pepper** poivron m; **b. tower** clocher m

belladonna [belə'dɒnə] n belladone f

bell-bottoms ['belbɒtəmz] npl pantalon m (à) pattes d'élé-phant

bellboy ['belbɔɪ] n Fam groom m

belle [bel] n beauté f; **the b. of the ball** la reine du bal

bellhop ['belhɒp] n Fam groom m

bellicose ['belɪkəʊs] adj belliqueux(euse)

belligerence [be'lɪdʒərəns] n agressivité f

belligerent [be'lɪdʒərənt] **1** n (in war) belligérant(e) m,f; (in dispute) partie f

2 adj (aggressive) agressif(ive), belliqueux(euse); (at war) belli-gérant(e)

bellow ['beləʊ] **1** n (of bull) beuglement m, mugissement m; (of person) braillement m

2 vi (of bull) beugler, mugir; (of person) brailler

bellows ['beləʊz] npl **(pair of) b.** soufflet m

bellringer ['belrɪŋə(r)] n carillonneur(euse) m,f

belly ['belɪ] (pl **bellies**) n ventre m; **to have a full/an empty b.** avoir le ventre plein/vide; Fam **to go b. up** (of company) faire faillite; Fam **b. button** nombril m; **b. dance** danse f du ventre; **b. dancer** danseuse f du ventre ou orientale; **b. laugh** gros rire m

bellyache ['belɪeɪk] Fam **1** n mal m au ventre

2 vi (complain) rouspéter, râler (**about sb/about sth** après qn/au sujet de qch)

belly-flop ['belɪflɒp] **1** n plat m

2 vi (pt & pp **belly-flopped**) faire un plat

bellyful ['belɪfʊl] n Fam **to have had a b. of sb/sth** en avoir marre ou ras le bol de qn/qch

belong [bɪ'lɒŋ] vi **(a)** **to b. to** (be property of) appartenir à; **that book belongs to me** ce livre m'appartient ou est à moi **(b)** **to b. to** (club, party) être membre de; (category) appartenir à **(c)** (have a proper place) aller; **to put sth back where it belongs** remettre qch à sa place; **the saucepans don't b. in that cup-board** les casseroles ne vont pas ou ne se rangent pas dans ce placard; **I feel I b. here** je me sens à ma place ici

belonging [bɪ'lɒŋɪŋ] n **to have a sense of b.** se sentir à sa place

belongings [bɪ'lɒŋɪŋz] npl affaires fpl

beloved 1 n [bɪ'lʌvɪd] Lit bien-aimé(e) m,f

2 adj [bɪ'lʌvd] bien-aimé(e)

below [bɪ'ləʊ] **1** prep **(a)** (line, age, temperature) au-dessous de; (bridge, ground) sous **(b)** (with numbers) moins de

2 adv au-dessous, en bas; (in text) ci-dessous; **on the floor b.** à l'étage du dessous; **it's 10 degrees b.** il fait moins 10

belt [belt] **1** n **(a)** (for trousers) ceinture f; Fig **to tighten one's b.** se serrer la ceinture; Fig **to have sth under one's b.** (dri-ver's license, degree) avoir qch en poche; (experience) avoir qch à son actif; Fig **that was a bit below the b.** (of remark, criticism) c'était un coup bas **(b)** (of machine) courroie f **(c)** (of land) ré-gion f, zone f **(d)** Fam (blow) coup m; **to give sb a b.** flanquer un gnon à qn

2 vt (hit) (ball) cogner dans; (person) flanquer un gnon à

3 vi Fam (move quickly) **to b. along** foncer; **she belted down the stairs** elle a descendu les escaliers quatre à quatre

▸**belt out** vt sep Fam (song) brailler

beltway ['beltweɪ] n (boulevard m) périphérique m

bemoan [bɪ'məʊn] vt (loss, somebody's death) pleurer; (one's fate) se lamenter sur

bemused [bɪ'mjuːzd] adj perplexe

bench [bentʃ] n (seat) & Pol banc m; (worktable) établi m; Sport **to be on the b.** être en réserve

benchmark ['bentʃmaːk] n repère m, (point m de) référence f

bend [bend] **1** n **(a)** (of road) virage m, tournant m; (of river) méandre m; (of pipe) coude m; Fam **around the b.** dingue **(b)** **the bends** (decompression sickness) la maladie des caissons

2 vt (pt & pp **bent** [bent]) (leg, arm, wire) plier; (head) baisser;

(light) réfracter; **do not b.** *(on envelope)* ne pas plier; **on bended knee** à genoux; **to b. the rules** faire une entorse au règlement

3 *vi (of road)* tourner; *(of river)* faire un coude; *(of branch)* plier
▸**bend down** *vi* se pencher
▸**bend over** *vi* se pencher; *Fig* **to b. over backward to do sth** se décarcasser pour faire qch

bender ['bendə(r)] *n Fam* beuverie *f*; **to go on a b.** prendre une cuite

beneath [bɪ'niːθ] **1** *prep* **(a)** *(physically)* sous **(b)** *(unworthy of)* **to marry b. one** faire une mésalliance; **she thinks it's b. her to work** elle pense que travailler est indigne d'elle; **b. contempt** parfaitement méprisable

2 *adv* dessous, au-dessous; **from b.** de dessous

Benedictine [benɪ'dɪktɪn] *adj Rel* bénédictin(e)
benediction [benɪ'dɪkʃən] *n Rel* bénédiction *f*
benefactor ['benɪfæktə(r)] *n* bienfaiteur *m*
benefactress ['benɪfæktrɪs] *n* bienfaitrice *f*
beneficent [bɪ'nefɪsənt] *adj (system)* bienfaisant(e); *(person)* bon (bonne)
beneficial [benɪ'fɪʃəl] *adj* bénéfique (**to** pour)
beneficiary [benɪ'fɪʃərɪ] *(pl* **beneficiaries)** *n* bénéficiaire *mf*
benefit ['benɪfɪt] **1** *n* **(a)** *(advantage)* profit *m*; **to have the b. of sth** pouvoir profiter de qch; **for sb's b., for the b. of sb** à l'intention de qn; **that remark was for my b.** cette remarque m'était destinée; **to give sb the b. of the doubt** accorder à qn le bénéfice du doute **(b)** *(charity event)* spectacle *m* de bienfaisance; **b. match** match *m* de bienfaisance **(c)** *(state payment)* allocation *f*; **to receive benefits** toucher une aide de l'État; **social security benefits** prestations *fpl* sociales

2 *vt (person, country)* profiter à; *(trade)* favoriser

3 *vi* **to b. from sth** tirer profit de qch; **you'll b. from a vacation** ça te fera du bien d'aller en vacances; **who stands to b. most?** à qui cela profitera-t-il le plus?

Benelux ['benɪlʌks] *n* Benelux *m*; **the B. countries** les pays du Benelux

benevolence [bɪ'nevələns] *n* bienveillance *f*
benevolent [bɪ'nevələnt] *adj* bienveillant(e); **b. society** association *f* de bienfaisance

Bengal [ben'gɔːl] *n* le Bengale
Bengali [ben'gɔːlɪ] **1** *n* **(a)** *(person)* Bengali *mf* **(b)** *(language)* bengali *m*

2 *adj* bengali

benign [bɪ'naɪn] *adj (attitude)* bienveillant(e); *(climate)* doux (douce); *(tumor)* bénin(igne)
Benin [be'niːn] *n* le Bénin
bent [bent] **1** *n (taste)* penchant *m*, inclination *f*; *(aptitude)* dispositions *fpl*; **to have a musical b.** avoir des dispositions pour la musique

2 *adj* **(a)** *(curved)* tordu(e); *(out of shape)* plié(e); *(person, back)* voûté(e) **(b)** **to be b. on doing sth** *(determined)* être résolu(e) à faire qch; **to be b. on sth** vouloir à tout prix qch

3 *pt & pp of* **bend**

benzene ['benziːn] *n Chem* benzène *m*
benzine ['benziːn] *n Chem* benzine *f*
bequeath [bɪ'kwiːð] *vt Formal* léguer (**to** à)
bequest [bɪ'kwest] *n Formal* legs *m*
berate [bɪ'reɪt] *vt* réprimander
Berber ['bɜːbə(r)] **1** *n* Berbère *mf*

2 *adj* berbère

bereaved [bɪ'riːvd] **1** *npl* **the b.** la famille du défunt (de la défunte)

2 *adj* en deuil; **recently b.** qui vient de perdre un être cher

bereavement [bɪ'riːvmənt] *n* deuil *m*; **b. counseling** = aide psychologique aux personnes en deuil

bereft [bɪ'reft] *adj* **to be b. of sth** être privé(e) de qch; **to feel b.** se sentir totalement seul(e)

beret ['bereɪ] *n* béret *m*
bergamot ['bɜːgəmɒt] *n* bergamote *f*
Berlin [bɜː'lɪn] *n* Berlin; **the B. Wall** le mur de Berlin
Berliner [bɜː'lɪnə(r)] *n* Berlinois(e) *m,f*
Bermuda [bə'mjuːdə] *n* les Bermudes *fpl*; **B. shorts** bermuda *m*
Bern(e) [bɜːn] *n* Berne
berry ['berɪ] *(pl* **berries)** *n* baie *f*
berserk [bə'zɜːk] *adj Fam* **to go b.** devenir fou furieux (folle furieuse)
berth [bɜːθ] **1** *n* **(a)** *(on train, ship)* couchette *f* **(b)** *(in harbor)* poste *m* à quai; *Fig* **to give sb a wide b.** éviter qn

2 *vt (boat)* amarrer à quai

3 *vi (of boat)* aborder *ou* se ranger à quai

beseech [bɪ'siːtʃ] *(pt & pp* **besought** [bɪ'sɔːt]) *vt Lit* supplier
beseeching [bɪ'siːtʃɪŋ] *adj* suppliant(e)
beset [bɪ'set] *(pt & pp* **beset)** *vt* assaillir; **to be beset by doubts** être assailli(e) par le doute; **to be beset with dangers/difficulties** être en proie à toutes sortes de dangers/difficultés
beside [bɪ'saɪd] *prep* **(a)** *(next to)* à côté de; *(sea, lake)* au bord de; **that's b. the point** cela n'a rien à voir; **to be b. oneself with joy/anger** être fou (folle) de joie/de colère **(b)** *(compared to)* à côté de, par rapport à
besides [bɪ'saɪdz] **1** *prep* à part; **other people b. ourselves** d'autres gens que nous; **what else can you do b. type?** à part taper, que savez-vous faire?; **b. being an excellent singer, she also plays the violin** non seulement elle chante très bien, mais en plus elle joue du violon; **b. which she was unwell** sans compter qu'elle ne se sentait pas bien

2 *adv* en plus; **many more b.** bien d'autres encore

besiege [bɪ'siːdʒ] *vt (castle, town)* assiéger; *Fig* **to b. sb with complaints/requests** assaillir qn de plaintes/demandes
besmirch [bɪ'smɜːtʃ] *vt Lit* souiller
besotted [bɪ'sɒtɪd] *adj* **to be b. with** *(person, car)* s'être entiché(e) de; *(idea)* être obsédé(e) par
besought [bɪ'sɔːt] *pt & pp of* **beseech**
bespatter [bɪ'spætə(r)] *vt* éclabousser (**with** de)
bespectacled [bɪ'spektəkəld] *adj* qui porte des lunettes, à lunettes
bespoke [bɪ'spəʊk], **bespoken** [bɪ'spəʊkən] *adj* (fait(e)) sur mesure; **b. tailor** tailleur *m* à façon
best [best] *(superlative of* **good, well)** **1** *n* **the b.** *(the best thing)* ce qu'il y a de mieux; **that's the b. I could find** c'est ce que j'ai trouvé de mieux; **at b.** au mieux; **the b. of it is...** le plus beau, c'est...; **at the b. of times** en temps normal; **to do one's b.** faire de son mieux (**to** pour); **to look one's b.** être à son avantage; **to be at one's b.** être au mieux de sa forme; **to bring out the b. in sb** révéler les qualités de qn; **to get the b. of the bargain** faire une bonne affaire; **to get the b. out of sth** tirer le meilleur parti de qch; **to make the b. of sth** s'accommoder de qch; **we are the b. of friends** nous sommes les meilleurs amis du monde; **to be in the b. of health** se porter à merveille; **to the b. of my knowledge** autant que je sache; **to the b. of one's ability** de son mieux; **he can sing with the b. of them** il chante aussi bien que n'importe qui; **to hope for the b.** avoir espoir; **to have** *or* **to get the b. of both worlds** gagner sur les deux tableaux; *Fam* **all the b.!** *(wishing somebody luck)* bonne chance!; *(at end of letter)* amitiés

2 *adj* meilleur(e); **my b. dress** ma plus belle robe; **she is b. at French** *(of group of people)* c'est la meilleure en français; **to put one's b. foot forward** partir du bon pied; **the b. part of a year** pratiquement un an; **I'm acting in your b. interests** j'agis au mieux de vos intérêts; **it is b. to...** le mieux, c'est de...; **the b. case scenario** le scénario le plus optimiste; **b. man** *(at wedding)* garçon *m* d'honneur; **may the b. man win** *(in contest)* que le meilleur gagne

3 *adv* le mieux; **as b. I could** du mieux que j'ai pu, de mon mieux; **you know b.** c'est vous qui êtes le mieux placé pour savoir; **do as you think b.** fais comme bon te semblera; **the b. dressed man** l'homme le mieux habillé; **she came off b.** *(in argument)* elle a eu le dessus

4 *vt (in contest, argument)* l'emporter sur

bestial ['bestɪəl] *adj* bestial(e)

bestiality [bestɪ'ælɪtɪ] *n* bestialité *f*

bestow [bɪ'stəʊ] *vt* accorder (**on** à)

bestseller [best'selə(r)] *n* best-seller *m*

bestselling [best'selɪŋ] *adj (book, author)* à succès

bet [bet] **1** *n* pari *m*; **to make** *or* **to place a b.** parier; *Fig* **my b. is that he'll come** je parie qu'il viendra; *Fig* **your best b. would be to…** ce que tu as de mieux à faire, c'est de…; *Fig* **it's a safe b.** il y a gros à parier

2 *vt (pt & pp* **bet** *or* **betted)** *also Fig* parier; *Fam Fig* **I b. you she'll win** je te parie qu'elle va gagner; *Fam Fig* **b. you I will!** chiche (que je le fais)!; **I'll b. you $10** je te parie 10 dollars

3 *vi* parier (**on** sur); **to b. on a horse** miser sur un cheval; *Fig* **I wouldn't b. on it!** je n'y compterais pas trop!; *Fam* **you b.!** et comment!; *Fam* **John says he's sorry – I b. (he does)!** John dit qu'il regrette – tu parles!

betel ['bi:təl] *n* bétel *m*; **b. nut** noix *f* d'arec

Bethlehem ['beθlɪhem] *n* Bethléem

betide [bɪ'taɪd] *vt Lit* **woe b. him/you!** malheur à lui/à toi!

betray [bɪ'treɪ] *vt also Fig* trahir; **to b. sb to the enemy** livrer qn à l'ennemi

betrayal [bɪ'treɪəl] *n* (**a**) *(of person, country)* trahison *f*; **b. of trust** abus *m* de confiance (**b**) *(of emotion)* indice *m*

betrothal [bɪ'trəʊðəl] *n Lit* fiançailles *fpl*

betrothed [bɪ'trəʊðd] *n & adj Lit* fiancé(e) *m,f*

better ['betə(r)] *(comparative of* **good, well)** **1** *n* **I expected b. of you** j'attendais mieux de ta part; **you should respect your (elders and) betters** il faut respecter ses aînés; **to change for the b.** *(of person)* changer en bien; *(of situation)* s'améliorer; **to get the b. of sb** avoir le dessus sur qn; **her shyness got the b. of her** sa timidité a été trop forte; **the sooner/faster the b.** le plus tôt/vite possible sera le mieux

2 *adj* meilleur(e); **to be b.** *(after sickness)* aller mieux; **to get b.** *(of person, wound)* aller mieux; *(of situation, weather)* s'arranger; **he's b. at math/running than his brother** il est meilleur en maths/à la course que son frère; **it would be b. for you to go** il vaudrait mieux que vous y alliez; **that's b.!** voilà qui est mieux!; **b. luck next time!** tu feras mieux la prochaine fois!; **the b. part of a week** pratiquement une semaine

3 *adv* mieux; **to look b.** *(of sick person)* avoir meilleure mine; **b. and b.** de mieux en mieux; **so much the b., all the b.** d'autant mieux; **for b. or for worse** pour le meilleur et pour le pire; **you had b. not stay** tu ferais mieux de ne pas rester; **to think b. of it** se raviser; **to be b. off** *(financially)* être plus à l'aise; *(in situation)* être mieux

4 *vt (improve)* améliorer; *(surpass)* faire mieux que; **to b. one-self** améliorer sa situation

betterment ['betəmənt] *n* amélioration *f*; *(of mankind)* progrès *m*

betting ['betɪŋ] *n (bets)* paris *mpl*; *Fam Fig* **the b. is that…** il y a fort à parier que…

between [bɪ'twi:n] **1** *prep* entre; **b. New York and Philadelphia** entre New York et Philadelphie; **(in) b. now and Monday** d'ici lundi; **we bought it b. us** nous l'avons acheté à nous deux/trois/*etc.*; **this is strictly b. you and me** que cela reste entre nous

2 *adv* **(in) b.** au milieu

bevel ['bevəl] **1** *n* biseau *m*

2 *vt* biseauter

beverage ['bevərɪdʒ] *n* boisson *f*

bevy ['bevɪ] *(pl* **bevies)** *n (group) (of people)* bande *f*; *(of birds)* volée *f*

bewail [bɪ'weɪl] *vt (loss)* pleurer; *(one's fate)* se lamenter sur

beware [bɪ'weə(r)] *vi* se méfier (**of** de); **b.!** attention!; **b. of the dog** *(sign)* chien méchant

bewilder [bɪ'wɪldə(r)] *vt* dérouter, laisser perplexe

bewildered [bɪ'wɪldəd] *adj* dérouté(e), perplexe

bewildering [bɪ'wɪldərɪŋ] *adj* déroutant(e)

bewilderment [bɪ'wɪldəmənt] *n* perplexité *f*; **to his b.** à son grand étonnement

bewitch [bɪ'wɪtʃ] *vt* ensorceler

bewitching [bɪ'wɪtʃɪŋ] *adj (smile, beauty)* enchanteur(eresse)

beyond [bɪ'jɒnd] **1** *prep* (**a**) *(in space, time)* au-delà de; **the house is b. the church** la maison est après l'église (**b**) *(surpassing)* **to live b. one's means** vivre au-dessus de ses moyens; **it's b. me (how they can do it)** ça me dépasse (qu'ils puissent faire ça); **due to circumstances b. our control** en raison de circonstances indépendantes de notre volonté; **it's b. my power** ça n'est pas en mon pouvoir; **I'm b. caring** ça m'est complètement égal; **it's b. doubt** cela ne fait aucun doute; **it's b. question** c'est incontestable; **it's b. a joke** ce n'est plus drôle; **b. belief** incroyable; **b. reach** hors de portée; **b. repair** irréparable (**c**) *(except)* à part

2 *adv* au-delà

3 *n* **the b.** l'au-delà *m*

Bhutan [bu:'tɑːn] *n* le Bhoutan

bias ['baɪəs] **1** *n* (**a**) *(inclination)* préjugé *m*, parti *m* pris (**against/towards** contre/en faveur de) (**b**) *(in sewing)* biais *m*

2 *vt (pt & pp* **bias(s)ed)** influencer (**against/towards** contre/en faveur de)

biased, biassed ['baɪəst] *adj (article, account)* partial(e); *(person)* de parti pris; *(opinion)* préconçu(e); **to be b. in sb's favor** avoir un préjugé en faveur de qn

bib [bɪb] *n (for baby)* bavoir *m*, bavette *f*; *(of apron, overalls)* bavette

bible ['baɪbəl] *n also Fig* bible *f*; **the B.** la Bible; **the B. Belt** = ensemble des États du sud des États-Unis où le fondamentalisme chrétien est très répandu; *Fam* **b. thumper** grenouille *f* de bénitier

biblical ['bɪblɪkəl] *adj* biblique; *Fam Hum* **to know sb in the b. sense** connaître qn au sens biblique du terme

bibliography [bɪblɪ'ɒgrəfɪ] *(pl* **bibliographies)** *n* bibliographie *f*

bibliophile ['bɪblɪəfaɪl] *n* bibliophile *mf*

bicameral [baɪ'kæmərəl] *adj Pol* bicaméral(e)

bicarbonate [baɪ'kɑːbəneɪt] *n* bicarbonate *m*; **b. of soda** bicarbonate de soude

bicentenary [baɪsen'tiːnərɪ], **bicentennial** [baɪsen'tenɪəl] **1** *n* bicentenaire *m*

2 *adj* bicentenaire

biceps ['baɪseps] *(pl* **biceps)** *n Anat* biceps *m*

bicker ['bɪkə(r)] *vi* se chamailler

bickering ['bɪkərɪŋ] *n* chamailleries *fpl*

bicycle ['baɪsɪkəl] *n* bicyclette *f*, vélo *m*; **to ride a b.** faire de la bicyclette *ou* du vélo; **b. clip** pince *f* à vélo; **b. kick** *(in soccer)* retourné *m* bicyclette; **b. shorts** cuissard *m*

bid[1] [bɪd] **1** *n* (**a**) *(offer)* offre *f*; *(at auction)* enchère *f*; **to make a b. (for sth)** faire une offre (pour qch); *(at auction)* faire une enchère (sur qch) (**b**) *(attempt)* tentative *f* (**for sth/to do sth** de qch/pour faire qch); **a rescue/suicide b.** une tentative de sauvetage/de suicide; **to make a b. for power** *(legally)* viser le pouvoir; *(illegally)* faire une tentative de coup d'État

2 *vt (pt & pp* **bid)** *(offer)* offrir; *(at auction)* faire une enchère de; **what am I bid for this table?** que m'offrez-vous pour cette table?

3 *vi* **to b. for sth** faire une offre pour qch; *(at auction)* faire une enchère sur qch

bid² [bɪd] (*pt* **bade** [bæd, beɪd] *or* **bid**, *pp* **bidden** [bɪdən] *or* **bid**) *vt Lit* **to b. sb welcome** souhaiter la bienvenue à qn; **to b. sb goodbye** faire ses adieux à qn

bidder ['bɪdə(r)] *n (at auction)* enchérisseur(euse) *m,f*; **the highest b.** le plus offrant

bidding¹ ['bɪdɪŋ] *n (at auction)* enchères *fpl*

bidding² ['bɪdɪŋ] *n Lit (command)* **at sb's b.** sur l'ordre de qn

bide [baɪd] *vt* **to b. one's time** attendre le bon moment

bidet ['biːdeɪ] *n* bidet *m*

biennial [baɪ'enɪəl] **1** *n (plant)* plante *f* bisannuelle
    2 *adj* bisannuel(elle)

bier [bɪə(r)] *n* brancards *mpl*

biff [bɪf] *Fam* **1** *n* gnon *m*
    2 *vt* flanquer un gnon à

bifocal [baɪ'fəʊkəl] **1** *n* **bifocals** lunettes *fpl* à double foyer
    2 *adj* à double foyer

big [bɪg] **1** *adj* **(a)** *(tall, large)* grand(e); *(fat)* gros (grosse); *(drop, increase)* fort(e); *(fashionable)* à la mode; **to get big(ger)** *(taller)* grandir; *(fatter)* grossir; **my b. brother** mon grand frère; **a b. problem** un gros problème; **to be a b. eater** être un gros mangeur (une grosse mangeuse); **a b. hand for our guest!** on applaudit bien fort notre invité!; **the B. Apple** = surnom de New York; **b. business** les milieux d'affaires; **b. game** *(in hunting)* gros gibier *m*; **b. spender** panier *m* percé; **b. toe** gros orteil *m*; **b. top** *(of circus)* chapiteau *m*
    (b) *(idioms)* **it's her b. day tomorrow** demain c'est son grand jour; **to have b. ideas** avoir de grands projets; **don't get any b. ideas!** ne t'excite pas trop!; *Fam* **what's the b. idea?** c'est quoi cette histoire?; **to earn b. money** gagner beaucoup d'argent; **to make it b.** réussir; **to be into sth in a b. way** adorer qch; *Ironic* **that's b. of you!** tu es trop bon!; **to be too b. for one's boots** ne plus se sentir; **to be b. on sth** tenir à qch; **to have a b. mouth** *(be indiscreet)* parler trop; *Fam* **b. deal!** la belle affaire!; *Fam* **b. gun** gros bonnet *m*; *Fig* **a b. name** un grand nom; *Fam* **b. shot** gros bonnet *m*; **the b. picture** une vue d'ensemble; **the b. time** le succès
    2 *adv* **to talk b.** faire l'important; **to think b.** voir grand

bigamist ['bɪgəmɪst] *n* bigame *mf*

bigamous ['bɪgəməs] *adj* bigame

bigamy ['bɪgəmɪ] *n* bigamie *f*

biggie, biggy ['bɪgɪ] *(pl* **biggies***) n Fam* **it's going to be a b.** *(storm, new movie)* ça va faire mal

bighead ['bɪghed] *n Fam* crâneur(euse) *m,f*

bigheaded [bɪg'hedɪd] *adj* crâneur(euse); **to get b.** commencer à avoir la grosse tête

bighearted [bɪg'hɑːtɪd] *adj* **to be b.** avoir le cœur sur la main

bigot ['bɪgət] *n* sectaire *mf*

bigoted ['bɪgətɪd] *adj* sectaire (**against** à l'égard de)

bigotry ['bɪgətrɪ] *n* sectarisme *m*

bigwig ['bɪgwɪg] *n Fam* gros bonnet *m*

bike [baɪk] **1** *n* vélo *m*; *(motorcycle)* moto *f*
    2 *vi (bicycle)* faire du vélo; *(motorcycle)* faire de la moto; **we biked there** nous y sommes allés à *ou* en vélo/moto

biker ['baɪkə(r)] *n Fam (motorcyclist)* motard(e) *m,f*; *(cyclist)* cycliste *mf*

bikini [bɪ'kiːnɪ] *n* bikini® *m*; **to have a b. wax** se faire faire une épilation maillot; **b. bottom** bas *m* de maillot; **b. top** haut *m* de maillot

bilateral [baɪ'lætərəl] *adj* bilatéral(e)

bilberry ['bɪlbərɪ] *(pl* **bilberries***) n* myrtille *f*

bile [baɪl] *n* bile *f*; *Fig (bitterness)* hargne *f*

bilge [bɪldʒ] *n Fam (nonsense)* bêtises *fpl*

bilingual [baɪ'lɪŋgwəl] *adj* bilingue

bilious ['bɪlɪəs] *adj* **(a)** *(nauseous)* nauséeux(euse); **b. attack** crise *f* de foie; **b. yellow** jaunâtre **(b)** *(bad-tempered)* hargneux(euse)

bill¹ [bɪl] *n (of bird)* bec *m*
    2 *vi Fam* **to b. and coo** roucouler

bill² [bɪl] *n* **(a)** *(for goods, services)* facture *f*; *(in hotel)* note *f*; *(in restaurant)* addition *f*; *Fin* **b. of exchange** lettre *f* de change **(b)** *(banknote)* billet *m* **(c)** *(notice)* affiche *f*; **(stick) no bills** *(sign)* défense d'afficher; *Theat* **to head** *or* **to top the b.** être en tête d'affiche **(d)** *(list)* **b. of fare** menu *m*; **to give sb a clean b. of health** trouver qn en parfaite santé; *Fam* **to fit the b.** faire l'affaire **(e)** *Pol (proposed law)* projet *m* de loi; **B. of Rights** = les dix premiers amendements à la Constitution américaine
    2 *vt* **(a)** *(give invoice to)* envoyer la facture à **(b)** *(publicize)* annoncer

billboard ['bɪlbɔːd] *n* panneau *m* d'affichage

billet ['bɪlɪt] *Mil* **1** *n* cantonnement *m*
    2 *vt* cantonner

billfold ['bɪlfəʊld] *n* portefeuille *m*

billiard ['bɪljəd] *n* **billiards** billard *m*; **b. ball/table** boule *f*/table *f* de billard

billion ['bɪljən] *n* milliard *m*; *Old-fashioned* billion *m*; *Fam* **I've got billions of things to do!** j'ai des tonnes de choses à faire!

billionaire [bɪljə'neə(r)] *n* milliardaire *mf*

billow ['bɪləʊ] **1** *n (of smoke)* nuage *m*
    2 *vi* ondoyer

billowy ['bɪləʊɪ] *adj* ondoyant(e); *(sea)* houleux(euse)

billposter ['bɪlpəʊstə] *n* **billposters will be prosecuted** *(sign)* ≃ défense d'afficher

billygoat ['bɪlɪgəʊt] *n* bouc *m*

bimbo ['bɪmbəʊ] *(pl* **bimbos***) n Fam Pej* minette *f*

bin [bɪn] *n (for coal, grain)* coffre *m*

binary ['baɪnərɪ] *adj Math & Comput* binaire; **b. code/number** code *m*/nombre *m* binaire

bind [baɪnd] **1** *n* **to be in a b.** avoir un embêtement
    2 *vt (pt & pp* **bound** [baʊnd]*)* **(a)** *(tie)* attacher; **to be bound hand and foot** être pieds et poings liés; **they are bound together by ties of friendship** ils sont unis par les liens de l'amitié **(b)** *(bandage)* bander **(c)** *(book)* relier **(d)** *(cause to stick)* lier **(e)** *(oblige)* **to be bound by sth** être lié(e) par qch; **she bound me to secrecy** elle m'a fait jurer de garder le secret; **you are bound to report any change in your income** vous êtes tenu de signaler tout changement dans vos revenus

▸**bind over** *vt sep Law* sommer

▸**bind up** *vt sep* **(a)** *(cut, wound)* bander **(b)** **to be bound up with sth** *(involved)* être lié(e) à qch

binder ['baɪndə(r)] *n* **(a)** *(for papers)* classeur *m* **(b)** *(bookbinder)* relieur(euse) *m,f* **(c)** *(farm machinery)* lieuse *f*

binding ['baɪndɪŋ] **1** *n* reliure *f*
    2 *adj (contract, promise)* qui engage *ou* lie

binge [bɪndʒ] *Fam* **1** *n (drinking spree)* beuverie *f*; **to go on a b.** prendre une cuite; **to go on a shopping b.** aller claquer du fric dans les magasins; **to have a chocolate b.** faire une orgie de chocolat
    2 *vi* **to b. on sth** *(drink)* s'enfiler des litres de qch; *(food)* s'empiffrer de qch

bingo ['bɪŋgəʊ] **1** *n* ≃ loto *m*; **b. hall** = salle où l'on joue au "bingo"
    2 *exclam* et voilà!

binoculars [bɪ'nɒkjʊləz] *npl* jumelles *fpl*

biochemical [baɪəʊ'kemɪkəl] *adj* biochimique

biochemist [baɪəʊ'kemɪst] *n* biochimiste *mf*

biochemistry [baɪəʊ'kemɪstrɪ] *n* biochimie *f*

biodegradable [baɪəʊdɪ'greɪdəbəl] *adj* biodégradable

biodiversity [baɪəʊdaɪ'vɜːsɪtɪ] *n* biodiversité *f*

biographer [baɪ'ɒgrəfə(r)] *n* biographe *mf*

biographic [baɪə'græfɪk], **biographical** [baɪə'græfɪkəl] *adj* biographique

biography [baɪ'ɒgrəfɪ] *(pl* **biographies***) n* biographie *f*

biological [baɪə'lɒdʒɪkəl] *adj* biologique; **b. clock** horloge *f* interne *ou* biologique; **my b. clock is ticking away** *(of woman)* mon temps est compté si je veux avoir des enfants; **b. warfare** guerre *f* bactériologique; **b. weapon** arme *f* biologique

biologist [baɪ'ɒlədʒɪst] *n* biologiste *mf*

biology [baɪ'ɒlədʒɪ] *n* biologie *f*

biometric [baɪə'metrɪk] *adj* biométrique; **b. identifier** identifiant *m* biométrique; **b. passport** passeport *m* biométrique

biopsy ['baɪɒpsɪ] *(pl* **biopsies***) n Med* biopsie *f*

biorhythm ['baɪəʊrɪðəm] *n* rythme *m* biologique

biosphere ['baɪəsfɪə(r)] *n* biosphère *f*

biotechnology [baɪəʊtek'nɒlədʒɪ] *n* biotechnologie *f*

bioterrorism [baɪəʊ'terərɪzəm] *n* bioterrorisme *m*

bioterrorist [baɪəʊ'terərɪst] *n* bioterroriste *mf*

bipartisan [baɪ'pɑːtɪzæn] *adj Pol* bipartite

biped ['baɪped] *n* bipède *m*

biplane ['baɪpleɪn] *n* biplan *m*

birch [bɜːtʃ] **1** *n* bouleau *m*; **to give sb the b.** fouetter qn **2** *vt (beat)* fouetter

bird [bɜːd] *n* (**a**) *(in general)* oiseau *m*; *(poultry)* volaille *f*; **b. of paradise** oiseau de paradis; **b. of prey** oiseau de proie, rapace *m*; **b. sanctuary** réserve *f* ornithologique; **b. table** mangeoire *f* pour oiseaux (**b**) *(idioms) Fam* **a little b. told me** c'est mon petit doigt qui me l'a dit; **the b. has flown** l'oiseau s'est envolé; *Prov* **a b. in the hand is worth two in the bush** un tiens vaut mieux que deux tu l'auras; *Prov* **birds of a feather flock together** qui se ressemble s'assemble; **to kill two birds with one stone** faire d'une pierre deux coups; *Euph* **it's time you told him about the birds and the bees** il serait temps de lui expliquer que les bébés ne naissent pas dans les choux; *Fam* **to give** *or* **to flip sb the b.** faire un doigt d'honneur à qn; **for the birds** *(worthless)* nul (nulle)

birdbath ['bɜːdbɑːθ] *n* vasque *f* pour les oiseaux

bird-brained ['bɜːdbreɪnd] *adj Fam (idea)* extravagant(e); **to be b.** *(of person)* avoir une cervelle d'oiseau

birdcage ['bɜːdkeɪdʒ] *n* cage *f* à oiseaux; *(in zoo)* volière *f*

birder ['bɜːdə(r)] *n (birdwatcher)* ornithologue *mf* amateur

birdhouse ['bɜːdhaʊs] *n (in yard)* abri *m* pour les oiseaux; *(in zoo)* volière *f*

birdie ['bɜːdɪ] *n* (**a**) *Fam (bird)* petit oiseau *m*; *Fig* **watch the b.!** *(when taking photo)* attention, le petit oiseau va sortir! (**b**) *(in golf)* birdie *m*

birdseed ['bɜːdsiːd] *n* graines *fpl* pour oiseaux

bird's-eye view ['bɜːdzaɪ'vjuː] *n* vue *f* d'ensemble

birdwatcher ['bɜːdwɒtʃə(r)] *n* ornithologue *mf* amateur

birdwatching ['bɜːdwɒtʃɪŋ] *n* **to go b.** aller observer les oiseaux

birth [bɜːθ] *n* naissance *f*; **to give b. (to)** accoucher (de); **at b.** à la naissance; **by b.** de naissance; **from b.** *(blind, deaf)* de naissance; **b. certificate** acte *m* de naissance; **b. control** contrôle *m* des naissances; *Fig* **b. pangs** accouchement *m* douloureux; **b. rate** taux *m* de natalité

birthday ['bɜːθdeɪ] *n* anniversaire *m*; *Fam* **to be in one's b. suit** *(of man)* être en costume d'Adam; *(of woman)* être en costume d'Ève; **b. card/present** carte *f*/cadeau *m* d'anniversaire

birthmark ['bɜːθmɑːk] *n* tache *f* de naissance, envie *f*

birthplace ['bɜːθpleɪs] *n* lieu *m* de naissance

birthright ['bɜːθraɪt] *n* droit *m* acquis à la naissance; *Fig* droit élémentaire

Biscay ['bɪskeɪ] *n see* **bay²**

biscuit ['bɪskɪt] *n* = petit gâteau que l'on mange avec un plat salé

bisect [baɪ'sekt] *vt* couper en deux

bisexual [baɪ'seksjʊəl] *n & adj* bisexuel(elle) *m,f*

bishop ['bɪʃəp] *n* évêque *m*; *(in chess)* fou *m*

bishopric ['bɪʃəprɪk] *n* évêché *m*

bison ['baɪsən] *n* bison *m*

bistro ['biːstrəʊ] *(pl* **bistros***) n* petit restaurant *m*

bit¹ [bɪt] *n* (**a**) *(in horseriding)* mors *m*; *Fig* **to get the b. between one's teeth** prendre le mors aux dents (**b**) *(for drill)* mèche *f*

bit² [bɪt] *n* (**a**) *(piece)* bout *m*; *(of movie, book)* passage *m*; **a b. of news** une nouvelle; **to take sth to bits** démonter qch; **to tear sth to bits** déchirer qch en petits morceaux; **to smash sth to bits** briser qch en mille morceaux; **he has eaten every b.** il a mangé jusqu'à la dernière miette; **to do one's b.** participer; **bits and pieces** *(personal belongings)* affaires *fpl*; *(small items)* trucs *mpl*

(**b**) **a b. (of)** *(expressing degree)* un peu (de); **a b. late/heavy/tired** un peu en retard/lourd(e)/fatigué(e); **we had a b. of difficulty in finding him** nous avons eu quelque difficulté à le trouver; **he's a b. of a know-it-all** il a un côté je-sais-tout; **b. by b.** petit à petit; **not a b. of it!** pas du tout!; **wait a b.!** attends une minute!; **it takes a b. of getting used to** il faut un moment pour s'y habituer; **a good b. older** nettement plus âgé(e); **a little b. (of)** un tout petit peu (de); **every b. as good/interesting as** tout aussi bon (bonne)/intéressant(e) que; *Fam* **that's a b. much!** ça c'est un peu fort!; **b. part** *(in play, movie)* petit rôle *m*

(**c**) *Comput* bit *m*

(**d**) *Fam (coin)* pièce *f*; **two bits** vingt-cinq cents *mpl*

bit³ [bɪt] *pt of* **bite**

bitch [bɪtʃ] **1** *n* (**a**) *(female dog)* chienne *f* (**b**) *very Fam Pej (woman)* garce *f*; **I've had a b. of a day!** j'ai eu une putain de journée!; **life's a b.!** chienne de vie! **2** *vi Fam (complain)* râler, rouspéter (**about** après)

bitchy ['bɪtʃɪ] *adj Fam* vache

bite [baɪt] **1** *n* (**a**) *(of person)* coup *m* de dent; *(of dog)* morsure *f*; *(of insect)* piqûre *f*; *(of snake)* morsure, piqûre (**b**) *(mouthful)* bouchée *f*; **to take a b. out of sth** mordre dans qch; **I haven't had a b. to eat all day** je n'ai rien mangé de la journée (**c**) *Fig (of speech, article)* mordant *m*; *(of sauce)* piquant *m* **2** *vt (pt* **bit** [bɪt], *pp* **bitten** ['bɪtən]) (**a**) *(of person, dog)* mordre; *(of insect)* piquer; *(of snake)* mordre, piquer; **the dog bit him in the leg** le chien l'a mordu à la jambe; **to b. one's nails** se ronger les ongles (**b**) *(idioms)* **to b. one's tongue** *(stay silent)* se mordre la langue; *Fam* **to b. the bullet** faire contre mauvaise fortune bon cœur; *Fam* **to b. the dust** *(of scheme, plan)* tomber à l'eau; **to b. the hand that feeds you** cracher dans la soupe; *Prov* **once bitten twice shy** chat échaudé craint l'eau froide **3** *vi* (**a**) *(of person, dog)* mordre; *(of insect)* piquer; *(of snake)* mordre, piquer; **to b. into sth** mordre dans qch (**b**) *Fig (be felt)* se faire sentir

▶**bite off** *vt sep* couper d'un coup de dent; *Fig* **to b. off more than one can chew** avoir les yeux plus gros que le ventre; *Fam Fig* **to b. sb's head off** rembarrer qn

biting ['baɪtɪŋ] *adj (wind, satire)* cinglant(e)

bitmap ['bɪtmæp] *n Comput* bitmap *m*

bitmapped ['bɪtmæpt] *adj Comput* pixélisé(e)

bitten ['bɪtən] *pp of* **bite**

bitter ['bɪtə(r)] *adj* (**a**) *(taste)* amer(ère); *Fig* **it was a b. pill to swallow** la pilule était amère, c'était dur à avaler (**b**) *(harsh) (wind, cold)* glacial(e); *(weather)* rigoureux(euse); *(opposition, resistance)* âpre; *(struggle)* implacable; *(tears, disappointment)* amer(ère); **to go on to the b. end** aller jusqu'au bout (**c**) *(resentful)* amer(ère); *(words)* acerbe; **to feel** *or* **to be b. about sth** éprouver de l'amertume à propos de qch

bitterly ['bɪtəlɪ] *adv* (**a**) *(extremely)* extrêmement; *(opposed)* résolument, farouchement; **to b. regret doing sth** regretter amèrement d'avoir fait qch; **it was b. cold** il faisait un froid de canard (**b**) *(resentfully)* avec amertume

bitterness ['bɪtənɪs] *n* amertume *f*

bittersweet ['bɪtəswiːt] *adj also Fig* doux-amer (douce-amère); **b. chocolate** chocolat *m* noir

bitty ['bɪtɪ] *adj Fam (tiny)* tout(e) petit(e); **a little b. town** une toute petite ville

bitumen ['bɪtjʊmɪn] *n* bitume *m*

bivouac ['bɪvʊæk] **1** *n* bivouac *m*

2 *vi (pt & pp bivouacked)* bivouaquer

biweekly [baɪ'wiːklɪ] **1** *adj (every two weeks)* bimensuel(elle); *(twice weekly)* bihebdomadaire

2 *adv (every two weeks)* deux fois par mois; *(twice weekly)* deux fois par semaine

bizarre [bɪ'zɑː(r)] *adj* bizarre

blab [blæb] *(pt & pp blabbed) Fam* **1** *vt* dire

2 *vi (chatter)* bavarder; *(betray secret)* vendre la mèche; **don't go blabbing to everybody** ne va pas le dire à tout le monde

black [blæk] **1** *n* **(a)** *(color)* noir *m*; **b. doesn't suit her** le noir ne lui va pas

(b) *(person)* Noir(e) *m,f*

(c) in the b. *(person)* solvable; *(account)* créditeur(trice)

(d) *(idioms)* **it says here in b. and white** c'est écrit noir sur blanc; **he sees everything in b. and white** avec lui, c'est ou tout l'un ou tout l'autre

2 *adj* **(a)** *(color)* noir(e); **a b. man** un Noir; **a b. woman** une Noire; **to be b. and blue** *(bruised)* être couvert(e) de bleus; **b. belt** *(in martial arts)* ceinture *f* noire; **b. box** *(flight recorder)* boîte *f* noire; **b. coffee** café *m* noir; **b. eye** œil *m* poché; *Astron* **b. hole** trou *m* noir; **b. humor** humour *m* noir; **b. ice** verglas *m*; **b. sheep** brebis *f* galeuse; **b. tie** *(bow tie)* = nœud papillon noir porté avec une tenue de soirée; *(on invitation)* tenue de soirée exigée

(b) *(evil, unfavorable)* noir(e); **to give sb a b. look** jeter à qn un regard noir; **the future is looking b.** l'avenir est sombre; **b. magic** magie *f* noire; **it was a b. mark against him** c'était un mauvais point pour lui

(c) *(unofficial)* **b. economy** économie *f* souterraine; **b. market** marché *m* noir

(d) *(in proper names)* **the B. Death** la peste noire; **the B. Forest** la Forêt-Noire; **B. Forest cake** forêt-noire *f*; **the B. Sea** la mer Noire

3 *vt (blacken)* noircir; **to b. one's face** se noircir le visage

▶**black out 1** *vt sep* **(a)** *(censor)* rayer *(d'un gros trait noir)* **(b)** *(city)* plonger dans l'obscurité **(c)** *(TV program)* interrompre

2 *vi (faint)* perdre connaissance, s'évanouir

black-and-white [blækən'waɪt] *adj (movie, photograph)* (en) noir et blanc *inv*; *(TV)* noir et blanc *inv*

blackball ['blækbɔːl] *vt* blackbouler

blackberry ['blækbərɪ] *(pl blackberries)* *n* mûre *f*

blackbird ['blækbɜːd] *n* merle *m* noir

blackboard ['blækbɔːd] *n* tableau *m* (noir)

blackcurrant ['blækkʌrənt] *n* cassis *m*

blacken ['blækən] *vt* noircir; *Fig* **to b. sb's character** calomnier qn

blackguard ['blægɑːd] *n Old-fashioned* fripouille *f*

blackhead ['blækhed] *n* point *m* noir

blackjack ['blækdʒæk] *n* **(a)** *(weapon)* nerf *m* de bœuf **(b)** *(card game)* black jack *m*, ≃ vingt-et-un *m*

blacklist ['blæklɪst] **1** *n* liste *f* noire

2 *vt* mettre sur la liste noire

blackmail ['blækmeɪl] **1** *n* chantage *m*; **emotional b.** chantage affectif

2 *vt* faire chanter

blackness ['blæknɪs] *n* noirceur *f*

blackout ['blækaʊt] *n* **(a)** *(during air raid)* black-out *m inv*; *Fig* **to impose a news b.** empêcher la divulgation d'une information **(b)** *(loss of consciousness)* évanouissement *m*

blacksmith ['blæksmɪθ] *n* forgeron *m*; *(who shoes horses)* maréchal-ferrant *m*

blacktop ['blæktɒp] *n (substance)* goudron *m*; *(surface)* route *f* goudronnée

bladder ['blædə(r)] *n* vessie *f*

blade [bleɪd] *n (of knife, sword)* lame *f*; *(of propeller, oar)* pale *f*; *(of grass)* brin *m*

blame [bleɪm] **1** *n* responsabilité *f*, faute *f*; **to place b. (for sth) on sb** faire porter à qn la responsabilité (de qch); **to take the b. for sth** endosser la responsabilité de qch

2 *vt* rendre responsable, faire porter la responsabilité à (**for** de); **to b. sb for doing sth** reprocher à qn d'avoir fait qch; **I am to b.** je suis fautif, c'est de ma faute; **the bad weather was to b.** c'était à cause du mauvais temps; **I b. myself for what happened** je m'en veux pour ce qui est arrivé; **I don't b. you for wanting to leave** je ne te reproche pas de vouloir partir; **she has nobody to b. but herself** elle n'a de reproche à faire qu'à elle-même

blameless ['bleɪmlɪs] *adj* irréprochable

blameworthy ['bleɪmwɜːðɪ] *adj (person)* coupable, blâmable; *(conduct)* répréhensible

blanch [blɑːntʃ] **1** *vt Culin* blanchir

2 *vi (go pale)* blêmir, pâlir

blancmange [blə'mɒnʒ] *n* blanc-manger *m*

bland [blænd] *adj (person, appearance)* terne; *(food)* insipide, fade; *(music)* sans intérêt; *(promise)* vain(e); **despite her b. assurances...** malgré ses protestations de politesse...

blandishments ['blændɪʃmənts] *npl* cajoleries *fpl*; **to resist sb's b.** ne pas se laisser amadouer par qn

blandly ['blændlɪ] *adv (speak, reply)* mielleusement

blank [blæŋk] **1** *n* **(a)** *(space)* blanc *m*; **fill in the blanks** remplissez les blancs *ou* les (espaces) vides; *Fig* **to draw a b.** faire chou blanc **(b)** *(rifle cartridge)* cartouche *f* à blanc; **to fire blanks** tirer à blanc

2 *adj (paper, screen)* blanc (blanche), vierge; *(face)* sans expression; **with a b. expression on his face** le visage sans expression; **to look b.** avoir l'air déconcerté *ou* ahuri; **my mind went b.** j'ai eu un trou; **b. cassette** cassette *f* vierge; **b. check** chèque *m* en blanc; *Fig* **to give sb a b. check** donner carte blanche à qn; **b. verse** vers *mpl* blancs

▶**blank out** *vt sep also Fig* effacer

blanket ['blæŋkɪt] **1** *n* couverture *f*; *Fig (of fog, cloud)* manteau *m*

2 *adj (general)* général(e), global(e); **the government imposed a b. ban on demonstrations** le gouvernement a interdit toutes les manifestations; **b. term** terme *m* général

blankly ['blæŋklɪ] *adv (without expression)* sans expression; *(without understanding)* l'air déconcerté; **she stared b. into space** elle avait le regard perdu dans le vide

blare ['bleə(r)] **1** *n* beuglements *mpl*

2 *vi (of TV, radio)* beugler

▶**blare out 1** *vt sep* beugler

2 *vi* beugler; **the music was blaring out** la musique était à fond

blarney ['blɑːnɪ] *n Fam* boniments *mpl*

blasé [blɑː'zeɪ] *adj* blasé(e); **she was very b. about the accident** l'accident ne lui avait fait ni chaud ni froid

blaspheme [blæs'fiːm] *vi* blasphémer

blasphemous ['blæsfəməs] *adj* blasphématoire

blasphemy ['blæsfəmɪ] *n* blasphème *m*

blast [blɑːst] **1** *n* **(a)** *(of wind)* coup *m*, rafale *f*; *(of heat)* bouffée *f*; *(of steam)* jet *m*; *(of whistle, horn)* coup *m*; **at full b.** *(radio, TV, heater)* à fond; **b. furnace** haut-fourneau *m* **(b)** *(explosion)* explosion *f*; *(shock wave)* souffle *m* d'une explosion; *Fam* **meeting her/hearing that song was a real b. from the past!** la rencontrer/cette chanson m'a ramené des années en arrière! **(c)** *Fam (good time)* **it was a b.** c'était génial; **we had a b.** on s'est super marrés

2 *vt* **(a)** *(hole, tunnel)* creuser *(en dynamitant)*; **the building**

had been blasted by a bomb le bâtiment avait été détruit par une bombe; *Fam* to b. sb's head off faire sauter la tête à qn (b) *Fam (criticize)* démolir (c) *Fam* b. (it)! zut alors!

▸**blast off** *vi (of space rocket)* décoller

blastoff ['blɑːstɒf] *n (of space rocket)* lancement *m*

blatant ['bleɪtənt] *adj* flagrant(e), manifeste; *(lie)* éhonté(e)

blatantly ['bleɪtəntlɪ] *adv* de façon flagrante; **b. obvious** tout à fait évident(e)

blather ['blæðə(r)] *vi Fam* parler à tort et à travers

blaze [bleɪz] **1** *n* (a) *(fire)* feu *m*; **many people died in the b.** beaucoup de gens ont péri dans les flammes (b) *(of color, light)* éclat *m*; **the movie was released in a b. of publicity** ils ont fait une publicité monstre pour la sortie du film; **to go out in a b. of glory** s'en aller plein(e) de gloire (c) *Fam* **what the blazes does he want?** mais qu'est-ce qu'il veut, bon sang?

  2 *vt Fig* **to b. a trail** ouvrir la voie

  3 *vi (of fire, sun)* flamboyer; *(of light)* être éclatant(e); **the house was blazing with lights** la maison était tout illuminée; **to b. with anger** *(of person)* fulminer; *(of eyes)* lancer des éclairs de colère

blazer ['bleɪzə(r)] *n* blazer *m*

blazing ['bleɪzɪŋ] *adj (burning)* en feu, enflammé(e); *Fig* **a b. argument** une violente dispute

bleach [bliːtʃ] **1** *n* (eau *f* de) Javel *f*

  2 *vt (clothes)* passer à l'eau de Javel *ou* à la Javel; *(hair)* décolorer

bleak [bliːk] *adj (landscape, weather)* morne, triste; *(outlook)* lugubre; *(prospect)* peu encourageant(e)

bleary ['blɪərɪ] *adj (eyes)* rouge

bleary-eyed [blɪərɪ'aɪd] *adj* **to be b.** *(from lack of sleep)* avoir de petits yeux; *(from hay fever, crying)* avoir les yeux rouges

bleat [bliːt] **1** *n (of sheep)* bêlement *m*

  2 *vi (of sheep)* bêler; *Fig (complain)* ronchonner (**about** à propos de)

bleed [bliːd] *(pt & pp* **bled** [bled]) **1** *vt Med* saigner; *(radiator)* purger; *Fig* **to b. sb dry** saigner qn à blanc

  2 *vi* saigner; **her nose is bleeding** elle saigne du nez; **to b. to death** saigner à mort

bleeding ['bliːdɪŋ] **1** *n* saignement *m*; **has the b. stopped?** est-ce que tu saignes/est-ce qu'il saigne/*etc.* toujours?

  2 *adj (wound)* qui saigne

bleep [bliːp] **1** *n* bip *m*

  2 *vi* faire bip

bleeper ['bliːpə(r)] *n (pager)* bip *m*

blemish ['blemɪʃ] **1** *n (mark)* marque *f*; *Fig* **it left a b. on her reputation** cela a entaché sa réputation

  2 *vt Fig (reputation)* entacher

blench [blentʃ] *vi* avoir un mouvement de recul

blend [blend] **1** *n* mélange *m*

  2 *vt* mélanger (**with** à *ou* avec)

  3 *vi* se mélanger, se mêler; **the colors b. together well** ces couleurs se marient bien *ou* vont bien ensemble

▸**blend in** *vi (with surroundings)* se fondre (**with** dans)

▸**blend into** *vt insep (surroundings)* se fondre dans; **to b. into the background** se fondre dans le décor

blender ['blendə(r)] *n* mixer *m*, mixeur *m*

bless [bles] *(pt & pp* **blessed** *or* **blest** [blest]) *vt* (a) *(say blessing for)* bénir; **God b. you!** que Dieu te bénisse!; **b. you!** *(when somebody sneezes)* à tes souhaits! (b) **to be blessed with sth** *(talent, beauty)* être doté(e) de qch; **they have been blessed with two fine children** ils ont deux beaux enfants

blessed ['blesɪd] *adj* (a) *(holy)* béni(e) (b) *Fam (for emphasis)* **the whole b. day** toute la sainte journée; **the whole b. lot** tout le bazar, tout le bataclan; **it's a b. nuisance having to...** quelle barbe d'avoir à...; **I can't see a b. thing!** je n'y vois absolument rien!

blessing ['blesɪŋ] *n* (a) *(religious)* bénédiction *f*; *Fig* **to give sb/sth one's b.** donner à qn/qch sa bénédiction (b) *(benefit,*

advantage) bienfait *m*; **it was a b. in disguise** finalement, ça a été une bonne chose; **it was a mixed b.** il y avait du bon et du mauvais; **to count one's blessings** s'estimer heureux de ce qu'on a

blest [blest] *pt & pp of* **bless**

blew [bluː] *pt of* **blow²**

blight [blaɪt] **1** *n (on cereals)* rouille *f*; *(on potatoes)* brunissure *f*; *Fig* **to cast a b. over sth** jeter un froid sur qch

  2 *vt Fig* assombrir; *(hopes)* anéantir

blind¹ [blaɪnd] **1** *npl* **the b.** les aveugles *mpl*; **school for the b.** école *f* pour aveugles; **they don't know what they're doing, it's like the b. leading the b.** ils ne savent pas ce qu'ils font, ils sont aussi nuls l'un que l'autre

  2 *adj also Fig* aveugle; **a b. man** un aveugle; **a b. woman** une aveugle; **b. in one eye** borgne, aveugle d'un œil; **as b. as a bat** myope comme une taupe; **to be b. to sth** ne pas voir qch; **to turn a b. eye to sth** fermer les yeux sur qch; **b. with fury** aveuglé(e) par la colère; *also Fig* **b. alley** impasse *f*; **b. date** = rencontre arrangée avec quelqu'un que l'on ne connaît pas; **b. man's buff** *or* **bluff** (jeu *m* de) colin-maillard *m*; **b. spot** *(for driver)* angle *m* mort; *Fig* **to have a b. spot for math** être nul (nulle) en maths

  3 *adv* **b. drunk** ivre mort(e)

  4 *vt* aveugler; *Fig* **love blinded her to his faults** aveuglée par l'amour, elle n'a pas vu ses défauts

blind² [blaɪnd] *n* (a) *(on window)* store *m* (b) *(for birdwatchers)* cachette *f*; *(for hunters)* affût *m*

blinders ['blaɪndəz] *npl (for horse)* œillères *fpl*; *Fig* **to be wearing b.** avoir des œillères

blindfold ['blaɪndfəʊld] **1** *n* bandeau *m*

  2 *vt* **to b. sb** mettre un bandeau à qn; **to be blindfolded** avoir les yeux bandés

blinding ['blaɪndɪŋ] *adj (light)* aveuglant(e); *Fig (intensity, realization)* affolant(e)

blindly ['blaɪndlɪ] *adv Fig* aveuglément

blindness ['blaɪndnɪs] *n* cécité *f*; *Fig* aveuglement *m*

bling (bling) [blɪŋ('blɪŋ)] *Fam* **1** *n (jewelry)* bijoux *mpl*, quincaillerie *f*

  2 *adj (ostentatious)* tape-à-l'œil; **that car is so b.!** cette voiture est vraiment tape-à-l'œil!

blink [blɪŋk] **1** *n (of eyes)* clignement *m* de paupières

  2 *vt* **to b. one's eyes** cligner des yeux

  3 *vi (of person)* cligner des yeux; *(of light)* clignoter

blinkered ['blɪŋkəd] *adj (approach, attitude)* borné(e); **to be b.** *(of person)* avoir des œillères

blinkers ['blɪŋkəz] = **blinders**

blinking ['blɪŋkɪŋ] *adj (light)* clignotant(e)

blip [blɪp] *n (on radar screen)* spot *m*; *Fam (temporary problem)* hic *m inv*, os *m*

bliss [blɪs] *n* bonheur *m*, béatitude *f*; **breakfast in bed, what b.!** le petit déjeuner au lit, quel bonheur!

blissful ['blɪsfʊl] *adj (person)* (bien)heureux(euse); *(vacation)* plein(e) de bonheur; **I'd rather remain in b. ignorance** j'aime autant ne pas savoir

blissfully ['blɪsfʊlɪ] *adv* merveilleusement; **b. happy** au comble du bonheur; **to be b. unaware that...** ne pas se douter le moins du monde que...

blister ['blɪstə(r)] **1** *n (on skin)* ampoule *f*, cloque *f*; *(on paint)* cloque

  2 *vt (skin)* provoquer des ampoules sur; *(paint)* faire des cloques sur

  3 *vi (of skin)* se couvrir d'ampoules; *(of paint)* cloquer

blistering ['blɪstərɪŋ] *adj (sun, heat)* brûlant(e); *(criticism, attack)* virulent(e)

blithe ['blaɪð] *adj (attitude, disregard)* désinvolte; *Lit (person)* joyeux(euse), allègre

blithely ['blaɪðlɪ] *adv (ignore, disregard)* avec une complète désinvolture; *Lit (happily)* joyeusement, allègrement

blithering ['blɪðərɪŋ] *adj* **a b. idiot** un(e) sombre idiot(e)

blitz [blɪts] *n (air bombardment)* blitz *m*, bombardement *m* aérien; *Fam* **to have a b. on sth** s'attaquer à qch

blizzard ['blɪzəd] *n* tempête *f* de neige

bloated ['bləʊtɪd] *adj (stomach, face)* gonflé(e); *(ego)* énorme

blob [blɒb] *n* **(a)** *(of cream, jam, paint)* tache *f*; *(of ink)* pâté *m* **(b)** *(indistinct shape)* silhouette *f*

bloc [blɒk] *n Pol* bloc *m*

block [blɒk] **1** *n* **(a)** *(of wood, stone)* bloc *m*; *(for execution, of butcher)* billot *m*; *Fam* **I'll knock your b. off!** je vais te casser la gueule!; **b. and tackle** *(for lifting)* palan *m*; **b. capitals** majuscules *fpl* en caractères d'imprimerie; **b. diagram** *(flow chart)* schéma *m* fonctionnel **(b)** *(group of buildings)* pâté *m* de maisons **(c)** *(of shares)* paquet *m*; **b. of seats** bloc-sièges *m inv*; **b. booking** réservation *f* ou location *f* de groupe; **b. vote** vote *m* groupé

2 *vt* **(a)** *(pipe, road, proposal)* bloquer; *(view)* cacher; **to b. sb's way** barrer *ou* bloquer le passage à qn; *Fin* **to b. a check** faire opposition à un chèque **(b)** *Comput (text)* sélectionner

▶**block off** *vt sep (road, exit)* barrer

▶**block out** *vt sep (light)* empêcher d'entrer *ou* de passer; *(a memory)* refouler; *(music, noise)* faire abstraction de

▶**block up** *vt sep (tunnel, passageway)* boucher; *(door, window)* murer

blockade [blɒ'keɪd] **1** *n* blocus *m* (**on** à)

2 *vt* bloquer, faire le blocus de

blockage ['blɒkɪdʒ] *n* obstruction *f*

blockbuster ['blɒkbʌstə(r)] *n (movie)* superproduction *f*; *(novel)* best-seller *m*

blockhead ['blɒkhed] *n Fam* lourdaud *m*

blog [blɒg] *n Comput (abbr* **weblog**) blog *m*

blogger ['blɒgə(r)] *n Comput* bloggeur(euse) *m,f*

blogging ['blɒgɪŋ] *n Comput* blogging *m*, création *f* de blogs

blonde [blɒnd] *n & adj* blond(e) *m,f*

blood [blʌd] **1** *n* **(a)** *(substance)* sang *m*; **to give b.** donner du sang; **b. bank** banque *f* du sang; **b. cell** globule *m* sanguin; **b. clot** caillot *m*; **b. count** numération *f* globulaire; **b. donor** donneur(euse) *m,f* de sang; **b. group** groupe *m* sanguin; **b. poisoning** septicémie *f*, toxémie *f*; **b. pressure** tension *f* (artérielle); **to have low/high b. pressure** avoir la tension basse/de la tension; **b. relation** parent(e) *m,f*; *Culin* **b. sausage** boudin *m* noir; **b. sport** la chasse; **b. test** prise *f* de sang; **b. transfusion** transfusion *f* sanguine; **b. vessel** vaisseau *m* sanguin **(b)** *(idioms)* **to have b. on one's hands** avoir du sang sur les mains; **it makes my b. boil** ça me fait bouillir; **it makes my b. run cold** ça me glace le sang; **in cold b.** de sang-froid; **he's after your b.** il en a après toi; **to have sth in one's b.** avoir qch dans le sang; **it's like trying to get b. out of a stone** c'est comme si on se heurtait à un mur; *Prov* **b. is thicker than water** la famille passe avant tout

2 *vt (initiate)* initier

bloodbath ['blʌdbɑːθ] *n* bain *m* de sang

bloodcurdling ['blʌdkɜːdlɪŋ] *adj* à vous tourner les sangs

bloodhound ['blʌdhaʊnd] *n* limier *m*

bloodless ['blʌdlɪs] *adj* **(a)** *(without bloodshed)* **it was a b. coup** le coup d'État s'est déroulé sans effusion de sang **(b)** *(pale)* exsangue

bloodletting ['blʌdletɪŋ] *n* **(a)** *Med* saignée *f* **(b)** *(slaughter, feud)* effusion *f* de sang

bloodshed ['blʌdʃed] *n* effusion *f* de sang; **without b.** sans verser le sang

bloodshot ['blʌdʃɒt] *adj (eyes)* injecté(e) de sang

bloodstain ['blʌdsteɪn] *n* tache *f* de sang

bloodstained ['blʌdsteɪnd] *adj* taché(e) de sang

bloodstream ['blʌdstriːm] *n* sang *m*

bloodsucker ['blʌdsʌkə(r)] *n also Fig* sangsue *f*

bloodthirsty ['blʌdθɜːstɪ] *adj (person)* sanguinaire; *(movie)* sanglant(e)

bloody ['blʌdɪ] *adj (bleeding, bloodstained)* ensanglanté(e); *(battle, revolution)* sanglant(e); *Fig* **to give sb a b. nose** mettre une raclée à qn

bloom [bluːm] **1** *n* fleur *f*; **in (full) b.** *(tree)* en fleur(s); *(flower)* éclos(e); **in the b. of youth** à *ou* dans la fleur de l'âge

2 *vi (of garden, flower, talent)* fleurir; *Fig* **to be blooming with health** être resplendissant(e) *ou* éclatant(e) de santé

bloomer ['bluːmə(r)] *n Fam (mistake)* bourde *f*

bloomers ['bluːməz] *npl* culotte *f* bouffante

blooper ['bluːpə(r)] *n Fam (mistake)* bourde *f*

blossom ['blɒsəm] **1** *n* fleur *f*; **in b.** en fleur(s)

2 *vi* fleurir; *Fig* s'épanouir; *Fig* **she had blossomed into a charming young woman** elle était devenue une charmante jeune femme

blot [blɒt] **1** *n (of ink)* pâté *m*; *Fig* **a b. on sb's reputation** une tache faite à la réputation de qn

2 *vt (pt & pp* **blotted**) *(stain)* tacher; *(with ink)* faire un pâté/ des pâtés sur; **to b. one's lipstick** fixer son rouge à lèvres *(en pressant les lèvres sur un mouchoir en papier)*

▶**blot out** *vt sep (sun, light)* masquer; *(memory)* effacer

blotch [blɒtʃ] *n (on skin)* tache *f*

blotchy ['blɒtʃɪ] *adj (skin)* couvert(e) de taches

blotter ['blɒtə(r)] *n* **(a)** *(with blotting paper)* buvard *m* **(b)** *(for police)* registre *m (provisoire)*

blotting paper ['blɒtɪŋpeɪpə(r)] *n* buvard *m*; **a sheet of b.** un buvard

blouse [blaʊz] *n* chemisier *m*, corsage *m*

blow[1] [bləʊ] *n* **(a)** *(hit)* coup *m*; **to come to blows (over sth)** en venir aux mains (pour *ou* au sujet de qch); *Fig* **to strike a b. for sth** remporter une victoire pour qch; *Fig* **to soften the b.** atténuer le choc **(b)** *(setback)* coup *m*; **this news was a b. to us** cette nouvelle a été pour nous un coup rude; **it was a b. to her pride** son orgueil en a pris un coup

blow[2] [bləʊ] *(pt* **blew** [bluː], *pp* **blown** [bləʊn]) **1** *vt* **(a)** *(of wind, person)* **the wind blew down the fence** le vent a renversé la barrière; **the wind blew the door open** le vent a fait s'ouvrir la porte; **to b. glass** souffler le verre; **to b. the horn** klaxonner; **to b. a whistle** donner un coup de sifflet; *Fig* **to b. the whistle on sb/sth** dénoncer qn/qch; **to b. the dust off sth** souffler sur qch pour en enlever la poussière; **to b. sb a kiss** envoyer un baiser à qn; **to b. bubbles** faire des bulles; **to b. one's nose** se moucher; *Fig* **to b. one's own trumpet** chanter ses propres louanges

(b) *Elec* **to b. a fuse** faire sauter un plomb; *Fig (of person)* disjoncter; *Fam Fig* **the Grand Canyon blew my mind!** quel pied, le Grand Canyon!; *Fam Fig* **the prices blew my mind!** j'ai été affolé par les prix!

(c) *Fam (waste) (chance)* gâcher; **you blew it!** tu as tout gâché!

(d) *Fam (money)* claquer (**on sth** pour s'acheter qch)

2 *vi* **(a)** *(of wind, person)* souffler; **to b. down** *or* **over** *(of fence, tree)* se renverser; **the door blew open/shut** le vent a ouvert/fermé la porte; **to b. on one's fingers** se souffler sur les doigts; *Fig* **to b. hot and cold** souffler le chaud et le froid

(b) *Elec (of fuse)* sauter

▶**blow away 1** *vt sep* **to b. sth away** *(of wind)* faire s'envoler qch; *Fam Fig* **to b. sb away** *(shoot dead)* descendre qn; *Fam Fig* **his latest movie blew me away!** son dernier film, c'est le pied!

2 *vi (of paper, hat)* s'envoler

▶**blow off 1** *vt sep* **(a)** *(of wind)* emporter; *Fam Fig* **to b. sb's head off** faire sauter la cervelle à qn **(b)** *Fig* **to b. off steam** dire ce qu'on a sur le cœur **(c)** *Fam* **to b. sb off** *(not show up)* poser un lapin à qn

2 *vi (of hat)* s'envoler

▶**blow out** vt sep (of wind) éteindre; (candle, match) souffler

▶**blow over** vi (of storm, argument) se calmer; **the scandal soon blew over** le scandale fut vite oublié

▶**blow up 1** vt sep (**a**) (balloon, tire) gonfler (**b**) (explode) faire sauter (**c**) (enlarge) (photograph) agrandir; Fig **the incident was blown up out of all proportion** on a fait une histoire incroyable autour de ce petit incident

2 vi (of bomb) exploser, sauter; Fig (lose one's temper) piquer une colère; **to b. up at sb/sth** se mettre en colère contre qn/qch

blow-by-blow ['bləʊbaɪ'bləʊ] adj (account) détaillé(e), minutieux(euse)

blow-dry ['bləʊdraɪ] **1** n brushing m

2 vt (pt & pp **blow-dried**) **to b. sb's hair** faire un brushing à qn

blowgun ['bləʊgʌn] n sarbacane f

blowhole ['bləʊhəʊl] n (of whale) évent m

blowjob ['bləʊdʒɒb] n Vulg pipe f; **to give sb a b.** tailler une pipe à qn

blown [bləʊn] pp of **blow²**

blowout ['bləʊaʊt] n (**a**) (of tire) éclatement m (**b**) Fam (big meal) gueuleton m

blowpipe ['bləʊpaɪp] n sarbacane f

blowsy = **blowzy**

blowtorch ['bləʊtɔːtʃ] n (for welding) chalumeau m, lampe f à souder; (for removing paint) brûloir m

blowzy ['blaʊzɪ] adj négligé(e)

blubber ['blʌbə(r)] **1** n (fat) graisse f

2 vi Fam (cry) pleurer comme une madeleine

bludgeon ['blʌdʒən] vt matraquer; Fig **to b. sb into doing sth** obliger brutalement qn à faire qch

blue [bluː] **1** n (**a**) (color) bleu m; Fig **out of the b.** à l'improviste; **her resignation came out of the b.** sa démission nous a pris par surprise (**b**) **the blues** (music) le blues; Fam **to have the blues** (be depressed) avoir le cafard

2 adj (**a**) (color) bleu(e); **b. with cold** bleu de froid; Fam **she can complain until she's b. in the face** elle peut se plaindre autant qu'elle veut; **once in a b. moon** tous les trente-six du mois; Fam **to scream b. murder** crier comme un putois; **b. blood** sang m bleu; **b. cheese** bleu m; **b. whale** baleine f bleue (**b**) Fam (sad) **to feel b.** avoir le cafard (**c**) Fam (obscene) (joke) grivois(e), paillard(e); (movie) porno; **to tell b. stories** en raconter des vertes et des pas mûres

bluebell ['bluːbel] n jacinthe f des bois

blueberry ['bluːbərɪ] (pl **blueberries**) n myrtille f, Can bleuet m

bluebird ['bluːbɜːd] n rouge-gorge m bleu

bluebottle ['bluːbɒtəl] n mouche f de la viande

blue-chip ['bluːtʃɪp] adj Fin **b. shares** valeurs fpl de père de famille; **b. company** affaire f de premier ordre

blue-collar ['bluːkɒlə(r)] adj **b. worker** col m bleu

bluejack ['bluːdʒæk] vt Tel = envoyer un SMS anonyme à

bluejacking ['bluːdʒækɪŋ] n Tel bluejacking m, = envoi de SMS anonymes à d'autres propriétaires de portables utilisant le protocole Bluetooth

blueprint ['bluːprɪnt] n Archit & Ind plan m; Fig projet m; **a b. for success** une garantie de succès

blue ribbon [bluː'rɪbən] **1** n = premier prix d'une compétition

2 adj de première classe

Bluetooth® ['bluːtuːθ] n Tel (technologie f) Bluetooth® m

bluff¹ [blʌf] **1** n (deception) bluff m; **to call sb's b.** (at cards) inviter qn à mettre les cartes sur la table; (in negotiation) prendre qn au mot

2 vt **you're bluffing me** tu bluffes; **to b. one's way out of a tricky situation** se tirer d'affaire par un coup de bluff

3 vi bluffer

bluff² [blʌf] n (cliff) à-pic m inv

bluff³ [blʌf] adj (manner) direct(e)

blunder ['blʌndə(r)] **1** n gaffe f

2 vi (make mistake) faire une gaffe; **to b. along** (move clumsily) avancer d'un pas maladroit; **to b. against** or **into sb/sth** heurter qn/à qch

blunderbuss ['blʌndəbʌs] n tromblon m

blunt [blʌnt] **1** adj (**a**) (blade) émoussé(e); (pencil) mal taillé(e) (**b**) (manner) brutal(e); (question, statement) direct(e); (refusal) net (nette); (person) brusque; **to be b.,...** pour parler franchement,...

2 vt (blade) émousser; (pencil) épointer; Fig (anger, enthusiasm) émousser, atténuer

bluntly ['blʌntlɪ] adv (frankly) franchement; **I told him b. that...** je lui ai dit tout net que...

bluntness ['blʌntnɪs] n (**a**) (of blade) manque m de tranchant (**b**) (of manner, statement) rudesse f; (of person) franchise f

blur [blɜː(r)] **1** n (vague shape) forme f vague; (unclear memory) vague souvenir m; **without my glasses, everything is a b.** sans mes lunettes, je suis complètement dans le brouillard; **to go by in a b.** (of time) passer à toute vitesse

2 vt (pt & pp **blurred**) brouiller, troubler

3 vi se brouiller; (of memories) s'estomper

blurb [blɜːb] n (on book cover) notice f publicitaire

blurred [blɜːd], **blurry** ['blɜːrɪ] adj (ink) qui a bavé; (writing) flou(e); (vision) trouble

▶**blurt out** [blɜːt] vt sep laisser échapper; **"I love him!" she blurted out** "je l'aime!" lâcha-t-elle

blush [blʌʃ] **1** n (**a**) (due to embarrassment) rougeur f; **to spare sb's blushes** éviter à qn un embarras (**b**) (make-up) blush m, fard m à joues (**c**) (wine) vin m rosé très léger

2 vi rougir; **to b. with shame** rougir de honte; **to b. at the thought of sth** rougir en pensant à qch; **I b. to admit it** j'ai honte de l'admettre

blusher ['blʌʃə(r)] n blush m, fard m à joues

bluster ['blʌstə(r)] **1** n protestations fpl véhémentes

2 vi protester avec véhémence

blustery ['blʌstərɪ] adj (day) venteux(euse), de grand vent; (wind) violent(e)

Blvd. abbr **Boulevard** bd, boul

BO [biː'əʊ] n Fam (abbr **body odor**) odeur f corporelle; **to have BO** sentir mauvais

boa ['bəʊə] n **b. (constrictor)** boa m (constricteur); **(feather) b.** boa m

boar ['bɔː(r)] n (male pig) verrat m; (wild pig) sanglier m

board [bɔːd] **1** n (**a**) (of wood) planche f; (for notices) panneau m; (for chess) échiquier m; (for checkers) damier m; (for Monopoly® etc.) tableau m; (blackboard) tableau; **to go by the b.** (of plan, system) être abandonné(e); **across the b.** globalement; **b. game** jeu m de société (avec des pions etc.)

(**b**) (of company) conseil m, comité m; **b. (of directors)** conseil d'administration; **b. of inquiry** commission f d'enquête; **b. of examiners** jury m d'examen; **b. meeting** réunion f du conseil

(**c**) (meals) **half b.** demi-pension f; **full b.** pension f complète; **b. and lodging** (in hotel) pension complète

(**d**) **on b.** à bord; **to go on b.** monter à bord; Fig **to take sth on b.** (idea, proposal) prendre qch en considération; (problem) tenir compte de qch

2 vt (ship, plane) embarquer; (train, bus) monter dans

3 vi (**a**) (lodge) être en pension (**with** chez); (at school) aller en pension

(**b**) Aviat **flight 123 is now boarding** l'embarquement du vol 123 a commencé

▶**board up** vt sep (house, window) condamner

boarder ['bɔːdə(r)] n (lodger) pensionnaire mf; (at school) interne mf, pensionnaire

boarding ['bɔːdɪŋ] n (a) **b. card** or **pass** carte f d'embarquement (b) **b. house** pension f de famille; **b. school** internat m

boardroom ['bɔːdruːm] n salle f de réunion (du conseil d'administration)

boardwalk ['bɔːdwɔːk] n = passage en bois sur la plage

boast [bəʊst] **1** n vantardise f

2 vt **the school boasts a wondeful library** l'école est fière de posséder une belle bibliothèque

3 vi se vanter (**about** de); **it's nothing to b. about!** il n'y a pas de quoi se vanter!

boastful ['bəʊstfʊl] adj vantard(e), fanfaron(onne)

boasting ['bəʊstɪŋ] n vantardise f, fanfaronnade f

boat [bəʊt] n bateau m; (small) canot m, embarcation f; **to come by b.** venir en bateau, prendre le bateau; Fig **we're all in the same b.** nous sommes tous dans le même cas

boatbuilder ['bəʊtbɪldə(r)] n constructeur m de bateaux

boater ['bəʊtə(r)] n (hat) canotier m

boathouse ['bəʊthaʊs] n hangar m pour bateaux

boating ['bəʊtɪŋ] n canotage m; **to go b.** faire du canotage

boatload ['bəʊtləʊd] n cargaison f; Fig **by the b.** par bateaux entiers

boatswain ['bəʊsən] n Naut maître m d'équipage

boatyard ['bəʊtjɑːd] n chantier m de construction pour canots et bateaux de plaisance

bob [bɒb] **1** n (a) (curtsey) petite révérence f (b) (hairstyle) (coupe f au) carré m (c) (bobsled) bobsleigh m

2 vt (pt & pp **bobbed**) (a) **to b. one's head** hocher la tête (b) **to have one's hair bobbed** se faire faire un carré

3 vi **to b. up and down** s'agiter; **to b. around** (on water) se balancer

bobbin ['bɒbɪn] n bobine f

bobble ['bɒbəl] n (on hat) pompon m

bobsled ['bɒbsled] n bobsleigh m

bod [bɒd] n Fam (body) corps m; **he's got a nice b.** il est bien foutu

bode [bəʊd] vi **to b. well/ill (for)** être de bon/mauvais augure (pour)

bodice ['bɒdɪs] n corsage m

bodily ['bɒdɪlɪ] **1** adj corporel(elle), physique; **b. functions** fonctions fpl corporelles; **b. needs** besoins mpl physiques

2 adv (grab) à bras-le-corps; **he was carried b. to the door** on l'a saisi à bras-le-corps et puis on l'a transporté jusqu'à la porte

body ['bɒdɪ] (pl **bodies**) n (a) (of person, animal) corps m; (dead) cadavre m, corps; **to have enough to keep b. and soul together** avoir juste de quoi vivre; Fam **over my dead b.!** plutôt crever!; **b. bag** = sac servant au transport des dépouilles mortelles; Fig **to deliver a b. blow (to)** porter un coup terrible (à); **b. builder** culturiste mf; **b. building** culturisme m; **b. count** (of casualties) comptage m des morts; (of those present) comptage des présents; **b. language** (of performer) gestuelle f; **I could tell by his b. language** je le savais d'après la façon dont il se tenait; **b. odor** odeur f corporelle; **b. piercing** piercing m; **b. stocking** (without legs) body m; (with legs) combinaison f collante

(b) (of wine) corps m; (of hair) volume m

(c) (group) corps m; **a large b. of people** une foule nombreuse; **b. of evidence** ensemble m de preuves; **b. of water** masse f d'eau; **public b.** organisme m public; **the b. politic** le corps politique

(d) (main part) (of car) carrosserie f; (of letter) corps m; (of argument) essentiel m; **b. shop** atelier m de carrosserie

(e) (garment) body m

bodyguard ['bɒdɪgɑːd] n (person) garde m du corps; (group) gardes mpl du corps

bodywork ['bɒdɪwɜːk] n (of car) carrosserie f

Boer ['bəʊə(r)] n Boer mf; **the B. War** la guerre des Boers

bog [bɒg] n (marsh) marécage m

▶**bog down** (pt & pp **bogged**) vt sep **to get bogged down (in)** (mud) s'enliser (dans), s'embourber (dans); (details) se perdre (dans)

bogey ['bəʊgɪ] (pl **bogeys**) n (cause of fear) hantise f

bogeyman, bogyman ['bəʊgɪmæn] n **the b.** le croquemitaine, le Père fouettard

boggle ['bɒgəl] vi Fam **to b. at doing sth** rechigner à faire qch; **the mind boggles!** ça laisse rêveur!

Bogotá [bɒgə'tɑː] n Bogotá

bogus ['bəʊgəs] adj faux (fausse); Fam **he's completely b.** c'est vraiment un faux jeton

bogyman = bogeyman

Bohemian [bəʊ'hiːmɪən] **1** n (native of Bohemia) Bohémien(enne) m,f; (artistic person) bohème mf

2 adj (from Bohemia) bohémien(enne); (person, lifestyle) bohème

boil¹ [bɔɪl] n (on skin) furoncle m

boil² [bɔɪl] **1** n **to come to the b.** arriver à ébullition; **to bring sth to the b.** amener qch à ébullition

2 vt faire bouillir; **to b. the kettle** mettre de l'eau à chauffer

3 vi bouillir; **the kettle's boiling** la bouilloire siffle; **the saucepan has boiled dry** l'eau de la casserole s'est complètement évaporée; **to b. with rage** bouillir (de colère)

▶**boil down** vt insep (sauce, soup) faire réduire; Fig (summarize) réduire à l'essentiel

▶**boil down to** vt insep Fam **it all boils down to...** ça revient à...

▶**boil over** vi (of milk, soup) déborder; Fig (of situation) empirer, s'aggraver

▶**boil up** vt sep (water, milk) faire bouillir

boiler ['bɔɪlə(r)] n chaudière f; **b. maker** chaudronnier m; **b. room** salle f des chaudières, chaufferie f; **b. suit** bleu m de chauffe

boiling ['bɔɪlɪŋ] **1** adj bouillant(e); Fam **I'm b.!** je crève de chaleur!; **b. point** point m d'ébullition; Fig **the situation has reached b. point** la situation est explosive

2 adv **it's b. hot** il fait une chaleur à crever

boisterous ['bɔɪstərəs] adj bruyant(e)

bold [bəʊld] adj (a) (brave) hardi(e), intrépide (b) (shameless) **as b. as brass** culotté(e) (c) (striking) (color) vif (vive); (handwriting) vigoureux(euse); Typ **b. type** caractères mpl gras

boldly ['bəʊldlɪ] adv (bravely) hardiment

boldness ['bəʊldnɪs] n (bravery) hardiesse f

Bolivia [bə'lɪvɪə] n la Bolivie

Bolivian [bə'lɪvɪən] **1** n Bolivien(enne) m,f

2 adj bolivien(enne)

bollard ['bɒlɑːd] n Naut bollard m

Bolshevik ['bɒlʃəvɪk] n & adj bolchevique mf

Bolshevism ['bɒlʃəvɪzəm] n bolchevisme m

bolster ['bəʊlstə(r)] **1** n (pillow) traversin m

2 vt (confidence, pride) renforcer, consolider

bolt [bəʊlt] **1** n (a) (on door) verrou m; (metal fastening) boulon m; Fam **he has shot his b.** il a échoué après avoir joué sa dernière carte (b) Fam (dash) **to make a b. for it** se sauver à toutes jambes; **she made a b. for the door** elle s'est précipitée vers la porte (c) **b. of lightning** foudre f; Fig **it came like a b. from the blue** ça a été comme un coup de tonnerre

2 adv **b. upright** droit(e) comme un i

3 vt (a) (lock) verrouiller; (fasten with bolts) boulonner (b) (food) engloutir

4 vi (of horse) s'emballer; (of person) décamper, déguerpir

▶**bolt down** vt sep (food) engloutir

bomb [bɒm] **1** n bombe f; **b.-disposal expert** démineur m; **b. scare** alerte f à la bombe

2 vt bombarder

3 vi Fam (fail) faire un bide

▶**bomb along** vi Fam (go quickly) foncer

bombard [bɒm'bɑːd] vt bombarder; Fig **to b. sb with questions** bombarder ou assaillir qn de questions

bombardment [bɒm'bɑːdmənt] n bombardement m

bombast ['bɒmbæst] n emphase f

bombastic [bɒm'bæstɪk] adj ampoulé(e), emphatique

bomber ['bɒmə(r)] n (aircraft) bombardier m; (person) poseur(euse) m,f de bombe; **b. jacket** blouson m d'aviateur

bombing ['bɒmɪŋ] n (aerial) bombardement m; (by terrorists) attentat m à la bombe

bombshell ['bɒmʃel] n obus m; Fig **to drop a b.** faire une révélation fracassante; Fam Fig **a blonde b.** une magnifique blonde

bombsite ['bɒmsaɪt] n zone f bombardée

bona fide ['bəʊnə'faɪdɪ] adj véritable

bonanza [bə'nænzə] n aubaine f; **a b. year** une année exceptionnelle

bonbon ['bɒnbɒn] n bonbon m

bond [bɒnd] **1** n (a) (attachment) lien m; **to feel a b. with sb** se sentir lié(e) à qn (b) Fin obligation f (c) Law caution f; Formal **my word is my b.** je n'ai qu'une parole (d) Com **in b.** en dépôt; **bonded warehouse** entrepôt m sous douane
2 vt (a) (stick) coller (b) Fig (unite) **to b. together** créer des liens entre
3 vi (a) (stick) adhérer (b) Fig (form attachment) créer des liens affectifs (**with sb** avec qn)

bondage ['bɒndɪdʒ] n (a) (slavery) esclavage m (b) (sexual) = pratique sexuelle où l'un des partenaires est attaché

bonding [bɒndɪŋ] n (emotional attachment) liens mpl affectifs; **male b.** amitié f virile; Fam Hum **they're doing some male b. at the bar** ils sont allés au bar entre hommes

bone [bəʊn] **1** n (a) (of person, animal) os m; (of fish) arête f; **b. china** porcelaine f tendre; **b. marrow** moëlle f; Med **b. marrow transplant** greffe f de moëlle; **b. meal** engrais m (de cendre d'os)
(b) (idioms) **to work one's fingers to the b.** se tuer au travail; **b. idle** or **lazy** paresseux(euse) comme une couleuvre; **I feel it in my bones** je le sens; **b. of contention** sujet m de dispute; Fam **to have a b. to pick with sb** avoir un compte à régler avec qn; **she made no bones about it** elle ne l'a pas caché; **close to the b.** (tactless, risqué) limite
2 vt (chicken, meat) désosser; (fish) ôter les arêtes de

▶**bone up on** vt insep Fam potasser

bone-dry ['bəʊn'draɪ] adj complètement sec (sèche)

bonfire ['bɒnfaɪə(r)] n (for burning trash) feu m; (for celebration) feu de joie

bong [bɒŋ] n (sound) bong m

bonhomie ['bɒnɒmiː] n bonhomie f

bonk [bɒŋk] vt Fam (hit) frapper

Bonn [bɒn] n Bonn

bonnet ['bɒnɪt] n (hat) bonnet m

bonsai ['bɒnsaɪ] n bonsaï m

bonus ['bəʊnəs] (pl **bonuses**) n (a) (money) prime f; **b. scheme** système m de primes de rendement (b) (advantage) avantage m; **b. number** (in lottery) numéro m supplémentaire

bony ['bəʊnɪ] adj (person, limb) maigre, décharné(e); (fish) plein(e) d'arêtes

boo [buː] **1** n (pl **boos**) huée f
2 vt (pt & pp **booed**) huer
3 exclam hou!

booby prize ['buːbɪpraɪz] n prix m décerné au dernier (en guise de plaisanterie)

booby trap ['buːbɪtræp] n (explosive device) objet m piégé; (practical joke) piège m

booby-trap ['buːbɪtræp] vt (pt & pp **booby-trapped**) piéger (en guise de farce)

booger ['buːgə(r)] n Fam crotte f de nez

book [bʊk] **1** n (a) (in general) livre m; (of stamps) carnet m; (of matches) pochette f; Fin **the books** (of company) les comptes mpl; **b. certificate** chèque-cadeau m pour des livres; **b. club** club m du livre; **b. end** serre-livres m inv (b) (idioms) **physics is a closed b. to me** je ne comprends absolument rien à la physique; **in my b.** à mon avis; **to be in sb's good books** être dans les petits papiers de qn, être bien vu(e) par qn; **to be in sb's bad books** être mal vu(e) par qn; **to bring sb to b.** forcer qn à rendre des comptes; **by** or **according to the b.** selon la procédure; **to throw the b. at sb** infliger la peine maximale à qn
2 vt (a) (seat, room, table, ticket) réserver; (performer) engager; **to b. sb on a flight** réserver une place pour qn sur un vol; **fully booked** (hotel, flight) complet(ète) (b) (for traffic offense) dresser une contravention à; (in soccer match) donner un carton jaune à

▶**book up 1** vt sep **the hotel is fully booked up** l'hôtel est complet; **I'm booked up for this evening** je suis pris toute la soirée
2 vi (make reservation) réserver

bookbinder ['bʊkbaɪndə(r)] n relieur(euse) m,f

bookbinding ['bʊkbaɪndɪŋ] n reliure f

bookcase ['bʊkkeɪs] n bibliothèque f

bookie ['bʊkɪ] n Fam (bookmaker) bookmaker m

booking ['bʊkɪŋ] n (reservation) réservation f; **to make a b.** effectuer une réservation

bookish ['bʊkɪʃ] adj (person) studieux(euse); Pej (approach, style) livresque

bookkeeping ['bʊkkiːpɪŋ] n Fin comptabilité f

booklet ['bʊklɪt] n brochure f

bookmaker ['bʊkmeɪkə(r)] n (in betting) bookmaker m

bookmark ['bʊkmɑːk] n (a) (for book) marque-page m inv (b) Comput (for Web page) signet m

bookseller ['bʊkselə(r)] n libraire mf

bookshelf ['bʊkʃelf] (pl **bookshelves** ['bʊkʃelvz]) n étagère f; **bookshelves** (furniture) bibliothèque f

bookshop ['bʊkʃɒp] n librairie f

bookstall ['bʊkstɔːl] n (in railroad station, airport) kiosque m à journaux; (selling second-hand books) étalage m de bouquiniste

bookstore ['bʊkstɔː(r)] n librairie f

bookworm ['bʊkwɜːm] n Fig passionné(e) m,f de lecture

boom[1] [buːm] n (a) Naut (barrier) estacade f; (for sail) bôme f (b) Cin & TV perche f

boom[2] [buːm] **1** n (economic) boom m; **b. town** ville f en plein essor économique
2 vi (of business, trade) être florissant(e)

boom[3] [buːm] **1** n (sound) détonation f
2 vi (of thunder, gun) gronder; (of person) tonitruer

boomerang ['buːməræŋ] n boomerang m

booming[1] ['buːmɪŋ] adj (business) prospère, en plein essor

booming[2] ['buːmɪŋ] adj (voice) tonitruant(e)

boon [buːn] n bénédiction f, aubaine f

boor ['bʊə(r)] n rustaud(e) m,f

boorish ['bʊərɪʃ] adj rustre, grossier(ère)

boost [buːst] **1** n **to give sth a b.** (production, economy) relancer qch; **to give sb's confidence a b.** redonner confiance à qn; **to give sb's morale a b.** remonter le moral à qn
2 vt (a) Tel (signal) régénérer; (production, economy) relancer; **to b. sb's hopes** redonner espoir à qn (b) Fam (steal) piquer; (break into) cambrioler

booster ['buːstə(r)] n (a) **b. (rocket)** fusée f de démarrage (b) Elec survolteur m (c) Med (injection) rappel m (d) **b. seat** (for child) réhausseur m

boot [buːt] **1** n (a) (footwear) (for walking) brodequin m; (for sports) chaussure f; (ankle-length) bottine f; (knee-length) botte f (b) (idioms) Fam **to give sb the b.** mettre qn à la porte; Fam **to get the b.** se faire mettre à la porte; **he's a liar and a thief to**

b. c'est un menteur et par-dessus le marché c'est un voleur

2 *vt* **(a)** *Fam (kick)* donner un coup de pied dans; **to b. sb out** mettre qn à la porte **(b)** *Comput* amorcer

3 *vi Comput* **to b. (up)** s'amorcer

bootee [buːˈtiː] *n* chausson *m* (*de bébé*)

booth [buːð] *n* (*at fair*) baraque *f*, stand *m*; (*for telephone*) cabine *f*; (*in voting*) isoloir *m*; (*in restaurant*) alcôve *f*

bootlace [ˈbuːtleɪs] *n* lacet *m* (*de botte*)

bootleg [ˈbuːtleg] *adj* (*alcohol*) de contrebande; (*recording*) pirate

bootstrap [ˈbuːtstræp] *n* **(a)** (*part of boot*) tirant *m* de botte; *Fig* **to pull oneself up by one's bootstraps** se faire tout(e) seul(e) **(b)** *Comput* routine *f* d'amorçage

booty [ˈbuːtɪ] *n* **(a)** (*loot*) butin *m* **(b)** *Fam (buttocks)* cul *m*, derche *m*; **to shake one's b.** s'éclater en dansant

booze [buːz] *Fam* **1** *n* alcool *m*

2 *vi* picoler

boozer [ˈbuːzə(r)] *n Fam (person)* poivrot(e) *m,f*

boozy [ˈbuːzɪ] *adj Fam (voice, breath)* aviné(e)

bop[1] [bɒp] *Fam* **1** *n (dance)* danse *f*

2 *vi* (*pt & pp* **bopped**) (*dance*) danser

bop[2] [bɒp] *Fam* **1** *n (blow)* léger coup *m*

2 *vt* (*pt & pp* **bopped**) (*hit*) donner un léger coup à

boracic [bəˈræsɪk] *adj Chem* borique

border [ˈbɔːdə(r)] **1** *n* **(a)** (*edge*) bord *m*; (*in garden*) plate-bande *f* **(b)** (*frontier*) frontière *f*; **b. guard** garde-frontière *m*; **b. town** ville *f* frontière *ou* frontalière

2 *vt (country)* avoir une frontière commune avec; (*road*) border

▶**border on** *vt insep (of country)* avoir une frontière commune avec; **to b. on insanity/the ridiculous** friser la folie/le ridicule

borderland [ˈbɔːdəlænd] *n* zone *f* frontalière

borderline [ˈbɔːdəlaɪn] *n* frontière *f*, ligne *f* de démarcation; **a b. case** un cas limite

bore[1] [ˈbɔː(r)] **1** *n (person)* raseur(euse) *m,f*; (*thing*) chose *f* ennuyeuse; **what a b.!** quelle barbe!

2 *vt* ennuyer

bore[2] [ˈbɔː(r)] **1** *n (caliber)* calibre *m*

2 *vt (with drill)* forer; **to b. a hole in sth** percer un trou dans qch

bore[3] [ˈbɔː(r)] *pt of* **bear**[2]

bored [bɔːd] *adj (sigh, look)* d'ennui; **to be b.** s'ennuyer; *Fam* **to be b. stiff** *or* **to tears** s'ennuyer à mourir

boredom [ˈbɔːdəm] *n* ennui *m*

boric [ˈbɔːrɪk] = **boracic**

boring [ˈbɔːrɪŋ] *adj* ennuyeux(euse)

born [bɔːn] **1** *adj* **to be a b. writer/leader** être un écrivain/ leader né

2 (*pp of* **bear**) **to be b.** naître; **I was b. in Miami/in 1975** je suis né à Miami/en 1975; *Fam* **I wasn't b. yesterday** je ne suis pas né de la dernière pluie

born-again [ˈbɔːnəgen] *adj* **b. Christian** chrétien(enne) *m,f* régénéré(e)

borne [bɔːn] *pp of* **bear**[2]

Borneo [ˈbɔːnɪəʊ] *n* Bornéo

borrow [ˈbɒrəʊ] **1** *vt* emprunter (**from sb** à qn); **to be living on borrowed time** (*of sick person, government*) ne plus en avoir pour longtemps

2 *vi* emprunter (**from sb** à qn)

borrower [ˈbɒrəʊə(r)] *n* emprunteur(euse) *m,f*

Bosnia(-Herzegovina) [ˈbɒznɪə(ˈhɜːtsəgəˈviːnə)] *n* la Bosnie(-Herzégovine)

Bosnian [ˈbɒznɪən] **1** *n* Bosniaque *mf*

2 *adj* bosniaque; **B. Croat/Muslim/Serb** Croate *mf*/ Musulman(e) *m,f*/Serbe *mf* de Bosnie

bosom [ˈbʊzəm] **1** *n (of woman)* poitrine *f*; *Fig* **in the b. of one's family** au sein de sa famille

2 *adj* **b. friend** ami(e) *m,f* intime

Bosphorus [ˈbɒsfərəs] *n* **the B.** le Bosphore

boss[1] [bɒs] *n (on shield)* ombon *m*, ombo *m*

boss[2] [bɒs] *Fam* **1** *n (at work)* patron(onne) *m,f*; **to be one's own b.** être son propre patron; **to show sb who's b.** montrer à qn qui commande

2 *vt* **to b. sb (about** *or* **around)** donner des ordres à qn

bossy [ˈbɒsɪ] *adj* autoritaire

bosun [ˈbəʊsən] *n Naut* maître *m* d'équipage

botanic [bəˈtænɪk], **botanical** [bəˈtænɪkəl] *adj* botanique; **b. garden(s)** jardin *m* botanique

botanist [ˈbɒtənɪst] *n* botaniste *mf*

botany [ˈbɒtənɪ] *n* botanique *f*

botch [bɒtʃ] *Fam* **1** *n* travail *m* salopé; **to make a b. of sth** (*job*) saloper qch; (*interview, test*) rater qch complètement

2 *vt* **to b. sth (up)** (*job*) saloper qch; (*interview, test*) rater complètement

botched [bɒtʃt] *adj Fam* raté(e); **a b. job** un travail de sagouin

both [bəʊθ] **1** *pron* les deux; **b. (of them) are dead** ils sont morts tous les deux; **b. of us saw it** nous l'avons vu tous les deux

2 *adj* les deux; **b. (the) brothers** les deux frères; **b. my parents** mes deux parents; **on b. sides** des deux côtés; **you can't have it b. ways** on ne peut pas tout avoir

3 *adv* **b. in Britain and in France** aussi bien en Grande-Bretagne qu'en France; **she is b. intelligent and beautiful** elle est à la fois intelligente et belle

bother [ˈbɒðə(r)] **1** *n (trouble)* ennui *m*; **if it's not too much b.** si cela ne vous dérange pas trop; **to go to the b. of doing sth** prendre la peine de faire qch

2 *vt* **(a)** (*annoy*) déranger; **my back's still bothering me** j'ai toujours des problèmes de dos; **I hate to b. you but...** je suis désolé de vous déranger mais... **(b)** (*care*) **to be bothered about sth** s'inquiéter de qch; *Fam* **I can't be bothered** ça ne me dit rien

3 *vi (care)* s'inquiéter (**about** de); **he didn't even b. to apologize** il n'a même pas pris la peine de s'excuser; **don't b.!** ce n'est pas la peine!

bothersome [ˈbɒðəsəm] *adj* ennuyeux(euse), gênant(e)

Botox® [ˈbəʊtɒks] *Pharm* **1** *n* Botox® *m*

2 *vt Fam* faire des injections de Botox® à

Botswana [bɒtˈswɑːnə] *n* le Botswana

bottle [ˈbɒtəl] **1** *n (container)* bouteille *f*; (*for perfume*) flacon *m*; (*for baby*) biberon *m*; *Fam* **to take to** *or* **to hit the b.** se mettre à picoler; **b. green** vert bouteille *inv*; **b. opener** ouvre-bouteilles *m inv*, décapsuleur *m*

2 *vt* mettre en bouteille

▶**bottle up** *vt sep (emotions, anger)* refouler, ravaler

bottled [ˈbɒtəld] *adj* en bouteille; **b. water** eau *f* minérale

bottle-feed [ˈbɒtəlfiːd] (*pt & pp* **bottle-fed** [ˈbɒtəlfed]) *vt* nourrir au biberon

bottleneck [ˈbɒtəlnek] *n (in road)* rétrécissement *m* de la chaussée; (*in traffic*) embouteillage *m* (*dû à un rétrécissement de la chaussée*); (*in production*) goulot *m* d'étranglement

bottom [ˈbɒtəm] **1** *n* **(a)** (*lowest part*) (*of well, box, sea*) fond *m*; (*of stairs, mountain, page*) bas *m*; (*of ship*) carène *f*, fond; **from the b. of one's heart** du fond du cœur; **to be at the b. of the class** être le (la) dernier(ère) de la classe; **to touch b.** (*of boat*) toucher le fond

(b) (*buttocks*) derrière *m*

(c) (*idioms*) **to be at the b. of sth** être à l'origine de qch; **to get to the b. of sth** aller au fond des choses; **at b.** au fond; **the b. has fallen out of the market** le marché s'est effondré; *Fam* **bottoms up!** cul sec!

2 *adj* du bas; **b. floor** rez-de-chaussée *m inv*; *Fam* **you can bet your b. dollar that...** vous pouvez être sûr que...; **the b. line** (*financially*) le solde final; *Fig* **the b. line is that he is unsuited to the job** le fait est qu'il n'est pas fait pour ce travail

▶**bottom out** *vi (of recession, slump)* atteindre son maximum; *(of price)* atteindre son minimum

bottomless ['bɒtəmlɪs] *adj (abyss)* sans fond; *(reserve)* inépuisable; *Fig* **a b. pit** un gouffre

bottommost ['bɒtəmməʊst] *adj* le (la) plus bas (basse)

botulism ['bɒtjʊlɪzəm] *n* botulisme *m*

boudoir ['buːdwɑː(r)] *n* boudoir *m*

bouffant ['buːfɒn] *adj (hair)* bouffant(e)

bough [baʊ] *n* branche *f*

bought [bɔːt] *pt & pp of* **buy**

boulder ['bəʊldə(r)] *n* gros bloc *m* de roche

boulevard ['buːləvɑːd] *n* boulevard *m*

bounce [baʊns] **1** *n* **(a)** *(of ball)* rebond *m* **(b)** *Fig (energy)* entrain *m*

2 *vt* **(a)** *(ball)* faire rebondir; *Fig* **to b. an idea off sb** soumettre une idée à qn *(de manière informelle)* **(b)** *Fam (check)* refuser d'honorer

3 *vi* **(a)** *(of ball)* rebondir (**off** contre); **to b. into/out of a room** *(of person)* entrer/sortir d'une pièce en sautillant **(b)** *Fam* **the check bounced** le chèque a été refusé *(parce qu'il était sans provision)*

▶**bounce back** *vi (after sickness, disappointment)* se remettre rapidement

bouncer ['baʊnsə(r)] *n Fam (doorman)* videur *m*

bouncing ['baʊnsɪŋ] *adj* **a b. baby** un bébé en pleine santé

bouncy ['baʊnsɪ] *adj* **(a)** *(ball)* qui rebondit bien; *(mattress)* élastique **(b)** *Fig (person)* plein(e) d'entrain

bound[1] [baʊnd] **1** *n (leap)* bond *m*; **at one b.** d'un bond

2 *vi (leap)* bondir

bound[2] [baʊnd] *adj* **(a)** *(destined)* **b. for** en route pour **(b)** *(in predictions)* **he's b. to come** il ne peut pas manquer de venir; **it was b. to happen** ça devait arriver

bound[3] [baʊnd] *pt & pp of* **bind**

boundary ['baʊndərɪ] *(pl* **boundaries**) *n* limite *f*

bounder ['baʊndə(r)] *n Fam Old-fashioned* goujat *m*

boundless ['baʊndlɪs] *adj* illimité(e), sans bornes

bounds [baʊndz] *npl (limit)* limites *fpl*; **out of b.** interdit(e); **it is not beyond the b. of possibility** c'est dans le domaine du possible; **to know no b.** *(of anger, ambition)* être sans bornes

bountiful ['baʊntɪfʊl] *adj* abondant(e)

bounty ['baʊntɪ] *(pl* **bounties**) *n* **(a)** *(reward)* récompense *f*; **b. hunter** chasseur *m* de primes **(b)** *(generosity)* générosité *f*

bouquet [buːˈkeɪ] *n (of flowers, wine)* bouquet *m*

bourbon ['bɜːbən] *n (whiskey)* bourbon *m*

bourgeois ['bʊəʒwɑː] *adj* bourgeois(e)

bourgeoisie [bʊəʒwɑːˈziː] *n* bourgeoisie *f*

bout [baʊt] *n* **(a)** *(of sickness)* accès *m*; *(of work, activity)* période *f* **(b)** *(boxing match)* combat *m*

boutique [buːˈtiːk] *n* boutique *f*

bovine ['bəʊvaɪn] *adj* bovin(e)

bow[1] [bəʊ] *n* **(a)** *(weapon)* arc *m*; *(for violin)* archet *m* **(b)** *(in hair, on dress)* nœud *m*; **b. tie** nœud papillon

bow[2] [baʊ] *n (of ship)* proue *f*, avant *m*

bow[3] [baʊ] **1** *n* salut *m*; **to take a b.** saluer

2 *vt* **to b. one's head** baisser la tête

3 *vi* **(a)** *(as greeting, sign of respect)* saluer; *Fig* **to b. down before sb** s'incliner devant qn **(b)** *Fig (yield)* **to b. to sb/sth** s'incliner devant qn/qch

▶**bow out** *vi (resign)* tirer sa révérence

bowdlerize ['baʊdləraɪz] *vt* expurger

bowed [baʊd] *adj (back)* voûté(e); *(head)* baissé(e); **b. with age** courbé(e) par le fardeau des ans

bowel ['baʊəl] *n* intestin *m*; *Lit* **the bowels of the earth** les entrailles *fpl* de la terre; **b. complaint** affection *f* intestinale; **b. movement** selles *fpl*; **to have a b. movement** aller à la selle

bower ['baʊə(r)] *n* tonnelle *f*

bowl [bəʊl] **1** *n* **(a)** *(small dish)* bol *m*; *(for salad)* saladier *m*; *(for soup)* assiette *f* creuse **(b)** *(of toilet)* cuvette *f*

2 *vi (in tenpins)* jouer au bowling

▶**bowl along** *vi (of car, bicycle)* rouler à toute vitesse

▶**bowl over** *vt sep (knock down)* renverser; *Fig (astound)* **to be bowled over by sth** être stupéfié(e) par qch

bow-legged [bəʊˈlegɪd] *adj* aux jambes arquées

bowler ['bəʊlə(r)] *n* **(a)** *(hat)* chapeau *m* melon **(b)** *(in tenpins)* joueur(euse) *m,f* de bowling

bowling ['bəʊlɪŋ] *n (game)* jeu *m* de boules; **b. alley** piste *f* de bowling; *(building)* bowling *m*; **b. green** terrain *m* de boules *(gazonné)*

box [bɒks] **1** *n* **(a)** *(container)* boîte *f*; *(larger)* caisse *f*; *(postal)* boîte postale; **b. camera** appareil *m* photo compact **(b)** *(on form)* case *f*; *(containing text)* encadré *m*; **(penalty) b.** *(in soccer, ice hockey)* surface *f* de réparation **(c)** *(in theater)* loge *f*

2 *vt* **(a)** *(place in box)* mettre en boîte/en caisse **(b)** **to b. sb's ears** gifler qn

3 *vi (fight)* boxer

boxcar ['bɒkskɑː(r)] *n* wagon *m* de marchandises

boxer ['bɒksə(r)] *n* **(a)** *(fighter)* boxeur *m*; **b. shorts, boxers** *(underwear)* caleçon *m* **(b)** *(dog)* boxer *m*

boxing ['bɒksɪŋ] *n* boxe *f*; **b. glove/match** gant *m*/match *m* de boxe; **b. ring** ring *m*

box-office ['bɒksɒfɪs] *n* bureau *m* de location; **a b. success** un succès au box-office

boy [bɔɪ] *n* garçon *m*; **a night out with the boys** une soirée avec les copains; *Fam* **oh b.!** ça alors!; *Fam* **boys will be boys** il faut bien que jeunesse se passe; **B. Scout** scout *m*

boyband ['bɔɪbænd] *n* boys band *m*

boycott ['bɔɪkɒt] **1** *n* boycott *m*

2 *vt* boycotter

boyfriend ['bɔɪfrend] *n* petit ami *m*

boyhood ['bɔɪhʊd] *n* enfance *f*

boyish ['bɔɪʃ] *adj (of man) (looks, behavior)* de garçon; *(of woman) (looks)* de garçon; *(behavior)* de garçon manqué

bra [brɑː] *n* soutien-gorge *m*

brace [breɪs] *n* **(a)** *(on teeth)* appareil *m* dentaire *ou* orthodontique **(b)** *(pair) (of birds, pistols)* paire *f* **(c)** **b. and bit** *(tool)* vilebrequin *m (avec mèche)*

2 *vt* **(a)** **to b. oneself** *(for impact)* s'accrocher; *Fig* **to b. oneself (for sth)** se préparer (à qch) **(b)** *(reinforce)* consolider

bracelet ['breɪslɪt] *n* bracelet *m*

bracing ['breɪsɪŋ] *adj (wind, weather)* vivifiant(e)

bracken ['brækən] *n* fougère *f*

bracket ['brækɪt] **1** *n* **(a)** *(for shelves)* équerre *f* **(b)** *(in writing)* parenthèse *f*; **in brackets** entre parenthèses **(c)** *(category) (of tax)* tranche *f*; *(of salaries)* fourchette *f*; **the fifteen-to-twenty age b.** les quinze à vingt ans

2 *vt* **(a)** *(word, phrase)* mettre entre parenthèses **(b)** *(classify)* associer; **to b. together** mettre dans la même catégorie

brackish ['brækɪʃ] *adj* saumâtre

brag [bræg] *(pt & pp* **bragged**) *vi* se vanter (**about** de)

braggart ['brægət] *n* vantard(e) *m,f*

braid [breɪd] **1** *n (of hair)* tresse *f*, natte *f*; *(of cloth)* galon *m*

2 *vt (hair, thread)* tresser

Braille [breɪl] *n* braille *m*

brain [breɪn] **1** *n* cerveau *m*; **brains** *(as food)* cervelle *f*; *Fam* **to have brains** être intelligent(e); *Fam* **she's the brains of the business** c'est elle le cerveau de l'entreprise; *Fam* **to have money/sex on the b.** être obsédé(e) par l'argent/le sexe; **b. damage** lésions *fpl* cérébrales; **b. dead** dans un coma dépassé; **the b. drain** la fuite des cerveaux; **b. surgeon** neurochirurgien(enne) *m,f*; **b. tumor** tumeur *f* au cerveau; *Fam* **b. wave** *(brilliant idea)* idée *f* de génie

2 *vt Fam (hit)* assommer

brainbox ['breɪnbɒks] *n Fam* cerveau *m*

brainchild ['breɪntʃaɪld] *n (idea, project)* idée *f*, trouvaille *f*

brainless ['breɪnlɪs] *adj* stupide

brainpower ['breɪnpaʊə(r)] *n* intelligence *f*

brainstorm ['breɪnstɔːm] *n Fam (brilliant idea)* idée *f* de génie

brainstorming ['breɪnstɔːmɪŋ] *n* brainstorming *m*, remue-méninges *m inv*

brainwash ['breɪnwɒʃ] *vt* faire un lavage de cerveau à; **to b. sb into doing sth** faire faire qch à qn à force d'endoctrinement

brainy ['breɪnɪ] *adj Fam* intelligent(e)

braise [breɪz] *vt* braiser

brake [breɪk] **1** *n* frein *m*; **to apply the brake(s)** freiner; *Fig* **to put the brakes on a project** ralentir l'exécution d'un projet; **b. fluid** liquide *m* de freins; **b. lights** feux *mpl* de stop; **b. pedal** pédale *f* de frein

2 *vi* freiner

braking distance ['breɪkɪŋ'dɪstəns] *n* distance *f* de freinage

bramble ['bræmbəl] *n* ronce *f*

bran [bræn] *n* son *m*

branch [brɑːntʃ] **1** *n* (**a**) *(of tree, family, subject)* branche *f*; *(of river)* bras *m*; *(of railroad, road)* embranchement *m*; **b. line** *(of railroad)* ligne *f* secondaire (**b**) *(of store)* succursale *f*; *(of bank)* agence *f*

2 *vi* bifurquer

▸**branch off** *vi (of discussion)* bifurquer (**into** vers)

▸**branch out** *vi* se diversifier; **to b. out into** étendre ses activités à

brand [brænd] **1** *n* (**a**) *(of product)* marque *f*; *Fig* **she has her own b. of humor** elle a un sens de l'humour particulier; **b. image** image *f* de marque; **b. leader** marque la plus vendue; **b. name** marque (**b**) *(on cattle)* marque *f (au fer rouge)*

2 *vt (cattle)* marquer au fer rouge; *Fig* **the image was branded on her memory** l'image était gravée dans sa mémoire; *Fig* **to b. sb (as) a liar/coward** coller à qn l'étiquette de menteur(euse)/lâche

brandish ['brændɪʃ] *vt* brandir

brand-new ['bræn(d)'njuː] *adj* flambant neuf (neuve)

brandy ['brændɪ] *(pl* **brandies**) *n (cognac)* cognac *m*; *(more generally)* eau-de-vie *f*; **cherry b.** cherry *m*

brash [bræʃ] *adj (person, behavior)* effronté(e); *(color, décor)* tape-à-l'œil *m*

brass [brɑːs] *n* (**a**) *(metal)* laiton *m* (**b**) *Mus (brass instruments)* cuivres *mpl*; **b. band** fanfare *f*

brassière ['bræzɪə(r)] *n* soutien-gorge *m*

brassy ['brɑːsɪ] *adj Fam (person, manner)* exubérant(e)

brat [bræt] *n Pej* morveux(euse) *m,f*

bravado [brə'vɑːdəʊ] *n* bravade *f*

brave [breɪv] **1** *n (Native American)* brave *m*

2 *adj* courageux(euse); **a b. effort** un bel effort; **a b. new world** un paradis; *Pej & Ironic* un monde utopique; **to put a b. face on it** faire bonne contenance

3 *vt* braver

bravely ['breɪvlɪ] *adv* courageusement

bravery ['breɪvərɪ] *n* courage *m*

bravo [brɑː'vəʊ] *exclam* bravo!

brawl [brɔːl] **1** *n* bagarre *f*; **a drunken b.** une querelle d'ivrognes

2 *vi* se bagarrer

brawn [brɔːn] *n Fam (strength)* muscle *m*; **he's all b. and no brain** il a du muscle mais rien dans la tête

brawny ['brɔːnɪ] *adj* musclé(e)

bray [breɪ] **1** *n (of donkey)* braiment *m*; *Fig (of person)* braillement *m*

2 *vi (of donkey)* braire; *Fig (of person)* brailler

brazen ['breɪzən] *adj* effronté(e), impudent(e); *(lie)* éhonté(e)

▸**brazen out** *vt sep* **to b. it out** s'en tirer au culot

brazier ['breɪzɪə(r)] *n* brasero *m*

Brazil [brə'zɪl] *n* le Brésil

brazil [brə'zɪl] *n* **b. (nut)** noix *f* du Brésil

Brazilian [brə'zɪlɪən] **1** *n* (**a**) *(person)* Brésilien(enne) *m,f* (**b**) *(bikini wax)* épilation *f* maillot brésilienne

2 *adj* brésilien(enne); **B. wax** épilation *f* maillot brésilienne

breach [briːtʃ] **1** *n* (**a**) *(in wall)* brèche *f*; *Fig* **to step into the b.** *(in emergency)* intervenir au pied levé (**b**) *(of agreement, contract)* rupture *f* (**of** de); *(of trust)* abus *m* (**of** de); *(of discipline)* manquement *m* (**of** à); *(of rules)* infraction *f* (**of** à); *Law* **b. of the peace** atteinte *f* à l'ordre public (**c**) *(in relationship)* **it caused a b. in their relationship** cela les a conduits à se brouiller

2 *vt* (**a**) *(defenses)* ouvrir une brèche dans (**b**) *(agreement, contract)* rompre; *(rules)* enfreindre

bread [bred] *n* (**a**) *(food)* pain *m*; **a loaf of b.** un pain; **b. and butter** du pain beurré; *Fig* gagne-pain *m*; *Fig* **he knows which side his b. is buttered on** il sait où est son intérêt; **b. box** boîte *f* à pain; **b. knife** couteau *m* à pain (**b**) *very Fam (money)* blé *m*, pognon *m*

bread-and-butter [bredən'bʌtə(r)] *adj Fam* **b. issues** questions *fpl* essentielles

breadbasket ['bredbɑːskɪt] *n* corbeille *f* à pain

breadboard ['bredbɔːd] *n* planche *f* à pain

breadcrumb ['bredkrʌm] *n* miette *f* de pain; **breadcrumbs** *(in recipe)* chapelure *f*; **fried in breadcrumbs** pané(e)

breadline ['bredlaɪn] *n* **on the b.** indigent(e), sans ressources

breadth [bredθ] *n* (**a**) *(width)* largeur *f* (**b**) *(of mind, opinions)* largeur *f*; *(of outlook, understanding)* ampleur *f*

breadwinner ['bredwɪnə(r)] *n* **to be the b.** faire bouillir la marmite

break [breɪk] **1** *n* (**a**) *(in bone)* fracture *f*; *(in wall, fence)* brèche *f*; *(in clouds)* trouée *f*; *(in electric circuit)* rupture *f*; **at b. of day** au point du jour; *Elec* **b. switch** disjoncteur *m*

(**b**) *(interval, rest)* pause *f*; *(vacation)* vacances *fpl*; **(commercial) b.** *(on TV, radio)* page *f* de publicité; **without a b.** sans interruption; **a b. in the weather** un changement de temps; *Fam* **give me a b.!** *(leave me in peace)* fiche-moi la paix deux minutes!; *(don't talk nonsense)* je t'en prie!

(**c**) *Fam (escape)* évasion *f*; **to make a b. for it** se faire la belle; **to make a b. for the exit** se précipiter vers la sortie

(**d**) *Fam (chance)* chance *f*; **to have a lucky b.** avoir de la veine; **this could be your big b.** ça pourrait être la chance de ta vie

2 *vt (pt* **broke** [brəʊk], *pp* **broken** ['brəʊkən]) (**a**) *(in general)* casser; **to b. one's arm** se casser le bras; **to b. sth into pieces** mettre qch en morceaux; **to b. the sound barrier** franchir le mur du son; *Fig* **to b. the ice** briser la glace; **to b. one's journey** s'arrêter en route; *Fig* **b. a leg!** *(good luck!)* bonne chance!

(**b**) *(cushion) (fall, force)* amortir

(**c**) *(destroy) (person, resistance, strike)* briser; *(health)* ruiner; **to b. sb's heart** briser le cœur à qn; **to b. sb's serve** *(in tennis)* prendre le service de qn

(**d**) *(infringe) (agreement, promise)* rompre; *(rule, speed limit)* enfreindre

(**e**) *(news, story)* annoncer (**to** à)

3 *vi* (**a**) *(of glass, machine, bone)* se casser; *(of weather)* changer; *(of day)* se lever; *(of waves)* se briser; *(of voice) (with emotion)* se briser; *(at puberty)* muer; **to b. in two** se casser en deux; **to b. loose** se détacher

(**b**) *(of news, story)* éclater

▸**break away** *vi* (**a**) **to b. away from** *(escape from) (person)* échapper à; *(place)* s'évader de (**b**) **to b. away from** *(cut ties with) (party, country)* quitter; *(family)* couper les ponts avec

▸**break down 1** *vt sep* (**a**) *(destroy) (resistance)* briser (**b**) *(analyze) (argument, figures)* décomposer (**into** en)

2 *vi* (**a**) *(of car, machine)* tomber en panne; *(of talks)* échouer; *(of argument)* s'effondrer; *(of person under pressure)* craquer; **to**

b. down (in tears) fondre en larmes (**b**) *(change chemically)* se décomposer (**into** en)

▸**break even** *vi* rentrer dans ses frais

▸**break in 1** *vt sep (horse)* dresser; *(new shoes)* faire; *(new recruit)* former; **to b. oneself in to sth** se faire à qch
   2 *vi (of burglar)* entrer par effraction

▸**break into** *vt insep* (**a**) *(of burglar)* entrer par effraction dans (**b**) *(begin suddenly)* **to b. into laughter** éclater de rire; **to b. into song/a run** se mettre à chanter/courir (**c**) *(show business)* percer dans; *(market)* percer sur

▸**break off 1** *vt sep* (**a**) *(detach) (twig, handle)* casser (**b**) *(terminate) (relations, engagement)* rompre
   2 *vi* (**a**) *(become detached)* se casser (**b**) *(stop talking, working)* s'interrompre

▸**break open 1** *vt sep (door)* enfoncer; *(lock, safe)* forcer
   2 *vi* s'ouvrir

▸**break out** *vi* (**a**) *(escape)* s'évader (**of** de) (**b**) *(of argument)* éclater; *(of disease)* se déclarer; **to b. out in a sweat** se mettre à transpirer; **to b. out in a rash** avoir une éruption de boutons

▸**break through 1** *vt insep (wall)* faire une brèche dans; *(barrier)* forcer; *Fig (someone's reserve, shyness)* vaincre
   2 *vi (of sun)* percer les nuages

▸**break up 1** *vt sep* (**a**) *(reduce to pieces)* couper en morceaux (**b**) *(estate, company)* morceler; *(machine)* démonter (**c**) *(fight, quarrel)* faire cesser
   2 *vi* (**a**) *(disintegrate)* se disloquer (**b**) *(end) (of talks)* cesser; *(of meeting, school semester)* se terminer; *(of school)* fermer; *(of pupils)* être en vacances; **to b. up with sb** *(end relationship)* rompre avec qn

▸**break with** *vt insep* rompre avec

breakable ['breɪkəbəl] **1** *n* **breakables** objets *mpl* fragiles
   2 *adj* fragile

breakage ['breɪkɪdʒ] *n* **was there any b.?** est-ce qu'il y a eu de la casse?; **all b. must be paid for** *(sign)* tout article cassé doit être payé

breakaway ['breɪkəweɪ] *adj* dissident(e)

breakdown ['breɪkdaʊn] *n* (**a**) *(of car, machine, computer)* panne *f*; *(of talks, in communication)* rupture *f*; **to have a b.** *(of motorist)* tomber en panne (**b**) *Psy* **(nervous) b.** dépression *f* nerveuse; **to have a b.** faire une dépression nerveuse (**c**) *(analysis) (of figures, costs)* détail *m*

breaker ['breɪkə(r)] *n (wave)* déferlante *f*

break-even point [breɪk'iːvənpɔɪnt] *n Fin* seuil *m* de rentabilité

breakfast ['brekfəst] **1** *n* petit déjeuner *m*; **to have b.** prendre son petit déjeuner, déjeuner; **b. cereal** céréales *fpl*
   2 *vi* prendre son petit déjeuner, déjeuner; **to b. on sth** manger qch au petit déjeuner

break-in ['breɪkɪn] *n* cambriolage *m*

breaking ['breɪkɪŋ] *n* (**a**) *Law* **b. and entering** entrée *f* par effraction (**b**) **b. point** *(of patience)* limite *f*; **to reach b. point** *(of person)* être à bout; *(of marriage)* être au bord de la rupture

breakneck ['breɪknek] *adj* **at b. speed** à toute allure

break-out ['breɪkaʊt] *n (from prison)* évasion *f*

breakthrough ['breɪkθruː] *n (discovery)* découverte *f* majeure; **there has been a b. in talks** un pas décisif a été franchi dans les négociations; **to make a b.** *(discovery)* faire une découverte majeure; *(in talks)* faire un pas décisif

breakthrough ['breɪkθruː] *n (discovery)* découverte *f* majeure; **there has been a b. in talks** un pas décisif a été franchi dans les négociations; **to make a b.** *(discovery)* faire une découverte majeure; *(in talks)* faire un pas décisif

break-up ['breɪkʌp] *n (of association)* dissolution *f*; *(of relationship)* rupture *f*; *(of meeting)* fin *f*

bream [briːm] *(pl* **bream**) *n* brème *f*

breast [brest] *n (of woman) & Lit (of man)* sein *m*; *(of chicken)* blanc *m*; **b. cancer** cancer *m* du sein; **b. implants** implants

mpl mammaires; **b. milk** lait *m* maternel; **b. pocket** poche *f* de poitrine

breastbone ['brestbəʊn] *n* sternum *m*

breast-feed ['brestfiːd] *(pt & pp* **breast-fed** ['brestfed]) *vt & vi* allaiter

breastplate ['brestpleɪt] *n* plastron *m (de cuirasse)*

breaststroke ['bres(t)strəʊk] *n* brasse *f*

breath [breθ] *n* souffle *m*; **to take a deep b.** inspirer profondément; **to pause for b.** s'arrêter pour reprendre sa respiration; **bad b.** mauvaise haleine *f*; **they are not to be mentioned in the same b.** on ne saurait les comparer; **in the next b.** aussitôt après; *also Fig* **to hold one's b.** retenir son souffle; *Fam* **don't hold your b.!** c'est pas demain la veille!; **to waste one's b.** gaspiller sa salive; **out of b.** à bout de souffle, hors d'haleine; **to get short of b.** s'essouffler; **to get one's b. back** reprendre haleine, reprendre son souffle; **under one's b.** à voix basse; *Fig* **to take sb's b. away** couper le souffle à qn; **a b. of wind/of air** un souffle de vent/d'air; **to go out for a b. of fresh air** sortir prendre l'air; *Fig* **she's a real b. of fresh air** elle apporte une bouffée d'air frais; **b. test** Alcotest® *m*

breathalyze ['breθəlaɪz] *vt* faire passer l'Alcotest® à

Breathalyzer® ['breθəlaɪzə(r)] *n* Alcotest® *m*

breathe [briːð] **1** *vt* (**a**) *(inhale)* respirer (**b**) *(idioms)* **to b. a sigh of relief** pousser un soupir de soulagement; *Lit* **to b. one's last** rendre son dernier soupir; **don't b. a word (of it)!** pas un mot!; **to b. fire** *(in anger)* jeter feu et flammes; **to b. new life into sth** *(project, scheme)* insuffler une force nouvelle à qch
   2 *vi* respirer; *(exhale)* souffler; **to b. heavily** *(noisily)* respirer bruyamment; *(with difficulty)* respirer avec difficulté; *Fig* **to b. easily again** respirer; *Fig* **to b. down sb's neck** *(follow)* talonner qn; *(nag)* être tout le temps sur le dos de qn

▸**breathe in 1** *vt* inhaler
   2 *vi* inspirer

▸**breathe out** *vi* expirer

breather ['briːðə(r)] *n Fam (rest)* pause *f*; **to take a b.** faire une pause

breathing ['briːðɪŋ] *n* respiration *f*; **b. apparatus** bouteille *f* d'oxygène et masque; *Fig* **to give sb some b. space** laisser respirer qn

breathless ['breθlɪs] *adj (person)* hors d'haleine, essoufflé(e); *(calm)* plat(e); *(silence)* profond(e)

breathtaking ['breθteɪkɪŋ] *adj (beauty, scenery)* à couper le souffle; *(speed)* vertigineux(euse); *(audacity)* sidérant(e)

breathy ['breθɪ] *adj (voice)* haletant(e)

bred [bred] *pt & pp of* **breed**

breech [briːtʃ] *n* (**a**) *Med* **b. delivery** *or* **birth** *(accouchement m par le)* siège *m* (**b**) *(of gun)* culasse *f*

breeches ['brɪtʃɪz] *npl* **(pair of) b.** culotte *f*

breed [briːd] **1** *n also Fig* race *f*
   2 *vt (pt & pp* **bred** [bred]) *(animals)* élever; *Fig (discontent)* engendrer
   3 *vi* se reproduire

breeder ['briːdə(r)] *n (of animals)* éleveur(euse) *m,f*; *Phys* **b. reactor** surgénérateur *m*

breeding ['briːdɪŋ] *n* (**a**) *(of animals)* élevage *m*; **b. ground** lieu *m* de reproduction; *Fig (of discontent, revolution)* foyer *m* (**b**) *(of person)* **(good) b.** éducation *f*, manières *fpl*

breeze [briːz] **1** *n* brise *f*
   2 *vi* **to b. in/out** *(quickly)* entrer/sortir en coup de vent; *(casually)* entrer/sortir avec désinvolture

breezy ['briːzɪ] *adj* (**a**) *(weather)* venteux(euse) (**b**) *(casual)* désinvolte

brethren ['breðrɪn] *npl Rel* frères *mpl*

Breton ['bretɒn] **1** *n* Breton(onne) *m,f*
   2 *adj* breton(onne)

breviary ['briːvɪərɪ] (*pl* **breviaries**) *n Rel* bréviaire *m*

brevity ['brevɪtɪ] *n* brièveté *f*

brew [bruː] **1** *n (beer)* bière *f*; *Fig (mixture)* mélange *m*
2 *vt (beer)* brasser; *(tea)* faire infuser, préparer
3 *vi (of beer)* fermenter; *(of tea)* infuser; **there's a storm brewing** il y a de l'orage dans l'air; *Fig* **there's something brewing** il se trame quelque chose; **there's trouble brewing** il va y avoir du grabuge

brewer ['bruːə(r)] *n* brasseur *m*

brewery ['brʊərɪ] (*pl* **breweries**) *n* brasserie *f (fabrique)*

briar ['braɪə(r)] *n (plant)* bruyère *f*; *(pipe)* pipe *f* de bruyère; **b. rose** églantine *f*

bribe [braɪb] **1** *n* pot-de-vin *m*
2 *vt* acheter; **to b. sb into doing sth** acheter qn pour qu'il fasse qch

bribery ['braɪbərɪ] *n* corruption *f*

bric-à-brac ['brɪkəbræk] *n* bric-à-brac *m*

brick [brɪk] *n (for building)* brique *f*; *Fig* **to drop a b.** faire une gaffe; **b. wall** mur *m* en briques; **you're banging your head against a b. wall** tu perds ton temps

▸**brick up** *vt sep* murer

bricklayer ['brɪkleɪə(r)] *n* maçon *m*

brickwork ['brɪkwɜːk] *n* briquetage *m*

bridal ['braɪdəl] *adj* nuptial(e); **b. dress** *or* **gown** robe *f* de mariée; **b. suite** suite *f* nuptiale

bride [braɪd] *n* mariée *f*; **the b. and groom** les mariés *mpl*

bridegroom ['braɪdgruːm] *n* marié *m*

bridesmaid ['braɪdzmeɪd] *n* demoiselle *f* d'honneur

bridge¹ [brɪdʒ] **1** *n (over river)* pont *m*; *(on ship)* passerelle *f*; *(on teeth)* bridge *m*; *(of nose)* arête *f*; *Fig* **we'll cross that b. when we come to it** chaque chose en son temps; *Fig* **b. building** réconciliation *f*; *Fin* **b. loan** prêt-relais *m*
2 *vt (river)* construire un pont sur; **to b. a gap** *(in knowledge)* combler une lacune; **to b. the gap between rich and poor** combler le fossé entre les riches et les pauvres

bridge² [brɪdʒ] *n (card game)* bridge *m*

bridgehead ['brɪdʒhed] *n Mil* tête *f* de pont

bridle ['braɪdəl] **1** *n* bride *f*; **b. path** piste *f* cavalière
2 *vt (horse)* brider
3 *vi (with anger)* s'indigner (**at** de)

brief [briːf] **1** *n Law* dossier *m*; *(instructions)* consignes *fpl*
2 *adj* bref (brève); *(garment)* court(e); **in b.,…, to be b.,…** en bref,…
3 *vt (inform)* mettre au courant (**on** de)

briefcase ['briːfkeɪs] *n* serviette *f*

briefing ['briːfɪŋ] *n (meeting)* briefing *m*; *(information)* instructions *fpl*

briefly ['briːflɪ] *adv* brièvement; *(hesitate, smile)* pendant un court instant; **(put) b.,…** en bref,…

briefs [briːfs] *npl (underwear)* slip *m*

brier = **briar**

brigade [brɪ'ɡeɪd] *n* brigade *f*

brigadier [brɪɡə'dɪə(r)] *n* **b. general** général *m* de brigade

brigand ['brɪɡənd] *n Lit* brigand *m*

bright [braɪt] **1** *adj* (**a**) *(sun, light)* brillant(e); *(day)* clair(e); *(color)* vif (vive); **to go b. red** *(blush)* devenir rouge comme une tomate (**b**) *(hopeful)* **the future looks b.** l'avenir s'annonce bien; **the situation is looking a bit brighter** la situation commence à s'améliorer; *Fig* **the only b. spot is…** la seule chose positive est…; **to look on the b. side (of things)** prendre les choses du bon côté (**c**) *(cheerful)* vif (vive) (**d**) *(smart) (person)* intelligent(e); *(idea)* lumineux(euse); **to be b. at sth** être doué(e) en qch
2 *adv* **b. and early** de bon matin

brighten ['braɪtən] **1** *vt (room, mood)* égayer
2 *vi (of weather, sky)* s'éclaircir; *(of face, eyes)* s'éclaircir; *(of prospects)* s'améliorer

▸**brighten up 1** *vt sep (room)* égayer
2 *vi (of person)* devenir plus gai(e); *(of weather, sky)* s'éclaircir; *(of face)* s'éclairer; *(of prospects)* s'améliorer

bright-eyed ['braɪtaɪd] *adj* aux yeux brillants; *Fig (eager)* enthousiaste; *Fam* **b. and bushy-tailed** frais (fraîche) et dispos(e)

brightly ['braɪtlɪ] *adv (say)* gaiement; *(lit, colored)* vivement; **the sun was shining b.** il faisait un soleil radieux; **to smile b.** faire un sourire radieux

brightness ['braɪtnɪs] *n (of light, sun, color)* éclat *m*; *(of lighting)* intensité *f*; *(on TV)* luminosité *f*

brilliance ['brɪljəns] *n* (**a**) *(of light, color)* éclat *m* (**b**) *(of person)* intelligence *f*; *(of idea)* ingéniosité *f*

brilliant ['brɪljənt] *adj* (**a**) *(light)* éclatant(e); *(sun, smile)* radieux(euse) (**b**) *(scientist, career, pupil)* brillant(e)

brilliantly ['brɪljəntlɪ] *adv* (**a**) *(colored, lit)* vivement (**b**) *(acted, played)* brillamment

brim [brɪm] **1** *n (of cup, glass, hat)* bord *m*; **to be full to the b. (with)** être plein(e) à ras bord (de)
2 *vi (pt & pp* **brimmed**) **to be brimming with sth** *(liquid)* être rempli(e) à ras bord de qch; *(enthusiasm, ideas)* déborder de qch; **eyes brimming with tears** yeux noyés de larmes

▸**brim over** *vi also Fig* déborder (**with** de)

brimful ['brɪmfʊl] *adj* plein(e) à ras bord; *Fig* **b. of health/ life** débordant(e) de santé/vie

brimstone ['brɪmstəʊn] *n Fig* **to preach fire and b.** menacer les fidèles des feux de l'enfer

brine [braɪn] *n* saumure *f*

bring [brɪŋ] (*pt & pp* **brought** [brɔːt]) *vt* (**a**) *(cause to come) (object, letter, news)* apporter; *(person, animal)* amener; **to b. sth to sb's attention** signaler qch à l'attention de qn; **what brings you to Boston?** qu'est-ce qui vous amène à Boston?; **to b. sth out of sth** *(box, bag)* sortir qch de qch; **to b. a child into the world** mettre un enfant au monde; *Law* **to b. an action against sb** intenter un procès à qn
(**b**) *(cause)* provoquer; **it has brought me great happiness** cela m'a procuré un grand bonheur; **to b. sb (good) luck/bad luck** porter bonheur/malheur à qn; **to b. new hope to sb** redonner de l'espoir à qn; **to b. tears to sb's eyes** faire venir les larmes aux yeux de qn
(**c**) *(to a particular condition)* **to b. sth into disrepute** discréditer qch; **to b. sth into question** remettre qch en question; **to b. sth to an end** mettre fin à qch; **to b. sth to light** *(crime, secret)* révéler qch; **to b. sth to mind** faire penser à qch; **I couldn't bring myself to do it** je n'ai pas pu me décider *ou* me résoudre à le faire
(**d**) *(be sold for)* rapporter

▸**bring about** *vt sep (cause)* entraîner, provoquer

▸**bring along** *vt sep (person)* amener; *(object)* apporter

▸**bring around** *vt sep* (**a**) *(revive)* ranimer, faire revenir à soi (**b**) *(persuade)* convaincre; **she brought him around to her point of view** elle l'a rallié à son point de vue (**c**) *(conversation)* amener (**to** sur)

▸**bring back** *vt sep* (**a**) *(person)* ramener; *(gift)* rapporter; **to b. sb back to life** ramener qn à la vie; **to b. sb back to health** rendre la santé à qn (**b**) *(memory)* rappeler (**c**) *(law, practice)* rétablir

▸**bring down** *vt sep* (**a**) *(from shelf, attic)* descendre (**b**) *(soldier, plane)* abattre; *(government)* faire tomber, renverser; *Fam* **her performance brought the house down** son interprétation lui a valu des applaudissements enthousiastes (**c**) *(lower) (price, temperature)* faire baisser

▸**bring forward** *vt sep* (**a**) *(proposal)* émettre; *(plan)* proposer; *(reasons, evidence)* avancer (**b**) *(advance time of)* avancer (**c**) *Com (in bookkeeping)* reporter

▸**bring in** *vt sep* (**a**) *(expert, consultant)* faire appel à; **the police brought him in for questioning** la police l'a emmené au poste pour l'interroger (**b**) *(earn) (of person)* gagner; *(of investment, sale)* rapporter (**c**) *(law, act)* introduire (**d**) *Law (verdict)* rendre

▸**bring off** *vt sep (accomplish)* réussir

▸**bring on** *vt sep (cause)* provoquer; **you've brought it on yourself** tu t'as cherché

▸**bring out** *vt sep* (**a**) *(publish)* sortir (**b**) *(cause to appear)* **to b. out the best/the worst in sb** faire ressortir les qualités/les défauts de qn; **strawberries b. out a rash in her** les fraises lui donnent de l'urticaire; **to b. sb out of their shell** faire sortir qn de sa coquille

▸**bring round** = **bring around**

▸**bring to** *vt sep (revive)* ranimer, faire revenir à soi

▸**bring together** *vt sep* réunir

▸**bring up** *vt sep* (**a**) *(subject)* soulever (**b**) *(child)* élever; **I was brought up to be polite** on m'a appris à être poli (**c**) *(vomit)* vomir

brink [brɪŋk] *n also Fig* bord *m*; *Fig* **to be on the b. of sth** *(war, ruin, disaster)* être au bord de qch; *(death, success)* être à deux doigts de qch; **to be on the b. of doing sth** être à deux doigts de faire qch

brinkmanship ['brɪŋkmənʃɪp] *n* politique *f* de la corde raide

brisk [brɪsk] *adj* (**a**) *(weather)* frais (fraîche); *(wind)* vivifiant(e) (**b**) *(person) (efficient)* énergique; *(dismissive)* vif (vive) (**c**) *(rapid)* **at a b. pace** *(work)* rapidement; *(walk)* d'un pas vif; **to go for a b. walk** se promener d'un pas vif; **business is b.** les affaires marchent bien

briskly ['brɪsklɪ] *adv* (**a**) *(efficiently)* énergiquement; *(dismissively)* vivement (**b**) *(rapidly) (walk)* d'un pas vif

bristle ['brɪsəl] **1** *n (of plant, brush, face)* poil *m*; *(of pig)* soie *f*
2 *vi* (**a**) *(of animal, animal's fur)* se hérisser; **to b. (with anger) (at)** se hérisser (à) (**b**) **to be bristling with** *(people)* grouiller de; *(difficulties)* être hérissé(e) de

Brit [brɪt] *n Fam* Britannique *mf*

Britain ['brɪtən] *n* la Grande-Bretagne

British ['brɪtɪʃ] **1** *npl* **the B.** les Britanniques *mpl*
2 *adj* britannique; **B. Columbia** la Colombie-Britannique; **the B. Isles** les îles *fpl* Britanniques

Briton ['brɪtən] *n* Britannique *mf*; *Hist* **ancient B.** Breton(onne) *m,f (de la Grande-Bretagne)*

Brittany ['brɪtənɪ] *n* la Bretagne

brittle ['brɪtəl] *adj (object, hair, voice)* cassant(e); *(bones)* friable

broach [brəʊtʃ] *vt (subject)* aborder

broad[1] [brɔːd] *adj (road, smile, sense, mind)* large; *(accent)* fort(e), prononcé(e); *(humor)* grossier(ère); *(hint)* appuyé(e); **in b. daylight** en plein jour; *Fig* au grand jour; **to be in b. agreement** être d'accord sur l'essentiel; **a b. outline** les grandes lignes *fpl*; **b. bean** fève *f*; **b. jump** saut *m* en longueur

broad[2] [brɔːd] *n Fam (woman)* gonzesse *f*

broadband ['brɔːdbænd] *Tel & Comput* **1** *n* connexion *f* à haut débit *ou* à large bande
2 *adj* à haut débit, à large bande

broadcast ['brɔːdkɑːst] **1** *n* émission *f*
2 *vt (pt & pp* **broadcast***)* diffuser; *Fam* **don't b. it!** ne va pas le crier sur les toits!
3 *vi (of station)* émettre

broadcaster ['brɔːdkɑːstə(r)] *n (person) (on TV, radio)* présentateur(trice) *m,f*; *(TV station)* chaîne *f* de télévision; *(radio station)* station *f* de radio

broadcasting ['brɔːdkɑːstɪŋ] *n (action)* diffusion *f*; **he works in b.** *(radio)* il travaille à la radio; *(TV)* il travaille à la télé

broaden ['brɔːdən] **1** *vt* élargir; **to b. one's horizons** élargir son horizon
2 *vi* **to b. (out)** s'élargir

broadly ['brɔːdlɪ] *adv (generally)* en gros; **to smile b.** faire un large sourire; **b. speaking** en gros

broad-minded [brɔːd'maɪndɪd] *adj (person)* large d'esprit; *(attitude)* ouvert(e)

broad-shouldered [brɔːd'ʃəʊldəd] *adj* large d'épaules; *Fig* **to be b.** *(resilient)* bien encaisser

broadside ['brɔːdsaɪd] **1** *n Naut* **to fire a b.** tirer une bordée; *Fig* **to fire a b. at sb/sth** attaquer violemment qn/qch
2 *adv* par le travers; **the truck hit us b.** le camion nous a heurtés sur le côté

brocade [brəʊ'keɪd] *n* brocart *m*

broccoli ['brɒkəlɪ] *n* brocolis *mpl*

brochure ['brəʊʃə(r)] *n* brochure *f*

brogue [brəʊg] *n (accent)* accent *m*

brogues [brəʊgz] *npl (shoes)* = chaussures solides souvent ornées de petits trous

broil [brɔɪl] *vt & vi* griller

broke [brəʊk] **1** *adj Fam* fauché(e); **to go for b.** jouer le tout pour le tout
2 *pt of* **break**

broken ['brəʊkən] **1** *adj (object, bone)* cassé(e); *(promise)* rompu(e); *(marriage, heart, person)* brisé(e); *(ground, surface)* irrégulier(ère); **to speak b. English** parler un mauvais anglais; **b. home** famille *f* désunie
2 *pp of* **break**

brokenhearted [brəʊkən'hɑːtɪd] *adj* **to be b.** avoir le cœur brisé

broker ['brəʊkə(r)] *n Fin (for shares, currency)* agent *m* de change; *Com (for goods, insurance)* courtier *m*

bromide ['brəʊmaɪd] *n Chem* bromure *m*; *Fig* banalité *f*

bronchial ['brɒŋkɪəl] *adj Anat* bronchique; **b. pneumonia** broncho-pneumonie *f*; **b. tubes** bronches *fpl*

bronchitic [brɒŋ'kɪtɪk] *adj* bronchitique

bronchitis [brɒŋ'kaɪtɪs] *n* bronchite *f*; **to have b.** avoir une bronchite

bronze [brɒnz] **1** *n* bronze *m*; **to win a b.** *(medal)* remporter une médaille de bronze; **the B. Age** l'âge *m* du bronze
2 *adj (material)* de *ou* en bronze; *(color)* couleur bronze *inv*

bronzed [brɒnzd] *adj* bronzé(e)

brooch [brəʊtʃ, bruːtʃ] *n* broche *f*

brood [bruːd] **1** *n (of birds)* couvée *f*; *Hum (of children)* progéniture *f*
2 *vi (of hen)* couver; *Fig* **to b. (over** or **about sth)** ruminer (qch)

broody ['bruːdɪ] *adj (hen)* couveuse *f*; *Fig (woman)* en mal d'enfant

brook[1] [brʊk] *n (stream)* ruisseau *m*

brook[2] [brʊk] *vt Formal (tolerate)* tolérer

broom [bruːm] *n* (**a**) *(plant)* genêt *m* (**b**) *(for cleaning)* balai *m*

broomstick ['bruːmstɪk] *n* manche *m* à balai

Bros *npl Com (written abbr* **Brothers***)* Richardson B. Richardson frères

broth [brɒθ] *n (soup) (thin)* bouillon *m*; *(thick)* potage *m*

brothel ['brɒθəl] *n* maison *f* close

brother ['brʌðə(r)] *n* frère *m*

brotherhood ['brʌðəhʊd] *n* fraternité *f*; *Rel* confrérie *f*; **the b. of man** la fraternité humaine

brother-in-law ['brʌðərɪnlɔː] *(pl* **brothers-in-law***) n* beau-frère *m*

brought [brɔːt] *pt & pp of* **bring**

brow [braʊ] *n* (**a**) *(forehead)* front *m*; *(eyebrow)* sourcil *m* (**b**) *(of hill)* sommet *m*

browbeat ['braʊbiːt] *(pt* **browbeat***, pp* **browbeaten** ['braʊbiːtən]*) vt* intimider; **to b. sb into doing sth** forcer qn à faire qch en usant d'intimidation

brown [braʊn] **1** *n* marron *m*
2 *adj* marron *inv*; *(hair)* brun(e); *(skin)* mat(e); *(tanned)* bronzé(e);

(bread, flour, rice) complet(ète); **b. paper** papier *m* kraft; **b. sugar** sucre *m* roux, cassonade *f*
3 *vt (in cooking)* faire dorer
4 *vi (in cooking)* dorer

brownfield site [ˈbraʊnfiːld'saɪt] *n* terrain *m* à bâtir *(après démolition de bâtiments préexistants)*

Brownie [ˈbraʊnɪ] *n* ≃ jeannette *f*; *Fig* **to win** *or* **to get b. points** se faire bien voir

brownie [ˈbraʊnɪ] *n (cake)* brownie *m*

brownnose, brown-nose [ˈbraʊnnəʊz] *vi Vulg* faire le lèche-cul

browse [braʊz] **1** *vt Comput* **to b. the Web** naviguer sur le Web
2 *vi* **(a)** *(in store)* regarder; **to b. through sth** *(collection, shelves)* jeter un œil sur qch; *(magazine)* feuilleter qch **(b)** *(of animal)* brouter

browser [ˈbraʊzə(r)] *n Comput* logiciel *m* de navigation, navigateur *m*

bruise [bruːz] **1** *n (on body)* bleu *m*; *(on fruit)* meurtrissure *f*
2 *vt (person)* faire un bleu à; *Fig (feelings, pride)* blesser; **to b. one's arm** se faire un bleu au bras
3 *vi (of person)* se faire des bleus; *(of fruit)* s'abîmer

bruiser [ˈbruːzə(r)] *n Fam* grosse brute *f*

bruising [ˈbruːzɪŋ] **1** *n (bruises)* bleus *mpl*
2 *adj (encounter, experience)* douloureux(euse)

brunch [brʌntʃ] *n* brunch *m*; **to have b.** bruncher

Brunei [bruːˈnaɪ] *n* le Brunei

brunette [bruːˈnet] *n* brune *f*

brunt [brʌnt] *n* **to bear** *or* **to take the b. of sth** *(attack)* essuyer le plus fort de qch; *(anger)* faire les frais de qch

bruschetta [brʊsˈketə] *n Culin* bruschetta *f*

brush [brʌʃ] **1** *n* **(a)** *(for clothes, hair)* brosse *f*; *(for sweeping)* balai *m*; *(for painting)* pinceau *m*
(b) *(action)* **to give sth a b.** donner un coup de brosse à qch; **to give the floor a b.** donner un coup de balai; **to give one's hair a b.** se donner un coup de brosse
(c) *(light touch)* effleurement *m*; *Fam* **to have a b. with the law** avoir des démêlés avec la justice
(d) *(of fox)* queue *f*
(e) *(undergrowth)* broussailles *fpl*
2 *vt* **(a)** *(clothes, shoes)* brosser; **to b. one's hair/teeth** se brosser les cheveux/les dents; **to b. the floor** balayer
(b) *(touch lightly)* effleurer
3 *vi* **to b. against sb/sth** effleurer qn/qch; **to brush past sb/sth** effleurer qn/qch en passant

▶**brush aside** *vt sep (objection, obstacle)* balayer; *(opponent)* écarter

▶**brush off** *vt sep* **(a)** *(from clothes, shoes)* enlever d'un coup de brosse **(b)** *(person)* envoyer promener; *(insult, incident)* ignorer

▶**brush up** *vt sep* **(a)** *(leaves, crumbs)* balayer **(b)** *Fam (subject, language)* **to b. up (on)** se remettre (à)

brushed [brʌʃt] *adj (nylon)* gratté(e); **b. cotton** pilou *m*, finette *f*

brush-off [ˈbrʌʃɒf] *n Fam* **to give sb the b.** envoyer promener qn

brushwood [ˈbrʌʃwʊd] *n (as fuel)* petit bois *m*; *(undergrowth)* broussailles *fpl*

brushwork [ˈbrʌʃwɜːk] *n Art* touche *f*

brusque [bruːsk] *adj* brusque

brusquely [ˈbruːsklɪ] *adv (behave)* avec brusquerie; *(say)* d'un ton brusque

Brussels [ˈbrʌsəlz] *n* Bruxelles; **B. sprout** chou *m* de Bruxelles

brutal [ˈbruːtəl] *adj* brutal(e); *(attack, crime)* sauvage

brutality [bruːˈtælɪtɪ] *n* brutalité *f*; *(of attack, crime)* sauvagerie *f*

brutalize [ˈbruːtəlaɪz] *vt (ill-treat)* brutaliser; *(make insensitive)* rendre insensible

brutally [ˈbruːtəlɪ] *adv* avec brutalité; *(beat, attack)* sauvagement

brute [bruːt] **1** *n (animal)* bête *f*; *(person)* brute *f*
2 *adj* **b. force** *or* **strength** force *f* brutale

brutish [ˈbruːtɪʃ] *adj* bestial(e)

BS [biːˈes], **BSc** [biːesˈsiː] *n (abbr* **Bachelor of Science**) to have a B. in computer science/physics avoir une licence d'informatique/de physique; **John Smith B.** John Smith, licencié en chimie/informatique/*etc.*

BSE [biːesˈiː] *n (abbr* **bovine spongiform encephalopathy**) EBS *f*, maladie *f* de la vache folle

bubble [ˈbʌbəl] **1** *n (of air, soap)* bulle *f*; *Fig* **the b. has burst** le rêve est terminé; **b. bath** bain *m* moussant; *Comput* **b.-jet printer** imprimante *f* à bulles
2 *vi (form bubbles)* bouillonner

▶**bubble over** *vi (of liquid)* déborder; *Fig* **to b. over with joy** ne plus se tenir de joie

bubblegum [ˈbʌbəlgʌm] *n* chewing-gum *m*

bubbly [ˈbʌblɪ] **1** *n Fam (champagne)* champ *m*
2 *adj* **(a)** *(liquid)* plein(e) de bulles **(b)** *(person)* débordant(e) de vitalité

bubonic [bjuːˈbɒnɪk] *adj* **b. plague** peste *f* bubonique

buccaneer [bʌkəˈnɪə(r)] *n* boucanier *m*

Bucharest [bʊkəˈrest] *n* Bucarest

buck [bʌk] **1** *n* **(a)** *Fam (dollar)* dollar *m*; **to make a fast** *or* **quick b.** faire du fric **(b)** *(of deer, rabbit)* mâle *m* **(c)** *Fam (responsibility)* **to pass the b.** refiler le bébé; **the b. stops here** *(with me)* en dernier ressort, c'est moi le responsable; *(with you)* en dernier ressort, c'est toi le responsable
2 *vt* **to b. the system/a trend** aller à l'encontre de l'ordre établi/d'une tendance
3 *vi (of horse)* faire le saut de mouton

▶**buck up** *Fam* **1** *vt sep (encourage)* remonter le moral à; **to b. one's ideas up** se prendre en main
2 *vi Fam (cheer up)* reprendre courage; *(hurry)* se grouiller

bucket [ˈbʌkɪt] *n* seau *m*

buckle [ˈbʌkəl] **1** *n* boucle *f*
2 *vt* **(a)** *(fasten)* boucler **(b)** *(deform)* déformer; *(wheel)* voiler
3 *vi (deform)* se déformer; *(of wheel)* se voiler; *(of knees)* flancher; **she buckled at the knees** ses jambes ont cédé sous elle

▶**buckle down** *vi* s'y mettre; **to b. down to a task** s'atteler à une tâche

▶**buckle up** *vi (fasten seatbelt)* attacher sa ceinture

buckshot [ˈbʌkʃɒt] *n* chevrotine *f*

buckskin [ˈbʌkskɪn] *n* daim *m (peau)*

buckteeth [bʌkˈtiːθ] *npl* dents *fpl* de lapin

bucktoothed [bʌkˈtuːθt] *adj* **to be b.** avoir des dents de lapin

buckwheat [ˈbʌkwiːt] *n* sarrasin *m*

bucolic [bjuːˈkɒlɪk] *adj Lit* bucolique

bud [bʌd] **1** *n (of leaf, branch)* bourgeon *m*; *(of flower)* bouton *m*
2 *vi (pt & pp* **budded**) *(of tree)* bourgeonner; *(of flowers)* être en boutons

Budapest [ˈbʊdəpest] *n* Budapest

Buddha [ˈbʊdə] *n* Bouddha

Buddhist [ˈbʊdɪst] **1** *n* bouddhiste *mf*
2 *adj (priest, doctrine)* bouddhiste; *(art, temple)* bouddhique

budding [ˈbʌdɪŋ] *adj (genius, actor)* en herbe; *(talent)* naissant(e)

buddy [ˈbʌdɪ] *(pl* **buddies**) *n Fam (friend)* pote *m*; **hey, b.!** dis donc, mec!

budge [bʌdʒ] **1** *vt (move)* bouger; *Fig (convince)* faire changer d'avis
2 *vi (move)* bouger; *Fig (yield)* céder

budgerigar [ˈbʌdʒərɪgɑː(r)] *n* perruche *f*

budget [ˈbʌdʒɪt] **1** *n* budget *m*; **to go over b.** dépasser le budget;

to be within b. être dans les limites du budget; **b. deficit/ surplus** déficit *m*/excédent *m* budgétaire

2 *vt (time, money)* gérer

3 *vi* **to b. for sth** prévoir qch

4 *adj (inexpensive)* économique, pour petits budgets; **b. prices** prix *mpl* avantageux

budgetary ['bʌdʒɪtərɪ] *adj Fin* budgétaire

budgie ['bʌdʒɪ] *n Fam* perruche *f*

Buenos Aires ['bwenɒ'saɪrɪz] *n* Buenos Aires

buff [bʌf] **1** *n* (**a**) *(color)* couleur *f* chamois (**b**) *Fam* **in the b.** *(naked)* à poil (**c**) *(enthusiast)* mordu(e) *m,f*; **movie b.** cinéphile *mf*

2 *adj* (couleur) chamois *inv*; *(envelope)* en papier kraft

3 *vt (polish)* lustrer

buffalo ['bʌfələu] *(pl* **buffalo** *or* **buffaloes)** *n* buffle *m*

buffer ['bʌfə(r)] *n Comput* mémoire *f* tampon; **to act as a b.** faire tampon; **b. state** Etat *m* tampon; **b. zone** zone *f* tampon

buffet¹ ['bʌfɪt] *vt (of wind)* secouer; *Fig* **to be buffeted by the waves/by events** être ballotté(e) par les vagues/par les événements

buffet² ['bʊfeɪ] *n* (**a**) *(sideboard)* buffet *m* (**b**) *(meal)* buffet *m*; **b. lunch/dinner** buffet

buffeting ['bʌfɪtɪŋ] *n* **to take a b.** *(of ship)* être violemment ballotté(e); *Fig (of person)* être fortement ébranlé(e)

buffoon [bə'fuːn] *n* bouffon *m*; **to play the b.** faire le pitre

bug [bʌg] **1** *n* (**a**) *(insect)* insecte *m*; *(bed bug)* punaise *f* (**b**) *Fam (sickness)* virus *m*, microbe *m*; **a stomach b.** un embarras gastrique; **there's a b. going around** il y a un virus qui traîne; *Fig* **the travel b.** le virus des voyages (**c**) *Comput* bug *m*, bogue *m* (**d**) *(listening device)* micro *m*

2 *vt (pt & pp* **bugged)** (**a**) *(telephone)* mettre sur écoute; *(building, room)* cacher des micros dans (**b**) *Fam (annoy)* taper sur les nerfs à; *(nag)* embêter; **stop bugging me about it!** arrête de m'embêter avec ça!

▸**bug off** *vt insep Fam (go away)* ficher le camp; **b. off!** dégage!, fiche le camp!

bugbear ['bʌgbeə(r)] *n Fam* cauchemar *m*

bug-eyed [bʌg'aɪd] *adj* aux yeux exorbités

bug-free [bʌg'friː] *adj Comput* sans bug

buggy ['bʌgɪ] *(pl* **buggies)** *n* (**a**) *(baby carriage)* landau *m* (**b**) *(carriage)* boghei *m*, buggy *m*

bugle ['bjuːgəl] *n* clairon *m*

bugler ['bjuːglə(r)] *n* (sonneur *m* de) clairon *m*

build [bɪld] **1** *n* carrure *f*

2 *vt (pt & pp* **built** [bɪlt]) construire; **to be built (out) of sth** être construit(e) en qch; **to b. sth into sth** *(include)* inclure qch dans qch; **to b. one's hopes on sth** fonder ses espoirs sur qch

▸**build on 1** *vt sep (add)* ajouter

2 *vt insep (success)* tirer parti de

▸**build up 1** *vt sep* (**a**) *(resources)* accumuler; **to b. up speed/ one's strength** prendre de la vitesse/des forces; **don't b. your hopes up** ne te fais pas d'illusions (**b**) *(custom)* se constituer; *(reputation)* se faire; *(company)* développer; **to b. up an immunity (to sth)** s'immuniser (contre qch) (**c**) *(hype)* faire du battage autour de

2 *vi (of clouds)* s'amasser; *(of hurricane, storm)* se préparer; *(of tension, pressure)* s'accumuler

builder ['bɪldə(r)] *n* maçon *m*; *(business owner)* entrepreneur *m* (dans le bâtiment)

building ['bɪldɪŋ] *n* (**a**) *(structure)* bâtiment *m*, immeuble *m* (**b**) *(action)* construction *f*; **the b. trade** le bâtiment; **b. block** cube *m*; *Fig* élément *m* essentiel

build-up ['bɪldʌp] *n (of tension, forces)* accumulation *f*; *(hype)* battage *m*; **the b. to Christmas/the match** la période précédant Noël/le match

built [bɪlt] *pt & pp of* **build**

built-in ['bɪl'tɪn] *adj (cupboard)* encastré(e); *(included)* com-

pris(e); **b. obsolescence** obsolescence *f* programmée

built-up ['bɪl'tʌp] *adj* **b. area** agglomération *f* urbaine

bulb [bʌlb] *n* (**a**) *(of plant)* bulbe *m* (**b**) *(light bulb)* ampoule *f*

bulbous ['bʌlbəs] *adj* bulbeux(euse); **a b. nose** un gros nez

Bulgaria [bʌl'geərɪə] *n* la Bulgarie

Bulgarian [bʌl'geərɪən] **1** *n* (**a**) *(person)* Bulgare *mf* (**b**) *(language)* bulgare *m*

2 *adj* bulgare

bulge [bʌldʒ] **1** *n* renflement *m*

2 *vi (of stomach)* être gonflé(e); *(of bag, pocket)* être bourré(e) (**with** de)

bulimia [bə'lɪmɪə] *n* boulimie *f*

bulk [bʌlk] *n* (**a**) *(mass)* masse *f*; **the b. (of sth)** la majeure partie (de qch) (**b**) *Com* **in b.** en gros; **b. purchase** achat *m* en gros

2 *vt* **to b. sth out** étoffer qch

3 *vi* **to b. large** *(of problem)* occuper une place importante

bulkhead ['bʌlkhed] *n Naut* cloison *f*

bulky ['bʌlkɪ] *adj* volumineux(euse), encombrant(e)

bull¹ [bʊl] *n* (**a**) *(animal)* taureau *m*; **b. elephant** éléphant *m* mâle; *Fin* **b. market** marché *m* à la hausse (**b**) *very Fam (nonsense)* conneries *fpl* (**c**) *(idioms)* **to take the b. by the horns** prendre le taureau par les cornes; **like a b. in a china shop** comme un éléphant dans un magasin de porcelaine

bull² [bʊl] *n Rel* bulle *f*

bulldog ['bʊldɒg] *n* bouledogue *m*

bulldoze ['bʊldəuz] *vt (land)* aplanir au bulldozer; *(building)* démolir au bulldozer; *Fig* **to b. sb into doing sth** forcer qn à faire qch

bulldozer ['bʊldəuzə(r)] *n* bulldozer *m*

bullet ['bʊlɪt] *n* balle *f*; **b. hole** impact *m* de balle; **b. wound** blessure *f* par balle

bulletin ['bʊlɪtɪn] *n* bulletin *m*; **b. board** panneau *m* d'affichage; *Comput* serveur *m* télématique, *Can* babillard *m*

bulletproof ['bʊlɪtpruːf] *adj (car, glass)* blindé(e); **b. vest** gilet *m* pare-balles

bullfight ['bʊlfaɪt] *n* corrida *f*, course *f* de taureaux; *(art)* tauromachie *f*

bullfighter ['bʊlfaɪtə(r)] *n* torero *m*

bullfighting ['bʊlfaɪtɪŋ] *n (bullfights)* courses *fpl* de taureaux; *(art)* tauromachie *f*

bullfinch ['bʊlfɪntʃ] *n* bouvreuil *m*

bullfrog ['bʊlfrɒg] *n* grenouille-taureau *f*, *Can* ouaouaron *m*

bullhorn ['bʊlhɔːn] *n* mégaphone *m*

bullion ['bʊljən] *n* **gold b.** lingots *mpl* d'or

bullish ['bʊlɪʃ] *adj Fin (market)* à la hausse; *Fig (optimistic)* optimiste

bullock ['bʊlək] *n* bœuf *m*

bullring ['bʊlrɪŋ] *n* arène *f*

bull's-eye ['bʊlzaɪ] *n* mille *m*; *also Fig* **to hit the b.** mettre dans le mille

bullshit ['bʊlʃɪt] *Vulg* **1** *n (nonsense)* conneries *fpl*

2 *exclam* c'est des conneries tout ça!

3 *vt (pt & pp* **bullshitted)** **to b. sb** raconter des conneries à qn; **she bullshitted her way into the job** elle a bluffé pour avoir le poste

4 *vi (talk nonsense)* dire des conneries

bully ['bʊlɪ] **1** *n (pl* **bullies)** *(child)* petite brute *f*; *(adult)* tyran *m*; **don't be such a b.** ne sois pas si tyrannique

2 *vt (pt & pp* **bullied)** maltraiter; **to b. sb into doing sth** forcer qn à faire qch

3 *exclam Ironic* **b. for you!** bravo!

bullyboy ['bʊlɪbɔɪ] *n* voyou *m*; **b. tactics** manœuvres *fpl* d'intimidation

bullying ['bʊlɪŋ] **1** *n* brimades *fpl*

2 *adj* brutal(e)

bulrush ['bʊlrʌʃ] *n* jonc *m*

bulwark ['bʊlwɜːk] *n also Fig* rempart *m* (**against** contre)

bum [bʌm] **1** *n (tramp)* clochard(e) *m,f*
2 *adj (of poor quality)* minable; **to get a b. deal** se faire avoir
3 *vt (pt & pp* **bummed**) **to b. a cigarette from** *or* **off sb** taxer une cigarette à qn; **to b. a ride** se faire prendre en stop

▸**bum around** *vi Fam (be idle)* glander; *(travel)* vadrouiller

bumblebee ['bʌmbəlbiː] *n* bourdon *m*

bumbling ['bʌmblɪŋ] *adj* **b. fool** *or* **idiot** imbécile *mf*

bummer ['bʌmə(r)] *n Fam* **what a b.!** quelle poisse!

bump [bʌmp] **1** *n* (**a**) *(jolt)* secousse *f*; **to land with a b.** tomber violemment par terre; *Fig* **to come back down to earth with a b.** redescendre brusquement sur terre (**b**) *(lump)* bosse *f*
2 *vt* cogner; **to b. one's head** se cogner la tête

▸**bump into** *vt insep (collide with)* rentrer dans; *Fam (meet by chance)* tomber sur

▸**bump off** *vt sep Fam (kill)* liquider

▸**bump up** *vt sep (price)* gonfler, augmenter

bumper¹ ['bʌmpə(r)] *n Aut* pare-chocs *m inv*; **b. car** auto *f* tamponneuse; **b. sticker** autocollant *(pour voiture)*

bumper² ['bʌmpə(r)] *adj* **b. crop** récolte *f* exceptionnelle; **b. issue** numéro *m* exceptionnel

bumpkin ['bʌmpkɪn] *n* (**country**) **b.** péquenaud(e) *m,f*

bumptious ['bʌmpʃəs] *adj* suffisant(e)

bumpy ['bʌmpɪ] *adj (road)* cahoteux(euse); *(journey)* agité(e); *(landing)* violent(e); *Fam Fig* **to give sb/sth a b. ride** malmener qn/qch

bun [bʌn] *n* (**a**) *(sweet)* petit gâteau *m* brioché; *(for burger)* petit pain *m* rond (**b**) *(hairstyle)* chignon *m*

bunch [bʌntʃ] *n (of flowers)* bouquet *m*; *(of bananas)* régime *m*; *(of grapes)* grappe *f*; *(of keys)* trousseau *m*; *(of people)* bande *f*; *(of cyclists)* peloton *m*; **he's the best of a bad b.** c'est le moins mauvais du lot; **she's the best** *or* **the pick of the b.** c'est la meilleure du lot; **a whole b. of things to do** tout un tas de choses à faire

▸**bunch together** *vi (of people)* se serrer

bundle ['bʌndəl] **1** *n (of clothes)* paquet *m*; *(of banknotes, papers)* liasse *f*; *(of straw)* botte *f*; *Fam Ironic* **you're a b. of laughs!** c'est fou ce que tu as l'air gai!; *Fam* **she's a b. of nerves** c'est un paquet de nerfs
2 *vt* **to b. sb out of the door** mettre qn dehors sans ménagement; **to b. sb into a car** embarquer qn dans une voiture

▸**bundle off** *vt sep (send)* expédier

▸**bundle up 1** *vt sep (dress warmly)* envelopper, couvrir
2 *vi (dress warmly)* se couvrir

bung [bʌŋ] **1** *n (plug)* bonde *f*
2 *vt (hole)* boucher

▸**bung up** *vt sep Fam* boucher; **my nose is bunged up** j'ai le nez bouché

bungalow ['bʌŋgələʊ] *n* pavillon *m* de plain-pied

bungee jumping ['bʌndʒiːdʒʌmpɪŋ] *n* saut *m* à l'élastique

bunghole ['bʌŋhəʊl] *n* bonde *f*

bungle ['bʌŋgəl] **1** *vt (attempt)* rater; *(job)* gâcher
2 *vi* se tromper

bunion ['bʌnjən] *n* oignon *m (au pied)*

bunk [bʌŋk] *n (bed)* lit *m*; *(in train, ship)* couchette *f*; **b. beds** lits superposés

bunker ['bʌŋkə(r)] *n* (**a**) *(for coal)* coffre *m* à charbon (**b**) *Mil* bunker *m*, blockhaus *m*; **nuclear b.** abri *m* antiatomique (**c**) *(on golf course)* bunker *m*

bunkum ['bʌŋkəm] *n Fam* âneries *fpl*

bunny ['bʌnɪ] *(pl* **bunnies**) *n Fam* **b.** (**rabbit**) petit lapin *m*

Bunsen burner ['bʌnsən'bɜːnə(r)] *n* bec *m* Bunsen

bunting ['bʌntɪŋ] *n (decorations)* guirlandes *fpl* de fanions

buoy [bɔɪ] *n* bouée *f*

▸**buoy up** *vt sep (person, prices)* soutenir

buoyancy ['bɔɪənsɪ] *n (in water)* flottabilité *f*; *Fig (of market)* stabilité *f*

buoyant ['bɔɪənt] *adj (in water)* qui flotte; *Fig (economy, prices)* stable; *Fig (person, mood)* plein(e) d'allant

burble ['bɜːbəl] *vi (of stream)* murmurer; *(of person)* marmonner

burden ['bɜːdən] **1** *n also Fig* fardeau *m*; **b. of taxation** pression *f* fiscale; *Law* **b. of proof** charge *f* de la preuve
2 *vt Fig* accabler (**with** de)

burdensome ['bɜːdənsəm] *adj* lourd(e)

bureau ['bjʊərəʊ] *(pl* **bureaux** ['bjʊərəʊz]) *n* (**a**) *(desk)* bureau *m*, secrétaire *m*; *(chest of drawers)* commode *f* (**b**) *(office)* bureau *m*; *(government department)* service *m*

bureaucracy [bjʊə'rɒkrəsɪ] *n* bureaucratie *f*

bureaucrat ['bjʊərəkræt] *n* bureaucrate *mf*

bureaucratic [bjʊərə'krætɪk] *adj* bureaucratique

bureaux ['bjʊərəʊz] *pl of* **bureau**

burgeon ['bɜːdʒən] *vi (of trade)* se développer; *(of crime)* augmenter; *(of relationship)* s'épanouir; **a burgeoning talent** un talent qui s'affirme

burger ['bɜːgə(r)] *n* hamburger *m*

burglar ['bɜːglə(r)] *n* cambrioleur(euse) *m,f*; **b. alarm** alarme *f* (de sécurité)

burglarize ['bɜːgləraɪz] *vt* cambrioler

burglarproof ['bɜːgləpruːf] *adj* inviolable

burglary ['bɜːglərɪ] *(pl* **burglaries**) *n* cambriolage *m*

burgle ['bɜːgəl] *vt* cambrioler

Burgundy ['bɜːgəndɪ] *n* la Bourgogne

burgundy ['bɜːgəndɪ] *adj (color)* bordeaux *inv*

burial ['berɪəl] *n* enterrement *m*; **b. ground** cimetière *m*

burka [bɜːkə] *n* burka *f*, burqa *f*

Burkina-Faso [bɜː'kiːnə'fæsəʊ] *n* le Burkina

burlesque [bɜː'lesk] **1** *n (caricature)* parodie *f*; *(style)* burlesque *m*
2 *adj* burlesque

burly ['bɜːlɪ] *adj* bien bâti(e)

Burma ['bɜːmə] *n Formerly* la Birmanie

Burmese [bɜː'miːz] **1** *npl* **the B.** les Birmans *mpl*
2 *n* (**a**) *(person)* Birman(e) *m,f* (**b**) *(language)* birman *m*
3 *adj* birman(e)

burn [bɜːn] **1** *n* brûlure *f*
2 *vt (pt & pp* **burned** *or* **burnt** [bɜːnt]) (**a**) *(fuel, building)* brûler; **to b. one's hand/one's finger** se brûler la main/le doigt; **to b. a hole in sth** faire un trou dans qch (**b**) *(idioms)* **to have money to b.** avoir de l'argent à ne plus savoir quoi en faire; **to b. one's bridges** brûler ses vaisseaux; **to b. the candle at both ends** brûler la chandelle par les deux bouts; **to b. the midnight oil** travailler tard
3 *vi* brûler; *(of light)* briller; **the fire is burning low** le feu baisse; *Fig* **to b. with desire** brûler de désir; **to b. with anger** bouillonner de colère; **to b. with enthusiasm** déborder d'enthousiasme

▸**burn down 1** *vt sep* incendier
2 *vi* être détruit(e) par le feu

▸**burn out 1** *vt sep* **to b. itself out** *(of fire)* s'éteindre; *Fig* **to b. oneself out** *(become exhausted)* s'épuiser
2 *vi (of fire)* s'éteindre

▸**burn up 1** *vt sep (energy)* dépenser
2 *vi (of rocket)* se désintégrer

burner ['bɜːnə(r)] *n* brûleur *m*

burning ['bɜːnɪŋ] *adj (on fire)* en feu; *(very hot)* brûlant(e); *(passion, ambition)* dévorant(e); **a b. issue** une question brûlante

burnish ['bɜːnɪʃ] *vt* polir, brunir

burnout ['bɜːnaʊt] *n* (**a**) *Elec* **what caused the b.?** qu'est-ce qui a fait griller les circuits? (**b**) *(exhaustion)* épuisement *m* total

burnt [bɜːnt] **1** *adj* brûlé(e)
2 *pt & pp of* **burn¹**

burnt-out ['bɜːntʾaʊt] *adj (building, car)* calciné(e); *Fig (person)* usé(e)

burp [bɜːp] **1** *n* rot *m*
2 *vi* roter

burqa = **burka**

burr[1] [bɜː(r)] *n (of plant)* bardane *f*; *(on tree trunk)* broussin *m*

burr[2] [bɜː(r)] *n* **to speak with a b.** grasseyer

burrow ['bʌrəʊ] **1** *n (of animal)* terrier *m*
2 *vi (of animal)* creuser la terre

bursar ['bɜːsə(r)] *n* Univ intendant(e) *m,f*

burst [bɜːst] **1** *n (of laughter)* éclat *m*; *(of enthusiasm)* élan *m*; **a b. of activity** une poussée d'activité; **a b. of applause** une salve d'applaudissements; **a b. of gunfire** une rafale; **a b. of speed** une pointe de vitesse
2 *vt (pt & pp* **burst***) (balloon, tire)* faire éclater; **to b. its banks** *(of river)* déborder, sortir de son lit
3 *vi (of balloon, bubble, tire, pipe)* éclater; *Fig* **to be bursting with pride** déborder de fierté; **to be bursting with impatience** bouillir d'impatience; **to be bursting to do sth** mourir d'envie de faire qch; **to be bursting (for the bathroom)** avoir un besoin pressant; *Fig* **to be bursting at the seams** *(of room)* être plein(e) à craquer

▸**burst into** *vt insep* **(a)** *(enter)* faire irruption dans **(b)** *(suddenly start)* **to b. into flames** prendre feu; **to b. into song** se mettre à chanter; **to b. into laughter/tears** éclater de rire/en sanglots

▸**burst open** *vi (of door)* s'ouvrir brusquement; *(of package)* éclater

▸**burst out** *vi* **to b. out laughing** éclater de rire; **to b. out crying** éclater en sanglots

Burundi [bə'rʊndɪ] *n* le Burundi

bury ['berɪ] *(pt & pp* **buried***) vt (body, treasure)* enterrer; *(of avalanche, mudslide) & Fig (hide)* ensevelir; **to b. oneself in one's work** se plonger dans son travail; **to b. one's face in one's hands** enfouir son visage dans ses mains; **to b. the hatchet** enterrer la hache de guerre

bus [bʌs] **1** *n (pl* **buses** *or* **busses***)* **(a)** *(vehicle)* bus *m*, autobus *m*; **by b.** en bus; **b. driver** chauffeur *m* de bus; **b. lane** couloir *m* de bus; **b. route** ligne *f* de bus; **b. shelter** Abribus® *m*; **b. station** gare *f* routière; **b. stop** arrêt *m* d'autobus **(b)** Comput bus *m*
2 *vt (pt & pp* **bused** *or* **bussed***)* transporter en autobus

bush [bʊʃ] *n (plant)* buisson *m*; **the b.** *(in Africa, Australia)* la brousse

bushed [bʊʃt] *adj Fam (exhausted)* vanné(e), claqué(e)

bushel ['bʊʃəl] *n* boisseau *m*; *Fig* **don't hide your light under a b.** ne cache pas ton talent

bushfire ['bʊʃfaɪə(r)] *n* feu *m* de brousse

bushy ['bʊʃɪ] *adj* touffu(e)

busily ['bɪzɪlɪ] *adv* **to be b. doing sth** être très occupé(e) à faire qch

business ['bɪznɪs] *n* **(a)** *(task, concern)* affaire *f*; **it's none of your b.** cela ne te regarde pas, ce ne sont pas tes affaires; **it's/it's not my b. to...** c'est/ce n'est pas à moi de...; **mind your own b.!** occupe-toi de tes affaires *ou* de ce qui te regarde!; **to make it one's b. to do sth** prendre sur soi de faire qch; **to go about one's b.** vaquer à ses occupations; **to get down to b.** se mettre au travail; **to mean b.** ne pas plaisanter; **I'm sick of the whole b.** j'en ai assez de toute cette histoire; **he was working like nobody's b.** il travaillait très dur; **she can tell jokes like nobody's b.** elle raconte très bien les histoires drôles
(b) *(individual company)* affaire *f*, entreprise *f*; *(commercial activity)* affaires; **to be in the entertainment b.** être dans le spectacle; **the travel b.** les métiers *ou* le secteur du tourisme; **I'm not in the b. of making compromises** ce n'est pas

mon genre de faire des compromis; **to be in b.** être dans les affaires; **to set up a b.** s'établir *ou* s'installer à son compte; **to go into b.** s'installer; **to go into b. with sb** monter une affaire avec qn; **to go out of b.** fermer; **to go to Chicago on b.** aller à Chicago pour affaires; **how's b.?** comment vont les affaires?; **it's good/bad for b.** c'est bon/mauvais pour les affaires; **to talk b.** parler affaires; **to do b. with sb** traiter avec qn; *Fin* **b. account** compte *m* professionnel; **b. card** carte *f* de visite; **b. class** *(on plane)* classe *f* affaires; **b. hours** *(of store)* heures *fpl* d'ouverture; *(of office)* heures de bureau; **b. lunch** déjeuner *m* d'affaires; **b. management** gestion *f* d'entreprise; **b. park** parc *m* d'activités; **b. school** école *f* de commerce; **b. studies** études *fpl* commerciales *ou* de commerce; **b. suit** complet *m* (-veston) *m*; **b. trip** voyage *m* d'affaires

businesslike ['bɪznɪslaɪk] *adj* professionnel(elle)

businessman ['bɪznɪsmæn] *n* homme *m* d'affaires; **to be a good b.** avoir le sens des affaires

businessperson ['bɪznɪspɜːsən] *n* homme *m*/femme *f* d'affaires; **to be a good b.** avoir le sens des affaires

businesswoman ['bɪznɪswʊmən] *n* femme *f* d'affaires; **to be a good b.** avoir le sens des affaires

busman ['bʌsmən] *n Fam* **a b.'s holiday** = vacances pendant lesquelles on fait la même chose qu'à son travail

bust[1] [bʌst] *n* **(a)** *(of woman)* poitrine *f*; **b. measurement** tour *m* de poitrine **(b)** *(statue)* buste *m*

bust[2] [bʌst] *Fam* **1** *adj* **(a)** *(broken)* fichu(e) **(b)** **to go b.** *(bankrupt)* faire faillite
2 *vt (pt & pp* **busted** *or* **bust***)* **(a)** *(break)* bousiller **(b)** *(arrest)* coffrer
3 *n Fam* **(a)** *(arrest)* arrestation *f*; *(police raid)* descente *f* **(b)** *(failure)* fiasco *m*

▸**bust out** *vi Fam (escape)* se tirer (**of** de)

▸**bust up** *vt sep Fam (disrupt) (event)* interrompre; *(relationship)* ficher en l'air

buster ['bʌstə(r)] *n Fam* **thanks, b.** merci, mon pote; **listen, b.** écoute, mec

bustle ['bʌsəl] **1** *n (commotion)* animation *f*
2 *vi* **to b. (around)** s'activer, s'affairer

bust-up ['bʌstʌp] *n Fam (dispute)* engueulade *f*; *(of relationship)* fin *f*; **to have a b.** *(argue)* s'engueuler

busy ['bɪzɪ] **1** *adj (person)* occupé(e); *(day, week)* chargé(e); *(road)* à grande circulation; *(telephone line)* occupé(e); **to keep sb b.** occuper qn; **to keep oneself b.** s'occuper; **to be b. doing sth** être occupé à faire qch; **the train was very b.** il y avait beaucoup de monde dans le train; **I got the b. signal** *(on telephone)* ça sonnait occupé
2 *vt (pt & pp* **busied***)* **to b. oneself with sth** s'occuper à qch

busybody ['bɪzɪbɒdɪ] *n (pl* **busybodies***) n Fam* fouineur(euse) *m,f*

but [bʌt] **1** *prep (except)* sauf, à part; **any day b. tomorrow** n'importe quand sauf demain; **it's nothing b. prejudice** ce ne sont rien que des préjugés; **she is anything b. stupid** elle est loin d'être bête; **b. for** sans; **the last b. one** l'avant-dernier(ère) *m,f*; **the next b. one** le (la) deuxième
2 *adv Formal* seulement; **he is b. a child** ce n'est qu'un enfant; **had I b. known!** si (seulement) j'avais su!; **one can b. try** on peut toujours essayer
3 *conj* mais; **not once b. twice** pas une fois, mais deux; **I told her to do it b. she refused** je lui ai dit de le faire mais elle a refusé; **b. I tell you I saw it!** mais puisque je te dis que je l'ai vu!; **I had no choice b. to go** je n'ai pas pu faire autrement que d'y aller; **what could I do b. invite him?** comment pouvais-je faire autrement que de l'inviter?
4 *n* **no buts!** il n'y a pas de "mais" qui tienne!

butane ['bjuːteɪn] *n* butane *m*

butch [bʊtʃ] *adj Fam* hommasse

butcher ['bʊtʃə(r)] **1** *n also Fig* boucher(ère) *m,f*; **b.'s** *(store)* boucherie *f*; **to go to the b.'s** aller chez le boucher *ou* à la boucherie

2 *vt (animal)* abattre; *Fig (person, song)* massacrer

butchery ['bʊtʃərɪ] *n also Fig* boucherie *f*

butler ['bʌtlə(r)] *n* majordome *m*, maître *m* d'hôtel

butt [bʌt] **1** *n* **(a)** *(of rifle)* crosse *f*; *(of cigarette)* mégot *m*; *Fig* **to be the b. of a joke** être la cible d'une plaisanterie **(b)** *Fam (buttocks)* fesses *fpl*

2 *vt (hit with head)* donner un coup de tête à

▸**butt in** *vi (interrupt)* intervenir

butter ['bʌtə(r)] **1** *n* beurre *m*; **she looks as if b. wouldn't melt in her mouth** on lui donnerait le bon Dieu sans confession; **b. bean** = gros haricot blanc; **b. dish** beurrier *m*; **b. knife** couteau *m* à beurre

2 *vt* beurrer

▸**butter up** *vt sep Fam (flatter)* passer de la pommade à

buttercup ['bʌtəkʌp] *n* bouton *m* d'or

butterfingers ['bʌtəfɪŋɡəz] *n Fam* empoté(e) *m,f*

butterfly ['bʌtəflaɪ] *(pl* **butterflies)** *n* papillon *m*; *Fig* **to have butterflies (in one's stomach)** avoir l'estomac noué; **b. (stroke)** *(in swimming)* (brasse *f*) papillon *m*

buttermilk ['bʌtəmɪlk] *n* babeurre *m*

butterscotch ['bʌtəskɒtʃ] *n* caramel *m* dur au beurre

buttock ['bʌtək] *n* fesse *f*

button ['bʌtən] **1** *n* **(a)** *(on shirt, machine)* bouton *m*; **b. mushroom** petit champignon *m* de Paris **(b)** *(badge)* badge *m*

2 *vt (shirt, dress)* boutonner; *Fam* **b. it!** la ferme!

▸**button up** *vt sep (shirt, dress)* boutonner

buttonhole ['bʌtənhəʊl] **1** *n* boutonnière *f*

2 *vt (detain)* coincer

buttress ['bʌtrɪs] **1** *n Archit* contrefort *m*; *Fig* pilier *m*

2 *vt Fig (support)* renforcer

buxom ['bʌksəm] *adj (plump)* plantureux(euse); *(full-bosomed)* à la poitrine généreuse

buy [baɪ] **1** *n* **a good/bad b.** une bonne/mauvaise affaire

2 *vt (pt & pp* **bought** [bɔːt]) **(a)** *(purchase)* acheter; **to b. sb sth, to b. sth for sb** acheter qch à qn; **to b. sth from sb** acheter qch à qn; *Fig* **to b. time** gagner du temps; **he's bought it** *(has died)* il a passé l'arme à gauche **(b)** *Fam (believe)* avaler

▸**buy into** *vt insep* **(a)** *(company, scheme)* acheter des parts de **(b)** *Fam (believe)* **to b. into sth** gober qch

▸**buy off** *vt sep Fam* acheter

▸**buy out** *vt sep Com* racheter la part de

▸**buy up** *vt sep (land, shares)* acheter; *(supplies)* faire des stocks de

buyer ['baɪə(r)] *n* acheteur(euse) *m,f*; **b.'s market** marché *m* demandeur

buyout ['baɪaʊt] *n Com* rachat *m*

buzz [bʌz] **1** *n* **(a)** *(noise)* bourdonnement *m*; *(of plane)* vrombissement *m*; **b. cut** *(hairstyle)* coupe *f* à ras; **b. saw** scie *f* mécanique *ou* circulaire; *Fam* **b. word** mot *m* à la mode **(b)** *Fam (thrill)* **to get a b. out of doing sth** prendre son pied à faire qch

2 *vt Fam (on intercom)* appeler à l'Interphone®; *(on pager)* biper

3 *vi (make noise)* bourdonner; *Fig* **to b. with excitement** *(of town)* bourdonner d'excitation; **my head was buzzing** j'avais la tête lourde

buzzard ['bʌzəd] *n* buse *f*

buzzer ['bʌzə(r)] *n (on intercom)* bouton *m* de l'Interphone®; *(on clock, oven)* sonnerie *f*

buzzing ['bʌzɪŋ] *n* bourdonnement *m*

by [baɪ] **1** *prep* **(a)** *(agent)* par; **he was arrested by the police** il a été arrêté par la police, la police l'a arrêté; **made by hand** fait(e) (à la) main; **a play by Shakespeare** une pièce de Shakespeare

(b) *(with manner, means)* **by train/car/plane** en train/voiture/avion; **by doing sth** en faisant qch; **to pay by credit card** payer par carte de crédit; **to have a child by sb** avoir un enfant de qn; **to take sb by the hand/arm** prendre qn par la main/le bras; **to know sb by name/sight** connaître qn de nom/de vue; **to earn one's living by teaching** gagner sa vie en enseignant

(c) *(close to)* près de; **by the fire** près du feu; **by the sea** au bord de la mer; **by the side of the road** sur le bord de la route

(d) *(via)* par; **by land/sea** par terre/mer

(e) *(past)* **to walk by sb/sth** passer devant qn/qch; **to drive by sb/sth** passer devant qn/qch (en voiture)

(f) *(at or before)* **she should be here by now** elle devrait être ici à l'heure qu'il est; **it'll be ready by tomorrow** ce sera prêt pour demain; **by 1980 they were all dead** en 1980 ils étaient déjà tous morts; **by then it was too late** il était déjà trop tard

(g) *(during)* **by day/night** de jour/nuit

(h) *(with measurements, quantities, numbers)* **to divide/to multiply by three** diviser/multiplier par trois; **10 ft by 6** ≃ 3 m sur 2; **to sell sth by weight** vendre qch au poids; **one by one** un par un

(i) *(according to)* **to go by appearances** se fier aux apparences; **to call sb by their first name** appeler qn par son prénom; **what do you mean by that?** qu'est-ce que tu entends par là?

(j) *(with reflexive pronouns)* **by oneself** tout(e) seul(e)

(k) *(as a result of)* **by accident/chance/mistake** par accident/hasard/erreur

2 *adv* **(a)** **by and large** dans l'ensemble; **by the way,...** au fait,...

(b) *(past)* **to go/to walk by** passer; **to drive by** passer (en voiture)

bye [baɪ] *exclam Fam* au revoir!, salut!; **b. for now!** à bientôt!

bye-bye ['baɪbaɪ] *exclam Fam* au revoir!, salut!

by-election, bye-election ['baɪɪlekʃən] *n Pol* élection *f* partielle

bylaw ['baɪlɔː] *n (of club, company)* statut *m*

Byelorussia [bɪeləʊ'rʌʃə] = **Belarus**

Byelorussian [bɪeləʊ'rʌʃən] **1** *n* Biélorusse *mf*

2 *adj* biélorusse

bygone ['baɪɡɒn] **1** *n* **let bygones be bygones** oublions le passé

2 *adj* révolu(e); **in b. days** autrefois

byline ['baɪlaɪn] *n (in newspaper)* signature *f*

bypass ['baɪpɑːs] **1** *n* **(a)** *(road)* rocade *f* **(b)** *(heart operation)* pontage *m*

2 *vt (of road) also Fig* contourner; *(middleman)* court-circuiter

by-product ['baɪprɒdʌkt] *n* sous-produit *m*, dérivé *m*; *Fig* conséquence *f* indirecte

bystander ['baɪstændə(r)] *n* passant(e) *m,f*

byte [baɪt] *n Comput* octet *m*

byway ['baɪweɪ] *n (road)* petite route *f*

byword ['baɪwɜːd] *n* **to be a b. for** être synonyme de

Byzantine ['baɪzəntiːn] *adj also Fig* byzantin(e)

C

C¹, c [siː] *n* (**a**) *(letter)* C, c *m inv* (**b**) *Mus* do *m*, ut *m* (**c**) *Sch (grade)* **to get a C** *(on test)* avoir mention passable; *(on homework, essay)* ≃ avoir 10 ou 11 sur 20

C² (**a**) *(abbr* **centigrade**) C (**b**) *(abbr* **century**) s.; **C.16** XVIᵉ s.

c, ca *(abbr* **circa**) *(approximately)* env.; *(with dates)* vers

cab [kæb] *n* (**a**) *(taxi)* taxi *m*; **c. driver** chauffeur *m* de taxi (**b**) *(of train, truck)* cabine *f*

cabaret ['kæbəreɪ] *n* cabaret *m*; **c. artist** artiste *mf* de cabaret

cabbage ['kæbɪdʒ] *n* chou *m*; **red c.** chou rouge; **c. butterfly** piéride *f* du chou

cabbie, cabby ['kæbɪ] *(pl* **cabbies**) *n Fam* (chauffeur *m* de) taxi *m*

cabin ['kæbɪn] *n (of ship, plane)* cabine *f*; *(hut)* cabane *f*; **c. boy** *(on ship)* mousse *m*; **c. crew** *(on plane)* équipage *m*

cabinet ['kæbɪnɪt] *n* (**a**) *(piece of furniture)* meuble *m* (à tiroirs); *(with glass front)* vitrine *f* (**b**) *Pol* cabinet *m*; **c. meeting** ≃ Conseil *m* des ministres; **c. member** ministre *m*, membre *m* du cabinet

cabinetmaker ['kæbɪnɪtmeɪkə(r)] *n* ébéniste *mf*

cable ['keɪbəl] **1** *n (electrical)* & *Tel* câble *m*; **c. car** téléphérique *m*; *Comput* **c. modem** modem-câble *m*; **c. (television)** (télévision *f* par) câble *m*
2 *vt (message)* câbler; **to c. sb** envoyer un câble à qn

caboodle [kə'buːdəl] *n Fam* **the whole (kit and) c.** tout le bazar *ou* bataclan

cacao [kə'kɑːəʊ] *n (plant)* cacaotier *m*, cacaoyer *m*; **c. bean** fève *f* de cacao

cache [kæʃ] *n* (**a**) *(of drugs, arms)* cache *f* (**b**) *Comput* mémoire-cache *f*

cackle ['kækəl] **1** *n* (**a**) *(of hen)* caquet *m* (**b**) *Fam (talking)* caquetage *m*; *(laugh)* gloussement *m*; **cut the c.!** arrête de jacasser!
2 *vi* (**a**) *(of hen)* caqueter (**b**) *Fam (laugh)* glousser

cacophonous [kə'kɒfənəs] *adj* cacophonique

cactus ['kæktəs] *(pl* **cacti** ['kæktaɪ] *or* **cactuses**) *n* cactus *m*

CAD [siːeɪ'diː] *n Comput (abbr* **computer-aided design**) CAO *f*

cad [kæd] *n Fam Old-fashioned* mufle *m*

cadaver [kə'dævə(r)] *n Formal* cadavre *m*

cadaverous [kə'dævərəs] *adj* cadavérique

caddy¹ ['kædɪ] *n (in golf)* caddie *m*

caddy² ['kædɪ] *(pl* **caddies**) *n* (**tea**) **c.** boîte *f* à thé

cadence ['keɪdəns] *n* cadence *f*, rythme *m*

cadet [kə'det] *n Mil* élève *m* officier; **c. corps** peloton *m* de préparation militaire

cadge [kædʒ] *vt Fam* quémander (**from** *or* **off** à); **to c. a meal off** *or* **from sb** se faire inviter à manger par qn; **can I c. a lift from you?** tu me déposes?

cadmium ['kædmɪəm] *n Chem* cadmium *m*

Caesarean, Caesarian = Cesarean, Cesarian

Caesar salad ['siːzə'sæləd] *n* = salade à base de romaine, de croûtons et d'une vinaigrette additionnée d'œuf

café, cafe ['kæfeɪ] *n* café *m*

cafeteria [kæfɪ'tɪərɪə] *n* cafétéria *f*

cafetiere [kæfə'tjeə(r)] *n* cafetière *f* (à piston)

caffeine ['kæfiːn] *n* caféine *f*; **c. free** décaféiné(e)

cage [keɪdʒ] **1** *n (for bird, animal)* cage *f*; *(of elevator)* cabine *f*
2 *vt* mettre en cage; **to feel caged in** se sentir prisonnier(ère)

cagey ['keɪdʒɪ] *adj (evasive)* évasif(ive) (**about** sur); *(cautious)* prudent(e)

cahoots [kə'huːts] *npl Fam* **to be in c. (with sb)** être de mèche (avec qn)

CAI [siːeɪ'aɪ] *n Comput (abbr* **computer-aided instruction**) EAO *m*

cairn ['keən] *n* cairn *m*

Cairo ['kaɪrəʊ] *n* Le Caire

cajole [kə'dʒəʊl] *vt* enjôler; **to c. sb into doing sth** amadouer qn pour qu'il fasse qch

cake [keɪk] **1** *n* (**a**) *(food)* gâteau *m*; *(pastry)* petit gâteau; **c. pan** moule *m* à gâteau (**b**) *(of soap)* pain *m* (**c**) *(idioms)* **it's a piece of c.** c'est du gâteau; **that takes the c.!** ça, c'est vraiment le bouquet!; *Prov* **you can't have your c. and eat it** on ne peut pas avoir le beurre et l'argent du beurre
2 *vt* **her shoes were caked with mud** ses chaussures étaient couvertes de boue

CAL [kæl] *n Comput (abbr* **computer-aided learning**) EAO *m*

calamity [kə'læmɪtɪ] *(pl* **calamities**) *n* calamité *f*

calcium ['kælsɪəm] *n* calcium *m*

calculate ['kælkjʊleɪt] **1** *vt* calculer; *(consequences, risk)* évaluer; **his remark was calculated to shock** sa remarque était destinée à choquer
2 *vi* **to c. on sth** compter sur qch; **to c. on doing sth** compter faire qch

calculated ['kælkjʊleɪtɪd] *adj (risk)* calculé(e); *(crime)* prémédité(e)

calculating ['kælkjʊleɪtɪŋ] *adj* calculateur(trice)

calculation [kælkjʊ'leɪʃən] *n* calcul *m*

calculator ['kælkjʊleɪtə(r)] *n* calculatrice *f*

calculus ['kælkjʊləs] *n Math* calcul *m*

calendar ['kælɪndə(r)] *n* calendrier *m*; **c. month** mois *m* civil; **c. year** année *f* civile

calf¹ [kɑːf] *(pl* **calves** [kɑːvz]) *n (animal)* veau *m*; **the cow is with c.** la vache est pleine; *Fig* **to kill the fatted c.** tuer le veau gras

calf² [kɑːf] *(pl* **calves** [kɑːvz]) *n (of leg)* mollet *m*

calfskin ['kɑːfskɪn] *n* veau *m*

caliber ['kælɪbə(r)] *n also Fig* calibre *m*

calibrate ['kælɪbreɪt] *vt* étalonner, calibrer

calico ['kælɪkəʊ] *n* calicot *m*

California [kælɪ'fɔːnɪə] *n* la Californie

calipers ['kælɪpəz] *npl* (**a**) *(for legs)* attelles *fpl* (**b**) *(measuring device)* compas *m*

calisthenics [kælɪs'θenɪks] *n* gymnastique *f* rythmique

call [kɔːl] **1** *n* (**a**) *(shout)* appel *m*, cri *m*
(**b**) *(appeal)* appel *m* (**for** à); **a c. to arms** un appel aux armes
(**c**) *(on phone)* appel *m*, coup *m* de téléphone; **to give sb a c.** passer un coup de téléphone à qn; **to make a c.** passer un coup de téléphone *ou* de fil; **to return sb's c.** rappeler qn; **c. center** centre *m* d'appels; **c. girl** call-girl *f*
(**d**) *(visit)* visite *f*; **to pay a c. on sb** rendre visite à qn
(**e**) *(demand)* demande *f*; **there are a lot of calls on my time** je suis très pris; **there's not much c. for it** il n'y a pas beaucoup de demande; **there's no c. for that kind of language!** inutile d'être impoli!; **to be on c.** *(of doctor)* être de garde
2 *vt* (**a**) *(shout to)* appeler
(**b**) *(summon)* appeler; **he's been called away** il a dû s'absenter; **he called me over to show me something** il m'a appelé pour que je vienne voir quelque chose; **to c. a meeting** décider d'organiser une réunion; **to c. a strike** appeler à la grève; **to c. sb's attention to sth** attirer l'attention de qn sur qch
(**c**) *(on phone)* appeler, téléphoner à; *(taxi)* appeler
(**d**) *(name)* appeler; **she's called Katy** elle s'appelle Katy; **to c. sb names** injurier qn; **to c. sb a liar/a thief** traiter qn de menteur/de voleur; **c. yourself a computer expert!** et moi qui te croyais bon en informatique!; **let's c. it $10** disons (que ce sera) 10 dollars; **do you c. that clean?** tu trouves vraiment que c'est propre?; **let's c. it a day** assez pour aujourd'hui
3 *vi* (**a**) *(shout)* appeler; **to c. to sb** appeler qn; **to c. for help** appeler au secours *ou* à l'aide
(**b**) *(on phone)* appeler, téléphoner; **to c. for an ambulance** appeler une ambulance; **who's calling?** qui est à l'appareil?
▶**call back** *vt sep & vi* rappeler
▶**call for** *vt insep* (**a**) *(require)* nécessiter; **this calls for a celebration!** il faut fêter ça!; **that wasn't called for!** c'était parfaitement déplacé! (**b**) *(demand)* réclamer (**c**) *(collect)* *(person)* passer chercher; *(object)* passer prendre
▶**call in 1** *vt sep* *(doctor, police)* appeler, faire venir; *(expert)* faire appel à
2 *vi (visit)* passer (**on sb** chez qn); **to c. in sick** *(to work)* téléphoner pour prévenir qu'on est malade
▶**call off** *vt sep* *(match, vacation)* annuler; *(search, strike)* mettre fin à; *(engagement)* rompre
▶**call on** *vt insep* (**a**) *(request)* **to c. on sb to do sth** *(urgently)* demander instamment à qn de faire qch; *(politely)* inviter qn à faire qch (**b**) *(visit)* rendre visite à (**c**) *Sch (of teacher)* interroger, poser une question à; **I was daydreaming when the teacher called on me** je rêvassais quand le prof m'a posé une question
▶**call out 1** *vt sep* (**a**) *(doctor, plumber, troops)* appeler; **to c. sb out on strike** donner l'ordre de grève à qn (**b**) *(shout)* appeler
2 *vi (shout)* crier
▶**call up** *vt sep* (**a**) *(on phone)* appeler, téléphoner à (**b**) *(memory, image)* évoquer (**c**) *Mil* appeler (sous les drapeaux)

caller [kɔːlə(r)] *n (visitor)* visiteur(euse) *m,f*; *(on phone)* correspondant(e) *m,f*; **next c., please** appel suivant, s'il vous plaît; **caller identification,** *Fam* **caller ID** identification *f* d'appel

calligraphy [kə'lɪgrəfɪ] *n* calligraphie *f*

calling ['kɔːlɪŋ] *n (vocation)* vocation *f*

callous ['kæləs] *adj* dur(e)

call-up ['kɔːlʌp] *n Mil* appel *m* (sous les drapeaux); **c. papers** ordre *m* d'incorporation

callus ['kæləs] *n* cal *m*

calm [kɑːm] **1** *n* calme *m*; *also Fig* **a dead c.** un calme plat; *also Fig* **the c. before the storm** le calme qui précède la tempête
2 *adj* calme, tranquille; *(sea)* calme; **to stay c.** rester calme; **to grow calmer** se calmer
3 *vt* calmer, apaiser; **to c. one's nerves** se calmer

▶**calm down 1** *vt sep* calmer
2 *vi* se calmer

calmly ['kɑːmlɪ] *adv* calmement

calorie ['kælərɪ] *n* calorie *f*

calumny ['kæləmnɪ] *(pl* **calumnies)** *n* calomnie *f*

calve [kɑːv] *vi (of cow)* vêler

calves [kɑːvz] *pl of* **calf**¹**, calf**²

calypso [kə'lɪpsəʊ] *(pl* **calypsos)** *n Mus* calypso *m*

CAM [siːeɪ'em] *n Comput (abbr* **computer-aided manufacturing)** FAO *f*

cam [kæm] *n Tech* came *f*

Cambodia [kæm'bəʊdɪə] *n* le Cambodge

Cambodian [kæm'bəʊdɪən] **1** *n* Cambodgien(enne) *m,f*
2 *adj* cambodgien(enne)

camcorder ['kæmkɔːdə(r)] *n* Caméscope® *m*

came [keɪm] *pt of* **come**

camel ['kæməl] *n* chameau *m*; *(female)* chamelle *f*; **c. coat** manteau *m* en poil de chameau; **c. driver** chamelier *m*; **c.'s hair** poil *m* de chameau

camelhair ['kæməlheə(r)] *n* poil *m* de chameau

camellia [kə'miːlɪə] *n* camélia *m*

cameo ['kæmɪəʊ] *(pl* **cameos)** *n* (**a**) *(jewelry)* camée *m*; **c. brooch** camée (**b**) *(in movie)* **c. (role)** brève apparition *f (d'un acteur connu)*

camera ['kæmərə] *n* (**a**) *(photographic)* appareil photo *m*; *TV & Cin* caméra *f*; *TV* **off c.** hors champ; **on c.** à l'écran; **c. crew** équipe *f* de prise de vue (**b**) *Law* **in c.** à huis clos

cameraman ['kæmərəmæn] *n* cameraman *m*

Cameroon [kæmə'ruːn] *n* le Cameroun

camisole ['kæmɪsəʊl] *n* caraco *m*, *Can & Suisse* camisole *f*

camomile ['kæməmaɪl, 'kæməmiːl] *n* camomille *f*; **c. tea** camomille

camouflage ['kæməflɑːʒ] **1** *n also Fig* camouflage *m*
2 *vt also Fig* camoufler

camp¹ [kæmp] **1** *n* (**a**) *(place)* camp *m*, campement *m*; **c. bed** lit *m* de camp; **c. site** *(establishment)* (terrain *m* de) camping *m*; *(in general)* campement (**b**) *(summer camp)* colonie *f* de vacances; **c. counselor** moniteur(trice) *m,f*
2 *vi* **to c. (out)** camper

camp² [kæmp] *adj* (**a**) *(effeminate)* efféminé(e) (**b**) *(theatrical)* *(person)* cabotin(e); *(behavior, manner)* théâtral(e) (**c**) *(in dubious taste)* kitsch *inv*

campaign [kæm'peɪn] **1** *n* campagne *f*
2 *vi* faire campagne (**for/against** pour/contre)

campaigner [kæm'peɪnə(r)] *n* militant(e) *m,f*; **to be a c. for/against sth** faire campagne pour/contre qch

camper ['kæmpə(r)] *n (person)* campeur(euse) *m,f*; *(vehicle)* camping-car *m*

campfire ['kæmpfaɪə(r)] *n* feu *m* de camp

campground ['kæmpgraʊnd] *n (commercial)* (terrain *m* de) camping *m*; *(wild)* emplacement *m* de camping

camphor ['kæmfə(r)] *n* camphre *m*

camping ['kæmpɪŋ] *n* camping *m*; **to go c.** faire du camping; **c. site** (terrain *m* de) camping

campus ['kæmpəs] *n* campus *m*

camshaft ['kæmʃɑːft] *n Aut* arbre *m* à cames

can¹ [kæn] **1** *n* (**a**) *(of food)* boîte *f*; *(of drink)* can(n)ette *f*; *(for gasoline)* bidon *m*; *(of paint)* pot *m*; *Fig* **to open a c. of worms** mettre à jour toutes sortes d'histoires désagréables; **c. opener** ouvre-boîte *m* (**b**) *very Fam (toilet)* chiottes *fpl*; *(prison)* taule *f*, tôle *f*
2 *vt (pt & pp* **canned)** (**a**) *(fruit, meat)* mettre en boîte *ou* en conserve; *Fig* **canned laughter** *(on radio, TV)* rires *mpl* préenregistrés (**b**) *Fam* **c. it!** *(keep quiet)* la ferme!

can² [kən, *stressed* kæn] *modal aux v (be able to)* pouvoir; **I c. go** je peux y aller; **I c. see/hear them** je les vois/entends; **we**

can't possibly do it nous ne pouvons en aucun cas le faire; **he'll do what he c.** il fera ce qu'il pourra; **how c. you tell?** à quoi vois-tu ça?; **it can't be done** c'est impossible à faire

(b) *(know how to)* savoir; **I c. swim** je sais nager; **c. you speak English?** parles-tu anglais?

(c) *(indicating possibility)* pouvoir; **it c. get very hot here** il peut faire très chaud ici; **it can't have been easy for her** ça n'a pas dû être facile pour elle; **you CAN'T be serious!** tu n'es pas sérieux!; **what c. it be?** qu'est-ce que ça peut bien être?

(d) *(with requests, permission)* pouvoir; **c. I ask you something?** je peux vous demander quelque chose?; **you can't smoke in here** on ne peut pas fumer ici

Canada ['kænədə] *n* le Canada

Canadian [kə'neɪdɪən] **1** *n* Canadien(enne) *m,f*
2 *adj* canadien(enne)

canal [kə'næl] *n* canal *m*

Canary [kə'neərɪ] *n* **the C. Islands, the Canaries** les (îles *fpl*) Canaries *fpl*

canary [kə'neərɪ] *(pl* **canaries***)* *n* canari *m*; **c. yellow** jaune canari *inv*

cancel ['kænsəl] **1** *vt* annuler; *(check)* faire opposition à
2 *vi* se décommander

▸**cancel out** *vt sep* annuler; **to c. each other out** s'annuler

cancellation [kænsə'leɪʃən] *n* annulation *f*; **c. fee** frais *mpl* d'annulation

Cancer ['kænsə(r)] *n* *(sign of zodiac)* le Cancer; **to be (a) C.** être (du) Cancer; *Geog* **the Tropic of C.** le tropique du Cancer

cancer ['kænsə(r)] *n* *(disease)* cancer *m*; **lung/skin c.** cancer du poumon/de la peau; **c. research** cancérologie *f*

cancerous ['kænsərəs] *adj Med* cancéreux(euse)

candelabra [kændɪ'lɑ:brə] *n* candélabre *m*

candid ['kændɪd] *adj* franc (franche)

candidacy ['kændɪdəsɪ] *n* candidature *f*

candidate ['kændɪdeɪt] *n* candidat(e) *m,f* **(for** à); **to run as a c.** poser sa candidature, se présenter

candidature ['kændɪdətʃə(r)] = **candidacy**

candidly ['kændɪdlɪ] *adv* franchement

candied ['kændɪd] *adj* glacé(e), confit(e); **c. peel** zeste *m* confit

candle ['kændəl] *n* bougie *f*; **he can't hold a c. to you** il ne t'arrive pas à la cheville; **it's not worth the c.** le jeu n'en vaut pas la chandelle

candlelight ['kændəllaɪt] *n* lumière *f* d'une bougie; **by c.** à la chandelle *ou* bougie

candlelit ['kændəllɪt] *adj* aux chandelles

candlestick ['kændəlstɪk] *n* bougeoir *m*; *(taller)* chandelier *m*

can-do ['kændu:] *adj* dynamique, entreprenant(e); **c. attitude** *or* **spirit** esprit *m* de battant *ou* de gagneur

candor ['kændə(r)] *n* franchise *f*

candy ['kændɪ] *(pl* **candies***)* *n* bonbon *m*; **some c.** des bonbons; **c. bar** barre *f* chocolatée; **c. store** confiserie *f*

cane [keɪn] **1** *n* *(of sugar, bamboo)* canne *f*, tige *f*; *(walking stick)* canne; *(for punishment)* verge *f*, baguette *f*; **to get the c.** recevoir des coups de verge *ou* de baguette; **c. furniture** meubles *mpl* en rotin; **c. sugar** sucre *m* de canne
2 *vt* *(beat)* frapper avec une verge *ou* une baguette

canine ['keɪnaɪn] **1** *n* **(a)** *(tooth)* canine *f* **(b)** *(animal)* canidé *m*
2 *adj* canin(e)

canister ['kænɪstə(r)] *n* boîte *f* (en métal); *(of gas)* bonbonne *f*

canker ['kæŋkə(r)] *n also Fig* chancre *m*

cannabis ['kænəbɪs] *n* cannabis *m*

cannery ['kænərɪ] *(pl* **canneries***)* *n* conserverie *f*

cannibal ['kænɪbəl] *n* cannibale *mf*

cannibalize ['kænɪbəlaɪz] *vt* cannibaliser

cannon ['kænən] *(pl* **cannons** *or* **cannon***)* *n* canon *m*; **c. fodder** chair *f* à canon; *Fam* **he's a loose c.** il n'en fait qu'à sa tête

cannonball ['kænənbɔ:l] *n* boulet *m* de canon

cannot ['kænɒt] = **can not**

canny ['kænɪ] *adj* rusé(e)

canoe [kə'nu:] *n* canoë *m*

canoeing [kə'nu:ɪŋ] *n* canoë-kayak *m*; **to go c.** faire du canoë-kayak

canoeist [kə'nu:ɪst] *n* canoéiste *mf*

canon ['kænən] *n* **(a)** *(religious decree)* & *Fig* canon *m*; **c. law** droit *m* canon **(b)** *(priest)* chanoine *m*

canonize ['kænənaɪz] *vt Rel* canoniser

canoodle [kə'nu:dəl] *vi Hum* se faire des mamours

canopy ['kænəpɪ] *(pl* **canopies***)* *n* *(above bed)* baldaquin *m*; *(outside store)* auvent *m*; *(parachute)* parachute *m*; *(of tree branches)* canopée *f*

cant [kænt] *n* *(hypocrisy)* langage *m* hypocrite

can't [kɑ:nt] = **can not**

cantaloup(e) ['kæntəlu:p] *n* melon *m* (cantaloup)

cantankerous [kæn'tæŋkərəs] *adj* revêche, acariâtre

canteen [kæn'ti:n] *n* **(a)** *(restaurant)* cantine *f* **(b)** *(water bottle)* gourde *f* **(c)** *(of cutlery)* ménagère *f*

canter ['kæntə(r)] **1** *n* *(on horse)* petit galop *m*
2 *vi* *(of horse)* aller au petit galop; *Fig* **to c. through a speech** expédier un discours

cantilever ['kæntɪli:və(r)] *n Tech* poutre *f* en porte-à-faux; **c. bridge** pont *m* cantilever

Cantonese [kæntə'ni:z] **1** *n* *(language)* cantonais *m*
2 *adj* cantonais(e)

canvas ['kænvəs] *n* **(a)** *(cloth)* (grosse) toile *f*; **under c.** *(in tent)* sous la tente; *Naut* sous voiles **(b)** *Art* toile *f*

canvass ['kænvəs] **1** *vt* **(a)** *Pol* **to c. sb** faire campagne auprès de qn **(b)** *Com (consumers)* sonder; *Fig* **to c. opinion** sonder l'opinion
2 *vi* **(a)** *Pol* faire du porte-à-porte *(dans le cadre d'une campagne électorale)* **(b)** *Com* faire du démarchage

canvasser ['kænvəsə(r)] *n Pol* = personne qui fait du porte-à-porte dans le cadre d'une campagne électorale

canyon ['kænjən] *n* canyon *m*, cañon *m*

canyoner ['kænjənə(r)] *n* canyoniste *mf*

canyoning ['kænjənɪŋ] *n Sport* canyoning *m*

cap [kæp] **1** *n* **(a)** *(hat)* *(without peak)* bonnet *m*; *(with peak)* casquette *f*; *Fig* **to go c. in hand to sb** se présenter chapeau bas devant qn **(b)** *(of bottle)* capsule *f*; *(of pen)* capuchon *m* **(c)** *(for toy gun)* amorce *f*
2 *vt* *(pt & pp* **capped***)* **(a)** *(cover)* recouvrir **(with** de) **(b)** **to have a tooth capped** se faire refaire l'émail d'une dent **(c)** *(surpass, do better than)* surpasser; **to c. it all,...** pour couronner le tout,.. **(d)** *(spending)* limiter

capability [keɪpə'bɪlɪtɪ] *(pl* **capabilities***)* *n* capacité *f* **(to do sth** de faire qch); **it is beyond our capabilities** c'est au-dessus de nos moyens

capable ['keɪpəbəl] *adj* capable; **to be c. of doing sth** être capable de faire qch; **the business is in c. hands** l'affaire est entre de bonnes mains

capably ['keɪpəblɪ] *adv* avec compétence

capacious [kə'peɪʃəs] *adj Formal* vaste, spacieux(euse)

capacitor [kə'pæsɪtə(r)] *n Elec* condensateur *m*

capacity [kə'pæsɪtɪ] *(pl* **capacities***)* *n* **(a)** *(of container, bus, theater)* & *Elec* capacité *f*; **the stadium has a c. of 50,000** le stade peut accueillir 50 000 spectateurs; **full to c.** plein(e); **there was a c. crowd at the match** le stade était bondé pour le match

(b) *(aptitude)* **to have a c. for sth** être capable de qch; **to be beyond sb's c.** dépasser les compétences de qn; **to be within sb's c.** être dans les possibilités de qn; **c. for work** capacité *f* de travail

(c) *(output)* capacité *f*; **at full c.** à plein

(d) *(role)* **in my c. as...** en ma qualité de...; **they are here in an official c.** ils sont ici à titre officiel

cape¹ [keɪp] *n (cloak)* pèlerine *f*, cape *f*

cape² [keɪp] *n Geog* cap *m*; **the C. of Good Hope** le cap de Bonne-Espérance; **C. Town** Le Cap

caper¹ ['keɪpə(r)] *n Culin* câpre *f*

caper² ['keɪpə(r)] **1** *n (prank)* cabriole *f*
2 *vi* **to c. (about)** faire des cabrioles

Cape Verde [keɪp'vɜːd] *n* le Cap-Vert

capillary [kə'pɪlərɪ] **1** *(pl* **capillaries)** *n* capillaire *m*
2 *adj* capillaire

capital ['kæpɪtəl] **1** *n* **(a)** *(letter)* majuscule *f*, capitale *f* **(b)** **c. (city)** capitale *f* **(c)** *Fin* capital *m*; *Fig* **to make c. out of sth** tirer parti de qch; **c. assets** actif *m* immobilisé; **c. expenditure** dépenses *fpl* en capital; **c.-gains tax** impôt *m* sur les plus-values (en capital); **c. goods** biens *mpl* d'équipement; **c. investment** investissement *m* de capitaux
2 *adj* **(a)** *(letter)* majuscule; **c. T** T majuscule; **he's rich with a c. R** il est vraiment très riche **(b)** *Law* **c. crime** *or* **offense** crime *m* capital *ou* puni de mort; **c. punishment** peine *f* capitale **(c)** *(important)* capital(e); **of c. importance** d'une importance capitale

capitalism ['kæpɪtəlɪzəm] *n* capitalisme *m*

capitalist ['kæpɪtəlɪst] *n & adj* capitaliste *mf*

capitalization [kæpɪtəlaɪ'zeɪʃən] *n Fin* capitalisation *f*

capitalize ['kæpɪtəlaɪz] *vt* **(a)** *Fin* capitaliser **(b)** *(initial letter)* écrire avec une majuscule; *(whole word)* écrire en majuscules
▸**capitalize on** *vt insep* profiter de, tirer parti de

Capitol ['kæpɪtəl] *n Pol* **the C.** le Capitole; **C. Hill** = la colline du Capitole, à Washington, où se trouve le Congrès américain

capitulate [kə'pɪtjʊleɪt] *vi* capituler (**to** devant)

capon ['keɪpən] *n Culin* chapon *m*

capper ['kæpə(r)] *n Fam* **that was the c.** *(the last straw)* c'est la goutte d'eau qui a fait déborder le vase; **that was the c. to a successful year** ça a été le couronnement d'une année faste

cappuccino [kæpʊ'tʃiːnəʊ] *(pl* **cappuccinos)** *n* cappuccino *m*

caprice [kə'priːs] *n* caprice *m*

capricious [kə'prɪʃəs] *adj* capricieux(euse)

Capricorn ['kæprɪkɔːn] *n (sign of zodiac)* le Capricorne; **to be (a) C.** être (du) Capricorne; *Geog* **the Tropic of C.** le tropique du Capricorne

capsicum ['kæpsɪkəm] *n Culin* poivron *m*

capsize [kæp'saɪz] **1** *vt* faire chavirer
2 *vi* chavirer

capstan ['kæpstən] *n Naut* cabestan *m*

capsule ['kæpsjuːl] *n (of medicine)* gélule *f*; **(space) c.** capsule *f* spatiale

Capt. *(abbr* **Captain)** Capt

captain ['kæptɪn] **1** *n* capitaine *m*
2 *vt* être le capitaine de; **he captained them to victory** il les a conduits à la victoire

caption ['kæpʃən] *n* **(a)** *(under illustration, photograph, cartoon)* légende *f* **(b)** *Cin & TV (subtitle)* sous-titre *m*
2 *vt* **(a)** *(illustration)* mettre une légende à, légender **(b)** *Cin & TV (subtitle)* sous-titrer

captioned ['kæpʃənd] *adj Cin & TV (subtitled)* = doté de sous-titres pour les malentendants

captivate ['kæptɪveɪt] *vt* fasciner

captivating ['kæptɪveɪtɪŋ] *adj* fascinant(e)

captive ['kæptɪv] *n & adj* captif(ive) *m,f*; **to be taken c.** être fait(e) prisonnier(ère); **he had a c. audience** *(spellbound)* son auditoire était subjugué; *(had no choice but to listen)* son auditoire était forcé de l'écouter

captivity [kæp'tɪvɪtɪ] *n* captivité *f*; **in c.** en captivité

captor ['kæptə(r)] *n* ravisseur(euse) *m,f*

capture ['kæptʃə(r)] **1** *n* capture *f*; *(of town, enemy, position)* prise *f*

2 *vt (person, animal)* capturer; *(town, enemy, position)* prendre (**from** à); *(in chess)* prendre; *Fig (mood)* rendre; **to c. sb's imagination** parler à l'imagination de qn; **to c. the moment** saisir l'instant

car [kɑː(r)] *n* **(a)** *(automobile)* voiture *f*, automobile *f*; **by c.** en voiture; **c. bomb** voiture piégée; **c. crash** accident *m* de voiture; **c. door** portière *f* de voiture; **c. industry** industrie *f* automobile; **c. phone** téléphone *m* de voiture; **c. pool** = groupe de personnes effectuant régulièrement un trajet dans la même voiture; **c. pooling** covoiturage *m*; **c. radio** autoradio *m*; **c. rental** location *f* de voitures **(b)** *(train wagon)* voiture *f*, wagon *m*

carafe [kə'ræf] *n* carafe *f*

caramel ['kærəməl] *n* caramel *m*

carat ['kærət] *n* carat *m*; **18-c. gold** or *m* (à) 18 carats

caravan ['kærəvæn] *n (of gipsy)* roulotte *f*; *(in desert)* caravane *f*; **to travel in c.** voyager en convoi

caraway ['kærəweɪ] *n* carvi *m*, cumin *m* des prés; **c. seeds** graines *fpl* de carvi

carbohydrate [kɑːbəʊ'haɪdreɪt] *n* hydrate *m* de carbone; *(in food)* glucide *m*; **low-/high-c. diet** régime *m* hypoglucidique/hyperglucidique

carbolic [kɑː'bɒlɪk] *adj Chem* **c. acid** phénol *m*

carbon ['kɑːbən] *n* carbone *m*; **c. copy** copie *f* (au carbone); *Fig* **she is a c. copy of her mother** c'est la copie conforme de sa mère; **c. dioxide** dioxyde de carbone, gaz *m* carbonique; **c. fiber** fibre *f* de carbone; **c. monoxide** monoxyde *m* de carbone; **c. paper** *(papier m)* carbone

carbonated ['kɑːbəneɪtɪd] *adj* gazéifié(e); *(naturally)* gazeux(euse)

carbonize ['kɑːbənaɪz] *vt* carboniser

carbuncle ['kɑːbʌŋkəl] *n Med* furoncle *m*

carburetor ['kɑːbjʊrətə(r)] *n* carburateur *m*

carcass ['kɑːkəs] *n (of animal)* carcasse *f*

carcinogenic [kɑːsɪnə'dʒenɪk] *adj Med* carcinogène *m*

card [kɑːd] *n* **(a)** *(for card game)* carte *f*; **to play cards** jouer aux cartes; **c. game** jeu *m* de cartes; **c. table** table *f* de jeux; **c. trick** tour *m* de cartes **(b)** *(with printed information)* carte *f*; *(postcard)* carte (postale); **c. index** *or* **file** fichier *m* **(c)** *(plastic)* carte *f* **(d)** *(cardboard)* carton *m* (fin) **(e)** *Comput* carte *f* **(f)** *(idioms)* **play your cards right and you could get promoted** si tu mènes bien ton jeu, tu seras peut-être promu; **to put one's cards on the table** jouer cartes sur table; **to have a c. up one's sleeve** avoir un atout dans son jeu; **it is in the cards that...** il est bien possible que...

cardamom ['kɑːdəməm] *n* cardamome *f*

cardboard ['kɑːdbɔːd] *n* carton *m*; **c. box** (boîte *f* en) carton; *Fig & Pej* **c. characters** personnages *mpl* sans aucune profondeur

card-carrying ['kɑːdkærɪŋ] *adj* **c. member** adhérent(e) *m,f*

cardholder ['kɑːdhəʊldə(r)] *n (of club, political party)* membre *m*, adhérent(e) *m,f*; *(of library)* abonné(e) *m,f*; *(of credit card)* titulaire *mf*

cardiac ['kɑːdɪæk] *adj* cardiaque; **c. arrest** arrêt *m* cardiaque

cardigan ['kɑːdɪgən] *n* cardigan *m*

cardinal ['kɑːdɪnəl] **1** *n* **(a)** *Rel* cardinal *m* **(b)** *(bird)* cardinal *m* rouge
2 *adj* cardinal(e); *Fig* **it's a c. sin** c'est impardonnable

cardiograph ['kɑːdɪəgræf] *n* cardiographe *m*

cardiologist [kɑːdɪ'ɒlədʒɪst] *n* cardiologue *mf*

cardiology [kɑːdɪ'ɒlədʒɪ] *n* cardiologie *f*

cardiovascular [kɑːdɪəʊ'væskjʊlə(r)] *adj* cardiovasculaire

cardsharp ['kɑːdʃɑːp], **cardsharper** ['kɑːdʃɑːpə(r)] *n* tricheur(euse) *m,f* professionnel(elle)

care [keə(r)] **1** *n* **(a)** *(worry)* souci *m*; **she doesn't have a c. in the world** elle n'a pas le moindre souci **(b)** *(attention)* soin *m*; *(medical treatment)* soins médicaux; **to**

put a lot of c. into sth apporter beaucoup de soin à qch; **to drive without due c.** conduire imprudemment; **to take c. of** s'occuper de; **to take c. of oneself** savoir se débrouiller tout(e) seul(e); *(healthwise)* prendre soin de sa santé; **to take c. to do sth** faire bien attention à faire qch; **take c.!** *(goodbye)* à bientôt!; **take good c. of yourself** fais bien attention à toi

(**c**) *(protection)* soins *mpl*; *(of clothes, machine)* entretien *m*; **to be in** *or* **under sb's c.** avoir été confié(e) à qn; **write to me c. of Mrs Wallace** écrivez-moi chez Mme Wallace *ou* aux bons soins de Mme Wallace

2 *vt* (**a**) *(mind)* **I don't c. what he says** peu m'importe ce qu'il en dit; **I don't c. whether he likes it or not** peu m'importe que cela lui plaise ou non

(**b**) *(like)* **would you c. to come with me?** aimeriez-vous m'accompagner?

3 *vi* (**a**) *(be concerned)* se préoccuper, se soucier (**about** de); **that's all he cares about** c'est tout ce qui l'intéresse; **to c. about sb** *(be fond of)* aimer qn

(**b**) *(mind)* **I don't c.** ça m'est égal; **who cares?** qu'est-ce que ça peut faire?; **I could be dead for all they c.!** ils se moquent éperdument de ce qui peut m'arriver!; **I couldn't c. less** je m'en moque éperdument

▶**care for** *vt insep* (**a**) *(look after)* soigner (**b**) *(like)* aimer

career [kə'rɪə(r)] **1** *n* carrière *f*; **it's a good/bad c. move** c'est bon/mauvais pour ma/ta/*etc.* carrière; **c. break** interruption *f* de carrière; **c. counselor** conseiller(ère) *m,f* d'orientation; **c. path** *(strategy)* plan *m* de carrière; *(prospects)* perspectives *fpl* de carrière; **c. service** service *m* d'orientation professionnelle

2 *vi* **to c. (along)** aller à vive allure; **the car careered off the road** la voiture a quitté la route à vive allure

careerist [kə'rɪərɪst] *n Pej* carriériste *mf*

carefree ['keəfriː] *adj* insouciant(e)

careful ['keəfʊl] *adj* (**a**) *(cautious)* prudent(e); **be c. of that step** fais attention à la marche; **(be) c.!** fais attention!; **to be c. to do sth** faire bien attention à faire qch; **she was c. not to mention his name** elle a bien fait attention à ne pas mentionner son nom; **be c. what you say** fais attention à ce que tu dis; **you can't be too c. these days** on n'est jamais trop prudent de nos jours (**b**) *(thorough)* *(work, inspection)* minutieux(euse); **after c. consideration** après mûre réflexion

carefully ['keəfʊlɪ] *adv* (**a**) *(cautiously)* prudemment (**b**) *(thoroughly)* soigneusement, avec soin; *(listen)* attentivement; **c. worded** aux termes choisis (avec soin)

caregiver ['keəgɪvə(r)] *n* *(professional)* aide *mf* à domicile; *(relative)* = personne qui s'occupant d'un parent malade ou âgé

careless ['keəlɪs] *adj* (**a**) *(negligent)* négligent(e); *(work)* négligé(e); **to be c. about one's appearance** être négligé; **a c. mistake** une faute d'inattention, une étourderie; **a c. remark** une remarque inconsidérée (**b**) *(unconcerned)* insouciant(e)

carelessly ['keəlɪslɪ] *adv* *(negligently)* négligemment

carelessness ['keəlɪsnɪs] *n* *(negligence)* négligence *f*

caress [kə'res] **1** *n* caresse *f*
2 *vt* caresser

caretaker ['keəteɪkə(r)] *n* concierge *mf*, gardien(enne) *m,f*; **c. government** gouvernement *m* intérimaire

careworn ['keəwɔːn] *adj* usé(e) par les soucis

cargo ['kɑːgəʊ] *(pl* **cargoes** *or* **cargos)** *n* cargaison *f*; **c. boat** *or* **ship** cargo *m*; **c. plane** avion-cargo *m*

Caribbean [kə'rɪbɪən] **1** *n* **the C. (Sea)** la mer des Caraïbes; **the C.** *(region)* la Caraïbe
2 *adj* caraïbe

caribou ['kærɪbuː] *n* caribou *m*

caricature ['kærɪkətjʊə(r)] **1** *n* caricature *f*
2 *vt* caricaturer

caricaturist [kærɪkə'tjʊərɪst] *n* caricaturiste *mf*

caries ['keəriːz] *n Med* carie *f*

caring ['keərɪŋ] *adj* *(society, personality)* humain(e); *(parent)* aimant(e); *(atmosphere)* chaleureux(euse)

carnage ['kɑːnɪdʒ] *n* carnage *m*

carnal ['kɑːnəl] *adj* charnel(elle)

carnation [kɑː'neɪʃən] *n* œillet *m*

carnival ['kɑːnɪvəl] *n* *(celebration)* carnaval *m*; *(amusement park)* fête *f* foraine

carnivore ['kɑːnɪvɔː(r)] *n* carnivore *m*

carnivorous [kɑː'nɪvərəs] *adj* carnivore

carob ['kærəb] *n* *(fruit)* caroube *f*; *(tree)* caroubier *m*

carol ['kærəl] *n* **(Christmas) c.** chant *m* de Noël; **c. service** = office religieux qui précède Noël

carouse [kə'raʊz] *vi* faire la fête

carousel [kærə'sel] *n* (**a**) *(at amusement park)* chevaux *mpl* de bois, manège *m* (**b**) *(at airport)* carrousel *m* (pour bagages) (**c**) *(for slides)* magasin *m*

carp¹ [kɑːp] *(pl* **carp)** *n* *(fish)* carpe *f*

carp² [kɑːp] *vi* se plaindre (**at** de)

Carpathians [kɑː'peɪθɪənz] *npl* **the C.** les Carpates *fpl*

carpenter ['kɑːpɪntə(r)] *n* menuisier *m*; *(on construction site)* charpentier *m*

carpentry ['kɑːpɪntrɪ] *n* menuiserie *f*; *(on construction site)* charpenterie *f*

carpet ['kɑːpɪt] **1** *n* (**a**) *(rug)* & *Fig* *(of flowers, snow)* tapis *m*; *(wall-to-wall)* moquette *f*; **c. bombing** bombardement *m* intensif; **c. shampoo** shampooing *m* pour moquette; **c. slippers** pantoufles *fpl*; **c. sweeper** balai *m* mécanique (**b**) *(idioms)* **to pull the c. out from under sb** faire un tour de cochon à qn
2 *vt* *(with rug)* recouvrir d'un tapis; *(with wall-to-wall carpet)* moquetter; *Fig* **to be carpeted with snow** être recouvert(e) de neige

carport ['kɑːpɔːt] *n* abri *m* pour voiture

carriage ['kærɪdʒ] *n* (**a**) *(vehicle)* voiture *f* (**b**) *(of typewriter)* chariot *m*; **c. return** retour-chariot *m* (**c**) *Com (transport)* transport *m*; *(cost)* frais *mpl* de port (**d**) *(bearing)* *(of person)* port *m*

carrier ['kærɪə(r)] *n* (**a**) *(of disease, germs)* porteur(euse) *m,f* (**b**) *Com (company, airline)* transporteur *m* (**c**) *(on bicycle)* porte-bagages *m inv* (**d**) **c. (bag)** sac *m* (en papier ou en plastique)

carrion ['kærɪən] *n* charogne *f*

carrot ['kærət] *n also Fig* carotte *f*; **a c.-and-stick approach** la carotte et le bâton

carry ['kærɪ] *(pt* & *pp* **carried)** **1** *vt* (**a**) *(transport, convey)* porter; *(goods, passengers)* transporter; *(electricity, fuel)* acheminer; *(gun, money)* avoir sur soi; *(a scar)* avoir; *(disease)* être porteur(euse) de; **the current carried the raft out to sea** le courant a emporté le radeau au large; **to c. an image in one's head** avoir une image en tête; **to be carrying sb's child** *(be pregnant)* porter l'enfant de qn

(**b**) *(involve)* *(risk)* comporter; **to c. a fine/penalty** être passible d'une amende/d'une peine; **to c. weight/authority** avoir du poids/de l'autorité

(**c**) *(develop)* **to c. sth too far** pousser qch trop loin; **to c. an argument to its logical conclusion** aller au bout d'un raisonnement

(**d**) *(capture, win)* **to c. all before one** *(be successful)* remporter tous les prix; *(win support, approval)* vaincre toutes les résistances; **his argument carried the day** son argument l'a emporté

(**e**) *(proposal, motion)* voter

(**f**) *(of newspaper, news program)* *(story)* faire état de; *(advertisement)* contenir

(**g**) *Com (keep in stock)* vendre

(**h**) **to c. oneself** *(behave)* se conduire

(**i**) *Math* **c. two** et je retiens deux

2 *vi (of sound)* porter; **her voice carries well** elle a une voix qui porte bien

▶**carry away** *vt sep* (**a**) *(take away)* emporter (**b**) **to get carried away** *(excited)* s'emballer

▶**carry forward** *vt sep Fin* reporter; **carried forward** report, à reporter

▶**carry off** *vt sep* (**a**) *(take away)* emporter; *(prize)* remporter (**b**) *(do successfully)* **she carried it off (well)** elle s'en est bien sortie

▶**carry on 1** *vt sep (tradition)* perpétuer; *(business, trade)* exercer; *(correspondence)* entretenir; *(conversation)* poursuivre
  2 *vi* (**a**) *(continue)* continuer, poursuivre; **to c. on doing sth** continuer de *ou* à faire qch (**b**) *Fam (behave badly)* mal se conduire; **I don't like the way she carries on** je n'aime pas ses façons (**c**) *Fam (have an affair)* avoir une liaison (**with** avec) (**d**) *(talk)* parler sans cesse (**about** de)

▶**carry out** *vt sep (plan, threat, decision)* mettre à exécution; *(experiment, test)* faire, effectuer; *(instructions)* exécuter

carryall ['kærɪɔːl] *n (bag)* fourre-tout *m inv*

carry-on ['kærɪɒn] *n Fam* ramdam *m*; **what a c.!** quel cirque!

carry-out ['kærɪaʊt] **1** *n (food)* plat *m* à emporter; *(restaurant)* restaurant *m* qui fait des plats à emporter
  2 *adj (food)* à emporter

carsick ['kɑːsɪk] *adj* **to be c.** avoir mal au cœur en voiture

cart [kɑːt] **1** *n (vehicle)* charrette *f*; *(for shopping etc.)* chariot *m*; *Fig* **to put the c. before the horse** mettre la charrue avant les bœufs
  2 *vt Fam (carry)* trimballer

▶**cart off** *vt sep Fam* **to c. sb off** emmener qn

carte blanche ['kɑːt'blɑ̃ʃ] *n* **to give sb c. (to do sth)** donner carte blanche à qn (pour faire qch)

cartel [kɑː'tel] *n Econ* cartel *m*

cartilage ['kɑːtɪlɪdʒ] *n* cartilage *m*

cartographer [kɑː'tɒɡrəfə(r)] *n* cartographe *mf*

cartography [kɑː'tɒɡrəfɪ] *n* cartographie *f*

carton ['kɑːtən] *n (of yoghurt, cream)* pot *m*; *(of milk, fruit juice)* brique *f*; *(of cigarettes)* cartouche *f*

cartoon [kɑː'tuːn] *n (drawing)* dessin *m* humoristique; *(movie)* dessin animé; **c. (strip)** bande *f* dessinée

cartoonist [kɑː'tuːnɪst] *n* dessinateur(trice) *m,f*

cartridge ['kɑːtrɪdʒ] *n* (**a**) *(for gun, pen, of film)* cartouche *f*; **c. belt** cartouchière *f* (**b**) **c. paper** papier *m* à cartouche

cartwheel ['kɑːtwiːl] *n* roue *f* de charrette; **to turn cartwheels** faire la roue

carve [kɑːv] *vt (wood, stone, statue)* sculpter; *(name)* graver; *(meat)* découper

▶**carve out** *vt sep* **to c. out a career for oneself** faire carrière; **the company carved out a niche for itself** la société s'est taillé une place sur le marché

▶**carve up** *vt sep Fig (territory)* découper

carving ['kɑːvɪŋ] *n* (**a**) *Art* sculpture *f* (**b**) **c. knife** *(for meat)* couteau *m* à découper

carwash ['kɑːwɒʃ] *n* = station de lavage automatique pour autos; *(sign)* lavage automatique

cascade [kæs'keɪd] **1** *n* cascade *f*
  2 *vi* tomber en cascade

case[1] [keɪs] *n* (**a**) *(instance, situation) & Med* cas *m*; **a c. in point** un cas d'espèce; **in c. of emergency/accident** en cas d'urgence/d'accident; **in c. he isn't there** au cas où il ne serait pas là; **I'll take it just in c.** je vais le prendre au cas où; **just in c. it rains** au cas où il pleuvrait; **in any c.** *(besides)* de toute façon; **in that c.** dans ce cas; **in such a c.** en pareil cas; **as the c. may be** suivant le cas; **if that's the c.** dans ce cas(-là), s'il en est ainsi; *Med* **c. history** antécédents *mpl*; **c. study** étude *f* de cas (**b**) *Law* affaire *f*; **the c. will be heard on January 5** l'audience aura lieu le 5 janvier; **the c. for the defense** la défense; **the c. for the prosecution** l'accusation *f*; *Fig* **the c. for sb/sth** les arguments *mpl* en faveur de qn/qch; *Fig* **she has a good c.** elle a de bons arguments; **c. law** droit *m* jurisprudentiel

case[2] [keɪs] *n* (**a**) *(container) (for eyeglasses, cigarettes, musical instrument)* étui *m*; *(for jewelry)* écrin *m*; (**packing**) **c.** caisse *f*; **a c. of wine** une caisse de vin; (**display** *or* **glass**) **c.** vitrine *f* (**b**) *(suitcase)* valise *f*; *(briefcase)* porte-documents *m inv* (**c**) *Typ* **lower/upper c.** bas *m*/haut *m* de casse

casement ['keɪsmənt] *n* **c. (window)** fenêtre *f* à deux battants

case-sensitive ['keɪs'sensɪtɪv] *adj Comput* qui distingue les majuscules des minuscules

cash [kæʃ] **1** *n (coins, banknotes)* liquide *m*; *Fam (money in general)* sous *mpl*; **to pay (in) c.** payer en liquide *ou* en espèces; **c. on delivery** paiement *m* à la livraison; **c. and carry** *(store)* magasin *m* de demi-gros; **c. in hand** fonds *m ou* argent *m* en caisse; **c. box** caisse *f*; **c. card** carte *f* de retrait; **c. cow** vache *f* à lait; **c. crop** culture *f* commerciale; **c. dispenser** *or* **machine** distributeur *m* automatique de billets; *Fin* **c. flow** trésorerie *f*; **c. price** prix *m* au comptant; **c. register** caisse enregistreuse
  2 *vt (check, money order)* encaisser

▶**cash in on** *vt insep Fam* profiter de, tirer profit de

cashbook ['kæʃbʊk] *n* livre *m ou* journal *m* de caisse

cashew ['kæʃuː] *n* **c. (nut)** noix *f* de cajou

cashier [kæ'ʃɪə(r)] *n* caissier(ère) *m,f*; **c.'s check** chèque *m* de banque

cashmere ['kæʃmɪə(r)] *n* cachemire *m*

casing ['keɪsɪŋ] *n Tech* boîtier *m*; *(of sausage)* boyau *m*

casino [kə'siːnəʊ] *(pl* **casinos**) *n* casino *m*

cask [kɑːsk] *n* fût *m*, tonneau *m*

casket ['kɑːskɪt] *n* (**a**) *(for jewelry)* coffret *m* (**b**) *(coffin)* cercueil *m*

Caspian Sea ['kæspɪən'siː] *n* **the C.** la mer Caspienne

cassava [kə'sɑːvə] *n* manioc *m*

casserole ['kæsərəʊl] *n (pot)* cocotte *f*; *(food)* ragoût *m*

cassette [kæ'set] *n* cassette *f*; **c. player** lecteur *m* de cassettes; **c. recorder** magnétophone *m* à cassettes

cassock ['kæsək] *n* soutane *f*

cast [kɑːst] **1** *n* (**a**) *(of play, movie) (actors)* acteurs *mpl*; *(list)* distribution *f*; *Cin & TV* **c. and credits** générique *f*
  (**b**) *(molded object)* moulage *m*; *Med* (**plaster**) **c.** plâtre *m*; *Fig* **c. of mind** tournure *f* d'esprit
  (**c**) **to have a c. in one's eye** *(squint)* avoir une coquetterie dans l'œil
  2 *vt (pt & pp* **cast**) (**a**) *(throw) (stone)* jeter, lancer; *(shadow, net, line)* jeter; **to c. one's eyes over sth** parcourir qch des yeux; **to c. doubt on sth** jeter un doute sur qch, faire planer un doute sur qch; *Fig* **to c. light on sth** permettre de comprendre qch; **to c. one's mind back to sth** revenir sur qch, se rappeler qch; **to c. its skin** *(of reptile)* muer; **to c. a spell over sb** envoûter qn
  (**b**) **to c. one's vote (for)** voter (pour)
  (**c**) *(film, movie)* faire la distribution de; **she was cast as** *or* **in the role of Desdemona** on l'a choisie pour le rôle de Desdémone
  (**d**) *(metal, statue)* couler; **c. iron** fonte *f*

▶**cast about, cast around** *vi* **to c. about** *or* **around for sth** chercher qch

▶**cast aside** *vt sep (idea, prejudice)* se défaire de

▶**cast away** *vt sep* **to be cast away** faire naufrage

▶**cast down** *vt sep* **to be cast down** être abattu(e) *ou* découragé(e)

▶**cast off 1** *vt sep (clothes, chains)* rejeter, enlever; *(chains)* se libérer de
  2 *vi* (**a**) *Naut* larguer les amarres (**b**) *(in knitting)* arrêter les mailles

▶**cast on** *vi (in knitting)* monter les mailles

castanets [kæstə'nets] *npl* castagnettes *fpl*

castaway ['kɑːstəweɪ] *n* naufragé(e) *m,f*

caste [kɑːst] *n (social rank)* caste *f*

castigate ['kæstɪgeɪt] *vt Formal* critiquer sévèrement

casting ['kɑːstɪŋ] **1** *n (of play, movie)* distribution *f*, casting *m*
   2 *adj* **c. vote** voix *f* prépondérante

cast-iron ['kɑːst'aɪən] *adj* en *ou* de fonte; *Fig (alibi, guarantee)* en béton

castle ['kɑːsəl] **1** *n* château *m; (in chess)* tour *f; Fig* **to build castles in the air** bâtir des châteaux en Espagne
   2 *vi (in chess)* roquer

castoff ['kɑːstɒf] **1** *n (garment)* vieux vêtement *m; (person)* laissé-pour-compte (laissée-pour-compte) *m,f*
   2 *adj* **c. clothing** vieux vêtements *mpl*

castor ['kɑːstə(r)] *n (on furniture)* roulette *f*

castor oil [kɑːstə'rɔɪl] *n* huile *f* de ricin

castrate [kæs'treɪt] *vt* châtrer, castrer

castration [kæs'treɪʃən] *n* castration *f*

casual ['kæʒjʊəl] *adj (a) (offhand) (remark, glance)* en passant **(b)** *(relaxed, informal)* décontracté(e); *(conversation)* à bâtons rompus; *(clothes)* sport *inv* **(c)** *(careless)* désinvolte **(d)** *(meeting)* fortuit(e) **(e)** *(employment, worker)* temporaire

casually ['kæʒjʊəlɪ] *adv (a) (remark, glance)* en passant **(b)** *(informally)* avec décontraction; *(dress)* sport **(c)** *(carelessly)* avec désinvolture **(d)** *(meet)* par hasard

casualty ['kæʒjʊəltɪ] *(pl* **casualties**) *n* victime *f*

cat [kæt] *n (a) (animal)* chat *m; (female)* chatte *f;* **the big cats** les grands fauves *mpl;* **c. burglar** monte-en-l'air *m inv;* **c. flap** chatière *f;* **c. litter** litière *f* pour chats **(b)** *(idioms)* **to play a c.-and-mouse game with sb** jouer au chat et à la souris avec qn; *Fam* **to be like a c. on a hot tin roof** *or* **on hot bricks** ne pas tenir en place; **to let the c. out of the bag** vendre la mèche; **to fight like c. and dog** être comme chien et chat; **to set the c. among the pigeons** jeter un pavé dans la mare; *Fam* **there isn't enough room to swing a c.** il n'y a même pas la place de se retourner; *Fam* **he thinks he's the cat's whiskers** il se croit sorti de la cuisse de Jupiter

cataclysm ['kætəklɪzəm] *n* cataclysme *m*

Catalan ['kætəlæn] **1** *n (a) (person)* Catalan(e) *m,f* **(b)** *(language)* catalan *m*
   2 *adj* catalan(e)

catalog, catalogue ['kætəlɒg] **1** *n* catalogue *m*
   2 *vt* inventorier

Catalonia [kætə'ləʊnɪə] *n* la Catalogne

catalyst ['kætəlɪst] *n also Fig* catalyseur *m*

catamaran [kætəmə'ræn] *n* catamaran *m*

catapult ['kætəpʌlt] **1** *n (hand-held)* fronde *f*, lance-pierre *m; (on aircraft carrier) & Hist (weapon)* catapulte *f*
   2 *vt* catapulter; **to c. sb to stardom** propulser qn vers la gloire

cataract ['kætərækt] *n (in river) & Med* cataracte *f*

catarrh [kə'tɑː(r)] *n* catarrhe *m*

catastrophe [kə'tæstrəfɪ] *n* catastrophe *f*

catastrophic [kætə'strɒfɪk] *adj* catastrophique

catatonic [kætə'tɒnɪk] *adj Med* catatonique

catcall ['kætkɔːl] *n* sifflet *m*

catch [kætʃ] **1** *n (a) (of ball)* prise *f* au vol; **good c.!** bien attrapé!
   (b) *(in fishing)* prise *f; (of a whole day)* pêche *f*
   (c) *(fastening) (of door)* loquet *m; (of window)* loqueteau *m; (of bracelet)* fermoir *m*
   (d) *(disadvantage)* **where's the c.?** c'est quoi le truc *ou* le piège?; **it's a c.-22 situation** c'est un cercle vicieux
   2 *vt (pt & pp* **caught** [kɔːt]) **(a)** *(ball, thief)* attraper; *(fish)* prendre; **caught you!** je t'y prends!; **to c. sb doing sth** surprendre qn en train de *ou* à faire qch; **you won't c. me doing that again** on ne m'y reprendra plus; **to be caught in a storm** être surpris(e) par un orage; **to c. the sun** *(of room, garden)* être ensoleillé(e); *(of person)* prendre des couleurs

   (b) *(bus, train)* prendre; *(movie)* voir
   (c) *(hear)* saisir
   (d) *(manage to find)* trouver; **you caught me at a bad time** tu arrives/me téléphones au mauvais moment; **(I'll) c. you later!** on se voit plus tard!
   (e) *(clothes)* accrocher **(on** à); **to c. one's fingers in the door** se prendre *ou* se coincer les doigts dans la porte
   (f) *(attention)* attirer; **to c. sb's eye** attirer l'attention de qn
   (g) *(disease)* attraper; **I caught this cold from you** c'est toi qui m'as passé ce rhume; **you'll c. your death out there!** tu vas attraper la mort!; **to c. fire** *or* **light** prendre feu
   (h) *(of blow, missile)* atteindre; **the stone caught her on the arm** la pierre l'a atteinte au bras; *Fam* **you'll c. it!** *(get into trouble)* ça va être ta fête!
   3 *vi (a) (of fire)* prendre
   (b) *(in door)* se prendre, se coincer; *(on a nail)* s'accrocher
   (c) *(of person)* **to c. at sth** s'accrocher à qch

▸**catch on** *vi (a) (of fashion)* prendre **(b)** *Fam (understand)* piger

▸**catch up** **1** *vt sep (a) (reach)* rattraper **(b)** **to get caught up in sth** *(discussion)* être entraîné(e) dans qch; *(book, movie)* être absorbé(e) par qch; *(traffic jam)* être pris(e) dans qch
   2 *vi (close gap, get closer)* **to c. up with sb** rattraper qn; **to c. up with sth** *(news, gossip)* se mettre au courant de qch; **to c. up with one's work** se mettre à jour dans son travail; **his past caught up with him** son passé a resurgi

catchall ['kætʃɔːl] *adj Fam* fourre-tout *inv*

catching ['kætʃɪŋ] *adj (disease, habit)* contagieux(euse)

catchment area ['kætʃmənteərɪə] *n (of school)* = zone desservie par une école; *(of hospital)* = zone desservie par un hôpital

catchphrase ['kætʃfreɪz] *n (political)* slogan *m; (of comedian)* formule *f* favorite

catchy ['kætʃɪ] *adj (tune, slogan)* facile à retenir

catechism ['kætəkɪzəm] *n* catéchisme *m*

categorical [kætɪ'gɒrɪkəl] *adj (denial, refusal)* catégorique; *(evidence)* formel(elle)

categorize ['kætɪgəraɪz] *vt* étiqueter (**as** comme)

category ['kætɪgərɪ] *(pl* **categories**) *n* catégorie *f*

cater ['keɪtə(r)] **1** *vi (a) (provide food)* s'occuper de la nourriture; **to c. to** *(guests)* fournir le repas pour; *(event)* fournir le(s) repas de **(b)** **to c. to** *(needs, tastes)* satisfaire; **we c. for the needs of small companies** nous répondons à la demande des petites entreprises
   2 *vt (party, event)* s'occuper de la nourriture pour

caterer ['keɪtərə(r)] *n* traiteur *m*

catering ['keɪtərɪŋ] *n (trade)* restauration *f;* **to do the c.** fournir les repas; **c. school** école *f* hôtelière

caterpillar ['kætəpɪlə(r)] *n* chenille *f;* **c. track** *(on tank, tractor)* chenille

catfish ['kætfɪʃ] *n* poisson-chat *m*

cathartic [kə'θɑːtɪk] *adj* cathartique

cathedral [kə'θiːdrəl] *n* cathédrale *f;* **c. city** ville *f* épiscopale, évêché *m*

catheter ['kæθɪtə(r)] *n Med* cathéter *m*

cathode ['kæθəʊd] *n Elec* cathode *f;* **c. ray tube** tube *m* cathodique

Catholic ['kæθlɪk] *Rel* **1** *n* catholique *mf;* **to be a C.** être catholique
   2 *adj* catholique

catholic ['kæθlɪk] *adj (wide-ranging)* éclectique

Catholicism [kə'θɒlɪsɪzəm] *n* catholicisme *m*

catkin ['kætkɪn] *n* chaton *m (d'arbre)*

catnap ['kætnæp] *n Fam* petit somme *m*

catsuit ['kætsuːt] *n* combinaison *f* collante

cattle ['kætəl] *npl* bétail *m;* **c. breeding** élevage *m* de bétail; **c. guard** = grille recouvrant une fosse et empêchant le passage du bétail; *also Fig* **c. market** marché *m ou* foire *f* aux bestiaux; **c. truck** bétaillère *f*

catty ['kætı] *adj Fam* vache; **c. remark** vacherie *f*

catwalk ['kætwɔːk] *n* podium *m*

Caucasian [kɔː'keɪʒən] **1** *n (white person)* Blanc (Blanche) *m,f (de type européen)*
2 *adj (in ethnology)* blanc (blanche) *(de type européen)*

Caucasus ['kɔːkəsəs] *n* **the C.** le Caucase

caucus ['kɔːkəs] *n Pol* caucus *m*

caught [kɔːt] *pt & pp of* **catch**

cauldron ['kɔːldrən] *n* chaudron *m*

cauliflower ['kɒlıflaʊə(r)] *n* chou-fleur *m*; **c. and cheese** chou-fleur au gratin; *Fam* **c. ear** oreille *f* en chou-fleur

cause [kɔːz] **1** *n* (**a**) *(origin)* cause *f*; **c. and effect** la cause et l'effet (**b**) *(reason)* raison *f*, motif *m*; **to have good c. for doing sth** avoir de bonnes raisons de faire qch; **and with good c.** et pour cause; **to give c. for complaint** donner lieu à des plaintes; **to give c. for concern** être inquiétant(e) (**c**) *(purpose, mission)* cause *f*; **to make common c. (with sb)** faire cause commune (avec qn); **it's all in a good c.** *(for charity)* c'est pour une bonne cause; *Fig* c'est pour la bonne cause
2 *vt* provoquer; *(trouble)* causer; **to c. sb grief** faire de la peine à qn; **to c. sb to do sth** faire faire qch à qn; **he caused the plan to fail** il a fait échouer le plan

causeway ['kɔːzweı] *n* chaussée *f (sur un marécage)*

caustic ['kɔːstık] *adj also Fig* caustique; **c. soda** soude *f* caustique

cauterize ['kɔːtəraız] *vt Med* cautériser

caution ['kɔːʃən] **1** *n* (**a**) *(prudence)* prudence *f*; **c.!** *(sign)* attention!; **to exercise c.** être prudent(e); **to throw c. to the wind(s)** abandonner toute prudence (**b**) *(warning)* avertissement *m*
2 *vt* (**a**) *(warn)* mettre en garde (**against sth** contre qch); **to c. sb against doing sth** déconseiller à qn de faire qch (**b**) *Sport* donner un avertissement à

cautionary ['kɔːʃənərı] *adj* **a c. tale** une histoire édifiante

cautious ['kɔːʃəs] *adj* prudent(e)

cautiously ['kɔːʃəslı] *adv* prudemment, avec prudence

cautiousness ['kɔːʃəsnıs] *n* prudence *f*

cavalier [kævə'lıə(r)] *adj* cavalier(ère)

cavalry ['kævəlrı] *n* cavalerie *f*

cave [keɪv] *n* grotte *f*; **c. dweller** *(contemporary)* troglodyte *m*; *(prehistoric)* homme *m* des cavernes; **c. paintings** peintures *fpl* rupestres

▶**cave in** *vi (of ground, structure)* s'affaisser; *Fig (stop resisting)* céder (**to** à)

caveman ['keɪvmæn] *n* homme *m* des cavernes

cavern ['kævən] *n* caverne *f*

cavernous ['kævənəs] *adj* immense

caviar(e) ['kævıɑː(r)] *n* caviar *m*

cavity ['kævıtı] *(pl* **cavities**) *n* cavité *f*

cavort [kə'vɔːt] *vi* faire des cabrioles; *Fig* batifoler

caw [kɔː] **1** *n* croassement *m*
2 *vi* croasser

cayenne [keɪ'en] *n* **c. (pepper)** (poivre *m* de) Cayenne *m*

CB [siː'biː] *n (abbr* **Citizens' Band**) CB *f*

cc [siː'siː] *n (abbr* **cubic centimeter(s)**) cm^3

CCTV ['siːsiː'tiː'viː] *n (abbr* **closed-circuit television**) télévision *f* en circuit fermé

CD [siː'diː] *n* (**a**) *(abbr* **compact disc**) CD *m inv*, compact *m*; **CD burner** graveur *m* de CD; **CD player** lecteur *m* laser *ou* de CD; **CD rack** casier *m* de rangement pour CD; **CD writer** graveur *m* de CD (**b**) *(abbr* **Corps Diplomatique**) CD

CDC [siːdiː'siː] *n Med (abbr* **Center for Disease Control and Prevention**) = institut fédéral de recherche sur les causes et la prévention des maladies

CDI [siːdiː'aı] *n Comput (abbr* **compact disc interactive**) CD-I *m inv*

CD-R [siːdiː'ɑː(r)] *n* (**a**) *(abbr* **compact disc recorder**) graveur *m* de disque compact (**b**) *(abbr* **compact disc recordable**) CD-R *m inv*

Cdr. *n (abbr* **Commander**) commandant *m*

Cdre. *n (abbr* **Commodore**) contre-amiral *m*

CD-ROM [siːdiː'rɒm] *n Comput (abbr* **compact disc read-only memory**) CD-ROM *m inv*

CD-RW [siːdiːɑː'dʌbəljuː] *n (abbr* **compact disc rewritable**) CD-RW *m inv*

cease [siːs] **1** *vt* cesser; **to c. doing sth** cesser de faire qch; **to c. fire** cesser le feu
2 *vi* cesser (**from doing sth** *or* **to do sth** de faire qch); **it never ceases to amaze me** ça ne laisse jamais de m'étonner

cease-fire ['siːsfaıə(r)] *n* cessez-le-feu *m inv*

ceaseless ['siːslıs] *adj* incessant(e), continuel(elle)

ceaselessly ['siːslıslı] *adv* sans cesse, continuellement

cedar ['siːdə(r)] *n (tree, wood)* cèdre *m*

cede [siːd] *vt Law (territory, property)* céder; **to c. a point** concéder un point

cedilla [sı'dılə] *n* cédille *f*

ceiling ['siːlıŋ] *n (of room) & Fig (limit)* plafond *m*; *Fig* **to hit the c.** piquer une crise; **c. price** prix *m* plafond

celeb [sə'leb] *n Fam* célébrité *f*

celebrant ['selıbrənt] *n Rel* officiant *m*

celebrate ['selıbreıt] **1** *vt (anniversary, victory, occasion)* célébrer, fêter; *(mass)* célébrer
2 *vi* faire la fête

celebrated ['selıbreıtıd] *adj* célèbre

celebration [selı'breıʃən] *n* célébration *f*; **celebrations** *(festivities)* festivités *fpl*; **in c. of sth** pour célébrer *ou* fêter qch; **this calls for a c.!** il faut fêter *ou* arroser ça!

celebrity [sı'lebrıtı] *(pl* **celebrities**) *n (person, fame)* célébrité *f*

celery ['selərı] *n* céleri *m*

celestial [sı'lestıəl] *adj* céleste

celibacy ['selıbəsı] *n (chastity)* absence *f* de rapports sexuels; *(by choice)* chasteté *f*; *Rel* célibat *m*

celibate ['selıbət] *adj* **to be c.** ne pas avoir de rapports sexuels; *(by choice)* être chaste; *Rel* être célibataire

cell [sel] *n* (**a**) *(in prison, monastery) & Biol* cellule *f* (**b**) *Fam (cellphone)* portable *m* (**c**) *(group)* cellule *f*; **a sleeper c.** une cellule (terroriste) dormante *ou* en sommeil

cellar ['selə(r)] *n* cave *f*

cellist ['tʃelıst] *n* violoncelliste *mf*

cello ['tʃeləʊ] *(pl* **cellos**) *n* violoncelle *m*

cellophane® ['seləfeın] *n* Cellophane® *f*

cellphone ['selfəʊn] *n Tel* téléphone *m* cellulaire, *Can* cellulaire *m*

cellular ['seljʊlə(r)] *adj* cellulaire; **c. phone** téléphone *m* cellulaire, *Can* cellulaire *m*

cellulite ['seljʊlaıt] *n* cellulite *f*

celluloid® ['seljʊlɔıd] *n* Celluloïd® *m*

cellulose ['seljʊləʊs] *n* cellulose *f*

Celsius ['selsıəs] *adj* Celsius; **ten degrees C.** dix degrés Celsius

Celt [kelt] *n* Celte *mf*

Celtic ['keltık] *adj* celte, celtique

cement [sı'ment] **1** *n* ciment *m*; **c. mixer** bétonnière *f*
2 *vt also Fig* cimenter

cemetery ['semətrı] *(pl* **cemeteries**) *n* cimetière *m*

cenotaph ['senətɑːf] *n* cénotaphe *m*

censor ['sensə(r)] **1** *n* censeur *m*; **the censors banned the movie** la censure a interdit le film
2 *vt* censurer

censorious [sen'sɔːrıəs] *adj* sévère (**of** vis-à-vis de)

censorship ['sensəʃɪp] *n* censure *f*

censure ['senʃə(r)] **1** *n* critique *f*; *Pol* **vote of c.** motion *f* de censure

2 *vt* blâmer; *(officially)* donner un blâme à

census ['sensəs] *n* recensement *m*

cent [sent] *n* cent *m*; *Fam* **I haven't got a c.** je n'ai pas un rond

centaur ['sentɔː(r)] *n* centaure *m*

centenarian [sentɪ'neərɪən] *n* centenaire *mf*

centennial [sen'tenɪəl] **1** *n* centenaire *m*

2 *adj* centenaire

center ['sentə(r)] **1** *n* centre *m*; *Sport (in football)* centre *m*; **in the c.** au centre; *Pol* **left/right of c.** du centre gauche/droit; **c. of gravity** centre de gravité; **c. of attention** centre d'attraction; **c. forward** *(in soccer)* avant-centre *m*

2 *vt (attention, interest)* concentrer (**on** sur)

▶**center on** *vt insep* se concentrer sur; *(conversation)* tourner autour de

centerfold ['sentəfəʊld] *n (in magazine)* double page *f* centrale détachable; *(nude photo)* photo *f* de pin-up

center-left [sentə'left] *adj Pol (politician, party, views)* du centre gauche

centerpiece ['sentəpiːs] *n (on table)* centre *m* de table; *(main attraction)* pièce *f* de résistance

center-right [sentə'raɪt] *adj Pol (politician, party, views)* du centre droite

centigrade ['sentɪgreɪd] *adj* centigrade; **ten degrees c.** dix degrés centigrades

centigram ['sentɪgræm] *n* centigramme *m*

centiliter ['sentɪliːtə(r)] *n* centilitre *m*

centime ['sɒntiːm] *n* centime *m*

centimeter ['sentɪmiːtə(r)] *n* centimètre *m*

centipede ['sentɪpiːd] *n* mille-pattes *m inv*

central ['sentrəl] *adj* central(e); **C. Manhattan** le centre de Manhattan; **our hotel is very c.** notre hôtel est dans le centre; **of c. importance** d'une importance capitale; **C. America** l'Amérique *f* centrale; **C. American** d'Amérique centrale; **c. bank** banque *f* centrale; **C. Europe** l'Europe *f* centrale; **C. European** d'Europe centrale; **c. government** gouvernement *m* central; **c. heating** chauffage *m* central; *Aut* **c. locking** verrouillage *m* centralisé; **c. nervous system** système *m* nerveux central; *Comput* **c. processing unit** unité *f* centrale; **C. Standard Time** heure *f* du centre de l'Amérique du Nord

Central African Republic ['sentrəl'æfrɪkənrɪ'pʌblɪk] *n* République *f* centrafricaine

centralize ['sentrəlaɪz] *vt* centraliser

centrally ['sentrəlɪ] *adv (funded, administered)* de façon centralisée; **c. located** central(e)

centrifugal [sentrɪ'fjuːgəl] *adj* centrifuge

century ['sentʃərɪ] *(pl* **centuries***) n* siècle *m*; **the 19th c.** le 19ᵉ siècle

CEO [siːiːˈəʊ] *n Com (abbr* **Chief Executive Officer***)* D.G. *m*; **President and C.** président(e)-directeur(trice) *m,f* général(e), P.-D.G. *m,f*

ceramic [sə'ræmɪk] **1** *n (material)* céramique *f*; **ceramics** *(art)* céramique *f*; *(objects)* céramiques *fpl*

2 *adj* en céramique

cereal ['sɪərɪəl] *n* céréale *f*; **(breakfast) c.** céréales

cerebellum [serɪ'beləm] *n Anat* cervelet *m*

cerebral ['serɪbrəl] *adj (intellectual) & Anat* cérébral(e); *Med* **c. palsy** paralysie *f* cérébrale

cerebrum ['serɪbrəm] *n Anat* cerveau *m*

ceremonial [serɪ'məʊnɪəl] **1** *n* cérémonial *m*

2 *adj* de cérémonie

ceremonious [serɪ'məʊnɪəs] *adj* cérémonieux(euse)

ceremony ['serɪmənɪ] *(pl* **ceremonies***) n* cérémonie *f*; **without c.** sans cérémonies; **to stand on c.** faire des cérémonies

certain ['sɜːtən] *adj* (**a**) *(sure) (failure, victory)* certain(e), assuré(e); *(cure, solution)* infaillible; **I can't say for c.** je ne peux pas l'affirmer; **I'll tell you next week for c.** je vous le dirai la semaine prochaine sans faute; **to know sth for c.** être certain(e) de qch; **to be c. of sth** être sûr(e) *ou* certain(e) de qch; **they're c. of winning** ils sont assurés de gagner; **to make c. of sth** *(find out)* s'assurer de qch; *(be sure to get)* s'assurer qch; **he is c. to come** il viendra à coup sûr (**b**) *(particular)* certain(e); **a c. Philip Thomas** un certain Philip Thomas

certainly ['sɜːtənlɪ] *adv* certainement; **c. not!** certainement pas!; **she's c. very clever, but...** certes elle est très intelligente, mais...

certainty ['sɜːtəntɪ] *(pl* **certainties***) n (strong likelihood)* certitude *f*; *(conviction)* conviction *f*; **there is no c. that we will win** il n'est pas certain que nous gagnions; **to know sth for a c.** être certain(e) de qch

certifiable ['sɜːtɪfaɪəbəl] *adj Fam (insane)* bon (bonne) pour l'asile

certificate [sə'tɪfɪkət] *n* certificat *m*; *(in education)* diplôme *m*

certify ['sɜːtɪfaɪ] *(pt & pp* **certified***) vt* (**a**) *(confirm)* certifier; **this is to c. that...** nous certifions par la présente que...; **to c. sb (insane)** déclarer que l'état de santé de qn nécessite l'internement psychiatrique (**b**) *(give certificate to)* délivrer un certificat à

certitude ['sɜːtɪtjuːd] *n* certitude *f*

cervical ['sɜːvɪkəl, sə'vaɪkəl] *adj* **c. cancer** cancer *m* du col de l'utérus

cervix ['sɜːvɪks] *(pl* **cervices** ['sɜːvɪsiːz]*) n Anat* col *m* de l'utérus

Cesarean, Cesarian [sɪ'zeərɪən] *n* **C. (section)** césarienne *f*

cessation [se'seɪʃən] *n* cessation *f*

cesspit ['sespɪt], **cesspool** ['sespuːl] *n* fosse *f* d'aisances; *Fig* cloaque *m*

Ceylon [sɪ'lɒn] *n Formerly* Ceylan

cf [siː'ef] *(abbr* **confer, compare***)* cf

CFC [siːef'siː] *(pl* **CFCs***) n (abbr* **chlorofluorocarbon***)* CFC *m*

CFO [siːef'əʊ] *n Com (abbr* **Chief Financial Officer***)* chef *m* comptable

CFP [siːef'piː] *n Fin (abbr* **certified financial planner***)* = conseiller(ère) *m,f* financier(ère) indépendant(e)

Chad [tʃæd] *n* le Tchad

chafe [tʃeɪf] **1** *vt (skin)* irriter; *(of shoes)* blesser

2 *vi (of skin)* être irrité(e); *(of shoes)* frotter (**against** contre); *Fig* **to c. at** *or* **against sth** *(resent)* s'irriter de qch

chaff [tʃɑːf] **1** *n* balle *f*; *Fig* **to separate the wheat from the c.** séparer le bon grain de l'ivraie

2 *vt (tease)* taquiner

chaffinch ['tʃæfɪntʃ] *n* pinson *m*

chagrin ['ʃægrɪn] *n Formal* dépit *m*

chain [tʃeɪn] **1** *n* chaîne *f*; *(for medallion)* chaînette *f*; **in chains** enchaîné(e); **c. gang** chaîne de forçats; **c. letter** = lettre faisant partie d'une chaîne; **c. mail** cotte *f* de mailles; **c. reaction** réaction *f* en chaîne; **c. saw** tronçonneuse *f*; **c. store** magasin *m* à succursales multiples

2 *vt (prisoner)* enchaîner; *(dog, bicycle)* attacher avec une chaîne (**to** à)

▶**chain up** *vt sep (prisoner)* enchaîner; *(dog, bicycle)* attacher avec une chaîne (**to** à)

chain-smoke ['tʃeɪnsməʊk] *vi* fumer cigarette sur cigarette

chair [tʃeə(r)] **1** *n* (**a**) *(seat)* chaise *f*; *(armchair)* fauteuil *m* (**b**) *(chairperson)* président(e) *m,f*; **to be in the c.** présider (**c**) *Univ (of professor)* chaire *f*

2 *vt (meeting)* présider

chairlift ['tʃeəlɪft] *n* télésiège *m*

chairman ['tʃeəmən] *n (of meeting, political party)* président *m*;

(of company) président-directeur *m* général, P.-D.G. *m*

chairmanship ['tʃeəmənʃɪp] *n* présidence *f*

chairperson ['tʃeəpɜːsən] *n* président(e) *m,f*

chairwoman ['tʃeəwʊmən] *n* présidente *f*

chalet ['ʃæleɪ] *n* chalet *m*

chalice ['tʃælɪs] *n Rel* calice *m*

chalk [tʃɔːk] **1** *n* craie *f*
   2 *vt (mark)* marquer à la craie; *(write)* écrire à la craie
►**chalk up** *vt sep (victory)* remporter

chalkboard ['tʃɔːkbɔːd] *n* tableau *m* (noir)

chalky ['tʃɔːkɪ] *adj (soil, complexion)* crayeux(euse); *(taste, texture)* plâtreux(euse)

challenge ['tʃælɪndʒ] **1** *n* défi *m* (**to** à); **the job presents a real c.** ce travail est très stimulant
   2 *vt* (**a**) *(of job)* mettre à l'épreuve, être stimulant(e) pour; **to c. sb to do sth** défier qn de faire qch; **he challenged me to a fight** il m'a défié de me battre contre lui (**b**) *(statement, authority)* contester (**c**) *Mil* interpeller

challenger ['tʃælɪndʒə(r)] *n Sport* challenger *m*

challenging ['tʃælɪndʒɪŋ] *adj (job)* stimulant(e)

chamber ['tʃeɪmbə(r)] *n* (**a**) *(hall)* chambre *f*; **C. of Commerce** Chambre de commerce; **c. music** musique *f* de chambre; **c. pot** pot *m* de chambre (**b**) *Law* **chambers** *(of judge)* cabinet *m* (au tribunal) (**c**) *(of heart)* cavité *f*; *(of revolver)* chambre *f*

chambermaid ['tʃeɪmbəmeɪd] *n* femme *f* de chambre

chameleon [kə'miːlɪən] *n* caméléon *m*

chamois *n* (**a**) ['ʃæmɪ] **c. (leather)** peau *f* de chamois (**b**) ['ʃæmwɑː] *(deer)* chamois *m*

chamomile = **camomile**

champ[1] [tʃæmp] *n Fam* champion(onne) *m,f*

champ[2] [tʃæmp] *vi Fig* **to c. at the bit** ronger son frein

champagne [ʃæm'peɪn] *n* champagne *m*

champion ['tʃæmpɪən] **1** *n (in sports, of cause)* champion(onne) *m,f*; **world/European c.** champion(onne) du monde/d'Europe
   2 *vt* défendre

championship ['tʃæmpɪənʃɪp] *n* championnat *m*

chance [tʃɑːns] **1** *n* (**a**) *(luck)* hasard *m*; **by c.** par hasard; **to leave nothing to c.** ne rien laisser au hasard; **by any c.** par hasard
   (**b**) *(opportunity)* occasion *f*; **to give sb a c.** donner une chance à qn; **she was trying to apologize but you didn't give her a c.** elle essayait de s'excuser mais tu ne lui en as pas laissé l'occasion; **now's your c.!** à toi de jouer!; **it's your last c.** c'est ta dernière chance
   (**c**) *(likelihood)* chance *f* (**of** de); **to have** *or* **to stand a c. of doing sth** avoir des chances de faire qch; **he never stood a c.** *(of escaping, surviving, etc.)* il n'avait aucune chance de s'en tirer; **there's no c. of that happening** il n'y a aucune chance que cela se produise; **(the) chances are (that)...** il y a fort à parier que...
   (**d**) *(risk)* risque *m*; **to take a c.** prendre un risque
   2 *adj (discovery)* accidentel(elle); *(meeting)* fortuit(e)
   3 *vt* **to c. doing sth** prendre le risque de faire qch
   4 *vi* **to c. to do sth** faire qch par hasard
►**chance on, chance upon** *vt insep* tomber (par hasard) sur

chancellor ['tʃɑːnsələ(r)] *n* (**a**) *Univ* président(e) *m,f* (**b**) *Pol (in Austria, Germany)* chancelier *m*; *(in Great Britain)* **C. (of the Exchequer)** Chancelier de l'Échiquier, ≃ ministre *m* des Finances

chancy ['tʃɑːnsɪ] *adj Fam (risky)* risqué(e)

chandelier [ʃændə'lɪə(r)] *n* lustre *m*

change [tʃeɪndʒ] **1** *n* (**a**) *(alteration)* changement *m*; **a c. for the better/worse** une amélioration/détérioration; **a c. of address** un changement d'adresse; **a c. of clothes** des vête-

ments *mpl* de rechange; **to have a c. of heart** changer d'avis; **for a c.** pour une fois; *Ironic* **pour changer**; **that makes a c.** ça change un peu; *Euph* **the c. (of life)** *(menopause)* le retour d'âge
   (**b**) *(money)* monnaie *f*; **small** *or* **loose c.** petite *ou* menue monnaie; **have you got c. for a $10 bill?** avez-vous la monnaie de 10 dollars *ou* sur un billet de 10 dollars?
   2 *vt* (**a**) *(alter)* changer; *(transform)* transformer (**into** en); **to c. one's mind** changer d'avis; **to c. the subject** changer de sujet
   (**b**) *(exchange)* changer (**for** pour *ou* contre); **to c. hands** *(of money, car)* changer de mains; **to c. trains** changer de train; **to c. places with sb** changer de place avec qn; *Fig* **I wouldn't like to c. places with him** je ne voudrais pas être à sa place
   (**c**) *(money)* changer; **to c. dollars into euros** changer des dollars en euros
   (**d**) **to get changed** *(put on other clothes)* se changer
   3 *vi* (**a**) *(alter)* changer; **to c. into sth** se transformer en qch
   (**b**) *(put on other clothes)* se changer
   (**c**) *(of passenger)* changer
►**change over** *vi* changer; **to c. over from sth to sth** passer de qch à qch; **to c. over to another channel** changer de chaîne

changeable ['tʃeɪndʒəbəl] *adj (person, mood)* changeant(e); *(weather)* variable

changeless ['tʃeɪndʒlɪs] *adj* immuable

changeover ['tʃeɪndʒəʊvə(r)] *n (to new system, currency)* passage *m* (**to** à); *(after election, appointment)* transition *f*

changing ['tʃeɪndʒɪŋ] *adj* changeant(e)

channel ['tʃænəl] **1** *n* (**a**) *(waterway)* chenal *m*; *(of communication, distribution)* canal *m*; **to go through the proper channels** suivre la filière officielle (**b**) *TV* chaîne *f*; *Rad* bande *f* de fréquences (**c**) **the (English) C.** la Manche; **the C. Islands** les îles *fpl* Anglo-Normandes; **the C. Tunnel** le tunnel sous la Manche
   2 *vt* canaliser (**to** vers)

channel-hop ['tʃænəlhɒp], **channel-surf** ['tʃænəlsɜːf] *vi Fam* zapper

chant [tʃɑːnt] **1** *n* (**a**) *(of demonstrators)* slogan *m* (**b**) *Rel* psalmodie *f*
   2 *vt* scander
   3 *vi (of demonstrators)* scander des slogans; *Rel* psalmodier

chaos ['keɪɒs] *n* chaos *m*; **our plans were thrown into c.** nos projets ont été bouleversés; **c. theory** théorie *f* du chaos

chaotic [keɪ'ɒtɪk] *adj* chaotique

chapel ['tʃæpəl] *n* chapelle *f*

chaperone ['ʃæpərəʊn] **1** *n* chaperon *m*
   2 *vt* chaperonner

chaplain ['tʃæplɪn] *n Rel* aumônier *m*

chaplaincy ['tʃæplɪnsɪ] *n* aumônerie *f*

chapped [tʃæpt] *adj (lips, skin)* gercé(e)

chapter ['tʃæptə(r)] *n* chapitre *m*; **a c. of accidents** une série noire; *Fig* **to quote c. and verse for sth** donner les références exactes de qch

char [tʃɑː(r)] *(pt & pp* **charred**) *vt (burn)* carboniser

character ['kærɪktə(r)] *n* (**a**) *(in novel, movie, play)* personnage *m*; **c. actor/actress** acteur(trice) *m,f* de genre *(qui se spécialise dans les rôles secondaires de personnages qui sont souvent comiques ou excentriques)* (**b**) *(personality)* caractère *m*; **his remark was in/out of c.** ça lui ressemble bien/ça ne lui ressemble pas d'avoir fait une remarque pareille; **to have/to lack c.** avoir du/manquer de caractère; **a person of good c.** une personne honorable; **c. assassination** diffamation *f*; **c. reference** *(when applying for job)* références *fpl*; *Law* **c. witness** témoin *m* de moralité (**c**) *(unusual person)* personnage *m*; **he's quite a c.!** c'est un personnage! (**d**) *(letter)* caractère *m*; *Comput* **c. set** jeu *m* de caractères

characteristic [kærɪktə'rɪstɪk] **1** *n* caractéristique *f*
2 *adj* caractéristique; **it's c. of him** ça lui ressemble bien, c'est bien de lui

characterization [kærɪktəraɪ'zeɪʃən] *n* (*of problem, situation*) description *f*; (*in novel*) psychologie *f* des personnages

characterize ['kærɪktəraɪz] *vt* (*describe*) décrire; (*be characteristic of*) caractériser

charade [ʃə'reɪd] *n* (*farce*) mascarade *f*; **charades** (*party game*) charades *fpl* mimées

charcoal ['tʃɑːkəʊl] *n* charbon *m* de bois; *Art* fusain *m*; **c. drawing** (dessin *m* au) fusain; **c. gray** anthracite *m inv*

charge [tʃɑːdʒ] **1** *n* (**a**) (*cost*) frais *mpl*; **free of c.** gratuitement; **it's free of c.** c'est gratuit; **c. account** compte *m* clients; **c. card** carte *f* de paiement (*de grand magasin*)
(**b**) *Law* chef *m* d'accusation; **to be arrested on a c. of...** être arrêté(e) pour...; **to bring a c. against sb** accuser qn
(**c**) (*responsibility*) **to take c. of sth** prendre qch en charge; **to be in c. of** être responsable de; **I'm in c. here!** c'est moi le chef ici!
(**d**) (*of explosive*) charge *f*
2 *vt* (**a**) (*price*) faire payer, demander; **to c. sb $10** faire payer 10 dollars à qn; **c. it to my account** mettez ça sur mon compte
(**b**) *Law* inculper (**with** de)
(**c**) (*attack*) attaquer
(**d**) *Elec* charger; *Fig* **a highly charged atmosphere** une atmosphère très tendue
3 *vi* (*rush*) charger; **to c. in/out** entrer/sortir en trombe

chariot ['tʃærɪət] *n* char *m*

charisma [kæ'rɪzmə] *n* charisme *m*

charismatic [kærɪz'mætɪk] *adj* charismatique

charitable ['tʃærɪtəbəl] *adj* (*person, action*) charitable; (*organization*) caritatif(ive); (*work*) pour une association caritative

charity ['tʃærɪtɪ] (*pl* **charities**) *n* (**a**) (*quality*) charité *f*; *Prov* **c. begins at home** charité bien ordonnée commence par soi-même (**b**) (*organization*) association *f* caritative

charlatan ['ʃɑːlətən] *n* charlatan *m*

charm [tʃɑːm] **1** *n* (**a**) (*attractiveness*) charme *m*; **to turn on the c.** faire le charmeur/la charmeuse (**b**) (*spell*) charme *m*; **it worked like a c.** ça a marché comme sur des roulettes; **c. offensive** offensive *f* de charme (**c**) (*lucky*) **c.** amulette *f*
2 *vt* charmer; **she charmed the money out of him** elle lui a extorqué son argent en lui faisant du charme; **to lead a charmed life** être né(e) sous une bonne étoile

charmer ['tʃɑːmə(r)] *n* charmeur(euse) *m,f*

charming ['tʃɑːmɪŋ] *adj also Ironic* charmant(e)

charred [tʃɑːd] *adj* carbonisé(e)

chart [tʃɑːt] **1** *n* (*graph*) diagramme *m*, graphique *m*; (*map*) carte *f*; **the charts** (*pop music*) le hit-parade
2 *vt* (**a**) (*on map*) porter sur une carte (**b**) *Fig* (*progress, rise*) retracer

charter ['tʃɑːtə(r)] **1** *n* (*of town*) charte *f*; (*of university*) statuts *mpl*; **c. flight** (vol *m*) charter *m*; **c. member** membre *m* fondateur
2 *vt* (*plane, ship*) affréter

chary ['tʃeərɪ] *adj* circonspect(e); **to be c. of doing sth** hésiter à faire qch

chase [tʃeɪs] **1** *n* (*pursuit*) poursuite *f*; **to give c. to sb** donner la chasse à qn
2 *vt* (*pursue*) poursuivre, donner la chasse à; (*sexually*) courir après
3 *vi* **to c. after sb** (*pursue*) poursuivre qn, donner la chasse à qn; (*sexually*) courir après qn

▶**chase up** *vt sep* (*person*) relancer; (*letter*) retrouver la trace de

chaser ['tʃeɪsə(r)] *n* = alcool bu après une bière ou vice versa

chasm ['kæzəm] *n also Fig* gouffre *m*, abîme *m*

chassis ['ʃæsɪ] *n* (*of car*) châssis *m*

chaste [tʃeɪst] *adj* chaste

chasten ['tʃeɪsən] *vt* rendre plus humble

chastise [tʃæs'taɪz] *vt* châtier; (*criticize*) fustiger

chastisement [tʃæs'taɪzmənt] *n* châtiment *m*; (*criticism*) fustigation *f*

chastity ['tʃæstɪtɪ] *n* chasteté *f*; **c. belt** ceinture *f* de chasteté

chat [tʃæt] **1** *n* (**a**) (*conversation*) discussion *f*; **to have a c. (with sb)** discuter *ou* bavarder (avec qn) (**b**) *Comput* (*on Internet*) bavardage *m*, chat *m*; **c. room** site *m* de bavardage, salon *m*, *Can* bavardoir *m*
2 *vi* (*pt & pp* **chatted**) bavarder; **to c. about sth** discuter de qch; *Comput* **to c. online** bavarder, tchater

chattel ['tʃætəl] *n Law* bien *m* meuble

chatter ['tʃætə(r)] **1** *n* bavardage *m*, papotage *m*
2 *vi* (*talk*) bavarder, papoter; **my teeth were chattering** je claquais des dents; *Pej* **the chattering classes** les intellectuels *mpl* qui s'écoutent parler

chatterbox ['tʃætəbɒks] *n Fam* pie *f*, moulin *m* à paroles

chatty ['tʃætɪ] *adj* (*person*) bavard(e); (*letter*) plein(e) de détails

chauffeur ['ʃəʊfə(r)] **1** *n* chauffeur *m*
2 *vt* conduire

chauvinism ['ʃəʊvɪnɪzəm] *n* (*patriotism*) chauvinisme *m*; (**male**) **c.** machisme *m*

chauvinist ['ʃəʊvɪnɪst] *n & adj* (*patriotic*) chauvin(e) *m,f*; (**male**) **c.** (*sexist*) macho *m*

chauvinistic [ʃəʊvɪ'nɪstɪk] *adj* (*patriotic*) chauvin(e); (*sexist*) macho

cheap [tʃiːp] **1** *n* **to do sth on the c.** faire qch à peu de frais *ou* pour pas cher
2 *adj* (**a**) (*inexpensive*) bon marché *inv*, pas cher (chère); **cheaper** meilleur marché *inv*, moins cher (chère); **c. rate** tarif *m* réduit (**b**) (*of little value*) de peu de valeur; (*vulgar*) de mauvais goût; **to feel c.** (*of person*) se sentir minable; **that was a c. shot** c'était vraiment mesquin comme critique
3 *adv Fam* **it was going c.** c'était bon marché

cheapen ['tʃiːpən] *vt* (*degrade*) gâcher; **to c. oneself** s'abaisser

cheaply ['tʃiːplɪ] *adv* (*buy*) (à) bon marché, à bas prix; (*live, travel*) à peu de frais, pour pas cher

cheapskate ['tʃiːpskeɪt] *n Fam* radin(e) *m,f*

cheat [tʃiːt] **1** *n* (*dishonest person*) escroc *m*; (*at games*) tricheur(euse) *m,f*; (*deception, trick*) tricherie *f*, triche *f*; *Fam* **c. sheet** antisèche *m or f*
2 *vt* duper, rouler; (*financially*) escroquer; **to c. sb out of sth** (*money*) escroquer qch à qn; (*chance*) priver qn de qch
3 *vi* tricher

▶**cheat on** *vt insep* (*be unfaithful to*) tromper

cheating ['tʃiːtɪŋ] *n* tricherie *f*, triche *f*; **that's c.!** c'est de la triche!

Chechenia, Chechnya ['tʃetʃnɪə] *n* la Tchétchénie

check¹ [tʃek] **1** *n* (**a**) (*inspection*) vérification *f*, contrôle *m* (**on** de); **to run a c. on sb** enquêter sur qn
(**b**) (*restraint*) **to keep sb in c.** tenir qn en échec; **to keep sth in c.** (*emotion, enemy advance*) contenir qch; *Pol* **checks and balances** équilibre *m* des pouvoirs
(**c**) *Fin* chèque *m*; **to make out** *or* **to write a c. (to sb)** faire un chèque (à l'ordre de qn); **a c. for $10** un chèque de 10 dollars
(**d**) (*restaurant bill*) addition *f*
(**e**) (*in chess*) échec *m*; **in c.** en échec
2 *vt* (**a**) (*verify, examine*) (*information, statement*) vérifier; (*passport, ticket*) contrôler; **to c. that...** vérifier *ou* s'assurer que...
(**b**) (*restrain*) (*inflation*) enrayer; (*emotion, impulse, enemy advance*) contenir
(**c**) (*coat, hat*) mettre au vestiaire; (*bag, luggage*) mettre à la consigne
3 *vi* vérifier; **to c. on sth** vérifier qch; **to c. on sb** surveiller

qn; **you'd better c. with her** vous feriez mieux de lui demander

▶**check in 1** vt sep (baggage) enregistrer

2 vi (at hotel) remplir le registre; (at airport) se présenter à l'enregistrement

▶**check off** vt sep cocher

▶**check out 1** vt sep (a) (investigate) (person) se renseigner sur; (information) vérifier (b) Fam (look at) viser

2 vi (leave hotel) quitter l'hôtel

▶**check up** vi vérifier; **to c. up on sb** surveiller qn

check² [tʃek] **1** n (pattern) carreaux mpl

2 adj à carreaux, Can carreauté(e)

checkbook ['tʃekbʊk] n carnet m de chèques, chéquier m; **c. journalism** = dans les milieux de la presse, pratique qui consiste à payer des sommes importantes pour le témoignage d'une personne impliquée dans une affaire

checkered ['tʃekəd] adj (patterned) à carreaux, Can carreauté(e); Fig **she's had a c. career** elle a eu une carrière en dents de scie

checkers ['tʃekəz] npl jeu m de dames

check-in ['tʃekɪn] n Aviat **c. (desk)** (comptoir m d')enregistrement m

checking account ['tʃekɪŋəkaʊnt] n compte m courant

checklist ['tʃeklɪst] n liste f de vérification

checkmate ['tʃekmeɪt] **1** n (in chess) échec m et mat

2 vt (in chess) faire échec et mat à; Fig (opponent) faire échec à

checkout ['tʃekaʊt] n (in supermarket) caisse f

checkpoint ['tʃekpɔɪnt] n (poste m de) contrôle m

checkroom ['tʃekruːm] n (for coats) vestiaire m; (for baggage) consigne f

checkup ['tʃekʌp] n Med bilan m complet

cheek [tʃiːk] n (a) (of face) joue f; **to dance c. to c.** danser joue contre joue; **c. by jowl (with sb)** coude à coude (avec qn); Fig **to turn the other c.** tendre l'autre joue (b) (buttock) fesse f (c) Fam (impudence) toupet m, culot m; **he's got some c.!** il est culotté ou gonflé!

cheekbone ['tʃiːkbəʊn] n pommette f

cheeky ['tʃiːkɪ] adj Fam effronté(e)

cheep [tʃiːp] vi (of bird) piailler

cheer [tʃɪə(r)] **1** n (a) (shout) hourra m; **cheers** acclamations fpl, bravos mpl; **three cheers for Mary!** un ban pour Mary! (b) Fam **cheers!** (when drinking) (à votre) santé! (c) Lit (good spirits) **to be of good c.** être de bonne humeur

2 vt (a) (applaud) acclamer (b) (make happier) remonter le moral à

3 vi (shout) pousser des hourras ou des acclamations

▶**cheer on** vt sep (support) encourager

▶**cheer up 1** vt sep (person) remonter le moral à; (room) égayer

2 vi (of person) reprendre courage; **c. up!** courage!

cheerful ['tʃɪəfʊl] adj (person) gai(e), de bonne humeur; (room, music, mood) gai(e); (conversation) enjoué(e)

cheerfully ['tʃɪəfʊlɪ] adv gaiement, avec entrain; Fam **I could c. strangle him!** je l'étranglerais volontiers!

cheerily ['tʃɪərɪlɪ] adv gaiement

cheerleader ['tʃɪəliːdə(r)] n pom-pom girl f

cheerless ['tʃɪəlɪs] adj morne; (room) triste

cheery ['tʃɪərɪ] adj joyeux(euse), gai(e)

cheese [tʃiːz] n fromage m; Fam **(say) c.!** (for photograph) souriez!; **c. sandwich/omelet** sandwich m/omelette f au fromage

▶**cheese off** vt sep Fam **to be cheesed off (with)** en avoir marre (de)

cheeseboard ['tʃiːzbɔːd] n (selection) plateau m de fromages

cheeseburger ['tʃiːzbɜːgə(r)] n cheeseburger m

cheesecake ['tʃiːzkeɪk] n gâteau m au fromage blanc

cheetah ['tʃiːtə] n guépard m

chef [ʃef] n chef m (cuisinier)

chemical ['kemɪkəl] **1** n produit m chimique

2 adj chimique; **c. warfare** guerre f chimique; **c. weapons** armes fpl chimiques

chemist ['kemɪst] n chimiste mf

chemistry ['kemɪstrɪ] n chimie f; Fig **there was a certain c. between them** il y avait une certaine affinité entre eux

chemo ['kiːməʊ] n Fam Med (abbr **chemotherapy**) chimio f; **to have c.** faire une chimio

chemotherapy [kiːməʊ'θerəpɪ] n Med chimiothérapie f; **to have c.** faire une chimiothérapie

cherish ['tʃerɪʃ] vt (memory, person) chérir; (hopes) caresser, nourrir

cherry ['tʃerɪ] (pl **cherries**) n (fruit) cerise f; **c. (tree)** cerisier m; **c. orchard** cerisaie f

cherub ['tʃerəb] (pl **cherubs** or **cherubim** ['tʃerəbɪm]) n chérubin m

chess [tʃes] n échecs mpl; **a game of c.** une partie d'échecs; **c. player** joueur(euse) m,f d'échecs

chessboard ['tʃesbɔːd] n échiquier m

chessman ['tʃesmæn], **chesspiece** ['tʃespiːs] n pièce f (de jeu d'échecs)

chest [tʃest] n (a) (of person) poitrine f; Fig **to get it off one's c.** dire ce qu'on a sur le cœur (b) (box) coffre m, caisse f; **c. of drawers** commode f

chestnut ['tʃesnʌt] **1** n (nut) châtaigne f; (tree, wood) châtaignier m; **(horse) c.** marron m d'Inde; Fam **an old c.** une plaisanterie usée

2 adj (hair) châtain; (horse) alezan(e)

chew [tʃuː] vt mâcher, mastiquer; (cigar, end of pen) mâchonner; **to c. one's nails** se ronger les ongles

▶**chew over** vt sep Fam réfléchir à, cogiter sur

chewing gum ['tʃuːɪŋgʌm] n chewing-gum m

chewy ['tʃuːɪ] adj (meat) caoutchouteux(euse); (candy) mou (molle)

chic [ʃiːk] adj élégant(e), chic

chick [tʃɪk] n (a) (young bird) oisillon m; (young chicken) poussin m (b) Fam (woman) nana f; **c. flick, c. movie** = film qui plaît particulièrement aux femmes

chicken ['tʃɪkɪn] **1** n (a) (bird) poulet m; Prov **don't count your chickens (before they are hatched)** il ne faut pas vendre la peau de l'ours avant de l'avoir tué; **c. feed** (food) nourriture f pour volaille; Fam Fig **that's c. feed!** c'est une misère! (b) Fam (coward) lâche mf, froussard(e) m,f

2 adj Fam (cowardly) froussard(e)

▶**chicken out** vi Fam se dégonfler

chickenpox ['tʃɪkɪnpɒks] n varicelle f

chickpea ['tʃɪkpiː] n pois m chiche

chide [tʃaɪd] (pt **chided** or **chid** [tʃɪd], pp **chided** or **chidden** ['tʃɪdən]) vt Lit réprimander

chief [tʃiːf] **1** n (of tribe) chef m; Fam **the c.** (boss) le patron; Mil **c. of staff** chef d'état-major; **(White House) C. of Staff** secrétaire m de la Maison-Blanche

2 adj (most important) principal(e); **c. assistant** principal(e) collaborateur(trice) m,f; Com **c. executive** directeur(trice) m,f général(e); **c. executive officer** directeur(trice) m,f général(e); Com **c. financial officer** chef m comptable; Law **c. justice** juge m à la Cour suprême

chiefly ['tʃiːflɪ] adv principalement, surtout

chieftain ['tʃiːftən] n (of clan) chef m

chiffon ['ʃɪfɒn] n mousseline f de soie

chilblain ['tʃɪlbleɪn] n engelure f

child [tʃaɪld] (pl **children** ['tʃɪldrən]) n enfant mf; **it's c.'s play** c'est un jeu d'enfant; **children's literature** littérature f enfantine ou pour enfants; **c. abuse** mauvais traitements mpl à enfant; (sexual) sévices mpl sexuels infligés à un enfant; **c. labor** travail m des enfants; **c. support** pension f alimentaire

child-bearing ['tʃaɪldbeərɪŋ] *n* maternité *f*; **of c. age** en âge d'avoir des enfants

childbirth ['tʃaɪldbɜːθ] *n* accouchement *m*; **to die in c.** mourir en couches

childcare ['tʃaɪldkeə(r)] *n* garde *f* d'enfants

childhood ['tʃaɪldhʊd] *n* enfance *f*

childish ['tʃaɪldɪʃ] *adj Pej* puéril(e); **don't be so c.!** ne fais pas l'enfant!

childless ['tʃaɪldlɪs] *adj* sans enfant(s)

childlike ['tʃaɪldlaɪk] *adj* enfantin(e)

childproof ['tʃaɪldpruːf] *adj* **c. lock** *(in car)* = serrure de sécurité pour enfants; **c. bottle** = bouteille pourvue d'une capsule de sécurité

children ['tʃɪldrən] *pl of* **child**

Chile ['tʃɪlɪ] *n* le Chili

Chilean ['tʃɪlɪən] **1** *n* Chilien(enne) *m,f*
 2 *adj* chilien(enne)

chili ['tʃɪlɪ] *(pl* **chilis** *or* **chilies)** *n (dish)* chili *m* con carne; **c. (pepper)** piment *m* (rouge); **c. powder** piment en poudre

chill [tʃɪl] **1** *n* coup *m* de froid; **to catch a c.** prendre froid; **a c. of fear** un frisson de peur; **there's a c. in the air** le fond de l'air est frais
 2 *adj* froid(e), glacé(e)
 3 *vt (wine, food)* mettre au frais; *(of wind)* glacer; **serve chilled** *(on product)* servir frais
 4 *vi Fam* se détendre; **c.!** on se calme!

▶**chill out** *vi Fam* se détendre; **c. out!** on se calme!

chilled [tʃɪld], **chilled-out** [tʃɪld'aʊt] *adj Fam (relaxed)* cool

chilli = **chili**

chilling ['tʃɪlɪŋ] *adj (frightening)* à vous donner le frisson

chill-out room ['tʃɪlaʊtruːm] *n* espace *m* chill-out

chilly ['tʃɪlɪ] *adj also Fig* froid(e)

chime [tʃaɪm] **1** *n (of bells)* carillon *m*
 2 *vt* **the clock chimed nine o'clock** le carillon de l'horloge sonna neuf heures
 3 *vi (of clock, bells)* carillonner

▶**chime in** *vi Fam (in conversation)* intervenir

chimney ['tʃɪmnɪ] *(pl* **chimneys)** *n* cheminée *f*; *Fam* **to smoke like a c.** *(of person)* fumer comme un pompier; **c. pot** tuyau *m* de cheminée; **c. sweep** ramoneur *m*

chimpanzee [tʃɪmpæn'ziː], *Fam* **chimp** [tʃɪmp] *n* chimpanzé *m*

chin [tʃɪn] *n* menton *m*; *Fig* **to keep one's c. up** tenir bon, tenir le coup

China ['tʃaɪnə] *n* la Chine

china ['tʃaɪnə] *n* porcelaine *f*; **c. clay** kaolin *m*

Chinese [tʃaɪ'niːz] **1** *npl* **the C.** *(people)* les Chinois *mpl*
 2 *n* (**a**) *(person)* Chinois(e) *m,f* (**b**) *(language)* chinois *m*
 3 *adj* chinois(e)

chink¹ [tʃɪŋk] *n (gap)* fente *f*, lézarde *f*; *Fig* **to find a c. in sb's armor** trouver le talon d'Achille de qn

chink² [tʃɪŋk] **1** *n (sound)* tintement *m*
 2 *vt (coins, glasses)* faire tinter
 3 *vi* tinter

chintz [tʃɪnts] *n* chintz *m*

chinwag ['tʃɪnwæg] *n Fam* **to have a c.** tailler une bavette

chip [tʃɪp] **1** *n* (**a**) *(of wood, glass)* éclat *m*; *(in plate, cup)* ébréchure *f*; **this cup has a c. in it** cette tasse est ébréchée
 (**b**) **(potato) chips** *(pommes fpl)* chips *mpl*, *Can* croustilles *fpl*
 (**c**) *(in gambling)* jeton *m*
 (**d**) *Comput* puce *f*
 (**e**) *(idioms)* **he's a c. off the old block** c'est son père tout craché; **to have a c. on one's shoulder** en vouloir à la terre entière; *Fam* **when the chips are down** dans les moments critiques
 2 *vt (pt & pp* **chipped)** (**a**) *(cut at) (stone, wood)* tailler; *(da-*

mage) (knife, plate) ébrécher; *(furniture)* écorner; **to c. one's tooth** se casser un petit bout de dent
 (**b**) *(in sports)* **to c. the ball** frapper la balle par en dessous
 3 *vi (of plate, cup)* s'ébrécher

▶**chip in** *vi Fam* (**a**) *(give money)* participer (**b**) *(in conversation)* mettre son grain de sel

chipboard ['tʃɪpbɔːd] *n* aggloméré *m*

chipmunk ['tʃɪpmʌŋk] *n* tamia *m* rayé, *Can* suisse *m*

chiropodist [kɪ'rɒpədɪst] *n* pédicure *mf*

chiropody [kɪ'rɒpədɪ] *n* pédicurie *f*

chirp [tʃɜːp] **1** *n (of birds)* gazouillis *m*, pépiement *m*; *(of grasshopper)* chant *m*
 2 *vt & vi (of bird)* gazouiller, pépier; *(of grasshopper)* chanter

chirpy ['tʃɜːpɪ] *adj* d'humeur joyeuse

chirrup ['tʃɪrəp] = **chirp**

chisel ['tʃɪzəl] **1** *n (tool)* ciseau *m*; *(for sculpture)* burin *m*
 2 *vt* (**a**) *(in woodwork, sculpture)* ciseler; *Fig* **chiseled features** visage délicatement ciselé (**b**) *very Fam (cheat)* rouler

chit [tʃɪt] *n* (**a**) *(memo, note)* note *f*; *(voucher)* bon *m* (**b**) *Fam Old-fashioned Pej* **a c. of a girl** une gamine

chitchat ['tʃɪttʃæt] *n Fam* bavardage *m*, papotage *m*

chivalrous ['ʃɪvəlrəs] *adj* chevaleresque; *(toward women)* galant(e)

chivalry ['ʃɪvəlrɪ] *n (courteous behavior)* courtoisie *f*; *(toward women)* galanterie *f*; *Hist* chevalerie *f*

chives [tʃaɪvz] *npl* ciboulette *f*

chiv(v)y ['tʃɪvɪ] *(pt & pp* **chiv(v)ied)** *vt Fam* harceler; **to c. sb into doing sth** harceler qn jusqu'à ce qu'il fasse qch; **to c. sb along** faire se presser qn

chloride ['klɔːraɪd] *n Chem* chlorure *m*

chlorinate ['klɔːrɪneɪt] *vt* chlorer

chlorine ['klɔːriːn] *n Chem* chlore *m*

chloroform ['klɒrəfɔːm] *n Chem* chloroforme *m*

chlorophyl(l) ['klɒrəfɪl] *n Biol* chlorophylle *f*

chock [tʃɒk] *n (for wheel of car, plane)* cale *f*

chockablock ['tʃɒkə'blɒk] *adj Fam (room)* plein(e) à craquer; *(container)* bourré(e); **the town is c. with tourists** la ville est archipleine de touristes

chocolate ['tʃɒklət] **1** *n* chocolat *m*; **hot c.** chocolat chaud
 2 *adj (made of chocolate)* en chocolat; *(chocolate-flavored)* au chocolat; **c. (colored)** chocolat *inv*

choice [tʃɔɪs] **1** *n* choix *m*; **to make a c.** choisir, faire un choix; **you have no c.** vous n'avez pas le choix; **I had no c. but to leave** je ne pouvais que partir; **there isn't much c.** il n'y a pas grand choix; **available in a wide c. of colors** disponible dans une large gamme de coloris
 2 *adj* (**a**) *(well chosen)* choisi(e); **she used some c. language** *(offensive)* elle a juré comme un charretier (**b**) *(food)* de choix; *(wine)* fin(e)

choir ['kwaɪə(r)] *n* chœur *m*

choirboy ['kwaɪəbɔɪ] *n* jeune choriste *m*

choke [tʃəʊk] **1** *n (of car)* starter *m*
 2 *vt* (**a**) *(strangle)* étrangler (**b**) *(block) (pipe, road)* boucher
 3 *vi* s'étrangler; **to c. with anger** s'étrangler de colère; **she choked on a fishbone** elle a failli s'étouffer en avalant une arête

▶**choke back** *vt sep (tears, words, anger)* ravaler

▶**choke up** *vt sep* (**a**) *(blocked) (pipe, road)* boucher (**b**) *Fam (emotionally)* toucher profondément; **she was all choked up** elle était bouleversée *ou* toute émue

choker ['tʃəʊkə(r)] *n (necklace)* collier *m* (court)

cholera ['kɒlərə] *n* choléra *m*

cholesterol [kə'lestərɒl] *n* cholestérol *m*

choose [tʃuːz] *(pt* **chose** [tʃəʊz], *pp* **chosen** ['tʃəʊzən]) **1** *vt* choisir; **to c. to do sth** choisir de faire qch; **there's not much to c. between them** ils se valent
 2 *vi* choisir (**between** entre); **I'll do as I c.** je ferai comme il me plaît

choosy ['tʃuːzɪ] *adj Fam* difficile

chop [tʃɒp] **1** *n* (**a**) *(with ax)* coup *m* (**b**) *(of lamb, pork)* côtelette *f* (**c**) **chops** *(of person)* joue *f*; *(of animal)* bajoues *fpl*; **to lick one's chops** se pourlécher les babines
2 *vt* (*pt & pp* **chopped**) *(wood)* couper; *(meat, vegetables)* couper en morceaux; *(finely)* hacher
▶**chop down** *vt sep (tree)* abattre
▶**chop off** *vt sep* trancher, couper; **to c. sb's head off** couper la tête à qn

chopper ['tʃɒpə(r)] *n* (**a**) *(cleaver)* couperet *m*; *(ax)* hachette *f* (**b**) *Fam (helicopter)* hélico *m*

chopping ['tʃɒpɪŋ] *n* **c. block** *(of butcher)* billot *m*; **c. board** planche *f* (à découper)

choppy ['tʃɒpɪ] *adj (sea, lake)* agité(e)

chopsticks ['tʃɒpstɪks] *npl* baguettes *fpl*

choral ['kɔːrəl] *adj* choral(e); **c. group** chorale *f*

chord [kɔːd] *n* (**a**) *Mus* accord *m*; *Fig* **her speech struck a c. with the electorate** son discours a trouvé un écho auprès des électeurs (**b**) *Math (of arc)* corde *f*

chore [tʃɔː(r)] *n* (**a**) **chores** *(in household)* travaux *mpl* ménagers (**b**) *(unwelcome task)* corvée *f*

choreograph ['kɒrɪəɡrɑːf] *vt* faire la chorégraphie de; *Fig* orchestrer

choreographer [kɒrɪ'ɒɡrəfə(r)] *n* chorégraphe *mf*

choreography [kɒrɪ'ɒɡrəfɪ] *n* chorégraphie *f*

chorister ['kɒrɪstə(r)] *n* choriste *mf*

chortle ['tʃɔːtəl] **1** *n* gloussement *m* (de joie)
2 *vi* glousser (de joie)

chorus ['kɔːrəs] **1** *n* (**a**) *(of song)* refrain *m* (**b**) *(group of singers, actors)* chœur *m*; *Fig* **a c. of protest** un concert de protestations; **c. girl** danseuse *f* de revue
2 *vt* dire en chœur

chose [tʃəʊz] *pt of* **choose**

chosen ['tʃəʊzən] **1** *adj* choisi(e); **the c. few** les heureux élus *mpl*; **the C. people** le peuple élu
2 *pp of* **choose**

Christ [kraɪst] **1** *n* le Christ *m*, Jésus-Christ *m*
2 *exclam very Fam* bon Dieu!; **C. Almighty!** nom de Dieu!

christen ['krɪsən] *vt (name)* baptiser

christening ['krɪsənɪŋ] *n* baptême *m*

Christian ['krɪstʃən] **1** *n* chrétien(enne) *m,f*; **to be a C.** être chrétien
2 *adj* chrétien(enne); **C. name** prénom *m*

Christianity [krɪstɪ'ænɪtɪ] *n* christianisme *m*

Christmas ['krɪsməs] *n* Noël *m*; **at C.** à Noël; **Merry C.!** joyeux Noël!; **C. card** carte *f* de Noël; **C. carol** chant *m* de Noël; **C. Day** jour *m* de Noël; **C. Eve** veille *f* de Noël; **C. tree** sapin *m* de Noël

chrome [krəʊm] *adj* chromé(e)

chromium ['krəʊmɪəm] *n Chem* chrome *m*

chromosome ['krəʊməsəʊm] *n Biol* chromosome *m*

chronic ['krɒnɪk] *adj (invalid, disease, unemployment)* chronique

chronicle ['krɒnɪkəl] **1** *n* chronique *f*; *Fig (of disasters)* suite *f*
2 *vt* faire la chronique de

chronological [krɒnə'lɒdʒɪkəl] *adj* chronologique

chronology [krə'nɒlədʒɪ] *n* chronologie *f*

chrysalis ['krɪsəlɪs] *n Zool* chrysalide *f*

chrysanthemum [krɪ'sænθəməm] *n* chrysanthème *m*

chubby ['tʃʌbɪ] *adj* potelé(e), dodu(e); *(face)* joufflu(e); **c.-cheeked** joufflu

chuck [tʃʌk] *vt Fam* (**a**) *(throw)* lancer, balancer (**b**) *(boyfriend, girlfriend)* plaquer; **to get chucked** se faire plaquer
▶**chuck away** *vt sep Fam* balancer; *Fig (opportunity)* foutre en l'air
▶**chuck out** *vt sep Fam (throw away)* balancer; *(from house, school, club)* vider

chuckle ['tʃʌkəl] **1** *n* petit rire *m*
2 *vi* rire tout bas

chug [tʃʌɡ] (*pt & pp* **chugged**) *vi* (**a**) *(of train)* haleter; *Fam* **he's still chugging along in the same job** il a toujours le même boulot pépère (**b**) *Fam (drink quickly)* descendre
▶**chug down** *vt sep Fam (drink)* descendre

chum [tʃʌm] *n Fam* copain (copine) *m,f*

chummy ['tʃʌmɪ] *adj Fam* copain (copine); **to be a bit too c.** être un peu trop familier(ère)

chump [tʃʌmp] *n Fam (foolish person)* idiot(e) *m,f*

chunk [tʃʌŋk] *n* gros morceau *m*; *(of bread)* quignon *m*; *(of time)* partie *f*

chunky ['tʃʌŋkɪ] *adj* (**a**) *(well-built)* bien bâti(e); *(fat)* grassouillet(ette); *(sweater)* gros (grosse) (**b**) *(stew, soup)* avec des morceaux

church [tʃɜːtʃ] *n* (**a**) *(building)* église *f*; *(French Protestant)* temple *m*; **to go to c.** aller à l'église/au temple (**b**) *(institution)* **the Presbyterian/Catholic C.** l'Église *f* presbytérienne/catholique

churchgoer ['tʃɜːtʃɡəʊə(r)] *n* pratiquant(e) *m,f*

churchyard ['tʃɜːtʃjɑːd] *n* cimetière *m*

churlish ['tʃɜːlɪʃ] *adj (rude)* grossier(ère); *(surly)* revêche

churn [tʃɜːn] **1** *n (for making butter)* baratte *f*; *(for milk)* bidon *m* à lait
2 *vt (butter)* battre; **the propeller churned up the water** l'eau bouillonnait sous l'action des hélices
3 *vi* **my stomach's churning** *(because of nervousness)* j'ai l'estomac noué
▶**churn out** *vt sep Fam (books)* pondre (en série); *(goods)* produire en série

chute [ʃuːt] *n* (**a**) *(for packages)* glissière *f*; **(garbage) c.** vide-ordures *m inv* (**b**) *(in swimming pool, playground)* toboggan *m*; **chutes and ladders** *(game)* ≃ jeu de l'oie; (**c**) *Fam (parachute)* parachute *m*

chutney ['tʃʌtnɪ] *n* chutney *m*

CIA [siːaɪ'eɪ] *n (abbr* **Central Intelligence Agency**) CIA *f*

cicada [sɪ'kɑːdə] *n* cigale *f*

CID [siːaɪ'diː] *n (abbr* **Criminal Investigation Department**) ≃ P.J.

cider ['saɪdə(r)] *n (apple juice)* jus *m* de pommes; **hard c.** cidre *m*; **c. apple** pomme *f* à cidre; **c. vinegar** vinaigre *m* de cidre

cigar [sɪ'ɡɑː(r)] *n* cigare *m*

cigarette [sɪɡə'ret] *n* cigarette *f*; **c. ash** cendre *f* de cigarette; **c. butt** *or* **end** mégot *m*; **c. case** étui *m* à cigarettes; **c. holder** fume-cigarette *m inv*; **c. lighter** briquet *m*; *(in car)* allume-cigare *m*; **c. machine** distributeur *m* automatique de cigarettes; **c. package** paquet *m* de cigarettes; **c. paper** papier *m* à cigarettes

cilantro [sɪ'læntrəʊ] *n Bot & Culin* coriandre *m*

C-in-C [siːɪn'siː] *n Mil & Naut (abbr* **Commander-in-Chief**) commandant *m* en chef

cinch [sɪntʃ] *n Fam* **it's a c.** c'est un jeu d'enfant

cinder ['sɪndə(r)] *n* **cinders** cendres *fpl*; **burned to a c.** complètement carbonisé(e)

Cinderella [sɪndə'relə] *n* Cendrillon

cine ['sɪnɪ] *pref* **c. camera** caméra *f*; **c. film** pellicule *f*

cinema ['sɪnəmə] *n* cinéma *m*

cinnamon ['sɪnəmən] *n* cannelle *f*

cipher ['saɪfə(r)] *n (code)* chiffre *m*, code *m*; *Fig* **he's a mere c.** c'est un zéro

circa ['sɜːkə] *prep (of time)* aux alentours de; *(of amount)* environ

circle ['sɜːkəl] **1** *n* (**a**) *(shape)* cercle *m*; **to sit in a c.** s'asseoir en cercle; *Fig* **to go around in circles** tourner en rond (**b**) *(movement)* **to come full c.** revenir à son point de départ (**c**) *(in theater)* balcon *m*; **dress c.** premier balcon (**d**) *(group)* cercle *m*, groupe *m*; **in certain circles** dans certains milieux

2 *vt* (**a**) *(go around)* tourner autour de (**b**) *(surround)* entourer (**with** de)

3 *vi (of plane, birds)* tourner, décrire des cercles

circuit ['sɜːkɪt] *n* (**a**) *(electric)* circuit *m*; **c. breaker** disjoncteur *m* (**b**) *(in motor racing) (course)* circuit *m*; *(lap)* tour *m*

circuitous [sə'kjuːɪtəs] *adj (route)* détourné(e); *(reasoning)* alambiqué(e)

circular ['sɜːkjʊlə(r)] **1** *n (letter)* circulaire *f*; *(advertisement)* prospectus *m*

2 *adj (movement, argument)* circulaire

circulate ['sɜːkjʊleɪt] **1** *vt* faire circuler

2 *vi* circuler

circulation [sɜːkjʊ'leɪʃən] *n (of air, blood, money)* circulation *f*; *(of newspaper)* tirage *m*; **for internal c. only** *(document)* à usage interne uniquement; *Fig* **to be out of c.** *(of person)* disparaître de la circulation

circumcise ['sɜːkəmsaɪz] *vt (boy)* circoncire; *(girl)* exciser

circumcision [sɜːkəm'sɪʒən] *n* circoncision *f*; **female c.** excision *f*

circumference [sə'kʌmfərəns] *n* circonférence *f*

circumflex ['sɜːkəmfleks] *n* accent *m* circonflexe

circumlocution [sɜːkəmlə'kjuːʃən] *n* circonlocution *f*, périphrase *f*

circumnavigate [sɜːkəm'nævɪgeɪt] *vt* **to c. sth** faire le tour de qch en bateau

circumscribe ['sɜːkəmskraɪb] *vt (limit)* limiter

circumspect ['sɜːkəmspekt] *adj* circonspect(e)

circumstances ['sɜːkəmstənsɪz] *npl* circonstances *fpl*; **in** *or* **under the c.** étant donné les circonstances; **in** *or* **under no c.** en aucun cas, sous aucun prétexte; **due to c. beyond our control** en raison de circonstances indépendantes de notre volonté

circumstantial [sɜːkəm'stænʃəl] *adj* **c. evidence** preuves *fpl* indirectes

circumvent [sɜːkəm'vent] *vt (law, rule)* contourner

circus ['sɜːkəs] *n* cirque *m*

cirrhosis [sɪ'rəʊsɪs] *n Med* cirrhose *f*

CIS [siːaɪ'es] *n (abbr* **Commonwealth of Independent States)** CEI *f*

cistern ['sɪstən] *n* citerne *f*; *(for toilet)* réservoir *m* de chasse d'eau

citadel ['sɪtədel] *n* citadelle *f*

citation [saɪ'teɪʃən] *n* citation *f*

cite [saɪt] *vt* citer

citizen ['sɪtɪzən] *n* citoyen(enne) *m,f*; *(of city)* habitant(e) *m,f*; **c.'s band (radio)** citizen band *f*

citizenship ['sɪtɪzənʃɪp] *n* citoyenneté *f*

citric acid ['sɪtrɪk'æsɪd] *n* acide *m* citrique

citrus fruit ['sɪtrəsfruːt] *n* agrumes *mpl*; **a c.** un agrume

city ['sɪtɪ] *(pl* **cities)** *n* (grande) ville *f*; **c. center** centre-ville *m*; **c. council** municipalité *f*; **c. hall** administration *f* (municipale); **c. planner** urbaniste *mf*; **c. planning** urbanisme *m*

city-dweller ['sɪtɪdwelə(r)] *n* citadin(e) *m,f*

civic ['sɪvɪk] *adj (duty, pride)* civique; *(building, authorities)* municipal(e); **c. center** centre *m* administratif et culturel

civil ['sɪvəl] *adj* (**a**) *(of society)* civil(e); **c. aviation** aviation *f* civile; **c. defense** protection *f* civile; **c. disobedience** résistance *f* passive; **c. engineering** génie *m* civil; **c. law** *(subject)* droit *m* civil; **c. liberties** libertés *fpl* civiques; *Law* **c. rights** droits civils; **c. servant** fonctionnaire *mf*; **the c. service** la fonction publique; **c. war** guerre *f* civile; **the (American) C. War** la guerre de Sécession (**b**) *(polite)* poli(e)

civilian [sɪ'vɪljən] **1** *n* civil *m*

2 *adj* civil(e)

civility [sɪ'vɪlɪtɪ] *(pl* **civilities)** *n* politesse *f*

civilization [sɪvɪlaɪ'zeɪʃən] *n* civilisation *f*

civilize ['sɪvɪlaɪz] *vt* civiliser

civilized ['sɪvɪlaɪzd] *adj* civilisé(e); **their divorce was very c.** leur divorce s'est passé sans heurts

CJD [siːdʒeɪ'diː] *n Med (abbr* **Creutzfeld-Jakob disease)** MCJ *f*; **new variant CJD** nouveau variant *m* de MCJ

cl *(abbr* **centiliter)** cl

clad [klæd] **1** *adj* **c. in** vêtu(e) de

2 *pt & pp of* **clothe**

claim [kleɪm] **1** *n* (**a**) *(demand) (for damages, compensation)* demande *f* d'indemnisation; *(as a right)* revendication *f*; **to lay c. to sth** revendiquer qch; **I have many claims on my time** je suis très pris; **it's his only c. to fame** c'est la seule façon dont il se soit distingué; **the town's only c. to fame** la seule chose pour laquelle cette ville soit connue

(**b**) *(assertion)* déclaration *f*; **she makes no c. to originality** elle ne prétend pas être originale

2 *vt* (**a**) *(as a right)* revendiquer; **to c. damages (from sb)** réclamer des dommages et intérêts (à qn); **to c. responsibility for sth** revendiquer qch

(**b**) *(assert)* **to c. that...** affirmer que...; **he claims to be an expert** il prétend être un expert

(**c**) *(lost property)* réclamer

(**d**) *(life)* **the epidemic has claimed thousands of lives** l'épidémie a fait des milliers de victimes

claimant ['kleɪmənt] *n (to throne)* prétendant(e) *m,f*; *Law (for social security, insurance)* demandeur(eresse) *m,f*

clairvoyant [kleə'vɔɪənt] **1** *n* voyant(e) *m,f*

2 *adj* extralucide

clam [klæm] *n* palourde *f*

▶**clam up** *(pt & pp* **clammed)** *vi Fam* se fermer comme une huître

clamber ['klæmbə(r)] *vi* **to c. up sth** escalader qch

clammy ['klæmɪ] *adj* moite

clamorous ['klæmərəs] *adj* bruyant(e)

clamor ['klæmə(r)] **1** *n (noise)* clameur *f*; *(protest)* tollé *m*

2 *vi* **to c. for sth** réclamer qch à grands cris

clamp [klæmp] **1** *n (tool)* serre-joint *m*; *(fixed to bench)* étau *m*; *Med* clamp *m*

2 *vt (fasten)* fixer; *(car)* mettre un sabot à

▶**clamp down on** *vt insep* faire la chasse à

clampdown ['klæmpdaʊn] *n* répression *f* (**on** de); **a c. on crime** un plan de lutte contre la criminalité

clan [klæn] *n also Fig* clan *m*

clandestine [klæn'destɪn] *adj* clandestin(e)

clang [klæŋ] **1** *n* bruit *m* métallique

2 *vi (of bell)* retentir; **the gate clanged shut** le portail se ferma avec un bruit métallique

clank [klæŋk] **1** *n* bruit *m* métallique

2 *vi* cliqueter

clap [klæp] *n* (**a**) *(with hands)* **to give sb a c.** applaudir qn; **a c. of thunder** un coup de tonnerre (**b**) *very Fam* **the c.** la chaude-pisse

2 *vt (pt & pp* **clapped)** (**a**) *(applaud)* applaudir; **to c. one's hands** applaudir; *(once)* frapper dans ses mains; **to c. sb on the back** donner une tape sur le dos à qn (**b**) *(put)* **he clapped his hat on** il enfonça son chapeau sur sa tête; *Fam* **to c. sb in prison** coller qn en prison; *Fam* **to c. eyes on sb/sth** voir qn/qch; **I've never clapped eyes on her before** je ne l'ai jamais vue de ma vie

3 *vi (applaud)* applaudir

clapper ['klæpə(r)] *n (of bell)* battant *m*

clapping ['klæpɪŋ] *n (applause)* applaudissements *mpl*

claptrap ['klæptræp] *n Fam* bêtises *fpl*

claret ['klærət] *n* bordeaux *m* (rouge)

clarification [klærɪfɪ'keɪʃən] *n* clarification *f*, éclaircissement *m*

clarify ['klærɪfaɪ] *(pt & pp* **clarified)** *vt* clarifier, éclaircir

clarinet [klærɪ'net] *n* clarinette *f*

clarity ['klærɪtɪ] *n* clarté *f*

clash [klæʃ] **1** *n* (**a**) *(of opinions, interests)* conflit *m*; *(between people, armies)* affrontement *m* (**b**) *(of metal objects)* fracas *m*

2 *vi* (**a**) *(come into conflict)* s'affronter; **to c. with sb** affronter qn; **police clashed with protesters** il y a eu des heurts entre la police et les manifestants (**b**) *(of evidence, explanations)* ne pas correspondre; *(of colors)* jurer (**c**) *(of events)* **to c. with** tomber en même temps que (**d**) *(of metal objects)* s'entrechoquer

clasp [klɑːsp] **1** *n (on necklace, handbag)* fermoir *m*; **c. knife** canif *m*

2 *vt (grip)* serrer; *(embrace)* étreindre; **to c. sb's hand** serrer la main à qn

class [klɑːs] **1** *n (in school, category, social group)* classe *f*; **to be in a c. of one's own** être insurpassable; **c. struggle** lutte *f* des classes

2 *vt (classify)* classer (**as** parmi)

classic ['klæsɪk] **1** *n* (**a**) *(book, movie, etc.)* classique *m* (**b**) *Sch & Univ* **classics** lettres *fpl* classiques

2 *adj* classique

classical ['klæsɪkəl] *adj* classique; **c. music** musique *f* classique

classification [klæsɪfɪ'keɪʃən] *n* classification *f*; *(of students)* classement *m*

classified ['klæsɪfaɪd] **1** *n* **the classifieds** *(in newspaper)* les petites annonces *fpl*

2 *adj* (**a**) *(secret)* confidentiel(elle) (**b**) **c. advertisements,** *Fam* **c. ads** *(in newspaper)* petites annonces *fpl*

classify ['klæsɪfaɪ] *(pt & pp* **classified)** *vt* classer

classmate ['klɑːsmeɪt] *n* camarade *mf* de classe

classroom ['klɑːsruːm] *n (salle f de)* classe *f*

classy ['klɑːsɪ] *adj Fam* qui a de la classe; *(bar)* chic

clatter ['klætə(r)] **1** *n (of shoes)* claquement *m*; *(of dishes)* fracas *m*

2 *vi* **the car clattered along the road** la voiture descendit la rue dans un bruit de ferraille; **to c. around** *(of person)* s'activer bruyamment

clause [klɔːz] *n (of contract)* clause *f*; *Gram* proposition *f*

claustrophobia [klɔːstrə'fəʊbɪə] *n* claustrophobie *f*

claustrophobic [klɔːstrə'fəʊbɪk] *adj (person)* claustrophobe; *(place, situation)* où l'on se sent claustrophobe

clavicle ['klævɪkəl] *n* clavicule *f*

claw [klɔː] **1** *n (of animal)* griffe *f*; *(of bird of prey)* serre *f*; *(of crab, lobster)* pince *f*; **c. hammer** arrache-clou *m*

2 *vt (scratch)* griffer; *Fig* **to c. one's way to the top** parvenir au sommet à force de travail

▸**claw back** *vt (money)* récupérer

clay [kleɪ] *n* argile *f*, *(terre f)* glaise *f*; **c. court** *(for tennis)* court *m* en terre battue; **c. pigeon** pigeon *m* d'argile; **c. pigeon shooting** ball-trap *m*

clean [kliːn] **1** *adj* (**a**) *(not dirty)* propre; *(piece of paper)* blanc (blanche); **a c. game/fight** un jeu/une bataille dans les règles; **c. living** vie *f* saine; **to have a c. driver's license** avoir tous ses points sur son permis de conduire (**b**) *(not obscene)* décent(e); **it's good c. fun** c'est innocent (**c**) *(clear) (shape, outline)* net (nette); **to make a c. break** *(of couple)* rompre une bonne fois pour toutes

2 *adv* (**a**) *(completely)* **to cut c. through sth** couper qch net; *Fam* **I c. forgot** j'ai complètement oublié (**b**) *Fam* **to come c.** dire la vérité

3 *vt* nettoyer; **to c. one's teeth/hands** se laver les dents/mains

▸**clean out** *vt sep* (**a**) *(cupboard, room)* nettoyer à fond (**b**) *Fam (leave without money)* nettoyer, plumer

▸**clean up 1** *vt sep* nettoyer

2 *vi* (**a**) *(neaten up)* nettoyer; *(wash oneself)* se laver (**b**) *Fam (win money)* toucher un gros paquet

clean-cut ['kliːn'kʌt] *adj (features)* net (nette), bien dessiné(e); *(person)* à l'apparence très soignée

cleaner ['kliːnə(r)] *n (person)* agent *m* de service; *(substance)* produit *m* de nettoyage; **c.'s** *(store)* pressing *m*; *Fam Fig* **to take sb to the c.'s** *(cheat)* nettoyer *ou* plumer qn

cleaning ['kliːnɪŋ] *n* nettoyage *m*; *(housework)* ménage *m*; **c. lady** femme *f* de ménage

cleanliness ['klenlɪnɪs] *n (of place, person)* propreté *f*

cleanly ['kliːnlɪ] *adv* proprement; *(fight)* dans les règles

cleanse [klenz] *vt* nettoyer; *(skin)* démaquiller

cleanser ['klenzə(r)] *n (for skin)* démaquillant *m*

clean-shaven ['kliːn'ʃeɪvən] *adj* rasé(e) de près

cleansing lotion ['klenzɪŋləʊʃən] *n* lait *m* démaquillant

clear [klɪə(r)] **1** *n* **to be in the c.** *(not under suspicion)* être lavé(e) de tout soupçon; *(out of danger)* être hors de danger

2 *adj* (**a**) *(liquid, image, directions)* clair(e); *(picture)* net (nette); *(glass)* transparent(e); *(skin)* net; **on a c. day** par temps clair; **all c.!** la voie est libre!; **to have a c. conscience** avoir la conscience tranquille; **as c. as a bell** *(of voice, sound)* cristallin(e); **c. profit** bénéfice *m* net; **c. winner** vainqueur *m* incontesté

(**b**) *(obvious)* clair(e), évident(e); **to make it c. to sb that...** bien faire comprendre à qn que...; **it is c. that...** il est clair *ou* évident que...; **to make oneself c.** se faire comprendre; **I wasn't c. (on) what she meant** je n'étais pas sûr d'avoir parfaitement compris ce qu'elle voulait dire

(**c**) *(space, road, passageway)* libre

(**d**) **to be c. of sth** *(rid of)* être débarrassé(e) de qch

3 *adv* **to steer c. of** éviter; **stand c. of the doors!** attention à la fermeture automatique des portières!

4 *vt* (**a**) *(road, area)* dégager; **the police cleared the square of demonstrators** la police a forcé les manifestants à évacuer la place; **to c. one's throat** se racler la gorge; **to c. the table** débarrasser la table; **to c. a debt** s'acquitter d'une dette; *Fig* **to c. the decks** déblayer le terrain; *Fig* **to c. the way for sth** ouvrir la voie à qch; *Fig* **to c. the air** *(ease tension)* détendre l'atmosphère; *(clarify matters)* mettre les choses au point

(**b**) *(exonerate)* disculper, innocenter; **to c. sb of blame** disculper qn; **to c. sb's name** blanchir (le nom de) qn

(**c**) *(jump over)* sauter, franchir

(**d**) *(authorize) (proposal, request)* approuver; **I'll need to c. it with the boss** il faut que j'obtienne la permission du patron

5 *vi* (**a**) *(of weather)* s'éclaircir; *(of sky)* se dégager; *(of fog)* se lever

(**b**) *(of check)* **the check hasn't cleared yet** le chèque n'a pas encore été viré

▸**clear away** *vt sep (dishes)* ranger; *(obstruction)* enlever

▸**clear out 1** *vt sep (cupboard)* vider; *(garage, shed)* débarrasser

2 *vi* *Fam (leave)* filer, se tirer

▸**clear up 1** *vt sep* (**a**) *(room)* ranger (**b**) *(doubt, misunderstanding)* dissiper; **to c. up a matter** tirer une affaire au clair

2 *vi* *(of weather)* s'éclaircir

clearance ['klɪərəns] *n* (**a**) *Com* **c. sale** liquidation *f* (**b**) *(authorization)* autorisation *f* (**c**) *(space)* espace *m* *(libre)*

clear-cut ['klɪə'kʌt] *adj (division, outline, feature)* net (nette); *(opinion)* tranché(e); **it's not as c. as that** ce n'est pas aussi simple que ça

clear-headed ['klɪə'hedɪd] *adj* lucide

clearing ['klɪərɪŋ] *n (in forest)* clairière *f*

clearing-house ['klɪərɪŋhaʊs] *n Fin* chambre *f* de compensation

clearly ['klɪəlɪ] *adv* (**a**) *(explain, write)* clairement; *(see)* bien (**b**) *(obviously)* évidemment; **he is c. wrong** il est évident qu'il a tort

clearness ['klɪənɪs] *n* clarté *f*; *(of image)* netteté *f*

clear-sighted ['klɪə'saɪtɪd] *adj (perceptive)* clairvoyant(e)

cleat [kliːt] *n (on shoe)* clou *m*, crampon *m*

cleavage ['kliːvɪdʒ] *n (of woman)* décolleté *m*

cleave [kli:v] (*pt* **cleaved** *or* **cleft** [kleft] *or* **clove** [kləʊv], *pp* **cleaved** *or* **cleft** *or* **cloven** ['kləʊvən]) *vt Lit* fendre

▸**cleave to** (*pt & pp* **cleaved**) *vt insep Formal* être fidèle à

cleaver ['kli:və(r)] *n* hachoir *m*

clef [klef] *n Mus* clé *f*, clef *f*

cleft [kleft] **1** *n* fissure *f*
2 *adj* fendu(e); **c. palate** division *f* palatine
3 *pt & pp of* **cleave**

clemency ['klemənsı] *n* clémence *f*

clementine ['klementi:n] *n* clémentine *f*

clench [klentʃ] *vt* **to c. one's fist/teeth** serrer le poing/les dents

Cleopatra ['kli:əʊ'pætrə] *pr n* Cléopâtre

clergy ['klɜ:dʒı] *n* clergé *m*

clergyman ['klɜ:dʒımən] *n* ecclésiastique *m*; (*Protestant*) pasteur *m*; (*Catholic*) prêtre *m*

cleric ['klerık] *n Rel* ecclésiastique *m*

clerical ['klerıkəl] *adj* (**a**) (*administrative*) **c. assistant** employé(e) *m,f* de bureau; **c. work** travail *m* de bureau (**b**) *Rel* clérical(e)

clerk [klɜ:rk] *n* (**a**) (*office worker*) employé(e) *m,f* de bureau (**b**) (*in store*) vendeur(euse) *m,f*

clever ['klevə(r)] *adj* (*intelligent*) intelligent(e); (*plan, idea*) ingénieux(euse); **to be c. with one's hands** être adroit(e) de ses mains

cleverly ['klevəlı] *adv* (*intelligently*) intelligemment; (*planned*) ingénieusement

cleverness ['klevənıs] *n* (*intelligence*) intelligence *f*; (*of plan*) ingéniosité *f*; (*skill*) adresse *f*

cliché ['kli:ʃeı] *n* cliché *m*

click [klık] **1** *n* (*sound*) petit bruit *m* sec; *Comput* clic *m*
2 *vt* (**a**) **to c. one's heels** claquer les talons; **to c. one's tongue** faire claquer sa langue (**b**) *Comput* cliquer (sur)
3 *vi* (**a**) (*make a sound*) faire un petit bruit sec (**b**) *Fam* (*become obvious*) faire tilt; **it suddenly clicked** tout à coup ça a fait tilt (**c**) *Fam* (*of people*) **we clicked straight away** ça a accroché tout de suite entre nous (**d**) *Comput* cliquer; **to c. on sth** cliquer sur qch

clickable ['klıkəbəl] *adj Ordinat* cliquable

client ['klaıənt] *n* client(e) *m,f*

clientele [kli:ən'tel] *n* clientèle *f*

cliff [klıf] *n* falaise *f*

cliffhanger ['klıfhæŋə(r)] *n* **it was a real c.** il y a eu du suspense jusqu'au bout

climactic [klaı'mæktık] *adj* qui constitue le point culminant

climate ['klaımət] *n* climat *m*

climatic [klaı'mætık] *adj* climatique

climax ['klaımæks] **1** *n* (*of series of events*) paroxysme *m*; (*of reign, career*) apogée *m*; (*of movie, book*) point *m* culminant; (*sexual*) orgasme *m*
2 *vi* (*of series of events*) atteindre son paroxysme; (*of reign, career*) atteindre son apogée; (*of movie, book*) atteindre son point culminant; (*sexually*) atteindre l'orgasme

climb [klaım] **1** *n* montée *f*, ascension *f*
2 *vt* (*tree*) grimper à; (*mountain*) faire l'ascension de; (*rock face*) escalader; (*stairs*) monter
3 *vi* (*of road, prices*) grimper; (*of plane*) prendre de l'altitude, monter; **to c. over sth** passer par-dessus qch

▸**climb down 1** *vt insep* (*descend*) descendre
2 *vi* (**a**) (*descend*) descendre (**b**) *Fig* (*in argument*) céder, en rabattre

climbdown ['klaımdaʊn] *n* dérobade *f*, reculade *f*

climber ['klaımə(r)] *n* (**a**) (*mountaineer*) alpiniste *mf* (**b**) (*plant*) plante *f* grimpante

climbing ['klaımıŋ] **1** *n* (*hiking*) randonnée *f* en montagne; (*of rockface*) escalade *f*; (*mountaineering*) alpinisme *m*
2 *adj* (*plant*) grimpant(e)

clinch [klıntʃ] **1** *n* (*of fighters*) corps à corps *m*; (*of lovers*) étreinte *f*
2 *vt* (*settle*) (*deal*) conclure; (*argument*) résoudre; **that clinches it!** voilà qui règle le problème une fois pour toutes!

cling [klıŋ] (*pt & pp* **clung** [klʌŋ]) *vi* **to c. to** (*rope, person*) s'accrocher à; *Fig* (*opinion*) persister dans; (*faith*) se raccrocher à

clinic ['klınık] *n* (*part of hospital*) service *m*

clinical ['klınıkəl] *adj* (**a**) *Med* clinique (**b**) (*unemotional*) froid(e), aseptisé(e)

clink[1] [klıŋk] **1** *n* (*sound*) tintement *m*
2 *vt* faire tinter; **to c. glasses with sb** trinquer avec qn
3 *vi* (*of glasses*) tinter

clink[2] [klıŋk] *n very Fam* (*prison*) taule *f*

clip[1] [klıp] **1** *n* (*for paper*) trombone *m*; (*for hair*) barrette *f*
2 *vt* (*pt & pp* **clipped**) (*paper*) attacher (*avec un trombone*) (**to** à)
3 *vi* **to c. together** s'emboîter

clip[2] [klıp] **1** *n* (**a**) *Fam* (*blow*) **to give sb a c. on the ear** flanquer une taloche à qn (**b**) (*of movie, program*) extrait *m*; *Comput* **c. art** clipart *m*
2 (*pt & pp* **clipped**) *vt* (**a**) (*hit*) **to c. sb on the ear** flanquer une taloche à qn (**b**) (*hedge*) tailler; (*ticket*) poinçonner; (*dog*) couper les poils à; (*hair, nails*) couper; *Fig* **to c. sb's wings** réduire la marge de manœuvre de qn

clipboard ['klıpbɔ:d] *n* planchette *f* porte-papiers (*à pince*)

clip-on ['klıpɒn] *adj* **c. earring** clip *m*; **c. microphone** micro-cravate *m*; **c. sunglasses** = verres teintés que l'on fixe à une autre paire de lunettes

clipped [klıpt] *adj* (*speech, tone*) saccadé(e)

clipper ['klıpə(r)] *n* (*ship*) clipper *m*

clippers ['klıpəz] *npl* (*for hair*) tondeuse *f*; (*for nails*) coupe-ongles *m inv*; (*for hedge*) cisaille *f*

clipping ['klıpıŋ] *n* (*from newspaper*) coupure *f*

clique [kli:k] *n* clique *f*

clitoris ['klıtərıs] *n* clitoris *m*

cloak [kləʊk] **1** *n* cape *f*; *Fig* **under the c. of darkness** sous le couvert de la nuit
2 *vt Fig* **cloaked in secrecy** enveloppé(e) de mystère

cloak-and-dagger [kləʊkən'dægə(r)] *adj* (*movie, book*) d'espionnage; *Fig* (*mysterious*) mystérieux(euse)

cloakroom ['kləʊkru:m] *n* vestiaire *m*

clobber [klɒbə(r)] *vt Fam* (*hit*) tabasser; (*defeat*) battre à plate couture

clock [klɒk] **1** *n* (**a**) (*large*) horloge *f*; (*small*) pendule *f*; **around the c.** 24 h sur 24; **a race against the c.** une course contre la montre; **to put the clocks forward/back** (*in spring, autumn*) avancer/retarder les pendules; *Fig* **to turn the c. back** revenir en arrière; **c. radio** radio-réveil *m* (**b**) *Fam* (*odometer*) compteur *m* kilométrique
2 *vt* (*measure speed of*) chronométrer; (*reach speed of*) atteindre

▸**clock in** *vi* pointer (*en arrivant sur son lieu de travail*)

▸**clock off** *vi* pointer (*en quittant son lieu de travail*)

▸**clock on** = clock in

▸**clock out** = clock off

▸**clock up** *vt sep* (*profits*) réaliser; (*votes*) totaliser; **this car has clocked up 10,000 miles** cette voiture a 10 000 miles au compteur

clockmaker ['klɒkmeıkə(r)] *n* horloger(ère) *m,f*

clockwise ['klɒkwaız] *adv* dans le sens des aiguilles d'une montre

clockwork ['klɒkwɜ:k] **1** *n* **to go like c.** (*of interview, ceremony*) marcher comme sur des roulettes; **to run like c.** (*of office, system*) être réglé(e) comme du papier à musique
2 *adj* (*toy*) mécanique

clod [klɒd] *n* (**a**) (*of earth*) motte *f* (**b**) (*stupid person*) crétin(e) *m,f*

clog [klɒg] **1** *n (shoe)* sabot *m*
  2 *vt (pt & pp* **clogged)** *(block)* boucher
  3 *vi* se boucher
▸**clog up 1** *vt sep* boucher
  2 *vi* se boucher

cloister ['klɔɪstə(r)] *n* cloître *m*

cloistered ['klɔɪstəd] *adj* **to lead a c. life** mener une vie de reclus(e)

clone [kləʊn] **1** *n also Fig* clone *m*
  2 *vt Biol* cloner

cloning ['kləʊnɪŋ] *n* clonage *m*

close¹ [kləʊs] **1** *adj* **(a)** *(in distance, time, relationship)* proche; **to be in c. contact with sb** être en contact étroit avec qn; **a c. friend** un ami intime; **a c. relative** un proche parent; **that was a c. call** *or* **shave** il s'en est fallu de peu; **at c. quarters** de près; **at c. range** de près; **c. combat** corps-à-corps *m* **(b)** *(inspection)* minutieux(euse); *(attention)* soutenu(e); **to keep a c. watch on sb/sth** surveiller qn/qch de près **(c)** *(weather)* lourd(e); *(room)* qui sent le renfermé **(d)** *(contest, election)* serré(e)
  2 *adv (near)* près; **to hold sb c.** serrer qn; **c. to** près de; **c. to tears** au bord des larmes; **c. to victory** proche de la victoire; **to come c. to death** frôler la mort; **to be c. to fifty** friser la cinquantaine; **to be c. to sb** *(emotionally)* être proche de qn; **c. at hand** à proximité; **to follow c. behind sb** suivre qn de près; **c. up** de près

close² [kləʊz] **1** *n (end)* fin *f*; **to draw to a c.** tirer à sa fin; **to bring sth to a c.** clore qch
  2 *vt* **(a)** *(door, eyes, book, road)* fermer; *Fig* **to c. ranks around sb** faire bloc autour de qn **(b)** *(meeting, debate)* clore; *(account)* fermer; *(deal)* conclure **(c)** *(business, store)* fermer
  3 *vi (of store, business)* fermer; *(of door)* se fermer
▸**close down 1** *vt (production, operations)* cesser; *(business, factory)* fermer
  2 *vi (of business, factory)* fermer; **Channel 6 closes down at midnight** les émissions sur Channel 6 se terminent à minuit
▸**close in** *vi (of night)* tomber
▸**close in on** *vi* **to c. in on sb** se rapprocher de qn
▸**close up 1** *vt sep (store)* fermer
  2 *vi* **(a)** *(of wound, hole)* se refermer **(b)** *(of store owner)* fermer

close-cropped ['kləʊs'krɒpt] *adj (hair)* coupé(e) ras

closed [kləʊzd] *adj* fermé(e); **behind c. doors** à huis clos; **c.-circuit television** télévision *f* en circuit fermé; *Ind* **c. shop** = usine ou société qui n'embauche que des travailleurs syndiqués

close-fitting ['kləʊs'fɪtɪŋ] *adj* bien ajusté(e)

close-knit ['kləʊs'nɪt] *adj (community, group)* très soudé(e); *(family)* très uni(e)

closely ['kləʊslɪ] *adv* **(a)** *(examine, listen, watch)* attentivement; *(resemble)* beaucoup; *(of concepts)* être étroitement liés(es); *(of people)* être proches parents; **c. contested** très serré(e) **(b)** *(populated)* densément; **c. packed** très serré(e)

closeness ['kləʊsnɪs] *n (physical proximity)* proximité *f*; *(of relationship, contact)* intimité *f*

close-set ['kləʊs'set] *adj (eyes)* rapproché(e)

closet ['klɒzɪt] **1** *n* placard *m*; *Fig* **to come out of the c.** révéler son homosexualité
  2 *adj* **c. homosexual** = personne qui cache son homosexualité; *Hum* **he's a c. Celine Dion fan** il n'ose pas avouer qu'il aime Celine Dion
  3 *vt* enfermer; **to c. oneself away** s'enfermer, s'isoler

close-up ['kləʊsʌp] *n* gros plan *m*; **in c.** en gros plan

closing ['kləʊzɪŋ] *n* fermeture *f*; **c. date** date *f* limite; **c. prices** cours *mpl* de clôture; **c. speech** discours *m* de clôture; **c. time** heure *f* de fermeture

closure ['kləʊʒə(r)] *n* **(a)** *(of company, store)* fermeture *f (définitive)* **(b)** *(emotional)* **it gave him a sense of c. after their**

break-up ça lui a permis de tourner la page après leur séparation

clot [klɒt] **1** *n (of blood)* caillot *m*
  2 *vi (pt & pp* **clotted)** *(of blood)* (se) coaguler

cloth [klɒθ] *n* **(a)** *(material)* tissu *m*; **a man of the c.** un membre du clergé **(b)** *(for cleaning or drying)* chiffon *m*

clothe [kləʊð] *(pt & pp* **clad** [klæd] *or* **clothed)** *vt* vêtir, habiller

clothes [kləʊðz] *npl* vêtements *mpl*; **to put one's c. on** s'habiller; **to take one's c. off** se déshabiller; **c. brush** brosse *f* à habits; **c. rack** séchoir *m* (à linge)

clotheshorse ['kləʊðhɔːs] *n (for laundry)* séchoir *m (à linge)*; *Fig Pej (model)* mannequin *m*

clothesline ['kləʊðzlaɪn] *n* corde *f* à linge

clothespin ['kləʊðzpɪn] *n* pince *f* à linge

clothing ['kləʊðɪŋ] *n (clothes)* vêtements *mpl*; **an article of c.** un vêtement; **the c. industry** l'industrie *f* du vêtement

cloud [klaʊd] **1** *n* **(a)** *(in sky)* nuage *m*; *Fig (of insects)* nuée *f* **(b)** *(idioms)* **to be under a c.** être en disgrâce; **to have one's head in the clouds** être dans les nuages; *Fam* **to be on c. nine** être aux anges
  2 *vt* **(a)** *(mirror)* embuer **(b)** *(happiness)* jeter une ombre sur; *(judgment)* affecter; **to c. the issue** embrouiller la question
▸**cloud over** *vi (of sky)* se couvrir

cloudburst ['klaʊdbɜːst] *n* averse *f*

cloudless ['klaʊdlɪs] *adj* sans nuages

cloudy ['klaʊdɪ] *adj* **(a)** *(sky, day)* nuageux(euse) **(b)** *(liquid)* trouble

clout [klaʊt] *Fam* **1** *n* **(a)** *(blow)* coup *m*; **to give sb a c. (with sth)** frapper qn (avec qch) **(b)** *(power, influence)* influence *f*; **to have a lot of c.** avoir le bras long
  2 *vt (hit)* flanquer une taloche à

clove¹ [kləʊv] *n (of garlic)* gousse *f*

clove² [kləʊv] *n (spice)* clou *m* de girofle

clove³ [kləʊv] *pt of* **cleave**

cloven ['kləʊvən] **1** *adj* **c. hoof** sabot *m* fendu
  2 *pp of* **cleave**

clover ['kləʊvə(r)] *n* trèfle *m*; *Fig* **to be in c.** être comme un coq en pâte

clown [klaʊn] **1** *n* clown *m*; **to act the c.** faire le clown
  2 *vi* **to c. around** faire le clown

cloying ['klɔɪɪŋ] *adj (taste, smell)* écœurant(e)

club [klʌb] **1** *n* **(a)** *(society)* club *m*; *Fam Fig* **join the c.!** tu n'es pas le seul/la seule!; **c. sandwich** sandwich *m* mixte *(à trois étages)*; **c. soda** eau *f* de Seltz **(b)** *(nightclub)* boîte *f* (de nuit) **(c)** *(weapon)* massue *f*, gourdin *m*; *(in golf)* club *m* **(d)** **clubs** *(in cards)* trèfle *m*; **ace of clubs** as *m* de trèfle
  2 *vt (pt & pp* **clubbed)** *(hit)* frapper avec une massue
  3 *vi* **to go clubbing** aller en boîte
▸**club together** *vi* se cotiser **(to buy** pour acheter)

clubhouse ['klʌbhaʊs] *n* pavillon *m*

cluck [klʌk] **1** *n* gloussement *m*
  2 *vi* glousser

clue [kluː] *n (in crime, mystery)* indice *m*; *(in crossword)* définition *f*; **to give sb a c.** donner un indice à qn, mettre qn sur la voie; **where's Lola? – I don't have a c.!** où est Lola? – je n'en ai pas la moindre idée!; *Fam* **he doesn't have a c.** *(is incompetent)* il est vraiment nul
▸**clue in** *vt sep Fam* **to be clued in (on sth)** être très calé(e) (en qch)

clueless ['kluːlɪs] *adj Fam* nul (nulle)

clump [klʌmp] **1** *n* **(a)** *(of bushes)* massif *m*; *(of people)* groupe *m* **(b)** *(sound)* bruit *m* bref et sourd
  2 *vi* **to c. around** marcher d'un pas lourd

clumsiness ['klʌmzɪnɪs] *n (of person, movement)* maladresse *f*

clumsy ['klʌmzɪ] *adj (person, movement)* maladroit(e)

clung [klʌŋ] *pt & pp of* **cling**

cluster ['klʌstə(r)] **1** *n (of grapes)* grappe *f; (of people, islands, houses)* groupe *m*
   2 *vi* **to c. around sb/sth** se grouper autour de qn/qch
clutch¹ [klʌtʃ] **1** *n (a) (in car)* embrayage *m;* **to let the c. in/out** embrayer/débrayer; **c. pedal** pédale *f* d'embrayage **(b)** *(grasp)* **to fall into sb's clutches** tomber entre les griffes de qn **(c)** *Fam* **to be in a c.** *(in a tricky situation)* être dans le pétrin
   2 *vt* tenir fermement
   3 *vi* **to c. at sth** s'agripper à qch; *Fig* **to c. at straws** se raccrocher à n'importe quoi
clutch² [klʌtʃ] *n (of eggs)* couvée *f*
clutter ['klʌtə(r)] **1** *n* désordre *m;* **in a c.** en désordre
   2 *vt* encombrer; **to be cluttered (up) with sth** être encombré(e) de qch
cluttered ['klʌtəd] *adj* encombré(e)
cm *n (abbr* **centimeter(s))** cm
C-note ['si:nəʊt] *n Fam* billet *m* de cent dollars
CO [si:'əʊ] *n Mil (abbr* **Commanding Officer)** chef *m* de corps
Co., co. [kəʊ] *n (abbr* **company)** Cie; *Fig* **Jane and co.** Jane et compagnie
c/o [si:'əʊ] *(abbr* **care of)** chez, aux bons soins de
coach [kəʊtʃ] **1** *n (a) (bus)* car *m; (horse-drawn carriage)* carrosse *m; (section of train)* voiture *f,* wagon *m;* **c. class** *(on airplane)* classe *f* économique **(b)** *(of athlete, team)* entraîneur(euse) *m,f*
   2 *vt (athlete, team)* entraîner; **to c. sb for a test** donner des leçons particulières à qn en préparation à un examen
coagulant [kəʊ'ægjʊlənt] *n Med* coagulant *m*
coagulate [kəʊ'ægjʊleɪt] *vi* coaguler
coal [kəʊl] *n* charbon *m;* **c. bunker** coffre *m* à charbon; **c. dealer** négociant *m* en charbon; **c. mine** mine *f* de charbon; **c. miner** mineur *m;* **c. mining** extraction *f* du charbon; **c. tar** goudron *m* de houille; *Fam* **to haul sb over the coals** passer un savon à qn
coalesce [kəʊə'les] *vi* s'unir
coalfield ['kəʊlfi:ld] *n* bassin *m* houiller
coalition [kəʊə'lɪʃən] *n* coalition *f*
coarse [kɔːs] *adj (a) (person, language)* grossier(ère), vulgaire **(b)** *(surface, texture)* grossier(ère); **to have c. hair** avoir les cheveux épais et rêches
coarsely ['kɔːslɪ] *adv (a) (vulgarly)* vulgairement **(b)** *(roughly)* **c. chopped/ground** haché(e)/moulu(e) grossièrement
coarseness ['kɔːsnɪs] *n (a) (of person, language)* grossièreté *f,* vulgarité *f* **(b)** *(of surface, texture)* grossièreté *f*
coast [kəʊst] **1** *n* côte *f; Fig* **the c. is clear** la voie est libre; **c. guard** garde-côte *m*
   2 *vi (in car, on bicycle)* avancer en roue libre; *Fig* **she coasted through her exams** elle a eu ses examens haut la main
coastal ['kəʊstəl] *adj* côtier(ère)
coaster ['kəʊstə(r)] *n (a) (for glass)* dessous *m* de verre **(b)** *(ship)* caboteur *m*
coastline ['kəʊstlaɪn] *n* littoral *m*
coast-to-coast ['kəʊsttəkəʊst] *adj* à l'échelle nationale
coat [kəʊt] **1** *n (a) (garment)* manteau *m;* **c. hanger** cintre *m;* **c. hook** patère *f* **(b)** *(of horse)* robe *f; (of dog)* pelage *m* **(c)** *(of snow, paint)* couche *f* **(d)** *(in heraldry)* **c. of arms** armoiries *fpl*
   2 *vt (with mud, paint)* couvrir **(with** de); *(with chocolate, sugar)* enrober **(with** de)
coating ['kəʊtɪŋ] *n (of paint, dust)* couche *f; (of chocolate)* enrobage *m*
coauthor [kəʊ'ɔːθə(r)] **1** *n* coauteur *m*
   2 *vt* **to c. a book with sb** écrire un livre en collaboration avec qn
coax [kəʊks] *vt* enjôler; **to c. sb to do** *or* **into doing sth**

amener qn à faire qch par des cajoleries; **to c. sth out of sb** obtenir qch de qn par des cajoleries
cob [kɒb] *n (a) (horse)* cob *m* **(b)** *(of corn)* épi *m*
cobalt ['kəʊbɔːlt] *n* cobalt *m;* **c. blue** bleu *m* de cobalt
cobble ['kɒbəl] **1** *n* pavé *m*
   2 *vt* paver
▶**cobble together** *vt sep* bricoler
cobbled ['kɒbəld] *adj (path, street)* pavé(e)
cobbler ['kɒblə(r)] *n* cordonnier *m*
cobblestone ['kɒbəlstəʊn] *n* pavé *m*
COBOL, Cobol ['kəʊbɒl] *n Comput (abbr* **Common Business Oriented Language)** Cobol *m*
cobra ['kəʊbrə] *n* cobra *m*
cobweb ['kɒbweb] *n* toile *f* d'araignée; *Fig* **to brush the cobwebs off sth** ressortir qch
cocaine [kəʊ'keɪn] *n* cocaïne *f*
cock [kɒk] **1** *n (a) (male fowl)* coq *m* **(b)** *Vulg (penis)* bi(t)te *f*
   2 *vt (gun)* armer; **to c. a snook at sb** faire la nique à qn; **to c. its ears** *(of horse, dog)* dresser les oreilles
cockade [kɒ'keɪd] *n* cocarde *f*
cock-a-doodle-doo ['kɒkədu:dəl'du:] *exclam* cocorico!
cock-a-hoop ['kɒkə'hu:p] *adj* enchanté(e)
cockatoo [kɒkə'tu:] *n* cacatoès *m*
cocked [kɒkt] *adj* **to knock sb into a c. hat** *(outclass)* surpasser qn
cockerel ['kɒkərəl] *n* jeune coq *m*
cocker spaniel [kɒkə'spænjəl] *n* cocker *m*
cockeyed ['kɒkaɪd] *adj Fam (decision, plan)* farfelu(e)
cockfight ['kɒkfaɪt] *n* combat *m* de coqs
cockle ['kɒkəl] *n (a) (shellfish)* coque *f* **(b)** *Fam* **it warmed the cockles of his heart** ça lui a réchauffé le cœur
Cockney ['kɒknɪ] **1** *n (a) (person)* cockney *mf* **(b)** *(dialect)* cockney *m*
   2 *adj* cockney
cockpit ['kɒkpɪt] *n* cabine *f* de pilotage, cockpit *m*
cockroach ['kɒkrəʊtʃ] *n* cafard *m*
cocksure ['kɒk'ʃʊə(r)] *adj (person, manner)* présomptueux(euse)
cocktail ['kɒkteɪl] *n also Fig* cocktail *m;* **c. dress** robe *f* de cocktail; **c. lounge** bar *m* confortable *(dans un restaurant, un hôtel);* **c. party** cocktail *m;* **c. shaker** shaker *m;* **c. stick** pique *f*
cocky ['kɒkɪ] *adj Fam* culotté(e)
cocoa ['kəʊkəʊ] *n (powder, drink)* cacao *m;* **c. butter** beurre *m* de cacao
coconut ['kəʊkənʌt] *n* noix *f* de coco; **c. milk** lait *m* de coco; **c. palm** cocotier *m*
cocoon [kə'ku:n] **1** *n also Fig* cocon *m*
   2 *vt Fig (protect)* couver
COD [si:əʊ'di:] *n Com (abbr* **cash** *or* **collect on delivery)** paiement *m* à la livraison
cod [kɒd] *(pl* **cod)** *n* morue *f;* **c. liver oil** huile *f* de foie de morue
coddle ['kɒdəl] *vt (child)* dorloter
code [kəʊd] **1** *n (a) (cipher)* code *m;* **in c.** codé(e); **c. book** code; **c. name** nom *m* de code; **c. number** numéro *m* de code **(b)** *(rules)* code *m;* **c. of conduct** déontologie *f,* code de conduite
   2 *vt (message)* coder
codeine ['kəʊdi:n] *n* codéine *f*
codify ['kəʊdɪfaɪ] *(pt & pp* **codified)** *vt* codifier
coed [kəʊ'ed] *Fam adj (a) (school)* mixte **(b)** *(female student)* étudiante *f (dans un établissement scolaire mixte)*
coeducational [kəʊedjʊ'keɪʃənəl] *adj (school)* mixte
coefficient [kəʊɪ'fɪʃənt] *n Math* coefficient *m*
coerce [kəʊ'ɜːs] *vt* forcer, contraindre; **to c. sb into doing sth** contraindre qn à faire qch

coercion [kəʊˈɜːʃən] n coercition f

coexist [kəʊɪgˈzɪst] vi coexister

coexistence [kəʊɪgˈzɪstəns] n coexistence f

coffee [ˈkɒfɪ] n café m; **c. bar** café; **c. bean** grain m de café; **c. break** pause-café f; **c. cup** tasse f à café; **c. grinder** moulin m à café; **c. grounds** marc m de café; **c. machine** (in café) percolateur m; (vending machine) machine f à café; (in home) cafetière f électrique; **c. mill** moulin à café; **c. pot** cafetière f; **c. shop** café m; **c. spoon** cuillère f à café; **c. table** table f basse; **c.-table book** grand livre m illustré

coffer [ˈkɒfə(r)] n (chest) coffre m; Fig **the coffers** (of company, country) les caisses fpl

coffin [ˈkɒfɪn] n cercueil m

cog [kɒg] n (tooth on gearwheel) dent f; (gearwheel) roue f dentée, rouage m; Fig **a c. in the machinery** un rouage dans la machine

cogent [ˈkəʊdʒənt] adj convaincant(e)

cogitate [ˈkɒdʒɪteɪt] vi Formal méditer, réfléchir

cognac [ˈkɒnjæk] n cognac m

cognition [kɒgˈnɪʃən] n cognition f

cohabit [kəʊˈhæbɪt] vi vivre en concubinage (**with** avec)

cohabitation [kəʊhæbɪˈteɪʃən] n concubinage m

coherence [kəʊˈhɪərəns] n cohérence f

coherent [kəʊˈhɪərənt] adj cohérent(e)

cohesion [kəʊˈhiːʒən] n cohésion f

cohesive [kəʊˈhiːsɪv] adj cohésif(ive)

coiffure [kwɑːˈfjʊə(r)] n coiffure f

coil [kɔɪl] **1** n (a) (of rope, wire) rouleau m; (electrical) bobine f; (contraceptive device) stérilet m (b) (single loop) anneau m
2 vt enrouler (**around** autour de)

▸**coil up** vi (of snake) se lover

coin [kɔɪn] **1** n pièce f (de monnaie); Fig **the other side of the c.** le revers de la médaille
2 vt (phrase, word) inventer; **to c. money** battre monnaie; Hum & Ironic ..., **to c. a phrase** ..., comme on dit

coinage [ˈkɔɪnɪdʒ] n (a) (coins) monnaie f (b) (word) mot m nouveau, néologisme m; (phrase) expression f nouvelle

coincide [kəʊɪnˈsaɪd] vi coïncider (**with** avec)

coincidence [kəʊˈɪnsɪdəns] n coïncidence f

coincidental [kəʊɪnsɪˈdentəl] adj fortuit(e)

coin-operated [ˈkɔɪnɒpəreɪtɪd] adj (machine) à pièces

coitus [ˈkɔɪtəs] n Formal coït m; **c. interruptus** coït interrompu

coke [kəʊk] n (a) (fuel) coke m (b) Fam (cocaine) coke f

col. (abbr **column**) col

colander [ˈkɒləndə(r)] n passoire f

cold [kəʊld] **1** n (a) (low temperature) froid m; **to feel the c.** être frileux(euse); Fig **to be left out in the c.** rester sur la touche (b) (sickness) rhume m; **to have a c.** avoir un rhume; **to catch a c.** attraper un rhume
2 adj also Fig froid(e); **I'm c.** j'ai froid; **it's c.** (weather) il fait froid; **to get c.** (of food) refroidir; (of weather) se refroidir; also Fig **to be in a c. sweat** avoir des sueurs froides; Fam **that leaves me c.** ça me laisse froid; **that's c. comfort** c'est une maigre consolation; Fig **to get c. feet (about sth)** hésiter (à faire qch) à la dernière minute; **to give sb the c. shoulder** snober qn; **c. cream** cold-cream m; Culin **c. cuts** assiette f anglaise; Met **c. front** front m froid; **c. meats** viandes fpl froides; **c. sore** bouton m de fièvre, Can feu m sauvage; **c. start** (of car) démarrage m à froid; **c. storage** conservation f par le froid; **c. war** guerre f froide
3 adv **to do sth c.** faire qch à froid; Fam Fig **to be out c.** être sans connaissance

cold-blooded [ˈkəʊldˈblʌdɪd] adj (animal) à sang froid; Fig (person) froid(e), insensible; **c. murder** meurtre m commis de sang-froid

cold-hearted [ˈkəʊldˈhɑːtɪd] adj (person, decision) impitoyable

coldly [ˈkəʊldlɪ] adv froidement

coldness [ˈkəʊldnɪs] n froideur f

cold-shoulder [ˈkəʊldˈʃəʊldə(r)] vt snober

coleslaw [ˈkəʊlslɔː] n = salade de chou blanc à la mayonnaise

colic [ˈkɒlɪk] n colique f

collaborate [kəˈlæbəreɪt] vi also Pej collaborer (**with** avec)

collaboration [kəlæbəˈreɪʃən] n also Pej collaboration f

collaborator [kəˈlæbəreɪtə(r)] n also Pej collaborateur(trice) m,f

collage [ˈkɒlɑːʒ] n collage m

collapse [kəˈlæps] **1** n (of building, prices) effondrement m
2 vi (of person, building, prices) s'effondrer, s'écrouler

collapsible [kəˈlæpsəbəl] adj (table, bed) pliant(e)

collar [ˈkɒlə(r)] **1** n (of shirt) col m; (for dog) collier m
2 vt Fam (seize) pincer

collarbone [ˈkɒləbəʊn] n clavicule f

collate [kəˈleɪt] vt rassembler

collateral [kəˈlætərəl] **1** n Fin nantissement m
2 adj Euph Mil **c. damage** dégâts mpl collatéraux, dommages mpl collatéraux

colleague [ˈkɒliːg] n collègue mf

collect [kəˈlekt] **1** adv **to call sb c.** appeler qn en PCV, Can faire un appel à frais virés à qn
2 vt (a) (stamps, paintings) collectionner, faire collection de (b) (gather) (belongings) rassembler; (information, news) recueillir; (garbage) ramasser; (taxes) lever; **to c. dust** (of ornament) prendre la poussière; **to c. sb** (pick up) passer prendre qn (c) (compose) **to c. one's thoughts** se concentrer; **to c. oneself** se calmer
3 vi (of people) se rassembler; (of things) s'amasser; (of dust) s'accumuler

collected [kəˈlektɪd] adj (a) (calm) calme (b) **c. works** œuvres fpl complètes

collection [kəˈlekʃən] n (a) (of stamps, paintings) collection f (b) (act of collecting) (of money) recouvrement m; (of garbage) ramassage m; (of taxes) levée f; **to take a c.** (for charity) faire une collecte; **c. plate** (in church) plat m de quête

collective [kəˈlektɪv] **1** n (group) collectif m; (farm) coopérative f agricole
2 adj collectif(ive); **c. bargaining** = négociations afin d'établir une convention collective; **c. noun** collectif m

collectively [kəˈlektɪvlɪ] adv collectivement

collectivize [kəˈlektɪvaɪz] vt collectiviser

collector [kəˈlektə(r)] n (a) (of stamps, paintings) collectionneur(euse) m,f; **c.'s item** pièce f de collection (b) **c. of taxes** percepteur m

college [ˈkɒlɪdʒ] n (university) université f; **to be at c.** être étudiant(e)

collide [kəˈlaɪd] vi entrer en collision (**with** avec)

collie [ˈkɒlɪ] n colley m

colliery [ˈkɒlɪərɪ] n (pl **collieries**) n houillère f, mine f de charbon

collision [kəˈlɪʒən] n collision f; Fig **to be on a c. course** aller droit au conflit

colloquial [kəˈləʊkwɪəl] adj familier(ère)

colloquialism [kəˈləʊkwɪəlɪzəm] n expression f familière

collude [kəˈluːd] vi être de connivence (**with** avec)

collusion [kəˈluːʒən] n collusion f; **to be in c. with sb** être de connivence avec qn

collywobbles [ˈkɒlɪwɒbəlz] npl Fam **to have the c.** avoir la trouille

cologne [kəˈləʊn] n eau f de Cologne

Colombia [kəˈlʌmbɪə] n la Colombie

Colombian [kəˈlʌmbɪən] **1** n Colombien(enne) m,f
2 adj colombien(enne)

colon [ˈkəʊlən] n (a) Anat côlon m (b) (punctuation mark) deux-points m

colonel ['kɜːnəl] n colonel m

colonial [kə'ləʊnɪəl] adj colonial(e)

colonialism [kə'ləʊnɪəlɪzəm] n colonialisme m

colonist ['kɒlənɪst] n colon m

colonize ['kɒlənaɪz] vt coloniser

colonnade [kɒlə'neɪd] n Archit colonnade f

colony ['kɒlənɪ] (pl **colonies**) n colonie f

colossal [kə'lɒsəl] adj colossal(e)

color ['kʌlə(r)] **1** n (a) (red, blue, etc.) couleur f; **what c. is it?** de quelle couleur est-ce?; **c. bar** (racial discrimination) discrimination f raciale; **c. blindness** daltonisme m; **c. line** (racial discrimination) discrimination f raciale; **c. scheme** coloris mpl, couleurs fpl; **c. television** télévision f couleur (b) (idioms) **the joke was off c.** la plaisanterie était d'un goût douteux; **to give c. to a story** rendre un récit plus vivant; **let's see the c. of your money** voyons la couleur de ton argent; **to pass with flying colors** être reçu(e) brillamment ou haut la main; **to show one's true colors** se montrer sous son vrai jour; **to nail one's colors to the mast** afficher ses opinions **2** vt (a) (of chemical, dye) colorer; (with felt-tips, crayons) colorier; **to c. one's hair** se faire une couleur (b) Fig (judgment, view) fausser **3** vi (blush) rougir

▸**color in** vt sep colorier

color-blind ['kʌləblaɪnd] adj daltonien(enne)

color-coded ['kʌləkəʊdɪd] adj différencié(e) par des couleurs

colored ['kʌləd] adj (a) (illustration) en couleurs; (pen, ink) de couleur; **brightly c.** aux couleurs vives; Fig **a highly c. narrative** un récit haut en couleurs (b) (person) de couleur

colorful ['kʌləfʊl] adj coloré(e); (vivid) coloré, pittoresque; **a c. character** un personnage haut en couleurs

coloring ['kʌlərɪŋ] n (a) (in food) colorants mpl (b) (complexion) teint m; **to have dark/fair c.** avoir le teint mat/clair (c) **c. book** album m à colorier

colorless ['kʌlələs] adj (a) (clear) incolore (b) Fig (dull) insipide, fade

colt [kəʊlt] n poulain m

Columbus [kə'lʌmbəs] pr n **Christopher C.** Christophe Colomb

column ['kɒləm] n (of troops, text, in building) colonne f; (newspaper feature) rubrique f

columnist ['kɒləmɪst] n (for newspaper, magazine) chroniqueur(euse) m,f

coma ['kəʊmə] n coma m; **to fall into a c.** tomber dans le coma; **to be in a c.** être dans le coma

comatose ['kəʊmətəʊs] adj also Fig comateux(euse)

comb [kəʊm] **1** n (a) (for hair) peigne m; **to run a c. through one's hair** se donner un coup de peigne (b) (of cock) crête f **2** vt (a) (hair) peigner; **to c. one's hair** se peigner (b) (search) ratisser, passer au peigne fin

combat ['kɒmbæt] **1** n combat m; **c. jacket** veste f de treillis; **c. pants** battle-dress m, pantalon m multi-poches; **c. zone** zone f de combat **2** vt (disease, prejudice, crime) combattre

combatant ['kɒmbətənt] n & adj combattant(e) m,f

combination [kɒmbɪ'neɪʃən] n combinaison f; **a c. of circumstances** un concours de circonstances; **c. lock** serrure f à combinaison; **c. skin** peau f mixte; Med **c. therapy** trithérapie f

combine 1 n ['kɒmbaɪn] (a) **c. (harvester)** moissonneuse-batteuse f (b) Econ cartel m **2** vt [kəm'baɪn] combiner, allier; **to c. business with pleasure** joindre l'utile à l'agréable **3** vi [kəm'baɪn] (of people) s'associer; (of companies) fusionner; (of chemical elements) se combiner

combustible [kəm'bʌstɪbəl] adj combustible

combustion [kəm'bʌstʃən] n combustion f; **c. chamber** chambre f de combustion

come [kʌm] (pt came [keɪm], pp come) vi (a) (move) venir (from de); (arrive) arriver; **to c. from France/Boston** venir de France/de Boston; **here he comes!** le voilà!; **coming!** j'arrive!; **c., c.!** allons, allons!; **she always comes to me for help** elle s'adresse toujours à moi quand elle a besoin d'aide; **she came running toward us** elle vint vers nous en courant, elle courut vers nous; **the rain came pouring down** il s'est mis à tomber des cordes; **nothing comes between her and her work** son travail passe avant tout; Fig **she has come a long way since then** elle a fait du chemin depuis; Fam **I don't know whether I'm coming or going!** je ne sais plus où j'en suis!

(b) (in time) **c. January** en janvier; **c. next summer** l'été prochain; **in the days/years to c.** dans les jours/années à venir; **it came as a shock/surprise to me** ça m'a fait un choc/une surprise; Fam **he had it coming (to him)** ça lui pendait au nez

(c) (happen) **to c. to do sth** finir par faire qch; **c. to think of it** maintenant que j'y pense; **to take things as they c.** prendre les choses comme elles viennent; **c. what may** quoi qu'il arrive; **how c....?** comment se fait-il que...? + subjunctive

(d) (in sequence) **to c. first/last** (in race, competition) finir premier/dernier; **October comes before November** octobre vient avant novembre; **what comes next?** qu'est-ce qui vient après?

(e) (exist, be available) **to c. in three sizes/colors** exister en trois tailles/couleurs; **work of that quality doesn't c. cheap** du travail de cette qualité, ça se paie; **he's as tough as they c.** il n'y a pas plus dur que lui

(f) (become) **to c. loose** se défaire; **to c. true** se réaliser; **to c. open** s'ouvrir; **to c. of age** devenir majeur(e)

(g) (reach) **to c. up/down to** arriver (jusqu')à

(h) very Fam (reach orgasm) jouir

▸**come about** vi se produire, arriver

▸**come across 1** vt insep (find) tomber sur **2** vi (make an impression) **to c. across well/badly** bien/mal passer; **he comes across as a nice person** il a l'air gentil

▸**come after** vt insep (chase) poursuivre

▸**come along** vi (a) **c. along!** allons, pressons! (b) (make progress) (of project, work) avancer; **his French is coming along well** il fait des progrès en français (c) (arrive) venir

▸**come around** vi (a) (visit) passer (b) (regain consciousness) reprendre connaissance (c) (accept) accepter; **to c. around to sb's way of thinking** se rallier à l'opinion de qn

▸**come at** vt insep (attack) attaquer

▸**come away** vi (become detached) se détacher

▸**come back** vi revenir; **it's all coming back to me** ça me revient; **to c. back to what I was saying...** pour revenir à ce que je disais...

▸**come by 1** vt insep (acquire) obtenir, trouver **2** vi (visit) passer

▸**come down** vi (a) (descend) descendre; (of temperature, prices) baisser; Fig **to c. down in the world** déchoir; **to c. down with the flu** attraper la grippe (b) (decide) **to c. down in favor of sb/sth** décider en faveur de qn/qch (c) **to c. down to** (be a matter of) se ramener à, se résumer à; **it comes down to the fact that...** le fait est que...

▸**come down on** vt insep (reprimand) passer un savon à

▸**come forward** vi se présenter; **no one has come forward with any suggestions** personne n'a fait de suggestions

▸**come in** vi (a) (of person) entrer; (of tide) monter; **c. in!** entrez!; **to c. in first/second** arriver premier/deuxième (b) (have a role) intervenir; **and where do I c. in?** et moi, qu'est-ce que je fais?; **to c. in useful** être utile

►**come in for** *vt insep* to c. in for criticism faire l'objet de critiques

►**come into** *vt insep* (**a**) *(room, city)* entrer dans; **to c. into the world** venir au monde; **to c. into existence** être créé(e); **to c. into force** *or* **effect** *(of law, ruling)* entrer en vigueur; **to c. into power** arriver au pouvoir; **luck didn't c. into it** la chance n'a rien à voir là-dedans (**b**) *(inherit)* hériter de

►**come of** *vi (result from)* **no good will c. of it** cela n'amènera rien de bon; **that's what comes of being too ambitious** c'est ce qui arrive lorsqu'on est trop ambitieux

►**come off 1** *vt insep* (**a**) *(fall from) (horse, bicycle)* tomber de (**b**) **c. off it!** arrête ton char!

2 *vi* (**a**) *(be removed) (of button)* se détacher; *(of paint)* s'écailler; *(of stain)* partir (**b**) *(succeed)* réussir; **to c. off well/badly** *(in contest)* bien/mal s'en tirer

►**come on** *vi* (**a**) **c. on!** allez! (**b**) *(make progress) (of project, work)* avancer; **his chess is coming on** il fait des progrès aux échecs; **I feel a cold coming on** je sens que je suis en train de m'enrhumer (**c**) *(of lights)* s'allumer; *(of heating)* se mettre en route

►**come on to** *vt insep* (**a**) *(proceed to consider)* aborder, passer à; **I want to c. on to the issue of epidemics** je veux passer à la question des épidémies (**b**) *Fam (flirt with)* draguer; **she was coming on to me in a big way** elle me draguait à fond

►**come out** *vi* (**a**) *(of person, magazine, movie)* sortir; *(of sun)* paraître; *(of truth)* se faire jour; **to c. out on strike** se mettre en grève; **to c. out in a rash** se couvrir de boutons; **to c. out in favor of/against sth** se prononcer pour/contre qch; **he came out of the deal well/badly** il a fait une bonne/mauvaise affaire; **to c. out with** *(remark, opinion)* sortir (**b**) *(of tooth, hair)* tomber; *(of screw)* se dévisser; *(of stain)* partir (**c**) *(as gay or lesbian)* déclarer son homosexualité

►**come over 1** *vt insep (affect)* **a strange feeling came over me** j'ai eu une sensation étrange; **what's come over you?** qu'est-ce qui te prend?

2 *vi* (**a**) *(visit)* passer (**b**) *(make impression)* **to c. over well/badly** bien/mal passer

►**come through 1** *vi (of message, news)* arriver

2 *vt insep (survive) (war, crisis, sickness)* survivre à

►**come to 1** *vt insep* (**a**) *(amount to)* s'élever à; **the scheme never came to anything** le projet n'a jamais abouti (**b**) *(reach)* **to c. to the point** en venir au fait; **to c. to a conclusion** arriver à une conclusion; **what is the world coming to?** où va-t-on?; **I never thought it would c. to this** je ne me doutais pas qu'on en arriverait là (**c**) *(be a matter of)* **when it comes to...** pour ce qui est de...; **if it comes to that...** à ce compte-là...

2 *vi (regain consciousness)* reprendre connaissance

►**come together** *vi (gather)* se rassembler

►**come up 1** *vt insep (stairs, hill)* monter

2 *vi* (**a**) *(of sun)* se lever; *(of opportunity, question, problem)* se présenter; **to c. up against a problem** rencontrer un problème; **there are some interesting movies coming up on television** il y a quelques films intéressants qui vont bientôt passer à la télévision; **I'll let you know if anything comes up** je te préviendrai si quelque chose se présente; **the case comes up (for trial) tomorrow** le procès commence demain (**b**) **to c. up with** *(funding, solution)* trouver; *(idea, theory)* proposer

►**come upon** *vt insep (find)* tomber sur

►**come up to** *vt insep* (**a**) *(approach)* s'approcher de (**b**) *(equal)* **the movie didn't c. up to my expectations** le film n'était pas à la hauteur de mes espérances

comeback ['kʌmbæk] *n* **to make a c.** *(of fashion)* revenir; *(of actor, athlete)* faire un come-back

comedian [kə'miːdɪən] *n* comique *mf*; *Fig (practical joker)* farceur(euse) *m,f*

comedienne [kəmiːdɪ'en] *n* comique *f*

comedown ['kʌmdaʊn] *n Fam* régression *f*

comedy ['kɒmɪdɪ] *(pl* **comedies)** *n (play, movie)* comédie *f*; *(of situation)* comique *m*; *(situation comedy)* sitcom *m*; **c. show** *(on TV)* spectacle *m* comique

come-on ['kʌmɒn] *n Fam (enticement)* appât *m*

comer ['kʌmə(r)] *n* **open to all comers** ouvert(e) à tous

comet ['kɒmɪt] *n* comète *f*

comeuppance [kʌm'ʌpəns] *n Fam* **to get one's c.** avoir ce qu'on mérite

comfort ['kʌmfət] **1** *n* (**a**) *(ease)* confort *m*; *(financial)* aisance *f*; **to do sth in the c. of one's own home** faire qch confortablement chez soi; **comforts** *(luxuries)* commodités *fpl*; **I like my home comforts** j'aime mon petit confort; **the bullets were too close for c.** les balles passaient un peu trop près à mon goût; **c. station** toilettes *fpl* publiques (**b**) *(consolation)* réconfort *m*, consolation *f*; **if it's any c.,...** si ça peut vous consoler,...; **to take c. from** *or* **in sth** trouver du réconfort dans qch

2 *vt (console)* réconforter, consoler

comfortable ['kʌmftəbəl] *adj* (**a**) *(place, bed, chair)* confortable; *(person)* bien *inv*, à l'aise; **to be c.** *(of patient)* ne pas souffrir; **to make oneself c.** se mettre à l'aise *ou* à son aise; **I wouldn't feel c. accepting that money** ça me mettrait mal à l'aise d'accepter cet argent (**b**) *(majority, income)* confortable; **to be in c. circumstances** mener une vie aisée

comfortably ['kʌmftəblɪ] *adv* (**a**) *(sit)* confortablement; **to live c.** mener une vie aisée (**b**) *(easily)* facilement; **to win c.** gagner avec une avance confortable

comforter ['kʌmfətə(r)] *n (quilt)* édredon *m*, *Can* confortable *m*

comforting ['kʌmfətɪŋ] *adj* réconfortant(e)

comfy ['kʌmfɪ] *adj Fam (place, bed, chair)* confortable; *(person)* bien *inv*, à l'aise

comic ['kɒmɪk] **1** *n* (**a**) *(performer)* comique *mf* (**b**) **c. (book)** bande *f* dessinée, BD *f*

2 *adj* comique; **c. opera** opéra-comique *m*; **to provide some c. relief** détendre l'atmosphère; **c. strip** bande *f* dessinée, BD *f*

comical ['kɒmɪkəl] *adj* comique

coming ['kʌmɪŋ] **1** *n (of person)* venue *f*, arrivée *f*; *(of night)* approche *f*; **comings and goings** allées *fpl* et venues; **c. of age** majorité *f*; **on his c. of age** à sa majorité

2 *adj (year, week)* prochain(e); *(elections, difficulties)* à venir

comma ['kɒmə] *n* virgule *f*

command [kə'mɑːnd] **1** *n* (**a**) *(order)* ordre *m*; *Comput* commande *f*; *Comput* **c. language** langage *m* de commandes

(**b**) *(authority, control)* commandement *m*; **to be in c. (of sth)** *(army, ship)* commander (qch); **to be in c. of the situation** maîtriser la situation; **to be at sb's c.** être aux ordres de qn; **to have sth at one's c.** avoir qch à sa disposition; **she has a good c. of English** elle a une bonne maîtrise de l'anglais; **c. economy** économie *f* planifiée

2 *vt* (**a**) *(give order to)* **to c. sb to do sth** ordonner *ou* commander à qn de faire qch

(**b**) *(ship, regiment)* commander

(**c**) *(have at one's disposal)* avoir à sa disposition

(**d**) *(respect, admiration, attention)* forcer; **to c. a high price** vendre cher

commandant [kɒmən'dænt] *n Mil* commandant *m*

commandeer [kɒmən'dɪə(r)] *vt* réquisitionner

commander [kə'mɑːndə(r)] *n Mil* commandant *m*; *Naut* capitaine *m* de frégate; **c.-in-chief** commandant en chef

commanding [kə'mɑːndɪŋ] *adj* (**a**) *Mil* **c. officer** chef *m* de corps (**b**) *(voice)* impérieux(euse); *(appearance)* qui en impose; *(position)* dominant(e); *(lead)* considérable

commandment [kə'mɑːndmənt] *n Rel* commandement *m*

commando [kə'mɑːndəʊ] *(pl* **commandos** *or* **commandoes)** *n Mil (soldier, unit)* commando *m*

commemorate [kə'meməreɪt] *vt* commémorer
commemoration [kəmemə'reɪʃən] *n* commémoration *f*
commemorative [kə'memərətɪv] *adj* commémoratif(ive)
commence [kə'mens] *vt & vi Formal* commencer; **to c. doing sth** commencer à faire qch
commencement [kə'mensmənt] *n* (**a**) *Formal (beginning)* commencement *m*, début *m* (**b**) *Univ* remise *f* des diplômes; **C. Day** jour *m* de la remise des diplômes
commend [kə'mend] *vt* (**a**) *(praise)* louer, féliciter; **to c. sb for bravery** louer qn pour sa bravoure (**b**) *(recommend)* recommander; **the train journey has little to c. it** je ne vous recommande pas le voyage en train (**c**) *Lit (entrust)* recommander (**to** à)
commendable [kə'mendəbəl] *adj* louable
commendation [kɒmen'deɪʃən] *n (praise)* éloges *mpl*; *(in competition)* mention *f* spéciale; *Mil* citation *f*
commensurate [kə'menʃərət] *adj Formal* proportionnel(elle) (**with** à)
comment ['kɒment] **1** *n* commentaire *m*, observation *f* (**on** sur); **no c.!** je n'ai rien à dire!
  2 *vt* **to c. that...** faire remarquer *ou* observer que...; **"how interesting," he commented** "comme c'est intéressant", remarqua-t-il *ou* observa-t-il
  3 *vi* faire des commentaires (**on** sur)
commentary ['kɒmentərɪ] *(pl* **commentaries**) *n* commentaire *m*
commentate ['kɒmenteɪt] *vi* faire le commentaire; **to c. on sth** commenter qch
commentator ['kɒmenteɪtə(r)] *n* commentateur(trice) *m,f*
commerce ['kɒmɜːs] *n* commerce *m*
commercial [kə'mɜːʃəl] **1** *n (advertisement)* publicité *f*, pub *f*
  2 *adj also Pej* commercial(e); **c. artist** graphiste *mf*; *Fin* **c. bank** banque *f* commerciale; **c. break** page *f* de publicité; **c. law** droit *m* commercial; **c. traveler** voyageur *m* de commerce; **c. value** valeur *f* marchande; **c. vehicle** véhicule *m* de commerce
commercialism [kə'mɜːʃəlɪzəm] *n Pej* mercantilisme *m*
commercialized [kə'mɜːʃəlaɪzd] *adj Pej* commercial(e)
commercially [kə'mɜːʃəlɪ] *adv* commercialement; **c. available** disponible dans le commerce
commie ['kɒmɪ] *n & adj Fam Pej* coco *mf*
commiserate [kə'mɪzəreɪt] *vi* **to c. with sb** *(show sympathy)* témoigner de la sympathie à qn; *(feel sympathy)* éprouver de la compassion pour qn
commiseration [kəmɪzə'reɪʃən] *n* commisération *f*; **you have my c.** je suis désolé pour vous
commission [kə'mɪʃən] **1** *n* (**a**) *Com (payment)* commission *f* (**b**) *(of work, painting)* commande *f* (**c**) *(investigating body)* commission *f* (**d**) *Naut* **in c.** armé(e); **out of c.** désarmé(e) (**e**) *Mil* brevet *m* d'officier
  2 *vt* (**a**) *(order) (work, painting)* commander; **to c. sb to do sth** charger qn de faire qch (**b**) *Mil* **to be commissioned** être nommé(e) officier
commissionaire [kəmɪʃə'neə(r)] *n* portier *m*
commissioner [kə'mɪʃənə(r)] *n* membre *m* d'une commission; *(of police)* ≃ commissaire *m* de police
commit [kə'mɪt] *(pt & pp* **committed**) **1** *vt* (**a**) *(error, crime)* commettre; **to c. suicide** se suicider
  (**b**) **to c. oneself** *(promise)* s'engager; **to c. oneself to sth/doing sth** s'engager à qch/faire qch; **to c. sth to sth** *(resources, troops)* engager qch dans qch
  (**c**) *(entrust)* confier (**to** à); **to c. sth to writing** coucher qch par écrit; **to c. sth to memory** apprendre qch par cœur
  (**d**) *(confine)* **to c. sb (to prison)** incarcérer qn; **to c. sb** *(to mental institution)* interner qn
  (**e**) *Law* **to c. sb for trial** mettre qn en accusation
  2 *vi (emotionally)* s'engager, s'investir

commitment [kə'mɪtmənt] *n* (**a**) *(obligation)* engagement *m*; **family/business commitments** obligations *fpl* familiales/professionnelles (**b**) *(dedication)* dévouement *m* (**to** à); **to make a c.** s'engager; **she lacks c.** elle ne s'investit pas assez
committed [kə'mɪtɪd] *adj* dévoué(e) (**to** à); *(Christian, Democrat)* convaincu(e); **to be c. (to one's work)** beaucoup s'impliquer (dans son travail)
committee [kə'mɪtɪ] *n* comité *m*, commission *f*
commode [kə'məʊd] *n* (**a**) *(chest of drawers)* commode *f* (**b**) *(toilet)* chaise *f* percée
commodious [kə'məʊdɪəs] *adj Formal* spacieux(euse)
commodity [kə'mɒdɪtɪ] *(pl* **commodities**) *n Econ* marchandise *f*, produit *m*; *Fin* matière *f* première; **to be a rare c.** être une denrée rare; **commodities market** marché *m* des matières premières
commodore ['kɒmədɔː(r)] *n Naut* ≃ contre-amiral *m*
common ['kɒmən] **1** *n* (**a**) **to have sth in c. (with)** avoir qch en commun (avec); **in c. with** *(similar to)* de même que
  (**b**) *(land)* terrain *m* communal
  2 *adj* (**a**) *(frequent)* commun(e), courant(e); **in c. use** d'usage courant
  (**b**) *(shared)* commun(e); **it is by c. consent the best** de l'avis de tous, c'est le meilleur; *Fin* **c. currency** monnaie *f* unique; *also Fig* **c. denominator** dénominateur *m* commun; **the c. good** le bien commun; *Fig* **c. ground** terrain *m* d'entente; **it's c. knowledge (that)...** tout le monde sait que...; **the C. Market** le Marché commun; *Sch* **c. room** *(for pupils)* salle *f* commune; *(for teachers)* salle des professeurs
  (**c**) *(average)* **the c. cold** le rhume; **the c. man** l'homme *m* de la rue; **the c. people** les gens *mpl* ordinaires; **c. sense** bon sens *m*
  (**d**) *Pej (vulgar)* vulgaire
commoner ['kɒmənə(r)] *n* roturier(ère) *m,f*
common-law ['kɒmənlɔː] *adj* **c. husband** concubin *m*; **c. marriage** concubinage *m*; **c. wife** concubine *f*
commonly ['kɒmənlɪ] *adv* communément
commonplace ['kɒmənpleɪs] **1** *n* lieu *m* commun
  2 *adj* courant(e)
commonwealth ['kɒmənwelθ] *n (country)* pays *m*; *(state)* État *m*; *(republic)* république *f*; **the (British) C.** le Commonwealth
commotion [kə'məʊʃən] *n (noise)* vacarme *m*; *(disruption)* agitation *f*
communal ['kɒmjʊnəl] *adj (bathroom, resource)* commun(e); *(life)* communautaire
commune 1 *n* ['kɒmjuːn] *(collective)* communauté *f*
  2 *vi* [kə'mjuːn] **to c. with nature** communier avec la nature
communicable [kə'mjuːnɪkəbəl] *adj (disease)* transmissible
communicant [kə'mjuːnɪkənt] *n Rel* communiant(e) *m,f*
communicate [kə'mjuːnɪkeɪt] **1** *vt* communiquer; *(illness)* transmettre
  2 *vi* communiquer (**with** avec)
communication [kəmjuːnɪ'keɪʃən] *n* communication *f*; **to be in c. with sb** être en contact avec qn
communicative [kə'mjuːnɪkətɪv] *adj* communicatif(ive)
communion [kə'mjuːnjən] *n Rel* communion *f*; **to take C.** communier
communism ['kɒmjʊnɪzəm] *n* communisme *m*
communist ['kɒmjʊnɪst] *n & adj* communiste *mf*
community [kə'mjuːnɪtɪ] *(pl* **communities**) *n* communauté *f*; **the business c.** le milieu des affaires; **c. center** foyer *m* municipal; **c. college** centre *m* universitaire (de premier cycle); **c. service** travail *m* d'intérêt général; **c. spirit** esprit *m* communautaire
commute [kə'mjuːt] **1** *vt Law* commuer (**to** en)
  2 *vi* **to c. (to work)** faire la navette entre son domicile et son travail

commuter [kə'mjuːtə(r)] *n* banlieusard(e) *m,f (qui fait la navette entre son domicile et son travail)*; **c. train** train *m* de banlieue

Comoros ['kɒmərɒs] *n* **the C. (Islands)** les Comores *fpl*

compact 1 *n* ['kɒmpækt] (**a**) *(for powder)* poudrier *m* (**b**) *(treaty)* accord *m* (**c**) *(car)* petite voiture *f*
2 *adj* [kəm'pækt] compact(e); **c. disk** disque *m* compact; **c. disk player** lecteur *m* de disques compacts
3 *vt* [kəm'pækt] compacter

companion [kəm'pænjən] *n (friend)* compagnon (compagne) *m,f*; *(of elderly woman)* dame *f* de compagnie; **traveling c.** compagnon de voyage

companionable [kəm'pænjənəbəl] *adj (person)* sociable; *(manner)* amical(e)

companionship [kəm'pænjənʃɪp] *n* compagnie *f*

company ['kʌmpənɪ] (*pl* **companies**) *n* (**a**) *(companionship)* compagnie *f*; **in his c.** en sa compagnie; **to keep sb c.** tenir compagnie à qn; **to be good c.** être d'agréable compagnie; **the dog is good c. for her** le chien lui fait de la compagnie; **to part c. with sb** *(split up)* se séparer de qn; *(disagree)* ne plus être d'accord avec qn; **to get into bad c.** avoir de mauvaises fréquentations; **to do sth in c.** *(in public)* faire qch en public; **to be expecting c.** *(guests)* attendre de la visite (**b**) *(business)* société *f*; **publishing c.** maison *f* d'édition; **Hobbs and C.** Hobbs et Compagnie; *Fam Fig* **Alex and c.** Alex et compagnie; **c. car** voiture *f* de fonction; **c. policy** politique *f* de la société; *Com* **c. secretary** secrétaire *mf* général(e) (**c**) *(army unit, theater group)* compagnie *f*

comparable ['kɒmpərəbəl] *adj* comparable (**to** à)

comparative [kəm'pærətɪv] **1** *n Gram* comparatif *m*
2 *adj* (**a**) *(relative) (cost, comfort, wealth)* relatif(ive); **she's a c. stranger to me** je la connais relativement peu (**b**) *(study, research)* comparatif(ive); *(psychology, literature)* comparé(e)

compare [kəm'peə(r)] **1** *vt* comparer (**with** *or* **to** avec *ou* à); **compared with** *or* **to** par rapport à, à côté de; *Fig* **to c. notes** échanger ses impressions
2 *vi* être comparable (**with** à); **to c. favorably with sth** ne le céder en rien à qch
3 *n Lit* **beyond c.** sans pareil(eille)

comparison [kəm'pærɪsən] *n* comparaison *f*; **in** *or* **by c.** (**with**) en comparaison (avec); **there is no c.** il n'y a pas de comparaison; **to draw** *or* **to make a c. between sth and sth** faire la comparaison entre qch et qch

compartment [kəm'pɑːtmənt] *n* compartiment *m*

compass ['kʌmpəs] *n* (**a**) *(for finding direction)* boussole *f*; *(of boat)* compas *m* (**b**) *Math* (**pair of**) **compasses** compas *m* (**c**) *(scope) (of mind)* portée *f*; *(of powers)* étendue *f*

compassion [kəm'pæʃən] *n* compassion *f*

compassionate [kəm'pæʃənət] *adj (person, attitude)* compatissant(e); *(by nature)* humain(e); **to be c. toward sb** éprouver de la compassion pour qn; **on c. grounds** pour raisons personnelles; **c. leave** congé *m* exceptionnel pour raisons personnelles

compatibility [kəmpætə'bɪlɪtɪ] *n* compatibilité *f*

compatible [kəm'pætəbəl] *adj* compatible (**with** avec)

compatriot [kəm'pætrɪət] *n* compatriote *mf*

compel [kəm'pel] (*pt & pp* **compelled**) *vt* forcer, obliger; **to c. sb to do sth** forcer *ou* obliger qn à faire qch; **to c. admiration/respect** forcer l'admiration/le respect

compelling [kəm'pelɪŋ] *adj (movie, performance)* captivant(e); *(argument)* convaincant(e); *(urge)* irrésistible

compendium [kəm'pendɪəm] *n (book)* précis *m*; *(of games)* sélection *f*

compensate ['kɒmpenseɪt] **1** *vt* dédommager (**for** de)
2 *vi* **to c. for sth** compenser qch

compensation [kɒmpen'seɪʃən] *n* compensation *f*; *(money)* dédommagement *m*, indemnité *f*

compensatory [kɒm'pensətɔːrɪ] *adj* compensatoire

compete [kəm'piːt] *vi* (**a**) *(contend)* rivaliser (**with** avec); *(of company)* être en concurrence (**with** avec); **to c. for sth** se disputer qch (**b**) *(in race, competition)* concourir (**for** pour)

competence ['kɒmpɪtəns] *n* (**a**) *(ability)* compétence *f*, compétences *fpl* (**b**) *Law* compétence *f*

competent ['kɒmpɪtənt] *adj (person)* compétent(e); **a c. piece of work** du bon travail

competition [kɒmpɪ'tɪʃən] *n* (**a**) *(contest)* concours *m*; *(in sports)* compétition *f* (**b**) *(rivalry)* rivalité *f*; *(between companies, candidates)* concurrence *f*; **to be in c. with sb** être en concurrence avec qn; **the c.** *(opponents) (in sports)* les adversaires *mpl*; *(in business)* la concurrence; **you're up against some tough c.** *(in sports)* vous êtes en face d'adversaires de taille; *(in business)* la concurrence est rude; **there's no c.!** il n'y a aucune comparaison!

competitive [kəm'petɪtɪv] *adj (person)* qui a l'esprit de compétition; *(atmosphere)* de compétition; *(price, company)* compétitif(ive); **c. sports** sports *mpl* de compétition; *Com* **c. tendering** appel *m* d'offres

competitor [kəm'petɪtə(r)] *n* concurrent(e) *m,f*

compilation [kɒmpɪ'leɪʃən] *n* compilation *f*

compile [kəm'paɪl] *vt (list)* dresser; *(dictionary)* rédiger

complacency [kəm'pleɪsənsɪ] *n* autosatisfaction *f*

complacent [kəm'pleɪsənt] *adj* content(e) de soi; **to be c. about sth** faire de l'autosatisfaction à propos de qch

complain [kəm'pleɪn] *vi* se plaindre (**about** de); **to c. of** *(sickness)* se plaindre de; **I can't c. about the service** je n'ai pas à me plaindre du service; **how are things? – can't c.** comment ça va? – je n'ai pas à me plaindre

complainant [kəm'pleɪnənt] *n Law* plaignant(e) *m,f*

complaint [kəm'pleɪnt] *n* (**a**) *(grievance)* récrimination *f*; *(official)* plainte *f*, réclamation *f*; **to have cause** *or* **grounds for c.** avoir des raisons de se plaindre; **to lodge** *or* **to make a c. against sb** porter plainte contre qn (**b**) *(sickness)* maladie *f*

complement 1 *n* ['kɒmplɪmənt] (**a**) *Gram* complément *m* (**b**) *Naut & Fig* **the full c.** l'effectif *m* complet
2 *vt* ['kɒmplɪment] compléter

complementary [kɒmplɪ'mentərɪ] *adj* complémentaire; **c. medicine** médecines *fpl* alternatives *ou* parallèles

complete [kəm'pliːt] **1** *adj* (**a**) *(whole)* complet(ète); *(utter)* total(e); **he is a c. fool** il est complètement idiot (**b**) *(finished)* achevé(e)
2 *vt* (**a**) *(finish)* achever; *(fill out) (form)* compléter (**b**) *(make whole)* compléter

completely [kəm'pliːtlɪ] *adv* complètement

completion [kəm'pliːʃən] *n* achèvement *m*; **on c.** *(of work)* à l'achèvement; **to near c.** toucher à sa fin

complex ['kɒmpleks] **1** *n (of buildings, psychological)* complexe *m*; **to have a c. about sth** être complexé(e) par qch
2 *adj* complexe

complexion [kəm'plekʃən] *n* teint *m*; **to have a fair c.** avoir le teint clair; *Fig* **that puts a different c. on things** voilà qui change tout

complexity [kəm'pleksɪtɪ] (*pl* **complexities**) *n* complexité *f*

compliance [kəm'plaɪəns] *n* observation *f* (**with** de); **in c. with** conformément à

compliant [kəm'plaɪənt] *adj* complaisant(e), accommodant(e)

complicate ['kɒmplɪkeɪt] *vt* compliquer

complicated ['kɒmplɪkeɪtɪd] *adj* compliqué(e)

complication [kɒmplɪ'keɪʃən] *n* complication *f*

complicity [kəm'plɪsɪtɪ] *n* complicité *f* (**in** dans)

compliment 1 *n* ['kɒmplɪmənt] compliment *m*; **to pay sb a c.** faire un compliment à qn; **with compliments** avec nos compliments; **compliments of the season** meilleurs vœux
2 *vt* ['kɒmplɪment] **to c. sb on sth** *(bravery, command of*

language) féliciter qn pour qch; *(dress, haircut)* faire des compliments à qn sur qch

complimentary [kɒmplɪˈmentərɪ] *adj* (a) *(praising)* élogieux(euse) (**about** à l'égard de) (b) *(free)* gratuit(e); **c. ticket** billet *m* de faveur

comply [kəmˈplaɪ] *(pt & pp* **complied)** *vi* **to c. with** *(rule)* se conformer à, se plier à; *(order)* obéir à; *(request)* accéder à

component [kəmˈpəʊnənt] **1** *n (electrical, chemical)* composant *m; Fig* composante *f*
2 *adj* **c. part** pièce *f* détachée; *Fig* composante *f*

compose [kəmˈpəʊz] *vt* (a) *(music, poetry)* composer (b) *(constitute)* **to be composed of** être composé(e) de, se composer de (c) *(calm)* **to c. oneself** se ressaisir

composed [kəmˈpəʊzd] *adj* calme

composer [kəmˈpəʊzə(r)] *n* compositeur(trice) *m,f*

composite [ˈkɒmpəzɪt] *adj (photograph)* composite

composition [kɒmpəˈzɪʃən] *n* composition *f; (essay)* rédaction *f*

compositor [kəmˈpɒzɪtə(r)] *n Typ* compositeur(trice) *m,f*

compost [ˈkɒmpɒst] *n* compost *m;* **c. heap** tas *m* de compost

composure [kəmˈpəʊʒə(r)] *n* sang-froid *m*

compound¹1 *n* [ˈkɒmpaʊnd] *Chem & Gram* composé *m*
2 *adj* [ˈkɒmpaʊnd] composé(e); *Med* **c. fracture** fracture *f* compliquée; *Fin* **c. interest** intérêts *mpl* composés
3 *vt* [kəmˈpaʊnd] *(problem, difficulty)* aggraver

compound² [ˈkɒmpaʊnd] *n (enclosure)* enceinte *f*

comprehend [kɒmprɪˈhend] *vt* comprendre

comprehensible [kɒmprɪˈhensəbəl] *adj* compréhensible

comprehension [kɒmprɪˈhenʃən] *n* compréhension *f;* **it is beyond my c.** cela dépasse mon entendement

comprehensive [kɒmprɪˈhensɪv] *adj (answer, program)* complet(ète); *(study)* exhaustif(ive); *(view)* d'ensemble; *(defeat, victory)* écrasant(e); *Fin* **c. insurance** assurance *f* tous risques

compress 1 *n* [ˈkɒmpres] *Med* compresse *f*
2 *vt* [kəmˈpres] *(air, gas)* comprimer; *Fig (text)* condenser

compression [kəmˈpreʃən] *n (of air, gas)* compression *f; Fig* raccourcissement *m*

compressor [kəmˈpresə(r)] *n* compresseur *m*

comprise [kəmˈpraɪz] *vt* comprendre, se composer de; **to be comprised of** comprendre, se composer de

compromise [ˈkɒmprəmaɪz] **1** *n* compromis *m;* **c. solution** solution *f* de compromis
2 *vt (person, security)* compromettre; *(principles)* transiger sur; **to c. oneself** se compromettre
3 *vi* transiger (**on** sur)

compromising [ˈkɒmprəmaɪzɪŋ] *adj* compromettant(e)

compulsion [kəmˈpʌlʃən] *n (urge)* besoin *m; (obligation)* contrainte *f;* **under c.** sous la contrainte; **to be under no c. to do sth** ne pas être obligé(e) de faire qch

compulsive [kəmˈpʌlsɪv] *adj (smoker, gambler, liar)* invétéré(e); **c. eating** boulimie *f;* **it's c. viewing** c'est captivant

compulsory [kəmˈpʌlsərɪ] *adj* obligatoire; **c. layoff** ≃ licenciement *m* sec; **c. retirement** mise *f* à la retraite d'office

compunction [kəmˈpʌŋkʃən] *n* remords *m*, scrupules *mpl*

computation [kɒmpjʊˈteɪʃən] *n* calcul *m*

compute [kəmˈpjuːt] *vt* calculer

computer [kəmˈpjuːtə(r)] *n* ordinateur *m;* **to be c. literate** avoir des connaissances en informatique; **c. game** jeu *m* électronique; **c. printout** impression *f;* **c. program** programme *m* informatique; **c. programmer** programmeur(euse) *m,f;* **c. programming** programmation *f;* **c. science** informatique *f;* **c. scientist** informaticien(enne) *m,f;* **c. simulation** simulation *f* par ordinateur

computer-aided [kəmˈpjuːtərˈeɪdɪd], **computer-assisted** [kəmˈpjuːtərəˈsɪstɪd] *adj* assisté(e) par ordinateur

computerization [kəmpjuːtəraɪˈzeɪʃən] *n* informatisation *f*

computerize [kəmˈpjuːtəraɪz] *vt* informatiser

computing [kəmˈpjuːtɪŋ] *n* informatique *f*

comrade [ˈkɒmreɪd] *n* camarade *mf*

comradeship [ˈkɒmreɪdʃɪp] *n* camaraderie *f*

con¹ [kɒn] *Fam* **1** *n (swindle)* arnaque *f;* **c. man** arnaqueur *m*
2 *vt (pt & pp* **conned)** *(swindle)* arnaquer; **to c. sth out of sb** arnaquer qn de qch; **to c. sb into doing sth** persuader qn de faire qch par la ruse

con² [kɒn] *n Fam (convict)* taulard(e) *m,f*

con³ [kɒn] *n (disadvantage) see* **pro²**

concave [kɒnˈkeɪv] *adj* concave

conceal [kənˈsiːl] *vt* cacher, dissimuler (**from** à)

concealer [kənˈsiːlə(r)] *n (make-up)* camoufleur *m*

concede [kənˈsiːd] **1** *vt* concéder; **to c. defeat** s'avouer vaincu(e); **to c. that...** admettre que...
2 *vi* s'incliner

conceit [kənˈsiːt] *n (vanity)* vanité *f*, suffisance *f*

conceited [kənˈsiːtɪd] *adj* vaniteux(euse), suffisant(e)

conceivable [kənˈsiːvəbəl] *adj* concevable, imaginable; **it is c. that...** il est concevable que... + *subjunctive*

conceivably [kənˈsiːvəblɪ] *adv* **we might c. get there by six** il se peut que nous soyons arrivés pour six heures; **she couldn't c. have done it** il est inconcevable qu'elle ait fait ça

conceive [kənˈsiːv] **1** *vt* (a) *(child, idea)* concevoir (b) *(understand)* concevoir
2 *vi* **to c. of sth** concevoir qch

concentrate [ˈkɒnsəntreɪt] **1** *n* concentré *m*
2 *vt* concentrer (**on** sur)
3 *vi* se concentrer (**on** sur); **to c. on doing sth** s'appliquer à faire qch

concentration [kɒnsənˈtreɪʃən] *n* concentration *f;* **to have a short c. span** ne pas avoir une grande capacité de concentration; **c. camp** camp *m* de concentration

concentric [kɒnˈsentrɪk] *adj Math* concentrique

concept [ˈkɒnsept] *n* concept *m*

conception [kənˈsepʃən] *n* (a) *(of child, idea)* conception *f* (b) *(understanding)* **to have no c. of sth** n'avoir aucune idée *ou* notion de qch

conceptual [kənˈseptjʊəl] *adj* conceptuel(elle)

conceptualize [kənˈseptjʊəlaɪz] *vt* conceptualiser

concern [kənˈsɜːn] **1** *n* (a) *(interest)* **it's no c. of mine/yours** cela ne me/vous regarde pas; **this is a matter of public c.** c'est une affaire qui nous concerne tous (b) *(worry, compassion)* inquiétude *f*, souci *m;* **to give cause for c.** être un sujet d'inquiétude; **there is no cause for c.** il n'y a pas de raison de s'inquiéter; **to show c.** se montrer inquiet(ète) (c) *(company)* entreprise *f*
2 *vt* (a) *(affect)* concerner; **to c. oneself with sth** se préoccuper *ou* se soucier de qch; **as far as I'm concerned,...** pour moi,..., en ce qui me concerne,...; **to whom it may c.** à qui de droit (b) *(worry)* inquiéter (c) *(be about) (of book)* traiter de; **it concerns your request for a transfer** c'est au sujet de votre demande de transfert

concerned [kənˈsɜːnd] *adj (worried)* inquiet(ète) (**about** au sujet de)

concerning [kənˈsɜːnɪŋ] *prep* au sujet de

concert [ˈkɒnsət] *n* (a) *(musical)* concert *m;* **c. hall** salle *f* de concert; **c. pianist** concertiste *mf* (b) *(cooperation)* **in c. (with)** de concert (avec)

concerted [kənˈsɜːtɪd] *adj* concerté(e)

concertina [kɒnsəˈtiːnə] *n* concertina *m*

concerto [kənˈtʃɜːtəʊ] *(pl* **concertos)** *n* concerto *m*

concession [kənˈseʃən] *n* (a) *(compromise, giving up)* concession *f* (b) **c. stand** *(for refreshments)* buvette *f*

conciliate [kənˈsɪlieɪt] *vt* apaiser

conciliation [kənsɪlɪˈeɪʃən] *n* conciliation *f; (in dispute)* conciliation, arbitrage *m;* **the dispute went to c.** le conflit a été soumis à l'arbitrage

conciliatory [kən'sɪliətəri] *adj* conciliant(e)

concise [kən'saɪs] *adj* concis(e)

conclude [kən'kluːd] **1** *vt* (**a**) *(speech, book, treaty)* conclure; *(conference, festival)* clore (**b**) *(deduce)* **to c. that...** conclure que...
  2 *vi* se conclure (**with** sur); *(of speaker)* conclure (**with** sur); *(of conference, festival)* se clore (**with** sur)

concluding [kən'kluːdɪŋ] *adj* final(e)

conclusion [kən'kluːʒən] *n* (**a**) *(inference)* conclusion *f*; **to come to** *or* **to reach a c.** arriver à une conclusion (**b**) *(end)* conclusion *f*; **in c.** pour conclure, en conclusion

conclusive [kən'kluːsɪv] *adj* concluant(e)

concoct [kən'kɒkt] *vt also Fig* concocter

concoction [kən'kɒkʃən] *n (drink, dish)* mixture *f*

concord ['kɒŋkɔːd] *n (harmony)* entente *f*

concordance [kən'kɔːdəns] *n (agreement)* accord *m*; **to be in c. with sth** être en accord avec qch

concourse ['kɒŋkɔːs] *n (in airport, train station)* hall *m*

concrete ['kɒŋkriːt] **1** *n* béton *m*; **c. jungle** univers *m* de béton; **c. mixer** bétonnière *f*
  2 *adj* en béton; *Fig (definite)* concret(ète)

concubine ['kɒŋkjʊbaɪn] *n* concubine *f*

concur [kən'kɜː(r)] *(pt & pp* **concurred**) *vi (of person)* être d'accord (**with** avec); *(of findings, results)* concorder (**with** avec)

concurrent [kən'kʌrənt] *adj* simultané(e), concordant(e)

concurrently [kən'kʌrəntlɪ] *adv* simultanément

concussed [kən'kʌst] *adj* commotionné(e)

concussion [kən'kʌʃən] *n* commotion *f* cérébrale

condemn [kən'dem] *vt* (**a**) *(disapprove of)* condamner (**b**) *Law (sentence)* condamner (**to** à) (**c**) *(building)* déclarer inhabitable

condemnation [kɒndem'neɪʃən] *n* condamnation *f*

condensation [kɒnden'seɪʃən] *n* (**a**) *(moisture) (on glass)* buée *f*; *(on walls)* condensation *f* (**b**) *(process)* condensation *f*

condense [kən'dens] **1** *vt* condenser; **condensed milk** lait *m* condensé
  2 *vi* se condenser

condenser [kən'densə(r)] *n Tech* condensateur *m*

condescend [kɒndɪ'send] *vi* **to c. to do sth** condescendre à faire qch; **to c. toward sb** se montrer condescendant(e) envers qn

condescending [kɒndɪ'sendɪŋ] *adj* condescendant(e)

condescension [kɒndɪ'senʃən] *n* condescendance *f*

condiment ['kɒndɪmənt] *n* condiment *m*

condition [kən'dɪʃən] **1** *n* (**a**) *(state)* état *m*; *(of person)* forme *f*; **in good/bad c.** *(of machine, road)* en bon/mauvais état; **you're in no c. to drive** tu n'es pas en état de conduire; **to be in good c./out of c.** *(of person)* être/ne pas être en forme
  (**b**) **conditions** *(circumstances)* conditions *fpl*; **working conditions** conditions de travail; **driving conditions** état *m* des routes; *Law* **conditions of employment** contrat *m* de travail
  (**c**) *(requirement)* condition *f*; **on (the) c. that...** à (la) condition que... + *subjunctive*; **on no c.** sous aucun prétexte, en aucun cas
  (**d**) *(disease)* maladie *f*; **heart c.** maladie du cœur
  2 *vt* (**a**) *(influence)* conditionner; **to be conditioned by** *(depend on)* dépendre de; **we have been conditioned to believe that...** on nous a appris que...; *Psy* **conditioned reflex** réflexe *m* conditionné
  (**b**) *(hair)* mettre de l'après-shampo(o)ing sur

conditional [kən'dɪʃənəl] **1** *n Gram* **the c.** le conditionnel
  2 *adj* conditionnel(elle); **to be c. on** dépendre de; *Law* **c. discharge** *or* **release** liberté *f* conditionnelle

conditionally [kən'dɪʃənəlɪ] *adv (accept, grant)* sous certaines conditions

conditioner [kən'dɪʃənə(r)] *n (for hair)* après-shampo(o)ing *m*

conditioning [kən'dɪʃənɪŋ] *n (psychological)* conditionnement *m*

condo ['kɒndəʊ] *(pl* **condos**) *n Fam (abbr* **condominium**) appartement *m* en copropriété

condolences [kən'dəʊlənsɪz] *npl* condoléances *fpl*

condom ['kɒndəm] *n* préservatif *m*

condominium [kɒndə'mɪnɪəm] *n (apartment)* appartement *m* en copropriété

condone [kən'dəʊn] *vt* excuser

condor ['kɒndɔː(r)] *n* condor *m*

conducive [kən'djuːsɪv] *adj* **to be c. to** être favorable *ou* propice à

conduct 1 *n* ['kɒndʌkt] *(behavior)* conduite *f*
  2 *vt* [kən'dʌkt] (**a**) *(business, orchestra)* diriger; *(campaign, inquiry, experiment)* mener; **to c. oneself** se conduire (**b**) *(guide)* guider; **we were conducted around the factory** on nous a fait visiter l'usine; **a conducted tour** une visite guidée (**c**) *(heat, electricity)* conduire
  3 *vi* [kən'dʌkt] *Mus* diriger

conductivity [kɒndʌk'tɪvɪti] *n Phys* conductivité *f*

conductor [kən'dʌktə(r)] *n* (**a**) *(on train)* chef *m* de train (**b**) *(of orchestra)* chef *m* d'orchestre (**c**) *Phys* conducteur *m*

conduit ['kɒndɪt] *n* conduit *m*

cone [kəʊn] *n* (**a**) *(shape)* cône *m* (**b**) *(of pine)* pomme *f* de pin (**c**) *(for ice cream)* cornet *m* (**d**) *(for traffic)* cône *m* de signalisation

cone-shaped ['kəʊnʃeɪpt] *adj* conique

confab ['kɒnfæb] *n Fam* **to have a c. about sth** discuter de qch

confectioner [kən'fekʃənə(r)] *n* confiseur(euse) *m,f*; **c.'s (store)** confiserie *f*; **c.'s sugar** sucre *m* glace

confectionery [kən'fekʃənəri] *n (candy)* confiserie *f*

confederacy [kən'fedərəsɪ] *n* confédération *f*; *Hist* **the C.** les États *mpl* confédérés *(pendant la guerre de Sécession américaine)*

confederate [kən'fedərət] **1** *n (accomplice)* complice *mf*; *Hist* **C.** sudiste *mf* *(pendant la guerre de Sécession américaine)*; **the Confederates** les Confédérés *mpl*
  2 *adj Pol* confédéré(e)

confederation [kənfedə'reɪʃən] *n* confédération *f*

confer [kən'fɜː(r)] *(pt & pp* **conferred**) **1** *vt (title, degree, powers)* octroyer (**on** à)
  2 *vi (discuss) (of several people)* se consulter; **to c. with sb about sth** discuter de qch avec qn

conference ['kɒnfərəns] *n* (**a**) conférence *f*, congrès *m*; *Com* **to be in c.** être en conférence; *Tel* **c. call** téléconférence *f* (**b**) *Sport (association)* association *f*, ligue *f*

confess [kən'fes] **1** *vt (crime, mistake)* confesser, avouer; *(feeling)* avouer; *Rel* confesser; **to c. that...** confesser *ou* avouer que...
  2 *vi* avouer; *Rel* se confesser; **to c. to sth** *(crime, mistake)* confesser *ou* avouer qch; *(feeling)* avouer qch

confession [kən'feʃən] *n* confession *f*, aveu *m*; *Rel* confession; **to go to c.** aller se confesser

confessional [kən'feʃənəl] *n Rel* confessionnal *m*

confessor [kən'fesə(r)] *n Rel* confesseur *m*

confetti [kən'feti] *n* confettis *mpl*

confidante [kɒnfɪ'dænt] *n* confident(e) *m,f*

confide [kən'faɪd] **1** *vt* **to c. sth to sb** confier qch à qn
  2 *vi* **to c. in sb** se confier à qn

confidence ['kɒnfɪdəns] *n* (**a**) *(trust)* confiance *f* (**in** en); **I have every c. that...** je ne doute pas un instant que...; **to take sb into one's c.** se confier à qn; **c. man** escroc *m*; **c. game** escroquerie *f* (**b**) *(self-assurance)* confiance *f* en soi (**c**) *(secret)* confidence *f*; **in c.** en confidence

confident ['kɒnfɪdənt] *adj* (**a**) *(self-assured) (person)* sûr(e) de soi; *(smile, exterior)* confiant(e) (**b**) *(certain)* certain(e); **to be c. of doing sth** être certain de faire qch

confidential [kɒnfɪ'denʃəl] *adj* confidentiel(elle)

confidentiality [kɒnfɪdenʃɪˈælɪtɪ] *n* confidentialité *f*

confidentially [kɒnfɪˈdenʃəlɪ] *adv* confidentiellement, en confidence

confidently [ˈkɒnfɪdəntlɪ] *adv* (**a**) *(with self-assurance)* avec assurance (**b**) *(with certainty)* avec confiance

configuration [kənfɪɡʊˈreɪʃən] *n* configuration *f*; *Comput* paramétrage *m*

confine [kənˈfaɪn] *vt* (**a**) *(imprison)* enfermer; **to be confined to bed** être alité(e); **to be confined to quarters** être consigné(e); **confined space** espace *m* restreint (**b**) *(limit)* **to c. oneself to sth/doing sth** se limiter *ou* s'en tenir à qch/à faire qch

confinement [kənˈfaɪnmənt] *n* (**a**) *(in prison)* emprisonnement *m* (**b**) *Old-fashioned Med (labor)* couches *fpl*

confines [ˈkɒnfaɪnz] *npl* *(of town)* confins *mpl*; *Fig (limits)* limites *fpl*; **within the c. of** dans les limites de

confirm [kənˈfɜːm] *vt* confirmer; *(power, position)* consolider, renforcer

confirmation [kɒnfəˈmeɪʃən] *n also Rel* confirmation *f*

confirmed [kənˈfɜːmd] *adj (smoker, liar)* invétéré(e); *(bachelor)* endurci

confiscate [ˈkɒnfɪskeɪt] *vt* confisquer (**from** à)

confiscation [kɒnfɪsˈkeɪʃən] *n* confiscation *f*

conflict 1 *n* [ˈkɒnflɪkt] conflit *m*; **to come into c. with** entrer en conflit avec; **c. of interest** conflit *m* d'intérêts
2 *vi* [kənˈflɪkt] être en contradiction (**with** avec)

conflicting [kənˈflɪktɪŋ] *adj (opinions)* opposé(e); *(reports, evidence)* contradictoire

confluence [ˈkɒnfluəns] *n (of rivers)* confluent *m*

conform [kənˈfɔːm] *vi* se plier aux règles; **to c. to** *(rules)* obéir à, se plier à; *(standards)* être en conformité avec; **to c. with** être conforme à

conformist [kənˈfɔːmɪst] *n & adj* conformiste *mf*

conformity [kənˈfɔːmɪtɪ] *n* conformité *f*; **in c. with** en conformité *ou* en accord avec

confound [kənˈfaʊnd] *vt* (**a**) *(puzzle)* laisser perplexe (**b**) *(frustrate) (plans)* faire échouer (**c**) *(surprise)* confondre (**d**) *Old-fashioned Fam (damn)* **c. it!** quelle barbe!; **c. him!** le diable l'emporte!

confront [kənˈfrʌnt] *vt* affronter, faire face à; **to be confronted by sth** être confronté(e) à qch; **to c. sb with sth** confronter qn à qch

confrontation [kɒnfrʌnˈteɪʃən] *n* affrontement *m*

confuse [kənˈfjuːz] *vt (bewilder)* embrouiller; *(mix up)* confondre (**with** avec)

confused [kənˈfjuːzd] *adj (person)* perdu(e); *(instructions, account, mind)* confus(e); **I'm c.** je m'y perds; **to get c.** s'embrouiller

confusing [kənˈfjuːzɪŋ] *adj (bewildering)* déroutant(e); *(muddled)* confus(e); **it's very c.** on s'y perd

confusion [kənˈfjuːʒən] *n (bewilderment)* perplexité *f*; *(disorder, lack of clarity)* confusion *f*; **to throw sth into c.** chambouler qch

congeal [kənˈdʒiːl] *vi (of blood)* (se) coaguler

congenial [kənˈdʒiːnɪəl] *adj* agréable

congenital [kənˈdʒenɪtəl] *adj* congénital(e); *Fig* **he's a c. liar** il ment tout le temps, c'est congénital

conger [ˈkɒŋɡə(r)] *n* **c. (eel)** congre *m*

congested [kənˈdʒestɪd] *adj (road)* encombré(e); *(area, town)* surpeuplé(e); *Med (lungs)* congestionné(e); *(nose)* bouché(e)

congestion [kənˈdʒestʃən] *n (of traffic)* encombrements *mpl*; *(of area, town)* surpeuplement *m*; *Med (of lungs)* congestion *f*

conglomerate [kənˈɡlɒmərət] *n* conglomérat *m*

Congo [ˈkɒŋɡəʊ] *n* **the C.** *(country)* le Congo

Congolese [kɒŋɡəˈliːz] **1** *n* Congolais(e) *m,f*
2 *adj* congolais(e)

congratulate [kənˈɡrætjʊleɪt] *vt* féliciter (**on** de); **to c. oneself on having done sth** se féliciter d'avoir fait qch

congratulations [kənɡrætjʊˈleɪʃənz] *npl* félicitations *fpl*; **c. on your promotion/passing your finals** félicitations pour votre promotion/vos examens

congratulatory [kənˈɡrætjʊleɪtərɪ] *adj* de félicitations

congregate [ˈkɒŋɡrɪɡeɪt] *vi* se rassembler, s'assembler

congregation [kɒŋɡrɪˈɡeɪʃən] *n (of church)* assemblée *f* des fidèles

congress [ˈkɒŋɡres] *n (conference)* congrès *m*; *Pol* **C.** le Congrès *(assemblée législative américaine)*

Congressman [ˈkɒŋɡresmən] *n Pol* membre *m* du Congrès

Congresswoman [ˈkɒŋɡreswʊmən] *n Pol* membre *m* du Congrès

conical [ˈkɒnɪkəl] *adj* conique

conifer [ˈkɒnɪfə(r)] *n* conifère *m*

coniferous [kəˈnɪfərəs] *adj (forest)* de conifères; **c. tree** conifère *m*

conjecture [kənˈdʒektʃə(r)] **1** *n* conjecture *f*; **it's sheer c.** ce ne sont que des suppositions
2 *vt* supposer
3 *vi* faire des conjectures

conjugal [ˈkɒndʒʊɡəl] *adj* conjugal(e)

conjugate [ˈkɒndʒʊɡeɪt] *Gram* **1** *vt* conjuguer
2 *vi* se conjuguer

conjugation [kɒndʒʊˈɡeɪʃən] *n Gram* conjugaison *f*

conjunction [kənˈdʒʌŋkʃən] *n* conjonction *f*; **in c. with** conjointement avec

conjunctivitis [kəndʒʌŋktɪˈvaɪtɪs] *n* conjonctivite *f*

conjure [ˈkʌndʒə(r)] *vi (do magic)* faire des tours de passe-passe; *Fig* **a name to c. with** un nom prestigieux
▸**conjure up** *vt sep* (**a**) *(produce)* faire apparaître; **she conjured up a meal** elle s'est débrouillée pour préparer un repas en un rien de temps; **to c. sth up out of nowhere** faire apparaître qch comme par magie (**b**) *(call to mind)* évoquer

conjurer [ˈkʌndʒərə(r)] *n* prestidigitateur *m*, illusionniste *mf*

conjuring [ˈkʌndʒərɪŋ] *n* prestidigitation *f*; **c. trick** tour *m* de prestidigitation *ou* de passe-passe

conjuror = **conjurer**

conk [kɒŋk] *vt Fam (hit)* cogner
▸**conk out** *vi Fam* (**a**) *(stop working) (of machine, TV)* flancher; **the car conked out on me** la voiture m'a claqué entre les doigts (**b**) *(fall asleep)* se mettre à pioncer

connect [kəˈnekt] **1** *vt* (**a**) *(pipes, wires, circuits)* relier (**to** à) (**b**) *(link, associate)* **to c. sb/sth to sb/sth** établir un lien entre qn/qch et qn/qch; **there is nothing to c. the two crimes** il n'y a aucun lien entre les deux crimes; **to be connected with** avoir un lien *ou* un rapport avec; **the two issues are not connected** les deux questions n'ont aucun rapport; **are they connected?** *(of people)* sont-ils parents?; **to be well connected** *(of person)* avoir des relations (**c**) *Tél* mettre en ligne *ou* en communication (**with** avec); **can you c. me with reservations?** pourriez-vous me passer le service des réservations?
2 *vi* (**a**) *(of pipes, wires, roads)* être relié(e) (**with** avec); *(of rooms)* communiquer (**with** avec)
(**b**) *(of train, plane)* assurer la correspondance (**with** avec)
(**c**) *(of blow)* atteindre son but; **the blow connected with his knee** le coup l'a atteint au genou
▸**connect up** *vt sep (pipes, wires)* raccorder

connection [kəˈnekʃən] *n* (**a**) *(link, association)* lien *m*, rapport *m*; **in c. with** à propos de; **in this c.** à ce propos (**b**) *(acquaintance)* relation *f*; **to have important connections** avoir des relations en haut lieu (**c**) *(of pipes, wires)* raccordement *m* (**d**) *(train, plane)* correspondance *f*

connivance [kəˈnaɪvəns] *n* connivence *f*

connive [kəˈnaɪv] *vi* (**a**) *(conspire)* comploter; **to c. with sb**

être de connivence avec qn (**b**) **to c. at sth** *(let happen)* laisser faire qch

conniving [kə'naɪvɪŋ] *adj* intrigant(e)

connoisseur [kɒnə'sɜː(r)] *n* connaisseur(euse) *m,f* (**of** en)

connotation [kɒnə'teɪʃən] *n* connotation *f*

conquer ['kɒŋkə(r)] *vt (country, someone's heart)* conquérir; *(difficulty, fears)* vaincre

conquering ['kɒŋkərɪŋ] *adj* victorieux(euse)

conqueror ['kɒŋkərə(r)] *n* vainqueur *m*

conquest ['kɒŋkwest] *n* conquête *f*; **to make a c. of sb** faire la conquête de qn

conscience ['kɒnʃəns] *n* conscience *f*; **to have a clear** *or* **clean c.** avoir la conscience tranquille; **to have a guilty c.** avoir mauvaise conscience; **to have sth on one's c.** avoir qch sur la conscience; **to have no c. about doing sth** ne pas avoir de scrupules à faire qch; **in all c.** raisonnablement

conscientious [kɒnʃɪ'enʃəs] *adj* consciencieux(euse); **c. objector** objecteur *m* de conscience

conscious ['kɒnʃəs] *adj* (**a**) *(awake)* conscient(e) (**b**) *(aware)* **to be c. of sth/that...** être conscient(e) de qch/que...; **to become c. of sth** prendre conscience de qch, s'apercevoir de qch; *Psy* **the c. mind** la conscience (**c**) *(intentional)* conscient(e); **to make a c. effort to do sth** faire un effort particulier pour faire qch; **to make a c. decision to do sth** chercher délibérément à faire qch

consciousness ['kɒnʃəsnɪs] *n* (**a**) *(wakefulness)* conscience *f*; **to lose/regain c.** perdre/reprendre connaissance (**b**) *(awareness)* conscience *f* (**of** de); **to raise people's c. of sth** sensibiliser les gens à qch

conscript 1 *n* ['kɒnskrɪpt] conscrit *m*
2 *vt* [kən'skrɪpt] enrôler; **to be conscripted** être appelé(e) (sous les drapeaux)

conscription [kən'skrɪpʃən] *n* conscription *f*

consecrate ['kɒnsɪkreɪt] *vt Rel & Fig* consacrer

consecration [kɒnsɪ'kreɪʃən] *n* consécration *f*

consecutive [kən'sekjʊtɪv] *adj* consécutif(ive); **on three c. days** trois jours consécutifs, trois jours de suite

consensus [kən'sensəs] *n* consensus *m*

consent [kən'sent] **1** *n* consentement *m*, assentiment *m*
2 *vi* **to c. to sth/to do sth** consentir à qch/à faire qch

consequence ['kɒnsɪkwəns] *n* (**a**) *(result)* conséquence *f*; **as a c., in c.** par conséquent; **to take the consequences** subir les conséquences (**b**) *(importance)* importance *f*; **of little c.** de peu d'importance; **of no c.** sans importance

consequent ['kɒnsɪkwənt] *adj* résultant(e); **c. upon sth** qui résulte de qch; **the war and its c. loss of life** la guerre et les pertes en vies humaines qui en résultent

consequently ['kɒnsɪkwəntlɪ] *adv* par conséquent

conservation [kɒnsə'veɪʃən] *n (of environment)* protection *f*; *(of energy)* économies *fpl*; *(nature reserve)* réserve *f* naturelle

conservationist [kɒnsə'veɪʃənɪst] *n* défenseur *m* de l'environnement

conservative [kən'sɜːvətɪv] **1** *n* conservateur(trice) *m,f*
2 *adj* conservateur(trice); *(conventional)* classique; **at a c. estimate** au bas mot

conservatory [kən'sɜːvətərɪ] *(pl* **conservatories)** *n* (**a**) *(room)* véranda *f* (**b**) *Mus* conservatoire *m*

conserve 1 *n* ['kɒnsɜːv] *(jam)* confiture *f*
2 *vt* [kən'sɜːv] *(monument, language, tradition)* préserver; *(water, energy)* faire des économies de

consider [kən'sɪdə(r)] *vt* (**a**) *(think over)* considérer; *(offer, matter)* étudier; **he was considering whether to go out when...** il était en train de se demander s'il allait sortir lorsque...; **to c. doing sth** envisager de faire qch; **to c. sb for a job** envisager qn pour un poste (**b**) *(take into account)* penser, réfléchir à; *(possibility)* envisager; *(person's feelings)* tenir compte de; **all things considered** tout bien considéré (**c**) *(re-*

gard) considérer; **I c. her a friend** je la considère comme une amie; **c. it done** considère que c'est déjà fait; **c. yourself dismissed** considère-toi comme renvoyé

considerable [kən'sɪdərəbəl] *adj* considérable; **after c. difficulty** après bien des difficultés

considerate [kən'sɪdərət] *adj* prévenant(e) (**toward** envers); **that wasn't very c. of you** ce n'était pas très aimable de ta part

consideration [kənsɪdə'reɪʃən] *n* (**a**) *(deliberation)* **to be under c.** être à l'étude; **after due c.** après mûre réflexion; **to take sth into c.** prendre qch en considération (**b**) *(factor)* facteur *m* (**c**) *(respect)* considération *f*; **show some c.!** tu pourrais faire preuve d'un peu de considération!; **out of c. for** par égard pour (**d**) *(payment)* contribution *f*; **for a small c.** en échange d'une modique somme

considering [kən'sɪdərɪŋ] **1** *prep* étant donné, vu
2 *conj* étant donné que; **c. (that) he is so young** étant donné son jeune âge
3 *adv (after all)* **not bad c.** pas mal après tout

consign [kən'saɪn] *vt* (**a**) *(dispose of)* reléguer (**to** à); **she was consigned to a life of loneliness** elle fut condamnée à une existence solitaire (**b**) *(entrust)* confier (**to** à) (**c**) *(send)* expédier (**to** à)

consignee [kɒnsaɪ'niː] *n* consignataire *mf*

consignment [kən'saɪnmənt] *n (of goods)* envoi *m*, expédition *f*; **c. store** dépôt-vente *m*

▸**consist in** [kən'sɪst] *vt insep* **to c. in doing sth** consister à faire qch; **to c. in sth** résider dans qch, se résumer à qch

▸**consist of** *vt insep* consister en, se composer de

consistency [kən'sɪstənsɪ] *n* (**a**) *(of substance, liquid)* consistance *f* (**b**) *(of arguments, ideas)* cohérence *f*; *(of behavior, person)* logique *f*; *(of performer, results)* régularité *f*

consistent [kən'sɪstənt] *adj (arguments, ideas)* cohérent(e); *(behavior, person)* logique; *(quality, standard)* constant(e); *(performer, results)* régulier(ère); *(refusal, failure)* persistant(e); **to be c. with** concorder avec

consistently [kən'sɪstəntlɪ] *adv (play, perform)* avec régularité; *(fail, deny, oppose)* toujours

consolation [kɒnsə'leɪʃən] *n* consolation *f*; **if it's any c.** si ça peut te consoler; **c. prize** prix *m* de consolation

console¹ ['kɒnsəʊl] *n (control panel)* console *f*

console² [kən'səʊl] *vt* consoler (**for** de); *(bereaved person)* réconforter

consolidate [kən'sɒlɪdeɪt] **1** *vt also Fig* consolider; *(position)* renforcer; *(power)* asseoir
2 *vi* se consolider

consolidation [kənsɒlɪ'deɪʃən] *n also Fig* consolidation *f*; *(of position, power)* renforcement *m*

consoling [kən'səʊlɪŋ] *adj* réconfortant(e)

consonant ['kɒnsənənt] **1** *n* consonne *f*
2 *adj Formal* **c.** en accord avec

consort ['kɒnsɔːt] *n (spouse of monarch)* époux (épouse) *m,f*; **(prince) c.** prince *m* consort

▸**consort with** [kən'sɔːt] *vt insep* frayer avec, fréquenter

consortium [kən'sɔːtɪəm] *(pl* **consortiums** *or* **consortia** [kən'sɔːtɪə]) *n Com* consortium *m*

conspicuous [kən'spɪkjʊəs] *adj (easily visible)* bien visible; *(bravery)* remarquable; **to look c.** ne pas passer inaperçu(e); **to make oneself c.** se faire remarquer; **in a c. position** en évidence; **to be c. by one's absence** briller par son absence; **c. consumption** consommation *f* ostentatoire

conspiracy [kən'spɪrəsɪ] *(pl* **conspiracies)** *n* conspiration *f*; **c. theory** = théorie postulant l'existence d'un complot pour expliquer des événements demeurés mystérieux

conspirator [kən'spɪrətə(r)] *n* conspirateur(trice) *m,f*

conspiratorial [kənspɪrə'tɔːrɪəl] *adj* de conspirateur; **a c. wink** un coup d'œil complice

conspire [kən'spaɪə(r)] *vi (of person)* se liguer (**against/with** contre/avec); *(for political reasons)* conspirer (**against/with** contre/avec); **circumstances conspired against me** les circonstances se sont liguées contre moi

constant ['kɒnstənt] **1** *n Math & Phys* constante *f*
2 *adj* (**a**) *(unchanging) (price, temperature)* constant(e); *(friend)* fidèle (**b**) *(continual) (attention, noise, care)* continuel(elle); *(questions, complaints)* incessant(e); **a c. stream of insults** un flot d'injures ininterrompu

constellation [kɒnstə'leɪʃən] *n* constellation *f*

consternation [kɒnstə'neɪʃən] *n* consternation *f*

constipated ['kɒnstɪpeɪtɪd] *adj also Fig* constipé(e)

constipation [kɒnstɪ'peɪʃən] *n* constipation *f*

constituency [kən'stɪtjʊənsɪ] *(pl* **constituencies***) n* circonscription *f* (électorale)

constituent [kən'stɪtjʊənt] **1** *n* (**a**) *Pol* électeur(trice) *m,f* (**b**) *(part)* élément *m* constitutif
2 *adj* constitutif(ive); **c. part** élément *m* constitutif

constitute ['kɒnstɪtjuːt] *vt* constituer

constitution [kɒnstɪ'tjuːʃən] *n* (**a**) *(of state, organization)* constitution *f* (**b**) *(of person)* constitution *f*; **to have a strong c.** avoir une santé de fer; **to have a weak c.** être de santé fragile

constitutional [kɒnstɪ'tjuːʃənəl] **1** *n (walk)* (courte) promenade *f*
2 *adj (reform, decision)* constitutionnel(elle); **c. law** droit *m* constitutionnel

constrain [kən'streɪn] *vt* contraindre, obliger (**to do** à faire); **to feel constrained to do sth** se sentir obligé(e) de faire qch

constraint [kən'streɪnt] *n* contrainte *f*; **to place constraints upon** imposer des contraintes à; **under c.** sous la contrainte

constrict [kən'strɪkt] *vt (blood vessel)* resserrer; *(movement)* gêner; **to feel constricted** se sentir à l'étroit

constriction [kən'strɪkʃən] *n (of blood vessel)* constriction *f*; *(of person)* gêne *f*

construct 1 *n* ['kɒnstrʌkt] *(idea)* concept *m*
2 *vt* [kən'strʌkt] construire

construction [kən'strʌkʃən] *n* (**a**) *(building)* & *Gram* construction *f*; **under c.** en construction; **the c. industry** l'industrie *f* du bâtiment, le bâtiment; **c. paper** papier *m* cartonné de couleur *(pour travaux manuels)*; **c. site** chantier *m* (de construction); **c. worker** ouvrier *m* du bâtiment (**b**) *(interpretation)* **to put a favorable/an unfavorable c. on sth** bien/mal interpréter qch

constructive [kən'strʌktɪv] *adj* constructif(ive)

construe [kən'struː] *vt* interpréter

consul ['kɒnsəl] *n* consul *m*

consular ['kɒnsjʊlə(r)] *adj* consulaire

consulate ['kɒnsjʊlət] *n* consulat *m*

consult [kən'sʌlt] *vt* consulter (**on** sur *ou* à propos de)
2 *vi* consulter (**with sb/about sth** qn/à propos de qch)

consultancy [kən'sʌltənsɪ] *(pl* **consultancies***) n* (**a**) *(of doctor)* poste *m* de spécialiste *(haut placé dans la hiérarchie hospitalière)* (**b**) *Com* conseil *m*; **to do c. work** être consultant(e)

consultant [kən'sʌltənt] *n* (**a**) *(doctor)* spécialiste *mf (pratiquant à l'hôpital)* (**b**) *(adviser)* consultant(e) *m,f*

consultation [kɒnsəl'teɪʃən] *n (reference)* consultation *f*; *(discussion)* délibération *f*; **to hold a c. with sb** s'entretenir avec qn; **in c. with sb** en consultation avec qn

consume [kən'sjuːm] *vt (food, fuel, power)* consommer; **to be consumed with jealousy/desire** brûler de jalousie/désir

consumer [kən'sjuːmə(r)] *n (of product)* consommateur(trice) *m,f*; **c. durables** biens *mpl* de consommation durables; **c. goods** biens de consommation; *Econ* **c. price index** indice *m* des prix de détails; **c. protection** la défense du consommateur; **c. research** étude *f* de marché; **c. society** société *f* de

consommation; **c. spending** dépenses *fpl* de consommation

consumerism [kən'sjuːmərɪzəm] *n* consumérisme *m*

consummate 1 *adj* [kən'sʌmɪt] *(linguist, cook)* de premier ordre; *(snob, hypocrite)* parfait(e)
2 *vt* ['kɒnsəmeɪt] *(marriage, relationship)* consommer

consumption [kən'sʌmpʃən] *n* (**a**) *(of goods, resources)* consommation *f*; **unfit for human c.** impropre à la consommation (**b**) *Old-fashioned Med (tuberculosis)* consomption *f*

cont. *(abbr* **continued***)* **c. on page 14** suite (à la) page 14

contact ['kɒntækt] **1** *n* (**a**) *(act of touching)* contact *m*; **to be in/come into c. with** être en/entrer en contact avec; **to make c. with sb** prendre contact avec qn; **to lose c. with sb** perdre contact avec qn; **to get in c. with sb** contacter qn; **c. lenses**, *Fam* **contacts** lentilles *fpl* (de contact) (**b**) *(acquaintance)* relation *f*; **he has lots of contacts** il connaît beaucoup de monde
2 *vt* se mettre en rapport avec, contacter

contagious [kən'teɪdʒəs] *adj (disease)* contagieux(euse); *(laughter)* communicatif(ive)

contain [kən'teɪn] *vt* (**a**) *(hold)* contenir, renfermer; *(include)* contenir (**b**) *(control)* contenir; **to c. oneself** se contenir; **he was unable to c. his laughter** il ne put s'empêcher de rire

container [kən'teɪnə(r)] *n (for storage)* récipient *m*; *(for transport)* conteneur *m*; **c. ship** (navire *m*) porte-conteneurs *m inv*

contaminate [kən'tæmɪneɪt] *vt also Fig* contaminer

contamination [kəntæmɪ'neɪʃən] *n* contamination *f*

contd. *(abbr* **continued***)* **c. on page 14** suite (à la) page 14

contemplate ['kɒntempleɪt] **1** *vt (look at)* contempler; *(consider)* réfléchir à; **to c. doing sth** envisager de *ou* songer à faire qch
2 *vi (consider)* méditer

contemplation [kɒntem'pleɪʃən] *n* contemplation *f*

contemplative [kən'templətɪv] *adj* contemplatif(ive)

contemporary [kən'tempərərɪ] *(pl* **contemporaries***) n & adj* contemporain(e) *m,f*

contempt [kən'tempt] *n* mépris *m*; **to hold sb/sth in c.** avoir du mépris pour qn/qch, mépriser qn/qch; **to be beneath c.** être des plus méprisables; *Law* **c. of court** outrage *m* au tribunal

contemptible [kən'temptəbəl] *adj* méprisable

contemptuous [kən'temptjʊəs] *adj* méprisant(e); **to be c. of sth** mépriser qch

contend [kən'tend] **1** *vt (maintain)* **to c. that...** prétendre *ou* soutenir que...
2 *vi* (**a**) *(struggle)* **to c. with sth** lutter contre qch; *(difficulties)* affronter qch; **they still had the chairman to c. with** il leur restait à régler le problème du P.D.-G. (**b**) *(compete)* **to c. for sth** se battre pour qch; *(for job, contract)* être en concurrence pour qch

contender [kən'tendə(r)] *n (in sports)* concurrent(e) *m,f*; *(in election, for job)* candidat(e) *m,f*

content[1] ['kɒntent] *n* (**a**) *(quantity)* teneur *f*; *(of book, speech, essay)* fond *m*; **protein/fiber c.** teneur en protéines/fibres (**b**) **contents** *(of pockets, drawer, house)* contenu *m*; **contents page** *(of book)* table *f* des matières

content[2] [kən'tent] **1** *adj (happy)* content(e), satisfait(e) (**with** de); **to be c. with one's lot** se contenter de son sort
2 *vt* contenter; **to c. oneself with sth/with doing sth** se contenter de qch/de faire qch

contented [kən'tentɪd] *adj (person)* content(e), satisfait(e) (**with** de); *(smile, sigh)* de satisfaction

contention [kən'tenʃən] *n* (**a**) *(dispute)* dispute *f* (**b**) *(competition)* **to be in c. (for sth)** être en compétition (pour qch) (**c**) *(opinion)* affirmation *f*; **it is my c. that...** j'affirme que...

contentious [kən'tenʃəs] *adj (issue, views)* controversé(e); *(person)* querelleur(euse)

contentment [kən'tentmənt] *n* contentement *m*

contest 1 n ['kɒntest] *(competition)* concours m; *(for job, presidency)* lutte f; *(in boxing)* combat m

2 vt [kən'test] *(right, ability, will)* contester; **to c. a seat** se porter candidat(e); **a fiercely contested election** une élection très disputée

contestant [kən'testənt] n *(in competition, game)* concurrent(e) m,f; *(in election)* candidat(e) m,f

context ['kɒntekst] n contexte m; **in/out of c.** en/hors contexte; **to put sth into c.** replacer qch dans son contexte

contextualize [kən'tekstjuːəlaɪz] vt contextualiser

continent¹ ['kɒntɪnənt] n *(land mass)* continent m

continent² ['kɒntɪnənt] adj Med continent(e)

continental [kɒntɪ'nentəl] adj **(a)** *(in geography)* continental(e); **c. drift** dérive f des continents; **c. shelf** plate-forme f continentale **(b) c. breakfast** = petit déjeuner se composant de tartines et d'une boisson chaude

contingency [kən'tɪndʒənsɪ] *(pl* **contingencies)** n éventualité f; **to allow for every c.** parer à toute éventualité; **c. fund** caisse f ou fond m de prévoyance; **c. plan** plan m d'urgence

contingent [kən'tɪndʒənt] adj contingent(e); **to be c. upon sth** dépendre de qch

continual [kən'tɪnjʊəl] adj continuel(elle), incessant(e)

continuation [kəntɪnjʊ'eɪʃən] n *(of story)* suite f; *(of action, work)* prolongation f; *(of road)* prolongement m

continue [kən'tɪnjuː] **1** vt *(activity, journey)* continuer, poursuivre; *(after interruption)* reprendre, continuer; *(tradition)* perpétuer; **to c. to do** or **doing sth** continuer à ou de faire qch; **to be continued** à suivre; **continued on page 30** suite (à la) page 30

2 vi continuer; *(of situation)* se prolonger; **to c. on one's way** continuer ou poursuivre son chemin; **she will c. as director until December** elle continuera d'assumer ses fonctions de directrice jusqu'en décembre; **the situation cannot c.** cette situation ne peut pas durer

continuity [kɒntɪ'njuːɪtɪ] n continuité f; **c. girl** scripte f

continuous [kən'tɪnjʊəs] adj continu(e); *Sch & Univ* **c. assessment** contrôle m continu; *Comput* **c. paper** or **stationery** papier m (en) continu; *Cin* **c. performance** cinéma m permanent

contort [kən'tɔːt] **1** vt tordre

2 vi se tordre (**with** de)

contortion [kən'tɔːʃən] n *(of features)* crispation f; *(of body)* contorsion f

contour ['kɒntʊə(r)] n contour m; **c. (line)** courbe f de niveau; **c. map** carte f en courbes de niveau

contraband ['kɒntrəbænd] n contrebande f; **c. goods** marchandises fpl de contrebande

contraception [kɒntrə'sepʃən] n contraception f

contraceptive [kɒntrə'septɪv] **1** n contraceptif m

2 adj **c. pill** pilule f contraceptive

contract 1 n ['kɒntrækt] contrat m; **to be under c.** être sous contrat; **to enter into a c.** passer un contrat; **to take out a c. on sb** *(hire assassin)* engager un tueur à gages pour assassiner qn; **c. killer** tueur m à gages

2 vt [kən'trækt] *(disease, debt)* contracter; **to c. to do sth** s'engager (par contrat) à faire qch

3 vi [kən'trækt] *(shrink)* se contracter

▸**contract out** vt sep *(work)* sous-traiter

contraction [kən'trækʃən] n contraction f

contractor [kən'træktə(r)] n *(businessman)* entrepreneur m (en bâtiment); *(worker)* ouvrier m (en bâtiment)

contractual [kən'træktjʊəl] adj contractuel(elle)

contradict [kɒntrə'dɪkt] vt *(disagree with)* contredire; *(deny)* démentir; **to c. oneself** se contredire

contradiction [kɒntrə'dɪkʃən] n contradiction f; **it's a c. in terms** c'est parfaitement contradictoire

contradictory [kɒntrə'dɪktərɪ] adj contradictoire

contralto [kən'ræltəʊ] *(pl* **contraltos)** n contralto mf

contraption [kən'træpʃən] n Fam machin m, truc m

contrary 1 n ['kɒntrərɪ] contraire m; **on the c.** au contraire; **unless you hear to the c.** sauf avis contraire; **there was no evidence to the c.** il n'y avait pas de preuve du contraire

2 adj **(a)** ['kɒntrərɪ] *(opposite)* contraire (**to** à); *(ideas, interests)* opposé(e) (**to** à); **c. to my expectations** contre mon attente; **c. to popular belief** contrairement à ce que croient la plupart des gens **(b)** [kən'treərɪ] *(awkward)* contrariant(e)

contrast 1 n ['kɒntrɑːst] contraste m (**between** entre); **in c. with** or **to** par opposition à; **by c.** par contraste

2 vt [kən'trɑːst] mettre en contraste (**with** avec)

3 vi [kən'trɑːst] faire contraste (**with** avec)

contrasting [kən'trɑːstɪŋ] adj *(attitudes, lifestyles)* qui fait contraste; *(colors)* opposé(e), contrasté(e)

contravene [kɒntrə'viːn] vt enfreindre

contravention [kɒntrə'venʃən] n *(of law)* infraction f (**of** à); **in c. of a treaty** en violation d'un traité

contribute [kən'trɪbjuːt] **1** vt *(money)* verser; *(time, clothes)* donner; **to c. an article to a newspaper** écrire un article pour un journal; **he didn't c. anything to the discussion** il n'a pas pris part à la discussion

2 vi **(a)** *(give money, goods, etc.)* contribuer (**to** à); *(to charity)* donner (**to** à); *(to newspaper)* collaborer (**to** à); **to c. to a discussion** prendre part à une discussion **(b)** *Fin (to pension fund)* cotiser (**to** à)

contribution [kɒntrɪ'bjuːʃən] n **(a)** *(of money, goods, etc.)* contribution f (**to** à); **the chocolate mousse was David's c.** c'est David qu'il faut remercier pour la mousse au chocolat **(b)** *Fin (to pension fund)* cotisation f

contributor [kən'trɪbjʊtə(r)] n *(to charity)* donateur(trice) m,f; *(to newspaper)* collaborateur(trice) m,f (**to** de)

contributory [kən'trɪbjʊtərɪ] adj *(cause, factor)* concourant(e); **to be a c. factor in sth** concourir à qch; *Law* **c. negligence** manque m de précautions; *Fin* **c. pension plan** système m de retraite par répartition

contrite ['kɒntraɪt] adj contrit(e)

contrition [kən'trɪʃən] n contrition f

contrivance [kən'traɪvəns] n *(device)* appareil m; *(scheme, plan)* système m

contrive [kən'traɪv] vt inventer; **to c. to do sth** trouver le moyen de faire qch

contrived [kən'traɪvd] adj forcé(e), qui manque de naturel

control [kən'trəʊl] **1** n **(a)** *(power, restriction)* contrôle m; **to impose controls on prices** imposer le contrôle des prix; **to take c. (of the situation)** prendre les choses en main; **to have c. over** *(power)* contrôler; *(authority)* avoir de l'autorité sur; **to be in c. of sth** contrôler qch; **to be back in c.** avoir repris le contrôle; **to get out of c.** devenir incontrôlable; **to let sth get out of c.** perdre le contrôle de qch; **to bring a fire under c.** maîtriser un incendie; **to keep one's feelings under c.** maîtriser ses émotions; **everything is under c.** je domine/nous dominons/*etc.* la situation; **to lose c. (of oneself)** ne plus être maître de soi; **to regain c. (of oneself)** se ressaisir; *Pej* **c. freak** = personne qui veut tout régenter; **c. group** groupe m témoin; **c. tower** *(at airport)* tour f de contrôle **(b)** *(device)* **the controls** les commandes fpl; **to be at the controls** être aux commandes; **c. panel** tableau m de bord

2 vt *(pt & pp* **controlled)** *(production, expenditure, prices)* contrôler; *(business)* diriger; *(child, pupils)* avoir de l'autorité sur; *(disease)* maintenir à un niveau raisonnable; *(vehicle)* garder le contrôle de; **to c. oneself** se maîtriser; **to c. one's anger** maîtriser sa colère

controlled [kən'trəʊld] adj *(person)* maître de soi, posé(e); *(experiment, explosion)* contrôlé(e)

controlling interest [kən'trəʊlɪŋ'ɪntrest] n *Fin* participation f majoritaire

controversial [kɒntrə'vɜːʃəl] *adj* **to be c.** *(of movie, decision)* être controversé(e); *(of person)* être provocateur(trice)

controversy ['kɒntrəvɜːsɪ, kən'trɒvəsɪ] *(pl* **controversies**) *n* controverse *f*, polémique *f*; **to cause a lot of c.** provoquer une grande controverse *ou* une vive polémique

conundrum [kə'nʌndrəm] *n (riddle)* devinette *f*; *(mystery)* énigme *f*

conurbation [kɒnɜː'beɪʃən] *n* conurbation *f*

convalesce [kɒnvə'les] *vi* être en convalescence

convalescence [kɒnvə'lesəns] *n* convalescence *f*

convalescent [kɒnvə'lesənt] *adj (patient)* convalescent(e); **c. home** maison *f* de repos

convection [kən'vekʃən] *n* convection *f*; **c. heater** convecteur *m*; **c. oven** four *m* à chaleur tournante

convene [kən'viːn] **1** *vt (meeting)* convoquer
2 *vi (of meeting, committee)* se réunir

convenience [kən'viːnɪəns] *n* commodité *f*; **at your c.** quand cela vous conviendra; *Formal* **at your earliest c.** dans les meilleurs délais; **c. food** aliments *mpl* tout prêts; **c. store** = supérette de quartier qui reste ouverte tard le soir, *Can* dépanneur *m*

convenient [kən'viːnɪənt] *adj (arrangement, method)* commode, pratique; **to be c. (for sb)** *(of arrangement)* être commode *ou* pratique (pour qn); *(of time)* convenir (à qn)

convent ['kɒnvənt] *n Rel* couvent *m*; **c. school** école *f* tenue par des sœurs

convention [kən'venʃən] *n* **(a)** *(conference)* convention *f*, congrès *m* **(b)** *(agreement)* convention *f* **(c)** *(established practice)* usage *m*; **the c. is that...** l'usage veut que...

conventional [kən'venʃənəl] *adj (behavior, ideas)* conventionnel(elle); *(person)* conformiste; **c. warfare** guerre *f* conventionnelle; **c. weapon** arme *f* conventionnelle; **c. wisdom** sagesse *f* populaire

converge [kən'vɜːdʒ] *vi* converger (**on** sur)

convergence [kən'vɜːdʒəns] *n* convergence *f*

conversant [kən'vɜːsənt] *adj* **to be c. with sth** s'y connaître en qch; *(with events, developments)* être au courant de qch

conversation [kɒnvə'seɪʃən] *n* conversation *f*; **to have a c. with sb** avoir une conversation avec qn; **to make the c.** faire la conversation; **the vase is quite a c. piece** le vase suscite bien des commentaires; *Fam* **to be a c. stopper** *or* **killer** arrêter net la conversation

conversational [kɒnvə'seɪʃənəl] *adj (style)* de la conversation; *Comput (mode)* dialogue; **in a c. tone** sur le ton de la conversation

conversationalist [kɒnvə'seɪʃənəlɪst] *n* **to be a good c.** avoir de la conversation; **I'm not much of a c.** je ne suis pas brillant causeur

converse¹ [kən'vɜːs] *vi (talk)* converser (**about** sur), s'entretenir (**about** de)

converse² ['kɒnvɜːs] *n (opposite)* **the c.** le contraire

conversely [kən'vɜːslɪ] *adv* inversement

conversion [kən'vɜːʃən] *n* **(a)** *(transformation)* conversion *f*; *(of building)* aménagement *m*; **c. table** *(for measurements)* table *f* de conversion **(b)** *(in football)* transformation *f*

convert 1 *n* ['kɒnvɜːt] *Rel & Fig* converti(e) *m,f* (**to** à)
2 *vt* [kən'vɜːt] **(a)** *Rel & Fig* convertir (**to** à); *(building)* aménager (**into** en) **(b)** *(in football)* **to c. after a touchdown** transformer un essai
3 *vi* [kən'vɜːt] *Rel & Fig* se convertir (**to** à)

convertible [kən'vɜːtəbəl] **1** *n (car)* décapotable *f*
2 *adj (sofa)* convertible; *(car)* décapotable; **c. currency** monnaie *f ou* devise *f* convertible

convex [kɒn'veks] *adj* convexe

convey [kən'veɪ] *vt* **(a)** *(communicate)* transmettre; **to c. one's meaning** communiquer sa pensée **(b)** *(transport)* transporter

conveyance [kən'veɪəns] *n* **(a)** *(of goods, passengers)* transport *m* **(b)** *Old-fashioned (vehicle)* véhicule *m*

conveyancing [kən'veɪənsɪŋ] *n Law* procédure *f* translative de propriété

conveyor belt [kən'veɪəbelt] *n* convoyeur *m*, tapis *m* roulant

convict 1 *n* ['kɒnvɪkt] détenu(e) *m,f*
2 *vt* [kən'vɪkt] **to c. sb (of)** déclarer qn coupable (de)

conviction [kən'vɪkʃən] *n* **(a)** *Law* condamnation *f*; **to have no previous convictions** n'avoir jamais été condamné(e) **(b)** *(belief)* conviction *f*; **to lack c.** manquer de conviction

convince [kən'vɪns] *vt* convaincre (**of/that** de/que); **I was convinced I was right** j'étais convaincu d'avoir raison

convincing [kən'vɪnsɪŋ] *adj* convaincant(e); *(defeat)* décisif(ive)

convivial [kən'vɪvɪəl] *adj (person)* chaleureux(euse); *(atmosphere)* joyeux(euse)

convoluted ['kɒnvəluːtɪd] *adj (argument, explanation)* compliqué(e)

convoy ['kɒnvɔɪ] *n* convoi *m*

convulse [kən'vʌls] *vt* secouer; **to be convulsed with laughter/pain** se tordre de rire/de douleur

convulsions [kən'vʌlʃənz] *npl Med* convulsions *fpl*; *Fig* **to be in c.** *(of laughter)* se tordre

coo [kuː] *(pt & pp* **cooed***) vi (of dove)* roucouler; *Fam* **to c. over sb/sth** s'extasier devant qn/qch

cook [kʊk] **1** *n* cuisinier(ère) *m,f*; *Prov* **too many cooks spoil the soup** *or* **stew** on n'arrive jamais à rien quand tout le monde met son grain de sel
2 *vt (meal)* préparer; *(food)* (faire) cuire; *Fig* **to c. the books** falsifier les comptes
3 *vi (of food)* cuire; *(of person)* faire la cuisine; *Fam* **what's cooking?** qu'est-ce qui se passe?

▶**cook up** *vt sep (excuse, story)* inventer

cookbook ['kʊkbʊk] *n* livre *m* de cuisine

cookery ['kʊkərɪ] *n* cuisine *f*

cookie ['kʊkɪ] *n* **(a)** biscuit *m*; *Fam* **that's the way the c. crumbles!** c'est la vie(, que veux-tu)!; **c. cutter** emporte-pièce *m*; **c. jar** bocal *m* à biscuits; *Fig* **to be caught with one's hand in the c. jar** être pris en flagrant délit **(b)** *Fam (person)* **a tough c.** un(e) dur(e) à cuire; **a smart c.** un(e) malin(igne) **(c)** *Comput* cookie *m*, cafteur *m*, *Can* témoin *m*

cooking ['kʊkɪŋ] *n (process)* cuisson *f*; *(activity)* cuisine *f*; **to do the c.** faire la cuisine; **c. apple** pomme *f* à cuire; **c. chocolate** chocolat *m* à cuire; **c. time** temps *m* de cuisson; **c. utensils** ustensiles *mpl* de cuisine

cookout ['kʊkaʊt] *n* barbecue *m*

cool [kuːl] **1** *n* **(a)** *(coldness)* fraîcheur *f*
(b) *(calm)* **to keep/to lose one's c.** garder/perdre son sang-froid
2 *adj* **(a)** *(wind, weather, drink)* frais (fraîche); *(coffee, bathwater)* tiède; **it's c. outside** il fait frais dehors; *Fam* **I lost a c. thousand** j'ai bien perdu mille dollars
(b) *(calm)* calme; *(unfriendly)* froid(e); **c. as a cucumber** parfaitement calme; **keep c.!** ne t'angoisse pas!; **to keep a c. head** garder la tête froide; **to be a c. customer** *(bold)* être culotté(e); *(self-possessed)* avoir beaucoup de sang-froid
(c) *Fam (good)* cool *inv*; *(trendy)* branché(e)
3 *adv Fam* **to play it c.** rester calme
4 *vt* rafraîchir, refroidir; *Fam* **c. it!** on se calme!; *Fam* **to c. one's heels** poireauter
5 *vi (of liquid)* refroidir; *(of anger)* passer; *(of passion, enthusiasm)* se refroidir

▶**cool down 1** *vt sep* **(a)** *(of cold drink)* rafraîchir **(b)** *(make calm)* calmer
2 *vi* **(a)** *(of weather)* se rafraîchir; *(of liquid)* refroidir **(b)** *(become calm)* se calmer

▶**cool off** *vi* **(a)** *(of person)* se rafraîchir **(b)** *(of passion, enthusiasm)* se refroidir; *(of angry person)* se calmer

coolant ['kuːlənt] *n* liquide *m* de refroidissement

cool-headed ['ku:l'hedɪd] *adj* calme; **to remain c.** garder la tête froide

cooling ['ku:lɪŋ] *adj (drink)* rafraîchissant(e); *(agent)* réfrigérant(e); *Ind & Com* **c.-off period** période *f* de réflexion; **c. tower** tour *f* de réfrigération

coop [ku:p] *n (for chickens)* poulailler *m*; *Fig* **to fly the c.** se faire la malle

▸**coop up** *vt sep* **to keep sb cooped up** tenir qn enfermé(e); **to feel cooped up** se sentir à l'étroit

co-op ['kəʊɒp] *n* coopérative *f*

cooperate [kəʊ'ɒpəreɪt] *vi* coopérer (**with** avec)

cooperation [kəʊɒpə'reɪʃən] *n* coopération *f*

cooperative [kəʊ'ɒpərətɪv] **1** *n* coopérative *f*
　2 *adj* coopératif(ive)

coopt [kəʊ'ɒpt] *vt* coopter (**onto** à)

coordinate 1 *n* [kəʊ'ɔ:dɪnət] (**a**) *Math* coordonnée *f* (**b**) **coordinates** *(clothes)* coordonnés *mpl*
　2 *vt* [kəʊ'ɔ:dɪneɪt] coordonner

coordination [kəʊɔ:dɪ'neɪʃən] *n* coordination *f*

coordinator [kəʊ'ɔ:dɪneɪtə(r)] *n* coordinateur(trice) *m,f*

co-owner ['kəʊ'əʊnə(r)] *n* copropriétaire *mf*

cop [kɒp] **1** *n Fam (policeman)* flic *m*; **to play cops and robbers** jouer aux gendarmes et aux voleurs
　2 *vt (pt & pp* **copped**) attraper, pincer; **to get copped** *(by police)* se faire pincer

▸**cop out** *vi Fam (avoid responsibility)* se défiler; *(choose easy solution)* choisir la solution de facilité; **to c. out of doing sth** ne pas avoir le cran de faire qch

coparent [kəʊ'peərənt] *n* coparent *m*

coparenthood [kəʊ'peərənthʊd] *n* coparentalité *f*

cope [kəʊp] *vi* se débrouiller, s'en tirer; **to c. with** *(demand, situation)* faire face à; *(problem, difficulty)* venir à bout de; **he can't c. with his job** il ne s'en sort pas dans son travail; **I just can't c.** je n'y arrive pas

Copenhagen [kəʊpən'heɪgən] *n* Copenhague

copier ['kɒpɪə(r)] *n (photocopier)* (photo)copieuse *f*

copilot ['kəʊpaɪlət] *n* copilote *m*

copious ['kəʊpɪəs] *adj* copieux(euse); *(tears, notes, amounts)* abondant(e)

cop-out ['kɒpaʊt] *n Fam* solution *f* de facilité

copper ['kɒpə(r)] **1** *n* (**a**) *(metal)* cuivre *m*; *Fam* **coppers** *(coins)* petite monnaie *f* (**b**) *Fam (policeman)* flic *m*
　2 *adj* **c.(-colored)** *(couleur)* cuivre *inv*, cuivré(e)

copperplate ['kɒpəpleɪt] *n* **c. (writing)** écriture *f* moulée

coppice ['kɒpɪs] *n* taillis *m*

coproduce [kəʊprə'dju:s] *vt Cin, Theat & TV* coproduire

coproducer ['kəʊprə'dju:sə(r)] *n Cin & TV* coproducteur(trice) *m,f*

coproduction ['kəʊprə'dʌkʃən] *n Cin & TV* coproduction *f*

copse [kɒps] *n* taillis *m*

copublish ['kəʊ'pʌblɪʃ] *vt* coéditer

copublisher ['kəʊ'pʌblɪʃə(r)] *n* coéditeur(trice) *m,f*

copublishing ['kəʊ'pʌblɪʃɪŋ] *n* coédition *f*

copulate ['kɒpjʊleɪt] *vi* copuler

copulation [kɒpjʊ'leɪʃən] *n* copulation *f*

copy ['kɒpɪ] **1** *(pl* **copies**) *n* (**a**) *(reproduction)* copie *f* (**b**) *(of letter, document)* copie *f*, double *m* (**c**) *(of book)* exemplaire *m*; *(of newspaper)* numéro *m* (**d**) *Journ (written material)* copie *f*; **the story made good c.** ça a fait un bon sujet d'article; **c. editor** *(in journalism)* secrétaire *mf* de rédaction; *(in publishing)* réviseur *m*
　2 *vt (pt & pp* **copied**) *(painting, document, text) & Comput* copier; **to c. sth to disk** copier qch sur disquette; **to c. and paste sth** faire un copier-coller sur qch
　3 *vi (on test)* copier

copy-and-paste ['kɒpɪənd'peɪst] *n Comput* copier-coller *m*

copybook ['kɒpɪbʊk] *n* cahier *m* d'écriture; **c. example** exemple *m* classique

copycat ['kɒpɪkæt] *Fam* **1** *n* copieur(euse) *m,f*
　2 *adj* **c. crime/murder** délit *m*/meurtre *m* inspiré par un autre

copyright ['kɒpɪraɪt] **1** *n* droit *m* d'auteur, copyright *m*; **to be out of c.** être tombé(e) dans le domaine public
　2 *adj* protégé(e) par le droit d'auteur

copywriter ['kɒpɪraɪtə(r)] *n* rédacteur(trice) *m,f* publicitaire

coquette [kɒ'ket] *n Lit* coquette *f*

coral ['kɒrəl] *n* corail *m*; **c. island** île *f* corallienne; **c. reef** récif *m* corallien; **the C. Sea** la mer de Corail

cord [kɔ:d] *n* (**a**) *(string)* grosse ficelle *f*; *(for curtains, pajamas)* cordon *m* (**b**) *(corduroy)* velours *m* côtelé; **a c. jacket** une veste en velours côtelé; **cords** pantalon *m* en velours côtelé

cordial ['kɔ:dɪəl] **1** *n (drink)* sirop *m*
　2 *adj (friendly)* cordial(e)

cordless ['kɔ:dlɪs] *adj* sans fil; **c. telephone** (téléphone *m*) sans-fil *m*

cordon ['kɔ:dən] *n* cordon *m*

▸**cordon off** *vt sep (road)* barrer; *(area)* boucler

corduroy ['kɔ:dərɔɪ] *n* velours *m* côtelé; **c. pants** pantalon *m* en velours côtelé

core [kɔ:(r)] **1** *n (of apple)* trognon *m*; *(of earth, magnet)* noyau *m*; *(of nuclear reactor)* centre *m*; *(of argument, problem)* cœur *m*; **hard c.** noyau dur; **he's rotten to the c.** il est pourri jusqu'à la moelle; *Sch* **c. curriculum** tronc *m* commun
　2 *vt (apple)* évider

Corfu [kɔ:'fu:] *n* Corfou

coriander [kɒrɪ'ændə(r)] *n* coriandre *f*

cork [kɔ:k] **1** *n (material)* liège *m*; *(stopper)* bouchon *m* (en liège)
　2 *vt (bottle)* boucher

corked [kɔ:kt] *adj (wine)* bouchonné(e)

corkscrew ['kɔ:kskru:] *n* tire-bouchon *m*

cormorant ['kɔ:mərənt] *n* cormoran *m*

corn¹ [kɔ:n] *n (maize)* maïs *m*; **c. on the cob** maïs en épi; **c. bread** pain *m* à la farine de maïs; **c. chip** tortilla *f*; **c. dog** = saucisse de Francfort enrobée de farine de maïs, frite et servie sur un bâtonnet; **c. meal** farine *f* de maïs; **c. oil** huile *f* de maïs

corn² [kɔ:n] *n (on foot)* cor *m*

cornea ['kɔ:nɪə] *n Anat* cornée *f*

corned beef ['kɔ:nd'bi:f] *n* corned-beef *m*

corner ['kɔ:nə(r)] **1** *n* (**a**) *(of room, street, page, screen)* coin *m*; **out of the c. of one's eye** du coin de l'œil; **it's just around the c.** c'est juste au coin; *Fig* **Christmas is just around the c.** on est tout près de Noël; **to turn the c.** tourner au coin de la rue; *Fig (of economy, company)* passer la période critique; **c. store** épicerie *f* du coin, *Can* dépanneur *m* (**b**) *(bend in road)* tournant *m*; *Fig* **to cut corners** *(with time)* faire les choses à la va-vite; *(with materials, money)* faire les choses à l'économie (**c**) *(in soccer)* **c. (kick)** corner *m*; **to take a c.** tirer un corner
　2 *vt* (**a**) *(person, animal)* acculer (**b**) *(market)* accaparer
　3 *vi (of car, driver)* prendre un virage

cornerstone ['kɔ:nəstəʊn] *n also Fig* pierre *f* angulaire

cornet [kɔ:'net] *n (musical instrument)* cornet *m* à pistons

cornfield ['kɔ:nfi:ld] *n (of maize)* champ *m* de maïs

cornflakes ['kɔ:nfleɪks] *npl* corn flakes *mpl*

cornflower ['kɔ:nflaʊə(r)] *n (plant)* bleuet *m*; **c. blue** bleu barbeau *inv*

cornice ['kɔ:nɪs] *n* corniche *f*

Cornish ['kɔ:nɪʃ] **1** *npl* **the C.** *(people)* les Cornouaillais *mpl*
　2 *n (language)* cornique *m*
　3 *adj* cornouaillais(e)

cornstarch ['kɔ:nstɑ:tʃ] *n Culin* fécule *f* de maïs

Cornwall ['kɔ:nwəl] *n* Cornouailles *f*

corny ['kɔːnɪ] *adj Fam (joke)* nul (nulle); *(movie, novel)* tarte

corollary [kə'rɒlərɪ] *(pl* **corollaries)** *n* corollaire *m*

coronary ['kɒrənərɪ] *Med* **1** *(pl* **coronaries)** *n* infarctus *m* (du myocarde)

2 *adj* coronarien(enne); **c. heart disease** maladie *f* coronarienne; **c. thrombosis** infarctus *m* du myocarde

coronation [kɒrə'neɪʃən] *n* couronnement *m*

coroner ['kɒrənə(r)] *n Law* coroner *m*

corporal[1] ['kɔːpərəl] *adj* corporel(elle); **c. punishment** châtiment *m* corporel

corporal[2] ['kɔːpərəl] *n Mil (in infantry)* caporal *m*; *(in artillery)* brigadier *m*

corporate ['kɔːpərət] *adj Com (of companies in general)* d'entreprise; *(of a specific company)* d'une société; **c. culture** culture *f* d'entreprise; **c. image** image *f* de marque de l'entreprise

corporation [kɔːpə'reɪʃən] *n Com* société *f*; **c. tax** impôt *m* sur les sociétés

corps [kɔː(r)] *(pl* **corps** [kɔːz]) *n Mil* corps *m*

corpse [kɔːps] *n* cadavre *m*; **a lifeless c.** un corps inerte

corpulent ['kɔːpjʊlənt] *adj* corpulent(e)

corpuscle ['kɔːpʌsəl] *n Anat* corpuscule *m*; **red/white (blood) corpuscles** globules *mpl* rouges/blancs

corral [kɒ'rɑːl] *n* corral *m*

correct [kə'rekt] **1** *adj* **(a)** *(accurate)* exact(e); **to prove c.** se vérifier, s'avérer juste; **if my memory is c.** si j'ai bonne mémoire; **he is c.** *(right)* il a raison; **that's c.** c'est exact **(b)** *(person, behavior)* correct(e), convenable; **it wasn't the c. thing to say/do** ce n'était pas la chose à dire/faire

2 *vt (homework, proofs, error)* corriger; *(misunderstanding)* dissiper; **c. me if I'm wrong, but...** reprenez-moi si je me trompe, mais...; **I stand corrected** j'avais tort

correction [kə'rekʃən] *n* correction *f*; **c. fluid** liquide *m* correcteur

corrective [kə'rektɪv] **1** *n* correctif *m*

2 *adj (action, measure)* rectificatif(ive), correctif(ive); **c. surgery** chirurgie *f* réparatrice

correlate ['kɒrɪleɪt] **1** *vt* mettre en rapport *ou* en corrélation (**with** avec); **they are closely correlated** ils sont étroitement liés

2 *vi* être en rapport *ou* en corrélation (**with** avec)

correlation [kɒrɪ'leɪʃən] *n* corrélation *f*

correspond [kɒrɪs'pɒnd] *vi* **(a)** *(be in accordance)* correspondre (**with** *or* **to** à) **(b)** *(be equivalent)* correspondre (**to** à), être l'équivalent (**to** de) **(c)** *(write letters)* correspondre (**with** avec)

correspondence [kɒrɪs'pɒndəns] *n* **(a)** *(relationship)* rapport *m* (**between** entre) **(b)** *(letter-writing)* correspondance *f*; **I don't get much c.** je ne reçois pas beaucoup de courrier; **c. course** cours *m* par correspondance

correspondent [kɒrɪs'pɒndənt] *n* correspondant(e) *m,f*

corresponding [kɒrɪ'spɒndɪŋ] *adj* correspondant(e)

corridor ['kɒrɪdɔː(r)] *n* couloir *m*, corridor *m*; *Fig* **the corridors of power** les hautes sphères *fpl* du pouvoir

corroborate [kə'rɒbəreɪt] *vt* corroborer, confirmer

corroboration [kərɒbə'reɪʃən] *n* corroboration *f*, confirmation *f*

corrode [kə'rəʊd] **1** *vt (metal)* corroder, attaquer; *Fig (society)* miner; *(optimism, friendship)* entamer

2 *vi (of metal)* se corroder

corrosion [kə'rəʊʒən] *n* corrosion *f*

corrosive [kə'rəʊsɪv] **1** *n* corrosif *m*

2 *adj* corrosif(ive)

corrugated ['kɒrəgeɪtɪd] *adj (cardboard)* ondulé(e); **c. iron** tôle *f* ondulée

corrupt [kə'rʌpt] **1** *adj (dishonest)* corrompu(e)

2 *vt* corrompre; *Comput* altérer; **to c. sb's morals** dépraver qn

corruption [kə'rʌpʃən] *n* corruption *f*

corset ['kɔːsɪt] *n* corset *m*

Corsica ['kɔːsɪkə] *n* la Corse

Corsican ['kɔːsɪkən] **1** *n* Corse *mf*

2 *adj* corse

cortege [kɔː'teʒ] *n* cortège *m*

cortex ['kɔːteks] *(pl* **cortices** ['kɔːtɪsiːz]) *n* cortex *m*

cortisone ['kɔːtɪzəʊn] *n* cortisone *f*

cos [kɒz] *conj Fam (abbr* **because)** parce que

cosmetic [kɒz'metɪk] **1** *n* cosmétique *m*, produit *m* de beauté; **to wear a lot of cosmetics** se maquiller beaucoup

2 *adj Fig (superficial)* superficiel(elle); **c. surgery** chirurgie *f* esthétique

cosmic ['kɒzmɪk] *adj* cosmique; *Fig* prodigieux(euse)

cosmonaut ['kɒzmənɔːt] *n* cosmonaute *mf*

cosmopolitan [kɒzmə'pɒlɪtən] *adj* cosmopolite

cosmos ['kɒzmɒs] *n* cosmos *m*

cosset ['kɒsɪt] *vt* couver, choyer

cost [kɒst] **1** *n* **(a)** *(price)* coût *m*; *Law* **costs** dépens *mpl*; *also Fig* **at little/great c.** à peu de/à grands frais; **at great c. to his health** au prix de sa santé; *Econ* **c. of living** coût de la vie; *Com* **c. of production** coût de production; *Fin* **c. accounting** comptabilité *f* analytique; *Econ* **c. benefit analysis** analyse *f* coûts-bénéfices; *Com* **c. price** prix *m* coûtant **(b)** *(idioms)* **to count the c. of sth** tirer la leçon de qch; **at all costs** à tout prix; **as I found out to my c.** comme je l'ai appris à mes dépens

2 *vt* **(a)** *(pt & pp* **cost)** *also Fig* coûter; **how much does it c.?** combien ça coûte?; **it costs $25** ça coûte *ou* c'est 25 dollars; **whatever it costs** quel qu'en soit le prix; *Fam* **to c. a fortune** *or* **the earth** coûter les yeux de la tête; **the attempt cost him his life** cette tentative lui a coûté la vie **(b)** *(pt & pp* **costed)** *Com (budget)* évaluer le coût de

co-star ['kəʊstɑː(r)] **1** *n (in movie)* partenaire *mf* à l'écran

2 *vt (pt & pp* **co-starred)** **the film co-stars Nicole Kidman** Nicole Kidman joue aussi dans ce film; **co-starring Ewan McGregor** avec Ewan McGregor

3 *vi* jouer dans un des rôles principaux

Costa Rica ['kɒstə'riːkə] *n* le Costa Rica

Costa Rican ['kɒstə'riːkən] **1** *n* Costaricien(enne) *m,f*

2 *adj* costaricien(enne)

cost-effective [kɒstɪ'fektɪv] *adj* rentable

costing ['kɒstɪŋ] *n Com (of job)* évaluation *f* du coût; *(of article)* évaluation *f* du prix de revient

costly ['kɒstlɪ] *adj* cher (chère), coûteux(euse); **it was a c. mistake** c'est une erreur qui a coûté cher

costume ['kɒstjʊm] *n* costume *m*; **c. drama** film *m*/pièce *f* en costumes d'époque; **c. jewelry** bijoux *mpl* fantaisie

cot [kɒt] *n (folding bed)* lit pliant

cottage ['kɒtɪdʒ] *n* = petite maison, généralement à la campagne; **thatched c.** chaumière *f*; **c. cheese** fromage *m* blanc (égoutté); **c. industry** industrie *f* artisanale; *(at home)* industrie familiale

cotton ['kɒtən] *n* coton *m*; **a c. shirt** une chemise en coton; **c. candy** barbe *f* à papa

▶**cotton on** *vi Fam* piger; **to c. on to sth** piger qch

▶**cotton to** *vi Fam* **(a)** *(take a liking to)* se prendre d'amitié pour; **I didn't c. to her at first** ça n'a pas accroché avec elle au début **(b)** *(approve of) (person)* avoir à la bonne; *(behaviour)* approuver de, voir d'un bon œil

couch [kaʊtʃ] **1** *n* divan *m*, canapé *m*; *(at doctor's)* lit *m*; *Fam* **to be a c. potato** passer sa vie devant la télé

2 *vt (express)* formuler

cougar ['kuːgə(r)] *n* cougar *m*, puma *m*

cough [kɒf] **1** *n* toux *f*; **to have a c.** tousser; **c. drop** pastille *f* pour la toux; **c. syrup** sirop *m* pour la toux

2 *vi* tousser

▶**cough up 1** *vt sep (phlegm, blood)* cracher; *Fam (money)* allonger

2 *vi Fam (pay)* allonger

could [kʊd] *modal aux v* (**a**) *(was able to)* **we couldn't do it** nous n'avons pas pu le faire; **he did what he c.** il a fait ce qu'il pouvait; **I c. hear them talking** je les entendais parler; **I c. have tried harder** j'aurais pu faire plus d'efforts; **he couldn't have been kinder** il a été on ne peut plus aimable; **how could you!** comment as-tu pu faire ça!; **I c. have hit him!** *(I was so angry)* je l'aurais battu!

(**b**) *(knew how to)* **I c. swim well at that age** à cet âge-là je savais déjà bien nager; **c. you speak French then?** tu parlais français à cette époque-là?

(**c**) *(indicating possibility)* **it c. be weeks before he's better** il pourrait se passer des semaines avant qu'il se rétablisse; **it c. have been worse** ça aurait pu être pire

(**d**) *(with requests)* **c. you get me some water?** est-ce que tu pourrais m'apporter de l'eau?

(**e**) *(in conditional, suggestions)* **(it) c. be** peut-être; **if I had more money I c. buy a new car** si j'avais plus d'argent je pourrais acheter une nouvelle voiture; **we c. always phone** on pourrait toujours téléphoner

couldn't ['kʊdənt] = **could not**

couldn't-care-less ['kʊdəntkeə'les] *adj* **c. attitude** je-m'en-foutisme *m*

council ['kaʊnsəl] *n* (**a**) *(assembly)* conseil *m* (**b**) *(local government)* municipalité *f*; **to be on the c.** être au conseil municipal

councilman ['kaʊnsɪlmæn] *n* conseiller *m* municipal

councilor ['kaʊnsɪlə(r)] *n* conseiller(ère) *m,f*, membre *m* du conseil

councilwoman ['kaʊnsɪlwʊmən] *n* conseillère *f* municipale

counsel ['kaʊnsəl] **1** *n* (**a**) *(advice)* conseil *m*, avis *m*; **to keep one's own c.** *(about plans)* garder ses projets pour soi; *(about opinions)* garder ses opinions pour soi (**b**) *(lawyer)* avocat(e) *m,f*; **c. for the defense** avocat *m* de la défense; **c. for the prosecution** procureur *m*

2 *vt (caution, patience)* conseiller; **to c. sb** *(advise)* conseiller qn; *(give psychological help to)* apporter une aide psychologique à qn; **to c. sb to do sth** conseiller à qn de faire qch

counseling ['kaʊnsəlɪŋ] *n* assistance *f* psychosociale

counselor ['kaʊnsələ(r)] *n* (**a**) *(adviser, therapist)* conseiller(ère) *m,f* (**b**) *Law* avocat(e) *m,f*

count[1] [kaʊnt] *n (nobleman)* comte *m*

count[2] [kaʊnt] **1** *n* (**a**) *(calculation)* compte *m*, comptage *m*; *(of votes)* dépouillement *m*; **at the last c.** au dernier comptage; **to keep c. of sth** tenir le compte de qch; **to lose c.** se perdre dans ses calculs; **I've lost c. of how many times I've asked you to...** je t'ai demandé je ne sais combien de fois de...

(**b**) *(in boxing)* & *Fig* **to be out for the c.** être K.-O.

(**c**) *Law* chef *m* d'accusation; *Fig* **on a number of counts** à plusieurs égards

2 *vt* (**a**) *(enumerate)* compter; **there were four of us counting/not counting the baby** nous étions quatre en comptant/sans compter le bébé

(**b**) *(consider)* considérer (**as** comme); **c. yourself lucky you weren't killed** estime-toi heureux de n'avoir pas été tué

3 *vi* (**a**) *(add up)* compter; **to c. (up) to ten** compter jusqu'à dix

(**b**) *(be important, valid)* compter; **that doesn't c.** ça ne compte pas; **it counts as one of my worst experiences** ça a été une de mes pires expériences

▶**count against** *vt insep* jouer contre

▶**count down** *vi* faire le compte à rebours

▶**count in** *vt sep (include)* compter; **c. me in!** j'en suis!

▶**count on** *vt insep* compter sur; **to c. on sb to do sth** compter sur qn pour faire qch

▶**count out** *vt sep* (**a**) *(money)* compter (**b**) *(exclude)* **c. me out!** ne comptez pas sur moi! (**c**) *(in boxing)* **to be counted out** être (mis(e)) K.-O.

▶**count up** *vt sep* compter

countable ['kaʊntəbəl] *adj* comptable

countdown ['kaʊntdaʊn] *n* compte *m* à rebours

countenance ['kaʊntɪnəns] *Formal* **1** *n* (**a**) *(face)* visage *m* (**b**) *(support)* **to give c. to** *(rumors)* accréditer; *(plans)* approuver

2 *vt (support)* approuver

counter[1] ['kaʊntə(r)] *n* (**a**) *(in store)* comptoir *m*; *(in supermarket)* rayon *m*; *(in bank)* guichet *m*; **available over the c.** *(medicine)* en vente libre; **to buy/to sell sth under the c.** acheter/vendre qch au noir (**b**) *(token in game)* jeton *m* (**c**) *(counting device)* compteur *m*

counter[2] ['kaʊntə(r)] **1** *adv* **c. to** contrairement à; **to run c. to** aller à l'encontre de

2 *vt* contrer; **to c. that...** riposter que...

3 *vi* riposter

counteract [kaʊntə'rækt] *vt (influence)* contrecarrer; *(rumors, effects)* neutraliser

counterattack ['kaʊntərətæk] **1** *n* contre-attaque *f*

2 *vt* & *vi* contre-attaquer

counterclockwise ['kaʊntə'klɒkwaɪz] **1** *adj* **in a c. direction** dans le sens inverse des aiguilles d'une montre

2 *adv* dans le sens inverse des aiguilles d'une montre

counterfeit ['kaʊntəfɪt] **1** *n* faux *m*

2 *adj* faux (fausse)

3 *vt* contrefaire

counterfoil ['kaʊntəfɔɪl] *n* talon *m*, souche *f*

counterintelligence ['kaʊntərɪn'telɪdʒəns] *n* contre-espionnage *m*

countermand ['kaʊntəmɑ:nd] *vt* annuler

countermeasure ['kaʊntəmeʒə(r)] *n* contre-mesure *f*

counteroffensive ['kaʊntərə'fensɪv] *n* contre-offensive *f*

counterpane ['kaʊntəpeɪn] *n* couvre-lit *m*

counterpart ['kaʊntəpɑ:t] *n (person)* homologue *mf*; *(system)* équivalent *m*

counterpoint ['kaʊntəpɔɪnt] *n Mus* contrepoint *m*

counterproductive ['kaʊntəprə'dʌktɪv] *adj* contre-productif(ive)

counterproposal ['kaʊntəprə'pəʊzəl] *n* contre-proposition *f*

counterrevolution ['kaʊntərevə'lu:ʃən] *n* contre-révolution *f*

counterrevolutionary ['kaʊntərevə'lu:ʃənərɪ] *n* & *adj* contre-révolutionnaire *mf*

countersign ['kaʊntəsaɪn] *vt* contresigner, viser

counterweight ['kaʊntəweɪt] *n* contrepoids *m*

countess ['kaʊntɪs] *n* comtesse *f*

countless ['kaʊntlɪs] *adj* innombrable; **on c. occasions** à maintes reprises; **c. times** un nombre incalculable de fois

country ['kʌntrɪ] *(pl* **countries)** *n* (**a**) *(land, nation)* pays *m*; *(homeland)* patrie *f* (**b**) *(as opposed to town)* campagne *f*; **in the c.** à la campagne; **c. and western (music)** country *m ou f*; **c. club** = club sportif ou de loisirs situé à la campagne

countryside ['kʌntrɪsaɪd] *n* campagne *f*

county ['kaʊntɪ] *(pl* **counties)** *n* comté *m*; **c. fair** fête *f* du comté; **c. seat** chef-lieu *m* de comté

coup [ku:] *n (surprising achievement)* (beau) coup *m*; *Pol* **c. (d'état)** coup *m* d'État

couple ['kʌpəl] **1** *n* (**a**) *(of things)* **a c. of** *(two)* deux; *(a few)* quelques (**b**) *(people)* couple *m*; **the happy c.** les heureux époux *mpl*

2 *vt* (**a**) *(associate)* associer (**with** à) (**b**) *(combine)* allier (**with** à)

3 *vi* s'accoupler

couplet ['kʌplɪt] *n* distique *m*

coupon ['ku:pɒn] *n (form)* coupon *m*; **(money-off) c.** *(for discount)* bon *m* de réduction

courage ['kʌrɪdʒ] *n* courage *m*; **to have the c. to do sth** avoir le courage de faire qch; **to have the c. of one's convictions** avoir le courage de ses opinions

courageous [kə'reɪdʒəs] *adj* courageux(euse)

courageously [kə'reɪdʒəslɪ] *adv* courageusement, avec courage

courier ['kʊrɪə(r)] *n (messenger)* messager *m*, coursier *m*; *(in tourism)* guide *mf*; *(drug smuggler)* passeur(euse) *m,f*

course [kɔːs] **1** *n* **(a)** *(of river, time, events)* cours *m*; **to be on c.** *Naut* suivre le cap; *Fig* être en bonne voie; *Naut* **to be off c.** dévier de son cap; **in the c. of time** *(gradually)* à la longue; *(eventually)* finalement; **in the c. of the evening** au cours de la soirée; **c. of action** ligne *f* de conduite; **to be in the c. of doing sth** être en train de faire qch; **in the normal c. of events** en temps normal; **to let things take** *or* **run their c.** laisser les choses suivre leur cours normal

(b) **of c.** naturellement, bien sûr; **of c. not** bien sûr que non

(c) *(at college)* cours *m* (**in** de); **c. of lectures** série *f* de conférences

(d) *Med* **c. of treatment** traitement *m*

(e) *(of meal)* plat *m*

(f) *(for race)* parcours *m*; *(for horseracing)* champ *m* de courses; *(for golf)* terrain *m*

2 *vi (of liquid)* couler

court [kɔːt] **1** *n* **(a)** *Law* cour *f*, tribunal *m*; **to go to c.** aller en justice; **to take sb to c.** faire un procès à qn; **to settle a case out of c.** arranger une affaire à l'amiable; **c. of appeals** cour d'appel; **c. of inquiry** commission *f* d'enquête; **c. of law** cour, tribunal; **c. appearance** comparution *f* en justice; *Mil* **c. martial** cour martiale; **c. order** ordonnance *f* du tribunal

(b) *(for tennis, squash)* court *m*

(c) *(royal)* cour *f*; *Fig* **to hold c.** tenir des discours à un entourage admiratif; **c. shoe** escarpin *m*

2 *vt* **(a)** *Old-fashioned (woo)* courtiser

(b) *(seek) (friendship, favor)* rechercher; *(death)* braver; *(disaster, danger)* aller au-devant de

3 *vi Old-fashioned* **to be courting** *(of couple)* se fréquenter

courteous ['kɜːtɪəs] *adj* courtois(e), poli(e)

courtesy ['kɜːtəsɪ] *(pl* **courtesies)** *n* courtoisie *f*, politesse *f*; **by c. of...** avec l'aimable autorisation de...; **to exchange courtesies** se faire des politesses; **c. call** visite *f* de politesse; **c. car** = voiture mise à la disposition d'un client par un hôtel ou un garage

courthouse ['kɔːthaʊs] *n* palais *m* de justice, tribunal *m*

courtier ['kɔːtɪə(r)] *n (man)* courtisan *m*; *(woman)* dame *f* de la cour

court-martial ['kɔːt'mɑːʃəl] *vt* faire passer en cour martiale; **to be court-martialed** passer en cour martiale

courtroom ['kɔːtruːm] *n Law* salle *f* d'audience

courtship ['kɔːtʃɪp] *n (of people)* cour *f*; *(of animals)* période *f* nuptiale; **c. display** parade *f* nuptiale

courtyard ['kɔːtjɑːd] *n* cour *f*

cousin ['kʌzən] *n* cousin(e) *m,f*

cove [kəʊv] *n* crique *f*

covenant ['kʌvənənt] *Law* **1** *n* convention *f*, contrat *m*

2 *vt* promettre par contrat

cover ['kʌvə(r)] **1** *n* **(a)** *(lid)* couvercle *m*

(b) *(soft covering) (for cushion, typewriter, chair)* housse *f*

(c) *(bedspread)* couvre-lit *m*; **covers** *(blankets)* couvertures *fpl*

(d) *(of book, magazine)* couverture *f*; **from c. to c.** de la première à la dernière page; **c. price** prix *m* de vente

(e) *(shelter)* **to take c.** s'abriter; **to break c.** sortir à découvert; *Fig* se manifester publiquement; **under c. of darkness** à la faveur de la nuit

(f) *(song)* **c. (version)** reprise *f*

(g) *(in restaurant)* **c. charge** couvert *m*; *(in bar, club)* prix *m* d'entrée

(h) **c. letter** *(for job application)* lettre *f* de motivation; *(sent with other documents)* lettre *f* d'accompagnement

2 *vt* **(a)** *(person, object)* couvrir (**with/in** de); **to c. one's eyes** se couvrir les yeux; **to c. a wall with paint** recouvrir un mur de peinture; **to c. oneself with glory** se couvrir de gloire; **to c. one's costs** couvrir ses frais; **to c. a song** *(of musician)* reprendre une chanson

(b) *(hide) (one's embarrassment, confusion)* dissimuler; **to c. one's tracks** brouiller les pistes

(c) *(travel over)* parcourir; **we covered 50 miles in one day** ≃ nous avons fait *ou* parcouru 80 km en un jour; *Fig* **to c. a lot of ground** traiter de nombreux problèmes

(d) *(include, deal with) (of book, lecture)* traiter de; **to c. a story** *(of journalist)* couvrir un sujet

(e) *Fin (with insurance)* couvrir (**for** *or* **against** contre); *Fig* **to c. oneself** *(take precautions)* se couvrir

▶**cover for** *vt insep (replace)* remplacer; *(provide excuses for)* couvrir

▶**cover up 1** *vt sep* **(a)** *(corruption, mistakes)* dissimuler; *(scandal)* étouffer **(b)** *(put cover on)* recouvrir

2 *vi (conceal the truth)* cacher la vérité (**for sb** pour protéger qn)

coverage ['kʌvərɪdʒ] *n* **(a)** *(on TV, in newspapers)* couverture *f* médiatique **(b)** *Fin (in insurance)* couverture *f*

coveralls ['kʌvərɔːlz] *npl* bleu *m ou* bleus *mpl* de travail

covering ['kʌvərɪŋ] *n (on furniture)* housse *f*; *(of snow, dust)* couche *f*; *(of chocolate)* nappage *m*

coverlet ['kʌvəlɪt] *n* dessus-de-lit *m inv*

covert ['kʌvət] *adj (operation)* secret(ète), clandestin(e); *(look)* furtif(ive)

cover-up ['kʌvərʌp] *n* **there was a c.** l'affaire a été étouffée

covet ['kʌvɪt] *vt Formal* convoiter

covetous ['kʌvɪtəs] *adj Formal* envieux(euse); **to be c. of sth** convoiter qch

cow[1] [kaʊ] *n (animal)* vache *f*; *(female elephant, whale)* femelle *f*; **till the cows come home** jusqu'à la saint-glinglin

cow[2] [kaʊ] *vt* intimider; **to look cowed** avoir un air de chien battu

coward ['kaʊəd] *n* lâche *mf*, poltron(onne) *m,f*

cowardice ['kaʊədɪs], **cowardliness** ['kaʊədlɪnəs] *n* lâcheté *f*, poltronnerie *f*

cowardly ['kaʊədlɪ] *adj* lâche

cowboy ['kaʊbɔɪ] *n* cow-boy *m*; **c. boots** santiags *fpl*; **c. hat** chapeau *m* de cow-boy

cower ['kaʊə(r)] *vi* se tapir; **to c. before sb** trembler devant qn

cowhide ['kaʊhaɪd] *n* peau *f* de vache

cowl [kaʊl] *n (on monk's habit, on chimney)* capuchon *m*; **c. neck** col *m* boule

coworker ['kəʊwɜːkə(r)] *n* collègue *mf*

cowshed ['kaʊʃed] *n* étable *f*

cox [kɒks] **1** *n (in rowing)* barreur(euse) *m,f*

2 *vt & vi* barrer

coy [kɔɪ] *adj (shy)* timide; *Pej (affectedly shy)* (faussement) timide (**about** à propos de)

coyote [kɔɪ'əʊtɪ] *n* coyote *m*

cozy ['kəʊzɪ] *adj (room, atmosphere)* douillet(ette), confortable; *(armchair, bar)* confortable; **to feel c.** *(in room)* être confortablement installé(e); *Fig & Pej* **they have a c. relationship** ils sont un peu trop copain-copain

CPA [si:pi:'eɪ] *n Com (abbr* **certified public accountant)** ≃ expert-comptable *m*

CPR [si:pi:'ɑː] *n Med (abbr* **cardiopulmonary resuscitation)** réanimation *f* cardiorespiratoire

CPU [si:pi:'ju:] *n Comput (abbr* **central processing unit)** unité *f* centrale

crab [kræb] *n* (**a**) *(crustacean)* crabe *m*; **c. cakes** croquettes *f* de crabe (**b**) *Fam (pubic louse)* morpion *m* (**c**) **c. apple** pomme *f* sauvage

crabbed ['kræbɪd] *adj (writing)* en pattes de mouche

crabby ['kræbɪ] *adj Fam* maussade, grincheux(euse)

crack [kræk] **1** *n* (**a**) *(in glass, porcelain)* fêlure *f*; *(in wood)* fente *f*; *(in wall)* lézarde *f*; *(in ice, rock)* fissure *f*; **at the c. of dawn** à la pointe du jour
(**b**) *(sound) (of branches, ice)* craquement *m*; *(of whip)* claquement *m*; *(of gunfire)* détonation *f*; *Fig* **to have** *or* **to take a c. at sth** tenter sa chance à qch
(**c**) *(blow)* coup *m* (**on** sur)
(**d**) *Fam (joke, insult)* plaisanterie *f*
(**e**) *(drug)* crack *m*
2 *adj Fam (team, regiment)* d'élite; **c. marksman** fin tireur *m*
3 *vt* (**a**) *(glass, porcelain)* fêler; *(wood)* fendre; *(wall)* lézarder; *(ice, rock)* fissurer
(**b**) *(make sound with) (whip)* faire claquer; *(fingers)* faire craquer; *Fig* **to c. the whip** faire le gendarme
(**c**) *Fam (hit)* **to c. sb over the head** assommer qn; **she cracked her head against the wall** elle s'est cogné la tête contre le mur
(**d**) *(solve) (problem)* résoudre; *(code)* décrypter
(**e**) *(break into) (safe)* percer; *(nut)* casser
(**f**) *Fam (joke)* raconter
4 *vi* (**a**) *(of glass, porcelain)* se fêler; *(of wood)* se fendre; *(of wall)* se lézarder; *(of ice, rock)* se fissurer; *(of paint)* se craqueler
(**b**) *(of voice)* se casser
(**c**) *(of person under pressure)* craquer
(**d**) *(make sound) (of branches, ice)* craquer; *(of whip)* claquer; *(of gunfire)* retentir; *Fam Fig* **to get cracking** se grouiller

▶**crack down** *vi* **to c. down (on)** prendre des mesures énergiques (contre)

▶**crack up** *Fam* **1** *vt sep* **it's not all it's cracked up to be** ce n'est pas aussi bien qu'on le dit
2 *vi* (**a**) *(go mad)* craquer (**b**) *(with laughter)* se tordre de rire

crackbrained ['krækbreɪnd] *adj Fam* dingue

crackdown ['krækdaʊn] *n* mesures *fpl* énergiques (**on** en matière de)

cracked [krækt] *adj Fam (mad)* dingue, cinglé(e)

cracker ['krækə(r)] *n* (**a**) *(biscuit)* biscuit *m* salé, cracker *m* (**b**) *(firecracker)* pétard *m* (**c**) *Fam Comput (excellent thing, person)* pirate *m* informatique

crackers ['krækəz] *adj Fam* dingue, cinglé(e)

crackle ['krækəl] **1** *n (of twigs)* craquement *m*; *(of shots, fire)* crépitement *m*; *(of frying)* grésillement *m*; *(of radio)* crachotement *m*
2 *vi (of twigs)* craquer; *(of shots, fire)* crépiter; *(of frying)* grésiller; *(of radio)* crachoter

crackling ['kræklɪŋ] *n* (**a**) *(of fire)* crépitement *m*; *(on radio)* crachotement *m* (**b**) *(pork skin)* couenne *f* grillée

crackpot ['krækpɒt] *Fam* **1** *n (person)* fêlé(e) *m,f*, cinglé(e) *m,f*
2 *adj (plan)* dingue

cradle ['kreɪdəl] **1** *n* (**a**) *(of child, civilization)* berceau *m*; **from the c. to the grave** du berceau à la tombe (**b**) *(for cleaning windows)* nacelle *f*
2 *vt (baby)* bercer *(dans ses bras)*; *(object)* tenir délicatement

craft¹ [krɑːft] **1** *n* (**a**) *(skill)* habileté *f*; *(professional)* métier *m*
(**b**) *(cunning)* ruse *f*
2 *vt (make)* travailler; **a beautifully crafted movie** un film magnifiquement travaillé

craft² [krɑːft] *(pl* **craft)** *n (boat)* (petite) embarcation *f*

craftsman ['krɑːftsmən] *n* artisan *m*; **this is the work of a real c.** c'est l'œuvre d'un spécialiste

craftsmanship ['krɑːftsmənʃɪp] *n* habileté *f* (manuelle); **a wonderful piece of c.** un pur chef-d'œuvre; **the c. is magnificent** c'est vraiment du beau travail

crafty ['krɑːftɪ] *adj* malin(igne)

crag [kræg] *n* rocher *m* à pic

craggy ['krægɪ] *adj (rocky)* rocheux(euse); *(features)* anguleux(euse)

cram [kræm] *(pt & pp* **crammed)** **1** *vt* fourrer, entasser (**into** dans); **to c. food into one's mouth** se gaver, s'empiffrer; **to be crammed (with)** être bourré(e) (de)
2 *vi* (**a**) *(crowd)* s'entasser (**into** dans) (**b**) *Fam (study)* bûcher

cramp [kræmp] **1** *n* crampe *f*
2 *vt (restrict)* gêner; *Fam* **to c. sb's style** priver qn de ses moyens

cramped [kræmpt] *adj (surroundings)* exigu(ë); **to be c. for space** être à l'étroit

cranberry ['krænbərɪ] *(pl* **cranberries)** *n* canneberge *f*; **c. sauce** sauce *f* à la canneberge

crane [kreɪn] **1** *n (lifting device, bird)* grue *f*; **c. fly** *(insect)* tipule *f*
2 *vt* **to c. one's neck** tendre le cou
3 *vi* **to c. forward** tendre le cou

cranium ['kreɪnɪəm] *(pl* **crania** ['kreɪnɪə]) *n Anat* boîte *f* crânienne

crank¹ [kræŋk] *n (gear mechanism)* manivelle *f*

crank² [kræŋk] *n Fam* (**a**) *(bad-tempered person)* grognon(onne) *m,f* (**b**) *(eccentric person)* excentrique *mf*; **a religious c.** un fanatique religieux

crankshaft ['kræŋkʃɑːft] *n Aut* vilebrequin *m*

cranky ['kræŋkɪ] *adj Fam (bad-tempered)* grognon(onne)

crap [kræp] **1** *n* (**a**) *Vulg (excrement)* merde *f*; **to take a c.** chier (**b**) *very Fam (junk)* saloperies *fpl*; *(nonsense)* conneries *fpl*; *(disgusting substance)* saloperie *f*; **don't talk c.!** ne dis pas de conneries!
2 *adj very Fam (bad)* nul (nulle)

crash [kræʃ] **1** *n* (**a**) *(noise)* fracas *m*
(**b**) *(accident) (in car)* accident *m*; *(in train, plane)* catastrophe *f*; **c. barrier** glissière *f* de sécurité; **c. helmet** casque *m*; **c. landing** atterrissage *m* en catastrophe
(**c**) *(financial)* krach *m*
2 *adj* **c. course** cours *m* intensif; **c. diet** régime *m* amaigrissant intensif
3 *vt* (**a**) **to c. one's car** avoir un accident de voiture
(**b**) *Fam* **to c. a party** = aller à une fête sans y être invité
4 *vi* (**a**) *(make noise)* s'écraser avec fracas; **to c. to the ground** s'écrouler avec fracas; **he was crashing around in the kitchen** il s'agitait bruyamment dans la cuisine
(**b**) *(of cars)* se percuter; **to c. into** rentrer dans
(**c**) *(of business)* faire faillite; *(of economy)* s'effondrer
(**d**) *Comput* tomber en panne
(**e**) *Fam (go to sleep)* s'écrouler

▶**crash out** *vi Fam (go to sleep)* s'écrouler; **he was crashed out on the sofa** il roupillait sur le divan

crashing ['kræʃɪŋ] *adj* **a c. bore** *(person)* une personne assommante

crash-land ['kræʃlænd] *vi* atterrir en catastrophe

crass [kræs] *adj* grossier(ère); **c. ignorance** ignorance *f* crasse; **c. stupidity** immense bêtise *f*

crate [kreɪt] *n (box)* caisse *f*; *(for fruit)* cageot *m*; *(for bottles)* casier *m*

crater ['kreɪtə(r)] *n* cratère *m*

cravat [krə'væt] *n* foulard *m*

crave [kreɪv] **1** *vt (cigarette)* avoir très envie de; *(affection)* être en manque de; *(opportunity)* attendre avec impatience
2 *vi* **to be craving for sth** *(cigarette)* avoir très envie de qch; *(affection)* être en manque de qch; *(opportunity)* attendre qch avec impatience

craving ['kreɪvɪŋ] *n* envie *f* irrésistible; **to have a c. for sth** *(cigarette)* avoir très envie de qch; *(affection)* être en manque de qch

crawl [krɔːl] **1** n (**a**) (slow pace) **to move at a c.** (of car, driver) rouler au pas; (of person) piétiner sur place (**b**) (swimming stroke) crawl m

2 vi (**a**) (of person) ramper; (of baby) marcher à quatre pattes; (of car) rouler au pas (**b**) Fam (be infested) **to be crawling with** grouiller de; **to make sb's skin c.** flanquer des boutons à qn (**c**) Fam (be obsequious) faire le lèche-bottes; **to c. to sb** lécher les bottes à qn

crayfish ['kreɪfɪʃ] n écrevisse f

crayon ['kreɪɒn] n (wax) crayon m gras

craze [kreɪz] n engouement m (**for** pour)

crazed [kreɪzd] adj (look, person) fou (folle)

crazy ['kreɪzɪ] adj fou (folle); **to go c.** devenir fou; **to drive sb c.** rendre qn fou; Fam **to be c. about sb/sth** être fou de qn/ qch; Fam **like c.** (run, work) comme un fou (une folle)

creak [kriːk] **1** n (of hinge) grincement m; (of floor, shoes) craquement m

2 vi (of hinge) grincer; (of floor, shoes) craquer

creaky ['kriːkɪ] adj (hinge) grinçant(e); (floor) qui craque; Fig (plot, dialogue) boiteux(euse)

cream [kriːm] **1** n (**a**) (of milk) crème f; **c. of tomato/chicken soup** crème de tomates/volaille; **c. cake** gâteau m à la crème; **c. cheese** fromage m frais à tartiner (**b**) Fig **the c.** (best part) la crème (de la crème) (**c**) (lotion) crème f (**d**) (color) crème m

2 adj **c.(-colored)** (de couleur) crème inv

3 vt Culin (butter) battre en crème

▸**cream off** vt sep Fig (money, profits) écrémer; **the universities c. off the best students** les universités sélectionnent les meilleurs étudiants

creamy ['kriːmɪ] adj (taste, consistency) crémeux(euse); (skin) laiteux(euse)

crease [kriːs] **1** n (in skin, fabric) pli m

2 vt (fabric) froisser; **to c. one's brow** plisser le front

3 vi (of fabric) se froisser; (of face, brow) se plisser

create [kriːˈeɪt] vt créer; **to c. a sensation/a good impression** faire sensation/bonne impression

creation [kriːˈeɪʃən] n création f

creative [kriːˈeɪtɪv] adj (person, activity) créatif(ive); (process, imagination) créateur(trice); Fin **c. accounting** manipulations fpl comptables; **c. writing** techniques fpl de l'écriture

creator [kriːˈeɪtə(r)] n créateur(trice) m,f; Rel **the C.** le Créateur

creature ['kriːtʃə(r)] n (person) créature f, être m; (animal) bête f; **to be a c. of habit** avoir ses petites habitudes; **c. comforts** confort m matériel; **to like one's c. comforts** aimer son confort

crèche [kreʃ] n (nursery) crèche f

credence ['kriːdəns] n **to lend** or **to give c. to sth** ajouter foi à qch

credentials [krɪˈdenʃəlz] npl (**a**) (proof of identity) pièces fpl justificatives d'identité; (of ambassador) lettres fpl de créance (**b**) (proof of ability) références fpl; Fig **to establish one's c.** faire ses preuves

credibility [kredɪˈbɪlɪtɪ] n crédibilité f; **c. gap** manque m de crédibilité

credible ['kredɪbəl] adj crédible; **it is hardly c. that...** il est difficile de croire que...

credit ['kredɪt] **1** n (**a**) (financial) crédit m; **to be in c.** (of person) avoir un compte créditeur; (of account) être créditeur(trice); **to give sb c.** faire crédit à qn; **to buy/sell sth on c.** acheter/ vendre qch à crédit; **c. card** carte f de crédit; Econ **c. control** encadrement m du crédit; **c. limit** plafond m de crédit; Fin **c. rating** degré m de solvabilité; Econ **c. squeeze** restrictions fpl de crédit; **c. union** société f de crédit

(**b**) (belief) **to give c. to sth** ajouter foi à qch; **to gain c.** (of theory) être accepté(e)

(**c**) (recognition) mérite m; **you have to give him c. for his honesty** tu es bien forcé de reconnaître qu'il est honnête; **to take the c. for sth** s'attribuer le mérite de qch; **to do sb c.** faire honneur à qn; **it does you c.** c'est tout à ton honneur; **c. where c.'s due** il faut rendre à César ce qui est à César; **to her c. she refused** elle a refusé, ce qui est tout à son honneur; **she is a c. to the school** elle fait honneur à l'école

(**d**) Univ unité f de valeur

(**e**) **credits** (of movie, TV program) générique m

2 vt (**a**) (money) virer (**to an account** sur un compte)

(**b**) (attribute) **to c. sb with sth** attribuer qch à qn

(**c**) (believe) croire; **would you c. it?** tu te rends compte?

creditable ['kredɪtəbəl] adj (praiseworthy) honorable; (efforts, attempt) louable

creditor ['kredɪtə(r)] n Fin créditeur(trice) m,f

credulity [krɪˈdjuːlɪtɪ] n crédulité f

credulous ['kredjʊləs] adj crédule

creed [kriːd] n also Fig principes mpl; **political c.** credo m politique

creek [kriːk] n (stream) ruisseau m; Fam Fig **to be up the c. (without a paddle)** être dans le pétrin

creep [kriːp] **1** n Fam (**a**) (unpleasant man) type m répugnant (**b**) **to give sb the creeps** faire froid dans le dos à qn

2 vi (pt & pp **crept** [krept]) (of animal, person) ramper; (of plants) ramper; (vertically) grimper; **to c. in/out** entrer/sortir à pas de loup; **to c. into bed** se glisser sous les draps; **old age has crept up on me** je me fais vieux; Fam **it makes my flesh c.** ça me flanque des boutons

creeper ['kriːpə(r)] n (plant) plante f rampante; (climbing) plante grimpante

creeping ['kriːpɪŋ] adj (gradual) progressif(ive)

creepy ['kriːpɪ] adj Fam sinistre

creepy-crawler ['kriːpɪˈkrɔːlə(r)], **creepy-crawly** ['kriːpɪˈkrɔːlɪ] n Fam bestiole f, insecte m

cremate [krɪˈmeɪt] vt incinérer

cremation [krɪˈmeɪʃən] n incinération f

crematorium [kreməˈtɔːrɪəm] (pl **crematoria** [kreməˈtɔːrɪə]), **crematory** ['kreməˈtɔrɪ] (pl **crematories** ['kreməˈtɒrɪz]) n crématorium m

creole ['kriːəʊl] **1** n (**a**) (person) Créole mf (**b**) (language) créole m

2 adj créole

creosote ['krɪəsəʊt] n créosote f

crêpe [kreɪp, krep] n (**a**) (textile) crêpe m; **c. paper** papier m crépon; **c.(-rubber) soles** semelles fpl de crêpe (**b**) (pancake) crêpe f

crept [krept] pt & pp of **creep**

crescendo [krɪˈʃendəʊ] (pl **crescendos**) n Mus & Fig crescendo m inv; **to rise to a c.** (of music, complaints) aller crescendo

crescent ['kresənt] **1** n (shape) croissant m; (street) rue f en croissant

2 adj **c.(-shaped)** en forme de croissant ou de demi-lune; **c. moon** croissant m de lune

cress [kres] n cresson m

crest [krest] n (of bird, wave, helmet) crête f; (of hill) sommet m; (coat of arms) armoiries fpl; Fig **to be on the c. of a wave** être dans une période faste

crestfallen ['krestfɔːlən] adj abattu(e), découragé(e)

Cretan ['kriːtən] **1** n Crétois(e) m,f

2 adj crétois(e)

Crete [kriːt] n la Crète

cretin ['kretɪn] n Fam crétin(e) m,f

crevice ['krevɪs] n (in rock) crevasse f, fissure f; (in wall) lézarde f

crew [kruː] **1** n (of ship, plane) équipage m; (of ambulance) équipe f; Fam (gang, group) bande f; **c. cut** (hairstyle) brosse f, cheveux *mpl* (coupés) en brosse; **c. neck** col *m* ras le *ou* du cou

2 *vt (ship)* **the ship was crewed by...** le bateau avait un équipage de...

crib [krɪb] **1** *n* **(a)** *(for baby)* lit *m* d'enfant; **c. death** mort *f* subite du nourrisson **(b)** *Fam* **c. (sheet)** *(in exam)* antisèche *f*

2 *vt (pt & pp* **cribbed)** *Fam (copy)* pomper

crick [krɪk] **1** *n* **to have a c. in one's neck** avoir un torticolis

2 *vt* **to c. one's neck** attraper un torticolis

cricket[1] ['krɪkɪt] *n (insect)* grillon *m*

cricket[2] ['krɪkɪt] *n (sport)* cricket *m*; **c. ball** balle *f* de cricket; **c. bat** batte *f* de cricket; **c. pitch** terrain *m* de cricket

crime [kraɪm] *n (act)* crime *m*; *Law* délit *m*; *(phenomenon)* criminalité *f*; **c. is on the increase** la criminalité augmente; *Fig* **it's a c. to waste money like that** c'est un crime de gaspiller de l'argent de cette façon; **c. wave** vague *f* de criminalité; **c. writer** auteur *m* de romans policiers

Crimea [kraɪ'mɪə] *n* la Crimée

Crimean [kraɪ'mɪən] *adj* de Crimée

criminal ['krɪmɪnəl] **1** *n* criminel(elle) *m,f*

2 *adj* criminel(elle); *Fig* **it's c. to knock down that building** c'est un crime de démolir ce bâtiment; **to go to c. court** être jugé(e) au pénal; **c. law** droit *m* pénal; **c. lawyer** avocat *m* au pénal; **c. offense** délit *m*; *(more serious)* crime *m*; **c. record** casier *m* judiciaire

criminalize ['krɪmɪnəlaɪz] *vt* criminaliser

criminology [krɪmɪ'nɒlədʒɪ] *n* criminologie *f*

crimp [krɪmp] *vt* **(a)** *(hair)* friser; *(pastry)* pincer **(b)** *(restrict)* gêner

crimson ['krɪmzən] **1** *n* pourpre *m*

2 *adj* pourpre; **to go c. with rage** devenir rouge de colère

cringe [krɪndʒ] *vi* **(a)** *(show fear)* avoir un mouvement de recul **(b)** *(be embarrassed)* avoir envie de rentrer sous terre; **it makes me c.** ça me donne envie de rentrer sous terre

cringing ['krɪndʒɪŋ] *adj (afraid)* craintif(ive); *(servile)* servile

crinkle ['krɪŋkəl] **1** *n (in paper, fabric)* pli *m*

2 *vt (paper, fabric)* froisser; **to c. one's nose** froncer le nez

3 *vi (of brow, nose)* se froncer; *(of face)* se rider

crinkly ['krɪŋklɪ] *adj (skin)* ridé(e); *(paper, fabric)* froissé(e)

cripple ['krɪpəl] **1** *n* estropié(e) *m,f*

2 *vt* estropier; *Fig (industry, system)* paralyser

crippling ['krɪplɪŋ] *adj* **(a)** *(disease)* invalidant(e) **(b)** *(effect, strike)* paralysant(e); *(taxes)* écrasant(e)

crisis ['kraɪsɪs] *(pl* **crises** ['kraɪsiːz]*) n* crise *f*; **to be in c.** être en (pleine) crise; **c. management** habileté *f* à gérer les situations de crise; **c. point** point *m* critique

crisp [krɪsp] *adj (apple, lettuce)* croquant(e); *(pastry)* croustillant(e); *(bill)* neuf (neuve); *(sheets)* frais (fraîche); *(snow)* qui crisse sous les pas; *(air, breeze)* vif (vive); *(style)* vif (vive) et précis(e); *(tone)* brusque, tranchant(e)

crispbread ['krɪspbred] *n* pain *m* suédois

crisply ['krɪsplɪ] *adv (say)* d'un ton brusque *ou* tranchant; *(write)* dans un style vif et précis

crispy ['krɪspɪ] *adj* croustillant(e)

criss-cross ['krɪskrɒs] **1** *vt* entrecroiser

2 *vi* s'entrecroiser

criterion [kraɪ'tɪərɪən] *(pl* **criteria** [kraɪ'tɪərɪə]*) n* critère *m*

critic ['krɪtɪk] *n (reviewer)* critique *mf*; *(opponent)* détracteur(trice) *m,f*

critical ['krɪtɪkəl] *adj* **(a)** *(judgmental)* critique (**of** à l'égard de); **to be c. of sb/sth** critiquer qn/qch **(b)** *(essay, study)* critique; **to be a c. success** être acclamé(e) par la critique **(c)** *(decisive)* critique; **the next few days will be c.** les prochains jours seront décisifs; **in a c. condition** *(of patient)* dans un état critique

criticism ['krɪtɪsɪzəm] *n* critique *f*

criticize ['krɪtɪsaɪz] **1** *vt* critiquer; **to c. sb for sth** reprocher

qch à qn; **to c. sb for doing sth** reprocher à qn de faire/ d'avoir fait qch

2 *vi* critiquer

critique [krɪ'tiːk] *n* critique *f*

croak [krəʊk] **1** *n (of frog)* coassement *m*; *(of raven)* croassement *m*

2 *vi* **(a)** *(of frog)* coasser; *(of raven)* croasser; *(of person)* parler d'une voix rauque **(b)** *Fam (die)* claquer

Croat ['krəʊæt] **1** *n (person)* Croate *mf*

2 *adj* croate

Croatia [krəʊ'eɪʃə] *n* la Croatie

Croatian [krəʊ'eɪʃən] = **Croat**

crochet ['krəʊʃeɪ] **1** *n* (travail *m* au) crochet *m*; **c. hook** crochet *m*

2 *vt (shawl, blanket)* faire au crochet

3 *vi* faire du crochet

crock [krɒk] *n* **(a)** *(pot)* pot *m* de terre; *very Fam* **that's a c. (of shit)!** tout ça, c'est des conneries! **(b)** *Fam* **old c.** *(person)* croulant(e) *m,f*

crockery ['krɒkərɪ] *n* vaisselle *f*

crocodile ['krɒkədaɪl] *n (animal)* crocodile *m*; **c. tears** larmes *fpl* de crocodile

crocus ['krəʊkəs] *n* crocus *m*

crone [krəʊn] *n Pej* **old c.** vieille bique *f*

crony ['krəʊnɪ] *(pl* **cronies***) n* copain (copine) *m,f*

crook [krʊk] **1** *n* **(a)** *(criminal)* escroc *m* **(b)** *(of shepherd)* houlette *f*; *(of bishop)* crosse *f* **(c)** *(curve)* coude *m*; **in the c. of one's arm** au creux du bras

2 *vt (finger, arm)* plier

crooked ['krʊkɪd] *adj* **(a)** *(not straight)* de travers; *(nose)* tordu(e); **a c. smile** un sourire en coin **(b)** *(dishonest, illegal)* malhonnête

croon [kruːn] *vt & vi* chantonner, fredonner

crop [krɒp] **1** *n* **(a)** *(of fruit, vegetables)* récolte *f*; *(of cereals)* moisson *f*; *Fig* **this year's c. of movies** la production cinématographique de cette année **(b)** *(handle of whip)* **(riding) c.** cravache *f* **(c)** *(of bird)* jabot *m* **(d)** *(short haircut)* coupe *f* très courte

2 *vt (pt & pp* **cropped)** **(a)** *(cut)* couper; *(hair)* couper ras; **cropped hair** cheveux *mpl* coupés ras **(b)** *(of cattle)* brouter

▸**crop up** *vi (of issue, question)* surgir; *(of problem, opportunity)* se présenter; *(of name)* être mentionné(e)

cropper ['krɒpə(r)] *n Fam* **to come a c.** se prendre une gamelle

croquet ['krəʊkeɪ] *n* croquet *m*

croquette [krɒ'ket] *n Culin* croquette *f*

cross [krɒs] **1** *n* **(a)** *(sign, shape)* croix *f*; **to make the sign of the c.** faire le signe de croix

(b) *(hybrid) & Fig* croisement *m* (**between** entre)

(c) *(in boxing)* coup *m* croisé; *(in soccer)* centre *m*

2 *adj (annoyed)* fâché(e); **to get c. (with sb)** se fâcher (contre qn); **to be c. with oneself** s'en vouloir; **we've never had a c. word** nous n'avons jamais eu un mot plus haut que l'autre

3 *vt* **(a)** *(river, road)* traverser; **to c. sb's path** se trouver sur le chemin de qn; **it crossed my mind that...** il m'est venu à l'esprit que...

(b) *(make into shape of cross)* croiser; **to c. oneself** se signer; **to c. one's legs/arms** croiser les jambes/bras; **to keep one's fingers crossed** croiser les doigts; **to c. one's eyes** loucher; *Fig* **to c. swords (with sb)** croiser le fer (avec qn); *Fig* **we must have got our wires crossed** nous avons dû mal nous comprendre; *Fam* **c. my heart (and hope to die)** croix de bois, croix de fer

(c) *(oppose)* contrecarrer

(d) *(animals, plants)* croiser (**with** avec)

(e) *(in writing)* **to c. one's t's** mettre une barre à ses t

4 *vi* **(a)** *(of roads, lines)* se croiser; **our letters crossed in the mail** nos lettres se sont croisées (**b**) *(go across)* traverser; **to c. from New York to South-ampton** faire la traversée de New York à Southampton

▶**cross off, cross out** *vt sep* barrer, rayer

crossbar ['krɒsbɑ:(r)] *n (on bike)* barre *f*; *(of goalposts)* barre transversale

crossbow ['krɒsbəʊ] *n* arbalète *f*

crossbreed ['krɒsbri:d] *n (of animals)* croisement *m*; *(of plants)* hybride *m*

cross-Channel ['krɒs'tʃænəl] *adj* transmanche *inv*

crosscheck ['krɒs'tʃek] **1** *n* vérification *f* (par recoupement) **2** *vt* vérifier par recoupement

cross-country ['krɒs'kʌntrɪ] *adj* **c. runner** coureur(euse) *m,f* de fond; **c. running** cross *m*

cross-examination ['krɒsɪgzæmɪ'neɪʃən] *n Law* contre-interrogatoire *m*; *Fig* interrogatoire *m* serré

cross-examine ['krɒsɪg'zæmɪn] *vt Law* soumettre à un contre-interrogatoire; *Fig* soumettre à un interrogatoire serré; **to c. sb about sth** interroger qn en détail sur qch

cross-eyed ['krɒsaɪd] *adj* **to be c.** loucher

crossfire ['krɒsfaɪə(r)] *n* feu *m* croisé; *Fig* **to be caught in the c.** être pris(e) entre deux feux

crossing ['krɒsɪŋ] *n* (**a**) *(of sea, river)* traversée *f* (**b**) *(in street)* passage *m* (pour) piétons, passage clouté

cross-legged ['krɒs'leg(ɪ)d] *adv* **to sit c.** être assis(e) en tailleur

cross-platform ['krɒs'plætfɔ:m] *adj Comput* multiplateforme

cross-purposes ['krɒs'pɜ:pəsɪz] *npl* **to be at c.** ne pas parler de la même chose

cross-reference ['krɒs'refərəns] *n* renvoi *m*

crossroads ['krɒsrəʊdz] (*pl* **crossroads**) *n* carrefour *m*, croisement *m*; *Fig (decisive moment)* point *m* crucial

cross-section ['krɒs'sekʃən] *n* coupe *f* ou section *f* transversale; *Fig (of population)* échantillon *m* représentatif

cross-trainer ['krɒs'treɪnə(r)] *n (gym equipment)* cross-trainer *m*

cross-training ['krɒs'treɪnɪŋ] *n Sport* cross-training *m*

crosswalk ['krɒswɔ:k] *n* passage *m* clouté

crosswind ['krɒswɪnd] *n* vent *m* de travers

crossword ['krɒswɜ:d] *n* **c. (puzzle)** mots *mpl* croisés

crotch [krɒtʃ] *n* entrejambe *m*

crotchet ['krɒtʃɪt] *n Mus* noire *f*

crotchety ['krɒtʃətɪ] *adj Fam* grognon

crouch [kraʊtʃ] *vi (of animal)* se tapir; *(of person)* s'accroupir

croupier ['kru:pɪə(r)] *n* croupier *m*

crow [krəʊ] **1** *n (bird)* corbeau *m*; **as the c. flies** à vol d'oiseau; **c.'s feet** *(on face)* pattes *fpl* d'oie; **c.'s nest** *(on ship)* nid-de-pie *m* **2** *vi* (**a**) *(of cock)* chanter (**b**) *(exult)* se vanter (**about** de)

crowbar ['krəʊbɑ:(r)] *n* levier *m*

crowd [kraʊd] **1** *n* (**a**) *(large number of people)* foule *f*; *(at sports event)* public *m*; **there was a c. at the movie theater** il y avait beaucoup de monde au cinéma; *Fig* **to stand out from the c.** se distinguer de la masse; *Fig* **to follow the c.** suivre le mouvement; **to be a c. puller** attirer les foules (**b**) *Fam (group)* bande *f* **2** *vt (people, objects)* entasser; *(streets, square)* envahir; **don't c. me!** laisse-moi respirer! **3** *vi* **to c. (together)** s'entasser; **to c. around sb** se presser autour de qn

▶**crowd out** *vt sep (of deal, market)* exclure (**of** de)

crowded ['kraʊdɪd] *adj (place)* bondé(e); *(day, schedule)* chargé(e)

crown [kraʊn] **1** *n* (**a**) *(of monarch)* couronne *f*; **the C.** *(the monarchy)* la Couronne; **c. jewels** joyaux *mpl* de la Couronne; **c. prince** prince *m* héritier (**b**) *(top) (of head)* sommet *m* de la tête; *(of hat)* haut *m*; *(of hill)* sommet *m*; *(of tooth)* couronne *f*

2 *vt also Fig* couronner; *Fam* **I'll c. you!** *(hit on the head)* je vais te flanquer une calotte!

crowning ['kraʊnɪŋ] *adj (achievement)* suprême; **c. glory** couronnement *m*

crucial ['kru:ʃəl] *adj (very important)* crucial(e)

crucible ['kru:sɪbəl] *n* creuset *m*; *Fig (test)* épreuve *f*

crucifix ['kru:sɪfɪks] *n* crucifix *m*

crucifixion [kru:sɪ'fɪkʃən] *n* crucifixion *f*

crucify ['kru:sɪfaɪ] *(pt & pp* **crucified**) *vt* crucifier; *Fig (criticize)* descendre en flammes; *(defeat)* écraser

crude [kru:d] *adj* (**a**) *(unsophisticated, unrefined)* grossier(ère); **c. (oil)** pétrole *m* brut (**b**) *(rude, vulgar)* vulgaire

cruel ['kru:əl] *adj* cruel(elle); *(winter)* rude; **you have to be c. to be kind** qui aime bien châtie bien

cruelty ['kru:əltɪ] *n* cruauté *f*

cruet ['kru:ɪt] *n Culin* **c. (stand** *or* **set)** service *m* à condiments

cruise [kru:z] **1** *n (on ship)* croisière *f*; **to go on a c.** faire une croisière; **c. missile** missile *m* de croisière; **c. ship** bateau *m* de croisière

2 *vi (of passengers)* être en croisière; *(of taxi)* être en maraude; *(of car)* rouler; *Fam (look for sexual partner)* draguer; **cruising speed** *(of ship, plane)* vitesse *f* de croisière

cruiser ['kru:zə(r)] *n (ship)* **(battle) c.** croiseur *m*; **(cabin) c.** yacht *m* de croisière

crumb [krʌm] *n also Fig* miette *f*; **my only c. of comfort is…** mon seul petit réconfort est…

crumble ['krʌmbəl] **1** *n (dessert)* crumble *m (dessert aux fruits recouvert de pâte sablée)* **2** *vt (bread, cake)* émietter **3** *vi (of stone)* s'effriter; *(of bread)* s'émietter; *Fig (of empire, hopes)* s'effondrer

crumbly ['krʌmblɪ] *adj* friable

crumpet ['krʌmpɪt] *n (teacake)* = petite crêpe épaisse mangée avec du beurre, de la confiture etc.

crumple ['krʌmpəl] **1** *vt (material, dress)* froisser, chiffonner; **to c. sth into a ball** mettre qch en boule **2** *vi (of material, dress)* se froisser, se chiffonner; *Fig (of face)* se crisper

crunch [krʌntʃ] **1** *n (sound)* craquement *m*; *(of snow, gravel)* crissement *m*; *Fig* **when it comes to the c.** au moment crucial; *Fig* **if it comes to the c.** au pire **2** *vt (with teeth)* croquer (dans) **3** *vi (of snow, gravel)* crisser; **to c. on sth** *(with teeth)* croquer (dans) qch

crunchy ['krʌntʃɪ] *adj* croquant(e); *(snow, gravel)* qui crisse sous les pas

crusade [kru:'seɪd] **1** *n also Fig* croisade *f* **2** *vi* **to c. for/against sth** se battre pour/contre qch

crusader [kru:'seɪdə(r)] *n Hist* croisé *m*; *Fig* militant(e) *m,f* (**for/against** pour/contre)

crush [krʌʃ] **1** *n* (**a**) *(crowd)* foule *f*; *(confusion)* bousculade *f* (**b**) *Fam (infatuation)* béguin *m*; **to have a c. on sb** avoir le béguin *ou* en pincer pour qn **2** *vt* écraser; *(grapes)* presser; *(ice)* piler; *(in a drawer, suitcase)* entasser; *Fig (opponent)* écraser; *(revolt)* étouffer, mater; *(hopes, person)* anéantir **3** *vi (be crammed)* s'entasser; *(crease)* se froisser

crushing ['krʌʃɪŋ] *adj (defeat)* écrasant(e); *(blow)* terrible; *(remark)* cinglant(e)

crust [krʌst] *n (of bread, pie, the earth)* croûte *f*

crustacean [krʌs'teɪʃən] *n* crustacé *m*

crusty ['krʌstɪ] *adj* (**a**) *(bread, roll)* croustillant(e) (**b**) *(person)* acariâtre

crutch [krʌtʃ] *n (for walking)* béquille *f*; *Fig (support)* soutien *m*; **to be on crutches** marcher avec des béquilles

crux [krʌks] *n (of matter, problem)* cœur *m*

cruzado [cru:'zɑ:dəʊ] *(pl* **cruzados**) *n* cruzado *m*

cry [kraɪ] **1** *n* (*pl* **cries**) (**a**) *(call) (of person, animal)* cri *m*; *(in demonstration)* slogan *m*; **to give a c.** pousser un cri; **a c. for help** un appel au secours; **to be a far c. from sth** n'avoir rien à voir avec qch (**b**) *(weeping)* **to have a good c.** pleurer un bon coup

2 *vt* (*pt & pp* **cried** [kraɪd]) (**a**) *(exclaim)* crier (**b**) *(weep)* **to c. oneself to sleep** s'endormir en pleurant

3 *vi* (**a**) *(weep)* pleurer; **to c. over sth** se lamenter sur qch; *Prov* **it's no use crying over spilled milk** ce qui est fait est fait (**b**) *(shout, call)* crier; **to c. for help** appeler à l'aide *ou* au secours

▶**cry out 1** *vt sep* (**a**) *(shout)* crier (**b**) *(weep)* **to c. one's eyes** *or* **heart out** pleurer toutes les larmes de son corps

2 *vi* *(shout)* pousser un cri; *Fam* **for crying out loud!** mais bon sang!; *Fam* **that wall is crying out for a coat of paint** ce mur aurait grand besoin d'une couche de peinture

crybaby ['kraɪbeɪbɪ] (*pl* **crybabies**) *n* *Fam* pleurnicheur(euse) *m,f*

crying ['kraɪɪŋ] **1** *n* *(weeping)* pleurs *mpl*
2 *adj* *(need)* urgent(e); **it's a c. shame that...** il est scandaleux que... + *subjunctive*

crypt [krɪpt] *n* crypte *f*

cryptic ['krɪptɪk] *adj* énigmatique

crystal ['krɪstəl] **1** *n* cristal *m*; **c. ball** boule *f* de cristal; **c. vase** vase *m* de *ou* en cristal
2 *adj* *(clear)* cristallin(e), limpide

crystal-clear ['krɪstəl'klɪə(r)] *adj* *(water)* limpide; *(explanation)* clair(e) comme de l'eau de roche

crystalize, crystallize ['krɪstəlaɪz] **1** *vt* *Chem* cristalliser; **crystallized fruit** fruits *mpl* confits
2 *vi* *Chem & Fig* se cristalliser

CST [siː'tiː] *n* (*abbr* **Central Standard Time**) = heure du centre de l'Amérique du Nord

cub [kʌb] *n* *(of fox)* renardeau *m*; *(of bear)* ourson *m*; *(of lion)* lionceau *m*; *(of wolf)* louveteau *m*; **c. reporter** jeune journaliste *mf*; **C. (Scout)** louveteau *m*

Cuba ['kjuːbə] *n* Cuba

Cuban ['kjuːbən] **1** *n* Cubain(e) *m,f*
2 *adj* cubain(e)

cubbyhole ['kʌbɪhəʊl] *n* cagibi *m*

cube [kjuːb] **1** *n* *(shape)* cube *m*; *(of sugar)* morceau *m*; *Math* **c. root** racine *f* cubique
2 *vt* *Math* élever au cube

cubic ['kjuːbɪk] *adj* cubique; **c. capacity** volume *m*; **c. meter** mètre *m* cube

cubicle ['kjuːbɪkəl] *n* *(in hospital, dormitory)* box *m*; *(in restroom)* W.-C. *m*

cubism ['kjuːbɪzəm] *n* *Art* cubisme *m*

cuckold ['kʌkəld] **1** *n* cocu *m*
2 *vt* cocufier, faire cocu

cuckoo ['kʊkuː] **1** *n* *(bird)* coucou *m*; **c. clock** coucou
2 *adj* *Fam* *(mad)* dingue

cucumber ['kjuːkʌmbə(r)] *n* concombre *m*

cud [kʌd] *n* **to chew the c.** ruminer

cuddle ['kʌdəl] **1** *n* câlin *m*; **to give sb a c.** faire un câlin à qn
2 *vt* câliner, faire des câlins à
3 *vi* se câliner, se faire des câlins; **to c. up to sb** se pelotonner *ou* se blottir contre qn

cuddly ['kʌdlɪ] *adj* *Fam* *(child, animal)* mignon(onne) à croquer; *Euph* *(plump)* rond(e)

cudgel ['kʌdʒəl] **1** *n* gourdin *m*, trique *f*
2 *vt* donner des coups de gourdin *ou* de trique à; **to c. one's brains** se creuser la cervelle

cue[1] [kjuː] *n* *(of actor)* réplique *f*; *Fig* *(signal)* signal *m*; **on c.** au bon moment; **to take one's c. from sb** prendre exemple sur qn; **c. card** *(for public speaker)* aide-mémoire *m inv*

cue[2] [kjuː] *n* *(in pool)* queue *f*; **c. ball** boule *f* blanche

cuff[1] [kʌf] *n* *(of shirt)* poignet *m*; *(of pants)* revers *m*; *Fam* **cuffs** *(handcuffs)* menottes *fpl*; *Fam* **off the c.** au pied levé; **c. links** boutons *mpl* de manchette

cuff[2] [kʌf] *Fam* **1** *n* *(blow)* calotte *f*
2 *vt* *(hit)* donner une calotte à

cuisine [kwɪ'ziːn] *n* cuisine *f*

cul-de-sac ['kʌldəsæk] *n* *also Fig* impasse *f*

culinary ['kʌlɪnərɪ] *adj* culinaire

cull [kʌl] **1** *n* *(of seals, deer)* abattage *m*
2 *vt* (**a**) *(herd)* réduire la taille de; *(animal)* abattre (**b**) *(select)* sélectionner (**from** parmi)

culminate ['kʌlmɪneɪt] *vi* **to c. in sth** aboutir à qch

culmination [kʌlmɪ'neɪʃən] *n* point *m* culminant

culottes [kuː'lɒts] *npl* jupe-culotte *f*

culpable ['kʌlpəbəl] *adj* coupable (**of** de)

culprit ['kʌlprɪt] *n* coupable *mf*

cult [kʌlt] *n* culte *m*; *(sect)* secte *f*; **c. figure** personnage *m* culte; **c. movie** film *m* culte

cultivate ['kʌltɪveɪt] *vt* *also Fig* cultiver

cultivated ['kʌltɪveɪtɪd] *adj* cultivé(e)

cultivation [kʌltɪ'veɪʃən] *n* culture *f*

cultivator ['kʌltɪveɪtə(r)] *n* *(for farm)* cultivateur *m*; *(for garden)* motoculteur *m*; *(person)* cultivateur(trice) *m,f*

cultural ['kʌltʃərəl] *adj* culturel(elle)

culture ['kʌltʃə(r)] *n* (**a**) *(artistic activity, refinement)* culture *f*; *Hum* **c. vulture** fou (folle) *m,f* de culture (**b**) *(society)* culture *f*; **c. shock** choc *m* culturel (**c**) *Biol* culture *f*

cultured ['kʌltʃəd] *adj* *(educated)* cultivé(e); **c. pearl** perle *f* de culture

cumbersome ['kʌmbəsəm] *adj* *(luggage, furniture)* encombrant(e); *(procedure, style)* lourd(e)

cumin ['kʌmɪn] *n* cumin *m*

cumulative ['kjuːmjʊlətɪv] *adj* cumulatif(ive)

cunning ['kʌnɪŋ] **1** *n* *(deviousness)* ruse *f*; *(ingenuity)* astuce *f*, ingéniosité *f*
2 *adj* *(devious)* rusé(e); *(ingenious)* astucieux(euse), ingénieux(euse)

cunt [kʌnt] *n* *Vulg* *(vagina)* chatte *f*; *(as insult)* enculé(e) *m,f*

cup [kʌp] **1** *n* (**a**) *(for drinking, measurement)* tasse *f*; *(plastic, paper)* gobelet *m*; *Fam Fig* **it's not my c. of tea** ce n'est pas ma tasse de thé; **it's not everyone's c. of tea** tout le monde n'aime pas (**b**) *(trophy)* coupe *f* (**c**) *(of bra)* bonnet *m*
2 *vt* (*pt & pp* **cupped**) **to c. one's hands around one's mouth** mettre ses mains en porte-voix; **to c. one's hand behind one's ear** mettre sa main en cornet

cupboard ['kʌbəd] *n* placard *m*; *Fam* **c. love** amour *m* intéressé; **c. space** rangements *mpl*

cupcake ['kʌpkeɪk] *n* = petit gâteau de Savoie

Cupid ['kjuːpɪd] *n* Cupidon *m*

curable ['kjʊərəbəl] *adj* guérissable

curate ['kjʊərət] *n* *Rel* vicaire *m*

curator [kjʊə'reɪtə(r)] *n* *(of exhibition)* conservateur(trice) *m,f*

curb [kɜːb] **1** *n* (**a**) *(limit)* **to put a c. on sth** mettre un frein à qch (**b**) *(of road)* bordure *f* de trottoir
2 *vt* *(spending)* réduire; *(emotions)* réfréner

curbside ['kɜːbsaɪd] *n* *(of road)* bord *m* du trottoir

curbstone ['kɜːbstəʊn] *n* bordure *f* de trottoir

curd [kɜːd] *n* **curd(s)** lait *m* caillé; **c. cheese** fromage *m* blanc battu

curdle ['kɜːdəl] **1** *vt* cailler
2 *vi* (se) cailler

cure ['kjʊə(r)] **1** *n* remède *m* (**for** contre); **there is no known c.** on n'a pas encore trouvé de remède; **beyond c.** *(person)* incurable; *(situation)* irrémédiable
2 *vt* (**a**) *(person)* guérir (**of** de) (**b**) *(preserve)* *(by salting)* saler; *(by smoking)* fumer; *(by drying)* sécher; *(hides)* traiter

cure-all ['kjʊərɔːl] *n* panacée *f*

curfew ['kɜːfjuː] *n* couvre-feu *m*

curio ['kjʊərɪəʊ] (*pl* **curios**) *n* curiosité *f*

curiosity [kjʊərɪ'ɒsɪtɪ] (*pl* **curiosities**) *n* curiosité *f*; *Prov* **c. killed the cat** la curiosité est un vilain défaut

curious ['kjʊərɪəs] *adj* (*inquisitive, strange*) curieux(euse); **to be c. to see/know** vouloir voir/savoir par curiosité

curl [kɜːl] **1** *n* (*of hair*) boucle *f*; (*of smoke*) volute *f*

2 *vt* (*hair*) boucler; (*tightly*) friser; **to c. one's lip** faire une moue dédaigneuse; **to c. oneself into a ball** se rouler en boule

3 *vi* (*of hair*) boucler; (*tightly*) friser; (*of paper, leaves*) se recroqueviller; (*of smoke*) s'élever en volutes

▶**curl up** *vi* (**a**) (*make oneself comfortable*) se pelotonner (**b**) (*protect oneself*) se rouler en boule (**c**) (*of paper, leaves*) se recroqueviller

curler ['kɜːlə(r)] *n* (*for hair*) bigoudi *m*

curlew ['kɜːljuː] *n* courlis *m*

curling ['kɜːlɪŋ] *n* (**a**) (*sport*) curling *m* (**b**) **c. iron** fer *m* à friser

curly ['kɜːlɪ] *adj* (*hair*) bouclé(e); (*tightly*) frisé(e)

currant ['kʌrənt] *n* raisin *m* de Corinthe

currency ['kʌrənsɪ] (*pl* **currencies**) *n* (**a**) (*money*) monnaie *f*; (*foreign*) devise *f*; **c. market** marché *m* monétaire (**b**) (*acceptance*) **to gain c.** (*of theory*) être accrédité(e); (*of idea, belief*) se répandre; **to give c. to a rumor** faire courir un bruit

current ['kʌrənt] **1** *n* (*of river, electricity*) & *Fig* (*trend*) courant *m*; *Fig* **to swim against the c.** aller à contre-courant

2 *adj* (**a**) (*existing, present*) actuel(elle); **c. affairs** actualité *f*; **c. issue** (*of magazine*) dernier numéro *m* (**b**) (*common*) courant(e)

currently ['kʌrəntlɪ] *adv* actuellement

curriculum [kə'rɪkjʊləm] (*pl* **curriculums** *or* **curricula** [kə'rɪkjʊlə]) *n Sch* programme *m*; **c. vitae** curriculum vitae *m inv*

curry¹ ['kʌrɪ] **1** *n* (*pl* **curries**) curry *m*; **chicken c.** curry de poulet; **c. powder** curry

2 *vt* (*pt & pp* **curried**) **curried lamb** agneau *m* au curry

curry² ['kʌrɪ] *vt* **to c. favor with sb** s'insinuer dans les bonnes grâces de qn

curse [kɜːs] **1** *n* (**a**) (*jinx, affliction*) malédiction *f*, mauvais sort *m*; (*swearword*) juron *m*; **to put a c. on sb** jeter un sort à qn (**b**) (*scourge*) fléau *m*

2 *vt* maudire; **to be cursed with sth** être affligé(e) de qch

3 *vi* jurer

cursor ['kɜːsə(r)] *n Comput* curseur *m*; **c. key** touche *f* de déplacement

cursory ['kɜːsərɪ] *adj* superficiel(elle)

curt [kɜːt] *adj* sec (sèche)

curtail [kɜː'teɪl] *vt* (*shorten*) abréger, écourter; (*limit*) réduire

curtain ['kɜːtən] *n* rideau *m*; **to draw the curtains** (*open*) ouvrir les rideaux; (*close*) fermer *ou* tirer les rideaux; *Fam Fig* **it's curtains for her** elle est fichue; *Theat* **c. call** rappel *m*; **c. raiser** *Theat* lever *m* de rideau; *Fig* prélude *m* (**to** à); **c. ring** anneau *m* de rideau; **c. rod** tringle *f* à rideau

▶**curtain off** *vt sep* séparer par un rideau

curts(e)y ['kɜːtsɪ] **1** *n* (*pl* **curtsies** *or* **curtseys**) révérence *f*

2 *vi* (*pt & pp* **curtsied** *or* **curtseyed**) faire la révérence (**to** à)

curvaceous [kɜː'veɪʃəs] *adj* pulpeux(euse)

curvature ['kɜːvətʃə(r)] *n* courbure *f*; **c. of the spine** scoliose *f*

curve [kɜːv] **1** *n* courbe *f*; (*in road*) tournant *m*, virage *m*; (*in river*) méandre *m*

2 *vi* (*of spine*) se courber; (*of road*) faire une courbe; (*of river*) serpenter

curved [kɜːvd] *adj* (*line*) courbe; (*spine*) courbé(e)

curvy ['kɜːvɪ] *adj* (**a**) (*road, line*) sinueux (**b**) *Fam* (*woman*) bien roulé(e)

cushion ['kʊʃən] **1** *n* (*on chair, of air*) coussin *m*; (*on billiard table*) bande *f*

2 *vt* (*blow, impact*) amortir; **to c. sb against sth** protéger qn contre qch

cushy ['kʊʃɪ] *adj Fam* pépère, peinard(e); **a c. number** une bonne planque

custard ['kʌstəd] *n* crème *f* renversée; **c. pie** (*in slapstick comedy*) tarte *f* à la crème

custodial [kʌs'təʊdɪəl] *adj* **c. parent** = parent auquel on a confié la garde des enfants

custodian [kʌs'təʊdɪən] *n* gardien(enne) *m,f*

custody ['kʌstədɪ] *n* (**a**) (*of children, important papers*) garde *f*; **to have c. of sb** avoir la garde de qn; **in safe c.** sous bonne garde (**b**) *Law* garde *f* à vue; **to take sb into c.** placer qn en garde à vue

custom ['kʌstəm] *n* (**a**) (*tradition, practice*) coutume *f*; **it was his c. to rise early** il avait l'habitude de se lever tôt (**b**) *Com* clientèle *f*; **to take one's c. elsewhere** aller se fournir ailleurs

customary ['kʌstəmərɪ] *adj* (*usual*) habituel(elle); (*traditional*) traditionnel(elle); **it is c. to...** il est d'usage de...

custom-built ['kʌstəmbɪlt] *adj* (*car, offices*) construit(e) sur mesure; (*kitchen units*) fabriqué(e) sur mesure

customer ['kʌstəmə(r)] *n* client(e) *m,f*; *Fam Fig* **he's an awkward c.** c'est un type pas commode; *Com* **c. services (department)** service *m* clientèle

customize ['kʌstəmaɪz] *vt* (*vehicle*) customiser; (*kitchen, computer*) personnaliser

custom-made ['kʌstəm'meɪd] *adj* (*fait(e)*) sur mesure

customs ['kʌstəmz] *npl* douane *f*; **to go through c.** passer la douane; **c. declaration** déclaration *f* en douane; **c. duty** droits *mpl* de douane; **c. officer** douanier(ère) *m,f*

cut [kʌt] **1** *n* (**a**) (*in flesh, text, movie*) coupure *f*; (*in wood, cloth*) entaille *f*; **c. of meat** morceau *m* (de viande); *Fam* **to be a c. above sb/sth** être un cran au-dessus de qn/qch

(**b**) (*in wages, prices*) réduction *f*

(**c**) (*blow*) coup *m*; **the c. and thrust of debate** les joutes *fpl* oratoires

(**d**) *Fam* (*share*) part *f*

(**e**) (*style*) (*of clothes, hair*) coupe *f*

2 *adj Fig* **c. and dried** (*clear*) simple; (*decided*) décidé(e); **c. flowers** fleurs *fpl* coupées; **c. glass** cristal *m* taillé

3 *vt* (*pt & pp* **cut**) (**a**) (*in general*) couper; (*into slices*) trancher, découper; (*meat, chicken*) découper; **to c. sb's finger/nails** se couper le doigt/les ongles; **to c. sb's hair** couper les cheveux à qn; **to have one's hair cut** se faire couper les cheveux; **to c. sth in two** *or* **in half** couper qch en deux; **to c. sth to pieces** couper qch en morceaux; **to c. oneself loose** *or* **free** se dégager, se libérer; **to c. a record** enregistrer un disque; *Comput* **to c. and paste sth** faire du couper-coller sur qch

(**b**) (*wages, prices*) réduire

(**c**) (*idioms*) **to c. a deal** conclure une affaire; **to c. one's losses** limiter les dégâts; **to c. corners** (*to economize*) faire des économies exagérées; **she doesn't believe in cutting corners** elle fait toujours les choses à fond; **to c. one's teeth on sth** se faire les dents sur qch; **to c. sb (dead)** faire semblant de ne pas voir qn; **it's cutting it** *or* **things (a bit) fine** ça fait (un peu) juste; **to c. sb short** couper la parole à qn; **to c. sth short** écourter qch; **to c. a long story short...** bref...

4 *vi* (**a**) (*of knife, scissors*) couper; (*of wind*) être cinglant(e); *Cin* **c.!** coupez!

(**b**) (*idioms*) **that's an argument that cuts both ways** c'est un argument à double tranchant; *Fam* **to c. and run** décamper

▶**cut across** *vt insep* (**a**) (*field*) couper à travers (**b**) (*transcend*) transcender

▶**cut back 1** *vt sep* (**a**) (*bush, tree*) tailler (**b**) (*costs, production*) réduire

2 *vi* **to c. back on sth** (*spending, time*) réduire qch; **to c. back on smoking/drinking** fumer/boire moins

▶**cut down 1** *vt sep* (**a**) *(tree, soldier)* abattre; **to be c. down in one's prime** être fauché(e) à la fleur de l'âge (**b**) *(speech, text)* abréger; *(spending, time)* réduire; *Fig* **to c. sb down to size** rabattre son caquet à qn
2 *vi* = **cut back**

▶**cut in** *vi* (**a**) *(interrupt conversation)* intervenir (**b**) *(in car)* **to c. in in front of sb** faire une queue de poisson à qn

▶**cut into** *vt insep (with knife)* entamer; *(of rope, handle)* blesser

▶**cut off** *vt sep* (**a**) *(remove)* couper; **to c. off sb's head** trancher la tête à qn, décapiter qn; *Fig* **that would be cutting off your nose to spite your face** ça va te retomber sur le nez (**b**) *(disconnect)* couper; **we've been c. off** *(had electricity disconnected)* on nous a coupé l'électricité; **I've been c. off** *(during phone conversation)* j'ai été coupé (**c**) *(isolate)* isoler; **to be c. off from** être coupé(e) de

▶**cut out 1** *vt sep* (**a**) *(picture, article)* découper; *(tumor)* enlever; *Fam* **to have one's work c. out** avoir du pain sur la planche; **to be c. out for sth** être fait(e) pour qch (**b**) *(stop)* supprimer; **to c. out smoking/desserts** arrêter de fumer/de manger des desserts; *Fam* **c. it out!** ça va maintenant! (**c**) *(exclude)* **to c. sb out of one's will** déshériter qn; **to c. sb out of a deal** évincer qn
2 *vi (of engine)* caler; *(of machine)* s'arrêter

▶**cut up** *vt sep* (**a**) *(food, paper)* couper; *(into slices)* découper (**b**) *Fam (upset)* **to be very c. up (about sth)** être complètement chamboulé(e) (par qch)

cut-and-paste ['kʌtənd'peɪst] *n Comput* couper-coller *m*

cutback ['kʌtbæk] *n* réduction *f*

cute [kjuːt] *adj* mignon(onne)

cuticle ['kjuːtɪkəl] *n* cuticule *f*

cutlery ['kʌtlərɪ] *n* couverts *mpl; Com* argenterie *f*

cutlet ['kʌtlɪt] *n* côtelette *f*

cutoff ['kʌtɒf] *n* **c. date** date *f* limite; **c. point** limite *f; (for tax)* seuil *m*

cutout ['kʌtaʊt] *n* (**a**) *(shape)* silhouette *f* (**b**) *Elec* disjoncteur *m*

cut-rate ['kʌt'reɪt] *adj (goods)* à prix réduit; *(rate)* réduit(e)

cutthroat ['kʌtθrəʊt] **1** *n* assassin *m*
2 *adj (competition)* acharné(e)

cutting ['kʌtɪŋ] **1** *n (of plant)* bouture *f*
2 *adj (wind, remark)* cinglant(e); **c. edge** tranchant *m; Fig* **to be at the c. edge of technology** être à la pointe du progrès

cuttlefish ['kʌtəlfɪʃ] *n* seiche *f*

CV [siː'viː] *n (abbr* **curriculum vitae**) CV *m*

cyanide ['saɪənaɪd] *n Chem* cyanure *m*

cybercafé ['saɪbəkæfeɪ] *n* cybercafé *m*

cybernetics [saɪbə'netɪks] *n Comput* cybernétique *f*

cybersex ['saɪbəseks] *n Comput* cybersexe *m*

cyberspace ['saɪbəspeɪs] *n Comput* cyberespace *m*

cybersquatter ['saɪbə'skwɒtə(r)] *n Comput* cybersquatteur *m*

cybersquatting ['saɪbəskwɒtɪŋ] *n Comput* cybersquatting *m, Offic* cybersquattage *m*

cyberstalker ['saɪbə'stɔːkə(r)] *n Comput* = personne qui en harcèle une autre par l'intermédiaire d'Internet

cyberstalking ['saɪbə'stɔːkɪŋ] *n Comput* cyberharcèlement *m*

cyberterrorism ['saɪbə'terərɪzəm] *n Comput* cyberterrorisme *m*

cyberterrorist ['saɪbə'terərɪst] *n Comput* cyberterroriste *mf*

cyclamen ['sɪkləmən] *(pl* **cyclamen**) *n* cyclamen *m*

cycle ['saɪkəl] **1** *n* (**a**) *(pattern)* cycle *m* (**b**) *(bicycle)* bicyclette *f*, vélo *m*; **c. lane** voie *f* réservée aux vélos; **c. path** piste *f* cyclable; **c. racing** course *f* cycliste
2 *vi* aller à bicyclette *ou* à vélo

cyclic ['saɪklɪk], **cyclical** ['saɪklɪkəl] *adj* cyclique

cycler ['saɪklə(r)] *n* cycliste *mf*

cycling ['saɪklɪŋ] *n* cyclisme *m*; **to go on a c. vacation** faire du cyclotourisme

cyclist ['saɪklɪst] *n* cycliste *mf*

cyclone ['saɪkləʊn] *n Met* cyclone *m*

cygnet ['sɪgnɪt] *n* jeune cygne *m*

cylinder ['sɪlɪndə(r)] *n (shape)* cylindre *m*; *(gas container)* bouteille *f*; **four-/eight-c. engine** moteur *m* à quatre/huit cylindres; **c. block** bloc-cylindres *m*; **c. head** culasse *f*

cylindrical [sɪ'lɪndrɪkəl] *adj* cylindrique

cymbal ['sɪmbəl] *n* cymbale *f*

cynic ['sɪnɪk] *n* cynique *mf*

cynical ['sɪnɪkəl] *adj* cynique (**about** sur)

cypress ['saɪprəs] *n* cyprès *m*

Cypriot ['sɪprɪət] **1** *n* Chypriote *mf*, Cypriote *mf*
2 *adj* chypriote, cypriote

Cyprus ['saɪprəs] *n* Chypre

cyst [sɪst] *n Med* kyste *m*

cystitis [sɪs'taɪtɪs] *n Med* cystite *f*

czar [zɑː(r)] *n* tsar *m*, czar *m*

czarist ['zɑːrɪst] *n & adj* tsariste *mf*

Czech [tʃek] **1** *n* (**a**) *(person)* Tchèque *mf* (**b**) *(language)* tchèque *m*
2 *adj* tchèque; **the C. Republic** la République tchèque

D

D¹, d [diː] *n* (**a**) *(letter)* D, d *m inv* (**b**) *Mus* ré *m* (**c**) *Sch (grade)* **to get a D** avoir entre 8 et 10 sur 20

D² *Pol (abbr* **Democrat** *or* **Democratic)** démocrate

DA [diːˈeɪ] *n Law (abbr* **district attorney)** ≃ procureur *m* de la République

DAB [ˈdiːeɪˈbiː] *n (abbr* **digital audio broadcasting)** diffusion *f* audionumérique

dab [dæb] **1** *n (of paint)* petit coup *m*; *(of glue)* point *m*; *(of perfume)* goutte *f*

2 *vt (pt & pp* **dabbed)** *(paint)* passer; *(eyes, wound)* tamponner

dabble [ˈdæbəl] **1** *vt* **to d. one's feet in the water** balancer ses pieds dans l'eau

2 *vi* **to d. in politics/journalism** faire vaguement de la politique/du journalisme

dabbler [ˈdæblə(r)] *n* amateur(trice) *m,f*

dachshund [ˈdækshʊnd] *n* teckel *m*

dad [dæd] *n Fam* papa *m*

daddy [ˈdædɪ] *(pl* **daddies)** *n Fam* papa *m*

daddy-longlegs [ˈdædɪˈlɒŋlegz] *(pl* **daddy-longlegs)** *n Fam* faucheur *m*, faucheux *m*

daffodil [ˈdæfədɪl] *n* jonquille *f*

dagger [ˈdægə(r)] *n* (**a**) *(weapon)* dague *f* (**b**) *(idioms)* **to be at daggers drawn (with sb)** être à couteaux tirés (avec qn); **to look daggers at sb** foudroyer qn du regard

dago [ˈdeɪgəʊ] *(pl* **dagoes** *or* **dagos)** *n very Fam Pej* = terme injurieux désignant un Espagnol, un Portugais, un Italien ou un Latino-Américain

dahlia [ˈdeɪlɪə] *n* dahlia *m*

daily [ˈdeɪlɪ] **1** *n (pl* **dailies)** *(newspaper)* quotidien *m*

2 *adj* quotidien(enne); **on a d. basis** *(paid, calculated)* à la journée; *(used)* quotidiennement; *Fam* **the d. grind** le train-train quotidien; **d. paper** quotidien *m*

3 *adv* tous les jours, quotidiennement; **twice d.** deux fois par jour

dainty [ˈdeɪntɪ] *adj* délicat(e)

dairy [ˈdeərɪ] *(pl* **dairies)** *n (store)* crémerie *f*; *(factory)* laiterie *f*; **d. cow** vache *f* laitière; **d. farm** = ferme spécialisée dans la production laitière; **d. farming** élevage *m* de vaches laitières; **d. products** produits *mpl* laitiers

dais [ˈdeɪɪs] *n* estrade *f*

daisy [ˈdeɪzɪ] *(pl* **daisies)** *n* pâquerette *f*; *(bigger)* marguerite *f*; *Fam* **to push up the daisies** manger les pissenlits par la racine; **d. chain** guirlande *f* de pâquerettes

daisywheel [ˈdeɪzɪwiːl] *n (on printer)* marguerite *f*

dale [deɪl] *n* vallée *f*

dalliance [ˈdælɪəns] *n Lit* badinage *m*

dally [ˈdælɪ] *(pt & pp* **dallied)** *vi (dawdle)* traîner, lambiner; **to d. over a decision** mettre du temps à se décider; **to d. with sb** flirter avec qn

Dalmatian [dælˈmeɪʃən] *n (dog)* dalmatien *m*

dam [dæm] **1** *n* barrage *m*

2 *vt (pt & pp* **dammed)** *(river, lake)* construire un barrage sur

▸**dam up** *vt sep (river, lake)* construire un barrage sur

damage [ˈdæmɪdʒ] **1** *n* (**a**) *(to machine, building)* dégâts *mpl*; *(to health, reputation)* mal *m*; **to do** *or* **to cause d. to** *(building)* faire des dégâts dans; *(health, reputation)* nuire à; *Fig* **the d. is done** le mal est fait; **we have to do some d. control** il faut limiter les dégâts (**b**) **damages** *(compensation)* dommages-intérêts *mpl*

2 *vt (machine, building)* abîmer, endommager; *(health, reputation)* nuire à; *(chances)* compromettre; *(person)* faire du tort à

damaging [ˈdæmɪdʒɪŋ] *adj* préjudiciable (**to** à)

Damascus [dəˈmæskəs] *n* Damas

damask [ˈdæməsk] *n* damas *m*

dame [deɪm] *n Fam (woman)* pépée *f*

damn [dæm] **1** *n very Fam* **I don't give a d.** j'en ai rien à fiche; **it's not worth a d.** ça ne vaut pas un clou

2 *adj very Fam* fichu(e); **you d. fool!** espèce d'idiot(e)!; **he's a d. nuisance!** qu'est-ce qu'il peut être casse-pieds!

3 *adv very Fam* sacrément; **you know d. well what I mean!** tu sais fichtrement bien ce que je veux dire!

4 *exclam very Fam* **d.!** zut!, mince!

5 *vt* (**a**) *(criticize severely)* éreinter; **to d. sb with faint praise** éreinter qn sous couleur d'éloge (**b**) *very Fam* **d. the expense!** au diable l'avarice!; **d. it!** zut!, mince!; **well I'll be damned!** ben mince alors!

damnation [dæmˈneɪʃən] **1** *n Rel* damnation *f*

2 *exclam Fam* **d.!** bon sang!

damned [dæmd] **1** *npl Rel* **the d.** les damnés *mpl*

2 *adj & adv very Fam* = **damn**

damn-fool [ˈdæmfuːl] *adj Fam* débile

damning [ˈdæmɪŋ] *adj (admission, revelation)* accablant(e)

damp [dæmp] **1** *n* humidité *f*

2 *adj* humide; *(skin)* moite

3 *vt (make wet)* humecter; **to d. down a fire** couvrir un feu

dampen [ˈdæmpən] *vt (make wet)* humecter; *Fig* **to d. sb's spirits** décourager qn

damper [ˈdæmpə(r)] *n Mus* étouffoir *m*; *Fig* **to put a d. on sth** jeter un froid sur qch

damsel [ˈdæmzəl] *n Lit* damoiselle *f*; *Hum* **a d. in distress** une belle éplorée

damson [ˈdæmzən] *n (fruit)* prune *f* de Damas; *(tree)* prunier *m* de Damas

dance [dɑːns] **1** *n* danse *f*; *(event)* soirée *f* dansante; *(for young people)* boum *f*; *(formal)* bal *m*; **d. band** orchestre *m* de danse; **d. floor** piste *f* de danse; **d. hall** salle *f* de bal; **d. music** *(in clubs)* dance (music) *f*

2 *vt (waltz, tango)* danser

3 *vi* danser; **they danced down the road** ils ont descendu la rue en dansant

dancer [ˈdɑːnsə(r)] *n* danseur(euse) *m,f*

dancing [ˈdɑːnsɪŋ] *n* danse *f*; **d. shoes** chaussons *mpl* de danse

dandelion [ˈdændɪlaɪən] *n* pissenlit *m*

dander [ˈdændə(r)] *n Fam* **to get sb's d. up** hérisser qn

dandruff ['dændrəf] n pellicules fpl

dandy ['dændɪ] **1** n (pl **dandies**) dandy m

2 adj Fam génial(e); **everything's just (fine and) d.** tout marche comme sur des roulettes

Dane [deɪn] n Danois(e) m,f

danger ['deɪndʒə(r)] n danger m; **in d.** en danger; **out of d.** hors de danger; **to be in d. of doing sth** risquer de faire qch; **there's no d. that...** il n'y a pas de danger que... + subjunctive; **d. pay** prime f de risque; Fig **d. sign** signal m d'alarme

dangerous ['deɪndʒərəs] adj dangereux(euse)

dangerously ['deɪndʒərəslɪ] adv dangereusement; **they came d. close to losing** ils ont bien failli perdre

dangle ['dæŋgəl] **1** vt balancer; Fig **to d. sth in front of sb** faire miroiter qch à qn

2 vi (of legs) pendre; (from rope, chain) se balancer; Fig **to keep sb dangling** laisser qn dans l'incertitude

Danish ['deɪnɪʃ] **1** n (language) danois m; (pastry) = sorte de chausson fourré

2 adj danois(e); **D. pastry** = sorte de chausson fourré

dank [dæŋk] adj humide et froid(e)

Danube ['dænju:b] n **the D.** le Danube

dapper ['dæpə(r)] adj soigné(e)

dappled ['dæpəld] adj tacheté(e); (horse) pommelé(e)

dare ['deə(r)] **1** n défi m; **to do sth for a d.** faire qch par défi

2 vt **to d. to do sth** oser faire qch; **to d. sb to do sth** défier qn de faire qch; **I d. you!** chiche!; **don't you d. (do that)!** ne t'avise pas de faire ça!; **how d. you!** comment oses-tu!; **I d. say** sans doute, c'est bien possible

daredevil ['deədevəl] **1** n casse-cou mf inv

2 adj (person) casse-cou inv; (stunt, escape) audacieux(euse)

daring ['deərɪŋ] **1** n audace f

2 adj audacieux(euse)

dark [dɑ:k] **1** n (a) (darkness) obscurité f; **before/after d.** avant/après la tombée de la nuit; **in the d.** dans le noir (b) (idioms) **to be in the d. (about)** ne pas être au courant (de); **to keep sb in the d. about sth** maintenir qn dans l'ignorance à propos de qch

2 adj (a) (not light) sombre; (skin, hair) foncé(e); **it's d. by six o'clock** il fait nuit à six heures; **it's getting d.** il commence à faire nuit; **d. glasses** lunettes fpl noires; Fig **d. horse** (competitor) outsider m; (in politics) candidat(e) m,f surprise; (secretive person) personne f pleine de mystère (b) Fig (thought) sombre, morose; (period) sombre; (look) noir(e); Hist **the D. Ages** le Haut Moyen Âge; Fig **to be in the D. Ages** être encore au Moyen Âge

darken ['dɑ:kən] **1** vt (sky, color) assombrir; **never d. my door again!** ne remettez plus les pieds chez moi!

2 vi (of sky, color, thoughts) s'assombrir

dark-haired ['dɑ:k'heəd] adj aux cheveux foncés

darkness ['dɑ:knɪs] n obscurité f; **in d.** dans l'obscurité

darkroom ['dɑ:kru:m] n chambre f noire

dark-skinned ['dɑ:k'skɪnd] adj à la peau mate

darling ['dɑ:lɪŋ] **1** n (term of address) (to woman) chérie f; (to man) chéri m; **she's the d. of the press** c'est la coqueluche des journaux

2 adj (dear) cher (chère); (charming) adorable

darn¹ [dɑ:n] vt (mend) repriser

darn² [dɑ:n] Fam **1** adj sacré(e); **it's a d. nuisance!** c'est vachement embêtant!

2 exclam **d. (it)!** zut!

darning ['dɑ:nɪŋ] n reprisage m; **d. needle** aiguille f à repriser

dart [dɑ:t] **1** n (a) (missile) flèche f; **darts** (game) fléchettes fpl (b) (movement) **to make a d. for sth** se ruer vers qch

2 vt **to d. a glance at sb** jeter un regard à qn

3 vi **to d. in/out** entrer/sortir comme une flèche

dartboard ['dɑ:tbɔ:d] n cible f (de jeu de fléchettes)

dash [dæʃ] **1** n (a) (of liquid) goutte f; (of humor, color) touche f

(b) (hyphen, in Morse code) tiret m

(c) (run) course f effrénée; **to make a d. for sth** se ruer vers qch; **to make a d. for it** s'enfuir

(d) (style) panache m; **to cut a d.** avoir fière allure

(e) (of car) tableau m de bord

2 vt (a) (throw) jeter; **to d. sth to the ground** jeter qch par terre

(b) (destroy) (hopes) réduire à néant

3 vi **to d. in/out** entrer/sortir comme une flèche; **I dashed around all day** j'ai couru toute la journée; Fam **I must d.** il faut que je file

▸**dash off 1** vt sep (letter) écrire en vitesse

2 vi (leave) filer

dashboard ['dæʃbɔ:d] n (of car) tableau m de bord

dashing ['dæʃɪŋ] adj (person) fringant(e); (appearance) élégant(e)

DAT [di:eɪ'ti:] n (abbr **digital audio tape**) DAT m

data ['deɪtə, 'dætə] n informations fpl; Comput données fpl; **an item** or **piece of d.** une information/donnée; **d. bank** banque f de données; Comput **d. processing** traitement m de l'information; **d. protection** protection f de l'information

database ['deɪtəbeɪs, 'dætəbeɪs] n Comput base f de données

date¹ [deɪt] n (fruit) datte f; **d. palm** palmier m dattier

date² [deɪt] **1** n (a) (day) date f; **d. of birth** date de naissance; **what's the d. (today)?** le combien sommes-nous aujourd'hui?; **to d.** à ce jour; **up to d.** (with work) à jour; (with events, news) au courant; (in fashion) à la mode; **out of d.** périmé(e); **d. stamp** tampon m ou timbre m à date (b) (with girlfriend, boyfriend) rendez-vous m; **d. rape** = viol commis par une connaissance de la victime (c) (girlfriend, boyfriend) ami(e) m,f

2 vt (a) (letter, ticket) dater (b) (go out with) sortir avec

3 vi (a) **to d. from** or **back to** (of custom, practice) remonter à; (of building) dater de (b) (go out of fashion) dater (c) (go out with people) sortir avec des filles/des garçons

datebook ['deɪtbʊk] n agenda m

dateline ['deɪtlaɪn] n date f et lieu m de rédaction

dating agency ['deɪtɪŋeɪdʒənsɪ] n agence f matrimoniale

dative ['deɪtɪv] n Gram datif m

daub [dɔ:b] vt barbouiller (**with** de)

daughter ['dɔ:tə(r)] n fille f

daughter-in-law ['dɔ:tərɪnlɔ:] n (pl **daughters-in-law**) belle-fille f

daunt [dɔ:nt] vt intimider; **nothing daunted** nullement découragé(e)

daunting ['dɔ:ntɪŋ] adj intimidant(e)

dawdle ['dɔ:dəl] vi traînasser, lambiner

dawn [dɔ:n] **1** n also Fig aube f; **at d.** à l'aube; **from d. to dusk** du lever au coucher du soleil; **the d. chorus** le chant des oiseaux à l'aube

2 vi (of day) se lever; Fig (of life, civilization) naître

▸**dawn on** vt insep **the truth finally dawned on her** la vérité a fini par lui apparaître; **it dawned on me that...** je me suis enfin rendu compte que...

day [deɪ] n (a) (period of daylight, twenty-four hours) jour m; (referring to duration) journée f; **once/twice a d.** une fois/deux fois par jour; **the d. before yesterday** avant-hier; **the d. after tomorrow** après-demain; **all d.** toute la journée; **d. after d.** jour après jour; **to change from d. to d.** changer d'un jour sur l'autre; **to live from d. to d.** vivre au jour le jour; **one d.,** **one of these days** un de ces jours; **any d. now** d'un jour à l'autre; **the other d.** l'autre jour; **every other d.** tous les deux jours, un jour sur deux; **a year ago to the d.** il y a un an jour pour jour; **from d. one** dès le début; **to take a d. off (work)** prendre un jour de congé; **to be paid by the d.** être payé(e) à la journée; **to work d. and night** travailler jour et nuit; Fam he's sixty if he's a d. il a soixante ans bien sonnés; **d. nursery** crèche *f*; **d. school** externat *m*; **d. shift** *(in factory)* équipe *f* de jour; **d. student** externe *mf*; **d. trip** excursion *f* d'une journée

(b) *(era)* **in my d.** de mon temps; **in this d. and age** à notre époque; **this government/TV has had its d.** ce gouvernement/cette télé a fait son temps; **in the days of...** du temps de...; **these days** de nos jours; **in those days** en ce temps-là; **those were the days!** c'était le bon temps!; **in days to come** à l'avenir

(c) *(idioms)* **it's all in a d.'s work** c'est la routine; **to make sb's d.** mettre qn de bonne humeur; *Fam* **let's call it a d.** ça suffit pour aujourd'hui; *Fam* **that'll be the d.!** c'est pas demain la veille!; **to name the d.** *(of wedding)* choisir la date de son mariage; **to carry** *or* **to win the d.** l'emporter

daybreak ['deɪbreɪk] *n* lever *m* du jour; **at d.** au lever du jour

daycare ['deɪkeə(r)] *n (for children)* service *m* de garderie; *(for elderly, disabled)* service *m* d'acceuil de jour

daydream ['deɪdriːm] **1** *n* rêverie *f*; *Pej* rêvasserie *f*
   2 *vi* rêver **(about** à); *Pej* rêvasser

daylight ['deɪlaɪt] *n* jour *m*, lumière *f*; **it was still d.** il faisait encore jour; *Fig* **it's d. robbery!** c'est du vol pur et simple!; **d. saving time** heure *f* d'été

daytime ['deɪtaɪm] *n* jour *m*, journée *f*; **in the d.** pendant la journée; **d. TV** = émissions de télévision diffusées pendant la journée

day-to-day ['deɪtə'deɪ] *adj* courant(e), quotidien(enne); **on a d. basis** au jour le jour

daze [deɪz] **1** *n* **in a d.** *(from news)* abasourdi(e); *(from drug, blow)* étourdi(e)
   2 *vt (of news)* abasourdir; *(of drug, blow)* étourdir

dazed [deɪzd] *adj (by news)* abasourdi(e); *(by drug, blow)* étourdi(e)

dazzle ['dæzəl] *vt also Fig* éblouir

dazzling ['dæzlɪŋ] *adj also Fig* éblouissant(e)

DC [diː'siː] *n* (a) *Elec (abbr* **direct current)** courant *m* continu
   (b) *(abbr* **District of Columbia)** DC

deacon ['diːkən] *n Rel* diacre *m*

deaconess [diːkə'nes] *n Rel* diaconesse *f*

dead [ded] **1** *adj* (a) *(not alive)* mort(e); **a d. man** un mort; **a d. woman** une morte; *Fig* **to be d. to the world** dormir d'un sommeil profond; *Fam* **over my d. body!** moi vivant, jamais!; *Fam* **I wouldn't be seen** *or* **caught d. in that dress!** je ne porterais cette robe pour rien au monde!; *Fam* **as d. as a doornail** *or* **a dodo** mort et bien mort; *Fig* **d. and buried** mort et enterré; *Fam* **if Dad finds out, you're d.** si Papa l'apprend, il va te tuer; **the D. Sea** la mer Morte; *Fam Fig* **d. duck** *(which will fail)* désastre *m* assuré; *(which has failed)* désastre *m*, fiasco *m*

   (b) *(numb) (limb)* engourdi(e); **to go d.** s'engourdir

   (c) *(voice, eyes)* éteint(e); *(phone)* sans tonalité; *(battery)* mort(e); **this place is d. in winter** cet endroit est mort en hiver; *also Fig* **d. end** cul-de-sac *m*; *Fig* **d. weight** poids *m* mort

   (d) *(absolute)* **d. calm** calme *m* plat; **d. heat** *(in race)* arrivée *f* ex aequo; *Fam* **it was a d. loss** ça n'a servi à rien; **he's a d. loss** c'est un bon à rien; *Fam* **to be a d. ringer for sb** être le sosie de qn

   2 *adv* (a) *(completely)* **to be d. set against sth** être totalement opposé(e) à qch; **to stop d.** s'arrêter net; *Fam* **d. beat** *or* **tired** crevé(e)

   (b) *(exactly)* **d. on six o'clock** à six heures précises

   3 *n* **in the d. of night** au plus profond de la nuit; **in the d. of winter** au cœur de l'hiver

   4 *npl* **the d.** les morts *mpl*; **to rise from the d.** ressusciter d'entre les morts; **the living d.** les morts-vivants *mpl*

deadbeat ['dedbiːt] *n Fam (good-for-nothing)* bon (bonne) *m,f* à rien; *(tramp)* épave *f*, loque *f*

deaden ['dedən] *vt (blow, sound)* amortir; *(pain)* calmer; **to become deadened to sth** devenir insensible à qch

dead-end ['ded'end] *adj (street)* sans issue; *Fig* **a d.** un travail qui n'offre aucune perspective d'avenir

deadline ['dedlaɪn] *n (day)* date *f* limite; *(time)* heure *f* limite; **to work to a d.** avoir un délai à respecter

deadlock ['dedlɒk] **1** *n* impasse *f*
   2 *vt* **to be deadlocked** *(of talks, negotiations)* être au point mort

deadly ['dedlɪ] **1** *adj (poison, blow, enemy)* mortel(elle); *(weapon)* meurtrier(ère); *(silence)* de mort; **d. nightshade** belladone *f*
   2 *adv (very)* **d. accurate** extrêmement précis(e); **d. boring** d'un ennui mortel; **to be d. serious** être on ne peut plus sérieux(euse)

deadpan ['dedpæn] *adj (expression)* figé(e); *(humor)* pince-sans-rire *inv*

deadwood ['dedwʊd] *n Fam* personnel *m* inutile

deaf [def] **1** *adj* sourd(e); **d. and dumb, d. mute** sourd-muet (sourde-muette); **to go d.** devenir sourd; **as d. as a post** sourd comme un pot; **to turn a d. ear to sb/sth** faire la sourde oreille à qn/qch; **the appeal fell on d. ears** l'appel n'a pas été entendu
   2 *npl* **the d.** les sourds *mpl*

deafen ['defən] *vt (make deaf)* rendre sourd(e); *(temporarily)* assourdir

deafening ['defənɪŋ] *adj* assourdissant(e)

deafness ['defnəs] *n* surdité *f*

deal [diːl] **1** *n* (a) *(agreement)* affaire *f*, marché *m*; **to do** *or Fam* **to cut a d.** conclure un marché; **it's a d.!** marché conclu!; **to get a good/bad d.** faire une bonne/mauvaise affaire; **he's had a raw d.** on ne lui a jamais fait de cadeaux; *Fam* **what's the d.?** qu'est ce qui se passe?; *Fam Ironic* **big d.!** la belle affaire!; **it's no big d.** ce n'est pas bien grave

   (b) *(amount)* **a good** *or* **great d.** beaucoup; **not a great d.** peu; **to have a great d. to do** avoir beaucoup à faire; **a good** *or* **great d. of my time** une grande partie de mon temps; **a good d. quicker/easier** beaucoup plus rapide/facile

   (c) *(in cards)* **whose d. is it?** c'est à qui de donner?; **your d.!** à vous de donner!

   2 *vt (pt & pp* **dealt** [delt]) (a) *(cards)* donner, distribuer
   (b) **to d. sb/sth a blow** donner un coup à qn/qch
   (c) *(drugs)* dealer, revendre

   3 *vi* (a) *(in card game)* donner, distribuer
   (b) *(trade)* **to d. in leather** faire le commerce des cuirs
   (c) *(sell drugs)* dealer, revendre de la drogue

▶**deal out** *vt sep (cards)* distribuer; **to d. out justice** rendre la justice

▶**deal with** *vt insep (subject)* traiter de; *(problem)* s'occuper de; **I know how to d. with him** je sais m'y prendre avec lui

dealer ['diːlə(r)] *n* (a) *(in card game)* donneur(euse) *m,f* (b) *Com* marchand(e) *m,f*; *(in cars)* concessionnaire *mf*; *(in drugs)* dealer *m*, revendeur(euse) *m,f*

dealership ['diːləʃɪp] *n Com & (for cars)* concession *f*

dealings ['diːlɪŋz] *npl* rapports *mpl*, relations *fpl*; **to have d. with sb** traiter avec qn

dealt [delt] *pt & pp of* deal²

dean [diːn] *n Rel & Univ* doyen *m*; *Univ* **d.'s list** = tableau d'honneur dans les universités américaines

dear [dɪə(r)] **1** **my d.** *(to man)* chéri; *(to woman)* chérie; **poor d.** mon pauvre/ma pauvre; *Fam* **an old d.** une grand-mère

   2 *adj* (a) *(loved)* cher (chère); **to hold sb/sth d.** tenir à qn/qch; **a d. friend** un bon ami/une bonne amie; **a place d. to the hearts of...** un endroit cher à...; *Fam* **to run for d. life** se sauver à toutes jambes

   (b) *(in letter)* **D. Sir** Monsieur; **D. Madam** Madame; **D. Sir or Madam, D. Sir/Madam** Monsieur, Madame; **D. Mr. Thomas** Cher M. Thomas; **D. Andrew** Cher Andrew; **My dearest Gertrude** Ma chère Gertrude

   (c) *(expensive)* cher (chère)

3 *adv (buy, sell)* cher; *Fig* **it cost me d.** ça m'a coûté cher

4 *exclam* **oh d.!** mon Dieu!

dearly ['dɪəlɪ] *adv (very much)* **to love sb d.** aimer qn de tout son cœur; **I would. love to know** j'aimerais vraiment savoir; *Fig* **she paid d. for her mistake** elle a payé très cher son erreur

dearth [dɜ:θ] *n* pénurie *f* (**of** de)

death [deθ] *n* (**a**) *(end of life)* mort *f*; **to put sb to d.** mettre qn à mort, exécuter qn; **a fight to the d.** une lutte à mort; **d. camp** camp *m* de la mort; **d. certificate** acte *m* de décès; **d. mask** masque *m* mortuaire; **d. penalty** peine *f* de mort; **d. rate** taux *m* de mortalité; **d. row** = quartier d'une prison où les condamnés attendent leur exécution; **d. sentence** condamnation *f* à mort; **d. squad** escadron *m* de la mort; **d. throes** agonie *f*; **d. toll** nombre *m* de morts; **D.Valley** la Vallée de la Mort; **d. warrant** ordre *m* d'exécution (**b**) *(idioms)* **to look like d. (warmed up)** avoir l'air d'un déterré/d'une déterrée; **to be sick to d. of sth** en avoir marre de qch; **to be scared to d.** être mort(e) de peur; **those children will be the d. of me!** ces enfants finiront par me tuer!; **you'll catch your d. (of cold)!** tu vas attraper la crève!; **to be at d.'s door** être à l'article de la mort; **to sound the d. knell for sth** sonner le glas de qch; **this house/car is a d. trap** cette maison/voiture est très dangereuse

deathbed ['deθbed] *n* lit *m* de mort

deathblow ['deθbləʊ] *n also Fig* coup *m* fatal; **to be the d. for sth** porter un coup fatal à qch

deathly ['deθlɪ] *adj (pallor)* mortel(elle); *(silence)* de mort

deathwatch beetle ['deθwɒtʃ'bi:təl] *n* vrillette *f*

debacle [deɪ'bɑːkəl] *n* débâcle *f*

debar [di:'bɑː(r)] *(pt & pp* **debarred**) *vt (from club)* exclure; **to d. sb from doing sth** interdire à qn de faire qch

debase [dɪ'beɪs] *vt (person)* rabaisser; *(reputation)* ternir; *(currency)* déprécier; **to d. oneself** se déprécier

debasement [dɪ'beɪsmənt] *n (of person)* rabaissement *m*; *(of currency)* dépréciation *f*

debatable [dɪ'beɪtəbəl] *adj* discutable

debate [dɪ'beɪt] **1** *n* discussion *f*; *(organized)* débat *m*; **after much d.** après bien des discussions

2 *vt (issue)* débattre de, discuter de; **he debated whether to do it** il se demandait s'il le ferait ou non

3 *vi* participer à des débats

debating society [dɪ'beɪtɪŋsəsaɪətɪ] *n* = société qui organise des débats

debauched [dɪ'bɔːtʃt] *adj* débauché(e)

debauchery [dɪ'bɔːtʃərɪ] *n* débauche *f*

debilitate [dɪ'bɪlɪteɪt] *vt* débiliter

debilitating [dɪ'bɪlɪteɪtɪŋ] *adj* débilitant(e)

debility [dɪ'bɪlɪtɪ] *n* débilité *f*

debit ['debɪt] *Fin* **1** *n* débit *m*; *Fig* **on the d. side,...** l'inconvénient, c'est que...; **d. card** = carte de paiement à débit immédiat, ≃ carte *f* Bleue®

2 *vt (person, account)* débiter (**with** de)

debonair [debə'neə(r)] *adj* élégant(e) et raffiné(e)

debrief [di:'briːf] *vt* débriefer, faire faire un compte rendu de fin de mission à

debriefing [di:'briːfɪŋ] *n* débriefing *m*, compte *m* rendu de fin de mission

debris ['debriː] *n (of building)* décombres *mpl*; *(of plane, car)* débris *mpl*

debt [det] *n* dette *f*; **to be in d.** avoir des dettes; *Fig* **I shall always be in your d.** je vous serai toujours redevable; **to owe sb a d. of gratitude** être redevable à qn; **d. collector** agent *m* de recouvrement

debtor ['detə(r)] *n* débiteur(trice) *m,f*

debug [di:'bʌg] *(pt & pp* **debugged**) *vt Comput (program)* déboguer

debunk [di:'bʌŋk] *vt Fam (theory)* discréditer; *(myth)* détruire

debut ['deɪbjuː] *n* début *m*; **to make one's d.** faire ses débuts

Dec. *(abbr* **December**) déc

decade ['dekeɪd] *n* décennie *f*

decadence ['dekədəns] *n* décadence *f*

decadent ['dekədənt] *adj* décadent(e)

decaf ['diːkæf] *n Fam (coffee)* déca *m*

decaffeinated [di:'kæfɪneɪtɪd] *adj* décaféiné(e)

decal ['diːkæl] *n* décalcomanie *f*; **to do decals** faire des décalcomanies

decant [dɪ'kænt] *vt* décanter

decanter [dɪ'kæntə(r)] *n* carafe *f*

decapitate [dɪ'kæpɪteɪt] *vt* décapiter

decathlon [dɪ'kæθlɒn] *n* décathlon *m*

decay [dɪ'keɪ] **1** *n* (**a**) *(of wood)* pourriture *f*; *(of teeth)* carie *f* (**b**) *(of civilization)* déclin *m*; *(of building)* délabrement *m*

2 *vi* (**a**) *(of wood)* pourrir; *(of teeth)* se carier (**b**) *(of civilization)* péricliter; *(of building)* se délabrer

decayed [dɪ'keɪd] *adj (food)* pourri(e); *(tooth)* carié(e); *(corpse)* décomposé(e)

decease [dɪ'siːs] *n Formal* décès *m*

deceased [dɪ'siːst] *Formal* **1** *n* **the d.** le défunt (la défunte)

2 *adj* décédé(e)

deceit [dɪ'siːt] *n* tromperie *f*, supercherie *f*

deceitful [dɪ'siːtfʊl] *adj (person)* fourbe; *(behavior)* malhonnête

deceive [dɪ'siːv] *vt* tromper, abuser; **to be deceived by appearances** se laisser abuser par les apparences; **to d. oneself** se mentir à soi-même; **to d. sb into doing sth** faire faire qch à qn en le manipulant; **I thought my eyes were deceiving me** je n'en croyais pas mes yeux

decelerate [di:'seləreɪt] *vi* ralentir

December [dɪ'sembə(r)] *n* décembre *m*; *see also* **May**

decency ['diːsənsɪ] *n (respectability)* décence *f*; **to have the common d. to do sth** avoir la décence de faire qch; **he didn't even have the d. to tell us first** il n'a même pas eu la politesse de nous avertir avant

decent ['diːsənt] *adj* (**a**) *(respectable)* respectable; *Fam* **are you d.?** es-tu visible? (**b**) *(of acceptable quality, size)* convenable, correct(e) (**c**) *(kind)* gentil(ille)

decently ['diːsəntlɪ] *adv* (**a**) *(respectably)* convenablement; **to dress d.** s'habiller décemment (**b**) *(to an acceptable degree)* convenablement, correctement (**c**) *(kindly)* gentiment

decentralization [di:sentrəlaɪ'zeɪʃən] *n* décentralisation *f*

decentralize [di:'sentrəlaɪz] *vt* décentraliser

deception [dɪ'sepʃən] *n* tromperie *f*, supercherie *f*

deceptive [dɪ'septɪv] *adj* trompeur(euse)

deceptively [dɪ'septɪvlɪ] *adv* **it looks d. easy** c'est moins facile que ça en a l'air; **she looks d. shy** c'est une fausse timide

decibel ['desɪbel] *n* décibel *m*

decide [dɪ'saɪd] **1** *vt (outcome, match, future)* décider de; **to d. to do sth** décider de faire qch; **it was decided to wait for her reply** il fut décidé d'attendre sa réponse; **that was what decided me** c'est ce qui m'a décidé; **that decides the matter** ça règle la question

2 *vi* décider; **to d. on sth** choisir qch; **to d. against doing sth** décider de ne pas faire qch; **they decided against going out** ils décidèrent de ne pas sortir; **to d. in favor of doing sth** décider de faire qch

decided [dɪ'saɪdɪd] *adj* (**a**) *(person)* décidé(e); *(opinion)* ferme (**b**) *(difference, preference, improvement)* net (nette)

decidedly [dɪ'saɪdɪdlɪ] *adv* (**a**) *(answer, say)* d'un ton résolu (**b**) *(very)* franchement; **he was d. unhelpful** il n'a pas été serviable du tout

deciding [dɪ'saɪdɪŋ] *adj* décisif(ive)

deciduous [dɪ'sɪdjʊəs] *adj* à feuilles caduques

decimal ['desɪməl] **1** *n* décimale *f*
2 *adj* décimal(e); **d. point** virgule *f*; **correct to five d. places** exact(e) jusqu'à la cinquième décimale
decimalization [desɪməlaɪ'zeɪʃən] *n* décimalisation *f*
decimate ['desɪmeɪt] *vt* décimer
decipher [dɪ'saɪfə(r)] *vt* déchiffrer
decision [dɪ'sɪʒən] *n* (**a**) *(of question)* décision *f* (**b**) *(resolve)* fermeté *f*, résolution *f*
decision-making [dɪ'sɪʒənmeɪkɪŋ] *n* prise *f* de décision
decisive [dɪ'saɪsɪv] *adj* (**a**) *(person, manner)* résolu(e) (**b**) *(action, event)* décisif(ive)
deck [dek] **1** *n* (**a**) *(of ship)* pont *m*; *(of bus)* niveau *m*, étage *m*; **on d.** sur le pont; **d. chair** transat *m* (**b**) **d. (of cards)** jeu *m* (de cartes)
2 *vt* **to d. oneself out in one's best attire** se mettre sur son trente et un
declaim [dɪ'kleɪm] *vt & vi* déclamer
declamatory [dɪ'klæmətərɪ] *adj* déclamatoire
declaration [deklə'reɪʃən] *n* déclaration *f*; **the D. of Independence** la Déclaration d'indépendance
declare [dɪ'kleə(r)] **1** *vt* déclarer; **to d. war (on)** déclarer la guerre (à); **anything to d.?** *(at customs)* avez-vous quelque chose à déclarer?
2 *vi* **to d. for/against sth** se déclarer en faveur de/contre qch; *Old-fashioned* **I do d.!** ça alors!
declassify [di:'klæsɪfaɪ] *(pt & pp* **declassified**) *vt (document)* ne plus considérer comme confidentiel
declension [dɪ'klenʃən] *n Gram* déclinaison *f*
decline [dɪ'klaɪn] **1** *n* déclin *m*; **to go into d.** *(of person, company, industry)* dépérir; *(of economy)* perdre de sa vigueur; *(of health)* se détériorer; **to be on the d.** *(of inflation, crime)* être en baisse
2 *vt* (**a**) *(offer, invitation)* décliner; **to d. to do sth** refuser de faire qch (**b**) *Gram* décliner
3 *vi* (**a**) *(refuse)* refuser (**b**) *(of health, influence)* décliner, baisser; **to d. in importance** perdre de son importance
declining [dɪ'klaɪnɪŋ] *adj (decreasing)* en baisse; *(deteriorating)* déclinant(e)
decode [di:'kəʊd] *vt* décoder
decompose [di:kəm'pəʊz] *vi* se décomposer
decomposition [di:kɒmpə'zɪʃən] *n* décomposition *f*
decompression [di:kəm'preʃən] *n* décompression *f*; **d. chamber** chambre *f* de décompression; **d. sickness** maladie *f* des caissons
decongestant [di:kən'dʒestənt] *n Med* décongestionnant *m*
decontaminate [di:kən'tæmɪneɪt] *vt* décontaminer
decor ['deɪkɔ:(r), 'dekɔ:(r)] *n* décor *m*
decorate ['dekəreɪt] *vt* (**a**) *(with decorations)* décorer (**with** de) (**b**) *(with paint)* peindre; *(with wallpaper)* tapisser (**c**) *(with medal)* décorer
decoration [dekə'reɪʃən] *n* (**a**) *(of room, cake)* décoration *f* (**b**) *(medal)* décoration *f*, médaille *f*
decorative ['dekərətɪv] *adj* décoratif(ive)
decorator ['dekəreɪtə(r)] *n* (**painter and**) **d.** (peintre *m*) décorateur *m*
decorous ['dekərəs] *adj Formal* bienséant(e)
decorum [dɪ'kɔ:rəm] *n* convenances *fpl*, décorum *m*
decoy 1 *n* ['di:kɔɪ] *also Fig* leurre *m*
2 *vt* [dɪ'kɔɪ] leurrer
decrease 1 *n* ['di:kri:s] diminution *f*, baisse *f* (**in** de); **to be on the d.** être en diminution
2 *vt* [dɪ'kri:s] réduire, baisser
3 *vi* [dɪ'kri:s] diminuer, baisser
decreasing [dɪ'kri:sɪŋ] *adj* décroissant(e), en baisse
decree [dɪ'kri:] **1** *n* décret *m*; *Law* **d. nisi** jugement provisoire
2 *vt* décréter

decrepit [dɪ'krepɪt] *adj (person)* décrépit(e); *(thing)* délabré(e)
decriminalize [di:'krɪmɪnəlaɪz] *vt* dépénaliser
decry [dɪ'kraɪ] *(pt & pp* **decried**) *vt* décrier
dedicate ['dedɪkeɪt] *vt (book, song)* dédier (**to** à); **to d. oneself to sth** se consacrer à qch; **she dedicated her life to helping the poor** elle a consacré sa vie aux pauvres
dedicated ['dedɪkeɪtɪd] *adj* (**a**) *(committed)* dévoué(e); **to be d. to sth** se consacrer à qch; **she is d. to helping the poor** elle se consacre aux pauvres; **he is d. to his family** il est entièrement dévoué à sa famille (**b**) *Comput* spécialisé(e); **d. word processor** machine *f* servant uniquement au traitement de texte
dedication [dedɪ'keɪʃən] *n* (**a**) *(of book, song)* dédicace *f* (**b**) *(devotion)* dévouement *m*
deduce [dɪ'dju:s] *vt* déduire (**from** de)
deduct [dɪ'dʌkt] *vt* déduire (**from** de)
deductible [dɪ'dʌktəbəl] *adj* déductible; *Fin* **d. for tax purposes** déductible des impôts
deduction [dɪ'dʌkʃən] *n* (**a**) *(subtraction)* déduction *f*; **after deductions** une fois les prélèvements effectués (**b**) *(conclusion)* déduction *f*; **by a process of d.** par déduction
deed [di:d] *n* (**a**) *(action)* acte *m*, action *f*; **to do one's good d. for the day** faire sa bonne action de la journée (**b**) *Law (document)* acte *m* notarié
deem [di:m] *vt Formal* juger, estimer
deep [di:p] **1** *n Lit* **the d.** l'océan *m*
2 *adj* (**a**) *(water, sleep, thinker, cut)* profond(e); **to be 10 ft d.** ≃ faire 3 m de profondeur; **two/four d.** sur deux/quatre rangs; *Fig* **to be in d. water** être dans le pétrin; **d. in debt** criblé(e) de dettes; **d. in thought** plongé(e) dans ses pensées; **d. end** *(of swimming pool)* côté *m* le plus profond; *Fig* **to go off the d. end (at sb)** s'emporter (contre qn); *Fig* **to be thrown in at the d. end** être mis(e) dans le bain; **d. freezer** congélateur *m*; **d. fryer** friteuse *f*; **the D. South** *(of United States)* le Sud profond (**b**) *(color)* foncé(e), sombre; *(sound)* grave
3 *adv* profondément; **to walk d. into the forest** pénétrer profondément dans la forêt; **to look d. into sb's eyes** pénétrer qn du regard; **to work d. into the night** travailler tard dans la nuit; **d. down he's very kind** au fond il est très gentil; **to run d.** *(of emotions, prejudice, mistrust)* être profond(e)
deep-dish ['di:pdɪʃ] *adj* **d. pie** tourte *f*; **d. pizza** pizza *f* à pâte épaisse
deepen ['di:pən] **1** *vt (well, ditch)* approfondir; *(sorrow, interest)* augmenter; **to d. sb's understanding of sth** permettre à qn de mieux comprendre qch
2 *vi* (**a**) *(of river, silence)* devenir plus profond(e); *(of conviction, belief)* augmenter; *(of mystery)* s'épaissir (**b**) *(of sound, voice)* devenir plus grave
deep-freeze ['di:p'fri:z] *vt (at home)* congeler; *(in factory)* surgeler
deep-fry ['di:p'fraɪ] *vt* faire cuire dans la friture
deep-fryer ['di:p'fraɪə(r)] *n* friteuse *f*
deep-rooted [di:p'ru:tɪd] *adj* profondément enraciné(e)
deep-sea ['di:p'si:] *adj* **d. diver** plongeur *m* sous-marin; **d. fishing** pêche *f* hauturière
deep-seated ['di:p'si:tɪd] *adj (dislike)* profond(e); *(belief, prejudice)* profondément enraciné(e)
deer ['dɪə(r)] *(pl* **deer**) *n (male)* daim *m*; *(female)* biche *f*
deerstalker ['dɪəstɔ:kə(r)] *n (hat)* chapeau *m* de chasse *(à la Sherlock Holmes)*
deface [dɪ'feɪs] *vt (monument, statue)* dégrader; *(poster, wall)* barbouiller
de facto [deɪ'fæktəʊ] *adj & adv* de facto
defamation [defə'meɪʃən] *n* diffamation *f*
defamatory [dɪ'fæmətərɪ] *adj* diffamatoire
defame [dɪ'feɪm] *vt* diffamer
default [dɪ'fɔ:lt] **1** *n* (**a**) *Law (failure to appear in court)* défaut *m*;

Fig **by d.** par défaut (**b**) *Comput* **d. drive** lecteur *m* par défaut; **d. font** police *f* par défaut

2 *vi Law* (**a**) *(fail to appear in court)* ne pas comparaître (**b**) *(fail to pay)* **to d. on alimony payments** manquer au versement de la pension alimentaire

defaulter [dɪˈfɔːltə(r)] *n Law* contumace *mf*; *(debtor)* débiteur(trice) *m,f* défaillant(e)

defeat [dɪˈfiːt] **1** *n* défaite *f*

2 *vt (army, opponent)* vaincre; *(government)* mettre en minorité; **that defeats the object** *or* **purpose** ça va à l'encontre du but recherché

defeatism [dɪˈfiːtɪzəm] *n* défaitisme *m*

defeatist [dɪˈfiːtɪst] *n & adj* défaitiste *mf*

defecate [ˈdefəkeɪt] *vi* déféquer

defect **1** *n* [ˈdiːfekt] défaut *m*

2 *vi* [dɪˈfekt] **to d. to the enemy** passer à l'ennemi

defection [dɪˈfekʃən] *n* défection *f*

defective [dɪˈfektɪv] *adj (machine, reasoning)* défectueux(euse); *(hearing)* déficient(e)

defector [dɪˈfektə(r)] *n* transfuge *mf*

defend [dɪˈfend] **1** *vt* défendre (**from** *or* **against** contre)

2 *vi (in sport)* défendre

defendant [dɪˈfendənt] *n Law* défendeur(eresse) *m,f*

defender [dɪˈfendə(r)] *n* défenseur *m*

defending [dɪˈfendɪŋ] *adj* **d. champion** champion(onne) *m,f* en titre

defense [dɪˈfens] *n* défense *f*; **to come to sb's d.** venir à l'aide de qn; **she said in her d. that...** elle a dit à sa décharge que...; *Law* **d. counsel** avocat *m* de la défense; **d. mechanism** *(psychological)* mécanisme *m* de défense; *Law* **witness for the d.** témoin *m* à décharge

defenseless [dɪˈfensləs] *adj* sans défense

defensible [dɪˈfensəbəl] *adj* défendable

defensive [dɪˈfensɪv] **1** *n* **on the d.** sur la défensive

2 *adj* défensif(ive); **to be/get d.** être/se mettre sur la défensive

defer [dɪˈfɜː(r)] (*pt & pp* **deferred**) **1** *vt (postpone)* différer, remettre

2 *vi* **to d. to** s'en remettre à

deference [ˈdefərəns] *n* déférence *f*; **out of** *or* **in d. to** par déférence pour

deferential [defəˈrenʃəl] *adj (person)* déférent(e); *(air, tone)* de déférence, respectueux(euse)

deferment [dɪˈfɜːmənt] *n* ajournement *m*, report *m*

defiance [dɪˈfaɪəns] *n* défi *m*; **in d. of** au mépris de

defiant [dɪˈfaɪənt] *adj (gesture, look)* de défi; *(person)* provocant(e)

deficiency [dɪˈfɪʃənsɪ] (*pl* **deficiencies**) *n* (**a**) *(lack) (of resources)* manque *m*; *(of vitamins, minerals)* carence *f* (**b**) *(flaw)* défaut *m*

deficient [dɪˈfɪʃənt] *adj* insuffisant(e); **to be d. in** manquer de

deficit [ˈdefɪsɪt] *n Fin* déficit *m*

defile [dɪˈfaɪl] *vt (memory)* salir; *(sacred place, tomb)* profaner

definable [dɪˈfaɪnəbəl] *adj* définissable

define [dɪˈfaɪn] *vt* définir

definite [ˈdefɪnɪt] *adj* (**a**) *(precise) (views, plan, date, answer)* précis(e); *(decision)* définitif(ive) (**b**) *(noticeable) (advantage, improvement)* net (nette) (**c**) *(certain)* certain(e); *(insistent)* catégorique; **I can't be d.** je n'en suis pas sûr (**d**) *Gram* **d. article** article *m* défini

definitely [ˈdefɪnɪtlɪ] *adv* (**a**) *(certainly)* sans aucun doute; **I'll d. be there** c'est sûr que j'y serai; **are you going? – d.!** est-ce que vous y allez? – absolument!; **d. not!** certainement pas! **he told me very d. that he didn't want to go** il m'a dit très clairement qu'il ne voulait pas y aller (**b**) *(noticeably) (improved, superior)* nettement

definition [defɪˈnɪʃən] *n* (**a**) *(of word)* définition *f*; **by d.** par

définition (**b**) *(of image)* définition *f*; *(of binoculars)* netteté *f*

definitive [dɪˈfɪnɪtɪv] *adj (book)* qui fait autorité; *(version)* définitif(ive); **she was the d. Juliet** elle était la Juliette idéale

deflate [diːˈfleɪt] **1** *vt* (**a**) *(ball, tire)* dégonfler (**b**) *Econ* **to d. the economy** pratiquer une politique déflationniste (**c**) *(person)* démonter

2 *vi (of tire)* se dégonfler

deflated [diːˈfleɪtɪd] *adj (person)* déprimé(e)

deflation [diːˈfleɪʃən] *n Econ* déflation *f*

deflationary [diːˈfleɪʃənərɪ] *adj Econ* déflationniste

deflect [dɪˈflekt] **1** *vt (ball, bullet)* (faire) dévier; *(sound)* renvoyer; *(criticism)* détourner; *Fig (person)* détourner (**from** de)

2 *vi (of ball, bullet)* dévier

deflection [dɪˈflekʃən] *n (of ball, bullet)* déviation *f*

deforestation [diːfɒrɪsˈteɪʃən] *n* déboisement *m*

deform [dɪˈfɔːm] *vt* déformer

deformation [diːfɔːˈmeɪʃən] *n* déformation *f*

deformity [dɪˈfɔːmɪtɪ] (*pl* **deformities**) *n* difformité *f*

defraud [dɪˈfrɔːd] *vt (IRS)* frauder; *(employer)* escroquer; **to d. sb of sth** escroquer qch à qn

defray [dɪˈfreɪ] *vt Formal* **to d. sb's expenses** défrayer qn; **to d. the cost of sth** rembourser les frais de qch

defrost [diːˈfrɒst] **1** *vt (refrigerator)* dégivrer; *(food)* décongeler; *(car windshield)* dégivrer

2 *vi (of refrigerator)* se dégivrer; *(of food)* se décongeler

defroster [diːˈfrɒstə(r)] *n* dégivreur *m*

deft [deft] *adj* adroit(e), habile

defunct [dɪˈfʌŋkt] *adj (person)* défunt(e); *(organization)* dissous(oute); *(law)* abandonné(e)

defuse [diːˈfjuːz] *vt also Fig* désamorcer

defy [dɪˈfaɪ] (*pt & pp* **defied**) *vt (authority, law)* braver; *(logic, analysis)* défier; **to d. description** défier toute description; **to d. sb to do sth** mettre qn au défi de faire qch

degenerate **1** *n & adj* [dɪˈdʒenərət] dégénéré(e) *m,f*

2 *vi* [dɪˈdʒenəreɪt] dégénérer (**into** en)

degeneration [dɪdʒenəˈreɪʃən] *n* dégénérescence *f*

degradation [degrəˈdeɪʃən] *n* avilissement *m*; *(squalor)* misère *f*

degrade [dɪˈgreɪd] *vt* avilir; **I won't d. myself by answering that** je ne m'abaisserai pas à répondre à cela

degrading [dɪˈgreɪdɪŋ] *adj* avilissant(e), dégradant(e)

degree [dɪˈgriː] *n* (**a**) *(extent)* degré *m*, point *m*; **to a d., to some d.** jusqu'à un certain point; **to such a d. that...** à (un) tel point que...; **by degrees** petit à petit; **a d. of risk** un certain risque; **a d. of truth** une part de vérité (**b**) *(of temperature, in geometry)* degré *m*; **it's 85 degrees** *(temperature)* ≃ il fait 30 degrés (**c**) *(at college, university)* diplôme *m* universitaire; *(bachelor's)* ≃ licence *f*; *(master's)* ≃ maîtrise *f*; *(PhD)* doctorat *m*; **to take a d.** préparer un diplôme

dehumanize [diːˈhjuːmənaɪz] *vt* déshumaniser

dehumidifier [diːhjuːˈmɪdɪfaɪə(r)] *n* déshumidificateur *m*

dehydrated [diːˈhaɪdreɪtɪd] *adj* déshydraté(e); **to get d.** se déshydrater

dehydration [diːhaɪˈdreɪʃən] *n* déshydratation *f*

deicer [diːˈaɪsə(r)] *n* dégivreur *m*

deify [ˈdiːɪfaɪ] (*pt & pp* **deified**) *vt* déifier

deign [deɪn] *vt* **to d. to do sth** condescendre à *ou* daigner faire qch

deindustrialization [diːɪndʌstrɪəlaɪˈzeɪʃən] *n* désindustrialisation *f*

deity [ˈdiːɪtɪ] (*pl* **deities**) *n* divinité *f*, dieu (déesse) *m,f*

dejected [dɪˈdʒektɪd] *adj* abattu(e), découragé(e)

dejection [dɪˈdʒekʃən] *n* abattement *m*, découragement *m*

delay [dɪˈleɪ] **1** *n* retard *m*; **without d.** sans délai; **an hour's**

d. une heure de retard; **all flights are subject to d.** tous les vols risquent d'avoir du retard

2 vt (**a**) (project, decision, act) retarder; (traffic) ralentir; **to be delayed** (of train, plane) avoir du retard; **delaying tactics** manœuvres fpl dilatoires (**b**) (put off) (decision, publication) différer; **we can't d. telling her any longer** on ne peut plus attendre davantage, nous devons le lui dire

3 vi tarder; **don't d.!** faites vite!

delayed-action [dɪleɪd'ækʃən] adj (drug, fuse, shutter) à retardement

delectable [dɪ'lektəbəl] adj délicieux(euse)

delegate 1 n ['delɪgət] délégué(e) m,f

2 vt ['delɪgeɪt] (power, responsibility) déléguer (**to** à); **to d. sb to do sth** déléguer qn pour faire qch

3 vi ['delɪgeɪt] déléguer

delegation [delɪ'geɪʃən] n délégation f

delete [dɪ'liːt] vt supprimer; **d. where inapplicable** rayer les mentions inutiles

deleterious [delɪ'tɪərɪəs] adj Formal délétère

deletion [dɪ'liːʃən] n suppression f

deli ['delɪ] n Fam (store) épicerie f fine; (café) restaurant-traiteur m

deliberate 1 adj [dɪ'lɪbərət] (**a**) (intentional) délibéré(e); **it wasn't d.** ça n'était pas voulu (**b**) (unhurried) (movement) mesuré(e); (person) méticuleux(euse)

2 vi [dɪ'lɪbəreɪt] (think) réfléchir (**on** sur); (discuss) délibérer (**on** sur)

deliberately [dɪ'lɪbərətlɪ] adv (**a**) (intentionally) délibérément; **she did it d.** elle l'a fait exprès (**b**) (unhurriedly) de façon mesurée

deliberation [dɪlɪbə'reɪʃən] n (**a**) (thought) réflexion f; (discussion) délibération f, débat m (**b**) (unhurriedness) mesure f; **with d.** posément

delicacy ['delɪkəsɪ] (pl **delicacies**) n (**a**) (quality) délicatesse f (**b**) (food) mets m délicat

delicate ['delɪkət] adj délicat(e)

delicately ['delɪkətlɪ] adv (**a**) (finely) délicatement (**b**) (tactfully) avec délicatesse

delicatessen [delɪkə'tesən] n (store) épicerie f fine; (café) restaurant-traiteur m

delicious [dɪ'lɪʃəs] adj délicieux(euse)

delight [dɪ'laɪt] **1** n plaisir m, joie f; **to my/her d.** à mon/son grand plaisir; **to take d. in sth** se réjouir de qch; **the car is a d. to drive** conduire cette voiture est un plaisir; **the delights of camping** les joies du camping; **the delights of Las Vegas** les charmes de La Vegas

2 vt ravir, réjouir

3 vi **to d. in doing sth** prendre plaisir à faire qch; Hum **he delights in the name of Fergus Fotherington** il répond au joli nom de Fergus Fotherington

delighted [dɪ'laɪtɪd] adj ravi(e), enchanté(e) (**with** de)

delightful [dɪ'laɪtful] adj (person, smile) charmant(e); (meal, evening) délicieux(euse)

delightfully [dɪ'laɪtfulɪ] adv (sing, write) merveilleusement

delimit [diː'lɪmɪt] vt délimiter

delineate [dɪ'lɪnɪeɪt] vt (plan, proposal) définir

delinquency [dɪ'lɪŋkwənsɪ] n délinquance f

delinquent [dɪ'lɪŋkwənt] n & adj délinquant(e) m,f

delirious [dɪ'lɪrɪəs] adj also Fig délirant(e); **to be d.** délirer

deliriously [dɪ'lɪrɪəslɪ] adv follement; **d. happy** fou (folle) de joie

delirium [dɪ'lɪrɪəm] n also Fig délire m; Med **d. tremens** delirium tremens m

deliver [dɪ'lɪvə(r)] **1** vt (**a**) (letter, package) remettre, distribuer (**to** à); (water, electricity, gas) distribuer; (goods) livrer; **to have sth delivered** faire livrer qch; Fig **to d. the goods** tenir ses engagements (**b**) (blow) donner; Sport (pass) faire; (speech, ver-

dict) prononcer; (ultimatum) poser; **to d. a service** proposer un service (**c**) (baby) mettre au monde

2 vi livrer; Fig (keep one's promise) tenir ses engagements; Com **we d.** nous livrons à domicile

deliverance [dɪ'lɪvərəns] n Formal délivrance f (**from** de)

delivery [dɪ'lɪvərɪ] (pl **deliveries**) n (**a**) (of letter, package) distribution f, remise f; (of goods) livraison f; **to take d. of sth** prendre livraison de qch; **d. date** date f de livraison; **d. man** livreur m; **d. van** camion m de livraison (**b**) (way of speaking) diction f (**c**) (of baby) accouchement m

delta ['deltə] n (of river, Greek letter) delta m inv; **d. wing** (of plane) aile f delta

delude [dɪ'luːd] vt tromper; **to d. oneself** se faire des illusions

deluge ['deljuːdʒ] **1** n also Fig déluge m

2 vt inonder (**with** de)

delusion [dɪ'luːʒən] n illusion f; **to be under a d.** se faire des illusions; **delusions of grandeur** mégalomanie f

deluxe [dɪ'lʌks] adj de luxe, haut de gamme inv

delve [delv] vi also Fig **to d. into** fouiller dans

demagog, demagogue ['deməgɒg] n démagogue mf

demand [dɪ'mɑːnd] **1** n (**a**) (request) demande f, exigence f; **to make demands on sb** exiger beaucoup de qn; **payable on d.** payable sur demande (**b**) (for goods) demande f (**for** de); **to be in d.** être demandé(e) ou recherché(e)

2 vt exiger, réclamer

demanding [dɪ'mɑːndɪŋ] adj (person) exigeant(e); (job) astreignant(e)

demarcation [diːmɑː'keɪʃən] n démarcation f; Ind **d. dispute** conflit m d'attributions; **d. line** ligne f de démarcation

demean [dɪ'miːn] vt humilier; **to d. oneself** s'abaisser

demeanor [dɪ'miːnə(r)] n comportement m

demented [dɪ'mentɪd] adj fou (folle)

dementia [dɪ'menʃɪə] n démence f

demerara sugar [demə'reərə'ʃugə(r)] n cassonade f

demigod ['demɪgɒd] n demi-dieu m

demilitarize [diː'mɪlɪtəraɪz] vt démilitariser

demise [dɪ'maɪz] n also Fig disparition f

demo ['deməʊ] (pl **demos**) n Fam (**a**) **d. (tape)** maquette f (**b**) (protest) manif f

demobilize [diː'məʊbɪlaɪz] vt démobiliser

democracy [dɪ'mɒkrəsɪ] (pl **democracies**) n démocratie f

Democrat ['deməkræt] n démocrate mf

democrat ['deməkræt] n démocrate mf

democratic [demə'krætɪk] adj démocratique; **the D. Republic of Congo** la République démocratique du Congo

democratically [demə'krætɪklɪ] adv démocratiquement

demographic [demə'græfɪk] adj démographique

demolish [dɪ'mɒlɪʃ] vt (building, theory) démolir; Fam (eat) engloutir; (in game) écraser

demolition [demə'lɪʃən] n démolition f

demon ['diːmən] n démon m

demonic [dɪ'mɒnɪk] adj démoniaque

demonstrable [dɪ'mɒnstrəbəl] adj démontrable

demonstrate ['demənstreɪt] **1** vt (fact, theory) démontrer; **to d. how sth works** montrer comment qch fonctionne

2 vi (protest) manifester (**for/against** pour/contre)

demonstration [demən'streɪʃən] n (**a**) (of fact, theory) démonstration f (**b**) (protest) manifestation f

demonstrative [dɪ'mɒnstrətɪv] adj also Gram démonstratif(ive)

demonstrator ['demənstreɪtə(r)] n (**a**) (protester) manifestant(e) m,f (**b**) (of machine) démonstrateur(trice) m,f

demoralize [dɪ'mɒrəlaɪz] vt démoraliser

demoralizing [dɪ'mɒrəlaɪzɪŋ] adj démoralisant(e)

demote [dɪ'məʊt] vt rétrograder

demotion [dɪ'məʊʃən] n rétrogradation f

demur [dɪ'mɜː(r)] (*pt & pp* **demurred**) *vi* soulever une objection

demure [dɪ'mjʊə(r)] *adj* réservé(e)

demystify [diː'mɪstɪfaɪ] (*pt & pp* **demystified**) *vt* démystifier

den [den] *n* (**a**) (*of lion, fox, bear*) antre *m*, tanière *f*; (*of Cub Scouts*) meute *f*; *Fig* **a d. of iniquity** un lieu de perdition; **a d. of thieves** un repaire de voleurs (**b**) (*room*) ≃ bureau *m*

denationalize [diː'næʃənəlaɪz] *vt* dénationaliser

denature [diː'neɪtʃə(r)] *vt* dénaturer

denial [dɪ'naɪəl] *n* (**a**) (*of request*) refus *m*; (*of right*) atteinte *f*; **d. of justice** déni *m* de justice (**b**) (*of accusation, rumor, guilt*) démenti *m* (**c**) (*psychological*) dénégation *f*; **to be in d.** refuser de se rendre à l'évidence

denigrate ['denɪgreɪt] *vt* dénigrer

denim ['denɪm] *n* (toile *f* de) jean *m*, denim *m*; **denims** (*jeans*) un jean; **d. skirt/shirt** jupe *f*/chemise *f* en jean

Denmark ['denmɑːk] *n* le Danemark

denomination [dɪnɒmɪ'neɪʃən] *n* (**a**) (*religious*) confession *f* (**b**) *Fin* valeur *f*

denominator [dɪ'nɒmɪneɪtə(r)] *n Math* dénominateur *m*

denote [dɪ'nəʊt] *vt* indiquer

dénouement [deɪ'nuːmɑ̃] *n* dénouement *m*

denounce [dɪ'naʊns] *vt* dénoncer

dense [dens] *adj* (**a**) (*smoke, fog, jungle, crowd*) dense (**b**) *Fam* (*stupid*) bouché(e)

densely ['denslɪ] *adv* **d. populated** fortement peuplé(e); **d. wooded** très boisé(e)

density ['densɪtɪ] *n* densité *f*

dent [dent] **1** *n* bosse *f*; *Fig* **the wedding put a d. in his savings** le mariage a fait un trou dans ses économies **2** *vt* cabosser; *Fig* (*confidence*) entamer

dental ['dentəl] *adj* dentaire; **d. appointment** rendez-vous *m* chez le dentiste; **d. floss** fil *m* dentaire; **d. hygiene** hygiène *f* dentaire; **d. hygienist** assistant(e) *m,f* dentaire; **d. surgeon** chirurgien-dentiste *m*

dentist ['dentɪst] *n* dentiste *mf*; **to go to the d.** *or* **d.'s** aller chez le dentiste

dentistry ['dentɪstrɪ] *n* dentisterie *f*

dentures ['dentʃəz] *npl* (**set of**) **d.** dentier *m*

denude [dɪ'njuːd] *vt* dénuder; **to be denuded of sth** être dépourvu(e) de qch

denunciation [dɪnʌnsɪ'eɪʃən] *n* dénonciation *f*

Denver boot ['denvə(r)buːt] *n* sabot *m* de Denver

deny [dɪ'naɪ] (*pt & pp* **denied**) *vt* (**a**) (*request*) refuser; **to d. sb his/her rights** priver qn de ses droits; **to d. oneself sth** se priver de qch (**b**) (*fact*) nier; (*rumor*) démentir; **to d. responsibility for sth** nier être responsable de qch; **to d. doing sth** nier avoir fait qch; **there's no denying that...** il est indéniable que...; **to d. all knowledge of sth** nier avoir connaissance de qch

deodorant [diː'əʊdərənt] *n* déodorant *m*; (*for room*) désodorisant *m*

depart [dɪ'pɑːt] *vi* (*leave*) partir (**from** de); **to d. from** (*tradition, subject, truth*) s'écarter de

department [dɪ'pɑːtmənt] *n* (*in company*) service *m*; (*in store*) rayon *m*; *Univ* département *m*; (*of government*) ministère *m*; *Fig* **that's my d.** c'est mon rayon; **d. store** grand magasin *m*

departmental [diːpɑːt'mentəl] *adj* (*manager*) de service

departure [dɪ'pɑːtʃə(r)] *n* (*from place*) départ *m*; (*from tradition*) écart *m*; (*from plan*) modification *f*; *Fig* **a new d.** un nouveau départ; **d. lounge** (*in airport*) salle *f* d'embarquement; **d. time** heure *f* de départ

depend [dɪ'pend] *vi* **to d. on** dépendre de; **that depends, it all depends** ça dépend; **to d. on sb** (*rely on*) compter sur qn; (*financially*) être à la charge de qn; **you can d. on it** tu peux compter là-dessus; **it depends on how much money I have** cela dépend de l'argent que j'ai; *Ironic* **you can d. on him to be late** tu peux compter sur lui pour être en retard

dependable [dɪ'pendəbəl] *adj* (*person, machine*) fiable; (*information*) sûr(e)

dependent [dɪ'pendənt] *n* personne *f* à charge

dependence [dɪ'pendəns] *n* (*reliance*) dépendance *f* (**on** à)

dependency [dɪ'pendənsɪ] (*pl* **dependencies**) *n* dépendance *f*; **d. culture** = situation d'une société dont les membres ont une mentalité d'assistés

dependent [dɪ'pendənt] *adj* (*child*) à charge; **to be d. on** dépendre de; **to be d. on sb** (*financially*) être à la charge de qn

depict [dɪ'pɪkt] *vt* (*of painting*) représenter; (*of movie, book*) décrire

depiction [dɪ'pɪkʃən] *n* (*in painting*) représentation *f*; (*in movie, book*) description *f*

depilatory [dɪ'pɪlətərɪ] *adj* dépilatoire

deplete [dɪ'pliːt] *vt* réduire, diminuer

depleted uranium [dɪ'pliːtdjʊ'reɪnjəm] *n* uranium *m* appauvri

depletion [dɪ'pliːʃən] *n* réduction *f*, diminution *f*

deplorable [dɪ'plɔːrəbəl] *adj* déplorable

deplore [dɪ'plɔː(r)] *vt* déplorer

deploy [dɪ'plɔɪ] *vt* déployer

deployment [dɪ'plɔɪmənt] *n* déploiement *m*

depopulate [diː'pɒpjʊleɪt] *vt* dépeupler

depopulation [diːpɒpjʊ'leɪʃən] *n* dépeuplement *m*

deport [dɪ'pɔːt] *vt* (*criminal*) déporter; (*immigrant*) expulser

deportation [diːpɔː'teɪʃən] *n* (*of criminal*) déportation *f*; (*of immigrant*) expulsion *f*

deportment [dɪ'pɔːtmənt] *n* (**a**) (*posture*) maintien *m* (**b**) (*behavior*) comportement *m*

depose [dɪ'pəʊz] *vt* déposer

deposit [dɪ'pɒzɪt] **1** *n* (**a**) (*in bank*) dépôt *m* (**b**) (*returnable*) caution *f*; (*first payment*) acompte *m*, arrhes *fpl*; **to put down a d. on sth** verser un acompte pour qch (**c**) (*of minerals*) gisement *m*; (*of wine*) dépôt *m* **2** *vt* déposer

deposition [diːpə'zɪʃən] *n Law* déposition *f*

depositor [dɪ'pɒzɪtə(r)] *n Fin* déposant(e) *m,f*

depot ['diːpəʊ, 'depəʊ] *n Mil & Com* dépôt *m*; (*bus station*) gare *f* routière

depravation [deprə'veɪʃən] *n* dépravation *f*

depraved [dɪ'preɪvd] *adj* dépravé(e)

depravity [dɪ'prævɪtɪ] *n* dépravation *f*

deprecate ['deprɪkeɪt] *vt* dévaloriser

deprecating ['deprɪkeɪtɪŋ], **deprecatory** ['deprɪkeɪtərɪ] *adj* désapprobateur(trice); **to be d. about sb/sth** dévaloriser qn/qch

depreciate [dɪ'priːʃɪeɪt] *vi* (*in value*) se déprécier

depreciation [dɪpriːʃɪ'eɪʃən] *n* (*in value*) dépréciation *f*

depress [dɪ'pres] *vt* (**a**) (*person*) déprimer; *Fig* (*prices*) faire baisser; (*economy, market*) affaiblir (**b**) (*press*) (*button, lever*) appuyer sur

depressed [dɪ'prest] *adj* (*person*) déprimé(e); *Fig* (*economy, market, region*) touché(e) par la crise; **to make sb d.** déprimer qn

depressing [dɪ'presɪŋ] *adj* déprimant(e)

depression [dɪ'preʃən] *n* (**a**) (*of person, economy*) dépression *f* (**b**) *Met* dépression *f* (**c**) (*hollow*) creux *m*; (*in landscape*) dépression *f*

deprivation [deprɪ'veɪʃən] *n* (*hardship*) privations *fpl*; **emotional d.** carence *f* affective

deprive [dɪ'praɪv] *vt* **to d. sb of sth** priver qn de qch

deprived [dɪ'praɪvd] *adj* défavorisé(e); (*childhood*) malheureux(euse)

dept. (*abbr* **department**) dép.

depth [depθ] *n* profondeur *f*; **in d.** (*investigate, discuss*) en profondeur; **to be out of one's d.** (*of swimmer*) ne plus avoir pied;

Fig ne pas être à la hauteur; **in the depths of winter** au cœur de l'hiver; **in the depths of despair** au plus profond du désespoir; *Naut* **d. charge** grenade *f* sous-marine; *Phot* **d. of field** profondeur de champ

deputation [depjʊ'teɪʃən] *n* délégation *f*

depute [dɪ'pjuːt] *vt* **to d. sb to do sth** charger qn de faire qch

deputize ['depjʊtaɪz] *vi* **to d. for sb** remplacer qn

deputy ['depjʊtɪ] (*pl* **deputies**) *n* (*second-in-command*) adjoint(e) *m,f*; (*replacement*) remplaçant(e) *m,f*; (*political representative*) député *m*; (*policeman*) shérif *m* adjoint

derail [dɪ'reɪl] **1** *vt Fig* (*project, plan*) faire avorter; **to be derailed** (*of train*) dérailler
    2 *vi* (*of train*) dérailler

derailment [dɪ'reɪlmənt] *n* déraillement *m*

deranged [dɪ'reɪndʒd] *adj* dérangé(e)

derby ['dɜːbɪ] (*pl* **derbies**) *n* (**a**) (*horse race*) derby *m* (**b**) (*local soccer match*) derby *m* (**c**) (*hat*) chapeau *m* melon

deregulate [diː'regjʊleɪt] *vt* (*economy, market*) déréguler; (*prices*) libérer; (*industry*) déréglementer

deregulation [diːregjʊ'leɪʃən] *n* (*of economy, market*) dérégulation *f*; (*of industry*) déréglementation *f*

derelict ['derəlɪkt] *adj* abandonné(e); (*ruined*) en ruines

dereliction [derɪ'lɪkʃən] *n* abandon *m*; **d. of duty** manquement *m* au devoir

deride [dɪ'raɪd] *vt* ridiculiser

derision [dɪ'rɪʒən] *n* dérision *f*

derisive [dɪ'raɪsɪv] *adj* moqueur(euse)

derisory [dɪ'raɪsərɪ] *adj* dérisoire

derivation [derɪ'veɪʃən] *n* (*source*) origine *f*

derivative [dɪ'rɪvətɪv] **1** *n Chem & Gram* dérivé *m*
    2 *adj* banal(e), sans originalité

derive [dɪ'raɪv] **1** *vt* dériver, provenir (**from** de); **to d. pleasure from sth** prendre plaisir à qch; **to be derived from** provenir de
    2 *vi* **to d. from** provenir de

dermatitis [dɜːmə'taɪtɪs] *n Med* dermite *f*, dermatite *f*

dermatologist ['dɜːmə'tɒlədʒɪst] *n Med* dermatologiste *mf*, dermatologue *mf*

dermatology [dɜːmə'tɒlədʒɪ] *n Med* dermatologie *f*

derogatory [dɪ'rɒgətərɪ] *adj* désobligeant(e)

derrick ['derɪk] *n* derrick *m*

desalination [diːsælɪ'neɪʃən] *n* dessalement *m*

descend [dɪ'send] **1** *vt* (*hill, stairs*) descendre
    2 *vi* (**a**) (*go down*) descendre; (*of darkness, dusk*) tomber; **in descending order** en ordre décroissant; **every summer tourists d. on the town** chaque été les touristes débarquent en ville; *Fig* **to d. to sb's level** s'abaisser au niveau de qn (**b**) **to d.** *or* **to be descended from sb** (*be related to*) descendre de qn

descent [dɪ'sent] *n* (**a**) (*of plane, from mountain*) descente *f* (**b**) (*ancestry*) **to be of Norman d.** être d'origine normande

describe [dɪs'kraɪb] *vt* décrire

description [dɪs'krɪpʃən] *n* description *f*; (*issued by police*) signalement *m*; **to answer** *or* **to fit the d.** répondre au signalement; **beyond d.** indescriptible; **birds of all descriptions** des oiseaux de toutes sortes

descriptive [dɪs'krɪptɪv] *adj* descriptif(ive)

desecrate ['desɪkreɪt] *vt* profaner

desecration [desɪ'kreɪʃən] *n* profanation *f*

desegregation [diːsegrɪ'geɪʃən] *n* déségrégation *f*

desert¹ ['dezət] *n* désert *m*; **d. island** île *f* déserte

desert² [dɪ'zɜːt] **1** *vt* abandonner; **to d. one's post** (*of soldier*) déserter son poste
    2 *vi* (*from army*) déserter

deserted [dɪ'zɜːtɪd] *adj* désert(e)

deserter [dɪ'zɜːtə(r)] *n* déserteur *m*

desertion [dɪ'zɜːʃən] *n Law* abandon *m* du domicile conjugal; *Mil* désertion *f*

deserts [dɪ'zɜːts] *npl* **he got his just d.** il a eu ce qu'il méritait

deserve [dɪ'zɜːv] *vt* mériter; **to d. to do sth** mériter de faire qch; **she deserves to be punished** elle mérite une punition

deserving [dɪ'zɜːvɪŋ] *adj* (*person*) méritant(e); (*action, cause*) méritoire; **to be d. of praise** être digne d'éloge

design [dɪ'zaɪn] **1** *n* (**a**) (*pattern*) (*on fabric, wallpaper*) motif *m* (**b**) (*style*) (*of car, furniture*) modèle *m*; (*of clothes*) coupe *f* (**c**) (*drawing*) (*of building, machine*) plan *m* (**d**) (*subject*) design *m*, stylisme *m* (**e**) (*planning*) (*of product, machine*) conception *f* (**f**) (*intention*) dessein *m*; **by d.** à dessein; **to have designs on** avoir des vues sur
    2 *vt* (*building, vehicle*) concevoir; (*clothes, furniture*) créer; **to be designed for sth/to do sth** (*intended*) être destiné(e) à qch/à faire qch

designate ['dezɪgneɪt] **1** *vt* désigner; **to d. sb to do sth** désigner qn pour faire qch; **this area has been designated a national park** cette zone a été classée parc national; **designated driver** = personne qui s'engage à ne pas boire pour pouvoir reconduire d'autres personnes en voiture
    2 *adj* désigné(e)

designation [dezɪg'neɪʃən] *n* (**a**) (*appointment*) nomination *f*; (*of funds*) affectation *f* (**b**) (*title*) désignation *f*

designer [dɪ'zaɪnə(r)] *n* concepteur(trice) *m,f*; (*of building*) architecte *mf*; (*of clothes*) styliste *mf* (de mode); (*of theater set*) décorateur(trice) *m,f*; **d. clothes** vêtements *mpl* de marque; **d. drugs** drogues *fpl* de synthèse; **d. label** griffe *f* de grande marque

desirable [dɪ'zaɪərəbəl] *adj* souhaitable; (*job, location*) attrayant(e); (*sexually*) désirable; **a d. residence** une belle résidence

desire [dɪ'zaɪə(r)] **1** *n* désir *m*, envie *f*; **I have no d. to go** je n'ai aucune envie d'y aller
    2 *vt* désirer; **to d. to do sth** désirer faire qch, avoir envie de faire qch; **it leaves a lot to be desired** ça laisse beaucoup à désirer

desirous [dɪ'zaɪərəs] *adj Formal* désireux(euse) (**of** de)

desist [dɪ'zɪst] *vi Formal* cesser; **to d. from doing sth** cesser de faire qch

desk [desk] *n* (*in school*) table *f*; (*with lid*) pupitre *m*; (*in office, home*) bureau *m*; (*hotel reception*) réception *f*; **d. diary** agenda *m*; **a d. job** un travail de bureau; **d. lamp** lampe *f* de bureau

desktop ['desktɒp] *n Comput* **d. computer** ordinateur *m* de bureau; **d. publishing** publication *f* assistée par ordinateur

desolate ['desələt] *adj* (*place*) désolé(e); (*future, prospect*) sombre; (*person*) abattu(e), affligé(e)

desolation [desə'leɪʃən] *n* désolation *f*; (*of person*) affliction *f*

despair [dɪs'peə(r)] **1** *n* désespoir *m*; **to be in d.** être désespéré(e); **to drive sb to d.** désespérer qn
    2 *vi* désespérer; **I d. of you** tu me désespères

despairing [dɪ'speərɪŋ] *adj* désespéré(e)

desperate ['despərət] *adj* désespéré(e); **to be in d. need of sth** avoir désespérément besoin de qch; **to be d. to do sth** vouloir à tout prix faire qch; **to be d. for sth** avoir désespérément besoin de qch

desperately ['despərətlɪ] *adv* désespérément; (*ill*) très gravement; **to be d. in love** être éperdument amoureux(euse); **to be d. sorry about sth** être affreusement désolé(e) de qch

desperation [despə'reɪʃən] *n* désespoir *m*; **in d.** par désespoir

despicable [dɪ'spɪkəbəl] *adj* méprisable

despise [dɪ'spaɪz] *vt* mépriser

despite [dɪs'paɪt] *prep* malgré

despondency [dɪs'pɒndənsɪ] *n* abattement *m*

despondent [dɪ'spɒndənt] *adj* abattu(e)

despot ['despɒt] *n* despote *m*

despotic [dɪs'pɒtɪk] *adj* despotique

despotism ['despɒtɪzəm] *n* despotisme *m*

dessert [dɪ'zɜːt] *n* dessert *m*; **d. wine** vin *m* doux

dessertspoon [dɪ'zɜːtspuːn] *n* cuillère *f* à dessert

destabilize [diː'steɪbəlaɪz] *vt* déstabiliser

destination [destɪ'neɪʃən] *n* destination *f*; **to reach one's d.** arriver à destination; *Comput* **d. disk/drive** disquette *f*/lecteur *m* cible

destine ['destɪn] *vt* destiner

destined ['destɪnd] *adj* (a) *(meant)* destiné(e); **to be d. to do sth** être destiné à faire qch; **he was d. to become famous** *(by fate)* il était destiné à devenir célèbre; *(reporting a fact)* il devait plus tard devenir célèbre (b) *(of plane, ship)* **d. for** à destination de

destiny ['destɪnɪ] *(pl* **destinies)** *n* destin *m*, destinée *f*

destitute ['destɪtjuːt] *adj* sans ressources; **to be utterly d.** être dans la misère

destress [diː'stres] *Fam* **1** *vt* **to d. oneself/one's life** se dé-stresser
2 *vi* déstresser

destressing ['diː'stresɪŋ] *adj Fam (treatment, experience)* déstressant(e)

destroy [dɪs'trɔɪ] *vt* (a) *(damage, ruin)* détruire (b) *(animal)* abattre; *(vermin)* éliminer

destroyer [dɪs'trɔɪə(r)] *n (ship)* contre-torpilleur *m*

destruction [dɪs'trʌkʃən] *n* destruction *f*; *(damage)* ravages *mpl*

destructive [dɪs'trʌktɪv] *adj* destructeur(trice)

desultory ['desəltərɪ] *adj (conversation)* décousu(e); *(attempt)* peu convaincant(e)

detach [dɪ'tætʃ] *vt* détacher (**from** de); **to d. oneself (from)** s'éloigner (de)

detachable [dɪ'tætʃəbəl] *adj* amovible

detached [dɪ'tætʃt] *adj* (a) *(separate)* détaché(e), séparé(e); **to become** *or* **to get d. from sth** se détacher de qch; *Med* **d. retina** décollement *m* de la rétine (b) *(disinterested) (tone)* détaché(e); **he's rather d.** il sait garder ses distances

detachment [dɪ'tætʃmənt] *n* (a) *(military unit)* détachement *m* (b) *(objectivity)* détachement *m*

detail ['diːteɪl] **1** *n* (a) *(item of information)* détail *m*; **to pay attention to d.** être minutieux(euse); **to go into detail(s)** entrer dans les détails; **in d.** en détail; **details** *(information)* renseignements *mpl*; *(address and phone number)* coordonnées *fpl* (b) *Mil* détachement *m*
2 *vt* (a) *(describe)* détailler (b) *Mil* **to d. sb to do sth** donner l'ordre à qn de faire qch

detailed ['diːteɪld] *adj (account, description)* détaillé(e); *(work)* minutieux(euse)

detain [dɪ'teɪn] *vt (in prison)* placer en détention; *(in a hospital)* garder; *(delay)* retenir; **such details need not d. us** ne nous laissons pas arrêter par de tels détails

detainee [diːteɪ'niː] *n* détenu(e) *m,f*

detangle [diː'tæŋgəl] *vt (hair)* démêler

detangler [diː'tæŋglə(r)] *n (for hair)* démêlant *m*

detect [dɪ'tekt] *vt (change, emotion, trace of substance)* déceler; *(error, pattern)* découvrir; *Med (disease)* dépister; *Mil (mines, etc.)* détecter

detection [dɪ'tekʃən] *n (of error)* découverte *f*; *Med (of disease)* dépistage *m*; *Mil (of mines, etc.)* détection *f*; **to escape d.** *(of mistake, change)* passer inaperçu(e); *(of burglar)* ne pas être découvert(e); **crime d.** le travail de détective

detective [dɪ'tektɪv] *n (private)* détective *m*; *(police officer)* ≃ inspecteur(trice) *m,f* de police; **d. story** roman *m* policier; **d. work** enquêtes *fpl*

detector [dɪ'tektə(r)] *n* détecteur *m*

détente, detente [deɪ'tɒnt] *n* détente *f*

detention [dɪ'tenʃən] *n* (a) *Law* détention *f*; *Law* **d. home** = centre de détention pour mineurs (b) *Sch* retenue *f*

deter [dɪ'tɜː(r)] *(pt & pp* **deterred)** *vt* dissuader; **to d. sb from doing sth** dissuader qn de faire qch

detergent [dɪ'tɜːdʒənt] *n (for cleaning)* produit *m* de nettoyage; *(for washing clothes)* lessive *f*

deteriorate [dɪ'tɪərɪəreɪt] *vi* se détériorer

deterioration [dɪtɪərɪə'reɪʃən] *n* détérioration *f*

determination [dɪtɜːmɪ'neɪʃən] *n* détermination *f*

determine [dɪ'tɜːmɪn] *vt* (a) *(decide)* **to d. to do sth** décider de faire qch; **to d. that...** décider que... (b) *(cause, date)* déterminer

determined [dɪ'tɜːmɪnd] *adj* déterminé(e), résolu(e); **to be d. to do sth** être déterminé *ou* résolu à faire qch; **I'm d. that we'll succeed** je suis déterminé à ce que nous réussissions

deterrent [dɪ'terənt] **1** *n* moyen *m* de dissuasion; **to act as a d.** avoir un effet dissuasif
2 *adj (effect)* dissuasif(ive)

detest [dɪ'test] *vt* détester

dethrone [dɪ'θrəʊn] *vt* détrôner

detonate ['detəneɪt] **1** *vt* faire exploser
2 *vi* exploser

detonation [detə'neɪʃən] *n* explosion *f*, détonation *f*

detonator ['detəneɪtə(r)] *n* détonateur *m*

detour ['diːtʊə(r)] *n* détour *m*

detoxification [diːtɒksɪfɪ'keɪʃən], *Fam* **detox** ['diːtɒks] *n* désintoxication *f*; **d. center/program** centre *m*/cure *f* de désintoxication

▸**detract from** [dɪ'trækt] *vt insep* diminuer; **I don't want to d. from her achievement, but...** je ne veux pas minimiser ce qu'elle a accompli, mais...

detractor [dɪ'træktə(r)] *n* détracteur(trice) *m,f*

detriment ['detrɪmənt] *n* **to the d. of** au détriment de; **without d. to** sans porter préjudice à

detrimental [detrɪ'mentəl] *adj* préjudiciable (**to** à); **to have a d. effect on** nuire à

detritus [dɪ'traɪtəs] *n* détritus *mpl*

deuce [djuːs] *n (in tennis)* égalité *f*

Deutschmark ['dɔɪtʃmɑːk] *n Formerly* (deutsche) mark *m*

devaluation [diːvæljʊ'eɪʃən] *n* (a) *(of currency)* dévaluation *f* (b) *(of person, achievement)* dévalorisation *f*

devalue [diː'væljuː] *vt* (a) *(currency)* dévaluer (b) *(person, achievement)* dévaloriser

devastate ['devəsteɪt] *vt (crops, village)* dévaster; *(person)* anéantir; **I was devastated by the news** la nouvelle m'a anéanti

devastating ['devəsteɪtɪŋ] *adj (storm, bombardment)* dévastateur(trice); *(news, findings, argument)* accablant(e); *(criticism)* cinglant(e); *(charm, beauty)* irrésistible

devastation [devəs'teɪʃən] *n* dévastation *f*

develop [dɪ'veləp] **1** *vt* (a) *(skills, theory, argument)* développer; *(product)* mettre au point (b) *(region)* développer; *(site)* aménager; **developed countries** pays *mpl* développés (c) *(acquire)* *(infection, disease)* attraper; *(habit)* prendre; **to d. a liking** *or* **taste for sth** se mettre à aimer qch (d) *(film)* développer
2 *vi* (a) *(grow)* se développer; **to d. into** devenir (b) *(become apparent)* apparaître

developer [dɪ'veləpə(r)] *n* (a) *(of real estate)* promoteur *m* (b) *Phot* révélateur *m*

developing [dɪ'veləpɪŋ] *adj (region, country)* en (voie de) développement; *(crisis)* en évolution

development [dɪ'veləpmənt] *n* (a) *(growth)* développement *m*; *(of idea)* évolution *f*; **d. aid** aide *f* au développement (b) *(progress, change)* développement *m*; **there have been some interesting developments** il y a eu quelques faits nouveaux intéressants; **the latest developments in medical research** les dernières découvertes médicales

deviant ['di:vɪənt] *adj* déviant(e)

deviate ['di:vɪeɪt] *vi* dévier (**from** de); *Fig* s'écarter (**from** de)

deviation [di:vɪ'eɪʃən] *n* déviation *f* (**from** par rapport à); *Fig* écart *m* (**from** par rapport à)

device [dɪ'vaɪs] *n* (**a**) *(mechanism)* dispositif *m*; *(gadget)* appareil *m*; (**explosive**) **d.** engin *m* explosif (**b**) *(method, scheme)* stratagème *m*; **to leave sb to their own devices** laisser qn se débrouiller

devil ['devəl] *n* (**a**) *(evil spirit)* diable *m*; **the D.** le Diable
(**b**) *Fam (person)* **poor d.!** pauvre diable!; **you little d.!** *(to child)* petit diable!; **you lucky d.!** veinard!
(**c**) *Fam (for emphasis)* **what the d. are you doing?** mais qu'est-ce que tu fabriques?; **how the d....?** comment diable...?; **we had a d. of a job moving it** nous avons eu un mal de chien à le déplacer
(**d**) *(idioms)* **he's a real d.** c'est un sacré numéro; **go on, be a d.!** allez, laisse-toi tenter!; **to work like the d.** travailler comme un(e) fou (folle); **to be (caught) between the d. and the deep blue sea** avoir à choisir entre la peste et le choléra; **speak of the d.!** quand on parle du loup!; *Prov* **better the d. you know (than the d. you don't)** on sait ce qu'on perd, on ne sait pas ce qu'on trouve; **to play d.'s advocate** se faire l'avocat du diable; *Culin* **d.'s food cake** gâteau *m* au chocolat noir

devilish ['devəlɪʃ] *adj* diabolique

devil-may-care ['devəlmeɪ'keə(r)] *adj* insouciant(e)

devious ['di:vɪəs] *adj (person, mind)* retors(e); *(scheme, route)* tortueux(euse); *(means)* détourné(e)

devise [dɪ'vaɪz] *vt* imaginer, élaborer

devoid [dɪ'vɔɪd] *adj* dénué(e), dépourvu(e) (**of** de)

devolution [di:və'lu:ʃən] *n Pol* décentralisation *f*

devolve [dɪ'vɒlv] **1** *vt* déléguer
2 *vi* **to d. on** incomber à; **power devolves on the regional assembly** le pouvoir appartient à l'assemblée régionale

devote [dɪ'vəʊt] *vt* consacrer (**to** à); **to d. oneself to** se consacrer à

devoted [dɪ'vəʊtɪd] *adj (parent)* dévoué(e); *(admirer)* fervent(e); **years of d. service** des années de bons et loyaux services; **they are d. to each other** ils sont très attachés l'un à l'autre

devotee [devəʊ'ti:] *n (of writer, artist)* admirateur(trice) *m,f*; *(of idea)* partisan *m*; *(of sports, music)* passionné(e) *m,f*

devotion [dɪ'vəʊʃən] *n (to cause, friend, family)* dévouement *m*; *(to god, saint)* dévotion *f*; **devotions** *(prayers)* prières *fpl*

devour [dɪ'vaʊə(r)] *vt also Fig* dévorer

devout [dɪ'vaʊt] *adj (person)* dévot(e); *(wish)* fervent(e)

dew [dju:] *n* rosée *f*

dewy-eyed [dju:ɪ'aɪd] *adj (loving)* ému(e); *(naive)* ingénu(e)

dexterity [deks'terɪtɪ] *n* dextérité *f*

dext(e)rous ['dekstrəs] *adj* adroit(e), habile

diabetes [daɪə'bi:ti:z] *n* diabète *m*

diabetic [daɪə'betɪk] *n & adj* diabétique *mf*; **d. chocolate** chocolat *m* pour diabétiques

diabolical [daɪə'bɒlɪkəl] *adj (evil)* diabolique

diadem ['daɪədem] *n* diadème *m*

diagnose ['daɪəgnəʊz] *vt also Fig* diagnostiquer

diagnosis [daɪəg'nəʊsɪs] (*pl* **diagnoses** [daɪəg'nəʊsi:z]) *n also Fig* diagnostic *m*

diagnostic [daɪəg'nɒstɪk] *adj* diagnostique

diagonal [daɪ'ægənəl] **1** *n* diagonale *f*
2 *adj* diagonal(e)

diagram ['daɪəgræm] *n* schéma *m*

dial ['daɪəl] **1** *n (of clock, phone)* cadran *m*; *(control knob)* bouton *m*; *Tel* **d. code** indicatif *m*; **d. tone** tonalité *f*
2 *vt (phone number)* composer; *(operator, country)* appeler

dialect ['daɪəlekt] *n* dialecte *m*

dialectic [daɪə'lektɪk], **dialectical** [daɪə'lektɪkəl] *adj* dialectique

dialog, dialogue ['daɪəlɒg] *n* dialogue *m*; *Comput* **d. box** boîte *f* de dialogue

dialysis [daɪ'ælɪsɪs] *n Med* dialyse *f*

diameter [daɪ'æmɪtə(r)] *n* diamètre *m*; **the wheel is 2 ft in d.** ≃ la roue a un diamètre de 60 cm

diametrically [daɪə'metrɪklɪ] *adv* diamétralement

diamond ['daɪəmənd] *n (gem)* diamant *m*; *(shape)* losange *m*; *(for baseball)* terrain *m* (de baseball); *(in cards)* carreau *m*; **ace of diamonds** as *m* de carreau; **d. jubilee** soixantième anniversaire *m*; **d. necklace/ring** collier *m*/bague *f* de *ou* en diamants

diaper ['daɪəpə(r)] *n* couche *f*

diaphanous [daɪ'æfənəs] *adj* diaphane

diaphragm ['daɪəfræm] *n* (**a**) *Anat* diaphragme *m* (**b**) *(contraceptive)* diaphragme *m*

diarrhea [daɪə'rɪə] *n* diarrhée *f*

diary ['daɪərɪ] (*pl* **diaries**) *n (personal)* journal *m* (intime); *(for appointments)* agenda *m*

diatribe ['daɪətraɪb] *n* diatribe *f* (**against** contre)

dice [daɪs] **1** *n (pl* **dice**) dé *m*; **to play d.** jouer aux dés; *Fam* **no d.!** des clous!, pas question!
2 *vt (food)* couper en dés
3 *vi* **to d. with death** jouer avec sa vie

dicey ['daɪsɪ] *adj Fam* risqué(e)

dichotomy [daɪ'kɒtəmɪ] (*pl* **dichotomies**) *n* dichotomie *f*

dick [dɪk] *n* (**a**) *Vulg (penis)* bite *f* (**b**) *Fam (detective)* privé *m*

dickhead ['dɪkhed] *n Vulg (idiot)* tête *f* de nœud

dictate 1 *n* ['dɪkteɪt] ordre *m*; **she followed the dictates of her conscience** elle fit ce que lui dictait sa conscience
2 *vt* [dɪk'teɪt] (**a**) *(letter, passage, conditions)* dicter (**b**) *(determine)* imposer; *(choice)* dicter
3 *vi* [dɪk'teɪt] (**a**) *(dictate text)* dicter (**b**) *(give orders)* **to d. to sb** donner des ordres à qn; **I won't be dictated to!** je n'ai pas d'ordres à recevoir!

dictation [dɪk'teɪʃən] *n* dictée *f*; **to take d.** écrire sous la dictée

dictator [dɪk'teɪtə(r)] *n* dictateur *m*

dictatorial [dɪktə'tɔ:rɪəl] *adj (power, regime)* dictatorial(e); *(manner, tone)* autoritaire

dictatorship [dɪk'teɪtəʃɪp] *n* dictature *f*

diction ['dɪkʃən] *n (pronunciation)* diction *f*; *(choice of words)* style *m*

dictionary ['dɪkʃənərɪ] (*pl* **dictionaries**) *n* dictionnaire *m*

did [dɪd] *pt of* **do²**

didactic [dɪ'dæktɪk] *adj* didactique

diddle ['dɪdəl] *vt Fam* rouler; **he diddled me out of $500** il m'a escroqué 500 dollars

didn't ['dɪdənt] = **did not**

die¹ [daɪ] *n* (**a**) *(pl* **dice** [daɪs]) *(in games)* dé *m*; **the d. is cast** les dés sont jetés (**b**) *(pl* **dies** [daɪz]) *(mold)* matrice *f*

die² [daɪ] *(pt & pp* **died**, *continuous* **dying**) **1** *vi* mourir (**from** *or* **of** de); **she is dying** elle est mourante; **to d. hard** *(of habit, rumor)* avoir la vie dure; *Fam* **never say d.!** il ne faut jamais désespérer!; *Fam* **I nearly died (of shame)** j'ai cru mourir de honte; *Fam* **to be dying to do sth** mourir d'envie de faire qch; *Fam* **I'm dying for a cigarette** je meurs d'envie de fumer une cigarette; **the engine died on me/us** le moteur a calé
2 *vt* **to d. a natural/violent death** mourir de mort naturelle/violente; *Fig* **to d. a death** *(of proposal)* tomber à l'eau; *(of performer)* faire un bide

▸**die away** *vi (of sound, voice)* s'affaiblir

▸**die down** *vi (of fire)* baisser; *(of wind)* tomber; *(of sound)* s'affaiblir; *(of excitement, scandal)* se calmer

▸**die off** *vi* mourir

▸**die out** *vi (of family, species)* s'éteindre

diehard ['daɪhɑ:d] **1** *n* réactionnaire *mf*
2 *adj* pur(e) et dur(e)

diesel ['di:zəl] **1** *n* *(fuel)* gas-oil *m*, gazole *m*; *(car, railroad engine)* diesel *m*
2 *adj (engine, train)* diesel; **d. oil** *or* **fuel** gas-oil *m*, gazole *m*

diet ['daɪət] **1** *n* *(usual food)* alimentation *f*; *(restricted food)* régime *m*; **to be/to go on a d.** être/se mettre au régime; **d. foods** aliments *mpl* allégés
2 *vi* être au régime

dietary ['daɪətərɪ] *adj* alimentaire; **d. fiber** fibres *fpl* (alimentaires)

dietician [daɪə'tɪʃən] *n* diététicien(enne) *m,f*

differ ['dɪfə(r)] *vi* **(a)** *(be different)* différer (**from** de); **to d. in size/color** être de taille/couleur différente **(b)** *(disagree)* ne pas être d'accord; **to d. with sb** ne pas être d'accord avec qn; **I beg to d.** permettez-moi d'être d'un autre avis; **to agree to d.** garder chacun son opinion

difference ['dɪfərəns] *n* **(a)** *(disparity)* différence *f* (**between/in** entre/de); **that doesn't make any d.** ça ne fait aucune différence; **it makes no d. to me** cela m'est égal; **that makes all the d.** voilà qui change tout; **a car with a d.** une voiture pas comme les autres **(b)** *(disagreement)* désaccord *m*, différend *m*; **d. of opinion** divergence *f* d'opinion; **we have to settle our differences** il faut nous mettre d'accord

different ['dɪfərənt] *adj* **(a)** *(not the same)* différent(e) (**from** de); **that's a d. matter** ça, c'est une autre affaire; **she feels like a d. person** elle ne se sent plus la même; **he just wants to be d.** il veut se singulariser **(b)** *(various)* différents(es), divers(es)

differential [dɪfə'renʃəl] **1** *n* *(in wages, prices)* écart *m*; *Math* **d. calculus** calcul *m* différentiel; *Aut* **d. (gear)** différentiel *m*
2 *adj* différentiel(elle)

differentiate [dɪfə'renʃɪət] **1** *vt* différencier (**from** de)
2 *vi* faire la différence (**between** entre)

differently ['dɪfərəntlɪ] *adv* différemment

differently-abled ['dɪfərəntlɪ'eɪbəld] *adj* *(in politically correct usage)* handicapé(e)

difficult ['dɪfɪkəlt] *adj* difficile; **to find it d. to do sth** avoir du mal à faire qch; **he's d. to get along with** il n'est pas commode; **you're just being d.** tu le fais exprès pour embêter le monde; **to make life d. for sb** compliquer la vie à qn

difficulty ['dɪfɪkəltɪ] *(pl* **difficulties)** *n* difficulté *f*; **to have d. in doing sth** avoir des difficultés *ou* du mal à faire qch; **to make difficulties for sb** créer des difficultés à qn

diffidence ['dɪfɪdəns] *n* manque *m* de confiance en soi

diffident ['dɪfɪdənt] *adj* peu sûr(e) de soi; **to be d. about doing sth** hésiter à faire qch

diffuse 1 *adj* [dɪ'fju:s] diffus(e)
2 *vt* [dɪ'fju:z] diffuser, répandre
3 *vi* [dɪ'fju:z] se diffuser, se répandre

dig [dɪg] **1** *n* **(a)** *(in archaeology)* fouilles *fpl*
(b) *(poke)* **a d. in the ribs** un coup de coude dans les côtes
(c) *(remark)* pique *f*; **to take a d. at sb** lancer une pique à qn
2 *vt* *(pt & pp* **dug** [dʌg]) **(a)** *(hole, grave, ditch)* creuser; *(garden)* bêcher; *Fig* **she is digging her own grave** elle est en train de creuser sa propre tombe
(b) *(thrust)* **to d. sth into sth** planter qch dans qch
(c) *Fam Old-fashioned (like)* **she really digs that kind of music** ce genre de musique, ça la botte
(d) *Fam Old-fashioned (look at)* mater; **d. that guy over there** mate un peu le mec, là-bas
(e) *Fam Old-fashioned (understand)* piger; **you d.?** tu piges?
3 *vi* *(of person, animal)* creuser; *(in archaeology)* faire des fouilles; **to d. for sth** creuser pour trouver qch

▶**dig in 1** *vt sep Fig* **to d. one's heels in** s'entêter
2 *vi* **(a)** *(of soldiers)* se retrancher **(b)** *Fam (eat)* attaquer

▶**dig out** *vt sep* **(a)** *(bullet, splinter)* extraire; *(person from ruins, snow drift)* dégager **(b)** *Fam (find) (information)* dénicher

▶**dig up** *vt sep* **(a)** *(plant)* arracher; *(treasure, body)* déterrer;

(road) excaver **(b)** *Fam (find) (information, person)* dénicher

digest 1 *n* ['daɪdʒest] *(summary)* condensé *m*
2 *vt* [dɪ'dʒest] *also Fig* digérer

digestible [dɪ'dʒestəbəl] *adj* digeste

digestion [dɪ'dʒestʃən] *n* digestion *f*

digestive [dɪ'dʒestɪv] *adj* digestif(ive); **d. system/tract** système *m*/tube *m* digestif

digger ['dɪgə(r)] *n* *(machine)* excavateur *m*

digicam ['dɪdʒɪkæm] *n* caméra *f* numérique

digit ['dɪdʒɪt] *n* **(a)** *(finger)* doigt *m*; *(toe)* orteil *m* **(b)** *(number)* chiffre *m*

digital ['dɪdʒɪtəl] *adj* numérique; *(clock, watch)* à affichage numérique; **d. camera** appareil *m* photo numérique; **d. recording** enregistrement *m* numérique; **d. signature** signature *f* numérique *ou* électronique; **d. television** *(technique)* télévision *f* numérique; *(appliance)* téléviseur *m* numérique

digitally ['dɪdʒɪtəlɪ] *adv* numériquement, sous forme digitale; *Mus* **d. recorded** enregistré(e) en numérique

digitize ['dɪdʒɪtaɪz] *vt Comput* numériser

digitized ['dɪdʒɪtaɪzd] *adj Comput* numérisé

dignified ['dɪgnɪfaɪd] *adj* digne

dignify ['dɪgnɪfaɪ] *(pt & pp* **dignified)** *vt* donner de la dignité à; **I won't d. that remark with a response!** je ne m'abaisserai pas à répondre à cette remarque!

dignitary ['dɪgnɪtərɪ] *(pl* **dignitaries)** *n* dignitaire *m*

dignity ['dɪgnɪtɪ] *n* dignité *f*; **she considered it beneath her d. to respond** elle estimait indigne d'elle de répondre

digress [daɪ'gres] *vi* faire une digression; **to d. from** s'écarter de; **..., but I d.** ..., mais je m'égare

digression [daɪ'greʃən] *n* digression *f*

dike [daik] *n* **(a)** *(barrier)* digue *f* **(b)** *very Fam (lesbian)* gouine *f*, = terme injurieux désignant une lesbienne

dilapidated [dɪ'læpɪdeɪtɪd] *adj* délabré(e)

dilapidation [dɪlæpɪ'deɪʃən] *n* délabrement *m*

dilate [daɪ'leɪt] **1** *vt* dilater
2 *vi* se dilater

dilation [daɪ'leɪʃən] *n* dilatation *f*

dilatory ['dɪlətərɪ] *adj Formal (reply)* dilatoire; **to be d. in doing sth** tarder à faire qch

dilemma [dɪ'lemə, daɪ'lemə] *n* dilemme *m*; **to be in a d.** être placé(e) devant un dilemme

dilettante [dɪlɪ'tɑːnt] *n* dilettante *mf*

diligence ['dɪlɪdʒəns] *n* application *f*, zèle *m*

diligent ['dɪlɪdʒənt] *adj* consciencieux(euse)

dill [dɪl] *n* aneth *m*; **d. pickle** cornichon *m* à l'aneth

dilly-dally ['dɪlɪ'dælɪ] *(pt & pp* **dilly-dallied)** *vi Fam (loiter)* traînasser; *(hesitate)* tergiverser

dilute [daɪ'luːt] **1** *adj* dilué(e)
2 *vt (liquid)* diluer; *Fig (policy, proposal)* édulcorer

dilution [daɪ'luːʃən] *n Fig (of policy, proposal)* édulcoration *f*

dim [dɪm] **1** *adj* **(a)** *(light, chance, hope)* faible; *(outline, memory)* vague; *(eyesight)* faible, trouble; *(future)* sombre; **to take a d. view of sth** avoir une piètre opinion de qch **(b)** *(stupid)* bête
2 *vt (pt & pp* **dimmed)** *(light)* baisser, atténuer
3 *vi (of light)* baisser

dime [daɪm] *n* *(pièce f de)* 10 cents *mpl*; *Fam* **it's not worth a d.** ça ne vaut pas un clou; *Fam* **they're a d. a dozen** il y en a à la pelle

dimension [daɪ'menʃən] *n also Fig* dimension *f*

diminish [dɪ'mɪnɪʃ] *vt & vi* diminuer; *Law* **diminished capacity** *or* **responsibility** responsabilité *f* atténuée

diminishing [dɪ'mɪnɪʃɪŋ] *adj* décroissant(e); **the law of d. returns** la loi des rendements décroissants

diminutive [dɪ'mɪnjʊtɪv] **1** *n Gram* diminutif *m*
2 *adj* minuscule

dimly ['dɪmlɪ] *adv (lit)* faiblement; *(remember, see)* vaguement

dimmer ['dɪmə(r)] n (a) (for lamp) **d. (switch)** variateur m (b) (for car headlights) basculeur m (de phares); **dimmers** (headlights) phares mpl code; (parking lights) feux mpl de position

dimple ['dɪmpəl] n fossette f

dimwit ['dɪmwɪt] n Fam andouille f

din [dɪn] n vacarme m

dine [daɪn] vi dîner, Belg, Can & Suisse souper

▸**dine out** vi dîner dehors

diner ['daɪnə(r)] n (a) (person) dîneur(euse) m,f (b) (restaurant) petit restaurant m

ding-dong ['dɪŋ'dɒŋ] **1** n (sound) ding dong m
2 adj Fam (argument, contest) acharné(e)

dinghy ['dɪŋgɪ] (pl **dinghies**) n (rubber) **d.** canot m pneumatique; **(sailing) d.** dériveur m

dingo ['dɪŋgəʊ] (pl **dingoes**) n dingo m

dingy ['dɪndʒɪ] adj (room, street) miteux(euse); (color) terne

dining ['daɪnɪŋ] n **d. car** (on train) wagon-restaurant m; **d. hall** (in school) réfectoire m; **d. room** salle f à manger; **d. table** table f de salle à manger

dinner ['dɪnə(r)] n dîner m, Belg, Can & Suisse souper m; **what's for d.?** qu'est-ce qu'on mange?; **to have d.** dîner; **d. jacket** smoking m; **d. party** dîner; **d. service** service m de table; **d. time** heure f du dîner

dinosaur ['daɪnəsɔː(r)] n also Fig dinosaure m

dint [dɪnt] n Formal **by d. of** à force de; **by d. of her efforts** grâce à ses efforts

diocese ['daɪəsɪs] n Rel diocèse m

diode ['daɪəʊd] n Elec diode f

dioxide [daɪ'ɒksaɪd] n Chem dioxyde m

dip [dɪp] **1** n (a) (slope) descente f; (hollow) dépression f; (in prices, figures) baisse f (b) (swim) baignade f; **to go for a d.** faire trempette (c) (sauce) = sauce dans laquelle on trempe des crudités, des biscuits salés, etc.
2 vt (pt & pp **dipped**) (a) (immerse) plonger (b) (lower) baisser
3 vi (of ground) descendre; (of prices, temperature) baisser; **the sun dipped below the horizon** le soleil descendit derrière l'horizon

▸**dip into** vt insep (savings, capital) puiser dans; (book) feuilleter

diphtheria [dɪf'θɪərɪə] n Med diphtérie f

diphthong ['dɪfθɒŋ] n Ling diptongue f

diploma [dɪ'pləʊmə] n diplôme m

diplomacy [dɪ'pləʊməsɪ] n also Fig diplomatie f

diplomat ['dɪpləmæt] n diplomate mf

diplomatic [dɪplə'mætɪk] adj diplomatique; Fig (person) diplomate; **d. corps** corps m diplomatique; **d. immunity** immunité f diplomatique; **d. pouch** valise f diplomatique

dipper ['dɪpə(r)] n (ladle) louche f; **the Big D.** (constellation) la Grande Ourse

dipsomaniac [dɪpsə'meɪnɪæk] n dipsomane mf

dipstick ['dɪpstɪk] n (a) Aut jauge f de niveau d'huile (b) Fam (idiot) abruti(e) m,f

dire ['daɪə(r)] adj (consequences) tragique; Fam (bad) épouvantable; **d. poverty** misère f noire; **to be in d. need of sth** avoir un besoin urgent de qch; **to be in d. straits** être dans une mauvaise passe

direct [dɪ'rekt, daɪ'rekt] **1** adj direct(e); (refusal, denial) catégorique; **the d. opposite** l'exact opposé; **to be a d. descendant of sb** descendre de qn en ligne directe; Elec **d. current** courant m continu; Fin **d. deposit** virement m automatique; **d. hit** coup m au but; **d. mail** publipostage m; Gram **d. object** complément m d'objet direct; Pol **d. rule** administration f centrale; Com **d. selling** vente f directe; Gram **d. speech** discours m direct; Fin **d. taxation** contributions fpl directes
2 adv directement; (broadcast) en direct (**from** de)
3 vt (a) (remark) adresser (**at** à); (gaze, light) diriger (**at** sur); (funds, effort) consacrer (**towards** à); **can you d. me to the station?** pouvez-vous m'indiquer le chemin de la gare? (b)

(company, actors) diriger; (traffic) régler; (play) mettre en scène; (movie) réaliser (c) (instruct) **to d. sb to do sth** ordonner à qn de faire qch; **as directed** selon les instructions

direction [dɪ'rekʃən] n (a) (way) direction f, sens m; **in the d. of** en direction de; **they ran off in all directions** ils sont partis en courant dans toutes les directions; **the town was surrounded by hills in all directions** la ville était entourée de tous côtés par des collines (b) (management) (of project) direction f; (of play) mise f en scène; (of movie) réalisation f; **under the d. of** (orchestra) sous la direction de (c) **directions** (to place) indications fpl; (for use) instructions fpl; **to ask for directions** demander son chemin

directive [dɪ'rektɪv] n (order) directive f

directly [dɪ'rektlɪ] adv (a) (go, write) directement; **to be d. descended from sb** descendre de qn en ligne directe (b) (exactly) juste; **d. opposite** juste en face de (c) (frankly) (answer, speak) ouvertement (d) (soon) immédiatement; **I'll be there d.** j'arrive tout de suite

director [dɪ'rektə(r)] n (manager) directeur(trice) m,f; (board member) administrateur(trice) m,f; (of movie) réalisateur(trice) m,f; (of play) metteur m en scène

directorate [dɪ'rektər(e)ɪt] n (board) conseil m d'administration

directorship [dɪ'rektəʃɪp] n direction f

directory [dɪ'rektərɪ] (pl **directories**) n (of phone numbers) annuaire m; Comput répertoire m; **(street) d.** index m (des rues)

dirge [dɜːdʒ] n chant m funèbre; Fam Fig chanson f lugubre

dirham [dɪ'ræm] n dirham m

dirt [dɜːt] n (a) (on clothes, body) saleté f; (mud) boue f; (soil) terre f; **to treat sb like d.** traiter qn comme un chien; Fam **dog d.** crotte f de chien; **d. road** chemin m de terre (b) Fam (scandal) cancans mpl, ragots mpl

dirtbag ['dɜːtbæg] n Fam nullard(e) m,f

dirt-cheap ['dɜːt'tʃiːp] Fam **1** adj donné(e)
2 adv pour trois fois rien

dirty ['dɜːtɪ] **1** adj (a) (unclean) (person, hands, clothes) sale; (with mud) crotté(e); **to get d.** se salir; also Fig **to get one's hands d.** se salir les mains; Fig **to wash one's d. linen in public** laver son linge sale en public
(b) Fig (unpleasant, unsavory) **it's a d. business** c'est une activité peu reluisante; **to give sb a d. look** regarder qn d'un sale œil; **d. work** sale boulot m
(c) (book, movie, joke) cochon(onne); (language, word) grossier(ère); **d. old man** vieux cochon m; **"communism" is a d. word nowadays** "communisme" est un mot tabou de nos jours
2 adv (a) (fight) déloyalement
(b) (obscenely) **to talk d.** dire des cochonneries
(c) Fam (for emphasis) vachement; **a d. big hole** un sacré grand trou
3 vt (pt & pp **dirtied**) salir

disability [dɪsə'bɪlɪtɪ] (pl **disabilities**) n handicap m, infirmité f; **d. payments** pension f d'invalidité

disable [dɪ'seɪbəl] vt (person) rendre infirme; (ship) désemparer; (alarm system) désactiver

disabled [dɪ'seɪbəld] **1** npl **the d.** les handicapés mpl
2 adj handicapé(e); **d. access** facilité f d'accès pour personnes handicapées; **d. restrooms** toilettes fpl pour handicapés

disabuse [dɪsə'bjuːz] vt Formal **to d. sb (of an idea)** détromper qn

disadvantage [dɪsəd'vɑːntɪdʒ] **1** n désavantage m, inconvénient m; **to be at a d.** être désavantagé(e); **to put sb at a d.** désavantager qn
2 vt désavantager

disadvantaged [dɪsəd'vɑːntɪdʒd] adj défavorisé(e)

disaffected [dɪsə'fektɪd] adj mécontent(e); (stronger) révolté(e)

disaffection [dɪsə'fekʃən] *n* désaffection *f*

disagree [dɪsə'griː] *vi* (**a**) *(quarrel)* ne pas être d'accord; **to d. with sb (about)** ne pas être d'accord avec qn (sur) (**b**) *(of reports, figures)* ne pas concorder (**c**) *(of climate, food)* **to d. with sb** ne pas réussir à qn

disagreeable [dɪsə'griːəbəl] *adj* désagréable

disagreement [dɪsə'griːmənt] *n* (**a**) *(failure to agree)* désaccord *m*; **to be in d. with sb** être en désaccord avec qn (**b**) *(quarrel)* différend *m* (**c**) *(discrepancy)* différence *f*

disallow [dɪsə'laʊ] *vt Formal (objection, claim)* rejeter; *(goal)* refuser

disappear [dɪsə'pɪə(r)] *vi* disparaître

disappearance [dɪsə'pɪərəns] *n* disparition *f*

disappoint [dɪsə'pɔɪnt] *vt* décevoir

disappointed [dɪsə'pɔɪntɪd] *adj* déçu(e) (**in** *or* **with** par)

disappointing [dɪsə'pɔɪntɪŋ] *adj* décevant(e)

disappointment [dɪsə'pɔɪntmənt] *n* déception *f*; **to be a d.** être décevant(e)

disapproval [dɪsə'pruːvəl] *n* désapprobation *f*

disapprove [dɪsə'pruːv] *vi* désapprouver; **to d. of sth** désapprouver qch; **he disapproves of them** ils ne lui plaisent pas

disapproving [dɪsə'pruːvɪŋ] *adj (tone, look)* désapprobateur(trice); **to be d. of sth** désapprouver qch

disarm [dɪs'ɑːm] *vt & vi* désarmer

disarmament [dɪs'ɑːməmənt] *n* désarmement *m*; **d. talks** conférence *f* sur le désarmement

disarming [dɪs'ɑːmɪŋ] *adj (smile, honesty)* désarmant(e)

disarray [dɪsə'reɪ] *n* désordre *m*; **in d.** en désordre

disaster [dɪ'zɑːstə(r)] *n* désastre *m*; *(earthquake, fire, crash)* catastrophe *f*; **d. area** région *f* sinistrée; *Fam Fig (person)* maladroit(e) *m,f*; **d. movie** film *m* catastrophe

disastrous [dɪ'zɑːstrəs] *adj* désastreux(euse)

disband [dɪs'bænd] **1** *vt (regiment)* supprimer; *(organization)* dissoudre

2 *vi (of organization)* se dissoudre; *(of regiment)* être supprimé(e)

disbar [dɪsbɑː(r)] *vt Law (attorney)* rayer du barreau

disbelief [dɪsbɪ'liːf] *n* incrédulité *f*; **in d.** *(listen, watch)* avec incrédulité

disbelieve [dɪsbɪ'liːv] *vt* ne pas croire

disburse [dɪs'bɜːs] *vt Formal* débourser

disc = **disk (b)**

discard [dɪs'kɑːd] *vt (person)* laisser tomber; *(plan, proposal)* abandonner; *(object)* se débarrasser de

discern [dɪ'sɜːn] *vt (shape, object)* discerner; *(sound, difference)* percevoir

discernible [dɪ'sɜːnɪbəl] *adj (shape, object)* discernable; *(sound, difference)* perceptible

discerning [dɪ'sɜːnɪŋ] *adj (person)* perspicace; *(taste)* fin(e)

discharge 1 *n* ['dɪstʃɑːdʒ] (**a**) *(of patient)* sortie *f*; *(authorization)* autorisation *f* de sortie; *(of prisoner)* mise *f* en liberté, libération *f*; *(of soldier)* libération *f*; *(for unfitness)* réforme *f*

(**b**) *(of firearm)* décharge *f*

(**c**) *(of gas, chemical)* dégagement *m*; *(of pus, fluid)* écoulement *m*

2 *vt* [dɪs'tʃɑːdʒ] (**a**) *(patient)* laisser sortir; *(prisoner)* libérer; *(employee)* congédier, renvoyer; *(soldier)* libérer; *(for unfitness)* réformer

(**b**) *(firearm)* décharger

(**c**) *(gas, chemical)* dégager; *(fluid)* déverser; **to d. pus** suppurer

(**d**) *(duty, debt)* s'acquitter de; *(fine)* payer

disciple [dɪ'saɪpəl] *n* disciple *mf*

disciplinarian [dɪsɪplɪ'neərɪən] *n* **to be a strict d.** être stricte en matière de discipline

disciplinary ['dɪsɪplɪnərɪ] *adj* disciplinaire

discipline ['dɪsɪplɪn] **1** *n* discipline *f*

2 *vt (punish)* punir; **to d. oneself** se discipliner

disclaim [dɪs'kleɪm] *vt (renounce)* renoncer à; *(deny)* démentir

disclaimer [dɪs'kleɪmə(r)] *n* démenti *m*

disclose [dɪs'kləʊz] *vt* révéler

disclosure [dɪs'kləʊʒə(r)] *n* révélation *f*

disco ['dɪskəʊ] *(pl* **discos**) *n* discothèque *f*, boîte *f* (de nuit)

discolor [dɪs'kʌlə(r)] *vt (fade)* décolorer; *(stain) (with age)* jaunir; *(with smoke)* noircir; **to become discolored** se décolorer

discomfiture [dɪs'kʌmfɪtʃə(r)] *n* embarras *m*

discomfort [dɪs'kʌmfət] *n (lack of comfort)* inconfort *m*; *(pain)* légère douleur *f*; **to be in some d.** éprouver une légère douleur

disconcert [dɪskən'sɜːt] *vt* déconcerter, décontenancer

disconcerted [dɪskən'sɜːtɪd] *adj* déconcerté

disconcerting [dɪskən'sɜːtɪŋ] *adj* déconcertant(e)

disconnect [dɪskə'nekt] *vt (gas, electricity, phone)* couper; *(machine, appliance)* débrancher

disconsolate [dɪs'kɒnsələt] *adj* désespéré(e) (**at** par)

discontent [dɪskən'tent] *n* mécontentement *m*

discontented [dɪskən'tentɪd] *adj* mécontent(e) (**with** de)

discontinue [dɪskən'tɪnjuː] *vt* interrompre; *Com* **discontinued line** fin *f* de série

discord ['dɪskɔːd] *n* discorde *f*

discordant [dɪs'kɔːdənt] *adj (opinions, sound)* discordant(e)

discotheque ['dɪskətek] *n* discothèque *f*, boîte *f* (de nuit)

discount 1 *n* ['dɪskaʊnt] remise *f*; **at a d.** au rabais

2 *vt* (**a**) ['dɪskaʊnt] *(price)* baisser; *(goods)* solder (**b**) [dɪs'kaʊnt] *(suggestion, rumors)* ignorer, ne pas tenir compte de; *(possibility, fact)* écarter

discourage [dɪs'kʌrɪdʒ] *vt* (**a**) *(dishearten)* décourager (**b**) *(dissuade)* **to d. sb from doing sth** dissuader qn de faire qch

discouragement [dɪs'kʌrɪdʒmənt] *n* (**a**) *(loss of enthusiasm)* découragement *m* (**b**) *(dissuasion)* **to act as** *or* **to be a d. (to sth)** avoir un effet dissuasif (sur qch)

discouraging [dɪs'kʌrɪdʒɪŋ] *adj* décourageant(e)

discourse *Formal* **1** *n* ['dɪskɔːs] *(speech)* discours *m*; *(conversation)* conversation *f*

2 *vi* [dɪs'kɔːs] **to d. (up)on sth** discourir sur qch

discourteous [dɪs'kɜːtɪəs] *adj* discourtois(e)

discourtesy [dɪs'kɜːtəsɪ] *n* impolitesse *f*

discover [dɪs'kʌvə(r)] *vt* découvrir

discovery [dɪs'kʌvərɪ] *(pl* **discoveries**) *n* découverte *f*

discredit [dɪs'kredɪt] **1** *n* discrédit *m*; **to be a d. to sb/sth** déshonorer qn/qch; **much to their d., they didn't even apologize** ils ne se sont même pas excusés, ce qui ne leur fait pas honneur

2 *vt (person, theory)* discréditer

discreet [dɪs'kriːt] *adj* discret(ète)

discrepancy [dɪs'krepənsɪ] *(pl* **discrepancies**) *n* décalage *m* (**between** entre)

discretion [dɪs'kreʃən] *n* (**a**) *(tact)* discrétion *f* (**b**) *(judgment)* jugement *m*; **at the manager's d.** à la discrétion du directeur; **to use one's own d.** juger par soi-même

discretionary [dɪs'kreʃənərɪ] *adj* discrétionnaire

discriminate [dɪs'krɪmɪneɪt] **1** *vt* distinguer (**from** de)

2 *vi* **to d. between** faire la différence entre; **to d. against** faire de la discrimination envers; **to be discriminated against** être victime de discrimination; **to d. in favor of** favoriser

discriminating [dɪs'krɪmɪneɪtɪŋ] *adj* perspicace

discrimination [dɪskrɪmɪ'neɪʃən] *n* (**a**) *(bias)* discrimination *f* (**b**) *(taste)* discernement *m* (**c**) *(differentiation)* différenciation *f*

discriminatory [dɪs'krɪmɪnətərɪ] *adj* discriminatoire

discursive [dɪs'kɜːsɪv] *adj* discursif(ive)

discus ['dɪskəs] *n* disque *m*

discuss [dɪs'kʌs] *vt (issue, problem)* discuter de; *(author, book,* *report)* examiner, parler de; **I don't wish to d. it** je ne veux pas en parler

discussion [dɪs'kʌʃən] *n* discussion *f*; **under d.** en discussion

disdain [dɪs'deɪn] **1** *n* dédain *m*
2 *vt* dédaigner; **to d. to do sth** dédaigner de faire qch

disdainful [dɪs'deɪnfʊl] *adj* dédaigneux(euse)

disease [dɪ'ziːz] *n* maladie *f*

diseased [dɪ'ziːzd] *adj* malade

disembark [dɪsem'bɑːk] *vt & vi* débarquer

disembodied [dɪsɪm'bɒdɪd] *adj* désincarné(e)

disenchanted [dɪsɪn'tʃɑːntɪd] *adj* désenchanté(e); **to be d. with sth** être déçu(e) par qch

disenchantment [dɪsɪn'tʃɑːntmənt] *n* désenchantement *m*

disengage [dɪsɪn'geɪdʒ] **1** *vt* dégager (**from** de); **to d. one-self from sth** se retirer de qch
2 *vi* se retirer (**from** de); *Mil* cesser le combat

disentangle [dɪsɪn'tæŋgəl] *vt* démêler

disfavor [dɪs'feɪvə(r)] *n* **to be in d.** être en défaveur; **to fall into d. (with sb)** tomber en disgrâce (auprès de qn)

disfigure [dɪs'fɪgə(r)] *vt* défigurer

disfigurement [dɪs'fɪgəmənt] *n* défigurement *m*

disgrace [dɪs'greɪs] **1** *n (shame)* honte *f*; **to be in d. (with sb)** être en disgrâce (auprès de qn); **to be a d. to one's fa-mily/country** déshonorer sa famille/son pays; **it's a d.!** c'est une honte!
2 *vt* déshonorer, couvrir de honte; **to d. oneself** se désho-norer

disgraceful [dɪs'greɪsfʊl] *adj* honteux(euse); **it's d.!** c'est honteux *ou* scandaleux!

disgracefully [dɪs'greɪsfʊlɪ] *adv* scandaleusement, honteu-sement

disgruntled [dɪs'grʌntəld] *adj* mécontent(e)

disguise [dɪs'gaɪz] **1** *n (costume)* déguisement *m*; **in d.** dégui-sé(e)
2 *vt* déguiser; **to d. oneself as** se déguiser en; **there is no disguising the fact that...** on ne peut pas cacher le fait que...

disgust [dɪs'gʌst] **1** *n* dégoût *m*; **to fill sb with d.** remplir qn de dégoût, écœurer qn; **in d.** dégoûté(e), écœuré(e)
2 *vt* dégoûter; **to be disgusted with oneself** se dégoûter

disgusting [dɪs'gʌstɪŋ] *adj* répugnant(e)

dish [dɪʃ] **1** *n (bowl, food)* plat *m*; **d. of the day** plat du jour; **dishes** *(plates, etc.)* vaisselle *f*; **to do the dishes** faire la vais-selle; *TV* **d. antenna** antenne *f* parabolique
2 *vt* **Fam to d. the dirt** tout raconter

▸**dish out** *vt sep (food)* servir; *(money, advice)* distribuer

disharmony [dɪs'hɑːmənɪ] *n* désaccord *m*

dishcloth ['dɪʃklɒθ] *n (for washing)* lavette *f*; *(for drying)* torch-on *m*

disheartening [dɪs'hɑːtənɪŋ] *adj* décourageant(e)

disheveled [dɪ'ʃevəld] *adj (person, appearance)* débraillé(e); *(hair)* ébouriffé(e); *(clothes)* en désordre

dishonest [dɪs'ɒnɪst] *adj* malhonnête

dishonesty [dɪs'ɒnɪstɪ] *n* malhonnêteté *f*

dishonor [dɪs'ɒnə(r)] **1** *n* déshonneur *m*
2 *vt* déshonorer

dishonorable [dɪs'ɒnərəbəl] *adj* déshonorant(e)

dishrag ['dɪʃræg] *n (for washing)* lavette *f*; *(for drying)* torchon *m*

dishtowel ['dɪʃtaʊəl] *n* torchon *m*

dishwasher ['dɪʃwɒʃə(r)] *n (person)* plongeur(euse) *m,f*; *(ma-chine)* lave-vaisselle *m inv*

dishwater ['dɪʃwɔːtə(r)] *n also Fig* eau *f* de vaisselle

disillusioned [dɪsɪ'luːʒənd] *adj* désillusionné(e); **to be d. with sb/sth** être déçu(e) par qn/qch; **to become d.** perdre ses illusions

disincentive [dɪsɪn'sentɪv] *n* **to be a d. (to sth)** avoir un ef-fet dissuasif (sur qch)

disinclination [dɪsɪŋklɪ'neɪʃən] *n* manque *m* d'enthousiasme (**to do sth** à faire qch)

disinclined [dɪsɪn'klaɪnd] *adj* **to be d. to do sth** être peu dis-posé(e) à faire qch

disinfect [dɪsɪn'fekt] *vt* désinfecter

disinfectant [dɪsɪn'fektənt] *n* désinfectant *m*

disinformation [dɪsɪnfə'meɪʃən] *n* désinformation *f*

disingenuous [dɪsɪn'dʒenjʊəs] *adj (person, answer)* peu sin-cère; *(manner, smile)* faux (fausse)

disinherit [dɪsɪn'herɪt] *vt* déshériter

disintegrate [dɪs'ɪntɪgreɪt] *vi* se désintégrer; *(of confidence)* s'effriter; *(of marriage, relationship)* se désagréger

disintegration [dɪsɪntɪ'greɪʃən] *n* désintégration *f*; *(of mar-riage, relationship)* désagrégation *f*

disinterest [dɪs'ɪntərɪst] *n (impartiality)* impartialité *f*; *(lack of interest)* désintérêt *m*, indifférence *f*

disinterested [dɪs'ɪntərɪstɪd] *adj (unbiased)* impartial(e); *(un-interested)* indifférent(e)

disinvestment [dɪsɪn'vestmənt] *n Fin* désinvestissement *m*

disjointed [dɪs'dʒɔɪntɪd] *adj (style, speech)* décousu(e); *(move-ments)* saccadé(e)

disk [dɪsk] *n* (**a**) *Comput* disque *m*; *(floppy)* disquette *f*; **d. drive** unité *f* de disques (**b**) disque *m*; *Aut* **d. brake** frein *m* à disque; **d. jockey** disc-jockey *m*

diskette [dɪs'ket] *n Comput* disquette *f*

dislike [dɪs'laɪk] **1** *n* aversion *f* (**of** *or* **for** pour); **we have the same likes and dislikes** nous avons les mêmes goûts; **to take a d. to sb/sth** prendre qn/qch en grippe
2 *vt* ne pas aimer; **I don't d. him** il ne me déplaît pas

dislocate ['dɪsləkeɪt] *vt* (**a**) *(shoulder, hip)* déboîter; **to d. one's shoulder** se déboîter l'épaule (**b**) *(plan, schedule)* pertur-ber

dislocation [dɪslə'keɪʃən] *n* (**a**) *(of shoulder, hip)* déboîtement *m* (**b**) *(of plan, schedule)* perturbation *f*

dislodge [dɪs'lɒdʒ] *vt (opponent, leader)* déloger (**from** de); *(brick, tile)* arracher; *(obstacle)* déplacer; *(something stuck)* dé-coincer

disloyal [dɪs'lɔɪəl] *adj* déloyal(e)

disloyalty [dɪs'lɔɪəltɪ] *n* déloyauté *f*

dismal ['dɪzməl] *adj (face, countryside)* lugubre; *(failure, perfor-mance)* lamentable; *(future)* sombre

dismantle [dɪs'mæntəl] *vt (empire, network)* démanteler; *(ma-chine)* démonter

dismay [dɪs'meɪ] **1** *n* consternation *f*; **in d.** consterné(e); **(much) to my d.** à ma grande consternation
2 *vt* consterner

dismember [dɪs'membə(r)] *vt also Fig* démembrer

dismiss [dɪs'mɪs] *vt* (**a**) *(from job)* renvoyer (**b**) *(send away)* con-gédier; *(pupils)* libérer; *Mil* **d.!** rompez! (**c**) *(thought, theory)* re-jeter; *(proposal, suggestion)* écarter; *(danger, threat)* ignorer; **she is dismissed as an airhead** elle est considérée comme une évaporée (**d**) *Law (case)* classer; *(appeal, charge)* rejeter

dismissal [dɪs'mɪsəl] *n* (**a**) *(of employee)* renvoi *m*, licencie-ment *m* (**b**) *Law (of case)* fin *f* de non-recevoir; *(of appeal, charge)* rejet *m*

dismissive [dɪs'mɪsɪv] *adj* dédaigneux(euse); **to be d. of sb/sth** faire peu de cas de qn/qch

dismount [dɪs'maʊnt] *vi (from horse, bicycle)* descendre, met-tre pied à terre

Disneyfication [dɪznɪfɪ'keɪʃən] *n (of place, culture, history)* disneylandisation *f*

Disneyfy ['dɪznɪfaɪ] *vt (place, culture, history)* disneylandiser

disobedience [dɪsə'biːdɪəns] *n* désobéissance *f*

disobedient [dɪsə'biːdɪənt] *adj* désobéissant(e); **to be d. to sb** désobéir à qn

disobey [dɪsə'beɪ] *vt (person, order)* désobéir à; *(law)* enfreindre

disorder [dɪs'ɔːdə(r)] *n* (**a**) *(confusion, unrest)* désordre *m*; **in d.** en désordre (**b**) *Med* troubles *mpl*; **a personality d.** trouble *m* de la personnalité

disordered [dɪs'ɔːdəd] *adj* désordonné(e)

disorderly [dɪs'ɔːdəlɪ] *adj (messy, unruly)* désordonné(e); *(crowd)* agité(e); *Law* **d. conduct** atteinte *f* à l'ordre public

disorganization [dɪsɔːɡənaɪ'zeɪʃən] *n* désorganisation *f*

disorganized [dɪs'ɔːɡənaɪzd] *adj* désorganisé(e)

disorient [dɪs'ɔːrɪənt], **disorientate** [dɪs'ɔːrɪənteɪt] *vt* désorienter

disorienting [dɪs'ɔːrɪəntɪŋ] *adj* déroutant(e)

disown [dɪs'əʊn] *vt* désavouer, renier

disparage [dɪs'pærɪdʒ] *vt* dénigrer

disparaging [dɪs'pærɪdʒɪŋ] *adj* désobligeant(e)

disparate ['dɪspərɪt] *adj* disparate

disparity [dɪs'pærɪtɪ] *(pl* **disparities**) *n* disparité *f*

dispassionate [dɪs'pæʃənət] *adj (calm)* calme; *(impartial)* impartial(e)

dispatch [dɪs'pætʃ] **1** *n* (**a**) *(of letter, package)* expédition *f*, envoi *m* (**b**) *(message)* dépêche *f*; *Mil* **to be mentioned in dispatches** être cité(e) à l'ordre du jour; **d. rider** *Mil* estafette *f*; *(courier)* coursier(ère) *m,f* (**c**) *Formal (promptness)* promptitude *f*; **with d.** promptement
2 *vt* (**a**) *(send)* envoyer (**b**) *(kill)* liquider

dispel [dɪs'pel] *(pt & pp* **dispelled**) *vt* dissiper

dispensable [dɪs'pensəbəl] *adj* dont on peut se passer

dispensary [dɪs'pensərɪ] *(pl* **dispensaries**) *n Med (in pharmacy)* officine *f*; *(in hospital)* pharmacie *f*

dispensation [dɪspen'seɪʃən] *n Law & Rel (exemption)* dispense *f* (**from** de)

dispense [dɪs'pens] *vt (justice)* rendre; *(advice)* prodiguer; *(medication)* préparer; *(of vending machine)* distribuer
▶**dispense with** *vt insep* se passer de; **to d. with the need for sth** rendre qch superflu(e)

dispersal [dɪs'pɜːsəl] *n* dispersion *f*

disperse [dɪs'pɜːs] **1** *vt (seeds, people)* disperser; *(knowledge, information)* propager
2 *vi (of crowd)* se disperser; *(of darkness, mist, clouds)* se dissiper

dispirited [dɪs'pɪrɪtɪd] *adj* découragé(e), abattu(e)

displace [dɪs'pleɪs] *vt* (**a**) *(shift)* déplacer; **displaced persons** personnes *fpl* déplacées (**b**) *(supplant)* remplacer, supplanter

displacement [dɪs'pleɪsmənt] *n* (**a**) *(of water, people)* déplacement *m* (**b**) *(substitution)* remplacement *m*

display [dɪs'pleɪ] **1** *n* (**a**) *(of goods)* étalage *m*; *(of handicrafts, paintings)* exposition *f*; **on d.** à l'étalage; *(sign, notice)* affiché(e); **d. cabinet** vitrine *f*; **d. copy** *(of book)* exemplaire *m* de démonstration; **d. window** vitrine *f* (**b**) *(demonstration)* démonstration *f* (**c**) *Comput* écran *m*
2 *vt* (**a**) *(goods)* exposer; *(sign, notice)* afficher (**b**) *(emotion)* manifester; *(talent, concern, ignorance)* faire preuve de

displease [dɪs'pliːz] *vt* mécontenter, contrarier; **to be displeased with sb/sth** ne pas être satisfait(e) de qn/qch

displeasure [dɪs'pleʒə(r)] *n* déplaisir *m*, mécontentement *m*

disposable [dɪs'pəʊzəbəl] *adj* (**a**) *(diaper, lighter, camera)* jetable (**b**) *(funds, income)* disponible

disposal [dɪs'pəʊzəl] *n* (**a**) *(getting rid of)* enlèvement *m*, élimination *f* (**b**) *(of property)* cession *f*, vente *f* (**c**) *(availability)* **to have sth at one's d.** avoir qch à sa disposition

dispose [dɪs'pəʊz] *vt Formal (arrange)* disposer
▶**dispose of** *vt insep* (**a**) *(garbage)* jeter, se débarrasser de; *(problem)* régler (**b**) *(kill)* se débarrasser de

disposed [dɪs'pəʊzd] *adj (willing)* **to be d. to do sth** être disposé(e) à faire qch

disposition [dɪspə'zɪʃən] *n* (**a**) *(temperament)* tempérament *m*, nature *f* (**b**) *(inclination)* tendance *f*; **to have a d. to do**

sth avoir tendance à faire qch (**c**) *Formal (arrangement)* disposition *f*

dispossess [dɪspə'zes] *vt* déposséder (**of** de)

disproportionate [dɪsprə'pɔːʃənət] *adj* disproportionné(e) (**to** à)

disprove [dɪs'pruːv] *(pp* **disproved**, *Law* **disproven** [dɪs'prəʊvən]) *vt* réfuter

dispute [dɪs'pjuːt] **1** *n (debate)* controverse *f*; *(argument)* dispute *f*; **the matter in d.** l'objet de la controverse; **it's beyond d.** c'est incontestable; **it's open to d.** c'est contestable
2 *vt (discuss)* discuter; *(call into question)* contester
3 *vi* se quereller (**with/about** avec/à propos de)

disqualification [dɪskwɒlɪfɪ'keɪʃən] *n (from competition)* disqualification *f*

disqualify [dɪs'kwɒlɪfaɪ] *(pt & pp* **disqualified**) *vt (from competition)* disqualifier (**from** de)

disquiet [dɪs'kwaɪət] *n Formal* inquiétude *f*

disregard [dɪsrɪ'ɡɑːd] **1** *n* mépris *m*
2 *vt* ignorer, ne tenir aucun compte de

disrepair [dɪsrɪ'peə(r)] *n* délabrement *m*; **in (a state of) d.** délabré(e); **to fall into d.** se délabrer

disreputable [dɪs'repjʊtəbəl] *adj (person)* peu recommandable; *(behavior)* peu honorable; *(neighborhood, bar)* mal famé(e)

disrepute [dɪsrɪ'pjuːt] *n* discrédit *m*; **to bring sb/sth into d.** discréditer qn/qch; **to fall into d.** tomber en discrédit

disrespect [dɪsrɪ'spekt] *n* irrespect *m*; **to treat sb with d.** manquer de respect à qn; **I meant no d.** je ne voulais pas être irrespectueux

disrespectful [dɪsrɪ'spektfʊl] *adj* irrespectueux(euse); **to be d. to sb** manquer de respect à qn

disrupt [dɪs'rʌpt] *vt* perturber

disruption [dɪs'rʌpʃən] *n (of traffic, life, routine)* perturbation *f*; *(of meeting)* interruption *f*

disruptive [dɪs'rʌptɪv] *adj* perturbateur(trice); **to be d.** faire du chahut

dissatisfaction [dɪsætɪs'fækʃən] *n* mécontentement *m* (**with** envers)

dissatisfied [dɪ'sætɪsfaɪd] *adj* mécontent(e) (**with** de)

dissect [dɪ'sekt] *vt also Fig* disséquer

dissemble [dɪ'sembəl] *vt & vi* dissimuler

disseminate [dɪ'semɪneɪt] **1** *vt* propager, répandre
2 *vi* se propager, se répandre

dissension [dɪ'senʃən] *n* dissension *f*

dissent [dɪ'sent] **1** *n* désaccord *m*
2 *vi* être en désaccord (**from** avec)

dissenter [dɪ'sentə(r)] *n Pol* dissident(e) *m,f*

dissenting [dɪ'sentɪŋ] *adj* dissident(e)

dissertation [dɪsə'teɪʃən] *n* mémoire *m*

disservice [dɪ'sɜːvɪs] *n* **to do sb/sth a d.** rendre un mauvais service à qn/qch

dissident ['dɪsɪdənt] *n & adj* dissident(e) *m,f*

dissimilar [dɪ'sɪmɪlə(r)] *adj* différent(e) (**to** de)

dissipate ['dɪsɪpeɪt] **1** *vt (fears, doubts)* dissiper; *(money, energy)* gaspiller
2 *vi (of mist, doubts)* se dissiper

dissipation [dɪsɪ'peɪʃən] *n (debauchery)* débauche *f*

dissociate [dɪ'səʊsɪeɪt] *vt* dissocier (**from** de); **to d. oneself from sb/sth** se dissocier *ou* se désolidariser de qn/qch

dissolute ['dɪsəluːt] *adj* dissolu(e)

dissolve [dɪ'zɒlv] **1** *vt* dissoudre
2 *vi* se dissoudre; **to d. into tears** fondre en larmes

dissuade [dɪ'sweɪd] *vt* **to d. sb from doing sth** dissuader qn de faire qch

distance ['dɪstəns] **1** *n* distance *f*; **from a d.** de loin; **in the d.** au loin; **within five minutes' walking d.** à cinq minutes de marche; **a short d. away** tout près; **some d. away** assez loin; **to keep one's d.** garder ses distances; **to keep sb at a d.** tenir qn à distance; *Sport & Fig* **to go the d.** tenir la distance; **d. learning** *or* **teaching** enseignement *m* à distance

2 *vt* **to d. oneself from sb/sth** prendre ses distances vis-à-vis de qn/qch

distant ['dɪstənt] *adj* **(a)** *(far-off)* lointain(e); **in the d. past** il y a très longtemps; **in the d. future** dans un avenir lointain; **10 miles d.** ≃ à 16 kilomètres de distance **(b)** *(reserved)* distant(e) **(c)** *(distracted)* distrait(e); **she had a d. look** son regard était perdu dans le vague

distantly ['dɪstəntlɪ] *adv* **(a) to be d. related to sb** être un parent éloigné de qn **(b)** *(distractedly)* distraitement

distaste [dɪs'teɪst] *n* dégoût *m* **(for** pour**)**

distasteful [dɪs'teɪstfʊl] *adj* déplaisant(e)

distemper¹ [dɪs'tempə(r)] *n* *(animal disease)* maladie *f* de Carré

distemper² [dɪs'tempə(r)] *n* *(paint)* détrempe *f*

distend [dɪs'tend] **1** *vt* distendre

2 *vi* se distendre

distill [dɪs'tɪl] *vt* distiller

distillery [dɪs'tɪlərɪ] *(pl* **distilleries)** *n* distillerie *f*

distinct [dɪs'tɪŋkt] *adj* **(a)** *(different)* distinct(e) **(from** de**); as d. from** par opposition à **(b)** *(clear)* clair(e); *(preference, improvement, difference)* net (nette); **it's a d. possibility** c'est fort possible

distinction [dɪs'tɪŋkʃən] *n* **(a)** *(difference)* distinction *f*; **to draw a d. between** faire une distinction entre **(b)** *(honor, excellence)* distinction *f*; *Ironic* **I had the d. of coming last** j'ai eu l'honneur de venir en dernier; **a writer/scientist of d.** un écrivain/scientifique réputé; **with d.** *(perform, serve)* brillamment **(c)** *(on test)* mention *f* très bien

distinctive [dɪs'tɪŋktɪv] *adj* distinctif(ive)

distinctly [dɪs'tɪŋktlɪ] *adv* **(a)** *(clearly) (speak, hear)* distinctement; *(remember)* très bien; **I d. told you not to do it** je t'ai clairement dit de ne pas le faire **(b)** *(decidedly) (better, easier)* nettement; *(stupid, rude)* vraiment

distinguish [dɪs'tɪŋgwɪʃ] **1** *vt* **(a)** *(recognize)* distinguer **(b)** *(characterize, differentiate)* distinguer **(from** de**); distinguishing marks** *(on passport)* signes *mpl* particuliers **(c) to d. oneself (by sth/by doing sth)** se distinguer (par qch/en faisant qch)

2 *vi* **to d. between** faire la distinction entre

distinguished [dɪs'tɪŋgwɪʃd] *adj* *(performance, career)* brillant(e); *(person, air)* distingué(e)

distort [dɪs'tɔ:t] *vt also Fig* déformer

distorted [dɪs'tɔ:tɪd] *adj also Fig* déformé(e)

distortion [dɪs'tɔ:ʃən] *n also Fig* distorsion *f*, déformation *f*

distract [dɪs'trækt] *vt* distraire; **to d. sb's attention** détourner l'attention de qn; **to be easily distracted** se laisser facilement distraire

distracted [dɪs'træktɪd] *adj* **(a)** *(with thoughts elsewhere)* distrait(e) **(b)** *(distraught)* affolé(e)

distracting [dɪs'træktɪŋ] *adj* gênant(e), qui distrait

distraction [dɪs'trækʃən] *n* **(a)** *(interruption, amusement)* distraction *f* **(b)** *(madness)* **to drive sb to d.** rendre qn fou (folle)

distraught [dɪs'trɔ:t] *adj* angoissé(e); **d. with grief** fou (folle) de douleur

distress [dɪs'tres] **1** *n* *(mental)* désarroi *m*; *(physical)* douleur *f*; **to be in d.** *(mentally)* être bouleversé(e); *(physically)* souffrir; *(of ship)* être en détresse; **d. signal** signal *m* de détresse

2 *vt* *(upset)* bouleverser

distressed [dɪs'trest] *adj* bouleversé(e)

distressing [dɪs'tresɪŋ] *adj* bouleversant(e)

distribute [dɪs'trɪbju:t] *vt* *(give out)* & *Com* *(supply)* distribuer; *(spread out)* répartir

distribution [dɪstrɪ'bju:ʃən] *n* *(giving out)* & *Com* *(supplying)* distribution *f*; *(spreading out)* répartition *f*; **d. of wealth** distribution des richesses; *Com* **d. cost** coût *m* de distribution; **d. rights** droits *mpl* de distribution

distributor [dɪs'trɪbjʊtə(r)] *n* **(a)** *(person, company)* distributeur(trice) *m,f*; *(of cars)* concessionnaire *mf* **(b)** *Aut* distributeur *m*

district ['dɪstrɪkt] *n* *(of country)* région *f*; *(of town, city)* quartier *m*; *(administrative)* district *m*; **d. attorney** ≃ procureur *m* de la République; **d. court** ≃ tribunal *m* d'instance (fédéral)

distrust [dɪs'trʌst] **1** *n* méfiance *f* **(of** à l'égard de**)**

2 *vt* se méfier de

distrustful [dɪs'trʌstfʊl] *adj* méfiant(e); **to be d. of** se méfier de

disturb [dɪs'tɜ:b] *vt* **(a)** *(interrupt)* déranger; *(criminal)* surprendre; *(someone's sleep)* troubler; *Law* **to d. the peace** troubler l'ordre public **(b)** *(worry)* perturber **(c)** *(disarrange) (papers, room)* déranger; *(surface of water)* agiter; *(ground)* remuer

disturbance [dɪs'tɜ:bəns] *n* **(a)** *(nuisance)* dérangement *m* **(b)** *(atmospheric, emotional)* perturbation *f* **(c)** *(fight)* bagarre *f*; *(riot)* émeute *f*; **to cause** *or* **to create a d.** semer le désordre; *Law* troubler l'ordre public; **d. of the peace** trouble *m* de l'ordre public

disturbed [dɪs'tɜ:bd] *adj* *(night, sleep)* agité(e); *(mentally, emotionally)* perturbé(e)

disturbing [dɪs'tɜ:bɪŋ] *adj* perturbant(e), troublant(e)

disunity [dɪs'ju:nɪtɪ] *n* désunion *f*

disuse [dɪs'ju:s] *n* **to fall into d.** tomber en désuétude

ditch [dɪtʃ] **1** *n* *(at roadside)* fossé *m*; *(as defense)* douve *f*; *(for drainage)* rigole *f*

2 *vt* *Fam* *(get rid of) (thing)* se débarrasser de; *(plan, idea)* abandonner; *(boyfriend, girlfriend)* plaquer

dither ['dɪðə(r)] *Fam vi* hésiter, tergiverser; **stop dithering!** décide-toi!

ditto ['dɪtəʊ] *adv* idem; *Fam* **I'm hungry – d.** j'ai faim – itou *ou* moi aussi

ditty ['dɪtɪ] *(pl* **ditties)** *n Fam* chansonnette *f*

diva ['di:və] *n* diva *f*

divan [dɪ'væn] *n* divan *m*; **d. bed** divan-lit *m*

dive [daɪv] **1** *n* **(a)** *(of swimmer)* plongeon *m*; *(of submarine, diver)* plongée *f*; **to make a d. for sth** *(rush)* se précipiter vers qch; **to go into a d.** *(of plane)* piquer du nez **(b)** *Fam Pej (place)* bouge *m*

2 *vi* *(pt* **dove** [dəʊv]**)** plonger; *(of plane)* piquer; **to d. for cover** plonger à couvert; **to d. for the exit/into the bar** se précipiter vers la sortie/au bar

diver ['daɪvə(r)] *n* plongeur(euse) *m,f*; *(deep sea)* scaphandrier *m*

diverge [daɪ'vɜ:dʒ] *vi* *(of rays, opinions)* diverger; *(of roads)* se séparer; *(of people)* avoir des opinions divergentes

divergence [daɪ'vɜ:dʒəns] *n* divergence *f*

divergent [daɪ'vɜ:dʒənt], **diverging** [daɪ'vɜ:dʒɪŋ] *adj* divergent(e)

diverse [daɪ'vɜ:s] *adj* divers(e)

diversification [daɪvɜ:sɪfɪ'keɪʃən] *n* diversification *f*

diversify [daɪ'vɜ:sɪfaɪ] *(pt & pp* **diversified)** **1** *vt* diversifier

2 *vi* se diversifier

diversion [daɪ'vɜ:ʃən] *n* **(a)** *(of plane, funds)* détournement *m*; **to create a d.** faire diversion **(b)** *(amusement)* distraction *f*

diversity [daɪ'vɜ:sɪtɪ] *n* diversité *f*

divert [daɪ'vɜ:t, dɪ'vɜ:t] *vt* **(a)** *(plane, funds, attention)* détourner **(b)** *(amuse)* **to d. oneself** se distraire

divest [daɪ'vest] *vt Formal* **to d. sb of sth** *(authority)* priver qn de qch; *(possession)* débarrasser qn de qch

divide [dɪ'vaɪd] **1** *vt* **(a)** *(money, food)* partager **(between/among** entre**); to d. sth in two/three** diviser qch en deux/

trois (**b**) *Math* diviser (**by** par) (**c**) *(separate)* séparer (**from** de)

2 *vi (of road)* bifurquer; *(of group)* se diviser; **to d. and rule** diviser pour régner

3 *n* fossé *m*

▸**divide up** *vt sep* partager

divided [dɪ'vaɪdɪd] *adj* divisé(e); **d. highway** route *f* à quatre voies

dividend ['dɪvɪdend] *n* dividende *m*; *Fig* **to pay dividends** porter ses fruits

dividers [dɪ'vaɪdəz] *npl (mathematical instrument)* compas *m* à pointe sèche

dividing [dɪ'vaɪdɪŋ] *adj* **d. line** ligne *f* de démarcation; **d. wall** mur *m* de séparation

divine [dɪ'vaɪn] **1** *adj also Fig* divin(e)

2 *vt* deviner

diving ['daɪvɪŋ] *n (in swimming pool)* plongeon *m*; *(underwater)* plongée *f*; **d. bell** cloche *f* à plongeur; **d. board** plongeoir *m*; **d. suit** scaphandre *m*

divinity [dɪ'vɪnɪtɪ] *(pl* **divinities**) *n* (**a**) *(divine nature, god)* divinité *f* (**b**) *(subject)* théologie *f*

divisible [dɪ'vɪzɪbəl] *adj* divisible

division [dɪ'vɪʒən] *n* (**a**) *(separation)* partage *m* (**b**) *(distribution)* répartition *f*, partage *m*; **d. of labor** division *f* du travail (**c**) *(discord)* division *f* (**d**) *(unit)* division *f*; **first/second d.** *(in sports league)* première/deuxième division

divisive [dɪ'vaɪsɪv] *adj* qui crée des divisions

divorce [dɪ'vɔːs] **1** *n* divorce *m*; **d. proceedings** procédure *f* de divorce

2 *vt* (**a**) *(husband, wife)* divorcer de; **to get divorced (from sb)** divorcer (de qn) (**b**) *Fig* séparer (**from** de)

3 *vi* divorcer

divorcee [dɪvɔː'siː] *n* divorcé(e) *m,f*

divulge [daɪ'vʌldʒ] *vt* divulguer

DIY [diːaɪ'waɪ] *n (abbr* **do-it-yourself**) bricolage *m*

dizzy ['dɪzɪ] *adj* (**a**) *(unsteady)* étourdi(e); **to feel d.** avoir le vertige; *Fig* **to reach the d. heights of...** atteindre les hauteurs vertigineuses de...; **d. spell** étourdissement *m* (**b**) *Fam (frivolous)* écervelé(e); **a d. blonde** une blonde évaporée

DJ ['diːdʒeɪ] *n (abbr* **disk jockey**) DJ *m*

Djibouti [dʒɪ'buːtɪ] *n* Djibouti

DMV [diːem'viː] *n (abbr* **Department of Motor Vehicles**) = service des immatriculations et des permis de conduire aux États-Unis

DNA [diːen'eɪ] *n (abbr* **deoxyribonucleic acid**) ADN *m*

do[1] [dəʊ] *n Mus* do *m*

do[2] [duː] **1** *v aux* (*3rd person singular* **does** [dʌz], *pt* **did** [dɪd], *pp* **done** [dʌn]) (**a**) *(in negatives)* **I don't speak French** je ne parle pas français; **I didn't see him** je ne l'ai pas vu

(**b**) *(in questions)* **do you speak French?** (est-ce que) tu parles français?; **did you see him?** (est-ce que) tu l'as vu?; **don't you speak French?** tu ne parles pas français?; **didn't you see him?** tu ne l'as pas vu?

(**c**) *(for emphasis)* **he DOES speak French!** mais oui, il parle français!; **I DIDN'T see him!** mais non, je ne l'ai pas vu!; **it doesn't matter – it DOES matter!** ce n'est pas grave – si, c'est grave!

(**d**) *(as substitute for main verb)* **she writes better than I do** elle écrit mieux que moi; **if you want to speak to her, do it now** si tu veux lui parler, fais-le tout de suite; **do you speak French? – yes, I do/no, I don't** parlez-vous français? – oui/non; **I like Paris – so do I** j'aime Paris – moi aussi; **you left the door unlocked – so I did** tu as laissé la porte ouverte – effectivement; **you said you would go – no, I didn't** tu as dit que tu irais – non, ce n'est pas vrai

(**e**) *(in tag questions)* **you speak French, don't you?** vous parlez français, n'est-ce pas *ou* non?; **John doesn't live there, does he?** John n'habite pas là, si?; **they said they'd come,**

didn't they? ils ont bien dit qu'ils viendraient, non?; **you didn't see her, did you?** est-ce que tu l'as vue ou pas?

2 *vt* (**a**) *(in general)* faire; **what do you do?** *(what's your job?)* que faites-vous dans la vie?; **don't do that again!** ne refais jamais ça!; **what are you going to do about it?** qu'est-ce que tu vas faire?

(**b**) *(activity)* faire; **to do the housework/the dishes** faire le ménage/la vaisselle; **to do one's hair** se coiffer; **to do one's teeth** se brosser les dents; *Fam* **to do drugs** se droguer; **they do good food here** ils font de la bonne cuisine ici; **it just isn't done!** ça ne se fait pas, c'est tout!; *Fam* **let's do lunch!** on se fait une bouffe?

(**c**) *(have effect on)* **to do sb good** faire du bien à qn; **that hairstyle does nothing/does a lot for her** cette coiffure ne la flatte pas/la flatte; **this music does nothing for me** cette musique ne me plaît pas tellement

(**d**) *(be enough for)* **will $10 do you?** est-ce que 10 dollars te suffiront?; **that'll do me** ça m'ira

(**e**) *(study)* faire; **to do French/physics** faire du français/de la physique

(**f**) *(with speed, distance)* **the car was doing 100 (miles per hour)** ≃ la voiture faisait du 160 (à l'heure)

3 *vi* (**a**) *(act)* **to do well/badly** bien/mal se débrouiller; **do as you're told** fais ce qu'on te dit; **you would do well to accept** tu ferais bien d'accepter; **how do you do?** enchanté(e); **how are you doing?** (comment) ça va?

(**b**) *(be enough)* **two bottles of wine will do** deux bouteilles de vin suffiront; **that'll do** *(is satisfactory)* ça ira; *(stop it)* ça suffit maintenant!

4 *n* **the do's and don'ts** les choses *fpl* à faire et à ne pas faire

▸**do away with** *vt insep* (**a**) *(abolish)* supprimer (**b**) *Fam (kill)* zigouiller

▸**do for** *vt insep Fam* **to be done for** être fichu(e)

▸**do in** *vt sep Fam* (**a**) *(murder)* zigouiller (**b**) *(exhaust)* **to be done in** être complètement crevé(e) (**c**) *(injure)* **to do one's back/knee in** se bousiller le dos/genou (**d**) *(cheat, swindle)* avoir; **I've been done in!** je me suis fait avoir!

▸**do out of** *vt sep Fam* **to do sb out of sth** *(job)* priver qn de qch; *(money)* faire perdre qch à qn

▸**do up 1** *vt sep* (**a**) *(fasten)* fermer; *(shoelaces)* attacher (**b**) *(wrap)* envelopper (**c**) *(improve appearance of)* restaurer; *(room, house)* rénover; *Fam* **to do oneself up** *(dress elegantly)* se faire beau (belle)

2 *vi (of clothes)* se fermer

▸**do with** *vt insep* (**a**) *(benefit from)* **I could do with a cup of tea** je prendrais bien une tasse de thé; **you could do with a haircut** tu aurais bien besoin de te faire couper les cheveux (**b**) *(be connected with)* **to have nothing to do with sb/sth** *(be unconnected with)* n'avoir rien à voir avec qn/qch; *(not get involved with)* n'avoir rien à faire avec qn/qch; **I had nothing to do with it** je n'ai rien à voir là-dedans; **it's nothing to do with you** *(not your business)* ça ne te regarde pas (**c**) *(finish using)* **to be done with sth** avoir fini avec qch; **are you done with the scissors yet?** est-ce que tu as fini avec les ciseaux?; **it's all over and done with** c'est du passé

▸**do without 1** *vt insep* se passer de

2 *vi* se priver

doc [dɒk] *n Fam (doctor)* toubib *m*

docile ['dəʊsaɪl] *adj* docile

dock[1] [dɒk] **1** *n (for ships)* dock *m*; **d. workers** dockers *mpl*

2 *vi (of ship)* accoster; *(of two spacecraft)* s'arrimer

dock[2] [dɒk] *n Law* banc *m* des accusés

dock[3] [dɒk] *vt* (**a**) *(tail)* couper (**b**) *(wages)* faire une retenue sur

docker ['dɒkə(r)] *n* docker *m*

dockyard ['dɒkjɑːd] *n* chantier *m* naval

doctor ['dɒktə(r)] **1** *n* (**a**) *(medical)* docteur *m*, médecin *m*; **to go to the d.** *or* **d.'s** aller chez le médecin; *Fam Fig* **just what**

the **d. ordered** exactement ce qu'il me fallait (**b**) *Univ* docteur *m*; **D. of Science** docteur ès sciences

    2 *vt Fam (accounts, evidence)* falsifier

doctorate ['dɒktərɪt] *n Univ* doctorat *m* (**in** en)

doctrinaire [dɒktrɪ'neə(r)] *adj* doctrinaire

doctrinal ['dɒktrɪnəl, dɒk'traɪnəl] *adj* doctrinal(e)

doctrine ['dɒktrɪn] *n* doctrine *f*

docudrama ['dɒkjʊdrɑːmə] *n TV* docudrame *m*

document1 *n* ['dɒkjʊmənt] document *m*; *Comput* **d. reader** lecteur *m* de documents

    2 *vt* ['dɒkjʊment] (**a**) *(show in detail)* présenter (**b**) *(support)* étayer; **the first documented case** le premier cas établi

documentary [dɒkjʊ'mentərɪ] **1** *n* (*pl* **documentaries**) *(TV program)* documentaire *m*

    2 *adj (movie)* documentaire; *(proof)* littéral(e)

documentation [dɒkjʊmen'teɪʃən] *n* documentation *f*

docusoap ['dɒkjʊsəʊp] *n TV* docu-soap *m*

dodder ['dɒdə(r)] *vi* marcher d'un pas hésitant

doddering ['dɒdərɪŋ] *adj (walk)* hésitant(e); **a d. old fool** un vieux gâteux (une vieille gâteuse)

dodge [dɒdʒ] **1** *n* (**a**) *(trick)* truc *m*, combine *f*; **tax d.** combine pour payer moins d'impôts (**b**) *(movement)* écart *m*

    2 *vt (blow, responsibility, question)* esquiver; *(person)* éviter; *(police)* échapper à

    3 *vi* **to d. (out of the way)** faire un bond de côté

dodo ['dəʊdəʊ] *(pl* **dodoes** *or* **dodos**) *n* dodo *m*, dronte *m*; **(as) dead as a d.** mort(e) et enterré(e)

doe [dəʊ] *n (deer)* biche *f*; *(rabbit)* lapine *f*

does [dʌz] *3rd person singular of* **do²**

doesn't ['dʌzənt] = **does not**

doff [dɒf] *vt* **to d. one's cap to sb** se découvrir devant qn

dog [dɒg] **1** *n* (**a**) *(animal)* chien *m*; **d. biscuit** biscuit *m* pour chien; **d. collar** collier *m* de chien; *Fam (of cleric)* col *m* blanc *(d'un religieux)*; **d. food** nourriture *f* pour chien; **d. handler** maître-chien *m*; **d. license** = permis nécessaire pour posséder un chien; **to do the d. paddle** nager comme un petit chien; **d. racing** courses *fpl* de lévriers; **d. show** exposition *f* canine; **d. tag** plaque *f* d'identité

    (**b**) *Fam (person)* **you lucky d.!** sacré veinard!; **dirty d.** sale type *m*

    (**c**) *Fam Pej (ugly woman)* cageot *m*

    (**d**) *(hot dog)* hot dog *m*

    (**e**) *Fam (foot)* panard *m*

    (**f**) *(idioms) Fam* **to lead a d.'s life** avoir une vie de chien; *Fam* **it's a d.-eat-d. world** c'est un monde sans pitié; *Fam* **to go to the dogs** *(of place)* aller à vau-l'eau; *(of person)* filer un mauvais coton; *Fam* **to be a d. in the manger** être un empêcheur de tourner en rond; *Prov* **you can't teach an old d. new tricks** les vieilles habitudes ont la vie dure; *Prov* **every d. has his day** tout le monde a son heure de gloire

    2 *vt (pt & pp* **dogged**) *(follow)* suivre de près; **to d. sb's footsteps** être sur les talons de qn; **to be dogged by scandal/misfortune** être poursuivi(e) par le scandale/la malchance

dog-eared ['dɒgɪəd] *adj (page)* corné(e); *(book)* aux pages cornées

dogfight ['dɒgfaɪt] *n (between planes)* combat *m* aérien; *(between people)* bagarre *f*

dogfish ['dɒgfɪʃ] *n* roussette *f*

dogged ['dɒgɪd] *adj* tenace

doggerel ['dɒgərəl] *n (comical)* poésie *f* burlesque; *(bad)* vers *mpl* de mirliton

doggy, doggie ['dɒgɪ] *(pl* **doggies**) *n Fam* toutou *m*; **d. bag** = petit sac fourni par certains restaurants pour que les clients puissent emporter les restes

doghouse ['dɒghaʊs] *n* (**a**) *(shelter)* chenil *m*, niche *f* (**b**) *Fam* **to be in the d.** ne pas être en odeur de sainteté

dogma ['dɒgmə] *n* dogme *m*

dogmatic [dɒg'mætɪk] *adj* dogmatique

do-gooder ['duː'gʊdə(r)] *n Fam Pej* âme *f* charitable

dog-tired ['dɒg'taɪəd] *adj Fam* claqué(e), crevé(e)

dogwood ['dɒgwʊd] *n* cornouiller *m*

doh [dəʊ] **1** *n Mus* do *m*

    2 *exclam* **d.!** que je suis bête!

doily ['dɔɪlɪ] *(pl* **doilies**) *n* napperon *m*

doing ['duːɪŋ] *n* (**a**) **this is his d.** c'est son œuvre; **it was none of my d.** je n'y étais pour rien; **that takes some d.** il faut le faire (**b**) **doings** faits *mpl* et gestes *mpl*

do-it-yourself [duːɪtjɔː'self] *n* bricolage *m*; **a d. enthusiast** un(e) adepte du bricolage

doldrums ['dɒldrəmz] *npl* **to be in the d.** *(of person)* broyer du noir; *(of economy)* être en plein marasme

▶**dole out** [dəʊl] *vt sep Fam* distribuer

doleful ['dəʊlfʊl] *adj* triste

doll [dɒl] *n* poupée *f*; **d. house** maison *f* de poupée

▶**doll up** *vt sep Fam* **to d. oneself up** se pomponner

dollar ['dɒlə(r)] *n* dollar *m*; **d. bill** billet *m* d'un dollar

dollop ['dɒləp] *n Fam (of cream, mashed potatoes)* bonne cuillerée *f*; *(of mud, clay)* tas *m*

dolly ['dɒlɪ] *(pl* **dollies**) *n* (**a**) *Fam (toy)* poupée *f* (**b**) *(for camera)* chariot *m*

dolphin ['dɒlfɪn] *n* dauphin *m*

dolt [dəʊlt] *n Fam* andouille *f*

domain [də'meɪn] *n also Fig & Comput* domaine *m*; *Comput* **d. name** nom *m* de domaine

dome [dəʊm] *n* dôme *m*

domestic [də'mestɪk] *adj* (**a**) *(appliance, use, tasks)* ménager(ère); *(animal)* domestique; **d. bliss** bonheur *m* familial; **d. servant** domestique *mf* (**b**) *(policy, flight, affairs)* intérieur(e); *(economy, currency)* national(e)

domesticate [də'mestɪkeɪt] *vt (animal)* domestiquer; *Hum* **to be domesticated** *(of person)* se débrouiller plutôt bien avec les travaux ménagers

domicile ['dɒmɪsaɪl] *n Law* domicile *m*

dominance ['dɒmɪnəns] *n (of disease, gene)* dominance *f*; *(of social group, political party)* prédominance *f*; *(of person)* supériorité *f*

dominant ['dɒmɪnənt] *adj* dominant(e); *(person, character)* dominateur(trice)

dominate ['dɒmɪneɪt] *vt & vi* dominer

domination [dɒmɪ'neɪʃən] *n* domination *f*

domineering [dɒmɪ'nɪərɪŋ] *adj* dominateur(trice)

Dominica [də'mɪnɪkə] *n* la Dominique

Dominican [də'mɪnɪkən] **1** *n* Dominicain(e) *m,f*

    2 *adj* dominicain(e); **the D. Republic** la République Dominicaine

dominion [də'mɪnjən] *n* domination *f*; *Can* **D. day** Fête *f* du Canada *(anniversaire de l'indépendance canadienne, le 1ᵉʳ juillet)*

domino ['dɒmɪnəʊ] *(pl* **dominos** *or* **dominoes**) *n* domino *m*; *Pol & Fig* **d. effect** effet *m* d'entraînement

don *(pt & pp* **donned**) *vt Formal (clothing)* mettre, revêtir

donate [dəʊ'neɪt] *vt* faire don de; **to d. blood** donner son sang

donation [dəʊ'neɪʃən] *n* donation *f*, don *m*

done [dʌn] *pp of* **do²**

donkey ['dɒŋkɪ] *(pl* **donkeys**) *n (animal) & Fam (person)* âne *m*; *Fam* **I haven't seen her for d.'s years** je ne l'ai pas vue depuis une éternité; *Fam* **to talk the hind legs off a d.** avoir la langue bien pendue

donkeywork ['dɒŋkɪwɜːk] *n Fam* travail *m* pénible

donor ['dəʊnə(r)] *n* donneur(euse) *m,f*; **d. card** carte *f* de donneur d'organe

don't [dəʊnt] = **do not**

donut ['dəʊnʌt] *n* beignet *m*, *Can* beigne *m*

doodle ['du:dəl] **1** *n* gribouillis *m*, gribouillage *m*
2 *vi* gribouiller

doom [du:m] **1** *n* destin *m* (funeste); **to be all d. and gloom** voir tout en noir
2 *vt* **to be doomed** *(of person) (unlucky)* être marqué(e) par le destin; *(about to die)* être perdu(e); **to be doomed (to failure)** *(of project)* être voué(e) à l'échec; **to be doomed to do sth** être condamné(e) à faire qch

doom-laden ['du:mleɪdən] *adj* de mauvais augure, sinistre

doomsday ['du:mzdeɪ] *n* jour *m* du Jugement dernier; *Fig* **till d.** indéfiniment

door [dɔ:(r)] *n* porte *f*; *(of train, car)* portière *f*; **to answer the d.** aller ouvrir (la porte); **to see sb to the d.** raccompagner qn à la porte; **to show sb the d.** mettre qn à la porte; **to shut the d. in sb's face** fermer la porte au nez de qn; **she lives two doors away** elle habite deux portes plus loin; *Fig* **to lay sth at sb's d.** imputer qch à qn; **out of doors** dehors, en plein air; **d. handle** poignée *f* de porte; **d. knocker** heurtoir *m*

doorbell ['dɔ:bel] *n* sonnette *f*

doorjamb ['dɔ:dʒæm] *n* montant *m* de porte

doorkeeper ['dɔ:ki:pə(r)] *n* portier *m*

doorknob ['dɔ:nɒb] *n* bouton *m* de porte

doorman ['dɔ:mən] *n* *(in hotel)* portier *m*; *(in apartment building)* concierge *m*

doormat ['dɔ:mæt] *n* paillasson *m*; *Fig* **to treat sb like a d.** traiter qn comme un moins que rien

doorpost ['dɔ:pəʊst] *n* montant *m* de porte

doorstep ['dɔ:step] *n* pas *m* de la porte, seuil *m*; *Fig* **on one's d.** à deux pas

doorstop ['dɔ:tɒp] *n* *(fixed)* butoir *m*; *(wedge)* cale-porte *m*

door-to-door ['dɔ:tə'dɔ:(r)] *adj* **d. canvassing** porte-à-porte *m* électoral; **d. salesman** démarcheur *m*

doorway ['dɔ:weɪ] *n* porte *f*; **in the d.** dans l'embrasure de la porte

dopamine ['dəʊpəmɪn] dopamine *f*

dope [dəʊp] **1** *n* (a) *very Fam (cannabis)* shit *m*; *Fam* **d. test** *(for athlete)* contrôle *m* antidopage (b) *Fam (idiot)* andouille *f*
2 *vt (person, horse) (to make faster)* doper; *(to make slower)* droguer; *(food, drink)* mettre une drogue dans

dopey ['dəʊpɪ] *adj Fam* idiot(e)

dorm [dɔ:m] *n Fam (dormitory)* dortoir *m*

dormant ['dɔ:mənt] **1** *adj (volcano)* en sommeil; *(conflict, emotion)* latent(e); *(idea)* qui sommeille
2 *adv* **to lie d.** être en sommeil

dormer window ['dɔ:mə'wɪndəʊ] *n* lucarne *f*

dormitory ['dɔ:mɪtərɪ] *(pl* **dormitories**) *n* (a) dortoir *m* (b) *Univ* résidence *f* universitaire

dormouse ['dɔ:maʊs] *(pl* **dormice** ['dɔ:maɪs]) *n* loir *m*

dorsal ['dɔ:səl] *adj* dorsal(e)

DOS [dɒs] *n Comput (abbr* **disk operating system**) DOS *m*

dose [dəʊs] **1** *n (amount)* dose *f*; **a bad d. of (the) flu** une bonne grippe; **to have a d. of measles** avoir la rougeole
2 *vt Fam* bourrer (**with** de); **to d. oneself (up) with pills** se bourrer de médicaments

dossier ['dɒsɪeɪ] *n* dossier *m*

dot [dɒt] **1** *n* point *m*; **on the d.** à l'heure pile; **at three o'clock on the d.** à trois heures pile; *Com* **d. com (company)** start-up *f*, jeune pousse *f*; *Comput* **d. matrix printer** imprimante *f* matricielle
2 *vt (pt & pp* **dotted**) parsemer (**with** de); **to d. an i/a j** mettre un point sur un i/un j; **dotted line** pointillé *m*; **to sign on the dotted line** ≃ signer à l'endroit indiqué; *Fig* donner son consentement; *Fig* **to d. the i's (and cross the t's)** peaufiner les détails

dotage ['dəʊtɪdʒ] *n* **to be in one's d.** être gâteux(euse)

dot-com [dɒt'kɒm] *adj* qui a trait à la netéconomie; **d. millionnaire** = personne qui a fait fortune en montant une start-up

dot-commer [dɒt'kɒmə(r)] *n* = personne qui travaille dans le secteur de la netéconomie

▶**dote on, dote upon** [dəʊt] *vt insep* adorer

dotty ['dɒtɪ] *adj Fam (person, idea)* toqué(e); **to be d. about sb** être fou (folle) de qn

double ['dʌbəl] **1** *n* (a) *(of person)* double *m*, sosie *m*
(b) *(hotel room)* chambre *f* pour deux personnes
(c) **doubles** *(in tennis)* double *m*; **a doubles match** un double
(d) **at** *or* **on the d.** à l'instant
(e) *(measure of drink)* double *m*
2 *adj* double; **d. m** *(when spelling)* deux m; **d. five two one** *(figure)* deux fois cinq deux un; *(phone number)* cinquante-cinq, vingt et un; **a d. whiskey** un double whisky; **d. agent** agent *m* double; **d. bass** contrebasse *f*; **d. bed** grand lit *m*, lit à deux personnes; **d. bill** *(at movies)* double programme *m*; **d. chin** double menton *m*; **to be in d. digits** *or* **figures** *(of statistic)* avoir atteint plus de dix; **inflation is now in d. digits** *or* **figures** l'inflation a passé la barre des 10 pour cent; **d. fault** *(in tennis)* double faute *f*; **d. glazing** double vitrage *m*; **to lead a d. life** mener une double vie; **d. meaning** double sens *m*; **d. room** chambre *f* pour deux personnes; **to have d. standards** faire deux poids, deux mesures; **to do a d. take** marquer un temps d'arrêt *(par surprise)*
3 *adv* **to see d.** voir double; **to fold sth d.** plier qch en deux; **to be bent d.** être plié(e) en deux
4 *vt* (a) *(multiply by two)* doubler
(b) *(fold)* plier en deux
5 *vi* (a) *(increase twofold)* doubler
(b) **to d. as sth** servir aussi de qch

▶**double back** *vi* rebrousser chemin

▶**double up** *vi (bend)* se plier en deux (**with** de)

double-barreled ['dʌbəl'bærəld] *adj (shotgun)* à deux coups

double-breasted ['dʌbəl'brestɪd] *adj (jacket, suit)* croisé(e)

double-check ['dʌbəl'tʃek] *vt & vi* bien vérifier

double-click ['dʌbəl'klɪk] **1** *n* double-clic *m*
2 *vi* **to d. on sth** double-cliquer *ou* faire un double-clic sur qch

double-cross ['dʌbəl'krɒs] *vt* trahir, doubler

double-dealing ['dʌbəl'di:lɪŋ] *n* fourberie *f*

double-edged ['dʌbəl'edʒd] *adj also Fig* à double tranchant

double-jointed [dʌbəl'dʒɔɪntɪd] *adj* désarticulé(e)

double-lock ['dʌbəl'lɒk] *vt* fermer à double tour

double-park ['dʌbəl'pɑ:k] *vi* se garer en double file

double-quick ['dʌbəl'kwɪk] *adv* en vitesse

doubly ['dʌblɪ] *adv* doublement; **to make d. sure of sth** bien vérifier qch; **d. difficult** deux fois plus difficile; **to be d. careful** redoubler de prudence

doubt [daʊt] **1** *n* doute *m*; **to have doubts about sth** avoir des doutes sur qch; **to be in d.** *(of person)* douter (**about** de); *(of outcome)* être incertain(e); **when in d.** en cas de doute, dans le doute; **beyond (a) d.** sans le moindre doute; **no d.** sans doute; **there is no d. that...** il ne fait aucun doute que...; **there is no d. about her guilt** sa culpabilité ne fait aucun doute; **there is some d. about...** il y a des doutes quant à...
2 *vt* douter de; **I d. it** j'en doute; **I d. if it makes him happy** je doute que cela le rende heureux

doubtful ['daʊtfʊl] *adj* (a) *(uncertain) (person)* dubitatif(ive); *(outcome)* incertain(e); **to be d. about sth** avoir des doutes sur qch (b) *(questionable)* douteux(euse)

dough [dəʊ] *n* (a) *(for bread)* pâte *f* (b) *Fam (money)* fric *m*

doughnut ['dəʊnʌt] = **donut**

dour [dʊə(r)] *adj* austère

douse [daʊs] *vt* (a) *(soak)* arroser (b) *(extinguish)* éteindre

dove¹ [dʌv] *n* colombe *f*

dove² [dəʊv] *pt of* **dive**

dovecot(e) ['dʌvkɒt] *n* colombier *m*

dovetail ['dʌvteɪl] *vi (fit closely)* concorder, cadrer (**with** avec)

dowager ['daʊədʒə(r)] n douairière f

dowdy ['daʊdɪ] adj (person) inélégant(e); (clothes, image) démodé(e)

dowel ['daʊəl] n cheville f

down¹ [daʊn] n (feathers) duvet m

down² [daʊn] 1 prep **to go d. the stairs/the street** descendre les escaliers/la rue; **to run d. the stairs/the street** descendre les escaliers/la rue en courant; **to fall d. the stairs** dégringoler les escaliers; **the tears ran d. her cheeks** les larmes coulaient sur ses joues

2 adv **(a)** (with motion) **to come/go d.** descendre; **to fall d.** tomber; **to bend d.** se pencher; **oil has come** ou **gone d. in price** le prix du pétrole a baissé; **I'll be d. in a minute** je descends tout de suite; **d. with traitors!** à bas les traîtres!

(b) (with position) en bas; **d. here/there** ici/là en bas; **further d.** plus bas; **gas is d. in price** le prix de l'essence a baissé; **one d., two to go!** et d'un! encore deux et c'est fini!; **everyone from the boss d.** tout le monde, même le chef

(c) (in crosswords) verticalement

(d) (idioms) **to be d. on sb/sth** avoir une dent contre qn/qch; **it's d. to her** (her decision) c'est à elle de décider; (her achievement) c'est grâce à elle; **I'm d. to my last dollar/cigarette** il ne me reste plus qu'un dollar/une cigarette

3 adj **(a)** (depressed) déprimé(e)

(b) to be d. (of computer, telephones) être en panne

4 vt **(a)** (aircraft) abattre

(b) (drink) descendre

down-and-out ['daʊnən'aʊt] Fam 1 n (tramp) clochard(e) m,f

2 adj sans le sou

downbeat ['daʊnbiːt] adj **(a)** (gloomy, pessimistic) triste, pessimiste **(b)** (restrained) réservé(e) **(about** sur)

downcast ['daʊnkɑːst] adj (eyes) baissé(e); (person) abattu(e), découragé(e)

downer ['daʊnə(r)] n Fam **(a)** (drug) tranquillisant m **(b)** (depressing situation) situation f déprimante; (depressing event) événement m déprimant

downfall ['daʊnfɔːl] n (of government) chute f; (of person) ruine f

downgrade 1 vt [daʊn'greɪd] rétrograder

2 n ['daʊngreɪd] descente f

downhearted [daʊn'hɑːtɪd] adj découragé(e)

downhill ['daʊn'hɪl] 1 adj (slope) en pente; **d. skiing** ski m alpin ou de descente

2 adv **to go d.** (of road, car) descendre; Fig (of person, career) être sur le déclin; (of business) péricliter

download ['daʊnləʊd] Comput 1 n téléchargement m

2 vt télécharger

3 vi effectuer un téléchargement; **graphic files take a long time to d.** le téléchargement de fichiers graphiques est très lent

downloading ['daʊnləʊdɪŋ] Comput n téléchargement m

downmarket [daʊn'mɑːkɪt] adj (product) bas de gamme inv; (area, place) populaire

down payment [daʊn'peɪmənt] n acompte m

downpour ['daʊnpɔː(r)] n averse f

downright ['daʊnraɪt] 1 adj (stupidity, dishonesty) véritable; **it's a d. lie!** c'est un mensonge flagrant!

2 adv (stupid, untrue) carrément

downsizing ['daʊnsaɪzɪŋ] n réduction f d'effectifs

Down's syndrome ['daʊnz'sɪndrəʊm] n trisomie f 21

downstairs 1 adj ['daʊnsteəz] (on a lower floor) de l'étage du dessous; (on ground floor) du rez-de-chaussée; **the d. apartment** l'appartement du dessous; **the d. bathroom** la salle de bains du bas

2 adv [daʊn'steəz] en bas; **to come/go d.** descendre; **he lives d.** il habite à l'étage au-dessous

downstream [daʊn'striːm] adv en aval; (with movement) vers l'aval

downswing ['daʊnswɪŋ] n Econ tendance f à la baisse

down-to-earth ['daʊntə'ɜːθ] adj terre à terre inv

downtown ['daʊn'taʊn] 1 n (city center) centre-ville m

2 adj du centre-ville; **d. New York** le centre de New York

3 adv au centre-ville

downtrodden ['daʊntrɒdən] adj opprimé(e)

downturn ['daʊntɜːn] n (in inflation) baisse f; (in economy) ralentissement m

downward ['daʊnwəd] 1 adj vers le bas; **a d. trend** une tendance à la baisse 2 adv vers le bas

downwards ['daʊnwədz] adv = **downward**

dowry ['daʊrɪ] (pl **dowries**) n dot f

doze [dəʊz] 1 n somme m; **to have a d.** faire un somme

2 vi somnoler

►**doze off** vi s'assoupir

dozen ['dʌzən] n douzaine f; **half a d./a d. eggs** une demi-douzaine/une douzaine d'œufs; Fam **dozens of times/people** des dizaines de fois/gens

dozy ['dəʊzɪ] adj **(a)** (sleepy) **to feel d.** avoir envie de dormir **(b)** Fam (stupid) abruti(e)

Dr. (abbr **Doctor**) Dr

drab [dræb] adj (person, color) terne; (atmosphere, city) morne

drachma ['drækmə] n Formerly drachme f

draconian [drə'kəʊnɪən] adj draconien(enne)

draft¹ [drɑːft] 1 n **(a)** (of letter) brouillon m; (of law, proposal) avant-projet m; (of novel) jet m **(b)** Fin traite f **(c)** (conscription) conscription f; **d. dodger** insoumis m

2 vt **(a)** (letter) faire le brouillon de; (proposal) rédiger; (law, bill) préparer **(b)** (recruit) **to d. sb in** détacher qn

draft² [drɑːft] n **(a)** (wind) courant m d'air **(b)** (of drink) gorgée f; (of air) bouffée f **(c) on d.** (beer) à la pression; **d. beer** bière f pression

draftee [drɑːf'tiː] n Mil recrue f

draftsman ['drɑːftsmən] n dessinateur(trice) m,f

drafty ['drɑːftɪ] adj plein(e) de courants d'air

drag [dræg] 1 n **(a)** (air resistance) traînée f; **d. racing** courses fpl de dragsters

(b) Fam (person) raseur(euse) m,f; (task) corvée f; **the party was a real d.** la soirée était vraiment rasante

(c) Fam (on cigarette) taffe f; **to take a d. on a cigarette** tirer une taffe sur une cigarette

(d) Fam (women's clothing worn by man) **to be in d.** être travesti; **d. artist** travesti m; **d. queen** travelo m

(e) Fam (street) **the main d.** la rue principale

2 vt (pt & pp **dragged**) **(a)** (pull) traîner; **to d. sb out of bed** tirer qn de son lit; Fig **to d. one's feet over doing sth** tarder à faire qch; Fig **to d. oneself away from sth** s'arracher à qch; **don't d. me into this!** ne me mêlez pas à vos histoires!; **to d. sb's name through the mud** traîner qn dans la boue

(b) (pond, canal) draguer

3 vi (of movie, day) traîner en longueur; (of conversation) languir

►**drag on** vi (of meeting, movie) traîner en longueur, s'éterniser

►**drag out** vt sep (meeting, speech) faire traîner

►**drag up** vt sep (refer to) ressortir

drag-and-drop ['drægən'drɒp] n Comput glisser-lâcher m

dragnet ['drægnet] n (in deep-sea fishing) seine f, senne f; Fig (to catch criminals) rafle f

dragon ['drægən] n also Fig dragon m

dragonfly ['drægənflaɪ] (pl **dragonflies**) n libellule f

dragoon [drə'guːn] 1 n (soldier) dragon m

2 vt **to d. sb into doing sth** forcer qn à faire qch

drain [dreɪn] 1 n **(a)** (for water, sewage) égout m; Fig **to throw money down the d.** jeter l'argent par les fenêtres; **that's five years' work down the d.** voilà cinq années de travail perdues; **that's my vacation down the d.** ce sont mes vacances qui tombent à l'eau (**b**) *(on resources)* ponction *f* (**on** sur); *(on strength)* perte *f* (**on** de)

2 *vt (liquid)* vider; *(vegetables)* égoutter; **to d. one's glass** finir son verre; *Fig* **to feel drained** être épuisé(e) *ou* vidé(e)

3 *vi (of liquid)* s'écouler; *(of dishes)* égoutter; *(of sink, washing machine)* se vider; *(of river)* se jeter; **the color drained from her face** elle est devenue blême

▸**drain away** *vi (of liquid)* s'écouler; *Fig (of strength, enthusiasm)* s'épuiser; *(of fear, tension)* s'apaiser

drainage ['dreɪnɪdʒ] *n* drainage *m*

drainpipe ['dreɪnpaɪp] *n* tuyau *m* d'écoulement; **drainpipes** *(pants)* pantalon *m* cigarette

drake [dreɪk] *n* canard *m* (mâle)

dram [dræm] *n (of whiskey)* goutte *f*

drama ['drɑːmə] *n* (**a**) *(art form)* théâtre *m*; *(play)* drame *m*; *Fig* **to make a d. out of sth** faire un drame de qch; *Fam* **d. queen** comédien(enne) *m,f*; **d. school** école *f* d'art dramatique (**b**) *(excitement)* action *f*

dramatic [drə'mætɪk] *adj* (**a**) *(work)* dramatique; *(actor)* de théâtre (**b**) *(significant)* spectaculaire (**c**) *(theatrical)* théâtral(e)

dramatically [drə'mætɪklɪ] *adv* (**a**) *(change, increase, drop)* de manière spectaculaire (**b**) *(theatrically) (act, speak)* de façon théâtrale

dramatist ['dræmətɪst] *n* auteur *m* dramatique, dramaturge *mf*

dramatize ['dræmətaɪz] *vt* (**a**) *(adapt) (for stage)* adapter pour la scène; *(for screen)* adapter pour l'écran (**b**) *(exaggerate)* dramatiser

drank [dræŋk] *pt of* **drink**

drape [dreɪp] **1** *npl* **drapes** *(curtains)* rideaux *mpl*

2 *vt (table, coffin)* draper (**with** de); **to d. sth over sth** draper qch sur qch

drastic ['dræstɪk] *adj (solution, change)* radical(e); *(improvement, decline)* spectaculaire; *(action)* énergique; *(shortage, difficulty)* dramatique

drat [dræt] *exclam Fam* **d.!** nom de nom!

draw [drɔː] **1** *n* (**a**) *(in match, argument)* match *m* nul (**b**) *(lottery)* loterie *f*, tombola *f*; *(for sports competition)* tirage *m* au sort (**c**) *(attraction)* attraction *f*

2 *vt (pt* **drew** [druː]*, pp* **drawn** [drɔːn]) (**a**) *(picture, diagram, map)* dessiner; *(circle, line)* tracer; **to d. sb's picture** faire le portrait de qn

(**b**) *(pull) (cart)* tirer; *(person)* attirer (**toward** vers); **to d. the curtains** *(open or shut)* tirer les rideaux; **to d. breath** souffler (**c**) *(extract)* retirer; *(pistol, sword)* dégainer; *(water, wine)* tirer; *Fig (strength, comfort)* retirer, puiser (**from** de); **to d. a knife on sb** menacer qn d'un couteau; **to d. a salary** toucher un salaire; **to d. blood** *(of dog)* mordre jusqu'au sang; *(of cat)* griffer jusqu'au sang; **to d. lots for sth** tirer qch au sort; **to d. a conclusion from sth** tirer une conclusion de qch; **they were drawn against the champions** *(in competition)* le tirage au sort a décidé qu'ils joueraient contre les champions

(**d**) *(attract)* attirer; **to d. a crowd** *(of incident)* créer un attroupement; *(of play)* attirer le public; **to feel drawn to sb/sth** se sentir attiré(e) par qn/qch; *Fig* **to d. sb's fire** s'attirer les foudres de qn

3 *vi* (**a**) *(make picture)* dessiner

(**b**) *(in game)* faire match nul (**with** avec)

(**c**) *(move)* **to d. ahead of sb** devancer qn; **to d. level with sb** rattraper qn; **to d. to an end** *or* **a close** tirer *ou* toucher à sa fin; **to d. near** (s')approcher; **to d. to a halt** s'arrêter

▸**draw back 1** *vt sep (sheet, veil)* retirer

2 *vi* reculer; **to d. back from doing sth** hésiter à faire qch

▸**draw in** *vi (of night)* raccourcir

▸**draw on 1** *vt insep (resources, savings)* tirer sur; *(experience)* se servir de

2 *vi (of evening)* approcher

▸**draw out** *vt sep* (**a**) *(encourage to talk)* faire parler (**b**) *(prolong)* faire durer

▸**draw up 1** *vt sep* (**a**) *(chair)* approcher; **she drew herself up to her full height** elle s'est dressée de toute sa hauteur (**b**) *(plan, document)* dresser; *(will)* rédiger

2 *vi (of vehicle)* s'arrêter

drawback ['drɔːbæk] *n* inconvénient *m*

drawbridge ['drɔːbrɪdʒ] *n* pont-levis *m*

drawer [drɔː(r)] *n* tiroir *m*

drawers [drɔːz] *npl Old-fashioned (for women)* culotte *f*; *(for men)* caleçon *m*

drawing ['drɔːɪŋ] *n* dessin *m*; **d. board** planche *f* à dessin; *Fig* **back to the d. board!** retour à la case départ!; **d. paper** papier *m* à dessin; **d. room** salon *m*

drawl [drɔːl] **1** *n* voix *f* traînante

2 *vi* parler d'une voix traînante

drawn [drɔːn] **1** *adj (face)* blême; *(features)* tiré(e); **to look d.** avoir les traits tirés

2 *pp of* **draw**

drawstring ['drɔːstrɪŋ] *n* cordon *m*

dread [dred] **1** *n* terreur *f*; **to have a d. of sth** avoir la hantise de qch

2 *vt* **to d. sth/doing sth** appréhender *ou* redouter qch/de faire qch; **I d. to think!** je n'ose pas imaginer!

dreaded ['dredɪd] *adj* redouté(e)

dreadful ['dredfʊl] *adj* (**a**) *(terrible)* épouvantable, affreux(-euse); **to feel d.** se sentir vraiment mal (**b**) *Fam (for emphasis)* terrible; **it's a d. bore/shame!** c'est vraiment rasant/dommage!

dreadfully ['dredfʊlɪ] *adv* (**a**) *(very badly)* affreusement (**b**) *Fam (extremely)* terriblement, horriblement

dreadlocks ['dredlɒks] *npl* dreadlocks *fpl*, coiffure *f* rasta

dream [driːm] **1** *n* rêve *m*; **to have a d. (about)** rêver (de); **to have a bad d.** faire un mauvais rêve; **a d. come true** un rêve devenu réalité; **it worked like a d.** ça a marché à merveille

2 *adj* de rêve; **my d. house** la maison de mes rêves; **d. world** monde *m* imaginaire; *Fig* **to live in a d. world** vivre en pleine utopie

3 *vt (pt & pp* **dreamt** [dremt] *or* **dreamed**) **to d. that...** rêver que...; *Fig* **I never dreamed you would take me seriously** je n'aurais jamais pensé que tu me prendrais au sérieux

4 *vi* rêver (**of** *or* **about** de); *Fam* **I wouldn't d. of it!** je n'y songerais même pas!

▸**dream up** *vt sep (scheme, excuse)* imaginer, inventer

dreamcatcher ['driːmkætʃə(r)] *n* attrapeur *m* de rêves

dreamer ['driːmə(r)] *n* rêveur(euse) *m,f*

dreamt [dremt] *pt & pp of* **dream**

dreamy ['driːmɪ] *adj* (**a**) *(person, expression)* rêveur(euse) (**b**) *Fam (wonderful)* magnifique, de rêve

dreary ['drɪərɪ] *adj* morne

dredge [dredʒ] *vt (canal, harbor)* draguer; *Fig* **to d. one's memory** fouiller dans ses souvenirs

▸**dredge up** *vt sep (body, object)* repêcher; *Fig (scandal, memory)* déterrer

dredger ['dredʒə(r)] *n (boat)* dragueur *m*

dregs [dregz] *npl (of wine)* lie *f*; *(of coffee)* marc *m*; *(in cup)* fond *m* de tasse; *Fig* **the d. of society** les bas-fonds *mpl* de la société

drench [drentʃ] *vt* tremper (**with** *or* **in** de); **drenched to the skin** trempé(e) jusqu'aux os

dress [dres] **1** *n* (**a**) *(for woman)* robe *f* (**b**) *(clothing)* tenue *f*; **to have good d. sense/no d. sense** savoir/ne pas savoir s'habiller; **d. circle** premier balcon *m*; **d. rehearsal** (répétition *f*) générale *f*; **d. shirt** chemise *f* de soirée

2 *vt* (**a**) *(person)* habiller, vêtir; **to d. oneself, to get dressed** s'habiller; **to be dressed in black/in rags** être vêtu(e) de noir/de haillons; **well/badly dressed** bien/mal habillé(e) (**b**) *(wound)* panser (**c**) *(salad)* assaisonner

3 *vi* s'habiller

▶**dress up** *vi (elegantly)* se faire beau (belle), s'habiller; *(in costume)* se déguiser (**as** en)

dresser ['dresə(r)] *n* (**a**) *(in kitchen)* vaisselier *m* (**b**) *(dressing table)* coiffeuse *f* (**c**) *Theat (person)* habilleur(euse) *m,f*

dressing ['dresɪŋ] *n* (**a**) **d. gown** robe *f* de chambre; **d. room** *(in theater)* loge *f*; *(in gym, sports center)* vestiaire *m*; *(in store)* cabine *f* d'essayage; **d. table** coiffeuse *f* (**b**) *(for wound)* pansement *m* (**c**) *(for salad)* assaisonnement *m*

dressing down ['dresɪŋ'daʊn] *n Fam* savon *m*; **to give sb a d.** passer un savon à qn

dressmaker ['dresmeɪkə(r)] *n* couturière *f*

dressmaking ['dresmeɪkɪŋ] *n* couture *f*

dressy ['dresɪ] *adj (clothes, party)* habillé(e), élégant(e)

drew [druː] *pt of* **draw**

drib [drɪb] *n* **in dribs and drabs** au compte-gouttes

dribble ['drɪbəl] **1** *n (saliva)* bave *f*; *(of blood, oil)* filet *m*
2 *vi* (**a**) *(of person)* baver (**b**) *(of liquid)* dégouliner; *Fig* **to d. in/out** *(of people)* entrer/sortir au compte-gouttes (**c**) *(of soccer or basketball player)* dribbler

drier ['draɪə(r)] *n (for clothes)* séchoir *m*; *(for hair) (on stand)* casque *m*; *(hand-held)* sèche-cheveux *m inv*

drift [drɪft] **1** *n* (**a**) *(of current)* direction *f*, sens *m*; *(of events)* cours *m*; **the d. toward home ownership** la tendance actuelle à l'accession à la propriété; **the d. from the land** l'exode *f* rurale; **d. net** *(for fishing)* filet *m* dérivant (**b**) *(meaning)* sens *m* général; *Fam* **I get the d.** j'ai compris (**c**) *(of snow)* congère *f*; *(of leaves)* amoncellement *m*; *(of fog, mist)* traînée *f*
2 *vi* (**a**) *(of boat)* dériver, aller à la dérive; *(of smoke)* flotter; *(of events)* tendre (**towards** vers); *(of person)* se laisser porter par les événements; **people drifted in and out** les gens entraient et sortaient nonchalamment; **to d. apart** *(of friends)* se perdre de vue; *(of couple)* devenir des étrangers l'un pour l'autre; **to d. into crime** sombrer peu à peu dans la délinquance (**b**) *(of sand, snow)* s'amonceler, s'entasser

drifter ['drɪftə(r)] *n (person)* **she's a bit of a d.** elle n'a pas vraiment de but dans la vie

driftwood ['drɪftwʊd] *n (in sea)* bois *m* flottant *ou* flotté; *(on shore)* bois rejeté par la mer

drill [drɪl] **1** *n* (**a**) *(tool)* foret *m*, mèche *f*; *(electric)* perceuse *f*; *(of dentist)* fraise *f*, roulette *f*; *(pneumatic)* marteau *m* piqueur; **d. bit** foret (**b**) *(training)* exercice *m*
2 *vt* (**a**) *(well)* forer; *(hole)* percer (**b**) *(train) (soldiers)* entraîner; *Fam* **to d. sth into sb** enfoncer qch dans la tête de qn
3 *vi* (**a**) *(for oil)* forer (**for** pour trouver); *(in wall, rock)* percer (**into** dans) (**b**) *(of troops)* faire l'exercice

drink [drɪŋk] **1** *n* boisson *f*; **to have a d.** prendre un verre, boire quelque chose; **to go for a d.** aller prendre un verre; **to pay for the drinks** payer les consommations; *Fam* **the d.** *(sea)* la baille; **to take to d.** se mettre à boire; **drinks machine** distributeur *m* automatique de boissons
2 *vt (pt* **drank** [dræŋk], *pp* **drunk** [drʌŋk]*)* boire; **she drank us all under the table** nous avions tous roulé sous la table depuis longtemps qu'elle était encore debout
3 *vi* boire; **to d. like a fish** boire comme un trou; **to d. to sb** *or* **to sb's health** boire à la santé de qn; *Fig* **to d. to sth** arroser qch; **to d. in the atmosphere** se pénétrer de l'atmosphère

▶**drink up 1** *vt sep* finir (de boire)
2 *vi* vider son verre

drinkable ['drɪŋkəbəl] *adj (water)* potable; *(wine, beer)* buvable

drinker ['drɪŋkə(r)] *n* buveur(euse) *m,f*; **to be a heavy d.** boire beaucoup

drinking ['drɪŋkɪŋ] *n* **d. is bad for you** l'alcool est mauvais pour la santé; **to have a d. problem** (trop) boire; **d. fountain** fontaine *f* publique; **d. straw** paille *f*; **d. water** eau *f* potable

drip [drɪp] **1** *n* (**a**) *(drop)* goutte *f*; *(sound)* bruit *m* de l'eau qui goutte (**b**) *(in hospital)* goutte-à-goutte *m inv*; **to be on a d.**

être sous perfusion (**c**) *Fam Pej (weak person)* mou (molle) *m,f*
2 *vt (pt & pp* **dripped***)* laisser tomber goutte à goutte; **you're dripping water everywhere!** tu mets de l'eau partout!
3 *vi (of liquid)* tomber goutte à goutte, goutter; *(of faucet)* fuire; **to be dripping with sweat/blood** ruisseler de sueur/sang; *Fig* **to be dripping with jewels** être couvert(e) de bijoux

drip-dry ['drɪp'draɪ] *adj (shirt, fabric)* ne nécessitant aucun repassage

dripping ['drɪpɪŋ] **1** *n* graisse *f* de rôti
2 *adj (faucet)* qui fuit
3 *adv* **d. wet** trempé(e)

drive [draɪv] **1** *n* (**a**) *(trip)* promenade *f* en voiture; **it's an hour's d. away** c'est à une heure en voiture; **to go for** *or* **to take a d.** aller faire une promenade en voiture
(**b**) *(of car)* **left-hand d.** conduite *f* à gauche; **four-wheel d.** *(car)* quatre-quatre *m inv*; *(system)* propulsion *f* à quatre roues motrices; **front-wheel d.** *(car, system)* traction *f* avant; **rear-wheel d.** *(car, system)* traction *f* arrière
(**c**) *Comput* lecteur *m*, unité *f*
(**d**) *(in golf, tennis)* drive *m*
(**e**) *(initiative)* énergie *f*, dynamisme *m*
(**f**) *(of house)* allée *f*
(**g**) *(campaign)* **sales/membership d.** campagne *f* pour attirer les acheteurs/de nouveaux membres
2 *vt (pt* **drove** [drəʊv], *pp* **driven** ['drɪvən]*)*
(**a**) *(car, train)* conduire; **to d. sb somewhere** conduire qn en voiture quelque part; **could you d. me home?** pourriez-vous me reconduire chez moi?
(**b**) *(direct, guide) (cattle)* mener, conduire; *(people)* chasser
(**c**) *(push)* **to d. sb to sth/to do sth** pousser qn à qch/à faire qch; **to d. sb crazy** rendre qn fou (folle); **to d. oneself too hard** trop exiger de soi-même; **to d. a hard bargain** ne pas faire de cadeau; **to d. prices up/down** faire monter/baisser les prix
(**d**) *(machine)* actionner, faire marcher; **to be driven by electricity** marcher à l'électricité
3 *vi (in car)* conduire; **can you d.?** savez-vous conduire?; **I don't d.** je n'ai pas mon permis; **to d. to work** aller au travail en voiture

▶**drive at** *vt insep* **what are you driving at?** où voulez-vous en venir?

▶**drive away 1** *vt sep* (**a**) *(in car)* emmener en voiture (**b**) *(force to leave)* chasser
2 *vi (in car)* s'en aller en voiture

▶**drive off 1** *vt sep (repel) (attackers)* chasser
2 *vi (in car)* s'en aller en voiture

▶**drive on** *vi (in car)* continuer (sa route)

drive-by ['draɪvbaɪ] *adj* **d. shooting** fusillade *f* exécutée d'une voiture en marche

drive-in ['draɪvɪn] *n (cinema)* drive-in *m*, *Can* ciné-parc *m*; *(restaurant)* = restaurant où on est servi dans sa voiture

drivel ['drɪvəl] *n Fam* bêtises *fpl*, balivernes *fpl*; **to talk d.** dire n'importe quoi

driven ['drɪvən] *pp of* **drive**

driver ['draɪvə(r)] *n* (**a**) *(of car, bus)* conducteur(trice) *m,f*; *(of truck, taxi)* chauffeur(euse) *m,f*; *(of train)* mécanicien(enne) *m,f*; **d.'s license** permis *m* de conduire; *Fig* **to be in the d.'s seat** être aux commandes (**b**) *(golf club)* driver *m*

driveway ['draɪvweɪ] *n* allée *f*

driving ['draɪvɪŋ] **1** *n (in car)* conduite *f*; **d. instructor** moniteur(trice) *m,f* d'auto-école; **d. lessons** leçons *fpl* de conduite; **d. school** auto-école *f*; **d. test** (examen *m* du) permis de conduire
2 *adj (rain)* battant(e); *Fig* **d. force** moteur *m*

drizzle ['drɪzəl] **1** *n* crachin *m*
2 *vi* bruiner

droll [drəʊl] *adj* drôle, comique; *Ironic* **oh, very d.!** très drôle!

dromedary ['drɒmədərɪ] (*pl* **dromedaries**) *n* dromadaire *m*

drone [drəʊn] **1** *n* (**a**) *(bee)* faux-bourdon *m* (**b**) *(of conversation, traffic, plane)* bourdonnement *m*

2 *vi* (**a**) *(of bee)* bourdonner (**b**) *(of person)* parler d'un ton monotone

▸**drone on** *vi* parler ad nauseam *(d'une voix monotone)* (**about** de)

drool [druːl] *vi (dribble)* baver; *Fig* **to d. over sb/sth** baver d'admiration devant qn/qch; *Fig* **she was drooling at the idea** elle en salivait d'avance

droop [druːp] *vi (of head)* pencher; *(of shoulders)* tomber; *(of flower)* pencher la tête; *Fig (of person)* perdre ses forces

drop [drɒp] **1** *n* (**a**) *(of liquid)* goutte *f*; **drops** *(for eyes, nose)* gouttes; **you've had a d. too much** *(to drink)* tu as bu un coup de trop; *Fig* **it's only a d. in the ocean** ce n'est qu'une goutte d'eau dans l'océan

(**b**) *(fall) (in prices, numbers)* chute *f*, baisse *f* (**in** de); *(by parachute)* parachutage *m*; **a d. of 30 feet** ≃ un à-pic *ou* escarpement de 10 mètres; *Fig* **at the d. of a hat** sans la moindre hésitation; *Sport* **d. kick** coup de pied tombé

2 *vt* (*pt & pp* **dropped**) (**a**) *(allow to fall)* laisser tomber; *(bomb)* lâcher; **to d. sb a line/a card** envoyer *ou* écrire un mot/une carte à qn; **I'll d. you (off) at the station** *(in car)* je te déposerai à la gare

(**b**) *(lower) (prices, one's eyes)* baisser

(**c**) *(abandon) (subject, idea, plan)* abandonner; **to d. sb** *(as friend)* laisser tomber qn; *(from team)* écarter qn; **to d. math/ French** *(of student)* arrêter les maths/le français; *Law* **to d. the charges** abandonner les poursuites; *Fam* **d. it!** laisse tomber!

(**d**) *(omit) (letter, syllable)* omettre, supprimer; *(when speaking)* ne pas prononcer

(**e**) *(lose) (points)* perdre

3 *vi* (**a**) *(of object)* tomber; *(of ground)* s'affaisser; **he dropped to sixth place** il est descendu à la sixième place; *Fam* **I'm ready to d.** *(with fatigue)* je tombe de fatigue; *Fam* **people are dropping like flies** les gens tombent comme des mouches; **to d. dead** tomber raide mort(e); *Fam* **d. dead!** va te faire voir!; *Fam* **let it d.!** laisse tomber!

(**b**) *(of prices, temperature, voice)* baisser; *(of wind)* tomber; *(of speed)* diminuer

▸**drop by** *vi (visit)* passer

▸**drop in** *vi* passer (**on sb** chez qn)

▸**drop off 1** *vt sep (person from car)* déposer

2 *vi* (**a**) **to d. off (to sleep)** s'assoupir, s'endormir (**b**) *(of membership, attendance)* diminuer

▸**drop out** *vi* (**a**) *(of object) (from pocket, bag)* tomber (**b**) *(of person) (from contest)* se retirer; *(from society)* devenir un(e) marginal(e); *(from college)* abandonner ses études

▸**drop round** = **drop by**

drop-kick ['drɒpkɪk] *vt Sport* **to d. the ball** donner un coup de pied tombé (au ballon)

droplet ['drɒplɪt] *n* gouttelette *f*

dropout ['drɒpaʊt] *n Fam (from society)* marginal(e) *m,f*; *(from college)* étudiant(e) *m,f* qui abandonne ses études

dropper ['drɒpə(r)] *n (for medicine)* compte-gouttes *m inv*

droppings ['drɒpɪŋz] *npl (of birds)* fiente *f*; *(of animals)* crottes *fpl*

dross [drɒs] *n Fam (nonsense)* rebut *m*; **I've never heard such d. in all my life** j'ai rarement entendu de telles bêtises

drought [draʊt] *n* sécheresse *f*

drove [drəʊv] **1** *n* **to arrive in droves** arriver en foule

2 *pt of* **drive**

drown [draʊn] **1** *vt* (**a**) *(in water)* noyer; **to d. oneself** se noyer; **to d. one's sorrows** noyer son chagrin dans l'alcool

(**b**) *(sound)* couvrir

2 *vi (die)* se noyer

▸**drown out** *vt sep (sound)* couvrir; *(person)* couvrir la voix de

drowse [draʊz] *vi* somnoler

drowsiness ['draʊzɪnɪs] *n* somnolence *f*

drowsy ['draʊzɪ] *adj* **to be** *or* **to feel d.** avoir envie de dormir

drudge [drʌdʒ] *n (man)* homme *m* de peine; *(woman)* bonne *f* à tout faire

drudgery ['drʌdʒərɪ] *n* travail *m* pénible *ou* ingrat

drug [drʌg] **1** *n (medicine)* médicament *m*; *(narcotic)* drogue *f*; **hard/soft drugs** drogues dures/douces; **to take drugs** se droguer; **d. abuse** usage *m* de stupéfiants; **d. addict** drogué(e) *m,f*; **d. dealer** *(large-scale)* trafiquant *m* de drogue; *(small-scale)* petit trafiquant de drogue, dealer *m*; **d. squad** brigade *f* des stupéfiants

2 *vt* (*pt & pp* **drugged**) droguer

druggist ['drʌgɪst] *n* pharmacien(enne) *m,f*

drugstore ['drʌgstɔː(r)] *n* pharmacie *f*

druid ['druːɪd] *n* druide *m*

drum [drʌm] **1** *n* (**a**) *(musical instrument)* tambour *m*; **drums** batterie *f* (**b**) *(container)* fût *m*; *(for oil)* bidon *m*

2 *vt* (*pt & pp* **drummed**) **to d. one's fingers** tambouriner de ses doigts; **to d. sth into sb** enfoncer qch dans la tête de qn

3 *vi (play drums)* jouer de la batterie; **the rain was drumming on the window panes** la pluie tambourinait contre les vitres

▸**drum up** *vt (support, enthusiasm)* chercher à susciter

drummer ['drʌmə(r)] *n (in pop band)* batteur(euse) *m,f*; *(in military band)* tambour *m*

drumstick ['drʌmstɪk] *n* (**a**) *(for playing drums)* baguette *f* de tambour (**b**) *(chicken leg)* pilon *m*

drunk [drʌŋk] **1** *n (man)* homme *m* soûl; *(woman)* femme *f* soûle; *(habitual)* ivrogne *mf*

2 *adj* ivre, soûl(e); **to get d.** se soûler; *Law* **d. and disorderly** = en état d'ivresse sur la voie publique; *Fig* **d. with joy/power** ivre de joie/puissance

3 *pp of* **drink**

drunkard ['drʌŋkəd] *n* ivrogne *mf*

drunk-driver ['drʌŋk'draɪvə(r)] *n* conducteur(trice) *m,f* ivre

drunk-driving ['drʌŋk'draɪvɪŋ] *n* conduite *f* en état d'ivresse

drunken ['drʌŋkən] *adj (person)* ivre; *(party)* bien arrosé(e); **in a d. stupor** hébété(e) par l'alcool; **d. brawl** querelle *f* d'ivrognes

dry [draɪ] **1** *adj* (**a**) *(weather, clothing, skin, hair, wine)* sec (sèche); *(day)* sans pluie; **to run** *or* **to go d.** *(of river)* s'assécher; *(of spring)* (se) tarir, s'épuiser; **d. as a bone** complètement sec; *Naut* **d. dock** cale *f* sèche; **d. goods** tissus *mpl* et articles *mpl* de bonneterie; **d. goods store** magasin *m* de tissus et d'articles de bonneterie; **d. ice** neige *f* carbonique; **d. land** terre *f* ferme; **d. rot** pourriture *f* sèche; **d. run** coup *m* d'essai, test *m*

(**b**) *(boring) (style, person)* ennuyeux(euse)

(**c**) *(humor)* pince-sans-rire *inv*

(**d**) *(where alcohol is banned)* où l'alcool est prohibé; *(where alcohol is not sold)* où on ne vend pas d'alcool

2 *vt* (*pt & pp* **dried**) sécher; *(clothes)* faire sécher; *(skin)* dessécher; *(dishes)* essuyer; **to d. oneself** se sécher; **to d. one's hair** se sécher les cheveux

3 *vi* sécher

▸**dry out** *vi* (**a**) *(of alcoholic)* se faire désintoxiquer (**b**) *(of wood, ground)* sécher; *(of skin)* se dessécher

▸**dry up** *vi* (**a**) *(of well, pool)* se dessécher, tarir (**b**) *(of funds, conversation)* tarir; *(of inspiration)* se tarir (**c**) *(forget one's lines)* oublier son texte; *(have nothing more to say)* ne plus rien avoir à dire

dry-clean ['draɪ'kliːn] *vt* nettoyer à sec

dry-cleaner's ['draɪ'kliːnəz] *n* teinturerie *f*, pressing *m*

dry-cleaning [draɪ'kliːnɪŋ] *n* (**a**) *(process)* nettoyage *m* à sec (**b**) *(clothes)* vêtements *mpl* laissés chez le teinturier

dryer = **drier**

DTP [diːtiː'piː] *n Comput (abbr* **desktop publishing**) PAO *f*

DTs [di:'ti:z] *npl* (*abbr* **delirium tremens**) **the D.** le delirium tremens

dual ['dju:əl] *adj* double; **d. carriageway** (*road*) route *f* à deux chaussées; **d. nationality** double nationalité *f*; **d. ownership** copropriété *f*

dual-band ['dju:əlbænd] *adj Tel* dual-band, bibande

dual-purpose ['dju:əl'pɜːpəs] *adj* à double emploi

dub [dʌb] (*pt & pp* **dubbed**) *vt* (**a**) (*movie*) doubler (**into** en) (**b**) (*nickname*) surnommer

dubbing ['dʌbɪŋ] *n* (*of movie*) doublage *m*

dubious ['dju:bɪəs] *adj* (**a**) (*uncertain*) incertain(e); **to be d. (about)** avoir quelques doutes (au sujet de) (**b**) (*questionable*) douteux(euse)

Dublin ['dʌblɪn] *n* Dublin

Dubliner ['dʌblɪnə(r)] *n* Dublinois(e) *m,f*

duchess ['dʌtʃɪs] *n* duchesse *f*

duchy ['dʌtʃɪ] (*pl* **duchies**) *n* duché *m*

duck [dʌk] **1** *n* canard *m*; (*female*) cane *f*; **to take to sth like a d. to water** faire qch comme si on l'avait fait toute sa vie; **criticism runs off him like water off a d.'s back** les critiques glissent sur lui; **d. pond** mare *f* aux canards
2 *vt* (**a**) (*head*) baisser subitement; **to d. sb** (*under water*) faire faire le plongeon à qn (**b**) (*avoid*) (*obligations*) se dérober à; **to d. the issue/question** se dérober
3 *vi* (*lower head*) baisser la tête, se baisser; (*under water*) plonger sous l'eau; **to d. behind a tree** se cacher derrière un arbre

►duck out of *vt insep* **to d. out of doing sth** éviter de faire qch; **he ducked out of the meeting** il s'est débrouillé pour ne pas assister à la réunion

duck-billed platypus ['dʌkbɪld'plætɪpəs] *n* ornithorynque *m*

duckling ['dʌklɪŋ] *n* (*male*) caneton *m*; (*female*) canette *f*

duct [dʌkt] *n* conduit *m*; **d. tape** ruban *m* adhésif en toile

dud [dʌd] *Fam* **1** *n* (*person*) incapable *mf*; (*shell*) obus *m* qui n'a pas éclaté; (*banknote*) faux *m*
2 *adj* (*shell*) qui n'a pas éclaté; (*check*) en bois

dude [du:d] *n Fam* type *m*

due [dju:] **1** *n* (**a**) (*what is owed*) dû *m*; **to give her her d., she did apologize** pour lui rendre justice, il faut reconnaître qu'elle s'est excusée
(**b**) **dues** (*membership fees*) cotisation *f*
2 *adj* (**a**) (*owed*) dû (due); **to fall d.** échoir, arriver à échéance; **are you d. any money from her?** vous doit-elle de l'argent?; **you're d. an apology** je vous dois/il vous doit/*etc.* une excuse; **d. to** par suite de, en raison de; **what is it d. to?** c'est dû à quoi?; *Fin* **d. date** échéance *f*
(**b**) (*merited, proper*) dû (due), mérité(e); **to give sb d. warning** avertir qn dans les formes; **after d. consideration** après mûre réflexion; **with all d. respect,...** avec tout le respect que je vous dois,...; **in d. course** (*when appropriate*) en temps voulu; (*eventually*) le moment venu
(**c**) (*expected*) **the train is d. (in** *or* **to arrive)** le train doit arriver d'un moment à l'autre; **when is he d. (in** *or* **to arrive)?** quand doit-il arriver?; **when is the baby d.?** pour quand la naissance est-elle prévue?; **she's d. back any minute** elle doit revenir d'un moment à l'autre; **the movie/book is d. out soon** le film/livre va sortir sous peu
3 *adv* **d. north/south** plein nord/sud

duel ['dju:əl] **1** *n* duel *m*; **to fight a d.** se battre en duel
2 *vi* se battre en duel

duet [dju:'et] *n* duo *m*; (*for piano*) morceau *m* à quatre mains

duffel, duffle ['dʌfəl] *n* **d. (coat)** duffle-coat *m*; **d. bag** sac *m* (de) marin

duffer ['dʌfə(r)] *n Fam* (*useless person*) gourde *f*; **to be a d. at sth** être nul en qch

dug [dʌg] *pt & pp of* **dig**

dugout ['dʌgaʊt] *n* (**a**) (*canoe*) pirogue *f* (**b**) (*shelter*) *Mil* tranchée-abri *f*; *Sport* banc *m* de touche

duke [dju:k] *n* duc *m*

dull [dʌl] **1** *adj* (**a**) (*boring*) ennuyeux(euse), terne; **as d. as dishwater** ennuyeux comme la pluie (**b**) (*unintelligent*) lent(e) (**c**) (*not sharp*) (*pain, sound*) sourd(e); (*blade, senses*) émoussé(e) (**d**) (*not bright*) (*color, surface*) terne; (*eyes*) sans éclat; (*weather, sky*) sombre, maussade
2 *vt* (**a**) (*pleasure*) rendre moins vif (vive); (*pain*) endormir, calmer; (*sound*) amortir, assourdir; (*blade, senses*) émousser (**b**) (*make less bright*) ternir

duly ['dju:lɪ] *adv* (**a**) (*properly*) dûment (**b**) (*as expected*) comme prévu

dumb [dʌm] *adj* (**a**) (*unable to speak*) muet(ette); **to be struck d.** (*with astonishment*) en rester muet; **d. animal** bête *f*; **d. insolence** silence *m* insolent (**b**) *Fam* (*stupid*) bête; **d. blonde** blonde *f* évaporée

►dumb down *vt sep* (*population, electorate*) infantiliser; (*media, program*) faire baisser le niveau de

dumbbell ['dʌmbel] *n* (**a**) (*with weights*) haltère *m* (**b**) *Fam* (*stupid person*) abruti(e) *m,f*

dumbfounded [dʌm'faʊndɪd] *adj* abasourdi(e), ébahi(e)

dumbing down ['dʌmɪŋ'daʊn] *n* (*of population, electorate*) infantilisation *f*; (*of media, program*) baisse *f* de niveau

dumbstruck ['dʌmstrʌk] = **dumbfounded**

dumbwaiter ['dʌmweɪtə(r)] *n* (*lift*) monte-plats *m inv*

dummy ['dʌmɪ] **1** *n* (*pl* **dummies**) (**a**) (*in store window*) mannequin *m*; (*of ventriloquist*) marionnette *f*; (*model, fake*) objet *m* factice (**b**) *Fam* (*idiot*) abruti(e) *m,f*
2 *adj* (*fake*) factice; **d. run** coup *m* d'essai

dump [dʌmp] **1** *n* (**a**) (*for refuse*) décharge *f*; *Fam Pej* (*town*) bled *m* paumé; (*house*) dépotoir *m*; **d. truck** tombereau *m*, dumper *m* (**b**) *Mil* (*store*) dépôt *m* (**c**) *Comput* vidage *m*
2 *vt* (**a**) (*put down*) déposer (**b**) (*dispose of*) se débarrasser de; (*waste*) déverser; *Fam* (*boyfriend, girlfriend*) plaquer (**c**) *Comput* (*memory*) vider

dumping ['dʌmpɪŋ] *n* (**a**) **no d.** (*sign*) décharge interdite; **d. ground** décharge *f*; *Fig* dépotoir *m* (**b**) *Econ* dumping *m*

dumpling ['dʌmplɪŋ] *n* (*in stew*) boulette *f* de pâte; **apple d.** pomme *f* en chausson

dumps [dʌmps] *npl Fam* **to be down in the d.** broyer du noir, avoir le cafard

Dumpster ['dʌmpstə(r)] *n* benne *f* à ordures

dumpy ['dʌmpɪ] *adj Fam* (*person, appearance*) boulot(otte)

dunce [dʌns] *n* (*at school*) âne *m*, cancre *m*; **d.'s cap** bonnet *m* d'âne

dune [dju:n] *n* dune *f*

dung [dʌŋ] *n* (*of cow*) bouse *f*; (*of horse*) crottin *m*; (*of wild animal*) fumées *fpl*

dungarees [dʌŋgə'ri:z] *npl* (**a pair of**) **d.** une salopette *f*; (*of workman*) un bleu de travail

dungeon ['dʌndʒən] *n* (*underground*) cachot *m*; *Hist* (*tower*) donjon *m*

dunghill ['dʌŋhɪl] *n* tas *m* de fumier

dunk [dʌŋk] *vt* (**a**) (*dip*) tremper (**b**) (*in basketball*) **to d. the ball** faire un lancer coulé

Dunkirk [dʌn'kɜːk] *n* Dunkerque

duo ['dju:əʊ] (*pl* **duos**) *n* (*in music*) duo *m*; (*two people*) couple *m*

duodenal [dju:əʊ'di:nəl] *adj* (*ulcer*) duodénal(e)

dupe [dju:p] **1** *n* dupe *f*
2 *vt* duper, tromper; **to d. sb into doing sth** faire faire qch à qn en le dupant

duplex ['dju:pleks] *n* = maison convertie en deux appartements

duplicate 1 ['dju:plɪkət] *n* (*of key*) double *m*; (*of letter, receipt*) double, duplicata *m*; **in d.** en double, en deux exemplaires
2 ['dju:plɪkət] *adj* **a d. key** un double de la clé; **a d. copy** un duplicata
3 *vt* ['dju:plɪkeɪt] (**a**) (*copy*) faire un double/duplicata de; (*on photocopier*) faire une photocopie de (**b**) (*do again*) refaire

duplication [djuːplɪˈkeɪʃən] n (**a**) (copying) reproduction f (**b**) (repetition) répétition f

duplicitous [djuːˈplɪsɪtəs] adj fourbe, faux (fausse)

duplicity [djuːˈplɪsɪtɪ] n duplicité f

durability [djʊərəˈbɪlɪtɪ] n (of material) résistance f; (of friendship) durabilité f

durable [ˈdjʊərəbəl] **1** n (**consumer**) **durables** biens mpl durables

2 adj (material) résistant(e); (friendship) durable

duration [djʊˈreɪʃən] n durée f; **for the d.** pour longtemps

duress [djʊˈres] n **under d.** sous la contrainte

during [ˈdjʊərɪŋ] prep pendant, durant; (in the course of) au cours de

dusk [dʌsk] n crépuscule m; **at d.** au crépuscule, à la tombée de la nuit

dust [dʌst] **1** n (**a**) (dirt, powder) poussière f; **d. cover** (for furniture) housse f; **d. cover** or **jacket** (for book) chemise f, jaquette f (**b**) (action) **to give sb a d.** passer un coup de chiffon sur qch (**c**) (idioms) **once the d. has settled** une fois que les choses se seront calmées

2 vt (**a**) (clean) dépoussiérer, épousseter (**b**) (sprinkle) (with flour, sugar) saupoudrer (**with** de)

3 vi (clean) épousseter

▸**dust off** vt sep (furniture) épousseter; Fig (legislation) dépoussiérer; (one's French) se remettre à

dustcloth [ˈdʌstklɒθ], **duster** [ˈdʌstə(r)] n (cloth) chiffon m (à poussière)

dustpan [ˈdʌstpæn] n pelle f (à poussière)

dust-up [ˈdʌstʌp] n Fam (brawl) bagarre f; **to have a d. with sb** se bagarrer avec qn

dusty [ˈdʌstɪ] adj poussiéreux(euse), couvert(e) de poussière; **to get d.** se couvrir de poussière

Dutch [dʌtʃ] **1** npl **the D.** (people) les Hollandais mpl

2 n (language) hollandais m

3 adj hollandais(e); Fam **I need some D. courage** j'ai besoin d'un verre pour me donner du courage

4 adv Fam **to go D.** payer chacun sa part

Dutchman [ˈdʌtʃmən] n Hollandais m, Néerlandais m

Dutchwoman [ˈdʌtʃwʊmən] n Hollandaise f, Néerlandaise f

dutiful [ˈdjuːtɪfʊl] adj (obedient) obéissant(e)

duty [ˈdjuːtɪ] (pl **duties**) n (**a**) (obligation) devoir m (**to** envers); **to do one's d.** faire son devoir; **to fail in one's d.** manquer à son devoir; **to make it one's d. to...** se faire un devoir de...; **it's your d. to...** il est de votre devoir de... (**b**) (task) **duties** fonctions fpl; **to take up** or **to assume one's duties** entrer en fonctions; **to carry out** or **to perform one's duties** exercer ses fonctions (**c**) (of soldier, employee) **to be on/off d.** être/ne pas être de service; **d. roster** tableau m de service (**d**) Fin (tax) droit m; **to pay d. on sth** payer une taxe sur qch

duty-free [ˈdjuːtɪˈfriː] **1** n marchandises fpl hors taxe

2 adj (cigarettes, wine, perfume) hors taxe; **d. store** magasin m hors taxe

duvet [ˈduːveɪ] n couette f; **d. cover** housse f decouette

DVD [diːviːˈdiː] n Comput (abbr **Digital Versatile Disc**, **Digital Video Disc**) DVD m inv, disque m vidéo numérique

DVD-ROM [ˈdiːviːˈdiːˈrɒm] n Comput (abbr **Digital Versatile Disc read-only memory**, **Digital Video Disc read-only memory**) DVD-ROM m inv

dwarf [dwɔːf] (pl **dwarfs** or **dwarves** [dwɔːvz]) **1** n & adj nain(e) m,f

2 vt (be taller than) écraser; Fig (achievements, success) éclipser

dwell [dwel] (pt & pp **dwelled** or **dwelt** [dwelt]) vi Lit (live) demeurer

▸**dwell on**, **dwell upon** vt insep remâcher, ressasser; **let's not d. on it** n'y pensons plus

dwelling [ˈdwelɪŋ] n Lit **d. (place)** demeure f, résidence f; **d. house** maison f d'habitation

dwelt [dwelt] pt & pp of **dwell**

dwindle [ˈdwɪndəl] vi diminuer; **to d. (away) to nothing** se réduire à rien

dwindling [ˈdwɪndəlɪŋ] adj (funds, membership) en baisse; (enthusiasm) faiblissant(e)

dye [daɪ] **1** n (for clothes, hair) teinture f

2 vt teindre; **to d. sth black/red** teindre qch en noir/rouge; **to d. one's hair** se teindre les cheveux

dyed-in-the-wool [ˈdaɪdɪnðəˈwʊl] adj (conservative, Marxist) bon teint inv

dying [ˈdaɪɪŋ] **1** npl **the d.** les mourants mpl, les moribonds mpl

2 adj (person) mourant(e), agonisant(e); (industry, tradition) moribond(e); **to my d. day** jusqu'à ma mort; **d. wish** dernières volontés fpl; **d. words** dernières paroles fpl

dyke = **dike**

dynamic [daɪˈnæmɪk] **1** n (driving force) dynamique f

2 adj also Fig dynamique

dynamics [daɪˈnæmɪks] npl dynamique f

dynamism [ˈdaɪnəmɪzəm] n (of person, society) dynamisme m

dynamite [ˈdaɪnəmaɪt] **1** n also Fig dynamite f; Fam **it's d.!** (excellent) c'est du tonnerre!

2 vt dynamiter

dynamo [ˈdaɪnəməʊ] (pl **dynamos**) n dynamo f

dynastic [dɪˈnæstɪk] adj dynastique

dynasty [ˈdɪnəstɪ] (pl **dynasties**) n dynastie f

dysentery [ˈdɪsəntrɪ] n dysenterie f

dysfunctional [dɪsˈfʌŋkʃənəl] adj **a d. family** une famille à problèmes

dyslexia [dɪsˈleksɪə] n dyslexie f

dyslexic [dɪsˈleksɪk] adj dyslexique

dystrophy [ˈdɪstrəfɪ] n Med dystrophie f

E

E, e [i:] *n* (**a**) *(letter)* E, e *m inv* (**b**) *Mus* mi *m* (**c**) *(abbr* **east**) E (**d**)
(abbr **ecstasy**) X *f*, ecsta *f*

each [i:tʃ] **1** *adj* chaque; **e. one of us** chacun(e) de nous *ou*
d'entre nous

2 *pron* (**a**) *(both, all)* chacun(e) *m,f*; **e. of us** chacun(e) de
nous *ou* d'entre nous; **we e. earn $300** nous gagnons chacun
300 dollars; **peaches at 50 cents e.** pêches à 50 cents cha-
cune *ou* 50 cents pièce; **a little of e.** un peu de chaque (**b**) *(reciprocal)* **e. other** *(two)* l'un l'autre (l'une l'autre); *(more than two)*
les uns les autres (les unes les autres); **separated from e.
other** séparé l'un de l'autre; **they hate e. other** ils se haïssent;
we write to e. other nous nous écrivons

eager ['i:gə(r)] *adj (look, voice)* avide; *(supporter)* fervent(e); *(desire, hope)* ardent(e), vif (vive); **to be e. for sth/to do sth** désirer vivement qch/faire qch; **to be e. to please** être
désireux(euse) de plaire; *Fam* **to be an e. beaver** être zélé(e)

eagerly ['i:gəli] *adv (listen)* avidement; *(work, talk)* avec enthousiasme; **e. awaited** attendu(e) avec impatience

eagerness ['i:gənɪs] *n* impatience *f*; *(to learn, please)* vif désir
m; **to show e. in doing sth** montrer un intérêt très vif à faire
qch

eagle ['i:gəl] *n* aigle *m*

eagle-eyed [i:gə'laɪd] *adj* aux yeux d'aigle

ear ['ɪə(r)] *n* (**a**) *(part of body)* oreille *f*; **to have an e. for music**
avoir l'oreille musicale; **to have an e. for languages** avoir
une bonne oreille pour les langues; *Med* **e., nose and throat
specialist** oto-rhino(-laryngologiste) *mf*; **e. lobe** lobe *m* de
l'oreille

(**b**) *(of wheat)* épi *m*

(**c**) *(idioms)* **to play it by e.** *(improvise)* improviser; **to have
sb's e.** avoir l'oreille de qn; **to keep one's e. to the ground**
être sur le qui-vive; **to go in one e. and out the other** *(of
words, information)* entrer par une oreille et sortir par l'autre;
Fam **to be up to one's ears in debt** être endetté(e) jusqu'au
cou; *Fam* **to be up to one's ears in work** être accablé(e) de
travail; *Fam* **to be thrown out on one's e.** se faire jeter dehors *ou* sur le pavé; **I'm all ears** je suis tout ouïe; **my ears
were burning** j'avais les oreilles qui sifflaient; **the house
was falling down around their ears** la maison s'écroulait
tout autour d'eux

earache ['ɪəreɪk] *n* mal *m* d'oreille(s); **to have an e.** avoir mal
à l'oreille/aux oreilles

earbud ['ɪəbʌd] *n* mini-écouteur *m*

eardrum ['ɪədrʌm] *n* tympan *m*

earful ['ɪəfʊl] *n Fam* **to give sb an e.** passer un savon à qn; **to
get an e.** se faire passer un savon

earl [ɜ:l] *n* comte *m*

earlier ['ɜːlɪə(r)] **1** *adj (previous)* plus ancien(enne); **I caught
an e. train** j'ai pris un train qui partait plus tôt; **her e. novels**
ses romans précédents

2 *adv* **e. (on)** avant; **a few days e.** quelques jours plus tôt;
no e. than tomorrow pas avant demain; **as we saw e.**
comme nous l'avons vu auparavant

earliest ['ɜːlɪəst] **1** *n* **at the e.** au plus tôt; **the e. I can be there
is four o'clock** je pourrai être là à quatre heures au plus tôt

2 *adj (opportunity, memory)* premier(ère); **from the e. times**
depuis les temps les plus reculés; **at the e. possible moment**
le plus tôt possible, dans les plus brefs délais

early ['ɜːlɪ] **1** *adj* (**a**) *(in the day)* matinal(e); **to have an e.
night** se coucher tôt; **to have an e. breakfast** déjeuner de
bonne heure; **to be an e. riser** être matinal, se lever de bon
matin; *Prov* **the e. bird catches the worm** l'avenir appartient à ceux qui se lèvent tôt

(**b**) *(at beginning of period of time)* **in (the) e. summer** au début de l'été; **at an e. age** tout jeune; **he's in his e. thirties** il a
la trentaine; **in the e. 1990s** au début des années 90; **an e.
example of...** un des premiers exemples de...

(**c**) *(ahead of time)* en avance; **half an hour e.** en avance
d'une demi-heure

(**d**) *(premature) (death)* prématuré(e); **e. retirement** préretraite *f*; *Mil* **e. warning system** système *m* radar de préalerte

(**e**) *(in future)* **at an e. date** prochainement

2 *adv* (**a**) *(in the day)* de bonne heure, tôt; **e. in the morning**
le matin de bonne heure; **e. in the evening** tôt dans la soirée;
as e. as possible le plus tôt possible

(**b**) *(at beginning of period of time)* **e. in the year** au début de
l'année; **e. on** dès l'abord; **e. in one's life** dans sa jeunesse; **e.
in one's career** au début de sa carrière

(**c**) *(ahead of time)* en avance; **too e.** trop tôt

(**d**) *(prematurely) (die)* prématurément; **to retire e.** prendre
une retraite anticipée

earmark ['ɪəmɑːk] *vt (funds)* assigner, affecter (**for** à); **the
building is earmarked for closure** il est prévu que ce bâtiment soit fermé

earn [ɜːn] *vt (money)* gagner; *(rest, respect)* mériter; **to e. sb's
love** gagner le cœur de qn; **to e. sb's praise** valoir des éloges
à qn; **to e. one's living** gagner sa vie

earner ['ɜːnə(r)] *n* (**wage**) **e.** salarié(e) *m,f*; **to be a big/small
e.** gagner beaucoup/peu; *Fam* **a nice little e.** une bonne petite
affaire

earnest ['ɜːnɪst] **1** *n* **in e.** sérieusement; **things have
started in e.** les choses ont vraiment commencé

2 *adj (person, effort, discussion)* sérieux(euse); *(expression)* pé-
nétré(e), grave; *(voice)* pressant(e); *(desire)* profond(e)

earnestly ['ɜːnɪstlɪ] *adv* sérieusement; *(desire)* profondément;
(hope, believe) sincèrement

earning power ['ɜːnɪŋ'paʊə(r)] *n* revenu *m* potentiel

earnings ['ɜːnɪŋz] *npl (of person)* salaire *m*; *(of company)* bénéfices *mpl*; **e. related** *(pensions, benefits)* proportionnel(elle) au
salaire

earphones ['ɪəfəʊnz] *npl* écouteurs *mpl*

earpiece ['ɪəpiːs] *n (of telephone)* écouteur *m*

earplug ['ɪəplʌg] *n* boule *f* Quiès®

earring ['ɪərɪŋ] *n* boucle *f* d'oreille

earshot ['ɪəʃɒt] *n* **within/out of e.** à portée/hors de portée
de voix

ear-splitting ['ɪəsplɪtɪŋ] *adj* à vous déchirer *ou* crever les tympans

earth [ɜ:θ] *n* (**a**) *(planet)* **the E.** la Terre; *Fam* **where/why on e....?** où/pourquoi diable...?; **to cost the e.** coûter les yeux de la tête; **to promise sb the e.** promettre la lune à qn; **e. mother** *(in mythology)* déesse *f* de la terre; *Fam Fig* mère *f* nourricière; **e. tremor** *(ground)* sol *m*; *(soil)* terre *f*; *Fig* **to come back to e. (with a bump)** revenir (brutalement) sur terre; *Fig* **to go to e.** *(of fugitive)* se terrer

earthenware ['ɜ:θənweə(r)] **1** *n* poterie *f* (de terre)
  2 *adj* en *ou* de terre cuite

earthling ['ɜ:θlɪŋ] *n* terrien(enne) *m,f*

earthly ['ɜ:θlɪ] *adj* (**a**) *(life, existence)* terrestre (**b**) *Fam (for emphasis)* **there's no e. reason why...** il n'y a absolument aucune raison pour que...; **she hasn't got an e. (chance)** elle n'a pas la moindre chance

earthquake ['ɜ:θkweɪk] *n* tremblement *m* de terre, séisme *m*

earth-shattering ['ɜ:θʃætərɪŋ] *adj Fam* stupéfiant(e)

earthworks ['ɜ:θwɜ:ks] *n* travaux *mpl* de terrassement; *Mil* fortifications *fpl* en terre

earthworm ['ɜ:θwɜ:m] *n* ver *m* de terre

earthy ['ɜ:θɪ] *adj* (**a**) *(of or like earth)* terreux(euse); **to have an e. smell** sentir la terre (**b**) *(coarse)* truculent(e); *(uninhibited)* direct(e)

earwax ['ɪəwæks] *n* cérumen *m*, cire *f*

earwig ['ɪəwɪg] *n (insect)* perce-oreille *m*

ease [i:z] **1** *n* (**a**) *(facility)* facilité *f*, aisance *f*; **with e.** avec facilité *ou* aisance (**b**) *(comfort)* tranquillité *f*, bien-être *m*; **at e.** à l'aise; **to put sb at (their) e.** mettre qn à l'aise; **to put** *or* **to set sb's mind at e.** rassurer qn; **a life of e.** une vie d'oisiveté
  2 *vt* (**a**) *(alleviate) (pain)* calmer, soulager; **to e. sb's mind** rassurer qn (**b**) *(relax) (pressure)* soulager; *(tension)* réduire; *(restrictions)* assouplir (**c**) *(move carefully, slowly)* déplacer doucement
  3 *vi (of pain, pressure)* s'atténuer; *(of wind, rain)* se calmer; *(of situation)* se détendre

▸**ease off, ease up** *vi (of pain, rain)* se calmer

easel ['i:zəl] *n* chevalet *m*

easily ['i:zɪlɪ] *adv* (**a**) *(without difficulty)* facilement, sans difficulté; **that's e. said** c'est facile à dire (**b**) *(undoubtedly)* **e. the best** de loin le meilleur/la meilleure; **he is e. forty** il a au moins quarante ans (**c**) *(comfortably)* à son aise

easiness ['i:zɪnɪs] *n* (**a**) *(of task)* facilité *f* (**b**) *(of manner)* décontraction *f*

east [i:st] **1** *n* est *m*; **to the e. (of)** à l'est (de); **the E.** *(the Orient)* l'Orient *m*; *(Eastern Europe)* l'Est
  2 *adj (coast, side)* est *inv*; *(wind)* d'est; **E. Africa** l'Afrique *f* orientale; *Formerly* **E. Germany** l'Allemagne *f* de l'Est; **the E. Side** = les quartiers est de New York
  3 *adv* à l'est; *(travel)* vers l'est; **e. of the Rhine** à l'est du Rhin; **to face e.** être orienté(e) à l'est

eastbound ['i:stbaʊnd] *adj (train, traffic)* en direction de l'est

Easter ['i:stə(r)] *n* Pâques *fpl*; **at E.** à Pâques; **E. egg** œuf *m* de Pâques; **E. Island** l'île *f* de Pâques; **E. Sunday** dimanche *m* *ou* jour *m* de Pâques; **E. week** *(following Easter)* semaine *f* de Pâques; *(Holy Week)* semaine sainte

easterly ['i:stəlɪ] **1** *n (wind)* vent *m* d'est
  2 *adj (point)* à l'est; *(wind)* d'est, qui vient de l'est; **in an e. direction** vers l'est

eastern ['i:stən] *adj* est *inv*; *(of Far East)* oriental(e); **e. France** l'est *m* de la France; **E. Europe** l'Europe *f* de l'est; **E. Standard Time** heure *f* de la côte est de l'Amérique du Nord

eastward ['i:stwəd] **1** *adj (in the east)* à l'est, dans l'est
  2 *adv (face, point)* à l'est; *(go, travel)* vers l'est

eastwards ['i:stwədz] *adv* = **eastward**

easy ['i:zɪ] **1** *adj* (**a**) *(not difficult)* facile; *(solution)* simple; **to be e. to please** ne pas être difficile; **e. to get on with** facile à

vivre; *Fam* **as e. as ABC** *or* **as pie** facile comme tout, simple comme bonjour; **the e. way out** la solution de facilité; *Fam* **e. money** argent *m* facile; **e. on the eye** agréable à regarder; *Com* **by e. payments, on e. terms** avec facilités de paiement; *Fam* **I'm e.** *(I don't mind)* ça m'est égal (**b**) *(comfortable, relaxed) (pace, life)* tranquille; *(manners)* libre, dégagé(e); *(style)* facile, naturel(elle); *Fam* **to be on e. street** ne pas avoir de problèmes financiers; **to have an e. time (of it)** avoir la vie facile; **e. chair** fauteuil *m*; *Mus* **e. listening** variété *f*; *very Fam* **she's e., she's an easy lay** elle couche avec tout le monde
  2 *adv* **to go e. on sb/sth** y aller doucement avec qn/qch; **to take things** *or* **it e.** *(lead a life of ease)* mener une vie tranquille; *(not overdo things)* ralentir; **take it e.!** *(calm down)* t'en fais pas!; **that's easier said than done** c'est plus facile à dire qu'à faire; **e. come, e. go** ça va, ça vient

easy-going ['i:zɪ'gəʊɪŋ] *adj (tolerant)* coulant(e), accommodant(e); *(calm)* décontracté(e)

eat [i:t] *(pt* ate [et, eɪt], *pp* eaten ['i:tən]) **1** *vt* (**a**) *(food)* manger; **to e. one's breakfast** prendre son petit déjeuner (**b**) *(idioms)* **to e. sb out of house and home** ruiner qn en nourriture; *Fam* **I could e. a horse!** j'ai une faim de loup!; *Fam* **he won't e. you!** il ne va pas te manger!; *Fam* **what's eating you?** qu'est-ce qui te tracasse?; **to e. one's words** se rétracter; *Fam* **if it works, I'll e. my hat** si ça réussit, je mange mon chapeau
  2 *vi* manger; *Fig* **you'll have them eating out of your hand** ils te mangeront dans la main

▸**eat away at** *vt insep (erode) (rocks, self-confidence)* éroder, miner; *(foundations)* saper

▸**eat into** *vt insep (erode)* ronger; *Fig (time, savings)* entamer

▸**eat out** *vi* manger au restaurant

▸**eat up 1** *vt sep* (**a**) *(food)* manger jusqu'à la dernière miette, finir (**b**) *(gas, money)* consommer beaucoup de
  2 *vi* finir son assiette; **e. up!** mange!

eaten ['i:tən] *pp of* **eat**

eater ['i:tə(r)] *n* mangeur(euse) *m,f*; **to be a fussy e.** être difficile (sur la nourriture)

eatery ['i:tərɪ] *(pl* **eateries**) *n* (café-)restaurant *m*

eats [i:ts] *npl Fam* bouffe *f*

eau de Cologne ['əʊdəkə'ləʊn] *n* eau *f* de Cologne

eaves [i:vz] *npl* avant-toit *m*

eavesdrop ['i:vzdrɒp] *(pt & pp* eavesdropped) *vi* **to e. (on sb/sth)** écouter (qn/qch) avec indiscrétion; **she was eavesdropping outside the door** elle écoutait à la porte

ebb [eb] **1** *n (of tide)* reflux *m*; **e. tide** marée *f* descendante; *Fig* **the e. and flow** *(of events)* les fluctuations *fpl*; *Fig* **to be at a low e.** *(of person)* ne pas avoir le moral; *(of spirits)* être bien bas; *(of finances, relations)* aller mal
  2 *vi (of tide)* baisser

▸**ebb away** *vi (of water)* s'écouler; *(of strength, enthusiasm)* faiblir, baisser

ebony ['ebənɪ] *n* ébène *f*

EBRD [i:bi:ɑ:'di:] *n (abbr* **European Bank for Reconstruction and Development**) BERD *f*

ebullience [ɪ'bʌlɪəns] *n* bouillonnement *m*, effervescence *f*

ebullient [ɪ'bʌlɪənt] *adj* bouillant(e), exubérant(e)

EC [i:'si:] *n (abbr* **European Community**) CE *f*

e-card ['i:kɑ:d] *n* carte *f* électronique

e-cash ['i:kæʃ] *n* argent *m* électronique, argent virtuel, e-cash *m*

eccentric [ek'sentrɪk] *n & adj* excentrique *mf*

eccentricity [eksen'trɪsɪtɪ] *n* excentricité *f*

ecclesiastic [ɪkli:zɪ'æstɪk] **1** *n* ecclésiastique *m*
  2 *adj* ecclésiastique

ECG [i:si:'dʒi:] *n Med (abbr* **electrocardiograph**) électrocardiographe *m*

echelon ['eʃəlɒn] *n* échelon *m*

echinacea [ekɪ'neɪʃə] *n Bot & Med* échinacée *f*

echo ['ekəʊ] **1** *n* (*pl* **echoes**) *also Fig* écho *m*
2 *vt* (*pt & pp* **echoed**) (*words*) répéter; (*opinion*) se faire l'écho de
3 *vi* résonner (**with** de)

eclair [eɪ'kleə(r)] *n* (*pastry*) éclair *m*; **chocolate e.** éclair au chocolat

eclectic [ə'klektɪk] *adj* (*tastes, style*) éclectique; (*blend*) hétérogène

eclipse [ɪ'klɪps] *also Fig* **1** *n* éclipse *f*
2 *vt* éclipser

eco-friendly ['i:kəʊfrendlɪ] *adj* (*product*) écologique, vert(e); (*lifestyle, person*) qui respecte l'environnement

ecological [i:kə'lɒdʒɪkəl] *adj* (*damage, balance*) écologique; (*campaign, activist*) écologiste

ecologist [ɪ'kɒlədʒɪst] *n* écologiste *mf*

ecology [ɪ'kɒlədʒɪ] *n* écologie *f*

e-commerce ['i:kɒmɜːs] *n* commerce *m* électronique

economic [i:kə'nɒmɪk] *adj* (**a**) *Econ* économique (**b**) (*profitable*) rentable; **to make sth e.** rentabiliser qch

economical [i:kə'nɒmɪkəl] *adj* (*cost-effective*) économique; (*style*) concis(e); **to be e. with the truth** ne dire la vérité qu'à moitié

economically [i:kə'nɒmɪklɪ] *adv* économiquement; (*written*) dans un style concis

economics [i:kə'nɒmɪks] **1** *n* économie *f*
2 *npl* (*financial aspects*) aspects *mpl* financiers

economist [ɪ'kɒnəmɪst] *n* économiste *mf*

economize [ɪ'kɒnəmaɪz] *vi* économiser (**on** sur)

economy [ɪ'kɒnəmɪ] *n* (*pl* **economies**) *n* économie *f*; **economies of scale** économies d'échelle; *Aviat* **e. class** classe *f* économique; **e. drive** politique *f* de réduction des dépenses; **e. measure** mesure *f* d'économie; **e. size** (*of package*) taille *f* économique

ecotax ['i:kəʊtæks] *n* écotaxe *f*

ecoterrorist ['i:kəʊterərɪst] *n* = militant ecologiste ayant recours à des actions violentes

ecotourism ['i:kəʊtʊərɪzəm] *n* écotourisme *m*

ecowarrior ['i:kəʊwɒrɪə(r)] *n* écoguerrier(ère) *m,f*

ecstasy ['ekstəsɪ] (*pl* **ecstasies**) *n* (**a**) (*emotional state*) extase *f*; **to go into ecstasies over sth** s'extasier devant qch (**b**) (*drug*) ecstasy *f*

ecstatic [ek'stætɪk] *adj* fou (folle) de joie; **he was e. about** *or* **over the news** la nouvelle l'a rendu fou de joie

ECT [i:si:'ti:] *n Med* (*abbr* **electroconvulsive therapy**) traitement *m* par électrochocs

ECU, ecu ['ekju:, 'i:kju:] *n* (*abbr* **European Currency Unit**) ÉCU *m*, écu *m*

Ecuador ['ekwədɔ:(r)] *n* l'Équateur *m*

ecumenical [i:kju'menɪkəl] *adj Rel* œcuménique

eczema ['eksɪmə] *n* eczéma *m*; **to have e.** avoir de l'eczéma

ed. [ed] (**a**) (*abbr* **edition**) éd., édit (**b**) (*abbr* **editor**) éd., édit

eddy ['edɪ] **1** *n* (*pl* **eddies**) tourbillon *m*
2 *vi* (*pt & pp* **eddied**) (*of water*) faire des remous; (*of wind, snow*) tourbillonner

Eden ['i:dən] *n* l'Éden *m*

edge [edʒ] **1** *n* (**a**) (*of table, road, river*) bord *m*; (*of wood*) lisière *f*; (*of book*) tranche *f*; **at the water's e.** au bord de l'eau; **to be on the e. of** (*new age*) être au seuil de; (*war*) être au bord de; *Fig* **to be on the e. of one's seat** retenir son souffle (**b**) (*of blade, tool*) tranchant *m*; (*of stone*) arête *f*; **to take the e. off** (*blade, appetite*) émousser; (*enjoyment*) gâter; *Fig* **to be on e.** être énervé(e); *Fig* **to set sb on e.** énerver qn (**c**) (*advantage*) **to have the e. (over sb)** être avantagé(e) (par rapport à qn)
2 *vt* (*in sewing*) border (**with** de)
3 *vi* (*move slowly*) **to e. past sb** passer lentement devant qn; **to e. toward** avancer lentement vers

▶**edge out** *vt sep* (*supplant*) évincer (**of** de)

edgeways ['edʒweɪz], **edgewise** ['edʒwaɪz] *adv* (*on its edge*) de chant; (*from side*) de côté; *Fam* **I can't get a word in e.** je ne peux pas en placer une

edgy ['edʒɪ] *adj* nerveux(euse); **to get e.** s'énerver

edible ['edɪbəl] *adj* (*safe to eat*) comestible; (*fit to eat*) mangeable

edict ['i:dɪkt] *n Formal* édit *m*

edification [edɪfɪ'keɪʃən] *n* édification *f*

edifice ['edɪfɪs] *n also Fig* édifice *m*

edify ['edɪfaɪ] (*pt & pp* **edified**) *vt* édifier

edifying ['edɪfaɪɪŋ] *adj* édifiant(e)

Edinburgh ['edɪnbrə] *n* Édimbourg

edit ['edɪt] *vt* (**a**) (*correct*) réviser; (*prepare for publication*) préparer pour la publication; **edited by** (*coordinated by*) sous la direction de (**b**) (*film*) monter (**c**) (*manage*) (*newspaper, magazine*) diriger (**d**) *Comput* éditer

▶**edit out** *vt sep* (*scene*) couper

editing ['edɪtɪŋ] *n Cin* montage *m*

edition [ɪ'dɪʃən] *n* (*of book, newspaper*) édition *f*; **in Tuesday's e. of the program** dans l'émission de mardi

editor ['edɪtə(r)] *n* (**a**) (*of published work*) (*author*) rédacteur(trice) *m,f*; (*in charge*) directeur(trice) *m,f* (**b**) (*of film*) monteur(euse) *m,f* (**c**) (*of newspaper, magazine*) rédacteur(trice) *m,f* en chef; (*of section*) rédacteur(trice) *m,f* (**d**) *Comput* (*software*) éditeur *m*

editorial [edɪ'tɔːrɪəl] **1** *n* éditorial *m*
2 *adj* de rédaction

EDP [i:di:'pi:] *n Comput* (*abbr* **electronic data processing**) traitement *m* électronique de l'information

educate ['edjʊkeɪt] *vt* éduquer, instruire; **he was educated at Harvard** il a fait ses études à Harvard

educated ['edjʊkeɪtɪd] *adj* instruit(e); **I made an e. guess** j'ai émis une hypothèse, mais je ne risquais guère de me tromper

education [edjʊ'keɪʃən] *n* (*process of learning, knowledge*) éducation *f*; (*process of teaching*) enseignement *m*; **to get (oneself) an e.** faire des études; **to complete one's e.** terminer ses études; *Fig* **it was an e. working over there** c'était instructif de travailler là-bas

educational [edjʊ'keɪʃənəl] *adj* (*system*) éducatif(ive); (*establishment, publisher*) scolaire; (*qualification*) d'enseignement; (*experience, visit*) instructif(ive)

Edwardian [ed'wɔːdɪən] *adj* (*architecture, furniture*) de l'époque d'Édouard VII; **the E. era** ≃ la Belle Époque

EEC [i:i:'si:] *n Formerly* (*abbr* **European Economic Community**) CEE *f*

eel [i:l] *n* anguille *f*

eerie ['ɪərɪ] *adj* (*atmosphere, cry*) sinistre; (*silence*) de mort; (*feeling*) étrange

eerily ['ɪərɪlɪ] *adv* étrangement

efface [ɪ'feɪs] *vt* effacer

effect [ɪ'fekt] **1** *n* (**a**) (*result*) effet *m* (**on** sur); **to take e.** (*of drug, medicine*) faire effet, agir; (*of law*) prendre effet; **to put sth into e.** mettre qch en application; **in e.** en fait; **or words to that e.** ou quelque chose d'approchant (**b**) (*impression*) effet *m*; **for e.** pour faire de l'effet (**c**) *Formal* **personal effects** effets *mpl* personnels
2 *vt Formal* (*cause*) (*change, rescue*) effectuer; (*saving, wish*) réaliser; (*solution*) apporter (**to** à)

effective [ɪ'fektɪv] *adj* (**a**) (*efficient, successful*) efficace; (*argument, speech*) convaincant(e) (**b**) (*actual, real*) (*profit, value*) réel(elle); **she will assume e. control of the business** c'est elle qui dirigera concrètement l'entreprise (**c**) *Law* (*in force*) **to be e.** prendre effet

effectively [ɪ'fektɪvlɪ] *adv* (**a**) (*efficiently*) avec efficacité; (*speak*) de façon convaincante (**b**) (*really*) en fait, en réalité;

they are e. the same en fait, ils sont identiques

effectiveness [ɪˈfektɪvnɪs] *n* efficacité *f*

effeminate [ɪˈfemɪnət] *adj* efféminé(e)

effervescent [efəˈvesənt] *adj also Fig* effervescent(e)

effete [ɪˈfiːt] *adj (person)* veule; *(gesture)* efféminé(e)

efficacious [efɪˈkeɪʃəs] *adj Formal* efficace

efficacy [ˈefɪkəsɪ] *n Formal* efficacité *f*

efficiency [ɪˈfɪʃənsɪ] *n* efficacité *f*; *(output, productivity)* rendement *m*

efficient [ɪˈfɪʃənt] *adj* efficace; *(productive)* performant(e); **to be e. at sth** faire qch avec compétence

efficiently [ɪˈfɪʃəntlɪ] *adv* efficacement

effigy [ˈefɪdʒɪ] *(pl* **effigies***) n* effigie *f*

effluent [ˈefluənt] *n* effluents *mpl*

effort [ˈefət] *n* (**a**) *(exertion)* effort *m*; **to make an e. (to do sth)** faire un effort (pour faire qch); **put some e. into it!** fais un effort!; **to be worth the e.** valoir la peine (**b**) *(attempt)* tentative *f* (**at doing sth** pour faire qch); **a good e.** un bel effort; **a poor e.** un effort insuffisant

effortless [ˈefətlɪs] *adj (victory, success)* facile; *(skill, grace)* naturel(elle)

effortlessly [ˈefətlɪslɪ] *adv* facilement, sans effort

effrontery [ɪˈfrʌntərɪ] *n* effronterie *f*

effusive [ɪˈfjuːsɪv] *adj (person)* démonstratif(ive), expansif(ive); *(welcome, speech)* enthousiaste

effusively [ɪˈfjuːsɪvlɪ] *adv (praise, welcome)* avec un enthousiasme débordant; *(thank)* avec effusion

EFL [iːeˈfel] *n (abbr* **English as a Foreign Language**) anglais *m* langue étrangère

EFT [iːefˈtiː] *n Comput (abbr* **electronic funds transfer**) transfert *m* de fonds électronique

EFTA [ˈeftə] *n (abbr* **European Free Trade Association**) AELE *f*

EFTPOS [ˈeftpɒs] *n Comput (abbr* **electronic funds transfer at point of sale**) transfert *m* de fonds électronique sur point de vente

e.g. [iːˈdʒiː] *adv (abbr* **exempli gratia**) p. ex.

egalitarian [ɪgælɪˈteərɪən] **1** *n* égalitariste *mf*
2 *adj (society)* égalitaire

egalitarianism [ɪgælɪˈteərɪənɪzəm] *n* égalitarisme *m*

egg [eg] *n* (**a**) *(of bird, fish, etc.)* œuf *m*; **e. flip** *(with milk)* lait *m* de poule; *(with alcohol)* lait de poule alcoolisé; *Culin* **e. roll** pâté *m* impérial; **e. timer** sablier *m*; **e. white** blanc *m* d'œuf; **e. yolk** jaune *m* d'œuf (**b**) *(idioms)* **a good e.** *(man)* un brave type; *(woman)* une brave fille; **a bad e.** *(man)* un sale type; *(woman)* une sale bonne femme; **to have e. on one's face** être ridicule; *Prov* **don't put all your eggs in one basket** il ne faut pas mettre tous ses œufs dans le même panier

▶**egg on** *vt sep* encourager (**to do sth** à faire qch)

eggcup [ˈegkʌp] *n* coquetier *m*

egghead [ˈeghed] *n Hum or Pej* intello *mf*

eggnog [ˈegnɒg] *n* lait *m* de poule alcoolisé

eggplant [ˈegplænt] *n* aubergine *f*

eggshell [ˈegʃel] *n* coquille *f* d'œuf

eggwhisk [ˈegwɪsk] *n* fouet *m*

egis [ˈiːdʒɪs] *n Formal* **under the e. of...** sous l'égide de...

ego [ˈiːgəʊ] *(pl* **egos***) n* ego *m*; **to have a big e.** être très imbu(e) de soi-même; **to give sb's e. a boost** flatter l'ego de qn; *Fam* **he's on an e. trip** il fait ça uniquement parce que ça flatte son ego

egocentric [iːgəʊˈsentrɪk] *adj* égocentrique

egoist [ˈiːgəʊɪst] *n* égoïste *mf*

egotism [ˈiːgəʊtɪzəm] *n* égocentrisme *m*

egotist [ˈiːgəʊtɪst] *n* égocentrique *mf*

egotistic [iːgəʊˈtɪstɪk], **egotistical** [iːgəʊˈtɪstɪkəl] *adj* égocentrique

e-government [ˈiːgʌvənmənt] *n Comput* administration *f* électronique

Egypt [ˈiːdʒɪpt] *n* l'Égypte *f*

Egyptian [ɪˈdʒɪpʃən] **1** *n* Égyptien(enne) *m,f*
2 *adj* égyptien(enne)

eiderdown [ˈaɪdədaʊn] *n* édredon *m*

eight [eɪt] **1** *n* huit *m inv*; **come at e.** venez à huit heures; **e. and e. are sixteen** huit et huit font seize; **there were e. of us** nous étions huit; **all e. of them left** tous les huit sont partis, ils sont partis tous les huit; **the e. of hearts** *(in cards)* le huit de cœur
2 *adj* huit; **e. cars** huit voitures; **e. dollars** huit dollars; **on page e.** (à la) page huit; **to be e. (years old)** avoir huit ans; **they live at number e.** ils habitent au numéro huit; **e. o'clock** huit heures; **it's e. minutes to five** il est cinq heures moins huit; *Tel* **e. hundred number** ≃ numéro *m* vert

eighteen [eɪˈtiːn] **1** *n* dix-huit *m inv*
2 *adj* dix-huit; *see also* **eight**

eighteenth [eɪˈtiːnθ] **1** *n* (**a**) *(fraction)* dix-huitième *m*; *(in series)* dix-huitième *mf* (**b**) *(of month)* dix-huit *m inv*
2 *adj* dix-huitième; *see also* **eighth**

eighth [eɪtθ] **1** *n* (**a**) *(fraction)* huitième *m*; *(in series)* huitième *mf*; **Edward the E.** Edouard Huit (**b**) *(of month)* huit *m inv*; **(on) May e.** le huit mai; **we're leaving on the e.** nous partons le huit
2 *adj* huitième; **e. floor** septième étage *m*; *Scol* **e. grade** = classe de lycée pour les 12-13 ans

eightieth [ˈeɪtɪθ] **1** *n (fraction)* quatre-vingtième *m*; *(in series)* quatre-vingtième *mf*
2 *adj* quatre-vingtième

eighty [ˈeɪtɪ] **1** *n* quatre-vingts *m inv*; **he was doing e.** *(in car)* il faisait du quatre-vingt (à l'heure); **in the eighties** *(decade)* dans les années quatre-vingt; **to be in one's eighties** avoir quatre-vingts ans passés; **the temperature was in the eighties** il faisait dans les vingt-cinq degrés
2 *adj* quatre-vingts; **e. cars/passengers** quatre-vingts voitures/passagers; **e. percent** quatre-vingt pour cent; **she's about e. (years old)** elle a dans les quatre-vingts ans

Eire [ˈeərə] *n* l'Eire *f*

either [ˈaɪðə(r), ˈiːðə(r)] **1** *adj* (**a**) *(one or the other)* l'un (l'une) ou l'autre; **I didn't like e. book** je n'ai aimé ni l'un ni l'autre de ces livres; **e. candidate may win** les deux candidats ont des chances de gagner (**b**) *(both)* les deux; **on e. side** des deux côtés; **in e. case** dans les deux cas
2 *pron (one or the other)* l'un (l'une) *m,f* ou l'autre; **e. (of them) will do** l'un ou l'autre fera l'affaire; **I don't want e. (of them)** je ne veux ni l'un ni l'autre; **I don't believe e. of you** je ne vous crois ni l'un ni l'autre
3 *conj* **e.... or...** ou... ou..., soit... soit...; **e. you or your brother** ou toi ou ton frère, soit toi soit ton frère; **she doesn't eat e. meat or fish** elle ne mange ni viande ni poisson; **e. come in or go out!** ou tu rentres ou tu sors!
4 *adv* **if you don't go, I won't go e.** si tu n'y vas pas, moi non plus; **I don't like him – I don't e.** je ne l'aime pas – moi non plus

either-or [ˈaɪðərɔː(r)] *adj* **it's an e. situation** c'est soit l'un soit l'autre

ejaculate [ɪˈdʒækjʊleɪt] *vi* (**a**) *(of man)* éjaculer (**b**) *Old-fashioned (exclaim)* s'écrier, s'exclamer

ejaculation [ɪdʒækjʊˈleɪʃən] *n* (**a**) *(of semen)* éjaculation *f* (**b**) *Old-fashioned (exclamation)* exclamation *f*

eject [ɪˈdʒekt] **1** *vt (cassette)* éjecter; *(troublemaker)* expulser
2 *vi (from plane)* s'éjecter

ejection [ɪˈdʒekʃən] *n (of cassette, from plane)* éjection *f*; *(of troublemaker)* expulsion *f*

ejector seat [ɪˈdʒektə(r)siːt] *n* siège *m* éjectable

▶**eke out** [i:k] *vt sep (money)* dépenser avec parcimonie; *(rations, supplies)* consommer avec parcimonie; **to e. out a living** gagner péniblement sa vie

elaborate1 *adj* [ɪ'læbərət] *(meal)* élaboré(e); *(drawing, description)* détaillé(e); *(excuse, scheme)* compliqué(e)
   2 *vt* [ɪ'læbəreɪt] *(formulate)* élaborer; *(flesh out)* développer
   3 *vi* [ɪ'læbəreɪt] être plus précis; **to e. on sth** donner plus de détails sur qch

elan [eɪ'lɑːn] *n Lit* impétuosité *f*

elapse [ɪ'læps] *vi* s'écouler

elastic [ɪ'læstɪk] **1** *n* élastique *m*
   2 *adj also Fig* élastique

elasticity [iːlæs'tɪsɪtɪ] *n also Fig* élasticité *f*

elasticized [ɪ'læstɪsaɪzd] *adj (garment, material)* extensible; *(waist)* élastique

elated [ɪ'leɪtɪd] *adj* transporté(e) (de joie)

elation [ɪ'leɪʃən] *n* exaltation *f*

elbow ['elbəʊ] **1** *n* coude *m*; **out at the elbows** *(of pullover, jacket)* troué(e) aux coudes; *Fig* **to give sb the e.** *(of employer)* se débarrasser de qn; *(of lover)* plaquer qn; *Fig* **to use some e. grease** mettre de l'huile de coude
   2 *vt* **to e. sb (in the ribs)** donner un coup de coude (dans les côtes) à qn; **to e. sb aside** écarter qn d'un coup de coude; *Fig* jouer des coudes pour évincer qn; **to e. one's way through** se frayer un passage en jouant des coudes

elbowroom ['elbəʊrʊm] *n Fam Fig* **to have enough e.** avoir assez de liberté

elder¹ ['eldə(r)] **1** *n* (**a**) *(older person)* aîné(e) *m,f*; **young people should respect their elders** les jeunes doivent le respect à leurs aînés (**b**) *(of tribe)* ancien(enne) *m,f*; *(of church)* = membre d'une congrégation protestante chargé de seconder le ministre dans certaines tâches
   2 *adj (brother, sister)* aîné(e); **e. statesman** grand homme *m* politique

elder² ['eldə(r)] *n (tree)* sureau *m*

elderberry ['eldəberɪ] *(pl* **elderberries**) *n* baie *f* de sureau

elderly ['eldəlɪ] **1** *npl* **the e.** les personnes *fpl* âgées
   2 *adj* âgé(e)

eldest ['eldɪst] **1** *n* **the e.** l'aîné(e) *m,f*
   2 *adj* aîné(e)

elect [ɪ'lekt] **1** *adj* élu(e)
   2 *vt* (**a**) *(councilor, Congressman)* élire (**b**) *Formal (choose)* **to e. to do sth** choisir de faire qch

election [ɪ'lekʃən] *n* élection *f*; **to hold an e.** procéder à une élection; **to run for e.** se présenter aux élections; **e. campaign** campagne *f* électorale

electioneering [ɪlekʃə'nɪərɪŋ] *n* propagande *f* électorale

elective [ɪ'lektɪv] **1** *n Univ (course)* option *f*
   2 *adj (assembly)* électoral(e); *Univ (course)* optionnel(elle); *Med* **e. surgery** chirurgie *f* de confort

elector [ɪ'lektə(r)] *n* électeur(trice) *m,f*

electoral [ɪ'lektərəl] *adj* électoral(e); **e. reform** réforme *f* du mode de scrutin; **e. roll** liste *f* électorale

electorate [ɪ'lektərət] *n* électorat *m*

electric [ɪ'lektrɪk] *adj* électrique; *Fig (atmosphere)* chargé(e) d'électricité; **e. blanket** couverture *f* chauffante; **e. blue** bleu *m* électrique; **e. chair** chaise *f* électrique; **e. cooker** cuisinière *f* électrique; **e. light** *(appliance)* lumière *f* électrique; *(lighting)* éclairage *m ou* lumière électrique; **e. shock** décharge *f* électrique; *Med* électrochoc *m*

electrical [ɪ'lektrɪkəl] *adj* électrique; **e. engineering** électrotechnique *f*

electrically [ɪ'lektrɪkəlɪ] *adv* **e. powered/operated** qui fonctionne à l'électricité; **e. charged** chargé(e) d'électricité

electrician [ɪlek'trɪʃən] *n* électricien(enne) *m,f*

electricity [ɪlek'trɪsɪtɪ] *n* électricité *f*

electrification [ɪlektrɪfɪ'keɪʃən] *n* électrification *f*

electrify [ɪ'lektrɪfaɪ] *(pt & pp* **electrified**) *vt* électrifier; *Fig (excite)* électriser

electrifying [ɪ'lektrɪfaɪɪŋ] *adj Fig* électrisant(e)

electrocardiogram [ɪlektrəʊ'kɑːdɪəʊgræm] *n Med* électrocardiogramme *m*

electrocardiograph [ɪlektrəʊ'kɑːdɪəʊgræf] *n Med* électrocardiographe *m*

electrocute [ɪ'lektrəkjuːt] *vt* électrocuter; **to e. oneself** s'électrocuter

electrocution [ɪlektrə'kjuːʃən] *n* électrocution *f*

electrode [ɪ'lektrəʊd] *n* électrode *f*

electrolysis [ɪlek'trɒlɪsɪs] *n* électrolyse *f*

electromagnet [ɪlektrəʊ'mægnɪt] *n* électroaimant *m*

electron [ɪ'lektrɒn] *n* électron *m*; **e. microscope** microscope *m* électronique

electronic [ɪlek'trɒnɪk] *adj* électronique; *Fin* **e. banking** bancatique *f*; *Comput* **e. mail** courrier *m* électronique; *Comput* **e. office** bureau *m* informatisé

electronically [ɪlek'trɒnɪklɪ] *adv* électroniquement

electronics [ɪlek'trɒnɪks] **1** *n (subject)* électronique *f*; **e. company** société *f* d'électronique; **the e. industry** l'industrie *f* (de l')électronique
   2 *npl* **the e.** *(of machine)* le système électronique

electroplated [ɪ'lektrəpleɪtɪd] *adj* plaqué(e) *(par électrodéposition)*

electroshock [ɪlektrəʊ'ʃɒk] *adj* **e. therapy** *or* **treatment** traitement *m* par électrochocs

elegance ['elɪgəns] *n* élégance *f*

elegant ['elɪgənt] *adj (person, appearance, movement)* élégant(e); *(reasoning)* clair(e) et simple

elegantly ['elɪgəntlɪ] *adv* avec élégance; **e. proportioned** aux proportions élégantes

elegy ['elɪdʒɪ] *(pl* **elegies**) *n* élégie *f*

element ['elɪmənt] *n* (**a**) *(constituent part)* part *f*; **an e. of danger/chance** une part de danger/chance; **this movie has all the elements of a hit movie** ce film réunit tous les ingrédients d'un grand succès (**b**) *(factor)* **the e. of surprise** l'effet *m* de surprise; **the human/time e.** le facteur humain/temps (**c**) *(in society)* élément *m*; **undesirable elements** éléments indésirables; **the hooligan e.** la frange constituée par les hooligans (**d**) *Chem* élément *m* (**e**) *(of kettle, electric fire)* résistance *f* (**f**) *(force of nature)* **the four elements** les quatre éléments; *Fig* **to brave the elements** braver les éléments; **to be in one's e.** être dans son élément

elemental [elɪ'mentəl] *adj* (**a**) *(basic)* fondamental(e) (**b**) *(primitive)* élémentaire, primitif(ive)

elementary [elɪ'mentərɪ] *adj* élémentaire; *(education)* primaire; **my Arabic is rather e.** je parle un arabe assez rudimentaire; **e. school** école *f* primaire

elephant ['elɪfənt] *n* éléphant *m*

elephantine [elɪ'fæntaɪn] *adj (movements)* lourd(e) et gauche; *(proportions)* éléphantesque

elevate ['elɪveɪt] *vt* élever (**to** à)

elevated ['elɪveɪtɪd] *adj (position, rank)* élevé(e); *(thoughts, discussion)* qui vole haut; *(language)* soutenu(e); **e. railway** métro *m* aérien

elevation [elɪ'veɪʃən] *n* (**a**) *(height)* altitude *f* (**b**) *(promotion)* élévation *f* (**to** à) (**c**) *Archit* élévation *f*

elevator ['elɪveɪtə(r)] *n* (**a**) *(for people)* ascenseur *m* (**b**) *(for goods)* élévateur *m* (**c**) *(on airplane wing)* gouvernail *m* de profondeur

eleven [ɪ'levən] **1** *n* onze *m inv*; **the French e.** *(football team)* le onze de France
   2 *adj* onze; *see also* **eight**

eleventh [ɪˈlevənθ] **1** *n* (**a**) *(fraction)* onzième *m*; *(in series)* onzième *mf* (**b**) *(of month)* onze *m inv*
   2 *adj* onzième; **at the e. hour** à la dernière minute; **e. floor** dixième étage *m*; *Scol* **e. grade** = classe de lycée pour les 15–16 ans; *see also* **eighth**

elf [elf] *(pl* **elves** [elvz]*)* *n* elfe *m*

elicit [ɪˈlɪsɪt] *vt (information, smile)* tirer (**from** de); *(reaction, response)* susciter (**from** de la part de)

eligibility [elɪdʒɪˈbɪlɪtɪ] *n (for grant, benefit)* droit *m* (**for** à); *(for job)* admissibilité *f*; *(to vote)* éligibilité *f*

eligible [ˈelɪdʒɪbəl] *adj (for job)* admissible; *(to vote)* éligible; **to be e. for a grant** avoir droit à une subvention; **e. bachelor** bon parti *m*

eliminate [ɪˈlɪmɪneɪt] *vt* éliminer

elimination [ɪlɪmɪˈneɪʃən] *n* élimination *f*; **by a process of e.** (en procédant) par élimination

elite [eɪˈliːt] **1** *n* élite *f*
   2 *adj* d'élite

elitism [eɪˈliːtɪzəm] *n* élitisme *m*

elitist [eɪˈliːtɪst] *n & adj* élitiste *mf*

elixir [ɪˈlɪksə(r)] *n Lit* élixir *m*

Elizabethan [ɪlɪzəˈbiːθən] **1** *n* = Anglais vivant sous le règne d'Élisabeth 1ère
   2 *adj* élisabéthain(e)

elk [elk] *n* élan *m*

ellipse [ɪˈlɪps] *n Math* ellipse *f*

ellipsis [ɪˈlɪpsɪs] *(pl* **ellipses** [ɪˈlɪpsiːz]*)* *n Gram* ellipse *f*

elliptical [ɪˈlɪptɪkəl] *adj* elliptique

elm [elm] *n* orme *m*

elocution [eləˈkjuːʃən] *n* élocution *f*, diction *f*

elongate [ˈiːlɒŋɡeɪt] *vt* allonger

elope [ɪˈləʊp] *vi* s'enfuir (pour se marier)

eloquence [ˈeləkwəns] *n* éloquence *f*

eloquent [ˈeləkwənt] *adj* éloquent(e)

else [els] *adv* **anyone e.** n'importe qui; *(in negative sentences)* personne d'autre; **is anyone e. interested?** quelqu'un d'autre est-il intéressé?; **someone e.** quelqu'un d'autre; **everyone e.** tous les autres; **no one e.** personne d'autre; **anything e.** n'importe quoi d'autre; *(in negative sentences)* rien d'autre; **do you have anything e. to do?** as-tu autre chose à faire?; **something e.** autre chose, quelque chose d'autre; **everything e.** tout le reste; **nothing e.** rien d'autre; **somewhere e.** autre part, ailleurs; **anywhere e.** (n'importe où) ailleurs; *(in negative sentences)* nulle part ailleurs; **everywhere e.** partout ailleurs; **nowhere e.** nulle part ailleurs; **who e. was there?** qui d'autre était là?; **who broke it? – Peter, who e.?** qui l'a cassé? – Peter, qui d'autre veux-tu que ce soit!; **what e.?** quoi d'autre?; **when e.?** à quel autre moment/quelle autre date?; **where e. did you go?** où êtes-vous allés encore?; **how e.?** de quelle autre manière?; **why e.?** pour quelle autre raison?; **little e.** pas grand-chose d'autre; **there isn't much e. we can do** nous ne pouvons pas faire grand-chose d'autre; **or e.** *(otherwise)* sinon; **do what I tell you or e.!** fais ce que je te dis ou sinon...!

elsewhere [ˈelsweə(r)] *adv* ailleurs, autre part

ELT [iːelˈtiː] *n (abbr* **English Language Teaching**) anglais *m* langue étrangère

elucidate [ɪˈluːsɪdeɪt] *vt (mystery)* élucider; *(reasons)* expliquer

elude [ɪˈluːd] *vt* échapper à

elusive [ɪˈluːsɪv] *adj (person)* insaisissable; *(concept)* difficile à saisir

elver [ˈelvə(r)] *n* civelle *f*

elves [elvz] *pl of* **elf**

emaciated [ɪˈmeɪsɪeɪtɪd] *adj* émacié(e)

e-mail [ˈiːmeɪl] **1** *n* courrier *m* électronique, mél *m*, *Can* courriel *m*; **e. address** adresse *f* électronique
   2 *vt (person)* envoyer un courrier électronique à; *(file, message)* envoyer par courrier électronique

emanate [ˈeməneɪt] **1** *vt* dégager
   2 *vi* émaner (**from** de)

emancipate [ɪˈmænsɪpeɪt] *vt* émanciper

emancipated [ɪˈmænsɪpeɪtɪd] *adj* émancipé(e)

emancipation [ɪmænsɪˈpeɪʃən] *n* émancipation *f*

e-marketing [ˈiːmɑːkɪtɪŋ] *n Comput* e-marketing *m*, web-marketing *m*

emasculate [ɪˈmæskjʊleɪt] *vt Fig* amputer

embalm [ɪmˈbɑːm] *vt* embaumer

embankment [ɪmˈbæŋkmənt] *n (beside railroad)* talus *m*; *(beside river)* berge *f*, quai *m*

embargo [emˈbɑːɡəʊ] *(pl* **embargoes**) **1** *n* embargo *m*; **to put an e. on** mettre un embargo sur
   2 *vt* mettre un embargo sur

embark [ɪmˈbɑːk] *vi* embarquer; *Fig* **to e. (up)on sth** s'embarquer dans qch

embarrass [ɪmˈbærəs] *vt* embarrasser, gêner; *(make ashamed)* faire honte à

embarrassed [ɪmˈbærəst] *adj (ashamed, uncomfortable)* embarrassé(e), gêné(e); *(financially)* gêné(e) (financièrement)

embarrassing [ɪmˈbærəsɪŋ] *adj* embarrassant(e), gênant(e); **how e.!** comme ça a dû être/c'est embarrassant!

embarrassment [ɪmˈbærəsmənt] *n* embarras *m*, gêne *f*; **much to my e.** à mon grand embarras; **to be an e. to sb** être une source d'embarras pour qn

embassy [ˈembəsɪ] *(pl* **embassies**) *n* ambassade *f*; **the French E.** l'ambassade de France

embattled [ɪmˈbætəld] *adj* assiégé(e) de toutes parts

embed [ɪmˈbed] *(pt & pp* **embedded**) *vt* (**a**) **to be embedded in sth** être fiché(e) dans qch; *(with cement)* être scellé(e) dans qch; *Fig* **to be embedded in sb's memory** être gravé(e) dans la mémoire de qn; *Fig* **embedded journalist/reporter** journaliste *mf* reporter *mf* embarqué(e) (**b**) *Comput* intégrer

embellish [ɪmˈbelɪʃ] *vt (room)* embellir (**with** de); *(account)* enjoliver

embers [ˈembəz] *npl* braises *fpl*

embezzle [ɪmˈbezəl] *vt* détourner (**from** de)

embezzlement [ɪmˈbezəlmənt] *n* **e. (of funds)** détournement *m* de fonds

embezzler [ɪmˈbezlə(r)] *n* escroc *m*

embitter [ɪmˈbɪtə(r)] *vt (person)* aigrir, remplir d'amertume

embittered [ɪmˈbɪtəd] *adj (person)* aigri(e)

emblazon [ɪmˈbleɪzən] *vt (shield)* orner (**with** de); *Fig (name, headline)* étaler

emblem [ˈembləm] *n* emblème *m*

embodiment [ɪmˈbɒdɪmənt] *n* incarnation *f*

embody [ɪmˈbɒdɪ] *(pt & pp* **embodied**) *vt* incarner

embolden [ɪmˈbəʊldən] *vt* enhardir; **to e. sb to do sth** donner à qn le courage de faire qch

embolism [ˈembəlɪzəm] *n Med* embolie *f*

embossed [ɪmˈbɒst] *adj (metal, leather)* repoussé(e); *(letter, wallpaper, design)* en relief

embrace [ɪmˈbreɪs] **1** *n* étreinte *f*
   2 *vt* (**a**) *(person)* étreindre; *Fig (belief, religion)* embrasser (**b**) *(include)* couvrir
   3 *vi* s'étreindre

embroider [ɪmˈbrɔɪdə(r)] *vt (cloth)* broder; *Fig (account, report)* enjoliver

embroidery [ɪmˈbrɔɪdərɪ] *n* broderie *f*

embroil [ɪmˈbrɔɪl] *vt* entraîner (**in** dans); **to get embroiled in sth** se laisser entraîner dans qch

embryo [ˈembrɪəʊ] *(pl* **embryos**) *n* embryon *m*; *Fig* **in e.** *(plan, idea)* à l'état embryonnaire

embryonic [embrɪˈɒnɪk] *adj Biol* embryonnaire; *(plan, idea)* à l'état embryonnaire

emend [ɪˈmend] *vt* corriger

emendation [iːmenˈdeɪʃən] *n* correction *f*

emerald [ˈemərəld] *n* émeraude *f*; **an e. necklace** un collier d'émeraudes; **e. (green)** (vert *m*) émeraude *m*; **the E. Isle** *(Ireland)* la verte Érin

emerge [ɪˈmɜːdʒ] *vi (of person, truth)* émerger (**from** de); **it later emerged that...** il est apparu par la suite que...

emergence [ɪˈmɜːdʒəns] *n (from hiding)* apparition *f*; *(of truth)* révélation *f*; *(of new state, new leader)* émergence *f*

emergency [ɪˈmɜːdʒənsɪ] *(pl* **emergencies)** *n* urgence *f*; **in an e., in case of e.** en cas d'urgence; **e. contraception** contraception *f* d'urgence; **e. exit** sortie *f* de secours; **e. landing** atterrissage *m* forcé; *Pol* **e. powers** pouvoirs *mpl* extraordinaires; *Med* **e. room** salle *f* des urgences; **e. services** services *mpl* d'urgence; **e. stop** arrêt *m* d'urgence; *Fin* **e. tax** impôt *m* extraordinaire

emergent [ɪˈmɜːdʒənt] *adj (talent, ability)* naissant(e); *(nation)* en voie de développement

emery [ˈemərɪ] *n* émeri *m*; **e. board** lime *f* à ongles *(en papier émeri)*; **e. paper** papier *m* émeri

emetic [ɪˈmetɪk] **1** *n* émétique *m*
  2 *adj* émétique

emigrant [ˈemɪɡrənt] **1** *n* émigrant(e) *m,f*; *(when settled)* émigré(e) *m,f*
  2 *adj* migrant(e); *(when settled)* émigré(e)

emigrate [ˈemɪɡreɪt] *vi* émigrer

emigration [emɪˈɡreɪʃən] *n* émigration *f*

émigré [ˈemɪɡreɪ] *n* émigré(e) *m,f*

eminence [ˈemɪnəns] *n* **(a)** *(importance)* position *f* éminente; *(of post)* distinction *f* **(b)** *(title of cardinal)* **Your E.** Votre Éminence

eminent [ˈemɪnənt] *adj* éminent(e)

eminently [ˈemɪnəntlɪ] *adv* éminemment

emirate [ˈemɪreɪt] *n* émirat *m*

emissary [ˈemɪsərɪ] *(pl* **emissaries)** *n* émissaire *m*

emission [ɪˈmɪʃən] *n (of gas, light, bank notes)* émission *f*

emit [ɪˈmɪt] *(pt & pp* **emitted)** *vt (heat, signal, sound)* émettre; *(smell)* dégager; *(sigh, cry)* pousser

emoticon [ɪˈməʊtɪkɒn] *n Comput* émoticon *m, Can* binette *f*

emotion [ɪˈməʊʃən] *n (strength of feeling)* émotion *f*; *(individual feeling)* sentiment *m*; **full of e.** ému(e)

emotional [ɪˈməʊʃənəl] *adj (person, reaction)* émotif(ive); *(problem, shock)* émotionnel(elle); *(movie, farewell)* émouvant(e); **to get e.** être ému(e)

emotionally [ɪˈməʊʃənəlɪ] *adv (thank, welcome)* avec effusion; **to be e. involved with sb** avoir une relation intime avec qn; **to get e. involved (with sb)** s'attacher (à qn); **e. deprived** en manque d'affection

emotive [ɪˈməʊtɪv] *adj (issue)* sensible; *(argument, words)* qui fait vibrer la corde sensible

empathize [ˈempəθaɪz] *vi* **to e. with** *(person)* comprendre; *(plight, problems)* compatir à

empathy [ˈempəθɪ] *n* affinité(s) *f(pl)*; *(power, ability)* capacité *f* à s'identifier à autrui

emperor [ˈempərə(r)] *n* empereur *m*

emphasis [ˈemfəsɪs] *(pl* **emphases** [ˈemfəsɪːz]) *n* accent *m*; **to lay** *or* **to place e. on sth** *(point, fact)* mettre l'accent sur qch; *(word, syllable)* appuyer sur qch

emphasize [ˈemfəsaɪz] *vt (point, fact)* insister sur; *(word, syllable)* appuyer sur

emphatic [ɪmˈfætɪk] *adj (denial, response, person)* catégorique; *(gesture, tone)* énergique

emphatically [ɪmˈfætɪkəlɪ] *adv (say)* énergiquement; *(refuse, deny)* catégoriquement; **most e.!** absolument!

empire [ˈempaɪə(r)] *n also Fig* empire *m*

empirical [emˈpɪrɪkəl] *adj* empirique

empiricism [emˈpɪrɪsɪzəm] *n* empirisme *m*

employ [ɪmˈplɔɪ] **1** *n Formal* **to be in sb's e.** être employé(e) par qn
  2 *vt (workers, force, skills)* employer; *(tool, means)* utiliser

employability [ɪmplɔɪəˈbɪlɪtɪ] *n* employabilité *f*

employable [ɪmˈplɔɪəbəl] *adj (person)* employable; *(method)* utilisable; **a good education makes you more e.** une bonne éducation donne plus de chances de trouver du travail

employee [emˈplɔɪiː] *n* employé(e) *m,f*; **employees** *(staff)* personnel *m*, salariés *mpl*

employer [ɪmˈplɔɪə(r)] *n* employeur(euse) *m,f*

employment [ɪmˈplɔɪmənt] *n* **(a)** *(work)* emploi *m*; **to be in e.** avoir un emploi; **to be without e.** être sans emploi; **to give e. to sb** employer qn; **e. agency** *or* **bureau** agence *f* ou bureau *m* de placement **(b)** *(use) (of money, force)* emploi *m*; *(of tool)* utilisation *f*

empower [ɪmˈpaʊə(r)] *vt* **to e. sb to do sth** habiliter qn à faire qch

empowering [ɪmˈpaʊərɪŋ] *adj (role, effect)* émancipateur(trice)

empress [ˈemprɪs] *n* impératrice *f*

emptiness [ˈemptɪnɪs] *n* vide *m*

empty [ˈemptɪ] **1** *n (pl* **empties)** *(bottle)* bouteille *f* vide
  2 *adj (container, existence)* vide; *(promise, threat, words)* en l'air; **on an e. stomach** l'estomac vide, à jeun
  3 *vt (pt & pp* **emptied)** vider
  4 *vi* se vider

▶**empty out** *vt sep (pockets)* vider

empty-handed [ˈemptɪˈhændɪd] *adv* les mains vides, bredouille

empty-headed [ˈemptɪˈhedɪd] *adj* sans cervelle; **to be e.** n'avoir rien dans la tête

EMS [iːemˈes] *n (abbr* **European Monetary System)** SME *m*

EMU [iːemˈjuː] *n (abbr* **Economic and Monetary Union)** union *f* économique et monétaire

emu [ˈiːmjuː] *n* émeu *m*

emulate [ˈemjʊleɪt] *vt* imiter

emulsion [ɪˈmʌlʃən] *n* émulsion *f*

enable [ɪˈneɪbəl] *vt* **(a)** *(allow)* **to e. sb to do sth** permettre à qn de faire qch **(b)** *Comput (function, device)* mettre en service

enact [ɪˈnækt] *vt (tragedy, play)* jouer; *(law)* promulguer

enamel [ɪˈnæməl] **1** *n* émail *m*
  2 *vt* émailler

enamored [ɪˈnæməd] *adj* **to be e. of** être entiché(e) de; **I'm not exactly e. of the idea** je ne peux pas dire que cette idée me ravisse

encampment [ɪnˈkæmpmənt] *n Mil* camp *m*, campement *m*

encapsulate [ɪnˈkæpsjʊleɪt] *vt* résumer

encase [ɪnˈkeɪs] *vt* envelopper; *(in concrete)* noyer

enchant [ɪnˈtʃɑːnt] *vt* **(a)** *(charm)* enchanter, ravir **(b)** *(put under a spell)* ensorceler

enchanting [ɪnˈtʃɑːntɪŋ] *adj (idea)* très séduisant(e); *(voice, person, smile)* charmant(e), ravissant(e)

enchantment [ɪnˈtʃɑːntmənt] *n* enchantement *m*

enchantress [ɪnˈtʃɑːntrɪs] *n* enchanteresse *f*

enchilada [entʃɪˈlɑːdə] *n Culin* enchilada *f*; *Fam* **big e.** *(person)* huile *f*; **the whole e.** *(everything)* tout le tremblement

encircle [ɪnˈsɜːkəl] *vt (of road, walls)* entourer; *(of army, police)* encercler, cerner

enclave [ˈenkleɪv] *n* enclave *f*

enclose [ɪnˈkləʊz] *vt* **(a)** *(surround)* entourer; **an enclosed space** un espace clos **(b)** *(include in letter)* joindre (**in** à); **enclosed please find..., please find enclosed...** veuillez trouver ci-joint *ou* ci-inclus...

enclosure [ɪnˈkləʊʒə(r)] *n* **(a)** *(area)* enceinte *f*; *(for animals)* enclos *m*; *(in horseracing)* paddock *m* (**b**) *(in letter)* pièce *f* jointe

encode [en'kəʊd] *vt* coder, chiffrer; *Comput* encoder

encompass [ɪn'kʌmpəs] *vt* englober, couvrir

encore ['ɒŋkɔ:(r)] *n* = chanson, morceau, etc. exécuté à la suite d'un rappel; **to call for an e.** bisser; **e.!** bis!

encounter [ɪn'kaʊntə(r)] **1** *n* rencontre *f*

   2 *vt (person, difficulty)* rencontrer; *(enemy)* affronter

encourage [ɪn'kʌrɪdʒ] *vt* encourager; **to e. sb to do sth** encourager qn à faire qch

encouragement [ɪn'kʌrɪdʒmənt] *n* encouragement *m*; **to give sb e.** encourager qn

encouraging [ɪn'kʌrɪdʒɪŋ] *adj* encourageant(e); *(smile)* d'encouragement

▶**encroach on, encroach upon** [ɪn'krəʊtʃ] *vt insep* empiéter sur; **the sea is encroaching on the land** la mer gagne du terrain

encrusted [ɪn'krʌstɪd] *adj* **e. with** *(jewels)* incrusté(e) de; *(mud)* couvert(e) de

encrypt [en'krɪpt] *vt Comput* crypter, encrypter, chiffrer

encumber [ɪn'kʌmbə(r)] *vt Formal* **to be encumbered with** être encombré(e) par

encumbrance [ɪn'kʌmbrəns] *n Formal* gêne *f*, embarras *m* (**to** pour)

encyclical [ɪn'sɪklɪkəl] *n Rel* encyclique *f*

encyclopedia [ɪnsaɪklə'pi:dɪə] *n* encyclopédie *f*

encyclopedic [ɪnsaɪklə'pi:dɪk] *adj* encyclopédique

end [end] **1** *n* (**a**) *(extremity)* bout *m*, extrémité *f*; **from one e. to the other** d'un bout à l'autre; **e. to e.** bout à bout; **to stand sth on e.** mettre qch debout; **his hair was standing on e.** ses cheveux se dressaient sur sa tête; *Fig* **to come to the e. of the road** *or* **line** être en fin de parcours

   (**b**) *(of month, book, meeting)* fin *f*; **for days on e.** pendant des jours entiers; **to put an e. to sth** mettre fin à qch; **to come to an e.** prendre fin; *Fig* **at the e. of the day** au bout du compte; **in the e.** finalement; **she gave me the money back in the e.** elle a fini par me rembourser; **it's not the e. of the world** ce n'est pas la fin du monde; *Fam* **no e. of** énormément de; **e. product** produit *m* fini; *Fig* résultat *m*; **e. user** utilisateur *m* final

   (**c**) *(aim, purpose)* fin *f*, but *m*; **an e. in itself** une fin en soi; **to what e.?** à quelle fin?, dans quel but?; **with this e. in view** dans ce but, à cette fin; **the e. justifies the means** la fin justifie les moyens

   (**d**) *(idioms) Fam* **to make ends meet** joindre les deux bouts; *Fam* **this job will be the e. of me!** ce boulot, j'y laisserai ma peau!; **we shall never hear the e. of it!** on n'a pas fini d'en entendre parler!

   2 *vt* finir, terminer; *(argument, uncertainty)* mettre fin à; *Fam* **to e. it all** *(commit suicide)* en finir

   3 *vi* finir, se terminer; *(of road, path)* s'arrêter; **it ended in a fight/a divorce** ça a fini en bagarre/par un divorce

▶**end up** *vi* finir; *(in particular place)* se retrouver; **to e. up doing sth** finir par faire qch

endanger [ɪn'deɪndʒə(r)] *vt (person, life)* mettre en danger; *(chances, future, health)* compromettre; **an endangered species** une espèce menacée

endear [ɪn'dɪə(r)] *vt* **to e. oneself to sb** se rendre sympathique aux yeux de qn; **these remarks did not e. her to the voters** ces réflexions ne lui ont pas gagné la faveur des électeurs

endearing [ɪn'dɪərɪŋ] *adj (person, personality)* attachant(e); *(smile, habit)* charmant(e)

endearment [ɪn'dɪəmənt] *n* **terms of e.** mots *mpl* tendres

endeavor [ɪn'devə(r)] *Formal* **1** *n* effort *m*

   2 *vt* **to e. to do sth** s'efforcer de faire qch

endemic [en'demɪk] *adj* endémique; *Fig* **e. to** propre à

ending ['endɪŋ] *n (of story)* fin *f*; *(of word)* terminaison *f*

endive ['endaɪv] *n* endive *f*

endless ['endlɪs] *adj (desert, number, possibilities)* infini(e); *(list, wait, task)* interminable

endocrine ['endəʊkraɪn] *adj Med* **e. gland** glande *f* endocrine

endocrinology [endəʊkraɪ'nɒlədʒɪ] *n* endocrinologie *f*

endorse [ɪn'dɔ:s] *vt* (**a**) *(document, check)* endosser (**b**) *(approve) (action)* approuver; *(opinion)* souscrire *ou* adhérer à; *(candidature)* appuyer (**c**) *(product)* faire de la publicité pour; **sportswear endorsed by top athletes** des vêtements de sport recommandés par des sportifs de haut niveau

endorsement [ɪn'dɔ:smənt] *n* (**a**) *(on document, check)* endos *m* (**b**) *(approval) (of action)* approbation *f* (**of** de); *(of opinion)* adhésion *f* (**of** à); *(of candidature)* appui *m* (**of** à) (**c**) *(of product)* **the movie star has made a fortune from her e. of cosmetic products** cette vedette du cinéma a gagné une fortune en faisant de la publicité pour des cosmétiques

endow [ɪn'daʊ] *vt* doter (**with** de)

endowment [ɪn'daʊmənt] *n* (**a**) *Fin* dotation *f* (**b**) *(talent)* don *m*, talent *m*

endurable [ɪn'djʊərəbəl] *adj* supportable

endurance [ɪn'djʊərəns] *n* endurance *f*; **beyond e.** au-delà des limites du supportable; **e. test** épreuve *f* d'endurance; *Fig* **this is a real e. test** ma patience est mise à rude épreuve

endure [ɪn'djʊə(r)] **1** *vt (violence, hardship)* endurer; *(person, insults)* supporter

   2 *vi (last)* survivre

enduring [ɪn'djʊərɪŋ] *adj* durable

enema ['enəmə] *n* lavement *m*

enemy ['enəmɪ] **1** *n (pl* **enemies***)* ennemi(e) *m,f*; **to make enemies** se faire des ennemis; **to be one's own worst e.** se desservir soi-même

   2 *adj (army, ship)* ennemi(e)

energetic [enə'dʒetɪk] *adj* énergique

energetically [enə'dʒetɪklɪ] *adv* énergiquement

energy ['enədʒɪ] *n* énergie *f*; **to save e.** faire des économies d'énergie; **e. crisis** crise *f* de l'énergie

energy-saving ['enədʒɪseɪvɪŋ] *adj* qui économise l'énergie

enervating ['enəveɪtɪŋ] *adj* débilitant(e)

enfeeble [ɪn'fi:bəl] *vt* affaiblir

enfold [ɪn'fəʊld] *vt* envelopper (**in** dans); **to e. sb in one's arms** serrer qn dans ses bras

enforce [ɪn'fɔ:s] *vt (regulation)* mettre en vigueur; *(rights)* faire valoir; **to e. the law** faire respecter la loi

enforcement [ɪn'fɔ:smənt] *n (of a law)* mise *f* en vigueur

enfranchise [ɪn'fræntʃaɪz] *vt* accorder le droit de vote à

engage [ɪn'geɪdʒ] **1** *vt* (**a**) *(employ)* engager; *(workmen)* embaucher (**b**) *(occupy) (person)* occuper; *(attention)* fixer; **to e. sb in conversation** engager la conversation avec qn; **to be engaged in doing sth** être occupé(e) à faire qch (**c**) *Mil (enemy)* attaquer (**d**) *(cog, gear)* mettre en prise; **to e. the clutch** embrayer

   2 *vi* (**a**) **to e. in** *(activity, sport)* s'adonner à (**b**) *(of cog wheel)* (s')engager

engaged [ɪn'geɪdʒd] *adj* (**a**) *(to be married)* fiancé(e) (**b**) *(busy)* occupé(e) (**in** à); **to be otherwise e.** avoir d'autres engagements

engagement [ɪn'geɪdʒmənt] *n* (**a**) *(to be married)* fiançailles *fpl*; **e. ring** bague *f* de fiançailles (**b**) *(appointment)* rendez-vous *m inv* (**c**) *(military action)* combat *m*, engagement *m*

engaging [ɪn'geɪdʒɪŋ] *adj* engageant(e), attrayant(e)

engender [ɪn'dʒendə(r)] *vt* faire naître, engendrer

engine ['endʒɪn] *n* (**a**) *(of car, plane, ship)* moteur *m*; **e. room** salle *f* des machines; **e. trouble** panne *f* de moteur (**b**) *(of train)* locomotive *f*; **e. driver** conducteur *m*, mécanicien *m*

engineer [endʒɪ'nɪə(r)] **1** *n* (**a**) *(technical specialist)* ingénieur *m*; *(mechanic)* dépanneur *m*; *(on ship)* mécanicien *m* (**b**) *(train*

driver) conducteur(trice) *m,f,* mécanicien(enne) *m,f*
 2 *vt (cause) (plan, downfall, defeat)* machiner, manigancer; *(situation)* manigancer

engineering [endʒɪˈnɪərɪŋ] *n* ingénierie *f*

England [ˈɪŋɡlənd] *n* l'Angleterre *f*

English [ˈɪŋɡlɪʃ] **1** *n (language)* anglais *m*; **E. class/teacher** cours *m*/professeur *m* d'anglais
 2 *npl* **the E.** les Anglais *mpl*
 3 *adj* anglais(e); **the E. Channel** la Manche

Englishman [ˈɪŋɡlɪʃmən] *n* Anglais *m*

Englishwoman [ˈɪŋɡlɪʃwʊmən] *n* Anglaise *f*

engrave [ɪnˈɡreɪv] *vt* graver

engraver [ɪnˈɡreɪvə(r)] *n* graveur *m*

engraving [ɪnˈɡreɪvɪŋ] *n* gravure *f*

engrossed [ɪnˈɡrəʊst] *adj* plongé(e) (**in** dans), absorbé(e) (**in** par)

engrossing [ɪnˈɡrəʊsɪŋ] *adj* absorbant(e), captivant(e)

engulf [ɪnˈɡʌlf] *vt (of waves, flames)* engloutir; *(of feeling)* s'emparer de

enhance [ɪnˈhɑːns] *vt (quality of life, chances)* améliorer; *(beauty, color)* rehausser, mettre en valeur; *(ability, effect)* renforcer; *(reputation, pleasure)* accroître; *(value)* augmenter

enigma [ɪˈnɪɡmə] *n* énigme *f*

enigmatic [enɪɡˈmætɪk] *adj* énigmatique

enjoy [ɪnˈdʒɔɪ] *vt* (**a**) *(take pleasure from)* prendre plaisir à; *(movie, book, concert)* aimer; *(food, drink)* savourer; **to e. doing sth** aimer faire qch; **to e. oneself** s'amuser (**b**) *(benefit from)* jouir de

enjoyable [ɪnˈdʒɔɪəbəl] *adj* agréable

enjoyment [ɪnˈdʒɔɪmənt] *n* plaisir *m*; **to get e. out of sth** retirer du plaisir de qch; **to get e. out of doing sth** prendre plaisir à faire qch

enlarge [ɪnˈlɑːdʒ] **1** *vt* agrandir; *(hole)* élargir
 2 *vi* s'agrandir; **to e. (up)on sth** s'étendre sur qch

enlargement [ɪnˈlɑːdʒmənt] *n* agrandissement *m*; *(of hole)* élargissement *m*

enlighten [ɪnˈlaɪtən] *vt* éclairer (**on** sur)

enlightened [ɪnˈlaɪtənd] *adj* éclairé(e)

enlightenment [ɪnˈlaɪtənmənt] *n (clarification)* éclaircissement *m*; **for your e.** pour votre édification; *Hist* **the E.** le Siècle des Lumières

enlist [ɪnˈlɪst] **1** *vt (support, help)* s'assurer; *(soldier)* enrôler, engager
 2 *vi (of soldier)* s'engager

enliven [ɪnˈlaɪvən] *vt* animer; *(party)* égayer, animer

en masse [ˈɒnˈmæs] *adv* en masse, tous ensemble

enmesh [ɪnˈmeʃ] *vt* **to be enmeshed in sth** être empêtré(e) dans qch

enmity [ˈenmɪtɪ] *n* inimitié *f*, hostilité *f*

enormity [ɪˈnɔːmɪtɪ] *n* énormité *f*

enormous [ɪˈnɔːməs] *adj (in physical size)* énorme; *(patience, gratitude, power, intelligence)* immense; *(strength)* colossal(e)

enormously [ɪˈnɔːməslɪ] *adv* énormément

enough [ɪˈnʌf] **1** *adj* assez de; **e. money/wine** assez d'argent/de vin; **more than e. food** plus de nourriture qu'il n'en faut
 2 *pron* assez; **to be e.** suffire; **more than e.** plus qu'il n'en faut; **that's e.!** ça suffit!; **e. is e.** il ne faut pas exagérer; **to have e. to live on** avoir de quoi vivre; **e. said!** je vois!; **to have had e. of sb/sth** en avoir assez de qn/qch
 3 *adv* (**a**) *(sufficiently)* assez; **good e.** assez bon (bonne); **he didn't try hard e.** il n'a pas vraiment essayé (**b**) *(reasonably)* assez; **she's a nice e. girl** c'est une fille assez sympa; **oddly** *or* **strangely e.,...** chose curieuse,...

enquire = **inquire**

enquiry = **inquiry**

enrage [ɪnˈreɪdʒ] *vt* rendre furieux(euse)

enrapture [ɪnˈræptʃə(r)] *vt* éblouir, émerveiller

enraptured [ɪnˈræptʃəd] *adj* ébloui(e), émerveillé(e)

enrich [ɪnˈrɪtʃ] *vt* enrichir

enroll [ɪnˈrəʊl] **1** *vt (soldier)* enrôler; *(student)* immatriculer; *(worker)* embaucher
 2 *vi (of soldier)* s'enrôler; *(of students)* s'inscrire

enrollment [ɪnˈrəʊlmənt] *n (of soldier)* enrôlement *m*; *(of student)* immatriculation *f*; *(of worker)* embauche *f*

ensconce [ɪnˈskɒns] *vt* **to e. oneself** s'installer confortablement (**in** dans)

ensemble [ɒnˈsɒmbəl] *n* ensemble *m*

enshrine [ɪnˈʃraɪn] *vt* **to be enshrined in sth** *(of belief, principle)* être enraciné(e) dans qch

ensign [ˈensaɪn] *n* (**a**) *(flag)* drapeau *m*; *Naut* pavillon *m* national (**b**) *(naval officer)* enseigne *m (de vaisseau de deuxième classe)*

enslave [ɪnˈsleɪv] *vt* réduire à l'esclavage, asservir

ensnare [ɪnˈsneə(r)] *vt (animal, criminal)* prendre au piège; *Fig (lover)* attirer dans ses filets

ensue [ɪnˈsjuː] *vi* s'ensuivre

ensuing [ɪnˈsjuːɪŋ] *adj (in the past)* qui a suivi; *(in the future)* qui suivra

en suite [ˈɒnˈswiːt] *adj* **e. bathroom** *(in hotel)* salle *f* de bains particulière; *(in house)* salle *f* de bains attenante

ensure [ɪnˈʃʊə(r)] *vt* assurer; **to e. that...** faire en sorte que... + *subjunctive*

ENT [iːenˈtiː] *n (abbr* **Ear, Nose and Throat**) ORL *f*; **E. specialist** ORL *mf*

entail [enˈteɪl] *vt* (**a**) *(involve)* entraîner, occasionner; *(difficulties)* comporter; **what does the job e.?** en quoi le travail consiste-t-il? (**b**) *Law* **to e. an estate** substituer un bien

entangle [ɪnˈtæŋɡəl] *vt* **to get** *or* **to become entangled in sth** *(of person, animal)* s'empêtrer dans qch; *(of hair, string, wires)* s'emmêler dans qch; *Fig* **he got entangled in the dispute** il s'est retrouvé impliqué dans la dispute

entanglement [ɪnˈtæŋɡəlmənt] *n* enchevêtrement *m*; **emotional entanglements** complications *fpl* sentimentales

enter [ˈentə(r)] **1** *vt* (**a**) *(house, country, army)* entrer dans; *(university)* entrer à; *(race, exam, competition)* participer à; **to e. sb for an exam** inscrire qn à un examen; **to e. sb for a race** inscrire qn au nombre des participants d'une course; **it never entered my head that...** il ne m'est jamais venu à l'esprit que...; **to e. a protest** protester formellement (**b**) *Comput (data)* entrer, introduire
 2 *vi (go in)* entrer; **to e. for a race** se faire inscrire pour une course

▸**enter into** *vt insep* (**a**) *(begin) (service, relationship)* entrer en; *(dispute)* entrer dans; *(negotiations)* entamer, engager; **to e. into partnership with sb** s'associer avec qn; **to e. into conversation with sb** engager une conversation avec qn (**b**) *(have a part in)* **money doesn't e. into it** l'argent n'entre pas en ligne de compte

enterprise [ˈentəpraɪz] *n* (**a**) *(undertaking, company)* entreprise *f* (**b**) *(initiative)* initiative *f*

enterprising [ˈentəpraɪzɪŋ] *adj* entreprenant(e); *(imaginative)* plein(e) d'imagination; *(solution)* ingénieux(euse)

entertain [entəˈteɪn] **1** *vt* (**a**) *(amuse)* divertir, amuser; **to e. guests** recevoir (des invités) (**b**) *(consider) (idea)* considérer; *(hope)* nourrir; *(fear, suspicion)* éprouver
 2 *vi (receive guests)* recevoir

entertainer [entəˈteɪnə(r)] *n* fantaisiste *mf*; *(comedian)* comique *mf*

entertaining [entəˈteɪnɪŋ] **1** *n (of guests)* **to do a lot of e.** recevoir beaucoup
 2 *adj (amusing)* divertissant(e), amusant(e)

entertainment [entəˈteɪnmənt] *n* (**a**) *(amusement)* divertissement *m*, amusement *m* (**b**) *(performances)* spectacle *m*, divertissement *m*; **the e. business** l'industrie *f* du spectacle; **e. guide** guide *m* des spectacles

enthrall [ɪn'θrɔːl] *vt* captiver, passionner; *(of object, beauty)* fasciner; *(of prospect, idea)* enthousiasmer

enthralling [ɪn'θrɔːlɪŋ] *adj* captivant(e), passionnant(e); *(object, beauty)* fascinant(e); *(prospect, idea)* enthousiasmant(e)

enthuse [ɪn'θjuːz] **1** *vt* enthousiasmer
2 *vi* s'enthousiasmer (**about** *or* **over** pour)

enthusiasm [ɪn'θjuːzɪæzəm] *n* enthousiasme *m*

enthusiast [ɪn'θjuːzɪæst] *n* passionné(e) *m,f*; **a golf e.** un passionné de golf

enthusiastic [ɪnθjuːzɪ'æstɪk] *adj* enthousiaste

enthusiastically [ɪnθjuːzɪ'æstɪklɪ] *adv* avec enthousiasme

entice [ɪn'taɪs] *vt* attirer, séduire; **to e. sb to do sth** inciter qn à faire qch; **to e. sb away from sb/sth** appâter qn pour qu'il quitte qn/qch

enticing [ɪn'taɪsɪŋ] *adj (offer, idea)* séduisant(e), tentant(e); *(dish)* alléchant(e); *(smile)* charmeur(euse)

entire [ɪn'taɪə(r)] *adj* (**a**) *(whole)* entier(ère), tout(e); **the e. day** toute la journée, la journée entière (**b**) *(intact)* intact(e)

entirely [ɪn'taɪəlɪ] *adv* entièrement, complètement

entirety [ɪn'taɪərətɪ] *n* intégralité *f*; **in its e.** dans son intégralité, intégralement

entitle [ɪn'taɪtəl] *vt* (**a**) *(allow)* **to e. sb to sth** donner à qn droit à qch; **to e. sb to do sth** permettre à qn de faire qch; **to be entitled to sth** avoir droit à qch; **to be entitled to do sth** avoir le droit de faire qch (**b**) *(book, chapter, song)* intituler

entitlement [ɪn'taɪtəlmənt] *n* droit *m* (**to** à); **holiday e.** congé *m* annuel *(auquel on a droit)*

entity ['entɪtɪ] *n (pl* **entities)** *n* entité *f*

entomologist [entə'mɒlədʒɪst] *n* entomologiste *mf*

entomology [entə'mɒlədʒɪ] *n* entomologie *f*

entourage ['ɒntuːrɑːʒ] *n* entourage *m*

entrails ['entreɪlz] *npl* entrailles *fpl*

entrance¹ ['entrəns] *n* (**a**) *(way in, act of entering)* entrée *f*; **to make one's e.** faire son entrée; **to gain e. to** s'introduire *ou* pénétrer dans (**b**) *(admission) (to club)* admission *f*; *(to movies)* entrée *f*; **e. examination** examen *m* d'entrée; **e. hall** *(in house)* vestibule *m*; *(in hotel)* hall *m*

entrance² [ɪn'trɑːns] *vt (charm)* ravir, transporter

entrancing [ɪn'trɑːnsɪŋ] *adj* ravissant(e), enchanteur(eresse)

entrant ['entrənt] *n (in race, competition)* inscrit(e) *m,f*; *(in examination)* candidat(e) *m,f*

entreat [ɪn'triːt] *vt* **to e. sb to do sth** implorer qn de faire qch

entreaty [ɪn'triːtɪ] *n (pl* **entreaties)** *n* prière *f*, supplication *f*

entrée ['ɒntreɪ] *n (dish before main course)* entrée *f*; *(main course)* plat *m* principal *ou* de résistance

entrenched [ɪn'trentʃd] *adj (views, ideas)* arrêté(e); *(customs)* enraciné(e)

entrepreneur [ɒntrəprə'nɜː(r)] *n* entrepreneur *m*

entrepreneurial [ɒntrəprə'nɜːrɪəl] *adj (person)* qui a l'esprit d'entreprise; *(skill, talents)* d'entrepreneur

entrepreneurship [ɒntrəprə'nɜːʃɪp] *n* entrepreneuriat *m*

entrust [ɪn'trʌst] *vt* **to e. sb with sth, to e. sth to sb** confier qch à qn

entry ['entrɪ] *n (pl* **entries)** *n* (**a**) *(way in, act of entering)* entrée *f*; **to make one's e.** faire son entrée; **to gain e. to** s'introduire *ou* pénétrer dans (**b**) *(of competitor)* inscription *f*; **e. form** feuille *f* d'inscription (**c**) *(in encyclopedia)* article *m*; *(in dictionary)* entrée *f*; *(in diary)* note *f*

entwine [ɪn'twaɪn] **1** *vt* entrelacer
2 *vi* s'entrelacer

enumerate [ɪ'njuːməreɪt] *vt* énumérer, détailler

enunciate [ɪ'nʌnsɪeɪt] *vt (sound, word)* prononcer, articuler; *(opinion, view)* énoncer

envelop [ɪn'veləp] *vt* envelopper (**in** dans)

envelope ['envələup, 'ɒnvələup] *n* enveloppe *f*

enviable ['envɪəbəl] *adj* enviable

envious ['envɪəs] *adj* envieux(euse); **to be e. of sb** envier qn

enviously ['envɪəslɪ] *adv* avec envie

environment [ɪn'vaɪrənmənt] *n* (**a**) *(surroundings)* milieu *m*; **a pleasant working e.** des conditions *fpl* de travail agréables; **a hostile e.** un climat d'hostilité, une ambiance hostile (**b**) *(nature)* **the e.** l'environnement *m*

environmental [ɪnvaɪrən'mentəl] *adj* **e. damage** dégâts *mpl* causés à l'environnement; **e. disaster** désastre *m* écologique; **e. policy** politique *f* de l'environnement; **E. Protection Agency** = agence américaine pour la protection de l'environnement; **e. science** science *f* de l'environnement

environmentalist [ɪnvaɪrən'mentəlɪst] *n* écologiste *mf*

environment-friendly [ɪn'vaɪrənmentfrendlɪ], **environmentally-friendly** [ɪnvaɪrən'mentəlɪ'frendlɪ] *adj (policy)* respectueux(euse) de l'environnement; *(technology, product)* non polluant(e)

environs [ɪn'vaɪrənz] *npl* environs *mpl*, alentours *mpl*

envisage [ɪn'vɪzɪdʒ], **envision** [en'vɪʒən] *vt* envisager

envoy ['envɔɪ] *n* envoyé(e) *m,f*

envy ['envɪ] **1** *n* envie *f*, jalousie *f*; **to be the e. of sb** être un objet d'envie pour qn
2 *vt (pt & pp* **envied)** envier; **to e. sb sth** envier qch à qn

enzyme ['enzaɪm] *n* enzyme *f*

eon ['iːən] *n* Fig période *f* incommensurable; **I haven't seen him in eons** je ne l'ai pas vu depuis une éternité *ou* des lustres

epaulet ['epələt] *n* épaulette *f*

e-petition ['iːpə'tɪʃən] *n* Comput e-pétition *f*

ephemeral [ɪ'femərəl] *adj* éphémère

epic ['epɪk] **1** *n (poem, novel)* épopée *f*; *(movie)* film *m* à grand spectacle
2 *adj* épique

epicenter ['epɪsentə(r)] *n* épicentre *m*

epicurean [epɪkjʊ'rɪən] *n & adj* épicurien(enne) *m,f*

epidemic [epɪ'demɪk] *also Fig* **1** *n* épidémie *f*
2 *adj* épidémique

epidermis [epɪ'dɜːmɪs] *n Anat* épiderme *m*

epidural [epɪ'djuːrəl] *n Med* péridurale *f*

epigram ['epɪgræm] *n* épigramme *f*

epilepsy ['epɪlepsɪ] *n* épilepsie *f*

epileptic [epɪ'leptɪk] **1** *n* épileptique *mf*
2 *adj* épileptique; **e. fit** crise *f* d'épilepsie

epilog, epilogue ['epɪlɒg] *n* épilogue *m*

Epiphany [ɪ'pɪfənɪ] *n* Épiphanie *f*

episcopal [ɪ'pɪskəpəl] *adj* épiscopal(e); **e. palace** évêché *m*

episcopalian [ɪpɪskə'peɪlɪən] *n & adj* épiscopalien(enne) *m,f*

episode ['epɪsəud] *n (part of story)* épisode *m*; *(incident)* incident *m*

epistle [ɪ'pɪsəl] *n also Hum* épître *f*

epitaph ['epɪtɑːf] *n* épitaphe *f*

epithet ['epɪθet] *n* épithète *f*

epitome [ɪ'pɪtəmɪ] *n* **to be the e. of sth** être l'exemple même de qch

epitomize [ɪ'pɪtəmaɪz] *vt* incarner

epoch ['iːpɒk] *n* époque *f*

epoch-making ['iːpɒkmeɪkɪŋ] *adj* qui fait date

eponymous [ɪ'pɒnɪməs] *adj* éponyme

EPS [iːpiː'es] *n (abbr* **earnings per share)** BPA *m*

equable ['ekwəbəl] *adj* constant(e); *(person)* à l'humeur égale

equal ['iːkwəl] **1** *n* égal(e) *m,f*; **to treat sb as an e.** traiter qn d'égal à égal
2 *adj* (**a**) *(identical)* égal(e) (**to** à); **all things being e.** en principe; **in e. measure** en quantité égale; **on e. terms** sur un pied d'égalité; **e. opportunities** égalité *f* des chances; **e.**

pay égalité des salaires; **e. rights** égalité des droits (**b**) (*good enough*) **to be e. to sth** être à la hauteur de qch

3 *vt* égaler

equality [ɪˈkwɒlɪtɪ] *n* égalité *f*

equalize [ˈiːkwəlaɪz] **1** *vt* égaliser; (*chances, forces*) équilibrer

2 *vi* (*in sport*) égaliser

equalizer [ˈiːkwəlaɪzə(r)] *n* (**a**) (*in sport*) but *m* égalisateur (**b**) *Elec* égaliseur *m* de potentiel

equally [ˈiːkwəlɪ] *adv* (**a**) (*to an equal degree*) tout aussi (**b**) (*in equal amounts*) (*share, divide*) en parts égales (**c**) (*likewise*) tout aussi bien, de la même manière

equanimity [ekwəˈnɪmɪtɪ] *n* sérénité *f*

equate [ɪˈkweɪt] *vt* assimiler (**with** avec)

equation [ɪˈkweɪʒən] *n* équation *f*; *Fig* **money doesn't even enter the e.** les questions d'argent n'entrent même pas en ligne de compte

equator [ɪˈkweɪtə(r)] *n* équateur *m*

equatorial [ekwəˈtɔːrɪəl] *adj* équatorial(e); **E. Guinea** la Guinée équatoriale

equestrian [ɪˈkwestrɪən] **1** *n* cavalier(ère) *m,f*; (*in circus*) écuyer(ère) *m,f*

2 *adj* (*sport, ability*) équestre

equidistant [ekwɪˈdɪstənt] *adj* équidistant(e)

equilateral [ekwɪˈlætərəl] *adj* équilatéral(e)

equilibrium [ekwɪˈlɪbrɪəm] *n* équilibre *m*

equinox [ˈekwɪnɒks] *n* équinoxe *m*

equip [ɪˈkwɪp] (*pt & pp* **equipped**) *vt* (**a**) (*provide with equipment*) équiper (**with** de); **the plane is equipped with the latest technology** l'avion est doté des équipements les plus modernes (**b**) (*prepare*) préparer (**for** pour)

equipment [ɪˈkwɪpmənt] *n* équipement *m*; (*in factory*) installations *fpl*, matériel *m*

equitable [ˈekwɪtəbəl] *adj* équitable

equity [ˈekwɪtɪ] (*pl* **equities**) *n* (**a**) (*fairness*) équité *f* (**b**) *Fin* (*of stockholders*) fonds *mpl ou* capitaux *mpl* propres; (*of company*) capital *m* actions; **equities** actions *fpl* ordinaires

equivalent [ɪˈkwɪvələnt] **1** *n* équivalent *m*

2 *adj* équivalent(e) (**to** à)

equivocal [ɪˈkwɪvəkəl] *adj* équivoque, ambigu(ë)

equivocate [ɪˈkwɪvəkeɪt] *vi* user d'équivoques *ou* de faux-fuyants

equivocation [ɪkwɪvəˈkeɪʃən] *n* paroles *fpl* équivoques, faux-fuyants *mpl*

ER [iːˈɑː(r)] *n* (*abbr* **Emergency Room**) urgences *fpl*

era [ˈɪərə] *n* ère *f*

eradicate [ɪˈrædɪkeɪt] *vt* éradiquer

erase [ɪˈreɪz] *vt* effacer; (*with eraser*) gommer

eraser [ɪˈreɪzə(r)] *n* gomme *f*

erect [ɪˈrekt] **1** *adj* droit(e), debout; (*penis, nipples*) en érection

2 *vt* (*building*) ériger; (*statue*) élever, ériger; (*scaffolding*) dresser

erection [ɪˈrekʃən] *n* (**a**) (*of building, statue*) construction *f*, érection *f* (**b**) (*erect penis*) érection *f*

ergonomic [ɜːɡəˈnɒmɪk] *adj* ergonomique

ergonomics [ɜːɡəˈnɒmɪks] *n* ergonomie *f*

Eritrea [errɪˈtreɪə] *n* l'Érythrée *f*

Eritrean [errɪˈtreɪən] **1** *n* Érythréen(enne) *m,f*

2 *adj* érythréen(enne)

ERM [iːɑːˈrem] *n* (*abbr* **Exchange Rate Mechanism**) mécanisme *m* de change (*du SME*)

ermine [ˈɜːmɪn] *n* hermine *f*

erode [ɪˈrəud] **1** *vt* (*rock, soil*) éroder; (*metal*) corroder, ronger; *Fig* (*confidence, power*) miner

2 *vi* (*of rock, soil*) s'éroder; (*of metal*) se corroder; *Fig* (*of confidence, power*) s'éroder peu à peu

erogenous [ɪˈrɒdʒɪnəs] *adj* érogène; **e. zone** zone *f* érogène

Eros [ˈɪərɒs] *n* Éros

erosion [ɪˈrəuʒən] *n* (*of rock, soil*) & *Fig* (*of confidence, power*) érosion *f*; (*of metal*) corrosion *f*

erotic [ɪˈrɒtɪk] *adj* érotique

eroticism [ɪˈrɒtɪsɪzəm] *n* érotisme *m*

err [ɜː(r)] *vi* (*make mistake*) faire erreur; **to e. on the side of caution** pécher par excès de prudence; *Prov* **to e. is human** l'erreur est humaine

errand [ˈerənd] *n* commission *f*, course *f*; **to run errands for sb** (aller) faire des commissions *ou* des courses pour qn; **I did** *or* **ran all the errands** j'ai fait toutes les commissions *ou* les courses; *Old-fashioned* **e. boy** garçon *m* de courses

erratic [ɪˈrætɪk] *adj* (*service, results, pulse*) irrégulier(ère); (*playing, performance*) inégal(e); (*behavior*) imprévisible; (*person*) lunatique; (*driving*) mal assuré(e)

erroneous [ɪˈrəunɪəs] *adj* erroné(e)

error [ˈerə(r)] *n* (*mistake*) erreur *f*, faute *f*; **to make an e.** faire une erreur; **in e.** par erreur; **an e. of judgment** une erreur de jugement; **to see the e. of one's ways** reconnaître ses erreurs

ersatz [ˈɜːzæts] *adj* **e. coffee** un succédané de café

erstwhile [ˈɜːstwaɪl] *adj* *Lit* ancien(enne)

erudite [ˈerudaɪt] *adj* érudit(e)

erudition [eruˈdɪʃən] *n* érudition *f*

erupt [ɪˈrʌpt] *vi* (*of volcano*) entrer en éruption; (*of person*) exploser; (*of anger, violence*) éclater; (*of pimple*) sortir

eruption [ɪˈrʌpʃən] *n* éruption *f*

escalate [ˈeskəleɪt] *vi* (*of prices*) monter en flèche; (*of conflict*) s'intensifier, s'aggraver

escalation [eskəˈleɪʃən] *n* (*of prices*) montée *f* en flèche; (*of conflict*) escalade *f*

escalator [ˈeskəleɪtə(r)] *n* escalier *m* roulant, Escalator® *m*

escalope [ˈeskəlɒp] *n* escalope *f*

escapade [ˈeskəpeɪd] *n* fredaine *f*, frasque *f*

escape [ɪsˈkeɪp] **1** *n* (*of person*) évasion *f*; (*of gas, water*) fuite *f*; **to make one's e.** s'échapper; *Com* **e. clause** clause *f* échappatoire; **e. route** (*from fire*) itinéraire *m* de sortie de secours; (*of criminal*) itinéraire *m* emprunté pour s'échapper

2 *vt* (*danger, punishment*) échapper à; **to e. sb's notice** échapper à l'attention de qn; **her name escapes me** son nom m'échappe

3 *vi* (*of person, gas, water*) s'échapper (**from** de); (*from prison*) s'évader (**from** de); **to e. unhurt** s'en tirer indemne; **he escaped to Italy** il s'est enfui en Italie; **to e. from reality** s'évader de la réalité

escapee [eskerˈpiː] *n* évadé(e) *m,f*

escapism [ɪsˈkeɪpɪzəm] *n* évasion *f* (hors de la réalité)

escapist [ɪsˈkeɪpɪst] **1** *n* personne *f* qui cherche à s'évader de la réalité

2 *adj* (*movie, literature*) d'évasion

escapologist [eskəˈpɒlədʒɪst] *n* prestidigitateur *m* spécialiste de l'évasion

escarpment [ɪsˈkɑːpmənt] *n* escarpement *m*

eschew [ɪsˈtʃuː] *vt* *Formal* éviter; **to e. sb's company** fuir *ou* éviter qn

escort 1 *n* [ˈeskɔːt] (**a**) (*for convoy*) escorte *f*; (*for tourists*) guide *m*; (*ship*) bâtiment *m* d'escorte; **under e.** sous escorte; *Mil* **e. duty** service *m* d'escorte (**b**) (*from agency*) (*woman*) hôtesse *f*; (*man*) cavalier *m*; **e. agency** agence *f* d'hôtesses

2 *vt* [ɪsˈkɔːt] escorter; (*prisoner*) conduire sous escorte

escudo [eˈskuːdəu] (*pl* **escudos**) *n* *Formerly* escudo *m*

e-signature *n* *Comput* signature *f* électronique, e-signature *f*

Eskimo [ˈeskɪməu] **1** *n* (*pl* **Eskimos**) Esquimau(aude) *m,f*

2 *adj* esquimau(aude), eskimo *inv*

esophagus [iːˈsɒfəgəs] (*pl* **esophagi** [iːˈsɒfəgaɪ]) *n* œsophage *m*

esoteric [esəuˈterɪk] *adj* ésotérique

ESP [iːesˈpiː] n (abbr **extrasensory perception**) perception f extra-sensorielle

especially [ɪsˈpeʃəlɪ] adv (a) (in particular) surtout (b) (more than normally) particulièrement; **we were e. lucky with the weather** le temps nous a été particulièrement favorable (c) (expressly) (tout) spécialement, exprès; **I did it e. for you** je l'ai fait spécialement ou exprès pour vous

Esperanto [espəˈræntəʊ] n l'Espéranto m

espionage [ˈespɪɑːnɑːʒ] n espionnage m

esplanade [espləˈneɪd] n esplanade f

espouse [ɪsˈpaʊz] vt épouser

espresso [esˈpresəʊ] (pl **espressos**) n express m, expresso m

Esq. (abbr **Esquire**) Derek Wilson, E. = Monsieur Derek Wilson

essay [ˈeseɪ] n (at school) composition f; (for younger pupils) rédaction f; (at university) dissertation f

essayist [ˈeseɪɪst] n essayiste mf

essence [ˈesəns] n (a) (most important part or quality) essence f; (of speech) essentiel m; (of question) fond m; **in e.** essentiellement, surtout; **the very e. of bravery** le courage même; **time is of the e.** le temps est le facteur prioritaire (b) Culin (extract) extrait m

essential [ɪˈsenʃəl] 1 npl **essentials** (basic foodstuffs) produits mpl de première nécessité; (basic issues) essentiel m; **just pack a few essentials** ne prends que l'essentiel
2 adj (a) (basic) essentiel(elle); **e. oil** huile f essentielle (b) (indispensable) essentiel(elle), indispensable (**to** or **for** à); **it is e. that...** il est essentiel que... + subjunctive

essentially [ɪˈsenʃəlɪ] adv essentiellement

EST [iːesˈtiː] n (abbr **Eastern Standard Time**) heure f de la côte est de l'Amérique du Nord

establish [ɪsˈtæblɪʃ] vt (a) (set up) (company) fonder; (custom) instaurer; (system, organization) établir; **to e. oneself in business** s'établir dans les affaires; **to e. a reputation** se faire une réputation; **the movie established her as an important director** avec ce film, elle s'est affirmée comme un metteur en scène important (b) (prove) établir

established [ɪsˈtæblɪʃt] adj établi(e); (fact) acquis(e)

establishment [ɪsˈtæblɪʃmənt] n (a) **the E.** (dominant group) l'establishment m; (prevailing values) l'ordre m établi (b) (hotel, restaurant) établissement m (c) (of company, organization) constitution f; (of fact) constatation f

estate [ɪsˈteɪt] n (a) Law (possessions) biens mpl; **e. tax** impôt sur les biens (b) (land) terre f, propriété f

esteem [ɪsˈtiːm] 1 n estime f, considération f; **to hold sb in high e.** tenir qn en haute estime; **to hold sb in low e.** avoir peu d'estime pour qn
2 vt (a) (person) estimer; (thing) priser (b) Formal (consider) considérer; **she esteemed it a great honor to be invited** elle se sentit fort honorée d'avoir été invitée

esthetic [iːsˈθetɪk] adj esthétique

esthetics [iːsˈθetɪks] n esthétique f

estimate 1 n [ˈestɪmət] (calculation) évaluation f, calcul m; Com devis m; **at a rough e.** à vue de nez
2 vt [ˈestɪmeɪt] estimer, évaluer; (value) estimer

estimation [estɪˈmeɪʃən] n (a) (calculation) estimation f, évaluation f (b) (judgment) jugement m, opinion f; **in my e.** à mon avis; **to go up/down in sb's e.** monter/descendre dans l'estime de qn

Estonia [esˈtəʊnɪə] n l'Estonie f

Estonian [esˈtəʊnɪən] 1 n (a) (person) Estonien(enne) m,f (b) (language) estonien m
2 adj estonien(enne)

estranged [ɪsˈtreɪndʒd] adj (couple) séparé(e); **her e. husband** son mari, dont elle est séparée; **their e. son** leur fils, avec qui ils sont brouillés

estrogen [ˈiːstrədʒən] n œstrogène m

estuary [ˈestjʊərɪ] (pl **estuaries**) n estuaire m

ETA [iːtiːˈeɪ] n (abbr **estimated time of arrival**) heure f d'arrivée prévue

e-tail [ˈiːteɪl] n vente f en ligne

et al [etˈæl] (abbr **et alii**) et autres

etc. [etˈsetrə] adv (abbr **et cetera**) etc.

etch [etʃ] vt graver à l'eau-forte; Fig **to be etched in sb's memory** être gravé(e) dans la mémoire de qn

etching [ˈetʃɪŋ] n (gravure f à l')eau-forte f

eternal [ɪˈtɜːnəl] adj éternel(elle); Fig (continual) continuel(elle), sans fin

eternally [ɪˈtɜːnəlɪ] adv éternellement

eternity [ɪˈtɜːnɪtɪ] n éternité f; Fam **to wait/to last an e.** attendre/durer une éternité; **e. ring** = bague entièrement sertie de pierres symbolisant l'éternité du mariage

ether [ˈiːθə(r)] n éther m

ethereal [ɪˈθɪərɪəl] adj éthéré(e); (fragile) léger(ère), impalpable

ethical [ˈeθɪkəl] adj éthique, moral(e)

ethically [ˈeθɪklɪ] adv sur le plan éthique; **to behave e.** suivre la déontologie

ethics [ˈeθɪks] npl éthique f, morale f; (of profession) déontologie f

Ethiopia [iːθɪˈəʊpɪə] n l'Éthiopie f

Ethiopian [iːθɪˈəʊpɪən] 1 n (person) Éthiopien(enne) m,f
2 adj éthiopien(enne)

ethnic [ˈeθnɪk] adj ethnique; **e. cleansing** purification f ethnique; **e. minority** minorité f ethnique

ethnically [ˈeθnɪklɪ] adv du point de vue ethnique

ethnocentric [eθnəʊˈsentrɪk] adj ethnocentrique

ethnography [eθˈnɒɡrəfɪ] n ethnographie f

ethnology [eθˈnɒlədʒɪ] n ethnologie f

ethos [ˈiːθɒs] n (of people) génie m; (of class) culture f

e-ticket [ˈiːtɪkɪt] n billet m électronique

etiquette [ˈetɪket] n étiquette f; **professional e.** usages mpl professionnels

Etruscan [ɪˈtrʌskən] 1 n (a) (person) Étrusque mf (b) (language) étrusque m
2 adj étrusque

etymological [etɪməˈlɒdʒɪkəl] adj étymologique

etymology [etɪˈmɒlədʒɪ] n étymologie f

EU [iːˈjuː] n (abbr **European Union**) UE f

eucalyptus [juːkəˈlɪptəs] n eucalyptus m

Eucharist [ˈjuːkərɪst] n **the E.** l'eucharistie f

eulogize [ˈjuːlədʒaɪz] vt faire l'éloge de

eulogy [ˈjuːlədʒɪ] (pl **eulogies**) n éloge m

eunuch [ˈjuːnək] n eunuque m

euphemism [ˈjuːfɪmɪzəm] n euphémisme m

euphemistic [juːfɪˈmɪstɪk] adj euphémique

euphoria [juːˈfɔːrɪə] n euphorie f

euphoric [juːˈfɔːrɪk] adj euphorique

Eurasian [jʊəˈreɪʒən] 1 n Eurasien(enne) m,f
2 adj eurasien(enne); (continent) eurasiatique

EURATOM [jʊəˈrætəm] n (abbr **European Atomic Energy Community**) CEEA f, EURATOM f

eureka [jʊəˈriːkə] exclam eurêka!

Euro, euro [ˈjʊərəʊ] (pl **Euros, euros**) n (European currency) euro m; **E. area, E. zone** zone f euro

Eurocrat [ˈjʊərəʊkræt] n eurocrate mf

Eurodollar [ˈjʊərəʊdɒlə(r)] n eurodollar m

Euro-election [ˈjʊərəʊɪˈlekʃən] n **the Euro-elections** les élections fpl européennes

Euroland [ˈjʊərəʊlænd] n Eurolande f, la zone euro

Euro-MP [ˈjʊərəʊempiː] n député(e) m,f européen(enne)

Europe [ˈjʊərəp] n l'Europe f

European [jʊərəˈpiːən] 1 n Européen(enne) m,f

2 *adj* européen(enne); **E. Commission** Commission *f* européenne; **E. Community** Communauté *f* européenne; **E. Court of Human Rights** Cour *f* européenne des droits de l'homme; **E. Court of Justice** Cour de justice européenne; **E. Currency Unit** unité *f* monétaire européenne; **E. Economic Community** Communauté *f* économique européenne; **E. Free Trade Association** Association *f* européenne de libre-échange; **E. Monetary System** Système *m* monétaire européen; **E. Parliament** Parlement *m* européen; **E. Union** Union *f* européenne

Europhile [ˈjʊərəʊˈfaɪl] *n* europhile *mf*, partisan *m* de l'Europe unie

Eurostar® [ˈjʊərəʊstɑː(r)] *n* Eurostar® *m*

Eustachian tube [juːsˈteɪʃənˈtjuːb] *n Anat* trompe *f* d'Eustache

euthanasia [juːθəˈneɪzɪə] *n* euthanasie *f*

evacuate [ɪˈvækjʊeɪt] *vt* évacuer

evacuation [ɪvækjʊˈeɪʃən] *n* évacuation *f*

evacuee [ɪvækjʊˈiː] *n* évacué(e) *m,f*

evade [ɪˈveɪd] *vt (blow)* esquiver, éviter; *(question)* éluder; *(pursuer)* échapper à; *(responsibilities)* se soustraire à, se dérober à; **to e. tax** frauder le fisc

evaluate [ɪˈvæljʊeɪt] *vt* évaluer

evaluation [ɪvæljʊˈeɪʃən] *n* évaluation *f*

evangelical [iːvænˈdʒelɪkəl] **1** *n* protestant(e) *m,f* évangélique **2** *adj* évangélique

evangelism [ɪˈvændʒɪlɪzəm] *n* évangélisme *m*

evangelist [ɪˈvændʒɪlɪst] *n* évangéliste *mf*

evangelize [ɪˈvændʒɪlaɪz] **1** *vt* évangéliser; *(person)* prêcher l'Évangile à **2** *vi* prêcher l'Évangile

evaporate [ɪˈvæpəreɪt] **1** *vt* faire évaporer; **evaporated milk** lait *m* condensé **2** *vi (of liquid)* s'évaporer; *Fig (of enthusiasm, hope)* s'envoler

evaporation [ɪvæpəˈreɪʃən] *n* évaporation *f*

evasion [ɪˈveɪʒən] *n (escape)* évasion *f*, fuite *f*; *(of pursuer, responsibilities, question)* dérobade *f*; **(tax) e.** fraude *f* fiscale

evasive [ɪˈveɪsɪv] *adj (person, reply)* évasif(ive); **to take e. action** faire une manœuvre d'évitement

eve [iːv] *n (day before)* veille *f*; **on the e. of** à la veille de

even [ˈiːvən] **1** *adj (a) (flat)* égal(e); *(smooth)* uni(e) **(b)** *(regular) (breathing, pace)* régulier(ère), égal(e); *(temperature)* constant(e); **to have an e. temper** être d'humeur égale; **e. number** nombre *m* pair **(c)** *(equal)* **to have an e. chance (of doing sth)** avoir une chance sur deux (de faire qch); *Fig* **to get e. with sb** prendre sa revanche sur qn **2** *adv* **(a)** même; *(with comparatives)* encore; **without e. speaking** sans même dire un mot; **I never e. saw it** je ne l'ai même pas vu; **e. bigger/more interesting** encore plus gros (grosse)/intéressant(e); **e. as I speak** au moment même où je parle **(b)** *(in phrases)* **e. if** même si; **e. now** même maintenant, aujourd'hui encore; **e. so** cependant, quand même; **e. then** *(already)* déjà (à cette époque); *(all the same)* même dans ces conditions; **e. though** bien que + *subjunctive* **3** *vt (make equal)* rendre égal(e); **to e. the odds** égaliser les chances

▸**even out 1** *vt sep (differences)* niveler; *(workload)* répartir plus également; *(inequalities)* réduire; **to e. things out** rendre les choses équitables **2** *vi (of differences)* se niveler; *(of workload)* être réparti(e) plus également; *(of inequalities)* se réduire

▸**even up** *vt sep* égaliser; **to e. things up** équilibrer les choses

even-handed [ˈiːvənˈhændɪd] *adj* juste, équitable

evening [ˈiːvnɪŋ] *n* soir *m*; *(referring to duration)* soirée *f*; **tomorrow e.** demain soir; **yesterday e.** hier soir; **good e.!**,

Fam **e.!** bonsoir!; **in the e.** le soir; **a musical/cultural e.** une soirée musicale/culturelle; **e. class** cours *m* du soir; **e. dress** *(for men)* tenue *f* de soirée; *(for women)* robe *f* du soir; **e. paper** journal *m* du soir; **e. performance** *(of play)* représentation *f* en soirée

evenly [ˈiːvənlɪ] *adv* **(a)** *(uniformly)* uniformément **(b)** *(regularly) (breathe)* régulièrement, de façon régulière; *(speak)* calmement **(c)** *(equally) (divide, distribute)* également, de façon égale; **e. matched** *(in size)* de grandeur égale; *(in strength)* de force égale

evensong [ˈiːvənsɒŋ] *n Rel* office *m* du soir

event [ɪˈvent] *n* **(a)** *(occurrence)* événement *m*; **in any e.** en tout cas; **in the e. of fire** en cas d'incendie; **in the e. of her refusing** au cas où elle refuserait; **after the e.** après coup; **e. manager** responsable *mf* d'événements; **e. organizer** organisateur(trice) *m,f* d'événements **(b)** *(in athletics)* épreuve *f*

even-tempered [ˈiːvənˈtempəd] *adj* d'humeur égale

eventful [ɪˈventfʊl] *adj (day, life)* mouvementé(e), riche en événements

eventual [ɪˈventjʊəl] *adj* final(e), définitif(ive)

eventuality [ɪventjʊˈælɪtɪ] *(pl* **eventualities)** *n* éventualité *f*; **in that e.** dans cette éventualité

eventually [ɪˈventjʊəlɪ] *adv (in the end)* finalement, en fin de compte; *(at a future date)* par la suite; **they e. reached the castle** ils ont fini par arriver au château; **he'll do it e.** il le fera tôt ou tard

ever [ˈevə(r)] *adv* **(a)** *(at any time)* **have you e. been to Spain?** es-tu déjà allé en Espagne?; **do you e. see Alan these days?** ça t'arrive de voir Alan?; **the worst/best e.** le pire/meilleur qui soit; **more than e.** plus que jamais; **she's a liar/fool if e. there was one** c'est une menteuse/idiote de première **(b)** *(always)* **e. since (then)/1960** depuis (lors)/1960; **all she e. does is criticize** elle ne fait que critiquer; **she was as friendly as e.** elle était toujours aussi aimable; **e. the gentleman, he opened the door for her** toujours galant, il lui ouvrit la porte; **for e.** pour toujours **(c)** *(with negative sense)* **not e.** jamais; **hardly e.** presque jamais; **nothing e. happens** il ne se passe jamais rien; **I don't think I'll e. see him again** je ne pense pas que je le reverrai; **I seldom if e. see her** je la vois peu ou pas du tout

evergreen [ˈevəgriːn] **1** *n (tree)* arbre *m* à feuilles persistantes; *(bush)* arbuste *m* à feuilles persistantes **2** *adj* à feuilles persistantes; *Fig* **e. topic** question *f* toujours d'actualité

everlasting [evəˈlɑːstɪŋ] *adj (eternal)* éternel(elle); *(continual)* continuel(elle), sans fin

evermore [evəˈmɔː(r)] *adv Formal* toujours; **for e.** à jamais

every [ˈevrɪ] *adj* **(a)** *(each)* chaque; **children of e. age** des enfants de tous âges; **at e. opportunity** à la moindre occasion; **from e. side** de tous côtés; **e. one of us** chacun(e) d'entre nous; **e. man for himself!** chacun pour soi! **(b)** *(indicating regular occurrence)* **e. week** chaque semaine, toutes les semaines; **e. ten years** tous les dix ans; **e. other** *or* **second day** tous les deux jours, un jour sur deux; **e. other line** une ligne sur deux; **e. so often, e. now and again** de temps en temps **(c)** *(for emphasis)* **you have e. right to be angry** vous avez tout lieu d'être mécontent; **e. bit as good/intelligent as...** tout aussi bon (bonne)/intelligent(e) que...; **she has e. chance of winning** elle a de très fortes chances de gagner

everybody [ˈevrɪbɒdɪ] *pron* tout le monde, chacun(e) *m,f*; **e. I know was there** tous ceux que je connais se trouvaient là; **e. else** tous les autres; **e. who is anybody** les gens qui comptent

everyday [ˈevrɪdeɪ] *adj* **(a)** *(daily)* journalier(ère), quotidien(enne); **it's an e. occurrence** ça se produit tous les jours **(b)** *(used every day)* de tous les jours; **for e. wear/use**

à porter/utiliser tous les jours; **e. expression** expression *f* courante (**c**) *(ordinary)* usuel(elle), ordinaire

everyone ['evrɪwʌn] = **everybody**

everything ['evrɪθɪŋ] *pron* tout; **e. I did seemed to go wrong** tout ce que je faisais semblait voué à l'échec; **he did e. possible** il a fait tout son possible; **money isn't e.** l'argent n'est pas tout

everywhere ['evrɪweə(r)] *adv* partout; **to look e.** regarder partout; **e. you go** où que vous alliez, partout où vous allez; **e. you look there is poverty** de quelque côté que l'on se tourne, on voit la misère

evict [ɪ'vɪkt] *vt* expulser

eviction [ɪ'vɪkʃən] *n* expulsion *f*; **e. order** avis *m* d'expulsion

evidence ['evɪdəns] **1** *n* (**a**) *(reason for belief)* évidence *f*; *(indication)* marque *f*, signe *m*; **to be in e.** être en évidence; **to show e. of** donner des signes de; **there was no e. of his stay in the house** rien ne montrait qu'il eût séjourné dans la maison (**b**) *(in court case)* preuve *f*; *(testimony)* témoignage *m*; **to give e.** témoigner; **to call sb in e.** appeler qn à la barre des témoins; **to turn State's e.** témoigner contre ses complices *(sous promesse de pardon)*
    2 *vt Formal* **as evidenced by...** comme en témoigne...

evident ['evɪdənt] *adj* évident(e), manifeste

evidently ['evɪdəntlɪ] *adv* (**a**) *(clearly)* manifestement, à l'évidence; **there have e. been some problems** il est clair *ou* évident qu'il y a eu des problèmes (**b**) *(apparently)* apparemment; **so she won't be coming? – e. not** alors elle ne vient pas? – il semble bien que non

evil ['iːvəl] **1** *n* mal *m*
    2 *adj (person, look)* mauvais(e), malveillant(e); *(influence, effect)* maléfique; *(spirit)* malfaisant(e), malin(igne); *(temper)* coléreux(euse)

evildoer ['iːvəlduːə(r)] *n Lit* homme (femme) *m,f* méchant(e)

evil-looking ['iːvəllʊkɪŋ] *adj* à l'aspect malfaisant

evil-minded ['iːvəl'maɪndɪd] *adj* malintentionné(e)

evil-smelling ['iːvəl'smelɪŋ] *adj* nauséabond(e)

evince [ɪ'vɪns] *vt Formal* faire montre de

evocation [evə'keɪʃən] *n* évocation *f*

evocative [ɪ'vɒkətɪv] *adj* évocateur(trice) (**of** de)

evoke [ɪ'vəʊk] *vt* (**a**) *(conjure up)* évoquer (**b**) *(provoke)* provoquer, susciter

evolution [iːvə'luːʃən] *n* évolution *f*, développement *m*

evolutionary [iːvə'luːʃənərɪ] *adj* évolutif(ive)

evolve [ɪ'vɒlv] **1** *vt (theory, plan)* élaborer, mettre au point
    2 *vi (of species, situation)* évoluer, se développer

ewe [juː] *n* brebis *f*

ex [eks] *n Fam (former husband, wife, girlfriend, boyfriend)* ex *mf*

ex- [eks] *pref (former)* ex-; **ex-minister/teacher** ancien ministre *m*/professeur *m*

exacerbate [eg'zæsəbeɪt] *vt* aggraver

exact [ɪg'zækt] **1** *adj* exact(e), précis(e); **at the e. moment when...** juste au moment où..., au moment précis où...; **those were her e. words** c'est ce qu'elle a dit mot pour mot; **the e. opposite** exactement le contraire; **on January 5, to be e.** le 5 janvier, pour être précis
    2 *vt (obedience, tax)* exiger (**from** de); *(promise)* extorquer (**from** à)

exacting [ɪg'zæktɪŋ] *adj* exigeant(e)

exactitude [ɪg'zæktɪtjuːd] *n Formal* exactitude *f*

exactly [ɪg'zæktlɪ] *adv* exactement; **not e.** pas tout à fait; *Ironic* pas vraiment

exaggerate [ɪg'zædʒəreɪt] *vt & vi* exagérer

exaggerated [ɪg'zædʒəreɪtɪd] *adj* exagéré(e)

exaggeration [ɪgzædʒə'reɪʃən] *n* exagération *f*

exalt [ɪg'zɔːlt] *vt Formal* exalter

exalted [ɪg'zɔːltɪd] *adj* (**a**) *(high) (rank)* élevé(e); *(person)* haut placé(e) (**b**) *Formal (joyful)* exalté(e)

exam [ɪg'zæm] *n* examen *m*; **to take an e.** passer un examen

examination [ɪgzæmɪ'neɪʃən] *n* examen *m*; *Med* examen médical; **to take an e.** passer un examen

examine [ɪg'zæmɪn] *vt (evidence, patient, question)* examiner; *(student)* faire passer un examen à; **to e. one's conscience** faire son examen de conscience

examinee [ɪgzæmɪ'niː] *n* candidat(e) *m,f*

examiner [ɪg'zæmɪnə(r)] *n* examinateur(trice) *m,f*

example [ɪg'zɑːmpəl] *n* exemple *m*; **for e.** par exemple; **to set an e. (to sb)** donner l'exemple (à qn); **to make an e. of sb** faire un exemple de qn; **to follow sb's e.** suivre l'exemple de qn; **to lead by e.** montrer l'exemple

exasperate [ɪg'zɑːspəreɪt] *vt* exaspérer; **to get exasperated** s'irriter

exasperating [ɪg'zɑːspəreɪtɪŋ] *adj* exaspérant(e)

exasperation [ɪgzɑːspə'reɪʃən] *n* exaspération *f*

excavate ['ekskəveɪt] *vt (hole, tunnel)* creuser; *(remains)* déterrer, exhumer; *(site)* faire des fouilles dans

excavation [ekskə'veɪʃən] *n* excavation *f*

excavator ['ekskəveɪtə(r)] *n (machine)* excavatrice *f*

exceed [ɪk'siːd] *vt* (**a**) *(limits)* excéder, dépasser; *(hopes, fears)* dépasser; *(one's authority)* outrepasser (**b**) *(number, amount)* dépasser

exceedingly [ɪk'siːdɪŋlɪ] *adv* extrêmement

excel [ɪk'sel] *(pt & pp excelled)* **1** *vt also Ironic* **to e. oneself** se surpasser
    2 *vi* exceller (**at** *or* **in** à *ou* en)

excellence ['eksələns] *n* excellence *f*

excellency ['eksələnsɪ] *n* **Your/His E.** Votre/Son Excellence *f*

excellent ['eksələnt] *adj* excellent(e)

except [ɪk'sept] **1** *prep* sauf, à l'exception de; **nobody e. him** personne excepté lui *ou* sauf lui; **I would go, e. I'm busy** j'irais bien, mais je suis occupé; **e. for** à part; **e. that** excepté que, si ce n'est que; **e. when** sauf *ou* à part quand
    2 *vt* excepter, exclure (**from** de); **present company excepted** les personnes présentes exceptées; **not excepting...** sans excepter...

exception [ɪk'sepʃən] *n* (**a**) *(thing excepted)* exception *f*; **to make an e. of sth/for sb** faire une exception pour qch/qn; **with the e. of...** à l'exception de..., exception faite de...; **without e.** sans exception; **the e. proves the rule** c'est l'exception qui confirme la règle (**b**) **to take e. to sth** *(be offended)* se formaliser *ou* s'offenser de qch; *(object)* trouver à redire à qch

exceptionable [ɪk'sepʃənəbəl] *adj Formal* critiquable; *(offensive)* offensant(e)

exceptional [ɪk'sepʃənəl] *adj* exceptionnel(elle)

exceptionally [ɪk'sepʃənəlɪ] *adv* exceptionnellement; *(in exceptional cases)* à titre exceptionnel

excerpt ['eksɜːpt] *n* extrait *m* (**from** de)

excess [ɪk'ses] *n* excès *m*; **to do sth to e.** faire qch à l'excès; **e. baggage** excédent *m* de bagages

excessive [ɪk'sesɪv] *adj* excessif(ive)

excessively [ɪk'sesɪvlɪ] *adv* extrêmement; *(eat, drink)* à l'excès

exchange [ɪks'tʃeɪndʒ] **1** *n* (**a**) *(of prisoners, ideas)* échange *m*; **in e. (for)** en échange (de); **a heated e.** un échange de paroles assez vives; **e. visit** échange (**b**) *Fin (of currency)* change *m*; **e. controls** contrôle *m* des changes; **e. rate** taux *m* de change; **e. rate mechanism** mécanisme *m* de change (**c**) **(Stock) E.** Bourse *f* (des valeurs) (**d**) **(telephone) e.** central *m* téléphonique
    2 *vt* échanger; **to e. sth for sth** échanger qch contre qch

exchangeable [ɪks'tʃeɪndʒəbəl] *adj* échangeable (**for** contre)

excise 1 *n* ['eksaɪz] **e. (duties)** *(tax)* droits *mpl* d'accise
    2 *vt* [ɪk'saɪz] *(remove) (tumor)* exciser; *(piece of text)* couper

excitable [ɪk'saɪtəbəl] *adj* nerveux(euse)

excite [ɪk'saɪt] *vt* (**a**) *(get worked up)* énerver, surexciter; *(arouse* *enthusiasm in)* enthousiasmer; *(stimulate)* exciter (**b**) *(give rise to) (admiration, desire)* provoquer; *(envy, interest)* susciter; *(curiosity)* piquer

excited [ɪkˈsaɪtɪd] *adj (worked up)* énervé(e), excité(e); *(enthusiastic)* enthousiaste; **to get e. (about)** s'exciter (pour); *(angry)* s'énerver (contre)

excitedly [ɪkˈsaɪtɪdlɪ] *adv (speak, laugh)* avec animation; *(wait)* avec une impatience fébrile

excitement [ɪkˈsaɪtmənt] *n (agitation)* agitation *f*; *(enthusiasm)* animation *f*, enthousiasme *m*; **to cause great e.** faire sensation

exciting [ɪkˈsaɪtɪŋ] *adj* passionnant(e); *(idea, prospect)* enthousiasmant(e)

exclaim [ɪksˈkleɪm] **1** *vt* **"it's beautiful!" she exclaimed** "c'est magnifique!" s'est-elle écrié
2 *vi* s'exclamer, s'écrier

exclamation [ɛksklə'meɪʃən] *n* exclamation *f*; **e. point** point *m* d'exclamation

exclamatory [ɛksˈklæmətərɪ] *adj* exclamatif(ive)

exclude [ɪksˈkluːd] *vt* exclure (**from** de); *(doubt, suspicion)* écarter; **excluding...** à l'exclusion de...

exclusion [ɪksˈkluːʒən] *n* exclusion *f* (**from** de); **to the e. of...** à l'exclusion de...

exclusive [ɪksˈkluːsɪv] **1** *n (in newspaper, on TV)* exclusivité *f*
2 *adj* (**a**) *(right, article, interview)* exclusif(ive) (**b**) *(chic)* huppé(e); *(club, social circle)* très fermé(e); *(clothing, jewelry)* de grande marque (**c**) *(only)* seul(e), unique

exclusively [ɪksˈkluːsɪvlɪ] *adv* exclusivement; *(in newspaper, on TV)* en exclusivité

excommunicate [ɛkskəˈmjuːnɪkeɪt] *vt* excommunier

excommunication [ɛkskəmjuːnɪˈkeɪʃən] *n* excommunication *f*

excrement [ˈɛkskrɪmənt] *n* excrément *m*

excrescence [ɛksˈkresəns] *n* excroissance *f*

excrete [ɪksˈkriːt] *vt Formal* excréter

excruciating [ɪksˈkruːʃɪeɪtɪŋ] *adj (pain, embarrassment)* atroce; **the whole evening was e.** *(embarrassing)* on a été gênés toute la soirée; *(boring)* on s'est horriblement ennuyés toute la soirée

excruciatingly [ɪksˈkruːʃɪeɪtɪŋlɪ] *adv (painful, embarrassing)* atrocement; *Fam* **e. funny** tordant(e)

excursion [ɪksˈkɜːʃən] *n* excursion *f*

excuse 1 *n* [ɪksˈkjuːs] excuse *f*; **that's no e.** ce n'est pas une excuse *ou* une raison; **a poor e. for a father/bus service** un père/un service d'autobus lamentable
2 *vt* [ɪksˈkjuːz] (**a**) *(forgive)* excuser, pardonner; **e. me!** pardon!, excusez-moi!; **e. me?** *(what did you say?)* pardon? (**b**) *(exempt)* exempter, dispenser (**from** de) (**c**) **to e. oneself** s'excuser

execrable [ˈɛksɪkrəbəl] *adj* exécrable, abominable

execute [ˈɛksɪkjuːt] *vt (prisoner, order)* exécuter; *(plan, operation)* mettre à exécution

execution [ɛksɪˈkjuːʃən] *n (of prisoner, order)* exécution *f*; **in the e. of one's duty** dans l'exercice de ses fonctions

executioner [ɛksɪˈkjuːʃənə(r)] *n* bourreau *m*

executive [ɪgˈzekjʊtɪv] **1** *n (businessman)* cadre *m*; *(committee)* bureau *m*, comité *m* central
2 *adj (post)* de cadre; *(car, suite)* de luxe; **e. director** directeur(trice) *m,f* administratif(ive)

executor [ɪgˈzekjʊtə(r)] *n Law* exécuteur(trice) *m,f* testamentaire

exemplary [ɪgˈzemplərɪ] *adj* exemplaire

exemplify [ɪgˈzemplɪfaɪ] *(pt & pp* **exemplified**) *vt* illustrer

exempt [ɪgˈzempt] **1** *adj* exempté(e), dispensé(e) (**from** de)
2 *vt* exempter, dispenser (**from** de)

exemption [ɪgˈzem(p)ʃən] *n* exemption *f*, dispense *f* (**from** de)

exercise [ˈeksəsaɪz] **1** *n* exercice *m*; **to take e.** faire de l'exercice; **e. bike** vélo *m* d'appartement
2 *vt* (**a**) *(body, mind)* exercer (**b**) *(right, influence)* exercer; *(caution, restraint)* user de
3 *vi* faire de l'exercice; *(train)* s'entraîner

exert [ɪgˈzɜːt] *vt (pressure, influence)* exercer; *(force)* faire usage de; **to e. oneself** se remuer, se donner du mal

exertion [ɪgˈzɜːʃən] *n (of force)* usage *m*, emploi *m*; *(effort)* effort *m*

exfoliant [eksˈfəʊlɪənt] *n* exfoliant *m*

exfoliate [eksˈfəʊlɪeɪt] **1** *vi* s'exfolier
2 *vt* exfolier

exhale [eksˈheɪl] *vi* expirer

exhaust [ɪgˈzɔːst] **1** *n (on car)* échappement *m*; **e. (fumes)** gaz *mpl* d'échappement; **e. fan** aérateur *m*; **e. pipe** tuyau *m* d'échappement
2 *vt (person, resources)* épuiser

exhausted [ɪgˈzɔːstɪd] *adj* épuisé(e)

exhausting [ɪgˈzɔːstɪŋ] *adj* épuisant(e)

exhaustion [ɪgˈzɔːstʃən] *n* épuisement *m*

exhaustive [ɪgˈzɔːstɪv] *adj (list)* exhaustif(ive); *(analysis, description)* détaillé(e), minutieux(euse); *(inquiry, search)* approfondi(e)

exhibit [ɪgˈzɪbɪt] **1** *n* (**a**) *(in art exhibition)* objet *m* exposé; *(in court case)* pièce *f* à conviction (**b**) = **exhibition (a)**
2 *vt* (**a**) *(object, goods)* exhiber, montrer (**b**) *(painting in exhibition)* exposer (**c**) *(show) (courage, judgment)* faire preuve de; **to e. signs of stress/wear** donner des signes de tension/d'usure

exhibition [eksɪˈbɪʃən] *n* (**a**) *(of paintings)* exposition *f*; *Fam Fig* **to make an e. of oneself** se donner en spectacle (**b**) *(of courage, bad manners)* démonstration *f*; **it was a disgraceful e.** ce fut un spectacle honteux

exhibitionist [eksɪˈbɪʃənɪst] *n* (**a**) *(show-off)* = personne qui aime se faire remarquer (**b**) *Psy* exhibitionniste *mf*

exhibitor [ɪgˈzɪbɪtə(r)] *n* exposant(e) *m,f*

exhilarated [ɪgˈzɪləreɪtɪd] *adj* grisé(e)

exhilarating [ɪgˈzɪləreɪtɪŋ] *adj (air, walk)* vivifiant(e); *(experience)* exaltant(e), grisant(e); *(news)* enthousiasmant(e)

exhort [ɪgˈzɔːt] *vt* exhorter, encourager (**to do sth** à faire qch)

exhortation [ɪgzɔːˈteɪʃən] *n* exhortation *f*

exhume [eksˈhjuːm] *vt* exhumer, déterrer

exigent [ˈeksɪdʒənt] *adj Formal* (**a**) *(urgent)* urgent(e), pressant(e) (**b**) *(demanding)* exigeant(e)

exile [ˈeksaɪl] **1** *n* (**a**) *(banishment)* exil *m*, bannissement *m*; **in e.** en exil (**b**) *(exiled person)* exilé(e) *m,f*
2 *vt* exiler

exist [ɪgˈzɪst] *vi* (**a**) *(be in existence)* exister; *(of conditions)* régner (**b**) *(survive)* se maintenir en vie, survivre (**on** avec)

existence [ɪgˈzɪstəns] *n* existence *f*; **in e.** existant(e), qui existe; **to come into e.** naître; **to go out of e.** disparaître, cesser d'exister

existential [egzɪsˈtenʃəl] *adj* existentiel(elle)

existentialism [egzɪsˈtenʃəlɪzəm] *n* existentialisme *m*

existentialist [egzɪsˈtenʃəlɪst] *n & adj* existentialiste *mf*

existing [ɪgˈzɪstɪŋ] *adj* existant(e), actuel(elle)

exit [ˈeksɪt] **1** *n* sortie *f*; **to make an e.** sortir; *Pol* **e. poll** = sondage effectué auprès des électeurs immédiatement après qu'ils ont voté; **e. visa** visa *m* de sortie
2 *vi (leave) & Comput* sortir

exodus [ˈeksədəs] *n* exode *m*

ex officio [ˈeksəˈfɪʃɪəʊ] *adj (member)* de droit

exonerate [ɪgˈzɒnəreɪt] *vt (absolve)* disculper, innocenter (**from** *or* **of** de)

exorbitant [ɪgˈzɔːbɪtənt] *adj* exorbitant(e)

exorcism [ˈeksɔːsɪzəm] *n* exorcisme *m*

exorcist ['eksɔːsɪst] *n* exorciste *mf*

exorcize ['eksɔːsaɪz] *vt* exorciser

exotic [ɪg'zɒtɪk] *adj* exotique

expand [ɪks'pænd] **1** *vt (production, output)* accroître; *(empire, company)* agrandir; *(mind, circle of friends)* élargir; *(range, idea)* développer

  2 *vi (of solid, gas)* se dilater; *(of company)* s'agrandir

▸**expand on, expand upon** *vt insep* développer

expanded [ɪks'pændɪd] *adj* étendu(e); *Comput (memory)* expansé(e); **e. polystyrene** polystyrène *m* expansé

expanding [ɪks'pændɪŋ] *adj (market, company)* en expansion, qui se développe; *(universe)* en expansion

expanse [eks'pæns] *n* étendue *f*

expansion [ɪks'pænʃən] *n* expansion *f*; *(of gas)* dilatation *f*; *Comput* **e. card** carte *f* d'extension

expansive [ɪks'pænsɪv] *adj (gas)* dilatable; *(person)* expansif(ive); **in an e. mood** d'humeur expansive

expat [eks'pæt] *n & adj Fam* expatrié(e) *m,f*

expatriate 1 *n* [eks'peɪtrɪət] expatrié(e) *m,f*

  2 *vt* [eks'peɪtrɪeɪt] expatrier

expect [ɪks'pekt] **1** *vt* **(a)** *(anticipate)* s'attendre à; **to e. to do sth** compter *ou* espérer faire qch; **to e. sb to do sth** s'attendre à ce que qn fasse qch; **I expected as much** je m'y attendais; **to e. the worst** s'attendre au pire; **to be expecting a baby** attendre un bébé **(b)** *(require)* **to e. sb to do sth** attendre de qn qu'il/elle fasse qch; **to e. sth from sb** attendre qch de qn; **I know what is expected of me** je sais ce qu'on attend de moi; **to e. too much from sb/sth** trop attendre de qn/qch

  2 *vi (be pregnant)* **to be expecting** attendre un bébé

expectancy [ɪks'pektənsɪ] *n* attente *f*; **an air of e.** l'air d'attendre quelque chose

expectant [ɪks'pektənt] *adj* impatient(e); **e. mother** future maman *f*

expectation [ekspek'teɪʃən] *n* espérance *f*; **in (the) e. of sth** dans l'attente de qch; **to have high expectations of sb/sth** attendre beaucoup de qn/qch; **to come up to expectations** se montrer à la hauteur; **to fall short of (sb's) expectations** décevoir (qn); **contrary to all expectations** contre toute attente

expected [ɪks'pektɪd] *adj* attendu(e); *(hoped for)* espéré(e)

expectorant [ɪks'pektərənt] **1** *n Med* expectorant *m*

  2 *adj* expectorant(e)

expediency [ɪks'piːdɪənsɪ] *n* opportunité *f*; *Pej (opportunism)* opportunisme *m*

expedient [ɪks'piːdɪənt] **1** *n* expédient *m*

  2 *adj* opportun(e), expédient(e)

expedite ['ekspɪdaɪt] *vt Formal* activer, accélérer

expedition [ekspə'dɪʃən] *n* expédition *f*; *Fam* **a shopping e.** une séance de shopping

expeditionary [ekspə'dɪʃənərɪ] *adj Mil* **e. force/corps** force *f*/corps *m* expéditionnaire

expel [ɪks'pel] *(pt & pp* **expelled***) vt* expulser; *(from school)* renvoyer

expendable [ɪks'pendəbəl] *adj (person)* qui n'est pas irremplaçable; *(troops)* que l'on peut sacrifier

expenditure [ɪks'pendɪtʃə(r)] *n (of money, energy)* dépense *f*

expense [ɪks'pens] *n* **(a)** *(cost)* dépense *f*, frais *mpl*; **to go to great e. (to do sth)** faire de grosses dépenses (pour faire qch); **no e. was spared** on n'a pas regardé à la dépense; **at the e. of one's health/sanity** aux dépens de sa santé/santé mentale; **to make a joke at sb's e.** faire une plaisanterie aux dépens de qn **(b)** *Com* **expenses** frais *mpl*, dépenses *fpl*; **it's on expenses** ça va sur la note de frais; **all expenses paid** tous frais payés; **e. account** note *f* de frais

expensive [ɪks'pensɪv] *adj (object, shop, restaurant)* cher (chère); *(procedure, habit)* coûteux(euse); *(tastes)* de luxe; *(mistake)* qui coûte cher

experience [ɪks'pɪərɪəns] **1** *n* expérience *f*; **to learn from e.** tirer les leçons d'une expérience; **in my e.** d'après mon expérience

  2 *vt (emotions, pain)* ressentir; *(hunger, success)* connaître, faire l'expérience de; *(difficulties, problems)* avoir; *(ill-treatment)* subir

experienced [ɪks'pɪərɪənst] *adj* expérimenté(e); **to be e. in sth** avoir de l'expérience en qch; *(observer)* averti(e)

experiment [ɪks'perɪmənt] **1** *n* expérience *f*; **as an e.** à titre d'essai

  2 *vi* expérimenter (**on** sur); **to e. with** *(technique, drugs)* essayer

experimental [ɪksperɪ'mentəl] *adj* expérimental(e)

expert ['ekspɜːt] **1** *n* expert *m*, spécialiste *mf*

  2 *adj* expert(e), habile; *(advice, opinion)* d'un expert; **to be e. in** *or* **at sth** être expert en qch; *Comput* **e. system** système *m* expert; *Law* **e. witness** expert *m* cité comme témoin

expertise [ekspɜː'tiːz] *n (technical, financial)* compétence *f*, connaissances *fpl*; *(as cook, carpenter)* savoir-faire *m*

expertly ['ekspɜːtlɪ] *adv* de manière experte

expiate ['ekspɪeɪt] *vt Formal* expier

expiration [ekspɪ'reɪʃən] *n* expiration *f*, fin *f*; **e. date** (date *f* d')échéance *f*, date d'expiration

expire [ɪks'paɪə(r)] *vi* **(a)** *(of law, deadline, passport)* expirer **(b)** *Lit (die)* expirer

explain [ɪks'pleɪn] **1** *vt* expliquer; **to e. oneself** *(make oneself clear)* s'expliquer; *(justify oneself)* se justifier

  2 *vi* donner des explications, expliquer; *(make oneself clear)* s'expliquer

▸**explain away** *vt sep (give explanation for)* donner une explication satisfaisante à; *(justify)* justifier

explanation [eksplə'neɪʃən] *n* explication *f*; **to give an e. of sth** *(make clear)* expliquer qch; *(justify)* justifier qch

explanatory [ɪks'plænətərɪ] *adj* explicatif(ive)

expletive ['eksplətɪv] *n* juron *m*

explicable [eks'plɪkəbəl] *adj* explicable

explicit [eks'plɪsɪt] *adj* explicite

explicitly [eks'plɪsɪtlɪ] *adv* de manière explicite

explode [ɪks'pləʊd] **1** *vt (bomb)* faire exploser; *Fig (idea, theory)* démontrer la fausseté de

  2 *vi (of bomb) & Fig (with anger)* exploser; *(of mine)* sauter; **to e. with laughter** éclater de rire

exploit 1 *n* ['eksplɔɪt] exploit *m*

  2 *vt* [eks'plɔɪt] **(a)** *(take unfair advantage of)* exploiter **(b)** *(use) (resources, scandal)* exploiter; *(talents)* mettre à profit

exploitation [eksplɔɪ'teɪʃən] *n* exploitation *f*

exploration [eksplə'reɪʃən] *n* exploration *f*

exploratory [ɪks'plɒrətərɪ] *adj (trip)* d'exploration; *(surgery, discussions, talks)* exploratoire

explore [ɪks'plɔː(r)] **1** *vt (area, countryside)* explorer; *(possibility, idea)* étudier

  2 *vi* partir en exploration

explorer [ɪks'plɔːrə(r)] *n* explorateur(trice) *m,f*

explosion [ɪks'pləʊʒən] *n also Fig* explosion *f*

explosive [ɪks'pləʊsɪv] **1** *n* explosif *m*

  2 *adj also Fig* explosif(ive)

exponent [ɪks'pəʊnənt] *n* **(a)** *(of theory, idea)* avocat(e) *m,f*; *(of piece of music)* interprète *mf* **(b)** *Math* exposant *m*

exponential [ekspəʊ'nenʃəl] *adj* exponentiel(elle)

export 1 *n* ['ekspɔːt] **(a)** *(product)* article *m* d'exportation; **exports** *(of country)* exportations *fpl* **(b)** *(activity)* exportation *f*; **e. duty** droit(s) *m(pl)* de sortie; **e. license** licence *f* d'exportation; **e. trade** exportations *fpl*

  2 *vt* [eks'pɔːt] *also Comput* exporter

exportation [ekspɔː'teɪʃən] *n* exportation *f*

exporter [eks'pɔːtə(r)] *n* exportateur(trice) *m,f*

expose [ɪks'pəʊz] *vt* **(a)** *(to air, cold, danger) & Phot* exposer (**to** à); *(wire)* mettre à jour; **to e. oneself to danger** s'exposer au danger (**b**) *(reveal) (secret)* éventer; *(crime)* dévoiler; *(criminal)* démasquer; *(feelings)* afficher; **to e. sb as a traitor/criminal** révéler que qn est un traître/criminel; **to e. oneself** *(of flasher)* s'exhiber

exposé [eks'pəʊzeɪ] *n (article, book)* exposé *m*; *(of scandal, corruption)* révélations *fpl*

exposed [ɪks'pəʊzd] *adj* exposé(e) (**to** à)

exposition [ekspə'zɪʃən] *n (explanation)* exposition *f*, exposé *m*

expostulate [ɪks'pɒstjʊleɪt] *vi Formal* vitupérer; **to e. with sb about sth** faire des remontrances à qn à propos de qch

exposure [ɪks'pəʊʒə(r)] *n* (**a**) *(to air, cold, danger)* exposition *f*; **to die of e.** mourir de froid (**b**) *(publicity)* couverture *f*; **to get a lot of e.** faire l'objet d'une importante couverture médiatique (**c**) *(of crime)* révélation *f*; *(of criminal, scandal)* dénonciation *f* (**d**) *Phot* pose *f*; **e. meter** posemètre *m*

expound [ɪks'paʊnd] *vt Formal* exposer

express [ɪks'pres] **1** *n (train)* express *m*, rapide *m*
2 *adj* (**a**) *(clear) (purpose, instruction)* exprès(esse); *(order)* formel(elle) (**b**) *(rapid) (letter, delivery)* exprès *inv*; *(train)* express *inv*
3 *adv* **to send sth e.** envoyer qch en exprès
4 *vt* exprimer; **to e. oneself** s'exprimer

expression [ɪks'preʃən] *n* expression *f*

expressionism [ɪks'preʃənɪzəm] *n* expressionnisme *m*

expressionist [ɪks'preʃənɪst] *n & adj* expressionniste *mf*

expressionless [ɪks'preʃənlɪs] *adj* sans expression

expressive [ɪks'presɪv] *adj* expressif(ive); *(gesture, silence)* éloquent(e)

expressly [ɪks'preslɪ] *adv* expressément

expropriate [eks'prəʊprɪeɪt] *vt* exproprier

expropriation [eksprəʊprɪ'eɪʃən] *n* expropriation *f*

expulsion [ɪks'pʌlʃən] *n* expulsion *f*; *(from school)* renvoi *m*

expunge [ɪks'pʌndʒ] *vt* effacer

expurgate ['ekspɜːgeɪt] *vt* expurger

exquisite [ek'skwɪzɪt] *adj* exquis(e); *(pleasure)* vif (vive)

exquisitely [eks'kwɪzɪtlɪ] *adv* d'une manière exquise

extant ['ekstænt] *adj* qui existe encore

extempore [ɪks'tempərɪ] **1** *adj (speech)* impromptu(e)
2 *adv* **to speak e.** improviser

extemporize [ɪks'tempəraɪz] *vi* improviser

extend [ɪks'tend] **1** *vt* (**a**) *(in space)* étendre, allonger; *(knowledge)* accroître; *(frontiers)* faire reculer; *(house)* agrandir (**b**) *(in time)* prolonger (**c**) *(give, offer) (one's hand)* tendre; *(thanks)* présenter; *(support)* offrir; *Fin* **to e. credit to sb** accorder un crédit à qn
2 *vi* (**a**) *(in space)* s'étendre (**b**) *(in time)* se prolonger, continuer

extended family [ɪks'tendɪd'fæmɪlɪ] *n* famille *f* élargie

extension [ɪks'tenʃən] *n* (**a**) *(to building)* annexe *f* (**b**) *(in time)* prolongation *f*; *(for essay)* délai *m* supplémentaire; **e. course** *or* **class** cours *m* de formation continue (**c**) *(for telephone)* poste *m* (**d**) **e. (cable)** rallonge *f* (**e**) **extensions** *(in hair)* rajouts *mpl*

extensive [ɪks'tensɪv] *adj (area, knowledge)* vaste, étendu(e); *(damage, repairs)* important(e); **to make e. use of sth** faire un usage considérable de qch

extensively [ɪks'tensɪvlɪ] *adv (travel, read)* énormément; *(revised, rewritten)* entièrement; *(damaged)* gravement; **to use sth e.** se servir beaucoup de qch

extent [ɪks'tent] *n* (**a**) *(of land, damage, knowledge)* étendue *f* (**b**) *(degree)* **to an e., to a certain e., to some e.** jusqu'à un certain point, dans une certaine mesure; **to a large e.** en grande partie, dans une large mesure; **to such an e. that...** à tel point que...; **to what e.?** jusqu'à quel point?

extenuating circumstances [ɪks'tenjʊeɪtɪŋ'sɜːkəmstænsɪz] *npl* circonstances *fpl* atténuantes

exterior [ɪks'tɪərɪə(r)] **1** *n (of building, car)* extérieur *m*; *(of person)* extérieur, dehors *mpl*
2 *adj* extérieur(e)

exterminate [ɪks'tɜːmɪneɪt] *vt* exterminer; *(disease)* éradiquer

extermination [ɪkstɜːmɪ'neɪʃən] *n* extermination *f*; *(of disease)* éradication *f*

external [ɪks'tɜːnəl] *adj (events, trade, debt)* extérieur(e); *(angle, damage, wall)* externe; *Pol* **e. affairs** affaires *fpl* étrangères *ou* extérieures; **for e. use only** *(on medicine)* à usage externe

extinct [ɪks'tɪŋkt] *adj (animal, species)* disparu(e), qui n'existe plus; *(volcano)* éteint(e)

extinction [ɪks'tɪŋkʃən] *n* extinction *f*; **to be threatened with e.** être en voie de disparition

extinguish [ɪks'tɪŋgwɪʃ] *vt (fire)* éteindre; *(hope)* anéantir

extinguisher [ɪks'tɪŋgwɪʃə(r)] *n* extincteur *m*

extirpate ['ekstɜːpeɪt] *vt Formal* extirper

extoll [ɪks'təʊl] *vt (virtues, merits)* exalter, vanter; *(beauty)* célébrer, chanter

extort [ɪks'tɔːt] *vt (money)* extorquer (**from** à); *(promise)* arracher (**from** à)

extortion [ɪks'tɔːʃən] *n* extorsion *f*

extortionate [ɪks'tɔːʃənɪt] *adj* exorbitant(e)

extra ['ekstrə] **1** *n (in movie)* figurant(e) *m,f*; *(on bill)* supplément *m*
2 *adj* (**a**) *(additional)* supplémentaire, de plus; **no e. charge** sans supplément de prix (**b**) *(spare)* de réserve, de rechange
3 *adv* (**a**) *(more than usual)* extrêmement; **to be e. careful** faire particulièrement attention; **e. large** *(clothing)* grand patron; **e. special** très spécial(e) (**b**) *(charge, pay)* en plus, en sus

extract 1 *n* ['ekstrækt] (**a**) *(concentrate)* extrait *m*, concentré *m* (**b**) *(from book, movie)* extrait *m*
2 *vt* [ɪks'trækt] *(tooth, raw material)* extraire (**from** de); *(confession, information)* arracher (**from** à)

extraction [ɪks'trækʃən] *n* (**a**) *(removal)* extraction *f* (**b**) *(origin) (social)* extraction *f*; *(geographical)* origine *f*; **she is of Danish e.** elle est d'origine danoise

extracurricular ['ekstrəkə'rɪkjʊlə(r)] *adj Sch* extrascolaire

extradite ['ekstrədaɪt] *vt* extrader

extradition [ekstrə'dɪʃən] *n* extradition *f*

extrajudicial ['ekstrədʒuː'dɪʃəl] *adj* extrajudiciaire

extramarital ['ekstrə'mærɪtəl] *adj* extraconjugal(e)

extraneous [ɪks'treɪnɪəs] *adj Formal (details)* sans rapport; *(considerations)* en dehors de la question

Extranet ['ekstrənet] *n Comput* Extranet *m*

extraordinarily [ɪks'trɔːdənərɪlɪ] *adv* extraordinairement

extraordinary [ɪks'trɔːdənərɪ] *adj* extraordinaire; **e. powers** pouvoirs *mpl* extraordinaires

extrapolate [ɪk'stræpəleɪt] *vt & vi* extrapoler (**from** à partir de)

extrapolation [ɪkstræpə'leɪʃən] *n* extrapolation *f*

extrasensory perception ['ekstrə'sensərɪpə'sepʃən] *n* perception *f* extrasensorielle

extraterrestrial ['ekstrətɪ'restrɪəl] *n & adj* extraterrestre *mf*

extravagance [ɪks'trævəgəns] *n* (**a**) *(excessive spending)* gaspillage *m* (**b**) *(extravagant purchase)* folie *f*

extravagant [ɪks'trævəgənt] *adj (person)* dépensier(ère); *(tastes)* dispendieux(euse); *(object)* hors de prix

extravaganza [ekstrævə'gænzə] *n (lavish production)* grand spectacle *m*

extreme [ɪks'triːm] **1** *n* extrême *m*; **in the e.** à l'extrême; **to go from one e. to the other** passer d'un extrême à l'autre; **to go to extremes** pousser les choses à l'extrême
2 *adj* extrême; *Pol* **the e. left** l'extrême gauche *f*; **e. sports** sports *mpl* extrêmes

extremely [ɪks'triːmlɪ] *adv* extrêmement

extremism [ɪks'triːmɪzəm] *n* extrémisme *m*

extremist [ɪks'triːmɪst] *n & adj* extrémiste *mf*

extremity [ɪks'tremɪtɪ] *(pl* **extremities**) *n* (**a**) *(end)* extrémité *f* (**b**) **extremities** *(of body)* extrémités *fpl* (**c**) *(extreme situation)* situation *f* extrême; *(extreme measure)* mesure *f* extrême

extricate ['ekstrɪkeɪt] *vt* dégager, tirer; **to e. oneself from** *(danger, difficulties)* se tirer de

extrovert ['ekstrəvɜːt] *n & adj* extraverti(e) *m,f*

exuberance [ɪg'zjuːbərəns] *n* exubérance *f*

exuberant [ɪg'zjuːbərənt] *adj* exubérant(e)

exude [ɪg'zjuːd] *vt (sweat, odor)* exsuder; *(health, confidence)* déborder de

exult [ɪg'zʌlt] *vi* exulter, se réjouir (**in** de)

exultant [ɪg'zʌltənt] *adj (mood)* joyeux(euse); *(cry)* de triomphe

eye [aɪ] **1** *n* (**a**) *(of person, storm)* œil *m*; *(of needle)* chas *m*; **to open/close one's eyes** ouvrir/fermer les yeux; **to look sb straight in the e.** regarder qn droit dans les yeux; **as far as the e. can see** à perte de vue; **to make e. contact with sb** regarder qn (droit) dans les yeux; *Fam* **e. candy** *(men)* beaux mecs *mpl*; *(women)* belles nanas *fpl*; **e. drops** *(medicine)* gouttes *fpl* pour les yeux; **at e. level** à la hauteur des yeux; **e. shadow** ombre *f* à paupières; **e. test** examen *m* de la vue

(**b**) *(idioms)* **in the eye(s) of the law** aux yeux de la loi; **to be in the public e.** occuper une position en vue; **to have an e. for a bargain** savoir reconnaître une bonne affaire; **to have an e. for detail/color** avoir l'œil pour les détails/les couleurs; **to look at sth with a critical e.** regarder qch d'un œil critique; **to see e. to e. with sb** voir les choses du même œil que qn; **for your eyes only** confidentiel(elle); **to keep one's eyes and ears open** rester en éveil; **to keep one's eyes peeled** *or* **skinned** ouvrir l'œil; **to open sb's eyes to sth** ouvrir *ou* dessiller les yeux à qn sur qch; **to shut** *or* **to close one's eyes to sth** fermer les yeux sur qch; **to do sth with one's eyes open** faire qch en connaissance de cause; **to catch sb's e.** attirer l'attention de qn; **to have eyes in** *or* **at the back of one's head** avoir des yeux derrière la tête; **he only has eyes for her** il n'a d'yeux que pour elle; **to set** *or* **to lay eyes on sth** poser les yeux sur qch; **I saw it with my own eyes** je l'ai vu de mes propres yeux; **to run** *or* **to cast one's e. over sth** jeter un coup d'œil sur qch; **to keep an e. on sb/sth** surveiller qn/qch; **to keep an e. out for sth** être à l'affût de qch; **to have one's e. on sb/sth** *(be watching)* avoir qn/qch à l'œil; *(have in mind)* avoir l'œil sur qn/qch; **to make eyes at sb** faire de l'œil à qn; **with an e. to...** en vue de...; **to be up to one's eyes in work** avoir du travail par-dessus la tête; **to be up to one's eyes in debt** être endetté(e) jusqu'au cou; *Fam* **that's one in the e. for him!** ça lui fera les pieds!; **an e. for an e.(, a tooth for a tooth)** œil pour œil(, dent pour dent)

2 *vt* regarder, observer

eyeball ['aɪbɔːl] *n* globe *m* oculaire

eyebrow ['aɪbraʊ] *n* sourcil *m*; *Fig* **to raise one's eyebrows** *(in surprise)* lever les sourcils

eye-catching ['aɪkætʃɪŋ] *adj* accrocheur(euse)

eyeful ['aɪfʊl] *n Fam* **to get an e. of sb/sth** *(look at)* reluquer qn/qch

eyeglass ['aɪglɑːs] *n* monocle *m*

eyeglasses ['aɪglɑːsɪz] *npl (spectacles)* lunettes *fpl*

eyelash ['aɪlæʃ] *n* cil *m*

eyelid ['aɪlɪd] *n* paupière *f*; *Fig* **she didn't bat an e.** elle n'a pas sourcillé

eyeliner ['aɪlaɪnə(r)] *n* eye-liner *m*

eye-opener ['aɪəʊpənə(r)] *n* révélation *f*; **it was an e. for him** ça lui a ouvert les yeux

eyepatch ['aɪpætʃ] *n* cache *m* (sur l'œil)

eyeshade ['aɪʃeɪd] *n* visière *f*

eyesight ['aɪsaɪt] *n* vue *f*

eyesore ['aɪsɔː(r)] *n* horreur *f*

eyestrain ['aɪstreɪn] *n* fatigue *f* oculaire

eyetooth ['aɪtuːθ] *n (pl* **eyeteeth** ['aɪtiːθ]) *n* canine *f*; **I'd give my eyeteeth to go with them** je donnerais n'importe quoi pour aller avec eux

eyewash ['aɪwɒʃ] *n (for eye)* collyre *m*; *Fig (nonsense)* boniment *m*, poudre *f* aux yeux

eyewitness ['aɪˈwɪtnɪs] *n* témoin *m* oculaire

eyrie ['ɪərɪ] *n* aire *f*

e-zine, ezine ['iːziːn] *n* ezine *m*, e-zine *m*, magazine *m* électronique

F

F, f [ef] *n* (**a**) *(letter)* F, f *m inv; Euph* **the F word** = euphémisme désignant le mot "fuck" (**b**) *Mus* fa *m*

fa [fɑː] *n Mus* fa *m*

fab [fæb] *adj Fam* sensass *inv*

fable ['feɪbəl] *n* fable *f*

fabled ['feɪbəld] *adj* légendaire; *Fig* fabuleux(euse)

fabric ['fæbrɪk] *n (cloth)* tissu *m*, étoffe *f*; *(of building)* structure *f*; *Fig* **the f. of society** le tissu social; **f. conditioner** *or* **softener** (produit *m*) assouplissant *m*

fabricate ['fæbrɪkeɪt] *vt (news, story, alibi)* forger, fabriquer; *(make)* fabriquer

fabulous ['fæbjʊləs] *adj* fabuleux(euse)

fabulously ['fæbjʊləslɪ] *adv (rich)* fabuleusement

façade [fæ'sɑːd] *n also Fig* façade *f*

face [feɪs] **1** *n* (**a**) *(of person)* visage *m*, figure *f; very Fam* **shut your f.!** ferme-la!, la ferme!; **I know that f.!** je connais cette tête-là!; **I told him to his f.** je le lui ai dit en face; **I shall never be able to look her in the f. again** je ne pourrai plus jamais la regarder en face; **to show one's f.** se montrer; **to set one's f. against sth** se braquer contre qch; **in the f. of** *(danger, threat, enemy)* devant, face à; *Fam* **in your f.** *(music, campaign)* percutant(e); **f. cloth** ≃ gant *m* de toilette; **f. cream** crème *f* pour le visage; **f. mask** *or* **pack** masque *m*; **f. powder** poudre *f*

(**b**) *(expression)* mine *f;* **to make** *or* **to pull faces** faire des grimaces; **to keep a straight f.** garder son sérieux; **to put a good f. on it** garder le sourire

(**c**) *(appearance)* **on the f. of it** à première vue; **to save f.** sauver la face; **to lose f.** perdre la face; **the changing f. of America** le visage changeant des États-Unis; **to take sth at f. value** prendre qch au pied de la lettre

(**d**) *(surface) (of the earth)* surface *f; (of clock)* cadran *m; (of coin, cliff)* face *f; Fig* **to disappear off the f. of the earth** se volatiliser; **f. down** *(person)* sur le ventre; *(document)* face imprimée dessous; *(playing card)* à l'envers; **f. up** *(person)* sur le dos; *(document)* face imprimée dessus; *(playing card)* à l'endroit

2 *vt* (**a**) *(confront) (difficulty, danger)* affronter, faire face à; **to be faced with sth** être confronté(e) à qch; **to f. facts** regarder les choses en face; **he faces six months in prison** il risque six mois de prison; **I can't f. going to work today** je n'ai pas le courage d'aller travailler aujourd'hui; **let's f. it** soyons réalistes; *Fig* **to f. the music** *(deal with situation)* faire front; *(accept consequences)* assumer ses responsabilités

(**b**) *(look toward)* faire face à; **to f. the front** regarder devant soi

3 *vi* **to f. north/south** *(of house)* être orienté(e) au nord/sud; **to f. toward** *(of person)* se tourner vers

▸**face up to** *vt insep (person)* tenir tête à; *(reality, fears)* affronter

faceless ['feɪslɪs] *adj* anonyme

face-lift ['feɪslɪft] *n (plastic surgery)* lifting *m; Fig (of building)* restauration *f;* **to have a f.** se faire faire un lifting

face-saving ['feɪsseɪvɪŋ] *adj* qui permet de sauver la face

facet ['fæsɪt] *n (of gem, character)* facette *f; (of problem, situation)* dimension *f*

facetious [fə'siːʃəs] *adj* facétieux(euse); **don't be f.!** ne plaisante pas!

face-to-face ['feɪstə'feɪs] **1** *adj* **a f. meeting** un face à face
2 *adv (meet)* face à face

facial ['feɪʃəl] **1** *n* soin *m* du visage; **to have a f.** se faire faire un soin du visage
2 *adj* facial(e); *(expression, hair)* du visage

facialist ['feɪʃəlɪst] *n* visagiste *mf*

facile ['fæsaɪl] *adj Pej* facile

facilitate [fə'sɪlɪteɪt] *vt* faciliter

facility [fə'sɪlɪtɪ] *(pl* **facilities**) *n* (**a**) *(ease)* facilité *f* (**b**) *(skill)* **to have a f. for sth** avoir un don pour qch (**c**) **facilities** *(equipment)* équipement *m; (place, building)* installations *fpl;* **shopping facilities** magasins *mpl;* **transport facilities** moyens *mpl* de transport; *Euph* **the facilities** *(toilets)* les toilettes (**d**) *(building)* **a detention f.** un établissement pénitentiaire (**e**) *(feature) (of computer, stereo)* fonction *f*

facsimile [fæk'sɪmɪlɪ] *n (copy)* fac-similé *m; (fax)* télécopie *f*

fact [fækt] *n* fait *m;* **in f.** en fait; **to distinguish f. from fiction** discerner la fiction de la réalité; **the f. is (that)...** le fait est que...; **it's a f. that...** c'est un fait que...; **to know for a f. (that)...** savoir pertinemment que...; **it's a f. of life** c'est une réalité; **to tell sb the facts of life** expliquer à qn comment on fait les enfants

fact-finding ['fæktfaɪndɪŋ] *adj* d'enquête; **f. mission** mission *f* d'information

faction ['fækʃən] *n* faction *f*

factor ['fæktə(r)] *n (aspect, in maths)* facteur *m*

factory ['fæktərɪ] *(pl* **factories**) *n* usine *f; (small)* fabrique *f;* **f. farming** élevage *m* industriel

factual ['fæktʃʊəl] *adj* basé(e) sur les faits

faculty ['fækltɪ] *(pl* **faculties**) *n (of mind, in university)* faculté *f;* **the f.** *(teaching staff)* le personnel enseignant

fad [fæd] *n* mode *f* (**for** de)

fade [feɪd] **1** *vt* faner
2 *vi (of flower, material, color)* se faner; *(of light)* baisser; *(of memory)* s'éteindre; *(of hope)* s'amenuiser; **to f. from memory** s'effacer de la mémoire

▸**fade away** *vi (of sound)* s'éteindre; *Fig (of person)* s'éteindre peu à peu

▸**fade out 1** *vt sep Cin* fermer en fondu; *(music)* terminer par un fondu
2 *vi* se terminer en fondu

faded ['feɪdɪd] *adj (flower, color)* fané(e); *(photograph, garment)* décoloré(e)

fading ['feɪdɪŋ] *adj (light)* pâlissant(e)

fag [fæg], **faggot** ['fægət] *very Fam (homosexual)* pédé *m*, = terme injurieux désignant un homosexuel

Fahrenheit ['færənhaɪt] *adj* Fahrenheit *inv*

fail [feɪl] **1** *n* (**a**) *(in exam)* échec *m* (**b**) **without f.** sans faute
2 *vt (exam, test)* échouer à, rater; *(candidate)* recaler; **to f. a**

drugs test être positif(ive) au contrôle anti-dopage; **words f. me** les mots me manquent; **his nerve failed him** le courage lui a fait défaut; **I won't f. you** vous pouvez compter sur moi
3 vi (of person, plan) échouer; (of business) faire faillite; (of engine) caler; (of memory, eyesight, light) baisser; (of brakes) lâcher; **to f. to do sth** (not succeed) ne pas arriver à faire qch; (forget) négliger de faire qch; **I f. to see what the problem is** je ne vois pas où est le problème; **if all else fails** en désespoir de cause; **to f. in one's duty** manquer à son devoir; **it never fails** (of strategy, excuse) ça marche à tous les coups

failed [feɪld] adj (artist, politician) raté(e)

failing ['feɪlɪŋ] **1** n (fault) faiblesse f, défaut m
2 adj (sight, strength) qui baisse; **to be in f. health** avoir une santé défaillante
3 prep à défaut de; **f. that** à défaut; **f. all else** en désespoir de cause

fail-safe ['feɪlseɪf] adj (mechanism) à sûreté intégrée

failure ['feɪljə(r)] n (**a**) (of plan, attempt) échec m; (of machine) panne f; (of company) faillite f; **to be a f.** (of show, movie) faire un bide; **f. to keep a promise** manquement m à une promesse; **f. to pay a bill** défaut m de paiement d'une facture (**b**) (person) raté(e) m,f

faint [feɪnt] **1** n **to fall down in a f.** s'évanouir
2 adj (**a**) (hope, light, sound) faible; (mark, writing) à peine visible; (color) pâle; (idea) vague; **I don't have the faintest idea** je n'en ai pas la moindre idée (**b**) (weak, unwell) **to feel** or **to be f.** (of person) se sentir mal
3 vi (lose consciousness) s'évanouir

faint-hearted ['feɪnt'hɑːtɪd] adj timoré(e); **not for the f.** à déconseiller aux âmes sensibles

faintly ['feɪntlɪ] adv (**a**) (remember, hear, see) vaguement; (shine) faiblement (**b**) (slightly) (uneasy, ridiculous) légèrement

fair¹ [feə(r)] n (**a**) (trade fair) foire f (**b**) (carnival) fête f foraine

fair² [feə(r)] **1** adj (**a**) (just) juste, équitable; (price) raisonnable; (fight) loyal(e); **it's not f.** ce n'est pas juste; **fair's f.!** ce n'est que justice!; **f. enough!** (OK) d'accord!; (rightly so) ça se comprend!; **it is f. to say (that)...** on peut dire que...; **to be f.,...** pour être honnête,...; **by f. means or foul** par tous les moyens; Prov **all's f. in love and war** tous les moyens sont bons; **to be f. game** être une proie facile; **f. play** fair-play m, Offic franc-jeu m; **to get one's f. share** recevoir son dû; **we've had our f. share of problems** nous avons eu notre lot de problèmes; Com **f. trade** commerce m équitable
(**b**) (quite good) assez bon (bonne); **a f. idea** une assez bonne idée; **at a f. pace** à une allure assez rapide; **a f. amount of** pas mal de
(**c**) (weather) beau (belle)
(**d**) (light-colored) (hair) blond(e); (skin) pâle
(**e**) (attractive) beau (belle); Old-fashioned **the f.** or **fairer sex** le beau sexe
2 adv (act, fight) loyalement; (play) jouer franc jeu; **to beat sb f. and square** battre qn à plates coutures

fairground ['feəgraʊnd] n parc m d'attractions

fair-haired ['feə'heəd] adj blond(e)

fairly ['feəlɪ] adv (**a**) (quite) assez; **it is f. certain (that)...** il est à peu près certain que... (**b**) (justly) équitablement; (play, fight) loyalement; (describe) objectivement (**c**) (for emphasis) **we f. raced home** nous sommes rentrés ventre à terre

fair-minded ['feə'maɪndɪd] adj équitable

fairness ['feənɪs] n (**a**) (of person, decision) impartialité f; **in all f.** en toute justice (**b**) (of hair) blondeur f; (of skin) pâleur f

fair-sized ['feə'saɪzd] adj assez grand(e)

fairway ['feəweɪ] n fairway m

fair-weather friend ['feəweðə'frend] n = ami qui n'est là que quand tout va bien

fairy ['feərɪ] (pl **fairies**) n (**a**) (magical being) fée f; **f. god-mother** bonne fée f; **f. lights** guirlande f lumineuse (pour sa-

pin de Noël) (**b**) very Fam (homosexual) tapette f, = terme injurieux désignant un homosexuel

fairytale ['feərɪteɪl] n conte m de fées; **a f. ending** une fin digne d'un conte de fées

faith [feɪθ] n foi f; **to have f. in sb** avoir foi en qn; **to be of the Catholic/Jewish f.** être de religion catholique/juive; **to keep f. with sb** tenir ses engagements envers qn; **in good f.** en toute bonne foi; **f. healer** guérisseur(euse) m,f

faith-based school ['feɪθbeɪst'skuːl] n école f confession-nelle

faithful ['feɪθfʊl] **1** npl **the f.** les fidèles mpl
2 adj fidèle

faithfully ['feɪθfʊlɪ] adv fidèlement; **yours f.** (in formal letter) recevez l'expression de mes/nos sentiments distingués

fake [feɪk] **1** n (object) faux m; (person) bluffeur m
2 adj faux (fausse); **f. tan** (product) autobronzant m
3 vt (signature) contrefaire; (result) truquer; **to f. an illness** feindre d'être malade

falafel [fə'læfəl] n Culin falafels mpl

falcon ['fælkən] n faucon m

falconry ['fælkənrɪ] n fauconnerie f

Falkland ['fɔːklənd] n **the F. Islands, the Falklands** les Malouines fpl, les Falkland fpl

fall [fɔːl] **1** n (**a**) (of person, prices, besieged city, snow) chute f; **to have a f.** tomber, faire une chute; Fig **to be heading for a f.** courir à sa perte; Fam **f. guy** (scapegoat) bouc m émissaire
(**b**) (autumn) automne m
(**c**) **falls** (waterfall) chutes fpl
2 vi (pt **fell** [fel], pp **fallen** ['fɔːlən]) (**a**) (drop, fall over) tomber; **to f. down a hole** tomber dans un trou; **to f. off a bicycle/chair** tomber d'un vélo/d'une chaise; Fig **to f. into a trap** tomber dans un piège; also Fig **to f. flat** tomber à plat; **to f. to pieces** (of object) tomber en morceaux; Fig (of person) craquer; **to f. short of doing sth** ne pas réussir à faire qch
(**b**) (decrease) (of price, temperature, standards) chuter, baisser
(**c**) (of government, city, soldier) tomber
(**d**) (of silence, darkness, light) tomber; **the responsibility falls on you** c'est à vous qu'en incombe la responsabilité; Formal **it falls to me to introduce...** j'ai l'honneur de vous présenter...
(**e**) (become) **to f. asleep** s'endormir; **to f. ill** tomber malade; **to f. in love (with)** tomber amoureux(euse) (de); **to f. silent** se taire; **to f. victim to an epidemic** être victime d'une épidémie; **the match fell victim to the weather** le match a dû être annulé en raison du mauvais temps
(**f**) (be classified) se classer; **to f. into two categories** se diviser en deux catégories; **suddenly everything fell into place** soudain tout est devenu clair
(**g**) (occur) **Christmas Day falls on a Thursday** Noël tombe un jeudi

▶**fall away** vi (of ground) descendre; (of attendance) diminuer

▶**fall back on** vt insep (resort to) se rabattre sur

▶**fall behind** vi (in race) se faire distancer; **to f. behind in the rent** être en retard pour payer son loyer

▶**fall down** vi (of person) tomber; (of building) s'écrouler, s'effondrer; **that's where your argument falls down** c'est par là que pèche ton raisonnement

▶**fall for** vt insep Fam (**a**) (fall in love with) tomber amoureux(euse) de (**b**) (trick) se laisser prendre à; **to f. for it** s'y laisser prendre

▶**fall in** vi (**a**) (of roof) s'écrouler, s'effondrer (**b**) Mil (of troops) former les rangs

▶**fall off** vi (**a**) (of object) tomber (**b**) (of profits, attendance) diminuer

▶**fall out** vi (**a**) (quarrel) se brouiller, se fâcher (**with** avec) (**b**) Mil rompre les rangs

▶**fall over 1** vi tomber (par terre)

2 vt insep (stumble on) trébucher sur; Fig **to be falling over oneself to do sth** (be very keen) se mettre en quatre pour faire qch

▶**fall through** vi (of plan, deal) tomber à l'eau

fallacious [fə'leɪʃəs] adj erroné(e)

fallacy ['fæləsɪ] (pl **fallacies**) n erreur f

fallen ['fɔːlən] **1** npl **the f.** les soldats mpl tombés au combat
2 adj (angel) déchu(e); (woman) perdu(e)
3 pp of **fall**

fallible ['fælɪbəl] adj faillible

Fallopian tube [fə'ləʊpɪən'tjuːb] n Anat trompe f de Fallope

fallout ['fɔːlaʊt] n (nuclear) retombées fpl radioactives; Fig (from scandal) retombées fpl; **f. shelter** abri m antiatomique

fallow ['fæləʊ] adj en jachère; **to lie f.** être en jachère; Fig **a f. period** un passage à vide

false [fɔːls] adj faux (fausse); **f. alarm** fausse alerte f; Fig **f. dawn** faux espoir m; **f. economy** fausse économie f; **f. friend** (in foreign language) faux ami m; Psy **f. memory syndrome** syndrome m des faux souvenirs; **f. modesty** fausse modestie f; Fig **to strike a f. note** (in movie) sonner faux; (of person) faire une gaffe; **f. pregnancy** grossesse f nerveuse; **under f. pretenses** (illegally) par des moyens frauduleux; (by lying) sous des prétextes fallacieux; **f. start** (in race) faux départ m; **f. teeth** dentier m; **to bear f. witness** faire un faux témoignage

falsehood ['fɔːlshʊd] n mensonge m

falsely ['fɔːlslɪ] adv (described) faussement; (accused) à tort; (smile) avec fausseté

falsetto [fɔːl'setəʊ] (pl **falsettos**) n Mus voix f de fausset

falsify ['fɔːlsɪfaɪ] (pt & pp **falsified**) vt (a) (forge) (records, document) falsifier (b) (disprove) (theory) prouver la fausseté de

falter ['fɔːltə(r)] vi also Fig vaciller; (of voice) hésiter

fame [feɪm] n renom m, renommée f; **to seek f. and fortune** rechercher la gloire et la fortune

famed [feɪmd] adj célèbre (**for** pour)

familiar [fə'mɪlɪə(r)] adj (a) (well-known) familier(ère) (**to** à) (b) (intimate) familier(ère), intime; **to be on f. terms with sb** avoir des rapports amicaux avec qn; **to get too f. with sb** se permettre trop de familiarités avec qn (c) (acquainted) **to be f. with sb/sth** bien connaître qn/qch

familiarity [fəmɪlɪ'ærɪtɪ] n (a) (intimacy) familiarité f; **f. breeds contempt** avec l'habitude vient la lassitude (b) (acquaintance) connaissance f (**with** de)

familiarize [fə'mɪlɪəraɪz] vt **to f. sb with sth** familiariser qn avec qch; **to f. oneself with sth** se familiariser avec qch

family ['fæmɪlɪ] (pl **families**) n famille f; **it runs in the f.** c'est de famille, ça tient de famille; **to start a f.** fonder une famille; **to treat sb as one of the f.** traiter qn comme un membre de la famille; Fam **to be in the f. way** être enceinte; **f. allowance** allocations fpl familiales; **f. business** entreprise f familiale; **f. doctor/life** docteur m/vie f de famille; **f. man** bon père m de famille; **f. planning** planning m familial; **f. planning clinic** (centre m de) planning familial; **f. resemblance** air m de famille; **f. room** (in hotel) chambre f familiale; (in house) salle f de séjour; **f. tree** arbre m généalogique

famine ['fæmɪn] n famine f; **f. relief** aide f aux victimes d'une famine

famished ['fæmɪʃd] adj affamé(e)

famous ['feɪməs] adj célèbre (**for** pour)

famously ['feɪməslɪ] adv Fam **to get on f. (with sb)** s'entendre à merveille (avec qn)

fan[1] [fæn] **1** n (cooling device) (hand-held) éventail m; (mechanical) ventilateur m; **f. belt** (of car) courroie f de ventilateur; **f. heater** radiateur m soufflant
2 vt (pt & pp **fanned**) (a) (face, person) éventer; **to f. oneself** s'éventer (b) (fire, passions) attiser

▶**fan out** vi se déployer en éventail

fan[2] [fæn] n (enthusiast) fan mf; (of sports team) supporter m; Fig **I'm not a f. of Chinese food** je n'aime pas trop la cuisine chinoise; **f. club** fan-club m; **f. mail** courrier m des admirateurs

fanatic [fə'nætɪk] n & adj fanatique mf

fanatical [fə'nætɪkəl] adj fanatique

fanciful ['fænsɪfʊl] adj (a) (unrealistic) (idea, project) chimérique; (person) qui se fait des idées (b) (design, style) plein(e) de fantaisie

fancy ['fænsɪ] **1** (pl **fancies**) n (a) (imagination) imagination f (b) (whim) fantaisie f, caprice m (c) (liking) **to take a f. to sb** prendre qn en affection; (sexually) s'enticher de qn; **to take a f. to sth** s'enticher de qch; **the house didn't take her f.** la maison ne lui a pas plu
2 adj (jewels, gadget, hat) fantaisie inv; (party, hotel) chic inv; (food, decoration) recherché(e); **f. dress** déguisement m; **f.-dress party** soirée f déguisée
3 vt (pt & pp **fancied**) (imagine) **to f. (that)...** croire ou penser que...; **I f. I've seen her before** j'ai l'impression de l'avoir déjà vue; **to f. oneself as a writer/musician** se prendre pour un écrivain/musicien; Fam **f. that!** ça alors!; **f. meeting you here!** si je m'attendais à te/vous rencontrer ici!

fanfare ['fænfeə(r)] n fanfare f

fanfic ['fænfɪk] n Fam fanfic f, fanfiction f

fang [fæŋ] n (of dog) croc m; (of snake) crochet m

fanny ['fænɪ] (pl **fannies**) n Fam (buttocks) derrière m, fesses fpl; **f. pack** banane f

fantasize ['fæntəsaɪz] vi fantasmer (**about** sur)

fantastic [fæn'tæstɪk] adj (a) Fam (excellent) formidable, fantastique (b) (enormous) (price) astronomique; (wealth, size) prodigieux(euse) (c) (unbelievable) (claim, story) grotesque, absurde (d) (strange) (creature) fantastique; (design) plein(e) de fantaisie

fantasy ['fæntəzɪ] (pl **fantasies**) n (a) (unrealistic idea) chimère f; (sexual) fantasme m (b) (imagination) fantaisie f (c) (literature) littérature f fantastique

FAO [efeɪ'əʊ] n (abbr **Food and Agriculture Organization**) FAO f

FAQ [efeɪ'kjuː] n Comput (abbr **frequently asked questions**) FAQ f

far [fɑː(r)] (comparative **farther** ['fɑːðə(r)] or **further** ['fɜːðə(r)], superlative **farthest** ['fɑːðɪst] or **furthest** ['fɜːðɪst]) **1** adj **in the f. distance** au loin, dans le lointain; **the f. end** l'autre bout; Pol **the f. left/right** l'extrême gauche f/droite f; **the F. East** l'Extrême-Orient m; **it's a f. cry from** ça n'a rien à voir avec
2 adv (a) (in distance) loin; **how f. is it to Toulouse?** combien y a-t-il jusqu'à Toulouse?; **f. away (from)** loin (de); **f. below/above** loin au-dessous/au-dessus; **as f. as** jusqu'à; also Fig **to go f.** aller loin; Fig **to go so f. as to do sth** aller jusqu'à faire qch; Fig **to go too f.** aller trop loin; also Fig **f. from...** loin de...; Fig **f. from it** loin de là; Fig **f. be it from me to...** loin de moi l'idée de...; **f. and wide** partout; Fig **as f. as I can see** pour autant que je puisse en juger; **as f. as I know** (pour) autant que je sache; **as f. as I'm concerned** en ce qui me concerne; Fig **as f. as possible** autant que possible
(b) (in time) **so f.** jusqu'ici, jusqu'à présent; **so f. so good** jusqu'ici tout va bien; **for as f. back as I can remember** d'aussi loin que je me souvienne; **to work f. into the night** travailler jusqu'à une heure avancée de la nuit
(c) (much) beaucoup; **f. better/bigger** beaucoup mieux/plus grand; **by f.** de loin; **f. and away the best** de loin le meilleur/la meilleure

faraway ['fɑːrəweɪ] adj lointain(e); (look) perdu(e) dans le vague

farce [fɑːs] n farce f; Fig **it's a f.!** c'est grotesque!

farcical ['fɑːsɪkəl] adj grotesque

fare [feə(r)] **1** n (a) (for journey) tarif m; **to pay one's f.** acheter son billet (**b**) *(taxi passenger)* client(e) *m,f* (**c**) *Formal (food)* chère *f*

2 *vi* se débrouiller

farewell [feə'wel] *n* adieu *m*; **to say** *or* **to make one's farewells** faire ses adieux; **f. dinner** dîner *m* d'adieu

far-fetched ['fɑː'fetʃt] *adj (idea, plan)* tiré(e) par les cheveux

far-flung ['fɑː'flʌŋ] *adj* lointain(e)

farm [fɑːm] **1** *n* ferme *f*; **f. animals** animaux *mpl* de ferme; **f. laborer** ouvrier *m* agricole; *Fam Fig* **to buy the f.** *(die)* clamser, claquer

2 *vt (land)* cultiver, exploiter

3 *vi* être cultivateur(trice)

▸**farm out** *vt sep (work)* confier en sous-traitance (**to** à); *(child)* confier (**to** à)

farmer ['fɑːmə(r)] *n* fermier(ère) *m,f*, agriculteur(trice) *m,f*

farmhouse ['fɑːmhaʊs] *n (corps m de)* ferme *f*

farming ['fɑːmɪŋ] *n (business)* agriculture *f*

farmland ['fɑːmlænd] *n* terres *fpl* arables

farmyard ['fɑːmjɑːd] *n* cour *f* de ferme

Faroe ['feərəʊ] *n* **the F. Islands, the Faroes** les îles *fpl* Féroé

far-off ['fɑːrɒf] *adj (country, time)* lointain(e); *(place)* éloigné(e)

far-out ['fɑːraʊt] *adj Fam (strange)* farfelu(e); *(avant-garde)* avant-gardiste; **f.!** *(fantastic)* génial!

far-reaching ['fɑː'riːtʃɪŋ] *adj (decision, change)* de grande envergure; *(consequences)* d'une grande portée

Farsi ['fɑːsiː] *n* farsi *m*

far-sighted ['fɑː'saɪtɪd] *adj* (**a**) *(forward-looking) (person)* prévoyant(e); *(decision)* avisé(e) (**b**) *(eyesight)* presbyte

fart [fɑːt] *Fam* **1** *n* (**a**) *(gas)* pet *m* (**b**) *(person)* birbe *m*; **he's a boring old f.** il est rasoir

2 *vi* péter

▸**fart about** *vi Fam (waste time)* glander

farther ['fɑːðə(r)] *comparative of* **far**

farthest ['fɑːðɪst] *superlative of* **far**

fascinate ['fæsɪneɪt] *vt* fasciner

fascinating ['fæsɪneɪtɪŋ] *adj* fascinant(e)

fascination [fæsɪ'neɪʃən] *n* fascination *f*

fascism ['fæʃɪzəm] *n* fascisme *m*

fascist ['fæʃɪst] *n & adj* fasciste *mf*

fashion ['fæʃən] **1** *n* (**a**) *(in clothes)* mode *f*; **in f.** à la mode; **out of f.** démodé(e), passé(e) de mode; **f. designer** styliste *mf*; *(big name)* couturier(ère) *m,f*; **f. house** maison *f* de couture; **f. plate** gravure *f* de mode; *Fig* élégant(e) *m,f*; **f. show** défilé *m* de mode; *Pej* **f. victim** esclave *mf* de la mode (**b**) *(manner)* manière *f*; **after a f.** tant bien que mal

2 *vt (form)* façonner; *(make)* confectionner

fashionable ['fæʃənəbəl] *adj* à la mode

fashionista [fæʃə'niːstə] *n* modeux(euse) *m,f*

fast[1] [fɑːst] **1** *adj* (**a**) *(rapid)* rapide; *Fam* **he pulled a f. one on me** il m'a joué un mauvais tour; **f. food** restauration *f* rapide; **f. food restaurant** fast-food *m*; **the f. lane** *(of highway)* la voie rapide; *Fig* **to live life in the f. lane** vivre à cent à l'heure (**b**) *(clock, watch)* **my watch is (five minutes) f.** ma montre avance (de cinq minutes) (**c**) *(secure) (grip)* ferme, solide; *(door, lid)* bien fermé(e); *(color)* résistant(e)

2 *adv* (**a**) *(rapidly)* vite, rapidement; **not so f.!** pas si vite!; **to play f. and loose with the facts** truquer les faits; **to play f. and loose with sb's emotions** jouer avec les sentiments de qn (**b**) *(securely)* solidement; **to hold f.** tenir bon; **f. asleep** profondément endormi(e)

fast[2] [fɑːst] **1** *n (lack of food)* jeûne *m*; *Rel* **f. day** jour *m* de jeûne

2 *vi* jeûner; *Med* être à la diète

fasten ['fɑːsən] **1** *vt (door, window)* fermer; *(belt, buttons)* attacher; *Fig* **to f. one's eyes on sth** fixer son regard sur qch

2 *vi (garment)* s'attacher

fastener ['fɑːsənə(r)] *n (of garment) (hook)* agrafe *f*; *(press stud)* bouton-pression *m*; *(of bag, jewelry)* fermoir *m*

fast-forward [fɑːst'fɔːwəd] **1** *n* avance *f* rapide

2 *vt (cassette)* mettre en avance rapide

fastidious [fæ'stɪdɪəs] *adj* difficile; *(about manners, hygiene, details)* pointilleux(euse) (**about** sur)

fast-moving ['fɑːst'muːvɪŋ] *adj* rapide

fat [fæt] **1** *n* (**a**) *(flesh)* graisse *f*; *(of cooked meat)* gras *m*; *(for cooking)* matière *f* grasse; **f. content** teneur *f* en graisse *ou* en lipides (**b**) *(idioms) Fam* **the f.'s in the fire!** ça va chauffer!; **to live off the f. of the land** vivre comme un coq en pâte; **to chew the f. (with sb)** tailler le bout de gras (avec qn)

2 *adj (person)* gros (grosse); *Fam (check, profit, salary)* gros; **to get f.** grossir; *Fig* **to grow f. at the expense of others** *(become rich)* s'engraisser aux dépens des autres; *Fam* **a f. lot of good that'll do you!** ça te fera une belle jambe!; *Fig* **f. cat** = personne touchant un salaire extrêmement élevé de façon injustifiée; *Fam* **f. camp, f. farm** centre *m* d'amaigrissement; *Fam* **f. chance!** tu parles!

fatal ['feɪtəl] *adj* mortel(elle)

fatalistic [feɪtə'lɪstɪk] *adj* fataliste

fatality [fə'tælɪtɪ] *(pl* **fatalities***)* *n* (**a**) *(person killed)* mort *m* (**b**) *(fate)* fatalité *f*

fatally ['feɪtəlɪ] *adv (wounded)* mortellement; **f. ill** condamné(e); **to be f. damaging to sth** causer un tort irréparable à qch

fate [feɪt] *n* destin *m*, sort *m*; **to suffer** *or* **to share the same f.** avoir le même sort; **it's a f. worse than death** c'est ce qu'on peut imaginer de pire

fated ['feɪtɪd] *adj* **to be f. to do sth** être destiné(e) à faire qch

fateful ['feɪtfʊl] *adj (words, day)* fatidique

father ['fɑːðə(r)] **1** *n (parent, priest)* père *m*; **from f. to son** de père en fils; **he was like a f. to me** il était comme un père pour moi; **like f., like son** tel père, tel fils; **Our F.** *(God)* Notre Père; **F.'s Day** la fête des pères; **to be a f. figure to sb** jouer le rôle du père pour qn

2 *vt (child)* engendrer

fatherhood ['fɑːðəhʊd] *n* paternité *f*

father-in-law ['fɑːðərɪnlɔː] *n* beau-père *m*

fatherly ['fɑːðəlɪ] *adj* paternel(elle)

fathom ['fæðəm] **1** *n (unit of measurement)* = 1,8 m, brasse *f*

2 *vt (understand)* comprendre

▸**fathom out** *vt sep (understand)* comprendre

fatigue [fə'tiːg] **1** *n* (**a**) *(tiredness)* fatigue *f*; **metal f.** fatigue des métaux (**b**) *Mil* **f. (duty)** corvée *f*; **fatigues** *(clothes)* treillis *m*

2 *vt (person)* fatiguer

fatso ['fætsəʊ] *(pl* **fatsos** *or* **fatsoes***)* *n Fam (man)* gros lard *m*; *(woman)* grosse vache *f*

▸**fatten up** ['fætən] *vt sep* faire grossir, engraisser

fatty ['fætɪ] **1** *n (pl* **fatties***)* *Fam* gros (grosse) *m,f*; **hey f.!** eh, bouboule!

2 *adj (food, meat)* gras (grasse); *(tissue)* adipeux(euse); **f. acid** acide *m* gras

fatuous ['fætjʊəs] *adj* idiot(e)

faucet ['fɔːsɪt] *n* robinet *m*

fault [fɔːlt] **1** *n* (**a**) *(flaw)* défaut *m*; *(in mechanism, on phone line)* problème *m*; **to find f. with** trouver à redire à; **to be generous to a f.** être généreux(euse) à l'excès (**b**) *(guilt)* faute *f*; **to be at f.** être en faute; **whose f. is it?** à qui la faute?; **it's my f.** c'est (de) ma faute; **through no f. of mine** sans que ce soit de ma faute (**c**) *(in tennis, squash)* faute *f* (**d**) *(geological)* faille *f*

2 *vt (person)* prendre en défaut; *(logic)* trouver une faille dans; **her attitude can't be faulted** il n'y a rien à redire à sa conduite

faultless ['fɔːltlɪs] *adj* impeccable

faulty ['fɔːltɪ] *adj* défectueux(euse)

faun [fɔːn] *n* faune *m*

fauna ['fɔːnə] *n* faune *f*

favor ['feɪvə(r)] **1** *n* (**a**) *(approval)* **to be in/out of f.** *(of person)* être bien/mal vu(e); *(of method)* être/ne plus être en faveur; **to look on sb/sth with f.** être bien disposé(e) envers qn/qch; **to find f. with sb** trouver grâce aux yeux de qn **(b)** *(act of kindness)* service *m*; **to do sb a f.** rendre service à qn; *Fam* **do me a f. and shut up!** ferme-la, tu veux?; **to ask sb a f., to ask a f. of sb** demander un service à qn **(c)** *(advantage)* **that's a point in her f.** c'est un élément en sa faveur; *Fin* **balance in your f.** solde *m* en votre faveur **(d) in f. of** *(in preference to)* en faveur de; **to be in f. of sth** être partisan(e) de qch/être favorable à qch

2 *vt* **(a)** *(prefer)* être pour, être partisan(e) de; **to f. sb** *(be biased toward)* favoriser qn **(b)** *(honor)* **to f. sb with sth** gratifier qn de qch

favorable ['feɪvərəbəl] *adj* favorable; *(terms)* avantageux(euse); **in a f. light** sous un jour favorable

favorite ['feɪvərɪt] **1** *n* favori(ite) *m,f*, préféré(e) *m,f*; *(in betting)* favori

2 *adj* favori(ite), préféré(e)

favoritism ['feɪvərɪtɪzəm] *n* favoritisme *m*

fawn¹ [fɔːn] **1** *n* **(a)** *(deer)* faon *m* **(b)** *(color)* fauve *m*

2 *adj* *(color)* fauve

fawn² [fɔːn] *vi* **to f. on sb** *(of person)* ramper devant qn; *(of dog)* faire fête à qn

fax [fæks] **1** *n* *(machine)* fax *m*, *Offic* télécopieur *m*; *(message)* fax *m*, *Offic* télécopie *f*; **f. modem** modem-fax *m*; **f. number** numéro *m* de fax

2 *vt* *(message, document)* faxer, envoyer par fax; *(person)* envoyer un fax à

faze [feɪz] *vt Fam* déconcerter

FBI [efbiː'aɪ] *n* *(abbr* **Federal Bureau of Investigation**) FBI *m*

fear [fɪə(r)] **1** *n* peur *f*; *(worry)* crainte *f*; **to be** *or* **to go in f. of** avoir peur de, redouter; **to go in f. of one's life** craindre pour sa vie; *Fam* **to put the f. of God into sb** faire une peur bleue à qn; **he didn't tell her for f. of her reaction** il ne lui a rien dit par peur de sa réaction; **for f. of doing sth** de peur de faire qch; **I didn't tell him, for f. that he'd be angry** je ne lui ai rien dit, de peur qu'il ne se mette en colère; *Fam* **no f.!** pas de danger!

2 *vt* craindre, redouter; **I f. there's been a misunderstanding** je crains qu'il (n')y ait eu un malentendu; **I f. so/not** je crains que oui/non; **to f. the worst** craindre le pire

3 *vi* **to f. for** craindre pour; **never f.!** ne crains rien!

fearful ['fɪəfʊl] *adj* **(a)** *(pain, consequence, noise)* épouvantable **(b)** *(person)* apeuré(e); **to be f. of doing sth** avoir peur de faire qch

fearless ['fɪəlɪs] *adj* intrépide

fearlessly ['fɪəlɪslɪ] *adv* avec intrépidité

fearsome ['fɪəsəm] *adj* effrayant(e)

feasibility [fiːzə'bɪlɪtɪ] *n* possibilité *f*; *(of plan)* faisabilité *f*; **f. study** étude *f* de faisabilité

feasible ['fiːzəbəl] *adj* faisable

feast [fiːst] **1** *n* festin *m*, banquet *m*; *Rel* **f. day** *(jour m de)* fête *f*

2 *vt* **to f. one's eyes on sth** repaître ses yeux de qch

3 *vi* **to f. on** se régaler de

feat [fiːt] *n* exploit *m*; **a f. of skill** un tour de force

feather ['feðə(r)] **1** *n* plume *f*; **you could have knocked me down with a f.** je n'en revenais pas; *Fig* **that's a f. in her cap** elle peut en être fière; **f. bed** lit *m* de plumes

2 *vt Fig* **to f. one's nest** faire son beurre

featherweight ['feðəweɪt] *n* *(in boxing)* poids *m* plume

feathery ['feðərɪ] *adj* doux (douce) et léger(ère) comme de la plume

feature ['fiːtʃə(r)] **1** *n* **(a)** *(of face)* trait *m* **(b)** *(characteristic)* caractéristique *f* **(c) f. (film)** long métrage *m* **(d)** *(in newspaper)* article *m* de fond; *(on television, radio)* reportage *m*; **f. writer** éditorialiste *mf*

2 *vt* *(of magazine, exhibition)* présenter; **a movie featuring...** un film ayant pour vedette...

3 *vi* *(appear)* figurer

featureless ['fiːtʃəlɪs] *adj* sans caractéristiques marquées

Feb. *(abbr* **February**) févr

febrile ['fiːbraɪl] *adj* fébrile

February ['februərɪ] *n* février *m*; *see also* **May**

feces ['fiːsiːz] *npl* fèces *fpl*

feckless ['feklɪs] *adj* **(a)** *(irresponsible)* irresponsable **(b)** *(ineffectual)* incapable

Fed [fed] *n* **(a)** *(abbr* **Federal Reserve Board**) banque *f* centrale (des États-Unis) **(b)** *(abbr* **Federal Reserve (System)**) (système *m* de) Réserve *f* fédérale

fed [fed] *pt & pp of* **feed**

federal ['fedərəl] *adj* fédéral(e)

federalism ['fedərəlɪzəm] *n* fédéralisme *m*

federalist ['fedərəlɪst] *n & adj* fédéraliste *mf*

federation [fedə'reɪʃən] *n* fédération *f*

fed up ['fedʌp] *adj Fam* **to be f. (with)** en avoir ras le bol (de), en avoir marre (de)

fee [fiː] *n* *(of lawyer, doctor)* honoraires *mpl*; *(for entrance)* droit *m* d'entrée; *(for membership)* cotisation *f*; **school fees** droits *mpl* d'inscription

feeble ['fiːbəl] *adj* faible; *(attempt)* peu convaincant(e)

feeble-minded ['fiːbəl'maɪndɪd] *adj* faible d'esprit

feebly ['fiːblɪ] *adv* faiblement; *(protest, reprimand)* mollement

feed [fiːd] **1** *n* **(a)** *(animal food)* nourriture *f* **(b)** *(for baby) (from breast)* tétée *f*; *(from bottle)* biberon *m*

2 *vt* *(pt & pp* **fed** [fed]) **(a)** *(give food to)* donner à manger à; *(baby) (from breast)* donner la tétée à; *(from bottle)* donner son biberon à; *(plant)* mettre de l'engrais à; **we were well fed** nous étions bien nourris; **to f. one's family** nourrir sa famille **(b)** *(supply)* **to f. a fire** alimenter un feu; **to f. coins into a machine** mettre des pièces dans une machine; **to f. sb with information** fournir des informations à qn

3 *vi* *(survive)* **to f. on** se nourrir de

feedback ['fiːdbæk] *n Elec* effet *m* Larsen; *Fig (response)* écho *m*, réactions *fpl*

feel [fiːl] **1** *n* **(a)** *(sensation)* toucher *m*; **the f. of silk against her skin** le contact de la soie contre sa peau; **the movie has an authentic f. to it** le film dégage une impression d'authenticité

(b) *(knack)* **to have a f. for translation/music** avoir un sens inné de la traduction/musique; **to get the f. of sth** s'habituer à qch

2 *vt* *(pt & pp* **felt** [felt]) **(a)** *(touch)* toucher; *(investigate)* tâter; **to f. one's way** *(in darkness)* avancer à tâtons; *Fig (in new situation)* essayer de s'habituer

(b) *(be physically aware of)* sentir; **I felt the floor tremble** *or* **trembling** j'ai senti le sol trembler

(c) *(experience) (relief, pain, despair)* ressentir, éprouver; **I f. it in my bones** *(have intuition)* je le sens

(d) *(believe)* **to f. (that)...** penser que...

3 *vi* **(a)** *(physically)* **to f. tired** se sentir fatigué(e); **to f. ill** ne pas se sentir bien; **to f. hot/cold/hungry/thirsty** avoir chaud/froid/faim/soif; **my foot feels better** j'ai moins mal au pied; **how are you feeling?** comment ça va *ou* te sens-tu?; **I don't f. myself** je ne suis pas dans mon assiette; **to f. up to doing sth** *(well enough)* se sentir assez bien pour faire qch; *(competent enough)* se sentir de taille à faire qch; **to f. (like) a new man/woman** se sentir comme neuf/neuve

(b) *(emotionally)* se sentir; **to f. strongly about sth** avoir des idées très arrêtées sur qch; **I f. bad about leaving her** cela m'ennuie de la quitter; **how would you f. if...?** comment est-ce que tu te sentirais si...?; **it feels strange** c'est étrange; **I felt as if I'd seen him before** j'avais l'impression de l'avoir déjà vu; **to f. like doing sth** avoir envie de faire qch; **I f. like a**

cup of tea *(would like)* j'ai envie d'une tasse de thé (**c**) *(have sympathy)* **to f. for sb** plaindre qn (**d**) *(of things)* **to f. hard/hot** être dur(e)/chaud(e); **it feels like (it's going to) rain** on dirait qu'il va pleuvoir (**e**) *(search)* **to f. in one's pockets for sth** chercher qch dans ses poches; **he felt on the ground for the key** il cherchait sa clé à tâtons sur le sol

feeler ['fiːlə(r)] *n (of insect)* antenne *f; (of snail)* corne *f; Fig* **to put out feelers** tâter le terrain

feelgood ['fiːlgʊd] *adj Fam* **a f. movie** un film qui donne la pêche; **the f. factor** l'optimisme *m* ambiant

feeling ['fiːlɪŋ] *n* (**a**) *(sense of)* **f.** toucher *m;* **to have no f. in one's arm** avoir le bras mort (**b**) *(sensation) (of cold, pain)* sensation *f* (**c**) *(emotion, impression)* sentiment *m;* **a f. of joy/anger** de la joie/colère; **to speak with f.** *(emotionally)* parler avec émotion; *(warmly)* parler avec chaleur; **I know the f.!** je sais ce que c'est!; **I had a f. I might find you here** je pensais bien vous trouver ici; **to hurt sb's feelings** blesser qn; **to have no feelings** n'avoir aucun cœur; **feelings were running high** les esprits étaient très échauffés; **no hard feelings!** sans rancune! (**d**) *(sensitivity)* sensibilité *f;* **to have a f. for sth** *(music, art)* être sensible à qch

feet [fiːt] *pl of* **foot**

feign [feɪn] *vt (anger, surprise)* feindre; **to f. illness/sleep** feindre d'être malade/de dormir

feint [feɪnt] **1** *n (in combat sports)* feinte *f* **2** *vi (in combat sports)* faire une feinte

feisty ['faɪstɪ] *adj Fam (lively)* plein(e) d'entrain; *(combative)* qui a du cran

felicitous [fɪ'lɪsɪtəs] *adj* heureux(euse)

feline ['fiːlaɪn] **1** *n* félin *m* **2** *adj* félin(e)

fell¹ [fel] *pt of* **fall**

fell² [fel] *vt (tree)* abattre, couper; *(opponent)* terrasser

fell³ [fel] *adj* **at one f. swoop** d'un seul coup

fellow ['feləʊ] *n* (**a**) *(comrade)* camarade *mf;* **f. citizen** concitoyen(enne) *m,f;* **f. countryman/countrywoman** compatriote *mf;* **f. passenger** compagnon *m* de voyage; **f. worker** collègue *mf;* **f. student** camarade d'études; **f. feeling** sympathie *f; Fig* **f. traveler** *(in politics)* compagnon de route (**b**) *(teacher)* professeur *m* titulaire; *(student)* boursier(ère) *m,f; (of academy, society)* membre *m* (**c**) *Fam (man)* gars *m*

fellowship ['feləʊʃɪp] *n* (**a**) *(friendship)* camaraderie *f* (**b**) *(association)* association *f,* corporation *f* (**c**) *(at university)* bourse *f* de recherche

felon ['felən] *n Law* criminel(elle) *m,f*

felony ['felənɪ] *(pl* **felonies**) *n Law* crime *m*

felt¹ [felt] *n (fabric)* feutre *m; (thinner)* feutrine *f*

felt² [felt] *pt & pp of* **feel**

felt-tip ['felt'tɪp] *n* **f. (pen)** *(crayon m)* feutre *m*

female ['fiːmeɪl] **1** *n (person)* femme *f; (animal, plant)* femelle *f* **2** *adj (person)* féminin(e); *(animal, plant)* femelle

feminine ['femɪnɪn] **1** *n Gram* féminin *m;* **in the f.** au féminin **2** *adj* féminin(e)

femininity [femɪ'nɪnɪtɪ] *n* féminité *f*

feminism ['femɪnɪzəm] *n* féminisme *m*

feminist ['femɪnɪst] *n & adj* féministe *mf*

femur ['fiːmə(r)] *n Anat* fémur *m*

fen [fen] *n (marshy land)* marais *m*

fence [fens] **1** *n* (**a**) *(barrier)* clôture *f; (more solid)* barrière *f; Fig* **to sit on the f.** ménager la chèvre et le chou; *Fig* **to get off the f.** se prononcer (**b**) *Fam (receiver of stolen property)* receleur(euse) *m,f* **2** *vi (as sport)* faire de l'escrime

▶**fence off** *vt sep* séparer par une clôture

fencing ['fensɪŋ] *n (sport)* escrime *f*

fend [fend] *vi* **to f. for oneself** se débrouiller (tout(e) seul(e))

▶**fend off** *vt sep (attack, blow)* parer; *(question)* éluder

fender ['fendə(r)] *n* (**a**) *(of car)* aile *f* (**b**) *(for fireplace)* garde-feu *m inv*

fennel ['fenəl] *n* fenouil *m*

ferment 1 *n* ['fɜːment] *(commotion)* agitation *f;* **in a (state of) f.** en effervescence **2** *vi* [fə'ment] *(of alcoholic drink)* fermenter

fermentation [fɜːmen'teɪʃən] *n* fermentation *f*

fern [fɜːn] *n* fougère *f*

ferocious [fə'rəʊʃəs] *adj* féroce

ferocity [fə'rɒsɪtɪ] *n* férocité *f*

ferret ['ferɪt] **1** *n* furet *m* **2** *vi* **to f. (about) for sth** fouiller à la recherche de qch

▶**ferret out** *vt sep (object, information)* dénicher

ferris wheel ['ferɪs'wiːl] *n* grande roue *f*

ferrous ['ferəs] *adj* ferreux(euse)

ferry ['ferɪ] **1** *n (pl* **ferries**) bac *m; (larger)* ferry *m* **2** *vt (pt & pp* **ferried**) transporter **3** *vi* **to f. back and forth** faire la navette

ferryman ['ferɪmən] *n* passeur *m*

fertile ['fɜːtaɪl] *adj also Fig* fertile

fertility [fɜː'tɪlɪtɪ] *n also Fig* fertilité *f;* **f. treatment** traitement *m* de la stérilité

fertilize ['fɜːtɪlaɪz] *vt (egg, plant)* féconder; *(soil)* fertiliser

fertilizer ['fɜːtɪlaɪzə(r)] *n* engrais *m*

fervent ['fɜːvənt] *adj (admirer, nationalist)* fervent(e); *(belief, desire)* ardent(e)

fervor ['fɜːvə(r)] *n* ferveur *f*

fester ['festə(r)] *vi (of wound)* s'infecter; *Fig (of situation)* s'envenimer; *(of dislike, resentment)* s'aviver

festival ['festɪvəl] *n* festival *m; (religious)* fête *f*

festive ['festɪv] *adj* de fête; **in f. mood** d'humeur festive

festivity [fes'tɪvɪtɪ] *(pl* **festivities**) *n (merriness)* gaieté *f;* **the festivities** *(celebrations)* les festivités *fpl*

festoon [fes'tuːn] *vt* orner (**with** de)

fetal ['fiːtəl] *adj* fœtal(e); **in the f. position** en position fœtale

fetch [fetʃ] *vt* (**a**) *(bring)* aller chercher (**b**) *(be sold for)* rapporter

▶**fetch up** *vi (end up) (of people)* se retrouver

fetching ['fetʃɪŋ] *adj (person, hat, smile)* ravissant(e)

fête [feɪt] **1** *n* fête *f* **2** *vt* fêter

fetid ['fetɪd] *adj* fétide

fetish ['fetɪʃ] *n (object)* fétiche *m;* **to have a f. for sth** faire une fixation sur qch

fetter ['fetə(r)] **1** *n* **fetters** *(on slave, prisoner)* fers *mpl; Fig (on rights, freedom)* entraves *fpl* **2** *vt (slave, prisoner)* enchaîner; *Fig (union, women)* entraver la liberté de

fettle ['fetəl] *n* **in good** *or* **fine f.** en condition

fetus ['fiːtəs] *n* fœtus *m*

feud [fjuːd] **1** *n* querelle *f* **2** *vi* se quereller (**with** avec)

feudal ['fjuːdəl] *adj* féodal(e); *Fig (approach, attitude)* moyenâgeux(euse)

feudalism ['fjuːdəlɪzəm] *n* le système féodal

fever ['fiːvə(r)] *n also Fig* fièvre *f;* **to have a f.** avoir de la fièvre; **excitement had risen to f. pitch** l'excitation était à son comble

feverish ['fiːvərɪʃ] *adj* fiévreux(euse); *Fig (atmosphere)* de fièvre

few [fjuː] **1** *adj* (**a**) *(not many)* peu de; **f. friends** peu d'amis; **too f. people/opportunities** trop peu de gens/d'occasions; **f. and far between** rarissime; **every f. minutes** toutes les deux ou trois minutes; **as f. as a dozen finished the race** seuls une douzaine d'entre eux ont terminé la course (**b**) *(some)* **a f.** quelques; **a f. friends** quelques amis; **a good f., quite a**

f. pas mal de; **in the next f. days** dans les jours qui suivent/
suivirent

2 *pron* (**a**) *(not many)* peu; **there are too f. of us** nous
sommes trop peu nombreux; **f. of them** peu d'entre eux; **f. if
any children** aucun enfant ou presque (**b**) *(some)* **a f.** quelques-uns (quelques-unes) *mpl, fpl*; **a f. of the survivors** quelques-uns des survivants; **a f. of them** quelques-uns d'entre eux

3 *n* **the f. who came** les rares personnes qui sont venues

fewer ['fjuːə(r)] *(comparative of few)* **1** *adj* moins de; **f.
friends** moins d'amis; **no f. than thirty** pas moins de trente;
the houses became f. les maisons devenaient plus rares; **f.
and f. people** de moins en moins de gens

2 *pron* moins; **there are f. (of them) than I thought** il y
en a moins que je ne pensais

fewest ['fjuːɪst] *(superlative of few)* **1** *adj* le moins de
2 *pron* le moins

fiasco [fɪ'æskəʊ] *(pl fiascos)* *n* fiasco *m*

fib [fɪb] *Fam* **1** *n* bobard *m*
2 *vi (pt & pp fibbed)* raconter des bobards

fibber ['fɪbə(r)] *n Fam* menteur(euse) *m,f*

fiber ['faɪbə(r)] *n* fibre *f*; *(in diet)* fibres *fpl*; **f. optics** technologie
f des fibres optiques

fiberglass ['faɪbəglɑːs] *n* fibre *f* de verre

fibrous ['faɪbrəs] *adj* fibreux(euse)

fickle ['fɪkəl] *adj (friend, fan)* inconstant(e); *(lover)* inconstant,
volage; *(weather)* changeant(e)

fiction ['fɪkʃən] *n (genre)* fiction *f*; *(books)* livres *mpl* de fiction;
(lie) invention *f*

fictional ['fɪkʃənəl] *adj* fictif(ive)

fictitious [fɪk'tɪʃəs] *adj* fictif(ive)

fiddle ['fɪdəl] **1** *n (violin)* violon *m*
2 *vt Fam (cheat)* combiner; **to f. the books** truquer les comptes
3 *vi* (**a**) *(play violin)* jouer du violon (**b**) *(fidget)* **to f. (about or
around) with sth** tripoter qch

fiddler ['fɪdlə(r)] *n* violoniste *mf*

fiddlesticks ['fɪdəlstɪks] *exclam Old-fashioned (nonsense)* balivernes!; *(expressing annoyance)* zut de zut!

fidelity [fɪ'delɪtɪ] *n* fidélité *f*

fidget ['fɪdʒɪt] **1** *n* **to be a f.** ne pas tenir en place
2 *vi* gigoter; **stop fidgeting!** arrête de gigoter!

fidgety ['fɪdʒɪtɪ] *adj* agité(e)

field [fiːld] **1** *n* (**a**) *(of farm)* & *Comput* champ *m*; *(for sports)*
terrain *m*; *(of oil, coal)* gisement *m*; **to work in the f.** *(not in
office)* travailler sur le terrain; **f. of vision** champ visuel; **f.
events** *(in athletics)* le saut et le lancer; **f. hockey** hockey *m*
sur gazon; **f. study** étude *f* sur le terrain; *Sch & Univ* **f. trip**
voyage *m* d'étude; **f. work** *(scientific)* recherches *fpl* sur le terrain (**b**) *Mil* **in the f.** en campagne; *Fig* **to have a f. day** s'en
donner à cœur joie; **f. glasses** jumelles *fpl*; **f. gun** canon *m* (de
campagne); **f. hospital** antenne *f* chirurgicale; **f. marshal** ≃
maréchal *m* de France (**c**) *(of knowledge)* domaine *m* (**d**) *(in race,
contest)* partants *mpl*; **to lead the f.** *Sport* mener le peloton; *Fig*
occuper la première place

2 *vt* (**a**) *(team)* composer (**b**) *(question)* répondre à

fieldmouse ['fiːldmaʊs] *(pl fieldmice* ['fiːldmaɪs]*)* *n* mulot *m*

fiend [fiːnd] *n (cruel person)* monstre *m*; *(demon)* démon *m*; **sex
f.** obsédé(e) *m,f* sexuel(elle); **jazz f.** fanatique *mf* de jazz

fiendish ['fiːndɪʃ] *adj (scheme, question)* diabolique; *(weather,
temper)* abominable

fiendishly ['fiːndɪʃlɪ] *adv (difficult)* horriblement

fierce ['fɪəs] *adj (animal, look)* féroce; *(appearance, person)* redoutable; *(wind, storm, criticism)* violent(e); *(heat)* torride; *(contest)* acharné(e)

fiercely ['fɪəslɪ] *adv (look)* d'un œil féroce; *(fight)* avec acharnement; *(criticize)* violemment

fiery ['faɪərɪ] *adj (red)* ardent(e); *(sky)* enflammé(e); *(taste)* très

épicé(e); *(person, character)* fougueux(euse)

fifteen [fɪf'tiːn] **1** *n (number)* quinze *m inv*
2 *adj* quinze; *see also* **eight**

fifteenth [fɪf'tiːnθ] **1** *n* (**a**) *(fraction)* quinzième *m* (**b**) *(in series)* quinzième *mf* (**c**) *(of month)* quinze *m inv*
2 *adj* quinzième; *see also* **eighth**

fifth [fɪfθ] **1** *n* (**a**) *(fraction)* cinquième *m* (**b**) *(in series)* cinquième *mf* (**c**) *(of month)* cinq *m inv*
2 *adj* cinquième; *Pol* **f. column** cinquième colonne *f*; **f. floor**
quatrième étage *m*; *Scol* **f. grade** ≃ classe du primaire pour les
9–10 ans; *Fig* **to be the f. wheel** tenir la chandelle; *see also*
eighth

fiftieth ['fɪftɪəθ] **1** *n* (**a**) *(fraction)* cinquantième *m* (**b**) *(in series)* cinquantième *mf*
2 *adj* cinquantième

fifty ['fɪftɪ] **1** *n* cinquante *m inv*
2 *adj* cinquante; *see also* **eighty**

fig [fɪg] *n (fruit)* figue *f*; *Fam* **she doesn't give** *or* **care a f.** elle
s'en fiche éperdument; **f. leaf** feuille *f* de figuier; *(in paintings)*
feuille de vigne; *Fig* **it's just a f. leaf** ce n'est qu'une couverture; **f. tree** figuier *m*

fig. [fɪg] *(abbr* **figure***)* fig

fight [faɪt] **1** *n* (**a**) *(physical)* bagarre *f*; *(verbal)* dispute *f*; *(boxing
match)* combat *m*; **to get into a f. with sb** *(physical)* se battre
avec qn; *(verbal)* se disputer avec qn; **to start a f. (with sb)**
provoquer une bagarre (avec qn); **to put up a good f.** bien se
défendre (**b**) *(spirit)* **to show some f.** résister; **there was no
f. left in him** il n'avait plus le cœur à se battre (**c**) *(struggle)*
lutte *f* (**for/against** pour/contre)
2 *vt (pt & pp fought* [fɔːt]*)* *(person)* se battre contre; *(decision,
enemy)* combattre; *(disease, fire, temptation)* lutter contre; *(election)* participer à; **to f. a war** être en guerre; *Law* **to f. a case**
(of lawyer) défendre une cause; *(of defendant)* être en procès; *Fig*
I'm not going to f. your battles for you c'est à vous de
vous débrouiller; **to f. one's way through a crowd** se frayer
un chemin à travers une foule
3 *vi* (**a**) *(physically)* se battre (**against** contre); *(verbally)* se
disputer; **to f. shy of doing sth** éviter à tout prix de faire qch
(**b**) *(struggle)* lutter (**for/against** pour/contre); **to f. for
breath** suffoquer

▸ **fight back 1** *vt sep (tears)* retenir; *(anger)* réprimer
2 *vi (retaliate)* se défendre

▸ **fight off** *vt sep (attacker)* repousser; *(illness)* combattre

▸ **fight out** *vt sep* **f. it out among yourselves** réglez ça entre
vous

fighter ['faɪtə(r)] *n (in fight)* combattant(e) *m,f*; *(for cause)* lut-
teur(euse) *m,f*; **she's a real f.** *(determined)* c'est une battante; **f.
(plane)** avion *m* de chasse; **f. squadron/pilot** escadron *m*/
pilote *m* de chasse

fighting ['faɪtɪŋ] **1** *n (scuffles)* bagarres *fpl*; *Mil* combat *m*
2 *adj* **to have a f. chance** avoir encore de bonnes chances;
to be f. fit être dans une forme éblouissante

figment ['fɪgmənt] *n* **it's a f. of your imagination** c'est le
fruit de ton imagination

figurative ['fɪgərətɪv] *adj (sense)* figuré(e); *(art)* figuratif(ive)

figuratively ['fɪgərətɪvlɪ] *adv* **f. speaking** métaphoriquement parlant

figure ['fɪgə(r)] **1** *n* (**a**) *(number)* chiffre *m*; **to be good at figures** être bon (bonne) en calcul; **to reach double figures** *(of
score)* atteindre la dizaine; *(of inflation, unemployment)* dépasser
la barre des dix pour cent

(**b**) *(body shape)* silhouette *f*; **to have a good f.** *(of woman)*
avoir une jolie silhouette; **to look after** *or* **to watch one's
figure** faire attention à sa ligne; **a fine f. of a man** un bel
homme; **to cut a sorry f.** avoir l'air pitoyable

(**c**) *(person, character)* personnage *m*; **a distinguished f.** une
personnalité

(d) *(illustration, geometric shape)* figure *f*
(e) *(expression)* **f. of speech** figure *f* de rhétorique; **it's just a f. of speech** c'est une façon de parler
2 *vt* **to f. (that)...** *(think)* penser que...; *(estimate)* supposer que...
3 *vi* **(a)** *(appear) (in list, book)* figurer
(b) *Fam (make sense)* **that figures!** ça se tient!; **go f.!** qui aurait imaginé ça?
▸**figure on** *vt insep* **to f. on doing sth** compter faire qch
▸**figure out** *vt sep (amount)* calculer; *(solution)* trouver; *(problem, person)* arriver à comprendre
figurehead ['fɪɡəhed] *n (on ship)* figure *f* de proue; *Fig (of country, party)* représentant(e) *m,f* nominal(e), *Pej* homme *m* de paille
Fiji ['fi:dʒi:] *n* les (îles *fpl*) Fidji *fpl*
Fijian [fi:'dʒi:ən] **1** *n* Fidjien(enne) *m,f*
2 *adj* fidjien(enne)
filament ['fɪləmənt] *n Elec* filament *m*
filch [fɪltʃ] *vt Fam* faucher (**from sb** à qn)
file¹ [faɪl] **1** *n (tool)* lime *f*
2 *vt (metal)* limer; **to f. one's nails** se limer les ongles
file² [faɪl] **1** *n* **(a)** *(folder)* chemise *f*; *(ring-bound)* classeur *m*; *(documents)* dossier *m* (**on** sur); **to have sth on f.** avoir qch dans ses dossiers; **f. cabinet** classeur *m* **(b)** *Comput* fichier *m*; **f. manager** gestionnaire *m* de fichiers; **f. server** serveur *m* de fichiers
2 *vt* **(a)** *(documents, letters)* classer **(b)** *(complaint, claim, request)* déposer
3 *vi* **to f. for divorce** demander le divorce
file³ [faɪl] **1** *n (line)* file *f*; **in single f.** en file indienne
2 *vi* **to f. past sb/sth** défiler devant qn/qch; **to f. in/out** entrer/sortir l'un(e) après l'autre
filial ['fɪlɪəl] *adj* filial(e)
filigree ['fɪlɪɡri:] *n* filigrane *m*
Filipino [fɪlɪ'pi:nəʊ] **1** *n* (*pl* **Filipinos**) Philippin(e) *m,f*
2 *adj* philippin(e)
fill [fɪl] **1** *n* **to eat one's f.** manger à sa faim; *Fig* **to have had one's f. of sth** en avoir assez de qch
2 *vt* **(a)** *(container)* remplir (**with** de); **to be filled with admiration/hope** être plein(e) d'admiration/d'espoir; **to have a tooth filled** se faire plomber une dent **(b)** *(occupy) (time)* occuper; **to f. a vacancy** *(of employer)* pourvoir à un poste vacant
3 *vi* se remplir (**with** de)
▸**fill in 1** *vt sep* **(a)** *(hole)* combler, boucher; *(form)* remplir; **to f. in time** occuper son temps **(b)** *Fam (inform)* **to f. sb in (on sth)** mettre qn au courant (de qch)
2 *vi* **to f. in for sb** remplacer qn
▸**fill out 1** *vt sep (form, application)* remplir
2 *vi (get fatter)* grossir
▸**fill up 1** *vt sep (glass)* remplir jusqu'au bord; *Fam* **f. her up!** *(with gas)* le plein!
2 *vi* **(a)** *(of tank, container)* se remplir **(b)** *(buy gas)* faire le plein
fillet ['fɪlɪt] **1** *n (of fish, beef)* filet *m*; **f. steak** filet de bœuf
2 *vt (fish)* découper en filets
filling ['fɪlɪŋ] **1** *n* **(a)** *(in tooth)* plombage *m*; *(in sandwich, pie)* garniture *f* **(b)** **f. station** station-service *f*
2 *adj (food, meal)* bourratif(ive); **it was very f.** cela m'a rassasié
filly ['fɪlɪ] (*pl* **fillies**) *n (horse)* pouliche *f*
film [fɪlm] **1** *n (movie)* film *m*; *(layer, for camera)* pellicule *f*; **a (roll of) f.** une pellicule, un rouleau de pellicule; **f. actor/actress** acteur *m*/actrice *f* de cinéma; **f. critic** critique *mf* de cinéma; **f. director** réalisateur(trice) *m,f*; **f. festival** festival *m* du cinéma; **the f. industry** l'industrie *f* cinématographique; **f. library** cinémathèque *f*; **f. maker** cinéaste *mf*; **f. script** scénario *m*, script *m*; **f. star** vedette *f* de cinéma, star *f*; **f. studio** studio *m* de cinéma
2 *vt & vi* filmer

Filofax® ['faɪləʊfæks] *n* Filofax® *m*
filter ['fɪltə(r)] **1** *n* filtre *m*; **f. coffee** café *m* filtre; **f. paper** papier *m* filtre
2 *vt* filtrer
3 *vi (move slowly)* **to f. in/out** entrer/sortir lentement
▸**filter out** *vt sep also Fig* éliminer
▸**filter through 1** *vt insep (of liquid, light)* passer à travers
2 *vi (of information)* filtrer
filth [fɪlθ] *n (dirt)* crasse *f*; *(in street)* immondices *fpl*; *(obscene words)* obscénités *fpl*; **it's f.** *(of book, movie)* c'est dégoûtant
filthy ['fɪlθɪ] **1** *adj* **(a)** *(very dirty)* dégoûtant(e) **(b)** *(very bad)* **in a f. temper** d'une humeur massacrante; **to give sb a f. look** regarder qn d'un sale œil; **f. weather** temps *m* de chien **(c)** *(obscene)* obscène
2 *adv Fam* **f. rich** pourri(e) de fric
fin [fɪn] *n (of fish)* nageoire *f*; *(of airplane)* empennage *m*; *(of swimmer)* palme *f*
final ['faɪnəl] **1** *n* **(a)** *(of competition)* **the f.** la finale **(b)** *Univ* **finals** examens *mpl* finaux
2 *adj* **(a)** *(last)* dernier(ère); **f. demand** dernier avis *m*; **f. warning** dernier avertissement *m* **(b)** *(definitive)* final(e); **the umpire's decision is f.** la décision de l'arbitre est sans appel; **and that's f.!** un point, c'est tout!
finale [fɪ'nɑ:lɪ] *n* finale *m*
finalist ['faɪnəlɪst] *n* finaliste *mf*
finalize ['faɪnəlaɪz] *vt (details, plans)* mettre au point; *(deal)* conclure
finally ['faɪnəlɪ] *adv* **(a)** *(lastly)* finalement **(b)** *(at last)* enfin; **she had f. met him** elle l'avait enfin rencontré **(c)** *(irrevocably)* définitivement; **it hasn't been f. decided yet** aucune décision définitive n'a encore été prise
finance ['faɪnæns, fɪ'næns] **1** *n* **(a)** *(subject)* finance *f*; **f. company** *or* **house** société *f* financière **(b)** **finances** *(funds)* finances *fpl*
2 *vt* financer
financial [faɪ'nænʃəl, fɪ'nænʃəl] *adj* financier(ère); **it was not a f. success** cela n'a pas rapporté beaucoup d'argent; **f. adviser** conseiller *m* financier; **f. market** marché *m* financier; **f. statement** bilan *m* financier
financially [faɪ'nænʃəlɪ, fɪ'nænʃəlɪ] *adv* financièrement
financier [faɪ'nænsɪə(r)] *n* financier *m*
finch [fɪntʃ] *n* fringillidé *m*
find [faɪnd] **1** *n* découverte *f*; **it's quite a f.** c'est une fameuse trouvaille
2 *vt* (*pt & pp* **found** [faʊnd]) **(a)** *(discover)* trouver; **to try to f. sth** chercher qch; **she was nowhere to be found** elle était introuvable; **I found her waiting in the hall** je l'ai trouvée qui attendait dans le vestibule; **this flower is commonly found in Canada** on trouve couramment cette fleur au Canada; **I found myself back where I'd started** je me suis retrouvé à mon point de départ; **you will f. that I'm right** tu verras que j'ai raison; **I was surprised to f. that...** j'ai découvert avec surprise que...; **he couldn't f. it in his heart to tell her** il n'avait pas le cœur à le lui dire; **to f. one's way** trouver son chemin; **to f. a way to do sth** trouver moyen de faire qch; **to f. oneself** *(spiritually)* se trouver
(b) *(experience)* trouver; **they will f. it easy/difficult** cela leur sera facile/difficile; **to f. it necessary to do sth** se trouver dans la nécessité de faire qch; **she found it impossible to understand him** elle avait beaucoup de mal à le comprendre; **how did you f. the meal?** le repas vous a-t-il plu?; **I found myself agreeing with her** il s'est trouvé que j'étais d'accord avec elle
(c) *Law* **to f. sb guilty/not guilty** déclarer qn coupable/non coupable
3 *vi Law* **to f. for/against sb** rendre un verdict en faveur de/contre qn

▶**find out 1** *vt sep* (a) *(discover)* découvrir (b) *(person)* prendre en défaut

2 *vi* **to f. out about sth** apprendre qch

finder ['faɪndə(r)] *n* **the f. of the money** la personne qui trouva/trouvera l'argent; *Fam* **finders keepers (losers weepers)** celui qui le trouve le garde

findings ['faɪndɪŋz] *npl* conclusions *fpl*; *Law (of jury, court)* verdict *m*

fine¹ [faɪn] **1** *n (penalty)* amende *f*

2 *vt* condamner à une amende; **to f. sb \$40** infliger une amende de 40 dollars à qn

fine² [faɪn] **1** *adj* (a) *(excellent)* excellent(e); *(foods, wine)* fin(e); *(weather)* beau; **to appeal to sb's finer feelings** faire appel aux bons sentiments de qn; **she's a f. woman** c'est une femme admirable; **f. art, the f. arts** les beaux-arts *mpl*; **she's got it down to a f. art** elle fait ça à la perfection

(b) *(satisfactory)* bien *inv*; **she's/everything's f.** elle/tout va bien; **that's f. by me** je n'y vois aucune objection

(c) *Ironic* **you're a f. one to talk!** tu peux bien parler!; **this is another f. mess you've got us into!** tu nous a encore mis dans un beau pétrin!

(d) *(thin) (hair, rain, line)* fin(e)

(e) *(subtle) (distinction)* subtil(e); **not to put too f. a point on it** pour parler carrément; **there's a f. line between eccentricity and madness** il n'y a qu'un pas de l'excentricité à la folie

2 *adv* très bien; **they get along f.** ils s'entendent (très) bien

finely ['faɪnlɪ] *adv* (a) *(judged)* soigneusement; *(written, painted)* admirablement; *Fig* **f. balanced** équilibré(e) (b) *(chopped, ground, grated)* finement

finery ['faɪnərɪ] *n* parure *f*; **she was dressed in all her f.** elle était habillée avec élégance

finesse [fɪ'nes] *n* finesse *f*

finger ['fɪŋgə(r)] *n* (a) *(of hand, glove)* doigt *m*; **to keep one's fingers crossed** croiser les doigts; **f. bowl** rince-doigts *m inv*; **f. food** *(snacks)* amuse-gueule *mpl* (b) *(measure)* **a f. of brandy** un doigt de cognac (c) *Aviat* passerelle *f* (d) *(idioms)* **he's got them (wrapped) around his little f.** il fait d'eux ce qu'il veut; **to have a f. in every pie** être mêlé(e) à tout; **don't you dare lay a f. on him** je vous défends de le toucher; **she never lifts a f. to help me** elle ne lève jamais le petit doigt pour m'aider; **I can't quite put my f. on it** je n'arrive pas à mettre le doigt dessus; **to get one's fingers burnt** se brûler les doigts; *Fam* **to give sb the f.** ≃ faire un bras d'honneur à qn

2 *vt* (a) *(feel)* tâter (b) *very Fam (inform on)* balancer

fingernail ['fɪŋgəneɪl] *n* ongle *m*

fingerprint ['fɪŋgəprɪnt] *n* empreinte *f* digitale

fingertip ['fɪŋgətɪp] *n* bout *m* du doigt; **to have sth at one's fingertips** savoir qch sur le bout des doigts

finicky ['fɪnɪkɪ] *adj (person)* tatillon(onne); *(job, device)* compliqué(e)

finish ['fɪnɪʃ] **1** *n* (a) *(end) (of day, meeting)* fin *f*; *(of race)* arrivée *f*; **f. line** ligne *f* d'arrivée (b) *(surface) (of fabric, leather)* apprêt *m*; **paint with a gloss/matt f.** peinture *f* vernie/mate (c) *(workmanship)* finition *f*

2 *vt* (a) *(end)* finir, terminer; **to f. doing sth** finir *ou* terminer de faire qch (b) *(kill) (person)* achever; *Fam* **he's finished!** il est fini!

3 *vi* finir, se terminer; **to f. fourth** *(in race, contest)* finir *ou* terminer quatrième

▶**finish off 1** *vt sep* (a) *(complete, use up)* finir, terminer (b) *(kill)* achever; *(ruin) (chances, hopes)* anéantir

2 *vi* finir, terminer

▶**finish up 1** *vt sep (use up)* finir

2 *vi (end up)* se retrouver; **to f. up doing sth** finir par faire qch

▶**finish with** *vt insep* (a) *(stop using)* **to f. with sth** finir de se servir de qch (b) *(boyfriend, girlfriend)* laisser tomber

finished ['fɪnɪʃt] *adj* (a) *(completed)* fini(e); *(supplies)* épuisé(e) (b) *(performance)* soigné(e)

finishing ['fɪnɪʃɪŋ] *adj* **to put the f. touches to sth** mettre la dernière main à qch; **f. school** = école d'arts d'agrément pour les jeunes filles

finite ['faɪnaɪt] *adj* limité(e); *Gram (verb)* conjugué(e)

Finland ['fɪnlənd] *n* la Finlande

Finn [fɪn] *n (person)* Finlandais(e) *m,f*, Finnois(e) *m,f*

Finnish ['fɪnɪʃ] **1** *n (language)* finlandais *m*, finnois *m*

2 *adj* finlandais(e), finnois(e)

fir [fɜː(r)] *n* **f. (tree)** sapin *m*; **f. cone** pomme *f* de pin

fire ['faɪə(r)] **1** *n* (a) *(in hearth)* feu *m*; *(large, destructive)* incendie *m*; **on f.** en feu; **to catch f.** prendre feu; **to set f. to sth, to set sth on f.** mettre le feu à qch; **f.!** au feu!; *Fig* **to play with f.** jouer avec le feu; *Fig* **to fight f. with f.** combattre le feu par le feu; **f. alarm** sirène *f* d'incendie; **f. department** sapeurs-pompiers *mpl*, pompiers *mpl*; **f. door** porte *f* coupe-feu; **f. drill** exercice *m* d'évacuation en cas d'incendie; **f. engine** voiture *f* de pompiers; **f. escape** escalier *m* de secours; **f. extinguisher** extincteur *m*; **to be a f. hazard** constituer un risque d'incendie; **f. hydrant** bouche *f* d'incendie; **f. insurance** assurance *f* contre l'incendie; **f. regulations** *(laws)* normes *fpl* de protection contre les incendies; *(instructions)* consignes *fpl* en cas d'incendie; **f. sale** = vente d'objets endommagés dans un incendie; **f. station** caserne *f* de pompiers

(b) *(of artillery)* tirs *mpl*; **to open f.** ouvrir le feu; **to hold one's f.** ne pas tirer; **to come under f.** être exposé(e) aux tirs; *Fig (be criticized)* être exposé à de sévères critiques; **f. power** puissance *f* de tir

(c) *Fig (enthusiasm)* fougue *f*, ardeur *f*

2 *vt* (a) *(shoot) (missile, flare)* lancer; **to f. a gun (at)** tirer un coup de fusil (sur); *Fig* **to f. a question at sb** poser une question à qn à brûle-pourpoint

(b) *(dismiss)* virer

(c) **oil-/gas-fired central heating** chauffage *m* central au mazout/au gaz; *Fig* **to f. sb's imagination** enflammer l'imagination de qn

(d) *(pottery)* cuire

3 *vi* (a) *(with gun)* tirer *(at* sur); *Fam Fig* **f. away!** *(to questioner)* allez-y!

(b) *(of engine)* tourner

firearm ['faɪərɑːm] *n* arme *f* à feu

firebrand ['faɪəbrænd] *n (torch)* tison *m*, brandon *m*; *Fig (person)* brandon de discorde

firecracker ['faɪəkrækə(r)] *n* pétard *m*

firefighter ['faɪəfaɪtə(r)] *n* pompier *m*

firefly ['faɪəflaɪ] *(pl* **fireflies***)* *n* luciole *f*

fireguard ['faɪəgɑːd] *n* garde-feu *m inv*

firelight ['faɪəlaɪt] *n* lumière *f* du feu

firelighter ['faɪəlaɪtə(r)] *n* allume-feu *m inv*

fireman ['faɪəmən] *n* pompier *m*

fireplace ['faɪəpleɪs] *n* cheminée *f*

fireproof ['faɪə'pruːf] *adj* ignifugé(e)

fireside ['faɪəsaɪd] *n* **by the f.** au coin du feu

firewall ['faɪəwɔːl] *n Comput* firewall *m*, pare-feu *m inv*

FireWire ['faɪəwaɪə(r)] *n Comput* FireWire *m*

firewood ['faɪəwʊd] *n* bois *m* de chauffage

firework ['faɪəwɜːk] *n* pièce *f* d'artifice; **fireworks** *(display)* feu *m* d'artifice; *Fig* **there'll be fireworks** il va y avoir du grabuge; **f. display** feu d'artifice

firing ['faɪərɪŋ] *n* tir *m*; *Fig* **to be in the f. line** être l'objet de violentes critiques; **f. squad** peloton *m* d'exécution

firm¹ [fɜːm] *n (company)* entreprise *f*, firme *f*

firm² [fɜːm] **1** *adj* (a) *(fruit, body, mattress, handshake)* ferme; *Fig (foundations, friendship)* solide; **the f. favorite** le/la grand(e) favori(ite); **it's my f. belief (that)...** j'ai la ferme conviction que... **(b)** *(strict)* ferme **(c)** *(definite) (decision)* ferme; *(date)* précis(e); *(evidence)* sérieux(euse)

2 *adv* **to stand f.** tenir bon *ou* ferme; **to hold f. to one's principles/beliefs** être fidèle à ses principes/croyances

firmly ['fɜːmlɪ] *adv* **(a)** *(securely)* solidement; **I f. believe (that)...** j'ai la ferme conviction que... **(b)** *(strictly)* fermement

first [fɜːst] **1** *n* **(a)** *(in series)* premier(ère) *m,f*; **we were the f. to arrive** nous étions les premiers arrivés; **it's the f. I've heard of it** c'est la première fois que j'en entends parler, première nouvelle; **Edward the F.** Edward Premier

(b) *(of month)* premier *m*; **we're leaving on the f.** nous partons le premier

(c) *(beginning)* **from f. to last** du début jusqu'à la fin; **from the f.** dès le début; **at f.** d'abord

(d) *(first gear)* première *f*

(e) *(unique event)* première *f*

2 *adj* premier(ère); **for the f. time** pour la première fois; **at f. hand** de première main; **f. things f.!** commençons par le commencement!; **I don't know the f. thing about motorcycles** je ne connais absolument rien aux motos; **f. thing (in the morning)** dès le matin; **at f. light** aux premières lueurs du jour; **at f. sight** à première vue; **in the f. place** d'abord; **f. aid** *(skill)* secourisme *m*; *(treatment)* premiers soins *mpl*; **f. cousin** cousin(e) *m,f* germain(e); **f. edition** édition *f* originale; **f. floor** rez-de-chaussée *m*; **f. gear** première *f* (vitesse *f*); *Scol* **f. grade** = classe du primaire pour les 5–6 ans; **the f. lady** première dame des États-Unis *(épouse du président)*; *Naut* **f. mate** second *m*; **f. name** prénom *m*; **f. night** *(of play)* première *f*; *Law* **f. offender** = personne qui commet un délit pour la première fois; **the F. World War** la Première Guerre mondiale

3 *adv* **(a)** *(firstly)* d'abord; **f. and foremost** avant toute chose; **f. of all** en premier lieu, d'abord

(b) *(for the first time)* pour la première fois; **I f. met her in London** je l'ai rencontrée pour la première fois à Londres

(c) *(before others)* le premier, la première; **you go f.!** *(in line)* passez devant!; **to come f.** *(in race)* arriver premier(ère); *(in exam)* être reçu(e) premier(ère); **my family comes f.** ma famille passe avant le reste; **f. come, f. served** les premiers arrivés sont les premiers servis; **ladies f.!** les femmes d'abord!; **I won't do it, I'd resign f.** plutôt démissionner que de faire ça

first-aid [fɜːst'eɪd] *adj* **f. certificate** brevet *m* de secourisme; **f. kit** trousse *f* de secours; **f. worker** secouriste *mf*

first-born ['fɜːstbɔːn] *n Lit* premier-né (première-née) *m,f*

first-class ['fɜːstklɑːs] **1** *adj* **(a)** *(compartment, ticket)* de première classe **(b)** **f. stamp** timbre *m* au tarif normal **(c)** *(excellent)* excellent(e)

2 *adv* **(a)** *(travel)* en première classe **(b)** *(post)* au tarif normal

first-degree ['fɜːstdɪ'griː] *adj* **(a)** *Med (burns)* au premier degré **(b)** *Law* **f. murder** assassinat *m*

first-hand ['fɜːst'hænd] *adj & adv* de première main

firstly ['fɜːstlɪ] *adv* premièrement, en premier lieu

first-rate ['fɜːstreɪt] *adj* excellent(e)

first-time buyer ['fɜːst'taɪm'baɪə(r)] *n* = personne achetant une propriété pour la première fois

fiscal ['fɪskəl] *adj* fiscal(e); **f. policy** politique *f* budgétaire; **f. year** année *f* fiscale *ou* d'exercice

fish [fɪʃ] **1** *n* *(pl* **fish** *or* **fishes)* **(a)** *(animal)* poisson *m*; **f. cake** croquette *f* de poisson; **f. farm** établissement *m* piscicole; **f. knife** couteau *m* à poisson; **f. sticks** bâtonnets *mpl* de poisson; **f. tank** aquarium *m* **(b)** *(idioms)* **there are plenty more f. in the sea** un de perdu, dix de retrouvés; **to have other f. to fry** avoir d'autres chats à fouetter; **to feel like a f. out of water** ne pas se sentir dans son élément; **to be neither f. nor fowl** n'être ni chair ni poisson

2 *vt* **(a)** *(river)* pêcher **(b)** *(remove)* **to f. sb/sth from somewhere** sortir qn/qch de quelque part

3 *vi* pêcher; *Fig* **to f. for compliments** rechercher les compliments; **she fished around in her pocket for some change** elle a fouillé dans sa poche pour trouver de la monnaie

fisherman ['fɪʃəmən] *n* pêcheur *m*

fish-hook ['fɪʃhʊk] *n* hameçon *m*

fishing ['fɪʃɪŋ] *n* pêche *f*; **to go f.** aller à la pêche; **f. boat** bateau *m* de pêche; **f. grounds** lieux *mpl* de pêche; **f. line** ligne *f*; **f. net** filet *m* de pêche; **f. port** port *m* de pêche; **f. pole** canne *f* à pêche

fishnet ['fɪʃnet] *adj (stockings, tights)* résille *inv*

fishy ['fɪʃɪ] *adj* **(a)** *(smell, taste)* de poisson **(b)** *Fam (suspicious)* louche

fission ['fɪʃən] *n* fission *f*

fissure ['fɪʃə(r)] *n (in mountain, rock)* fissure *f*; *Med* scissure *f*

fist [fɪst] *n* poing *m*

fistfight ['fɪstfaɪt] *n* bagarre *f*, baston *f*

fistful ['fɪstfʊl] *n* poignée *f*

fisticuffs ['fɪstɪkʌfs] *npl Hum* coups *mpl* de poing

fit¹ [fɪt] *n (seizure)* attaque *f*; **to have a f.** avoir une attaque; *Fam Fig* **to have** *or* **to throw a f.** piquer une crise; **in a f. of temper** dans un accès de colère; **a f. of coughing** une quinte de toux; **a f. of crying** une crise de larmes; **to be in fits (of laughter)** se tordre de rire; **in fits and starts** par à-coups

fit² [fɪt] **1** *n* **the jacket is a good f.** cette veste me/te/*etc.* va bien; **comfortable/tight f.** coupe *f* confortable/ajustée; **these trousers are a bit of a tight f.** ce pantalon est un peu juste

2 *adj* **(a)** *(appropriate)* **f. to eat** mangeable; **f. to drink** buvable; **f. for human consumption** propre à la consommation; **a meal f. for a king** un repas digne d'un *ou* de roi; **do as you see** *or* **think f.** faites comme bon vous semblera; **to see f. to do sth** juger bon de faire qch; **that's all he's f. for** il n'est bon qu'à cela; **to be f. to do sth** *(worthy of)* être digne de faire qch; **to be f. to drop** tomber de fatigue

(b) *(healthy)* en forme; **to get f.** retrouver la forme; **to keep f.** se maintenir en forme; **to be f. to do sth** *(healthy enough)* être en état de faire qch; *Fam* **to be as f. as a fiddle** péter la forme

3 *vt* *(pt & pp* **fitted)** **(a)** *(match)* correspondre à; **to make the punishment f. the crime** proportionner la peine au délit

(b) *(be the right size for)* **to f. sb** aller à qn; **this key fits the lock** cette clé rentre dans la serrure

(c) *(install)* adapter (**to/on** à/sur); **to f. sth with sth** équiper *ou* pourvoir qch de qch

(d) *(insert)* **to f. sth into/onto sth** faire rentrer qch dans/sur qch; **we can f. another two people inside** il y a encore de la place pour deux personnes

4 *vi* **(a)** *(be the right size) (of lid, key, plug)* aller; **to f. together** s'adapter; **to f. into sth** rentrer dans qch

(b) *(of clothes)* **it fits perfectly** ça me/te/*etc.* va parfaitement

▶**fit in 1** *vt sep (in schedule)* caser

2 *vi* **(a)** *(go into place)* aller **(b)** *(of person) (in company, group)* s'intégrer; **you don't f. in here** tu n'es pas à ta place ici

▶**fit out** *vt sep (ship)* armer; *(person)* équiper

fitful ['fɪtfʊl] *adj (sleep)* agité(e); **to make f. progress** progresser par à-coups

fitness ['fɪtnɪs] *n* **(a)** *(health)* forme *f*; **f. center** club *m* de gym; **f. room** salle *f* de musculation **(b)** *(suitability)* aptitude *f* (**for** à)

fitted ['fɪtɪd] *adj (jacket, dress)* ajusté(e); **f. sheet** drap-housse *m*

fitting ['fɪtɪŋ] **1** *n (of clothes)* essayage *m*; **f. room** cabine *f* d'essayage

2 *adj* approprié(e) (**to** à)

five [faɪv] **1** *n* cinq *m inv*

2 *adj* cinq; **f. o'clock shadow** barbe *f* d'un jour; *see also* **eight**

fiver ['faɪvə(r)] n Fam (bill) billet m de cinq dollars

fix [fɪks] **1** n (a) Fam (difficulty) **to be in a f.** être dans le pétrin; **to get into a f.** se fourrer dans le pétrin (b) Fam (of drug) dose f; Fig **she needs her daily f. of chocolate** il lui faut sa dose quotidienne de chocolat (c) Fam **to be a f.** (of election, contest) être truqué(e)

2 vt (a) (attach securely) fixer (**to** à); **to f. sth in one's memory** graver qch dans sa mémoire; **to f. one's attention on sth** fixer son attention sur qch; **to f. one's eyes on sb/sth** fixer qn/qch (b) (decide) (limit, price) fixer (c) (repair) arranger, réparer (d) (arrange) (meeting) arranger; **to f. one's hair** se coiffer; Fam **I'll f. him!** je vais lui faire son affaire! (e) (prepare) (food, drink) préparer (f) Fam (election, contest) truquer

▸**fix up** vt sep (a) (arrange) arranger (b) (provide) **to f. sb up with a job/apartment** trouver un emploi/appartement à qn; **I fixed you up with a date** je t'ai arrangé un rendez-vous galant

fixation [fɪk'seɪʃən] n fixation f; **to have a f. about sth** faire une fixation sur qch

fixed [fɪkst] adj (a) (price, costs, income) fixe; **f. assets** immobilisations fpl (b) (definite) (ideas) bien arrêté(e); (plans) précis(e) (c) Fam **how are you f. for money/time?** tu as de l'argent/le temps? (d) Fam (election, contest) truqué(e)

fixer ['fɪksə(r)] n Fam combinard(e) m,f

fixture ['fɪkstʃə(r)] n **fixtures** (in house, office) installations fpl fixes; **bathroom fixtures** sanitaires mpl; Fam **to be a f.** (of person) faire partie des meubles

fizz [fɪz] **1** n (a) (sound) pétillement m; (bubbles) gaz m (b) Fam (soda) boisson f gazeuse; (champagne) champ m

2 vi (of champagne) pétiller

▸**fizzle out** ['fɪzəl] vi Fam (of plan) tomber à l'eau; (of enthusiasm, interest) retomber; (of relationship) partir en eau de boudin

fizzy ['fɪzɪ] adj (soda) gazeux(euse); (wine) mousseux(euse)

fjord [fjɔːd] n fjord m

flab [flæb] n Fam (fat) graisse f

flabbergasted ['flæbəgɑːstɪd] adj Fam abasourdi(e)

flabby ['flæbɪ] adj (person, features) bouffi(e); (limbs) mou (molle); Fig (argument, reasoning) qui manque de rigueur

flaccid ['flæsɪd] adj flasque

flag [flæg] **1** n drapeau m; Naut pavillon m; **F. Day** (June 14) = le 14 juin, fête commémorant l'adoption du drapeau américain; **f. stop** (for bus) arrêt m facultatif

2 vt (pt & pp **flagged**) marquer; (mark) signaler; **to f. (down) a taxi** héler un taxi

3 vi (of person, conversation, interest) faiblir; (of strength, spirits) baisser

flagellate ['flædʒəleɪt] vt flageller

flagpole ['flægpəʊl] n mât m (de drapeau)

flagrant ['fleɪgrənt] adj flagrant(e)

flagrantly ['fleɪgrəntlɪ] adv de façon flagrante; **f. dishonest** d'une malhonnêteté flagrante

flagship ['flægʃɪp] n (of fleet) navire m amiral; Fig (of range of products, party) fleuron m; **f. store** magasin m vitrine

flagstone ['flægstəʊn] n dalle f

flail [fleɪl] **1** n (tool) fléau m

2 vt agiter

3 vi (of rope, cable) se balancer; (of arms, legs) s'agiter dans tous les sens

▸**flail about, flail around** vi (of arms, legs) s'agiter dans tous les sens; (of person) se débattre

flair [fleə(r)] n don m (**for** pour); **to do sth with f.** faire qch avec style; **to have a f. for business** avoir le sens des affaires; **to have a f. for doing sth** avoir le don de faire qch

flak [flæk] n tir m antiaérien ou de DCA; Fig critiques fpl; **she got a lot of f. for her decision** sa décision a été très critiquée; **f. jacket** gilet m pare-balles

flake [fleɪk] **1** n (of snow, cereal) flocon m; (of paint) écaille f; (of soap) paillette f; **a f. of skin** un bout de peau morte

2 vi (of paint) s'écailler; **my skin is flaking** je pèle

▸**flake out** vi Fam s'effondrer de fatigue

flaky ['fleɪkɪ] adj (a) (paint) écaillé(e); (pastry) feuilleté(e) (b) (eccentric) loufoque

flamboyant [flæm'bɔɪənt] adj (person, behavior) extravagant(e); (gesture) théâtral(e); (clothes, colors) voyant(e)

flame [fleɪm] **1** n flamme f; **to go up in flames** prendre feu; Fig (of hopes, chances) partir en fumée; **to burst into flames** s'enflammer; Fam **an old f.** (man) un ancien amoureux; (woman) une ancienne amoureuse

2 vt Comput descendre en flammes

3 vi (a) (of fire) flamber (b) Comput rédiger un message injurieux

flamenco [flə'meŋkəʊ] n flamenco m

flameproof ['fleɪmpruːf] adj ignifugé(e); (dish) qui va sur le feu

flamethrower ['fleɪmθrəʊə(r)] n lance-flammes m inv

flaming ['fleɪmɪŋ] **1** adj (burning) enflammé(e); Fig (sunset) flamboyant(e); **a f. temper** une colère noire

2 n Comput envoi m de messages injurieux

flamingo [flə'mɪŋgəʊ] (pl **flamingos**) n flamant m

flammable ['flæməbəl] adj inflammable

Flanders ['flɑːndəz] n les Flandres fpl, la Flandre

flank [flæŋk] **1** n flanc m; (of beef, mutton) flanchet m

2 vt flanquer (**with** or **by** de)

flannel ['flænəl] n (fabric) flanelle f; **(pair of) flannels** pantalon m en flanelle

flap [flæp] **1** n (a) (of envelope, book cover, tent) rabat m; (of airplane) volet m (b) Fam (panic) **to be in a f.** être affolé(e), paniquer

2 vt (pt & pp **flapped**) **to f. its wings** (of bird) battre des ailes; **to f. one's arms** agiter les bras

3 vi (of wings, flag) battre

flapjack ['flæpdʒæk] n (pancake) = petite crêpe épaisse

flare [fleə(r)] **1** n (a) (signal) signal m lumineux; (rocket) fusée f éclairante (b) **(pair of) flares** pantalon m (à) pattes d'éléphant

2 vt (nostrils) dilater

3 vi (of fire) flamboyer; Fig **tempers flared at the meeting** le ton est monté à la réunion

▸**flare up** vi (of fire) s'embraser; (of medical condition) se déclencher; (of anger, trouble) éclater

flash [flæʃ] **1** n (a) (of light) éclair m; **a f. of lightning** un éclair; **f. of wit** trait m d'esprit; **f. of inspiration** éclair de génie; **in a f.** (very quickly) en un clin d'œil; Fig **a f. in the pan** un feu de paille; Comput **f. drive** clef f USB; **f. flood** crue f subite; **f. point** (of situation) point m de rupture; (region) point chaud (b) (in photography) flash m; **f. photography** photographie f au flash

2 vt (a) (smile, look) lancer (**at** à); (card, badge) montrer rapidement (**at** à); **to f. one's headlights at sb** faire un appel de phares à qn (b) Fam (expose oneself to) s'exhiber devant

3 vi (a) (of diamond) briller; (of light) clignoter (b) (move quickly) **to f. past** passer comme un éclair; **my life flashed before me** ma vie a défilé devant mes yeux (c) Fam (expose oneself) s'exhiber (**at** devant)

flashback ['flæʃbæk] n (in novel, movie) flash-back m inv, retour m en arrière

flasher ['flæʃə(r)] n Fam (man exposing himself) exhibitionniste m

flashing ['flæʃɪŋ] adj (light) clignotant(e)

flashlight ['flæʃlaɪt] n torche f électrique

flashy ['flæʃɪ] adj Fam (clothes, car, jewelry) tape-à-l'œil inv; (person) aux goûts tapageurs

flask [flɑːsk] n (for alcohol) flasque f; (in chemistry) fiole f; **(Thermos®) f.** (bouteille f) Thermos® f

flat [flæt] **1** n Fam (flat tire) pneu m à plat; (punctured) pneu crevé

2 adj (**a**) (surface) plat(e); (nose) camus; **as f. as a pancake** plat comme une galette; Fam (flat-chested) plate comme une limande; **f. racing** plat m; **f. rate** tarif m unique; Comput & TV **f. screen** écran m plat; **f. tire** pneu m à plat; (punctured) pneu crevé

(**b**) (refusal) **to give a f. refusal** refuser net

(**c**) (existence) monotone; (voice) terne; (battery) à plat; (drink) éventé(e)

(**d**) (in music) (a semitone lower) bémol; (out of tune) en dessous du ton; **B f.** si m inv bémol

3 adv (**a**) (level) à plat; **to fall f. on one's face** tomber à plat ventre; Fig se casser le nez; Fig **to fall f.** (of joke) tomber à plat; **he pressed himself f. against the wall** il s'est plaqué contre le mur

(**b**) (completely) **to turn sb down f.** opposer un refus catégorique à qn; **in twenty seconds f.** en vingt secondes pile; **to work f. out** travailler d'arrache-pied; Fam **to be f. broke** être complètement fauché(e)

flat-chested ['flæt'tʃestɪd] adj **to be f.** avoir peu de poitrine

flatfish ['flætfɪʃ] n poisson m plat

flat-footed ['flæt'fʊtɪd] adj **to be f.** avoir les pieds plats

flatly ['flætlɪ] adv (refuse, deny) catégoriquement

flatten ['flætən] vt aplatir; **to f. oneself against a wall** s'aplatir contre un mur; Fam **to f. sb** casser la tête à qn

flatter ['flætə(r)] vt (of person, clothes) flatter; Fam **don't f. yourself!** ne te fais pas trop d'illusions!

flattering ['flætərɪŋ] adj (words, photo) flatteur(euse); (clothes, color) qui avantage

flattery ['flætərɪ] n flatterie f

flatulence ['flætjʊləns] n Med flatulence f

flaunt [flɔːnt] vt (knowledge, wealth) étaler; (jewels) exhiber; Fig (ignorance, bad manners) étaler sans complexes

flavor ['fleɪvə(r)] **1** n (**a**) (of food) goût m; (of ice cream, yoghurt) parfum m (**b**) (characteristic) note f; **her stories have a Provençal f.** ses histoires fleurent bon la Provence

2 vt (savory food) relever (**with** de); (sweet food) parfumer (**with** à); **vanilla flavored** parfumé(e) à la vanille

flavoring ['fleɪvərɪŋ] n parfum m; **artificial f.** arôme m artificiel

flavorless ['fleɪvəlɪs] adj sans saveur, insipide

flaw [flɔː] n défaut m; (in plan, argument) faille f

flawed [flɔːd] adj qui a un défaut/des défauts; (plan, argument) bancal(e)

flawless ['flɔːlɪs] adj parfait(e)

flax [flæks] n lin m

flay [fleɪ] vt (flog) fouetter; Fig (criticize) éreinter

flea [fliː] n puce f; **f. market** (marché m aux) puces fpl

fleabite ['fliːbaɪt] n piqûre f de puce

flea-bitten ['fliːbɪtən] adj (person, animal) plein(e) de puces; Fam (shabby) miteux(euse)

fleck [flek] **1** n (of color, light) petite tache f; (of dust) grain m **2** vt tacheter (**with** de); **hair flecked with gray** cheveux mpl grisonnants

fled [fled] pt & pp of **flee**

fledgling ['fledʒlɪŋ] **1** n (young bird) oisillon m **2** adj Fig (person) novice, débutant(e); (company, state) naissant(e)

flee [fliː] (pt & pp **fled** [fled]) vi fuir, s'enfuir; **to f. from persecution** fuir la persécution

fleece [fliːs] **1** n (**a**) (of sheep) toison f (**b**) (garment) fourrure f polaire **2** vt Fam (cheat) estamper

fleecy ['fliːsɪ] adj duveteux(euse)

fleet [fliːt] n (of ships) flotte f; (of taxis, buses) parc m; Fig (convoy) file f

fleet-footed ['fliːt'fʊtɪd] adj Lit au pied léger

fleeting ['fliːtɪŋ] adj (moment, happiness, glance) fugace; (beauty) éphémère; (visit) court(e), rapide; **to catch a f. glimpse of sb/sth** entrevoir qn/qch

Flemish ['flemɪʃ] **1** n (language) flamand m **2** adj flamand(e)

flesh [fleʃ] n chair f; **in the f.** en chair et en os; **to make sb's f. creep** or **crawl** donner la chair de poule à qn; **his own f. and blood** (children) la chair de sa chair; (close family) les siens mpl; **f. wound** blessure f superficielle

▸**flesh out** vt sep (plan, remarks) étoffer

fleshy ['fleʃɪ] adj charnu(e)

flew [fluː] pt of **fly**[3]

flex [fleks] vt (arms, knees) fléchir; (muscles) faire jouer; Fig **they're just flexing their muscles** ce n'est qu'une démonstration d'autorité de leur part

flexible ['fleksɪbəl] adj (material, approach, timetable) flexible; (person's character) souple

flexitime ['fleksɪtaɪm], **flextime** ['flekstaɪm] n horaires mpl flexibles ou à la carte

flick [flɪk] **1** n (with finger) pichenette f; (of whip, tail) petit coup m; **at the f. of a switch** en appuyant juste sur un bouton **2** vt (with finger) donner une chiquenaude à; **he flicked the cigarette ash onto the carpet** il fit tomber la cendre de sa cigarette sur le tapis; **to f. the hair out of one's eyes** écarter les cheveux de ses yeux

▸**flick through** vt insep (book, magazine) feuilleter; (photographs) passer rapidement en revue

flicker ['flɪkə(r)] **1** n (of flame) vacillement m; Fig (of hope) lueur f; (of interest, annoyance) pointe f; **a f. of light** une lueur vacillante **2** vi (of flame, light) vaciller

flier ['flaɪə(r)] n (**a**) (passenger) = personne qui voyage en avion (**b**) (leaflet) prospectus m

flight [flaɪt] n (**a**) (act of flying, specific trip) vol m; **it's a two-hour f. from Chicago** c'est à deux heures de vol de Chicago; Fig **f. of fancy** lubie f; **f. attendant** (male) steward m; (female) hôtesse f de l'air; **f. deck** (of aircraft) poste m ou cabine f de pilotage; **f. path** trajectoire f de vol; **f. recorder** enregistreur m de vol; **f. simulator** simulateur m de vol; **f. socks** chaussettes fpl de contention (**b**) (group of birds) vol m, volée f; Fig **in the top f.** parmi les tout premiers (**c**) **f. (of stairs)** escalier m; **two flights up from me** deux étages au-dessus de chez moi (**d**) (escape) fuite f; **to put sb to f.** mettre qn en fuite

flightless ['flaɪtlɪs] adj coureur(euse)

flighty ['flaɪtɪ] adj (fickle) volage

flimsy ['flɪmzɪ] adj (structure, fence) peu solide; (dress, excuse, plot) léger(ère); (evidence) ténu(e)

flinch [flɪntʃ] vi (with pain) tressaillir; (at an idea) frémir; **to do sth without flinching** faire qch sans broncher; **to f. from doing sth** hésiter à faire qch

fling [flɪŋ] **1** n Fam (affair) aventure f **2** vt (pt & pp **flung** [flʌŋ]) jeter; (ball) lancer; **to f. oneself into an armchair** se jeter dans un fauteuil; **to f. one's arms around sb** prendre qn dans ses bras; Fig **to f. oneself into a task** se lancer dans une tâche

▸**fling out** vt sep (object) jeter; (person) mettre à la porte; (proposal, case) rejeter

flint [flɪnt] n (stone) silex m; (of lighter) pierre f (à briquet)

flip [flɪp] **1** n Fam **the f. side** (of record) la face B; Fig (of situation) le revers de la médaille **2** vt (pt & pp **flipped**) (record, pancake, card) retourner; **to f. the switch** appuyer sur l'interrupteur; **to f. a coin** jouer à pile ou face; Fam **to f. one's lid** (get angry) piquer une crise; (go mad) perdre la boule **3** vi Fam (get angry) piquer une crise; (go mad) perdre la boule

▸**flip through** vt insep (book, magazine) feuilleter; (photos, samples) jeter un coup d'œil à

flipboard ['flɪpbɔːd], **flipchart** ['flɪptʃɑːt] *n* tableau *m* à feuilles (mobiles)

flip-flops ['flɪpflɒps] *npl* (**a pair of**) f. des tongs *fpl*

flippant ['flɪpənt] *adj* désinvolte, cavalier(ère)

flipper ['flɪpə(r)] *n* (*of animal*) nageoire *f*; (*of diver*) palme *f*

flip-top *adj* (*carton, pack*) à rabat; (*cellphone*) à clapet

flirt [flɜːt] **1** *n* charmeur(euse) *m,f*
2 *vi* flirter (**with** avec); *Fig* **to f. with an idea** caresser une idée

flirtatious [flɜːˈteɪʃəs] *adj* (*look, smile*) charmeur(euse); **to be f.** aimer flirter; **to be f. with sb** flirter avec qn

flit [flɪt] *vi* (*pt & pp* **flitted**) **to f. about** (*of bird*) voleter; *Fig* **to f. from one thing to another** (*of person*) s'éparpiller

float [fləʊt] **1** *n* (**a**) (*on fishing line*) bouchon *m*; (*for swimming, on net*) flotteur *m* (**b**) (*in procession*) char *m* (**c**) (*money*) fonds *m* de caisse
2 *vt* (**a**) (*ship*) mettre à flot (**b**) (*idea, proposal*) émettre; (*company*) introduire en Bourse
3 *vi* flotter; **to f. to the surface** remonter à la surface; **to f. on one's back** (*of swimmer*) faire la planche; **the bottle floated out to sea** la bouteille a été emportée vers le large; *Fam Fig* **he's floating around somewhere** il traîne par là

floating ['fləʊtɪŋ] *adj* flottant(e); (*population*) fluctuant(e); **f. voter** électeur(trice) *m,f* indécis(e)

flock [flɒk] **1** *n* (*of sheep*) troupeau *m*; (*of birds*) vol *m*, volée *f*; *Rel* (*congregation*) ouailles *fpl*; *Fig* (*of people*) foule *f*
2 *vi* (*gather*) **to f. around sb** s'attrouper autour de qn; **people are flocking to the exhibition** les gens vont en masse *ou* en foule voir l'exposition

flog [flɒg] (*pt & pp* **flogged**) *vt* (*beat*) fouetter; *Fam* **to be flogging a dead horse** se dépenser en pure perte; *Fam* **to f. a subject to death** s'étendre indéfiniment sur un sujet

flood [flʌd] **1** *n* inondation *f*; (*of light*) flot *m*; **the F.** (*in the Bible*) le Déluge; **to be in floods (of tears)** verser des torrents de larmes
2 *vt* (*land, bathroom*) inonder; **to be flooded with light** être inondé(e) de lumière; **the river flooded its banks** la rivière a débordé *ou* est sortie de son lit; **to f. the market (with sth)** inonder le marché (de qch); **to be flooded with complaints/telephone calls** être submergé(e) de réclamations/ de coups de fil
3 *vi* (*of river*) déborder; **the sun's rays came flooding through the window** les rayons du soleil entraient à flots par la fenêtre; **letters came flooding in** nous avons/ils ont/*etc.* été submergés de lettres; **it all came flooding back** tout m'/lui/*etc.* est revenu d'un coup

floodgate ['flʌdgeɪt] *n Fig* **to open the floodgates to sth** laisser la porte ouverte à qch

flooding ['flʌdɪŋ] *n* inondation(s) *f(pl)*

floodlight ['flʌdlaɪt] *n* projecteur *m*; **by f.** à la lumière des projecteurs

floodlit ['flʌdlɪt] *adj* (*stadium, match*) éclairé(e) aux projecteurs; (*building*) illuminé(e)

floor [flɔː(r)] **1** *n* (**a**) (*of room, forest*) sol *m*; (*of Stock Exchange*) parquet *m*; (*of ocean*) fond *m*; **f. show** spectacle *m* de cabaret (**b**) (*at meeting, debate*) **to give sb the f.** donner la parole à qn; **to take the f.** prendre la parole; **questions from the f.** questions *fpl* du public (**c**) (*story*) étage *m*; **to live ten floors up** habiter au dixième étage
2 *vt* (*knock down*) envoyer au tapis; *Fig* (*of question, criticism*) désarçonner

floorboard ['flɔːbɔːd] *n* latte *f* de plancher

floozie, floozy ['fluːzɪ] (*pl* **floozies**) *n very Fam Pej* pouffiasse *f*

flop [flɒp] **1** *n* (*failure*) fiasco *m*, bide *m*; **to be a f.** (*of movie*) faire un bide; (*of party*) être un bide

2 *vi* (*pt & pp* **flopped**) (**a**) (*fall*) (*into water*) tomber; (*onto seat*) s'affaler (**b**) (*fail*) échouer; (*of movie*) faire un bide; (*of party*) être un bide

floppy ['flɒpɪ] **1** *n* (*pl* **floppies**) *Comput* disquette *f*
2 *adj* (*ears*) pendant(e); (*garment*) flottant(e); (*hat*) mou (molle); *Comput* **f. disk** disquette *f*

flora ['flɔːrə] *n* (*plant life*) flore *f*

floral ['flɔːrəl] *adj* floral(e); **f. tribute** (*at funeral*) couronne *f* de fleurs

Florence ['flɒrəns] *n* Florence

florid ['flɒrɪd] *adj* (*style*) fleuri(e); (*complexion*) rubicond(e)

Florida ['flɒrɪdə] *n* la Floride

florist ['flɒrɪst] *n* fleuriste *mf*; **f.'s (shop)** fleuriste *m*

floss [flɒs] **1** *n* (**dental**) **f.** fil *m* dentaire
2 *vt* nettoyer avec du fil dentaire
3 *vi* se nettoyer les dents au fil dentaire

flotation [fləʊˈteɪʃən] *n Com* (*of company*) lancement *m*

flotsam ['flɒtsəm] *n* **f. (and jetsam)** débris *mpl* refoulés par la mer; *Fig* **the f. of society** les laissés-pour-compte *mpl* de la société

flounce [flaʊns] **1** *n* (*in sewing*) volant *m*
2 *vi* **to f. in/out** entrer/sortir de façon théâtrale

flounder ['flaʊndə(r)] **1** *n* (*fish*) flet *m*
2 *vi* (*in water, mud*) patauger; (*in job, course, speech*) perdre pied

flour ['flaʊə(r)] **1** *n* farine *f*
2 *vt* fariner

flourish ['flʌrɪʃ] **1** *n* (*gesture*) grand geste *m* théâtral; (*musical, in writing*) fioriture *f*
2 *vt* (*brandish*) brandir
3 *vi* (*of plant, person*) prospérer; (*of business, arts*) être florissant(e)

flourishing ['flʌrɪʃɪŋ] *adj* (*plant*) qui prospère; (*business*) florissant(e)

flout [flaʊt] *vt* (*rule, instruction*) faire fi de; (*person*) défier l'autorité de; (*authority*) défier

flow [fləʊ] **1** *n* (*of liquid*) écoulement *m*; (*of electrical current, information*) circulation *f*; (*of tide, capital*) flux *m*; **f. of traffic** circulation; *Fig* **in full f.** en plein discours; *Fig* **to follow the f. of an argument** suivre (le fil d')un raisonnement; *Fig* **to go with the f.** suivre le mouvement; **f. chart, f. diagram** organigramme *m*
2 *vi* (**a**) (*of liquid*) couler; (*of electrical current*) circuler; (*of traffic*) s'écouler; *Fig* (*of writing*) couler bien; (*of ideas*) affluer; **to f. into the sea** (*of river*) se jeter dans la mer (**b**) **to f. from** (*result from*) découler de

flower ['flaʊə(r)] **1** *n* fleur *f*; **to be in f.** être en fleur(s); *Fig* **in the first f. of youth** dans la fleur de l'âge; **f. arranging** art *m* floral; **f. garden** jardin *m* d'agrément; **f. girl** = jeune demoiselle d'honneur; **f. store** fleuriste *m*; **f. show** exposition *f* florale
2 *vi* fleurir

flowerbed ['flaʊəbed] *n* parterre *m* de fleurs

flowerpot ['flaʊəpɒt] *n* pot *m* de fleurs

flowing ['fləʊɪŋ] *adj* (*hair*) flottant(e); (*movement, style*) fluide

flown [fləʊn] *pp of* **fly³**

flu [fluː] *n* grippe *f*; **a dose** *or* **bout of (the) f.** une grippe; **to have (the) f.** avoir la grippe

fluctuate ['flʌktjʊeɪt] *vi* (*of prices*) fluctuer; (*of pulse, temperature*) varier

fluctuation [flʌktjʊˈeɪʃən] *n* (*of prices*) fluctuation *f*; (*of pulse, temperature*) variation *f*

flue [fluː] *n* (*of heater, chimney*) tuyau *m*

fluency ['fluːənsɪ] *n* aisance *f* (**of/in** de/en)

fluent ['fluːənt] *adj* (*speech, style*) fluide; **he is f. in French, he speaks f. French** il parle couramment français

fluently ['fluːəntlɪ] *adv* (*express oneself*) avec facilité *ou* aisance; (*speak language*) couramment

fluff [flʌf] **1** *n* peluche *f*; **a bit of f.** une peluche

2 *vt* (**a**) **to f. sth (up)** *(pillow, duvet)* remettre qch en forme *(en le secouant)* (**b**) *Fam (botch)* rater

fluffy ['flʌfɪ] *adj* duveteux(euse); *(clouds)* cotonneux(euse)

fluid ['fluːɪd] **1** *n* fluide *m*, liquide *m*; **bodily fluids** sécrétions *fpl*

2 *adj (substance)* fluide, liquide; *(style, movement)* fluide; *(situation, plans)* mal défini(e); **f. ounce** = 0,03 l

fluidity [fluːˈɪdɪtɪ] *n (of style, movement)* fluidité *f*; *(of situation, plans)* imprécision *f*

fluke [fluːk] *n Fam (stroke of luck)* coup *m* de veine *ou* de bol; *(coincidence)* hasard *m*; **by a f.** par hasard; **his success was a pure f.** c'est un hasard qu'il ait réussi

fluk(e)y ['fluːkɪ] *Fam adj* (**a**) *(lucky) (person)* veinard(e); *(guess, shot)* heureux(euse) (**b**) *(strange)* bizarre

flummox ['flʌməks] *vt Fam* scier

flung [flʌŋ] *pt & pp of* **fling**

flunk [flʌŋk] *Fam* **1** *vt (exam)* rater; *(student)* recaler, coller

2 *vi (in exam)* être recalé(e) *ou* collé(e)

flunkey ['flʌŋkɪ] *(pl* **flunkeys**) *n Fam Pej* larbin *m*

fluorescent [fluəˈresənt] *adj* fluorescent(e)

fluoride ['fluəraɪd] *n* fluorure *m*; **f. toothpaste** dentifrice *m* au fluor

flurry ['flʌrɪ] *(pl* **flurries**) *n (of snow)* bourrasque *f*; **a f. of activity/excitement** une soudaine activité/excitation

flush [flʌʃ] **1** *n* (**a**) *(beginning)* **in the first f. of youth** dans tout l'éclat de sa jeunesse (**b**) *(in cards)* flush *m* (**c**) *(in toilet)* chasse *f* (d'eau)

2 *adj* (**a**) *(even)* de niveau (**with** avec) (**b**) *Fam (rich)* plein(e) aux as

3 *vt* **to f. the toilet** tirer la chasse (d'eau)

4 *vi* (**a**) *(of person)* rougir (**with** de) (**b**) *(of toilet)* **the toilet isn't flushing properly** la chasse d'eau ne fonctionne pas bien

▸**flush out** *vt sep (force to emerge)* déloger

flushed [flʌʃd] *adj (person, face)* rouge (**with** de)

fluster ['flʌstə(r)] *vt* démonter; **to get flustered** se démonter

flute [fluːt] *n* (**a**) *Mus* flûte *f* traversière (**b**) *(glass)* flûte *f*

flutist ['fluːtɪst] *n* flûtiste *mf*

flutter ['flʌtə(r)] **1** *n (of wings, eyelashes, heart)* battement *m*; *Fig* **to be in a f.** *(of excitement)* être en émoi

2 *vt* **to f. its wings** *(of bird)* battre des ailes; **to f. one's eyelashes at sb** regarder qn en battant des cils

3 *vi (of birds, insects)* voleter; *(of heart)* battre; *(of flag)* flotter

flux [flʌks] *n* **to be in a state of f.** changer perpétuellement

fly¹ [flaɪ] *n (of pants)* braguette *f*

fly² [flaɪ] *(pl* **flies**) *n (insect)* mouche *f*; **he wouldn't hurt a f.** il ne ferait pas de mal à une mouche; **they were dropping like flies** ils tombaient comme des mouches; *Fig* **a f. in the ointment** un os; *Fam Fig* **there are no flies on her** elle est loin d'être bête; *Fam* **to live on the f.** vivre à cent à l'heure

fly³ [flaɪ] *(pt* **flew** [fluː], *pp* **flown** [fləʊn]) **1** *vt* (**a**) *(plane)* piloter; *(goods)* transporter en avion; *(route)* emprunter; **to f. Air India** voyager avec Air India (**b**) *(kite)* faire voler; **to f. a flag** *(of ship)* arborer un pavillon; *Fig* **to f. the flag (for one's country)** défendre les couleurs de son pays (**c**) *(flee)* s'enfuir de; *Fig* **to f. the nest** *(of child)* quitter le foyer familial

2 *vi* (**a**) *(of bird, plane)* voler; *(of passenger)* voyager en avion, prendre l'avion; **to f. over New York** survoler New York; **to f. across the Atlantic** traverser l'Atlantique en avion (**b**) *(of flag, hair)* flotter (**c**) *(move quickly)* **I must f.** il faut que je file; **to f. to sb's help** voler au secours de qn; **how time flies!** comme le temps passe! **the door flew open** la porte s'est ouverte brusquement; **to f. into a rage** sortir de ses gonds; *Fam* **to send sb/sth flying** envoyer rouler qn/qch; **to f. in the face of reason/logic** défier la raison/toute logique

▸**fly away** *vi (of bird, papers)* s'envoler

▸**fly in 1** *vt sep (troops, rescuers)* transporter en avion

2 *vi (of passenger)* arriver en avion

▸**fly out 1** *vt sep (survivors)* transporter en avion

2 *vi (of passenger)* partir en avion

flyby ['flaɪbaɪ] *n Aviat* défilé *m* aérien

fly-by-night ['flaɪbaɪnaɪt] *adj Fam Pej (company)* véreux(euse)

flyer = **flier**

flying ['flaɪɪŋ] **1** *n (as pilot)* pilotage *m*; *(as passenger)* voyages *mpl* en avion; **she loves f.** *(as pilot)* elle adore piloter; *(as passenger)* elle adore prendre l'avion; **f. club** aéro-club *m*; **f. lessons** leçons *fpl* de pilotage; **f. time** heures *fpl* de vol

2 *adj* (**a**) *(bird, fish)* volant(e); **they were hurt by f. glass** ils ont été blessés par des éclats de verre; **to pass with f. colors** réussir haut la main; **f. boat** hydravion *m*; **f. doctor** médecin *m* volant; **f. saucer** soucoupe *f* volante (**b**) *(rapid)* **a f. visit** une visite éclair; **to get off to a f. start** très bien démarrer

flyleaf ['flaɪliːf] *(pl* **flyleaves** ['flaɪliːvz]) *n* page *f* de garde

flyover ['flaɪəʊvə(r)] *n Aviat* défilé *m* aérien

flypaper ['flaɪpeɪpə(r)] *n* papier *m* tue-mouches, *Can* collant *m* à mouches

flyweight ['flaɪweɪt] *n (in boxing)* poids *m* mouche

FM [eˈfem] *n (abbr* **frequency modulation**) FM *f*

foal [fəʊl] **1** *n (horse)* poulain *m*; *(female)* pouliche *f*

2 *vi* pouliner

foam [fəʊm] **1** *n (on sea)* écume *f*; *(on beer, bath)* mousse *f*; **f. rubber** caoutchouc *m* Mousse®

2 *vi (of sea)* écumer; *(of beer, bath)* mousser; **to f. at the mouth** baver; *Fig* écumer de rage

foamy ['fəʊmɪ] *adj (sea)* écumeux(euse); *(beer)* moussant(e)

fob [fɒb] *n* chaîne *f* (de montre); **f. watch** montre *f* de gousset

▸**fob off** *(pt & pp* **fobbed**) *vt sep Fam* **to f. sb off with an excuse** se débarrasser de qn en lui racontant des salades; **to f. sth off on sb** refiler *ou* fourguer qch à qn

focal ['fəʊkəl] *adj* focal(e); **f. point** foyer *m*; *Fig (of discussion)* point *m* central

focus ['fəʊkəs] **1** *n (pl* **focuses** *or* **foci** ['fəʊkaɪ]) *(of lens)* foyer *m*; *Fig (of discontent)* cible *f*; *(of interest, attention)* centre *m*; *Com & Pol* **f. group** *(of customers)* groupe *m* témoin; **to be in f.** être au point; **to be out of f.** ne pas être au point

2 *vt (lens, camera)* mettre au point; *(rays, attention, energy)* concentrer (**on** sur); **all eyes were focused on him** tous les regards étaient tournés vers lui

3 *vi* **to f. on sth** *(with camera)* faire la mise au point sur qch; *(with eyes)* fixer qch; *Fig (of debate, speaker)* se concentrer sur qch

fodder ['fɒdə(r)] *n* fourrage *m*

foe [fəʊ] *n* ennemi *m*

fog [fɒg] *n* brouillard *m*; *Fig* **to be in a f.** *(confused)* être dans le brouillard; **f. light** *(on car)* (phare *m*) antibrouillard *m*

▸**fog up** *(pt & pp* **fogged**) *vi (of windows, glasses)* s'embuer

fogbound ['fɒgbaʊnd] *adj (port, airport)* bloqué(e) en raison du brouillard

fogey ['fəʊgɪ] *(pl* **fogies**) *n Fam* **old f.** vieux (vieille) schnock *m,f*

foggy ['fɒgɪ] *adj* brumeux(euse); **it's f.** il y a du brouillard; *Fam* **I don't have the foggiest (idea)!** je n'en ai pas la moindre idée!

foghorn ['fɒghɔːn] *n (on ship)* corne *f* de brume; *Fam* **a voice like a f.** une voix de stentor

fogy *(pl* **fogies**) = **fogey**

foible ['fɔɪbəl] *n (habit)* manie *f*; *(weakness)* point *m* faible

foil [fɔɪl] **1** *n* (**a**) *(metal sheet)* feuille *f*; **(cooking** *or* **kitchen) f.** papier *m* alu(minium) (**b**) *(complement)* **to act as a f. (to** *or* **for)** servir de repoussoir (à) (**c**) *(sword)* fleuret *m*

2 *vt (plan, ambitions)* contrecarrer; *(attempt, coup)* faire échouer

foist [fɔɪst] *vt* refiler (**on** à); *(ideas)* imposer (**on** à)

fold¹ [fəʊld] *n* (**sheep**) **f.** parc *m* à moutons

fold² [fəʊld] **1** *n* pli *m*; *(of fat)* bourrelet *m*

2 *vt* (**a**) *(bend)* plier; **to f. sth in two** *or* **in half** plier qch en deux; **to f. one's arms** croiser les bras (**b**) *(in cooking)* mélanger délicatement

3 *vi* (**a**) *(of chair, table)* se plier, se replier (**b**) *Fam (of business)* plier boutique

▸**fold up 1** *vt sep* plier, replier

2 *vi (of map, chair)* se plier, se replier

foldaway ['fəʊldəweɪ] *adj (table, bed)* pliant(e)

folder ['fəʊldə(r)] *n (file, document wallet)* chemise *f*; *(ring binder)* classeur *m*; *Comput* répertoire *m*

folding ['fəʊldɪŋ] *adj (chair, table)* pliant(e); **f. door** porte *f* en accordéon

foliage ['fəʊlɪdʒ] *n* feuillage *m*

folio ['fəʊlɪəʊ] *(pl* **folios**) *n* folio *m*

folk [fəʊk] **1** *npl Fam (people)* gens *mpl*; **my/your folks** *(family)* ma/ta famille

2 *adj (traditional)* folklorique; **f. (music)** (musique *f*) folk *m*; **f. singer** chanteur(euse) *m,f* folk; **f. song** chanson *f* folk

folklore ['fəʊklɔː(r)] *n* folklore *m*

follow ['fɒləʊ] **1** *vt* suivre; *(act, performance)* passer après; *(career)* poursuivre; **the road follows the coast** la route longe la côte; **to f. one's nose** *(go straight ahead)* aller tout droit; *(act instinctively)* y aller à l'instinct

2 *vi* (**a**) *(come after)* suivre; **proceed as follows** procéder comme suit (**b**) *(result)* s'ensuivre; **it follows that...** il s'ensuit que... (**c**) *(understand)* suivre

▸**follow on** *vi* (**a**) *(go after)* **you go ahead, we'll f. on** pars devant, nous te suivons (**b**) *(continue)* **to f. on from sth** découler de qch

▸**follow through 1** *vt sep (project, plan)* mener à son terme

2 *vi* **he's full of ideas but he seldom follows through** il a beaucoup d'idées, mais il les met rarement à exécution

▸**follow up** *vt sep (advantage, success)* exploiter; *(opportunity)* saisir; *(contact)* garder; *(clue)* suivre

follower ['fɒləʊə(r)] *n (of team)* supporter *m*; *(of ideas, politician)* partisan(e) *m,f*; *(of philosopher)* disciple *m*

following ['fɒləʊɪŋ] **1** *n (supporters) (of team)* supporters *mpl*; *(of ideas, politician)* partisans *mpl*; *(of program)* public *m*

2 *pron* **the f.** *(things, points)* ce qui suit; *(people)* les personnes *fpl* suivantes

3 *adj* suivant(e); (**on**) **the f. day** le jour suivant, le lendemain

4 *prep* après

follow-up ['fɒləʊʌp] *n Com (of orders)* suivi *m*

folly ['fɒlɪ] *n* folie *f*; **an act of f.** une folie

foment [fə'ment] *vt Lit* fomenter

fond [fɒnd] *adj* (**a**) **to be f. of sb/sth** aimer bien qn/qch; **to become f. of sb** s'attacher à qn; **to become f. of sth** prendre goût à qch; **to be f. of doing sth** aimer bien faire qch (**b**) *(loving)* tendre, affectueux(euse); **f. memories (of)** de bons souvenirs (de) (**c**) *(hope)* naïf(ïve)

fondle ['fɒndəl] *vt* caresser

fondly ['fɒndlɪ] *adv* (**a**) *(lovingly)* tendrement, affectueusement (**b**) *(naively)* naïvement

fondness ['fɒndnɪs] *n* (**a**) *(affection)* tendresse *f*, affection *f* (**for** pour) (**b**) *(liking)* penchant *m* (**for** pour)

font [fɒnt] *n* (**a**) *Rel* fonts *mpl* baptismaux (**b**) *Typ & Comptr* police *f* de caractères, fonte *f*

food [fuːd] *n* nourriture *f*; **Chinese/Mexican f.** la cuisine chinoise/mexicaine; **to be off one's f.** ne pas avoir d'appétit; **to give sb f. for thought** donner à penser *ou* à réfléchir à qn; *Biol* **f. chain** chaîne *f* alimentaire; **f. industry** industrie *f* alimentaire; **f. poisoning** intoxication *f* alimentaire; **f. processor** robot *m* de cuisine

foodstuffs ['fuːdstʌfs] *npl* produits *mpl* alimentaires

fool [fuːl] **1** *n (stupid person)* imbécile *mf*, idiot(e) *m,f*; *(jester)* fou *m*; **you'd be a f. to buy it** tu serais bien bête de l'acheter; **any f. knows that** le premier imbécile venu sait ça; **a f. of a doctor** un imbécile de docteur; **to play** *or* **to act the f.** faire l'idiot; **to make a f. of sb** *(make look ridiculous)* ridiculiser qn; *(tease)* se moquer de qn; **to make a f. of oneself** se couvrir de ridicule; **the more f. you!** tu es vraiment bête!; **I felt such a f.** je me suis senti vraiment bête; **she's no** *or* **nobody's f.** on ne la lui fait pas, elle est maligne; **to live in a f.'s paradise** se bercer d'illusions; *Fam* **there's no f. like an old f.** il n'y a pire fou qu'un vieux fou

2 *vt (deceive)* avoir, duper; **you can't f. me** on ne m'a pas comme ça; **to let oneself be fooled by sth** se laisser avoir par qch; **you could have fooled me!** je ne l'aurais pas cru!

▸**fool about, fool around** *vi* (**a**) *(act foolishly)* faire l'imbécile; **to f. about** *or* **around with sth** *(clumsily, for fun)* jouer avec qch; *(fiddle)* tripoter qch (**b**) *(waste time)* perdre son temps (**c**) *(have affair(s))* avoir une aventure/des aventures

foolhardy ['fuːlhɑːdɪ] *adj* téméraire, imprudent(e)

foolish ['fuːlɪʃ] *adj (stupid)* idiot(e); *(imprudent)* insensé(e); **to make sb look f.** ridiculiser qn

foolishly ['fuːlɪʃlɪ] *adv (stupidly)* bêtement; *(imprudently)* imprudemment

foolproof ['fuːlpruːf] *adj (method, plan)* infaillible; *(device)* indétraquable

foosball ['fuːsbɔːl] *n* baby-foot *m inv*

foot [fʊt] *(pl* **feet** [fiːt]) **1** *n* (**a**) *(of person, horse, chair)* pied *m*; *(of other animal)* patte *f*; **to put one's feet up** *(have a rest)* se reposer; **to set f. on** poser le pied sur; **I shall never set f. in his house again** je ne remettrai jamais plus les pieds chez lui; **to be on one's feet all day** être debout du matin au soir; **to be on one's feet again** *(after illness)* être de nouveau sur pied; **on f.** à pied; **under f.** sous les pieds; *Mil* **f. patrol** patrouille *f* à pied; **f. pump** pompe *f* à pied; **f. soldier** fantassin *m*, soldat *m* d'infanterie

(**b**) *(of mountain, stairs)* pied *m*; *(of page)* bas *m*; *(of bed, table)* bout *m*

(**c**) *(in poetry)* pied *m*

(**d**) *(unit of measurement)* = 0,3048 m, pied *m* (anglais); **three f.** *or* **feet six (inches)** trois pieds six pouces, ≃ 1 m

(**e**) *(idioms)* **to have one's feet firmly on the ground** avoir les pieds sur terre; **to have one f. in the grave** avoir un pied dans la tombe; **to have a f. in both camps** avoir un pied dans chaque camp; **she hasn't put a f. wrong** elle n'a pas commis la moindre erreur; **to put one's f. down** *(be firm)* faire preuve de fermeté; *(refuse)* mettre le holà; *Fam* **to put one's f. in one's mouth** mettre les pieds dans le plat, faire une gaffe; **to find one's feet** s'adapter; **to get a f. in the door** avoir un pied dans la place; *Fam* **my f.!** mon œil!

2 *vt* **to f. the bill** payer la note

footage ['fʊtɪdʒ] *n Cin* séquences *fpl*, images *fpl*

foot-and-mouth disease [fʊtən'maʊθdɪ'ziːz] *n* fièvre *f* aphteuse

football ['fʊtbɔːl] *n* football *m* américain; *(ball)* ballon *m* (de football américain); **f. fan** supporter *m* d'une équipe de football américain; **f. field** terrain *m* de football américain; **f. player** joueur *m* de football américain; **f. supporter** supporter *m* d'une équipe de football américain; **f. team** équipe *f* de football américain

footballer ['fʊtbɔːlə(r)] *n* joueur *m* de football américain

footbridge ['fʊtbrɪdʒ] *n* passerelle *f*

foothills ['fʊthɪlz] *npl* contreforts *mpl*

foothold ['fʊthəʊld] *n* prise *f* (pour le pied); *Fig* **to gain a f.** *(of theory, feeling)* se propager

footing ['fʊtɪŋ] *n* (**a**) *(balance)* **to lose one's f.** perdre l'équilibre (**b**) *(level)* **on an equal f.** sur un pied d'égalité; **to be on a friendly f. with sb** avoir des rapports amicaux avec qn

footlights ['fʊtlaɪts] *npl Theat* rampe *f*

footloose ['fotluːs] *adj* libre; **to be f. and fancy-free** être libre comme l'air

footman ['fotmən] *n* valet *m* de pied

footnote ['fotnəʊt] *n* note *f* de bas de page; *Fig* détail *m*

footpath ['fotpɑːθ] *n* sentier *m*

footprint ['fotprɪnt] *n* trace *f* de pas; *(of bare foot)* empreinte *f* de pied

footrest ['fotrest] *n* repose-pieds *m inv*

footsie ['fotsɪ] *n Fam* **to play f. with sb** faire du pied à qn

footsore ['fotsɔː(r)] *adj* **to be f.** avoir mal aux pieds

footstep ['fotstep] *n* pas *m*; *Fig* **to follow in sb's footsteps** suivre les traces de qn

footwear ['fotweə(r)] *n* chaussures *fpl*

footwork ['fotwɜːk] *n* jeu *m* de jambes; *Fig* **it required some rather fancy f.** il a fallu faire des pieds et des mains

fop [fɒp] *n* dandy *m*

foppish ['fɒpɪʃ] *adj* de dandy

for [fɔː(r), *unstressed* fə(r)] **1** *prep* **(a)** *(expressing purpose, destination)* pour; **to leave f. France** partir pour la France; **there's no time f. that** il n'y a pas de temps pour ça; **what's it f.?** c'est pour quoi faire?; **can you give me something f. the pain?** pouvez-vous me donner quelque chose contre la douleur?

(b) *(because of)* pour, en raison de; **she couldn't sleep f. the pain** elle ne pouvait pas dormir à cause de la douleur

(c) *(expressing cost, amount)* **I bought it f. $10** je l'ai acheté 10 dollars; **a check f. $50** un chèque de 50 dollars

(d) *(considering)* pour; **he is big f. his age** il est grand pour son âge; **f. all the good it will do** pour ce que ça changera; **f. all his wealth, he was still unhappy** en dépit de toutes ses richesses, il était toujours malheureux

(e) *(representing)* **A f. Anne** A comme Anne; **what's the French f. "book"?** comment dit-on "book" en français?

(f) *(duration)* **I was there f. a month** je suis resté là-bas (pendant) un mois; **I've been here f. a month** il y a un mois que je suis ici, je suis ici depuis un mois; **I will be here f. a month** je serai ici pendant un mois; **I haven't been there f. a month** je n'y suis pas allé depuis un mois; **I'm going away f. a week** je pars pour une semaine; **we have enough food f. two days** nous avons suffisamment à manger pour deux jours

(g) *(with point in time)* **f. the first/last time** pour la première/dernière fois; **I need it f. Friday** j'en ai besoin pour vendredi

(h) *(as compared to)* pour; **they sell ten red bikes f. every black one** ils vendent dix vélos rouges pour un noir

(i) *(in favor of)* **to be f. sth** être pour qch, être favorable à qch; *Fam* **I'm all f. it!** je suis tout à fait pour!

(j) *(introducing an infinitive clause)* **it is too early f. me to decide** il est trop tôt pour que je prenne une décision; **it will be difficult f. her to come** il lui sera difficile de venir; **it took an hour f. us to get there** il nous a fallu une heure pour arriver là-bas

(k) *(idioms)* **f. all I know** pour ce que j'en sais; **that's men f. you!** c'est bien les hommes!; *Fam* **he's in f. it!** qu'est-ce qu'il va prendre!

2 *conj Lit (because)* car

forage ['fɒrɪdʒ] **1** *n (animal food)* fourrage *m*

2 *vi* **to f. for sth** fouiller pour trouver qch

foray ['fɒreɪ] *n* incursion *f* (**into** dans)

forbear [fɔːˈbeə(r)] *(pt* **forbore** [fɔːˈbɔː(r)], *pp* **forborne** [fɔːˈbɔːn]) *vi Formal* **to f. to do sth** s'abstenir de faire qch

forbearance [fɔːˈbeərəns] *n Formal* patience *f*

forbid [fəˈbɪd] *(pt* **forbade** [fəˈbæd, fəˈbeɪd], *pp* **forbidden** [fəˈbɪdən]) *vt* interdire; **to f. sb to do sth** interdire à qn de faire qch; **smoking is forbidden** il est interdit de fumer; **God f.!** Dieu m'en/nous en préserve!

forbidding [fəˈbɪdɪŋ] *adj (appearance, look, landscape)* sinistre; *(task)* rébarbatif(ive)

force [fɔːs] **1** *n* **(a)** *(strength, power, influence)* force *f*; **by sheer** *or* **brute f.** par la force; **by f. of circumstance(s)** par la force des circonstances; **f. of habit** la force de l'habitude; **several forces conspired to bring about his downfall** plusieurs facteurs ont contribué à provoquer sa chute **(b)** *Mil* **the (armed) forces** les forces *fpl* armées; **to join forces (to do sth)** joindre ses efforts (pour faire qch); **they turned out in (full) f.** ils sont venus en masse **(c)** *(effect)* **to come into f.** entrer en vigueur

2 *vt* **(a)** *(compel)* **to f. sb to do sth** *or* **into doing sth** forcer *ou* obliger qn à faire qch; **to f. sth on sb** imposer qch à qn; **they forced the enemy back** ils ont repoussé l'ennemi **(b)** *(obtain by effort)* **to f. the issue** précipiter les choses; **to f. sb's hand** forcer la main à qn; **to f. one's way through a crowd** se frayer un passage à travers la foule; **to f. oneself on sb** *(sexually)* essayer d'abuser de qn physiquement

▸ **force down** *vt sep* **(a)** *(aircraft)* obliger à atterrir **(b)** *(food)* se forcer à avaler

▸ **force open** *vt sep (door, window, lock)* forcer

forced [fɔːst] *adj (manner, laugh)* forcé(e), artificiel(elle); **f. labor** travail *m* forcé; *Aviat* **f. landing** atterrissage *m* forcé; *Mil* **f. march** marche *f* forcée

force-feed ['fɔːsfiːd] *(pt & pp* **force-fed** ['fɔːsˈfed]) *vt (person)* nourrir de force; *(livestock)* gaver

forceful ['fɔːsfʊl] *adj (person, language)* énergique; *(argument)* puissant(e)

forceps ['fɔːseps] *npl* forceps *mpl*; **f. delivery** accouchement *m* aux forceps

forcible ['fɔːsɪbəl] *adj* **(a)** *Law* **f. entry** entrée *f* par effraction **(b)** *(argument)* puissant(e); *(reminder)* brutal(e)

forcibly ['fɔːsɪblɪ] *adv* **(a)** *(by force)* de force **(b)** *(argue)* vigoureusement

ford [fɔːd] **1** *n* gué *m*

2 *vt* traverser à gué

fore [fɔː(r)] **1** *n* **to come to the f.** *(of person)* commencer à être connu(e); *(of issue)* être mis(e) en évidence

2 *adj Naut* à l'avant

forearm ['fɔːrɑːm] *n* avant-bras *m inv*

forebear ['fɔːbeə(r)] *n* ancêtre *mf*

foreboding [fɔːˈbəʊdɪŋ] *n (mauvais)* pressentiment *m*

forecast ['fɔːkɑːst] **1** *n* prévisions *fpl*; *(in horseracing)* pronostics *mpl* (des courses); **(weather) f.** prévisions météorologiques, météo *f*

2 *vt (pt & pp* **forecast(ed))** prévoir; *(in horseracing)* pronostiquer

foreclose [fɔːˈkləʊz] *vt Fin* **to f. a mortgage** saisir un immeuble hypothéqué

forecourt ['fɔːkɔːt] *n (of gas station)* devant *m*

forefathers ['fɔːfɑːðəz] *npl* aïeux *mpl*

forefinger ['fɔːfɪŋɡə(r)] *n* index *m*

forefront ['fɔːfrʌnt] *n* **to be in the f. of** être au premier plan de

forego [fɔːˈɡəʊ] *(pt* **forewent** [fɔːˈwent], *pp* **foregone** [fɔːˈɡɒn]) *vt* renoncer à

foregone ['fɔːɡɒn] **to be a f. conclusion** être couru(e) d'avance

foreground ['fɔːɡraʊnd] **1** *n* premier plan *m*; **in the f.** au premier plan

2 *vt* mettre au premier plan

forehand ['fɔːhænd] *n (in tennis)* coup *m* droit; **f. volley** volée *f* de face

forehead ['fɒrɪd, 'fɔːhed] *n* front *m*

foreign ['fɒrɪn] *adj* étranger(ère); **f. affairs** les affaires *fpl* étrangères; **f. aid** aide *f* aux pays étrangers; *(from point of view of recipient)* aide de l'étranger; *Med* **f. body** corps *m* étranger;

Journ **f. correspondent** correspondant(e) *m,f* à l'étranger; **f. currency** devises *fpl* étrangères; **f. legion** légion *f* étrangère; *Pol* **F. Minister** ministre *m* des Affaires étrangères; *Pol* **f. policy** politique *f* étrangère *ou* extérieure; *Pol* **f. service** service *m* diplomatique; **f. trade** commerce *m* extérieur

foreigner ['fɒrɪnə(r)] *n* étranger(ère) *m,f*

foreleg ['fɔːleg] *n* patte *f* de devant; *(of horse)* membre *m* antérieur

foreman ['fɔːmən] *n (of workers)* contremaître *m*; *(of jury)* président *m*

foremost ['fɔːməʊst] *adj* le (la) plus important(e)

forename ['fɔːneɪm] *n* prénom *m*

forensic [fəˈrensɪk] *adj Law* légal(e); **f. evidence** résultats *mpl* des expertises médico-légales; **f. medicine** médecine *f* légale; **f. scientist** médecin *m* légiste

foreplay ['fɔːpleɪ] *n* préliminaires *mpl* amoureux

forerunner ['fɔːrʌnə(r)] *n* (**a**) *(person)* précurseur *m* (**of** de) (**b**) *(sign)* signe *m* précurseur (**of** de)

foresee [fɔːˈsiː] *(pt* foresaw [fɔːˈsɔː], *pp* foreseen [fɔːˈsiːn]) *vt* prévoir

foreseeable [fɔːˈsiːəbəl] *adj* prévisible; **in the f. future** dans un avenir proche; **for the f. future** dans l'immédiat

foreshadow [fɔːˈʃædəʊ] *vt* annoncer

foresight ['fɔːsaɪt] *n* prévoyance *f*

foreskin ['fɔːskɪn] *n Anat* prépuce *m*

forest ['fɒrɪst] *n* forêt *f*; **f. fire** incendie *m* de forêt; **f. ranger** garde *m* forestier; **the F. Service** organisme américain de gestion des forêts domaniales, ≃ les eaux et forêts *fpl*

forestall [fɔːˈstɔːl] *vt* devancer

forester ['fɒrɪstə(r)] *n* (garde *m*) forestier *m*

forestry ['fɒrɪstrɪ] *n* sylviculture *f*; **f. worker** *(forester)* forestier *m*; *(lumberjack)* bûcheron *m*

foretaste ['fɔːteɪst] *n* avant-goût *m* (**of** de)

foretell [fɔːˈtel] *(pt & pp* foretold [fɔːˈtəʊld]) *vt* prédire

forethought ['fɔːθɔːt] *n* prévoyance *f*

forever [fəˈrevə(r)] *adv* (**a**) *(eternally)* pour toujours; **nothing lasts f.** tout a une fin; **the journey seemed to last f.** il semblait que le voyage ne finirait jamais (**b**) *(repeatedly)* sans cesse; **he was f. changing his mind** il changeait sans cesse *ou* constamment d'avis (**c**) *Fam (a long time)* une éternité; **to take f. (to do sth)** mettre un temps infini (à faire qch)

forewarn [fɔːˈwɔːn] *vt* prévenir, avertir; *Prov* **forewarned is forearmed** un homme averti en vaut deux

forewent [fɔːˈwent] *pt of* **forego**

foreword ['fɔːwɜːd] *n* avant-propos *m inv,* préface *f*

forfeit ['fɔːfɪt] **1** *n (in game)* gage *m*; *Law* amende *f*
2 *vt (rights)* être déchu(e) de; *(property)* se faire confisquer; *(someone's respect)* perdre

forgave [fəˈgeɪv] *pt of* **forgive**

forge [fɔːdʒ] **1** *n* forge *f*
2 *vt* (**a**) *(metal, alliance)* forger (**b**) *(check, signature, bill)* contrefaire; **to f. a document/passport** faire un faux document/passeport

▶**forge ahead** *vi* (**a**) *(make progress)* faire des progrès; *(of company)* aller de l'avant (**b**) *(outstrip competitors)* prendre de l'avance (**of** sur)

forged [fɔːdʒd] *adj* faux (fausse)

forgery ['fɔːdʒərɪ] *(pl* forgeries) *n* (**a**) *(activity)* contrefaçon *f*; *(of document, bill)* falsification *f* (**b**) *(thing forged)* faux *m*

forget [fəˈget] *(pt* forgot [fəˈgɒt], *pp* forgotten [fəˈgɒtən]) **1** *vt* oublier; **to f. to do sth** oublier de faire qch; **to f. how to do sth** oublier comment on fait qch, ne plus savoir faire qch; **to be forgotten** tomber dans l'oubli; **f. it!** *(in reply to apology, thanks)* il n'y a pas de quoi!; *(stop talking about it)* laisse tomber!
2 *vi* oublier; **to f. about sb/sth** oublier qn/qch; **you can f. about going to London!** tu peux faire une croix sur ton voyage à Londres!; **let's f. about it** n'y pensons plus

forgetful [fəˈgetfʊl] *adj* **to be f.** avoir mauvaise mémoire

forget-me-not [fəˈgetmiːnɒt] *n* myosotis *m*

forgivable [fəˈgɪvəbəl] *adj* excusable, pardonnable

forgive [fəˈgɪv] *(pt* forgave [fəˈgeɪv], *pp* forgiven [fəˈgɪvən]) **1** *vt* pardonner; **to f. sb for sth** pardonner qch à qn; **if you'll f. the pun** pardonnez-moi ce jeu de mots; **f. me for interrupting** pardonnez-moi de vous interrompre
2 *vi* pardonner; **to f. and forget** oublier sa rancune

forgiveness [fəˈgɪvnɪs] *n* pardon *m*

forgiving [fəˈgɪvɪŋ] *adj* indulgent(e)

forgo = **forego**

forgot [fəˈgɒt] *pt of* **forget**

forgotten [fəˈgɒtən] *pp of* **forget**

fork [fɔːk] **1** *n* (**a**) *(for food)* fourchette *f* (**b**) *(for gardening)* fourche *f* (**c**) *(in road, path)* bifurcation *f*
2 *vi (of road, path)* bifurquer

▶**fork out** *Fam* **1** *vt sep (money)* allonger
2 *vi* casquer (**for** pour)

forked [fɔːkt] *adj (stick, tongue)* fourchu(e); **f. lightning** éclairs *mpl*

fork-lift truck ['fɔːklɪftˈtrʌk] *n* chariot *m* (élévateur) à fourche

forlorn [fəˈlɔːn] *adj (person, look)* triste, malheureux(euse); *(hope, attempt)* désespéré(e)

form [fɔːm] **1** *n* (**a**) *(shape)* *(of object, animal)* forme *f*; *(of person)* silhouette *f*; **to take the f. of sth** prendre la forme de qch
(**b**) *(type)* forme *f*; **in the f. of** sous forme de; **f. of address** titre *m* de politesse
(**c**) *(politeness)* **as a matter of f., for f.'s sake** pour la forme, par pure formalité; **it's good/bad f. to...** cela se fait/ne se fait pas de...
(**d**) *(for applications, orders)* formulaire *m*
(**e**) *(condition, performance)* forme *f*; *(in horseracing)* performances *fpl*; **to be in good f.** être en forme; **on present f.** si l'on en juge par la situation actuelle
2 *vt (government, character)* former; *(idea)* avoir; *(opinion)* se faire, se former; *(relationship, friendship)* nouer; *(organization, obstacle)* constituer; **to f. a plan to do sth** projeter de faire qch; **to f. part of sth** faire partie de qch
3 *vi* se former

formal ['fɔːməl] *adj (manner)* cérémonieux(euse); *(offer, occasion, invitation)* officiel(elle); *(language)* soutenu(e); **f. dress** tenue *f* de soirée

formality [fɔːˈmælɪtɪ] *(pl* formalities) *n (procedure)* formalité *f*

formalize ['fɔːməlaɪz] *vt* officialiser

formally ['fɔːməlɪ] *adv (behave)* de façon cérémonieuse; *(invite, announce)* officiellement; **to dress f.** *(for evening reception)* porter une tenue de soirée

format ['fɔːmæt] **1** *n* format *m*
2 *vt (pt & pp* formatted) *Comput* formater

formation [fɔːˈmeɪʃən] *n (act, arrangement)* formation *f*; *(of idea, plan)* élaboration *f*; **f. flying** vol *m* de groupe

formative ['fɔːmətɪv] *adj* formateur(trice); **the f. years** les années *fpl* de formation

former ['fɔːmə(r)] **1** *pron* **the f.** le premier (la première), celui-là (celle-là); *(plural)* les premiers (les premières), ceux-là (celles-là)
2 *adj (pupil, colleague, job)* ancien(enne) *(before noun)*; **in f. times** autrefois; **in a f. life** dans une vie antérieure

formerly ['fɔːməlɪ] *adv* autrefois; **Mrs Connelly, f. Miss Paton** Mme Connelly, née Paton; **Zambia, f. Northern Rhodesia** la Zambie, ancienne Rhodésie du Nord

formidable ['fɔːmɪdəbəl] *adj (opponent, difficulty)* redoutable; *(performance, talent)* formidable

formula ['fɔːmjʊlə] *(pl* formulas *or* formulae ['fɔːmjʊliː]) *n* (**a**) *(scheme, in math, chemistry)* formule *f*; **the f. for success** la clé de la réussite; **a peace f.** une solution en faveur de la paix; *Aut* **F. 1** formule 1 (**b**) *(baby food)* lait *m* en poudre

formulate ['fɔːmjʊleɪt] *vt (plan, proposal)* élaborer; *(thought, opinion)* formuler

fornication [fɔːnɪ'keɪʃən] *n Formal* fornication *f*

forsake [fə'seɪk] *(pt* **forsook** [fə'sʊk], *pp* **forsaken** [fə'seɪkən]) *vt Lit* (**a**) *(abandon)* abandonner (**b**) *(renounce)* renoncer à

forswear [fɔː'sweə(r)] *(pt* **forswore** [fɔː'swɔː(r)], *pp* **forsworn** [fɔː'swɔːn]) *vt Lit* renoncer à

fort [fɔːt] *n* fort *m*, forteresse *f*; *Fig* **to hold the f.** monter la garde

forte ['fɔːtɪ] *n* fort *m*

forth [fɔːθ] *adv* en avant; **to go f.** avancer; **to walk back and f.** marcher de long en large, faire les cent pas; **from that day f.** à dater de ce jour; **and so f.** et cetera, et ainsi de suite

forthcoming [fɔːθ'kʌmɪŋ] *adj* (**a**) *(election)* prochain(e); *(book, movie)* qui sortira bientôt (**b**) *(available)* **no money was f.** l'argent n'est pas arrivé (**c**) *(informative)* expansif(ive) (**about** sur)

forthright ['fɔːθraɪt] *adj* franc (franche)

forthwith [fɔːθ'wɪθ] *adv Formal* immédiatement, sur-le-champ

fortieth ['fɔːtɪəθ] **1** *n* (**a**) *(fraction)* quarantième *m* (**b**) *(in series)* quarantième *mf*
2 *adj* quarantième

fortification [fɔːtɪfɪ'keɪʃən] *n* fortification *f*

fortified ['fɔːtɪfaɪd] *adj* (**a**) *(town)* fortifié(e) (**b**) **f. wine** vin *m* doux (naturel), vin de liqueur

fortify ['fɔːtɪfaɪ] *(pt & pp* **fortified**) *vt Mil* fortifier; **to f. oneself** se prémunir

fortitude ['fɔːtɪtjuːd] *n* force *f* morale

fortress ['fɔːtrɪs] *n* forteresse *f*

fortuitous [fɔː'tjuːɪtəs] *adj Formal* fortuit(e)

fortunate ['fɔːtʃənət] *adj* heureux(euse); **to be f.** avoir de la chance; **to be f. enough to do sth** avoir la chance de faire qch

fortunately ['fɔːtʃənətlɪ] *adv* heureusement, par bonheur

fortune ['fɔːtʃən] *n* (**a**) *(riches)* fortune *f*; **to make a** *or* **one's f.** faire fortune; *Fam* **to cost a (small) f.** coûter une fortune *ou* les yeux de la tête (**b**) *(luck)* chance *f*; **good f.** chance *f*; **bad f.** malchance *f*; **to tell sb's f.** dire la bonne aventure à qn

fortune-teller ['fɔːtʃəntelə(r)] *n* diseur(euse) *m,f* de bonne aventure

forty ['fɔːtɪ] **1** *n* quarante *m inv*
2 *adj* quarante; *Fam* **to take f. winks** piquer *ou* faire un petit somme; *see also* **eighty**

forum ['fɔːrəm] *n* forum *m*; *Comput (on Internet)* groupe *m* de discussion; **a f. for debate** un lieu de débat

forward ['fɔːwəd] **1** *n (in sport)* avant *m*
2 *adj* (**a**) *(position)* avant *inv*; *(movement)* en avant, vers l'avant; **f. planning** planification *f*; *Fin* **f. market** marché *m* à terme (**b**) *(impudent, bold)* effronté(e), hardi(e)
3 *adv* (**a**) *(of time)* **from this/that day f.** à partir d'aujourd'hui/de ce jour-là; **to put the clocks f.** avancer les pendules (**b**) *(of direction)* en avant; **to walk f.** avancer (**c**) *(of position)* à l'avant; **we're sitting too far f.** *(at movies, in theater)* nous sommes assis trop près; **the seat is too far f.** le siège est trop avancé
4 *vt* (**a**) *(letter)* faire suivre; *(complaint, query)* faire passer (**to** à) (**b**) *(one's career, interests)* favoriser

forwarding agent ['fɔːwədɪŋ'eɪdʒənt] *n Com* (agent *m*) transitaire *m*

forward-looking ['fɔːwədlʊkɪŋ] *adj* progressiste

forwards ['fɔːwədz] *adv* = **forward**

fossil ['fɒsəl] *n* fossile *m*; *Fam* **an old f.** *(man)* un vieux croûton; *(woman)* une vieille bique; **f. fuel** combustible *m* fossile

fossilized ['fɒsɪlaɪzd] *adj* fossilisé(e); *Fig* sclérosé(e)

foster ['fɒstə(r)] **1** *adj* **f. child** = enfant placé dans une famille d'accueil; **f. parents** famille *f* d'accueil, parents *mpl* nourriciers
2 *vt* (**a**) *(child)* prendre en famille d'accueil (**b**) *(idea, hope)* nourrir, entretenir; *(friendship)* stimuler

fought [fɔːt] *pt & pp of* **fight**

foul [faʊl] **1** *n (in sport)* faute *f*
2 *adj* (**a**) *(disgusting) (smell, taste)* infect(e), nauséabond(e); *(weather)* sale; *(air)* vicié(e); *(language)* ordurier(ère); **to be in a f. mood** être d'une humeur massacrante (**b**) *(illegal)* **f. play** *Sport* jeu *m* irrégulier; *Law* acte *m* criminel; **f. play is not suspected** on ne croit pas à un meurtre
3 *adv* (**a**) **to smell f.** puer; **to taste f.** avoir un goût infect (**b**) **to fall f. of the law** avoir des démêlés avec la justice
4 *vt* (**a**) *(pollute)* salir (**b**) *(entangle)* s'enchevêtrer autour de (**c**) *(in sport)* commettre une faute contre

▸ **foul up** *vt sep Fam (ruin)* gâcher

foul-mouthed ['faʊl'maʊðd] *adj* grossier(ère), mal embouché(e)

found[1] [faʊnd] *vt* (**a**) *(city, organization)* fonder; *(company)* créer; *(empire)* établir (**b**) *(base)* baser, fonder (**on** sur)

found[2] [faʊnd] *pt & pp of* **find**

foundation [faʊn'deɪʃən] *n* (**a**) *(of city, organization)* fondation *f*; *(of company)* création *f* (**b**) *(basis)* fondement *m*, base *f*; **to be without f.** être dénué(e) de fondement (**c**) **foundations** *(of building, society)* fondations *fpl* (**d**) *(make-up)* **f. (cream)** fond *m* de teint

founder[1] ['faʊndə(r)] *n (of hospital, school)* fondateur(trice) *m,f*; **f. member** membre *m* fondateur

founder[2] ['faʊndə(r)] *vi (of ship)* s'échouer; *Fig (of project, talks)* avorter

founding father ['faʊndɪŋ'fɑːðə(r)] *n* père *m* fondateur

foundling ['faʊndlɪŋ] *n Old-fashioned* enfant *mf* trouvé(e)

foundry ['faʊndrɪ] *(pl* **foundries**) *n* fonderie *f*

fount [faʊnt] *n Lit & Fig* source *f*

fountain ['faʊntɪn] *n* fontaine *f*; **f. pen** stylo *m* (à) plume

four [fɔː(r)] **1** *n* quatre *m inv*; **on all fours** à quatre pattes
2 *adj* quatre; **to the f. corners of the earth** aux quatre coins du monde; *see also* **eight**

four-eyes ['fɔːraɪz] *n Fam* binoclard(e) *m,f*

four-figure ['fɔː'fɪgə(r)] *adj* **f. sum** un montant de quatre chiffres

fourfold ['fɔːfəʊld] **1** *adj* **a f. increase** une augmentation au quadruple
2 *adv* **to increase f.** quadrupler

four-legged ['fɔː'legɪd] *adj* quadrupède; *Hum* **f. friend** ami *m* à quatre pattes

four-letter word ['fɔːletə'wɜːd] *n* gros mot *m*

four-poster ['fɔː'pəʊstə(r)] *n* **f. (bed)** lit *m* à baldaquin

foursome ['fɔːsəm] *n* groupe *m* de quatre personnes

fourteen ['fɔːtiːn] **1** *n* quatorze *m inv*
2 *adj* quatorze; *see also* **eight**

fourteenth [fɔː'tiːnθ] **1** *n* (**a**) *(fraction)* quatorzième *m* (**b**) *(in series)* quatorzième *mf* (**c**) *(of month)* quatorze *m inv*
2 *adj* quatorzième; *see also* **eighth**

fourth [fɔːθ] **1** *n* (**a**) *(fraction)* quatrième *m* (**b**) *(in series)* quatrième *mf* (**c**) *(of month)* quatre *m inv*
2 *adj* quatrième; **f. floor** troisième étage; *Scol* **f. grade** = classe du primaire pour les 8–9 ans; *see also* **eighth**

fourthly ['fɔːθlɪ] *adv* quatrièmement

fowl [faʊl] *(pl* **fowl**) *n* volaille *f*

fox [fɒks] **1** *n* renard *m*; *Fig* **a sly old f.** *(cunning person)* un vieux renard; **f. cub** renardeau *m*; **f. hunt** chasse *f* au renard
2 *vt (perplex)* laisser perplexe; *(deceive)* duper

foxglove ['fɒksglʌv] *n* digitale *f* (pourprée)

fox-hunting ['fɒkshʌntɪŋ] *n* chasse *f* au renard

foxtrot ['fɒkstrɒt] *n* fox-trot *m inv*

foxy ['fɒksɪ] *adj Fam* (**a**) *(sly)* rusé(e) (**b**) *(sexy)* sexy *inv*

foyer ['fɔɪeɪ] *n (in theater)* foyer *m*; *(in movie theater, hotel)* hall *m*

fraction ['frækʃən] *n (in math)* fraction *f*; *Fig (small part)* petite partie *f*; **a f. too small/large** un tout petit peu trop petit(e)/grand(e)

fractional ['frækʃənəl] *adj (very small)* infime

fractious ['frækʃəs] *adj (adult)* de mauvaise humeur; *(baby)* pleurnicheur(euse); *(tone, expression)* irrité(e)

fracture ['fræktʃə(r)] **1** *n* fracture *f*
2 *vt (bone)* fracturer; *(pipe)* fendre
3 *vi (of bone)* se fracturer; *(of pipe)* se fendre

fragile ['frædʒaɪl] *adj* fragile; *Fam* **I'm feeling a bit f. this morning** *(after drinking)* j'ai un peu la gueule de bois ce matin

fragility [frə'dʒɪlɪtɪ] *n* fragilité *f*

fragment 1 *n* ['frægmənt] fragment *m*; **I only heard a f. of what was said** je n'ai entendu que des bribes de la conversation
2 *vi* [fræg'ment] *(of object)* se fragmenter; *(of organization)* éclater

fragrance ['freɪgrəns] *n* parfum *m*

fragrant ['freɪgrənt] *adj* odorant(e), parfumé(e)

frail [freɪl] *adj (person)* frêle; *(object)* fragile

frailty ['freɪltɪ] *n* faiblesse *f*

frame [freɪm] **1** *n* (**a**) *(of picture)* cadre *m*, encadrement *m*; *(of door, window)* encadrement (**b**) *(of person, animal)* ossature *f*; *(of building, bridge)* charpente *f*; *(of bicycle)* cadre *m*; *(of eyeglasses)* monture *f* (**c**) **f. of mind** état *m* d'esprit; **f. of reference** système *m* de référence
2 *vt* (**a**) *(surround)* encadrer (**b**) *(compose) (answer)* formuler; *(law)* rédiger (**c**) *Fam (falsely incriminate)* monter un coup contre

framework ['freɪmwɜːk] *n (structure)* cadre *m*, structure *f*; *(of building, construction)* charpente *f*; *Fig* **within the f. of** dans le cadre de

franc [fræŋk] *n (currency)* franc *m*; *Formerly* **Belgian/French f.** franc belge/français; **Swiss f.** franc suisse

France [frɑːns] *n* la France

franchise ['fræntʃaɪz] **1** *n* (**a**) *Com* franchise *f* (**b**) *Pol* droit *m* de vote
2 *vt Com* franchiser

francophile ['fræŋkəʊfaɪl] *n & adj* francophile *mf*

francophone ['fræŋkəʊfəʊn] *n & adj* francophone *mf*

frank [fræŋk] **1** *adj* franc (franche); **to be f....** pour être franc...
2 *vt (letter)* affranchir

Frankfurt ['fræŋkfɜːt] *n* Francfort

frankfurter ['fræŋkfɜːtə(r)] *n* saucisse *f* de Francfort

frankincense ['fræŋkɪnsens] *n* encens *m*

frankly ['fræŋklɪ] *adv* franchement

frantic ['fræntɪk] *adj (rush, pace)* frénétique; *(attempt, effort)* désespéré(e); **f. with worry** fou (folle) d'inquiétude

frantically ['fræntɪklɪ] *adv* frénétiquement; *(work, write)* avec frénésie; *(try)* désespérément

fraternal [frə'tɜːnəl] *adj* fraternel(elle)

fraternity [frə'tɜːnɪtɪ] *(pl* **fraternities***) n* (**a**) *(brotherliness)* fraternité *f* (**b**) *(group)* confrérie *f*; **the banking/medical f.** la confrérie des banquiers/médecins (**c**) *Univ* = organisation d'étudiants; **f. house** = maison communautaire (d'étudiants d'une même organisation)

fraternize ['frætənaɪz] *vi* fraterniser (**with** avec)

fraud [frɔːd] *n* (**a**) *(person)* imposteur *m* (**b**) *(deception)* supercherie *f*; *(crime)* fraude *f*

fraudulent ['frɔːdjʊlənt] *adj (charge, accusation, feelings)* faux (fausse); *(claim, transaction)* frauduleux(euse)

fraught [frɔːt] *adj* (**a**) **f. with danger** rempli(e) d'embûches; **f. with emotion** chargé(e) d'émotion

fray¹ [freɪ] *n (brawl)* bagarre *f*; **to enter the f.** entrer dans l'arène

fray² [freɪ] **1** *vt (material)* user
2 *vi (of material)* s'user; *(of tempers)* s'échauffer; *(of nerves)* craquer

frazzle ['fræzəl] *n* **to be burnt to a f.** *(of food)* être carbonisé(e); *Fam (of person)* être brûlé(e) par le soleil

frazzled ['fræzəld] *adj Fam (person)* lessivé(e), épuisé(e); *(nerves)* à plat

freak [friːk] **1** *n* (**a**) *(strange being)* monstre *m*, phénomène *m*; **f. show** exhibition *f* de monstres (**b**) *(strange event)* **by a f. of fortune** par un coup de chance; **f. accident** accident *m* imprévisible; **f. storm** orage *m* inattendu (**c**) *(enthusiast)* fana *mf*; **jazz/movie f.** fana de jazz/cinéma
2 *vi* = **freak out** *vi*

freak out *Fam* **1** *vt sep (shock, scare)* faire flipper
2 *vi (panic)* paniquer; *(become angry)* piquer une crise

freckle ['frekəl] *n* tache *f* de rousseur

free [friː] **1** *adj* (**a**) *(unrestricted)* libre (**from** *or* **of** de); *(movement)* dégagé(e); **to be f. of sb** être débarrassé(e) de qn; **f. from worry** sans souci; **to be f. to do sth** être libre de faire qch; **to set sb f.** rendre sa liberté à qn; **f. and easy** décontracté(e); *Fam* **feel f. to borrow the car** n'hésitez pas à emprunter la voiture; (**as**) **f. as a bird** libre comme l'air; **to be a f. agent** être libre (de ses mouvements); *Fig* **to have a f. hand** avoir pleine liberté d'action; *Econ* **f. enterprise** libre entreprise *f*; **f. fall** *(of parachutist, economy)* chute *f* libre; **f. kick** *(in soccer)* coup *m* franc; *Econ* **f. market** économie *f* de marché; **f. speech** liberté *f* d'expression; **f. throw** *(in basketball)* lancer *m* franc; **f. trade** libre-échange *m*; **f. verse** vers *mpl* libres; **f. will** libre arbitre *m*; **to do sth of one's own f. will** faire qch de son plein gré
(**b**) *(unoccupied) (person, seat, table, time)* libre
(**c**) *(without charge)* gratuit(e); **f. gift** cadeau *m*
(**d**) *(generous)* **to be f. with one's advice** être prodigue en conseils
2 *adv (without charge)* gratuitement; **to do sth for f.** faire qch gratuitement
3 *vt (pt & pp* **freed** [friːd]*) (prisoner, time, place)* libérer (**from** de); *(something stuck)* dégager (**from** de); **to f. oneself from** *or* **of sth** se libérer de qch

freedom ['friːdəm] *n* liberté *f*; **to have the f. to do sth** être libre de faire qch; **f. of information** libre accès *m* à l'information; **f. of speech/worship** liberté d'expression/de culte; **to give sb the f. of the city** nommer qn citoyen(enne) d'honneur de la ville; **f. fighter** guérillero *m*, révolutionnaire *mf*

free-for-all ['friːfərɔːl] *n Fam* bagarre *f*

freehold ['friːhəʊld] *n Law* propriété *f* foncière perpétuelle et libre

freeholder ['friːhəʊldə(r)] *n* propriétaire *m* foncier (à perpétuité)

freelance ['friːlɑːns] **1** *n* travailleur(euse) *m,f* indépendant(e)
2 *adj* indépendant(e), free-lance *inv*
3 *adv* **to work f.** travailler en indépendant(e) *ou* en free-lance
4 *vi* travailler en indépendant(e) *ou* en free-lance

freelancer ['friːlɑːnsə(r)] *n* travailleur(euse) *m,f* indépendant(e)

freeloader ['friːləʊdə(r)] *n Fam* pique-assiette *mf inv*, parasite *m*

freely ['friːlɪ] *adv (give)* sans compter; *(speak)* en toute liberté; *(spend)* libéralement; **f. available** *(for sale)* en vente libre; *(easy to get hold of)* qu'on peut se procurer facilement

freemason ['friːmeɪsən] *n* franc-maçon *m*

freemasonry ['friːmeɪsənrɪ] *n* franc-maçonnerie *f*

free-range ['friːˈreɪndʒ] *adj (chicken)* fermier(ère); **f. eggs** œufs *mpl* de poules élevées en plein air

freestyle ['friːstaɪl] **1** *n (in swimming)* nage *f* libre
2 *adj (skateboarding, snowboarding, etc.)* free-style; **f. skiing** ski *m* artistique

freethinker ['friːθɪŋkə(r)] *n* libre-penseur(euse) *m,f*

freeware ['friːweə(r)] *n Comput* logiciel *m* (du domaine) public, gratuiciel *m*

freeway ['friːweɪ] *n* autoroute *f*

freewheel ['friːwiːl] *vi (on bicycle)* être en roue libre; *(in car)* rouler au point mort

freeze [friːz] **1** *n (in weather)* gel *m*, gelée *f*; **price/wage f.** gel des prix/salaires

2 *vt (pt* **froze** [frəʊz], *pp* **frozen** ['frəʊzən]) *(food)* congeler; *(prices, assets)* geler; **to be frozen to death** être mort(e) de froid

3 *vi* (**a**) *(of weather)* **it's freezing** *(below zero)* il gèle; *Fig (very cold)* on gèle (**b**) *(of liquid, food)* geler; **to f. to death** mourir de froid; *Fam* **I'm freezing** je suis gelé (**c**) *(stand still)* s'arrêter net, se figer; **f.!** ne bougez plus!

▸**freeze out** *vt sep Fam* **to f. sb out** *(of conversation, deal)* exclure qn; *Com* **to f. out the competition** évincer les concurrents

▸**freeze over** *vi (of pond, river)* geler

▸**freeze up** *vi (of pond, mechanism)* geler

freeze-dried ['friːzdraɪd] *adj (coffee, herbs)* lyophilisé(e)

freeze-frame ['friːzfreɪm] *n Cin* arrêt *m* sur image

freezer ['friːzə(r)] *n* congélateur *m*

freezing ['friːzɪŋ] *adj* **f.** (**cold**) *(room, weather, temperature)* glacial(e); *(water)* glacé(e); **it's f. cold in here** on meurt de froid ici

freight [freɪt] *Com* **1** *n (transport)* fret *m*, transport *m* de marchandises; *(goods)* cargaison *f*; *(price)* prix *m* de transport; **f. train** train *m* de marchandises

2 *vt (goods)* transporter

freighter ['freɪtə(r)] *n (ship)* cargo *m*

French [frentʃ] **1** *n (language)* français *m*; *Hum* **pardon my F.** *(after swearing)* excusez mon langage; **F. class/teacher** classe *f*/professeur *m* de français

2 *npl* **the F.** *(people)* les Français *mpl*

3 *adj* français(e); **F. Canadian** *(person)* Canadien(enne) *m,f* français(e); **F. fries** frites *fpl*; **F. horn** cor *m* d'harmonie; **F. kiss** baiser *m* avec la langue; **F. loaf** baguette *f*; **F. Polynesia** la Polynésie française; **F. door** *or* **window** porte-fenêtre *f*

French-Canadian [frentʃkə'neɪdjən] *n* canadien(enne) français(e)

Frenchman ['frentʃmən] *n* Français *m*

French-speaking ['frentʃ'spiːkɪŋ] *adj* francophone

Frenchwoman ['frentʃwʊmən] *n* Française *f*

frenetic [frə'netɪk] *adj* frénétique

frenzied ['frenzɪd] *adj (person)* affolé(e); *(attack)* déchaîné(e); *(activity)* frénétique; **f. with rage/worry** fou (folle) de rage/ d'inquiétude

frenzy ['frenzɪ] *(pl* **frenzies**) *n* frénésie *f*, folie *f*; **to work oneself into a f.** se mettre dans tous ses états

frequency ['friːkwənsɪ] *(pl* **frequencies**) *n* fréquence *f*; **f. band** bande *f* de fréquences

frequent 1 *adj* ['friːkwənt] fréquent(e); **it's a f. occurrence** cela se produit souvent

2 *vt* [frɪ'kwent] fréquenter

frequently ['friːkwəntlɪ] *adv* fréquemment, souvent

fresco ['freskəʊ] *(pl* **frescos** *or* **frescoes**) *n* fresque *f*

fresh [freʃ] **1** *adj* (**a**) *(food, news)* frais (fraîche); **to smell f.** sentir bon le frais; **to get some f. air** s'aérer; **f. water** *(not salty)* eau *f* douce; **it's still f. in my mind** c'est encore frais dans ma mémoire; **as f. as a daisy** frais et dispos *inv* (**b**) *(page, attempt, drink)* nouveau(elle) *(before noun)*; **to make a f. start** recommencer à zéro (**c**) *(original) (approach, writing)* nouveau(elle), original(e) (**d**) *Fam (cheeky)* insolent(e); **to get f. with sb** *(sexually)* faire des avances à qn

2 *adv* **f. from** *(school, university)* frais émoulu(e) de; **we're f. out of lemons** nous n'avons plus de citrons

freshen ['freʃən] *vi (of wind, weather)* rafraîchir

▸**freshen up** *vi (wash)* faire un brin de toilette

freshly ['freʃlɪ] *adv* fraîchement; **f. baked** sortant du four; **f. made** qui vient d'être fait

freshman ['freʃmən] *n Sch & Univ* étudiant(e) *m,f* de première année

freshness ['freʃnɪs] *n* (**a**) *(of food)* fraîcheur *f* (**b**) *(originality)* nouveauté *f*, originalité *f*

freshwater ['freʃwɔːtə(r)] *adj (fish)* d'eau douce

fret [fret] *(pt & pp* **fretted**) *vi (worry)* s'inquiéter, se tourmenter

fretful ['fretfʊl] *adj* inquiet(ète)

Freudian ['frɔɪdɪən] *adj* freudien(enne); **F. slip** lapsus *m*

FRG [efɑː'dʒiː] *n Formerly (abbr* **Federal Republic of Germany**) **the F.** la RFA *f*

Fri. *(abbr* **Friday**) ven

friar ['fraɪə(r)] *n* religieux *m*, moine *m*

fricassee [frɪkə'siː] *n* fricassée *f*

friction ['frɪkʃən] *n also Fig* friction *f*; **f. tape** chatterton *m*

Friday ['fraɪdɪ] *n* vendredi *m*; *see also* **Saturday**

fridge [frɪdʒ] *n* frigo *m*

fried [fraɪd] *adj* frit(e)

friend [frend] *n* ami(e) *m,f*; **to be friends with sb** être ami avec qn; **to make friends with sb** devenir ami avec qn; **that's what friends are for** c'est à ça que servent les amis; **we're just good friends** nous sommes bons amis, c'est tout; **he's no f. of mine** ce n'est pas un ami; **to have friends in high places** avoir des amis bien placés; **to be a f. of the arts** être un défenseur des beaux-arts; *Prov* **a f. in need is a f. indeed** c'est dans le besoin que l'on connaît ses amis

friendless ['frendlɪs] *adj (person)* sans amis; *(childhood)* solitaire

friendly ['frendlɪ] *adj* amical(e); **f. advice** conseils *mpl* d'ami; **a f. nation** un pays ami; **to be f. with sb** être ami(e) avec qn; **to be on f. terms with sb** être en bons termes avec qn; *Mil* **f. fire** tirs *mpl* provenant de son propre camp

friendship ['frendʃɪp] *n* amitié *f*

fries [fraɪz] *npl* (**French**) **f.** frites *fpl*

frieze [friːz] *n Art & Archit* frise *f*

frigate ['frɪgət] *n* frégate *f*

fright [fraɪt] *n* peur *f*, effroi *m*; **to take f.** prendre peur; **to get a f.** avoir peur; **to give sb a f.** faire peur à qn; *Fam* **to look a f.** être à faire peur

frighten ['fraɪtən] **1** *vt* effrayer, faire peur à; **to f. sb into doing sth** faire peur à qn jusqu'à ce qu'il fasse qch; *Fam* **to f. the life** *or* **the wits out of sb** rendre qn fou (folle) de peur

2 *vi* **I don't f. easily** je ne me laisse pas effrayer facilement

frightened ['fraɪtənd] *adj* apeuré(e); **to be f. (of)** avoir peur (de); **to be f. to do sth** avoir peur de faire qch

frightening ['fraɪtənɪŋ] *adj* effrayant(e)

frightful ['fraɪtfʊl] *adj* épouvantable, affreux(euse)

frigid ['frɪdʒɪd] *adj (sexually)* frigide; *(smile, atmosphere)* glacial(e)

frill [frɪl] *n* volant *m*; *Fig* **with no frills** *(ceremony)* sans chichis; *(vacation)* rudimentaire

frilly ['frɪlɪ] *adj* à volants

fringe [frɪndʒ] *n* (**a**) *(on clothes, lampshade)* frange *f* (**b**) *(edge) (of forest)* lisière *f*; *(of town)* abords *mpl*; **on the fringes of society** en marge de la société; **f. benefits** avantages *mpl* divers; *Pol* **f. group** groupuscule *m*

frisk [frɪsk] **1** *vt (search)* fouiller

2 *vi* **to f. about** gambader

frisky ['frɪskɪ] *adj (person)* plein(e) d'entrain; *(horse)* nerveux(euse)

fritter ['frɪtə(r)] *n Culin* beignet *m*

▸**fritter away** *vt sep* gaspiller

frivolity [frɪ'vɒlɪtɪ] (*pl* **frivolities**) *n* frivolité *f*

frivolous ['frɪvələs] *adj* frivole; *(remark)* futile

frizzy ['frɪzɪ] *adj* crépu(e)

fro [frəʊ] *adv* **to go to and f.** aller et venir

frock [frɒk] *n Old-fashioned (dress)* robe *f*; **f. coat** redingote *f*

frog [frɒg] *n* (**a**) *(animal)* grenouille *f*; *Fam* **to have a f. in one's throat** avoir un chat dans la gorge (**b**) *Fam (French person)* = terme xénophobe, souvent humoristique, désignant un Français

frogman ['frɒgmən] *n* homme-grenouille *m*

frogmarch ['frɒgmɑːtʃ] *vt* emmener de force

frogspawn ['frɒgspɔːn] *n* œufs *mpl* de grenouille

frolic ['frɒlɪk] (*pt & pp* **frolicked**) *vi* s'ébattre

from [frɒm, *unstressed* frəm] *prep* (**a**) *(expressing place of origin)* de; **where are you f.?, where do you come f.?** d'où êtes-vous?, d'où venez-vous?; **she's f. Portugal** elle vient du Portugal; **f. New York to Boston** de New York à Boston; **the train f. Chicago** le train de Chicago; **5 miles f. Paris** ≃ à 8 km de Paris

(**b**) *(expressing time)* à partir de; **f. tomorrow** à partir de demain; **f. then (on)** depuis ce jour-là; **f. the beginning** dès le début; **f. six to seven o'clock** de six heures à sept heures; **f. morning to** *or* **till night** du matin au soir; **five years f. now** dans cinq ans; **blind f. birth** aveugle de naissance

(**c**) *(expressing range, change)* **f.... to...** de... à...; **children f. seven to nine years** les enfants de sept à neuf ans; **wine f. $10 a bottle** du vin à partir de 10 dollars la bouteille

(**d**) *(expressing source)* de; **to buy sth f. sb** acheter qch à qn; **to drink f. a cup** boire dans une tasse; **a quotation f. the Bible** une citation tirée de la Bible; **made f. rubber** en caoutchouc

(**e**) *(expressing removal)* de; **to take sth f. sb** prendre qch à qn; **he was banned f. the club** il a été exclu du club

(**f**) *(on the basis of)* **f. what I heard/saw...** d'après ce que j'ai entendu/vu...

frond [frɒnd] *n (of fern)* fronde *f*; *(of palm)* feuille *f*

front [frʌnt] **1** *n* (**a**) *(not back)* devant *m*; *(of car, plane, boat)* avant *m*; *(of building)* façade *f*; **on the f. of the book** sur la couverture du livre; **at the f. of the book** au début du livre; **I sat in (the) f.** *(of car)* j'étais assis devant

(**b**) *(outward appearance)* **his kindness is only a f.** sa gentillesse n'est qu'une façade; **the company is a f. for their arms dealing** l'entreprise sert de couverture à leur trafic d'armes; **f. man** *(of pop group, organization)* leader *m*

(**c**) *Mil, Pol & Met* front *m*; *Fig* **on all fronts** sur tous les fronts; *Met* **warm/cold f.** front chaud/froid

(**d**) **in f.** devant; *(in race, contest)* en tête; **in f. of** devant

(**e**) *Fam* **to pay up f.** payer d'avance; **to be up f. about sth** être franc (franche) au sujet de qch

2 *adj* de devant; **f. door** porte *f* d'entrée; *Mil* **f. line** front *m*; **f. cover** couverture *f*; **f. page** *(of newspaper)* première page *f*; **f. room** *(lounge)* salon *m*; **f. row** premier rang *m*; **to have a f.-row seat** *(in theater)* être (assis(e)) au premier rang; *Fig* être aux premières loges; **f. seat** *(in car)* siège *m* avant; **f. teeth** dents *fpl* de devant; **f. view** vue *f* de face; **f. yard** jardin *m* (devant une maison)

3 *vt (organization, pop group)* être à la tête de; *(government)* diriger

4 *vi (of building)* **the house fronts onto the river** la maison donne sur le fleuve

frontage ['frʌntɪdʒ] *n (of building)* façade *f*; *(of shop)* devanture *f*

frontal ['frʌntəl] *adj Anat* frontal(e); *Mil (attack)* de front

frontier [frʌn'tɪə(r)] *n* frontière *f*; **the frontiers** *(of knowledge, science)* les limites *fpl*; **f. guard** garde-frontière *m*; **f. town** ville *f* frontalière

frontispiece ['frʌntɪspiːs] *n* frontispice *m*

frontrunner ['frʌntrʌnə(r)] *n* favori(ite) *m,f*

frost [frɒst] *n* gel *m*; **there was a f.** il a gelé

▶**frost over, frost up** *vi (of window)* se couvrir de givre

frostbite ['frɒstbaɪt] *n* gelure *f*

frostbitten ['frɒstbɪtən] *adj* gelé(e)

frosted ['frɒstɪd] *adj* (**a**) *(glass)* dépoli(e) (**b**) *(cake)* glacé(e)

frosting ['frɒstɪŋ] *n (on cake)* glaçage *m*

frosty ['frɒstɪ] *adj (night, air)* glacé(e); *Fig (welcome, smile)* glacial(e)

froth [frɒθ] **1** *n (on beer, cappuccino)* mousse *f*; *(on waves)* écume *f*

2 *vi (of liquid)* mousser; **he was frothing at the mouth** il bavait; *(with anger)* il écumait de rage

frothy ['frɒθɪ] *adj (beer, cappuccino)* mousseux(euse)

frown [fraʊn] **1** *n* froncement *m* de sourcils

2 *vi* froncer les sourcils; **to f. at sb** regarder qn en fronçant les sourcils

▶**frown on, frown upon** *vt insep (disapprove of)* désapprouver

froze [frəʊz] *pt of* **freeze**

frozen ['frəʊzən] **1** *adj (food)* congelé(e), surgelé(e); *(lake, hands)* gelé(e)

2 *pp of* **freeze**

fructose ['frʌktəʊs] *n* fructose *m*

frugal ['fruːgəl] *adj* frugal(e)

fruit [fruːt] *n* fruit *m*; **some f.** *(several pieces)* des fruits; *(one piece)* un fruit; *Fig* **to bear f.** *(of plan, investment)* porter ses fruits; **fruits of the forest** fruits des bois; **f. bowl** coupe *f* à fruits; **f. juice** jus *m* de fruit; **f. salad** salade *f* de fruits; **f. tree** arbre *m* fruitier

fruitcake ['fruːtkeɪk] *n* cake *m*; *Fam (mad person)* fou (folle) *m,f*

fruitful ['fruːtfʊl] *adj (discussion)* fructueux(euse)

fruition [fruː'ɪʃən] *n* **to come to f.** *(of plan, effort)* porter ses fruits

fruitless ['fruːtlɪs] *adj (attempt, search, trip)* infructueux(euse)

fruity ['fruːtɪ] *adj (taste)* fruité(e); *Fam (voice)* étoffé(e)

frump [frʌmp] *n Fam* **she's a f.** elle fait mémère

frumpish ['frʌmpɪʃ], **frumpy** ['frʌmpɪ] *adj Fam* **to be f.** faire mémère

frustrate [frʌs'treɪt] *vt (person)* décevoir, frustrer; *(plan)* contrarier

frustrated [frʌs'treɪtɪd] *adj* frustré(e)

frustrating [frʌs'treɪtɪŋ] *adj* frustrant(e)

frustration [frʌs'treɪʃən] *n* frustration *f*

fry [fraɪ] (*pt & pp* **fried**) **1** *vt* faire frire

2 *vi* frire

frying pan [fraɪŋpæn], **frypan** ['fraɪpæn] *n* poêle *f* (à frire); **to jump out of the f. into the fire** tomber de Charybde en Scylla

ft *(abbr* **foot** *or* **feet**) p., pd.

FTP [eftiː'piː] *n Comput (abbr* **File Transfer Protocol**) FTP

fuchsia ['fjuːʃə] *n* fuchsia *m*

fuck [fʌk] *Vulg* **1** *n (intercourse)* baise *f*; **to have a f.** baiser; **I don't give a f.** j'en ai rien à foutre; **what the f. do you think you're doing?** putain, mais qu'est-ce que tu fous?; **f. knows why he came!** mais pourquoi il est venu, bordel!; **f.!** bordel!, merde!

2 *vt* baiser; **f. it!** et merde!; **f. you!** va te faire foutre!

3 *vi* baiser

▶**fuck about, fuck around** *vi Vulg (play the fool)* déconner; *(waste time)* glander

▶**fuck off** *vi Vulg (go away)* se casser; **f. off!** va te faire foutre!

fuck-all ['fʌk'ɔːl] *n Vulg* **he's done f. this week** il a fait que dalle cette semaine; **she knows f. about it** elle en sait que dalle

fucked [ˈfʌkt] *adj Vulg (broken)* foutu(e)

fucking [ˈfʌkɪŋ] *Vulg* **1** *adj* **he's a f. idiot!** c'est un connard!; **where's the f. car?** où est cette putain de voiture?
2 *adv (cold, brilliant, stupid)* foutrement

fuddy-duddy [ˈfʌdɪdʌdɪ] *(pl* **fuddy-duddies***) n* **an old f.** *(man)* un vieux schnock; *(woman)* une vieille mémère

fudge [fʌdʒ] **1** *n (candy)* caramel *m* mou
2 *vt* **to f. the issue** éluder la question

fuel [ˈfjʊəl] **1** *n* combustible *m; (for engine)* carburant *m; Fig* **to add f. to the flames** jeter de l'huile sur le feu; **f. consumption** *(of car)* consommation *f* (d'essence); **f. gauge** jauge *f* de carburant; **f. injection** injection *f* de carburant; **f. pump** pompe *f* d'alimentation; **f. tank** réservoir *m*
2 *vt Fig (hatred)* attiser; *(speculation)* nourrir

fugitive [ˈfjuːdʒɪtɪv] *n* fugitif(ive) *m,f*

fugue [fjuːg] *n Mus* fugue *f*

fulcrum [ˈfʌlkrəm] *n* pivot *m*

fulfill [fʊlˈfɪl] *vt (plan, ambition)* réaliser; *(condition, duty)* remplir; *(need)* répondre à; **to feel fulfilled** *(of person)* se sentir épanoui(e)

fulfillment [fʊlˈfɪlmənt] *n (of plan, condition)* réalisation *f; (satisfaction)* épanouissement *m;* **to find** *or* **to achieve f.** s'épanouir

full [fʊl] **1** *adj* **(a)** *(container)* plein(e) **(of** de); *(hotel, bus, parking lot)* complet(ète); *(day)* chargé(e); **to be f. of praise for sb** ne pas tarir d'éloges sur qn; **to be f. of oneself** être imbu(e) de soi-même; **f. to the brim** plein à ras bords; **don't speak with your mouth f.!** ne parle pas la bouche pleine!; **to be f. (up)** *(of person)* être rassasié(e); **on a f. stomach** le ventre plein
(b) *(complete) (amount)* intégral(e); *(explanation, recovery)* complet(ète); *(support)* total(e); **to take f. responsibility for sth** assumer l'entière responsabilité de qch; **she gave me the f. story** elle m'a raconté toute l'histoire; **the f. horror** toute l'horreur; **to lead a f. life** avoir une vie bien remplie; **I waited two f. hours** *or* **a f. two hours** j'ai attendu deux bonnes heures; **in f. flow** *(speaker)* en plein discours; **to be in f. swing** *(of party, sales)* battre son plein; **in f. view** of sous les yeux; **f. board** pension *f* complète; *Phot* **in f. color** en couleur; **f. fare** plein tarif *m;* **f. house** *(in theater)* salle *f* comble; *(in cards)* main *f* pleine; **f. moon** pleine lune *f;* **f. name** nom *m* et prénom *m;* **f. price** plein tarif
(c) *(maximum)* **at f. speed** à toute vitesse; **at f. stretch** *(work)* à plein rendement
(d) *(skirt, sleeve)* bouffant(e); **a f. figure** *(of woman)* un corps épanoui; **f. lips** lèvres *fpl* charnues *ou* pleines
2 *adv* **you know f. well that...** tu sais parfaitement que...; **it hit him f. in the face** il a reçu le coup en pleine figure
3 *n* **to pay in f.** payer intégralement; **name in f.** nom et prénoms; **to live life to the f.** vivre pleinement

fullback [ˈfʊlbæk] *n (in football, rugby)* arrière *m*

full-blown [ˈfʊlˈbləʊn] *adj (row)* vrai(e); *(crisis)* de grande envergure; **to have f. AIDS** avoir le sida

full-bodied [ˈfʊlˈbɒdɪd] *adj (wine)* corsé(e)

full-fledged [ˈfʊlˈfledʒd] *adj Fig* qualifié(e)

full-grown [ˈfʊlˈgrəʊn] *adj* adulte

full-length [ˈfʊlˈleŋθ] *adj (portrait, mirror)* en pied; *(dress)* long (longue); **f. movie** long métrage *m*

fullness [ˈfʊlnɪs] *n* **in the f. of time** avec le temps

full-page [ˈfʊlˈpeɪdʒ] *adj (advertisement, illustration)* pleine page

full-scale [ˈfʊlˈskeɪl] *adj* **(a)** *(model)* grandeur nature *inv* **(b)** *(search)* de grande envergure; **f. war** guerre *f* généralisée

full-size [ˈfʊlˈsaɪz], **full-sized** [ˈfʊlˈsaɪzd] *adj (animal, plant)* adulte; *(drawing, model)* grandeur nature *inv;* **f. car** grosse voiture *f*

full-time [ˈfʊlˈtaɪm] *adj & adv* à temps complet, à plein temps; *Fig* **looking after the baby is a f. job** s'occuper du bébé ne laisse pas une minute de libre; **to be in f. employment** travailler à plein temps

full-timer [ˈfʊlˈtaɪmər] *n* travailleur(euse) *m,f* à temps complet *ou* à plein temps

fully [ˈfʊlɪ] *adv* **(a)** *(completely)* complètement, entièrement; *(understand, be aware)* parfaitement, tout à fait; **f. booked** complet(ète); **f. grown** adulte **(b)** *(at least)* **it takes f. two hours** cela prend au moins deux heures

fulminate [ˈfʌlmɪneɪt] *vi* fulminer (**against** contre)

fulsome [ˈfʊlsəm] *adj (apology, thanks)* excessif(ive), outré(e); *(compliments)* outré(e); **to be f. in one's praise of sb/sth** porter qn/qch aux nues

fumble [ˈfʌmbəl] **1** *vt (ball)* mal attraper
2 *vi* fouiller; **to f. for sth** fouiller pour trouver qch; *(in dark)* tâtonner pour trouver qch; **to f. for words** chercher ses mots; **he fumbled with the switch** il a essayé maladroitement de faire fonctionner l'interrupteur

fume [fjuːm] **1** *npl* **fumes** émanations *fpl; (from car exhaust)* gaz *mpl* d'échappement; **gas fumes** vapeurs *fpl* d'essence
2 *vi* **(a)** *(give off fumes)* fumer **(b)** *(be angry)* **to be fuming** rager, être furieux(euse)

fumigate [ˈfjuːmɪgeɪt] *vt* désinfecter par fumigation

fun [fʌn] *n* plaisir *m;* **to have f.** s'amuser; **it's/he's great f.** c'est/il est très amusant; **there'll be f. and games** *(trouble)* il va y avoir du grabuge; **it's no f. having to stay at home** ce n'est pas drôle de devoir rester à la maison; **to make f. of** se moquer de; **to be a figure of f.** être la risée de tous; **to say sth in f.** dire qch pour rire *ou* en plaisantant; **to do sth for f.** *or* **for the f. of it** faire qch pour s'amuser; *Ironic* **what f.!** c'est drôle!; **f. fur** fourrure *f* fantaisie

function [ˈfʌŋkʃən] **1** *n* **(a)** *(role) & Math* fonction *f; Comput* **f. key** touche *f* de fonction **(b)** *(party)* réception *f; (public)* cérémonie *f*
2 *vi* fonctionner; **to f. as** jouer le rôle de, faire fonction de

functional [ˈfʌŋkʃənəl] *adj* **(a)** *(practical)* fonctionnel(elle) **(b)** *(operational)* opérationnel(elle)

functionary [ˈfʌŋkʃənərɪ] *(pl* **functionaries***) n* fonctionnaire *mf*

fund [fʌnd] **1** *n* **(a)** *(of money)* fonds *m;* **funds** fonds *mpl*, capitaux *mpl;* **to be in funds** être en fonds; *Fin* **f. manager** gestionnaire *mf* de fonds **(b)** *(of information)* mine *f*
2 *vt* financer

fundamental [fʌndəˈmentəl] **1** *n* **fundamentals** principes *mpl*, fondements *mpl*
2 *adj* fondamental(e), essentiel(elle); **her f. honesty** sa profonde honnêteté

fundamentalist [fʌndəˈmentəlɪst] *n & adj (religious)* intégriste *mf*, fondamentaliste *mf*

fundamentally [fʌndəˈmentəlɪ] *adv* fondamentalement

funding [ˈfʌndɪŋ] *n* financement *m*

fund-raiser [ˈfʌndreɪzə(r)] *n (person)* collecteur(trice) *m,f* de fonds; *(event)* = manifestation organisée au profit d'une œuvre de bienfaisance

funeral [ˈfjuːnərəl] *n* enterrement *m; (formal)* funérailles *fpl*, obsèques *fpl; Fam* **that's your f.!** c'est ton problème!; **f. director** entrepreneur *m* de pompes funèbres; *Mus* **f. march** marche *f* funèbre; **f. parlor** établissement *m* de pompes funèbres; **f. procession** cortège *m* funèbre; **f. service** service *m* funèbre

fungal [ˈfʌŋgəl] *adj* **f. infection** mycose *f*

fungus [ˈfʌŋgəs] *(pl* **fungi** [ˈfʌŋgaɪ]*) n (mushroom, toadstool)* champignon *m; (on walls)* moisissure *f; Med* fongus *m*

funk [fʌŋk] *n* **(a)** *Fam Old-fashioned (fright)* **to be in a f.** avoir une peur bleue **(b)** *(music)* funk *m*

funky [ˈfʌŋkɪ] *adj very Fam (clothing, bar, music)* cool *inv*

funnel [ˈfʌnəl] **1** *n* **(a)** *(of locomotive, steamship)* cheminée *f* **(b)** *(for filling)* entonnoir *m*

2 *vt (direct) (funds)* acheminer (**to** vers); **to f. liquid into sth** verser un liquide dans qch

funnies ['fʌnɪz] *npl Fam* **the f.** les bandes *fpl* dessinées *(dans un journal)*

funnily ['fʌnɪlɪ] *adv (strangely)* bizarrement; **f. enough,...** bizarrement,...

funny ['fʌnɪ] *adj* **(a)** *(amusing)* drôle, amusant(e); **are you trying to be f.?** tu te crois drôle?; *Ironic* **very f.!** très drôle!; *Fam* **f. bone** petit juif *m* **(b)** *(strange)* bizarre, drôle; **I feel a bit f.** *(ill)* je me sens un peu bizarre; **to taste/smell f.** avoir un drôle de goût/une drôle d'odeur; **f., I thought I'd locked the door** c'est curieux, je croyais avoir fermé la porte à clé; **(it's) f. you should say that** c'est drôle que tu dises ça; *Fam* **he's a bit f. in the head** il est un peu bizarre; *Fam* **I don't want any f. business!** et pas de blagues!; *Fam* **f. farm** maison *f* de fous

fur [fɜː(r)] *n (hair)* poils *mpl; (animal skin)* fourrure *f; Fig* **the f. was flying** ça chauffait; **f. coat** manteau *m* de fourrure; **f. trade** commerce *m* de fourrures

furious ['fjʊərɪəs] *adj (person)* furieux(euse) (**with** contre); *(quarrel, storm)* violent(e); **to be f. with oneself** être en colère contre soi-même; **at a f. speed** à une vitesse folle

furiously ['fjʊərɪəslɪ] *adv* furieusement; *(work, write)* frénétiquement

furlong ['fɜːlɒŋ] *n* = 201 m, furlong *m*

furnace ['fɜːnɪs] *n* fourneau *m; Fig* **it's like a f. in here!** quelle fournaise!

furnish ['fɜːnɪʃ] *vt* **(a)** *(house, apartment)* meubler **(b)** *Formal (provide)* fournir; **to f. sb with sth** fournir qch à qn

furnished ['fɜːnɪʃd] *adj (room, apartment)* meublé(e); **f. accommodations** *(logement m)* meublé *m*

furnishings ['fɜːnɪʃɪŋz] *npl* ameublement *m*

furniture ['fɜːnɪtʃə(r)] *n* meubles *mpl*, mobilier *m;* **a piece of f.** un meuble; **f. polish** encaustique *f* pour les meubles; **f. mover** déménageur *m;* **f. store** magasin *m* de meubles *ou* d'ameublement; **f. van** camion *m* de déménagement

furor ['fjʊərɔː(r)] *n (uproar)* scandale *m*

furrow ['fʌrəʊ] **1** *n (in field)* sillon *m; (on face)* ride *f* profonde
2 *vt Lit* **his brow was furrowed with worry** son front était plissé par l'inquiétude

furry ['fɜːrɪ] *adj (animal)* à poil; **f. toy** peluche *f;* **to have a f. tongue** avoir la langue chargée

further ['fɜːðə(r)] *(comparative of* **far)** **1** *adj* **(a)** *(more distant)* plus loin **(b)** *(additional)* supplémentaire; **upon f. consideration** après plus ample réflexion; **until f. notice** jusqu'à nouvel ordre; **without f. delay** sans plus attendre
2 *adv* **(a)** *(in general)* plus loin; **this mustn't go any f.** *(don't tell anyone else)* il faut que cela reste entre nous; **I didn't question him any f.** je ne l'ai pas interrogé davantage; **that doesn't get us much f.** ça ne nous avance pas beaucoup; **f. back** *(in space)* plus loin en arrière; *(in time)* plus loin dans le temps; **f. on** *(in space)* plus loin; *(in time)* plus tard **(b)** *Formal (moreover)* de plus; **f. to your letter...** suite à votre lettre...
3 *vt (cause, career)* faire avancer

furthermore [fɜːðə'mɔː(r)] *adv Formal* en outre, de plus

furthermost ['fɜːðəməʊst] *adj Lit* le (la) plus reculé(e)

furthest ['fɜːðɪst] *(superlative of* **far)** **1** *adj* le (la) plus éloigné(e)
2 *adv* le plus loin

furtive ['fɜːtɪv] *adj* sournois(e)

fury ['fjʊərɪ] *n (of person, storm)* fureur *f;* **to be in a f.** *(of person)* être furieux(euse); *Fam* **to work like f.** travailler avec acharnement

fuse [fjuːz] **1** *n* **(a)** *(for plug)* fusible *m;* **f. box** boîte *f* à fusibles; **f. wire** fusible *m* **(b)** *(for dynamite)* détonateur *m; (in bomb)* amorce *f; Fam Fig* **to have a short f.** *(be short-tempered)* se mettre facilement en colère
2 *vt (melt)* fondre; *(join)* fusionner
3 *vi* **(a)** *(of metals)* fondre; **to f. together** fusionner **(b)** *(of organizations, parties)* fusionner

fused [fjuːzd] *adj Elec (plug, appliance)* muni(e) d'un fusible

fuselage ['fjuːzəlɑːʒ] *n* fuselage *m*

fusillade [fjuːzɪ'leɪd] *n (of bullets)* fusillade *f; Fig (of criticism, questions)* avalanche *f*

fusion ['fjuːʒən] *n* fusion *f*

fuss [fʌs] **1** *n* histoires *fpl;* **what's all the f. about?** qu'est-ce que c'est que toutes ces histoires?; **I don't want any f.** pas de cérémonie; **a lot of f. about** *or* **over nothing** beaucoup d'histoires pour pas grand-chose; **I don't see what all the f. is about** je ne vois pas pourquoi on en fait un tel cas; **to kick up** *or* **to make a f.** faire des histoires; **to make a f. of sb** être aux petits soins pour qn
2 *vi* faire des histoires; **to f. about** s'activer

fussbudget ['fʌsbʌdʒɪt], **fusspot** ['fʌspɒt] *n Fam* chichiteux(euse) *m,f*

fussy ['fʌsɪ] *adj* **(a)** *(person)* difficile, exigeant(e); **I'm not f.** *(I don't mind)* ça m'est égal **(b)** *(dress, décor)* surchargé(e)

futile ['fjuːtaɪl, 'fjuːtəl] *adj (attempt, protest)* vain(e); *(remark, suggestion)* futile

futility [fjuː'tɪlɪtɪ] *n* futilité *f*

futon ['fuːtɒn] *n* futon *m*

future ['fjuːtʃə(r)] **1** *n* **(a)** *(in time)* avenir *m;* **in (the) f.** à l'avenir; **in the near/distant f.** dans un avenir proche/lointain; **she's got a job with a (good) f.** elle a une situation pleine d'avenir **(b)** *Fin* **futures** opérations *fpl* à terme **(c)** *Gram* futur *m;* **the f. perfect** le futur antérieur
2 *adj* futur(e); **at some f. date** à une date ultérieure; **for f. reference** à titre d'information

futuristic ['fjuːtʃə'rɪstɪk] *adj* futuriste

fuze = **fuse**

fuzed = **fused**

fuzz [fʌz] *n* **(a)** *(on fabric)* peluches *fpl; (on peach, skin)* duvet *m* **(b)** *Fam* **the f.** *(police)* les flics *mpl*

fuzzy ['fʌzɪ] *adj (outline, photo)* flou(e); *(idea)* vague; *(hair)* crépu(e); **f. logic** logique *f* floue

FYI [efwaɪ'aɪ] *(abbr* **for your information)** à titre indicatif

G

G, g¹ [dʒiː] n (**a**) (letter) G, g m inv (**b**) Mus sol m

g² (abbr **gram**) gr

gab [gæb] (pt & pp **gabbed**) vi Fam (talk) papoter; (gossip) jaser

gabardine [gæbəˈdiːn] n gabardine f

gabble [ˈgæbəl] **1** n a g. of conversation un bruit de conversation

2 vi (incoherently) bredouiller; **to g. on** papoter

gable [ˈgeɪbəl] n pignon m; **g. end** (wall) pignon m

Gabon [ˈgæbən] n le Gabon

Gabonese [gæbəˈniːz] **1** n Gabonais(e) m,f

2 adj gabonais(e)

▶**gad about** [gæd] (pt & pp **gadded**) vi Fam être en vadrouille

gadfly [ˈgædflaɪ] (pl **gadflies**) n (insect) taon m; Fig (person) casse-pieds mf inv

gadget [ˈgædʒɪt] n gadget m

Gaelic [ˈgeɪlɪk] **1** n gaélique m

2 adj gaélique

Gaels [geɪlz] npl the G. les Gaëls mpl

gaff [gæf] n (in fishing) gaffe f

gaffe [gæf] n (blunder) gaffe f

gaffer [ˈgæfə(r)] n (**a**) Fam (old man) **an old g.** un vieux bonhomme (**b**) Cin chef m électricien, gaffer m

gag [gæg] **1** n (**a**) (on mouth) bâillon m (**b**) Fam (joke) blague f

2 vt (pt & pp **gagged**) (person) bâillonner; Fig (media, opposition) museler

3 vi (retch) avoir des haut-le-cœur

gaga [ˈgɑːgɑː] adj Fam gâteux(euse), gaga inv

gage = **gauge**

gaggle [ˈgægəl] n also Fig troupeau m

gaiety [ˈgeɪətɪ] n gaieté f

gaily [ˈgeɪlɪ] adv (happily) joyeusement; (laugh) de bon cœur; **g. colored** aux couleurs gaies

gain [geɪn] **1** n (**a**) (profit) gain m, profit m; **for personal g.** par intérêt personnel (**b**) (increase) augmentation f (**in** de); Fin (on stock market) hausse f; **to make gains** (progress) progresser; Fin (of shares) augmenter

2 vt (**a**) (advantage, degree) obtenir; (victory, prize) remporter; (reputation, experience) acquérir; (sympathy, respect) gagner; **to g. entrance (to)** entrer (dans); (of burglar) s'introduire (dans) (**b**) (increase) **to g. weight/speed** prendre du poids/de la vitesse; also Fig **to g. ground on** gagner du terrain sur; **to g. time** gagner du temps

3 vi (**a**) (benefit) **to g. by sth** bénéficier de qch (**b**) (increase) **to g. in confidence** gagner de l'assurance; **to g. in popularity** devenir populaire (**c**) (of clock) avancer

▶**gain on** vt insep also Fig gagner du terrain sur

gainful [ˈgeɪnfʊl] adj **g. employment** un emploi rémunéré

gainfully [ˈgeɪnfʊlɪ] adv **to be g. employed** avoir un emploi rémunéré

gainsay [geɪnˈseɪ] (pt & pp **gainsaid** [geɪnˈsed]) vt Formal contredire; **there's no gainsaying her ability** son talent est indéniable

gait [geɪt] n démarche f

gal [gæl] n Fam Old-fashioned fille f

gala [ˈgɑːlə] n gala m; **swimming g.** compétition f de natation; **g. evening/performance** soirée f/représentation f de gala

galactic [gəˈlæktɪk] adj galactique

Galapagos [gəˈlæpəgəs] npl the G. (Islands) les (îles fpl) Galapagos fpl

galaxy [ˈgæləksɪ] (pl **galaxies**) n galaxie f; Fig **a g. of stars** une pléiade de vedettes

gale [geɪl] n (strong wind) vent m violent; Fig **a g. of laughter** un éclat de rire

gall [gɔːl] **1** n (**a**) Med bile f; **g. bladder** vésicule f biliaire (**b**) (impudence) culot m

2 vt (annoy) irriter, exaspérer

gallant [ˈgælənt] adj (brave) brave, vaillant(e); (polite) galant(e)

gallantry [ˈgæləntrɪ] n (bravery) bravoure f; (politeness) galanterie f

galleon [ˈgælɪən] n galion m

gallery [ˈgælərɪ] (pl **galleries**) n (**a**) (art) g. (for sale) galerie f (d'art); (for exhibition) musée m (**b**) (in theater) galerie f; Fig **to play to the g.** (of politician) chercher à épater la galerie

galley [ˈgælɪ] (pl **galleys**) n (**a**) (ship) galère f; **g. slave** galérien m (**b**) (ship's kitchen) cuisine f (**c**) Typ **g. (proof)** placard m

Gallic [ˈgælɪk] adj (French) français(e); Hist (of Gaul) gaulois(e)

galling [ˈgɔːlɪŋ] adj humiliant(e)

▶**gallivant about, gallivant around** [ˈgælɪvænt] vi être en vadrouille

gallon [ˈgælən] n = 3,78 l, gallon m

gallop [ˈgæləp] **1** n galop m; **at a g.** au galop

2 vi galoper; Fig **to g. through one's work** expédier son travail

gallows [ˈgæləʊz] n potence f, gibet m; **g. humor** humour m noir

gallstone [ˈgɔːlstəʊn] n calcul m biliaire

galore [gəˈlɔː(r)] adv Fam à profusion, à gogo

galoshes [gəˈlɒʃɪz] npl bottes fpl en caoutchouc

galvanize [ˈgælvənaɪz] vt also Fig galvaniser; **to g. sb into action** pousser qn à agir

galvanized [ˈgælvənaɪzd] adj galvanisé(e)

Gambia [ˈgæmbɪə] n the G. la Gambie

Gambian [ˈgæmbɪən] **1** n Gambien(enne) m,f

2 adj gambien(enne)

gambit [ˈgæmbɪt] n (in chess) gambit m; (in negotiation, diplomacy) tactique f; **opening g.** (in negotiation, diplomacy) manœuvre f d'approche

gamble [ˈgæmbəl] **1** n (risk) risque m; **to take a g.** prendre un risque

2 vt (money) jouer, parier

3 vi jouer (de l'argent); **to g. on the horses** jouer aux courses; **she gambled on nobody noticing** elle comptait sur le fait que personne ne s'en apercevrait

gambler ['gæmblə(r)] *n* joueur(euse) *m,f*

gambling ['gæmblɪŋ] *n* jeux *mpl* d'argent; **g. debts** dettes *fpl* de jeu; **g. den** tripot *m*

gambol ['gæmbəl] *vi* gambader

game [geɪm] **1** *n* (**a**) *(activity, sport)* jeu *m*; *(of cards, pool, chess)* partie *f*; *(match)* match *m*; **to have a g. of tennis/soccer** faire une partie de tennis/foot(ball); **g., set and match** *(in tennis)* jeu, set et match; **politics is just a g. to them** pour eux, la politique n'est qu'un jeu; **g. show** jeu *m* télévisé (**b**) *(animals, food)* gibier *m*; **g. reserve** réserve *f* de gibier (**c**) *(idioms)* **to play the g.** jouer le jeu; **two can play at that g.** on peut jouer à deux à ce petit jeu-là; **to beat sb at his own g.** battre qn à son propre jeu; **to play games with sb** jouer avec qn; **to give the g. away** vendre la mèche; **what's his g.?** où veut-il en venir?; **I know what your g. is!** je sais bien où vous voulez en venir!; **the g.'s up for him** c'est fichu pour lui; **I've been in this g. a long time** ça fait longtemps que je suis de la partie; **to be ahead of the g.** mener le jeu; **it's a whole new g.** c'est une toute autre histoire; **that's the name of the g.!** c'est comme ça!; **money is the name of the g.** c'est une affaire d'argent; **g. plan** stratégie *f*
2 *adj* (**a**) *(brave)* courageux(euse); **to be g. (to do sth)** *(willing)* être partant(e) (pour faire qch) (**b**) *(lame)* estropié(e); **to have a g. leg** avoir une jambe estropiée

gamekeeper ['geɪmkiːpə(r)] *n* garde-chasse *m*

gamely ['geɪmlɪ] *adv* courageusement

gamer ['geɪmə(r)] *n Comput* = amateur de jeux vidéo

gaming ['geɪmɪŋ] *n* (**a**) *(gambling)* jeu *m*; **g. room** salle *f* de jeu; **g. table** table *f* de jeu (**b**) *(playing of computer games)* (pratique *f* des) jeux *mpl* électroniques

gamma ['gæmə] *n* gamma *m*; *Phys* **g. rays** rayons *mpl* gamma

gamut ['gæmət] *n* gamme *f*; **to run the g. of** *(emotions)* passer par toute la gamme de

gamy ['geɪmɪ] *adj (flavor)* faisandé(e)

gander ['gændə(r)] *n* (**a**) *(male goose)* jars *m* (**b**) *very Fam* **to take a g. (at)** *(look)* jeter un coup d'œil (à)

gang [gæŋ] *n (of criminals, children, friends)* bande *f*; *(of workers)* équipe *f*

▸**gang up** *vi* **to g. up on sb** se liguer contre qn; **to g. up with sb** s'allier avec qn

gangbang ['gæŋbæŋ] *n very Fam (group rape)* viol *m* collectif, tournante *f*

Ganges ['gændʒiːz] *n* **the G.** le Gange

gangland ['gæŋlænd] *n (underworld)* milieu *m*, pègre *f*; **g. boss/killer** caïd *m*/tueur *m* du milieu; **g. killing** règlement *m* de compte *(entre gangsters)*

gangling ['gæŋglɪŋ] *adj* dégingandé(e)

ganglion ['gæŋglɪən] *(pl* **ganglia** ['gæŋglɪə]*) n* ganglion *m*

gangmaster ['gæŋmɑːstə(r)] *n* contremaître *m*

gangplank ['gæŋplæŋk] *n* passerelle *f*

gang-rape ['gæŋreɪp] **1** *n* viol *m* collectif
2 *vt* commettre un viol collectif sur

gangrene ['gæŋgriːn] *n* gangrène *f*; **to have g.** avoir la gangrène

gangrenous ['gæŋgrɪnəs] *adj* gangreneux(euse)

gangster ['gæŋstə(r)] *n* gangster *m*; **g. movie** film *m* de gangsters

gangway ['gæŋweɪ] *n (on ship)* passerelle *f*; **g.!** dégagez, s'il vous plaît!

gannet ['gænɪt] *n (bird)* fou *m* de Bassan

gantry ['gæntrɪ] *n (pl* **gantries**) *n (for crane, over railroad)* portique *m*; *(for rocket)* tour *f* de lancement

gap [gæp] *n* (**a**) *(space)* espace *m*; *(narrower)* interstice *m*; *(in wall)* brèche *f*; *(in text)* blanc *m* (**b**) *(difference)* *(in age, ability)* écart *m*; **the g. between rich and poor** le fossé entre les riches et les pauvres (**c**) *(in knowledge)* lacune *f*; **his death**

leaves a g. in all our lives sa mort nous laisse un vide; *Com* **a g. in the market** un créneau (**d**) *(in time)* intervalle *m* (**e**) *(mountain pass)* col *m*

gape [geɪp] *vi* (**a**) *(stare)* rester bouche bée; **to g. at sb/sth** regarder qn/qch bouche bée (**b**) **to g. (open)** *(of door, blouse)* s'ouvrir tout(e) grand(e); *(of wound, hole)* être béant(e)

gaping ['geɪpɪŋ] *adj* béant(e)

garage [gə'rɑːʒ] *n (for storing or repairing car)* garage *m*; *(gas station)* station-service *f*

garb ['gɑːb] *n Lit* costume *m*

garbage ['gɑːbɪdʒ] *n* (**a**) *(rubbish)* ordures *fpl*; **g. bag** sac-poubelle *m*; **g. can** poubelle *f*; **g. collector** éboueur *m*; **g. heap** tas *m* d'ordures; **g. pail** poubelle *f* (**b**) *(nonsense)* âneries *fpl*; **to talk g.** dire n'importe quoi

garbanzo [gɑː'bænzəʊ] *(pl* **garbanzos***) n* pois *m* chiche

garbled ['gɑːbəld] *adj* confus(e)

garden ['gɑːdən] **1** *n* jardin *m*; *Fig* **to lead sb up the g. path** faire marcher qn; **g. center** jardinerie *f*; **g. furniture** meubles *mpl* de jardin; **g. gnome** nain *m* de jardin; **g. party** réception *f* en plein air, garden-party *f*; **g. shed** resserre *f*
2 *vi* jardiner, faire du jardinage

gardener ['gɑːdnə(r)] *n* jardinier(ère) *m,f*

gardening [gɑːdnɪŋ] *n* jardinage *m*; **to do the g.** s'occuper du jardin

gargantuan [gɑː'gæntjʊən] *adj* gargantuesque

gargle ['gɑːgəl] *vi* se gargariser (**with** avec)

gargoyle ['gɑːgɔɪl] *n* gargouille *f*

garish ['geərɪʃ] *adj (clothes)* voyant(e); *(taste)* vulgaire; *(colors)* criard(e); *(light)* cru(e)

garland ['gɑːlənd] **1** *n* guirlande *f*
2 *vt* enguirlander (**with** de)

garlic ['gɑːlɪk] *n* ail *m*; **g. bread** = pain chaud au beurre d'ail; **g. butter** beurre *m* d'ail; **g. sausage** saucisson *m* à l'ail

garment ['gɑːmənt] *n* vêtement *m*

garnet ['gɑːnɪt] *n* grenat *m*

garnish ['gɑːnɪʃ] **1** *n* garniture *f*
2 *vt* garnir (**with** avec)

garret ['gærət] *n* mansarde *f*

garrison ['gærɪsən] **1** *n* garnison *f*; **g. duty** service *m* de garnison; **g. town** ville *f* de garnison
2 *vt (troops)* mettre en garnison

garrote [gə'rɒt] **1** *n* garrot *m*
2 *vt* exécuter au garrot

garrulous ['gærʊləs] *adj (person)* loquace, bavard(e); *(account, letter)* verbeux(euse)

garter ['gɑːtə(r)] *n* jarretière *f*; **g. belt** porte-jarretelles *m inv*; **g. snake** couleuvre *f*

gas [gæs] **1** *n* (**a**) *(substance, fuel)* gaz *m inv*; *Med (gaz)* anesthétique *m*; **g. bill** note *f* de gaz; **g. chamber** chambre *f* à gaz; **g. cooker** cuisinière *f* à gaz; **g. cylinder** bouteille *f* de gaz; **g. lamp** lampe *f* à gaz; **g. mask** masque *m* à gaz (**b**) *(gasoline)* essence *f*; *Fam* **to step on the g.** appuyer sur le champignon; **g. station** station-service *f*; **g. tank** réservoir *m* (**c**) *Fam (amusing situation)* **to have a g.** rigoler; **what a g.!** quelle rigolade!
2 *vt (pt & pp* **gassed***) (person)* asphyxier; *(deliberately)* gazer; **to g. oneself** se suicider au gaz
3 *vi Fam (chat)* jacasser

gasbag ['gæsbæg] *n Fam (chatterbox)* bavard(e) *m,f*; *(boaster)* vantard(e) *m,f*

gaseous ['gæsɪəs] *adj* gazeux(euse)

gash [gæʃ] **1** *n (in skin, wood)* entaille *f*; *(in metal)* fente *f*
2 *vt* entailler

gasket ['gæskɪt] *n (in engine)* joint *m* de culasse; *Fam* **to blow a g.** piquer une colère

gasoline ['gæsəliːn] *n* essence *f*

gasometer [gæ'sɒmɪtə(r)] *n* gazomètre *m*

gasp [gɑːsp] **1** *n (of surprise)* sursaut *m*; **to be at one's last g.**

être sur le point de rendre son dernier soupir

2 *vi* avoir le souffle coupé (**with** *or* **in** de); **to make sb g.** couper le souffle à qn; **to g. for breath** *or* **for air** haleter, suffoquer; *Fam* **to be gasping for a cigarette/a drink** mourir d'envie de fumer une cigarette/de boire un verre

gassy ['gæsɪ] *adj* gazeux(euse)

gastric ['gæstrɪk] *adj* gastrique; **g. flu** grippe *f* gastro-intestinale; **g. juices** sucs *mpl* gastriques; **g. ulcer** ulcère *m* à l'estomac

gastritis [gæs'traɪtɪs] *n* gastrite *f*; **to have g.** avoir une gastrite

gastro-enteritis [gæstrəʊəntə'raɪtɪs] *n* gastro-entérite *f*; **to have g.** avoir une gastro-entérite

gastronomic [gæstrə'nɒmɪk] *adj* gastronomique

gastronomy [gæs'trɒnəmɪ] *n* gastronomie *f*

gasworks ['gæswɜːks] *n* usine *f* à gaz

gate [geɪt] *n* (**a**) *(in garden, field)* barrière *f*; *(of city, in airport)* porte *f* (**b**) *Sport (spectators)* nombre *m* de spectateurs; *(takings)* recette *f*

gatecrash ['geɪtkræʃ] *vt Fam* **to g. a party** aller à une fête sans y être invité(e)

gatecrasher ['geɪtkræʃə(r)] *n Fam* intrus(e) *m,f*

gated community ['geɪtɪdkə'mjuːnɪtɪ] *n* = quartier de riches, sous la surveillance de vigiles, dans une ville où il y a beaucoup de ghettos pauvres

gatehouse ['geɪthaʊs] *n* loge *f*

gatekeeper ['geɪtkiːpə(r)] *n* gardien(enne) *m,f*

gatepost ['geɪtpəʊst] *n* montant *m* (de porte)

gateway ['geɪtweɪ] *n* entrée *f*; *Fig* **the g. to the East** la porte de l'Orient; **the g. to success** la voie de la réussite

gather ['gæðə(r)] **1** *vt* (**a**) *(collect) (people, belongings)* rassembler; *(information)* recueillir; *(wood, papers)* ramasser; *(fruit, flowers)* cueillir; *(harvest)* rentrer; **to g. one's thoughts** rassembler ses idées; **to g. sb in one's arms** serrer qn dans ses bras (**b**) *(accumulate)* **to g. dirt** s'encrasser; *also Fig* **to g. dust** ramasser de la poussière; **to g. speed** prendre de la vitesse (**c**) *(conclude, understand)* **to g. that...** croire comprendre que...; **as you may already have gathered,...** comme vous avez déjà dû le deviner,...

2 *vi (of people)* se rassembler; *(of things)* s'accumuler; *(of storm)* se préparer

▸**gather round 1** *vt insep* se rassembler autour de

2 *vi* se rassembler

▸**gather together 1** *vt sep (belongings)* rassembler; *(evidence)* recueillir

2 *vi (of people)* se rassembler

▸**gather up** *vt sep* ramasser

gathering ['gæðərɪŋ] **1** *n (group)* attroupement *m*; *(meeting)* réunion *f*

2 *adj (darkness, speed)* croissant(e); *also Fig* **the g. storm** l'orage qui se prépare

GATT [gæt] *n (abbr* **General Agreement on Tariffs and Trade)** GATT *m*

gauche [gəʊʃ] *adj* gauche, maladroit(e)

gaudily ['gɔːdɪlɪ] *adv* de façon criarde

gaudy ['gɔːdɪ] *adj* tape-à-l'œil *inv*; *(colors)* criard(e)

gauge [geɪdʒ] **1** *n* (**a**) *(size) (of screw, wire, gun)* calibre *m*; *(of railroad track)* écartement *m* (**b**) *(measuring device)* jauge *f* (**c**) *Fig (indicator)* signe *m*, indicateur *m* (**of** de)

2 *vt* évaluer

Gaul [gɔːl] *n Hist (region)* la Gaule; *(inhabitant)* Gaulois(e) *m,f*

gaunt [gɔːnt] *adj* décharné(e)

gauntlet ['gɔːntlɪt] *n (glove)* gant *m* à manchette; *Hist* gantelet *m*; *Fig* **to throw** *or* **to fling down the g. (to sb)** jeter le gant (à qn); *Fig* **to take up the g.** relever le gant; *Fig* **to run the g. of sth** s'exposer à qch

gauze [gɔːz] *n* gaze *f*

---

gave [geɪv] *pt of* **give**

gavel ['gævəl] *n* marteau *m*

gawk [gɔːk] *vi Fam* rester bouche bée; **to g. at sb/sth** rester bouche bée à regarder qn/qch

gawky ['gɔːkɪ] *adj Fam* gauche, empoté(e)

gawp [gɔːp] *vi Fam* rester bouche bée; **to g. at sb/sth** rester bouche bée à regarder qn/qch

gay [geɪ] **1** *n (homosexual)* homosexuel(elle) *m,f*

2 *adj* (**a**) *(homosexual)* homosexuel(elle), gay *inv*; **g. rights** les droits *mpl* des homosexuels (**b**) *Old-fashioned (happy)* gai(e); **with g. abandon** avec insouciance

Gaza ['gɑːzə] *n* Gaza; **the G. Strip** la Bande de Gaza

gaze [geɪz] **1** *n* regard *m*; **to meet** *or* **to return sb's g.** regarder qn dans les yeux

2 *vi* **to g. at sb/sth** regarder fixement qn/qch; **to g. into space** regarder dans le vague

gazelle [gə'zel] *n* gazelle *f*

gazette [gə'zet] *n* journal *m* officiel

gazetteer [gæzɪ'tɪə(r)] *n* index *m* géographique

GB ['dʒiː'biː] *n (abbr* **Great Britain)** GB *f*

GBH [dʒiːbiː'eɪtʃ] *n Law (abbr* **grievous bodily harm)** coups *mpl* et blessures *fpl*

GDP [dʒiːdiː'piː] *n Econ (abbr* **gross domestic product)** PIB *m*

GDR [dʒiːdiː'ɑː(r)] *n Formerly (abbr* **German Democratic Republic)** **the G.** la RDA

gear [gɪə(r)] *n* (**a**) *(on car, bicycle)* vitesse *f*; *Fig* **to put sb's plans out of g.** perturber les projets de qn; **first/second g.** première *f*/seconde *f* (vitesse); **g. lever** changement *m* de vitesse (**b**) *Fam (equipment)* attirail *m*; *(belongings)* affaires *fpl* (**c**) *Fam (clothes)* fringues *fpl*

▸**gear to** *vt sep* **to g. sth to sth** adapter qch à qch

▸**gear toward** *vt sep* **to be geared toward sb/sth** s'adresser à qn/qch

gearstick ['gɪəstɪk] *n* changement *m* de vitesses

gee [dʒiː] *exclam* **g. (whiz)!** mince alors!

geek [giːk] *n Fam* ringard(e) *m,f*, bouffon *m*

geeky ['giːkɪ] *adj Fam* ringard(e)

geese [giːs] *pl of* **goose**

geezer ['giːzə(r)] *n Fam* **old g.** vieux bonhomme *m*

Geiger counter ['gaɪgə'kaʊntə(r)] *n* compteur *m* Geiger

gel [dʒel] **1** *n Chem & (for hair)* gel *m*

2 *vi (of liquid)* se gélifier; *Fig (of ideas, plans)* prendre forme; *(of team)* se souder

gelatin ['dʒelətiːn] *n* gélatine *f*

gelatinous [dʒɪ'lætɪnəs] *adj* gélatineux(euse)

gelding ['geldɪŋ] *n* hongre *m*

gelignite ['dʒelɪgnaɪt] *n* gélignite *f*

gem [dʒem] *n (precious stone)* pierre *f* précieuse; *Fig (person)* perle *f*; *(movie, joke, goal)* pure merveille *f*

Gemini ['dʒemɪnaɪ] *n (sign of zodiac)* les Gémeaux *mpl*; **to be (a) G.** être (des) Gémeaux

gemstone ['dʒemstəʊn] *n* pierre *f* gemme

gender ['dʒendə(r)] *n* (**a**) *Gram* genre *m* (**b**) *(sex)* sexe *m*

gene [dʒiːn] *n Biol* gène *m*; *Fig* **it's in his genes** *(of talent, characteristic)* c'est héréditaire; **g. pool** patrimoine *m* génétique; **g. therapy** thérapie *f* génétique, génothérapie *f*

genealogy [dʒiːnɪ'ælədʒɪ] *n* généalogie *f*

genera ['dʒenərə] *pl of* **genus**

general ['dʒenərəl] **1** *n* (**a**) **in g.** en général (**b**) *Mil* général *m*

2 *adj* général(e); **as a g. rule** en règle générale; **in g. terms** en termes généraux; **g. anesthetic** anesthésie *f* générale; **G. Assembly** *(of United Nations)* Assemblée *f* générale; **g. delivery** poste *f* restante; *Mil* **G. Headquarters** (grand) quartier *m* général; **g. knowledge** culture *f* générale; **g. manager** directeur(trice) *m,f* général(e); **g. meeting** assemblée *f* générale; **g.**

practice *(in medicine)* médecine *f* générale; **g. practitioner** *(doctor)* médecin *m* généraliste; **the g. public** le grand public; **g. store** bazar *m*; **g. strike** grève *f* générale

generality [dʒenə'ralıtı] *(pl* **generalities)** *n* généralité *f*

generalization [dʒenərəlaı'zeıʃən] *n* généralisation *f*

generalize ['dʒenərəlaız] **1** *vt* **to become generalized** *(of practice, belief)* se généraliser
2 *vi* généraliser

generally ['dʒenrəlı] *adv (taken overall)* dans l'ensemble; *(as a general rule)* généralement, en général; **g. speaking** d'une manière générale

generate ['dʒenəreıt] *vt (electricity, heat)* produire; *(income)* créer; *(reaction, response)* provoquer; *(interest, ideas)* faire naître

generation [dʒenə'reıʃən] *n* **(a)** *(of people, products)* génération *f*; **from g. to g.** de génération en génération; **the younger/older g.** la jeune/l'ancienne génération; **the g. gap** le fossé entre les générations **(b)** *(of electricity)* production *f*

generator ['dʒenəreıtə(r)] *n Elec* générateur *m*

generic [dʒı'nerık] *adj* générique

generosity [dʒenə'rɒsıtı] *n* générosité *f*

generous ['dʒenərəs] *adj* généreux(euse)

generously ['dʒenərəslı] *adv* généreusement

genesis ['dʒenısıs] *n* genèse *f*; **(the Book of) G.** la Genèse

genetic [dʒı'netık] *adj* génétique; **g. code** code *m* génétique; **g. engineering** génie *m* génétique; **g. fingerprinting** empreinte *f* génétique

genetically [dʒı'netıklı] *adv* génétiquement; **g. modified** génétiquement modifié(e)

genetics [dʒı'netıks] *n* génétique *f*

Geneva [dʒı'ni:və] *n* Genève; **Lake G.** le Lac de Genève, le Lac Léman; **the G. Convention** la Convention de Genève

genial ['dʒi:nıəl] *adj* cordial(e)

geniality [dʒi:nı'ælıtı] *n* cordialité *f*

genially ['dʒi:nıəlı] *adv* cordialement

genie ['dʒi:nı] *(pl* **genii** ['dʒi:nıaı]) *n* génie *m*

genital ['dʒenıtəl] **1** *npl* **genitals** organes *mpl* génitaux
2 *adj* génital(e)

genitive ['dʒenıtıv] *Gram* **1** *n* génitif *m*; **in the g.** au génitif
2 *adj* génitif(ive)

genius ['dʒi:nıəs] *n* génie *m*; *Ironic* **to have a g. for sth/doing sth** avoir le génie de qch/de faire qch; **man/work of g.** homme *m*/œuvre *f* de génie

Genoa ['dʒenəʊə] *n* Gênes

genocide ['dʒenəsaıd] *n* génocide *m*

genre ['ʒɒnrə] *n (of movie, novel)* genre *m*

gent [dʒent] *n Fam (well-bred man)* gentleman *m*

genteel [dʒen'ti:l] *adj (refined)* distingué(e); *(respectable)* comme il faut; *Pej (affected)* maniéré(e)

Gentile ['dʒentaıl] *n* gentil *m*

gentle ['dʒentəl] *adj (person, manner)* doux (douce); *(push, breeze, rise, slope)* léger(ère); *(hint)* discret(ète); *(exercise)* modéré(e); **to be g. with sb** être doux avec qn; **to be g. with sth** faire attention à qch; *Fam* **a g. giant** un agneau sous des airs de brute

gentleman ['dʒentəlmən] *n* **(a)** *(well-bred man)* gentleman *m*; **g.'s agreement** gentleman's agreement *m* **(b)** *(man)* homme *m*; **Ladies and Gentlemen!** mesdames et messieurs!

gentlemanly ['dʒentəlmənlı] *adj* bien élevé(e)

gentleness ['dʒentəlnıs] *n* douceur *f*

gently ['dʒentlı] *adv (speak, remind)* gentiment; *(slope)* en pente douce; **g. (does it)!** allez-y doucement!

gentrification [dʒentrıfı'keıʃən] *n* embourgeoisement *m*

gentrify ['dʒentrıfaı] *vt* embourgeoiser

gentry ['dʒentrı] *n* petite noblesse *f*

genuflect ['dʒenjʊflekt] *vi Formal* faire une génuflexion

genuine ['dʒenjʊın] *adj* **(a)** *(manuscript, painting)* authentique;

(gold, leather) véritable; *(excuse)* valable; *(offer)* sérieux(euse) **(b)** *(sincere)* sincère; **it was a g. mistake** ce n'était pas intentionnel

genuinely ['dʒenjʊınlı] *adv (sincerely)* sincèrement, vraiment

genus ['dʒi:nəs] *(pl* **genera** ['dʒenərə]) *n Biol* genre *m*

geo- ['dʒi:əʊ] *pref* géo-

geographer [dʒı'ɒgrəfə(r)] *n* géographe *mf*

geographic [dʒıə'græfık], **geographical** [dʒıə'græfıkəl] *adj* géographique

geography [dʒı'ɒgrəfı] *n* géographie *f*

geological [dʒıə'lɒdʒık], geological [dʒıə'lɒdʒıkəl] *adj* géologique

geologist [dʒı'ɒlədʒıst] *n* géologue *mf*

geology [dʒı'ɒlədʒı] *n* géologie *f*

geometric [dʒıə'metrık], **geometrical** [dʒıə'metrıkəl] *adj* géométrique

geometry [dʒı'ɒmıtrı] *n* géométrie *f*

geophysics [dʒıəʊ'fızıks] *n* géophysique *f*

geopolitics [dʒıəʊ'pɒlıtıks] *n* géopolitique *f*

Georgia ['dʒɔ:dʒə] *n (country, US state)* la Géorgie

Georgian ['dʒɔ:dʒən] **1** *n* **(a)** *(person)* Géorgien(enne) *m,f* **(b)** *(language)* géorgien *m*
2 *adj* géorgien(enne)

geothermal [dʒi:əʊ'θɜ:məl] *adj* géothermique

geranium [dʒə'reınıəm] *n* géranium *m*

gerbil ['dʒɜ:bıl] *n* gerbille *f*

geriatric [dʒerı'ætrık] **1** *n* malade *mf* gériatrique; *Fam Pej (old person)* gâteux(euse) *m,f*
2 *adj (hospital)* gériatrique; *(care)* aux vieillards; **g. medicine** gériatrie *f*

geriatrics [dʒerı'ætrıks] *n* gériatrie *f*

germ [dʒɜ:m] *n* **(a)** *(causing disease)* microbe *m*; **g. warfare** guerre *f* bactériologique **(b)** *(of seed) & Fig (of idea)* germe *m*

German ['dʒɜ:mən] **1** *n* **(a)** *(person)* Allemand(e) *m,f* **(b)** *(language)* allemand *m*; **G. class/teacher** cours *m*/professeur *m* d'allemand
2 *adj* allemand(e); **G. measles** rubéole *f*; **G. shepherd** berger *m* allemand

germane [dʒɜ:'meın] *adj Formal* approprié(e); **to be g. to sth** avoir rapport à qch

Germanic [dʒɜ:'mænık] *adj* germanique

Germany ['dʒɜ:mənı] *n* l'Allemagne *f*

germinate ['dʒɜ:mıneıt] *vi* germer

germination [dʒɜ:mı'neıʃən] *n* germination *f*

gerrymandering ['dʒerımændərıŋ] *n Pol* charcutage *m* électoral

gerund ['dʒerənd] *n Gram* gérondif *m*

gestation [dʒes'teıʃən] *n also Fig* gestation *f*; **g. period** période *f* de gestation

gesticulate [dʒes'tıkjʊleıt] *vi* gesticuler

gesture ['dʒestʃə(r)] **1** *n also Fig* geste *m*; *Fig* **as a g. of friendship** en témoignage d'amitié
2 *vi (single action)* faire un geste; *(repeatedly)* faire des gestes; **to g. to sb** faire signe à qn; **to g. toward sb/sth** désigner qn/qch d'un geste

get [get] *(pt & pp* **got** [gɒt], *pp* **got** *or* **gotten** ['gɒtən]) **1** *vt* **(a)** *(obtain)* obtenir; *(job)* trouver; **to g. sth for sb** obtenir qch pour qn; **I got the idea from a book** j'ai trouvé l'idée dans un livre; **to g. the right answer** trouver la solution; **to g. the wrong answer** se tromper
(b) *(buy)* acheter; **to g. sth for sb** acheter qch à qn
(c) *(receive) (present, reply)* recevoir; *(surprise, shock)* avoir; **we can't g. Radio 4 here** on ne reçoit pas Radio 4 ici; **to g. $50,000 a year** gagner 50 000 dollars par an; **we don't g. many visitors here** nous ne recevons pas beaucoup de visites ici
(d) *(catch) (person, disease)* attraper; *(train, bus)* prendre; *Fam* **I'll g. you for that** je t'aurai

(**e**) *(fetch)* aller chercher; **to g. sth for sb** aller chercher qch pour qn; **can I g. you anything?** je te rapporte quelque chose?

(**f**) *Fam (annoy)* énerver

(**g**) *Fam (understand)* piger; **do you g. my meaning?** tu vois ce que je veux dire?; **to g. the point** piger; **to g. a joke** saisir une blague

(**h**) *(send)* **to g. sth to sb** faire parvenir qch à qn

(**i**) *(cause to be in a certain state)* **to g. sth dry/wet** sécher/mouiller qch; **to g. sth clean/dirty** nettoyer/salir qch; **you've got him worried** tu l'as fait s'inquiéter; **to g. sb pregnant** mettre qn enceinte; **to g. the children to bed** envoyer les enfants au lit

(**j**) *(cause to be done)* **to g. sth done** faire faire qch; **to g. the house painted** faire peindre la maison; **she got her work finished** elle a terminé son travail

(**k**) *(cause to do)* **to g. sb to do sth** faire faire qch à qn; **she got me to help her** elle m'a persuadé de l'aider; **you can g. them to wrap it for you** tu peux leur demander de te l'emballer

(**l**) *(do gradually)* **to g. to know sb** apprendre à connaître qn; **you'll g. to like him** tu finiras par l'apprécier; **she soon got to thinking that...** elle se mit bientôt à penser que...

(**m**) *(have opportunity)* **to g. to do sth** avoir l'occasion de faire qch

(**n**) *(possess) (with have)* **she hasn't got a car** elle n'a pas de voiture; **she's got the measles/AIDS** elle a la rougeole/le sida; **what's that got to do with it?** qu'est-ce que ça a à voir?

(**o**) *(must) (with have)* **I've got to go** il faut que j'y aille; **it's got to be done** il faut que ce soit fait

2 *vi* (**a**) *(arrive)* arriver; **to g. home** arriver chez soi; **to g. back** arriver; **how do you g. there?** comment fait-on pour y aller?; **he got as far as chapter five** il est allé jusqu'au chapitre cinq; **it got to the point where...** ça en est arrivé à un point où...

(**b**) *(move) also Fig* **to g. in sb's way** se mettre sur le chemin de qn; **where has he got to?** où est-il passé?; **we're getting nowhere** on n'avance pas

(**c**) *(become)* **to g. angry** se mettre en colère; **to g. better** s'améliorer; **to g. drunk** se soûler; **to g. old** vieillir

(**d**) *(with past participle)* **to g. broken** être cassé(e); **to g. stolen** être volé(e); **to g. killed** se faire tuer; **to g. dressed** s'habiller; **to g. married** se marier

(**e**) *(start)* **to g. going** *(leave)* se mettre en route; *(start working)* se mettre au travail; **to g. talking with sb** entrer en conversation avec qn

▶**get about** *vi (of person)* se déplacer; *(of news, rumor)* circuler

▶**get across** *vt sep (ideas, message)* faire passer

▶**get ahead** *vi* avancer

▶**get along** *vi* (**a**) *(leave)* s'en aller, partir (**b**) *(progress)* **how are you getting along in your new job?** comment ça va, votre nouveau travail?; **we can g. along without them** nous pouvons très bien nous passer d'eux (**c**) *(have good relationship)* s'entendre

▶**get around 1** *vt insep (problem, difficulty)* contourner; **there's no getting around it, we'll have to tell her** on n'a pas le choix, il va falloir lui dire

2 *vi* = **get about**

▶**get around to** *vt insep* **to g. around to doing sth** trouver le temps de faire qch

▶**get at** *vt insep* (**a**) *(have access to)* accéder à; *(reach)* atteindre; **to g. at the truth** découvrir la vérité (**b**) *(imply)* **what are you getting at?** où veux-tu en venir? (**c**) *Fam (criticize)* s'en prendre à

▶**get away** *vi (escape, leave)* se sauver; *(take a vacation)* s'échapper

▶**get away with** *vt insep* (**a**) *(fine, warning)* s'en tirer avec (**b**) *(crime)* **he stole the money and got away with it** il a volé

l'argent et il ne s'est pas fait prendre; *Fig* **that child gets away with murder** on lui passe tout à ce gosse

▶**get back 1** *vt sep (recover)* récupérer; *(strength)* reprendre

2 *vi (return)* revenir

▶**get back at** *vt insep* **to g. back at sb (for sth)** se venger de qn (pour qch)

▶**get behind 1** *vt insep (support)* soutenir

2 *vi (become delayed)* prendre du retard (**with** *or* **in** dans)

▶**get by** *vi (manage)* se débrouiller, s'en tirer (**on/in** avec/en)

▶**get down 1** *vt sep* (**a**) *(reduce) (weight)* perdre; *(costs, temperature)* faire baisser (**b**) *(depress)* déprimer (**c**) *(fetch)* descendre

2 *vi (descend)* descendre (**from** de)

▶**get down to** *vt insep* en arriver à; **to g. down to the facts** en venir aux faits

▶**get in 1** *vt sep* (**a**) *(bring inside)* rentrer (**b**) *(insert)* **I couldn't g. a word in** je n'ai pas pu en placer une (**c**) *(stock up with)* faire provision de

2 *vi* (**a**) *(gain entrance)* entrer (**b**) *(arrive)* arriver (**c**) *(be elected)* être élu(e)

▶**get into** *vt insep* (**a**) *(house)* entrer dans; *(car)* monter dans; **to g. into Congress** être élu(e) député; **to g. into trouble** s'attirer des ennuis; *Fam* **I don't know what's got into her** je ne sais pas ce qui lui prend (**b**) *(clothes, boots)* enfiler; **I can't g. into my dress any more** je n'entre plus dans ma robe (**c**) *Fam (become interested in) (activity)* commencer à s'intéresser à; *(book)* rentrer dans

▶**get in with** *vt insep (group of people)* se mettre bien avec

▶**get off 1** *vt sep* (**a**) **to g. sb off** *(save from punishment)* tirer qn de là (**b**) *(send)* **to g. the children off to school** envoyer les enfants à l'école

2 *vi (train, bus)* descendre de

3 *vi* (**a**) *(from train, bus)* descendre; *Fig* **I told him where to g. off** je l'ai envoyé promener (**b**) *(go unpunished)* s'en tirer (**c**) *(begin)* **to g. off to sleep** s'endormir; **to g. off to a good/bad start** commencer bien/mal

▶**get off on** *vt insep very Fam* **to g. off on sth** être excité(e) par qch; **to g. off on doing sth** prendre son pied à faire qch

▶**get on 1** *vt sep* (**a**) *(clothes)* mettre, enfiler (**b**) *Fam* **to g. it on (with sb)** *(have sex)* s'envoyer en l'air (avec qn)

2 *vt insep (train, bus, plane)* monter dans

3 *vi* (**a**) *(enter train, bus)* monter (**b**) *(have good relationship)* s'entendre; **to g. on well/badly with sb** s'entendre bien/mal avec qn (**c**) *(age)* **to be getting on (in years)** se faire vieux (vieille)

▶**get onto** *vt insep (move onto subject of)* en arriver à; **they eventually got onto (the subject of) money** ils en vinrent finalement à parler d'argent

▶**get out 1** *vt sep* (**a**) *(bring out)* sortir (**b**) *(remove) (nail, splinter)* retirer; *(stain)* faire partir

2 *vi* (**a**) *(leave)* sortir (**b**) *(of secret, news)* transpirer

▶**get out of** *vt insep (vehicle)* sortir de; **to g. out of the way** s'écarter; **g. out of here!** *(go away)* va-t-en!; *Fam (I don't believe you)* arrête de dire des bêtises!; **to g. out of doing sth** s'arranger pour ne pas faire qch

▶**get over 1** *vt sep (idea, information)* faire passer; *(facts)* expliquer

2 *vt insep* (**a**) *(road, river)* traverser, franchir; *(wall, fence)* passer par-dessus (**b**) *(illness, trauma)* se remettre de

▶**get over with** *vt sep* **to g. sth over with** en finir avec qch

▶**get through 1** *vt sep (communicate)* **to g. sth through to sb** faire comprendre qch à qn

2 *vt insep* (**a**) *(pass through) (hole, roof)* passer à travers (**b**) *(survive) (test, interview)* survivre à; *(period of time)* tenir (**c**) *(finish)* achever (**d**) *(consume) (food, drink)* consommer; *(money)* dépenser

3 *vi* (**a**) *(arrive) (of news)* parvenir; *(of messenger)* arriver (**b**) **to**

g. through to sb *(on telephone)* obtenir la communication avec qn; *Fig (make understand)* se faire comprendre par qn

▶**get together 1** *vt sep (money)* réunir; *(belongings, ideas)* rassembler

   2 *vi (of people)* se réunir

▶**get up 1** *vt sep* **(a)** *(out of bed)* faire lever **(b)** *(dress up)* **he got himself up in his best clothes** il a mis ses plus beaux vêtements **(c)** *very Fam (achieve erection)* **he couldn't g. it up** il n'a pas réussi à bander

   2 *vt insep Fig* **to g. up sb's nose** taper sur les nerfs à qn

   3 *vi (rise)* se lever

▶**get up to** *vt insep (do)* **what have you been getting up to recently?** qu'est-ce que tu as fait ces derniers temps?; **to g. up to mischief** faire des bêtises; **he's been getting up to his old tricks** il a encore fait des siennes

getaway ['getəweɪ] *n* fuite *f*; **to make one's g.** prendre la fuite; **g. car** = voiture utilisée pour la fuite

get-rich-quick ['get'rɪtʃ'kwɪk] *adj Fam* **a g. scheme** un moyen de devenir riche rapidement

get-together ['gettəgeðə(r)] *n Fam* réunion *f* (entre amis)

get-up ['getʌp] *n Fam (clothes)* accoutrement *m*; *(fancy dress)* déguisement *m*

get-up-and-go ['getʌpənd'gəʊ] *n Fam* énergie *f*

get-well card ['get'wel'kɑːd] *n* carte *f* de prompt rétablissement

geyser ['gaɪzə(r)] *n (spring)* geyser *m*

Ghana ['gɑːnə] *n* le Ghana

Ghanaian [gɑː'neɪən] **1** *n* Ghanéen(enne) *m,f*

   2 *adj* ghanéen(enne)

ghastly ['gɑːstlɪ] *adj (terrible)* horrible, épouvantable; *(mistake)* monstrueux(euse)

Ghent [gent] *n* Gand

gherkin ['gɜːkɪn] *n* cornichon *m*

ghetto ['getəʊ] *(pl* **ghettoes** *or* **ghettos)** *n* ghetto *m*; *Fam* **g. blaster** grand radiocassette *m* portatif

ghost [gəʊst] **1** *n* fantôme *m*; **you look as though you've seen a g.** on dirait que tu as vu un revenant; **not the g. of a chance** pas la moindre chance; **to give up the g.** *(of person, machine)* rendre l'âme; **g. story** histoire *f* de fantôme; **g. town** ville *f* fantôme

   2 *vt* **to g. a book** servir de nègre pour un livre

ghostly ['gəʊstlɪ] *adj* spectral(e)

ghostwrite ['gəʊstraɪt] *vt* **to g. a book** servir de nègre pour un livre

ghostwriter ['gəʊstraɪtə(r)] *n* nègre *m*

ghoul [guːl] *n (evil spirit)* goule *f*; *Fig (morbid person)* personne *f* morbide

ghoulish ['guːlɪʃ] *adj (humor, remark)* morbide; *(scene)* macabre

GHQ [dʒiːeɪtʃ'kjuː] *n Mil (abbr* **General Headquarters)** QG *m inv*

GI [dʒiː'aɪ] *n Fam* GI *m inv*

giant ['dʒaɪənt] **1** *n* géant(e) *m,f*; **g. killer** *(in sport)* vainqueur *m* surprise

   2 *adj* géant(e)

gibber ['dʒɪbə(r)] *vi* baragouiner

gibbering ['dʒɪbərɪŋ] *adj* au discours incohérent; *Fam* **a g. idiot** un(e) pauvre idiot(e)

gibberish ['dʒɪbərɪʃ] *n* charabia *m*; **to talk g.** dire n'importe quoi

gibbet ['dʒɪbɪt] *n* gibet *m*, potence *f*

gibbon ['gɪbən] *n* gibbon *m*

gibe [dʒaɪb] **1** *n* moquerie *f*

   2 *vi* **to g. at sb** se moquer de qn

giblets ['dʒɪblɪts] *npl* abats *mpl*

Gibraltar [dʒɪ'brɔːltə(r)] *n* Gibraltar

giddiness ['gɪdɪnɪs] *n* étourdissement *m*, vertige *m*

giddy ['gɪdɪ] *adj* **to be** *or* **to feel g.** avoir le vertige; **it makes me (feel) g.** ça me donne le vertige; *Fig* **the g. heights** les hautes sphères *fpl*

GIF [dʒɪf] *n Comput (abbr* **Graphic Information Format)** GIF *m*

gift [gɪft] *n* **(a)** *(present)* cadeau *m*; *Prov* **never look a g. horse in the mouth** à cheval donné on ne regarde pas la bouche; **g. store** boutique *f* de cadeaux; **g. token** chèque-cadeau *m* **(b)** *(talent)* don *m*; **to have a g. for sth** être doué(e) pour qch; **to have the g. of the gab** *(be talkative)* avoir la langue bien pendue; *(speak persuasively)* avoir du bagout

gifted ['gɪftɪd] *adj* doué(e); *(artist, musician)* de talent

gift-wrapped ['gɪftræpt] *adj* sous paquet-cadeau

gig [gɪg] *n* **(a)** *(carriage)* cabriolet *m* **(b)** *Fam (pop concert)* concert *m*

gigabyte ['dʒɪgəbaɪt] *n Comput* gigaoctet *m*

gigantic [dʒaɪ'gæntɪk] *adj* colossal(e), gigantesque

giggle ['gɪgəl] **1** *n (laugh)* petit rire *m* idiot; **to have (a fit of) the giggles** avoir le fou rire

   2 *vi* rire (nerveusement)

giggly ['gɪgəlɪ] *adj* **to be g.** pouffer de rire

gigolo ['dʒɪgələʊ] *(pl* **gigolos)** *n* gigolo *m*

gild [gɪld] *(pt & pp* **gilded** *or* **gilt** [gɪlt]) *vt* dorer; *Fig* **to g. the lily** surcharger

gill [dʒɪl] *n (liquid measure)* = 0,142 l, quart *m* de pinte

gills [gɪlz] *npl (of fish)* ouïes *fpl*, branchies *fpl*; *Fig* **to be green about the g.** avoir le teint verdâtre; *Fam* **to be stuffed to the g.** être rassasié(e)

gilt [gɪlt] **1** *n* dorure *f*; *Fin* **gilts** titres *mpl ou* fonds *mpl* d'État

   2 *adj* doré(e)

   3 *pt & pp of* **gild**

gilt-edged ['gɪltedʒd] *adj* **(a)** *Fin* **g. securities** *or* **stocks** titres *mpl ou* fonds *mpl* d'État **(b)** *Fig (opportunity)* en or

gimlet ['gɪmlɪt] *n (tool)* vrille *f*; *Fig* **g. eyes** yeux *mpl* perçants

gimme ['gɪmi:] *very Fam =* **give me**

gimmick ['gɪmɪk] *n* truc *m*, astuce *f*

gimmicky ['gɪmɪkɪ] *adj* artificiel(elle), qui relève du procédé

gin [dʒɪn] *n* gin *m*; **a g. and tonic** un gin tonic

ginger ['dʒɪndʒə(r)] **1** *n* gingembre *m*; **g. ale** = boisson gazeuse au gingembre pouvant servir à couper un alcool; **g. beer** limonade *f* au gingembre

   2 *adj (hair)* roux (rousse)

gingerbread ['dʒɪndʒəbred] *n* pain *m* d'épice; **g. man** = bonhomme en biscuit parfumé au gingembre

gingerly ['dʒɪndʒəlɪ] *adv* avec précaution

gingham ['gɪŋəm] *n* vichy *m*

gingivitis [dʒɪndʒɪ'vaɪtɪs] *n Med* gingivite *f*

ginseng ['dʒɪnseŋ] *n* ginseng *m*

gipsy ['dʒɪpsɪ] *(pl* **gipsies)** *n (Eastern European)* tzigane *mf*; *(Spanish)* gitan(e) *m,f*; **g. caravan** roulotte *f*

giraffe [dʒɪ'rɑːf] *n* girafe *f*

gird [gɜːd] *(pt & pp* **girded** *or* **girt** [gɜːt]) *vt Lit* **to g. one's loins** se ceindre les reins

girder ['gɜːdə(r)] *n* poutre *f* (métallique)

girdle ['gɜːdəl] **1** *n (corset)* gaine *f*

   2 *vt Lit (surround)* ceindre, entourer

girl [gɜːl] *n* fille *f*; **a French g.** une (jeune) Française; **girl band** girls band *m*; **G. Scout** éclaireuse *f*

girlfriend ['gɜːlfrend] *n (lover)* petite amie *f*; *(friend)* amie *f*

girlhood ['gɜːlhʊd] *n* enfance *f*, jeunesse *f*

girlie ['gɜːlɪ] *n Fam* **g. mag** magazine *m* érotique

girlish ['gɜːlɪʃ] *adj (of girl)* de fille; *(of woman, effeminate man)* de jeune fille; **g. laughter** rire *m* de jeune fille

girt [gɜːt] *pt & pp of* **gird**

girth [gɜːθ] *n (of tree)* circonférence *f*; *(of person)* corpulence *f*

gist [dʒɪst] *n* essentiel *m*; **to get the g.** saisir l'essentiel

give [gɪv] **1** *vt* (*pt* **gave** [geɪv], *pp* **given** ['gɪvən]) (**a**) (*in general*) donner; (*as present*) offrir; **to g. sth to sb, to g. sb sth** donner qch à qn; (*as present*) offrir qch à qn; **to g. sb a dirty look** lancer un regard noir à qn; **he was given ten years/a fine** il a été condamné à dix ans de prison/à une amende; **g. her my love** embrasse-la pour moi; **she gave her age as twenty** elle a déclaré qu'elle avait vingt ans; **she gave me to understand that...** elle m'a fait comprendre que...; **g. or take a few minutes/cents** à quelques minutes/cents près
(**b**) (*with noun to form verbal expressions*) **to g. a laugh** partir d'un éclat de rire; **to g. a sigh** pousser un soupir; **to g. sb a smile** sourire à qn; **to g. sb a fright** faire peur à qn; **to g. sb a kiss** embrasser qn; **he gave his face a wash** il s'est lavé le visage; **she gave the soup a stir** elle a remué la soupe
2 *vi* (**a**) (*donate*) donner; **please g. generously** soyez généreux, s'il vous plaît; **to g. of one's time** donner de son temps
(**b**) (*yield, break*) (*of cloth, shoes*) se faire; (*of rope*) lâcher; (*of support, door*) céder
(**c**) *Fam* **what gives?** quoi de neuf ?
3 *n* (*of fabric*) élasticité *f*

▶**give away** *vt sep* (**a**) (*give for nothing*) donner (**b**) (*prize*) distribuer; **to g. the bride away** conduire la mariée à l'autel (**c**) (*reveal*) trahir

▶**give back** *vt sep* rendre

▶**give in 1** *vt sep* (*hand over*) remettre
2 *vi* (*surrender*) céder (**to** à); (*admit defeat*) abandonner

▶**give off** *vt sep* (*smell, heat*) dégager

▶**give onto** *vt insep* **the house gives directly onto the street** la maison donne directement sur la rue

▶**give out 1** *vt sep* (**a**) (*money, food*) distribuer; (*information*) donner (**b**) (*noise*) émettre; (*heat*) répandre
2 *vi* (*of supplies, patience*) s'épuiser; (*of luck*) tourner

▶**give over** *vt sep* (*money, objects*) remettre; (*devote*) consacrer (**to** à)

▶**give up 1** *vt sep* (*possessions*) renoncer à; (*activity, hope*) abandonner; **to g. up smoking** arrêter de fumer; **to g. up one's job** quitter son emploi; **to g. sb up for dead** considérer qn comme mort(e)
2 *vi* abandonner; **to g. up on sb** perdre tout espoir en qn; (*of doctors*) perdre tout espoir en ce qui concerne qn; **to g. up on sth** laisser tomber qch

▶**give way** *vi* (**a**) (*collapse*) (*of support*) céder; (*of floor, ceiling*) s'effondrer; (*of rope, legs*) lâcher; (*of ground*) se dérober (**b**) (*yield*) (*in argument*) céder (**to** à); (*in car*) céder le passage (**to** à); **her tears gave way to laughter** ses larmes ont cédé la place au rire

give-and-take ['gɪvən'teɪk] *n* concessions *fpl* (mutuelles); **there has to be some g.** il faut que chacun y mette du sien

giveaway ['gɪvəweɪ] *n Fam* (**a**) (*revelation*) **what she said about the night before was the g.** ce qu'elle a dit sur la soirée précédente l'a trahie; **it was a dead g.** cela en disait long (**b**) (*free gift*) cadeau *m*; **g. price** prix *m* imbattable

given ['gɪvən] **1** *adj* (**a**) (*specific*) (*time, place*) donné(e); **at a g. point** à un moment donné; **g. name** prénom *m* (**b**) (*apt, likely*) **to be g. to doing sth** avoir tendance à faire qch
2 *conj* (**a**) (*considering*) étant donné; **g. that...** étant donné que...; **g. the nature of the case** étant donné la nature de l'affaire (**b**) **g. the chance again** si l'occasion se représentait
3 *pp of* **give**

gizmo ['gɪzməʊ] (*pl* **gizmos**) *n Fam* truc *m*, machin *m*

gizzard ['gɪzəd] *n* gésier *m*

glacé cherry ['glæseɪ'tʃerɪ] *n* cerise *f* confite

glacial ['gleɪsɪəl] *adj* glaciaire; *Fig* glacial(e)

glacier ['glæsɪə(r)] *n* glacier *m*

glad [glæd] *adj* heureux(euse), content(e) (**about** de); **I would be g. to assist you** je serais ravi de pouvoir vous ai-

der; **to be g. of sth** (*grateful for*) être heureux d'avoir qch; *Fig* **to give sb the g. eye** faire de l'œil à qn; *Fam* **to put on one's g. rags** se mettre sur son trente et un

gladden ['glædən] *vt* réjouir

glade [gleɪd] *n Lit* clairière *f*

gladiator ['glædɪeɪtə(r)] *n* gladiateur *m*

gladiolus [glædɪ'əʊləs] (*pl* **gladioli** [glædɪ'əʊlaɪ]) *n* glaïeul *m*

gladly ['glædlɪ] *adv* avec plaisir, volontiers

glamor ['glæmə(r)] *n* (*of person*) élégance *f*; (*of job, image, lifestyle*) prestige *m*; (*of place*) chic *m inv*, élégance; *Fam* **g. girl** belle fille *f*, pin-up *f*

glamorize ['glæməraɪz] *vt* (*lifestyle*) rendre séduisant(e); (*violence*) esthétiser; (*person*) idéaliser

glamorous ['glæmərəs] *adj* (*person*) élégant(e); (*job, image, lifestyle*) prestigieux(euse); (*place*) chic *inv*, élégant(e); (*dress*) magnifique

glance [glɑːns] **1** *n* coup *m* d'œil; **to have a g. at sth** jeter un coup d'œil à qch; **at a g.** d'un coup d'œil; **at first g.** au premier coup d'œil
2 *vi* **to g. at** regarder brièvement, jeter un coup d'œil à; **to g. through sth** parcourir qch rapidement

▶**glance off** *vt insep* (*of blow, missile*) ricocher sur

glancing ['glɑːnsɪŋ] *adj* (*blow*) oblique

gland [glænd] *n* glande *f*

glandular ['glændjʊlə(r)] *adj* glandulaire; **g. fever** mononucléose *f* infectieuse

glare [gleə(r)] **1** *n* (**a**) (*angry stare*) regard *m* furieux (**b**) (*bright light*) éclat *m*, lumière *f* éblouissante; *Fig* **in the full g. of publicity** sous les feux de médias
2 *vi* (*stare angrily*) **to g. at sb/sth** fixer qn/qch d'un air furieux

glaringly ['gleərɪŋlɪ] *adv* **it's g. obvious** ça saute aux yeux

glass [glɑːs] *n* verre *m*; (*glassware*) verrerie *f*; **a g. of wine** un verre de vin; **g. bottle** bouteille *f* en verre; **g. case** vitrine *f*; **g. door** porte *f* vitrée; **g. eye** œil *m* de verre; **g. wool** laine *f* de verre

glass-blowing ['glɑːsbləʊɪŋ] *n* soufflage *m* du verre

glasses ['glɑːsɪz] *npl* (*eyeglasses*) lunettes *fpl*

glassful ['glɑːsfʊl] *n* verre *m*

glasspaper ['glɑːspeɪpə(r)] *n* papier *m* de verre

glassware ['glɑːsweə(r)] *n* verrerie *f*

glassworks ['glɑːswɜːks] *n* verrerie *f*; (*for crystal*) crystallerie *f*

glassy ['glɑːsɪ] *adj* (*eyes, look*) vitreux(euse); (*water*) immobile

glaucoma [glɔː'kəʊmə] *n* glaucome *m*; **to have g.** avoir un glaucome

glaze [gleɪz] **1** *n* (*on pottery*) vernis *m*; (*on pastry*) glaçage *m*
2 *vt* (**a**) (*window*) vitrer (**b**) (*pottery*) vernisser; (*pastry*) glacer

▶**glaze over** *vi* (*of eyes*) devenir vitreux(euse)

glazed [gleɪzd] *adj* (**a**) (*pottery*) vernissé(e) (**b**) (*eyes, look*) vitreux(euse), terne

glazier ['gleɪzɪə(r)] *n* vitrier *m*

gleam [gliːm] **1** *n* (*of light*) rayon *m*; *Fig* **a g. of hope** une lueur d'espoir
2 *vi* luire, briller; (*of water*) miroiter

gleaming ['gliːmɪŋ] *adj* étincelant(e)

glean [gliːn] *vt* glaner

glee [gliː] *n* (*delight*) joie *f*; (*malicious pleasure*) jubilation *f*

gleeful ['gliːfʊl] *adj* (*happy*) joyeux(euse); **to be g.** (*maliciously happy*) jubiler

glib [glɪb] *adj* (*person, excuse*) désinvolte; (*reply*) spécieux(euse)

glibly ['glɪblɪ] *adv* (*reply*) de façon désinvolte; (*speak*) avec aisance

glide [glaɪd] *vi* (*move smoothly*) glisser; (*of aircraft, bird*) planer

glider ['glaɪdə(r)] *n* (*aircraft*) planeur *m*

gliding ['glaɪdɪŋ] *n* (*sport*) vol *m* à voile

glimmer ['glɪmə(r)] **1** *n* faible lueur *f*; (*of water*) reflet *m*; *Fig* **a g. of hope** une lueur d'espoir
2 *vi* (*of light*) luire; (*of water*) miroiter; (*of metal*) étinceler

glimpse [glɪmps] **1** *n* **to catch a g. of** entrevoir; **a g. of the future** un aperçu de (ce que sera) l'avenir
2 *vt* entrevoir

glint [glɪnt] **1** *n* (of light) (flash) éclat *m*; (continuous) scintillement *m*; (of water) reflet *m*; **with a g. in her eye** avec une lueur dans le regard
2 *vi* (of light, eye) briller; (of water, metal) scintiller

glisten ['glɪsən] *vi* (of water, metal) scintiller; **his forehead glistened with sweat** la sueur perlait sur son front

glitter ['glɪtə(r)] **1** *n* (a) (sparkle) scintillement *m*; *Fig* (of occasion) éclat *m*, faste *m* (b) (decoration, make-up) paillettes *fpl*
2 *vi* scintiller; *Prov* **all that glitters is not gold** tout ce qui brille n'est pas d'or

glittering ['glɪtərɪŋ] *adj* (jewels) scintillant(e); *Fig* (occasion, career) brillant(e)

glitz [glɪts] *n* clinquant *m*, tape-à-l'œil *m inv*

glitzy ['glɪtsɪ] *adj Fam* tape-à-l'œil *m inv*

gloat [gləʊt] *vi* (at one's own success) jubiler (**at** à l'idée de); (about somebody else's misfortune) se réjouir (**about** *or* **over** de); **I don't like to g., but...** ce n'est pas que ça me réjouisse, mais...

global ['gləʊbəl] *adj* (comprehensive) global(e); (worldwide) mondial(e); **g. economy** économie *f* mondiale; **g. village** village *m* planétaire; **g. warming** réchauffement *m* de la planète

globalization ['gləʊbəlaɪ'zeɪʃən] *n Econ* mondialisation *f*

globally ['gləʊbəlɪ] *adv* (comprehensively) globalement; (worldwide) mondialement

globe [gləʊb] *n* (sphere) globe *m*; (with map) globe terrestre; **the g.** (the earth) le globe terrestre; **to travel the g.** voyager dans le monde entier

globetrotter ['gləʊbtrɒtə(r)] *n Fam* globe-trotter *mf*

globule ['glɒbjuːl] *n* gouttelette *f*

gloom [gluːm] *n* (a) (darkness) obscurité *f* (b) (sadness) morosité *f*

gloomily ['gluːmɪlɪ] *adv* (sadly) sombrement

gloomy ['gluːmɪ] *adj* (a) (dark) sombre; (weather) morose (b) (sad) triste (c) (pessimistic) pessimiste; **g. thoughts** idées *fpl* noires

glorified ['glɔːrɪfaɪd] *adj* **she's just a g. secretary** elle n'est rien de plus qu'une secrétaire; **it's just a g. motor scooter** ce n'est qu'un scooter amélioré

glorify ['glɔːrɪfaɪ] (*pt & pp* **glorified**) *vt* (a) (extoll) célébrer; *Rel* **to g. God** rendre gloire à Dieu (b) (war, violence) glorifier

glorious ['glɔːrɪəs] *adj* (a) (reign, victory) glorieux(euse) (b) (view, sunshine) magnifique

gloriously ['glɔːrɪəslɪ] *adv* (a) (die, reign) avec gloire (b) (beautifully) superbement; **it was g. sunny** il faisait un soleil splendide

glory ['glɔːrɪ] *n* (a) (honor) gloire *f* (b) (splendor) splendeur *f*

►**glory in** (*pt & pp* **gloried**) *vt insep* se glorifier de

gloss[1] [glɒs] *n* (in text) glose *f*

gloss[2] [glɒs] *n* (shine) lustre *m*; *Fig* vernis *m*; *Fig* **to take the g. off sth** gâcher qch; **g. paint** peinture *f* brillante

►**gloss over** *vt insep* passer sur

glossary ['glɒsərɪ] (*pl* **glossaries**) *n* glossaire *m*

glossy ['glɒsɪ] *adj* (hair) brillant(e); (fur, leather) luisant(e), lustré(e); (surface) brillant, poli(e); **g. brochure** brochure *f* luxueuse; **g. magazine** magazine *m* de luxe; **g. paper** papier *m* glacé

glottal stop ['glɒtəl'stɒp] *n Ling* coup *m* de glotte

glove [glʌv] *n* gant *m*; *Fig* **the gloves are off** tous les coups sont permis; **g. box, g. compartment** (in car) boîte *f* à gants; **g. puppet** marionnette *f* à gaine

glow [gləʊ] **1** *n* (light) lueur *f*; (on cheeks) couleurs *fpl*; **the g. of the setting sun** l'embrasement du couchant; *Fig* **a g. of pride/satisfaction** un vif sentiment de fierté/satisfaction
2 *vi* (of light, fire) rougeoyer; *Fig* **to be glowing with health** être resplendissant(e) de santé; *Fig* **to g. with pride/pleasure** rayonner de fierté/plaisir

glower ['glaʊə(r)] *vi* **to g. at sb** lancer des regards noirs à qn

glowing ['gləʊɪŋ] *adj* (cigarette, coal) incandescent(e); (metal) chauffé(e) au rouge; *Fig* (praise, words) chaleureux(euse); (description, report) enthousiaste; *Fig* **to paint sth in g. colors** présenter qch sous un jour très favorable

glow-worm ['gləʊwɜːm] *n* ver *m* luisant

glucose ['gluːkəʊs] *n* glucose *m*

glue [gluː] **1** *n* colle *f*
2 *vt* coller (**to** à); *Fig* **to be glued to the television** être cloué(e) devant la télévision

glue-sniffing ['gluːsnɪfɪŋ] *n* inhalation *f* de colle

glum [glʌm] *adj* triste, morose

glut [glʌt] **1** *n* (of goods) encombrement *m*
2 *vt* (*pt & pp* **glutted**) (a) (market, economy) encombrer, inonder (b) **to g. oneself (on)** se gaver (de)

glutinous ['gluːtɪnəs] *adj* gluant(e)

glutton ['glʌtən] *n* (greedy person) goinfre *mf*, glouton(onne) *m,f*; *Fig* **to be a g. for punishment** être masochiste

gluttony ['glʌtənɪ] *n* goinfrerie *f*, gloutonnerie *f*

glycemia [glaɪˈsiːmɪə] *n Med* glycémie *f*

glycemic index [glaɪˈsiːmɪkˈɪndeks] *n Med* index *m* glycémique

glycerin ['glɪsərɪn], **glycerol** ['glɪsərɒl] *n* glycérine *f*

GM [dʒiːˈem] *adj* (abbr **genetically modified**) génétiquement modifié(e); **GM foods** aliments *mpl* génétiquement modifiés

GMO [dʒiːemˈəʊ] *n* (abbr **genetically modified organism**) OGM *m*

GMT [dʒiːemˈtiː] *n* (abbr **Greenwich Mean Time**) GMT *m*

gnarled [nɑːld] *adj* noueux(euse)

gnash [næʃ] *vt* **to g. one's teeth** grincer des dents

gnat [næt] *n* moucheron *m*

gnaw [nɔː] **1** *vt* (of rodent) ronger
2 *vi* (a) (of rodent) **to g. through sth** ronger qch (b) *Fig* (of doubt, guilt) **to g. away at sb** ronger qn

gnome [nəʊm] *n* gnome *m*

GNP [dʒiːenˈpiː] *n Econ* (abbr **Gross National Product**) PNB *m*

gnu [nuː] *n* gnou *m*

go [gəʊ] **1** *vi* (3rd person singular **goes** [gəʊz], *pt* **went** [went], *pp* **gone** [gɒn]) (a) (move) aller; **to go to France** aller en France; **to go to the doctor** aller chez le docteur; **to go home** rentrer chez soi; **to go swimming/skiing** (aller) nager/skier; **the proceeds will go to charity** l'argent recueilli sera versé à des œuvres de charité; *Fig* **where do we go from here?** et maintenant, qu'est-ce qu'on fait?
(b) (leave) partir, s'en aller; **I've got to go** il faut que j'y aille; **let's go!** allons-y!
(c) (function) marcher; (of bell) sonner; **to keep the conversation going** entretenir la conversation
(d) (progress) aller; **to go well/badly** bien/mal se passer; *Fam* **how's it going?** comment ça va?; **how does the tune/story go?** c'est quoi, l'air/l'histoire, déjà?
(e) (of time) passer; **the time went quickly/slowly** le temps a passé vite/lentement; **it has just gone eight** il est huit heures à peine passées; **there are only five minutes to go** il ne reste que cinq minutes
(f) (disappear, deteriorate) disparaître; (of light bulb) griller; (of fuse) sauter; (of batteries) s'user; **her sight/voice is going** elle est en train de perdre la vue/la voix; **most of my money goes on food** l'essentiel de mon argent passe dans la nourriture
(g) (forming future) **to be going to do sth** aller faire qch; **I was going to walk** j'allais y aller à pied; **it's going to rain** il va pleuvoir

(h) *(match)* aller (**with** avec); **these colors go/don't go** ces couleurs vont bien/ne vont pas ensemble

(i) *(be available)* **there's a job going at the factory** il y a une place à l'usine; **is there any wine going?** est-ce qu'il y a du vin?; **it went for \$12** on l'a vendu 12 dollars

(j) *(fit)* entrer; **the piano won't go through the door** le piano ne passera pas par la porte; **four into three won't go** trois n'est pas divisible par quatre

(k) *(belong)* aller; **the cups go on that shelf** les tasses vont sur cette étagère

(l) *(become)* devenir; **to go crazy** devenir fou (folle); **to go red** rougir; **to go cold** refroidir

(m) *(be the rule)* **what she says goes** c'est elle qui commande

(n) *Fam (urinate)* aller aux toilettes

(o) **two burgers to go** *(to take out)* deux hamburgers à emporter

2 *vt* **(a)** *(make sound)* & *Fam (say)* faire; **cows go moo** la vache fait meuh; **to go bang/plop** faire paf/plouf

(b) *(idioms)* **to go it alone** se lancer en solo; **to go one better than sb** faire mieux que qn, surenchérir sur qn; *Fam* **I could really go a beer!** je me ferais bien une bière!

3 *n* (*pl* **goes**) **(a)** *(expressing activity)* **to be on the go** ne pas arrêter; **she had three boyfriends on the go at the same time** elle avait trois copains en même temps; **it's all go** ça n'arrête pas; **from the word go** dès le début

(b) *(energy)* **to be full of go** être très dynamique

(c) *(success)* **to make a go of sth** réussir qch

(d) *(turn)* tour *m*; **(it's) your go!** *(in game)* c'est ton tour!, c'est à toi!; **to have a go at doing sth** essayer de faire qch; *Fam* **let's have a go!** allons-y!; *(let me try)* laisse-moi essayer!; **at one go** d'un coup; **\$2 a go** *(at amusement park)* 2 dollars le tour

▸**go about, go around 1** *vi (circulate) (of person)* se promener; *(of rumor)* circuler; **you can't go about saying things like that!** il ne faut pas raconter des choses pareilles!; **there's a bug going around** il y a un microbe qui se promène

2 *vt insep* **(a)** *(travel) (country)* parcourir **(b)** *(tackle) (task)* vaquer à; **to go about doing sth** s'y prendre pour faire qch; **how do I go about getting a license?** que dois-je faire pour obtenir un permis?

▸**go across** *vt insep & vi* traverser

▸**go after** *vt insep (pursue)* **to go after sb** courir après qn; **to go after sth** essayer d'obtenir qch

▸**go against** *vt insep* **(a)** *(contradict) (principles, instincts)* aller à l'encontre de **(b)** *(be unfavorable to)* **the decision went against him** la décision lui a été défavorable

▸**go ahead** *vi* **(a)** *(take place)* avoir lieu; **to go ahead with sth** commencer *ou* entreprendre qch; **may I say something? – go ahead** puis-je dire quelque chose? – allez-y **(b)** *(go in front)* passer devant; **to go ahead of sb** devancer qn

▸**go along** *vi (proceed)* se dérouler; **as we go along** en chemin; **to do sth as one goes along** faire qch au fur et à mesure

▸**go along with** *vt insep (suggestion, plan)* approuver, être d'accord avec

▸**go around** *vi* **(a)** *(circulate) (of rumor)* circuler; *(of cold, flu)* se promener **(b)** *(be enough)* **there was enough food/drink to go around** il y avait assez à manger/boire pour tout le monde

▸**go at** *vt insep (person, task)* s'attaquer à

▸**go away** *vi (leave)* partir; *(disappear)* disparaître; **go away!** allez-vous-en!; **to go away on business/for the weekend** partir en voyage d'affaires/en week-end

▸**go back** *vi* **(a)** *(return)* revenir; **to go back to doing sth** se remettre à faire qch; **to go back to sleep** se rendormir; **to go back to one's old ways** reprendre ses anciennes habitudes **(b)** *(in time)* **to go back to** remonter à; *Fam* **we go back a long way** ça fait longtemps qu'on se connaît

▸**go back on** *vt insep (promise)* revenir sur

▸**go before 1** *vi (precede)* précéder

2 *vt insep* **to go before the court** *(of defendant, case)* passer au tribunal

▸**go by 1** *vi* **(a)** *(pass)* passer; **to watch the world go by** regarder passer les gens **(b)** *(of time)* s'écouler

2 *vt insep* **(a)** *(be guided by)* **to go by appearances** juger d'après les apparences; **to go by the rules** respecter les règles **(b)** *(be known by)* **to go by the name of** être connu(e) sous le nom de

▸**go down 1** *vt insep (descend)* descendre

2 *vi* **(a)** *(descend)* descendre; *(of sun)* se coucher; *(of ship)* sombrer; **to go down on one's knees** s'agenouiller; *Fig* se mettre à genoux; **to go down with an illness** tomber malade **(b)** *(be defeated)* être vaincu(e); **I'm not going to go down without a fight** je me battrai jusqu'au bout **(c)** *(of level, temperature, prices)* baisser; *(of tire, balloon)* se dégonfler **(d)** *(be received)* **to go down well/badly** être bien/mal reçu(e); **he has gone down in history as a tyrant** l'histoire a retenu de lui l'image d'un tyran

▸**go for** *vt insep* **(a)** *(attack)* attaquer; **if you really want the job, go for it!** si tu veux vraiment le poste, bats-toi!; *Fam* **go for it!** vas-y! **(b)** *(like)* avoir un faible pour **(c)** *(choose)* prendre **(d)** **he has got a lot going for him** il a bien des atouts **(e)** *(apply to)* s'appliquer à; **the same goes for you** ça vaut aussi pour toi

▸**go in** *vi (enter)* entrer; *(fit)* rentrer; *(of sun)* se cacher

▸**go in for** *vt insep* **(a)** *(competition)* s'inscrire à **(b)** *(like)* **she doesn't go in for cooking/sports** elle n'est pas très portée sur la cuisine/les sports

▸**go into** *vt insep* **(a)** *(enter)* entrer dans **(b)** *(examine)* examiner

▸**go off 1** *vi* **(a)** *(leave)* partir (**with** avec) **(b)** *(of bomb)* exploser; *(of alarm)* se déclencher; **the gun went off** le coup est parti **(c)** *(of event)* **to go off well** *or* **smoothly** se dérouler bien **(d)** *(stop working)* **the power went off** l'électricité a été coupée; **the light went off** la lumière s'est éteinte

2 *vt insep (lose liking for)* ne plus aimer, se lasser de; **I've gone off the idea** l'idée ne me séduit plus

▸**go on 1** *vi* **(a)** *(continue)* continuer; **to go on doing sth** continuer à faire qch; **as time went on** avec le temps **(b)** *(proceed)* **to go on to sth** passer à qch; **to go on to do sth** poursuivre en faisant qch **(c)** *(talk excessively)* **don't go on about it!** arrête de parler de ça!; **he does go on a bit** il est un peu soûlant; **to go on at sb** s'en prendre à qn **(d)** *(happen)* se passer; **what's going on here?** qu'est-ce qui se passe ici? **(e)** *(of electricity, light, heating)* s'allumer

2 *vt insep* **(a)** *(be guided by)* se fonder sur; **the police have nothing to go on** la police n'a rien sur quoi se fonder **(b)** *(approach)* **she's two going on three** elle va sur ses trois ans; *Hum* **he's fifteen going on forty** *(wise)* il a quinze ans mais il est déjà très mûr; *(old beyond his years)* il a quinze ans mais il est vieux avant l'âge

▸**go out** *vi* **(a)** *(leave)* sortir; **to go out for a meal** aller au restaurant; **to go out on strike** se mettre en grève **(b)** *(date)* sortir ensemble; **to go out with sb** sortir avec qn **(c)** *(of fire, light)* s'éteindre **(d)** *(become unfashionable)* passer de mode **(e)** *(be eliminated)* être éliminé(e) **(f)** *(of TV, radio program)* être diffusé(e)

▸**go over 1** *vi* **(a)** *(cross)* **to go over to sb** aller vers qn **(b)** *(switch)* **to go over to sth** passer à qch **(c)** *(of suggestion, joke)* **to go over well/badly** être bien/mal reçu(e)

2 *vt insep* **(a)** *(bridge)* passer; *(road)* traverser; **the ball went over the wall** la balle est passée par-dessus le mur **(b)** *(examine)* passer en revue; *(figures, accounts)* vérifier; **to go over sth in one's mind** repasser qch dans son esprit

▸**go round** = **go around**

▸**go through 1** *vt insep* **(a)** *(penetrate)* traverser **(b)** *(suffer)* subir **(c)** *(complete) (formalities)* accomplir **(d)** *(examine)* passer en revue; *(one's notes, speech)* revoir; *(suitcase, house)* fouiller; **to go through sb's pockets** fouiller les poches de qn (**e**) *(use up) (money)* dépenser; *(food)* consommer; **we've gone through six cartons of milk** nous avons bu six briques de lait

2 *vi (be completed) (of deal)* être conclu(e); *(of bill)* passer; *(of divorce)* être prononcé(e)

▶**go through with** *vt insep* aller jusqu'au bout de; **I can't go through with the wedding** finalement, je ne me marie plus; **I can't go through with it** je ne peux pas le faire

▶**go under** *vi (of ship)* couler; *Fig (of firm)* faire faillite

▶**go up 1** *vt insep* monter

2 *vi* (**a**) *(climb, rise)* monter; *(of theater curtain)* se lever; **to go up to bed** monter se coucher; **a shout went up from the crowd** un cri s'éleva de la foule; *Fig* **to go up in the world** *(socially)* faire son chemin (**b**) *(of prices, temperature)* monter, grimper; **to go up in sb's estimation** monter dans l'estime de qn (**c**) *(explode)* sauter

▶**go up to** *vt insep* (**a**) *(approach)* se diriger vers (**b**) *(reach)* aller jusqu'à

▶**go with** *vt insep* (**a**) *(accompany)* aller (de pair) avec; **a company car goes with the job** le poste donne droit à une voiture de fonction (**b**) *(harmonize with)* aller avec

▶**go without 1** *vi* se priver; **I'd rather go without** je préfère m'en passer

2 *vt insep* se passer de

goad [gəʊd] **1** *n Fig (remark, criticism)* aiguillon *m*

2 *vt Fig (person)* provoquer; **to g. sb into doing sth** harceler qn jusqu'à ce qu'il fasse qch

▶**goad on** *vt sep* aiguillonner

▶**go-ahead** ['gəʊəhed] **1** *n* **to give sb/sth the g.** donner le feu vert à qn/qch

2 *adj (enterprising)* entreprenant(e), dynamique

goal [gəʊl] *n* (**a**) *(aim)* but *m*, objectif *m* (**b**) *(in soccer, hockey)* but *m*; **g. kick** coup *m* de pied de but; **g. line** ligne *f* de but; **g. scorer** buteur(euse) *m,f*

goalkeeper ['gəʊlki:pə(r)], *Fam* **goalie** ['gəʊli] *n* gardien *m* de but, goal *m*

goalless ['gəʊllɪs] *adj* **g. draw** match *m* nul

goalmouth ['gəʊlmaʊθ] *n (in soccer, hockey)* (entrée *f* du) but *m*

goalpost ['gəʊlpəʊst] *n* poteau *m* de but; **the goalposts** les buts *mpl*; *Fig* **to move** *or* **to shift the goalposts** changer les règles du jeu

goat [gəʊt] *n* chèvre *f*; **g.'s milk** lait *m* de chèvre; *Fam* **it really gets my g.!** ça me tape vraiment sur les nerfs!

goatherd ['gəʊthɜːd] *n* chevrier(ère) *m,f*

goatskin ['gəʊtskɪn] *n* peau *f* de chèvre

gobble ['gɒbəl] **1** *vt (eat)* engloutir

2 *vi (of turkey)* glouglouter

▶**gobble up** *vt sep also Fig* engloutir

gobbledygook ['gɒbəldɪguːk] *n Fam* charabia *m*

go-between ['gəʊbɪtwiːn] *n* intermédiaire *mf*

goblet ['gɒblɪt] *n* verre *m* à pied; *(in medieval times)* coupe *f*

goblin ['gɒblɪn] *n* lutin *m*

go-cart = go-kart

god [gɒd] *n (divine being)* dieu *m*; **G.** Dieu *m*; **G. forbid!** Dieu m'en garde!; **G. willing** si Dieu le veut; **I wish to G. I hadn't told him** si seulement je ne lui avais rien dit; **in G.'s name** au nom du Ciel; *Fam* (**oh**) **my G.!** mon Dieu!; *Fam* **for G.'s sake!** pour l'amour du ciel!; *Fam* **G. knows** Dieu seul le sait; *Fam* **he thinks he's G.'s gift to women** il s'imagine que toutes les femmes sont folles de lui

godchild ['gɒdtʃaɪld] *n* filleul(e) *m,f*

goddam(n) ['gɒdæm] *very Fam* **1** *adj* sacré(e), fichu(e); **that g. dog!** ce sacré chien!

2 *adv* vachement

3 *exclam* nom de Dieu!

goddaughter ['gɒddɔːtə(r)] *n* filleule *f*

goddess ['gɒdɪs] *n* déesse *f*

godfather ['gɒdfɑːðə(r)] *n* parrain *m*

god-fearing ['gɒdfɪːrɪŋ] *adj* pieux(euse)

godforsaken ['gɒdfəseɪkən] *adj* perdu(e)

godless ['gɒdlɪs] *adj* impie

godmother ['gɒdmʌðə(r)] *n* marraine *f*

godparent ['gɒdpeərənt] *n (godfather)* parrain *m*; *(godmother)* marraine *f*; **my godparents** mon parrain et ma marraine

godsend ['gɒdsend] *n* aubaine *f*

godson ['gɒdsʌn] *n* filleul *m*

gofer ['gəʊfə(r)] *n Fam (male assistant)* homme *m* à tout faire; *(female assistant)* bonne *f* à tout faire

go-getter ['gəʊgetə(r)] *n Fam* battant(e) *m,f*

goggle ['gɒgəl] *vi* ouvrir des yeux ronds; **to g. at sb/sth** regarder qn/qch avec des yeux ronds

goggle-eyed ['gɒgəlaɪd] *adv Fam* avec des yeux ronds

goggles ['gɒgəlz] *npl (for swimming)* lunettes *fpl* de plongée; *(for skiing)* lunettes de ski; *(for worker)* lunettes protectrices

go-go dancer ['gəʊgəʊ'dɑːnsə(r)] *n* danseuse *f* de boîte de nuit

going ['gəʊɪŋ] **1** *n* (**a**) *(progress)* **that's very good g.!** voilà qui n'est pas mal du tout!; **it's slow g.** *(at work)* ça n'avance pas vite (**b**) *(condition of ground)* terrain *m*; *Fig* **the book/movie was pretty heavy g.** le livre/film était plutôt indigeste; *Fig* **to get out while the g. is good** se retirer tant que la chance nous/leur/etc. est favorable

2 *adj* (**a**) *(successful)* **a g. concern** une affaire qui tourne (**b**) *(current) (price, rate)* courant(e), actuel(elle)

going-away ['gəʊɪŋə'weɪ] *adj* **g. outfit** = tenue de voyage de noces; **g. party/present** fête *f*/cadeau *m* d'adieu

going-over ['gəʊɪŋ'əʊvə(r)] *n Fam* **to give sb a g.** *(beating)* tabasser qn; *(criticism)* sonner les cloches à qn

goings-on ['gəʊɪŋzɒn] *npl Fam (activities)* activités *fpl*; *(events)* événements *mpl*

goiter ['gɔɪtə(r)] *n* goitre *m*

go-kart ['gəʊkɑːt] *n (child's toy)* petit chariot *m*; *(with engine)* kart *m*; **g. racing** karting *m*

gold [gəʊld] **1** *n* or *m*; **g. bullion** or en barre; **g. dust** poussière *f* d'or; **tickets are like g. dust** les billets valent de l'or; **g. leaf** *or* **foil** feuille *f* d'or; **g. medal** médaille *f* d'or; *also Fig* **g. mine** mine *f* d'or; **g. plate** orfèvrerie *f*; *Fin* **g. reserves** réserves *fpl* d'or; *Hist* **the G. Rush** la ruée vers l'or

2 *adj (made of gold)* en or; *(gold-colored)* doré(e)

gold-digger ['gəʊld'dɪgə(r)] *n Fam Pej (woman)* croqueuse *f* de diamants

golden ['gəʊldən] *adj (made of gold)* en or; *(gold-colored)* doré(e); **a g. opportunity** une occasion en or; **the g. age** l'âge *m* d'or; **g. boy** enfant *m* chéri; **g. eagle** aigle *m* royal; **g. girl** enfant *f* chérie; **g. handshake** *(retirement bonus)* indemnité *f* de départ; **g. jubilee** jubilé *m*; **g. rule** règle *f* d'or; *Fin* **g. share** action *f* privilégiée; **g. wedding** noces *fpl* d'or

goldfinch ['gəʊldfɪntʃ] *n* chardonneret *m*

goldfish ['gəʊldfɪʃ] *(pl goldfish)* *n* poisson *m* rouge; **g. bowl** bocal *m* à poissons rouges; **it's like living in a g. bowl** c'est comme vivre en vitrine

gold-plated ['gəʊld'pleɪtɪd] *adj* plaqué(e) or

goldsmith ['gəʊldsmɪθ] *n* orfèvre *m*

golf [gɒlf] *n* golf *m*; **g. ball** balle *f* de golf; **g. club** *(stick, association)* club *m* de golf; **g. course** terrain *m* de golf

golfer ['gɒlfə(r)] *n* joueur(euse) *m,f* de golf

golfing ['gɒlfɪŋ] *n* golf *m*; **g. umbrella** grand parapluie *m* (de golf)

golly ['gɒlɪ] *exclam Fam Old-fashioned* fichtre!

gondola ['gɒndələ] *n* (**a**) *(boat)* gondole *f* (**b**) *(cable car)* cabine *f* de téléphérique

gondolier [gɒndə'lɪə(r)] *n* gondolier *m*

gone [gɒn] **1** *adj Fam* **to be six months g.** *(pregnant)* être enceinte de six mois; *Fam* **to be pretty far g.** *(drunk)* être complètement bourré(e); *Fam* **to be g. on sb** *(infatuated)* avoir le béguin pour qn

2 *pp of* **go**

goner ['gɒnə(r)] *n Fam* **I thought she was a g.** *(would die)* j'ai cru qu'elle allait y passer; **I'm a g. if he finds out** si elle l'apprend, je suis mort

gong [gɒŋ] *n* gong *m*

gonna ['gɒnə] *Fam* = **going to**

gonorrhea [gɒnə'rɪə] *n* blennorragie *f*; **to have g.** avoir une blennorragie

goo [gu:] *n Fam* **(a)** *(sticky substance)* substance *f* visqueuse **(b)** *(sentimentality)* guimauve *f*

good [gʊd] **1** *n* **(a)** bien *m*; **to do g.** faire le bien; **he's up to no g.** il prépare un mauvais coup; **to see the g. in sb/sth** voir les bons côtés de qn/qch

(b) *(benefit)* **I did it for your own g.** je l'ai fait pour ton bien; **it was all to the g.** c'était tout bénéfice; **we were $100 to the g.** nous avons fait 100 dollars de bénéfice; **for the g. of one's health** pour sa santé; **for the common g.** dans l'intérêt général; **it will do you g.** cela te fera du bien; **it won't do any g.** cela ne servira à rien; **what's the g. of that?** à quoi bon?; **it's no g.** ça ne sert à rien; **it's no g. complaining** cela ne sert à rien de se plaindre; **he's no g.** *(incompetent)* il est nul; *(morally bad)* il ne vaut pas grand-chose

(c) **for g.** *(permanently)* pour toujours; **she is gone for g.** elle est partie pour de bon

2 *adj (comparative* **better** ['betə(r)], *superlative* **best** [best]) **(a)** *(in quality)* bon (bonne); *(weather, handwriting)* beau (belle); **she looks g. in that hat** ce chapeau lui va bien, elle est bien avec ce chapeau; **to taste g.** avoir bon goût; **(that) sounds g.!** bonne idée!; **g. to eat** comestible; **it's g. to see you** ça fait plaisir de vous voir; *Fam* **that's a g. one!** *(of story, joke)* elle est bien bonne!; **he thinks he's too g. for us** il se croit trop bien pour nous; **to earn g. money** bien gagner sa vie; **you've got a g. chance** tu as tes chances; **to be on to a g. thing** être sur un bon filon; **to have a g. time** s'amuser; **to show sb a g. time** faire passer un bon moment à qn; **all in g. time** chaque chose en son temps; **too g. to be true** trop beau pour être vrai; **as g. as new** comme neuf (neuve); **he as g. as called me a liar** pour un peu, il m'aurait traité de menteur; **the g. old days** le bon vieux temps; **g. afternoon!** bonjour!; **the G. Book** la sainte Bible; **he's a g. friend** c'est un ami; **G. Friday** le Vendredi Saint; *Fam* **g. grief!** fichtre!; **the g. life** la belle vie; *Fam* **g. Lord!, g. heavens!, g. gracious!** bon sang!; **g. morning!** bonjour!; **g. night!** bonne nuit!; **the G. Samaritan** le bon Samaritain

(b) *(advantageous)* **a g. opportunity** une bonne occasion; **to be in a g. position to do sth** être bien placé(e) pour faire qch; **it's looking g.** ça se présente bien

(c) *(beneficial)* bon (bonne); **he doesn't know what's g. for him** il n'a pas un sou de bon sens; **to be g. for business** être bon pour les affaires; **it's a g. thing we were here** heureusement que nous étions là; **g. riddance!** bon débarras!

(d) *(skillful)* bon (bonne) **(at en)**; **to be g. with one's hands** être habile de ses mains; **to be g. with children** savoir y faire avec les enfants; **to be g. in bed** être bon au lit amour

(e) *(well-behaved)* sage; **be g.!** *(to child)* sois sage!; **to be as g. as gold** être sage comme une image; **to lead a g. life** mener une vie respectable; **g. conduct** *or* **behavior** bonne conduite *f*

(f) *(kind)* gentil(ille); **that's very g. of you** c'est bien aimable *ou* très gentil de votre part; **he was very g. about it** il s'est montré très compréhensif; **to do sb a g. turn** rendre un service à qn

(g) *(valid)* **a g. reason** une bonne raison, une raison valable; **he's g. for $10,000** *(has in credit)* il dispose de 10 000 dollars

(h) *(for emphasis)* bon (bonne); **a g. two hours** deux bonnes heures; **a g. deal of, a g. many** beaucoup de; **to have a g. look at sb/sth** bien regarder qn/qch; **to have a g. cry** pleurer un bon coup; **a g. long time** un bien long moment

(i) **to make g.** *(of person)* faire son chemin; **to make g. one's losses** compenser ses pertes; **to make g. one's promise** tenir sa promesse; **he made g. his escape** il a réussi son évasion

3 *adv* **(a)** **I like my coffee g. and strong** j'aime le café bien fort; **I'll do it when I'm g. and ready** je le ferai quand ça me chantera

(b) *(as comment, answer)* bien; **I feel better today – g.** je me sens mieux aujourd'hui – tant mieux

goodbye [gʊd'baɪ] *n* au revoir *m*; **g.!** au revoir!; **to say g. to sb** dire au revoir à qn; **he can say g. to his hopes of winning** il peut dire adieu à ses espoirs de victoire

good-for-nothing ['gʊdfənʌθɪŋ] *n* bon (bonne) *m,f* à rien

good-humored [gʊd'hju:məd] *adj (debate, meeting)* détendu(e); **to be g.** *(of person)* avoir un caractère enjoué

good-looking ['gʊdlʊkɪŋ] *adj* beau (belle)

good-natured [gʊd'neɪtʃəd] *adj (person)* d'un caractère agréable; *(remarks, laugh)* bon enfant *inv*

goodness ['gʊdnɪs] *n* **(a)** *(of person)* bonté *f* **(b)** *(of food)* qualités *fpl* nutritives **(c)** *(in exclamations)* **g. (me)!** mon Dieu!; **thank g.!** Dieu merci!; **for g. sake!** pour l'amour de Dieu!

goods [gʊdz] *npl* **(a)** *Law* biens *mpl* **(b)** *(articles)* articles *mpl*, marchandises *fpl*; *Fig* **to deliver the g.** remplir ses engagements; *Fig* **to come up with the g.** faire le nécessaire; **g. train/depot** train *m*/dépôt *m* de marchandises

good-tempered [gʊd'tempəd] *adj (person)* d'un caractère facile; *(discussion)* aimable

goodwill [gʊd'wɪl] *n* **(a)** *(benevolence)* bienveillance *f*; *(willingness)* bonne volonté *f* **(b)** *Com* fonds *m* de commerce

goody ['gʊdɪ] *Fam* **1** *n* (*pl* **goodies**) **(a)** *(person)* bon *m*; **the goodies and the baddies** les bons *mpl* et les méchants *mpl* **(b)** **goodies** *(nice food)* bonnes choses *fpl*; *(nice things)* petits cadeaux *mpl*

2 *exclam* chouette!

goody-goody ['gʊdɪgʊdɪ] *Fam Pej* **1** *n* (*pl* **goody-goodies**) fayot *m*

2 *adj* fayot

goody-two-shoes ['gʊdɪtu:ʃu:z] *n Fam Pej* petit(e) saint(e) *m,f*; *Hum* modèle *m* de vertu

gooey ['gu:ɪ] *adj Fam* **(a)** *(sticky)* gluant(e) **(b)** *(sentimental)* à la guimauve

goof [gu:f] *Fam* **1** *n* **(a)** *(blunder)* gaffe *f*, bourde *f* **(b)** *(idiot)* cave *m*

2 *vi* **(a)** *(blunder)* faire une gaffe *ou* une bourde **(b)** *(joke)* rigoler **(c)** *(stare)* **to g. at sb/sth** regarder qn/qch bêtement

▸**goof about, goof around** *vi Fam* faire l'idiot(e)

▸**goof off** *vi Fam* flemmarder, glandouiller

▸**goof up** *Fam* **1** *vt sep* bousiller, saloper

2 *vi* merder

goofball ['gu:fbɔːl] *n Fam* **(a)** *(fool)* crétin(e) *m,f*, andouille *f* **(b)** *(barbiturate)* barbiturique *m*

goofy ['gu:fɪ] *adj Fam (stupid)* loufoque

google ['gu:gəl] *Fam Comput* **1** *vt* **to g. sb/sth** faire une recherche sur qn/qch sur Internet

2 *vi* **to g. (for sb/sth)** faire une recherche (sur qn/qch) sur Internet

goon [gu:n] *n Fam* **(a)** *(stupid person)* imbécile *mf* **(b)** *(thug)* gorille *m*

goose [gu:s] *(pl* **geese** [gi:s]) *n* oie *f*; *Fig* **his g. is cooked** il est fichu; **to kill the g. that lays the golden egg** tuer la poule aux œufs d'or; **g. bumps** chair *f* de poule

gooseberry ['gʊzbərɪ] *(pl* **gooseberries**) *n* groseille *f* à maquereau

gooseflesh ['gu:sfleʃ] n chair f de poule

goose-step ['gu:sstep] **1** n pas m de l'oie

2 vi (pt & pp **goose-stepped**) marcher au pas de l'oie

gopher ['gəʊfə(r)] n (animal) spermophile m

gore [gɔ:(r)] **1** n (blood) sang m (versé)

2 vt (of bull) encorner; **to be gored to death** être tué(e) à coups de corne

gorge [gɔ:dʒ] **1** n (valley) gorge f, défilé m

2 vt **to g. oneself** se gorger, se gaver (**on** de)

3 vi se gorger, se gaver (**on** de)

gorgeous ['gɔ:dʒəs] adj magnifique; (meal, food) excellent(e)

gorilla [gə'rɪlə] n gorille m

gorse [gɔ:s] n ajoncs mpl

gory ['gɔ:rɪ] adj (movie, crime, war) sanglant(e); (covered in blood) ensanglanté(e); Fig & Hum **in g. detail** avec tous les détails

gosh [gɒʃ] exclam Fam ça alors!

goshawk ['gɒshɔ:k] n autour m

gosling ['gɒzlɪŋ] n oison m

gospel ['gɒspəl] n évangile m; **to take sth as g.** accepter qch comme parole d'évangile; **g. (music)** gospel m; **g. singer** chanteur(euse) m,f de gospel

gossamer ['gɒsəmə(r)] n (a) (spider's web) fils mpl de la Vierge (b) (fabric) gaze f légère

gossip ['gɒsɪp] **1** n (a) (person) bavard(e) m,f; (ill-natured) commère f (b) (talk) bavardages mpl; (ill-natured) commérage(s) m(pl); **have you heard the latest g.?** tu sais la nouvelle?; **to have a g. (about)** bavarder (à propos de); **g. column** (in newspaper) chronique f mondaine; **g. columnist** échotier(ère) m,f

2 vi bavarder; (ill-naturedly) colporter des commérages

gossipy ['gɒsɪpɪ] adj (person) bavard(e); (ill-natured) cancanier(ère); (letter, conversation) plein(e) de petits potins

got [gɒt] pt & pp of **get**

Gothic ['gɒθɪk] **1** n (artistic style, language) gothique m
2 adj gothique

gotta ['gɒtə] very Fam = **got to**

gotten ['gɒtən] pp of **get**

▶**gouge out** [gaʊdʒ] vt sep (hole, path) creuser; **to g. sb's eye out** arracher l'œil à qn

goulash ['gu:læʃ] n goulasch m

gourd [gʊəd] n gourde f

gourmet ['gʊəmeɪ] n gourmet m, gastronome mf; **g. restaurant** restaurant m gastronomique

gout [gaʊt] n (disease) goutte f

Gov. (a) (abbr **government**) gouvernement m (b) (abbr **governor**) gouverneur m

govern ['gʌvən] vt (a) (state, country) gouverner (b) (of scientific law) régir (c) (emotions) maîtriser, contenir

governess ['gʌvənɪs] n gouvernante f

governing ['gʌvənɪŋ] adj (party, coalition) au pouvoir; (concept, principle) directeur(trice); **g. body** conseil m d'administration

government ['gʌvənmənt] n gouvernement m; **g. intervention** intervention f du gouvernement

governmental [gʌvən'mentəl] adj gouvernemental(e)

governor ['gʌvənə(r)] n (of colony, US state) gouverneur m; **g. general** gouverneur m général

governorship ['gʌvənəʃɪp] n (post) poste m de gouverneur; (function) fonctions fpl de gouverneur

Govt. (abbr **government**) gouvernement m

gown [gaʊn] n (of woman) robe f; (of magistrate, academic) robe f, toge f; (of surgeon) blouse f

GP [dʒi:'pi:] n (abbr **general practitioner**) (médecin m) généraliste mf

gr (abbr **gram(s)**) g

grab [græb] **1** n **to make a g. at** or **for sth** essayer d'attraper

qch; Fam **to be up for grabs** être à qui veut le prendre; (be for sale) être à qui veut l'acheter

2 vt (pt & pp **grabbed**) (a) (seize) **to g. (hold of) sb/sth** saisir qn/qch; (more tightly) empoigner qn/qch; **I'll g. a sandwich later** j'avalerai un sandwich plus tard (b) Fam (attract) **the idea doesn't g. me** ça ne me dit rien; **how does that g. you?** ça te dit?

3 vi **to g. at sb** essayer de s'agripper à qn; **to g. at sth** essayer d'attraper qch

grace [greɪs] **1** n (a) (of movement, dancer, manners) grâce f; **to do sth with good/bad g.** faire qch de bonne/mauvaise grâce; **to have the (good) g. to do sth** avoir la grâce de faire qch (b) (favor) **to be in sb's good graces** être dans les bonnes grâces de qn (c) Rel **in a state of g.** en état de grâce; **to fall from g.** perdre la grâce; Fig tomber en disgrâce; **there, but for the g. of God, go I** je remercie le ciel de m'avoir épargné (d) (for payment of a bill) **seven days' g.** sept jours de délai ou de grâce (e) (prayer before meal) bénédicité m (f) (form of address) **Your G.** (to bishop) Monseigneur; (to duke) Monsieur le duc; (to duchess) Madame la duchesse

2 vt (a) (honor) honorer (**with** de) (b) (decorate) embellir, enjoliver

graceful ['greɪsfʊl] adj (person, movement) gracieux(euse); (speech, style) élégant(e)

gracefully ['greɪsfʊlɪ] adv avec grâce, gracieusement

graceless ['greɪslɪs] adj (a) (inelegant) disgracieux(euse) (b) (rude) effronté(e)

gracious ['greɪʃəs] **1** adj (a) (kind, polite) poli(e), affable; (in victory) courtois(e) (b) (elegant) pleine(e) de raffinement

2 exclam **g. (me)!, goodness g.!** mon Dieu!

graciously ['greɪʃəslɪ] adv avec grâce; (accept, invite) de bonne grâce

gradation [grə'deɪʃən] n (of colors) gradation f; (on thermometer) degré m; (of meaning) nuance f

grade [greɪd] **1** n (a) (rank) grade m, rang m; (in profession) échelon m; **g. crossing** passage m à niveau (b) (quality) qualité f; (of vegetable, fruit) calibre m; Fig **to make the g.** se montrer à la hauteur (c) Sch (mark) note f; (year) classe f; **g. school** ≃ école f primaire

2 vt (a) (classify) classer; (fruit, vegetables) calibrer (b) (essay, exercise) noter

gradient ['greɪdɪənt] n (a) (of slope) dénivellation f (b) (of temperature) gradient m

gradual ['grædjʊəl] adj progressif(ive), graduel(elle)

gradualism ['grædjʊəlɪzm] n gradualisme m

gradually ['grædjʊəlɪ] adv progressivement, peu à peu

graduate 1 n ['grædjʊət] (from university) ≃ licencié(e) m,f; (from high school) bachelier(ère) m,f

2 adj ['grædjʊət] (postgraduate) **g. school** = école où l'on poursuit ses études après la licence; **g. studies** études fpl de troisième cycle

3 vi ['grædjʊeɪt] (a) (from university) obtenir sa licence; (from high school) avoir son bac (b) (progress) **to g. from sth to sth** passer de qch à qch

4 vt ['grædjʊeɪt] **to g. college** obtenir sa licence; **to g. high school** avoir son bac

graduated ['grædjʊeɪtɪd] adj (thermometer) gradué(e); (pay rise) progressif(ive)

graduation [grædjʊ'eɪʃən] n (from school, university) remise f des diplômes; **g. ceremony** cérémonie f de remise des diplômes

graffiti [græ'fi:ti:] n graffiti mpl; **a piece of g.** un graffiti

graft¹ [grɑ:ft] **1** n (technique) greffe f; (thing grafted) greffon m
2 vt greffer (**onto** sur)

graft² [grɑ:ft] n Fam (bribe) pot-de-vin m

grain [greɪn] n (a) (of wheat, salt, sand) grain m; **a g. of truth** une once de vérité; Fig **to take sth with a g. of salt** ne pas prendre qch pour argent comptant (**b**) *(in photo, wood)* grain *m*; *(in meat, material)* fil *m*; *Fig* **it goes against the g. for me to do it** ce n'est pas dans ma nature de le faire (**c**) *(cereals)* céréales *fpl*

grainy ['greɪnɪ] *adj* granuleux(euse)

gram [græm] *n* gramme *m*

grammar ['græmə(r)] *n* grammaire *f*; **g. (book)** (livre *m* de) grammaire

grammarian [grə'meərɪən] *n* grammairien(enne) *m,f*

grammatical [grə'mætɪkəl] *adj* grammatical(e)

grammatically [grə'mætɪklɪ] *adv* grammaticalement

gramme = **gram**

granary ['grænərɪ] *(pl* **granaries**) *n* grenier *m*

grand [grænd] **1** *adj* (**a**) *(imposing)* grandiose, imposant(e); **to do things on a g. scale** faire les choses en grand; *Mus & Fig* **g. finale** apothéose *f*; **g. jury** = jury qui décide si une affaire doit être portée ou non devant les tribunaux; **g. master** *(in chess)* grand maître *m*; **g. piano** piano *m* à queue; **g. slam** grand chelem *m*; **g. total** somme *f* totale (**b**) *Fam (excellent)* excellent(e)

   2 *n (pl* **grand**) *Fam (thousand dollars)* mille dollars *mpl*

grandchild ['grænt∫aɪld] *(pl* **grandchildren** ['grænt∫ɪldrən]) *n (boy)* petit-fils *m*; *(girl)* petite fille *f*; **grandchildren** petits-enfants *mpl*

grandad ['grændæd] *n Fam* (**a**) *(grandfather)* grand-père *m*; *(term of address)* papy *m*, pépé *m* (**b**) *Pej (old man)* pépé *m*

grand-dad ['grændæd], **grandaddy** ['grændædɪ] *(pl* **grandaddies**) *n Fam* grand-père *m*; *(term of address)* papy *m*, pépé *m*

granddaughter ['grændɔ:tə(r)] *n* petite fille *f*

grandeur ['grændjə(r)] *n (of person)* grandeur *f*, noblesse *f*; *(of building, surroundings)* splendeur *f*, magnificence *f*

grandfather ['grænfɑ:ðə(r)] *n* grand-père *m*; **g. clock** horloge *f* (de parquet)

grandiloquent [græn'dɪləkwənt] *adj* grandiloquent(e)

grandiose ['grændɪəʊs] *adj (building)* monumental(e); *(term, title)* pompeux(euse); *(idea, scheme)* démesuré(e)

grandly ['grændlɪ] *adv (impressively)* de façon grandiose; *(pompously)* de façon pompeuse

grandma ['grænmɑ:] *n Fam* grand-mère *f*; *(term of address)* mamie *f*, mémé *f*

grandmother ['grænmʌðə(r)] *n* grand-mère *f*

grandpa ['grænpɑ:] *n Fam* grand-père *m*; *(term of address)* papy *m*, pépé *m*

grandparent ['grænpeərənt] *n* grand-parent *m*

grandson ['grænsʌn] *n* petit-fils *m*

grandstand ['grænstænd] *n* tribune *f* d'honneur; *Fig* **to have a g. view of sth** être bien placé(e) pour voir qch

granite ['grænɪt] *n* granit *m*

granny ['grænɪ] *(pl* **grannies**) *n Fam* grand-mère *f*; *(term of address)* mamie *f*, mémé *f*; **g. knot** double nœud *m*

grant [grɑ:nt] **1** *n (financial aid)* subvention *f*; *(for student)* bourse *f* (d'études)

   2 *vt* (**a**) *(allow) (permission)* donner; *(interview, request)* accorder; **to take sth for granted** considérer qch comme allant de soi ou comme étant dû; **to take sb for granted** croire que qn sera toujours là (**b**) *(award) (money, subsidy)* accorder, allouer (**c**) *(admit)* admettre; **I g. that he's talented** je reconnais qu'il a du talent

granular ['grænjʊlə(r)] *adj* granuleux(euse)

granulated sugar ['grænjʊleɪtɪd'∫ʊgə(r)] *n* sucre *m* semoule

granule ['grænjʊl] *n (of salt, sand)* grain *m*; *(of coffee)* granule *m*

grape [greɪp] *n* grain *m* de raisin; **some grapes** du raisin; **g. harvest** vendange(s) *f(pl)*; **g. juice** jus *m* de raisin; **g. picker** vendangeur(euse) *m,f*

grapefruit ['greɪpfru:t] *n* pamplemousse *m*; **g. juice** jus *m* de pamplemousse

grapevine ['greɪpvaɪn] *n* vigne *f*; *(climbing)* treille *f*; *Fam* **I heard on the g. that...** j'ai entendu par le téléphone arabe que...

graph [grɑ:f] *n* graphique *m*, diagramme *m*; **g. paper** papier *m* millimétré

graphic ['græfɪk] *adj* (**a**) *(vivid)* très détaillé(e); *(language)* cru(e); **in g. detail** de façon très détaillée (**b**) **g. artist** graphiste *mf*; **g. arts** arts *mpl* graphiques; **g. design** conception *f* graphique; **g. designer** graphiste *mf*; **g. equalizer** égalisateur *m* graphique; **g. novel** bande *f* dessinée (pour adultes)

graphically ['græfɪklɪ] *adv (describe)* de façon très détaillée

graphics ['græfɪks] **1** *n (art)* arts *mpl* graphiques

   2 *npl Comput* graphismes *mpl*, graphiques *mpl*

graphite ['græfaɪt] *n* graphite *m*, mine *f* de plomb

graphology [græ'fɒlədʒɪ] *n* graphologie *f*

grapnel ['græpnəl] *n Naut* grappin *m*

grapple ['græpəl] *vi (fight)* lutter corps à corps (**with** avec); *Fig (with problem)* se débattre (**with** avec)

grappling hook ['græplɪŋ'hʊk], **grappling iron** ['græplɪŋ'aɪən] *n Naut* grappin *m*

grasp [grɑ:sp] **1** *n* (**a**) *(hold)* prise *f*; *Fig* **to have sth within one's g.** avoir qch à sa portée (**b**) *(understanding)* compréhension *f* (**of** de)

   2 *vt* (**a**) *(hold firmly)* saisir; *(more tightly)* empoigner; **to g. sb's arm** saisir qn par le bras; *Fig* **to g. the opportunity** saisir l'occasion (**b**) *(understand)* saisir, comprendre

grasping ['grɑ:spɪŋ] *adj (mean)* avide, cupide

grass [grɑ:s] *n* (**a**) *(plant)* herbe *f*; *Fig* **she doesn't let the g. grow under her feet** elle ne perd pas de temps; **the g. is always greener (on the other side of the fence)** c'est toujours mieux ailleurs; *Fig* **g. roots** *(of organization)* base *f*; **g.-roots support/opposition** soutien *m*/opposition *f* de la base; **g. snake** couleuvre *f* (à collier); **g. widow** = femme dont le mari est souvent en déplacement (**b**) *(lawn)* pelouse *f*, gazon *m*; **keep off the g.** *(sign)* pelouse interdite; **g. court** *(in tennis)* court *m* en gazon (**c**) *(pasture)* herbage *m*; *Fig* **to put sb out to g.** mettre qn à la retraite (**d**) *Fam (marijuana)* herbe *f*

grass-green ['grɑ:s'gri:n] *adj* vert gazon *inv*

grasshopper ['grɑ:shɒpə(r)] *n* sauterelle *f*

grassland ['grɑ:slænd] *n* prairie *f*, pré *m*

grassy ['grɑ:sɪ] *adj* herbu(e), herbeux(euse)

grate[1] [greɪt] *n (of hearth)* grille *f*; *(fireplace)* foyer *m*

grate[2] [greɪt] **1** *vt (cheese, nutmeg)* râper

   2 *vi (of machinery)* grincer; **to g. on the ear** *(of voice)* écorcher les oreilles; *(of sound)* faire mal aux oreilles; **it really grates on me** *or* **on my nerves** ça me tape vraiment sur les nerfs

grateful ['greɪtfʊl] *adj* reconnaissant(e) (**for** de); **I would be g. if you could let me know** je vous serais reconnaissant de m'en informer

gratefully ['greɪtfʊlɪ] *adv* avec reconnaissance

grater ['greɪtə(r)] *n* râpe *f*

gratification [grætɪfɪ'keɪ∫ən] *n* satisfaction *f*

gratified ['grætɪfaɪd] *adj* satisfait(e), content(e)

gratify ['grætɪfaɪ] *(pt & pp* **gratified**) *vt (person)* faire plaisir à; *(wish, desire)* satisfaire

gratifying ['grætɪfaɪɪŋ] *adj* satisfaisant(e)

grating[1] ['greɪtɪŋ] *adj (noise)* grinçant(e); *(voice)* éraillé(e)

grating[2] ['greɪtɪŋ] *n (in grille)* grille *f*

gratis ['grɑ:tɪs] *adv* gratis

gratitude ['grætɪtju:d] *n* gratitude *f*, reconnaissance *f*

gratuitous [grə'tju:ɪtəs] *adj* gratuit(e)

gratuitously [grə'tju:ɪtəslɪ] *adv* gratuitement, sans raison

gratuity [grə'tju:ɪtɪ] *(pl* **gratuities**) *n Formal (tip)* pourboire *m*

grave[1] [greɪv] **1** *n* tombe *f*; *Fig* **it would make him turn in his g.** ça le ferait se retourner dans sa tombe; **to have one foot in the g.** avoir un pied dans la tombe

   2 *adj (manner, voice)* solennel(elle); *(situation)* grave; **to make a g. mistake** se tromper lourdement

gravedigger ['greɪvdɪgə(r)] *n* fossoyeur *m*

gravel ['grævəl] *n* gravier *m*; **g. path** allée *f* de gravier; **g. pit** carrière *f* de gravier

gravelly ['grævəlɪ] *adj (sand, soil)* graveleux(euse); *(voice)* râpeux(euse)

gravely ['greɪvlɪ] *adv* gravement

graven ['greɪvən] *adj* **g. image** idole *f*

graveside ['greɪvsaɪd] *n* **at the g.** près de la tombe

gravestone ['greɪvstəun] *n* pierre *f* tombale

graveyard ['greɪvjɑːd] *n* cimetière *m*

gravitate ['græviteɪt] *vi* **to g. toward sth** *(of person)* être attiré(e) par qch; **most of the guests had gravitated toward the bar** la plupart des invités s'étaient rapprochés du bar

gravitational [grævɪ'teɪʃənəl] *adj* gravitationnel(elle); **g. pull** gravitation *f*

gravity ['grævɪtɪ] *n* **(a)** *(physical force)* gravité *f*, pesanteur *f* **(b)** *(seriousness)* gravité *f*

gravy ['greɪvɪ] *n* = sauce à base de jus de viande; **g. boat** saucière *f*; *Fam* **g. train** assiette *f* au beurre; **to get on the g. train** trouver un filon

gray [greɪ] **1** *n (color)* gris *m*
2 *adj* gris(e); *Fig (dull)* morne; **to go g.** *(gray-haired)* grisonner; *Fig* **a g. area** une zone d'ombre; **g. matter** *(brain)* matière *f* grise
3 *vi (of hair)* grisonner

gray-haired ['greɪheəd] *adj* aux cheveux gris

graying ['greɪɪŋ] *adj (hair)* grisonnant(e)

graze¹ [greɪz] **1** *vt (of farmer) (cattle)* faire paître
2 *vi (of cattle)* paître

graze² [greɪz] **1** *n* écorchure *f*; *(less serious)* égratignure *f*
2 *vt* écorcher; *(less seriously)* égratigner

grease [griːs] **1** *n* graisse *f*; **g. gun** pistolet *m* graisseur
2 *vt (machine)* graisser, lubrifier; *(cake pan)* beurrer; **to g. back one's hair** se gominer les cheveux; *Fam Fig* **to g. sb's palm** graisser la patte à qn; *Fam* **like greased lightning** en quatrième vitesse

greasepaint ['griːspeɪnt] *n* maquillage *m* de théâtre

greasy ['griːsɪ] *adj* **(a)** *(covered in grease)* graisseux(euse); *(hair, skin, food)* gras (grasse) **(b)** *Fam Pej (manner)* mielleux(euse)

great [greɪt] **1** *n* grand nom *m*
2 *adj* **(a)** *(large, important)* grand(e); **a g. many people** beaucoup de monde; **to reach a g. age** parvenir à un âge avancé; **to take g. care (of)** prendre grand soin (de); **they are g. friends** ce sont de grands amis
(b) *(in proper names)* **G. Britain** la Grande-Bretagne; **G. Dane** danois *m*; **the G. Lakes** les Grands Lacs *mpl*; **Greater London** Londres et son agglomération; *Hist* **the G. War** la Grande Guerre
(c) *Fam (very good)* formidable, génial(e); **to have a g. time** bien s'amuser
(d) *(enthusiastic)* **to be a g. knitter/reader** adorer tricoter/la lecture; **to be a g. believer in doing sth** être partisan(e) de faire qch; *Fam* **she's a g. one for having everything planned in advance** avec elle, on peut être sûr que tout sera préparé à l'avance
3 *adv Fam* **(a)** *(well)* très bien; **to feel g.** se sentir en super forme
(b) *(for emphasis)* **a g. big dog** un chien énorme; **you g. fat slob!** espèce de gros tas!

great-aunt ['greɪtɑːnt] *n* grand-tante *f*

greatcoat ['greɪtkəut] *n* pardessus *m*

great-grandchild ['greɪt'græntʃaɪld] *(pl* **great-grandchildren** ['greɪt'græntʃɪldrən] *) n (boy)* arrière-petit-fils *m*; *(girl)* arrière-petite-fille *f*; **great-grandchildren** arrière-petits-enfants *mpl*

great-granddaughter ['greɪt'grændɔːtə(r)] *n* arrière-petite-fille *f*

great-grandfather ['greɪt'grænfɑːðə(r)] *n* arrière-grand-père *m*

great-grandmother ['greɪt'grænmʌðə(r)] *n* arrière-grand-mère *f*

great-grandparents ['greɪt'grænpeərənts] *npl* arrière-grands-parents *mpl*

great-grandson ['greɪt'grænsʌn] *n* arrière-petit-fils *m*

greatly ['greɪtlɪ] *adv* très

greatness ['greɪtnɪs] *n* **(a)** *(of person, action)* grandeur *f*; **to achieve g.** rejoindre les plus grands **(b)** *(of thing, problem)* importance *f*

great-uncle ['greɪtʌŋkəl] *n* grand-oncle *m*

grebe [griːb] *n* grèbe *m*

Grecian ['griːʃən] *adj* grec (grecque)

Greece [griːs] *n* la Grèce

greed [griːd] *n (for food)* gourmandise *f*; *(for money)* avidité *f*, cupidité *f*; *(for fame, power)* recherche *f* avide (**for** de)

greedily ['griːdɪlɪ] *adv (eat)* goulûment; *(look, say)* avec gourmandise

greediness ['griːdɪnɪs] = **greed**

greedy ['griːdɪ] *adj (for food)* gourmand(e); *(for money, fame, power)* avide

Greek [griːk] **1** *n* **(a)** *(person)* Grec (Grecque) *m,f* **(b)** *(language)* grec *m*; **modern G.** le grec moderne; *Fam* **it's all G. to me** c'est de l'hébreu pour moi
2 *adj* grec (grecque); **G. salad** salade *f* grecque

green [griːn] **1** *n* **(a)** *(color)* vert *m* **(b)** **greens** *(vegetables)* légumes *mpl* verts **(c)** *(grassy area)* pelouse *f*, gazon *m*; *(in golf)* green *m* **(d)** *(environmentalist)* écologiste *mf*
2 *adj* **(a)** *(color)* vert(e); **to go** *or* **to turn g.** *(of traffic lights)* passer au vert; *(of person, fields)* verdir; **to be g. with envy** être vert de jalousie; *Fig* **to give sb the g. light (to do sth)** donner le feu vert à qn (pour faire qch); **to have a g. thumb** avoir la main verte; **g. beans** haricots *mpl* verts; **g. belt** zone *f* verte; **g. card** ≃ carte *f* de séjour; **g. salad** salade *f* verte **(b)** *(young, inexperienced)* jeune, inexpérimenté(e); *(naive)* naïf (naïve) **(c)** *(environmentalist)* écologiste; **the G. Party** le parti écologiste, les Verts *mpl*

greenback ['griːnbæk] *n Fam* billet *m* vert

greenery ['griːnərɪ] *n* verdure *f*

green-eyed ['griːnaɪd] *adj* aux yeux verts; **the g. monster** la jalousie

greenfield ['griːnfiːld] *n* **g. site** terrain *m* non-bâti *(à l'extérieur d'une ville)*

greenfly ['griːnflaɪ] *(pl* **greenflies**) *n* puceron *m*

greengage ['griːngeɪdʒ] *n* reine-claude *f*

greenhouse ['griːnhaʊs] *n* serre *f*; **g. effect** effet *m* de serre

Greenland ['griːnlənd] *n* le Groenland

Greenlander ['griːnləndə(r)] *n* Groenlandais(e) *m,f*

Greenwich Mean Time ['grenɪtʃ'miːntaɪm] *n* temps *m* universel

greet [griːt] *vt (say hello to)* saluer; *(welcome) (person, idea)* accueillir

greeting ['griːtɪŋ] *n* salut *m*; *(more formal)* salutation *f*; **New Year greetings** vœux *mpl* de bonne année; **g. card** carte *f* de vœux

gregarious [grɪ'geərɪəs] *adj* sociable

gremlin ['gremlɪn] *n Fam* diablotin *m*

Grenada [grə'neɪdə] *n* la Grenade

grenade [grə'neɪd] *n* grenade *f*

grenadier [grenə'dɪə(r)] *n* grenadier *m*

grenadine ['grenədiːn] *n* grenadine *f*

grew [gruː] *pt of* **grow**

grey = **gray**

greyhound ['greɪhaʊnd] *n* lévrier *m*; **g. racing** courses *fpl* de lévriers; **g. stadium** cynodrome *m*

grid [grɪd] *n* (**a**) *(bars)* grille *f*, grillage *m* (**b**) *(on map)* quadrillage *m*; **g. layout** *(of town)* quadrillage, damier *m*; **g. reference** coordonnées *fpl*

griddle ['grɪdəl] *n (for cooking)* tôle *f*

gridiron ['grɪdaɪən] *n* (**a**) *(for cooking)* gril *m* (**b**) *(football)* football *m* américain; *(playing field)* terrain *m* de football

gridlock ['grɪdlɒk] *n* embouteillage *m* monstre

gridlocked ['grɪdlɒkt] *adj (road, negotiations)* bloqué(e)

grief [griːf] *n* (**a**) *(pain)* chagrin *m*; **to come to g.** échouer; *Fam* **good g.!** mon Dieu!; **g. counselor** = personne apportant une aide psychologique aux personnes frappées par un deuil (**b**) *Fam (hassle)* **to give sb g.** embêter qn

grief-stricken ['griːfstrɪkən] *adj* accablé(e) de douleur *ou* de chagrin

grievance ['griːvəns] *n* (**a**) *(resentment)* grief *m* (**b**) *(complaint)* doléance *f*; **to air one's grievances** exprimer ses doléances; *Ind* **g. procedure** procédure *f* pour porter plainte

grieve [griːv] **1** *vt* chagriner, affliger
2 *vi* **to g. for sb/over sth** pleurer qn/qch

grieving ['griːvɪŋ] *adj* éploré(e)

grievous ['griːvəs] *adj Formal* grave; *Law* **g. bodily harm** coups *mpl* et blessures *fpl*

grievously ['griːvəslɪ] *adv (seriously)* gravement; **you are g. mistaken** vous commettez une grave erreur

griffin ['grɪfɪn] *n* griffon *m*

grill [grɪl] **1** *n (for cooking)* gril *m*
2 *vt* (**a**) *(cook)* griller (**b**) *Fam (interrogate)* cuisiner

grille [grɪl] *n (bars)* grille *f*; (**radiator**) **g.** *(on car)* calandre *f*

grilling ['grɪlɪŋ] *n Fam (interrogation)* **to give sb a g.** cuisiner qn

grim [grɪm] *adj* (**a**) *(stern)* sévère; *(gloomy) (place)* sinistre; *(news, report)* sombre; **to hang on like g. death** se cramponner; **to look g.** *(of person) (serious)* avoir l'air sombre; *(ill)* avoir très mauvaise mine (**b**) *Fam (bad)* lamentable; **how do you feel? – pretty g.!** comment te sens-tu? – pas terrible!

grimace ['grɪməs] **1** *n* grimace *f*
2 *vi* grimacer, faire la grimace

grime [graɪm] *n* saleté *f*

grimly ['grɪmlɪ] *adv (fight, hold on)* avec acharnement

grimy ['graɪmɪ] *adj* encrassé(e)

grin [grɪn] **1** *n* grand sourire *m*
2 *vi (pt & pp* **grinned**) faire un grand sourire (**at** à); *Fig* **to g. and bear it** tâcher de garder le sourire

grind [graɪnd] **1** *n Fam (work)* corvée *f*; **the daily g.** le train-train quotidien
2 *vt (pt & pp* **ground** [graʊnd]) (**a**) *(grain, coffee)* moudre; **to g. one's teeth** grincer des dents (**b**) *(glass, gems)* dépolir
3 *vi (of wheels, gears)* grisser; **to g. to a halt** *(of car, machine)* s'immobiliser; *(of project, economy)* s'arrêter

▶**grind down** *vt sep Fig* venir à bout de

▶**grind on** *vi (proceed relentlessly)* ne pas en finir

▶**grind out** *vt sep (article, novel)* pondre

grinder ['graɪndə(r)] *n (for coffee, pepper)* moulin *m*; *(for polishing)* polissoire *f*; *(for sharpening)* meule *f*

grinding ['graɪndɪŋ] *adj (poverty)* extrême; **to come to a g. halt** *(of car, machine)* s'immobiliser; *(of project, economy)* s'arrêter

grindstone ['graɪndstəʊn] *n* meule *f*; *Fig* **to keep one's nose to the g.** travailler dur

gringo ['grɪŋgəʊ] *(pl* **gringos**) *n Fam* gringo *m*

grip [grɪp] **1** *n* (**a**) *(hold, grasp)* prise *f*; **to have a strong g.** avoir une bonne poigne; **to get a g. on sth** avoir prise sur qch; *Fig* **to get to grips with sth** s'attaquer à qch; *Fig* **to get a g. on oneself** se ressaisir; *Fig* **get a g.!** reprends-toi!, ressaisis-toi!; *Fig* **to have a firm g. on a situation** avoir la situation bien en main; **to lose one's g.** lâcher prise; **to lose one's g. on sth** lâcher qch; *Fig* **to lose one's g. on reality**

perdre pied avec la réalité; *Fig* **to be in the g. of a disease/a crisis** être en proie à une maladie/une crise (**b**) *(handle)* poignée *f* (**c**) *(bag)* mallette *f*
2 *vt (pt & pp* **gripped**) *(seize)* saisir, prendre; *(hold)* empoigner, agripper; *(of tires)* adhérer à; *Fig* **to be gripped by panic** être pris(e) de panique; *Fig* **the audience was gripped by the play** la pièce a captivé les spectateurs
3 *vi (of tire)* adhérer

gripe [graɪp] **1** *n* (**a**) *Fam (complaint)* **to have a g. about sth** avoir à se plaindre de qch; **what's your g.?** de quoi te plains-tu? (**b**) *(pain)* **gripes** coliques *fpl*; **g. water** = médicament pour coliques infantiles
2 *vi Fam (complain)* ronchonner, râler (**about** à propos de)

gripping ['grɪpɪŋ] *adj* passionnant(e), palpitant(e)

grisly ['grɪzlɪ] *adj* macabre, sinistre

grist [grɪst] *n* **it's all g. to the mill** cela apporte de l'eau à mon/ton/*etc.* moulin

gristle ['grɪsəl] *n* nerfs *mpl*

gristly ['grɪslɪ] *adj* nerveux(euse)

grit [grɪt] **1** *n* (**a**) *(gravel)* gravillons *mpl*; *(in eye)* poussière *f*; *(for icy roads)* sable *m* (**b**) *(courage, determination)* cran *m* (**c**) **grits** gruau *m* de maïs
2 *vt (pt & pp* **gritted**) (**a**) *(road)* sabler (**b**) *(clench)* **to g. one's teeth** grincer des dents; *Fig* serrer les dents

gritty ['grɪtɪ] *adj* (**a**) *(soil, road)* plein(e) de gravillons (**b**) *(determined)* qui a du cran, résolu(e) (**c**) **g. realism** réalisme *m* cru

grizzled ['grɪzəld] *adj (hair, person)* grisonnant(e)

grizzly ['grɪzlɪ] *n (pl* **grizzlies**) **g. (bear)** grizzly *m*
2 *adj (hair, person)* grisonnant(e)

groan [grəʊn] **1** *n (of pain)* gémissement *m*; *(of disappointment, dismay)* grognement *m*; *(of chair, floor)* grincement *m*
2 *vi (in pain)* gémir, pousser un gémissement; *(in disappointment, dismay)* grogner, pousser un grognement; **to g. under the weight of sth** *(of shelf, chair)* se creuser sous le poids de qch

grocer ['grəʊsə(r)] *n* épicier(ère) *m,f*; **g.'s (shop)** épicerie *f*

groceries ['grəʊsərɪz] *npl (provisions)* provisions *fpl*

grocery ['grəʊsərɪ] *(pl* **groceries**) *n* **g. (store)** épicerie *f*

grog [grɒg] *n Fam* grog *m*

groggy ['grɒgɪ] *adj Fam* groggy *inv*

groin [grɔɪn] *n* aine *f*

groom [gruːm] **1** *n* (**a**) *(of horse)* palefrenier *m* (**b**) *(at wedding)* marié *m*
2 *vt (horse)* panser; *(dog)* toiletter; *Fig (candidate)* préparer

groomed [gruːmd] *adj* soigné(e); **to be well-g.** *(of person)* être soigné(e) de sa personne; *(of horse)* être bien entretenu(e)

groove [gruːv] *n (in wood, metal)* rainure *f*; *(in record)* sillon *m*; *Fig* **to get stuck in a g.** s'encroûter

groovy ['gruːvɪ] *adj Fam* chouette

grope [grəʊp] **1** *vt* (**a**) **to g. one's way forward** avancer à tâtons (**b**) *Fam (sexually)* peloter, tripoter
2 *vi* **to g. (about) for sth** chercher qch à tâtons

gross [grəʊs] **1** *n (pl* **gross**) *(quantity)* grosse *f*, douze douzaines *fpl*
2 *adj* (**a**) *(fat)* obèse (**b**) *(blatant) (error)* grossier(ère); *(ignorance)* crasse; *(abuse)* choquant(e); *(injustice)* flagrant(e); *Law* **g. negligence** négligence *f* coupable (**c**) *(vulgar)* grossier(ère) (**d**) *(profit, income, weight)* brut(e); *Econ* **g. domestic product** produit *m* intérieur brut; **g. national product** produit national brut (**e**) *Fam (disgusting)* dégueulasse
3 *vt (profit)* gagner brut; **to g. $40,000 a year** gagner brut 40 000 dollars par an

▶**gross out** *vt sep Fam* dégoûter, débecter

grossly ['grəʊslɪ] *adv (exaggerated)* grossièrement; *(negligent)* extrêmement; *(unfair)* vraiment; **g. overweight** obèse

grotesque [grəʊ'tesk] *adj* grotesque

grotto ['grɒtəʊ] (*pl* **grottoes** *or* **grottos**) *n* grotte *f*

grouch [graʊtʃ] *Fam* **1** *n* (**a**) *(person)* râleur(euse) *m,f* (**b**) *(complaint)* plainte *f*

2 *vi* râler, ronchonner (**about** à propos de)

grouchy ['graʊtʃɪ] *adj Fam* râleur(euse), ronchon(onne)

ground [graʊnd] **1** *n* (**a**) *(earth)* sol *m*, terre *f*; **to sit on the g.** s'asseoir par terre; **above g.** en surface; **below g.** sous terre; **burnt to the g.** entièrement brûlé(e); *Fig* **to get off the g.** *(of project)* démarrer; *Fig* **to work oneself into the g.** se tuer au travail; **to go to g.** se cacher; **to run sb to g.** traquer qn; **g. control** contrôle *m* au sol; **g. crew** personnel *m* au sol; **g. floor** rez-de chaussée *m*; *Mil* **g. forces** forces *fpl* au sol; **g. frost** gelée *f* blanche; **at g. level** au rez-de-chaussée; **g. rules** règles *fpl* de base

(**b**) *(land)* terrain *m*; *Fig* **to find common g. for negotiations** trouver un terrain d'entente en vue de négociations; **to be sure of one's g.** être sûr(e) de son fait; *Fig* **to be on shaky g.** être en terrain miné; *Fig* **to change** *or* **to shift one's g.** changer de tactique; *Fig* **to break new g.** faire œuvre de pionnier; *Fig* **to cover a lot of g.** *(of book, lecture)* couvrir de très nombreux domaines; *Fig* **to gain g. on sb** gagner du terrain sur qn; *Fig* **to lose g.** se perdre du terrain sur qn; *Fig* **to stand** *or* **to hold one's g.** tenir bon

(**c**) **grounds** *(of school, hospital, country house)* parc *m*

(**d**) **grounds** *(reasons)* raisons *fpl*, motifs *mpl*; **to have (good) grounds for doing sth** avoir de bonnes raisons de faire qch; **on grounds of ill-health** pour raisons de santé; *Law* **grounds for divorce** motif *m* de divorce

2 *adj (coffee, pepper)* moulu(e); **g. meat** viande *f* hachée

3 *vt* (**a**) *(base)* baser, appuyer (**on** sur)

(**b**) *(educate)* **to g. sb in sth** former qn à qch

(**c**) *(electrical current)* mettre à la masse

(**d**) *(airplane)* interdire de vol

(**e**) *(prevent from going out)* priver de sortie; **you're grounded** tu n'as pas le droit de sortir

4 *pt & pp of* **grind**

ground-breaking ['graʊndbreɪkɪŋ] *adv* révolutionnaire

groundhog ['graʊndhɒg] *n* marmotte *f* d'Amérique

grounding ['graʊndɪŋ] *n* (**a**) *(basis)* fondement *m* (**b**) *(basic knowledge)* bases *fpl* (**in** de *ou* en)

groundless ['graʊndlɪs] *adj* sans fondement

groundsheet ['graʊndʃiːt] *n* tapis *m* de sol

groundskeeper ['graʊndzkiːpə(r)] *n* = responsable de l'entretien d'un terrain de sport

groundswell ['graʊndswel] *n* **a g. of support** un raz-de-marée

groundwork ['graʊndwɜːk] *n* travail *m* préparatoire; **to do** *or* **to lay the g. (for sth)** préparer le terrain (pour qch)

group [gruːp] **1** *n* groupe *m*; **g. booking** réservation *f* de groupe; **g. decision** décision *f* collective; **g. dynamics** dynamique *f* de groupe; **g. photograph** photographie *f* de groupe; **g. therapy** thérapie *f* de groupe

2 *vt* grouper

3 *vi* se grouper

groupie ['gruːpɪ] *n Fam* groupie *f*

grouping ['gruːpɪŋ] *n (of people)* groupe *m*

grouse[1] [graʊs] (*pl* **grouse**) *n (bird)* tétras *m*, grouse *f*

grouse[2] [graʊs] *Fam* **1** *n (complaint)* **to have a g. (about sth)** avoir des raisons de se plaindre (de qch)

2 *vi* ronchonner, grogner (**about** au sujet de)

grout [graʊt] *n* mastic *m*

grove [grəʊv] *n* bosquet *m*

grovel ['grɒvəl] *vi (on ground)* être à quatre pattes; **to g. to sb** ramper *ou* s'aplatir devant qn

groveling ['grɒvəlɪŋ] *adj* obséquieux(euse)

grow [grəʊ] (*pt* **grew** [gruː], *pp* **grown** [grəʊn]) **1** *vt* (**a**) *(vegetables)* cultiver; *(flowers)* faire pousser; **to g. a beard** se laisser

pousser la barbe; **to g. one's hair** se laisser pousser les cheveux (**b**) *Com (company)* développer

2 *vi* (**a**) *(increase in size)* *(plant)* pousser; *(person, animal)* grandir; *(problem)* s'aggraver; *(economy, feeling)* croître; *Fam* **it'll g. on you** *(of music, book)* tu finiras par t'y intéresser (**b**) grow *(become)* devenir; **to g. old** vieillir; **to g. angry** se fâcher (**c**) *(come eventually)* **to g. to like sth** finir par aimer qch

▸**grow apart** *vi (of people)* s'éloigner

▸**grow out of** *vt insep* (**a**) *(become too big for)* **he's grown out of his shoes** ses chaussures sont maintenant trop petites pour lui (**b**) *(become too old for)* **she grew out of her dolls** elle a passé l'âge de jouer à la poupée; **most children g. out of such behavior** la plupart des enfants cessent de se conduire ainsi en grandissant

▸**grow up** *vi (become adult)* grandir; **when I g. up** quand je serai grand; **when I was growing up** quand j'étais petit; *Fam* **g. up!** ne fais pas l'enfant!

grower ['grəʊə(r)] *n (person)* cultivateur(trice) *m,f*; *(of trees, flowers)* horticulteur(trice) *m,f*

growing ['grəʊɪŋ] *adj (child)* en pleine croissance; *(town, population)* en pleine expansion; *(debt)* qui augmente, qui va croissant; *(discontent)* croissant(e); **there was a g. fear that...** on craignait de plus en plus que...; **g. pains** *(of child)* douleurs *fpl* de croissance; *Fig (of firm, country)* difficultés *fpl* de croissance

growl [graʊl] **1** *n (of dog)* grondement *m*

2 *vi (of dog)* gronder; *(of person)* grogner, grommeler (**at** contre)

growling ['graʊlɪŋ] *n (of dog)* grondement *m*

grown [grəʊn] **1** *adj* grand(e); **a g. woman** une adulte; **to be fully g.** avoir atteint sa taille adulte

2 *pp of* **grow**

grown-up 1 *n* ['grəʊnʌp] grand(e) *m,f*, grande personne *f*; **the grown-ups** les grands, les grandes personnes

2 *adj* [grəʊn'ʌp] *(person, topic)* adulte; **he was very g. about it** il a fait preuve de beaucoup de maturité

growth [grəʊθ] *n* (**a**) *(of person, plant, economy)* croissance *f*; *(of population, demand)* augmentation *f*; **a week's g. of beard** une barbe d'une semaine; **g. area** secteur *m* en expansion; **g. industry** industrie *f* en expansion (**b**) *(tumor)* grosseur *f*

grub [grʌb] *n* (**a**) *(larva)* larve *f* (**b**) *Fam (food)* bouffe *f*

▸**grub about, grub around** (*pt & pp* **grubbed**) *vi Fam* farfouiller (**for sth** pour trouver qch)

grubby ['grʌbɪ] *adj* crasseux(euse)

grudge [grʌdʒ] **1** *n* rancune *f*; **to bear sb a g.** en vouloir à qn

2 *vt* (**a**) *(give unwillingly)* **to g. sb sth** donner qch à qn à contrecœur (**b**) *(resent)* **to g. doing sth** faire qch à contrecœur; **she grudges him his success** elle lui en veut parce qu'il a réussi

grudging ['grʌdʒɪŋ] *adj* accordé(e) à contrecœur; **to be g. in one's praise** être avare de compliments

grudgingly ['grʌdʒɪŋlɪ] *adv* à contrecœur

gruel ['gruːəl] *n* gruau *m*

grueling ['gruːəlɪŋ] *adj (journey, experience)* épuisant(e)

gruesome ['gruːsəm] *adj* abominable, horrible; **to relate sth in g. detail** raconter qch jusqu'aux détails les plus horribles

gruesomely ['gruːsəmlɪ] *adv* abominablement

gruff [grʌf] *adj (tone, manner)* bourru(e); *(voice)* gros (grosse)

gruffly ['grʌflɪ] *adv* d'un ton bourru

grumble ['grʌmbəl] **1** *n* grommellement *m*, grognement *m*; **she obeyed without so much as a g.** elle a obéi sans la moindre protestation

2 *vi (of person)* grommeler; *(of stomach)* gargouiller; **to g. about sth** rouspéter contre qch; **(I) mustn't g.** il ne faut pas se plaindre

grumbler ['grʌmblə(r)] *n* grincheux(euse) *m,f*

grumbling ['grʌmblɪŋ] **1** *n* ronchonnements *mpl*

2 *adj* grognon(onne); **g. appendix** appendicite *f* chronique

grump [grʌmp] n Fam grincheux(euse) m,f

grumpily ['grʌmpɪlɪ] adv en ronchonnant

grumpy ['grʌmpɪ] adj grognon(onne)

grunge [grʌndʒ] n (music, fashion) grunge m

grunt [grʌnt] **1** n (**a**) (of pig, person) grognement m; **to give a g.** pousser un grognement (**b**) Fam Mil (soldier) troufion m
2 vi (of pig, person) grogner

GSM ['dʒi:es'em] n Tel (abbr **global system for mobile communication**) GSM m

Guadeloupe [gwɑːdə'luːp] n la Guadeloupe

guarantee [gærən'tiː] **1** n (spoken, written) garantie f; **she gave me her g. that it wouldn't happen again** elle m'a assuré que cela ne se reproduirait plus; **there's no g. that she'll come** ce n'est pas sûr qu'elle vienne; Com **under g.** sous garantie
2 vt garantir; **I can't g. that she'll come** je ne garantis pas qu'elle viendra; **the watch is guaranteed for two years** cette montre est garantie deux ans; Fin **to g. sb against loss** garantir qn contre les pertes

guaranteed [gærən'tiːd] adj garanti(e)

guarantor [gærən'tɔː(r)] n garant(e) m,f

guard [gɑːd] **1** n (**a**) (defenses) **to be on one's g.** être sur ses gardes; **to put sb on his g.** mettre qn en garde; **to put sb off his g.** déjouer la vigilance de qn; **to catch sb off his g.** prendre qn au dépourvu; **his g. was down** il ne se méfiait pas (**b**) (supervision) garde f; **to keep sb under g.** garder qn sous surveillance; **to be on g. duty** être de garde; **g. dog** chien m de garde (**c**) (sentry) garde m; (in prison) gardien m; Mil (group of sentries) garde f; **g. of honor** garde f d'honneur (**d**) (device) (on machine) protection f (**e**) (in basketball) défenseur m
2 vt garder; **to g. sb from danger** protéger qn d'un danger
▸**guard against** vt insep se prémunir contre; **he was keen to g. against any further mistakes** il prenait garde de ne pas commettre de nouvelles erreurs

guarded ['gɑːdɪd] adj circonspect(e), prudent(e)

guardedly ['gɑːdɪdlɪ] adv avec circonspection, avec prudence

guardhouse ['gɑːdhaʊs] n Mil poste m de garde; (prison) prison f

guardian ['gɑːdɪən] n (of standards) gardien(enne) m,f; Law (of minor) tuteur(trice) m,f; **g. angel** ange m gardien

guardianship ['gɑːdɪənʃɪp] n Law (of minor) tutelle f

guardrail ['gɑːdreɪl] n garde-fou m, parapet m; (on ship) bastingage m

guardroom ['gɑːdruːm] n corps m de garde

Guatemala [gwætɪ'mɑːlə] n le Guatemala

Guatemalan [gwætɪ'mɑːlən] **1** n Guatémaltèque mf
2 adj guatémaltèque

guava ['gwɑːvə] n goyave f; **g. tree** goyavier m

guerrilla [gə'rɪlə] n guérillero m; **g. warfare** guérilla f

guess [ges] **1** n estimation f; **to have** or **to make a g.** deviner; Ironic **I'll give you three guesses!** devine!; **at a g., (I'd say) three hundred** je dirais environ trois cents; **your g. is as good as mine** j'en ai pas la moindre idée; **it's anybody's g.** qui sait?
2 vt (**a**) (attempt to answer) deviner; **g. who I saw!** devine qui j'ai vu!; **g. what!** tu sais quoi?; **you've guessed it!** tu as deviné! (**b**) (suppose) supposer, croire; **I g. you're right** tu dois avoir raison
3 vi deviner; **to g. right** deviner juste; **to g. wrong** se tromper; **to keep sb guessing** laisser qn dans l'ignorance; **to g. at sth** essayer de deviner qch

guessing game ['gesɪŋ geɪm] n jeu m de devinettes; Fig **it's a bit of a g.** on ne peut que spéculer

guesstimate ['gestɪmɪt] n Fam calcul m au pif

guesswork ['geswɜːk] n conjecture f; **it's pure** or **sheer g.** c'est de la pure conjecture

guest [gest] n (at home, party, on TV show) invité(e) m,f; (at hotel) client(e) m,f; **be my g.!** je t'en prie!; **to make a g. appearance** (on TV show) passer en invité vedette; (in movie) participer à titre exceptionnel; **g. artist** invité vedette; **g. room** chambre f d'amis; **g. speaker** conférencier(ère) m,f (invité par une organisation ou une association); **g. star** invité(e) m,f vedette; **g. worker** travailleur(euse) m,f immigré(e)

guesthouse ['gesthaʊs] n pension f de famille

guff [gʌf] n Fam âneries fpl

guffaw [gʌ'fɔː] **1** n gros rire m
2 vi s'esclaffer

GUI ['guːɪ] n Comput (abbr **Graphical User Interface**) interface f utilisateur graphique

Guiana [gaɪ'ɑːnə] n la Guyane

guidance ['gaɪdəns] n direction f; **under the g. of** sous la direction de; **for your g.** à titre d'information; **g. counselor** conseiller(ère) m,f d'orientation

guide [gaɪd] **1** n (**a**) (person) guide m; **g. dog** chien m d'aveugle (**b**) (book) guide m (**to** de) (**c**) (indication) indication f (**to** sur); **as a g.** à titre indicatif
2 vt guider; **to be guided by sth** suivre qch

guidebook ['gaɪdbʊk] n guide m

guided ['gaɪdɪd] adj **g. missile** missile m guidé; **g. tour** visite f guidée

guideline ['gaɪdlaɪn] n (indication) indication f; **guidelines** directives fpl; **as a general g.** en règle générale

guiding ['gaɪdɪŋ] adj (principle, concept) directeur(trice)

guild [gɪld] n (association) association f

guilder ['gɪldə] n florin m

guile [gaɪl] n ruse f

guileless ['gaɪllɪs] adj candide

guillemot ['gɪlɪmɒt] n guillemot m

guillotine ['gɪləti:n] **1** n (for execution) guillotine f; (for cutting paper) massicot m
2 vt (execute) guillotiner

guilt [gɪlt] n culpabilité f; **to feel g.** se sentir coupable; **g. complex** complexe m de culpabilité; **to be on a g. trip** culpabiliser

guiltily ['gɪltɪlɪ] adv d'un air coupable

guiltless ['gɪltlɪs] adj innocent(e)

guilty ['gɪltɪ] adj coupable; **to find sb g./not g.** déclarer qn coupable/non coupable; **to feel g.** se sentir coupable; **to have a g. conscience** avoir mauvaise conscience; **g. secret** secret m inavouable

Guinea ['gɪnɪ] n la Guinée

guinea ['gɪnɪ] n **g. fowl** pintade f; **g. pig** cobaye m, cochon m d'Inde; Fig **to be a g. pig** servir de cobaye

Guinea-Bissau ['gɪnɪbɪ'saʊ] n la Guinée-Bissau

Guinean [gɪ'neɪən] **1** n Guinéen(enne) m,f
2 adj guinéen(enne)

guise [gaɪz] n apparence f; **in** or **under the g. of** sous l'apparence de; **in a different g.** sous une autre forme

guitar [gɪ'tɑː(r)] n guitare f

guitarist [gɪ'tɑːrɪst] n guitariste mf

gulch [gʌltʃ] n ravin m

gulf [gʌlf] n (**a**) (bay) golfe m; **the (Persian) G.** le golfe Persique; **the G. of Mexico** le golfe du Mexique; **the G. Stream** le Gulf Stream; **the G. War** la guerre du Golfe; **G. War syndrome** syndrome m de la guerre du Golfe (**b**) (between people, ideas) abîme m, gouffre m (**between** entre)

gull [gʌl] n mouette f, goéland m

gullet ['gʌlɪt] n gosier m

gullibility [gʌlɪ'bɪlɪtɪ] n crédulité f

gullible ['gʌlɪbəl] adj crédule

gully ['gʌlɪ] n (pl **gullies**) n petit ravin m

gulp [gʌlp] **1** n (**a**) (of food) bouchée f; (of drink) gorgée f; **in** or **at one g.** d'un coup (**b**) (of surprise) serrement m de gorge

2 vt *(food, drink)* engloutir

3 vi *(with surprise)* avoir un serrement de gorge

►**gulp down** vt sep *(food, drink)* engloutir

gum [gʌm] **1** n (**a**) *(in mouth)* gencive f; **g. disease** gingivite f (**b**) *(adhesive)* colle f (**c**) **(chewing) g.** chewing gum m (**d**) *(resin)* **g. arabic** gomme f arabique; **g. tree** gommier m

2 vt *(pt & pp* **gummed***) (stick)* coller

►**gum up** vt sep *(mechanism)* enrayer; *(eyes)* coller

gumboot ['gʌmbuːt] n botte f de caoutchouc

gummed [gʌmd] adj gommé(e)

gummy ['gʌmɪ] adj collant(e)

gumption ['gʌmʃən] n Fam *(common sense)* jugeote f; *(courage)* cran m

gumshield ['gʌmʃiːld] n protège-dents m inv

gumshoe ['gʌmʃuː] n (**a**) *(rubber overshoe)* caoutchouc m (**b**) Fam *(private detective)* privé m

gun [gʌn] **1** n (**a**) *(pistol)* pistolet m; *(rifle)* fusil m; *(artillery piece)* canon m; **g. carriage** affût m de canon; **g. control** contrôle m du port d'armes; **g. dog** chien m d'arrêt; **g. laws** législation f sur les armes à feu; **g. license** permis m de port d'armes (**b**) *(idioms)* Fam **big g.** huile f; Fam **to be going great guns** marcher très fort; **to stick to one's guns** tenir bon; **to jump the g.** s'emballer

2 vt *(pt & pp* **gunned***) (engine)* accélérer

►**gun down** vt sep abattre

►**gun for** vt insep **to be gunning for sb** en avoir après qn; **she's gunning for his job** elle fait tout ce qu'elle peut pour lui prendre son poste

gunboat ['gʌnbəʊt] n cannonière f; **g. diplomacy** politique f de la cannonière

gunfight ['gʌnfaɪt] n fusillade f

gunfire ['gʌnfaɪə(r)] n *(of artillery)* tirs mpl d'artillerie; *(of smaller guns)* coups mpl de feu

gung-ho [gʌŋ'həʊ] adj (**a**) *(overly enthusiastic)* d'un enthousiasme irritant (**b**) *(keen for war)* va-t-en-guerre inv

gunk [gʌŋk] n Fam matière f gluante

gunman ['gʌnmən] n homme m armé

gunner ['gʌnə(r)] n artilleur m

gunpoint ['gʌnpɔɪnt] n **at g.** sous la menace d'une arme à feu

gunpowder ['gʌnpaʊdə(r)] n poudre f (à canon)

gunrunner ['gʌnrʌnə(r)] n trafiquant(e) m,f d'armes

gunrunning ['gʌnrʌnɪŋ] n trafic m d'armes

gunship ['gʌnʃɪp] n (**helicopter**) **g.** hélicoptère m de combat

gunshot ['gʌnʃɒt] n coup m de feu; **g. wound** blessure f par balle

gunsmith ['gʌnsmɪθ] n armurier m

gunwale ['gʌnəl] n Naut plat-bord m

gurgle ['gɜːgəl] **1** n *(of liquid)* gargouillement m; *(of baby)* gazouillis m

2 vi *(of liquid)* gargouiller; *(of baby)* gazouiller

gurney ['gɜːnɪ] n chariot m d'hôpital

guru ['gʊruː] n gourou m

gush [gʌʃ] **1** n *(of water)* jaillissement m; Fig *(of words)* flot m

2 vi (**a**) *(of water)* jaillir; **tears gushed from her eyes** elle

pleurait à chaudes larmes (**b**) Pej *(talk effusively)* s'extasier (**over** or **about** devant)

gushing ['gʌʃɪŋ] adj Pej *(person, praise)* exubérant(e)

gusset ['gʌsɪt] n soufflet m

gust [gʌst] **1** n *(of wind)* rafale f; *(of hot air)* bouffée f

2 vi *(of wind)* souffler par rafales

gusto ['gʌstəʊ] n enthousiasme m; **with (great) g.** avec (beaucoup d')enthousiasme

gusty ['gʌstɪ] adj *(wind)* qui souffle par rafales; *(day, weather)* de grand vent

gut [gʌt] **1** n (**a**) *(intestine)* intestin m; Fam **guts** *(of person, machine)* entrailles fpl; Fam **to sweat** or **to work one's guts out** se tuer à la tâche; Fam **to hate sb's guts** ne pas pouvoir sentir qn; **a g. feeling** une intuition; **g. reaction** réaction f viscérale (**b**) Fam *(stomach)* bide m (**c**) Fam **guts** *(courage)* cran m; **I didn't have the guts to tell them** je n'ai pas eu le courage de le leur dire

2 vt *(pt & pp* **gutted***)* (**a**) *(fish)* vider (**b**) *(building)* *(of fire)* ravager; *(of builder)* vider entièrement

gutless ['gʌtlɪs] adj Fam lâche

gutsy ['gʌtsɪ] adj Fam courageux(euse), qui a du cran

gutter ['gʌtə(r)] **1** n *(in street)* caniveau m; *(on roof)* gouttière f; Fig **to end up in the g.** finir sous les ponts; Fig **to drag oneself out of the g.** se sortir de la misère; Fam Pej **g. press** presse f à scandales

2 vi *(of candle)* vaciller

guttural ['gʌtərəl] adj guttural(e)

guy[1] [gaɪ] n Fam (**a**) *(man)* type m, mec m; **a tough g.** un dur (**b**) *(person)* **hi guys!** salut la compagnie!

guy[2] [gaɪ] n **g. (rope)** *(for tent)* tendeur m

Guyana [gaɪ'ænə] n le Guyana

Guyanese [gaɪə'niːz] **1** n Guyanais(e) m,f

2 adj guyanais(e)

guzzle ['gʌzəl] vt Fam *(food)* engloutir; *(drink)* siffler

gym [dʒɪm] n *(gymnasium)* gymnase m; *(gymnastics)* gym f; **g. shoes** chaussures fpl de gym

gymkhana [dʒɪm'kɑːnə] n concours m hippique

gymnasium [dʒɪm'neɪzɪəm] n gymnase m

gymnast ['dʒɪmnæst] n gymnaste mf

gymnastic [dʒɪm'næstɪk] adj gymnastique

gymnastics [dʒɪm'næstɪks] **1** n gymnastique f

2 npl Fig **mental/verbal g.** gymnastique f intellectuelle/verbale

gynecological [gaɪnɪkə'lɒdʒɪkəl] adj gynécologique

gynecologist [gaɪnɪ'kɒlədʒɪst] n gynécologue mf

gynecology [gaɪnɪ'kɒlədʒɪ] n gynécologie f

gypsum ['dʒɪpsəm] n gypse m

gypsy = **gipsy**

gyrate [dʒaɪ'reɪt] vi *(of planet, sphere)* tourner; *(of dancer)* tournoyer

gyration [dʒaɪ'reɪʃən] n giration f

gyro ['dʒaɪrəʊ] n *(kebab)* sandwich m grec

gyroscope ['dʒaɪrəskəʊp] n gyroscope m

H

H, h [eɪtʃ] *n (letter)* H, h *m inv;* **H bomb** bombe *f* H

haberdashery ['hæbədæʃərɪ] *(pl* **haberdasheries)** *n (men's clothes, store)* chemiserie *f*

habit ['hæbɪt] *n* (**a**) *(custom, practice)* habitude *f;* **to be in the h. of doing sth** avoir l'habitude de faire qch; **to get into the h. of doing sth** prendre l'habitude de faire qch; **to get out of the h. of doing sth** perdre l'habitude de faire qch; **don't make a h. of it!** que cela ne devienne pas une habitude!; **from force of h.** par habitude (**b**) *Fam (addiction to drugs)* accoutumance *f;* **to kick the h.** décrocher (**c**) *(of monk, nun)* habit *m*

habitable ['hæbɪtəbəl] *adj* habitable

habitat ['hæbɪtæt] *n* habitat *m*

habitation [hæbɪ'teɪʃən] *n* habitation *f;* **there were no signs of h.** l'endroit semblait inhabité; **fit for h.** habitable; **unfit for h.** inhabitable

habitual [hə'bɪtjʊəl] *adj (generosity, rudeness)* habituel(elle); *(liar, drunk)* invétéré(e)

habitually [hə'bɪtjʊəlɪ] *adv* habituellement

habituate [hə'bɪtjʊeɪt] *vt Formal* habituer (**to** à); **to become habituated to sth** s'habituer à qch

hacienda [hæsɪ'endə] *n* ranch *m,* hacienda *f*

hack¹ [hæk] **1** *vt* (**a**) *(cut)* tailler, taillader; **to h. sb/sth to pieces** tailler qn/qch en pièces; **to h. one's way through the jungle** se frayer un chemin dans la jungle à la machette (**b**) *very Fam (cope with)* **he can't h. it** il ne s'en sort pas
2 *vi* (**a**) *(cut)* **to h. at sth** taillader qch (**b**) *(cough)* tousser d'une toux sèche

▸**hack down** *vt sep* abattre

▸**hack into** *vt insep Comput* **to hack into a system** entrer dans un système par effraction

▸**hack off** *vt sep* (**a**) *(branch, limb)* couper (**b**) *Fam* **to be hacked off (with sb/sth)** en avoir marre (de qn/qch)

hack² [hæk] *n* (**a**) *Fam Pej (journalist)* journaliste *mf* besogneux(euse); *(political activist)* militant(e) *m,f* (**b**) *(horseride)* **to go for a h.** aller faire une promenade à cheval (**c**) *Fam (taxi)* taxi *m*

hacker ['hækə(r)] *n Comput* pirate *m* informatique

hackles ['hækəlz] *npl (of dog)* poils *mpl* du cou; *(of bird)* plumes *fpl* du cou; *Fig* **to make sb's h. rise** hérisser qn

hackney ['hæknɪ] *n Formal* **h. cab** *or* **carriage** *or* **coach** *(taxi)* fiacre *m*

hackneyed ['hæknɪd] *adj (argument)* rebattu(e); *(language)* banal(e); **h. expression** lieu *m* commun

hacksaw ['hæksɔː] *n* scie *f* à métaux

had [hæd] *pt & pp of* **have**

haddock ['hædək] *(pl* **haddock** *or* **haddocks)** *n* églefin *m*

hadn't ['hædənt] = **had not**

hag [hæg] *n Pej* vieille taupe *f*

haggard ['hægəd] *adj* hâve

haggis ['hægɪs] *n* = panse de brebis farcie *(plat national écossais)*

haggle ['hægəl] *vi* marchander (**with sb** avec qn); **to h. over sth** marchander qch; **to h. about** *or* **over the price of sth** chicaner sur le prix de qch

hagiography [hægɪ'ɒgrəfɪ] *n* hagiographie *f*

Hague [heɪg] *n* **the H.** La Haye

hail¹ [heɪl] **1** *n* grêle *f; Fig* **a h. of bullets/insults** une pluie de balles/d'injures; **a h. of blows** une volée de coups
2 *vi* **it's hailing** il grêle

hail² [heɪl] *vt* (**a**) *(attract attention of)* héler (**b**) *(acclaim)* saluer (**as** comme)

▸**hail from** *vt insep* être originaire de

hailstone ['heɪlstəʊn] *n* grêlon *m*

hailstorm ['heɪlstɔːm] *n* averse *f* de grêle

hair [heə(r)] *n (on head)* cheveux *mpl; (on body, animal)* poils *mpl; (single hair) (on head)* cheveu *m; (on body, animal)* poil *m;* **to have fair/long h.** avoir les cheveux clairs/longs; **to do one's h.** se coiffer; **to comb one's h.** se peigner; **to brush one's h.** se brosser les cheveux; **to have** *or* **to get one's h. cut** se faire couper les cheveux; **if you harm** *or* **touch a h. on that child's head...** si tu touches à un cheveu de la tête de cet enfant...; **to make sb's h. stand on end** faire dresser les cheveux sur la tête à qn; *Fam* **keep your h. on!** calmez-vous!; *Fam* **get in sb's h.** enquiquiner qn; *Fig* **to let one's h. down** se laisser aller; *Fam Hum* **that'll put hairs on your chest!** ça va te donner du poil de la bête!; *Fam* **h. of the dog** *(for hangover)* = verre d'alcool pris pour calmer la gueule de bois; **h. gel** gel *m* pour les cheveux; **h. products** produits *mpl* pour les cheveux; **hair remover** *(cream)* crème *f* dépilatoire; **h. straighteners** défriseur *m*

hairband ['heəbænd] *n* bandeau *m*

hairbrush ['heəbrʌʃ] *n* brosse *f* à cheveux

haircut ['heəkʌt] *n* coupe *f* de cheveux; **to have a h.** se faire couper les cheveux

hairdo ['heəduː] *(pl* **hairdos)** *n Fam* coiffure *f*

hairdresser ['heədresə(r)] *n* coiffeur(euse) *m,f;* **to go to the h.'s** aller chez le coiffeur

hairdressing ['heədresɪŋ] *n* coiffure *f;* **h. salon** salon *m* de coiffure

hairdryer ['heədraɪə(r)] *n* sèche-cheveux *m inv*

hairless ['heəlɪs] *adj (face)* glabre; *(puppy)* sans poils

hairline ['heəlaɪn] *n* (**a**) *(of person)* naissance *f* des cheveux; **to have a receding h.** avoir le front qui se dégarnit (**b**) **h. crack** *(in pipe, wall)* légère fêlure *f;* **h. fracture** *(of bone)* fêlure *f*

hairnet ['heənet] *n* résille *f,* filet *m* à cheveux

hairpiece ['heəpiːs] *n* postiche *m*

hairpin ['heəpɪn] *n* épingle *f* à cheveux; **h. turn** *(on road)* virage *m* en épingle à cheveux

hair-raising ['heəreɪzɪŋ] *adj* à faire dresser les cheveux sur la tête

hair's-breadth ['heəzbredθ] *n* **by a h.** *(win, lose)* de justesse; **the car missed him by a h.** la voiture l'a frôlé; **to be within a h. of** être à deux doigts de

hairspray ['heəspreɪ] *n* laque *f*

hairstyle ['heəstaɪl] n coiffure f

hairy ['heərɪ] adj (a) (covered in hair) velu(e), poilu(e) (b) Fam (scary) effrayant(e)

Haiti ['heɪtɪ] n Haïti

Haitian ['heɪʃən] 1 n Haïtien(enne) m,f
2 adj haïtien(enne)

hake [heɪk] (pl **hake** or **hakes**) n merlu m, colin m

halcyon days ['hælsɪən'deɪz] npl Lit jours mpl heureux

hale [heɪl] adj vigoureux(euse); **to be h. and hearty** être en pleine forme

half [hɑːf] 1 n (pl **halves** [hɑːvz]) (a) (in general) moitié f; **h. an hour** une demi-heure; **h. past** or **after ten** dix heures et demie; **it's h. past** il est la demie; **to fold/cut sth in h.** plier/couper qch en deux; **h. a dozen** une demi-douzaine; **h. of them** la moitié d'entre eux; **to have h. a mind to do sth** avoir bien envie de faire qch; Hum **my better** or **other h.** ma moitié; **to go halves with sb** partager avec qn; Fam **you don't know the h. of it!** tu ne sais pas tout!
(b) (fraction) demie f, moitié f; **three and a h.** trois et demi
(c) **first/second h.** (in match) première/deuxième mi-temps f
2 adj demi(e); **h. board** demi-pension f; **h. day** demi-journée f; **h. hour** demi-heure f; **every h. hour** toutes les demi-heures; **h. price** demi-tarif m; **at h. price** à moitié prix
3 adv à moitié; **to h. do sth** faire qch à moitié; **h. full/empty** à moitié plein(e)/vide; **you're h. right** tu n'as pas tout à fait tort

half- [hɑːf] pref **h.-asleep** à moitié endormi(e); **h.-dead** à moitié mort(e); **h.-naked** à moitié nu(e)

half-baked [hɑːf'beɪkt] adj Fam bancal(e)

halfbreed ['hɑːfbriːd] n métis(isse) m,f

half-brother ['hɑːfbrʌðə(r)] n demi-frère m

half-caste ['hɑːfkɑːst] n métis(isse) m,f

half-cocked ['hɑːf'kɒkt] adj (gun) à moitié armé(e); Fam Fig **to go off h.** (of plan, event) avorter, échouer

half-hearted ['hɑːf'hɑːtɪd] adj (effort, performance) timide, hésitant(e); (belief, support) peu enthousiaste

half-heartedly ['hɑːf'hɑːtɪdlɪ] adv sans grand enthousiasme, sans conviction

half-hourly [hɑːf'aʊəlɪ] adv toutes les demi-heures

half-life ['hɑːflaɪf] n Phys demi-vie f

half-mast ['hɑːf'mɑːst] 1 n **at h.** (flag) en berne; Fam (socks) en accordéon

half-sister ['hɑːf'sɪstə(r)] n demi-sœur f

half-size ['hɑːf'saɪz] n (in shoes) demi-pointure f

half-timbered [hɑːf'tɪmbəd] adj Archit & Constr à colombages

half time ['hɑːf'taɪm] n (in match) mi-temps f

half-truth ['hɑːf'truːθ] n demi-vérité f

halfway [hɑːf'weɪ] 1 adj **at the h. point** (in space) à mi-chemin; (in time) à la moitié; **h. house** (for rehabilitation) centre m de réadaptation (pour anciens détenus, malades mentaux, drogués, etc.); Fig compromis m; **h. line** (on sports pitch) ligne f médiane
2 adv à mi-chemin; Fig **to meet sb h.** faire un compromis avec qn

halfwit ['hɑːfwɪt] n simple mf d'esprit

halfwitted [hɑːf'wɪtɪd] adj stupide

half-yearly ['hɑːf'jɪəlɪ] adj semestriel(elle)

halibut ['hælɪbət] (pl **halibut** or **halibuts**) n flétan m

halitosis [hælɪ'təʊsɪs] n mauvaise haleine f

hall [hɔːl] n (a) (entrance room) entrée f; (corridor) couloir m (b) (for concerts, meetings) salle f

hallmark ['hɔːlmɑːk] n (on metal) poinçon m; Fig (typical quality) signe m

hallowed ['hæləʊd] adj saint(e), béni(e)

Hallowe'en [hæləʊ'iːn] n Halloween, = veille de la Toussaint

hallucinate [hə'luːsɪneɪt] vi avoir des hallucinations

hallucination [həluːsɪ'neɪʃən] n hallucination f

hallucinatory [hə'luːsɪnətərɪ] adj hallucinatoire

hallucinogenic [həluːsɪnəʊ'dʒenɪk] adj hallucinogène

hallway ['hɔːlweɪ] n (entrance room) entrée f; (corridor) couloir m

halo ['heɪləʊ] (pl **haloes** or **halos**) n auréole f

halt [hɒlt] 1 n halte f, arrêt m; **to come to a h.** s'arrêter; **to bring sth to a h.** interrompre ou faire cesser qch; **to call a h. to sth** mettre fin à qch
2 vt interrompre
3 vi s'arrêter

halter ['hɔːltə(r)] n (a) (for horse) licou m (b) **h. top** bain m de soleil

halting ['hɔːltɪŋ] adj (voice, progress) hésitant(e)

halve [hɑːv] vt (a) (divide in two) diviser en deux; (cake, fruit) couper en deux (b) (reduce by half) réduire de moitié

halves [hɑːvz] pl of **half**

ham [hæm] 1 n (a) (meat) jambon m (b) Fam (actor) cabotin(e) m,f; **h. acting** cabotinage m
2 vt (pt & pp **hammed**) Fam (of actor) **to h. it up** en faire trop

Hamburg ['hæmbɜːg] n Hambourg

hamburger ['hæmbɜːgə(r)] n (a) (sandwich) hamburger m (b) (ground meat) viande f hachée

ham-fisted ['hæm'fɪstɪd] adj Fam maladroit(e)

hamlet ['hæmlɪt] n hameau m

hammer ['hæmə(r)] 1 n marteau m; **to come under the h.** (be auctioned) être mis(e) aux enchères; Fam **to go at it h. and tongs** mettre le paquet; **the h. and sickle** la faucille et le marteau
2 vt (a) (hit with hammer) (nail) enfoncer (**into** dans); (wall) taper à coups de marteau; Fig **to h. one's point home** insister lourdement (b) (hit with fist) (object) frapper du poing; (person) frapper à coups de poing (c) Fam (defeat) écraser

▶**hammer away at** vt insep Fig (problem) travailler avec acharnement sur

▶**hammer out** vt sep Fig (plan, compromise) mettre au point

hammering ['hæmərɪŋ] n (a) (noise) martèlement m (b) Fam (defeat) raclée f; **they gave us a real h.** ils nous ont mis une vraie raclée

hammock ['hæmək] n hamac m

hamper ['hæmpə(r)] 1 n (for laundry) panier m à linge sale
2 vt (hinder) gêner, entraver

hamster ['hæmstə(r)] n hamster m

hamstring ['hæmstrɪŋ] 1 n tendon m du jarret
2 vt (pt & pp **hamstrung** ['hæmstrʌŋ]) (incapacitate) paralyser

hand [hænd] 1 n (a) (part of body) main f; (of clock, watch) aiguille f; **to hold hands** se tenir par la main; **h. in h.** la main dans la main; **to hold sth in one's h.** tenir qch à la main; **to take sb by the h.** prendre qn par la main; **on one's hands and knees** à quatre pattes; **by h.** (make, wash) à la main; (on envelope) en ville, E.V.; **hands off!** pas touche!; **hands up!** haut les mains!; **h. baggage** bagages mpl à main; **h. basin** lavabo m; **h. cream** crème f pour les mains; **h. grenade** grenade f
(b) (worker) ouvrier(ère) m,f; (sailor) matelot m; **to be an old h. at sth** avoir une expérience considérable de qch
(c) (handwriting) **in his own h.** de sa main
(d) (in cards) main f, jeu m; Fig **to show one's h.** dévoiler son jeu; **to overplay one's h.** présumer de ses forces
(e) (idioms) **at** or **on h.** disponible; **to have sth to h.** avoir qch sous la main; **to ask for sb's h. (in marriage)** demander la main de qn; **to be in good hands** être en de bonnes mains; **to fall into the wrong hands** tomber en de mauvaises mains; **it's out of my hands** ça ne dépend plus de moi; **to change hands** (of money, car) changer de mains; **to have a h. in sth** être impliqué(e) dans qch; **to go h. in h. with sth**

aller de pair avec qch; **to try one's h. at sth** s'essayer à qch; **to turn one's h. to sth** s'essayer à qch; **to keep one's h. in** garder la main; **to give** or **to lend sb a h.** donner un coup de main à qn; **to give sb a big h.** (applaud) applaudir qn bien fort; **to suffer at sb's hands** souffrir aux mains de qn; **on (the) one h.** d'une part; **on the other h.** d'autre part; **to have time on one's hands** avoir du temps à soi; **to have a situation in h.** maîtriser une situation; **to take sb in h.** prendre qn en main; **to get out of h.** devenir incontrôlable; **to dismiss a suggestion out of h.** rejeter une proposition sur-le-champ; **to have one's hands full** être débordé(e); **to have one's hands tied** avoir les mains liées; **to be h. in glove with sb** être de mèche avec qn; **to live from h. to mouth** mener une existence précaire; **to lose money h. over fist** perdre des sommes considérables; **to make money h. over fist** gagner une fortune; **to win hands down** gagner haut la main

2 vt donner, passer; **he handed her the letter to read** il lui a passé la lettre pour qu'elle la lise; Fig **to h. sth to sb on a plate** apporter qch à qn sur un plateau; Fig **you've got to h. it to him** c'est une qualité qu'il faut lui reconnaître

▶**hand around** vt sep faire circuler

▶**hand back** vt sep rendre, repasser

▶**hand down** vt sep (a) (jewelry, tradition, skill) transmettre (b) (give) passer

▶**hand in** vt sep remettre; **to h. in one's resignation** donner sa démission

▶**hand on** vt sep transmettre

▶**hand out** vt sep distribuer

▶**hand over** vt sep donner

handbag ['hændbæg] n sac m à main

handball ['hændbɔːl] n (a) (game) handball m (b) (soccer offense) main f

handbook ['hændbʊk] n guide m, manuel m

handbrake ['hændbreɪk] n frein m à main

handcuff ['hændkʌf] vt passer les menottes à

handcuffs ['hændkʌfs] npl menottes fpl

handful ['hændfʊl] n (of sand, rice, people) poignée f; Fig **that child is a real h.** cet enfant n'est pas facile

handgun ['hændgʌn] n revolver m, pistolet m

handicap ['hændɪkæp] **1** n handicap m

2 vt (pt & pp **handicapped**) handicaper

handicapped ['hændɪkæpt] **1** npl **the h.** les handicapés mpl

2 adj handicapé(e)

handicraft ['hændɪkrɑːft] n (skill) artisanat m; (object) objet m artisanal

handiwork ['hændɪwɜːk] n travail m manuel; Hum **this looks like Jane's h.!** ça, c'est signé Jane!

handkerchief ['hæŋkətʃɪf] n mouchoir m

handle ['hændəl] **1** n (of broom, knife, saucepan) manche m; (of suitcase, door) poignée f; (of cup) anse f; Fig **to fly off the h.** piquer une colère; Fig **to get a h. on sth** piger qch

2 vt (a) (touch, hold) manipuler, toucher à; **h. with care** (on parcel) ≃ fragile (b) Fam (cope with) (situation, crisis) faire face à (c) Com (business, contract, client) s'occuper de

3 vi (of car, boat) **to h. well** être maniable

handlebars ['hændəlbɑːz] npl guidon m

handmade ['hænd'meɪd] adj fait(e) à la main

hand-me-downs ['hændmɪdaʊnz] npl Fam **I wear my brother's h.** je mets les vieilles frusques de mon frère

handout ['hændaʊt] n (a) (donation) don m (b) (leaflet) prospectus m

hand-picked ['hænd'pɪkt] adj (person, team) trié(e) sur le volet

handrail ['hændreɪl] n rampe f

handset ['hændset] n (of telephone) combiné m

hands-free [hændz'friː] adj Tel mains libres; **h. kit** kit m mains libres

handshake ['hændʃeɪk] n poignée f de main

hands-off ['hæn'zɒf] adj (approach, style) non-interventionniste

handsome ['hænsəm] adj (a) (physically attractive) beau (belle) (b) (praise) sincère; (price, profit) considérable; (reward) beau (belle)

handsomely ['hænsəmlɪ] adv (a) (dressed, furnished) élégamment (b) (rewarded, paid) généreusement

hands-on ['hæn'zɒn] adj **the director has a h. style of management** le directeur n'a pas peur de mettre la main à la pâte; **h. training** formation f pratique

handstand ['hændstænd] n **to do a h.** faire un équilibre sur les mains

hand-to-hand ['hæntə'hænd] adj (combat) au corps à corps

hand-to-mouth ['hæntə'maʊθ] **1** adj (existence) précaire

2 adv **to live h.** tirer le diable par la queue

handwriting ['hændraɪtɪŋ] n écriture f

handwritten ['hændrɪtən] adj manuscrit(e)

handy ['hændɪ] adj (a) (useful) pratique; **to come in h.** être utile (b) (convenient) commode; **my apartment is very h. for the stores** mon appartement est tout près des commerces (c) (within reach) à portée de la main; **have you got a pen h.?** est-ce que tu as un stylo à portée de la main? (d) (skillful) bricoleur(euse); **he's very h. in the kitchen** il est bon cuisinier

handyman ['hændɪmæn] n homme m à tout faire

hang [hæŋ] **1** n Fam **to get the h. of sth** piger qch

2 vt (pt & pp **hung** [hʌŋ]) (a) (suspend) (from ceiling) pendre, suspendre; (on wall) accrocher (b) **to h. one's head** baisser la tête; **he hung his head in shame** il baissa la tête sous l'effet de la honte (c) (pt & pp **hanged**) (criminal) pendre

3 vi (a) (be suspended) (from ceiling) être suspendu(e); (on wall) être accroché(e); Fig **she hung on his every word** elle était pendue à ses lèvres (b) (be executed) être pendu(e) (c) (of clothes) tomber

▶**hang about, hang around** vi Fam (wait) poireauter; **to keep sb hanging about** or **around** faire poireauter qn

▶**hang back** vi hésiter

▶**hang in** vi Fam **h. in there!** accroche-toi!, tiens bon!

▶**hang on 1** vi (a) Fam (wait) patienter, attendre (b) (survive) tenir le coup

2 vt insep (depend on) dépendre de

▶**hang on to** vt insep garder

▶**hang out 1** vt sep (washing) étendre

2 vi (a) (from pocket, box) dépasser (b) Fam (spend time) traîner

▶**hang together** vi (of argument, statements) se tenir

▶**hang up 1** vt sep (hat, picture) accrocher

2 vi (on telephone) raccrocher; **to h. up on sb** raccrocher au nez de qn

hangar ['hæŋə(r)] n hangar m

hangdog ['hæŋdɒg] adj (look, expression) de chien battu

hanger ['hæŋə(r)] n (for clothes) cintre m

hanger-on [hæŋə'rɒn] n (pl **hangers-on**) parasite m, pique-assiette m inv

hang-glider ['hæŋglaɪdə(r)] n (a) (object) deltaplane m (b) (person) deltiste mf

hang-gliding ['hæŋglaɪdɪŋ] n deltaplane m; **to go h.** faire du deltaplane

hanging ['hæŋɪŋ] n (execution) pendaison f

hangman ['hæŋmən] n bourreau m

hangnail ['hæŋneɪl] n envie f

hang-out ['hæŋaʊt] n Fam repaire m

hangover ['hæŋəʊvə(r)] n (a) (from drinking) gueule f de bois (b) (practice, belief) reste m, vestige m

hang-up ['hæŋʌp] n Fam complexe m; **to have a h. about sth** être complexé(e) à propos de qch

hanker ['hæŋkə(r)] *vi* **to h. after** *or* **for sth** avoir très envie de qch

hankering ['hæŋkərɪŋ] *n* **to have a h. for sth** avoir très envie de qch

hankie, hanky ['hæŋkɪ] (*pl* **hankies**) *n Fam* mouchoir *m*

hanky-panky ['hæŋkɪ'pæŋkɪ] *n Fam* (**a**) *(sexual activity)* galipettes *fpl* (**b**) *(underhand behavior)* entourloupettes *fpl*

Hanover ['hænəʊvə(r)] *n* Hanovre

haphazard [hæp'hæzəd] *adj (choice, decision)* pris(e) au hasard; *(attempt)* mal organisé(e)

haphazardly [hæp'hæzədlɪ] *adv* n'importe comment

hapless ['hæplɪs] *adj Formal* infortuné(e)

happen ['hæpən] *vi* arriver, se produire; **it happened ten years ago** c'est arrivé il y a dix ans; **what happened?** que s'est-il passé?; **to h. again** se reproduire; **it so happens (that)...** il se trouve justement que...; **as if nothing had happened** comme si de rien n'était; **as it happens,...** justement...; **what has happened to him?** que lui est-il arrivé?; **to h. to meet sb** rencontrer qn par hasard; **I h. to know (that)...** il se trouve que je sais que...; **do you h. to know whether...?** savez-vous par hasard si...?

▶**happen on, happen upon** *vt insep* tomber sur

happening ['hæpənɪŋ] **1** *n* événement *m*
2 *adj Fam (town) (lively)* dynamique; *(trendy)* branché(e), dans le coup

happily ['hæpɪlɪ] *adv* (**a**) *(play)* gentiment; *(chat)* tranquillement; **a h. married couple** un ménage heureux; **they lived h. ever after** ≃ ils vécurent heureux et eurent beaucoup d'enfants (**b**) *(fortunately)* heureusement, par bonheur (**c**) *(willingly)* volontiers

happiness ['hæpɪnɪs] *n* bonheur *m*

happy ['hæpɪ] *adj* (**a**) *(content, cheerful)* heureux(euse); **to be h. with sth** être satisfait(e) de qch; **to make sb h.** rendre qn heureux; **to keep sb h.** satisfaire qn; **a story with a h. ending** une histoire qui finit bien; **a h. medium** le juste milieu; **h. birthday!** joyeux anniversaire!; **h. New Year!** bonne année! (**b**) *(fortunate) (choice, phrase)* heureux(euse) (**c**) *(willing)* **to be h. to do sth** être heureux(euse) de faire qch

happy-go-lucky ['hæpɪgəʊ'lʌkɪ] *adj* insouciant(e)

harangue [hə'ræŋ] **1** *n* harangue *f*
2 *vt* haranguer (**about** au sujet de)

harass [hə'ræs, 'hærəs] *vt* harceler

harassed [hə'ræst, 'hærəst] *adj* stressé(e)

harassment ['hærəsmənt, hə'ræsmənt] *n* harcèlement *m*; **police h.** harcèlement policier

harbor ['hɑːbə(r)] **1** *n* port *m*
2 *vt (fugitive)* cacher; *(hope, suspicion)* nourrir; **to h. a grudge against sb** garder rancune à qn

hard [hɑːd] **1** *adj* (**a**) *(substance)* dur(e); *(fact, evidence)* tangible; *Fig* **to be as h. as nails** être un(e) dur(e) à cuire; **h. candy** bonbon *m* à sucer; **in h. cash** en liquide; **h. cider** cidre *m*; *Comput* **h. copy** copie *f* sur papier; **h. core** *(of group)* noyau *m* dur; **h. court** *(for tennis)* court *m* en dur; *Comput* **h. disk, h. drive** disque *m* dur; **h. drugs** drogues *fpl* dures; *Pol* **h. left/right** extrême gauche *f*/droite *f*; **h. liquor** spiritueux *mpl*; *Comput* **h. return** retour *m* chariot obligatoire
(**b**) *(difficult)* difficile; *(strenuous)* pénible; **it was h. work persuading him to come** ça n'a pas été facile de le convaincre de venir; **it's h. to say...** il est difficile de dire...; **to be h. to please** être difficile (à satisfaire); **to learn sth the h. way** apprendre qch à ses dépens; **to do things the h. way** se compliquer la vie; **h. of hearing** dur(e) d'oreille
(**c**) *(harsh) (person, conditions, life)* dur(e); **to be h. on sb** être dur avec qn; **to have a h. time (of it)** en baver; **to give sb a h. time** mener la vie dure à qn; **a h. winter** un hiver rigoureux; **no h. feelings?** sans rancune?; **to take a h. line on sth** prendre une position très ferme sur qch

(**d**) *(intense)* **to be a h. worker** travailler dur; *Law* **h. labor** travaux *mpl* forcés; *Com* **to give sb the h. sell** essayer de convaincre qn d'acheter à toute force
(**e**) *(water)* calcaire
2 *adv* (**a**) *(work)* dur; *(push, hit)* fort; **to try h.** faire de son mieux; **to look h. at sb/sth** regarder qn/qch fixement; **to think h.** bien réfléchir; **to be h. at work** être en plein travail; **it's raining h.** il pleut à verse; *Fam* **h. up** *(short of money)* fauché(e)
(**b**) *(near)* **h. by** tout près de; **to follow h. upon sb/sth** suivre qn/qch de près

hard-and-fast ['hɑːdən'fɑːst] *adj (rule)* absolu(e)

hardback ['hɑːdbæk] *n* livre *m* relié

hardball ['hɑːdbɔːl] *n* (game) baseball *m*; (ball) balle *f* de baseball; *Fam Fig* **to play h.** employer les grands moyens

hard-bitten [hɑːd'bɪtən] *adj* endurci(e)

hardboard ['hɑːdbɔːd] *n* aggloméré *m*

hard-boiled [hɑːd'bɔɪld] *adj (egg)* dur(e); *Fig (person)* dur à cuire

hard-core ['hɑːdkɔː(r)] *adj (supporter)* inconditionnel(elle); *(pornography)* hard *inv*; *(punk)* hard-core *inv*

hard-earned [hɑːd'ɜːnd] *adj* durement gagné(e)

harden ['hɑːdən] **1** *vt* endurcir; **to h. oneself to sth** s'endurcir à qch
2 *vi (of substance, attitude)* durcir

hardened ['hɑːdənd] *adj (steel)* trempé(e); *(drinker)* invétéré(e); *(criminal)* endurci(e)

hard-fought [hɑːd'fɔːt] *adj (election, contest)* âprement disputé(e)

hard-headed [hɑːd'hedɪd] *adj (attitude, person)* réaliste

hard-hearted [hɑːd'hɑːtɪd] *adj* dur(e)

hard-hitting [hɑːd'hɪtɪŋ] *adj (criticism, report)* sans indulgence

hardliner [hɑːd'laɪnə(r)] *n (politician, activist)* jusqu'au-boutiste *mf*, dur(e) *m,f*

hardly ['hɑːdlɪ] *adv (scarcely)* à peine; **h. had I arrived when...** j'étais à peine arrivé que...; **you can h. expect me to do that** vous ne vous attendez tout de même pas à ce que je fasse ça; **I can h. believe it** j'ai du mal à y croire; *also Ironic* **I can h. wait** j'ai hâte d'y être; **h. ever** presque jamais; **h. anyone/anything** presque personne/rien

hardness ['hɑːdnɪs] *n* (**a**) *(of substance)* dureté *f* (**b**) *(of problem)* difficulté *f*

hard-on ['hɑːdɒn] *n Vulg* **to have/to get a h.** bander

hard-pressed [hɑːd'prest], **hard-pushed** [hɑːd'pʊʃt] *adj* en difficulté; **to be h. for time/money** manquer de temps/d'argent; **to be h. to do sth** avoir du mal à faire qch

hardship ['hɑːdʃɪp] *n* épreuve *f*; **to live in h.** vivre dans la misère

hardware ['hɑːdweə(r)] *n* (**a**) *(tools)* matériel *m*; (**military**) **h.** *(weapons)* matériel militaire, armement *m*; **h. store** quincaillerie *f* (**b**) *Comput* matériel *m*, hardware *m*

hard-wearing [hɑːd'weərɪŋ] *adj* résistant(e)

hard-won [hɑːd'wʌn] *adj* durement acquis(e)

hard-working ['hɑːd'wɜːkɪŋ] *adj* travailleur(euse)

hardy ['hɑːdɪ] *adj* résistant(e), robuste

hare [heə(r)] *n* lièvre *m*

harebrained ['heəbreɪnd] *adj* écervelé(e)

harelip ['heəlɪp] *n* bec-de-lièvre *m*

harem [hɑː'riːm] *n* harem *m*

haricot ['hærɪkəʊ] *n* **h. (bean)** haricot *m* blanc

hark [hɑːk] *exclam Lit* écoutez!

▶**hark back** *vi* **to h. back to sth** évoquer qch; **he's always harking back to that mistake I made** il revient toujours sur l'erreur que j'ai faite

harlot ['hɑːlət] *n Lit* prostituée *f*

harm [hɑːm] **1** *n* mal *m*; *(to reputation)* tort *m*; **to do sb h.** faire du mal à qn; **to do oneself h.** se faire du tort; **it will do more h. than good** cela va faire plus de mal que de bien; **I can't see any h. in it** je ne vois pas de mal à ça; **there's no h. in trying** ça ne coûte rien d'essayer; **you will come to no h.** il ne t'arrivera rien (de mal); **out of h.'s way** en sûreté, en lieu sûr
2 *vt (physically)* faire du mal à; *(health, reputation, cause)* nuire à; *(skin, fabric)* abîmer

harmful ['hɑːmfʊl] *adj (influence, activity)* néfaste; *(substance, ray)* nocif(ive)

harmless ['hɑːmlɪs] *adj (person, animal)* inoffensif(ive); *(joke)* innocent(e); **it's just a bit of h. fun** ça ne fait de mal à personne

harmonica [hɑːˈmɒnɪkə] *n* harmonica *m*

harmonious [hɑːˈməʊnɪəs] *adj* harmonieux(euse)

harmonization [hɑːmənaɪˈzeɪʃən] *n* harmonisation *f*

harmonize ['hɑːmənaɪz] **1** *vt* harmoniser
2 *vi* s'harmoniser (**with** avec)

harmony ['hɑːmənɪ] *(pl* **harmonies***) n also Fig* harmonie *f*; **in h. with** en harmonie *ou* en accord avec; **to live in h. (with)** vivre en harmonie (avec)

harness ['hɑːnɪs] **1** *n* **(a)** *(for horse, baby, of parachute)* harnais *m*; *(for climber)* baudrier *m* **(b)** *(idioms)* **to work in h. (with)** travailler en équipe (avec); **to die in h.** mourir à la tâche
2 *vt (horse)* harnacher; *(to a cart)* atteler; *(resources)* exploiter

harp [hɑːp] *n* harpe *f*
▸**harp on** *vi* **to h. on about sth** revenir sans arrêt sur qch

harpist ['hɑːpɪst] *n* harpiste *mf*

harpoon [hɑːˈpuːn] **1** *n* harpon *m*
2 *vt* harponner

harpsichord ['hɑːpsɪkɔːd] *n* clavecin *m*

harpy ['hɑːpɪ] *(pl* **harpies***) n* harpie *f*

harrow ['hærəʊ] *n* herse *f*

harrowing ['hærəʊɪŋ] *adj (experience, sight)* pénible; *(account, image)* déchirant(e)

harry ['hærɪ] *(pt & pp* **harried***) vt* harceler

harsh [hɑːʃ] *adj (voice, sound)* strident(e); *(climate)* rude; *(treatment, person)* dur(e)

harshly ['hɑːʃlɪ] *adv (answer, speak, treat)* durement

harvest ['hɑːvɪst] **1** *n (of fruit)* récolte *f*; *(of crops)* moisson *f*; *(of grapes)* vendange *f*; **h. festival** = fête religieuse pour célébrer la fin de la moisson
2 *vt (fruit)* récolter; *(crops)* moissonner; *(grapes)* vendanger; *Fig (information)* récolter

has [hæz] *3rd pers singular of* **have**

has-been ['hæzbiːn] *n Fam Pej* has been *mf inv*

hash [hæʃ] *n* **(a)** *(stew)* hachis *m*; **h. browns** = pommes de terre râpées et sautées *(présentées parfois sous forme de galette)* **(b)** *very Fam (hashish)* hasch *m* **(c)** *(symbol)* **h. mark, h. sign** dièse *m*

hashish ['hæʃiːʃ] *n* haschich *m*

hasn't ['hæznt] = **has not**

hassle ['hæsəl] *Fam* **1** *n* embêtements *mpl*; **it's too much h.** c'est trop de tintouin; **it's a real h. buying a house** l'achat d'une maison est un vrai casse-tête; **to give sb a h.** faire des histoires à qn
2 *vt* embêter, harceler; **don't h. me!** arrête de m'embêter!

haste [heɪst] *n* hâte *f*; **in h.** en hâte, à la hâte; **to make h.** se dépêcher, se hâter; *Prov* **more h. less speed** hâtez-vous lentement

hasten ['heɪsən] **1** *vt (accelerate)* précipiter; **to h. sb's departure** avancer *ou* hâter le départ de qn
2 *vi* se presser; **I h. to add...** je m'empresse d'ajouter...

hastily ['heɪstɪlɪ] *adv (write, prepare)* hâtivement; *(say, eat)* précipitamment; **too h.** trop vite

hasty ['heɪstɪ] *adj (departure, removal)* précipité(e); *(meal)* rapide;

(reply, decision) irréfléchi(e); **to jump to a h. conclusion** conclure à la légère

hat [hæt] *n* chapeau *m*; *also Fig* **to take one's h. off to sb** tirer son chapeau à qn; *Fig* **to pass the h. around** *(collect money)* faire la quête; *Fig* **to throw one's h. in the ring** *(enter contest)* se porter candidat(e); *Fam Fig* **to keep sth under one's h.** garder qch pour soi; *Fig* **I'm speaking with my lawyer's h. on** je parle en ma qualité de juriste; **h. stand** portemanteau *m*; **h. trick** *(of goals)* = trois buts marqués par le même joueur; *(of victories)* triplé *m*

hatch[^1] [hætʃ] *n (of ship)* écoutille *f*; *Fam* **down the h.!** cul sec!; **(serving) h.** passe-plat *m*

hatch[^2] [hætʃ] **1** *vt (egg)* faire éclore; *Fig (scheme, plot)* tramer
2 *vi (of egg)* éclore

hatchback ['hætʃbæk] *n (car) (three-door)* voiture *f* à trois portes, trois-portes *f inv*; *(five-door)* voiture *f* à cinq portes, cinq-portes *f inv*

hatchet ['hætʃɪt] *n* hachette *f*; *Fam* **to do a h. job on sb/sth** *(of critic, reviewer)* démolir qn/qch; *Fam* **h. man** homme *m* de main

hate [heɪt] **1** *n* haine *f*; **h. mail** lettres *fpl* d'injures
2 *vt* détester, haïr; **to h. doing sth** détester faire qch, avoir horreur de faire qch; **she hates to be contradicted** elle a horreur qu'on la contredise; *Fam* **I h. to tell you, but I think you've missed your train** ça m'ennuie de te le dire, mais je pense que tu as raté ton train

hateful ['heɪtfʊl] *adj* odieux(euse)

hatpin ['hætpɪn] *n* épingle *f* à chapeau

hatred ['heɪtrɪd] *n* haine *f* (**of**/**for** de/pour)

haughty ['hɔːtɪ] *adj* hautain(e)

haul [hɔːl] **1** *n* **(a)** *(fish caught)* prise *f*; *(loot)* butin *m*; *(of drugs, stolen goods)* saisie *f* **(b)** *Fam (journey)* parcours *m*, trajet *m*; **it's a long h.** la route est longue; *Fig* c'est un travail de longue haleine
2 *vt* **(a)** *(pull)* tirer; *(tow)* remorquer; *Fam* **he was hauled in for questioning** on l'a emmené pour l'interroger; *Fam Fig* **to h. sb over the coals** *(reprimand)* passer un savon à qn; **she was hauled up before the principal** elle a été convoquée chez le proviseur **(b)** *(transport)* transporter par camion

haulage ['hɔːlɪdʒ] *n (transportation)* transport *m* (routier); *(costs)* (frais *mpl* de) transport; **h. firm** entreprise *f* de transports routiers

hauler ['hɔːlə(r)] *n (company)* entreprise *f* de transports routiers

haunch [hɔːntʃ] *n (of person)* hanche *f*; *(of venison)* cuissot *m*; **to sit** *or* **to squat on one's haunches** être accroupi(e)

haunt [hɔːnt] **1** *n (of criminals)* repaire *m*; *(of group of people)* (lieu *m* de) rendez-vous *m*; **it's one of his favorite haunts** *(favorite places)* c'est un des endroits qu'il fréquente habituellement
2 *vt also Fig* hanter

haunted ['hɔːntɪd] *adj (castle, room)* hanté(e); *Fig* **he has a h. look** il a l'air égaré

haunting ['hɔːntɪŋ] *adj* obsédant(e)

Havana [həˈvænə] *n* la Havane; **H. (cigar)** havane *m*

have [hæv] **1** *vt (pt & pp* **had***)* **(a)** *(own)* avoir; **they've (got) a big house** ils ont une grande maison; **she doesn't h.** *or* **hasn't got a car** elle n'a pas de voiture; **I've (got) things to do** j'ai des choses à faire; **you can h. it back tomorrow** je te le rendrai demain; **to h. sb in one's power** tenir qn à sa merci; **to h. it on good authority that...** tenir de source sûre que...
(b) *(with noun to denote activity)* **to h. a swim** se baigner; **to h. a shave** se raser; **to h. a bath** prendre un bain; **to h. lunch** déjeuner; **to h. a cigarette** fumer une cigarette; **to h. a drink** prendre un verre; **to h. a good/bad time** passer un bon/mauvais moment
(c) *(with illnesses)* **to h. a cold** être enrhumé(e); **to h. the flu/cancer** avoir la grippe/un cancer

(**d**) *(cause to do, to be done)* **to h. sb do sth** faire faire qch à qn; **to h. sth done** faire faire qch; **to h. one's hair cut** se faire couper les cheveux; **h. him call me** dis-lui de m'appeler; **I'll h. you know that…!** je vous signale que…!

(**e**) *(in passive constructions)* **I had my watch stolen** on m'a volé ma montre; **three houses had their windows broken** il y a des fenêtres brisées dans trois maisons

(**f**) *(allow)* **I won't h. it!** je n'accepte pas ça!; **I won't h. you causing trouble!** pas question que tu fasses des histoires!

(**g**) *(be compelled)* **to h. (got) to do sth** devoir faire qch; **I h. or I've got to go** je dois y aller; **you don't h. to come with me** tu n'es pas obligé de venir avec moi; **do you h. or h. you got to work?** est-ce qu'il faut vraiment que tu travailles?; **it has or it's got to be done** il faut que ce soit fait

(**h**) *Fam (idioms)* **to be had** *(cheated)* se faire avoir; **to h. had it** être fichu(e); **to h. had it with sb/sth** en avoir marre de qn/qch; **he had it coming** ça lui pendait au nez

2 *v aux* avoir/être

Most French verbs will conjugate with **avoir** to form the perfect tense. However, all reflexive verbs and many intransitive verbs – mainly of motion – will conjugate with **être**.

---

to h. seen avoir vu; **to h. left** être parti(e); **to h. hurt oneself** s'être blessé(e); **I've worked here for three years** je travaille ici depuis trois ans; **we've seen this movie before – no, we haven't!** nous avons déjà vu ce film – mais non!; **you haven't done the dishes – yes, I h.!** tu n'as pas fait la vaisselle – si, je l'ai faite!; **you h. told him, haven't you?** tu le lui as dit, n'est-ce pas *ou* non?; **you haven't forgotten, h. you?** tu n'as pas oublié, n'est-ce pas *ou* hein?

3 *n* **the haves and the have-nots** les riches *mpl* et les pauvres

▶**have in** *vt sep Fam* **to h. it in for sb** en avoir après qn

▶**have on** *vt sep (be wearing)* porter; **to h. nothing on** être nu(e)

▶**have out** *vt sep* (**a**) *(have removed)* **to h. a tooth out** se faire arracher une dent; **to h. one's appendix out** se faire opérer de l'appendicite (**b**) *(resolve)* **to h. it out with sb** s'expliquer avec qn

haven ['heɪvən] *n* refuge *m*

haven't ['hævənt] = **have not**

haversack ['hævəsæk] *n* sac *m* à dos

havoc ['hævək] *n* (**a**) *(damage)* ravages *mpl*, dégâts *mpl*; **to cause** *or* **to wreak h.** faire des ravages (**b**) *(confusion)* pagaille *f*; **to play h. with sth** *(plans)* chambouler qch

Hawaii [hə'waɪiː] *n* Hawaii

Hawaiian [hə'waɪən] **1** *n* Hawaiien(enne) *m,f*

2 *adj* hawaiien(enne)

hawk¹ [hɔːk] *n also Pol* faucon *m*; **to watch sb/sth like a h.** ne pas quitter qn/qch du regard

hawk² [hɔːk] *vt* **to h. one's wares** *(in market, street)* vendre ses marchandises à la criée; *(from door to door)* faire du porte-à-porte

hawk-eyed ['hɔːkaɪd] *adj* **to be h.** avoir des yeux de lynx

hawkish ['hɔːkɪʃ] *adj Pol* belliciste

hawser ['hɔːzə(r)] *n* aussière *f*

hawthorn ['hɔːθɔːn] *n* aubépine *f*

hay [heɪ] *n* foin *m*; **to make h.** faire les foins; *Fig* **to make h. while the sun shines** en profiter tant que ça dure

hayfever ['heɪfiːvə(r)] *n* rhume *m* des foins

hayloft ['heɪlɒft] *n* fenil *m*

hayseed ['heɪsiːd] *n Fam (hick)* péquenaud(e) *m,f*, plouc *m*

haystack ['heɪstæk] *n* meule *f* de foin

haywire ['heɪwaɪə(r)] *adv Fam* **to go h.** *(of plan)* mal tourner; *(of mechanism)* se détraquer

hazard ['hæzəd] **1** *n (danger)* danger *m*, risque *m*; **a fire h.** un risque d'incendie; **a health h.** un danger pour la santé; **h. lights** feux *mpl* de détresse

2 *vt (one's life, fortune)* risquer; *(opinion)* hasarder; **to h. a guess** essayer de deviner

hazardous ['hæzədəs] *adj* dangereux(euse); *(financial venture)* hasardeux(euse)

haze¹ [heɪz] *n (mist)* brume *f*; *(of doubt, confusion)* atmosphère *f*; **my mind was in a h.** j'avais l'esprit embrouillé

haze² [heɪz] *vt Univ* bizuter

hazel ['heɪzəl] **1** *n (color)* (couleur *f*) noisette *f*; **h. (tree)** noisetier *m*

2 *adj (color)* noisette *inv*; **h. eyes** yeux *mpl* (couleur) noisette

hazelnut ['heɪzəlnʌt] *n* noisette *f*

hazily ['heɪzɪlɪ] *adv* vaguement

hazing ['heɪzɪŋ] *n Univ* bizutage *m*

hazy ['heɪzɪ] *adj (weather)* brumeux(euse); *(image, memory)* flou(e), vague; **to be h. about sth** *(remember vaguely)* n'avoir qu'un vague souvenir de qch

he [hiː] **1** *pron* il; **he's Scottish** il est écossais; HE **hasn't got it!** ce n'est pas lui qui l'a!

2 *n* **it's a he** *(of animal)* c'est un mâle

head [hed] **1** *n* (**a**) *(part of body)* tête *f*; **a fine h. of hair** une belle chevelure; **from h. to foot** *or* **toe** de la tête aux pieds; **to stand on one's h.** faire le poirier; *Fig* **to stand sth on its h.** retourner qch; **to win by a h.** *(of horse)* gagner d'une tête; *Fig* **she's h. and shoulders above the other candidates** les autres candidats ne lui arrivent pas à la cheville; **h. cold** rhume *m* de cerveau; **h. start** *(advantage)* avantage *m*; *(in race)* avance *f*

(**b**) *(intellect, mind)* tête *f*; **to do sums in one's h.** calculer de tête; **to have a good h. on one's shoulders** avoir la tête sur les épaules; **to have a good h. for business** avoir le sens des affaires; **to have a good h. for figures** être à l'aise avec les chiffres; **to have a (good) h. for heights** ne pas avoir le vertige; **to take it into one's h. to do sth** se mettre en tête de faire qch; **to take it into one's h. that…** se mettre dans la tête que…; **it never entered my h. that…** il ne m'est jamais venu à l'esprit que…; **to put ideas into sb's h.** donner des idées à qn; *Fam* **he's not right in the h.** il a un grain

(**c**) *(of pin, hammer, list, bed)* tête *f*; *(of arrow)* pointe *f*; *(of page, stairs)* haut *m*; *(of table)* bout *m*; *(on beer)* mousse *f*; *(on tape recorder)* tête; **a h. of lettuce/cabbage** un pied de laitue/chou; **heads or tails?** *(when tossing coin)* pile ou face?; **to build up a h. of steam** *(of campaign)* s'intensifier; *(of person)* progresser rapidement; **to come to a h.** *(of conflict, crisis)* atteindre un paroxysme

(**d**) *(person in charge) (of family, the Church, business)* chef *m*; **h. of state** chef d'État; **h. office** siège *m* (social); **h. waiter** maître *m* d'hôtel

(**e**) *(unit)* **$10 per h.** *or* **a h.** 10 dollars par personne; **six h. of cattle** six têtes de bétail

(**f**) *(idioms)* **we put our heads together** nous nous y sommes tous mis; **they'll have your h. (on a plate) for this** cela te coûtera ta tête; **to bury** *or* **to have one's h. in the sand** pratiquer la politique de l'autruche; **on your own h. be it** à tes risques et périls; **to go over sb's h.** *(appeal to higher authority)* ne pas consulter qn *(en suivant la voie hiérarchique)*; *Fam* **to shout one's h. off** crier à tue-tête; **the wine/praise went to his h.** le vin/compliment lui est monté à la tête; *Prov* **two heads are better than one** deux avis valent mieux qu'un; **off the top of one's h.** au hasard; **it was** *or* **went over my h.** ça m'a dépassé; **I can't make h. nor tail of this** ça n'a ni queue ni tête; *Fam* **to lose one's h.** *(panic)* perdre la tête; *(get angry)* perdre son calme; *Fam* **to keep one's h.** garder son calme; *Fam* **to be out of one's h.** avoir perdu la boule; **to fall h. over heels in love with sb** tomber éperdument amoureux de qn; *Vulg* **to give sb h.** faire une pipe à qn

2 *vt* (**a**) *(lead) (organization, campaign)* diriger; *(list)* venir en tête de

(**b**) *(steer)* diriger; **one of the locals headed me in the**

right direction un des habitants m'a indiqué la bonne direction
(**c**) *(put a title on) (page, chapter)* intituler
(**d**) *(in soccer)* **to h. the ball** faire une tête
3 *vi (move)* se diriger; **they were heading out of town** ils sortaient de la ville

▸**head for** *vt insep* se diriger vers; **you're heading for disaster** tu vas droit au désastre; **you're heading for trouble** tu vas avoir des ennuis

▸**head off 1** *vt sep (divert)* éviter
2 *vi (depart)* partir

headache ['hedeɪk] *n* mal *m* de tête; *Fig (problem)* casse-tête *m inv*; **to have a h.** avoir mal à la tête

headband ['hedbænd] *n* bandeau *m*

headboard ['hedbɔːd] *n* tête *f* de lit

headcase ['hedkeɪs] *n Fam* cinglé(e) *m,f*

headdress ['heddres] *n* coiffure *f*

headed ['hedɪd] *adj* **h. (note)paper** papier *m* à en-tête

header ['hedə(r)] *n* (**a**) *Typ* en-tête *m* (**b**) *(in soccer)* (coup *m* de) tête *f*

headfirst ['hed'fɜːst] *adv* la tête la première

headgear ['hedgɪə(r)] *n* couvre-chef *m*

head-hunt ['hed'hʌnt] *vt Com* **to be head-hunted** être recruté(e) par un chasseur de têtes

head-hunter ['hedhʌntə(r)] *n Com* chasseur *m* de têtes

heading ['hedɪŋ] *n (of chapter, article)* titre *m*; *(of letter)* en-tête *m*; **it comes** *or* **falls under the h. of...** c'est à mettre sous la rubrique de...

headland ['hedlənd] *n* cap *m*, pointe *f*

headlight ['hedlaɪt] *n (on car)* phare *m*

headline ['hedlaɪn] **1** *n (of TV news)* titre *m*; *(of newspaper)* (gros) titre; **to hit the headlines** faire la une des journaux; **to be h. news** faire la une des journaux
2 *vt (article, story)* intituler

headlong ['hedlɒŋ] **1** *adj* **there was a h. rush for the bar** tout le monde s'est rué vers le bar
2 *adv (fall)* la tête la première; *(rush)* tête baissée

head-on ['hed'ɒn] *adj & adv* de front; **to meet sb h.** aborder qn de front; **a h. collision** une collision frontale

headphones ['hedfəʊnz] *npl* écouteurs *mpl*

headquarters [hed'kwɔːtəz] *npl (of organization)* siège *m* (social); *Mil* quartier *m* général

headrest ['hedrest] *n* appui-tête *m inv*

headroom ['hedruːm] *n (under bridge, inside car)* hauteur *f*

headscarf ['hedskɑːf] *(pl* **headscarves** ['hedskɑːvz]*) n* foulard *m*

headset ['hedset] *n* écouteurs *mpl*; *(providing commentary in museum, etc.)* audioguide *f*

headstone ['hedstəʊn] *n (on grave)* pierre *f* tombale

headstrong ['hedstrɒŋ] *adj* têtu(e), entêté(e)

heads-up ['hedzʌp] *n Fam* **to give sb a h.** *(warning)* tuyauter qn

headway ['hedweɪ] *n* **to make h.** avancer, faire des progrès

headwind ['hedwɪnd] *n* vent *m* contraire; *Naut* vent debout

heady ['hedɪ] *adj (atmosphere)* enivrant(e); *(wine, perfume)* capiteux(euse); *(heights, days)* grisant(e)

heal [hiːl] **1** *vt (wound, person)* guérir; *(disagreement)* régler; *Fig* **wounds which only time would h.** des blessures que seul le temps cicatriserait
2 *vi (of wound)* **to h. (up** *or* **over)** cicatriser

health [helθ] *n* santé *f*; **to be in good/poor h.** être en bonne/ mauvaise santé; *Fig* **the economy is in good h.** l'économie se porte bien; **the Department of H. and Human Services** ≃ le ministère de la Santé; **to drink (to) sb's h.** boire à la santé de qn; **h. club** club *m* de remise en forme; **h. farm** centre *m* de remise en forme; **h. food** produits *mpl* biologiques; **h.-food store** magasin m de produits diététiques; **h. ha-**

zard *or* **risk** risque *m* pour la santé; **h. insurance** assurance maladie; **h. resort** station *f* climatique; *(by sea)* station balnéaire; **h. services** services *mpl* de santé

healthcare ['helθkeə(r)] *n* soins *mpl ou* services *mpl* médicaux; **h. provider** professionnel(elle) *m,f* de (la) santé

healthy ['helθɪ] *adj (person)* en bonne santé; *(climate)* salubre; *(food, habit, economy)* sain(e); **a h. appetite** un bon appétit; **it is a h. sign that...** c'est bon signe que...; **he has a h. respect for his opponents** il apprécie ses adversaires à leur juste valeur

heap [hiːp] **1** *n* tas *m*; *Fig* **people at the top/bottom of the h.** ceux qui sont en haut/bas de l'échelle sociale; *Fam* **she's got heaps of money** elle a plein d'argent; *Fam* **we've got heaps of time** on a largement le temps
2 *vt* entasser; **his plate was heaped with food** son assiette était remplie de nourriture; **to h. sth with** remplir qch de; **a heaped spoonful** *(in recipe)* une cuillerée bien pleine; **to h. riches/praise on sb** couvrir qn de richesses/d'éloges; **to h. insults on sb** abreuver qn d'injures

hear [hɪə(r)] *(pt & pp* **heard** [hɜːd]*)* **1** *vt* (**a**) *(perceive)* entendre; **to h. sb speak** entendre qn parler; **I can hardly h. myself think!** on ne s'entend pas ici!; **to make oneself heard** se faire entendre; **let's h. it for...** applaudissons bien fort...; **have you heard the one about...?** est-ce que tu connais celle de...? (**b**) *(listen to)* écouter; **h., h.!** *(at meeting)* bravo!; *Law* **to h. a case** juger une affaire (**c**) *(find out)* entendre (dire), apprendre; **have you heard the news?** tu connais la nouvelle?; **I h. you're getting married** j'ai entendu dire que tu te mariais
2 *vi* entendre; **I can't h. properly** je n'entends pas bien; **to h. from sb** avoir des nouvelles de qn; **you'll be hearing from my lawyer!** mon avocat vous contactera!; **to h. of** *or* **about sth** entendre parler de qch; **I won't h. of it!** je ne veux pas en entendre parler!

▸**hear out** *vt sep* **to h. sb out** écouter qn jusqu'au bout

hearing ['hɪərɪŋ] *n* (**a**) *(sense)* ouïe *f*, audition *f*; **h. aid** audiophone *m* (**b**) *(earshot)* **to be within/out of h.** être à portée/ hors de portée de voix (**c**) *(chance to explain)* **to give sb a fair h.** laisser parler qn, laisser qn s'expliquer (**d**) *Law (inquiry)* audition *f*

hearsay ['hɪəseɪ] *n* ouï-dire *m inv*, on-dit *m inv*; *Law* **h. evidence** déposition *f* sur la foi d'autrui

hearse [hɜːs] *n* corbillard *m*

heart [hɑːt] *n* (**a**) *(organ)* cœur *m*; **to have h. trouble, to have a weak** *or* **bad h.** être cardiaque; **h. attack** crise *f* cardiaque; **h. disease** maladie *f* cardiaque; **h. failure** arrêt *m* cardiaque; **h. surgeon** chirurgien(enne) *m,f* cardiologique; **h. surgery** chirurgie *f* cardiaque; **h. transplant** transplantation *f* cardiaque
(**b**) *(seat of the emotions)* cœur *m*; **to have a big h.** avoir bon cœur; **a h. of gold** un cœur d'or; **a h. of stone** un cœur de pierre; **have a h.!** ayez un peu de cœur!; **her h.'s in the right place** elle a bon cœur; **with a heavy h.** le cœur gros; **my h. sank** j'ai été très déçu; **to have one's h. in one's mouth** être terrorisé(e); **to break sb's h.** briser le cœur à qn; **to wear one's h. on one's sleeve** ne pas cacher ses sentiments; **affairs** *or* **matters of the h.** affaires *fpl* de cœur; *Ironic* **my h. bleeds for you** ça me fait de la peine pour toi; **in my h. of hearts** au fond de mon cœur; **from the bottom of one's h.** du fond du cœur; **he loved her with all his h.** il l'aimait de toute son âme; **at h.** au fond; **to have sb's welfare/interests at h.** avoir le bien-être/les intérêts de qn à cœur; **to take sth to h.** prendre qch à cœur; **to set one's h. on sth** vouloir qch à tout prix; **he's a man after my own h.** il est comme moi; **to one's h.'s content** tout son soûl
(**c**) *(enthusiasm, courage)* **to take h.** reprendre courage; **to lose h.** se décourager; **he tried to convince them but his h. wasn't in it** il a essayé de les convaincre mais le cœur n'y

était pas; **I didn't have the h. to tell him** je n'ai pas eu le cœur de lui dire

(**d**) **by h.** *(know, learn)* par cœur

(**e**) *(center) (of city, forest)* cœur *m*; **the h. of the matter** le fond du problème

(**f**) *(in cards)* **hearts** cœur *m*; **ace of hearts** as *m* de coeur

heartache ['hɑːteɪk] *n* chagrin *m*, peine *f*

heartbeat ['hɑːtbiːt] *n (rhythm)* pouls *m*; *(single beat)* battement *m* de cœur

heartbreaking ['hɑːtbreɪkɪŋ] *adj* déchirant(e), navrant(e)

heartbroken ['hɑːtbrəʊkən] *adj* **to be h.** avoir le cœur brisé

heartburn ['hɑːtbɜːn] *n (indigestion)* brûlures *fpl* d'estomac

hearten ['hɑːtən] *vt* encourager

heartening ['hɑːtənɪŋ] *adj* encourageant(e)

heartfelt ['hɑːtfelt] *adj* sincère, qui vient du cœur

hearth [hɑːθ] *n (fireplace, home)* foyer *m*

hearthrug ['hɑːθrʌg] *n* devant *m* de foyer

heartily ['hɑːtɪlɪ] *adv (welcome, applaud)* chaleureusement; *(agree)* de tout cœur; *(eat)* avec appétit; **to be h. sick of sth** être profondément dégoûté(e) de qch

heartlands ['hɑːtlændz] *npl* centre *m*, cœur *m*

heartless ['hɑːtlɪs] *adj* sans cœur, cruel(elle)

heartrending ['hɑːtrendɪŋ] *adj* déchirant(e), navrant(e)

heart-searching ['hɑːtsɜːtʃɪŋ] *n* **after much h.** après avoir longuement réfléchi

heartstrings ['hɑːtstrɪŋz] *npl* **to tug at sb's h.** jouer sur la corde sensible de qn

heartthrob ['hɑːtθrɒb] *n Fam* idole *f*

heart-to-heart ['hɑːtəˈhɑːt] **1** *n* **to have a h. with sb** avoir une conversation à cœur ouvert avec qn

2 *adj* **a h. talk** une conversation à cœur ouvert

heart-warming ['hɑːtwɔːmɪŋ] *adj* réconfortant(e), qui réchauffe le cœur

hearty ['hɑːtɪ] *adj* (**a**) *(person, laugh)* jovial(e); *(approval, welcome)* chaleureux(euse); **to have a h. dislike of sth** avoir une sainte horreur de qch; **my heartiest congratulations** mes plus sincères félicitations (**b**) *(substantial) (meal, appetite)* solide

heat [hiːt] **1** *n* (**a**) *(high temperature)* chaleur *f*; **to give out h.** dégager de la chaleur; **to cook at a moderate/low h.** faire cuire à feu moyen/doux; **h. exhaustion** coup *m* de chaleur; **h. haze** brume *f* de chaleur; **h. loss** déperdition *f* de chaleur; **h. rash** boutons *mpl* de chaleur; *Med* **h. treatment** thermothérapie *f* (**b**) *(passion)* feu *m*; **in the h. of the moment/argument** dans le feu de l'action/de la discussion (**c**) *Fam (pressure)* **to turn up the h.** mettre la pression; **the h. is on** la tension est à son comble (**d**) *(of female animal)* **in h.** en chaleur (**e**) *(in sports)* éliminatoire *f*

2 *vt (food, water)* faire chauffer; *(room, building)* chauffer

▶**heat up 1** *vt sep* réchauffer

2 *vi (of water)* chauffer; *(of room)* se réchauffer; *Fig (of argument, contest)* s'animer

heated ['hiːtɪd] *adj* (**a**) *(room, building, swimming pool)* chauffé(e) (**b**) *(argument)* animé(e); **to become h.** *(of person)* s'échauffer

heater ['hiːtə(r)] *n* radiateur *m*

heath [hiːθ] *n (land)* lande *f*

heathen ['hiːðən] *n Rel* païen(enne) *m,f*; *Hum* barbare *mf*

heather ['heðə(r)] *n* bruyère *f*

heating ['hiːtɪŋ] *n* chauffage *m*

heatproof ['hiːtpruːf] *adj* résistant(e) à la chaleur; *(clothing)* isolant(e)

heatstroke ['hiːtstrəʊk] *n* coup *m* de chaleur

heatwave ['hiːtweɪv] *n* vague *f* de chaleur, canicule *f*

heave [hiːv] **1** *n* effort *m*

2 *vt* (**a**) *(pull)* tirer fort; *(push)* pousser fortement; *(lift)* soulever avec effort; **she heaved herself out of her chair** elle

s'extirpa de sa chaise; **to h. a sigh of relief** pousser un soupir de soulagement (**b**) *Fam (throw)* balancer

3 *vi* (**a**) *(pull)* **they heaved on the rope** ils tirèrent sur la corde fortement (**b**) *(of deck, ground)* tanguer, se soulever; *(of bosom)* se soulever (**c**) *(retch)* avoir des haut-le-cœur; *(vomit)* vomir (**d**) *(pt & pp* **hove** [həʊv]) *also Fig* **to h. into view** paraître à l'horizon

▶**heave to** *(pt & pp* **hove** [həʊv]) *vi Naut* se mettre en panne

heaven ['hevən] *n* paradis *m*, ciel *m*; **in h.** au paradis, au ciel; *Fig (overjoyed)* aux anges; **this is h.!** c'est le paradis!; **to move h. and earth to do sth** remuer ciel et terre pour faire qch; **the heavens opened** il s'est mis à pleuvoir à torrents; *Fam* **it stinks to high h.** ça pue; **(good) heavens!, heavens above!** juste ciel!, mon Dieu!; **thank h. (for that)!** Dieu merci!; **h. knows why…** Dieu seul sait pourquoi…; **for h.'s sake!** pour l'amour du ciel!; **h. forbid!** que le ciel nous en préserve!

heavenly ['hevənlɪ] *adj* (**a**) **h. body** corps *m* céleste (**b**) *Fam (weather, food)* divin(e)

heaven-sent ['hevənsent] *adj* providentiel(elle)

heavily ['hevɪlɪ] *adv (fall, walk, tax)* lourdement; *(sleep)* profondément; *(breathe)* bruyamment; **to drink/to smoke h.** boire/fumer beaucoup; **it was raining h.** il pleuvait à torrents; **to rely** *or* **to depend h. on** dépendre beaucoup de; **h. built** solidement charpenté(e); **to be h. defeated** subir une lourde défaite

heavy ['hevɪ] **1** *n (pl* **heavies**) *Fam (tough guy)* dur *m*

2 *adj* (**a**) *(in weight, food)* lourd(e); **how h. is it?** combien est-ce que ça pèse?; **a h. blow** un coup violent; *Fig* un coup rude; *Culin* **h. cream** ≃ crème *f* fraîche épaisse; **h. industry** industrie *f* lourde; **h. metal** *Chem* métal *m* lourd; *(music)* heavy metal *m*

(**b**) *(large, thick) (coat, shoes)* gros (grosse); **h. losses** lourdes pertes *fpl*

(**c**) *(intense) (fighting)* violent(e); *(rain, showers)* fort(e); *(drinker, smoker)* gros (grosse); **a h. cold** un gros rhume; **there was h. traffic** il y avait beaucoup de circulation; **to be a h. sleeper** avoir le sommeil lourd; **to come under h. fire** essuyer un feu nourri

(**d**) *(oppressive) (smell)* fort(e); *(sky, fine, sentence)* lourd(e); **h. responsibility** lourde responsabilité *f*

(**e**) *(hard) (work, day, breathing)* pénible; **it was h. going** c'était difficile *ou* ardu; **h. seas** grosse mer *f*

(**f**) *Fam (threatening) (situation)* difficile, pénible

(**g**) *Fam (serious) (book, article)* intello

heavy-duty [hevɪ'djuːtɪ] *adj (machine)* à usage industriel; *(clothing, boots)* résistant(e)

heavy-handed [hevɪ'hændɪd] *adj (clumsy)* maladroit(e); *(government, policy)* autoritaire; **the police responded in a h. way** la police est intervenue de façon très agressive

heavyweight ['hevɪweɪt] *n (in boxing)* poids *m* lourd; *Fig* **a political h.** un grand ponte de la politique; **an intellectual h.** un grand intellectuel

Hebrew ['hiːbruː] **1** *n (language)* hébreu *m*

2 *adj* hébraïque

Hebrides ['hebrɪdiːz] *npl* **the H.** les (îles *fpl*) Hébrides *fpl*

heck [hek] *n Fam* **h.!** zut!; **what the h. are you doing here?** qu'est-ce que tu fiches là?; **what the h.!** et puis flûte!; **a h. of a lot** des masses

heckle ['hekəl] **1** *vt* interpeller, interrompre

2 *vi* chahuter

heckler ['heklə(r)] *n* chahuteur(euse) *m,f*

heckling ['heklɪŋ] *n* chahut *m*

hectare ['hektɑː(r)] *n* hectare *m*

hectic ['hektɪk] *adj (busy)* agité(e); *(eventful)* mouvementé(e); **a h. life** une vie trépidante

hector ['hektə(r)] *vt* rudoyer

hectoring ['hektərɪŋ] *adj* autoritaire

he'd [hi:d] = **he had, he would**

hedge [hedʒ] **1** *n* (**a**) *(in field, garden)* haie *f* (**b**) *(barrier)* **a h. against inflation** une protection contre l'inflation; *Fin* **h. fund** société *f* d'investissement **2** *vt* (**a**) *(field)* entourer d'une haie (**b**) **to h. one's bets** se couvrir **3** *vi (in discussion)* ne pas se mouiller

hedgehog ['hedʒhɒg] *n* hérisson *m*

hedgerow ['hedʒrəʊ] *n* haie *f*

hedonism ['hi:dənɪzəm] *n* hédonisme *m*

hedonist ['hi:dənɪst] *n* & *adj* hédoniste *mf*

heed [hi:d] **1** *n* **to pay (no) h. to, to take (no) h. of** (ne pas) tenir compte de **2** *vt (warning, advice)* tenir compte de

heedless ['hi:dlɪs] *adj* **to be h. of** ne pas tenir compte de

heel [hi:l] **1** *n (of foot, shoe, sock)* talon *m*; **high heels** talons hauts; **he had the police at his heels** il avait la police sur les talons *ou* à ses trousses; **to take to one's heels** prendre ses jambes à son cou; **to turn on one's h.** tourner les talons; *Fam* **to cool** *or* **to kick one's heels** *(wait)* poireauter; *Fig* **to bring sb to h.** *(bring under control)* mettre qn au pas; **to be down at the heels** *(shoes)* être éculé(e); *Fig (person)* avoir l'air miteux **2** *vt (shoe)* réparer le talon de

hefty ['heftɪ] *adj Fam (person)* costaud(e); *(suitcase, box)* lourd(e); *(blow)* puissant(e); *(bill, fine)* gros (grosse)

heifer ['hefə(r)] *n* génisse *f*

height [haɪt] *n (of building, tree)* hauteur *f*; *(of mountain)* altitude *f*; *(of person)* taille *f*; **what h. are you?** combien mesurez-vous?; **to gain/lose h.** *(of plane)* prendre/perdre de l'altitude; **to be afraid of heights** avoir le vertige; **she's at the h. of her powers** elle est au maximum de ses capacités; **she's at the h. of her career** elle est à l'apogée de sa carrière; **the h. of fashion** la dernière mode; **it's the h. of madness!** c'est le comble de la folie pure!; **at the h. of the storm** au plus fort de l'orage; **the season is at its h.** la saison bat son plein

heighten ['haɪtən] *vt (sensation)* intensifier; *(tension)* augmenter; **to h. public awareness** sensibiliser l'opinion

heinous ['heɪnəs] *adj Formal (crime)* abominable, atroce

heir [eə(r)] *n* héritier(ère) *m,f*; **to be h. to sth** être l'héritier de qch; **h. apparent** héritier présomptif

heiress ['eərɪs] *n* héritière *f*

heirloom ['eəlu:m] *n* **a family h.** un objet de famille

held [held] *pt* & *pp of* **hold**

helicopter ['helɪkɒptə(r)] *n* hélicoptère *m*

helipad ['helɪpæd], **heliport** ['helɪpɔ:t] *n* héliport *m*

heliskiing ['helɪski:ɪŋ] *n* héliski *m*

helium ['hi:lɪəm] *n* hélium *m*

hell [hel] *n* (**a**) *Rel* enfer *m*; *Fam* **h.!** zut alors! (**b**) *Fam (for emphasis)* **a h. of a price** un prix salé; **what the h. do you think you're doing?** qu'est-ce que tu fous?; **who the h. are you?** qui diable êtes-vous?; **she put up a h. of a fight** elle s'est bien défendue; **to have a h. of a time** *(good)* s'éclater; *(bad)* en baver; **a h. of a lot of...** énormément de...; **he's one** *or* **a h. of a guy** c'est un brave type (**c**) *Fam (idioms)* **it was h.** c'était l'enfer; **to feel like h.** se sentir horriblement mal; **to make sb's life h.** faire de la vie de qn un enfer; **these shoes are giving me h.** ces chaussures me font un mal de chien; **all h. was let** *or* **broke loose** ce fut le chaos; **there'll be h. to pay if...** ça va barder si...; **go to h.!** va te faire voir!; **to run like h.** courir comme un dératé; **like h. (I will)!** certainement pas!; **until h. freezes over** jusqu'à la saint-glinglin; **come h. or high water** quoi qu'il arrive; **to run h. for leather** courir ventre à terre; **to do sth for the h. of it** faire qch sans raison particulière

he'll [hi:l] = **he will, he shall**

hellbent ['helbent] *adj Fam* **to be h. on doing sth** vouloir à tout prix faire qch

hellhole ['helhəʊl] *n Fam (bar, club)* bouge *m*; *(prison)* enfer *m*

hellish ['helɪʃ] *adj Fam* infernal(e)

hello [he'ləʊ] *exclam* bonjour!; *(on phone)* allô!; **to say h. to sb** dire bonjour à qn

hell-raiser ['helreɪzə(r)] *n Fam* perturbateur(trice) *m,f*

helm [helm] *n (of ship)* barre *f*; *also Fig* **to be at the h.** être à la barre

helmet ['helmɪt] *n* casque *m*

helmsman ['helmzmən] *n* timonier *m*

help [help] **1** *n* (**a**) *(aid)* aide *f*; **to shout for h.** crier à l'aide; **h.!** à l'aide!, au secours!; **to be of h. to sb** aider qn; **thank you, you've been a great h.** merci beaucoup de votre aide; **there was no h. for it** il n'y avait rien à faire; **with the h. of sb** avec l'aide de qn; **with the h. of sth** *(implement)* à l'aide de qch; *Comput* **h. desk** service *m* d'assistance; *Comput* **h. file** fichier *m* d'aide (**b**) *(employees)* employés *mpl*; *(cleaning woman)* femme *f* de ménage; **h. wanted** *(ad)* cherchons employés **2** *vt* (**a**) *(aid)* aider; **to h. sb (to) do sth** aider qn à faire qch; **to h. sb to their feet** aider qn à se mettre debout; **to h. sb on/off with his coat** aider qn à mettre/enlever son manteau; **to h. one another** s'entraider; **to h. oneself to sth** se servir en *ou* de qch; **h. yourself!** servez-vous! (**b**) *(prevent)* **I can't h. it** je ne peux pas m'en empêcher; **it can't be helped** on n'y peut rien; **I couldn't h. laughing/overhearing** je ne pouvais pas m'empêcher de rire/d'écouter; **he can't h. being bald** ce n'est pas de sa faute s'il est chauve; **not if I can h. it!** pas si je peux l'éviter! **3** *vi* aider; **can I h.?** puis-je vous aider?; **that doesn't h. very much** cela ne nous avance pas beaucoup

▸ **help out** *vt sep* & *vi* aider

helper ['helpə(r)] *n* aide *mf*, assistant(e) *m,f*

helpful ['helpfʊl] *adj (person)* serviable; *(advice, device, book)* utile; **to be h.** *(of person)* se rendre utile, aider

helpfully ['helpfʊlɪ] *adv* obligeamment

helping ['helpɪŋ] **1** *n (portion)* part *f*, portion *f*; **I had a second h. of spaghetti** je me suis resservi des spaghettis **2** *adj* **to lend a h. hand** donner un coup de main

helpless ['helplɪs] *adj (powerless)* impuissant(e); *(invalid)* impotent(e); **we were h. to prevent it** nous n'avons pas pu l'empêcher; **to be h. with laughter** être plié(e) de rire

helplessly ['helplɪslɪ] *adv (watch)* sans pouvoir agir; *(struggle)* en vain

helpline ['helplaɪn] *n* service *m* d'assistance téléphonique

Helsinki [hel'sɪŋkɪ] *n* Helsinki

helter-skelter ['heltə'skeltə(r)] *adv* **to run h.** courir comme un fou (une folle); **to fall h.** faire une chute spectaculaire

hem [hem] **1** *n* ourlet *m* **2** *vt (pt* & *pp* **hemmed)** ourler **3** *vi* **to h. and haw** hésiter

▸ **hem in** *vt sep (surround)* cerner

he-man ['hi:mæn] *n Fam* homme *m* viril

hemisphere ['hemɪsfɪə(r)] *n* hémisphère *m*

hemline ['hemlaɪn] *n* ourlet *m*

hemlock ['hemlɒk] *n* ciguë *f*

hemoglobin [hi:məʊ'gləʊbɪn] *n* hémoglobine *f*

hemophilia [hi:məʊ'fɪlɪə] *n* hémophilie *f*

hemophiliac [hi:məʊ'fɪlɪæk] *n* hémophile *mf*

hemorrhage ['hemərɪdʒ] **1** *n also Fig* hémorragie *f* **2** *vi Med* faire une hémorragie; *Fig (of support, funds)* diminuer

hemp [hemp] *n* chanvre *m*

hen [hen] *n* poule *f*

hence [hens] *adv* (**a**) *(thus)* d'où; **h. his anger** d'où sa colère (**b**) *(from now)* d'ici; **five years h.** d'ici cinq ans

henceforth [hens'fɔ:θ] *adv Formal* dès lors, désormais

henchman ['henʃmən] *n Pej* acolyte *m*

hencoop ['henku:p] *n* cage *f* à poules

henhouse ['henhaʊs] *n* poulailler *m*

henna ['henə] **1** *n* henné *m*; **h. tattoo** tatouage *m* au henné
2 *vt* teindre au henné; **to h. one's hair** se faire un henné

henpecked ['henpekt] *adj* mené(e) par le bout du nez

hepatitis [hepə'taɪtɪs] *n* hépatite *f*

her [*unstressed* hə(r), *stressed* hɜ:(r)] **1** *pron* (**a**) *(direct object)* la; **I hate h.** je la déteste; **I love h.** je l'aime; **I can understand her son but not** HER je comprends son fils, mais elle, je ne la comprends pas (**b**) *(indirect object)* lui; **I gave h. the book** je lui ai donné le livre; **I gave it to h.** je le lui ai donné (**c**) *(after preposition)* elle; **I'm thinking of h.** je pense à elle (**d**) *(as complement of verb* to be) elle; **it's h.!** c'est elle!; **it was h. who did it** c'est elle qui l'a fait
2 *possessive adj* (**a**) *(singular)* son (sa); *(plural)* ses; **h. husband** son mari; **h. family** sa famille; **h. parents** ses parents; **it wasn't** HER **idea!** ce n'est pas elle qui en a eu l'idée! (**b**) *(for parts of body)* **she hit h. head** elle s'est cogné la tête

herald ['herəld] **1** *n (messenger)* héraut *m*; *Fig (sign)* signe *m* avant-coureur
2 *vt* annoncer

heraldry ['herəldrɪ] *n* héraldique *f*

herb [ɜ:b, hɜ:b] *n* herbe *f* aromatique

herbal ['ɜ:bəl, 'hɜ:bəl] *adj* à base de plantes; **h. tea** tisane *f*

herbalist [ɜ:bəlɪst, 'hɜ:bəlɪst] *n* herboriste *mf*

herbicide ['ɜ:bɪsaɪd, 'hɜ:bɪsaɪd] *n* herbicide *m*

herbivorous [ɜ:'bɪvərəs, hɜ:'bɪvərəs] *adj* herbivore

herd [hɜ:d] **1** *n (of cattle, sheep, elephants)* troupeau *m*; *(of horses)* troupe *f*; *(of people)* groupe *m*; *Pej* troupeau; **the h. instinct** l'instinct grégaire
2 *vt (cattle, people)* rassembler

herdsman ['hɜ:dzmən] *n* gardien *m* de troupeau

here [hɪə(r)] **1** *adv* ici; **over h.** par ici; **h. it/he is** le voilà; **h.!** *(at roll call)* présent!; **come h.!** viens ici!; **h., come and look at this!** eh! viens voir ça!; **she's not h.** elle n'est pas là; **h. she comes** la voilà; **h. and now** immédiatement; **h. and there** çà et là; *Fig* **that's neither h. nor there** ça n'a aucun rapport; **what have we h.?** qu'est-ce que c'est que ça?; **h.'s what you have to do** voilà ce que tu as à faire; **h. goes!** allons-y!; **h.'s to the future!** à l'avenir!
2 *n* **the h. and now** le présent

hereafter [hɪər'ɑ:ftə(r)] **1** *n Lit* **the h.** l'au-delà *m*
2 *adv Formal (below)* ci-après; *(in the future)* dorénavant

hereby [hɪə'baɪ] *adv Formal (in writing)* par la présente; *(in speech)* solennellement

hereditary [hɪ'redɪtərɪ] *adj* héréditaire

heredity [hɪ'redɪtɪ] *n* hérédité *f*

heresy ['herəsɪ] *(pl* **heresies**) *n* hérésie *f*

heretic ['herətɪk] *n* hérétique *mf*

heretical [hɪ'retɪkəl] *adj* hérétique

heritage ['herɪtɪdʒ] *n* patrimoine *m*

hermaphrodite [hɜ:'mæfrədaɪt] *n & adj* hermaphrodite *mf*

hermetic [hɜ:'metɪk] *adj* hermétique

hermetically [hɜ:'metɪklɪ] *adv* hermétiquement

hermit ['hɜ:mɪt] *n* ermite *m*; **h. crab** bernard-l'ermite *m inv*

hernia ['hɜ:nɪə] *n* hernie *f*

hero ['hɪərəʊ] *(pl* **heroes**) *n* héros *m*; **h. worship** adulation *f*, idolâtrie *f*

heroic [hɪ'rəʊɪk] *adj* héroïque

heroically [hɪ'rəʊɪklɪ] *adv* héroïquement

heroics [hɪ'rəʊɪks] *npl* coup *m* d'éclat

heroin ['herəʊɪn] *n (drug)* héroïne *f*; **h. addict** héroïnomane *mf*

heroine ['herəʊɪn] *n (female hero)* héroïne *f*

heroism ['herəʊɪzəm] *n* héroïsme *m*

heron ['herən] *n* héron *m*

hero-worship ['hɪərəʊwɜ:ʃɪp] *vt* idolâtrer

herpes ['hɜ:pi:z] *n* herpès *m*

herring ['herɪŋ] *(pl* **herring** *or* **herrings**) *n* hareng *m*

hers [hɜ:z] *possessive pron* (**a**) *(singular)* le sien (la sienne) *m,f*; *(plural)* les siens (les siennes) *mpl, fpl*; **my house is big, but h. is bigger** j'ai une grande maison, mais la sienne est plus grande encore (**b**) *(used attributively)* **this book is h.** ce livre est à elle; **a friend of h.** un de ses amis; **where's that brother of h.?** où son frère a-t-il bien pu passer?

herself [hɜ:'self] *pron* (**a**) *(reflexive)* **she spoils h.** elle se gâte; **she hurt h.** elle s'est blessée (**b**) *(emphatic)* elle-même; **she h. has never...** elle-même n'a jamais...; **she told me h.** elle me l'a dit elle-même; **she's not h. today** elle n'est pas dans son état normal aujourd'hui (**c**) *(after preposition)* **she lives by h.** elle vit seule; **she bought it for h.** elle se l'est acheté; **she talks to h.** elle parle toute seule

he's [hi:z] = **he is, he has**

hesitancy ['hezɪtənsɪ] *n* hésitation *f*

hesitant ['hezɪtənt] *adj* hésitant(e); **to be h. about doing sth** hésiter à faire qch

hesitate ['hezɪteɪt] *vi* hésiter

hesitation [hezɪ'teɪʃən] *n* hésitation *f*; **without h.** sans hésitation, sans hésiter

heterogeneous [hetərə'dʒi:nɪəs] *adj* hétérogène

heterosexual [hetərəʊ'seksjʊəl] *n & adj* hétérosexuel(elle) *m,f*

heterosexuality [hetərəʊseksjʊ'ælɪtɪ] *n* hétérosexualité *f*

heuristics [hu:'rɪstɪks] *npl* heuristique *f*

hew [hju:] *(pp* **hewn** [hju:n] *or* **hewed**) *vt (wood)* couper; *(rock)* tailler

hexagon ['heksəgən] *n* hexagone *m*

hexagonal [hek'sægənəl] *adj* hexagonal(e)

hey [heɪ] *exclam (for atttention)* eh!; *(in surprise)* tiens!; **h. (there)!** *(as greeting)* salut!

heyday ['heɪdeɪ] *n* apogée *m*; **in its h.** à son apogée; **in his h.** au sommet de sa gloire

hi [haɪ] *exclam Fam* salut!

hiatus [haɪ'eɪtəs] *n (interruption)* interruption *f*; *(in conversation)* silence *m*; *(in manuscript, records)* lacune *f*

hibernate ['haɪbəneɪt] *vi* hiberner

hibernation [haɪbə'neɪʃən] *n* hibernation *f*; **to go into h.** entrer en hibernation

hiccup ['hɪkʌp] **1** *n* hoquet *m*; *Fig (in plan)* accroc *m*; **to have (the) hiccups** avoir le hoquet
2 *vi* avoir le hoquet; *(once)* avoir un hoquet

hick [hɪk] *n Fam* péquenaud(e) *m,f*

hickory ['hɪkərɪ] *(pl* **hickories**) *n (tree, wood)* hickory *m*, noyer *m* blanc d'Amérique

hid [hɪd] *pt of* **hide**[1]

hidden ['hɪdən] **1** *adj* caché(e); **h. agenda** programme *m* secret
2 *pp of* **hide**[1]

hide[1] [haɪd] **1** *n (for birdwatching)* affût *m*
2 *vt (pt* **hid** [hɪd], *pp* **hidden** ['hɪdən]) cacher (**from** à); **to have nothing to h.** n'avoir rien à cacher; **to be hidden from sight** être caché(e); **to h. oneself** se cacher
3 *vi* se cacher (**from** de)

hide[2] [haɪd] *n (skin)* peau *f*; *Fig* **to save one's h.** sauver sa peau; **I haven't seen h. nor hair of her** je ne l'ai pas vue du tout

hide-and-seek [haɪdən'si:k] *n* cache-cache *m*; **to play h.** jouer à cache-cache

hidebound ['haɪdbaʊnd] *adj* rigide, borné(e)

hideous ['hɪdɪəs] *adj (ugly)* hideux(euse); *(horrific)* horrible

hideously ['hɪdɪəslɪ] *adv* horriblement, affreusement

hide-out ['haɪdaʊt] *n* cachette *f*

hiding[1] ['haɪdɪŋ] *n (concealment)* **to be in h.** se cacher; **to go into h.** se cacher; **to come out of h.** sortir de sa cachette; *(after war)* sortir de la clandestinité; **h. place** cachette *f*

hiding[2] ['haɪdɪŋ] *n Fam (beating)* raclée *f*; **to give sb a h.** donner une raclée à qn

hierarchical [haɪə'rɑːkɪkəl] *adj* hiérarchique

hierarchy ['haɪərɑːkɪ] (*pl* **hierarchies**) *n* hiérarchie *f*

hieroglyphics [haɪərə'glɪfɪks] *npl* hiéroglyphes *mpl*

hi-fi ['haɪfaɪ] *n* hi-fi *f inv*; *(stereo system)* chaîne *f* (hi-fi)

higgledy-piggledy ['hɪgəldɪ'pɪgəldɪ] *Fam* **1** *adj* en désordre **2** *adv* pêle-mêle

high [haɪ] **1** *n* (**a**) *(peak) (in career, performance)* sommet *m*; *(in quantity, degree)* maximum *m*; **unemployment has reached a new h.** le chômage a atteint un nouveau record; **to be on a h.** *(from drugs)* planer; *(from success)* être sur un petit nuage; **the highs and lows** les hauts *mpl* et les bas *mpl*
(**b**) *(weather front)* anticyclone *m*
2 *adj* (**a**) *(mountain, building)* haut(e), élevé(e); **to be five feet h.** ≃ faire 1,50 mètres de haut; *Fam* **to be left h. and dry** être laissé(e) en plan; *Aut* **h. beams** phares *mpl*; *Aut* **h. gear** quatrième *f* (vitesse *f*); *(fifth)* cinquième *f* (vitesse *f*); *Fig* **to move into h. gear** se dépêcher; **h. jump** saut *m* en hauteur; **h. jumper** sauteur(euse) *m,f* en hauteur; **h. tide** marée *f* haute; **h. wire** corde *f* raide
(**b**) *(price, speed, standards)* élevé(e); *(quality)* premier(ère); **to have a h. opinion of sb** avoir une haute opinion de qn; **h. explosive** explosif *m* puissant; **h. point** point *m* culminant; **in h. spirits** plein(e) d'entrain; *Law* **h. treason** haute trahison *f*; **h. winds** vents *mpl* forts
(**c**) *(rank, position)* haut(e); **to act all h. and mighty** agir avec beaucoup d'arrogance; *Mil* **h. command** haut commandement *m*; **H. Commission** haut-commissariat *m*; **h. court** ≃ Cour *f* suprême; **H. Mass** grand-messe *f*; **h. school** = école secondaire qui accueille les élèves de 11 à 18 ans; **h. society** haute société *f*
(**d**) *(in tone, pitch)* aigu(ë); *Fig* **h. note** *(of career, performance)* point *m* culminant
(**e**) *(with time)* **it's h. time you got yourself a job** il est grand temps que tu trouves un travail; **h. noon** plein midi; **h. summer** plein été
(**f**) *(meat)* avancé(e)
(**g**) *Fam* **to be h.** *(on drugs)* planer; *Fig (on success, excitement)* être euphorique
3 *adv (aim, jump)* haut; **to hunt h. and low for sth** remuer ciel et terre pour trouver qch; **feelings were running h.** la tension montait

highbrow ['haɪbraʊ] *adj* intellectuel(elle)

highchair ['haɪtʃeə(r)] *n* chaise *f* haute

higher education ['haɪəredjʊ'keɪʃən] *n* enseignement *m* supérieur

high-flier, high-flyer ['haɪ'flaɪə(r)] *n (person)* battant(e) *m,f*; *(company)* société *f* qui va de l'avant

high-flying ['haɪ'flaɪɪŋ] *adj* ambitieux(euse)

high-frequency [haɪ'friːkwənsɪ] *adj* (à) haute fréquence *inv*

high-handed [haɪ'hændɪd] *adj* autoritaire, despotique

high-heeled ['haɪ'hiːld] *adj* à talons hauts

Highlands ['haɪləndz] *npl* **the H.** *(of Scotland)* les Highlands *fpl*

high-level ['haɪlevəl] *adj (talks)* à haut niveau; *(delegation)* de haut niveau

highlight ['haɪlaɪt] **1** *n* (**a**) *(of performance, career)* point *m* culminant; **highlights** *(of match, event)* moments *mpl* forts (**b**) **highlights** *(in hair) (artificial)* mèches *fpl*; *(natural)* reflets *mpl*
2 *vt* (**a**) *(problem, difference)* mettre en évidence, souligner (**b**) *(with highlighter)* surligner; *Comput (block of text)* sélectionner

highlighter ['haɪlaɪtə(r)] *n (pen)* surligneur *m*

highly ['haɪlɪ] *adv* (**a**) *(very)* très, extrêmement; **h. paid** très bien payé(e); **h. seasoned** fortement assaisonné(e) (**b**) *(favorably)* **to think h. of sb** avoir une haute opinion de qn; **to speak h. of sb** parler de qn en termes élogieux

high-minded ['haɪ'maɪndɪd] *adj (sentiments, behavior)* noble; *(person)* qui a des principes

Highness ['haɪnɪs] *n* **His/Her Royal H.** Son Altesse *f*

high-pitched ['haɪpɪtʃt] *adj* aigu(ë)

high-powered ['haɪ'paʊəd] *adj (engine, car, telescope)* très puissant(e); *(job)* à hautes responsabilités; *(person)* qui occupe un poste à hautes responsabilités

high-pressure ['haɪ'preʃə(r)] *adj* (**a**) *(cylinder, gas, machine)* à haute pression (**b**) *(salesman)* agressif(ive)

high-profile ['haɪ'prəʊfaɪl] *adj (person)* très en vue; *(campaign)* de grande envergure

high-resolution ['haɪrezə'luːʃən] *adj Comput (screen, graphics)* à haute résolution

high-rise ['haɪ'raɪz] **1** *n (apartment block)* tour *f*
2 *adj* **h. building** tour *f*

high-risk ['haɪrɪsk] *adj (strategy, investment)* à haut risque

highroad ['haɪrəʊd] *n Old-fashioned* grand-route *f*; *Fig* **the h. to success** la voie du succès

high-speed ['haɪ'spiːd] *adj* ultrarapide; *(train)* à grande vitesse; **h. chase** course-poursuite *f* infernale

high-spirited [haɪ'spɪrɪtɪd] *adj* plein(e) d'entrain

high-strung [haɪ'strʌŋ] *adj* hypersensible

high-tech ['haɪ'tek] *adj (appliance)* perfectionné(e); *(industry)* de pointe; *(approach, solution)* qui a recours à une technologie de pointe

high-up ['haɪʌp] *adj Fam (important)* haut placé(e)

highway ['haɪweɪ] *n (main road)* (route *f*) nationale *f*; *(freeway)* autoroute *f*; **h. patrol** police *f* de la route; **h. robbery** banditisme *m* de grand chemin; *Fam Fig* **that's h. robbery!** c'est du vol!

highwayman ['haɪweɪmən] *n* bandit *m* de grand chemin

hijack ['haɪdʒæk] *vt (plane)* détourner; *(car, truck)* s'emparer de force de; *(idea)* s'approprier

hijacker ['haɪdʒækə(r)] *n (of plane)* pirate *m* de l'air

hike [haɪk] **1** *n* (**a**) *(walk)* randonnée *f*; **to go on** or **for a h.** faire une randonnée; *Fam Fig* **go take a h.!** lâche-moi les baskets! (**b**) *(in prices)* hausse *f*
2 *vt (prices)* augmenter
3 *vi (walk)* faire de la randonnée

hiker ['haɪkə(r)] *n* randonneur(euse) *m,f*

hiking ['haɪkɪŋ] *n* randonnée *f*; **to go h.** faire de la randonnée; **h. boots** chaussures *fpl* de marche

hilarious [hɪ'leərɪəs] *adj* hilarant(e)

hilariously [hɪ'leərɪəslɪ] *adv* **h. funny** à se tordre de rire; **to laugh h.** se tordre de rire

hilarity [hɪ'lærɪtɪ] *n* hilarité *f*; **his suggestion was greeted with much h.** sa suggestion déclencha l'hilarité générale

hill [hɪl] *n* (**a**) *(small mountain)* colline *f*; *Fig* **to be over the h.** commencer à se faire vieux (vieille) (**b**) *(slope)* côte *f*, pente *f*; **to go down/up the h.** descendre/monter la côte

hillbilly ['hɪlbɪlɪ] (*pl* **hillbillies**) *n Pej* péquenaud(e) *m,f*

hillock ['hɪlək] *n* butte *f*

hillside ['hɪlsaɪd] *n* coteau *m*

hilltop ['hɪltɒp] *n* sommet *m* de la colline

hillwalker ['hɪlwɔːkə(r)] *n* randonneur(euse) *m,f*

hillwalking ['hɪlwɔːkɪŋ] *n* randonnée *f* en basse montagne

hilly ['hɪlɪ] *adj* vallonné(e)

hilt [hɪlt] *n (of sword)* poignée *f*; *(of knife, dagger)* manche *m*; *Fig* **to back sb to the h.** soutenir qn sans réserve

him [hɪm] *pron* (**a**) *(direct object)* le; **I hate h.** je le déteste; **I love h.** je l'aime; **I can understand his son but not** HIM je comprends son fils, mais lui, je ne le comprends pas (**b**) *(indirect* *object)* lui; **I gave h. the book** je lui ai donné le livre; **I gave it to h.** je le lui ai donné (**c**) *(after preposition)* lui; **I'm thinking of h.** je pense à lui (**d**) *(as complement of verb to be)* lui; **it's h.!** c'est lui!; **it was h. who did it** c'est lui qui l'a fait

Himalayan [hɪmə'leɪən] *adj* himalayen(enne)

Himalayas [hɪmə'leɪəz] *npl* **the H.** l'Himalaya *m*

himself [hɪm'self] *pron* (**a**) *(reflexive)* **he spoils h.** il se gâte; **he hurt h.** il s'est blessé (**b**) *(emphatic)* lui-même; **he h. has never…** lui-même n'a jamais…; **he told me h.** il me l'a dit lui-même; **he's not h. today** il n'est pas dans son état normal aujourd'hui (**c**) *(after preposition)* **he lives by h.** il vit seul; **he bought it for h.** il se l'est acheté; **he talks to h.** il parle tout seul

hind¹ [haɪnd] *adj (back)* de derrière; **h. legs** pattes *fpl* de derrière

hind² [haɪnd] *n (female deer)* daim *m* femelle

hinder ['hɪndə(r)] *vt (impede)* gêner; *(delay)* retarder; **to h. sb from doing sth** empêcher qn de faire qch

Hindi ['hɪndɪ] *n (language)* hindi *m*

hindquarters ['haɪndkwɔːtəz] *npl* arrière-train *m*

hindrance ['hɪndrəns] *n* entrave *f*, obstacle *m*

hindsight ['haɪndsaɪt] *n* recul *m*; **with (the benefit of) h.** avec le recul

Hindu ['hɪndu:] **1** *n* Hindou(e) *m,f*
2 *adj* hindou(e)

Hinduism ['hɪndu:ɪzəm] *n* hindouisme *m*

hinge [hɪndʒ] *n* charnière *f*, gond *m*; **to come off its hinges** sortir de ses gonds

▶**hinge on, hinge upon** *vt insep (depend on)* dépendre de

hinky ['hɪŋkɪ] *adj Fam* bizarre, louche; **it tastes h.** ça a un drôle de goût

hint [hɪnt] **1** *n* (**a**) *(allusion)* allusion *f*; *(clue)* indice *m*; **to drop sb a h.** faire une allusion à l'intention de qn; **to take the h.** comprendre l'allusion; **he can't take a h.** il faut lui mettre les points sur les i (**b**) *(sign)* signe *m* (**c**) *(small amount)* soupçon *m* (**d**) *(piece of advice)* truc *m*, conseil *m*
2 *vt* **to h. that…** insinuer *ou* laisser entendre que…

▶**hint at** *vt insep* faire allusion à

hinterland ['hɪntəlænd] *n* arrière-pays *m inv*

hip¹ [hɪp] *n (part of body)* hanche *f*; **to break one's h.** se casser le col du fémur; **h. flask** flasque *f*; **h. joint** articulation *f* de la hanche; **h. pocket** poche *f* revolver

hip² [hɪp] *adj Fam (fashionable)* branché(e)

hip-hop ['hɪphɒp] *n (music)* hip-hop *m inv*

hiphuggers ['hɪphʌgəz] *npl* pantalon *m* à taille basse

hippo ['hɪpəʊ] *(pl* **hippos***) n Fam* hippopotame *m*

hippopotamus [hɪpə'pɒtəməs] *(pl* **hippopotami** [hɪpə'pɒtəmaɪ]*) n* hippopotame *m*

hippy ['hɪpɪ] *(pl* **hippies***) n* hippie *mf*

hire [haɪə(r)] *vt (lawyer, worker)* engager

▶**hire out** *vt sep (one's services)* offrir

hired ['haɪəd] *adj* **h. hand** *(on farm)* ouvrier(ère) *m,f* agricole

hirsute ['hɜːsjuːt] *adj Lit* velu(e)

his [hɪz] **1** *possessive adj* (**a**) *(singular)* son (sa); *(plural)* ses; **h. job** son travail; **h. wife** sa femme; **h. parents** ses parents; **it wasn't HIS idea!** ce n'est pas lui qui en a eu l'idée! (**b**) *(for parts of body)* **he hit h. head** il s'est cogné la tête
2 *possessive pron* (**a**) *(singular)* le sien (la sienne) *m,f*; *(plural)* les siens (les siennes) *mpl, fpl*; **my house is big, but h. is bigger** j'ai une grande maison, mais la sienne est plus grande encore (**b**) *(used attributively)* **this book is h.** ce livre est à lui; **a friend of h.** un de ses amis; **where's that brother of h.?** où son frère a-t-il bien pu passer?

Hispanic [hɪs'pænɪk] **1** *n* Latino-Américain(e) *m,f*
2 *adj* hispanique

hiss [hɪs] **1** *n (sound)* sifflement *m*; *(to express disapproval)* sifflet *m*
2 *vt & vi* siffler

histogram ['hɪstəgræm] *n* histogramme *m*

historian [hɪs'tɔːrɪən] *n* historien(enne) *m,f*

historic [hɪs'tɒrɪk] *adj* historique

historical [hɪs'tɒrɪkəl] *adj* historique

historically [hɪs'tɒrɪklɪ] *adv* historiquement

history ['hɪstərɪ] *(pl* **histories***) n* (**a**) *(the past)* histoire *f*; **to go down in h., to make h.** *(of event)* faire date; *(of person)* entrer dans l'histoire; *Fig* **that's (ancient) h.** c'est de l'histoire ancienne; **h. book/teacher** livre *m*/professeur *m* d'histoire (**b**) *(medical record)* antécédents *mpl*; **there is a h. of diabetes in his family** il y a des cas de diabète dans sa famille

histrionic [hɪstrɪ'ɒnɪk] *adj Pej* théâtral(e)

histrionics [hɪstrɪ'ɒnɪks] *npl Pej* comédie *f*, cinéma *m*; **to have h.** faire une scène *ou* du cinéma

hit [hɪt] **1** *n* (**a**) *(blow)* coup *m*; *(in shooting)* tir *m* réussi; **to score a direct h.** taper dans le mille; **h. list** *(of targets)* liste *f* noire; **h. man** tueur *m* à gages
(**b**) *(success)* succès *m*; **to be a h. with sb** avoir beaucoup de succès auprès de qn; **h. (record)** hit *m*
(**c**) *Comput (visit to website)* hit *m*, accès *m*; **this website counted 5,000 hits last week** ce site Web a été consulté 5 000 fois la semaine dernière
2 *adj (movie, play)* à succès
3 *vt (pt & pp* **hit***)* (**a**) *(of person)* frapper; *(of bullet)* atteindre; *(of car)* percuter; *Comput (key)* frapper, appuyer sur; **to h. one's head (on sth)** se cogner la tête (contre qch); *Fig* **it suddenly hit me that…** j'ai réalisé tout d'un coup que…; *Fig* **he didn't know what had hit him** il n'a pas eu le temps de se rendre compte de ce qui lui arrivait
(**b**) *(reach)* (barrier, difficulty) se heurter à; **to h. a note** atteindre une note; **to h. 90 (miles an hour)** ≃ faire du 140 (à l'heure); **to h. an all-time low** *(of investment, relationship)* être au plus bas; **the circus hits town tomorrow** le cirque arrive en ville demain; **it hits the stores next week** c'est en vente la semaine prochaine; *Fam* **to h. the road** *(leave)* se mettre en route; *Fam* **to h. the ceiling** *or* **the roof** sortir de ses gonds; *Fam* **to h. the hay** aller se pieuter; *Fam* **that really hits the spot!** *(of food, drink)* c'est juste ce dont j'avais besoin!; *Fam* **when it** *or Vulg* **the shit hits the fan** quand nous serons dans la merde (jusqu'au cou)
(**c**) *(affect)* toucher; **to be hard hit by sth** être durement touché(e) par qch
4 *vi* frapper

▶**hit back 1** *vt sep* **to h. sb back** rendre un coup à qn
2 *vi also Fig* riposter (**at** à)

▶**hit off** *vt sep Fam* **to h. it off** accrocher

▶**hit on** *vt insep* (**a**) *(idea, solution)* trouver (**b**) *Fam* **to h. on sb** *(make sexual advances)* draguer qn

▶**hit out** *vi* **to h. out at sb** *(physically)* frapper qn; *(verbally)* s'en prendre à qn

▶**hit upon** = hit on

hit-and-run ['hɪtən'rʌn] *n* **h. (accident)** accident *m* avec délit de fuite

hitch [hɪtʃ] **1** *n* (**a**) *(difficulty)* problème *m*; **without a h.** sans anicroche (**b**) *(knot)* nœud *m*
2 *vt* (**a**) *(attach)* attacher (**to** à); *Fam Fig* **to get hitched** *(married)* passer devant Monsieur le Maire (**b**) *Fam* **to h. a lift** faire du stop
3 *vi Fam* faire du stop; **to h. to LA** aller à Los Angeles en stop

▶**hitch up** *vt sep (pants, skirt)* remonter

hitchhike ['hɪtʃhaɪk] *vi* faire de l'auto-stop; **to h. to LA** aller à Los Angeles en auto-stop

hitchhiker ['hɪtʃhaɪkə(r)] *n* auto-stoppeur(euse) *m,f*

hi-tech = high-tech

hither ['hɪðə(r)] *adv Lit* ici; **h. and thither** çà et là

hitherto ['hɪðə'tuː] *adv* jusqu'ici, jusqu'à présent

hit-or-miss ['hɪtɔː'mɪs] *adj* aléatoire, approximatif(ive)

HIV [eɪtʃɑɪ'viː] *n* (*abbr* **human immunodeficiency virus**) VIH *m*, HIV *m*; **to be H. positive/negative** être séropositif(ive)/séronégatif(ive)

hive [haɪv] *n* ruche *f*; *Fig* **a h. of activity** une véritable ruche

▶**hive off** *vt sep* (*money, profits*) séparer

hives [haɪvz] *npl Med* urticaire *f*; **to have h.** avoir de l'urticaire

hoard [hɔːd] **1** *n* (*of food*) réserve *f*, provisions *fpl*; (*of money*) trésor *m*

  2 *vt* (*food*) amasser, stocker; (*money*) amasser, thésauriser

hoarder ['hɔːdə(r)] *n* personne *f* qui fait des réserves; **she's a real h.** elle ne jette rien

hoarding ['hɔːdɪŋ] *n* (*of food*) stockage *m*

hoarfrost ['hɔːfrɒst] *n* givre *m*, gelée *f* blanche

hoarse [hɔːs] *adj* enroué(e); **to shout oneself h.** s'enrouer à force de crier

hoary ['hɔːrɪ] *adj* (*story*) vieux (vieille); (*joke*) éculé(e)

hoax [həʊks] **1** *n* canular *m*; **to play a h. on sb** faire un canular à qn; (**bomb**) **h.** fausse alerte *f* à la bombe; **h. caller** auteur *m* de canular(s) téléphonique(s)

  2 *vt* faire un canular à

hobble ['hɒbəl] *vi* boitiller

hobby ['hɒbɪ] (*pl* **hobbies**) *n* passe-temps *m inv*; hobby *m*

hobbyhorse ['hɒbɪhɔːs] *n* (*toy*) cheval *m* de bois (*tête emmanchée sur un bâton*); *Fig* (*favorite subject*) dada *m*

hobnail boot ['hɒbneɪl'buːt] *n* chaussure *f* ferrée

hobnob ['hɒbnɒb] (*pt & pp* **hobnobbed**) *vi Fam* **to h. with sb** frayer avec qn

hock[1] [hɒk] *n* (*wine*) vin *m* du Rhin

hock[2] [hɒk] *Fam* **1** *n* **to be in h.** (*of object*) être au clou; (*of person*) être endetté(e)

  2 *vt* mettre au clou

hockey ['hɒkɪ] *n* (*on ice*) hockey *m* (sur glace); **field h.** hockey (sur gazon); **h. stick** crosse *f* de hockey

hocus-pocus ['həʊkəs'pəʊkəs] *n* (*trickery*) tromperie *f*, supercherie *f*; (*talk*) paroles *fpl* trompeuses

hodgepodge ['hɒdʒpɒdʒ] *n Fam* mélange *m*

hoe [həʊ] **1** *n* houe *f*, binette *f*

  2 *vt* (*pt & pp* **hoed**) biner, sarcler

hog [hɒg] **1** *n* (**a**) (*pig*) porc *m* châtré; *Fam* **to go the whole h.** aller jusqu'au bout (**b**) (*glutton*) glouton(onne) *m,f*, goinfre *mf*

  2 *vt* (*pt & pp* **hogged**) *Fam* (*monopolize*) monopoliser; **to h. the limelight** monopoliser l'attention

Hogmanay ['hɒgmə'neɪ] *n* (*in Scotland*) la Saint-Sylvestre

hogwash ['hɒgwɒʃ] *n Fam* âneries *fpl*

hoist [hɔɪst] **1** *n* (*device*) appareil *m* de levage

  2 *vt* hisser; **he hoisted himself on to the wall** il s'est hissé sur le mur; *Fig* **to be hoist with one's own petard** se faire prendre à son propre piège

hoity-toity ['hɔɪtɪ'tɔɪtɪ] *adj* **to be h.** se donner de grands airs

hold [həʊld] **1** *n* (**a**) (*grip*) prise *f*; **to have h. of sb/sth** tenir qn/qch; **to catch** *or* **to take h. of sth** saisir qch; *Fig* **to get h. of sb** (*find*) trouver qn; (*on phone*) joindre qn; *Fig* **to get h. of sth** se procurer qch; **to let go one's h.** relâcher son étreinte, lâcher prise; **to lose one's h. on reality** perdre le sens des réalités; *Fig* **to have a h. on** *or* **over sb** avoir de l'emprise sur qn

  (**b**) (*in wrestling*) prise *f*; *Fig* **no holds barred** tous les coups sont permis

  (**c**) **to be on h.** (*of project*) être en suspens; (*of telephone caller*) être en attente; **to put sth on h.** mettre qch en suspens; **to put sb on h.** (*on telephone*) mettre qn en attente

  (**d**) (*of ship*) cale *f*; (*of plane*) soute *f*

  2 *vt* (*pt & pp* **held** [held]) (**a**) (*grip*) tenir; **to h. sb/sth tight** tenir qn/qch serré(e), serrer qn/qch; **to h. hands** se tenir (par) la main; **to h. sth in position** maintenir qch en place; **to h. sb prisoner** retenir qn prisonnier(ère); **the police are holding him for questioning** il a été placé en garde à vue; **to h.**

sb's interest/attention retenir l'intérêt/l'attention de qn; **to h. sb to his promise** obliger qn à tenir sa promesse; **to h. one's breath** retenir sa respiration *ou* son souffle; *Fig* **don't h. your breath!** ce n'est pas pour demain! **there's no holding her** il n'y a pas moyen de l'arrêter; **h. your tongue!** tais-toi!; *Fam* **h. it!, h. your horses!** attendez!, minute!; **to h. a note** (*of singer*) tenir une note; **h. the line!** (*on telephone*) ne quittez pas!; *Fam* **h. the mayo/onions!** (*in restaurant*) sans mayonnaise/oignons!

  (**b**) (*keep*) (*town, position*) tenir; (*ticket, room*) réserver; **to h. one's ground** tenir bon; **to h. one's own** se défendre

  (**c**) (*carry*) **to h. one's head high** garder la tête haute; **to h. oneself well** se tenir bien

  (**d**) (*contain*) contenir; *Fig* **to h. water** (*of theory, story*) tenir la route; **nobody knows what the future holds** personne ne sait ce que l'avenir nous réserve; **it holds no interest for me** ça ne présente aucun intérêt pour moi

  (**e**) (*conduct*) (*negotiations*) mener; (*meeting*) organiser; (*conversation*) avoir

  (**f**) (*possess*) (*title, rank, opinion*) avoir; (*job, position*) occuper; (*record*) détenir; **to h. office** être en fonction

  (**g**) (*consider*) **to h. sb responsible** tenir qn pour responsable; **to h. sb in respect** respecter qn; **to h. that...** soutenir que...

  3 *vi* (**a**) (*of rope*) tenir; **h. tight!** tiens bon!

  (**b**) (*of agreement, weather*) durer; (*of luck*) persister; **the same holds (true) for you** cela vaut aussi pour toi

  (**c**) *Tel* attendre; **please h.** ne quittez pas

▶**hold against** *vt sep* **to h. sth against sb** reprocher qch à qn

▶**hold back 1** *vt sep* (**a**) (*restrain*) (*person, emotion*) retenir; (*progress, project*) ralentir, freiner (**b**) (*conceal*) cacher

  2 *vi* (*refrain*) se retenir (**from doing** de faire)

▶**hold down** *vt sep* (**a**) (*restrain*) (*person*) immobiliser; (*taxes, prices*) bloquer (**b**) (*job*) (*occupy*) avoir; (*keep*) garder

▶**hold forth** *vi* disserter, pérorer (**about** *or* **on** sur)

▶**hold off 1** *vt sep* (**a**) (*keep at bay*) tenir à distance (**b**) (*delay*) remettre à plus tard, repousser; **to h. off making a decision** remettre une décision à plus tard

  2 *vi* (*delay*) attendre

▶**hold on** *vi* (**a**) (*last*) tenir (**b**) (*wait*) patienter; **h. on!** attendez!; (*on telephone*) ne quittez pas! (**c**) (*not let go*) s'accrocher

▶**hold on to** *vt insep* (**a**) (*rope, handle*) s'agripper à; *Fig* (*idea, hope*) s'accrocher à (**b**) (*keep*) garder

▶**hold out 1** *vt sep* (*one's hand*) tendre; (*hope, opportunity*) offrir

  2 *vi* (**a**) (*resist*) tenir (le coup) (**b**) (*wait*) **to h. out for a better offer** attendre une meilleure offre (**c**) (*last*) durer

▶**hold over** *vt sep* remettre, reporter

▶**hold together 1** *vt sep* **to h. sth together** faire tenir qch; **to be held together with sth** tenir avec qch

  2 *vi* (*of party, group of people*) rester uni(e); (*of marriage, relationship*) tenir

▶**hold up 1** *vt sep* (**a**) (*support*) soutenir (**b**) (*raise*) lever; *Fig* **to h. sb/sth up as an example** montrer *ou* citer qn/qch en exemple; *Fig* **to h. sb/sth up to ridicule** tourner qn/qch en ridicule (**c**) (*delay*) retarder (**d**) (*rob*) attaquer

  2 *vi* (*of theory, alibi*) (se) tenir; (*of good weather*) se maintenir; **she's holding up well under the pressure** elle tient bien le coup

▶**hold with** *vt insep* (*agree with*) être d'accord avec; (*approve of*) approuver

holder ['həʊldə(r)] *n* (**a**) (*of license, ticket, record, trophy*) détenteur(trice) *m,f*; (*of passport, degree*) titulaire *mf*; (*of belief, opinion*) tenant *m* (**b**) (*device*) support *m*

holding ['həʊldɪŋ] *n* (**a**) (*property*) propriété *f* (**b**) (*of shares*) participation *f*; *Com* **h. company** holding *m* (**c**) *Fig* **h. operation** opération *f* destinée à gagner du temps

hold-up ['həʊldʌp] *n* (**a**) (*delay*) (*in plan*) retard *m*; (*of traffic*) ralentissement *m* (**b**) *(armed robbery)* hold-up *m inv*, attaque *f* à main armée

hole [həʊl] **1** *n* (**a**) *(opening)* trou *m*; *(of rabbit, fox)* terrier *m*; *also Fig* **to make a h. in sth** faire un trou dans qch; *Fig* **to pick holes in sth** relever les failles de qch; *Fig* **a h. in the law** un vide juridique; **to get a h. in one** *(in golf)* faire un trou en un; *Fam Fig* **to be in a h.** *(in difficulty)* être dans le pétrin (**b**) *Fam Pej (room, house)* taudis *m*; *(town)* trou *m*
2 *vt (ship)* faire une brèche dans; *(in golf)* **to h. a putt** faire le trou

▶**hole up** *vi Fam (hide)* se terrer

holiday ['hɒlɪdeɪ] *n* (**a**) *(day off)* (jour *m* de) congé *m* (**b**) *(public)* jour *m* férié (**c**) *(vacation)* vacances *fpl*; **a month's h.** un mois de vacances; **to be on h.** être en vacances; **to go on h.** aller *ou* partir en vacances

holiness ['həʊlɪnɪs] *n* sainteté *f*; **Your H.** Votre Sainteté

holistic [həʊ'lɪstɪk] *adj* holistique

Holland ['hɒlənd] *n* la Hollande

holler ['hɒlə(r)] *vi Fam* brailler

hollow ['hɒləʊ] **1** *n* creux *m*
2 *adj* (**a**) *(container, cheeks)* creux(euse); *(eyes)* cave (**b**) *(sound)* creux(euse); *(voice)* blanc (blanche); *(laugh)* forcé(e) (**c**) *(promise, guarantee)* vain(e); *(victory)* sans signification
3 *adv* (**a**) **to sound h.** sonner creux (**b**) *Fam* **to beat sb h.** battre qn à plate(s) couture(s)

▶**hollow out** *vt sep* évider

holly ['hɒlɪ] *n* houx *m*

hollyhock ['hɒlɪhɒk] *n* rose *f* trémière

holocaust ['hɒləkɔːst] *n* holocauste *m*

hologram ['hɒləgræm] *n* hologramme *m*

holster ['həʊlstə(r)] *n* étui *m* de revolver

holy ['həʊlɪ] *adj* saint(e); *Fam* **h. cow** *or* **smoke!** ça alors!; *Vulg* **h. shit!** merde alors!; **the H. Bible** la Sainte Bible; **H. Communion** communion *f*; **the H. Father** le saint-père; **the H. Ghost** *or* **Spirit** le Saint-Esprit; *Fam Pej* **H. Joe** grenouille *f* de bénitier; **the H. Land** la Terre Sainte; **h. orders** ordres *mpl*; **h. war** guerre *f* sainte; **h. water** eau *f* bénite; **H. Week** la semaine sainte

homage ['hɒmɪdʒ] *n* hommage *m*; **to pay h. to sb** rendre hommage à qn

home [həʊm] **1** *n* (**a**) *(house)* maison *f*; *(of animal, plant)* habitat *m*; **at h.** à la maison, chez soi; **to feel at h.** se sentir chez soi; **make yourself at h.** faites comme chez vous; **to leave h.** *(in the morning)* partir de chez soi; *(one's parents' home)* partir de chez ses parents; **to be away from h.** être en déplacement; **to work at** *or* **from h.** travailler à domicile; **to be a h. away from h.** être un second chez-soi; **to make one's h. in France** s'établir en France; **old people's h.** maison *f* de retraite; **children's h.** foyer *m* pour enfants; **h. address** adresse *f* personnelle, domicile *m*; **h. banking** banque *f* à domicile; **h. brew** bière *f* maison; **h. cooking** cuisine *f* familiale; **h. economics** *(school subject)* arts *mpl* ménagers; **h. helper** aide *f* ménagère; **h. improvements** travaux *mpl* de rénovation; **h. improvement store** magasin *m* de bricolage; **h. life** vie *f* de famille; *Fin* **h. loan** prêt *m* immobilier; **h. movie** film *m* amateur; *Sch* **h. room** = salle où l'on fait l'appel; **h. run** *(in baseball)* tour *m* complet; *Sport & Fig* **the h. stretch** la dernière ligne droite; **h. town** ville *f* natale; **to tell sb a few h. truths** dire ses quatre vérités à qn (**b**) *(country, region)* patrie *f*; **at h. and abroad** dans notre pays et à l'étranger; **an example nearer h.** un exemple qui nous concerne plus; **Milan, the h. of fashion** Milan, capitale de la mode; **h. front** arrière *m*; **h. news** nouvelles *fpl* nationales; *Pol* **h. rule** régime *m* d'autonomie politique
2 *adv* (**a**) *(to or at one's house)* à la maison, chez soi; *Fig* **to bring sth h. to sb** faire comprendre qch à qn; **to send sb h.** *(to house)* renvoyer qn chez soi; *(to home country)* rapatrier qn

(**b**) *(all the way)* **he hammered the nail h.** il enfonça complètement le clou; **the bolt slid h.** le verrou se ferma

▶**home in on** *vt insep (target)* se diriger vers; *(mistake, evidence)* relever

homecoming ['həʊmkʌmɪŋ] *n (to one's house)* retour *m* (au foyer); *(to one's country)* retour au pays; *Sch & Univ* **H.** = fête donnée en l'honneur de l'équipe de football d'une école ou d'une université, à laquelle sont invités les anciens élèves

home-grown ['həʊm'grəʊn] *adj (vegetables)* du jardin; *Fig (not imported)* national(e)

homeland ['həʊmlænd] *n* patrie *f*, pays *m* (d'origine)

homeless ['həʊmlɪs] **1** *npl* **the h.** les sans-abri *mpl*
2 *adj* sans abri

homely ['həʊmlɪ] *adj (plain)* sans charme

home-made ['həʊm'meɪd] *adj* fait(e) maison

homemaker ['həʊmmeɪkə(r)] *n* femme *f* au foyer

homeopath ['həʊmɪəʊpæθ] *n* homéopathe *mf*

homeopathic [həʊmɪəʊ'pæθɪk] *adj* homéopathique

homeopathy [həʊmɪ'ɒpəθɪ] *n* homéopathie *f*

homeowner ['həʊməʊnə(r)] *n* propriétaire *mf*

homesick ['həʊmsɪk] *adj* **to be** *or* **to feel h.** avoir le mal du pays; *(of child)* s'ennuyer de ses parents; **to be h. for sth** avoir la nostalgie de qch

homesickness ['həʊmsɪknɪs] *n* mal *m* du pays

homespun ['həʊmspʌn] *adj Fig (wisdom, advice)* simple

homestead ['həʊmsted] *n* propriété *f*; *(farm)* ferme *f*

homeward ['həʊmwəd] **1** *adj* de retour
2 *adv (to one's house)* vers sa maison; *(to one's country)* vers son pays; **to be h.-bound** être sur le chemin du retour

homewards ['həʊmwədz] *adv* = **homeward**

homework ['həʊmwɜːk] *n Sch* devoirs *mpl*; **to do one's h.** faire ses devoirs; *Fig* faire ses recherches

homey[1] ['həʊmɪ] *adj (comfortable)* accueillant(e), confortable

homey[2] ['həʊmɪ] *n Fam (from one's home town)* compatriote *mf*, *(friend)* copain (copine) *m,f*; *(fellow gang member)* = membre de la même bande

homicidal [hɒmɪ'saɪdəl] *adj* meurtrier(ère)

homicide ['hɒmɪsaɪd] *n* homicide *m*

homily ['hɒmɪlɪ] *(pl* **homilies**) *n* homélie *f*, sermon *m*

homing ['həʊmɪŋ] *adj* **h. device** mécanisme *m* d'autoguidage; **h. pigeon** pigeon *m* voyageur

homogeneous [hɒmə'dʒiːnɪəs, hə'mɒdʒɪnəs] *adj* homogène

homogenize [hə'mɒdʒənaɪz] *vt* homogénéiser

homonym ['hɒmənɪm] *n* homonyme *m*

homophobia [hɒmə'fəʊbɪə] *n* homophobie *f*

homosexual [hɒmə'seksjʊəl] *n & adj* homosexuel(elle) *m,f*

homosexuality [hɒməseksjʊ'ælɪtɪ] *n* homosexualité *f*

homy = **homey**[1]

honcho ['hɒntʃəʊ] *(pl* **honchos**) *n Fam* **the head h.** le boss

Honduras [hɒn'djʊərəs] *n* le Honduras

hone [həʊn] *vt (skill)* peaufiner

honest ['ɒnɪst] *adj* honnête (**with** avec); **she has an h. face** elle a un visage franc; **the h. truth** la vérité vraie; **to be h., I don't know** honnêtement *ou* à dire vrai, je ne sais pas; **to earn an h. living** gagner honnêtement sa vie; *Hum* **to make an h. woman of sb** *(marry)* faire de qn une honnête femme

honestly ['ɒnɪstlɪ] *adv* (**a**) *(legitimately, sincerely)* honnêtement; **to obtain sth h.** obtenir qch par des moyens honnêtes; **I can h. say that...** honnêtement, je peux dire que... (**b**) *(expressing indignation)* **well h.!** franchement!; **h.! some people!** il y a des gens, je te jure!

honesty ['ɒnɪstɪ] *n* honnêteté *f*; **in all h.** en toute honnêteté; *Prov* **h. is the best policy** l'honnêteté est toujours récompensée

honey ['hʌnɪ] *n* (**a**) *(food)* miel *m* (**b**) *Fam (term of endearment)* chéri(e) *m,f*

honeycomb ['hʌnɪkəʊm] **1** *n* rayon *m* de miel

2 *vt* **the mountain is honeycombed with tunnels** la montagne est truffée de tunnels

honeymoon ['hʌnɪmuːn] **1** *n* voyage *m* de noces; *Fig* **the h. is over** l'état de grâce est terminé

2 *vi* partir en voyage de noces

honeysuckle ['hʌnɪsʌkəl] *n* chèvrefeuille *m*

Hong Kong ['hɒŋ'kɒŋ] *n* Hongkong

honk [hɒŋk] **1** *n* (*of goose*) cri *m*; (*of car horn*) coup *m* de Klaxon®

2 *vi* (*of goose*) cacarder; (*of car driver*) klaxonner

honky ['hɒŋkɪ] (*pl* **honkies**) *n very Fam* sale Blanc (Blanche) *m,f*, = terme injurieux désignant un Blanc

honky-tonk ['hɒŋkɪtɒŋk] *adj Fam* (*unsavory*) louche

honor ['ɒnə(r)] **1** *n* (**a**) (*respect*) honneur *m*; **in h. of** en l'honneur de; **in h. of the occasion** pour l'occasion; **to have the h. of doing sth** avoir l'honneur de faire qch; *Hum* **to what do I owe this h.?** qu'est-ce qui me vaut cet honneur?; **Your H.** (*judge*) Votre Honneur (**b**) (*good name*) honneur *m*; **to feel h. bound to do sth** se sentir tenu(e) par l'honneur de faire qch; **on my (word of) h.!** parole d'honneur!; *Prov* **(there is) h. among thieves** les loups ne se mangent pas entre eux (**c**) (*award, distinction*) **he was buried with full military honors** il a été enterré avec tous les honneurs militaires; *Hum* **to do the honors** (*serve food or drink*) faire les honneurs; (*make introductions*) faire les présentations

2 *vt* honorer; **I felt honored that they had invited me** je me suis senti honoré par leur invitation

honorable ['ɒnərəbəl] *adj* honorable

honorably ['ɒnərəblɪ] *adv* honorablement

honorary ['ɒnərərɪ] *adj* (*member*) honoraire; (*title*) honorifique; *Univ* **h. degree** grade *m* honoris causa

hooch [huːtʃ] *n Fam* (*liquor*) gnôle *f*

hood [hʊd] *n* (**a**) (*of coat, sweater*) capuche *f*; (*with eye-holes*) cagoule *f*; (*of car*) capot *m*; (*over stove, fireplace*) hotte *f* (**b**) *Fam* (*gangster*) truand *m*; (*neighborhood*) quartier *m*

hooded ['hʊdɪd] *adj* (*clothing*) à capuchon; (*person*) encapuchonné; (*executioner, thief*) au visage masqué; *Fig* **h. eyes** yeux *mpl* aux paupières tombantes

hoodie ['hʊdɪ] *n Fam* sweatshirt *m* à capuche

hoodlum ['huːdləm] *n Fam* voyou *m*

hoodwink ['hʊdwɪŋk] *vt Fam* embobiner; **to h. sb into doing sth** embobiner qn pour qu'il fasse qch

hoof [huːf] **1** *n* (*pl* **hooves** [huːvz]) sabot *m*

2 *vt Fam* **to h. it** aller à pinces

hook [hʊk] **1** *n* (**a**) (*for hanging*) (*in general*) crochet *m*; (*for coats*) patère *f*; (*for meat*) croc *m*; (*on clothes*) agrafe *f*; (*for fishing*) hameçon *m*; **to leave the phone off the h.** (*on purpose*) laisser le téléphone décroché; (*accidentally*) mal raccrocher son téléphone; *Fam Fig* **to get** *or* **to let sb off the h.** tirer qn d'affaire; *Fam* **he swallowed it h., line and sinker** (*believed it*) il a tout gobé; *Fam* **by h. or by crook** coûte que coûte (**b**) (*in boxing*) crochet *m*

2 *vt* accrocher; **to h. a fish** attraper un poisson

▸**hook up 1** *vt sep Comput* connecter (**to** à)

2 *vi* (**a**) (*of dress*) s'agrafer (**b**) *Comput* se connecter; *TV* **to h. up with** faire une émission en duplex avec (**c**) *Fam* (*meet*) se rencontrer, se donner rendez-vous; **to h. up with sb** (*go out with*) sortir avec qn

hooked [hʊkt] *adj* (**a**) **h. nose** nez *m* crochu (**b**) *Fam* (*addicted*) **to be h. (on)** être accro (à); (*on movies, jazz*) être mordu(e) (de)

hooker [hʊkər] *n Fam* (*prostitute*) pute *f*

hook(e)y ['hʊkɪ] *n Fam* **to play h.** sécher les cours

hooligan ['huːlɪgən] *n* hooligan *m*, vandale *m*

hooliganism ['huːlɪgənɪzəm] *n* hooliganisme *m*, vandalisme *m*

hoop [huːp] *n* cerceau *m*; (*in croquet*) arceau *m*; *Fig* **to put sb**

through the hoops mettre qn à l'épreuve

hooray [hʊ'reɪ] *exclam* hourra!

hoot [huːt] **1** *n* (**a**) (*of owl*) hululement *m*; (*of ship, factory whistle*) mugissement *m*; **hoots of laughter** éclats *mpl* de rire; *Fam Fig* **I don't give a h.** *or* **two hoots** je m'en fiche comme de l'an quarante (**b**) *Fam* **she's a h.!** elle est tordante!; **it was a h.!** c'était tordant!

2 *vt* (*person*) huer; **he was hooted off the stage** il a quitté la scène sous les huées

3 *vi* (*of owl*) hululer; (*of train*) siffler; **to h. with laughter** hurler de rire

hooves [huːvz] *pl of* **hoof**

hop [hɒp] **1** *n* (*jump*) saut *m*; *Fam* (*dance*) bal *m*; **a short h.** (*journey*) un petit voyage; *Fam Fig* **to catch sb on the h.** prendre qn de court *ou* au dépourvu

2 *vi* (*pt & pp* **hopped**) (*jump*) sautiller; (*on one leg*) sauter à cloche-pied; *Fam* **h. in!** (*to car*) allez, grimpe!; **he hopped onto the first train** il a sauté dans le premier train; *Fam* **h. to it!** grouille!

▸**hop off** *vi Fam* ficher le camp

hope [həʊp] **1** *n* espoir *m*; **in the h. of doing sth** dans l'espoir de faire qch; **in the h. that...** dans l'espoir que...; **to have little h. of doing sth** avoir peu de chances de faire qch; **to have hopes of doing sth** avoir l'espoir de faire qch; **don't get your hopes up** n'espère pas trop; **to raise hopes of sth** faire naître l'espoir de qch; **she doesn't have a h. of winning** elle n'a aucun espoir de gagner; *Ironic* **some h.!** tu peux toujours rêver!; *Fam* **we live in h.!** l'espoir fait vivre!

2 *vt* **to h. to do sth** espérer faire qch; **to h. (that)...** espérer que...; **I h. you're right** j'espère que tu as raison; **I h. and pray that...** je prie le ciel que...; **I h. so** j'espère (bien); **I h. not** j'espère que non

3 *vi* espérer; **to h. for sth** espérer qch; **don't h. for too much** n'en attends pas trop; **we'll just have to h. for the best** espérons que tout se passe bien; **to h. against h.** espérer malgré tout

hopeful ['həʊpfʊl] **1** *n Fam* **a young h.** un jeune espoir

2 *adj* (*situation*) encourageant(e); (*person*) optimiste; **to be h. that...** avoir bon espoir que...

hopefully ['həʊpfʊlɪ] *adv* (**a**) (*with luck*) avec un peu de chance; **h. not** espérons que non (**b**) (*in a hopeful manner*) **to do sth h.** faire qch plein(e) d'espoir

hopeless ['həʊplɪs] *adj* (**a**) (*without hope*) (*person, cause, situation*) désespéré(e); **it's h.!** ça ne sert à rien! (**b**) *Fam* (*very bad*) nul (nulle) (**at** en)

hopelessly ['həʊplɪslɪ] *adv* (**a**) (*inconsolably*) avec désespoir (**b**) (*completely*) complètement; **he was h. in love with her** il était éperdument amoureux d'elle

hopping ['hɒpɪŋ] *adv Fam* **to be h. mad** être fou (folle) de rage

hops [hɒps] *npl* (*for making beer*) houblon *m*

hopscotch ['hɒpskɒtʃ] *n* marelle *f*

horde [hɔːd] *n* horde *f*

horizon [hə'raɪzən] *n* horizon *m*; **on the h.** à l'horizon; *Fig* en vue

horizontal [hɒrɪ'zɒntəl] **1** *n* horizontale *f*

2 *adj* horizontal(e)

horizontally [hɒrɪ'zɒntəlɪ] *adv* horizontalement

hormonal [hɔː'məʊnəl] *adj* hormonal(e)

hormone ['hɔːməʊn] *n* hormone *f*; **h. replacement therapy** hormonothérapie *f* de substitution

horn [hɔːn] *n* (**a**) (*of animal*) corne *f*; (*of insect*) antenne *f* (**b**) (*musical instrument*) cor *m*; (*on car*) Klaxon® *m*; **to honk one's h.** klaxonner (**c**) (*idioms*) **to be on the horns of a dilemma** être en proie à un dilemme

▸**horn in** *vi Fam* (*on conversation*) mettre son grain de sel; (*on a deal*) s'immiscer

horned [hɔːnd] *adj* à cornes

hornet ['hɔːnɪt] *n* frelon *m*; *Fig* **to stir up a h.'s nest** mettre le feu aux poudres

hornpipe ['hɔːnpaɪp] *n* matelote *f*

horn-rimmed ['hɔːnrɪmd] *adj* **h. glasses** lunettes *fpl* à monture d'écaille

horny ['hɔːnɪ] *adj* **(a)** *(hands)* calleux(euse) **(b)** *very Fam (sexually aroused)* excité(e); *(sexually attractive)* bandant(e)

horoscope ['hɒrəskəʊp] *n* horoscope *m*

horrendous [hɒ'rendəs] *adj* horrible, affreux(euse)

horrendously [hɒ'rendəslɪ] *adv* horriblement, affreusement

horrible ['hɒrəbəl] *adj* **(a)** *(unpleasant)* horrible, affreux(euse); **how h.!** quelle horreur! **(b)** *(unkind)* méchant(e) (**to** avec)

horribly ['hɒrɪblɪ] *adv* horriblement; **to behave h.** se conduire horriblement mal

horrid ['hɒrɪd] *adj* **(a)** *(unpleasant)* affreux(euse) **(b)** *(unkind)* méchant(e) (**to** avec)

horrific [hɒ'rɪfɪk] *adj* horrible

horrify ['hɒrɪfaɪ] *(pt & pp* **horrified)** *vt* horrifier

horrifying ['hɒrɪfaɪɪŋ] *adj* horrifiant(e)

horror ['hɒrə(r)] *n* horreur *f*; **to my h.,...** à ma grande horreur,...; **to have a h. of sth** avoir horreur de qch; **it gives me the horrors** ça me donne le frisson; *Fam* **that child's a little h.** cet enfant est un petit monstre; **h. movie** film *m* d'horreur; *Fig* **h. story** histoire *f* épouvantable

horror-stricken ['hɒrəstrɪkən], **horror-struck** ['hɒrəstrʌk] *adj* frappé(e) d'horreur

horse [hɔːs] *n* **(a)** *(animal)* cheval *m*; **h. chestnut** *(tree)* marronnier *m*; *(fruit)* marron *m*; **h. racing** courses *fpl* de chevaux; **h. riding** équitation *f*; **h. show** concours *m* hippique; **h. trading** *(in negotiation)* maquignonnage *m* **(b)** *(in gymnastics)* cheval *m* d'arçons **(c)** *(idioms)* **to get on one's high h.** monter sur ses grands chevaux; *Fam* **I could eat a h!** j'ai une faim de loup!; **to eat like a h.** manger comme quatre; **to hear sth straight from the h.'s mouth** entendre qch de la bouche de l'intéressé

▶**horse about, horse around** *vi* chahuter

horseback ['hɔːsbæk] *n* **on h.** à cheval; **h. riding** équitation; **do you like h. riding?** tu aimes monter à cheval?

horsecar ['hɔːskɑː(r)] *n* van *m*

horse-drawn ['hɔːsdrɔːn] *adj* tiré(e) par des chevaux

horsefly ['hɔːsflaɪ] *(pl* **horseflies)** *n* taon *m*

horsehair ['hɔːsheə(r)] *n* crin *m* (de cheval)

horseman ['hɔːsmən] *n* cavalier *m*

horsemanship ['hɔːsmənʃɪp] *n (skill)* talent *m* de cavalier

horseplay ['hɔːspleɪ] *n* chahut *m*

horsepower ['hɔːspaʊə(r)] *n* puissance *f* (en chevaux); *(unit)* cheval-vapeur *m*

horseradish ['hɔːsrædɪʃ] *n* raifort *m*

horseshoe ['hɔːsʃuː] *n* fer *m* à cheval

horsewhip ['hɔːswɪp] **1** *n* cravache *f*
2 *vt (pt & pp* **horsewhipped)** cravacher

horsewoman ['hɔːswʊmən] *n* cavalière *f*

hors(e)y ['hɔːsɪ] *adj* **(a)** *(horse-like)* chevalin(e) **(b)** *(keen on horses)* passionné(e) de chevaux

horticultural [hɔːtɪ'kʌltʃərəl] *adj* horticole

horticulture ['hɔːtɪkʌltʃə(r)] *n* horticulture *f*

hose [həʊz] **1** *n (pipe)* tuyau *m*
2 *vt* arroser (au jet d'eau)

▶**hose down** *vt sep* laver au jet

hosepipe ['həʊzpaɪp] *n* tuyau *m* d'arrosage

hosiery ['həʊzɪərɪ] *n* bonneterie *f*

hospice ['hɒspɪs] *n (hospital)* = établissement pour malades en phase terminale

hospitable [hɒs'pɪtəbəl] *adj* hospitalier(ère)

hospitably [hɒs'pɪtəblɪ] *adv* avec hospitalité

hospital ['hɒspɪtəl] *n* hôpital *m*; **in the h.** à l'hôpital; **h. bed/food** lit *m*/nourriture *f* d'hôpital; **h. care** soins *mpl* hospitaliers

hospitality [hɒspɪ'tælɪtɪ] *n* hospitalité *f*

hospitalize ['hɒspɪtəlaɪz] *vt* **to be hospitalized** être hospitalisé(e)

host[1] [həʊst] **1** *n* **(a)** *(at home, party)* hôte *m*; *(on TV, radio)* animateur(trice) *m,f*; **h. city/country** ville *f*/pays *m* d'accueil **(b)** *Biol (of parasite)* hôte *m* **(c)** *Comput (of website)* hébergeur *m*
2 *vt* **(a)** *(party)* donner, organiser; *(TV, radio show)* animer **(b)** *Comput (website)* héberger

host[2] [həʊst] *n (great number)* **a (whole) h. of** (toute) une foule de

host[3] [həʊst] *n Rel* hostie *f*

hostage ['hɒstɪdʒ] *n* otage *m*; **to take/hold sb h.** prendre/garder qn en otage; **to offer a h. to fortune** hypothéquer l'avenir

hostel ['hɒstəl] *n (for homeless people, students)* foyer *m*; *(youth hostel)* auberge *f* de jeunesse

hostess ['həʊstɪs] *n (at home, party)* hôtesse *f*; *(on TV, radio)* animatrice *f*

hostile ['hɒstaɪl] *adj* hostile (**to** à); *Com* **h. takeover bid** OPA *f* hostile

hostility [hɒs'tɪlɪtɪ] *(pl* **hostilities)** *n* hostilité *f* (**towards** envers); **hostilities** *(fighting)* hostilités

hot [hɒt] *adj* **(a)** *(having high temperature)* chaud(e); **to get h.** *(of person)* commencer à avoir chaud; **to be h.** *(of person)* avoir chaud; *(of thing)* être chaud; **it's h.** *(of weather)* il fait chaud; *Med* **h. flashes** bouffées *fpl* de chaleur; **h. tub** = sorte de Jacuzzi® que l'on installe dehors
(b) *(spicy) (food)* épicé(e); *(pepper, mustard)* fort(e)
(c) *(close)* **you're getting h.** *(in guessing game)* tu brûles; **to be h. on sb's trail** être aux trousses de qn
(d) *Fam (good)* **it wasn't such a h. idea** l'idée n'était pas si géniale; **how are you? – not so h.** comment ça va? – pas terrible; **to be h. stuff (at)** être un as (en)
(e) *Fam (sexy)* sexy *inv*
(f) *Fam (stolen)* chouré(e)
(g) *(idioms)* **h. off the press** *(of news)* de dernière minute; *(of book)* qui vient juste de paraître; **too h. to handle** *(issue)* brûlant(e); **to have a h. temper** s'emporter facilement; **to get h. under the collar** se mettre en colère; **a h. favorite** *(in race)* un grand favori; *Fam* **it's all just h. air** tout ça, c'est du vent; **they're selling like h. cakes** ils se vendent comme des petits pains; **h. desking** = pratique qui consiste à ne pas assigner de bureaux individuels aux employés, ces derniers étant libres de s'installer à n'importe quel poste de travail inoccupé; **the h. gossip** les derniers potins *mpl*; **h. line** *(telephone number)* permanence *f* téléphonique; **h. news** les toutes dernières nouvelles; *Fam* **h. potato** *(controversial issue)* sujet *m* brûlant; **to be in the h. seat** *(of politician, manager)* avoir toutes les responsabilités; **h. spot** *(trouble spot)* point *m* chaud; *Fam* **to get into h. water** *(in difficult situation)* s'attirer des ennuis

hot-air balloon ['hɒteəbə'luːn] *n* montgolfière *f*

hotbed ['hɒtbed] *n* **a h. of rebellion/intrigue** un foyer de rébellion/d'intrigue

hot-blooded ['hɒt'blʌdɪd] *adj* au sang chaud, passionné(e)

hot-button ['hɒt'bʌtən] *adj Fig* **a h. issue** un sujet brûlant

hotdog ['hɒtdɒg] *n* hot dog *m*

hotel [həʊ'tel] *n* hôtel *m*; **h. room/manager** chambre *f*/gérant(e) *m,f* d'hôtel; **the h. trade** l'industrie *f* hôtelière

hotelier [həʊ'teljeɪ] *n* hôtelier(ère) *m,f*

hotfoot ['hɒt'fʊt] *Fam***1** *adv* en vitesse
2 *vt* **to h. it** aller à toute vitesse

hothead ['hɒthed] *n* tête *f* brûlée

hotheaded ['hɒt'hedɪd] *adj* exalté(e)

hothouse ['hɒthaʊs] *n* serre *f* (chaude)

hotly ['hɒtlɪ] *adv (reply, protest)* vivement; **h. contested** âprement disputé(e)

hotplate ['hɒtpleɪt] *n (on cooker)* plaque *f* (chauffante); *(for keeping food warm)* chauffe-plat *m*

hots ['hɒts] *npl very Fam* **to have the h. for sb** craquer pour qn

hotshot ['hɒtʃɒt] *n Fam (expert)* as *m*, crack *m*; *(self-important person)* gros bonnet *m*

hotspot ['hɒtspɒt] *n Comput (for WiFi access)* point *m* chaud

hot-tempered ['hɒt'tempəd] *adj* colérique, coléreux(euse)

hot-water [hɒt'wɔːtə(r)] *adj* d'eau chaude; **h. bottle** bouillotte *f*

hound [haʊnd] **1** *n (dog)* chien *m* de chasse
  2 *vt (persecute)* traquer, pourchasser

hour ['aʊə(r)] *n* heure *f*; **an h. and a half** une heure et demie; **half an h.** une demi-heure; **to pay sb by the h.** payer qn à l'heure; **to take hours over sth** mettre des heures à faire qch; **we've been waiting for hours** ça fait des heures que nous attendons; **to work long hours** faire de longues journées (de travail); **to keep late hours** *(of person)* se coucher tard; **till all hours** jusqu'à très tard; **where were you in my h. of need?** où étais-tu quand j'avais besoin de toi?; **h. hand** *(of watch, clock)* petite aiguille *f*

hourglass ['aʊəglɑːs] *n* sablier *m*; **an h. figure** une taille de guêpe

hourly ['aʊəlɪ] **1** *adj* **at h. intervals** toutes les heures; **h. rate** taux *m* horaire
  2 *adv (every hour)* toutes les heures; *(at any time)* d'un moment à l'autre

house 1 *n* [haʊs] **(a)** *(dwelling)* maison *f*; **to stay at sb's h.** loger chez qn; **from h. to h.** de porte à porte; **they keep open h.** leur maison est toujours ouverte; *Fig* **to put one's h. in order** balayer devant sa porte; **to get on like a h. on fire** *(very well)* s'entendre comme larrons en foire; **the H. of Commons/Lords** *(in England)* la Chambre des communes/lords; **the Houses of Parliament** *(in England)* le Parlement; **the H. of Representatives** la Chambre des représentants; *Law* **to be under h. arrest** être assigné(e) à résidence; **h. guest** invité(e) *m,f*; **h. martin** hirondelle *f* de fenêtre; **h. painter** peintre *m* en bâtiment; **h. party** partie *f* de campagne; **h. plant** plante *f* d'intérieur *ou* d'appartement; **h. spider** araignée *f* commune
  (b) *Com (company)* maison *f*; **h. style** style *m* maison
  (c) *(restaurant)* **on the h.** aux frais de la maison; **h. wine** vin *m* de la maison
  (d) *Theat* **an empty/good h.** une salle vide/pleine
  (e) **h. (music)** house music *f*
  2 *vt* [haʊz] *(person)* loger; *(collection, mechanism)* contenir, recevoir

houseboat ['haʊsbəʊt] *n* péniche *f* aménagée

housebound ['haʊsbaʊnd] *adj* confiné(e) chez soi

housebreak ['haʊsbreɪk] *vt (pet)* dresser à la propreté

housebreaker ['haʊsbreɪkə(r)] *n* cambrioleur(euse) *m,f*

housebreaking ['haʊsbreɪkɪŋ] *n* cambriolage *m*

housebroken ['haʊsbrəʊkən] *adj (pet)* propre

housecoat ['haʊskəʊt] *n* robe *f* d'intérieur

housefly ['haʊsflaɪ] *(pl* **houseflies***)* *n* mouche *f* domestique

household ['haʊshəʊld] *n* ménage *m*; **h. appliance** appareil *m* électroménager; **h. chores** tâches *fpl* ménagères; **he's a h. name** tout le monde connaît son nom

householder ['haʊshəʊldə(r)] *n (owner)* propriétaire *mf*; *(tenant)* locataire *mf*

househusband ['haʊshʌzbənd] *n* homme *m* au foyer

housekeeper ['haʊskiːpə(r)] *n (private)* gouvernante *f*; *(in institution)* intendante *f*

housekeeping ['haʊskiːpɪŋ] *n* **h. (money)** argent *m* du ménage

housemaid ['haʊsmeɪd] *n* bonne *f*, femme *f* de chambre; **h.'s knee** *(inflammation)* inflammation *f* du genou

house-sitter ['haʊssɪtə(r)] *n* = personne qui garde la maison en l'absence de ses occupants

house-to-house ['haʊstə'haʊs] *adj* **to make a h. search** fouiller chaque maison

housewarming ['haʊswɔːmɪŋ] *n* **h. (party)** pendaison *f* de crémaillère; **to have a h. party** pendre la crémaillère

housewife ['haʊswaɪf] *(pl* **housewives** ['haʊswaɪvz]*)* *n* femme *f* au foyer

housework ['haʊswɜːk] *n* ménage *m*

housing ['haʊzɪŋ] *n* logement *m*; **the h. market** le marché de l'immobilier; **h. project** cité *f* HLM

hove [həʊv] *pt & pp of* **heave**

hovel ['hɒvəl] *n* taudis *m*

hover ['hɒvə(r)] *vi* **(a)** *(of bird)* planer; *(of helicopter)* effectuer un vol stationnaire **(b)** *(of person)* **to h. near sb** être derrière le dos de qn

hovercraft ['hɒvəkrɑːft] *n* hovercraft *m*, aéroglisseur *m*

how [haʊ] *adv* **(a)** *(in what way, by what means)* comment; **h. did they find out?** comment l'ont-ils appris?; **h. do you spell this word?** comment s'écrit ce mot?; *Fam* **h. come?** comment ça se fait?; *Fam* **and h.!** et comment!
  (b) *(to what extent)* **h. much money?** combien d'argent?; **h. many people?** combien de gens?; **h. old are you?** quel âge as-tu?; **h. big is it?** c'est grand comment?; **h. long have you been here?** depuis combien de temps êtes-vous ici?; **h. often do you see him?** tu le vois tous les combien?; **you know h. difficult it is** tu sais à quel point c'est difficile; **h. useful will it be?** est-ce que ce sera très utile?
  (c) *(greetings, inquiries after health)* **h. are you?** comment vas-tu?; *Fam* **h. are things?** ça va?; **h.'s business?** comment vont les affaires?
  (d) *(in exclamations)* que, comme; **h. pretty she is!** qu'elle est jolie!, comme elle est jolie!; **h. disgusting!** c'est vraiment dégoûtant!; **h. true!** c'est bien vrai!; **h. she's changed!** comme elle a changé!
  (e) *(in suggestions)* **h. about a game of cards?** et si on faisait une partie de cartes?; **h. about going out for a meal?** et si on allait manger quelque part?; **h. about it?** ça te dirait?; **h. about you?** et toi?

howdy ['haʊdɪ] *exclam Fam* salut!

however [haʊ'evə(r)] **1** *adv* **(a)** *(in whatever degree)* si... que + *subjunctive*; **h. clever she is** si intelligente qu'elle soit; **h. hard she tried, she couldn't do it** elle avait beau essayer, elle n'y arrivait pas **(b)** *(in whatever way)* **h. you look at it...** de quelque façon qu'on envisage la chose... **(c)** *(in what way)* comment; **h. did she find out?** comment a-t-elle bien pu l'apprendre?
  2 *conj* pourtant, cependant; **h., this does not explain why she...** ceci n'explique pourtant pas pourquoi elle...

howl [haʊl] **1** *n (of animal, person)* hurlement *m*; **howls of derision** des huées *fpl*
  2 *vi (of animal, person)* hurler; **to h. with laughter** hurler de rire

▸**howl down** *vt sep* huer

howler ['haʊlə(r)] *n Fam (mistake)* bourde *f*

howling ['haʊlɪŋ] **1** *n (of wind, wolf)* hurlement *m*; *(of baby)* hurlements
  2 *adj (wolf)* qui hurle; *(gale, wind)* furieux(euse); *Fam* **it wasn't exactly a h. success** ça n'a pas vraiment eu un succès fou

HP, hp [eɪtʃ'piː] *n (abbr* **horsepower***)* CV *m*

HQ [eɪtʃ'kjuː] *n (abbr* **headquarters***)* QG *m*

hr. *(abbr* **hour***)* h

HRM [eɪtʃɑː'rem] *n (abbr* **human resource management***)* GRH *f*

HRT [eɪtʃɑːˈtiː] *n Med (abbr* **hormone replacement therapy**) hormonothérapie *f* de substitution

HTML [eɪtʃtiːemˈel] *n Comput (abbr* **Hyper Text Markup Language**) HTML

HTTP [eɪtʃtiːtiːˈpiː] *n Comput (abbr* **Hyper Text Transfer Protocol**) HTTP

hub [hʌb] *n* (**a**) *(of wheel)* moyeu *m* (**b**) *(of community)* centre *m*; **h. airport** plate-forme *f* aéroportuaire

hubbub [ˈhʌbʌb] *n* brouhaha *m*

hubby [ˈhʌbɪ] *(pl* **hubbies**) *n Fam* petit mari *m*

hubcap [ˈhʌbkæp] *n (of wheel)* enjoliveur *m*

huckleberry [ˈhʌkəlbərɪ] *n (pl* **huckleberries**) *n* airelle *f*, myrtille *f*

huddle [ˈhʌdəl] **1** *n (of people)* petit groupe *m*; *(of things)* tas *m*; **to go into a h.** se réunir en petit comité
2 *vi* se blottir

►**huddle together** *vi* se blottir les uns contre les autres; *(to talk)* se mettre en petit groupe serré

►**huddle up** *vi* se blottir

Hudson Bay [hʌdsənˈbeɪ] *n* la baie d'Hudson

hue¹ [hjuː] *n (color)* teinte *f*

hue² [hjuː] *n* **h. and cry** tollé *m*; **to raise a h. and cry about sth** crier haro sur qch

huff [hʌf] **1** *n Fam* **to be in a h.** faire la tête
2 *vi* **to h. and puff** *(blow)* souffler; *Fig (show annoyance)* maugréer

huffy [ˈhʌfɪ] *adj Fam (sulky)* susceptible

hug [hʌg] **1** *n* étreinte *f*; **to give sb a h.** serrer qn (dans ses bras)
2 *vt (pt & pp* **hugged**) (**a**) *(embrace)* serrer (dans ses bras) (**b**) *Fig (shore, curb)* serrer; *(ground)* raser

huge [hjuːdʒ] *adj (very big)* énorme; *(very tall, long)* immense

hugely [ˈhjuːdʒlɪ] *adv* énormément, extrêmement

hulk [hʌlk] *n* (**a**) *(of ship)* épave *f* (**b**) *(person)* mastodonte *m*

hulking [ˈhʌlkɪŋ] *adj Fam* **a h. great man** une armoire à glace

hull [hʌl] *n* (**a**) *(of ship)* coque *f* (**b**) *(of pea)* cosse *f*
2 *vt (peas)* écosser

hullabaloo [hʌləbəˈluː] *(pl* **hullabaloos**) *n Fam* raffut *m*

hum [hʌm] **1** *n* bourdonnement *m*
2 *vt (pt & pp* **hummed**) *(tune)* fredonner
3 *vi (of person)* fredonner; *(of insect, computer)* bourdonner; *(of engine, refrigerator)* ronronner; **to h. with activity** bourdonner d'activité

human [ˈhjuːmən] **1** *n* (être *m*) humain *m*
2 *adj* humain(e); **h. being** être *m* humain; **h. cloning** clonage *m* humain; **h. error** erreur *f* humaine; **h. nature** la nature humaine; **h. resources** ressources *fpl* humaines; **h. rights** droits *mpl* de l'homme; **h. shield** bouclier *m* humain

humane [hjʊˈmeɪn] *adj* humain(e)

humanely [hjʊˈmeɪnlɪ] *adv* humainement

humanism [ˈhjuːmənɪzəm] *n* humanisme *m*

humanistic [hjuːməˈnɪstɪk] *adj* humaniste

humanitarian [hjʊmænɪˈteərɪən] **1** *n* philanthrope *mf*
2 *adj* humanitaire

humanity [hjʊˈmænɪtɪ] *n* humanité *f*; *Univ* **humanities** lettres *fpl*

humanize [ˈhjuːmənaɪz] *vt* humaniser

humankind [hjʊmənˈkaɪnd] *n* humanité *f*

humanly [ˈhjuːmənlɪ] *adv* **to do everything h. possible** faire tout ce qui est humainement possible

humble [ˈhʌmbəl] **1** *adj (meek)* humble; *(unpretentious)* modeste; **in my h. opinion** à mon humble avis; *Fig* **to eat h. pie** reconnaître qu'on a tort
2 *vt* humilier

humbling [ˈhʌmbəlɪŋ] *adj* humiliant(e)

humbly [ˈhʌmbəlɪ] *adv (meekly)* humblement; *(modestly)* modestement

humbug [ˈhʌmbʌg] *n* (**a**) *(nonsense)* balivernes *fpl* (**b**) *(hypocrite)* charlatan *m*

humdinger [ˈhʌmdɪŋə(r)] *n Fam* **a h. of a movie/book** un film/livre extra

humdrum [ˈhʌmdrʌm] *adj* monotone

humerus [ˈhjuːmərəs] *(pl* **humeri** [ˈhjuːməraɪ]) *n Anat* humérus *m*

humid [ˈhjuːmɪd] *adj* humide

humidifier [hjʊˈmɪdɪfaɪə(r)] *n* humidificateur *m*

humidity [hjʊˈmɪdɪtɪ] *n* humidité *f*

humiliate [hjʊˈmɪlɪeɪt] *vt* humilier

humiliating [hjʊˈmɪlɪeɪtɪŋ] *adj* humiliant(e)

humiliation [hjʊmɪlɪˈeɪʃən] *n* humiliation *f*

humility [hjʊˈmɪlɪtɪ] *n* humilité *f*

Hummer® [hʌmə(r)] *n Aut* Hummer® *m*

hummingbird [ˈhʌmɪŋbɜːd] *n* colibri *m*

hummus [ˈhʊmʊs, ˈhʌməs] *n* houmous *m*

humor [ˈhjuːmə(r)] **1** *n* (**a**) *(fun)* humour *m* (**b**) *Formal (mood)* humeur *f*
2 *vt (indulge)* faire plaisir à

humorless [ˈhjuːmələs] *adj* dépourvu(e) d'humour

humorous [ˈhjuːmərəs] *adj (situation)* drôle, comique; *(writer, drawing, remark)* humoristique

humorously [ˈhjuːmərəslɪ] *adv* avec humour

hump [hʌmp] **1** *n (on back, road)* bosse *f*
2 *vt Vulg (have sex with)* sauter

humpback [ˈhʌmpbæk] *n* **h. bridge** pont *m* en dos d'âne; **h. whale** baleine *f* à bosse

humus [ˈhjuːməs] *n* humus *m*

hunch [hʌntʃ] **1** *n (intuition)* intuition *f*; **to have a h. that...** avoir l'intuition que...
2 *vt* **to h. one's shoulders** rentrer les épaules

hunchback [ˈhʌntʃbæk] *n* bossu(e) *m,f*

hundred [ˈhʌndrəd] **1** *n* cent *m*; **one** *or* **a h.** cent; **a h. and twenty-five pages** cent vingt-cinq pages; **two h. pages** deux cents pages; **I've told you hundreds of times** je te l'ai dit des centaines de fois; **to live to be a h.** vivre jusqu'à cent ans
2 *adj* cent; **a h. miles an hour** ≃ 160 km à l'heure; **one** *or* **a h. per cent** cent pour cent; **to be a h. per cent certain** être sûr(e) à cent pour cent; **I'm not feeling a h. per cent** je ne me sens pas au mieux de ma forme; **the h. meters** *(in track and field)* le cent mètres

hundredfold [ˈhʌndrədfəʊld] *adv* **to increase a h.** centupler

hundredth [ˈhʌndrədθ] **1** *n* (**a**) *(fraction)* centième *m* (**b**) *(in series)* centième *mf*
2 *adj* centième; *Fam* **for the h. time, no!** pour la centième fois, non!; *see also* **eighth**

hung [hʌŋ] **1** *adj* **h. jury** jury *m* sans majorité
2 *pt & pp of* **hang**

Hungarian [hʌŋˈgeərɪən] **1** *n* (**a**) *(person)* Hongrois(e) *m,f* (**b**) *(language)* hongrois *m*
2 *adj* hongrois(e)

Hungary [ˈhʌŋgərɪ] *n* la Hongrie

hunger [ˈhʌŋgə(r)] *n* faim *f*; *Fig (for power)* soif *f* (**for** de); **h. strike** grève *f* de la faim

►**hunger after, hunger for** *vt insep Fig* avoir soif de

hungrily [ˈhʌŋgrɪlɪ] *adv also Fig* avidement

hungry [ˈhʌŋgrɪ] *adj* **to be h.** avoir faim; **to be h. for knowledge** être avide de connaissances

hunk [hʌŋk] *n* (**a**) *(of bread, meat)* gros morceau *m* (**b**) *Fam (attractive man)* beau mec *m*

hunky [ˈhʌŋkɪ] *adj Fam (man)* bien foutu

hunt [hʌnt] **1** *n (for animals)* chasse *f*; *(for person, work)* recherche *f*

2 *vt (animal)* chasser; *(criminal)* pourchasser

3 *vi* (**a**) *(search)* **to h. for** rechercher (**b**) *(kill animals)* chasser

►**hunt down** *vt sep (animal, person)* traquer; *(information)* dénicher

►**hunt out** *vt sep (find) (person)* retrouver; *(thing)* dénicher

hunted ['hʌntɪd] *adj (look)* hagard(e)

hunter ['hʌntə(r)] *n* chasseur *m*

hunting ['hʌntɪŋ] *n* chasse *f*; **to go h.** aller à la chasse; **h. ground** terrain *m* de chasse; **h. lodge** pavillon *m* de chasse

huntsman ['hʌntsmən] *n* chasseur *m*

hurdle ['hɜːdəl] **1** *n (in race)* haie *f*; *Fig (obstacle)* obstacle *m*

2 *vt (jump over)* sauter, franchir

hurdler ['hɜːdlə(r)] *n Sport* coureur(euse) *m,f* de haies

hurdling ['hɜːdəlɪŋ] *n Sport* course *f* de haies

hurl [hɜːl] **1** *vt* jeter, lancer (**at** sur); *(insults)* lancer (**at** à); **to h. oneself at sb** se jeter *ou* se ruer sur qn

2 *vi Fam (vomit)* dégobiller

hurly-burly ['hɜːlɪ'bɜːlɪ] *n Fam* tohu-bohu *m inv*

hurrah [hʊ'rɑː], **hurray** [hʊ'reɪ] *exclam* hourra!

hurricane ['hʌrɪkeɪn] *n* ouragan *m*; **h. lamp** lampe *f* tempête

hurried ['hʌrɪd] *adj (gesture, conversation, meal)* rapide; *(departure)* précipité(e); *(work)* fait(e) à la hâte; *(decision, choice)* pris(e) à la hâte

hurriedly ['hʌrɪdlɪ] *adv* précipitamment

hurry ['hʌrɪ] **1** *n* hâte *f*; **to be in a h. (to do sth)** être pressé(e) (de faire qch); **to do sth in a h.** faire qch à la hâte; **to leave in a h.** partir à la hâte; **I won't do that again in a h.** je ne suis pas prêt de recommencer; **there's no h.** rien ne presse; **what's the h.?** qu'est-ce qui presse?

2 *vt (pt & pp* **hurried)** *(person)* presser; *(work)* hâter

3 *vi* se dépêcher, se presser; **to h. to do sth** se dépêcher *ou* se presser de faire qch; **to h. into/out of a room** se précipiter dans une/hors d'une pièce

►**hurry along 1** *vt sep (person)* faire se dépêcher; *(work)* accélérer

2 *vi* se presser

►**hurry back** *vi* se dépêcher de revenir

►**hurry on 1** *vt sep (person)* faire circuler; *(work)* faire accélérer

2 *vi (leave)* partir en hâte

►**hurry up 1** *vt sep* faire accélérer

2 *vi* se dépêcher; **h. up!** vite!, dépêche-toi!

hurt [hɜːt] **1** *n (emotional)* blessure *f*

2 *adj* blessé(e)

3 *vt (pt & pp* **hurt)** (**a**) *(physically)* faire mal à; *(reputation, chances)* nuire à; **to h. oneself** se faire mal; **to h. one's foot** se faire mal au pied; **to get h.** se blesser; *Fig* **it won't h. him to have to wait** ça ne lui fera pas de mal d'attendre un peu (**b**) *(emotionally)* faire du mal *ou* de la peine à; **to h. sb's feelings** blesser qn

4 *vi* (**a**) *(cause pain)* faire mal; **where does it h.?** où est-ce que ça fait mal?; **my foot hurts** j'ai mal au pied, mon pied me fait mal (**b**) *(emotionally)* faire mal

hurtful ['hɜːtfʊl] *adj* blessant(e)

hurtle ['hɜːtəl] *vi* **to h. along** avancer à toute vitesse; **to h. down the street** dévaler la rue; **to h. toward** foncer sur

husband ['hʌzbənd] **1** *n* mari *m*

2 *vt Formal (one's resources)* ménager

husbandry ['hʌzbəndrɪ] *n* agriculture *f*; **animal h.** élevage *m*

hush [hʌʃ] **1** *n (quiet)* silence *m*; **h.!** chut!

2 *vt* calmer

►**hush up** *vt sep (scandal)* étouffer

hushed [hʌʃt] *adj (conversation)* étouffé(e); *(silence)* profond(e); **to talk in h. tones** parler à voix basse

hush-hush ['hʌʃhʌʃ] *adj Fam* top secret *inv*

husk [hʌsk] **1** *n (of seed)* enveloppe *f*; *(of pea)* cosse *f*; *(of nut)* brou *m*

2 *vt (grain)* décortiquer

husky[1] ['hʌskɪ] *adj (voice)* rauque

husky[2] ['hʌskɪ] *(pl* **huskies)** *n (dog)* husky *m*

hussar [hʊ'zɑː(r)] *n Mil* hussard *m*

hussy ['hʌsɪ] *(pl* **hussies)** *n Old-fashioned or Hum* gourgandine *f*

hustle ['hʌsəl] **1** *n* **h. (and bustle)** effervescence *f*

2 *vt (shove, push)* **to h. sb away** emmener qn de force; **I was hustled into a small room** on m'a poussé dans une petite pièce

hustler ['hʌslə(r)] *n Fam (swindler)* arnaqueur(euse) *m,f*; *(prostitute)* prostitué(e) *m,f*

hut [hʌt] *n (shed)* cabane *f*; *(dwelling)* hutte *f*

hutch [hʌtʃ] *n (for rabbit)* clapier *m*

hyacinth ['haɪəsɪnθ] *n* jacinthe *f*

hybrid ['haɪbrɪd] **1** *n* hybride *m*

2 *adj* hybride

hydrangea [haɪ'dreɪndʒə] *n* hortensia *m*

hydrant ['haɪdrənt] *n* prise *f* d'eau; **fire h.** bouche *f* d'incendie

hydraulic [haɪ'drɔːlɪk] *adj* hydraulique; **h. engineering** hydraulique *f*

hydraulics [haɪ'drɔːlɪks] *n* hydraulique *f*

hydrocarbon [haɪdrəʊ'kɑːbən] *n* hydrocarbure *m*

hydrochloric acid [haɪdrəʊ'klɒrɪk'æsɪd] *n* acide *m* chlorhydrique

hydroelectric [haɪdrəʊɪ'lektrɪk] *adj* hydroélectrique

hydroelectricity [haɪdrəʊɪlek'trɪsɪtɪ] *n* hydroélectricité *f*

hydrofoil ['haɪdrəfɔɪl] *n* hydrofoil *m*, hydroptère *m*

hydrogen ['haɪdrədʒən] *n* hydrogène *m*; **h. bomb** bombe *f* à hydrogène

hydrolysis [haɪ'drɒlɪsɪs] *n* hydrolyse *f*

hydrophobia [haɪdrə'fəʊbɪə] *n Med (rabies)* rage *f*

hydroplane ['haɪdrəpleɪn] *n (boat)* hydroglisseur *m*; *(seaplane)* hydravion *m*

hydroxide [haɪ'drɒksaɪd] *n* hydroxyde *m*

hyena [haɪ'iːnə] *n* hyène *f*

hygiene ['haɪdʒiːn] *n* hygiène *f*

hygienic [haɪ'dʒiːnɪk] *adj* hygiénique

hymen ['haɪmen] *n* hymen *m*

hymn [hɪm] *n* cantique *m*; **h. book** livre *m* de cantiques

hymnal ['hɪmnəl] *n* livre *m* de cantiques

hype [haɪp] *Fam* **1** *n (publicity)* battage *m* publicitaire

2 *vt (publicize)* faire du battage publicitaire pour

hype up *vt sep Fam* (**a**) *(publicize)* faire du battage publicitaire pour (**b**) **to be hyped up** *(excited)* être surexcité(e)

hyper ['haɪpə(r)] *adj Fam (overexcited)* surexcité(e); **she's really h.** elle est très speed

hyperactive [haɪpə'ræktɪv] *adj* hyperactif(ive)

hyperbola [haɪ'pɜːbələ] *n Math* hyperbole *f*

hyperbole [haɪ'pɜːbəlɪ] *n* hyperbole *f*

hypercritical [haɪpə'krɪtɪkəl] *adj* hypercritique

hyperinflation [haɪpərɪn'fleɪʃən] *n Econ* hyperinflation *f*

hyperlink ['haɪpəlɪŋk] *n Comput* hyperlien *m*

hypermarket ['haɪpəmɑːkɪt] *n* hypermarché *m*

hypersensitive [haɪpə'sensɪtɪv] *adj* hypersensible

hypertension [haɪpə'tenʃən] *n Med* hypertension *f*

hypertext ['haɪpətekst] *n Comput* hypertexte *m*; **h. link** lien *m* hypertexte

hyphen ['haɪfən] *n* trait *m* d'union

hyphenate ['haɪfəneɪt] *vt (word)* mettre un trait d'union à; **a hyphenated word** un mot à trait d'union; **hyphenated American** étranger(ère) *m,f* naturalisé(e)

hypnosis [hɪp'nəʊsɪs] *n* hypnose *f*

hypnotic [hɪp'nɒtɪk] *adj* hypnotique

hypnotism ['hɪpnətɪzəm] *n* hypnotisme *m*

hypnotist ['hɪpnətɪst] *n* hypnotiseur(euse) *m,f*

hypnotize ['hɪpnətaɪz] *vt* hypnotiser

hypoallergenic [haɪpəʊælə'dʒenɪk] *adj* hypoallergénique

hypochondria [haɪpə'kɒndrɪə] *n* hypocondrie *f*

hypochondriac [haɪpə'kɒndrɪæk] *n* hypocondriaque *mf*

hypocrisy [hɪ'pɒkrɪsɪ] *n* hypocrisie *f*

hypocrite ['hɪpəkrɪt] *n* hypocrite *mf*

hypocritical [hɪpə'krɪtɪkəl] *adj* hypocrite

hypodermic [haɪpə'dɜːmɪk] **1** *n* seringue *f* hypodermique
    2 *adj* hypodermique

hypotenuse [haɪ'pɒtənjuːz] *n* Math hypoténuse *f*

hypothermia [haɪpəʊ'θɜːmɪə] *n* hypothermie *f*; **to have h.**
    faire de l'hypothermie

hypothesis [haɪ'pɒθəsɪs] (*pl* **hypotheses** [haɪ'pɒθəsiːz]) *n*
    hypothèse *f*

hypothesize [haɪ'pɒθəsaɪz] **1** *vt* **to h. that...** émettre l'hy-
    pothèse que...
    2 *vi* faire des hypothèses

hypothetical [haɪpə'θetɪkəl] *adj* hypothétique

hysterectomy [hɪstə'rektəmɪ] (*pl* **hysterectomies**) *n* hys-
    térectomie *f*; **to have a h.** subir une hystérectomie

hysteria [hɪs'tɪərɪə] *n* (**a**) *(panic)* hystérie *f* (**b**) *(laughter)* fou
    rire *m*

hysterical [hɪs'terɪkəl] *adj* (**a**) *(uncontrolled)* hystérique; **to be
    h.** faire une crise de nerfs; **h. laughter** fou rire *m* (**b**) *(very
    funny)* tordant(e)

hysterically [hɪs'terɪklɪ] *adv* (**a**) *(uncontrolledly)* sans pouvoir
    se contrôler; **to laugh h.** avoir le fou rire (**b**) **h. funny** tor-
    dant(e)

hysterics [hɪs'terɪks] *npl* (**a**) *(panic)* crise *f* de nerfs; **to go
    into** *or* **to have h.** avoir une crise de nerfs (**b**) *(laughter)* fou
    rire *m*; **to be in h.** avoir le fou rire

I

I¹, i [aɪ] *n (letter)* I, i *m inv*

I² [aɪ] *pron* je; **I'm American** je suis américain; **I haven't got it!** ce n'est pas moi qui l'ai!

IAEA [aɪeɪiː'eɪ] *n (abbr* **International Atomic Energy Agency)** AIEA *f*

IAP [aɪeɪ'piː] *n Comput (abbr* **Internet Access Provider)** fournisseur *m* d'accès à l'Internet

Iberian [aɪ'biːrɪən] *adj* ibérique; **the I. Peninsula** la péninsule Ibérique

ibex ['aɪbeks] *n* bouquetin *m*

ibid ['ɪbɪd] *adv (abbr* **ibidem)** ibid

IBM [aɪbiː'em] *n (abbr* **intercontinental ballistic missile)** MBI *m*

IBRD [aɪbiːɑː'diː] *n (abbr* **International Bank for Reconstruction and Development)** BIRD *f*

IBS [aɪbiː'es] *n (abbr* **irritable bowel syndrome)** colopathie *f* fonctionnelle

ice [aɪs] **1** *n* **(a)** *(frozen water)* glace *f*; *(on road)* verglas *m*; **i. age** période *f* glaciaire; **i. bucket** seau *m* à glace; **i. cube** glaçon *m*; **i. floe** banquise *f*; **i. pack** sachet *m* de glace; **i. pick** pic *m* à glace; **i. rink** patinoire *f* **(b)** *(idioms)* **to put a project on i.** geler un projet; **to break the i.** rompre la glace; **to be skating on thin i.** avancer sur un terrain glissant; **that cuts no i. with me** ça ne marche pas avec moi
  2 *vt (cake)* glacer

▸**ice over** *vi* geler

▸**ice up** *vi* se givrer

iceberg ['aɪsbɜːg] *n* iceberg *m*; *Fig* **that's just the tip of the i.** ce n'est que la partie visible de l'iceberg; **i. lettuce** = variété croquante de laitue de serre

icebound ['aɪsbaʊnd] *adj* bloqué(e) par les glaces

icebox ['aɪsbɒks] *n (fridge)* réfrigérateur *m*

icebreaker ['aɪsbreɪkə(r)] *n (ship)* brise-glace *m inv*; *Fig (at party, in conversation)* **it's a good i.** c'est un bon moyen de briser la glace

icecap ['aɪskæp] *n* calotte *f* glaciaire

ice-cold ['aɪs'kəʊld] *adj* glacé(e); *(wind)* glacial(e)

ice-cream ['aɪs'kriːm] *n* glace *f*; **i. cone** cornet *m* de glace; **i. maker** sorbetière *f*; **i. parlor** salon *m* de dégustation de glaces; **i. van** camionnette *f* de vendeur de glaces

iced [aɪst] *adj* **(a)** *(water)* avec des glaçons **(b)** *(cake)* glacé(e)

Iceland ['aɪslənd] *n* l'Islande *f*

Icelander ['aɪsləndə(r)] *n* Islandais(e) *m,f*

Icelandic [aɪs'lændɪk] **1** *n (language)* islandais *m*
  2 *adj* islandais(e)

ice-skate ['aɪs'skeɪt] **1** *n* patin *m* à glace
  2 *vi* faire du patin à glace

ice-skating ['aɪs'skeɪtɪŋ] *n* patinage *m* (sur glace); **to go i.** faire du patin à glace

icicle ['aɪsɪkəl] *n* glaçon *m (qui pend d'une gouttière etc.)*

icing ['aɪsɪŋ] *n (on cake)* glaçage *m*; *Fig* **the i. on the cake** la cerise sur le gâteau

icon ['aɪkɒn] *n Rel & Comput* icône *f*; *Fig* **gay i.** idole *f* gay

iconoclastic [aɪkɒnəʊ'klæstɪk] *adj* iconoclaste

icy ['aɪsɪ] *adj* **(a)** *(road)* verglacé(e); *(ground)* gelé(e); *(water, hands)* glacé(e); *(wind)* glacial(e) **(b)** *Fig (expression, reply)* glacial(e)

ID ['aɪ'diː] *n (abbr* **identification)** papiers *mpl* (d'identité); **ID card** carte *f* d'identité

I'd [aɪd] = **I had, I would**

idea [aɪ'dɪə] *n* **(a)** *(individual notion)* idée *f*; **to put an i. into sb's head** mettre une idée dans la tête de qn; **the very i.!** quelle idée!; *Fam* **what's the big i.?** qu'est-ce qui te prend?; **where did you get the i. for your book?** d'où vous est venue l'idée de votre livre? **(b)** *(concept)* conception *f*; **to have an i. that...** avoir l'impression que...; **that's not my i. of fun** ce n'est pas vraiment comme ça que je m'amuserais; **it's her i. of a joke** elle trouve ça drôle; **I have no i.** je n'ai aucune idée; **I had no i. that...** je ne savais pas que...; **I thought the i. was for them to come here** je croyais qu'il était prévu qu'ils viennent ici; **the general i. is to...** l'idée est de...; **the i. of the game is to...** le but du jeu est de...

ideal [aɪ'dɪəl] **1** *n* idéal *m*
  2 *adj* idéal(e) **(for** pour)

idealism [aɪ'dɪəlɪzəm] *n* idéalisme *m*

idealist [aɪ'dɪəlɪst] *n* idéaliste *mf*

idealistic [aɪdɪə'lɪstɪk] *adj* idéaliste

idealize [aɪ'dɪəlaɪz] *vt* idéaliser

ideally [aɪ'diːəlɪ] *adv* **(a)** *(extremely well)* idéalement; **they're i. matched** ils vont parfaitement bien ensemble **(b)** *(in an ideal situation)* dans l'idéal

identical [aɪ'dentɪkəl] *adj* identique; **i. twins** *(boys)* vrais jumeaux *mpl*; *(girls)* vraies jumelles *fpl*

identification [aɪdentɪfɪ'keɪʃən] *n* **(a)** *(of body, criminal)* identification *f* **(b)** *(documents)* papiers *mpl* (d'identité)

identifier [aɪ'dentɪfaɪə(r)] *n Comput* identifiant *m*

identify [aɪ'dentɪfaɪ] *(pt & pp* **identified)** **1** *vt* **(a)** *(recognize)* identifier **(b)** *(associate)* **to i. sth with sth** identifier qch à qch
  2 *vi* s'identifier **(with sb** à qn); **I can't i. with his problems** j'ai du mal à comprendre ses problèmes

identifying mark [aɪ'dentɪfaɪɪŋ'mɑːk] *n* signe *m* particulier

Identikit® [aɪ'dentɪkɪt] *n* **I.** *(picture)* portrait-robot *m*

identity [aɪ'dentɪtɪ] *(pl* **identities)** *n* identité *f*; **it was a case of mistaken i.** il y a eu erreur sur la personne; **i. card** carte *f* d'identité; **i. crisis** crise *f* d'identité

ideological [aɪdɪə'lɒdʒɪkəl] *adj* idéologique

ideology [aɪdɪ'ɒlədʒɪ] *(pl* **ideologies)** *n* idéologie *f*

idiocy ['ɪdɪəsɪ] *n* idiotie *f*

idiom ['ɪdɪəm] *n (expression)* expression *f*, locution *f*; *(dialect)* idiome *m*

idiomatic [ɪdɪə'mætɪk] *adj* idiomatique

idiosyncrasy [ɪdɪəʊ'sɪŋkrəsɪ] *(pl* **idiosyncrasies)** *n* particularité *f*; *(foible)* petite manie *f*

idiosyncratic [ɪdɪəʊsɪŋ'krætɪk] *adj* particulier(ère)

idiot ['ɪdɪət] n idiot(e) m,f

idiotic [ɪdɪ'ɒtɪk] adj idiot(e)

idle ['aɪdəl] **1** adj (**a**) (unoccupied) (factory, machine) arrêté(e); (person) désœuvré(e); **an i. moment** un moment libre (**b**) (lazy) oisif(ive) (**c**) (futile) (threat, boast) vain(e); (gossip, rumor) pour passer le temps; (curiosity) simple

2 vi (of engine) tourner au ralenti

▶**idle away** vt sep (time) passer à ne rien faire; **we idled the afternoon away chatting** nous avons passé l'après-midi à bavarder

idleness ['aɪdəlnɪs] n (**a**) (inaction) inactivité f (**b**) (laziness) oisiveté f

idler ['aɪdlə(r)] n (lazy person) paresseux(euse) m,f

idly ['aɪdəlɪ] adv (**a**) (inactively) sans rien faire (**b**) (casually) négligemment

idol ['aɪdəl] n idole f; **a teen idol** une idole des jeunes

idolatry [aɪ'dɒlətrɪ] n idolâtrie f

idolize ['aɪdəlaɪz] vt idolâtrer

idyll ['aɪdɪl] n (situation) situation f idyllique; (place) endroit m idyllique

idyllic [aɪ'dɪlɪk] adj idyllique

ie ['aɪ'iː] (abbr **id est**) c.-à-d.

if [ɪf] **1** conj (**a**) (conditional) si; **if I were rich...** si j'étais riche...; **if I were you...** si j'étais toi..., à ta place...

(**b**) (conceding) **the movie was good, if rather long** le film était un peu long, mais bien; **if anything it's better** c'est presque mieux

(**c**) (whether) si; **I asked if it was true** j'ai demandé si c'était vrai

(**d**) (in phrases) **if not** sinon; **there were hundreds, if not thousands, of people** il y avait des centaines de gens, voire des milliers; **if so** si c'est le cas; **if only I had more money...** si seulement j'avais plus d'argent...; **if and when they arrive...** quand ils arriveront, s'ils arrivent...; **she sees them rarely, if at all** or **if ever** elle ne les voit jamais, ou alors très rarement

2 n **ifs, ands** or **buts** restrictions fpl; **it's a big if** c'est un grand point d'interrogation

IFA [aɪef'eɪ] n Fin (abbr **independent financial adviser**) conseiller(ère) m,f financier(ère) indépendant(e)

iffy ['ɪfɪ] adj Fam (doubtful) incertain(e); (suspect) louche

igloo ['ɪgluː] (pl **igloos**) n igloo m

ignite [ɪg'naɪt] **1** vt (fire) allumer; (paper) enflammer; Fig (conflict) déclencher

2 vi (of fire) prendre; (of paper) s'enflammer; Fig (of conflict) se déclencher

ignition [ɪg'nɪʃən] n (of car) allumage m; **to switch on/off the i.** mettre/couper le contact; **i. key** clé f de contact

ignoble [ɪg'nəʊbəl] adj ignoble

ignominious [ɪgnə'mɪnɪəs] adj ignominieux(euse)

ignoramus [ɪgnə'reɪməs] n ignorant(e) m,f, ignare mf

ignorance ['ɪgnərəns] n (**a**) (lack of knowledge) ignorance f; **out of** or **through i.** par ignorance (**b**) (ill manners) manque m d'éducation

ignorant ['ɪgnərənt] adj (**a**) (lacking knowledge) (person) ignorant(e); (remark) d'ignorant; **to be i. of sth** ignorer qch (**b**) (ill-mannered) mal élevé(e)

ignore [ɪg'nɔː(r)] vt ignorer; **just i. him!** ne fais pas attention à lui!

iguana [ɪg'wɑːnə] n iguane m

ilk [ɪlk] n **of that i.** de ce genre

ill [ɪl] **1** npl **ills** maux mpl

2 adj (**a**) (unwell) malade; **to feel i.** ne pas se sentir bien; **to fall** or **to be taken i.** tomber malade (**b**) (bad, poor) **i. effects** effets mpl néfastes; **i. feeling** animosité f; **i. fortune** malchance f; **to be in i. health** être en mauvaise santé; **i. at ease** mal à l'aise; **of i. repute** mal famé(e); **i. will** malveillance f

3 adv mal; **I can i. afford it** je peux difficilement me le permettre; **to speak/to think i. of sb** dire/penser du mal de qn

I'll [aɪl] = **I will, I shall**

ill-advised ['ɪləd'vaɪzd] adj (person) malavisé(e); (decision, comment) peu judicieux(euse); **to be i. to do sth** être malavisé de faire qch

ill-bred ['ɪl'bred] adj mal élevé(e)

ill-concealed ['ɪlkən'siːld] adj mal dissimulé(e)

ill-considered ['ɪlkən'sɪdəd] adj irréfléchi(e)

ill-disposed ['ɪldɪs'pəʊzd] adj **to be i. toward sb/sth** être mal disposé(e) envers qn/qch

illegal [ɪ'liːgəl] adj illégal(e); (immigrant) clandestin(e)

illegality [ɪlɪ'gælɪtɪ] n illégalité f

illegible [ɪ'ledʒɪbəl] adj illisible

illegitimate [ɪlɪ'dʒɪtɪmət] adj illégitime

ill-equipped ['ɪlɪ'kwɪpd] adj mal équipé(e); Fig **to be i. to do sth** ne pas être apte à faire qch

ill-fated ['ɪl'feɪtɪd] adj (day, occasion) fatal(e); (person, enterprise) malheureux(euse)

ill-founded ['ɪl'faʊndɪd] adj sans fondement

ill-gotten gains ['ɪlgɒtən'gaɪnz] npl biens mpl mal acquis

illiberal [ɪ'lɪbərəl] adj (person) intolérant(e); (measure) restrictif(ive)

illicit [ɪ'lɪsɪt] adj illicite

ill-informed [ɪlɪn'fɔːmd] adj mal informé(e); (idea) inexact(e)

ill-intentioned ['ɪlɪn'tenʃənd] adj malintentionné(e)

illiteracy [ɪ'lɪtərəsɪ] n analphabétisme m

illiterate [ɪ'lɪtərət] **1** n analphabète mf

2 adj analphabète

ill-mannered ['ɪl'mænəd] adj grossier(ère)

ill-natured ['ɪl'neɪtʃəd] adj désagréable

illness ['ɪlnɪs] n maladie f

illogical [ɪ'lɒdʒɪkəl] adj illogique

ill-suited ['ɪl'suːtɪd] adj inapproprié(e) (**to** à); (person) inapte (**to** à)

ill-tempered ['ɪl'tempəd] adj (person) qui a mauvais caractère; (remark) désagréable

ill-timed ['ɪl'taɪmd] adj inopportun(e)

ill-treat ['ɪl'triːt] vt maltraiter

illuminate [ɪ'luːmɪneɪt] vt (**a**) (light up) (room) éclairer; (building) illuminer (**b**) (clarify) éclairer

illuminating [ɪ'luːmɪneɪtɪŋ] adj éclairant(e)

illumination [ɪluːmɪ'neɪʃən] n (**a**) (lighting) éclairage m; **illuminations** (decorative lights) illuminations fpl (**b**) (clarification) éclaircissements mpl

ill-use 1 n ['ɪl'juːs] mauvais traitement m

2 vt ['ɪl'juːz] maltraiter

illusion [ɪ'luːʒən] n illusion f; **to be under the i. that...** s'imaginer que...; **to be under** or **to have no illusions about sb/sth** ne se faire aucune illusion sur qn/qch

illusory [ɪ'luːsərɪ] adj illusoire

illustrate ['ɪləstreɪt] vt illustrer

illustration [ɪləs'treɪʃən] n illustration f

illustrator ['ɪləstreɪtə(r)] n illustrateur(trice) m,f

illustrious [ɪ'lʌstrɪəs] adj illustre

ILO [aɪe'ləʊ] n (abbr **International Labor Organization**) OIT f

IM [aɪ'em] n Comput (abbr **instant messaging**) messagerie f instantanée

I'm [aɪm] = **I am**

image ['ɪmɪdʒ] n image f; **to be the i. of sb** être le portrait de qn

imagery ['ɪmɪdʒərɪ] n imagerie f, images fpl

imaginary [ɪ'mædʒɪnərɪ] adj imaginaire

imagination [ɪmædʒɪ'neɪʃən] n imagination f; **it's (all in) your i.** tu te fais des idées; **use your i.!** fais preuve d'un peu d'imagination!

imaginative [ɪˈmædʒɪnətɪv] *adj (person)* imaginatif(ive); *(excuse, solution)* original(e)

imagine [ɪˈmædʒɪn] *vt* imaginer; **to i. doing sth** s'imaginer faire qch; **to i. sb doing sth** imaginer qn faisant qch; **I can't i. why…** je n'arrive pas à comprendre pourquoi…; **you're imagining things** tu te fais des idées; **you must have imagined it** tu as dû rêver

imbalance [ɪmˈbæləns] *n* déséquilibre *m*

imbecile [ˈɪmbɪsɪl] *n* imbécile *mf*

imbibe [ɪmˈbaɪb] *vt Formal (drink)* absorber; *Fig (knowledge, ideas)* absorber, assimiler

imbue [ɪmˈbjuː] *vt Formal* **to i. sb with sth** imprégner qn de qch; **to be imbued with scorn/fervor** *(of speech, book)* être empreint(e) de mépris/ferveur

IMF [aɪeˈmef] *n (abbr* **International Monetary Fund**) FMI *m*

imitate [ˈɪmɪteɪt] *vt* imiter

imitation [ɪmɪˈteɪʃən] *n (action, copy)* imitation *f*; **in i. of** à l'imitation de; **i. jewelry** faux bijoux *mpl*; **i. leather** simili-cuir *m*, imitation cuir

imitative [ˈɪmɪtətɪv] *adj* imitatif(ive)

imitator [ˈɪmɪteɪtə(r)] *n* imitateur(trice) *m,f*

immaculate [ɪˈmækjʊlət] *adj* impeccable; *Rel* **the I. Conception** l'Immaculée Conception *f*

immaterial [ɪməˈtɪərɪəl] *adj* sans importance

immature [ɪməˈtjʊə(r)] *adj* immature

immaturity [ɪməˈtjʊərɪtɪ] *n* immaturité *f*

immeasurable [ɪˈmeʒərəbəl] *adj* incommensurable

immediacy [ɪˈmiːdɪəsɪ] *n* immédiateté *f*; *(of danger, disaster)* imminence *f*

immediate [ɪˈmiːdɪət] *adj* (**a**) *(instant)* immédiat(e); *(danger)* imminent(e) (**b**) *(nearest) (vicinity)* proche; *(future)* immédiat(e); **the i. family** les proches parents *mpl*

immediately [ɪˈmiːdɪətlɪ] **1** *adv* immédiatement, tout de suite

2 *conj* dès que

immemorial [ɪmɪˈmɔːrɪəl] *adj* **from time i.** depuis des temps immémoriaux

immense [ɪˈmens] *adj* immense

immensely [ɪˈmenslɪ] *adv (interesting, painful)* extrêmement; *(rich)* immensément; *(enjoy oneself)* énormément

immensity [ɪˈmensɪtɪ] *n* immensité *f*; *(of problem, task)* énormité *f*

immerse [ɪˈmɜːs] *vt also Fig* plonger (**in** dans); **to i. oneself in sth** se plonger dans qch

immigrant [ˈɪmɪɡrənt] *n & adj* immigré(e) *m,f*

immigrate [ˈɪmɪɡreɪt] *vi* immigrer

immigration [ɪmɪˈɡreɪʃən] *n* immigration *f*; **to go through i.** passer (à) l'immigration; **i. control** services *mpl* de l'immigration; **i. officer** agent *m* des services de l'immigration

imminent [ˈɪmɪnənt] *adj* imminent(e)

immobile [ɪˈməʊbaɪl] *adj* immobile

immobilize [ɪˈməʊbɪlaɪz] *vt* immobiliser

immoderate [ɪˈmɒdərət] *adj* immodéré(e)

immodest [ɪˈmɒdɪst] *adj (vain)* présomptueux(euse); *(indecent)* impudique

immoral [ɪˈmɒrəl] *adj* immoral(e); **i. earnings** gains *mpl* du proxénétisme

immorality [ɪməˈrælɪtɪ] *n* immoralité *f*

immortal [ɪˈmɔːtəl] **1** *n* immortel(elle) *m,f*

2 *adj* immortel(elle); *(memory)* impérissable

immortality [ɪmɔːˈtælɪtɪ] *n* immortalité *f*

immovable [ɪˈmuːvəbəl] *adj (object)* fixe; *Fig (person, opposition)* inébranlable

immune [ɪˈmjuːn] *adj (to disease)* immunisé(e) (**to** contre); *Fig (to criticism)* imperméable (**to** à); **i. from taxation** exonéré(e)

d'impôts; *Med* **i. deficiency** immunodéficience *f*; *Med* **i. system** système *m* immunitaire

immunity [ɪˈmjuːnɪtɪ] *n (to disease)* immunité *f*; *(from taxation)* exonération *f*; *Law* **i. (from prosecution)** immunité

immunization [ɪmjʊnaɪˈzeɪʃən] *n* immunisation *f*

immunize [ˈɪmjʊnaɪz] *vt* immuniser (**against** contre)

immunosuppression [ˈɪmjuːnəʊsəˈpreʃən] *n Med* immunosuppression *f*

immutable [ɪˈmjuːtəbəl] *adj* immuable

imp [ɪmp] *n (sprite)* lutin *m*; *Fig (mischievous child)* garnement *m*

impact 1 *n* [ˈɪmpækt] impact *m*; **to make an i. on sb/sth** avoir un impact sur qn/qch; **on i.** au moment de l'impact

2 *vt* [ɪmˈpækt] *(collide with)* heurter; *(influence)* avoir un impact sur

impacted [ɪmˈpæktɪd] *adj (tooth)* inclus(e)

impair [ɪmˈpeə(r)] *vt (sight, hearing)* affaiblir; *(relations, chances)* compromettre

impale [ɪmˈpeɪl] *vt* empaler (**on** sur)

impart [ɪmˈpɑːt] *vt Formal (heat, light, quality)* donner; *(knowledge, news)* transmettre

impartial [ɪmˈpɑːʃəl] *adj* impartial(e)

impartiality [ɪmpɑːʃɪˈælɪtɪ] *n* impartialité *f*

impassable [ɪmˈpɑːsəbəl] *adj (river, barrier)* infranchissable; *(road)* impraticable

impasse [ˈæmpɑːs] *n* impasse *f*; **to have reached an i.** être dans une impasse

impassioned [ɪmˈpæʃənd] *adj* passionné(e)

impassive [ɪmˈpæsɪv] *adj* impassible

impassively [ɪmˈpæsɪvlɪ] *adv* impassiblement

impatience [ɪmˈpeɪʃəns] *n* impatience *f*

impatient [ɪmˈpeɪʃənt] *adj* impatient(e); **to be i. to do sth** être impatient de faire qch; **to be i. for sth** avoir soif de qch; **to get i. (with sb)** s'impatienter (contre qn)

impatiently [ɪmˈpeɪʃəntlɪ] *adv* avec impatience

impeach [ɪmˈpiːtʃ] *vt Law & Pol* entamer une procédure d'"impeachment" contre

impeachment [ɪmˈpiːtʃmənt] *n Law & Pol* = mise en accusation d'un élu devant le Congrès

impeccable [ɪmˈpekəbəl] *adj* impeccable

impede [ɪmˈpiːd] *vt* gêner

impediment [ɪmˈpedɪmənt] *n* (**a**) *(obstacle)* obstacle *m* (**b**) *(disability)* handicap *m*

impel [ɪmˈpel] *(pt & pp* **impelled**) *vt* (**a**) *(oblige)* obliger; *(incite)* pousser (**b**) *(push)* propulser

impending [ɪmˈpendɪŋ] *adj* imminent(e)

impenetrable [ɪmˈpenɪtrəbəl] *adj (defenses, mystery)* impénétrable; *(jargon)* incompréhensible

imperative [ɪmˈperətɪv] **1** *n Gram* impératif *m*; **in the i.** à l'impératif

2 *adj* impératif(ive); **it is i. that he should come** il faut impérativement qu'il vienne

imperceptible [ɪmpəˈseptɪbəl] *adj* imperceptible

imperfect [ɪmˈpɜːfɪkt] **1** *n Gram* **the i.** l'imparfait *m*; **in the i.** à l'imparfait

2 *adj (not perfect)* imparfait(e); *Gram* de l'imparfait; **i. tense** imparfait *m*

imperfection [ɪmpəˈfekʃən] *n* imperfection *f*

imperial [ɪmˈpɪərɪəl] *adj (of empire)* impérial(e)

imperialism [ɪmˈpɪərɪəlɪzəm] *n* impérialisme *m*

imperialist [ɪmˈpɪərɪəlɪst] *n & adj* impérialiste *mf*

imperil [ɪmˈperɪl] *vt* mettre en péril

imperious [ɪmˈpɪərɪəs] *adj* impérieux(euse)

impermanent [ɪmˈpɜːmənənt] *adj* temporaire

impersonal [ɪmˈpɜːsənəl] *adj* impersonnel(elle)

impersonate [ɪmˈpɜːsəneɪt] *vt (pretend to be)* se faire passer pour; *(imitate)* imiter

impersonation [ɪmpɜːsə'neɪʃən] n (pretense of being) usurpation f d'identité; (imitation) imitation f

impersonator [ɪm'pɜːsəneɪtə(r)] n (impostor) imposteur m; (mimic) imitateur(trice) m,f

impertinence [ɪm'pɜːtɪnəns] n impertinence f

impertinent [ɪm'pɜːtɪnənt] adj impertinent(e)

imperturbable [ɪmpə'tɜːbəbəl] adj imperturbable

impervious [ɪm'pɜːvɪəs] adj also Fig imperméable (to à)

impetuous [ɪm'petjʊəs] adj impétueux(euse)

impetus ['ɪmpɪtəs] n élan m

▸ **impinge on** [ɪm'pɪndʒ] vt insep affecter, avoir un effet sur

impious ['ɪmpɪəs] adj impie

impish ['ɪmpɪʃ] adj espiègle

implacable [ɪm'plækəbəl] adj implacable

implant 1 n ['ɪmplɑːnt] Med implant m
  2 vt [ɪm'plɑːnt] (a) Med implanter (b) (opinion, belief) inculquer

implausible [ɪm'plɔːzɪbəl] adj peu plausible, invraisemblable

implement 1 n ['ɪmplɪmənt] instrument m; (for cooking) ustensile m; (for gardening, home improvement) outil m
  2 vt [ɪm'plɪment] (plan, agreement) mettre en application

implementation [ɪmplɪmen'teɪʃən] n (of plan, agreement) mise f en œuvre, application f

implicate ['ɪmplɪkeɪt] vt impliquer

implication [ɪmplɪ'keɪʃən] n implication f; **by i.** implicitement

implicit [ɪm'plɪsɪt] adj (a) (implied) implicite; **it was i. in her remarks** c'était impliqué dans ses remarques (b) (absolute) absolu(e); **i. faith** confiance f aveugle

implied [ɪm'plaɪd] adj implicite

implore [ɪm'plɔː(r)] vt implorer; **to i. sb to do sth** implorer qn de faire qch

imploring [ɪm'plɔːrɪŋ] adj implorant(e)

imply [ɪm'plaɪ] (pt & pp implied) vt (a) (insinuate) insinuer, sous-entendre (b) (involve) impliquer; (presuppose) supposer

impolite [ɪmpə'laɪt] adj impoli(e)

impoliteness [ɪmpə'laɪtnɪs] n impolitesse f

imponderable [ɪm'pɒndərəbəl] **1** n impondérable m
  2 adj impondérable

import 1 n ['ɪmpɔːt] (a) (item, activity) importation f; **i. duty** droit m de douane à l'importation (b) Formal (importance) importance f
  2 vt [ɪm'pɔːt] also Comput importer

importance [ɪm'pɔːtəns] n importance f; **of the utmost i.** de la plus haute importance; **it is of no great i.** ça n'a pas grande importance; **to attach i. to sth** attacher de l'importance à qch; **to be full of one's own i.** être imbu(e) de sa personne

important [ɪm'pɔːtənt] adj important(e); **to be i. to sb** être important pour qn; **to become more i.** prendre de l'importance; **it's not i.** c'est sans importance

importantly [ɪm'pɔːtəntlɪ] adv (speak) d'un air important; **but, more i....** mais, plus important...

importation [ɪmpɔː'teɪʃən] n importation f

importer [ɪm'pɔːtə(r)] n importateur(trice) m,f

import-export ['ɪmpɔːt'eks_pɔːt] n **i. (trade)** import-export m

importune [ɪm'pɔːtjuːn] vt Formal importuner

impose [ɪm'pəʊz] **1** vt (silence, one's will, restrictions) imposer (on à); **to i. a tax on sth** taxer qch; **to i. a fine on sb** condamner qn à (payer) une amende
  2 vi (take advantage) s'imposer

▸ **impose on, impose upon** vt insep (take advantage of) abuser de; **to i. on** or **upon sb** abuser de la gentillesse de qn

imposing [ɪm'pəʊzɪŋ] adj imposant(e)

imposition [ɪmpə'zɪʃən] n (a) (of tax, fine) imposition f (b) (unfair demand) **it was a bit of an i.** il y avait de l'abus

impossibility [ɪmpɒsɪ'bɪlɪtɪ] (pl **impossibilities**) n impossibilité f; **it's a physical i.** c'est matériellement impossible

impossible [ɪm'pɒsɪbəl] **1** n **the i.** l'impossible m; **to do/achieve the i.** faire/réussir l'impossible
  2 adj impossible; **to make it i. for sb to do sth** mettre qn dans l'impossibilité de faire qch

impossibly [ɪm'pɒsɪblɪ] adv (extremely) incroyablement

impostor [ɪm'pɒstə(r)] n imposteur m

impotence ['ɪmpətəns] n impuissance f

impotent ['ɪmpətənt] adj impuissant(e)

impound [ɪm'paʊnd] vt Law saisir; (car) mettre à la fourrière

impoverish [ɪm'pɒvərɪʃ] vt appauvrir

impoverished [ɪm'pɒvərɪʃd] adj appauvri(e)

impracticable [ɪm'præktɪkəbəl] adj impraticable, irréalisable

impractical [ɪm'præktɪkəl] adj (suggestion) irréaliste; (person) qui manque de sens pratique

imprecise [ɪmprɪ'saɪs] adj imprécis(e)

imprecision [ɪmprɪ'sɪʒən] n imprécision f

impregnable [ɪm'pregnəbəl] adj (fortress) imprenable; Fig (argument) irréfutable, inattaquable

impregnate [ɪm'pregneɪt] vt (a) (fertilize) féconder (b) (soak) imprégner (with de)

impresario [ɪmpre'sɑːrɪəʊ] (pl **impresarios** or **impresari** [ɪmpre'sɑːriː]) n imprésario m

impress [ɪm'pres] vt (a) (make an impression on) impressionner; **to be impressed with** or **by sb/sth** être impressionné(e) par qn/qch; **to i. sb favorably/unfavorably** faire une impression favorable/défavorable à qn (b) (emphasize) **to i. sth on sb** faire comprendre qch à qn (c) (imprint) **to i. sth on sth** imprimer qch sur qch

impression [ɪm'preʃən] n (a) (effect) impression f; **to make an i. on sb** marquer qn; **to make an i. on sth** avoir un impact sur qch; **to make a good/bad i. (on sb)** faire bonne/mauvaise impression (à qn); **to create a false i.** donner une fausse impression; **to be under the i. that...** avoir l'impression que...; **to give the i. that...** donner l'impression que... (b) (imprint) (in wax, snow) empreinte f (c) (of book) réimpression f (d) (imitation) imitation f; **to do impressions** faire des imitations; **to do an i. of sb** imiter qn

impressionable [ɪm'preʃənəbəl] adj impressionnable

impressionism [ɪm'preʃənɪzəm] n Art impressionnisme m

impressionist [ɪm'preʃənɪst] **1** n (a) Art impressionniste mf (b) (mimic) imitateur(trice) m,f
  2 adj Art impressionniste

impressionistic [ɪmpreʃə'nɪstɪk] adj vague

impressive [ɪm'presɪv] adj impressionnant(e)

imprint 1 n ['ɪmprɪnt] empreinte f
  2 vt [ɪm'prɪnt] imprimer (on sur); **her words are imprinted on my memory** ses mots restent gravés dans ma mémoire

imprison [ɪm'prɪzən] vt emprisonner

imprisonment [ɪm'prɪzənmənt] n emprisonnement m

improbability [ɪmprɒbə'bɪlɪtɪ] (pl **improbabilities**) n improbabilité f

improbable [ɪm'prɒbəbəl] adj (unlikely) improbable; (unbelievable) invraisemblable

impromptu [ɪm'prɒmptuː] **1** adj (speech, party) improvisé(e)
  2 adv (unexpectedly) à l'improviste; (ad lib) au pied levé

improper [ɪm'prɒpə(r)] adj (a) (use, purpose) mauvais(e); (behavior) déplacé(e); Law **i. practices** pratiques fpl malhonnêtes (b) (lewd) indécent(e)

impropriety [ɪmprə'praɪətɪ] n inconvenance f; (of language) impropriété f

improve [ɪm'pruːv] **1** vt améliorer; (invention, technique) perfectionner; **to i. one's mind** se cultiver
  2 vi s'améliorer; (of business) reprendre

▶**improve on, improve upon** *vt insep* améliorer; **to i. on a bid** surenchérir

improved [ɪmˈpruːvd] *adj (system, design)* perfectionné(e)

improvement [ɪmˈpruːvmənt] *n* amélioration *f* (**in** de); *(of invention, technique)* perfectionnement *m*; **to be an i. on** être meilleur(e) que; **there's room for i.** on peut faire mieux; **to make improvements (to a house)** faire des travaux d'aménagement (dans une maison)

improvident [ɪmˈprɒvɪdənt] *adj Formal (person)* imprévoyant(e)

improvisation [ɪmprəvɪˈzeɪʃən] *n* improvisation *f*

improvise [ˈɪmprəvaɪz] *vt & vi* improviser

imprudent [ɪmˈpruːdənt] *adj* imprudent(e)

impudence [ˈɪmpjʊdəns] *n* impudence *f*, insolence *f*

impudent [ˈɪmpjʊdənt] *adj* impudent(e), insolent(e)

impugn [ɪmˈpjuːn] *vt Formal* mettre en doute

impulse [ˈɪmpʌls] *n* impulsion *f*; **to feel an i. to do sth** avoir une soudaine envie de faire qch; **on i.** sur un coup de tête; **i. buying** achat *m* d'impulsion

impulsive [ɪmˈpʌlsɪv] *adj* impulsif(ive)

impunity [ɪmˈpjuːnɪtɪ] *n* impunité *f*; **with i.** en toute impunité

impure [ɪmˈpjʊə(r)] *adj* impur(e)

impurity [ɪmˈpjʊərətɪ] *(pl* **impurities***) n* impureté *f*

impute [ɪmˈpjuːt] *vt Formal* **to i. sth to sb** imputer *ou* attribuer qch à qn

in [ɪn] **1** *prep* **(a)** *(with place)* dans; **in the garden** dans le jardin; **in France** en France; **in Japan** au Japon; **in the USA** aux États-Unis; **in Paris** à Paris; **in the hospital** à l'hôpital; **in town** en ville; **in bed** au lit; **in here** ici; **in there** là
(b) *(with expressions of time)* **in 1927/April** en 1927/avril; **in (the) spring** au printemps; **in (the) summer** en été; **in the afternoon** l'après-midi; **in the 70s** dans les années 70
(c) *(expressing manner)* **in French** en français; **to write in pen** écrire au stylo; **in a loud voice** d'une voix forte; **in this way** ainsi, de cette façon
(d) *(within, during)* **she did it in three hours** elle l'a fait en trois heures; **he'll be here in three hours** il sera ici dans trois heures; **I haven't seen him in years** ça fait des années que je ne l'ai pas vu
(e) *(with situation, arrangement)* **in the rain** sous la pluie; **in the sun** au soleil; **dressed in white** habillé(e) en blanc; **in danger** en danger; **in twos** deux par deux; **in a circle/line** en rond/rang
(f) *(with numbers, quantities, ratios)* **one in ten** un sur dix; **in small/large quantities** en petite/grande quantité; **3 ft in length/height/width** ≃ 1 m de long/de haut/de large; **she's in her sixties** elle a la soixantaine; **the temperature was in the nineties** ≃ il faisait dans les trente degrés
(g) *(with gerund)* **to have no difficulty in doing sth** ne pas avoir de mal à faire qch; **in saying this...** en disant cela...
(h) *(with field of activity)* **to be in insurance/publishing** être dans les assurances/l'édition
(i) *(idioms)* **I didn't think she had it in her to...** je ne l'aurais pas crue capable de...

2 *adv* **(a)** *(inside)* dedans; **to go in** entrer, rentrer
(b) *(not out)* là; **is your mother in?** est-ce que ta mère est là?; **to stay in** *(at home)* rester à la maison
(c) **to be in** *(of plane, train)* être arrivé(e)
(d) *(fashionable)* à la mode
(e) **in that...** puisque..., vu que...
(f) *(idioms)* **to have it in for sb** en vouloir à qn; **she's in for a shock/surprise** elle va avoir un choc/une surprise; **to be in on a plan/secret** être dans le coup; **he's in for it** ça va être sa fête

3 *adj* **the in crowd** les branchés *mpl*

4 *n* **the ins and outs** *(of question)* les tenants *mpl* et les aboutissants; *(of plot)* les subtilités *fpl*

inability [ɪnəˈbɪlɪtɪ] *n* incapacité *f* (**to do sth** à faire qch)

inaccessibility [ɪnæksesɪˈbɪlɪtɪ] *n* inaccessibilité *f*

inaccessible [ɪnækˈsesɪbəl] *adj* inaccessible (**to** à)

inaccuracy [ɪnˈækjʊrəsɪ] *(pl* **inaccuracies***) n (of estimate, translation, report)* inexactitude *f*; *(of rifle, instrument)* manque *m* de précision

inaccurate [ɪnˈækjʊrət] *adj (estimate, translation, report)* inexact(e); *(rifle, instrument)* qui manque de précision

inaction [ɪnˈækʃən] *n* inaction *f*

inactive [ɪnˈæktɪv] *adj* inactif(ive)

inactivity [ɪnækˈtɪvɪtɪ] *n* inactivité *f*

inadequacy [ɪnˈædɪkwəsɪ] *(pl* **inadequacies***) n* insuffisance *f*; **a feeling of i.** un complexe d'infériorité

inadequate [ɪnˈædɪkwət] *adj* insuffisant(e); **to feel i.** ne pas se sentir à la hauteur

inadmissible [ɪnədˈmɪsɪbəl] *adj Law (evidence)* irrecevable

inadvertent [ɪnədˈvɜːtənt] *adj* involontaire

inadvertently [ɪnədˈvɜːtəntlɪ] *adv* par inadvertance

inadvisable [ɪnədˈvaɪzəbəl] *adj* déconseillé(e)

inalienable [ɪnˈeɪlɪənəbəl] *adj Formal* inaliénable

inane [ɪˈneɪn] *adj* idiot(e), stupide

inanimate [ɪnˈænɪmət] *adj* inanimé(e)

inanity [ɪˈnænɪtɪ] *n* ineptie *f*

inapplicable [ɪnˈæplɪkəbəl] *adj* inapplicable (**to** à); **delete where i.** *(sign)* rayer la mention inutile

inappropriate [ɪnəˈprəʊprɪət] *adj (behavior, remark)* déplacé(e); *(dress)* peu approprié(e) (**to** à); *(time)* inopportun(e)

inapt [ɪnˈæpt] *adj* peu approprié(e)

inarticulate [ɪnɑːˈtɪkjʊlɪt] *adj (sound)* inarticulé(e); **to be i.** *(of person)* avoir du mal à s'exprimer; **to be i. with rage** bégayer de rage

inasmuch as [ɪnəzˈmʌtʃəz] *conj Formal* dans la mesure où

inattention [ɪnəˈtenʃən] *n* inattention *f*

inattentive [ɪnəˈtentɪv] *adj* inattentif(ive) (**to** à)

inaudible [ɪnˈɔːdɪbəl] *adj* inaudible

inaugural [ɪˈnɔːgjʊrəl] *adj* inaugural(e)

inaugurate [ɪˈnɔːgjʊreɪt] *vt (building, exhibition)* inaugurer; *(president)* investir

inauguration [ɪnɔːgjʊˈreɪʃən] *n (of building, exhibition)* inauguration *f*; *(of president)* cérémonie *f* de prise de fonctions

inauspicious [ɪnɔːsˈpɪʃəs] *adj* peu propice; **to get off to an i. start** mal commencer

inauthentic [ɪnɔːˈθentɪk] *adj* inauthentique

in-between [ɪnbɪˈtwiːn] *adj* intermédiaire

inborn [ˈɪnbɔːn] *adj* inné(e)

inbound [ˈɪnbaʊnd] *adj (flight, passenger)* à l'arrivée

inbox [ˈɪnbɒks] *n Comput (for e-mail)* boîte *f* de réception, corbeille *f* d'arrivée

inbred [ˈɪnbred] *adj (person)* de parents consanguins; *(distrust, confidence)* inné(e)

in-built [ˈɪnbɪlt] *adj (trait)* inhérent(e); **his height gives him an i. advantage** sa taille lui donne un avantage dès le départ

Inc. [ɪŋk] *adj (abbr* **Incorporated**) ≃ SARL

Inca [ˈɪŋkə] **1** *n* Inca *mf*
2 *adj* inca

incalculable [ɪnˈkælkjʊləbəl] *adj (consequences, damage)* incalculable; *(help, value)* inestimable

incandescent [ɪnkænˈdesənt] *adj* incandescent(e); *Fig* **i. with rage** fou (folle) de rage

incantation [ɪnkænˈteɪʃən] *n* incantation *f*

incapable [ɪnˈkeɪpəbəl] *adj* incapable (**of** de); *(through illness)* impotent(e); *(through drink)* ivre mort(e); **to be i. of doing sth** être incapable de faire qch

incapacitate [ɪnkəˈpæsɪteɪt] *vt* rendre impotent(e); **to be incapacitated for work** être inapte au travail

incapacity [ɪnkə'pæsɪtɪ] *n* incapacité *f*; **i. to do sth** incapacité à faire qch

incarcerate [ɪn'kɑːsəreɪt] *vt Formal* incarcérer

incarceration [ɪnkɑːsə'reɪʃən] *n Formal* incarcération *f*

incarnate [ɪn'kɑːneɪt] *adj* incarné(e)

incarnation [ɪnkɑː'neɪʃən] *n* incarnation *f*; **in a previous i.** dans une vie antérieure

incautious [ɪn'kɔːʃəs] *adj* imprudent(e)

incendiary [ɪn'sendɪərɪ] **1** *n* (*pl* **incendiaries**) *(arsonist)* incendiaire *mf*; *(bomb)* bombe *f* incendiaire

2 *adj also Fig* incendiaire

incense[1] ['ɪnsens] *n* encens *m*

incense[2] [ɪn'sens] *vt (anger)* rendre furieux(euse)

incentive [ɪn'sentɪv] *n (stimulus)* motivation *f*; *(payment)* prime *f*; **there is no i. for students to work hard** il n'y a rien qui encourage les étudiants à travailler dur; **i. bonus** *or* **payment** prime *f* de rendement; **i. program** *(for workers)* système *m* de primes

inception [ɪn'sepʃən] *n* début *m*

incessant [ɪn'sesənt] *adj* incessant(e)

incest ['ɪnsest] *n* inceste *m*

incestuous [ɪn'sestjʊəs] *adj* incestueux(euse); *Fig (environment, group)* très fermé(e)

inch [ɪntʃ] *n* **(a)** *(unit of measurement)* = 2,54 cm, pouce *m*; **i. by i.** petit à petit, peu à peu **(b)** *(idioms)* **I know every i. of this town** je connais cette ville comme ma poche; **he's every i. the gentleman** c'est le parfait gentleman; **to miss sth by inches** manquer qch d'un cheveu; **to be within an i. of doing sth** être à deux doigts de faire qch; **she won't give an i.** elle ne cédera pas d'un pouce; **give her an i. and she'll take a mile** tu lui en donnes jusqu'au coude, elle en demande long comme le bras

▶**inch along, inch forward** *vi* avancer tout doucement

incidence ['ɪnsɪdəns] *n (frequency)* taux *m*; *(of disease)* incidence *f*

incident ['ɪnsɪdənt] *n* incident *m*; *(in book, movie)* scène *f*; **full of i.** riche en incidents

incidental [ɪnsɪ'dentəl] *adj (minor)* accessoire (**to** par rapport à); **i. expenses** faux frais *mpl*; **i. music** *(in movie)* musique *f*

incidentally [ɪnsɪ'dentəlɪ] *adv (by the way)* au fait

incinerate [ɪn'sɪnəreɪt] *vt* incinérer; *Fig* carboniser

incineration [ɪnsɪnə'reɪʃən] *n* incinération *f*

incinerator [ɪn'sɪnəreɪtə(r)] *n* incinérateur *m*

incipient [ɪn'sɪpɪənt] *adj Formal* naissant(e)

incision [ɪn'sɪʒən] *n* incision *f*

incisive [ɪn'saɪsɪv] *adj* incisif(ive)

incisor [ɪn'saɪzə(r)] *n* incisive *f*

incite [ɪn'saɪt] *vt (violence, unrest)* inciter à; **to i. sb to do sth** inciter qn à faire qch

incitement [ɪn'saɪtmənt] *n* incitation *f* (**to** à)

incivility [ɪnsɪ'vɪlɪtɪ] *(pl* **incivilities**) *n Formal* incivilité *f*

inclement [ɪn'klemənt] *adj Formal (weather)* inclément(e)

inclination [ɪnklɪ'neɪʃən] *n* **(a)** *(liking)* inclination *f*, penchant *m* (**for** pour); *(desire)* envie *f*; **to have an i. to do sth** avoir envie de faire qch **(b)** *(tendency)* tendance *f* (**towards** à); **to have an i. to do sth** avoir tendance à faire qch; **by i.** de *ou* par nature **(c)** *(angle)* inclinaison *f*

incline 1 *n* ['ɪnklaɪn] *(slope)* pente *f*

2 *vt* [ɪn'klaɪn] **(a)** *(cause)* **to i. sb to do sth** inciter qn à faire qch **(b)** *(lean)* incliner; **to i. one's head** incliner la tête **(c)** **to be inclined to do sth** *(tend)* avoir tendance à faire qch; **I'm inclined to agree** j'aurais tendance à être d'accord

3 *vi* [ɪn'klaɪn] *(lean)* s'incliner; *(tend)* **to i. to** *or* **toward** pencher pour; **to i. to the belief that...** être porté(e) à croire que...

include [ɪn'kluːd] *vt* inclure, comprendre; *(in letter)* joindre; **the price does not i. accommodations** le logement n'est pas compris dans le prix

including [ɪn'kluːdɪŋ] *prep* y compris; **seven not i. the children** sept sans compter les enfants; **up to and i. page 40** jusqu'à la page 40 incluse

inclusion [ɪn'kluːʒən] *n* inclusion *f*

inclusive [ɪn'kluːsɪv] *adj (price, sum)* net (nette); **to be i. of** comprendre; **i. of VAT** TVA comprise; **from February 4 through 12 i.** du 4 au 12 février inclus

incognito [ɪnkɒg'niːtəʊ] *adv* incognito

incoherence [ɪnkəʊ'hɪərəns] *n* incohérence *f*

incoherent [ɪnkəʊ'hɪərənt] *adj* incohérent(e)

income ['ɪnkʌm] *n* revenu *m*; **i. tax** impôt *m* sur le revenu

incoming ['ɪnkʌmɪŋ] *adj (government, president)* nouveau(elle); *(plane, train)* à l'arrivée; *(phone call)* de l'extérieur; *(tide)* montant(e); **i. mail** courrier *m* (du jour)

incommensurate [ɪnkə'menʃərɪt] *adj* **to be i. with** ne pas être proportionné(e) à

incommunicado [ɪnkəmjuːnɪ'kɑːdəʊ] *adj (uncontactable)* injoignable

incomparable [ɪn'kɒmpərəbəl] *adj* incomparable

incompatible [ɪnkəm'pætɪbəl] *adj* incompatible (**with** avec)

incompetence [ɪn'kɒmpɪtəns] *n* incompétence *f*

incompetent [ɪn'kɒmpɪtənt] *adj* incompétent(e)

incomplete [ɪnkəm'pliːt] *adj* **(a)** *(not whole)* incomplet(ète) **(b)** *(not finished)* inachevé(e)

incomprehensible [ɪnkɒmprɪ'hensɪbəl] *adj* incompréhensible

incomprehension [ɪnkɒmprɪ'henʃən] *n* incompréhension *f*

inconceivable [ɪnkən'siːvəbəl] *adj* inconcevable

inconclusive [ɪnkən'kluːsɪv] *adj (evidence, results)* peu concluant(e); **the meeting/investigation was i.** la réunion/ l'enquête n'a abouti à rien

incongruity [ɪnkɒŋ'gruːɪtɪ] *(pl* **incongruities**) *n* incongruité *f*

incongruous [ɪn'kɒŋgrʊəs] *adj* incongru(e)

inconsequential [ɪnkɒnsɪ'kwenʃəl] *adj* insignifiant(e), sans importance

inconsiderate [ɪnkən'sɪdərɪt] *adj (person)* sans égards pour les autres; *(remark)* déplacé(e); **it was i. of you not to invite her** ce n'est pas gentil de ta part de ne pas l'avoir invitée

inconsistency [ɪnkən'sɪstənsɪ] *(pl* **inconsistencies**) *n (in argument)* incohérence *f*; *(between reports, descriptions)* contradiction *f*; *(uneven quality)* irrégularité *f*

inconsistent [ɪnkən'sɪstənt] *adj (person)* incohérent(e); *(uneven)* irrégulier(ère); **to be i. with** ne pas concorder *ou* cadrer avec

inconsolable [ɪnkən'səʊləbəl] *adj* inconsolable

inconspicuous [ɪnkən'spɪkjʊəs] *adj* qui passe inaperçu(e)

incontestable [ɪnkən'testəbəl] *adj* incontestable

incontinence [ɪn'kɒntɪnəns] *n* incontinence *f*

incontinent [ɪn'kɒntɪnənt] *adj* incontinent(e)

incontrovertible [ɪnkɒntrə'vɜːtɪbəl] *adj Formal* incontestable

inconvenience [ɪnkən'viːnjəns] **1** *n* désagrément *m*; **to be an i. to sb** déranger qn

2 *vt* déranger

inconvenient [ɪnkən'viːnjənt] *adj (time)* mauvais(e); *(place, arrangement)* peu commode; **if it's not i.** si cela ne vous dérange pas; **it's a bit i. just now** ça ne tombe pas très bien en ce moment

incorporate [ɪn'kɔːpəreɪt] *vt* incorporer; *(have as quality)* comprendre

incorrect [ɪnkə'rekt] *adj* incorrect(e)

incorrigible [ɪn'kɒrɪdʒɪbəl] *adj* incorrigible

incorruptible [ɪnkə'rʌptɪbəl] *adj* incorruptible

increase 1 *n* ['ɪnkriːs] *(in price, rate, sales)* augmentation *f*, hausse *f* (**in** de); *(in salary)* augmentation (de salaire); *(in pain, population)* accroissement *m* (**in** de); **to be on the i.** être en hausse

2 *vt* [ɪnˈkriːs] augmenter; **to i. one's efforts** redoubler d'efforts; **to i. one's speed** accélérer

3 *vi* [ɪnˈkriːs] augmenter; **to i. in price** augmenter; **to i. in value** prendre de la valeur

increasing [ɪnˈkriːsɪŋ] *adj* croissant(e)

increasingly [ɪnˈkriːsɪŋlɪ] *adv* de plus en plus

incredible [ɪnˈkredɪbəl] *adj* (**a**) *(unbelievable)* incroyable (**b**) *Fam (excellent)* génial(e)

incredibly [ɪnˈkredɪblɪ] *adv* (**a**) *(extremely)* incroyablement; *Fam* **i. good** génial(e) (**b**) *(unbelievably)* **i., no one was hurt** aussi incroyable que cela puisse paraître, personne n'a été blessé

incredulous [ɪnˈkredjʊləs] *adj* incrédule

increment [ˈɪnkrɪmənt] *n* augmentation *f*

incremental [ɪnkrɪˈmentəl] *adj (increasing)* croissant(e); **i. increases** augmentations *fpl* régulières

incriminate [ɪnˈkrɪmɪneɪt] *vt* incriminer, mettre en cause

incriminating [ɪnˈkrɪmɪneɪtɪŋ] *adj* compromettant(e)

incubate [ˈɪnkjʊeɪt] *vt (of bird)* couver; *(baby)* mettre en couveuse

incubation [ɪnkjʊˈbeɪʃən] *n* incubation *f*; *Med* **i. period** *(of infection)* durée *f* d'incubation

incubator [ˈɪnkjʊbeɪtə(r)] *n (for babies)* couveuse *f*; *(for eggs)* incubateur *m*

inculcate [ˈɪnkʌlkeɪt] *vt Formal* **to i. sth in sb, to i. sb with sth** inculquer qch à qn

incumbent [ɪnˈkʌmbənt] *Formal* **1** *n* **the present i. (of the presidency)** le président en exercice

2 *adj* **it is i. on sb to do sth** il incombe *ou* appartient à qn de faire qch

incur [ɪnˈkɜː(r)] *(pt & pp* **incurred**) *vt (blame, expense)* encourir; *(loss)* subir; *(risk)* courir; *(person's anger)* s'attirer; *(debt)* contracter

incurable [ɪnˈkjʊərəbəl] *adj also Fig* incurable

incurious [ɪnˈkjʊərɪəs] *adj* peu curieux(euse)

incursion [ɪnˈkɜːʃən] *n Formal* incursion *f*

indebted [ɪnˈdetɪd] *adj (financially)* endetté(e); *(for help, advice)* redevable (**to** à); **I am i. to my family for all their support** je suis reconnaissant à ma famille pour son soutien

indebtedness [ɪnˈdetɪdnɪs] *n (financial)* endettement *m*; *(for help, advice)* dette *f* (**to** envers)

indecency [ɪnˈdiːsənsɪ] *n* indécence *f*; *Law* attentat *m* à la pudeur

indecent [ɪnˈdiːsənt] *adj* indécent(e); **to do sth with i. haste** mettre un empressement déplacé à faire qch; *Law* **i. assault** attentat *m* à la pudeur; *Law* **i. exposure** outrage *m* public à la pudeur

indecipherable [ɪndɪˈsaɪfərəbəl] *adj* indéchiffrable

indecision [ɪndɪˈsɪʒən] *n* indécision *f*

indecisive [ɪndɪˈsaɪsɪv] *adj (person)* indécis(e); *(battle, election)* à l'issue peu claire

indecorous [ɪnˈdekərəs] *adj Formal* peu digne

indeed [ɪnˈdiːd] *adv* (**a**) *(used with 'very')* vraiment; **very big i.** vraiment très grand; **thank you very much i.** merci mille fois (**b**) *(in confirmation)* en effet, effectivement; *(certainly)* certainement (**c**) *(what's more)* en fait, et même; **I think so, i. I'm sure of it** je pense que oui, en fait j'en suis sûr (**d**) *(expressing ironic surprise)* **have you i.?** vraiment?

indefatigable [ɪndɪˈfætɪgəbəl] *adj Formal* infatigable

indefensible [ɪndɪˈfensɪbəl] *adj (behavior, attitude)* injustifiable, impardonnable; *(theory)* indéfendable

indefinable [ɪndɪˈfaɪnəbəl] *adj* indéfinissable

indefinite [ɪnˈdefɪnɪt] *adj* (**a**) *(period of time, number)* indéterminé(e) (**b**) *(idea, plan)* mal défini(e) (**c**) *Gram* indéfini(e)

indefinitely [ɪnˈdefɪnɪtlɪ] *adv* indéfiniment

indelible [ɪnˈdelɪbəl] *adj also Fig* indélébile

indelicate [ɪnˈdelɪkət] *adj* indélicat(e)

indemnify [ɪnˈdemnɪfaɪ] *(pt & pp* **indemnified**) *vt* **to i. sb for sth** *(compensate)* indemniser *ou* dédommager qn de qch; **to i. sb against sth** *(give security)* assurer qn contre qch

indemnity [ɪnˈdemnɪtɪ] *(pl* **indemnities**) *n (guarantee)* garantie *f*, assurance *f*; *(money)* indemnité *f*, dédommagement *m*

indent *Typ* **1** *n* [ˈɪndent] alinéa *m*

2 *vt* [ɪnˈdent] mettre en retrait

indentation [ɪndenˈteɪʃən] *n (mark)* trace *f*, empreinte *f*; *(in coastline)* découpure *f*; *Typ* alinéa *m*

independence [ɪndɪˈpendəns] *n* indépendance *f* (**from** par rapport à); **I. Day** fête *f* nationale de l'Indépendance

independent [ɪndɪˈpendənt] *adj* indépendant(e) (**of** de); *Fin* **i. financial adviser** conseiller(ère) *m,f* financier(ère) indépendant(e)

independently [ɪndɪˈpendəntlɪ] *adv* indépendamment; **i. of** indépendamment de; **to live i.** être indépendant(e)

in-depth [ˈɪndepθ] *adj* approfondi(e), en profondeur

indescribable [ɪndɪsˈkraɪbəbəl] *adj* indescriptible

indestructible [ɪndɪsˈtrʌktəbəl] *adj* indestructible

indeterminate [ɪndɪˈtɜːmɪnət] *adj* indéterminé(e)

index [ˈɪndeks] **1** *n (of book)* index *m*; *(in library)* fichier *m*; **i. finger** index; *Fin* **i. fund** fonds *m* indiciel

2 *vt* (**a**) *(book)* dresser l'index de (**b**) *Fin (wages)* indexer (**to** sur)

index-linked [ˈɪndeksˈlɪŋkt] *adj Fin* indexé(e)

India [ˈɪndɪə] *n* l'Inde *f*

Indian [ˈɪndɪən] **1** *n* (**a**) *(from India)* Indien(enne) *m,f* (**b**) *(Native American)* Indien(enne) *m,f* d'Amérique

2 *adj* indien(enne); **I. elephant** éléphant *m* d'Asie; **in I. file** en file indienne; **the I. Ocean** l'océan *m* Indien; **I. summer** été *m* indien

indicate [ˈɪndɪkeɪt] *vt* (**a**) *(point to, show)* indiquer (**b**) *(intention, opposition, willingness)* signaler

indication [ɪndɪˈkeɪʃən] *n (sign)* signe *m*; *(information)* indication *f*; **she gave no i. of her feelings** elle n'a rien laissé voir de ses sentiments; **there is every i. that..., all the indications are that...** tout porte à croire que...

indicative [ɪnˈdɪkətɪv] **1** *n Gram* indicatif *m*; **in the i.** à l'indicatif

2 *adj* **to be i. of** être symptomatique de

indicator [ˈɪndɪkeɪtə(r)] *n (sign)* indice *m*; **economic indicators** indicateurs *mpl* économiques

indict [ɪnˈdaɪt] *vt Law* inculper (**for** de)

indictable [ɪnˈdaɪtəbəl] *adj Law* **i. offense** délit *m*

indictment [ɪnˈdaɪtmənt] *n Law* inculpation *f*; *Fig* **it is an i. of our society** c'est une preuve accablante de l'état de notre société

indie [ˈɪndɪ] *adj Fam (music, band, movie company)* indé *inv*

indifference [ɪnˈdɪfərəns] *n* indifférence *f* (**to** pour); **it's a matter of complete i. to me** cela m'est complètement indifférent

indifferent [ɪnˈdɪfərənt] *adj* (**a**) *(not interested)* indifférent(e) (**to** à); **I am** *or* **feel i. about him** il m'est indifférent (**b**) *(mediocre)* médiocre

indigenous [ɪnˈdɪdʒɪnəs] *adj* indigène

indigestible [ɪndɪˈdʒestɪbəl] *adj also Fig* indigeste

indigestion [ɪndɪˈdʒestʃən] *n* troubles *mpl* digestifs; **to have an attack of i.** avoir des troubles digestifs

indignant [ɪnˈdɪgnənt] *adj* indigné(e); **to get i. about sth** s'indigner de qch

indignation [ɪndɪgˈneɪʃən] *n* indignation *f*

indignity [ɪnˈdɪgnɪtɪ] *n* indignité *f*

indigo [ˈɪndɪgəʊ] **1** *n* indigo *m*

2 *adj* indigo *inv*

indirect [ɪndɪˈrekt] *adj* indirect(e); *(person)* pas direct(e); *Com* **i. costs** frais *mpl* indirects; *Gram* **i. object** complément *m* d'objet indirect; *Gram* **i. discourse** discours *m* indirect

indirectly [ɪndɪˈrektlɪ] *adv* indirectement

indiscernible [ɪndɪˈsɜːnɪbəl] *adj (reason)* obscur(e); *(difference)* imperceptible

indiscipline [ɪnˈdɪsɪplɪn] *n* indiscipline *f*

indiscreet [ɪndɪsˈkriːt] *adj* indiscret(ète)

indiscretion [ɪndɪsˈkreʃən] *n* indiscrétion *f*

indiscriminate [ɪndɪsˈkrɪmɪnɪt] *adj* **i. killing** tuerie *f* générale; **to be i. in one's praise** distribuer les compliments à tort et à travers

indispensable [ɪndɪsˈpensəbəl] *adj* indispensable

indisposed [ɪndɪsˈpəʊzd] *adj Formal (sick)* indisposé(e)

indisputable [ɪndɪsˈpjuːtəbəl] *adj (evidence, argument)* incontestable; *(leader)* incontesté(e)

indissoluble [ɪndɪˈsɒljʊbəl] *adj Formal* indissoluble

indistinct [ɪndɪsˈtɪŋkt] *adj* indistinct(e)

indistinguishable [ɪndɪsˈtɪŋgwɪʃəbəl] *adj* impossible à distinguer (**from** de)

individual [ɪndɪˈvɪdjʊəl] **1** *n (person)* individu *m*; **a private i.** un particulier
    2 *adj* (**a**) *(of or for one person)* individuel(elle); *(bathroom)* privé(e) (**b**) *(characteristic)* personnel(elle)

individualist [ɪndɪˈvɪdjʊəlɪst] *n* individualiste *mf*

individuality [ɪndɪvɪdjʊˈælɪtɪ] *n* individualité *f*

individually [ɪndɪˈvɪdjʊəlɪ] *adv* individuellement

indivisible [ɪndɪˈvɪzɪbəl] *adj* indivisible

Indochina [ɪndəʊˈtʃaɪnə] *n* l'Indochine *f*

indoctrinate [ɪnˈdɒktrɪneɪt] *vt* endoctriner; **to i. sb with an idea** inculquer une idée à qn

indoctrination [ɪndɒktrɪˈneɪʃən] *n* endoctrinement *m*

indolent [ˈɪndələnt] *adj Formal* paresseux(euse)

indomitable [ɪnˈdɒmɪtəbəl] *adj* indomptable

Indonesia [ɪndəʊˈniːzə] *n* l'Indonésie *f*

Indonesian [ɪndəʊˈniːzən] **1** *n* (**a**) *(person)* Indonésien(enne) *m,f* (**b**) *(language)* indonésien *m*
    2 *adj* indonésien(enne)

indoor [ˈɪndɔː(r)] *adj (swimming pool, tennis court)* couvert(e); *(plant)* d'appartement; *(photography)* d'intérieur; **i. athletics** athlétisme *m* en salle

indoors [ɪnˈdɔːz] *adv* à l'intérieur; **to go i.** rentrer; **I've been i. all day** je suis resté enfermé toute la journée

induce [ɪnˈdjuːs] *vt* (**a**) *(persuade)* **to i. sb to do sth** persuader qn de faire qch (**b**) *(cause)* provoquer (**c**) *Med* **to i. labor** provoquer l'accouchement; **she's had to be induced** il a fallu provoquer l'accouchement

inducement [ɪnˈdjuːsmənt] *n (incentive)* incitation *f*; *(financial)* avantage *m* financier

induct [ɪnˈdʌkt] *vt* (**a**) *(into job)* installer (**b**) *Elec* induire (**c**) *Mil (draft)* appeler (sous les drapeaux)

induction [ɪnˈdʌkʃən] *n* (**a**) *(into job)* période *f* d'introduction (**b**) *Med (of labor)* déclenchement *m* (**c**) *Elec* induction *f* (**d**) *Mil (drafting)* appel *m* sous les drapeaux, conscription *f*

inductive [ɪnˈdʌktɪv] *adj (reasoning)* inductif(ive)

indulge [ɪnˈdʌldʒ] **1** *vt (child)* gâter; *(passion)* donner libre cours à; **they indulged his every whim** ils lui passaient tous ses caprices; **to i. oneself** se faire plaisir; **go on, i. me!** allez, fais-moi plaisir!
    2 *vi* **to i. in sth** *(as a habit)* se livrer à qch; *(as a treat)* s'offrir qch

indulgence [ɪnˈdʌldʒəns] *n* (**a**) *(leniency)* indulgence *f* (**b**) *(treat)* gâterie *f*

indulgent [ɪnˈdʌldʒənt] *adj* indulgent(e) (**to** avec)

industrial [ɪnˈdʌstrɪəl] *adj* industriel(elle); **i. accident** accident *m* du travail; **i. disease** maladie *f* professionnelle; **i.**

espionage espionnage *m* industriel; **i. park** zone *f* industrielle; **i. relations** relations *fpl* entre les travailleurs et le patronat; **the I. Revolution** la révolution industrielle; **i. school** école *f* technique; **i. waste(s)** déchets *mpl* industriels

industrialist [ɪnˈdʌstrɪəlɪst] *n* industriel *m*

industrialize [ɪnˈdʌstrɪəlaɪz] *vt* industrialiser

industrious [ɪnˈdʌstrɪəs] *adj* travailleur(euse)

industry [ˈɪndʌstrɪ] *(pl* **industries**) *n* (**a**) *(economic sector)* industrie *f*; **heavy/light i.** l'industrie lourde/légère; **the aircraft/mining i.** l'industrie aéronautique/minière; **the tourist/entertainment i.** l'industrie du tourisme/du spectacle (**b**) *(hard work)* assiduité *f*

inebriated [ɪnˈiːbrɪeɪtɪd] *adj Formal or Hum* ivre

inedible [ɪnˈedɪbəl] *adj (plant, mushroom)* non comestible; *(food)* immangeable

ineffable [ɪnˈefəbəl] *adj Formal* ineffable

ineffective [ɪnɪˈfektɪv] *adj* inefficace

ineffectual [ɪnɪˈfektjʊəl] *adj* inefficace

inefficiency [ɪnɪˈfɪʃənsɪ] *n* inefficacité *f*, manque *m* d'efficacité

inefficient [ɪnɪˈfɪʃənt] *adj* inefficace

inelegant [ɪnˈelɪgənt] *adj* inélégant(e)

ineligible [ɪnˈelɪdʒɪbəl] *adj* **to be i. for sth** ne pas avoir droit à qch; **to be i. to do sth** ne pas avoir le droit de faire qch

inept [ɪnˈept] *adj (person)* incompétent(e); *(remark)* inepte

ineptitude [ɪnˈeptɪtjuːd] *n* incompétence *f*

inequality [ɪnɪˈkwɒlɪtɪ] *(pl* **inequalities**) *n* inégalité *f*

inequitable [ɪnˈekwɪtəbəl] *adj Formal* inéquitable

inert [ɪˈnɜːt] *adj* inerte

inertia [ɪˈnɜːʃɪə] *n* inertie *f*

inescapable [ɪnɪˈskeɪpəbəl] *adj (conclusion)* incontournable; *(resemblance)* indéniable; **it's an i. fact that...** il est indéniable que...

inessential [ɪnɪˈsenʃəl] *adj* non essentiel(elle)

inestimable [ɪnˈestɪməbəl] *adj* inestimable

inevitability [ɪnevɪtəˈbɪlɪtɪ] *n* caractère *m* inévitable

inevitable [ɪnˈevɪtəbəl] **1** *n* **the i.** l'inévitable *m*
    2 *adj* inévitable; *(conclusion)* incontournable

inevitably [ɪnˈevɪtəblɪ] *adv* inévitablement

inexact [ɪnɪgˈzækt] *adj (memory, estimate)* imprécis(e)

inexcusable [ɪnɪksˈkjuːzəbəl] *adj* inexcusable

inexhaustible [ɪnegˈzɔːstɪbəl] *adj* inépuisable

inexorable [ɪnˈeksərəbəl] *adj* inexorable

inexpensive [ɪnɪksˈpensɪv] *adj* pas cher (chère), bon marché *inv*

inexperience [ɪnɪksˈpɪərɪəns] *n* inexpérience *f*

inexperienced [ɪnɪksˈpɪərɪənst] *adj* (**a**) *(person)* inexpérimenté(e); **to be i. in doing sth** ne pas avoir l'habitude de faire qch (**b**) *(ear, eye)* inexercé(e)

inexplicable [ɪnɪksˈplɪkəbəl] *adj* inexplicable

inexpressible [ɪnɪksˈpresɪbəl] *adj* inexprimable

inexpressive [ɪnɪksˈpresɪv] *adj* inexpressif(ive)

inextricably [ɪneksˈtrɪkəblɪ] *adv* inextricablement

infallibility [ɪnfælɪˈbɪlɪtɪ] *n* infaillibilité *f*

infallible [ɪnˈfælɪbəl] *adj* infaillible

infamous [ˈɪnfəməs] *adj (well-known)* tristement célèbre; *(crime, rumor)* infâme

infamy [ˈɪnfəmɪ] *n Formal* infamie *f*

infancy [ˈɪnfənsɪ] *n (childhood)* petite enfance *f*; *Fig* **when medicine was still in its i.** alors que la médecine en était encore à ses balbutiements

infant [ˈɪnfənt] *n* bébé *m*; **i. mortality** mortalité *f* infantile

infanticide [ɪnˈfæntɪsaɪd] *n* infanticide *m*

infantile [ˈɪnfəntaɪl] *adj Pej* infantile, puéril(e)

infantry [ˈɪnfəntrɪ] *n* infanterie *f*

infantryman [ˈɪnfəntrɪmən] *n* soldat *m* d'infanterie, fantassin *m*

infatuated [ɪnˈfætjʊeɪtɪd] *adj* **to be i. with sb** être entiché(e) de qn

infatuation [ɪnfætjʊˈeɪʃən] *n (with person)* tocade *f*, passade *f* (**with** pour)

infect [ɪnˈfekt] *vt (water, food)* contaminer; *(with prejudice)* corrompre; **to become infected** *(of wound)* s'infecter; **to i. sb with sth** transmettre qch à qn; **her enthusiasm infected us all** elle nous a communiqué son enthousiasme

infection [ɪnˈfekʃən] *n* infection *f*

infectious [ɪnˈfekʃəs] *adj* (**a**) *(disease)* infectieux(euse); *(person)* contagieux(euse) (**b**) *(laughter, enthusiasm)* communicatif(ive)

infer [ɪnˈfɜː(r)] *(pt & pp* **inferred**) *vt* déduire (**from** de)

inference [ˈɪnfərəns] *n* conclusion *f*; **by i.** par déduction

inferior [ɪnˈfɪərɪə(r)] **1** *n* inférieur(e) *m,f*; **to be sb's i.** être inférieur à qn
  2 *adj* inférieur(e) (**to** à)

inferiority [ɪnfɪərɪˈɒrɪtɪ] *n* infériorité *f*; **i. complex** complexe *m* d'infériorité

infernal [ɪnˈfɜːnəl] *adj* (**a**) *(diabolical)* infernal(e), diabolique (**b**) *Fam (for emphasis)* **it's an i. nuisance** c'est diablement embêtant; **that i. idiot!** cette espèce d'idiot!

inferno [ɪnˈfɜːnəʊ] *(pl* **infernos**) *n (hell)* enfer *m*; *(blaze)* brasier *m*

infertile [ɪnˈfɜːtəl] *adj* stérile

infertility [ɪnfɜːˈtɪlɪtɪ] *n* stérilité *f*

infest [ɪnˈfest] *vt* **to be infested with** *or* **by sth** être infesté(e) de qch

infidelity [ɪnfɪˈdelɪtɪ] *n* infidélité *f*

infighting [ˈɪnfaɪtɪŋ] *n* querelles *fpl* intestines

infiltrate [ˈɪnfɪltreɪt] **1** *vt* infiltrer
  2 *vi* s'infiltrer

infiltration [ɪnfɪlˈtreɪʃən] *n* infiltration *f*

infinite [ˈɪnfɪnɪt] **1** *n* **the i.** l'infini *m*
  2 *adj* infini(e); *Rel & Hum* **in her i. wisdom** dans son infinie sagesse

infinitely [ˈɪnfɪnɪtlɪ] *adv* infiniment

infinitesimal [ɪnfɪnɪˈtesɪməl] *adj* infinitésimal(e)

infinitive [ɪnˈfɪnɪtɪv] *n Gram* infinitif *m*; **in the i.** à l'infinitif

infinity [ɪnˈfɪnɪtɪ] *n* infinité *f*; *Math* infini *m*

infirm [ɪnˈfɜːm] *adj* infirme

infirmary [ɪnˈfɜːmərɪ] *(pl* **infirmaries**) *n (hospital)* hôpital *m*; *(in school, prison)* infirmerie *f*

infirmity [ɪnˈfɜːmɪtɪ] *(pl* **infirmities**) *n (weakness)* infirmité *f*

inflame [ɪnˈfleɪm] *vt* (**a**) *(desire)* allumer; *(curiosity)* attiser; *(crowd)* enflammer (**b**) **to become inflamed** *(of wound)* s'enflammer

inflammable [ɪnˈflæməbəl] *adj (substance)* inflammable; *Fig (situation)* explosif(ive)

inflammation [ɪnfləˈmeɪʃən] *n* inflammation *f*

inflammatory [ɪnˈflæmətɒrɪ] *adj* incendiaire

inflatable [ɪnˈfleɪtəbəl] **1** *n (rubber dinghy)* canot *m* pneumatique
  2 *adj* gonflable; **i. castle** château *m* gonflable

inflate [ɪnˈfleɪt] **1** *vt* (**a**) *(tire, lifejacket)* gonfler (**b**) *(prices)* faire monter
  2 *vi* se gonfler

inflated [ɪnˈfleɪtɪd] *adj (tire, lifejacket)* gonflé(e); **to have an i. opinion of oneself** avoir une opinion trop flatteuse de soi-même

inflation [ɪnˈfleɪʃən] *n Econ* inflation *f*

inflationary [ɪnˈfleɪʃənrɪ] *adj Econ* inflationniste

inflect [ɪnˈflekt] **1** *vt* (**a**) *(voice)* moduler (**b**) *Gram* ajouter la désinence de
  2 *vi Gram* prendre une désinence

inflexibility [ɪnfleksɪˈbɪlɪtɪ] *n* rigidité *f*

inflexible [ɪnˈfleksɪbəl] *adj* rigide

inflict [ɪnˈflɪkt] *vt (suffering, punishment, defeat)* infliger (**on** à); *(damage)* causer (**on** à); **to i. oneself on sb** infliger sa présence à qn

in-flight [ˈɪnflaɪt] *adj* **i. entertainment** distractions *fpl* en vol; **i. meal** repas *m* servi pendant le vol

influence [ˈɪnflʊəns] **1** *n* influence *f* (**on** sur); **to be a good/bad i.** (**on sb**) avoir une bonne/mauvaise influence (sur qn); **to have i. over sb** avoir de l'influence sur qn; **under the i. of drink/drugs** sous l'empire de la boisson/de la drogue
  2 *vt* influencer; **to be easily influenced** être influençable

influential [ɪnflʊˈenʃəl] *adj* influent(e)

influenza [ɪnflʊˈenzə] *n* grippe *f*

influx [ˈɪnflʌks] *n* afflux *m*

info [ˈɪnfəʊ] *n Fam* renseignements *mpl*

infomercial [ɪnfəʊˈmɜːʃəl] *n* infomercial *m*, publi-information *f*

inform [ɪnˈfɔːm] **1** *vt* informer (**of** *or* **about** de); **to keep sb informed of sth** tenir qn au courant de qch
  2 *vi* **to i. on sb** dénoncer qn

informal [ɪnˈfɔːməl] *adj* (**a**) *(unaffected)* simple (**b**) *(casual)* décontracté(e); *(word, language)* familier(ère) (**c**) *(unofficial) (meeting, talks)* officieux(euse)

informality [ɪnfɔːˈmælɪtɪ] *n* (**a**) *(unaffectedness)* simplicité *f* (**b**) *(casualness)* décontraction *f* (**c**) *(of talks)* caractère *m* officieux

informally [ɪnˈfɔːməlɪ] *adv* (**a**) *(unaffectedly)* avec simplicité (**b**) *(casually)* avec décontraction (**c**) *(hold talks)* officieusement

informant [ɪnˈfɔːmənt] *n* informateur(trice) *m,f*

information [ɪnfəˈmeɪʃən] *n* (**a**) *(news, facts)* renseignements *mpl*; **a piece of i.** un renseignement; **for further i.** pour de plus amples renseignements; **i. bureau** bureau *m* des renseignements; **i. desk** accueil *m*; **i. officer** *(press officer)* responsable *mf* de la communication; *(archivist)* documentaliste *mf*; **i. pack** dossier *m* d'information (**b**) *(telephone service)* renseignements *mpl*; **to call i.** appeler les renseignements (**c**) *Comput* **i. processing** traitement *m* de l'information; **i. retrieval** recherche *f* documentaire; **i. science** informatique *f*; **the i. superhighway** l'autoroute *f* de l'information, *Can* l'inforoute *f*; **i. technology** informatique *f*

informative [ɪnˈfɔːmətɪv] *adj* instructif(ive); **she was very i.** elle nous a appris beaucoup de choses

informed [ɪnˈfɔːmd] *adj (person)* bien renseigné(e), bien informé(e); **my i. guess is that…** en me basant sur ce que je sais, je dirais que…; **an i. decision** une décision prise en connaissance de cause

informer [ɪnˈfɔːmə(r)] *n* indicateur *m*

infra dig [ˈɪnfrəˈdɪg] *adj Fam* rabaissant(e), dégradant(e)

infrared [ɪnfrəˈred] *adj* infrarouge; **i. camera** caméra *f* infrarouge

infrastructure [ˈɪnfrəstrʌktʃə(r)] *n* infrastructure *f*

infrequent [ɪnˈfriːkwənt] *adj* rare, peu fréquent(e)

infringe [ɪnˈfrɪndʒ] *vt (rule, law)* enfreindre; *(right)* empiéter sur
▸ **infringe on** *vt insep* empiéter sur

infringement [ɪnˈfrɪndʒmənt] *n (of rule, law)* infraction *f* (**of** à); *(of right)* atteinte *f* (**of** à)

infuriate [ɪnˈfjuːrɪeɪt] *vt* exaspérer

infuriating [ɪnˈfjuːrɪeɪtɪŋ] *adj* exaspérant(e)

infuse [ɪnˈfjuːz] **1** *vt* (**a**) *(tea)* faire infuser (**b**) *Fig (energy, hope)* insuffler (**into** à)
  2 *vi (of tea)* infuser

infusion [ɪnˈfjuːʒən] *n* (**a**) *(drink)* infusion *f* (**b**) *Fig (of energy, hope)* injection *f*

ingenious [ɪnˈdʒiːnɪəs] *adj* ingénieux(euse)

ingenuity [ɪndʒɪˈnjuːɪtɪ] *n* ingéniosité *f*

ingenuous [ɪn'dʒenʊəs] *adj (naive)* ingénu(e); *(frank)* franc (franche)

inglorious [ɪn'glɔːrɪəs] *adj* déshonorant(e), honteux(euse)

ingot ['ɪŋgət] *n* lingot *m*

ingrained [ɪn'greɪnd] *adj (prejudice, habit)* enraciné(e); **i. dirt** crasse *f*

ingratiate [ɪn'greɪʃɪeɪt] *vt* **to i. oneself (with sb)** se faire bien voir (de *ou* par qn)

ingratiating [ɪn'greɪʃɪeɪtɪŋ] *adj* doucereux(euse)

ingratitude [ɪn'grætɪtjuːd] *n* ingratitude *f*

ingredient [ɪn'griːdɪənt] *n also Fig* ingrédient *m; Fig* **the missing i.** l'élément *m* manquant

ingrowing ['ɪngrəʊɪŋ], **ingrown** ['ɪngrəʊn] *adj* **i. toenail** ongle *m* incarné

inhabit [ɪn'hæbɪt] *vt* habiter

inhabitable [ɪn'hæbɪtəbəl] *adj* habitable

inhabitant [ɪn'hæbɪtənt] *n* habitant(e) *m,f*

inhabited [ɪn'hæbɪtɪd] *adj* habité(e) (**by** par)

inhale [ɪn'heɪl] **1** *vt (gas, fumes)* inhaler; *(cigarette smoke)* avaler
2 *vi* inspirer; *(in smoking)* avaler la fumée

inhaler [ɪn'heɪlə(r)] *n (for asthmatics)* inhalateur *m*

inherent [ɪn'herənt] *adj* inhérent(e) (**in** à)

inherit [ɪn'herɪt] *vt* hériter (**from** de)

inheritance [ɪn'herɪtəns] *n* héritage *m*; **i. tax** droits *mpl* de succession

inhibit [ɪn'hɪbɪt] *vt (progress, growth)* entraver; *(person)* inhiber

inhibited [ɪn'hɪbɪtɪd] *adj (person)* inhibé(e)

inhibition [ɪnɪ'bɪʃən] *n* inhibition *f*; **to have no inhibitions about doing sth** n'avoir aucune honte à faire qch

inhospitable [ɪnhɒ'spɪtəbəl] *adj* inhospitalier(ère)

in-house ['ɪn'haʊs] **1** *adj (training)* interne; *(staff)* qui travaille sur place
2 *adv* sur place

inhuman [ɪn'hjuːmən] *adj* inhumain(e)

inhumane [ɪnhjuː'meɪn] *adj* inhumain(e)

inhumanity [ɪnhjuː'mænɪtɪ] *n* inhumanité *f*, cruauté *f*

inimical [ɪ'nɪmɪkəl] *adj Formal (people)* ennemi(e), hostile; *(conditions)* contraire (**to** à)

inimitable [ɪ'nɪmɪtəbəl] *adj* inimitable

iniquitous [ɪ'nɪkwɪtəs] *adj* inique

iniquity [ɪ'nɪkwɪtɪ] *(pl* **iniquities)** *n* iniquité *f*

initial [ɪ'nɪʃəl] **1** *n* initiale *f*; **initials** *(signature)* paraphe *m*
2 *adj* initial(e), premier(ère); **in the i. stages of sth** au stade initial de qch
3 *vt* parapher

initially [ɪ'nɪʃəlɪ] *adv* au début

initiate [ɪ'nɪʃɪeɪt] *vt* **(a)** *(negotiations)* amorcer; *(rumor, project)* lancer; *Law* **to i. proceedings (against sb)** entamer des poursuites (contre qn) **(b)** **to i. sb into a secret society/gang** faire subir à qn les épreuves initiatiques d'une société secrète/d'un gang

initiation [ɪnɪʃɪ'eɪʃən] *n* **(a)** *(beginning)* commencement *m*, début(s) *m(pl)* **(b)** *(induction)* initiation *f*; **i. ceremony** rite *m* d'initiation

initiative [ɪ'nɪʃətɪv] *n* initiative *f*; **to take the i. (in doing sth)** prendre l'initiative (de faire qch); **to use one's i.** faire preuve d'initiative; **on one's own i.** de sa propre initiative

inject [ɪn'dʒekt] *vt (drug, money)* injecter; *(enthusiasm)* communiquer; **to i. new life into sth** donner un nouvel essor à qch

injection [ɪn'dʒekʃən] *n* injection *f*, piqûre *f*; *Fig* injection; **polio i.** vaccin *m* contre la polio; **to give sb an i.** faire une piqûre à qn

injudicious [ɪndʒuː'dɪʃəs] *adj* peu judicieux(euse), malavisé(e)

injunction [ɪn'dʒʌŋkʃən] *n Law* arrêt *m*, jugement *m*; **to take out an i. against sb** mettre qn en demeure

injure ['ɪndʒə(r)] *vt (person)* blesser; *(reputation, interests)* nuire

à; **to i. oneself** se blesser; **to i. one's leg** se blesser à la jambe; **her pride is injured** elle est blessée dans son orgueil

injured ['ɪndʒəd] **1** *n* **the i.** les blessés *mpl*
2 *adj* blessé(e); *(look, voice)* offensé(e); *Law* **the i. party** la partie lésée

injurious [ɪn'dʒʊrɪəs] *adj* nuisible, préjudiciable (**to** à)

injury ['ɪndʒərɪ] *(pl* **injuries)** *n (physical)* blessure *f*; **to do oneself an i.** se blesser; **i. time** *(in soccer game)* arrêts *mpl* de jeu

injustice [ɪn'dʒʌstɪs] *n* injustice *f*; **to do sb an i.** être injuste envers qn

ink [ɪŋk] *n* encre *f*; **i. pad** tampon *m* (encreur)

ink-jet ['ɪŋkdʒet] *adj Comput* **i. (printer)** imprimante *f* à jet d'encre

inkling ['ɪŋklɪŋ] *n* soupçon *m*; **to have an i. of sth** se douter de qch

inkwell ['ɪŋkwel] *n* encrier *m (de pupitre)*

inky ['ɪŋkɪ] *adj* **(a)** *(stained with ink)* taché(e) d'encre **(b)** **i. (black)** noir(e) comme (de) l'encre

inlaid [ɪn'leɪd] *adj (with wood)* marqueté(e); *(with jewels)* incrusté(e) (**with** de)

inland 1 *adj* ['ɪnlənd] intérieur(e)
2 *adv* [ɪn'lænd] *(travel)* vers l'intérieur; *(live)* dans les terres

in-laws ['ɪnlɔːz] *npl (spouse's parents)* beaux-parents *mpl*; *(spouse's family)* belle-famille *f*

inlet ['ɪnlet] *n* **(a)** *(of sea)* petit bras *m* de mer **(b)** *(of pipe, machine)* (orifice *m* d')entrée *f*

in-line [ɪn'laɪn] *adj* **i. skates** rollers *mpl*; **i. skating** roller *m*; **to go i. skating** faire du roller

inmate ['ɪnmeɪt] *n (in prison)* détenu(e) *m,f*; *(in mental hospital)* interné(e) *m,f*

inn [ɪn] *n* auberge *f*

innards ['ɪnədz] *npl* entrailles *fpl*

innate [ɪ'neɪt] *adj* inné(e)

inner ['ɪnə(r)] *adj* **(a)** *(chamber, lining)* intérieur(e); **i. circle** *(of party, association)* initiés *mpl*; **i. city** quartiers *mpl* déshérités du centre-ville; **i. ear** oreille *f* interne; **i. tube** chambre *f* à air **(b)** *(thought, feeling)* intime; *(peace)* intérieur(e)

innermost ['ɪnəməʊst] *adj (part)* le (la) plus profond(e); *(thoughts, feelings)* le (la) plus secret(ète)

inning ['ɪnɪŋ] *n (in baseball)* tour *m* de batte

innkeeper ['ɪnkiːpə(r)] *n* aubergiste *mf*

innocence ['ɪnəsəns] *n* innocence *f*

innocent ['ɪnəsənt] **1** *n* innocent(e) *m,f*; **to act the i.** faire l'innocent
2 *adj* innocent(e)

innocuous [ɪ'nɒkjʊəs] *adj* inoffensif(ive); *(remark)* anodin(e)

innovate ['ɪnəveɪt] *vi* innover

innovation [ɪnə'veɪʃən] *n* innovation *f*

innovative ['ɪnəvɪtɪv] *adj* (in)novateur(trice)

innovator ['ɪnəveɪtə(r)] *n* (in)novateur(trice) *m,f*

innuendo [ɪnjʊ'endəʊ] *(pl* **innuendos** *or* **innuendoes)** *n (insinuation)* insinuation *f*; *(in jokes)* allusion *f* grivoise

innumerable [ɪ'njuːmərəbəl] *adj* innombrable

inoculate [ɪ'nɒkjʊleɪt] *vt* vacciner; **to i. sb with sth** inoculer qch à qn; **to i. sb against sth** vacciner qn contre qch

inoculation [ɪnɒkjʊ'leɪʃən] *n* inoculation *f*

inoffensive [ɪnə'fensɪv] *adj (animal, person)* inoffensif(ive); *(remark, humor)* qui n'a rien d'offensant; *(odor)* qui n'a rien de désagréable

inoperable [ɪn'ɒpərəbəl] *adj* inopérable

inoperative [ɪn'ɒpərətɪv] *adj (rule)* inopérant(e); *(machine)* arrêté(e)

inopportune [ɪn'ɒpətjuːn] *adj* inopportun(e)

inordinate [ɪn'ɔːdɪnət] *adj* démesuré(e)

inorganic [ɪnɔː'gænɪk] *adj* inorganique

in-patient ['ɪnpeɪʃənt] *n* patient(e) *m,f* hospitalisé(e)

input ['ɪnpʊt] **1** *n* (**a**) *Elec* puissance *f* d'alimentation; *(terminal)* entrée *f*; *Comput* entrée, introduction *f* (**b**) *(contribution)* contribution *f*
   2 *vt (pt & pp* **input**) *Comput (data)* entrer

inquest ['ɪnkwest] *n Law* enquête *f*; *Fig (in politics, business)* analyse *f*; **to hold an i.** *Law (of coroner)* mener une enquête (**into** sur); *(in politics, business)* faire une analyse (**into** de)

inquire [ɪn'kwaɪə(r)] **1** *vt* demander
   2 *vi* se renseigner (**about** sur); **i. within** *(sign)* s'adresser ici

▸**inquire after** *vt insep* demander des nouvelles de

▸**inquire into** *vt insep* faire des recherches sur

inquiring [ɪn'kwaɪrɪŋ] *adj (mind)* curieux(euse); *(look, voice)* interrogateur(trice)

inquiry [ɪn'kwaɪrɪ] *(pl* **inquiries**) *n* (**a**) *(official investigation)* enquête *f*; **to hold an i. (into sth)** faire une enquête (sur qch) (**b**) *(request for information)* demande *f* de renseignements; **to make inquiries (about sth)** se renseigner (sur qch); **i. desk** bureau *m* de(s) renseignements

Inquisition [ɪnkwɪ'zɪʃən] *n* **the I.** l'Inquisition *f*

inquisitive [ɪn'kwɪzɪtɪv] *adj (person, mind)* curieux(euse); *(look)* interrogateur(trice)

inroads ['ɪnrəʊdz] *npl* **to make i. into** *(capital, savings)* entamer; *(market)* pénétrer

insane [ɪn'seɪn] *adj (person)* dément(e); *Fam (desire, scheme)* fou (folle); **to go i.** devenir fou, perdre la raison; **to be i. with grief/jealousy** être fou de douleur/jalousie

insanely [ɪn'seɪnlɪ] *adv* comme un fou (une folle); **i. jealous** d'une jalousie maladive

insanitary [ɪn'sænɪtrɪ] *adj* insalubre, malsain(e)

insanity [ɪn'sænɪtɪ] *n (of person)* démence *f*; *Fam (of desire, scheme)* folie *f*

insatiable [ɪn'seɪʃəbəl] *adj* insatiable

inscribe [ɪn'skraɪb] *vt (write)* écrire; *(engrave)* inscrire, graver

inscription [ɪn'skrɪpʃən] *n (on stone, coin)* inscription *f*; *(in book)* dédicace *f*

inscrutable [ɪn'skru:təbəl] *adj (look, face)* impénétrable; *(remark)* énigmatique

insect ['ɪnsekt] *n* insecte *m*; **i. bite** piqûre *f* d'insecte; **i. repellent** anti-moustiques *m inv*

insecticide [ɪn'sektɪsaɪd] *n* insecticide *m*

insecure [ɪnsɪ'kjʊə(r)] *adj* (**a**) *(person) (generally)* pas sûr(e) de soi, qui manque d'assurance; *(temporarily)* angoissé(e) (**b**) *(government)* fragile; *(job, future)* précaire; **to be financially i.** être dans une situation financière précaire

insecurity [ɪnsɪ'kjʊərɪtɪ] *n* (**a**) *(of person) (lack of confidence)* manque *m* d'assurance; *(anxiety)* angoisse *f* (**b**) *(of job, future)* précarité *f*

insemination [ɪnsemɪ'neɪʃən] *n* insémination *f*

insensible [ɪn'sensɪbəl] *adj Formal (unaware, unconscious)* inconscient(e) (**to** de)

insensitive [ɪn'sensɪtɪv] *adj (person)* insensible (**to** à); *(remark)* indélicat(e)

insensitivity [ɪnsensɪ'tɪvɪtɪ] *n* insensibilité *f*

inseparable [ɪn'sepərəbəl] *adj* inséparable

insert¹ *n* ['ɪnsɜːt] *(in magazine)* encart *m*
   2 *vt* [ɪn'sɜːt] *(key, finger)* introduire (**into** dans); *(clause)* insérer (**in** dans); *(advertisement)* mettre (**in** dans)

insertion [ɪn'sɜːʃən] *n* insertion *f*

inset ['ɪnset] *n (in map, picture)* médaillon *m*

inshore [ɪn'ʃɔ:(r)] **1** *adj (navigation, fishing)* côtier(ère)
   2 *adv (be situated)* sur la côte; *(travel)* vers la côte, vers les terres

inside¹ *n* ['ɪn'saɪd] (**a**) *(of house)* intérieur *m*; **on/from the i.** à/de l'intérieur (**b**) *Fam* **insides** *(internal organs)* entrailles *fpl* (**c**) *(in phrases)* **i. out** *(clothes)* à l'envers; *Fig* **to know sth i. out** connaître qch comme sa poche
   2 *adj* ['ɪnsaɪd] intérieur(e); **to have i. information** avoir des

informations de première main; *Fam* **it's an i. job** c'est quelqu'un de la maison qui a fait ça; **i. lane** file *f* de gauche; **to know the i. story** connaître les dessous de l'affaire
   3 *adv* [ɪn'saɪd] (**a**) *(indoors)* à l'intérieur; **come i.!** entrez! (**b**) *(within oneself)* en son for intérieur (**c**) *Fam (in prison)* en taule
   4 *prep* [ɪn'saɪd] (**a**) *(place)* à l'intérieur de, dans (**b**) *(with time)* **i. (of) a week/an hour** en moins d'une semaine/heure

insider [ɪn'saɪdə(r)] *n* initié(e) *m,f*; *Fin* **i. dealing, i. trading** délit *m* d'initié

insidious [ɪn'sɪdɪəs] *adj* insidieux(euse)

insight ['ɪnsaɪt] *n* (**a**) *(perspicacity)* perspicacité *f* (**b**) *(understanding)* aperçu *m*; **to get an i. into sth** avoir un aperçu de qch

insignia [ɪn'sɪgnɪə] *n* insigne *m*

insignificance [ɪnsɪg'nɪfɪkəns] *n* insignifiance *f*; **to pale into i. (beside sth)** sembler totalement insignifiant(e) (à côté de qch)

insignificant [ɪnsɪg'nɪfɪkənt] *adj* insignifiant(e)

insincere [ɪnsɪn'sɪə(r)] *adj* peu sincère, faux (fausse)

insincerity [ɪnsɪn'serɪtɪ] *n* manque *m* de sincérité, fausseté *f*

insinuate [ɪn'sɪnjʊeɪt] *vt* insinuer; **to i. oneself into sb's favor** s'insinuer dans les bonnes grâces de qn

insinuation [ɪnsɪnjʊ'eɪʃən] *n* insinuation *f*

insipid [ɪn'sɪpɪd] *adj* insipide

insist [ɪn'sɪst] **1** *vt* (**a**) *(maintain)* **to i. that...** soutenir *ou* maintenir que... (**b**) *(demand)* **to i. (that) sb does sth** insister pour que qn fasse qch
   2 *vi* insister; **to i. on sth** exiger qch; **to i. on doing sth** tenir à faire qch

insistence [ɪn'sɪstəns] *n* insistance *f* (**on** à); **I stayed at her i.** elle insista, et je restai

insistent [ɪn'sɪstənt] *adj (person, demand)* pressant(e); **to be i.** se montrer pressant; **to be i. about sth** insister sur qch

insofar as ['ɪnsəʊ'fɑ:rəz] *adv* dans la mesure où

insole ['ɪnsəʊl] *n* semelle *f* intérieure

insolence ['ɪnsələns] *n* insolence *f* (**to** envers)

insolent ['ɪnsələnt] *adj* insolent(e) (**to** envers)

insoluble [ɪn'sɒljʊbəl] *adj* insoluble

insolvency [ɪn'sɒlvənsɪ] *n Fin (of person)* insolvabilité *f*; *(of company)* faillite *f*

insolvent [ɪn'sɒlvənt] *adj Fin (person)* insolvable; *(company)* en faillite

insomnia [ɪn'sɒmnɪə] *n* insomnie *f*

insomniac [ɪn'sɒmnɪæk] *n* insomniaque *mf*

inspect [ɪn'spekt] *vt (passport, luggage, picture)* examiner; *(school, factory)* inspecter; *(troops)* passer en revue

inspection [ɪn'spekʃən] *n (of passport, luggage, picture)* examen *m*; *(of school, factory)* visite *f* d'inspection *f*; *(of troops)* revue *f*; **on closer i.** en y regardant de plus près

inspector [ɪn'spektə(r)] *n (of schools, factories)* inspecteur(trice) *m,f*; **(police) i.** inspecteur *m* de police

inspiration [ɪnspɪ'reɪʃən] *n* inspiration *f*; **to be an i. to sb** inspirer qn

inspire [ɪn'spaɪə(r)] *vt* inspirer; **to i. sb to do sth** pousser qn à faire qch; **to i. sth in sb, to i. sb with sth** inspirer qch à qn

inspired [ɪn'spaɪəd] *adj* inspiré(e)

inspiring [ɪn'spaɪərɪŋ] *adj (music, speech)* exaltant(e); *(leader)* enthousiasmant(e); **the menu wasn't very i.** le menu n'avait rien de bien tentant

instability [ɪnstə'bɪlɪtɪ] *n* instabilité *f*

install [ɪn'stɔːl] *vt* installer; **to i. sb in a post** mettre qn à un poste; **to i. oneself in an armchair** s'installer dans un fauteuil

installation [ɪnstə'leɪʃən] *n* installation *f*

installment [ɪn'stɔːlmənt] *n* (**a**) *(part payment)* versement *m*; **to pay by installments** payer par versements échelonnés (**b**) *(of radio, TV program)* épisode *m*

instance ['ɪnstəns] *n (example)* cas *m*; **for i.** par exemple; **in the first i.** en (tout) premier lieu

instant ['ɪnstənt] **1** *n (moment)* instant *m*, moment *m*; **this i.** immédiatement; **not an i. too soon** juste à temps; **the i. I saw her** dès que je l'ai vue
   2 *adj* (**a**) *(reply, success, dislike)* immédiat(e); *(solution)* instantané(e); *Comput* **i. messaging** messagerie *f* instantanée; *TV* **i. replay** reprise *f* de l'action (**b**) *(coffee, soup)* instantané(e)

instant-access [ɪnstənt'ækses] *adj (bank account)* à accès immédiat

instantaneous [ɪnstən'teɪnɪəs] *adj* instantané(e)

instantly ['ɪnstəntlɪ] *adv* instantanément

instead [ɪn'sted] *adv (in place of something)* à la place; *(in place of somebody)* à ma/sa/etc. place; **i. of** *(thing)* au lieu de; *(person)* à la place de; **i. of doing sth** au lieu de faire qch

instep ['ɪnstep] *n (of foot)* cou-de-pied *m*; *(of shoe)* cambrure *f*

instigate ['ɪnstɪgeɪt] *vt* être à l'origine de

instigation ['ɪnstɪgeɪʃən] *n* instigation *f*; **at sb's i.** à l'instigation de qn

instigator ['ɪnstɪgeɪtə(r)] *n* instigateur(trice) *m,f*

instill [ɪn'stɪl] *vt (courage, pride)* inspirer (**in** à); *(doubt, jealousy)* instiller (**in** à); *(idea)* inculquer (**into** à)

instinct ['ɪnstɪŋkt] *n* instinct *m*; **he has an i. for the game** ce jeu, chez lui, c'est instinctif

instinctive [ɪn'stɪŋktɪv] *adj* instinctif(ive)

institute ['ɪnstɪtjuːt] **1** *n* institut *m*
   2 *vt (system, procedure)* établir, instituer; *(search)* lancer; *Law (inquiry)* ordonner; **to i. proceedings (against sb)** entamer *ou* engager des poursuites (contre qn)

institution [ɪnstɪ'tjuːʃən] *n (organization)* institution *f*; *(public, financial)* établissement *m*; *(for old people)* hospice *m*; *(for mental patients)* asile *m*; *Fig* **to become a national i.** *(of event, TV program)* devenir une institution nationale

institutional [ɪnstɪ'tjuːʃənəl] *adj* institutionnel(elle)

institutionalize [ɪnstɪ'tjuːʃənəlaɪz] *vt* (**a**) *(put in a home)* placer dans un établissement spécialisé; **to become institutionalized** *(of prisoner, patient)* devenir complètement dépendant(e) (**b**) *(turn into an institution)* institutionnaliser

instruct [ɪn'strʌkt] *vt* (**a**) *(teach)* enseigner; **to i. sb in sth** enseigner qch à qn (**b**) *(command)* ordonner; **to i. sb to do sth** ordonner à qn de faire qch

instruction [ɪn'strʌkʃən] *n* (**a**) *(training)* instruction *f*, enseignement *m* (**b**) **instructions** *(orders)* instructions *fpl*, directives *fpl* (**c**) **instructions (for use)** notice *f* (d'emploi); **i. manual** manuel *m* d'entretien

instructive [ɪn'strʌktɪv] *adj* instructif(ive)

instructor [ɪn'strʌktə(r)] *n* (**a**) *(of sporting activity, driving)* moniteur(trice) *m,f* (**b**) *(university lecturer)* professeur *m*

instrument ['ɪnstrʊmənt] *n* instrument *m*; **i. board** *or* **panel** *(in plane, car)* tableau *m* de bord

instrumental [ɪnstrʊ'mentəl] **1** *n (music without words)* instrumental *m*
   2 *adj* (**a**) *(contributory)* **to be i. in sth** jouer un rôle décisif dans qch (**b**) *(in music)* instrumental(e)

instrumentalist [ɪnstrʊ'mentəlɪst] *n* instrumentiste *mf*

instrumentation [ɪnstrʊmen'teɪʃən] *n* instrumentation *f*

insubordinate [ɪnsə'bɔːdɪnət] *adj* insubordonné(e)

insubordination [ɪnsəbɔːdɪ'neɪʃən] *n* insubordination *f*

insubstantial [ɪnsəb'stænʃəl] *adj (structure, argument)* peu solide; *(meal)* frugal(e); *(book)* creux(euse), qui manque de substance

insufferable [ɪn'sʌfrəbəl] *adj* insupportable, intolérable

insufficient [ɪnsə'fɪʃənt] *adj* insuffisant(e)

insular ['ɪnsjʊlə(r)] *adj* borné(e); *(climate)* insulaire

insulate ['ɪnsjʊleɪt] *vt* isoler; *Fig* **to be insulated from sth** être protégé(e) de qch

insulating tape [ɪnsjʊleɪtɪŋ'teɪp] *n* chatterton *m*

insulation [ɪnsjʊ'leɪʃən] *n* isolation *f*

insulin ['ɪnsjʊlɪn] *n* insuline *f*

insult 1 *n* ['ɪnsʌlt] *(words, action)* insulte *f*; **to add i. to injury** aggraver les choses
   2 *vt* [ɪn'sʌlt] insulter

insulting [ɪn'sʌltɪŋ] *adj* insultant(e)

insuperable [ɪn'suːpərəbəl] *adj* insurmontable

insurance [ɪn'ʃʊərəns] *n* assurance *f*; *Fig (protection)* garantie *f*; **to take out i.** prendre une assurance; **i. broker** courtier *m* en assurances; **i. claim** demande *f* d'indemnité; *(for more serious damage)* déclaration *f* de sinistre; **i. company** companie *f* d'assurances; **i. policy** police *f* d'assurance; **i. premium** prime *f* d'assurance

insure [ɪn'ʃʊə(r)] *vt* assurer (**against** contre); **to i. one's life** s'assurer sur la vie

insured [ɪn'ʃʊəd] *adj* assuré(e) (**against** contre); **i. value** valeur *f* assurée

insurer [ɪn'ʃʊərə(r)] *n* assureur *m*

insurgent [ɪn'sɜːdʒənt] *n* insurgé(e) *m,f*

insurmountable [ɪnsə'maʊntəbəl] *adj* insurmontable

insurrection [ɪnsə'rekʃən] *n* insurrection *f*

intact [ɪn'tækt] *adj* intact(e)

intake ['ɪnteɪk] *n* (**a**) *(of alcohol, food)* consommation *f*; *(of calories)* absorption *f* (**b**) *Tech* admission *f*

intangible [ɪn'tændʒɪbəl] *adj* impalpable

integer ['ɪntɪdʒə(r)] *n* Math nombre *m* entier

integral ['ɪntɪgrəl] *adj (essential)* indispensable; **to be an i. part of sth** faire partie intégrante de qch; *Math* **i. calculus** calcul *m* intégral

integrate ['ɪntɪgreɪt] **1** *vt* intégrer (**into** à)
   2 *vi* s'intégrer (**into** à)

integrated ['ɪntɪgreɪtɪd] *adj* intégré(e); *(school)* qui pratique la déségrégation raciale

integration [ɪntɪ'greɪʃən] *n* intégration *f*

integrity [ɪn'tegrɪtɪ] *n* intégrité *f*

intellect ['ɪntɪlekt] *n* intellect *m*, intelligence *f*

intellectual [ɪntɪ'lektjʊəl] **1** *n* intellectuel(elle) *m,f*
   2 *adj* intellectuel(elle)

intelligence [ɪn'telɪdʒəns] *n* (**a**) *(faculty)* intelligence *f*; *Psy* **i. quotient** quotient *m* intellectuel; **i. test** test *m* d'intelligence (**b**) *(secret service)* services *mpl* secrets; **i. officer** agent *m* de renseignements; **i. service** services secrets

intelligent [ɪn'telɪdʒənt] *adj* intelligent(e)

intelligentsia [ɪntelɪ'dʒensɪə] *n* intelligentsia *f*

intelligible [ɪn'telɪdʒɪbəl] *adj* intelligible

intemperate [ɪn'tempərət] *adj* Formal *(climate)* rude; *(person, behavior)* intempérant(e)

intend [ɪn'tend] *vt* **to i. to do sth** avoir l'intention de faire qch; **to i. sth for sb** destiner qch à qn; **was that intended?** était-ce intentionnel?; **it was intended as a compliment/a joke** c'était un compliment/pour plaisanter; **I didn't i. her to see it yet** il n'était pas dans mes intentions qu'elle le voie si tôt

intended [ɪn'tendɪd] **1** *n* Old-fashioned or Hum *(future spouse)* futur(e) *m,f*
   2 *adj (consequence, outcome)* prévu(e); *(effect)* escompté(e); *(insult, mistake)* voulu(e)

intense [ɪn'tens] *adj* intense; *(interest, anger)* vif (vive); *(person)* passionné(e)

intensely [ɪn'tenslɪ] *adv* (**a**) *(amusing, boring)* extrêmement (**b**) *(look at, speak)* intensément, avec intensité

intensify [ɪn'tensɪfaɪ] *(pt & pp* **intensified***)* **1** *vt (search, effort)* intensifier; *(pressure)* augmenter
   2 *vi* s'intensifier

intensity [ɪn'tensɪtɪ] *n* intensité *f*

intensive [ɪn'tensɪv] *adj* intensif(ive); *Med* **i. care** soins *mpl* intensifs; *Med* **i.-care unit** unité *f* de soins intensifs

intent [ɪn'tent] **1** *n* intention *f*; **to all intents and purposes** quasiment

2 *adj (look)* intense; **to be i. on doing sth** être résolu(e) *ou* déterminé(e) à faire qch

intention [ɪn'tenʃən] *n* intention *f*; **to have every i. of doing sth** avoir la ferme intention de faire qch; **to have no i. of doing sth** n'avoir nullement l'intention de faire qch

intentional [ɪn'tenʃənəl] *adj* intentionnel(elle), voulu(e)

intentionally [ɪn'tenʃənəlɪ] *adv* intentionnellement; **I didn't do it i.** je ne l'ai pas fait exprès

intently [ɪn'tentlɪ] *adv (listen, look at)* attentivement

inter [ɪn'tɜː(r)] *(pt & pp* **interred)** *vt* inhumer, enterrer

interact [ɪntə'rækt] *vi* **(a)** *(of person)* communiquer (**with** avec); *(of two or more people)* communiquer entre eux (elles) **(b)** *(of chemical)* réagir (**with** avec); *(of two or more chemicals)* réagir entre eux (elles)

interaction [ɪntə'rækʃən] *n* interaction *f*

interactive [ɪntə'ræktɪv] *adj* interactif(ive); **i. whiteboard** tableau *m* interactif

intercede [ɪntə'siːd] *vi* intercéder (**with/for** auprès de/en faveur de)

intercept [ɪntə'sept] *vt* intercepter

interception [ɪntə'sepʃən] *n* interception *f*

intercession [ɪntə'seʃən] *n* intercession *f*

interchange 1 *n* ['ɪntətʃeɪndʒ] *(exchange)* échange *m*; *(on highway)* échangeur *m*

2 *vt* [ɪntə'tʃeɪndʒ] *(exchange)* échanger; *(transpose)* intervertir

interchangeable [ɪntə'tʃeɪndʒəbəl] *adj* interchangeable

intercom ['ɪntəkɒm] *n* Interphone® *m*

interconnect [ɪntəkə'nekt] *vt* interconnecter

intercontinental [ɪntəkɒntɪ'nentəl] *adj* intercontinental(e); **i. ballistic missile** missile *m* balistique intercontinental

intercourse ['ɪntəkɔːs] *n* **(a) (sexual) i.** rapports *mpl* (sexuels) **(b)** *Formal (dealings)* commerce *m*, relations *fpl*

interdependent ['ɪntədɪ'pendənt] *adj* interdépendant(e)

interest ['ɪntrest] **1** *n* **(a)** *(curiosity)* intérêt *m*; *(hobby)* centre *m* d'intérêt; **of i.** intéressant(e); **of historical i.** intéressant du point de vue historique; **to be of i. to sb** intéresser qn; **to take an i. in sth** s'intéresser à qch; **to lose i. (in sth)** se désintéresser (de qch) **(b)** *(stake)* intérêt *m*; **to have a financial i. in sth** avoir investi financièrement dans qch **(c)** *(benefit)* intérêt *m*; **to act in sb's interests** agir dans l'intérêt de qn; **the public i.** l'intérêt public; **it's in my i. to do it** j'ai tout intérêt à le faire; **in the interests of...** dans l'intérêt de... **(d)** *(on loan, investment)* intérêt(s) *m(pl)*

2 *vt* intéresser; **to i. sb in sth** intéresser qn à qch; **can I i. you in a drink?** je peux vous offrir un verre?

interested ['ɪntrestɪd] *adj* intéressé(e); **to be interested in sth** s'intéresser à qch; **he seemed i. in the proposal** il a semblé intéressé par cette proposition

interest-free ['ɪntrest'friː] *adj (loan)* sans intérêt; *(credit)* gratuit(e)

interesting ['ɪntrestɪŋ] *adj* intéressant(e)

interface ['ɪntəfeɪs] *n Comput* interface *f*

interfere [ɪntə'fɪə(r)] *vi* **(a)** *(meddle)* se mêler (**in** de); **he's always interfering** il est toujours à se mêler de ce qui ne le regarde pas; **don't i. with my papers** ne touche pas à mes papiers **(b)** **to i. with sth** *(hinder)* gêner qch

interference [ɪntə'fɪərəns] *n* **(a)** *(meddling)* ingérence *f* **(b)** *Rad & TV* interférences *fpl*

interfering [ɪntə'fɪərɪŋ] *adj* importun(e)

interim ['ɪntərɪm] **1** *n* **in the i.** entre-temps

2 *adj (agreement, report)* provisoire

interior [ɪn'tɪərɪə(r)] **1** *n* intérieur *m*

2 *adj* intérieur(e); **i. decorator** décorateur(trice) *m,f* (d'intérieurs); **i. designer** architecte *mf* d'intérieur

interject [ɪntə'dʒekt] *vt (remark)* lancer; *(protest)* émettre

interjection [ɪntə'dʒekʃən] *n* interjection *f*

interlocking [ɪntə'lɒkɪŋ] *adj (parts)* emboîtable; *(gears)* qui s'enclenchent

interlocutor [ɪntə'lɒkjuːtə(r)] *n Formal* interlocuteur (trice) *m,f*

interloper ['ɪntələʊpə(r)] *n* intrus(e) *m,f*

interlude ['ɪntəluːd] *n also Fig* intermède *m*

intermarriage [ɪntə'mærɪdʒ] *n (within a family)* mariage *m* consanguin; *(with member of another group)* mariage

intermarry [ɪntə'mærɪ] *(pt & pp* **intermarried)** *vi* se marier *(au sein de la même famille)*

intermediary [ɪntə'miːdɪərɪ] *(pl* **intermediaries)** *n* intermédiaire *mf*

intermediate [ɪntə'miːdɪət] *adj* intermédiaire; *(student)* de niveau moyen

interminable [ɪn'tɜːmɪnəbəl] *adj* interminable

intermingle [ɪntə'mɪŋgəl] **1** *vt* mélanger (**with** avec)

2 *vi* se mêler (**with** à), se mélanger (**with** avec)

intermission [ɪntə'mɪʃən] *n* entracte *m*

intermittent [ɪntə'mɪtənt] *adj* intermittent(e)

intern 1 *n* ['ɪntɜːn] *Med* interne *mf*; *(in firm)* stagiaire *mf*

2 *vt* [ɪn'tɜːn] interner

3 *vi* ['ɪntɜːn] *Med* faire son internat; *(in firm)* faire un stage (en entreprise)

internal [ɪn'tɜːnəl] *adj* interne; *(flight)* intérieur(e); **i. combustion engine** moteur *m* à combustion interne; *Fin* **the I. Revenue Service** ≃ le fisc, la Direction Générale des Impôts

internalize [ɪn'tɜːnəlaɪz] *vt* intérioriser

internally [ɪn'tɜːnəlɪ] *adv* intérieurement; **not to be taken i.** *(on medicine container)* à usage externe

international [ɪntə'næʃənəl] *adj* international(e); **i. reply coupon** coupon-réponse *m* international; **I. Date Line** ligne *f* de changement de date; *Fin* **I. Monetary Fund** Fonds *m* monétaire international

internee [ɪntɜː'niː] *n* interné(e) *m,f*

Internet ['ɪntənet] *n Comput* **the I.** l'Internet *m*; **I. access** accès *m* (à l')Internet; **I. banking** opérations *fpl* bancaires par l'Internet; **I. dating** rencontres *fpl* sur Internet; **I. protocol** protocole *m* Internet; **I. relay chat** service *m* de bavardage; **I. service provider** fournisseur *m* d'accès à l'Internet; **I. user** internaute *mf*

internment [ɪn'tɜːnmənt] *n* internement *m*

interpersonal [ɪntə'pɜːsənəl] *adj* interpersonnel(elle)

interplay ['ɪntəpleɪ] *n* interaction *f* (**of** *or* **between** entre)

Interpol ['ɪntəpɒl] *n* Interpol

interpolate [ɪn'tɜːpəleɪt] *vt Formal (remark, question)* glisser; *(word, passage)* intercaler

interpose [ɪntə'pəʊz] *vt* interposer (**between** entre)

interpret [ɪn'tɜːprɪt] **1** *vt* interpréter

2 *vi* faire l'interprète

interpretation [ɪntɜːprɪ'teɪʃən] *n* interprétation *f*

interpreter [ɪn'tɜːprɪtə(r)] *n* interprète *mf*

interracial [ɪntə'reɪʃəl] *adj* interracial(e)

interrelated [ɪntərɪ'leɪtɪd] *adj* lié(e)

interrogate [ɪn'terəgeɪt] *vt* interroger

interrogation [ɪnterə'geɪʃən] *n* interrogatoire *m*

interrogative [ɪnte'rɒgətɪv] **1** *n Gram* interrogatif *m*; *(question mark)* point *m* d'interrogation

2 *adj (look, tone)* interrogateur(trice); *Gram* interrogatif(ive)

interrogator [ɪn'terəgeɪtə(r)] *n* interrogateur(trice) *m,f*

interrupt [ɪntə'rʌpt] **1** *vt* interrompre

2 *vi* **it's rude to i.** ce n'est pas poli d'interrompre les gens; **I'm sorry to i.** je suis désolé de vous interrompre

interruption [ɪntə'rʌpʃən] n interruption f
intersect [ɪntə'sekt] **1** vt couper
  2 vi se couper
intersection [ɪntə'sekʃən] n (**a**) (of roads) carrefour m (**b**) Math intersection f
intersperse [ɪntə'spɜːs] vt **to be interspersed with sth** être parsemé(e) de qch; **sunshine interspersed with showers** temps ensoleillé entrecoupé d'averses
intertwine [ɪntə'twaɪn] **1** vt entremêler (**with** de); **to be intertwined** (of two things) être entrelacés(ées)
  2 vi s'entrelacer
interval ['ɪntəvəl] n intervalle m; **at regular intervals** à intervalles réguliers; **at weekly intervals** toutes les semaines; **sunny intervals** éclaircies fpl
intervene [ɪntə'viːn] vi (of person) intervenir (**in** dans); (of event) survenir
intervening [ɪntə'viːnɪŋ] adj intermédiaire; **in the i. period** entre-temps, dans l'intervalle
intervention [ɪntə'venʃən] n intervention f
interview ['ɪntəvjuː] **1** n (for job) entretien m; TV & Journ interview f
  2 vt (for job) faire passer un entretien à; TV & Journ interviewer
interviewee [ɪntəvjuː'iː] n (for job) candidat(e) m,f (à qui l'on fait passer un entretien); TV & Journ personne f interviewée
interviewer ['ɪntəvjuːə(r)] n (for job) = personne qui fait passer un entretien; TV & Journ intervieweur(euse) m,f
intestate [ɪn'testeɪt] adj Law **to die i.** mourir intestat
intestinal [ɪntes'taɪnəl] adj intestinal(e)
intestine [ɪn'testɪn] n intestin m; **large i.** gros intestin; **small i.** intestin grêle
intimacy ['ɪntɪməsɪ] n (of relationship, atmosphere) intimité f; Euph (sexual) relations fpl intimes
intimate 1 n ['ɪntɪmət] intime mf
  2 adj ['ɪntɪmət] (friend, restaurant) intime; (knowledge) approfondi(e); Euph **to be i. with sb** (sexually) avoir des relations intimes avec qn
  3 vt ['ɪntɪmeɪt] Formal (hint at) faire comprendre; (make known) signifier
intimately ['ɪntɪmətlɪ] adv intimement
intimidate [ɪn'tɪmɪdeɪt] vt intimider; **to i. sb into doing sth** forcer qn à faire qch en usant d'intimidation
intimidation [ɪntɪmɪ'deɪʃən] n intimidation f
into ['ɪntʊ] prep (**a**) (with motion, direction) dans; **to go i. a house** entrer dans une maison; **to get i. bed** se mettre au lit; **to crash i. sth** rentrer dans qch (**b**) (expressing change) en; **to change i. sth** se changer en qch; **to translate sth i. English** traduire qch en anglais; **to break sth i. pieces** mettre qch en morceaux (**c**) (in division) **three i. six goes twice** six divisé par trois donne deux (**d**) Fam (keen on) **to be i. jazz** être branché(e) jazz; **he's really i. my sister** il en pince vraiment pour ma sœur
intolerable [ɪn'tɒlərəbəl] adj intolérable
intolerance [ɪn'tɒlərəns] n intolérance f
intolerant [ɪn'tɒlərənt] adj **to be i. of sb** être intolérant(e) à l'égard de qn; **to be i. of sth** ne pas tolérer qch
intonation [ɪntə'neɪʃən] n intonation f
intone [ɪn'təʊn] vt (speak) débiter; (of preacher) psalmodier
intoxicated [ɪn'tɒksɪkeɪtɪd] adj (drunk) ivre; Fig **i. with power/fame** ivre de puissance/gloire
intoxication [ɪntɒksɪ'keɪʃən] n also Fig ivresse f
intractable [ɪn'træktəbəl] adj (person) intraitable; (problem) très délicat(e)
Intranet ['ɪntrənet] n Comput Intranet m
intransigence [ɪn'trænzɪdʒəns] n Formal intransigeance f (**over** sur)
intransigent [ɪn'trænzɪdʒənt] adj Formal intransigeant(e) (**over** sur)

intransitive [ɪn'trænzɪtɪv] adj Gram intransitif(ive)
intrauterine device ['ɪntrə'juːtəraɪndɪ'vaɪs] n Med stérilet m
intravenous ['ɪntrə'viːnəs] adj Med (drip) veineux(euse); **i. injection** intraveineuse f
intravenously ['ɪntrə'viːnəslɪ] adv Med par voie intraveineuse
in-tray ['ɪntreɪ] n bac m du courrier à traiter
intrepid [ɪn'trepɪd] adj intrépide
intricacy ['ɪntrɪkəsɪ] (pl **intricacies**) n complexité f; **the intricacies of the law** les subtilités du droit
intricate ['ɪntrɪkət] adj compliqué(e)
intrigue 1 n ['ɪntriːg] intrigue f
  2 vt [ɪn'triːg] (interest) intriguer
intrinsic [ɪn'trɪnsɪk] adj intrinsèque
introduce [ɪntrə'djuːs] vt (**a**) (person) présenter (**to** à); **to i. oneself** se présenter; **to i. sb to sth** initier qn à qch (**b**) (reform, practice) introduire
introduction [ɪntrə'dʌkʃən] n (**a**) (of person) présentation f; **to make the introductions** faire les présentations (**b**) (to book) avant-propos m inv, introduction f (**c**) (of reform, practice) introduction f (**d**) (first experience) initiation f (**to** à)
introductory [ɪntrə'dʌktərɪ] adj d'introduction; (price, offer) de lancement
introspection [ɪntrə'spekʃən] n introspection f
introspective [ɪntrə'spektɪv] adj (person) introverti(e); (mood) introspectif(ive)
introvert ['ɪntrəvɜːt] n introverti(e) m,f
introverted [ɪntrə'vɜːtɪd] adj introverti(e)
intrude [ɪn'truːd] vi (**a**) (impose oneself) déranger (**b**) (interfere) **her work intrudes on her family life** son travail empiète sur sa vie de famille; **to i. on sb's privacy** s'immiscer dans la vie privée de qn
intruder [ɪn'truːdə(r)] n intrus(e) m,f
intrusion [ɪn'truːʒən] n intrusion f
intrusive [ɪn'truːsɪv] adj importun(e)
intuition [ɪntjuː'ɪʃən] n intuition f
intuitive [ɪn'tjuːɪtɪv] adj intuitif(ive)
Inuit ['ɪnɔɪt] **1** n Inuit mf
  2 adj inuit
inundate ['ɪnʌndeɪt] vt inonder (**with** de); Fig (with phone calls, letters) submerger (**with** de)
invade [ɪn'veɪd] vt envahir; **to i. sb's privacy** s'immiscer dans la vie privée de qn
invader [ɪn'veɪdə(r)] n envahisseur(euse) m,f
invalid¹ [ɪn'vælɪd] adj (document, argument) non valable; (marriage) non valide
invalid² ['ɪnvəlɪd] n (disabled person) invalide mf, infirme mf; (sick person) malade mf
invalidate [ɪn'vælɪdeɪt] vt (theory) infirmer; (document, contract) invalider
invaluable [ɪn'væljʊəbəl] adj précieux(euse)
invariable [ɪn'veərɪəbəl] adj invariable
invariably [ɪn'veərɪəblɪ] adv invariablement
invasion [ɪn'veɪʒən] n invasion f
invasive [ɪn'veɪsɪv] adj (**a**) (army) d'invasion; Fig envahissant(e) (**b**) (surgery) **i. surgery** chirurgie f invasive
invective [ɪn'vektɪv] n invectives fpl
inveigh [ɪn'veɪ] vi Formal **to i. against** invectiver contre
inveigle [ɪn'veɪgəl] vt **to i. sb into doing sth** entortiller qn pour qu'il fasse qch
invent [ɪn'vent] vt inventer
invention [ɪn'venʃən] n (**a**) (action, thing invented) invention f (**b**) (creativity) inventivité f
inventive [ɪn'ventɪv] adj inventif(ive)
inventiveness [ɪn'ventɪvnəs] n inventivité f

inventor [ɪnˈventə(r)] n inventeur(trice) m,f

inventory [ˈɪnventərɪ] (pl **inventories**) n (list) inventaire m; (stock) stock(s) m(pl)

inverse [ˈɪnvɜːs] adj inverse

invert [ɪnˈvɜːt] vt (turn upside down) renverser; (reverse) inverser, intervertir

invertebrate [ɪnˈvɜːtɪbrɪt] **1** n invertébré m
   2 adj invertébré(e)

inverted [ɪnˈvɜːtɪd] adj (upside down) renversé(e); (reversed) inversé(e); **to be an i. snob** faire du snobisme à l'envers

invest [ɪnˈvest] **1** vt (a) (money, time) investir (**in** dans) (**b**) (right, power) investir (**with** de)
   2 vi investir (**in** dans)

investigate [ɪnˈvestɪɡeɪt] vt (crime) enquêter sur; (question) examiner

investigation [ɪnvestɪˈɡeɪʃən] n enquête f

investigative [ɪnˈvestɪɡətɪv] adj (journalism) d'investigation

investigator [ɪnˈvestɪɡeɪtə(r)] n enquêteur(euse) m,f

investment [ɪnˈvestmənt] n investissement m; **i. account** compte m d'investissement; **i. analyst** analyste mf en placements; **i. bank** banque f d'affaires; **i. fund** fonds m commun de placement, fonds d'investissement; **i. income** revenu m provenant d'investissements; **i. trust** société f de placement

investor [ɪnˈvestə(r)] n investisseur m

inveterate [ɪnˈvetərɪt] adj (gambler, drunkard, liar) invétéré(e); (critic) acharné(e)

invidious [ɪnˈvɪdɪəs] adj (choice, comparison) inéquitable; (position, task) peu enviable

invigorating [ɪnˈvɪɡəreɪtɪŋ] adj vivifiant(e)

invincible [ɪnˈvɪnsɪbəl] adj invincible

inviolable [ɪnˈvaɪələbəl] adj Formal inviolable

inviolate [ɪnˈvaɪələt] adj Formal inviolé(e)

invisible [ɪnˈvɪzɪbəl] adj invisible (**to** à); **i. earnings** invisibles mpl; **i. ink** encre f sympathique

invitation [ɪnvɪˈteɪʃən] n invitation f

invite 1 n [ˈɪnvaɪt] Fam invit f
   2 vt [ɪnˈvaɪt] (**a**) (guest) inviter; **to i. sb in/up** inviter qn à entrer/monter; **to i. sb to do sth** inviter qn à faire qch; **applications are invited for the post of…** ≃ nous recrutons un… (**b**) (trouble, criticism) (of person) aller au-devant de

inviting [ɪnˈvaɪtɪŋ] adj attrayant(e); (food) appétissant(e)

in vitro fertilization [ɪnˈviːtrəʊfɜːtɪlaɪˈzeɪʃən] n fécondation f in vitro

invoice [ˈɪnvɔɪs] Com **1** n facture f; **to make out an i.** établir une facture
   2 vt (goods) facturer; (person, company) envoyer la facture à

invoke [ɪnˈvəʊk] vt Formal (God, law) invoquer; (spirit, feeling) évoquer; **to i. sb's aid** appeler qn à son secours

involuntary [ɪnˈvɒlʌntərɪ] adj involontaire

involve [ɪnˈvɒlv] vt (**a**) (implicate) **to i. sb in sth** impliquer qn dans qch; **this doesn't i. you** ça ne te concerne pas (**b**) (entail) (work, expense) impliquer, entraîner; **my job involves a lot of travel** je suis amené à voyager pour mon travail

involved [ɪnˈvɒlvd] adj (**a**) (implicated) **to be/to get i. in sth** (crime, affair) être impliqué(e) dans qch; **to be i. in an accident** avoir un accident; **to be i. in teaching/banking** être dans l'enseignement/la banque; **50 people were i. in the project** 50 personnes ont pris part au projet; **the police became i.** la police est intervenue; **don't get i.!** ne te mêle pas de ça!; **how much money is i.?** de combien d'argent s'agit-il? (**b**) (emotionally) **to be/to get i. with sb** sortir avec qn; **I don't want to get i.** je ne veux pas m'engager (**c**) (engrossed) **to get i. in a book/movie** s'absorber dans un livre/film; **I'm getting really i. in this job** je commence à trouver ce travail vraiment intéressant (**d**) (complicated) compliqué(e)

involvement [ɪnˈvɒlvmənt] n (**a**) (participation) participation f (**in** à) (**b**) (commitment) engagement m (**in** dans)

invulnerable [ɪnˈvʌlnərəbəl] adj invulnérable (**to** à)

inward [ˈɪnwəd] **1** adj (**a**) (thoughts, feelings) intime (**b**) (movement) vers l'intérieur
   2 adv vers l'intérieur

inward-looking [ɪnwədˈlʊkɪŋ] adj replié(e) sur soi-même

inwards [ˈɪnwədz] adv = **inward**

in-your-face [ˈɪnjɔːˈfeɪs] adj Fam (movie, advertisement) cru(e); (attitude, personality) agressif(ive)

iodine [ˈaɪədaɪn] n Chem iode m; (antiseptic) teinture f d'iode

ion [ˈaɪən] n ion m

Ionian [aɪˈəʊnɪən] n **the I. (Sea)** la mer Ionienne

ionize [ˈaɪənaɪz] vt ioniser

iota [aɪˈəʊtə] n iota m; **she hadn't changed one i.** elle n'avait pas du tout changé; **not an i. of truth** pas une once de vérité

IOU [aɪəʊˈjuː] n (= I owe you) reconnaissance f de dette

IP [aɪˈpiː] n Comput (abbr **Internet Protocol**) IP **address** adresse f IP

IPA [aɪpiːˈeɪ] n (abbr **International Phonetic Alphabet**) API m

iPod® [ˈaɪpɒd] n iPod® m

IQ [aɪˈkjuː] n (abbr **intelligence quotient**) QI m

IRA [aɪɑːˈreɪ] n (abbr **Irish Republican Army**) IRA f

Iran [ɪˈrɑːn] n l'Iran m

Iranian [ɪˈreɪnɪən] **1** n (**a**) (person) Iranien(enne) m,f (**b**) (language) iranien m
   2 adj iranien(enne)

Iraq [ɪˈrɑːk] n l'Irak m

Iraqi [ɪˈrɑːkɪ] **1** n Irakien(enne) m,f, Iraquien(enne) m,f
   2 adj irakien(enne), iraquien(enne)

irascible [ɪˈræsɪbəl] adj (person) irascible; (temperament) colérique

irate [aɪˈreɪt] adj furieux(euse)

IRC [aɪɑːˈsiː] n Comput (abbr **Internet Relay Chat**) IRC, service m de bavardage Internet

ire [ˈaɪə(r)] n Lit courroux m

Ireland [ˈaɪələnd] n l'Irlande f

iris [ˈaɪrɪs] n iris m

Irish [ˈaɪrɪʃ] **1** npl (people) **the I.** les Irlandais mpl
   2 n (language) irlandais m
   3 adj irlandais(e); **I. coffee** Irish coffee m; **the I. Sea** la mer d'Irlande; **I. stew** = ragoût de mouton, aux pommes de terre et aux oignons

Irishman [ˈaɪrɪʃmən] n Irlandais m

Irishwoman [ˈaɪrɪʃwʊmən] n Irlandaise f

irk [ɜːk] vt agacer

irksome [ˈɜːksəm] adj agaçant(e)

iron [ˈaɪən] **1** n (**a**) (metal, golf club) fer m; **made of i.** en fer; **to have an i. constitution** avoir une santé de fer; **an i. will** une volonté de fer; **i. discipline** discipline f de fer; **the I. Age** l'âge m de fer; Hist **the I. Curtain** le rideau de fer; **i. lung** poumon m d'acier; **i. ore** minerai m de fer (**b**) (for clothes) fer m (à repasser); Fig **to have several irons in the fire** avoir plusieurs fers au feu
   2 vt & vi (clothes) repasser

▸**iron out** vt sep (difficulty) aplanir; (problem) résoudre

ironic [aɪˈrɒnɪk], **ironical** [aɪˈrɒnɪkəl] adj ironique

ironing [ˈaɪənɪŋ] n repassage m; **to do the i.** repasser, faire le repassage; **i. board** planche f ou table f à repasser

irony [ˈaɪrənɪ] (pl **ironies**) n ironie f; **the i. is that…** ce qu'il y a d'ironique, c'est que…

irrational [ɪˈræʃənəl] adj irrationnel(elle)

irreconcilable [ɪrekənˈsaɪləbəl] adj (enemy) irréconciliable; (hatred) implacable; (belief, idea) incompatible, inconciliable

irredeemable [ɪrɪ'diːməbəl] *adj (fault)* irréparable; *(situation)* irrémédiable

irrefutable [ɪrɪ'fjuːtəbəl] *adj* irréfutable

irregular [ɪ'regjʊlə(r)] *adj* irrégulier(ère)

irregularity [ɪregjʊ'lærɪtɪ] *(pl* **irregularities***) n* irrégularité *f*

irrelevance [ɪ'reləvəns], **irrelevancy** [ɪ'reləvənsɪ] *(pl* **irrelevancies***) n (of remark, advice)* manque *m* d'à-propos

irrelevant [ɪ'reləvənt] *adj (remark, advice)* hors de propos; **that's i.** cela n'a rien à voir (avec la question)

irreligious [ɪrɪ'lɪdʒəs] *adj* irréligieux(euse)

irremediable [ɪrɪ'miːdɪəbəl] *adj Formal (situation, loss)* irrémédiable; *(mistake)* irréparable

irreparable [ɪ'repərəbəl] *adj* irréparable

irreplaceable [ɪrɪ'pleɪsəbəl] *adj* irremplaçable

irrepressible [ɪrɪ'presɪbəl] *adj (urge)* irrépressible; *(good humor)* à toute épreuve; **he's i.** rien n'entame sa bonne humeur

irreproachable [ɪrɪ'prəʊtʃəbəl] *adj* irréprochable

irresistible [ɪrɪ'zɪstɪbəl] *adj* irrésistible

irresolute [ɪ'rezəluːt] *adj* irrésolu(e), indécis(e)

irrespective of [ɪrɪ'spektɪvəv] *prep* indépendamment de, sans tenir compte de

irresponsible [ɪrɪ'spɒnsɪbəl] *adj* irresponsable

irretrievable [ɪrɪ'triːvəbəl] *adj (loss)* irrémédiable; *(money)* irrécupérable; *(mistake, situation)* irréparable

irreverent [ɪ'revərənt] *adj* irrévérencieux(euse)

irreversible [ɪrɪ'vɜːsɪbəl] *adj (decision, process)* irréversible

irrevocable [ɪ'revəkəbəl] *adj* irrévocable

irrigate ['ɪrɪgeɪt] *vt* irriguer

irrigation [ɪrɪ'geɪʃən] *n* irrigation *f*; **i. canal** *or* **ditch** canal *m* d'irrigation

irritable ['ɪrɪtəbəl] *adj* irritable; *Med* **i. bowel syndrome** colopathie *f* fonctionnelle

irritant ['ɪrɪtənt] *n (to eyes, skin)* irritant *m*; *(to person, government)* empêcheur(euse) *m,f* de tourner en rond

irritate ['ɪrɪteɪt] *vt (annoy)* agacer, irriter; *Med* irriter

irritating ['ɪrɪteɪtɪŋ] *adj* agaçant(e), irritant(e)

irritation [ɪrɪ'teɪʃən] *n* agacement *m*, irritation *f*; *Med* irritation *f*

IRS [aɪɑː'res] *n (abbr* **Internal Revenue Service***)* **the I.** le fisc

IS [aɪ'es] *n (abbr* **information system***)* système *m* informatique

is [ɪz] *3rd pers singular of* **be**

ISBN [aɪesbiː'en] *n (abbr* **International Standard Book Number***)* ISBN *m*

Islam ['ɪzlɑːm] *n* l'Islam *m*

Islamic [ɪz'læmɪk] *adj* islamique

Islamophobia [ɪzlæmə'fəʊbɪə] *n* islamophobie *f*

Islamophobic [ɪzlæmə'fəʊbɪk] *adj* islamophobe

island ['aɪlənd] *n* île *f*; *(small)* îlot *m*; *(in road)* refuge *m*

islander ['aɪləndə(r)] *n (in general)* insulaire *mf*; *(of specific island)* habitant(e) *m,f* de l'île

isle [aɪl] *n* île *f*

isn't ['ɪzənt] = **is not**

ISO [aɪes'əʊ] *n (abbr* **International Standards Organization***)* ISO *f*

isobar ['aɪsəʊbɑː(r)] *n* isobare *f*

isolate ['aɪsəleɪt] *vt* isoler (**from** de)

isolated ['aɪsəleɪtɪd] *adj* isolé(e)

isolation [aɪsə'leɪʃən] *n* isolement *m*; **in i. (from)** isolément (de); **i. ward** salle *f* des contagieux

isotope ['aɪsəʊtəʊp] *n Phys* isotope *m*

ISP [aɪes'piː] *n Comput (abbr* **Internet Service Provider***)* fournisseur *m* d'accès à l'Internet

Israel ['ɪzreɪəl] *n* Israël *m*

Israeli [ɪz'reɪlɪ] **1** *n* Israélien(enne) *m,f*
  2 *adj* israélien(enne)

Israelite ['ɪzrəlaɪt] *n Hist* Israélite *mf*

issue ['ɪsjuː, 'ɪʃuː] **1** *n* **(a)** *(topic)* problème *m*, question *f*; **the issues of the day** les questions du jour; **that's not the i.** ce n'est pas (là) le problème; **to avoid the i.** esquiver le problème; **to confuse the i.** compliquer les choses; **to make an i. of sth** faire toute une affaire de qch; **at i.** en cause; **to take i. with sb** exprimer son désaccord avec qn **(b)** *(of banknotes, stamps)* émission *f* **(c)** *(of magazine)* numéro *m*
  2 *vt (banknote, stamp)* émettre; *(order)* donner; **to i. sb with sth** délivrer qch à qn; **to i. a statement** faire une déclaration; *Law* **to i. a summons** notifier une citation
  3 *vi Formal (of blood, smoke, water)* s'échapper (**from** de); *(of noise)* provenir (**from** de)

Istanbul [ɪstæn'bʊl] *n* Istanbul

isthmus ['ɪsməs] *n* isthme *m*

IT [aɪ'tiː] *n Comput (abbr* **information technology***)* l'informatique *f*

it [ɪt] *pron* **(a)** *(subject)* il (elle) *m,f*; **where's the book? – it's on the shelf** où est le livre? – il est sur l'étagère; **put the TV on – it's not working** allume la télé – elle est en panne; **it's a big house** c'est une grande maison; **it's the best movie I've ever seen** c'est le meilleur film que j'aie jamais vu
  (b) *(direct object)* le (la) *m,f*; **I can do it** je peux le/la faire; **I saw it** je l'ai vu
  (c) *(indirect object)* lui; **give it something to eat** donne-lui à manger
  (d) *(prepositional object)* **on it** dessus; **under it** dessous; **beside it** à côté; **I forgot about it** j'ai oublié
  (e) *(as impersonal subject)* **it's raining** il pleut; **it's ten o'clock** il est dix heures; **it's cold today** il fait froid aujourd'hui; **it's impossible to work in this heat** il est impossible de travailler avec cette chaleur; **it's me** c'est moi
  (f) *(as complement of verb* **to be***)* **that's it** *(that's all)* c'est tout

Italian [ɪ'tælɪən] **1** *n* **(a)** *(person)* Italien(enne) *m,f* **(b)** *(language)* italien *m*; **I. class/teacher** classe *f*/professeur *m* d'italien
  2 *adj* italien(enne)

italic [ɪ'tælɪk] *Typ* **1** *n* italic(s) italique *m*
  2 *adj* italique

Italy ['ɪtəlɪ] *n* l'Italie *f*

itch [ɪtʃ] **1** *n* démangeaison *f*; *Fig* **to have an i. to do sth** brûler d'envie de faire qch
  2 *vi (of person)* éprouver des démangeaisons; **my hand itches** j'ai la main qui me démange; *Fig* **to be itching to do sth** brûler d'envie de faire qch

itchy ['ɪtʃɪ] *adj* **I've got an i. hand, my hand's i.** j'ai la main qui me démange; *Fig* **to have i. feet** avoir la bougeotte

it'd ['ɪtəd] = **it would, it had**

item ['aɪtəm] *n (in collection, list)* article *m*; *(in news)* entrefilet *m*; *(longer)* article *m*; **an i. of clothing** un vêtement; **personal items** objets *mpl* personnels; *Fam* **they're an i.** ils sortent ensemble

itemize ['aɪtəmaɪz] *vt* détailler

iterative ['ɪtərətɪv] *adj Comput* itératif(ive)

itinerant [ɪ'tɪnərənt] *adj (preacher)* itinérant(e); *(salesman, musician)* ambulant(e)

itinerary [aɪ'tɪnərərɪ] *(pl* **itineraries***) n* itinéraire *m*

it'll ['ɪtəl] = **it will**

its [ɪts] *possessive adj* **(a)** *(singular)* son (sa); *(plural)* ses; **i. bone** son os; **i. litter** sa litière; **i. kittens** ses châtons **(b)** *(for parts of body)* **the bear hurt i. paw** l'ours s'est blessé à la patte

it's [ɪts] = **it is, it has**

itself [ɪt'self] *pron* **(a)** *(reflexive)* **the dog hurt i.** le chien s'est blessé **(b)** *(emphatic)* **this method is simplicity i.** cette méthode est la simplicité même; **the town i. isn't very interesting** la ville (elle-)même n'est pas d'un grand intérêt (**c**) *(after preposition)* **by i.** tout(e) seul(e); **in i.** en soi

IUD [aɪjuːˈdiː] *n Med (abbr* **intra-uterine device**) stérilet *m*

I've [aɪv] = **I have**

IVF [aɪviːˈef] *n Med (abbr* **in vitro fertilization**) FIV *f*

ivory [ˈaɪvərɪ] *n* ivoire *m*; **the I. Coast** la Côte d'Ivoire; *Fig* **i. tower** tour *f* d'ivoire

ivy [ˈaɪvɪ] *n (plant)* lierre *m*; **I. League** = ensemble des huit universités les plus prestigieuses du nord-est des États-Unis

J

J, j [dʒeɪ] *n (letter)* J, j *m inv*

jab [dʒæb] **1** *n (with elbow, finger)* coup *m*; *(in boxing)* direct *m*
2 *vt (pt & pp* **jabbed**) **he jabbed her in the leg with a pencil** il lui a enfoncé un crayon dans la jambe; **to j. a finger at sb** agiter son doigt sous le nez de qn

jabber ['dʒæbə(r)] *vi Fam (talk unclearly)* marmonner; *(chatter)* jacasser

Jack [dʒæk] *n* **J. Frost** le Bonhomme Hiver

jack [dʒæk] *n* (**a**) *(person)* **every man j. of them** absolument tout le monde; **j. of all trades** touche-à-tout *mf* (**b**) *(for car)* cric *m* (**c**) *(in cards)* valet *m* (**d**) *(electric plug)* prise *f ou* fiche *f* mâle

▸**jack off** *vi Vulg (masturbate)* se branler

▸**jack up** *vt sep Fam (price, salaries)* augmenter

jackal ['dʒækəl] *n* chacal *m*

jackass ['dʒækæs] *n also Fig* âne *m*

jackboot ['dʒækbuːt] *n* botte *f* de cavalier; *Fig* **under the j. of** sous la botte de

jackdaw ['dʒækdɔː] *n* choucas *m*

jacket ['dʒækɪt] *n (coat)* veste *f*; *(of book)* jaquette *f*; *(of boiler)* chemise *f*, enveloppe *f*

jackhammer ['dʒækhæmə(r)] *n* marteau-piqueur *m*

jack-in-the-box ['dʒækɪnðəbɒks] *n* diable *m* à ressort

jackknife ['dʒæknaɪf] **1** *n (pl* **jackknives**) couteau *m* de poche
2 *vi (of trailer truck)* **the trailer jackknifed** la remorque du camion s'est soudain mise en travers de la route

jack-o'-lantern ['dʒækəˈlæntən] *n* = lanterne faite dans une citrouille sur laquelle on a creusé un visage

jackpot ['dʒækpɒt] *n (in lottery)* gros lot *m*; **to hit** *or* **to win the j.** gagner le gros lot

jack rabbit ['dʒækræbɪt] *n* = gros lièvre commun en Amérique du Nord

Jacobean [dʒækəˈbɪən] *adj* = de l'époque de Jacques 1ᵉʳ (1603–1625)

Jacobite ['dʒækəbaɪt] *n & adj* Jacobite *mf*

Jacuzzi® [dʒəˈkuːzɪ] *n* Jacuzzi® *m*

jade [dʒeɪd] **1** *n (stone, color)* jade *m*
2 *adj (color)* **j.(-green)** vert jade *inv*

jaded ['dʒeɪdɪd] *adj (tired)* las (lasse); *(bored)* blasé(e); **to be j. with sth** être las de qch; **to have a j. palate** avoir le palais blasé

Jag [dʒæg] *n Fam (car)* Jaguar *m*

jag [dʒæg] *n Fam* **to go on a (drinking) j.** prendre une cuite; **to have a crying j.** avoir une crise de larmes

jagged ['dʒægɪd] *adj (coastline, mountain top)* déchiqueté(e), découpé(e); *(blade)* ébréché(e)

jaguar ['dʒægwɑː(r)] *n Zool* jaguar *m*

jail [dʒeɪl] **1** *n* prison *f*; **to be in j.** être en prison; **to go to j.** aller en prison
2 *vt* emprisonner, mettre en prison

jailbait ['dʒeɪlbeɪt] *n Fam* mineur(e) *m,f*; **she's j.** c'est un coup à se retrouver en taule *(pour détournement de mineur)*

jailbird ['dʒeɪlbɜːd] *n Fam (in prison)* taulard(e) *m,f*; *(recidivist)* cheval *m* de retour

jailbreak ['dʒeɪlbreɪk] *n* évasion *f*

jailer ['dʒeɪlə(r)] *n* geôlier(ère) *m,f*

jailhouse ['dʒeɪlhaʊs] *n* prison *f*

jailor = **jailer**

Jakarta [dʒəˈkɑːtə] *n* Djakarta

jalopy [dʒəˈlɒpɪ] *(pl* **jalopies**) *n Fam* vieille guimbarde *f*, vieux tacot *m*

jam¹ [dʒæm] **1** *n* (**a**) *(crowd) (of people)* foule *f*; *(of traffic)* encombrement *m* (**b**) *Fam (difficult situation)* **to be in/to get into a (bit of a) j.** être/se fourrer dans le pétrin (**c**) *(improvised performance)* **j. (session)** jam-session *f*, bœuf *m*
2 *vt (pt & pp* **jammed**) (**a**) *(pack tightly) (objects)* entasser (**into** dans); *(container)* bourrer (**with** de); **people/cars jammed the street** la rue était noire de monde/embouteillée (**b**) *(immobilize) (drawer, mechanism)* coincer, bloquer; *(radio broadcast, station)* brouiller; *(switchboard)* saturer
3 *vi* (**a**) *(of drawer, mechanism)* se coincer, se bloquer (**b**) *(of crowd)* s'entasser (**into** dans) (**c**) *(of musicians)* improviser

▸**jam on** *vt sep* **to j. on the brakes** écraser la pédale de frein

jam² [dʒæm] *n (fruit preserve)* confiture *f*; **j. tart** tarte *f* à la confiture

Jamaica [dʒəˈmeɪkə] *n* la Jamaïque

Jamaican [dʒəˈmeɪkən] **1** *n* Jamaïcain(e) *m,f*
2 *adj* jamaïcain(e)

jamb [dʒæm] *n* montant *m*

jamboree [dʒæmbəˈriː] *n (Scouts' meeting)* jamboree *m*; *Fam (celebration)* fête *f*

jamming ['dʒæmɪŋ] *n (of radio broadcast, station)* brouillage *m*

jammy ['dʒæmɪ] *adj (covered with jam)* plein(e) de confiture

jam-packed [dʒæm'pækd] *adj* plein(e) à craquer; *(street)* noir(e) de monde, bondé(e)

Jan. *(abbr* **January**) janv

jangle ['dʒæŋgəl] **1** *n* cliquetis *m*
2 *vt* faire cliqueter
3 *vi* cliqueter; *Fig* **her voice made his nerves j.** sa voix lui mettait les nerfs en pelote

janitor ['dʒænɪtə(r)] *n (superintendent)* concierge *mf*

January ['dʒænjʊərɪ] *n* janvier *m*; *see also* **May**

Jap [dʒæp] *n very Fam* Jap *mf*, = terme raciste désignant un Japonais

Japan [dʒəˈpæn] *n* le Japon

Japanese [dʒæpəˈniːz] **1** *npl (people)* **the J.** les Japonais *mpl*
2 *n* (**a**) *(person)* Japonais(e) *m,f* (**b**) *(language)* japonais *m*; **J. class/teacher** classe *f*/professeur *m* de japonais
3 *adj* japonais(e)

jape [dʒeɪp] *n* blague *f*

jar¹ [dʒɑː(r)] **1** *n (jolt)* choc *m*, secousse *f*
2 *vt (pt & pp* **jarred**) *also Fig* secouer; **someone jarred my elbow** quelqu'un m'a cogné le coude

3 *vi* (**a**) *(make unpleasant sound)* rendre un son discordant; **to j. on the ears** écorcher les oreilles; **to j. on the nerves** taper sur les nerfs (**b**) *(of colors)* jurer; *(of ideas)* être en contradiction

jar² [dʒɑː(r)] *n (container)* pot *m*; *(earthenware)* jarre *f*

jargon ['dʒɑːgən] *n Pej* jargon *m*

jarring ['dʒɑːrɪŋ] *adj (noise, voice)* discordant(e); *(blow)* qui ébranle tout le corps

jasmine ['dʒæzmɪn] *n* jasmin *m*

jaundice ['dʒɔːndɪs] *n* jaunisse *f*

jaundiced ['dʒɔːndɪst] *adj Fig (attitude, view)* aigu(ë), amer(ère); **to take a j. view of sth** voir qch d'un mauvais œil

jaunt [dʒɔːnt] *n* excursion *f*, sortie *f*

jauntiness ['dʒɔːntɪnɪs] *n (cheerfulness)* enjouement *m*; *(carefreeness)* insouciance *f*

jaunty ['dʒɔːntɪ] *adj (cheerful)* enjoué(e); *(carefree)* insouciant(e)

Java¹ ['dʒɑːvə] *n Geog* Java

Java²® ['dʒɑːvə] *n Comput* Java *m*; **J. script** (langage *m*) Java-script® *m*

javelin ['dʒævlɪn] *n* javelot *m*

jaw [dʒɔː] **1** *n* mâchoire *f*; **jaws** *(of animal)* gueule *f*; **the jaws of death** les griffes *fpl* de la mort

2 *vi Fam (chat)* papoter

jawbone ['dʒɔːbəʊn] *n* maxillaire *m*

jawbreaker ['dʒɔːbreɪkə(r)] *n* (**a**) *Fam (word)* mot *m* imprononçable; *(name)* nom *m* à coucher dehors (**b**) *(candy)* = sorte de bonbon dur

jay [dʒeɪ] *n* geai *m*

jaywalker ['dʒeɪwɔːkə(r)] *n* = piéton qui traverse en dehors des passages cloutés

jaywalking ['dʒeɪwɔːkɪŋ] *n* = fait de traverser en dehors des passages cloutés

jazz [dʒæz] *n* jazz *m*; *Fam* **and all that j.** et tout le tremblement *ou* le bazar

▸**jazz up** *vt sep Fam (enliven) (clothes, room, style)* égayer; *(party)* animer; *(taste)* relever

jazzy ['dʒæzɪ] *adj (tune)* jazzy *inv*; *(clothes, pattern)* aux couleurs vives

jealous ['dʒeləs] *adj* jaloux(ouse); **to be j. of sb** être jaloux de qn

jealously ['dʒeləslɪ] *adv* jalousement; **to guard sth j.** veiller jalousement sur qch

jealousy ['dʒeləsɪ] *n* jalousie *f*

jeans [dʒiːnz] *npl* jeans *m*

Jeep® [dʒiːp] *n* Jeep® *f*

jeer [dʒɪə(r)] **1** *n (mocking)* moquerie *f*; **the jeers of the crowd** *(booing)* les huées *fpl* de la foule

2 *vt (boo)* huer; *(mock)* se moquer de

3 *vi* **to j. at sb/sth** *(boo)* huer qn/qch; *(mock)* se moquer de qn/qch

jeering ['dʒɪərɪŋ] **1** *n (booing)* huées *fpl*; *(mocking)* moqueries *fpl*

2 *adj* railleur(euse), moqueur(euse)

jeez [dʒiːz] *exclam Fam* mince alors!

Jehovah [dʒɪ'həʊvə] *n* Jéhovah; **J.'s Wɪᴛɴᴇss** témoin *m* de Jéhovah

jell [dʒel] *vi (of liquid)* se gélifier; *Fig (of ideas, plans)* prendre forme; *Fig (of team)* se souder

Jell-O® ['dʒeləʊ] *n (dessert)* ≃ gelée *f*

jelly ['dʒelɪ] *n (pl jellies) (jam)* gelée *f*; **j. roll** gâteau *m* roulé

jellybean ['dʒelɪbiːn] *n* = bonbon couvert de sucre, en forme de haricot

jellyfish ['dʒelɪfɪʃ] *n* méduse *f*

jeopardize ['dʒepədaɪz] *vt* compromettre; *(life)* mettre en danger

jeopardy ['dʒepədɪ] *n* **in j.** en danger, en péril; **to put sb/sth in j.** mettre qn/qch en danger *ou* en péril

jerk¹ [dʒɜːk] **1** *n (sudden pull)* secousse *f*, coup *m* sec; **to give sth a j.** tirer sur qch d'un coup sec

2 *vt (pull)* tirer brusquement; *(in order to move)* déplacer par à-coups

3 *vi* **to j. forward** *(of car)* faire un bond en avant; *(of head)* partir en avant; **to j. to a halt** s'arrêter avec des soubresauts

jerk² [dʒɜːk] *n Fam (person)* abruti(e) *m,f*

▸**jerk off** *vi Vulg (masturbate)* se branler

jerkily ['dʒɜːkɪlɪ] *adv* de manière saccadée

jerky ['dʒɜːkɪ] *adj (movement)* saccadé(e); *(style)* hâché(e)

jerrican ['dʒerɪkæn] *n* jerrican *m*

jerry-built ['dʒerɪbɪlt] *adj* construit(e) à la va-vite

Jersey ['dʒɜːzɪ] *n (island)* Jersey; **J. (cow)** jersiaise *f*

jersey ['dʒɜːzɪ] *(pl jerseys) n (garment)* pull(-over) *m*, tricot *m*

Jerusalem [dʒə'ruːsələm] *n* Jérusalem; **J. artichoke** topinambour *m*

jest [dʒest] **1** *n* plaisanterie *f*; **in j.** pour plaisanter

2 *vi* plaisanter

jester ['dʒestə(r)] *n* farceur(euse) *m,f*; *Hist* **(court) j.** fou *m* (du roi)

jesting ['dʒestɪŋ] *adj (remark)* pour rire; *(tone)* de la plaisanterie

Jesuit ['dʒezjʊɪt] *n* jésuite *m*

Jesuitical [dʒezjʊ'ɪtɪkəl] *adj Pej (argument, reasoning)* de jésuite

Jesus ['dʒiːzəs] **1** *n* Jésus *m*; **J. Christ** Jésus-Christ

2 *exclam Fam* **J. (Christ)!** nom de Dieu!

jet¹ [dʒet] **1** *n* (**a**) *(plane)* jet *m*, avion *m* à réaction; **j. engine** réacteur *m*, moteur *m* à réaction; **j. fighter** chasseur *m* à réaction; **j. propulsion** propulsion *f* par réaction; **the j. set** la jet-set; **j. ski** scooter *m* des mers, jet-ski *m* (**b**) *(nozzle, of liquid)* jet *m*

2 *vi (pt & pp jetted) Fam (travel by plane)* **to j. in** venir en avion; **to j. off** s'envoler; **to j. around the world** passer son temps dans les avions

jet² [dʒet] **1** *n (stone)* jais *m*

2 *adj* **j. (black)** de jais

jetlag ['dʒetlæg] *n* fatigue *f* due au décalage horaire

jetlagged ['dʒetlægd] *adj* fatigué(e) par le décalage horaire

jet-powered [dʒet'paʊəd], **jet-propelled** [dʒetprə'peld] *adj* à réaction

jettison ['dʒetɪsən] *vt (cargo)* jeter à la mer *ou* par-dessus bord; *(plan, tradition)* abandonner

jetty ['dʒetɪ] *n (pl jetties)* jetée *f*; *(for landing)* embarcadère *m*

Jew [dʒuː] *n* Juif (Juive) *m,f*

jewel ['dʒuːəl] *n (gem, piece of jewelry)* bijou *m*; *Fig (person)* perle *f*

jeweler ['dʒuːələ(r)] *n* bijoutier(ère) *m,f*

jewelry ['dʒuːəlrɪ] *n* bijoux *mpl*; **a piece of j.** un bijou; **j. store** bijouterie *f*

Jewess ['dʒuːɪs] *n Old-fashioned* Juive *f*

Jewish ['dʒuːɪʃ] *adj* juif (juive)

Jewry ['dʒuːərɪ] *n* communauté *f* juive

jib¹ [dʒɪb] *n* (**a**) *(sail)* foc *m* (**b**) *(of crane)* flèche *f*

jib² [dʒɪb] *(pt & pp jibbed) vi* **to j. at sth/at doing sth** rechigner à qch/à faire qch

jibe [dʒaɪb] **1** *n* moquerie *f*

2 *vi* **to j. at sb** se moquer de qn

jiffy ['dʒɪfɪ] *n Fam* **in a j.** dans un instant, tout de suite

jig [dʒɪg] **1** *n (dance, music)* gigue *f*

2 *vi (pt & pp jigged) (dance)* danser la gigue

jiggle ['dʒɪgəl] **1** *vt* secouer rapidement

2 *vi* remuer dans tous les sens

▸**jiggle about, jiggle around** *vt sep & vi* = **jiggle**

jigsaw ['dʒɪgsɔː] *n* (**a**) *(saw)* scie *f* sauteuse (**b**) *(game)* **j. (puzzle)** puzzle *m*

jihad [dʒɪ'hæd] *n* djihad *m*

jilt [dʒɪlt] *vt (lover)* plaquer

jingle ['dʒɪŋgəl] **1** *n* (**a**) *(of bells, coins)* tintement *m*; *(of keys)* cliquetis *m* (**b**) *(catchy tune)* jingle *m*; *Rad & TV (in advertisement)* jingle *m*, *Offic* sonal *m*
  2 *vt (bells, coins)* faire tinter; *(keys)* faire cliqueter
  3 *vi (of bells, coins)* tinter; *(of keys)* cliqueter

jingoism ['dʒɪŋgəʊɪzəm] *n Pej* chauvinisme *m*

jingoistic ['dʒɪŋgəʊ'ɪstɪk] *adj Pej* chauvin(e)

jinx [dʒɪŋks] *Fam* **1** *n (spell, curse)* (mauvais) sort *m*; **to put a j. on sb/sth** jeter un sort à qn/qch
  2 *vt* **to be jinxed** avoir la poisse

JIT [dʒɪt] *adj Com (abbr* **just in time)** juste à temps

jitters ['dʒɪtəz] *npl Fam* **to have** *or* **to get the j.** être à cran

jittery ['dʒɪtərɪ] *adj Fam* à cran

jive [dʒaɪv] **1** *n (music, dance)* swing *m*
  2 *vi (dance)* danser le swing

Jnr (*abbr* **Junior**) **Thomas Smith, J.** Thomas Smith fils

job [dʒɒb] *n* (**a**) *(employment, post)* travail *m*, emploi *m*; **to be out of a j.** être sans travail *ou* emploi; **j. creation** création *f* d'emplois; **j. description** description *f* de poste; **to go j. hunting** chercher du travail; **j. losses** suppressions *fpl* d'emplois; **j. offer** offre *f* d'emploi; **j. opportunities** débouchés *mpl*; **j. satisfaction** satisfaction *f* dans le travail; **j. security** sécurité *f* de l'emploi; **j. sharing** partage *m* de poste; **j. title** fonction *f* (**b**) *(piece of work, task)* tâche *f*; **to do a good j.** faire du beau travail; *Fig* **to do the j.** *(serve purpose)* convenir, faire l'affaire; **it was quite a j. getting her to come** la convaincre de venir n'a pas été une mince affaire; *Com* **j. lot** lot *m* (**c**) *(responsibility, duty)* travail *m*; **to have the j. of doing sth** être chargé(e) de faire qch (**d**) *Fam (crime)* coup *m* (**e**) *(idiom)* **that's just the j.!** c'est juste ce qu'il faut!

jobless ['dʒɒblɪs] **1** *npl* **the j.** les sans-emploi *mpl*
  2 *adj* sans emploi

job-share ['dʒɒbʃeə(r)] *vi* partager un poste

jockey ['dʒɒkɪ] **1** *n (pl* **jockeys)** jockey *m*; **j. shorts** slip *m*
  2 *vi* **to j. for position** jouer des coudes

jockstrap ['dʒɒkstræp] *n* slip *m* à coquille

jocular ['dʒɒkjʊlə(r)] *adj* enjoué(e)

jodhpurs ['dʒɒdpəz] *npl* jodhpurs *mpl*

Joe [dʒəʊ] *n Fam* **he's an ordinary J.** c'est un mec ordinaire; **J. Schmo** Monsieur Tout-le-monde

jog [dʒɒg] **1** *n* (**a**) *(push)* secousse *f*; *(with elbow)* coup *m* de coude; **to give sb's memory a j.** rafraîchir la mémoire de qn (**b**) *(run)* course *f* (à petites foulées); **to break into a j.** se mettre à courir (à petites foulées); **to go for a j.** aller faire un jogging
  2 *vt (pt & pp* **jogged)** *(push)* pousser; **to j. sb's elbow** donner un coup de coude à qn; **to j. sb's memory** rafraîchir la mémoire à qn
  3 *vi (run)* faire du jogging; **to go jogging** aller faire un jogging

►**jog along** *vi (run)* courir à petites foulées; *Fig (in job, life)* aller son petit bonhomme de chemin

jogger ['dʒɒgə(r)] *n* joggeur(euse) *m,f*

jogging ['dʒɒgɪŋ] *n* jogging *m*; **j. pants** pantalon *m* de jogging; **j. suit** tenue *f* de jogging

joggle ['dʒɒgəl] *vt* secouer légèrement

Johannesburg [dʒəʊ'hænɪzbɜːg] *n* Johannesburg

john [dʒɒn] *n Fam (lavatory)* petit coin *m*

join [dʒɔɪn] **1** *n* raccord *m*; *(in fabric)* couture *f*
  2 *vt* (**a**) *(unite, connect)* relier; *(planks)* joindre; **to j. two things together** relier une chose à une autre; **to j. battle** engager le combat; **to j. forces (with sb)** s'unir (à qn) (**b**) *(club, political party)* adhérer à; *(army)* s'engager dans; *(discussion, game)* se joindre à; **to j. a union** se syndiquer; **to j. the line**
se mettre dans la queue (**c**) *(meet with)* rejoindre; **may I j. you?** *(to somebody at table)* puis-je me joindre à vous? (**d**) *(of river, road)* rejoindre; **where the river joins the sea** où le fleuve se jette dans la mer
  3 *vi* (**a**) *(of pipes, roads, rivers)* se rejoindre (**b**) *(in club, political party)* adhérer; *(in union)* devenir membre

►**join in 1** *vt insep* participer à, prendre part à
  2 *vi* participer

►**join up** *vi Mil* s'engager

joint [dʒɔɪnt] **1** *n* (**a**) *(in body)* articulation *f*; **out of j.** déboîté(e) (**b**) *(in woodwork)* assemblage *m*; *(in metalwork)* joint *m* (**c**) *Fam (nightclub)* boîte *f*; *(restaurant)* resto *m* (**d**) *Fam (cannabis cigarette)* joint *m*
  2 *adj* commun(e); *(effort)* conjugué(e); **j. account** compte *m* joint; **j. custody** garde *f* conjointe; **j. ownership** copropriété *f*; **j. stock company** société *f* par actions; **j. venture** *(undertaking)* entreprise *f* commune; *(company)* société *f* commune *ou* en participation

jointly ['dʒɔɪntlɪ] *adv* conjointement

joist [dʒɔɪst] *n* solive *f*

joke [dʒəʊk] **1** *n* (**a**) *(remark)* plaisanterie *f*, blague *f*; *(prank, trick)* tour *m*, farce *f*; **to tell** *or* **to crack a j. (about sth)** raconter une blague (sur qch); **to make a j. (about sth)** faire une plaisanterie (sur qch); **to make a j. of sth** rire de qch; **to say/do sth for a j.** dire/faire qch pour rire; **the j. was on him** la plaisanterie s'est retournée contre lui; **she can't take a j.** elle n'aime pas la plaisanterie; **it's no j.!** ce n'est pas une mince affaire!; **it's no j. waiting for hours** ce n'est pas drôle d'attendre pendant des heures; **it's getting beyond a j.** ça n'est plus drôle, la plaisanterie a assez duré; **to play a j. on sb** jouer un tour à qn (**b**) *Fam* **to be a j.** *(ridiculous)* être lamentable
  2 *vi* plaisanter; **to j. about sth** plaisanter sur qch; **I was only joking** je plaisantais; **you're joking!, you must be joking!** tu plaisantes!, tu veux rire!; **joking apart...** blague à part...

joker ['dʒəʊkə(r)] *n* (**a**) *(clown)* farceur(euse) *m,f*; *(incompetent person)* plaisantin *m*; *(stupid person)* abruti *m*; **some j. has stolen my umbrella** il y a un abruti qui m'a piqué mon parapluie (**b**) *(in cards)* joker *m*; *Fig* **the j. in the pack** la grande inconnue

jokey = **joky**

jokily ['dʒəʊkɪlɪ] *adv* en plaisantant

jokingly ['dʒəʊkɪŋlɪ] *adv* en plaisantant

joky ['dʒəʊkɪ] *adj (person)* blagueur(euse); *(mood, conversation)* jovial(e); *(remark, comment)* moqueur(euse)

jolly ['dʒɒlɪ] *adj (cheerful)* joyeux(euse), gai(e); **the J. Roger** le pavillon noir

jolt [dʒəʊlt] **1** *n* (**a**) *(shake)* secousse *f* (**b**) *(shock, surprise)* choc *m*, coup *m*; **to give sb a j.** faire un choc *ou* un coup à qn
  2 *vt (shake)* secouer; *(shock, surprise)* ébranler; **to j. sb into action** secouer les puces à qn; **to j. sb out of a depression** faire sortir qn de son état dépressif
  3 *vi (shake)* secouer; **to j. along** *(of vehicle)* cahoter; **to j. to a stop** *(of vehicle)* s'arrêter avec des à-coups; **his head jolted forward/back** sa tête est partie en avant/en arrière

Jordan ['dʒɔːdən] *n (country)* la Jordanie; **the (River) J.** le Jourdain

Jordanian [dʒɔː'deɪnɪən] **1** *n* Jordanien(enne) *m,f*
  2 *adj* jordanien(enne)

josh [dʒɒʃ] *vt Fam* mettre en boîte

joss stick ['dʒɒsstɪk] *n* bâton *m* d'encens

jostle ['dʒɒsəl] **1** *vt* bousculer; **to j. sb out of the way** écarter qn en jouant des coudes
  2 *vi (push)* se bousculer; **to j. for position** *(in contest, job)* jouer des coudes

jot [dʒɒt] *n* **he doesn't care a j.** il s'en fiche complètement; **there isn't a j. of truth in what you say** il n'y a pas une once de vérité dans ce que vous dites; **it doesn't make a j.**

of difference ça ne fait pas la moindre différence

▶**jot down** (*pt & pp* **jotted**) *vt sep* noter

jottings ['dʒɒtɪŋz] *npl* notes *fpl*

joule [dʒu:l] *n Phys* joule *m*

journal ['dʒɜ:nəl] *n (publication)* revue *f*; *(diary)* journal *m*; **to keep a j.** tenir un journal

journalese [dʒɜ:nə'li:z] *n Fam Pej* jargon *m* journalistique

journalism ['dʒɜ:nəlɪzəm] *n* journalisme *m*

journalist ['dʒɜ:nəlɪst] *n* journaliste *mf*

journalistic [dʒɜ:nə'lɪstɪk] *adj* journalistique

journey ['dʒɜ:nɪ] **1** *n (pl* **journeys)** voyage *m*; *(short)* trajet *m*; **a train j.** un voyage en train; **to make a j.** faire un voyage; **to go (away) on a j.** partir en voyage; **to get to** *or* **to reach the end of one's j.** arriver à destination; **j. time** durée *f* du voyage; *(shorter distance)* durée du trajet

  2 *vi* voyager

joust [dʒaʊst] *vi Hist* jouter; *Fig (compete)* se chamailler

jovial ['dʒəʊvɪəl] *adj* jovial(e), enjoué(e)

jovially ['dʒəʊvɪəlɪ] *adv* jovialement

jowl [dʒaʊl] *n (jaw)* mâchoire *f*; *(cheek)* bajoue *f*

joy [dʒɔɪ] *n* (a) *(happiness)* joie *f* (b) *(pleasure)* plaisir *m*; **she's a j. to be with** c'est un plaisir d'être avec elle

joyful ['dʒɔɪfʊl] *adj (occasion, news)* heureux(euse); *(person, party)* joyeux(euse)

joyfully ['dʒɔɪfəlɪ] *adv* joyeusement

joyless ['dʒɔɪlɪs] *adj* triste

joyous ['dʒɔɪəs] *adj (occasion, news)* heureux(euse); *(person, party)* joyeux(euse)

joyride ['dʒɔɪraɪd] **1** *n (in stolen car)* = virée dans une voiture volée; **to go for a j.** = faire une virée dans une voiture volée

  2 *vt* **to go joyriding** = faire une virée dans une voiture volée

joyrider ['dʒɔɪraɪdə(r)] *n* = chauffard qui conduit une voiture volée

joystick ['dʒɔɪstɪk] *n (in aircraft)* manche *m* à balai; *(for computer)* manette *f*

JP [dʒeɪ'pi:] *n Law (abbr* **Justice of the Peace)** juge *m* de paix

Jr. *(abbr* **Junior) Thomas Smith, Jr.** Thomas Smith fils

jubilant ['dʒu:bɪlənt] *adj (shouts)* de joie; *(expression)* réjoui(e); *(person)* exultant(e); *(celebration)* joyeux(euse); **to be j. (at** *or* **about sth)** être transporté(e) de joie (par qch)

jubilation [dʒu:bɪ'leɪʃən] *n (grande)* joie *f*, jubilation *f*

jubilee ['dʒu:bɪli:] *n* **(golden) j.** cinquantième anniversaire *m*, jubilé *m*; **silver/diamond j.** vingt-cinquième/soixantième anniversaire

Judaic [dʒu:'deɪɪk] *adj* judaïque

Judaism ['dʒu:deɪɪzəm] *n* judaïsme *m*

Judas ['dʒu:dəs] *n (traitor)* Judas *m*

judge [dʒʌdʒ] **1** *n* (a) *(in law, sport)* juge *m*; *(in competition)* membre *m* du jury (b) *(expert)* **to be a good/poor j. of sth** s'y connaître/ne pas s'y connaître en qch; **I will be the j. of that** c'est moi qui (en) jugerai

  2 *vt* (a) *(in law, sport)* juger (b) *(assess critically)* juger; **to j. sb by** *or* **on sth** juger qn sur *ou* d'après qch; **to j. sb/sth a success/failure** considérer que qn/qch a réussi/échoué; **to j. it necessary to do sth** estimer *ou* juger nécessaire de faire qch; **don't j. a book by its cover** l'habit ne fait pas le moine (c) *(estimate)* estimer, évaluer

  3 *vi* juger; **to j. by appearances** juger d'après les apparences; **to j. for oneself** juger par soi-même; **judging by...** à en juger par...

judgment ['dʒʌdʒmənt] *n* (a) *(decision)* jugement *m*; **to sit in j.** *(of judge, court)* siéger; **to pass j.** *(of judge, court)* rendre un jugement; *Fig* **to pass j. on sb** porter des jugements sur qn, juger qn; *Rel* **J. Day** le (jour du) Jugement dernier (b) *(opinion)* avis *m*, opinion *f*; **to form a j.** se faire un avis *ou* une opinion (c) *(discernment)* jugement *m*; **to have good j.** faire

preuve de jugement; **to have poor j.** manquer de jugement; **to trust sb's j.** s'en remettre au jugement de qn; **in my j.** à mon sens; **against my better j.** en sachant que c'est/c'était une erreur

judgmental [dʒʌdʒ'mentəl] *adj* critique

judicial [dʒu:'dɪʃəl] *adj* judiciaire

judiciary [dʒu:'dɪʃɪərɪ] *n (judges)* magistrature *f*; *(branch of government)* pouvoir *m* judiciaire

judicious [dʒu:'dɪʃəs] *adj* judicieux(euse)

judiciously [dʒu:'dɪʃəslɪ] *adv* judicieusement

judiciousness [dʒu:'dɪʃəsnɪs] *n* bon sens *m*

judo ['dʒu:dəʊ] *n* judo *m*

jug [dʒʌg] *n* (a) *(for cream, milk)* pot *m* (b) *very Fam (prison)* **in the j.** en taule

juggle ['dʒʌgəl] **1** *vt also Fig* jongler avec

  2 *vi also Fig* jongler (**with** avec)

juggler ['dʒʌglə(r)] *n* jongleur(euse) *m,f*

juggling ['dʒʌglɪŋ] *n also Fig* jonglerie *f*

jugular ['dʒʌgjʊlə(r)] **1** *n* jugulaire *f*; *Fig* **to go for the j.** frapper au point sensible

  2 *adj* jugulaire

juice [dʒu:s] *n* (a) *(of fruit, meat)* jus *m*; *(of plant)* suc *m*; **j. bar** = bar où l'on sert des jus de fruit; **j. extractor** centrifugeuse *f* (b) *Fam (gas)* jus *m*; *(electricity)* jus *m* (c) *Fam (alcohol)* alcool *m*

juicer ['dʒu:sə(r)] *n* centrifugeuse *f*

juicy ['dʒu:sɪ] *adj* (a) *(fruit)* juteux(euse); *(meat)* qui rend du jus (b) *Fig (contract, deal)* juteux(euse); *(story)* croustillant(e)

jukebox ['dʒu:kbɒks] *n* juke-box *m*

Jul. *(abbr* **July)** juill

July [dʒu:'laɪ] *n* juillet *m*; *see also* **May**

jumble ['dʒʌmbəl] **1** *n (of things)* tas *m*; *(of ideas, words)* fatras *m*; **in a j.** *(things)* en désordre, en pagaïe; *(ideas, words)* embrouillé(e)

  2 *vt (things)* mélanger; *(ideas, words)* embrouiller

jumbo ['dʒʌmbəʊ] *adj* **j. (sized)** énorme, géant(e); **j. jet** jumbo jet *m*, gros-porteur *m*

jump [dʒʌmp] **1** *n* (a) *(leap)* saut *m*; *Fig* **to be one j. ahead** avoir une longueur d'avance; **j. cables** câbles *mpl* de démarrage; **j. jet** ADAV *m*; **j. rope** corde *f* à sauter; **j. suit** combinaison *f*

  (b) *(rise)* hausse *f* soudaine (**in** de)

  (c) *(on racecourse)* obstacle *m*

  (d) *(idioms)* **to have the j. on sb** avoir une longueur d'avance sur qn; **to get the j. on sb** devancer qn

  2 *vt (hedge, ditch)* sauter; *Fam* **to j. sb** attaquer qn; **to j. bail** se dérober à la justice *(alors qu'on est en liberté provisoire)*; **to j. the gun** *(in race)* faire un faux départ; *Fig* anticiper, agir prématurément; **to j. the lights** *(in car)* brûler un feu rouge; **to j. rope** sauter à la corde; **to j. ship** déserter le navire

  3 *vi* (a) *(leap)* sauter; **to j. to one's feet** se lever d'un bond; **to j. for joy** sauter de joie; **to j. onto a train** sauter dans un train; **to j. out (of) the window** sauter par la fenêtre; **to j. to conclusions** tirer des conclusions hâtives; *Fam* **to j. down sb's throat** rabrouer qn; *Fig* **to j. out at sb** *(of mistake, surprising detail)* sauter aux yeux de qn

  (b) *(go directly)* **to j. from one subject to another** *or* **to the next** sauter d'un sujet à l'autre; **the movie then jumps to the present** le film passe d'un seul coup au présent

  (c) *(of unemployment, inflation)* faire un bond

  (d) *(make a sudden movement)* *(of person)* sursauter; *(of heart)* faire un bond; *(of record player needle)* sauter; **we nearly jumped out of our skins** ça nous a fichu un coup

▶**jump at** *vt insep (offer, chance)* sauter sur

▶**jump on** *vt insep Fam (reprimand)* sauter sur (**for doing** d'avoir fait)

jumper ['dʒʌmpə(r)] *n (sleeveless dress)* robe-chasuble *f*

jumping ['dʒʌmpɪŋ] *adj* (a) **j. jack** *(puppet)* pantin *m*; *(exercise)*

= saut avec extension latérale des membres (**b**) *Fam (very lively)* hyper animé(e)

jumping-off place ['dʒʌmpɪŋ'ɒf'pleɪs], **jumping-off point** ['dʒʌmpɪŋ'ɒf'pɔɪnt] *n* point *m* de départ; *Fig* tremplin *m*

jump-start ['dʒʌmpstɑːt] *vt Aut* faire démarrer avec des câbles de démarrage; *Fig (economy)* donner un sérieux coup de pouce à

jumpy ['dʒʌmpɪ] *adj* nerveux(euse)

Jun. (*abbr* **June**) juin

junction ['dʒʌŋkʃən] *n (of roads, railroad lines)* embranchement *m*; *Elec* **j. box** boîte *f* de dérivation

juncture ['dʒʌŋktʃə(r)] *n Formal* **at this j.** à ce moment(-là)

June [dʒuːn] *n* juin *m*; *see also* **May**

jungle ['dʒʌŋgəl] *n also Fig* jungle *f*; **j. gym** cage *f* à poules

junior ['dʒuːnjə(r)] **1** *n* (**a**) *(in age)* **to be sb's j.** être plus jeune que qn; **he's three years my j.** il a trois ans de moins que moi (**b**) *(in rank)* subalterne *mf* (**c**) *Sch & Univ* étudiant(e) *m,f* de troisième année

  2 *adj* (**a**) *(in age)* **to be j. to sb** être plus jeune que qn; **Thomas Smith, J.** Thomas Smith fils; **j. high (school)** ≃ collège *m* d'enseignement secondaire; *Sch & Univ* **j. year** avant-dernière année *f* (**b**) *(in rank)* subalterne; **to be j. to sb** être au-dessous de qn; **j. teacher/executive** jeune professeur *m*/ cadre *m*; **j. doctor** interne *mf*

juniper ['dʒuːnɪpə(r)] *n* **j. (tree)** genévrier *m*, genièvre *m*; **j. berry** baie *f* de genièvre

junk¹ [dʒʌŋk] **1** *n (unwanted objects)* bric-à-brac *m*; *(inferior goods)* camelote *f*; *Fin* **j. bond** obligation *f* à risque; **j. food** cochonneries *fpl*; **j. mail** prospectus *mpl*; **j. shop** brocante *f*

  2 *vt Fam (discard) (objects)* bazarder; *(plan)* laisser tomber

junk² [dʒʌŋk] *n (boat)* jonque *f*

junket ['dʒʌŋkɪt] *n* (**a**) *(food)* lait *m* caillé (**b**) *Pej (trip by public official)* voyage *m* aux frais du contribuable

junkie, junky ['dʒʌŋkɪ] (*pl* **junkies**) *n Fam (drug addict)* drogué(e) *m,f*; **a fast-food/game-show j.** un accro des fast-food/jeux télévisés

junkyard ['dʒʌŋkjɑːd] *n (for metal)* ferraille *f*; **at the j.** chez le ferrailleur

junta ['dʒʌntə] *n* junte *f*

Jupiter ['dʒuːpɪtə(r)] *n (planet)* Jupiter

jurisdiction [dʒʊərɪs'dɪkʃən] *n* juridiction *f*; **to have j. over sb** avoir autorité sur qn; **to come within** *or* **under the j. of...** être sous la juridiction de...

jurisprudence [dʒʊərɪs'pruːdəns] *n* jurisprudence *f*

jurist ['dʒʊərɪst] *n (legal expert)* juriste *mf*

juror ['dʒʊərə(r)] *n Law* juré(e) *m,f*

jury ['dʒʊərɪ] (*pl* **juries**) *n Law* jury *m*; **to be** *or* **to serve on the j.** être membre *ou* faire partie du jury; **to be on j. duty** *or* **service** être convoqué(e) pour faire partie d'un jury; *Fig* **the j. is still out on that one** ça reste à voir; **j. box** banc *m* des jurés

just [dʒʌst] **1** *adj (fair)* juste; **it's only j. that...** c'est normal que... + *subjunctive*; **to get one's j. deserts** n'avoir que ce que l'on mérite

  2 *adv* (**a**) *(exactly)* exactement; **that's j. what I told her** c'est exactement ce que je lui ai dit; **j. how many are there?** combien y en a-t-il au juste?; **that's j. the point!** justement!, précisément!; **j. my luck!** c'est bien ma chance!; **it's j. as good/difficult as...** c'est tout aussi bon/difficile que...; **j. then** juste à ce moment-là; **j. now** en ce moment; **j. as I was leaving...** juste au moment où je partais...; **I can j. see her as a doctor** je la vois très bien médecin

  (**b**) *(only)* juste; **she's j. a baby** ce n'est qu'un bébé; **it costs j. $10** ça coûte juste 10 dollars

  (**c**) *(barely)* juste; **j. before/after** juste avant/après; **j. over/under $50** à peine plus/moins de 50 dollars; **j. in time** juste à temps; **it's only j. big enough** c'est tout juste assez grand; **they j. caught the train** ils ont eu le train de justesse; **they j. missed the train** ils ont raté le train d'un cheveu

  (**d**) *(recently)* **to have j. done sth** venir de faire qch; **j. yesterday/last year** pas plus tard qu'hier/que l'année dernière

  (**e**) *(simply)* **it was j. wonderful/dreadful!** c'était tout simplement merveilleux/affreux!; **he j. refuses to listen!** il refuse carrément d'écouter!; **j. ask if you need money** si tu as besoin d'argent, tu n'as qu'à demander

  (**f**) *(in threats, exhortations)* **j. (you) try/wait!** essaie/attends un peu pour voir!; **(that's) j. as well!** heureusement!

  (**g**) **j. about** *(almost)* à peu près; **they're j. about the same** ils se valent; **I can j. about manage** j'y arrive tout juste; **to be j. about to do sth** être sur le point de faire qch

justice ['dʒʌstɪs] *n* (**a**) *(power of law)* justice *f*; **to bring sb to j.** traduire qn en justice (**b**) *(fairness)* légitimité *f*; **this photograph doesn't do him j.** cette photo ne le met pas en valeur; **to do j. to a meal** faire honneur à un repas; **to do oneself j.** se montrer sous son meilleur jour (**c**) *(judge)* juge *m*; **j. of the peace** juge *m* de paix

justifiable ['dʒʌstɪfaɪəbəl] *adj* justifié(e), légitime; **j. homicide** légitime défense *f*

justifiably ['dʒʌstɪfaɪəblɪ] *adv* à juste titre

justification [dʒʌstɪfɪ'keɪʃən] *n* justification *f*; **in j. of sth** pour justifier qch

justify ['dʒʌstɪfaɪ] (*pt & pp* **justified**) *vt* (**a**) *(act, behavior)* justifier; **to be justified in doing sth** avoir de bonnes raisons de faire qch (**b**) *Comput & Typ (text)* justifier

justly ['dʒʌstlɪ] *adv (fairly)* avec justice; *(deservedly)* à juste titre

▸**jut out** [dʒʌt] (*pt & pp* **jutted**) **1** *vt sep (chin)* avancer

  2 *vi (of balcony, rock)* faire saillie; **to j. out over sth** surplomber qch; **to j. out into the sea** s'avancer dans la mer

jute [dʒuːt] *n* jute *m*

juvenile ['dʒuːvɪnəl] **1** *n Law* mineur(e) *m,f*

  2 *adj* (**a**) *Law (crime, delinquency)* juvénile; **j. court** tribunal *m* pour enfants; **j. delinquent** jeune délinquant(e) *m,f* (**b**) *Pej (childish)* puéril(e)

juxtapose [dʒʌkstə'pəʊz] *vt* mettre en juxtaposition (**with** avec)

juxtaposition [dʒʌkstəpə'zɪʃən] *n* juxtaposition *f*

K

K, k [keɪ] *n* (**a**) *(letter)* K, k *m inv* (**b**) *(abbr* **thousand, thousand dollars**) **he earns 30K** il gagne 30 000 dollars (**c**) *Comput (abbr* **kilobyte**) KO

Kabul [ˈkɑːbʊl] *n* Kaboul

kaftan [ˈkæftæn] *n* caf(e)tan *m*

kalashnikov [kəˈlæʃnɪkɒv] *n* kalachnikov *m ou f*

kale [keɪl] *n* chou *m* frisé

kaleidoscope [kəˈlaɪdəskəʊp] *n* kaléidoscope *m*

kamikaze [kæmɪˈkɑːzɪ] **1** *n also Fig* kamikaze *m*
2 *adj* kamikaze

Kampuchea [kæmpʊˈtʃɪə] *n Formerly* le Kampuchéa

kangaroo [kæŋgəˈruː] *n* kangourou *m;* **k. court** tribunal *m* irrégulier

kaput [kəˈpʊt] *adj Fam* kaput *inv*

karaoke [kærɪˈəʊkɪ] *n* karaoké *m*

karate [kəˈrɑːtɪ] *n* karaté *m;* **k. chop** coup *m* de karaté

Kashmir [kæʃˈmɪə(r)] *n* Cachemire

Kashmiri [kæʃˈmɪərɪ] **1** *n* (**a**) *(person)* Cachemirien (enne) *m,f* (**b**) *(language)* cachemirien *m*
2 *adj* cachemirien(enne)

Katmandu [kætmænˈduː] *n* Katmandou

kayak [ˈkaɪæk] *n* kayak *m*

Kazak(h)stan [kæzækˈstɑːn] *n* Kazakhstan *m*

KB [keɪˈbiː] *n Comput (abbr* **kilobyte**) Ko *m*

kebab [kəˈbæb] *n* brochette *f;* **shish k.** chiche-kébab *m;* **doner k.** sandwich *m* grec

keel [kiːl] *n (of ship)* quille *f; Fig* **to be on an even k.** être stable
▸**keel over** *vi (of boat)* chavirer; *Fam (of person)* s'écrouler

keen [kiːn] *adj* (**a**) *(enthusiastic)* enthousiaste; *(student)* assidu(e); **to be k. to do sth** avoir très envie de faire qch; **to be k. for sth to happen** tenir beaucoup à ce que qch arrive; **to take a k. interest in sth** s'intéresser de très près à qch (**b**) *(eye, mind, look)* vif (vive); *(price)* compétitif(ive); **to have a k. eye for detail** remarquer jusqu'au moindre détail (**c**) *(intense)* vif (vive); *(remorse)* cuisant(e); *(competition)* intense

keenly [ˈkiːnlɪ] *adv* (**a**) *(enthusiastically)* avec enthousiasme (**b**) *(intensely)* profondément; **to be k. aware of sth** avoir une conscience aiguë de qch; **k. contested** âprement disputé(e)

keep [kiːp] **1** *n* (**a**) **to pay for one's k.** payer sa pension; **to earn one's k.** *(make a living)* gagner sa vie; *(pay one's way)* payer sa pension
(**b**) *(of castle)* donjon *m*
(**c**) *Fam* **for keeps** pour de bon
2 *vt (pt & pp* **kept** [kept]) (**a**) *(retain)* garder; *(store)* ranger; **to k. sth from sb** dissimuler qch à qn; **to k. its shape/color** *(of garment)* ne pas se déformer/déteindre; **to k. sb's attention** retenir l'attention de qn; **k. the change** gardez la monnaie
(**b**) *(maintain)* **to k. a journal** tenir un journal; **to k. order** maintenir l'ordre; **to k. a record of sth** garder une trace écrite de qch; **to k. a secret** garder un secret
(**c**) *(maintain in a certain condition)* **to k. sth secret** garder qch secret; **to k. sb awake** empêcher qn de (s'en)dormir; **to k. sb waiting** faire attendre qn; **she keeps her apartment clean** son appartement est toujours bien tenu
(**d**) *(look after) (poultry, cows)* élever; *(shop)* tenir; *(family, mistress)* entretenir; **a kept woman** une femme entretenue
(**e**) *(detain)* retenir; **what kept you?** pourquoi ce retard ?
(**f**) *(observe)* respecter; *(promise)* tenir; **to k. late hours** se coucher tard; **to k. one's word** tenir parole
3 *vi* (**a**) *(remain)* rester; **to k. well** rester en bonne santé; **to k. quiet** se tenir tranquille; **how are you keeping?** comment allez-vous?
(**b**) *(continue)* **to k. straight on** continuer tout droit; **k. (to the) left/right** serrez à gauche/à droite; **to k. doing sth** ne pas arrêter de faire qch; **to k. smiling** garder le sourire; **to k. going** tenir le coup
(**c**) *(of food)* se conserver; *Fig* **it will k.** *(of problem)* ça peut attendre
▸**keep away 1** *vt sep* **to k. sb away (from sb/sth)** empêcher qn de s'approcher (de qn/qch)
2 *vi* **to k. away from sb/sth** ne pas s'approcher de qn/qch
▸**keep back 1** *vt sep* (**a**) *(crowd, tears)* retenir; **to k. sth back from sb** cacher qch à qn (**b**) *(delay)* retarder
2 *vi (not approach)* ne pas s'approcher
▸**keep down 1** *vt sep* (**a**) *(head)* baisser; **to k. one's voice down** parler moins fort; **to k. the noise down** faire moins de bruit; *Fig* **to k. one's head down** ne pas se faire remarquer; **I can't k. my food down** je vomis tout ce que je mange (**b**) *(repress) (people)* opprimer; *(prices)* empêcher d'augmenter
2 *vi (not stand up)* se tapir
▸**keep from** *vt sep* **to k. sb from doing sth** empêcher qn de faire qch; **to k. sb from his work** empêcher qn de travailler
▸**keep in** *vt sep (pupil)* garder en retenue; **to k. sb in overnight** *(in hospital)* garder qn pour la nuit
▸**keep off 1** *vt sep* **to k. one's hands off sb/sth** ne pas toucher à qn/qch
2 *vt insep* **k. off the grass** *(sign)* Pelouse interdite
3 *vi (stay away)* ne pas intervenir
▸**keep on 1** *vt sep (clothing, employee)* garder; *(lights, TV)* laisser allumé(es); *Fam* **k. your hair on!** on se calme!
2 *vi* continuer; **to k. on doing sth** continuer de faire qch; **to k. on about sth** insister constamment sur qch
▸**keep out 1** *vt sep (not allow to enter)* empêcher d'entrer
2 *vi (stay away from)* **to k. out of sth** éviter qch; **to k. out of sb's way** éviter qn; **to k. out of danger** rester à l'abri du danger; **to k. out of trouble** ne pas s'attirer d'ennuis; **to k. out of an argument** rester en dehors d'une dispute; **k. out** *(sign)* défense d'entrer
▸**keep to 1** *vt sep* (**a**) *(hold)* **to k. sb to a promise** faire tenir une promesse à qn; **to k. sth to a minimum** minimiser qch (**b**) *(not reveal)* **to k. sth to oneself** garder qch pour soi; **to k. oneself to oneself** rester à l'écart
2 *vt insep (promise)* tenir; *(contract, agreement)* respecter; *(subject)* s'en tenir à; **to k. to one's bed** garder le lit
▸**keep up 1** *vt sep* (**a**) *(custom)* conserver; **to k. up the payments** continuer à payer; **to k. it up** *(continue to do well)*

continuer comme ça; **k. up the good work!** continuez à bien travailler; **to k. up appearances** sauver les apparences **(b)** *(keep awake)* empêcher de dormir

2 *vi* **(a)** *(of rain, snow)* continuer **(b)** *(remain level)* tenir le rythme; **to k. up with sb** aller à la même allure que qn; **to k. up with the Joneses** rivaliser de standing avec ses voisins; **to k. up with events** se tenir informé(e) de l'actualité; **to k. up with the times** être à la page

keeper ['ki:pə(r)] *n (in zoo, park, museum)* gardien(enne) *m,f*; *(gamekeeper)* garde-chasse *m*; *Fam (goalkeeper)* goal *m*

keeping ['ki:pɪŋ] *n (a) (care)* garde *f*; **to have sb/sth in one's k.** avoir qn/qch sous sa garde **(b)** *(conformity)* **in k. with** conformément à; **out of k. with** en désaccord avec

keepsake ['ki:pseɪk] *n* souvenir *m*

keg [keg] *n* baril *m*

ken [ken] *n* **to be beyond sb's k.** être en dehors des compétences de qn

kennel ['kenəl] *n (for dogs)* chenil *m*

Kenya ['kenjə, 'ki:njə] *n* Kenya *m*

Kenyan ['kenjən] **1** *n* Kenyan(e) *m,f*
2 *adj* kenyan(e)

kept [kept] *pt & pp of* **keep**

kernel ['kɜ:nəl] *n (of nut)* amande *f*; *(of grain)* grain *m*; *Fig (of problem)* fond *m*, essentiel *m*

kerosene ['kerəsi:n] *n (a) (for lamps, stoves)* pétrole *m* (lampant); **k. lamp** lampe *f* à pétrole **(b)** *(aircraft fuel)* kérosène *m*

kestrel ['kestrəl] *n* faucon *m* crécerelle

ketchup ['ketʃəp] *n* **(tomato) k.** ketchup *m*

kettle ['ketəl] *n* bouilloire *f*; **to put the k. on** mettre l'eau à chauffer; *Fam* **that's a different k. of fish** c'est une autre paire de manches

kettledrum ['ketəldrʌm] *n* timbale *f*

key [ki:] **1** *n* **(a)** *(of door, clock, toy)* clé *f*; *(of piano, typewriter)* touche *f*; *Fig* **the k. to happiness/success** la clé du bonheur/de la réussite **(b)** *(to map)* légende *f*; *(to exercise)* solutions *fpl* **(c)** *(in music)* ton *m*; **in the k. of C** en ut; **to be off k.** *(of singer)* chanter faux; *(of musician)* jouer faux
2 *adj (role, factor, figure)* clé; *(influence, consideration)* capital(e); **k. person** pivot *m*

►**key in** *vt sep (data)* saisir

keyboard ['ki:bɔ:d] *n (of piano, computer)* clavier *m*

keyboarder ['ki:bɔ:də(r)] *n* claviste *mf*, opérateur(trice) *m,f* de saisie

keycard ['ki:kɑ:d] *n* carte *f* magnétique *(servant à ouvrir la porte d'une chambre d'hôtel)*

keyhole ['ki:həʊl] *n* trou *m* de serrure; **k. surgery** chirurgie *f* à incision minimale

keynote ['ki:nəʊt] **1** *n* tonique *f*; *Fig (of speech, approach)* point *m* essentiel
2 *adj (speech)* programme; *(speaker)* principal(e)

keypad ['ki:pæd] *n Comput* pavé *m*

keyring ['ki:rɪŋ] *n* porte-clés *m inv*

keystone ['ki:stəʊn] *n also Fig* clef *f* de voûte

keystroke ['ki:strəʊk] *n Comput* touche *f*

kg *(abbr* **kilogram)** kg

KGB [keɪdʒi:'bi:] *n Formerly* KGB *m*

khaki ['kɑ:kɪ] **1** *n* **(a)** *(color)* kaki *m* **(b)** **khakis** *(pants)* pantalon *m* de treillis
2 *adj* kaki *inv*

Khartoum [kɑ:'tu:m] *n* Khartoum

kHz *(abbr* **kilohertz)** kHz

kibbutz [kɪ'bʊts] *n (pl* **kibbutzim** [kɪbʊt'si:m]) *n* kibboutz *m*

kibosh ['kaɪbɒʃ] *n Fam* **to put the k. on sth** faire tomber qch à l'eau

kick [kɪk] **1** *n* **(a)** *(with foot)* coup *m* de pied; *(of horse)* ruade *f*; *(of gun)* recul *m*; **to give sb/sth a k.** donner un coup de pied à

qn/dans qch; *Fam Fig* **she needs a k. in the backside** elle a besoin d'un bon coup de pied au derrière; *Fig* **that was a k. in the teeth for him** ça lui a fait un sacré coup; **that drink has a real k. to it!** cette boisson est vraiment traître!; **k. boxing** boxe *f* française **(b)** *Fam (thrill)* **to get a k. out of doing sth** prendre son pied à faire qch; **to do sth for kicks** faire qch pour s'amuser

2 *vt* donner un coup/des coups de pied à; *(football)* taper dans; **to get kicked** recevoir un coup/des coups de pied; *Fam Fig* **to k. the bucket** casser sa pipe; *Fig* **to k. a man when he's down** s'acharner sur qn qui a perdu ses moyens; **I could have kicked myself** je me serais donné des gifles; **to k. the habit** *(stop smoking, taking drugs)* arrêter (la drogue)

3 *vi* donner un coup/des coups de pied; *(of horse)* ruer; *(of gun)* reculer; *Fam Fig* **to k. against sth** regimber contre qch

►**kick about, kick around 1** *vt sep (ball)* taper dans; *Fam (idea)* tester; **don't let them k. you around** tu ne devrais pas les laisser te traiter comme ça

2 *vi Fam (hang around)* traîner; **there are plenty of people like that kicking around** des gens comme ça, ce n'est pas ce qui manque

►**kick in 1** *vt sep (door)* enfoncer à coups de pied; *Fam* **to k. sb's head in** casser la tête à qn

2 *vi Fam* entrer en action; **the painkillers haven't kicked in yet** les analgésiques n'ont pas encore fait effet

►**kick off** *vi (in football)* donner le coup d'envoi; *Fam Fig (in meeting, debate)* démarrer

►**kick out** *vt sep Fam* mettre à la porte

►**kick up** *vt sep Fam* **to k. up a fuss** faire tout un plat *ou* toute une histoire; **to k. up a row** *or* **a racket** faire du boucan

kickback ['kɪkbæk] *n Fam (payment)* pot-de-vin *m*

kickoff ['kɪkɒf] *n (in football)* coup *m* d'envoi

kick-start ['kɪkstɑ:t] **1** *n (on motorcycle)* kick *m*
2 *vt (motorcycle)* démarrer au kick; *Fig (economy)* donner un sérieux coup de pouce à

kid [kɪd] **1** *n* **(a)** *Fam (child)* gamin(e) *m,f*, gosse *mf*; **my k. brother** mon petit frère; **it's k.'s stuff** *(easy)* c'est un jeu d'enfant; *(childish)* c'est bon pour les gosses **(b)** *(young goat)* chevreau *m*; *(female)* chevrette *f*; *(skin)* chevreau *m*; **k. gloves** gants *mpl* en chevreau; *Fig* **to handle sb with k. gloves** prendre des gants avec qn

2 *vt (pt & pp* **kidded)** *Fam (fool)* faire marcher; **to k. oneself** se faire des illusions; **who do you think you're kidding?** tu te fous de moi?

3 *vi* **to be kidding** plaisanter; **no kidding!** sans blague!

kidnap ['kɪdnæp] *vt (pt & pp* **kidnaped** *or* **kidnapped)** kidnapper, enlever

kidnap(p)er ['kɪdnæpə(r)] *n* ravisseur(euse) *m,f*, kidnappeur(euse) *m,f*

kidnap(p)ing ['kɪdnæpɪŋ] *n* enlèvement *m*, kidnapping *m*

kidney ['kɪdnɪ] *(pl* **kidneys)** *n (of person)* rein *m*; *(meat)* rognon *m*; **k. bean** haricot *m* rouge; **k. donor** donneur(euse) *m,f* de rein; **k. machine** rein artificiel

kill [kɪl] **1** *n (in hunting) (action)* mise *f* à mort; *(animals killed)* tableau *m* de chasse; **to be in at the k.** assister à la mise à mort; *Fig* assister au dénouement

2 *vt* **(a)** *(person, animal)* tuer; **to k. oneself** se tuer; *Fam* **to k. oneself laughing** mourir de rire; *Ironic* **don't k. yourself!** surtout, ne te surmène pas!; *Fam* **this one'll k. you** *(of joke)* ça va te faire mourir de rire; **to k. two birds with one stone** faire d'une pierre deux coups; *Fam* **my feet/these shoes are killing me** mes pieds/ces chaussures me font un mal de chien **(b)** *Fig (friendship)* détruire; *(sound)* amortir; *(pain)* calmer; *(chances)* anéantir; *Journ* **to k. a story** retirer une information; **to k. time** tuer le temps

3 *vi* tuer; **to shoot to k.** tirer dans l'intention de tuer; *Rel* **thou shalt not k.** tu ne tueras point

▶**kill off** *vt sep (people)* tuer; *(character in movie, novel)* faire mourir; *Fig (hope)* anéantir

killer ['kɪlə(r)] *n* tueur(euse) *m,f*; **he knew his k.** il connaissait son meurtrier; *Fam Fig* **those steps were a k.!** ces escaliers m'ont tué!; *Fam Fig* **this one's a k.** *(joke)* celle-ci est à mourir de rire; **k. (disease)** maladie *f* meurtrière; *Fig* **to have the k. instinct** être impitoyable; **k. whale** épaulard *m*

killing ['kɪlɪŋ] **1** *n (of person)* meurtre *m*; *(of animals)* destruction *f*; *Fam* **to make a k.** faire un bénéfice énorme
  2 *adj Fam (exhausting)* tuant(e); *(very amusing)* tordant(e)

killjoy ['kɪldʒɔɪ] *n* rabat-joie *m inv*

kiln [kɪln] *n* four *m*

kilo ['kiːləʊ] *(pl* **kilos**) *n* kilo *m*

kilobyte ['kɪləbaɪt] *n Comput* kilo-octet *m*

kilogram ['kɪləgræm] *n* kilogramme *m*

kilohertz ['kɪləʊhɜːts] *(pl* **kilohertz**) *n* kilohertz *m*

kilometer [kɪ'lɒmɪtə(r)] *n* kilomètre *m*

kilowatt ['kɪləwɒt] *n* kilowatt *m*; **k.-hour** kilowatt-heure *m*

kilt [kɪlt] *n* kilt *m*

kilter ['kɪltə(r)] *n Fam* **out of k.** *(of machine part)* déréglé(e) (**with** par rapport à); *(of budget)* déséquilibré(e)

kimono [kɪ'məʊnəʊ] *(pl* **kimonos**) *n* kimono *m*

kin [kɪn] *n Formal* parents *mpl*

kind¹ [kaɪnd] *n* (**a**) *(sort)* genre *m*, espèce *f*; **all kinds of...** toutes sortes de...; **something of the k.** quelque chose comme ça, quelque chose de ce genre; **I said nothing of the k.!** je n'ai jamais dit ça!; **she's really boring – she's nothing of the k.!** elle est vraiment ennuyeuse – mais pas du tout!; **in a k. of way** d'une certaine manière; **well, it's coffee of a k. I suppose** je suppose qu'on peut appeler ça du café; **we're two of a k.** nous sommes pareils; **it's the only one of its k.** c'est le seul de ce genre; **he's that k. of person** il est comme ça; **this is my k. of party!** voilà le genre de soirée que j'aime!; **this k. of thing** ce genre de chose (**b**) **in k.** *(payment)* en nature (**c**) *Fam* **you look k. of tired** tu as l'air un peu fatigué!; **I k. of expected this** je m'y attendais un peu; **do you like it? – k. of** ça te plaît? – oui, plus ou moins; **it was a k. of saucer-shaped thing** c'était quelque chose qui ressemblait à une soucoupe

kind² [kaɪnd] *adj* gentil(ille); **to be k. to sb** être gentil avec qn; *Formal* **would you be k. enough to** *or* **so k. as to...?** auriez-vous la bonté de...?; **you are really too k.** vous êtes vraiment trop aimable; **k. to the skin** *(of detergent, soap)* qui n'irrite pas la peau; **by k. permission of...** avec l'aimable autorisation de...

kinda ['kaɪndə] *Fam* = **kind of**

kindergarten ['kɪndəgɑːtən] *n* jardin *m* d'enfants

kind-hearted ['kaɪnd'hɑːtɪd] *adj (person)* qui a bon cœur; *(action)* généreux(euse)

kindle ['kɪndəl] *vt (flame)* allumer; *Fig (emotions)* éveiller

kindling ['kɪndlɪŋ] *n* petit bois *m*

kindly ['kaɪndlɪ] **1** *adv* gentiment; **to speak k. of sb** dire du bien de qn; *Formal* **(would you) k. be quiet!** voudriez-vous avoir la bonté de vous taire!; **she didn't take k. to being criticized** elle n'a pas apprécié qu'on la critique
  2 *adj (person)* gentil(ille); *(tone, advice)* bienveillant(e)

kindness ['kaɪndnɪs] *n* gentillesse *f*; **to do sth out of the k. of one's heart** faire qch par bonté d'âme; **to do sb a k.** rendre service à qn

kindred ['kɪndrɪd] *adj* du même genre, de la même nature; **we are k. spirits** c'est mon alter ego

kinetic [kɪ'netɪk] *adj* cinétique

king [kɪŋ] *n* roi *m*; **K. Charles the First** le roi Charles Iᵉʳ; *Bible* **the three kings** les Rois mages; **the k. of the beasts** le roi des animaux; *Fig* **to live like a k.** vivre en grand seigneur; **the K.'s English** le bon anglais

kingdom ['kɪŋdəm] *n* royaume *m*; **the k. of heaven** le royaume des cieux; **the animal/plant k.** le règne animal/

végétal; *Fam* **until** *or* **till k. come** jusqu'à la saint-glinglin; *Fam* **to send sb to k. come** envoyer qn ad patres

kingfisher ['kɪŋfɪʃə(r)] *n* martin-pêcheur *m*

kingpin ['kɪŋpɪn] *n Fig (of organization, company)* cheville *f* ouvrière

king-size ['kɪŋsaɪz], **king-sized** ['kɪŋsaɪzd] *adj* (**a**) *(cigarette)* long (longue); **a k. bed** = un lit d'1 m 95 de large (**b**) *Fam (headache, problem)* sacré(e)

kink [kɪŋk] *n (in wire, rope)* boucle *f*; *(in hair)* frisette *f*; *(in character)* bizarrerie *f*

kinky ['kɪŋkɪ] *adj* (**a**) *(hair)* frisotté(e) (**b**) *Fam (person) (sexually)* qui a des goûts sexuels bizarres; *(eccentric)* extravagant(e); *(garment)* sexy *inv*; *(behavior, practice)* pervers(e)

kinship ['kɪnʃɪp] *n* parenté *f*

kinsman ['kɪnzmən] *n Lit* parent *m*

kinswoman ['kɪnzwʊmən] *n Lit* parente *f*

kiosk ['kiːɒsk] *n* kiosque *m*

kipper ['kɪpə(r)] *n* hareng *m* salé et fumé

Kirg(h)izia [kɜː'giːzɪə], **Kirg(h)izstan** [kɜːgɪz'stæn] *n* le Kirghizistan

kiss [kɪs] **1** *n* baiser *m*; **to give sb a k.** donner un baiser à qn; **to give sb the k. of life** faire du bouche-à-bouche à qn; *Fig* **to be the k. of death for sth** porter un coup fatal à qch
  2 *vt* embrasser; **to k. sb goodbye** dire au revoir à qn en l'embrassant; **he kissed her on the mouth/hand** il l'a embrassée sur la bouche/lui a baisé la main; *Fig* **you can k. your promotion goodbye** tu peux dire adieu à ta promotion
  3 *vi* s'embrasser; **to k. and make up** se réconcilier; **to k. and tell** dévoiler à la presse ses secrets d'alcôve *(impliquant généralement une personne célèbre)*

kissogram ['kɪsəgræm] *n* = service permettant de faire délivrer un message, un poème, une chanson etc, souvent grivois, accompagnés d'un baiser, pour une occasion particulière

kit [kɪt] *n (for assembly)* **(model) k.** maquette *f*; **to make sth from a k.** faire qch à partir de pièces détachées; **in k. form** en kit

kitbag ['kɪtbæg] *n* sac *m* de marin; *Mil* sac à paquetage

kitchen ['kɪtʃɪn] *n* cuisine *f*; **k. knife** couteau *m* de cuisine; **k. sink** évier *m*; *Fam* **to take everything but the k. sink** emporter des tonnes de choses; *(of thief)* ne laisser que les murs; **k. unit** élément *m* de cuisine

kitchenette [kɪtʃɪ'net] *n* coin-cuisine *m*, kitchenette *f*, *Offic* cuisinette *f*

kitchenware ['kɪtʃɪnweə(r)] *n* vaisselle *f* et ustensiles *mpl* de cuisine

kite [kaɪt] *n* (**a**) *(toy)* cerf-volant *m*; **to fly a k.** faire voler un cerf-volant; *Fig* lancer un ballon d'essai; *Fam* **go fly a k.!** va voir là-bas si j'y suis!; *Fam* **to be as high as a k.** *(excited)* être excité(e) comme une puce; *(on drugs)* planer (**b**) *(bird)* milan *m*

kith [kɪθ] *n Lit* **k. and kin** parents *mpl* et amis *mpl*

kitsch [kɪtʃ] *n* kitsch *m*

kitten ['kɪtən] *n* chaton *m*

kitty ['kɪtɪ] *(pl* **kitties**) *n* (**a**) *Fam (cat)* minou *m* (**b**) *(for bills, in cards)* cagnotte *f*

kiwi ['kiːwiː] *n* (**a**) *(bird)* kiwi *m*; **k. fruit** kiwi (**b**) *Fam* **K.** *(New Zealander)* Néo-Zélandais(e) *m,f*

kleptomania [kleptə'meɪnɪə] *n* kleptomanie *f*

kleptomaniac [kleptə'meɪnɪæk] *n* kleptomane *mf*

km *(abbr* **kilometer***)* km

kmph *(abbr* **kilometers per hour***)* km/h

knack [næk] *n* talent *m*; *(for manual activity)* tour *m* de main; **to have the k. of** *or* **a k. for doing sth** avoir un don pour faire qch; *Ironic* avoir le don de faire qch; **to get the k. (of doing sth)** attraper le tour de main *(pour faire qch)*

knapsack ['næpsæk] *n* sac *m* à dos

knave [neɪv] *n* (**a**) *(in cards)* valet *m* (**b**) *Lit (scoundrel)* coquin *m*, fripon *m*

knead [ni:d] *vt (dough)* pétrir; *(muscles)* masser

knee [ni:] **1** *n* genou *m*; **to go down on one's knees** s'agenouiller; *Fig* **to bring sb to his knees** obliger qn à capituler
2 *vt (hit with knee)* donner un coup de genou à

kneecap ['ni:kæp] **1** *n* rotule *f*
2 *vt (pt & pp* **kneecapped)** tirer dans les rotules à

knee-deep ['ni:'di:p] *adj* **to be k. in sth** *(in water, snow)* être enfoncé(e) jusqu'aux genoux dans qch; *Fig (in problems)* avoir qch jusqu'au cou; *(in work)* être débordé(e) de qch

knee-high ['ni:'haɪ] *adj* **to be k.** *(of water, snow)* arriver à hauteur du genou; *Fam* **when I was k. to a grasshopper** quand j'étais haut comme trois pommes

kneejerk ['ni:dʒɜ:k] *adj (reaction, response)* instinctif(ive)

kneel [ni:l] *(pt & pp* **knelt** [nelt]) *vi* s'agenouiller, se mettre à genoux (**before/to** devant)

knee-length ['ni:leŋθ] *adj (skirt)* qui descend jusqu'aux genoux; *(boots, socks)* qui monte jusqu'aux genoux

knell [nel] *n Lit* glas *m*; **to toll the k. for sb** signer l'arrêt de mort de qn; **to toll the k. for sth** sonner le glas de qch

knelt [nelt] *pt & pp of* **kneel**

knew [nju:] *pt of* **know**

knickerbockers ['nɪkəbɒkəz] *npl* knickers *mpl*

knickers ['nɪkəz] *npl (breeches)* knickers *mpl*

knick-knack ['nɪknæk] *n Fam* babiole *f*

knife [naɪf] **1** *n (pl* **knives** [naɪvz]) couteau *m*; **k. and fork** couvert *m*; *Fig* **the knives are out** ils sont/nous sommes/*etc.* à couteaux tirés *ou* en guerre ouverte; **k. sharpener** aiguisoir *m*
2 *vt (stab)* donner un coup de couteau à, poignarder

knife-edge ['naɪfedʒ] *n Fig* **to be on a k.** *(of person)* être sur les nerfs; **to be balanced on a k.** *(of situation, game)* ne tenir qu'à un fil

knife-point ['naɪfpɔɪnt] *n* **at k.** sous la menace d'un couteau

knifing ['naɪfɪŋ] *n* agression *f* au couteau

knight [naɪt] **1** *n* chevalier *m*; *(in chess)* cavalier *m*
2 *vt* faire chevalier

knighthood ['naɪthʊd] *n (title)* **to be given a k.** être fait chevalier

knit [nɪt] *(pt & pp* **knitted** *or* **knit) 1** *vt (sweater)* tricoter; **to k. one's brows** froncer les sourcils
2 *vi* tricoter, faire du tricot

▸**knit together** *vi (of broken bones)* se ressouder

knitted ['nɪtəd] *adj* tricoté(e)

knitting ['nɪtɪŋ] *n (item produced)* tricot *m*; **to do some k.** tricoter; **k. machine** machine *f* à tricoter; **k. needle** aiguille *f* à tricoter

knitwear ['nɪtweə(r)] *n* lainages *mpl*

knives [naɪvz] *pl of* **knife**

knob [nɒb] *n (on cane)* pommeau *m*; *(on banisters)* pomme *f*; *(on drawer, door)* poignée *f*; *(on radio)* bouton *m*

knobbly ['nɒblɪ], **knobby** ['nɒbɪ] *adj* couvert(e) de bosses; *(tree)* noueux(euse); **k. knees** genoux *mpl* cagneux

knock [nɒk] *n (blow)* coup *m*; **there was a k. at the door** on frappa à la porte
2 *vt* **(a)** *(hit)* frapper, heurter; **to k. sb to the ground** faire tomber qn en le frappant; **to k. sb unconscious** assommer qn; **to k. one's head against sth** se cogner la tête contre qch; **to k. a hole in sth** faire un trou dans qch; **to k. holes in an argument** démolir un argument; **to k. some sense into sb** apprendre à vivre à qn; *Fig* **to k. sb into shape** mettre qn au pas **(b)** *Fam (criticize)* débiner; **don't k. it until you've tried it** il faut essayer avant de critiquer
3 *vi* **(a)** *(hit)* frapper; **to k. at the door** frapper à la porte; **k. against/on sth** heurter qch; **his knees were knocking** ses genoux s'entrechoquaient **(b)** *(of engine)* cogner

▸**knock about, knock around 1** *vt sep* **(a)** *(mistreat)* malmener; *(beat up)* battre **(b)** *Fam (idea, suggestion)* discuter de

2 *vi Fam (hang around)* traîner; **to k. about with sb** fréquenter qn
3 *vt insep Fam (spend time in)* **to k. about the world** rouler sa bosse; **she spent a year knocking about Europe** elle a passé une année à se balader en Europe

▸**knock back** *vt sep Fam (drink)* s'envoyer

▸**knock down** *vt sep* **(a)** *(pedestrian)* renverser **(b)** *(building)* abattre **(c)** *(price)* baisser

▸**knock off 1** *vt sep* **(a)** *(cause to fall off)* faire tomber; **he was knocked off his bike by a car** une voiture a heurté son vélo et il est tombé; *Fam* **to k. sb's head** *or* **block off** casser la figure à qn; *Fam* **to k. sth off the price** baisser un peu le prix **(b)** *Fam (kill)* zigouiller **(c)** *Fam* **k. it off!** *(stop it)* ça suffit!, arrête! **(d)** *Fam (produce quickly)* expédier
2 *vi Fam (finish work)* cesser le travail, finir

▸**knock out** *vt sep* **(a)** *(make unconscious)* mettre K.-O.; *Fam* **to k. sb's brains** *or* **teeth out** arranger le portrait à qn **(b)** *(eliminate from competition)* éliminer

▸**knock over** *vt sep* faire tomber

▸**knock up** *vt sep very Fam (make pregnant)* mettre en cloque

knockdown price ['nɒkdaʊn'praɪs] *n Fam* **at a k.** à très bas prix

knocker ['nɒkə(r)] *n* **(a)** *(on door)* heurtoir *m* **(b)** *very Fam* **knockers** *(breasts)* nichons *mpl*

knocking ['nɒkɪŋ] *n (at door)* coups *mpl*; *(of engine)* cognement *m*

knock-kneed ['nɒk'ni:d] *adj* **to be k.** avoir les genoux en dedans

knockoff ['nɒkɒf] *n (copy)* imitation *f*

knock-on effect ['nɒkɒn'fekt] *n* répercussions *fpl* en chaîne

knockout ['nɒkaʊt] **1** *n* **(a)** *(in boxing)* knock-out *m inv*; *Fig* coup *m* de grâce **(b)** *Fam* **he's/she's a k.** *(attractive)* il/elle est canon
2 *adj* **(a)** **k. blow** *(in boxing)* coup *m* qui provoque un K.-O.; *Fig* coup de grâce; *Fig* **to deliver the k. blow** donner le coup de grâce **(b)** **k. competition** compétition *f* avec épreuves éliminatoires

knot [nɒt] **1** *n* **(a)** *(in general)* nœud *m*; **to tie/to untie a k.** faire/défaire un nœud; *Fam Fig* **to tie the k.** *(get married)* se marier **(b)** *Naut (unit of speed)* nœud *m* **(c)** *(group of people)* petit groupe *m*
2 *vt (pt & pp* **knotted)** *(rope, string)* nouer

knotty ['nɒtɪ] *adj (problem)* épineux(euse)

know [nəʊ] **1** *n Fam* **to be in the k.** être au courant
2 *vt (pt* **knew** [nju:], *pp* **known** [nəʊn]) **(a)** *(be acquainted with)* connaître; **to k. sb** apprendre à connaître qn; **when I first knew her** quand j'ai fait sa connaissance; **I've never known anything like it** je n'ai jamais rien vu de tel; **I k. her to say hello to** nous nous saluons, c'est tout; **knowing him...** le connaissant...
(b) *(have knowledge of)* savoir; **she thinks she knows all the answers** elle croit avoir réponse à tout; **to k. Spanish** connaître l'espagnol; **to k. a lot/a little about sth** bien s'y connaître/s'y connaître un peu en qch; **she knows what she is talking about** elle sait de quoi elle parle; **to k. how to do sth** savoir faire qch; *Fam* **to k. a thing or two** être malin(igne); **to k. one's own mind** savoir ce que l'on veut; **heaven** *or* **God knows!** Dieu seul le sait!
(c) *(recognize)* reconnaître (**by** à); *(distinguish)* distinguer (**from** de); **to k. right from wrong** savoir faire la distinction entre le bien et le mal
3 *vi* savoir; **to k. about sth** être au courant de qch; **to get to k. of sth** apprendre qch; **as far as I k.** (pour) autant que je sache; **how should I k.?** comment le saurais-je?; **you never k.** on ne sait jamais; **not that I k. of** pas que je sache; **to k. better than to do sth** savoir qu'il ne faut pas faire qch; **you k....** tu sais...

know-how ['nəʊhaʊ] *n Fam* savoir-faire *m*; *(technical)* know-how *m*

knowing ['nəʊɪŋ] **1** *n* there's no k. c'est impossible à savoir **2** *adj (look, smile)* entendu(e), complice

know-it-all ['nəʊɪtɔːl] *n Fam* monsieur *m*/madame *f* je-sais-tout

knowledge ['nɒlɪdʒ] *n* **(a)** *(of fact)* connaissance *f*; **(not) to my k.** (pas) à ma connaissance; **to have no k. of sth** ignorer qch; **to have full k. of sth** avoir pleine connaissance de qch; **it is common k. that...** c'est un fait notoire que...; *Formal* **it has recently come to our k. that...** il a été récemment porté à notre connaissance que... **(b)** *(learning)* savoir *m*, connaissances *fpl*; *Prov* **k. is power** savoir c'est pouvoir; *Comput* **k.-based system** système *m* basé sur les connaissances; **k. economy** économie *f* de la connaissance

knowledgeable ['nɒlɪdʒəbəl] *adj* savant(e); **to be k. about sth** bien s'y connaître en qch

known [nəʊn] **1** *adj* connu(e); *(notorious)* notoire **2** *pp of* **know**

knuckle ['nʌkəl] *n* articulation *f ou* jointure *f* (du doigt)

▸**knuckle down** *vi Fam* se mettre au boulot; **to k. down to sth** se mettre à qch

▸**knuckle under** *vi Fam* mettre les pouces

knuckle-duster ['nʌkəldʌstə(r)] *n* coup-de-poing *m* américain

KO ['keɪ'əʊ] *Fam* **1** *n (pl* KO's ['keɪ'əʊz]) *(in boxing)* K.-O. *m* **2** *vt (pt & pp* KO'd ['keɪ'əʊd]) *(in boxing)* mettre K.-O.

koala [kəʊ'ɑːlə] *n* **k. (bear)** koala *m*

kopeck ['kəʊpek] *n* kopeck *m*

Koran [kə'rɑːn] *n* **the K.** le Coran

Koranic [kə'rænɪk] *adj* coranique

Korea [kə'rɪə] *n* la Corée; **North/South K.** la Corée du Nord/du Sud

Korean [kə'rɪən] **1** *n* **(a)** *(person)* Coréen(enne) *m,f* **(b)** *(language)* coréen *m* **2** *adj* coréen(enne); **the K. War** la guerre de Corée

kosher ['kəʊʃə(r)] *adj* **(a)** *(in Judaism)* casher *inv*, kasher *inv* **(b)** *Fam (legitimate)* réglo *inv*

Kosovan ['kɒsəvən] **1** *n* Kosovar *mf* **2** *adj* kosovar(e)

Kosovo ['kɒsəvəʊ] *n* le Kosovo

kowtow ['kaʊ'taʊ] *vi* **to k. to sb** faire des courbettes devant qn

Kraut [kraʊt] *n very Fam* Boche *mf*, = terme injurieux désignant un Allemand

Kremlin ['kremlɪn] *n* **the K.** le Kremlin

krona ['krəʊnə] *(pl* **kronor** ['krəʊnɔː(r)]) *n* couronne *f*

krone ['krəʊnə] *(pl* **kroner** ['krəʊnə(r)]) *n* couronne *f*

kudos ['kjuːdɒs] *n (prestige)* prestige *m*; *(fame)* célébrité *f*

Kurd [kɜːd] **1** *n* Kurde *mf* **2** *adj* kurde

Kurdish ['kɜːdɪʃ] **1** *n (language)* kurde *m* **2** *adj* kurde

Kurdistan [kɜːdɪ'stæn] *n* le Kurdistan

Kuwait [kʊ'weɪt] *n* le Koweït

Kuwaiti [kʊ'weɪtɪ] **1** *n* Koweïtien(enne) *m,f* **2** *adj* koweïtien(enne)

kW *(abbr* **kilowatt**) kW

L

L, l [el] *n (letter)* L, l *m inv*
LA [el'eɪ] *n (abbr* **Los Angeles***)* Los Angeles
lab [læb] *n Fam (abbr* **laboratory***)* labo *m*
label ['leɪbəl] **1** *n* (**a**) *also Fig* étiquette *f* (**b**) *(of record company)* label *m*
  2 *vt also Fig* étiqueter; *Fig* **to l. sb a liar** qualifier qn de menteur(euse)
labor ['leɪbə(r)] **1** *n* (**a**) *(work)* labeur *m*; **l. camp** camp *m* de travail (**b**) *(workers)* main-d'œuvre *f*; **l. costs** coût *m* de la main-d'œuvre; **L. Day** fête *f* du travail *(aux États-Unis, célébrée le premiere lundi de septembre)*; **l. dispute** conflit *m* du travail; **l. force** effectifs *mpl*; **l. market** marché *m* du travail; **l. shortage** pénurie *f* de main-d'œuvre (**c**) *(task)* effort *m*; **to do sth as a l. of love** faire qch pour le plaisir (**d**) *(childbirth)* travail *m*; **to be in l.** être en travail; **l. pains** douleurs *fpl* de l'accouchement
  2 *vt* **to l. a point** s'étendre sur un sujet
  3 *vi* (**a**) *(of person)* peiner (**over** sur); **to l. in vain** s'échiner en vain; **to be laboring under a misapprehension** être dans l'erreur (**b**) *(of engine)* peiner
laboratory ['læbrətɒrɪ] *(pl* **laboratories***) n* laboratoire *m*; **l. assistant** laborantin(e) *m,f*
labored ['leɪbəd] *adj* laborieux(euse); *(breathing)* pénible, difficile
laborer ['leɪbərə(r)] *n* manœuvre *m*; *(on farm)* ouvrier(ère) *m,f* agricole
labor-intensive [leɪbərɪn'tensɪv] *adj* qui demande une main-d'œuvre importante
laborious [lə'bɔːrɪəs] *adj (work)* pénible, fatigant(e); *(explanation)* laborieux(euse)
laboriously [lə'bɔːrɪəslɪ] *adv* laborieusement
labor-saving ['leɪbəseɪvɪŋ] *adj* qui simplifie la tâche
Labour ['leɪbə(r)] *n Pol* **the L. Party** *(in Great Britain)* le parti travailliste, les travaillistes *mpl*
labrador ['læbrədɔː(r)] *n* labrador *m*
laburnum [lə'bɜːnəm] *n* cytise *m*
labyrinth ['læbərɪnθ] *n* labyrinthe *m*
labyrinthine [læbe'rɪnθaɪn] *adj Archit* en labyrinthe; *Fig* labyrinthique
lace [leɪs] **1** *n* (**a**) *(cloth)* dentelle *f*; **l. curtain** rideau *m* en *ou* de dentelle (**b**) *(of shoe)* lacet *m*
  2 *vt* (**a**) *(shoes)* **to l. (up)** lacer (**b**) *(drink)* ajouter de l'alcool à; *Fig (story)* entremêler (**with** de); **to l. a drink with sth** ajouter qch dans une boisson
lacerate ['læsəreɪt] *vt* lacérer
laceration [læsə'reɪʃən] *n* lacération *f*
lace-up ['leɪsʌp] **1** *n (shoe)* chaussure *f* à lacets
  2 *adj (shoe)* à lacets
lachrymose ['lækrɪməʊs] *adj Lit* larmoyant(e)
lack [læk] **1** *n* manque *m* (**of** de); **for l. of...** faute de...; **there's no l. of volunteers** ce ne sont pas les volontaires qui manquent
  2 *vt* manquer de
  3 *vi* **to be lacking in sth** manquer de qch

lackadaisical [lækə'deɪzɪkəl] *adj* désinvolte
lackey ['lækɪ] *(pl* **lackeys***) n Pej* larbin *m*
lackluster ['læklʌstə(r)] *adj* terne
laconic [lə'kɒnɪk] *adj* laconique
lacquer ['lækə(r)] **1** *n* laque *f*
  2 *vt* laquer
lacrosse [lə'krɒs] *n Sport* crosse *f*
lacuna [lə'kjuːnə] *(pl* **lacunae** [lə'kjuːniː] *or* **lacunas***) n* lacune *f*
lad [læd] *n Fam (young man)* jeune gars *m*; *(boy)* garçon *m*; **he's a big l.** c'est un grand gaillard
ladder ['lædə(r)] *n* échelle *f*; **the social l.** l'échelle sociale; *Fig* **to get one's foot on the l.** mettre un pied à l'étrier; *Fig* **to reach the top of the l.** atteindre le sommet de l'échelle
laden ['leɪdən] *adj* chargé(e) (**with** de)
ladle ['leɪdəl] **1** *n* louche *f*
  2 *vt (soup)* servir (à la louche)
▸**ladle out** *vt sep (soup)* servir (à la louche); *Fig* **to l. out advice/praise** distribuer les conseils/les compliments
lady ['leɪdɪ] *(pl* **ladies***) n* (**a**) *(woman)* dame *f*; **a young l.** *(unmarried)* une jeune fille; *(married)* une jeune dame; **the l. of the house** la maîtresse de maison; **she's no l.** elle n'a aucune classe; **ladies and gentlemen!** mesdames et messieurs!; **ladies' man** homme *m* à femmes; **ladies' (room)** toilettes *fpl* (des dames); **l. friend** amie *f* (**b**) **Our L.** Notre-Dame *f* (**c**) *(title)* **L. Browne** lady Browne *(titre de noblesse féminin)*; **l. of the manor** châtelaine *f*; **my L.** Madame la Marquise/la Baronne*/etc*; **L. Luck** la chance
ladybug ['leɪdɪbʌg] *n* coccinelle *f*
lady-in-waiting ['leɪdɪɪn'weɪtɪŋ] *(pl* **ladies-in-waiting***) n* dame *f* d'honneur
lady-killer ['leɪdɪkɪlə(r)] *n Fam* bourreau *m* des cœurs
ladylike ['leɪdɪlaɪk] *adj (woman)* comme il faut; *(air, behavior)* distingué(e)
ladyship ['leɪdɪʃɪp] *n also Ironic* **Her/Your L.** madame
lag [læg] **1** *n (gap)* décalage *m*
  2 *vt (pt & pp* **lagged***) (pipes, boiler)* isoler
  3 *vi (of person, economy)* **to l. behind** être à la traîne; **to l. behind sb/sth** être à la traîne derrière qn/qch
lager ['lɑːgə(r)] *n* bière *f* blonde; *Fam* **l. lout** = voyou imbibé de bière
laggard ['lægəd] *n* traînard(e) *m,f*
lagoon [lə'guːn] *n* lagune *f*; *(of atoll)* lagon *m*
laid [leɪd] *pt & pp of* **lay²**
laid-back [leɪd'bæk] *adj Fam* cool *inv*, relax *inv*
lain [leɪn] *pp of* **lie²**
lair [leə(r)] *n* repaire *m*
laissez-faire [leseɪ'feə(r)] **1** *n* laisser-faire *m*
  2 *adj* de laisser-faire
laity ['leɪɪtɪ] *n* **the l.** les laïques *mpl*
lake [leɪk] *n* lac *m*; **L. Geneva** le lac de Genève, le lac Léman; **L. Superior** le lac Supérieur; **the L. District** la région des lacs *(dans le nord-ouest de l'Angleterre)*

lamb [læm] *n* agneau *m*; **poor l.!** pauvre biquet!; **like lambs to the slaughter** comme des veaux que l'on mène à l'abattoir; **l. chop** côtelette *f* d'agneau

lambast, lambaste [læm'bæst] *vt* fustiger

lambing ['læmɪŋ] *n* agnelage *m*

lambskin ['læmskɪn] *n* peau *f* d'agneau

lambswool ['læmswʊl] **1** *n* lambswool *m*
2 *adj* en lambswool

lame [leɪm] **1** *adj* (**a**) *(person, horse)* boiteux(euse); *Fig (excuse)* bancal(e); *(plot, argument)* boiteux; **to be l.** boiter; **to go l.** se mettre à boiter; *Fig* **l. duck** canard *m* boiteux (**c**) *Fam (stupid)* cloche, nouille
2 *vt* rendre boiteux(euse)

lamé ['lɑːmeɪ] *n* lamé *m*; **a l. dress** une robe en lamé

lamely ['leɪmlɪ] *adv* maladroitement

lament [lə'ment] **1** *n* lamentation *f*; *Mus* complainte *f*
2 *vt* se lamenter sur; **the late lamented Mr Jones** le regretté M. Jones
3 *vi* se lamenter (**over** sur)

lamentable ['læməntəbəl] *adj* lamentable; *(decision, loss)* déplorable

lamentably ['læməntəblɪ] *adv* lamentablement

lamentation [læmən'teɪʃən] *n* lamentation *f*

laminate ['læmɪneɪt] *n* stratifié *m*

laminated ['læmɪneɪtəd] *adj* (**a**) *(glass)* feuilleté(e); *(wood, plastic)* stratifié(e) (**b**) *(paper, identity card)* plastifié(e)

lamp [læmp] *n* lampe *f*

lamplight ['læmplaɪt] *n* **by l.** à la lumière d'une lampe

lampoon [læm'puːn] **1** *n* pamphlet *m*
2 *vt* brocarder

lamppost ['læmppəʊst] *n* réverbère *m*

lamprey ['læmprɪ] *(pl* **lampreys***)* *n* lamproie *f*

lampshade ['læmpʃeɪd] *n* abat-jour *m inv*

lampstand ['læmpstænd] *n* pied *m* de lampe

LAN [eleɪ'en] *n Comput (abbr* **local area network***)* réseau *m* local

lance [lɑːns] **1** *n (weapon)* lance *f*
2 *vt (abscess)* percer, inciser

lancer ['lɑːnsə(r)] *n (soldier)* lancier *m*

lancet ['lɑːnsɪt] *n* lancette *f*

land [lænd] **1** *n* (**a**) *(ground, earth)* terre *f*; **on l.** sur terre; **to live off the l.** vivre du produit de la terre; **to be in the l. of the living** être toujours de ce monde; *Mil* **l. forces** armée *f* de terre; **l. reclamation** mise *f* en valeur des sols; **l. reform** réforme *f* agraire
(**b**) *(property)* terres *fpl*; **a piece of l.** *(for farming)* un lopin de terre; *(for building)* un terrain (à bâtir)
(**c**) *Lit or Formal (nation)* pays *m*; **distant lands** pays lointains
2 *vt* (**a**) *(passengers, cargo)* débarquer
(**b**) *(plane)* poser
(**c**) *(fish)* sortir de l'eau
(**d**) *Fam (job, prize)* décrocher
(**e**) *Fam (put)* **to l. sb in prison/court** mener qn en prison/au tribunal; **to l. sb in trouble** attirer des ennuis à qn
(**f**) *Fam* **to be landed with sth** rester avec qch sur les bras; **I got landed with doing the dishes** c'est moi qui ai dû me taper la vaisselle
(**g**) *Fam (hit)* **to l. sb one** en coller une à qn
3 *vi (of plane)* atterrir; *(of gymnast)* se réceptionner; *Fig* **to l. on one's feet** retomber sur ses pieds
▶**land up** *vi* atterrir

landed [lændəd] *adj* **l. gentry** noblesse *f* terrienne; **l. proprietor** propriétaire *mf* terrien(enne)

landfall ['lændfɔːl] *n Naut* **to make l.** arriver en vue des côtes

landfill site ['lændfɪl'saɪt] *n* décharge *f* publique

landing ['lændɪŋ] *n* (**a**) *(of cargo, troops)* débarquement *m*; **l. card** carte *f* de débarquement; **l. craft** navire *m* de débarque-

ment; **l. stage** débarcadère *m* (**b**) *(of aircraft)* atterrissage *m*; **l. gear** train *m* d'atterrissage; **l. lights** phares *mpl* d'atterrissage; **l. strip** piste *f* d'atterrissage (**c**) *(of staircase)* palier *m*

landlady ['lændleɪdɪ] *(pl* **landladies***)* *n* (**a**) *(of rented accommodations)* propriétaire *f* (**b**) *(of small hotel)* logeuse *f*

landlocked ['lændlɒkt] *adj* sans accès à la mer

landlord ['lændlɔːd] *n (of rented accommodations)* propriétaire *m*

landmark ['lændmɑːk] *n (distinctive feature)* point *m* de repère; *Fig (important event)* événement *m* marquant

landmass ['lændmæs] *n* masse *f* continentale

landmine ['lændmaɪn] *n* mine *f* terrestre

landowner ['lændəʊnə(r)] *n* propriétaire *mf* foncier(ère)

landowning ['lændəʊnɪŋ] *adj* **the l. classes** la propriété foncière

landscape ['lændskeɪp] **1** *n* paysage *m*; **l. design** aménagement *m* d'espaces verts; **l. gardener** jardinier(ère) *m,f* paysagiste; *Comput* **l. (orientation)** format *m* paysage; **l. painter** paysagiste *mf*
2 *vt* aménager en espaces verts

landslide ['lændslaɪd] *n* (**a**) *(of earth, rocks)* glissement *m* de terrain (**b**) *(election victory)* raz *m inv* de marée électoral; **to win by a l.** gagner avec une majorité écrasante

landslip ['lændslɪp] *n* glissement *m* de terrain

landward ['lændwəd] **1** *adj (wind)* marin(e); **on the l. side** du côté des terres
2 *adv* vers la terre

lane [leɪn] *n* (**a**) *(in country)* chemin *m*; *(in town)* ruelle *f*, passage *m* (**b**) *(on road)* voie *f*, file *f* (**c**) *(for runner, swimmer)* couloir *m*

language ['læŋgwɪdʒ] *n* (**a**) *(of a people)* langue *f*; *Fam Fig* **we don't speak the same l.** nous ne parlons pas la même langue; **l. laboratory** laboratoire *m* de langues; **l. learning/teaching** apprentissage *m*/enseignement *m* des langues (**b**) *(style of speech or writing)* langage *m*

languid ['læŋgwɪd] *adj* alangui(e)

languidly ['læŋgwɪdlɪ] *adv* paresseusement

languish ['læŋgwɪʃ] *vi* languir (**for** après); **to l. in jail** moisir en prison

languor ['læŋgə(r)] *n* langueur *f*

languorous ['læŋgərəs] *adj* alangui(e)

lank [læŋk] *adj (hair)* terne

lanky ['læŋkɪ] *adj* dégingandé(e)

lanolin(e) ['lænəlɪn] *n* lanoline *f*

lantern ['læntən] *n* lanterne *f*

Laos [laʊs] *n* le Laos

Laotian ['laʊʃɪən] **1** *n* Laotien(enne) *m,f*
2 *adj* laotien(enne)

lap¹ [læp] *n* (**a**) *(part of body)* genoux *mpl*; **to sit on sb's l.** s'asseoir sur les genoux de qn; **l. dancer** = entraîneuse qui danse nue pour un client (**b**) *(idioms)* **it's in the l. of the gods** on ne peut que s'en remettre au sort; **she expects everything to fall into her l.** elle s'attend à ce que tout lui tombe tout cuit dans le bec; **to live in the l. of luxury** vivre dans le luxe

lap² [læp] **1** *n (in race)* tour *m*; **l. of honor** tour d'honneur
2 *vt (pt & pp* **lapped***) (overtake)* prendre un tour d'avance sur

lap³ [læp] *(pt & pp* **lapped***)* *vi (of animal)* laper; **to l. against sth** *(of waves)* clapoter contre qch
▶**lap up** *vt sep (drink)* laper; *Fam Fig (enjoy indiscriminately)* se délecter de; *(believe)* gober, avaler

laparotomy [læpə'rɒtəmɪ] *(pl* **laparotomies***)* *n Med* laparotomie *f*

lapdog ['læpdɒg] *n* chien *m* d'appartement; *Fig* toutou *m*

lapel [lə'pel] *n* revers *m*

Lapland ['læplænd] *n* la Laponie

Laplander ['læplændə(r)] *n* Lapon(one) *m,f*

Lapp [læp] **1** n (**a**) (person) Lapon(one) m,f (**b**) (language) lapon m
2 adj lapon(one)

lapse [læps] **1** n (**a**) (of time) laps m de temps (**b**) (in standards, concentration) baisse f (**in** de); (in behavior) écart m (**in** de)
2 vi (**a**) (of concentration, standards) baisser; (of person) retomber dans un travers; **to l. into silence** se taire (**b**) (of permit, membership) expirer

lapsed [læpst] adj (Catholic) qui ne pratique plus

laptop ['læptɒp] n Comput portable m

lapwing ['læpwɪŋ] n vanneau m

larceny ['lɑːsənɪ] n Law vol m

larch [lɑːtʃ] n mélèze m

lard [lɑːd] **1** n (fat) saindoux m
2 vt Fam Fig **to l. one's writings with quotations** truffer ses écrits de citations

larder ['lɑːdə(r)] n garde-manger m inv

large [lɑːdʒ] **1** n **to be at l.** être en liberté; **people at l., the public at l.** le grand public
2 adj (**a**) (big) grand(e); (fat, bulky) gros (grosse); (audience) nombreux(euse); **to grow** or **to get larger** s'agrandir; (of person) grossir; **to make sth larger** agrandir qch; **as l. as life** en chair et en os; **larger than life** haut(e) en couleur (**b**) (extensive, significant) **to a l. extent** en grande partie; **a l. part of** une grande partie de
3 adv **by and l.** dans l'ensemble

largely ['lɑːdʒlɪ] adv en grande partie

large-scale ['lɑːdʒ'skeɪl] adj (map) à grande échelle; (undertaking) ambitieux(euse); (disaster) immense

largesse [lɑː'ʒes] n largesse f

lark[1] [lɑːk] n (bird) alouette f; **to rise with the l.** se lever au chant du coq

lark[2] [lɑːk] n (joke) rigolade f; **to do sth for a l.** faire qch pour rire

▸**lark about, lark around** vi faire le fou (la folle)

larva ['lɑːvə] (pl **larvae** ['lɑːviː]) n larve f

laryngitis [lærɪn'dʒaɪtɪs] n laryngite f; **to have l.** avoir une laryngite

larynx ['lærɪŋks] n larynx m

lasagne [lə'sænjə] n lasagnes fpl

lascivious [lə'sɪvɪəs] adj lascif(ive)

laser ['leɪzə(r)] n laser m; **l. beam** rayon m laser; **l. disk** disque m laser; **l. printer** imprimante f laser; **l. surgery** chirurgie f au laser

lash [læʃ] **1** n (**a**) (eyelash) cil m (**b**) (of whip) coup m de fouet
2 vt (**a**) (with whip) cingler; (of rain, waves) fouetter (**b**) (tie) lier, attacher
3 vi **the rain** or **it was lashing down** il pleuvait dru

▸**lash out** vi (attack) **to l. out at sb** (physically) donner un coup/des coups à qn; (verbally) s'en prendre violemment à qn

lass [læs] n jeune fille f

lassitude ['læsɪtjuːd] n (weariness) lassitude f; (laziness) paresse f

lasso ['læsəʊ] **1** n (pl **lassoes** or **lassos**) lasso m
2 vt (pt & pp **lassoed**) attraper au lasso

last[1] [lɑːst] **1** n **the l.** le dernier (la dernière) m,f; **the l. but one** l'avant-dernier(ère) m,f; **we'll never hear the l. of it** on n'a pas fini d'en entendre parler; **I don't think we've heard the l. of him** je crois que nous n'en sommes pas encore débarrassés; **that's the l. I saw of her** je ne l'ai pas revue depuis; **that's the l. of the wine** on a fini le vin; **to** or **till the l.** jusqu'à la fin; **at (long) l.** enfin
2 adj (**a**) (final) dernier(ère); **you are my l. hope** vous êtes mon dernier espoir; **to have the l. word** avoir le dernier mot; **the l. word in comfort/style** le summum du confort/de l'élégance; **at the l. moment** or **minute** au dernier moment, à la dernière minute; **l. thing at night** avant de se coucher; **to**

be on one's l. legs être au bout du rouleau; **he's the l. person I'd ask to help me** c'est (bien) la dernière personne à qui je demanderais de m'aider; **that's the l. thing I'd do** c'est (bien) la dernière chose que je ferais; **as a l. resort** en dernier recours; **the L. Judgment** le Jugement dernier; **l. name** nom m de famille; **l. rites** derniers sacrements mpl; Fig **the l. straw** la goutte d'eau qui a fait déborder le vase
(**b**) (most recent) dernier(ère); **the l. time I saw him** la dernière fois que je l'ai vu; **l. January** en janvier (dernier); **l. night** (during the night) la nuit dernière; (in the evening) hier (au) soir; **l. Tuesday** mardi dernier; **l. week** la semaine dernière
3 adv **to arrive/to finish l.** arriver/finir dernier; **when I l. saw him** la dernière fois que je l'ai vu; **l. but not least** enfin

last[2] [lɑːst] n (for shoe) forme f (à chaussure)

last[3] [lɑːst] **1** vt **that watch will l. you a lifetime** vous pourrez garder cette montre toute votre vie; **it has lasted him well** ça lui a fait de l'usage; **have we got enough to l. us until tomorrow?** en avons-nous assez pour tenir jusqu'à demain?
2 vi durer; **it's too good to l.** c'est trop beau pour durer; **the supplies won't l. two months** les provisions ne seront pas suffisantes pour deux mois; **he won't l. long in that job** il ne tiendra pas très longtemps à ce poste; **she won't l. the night** elle ne passera pas la nuit

▸**last out 1** vt sep **to l. the year out** (of person) survivre jusqu'à la fin de l'année; (of supplies) suffire pour l'année
2 vi (of person) tenir le coup; (of supplies) suffire

last-ditch [lɑːst'dɪtʃ] adj ultime; **a l. attempt** un ultime effort

lasting ['lɑːstɪŋ] adj durable

lastly ['lɑːstlɪ] adv pour finir, en dernier lieu

last-minute [lɑːst'mɪnɪt] adj de dernière minute

latch [lætʃ] n loquet m

▸**latch onto** vt insep Fam (**a**) (attach oneself to) **to l. onto sb/sth** s'accrocher à qn/qch (**b**) (understand) **to l. onto sth** piger qch

latchkey ['lætʃkiː] (pl **latchkeys**) n clef f de la porte d'entrée; **l. child** = enfant dont les parents travaillent et qui doit rentrer seul après l'école

late [leɪt] **1** adj (**a**) (not on time) en retard; **to be l. (for sth)** être en retard (pour qch); **to be ten minutes l.** avoir dix minutes de retard
(**b**) (far on in time) tard; **it's getting l.** il se fait tard; **to keep l. hours** se coucher tard; **in the l. afternoon** en fin d'après-midi; **in l. summer** vers la fin de l'été; **to be in one's l. thirties** approcher de la quarantaine; **in the l. eighties** vers la fin des années 80; Fig **it's a bit l. in the day to...** il est un peu tard pour...; **l. booking** réservation f de dernière minute
(**c**) (dead) feu(e); **my l. husband** feu mon mari
2 adv (**a**) (in general) tard; **to work l.** travailler tard; **l. into the night** jusqu'à une heure avancée de la nuit; **l. in the year** vers la fin de l'année; **l. in life** sur le tard; Prov **better l. than never** mieux vaut tard que jamais
(**b**) (recently) **as l. as last week** pas plus tard que la semaine dernière; **of l.** récemment

latecomer ['leɪtkʌmə(r)] n retardataire mf

lately ['leɪtlɪ] adv dernièrement, récemment; **until l.** jusqu'à ces derniers temps

lateness ['leɪtnɪs] n (of person, train) retard m; **the l. of the hour** l'heure f tardive

latent ['leɪtənt] adj (disease, tendency) latent(e); (period) de latence

later ['leɪtə(r)] **1** adj ultérieur(e); **I caught a l. train** j'ai pris un train qui partait plus tard; **l. events proved that...** la suite des événements a prouvé que...; **her l. novels** ses derniers romans; **in l. life** avec l'âge
2 adv **l. (on)** plus tard; **a few days l.** quelques jours plus tard; **no l. than tomorrow** demain au plus tard; **as we shall**

see l. comme nous le verrons par la suite; *Fam* **see you l.!** à plus tard!

lateral ['lætərəl] *adj* latéral(e); **l. thinking** approche *f* originale

latest ['leɪtɪst] **1** *n* **at the l.** au plus tard; **the l. I can stay is four o'clock** je peux rester jusqu'à quatre heures au plus tard; **have you heard the l.?** vous savez la dernière?

    2 *adj (most recent)* dernier(ère)

latex ['leɪteks] *n* latex *m*

lathe [leɪð] *n* tour *m*

lather ['læðə(r)] **1** *n* mousse *f*; *Fam* **to work oneself** *or* **to get into a l. (about sth)** se mettre dans tous ses états (à propos de qch)

    2 *vt* savonner

Latin ['lætɪn] **1** *n* **(a)** *(person) (European)* Latin(e) *m,f*; *(Latin American)* Latino-Américain(e) *m,f* **(b)** *(language)* latin *m*

    2 *adj* latin(e); **L. America** l'Amérique *f* latine; **L. American** latino-américain(e)

Latino [læ'ti:nəʊ] *(pl* **Latinos)** *n* latino *mf*

latitude ['lætɪtju:d] *n also Fig* latitude *f*

latrine [lə'tri:n] *n* latrines *fpl*

latte ['læteɪ] *n* café *m* au lait

latter ['lætə(r)] **1** *n (of two)* **the l.** le second (la seconde)

    2 *adj* **(a)** *(of two)* second(e) **(b)** *(last)* dernier(ère); **the l. half** *or* **part of June** la deuxième moitié de juin

latter-day ['lætə'deɪ] *adj* moderne; *Rel* **the L. Saints** les mormons *mpl*

latterly ['lætəlɪ] *adv (recently)* dernièrement, récemment; *(toward the end of a period)* vers la fin

lattice ['lætɪs] *n* treillis *m*; **l. window** fenêtre *f* à croisillons de plomb

latticework ['lætɪswɜ:k] *n* treillis *m*

Latvia ['lætvɪə] *n* la Lettonie

Latvian ['lætvɪən] **1** *n* **(a)** *(person)* Letton(onne) *m,f* **(b)** *(language)* letton *m*

    2 *adj* letton(onne)

laudable ['lɔ:dəbəl] *adj* louable, digne de louanges

laudanum ['lɔ:dənəm] *n* laudanum *m*

laugh [lɑ:f] **1** *n* rire *m*; *Fam* **to have a good l.** bien se marrer; *Fam* **to do sth for a l.** faire qch pour rire; *Ironic* **that's a l.!** la bonne blague!; *Fam* **he's a good l.** on se marre avec lui; **to have the last l.** être bien vengé(e)

    2 *vi* rire (**at** de); *Fam* **don't make me l.!** laisse-moi rire!; *Fam* **to l. one's head off** être mort(e) de rire; **he'll be laughing on the other side of his face when…** il rira jaune quand…; *Fam* **to l. all the way to the bank** s'en mettre plein les poches; *Prov* **he who laughs last laughs longest** rira bien qui rira le dernier

    3 *vt* **to l. oneself silly** se tordre de rire; **you'll be laughed out of court** vous vous couvrirez de ridicule

▸**laugh off** *vt sep* tourner en plaisanterie

laughable ['lɑ:fəbəl] *adj* ridicule

laughing ['lɑ:fɪŋ] **1** *n* rires *mpl*

    2 *adj* rieur(euse); **it's no l. matter** ce n'est pas à prendre à la légère; **she was in no l. mood** elle n'était pas d'humeur à rire; **l. gas** gaz *m* hilarant; **l. stock** risée *f*; **to make sb a l. stock** faire de qn un sujet de plaisanterie

laughter ['lɑ:ftə(r)] *n* rires *mpl*

launch [lɔ:ntʃ] **1** *n* **(a)** *(boat)* chaloupe *f*; **(motor) l.** vedette *f* **(b)** *(of ship, rocket, product)* lancement *m*; **l. pad** plate-forme *f* de lancement

    2 *vt (ship, rocket, product)* lancer; *(inquiry)* ouvrir; **to l. sb on a career** *(of event)* marquer le début de la carrière de qn

▸**launch into** *vt insep (attack, story, complaint)* se lancer dans

launching ['lɔ:ntʃɪŋ] *n (of ship, rocket, product)* lancement *m*; *(of inquiry)* ouverture *f*; **l. pad** plate-forme *f* de lancement

launder ['lɔ:ndə(r)] *vt also Fig* blanchir

Laundromat ['lɔ:ndrəmæt] *n* laverie *f* automatique

laundry ['lɔ:ndrɪ] *n* linge *m*; **to do the l.** faire la lessive; **l. basket** panier *m* à linge

laurel ['lɒrəl] *n* laurier *m*; *Fig* **to rest on one's laurels** se reposer sur ses lauriers; **l. wreath** couronne *f* de lauriers

lava ['lɑ:və] *n* lave *f*

lavatory ['lævətrɪ] *(pl* **lavatories)** *n* toilettes *fpl*; **to go to the l.** aller aux toilettes; **l. paper** papier *m* hygiénique

lavender ['lævɪndə(r)] **1** *n (shrub)* lavande *f*; **l. water** (eau *f* de Cologne à la) lavande

    2 *adj (color)* bleu lavande *inv*

lavish ['lævɪʃ] **1** *adj* **(a)** *(person)* prodigue (**with/in** de) **(b)** *(gift, meal, décor)* somptueux(euse); *(spending)* extravagant(e); *(portion)* généreux(euse)

    2 *vt* **to l. sth on sb** couvrir qn de qch

lavishly ['lævɪʃlɪ] *adv* somptueusement; **to spend l.** dépenser sans compter; **to praise sb l.** couvrir qn d'éloges

law [lɔ:] *n* **(a)** *(rule)* loi *f*; **there's no l. against it** aucune loi ne l'interdit; **the laws of gravity** les lois de la pesanteur; **to be a l. unto oneself** n'en faire qu'à sa tête **(b)** *(set of rules)* loi *f*; **to be against the l.** être illégal(e); **to break the l.** enfreindre la loi; **to be above the l.** être au-dessus des lois; **to take the l. into one's own hands** se faire justice soi-même; **l. and order** l'ordre *m* public; **l. enforcement** le respect de la loi; **l. firm** cabinet *m* d'avocats **(c)** *(system of justice, subject)* droit *m*; **to practice l.** exercer une profession juridique; **l. school** faculté *f* de droit **(d)** *Fam* **the l.** *(police)* les flics *mpl*

law-abiding ['lɔ:əbaɪdɪŋ] *adj* respectueux(euse) des lois

lawbreaker ['lɔ:breɪkə(r)] *n* personne *f* qui transgresse la loi

lawcourt ['lɔ:kɔ:t] *n* cour *f* de justice

lawful ['lɔ:fʊl] *adj (legal)* légal(e); *(rightful)* légitime

lawless ['lɔ:lɪs] *adj (country, society)* livré(e) à l'anarchie; *(mob)* sans foi ni loi

lawlessness ['lɔ:lɪsnɪs] *n* anarchie *f*

lawmaker ['lɔ:meɪkə(r)] *n* législateur(trice) *m,f*

lawn [lɔ:n] *n* pelouse *f*, gazon *m*; **l. bowling** boules *fpl*; **l. tennis** tennis *m*

lawnmower ['lɔ:nməʊə(r)] *n* tondeuse *f* (à gazon)

lawsuit ['lɔ:su:t] *n* action *f* en justice; **to bring a l. against sb** intenter une action en justice contre qn

lawyer ['lɔ:jə(r)] *n* avocat(e) *m,f*; *(for wills, conveyancing)* notaire *m*; *(in company)* conseiller(ère) *m,f* juridique

lax [læks] *adj (discipline, principles, conduct)* relâché(e); *(person)* laxiste

laxative ['læksətɪv] **1** *n* laxatif *m*

    2 *adj* laxatif(ive)

laxity ['læksɪtɪ], **laxness** ['læksnɪs] *n (of discipline, principles, conduct)* relâchement *m*; *(of person)* laxisme *m*

lay[1] [leɪ] *adj Rel* laïque; **l. preacher** prédicateur *m* laïque

lay[2] [leɪ] *(pt & pp* **laid** [leɪd]*)* **1** *vt* **(a)** *(place)* mettre, poser; **to l. sb flat** coucher *ou* étendre qn; **to l. sth flat** poser *ou* coucher qch à plat; **to l. sb to rest** inhumer qn; **to l. one's hands on sth** mettre la main sur qch; **she reads everything she can l. her hands on** elle lit tout ce qui lui tombe sous la main; **if you l. a finger on her…** si tu touches à un seul cheveu de sa tête…; **to have nowhere to l. one's head** n'avoir nulle part où dormir; **to l. eyes on sb/sth** poser les yeux sur qn/qch; **to l. emphasis on sth** insister sur qch; **to l. the facts before sb** exposer les faits à qn; **to l. claim to sth** prétendre à qch; **to l. the blame on sb** faire porter la responsabilité à qn; **to l. sth bare** mettre qch à nu; **to l. oneself open to criticism** s'exposer à la critique; **to l. sb's fears to rest** apaiser les craintes de qn

    (b) *(foundations, carpet, trap, cable)* poser

    (c) *(egg)* pondre

    (d) **to l. a bet (on)** parier (sur)

    (e) *very Fam* **to get laid** s'envoyer en l'air

2 *vi (of bird)* pondre
3 *pt of* **lie²**
4 *n very Fam* **he's/she's a good l.** c'est un bon coup

▶**lay aside** *vt sep* (**a**) *(money)* mettre de côté (**b**) *(prejudices, doubt)* oublier

▶**lay by** *vt sep (money)* mettre de côté

▶**lay down** *vt sep* (**a**) **to l. down one's arms** rendre *ou* déposer les armes; **to l. down one's life** sacrifier sa vie (**b**) *(principle, rule)* établir, poser; **to l. down the law** dicter sa loi

▶**lay in** *vt sep (supplies, food)* stocker

▶**lay into** *vt insep Fam (physically)* rosser; *(verbally)* voler dans les plumes à

▶**lay off 1** *vt sep (cease to employ)* licencier; *(temporarily)* mettre en chômage technique
2 *vt insep Fam* (**a**) *(abstain from)* arrêter; **to l. off drink** arrêter de boire (**b**) *(leave alone)* ficher la paix à
3 *vi Fam (desist)* arrêter

▶**lay out** *vt sep* (**a**) *(arrange, display)* arranger, disposer; *(dead body)* faire la toilette de (**b**) *(house, town)* concevoir

▶**lay over** *vi* faire escale

layer ['leɪə(r)] **1** *n* couche *f*; **l. cake** génoise *f*
2 *vt (hair)* dégrader; **to have one's hair layered** se faire faire un dégradé

layman ['leɪmən] *n Rel* laïque *mf*; *(non-specialist)* profane *mf*, non-initié(e) *m,f*

lay-off ['leɪɒf] *n* licenciement *m*; *(temporary)* mise *f* en chômage technique

layout ['leɪaʊt] *n (of town)* plan *m*; *(of building)* agencement *m*; *(of text)* mise *f* en page

layover ['leɪəʊvə(r)] *n* escale *f*; **we had a three-hour l. in Miami** nous avons eu *ou* fait une escale de trois heures à Miami

laywoman ['leɪwʊmən] *n Rel* laïque *f*; *(non-specialist)* profane *f*, non-initiée *f*

laze [leɪz] *vi* **to l. (about** *or* **around)** paresser, fainéanter

laziness ['leɪzɪnɪs] *n* paresse *f*, fainéantise *f*

lazy ['leɪzɪ] *adj (person)* paresseux(euse), fainéant(e); *(afternoon)* passé(e) à ne rien faire

lazybones ['leɪzɪbəʊnz] *(pl* **lazybones**) *n Fam* flemmard(e) *m,f*

lb *(abbr* **pound**) livre *f*

LCD [elsi:'di:] *n (abbr* **liquid crystal display**) affichage *m* à cristaux liquides

LDC [eldi:'si:] *n Econ (abbr* **less developed country**) PVD *m*

lead¹ [led] *n* (**a**) *(metal)* plomb *m*; **l. poisoning** saturnisme *m* (**b**) *(for pencil)* mine *f* (**c**) *(idioms)* **to go down like a l. balloon** tomber à plat; *Fam* **to fill sb full of l.** truffer qn de plomb

lead² [li:d] **1** *n* (**a**) *(advantage)* avance *f*; **to be in the l.** être en tête; **to take** *or* **to go into the l.** *(in race)* prendre la tête; *(in match)* mener; **to have a 10-point l.** avoir 10 points d'avance; *Ind* **l. time** *(for production)* délai *m* de production; *(for delivery)* délai de livraison
(**b**) *(example)* exemple *m*; **to follow sb's l.** suivre l'exemple de qn
(**c**) *(clue)* indice *m*
(**d**) *(in card game)* **it's your l.** à vous de jouer
(**e**) *(in movie, play)* premier rôle *m*, rôle principal
(**f**) *(cable)* câble *m* ou fil *m* (électrique)
2 *vt (pt & pp* **led** [led]*)* (**a**) *(guide)* mener, conduire; **you l. the way** montrez-nous le chemin; **to l. the conversation away from a subject** détourner la conversation; **to be easily led** être très influençable; **that leads me to believe that...** cela m'amène à penser que...
(**b**) **to l. a happy/sad life** mener une vie heureuse/triste
(**c**) *(be leader of)* mener

(**d**) *(be ahead of)* **to l. the field** mener; *Fig* **to l. the field in sth** être en tête dans le domaine de qch; **to l. sb by eight points** avoir une avance de huit points sur qn
3 *vi* (**a**) *(of road)* mener, conduire (**to** à)
(**b**) **to l. to sth** *(cause)* mener à qch
(**c**) *(in competition, race)* mener; *(in card game)* jouer le premier; **you l. and I'll follow** vas-y, je te suis

▶**lead away** *vt sep* emmener

▶**lead off** *vi* (**a**) *(road, corridor)* partir (**from** de) (**b**) *(in discussion)* commencer

▶**lead on** *vt sep (deceive)* tromper, duper

▶**lead up to** *vt insep (of person)* en venir à; *(of event)* précéder; **what are you leading up to?** où veux-tu en venir?

leaded ['ledɪd] *adj* **1. window** fenêtre *f* à croisillons de plomb; **l. gas** essence *f* au plomb

leaden ['ledən] *adj (heavy)* lourd(e)

leader ['li:də(r)] *n (of group)* chef *m*; *Pol* chef, leader *m*, dirigeant(e) *m,f*; *(of riot)* meneur(euse) *m,f*; *(in race)* premier(ère) *m,f*; **to be a born l.** être fait(e) pour commander

leadership ['li:dəʃɪp] *n (people in charge)* dirigeants *mpl*; *(position)* direction *f*; *(quality)* qualités *fpl* d'encadrement

lead-free [led'fri:] *adj (gas, paint)* sans plomb

lead-in ['li:dɪn] *n TV & Rad* introduction *f*

leading ['li:dɪŋ] *adj* (**a**) *(best, most important)* principal(e); **l. lady** *(in movie, play)* premier rôle *m* féminin; *Fig* **l. light** personnalité *f* de premier plan; **l. man** *(in movie, play)* premier rôle masculin; **l. role** *(in movie, play)* premier rôle (**b**) *(team, runner)* de tête (**c**) **l. question** question *f* tendancieuse

leaf [li:f] *(pl* **leaves** [li:vz]*)* *n* (**a**) *(of plant)* feuille *f*; *(of book)* feuillet *m*; *Fig* **to turn over a new l.** s'acheter une conduite; *Fig* **to take a l. out of sb's book** prendre exemple sur qn (**b**) *(of table) (inserted)* rallonge *f*; *(hinged)* battant *m*

▶**leaf through** *vt insep (book, magazine)* feuilleter

leaflet ['li:flɪt] **1** *n* prospectus *m*; *(political)* tract *m*; *(folded)* dépliant *m*
2 *vt (area)* distribuer des prospectus dans

leafy ['li:fɪ] *adj (tree)* feuillu(e); *(street)* ombragé(e); **a l. suburb** une banlieue verte

league [li:g] *n* ligue *f*; *(in sport)* championnat *m*; **to be in l. with sb** être de mèche avec qn; *Fig* **to be in a different l.** être hors classe; *Fig* **they're not in the same l.** ils ne sont pas du même niveau; **l. champions** vainqueurs *mpl* du championnat

leak [li:k] **1** *n also Fig* fuite *f*; *(in boat)* voie *f* d'eau; *Fam* **to take a l.** pisser un coup
2 *vt (information)* divulguer (**to** à); **the pipe was leaking gas/water** du gaz/de l'eau fuyait du tuyau
3 *vi* fuir; *(of shoe)* prendre l'eau; *(of boat)* faire eau; **the roof is leaking** il y a une fuite dans le toit

leakage ['li:kɪdʒ] *n* fuite *f*

leaky ['li:kɪ] *adj (bucket, pipe, faucet)* qui fuit; *(roof)* qui a une fuite; *(shoe)* qui prend l'eau; *(boat)* qui fait eau

lean¹ [li:n] *adj* (**a**) *(person, face)* mince; *(meat)* maigre (**b**) *(harvest)* maigre; *(year)* de vaches maigres

lean² [li:n] *(pt & pp* **leant** [lent] *or* **leaned**) **1** *vt* **to l. sth on/against sth** appuyer qch sur/contre qch
2 *vi (of building)* pencher; **to l. on/against sth** s'appuyer sur/contre qch; *Fig* **to l. on sb** *(rely on)* s'appuyer sur qn; *(put pressure on)* faire pression sur qn; **the Leaning Tower of Pisa** la tour de Pise; **to l. out of the window** se pencher à la fenêtre

▶**lean back** *vi* se pencher en arrière

▶**lean over 1** *vt insep* **to l. over sb/sth** se pencher par-dessus qn/qch
2 *vi* se pencher

leaning ['li:nɪŋ] *n (tendency)* inclination *f*, penchant *m* (**towards** pour); **to have artistic leanings** avoir des dispositions artistiques

leant [lent] *pt & pp of* **lean²**

lean-to ['li:ntu:] *(pl* **lean-tos***) n* appentis *m*

leap [li:p] **1** *n* saut *m*, bond *m; Fig* **to take a l. in the dark** faire un saut dans l'inconnu; *Fig* **to advance by leaps and bounds** avancer à pas de géant; **l. year** année *f* bissextile

2 *vt (pt & pp* **leapt** [lept] *or* **leaped)** franchir d'un bond *ou* d'un saut

3 *vi* sauter, bondir; **to l. to one's feet** se lever d'un bond; **to l. at the chance** sauter sur l'occasion; **to l. for joy** sauter de joie

leapfrog ['li:pfrɒg] **1** *n* saute-mouton *m;* **to play l.** jouer à saute-mouton

2 *vt (pt & pp* **leapfrogged)** *Fig* passer avant

leapt [lept] *pt & pp of* **leap**

learn [lɜ:n] *(pt & pp* **learnt** [lɜ:nt] *or* **learned) 1** *vt* apprendre

2 *vi* apprendre; **to l. of** *or* **about sth** apprendre qch; **to l. from one's mistakes** tirer un enseignement de ses erreurs

learned ['lɜ:nɪd] *adj* savant(e), érudit(e)

learner ['lɜ:nə(r)] *n (beginner)* débutant(e) *m,f; (student)* étudiant(e) *m,f;* **to be a quick/slow l.** apprendre vite/lentement

learning ['lɜ:nɪŋ] *n (act of learning)* apprentissage *m; (knowledge)* savoir *m,* connaissances *fpl;* **l. curve** courbe *f* d'assimilation; **it was a steep l. curve** l'apprentissage a été difficile

learnt [lɜ:nt] *pt & pp of* **learn**

lease [li:s] **1** *n* bail *m; Fig* **to give sb a new l. on life** redonner à qn goût à la vie; **to get a new l. on life** *(of person)* renaître à la vie; *(of industry, town)* retrouver un nouveau souffle

2 *vt* louer **(from/to** à)

leasehold ['li:shəʊld] *n (contract)* bail *m; (property)* location *f* à bail

leaseholder ['li:shəʊldə(r)] *n* locataire *mf*

leash [li:ʃ] *n (for dog)* laisse *f; Fig* **to keep sb on a tight l.** tenir la bride haute à qn

leasing ['li:sɪŋ] *n Com* location-vente *f*

least [li:st] **1** *n* **the l.** le moins; **..., to say the l.** le moins qu'on puisse dire, c'est que...; **it's the l. I can do** c'est la moindre des choses; **that's the l. of my worries** c'est le cadet de mes soucis; **at l.** au moins; **he's leaving, at l. that's what I've heard** il part, du moins c'est ce que j'ai entendu dire; **at l. as old as...** au moins aussi vieux que...; **at the very l. they should pay your expenses** ce serait vraiment la moindre des choses qu'ils te remboursent tes frais; **not in the l.** pas du tout; **it doesn't matter in the l.** cela n'a pas la moindre importance

2 *adj (superlative of* **little)** *(smallest)* moindre; **the l. thing annoys her** un rien l'agace

3 *adv* **the l. difficult** le (la) moins difficile; **l. of all her** elle encore moins que les autres; **when I was l. expecting it** au moment où je m'y attendais le moins

leather ['leðə(r)] **1** *n* cuir *m*

2 *vt Fam (beat)* tanner le cuir à

leather-bound ['leðəbaʊnd] *adj (book)* relié(e) en cuir

leathery ['leðərɪ] *adj (face, skin)* tanné(e); *(meat)* coriace

leave [li:v] **1** *n* **(a)** *(permission)* permission *f,* autorisation *f;* **to ask l. to do sth** demander la permission *ou* l'autorisation de faire qch; **to grant** *or* **to give sb l. to do sth** accorder *ou* donner à qn l'autorisation de faire qch

(b) *(vacation)* congé *m;* **to be on l.** *(from work)* être en congé; *(from army)* être en permission; **l. of absence** *(from work)* congé exceptionnel; *(from army)* permission *f* exceptionnelle

(c) *(farewell)* **to take one's l. (of sb)** prendre congé (de qn); **to take l. of one's senses** perdre l'esprit

2 *vt (pt & pp* **left** [left]) **(a)** *(depart from)* quitter; **to l. the table** se lever de table; **the car left the road** la voiture a quitté la route

(b) *(put, deposit)* **to l. sth somewhere** *(on purpose)* laisser qch quelque part; *(accidentally)* oublier qch quelque part; **take**

it or **l. it** *(of offer)* c'est à prendre ou à laisser; **to l. a message for sb** laisser un message pour qn

(c) *(allow to remain)* laisser; **to l. the door open** laisser la porte ouverte; **to l. oneself open to criticism** laisser la porte ouverte aux critiques; **to l. sth unfinished** laisser qch inachevé(e); **to l. sb to do sth** laisser qn faire qch; **l. it to me** laisse-moi faire; **to l. much** *or* **a lot to be desired** laisser beaucoup à désirer; **let's l. it at that** restons-en là; **to l. well alone** ne pas s'en mêler; **l. me alone!** fiche-moi la paix!

(d) *(bequeath)* laisser **(to** à); **he leaves a wife and three children** *(after dying)* il laisse une femme et trois enfants

(e) **to be left** *(remain)* rester; **there are a few chocolates left** il reste quelques chocolats; **three from seven leaves four** sept moins trois égale quatre

3 *vi (depart)* partir

►**leave behind** *vt sep* **to l. sth behind** *(on purpose)* laisser qch; *(accidentally)* oublier qch; **to l. sb behind** partir sans qn

►**leave off 1** *vt insep Fam* **to l. off doing sth** arrêter de faire qch; **to l. off work** cesser le travail

2 *vi* s'arrêter

►**leave on** *vt sep (light, TV)* laisser allumé(e)

►**leave out** *vt sep* **(a)** *(omit)* omettre **(b)** *(not involve)* **to l. sb out of sth** laisser qn en dehors de qch; **to feel left out** se sentir exclu(e) **(c)** *(leave ready, available)* **I'll l. your dinner out on the table for you** je laisserai ton dîner sur la table; **l. the disks out where I can see them** laisse les disquettes en évidence **(d)** *(leave outside)* laisser dehors; **who left the milk out?** qui a oublié de mettre le lait au frigo?

►**leave over** *vt sep* **to be left over** *(of food, money)* rester; **there's some lasagne left over** il reste des lasagnes

leaven ['levən] *n* levain *m*

leaves [li:vz] *pl of* **leaf**

leave-taking ['li:vteɪkɪŋ] *n* adieux *mpl*

Lebanese [lebə'ni:z] **1** *npl (people)* **the L.** les Libanais *mpl*

2 *n (person)* Libanais(e) *m,f*

3 *adj* libanais(e)

Lebanon ['lebənən] *n* **le Liban**

lecher ['letʃə(r)] *n* obsédé *m*

lecherous ['letʃərəs] *adj* lubrique

lechery ['letʃərɪ] *n* lubricité *f*

lectern ['lektən] *n* lutrin *m*

lecture ['lektʃə(r)] **1** *n* **(a)** *(talk)* conférence *f; (at university)* cours *m* magistral; **l. hall** amphithéâtre *m* **(b)** *Fam (reprimand)* sermon *m;* **to give sb a l.** faire la morale à qn

2 *vt Fam (reprimand)* faire la morale à

3 *vi (give public lectures)* donner une conférence/des conférences; *(at university)* donner un cours magistral/des cours magistraux

LED [eli:'di:] *n Elec (abbr* **light-emitting diode)** LED *f*

led [led] *pt & pp of* **lead²**

ledge [ledʒ] *n (on cliff)* corniche *f; (of window, on building)* rebord *m*

ledger ['ledʒə(r)] *n* grand livre *m*

leech [li:tʃ] *n also Fig* sangsue *f;* **to cling to sb like a l.** se cramponner à qn comme une sangsue

leek [li:k] *n* poireau *m*

leer ['lɪə(r)] **1** *n (lustful)* regard *m* lubrique; *(cruel)* regard sadique

2 *vi* **to l. at sb** *(lustfully)* regarder qn d'un air lubrique; *(cruelly)* regarder qn d'un air sadique

lees [li:z] *npl (of wine)* lie *f*

leeward ['li:wəd] **1** *n* côté *m* sous le vent

2 *adj* sous le vent; **the L. Islands** les îles *fpl* Sous-le-Vent

leeway ['li:weɪ] *n* marge *f* de manœuvre

left¹ [left] **1** *n* gauche *f;* **on** *or* **to the l.** à gauche; **on my l.** à ma gauche

2 *adj* gauche; **the l. wing** *(of party)* l'aile *f* gauche

3 *adv* à gauche

left² [left] *pt & pp of* **leave**

left-field ['left'fi:ld] adj Fam (bizarre) bizarroïde

left-hand ['left'hænd] adj de gauche; (corner, side) gauche; **l. drive** conduite f à gauche; **on the l. side** à gauche

left-handed [left'hændid] **1** adj gaucher(ère)
2 adv de la main gauche

left-hander [left'hændə(r)] n (person) gaucher(ère) m,f

leftover ['leftəʊvə(r)] **1** adj **l. food/paint** un reste de nourriture/de peinture
2 n leftovers restes mpl

left-wing ['leftwiŋ] adj de gauche

left-winger ['left'wiŋə(r)] n homme (femme) m,f de gauche

lefty ['lefti] (pl lefties) n Fam (a) (left-handed person) gaucher(ère) m,f (b) Pol (left-winger) homme (femme) m,f de gauche

leg [leg] **1** n (a) (of person, trousers) jambe f; (of animal) patte f; (of table, chair) pied m (b) Culin (of lamb) gigot m; (of chicken) cuisse f; (of pork) rôti m (c) (of journey, race) étape f (d) (idioms) **to pull sb's l.** faire marcher qn; **to show a l.** se lever; **to shake a l.** se remuer; **you don't have a l. to stand on** tu n'as rien sur quoi t'appuyer; **to give sb a l. up** donner un coup de pouce à qn; very Fam **to get one's l. over** s'envoyer en l'air
2 vt (pt & pp legged) Fam **to l. it** jouer des gambettes

legacy ['legəsi] (pl legacies) n also Fig legs m; **to come into a l.** faire un héritage

legal ['li:gəl] adj légal(e); **to take l. action (against sb)** intenter une action (contre qn); **to take l. advice** consulter un avocat; **l. aid** aide f juridique; **l. holiday** jour m férié; **the l. profession** les professions fpl juridiques; **to be l. tender** avoir cours (légal)

legality [li'gæliti] n légalité f

legalization [li:gəlai'zeiʃən] n légalisation f

legalize ['li:gəlaiz] vt légaliser

legally ['li:gəli] adv légalement

legate ['legit] n Rel légat m

legation [li'geiʃən] n légation f

legend ['ledʒənd] n légende f; **to be a l. in one's own lifetime** être une légende vivante

legendary ['ledʒəndəri] adj légendaire

leggings ['legiŋz] npl (of woman) caleçon m; (of cowboy) jambières fpl

leggy ['legi] adj (person) tout en jambes

legible ['ledʒibəl] adj lisible

legion ['li:dʒən] n légion f

legionary ['li:dʒənəri] (pl legionaries) n légionnaire m

legionnaire [li:dʒə'neə(r)] n légionnaire m; **l.'s disease** maladie f du légionnaire

legislate ['ledʒisleit] vi légiférer (**against** contre)

legislation [ledʒis'leiʃən] n (laws) législation f; (action) élaboration f des lois

legislative ['ledʒislətiv] adj législatif(ive)

legislator ['ledʒisleitə(r)] n législateur(trice) m,f

legislature ['ledʒislətʃə(r)] n corps m législatif

legitimacy [li'dʒitiməsi] n légitimité f

legitimate 1 adj [li'dʒitimət] légitime
2 vt [li'dʒitimeit] légitimer

legitimately [li'dʒitimətli] adv légitimement

legroom ['legrom] n place f pour les jambes

legume ['legju:m] n Bot légumineuse f

legwarmers ['legwɔ:məz] npl jambières fpl

leisure ['li:ʒər] n loisirs mpl; **to do sth at one's l.** faire qch à son rythme; **a life of l.** une vie de loisirs; **l. activities** activités fpl de loisirs; **l. center** centre m de loisirs; **l. club** club m de loisirs; **l. industry** industrie f des loisirs; **l. time** temps m libre

leisurely ['li:ʒərli] adj (weekend) relax inv; **at a l. pace** sans se presser; **to make l. progress** avancer à son rythme; **to go for a l. stroll** se promener tranquillement

leisurewear ['li:ʒəweər] n vêtements mpl décontractés

lemming ['lemiŋ] n lemming m; **to follow sb like lemmings** suivre qn comme des moutons

lemon ['lemən] **1** n (a) (fruit, color) citron m; Fam **I felt like a real l.** j'ai vraiment eu l'air malin; **l. sole** limande-sole f; **l. squeezer** presse-citron m; **l. tea** thé m au citron; **l. tree** citronnier m (b) Fam (defective car) navet m, voiture f de mauvaise qualité
2 adj **l. (colored)** jaune citron inv

lemonade [lemə'neid] n (freshly squeezed) citronnade f, citron m pressé

lemur ['li:mə(r)] n maki m

lend [lend] (pt & pp lent [lent]) vt (money, book, pen) prêter; (support) apporter (**to** à); **to l. credibility to sth** rendre qch crédible; **to l. sb a (helping) hand** donner un coup de main à qn; **to l. an ear or one's ear to...** prêter l'oreille à...; **her work doesn't l. itself to dramatization** son œuvre ne se prête pas à une adaptation théâtrale

lender ['lendə(r)] n prêteur(euse) m,f

lending ['lendiŋ] n prêt m; **l. library** bibliothèque f de prêt; **l. rate** taux m (d'un prêt)

length [leŋθ] n (a) (in space) longueur f; **it's 3 ft in l.** ≃ ça fait 1 m de long; **the l. and breadth of the country** dans tout le pays (b) (in time) durée f; **at (great) l.** longuement; **a great l. of time** longtemps; **l. of service** ancienneté f (c) **to go to the l. of doing sth** aller jusqu'à faire qch; **to go to great lengths to do sth** se donner beaucoup de mal pour faire qch; **he would go to any lengths (to do sth)** il ne reculerait devant rien (pour faire qch) (d) (of wood, string) morceau m

lengthen ['leŋθən] **1** vt allonger, rallonger
2 vi (of days) allonger, rallonger; (of shadows) s'allonger

lengthily ['leŋθili] adv longuement

lengthways ['leŋθweiz], **lengthwise** ['leŋθwaiz] adv dans le sens de la longueur

lengthy ['leŋθi] adj long (longue)

lenient ['li:niənt] adj indulgent(e)

Leningrad ['leniŋgræd] n Formerly Leningrad

lens [lenz] (pl lenses) n (of eyeglasses) verre m; (of camera) objectif m; (of eye) cristallin m; **(contact) l.** lentille f (de contact); **l. cap** capuchon m d'objectif

Lent [lent] n Rel carême m; **to keep L.** faire carême

lent [lent] pt & pp of **lend**

lentil ['lentil] n lentille f

Leo ['li:əʊ] (pl Leos) n (sign of zodiac) le Lion; **to be (a) L.** être (du) Lion

leopard ['lepəd] n léopard m

leotard ['li:ətɑ:d] n justaucorps m

leper ['lepə(r)] n lépreux(euse) m,f; **l. colony** léproserie f

leprechaun ['leprəkɔ:n] n lutin m, farfadet m

leprosy ['leprəsi] n lèpre f; **to have l.** avoir la lèpre

lesbian ['lezbiən] **1** n lesbienne f
2 adj lesbien(enne)

lesion ['li:ʒən] n lésion f

Lesotho [li'su:tu:] n le Lesotho

less [les] **1** adj (comparative of little) moins de; **it's l. than a week's work** cela représente moins d'une semaine de travail; **the distance is l. than I thought** c'est moins loin que je ne pensais
2 prep moins; **a year l. two days** un an moins deux jours; **I've got $50, l. what I spent on the train ticket** j'ai 50 dollars, moins ce que j'ai dépensé pour le billet de train
3 pron moins; **I don't think any (the) l. of you** tu n'as pas baissé dans mon estime; **I see l. of her nowadays** je la vois moins ces temps-ci; **in l. than an hour** en moins d'une heure; **the l. said about it the better** moins on en parle mieux c'est
4 adv moins; **l. and l.** de moins en moins; **no more, no l.** ni plus ni moins; **still l., even l.** encore moins; **nothing l. than**

total obedience rien moins qu'une obéissance totale; **she was driving a Rolls, no l.!** elle conduisait une Rolls, rien que ça!; **I expected no l. from you** je n'en attendais pas moins de vous; **they don't have a refrigerator, much l. a freezer** ils n'ont pas de réfrigérateur et encore moins de congélateur

lessen ['lesən] **1** *vt (importance, cost)* diminuer, réduire; *(noise)* atténuer; *(enthusiasm, pain)* calmer
2 *vi (of pain, anger)* se calmer; *(of noise)* s'atténuer

lesser ['lesə(r)] *adj (in size)* plus petit(e); *(in importance)* moindre; **the l. of two evils** un moindre mal; **to a l. extent** *or* **degree** dans une moindre mesure

lesson ['lesən] *n* leçon *f*; **to give English lessons** donner des cours d'anglais; *Fig* **he has learned his l.** ça lui a servi de leçon; *Fig* **to teach sb a l.** *(of person)* donner une bonne leçon à qn; *(of event, experience)* servir de leçon à qn

lest [lest] *conj Formal* de peur *ou* de crainte que + *subjunctive*; **l. we forget** *(on war memorial)* pour ne pas oublier

let¹ [let] *n (in tennis)* let *m*

let² [let] *vt (pt & pp* **let**) *(rent out)* louer; **(house) to l.** *(maison)* à louer

let³ [let] *(pt & pp* **let**) *vt* **(a)** *(allow)* **to l. sb do sth** laisser qn faire qch, permettre à qn de faire qch; **l. me see** voyons un peu; *(show me)* fais(-moi) voir; **to l. sb know sth** faire savoir qch à qn; **to l. sth pass** laisser passer qch; **to l. sth go** lâcher qch; **to l. oneself go** se laisser aller; **to l. sb go** laisser partir qn; *(lay off)* se séparer de qn; **don't l. it get you down/get to you** ne te laisse pas abattre/affecter par ça; **don't l. me see you here again!** que je ne vous retrouve plus ici!; **can you l. me have it back tomorrow?** pouvez-vous me le rendre demain?; *Math* **l. AB be equal to CD** soit AB égal à CD **(b)** *(with suggestions)* **l.'s go!** allons-y!; **l.'s hurry!** dépêchons-nous!; **l.'s not have an argument about it!** on ne va pas se disputer pour ça!; **now, don't l.'s have any nonsense!** allons, pas de bêtises!

▶**let by** *vt sep (allow to pass)* laisser passer

▶**let down** *vt sep* **(a)** *(hem)* rallonger; *Fig* **to l. one's hair down** se défouler **(b)** *Fam (disappoint, fail)* décevoir; **the car l. us down again** la voiture nous a encore lâchés

▶**let in** *vt sep* **(a)** *(allow to enter)* laisser entrer; **to l. oneself in** *(to house)* entrer; **to l. in the light** laisser entrer *ou* passer la lumière; **to l. in water** *(of shoes)* prendre l'eau **(b)** **to l. sb in on a plan** mettre qn au courant d'un projet; **to l. sb in on a secret** mettre qn dans le secret **(c)** *Fam* **to l. oneself in for a hard time** aller au-devant de grandes difficultés; **what are you letting yourself in for?** est-ce que tu sais à quoi tu t'exposes?

▶**let into** *vt sep* **to l. sb into the house** faire entrer qn; **to l. sb into a secret** mettre qn dans le secret

▶**let off** *vt sep* **(a)** *(bomb)* lâcher; *(firework)* tirer; *Fig* **to l. off steam** se défouler **(b)** *(excuse)* ne pas sanctionner; **I'll l. you off this time** ça va pour cette fois; **they l. him off with a fine** il s'en est tiré avec une amende

▶**let on** *vt sep Fam* **(a)** *(tell)* dire; **don't l. on that I was there** n'allez pas dire que j'y étais **(b)** *(claim)* prétendre; **he wasn't as ill as he l. on** il n'était pas aussi malade qu'il le prétendait

▶**let out 1** *vt sep* **(a)** *(release) (person)* laisser sortir; *(prisoner)* libérer; *(air, yell)* laisser échapper; *(secret)* divulguer **(b)** *(jacket, trousers)* élargir
2 *vi (school, performance)* finir

▶**let up** *vi (lessen)* diminuer; *(stop)* cesser; **once he's started, he never lets up** une fois lancé, il ne s'arrête plus

let-down ['letdaʊn] *n Fam* déception *f*

lethal ['li:θəl] *adj* mortel(elle); *Fam* **that vodka's l.!** elle est mortelle, cette vodka!; **l. dose** dose *f* létale *ou* mortelle; **l. weapon** arme *f* meurtrière

lethargic [lɪ'θɑ:dʒɪk] *adj* mou (molle)

lethargy ['leθədʒɪ] *n* mollesse *f*

letter ['letə(r)] *n* lettre *f*; **the l. of the law** la lettre de la loi; **to do sth to the l.** faire qch à la lettre; **to publish a writer's letters** publier la correspondance d'un écrivain; *Com* **l. of credit/exchange** lettre de crédit/de change; **l. of acknowledgment** accusé *m* de réception; **l. bomb** lettre piégée; **l. box** boîte *f* aux lettres; **l. opener** coupe-papier *m inv*

letterhead ['letəhed] *n* en-tête *m*; *(paper)* papier *m* à en-tête

lettuce ['letɪs] *n* salade *f* (verte)

let-up ['letʌp] *n (in conflict)* trêve *f*; *(in weather)* accalmie *f*; *(in pressure)* relâchement *m*; **to work fifteen hours without a l.** travailler quinze heures sans répit

leukemia [lu:'ki:mɪə] *n* leucémie *f*

level ['levəl] **1** *n* niveau *m*; **at eye l.** à (la) hauteur des yeux; **to be on a l. with sb** être sur un pied d'égalité avec qn; *Fam* **on the l.** régulier(ère); **to come down to sb's l.** se mettre à la portée de qn; **to sink to sb's l.** tomber au niveau de qn; **at governmental/international l.** à l'échelon gouvernemental/international
2 *adj* **(a)** *(not sloping)* plat(e); *Fig* **a l. playing field** une situation qui ne défavorise personne **(b)** **to be l. with sb/sth** *(physically)* être au niveau de qn/qch; *(in race, ability, progress)* être au même niveau que qn/qch; **to draw l. with** *(in race, match)* rattraper; **to do one's l. best** faire tout son possible; **l. spoonful** cuillerée *f* rase **(c)** *(voice, tone)* égal(e); **to keep a l. head** garder son sang-froid
3 *vt* **(a)** *(make level)* niveler, égaliser; *(building)* raser **(b)** *(aim) (blow)* porter (**at** à); *(criticism)* adresser (**at** à); *(accusation)* porter (**at** contre)
4 *vi Fam* **to l. with sb** parler franchement à qn

▶**level off, level out** *vi (of ground)* s'aplanir; *(of prices, demand)* se stabiliser; *(of aircraft)* se redresser

level-headed ['levəl'hedɪd] *adj* pondéré(e)

lever ['levə(r)] **1** *n also Fig* levier *m*
2 *vt* **to l. sth open** ouvrir qch au moyen d'un levier

leverage ['levərɪdʒ] *n (power)* effet *m* de levier; *Fig (influence)* pression *f*

leveraged buyout ['levərɪdʒd'baɪaʊt] *n Fin* OPA *f* à crédit

levitate ['levɪteɪt] *vi* léviter

levitation [levɪ'teɪʃən] *n* lévitation *f*

levity ['levɪtɪ] *n* légèreté *f*

levy ['levɪ] **1** *n (pl* **levies**) taxe *f* (**on** sur)
2 *vt (pt & pp* **levied**) lever, percevoir (**on** sur)

lewd [lu:d] *adj* obscène

lexical ['leksɪkəl] *adj* lexical(e)

lexicographer [leksɪ'kɒɡrəfə(r)] *n* lexicographe *mf*

lexicography [leksɪ'kɒɡrəfɪ] *n* lexicographie *f*

liability [laɪə'bɪlɪtɪ] *n (pl* **liabilities**) **(a)** *Law (responsibility)* responsabilité *f* (**for** de); *Fin* **liabilities** passif *m* **(b)** *(disadvantage)* handicap *m* (**to** pour)

liable ['laɪəbəl] *adj* **(a)** *Law (responsible)* responsable (**for** de) **(b)** *(to tax)* assujetti(e) (**to** à); *(to fine)* passible (**to** de) **(c)** *(likely)* **to be l. to do sth** risquer de faire qch

liaise [li:'eɪz] *vi* **to l. with sb** *(be in contact with)* assurer la liaison avec qn; *(work together with)* collaborer avec qn

liaison [lɪ'eɪzɒn] *n* **(a)** *(contact)* liaison *f*; *(co-operation)* collaboration *f*; *Mil* **l. officer** officier *m* de liaison **(b)** *(love affair)* liaison *f*

liar ['laɪə(r)] *n* menteur(euse) *m,f*

libel ['laɪbəl] *Law* **1** *n* diffamation *f*; **l. action** procès *m* en diffamation; **l. laws** lois *fpl* contre la diffamation
2 *vt* diffamer (par écrit)

libelous ['laɪbələs] *adj* diffamatoire

liberal ['lɪbərəl] **1** *n Pol* **L.** libéral(e) *m,f*
2 *adj* **(a)** *(tolerant)* libéral(e) **(b)** *(generous, abundant)* généreux(euse); **to be l. with one's praise/advice** ne pas être avare de compliments/de conseils **(c)** *Pol* **L.** libéral(e); **the L.**

Democrats *(in Great Britain)* parti *m* libéral démocrate *(parti politique britannique de tendance centriste)*

liberalism ['lɪbərəlɪzəm] *n* libéralisme *m*

liberalize ['lɪbərəlaɪz] *vt* libéraliser; *(law)* assouplir

liberally ['lɪbərəlɪ] *adv* libéralement, généreusement

liberate ['lɪbəreɪt] *vt* libérer

liberated ['lɪbəreɪtɪd] *adj (person)* libéré(e); *(views, ideas)* progressiste

liberating ['lɪbəreɪtɪŋ] *adj* libérateur(trice)

liberation [lɪbə'reɪʃən] *n* libération *f*; **l. movement** mouvement *m* de libération

liberator ['lɪbəreɪtə(r)] *n* libérateur(trice) *m,f*

Liberia [laɪ'bɪərɪə] *n* le Liberia

Liberian [laɪ'bɪərɪən] **1** *n* Libérien(enne) *m,f*
2 *adj* libérien(enne)

libertarian [lɪbə'teərɪən] *n & adj* libertaire *mf*

liberty ['lɪbətɪ] *(pl* **liberties)** *n* liberté *f*; **at l.** en liberté; **to be at l.** to do sth être libre de faire qch; **to take the l. of doing sth** prendre la liberté de faire qch; **to take liberties with sb/sth** prendre des libertés avec qn/qch

libido [lɪ'bi:dəʊ] *n* libido *f*

Libra ['li:brə] *n (sign of zodiac)* la Balance; **to be (a) L.** être (de la) Balance

librarian [laɪ'breərɪən] *n* bibliothécaire *mf*

library ['laɪbrərɪ] *(pl* **libraries)** *n* bibliothèque *f*; **l. book** livre *m* de bibliothèque; **l. card** carte *f* de bibliothèque

libretto [lɪ'bretəʊ] *(pl* **librettos** or **libretti** [lɪ'breti:]) *n Mus* livret *m*

Libya ['lɪbɪə] *n* la Libye

Libyan ['lɪbɪən] **1** *n* Libyen(enne) *m,f*
2 *adj* libyen(enne)

lice [laɪs] *pl* of **louse**

license¹ ['laɪsəns] *n* (a) *(permit)* permis *m*; *(for trade, bar)* licence *f*; *Com* **under l.** sous licence; **(driver's) l.** permis de conduire; **l. number** *(of car)* numéro *m* d'immatriculation; **l. plate** plaque *f* d'immatriculation (b) *(freedom)* liberté *f*; *(excessive freedom)* licence *f*

license² ['laɪsəns] *vt Com* accorder une licence à; **to be licensed to carry a gun** avoir un permis de port d'armes

licentious [laɪ'senʃəs] *adj* licencieux(euse)

lichen ['laɪkən] *n* lichen *m*

lick [lɪk] **1** *n* (a) *(with tongue)* coup *m* de langue; *Fam* **a l. of paint** un petit coup de peinture (b) *Fam* **at a great l., at full l.** à toute allure
2 *vt* (a) *(with tongue)* lécher; **to l. one's lips** se lécher les lèvres; *Fig* se (pour)lécher les babines; *Fig* **to l. one's wounds** panser ses blessures; *Fam Fig* **to l. sb's boots** lécher les bottes à qn; *Vulg* **to l. sb's ass** faire du lèche-cul à qn; *Fam* **to l. sb into shape** dresser qn (b) *Fam (defeat)* mettre une raclée à

licorice ['lɪkərɪs] *n* réglisse *f*

lid [lɪd] *n* (a) *(of pot, jar)* couvercle *m* (b) *(idioms)* **to take the l. off sth** exposer qch au grand jour; **to keep the l. on sth** étouffer qch

lie¹ [laɪ] **1** *n* mensonge *m*; **to tell a l.** dire un mensonge; **to give the l. to sth** démentir qch; **l. detector** détecteur *m* de mensonges
2 *vi* mentir; **to l. through one's teeth** mentir effrontément

lie² [laɪ] *vi (pt* **lay** [leɪ]*, pp* **lain** [leɪn]) (a) *(of person, animal) (be in a lying position)* être couché(e) ou allongé(e); *(get down)* se coucher, s'allonger; **here lies...** *(on gravestone)* ci-gît...; **to l. in bed** rester au lit; **I lay awake all night** je n'ai pas dormi de la nuit; *Fig* **to l. low** garder un profil bas; *Fig* **to l. in wait for sb** guetter l'arrivée de qn (b) *(of object)* être, se trouver; **snow lay on the hills** il y avait de la neige sur les collines; **to l. in ruins** *(of building)* être en ruines; *(of career, hopes)* être détruit(e) (c) *(of abstract thing)* **the responsibility lies with the author** la responsabilité incombe à l'auteur; **to know where one's in-**

terests l. savoir où se trouve son intérêt; **the difference lies in that...** la différence réside dans le fait que...; **a brilliant future lies before her** un brillant avenir s'ouvre devant elle; **what lies behind this uncharacteristic generosity?** que cache cette générosité inhabituelle?

▸**lie back** *vi* s'allonger

▸**lie down** *vi* se coucher, s'étendre; *Fig* **to take criticism/an insult lying down** se laisser critiquer/insulter sans réagir; **I'm not going to take this lying down** je ne vais pas me laisser faire

Liechtenstein ['lɪktenstaɪn] *n* le Liechtenstein

lieu [lu:] *n* **in l.** à la place; **in l. of** au lieu de

lieutenant [lu:'tenənt] *n Mil* lieutenant *m*; *Naut* lieutenant de vaisseau; *(police officer)* inspecteur *m* de police; *Fig (helper)* lieutenant; **l. colonel** lieutenant-colonel *m*

life [laɪf] *(pl* **lives** [laɪvz]) *n* (a) *(existence)* vie *f*; **to take sb's l.** tuer qn; **to take one's own l.** se suicider; **to bring sb back to l.** ramener qn à la vie; **a matter of l. and death** une question de vie ou de mort; **l. after death** la vie après la mort; **to risk one's l., to risk l. and limb** risquer sa vie ou sa peau; **to escape with one's l.** avoir la vie sauve; **to lose one's l.** perdre la vie; **no lives were lost** on ne déplore aucune victime; **he held on to the rope for dear l.** il s'accrochait au cordage avec l'énergie du désespoir; **run for your lives!** sauve qui peut!; *Fam* **not on your l.!** jamais de la vie!; *Fam* **I couldn't for the l. of me remember** je n'arrivais absolument pas à me rappeler; **from l.** *(to draw, paint)* d'après nature; **bird l.** oiseaux *mpl*; **plant l.** végétaux *mpl*; **l. belt** ceinture *f* de sauvetage; **l. coach** coach *m*; **l. cycle** cycle *m* de vie; **l. drawing** dessin *m* d'après modèle; **l. force** force *f* vitale; **l. form** forme *f* de vie; **l. jacket** gilet *m* de sauvetage; **l. sciences** sciences *fpl* de la vie; **l. vest** gilet *m* de sauvetage

(b) *(period of existence)* vie *f*; **she had worked all her l.** elle avait travaillé toute sa vie; **never in (all) my l.** jamais de ma vie; **a l. of Tolstoy** une biographie de Tolstoï; *Fam* **to get l.** en prendre pour perpète; **l. annuity** rente *f* viagère; **l. expectancy** espérance *f* de vie; **l. imprisonment** emprisonnement *m* à vie; **l. insurance** assurance-vie *f*; **l. member** membre *m* à vie; **l. pension** pension *f* à vie; **l. sentence** condamnation *f* à perpétuité; **l. span** *(of person, animal)* espérance *f* de vie; *(of machine)* durée *f* de vie; **to write one's l. story** écrire son autobiographie

(c) *(mode of existence)* vie *f*; *Fam* **to live** or **to lead the l. of Riley** se la couler douce; **to make a new l. for oneself** refaire sa vie; **way of l.** style *m* de vie; **he makes her l. a misery** il lui rend la vie insupportable; **to make l. worth living** donner un sens à l'existence; *Fam* **how's l.?** comment ça va?; **what a l.!** quelle vie!; **such is** or **that's l.!** c'est la vie!; **this is the l.!** voilà ce que j'appelle vivre!; *Fam* **get a l.!** t'es vraiment nul!

(d) *(liveliness)* **to come to l.** s'animer; **to bring sb to l.** *(of book, author)* donner vie à qn; **the l. and soul of the party** le boute-en-train de la soirée; **there's l. in the old dog yet** il n'a pas encore dit son dernier mot, le vieux

lifeblood ['laɪfblʌd] *n (of person)* souffle *m* vital; *Fig (of economy, society)* moteur *m*

lifeboat ['laɪfbəʊt] *n* canot *m* de sauvetage

life-giving ['laɪfgɪvɪŋ] *adj (sun, water)* nourricier(ère); *(aid)* vital(e)

lifeguard ['laɪfgɑːd] *n (at the seaside)* surveillant(e) *m,f* de baignade; *(at swimming pool)* maître *m* nageur

lifeless ['laɪflɪs] *adj* sans vie; *(performance, style)* qui manque de vie

lifelessly ['laɪflɪslɪ] *adv* sans vie

lifelike ['laɪflaɪk] *adj (portrait)* très ressemblant(e)

lifeline ['laɪflaɪn] *n Fig* planche *f* (de salut); **to throw sb a l.** offrir ou tendre à qn une planche (de salut)

lifelong ['laɪflɒŋ] *adj* de toujours

lifer ['laɪfə(r)] *n Fam (prisoner)* condamné(e) *m,f* à perpète

life-saver ['laɪfseɪvə(r)] *n Fam* **seatbelts can be life-savers** le port de la ceinture de sécurité peut sauver des vies; *Fig* **you're a l.!** tu me sauves la vie!

life-saving ['laɪfseɪvɪŋ] *adj* salvateur(trice); *(equipment)* de réanimation; **she needed a l. operation** elle devait se faire opérer, c'était une question de vie ou de mort

life-size ['laɪfsaɪz], **life-sized** ['laɪfsaɪzd] *adj* grandeur nature *inv*

lifestyle ['laɪfstaɪl] *n* style *m ou* mode *m* de vie

life-support ['laɪfsəpɔːt] *adj* **l. system** *or* **machine** respirateur *m* artificiel

life-threatening ['laɪfθretnɪŋ] *adj (disease)* potentiellement mortel(elle); **to be in a l. situation** être en danger de mort

lifetime ['laɪftaɪm] *n (of person)* vie *f*; **in my l.** de mon vivant; **it's the chance of a l.** une telle chance ne se présente qu'une fois dans la vie; **the vacation of a l.** des vacances exceptionnelles

lift [lɪft] **1** *n* **(a)** *(elevator)* ascenseur *m*; **(goods) l.** montecharge *m inv* **(b)** *(car ride)* **to give sb a l.** prendre *ou* emmener qn en voiture; **could you give me a l. to the station?** est-ce que tu peux m'emmener à la gare? **(c)** *Fam* **to give sb a l.** *(cheer up)* remonter le moral à qn

2 *vt* **(a)** *(one's head, eyes, arm)* lever; **he won't l. a finger to help** il ne lèvera pas le petit doigt; **to l. sb (up)** *(after fall)* aider qn à se relever; **to l. a child up** prendre un enfant dans ses bras **(b)** *Fam (take, steal)* piquer; *(arrest)* choper **(c)** *(restrictions, siege)* lever

3 *vi (of mist, fog)* se lever, se dissiper

▸**lift off** *vi (of rocket)* décoller

liftoff ['lɪftɒf] *n (of rocket)* décollage *m*

ligament ['lɪgəmənt] *n* ligament *m*

light¹ [laɪt] **1** *n* **(a)** *(illumination)* lumière *f*; **by the l. of the moon** à la clarté de la lune; **things will look different in the cold l. of day** demain vous verrez les choses sous un autre jour; **to be in sb's l.** faire de l'ombre à qn; *Comput* **l. pen** crayon *m* optique; **l. year** année-lumière *f* **(b)** *(lamp)* lumière *f*; *Fam* **to go out like a l.** s'endormir aussitôt couché(e); **(traffic) lights** feux *mpl* de circulation; **l. bulb** ampoule *f* **(c)** *(fire)* **to set l. to sth** mettre le feu à qch; **have you got a l.?** vous avez du feu? **(d)** *(idioms)* **the l. at the end of the tunnel** le bout du tunnel; **to throw** *or* **to cast l. on sth** faire la lumière sur qch; **to bring sth to l.** mettre qch en lumière; **to come to l.** être découvert(e); **to see sb/sth in a new/different l.** voir qn/qch sous un jour nouveau/différent; **in (the) l. of...** *(considering)* à la lumière de...

2 *adj (not dark)* clair(e); **it will soon be l.** il fera bientôt jour **3** *vt (pt & pp* **lit** [lɪt]*)* **(a)** *(fire, cigarette)* allumer **(b)** *(room, street)* éclairer, illuminer

light² [laɪt] **1** *adj* **(a)** *(not heavy)* léger(ère); **to be l. on one's feet** avoir le pas léger; **to be a l. sleeper** avoir le sommeil léger; **to have a l. touch** avoir la main légère; **l. aircraft** avion *m* petit porteur; **l. artillery** artillerie *f* légère; *Culin* **l. cream** crème *f* liquide; **l. industry** industrie *f* légère; **l. infantry** infanterie *f* légère **(b)** *(not severe) (job, exercise)* facile, peu fatigant(e); *(rain)* fin(e); *(prison sentence)* léger(ère) **(c)** *(not serious)* léger(ère); **to make l. of sth** prendre qch à la légère; **l. entertainment** variétés *fpl*; **l. reading** lectures *fpl* récréatives; **l. verse** poésie *f* facile

2 *adv* **to travel l.** voyager léger

▸**light on** *(pt & pp* **lighted**) *vt insep* tomber sur

▸**light up 1** *vt sep (house, room)* éclairer; *(cigarette)* allumer **2** *vi* s'éclairer; *Fam (of smoker)* allumer une cigarette

lighten¹ ['laɪtən] **1** *vt (make less dark)* éclaircir **2** *vi (of sky)* s'éclaircir

lighten² ['laɪtən] *vt (make less heavy)* alléger; *Fig* **to l. sb's load** soulager qn

▸**lighten up** *vi Fam* se détendre

lighter ['laɪtə(r)] *n* briquet *m*; **l. fluid** *or* **fuel** essence *f* à briquet

light-fingered [laɪt'fɪŋgəd] *adj Fam* **to be l.** être chapardeur(euse)

light-headed [laɪt'hedɪd] *adj* étourdi(e)

light-hearted [laɪt'hɑːtɪd] *adj (person, discussion)* enjoué(e); *(remark)* badin(e); **to take a l. look at sth** poser un regard amusé sur qch

lighthouse ['laɪthaʊs] *n* phare *m*; **l. keeper** gardien *m* de phare

lighting ['laɪtɪŋ] *n (act, system)* éclairage *m*

lightly ['laɪtlɪ] *adv* légèrement; **to sleep l.** avoir le sommeil léger; **to get off l.** s'en tirer à bon compte; **to speak l. of sth** parler de qch à la légère; **to speak l. of sb** parler de qn sur un ton léger; **to take a decision l.** prendre une décision à la légère

lightness ['laɪtnɪs] *n* **(a)** *(brightness)* clarté *f* **(b)** *(in weight)* légèreté *f*

lightning ['laɪtnɪŋ] *n* **(a)** *(bolt)* éclairs *mpl*, foudre *f*; **l. rod** paratonnerre *m* **(b)** *(idioms)* **as quick as l.**, **with l. speed** rapide comme l'éclair; **l. attack** attaque *f* éclair; **l. visit** visite *f* éclair

lightweight ['laɪtweɪt] **1** *n (in boxing)* poids *m* léger; *Fig & Pej (in character, intellect)* personne *f* qui manque d'envergure **2** *adj (garment, fabric)* léger(ère)

lignite ['lɪgnaɪt] *n* lignite *m*

like¹ [laɪk] **1** *n* **he and his l.** lui et ses semblables; **it's not for the likes of me** ce n'est pas pour des gens comme moi; **music, painting and the l.** la musique, la peinture et autres choses du même genre; **I've never seen the l. of it** je n'ai jamais vu une chose pareille

2 *adj* semblable, pareil(eille); **they are as l. as two peas (in a pod)** ils se ressemblent comme deux gouttes d'eau

3 *prep* **(a)** *(similar to)* **to be l. sb/sth** être semblable à qn/qch; ressembler à qn/qch; **to taste l. sth** avoir le même goût que qch; **to look l. sb/sth** ressembler à qn/qch; **what's the weather l.?** quel temps fait-il?; **people l. you** des gens comme vous; **you know what she's l.** tu sais comment elle est; **it costs something l. \$30** cela coûte dans les 30 dollars; **that's more l. it** voilà qui est mieux; **we don't have anything l. as many as that** on est loin d'en avoir autant; **there's nothing l. it!** il n'y a rien de tel!; **she is nothing l. as intelligent as you** elle est loin d'être aussi intelligente que vous; **that's not l. her** cela ne lui ressemble pas; **that's just l. him!** c'est bien de lui!; *Prov* **l. father, l. son** tel père, tel fils **(b)** *(in the manner of)* comme; *Fam* **don't be l. that!** ne fais pas l'idiot! **(c)** *(such as)* tel (telle) que; **take more exercise, l. jogging** fais plus d'exercice, du jogging par exemple

4 *adv Fam* **as l. as not** à coup sûr

5 *conj Fam* **do it l. I said** fais comme je t'ai dit; **he looked l. he'd seen a ghost** on aurait dit qu'il avait vu un fantôme; **it's not l. he's ill or anything** ce n'est pas comme s'il était malade ou quoi que ce soit

like² [laɪk] **1** *n* **likes** goûts *mpl*, préférences *fpl*; **likes and dislikes** préférences

2 *vt* **(a)** *(person)* bien aimer; **she is well liked** elle est très appréciée **(b)** *(enjoy)* aimer; **whether she likes it or not,...** que ça lui plaise ou non,...; **I l. to think my father would have agreed** j'aime à penser que mon père aurait approuvé; *Fam Ironic* **well, I l. that!** elle est bien bonne, celle-là! **(c)** *(want)* **would you l. a coffee?** est-ce que tu aimerais un café?; **I would very much l. to go** j'aimerais beaucoup y aller; **I would l. nothing better than...** rien ne me ferait plus plaisir que...; **he doesn't l. people to talk about it** il n'aime pas que l'on en parle; **he thinks he can do anything he likes** il se croit tout permis; **if/when you l.** si/quand vous voulez; **as much as you l.** tant que vous voulez; **as often as you l.** aussi souvent que vous voulez; **I didn't l. to mention it** j'ai préféré ne pas le mentionner

likeable ['laɪkəbəl] *adj* sympathique

likelihood ['laɪklɪhʊd] *n* probabilité *f*; **in all l.** selon toute vrai-semblance *ou* probabilité; **there is little l. of finding it** il y a peu de chance pour qu'on le trouve; **the l. is that...** il est probable que... + *subjunctive*

likely ['laɪklɪ] **1** *adj* (**a**) *(probable)* probable; **it's more than l.** c'est plus que probable; **it's l. to rain** il est probable qu'il pleuve, il pleuvra probablement; *Ironic* **a l. story!** à d'autres! (**b**) *(suitable)* approprié(e)
  2 *adv* **very l.** très probablement; **as l. as not** sûrement; *Fam* **not l.!** tu plaisantes?

like-minded [laɪk'maɪndɪd] *adj* du même avis; *(having same tastes)* qui ont les mêmes goûts

liken ['laɪkən] *vt* comparer (**to** à)

likeness ['laɪknɪs] *n* (**a**) *(similarity)* ressemblance *f*; **family l.** air *m* de famille (**b**) *(portrait)* portrait *m*

likewise ['laɪkwaɪz] *adv* *(similarly)* de même, aussi; **to do l.** en faire autant

liking ['laɪkɪŋ] *n* goût *m*, penchant *m*; **is it to your l.?** cela est-il à votre goût?; **to have a l. for sth** avoir du goût pour qch, aimer qch; **to take a l. to sth** prendre goût à qch; **to take a l. to sb** se prendre d'amitié pour qn

lilac ['laɪlək] **1** *n* lilas *m*
  2 *adj* lilas *inv*

lilt [lɪlt] *n (of voice)* inflexions *fpl*

lilting ['lɪltɪŋ] *adj* chantant(e)

lily ['lɪlɪ] *(pl* **lilies)** *n* lis *m*; **l. of the valley** muguet *m*

lily-livered ['lɪlɪlɪvəd] *adj Fam* froussard(e)

lima bean ['liːmə'biːn] *n* haricot *m* de Lima

limb [lɪm] *n* (**a**) *(of body)* membre *m*; **to tear sb l. from l.** dé-chiqueter qn, mettre qn en pièces (**b**) *(of tree)* grosse branche *f*; *Fig* **to be out on a l.** *(be in dangerous position)* être dans une situation délicate; *(be alone)* être en plan; **to go out on a l.** prendre des risques

limber ['lɪmbə(r)] *adj* souple
▶limber up *vi* s'échauffer

limbo ['lɪmbəʊ] *(pl* **limbos)** *n* (**a**) *Rel* les limbes *mpl*; *Fig* **to be in l.** être dans les limbes (**b**) *(dance)* limbo *m*

lime¹ [laɪm] *n (fruit)* citron *m* vert; *(citrus tree)* limettier *m*; *(lin-den tree)* tilleul *m*; **l. green** vert *m* jaune; **l. juice** jus *m* de citron vert

lime² [laɪm] *n Chem* chaux *f*

limelight ['laɪmlaɪt] *n* **to be in the l.** être sous les projecteurs; **to steal the l.** voler la vedette

limerick ['lɪmərɪk] *n* = poème burlesque en cinq vers

limestone ['laɪmstəʊn] *n* calcaire *m*

limey ['laɪmɪ] *(pl* **limeys)** *n Fam (British person)* Rosbif *m*

limit ['lɪmɪt] **1** *n* limite *f*; **within limits** jusqu'à un certain point; **off limits (to)** inaccessible (à); *(forbidden)* interdit(e) (à); **to know no limits** être sans limites; **that's the l.!** ce n'est plus possible!; **he's the l.!** il est impossible!
  2 *vt* limiter; **to l. oneself to sth/to doing sth** se limiter à qch/à faire qch

limitation [lɪmɪ'teɪʃən] *n* limitation *f*; **to know one's limita-tions** connaître ses limites

limited ['lɪmɪtəd] *adj* limité(e); **l. company** société *f* à responsabilité limitée; **l. edition** édition *f* à tirage limité; *Law* **l. liability** responsabilité *f* limitée

limitless ['lɪmɪtlɪs] *adj (wealth, amount, supply)* illimité(e); *(generosity)* sans bornes

limo ['lɪməʊ] *(pl* **limos)** *n Fam* limousine *f*

limousine [lɪmə'ziːn] *n* limousine *f*

limp¹ [lɪmp] **1** *n* boitement *m*; **to have a l.** boiter
  2 *vi* boiter

limp² [lɪmp] *adj* mou (molle); **to go l.** s'affaisser

limpet ['lɪmpɪt] *n* bernique *f*, patelle *f*; *Fig* **to stick to sb like a l.** ne pas lâcher qn; *Mil* **l. mine** mine *f* magnétique

limpid ['lɪmpɪd] *adj* limpide

limply ['lɪmplɪ] *adv* mollement

linchpin ['lɪntʃpɪn] *n Fig (person)* cheville *f* ouvrière; *(thing)* clé *f* de voûte

linden ['lɪndən] *n* **l. (tree)** tilleul *m*

line¹ [laɪn] **1** *n* (**a**) *(mark)* ligne *f*; *(drawn)* trait *m*; *(on face)* ride *f*; *Fig* **to draw the l. at doing sth** se refuser à faire qch; **l. drawing** dessin *m* au trait
  (**b**) *(row)* ligne *f*, rangée *f*; *(one behind the other)* file *f*; *(queue)* queue *f*; **to stand in a l.** être en rang; *(one behind the other)* être en file; **to stand** *or* **to wait in l.** *(queue)* faire la queue; *Fig* **to be out of l.** dépasser les bornes; **to be in l. with sth** être conforme à qch; *Fig* **to be in l. for promotion** être sur la liste des promotions; *Fig* **to be on the l.** *(of one's job, reputation)* être en jeu; **l. dancing** = danse de style country effectuée en rangs; *Com & Ind* **l. manager** chef *m* d'équipe
  (**c**) *(rope)* ligne *f*; *(for clothes)* corde *f* à linge
  (**d**) *(railroad track)* voie *f*; *(railroad route)* ligne *f*
  (**e**) *(direction)* **l. of argument** raisonnement *m*; **l. of attack** plan *m* d'attaque; **to be in the l. of fire** être dans la ligne de tir; *Fig* être en butte aux critiques; **something along the lines of...** quelque chose dans le genre de...
  (**f**) *(policy)* ligne *f*; **the party l.** la ligne du parti; **to take a firm l. with sb** se montrer ferme avec qn
  (**g**) *(of text)* ligne *f*; *(of poem)* vers *m*; **to drop sb a l.** écrire un mot à qn; **to learn one's lines** apprendre son rôle; *Fig* **to read between the lines** lire entre les lignes
  (**h**) *(family)* lignée *f*; **in a direct l.** en ligne directe
  (**i**) *(telephone connection)* ligne *f*
  (**j**) *Fam (job)* **what l. (of business) are you in?** vous travail-lez dans quelle branche?
  (**k**) *Com (of goods)* ligne *f*
  2 *vt (road, river)* border; **the crowd lined the street** la foule s'alignait le long du trottoir
▶line up 1 *vt sep* (**a**) *(form into a line)* mettre en ligne, aligner (**b**) *(prepare)* **to have sb lined up for sth** avoir qn en vue pour qch; **have you got anything lined up for this evening?** avez-vous quelque chose de prévu pour ce soir?
  2 *vi (form a line)* se mettre en rang

line² [laɪn] *vt (coat, curtain)* doubler (**with** de); *(box, drawer)* ta-pisser (**with** de); *Fig* **to l. one's pockets** se remplir les poches

lineage ['lɪnɪɪdʒ] *n* lignée *f*

linear ['lɪnɪə(r)] *adj* linéaire; *Math* **l. equation** équation *f* li-néaire; *Comput* **l. programming** programmation *f* linéaire

lined¹ [laɪnd] *adj (paper)* réglé(e); *(face)* ridé(e)

lined² [laɪnd] *adj (coat, curtain)* doublé(e) (**with** de)

linen ['lɪnɪn] *n* (**a**) *(fabric)* lin *m*; **a l. dress** une robe en lin (**b**) *(clothes)* linge *m*; *(sheets, tablecloths, etc.)* linge (de maison); *Fig* **don't wash your dirty l. in public** il faut laver son linge sale en famille; **l. basket** panier *m* à linge

liner ['laɪnə(r)] *n (ship)* (paquebot *m*) transatlantique *m*

linesman ['laɪnzmən] *n (in tennis)* juge *m* de ligne; *(in soccer)* juge de touche

line-up ['laɪnʌp] *n* (**a**) *(of team)* composition *f*; *(on TV show)* plateau *m* (**b**) *(police identification)* séance *f* d'identification

linger ['lɪŋgə(r)] *vi (of person)* s'attarder; *(of smell, custom)* sub-sister, persister; **to l. behind** rester en arrière; **to l. over do-ing sth** prendre son temps pour faire qch

lingerie ['lɔːnʒərɪ] *n* lingerie *f*

lingering ['lɪŋgrɪŋ] *adj (look)* long (longue); *(doubt)* persis-tant(e); *(death)* lent(e)

lingo ['lɪŋgəʊ] *(pl* **lingoes)** *n Fam (language)* langue *f*; *(jargon)* charabia *m*

lingua franca ['lɪŋgwə'fræŋkə] *n* langue *f* véhiculaire

linguist ['lɪŋgwɪst] n (**a**) (specialist in linguistics) linguiste mf (**b**) (polyglot) **to be a l.** être doué(e) pour les langues

linguistic [lɪŋ'gwɪstɪk] adj linguistique

linguistics [lɪŋ'gwɪstɪks] n linguistique f

lining ['laɪnɪŋ] n (of coat, curtain) doublure f; (of brakes) garniture f; (of stomach) paroi f

link [lɪŋk] **1** n (**a**) (of chain) chaînon m, maillon m; Fig **the weak l.** (in argument) le point faible; (in team) l'élément m faible (**b**) (connection) lien m (**between** entre) (**c**) Comput lien m (**to** avec)
2 vt (physically) relier; (by association) lier; **to l. hands** se donner la main
▶**link up 1** vt relier
2 vi (of roads, travelers) se rejoindre

linoleum [lɪ'nəʊlɪəm] n linoléum m

linseed ['lɪnsi:d] n graine f de lin; **l. oil** huile f de lin

lintel ['lɪntəl] n linteau m

Linux ['laɪnəks, 'lɪnəks] n Comput Linux m

lion ['laɪən] n lion m; Fig **the l.'s share** la part du lion; **l. cub** lionceau m; **l. tamer** dresseur m de lions

lioness ['laɪənes] n lionne f

lion-hearted ['laɪən'hɑːtɪd] adj courageux(euse) comme un lion

lip [lɪp] n (**a**) (of person) lèvre f; (of animal) babine f; **to read sb's lips** lire sur les lèvres de qn; **to pay l. service to sth** faire semblant de s'intéresser à qch; **l. balm** baume m pour les lèvres; **l. gloss** brillant m à lèvres (**b**) (of pitcher) bec m (**c**) Fam (impudence) insolence f; **less of your l.!** sois un peu moins insolent(e)!

liposuction ['lɪpəʊsʌkʃən] n lipposuccion f

lip-read ['lɪpriːd] (pt & pp **lip-read** ['lɪpred]) **1** vt lire sur les lèvres de
2 vi lire sur les lèvres

lipstick ['lɪpstɪk] n rouge m à lèvres

liquefy ['lɪkwɪfaɪ] (pt & pp **liquefied**) **1** vt liquéfier
2 vi se liquéfier

liqueur [lɪ'kɜː(r)] n liqueur f

liquid ['lɪkwɪd] **1** n liquide m
2 adj liquide; Fin **l. assets** liquidités fpl; **l. crystal display** affichage m à cristaux liquides

liquidate ['lɪkwɪdeɪt] vt (**a**) Fin (company, debt) liquider; (capital) mobiliser (**b**) Fam (kill) liquider

liquidation [lɪkwɪ'deɪʃən] n Fin (of company, debt) liquidation f; (of capital) mobilisation f; **to go into l.** entrer en liquidation

liquidity [lɪ'kwɪdɪtɪ] n Fin liquidité f; **l. ratio** ratio m de liquidité

liquidize ['lɪkwɪdaɪz] vt (gas, solid) liquéfier

liquor ['lɪkə(r)] n alcool m; **l. store** magasin m de vins et spiritueux

lira ['lɪərə] (pl **lire** ['lɪərə]) n lire f

Lisbon ['lɪzbən] n Lisbonne

lisp [lɪsp] **1** n zézaiement m; **to have a l.** avoir un cheveu sur la langue
2 vi avoir un cheveu sur la langue, zézayer

list¹ [lɪst] **1** n liste f; **l. price** prix m de vente
2 vt (enter in list) faire une liste de; **her phone number isn't listed (in the directory)** son numéro de téléphone ne figure pas dans l'annuaire; **to be listed on the Stock Exchange** être coté(e) en Bourse; **listed building** immeuble m classé

list² [lɪst] **1** n (of ship) bande f, gîte f
2 vi (of ship) donner de la bande ou de la gîte

listen ['lɪsən] vi écouter; **to l. to sb/sth** écouter qn/qch; **to l. for sth** tendre l'oreille afin d'entendre qch; **to l. (out) for the phone** guetter la sonnerie du téléphone; **to l. to reason** entendre raison; **he wouldn't l.** il n'a rien voulu savoir
▶**listen in** vi **to l. in (on sth)** écouter (qch)

listener ['lɪsnə(r)] n (**a**) **to be a good l.** savoir écouter (**b**) (to radio program) auditeur(trice) m,f

listing ['lɪstɪŋ] n (list) liste f; **listings** (in newspaper) rubrique f des spectacles

listless ['lɪstlɪs] adj apathique

lit [lɪt] pt & pp of **light¹**

litany ['lɪtənɪ] (pl **litanies**) n litanie f

liter ['liːtə(r)] n litre m

literacy ['lɪtərəsɪ] n alphabétisation f; **l. rate** taux m d'alphabétisation

literal ['lɪtərəl] adj littéral(e)

literally ['lɪtərəlɪ] adv littéralement; **to take sth l.** prendre qch au pied de la lettre

literary ['lɪtərərɪ] adj littéraire

literate ['lɪtərɪt] adj **to be l.** (able to read and write) savoir lire et écrire; (educated) être cultivé(e)

literature ['lɪtərɪtʃə(r)] n (**a**) (fiction, poetry) littérature f (**b**) (information) documentation f

lithe [laɪð] adj agile

lithium ['lɪθɪəm] n lithium m

lithograph ['lɪθəgræf] n lithographie f

Lithuania [lɪθjʊ'eɪnɪə] n la Lituanie

Lithuanian [lɪθjʊ'eɪnɪən] **1** n (**a**) (person) Lituanien(enne) m,f (**b**) (language) lituanien m
2 adj lituanien(enne)

litigant ['lɪtɪgənt] n Law partie f

litigate ['lɪtɪgeɪt] vi Law intenter une action en justice

litigation [lɪtɪ'geɪʃən] n Law action f en justice

litigious [lɪ'tɪdʒəs] adj (**a**) Law (matter) litigieux(euse), contentieux(euse) (**b**) Pej (fond of lawsuits) procédurier(ère)

litmus ['lɪtməs] n **l. paper** papier m (de) tournesol; Fig **l. test** test m décisif

litter ['lɪtə(r)] **1** n (**a**) (rubbish) détritus mpl, ordures fpl (**b**) (of animal) portée f (**c**) (for cat) litière f; **l. tray** caisse f (pour litière) (**d**) Hist (conveyance) litière f
2 vt **to be littered with** être couvert(e) ou jonché(e) de

litterbug ['lɪtəbʌg] n Fam = personne qui jette des détritus n'importe où

little ['lɪtəl] **1** n peu m; **to eat l. or nothing** manger peu ou pas du tout; **he knows very l.** il ne sait pas grand-chose; **a l. more** un peu plus; **a l. hot/slow** un peu chaud(e)/lent(e); **every l. helps** les petits ruisseaux font les grandes rivières
2 adj (**a**) (small) petit(e); **a l. while** un petit moment; **l. finger** petit doigt m (**b**) (comparative **less**, superlative **least**) (not much) peu de; **l. money** peu d'argent; **a l. money** un peu d'argent; **it makes l. sense** ça n'a pas beaucoup de sens
3 adv (comparative **less**, superlative **least**) peu; **l. by l.** peu à peu; **l. more than an hour ago** il y a à peine une heure; **that's l. short of bribery** ça frise la corruption; **l. did I think that...** j'étais loin de penser que...

littoral ['lɪtərəl] **1** n littoral m
2 adj littoral(e)

liturgy ['lɪtədʒɪ] (pl **liturgies**) n liturgie f

live¹ [laɪv] **1** adj (**a**) (person, animal) vivant(e), en vie; Fam **a real l. movie star** une vedette de cinéma en chair et en os; **a l. issue** un sujet brûlant (**b**) (performance, broadcast) en direct (**c**) (bomb) non explosé(e); **l. ammunition** balles fpl réelles; **l. wire** fil m sous tension; Fig **to be a l. wire** déborder de vie (**d**) (volcano) actif(ive)
2 adv (broadcast) en direct; **to perform l.** (of comedian, dancer) être sur scène; (of band) jouer en concert

live² [lɪv] **1** vt vivre; **to l. a long life** vivre longtemps; **to l. a happy life** mener une vie heureuse; **to l. a lie** vivre dans le mensonge; **it makes life worth living** cela donne un sens à la vie
2 vi vivre; (reside) habiter, vivre; **to l. with sb** vivre avec qn; **as long as I l.** tant que je vivrai; **to l. a little** profiter un peu de la vie; **l. and let l.!** un peu de tolérance!; **you l. and learn** on en apprend tous les jours

▶**live down** *vt sep (mistake, one's past)* faire oublier; **I'll never l. it down!** je n'ai pas fini d'en entendre parler!

▶**live off** *vt insep* **to l. off sth** vivre de qch; **to l. off sb** vivre aux crochets de qn

▶**live on 1** *vt insep (food)* se nourrir de; *(capital)* vivre sur; **it's not enough to l. on** ce n'est pas suffisant pour vivre
  2 *vi (of person)* continuer à vivre; *(of memory)* survivre

▶**live out** *vt sep* **to l. out one's life** *or* **days** passer ses jours; **to l. out a fantasy** réaliser un fantasme

▶**live through** *vt insep* connaître, vivre

▶**live together** *vi* vivre ensemble

▶**live up** *vt sep Fam* **to l. it up** faire la fête

▶**live up to** *vt insep* **to l. up to sb's expectations** répondre aux attentes de qn; **to fail to l. up to expectations** ne pas tenir ses promesses; **to l. up to one's reputation** être à la hauteur de sa réputation

live-in ['lɪvɪn] *adj (chauffeur, nanny)* logé(e) et nourri(e); **l. lover** compagnon (compagne) *m,f*

livelihood ['laɪvlɪhʊd] *n* gagne-pain *m inv*; **to earn one's l.** gagner sa vie

liveliness ['laɪvlɪnɪs] *n* vivacité *f*

lively ['laɪvlɪ] *adj (person)* plein(e) de vie; *(place, party, conversation)* animé(e); *(music)* entraînant(e); *(imagination)* fertile; **to take a l. interest in sth** s'intéresser vivement à qch

▶**liven up** ['laɪvən] **1** *vt sep (person)* égayer; *(place, party, conversation)* animer; *(proceedings)* activer
  2 *vi (of person)* s'égayer; *(of place, party, conversation)* s'animer

liver ['lɪvə(r)] *n* foie *m*; **l. spot** tache *f* de vieillesse

livery ['lɪvərɪ] *n* livrée *f*

lives [laɪvz] *pl of* **life**

livestock ['laɪvstɒk] *n* bétail *m*

livid ['lɪvɪd] *adj* **(a)** *(angry)* furieux(euse) **(b)** *(bluish-gray)* livide, blême

living ['lɪvɪŋ] **1** *n* vie *f*; **to earn one's l.** gagner sa vie; **what does she do for a l.?** qu'est-ce qu'elle fait dans la vie?; **l. conditions** conditions *fpl* de vie; **l. expenses** faux frais *mpl*; **l. room** (salle *f* de) séjour *m*, salon *m*; **l. standards** niveau *m* de vie
  2 *adj* vivant(e); **there is not a l. soul to be seen** il n'y a pas âme qui vive; **within l. memory** de mémoire d'homme

lizard ['lɪzəd] *n* lézard *m*

llama ['lɑːmə] *n* lama *m*

lo [ləʊ] *exclam Lit or Hum* **lo and behold...** ô surprise...

load [ləʊd] **1** *n* **(a)** *(burden)* fardeau *m*, charge *f*; **to share** *or* **to spread the l.** répartir le travail; **that's a l. off my mind!** cela m'enlève un poids! **(b)** *Fam (lot)* **a l. of, loads of** plein de; **it's a l. of garbage!** c'est n'importe quoi!; **we've got loads of time** on a largement le temps
  2 *vt (truck, gun, camera)* charger; *(software)* installer; *(washing machine)* remplir
  3 *vi (of truck)* prendre un chargement

▶**load up 1** *vt sep* charger
  2 *vi* prendre un chargement

loaded ['ləʊdɪd] *adj* **(a)** *(truck, gun, camera)* chargé(e) **(b)** *(dice)* pipé(e); *(question)* insidieux(euse) **(c)** *Fam (rich)* plein(e) aux as **(d)** *Fam (drunk)* bourré(e); *(on drugs)* défoncé(e)

loading ['ləʊdɪŋ] *n* chargement *m*; **l. bay** aire *f* de chargement

loaf [ləʊf] *(pl* **loaves** [ləʊvz]*)* *n* **a l. (of bread)** un pain

▶**loaf about, loaf around** *vi* traîner

loafer ['ləʊfə(r)] *n* **(a)** *(person)* fainéant(e) *m,f* **(b)** *(shoe)* mocassin *m*

loam [ləʊm] *n* terreau *m*

loan [ləʊn] **1** *n (from lender's point of view)* prêt *m*; *(from borrower's point of view)* emprunt *m*; **to give sb a l. of sth** prêter qch à qn; **to take out a l.** faire un emprunt; *Fam* **l. shark** usurier(ère) *m,f*
  2 *vt (money)* prêter

loath [ləʊθ] *adj* **to be l. to do sth** répugner à faire qch

loathe [ləʊð] *vt* détester; **to l. doing sth** détester faire qch

loathing ['ləʊðɪŋ] *n* dégoût *m*, répugnance *f*

loathsome ['ləʊðsəm] *adj* répugnant(e)

loaves [ləʊvz] *pl of* **loaf**

lob [lɒb] **1** *n (in tennis)* lob *m*
  2 *vt (pt & pp* **lobbed***)* **(a)** *(in tennis)* lober **(b)** *Fam (throw)* balancer

lobby ['lɒbɪ] **1** *n (pl* **lobbies***)* **(a)** *(of hotel)* hall *m*; *(of theater)* foyer *m* **(b)** *(pressure group)* groupe *m* de pression, lobby *m*
  2 *vt (pt & pp* **lobbied***)* faire pression sur
  3 *vi* **to l. for/against sth** faire pression en faveur de/contre qch

lobbyist ['lɒbɪɪst] *n* membre *m* d'un groupe de pression

lobe [ləʊb] *n* lobe *m*

lobotomy [lə'bɒtəmɪ] *(pl* **lobotomies***)* *n* lobotomie *f*

lobster ['lɒbstə(r)] *n* homard *m*; **as red as a l.** *(sunburnt)* rouge comme une écrevisse; **l. pot** casier *m* à homards

local ['ləʊkəl] **1** *n (person)* **the locals** les gens *mpl* du coin
  2 *adj* local(e); **l. anesthetic** anesthésie *f* locale; **l. color** couleur *f* locale; **l. government** ≃ administration *f* municipale; **l. time** heure *f* locale

locale [ləʊ'kɑːl] *n (of events)* lieu *m*; *(for a movie)* lieu de tournage

locality [ləʊ'kælɪtɪ] *(pl* **localities***)* *n* voisinage *m*, environs *mpl*

localization [ləʊkəlaɪ'zeɪʃən] *n* localisation *f*

localize ['ləʊkəlaɪz] *vt* localiser; **to become localized** *(disease, pain)* se localiser

locally ['ləʊkəlɪ] *adv (in neighborhood)* dans le quartier; *(in region)* dans la région

locate [ləʊ'keɪt] **1** *vt (find)* localiser; *(situate)* situer
  2 *vi (of company)* s'installer

location [ləʊ'keɪʃən] *n* **(a)** *(place)* emplacement *m*; *Cin* **on l.** en extérieur; *Cin* **l. shot** plan *m* en extérieur **(b)** *(act of finding)* localisation *f*

loch [lɒx] *n (Scottish lake)* loch *m*, lac *m*

lock¹ [lɒk] **1** *n* **(a)** *(on door)* serrure *f*; **under l. and key** *(object)* sous clef; *(person)* sous les verrous; *Fig* **l., stock and barrel** en entier **(b)** *(in wrestling)* clef *f* **(c)** *(on canal)* écluse *f*
  2 *vt (door, padlock)* fermer à clef; **to be locked in each other's arms** être étroitement enlacés(ées); *Fig* **to l. horns with sb** livrer bataille à qn
  3 *vi (of door)* se fermer; *(of car wheels)* se bloquer

▶**lock in** *vt sep* enfermer à clef

▶**lock out** *vt sep* enfermer dehors; **I locked myself out of my house** je me suis enfermé dehors

▶**lock up 1** *vt sep (person, valuables)* enfermer; *(house)* fermer à clef
  2 *vi* fermer

lock² [lɒk] *n (of hair)* mèche *f*

locker ['lɒkə(r)] *n* casier *m*; **l. room** vestiaire *m*

locket ['lɒkɪt] *n* médaillon *m*

lockjaw ['lɒkdʒɔː] *n Old-fashioned* tétanos *m*

lock-out ['lɒkaʊt] *n* lock-out *m inv*

locksmith ['lɒksmɪθ] *n* serrurier *m*

lockup ['lɒkʌp] *n Fam (police cells)* violon *m*, bloc *m*

loco ['ləʊkəʊ] *adj Fam (crazy)* dingue, cinglé(e)

locomotion [ləʊkə'məʊʃən] *n* locomotion *f*

locomotive [ləʊkə'məʊtɪv] **1** *n (train)* locomotive *f*
  2 *adj* locomotif(ive)

locust ['ləʊkəst] *n* sauterelle *f*

locution [ləʊ'kjuːʃən] *n* locution *f*

lodge [lɒdʒ] **1** *n (of porter, caretaker, masons)* loge *f*; *(small house)* pavillon *m*
  2 *vt* **(a)** *(accommodate)* loger, héberger **(b)** *Law* **to l. an appeal**

faire appel; **to l. a complaint** porter plainte

3 vi (**a**) (live) loger (**b**) (become fixed) se loger; **to be lodged in sb's memory** être gravé(e) dans la mémoire de qn

lodger ['lɒdʒə(r)] n locataire mf (en meublé); (who has meals provided) pensionnaire mf

lodging ['lɒdʒɪŋ] n logement m; **lodgings** chambre f meublée; Old-fashioned **l. house** (hôtel m) garni m

loft [lɒft] n grenier m

lofty ['lɒftɪ] adj (**a**) (aim, desire) noble (**b**) Lit (high) haut(e)

log [lɒg] **1** n (**a**) (of wood) bûche f; **to sleep like a l.** dormir comme une souche; **l. cabin** hutte f en rondins; **l. fire** feu m de bois (**b**) (record) registre m; (of ship, traveler) journal m de bord; (of plane) carnet m de vol

2 vt (pt & pp **logged**) (record) enregistrer; (in ship's, traveler's log) noter dans le journal de bord; (in plane's log) noter dans le carnet de vol

▸**log in** vi Comput entrer

▸**log off** vi Comput sortir

▸**log on** vi Comput entrer

▸**log out** vi Comput sortir

logarithm ['lɒgərɪθəm] n logarithme m

logbook ['lɒgbʊk] n (of ship, traveler) journal m de bord; (of plane) carnet m de vol

loggerheads ['lɒgəhedz] n Fam **to be at l. with sb** être en conflit avec qn

logic ['lɒdʒɪk] n logique f

logical ['lɒdʒɪkəl] adj logique

logically ['lɒdʒɪklɪ] adv logiquement

logistic [lə'dʒɪstɪk], **logistical** [lə'dʒɪstɪkəl] adj logistique

logistics [lə'dʒɪstɪks] npl logistique f; **the l. of the situation** les données logistiques de la situation

logjam ['lɒgdʒæm] n impasse f

logo ['ləʊgəʊ] (pl **logos**) n sigle m, logo m

loin [lɔɪn] n (**a**) (of beef) aloyau m; (of mutton, pork) filet m; (of veal) longe f; **l. chop** côtes fpl premières (**b**) **loins** (of person) reins mpl

loincloth ['lɔɪnklɒθ] n pagne m

loiter ['lɔɪtə(r)] vi traîner; (suspiciously) rôder; Law **to l. with intent** = rôder d'une manière suspecte

loll [lɒl] vi (of person) se prélasser; (of head) tomber en avant; (of tongue) pendre

lollipop ['lɒlɪpɒp] n sucette f

lollop ['lɒləp] vi Fam **to l. along** courir lourdement

London ['lʌndən] n Londres

Londoner ['lʌndənə(r)] n Londonien(enne) m,f

lone [ləʊn] adj (single, solitary) solitaire; Fig **a l. wolf** un(e) solitaire

loneliness ['ləʊnlɪnɪs] n (feeling) solitude f; (of place) isolement m

lonely ['ləʊnlɪ] adj (person) seul(e); (life, job) solitaire; (place) isolé(e); **to feel l.** se sentir seul; **l. hearts club** club m de rencontres; **l. hearts column** rubrique f rencontres

loner ['ləʊnə(r)] n solitaire mf

lonesome ['ləʊnsəm] **1** n Fam **to be on one's l.** être abandonné(e) à son triste sort

2 adj solitaire, seul(e)

long¹ [lɒŋ] **1** n **the l. and the short of it is that...** bref,...

2 adj (**a**) (in size) long (longue); **how l. is the table?** quelle est la longueur de la table?; **to be 3 ft l.** ≃ faire 1 m de long; **to go the l. way (around)** prendre le chemin le plus long; Fig **the best by a l. way** de loin le meilleur (la meilleure); Fig **she'll go a l. way** elle ira loin; Fig **to go a l. way toward doing sth** beaucoup contribuer à faire qch; Fam **to be l. on charm/good ideas** être plein(e) de charme ou de bonnes idées; **the l. arm of the law** (le bras de) la justice; Fig **to have a l. face** faire une tête de six pieds de long; **it's a l. shot** ça n'a pas beaucoup de chances de réussir; **not by a l. shot** loin s'en

faut; **l. johns** caleçon m long; Sport **l. jump** saut m en longueur; Rad **l. wave** grandes ondes fpl

(**b**) (in time) long (longue); **a l. time ago** il y a longtemps; **it's been a l. day** ça a été une longue journée; **the days are getting longer** les jours rallongent; **to take a l. look at sth** regarder longuement qch; **in the l. term** or **run** à long terme, à longue échéance; **to have a l. memory** avoir bonne mémoire; **to take the l. view** envisager les choses à long terme; **l. weekend** long week-end m, week-end prolongé

3 adv (**a**) (for a long period) longtemps; **l. live the King/Queen!** vive le roi/la reine!; **as l. as** (providing) du moment que, tant que; (while) tant que; **to think l. and hard (about sth)** réfléchir longuement (à qch); **she won't be l.** elle ne tardera pas; (will soon have finished) elle n'en a pas pour longtemps; **I have l. been convinced of it** j'en suis convaincu depuis longtemps; **how l. have you known her?** depuis combien de temps la connais-tu?; Fam **so l.!** au revoir!, à bientôt!; **l. before/after** longtemps avant/après; **l. ago** il y a longtemps

(**b**) (for the duration of) **all day l.** toute la journée

(**c**) **I could no longer hear him** je ne l'entendais plus; **I couldn't wait any longer** je ne pouvais plus attendre; **five minutes longer** cinq minutes de plus

long² [lɒŋ] vi **to l. to do sth** rêver de faire qch; **to l. for sth** rêver de qch; (look forward to) attendre qch avec impatience; **we're longing for them to leave** il nous tarde qu'ils partent; **a longed-for vacation** des vacances fpl très attendues

long³ [lɒŋ] (abbr **longitude**) long

longboat ['lɒŋbəʊt] n chaloupe f

longbow ['lɒŋbəʊ] n arc m

long-distance ['lɒŋ'dɪstəns] **1** adj (runner, race) de fond; (telephone call) longue distance

2 adv **to telephone l.** faire un appel longue distance

longevity [lɒn'dʒevɪtɪ] n longévité f

long-forgotten ['lɒŋfə'gɒtən] adj depuis longtemps oublié(e)

longhaired ['lɒŋ'heəd] adj (cat, dog) à poil(s) long(s); (person) aux cheveux longs

long-haul ['lɒŋ'hɔːl] adj long-courrier

longing ['lɒŋɪŋ] n profond désir m, grande envie f (**for** de)

longingly ['lɒŋɪŋlɪ] adv avec envie

longitude ['lɒndʒɪtjuːd] n longitude f

longitudinal [lɒndʒɪ'tjuːdɪnəl] adj longitudinal(e)

long-lasting ['lɒŋ'lɑːstɪŋ] adj durable, qui dure longtemps

long-life ['lɒŋ'laɪf] adj (juice, milk) longue conservation inv; (battery) longue durée inv

long-lost ['lɒŋ'lɒst] adj perdu(e) depuis longtemps; (relative) perdu de vue depuis longtemps

long-range ['lɒŋ'reɪndʒ] adj (missile) longue portée; (forecast) à long terme; (plane) à long rayon d'action

longshoreman ['lɒŋ'ʃɔːmən] n docker m

long-sleeved ['lɒŋ'sliːvd] adj à manches longues

long-standing ['lɒŋ'stændɪŋ] adj (arrangement, friendship) de longue date

long-suffering ['lɒŋ'sʌfərɪŋ] adj patient(e)

long-term ['lɒŋtɜːm] adj (prisoner) condamné(e) à une longue peine; (loan, planning) à long terme; **the l. unemployed** les chômeurs mpl de longue durée

long-winded [lɒŋ'wɪndɪd] adj verbeux(euse)

loofah ['luːfə] n loofa m, luffa m

look [lʊk] **1** n (**a**) (act of looking) **to have** or **to take a l. at sth** regarder qch; (quickly) jeter un coup d'œil à ou sur qch; **to have a l. for sth** chercher qch; **let me have a l.** fais(-moi) voir; **to have a l. around the town** faire un tour dans la ville; **to have a l. through some magazines** jeter un coup d'œil à des magazines

(**b**) (glance) regard m; **to give sb. a dirty l.** jeter un regard noir à qn; **if looks could kill** il y a des regards qui tuent

(c) *(appearance)* air *m*; **I don't like the l. of this** cela ne me dit rien qui vaille; **I don't like the l. of him** sa tête ne me revient pas; **by the l. of it,...** on dirait bien que...

(d) **(good) looks** beauté *f*; **to have lost one's looks** être moins beau (belle); **looks don't matter** le physique n'a pas d'importance

2 *vt* **to l. sb in the face** regarder qn en face *ou* dans les yeux; **to l. sb up and down** toiser qn; **l. what you've done!** regarde ce que tu as fait!; **l. where you're going!** vous ne pouvez pas faire attention, non?

3 *vi* **(a)** *(in general)* regarder; **to l. at sb/sth** regarder qn/qch; **he's not much to l. at** il n'est pas très beau; *Fig* **to l. the other way** fermer les yeux; **I'm just looking, thank you** *(in store)* je ne fais que regarder, merci; **to l. on the bright side** voir les choses du bon côté; **l. here!** dites donc!; **I don't l. at it that way** je ne vois pas les choses comme ça; *Prov* **l. before you leap** il faut réfléchir avant d'agir

(b) *(search)* **to l. for sb/sth** chercher qn/qch; **we've looked everywhere** nous avons cherché partout

(c) *(seem, appear)* avoir l'air, paraître; **to l. old** avoir l'air vieux (vieille); **things are looking bad** les choses prennent une mauvaise tournure; **things are looking good** ça a l'air de bien se passer; **to l. one's age** faire son âge; **to l. the part** avoir l'allure qui convient; **what does she l. like?** comment est-elle?; **to l. like sb** ressembler à qn; **it looks like** *or* **as if...** on dirait que...; **it looks like rain** on dirait qu'il va pleuvoir; **you l. as if you've slept badly** vous avez l'air d'avoir mal dormi

▸**look after** *vt insep* *(take care of)* s'occuper de; **to l. after oneself** se débrouiller tout(e) seul(e); **to l. after sb's house/bag** surveiller la maison/le sac de qn; **can you l. after the children tomorrow?** tu peux garder les enfants demain?

▸**look around 1** *vt insep* *(town, stores)* faire un tour dans

2 *vi* *(in town)* faire un tour; *(in store)* jeter un coup d'œil; **to l. around for sth** essayer de trouver qch

▸**look back** *vi* **(a)** *(in space)* regarder en arrière *ou* derrière soi **(b)** *(in time)* **to l. back on sth** revenir sur qch; **she has never looked back since that day** depuis ce jour sa situation n'a cessé de s'améliorer

▸**look down** *vi* *(from above)* regarder en bas *ou* vers le bas; *(lower one's eyes)* baisser les yeux; *Fig* **to l. down on sb** regarder qn de haut

▸**look forward to** *vt insep* **to l. forward to sth** attendre qch avec impatience; **I'm looking forward to seeing her again** il me tarde de la revoir; **I l. forward to hearing from you** *(in letter)* dans l'attente de vous lire

▸**look in** *vi* **to l. in (on sb)** passer (voir qn)

▸**look into** *vt insep* examiner

▸**look on 1** *vt insep* *(consider)* **to l. on sb/sth as** considérer qn/qch comme

2 *vi* *(watch)* regarder

▸**look out** *vi* **(a)** *(from indoors)* regarder dehors; **to l. out of the window** regarder par la fenêtre **(b)** *(be careful)* faire attention; **l. out!** attention!

▸**look out for** *vt insep* **(a)** *(look for)* *(person)* guetter; *(thing)* chercher **(b)** *(be on guard for)* faire attention à

▸**look over** *vt insep* jeter un coup d'œil sur

▸**look through** *vt insep* **(a)** *(inspect)* *(written material)* parcourir; *(clothes, CDs)* passer en revue **(b)** *(not see)* **to l. straight through sb** regarder qn sans le voir; *(deliberately)* ignorer qn

▸**look to** *vt insep* **(a)** *(rely on)* **to l. to sb (for sth)** compter sur qn (pour qch) **(b)** **to l. to the future** se tourner vers l'avenir

▸**look up 1** *vt sep* *(word, address)* chercher; *(person)* passer voir

2 *vi* *(from below)* regarder vers le haut; *(raise one's eyes)* lever les yeux; *Fig* **things are looking up** la situation s'améliore

▸**look upon** *vt insep* *(consider)* **to l. upon sb/sth as** considérer qn/qch comme

▸**look up to** *vt insep* respecter, estimer

lookalike ['lʊkəlaɪk] *n* sosie *m*

looking-glass ['lʊkɪŋglɑːs] *n Old-fashioned* miroir *m*

lookout ['lʊkaʊt] *n* *(person)* guetteur *m*; *(on ship)* vigie *f*; **to keep a l. for sb/sth** guetter qn/qch; **to be on the l. for sb/sth** être à la recherche de qn/qch; **l. post/tower** poste *m*/tour *f* de guet

loom¹ [luːm] *n* *(for making cloth)* métier *m* à tisser

loom² [luːm] *vi* *(of person, building)* se dresser; *(of danger, event)* être imminent(e); **to l. large** être très présent(e)

loony ['luːnɪ] *Fam* **1** *n* *(pl* **loonies**) dingue *mf*; **l. bin** maison *f* de fous

2 *adj* dingue

loop [luːp] **1** *n* boucle *f*

2 *vt* faire une boucle/des boucles à; **to l. sth around sth** enrouler qch autour de qch; **to l. the loop** *(in plane)* faire un looping

loophole ['luːphəʊl] *n* *(in law, regulations, etc.)* point *m* faible; **to find a l.** trouver une échappatoire; **legal l.** vide *m* juridique

loopy ['luːpɪ] *adj Fam* barjo(t)

loose [luːs] **1** *n* **to be on the l.** *(of prisoner)* être en cavale; *(of animal)* être en liberté

2 *adj* *(animal)* qui s'est échappé(e); *(tooth, plank)* qui bouge; *(piece of clothing)* large, ample; *(skin)* flasque; *(alliance, network)* peu structuré(e); *(translation)* approximatif(ive); *(morals, lifestyle)* dissolu(e); **to come l.** *(of knot)* se défaire; *(of screw)* se desserrer; **to let sb l.** relâcher qn; **to let sb l. on sth** laisser qn toucher à qch; **don't let him l. in the kitchen!** ne le laisse pas faire la cuisine tout seul!; **to let l. a torrent of abuse** lâcher des torrents d'injures; **to buy sth l.** acheter qch en vrac; **l. change** petite *ou* menue monnaie *f*; **l. connection** *(in appliance)* faux contact *m*; **to be at l. ends** ne pas savoir quoi faire; *Fig* **to tie up the l. ends** régler les derniers détails; **l. talk** propos *mpl* irréfléchis; **to have a l. tongue** ne pas savoir tenir sa langue; **a l. woman** une femme de mauvaise vie

3 *vt Lit* *(arrow)* décocher; *(bullet)* tirer

loose-fitting ['luːsfɪtɪŋ] *adj* ample, large

loose-leaf ['luːsliːf] *adj* à feuilles mobiles; **l. binder** classeur *m*

loose-limbed ['luːs'lɪmd] *adj* souple

loosely ['luːslɪ] *adv* **(a)** *(attached)* de façon lâche; **l. packed** *(snow)* poudreux(euse) **(b)** *(roughly)* de façon approximative; **to be l. connected** avoir un lointain rapport; **l. speaking** en gros; **l. translated** traduit librement

loosen ['luːsən] **1** *vt* *(screw, knot, belt)* desserrer; *(restrictions)* assouplir; **to l. one's grip** relâcher son étreinte; **to l. sb's tongue** délier la langue à qn

2 *vi* se desserrer

▸**loosen up** *vi* *(relax)* se détendre

loot [luːt] **1** *n* *(booty)* butin *m*; *Fam* *(money)* oseille *f*

2 *vt* piller

looter ['luːtə(r)] *n* pillard(e) *m,f*

looting ['luːtɪŋ] *n* pillage *m*

lopsided [lɒp'saɪdɪd] *adj* *(face)* asymétrique; *(picture)* de guingois, de travers; *(grin)* en coin

loquacious [lə'kweɪʃəs] *adj Formal* loquace

lord [lɔːd] **1** *n* **(a)** *(aristocrat)* noble *m*; *(feudal)* seigneur *m*; **L. Browne** lord Browne *(titre de noblesse masculin)*; **l. of the manor** châtelain *m*; **the L. Mayor** le lord-maire; **my L.** *(to noble)* Monsieur le Marquis/le Baron/*etc*; *(to judge)* Monsieur le juge **(b)** *Rel* **the L.** le Seigneur; **the L.'s Prayer** le Notre Père; *Fam* **good L.!** mon Dieu!; *Fam* **L. knows** Dieu seul le sait

2 *vt* **to l. it over sb** traiter qn de haut

lordly ['lɔːdlɪ] *adj* *(noble)* altier(ère); *Pej* *(arrogant)* hautain(e)

lordship ['lɔːdʃɪp] *n* autorité *f*; *also Ironic* **His/Your L.** monsieur; *(to judge)* son/votre Honneur

lore [lɔː(r)] *n* tradition *f* orale

Los Angeles [lɒsˈændʒəliːz] *n* Los Angeles

lose [luːz] (*pt & pp* **lost** [lɒst]) **1** *vt* perdre; **to have nothing to l.** n'avoir rien à perdre; **he had lost interest in his work** son travail ne l'intéressait plus; **it loses something in translation** ça perd à la traduction; **to be lost at sea** périr en mer; **the joke was lost on him** il n'a pas saisi la plaisanterie; **that clock loses five minutes a day** cette pendule retarde de cinq minutes par jour; **that mistake lost her the match** cette erreur lui a coûté le match; **to l. one's way, to get lost** se perdre; *Fam* **get lost!** va te faire voir!; **to l. one's balance** perdre l'équilibre; **to l. sight of sb/sth** perdre qn/qch de vue; *Fam Fig* **you've lost me!** je ne vous suis plus!; **to l. weight** perdre du poids; **we lost him in the crowd** nous avons été séparés dans la cohue; **to l. oneself in a book/one's work** se plonger dans un livre/son travail

2 *vi (in contest)* perdre

▶**lose out** *vi* être perdant(e) (**to sb** par rapport à qn); **to l. out on a deal** être perdant(e) dans une affaire

loser [ˈluːzə(r)] *n* **(a)** *(in contest)* perdant(e) *m,f*; **to be a bad l.** être mauvais(e) perdant(e) **(b)** *Fam (unsuccessful person)* raté(e) *m,f*, minable *mf*; **a born l.** un(e) vrai(e) raté(e)

losing [ˈluːzɪŋ] *adj* **to fight a l. battle** être battu(e) d'avance; **the l. side** *(in war)* les vaincus *mpl*; *(in contest)* l'équipe *f* perdante

loss [lɒs] *n* **(a)** *(in contest, war)* perte *f*; **there was a great l. of life** il y a eu de grosses pertes en vies humaines; **to suffer heavy losses** subir de grosses pertes; **it's no great l.** ce n'est pas une grosse perte; *Fam* **it's your l.!** tu ne sais pas ce que tu perds!; **without l. of face** sans perdre la face; **to be at a l. to do sth** être incapable de faire qch; **she's never at a l. for an answer** elle a toujours réponse à tout **(b)** *(financial)* **to make a l.** perdre de l'argent, être déficitaire; **to sell at a l.** vendre à perte; *Fig* **to cut one's losses** sauver les meubles; **l. leader** article *m ou* produit *m* d'appel

loss-making [ˈlɒsmeɪkɪŋ] *adj* déficitaire

lost [lɒst] **1** *adj* perdu(e); **to give sb/sth up for l.** abandonner tout espoir de retrouver qn/qch; **l. cause** cause *f* perdue; **l. soul** âme *f* en peine

2 *pt & pp of* **lose**

lost-and-found (office) [ˈlɒstəndˈfaʊnd(ɒfɪs)] *n* bureau *m* des objets trouvés

lot [lɒt] **1** *n* **(a)** *(large quantity)* **a l., lots** beaucoup; **the l.** tout; **I bought the l.** j'ai tout acheté; **a l. of *or* lots of people** beaucoup de monde; **I see quite a l. of her** je la vois assez souvent; **we had a l. of *or* lots of fun** nous nous sommes bien amusés **(b)** *(destiny)* sort *m*, destin *m*; **to draw *or* to cast lots for sth** tirer qch au sort; **to throw in one's l. with sb** partager le sort de qn **(c)** *(piece of land)* (lot *m* de) terrain *m*; *(at auction)* lot *m*

2 *adv* **a l.** beaucoup; **a l. bigger** beaucoup *ou* bien plus grand(e); **thanks a l.** merci beaucoup

lotion [ˈləʊʃən] *n* lotion *f*

lottery [ˈlɒtərɪ] *(pl* **lotteries)** *n also Fig* loterie *f*

lotto [ˈlɒtəʊ] *n* loto *m*

lotus [ˈləʊtəs] *n* lotus *m*; **l. position** (position *f* du) lotus

loud [laʊd] **1** *adj* **(a)** *(noise)* bruyant(e); *(voice, music)* fort(e); *Pej (person)* fort(e) en gueule; **to be l. in one's praise/condemnation of sth** louer/condamner qch avec force **(b)** *(color, clothes)* voyant(e)

2 *adv* fort; **to think out l.** penser tout haut; **l. and clear** parfaitement

loudly [ˈlaʊdlɪ] *adv* fort; *(complain)* bruyamment

loudmouth [ˈlaʊdmaʊθ] *n Fam* **to be a l.** être *ou* avoir une grande gueule

loudmouthed [ˈlaʊdmaʊðd] *adj Fam* fort(e) en gueule

loudness [ˈlaʊdnɪs] *n (of noise, voice)* volume *m*

loudspeaker [laʊdˈspiːkə(r)] *n* haut-parleur *m*

Louisiana [luːiːzɪˈænə] *n* la Louisiane

lounge [laʊndʒ] **1** *n (in house, hotel)* salon *m*

2 *vi* fainéanter

▶**lounge about, lounge around** *vi* traîner

louse [laʊs] *n* **(a)** *(pl* **lice** [laɪs]) *(insect)* pou *m* **(b)** *Fam (pl* **louses)** *(person)* salaud *m*

lousy [ˈlaʊzɪ] *adj Fam* nul (nulle); *(weather)* dégueulasse; *(trick)* sale; **to feel l.** se sentir vraiment mal; **we had a l. time on vacation** nous avons passé des vacances nulles

lout [laʊt] *n* voyou *m*

loutish [ˈlaʊtɪʃ] *adj* de voyou

louver door [ˈluːvəˈdɔː(r)] *adj* porte *f* à persiennes

lovable [ˈlʌvəbəl] *adj* attachant(e)

love [lʌv] **1** *n* **(a)** *(for family, country)* amour *m* (**of** *ou* **for** de *ou* pour); **give my l. to your parents** embrasse tes parents pour moi; **with l. from...** *(at end of letter)* affectueusement,...; **Bill sends (you) his l.** Bill t'embrasse; **there's no l. lost between them** ils ne peuvent pas se sentir; **I wouldn't do it for l. or money** je ne le ferais pour rien au monde; **to do sth for the l. of it** faire qch pour le plaisir

(b) *(between lovers)* amour *m*; **to be/fall in l. with sb** être/tomber amoureux(euse) de qn; **to make l. with *or* to sb** faire l'amour avec qn; **the l. of my life** l'homme (la femme) de ma vie; **it was l. at first sight** ce fut le coup de foudre; **(my) l.** *(term of endearment)* mon amour; **a l.-hate relationship** une relation faite à la fois d'amour et de haine; **l. affair** liaison *f* (amoureuse); *Fig* passion *f*; **his l. affair with Paris** sa passion pour Paris; *Euph* **l. child** enfant *mf* de l'amour; **l. letter** lettre *f* d'amour; **l. life** vie *f* amoureuse; **l. match** mariage *m* d'amour; **l. nest** nid *m* d'amour; **l. triangle** ménage *m* à trois

(c) *(in tennis)* **15 l.** 15 à rien; **l. game** jeu *m* blanc

2 *vt (person)* aimer; *(thing)* adorer; **I l. Chinese food** j'adore manger chinois; **to l. to do *or* doing sth** adorer faire qch; **I'd l. to come** j'aimerais beaucoup venir

lovebird [ˈlʌvbɜːd] *n Fam Fig* **a pair of lovebirds** un couple de tourtereaux

lovebite [ˈlʌvbaɪt] *n* suçon *m*

loveless [ˈlʌvlɪs] *adj* sans amour

lovely [ˈlʌvlɪ] *adj (idea, smell)* très bon (bonne); *(weather)* beau (belle); *(person)* charmant(e); **to have a l. time** passer un bon moment

lovemaking [ˈlʌvmeɪkɪŋ] *n (sexual intercourse)* ébats *mpl* amoureux

lover [ˈlʌvə(r)] *n (of person) (man)* amant *m*; *(woman)* maîtresse *f*; *(of nature, good food)* amoureux(euse) *m,f*

lovesick [ˈlʌvsɪk] *adj* qui languit d'amour

lovey-dovey [ˈlʌvɪˈdʌvɪ] *adj Fam (talk)* mièvre, à la guimauve; *(person)* roucoulant(e)

loving [ˈlʌvɪŋ] *adj* affectueux(euse), tendre

low¹ [ləʊ] **1** *n* **(a)** **to reach a new *or* an all-time l.** atteindre son niveau le plus bas

(b) *(weather front)* zone *f* de basse pression

2 *adj* **(a)** *(not high, not loud)* bas (basse); *(neckline)* profond(e); **fuel is getting l.** on n'a plus beaucoup d'essence; **to cook sth over a l. heat** cuire qch à feu doux; **of l. birth** de basse extraction; **the lower classes** les classes les moins aisées; **lower ranks** *(in army)* rangs *mpl* inférieurs; **to have a l. opinion of sb** avoir une mauvaise opinion de qn; *Aut* **l. beams** codes *mpl*; *Fig* **a l. blow** un coup bas; **the L. Countries** les Pays-Bas *mpl*; **l. tide** marée *f* basse

(b) *(depressed)* déprimé(e)

(c) *(ignoble)* **the lowest of the l.** le dernier des derniers (la dernière des dernières); **that's a l. trick!** c'est vraiment un coup vache!

3 *adv* bas; **the l. paid** les petits salaires *mpl*; **turn the music/the lights down l.** baisse la musique/la lumière; **to be running l. on sth** être presque à court de qch

low² [ləʊ] vi (of cattle) meugler

lowbrow ['ləʊbraʊ] adj Pej (tastes, interests) peu intellectuel(elle)

low-budget [ləʊ'bʌdʒɪt] adj (movie) à petit budget; (vacation) bon marché inv

low-calorie [ləʊ'kælərɪ] adj basses calories, hypocalorique

low-cost [ləʊ'kɒst] adj économique; (housing) à loyer modéré; l. airline low-cost m

low-cut [ləʊ'kʌt] adj décolleté(e)

low-down ['ləʊdaʊn] n Fam to give sb the l. on sth tuyauter qn sur qch; what's the l. on Peter's resignation? tu as des tuyaux sur la démission de Peter?

lower¹ ['ləʊə(r)] vt (a) (eyes, blind, head, window) baisser; (sail) amener; also Fig to l. one's guard baisser sa garde; to l. one's voice baisser la voix; to l. oneself into/onto sth se laisser glisser dans/sur qch (b) (morally) to l. oneself (to do sth) s'abaisser (à faire qch)

lower² ['ləʊə(r)] vi (of sky) se couvrir; to l. at sb (of person) lancer des regards noirs à qn

low-fat ['ləʊ'fæt] adj (yoghurt, potato chips) allégé(e); (milk) demi-écrémé

low-flying ['ləʊ'flaɪɪŋ] adj volant à basse altitude

low-grade ['ləʊ'greɪd] adj de qualité inférieure

low-key [ləʊ'kiː] adj (approach, debate) modéré(e); (movie, style) sobre, dépouillé(e); (person) réservé(e)

lowlands ['ləʊləndz] npl basses terres fpl; the L. (of Scotland) les Basses Terres de l'Écosse

low-level ['ləʊ'levəl] adj (a) (discussion) à bas niveau (b) (radiation) de faible intensité

lowly ['ləʊlɪ] adj humble, modeste

low-lying ['ləʊ'laɪɪŋ] adj de basse altitude

low-salt [ləʊ'sɔːlt] adj à faible teneur en sel

low-spirited ['ləʊ'spɪrɪtɪd] adj abattu(e)

low-tech ['ləʊtek] adj rudimentaire

lox [lɒks] n Culin saumon m fumé

loyal ['lɔɪəl] adj (friend) loyal(e), dévoué(e); to be l. to sb/sth être fidèle à qn/qch

loyalist ['lɔɪəlɪst] n & adj loyaliste mf

loyally ['lɔɪəlɪ] adv loyalement

loyalty ['lɔɪəltɪ] (pl loyalties) n loyauté f; you'll have to decide where your loyalties lie il faudra que vous décidiez de quel côté vous êtes; to have divided loyalties être partagé(e)

lozenge ['lɒzɪndʒ] n (shape) losange m; (cough sweet) pastille f

LP [el'piː] n (abbr long playing record) 33 tours m

LSD [eles'diː] n (abbr lysergic acid diethylamide) LSD m

Lt. (abbr Lieutenant) lt

Ltd. (abbr limited) ≃ SARL, Can limité

lubricant ['luːbrɪkənt] n lubrifiant m

lubricate ['luːbrɪkeɪt] vt lubrifier

lubrication [luːbrɪ'keɪʃən] n lubrification f

lucid ['luːsɪd] adj lucide; (explanation) clair(e)

luck [lʌk] n chance f; (good) l. bonheur m, chance; good l.! bonne chance!; bad l. malchance f; bad l.! pas de chance!; to wish sb l. souhaiter bonne chance à qn; to be in l. avoir de la chance; to be out of l. ne pas avoir de chance; to be down on one's l. être sur la paille; to try one's l. tenter sa chance; don't push your l.! ne pousse pas le bouchon trop loin!; some people have all the l. il y a vraiment des gens qui ont de la veine; just my l.! c'est bien ma chance!; no such l.! je n'ai pas (eu) cette chance!; with any l. avec un peu de chance

▸**luck out** vi Fam avoir de la veine

luckily ['lʌkɪlɪ] adv par bonheur, heureusement

lucky ['lʌkɪ] adj (person) to be l. avoir de la chance; to make a l. guess tomber juste; to have a l. escape l'échapper belle; l. you! veinard(e)!; Fam l. devil, l. beggar sacré(e) veinard(e)

m,f; Ironic you should be so l.! tu peux toujours courir!; it's you came when you did c'est une chance que tu sois arrivé à ce moment-là; she's l. to be alive elle a de la chance d'être encore en vie; my l. number mon chiffre porte-bonheur; it's not my l. day ce n'est pas mon jour de chance; that was l. ça a été un coup de chance; to strike it l. décrocher le gros lot; l. charm porte-bonheur m inv; you can thank your l. stars she didn't see you! tu peux t'estimer heureux qu'elle ne t'ait pas vu!

lucrative ['luːkrətɪv] adj lucratif(ive)

lucre ['luːkə(r)] n Pej or Hum lucre m

ludicrous ['luːdɪkrəs] adj risible, ridicule

lug [lʌg] (pt & pp lugged) vt Fam trimbaler

luggage ['lʌgɪdʒ] n bagages mpl; l. label étiquette f à bagages; l. locker consigne f automatique; l. rack (in train) porte-bagages m inv; (on car) galerie f

lugubrious [luː'guːbrɪəs] adj lugubre

lukewarm ['luːkwɔːm] adj also Fig tiède; she was rather l. about my suggestion ma suggestion ne l'a pas enthousiasmée

lull [lʌl] 1 n (in fighting) accalmie f; (in conversation) pause f; Fig the l. before the storm le calme avant la tempête
2 vt to l. sb to sleep endormir qn en le berçant; they were lulled into a false sense of security ils se sont laissés aller à un sentiment de sécurité illusoire

lullaby ['lʌləbaɪ] (pl lullabies) n berceuse f

lumbago [lʌm'beɪgəʊ] n lumbago m

lumbar ['lʌmbə(r)] adj Anat lombaire

lumber ['lʌmbə(r)] 1 n (wood) bois m de charpente ou de construction
2 vt to get lumbered with sth se taper ou se coltiner qch; I got lumbered with a huge bill je me suis retrouvé avec une facture gratinée
3 vi to l. about or around avancer d'un pas lourd

lumbering ['lʌmbərɪŋ] adj (walk) lourd(e), pesant(e)

lumberjack ['lʌmbədʒæk] n bûcheron m

luminary ['luːmɪnərɪ] (pl luminaries) n Lit sommité f

luminescent [luːmɪ'nesənt] adj luminescent(e)

luminous ['luːmɪnəs] adj (paint, road sign, color) fluorescent(e)

lump [lʌmp] 1 n (a) (of earth) motte f; (of stone, coal) morceau m; (in sauce) grumeau m; (on body) grosseur f; a l. of sugar un sucre; Fig it brought a l. to my throat (made me sad) ma gorge se serra; Fin l. sum somme f forfaitaire; to pay in a l. sum payer en une seule fois (b) Fam Pej (person) empoté(e) m,f
2 vt (a) (group) to l. (together) regrouper; Pej mettre dans le même sac (b) Fam (endure) you'll just have to (like it or) l. it! il faudra que tu fasses avec!

lumpy ['lʌmpɪ] adj (sauce) grumeleux(euse); (mattress) bosselé(e)

lunacy ['luːnəsɪ] n folie f

lunar ['luːnə(r)] adj lunaire; l. eclipse éclipse f de lune; l. landing alunissage m

lunatic ['luːnətɪk] 1 n fou (folle) m,f; l. asylum asile m d'aliénés
2 adj (idea, behavior) dément(e); l. fringe extrémistes mpl fanatiques

lunch [lʌntʃ] 1 n déjeuner m, Can dîner m; to have l. prendre son déjeuner, déjeuner; Fam Fig to be out to l. (be crazy) déblocquer; l. hour heure f du déjeuner
2 vi déjeuner, Can dîner (on de)

luncheon ['lʌntʃən] n Formal déjeuner m

lunchtime ['lʌntʃtaɪm] n heure f du déjeuner

lung [lʌŋ] n poumon m; l. cancer cancer m des poumons

lunge [lʌndʒ] 1 n mouvement m brusque en avant; to make a l. for se ruer vers
2 vi se ruer (at vers)

lupin ['luːpɪn] n lupin m

lupus ['luːpəs] *n Med* lupus *m*

lurch [lɜːtʃ] **1** *n (of ship, car)* embardée *f*; **a l. to the left/right** *(of politician, party)* un virage à gauche/droite; *Fam* **to leave sb in the l.** laisser qn dans le pétrin

2 *vi (of ship, car)* faire une embardée; *(of person)* tituber; **to l. to the left/right** *(of politician, party)* virer à gauche/droite

lure ['lʊə(r)] **1** *n (attraction)* attrait *m*

2 *vt (into trap, ambush)* attirer; **nothing could l. her away from her computer** rien ne pouvait l'éloigner de son ordinateur

lurid ['lʊərɪd] *adj* **(a)** *(story, description)* cru(e); *(headline)* sensationnel(elle); **she described it in l. detail** elle en a fait une description qui ne laissait rien à l'imagination **(b)** *(gaudy)* criard(e)

lurk [lɜːk] *vi* être tapi(e); *(of doubt, fear)* subsister

luscious ['lʌʃəs] *adj (woman)* appétissant(e); *(lips)* pulpeux(euse); *(fruit)* succulent(e)

lush [lʌʃ] *adj (plant, vegetation)* luxuriant(e); *Fig (surroundings)* luxueux(euse)

lust [lʌst] *n (sexual)* désir *m* (charnel); *Fig (for power, knowledge)* soif *f* (**for** de)

▶**lust after** *vt insep* convoiter

luster ['lʌstə(r)] *n* lustre *m*, éclat *m*

lustful ['lʌstfʊl] *adj* lubrique

lustrous ['lʌstrəs] *adj* brillant(e)

lusty ['lʌstɪ] *adj (person)* vigoureux(euse); *(cry, blow)* puissant(e)

lute [luːt] *n* luth *m*

Luxemb(o)urg ['lʌksəmbɜːg] *n* le Luxembourg

Luxemb(o)urger ['lʌksəmbɜːgə(r)] *n* Luxembourgeois(e) *m,f*

luxuriant [lʌg'zjʊərɪənt] *adj* luxuriant(e)

luxuriate [lʌg'zjʊərɪeɪt] *vi* se prélasser (**in** dans)

luxurious [lʌg'zjʊərɪəs] *adj* somptueux(euse)

luxury ['lʌkʃərɪ] **1** *n (pl* **luxuries)** luxe *m*; **to lead a life of l.** vivre dans le luxe

2 *adj* de luxe

lychee [laɪ'tʃiː] *n* litchi *m*

lying ['laɪɪŋ] **1** *n* mensonges *mpl*

2 *adj (person)* menteur(euse)

lymph [lɪmf] *n Anat* lymphe *f*; **l. node** ganglion *m* lymphatique

lymphatic [lɪm'fætɪk] *adj* lymphatique

lymphoma [lɪm'fəʊmə] *n Med* lymphome *m*

lynch [lɪntʃ] *vt* lyncher

lynching ['lɪntʃɪŋ] *n* lynchage *m*

lynx [lɪŋks] *n* lynx *m*

Lyons ['liːɒn] *n* Lyon

lyre ['laɪə(r)] *n* lyre *f*

lyric ['lɪrɪk] *adj* lyrique

lyrical ['lɪrɪkəl] *adj* lyrique

lyricism ['lɪrɪsɪzəm] *n* lyrisme *m*

lyricist ['lɪrɪsɪst] *n* parolier(ère) *m,f*

lyrics ['lɪrɪks] *npl (of song)* paroles *fpl*

M

M, m¹ [em] *n (letter)* M, m *m inv*
m² (**a**) *(abbr* **meter(s)**) m (**b**) *(abbr* **mile(s)**) mile(s)
MA [ɛm'eɪ] *n Univ (abbr* **Master of Arts**) to have an MA in linguistics ≃ avoir une maîtrise de linguistique; **John Smith MA** John Smith, titulaire d'une maîtrise de lettres/droit/*etc.*

ma [mɑː] *n Fam* maman *f*
ma'am [mɑːm] *n* madame *f*
mac [mæk] *n Fam (term of address)* chef *m*
macabre [mə'kɑːbə(r)] *adj* macabre
macaque [mə'kɑːk] *n Zool* macaque *m*
macaroni [mækə'rəʊnɪ] *n* macaronis *mpl*; **m. and cheese** gratin *m* de macaronis
macaroon [mækə'ruːn] *n* macaron *m*
macaw [mə'kɔː] *n* ara *m*
Mace® [meɪs] **1** *n (spray)* gaz *m* lacrymogène
2 *vt Fam* bombarder au gaz lacrymogène
mace¹ [meɪs] *n (weapon, symbol of office)* masse *f*
mace² [meɪs] *n (spice)* macis *m*
Macedonia [mæsə'dəʊnɪə] *n* la Macédoine
Macedonian [mæsə'dəʊnɪən] **1** *n* (**a**) *(person)* Macédonien(enne) *m,f* (**b**) *(language)* macédonien *m*
2 *adj* macédonien(enne)
Mach [mæk] *n Phys* **M. (number)** (nombre *m* de) Mach
machete [mə'ʃetɪ] *n* machette *f*
Machiavellian [mækɪə'velɪən] *adj* machiavélique
machinations [mæʃɪ'neɪʃənz] *npl* machinations *fpl*, manœuvres *fpl*
machine [mə'ʃiːn] **1** *n* machine *f*; *Fig (person)* robot *m*; **party/propaganda m.** appareil *m* du parti/de la propagande; *Comput* **m. code** code *m* machine; **m. gun** mitrailleuse *f*; *Comput* **m. language** langage *m* machine; **m. shop** atelier *m* d'usinage; **m. tool** machine-outil *f*; **m. translation** traduction *f* assistée par ordinateur
2 *vt* (**a**) *Ind* usiner (**b**) *(with sewing machine)* coudre *ou* piquer à la machine
machine-gun [mə'ʃiːngʌn] *vt* mitrailler
machine-readable [mə'ʃiːn'riːdəbəl] *adj Comput* lisible par ordinateur
machinery [mə'ʃiːnərɪ] *n (machines)* machines *fpl*, machinerie *f*; *Fig (of organization)* rouages *mpl*
machinist [mə'ʃiːnɪst] *n (on sewing machine)* mécanicienne *f*; *(on machine tool)* ouvrier(ère) *m,f*
machismo [mæ'tʃɪzməʊ] *n* machisme *m*
macho ['mætʃəʊ] *adj* macho *inv*
mackerel ['mækrəl] *n* maquereau *m*
macro ['mækrəʊ] *(pl* **macros**) *n Comput* macro *f*, macrocommande *f*
macrobiotic ['mækrəʊbaɪ'ɒtɪk] *adj* macrobiotique
macrobiotics ['mækrəʊbaɪ'ɒtɪks] *n* macrobiotique *f*
macrocosm ['mækrəʊkɒzəm] *n* macrocosme *m*
macroeconomics ['mækrəʊiːkə'nɒmɪks] *n* macro-économie *f*

mad [mæd] *adj* (**a**) *(insane) (person)* fou (folle); *(idea, plan)* insensé(e); *(dog)* enragé(e); **to go m.** devenir fou; **as m. as a hatter** fou à lier; **m. with fear** mort(e) de peur; **there was a m. rush for the door** les gens se ruèrent vers la porte; *Fam* **to run/to work like m.** courir/travailler comme un fou (une folle); *Fam* **m. cow disease** maladie *f* de la vache folle (**b**) *Fam (enthusiastic)* **to be m. about sth** être fou (folle) de qch; **the crowd went m.** ce fut le délire parmi les spectateurs (**c**) *Fam (angry)* furieux(euse) (**with** *or* **at** contre); **to get m.** piquer une colère
Madagascan [mædə'gæskən] **1** *n* Malgache *mf*
2 *adj* malgache
Madagascar [mædə'gæskə(r)] *n* Madagascar
madam ['mædəm] *n (as form of address)* madame *f*
madcap ['mædkæp] *adj* insensé(e)
madden ['mædən] *vt* exaspérer
maddening ['mædənɪŋ] *adj* exaspérant(e)
made [meɪd] *pt & pp of* **make**
Madeira [mə'dɪərə] *n (island)* Madère *f*; *(wine)* madère *m*
made-up [meɪ'dʌp] *adj* (**a**) *(story, excuse)* inventé(e) de toutes pièces (**b**) *(wearing make-up)* maquillé(e)
madhouse ['mædhaʊs] *n Fam* maison *f* de fous
madly ['mædlɪ] *adv* (**a**) *(insanely, desperately)* comme un fou (une folle) (**b**) *Fam (exciting, interested, jealous)* follement; **m. in love** follement *ou* éperdument amoureux(euse)
madman ['mædmən] *n* fou *m*, dément *m*
madness ['mædnɪs] *n* folie *f*, démence *f*; **it's sheer m.!** c'est de la folie pure!
madonna [mə'dɒnə] *n* madone *f*
Madrid [mə'drɪd] *n* Madrid
madwoman ['mædwʊmən] *n* folle *f*, démente *f*
maelstrom ['meɪlstrəm] *n (confusion)* tourbillon *m*
maestro ['maɪstrəʊ] *(pl* **maestros**) *n* maestro *m*
Mafia ['mæfɪə] *n* **the M.** la Mafia
mag [mæg] *n Fam* magazine *m*, revue *f*
magazine [mægə'ziːn] *n* (**a**) *(publication)* magazine *m*, revue *f* (**b**) *(on radio, TV)* **m. (show)** magazine *m* (**c**) *(for gun)* magasin *m*; *(ammunition store)* dépôt *m* de munitions
magenta [mə'dʒentə] **1** *n* magenta *m*
2 *adj* magenta *inv*
maggot ['mægət] *n* asticot *m*
Maghreb [mæ'greb] *n* **the M.** le Maghreb
Magi ['meɪdʒaɪ] *npl* **the M.** les Rois *mpl* mages
magic ['mædʒɪk] **1** *n* magie *f*; **as if by m.** comme par enchantement; **black/white m.** magie noire/blanche
2 *adj (supernatural)* magique; **m. carpet** tapis *m* volant; *Fam* **m. mushrooms** champignons *mpl* (hallucinogènes); **m. wand** baguette *f* magique
►magic away *(pt & pp* **magicked**) *vt sep* faire disparaître comme par enchantement
magical ['mædʒɪkəl] *adj* magique
magician [mə'dʒɪʃən] *n* magicien(enne) *m,f*

magisterial [mædʒɪsˈtɪərɪəl] *adj* magistral(e); *Law* de magistrat

magistrate [ˈmædʒɪstreɪt] *n Law* magistrat *m*

magnanimity [mægnəˈnɪmɪtɪ] *n* magnanimité *f*

magnanimous [mægˈnænɪməs] *adj* magnanime

magnate [ˈmægneɪt] *n* magnat *m*

magnesium [mægˈniːzɪəm] *n Chem* magnésium *m*

magnet [ˈmægnɪt] *n* aimant *m*; *Fig (for tourists, investors)* pôle *m* d'attraction

magnetic [mægˈnetɪk] *adj also Fig* magnétique; **m. card** carte *f* magnétique; **m. compass** boussole *f*; **m. tape** bande *f* magnétique

magnetism [ˈmægnɪtɪzəm] *n also Fig* magnétisme *m*

magnification [mægnɪfɪˈkeɪʃən] *n* grossissement *m*; *(of sound)* amplification *f*

magnificence [mægˈnɪfɪsəns] *n* magnificence *f*

magnificent [mægˈnɪfɪsənt] *adj* magnifique; *(meal, wine)* excellent(e)

magnify [ˈmægnɪfaɪ] *(pt & pp **magnified**) vt (image)* grossir, agrandir; *(sound)* amplifier; *Fig (importance, problem)* exagérer

magnifying glass [ˈmægnɪfaɪɪŋˈglɑːs] *n* loupe *f*

magnitude [ˈmægnɪtjuːd] *n* ampleur *f*; **a problem of the first m.** un problème majeur

magnolia [mægˈnəʊlɪə] **1** *n (tree)* magnolia *m*
   2 *adj* couleur magnolia *(inv)*, blanc rosé *(inv)*

magnum [ˈmægnəm] *n (of champagne)* magnum *m*

magpie [ˈmægpaɪ] *n* pie *f*; *Fig* **he's a bit of a m.** il a quelque chose du collectionneur fou

mahogany [məˈhɒgənɪ] **1** *n (wood, color)* acajou *m*
   2 *adj* en acajou

maid [meɪd] *n (servant)* bonne *f*, domestique *f*; **m. of honor** *(at wedding)* première demoiselle d'honneur; *(to queen)* demoiselle *f* d'honneur

maiden [ˈmeɪdən] **1** *n Lit (girl)* jeune fille *f*
   2 *adj (flight, voyage)* inaugural(e); **m. aunt** tante *f* célibataire; **m. name** nom *m* de jeune fille

mail[1] [meɪl] **1** *n* (**a**) *(letters, packages)* courrier *m*; **it came in the m.** c'est arrivé au courrier; **m. bomb** *(letter)* lettre *m* piégé; *(package)* colis *m* piégé
   (**b**) *(system)* poste *f*; **by m.** par la poste; *Comput* **m. merge** publipostage *m*; *Com* **m. order catalog/company** catalogue *m*/entreprise *f* de vente par correspondance; **by m. order** par correspondance; **m. train** train *m* postal; **m. truck** camionnette *f* ou fourgonnette *f* des postes
   (**c**) *Comput* courrier *m* électronique, mél *m*, *Can* courriel *m*
   2 *vt* (**a**) *(letter)* poster; *(package)* envoyer *ou* expédier par la poste
   (**b**) *Comput (message, document)* envoyer par courrier électronique; *(person)* envoyer un courrier électronique à

mail[2] [meɪl] *n (armor)* mailles *fpl*

mailbag [ˈmeɪlbæg] *n* sac *m* postal; **she gets a huge m.** *(of celebrity, politician)* elle reçoit énormément de courrier

mailbox [ˈmeɪlbɒks] *n also Comput* boîte *f* aux lettres

mailing [ˈmeɪlɪŋ] *n Mktg* publipostage *m*, mailing *m*; **m. list** fichier *m* d'adresses

mailman [ˈmeɪlmæn] *n* facteur *m*

mailshot [ˈmeɪlʃɒt] *n* publipostage *m*, mailing *m*

maim [meɪm] *vt* mutiler, estropier

main [meɪn] **1** *n* (**a**) *(pipe)* conduite *f* (principale); **the mains** *(electricity)* le secteur; **to turn the water off at the mains** couper l'arrivée d'eau; **gas from the mains** gaz de ville (**b**) **in the m.** *(generally)* en général, en gros
   2 *adj* principal(e); **the m. thing is to...** l'essentiel est de...; *Gram* **m. clause** proposition *f* principale; **m. course** plat *m* de résistance; **m. entrance** entrée *f* principale; *Rail* **m. line** grande ligne *f*; **m. road** grande route *f*; *Fam* **m. squeeze** petit(e) ami(e) *m,f*; **m. street** rue *f* principale

mainframe [ˈmeɪnfreɪm] *n Comput* ordinateur *m* central

mainland [ˈmeɪnlænd] *n* continent *m*; **m. Europe** l'Europe continentale

mainline [ˈmeɪnlaɪn] *vi Fam (inject drugs)* se piquer

mainly [ˈmeɪnlɪ] *adv* principalement; **the passengers were m. Spanish** la plupart des passagers étaient espagnols

mainspring [ˈmeɪnsprɪŋ] *n Fig (of change, revolution)* moteur *m*

mainstay [ˈmeɪnsteɪ] *n (of economy, philosophy)* pilier *m*, base *f*

mainstream [ˈmeɪnstriːm] **1** *n* courant *m* principal
   2 *adj* ordinaire

maintain [meɪnˈteɪn] *vt* (**a**) *(preserve)* (order, reputation) maintenir; *(silence, attitude)* garder; **to m. one's enthusiasm** rester enthousiaste (**b**) *(building, machine, road)* entretenir (**c**) *(family)* subvenir aux besoins de (**d**) *(state)* **to m. that...** soutenir que...

maintenance [ˈmeɪntɪnəns] *n (of car, building, roads)* entretien *m*; **m. costs** frais *mpl* d'entretien

Maj. (**a**) *Mil (abbr **Major**)* Cdt (**b**) *Mus (abbr **Major**)* M

majestic [məˈdʒestɪk] *adj* majestueux(euse)

majesty [ˈmædʒəstɪ] *n* majesté *f*; **His/Her M.** Sa Majesté le Roi/la Reine

major [ˈmeɪdʒə(r)] **1** *n* (**a**) *Mil (in air force)* ≃ commandant *m*, *Can & Belg* ≃ major *m*; *(in infantry)* chef *m* de bataillon; *(in cavalry)* chef *m* d'escadron; **m. general** général *m* de division (**b**) *Univ (subject)* matière *f* principale; **she's a physics m.** elle fait des études de physique
   2 *adj* (**a**) *(important)* majeur(e); *(most important)* principal(e); *(accident, illness)* très grave; **of m. importance** de la plus haute importance (**b**) *Mus* majeur(e)
   3 *vi Univ* **to m. in sth** se spécialiser en qch

Majorca [məˈjɔːkə] *n* Majorque *f*

Majorcan [məˈjɔːkən] **1** *n* Majorquin(e) *m,f*
   2 *adj* majorquin(e)

majority [məˈdʒɒrɪtɪ] *(pl **majorities**) n* (**a**) *(in vote)* majorité *f*; **to be in a** *or* **the m.** être majoritaire; **m. decision** décision *f* prise à la majorité; *Pol* **m. rule** système *m* majoritaire; *Law* **m. verdict** verdict *m* de la majorité; *Pol* **there was a m. vote in favor of...** on a voté à la majorité pour... (**b**) *Law (age)* majorité *f*

make [meɪk] **1** *vt (pt & pp **made** [meɪd])* (**a**) *(produce, perform)* faire; *(payment)* effectuer; *(decision)* prendre; **made in Spain** fabriqué(e) en Espagne; **made from** *or* **of stone/wood** en pierre/bois; **I'll show them what I'm made of!** je vais leur montrer de quel bois je me chauffe!; **I'm not made of money!** je ne suis pas millionnaire!; **to m. something of oneself** faire quelque chose de sa vie; **2 and 2 m. 4** 2 et 2 font 4; **to m. a choice** prendre une décision; **it doesn't m. any difference** cela ne change rien; **to m. a noise** faire du bruit
   (**b**) *(earn)* gagner; **to m. a living** gagner sa vie; **to m. a name for oneself** se faire un nom
   (**c**) *(make successful)* **this is the book that made her** ce livre l'a rendue célèbre; *Fam* **to m. it** *(be successful)* réussir; **you've got it made** tu as la belle vie; **it's m. or break** ça passe ou ça casse; **it made my day** il m'a fait très plaisir
   (**d**) *(cause to be)* **to m. sb happy/sad** rendre qn heureux(euse)/triste; **to m. sb hungry** donner faim à qn; **to m. sb tired** fatiguer qn
   (**e**) *(compel)* **to m. sb do sth** faire faire qch à qn; **don't m. me laugh!** tu me fais rire!
   (**f**) *(reach)* **to m. it** *(arrive in time)* arriver à temps; *(finish in time)* finir à temps; **to m. the final** *(of team, competitor)* arriver en finale; **to m. the first team** être sélectionné(e) pour jouer dans la première équipe
   (**g**) *(become, be)* **she'll m. a good doctor/singer** elle fera un bon médecin/une bonne chanteuse; **the report makes interesting reading** le rapport est intéressant à lire

(**h**) *(manage to attend) (show, meeting)* assister à; **I can m. two o'clock** je peux être là à deux heures

2 *vi* (**a**) **to m. as if** *or* **as though to do sth** *(get ready to)* s'apprêter à faire qch; *(pretend)* faire semblant de faire qch

(**b**) **to m. do** *(cope)* se débrouiller; **to m. do with** se contenter de; **to m. believe (that)...** imaginer que...

(**c**) **to m. sure** *or* **certain of** s'assurer de

3 *n* (**a**) *(brand)* marque *f*

(**b**) *Fam* **to be on the m.** *(financially)* chercher à s'en mettre plein les poches; *(sexually)* draguer

▸**make after** *vt insep (chase)* se lancer à la poursuite de

▸**make for** *vt insep* (**a**) *(head toward)* se diriger vers (**b**) *(contribute to)* contribuer à

▸**make of** *vt sep* **what do you m. of the new manager?** que pensez-vous du nouveau directeur?; **I don't know what to m. of that remark** je ne sais pas comment interpréter cette remarque

▸**make off** *vi Fam (leave)* filer, décamper

▸**make off with** *vt insep Fam (steal)* filer avec

▸**make out** *vt sep* (**a**) *(understand, decipher)* comprendre; *(see, hear)* distinguer; *(handwriting)* déchiffrer (**b**) *(write) (list, check)* faire (**c**) *Fam (claim)* **to m. out (that)...** prétendre que...

2 *vi Fam (sexually)* se peloter; **to m. out with sb** peloter qn

▸**make over** *vt sep* (**a**) *(transfer)* céder (**to** à) (**b**) *(transform)* transformer

▸**make up 1** *vt sep* (**a**) *(story, excuses)* inventer (**b**) *(deficit, loss)* combler; **I'll m. it up to you later, I promise** je te le revaudrai, je te le promets (**c**) *(complete) (team, amount)* compléter (**d**) *(form)* constituer, composer; **to m. up one's mind** se décider (**e**) *(put together) (list)* faire; *(package, bed)* faire; **to m. up a prescription** préparer les médicaments prescrits sur une ordonnance (**f**) *(apply make-up to)* maquiller; **to m. oneself up** se maquiller

2 *vi (end quarrel)* se réconcilier

▸**make up for** *vt insep* compenser; *(lost time)* rattraper

make-believe ['meɪkbɪliːv] **1** *n* fantaisie *f*; **to live in a land of m.** ne pas avoir le sens des réalités

2 *adj* imaginaire

makeover ['meɪkəʊvə(r)] *n (of appearance)* séance *f* de maquillage; *Fig* transformation *f*

maker ['meɪkə(r)] *n* (**a**) *(manufacturer)* fabricant *m*; *(of planes, cars)* constructeur *m* (**b**) **to meet one's M.** monter au ciel

makeshift ['meɪkʃɪft] *adj* de fortune

make-up ['meɪkʌp] *n* (**a**) *(cosmetics)* maquillage *m*; **m. artist** maquilleur(euse) *m,f*; **m. bag** trousse *f* à maquillage; **m. remover** démaquillant *m* (**b**) *(composition) (of team, group)* composition *f*; *(of person)* caractère *m*

making ['meɪkɪŋ] *n (of goods)* fabrication *f*; **the film was three years in the m.** le tournage du film a duré trois ans; **history in the m.** l'histoire en train de se faire; **a poet in the m.** un poète en herbe; **the problem is of her own m.** c'est un problème qu'elle s'est elle-même créé; **he has the makings of an actor** il a tout ce qu'il faut pour devenir acteur

maladjusted [mælə'dʒʌstɪd] *adj* inadapté(e)

maladroit [mælə'drɔɪt] *adj* maladroit(e)

malady ['mælədɪ] *(pl* **maladies**) *n Fig* mal *m*

Malagasy ['mæləɡæsɪ] **1** *n (language)* malgache *m*

2 *adj* malgache

malaise [mæ'leɪz] *n* malaise *m*

malaria [mə'leərɪə] *n* malaria *f*, paludisme *m*

Malawi [mə'lɑːwɪ] *n* le Malawi

Malawian [mə'lɑːwɪən] **1** *n* Malawien(enne) *m,f*

2 *adj* malawien(enne)

Malay [mə'leɪ] **1** *n* (**a**) *(person)* Malais(e) *m,f* (**b**) *(language)* malais *m*

2 *adj* malais(e)

Malaysia [mə'leɪzɪə] *n* la Malaisie

Malaysian [mə'leɪən] **1** *n* Malais(e) *m,f*

2 *adj* malais(e)

Maldives ['mɔːldiːvz] *npl* **the M.** les (îles *fpl*) Maldives *fpl*

male [meɪl] **1** *n (person)* homme *m*; *(animal)* mâle *m*

2 *adj* mâle; *(sex, attitude, public)* masculin(e); **m. chauvinist pig** phallocrate *m*; **m. nurse** infirmier *m*

malefactor ['mælɪfæktə(r)] *n Lit* malfaiteur(trice) *m, f*

malevolence [mə'levələns] *n* malveillance *f*

malevolent [mə'levələnt] *adj* malveillant(e)

malformed [mæl'fɔːmd] *adj* difforme

malfunction [mæl'fʌŋkʃən] **1** *n* mauvais fonctionnement *m*

2 *vi* mal fonctionner

Mali ['mɑːlɪ] *n* le Mali

malice ['mælɪs] *n* méchanceté *f*; *Law* **with m. aforethought** avec préméditation

malicious [mə'lɪʃəs] *adj* méchant(e), malveillant(e)

maliciously [mə'lɪʃəslɪ] *adv* méchamment, avec malveillance

malign [mə'laɪn] **1** *adj* pernicieux(euse)

2 *vt* calomnier, diffamer

malignant [mə'lɪɡnənt] *adj (person)* malveillant(e), méchant(e); *(tumor)* malin(igne)

malinger [mə'lɪŋɡə(r)] *vi* faire semblant d'être malade

malingerer [mə'lɪŋɡərə(r)] *n* simulateur(trice) *m,f*

mall [mɔːl] *n* (**shopping**) **m.** centre *m* commercial

mallard ['mælɑːd] *n* colvert *m*

malleable ['mælɪəbəl] *adj also Fig* malléable

mallet ['mælɪt] *n* maillet *m*

malnourished [mæl'nʌrɪʃt] *adj* sous-alimenté(e)

malnutrition [mælnjuː'trɪʃən] *n* malnutrition *f*

malpractice [mæl'præktɪs] *n* faute *f* professionnelle

malt [mɔːlt] *n* malt *m*; **m. vinegar** vinaigre *m* de malt; **m. whiskey** whisky *m* de malt

Malta ['mɔːltə] *n* Malte *f*

Maltese [mɔːl'tiːz] **1** *n* (**a**) *(person)* Maltais(e) *m,f*; **the M.** les Maltais *mpl* (**b**) *(language)* maltais *m*

2 *adj* maltais(e); **the M. cross** la croix de Malte

maltreat [mæl'triːt] *vt* maltraiter

maltreatment [mæl'triːtmənt] *n* mauvais traitements *mpl*

malware ['mælweə(r)] *n Comput* code *m* malicieux, malware *m*

mammal ['mæməl] *n* mammifère *m*

mammary ['mæmərɪ] *adj Anat* mammaire; **m. glands** glandes *fpl* mammaires

mammography [mæ'mɒɡrəfɪ] *n Med* mammographie *f*

mammoth ['mæməθ] **1** *n (animal)* mammouth *m*

2 *adj (huge)* gigantesque

mammy ['mæmɪ] *(pl* **mammies**) *n Fam* maman *f*

man [mæn] **1** *n (pl* **men** [men]) (**a**) *(adult male)* homme *m*; *Fam* **hey, m.!** eh toi!; *Fam* **how are you doing, m.?** comment ça va, vieux?; **a m.'s jacket/bicycle** une veste/bicyclette d'homme; **the army will make a m. of him** l'armée en fera un homme; **he took it like a m.** il a pris ça courageusement; **this will separate the men from the boys** c'est là qu'on verra les vrais hommes; **to be m. enough to do sth** être assez courageux pour faire qch; **to talk to sb m. to m.** parler à qn d'homme à homme; **he's just the m. for the job** c'est l'homme qu'il nous faut; **to be one's own m.** être son (propre) maître; **he's a m.'s m.** il aime bien être avec ses copains; **the m. in the street** l'homme de la rue; **a m. of God** un homme d'église; **a m. of the world** un homme d'expérience

(**b**) *(individual, person)* homme *m*; **any m.** n'importe qui; **few men** peu d'hommes; **to reply as one m.** répondre d'une seule voix; **they were patriots to a m.** ils étaient tous patriotes

(**c**) *(husband, partner)* **my m.** mon homme

(**d**) *(humanity)* l'homme *m*

(**e**) *(employee) (in factory)* homme *m*, ouvrier *m*; *(servant)* valet *m*, domestique *m*; *(soldier)* homme, soldat *m*; **our m. in Rome** *(diplomat)* notre envoyé à Rome; *(spy)* notre agent à Rome; *(reporter)* notre correspondant à Rome

(**f**) *(in chess)* pièce *f*; *(in drafts)* pion *m*

2 *vt (pt & pp* **manned**) *(machine)* assurer le fonctionnement de; *(plane, boat)* être membre de l'équipage de; **to m. the phone** répondre au téléphone; **a manned flight** un vol habité

manacles ['mænəkəlz] *npl* menottes *fpl*

manage ['mænɪdʒ] **1** *vt* (**a**) *(company, project)* diriger; *(store, hotel)* être le gérant de; *(economy, resources, money, time)* gérer (**b**) *(deal with) (situation)* gérer; **to know how to m.** savoir (comment) prendre qn; **to m. to do sth** *(succeed)* réussir *ou* arriver à faire qch; **I can't m. three suitcases** je ne peux pas porter trois valises; **$50 is the most that I can m.** *(to pay)* je ne peux pas aller au-delà de 50 dollars; **can you m. dinner on Thursday?** est-ce que vous pouvez venir dîner jeudi?

2 *vi (cope)* se débrouiller (**with** avec); **to m. without sb/sth** pouvoir se passer de qn/qch; **he'll never m. on his own** il n'y arrivera pas tout seul

manageable ['mænɪdʒəbəl] *adj (object, size, vehicle)* maniable; *(hair)* facile à coiffer

management ['mænɪdʒmənt] *n* (**a**) *(activity) (of company, project)* gestion *f*, direction *f*; *(of economy, resources, store, hotel)* gestion; **m. consultant** conseiller(ère) *m,f* en gestion; **m. studies** études *fpl* de gestion (**b**) *(managers, employers)* direction *f*; **under new m.** *(sign)* changement de propriétaire; **m. buyout** = rachat d'une société par la direction; **m. team** équipe *f* dirigeante

manager ['mænɪdʒə(r)] *n (of bank, company)* directeur(trice) *m,f*; *(of store, hotel, bar)* gérant(e) *m,f*; *(of boxer, singer, sports team)* manager *m*

manageress [mænɪdʒə'res] *n (of bank, company)* directrice *f*; *(of store, hotel, bar)* gérante *f*

managerial [mænɪ'dʒɪərɪəl] *adj* directorial(e); **m. staff** cadres *mpl*; **m. skills** qualités *fpl* de gestionnaire

managing director ['mænɪdʒɪŋdaɪ'rektə(r)] *n* directeur(trice) *m,f* général(e)

Mandarin ['mændərɪn] *n (language)* mandarin *m*

mandarin ['mændərɪn] *n* (**a**) *(fruit)* mandarine *f* (**b**) *(official)* mandarin *m*

mandate ['mændeɪt] *n* mandat *m*

mandatory ['mændətərɪ] *adj* obligatoire

mandible ['mændɪbəl] *n (of insect)* mandibule *f*; *(of vertebrate)* mâchoire *f* inférieure

mandolin ['mændəlɪn] *n* mandoline *f*

mane [meɪn] *n* crinière *f*

man-eater ['mæniːtə(r)] *n* (**a**) *(animal)* mangeur *m* d'hommes (**b**) *Hum (woman)* mangeuse *f* d'hommes

man-eating ['mæniːtɪŋ] *adj* mangeur(euse) d'hommes

maneuver [mə'nuːvə(r)] **1** *n also Fig* manœuvre *f*; *Fig* **there wasn't much room for m.** la marge de manœuvre était assez limitée; **to be on maneuvers** *(of soldiers)* être en manœuvre(s)

2 *vt* manœuvrer; **she maneuvered the car into the space** elle a garé la voiture dans l'emplacement

3 *vi* manœuvrer

maneuverable [mə'nuːvrəbəl] *adj* maniable

manfully ['mænfʊlɪ] *adv* courageusement, vaillamment

manganese [mæŋgə'niːz] *n Chem* manganèse *m*

mange [meɪndʒ] *n* gale *f*

manger ['meɪndʒə(r)] *n* mangeoire *f*

mangle ['mæŋgəl] **1** *n (for clothes)* essoreuse *f* (à rouleaux)

2 *vt (body)* mutiler; *(car)* broyer; *(text)* massacrer

mango ['mæŋgəʊ] *(pl* **mangoes**) *n* mangue *f*

mangrove ['mæŋgrəʊv] *n* palétuvier *m*; **m. swamp** mangrove *f*

mangy ['meɪndʒɪ] *adj (animal)* galeux(euse); *(carpet, coat)* minable, miteux(euse)

manhandle ['mænhændəl] *vt (person)* malmener; *(large object)* transporter à la force des bras

manhole ['mænhəʊl] *n (in road)* bouche *f* d'égout; **m. cover** plaque *f* d'égout

manhood ['mænhʊd] *n* (**a**) *(maturity)* âge *m* d'homme; **to reach m.** devenir un homme (**b**) *(masculinity)* virilité *f* (**c**) *(men collectively)* **American m.** les hommes américains

man-hour ['mænaʊə(r)] *n Econ* heure *f* de travail

manhunt ['mænhʌnt] *n* chasse *f* à l'homme

mania ['meɪnɪə] *n (liking)* passion *f* (**for** pour); *(psychological)* manie *f*; **to have a m. for doing sth** avoir la manie de faire qch

maniac ['meɪnɪæk] *n* fou (folle) *m,f*; **to drive like a m.** conduire comme un fou

manic ['mænɪk] *adj Fig (person)* stressé(e); *(activity)* frénétique

manic-depressive ['mænɪkdɪ'presɪv] *n & adj Psy* maniaco-dépressif(ive) *m,f*

manicure ['mænɪkjʊə(r)] **1** *n* manucure *f*; **to have a m.** se faire faire les ongles

2 *vt* **to m. one's nails** se faire les ongles

manifest ['mænɪfest] **1** *n (of ship, aircraft)* manifeste *m*

2 *adj* manifeste, évident(e)

3 *vt* manifester

manifestation [mænɪfes'teɪʃən] *n* manifestation *f*

manifestly ['mænɪfestlɪ] *adv* manifestement

manifesto [mænɪ'festəʊ] *(pl* **manifestos**) *n Pol* manifeste *m*

manifold ['mænɪfəʊld] **1** *n Aut* collecteur *m*

2 *adj Lit (numerous)* multiple, nombreux(euse)

Manila [mə'nɪlə] *n* Manille

mani(l)la envelope [mə'nɪlə'envələʊp] *n* enveloppe *f* en papier kraft

manipulate [mə'nɪpjʊleɪt] *vt also Fig* manipuler

manipulation [mənɪpjʊ'leɪʃən] *n also Fig* manipulation *f*

manipulative [mə'nɪpjʊlətɪv] *adj Pej* manipulateur (trice)

mankind [mæn'kaɪnd] *n* l'humanité *f*

manliness ['mænlɪnɪs] *n* virilité *f*

manly ['mænlɪ] *adj* viril(e)

man-made ['mænmeɪd] *adj (fabric, product)* synthétique; *(lake, beach)* artificiel(elle); **a m. disaster** un désastre provoqué par l'homme

mannequin ['mænɪkɪn] *n* mannequin *m*

manner ['mænə(r)] *n* (**a**) *(way, method, style)* manière *f*, façon *f*; **the m. in which...** la manière *ou* façon dont...; **in a m. of speaking** pour ainsi dire, en quelque sorte (**b**) **manners** *(etiquette)* manières *fpl*; **it's bad manners to stare** il est mal élevé de dévisager les gens; **he's got no manners** il ne sait pas se tenir (**c**) *(type)* **all m. of people/things** toutes sortes de gens/choses; **by no m. of means, not by any m. of means** absolument pas (**d**) *(attitude, behavior)* **I don't like his m.** je n'aime pas sa façon d'être; **she has a very abrasive m.** elle est très acerbe (**e**) **manners** *(social usages)* mœurs *fpl*

mannered ['mænəd] *adj* maniéré(e)

mannerism ['mænərɪzəm] *n* manie *f*, tic *m*

manor ['mænə(r)] *n* **m. (house)** manoir *m*

manpower ['mænpaʊə(r)] *n* main-d'œuvre *f*

mansion ['mænʃən] *n (in country)* château *m*; *(in town)* hôtel *m* particulier

manslaughter ['mænslɔːtə(r)] *n Law* homicide *m* involontaire

mantelpiece ['mæntəlpiːs] *n* dessus *m* de cheminée; **on the m.** sur la cheminée

mantis ['mæntɪs] *n* mante *f* religieuse

mantle ['mæntəl] *n* (**a**) *Lit (of snow)* manteau *m*; *Fig* **to take on the m. of office** assumer les responsabilités qui incombent au poste (**b**) *(of gas lamp)* manchon *m* (**c**) *Geol* manteau *m*

man-to-man [mæntə'mæn] *adj & adv* d'homme à homme

manual ['mænjʊəl] **1** *n (handbook)* manuel *m*
2 *adj (work, worker)* manuel(elle); **m. dexterity** dextérité *f*

manually ['mænjʊəlɪ] *adv* manuellement

manufacture [mænjʊ'fæktʃə(r)] **1** *n* fabrication *f*; *(of vehicles)* construction *f*
2 *vt* fabriquer; *(vehicles)* construire; *(clothes)* confectionner; *Fig (evidence)* fabriquer (de toutes pièces)

manufacturer [mænjʊ'fæktʃərə(r)] *n Ind* fabricant *m*; *(of vehicles)* constructeur *m*

manufacturing [mænjʊ'fæktʃərɪŋ] *Ind* **1** *n* l'industrie *f* (manufacturière)
2 *adj (center, sector)* industriel(elle); **m. capacity** capacité *f* de production; **m. industries** industries *fpl* manufacturières

manure [mə'njʊə(r)] **1** *n* fumier *m*; **liquid m.** purin *m*
2 *vt* engraisser

manuscript ['mænjʊskrɪpt] *n* manuscrit *m*

many ['menɪ] *(comparative* **more** [mɔː(r)], *superlative* **most** [məʊst]) **1** *pron* beaucoup; **m. of us/them** beaucoup d'entre nous/eux; **not m.** pas beaucoup; **too m.** trop; **as m. as you like** autant que vous voulez; **there were as m. as 100 people there** il y avait bien jusqu'à 100 personnes; *Fam* **to have had one too m.** avoir bu un coup de trop
2 *adj* beaucoup de; **m. people** beaucoup de gens; **m. times** souvent, bien des fois; **not m.** pas beaucoup de; **in m. ways** de bien des façons; **not in so m. words** pas aussi explicitement; **there were so m. people that...** il y avait tant de gens que...; **a good m. people** un bon nombre de gens; **too m.** trop de; **as m.... as** autant de... que; **m.'s the time I've done that** j'ai fait ça bien des fois; *Prov* **m. hands make light work** à plusieurs, l'ouvrage avance vite

many-colored ['menɪ'kʌləd] *adj* multicolore

Maori ['maʊrɪ] **1** *n* Maori(e) *m,f*
2 *adj* maori(e)

map [mæp] **1** *n* carte *f*; *(of subway, town)* plan *m*; *Fig* **this will put Stonybridge on the m.** cela va faire parler de Stonybridge; **m. reference** coordonnées *fpl*
2 *vt (pt & pp* **mapped**) *(region)* dresser une carte de
▸**map out** *vt sep (route)* tracer; *(plan, program)* élaborer; **she had her career all mapped out** sa carrière était toute tracée

maple ['meɪpəl] *n* érable *m*; **m. leaf** feuille *f* d'érable; **m. syrup** sirop *m* d'érable

mar [mɑː(r)] *(pt & pp* **marred**) *vt* gâcher

Mar. *(abbr* **March**) mars

maracas [mə'rækəz] *npl Mus* maracas *fpl*

marathon ['mærəθən] *n also Fig* marathon *m*; **a m. speech** un discours-marathon; **m. runner** marathonien(enne) *m,f*

marauder [mə'rɔːdə(r)] *n* maraudeur(euse) *m,f*

marauding [mə'rɔːdɪŋ] *adj* en maraude

marble ['mɑːbəl] *n* (**a**) *(stone)* marbre *m* (**b**) *(glass ball)* bille *f*; **to play marbles** jouer aux billes; *Fam Fig* **to lose one's marbles** *(go mad)* perdre la boule

marbled ['mɑːbəld] *adj* marbré(e)

March [mɑːtʃ] *n* mars *m*; *see also* **May**

march [mɑːtʃ] **1** *n* marche *f*; *Fig* **the m. of time** la marche du temps; **on the m.** en marche; **m. past** défilé *m*
2 *vt (soldiers)* faire défiler; **he was marched off to prison** il a été emmené en prison
3 *vi (of soldiers)* marcher au pas; *(of soldiers on parade, demonstrators)* défiler; **to m. off** partir; **to m. by** *or* **past (sb/sth)** défiler (devant qn/qch)

marcher ['mɑːtʃə(r)] *n (demonstrator)* manifestant(e) *m,f*

mare [meə(r)] *n* jument *f*

margarine [mɑːdʒə'riːn] *n* margarine *f*

margin ['mɑːdʒɪn] *n* (**a**) *(on page)* marge *f*; **in the m.** dans la marge (**b**) *(edge) (of forest)* orée *f*; **on the margin(s) of society** en marge de la société (**c**) *(gap)* **to win by a narrow m.** gagner de justesse; **to win by an enormous m.** gagner haut la main; **a m. of error** une marge d'erreur (**d**) *Com* marge *f* bénéficiaire

marginal ['mɑːdʒɪnəl] *adj* (**a**) *(improvement, increase)* léger(ère) (**b**) *(note)* en marge

marginalize ['mɑːdʒɪnəlaɪz] *vt* marginaliser

marginally ['mɑːdʒɪnəlɪ] *adv* légèrement

marigold ['mærɪɡəʊld] *n* souci *m*

marihuana, marijuana [mærɪ'wɑːnə] *n* marijuana *f*

marina [mə'riːnə] *n* port *m* de plaisance

marinade ['mærɪneɪd] *Culin* **1** *n* marinade *f*
2 *vt (faire)* mariner

marinate ['mærɪneɪt] *vt Culin (faire)* mariner

marine [mə'riːn] **1** *n (soldier)* fusilier *m* marin; *Fam* **(go) tell it to the marines!** (allez dire ça) à d'autres!
2 *adj (life, biology)* marin(e); **m. engineering** génie *m* maritime

mariner ['mærɪnə(r)] *n Lit* marin *m*

marionette [mærɪə'net] *n* marionnette *f* à fils

marital ['mærɪtəl] *adj* conjugal(e); **m. status** situation *f* de famille

maritime ['mærɪtaɪm] *adj* maritime

marjoram ['mɑːdʒərəm] *n* marjolaine *f*

mark [mɑːk] **1** *n* (**a**) *(scratch, stain)* tache *f*, marque *f*
(**b**) *(symbol)* marque *f*
(**c**) *(sign, proof)* signe *m*; **as a m. of respect** en signe de respect; **years of imprisonment had left their m. on him** ses années de captivité l'avaient marqué; **to make one's m.** *(succeed)* faire ses preuves
(**d**) *(target)* **his comments hit the m.** ses remarques ont touché en plein dans le mille; **unemployment has passed the 3 million m.** le nombre des chômeurs a dépassé la barre des 3 millions; **her accusation was wide of the m.** son accusation était complètement à côté de la plaque; **he's not up to the m.** il n'est pas à la hauteur
(**e**) *(in test, exam)* note *f*; **full marks** la note maximale
(**f**) *(in race)* **on your mark(s)! get set! go!** à vos marques! prêts! partez!
(**g**) *(model, of machine)* **m. II/III** série II/III
2 *vt* (**a**) *(put mark on)* marquer
(**b**) *(homework, exam)* noter; **to m. sth right/wrong** compter qch comme juste/faux
(**c**) *(indicate)* indiquer; *(anniversary, end, occasion)* marquer; **this decision marks a change in policy** cette décision est le signe d'un changement de politique; *Fig* **to m. time** *(wait)* piétiner
(**d**) *(characterize)* caractériser; **his comments were marked by their sarcasm** ses commentaires étaient empreints de sarcasme
(**e**) *(in sport) (opponent)* marquer
(**f**) *(pay attention to)* **m. my words** notez bien ce que je vais dire
▸**mark down** *vt sep* (**a**) *(make note of)* noter; **they had him marked down as a troublemaker** ils l'avaient étiqueté comme fauteur de troubles (**b**) *Com (price)* baisser; *(goods)* démarquer
▸**mark off** *vt sep* (**a**) *(area)* délimiter (**b**) *(tick off)* cocher
▸**mark out** *vt sep* **to m. sb out** distinguer qn
▸**mark up** *vt sep (price)* augmenter, majorer; **to be marked up** *(of goods)* avoir augmenté

marked [mɑːkt] *adj* (**a**) *(difference, improvement)* marqué(e), sensible (**b**) *(bearing a mark)* **m. cards** cartes truquées *ou* marquées; **to be a m. man** être surveillé

markedly ['mɑːkɪdlɪ] *adv* nettement

marker ['mɑːkə(r)] n (a) (of essay, exam) correcteur(trice) m,f (b) **m. (pen)** marqueur m (c) (flag, post) balise f; **m. buoy** bouée f de balisage

market ['mɑːkɪt] 1 n marché m; **to put sth on the m.** mettre qch en vente; Fin **m. analyst** analyste mf du marché; **m. day** jour m de marché; Econ **(free) m. economy** économie f de marché; Econ **m. forces** tendances fpl du marché; Com **m. leader** leader m du marché; Econ **m. price** prix m du marché; Com **m. research** étude f de marché; Com **m. share** part f de marché; Com **m. survey** étude f de marché; **m. town** ville f de marché
  2 vt commercialiser

marketable ['mɑːkɪtəbəl] adj commercialisable

marketing ['mɑːkɪtɪŋ] n Com (study, theory) marketing m, mercatique f; (of product) commercialisation f; **m. campaign** campagne f de marketing; **m. department** service m de marketing; **m. manager** responsable mf ou directeur(trice) m,f du marketing; **m. strategy** stratégie f marketing

marketplace ['mɑːkɪtpleɪs] n (a) (in village, town) place f du marché (b) Econ marché m; **in the m.** sur le marché

marking ['mɑːkɪŋ] n (a) **markings** (on animal) (spots) taches fpl; (stripes) rayures fpl; (on plane) insignes mpl (b) (of essay, exam) correction f; **I've got a lot of m. to do** j'ai beaucoup de copies à corriger

marksman ['mɑːksmən] n tireur m d'élite

mark-up ['mɑːkʌp] n (on price) majoration f

marmalade ['mɑːməleɪd] n confiture f d'oranges

maroon[1] [mə'ruːn] n (color) bordeaux m

maroon[2] [mə'ruːn] vt abandonner; **we were marooned by the floods** nous étions isolés à cause des inondations

marquee [mɑː'kiː] n grande tente f; (at circus) chapiteau m

marquis ['mɑːkwɪs] n marquis m

Marrakesh ['mærəkeʃ] n Marrakech

marriage ['mærɪdʒ] n also Fig mariage m; **a happy m.** un ménage heureux; **she's my aunt by m.** c'est ma tante par alliance; **m. of convenience** mariage de convenance; Fig **it was a m. of minds** c'était la rencontre de deux esprits; **m. certificate** certificat m de mariage; **m. counselor** conseiller(ère) m,f conjugal(e); **m. vows** vœux mpl du mariage

marriageable ['mærɪdʒəbəl] adj **a girl of m. age** une fille en âge de se marier

married ['mærɪd] adj marié(e); **to get m. (to)** se marier (avec); **m. life** la vie maritale; **m. name** nom m de femme mariée; Mil **m. quarters** logements mpl pour familles

marrow ['mærəʊ] n (a) (of bone) moelle f (b) (vegetable) courge f

marrowbone ['mærəʊbəʊn] n os m à moelle

marrowfat pea ['mærəʊfæt'piː] n pois m carré

marry ['mærɪ] (pt & pp married) 1 vt (a) (get married to) épouser, se marier avec; (of priest, parent) marier; **will you m. me?** veux-tu m'épouser?; Fig **he's married to his job** il n'y a que son travail qui compte (b) (combine) marier
  2 vi se marier

▶**marry off** vt sep marier

Mars [mɑːz] n (planet) Mars f

Marseilles [mɑː'seɪ] n Marseille

marsh [mɑːʃ] n marais m, marécage m

marshal ['mɑːʃəl] 1 n (a) (army officer) maréchal m (b) (at race, demonstration) membre m du service d'ordre
  2 vt (vehicles, troops) rassembler; (crowd) canaliser; (arguments, thoughts) mettre en ordre

marshland ['mɑːʃlænd] n région f marécageuse

marshmallow [mɑːʃ'mæləʊ] n guimauve f

marshy ['mɑːʃɪ] adj marécageux(euse)

marsupial [mɑː'suːpɪəl] n marsupial m

martial ['mɑːʃəl] adj martial(e); **m. arts** arts mpl martiaux; **to declare m. law** proclamer la loi martiale

Martian ['mɑːʃən] n Martien(enne) m,f

martyr ['mɑːtə(r)] 1 n martyr(e) m,f; Fig **to be a m. to rheumatism** souffrir le martyre à cause de rhumatismes
  2 vt martyriser

martyrdom ['mɑːtədəm] n martyre m

marvel ['mɑːvəl] 1 n merveille f; **to work marvels** faire des merveilles; **it's a m. they survived** c'est un miracle qu'ils soient encore vivants; Fam **you're a m.!** tu es un as!
  2 vi s'émerveiller (at de)

marvelous ['mɑːvələs] adj merveilleux(euse); Ironic **(isn't it) m.!** ça, c'est le bouquet ou le comble!

Marxism ['mɑːksɪzəm] n marxisme m

Marxist ['mɑːksɪst] n & adj marxiste mf

marzipan ['mɑːzɪpæn] n pâte f d'amandes

mascara [mæs'kɑːrə] n mascara m

mascot ['mæskət] n mascotte f

masculine ['mæskjʊlɪn] 1 n Gram masculin m; **in the m.** au masculin
  2 adj masculin(e)

masculinity [mæskjʊ'lɪnɪtɪ] n masculinité f

mash [mæʃ] 1 n (for pigs, poultry) pâtée f
  2 vt **to m. (up)** broyer; (vegetables) écraser

mashed potatoes [mæʃtpə'teɪtəʊz] n purée f de pommes de terre

mask [mɑːsk] 1 n masque m; (for eyes only) loup m
  2 vt (conceal) dissimuler

masked [mɑːskt] adj masqué(e)

masking tape ['mɑːskɪŋteɪp] n ruban m de papier adhésif

masochism ['mæsəkɪzəm] n masochisme m

masochist ['mæsəkɪst] n masochiste mf

masochistic [mæsə'kɪstɪk] adj masochiste

mason ['meɪsən] n (builder) maçon m; (freemason) franc-maçon m

masonry ['meɪsənrɪ] n (stonework) maçonnerie f

masquerade [mæskə'reɪd] 1 n (a) Fig (disguise) mascarade f (b) (dance) bal m masqué
  2 vi **to m. as sb** se faire passer pour qn

mass[1] [mæs] 1 n (a) (large number) foule f, multitude f; **m. culture** culture f de masse; **m. demonstration** grande manifestation f; **m. grave** charnier m; **m. hysteria** hystérie f collective; **m. media** (mass) médias mpl; **m. meeting** grand rassemblement m; **m. murderer** tueur m fou; **m. production** fabrication f en série; **m. protest** protestation f en masse; **m. unemployment** chômage m sur une grande échelle (b) (shapeless substance) masse f (c) Pol **the masses** le peuple m (d) Phys masse f
  2 vi (of troops, people, clouds) se masser

mass[2] [mæs] n Rel messe f; **to go to m.** aller à la messe

massacre ['mæsəkə(r)] 1 n massacre m; Fam Fig **it was a m.** (in sports, election) ça a été le massacre
  2 vt also Fig massacrer

massage [mə'sɑːʒ] 1 n massage m; **m. parlor** salon m de massage; **m. therapist** masseur(euse) m,f
  2 vt (body) masser; Fig **to m. the figures** manipuler les chiffres

masseur [mæ'sʊə(r)] n masseur m

masseuse [mæ'suːz] n masseuse f

massive ['mæsɪv] adj (increase, scale, dose) massif(ive); (amount, building, obstacle) énorme; (room) immense; (heart attack, stroke) foudroyant(e)

mass-produce [mæsprə'djuːs] vt fabriquer en série

mast [mɑːst] n (of ship) mât m; (of radio, TV transmitter) pylône m

mastectomy [mæs'tektəmɪ] (pl **mastectomies**) n Med mastectomie f

master ['mɑːstə(r)] 1 n (a) (man in charge) maître m; (of ship) capitaine m; **the m. of the house** le maître de maison; **to be**

one's own m. être son propre maître; **to be m. of the situation** être maître de la situation; **m. of ceremonies** maître des cérémonies; *(for TV program)* présentateur *m*; **m. bedroom** chambre *f* principale; **m. copy** original *m*; **m. key** passe-partout *m*; **m. plan** plan *m* d'ensemble; **m. race** race *f* supérieure

(**b**) *(skilled person)* maître *m*, expert(e) *m,f*; *Univ* **M. of Arts** *(qualification)* ≃ maîtrise *f* ès lettres; *(person)* ≃ maître ès lettres; *Univ* **M. of Science** *(qualification)* ≃ maîtrise *f* ès sciences; *(person)* ≃ maître ès sciences; **m. mason/builder** maître maçon/d'œuvre; *Mus* **m. class** cours *m* de maître; *Univ* **m.'s (degree)** ≃ maîtrise *f* (**in** de)

(**c**) *(teacher)* professeur *m*; **fencing/dancing m.** maître d'escrime/de ballet

(**d**) *(young boy)* **M. David Thomas** Monsieur David Thomas

(**e**) *Art* **an old m.** une œuvre de maître

2 *vt* maîtriser; *(situation)* dominer

masterful ['mɑːstəfʊl] *adj* autoritaire

masterly ['mɑːstəlɪ] *adj* magistral(e)

mastermind ['mɑːstəmaɪnd] **1** *n* cerveau *m*

2 *vt (project)* diriger, organiser; *(plot, crime)* échafauder

masterpiece ['mɑːstəpiːs] *n* chef-d'œuvre *m*

masterstroke ['mɑːstəstrəʊk] *n* coup *m* de maître

mastery ['mɑːstərɪ] *n* maîtrise *f*

mastiff ['mæstɪf] *n* mastiff *m*

mastitis [mæs'taɪtəs] *n Med* mastite *f*

masturbate ['mæstəbeɪt] *vi* se masturber

masturbation [mæstə'beɪʃən] *n* masturbation *f*

mat [mæt] *n (on floor)* tapis *m*; *(of straw)* natte *f*; *(at door)* paillasson *m*; **(table) m.** *(for plates)* set *m* de table; *(for dishes)* dessous-de-plat *m inv*

match¹ [mætʃ] *n (for lighting fire, cigarette)* allumette *f*

match² [mætʃ] **1** *n* (**a**) *(in sports)* match *m*; **m. point** *(in tennis)* balle *f* de match (**b**) **they're a good m.** *(of clothes)* ils vont bien ensemble; *(marriage)* **to make a good m.** faire un bon mariage; **to meet one's m.** trouver son maître; **to be no m. for sb** ne pas être à l'hauteur par rapport à qn

2 *vt* (**a**) *(equal)* égaler (**b**) *(of colors, clothes)* être assorti(e) à; *(of description, account)* concorder avec (**c**) **we can't m. their prices** nous ne pouvons pas rivaliser avec leurs prix; **to m. sb against sb** opposer qn à qn; **to be well matched** *(of teams, players)* être de même niveau; **a well-matched couple** un couple bien assorti

3 *vi (of colors, clothes)* être assortis(ties); *(of descriptions, accounts)* concorder

▶**match up 1** *vt sep (colors, clothes)* assortir

2 *vi (of clothes, colors)* être assortis(ties); *(of explanations)* concorder; **to m. up to sb's expectations** répondre à l'attente de qn

matchbox ['mætʃbɒks] *n* boîte *f* d'allumettes

matching ['mætʃɪŋ] *adj* assorti(e)

matchless ['mætʃlɪs] *adj* sans pareil

matchmaker ['mætʃmeɪkə(r)] *n* marieur(euse) *m,f*

matchstick ['mætʃstɪk] *n* allumette *f*; **m. man** *or* **figure** bonhomme *m* dessiné de simples traits

mate¹ [meɪt] **1** *n* (**a**) *(sexual partner) (male animal)* mâle *m*; *(female animal)* femelle *f*; *(person)* partenaire *mf* (**b**) *(assistant)* assistant(e) *m,f* (**c**) *(on ship)* officier *m*; **(first) m.** second *m*

2 *vt (animals)* accoupler

3 *vi (of animals)* s'accoupler

mate² [meɪt] **1** *n (in chess)* mat *m*

2 *vt (in chess)* mettre mat

material [mə'tɪərɪəl] **1** *n* (**a**) *(substance)* matériau *m*, matière *f*; *Fig* **he isn't officer m.** il n'a pas l'étoffe d'un officier (**b**) *(for book, article)* matériaux *mpl*; **reading m.** de quoi lire; **she writes all her own m.** *(of singer)* elle écrit ses chansons elle-même (**c**) *(cloth)* tissu *m* (**d**) **materials** *(equipment)* matériel *m*

2 *adj* (**a**) *(needs, possessions)* matériel(elle) (**b**) *(important, relevant)* essentiel(elle); *(fact)* pertinent(e); **the point is m. to my argument** c'est un point essentiel de mon argumentation

materialism [mə'tɪərɪəlɪzəm] *n* matérialisme *m*

materialistic [mətɪərɪə'lɪstɪk] *adj* matérialiste

materialize [mə'tɪərɪəlaɪz] *vi (of hope, threat)* se réaliser; *(of event)* avoir lieu; *(of spirit)* apparaître

materially [mə'tɪərɪəlɪ] *adv* (**a**) *(in money, goods)* matériellement (**b**) *(appreciably)* sensiblement

maternal [mə'tɜːnəl] *adj* maternel(elle)

maternity [mə'tɜːnɪtɪ] *n* maternité *f*; **m. dress** robe *f* de grossesse; **m. hospital** maternité; **m. leave** congé *m* de maternité; **m. ward** maternité

math [mæθ] *n* maths *fpl*

mathematical [mæθə'mætɪkəl] *adj* mathématique

mathematician [mæθəmə'tɪʃən] *n* mathématicien(enne) *m,f*

mathematics [mæθə'mætɪks] *n (subject)* mathématiques *fpl*; *(calculations)* calculs *mpl*

matinée ['mætɪneɪ] *n (of play, film)* matinée *f*

mating ['meɪtɪŋ] *n* accouplement *m*; **m. call** appel *m* du mâle; **m. ritual** parade *f* nuptiale; **m. season** saison *f* des amours

matriarch ['meɪtrɪɑːk] *n* = femme ayant le statut de chef de famille

matriarchal ['meɪtrɪɑːkəl] *adj* matriarcal(e)

matriculate [mə'trɪkjʊleɪt] *vi* s'inscrire

matriculation [mətrɪkjʊ'leɪʃən] *n* inscription *f*

matrimonial [matrɪ'məʊnɪəl] *adj* matrimonial(e)

matrimony ['mætrɪmənɪ] *n* mariage *m*

matrix ['meɪtrɪks] *(pl* **matrixes** ['meɪtrɪksɪz] *or* **matrices** ['meɪtrɪsiːz]) *n Math & Tech* matrice *f*

matron ['meɪtrən] *n* (**a**) *(older woman)* matrone *f* (**b**) *(in prison)* gardienne *f* (**c**) **m. of honor** *(at wedding)* dame *f* d'honneur

matt [mæt] *adj* mat(e)

matted ['mætɪd] *adj (hair)* emmêlé(e)

matter ['mætə(r)] **1** *n* (**a**) *(affair, issue)* question *f*, problème *m*; **that's a m. of opinion/taste** c'est une question d'opinion/de goût; **it's no easy m.** ce n'est pas simple; **that's quite another m.** ce n'est pas du tout la même chose; **within a m. of hours** en quelques heures; **for that m.** d'ailleurs; **as a m. of course** bien évidemment; **as a m. of fact** en fait; **as matters stand** au point où en sont les choses; **and to make matters worse...** et pour aggraver les choses...; **military matters** questions *fpl* militaires; **business matters** affaires *fpl*

(**b**) *(problem)* **what's the m.?** qu'est-ce qu'il y a?; **what's the m. with you?** qu'est-ce que tu as?; **there's something the m. with the car/my foot** j'ai un problème avec la voiture/mon pied

(**c**) *(substance)* matière *f*

(**d**) *(with no)* **no m.!** peu importe!; **no m. who/where** qui/où que ce soit; **no m. how hard I try...** j'ai beau essayer...; **no m. what I do** quoi que je fasse

2 *vi* avoir de l'importance (**to** pour); **it doesn't m.** cela n'a pas d'importance, ça ne fait rien; **nothing else matters** le reste est sans importance; **it doesn't m. to me** ça m'est égal

Matterhorn ['mætəhɔːn] *n* **the M.** le mont Cervin

matter-of-fact ['mætərə'fækt] *adj (person, statement)* terre à terre; *(tone, voice)* neutre; **he was very m. about it** il avait l'air très détaché

matting ['mætɪŋ] *n* tapis *m* de sol tressé

mattress ['mætrɪs] *n* matelas *m*

mature [mə'tjʊə(r)] **1** *adj (person, fruit)* mûr(e); *(hard cheese)* fort(e); **m. garden** jardin *m* planté depuis plusieurs années

2 *vt (wine)* faire vieillir

3 *vi (of person, fruit)* mûrir; *(of wine)* vieillir; *Fin (of investment)* arriver à échéance

maturity [mə'tjʊərɪtɪ] n maturité f; Fin **on m.** à l'échéance

maudlin ['mɔ:dlɪn] adj larmoyant(e)

maul [mɔ:l] vt (of lion, tiger) mutiler; Fig (criticize) tailler en pièces

Mauritania [mɒrɪ'teɪnɪə] n la Mauritanie

Mauritanian [mɒrɪ'teɪnɪən] **1** n Mauritanien(enne) m,f
2 adj mauritanien(enne)

Mauritian [mə'rɪʃən] **1** n Mauricien(enne) m,f
2 adj mauricien(enne)

Mauritius [mə'rɪʃəs] n l'île f Maurice

mausoleum [mɔ:sə'li:əm] n mausolée m

mauve [məʊv] **1** n mauve m
2 adj mauve

maverick ['mævərɪk] n franc-tireur m, non-conformiste mf

mawkish ['mɔ:kɪʃ] adj Pej mièvre

max [mæks] (abbr **maximum**) **1** n max
2 adv Fam maximum; **it'll take three days m.** ça prendra trois jours maximum

▸**max out** Fam **1** vt sep **to m. out one's credit card** = dépenser le maximum autorisé avec sa carte de crédit
2 vi **to m. out on chocolate** se gaver de chocolat; **to m. out on booze** picoler un max

maxim ['mæksɪm] n maxime f

maximize ['mæksɪmaɪz] vt maximaliser

maximum ['mæksɪməm] **1** n (pl **maximums** or **maxima** ['mæksɪmə]) maximum m; **to the m.** au maximum
2 adj maximum inv, maximal(e)

May [meɪ] n mai m; **in M.** en mai, au mois de mai; **at the beginning/end of M.** début/fin mai; **during M.** en mai; **each** or **every M.** chaque année en mai; **in the middle of M.** mimai; **last/next M.** en mai dernier/prochain; **on M. sixteenth** le seize mai; **she was born on M. 22, 1953** elle est née le 22 mai 1953; **M. Day** le Premier Mai

may [meɪ] v aux (3rd person singular **may**, pt **might** [maɪt]) (a) (expressing possibility) **he m. return at any moment** il pourrait rentrer à tout moment; **he m. have lost it** il se peut ou se pourrait qu'il l'ait perdu; **it m. be that…** il se peut ou se pourrait que… + subjunctive; **you m. be wondering why…** vous vous demandez peut-être pourquoi…; **you m. well ask!** bonne question!; **we m. as well go** autant y aller; **you m. as well tell them the truth** autant que tu leur dises la vérité (b) Formal (asking for or giving permission) **m. I come in?** puis-je entrer?; **if I m. say so** si je peux me permettre; **m. I?** (when borrowing) vous permettez? (c) Formal (expressing wish, purpose) **m. she rest in peace!** paix à son âme!; **m. the best man win!** que le meilleur gagne! (d) (with concessions) **he m. be very talented but I still don't like him** il est peut-être très doué, mais il me déplaît quand même; **be that as it m., that's as m. be** quoi qu'il en soit

Mayan ['maɪən] **1** n Maya mf
2 adj maya

maybe ['meɪbi:] adv peut-être; **m. she won't accept** elle n'acceptera peut-être pas

Mayday ['meɪdeɪ] n (distress signal) signal m de détresse, SOS m; **M.!** mayday!

mayhem ['meɪhem] n **it was m.** c'était la pagaille

mayonnaise [meɪə'neɪz] n mayonnaise f

mayor ['meə(r)] n maire m

mayoress ['meəres] n mairesse f; (mayor's wife) femme f du maire

maypole ['meɪpəʊl] n = mât autour duquel les gens dansent pour célébrer le Premier Mai

maze [meɪz] n labyrinthe m; Fig dédale m

MBA [embi:'eɪ] n Univ (abbr **Master of Business Administration**) MBA m

MBO [embi:'əʊ] n Com (abbr **management buyout**) = rachat d'une entreprise par ses cadres

MC [em'si:] n (abbr **Master of Ceremonies**) maître m des cérémonies; (for TV program) présentateur m

MD [em'di:] n (a) Med (abbr **Doctor of Medicine**) docteur m en médecine (b) Com (abbr **Managing Director**) directeur(trice) m,f général(e)

ME [e'mi:] n Med (abbr **myalgic encephalomyelitis**) encéphalomyélite f myalgique

me¹ [unstressed mɪ, stressed mi:] pron (a) (direct object) me; **she hates me** elle me déteste; **she loves me** elle m'aime; **she can understand my son but not ME** elle comprend mon fils, mais moi, elle ne me comprend pas
(b) (indirect object) **she gave me the book** elle m'a donné le livre; **she gave it to me** elle me l'a donné
(c) (after preposition) moi; **she's thinking of me** elle pense à moi
(d) (as complement of verb to be) moi; **it's me!** c'est moi!; **it was me who did it** c'est moi qui l'ai fait
(e) (with interjections) **silly me!** que je suis bête!; **poor me!** pauvre de moi!

me² [mi:] n Mus mi m

meadow ['medəʊ] n prairie f, pré m

meager ['mi:gə(r)] adj maigre

meal¹ [mi:l] n repas m; Fig **to make a m. of sth** faire tout un plat de qch; **m. ticket** ticket m restaurant; Fam Fig (source of income) **I can't leave Harry, he's my m. ticket** je ne peux pas quitter Harry, c'est lui qui fait bouillir la marmite

meal² [mi:l] n (flour) farine f

mealtime ['mi:ltaɪm] n heure f du repas

mealy ['mi:lɪ] adj farineux(euse)

mealy-mouthed [mi:lɪ'maʊðd] adj Pej mielleux(euse)

mean¹ [mi:n] **1** n (average) moyenne f
2 adj (average) moyen(enne)

mean² [mi:n] adj (a) (nasty) méchant(e); **she has a m. streak** elle peut être méchante quand elle veut; **that was a m. thing to do/say** ce n'est pas chic d'avoir dit ça/fait ça (b) (miserly) mesquin(e), avare (c) (poor) **she's no m. photographer** c'est une sacrée photographe; **it was no m. feat** ce n'est pas un mince exploit (d) Fam (good) **he plays a m. game of pool** c'est un as du billard

mean³ [mi:n] (pt & pp **meant** [ment]) vt (a) (signify) (of word, event) signifier; (of person) vouloir dire; **what does the word "tacky" m.?** que signifie le mot "tacky"?; **this is Tim, I m. Tom** je vous présente Tim, je veux dire Tom; **I know what you m.** je comprends; **what do you m.?** qu'est-ce que tu veux dire?; **it doesn't m. anything** ça ne veut rien dire
(b) (be serious about) **do you think he meant what he said?** pensez-vous qu'il l'ait dit sérieusement?; **I didn't m. that** ce n'est pas ce que je voulais dire; **I m. it** je parle sérieusement; **you don't m. it!** tu plaisantes!
(c) (be of importance) **the price means nothing to him** le prix importe peu pour lui; **it means a lot to me** c'est très important pour moi
(d) (intend) **to m. to do sth** avoir l'intention de faire qch; **I didn't m. to do it** je ne l'ai pas fait exprès; **I m. him no harm** je ne lui veux pas de mal; **she means well** ses intentions sont bonnes; **I m. to succeed** je veux réussir; **she meant you to have this ring** elle voulait que tu aies cette bague; **it was meant as a joke/compliment** c'était une blague/un compliment; **this portrait is meant to be of the duke** ce portrait est censé représenter le duc; **you were meant to be here at eight** vous étiez censé arriver à huit heures; **it's meant to be a good film** il paraît que c'est un bon film; **they were meant for each other** ils sont faits l'un pour l'autre

meander [mɪ'ændə(r)] **1** n méandre m
2 vi (of river, road) serpenter; (of person) flâner

meaning ['mi:nɪŋ] *n* sens *m*, signification *f*; *Fam* **if you get my m.** si tu vois ce que je veux dire; **what's the m. of this?** *(expressing indignation)* qu'est-ce que ça signifie?; **the m. of life** le sens de la vie

meaningful ['mi:nɪŋfʊl] *adj* significatif(ive); *(relationship)* sérieux(euse)

meaningless ['mi:nɪŋlɪs] *adj* vide de sens, sans signification

meanness ['mi:nnɪs] *n* (**a**) *(miserliness)* avarice *f* (**b**) *(nastiness)* mesquinerie *f*

means [mi:nz] **1** *n* (*pl* **means**) *(method)* moyen *m*; **by m. of...** au moyen de..., à l'aide de...; **there is no m. of escape** il n'y a aucun moyen de s'échapper; **by some m. or other** d'une manière ou d'une autre; **a m. to an end** un moyen (d'arriver à ses fins); **by all m.** *(certainly)* je vous en prie; **by no m.** pas du tout, nullement; **she is by no m. stupid** elle est loin d'être bête; **m. of communication** moyen de communication; **m. of production** moyens de production; **m. of transport** moyen de transport
    2 *npl (income, wealth)* moyens *mpl*, ressources *fpl*; **a man of m.** un homme fortuné; **to live beyond/within one's m.** vivre au-dessus de/selon ses moyens; **m. test** *(for state benefit)* enquête *f* sur les revenus

meant [ment] *pt & pp of* **mean**[1]

meantime ['mi:ntaɪm], **meanwhile** ['mi:nwaɪl] **1** *n* **in the m.** *(at the same time)* pendant ce temps; *(between two events)* entre-temps
    2 *adv (at the same time)* pendant ce temps; *(between two events)* entre-temps

measles ['mi:zəlz] *n* rougeole *f*; **to have (the) m.** avoir la rougeole

measly ['mi:zlɪ] *adj Fam* minable

measurable ['meʒərəbəl] *adj* mesurable; *Fig (difference, improvement)* notable, sensible

measure ['meʒə(r)] **1** *n* (**a**) *(measurement, quantity)* mesure *f*; **this was a m. of how serious the situation was** cela montrait à quel point la situation était sérieuse; **they allowed her a m. of freedom** on lui accordait une certaine liberté; **to get the m. of sb** jauger qn; **then he called me a liar for good m.** par-dessus le marché, il m'a traité de menteur (**b**) *(degree)* **in some m.** dans une certaine mesure (**c**) *(action, step)* mesure *f*; **to take measures to do sth** prendre des mesures pour faire qch
    2 *vt & vi* mesurer

▸**measure up** *vi* être à la hauteur (**to** de)

measured ['meʒəd] *adj* mesuré(e)

measurement ['meʒəmənt] *n* mesure *f*

measuring ['meʒərɪŋ] *n* **m. cup** gobelet *m* doseur; **m. spoon** cuillère-mesure *f*; **m. tape** mètre *m* ruban

meat [mi:t] *n* (**a**) *(food)* viande *f*; **m. loaf** pain *m* de viande (**b**) *Fig (substantial content)* substance *f*

meatball ['mi:tbɔ:l] *n* boulette *f* de viande

meaty ['mi:tɪ] *adj (taste, smell)* de viande; *Fig (book, film)* riche

Mecca ['mekə] *n* La Mecque; *Fig* paradis *m*

mechanic [mɪ'kænɪk] *n* mécanicien(enne) *m,f*

mechanical [mɪ'kænɪkəl] *adj also Fig* mécanique; **m. engineer** ingénieur *m* mécanicien; **m. engineering** construction *f* mécanique

mechanics [mɪ'kænɪks] **1** *n* (**a**) *(science)* mécanique *f* (**b**) *(working parts)* mécanisme *m*
    2 *npl Fig (processes)* mécanisme *m*

mechanism ['mekənɪzəm] *n* mécanisme *m*

mechanize ['mekənaɪz] *vt* mécaniser

mechanized ['mekənaɪzd] *adj* **m. industry** industrie *f* mécanisée; **m. troops** troupes *fpl* motorisées

MEd [e'med] *n Univ (abbr* **Master of Education**) maîtrise *f* en sciences de l'éducation

medal ['medəl] *n* médaille *f*

medalist ['medəlɪst] *n* médaillé(e) *m,f*

medallion [mɪ'dæljən] *n* médaillon *m*

meddle ['medəl] *vi (interfere)* se mêler (**in** de); *(tamper)* toucher (**with** à)

meddler ['medlə(r)] *n* indiscret(ète) *m,f*

meddlesome ['medəlsəm] *adj* indiscret(ète)

media ['mi:dɪə] *n* (**a**) *(TV, press)* médias *mpl*; **m. circus** cirque *m* médiatique; **m. coverage** couverture *f* médiatique; **m. studies** études *fpl* de communication (**b**) *pl of* **medium**

median ['mi:dɪən] **1** *n* (**a**) *Math* médiane *f* (**b**) *(on highway)* terre-plein *m* central
    2 *adj* (**a**) *Math* médian(e) (**b**) **m. strip** terre-plein *m* central

mediate ['mi:dɪeɪt] *vi* servir de médiateur (**for/between** pour/entre)

mediation [mi:dɪ'eɪʃən] *n* médiation *f*; **to go to m.** recourir à une médiation

mediator ['mi:dɪeɪtə(r)] *n* médiateur(trice) *m,f*

medic ['medɪk] *n (doctor)* médecin *m*

medical ['medɪkəl] *adj (record, treatment, profession)* médical(e); *(book)* de médecine; *(student)* en médecine; **to seek m. advice** consulter un médecin; **m. board** commission *f* médicale; **m. care** soins *mpl* médicaux; **m. certificate** certificat *m* médical; **m. examination** visite *f* médicale; **m. insurance** assurance *f* maladie; **m. practitioner** (médecin *m*) généraliste *mf*; **m. records** dossier *m* médical

medicated ['medɪkeɪtɪd] *adj (soap)* médical(e); *(shampoo)* traitant(e)

medication [medɪ'keɪʃən] *n* médicaments *mpl*; **to be on m.** être sous traitement

medicinal [me'dɪsɪnəl] *adj* médicinal(e)

medicine ['medsɪn] *n* (**a**) *(science)* médecine *f*; **to practice m.** exercer la médecine; **to study m.** faire des études de médecine (**b**) *(drugs)* médicament *m*; *Fig* **to give sb a taste of his own m.** rendre à qn la monnaie de sa pièce; **m. chest** *or* **cabinet** (armoire *f* à) pharmacie *f*; **m. man** *(traditional healer)* sorcier *m*, guérisseur *m*

medieval [medɪ'i:vəl] *adj* médiéval(e)

mediocre [mi:dɪ'əʊkə(r)] *adj* médiocre

mediocrity [mi:dɪ'ɒkrɪtɪ] *n* médiocrité *f*

meditate ['medɪteɪt] *vi* méditer (**on** sur)

meditation [medɪ'teɪʃən] *n* méditation *f*

Mediterranean [medɪtə'reɪnɪən] **1** *n* **the M.** la (mer) Méditerranée
    2 *adj* méditerranéen(enne); **the M. Sea** la mer Méditerranée

medium ['mi:dɪəm] **1** *n* (**a**) (*pl* **media** ['mi:dɪə] *or* **mediums**) *(means of communication)* moyen *m* de communication; *(means of expression)* moyen d'expression; **through the m. of the press** par voie de presse (**b**) *(in spiritualism)* médium *mf*
    2 *adj* moyen(enne); **of m. height** de taille moyenne; **in the m. term** à moyen terme; **m. dry** demi-sec; **m. rare** à point; **m. wave** ondes *fpl* moyennes

medley ['medlɪ] (*pl* **medleys**) *n (mixture)* mélange *m*; *(in music)* pot-pourri *m*; **the 400 meters m.** *(in swimming)* le 400 mètres quatre nages

meek [mi:k] *adj* docile; **m. and mild** doux (douce) comme un agneau

meekly ['mi:klɪ] *adv* docilement

meet [mi:t] (*pt & pp* **met** [met]) **1** *vt* (**a**) *(encounter) (by accident)* rencontrer; *(by arrangement)* rejoindre, retrouver; *(collect)* attendre, aller chercher; **his eyes met mine** nos regards se sont croisés; **a remarkable sight met our eyes** un spectacle extraordinaire s'offrait à nos yeux; **there's more to this than meets the eye** on ne connaît pas les dessous de cette affaire; **there's more to her than meets the eye** elle cache bien son jeu
    (**b**) *(become acquainted with)* rencontrer, faire la connaissance de; **have you met my husband?** connaissez-vous mon

mari?; **m. Mr Ford** je vous présente M. Ford

(**c**) *(join with) (river)* se jeter dans; *(road)* rejoindre

(**d**) *(satisfy) (demand, order)* satisfaire; *(condition, requirement)* satisfaire à; *(objection, criticism)* répondre à; *(cost, expense)* prendre en charge, payer

(**e**) *(danger)* affronter; *(difficulties)* rencontrer; **to m. one's death** trouver la mort; **to m. one's match** trouver son maître

2 *vi* (**a**) *(encounter) (by accident)* se rencontrer; *(by arrangement)* se retrouver; **our eyes met** nos regards se sont croisés

(**b**) *(become acquainted)* se rencontrer

(**c**) *(of society, assembly)* se réunir

(**d**) *(join)* se rencontrer; *(of rivers, roads)* se rejoindre

3 *n (for sports)* rencontre *m*

▶**meet up** *vi (by accident)* se rencontrer; *(by arrangement)* se retrouver; **to m. up with sb** *(by accident)* rencontrer qn; *(by arrangement)* retrouver qn

▶**meet with** *vt insep* (**a**) *(encounter) (by accident)* rencontrer; *(by arrangement)* retrouver (**b**) *(difficulty, refusal)* se heurter à; *(danger)* affronter; **to m. with disaster** se solder par un désastre; **to m. with failure** échouer; **to m. with an accident** avoir un accident; **to m. with sb's approval** recevoir l'accord de qn

meeting ['miːtɪŋ] *n* (**a**) *(encounter) (by accident)* rencontre *f*; *(by arrangement)* rendez-vous *m*; **m. place** (lieu *m* de) rendez-vous (**b**) *(for business, discussion)* réunion *f*; *(of shareholders)* assemblée *f*; **to be in a m.** être en réunion; **to hold a m.** se réunir

meet-up ['miːtʌp] *n Comput* rencontre *f* organisée sur Internet

megabyte ['megəbaɪt] *n Comput* mégaoctet *m*

megahertz ['megəhɜːts] *(pl* **megahertz***) n Elec* mégahertz *m*

megalomania [megələʊ'meɪnɪə] *n* mégalomanie *f*

megalomaniac [megələʊ'meɪnɪæk] *n* mégalomane *mf*

megaphone ['megəfəʊn] *n* mégaphone *m*, porte-voix *m inv*

megaton ['megətʌn] *n* mégatonne *f*

megawatt ['megəwɒt] *n Elec* mégawatt *m*

melancholy ['melənkəlɪ] **1** *n* mélancolie *f*

2 *adj (person)* mélancolique; *(atmosphere, news)* triste

melanin ['melənɪn] *n* mélanine *f*

melanoma [melə'nəʊmə] *n Med* mélanome *m*

melee ['meleɪ] *n* mêlée *f*

mellifluous [mə'lɪfluəs] *adj* mélodieux(euse)

mellow ['meləʊ] **1** *adj (flavor)* suave; *(voice, color)* chaud(e); *(wine)* moelleux(euse); *(light)* doux (douce); *(person)* détendu(e), serein(e)

2 *vi* s'adoucir

melodic [mɪ'lɒdɪk] *adj* mélodique

melodious [mɪ'ləʊdɪəs] *adj* mélodieux(euse)

melodrama ['melədrɑːmə] *n* mélodrame *m*

melodramatic [melədrə'mætɪk] *adj* mélodramatique

melody ['melədɪ] *(pl* **melodies***) n* mélodie *f*

melon ['melən] *n* melon *m*

melt [melt] **1** *vt also Fig* faire fondre

2 *vi* fondre; **to m. into thin air** s'évaporer, disparaître; **to m. into the crowd** se fondre dans la foule

▶**melt away** *vi (of snow)* fondre; *(of clouds, vapor)* se dissiper; *(of crowd)* se disperser; *(of objections, opposition)* s'évanouir

▶**melt down** *vt sep (metal)* fondre

meltdown ['meltdaʊn] *n Phys* fusion *f*

melting ['meltɪŋ] *n* **m. point** point *m* de fusion; *Fig* **m. pot** melting-pot *m*, creuset *m*

member ['membə(r)] **1** *n* membre *m*; *Pol (in Great Britain and Canada)* **M. of Parliament** député(e) *m,f*

2 *adj* **m. country/state** pays *m*/État *m* membre

membership ['membəʃɪp] *n* (**a**) *(state)* adhésion *f*; **m. card** carte *f* de membre *ou* d'adhérent; **m. fee** cotisation *f* (**b**) *(members)* membres *mpl*, adhérents *mpl*; **a large/small m.** une forte/faible adhésion

membrane ['membreɪn] *n* membrane *f*

memento [mɪ'mentəʊ] *(pl* **mementos** *or* **mementoes***) n* souvenir *m*

memo ['meməʊ] *(pl* **memos***) n* note *f* de service; **m. pad** bloc-notes *m*

memoir ['memwɑː(r)] *n (essay)* mémoire *m*; *(biography)* biographie *f*; **memoirs** *(autobiography)* mémoires *mpl*

memorable ['memərəbəl] *adj* mémorable

memorandum [memə'rændəm] *(pl* **memoranda** [memə'rændə] *or* **memorandums***) n* note *f* de service

memorial [mɪ'mɔːrɪəl] **1** *n (monument)* mémorial *m*

2 *adj* commémoratif(ive)

memorize ['meməraɪz] *vt* mémoriser

memory ['memərɪ] *(pl* **memories***) n* (**a**) *(faculty) & Comput* mémoire *f*; **to have a good/bad m.** avoir (une) bonne/mauvaise mémoire; **if my m. serves me right** si ma mémoire est bonne; **from m.** de mémoire; **to lose one's m.** perdre la mémoire; **to commit sth to m.** apprendre qch par cœur; **within living m.** de mémoire d'homme (**b**) *(thing remembered)* souvenir *m*; **in m. of...** en souvenir de..., à la mémoire de...; **to take a trip down m. lane** se remémorer le passé

men [men] *pl of* **man**

menace ['menɪs] **1** *n (threat)* menace *f*; *(danger)* danger *m*; *Fam Fig (pest)* plaie *f*

2 *vt* menacer

menacing ['menəsɪŋ] *adj* menaçant(e)

menagerie [mɪ'nædʒərɪ] *n* ménagerie *f*

mend [mend] **1** *vt (repair)* réparer; *(clothing)* raccommoder; **to m. one's ways** s'amender

2 *vi (of broken bone)* se ressouder

3 *n Fam* **to be on the m.** aller mieux

menfolk ['menfəʊk] *npl* **the m.** les hommes *mpl*

menial ['miːnɪəl] **1** *n Pej* laquais *m*

2 *adj (job)* subalterne; **m. tasks** corvées *fpl*

meningitis [menɪn'dʒaɪtɪs] *n* méningite *f*; **to have m.** avoir la méningite

menopause ['menəpɔːz] *n* ménopause *f*

menstrual ['menstrʊəl] *adj* menstruel(elle)

menstruate ['menstrʊeɪt] *vi* avoir ses règles

menstruation [menstrʊ'eɪʃən] *n* menstruation *f*

menswear ['menzweə(r)] *n* vêtements *mpl* pour hommes

mental ['mentəl] *adj* (**a**) *(state, age)* mental(e); **to make a m. note of sth/to do sth** essayer de se souvenir de qch/de faire qch; **to have a m. block about sth** faire un blocage sur qch; **m. arithmetic** calcul *m* mental; **m. breakdown** dépression *f* (nerveuse); **m. health** santé *f* mentale; **m. hospital** hôpital *m* psychiatrique; **m. illness** maladie *f* mentale; **m. patient** malade *mf* mental(e) (**b**) *very Fam (mad)* malade, dingue; **to go m.** *(lose one's temper)* devenir dingue

mentality [men'tælɪtɪ] *(pl* **mentalities***) n* mentalité *f*

mentally ['mentəlɪ] *adv* mentalement; **to be m. handicapped** être handicapé(e) mental(e); **to be m. ill** avoir une maladie mentale

menthol ['menθɒl] *n* menthol *m*; **m. cigarettes** cigarettes *fpl* mentholées

mention ['menʃən] **1** *n* mention *f*; **he gets a brief m. in her autobiography** elle le mentionne brièvement dans son autobiographie; **to make no m. of sth** ne pas faire référence à qch

2 *vt* parler de; *(allude to)* mentionner; **to m. that...** dire que...; **to m. sb in one's will** coucher qn sur son testament; **to be mentioned in dispatches** être cité(e) à l'ordre du jour; **not to m....** sans parler de...; **now (that) you m. it** maintenant que tu le dis; **don't m. it!** il n'y a pas de quoi!

mentor ['mentɔː(r)] **1** *n* mentor *m*

2 *vt* jouer les mentors auprès de

mentoring ['mentərɪŋ] *n* mentoring *m (relation de conseil et de soutien entre une personne expérimentée et un débutant)*

menu ['menju:] n (a) (in restaurant) (set) menu m; (à la carte) carte f (b) Comput menu m; **m. bar** barre f de menu; **m. item** élément m de menu

meow [mɪ'aʊ] 1 n miaulement m; **m.!** miaou!
2 vi miauler

MEP [emiː'piː] n Pol (abbr **Member of the European Parliament**) député m au Parlement européen

mercantile ['mɜːkəntaɪl] adj commercial(e)

mercenary ['mɜːsɪnərɪ] 1 n (pl **mercenaries**) mercenaire m
2 adj Pej intéressé(e)

merchandise ['mɜːtʃəndaɪz] 1 n marchandises fpl
2 vt marchandiser

merchandising ['mɜːtʃəndaɪzɪŋ] n merchandising m, marchandisage m

merchant ['mɜːtʃənt] n (retail) marchand(e) m,f; (wholesale) négociant(e) m,f; **m. bank** banque f d'affaires; **m. marine** marine f marchande; **m. seaman** marin m de la marine marchande; **m. ship** navire m marchand

merchantman ['mɜːtʃəntmən] n (ship) navire m marchand

merciful ['mɜːsɪfʊl] adj (person) clément(e); (act) charitable

mercifully ['mɜːsɪfʊlɪ] adv (a) (showing mercy) avec clémence (b) (fortunately) heureusement

merciless ['mɜːsɪlɪs] adj sans pitié, impitoyable

mercurial [mɜː'kjʊərɪəl] adj (lively) vif (vive); (changeable) changeant(e), lunatique

Mercury ['mɜːkjʊrɪ] n (planet) Mercure f

mercury ['mɜːkjʊrɪ] n (metal) mercure m

mercy ['mɜːsɪ] (pl **mercies**) n (a) (clemency) pitié f, clémence f; **to have m. on sb** avoir pitié de qn; **to beg for m.** demander grâce; **at the m. of** à la merci de; **m. killing** acte m d'euthanasie (b) (blessing) bonheur m, chance f; **it's a m. that...** c'est une chance que...; **to be thankful** or **grateful for small mercies** apprécier ce dont on dispose

mere [mɪə(r)] adj simple; **he's a m. child** ce n'est qu'un enfant

merely ['mɪəlɪ] adv simplement, seulement

merge [mɜːdʒ] 1 vt (companies) & Comput fusionner
2 vi (of colors, sounds) se fondre, se confondre; (of companies) fusionner; **to m. into the background** se fondre dans le décor

merger ['mɜːdʒə(r)] n fusion f; **mergers and acquisitions** fusions fpl et acquisitions fpl

meridian [mə'rɪdɪən] n méridien m

meringue [mə'ræŋ] n meringue f

merit ['merɪt] 1 n (advantage, worth) mérite m; **of little/great m.** de peu de/grande valeur; **to judge sth on its merits** juger qch pour ce qu'il vaut; **in order of m.** par ordre de mérite
2 vt mériter

meritocracy [merɪ'tɒkrəsɪ] (pl **meritocracies**) n méritocratie f

meritorious [merɪ'tɔːrɪəs] adj Formal méritoire, louable

mermaid ['mɜːmeɪd] n sirène f

merrily ['merɪlɪ] adv joyeusement, gaiement

merriment ['merɪmənt] n gaieté f

merry ['merɪ] adj (a) (happy) joyeux(euse), gai(e); **to make m.** s'amuser; **M. Christmas!** Joyeux Noël!; **the more the merrier** plus on est de fous, plus on rit (b) (slightly drunk) gai(e)

merry-go-round ['merɪɡəʊraʊnd] n manège m, Can, Belg & Suisse carrousel m

mesh [meʃ] 1 n (of net, sieve) mailles fpl
2 vi (of gears) s'engrener

mesmerize ['mezməraɪz] vt hypnotiser

mess [mes] 1 n (a) (disorder) désordre m; **you look a m.!** tu es dans un triste état!; **to be (in) a m.** (of room) être en désordre; Fig (of person) être dans le pétrin; (of one's life) être un désastre; **he's a m.** il est dans un triste état; Fig **to make a m. of sth** (essay, job) saloper qch (b) (dirt) saletés fpl; **to make a m. of** sth salir qch; **the dog's made a m. on the carpet** le chien a fait ses besoins sur le tapis (c) Mil (for officers) mess m; (for soldiers) réfectoire m; **m. kit** gamelle f
2 vi Fam (of dog, cat) faire ses besoins

▸**mess about, mess around** vi (a) (fool about) faire l'imbécile; (waste time) traîner (b) (tinker) **to m. about** or **around with sth** tripoter qch

▸**mess up** 1 vt sep (hair, room, papers) mettre en désordre; (plans) ficher en l'air
2 vi tout rater

message ['mesɪdʒ] n message m; **to leave a m. for sb** laisser un message pour qn; Fam Fig **to get the m.** piger

messaging ['mesɪdʒɪŋ] n Comput messagerie f électronique

messenger ['mesɪndʒə(r)] n messager(ère) m,f; **m. boy** garçon m de courses, coursier m

Messiah [mɪ'saɪə] n Rel Messie m

messianic [mesɪ'ænɪk] adj messianique

messily ['mesɪlɪ] adv salement; Fig **to end m.** (of relationship) mal terminer

Messrs ['mesəz] (abbr **Messieurs**) MM

messy ['mesɪ] adj (a) (dirty) sale; (job) salissant(e); **to be a m. eater** manger salement (b) (untidy) (room, hair) en désordre; (handwriting) peu soigné(e); (appearance) négligé(e) (c) (unpleasantly complex) (affair, situation) embrouillé(e); (private life) troublé(e)

met [met] pt & pp of **meet**

metabolic [metə'bɒlɪk] adj métabolique

metabolism [mɪ'tæbəlɪzəm] n métabolisme m

metal ['metəl] 1 n métal m; **m. detector** détecteur m de métaux
2 adj en métal

metallic [mɪ'tælɪk] adj (sound, voice) métallique; (paint) métallisé(e); (taste) de métal

metallurgy [me'tælədʒɪ] n métallurgie f

metalwork ['metəlwɜːk] n ferronnerie f

metamorphosis [metə'mɔːfəsɪs] (pl **metamorphoses** [metə'mɔːfəsiːz]) n métamorphose f

metaphor ['metəfə(r)] n métaphore f

metaphoric [metə'fɒrɪk], **metaphorical** [metə'fɒrɪkəl] adj métaphorique

metaphysical [metə'fɪzɪkəl] adj métaphysique

metaphysics [metə'fɪzɪks] n métaphysique f

▸**mete out** [miːt] vt sep (punishment) infliger (**to** à); (justice) rendre

meteor ['miːtɪə(r)] n météore m

meteoric [miːtɪ'ɒrɪk] adj météorique; Fig **a m. rise** une ascension fulgurante

meteorite ['miːtɪəraɪt] n météorite f

meteorological [miːtɪərə'lɒdʒɪkəl] adj météorologique

meteorology [miːtɪə'rɒlədʒɪ] n météorologie f

meter[1] ['miːtə(r)] n compteur m; **to read the m.** relever le compteur; **(parking) m.** parcmètre m; Fam **m. maid** contractuelle f; Fam **m. man** contractuel m

meter[2] ['miːtə(r)] n (measurement) mètre m

meter[3] ['miːtə(r)] n (of poetry) mètre m

methane ['miːθeɪn] n méthane m

method ['meθəd] n méthode f; **there's m. in his madness** il n'est pas aussi fou qu'il en a l'air; **m. acting** méthode de Stanislavski

methodical [mɪ'θɒdɪkəl] adj méthodique

Methodism ['meθədɪzəm] n Rel méthodisme m

Methodist ['meθədɪst] n Rel méthodiste mf

methodology [meθə'dɒlədʒɪ] n méthodologie f

methylated spirits ['meθɪleɪtɪd'spɪrɪts] n alcool m à brûler

meticulous [mɪ'tɪkjʊləs] adj méticuleux(euse)

metric ['metrɪk] adj métrique; **the m. system** le système métrique

metronome ['metrənəʊm] n métronome m

metropolis [mɪ'trɒpəlɪs] n métropole f

metropolitan [metrə'pɒlɪtən] adj urbain(e); **M. France** la France métropolitaine

metrosexual [metrəʊ'sekʃuːəl] **1** n métrosexuel m
2 adj métrosexuel

mettle ['metəl] n (courage) courage m; **to be on one's m.** être fin prêt(e); **to show one's m.** montrer de quoi on est capable

mew [mjuː] **1** n miaulement m
2 vi miauler

mews [mjuːz] (pl **mews**) n ruelle f; **m. cottage** = maison luxueuse aménagée dans une ancienne écurie

Mexican ['meksɪkən] **1** n Mexicain(e) m,f
2 adj mexicain(e); **M. wave** ola f

Mexico ['meksɪkəʊ] n le Mexique; **M. City** Mexico

mezzanine ['metsəniːn] n **m. (floor)** mezzanine f

mg [em'dʒiː] n (abbr **milligram(s)**) mg

Mgr. (abbr **Monsignor**) Mgr

MHz (abbr **megahertz**) MHz

mi [miː] n Mus mi m

mica ['maɪkə] n mica m

mice [maɪs] pl of **mouse**

Michelangelo [maɪkəl'ændʒələʊ] n Michel-Ange

Mickey Mouse ['mɪkɪ'maʊs] adj Fam Pej (job, studies, qualification) à la noix

micro ['maɪkrəʊ] (pl **micros**) n micro m

microbe ['maɪkrəʊb] n microbe m

microbiology [maɪkrəʊbaɪ'ɒlədʒɪ] n microbiologie f

microchip ['maɪkrəʊtʃɪp] n microprocesseur m

microcomputer ['maɪkrəʊkəm'pjuːtə(r)] n micro-ordinateur m

microcomputing ['maɪkrəʊkəm'pjuːtɪŋ] n micro-informatique f

microcosm ['maɪkrəʊkɒzəm] n microcosme m

microfiche ['maɪkrəʊfiːʃ] n microfiche f

microfilm ['maɪkrəʊfɪlm] **1** n microfilm m
2 vt microfilmer

micrometer [maɪ'krɒmɪtə(r)] n micromètre m

microphone ['maɪkrəfəʊn] n microphone m

microprocessor ['maɪkrəʊ'prəʊsesə(r)] n micro-processeur m

microscope ['maɪkrəskəʊp] n microscope m

microscopic [maɪkrə'skɒpɪk] adj microscopique

microsurgery [maɪkrəʊ'sɜːdʒərɪ] n microchirurgie f

microwave ['maɪkrəʊweɪv] **1** n Phys micro-onde f; **m. (oven)** (four m à) micro-ondes m inv
2 vt faire cuire au micro-ondes

mid [mɪd] adj **in m. ocean** au milieu de l'océan; **m. June** mi-juin; **he stopped in m. sentence** il s'est arrêté au milieu d'une phrase

midair [mɪd'eə(r)] **1** n **in m.** en plein ciel
2 adj (collision) en plein ciel

mid-Atlantic accent [mɪdət'læntɪk'æksent] n accent m mi-américain mi-britannique

midday ['mɪd'deɪ] n midi m; **m. meal** déjeuner m; **the m. sun** le soleil de midi

middle ['mɪdəl] **1** n (a) (center) milieu m; **to be in the m. of doing sth** être en train de faire qch; **in the m. of the night** en pleine nuit; **in the m. of nowhere** dans un coin perdu; Fig **to split sth down the m.** partager qch en deux (b) (waist) taille f
2 adj du milieu; **m. age** l'âge m mûr; Hist **the M. Ages** le Moyen Âge; Mus **m. C** do m du milieu du clavier; **the m. class(es)** les classes mpl moyennes; Fig **to steer a m. course** adopter une solution intermédiaire; **in the m. distance** au

second plan; **the M. East** le Moyen-Orient; **M. Eastern** du Moyen-Orient; Pol **the m. ground** le centre; **m. management** cadres mpl moyens; **m. name** deuxième prénom m; Fam **"generosity" isn't exactly his m. name!** on ne peut pas dire qu'il soit particulièrement généreux!

middle-aged [mɪdəl'eɪdʒd] adj d'âge mûr; **he was already m. when...** il avait déjà un certain âge quand...

middlebrow ['mɪdəlbraʊ] adj moyen(enne); **a m. novelist** un romancier sans prétentions

middle-class [mɪdəl'klɑːs] adj bourgeois(e)

middleman ['mɪdəlmæn] n intermédiaire mf

middle-of-the-road ['mɪdləvðə'rəʊd] adj (policy) modéré(e); (music) grand public inv

middle-sized ['mɪdəl'saɪzd] adj de taille moyenne

middleweight ['mɪdəlweɪt] n (in boxing) poids m moyen

middling ['mɪdlɪŋ] adj (fairly good) moyen(enne); (mediocre) médiocre

midge [mɪdʒ] n moucheron m

midget ['mɪdʒɪt] **1** n (small person) nain(e) m,f
2 adj (miniature) miniature

midi system ['mɪdɪsɪstəm] n (stereo) chaîne f midi

midlife crisis ['mɪdlaɪf'kraɪsɪs] n crise f aux alentours de la cinquantaine

midmorning [mɪd'mɔːnɪŋ] n milieu m de matinée

midnight ['mɪdnaɪt] n minuit m; **to burn the m. oil** travailler tard dans la nuit

midriff ['mɪdrɪf] n ventre m

midshipman ['mɪdʃɪpmən] n aspirant m de marine

midst [mɪdst] n milieu m, cœur m; **in the m. of** au milieu de; **in our/their m.** parmi nous/eux

midstream [mɪd'striːm] n **in m.** au milieu du courant; Fig (when speaking) en plein milieu d'une phrase

midsummer ['mɪdsʌmə(r)] n milieu m de l'été; **M.'s Day** la Saint-Jean

midterm ['mɪd'tɜːm] n (a) Pol **m. elections** = élections qui ont lieu au milieu du mandat présidentiel (b) Sch & Univ milieu m du trimestre; **m. break** vacances fpl de milieu de trimestre; **m. exams, midterms** examens mpl du milieu du trimestre

midway ['mɪdweɪ] **1** adj **at the m. point** (in space) à la mi-chemin; (in time) à la moitié
2 adv à mi-chemin

midweek [mɪd'wiːk] adv en milieu de semaine

Midwest ['mɪd'west] n Midwest m

Midwestern [mɪd'westən] adj du Midwest

midwife ['mɪdwaɪf] (pl **midwives** [mɪdwaɪvz]) n sage-femme f

midwifery [mɪd'wɪfərɪ] n profession f de sage-femme

midwinter ['mɪd'wɪntə(r)] n milieu m de l'hiver

might¹ [maɪt] n (strength) force f; **with all one's m.** de toutes ses forces; Prov **m. is right** la raison du plus fort est toujours la meilleure

might² [maɪt] v aux (a) (expressing possibility) **it m. be difficult** il se peut ou se pourrait que ce soit difficile; **it m. be better to phone first** il vaudrait peut-être mieux téléphoner d'abord; **it m. be that...** il se peut ou se pourrait que... + subjunctive; **you m. want to...** tu pourrais peut-être...; **we m. as well go home** autant rentrer; **you m. as well stay here** autant que vous restiez ici; **I m. as well be talking to myself!** autant parler à un mur!

(b) (as past form of may) **I knew he m. be angry** je me doutais qu'il pourrait se fâcher; **he said he m. be late** il a dit qu'il se pourrait qu'il soit en retard

(c) Formal (asking for permission) **m. I have a word with you?** pourrais-je vous parler un instant?

(d) (with concessions) **it might not be the fastest car in the world, but...** ce n'est peut-être pas la voiture la plus rapide du monde, mais...

mightily ['maɪtɪlɪ] *adv* (**a**) *(powerfully)* avec force, vigoureusement (**b**) *Fam (for emphasis)* drôlement

mightn't ['maɪtənt] = **might not**

might've ['maɪtəv] = **might have**

mighty ['maɪtɪ] **1** *adj* (**a**) *(powerful) (nation, army)* puissant(e); *(blow)* grand(e) (**b**) *(large, imposing)* majestueux(euse)
2 *adv Fam (for emphasis)* drôlement

migraine ['maɪgreɪn] *n* migraine *f*; **to have a m.** avoir la migraine

migrant ['maɪgrənt] **1** *n (person)* migrant(e) *m,f*; *(bird)* (oiseau *m*) migrateur *m*
2 *adj (bird)* migrateur(trice); **m. worker** travailleur(euse) *m,f* immigré(e)

migrate [maɪ'greɪt] *vi (of bird)* migrer; *(of person)* émigrer

migration [maɪ'greɪʃən] *n (of birds)* migration *f*; *(of people)* émigration *f*

migratory ['maɪgrətrɪ] *adj* migratoire; *(bird)* migrateur(trice)

mike [maɪk] *n Fam (microphone)* micro *m*

mild [maɪld] *adj (person, climate, soap, cheese)* doux (douce); *(curry)* peu épicé(e); *(punishment, annoyance, amusement, criticism)* léger(ère); *(illness)* bénin(igne)

mildew ['mɪldju:] *n* moisissure *f*

mildly ['maɪldlɪ] *adv* (**a**) *(say)* doucement; **...to put it m.** ...pour ne pas dire plus (**b**) *(moderately)* légèrement

mildness ['maɪldnɪs] *n (of person, weather, punishment)* douceur *f*; *(of criticism)* modération *f*

mile [maɪl] *n (distance)* = 1609 m, mile *m*; **a 200-m. journey** ≃ un voyage de 320 km; **to see for miles** voir à des kilomètres; **it's miles from anywhere** c'est loin de tout; **miles per hour** ≃ kilomètres à l'heure; **he lives miles away** il habite très loin d'ici; *Fam Fig* **to be miles away** être dans la lune; *Fam* **miles better** cent fois mieux; *Fam* **it sticks** *or* **stands out a m.** ça crève les yeux

mileage ['maɪlɪdʒ] *n* (**a**) *(distance traveled)* ≃ kilométrage *m*; **m. allowance** ≃ indemnité *f* kilométrique (**b**) *(rate of fuel consumption)* consommation *f*; *Fig* **to get a lot of m. out of sth** tirer le maximum de qch

milestone ['maɪlstəʊn] *n (on road)* ≃ borne *f* kilométrique; *Fig (in career, history)* étape *f* importante

milieu [mi:'ljʊ:] *n* milieu *m*

militant ['mɪlɪtənt] *adj & n* militant(e) *m,f*

militarism ['mɪlɪtərɪzəm] *n* militarisme *m*

military ['mɪlɪtərɪ] **1** *adj* militaire; **m. academy** école *f* militaire; **m. man** militaire *m*; **m. police** police *f* militaire; **m. service** service *m* militaire
2 *npl* **the m.** les militaires *mpl*, l'armée *f*

militate ['mɪlɪteɪt] *vi* **to m. against sth** compromettre qch

militia [mɪ'lɪʃə] *n* milice *f*

milk [mɪlk] **1** *n* lait *m*; **m. of magnesia** lait *m* de magnésie; **m. bottle** bouteille *f* de lait; **m. chocolate** chocolat *m* au lait; **m. can** bidon *m* à lait; **m. pitcher** pot *m* à lait; **m. tooth** dent *f* de lait; **m. train** premier train *m* (du matin); **m. truck** camionnette *f* du laitier
2 *vt (cow)* traire; *Fam Fig* **to m. sb dry** dépouiller qn; *Fig* **they milked the story for all it was worth** ils ont tiré tout ce qu'ils ont pu de l'histoire

milking ['mɪlkɪŋ] *n* traite *f*; **m. machine** trayeuse *f*

milkman ['mɪlkmən] *n* = homme qui livre le lait à domicile

milkshake [mɪlk'ʃeɪk] *n* milk-shake *m*

milky ['mɪlkɪ] *adj (drink)* avec du lait; *(taste)* de lait; *(color)* laiteux(euse); **the M. Way** la Voie lactée

mill [mɪl] **1** *n* (**a**) *(grinder)* moulin *m*; *Fam* **to put sb through the m.** en faire baver à qn (**b**) *(textile factory)* filature *f*
2 *vt (grain)* moudre

▶**mill about, mill around** *vi (of crowd)* grouiller; *(of thoughts, ideas)* se bousculer

millennium [mɪ'lenɪəm] *n* millénaire *m*; *Comput* **m. bug** bogue *m* de l'an deux mille

miller ['mɪlə(r)] *n* meunier(ère) *m,f*

millet ['mɪlɪt] *n* millet *m*

milligram ['mɪlɪgræm] *n* milligramme *m*

milliliter ['mɪlɪli:tə(r)] *n* millilitre *m*

millimeter ['mɪlɪmi:tə(r)] *n* millimètre *m*

milliner ['mɪlɪnə(r)] *n* modiste *mf*

million ['mɪljən] *n* million *m*; **two m. men** deux millions d'hommes; *Fam* **I've told him a m. times** je le lui ai dit mille fois; *Fam* **thanks a m.!** merci mille fois!; *Fam* **she's one in a m.** elle est unique

millionaire [mɪljə'neə(r)] *n* millionnaire *m*

millionairess [mɪljə'neərɪs] *n* millionnaire *f*

millionth ['mɪljənθ] **1** *n* (**a**) *(fraction)* millionième *m* (**b**) *(in series)* millionième *mf*
2 *adj* millionième; *see also* **eighth**

millipede ['mɪlɪpi:d] *n* mille-pattes *m inv*

millpond ['mɪlpɒnd] *n* **as calm as a m.** *(of sea)* d'huile

millstone ['mɪlstəʊn] *n* meule *f*; *Fig* **it's a m. around my neck** c'est un boulet que je traîne

milometer [maɪ'lɒmɪtə(r)] *n (in car)* ≃ compteur *m* (kilométrique)

mime [maɪm] **1** *n* mime *m*; **m. (artist)** mime *mf*
2 *vt* mimer
3 *vi* mimer; *(of singer)* chanter en play-back

mimic ['mɪmɪk] **1** *n* imitateur(trice) *m,f*
2 *vt (pt & pp* **mimicked***)* imiter

mimicry ['mɪmɪkrɪ] *n* imitation *f*

Min. *Mus (abbr* **Minor***)* m

min. (**a**) *(abbr* **minute(s)***)* min (**b**) *(abbr* **minimum***)* min

minaret [mɪnə'ret] *n* minaret *m*

mince [mɪns] **1** *vt (chop up)* hacher; *Fig* **she doesn't m. her words** elle ne mâche pas ses mots
2 *vi (walk)* marcher à petits pas

mincemeat ['mɪnsmi:t] *n* = mélange de fruits secs et d'épices utilisé en pâtisserie; *Fam Fig* **to make m. of sb** faire de la chair à pâté de qn

mincing ['mɪnsɪŋ] *adj (walk, voice)* affecté(e)

mind [maɪnd] **1** *n* (**a**) *(thoughts)* esprit *m*; **in one's m.'s eye** en imagination; **to put** *or* **to set sb's m. at rest** rassurer qn; **to bear** *or* **to keep sth in m.** garder qch à l'esprit *ou* en tête; **it went completely** *or* **clean out of my m.** ça m'est complètement sorti de l'esprit *ou* de la tête; **to have sth on one's m.** être préoccupé(e) par qch; **to take sb's m. off sth** distraire qn de qch; **I couldn't get it off my m.** je ne pouvais pas m'empêcher d'y penser; **it puts me in m. of sb/sth** ça me rappelle qn/qch
(**b**) *(opinion)* **to my m.** à mon avis; **to speak one's m.** dire ce qu'on pense; *Fam* **to give sb a piece of one's m.** dire à qn sa façon de penser; **to be of one m., to be of the same m.** être du même avis
(**c**) *(will)* **to know one's own m.** savoir ce qu'on veut; **to have a m. of one's own** savoir penser par soi-même; **to make up one's m.** se décider; **to be of two minds (about sth/about doing sth)** hésiter (sur qch/à faire qch); **to have a good m./half a m. to do sth** avoir bien envie/presque envie de faire qch; **this shopping cart has a m. of its own** ce caddie n'en fait qu'à sa tête; **to have sb in m.** avoir qn en vue; **to have sth in m.** avoir qch en tête
(**d**) *(attention)* **to keep one's m. on sth** se concentrer sur qch; **my m. isn't on the job** je n'ai pas la tête à ce que je fais; **if you put your m. to it you could do it** si tu t'y mettais, tu pourrais le faire
(**e**) *(reason)* raison *f*; **her m. is going** elle perd la raison; *Fam* **to be out of one's m.** avoir perdu la tête; **to be bored out of one's m.** s'ennuyer à mourir; **to be out of one's m. with**

worry être fou (folle) d'inquiétude; **no one in his right m. would do that** aucune personne saine d'esprit ne ferait ça

(**f**) *(person)* esprit *m*; *Prov* **great minds think alike** les grands esprits se rencontrent

2 *vt* (**a**) *(pay attention to)* faire attention à; **m. you don't fall** fais attention à ne pas tomber; **m. you're not late!** fais en sorte de ne pas être en retard!; **m. the step!** attention à la marche!; **to m. one's language/manners** surveiller son langage/ses manières

(**b**) *(concern oneself with)* **never m. the car/money** ne t'inquiète pas pour la voiture/l'argent; **m. you,...** remarque,...

(**c**) *(object to)* **what I m. is...** ce qui me gêne, c'est...; **I don't m. the cold** le froid ne me gêne pas; **I don't m. trying** je veux bien essayer; **if you don't m. my asking,...** si je peux me permettre,...; **would you m. not doing that?** pourrais-tu arrêter ça?; **I wouldn't m. a cup of tea** je prendrais bien une tasse de thé

(**d**) *(look after)* s'occuper de, garder

3 *vi* (**a**) *(object)* **I don't m.** ça m'est égal; **do you m.!** dites donc!; **do you m. if I smoke?** ça vous dérange si je fume?; **I don't m. if I do!** *(accepting offer)* ce n'est pas de refus!

(**b**) *(concern oneself)* **never m.!** ça ne fait rien!; **never m. about that now** ne t'inquiète pas de ça maintenant; *Fam* **never you m.!** occupe-toi de tes oignons!

mind-boggling ['maɪndbɒglɪŋ], **mind-blowing** ['maɪndbləʊɪŋ] *adj Fam* époustouflant(e)

minded ['maɪndɪd] *adj* **to be m. to do sth** vouloir faire qch; **to be mechanically m.** avoir le sens de la mécanique; **to be scientifically m.** avoir l'esprit scientifique

mindful ['maɪndfʊl] *adj* **to be m. of sth** être soucieux(euse) de qch

mindless ['maɪndlɪs] *adj (destruction, violence)* gratuit(e); *(task, job)* abrutissant(e)

mind-numbing ['maɪndnʌmɪŋ] *adj* abêtissant(e)

mind-reader ['maɪndriːdə(r)] *n Fam Hum* **I'm not a m.!** je ne suis pas devin!

mine¹ [maɪn] **1** *n* (**a**) *(for coal, tin, diamonds)* mine *f*; *Fig* **a m. of information** une mine d'informations; **m. shaft** puits *m* de mine (**b**) *(bomb)* **(land) m.** mine *f*; **m. detector** détecteur *m* de mines

2 *vt* (**a**) *(coal, gold)* extraire; *(seam)* exploiter (**b**) *(place mines in)* miner

3 *vi* **to m. for coal/gold** extraire du charbon/de l'or

mine² [maɪn] *possessive pron* (**a**) *(singular)* le mien (la mienne) *m,f*; *(plural)* les miens (les miennes) *mpl,fpl*; **her house is big but m. is bigger** elle a une grande maison, mais la mienne est plus grande encore (**b**) *(used attributively)* **this book is m.** c'est livre est à moi; **a friend of m.** un de mes amis; **where's that brother of m.?** où mon frère a-t-il bien pu passer?

minefield ['maɪnfiːld] *n* champ *m* de mines; *Fig* terrain *m* miné

miner ['maɪnə(r)] *n* mineur *m*

mineral ['mɪnərəl] *n* minéral *m*; *(extracted)* minerai *m*; **m. water** eau *m* minérale

minesweeper ['maɪnswiːpə(r)] *n* dragueur *m* de mines

mingle ['mɪŋgəl] **1** *vt* mélanger, mêler

2 *vi (of things)* se mélanger, se mêler; *(of person)* parler un peu à tout le monde; **to m. with the crowd** se mêler à la foule

mini ['mɪnɪ] *n (miniskirt)* minijupe *f*

miniature ['mɪnɪtʃə(r)] **1** *n* miniature *f*

2 *adj* miniature

miniaturize ['mɪnɪtʃəraɪz] *vt* miniaturiser

minibus ['mɪnɪbʌs] *n* minibus *m*

MiniDisc® ['mɪnɪdɪsk] *n* MiniDisc® *m*

minidish ['mɪnɪdɪʃ] *n* mini antenne *f* parabolique

minidisk ['mɪnɪdɪsk] *n* mini-disquette *f*

minigolf ['mɪnɪgɒlf] *n* minigolf *m*

minim ['mɪnɪm] *n Mus* blanche *f*

minimal ['mɪnɪməl] *adj* minime

minimize ['mɪnɪmaɪz] *vt (importance)* minimiser; *(noise, risk)* réduire au minimum

minimum ['mɪnɪməm] **1** *n* minimum *m*; **to keep sth to a m.** réduire qch au minimum

2 *adj* minimum *inv*; minimal(e); *Fin* **m. lending rate** taux *m* de base; **m. wage** salaire *m* minimum

mining ['maɪnɪŋ] *n* exploitation *f* minière; **m. engineer** ingénieur *m* des mines; **m. industry** industrie *f* minière

minion ['mɪnjən] *n* esclave *mf*

miniskirt ['mɪnɪskɜːt] *n* minijupe *f*

minister ['mɪnɪstə(r)] **1** *n* (**a**) *Pol* ministre *m* (**b**) *Rel* pasteur *m*

2 *vi* **to m. to sb** s'occuper de qn; **to m. to sb's needs** pourvoir aux besoins de qn

ministerial [mɪnɪ'stɪərɪəl] *adj Pol* ministériel(elle)

ministry ['mɪnɪstrɪ] *(pl* **ministries)** *n* (**a**) *Pol* ministère *m* (**b**) *Rel* **the m.** le sacerdoce

mink [mɪŋk] *n* vison *m*; **m. (coat)** *(manteau m* de) vison

minnow ['mɪnəʊ] *n (fish)* vairon *m*; *Fig (menu)* fretin *m*

minor ['maɪnə(r)] **1** *adj* (**a**) *(unimportant)* mineur(e); *(operation)* bénin(igne); *(road)* secondaire (**b**) *Mus* mineur(e)

2 *n Law* mineur(e) *m,f*

Minorca [mɪ'nɔːkə] *n* Minorque

Minorcan [mɪ'nɔːkən] **1** *n* Minorquin(e) *m,f*

2 *adj* minorquin(e)

minority [maɪ'nɒrɪtɪ] *(pl* **minorities)** *n* minorité *f*; **to be in a** *or* **the m.** être en minorité; **m. party/government** parti *m*/gouvernement *m* minoritaire

minstrel ['mɪnstrəl] *n* ménestrel *m*

mint¹ [mɪnt] *n (plant)* menthe *f*; *(sweet)* bonbon *m* à la menthe; **m. tea** infusion *f* de menthe

mint² [mɪnt] **1** *n (where coins are made)* l'Hôtel *m* de la Monnaie, la Monnaie; *Fam* **to make a m.** gagner une fortune; **in m. condition** à l'état neuf

2 *vt (coins)* frapper

minuet [mɪnjʊ'et] *n Mus* menuet *m*

minus ['maɪnəs] **1** *n (sign)* moins *m*; *(negative aspect)* inconvénient *m*

2 *adj (quantity, number)* négatif(ive); **B m.** *(grade)* B moins; **on the m. side** quant aux inconvénients; **m. sign** signe *m* moins

3 *prep* moins; **10 m. 8 leaves 2** 10 moins 8 égale 2; **it's m. 12 (degrees)** il fait moins 12; **he managed to escape, but m. his luggage** il a réussi à s'enfuir, mais sans ses bagages

minuscule ['mɪnəskjuːl] *adj* minuscule

minute¹ ['mɪnɪt] **1** *n* (**a**) *(of time)* minute *f*; **ten minutes past/to three** trois heures dix/moins dix; **wait a m.!** attendez une minute!; **go downstairs this m.!** descends immédiatement!; **just a m.** une minute; **the m. my back was turned** dès que j'ai eu le dos tourné; **any m.** d'une minute à l'autre; **in a m.** dans une minute; **at the last m.** à la dernière minute; **m. hand** *(of watch)* grande aiguille *f*; **m. steak** steak *m* minute (**b**) *(note)* note *f*; **minutes** *(of meeting)* compte rendu *m*

2 *vt (make note of)* inscrire au procès-verbal

minute² [maɪ'njuːt] *adj* (**a**) *(small)* infime, minuscule (**b**) *(detailed)* minutieux(euse)

minutely [maɪ'njuːtlɪ] *adv* minutieusement

mips [mɪps] *n Comput (abbr* **million instructions per second)** MIPS *m*

miracle ['mɪrəkəl] *n also Fig* miracle *m*; **to perform** *or* **to work miracles** faire des miracles; **by a** *or* **some m.** par miracle; **m. worker** faiseur(euse) *m,f* de miracles

miraculous [mɪ'rækjʊləs] *adj also Fig* miraculeux(euse)

mirage [mɪ'rɑːʒ] *n* mirage *m*

mire [maɪə(r)] *n (mud)* boue *f*; *Fig* bourbier *m*

mirror ['mɪrə(r)] **1** *n* miroir *m*, glace *f*; *Fig* **to hold a m. to sth**

refléter qch; **m. image** *(reversed image)* image *f* inversée; *(exact copy)* copie *f* conforme

2 *vt also Fig* refléter

mirth [mɜːθ] *n* gaieté *f*, joie *f*

misadventure [mɪsəd'ventʃə(r)] *n* mésaventure *f*; *Law* **death by m.** mort *f* accidentelle

misanthropic [mɪsən'θrɒpɪk] *adj* misanthrope

misanthropist [mɪ'sænθrəpɪst] *n* misanthrope *mf*

misapprehension [mɪsæprɪ'henʃən] *n* malentendu *m*; **to be (laboring) under a m.** se méprendre

misappropriation ['mɪsəprəʊprɪ'eɪʃən] *n* détournement *m*

misbehave [mɪsbɪ'heɪv] *vi* se conduire mal

misbehavior [mɪsbɪ'heɪvjə(r)] *n* mauvaise conduite *f*

misc. *(abbr* **miscellaneous)** divers

miscalculate [mɪs'kælkjʊleɪt] **1** *vt* mal calculer; *Fig* mal évaluer

2 *vi* faire une erreur de calcul; *Fig* faire un mauvais calcul

miscalculation [mɪskælkjʊ'leɪʃən] *n* erreur *f* de calcul; *Fig* mauvais calcul *m*

miscarriage [mɪs'kærɪdʒ] *n* **(a)** *Med* fausse couche *f*; **to have a m.** faire une fausse couche **(b)** *Law* **m. of justice** erreur *f* judiciaire

miscarry [mɪs'kærɪ] *(pt & pp* **miscarried)** *vi* **(a)** *(of woman)* faire une fausse couche **(b)** *Fig (of plan)* avorter

miscast [mɪs'kɑːst] *(pt & pp* **miscast)** *vt* **to m. an actor** = donner à un acteur un rôle qui ne lui convient pas

miscellaneous [mɪsə'leɪnɪəs] *adj* divers(es)

miscellany [mɪ'selənɪ] *(pl* **miscellanies)** *n* mélange *m*

mischief ['mɪstʃɪf] *n* **(a)** *(naughtiness)* espièglerie *f*; **to get up to m.** faire des bêtises; *Hum* **to keep sb out of m.** occuper qn **(b)** *(trouble)* problèmes *mpl*; **to make m. (for sb)** créer des problèmes (à qn) **(c)** *Fam (injury)* **to do oneself a m.** se faire mal

mischievous ['mɪstʃɪvəs] *adj (naughty)* espiègle; *(malicious)* malveillant(e)

misconception [mɪskən'sepʃən] *n* idée *f* fausse

misconduct [mɪs'kɒndʌkt] *n* inconduite *f*

misconstrue [mɪskən'struː] *vt* mal interpréter

misdemeanor [mɪsdɪ'miːnə(r)] *n Law* délit *m*

misdiagnose [mɪsdaɪəg'nəʊz] *vt* mal diagnostiquer

misdirect [mɪsdɪ'rekt] *vt* **(a)** *(person)* mal orienter **(b)** *(letter)* mal adresser

miser ['maɪzə(r)] *n* avare *mf*

miserable ['mɪzərəbəl] *adj* **(a)** *(unhappy)* malheureux(euse), triste; **to make sb's life m.** faire de la vie de qn un enfer **(b)** *(unpleasant)* déplorable; *(weather)* épouvantable **(c)** *(wretched)* misérable; **I only got a m. $20** je n'ai eu que 20 malheureuses dollars

miserably ['mɪzərəblɪ] *adv* **(a)** *(unhappily)* tristement **(b)** *(wretchedly)* misérablement **(c)** *(very badly)* lamentablement

miserly ['maɪzəlɪ] *adj* avare

misery ['mɪzərɪ] *(pl* **miseries)** *n (unhappiness)* détresse *f*; *(suffering)* malheur *m*; **to make sb's life a m.** faire de la vie de qn un enfer; **to put an animal out of its m.** achever un animal; *Hum* **to put sb out of his m.** *(tell secret)* mettre fin au supplice de qn

misfire [mɪs'faɪə(r)] *vi (of gun)* faire long feu; *Fig (of plan)* rater

misfit ['mɪsfɪt] *n* inadapté(e) *m,f*

misfortune [mɪs'fɔːtʃən] *n* malheur *m*, malchance *f*

misgiving [mɪs'gɪvɪŋ] *n* doute *m*; **to have misgivings (about sth)** avoir des doutes (sur qch)

misgovern [mɪs'gʌvən] *vt* mal gouverner

misguided [mɪs'gaɪdɪd] *adj (person, decision)* mal inspiré(e); *(attempt)* malencontreux(euse); *(energy, idealism)* mal placé(e)

mishandle [mɪs'hændəl] *vt (device)* mal utiliser; *(situation)* mal gérer; *(person)* malmener

mishap ['mɪshæp] *n* incident *m*; **without m.** sans encombre

mishear [mɪs'hɪə(r)] *(pt & pp* **misheard** [mɪs'hɜːd]) *vt & vi* mal comprendre

mishmash ['mɪʃmæʃ] *n Fam* méli-mélo *m*

misinterpret [mɪsɪn'tɜːprɪt] *vt (words)* mal interpréter; *(person)* mal interpréter les paroles de

misjudge [mɪs'dʒʌdʒ] *vt (person)* mal juger; *(distance, situation)* mal évaluer

misjudg(e)ment [mɪs'dʒʌdʒmənt] *n* erreur *f* de jugement

mislay [mɪs'leɪ] *(pt & pp* **mislaid** [mɪs'leɪd]) *vt* égarer

mislead [mɪs'liːd] *(pt & pp* **misled** [mɪs'led]) *vt* induire en erreur, tromper

misleading [mɪs'liːdɪŋ] *adj* trompeur(euse)

misled [mɪs'led] *pt & pp of* **mislead**

mismanage [mɪs'mænɪdʒ] *vt* mal gérer

mismanagement [mɪs'mænɪdʒmənt] *n* mauvaise gestion *f*

misnomer [mɪs'nəʊmə(r)] *n* terme *m* mal approprié

miso ['miːsəʊ] *n Culin* miso *m*

misogynist [mɪ'sɒdʒɪnɪst] *n* misogyne *mf*

misplace [mɪs'pleɪs] *vt* **(a)** *(mislay)* égarer **(b)** *(trust, confidence)* mal placer

misprint ['mɪsprɪnt] *n* faute *f* d'impression, coquille *f*

mispronounce [mɪsprə'naʊns] *vt* mal prononcer

mispronunciation [mɪsprənʌnsɪ'eɪʃən] *n* mauvaise prononciation *f*

misquote [mɪs'kwəʊt] *vt* citer incorrectement

misread [mɪs'riːd] *(pt & pp* **misread** [mɪs'red]) *vt* **(a)** *(notice, timetable)* mal lire **(b)** *(misinterpret)* mal interpréter

misrepresent [mɪsreprɪ'zent] *vt (facts, theory)* dénaturer, déformer; *(person)* présenter sous un faux jour

misrepresentation [mɪsreprɪzen'teɪʃən] *n* déformation *f*

misrule [mɪs'ruːl] *n* mauvais gouvernement *m*

Miss [mɪs] *n* Mademoiselle *f*; **M. World** Miss Monde

miss [mɪs] **1** *n* coup *m* manqué; *Fam* **to give sth a m.** *(event)* s'abstenir d'aller à

2 *vt* **(a)** *(target, bus, chance)* manquer, rater; *Fig* **to m. the boat** louper le coche; **you're missing the point** ce n'est pas le problème; **you've just missed him** tu l'as loupé de peu **(b)** *(not hear)* ne pas entendre; **she doesn't m. a thing** rien ne lui échappe **(c)** *(feel lack of)* **I m. you** tu me manques; **do you m. me?** est-ce que je te manque? **(d)** *(avoid)* **the car just missed me** la voiture m'a évité de peu; **she just missed being killed** elle a failli *ou* manqué être tuée **(e)** *(word, line)* sauter **(f)** *(lack)* **the table is missing one of its legs** il manque un pied à la table

3 *vi (miss target)* rater *ou* manquer son coup

▶**miss out** **1** *vi (not benefit)* **to m. out on sth** rater qch; **you missed out there** tu as raté quelque chose

missal ['mɪsəl] *n Rel* missel *m*

misshapen [mɪs'ʃeɪpən] *adj* difforme

missile ['mɪsəl] *n (rocket)* missile *m*; *(object thrown)* projectile *m*; **m. launcher** lance-missiles *m inv*

missing ['mɪsɪŋ] *adj (person) (lost)* disparu(e); *(absent)* absent(e); *(object)* manquant(e); **nothing is m.** il ne manque rien; **m. link** chaînon *m* manquant; **m. person** personne *f* disparue

mission ['mɪʃən] *n* mission *f*

missionary ['mɪʃənərɪ] *(pl* **missionaries)** *n Rel* missionnaire *mf*; **the m. position** la position du missionnaire

missive ['mɪsɪv] *n Formal* missive *f*

misspell [mɪs'spel] *(pt & pp* **misspelt** ['mɪs'spelt]) *vt* mal écrire

misspent ['mɪs'spent] *adj (time, money)* gaspillé(e); **m. youth** jeunesse *f* dissipée

mist [mɪst] *n (fog)* brume *f; (condensation)* buée *f*

▸**mist over, mist up** *vi (of mirror, glasses)* s'embuer

mistakable [mɪsˈteɪkəbəl] *adj* facile à confondre (**for** avec)

mistake [mɪsˈteɪk] **1** *n* erreur *f; (in grammar, spelling)* faute *f;* **to make a m.** faire *ou* commettre une erreur; **by m.** par erreur; *Fam* **this is hard work and no m.!** pas de doute, c'est vraiment très dur!

2 *vt (pt* **mistook** [mɪsˈtʊk], *pp* **mistaken** [mɪsˈteɪkən]) **(a)** *(misunderstand)* se tromper sur **(b)** *(confuse)* **to m. sb for** prendre qn pour; **there's no mistaking a voice like that!** avec une voix pareille, on ne peut pas se tromper!

mistakeable = **mistakable**

mistaken [mɪsˈteɪkən] *adj (belief, impression)* erroné(e), faux (fausse); **to be m.** se tromper

Mister [ˈmɪstə(r)] *n* Monsieur *m*

mistime [mɪsˈtaɪm] *vt* mal calculer

mistletoe [ˈmɪsəltəʊ] *n* gui *m*

mistranslation [mɪstrænsˈleɪʃən] *n* erreur *f* de traduction

mistreat [mɪsˈtriːt] *vt* maltraiter

mistress [ˈmɪstrɪs] *n* maîtresse *f; (in secondary school)* professeur *m*

mistrial [mɪsˈtraɪəl] *n Law* = procès dans lequel le jury ne parvient pas à prendre de décision

mistrust [mɪsˈtrʌst] **1** *n* méfiance *f* (**of** à l'égard de)
2 *vt* se méfier de, ne pas avoir confiance en

mistrustful [mɪsˈtrʌstfʊl] *adj* méfiant(e); **to be m. of** se méfier de

misty [ˈmɪstɪ] *adj (place, weather)* brumeux(euse); *(outline, shape)* flou(e)

misunderstand [mɪsʌndəˈstænd] *(pt & pp* **misunderstood** [mɪsʌndəˈstʊd]) *vt & vi* mal comprendre

misunderstanding [mɪsʌndəˈstændɪŋ] *n* **(a)** *(misconception)* malentendu *m* (**about** sur) **(b)** *(disagreement)* mésentente *f*

misunderstood [mɪsʌndəˈstʊd] *pt & pp of* **misunderstand**

misuse 1 *n* [mɪsˈjuːs] *(of equipment, resources)* mauvais emploi *m; (of authority)* abus *m; (of funds)* détournement *m*
2 *vt* [mɪsˈjuːz] *(equipment, resources)* mal employer; *(authority)* abuser de; *(funds)* détourner

mite [maɪt] *n* **(a)** *(bug)* acarien *m* **(b)** *Fam (child)* **poor little m.!** pauvre petit! **(c)** *Fam (little bit)* **a m. expensive/tired** un tantinet cher (chère)/fatigué(e)

miter [ˈmaɪtə(r)] *n Rel* mitre *f*

mitigate [ˈmɪtɪgeɪt] *vt* atténuer; *Law* **mitigating circumstances** *fpl* atténuantes

mitigation [mɪtɪˈgeɪʃən] *n* atténuation *f; Law* **to say sth in m.** dire qch pour sa défense

mitt [mɪt] *n* **(a)** *(mitten)* moufle *f;* **baseball m.** gant *m* de baseball **(b)** *Fam (hand)* patte *f*

mitten [ˈmɪtən] *n (glove)* moufle *f*

mix [mɪks] **1** *vt* mélanger; *(drink)* préparer; **to m. business with pleasure** mélanger les affaires et le plaisir
2 *vi* **(a)** *(blend)* se mélanger (**with** avec) **(b)** *(socially)* **to m. with** fréquenter
3 *n* mélange *m; (in music)* remix *m*

▸**mix up** *vt sep* **(a)** *(ingredients, papers)* mélanger **(b)** *(people, dates)* confondre **(c)** *Fam* **to be mixed up in sth** *(involved)* être mêlé(e) à qch, être impliqué(e) dans qch; **to get mixed up with sb** se mettre à fréquenter qn

mixed [mɪkst] *adj* mélangé(e); *Fam* **it was a m. bag** il y avait de tout; **to have m. feelings (about sth)** avoir des sentiments mitigés (envers qch); **a man/a woman of m. race** un métis/une métisse; **m. doubles** *(in tennis)* double *m* mixte; **m. grill** assortiment *m* de grillades; **m. marriage** mariage *m* mixte

mixed-up [mɪksˈtʌp] *adj Fam (person)* déboussolé(e)

mixer [ˈmɪksə(r)] *n* **(a)** *(for cooking)* mixe(u)r *m* **(b)** *(socially)* **to**

be a good m. être très sociable **(c)** *(drink)* = boisson servant à allonger un alcool

mixing bowl [ˈmɪksɪŋˈbəʊl] *n* saladier *m*

mixture [ˈmɪkstʃə(r)] *n* mélange *m*

mix-up [ˈmɪksʌp] *n* confusion *f* (**over** *or* **with** dans)

mktg *Com (abbr* **marketing**) marketing

ml *(abbr* **milliliter(s))** ml

MLR [emelˈɑː(r)] *n Fin (abbr* **minimum lending rate**) taux *m* de base

mm *(abbr* **millimeter(s))** mm

MMS [ememˈes] *n Tel (abbr* **multimedia message service**) MMS *m*

mnemonic [nɪˈmɒnɪk] *n* moyen *m* mnémotechnique

moan [məʊn] **1** *n* **(a)** *(sound)* gémissement *m* **(b)** *(complaint)* plainte *f*
2 *vi* **(a)** *(make sound)* gémir **(b)** *(complain)* ronchonner; **to m. about sth** se plaindre de qch

moat [məʊt] *n* douve *f*

mob [mɒb] **1** *n (crowd)* foule *f; Fam* **the M.** la Mafia; **m. rule** loi *f* de la rue
2 *vt (pt & pp* **mobbed**) prendre d'assaut

mobile [ˈməʊbaɪl] **1** *adj* mobile; **m. home** mobile home *m;* **m. phone** téléphone *m* portable *ou* mobile, *Can* cellulaire *m*
2 *n* **(a)** *(hanging ornament)* mobile *m* **(b)** *Fam (mobile phone)* (téléphone *m*) portable *m ou* mobile *m, Can* cellulaire *m*

mobility [məʊˈbɪlɪtɪ] *n* mobilité *f*

mobilize [ˈməʊbɪlaɪz] *vt* mobiliser

mobster [ˈmɒbstə(r)] *n Fam* gangster *m*

moccasin [ˈmɒkəsɪn] *n* mocassin *m*

mock [mɒk] **1** *adj* faux (fausse), factice
2 *vt (ridicule)* se moquer de

mockery [ˈmɒkərɪ] *n* **(a)** *(ridicule)* moqueries *fpl* **(b)** *(travesty)* parodie *f;* **to make a m. of sb** ridiculiser qn; **to make a m. of sth** faire perdre toute crédibilité à qch

mockingbird [ˈmɒkɪŋbɜːd] *n* moqueur *m*

mock-up [ˈmɒkʌp] *n* maquette *f*

mode [məʊd] *n* mode *m*

model [ˈmɒdəl] **1** *n* **(a)** *(small version)* maquette *f*, modèle *m* réduit; **m. aircraft** maquette d'avion **(b)** *(example, paragon)* modèle *m;* **m. home** maison *f* témoin; **m. pupil** élève *mf* modèle **(c)** *(fashion model)* mannequin *m; (for artist)* modèle *m*
2 *vt* **(a)** **to m. oneself on sb** prendre exemple sur qn **(b)** **to m. clothes** être mannequin **(c)** *Comput* modéliser
3 *vi (on catwalk, for photographer)* travailler comme mannequin; *(for artist)* poser

modeling [ˈmɒdəlɪŋ] **1** *n* **(a)** *(building models)* modelage *m; (as a hobby)* construction *f* de maquettes **(b)** *(being a fashion model)* mannequinat *m*
2 *adj* **m. clay** pâte *f* à modeler

modem [ˈməʊdem] *n Comput* modem *m;* **m. cable** câble *m* modem; **m. card** carte *f* modem

moderate 1 *n* [ˈmɒdərɪt] *Pol* modéré(e) *m,f*
2 *adj* [ˈmɒdərɪt] modéré(e)
3 *vt* [ˈmɒdəreɪt] modérer
4 *vi* [ˈmɒdəreɪt] *Formal* présider

moderately [ˈmɒdərɪtlɪ] *adv* **(a)** *(in moderation)* modérément **(b)** *(quite)* assez

moderation [mɒdəˈreɪʃən] *n* modération *f;* **in m.** avec modération

modern [ˈmɒdən] *adj* moderne; **m. art** art *m* moderne; **with all m. conveniences** *(house)* tout confort; *(car)* avec toutes les options; **m. languages** langues *fpl* vivantes

modernism [ˈmɒdənɪzəm] *n* modernisme *m*

modernization [mɒdənaɪˈzeɪʃən] *n* modernisation *f*

modernize [ˈmɒdənaɪz] **1** *vt* moderniser
2 *vi* se moderniser

modest ['mɒdɪst] *adj* **(a)** *(unassuming, moderate)* modeste **(b)** *(chaste)* pudique

modestly ['mɒdɪstlɪ] *adv* **(a)** *(unassumingly)* modestement **(b)** *(moderately)* assez, moyennement

modesty ['mɒdɪstɪ] *n* modestie *f*

modicum ['mɒdɪkəm] *n* **a m. of** un minimum de

modification [mɒdɪfɪ'keɪʃən] *n* modification *f*; **to make modifications to sth** apporter des modifications à qch

modify ['mɒdɪfaɪ] *(pt & pp* **modified**) *vt* modifier

modular ['mɒdjʊlə(r)] *adj* modulaire

modulate ['mɒdjʊleɪt] *vt* moduler

modulation [mɒdjʊ'leɪʃən] *n* modulation *f*

module ['mɒdjuːl] *n* module *m*

mogul ['məʊgəl] *n Fig* magnat *m*

mohair ['məʊheə(r)] *n* mohair *m*; **m. sweater** pull *m* en mohair

Mohammed [məʊ'hæmɪd] *n* Mahomet

moist [mɔɪst] *adj* humide; *(skin, hand)* moite; *(cake)* moelleux(euse)

moisten ['mɔɪsən] *vt* humecter

moisture ['mɔɪstʃə(r)] *n* humidité *f*

moisturize ['mɔɪstʃəraɪz] *vt* hydrater

moisturizer ['mɔɪstʃəraɪzə(r)] *n* crème *f* hydratante

mojito [məʊ'hiːtəʊ] *n (cocktail)* mojito *m*

molar ['məʊlə(r)] *n* molaire *f*

molasses [mə'læsɪz] *n* mélasse *f*

mold¹ [məʊld] *n (fungus)* moisissure *f*

mold² [məʊld] **1** *n (in art, cooking)* moule *m*; *Fig* **cast in the same m.** fait(e) dans le même moule; *Fig* **a star in the John Wayne m.** une star dans le style John Wayne; *Fig* **to break the m.** rompre avec la tradition
2 *vt (plastic, person's character)* modeler, façonner

Moldavia [mɒl'deɪvɪə], **Moldova** [mɒl'dəʊvə] *n* la Moldavie

Moldavian [mɒl'deɪvɪən], **Moldovan** [mɒl'dəʊvən] **1** *n* Moldave *mf*
2 *adj* moldave

molder ['məʊldə(r)] *vi (of food)* moisir; *(of building)* se délabrer

molding ['məʊldɪŋ] *n Archit* moulure *f*

moldy ['məʊldɪ] *adj* moisi(e)

mole¹ [məʊl] *n (birthmark)* grain *m* de beauté

mole² [məʊl] *n (animal, spy)* taupe *f*

molecular [mə'lekjʊlə(r)] *adj* moléculaire

molecule ['mɒlɪkjuːl] *n* molécule *f*

molehill ['məʊlhɪl] *n* taupinière *f*

molest [mə'lest] *vt (pester)* importuner; *(sexually)* agresser (sexuellement)

mollify ['mɒlɪfaɪ] *(pt & pp* **mollified**) *vt* calmer, apaiser

mollusk ['mɒləsk] *n* mollusque *m*

mollycoddle ['mɒlɪkɒdəl] *vt Fam* dorloter

molten ['məʊltən] *adj* en fusion

mom [mɒm] *n Fam* maman *f*

moment ['məʊmənt] *n* moment *m*, instant *m*; **at the m.** en ce moment; **at the last m.** au dernier moment; **for the m.** pour le moment *ou* l'instant; **in a m.** dans un instant; **any m.** d'un instant à l'autre; **wait a m.!, one m.!** un moment!, un instant!; **the m. he arrives** dès qu'il arrive; **without a m.'s hesitation** sans une seconde d'hésitation; **to live for the m.** profiter du moment présent; **the man of the m.** l'homme du moment; **the m. of truth** le moment de vérité; **he's not a genius, but he has his moments** ce n'est pas un génie, mais il a parfois des moments d'inspiration

momentary ['məʊməntərɪ] *adj* momentané(e)

momentous [məʊ'mentəs] *adj* capital(e)

momentum [məʊ'mentəm] *n Phys* moment *m*; **to gather m.** *(of campaign)* prendre de l'ampleur; **to lose m.** *(of campaign)* s'essouffler

mommy ['mɒmɪ] *(pl* **mommies**) *n Fam* maman *f*

Mon. *(abbr* **Monday**) lundi

Monaco ['mɒnəkəʊ] *n* Monaco

monarch ['mɒnək] *n* monarque *m*

monarchist ['mɒnəkɪst] *n* monarchiste *mf*

monarchy ['mɒnəkɪ] *(pl* **monarchies**) *n* monarchie *f*

monastery ['mɒnəstrɪ] *(pl* **monastries**) *n* monastère *m*

monastic [mə'næstɪk] *adj* monastique, monacal(e)

Monday ['mʌndɪ] *n* lundi *m*; *see also* **Saturday**

monetarism ['mʌnɪtərɪzm] *n* monétarisme *m*

monetarist ['mʌnɪtərɪst] *n & adj* monétariste *mf*

monetary ['mʌnɪtərɪ] *adj* monétaire

money ['mʌnɪ] *n* argent *m*; **to do sth for the m.** faire qch pour l'argent; **to make m.** *(of person)* gagner de l'argent; *(of business)* rapporter de l'argent; **to be worth a lot of m.** *(of thing)* valoir cher; *(of person)* être très riche; **there's no m. in it** ça ne paie pas; *Fam* **to be in the m.** être plein(e) aux as; **to get one's m.'s worth** en avoir pour son argent; **to put one's m. where one's mouth is** joindre le geste à la parole; *Fam* **to spend m. like water** dépenser sans compter; *Fam* **m. doesn't grow on trees!** l'argent ne se trouve pas sous le sabot d'un cheval!; **for my m.,...** à mon avis,...; **m. laundering** blanchiment *m* d'argent; *Fin* **m. market** marché *m* monétaire; *Econ* **m. supply** masse *f* monétaire

moneybags ['mʌnɪbægz] *n Fam (person)* richard(e) *m,f*

moneyed ['mʌnɪd] *adj* fortuné(e)

moneylender ['mʌnɪlendə(r)] *n* prêteur(euse) *m,f*; *(usurer)* usurier(ère) *m,f*

moneymaker ['mʌnɪmeɪkə(r)] *n* **to be a m.** *(of store, business, product)* rapporter

moneymaking ['mʌnɪmeɪkɪŋ] *adj* qui rapporte

Mongol ['mɒŋgəl] *Hist* **1** *n* Mongol(e) *m,f*
2 *adj* mongol(e)

Mongolia [mɒŋ'gəʊlɪə] *n* la Mongolie

Mongolian [mɒŋ'gəʊlɪən] **1** *n* Mongol(e) *m,f*
2 *adj* mongol(e)

mongoose ['mɒŋguːs] *n* mangouste *f*

mongrel ['mʌŋgrəl] *n* bâtard *m*

monitor ['mɒnɪtə(r)] **1** *n* **(a)** *(supervisor)* superviseur *m* **(b)** *TV & Comput (screen)* moniteur *m*
2 *vt (broadcast, conversation)* écouter; *(patient's condition, operation, results)* surveiller; *(performance)* suivre

monk [mʌŋk] *n* moine *m*

monkey ['mʌŋkɪ] *(pl* **monkeys**) *n (animal)* singe *m*; *Fam Fig (naughty child)* petit(e) diable(esse) *m,f*; *Fam* **to make a m. out of sb** se payer la tête de qn; *Fam* **m. business** *(dishonest behavior)* magouilles *fpl*; *(mischief)* bêtises *fpl*; **m. puzzle (tree)** désespoir *m* des singes; **m. wrench** clef *f* anglaise *ou* à molette

▸**monkey about, monkey around** *vi Fam (fool around)* faire l'imbécile

monkfish ['mʌŋkfɪʃ] *n* lotte *f*

mono ['mɒnəʊ] *n* mono *f*

monochrome ['mɒnəkrəʊm] *adj* monochrome; *(photo)* en noir et blanc

monocle ['mɒnəkəl] *n* monocle *m*

monogamous [mɒ'nɒgəməs] *adj* monogame

monogamy [mɒ'nɒgəmɪ] *n* monogamie *f*

monogram ['mɒnəgræm] *n* monogramme *m*

monograph ['mɒnəgræf] *n* monographie *f*

monolingual [mɒnəʊ'lɪŋgwəl] *adj* monolingue

monolithic [mɒnə'lɪθɪk] *adj* monolithique

monolog, monologue ['mɒnəlɒg] *n* monologue *m*

mononucleosis ['mɒnəʊnjuːklɪ'əʊsɪs] *n Med* mononucléose *f* (infectieuse)

monopolize [mə'nɒpəlaɪz] *vt also Fig* monopoliser

monopoly [mə'nɒpəli] (*pl* **monopolies**) *n also Fig* monopole *m*; **to have a m. on sth** avoir le monopole de qch

monorail ['mɒnəʊreɪl] *n* monorail *m*

monoski ['mɒnəʊski:] *n* monoski *m*

monosyllabic [mɒnəʊsɪ'læbɪk] *adj (word)* monosyllabique; *(reply)* laconique

monosyllable [mɒnəʊ'sɪləbəl] *n* monosyllabe *m*

monotone ['mɒnətəʊn] *n* ton *m* monotone; **to speak in a m.** parler d'une voix monotone

monotonous [mə'nɒtənəs] *adj* monotone

monotony [mə'nɒtənɪ] *n* monotonie *f*

Monsignor [mɒn'si:njə(r)] *n* Monseigneur

monsoon [mɒn'su:n] *n* mousson *f*

monster ['mɒnstə(r)] **1** *n* monstre *m*
2 *adj Fam (enormous)* monstre, colossal(e)

monstrosity [mɒn'strɒsɪtɪ] (*pl* **monstrosities**) *n* monstruosité *f*

monstrous ['mɒnstrəs] *adj* monstrueux(euse)

montage ['mɒntɑ:ʒ] *n* montage *m*

month [mʌnθ] *n* mois *m*; **in the m. of August** au mois d'août; *Fam* **never in a m. of Sundays** jamais de la vie

monthly ['mʌnθlɪ] **1** *n* (*pl* **monthlies**) *(magazine)* mensuel *m*
2 *adj* mensuel(elle); **m. payment** *or* **installment** mensualité *f*
3 *adv* tous les mois

monument ['mɒnjʊmənt] *n also Fig* monument *m* (**to** à)

monumental [mɒnjʊ'mentəl] *adj* monumental(e); *(importance)* capital(e)

moo [mu:] **1** *n* (*pl* **moos**) meuglement *m*, beuglement *m*; **m.!** meuh!
2 *vi* (*pt & pp* **mooed**) meugler, beugler

mooch [mu:tʃ] *Fam* **1** *vi (cadge)* taxer; **he's always mooching off** *or* **on people** il est toujours en train de taper quelqu'un
2 *vt* (a) *(cadge)* taper; **to m. ten dollars off or from sb** taper qn de dix dollars (b) *(steal)* chiper, piquer

▸**mooch about, mooch around** *vi Fam* traîner

mood [mu:d] *n* (a) *(state of mind)* humeur *f*; **to be in a good/bad m.** être de bonne/mauvaise humeur; **she's in one of her moods** elle est de mauvaise humeur; **to be in the m. for sth** avoir envie de qch; **to be in the m. for doing sth** être d'humeur à faire qch (b) *Gram* mode *m*

moodily ['mu:dɪlɪ] *adv (answer, speak)* d'un ton maussade

moody ['mu:dɪ] *adj* (a) *(sulky)* maussade (b) *(changeable)* lunatique

moon [mu:n] **1** *n* lune *f*; **the M.** la Lune; *Fam* **to ask for the m.** demander la lune; *Fam* **to promise sb the m.** promettre la lune à qn; *Fam* **to be over the m.** être aux anges; **m. landing** alunissage *m*
2 *vi Fam (expose one's buttocks)* montrer ses fesses

▸**moon about, moon around** *vi* musarder, flâner

moonbeam ['mu:nbi:m] *n* rayon *m* de lune

moonlight ['mu:nlaɪt] **1** *n* clair *m* de lune; **in the m., by m.** au clair de lune
2 *vi Fam (work illegally)* travailler au noir

moonlighting ['mu:nlaɪtɪŋ] *n Fam* travail *m* au noir

moonlit ['mu:nlɪt] *adj* éclairé(e) par la lune

moonshine ['mu:nʃaɪn] *n Fam* (a) *(nonsense)* balivernes *fpl*, bêtises *fpl* (b) *(illegal alcohol)* alcool *m* de contrebande

Moor [mʊə(r)] *n* Maure *mf*

moor¹ [mʊə(r)] *n (heath)* lande *f*

moor² [mʊə(r)] *vt (ship)* amarrer

mooring ['mʊərɪŋ] *n* (a) *(place)* mouillage *m* (b) **moorings** *(chains, ropes)* amarres *fpl*

Moorish ['mʊərɪʃ] *adj* maure, mauresque

moorland ['mʊələnd] *n* lande *f*

moose [mu:s] (*pl* **moose**) *n* orignal *m*

moot [mu:t] **1** *adj* **it's a m. point** c'est difficile à dire
2 *vt (suggest)* suggérer

mop [mɒp] **1** *n (for floor)* balai *m* à franges; *(with sponge)* balai-éponge *m*; *Fam* **m. (of hair)** tignasse *f*
2 *vt (pt & pp* **mopped**) **to m. the floor** laver par terre; **to m. one's brow** s'éponger le front

▸**mop up** *vt sep (liquid)* éponger; *Fig (enemy forces)* liquider

▸**mope about, mope around** [məʊp] *vi* broyer du noir

moped ['məʊped] *n (motorbike)* Mobylette® *f*

moral ['mɒrəl] **1** *n* (a) *(of story)* morale *f* (b) **morals** *(principles)* moralité *f*
2 *adj* moral(e); **m. fiber** force *f* de caractère; **the m. majority** les néo-conservateurs *mpl* (surtout aux États-Unis); **m. support** soutien *m* moral; **m. victory** victoire *f* morale

morale [mɒ'rɑ:l] *n* moral *m*; **to be good/bad for m.** être bon (bonne)/mauvais(e) pour le moral

moralistic [mɒrə'lɪstɪk] *adj* moraliste

morality [mə'rælɪtɪ] *n* moralité *f*

moralize ['mɒrəlaɪz] *vi* faire la morale, moraliser

morally ['mɒrəlɪ] *adv* moralement; **m. right** moralement correct(e); **m. wrong** contraire à la morale

morass [mə'ræs] *n (marsh)* marais *m*; *Fig (of detail, despair)* bourbier *m*

moratorium [mɒrə'tɔ:rɪəm] (*pl* **moratoria** [mɒrə'tɔ:rɪə] *or* **moratoriums**) *n* moratoire *m* (**on** sur)

morbid ['mɔ:bɪd] *adj* morbide

morbidly ['mɔ:bɪdlɪ] *adv* de façon morbide

mordant ['mɔ:dənt] *adj Formal (sarcasm, wit)* mordant(e)

more [mɔ:(r)] *(comparative of* **many, much**) **1** *pron* plus; **there are m. of us** nous sommes plus nombreux; **have (some) m.** reprenez-en; **there's no m.** il n'y en a plus; **let's say no m. about it** n'en parlons plus; **she knows m. than you** elle en sait plus long que toi; **we should see m. of each other** nous devrions nous voir plus souvent; **it's just m. of the same** c'est encore et toujours la même chose; **the m. I see her, the m. I like her** plus je la vois, plus elle me plaît; **what's m.,...** qui plus est,...; **what m. can I say?** que puis-je dire de plus?
2 *adj* (a) *(larger quantity or number of)* plus de; **m. water/children** plus d'eau/d'enfants; **m. than a hundred people were there** il y avait plus de cent personnes; **he has m. patience than I have** il a plus de patience que moi; **there are m. and m. accidents every year** chaque année, il y a de plus en plus d'accidents
(b) *(additional quantity or number of)* **one m. month** un mois de plus; **is there any m. bread?** est-ce qu'il y a encore du pain?; **I've no m. money** je n'ai plus d'argent; **I need m. time** il me faut plus de temps
3 *adv* (a) *(to form comparative of adjectives and adverbs)* plus (**than** que); **m. interesting** plus intéressant(e); **m. easily** plus facilement; **things are getting m. and m. difficult** les choses deviennent de plus en plus difficiles
(b) *(to a greater extent)* plus; **you should eat m.** tu devrais manger plus; **I'm m. than satisfied** je suis plus que satisfait; **he was m. surprised than annoyed** il était plus surpris que fâché; **I like her m. than I used to** je l'aime plus qu'avant; **that's m. like it!** voilà qui est mieux!; **m. or less** plus ou moins
(c) *(with time)* **once/twice m.** une/deux fois de plus; **he doesn't drink any m.** il ne boit plus; **I can't see you any m.** nous ne pouvons plus nous voir

moreover [mɔ:'rəʊvə(r)] *adv* de plus

mores ['mɔ:reɪz] *npl Formal* mœurs *fpl*

morgue [mɔ:g] *n* morgue *f*; *Fig* **this place is like a m.** c'est complètement mort ici

moribund ['mɒrɪbʌnd] *adj* moribond(e)

Mormon ['mɔ:mən] *n Rel* mormon(e) *m,f*

morning ['mɔːnɪŋ] *n* matin *m*; *(referring to duration)* matinée *f*; **tomorrow m.** demain matin; **yesterday m.** hier matin; **the next m., the m. after** le lendemain matin; **the m. before** la veille au matin; *Fam* **it's the m. after (the night before)** c'est un lendemain de cuite; **m., noon and night** du matin au soir; **in the m.** le matin; **on Wednesday m.** mercredi matin; **good m.!,** *Fam* **m.!** bonjour!; **m. sickness** nausées *fpl* matinales; **m. star** étoile *f* du matin

morning-after pill ['mɔːnɪŋˈɑːftəpɪl] *n* pilule *f* du lendemain

Moroccan [məˈrɒkən] **1** *n* Marocain(e) *m,f*
2 *adj* marocain(e)

Morocco [məˈrɒkəʊ] *n* le Maroc

moron ['mɔːrɒn] *n* crétin(e) *m,f*

moronic [məˈrɒnɪk] *adj* débile

morose [məˈrəʊs] *adj* morose

morph [mɔːf] *Comput* **1** *vt* transformer par morphing
2 *vi* **to m. into sth** se transformer en qch

morphing ['mɔːfɪŋ] *n Comput* morphing *m*

Morse [mɔːs] *n* **M. (code)** morse *m*

morsel ['mɔːsəl] *n* morceau *m*

mortal ['mɔːtəl] **1** *n* mortel(elle) *m,f*; *Fig & Ironic* **mere mortals** de simples mortels
2 *adj* mortel(elle); **m. enemy** ennemi *m* mortel; **m. remains** dépouille *f* mortelle; **m. sin** péché *m* mortel; **m. wound** blessure *f* mortelle

mortality [mɔːˈtælɪtɪ] *n* mortalité *f*

mortally ['mɔːtəlɪ] *adv* mortellement

mortar ['mɔːtə(r)] *n* mortier *m*

mortgage ['mɔːgɪdʒ] **1** *n (from lender's point of view)* prêt *m* immobilier; *(from borrower's point of view)* emprunt *m* immobilier; **m. broker** courtier *m* en prêts hypothécaires; **m. (re)payments** remboursements *mpl* d'emprunt; **m. rate** taux *m* de crédit immobilier
2 *vt (property, one's future)* hypothéquer

mortician [mɔːˈtɪʃən] *n (undertaker)* entrepreneur *m* de pompes funèbres

mortification [mɔːtɪfɪˈkeɪʃən] *n Rel* mortification *f*; *Fig (embarrassment)* honte *f*

mortify ['mɔːtɪfaɪ] *(pt & pp* **mortified***) vt Rel* mortifier; *Fig* **to be mortified** être mort(e) de honte

mortise ['mɔːtɪs] *n* mortaise *f*; **m. lock** serrure *f* encastrée

mortuary ['mɔːtjʊərɪ] *(pl* **mortuaries***) n* morgue *f*

mosaic [məʊˈzeɪk] *n also Fig* mosaïque *f*

Moscow ['mɒskəʊ] *n* Moscou

Moses ['məʊzɪz] *n* Moïse

Moslem ['mɒzləm] *n & adj* musulman(e) *m,f*

mosque [mɒsk] *n* mosquée *f*

mosquito [məsˈkiːtəʊ] *(pl* **mosquitos** *or* **mosquitoes***) n* moustique *m*; **m. bite** piqûre *f* de moustique; **m. net** moustiquaire *f*; **m. repellent** produit *m* antimoustique

moss [mɒs] *n* mousse *f*

most [məʊst] *(superlative of* **many, much***)* **1** *pron* **(a)** *(the majority)* la plupart; **m. of the people/time** la plupart des gens/du temps; **m. of us/them** la plupart d'entre nous/eux; **he is more interesting than m.** il est plus intéressant que la plupart des gens
(b) *(greatest amount)* **the m.** le plus; **he earns the m.** c'est lui qui gagne le plus; **at the (very) m.** au maximum; **to make the m. of sth** *(situation, talents)* tirer le meilleur parti de qch; *(time, vacation)* profiter au maximum de qch
2 *adj* **(a)** *(the majority of)* la plupart de; **m. women** la plupart des femmes
(b) *(greatest amount of)* **the m.** le plus de; **he has the m. money** c'est lui qui a le plus d'argent; **for the m. part** dans l'ensemble
3 *adv* **(a)** *(to form superlative of adjectives and adverbs)* plus; **the m. interesting book** le livre le plus intéressant; **the m.**
beautiful woman la plus belle femme; **these are the m. expensive** ce sont les plus chers; **those who answered m. honestly** ceux qui ont répondu le plus franchement
(b) *(to the greatest extent)* le plus; **the one who works (the) m. is...** celui qui travaille le plus est...; **that's what worries me (the) m.** c'est ce qui m'inquiète le plus; **who do you like m.?** qui préfères-tu?; **what I want m.** ce que je veux par-dessus tout
(c) *(very)* extrêmement; **m. unhappy** extrêmement malheureux(euse)

mostly ['məʊstlɪ] *adv* **(a)** *(in the main)* principalement, surtout
(b) *(most often)* le plus souvent, la plupart du temps

motel [məʊˈtel] *n* motel *m*

moth [mɒθ] *n* papillon *m* de nuit; *(in clothes)* mite *f*

mothball ['mɒθbɔːl] *n* boule *f* de naphtaline; *Fig* **to put a project in mothballs** mettre un projet au placard

moth-eaten ['mɒθiːtən] *adj* mité(e); *Fam (in poor condition)* miteux(euse)

mother ['mʌðə(r)] **1** *n* mère *f*; **M.'s Day** la fête des Mères; **m. country** patrie *f*; **M. Nature** Dame Nature *f*; *Rel* **M. Superior** Mère supérieure; **m. tongue** langue *f* maternelle
2 *vt* materner

motherboard ['mʌðəbɔːd] *n Comput* carte *f* mère

motherhood ['mʌðəhʊd] *n* maternité *f*

mother-in-law ['mʌðərɪnlɔː] *(pl* **mothers-in-law***) n* belle-mère *f*

motherland ['mʌðəlænd] *n* patrie *f*

mother-of-pearl ['mʌðərəvˈpɜːl] *n* nacre *f*

mother-to-be ['mʌðətəˈbiː] *(pl* **mothers-to-be***) n* future mère *f*

motif [məʊˈtiːf] *n* motif *m*

motion ['məʊʃən] **1** *n* **(a)** *(movement)* mouvement *m*; **to set sth in m.** *(machine)* mettre qch en marche; *(process)* déclencher qch; *Fig* **to go through the motions** agir machinalement; **m. picture** film *m* **(b)** *(in meeting, debate)* motion *f*; **to propose/to second a m.** présenter/appuyer une motion
2 *vt* **to m. sb to do sth** faire signe à qn de faire qch
3 *vi* **to m. to sb to do sth** faire signe à qn de faire qch

motionless ['məʊʃənlɪs] *adj* immobile

motivate ['məʊtɪveɪt] *vt* motiver

motivation [məʊtɪˈveɪʃən] *n* motivation *f*

motive ['məʊtɪv] **1** *n (reason)* motif *m*; *Law (for crime)* mobile *m*
2 *adj* **m. force** *or* **power** force *f* motrice

motley ['mɒtlɪ] *adj* hétéroclite; **m. crew** groupe *m* hétéroclite

motor ['məʊtə(r)] **1** *n (engine)* moteur *m*; **m. industry** industrie *f* automobile; **m. insurance** assurance *f* automobile; *Med* **m. neurone disease** maladie *f* de Charcot; **m. racing** courses *fpl* automobiles; **m. show** salon *m* de l'automobile; **m. vehicle** véhicule *m* automobile
2 *vi* voyager en voiture

motorbike ['məʊtəbaɪk] *n* moto *f*

motorboat ['məʊtəbəʊt] *n* canot *m* à moteur

motorcade ['məʊtəkeɪd] *n* cortège *m* de voitures

motorcar ['məʊtəkɑː(r)] *n* voiture *f*

motorcycle ['məʊtəsaɪkəl] *n* moto *f*, motocyclette *f*

motorcyclist ['məʊtəsaɪklɪst] *n* motocycliste *mf*

motoring ['məʊtərɪŋ] *n* conduite *f*

motorist ['məʊtərɪst] *n* automobiliste *mf*

motorize ['məʊtəraɪz] *vt* motoriser

motorized ['məʊtəraɪzd] *adj* motorisé(e)

motorway ['məʊtəweɪ] *n (in Great Britain)* autoroute *f*

mottled ['mɒtəld] *adj (skin)* marbré(e); *(coat, surface)* tacheté(e), moucheté(e)

motto ['mɒtəʊ] *(pl* **mottoes***) n* devise *f*

molt [məʊlt] *vi (of bird)* muer; *(of cat, dog)* perdre ses poils

mound [maʊnd] *n (hill)* butte *f*; *(of earth, sand)* tas *m*

mount[1] [maʊnt] *n* (*mountain*) mont *m*; **M. Everest** le mont Everest, l'Everest *m*; **M. Vesuvius** le Vésuve

mount[2] [maʊnt] **1** *n* (**a**) (*for painting*) carton *m* de montage; (*for slide*) cadre *m* (**b**) (*horse*) monture *f*

2 *vt* (**a**) (*bicycle, horse*) monter sur, enfourcher; (*stairs*) monter; (*ladder*) monter à (**b**) (*photograph, exhibition*) monter; (*machine gun*) installer; (*offensive*) lancer; **to m. guard** monter la garde

3 *vi* (**a**) (*get onto horse*) se mettre en selle (**b**) (*increase*) monter, augmenter

▶**mount up** *vi* (*of cost, debts*) monter, augmenter

mountain ['maʊntɪn] *n also Fig* montagne *f*; **to make a m. out of a molehill** faire une montagne d'un rien; **m. bike** vélo *m* tout terrain; **m. climbing** alpinisme *m*; **m. lion** puma *m*; **m. range** chaîne *f* de montagnes; **m. rescue team** équipe *f* de secours en montagne; **M. Standard Time** heure *f* des montagnes Rocheuses

mountaineer [maʊntɪ'nɪə(r)] *n* alpiniste *mf*

mountaineering [maʊntɪ'nɪərɪŋ] *n* alpinisme *m*

mountainous ['maʊntɪnəs] *adj* montagneux(euse)

mounted ['maʊntɪd] *adj* monté(e), à cheval; **the m. police** la police montée

mounting ['maʊntɪŋ] **1** *n* (*for engine, gun*) support *m*

2 *adj* (*increasing*) croissant(e)

mourn [mɔːn] **1** *vt* pleurer

2 *vi* **to m. for sb/sth** pleurer qn/qch

mourner ['mɔːnə(r)] *n* = personne assistant aux obsèques

mournful ['mɔːnfʊl] *adj* triste

mourning ['mɔːnɪŋ] *n* deuil *m*; **to be in m. (for sb)** être en deuil (de qn); **to go into m.** prendre le deuil

mouse [maʊs] (*pl* **mice** [maɪs]) *n also Comput* souris *f*; **m. mat, m. pad** tapis *m* de souris

mousetrap ['maʊstræp] *n* tapette *f*, souricière *f*

mousse [muːs] *n* mousse *f*; **chocolate m.** mousse au chocolat

mousy ['maʊsɪ] *adj* (**a**) (*hair*) châtain terne *inv* (**b**) (*person, manner*) timide, effacé(e)

mouth 1 *n* [maʊθ], *pl* [maʊðz] (*of person, horse*) bouche *f*; (*of other animal*) gueule *f*; (*of tunnel*) entrée *f*; (*of river*) embouchure *f*; **we have seven mouths to feed** nous avons sept bouches à nourrir; *Fam* **keep your m. shut about this** garde ça pour toi; *Fam Fig* **to have a big m.** avoir une grande gueule; *Fam* **he's all m.** c'est une grande gueule; **don't put words into my m.** ne me fais pas dire ce que je n'ai pas dit; **m. organ** harmonica *m*

2 *vt* [maʊð] (*insincerely*) débiter; (*silently*) articuler silencieusement

▶**mouth off** *vi* se montrer insolent(e)

mouthful ['maʊθfʊl] *n* (*of food*) bouchée *f*; (*of drink*) gorgée *f*; *Fam Fig* (*long word*) = mot long et difficile à prononcer; (*long name*) nom *m* à coucher dehors; *Fam* **you said a m.!** ça, tu peux le dire!, tu l'as dit, bouffi!

mouthpiece ['maʊθpiːs] *n* (**a**) (*of musical instrument*) embouchure *f*; (*of telephone*) microphone *m* (**b**) (*of government, political party*) porte-parole *m inv*

mouth-to-mouth (resuscitation) ['maʊθtə'maʊθ-(rɪsʌsɪ'teɪʃən)] *n* bouche-à-bouche *m inv*

mouthwash ['maʊθwɒʃ] *n* bain *m* de bouche

mouthwatering ['maʊθwɔːtərɪŋ] *adj* (*smell*) appétissant(e); (*prospect*) alléchant(e)

movable ['muːvəbəl] *adj* mobile; *Rel* **m. feast** fête *f* mobile

move [muːv] **1** *n* (**a**) (*motion*) mouvement *m*; **to make a m.** (*leave*) partir; **to make a m. toward sb/sth** se diriger vers qn/qch; **on the m.** en mouvement; *Fam* **to get a m. on** se grouiller, se magner

(**b**) (*action, step*) pas *m*, démarche *f*; **to make the first m.** faire le premier pas

(**c**) (*from home*) déménagement *m*; (*from job*) changement *m* de poste

(**d**) (*in games*) coup *m*; (**it's**) **your m.** (c'est) à toi de jouer

2 *vt* (**a**) (*change position of*) déplacer; (*set in motion*) remuer; (*employee*) muter; *Fam* **to m. oneself** se remuer

(**b**) *Fig* (*sway*) faire changer d'avis; **to feel moved to do sth** se sentir obligé(e) de faire qch

(**c**) (*affect emotionally*) émouvoir; **to m. sb to anger** provoquer la colère de qn; **to m. sb to tears** émouvoir qn jusqu'aux larmes

(**d**) (*in debate*) proposer

3 *vi* (**a**) (*change position*) se déplacer; (*stir*) bouger; (*progress, advance*) avancer; (*leave*) partir; **to get things moving** faire avancer les choses; **could you m., please?** pourriez-vous vous pousser, s'il vous plaît?; *Fam* **come on, m.!** allez, remue-toi!

(**b**) (*act*) agir

(**c**) (*to new home, office*) emménager; **to m. to another job** changer de travail; **to m. to the country** s'installer à la campagne

(**d**) *Fig* (*be swayed*) céder

(**e**) (*in games*) (*of player*) jouer; (*of piece*) avancer

▶**move about, move around 1** *vt sep* (*furniture*) déplacer; (*employee*) muter, transférer

2 *vi* (*change position*) se déplacer; (*stir*) bouger; **he moves around a lot** (*in job*) il est souvent en déplacement

▶**move along** = **move on**

▶**move away 1** *vt sep* éloigner, écarter (**from** de)

2 *vi* (*from window, person*) s'éloigner, s'écarter (**from** de); (*from home*) déménager

▶**move back 1** *vt sep* (*further away*) reculer; (*to former position*) remettre en place

2 *vi* (*retreat*) s'écarter, (se) reculer; (*to former position*) retourner (**to** à)

▶**move forward 1** *vt sep* (*object, date, meeting*) avancer; (*troops*) faire avancer

2 *vi* (*of person, car*) (s')avancer

▶**move in** *vi* (*take up residence*) emménager

▶**move off** *vi* (*go away*) partir, s'éloigner; (*start journey*) se mettre en marche; (*of car*) démarrer

▶**move on 1** *vt sep* (*crowd*) faire circuler

2 *vi* (**a**) **time's moving on** il se fait tard; **it's time we were moving on** il est temps de partir (**b**) (*change subject*) passer à autre chose; **to m. on to sth** passer à qch (**c**) (*progress, develop*) changer

▶**move out** *vi* (*leave home*) déménager

▶**move over** *vi* (*make room*) se pousser

▶**move up** *vi* (**a**) (*make room*) se pousser (**b**) (*be promoted*) avoir de l'avancement

moveable = **movable**

movement ['muːvmənt] *n* mouvement *m*; **to watch sb's movements** surveiller les faits et gestes de qn; (**bowel**) **m.** selles *fpl*

mover ['muːvə(r)] *n* (**a**) (*for moving*) déménageur *m* (**b**) (*in debate*) auteur *m* d'une motion; **the movers and shakers** les grands pontes *mpl*

movie ['muːvɪ] *n* film *m*; **to go to the movies** aller au cinéma; **to be in the movies** faire du cinéma; **m. actor/actress** acteur *m*/actrice *f* de cinéma; **m. camera** caméra *f*; **m. house** cinéma *m*; **m. industry** industrie *f* cinématographique; **m. star** vedette *f* de cinéma; **m. theater** cinéma *m*

moviegoer ['muːvɪɡəʊə(r)] *n* spectateur(trice) *m, f* de cinéma

moving ['muːvɪŋ] *adj* (**a**) (*in motion*) en mouvement; (*train, vehicle*) en marche; (*parts*) mobile; **m. staircase** escalier *m* mécanique (**b**) (*touching*) émouvant(e)

mow [məʊ] (*pp* **mown** [məʊn]) *vt* (*lawn*) tondre; (*hay*) faucher

▶**mow down** *vt sep* (*slaughter*) faucher

Mozambican [məʊzæm'bi:kən] **1** *n* Mozambicain(e) *m,f*
2 *adj* mozambicain(e)

Mozambique [məʊzæm'bi:k] *n* le Mozambique

MP [em'pi:] *n* (**a**) *Pol (in Great Britain, Canada)* (*abbr* **Member of Parliament**) député(e) *m,f* (**b**) *Mil* (*abbr* **Military Police**) police *f* militaire

mpg [empi:'dʒi:] *n* (*abbr* **miles per gallon**) ≃ litre *m* aux cent (kilomètres)

mph [empi:'eɪtʃ] *n* (*abbr* **miles per hour**) ≃ km/h

MP3 [empi:'θri:] *n Comput* (format *m*) MP3 *m*; **MP3 player** lecteur *m* MP3

Mr. ['mɪstə(r)] (*abbr* **Mister**) Mr. McLean M. McLean; **Mr. Right** *(ideal husband)* l'homme *m* idéal

Mrs. ['mɪsɪz] (*abbr* **Mistress**) Mrs. Sole Mme Sole

MS [em'es] *n* (**a**) *Univ* (*abbr* **Master of Science**) **to have an MS in chemistry** ≃ avoir une maîtrise de chimie; **John Smith MS** John Smith, titulaire d'une maîtrise de sciences (**b**) (*abbr* **multiple sclerosis**) sclérose *f* en plaques (**c**) (*abbr* **manuscript**) manuscrit *m*

ms (*abbr* **millisecond**) millième *m* de seconde

Ms. [mɪz] ≃ Mme *(ne donne pas d'indications sur le statut de famille)*

MSc [emes'si:] *n Univ* (*abbr* **Master of Science**) **to have an M. in chemistry** ≃ avoir une maîtrise de chimie; **John Smith M.** John Smith, titulaire d'une maîtrise de sciences

MSG [emes'dʒi:] *n Culin* (*abbr* **monosodium glutamate**) glutamate *m* de sodium

MST [emes'ti:] *n* (*abbr* **Mountain Standard Time**) heure *f* d'hiver des montagnes Rocheuses

Mt. (*abbr* **Mount**) Mt.

much [mʌtʃ] (*comparative* **more** [mɔ:(r)], *superlative* **most** [məʊst]) **1** *pron* beaucoup; **there isn't m. left** il n'en reste pas beaucoup; **it's not worth m.** ça ne vaut pas grand-chose; *Formal* **m. has happened since you left** il s'est passé beaucoup de choses depuis ton départ; **I'll say this m. for him, he's very polite** je dois reconnaître une chose, c'est qu'il est très poli; **I don't think m. of him** je n'ai pas grande estime pour lui; **it didn't come as m. of a surprise** ça n'a pas été une grande surprise; **she isn't m. of a singer** comme chanteuse, elle n'est pas très bonne; **twice as m.** deux fois plus; **I thought as m.** c'est ce que je pensais; **as m. as possible** autant que possible; **it was as m. as we could do to stay upright** nous n'avions déjà assez de mal à rester debout; **he left without so m. as saying goodbye** il est parti sans même dire au revoir; **he has drunk so m. that...** il a tellement bu que...; **so m. the better** tant mieux; **so m. so that...** à tel point que...; **so m. for her promises of help!** c'était bien la peine de promettre qu'elle m'/nous/*etc.* aiderait!; *Fam* **that's a bit m.!** c'est un peu fort!

2 *adj* **how m. money?** combien d'argent?; **there isn't m. traffic** il n'y a pas beaucoup de circulation; **too m. work** trop de travail; **so m. time** tant de temps; **as m. food as** autant de nourriture que; *Formal* **m. work still needs to be done** il reste encore beaucoup de travail à faire

3 *adv* beaucoup; **I don't like it m.** ça ne me plaît pas beaucoup; **m. better** bien meilleur(e); **m. more difficult** beaucoup plus difficile; **m. the best** de loin le meilleur (la meilleure); **m. the most interesting** de loin le (la) plus intéressant(e); **thank you very m.** merci beaucoup; **m. the same** presque pareil(eille); **m. to my astonishment** à mon grand étonnement; **m. as I like him, I don't really trust him** j'ai beau l'apprécier, je ne lui fais pas vraiment confiance; **the result was m. as I expected** le résultat correspondait assez à mes attentes; **so m.** autant; **I love him so m.** je l'aime tellement; **too m.** trop; **ten dollars too m.** dix dollars de trop; **this is (really) too m.!** trop c'est trop!

muchness ['mʌtʃnɪs] *n Fam* **they're much of a m.** ils se valent

muck [mʌk] *n Fam (dirt)* saleté *f*; *(manure)* fumier *m*; *(bad food)* cochonneries *fpl*; *(bad quality book, TV program)* idioties *fpl*
▸**muck about, muck around** *vi Fam* (**a**) *(fool about)* faire l'imbécile; *(waste time)* traîner (**b**) *(tinker)* **to m. about or around with sth** tripoter qch

muckraking ['mʌkreɪkɪŋ] *n Fam (in journalism)* = pratique consistant à révéler et exploiter à fond des scandales

mucous ['mju:kəs] *adj* muqueux(euse)

mucus ['mju:kəs] *n* mucus *m*, mucosités *fpl*

mud [mʌd] *n* boue *f*; *Fig* **to throw m. at sb** couvrir qn de boue; *Fam* **his name is m.** il n'a pas la cote; **m. hut** hutte *f* en terre; **m. wrestling** catch *m* dans la boue

mudbank ['mʌdbæŋk] *n* banc *m* de vase

mudflat ['mʌdflæt] *n* banc *m* de boue

muddle ['mʌdəl] **1** *n* confusion *f*; **to be in a m.** *(of things)* être en désordre; *(of person)* ne plus s'y retrouver; **to get into a m.** *(of things)* se mélanger; *(of person)* s'embrouiller
2 *vt* (**a**) *(put in disorder)* mélanger (**b**) *(bewilder)* embrouiller; **to get muddled** s'embrouiller
▸**muddle along** *vi* se débrouiller tant bien que mal
▸**muddle through** *vi* se débrouiller
▸**muddle up** *vt sep* (**a**) *(put in disorder)* mélanger (**b**) *(confuse)* embrouiller; **to get muddled up** s'embrouiller

muddleheaded [mʌdəl'hedɪd] *adj (person)* brouillon(onne); *(thinking)* confus(e)

muddy ['mʌdɪ] **1** *adj (path, water)* boueux(euse); *(clothing, hands)* couvert(e) de boue; *(complexion)* terreux(euse); *(color)* sale
2 *vt (pt & pp* **muddied***)* salir; *Fig* **to m. the waters** brouiller les pistes

mudguard ['mʌdgɑ:d] *n* garde-boue *m inv*

mudpack ['mʌdpæk] *n* masque *m* à l'argile

mudslinging ['mʌdslɪŋɪŋ] *n Fam* = fait de dénigrer systématiquement ses adversaires

muesli ['mju:zlɪ] *n* muesli *m*

muff [mʌf] *n (for hands)* manchon *m*

muffin ['mʌfɪn] *n* muffin *m*

muffle ['mʌfəl] *vt* (**a**) *(sound)* assourdir, étouffer (**b**) **to m. oneself up** s'emmitoufler

muffled ['mʌfəld] *adj (sound, footstep)* assourdi(e), étouffé(e)

muffler ['mʌflə(r)] *n* (**a**) *(scarf)* cache-nez *m inv* (**b**) *(of car)* silencieux *m*

mufti ['mʌftɪ] *n Fam* **in m.** *(soldier)* en civil

mug [mʌg] **1** *n* (**a**) *(cup)* grande tasse *f* (**b**) *Fam (face)* gueule *f*; **m. shot** photo *f* d'identité judiciaire (**c**) *Fam (gullible person)* poire *f*; **it's a m.'s game** on est toujours perdant à ce jeu-là
2 *vt (pt & pp* **mugged***) (attack)* agresser

mugger ['mʌgə(r)] *n* agresseur *m*

mugging ['mʌgɪŋ] *n* agression *f*

muggy ['mʌgɪ] *adj* lourd(e), étouffant(e)

mulatto [mju:'lætəʊ] *(pl* **mulattos** *or* **mulattoes***) n* mulâtre *mf*

mulberry ['mʌlbərɪ] *(pl* **mulberries***) n (fruit)* mûre *f*; *(tree)* mûrier *m*

mule [mju:l] *n* mulet *m*; *(female)* mule *f*
▸**mull over** [mʌl] *vt sep (consider)* **to m. sth over** retourner qch dans sa tête

mulled wine ['mʌld'waɪn] *n* vin *m* chaud épicé

mullet ['mʌlɪt] *n* **gray m.** mulet *m* gris; **red m.** rouget *m*

multi-access ['mʌltɪ'ækses] *adj Comput* à accès multiple

multicolored ['mʌltɪkʌləd] *adj* multicolore

multicultural [mʌltɪ'kʌltʃərəl] *adj* multiculturel(elle)

multidisciplinary [mʌltɪdɪsɪ'plɪnərɪ] *adj* pluridisciplinaire

multifarious [mʌltɪ'feərɪəs] *adj* varié(e), divers(e)

multifunctional [mʌltɪ'fʌŋkʃənəl] *adj* multifonctions *inv*

multilateral [mʌltɪ'lætərəl] *adj* multilatéral(e)

multilingual [mʌltɪ'lɪŋgwəl] *adj* multilingue

multimedia [mʌltɪ'miːdɪə] *adj* multimédia

multimillionaire [mʌltɪmɪljə'neə(r)] *n* multimillionnaire *mf*

multinational [mʌltɪ'næʃənəl] **1** *n* multinationale *f*
   2 *adj* multinational(e)

multiparty [mʌltɪ'pɑːtɪ] *adj* **m. system** pluripartisme *m*

multiplayer [mʌltɪ'pleɪə(r)] *adj* multijoueur

multiple ['mʌltɪpəl] **1** *n Math* multiple *m*
   2 *adj* multiple; **m. sclerosis** sclérose *f* en plaques

multiple-choice ['mʌltɪpl'tʃɔɪs] *adj* à choix multiples

multiplex ['mʌltɪpleks] *n Cin* multiplexe *m*, complexe *m* multi-salles

multiplication [mʌltɪplɪ'keɪʃən] *n* multiplication *f*; **m. table** table *f* de multiplication

multiplicity [mʌltɪ'plɪsɪtɪ] *n* multiplicité *f*

multiply ['mʌltɪplaɪ] (*pt & pp* **multiplied**) **1** *vt* multiplier (**by** par)
   2 *vi (reproduce)* se multiplier

multipurpose [mʌltɪ'pɜːpəs] *adj* polyvalent(e)

multiracial [mʌltɪ'reɪʃəl] *adj* multiracial(e)

multistory [mʌltɪ'stɔːrɪ] *adj* à étages; **m. (parking lot)** parking *m* à plusieurs niveaux

multitude ['mʌltɪtjuːd] *n* multitude *f*

multivitamin [mʌltɪ'vaɪtəmɪn] *n* multivitamine *f*

mumble ['mʌmbəl] **1** *n* marmonnement *m*
   2 *vt & vi* marmonner

mumbo jumbo ['mʌmbəʊ'dʒʌmbəʊ] *n (nonsense)* âneries *fpl*; *(jargon)* charabia *m*

mummify ['mʌmɪfaɪ] (*pt & pp* **mummified**) *vt* momifier

mummy ['mʌmɪ] (*pl* **mummies**) *n (embalmed body)* momie *f*

mumps [mʌmps] *n (illness)* oreillons *mpl*; **to have the m.** avoir les oreillons

munch [mʌntʃ] *vt* mâcher

munchies ['mʌntʃɪz] *npl Fam* **(a)** *(snacks)* amuse-gueule *mpl*
   (b) *(desire to eat)* **to have the m.** avoir la fringale

mundane [mʌn'deɪn] *adj* banal(e), ordinaire

municipal [mjuː'nɪsɪpəl] *adj* municipal(e)

municipality [mjuː'nɪsɪ'pælɪtɪ] (*pl* **municipalities**) *n* municipalité *f*

munitions [mjuː'nɪʃənz] *npl* munitions *fpl*

mural ['mjʊərəl] *n* peinture *f* murale

murder ['mɜːdə(r)] **1** *n* **(a)** *(killing)* meurtre *m*; *Fig* **she gets away with m.** elle peut tout se permettre; **m. case** affaire *f* de meurtre; **m. inquiry** enquête *f* sur une affaire de meurtre **(b)** *Fam Fig (difficult task)* cauchemar *m*, enfer *m*; **finding a parking place on a Saturday is m.** c'est l'enfer pour trouver à se garer le samedi
   2 *vt* **(a)** *(kill)* assassiner; *Fam Fig* **I'll m. you!** je vais te tuer! **(b)** *Fig (song, tune)* massacrer

murderer ['mɜːdərə(r)] *n* meurtrier(ère) *m,f*, assassin *m*

murky ['mɜːkɪ] *adj (weather, sky)* sombre; *(details, past)* trouble

murmur ['mɜːmə(r)] **1** *n* murmure *m*; **to do sth without a m.** faire qch sans broncher
   2 *vi also Fig* murmurer

muscle ['mʌsəl] *n* muscle *m*; *Fig (power)* poids *m*; **not to move a m.** rester immobile

▶**muscle in** *vi* intervenir (**on** dans)

muscleman ['mʌsəlmæn] *n* Monsieur *m* muscle

Muscovite ['mʌskəvaɪt] **1** *n* Moscovite *mf*
   2 *adj* moscovite

muscular ['mʌskjʊlə(r)] *adj (tissue, pain)* musculaire; *(person)* musclé(e); **m. dystrophy** myopathie *f*

Muse [mjuːz] *n (in mythology)* Muse *f*; *(of poet)* muse *f*

muse [mjuːz] *vi* rêvasser, songer (**on** *or* **about** à)

museum [mjuː'zɪəm] *n* musée *m*

mush [mʌʃ] *n* **(a)** *(pulp)* bouillie *f* **(b)** *Fig (sentimentality)* mièvrerie *f*

mushroom ['mʌʃrʊm] **1** *n* champignon *m*; **m. cloud** champignon atomique
   2 *vi (of costs, prices)* grimper (en flèche); *(of town)* se développer; *(of houses, factories)* pousser comme des champignons

mushy ['mʌʃɪ] *adj* **(a)** *(food)* en bouillie; *(ground)* détrempé(e) **(b)** *Fam Fig Pej (sentimental)* à l'eau de rose, mièvre

music ['mjuːzɪk] *n* musique *f*; *Fig* **those words were m. to her ears** elle était ravie d'entendre ces mots; **m. box** boîte *f* à musique; **m. hall** music-hall *m*; **m. stand** pupitre *m* (à musique); **m. teacher** professeur *m* de musique

musical ['mjuːzɪkəl] **1** *n (show, film)* comédie *f* musicale
   2 *adj (tuneful)* musical(e); *(musically gifted)* musicien(enne); **m. chairs** (jeu *m* des) chaises *fpl* musicales; *also Fig* **to play m. chairs** jouer aux chaises musicales; **m. comedy** comédie *f* musicale; **m. instrument** instrument *m* de musique

musician [mjuː'zɪʃən] *n* musicien(enne) *m,f*

musicologist [mjuːzɪ'kɒlədʒɪst] *n* musicologue *mf*

musings ['mjuːzɪŋz] *npl* rêverie(s) *f(pl)*

musk [mʌsk] *n* musc *m*

musket ['mʌskɪt] *n* mousquet *m*

musketeer [mʌskə'tɪə(r)] *n* mousquetaire *m*

muskrat ['mʌskræt] *n* rat *m* musqué

Muslim ['mʊzlɪm] *n & adj* musulman(e) *m,f*

muslin ['mʌzlɪn] *n* mousseline *f*

mussel ['mʌsəl] *n* moule *f*; **m. bed** parc *m* à moules

must [mʌst] **1** *modal aux v* **(a)** *(expressing obligation)* devoir; **you m. do it** tu dois le faire, il faut que tu le fasses; **they mustn't find out** il ne faut pas qu'ils l'apprennent; **you mustn't tell anyone** surtout, n'en parle à personne; **this plant m. be watered daily** cette plante doit être arrosée chaque jour; **I m. say I thought it was rather good** je dois avouer que j'ai trouvé ça plutôt bon; **will you come with me? – if I m.** tu viens avec moi? – s'il le faut; **take it if you m.** prends-le, si tu le veux vraiment; **m. you be so silly?** tu te sens obligé d'être aussi bête?
   (b) *(suggesting, inviting)* **you m. come and visit us** il faut vraiment que vous nous rendiez visite; **we m. go out for a drink sometime** il faudrait que nous allions prendre un verre, un de ces jours
   (c) *(expressing probability)* devoir; **you m. be hungry** vous devez avoir faim; **I m. have made a mistake** j'ai dû faire une erreur; **you m. be joking!** tu veux rire!
   2 *n Fam* **(a)** *(necessity)* **to be a m.** être une nécessité; **sunglasses/hiking boots are a m.** il faut absolument emporter des lunettes de soleil/des chaussures de marche
   (b) *(thing not to be missed)* **this film's a m.** ce film est un must

mustache ['mʌstæʃ] *n* moustache *f*

mustard ['mʌstəd] *n* moutarde *f*; *Fam Fig* **he couldn't cut the m.** il n'a pas été à la hauteur; **m. bath** bain *m* sinapisé; **m. gas** gaz *m* moutarde

muster ['mʌstə(r)] **1** *n Fig* **to pass m.** être acceptable
   2 *vt (gather)* rassembler; **to m. one's strength/courage** rassembler ses forces/son courage

musty ['mʌstɪ] *adj (smell)* de moisi; **to have a m. smell** *(of room)* sentir le renfermé

mutant ['mjuːtənt] *n & adj* mutant(e) *m,f*

mutate [mjuː'teɪt] *vi* muter

mutation [mjuː'teɪʃən] *n* mutation *f*

mute [mjuːt] **1** *n* **(a)** *(dumb person)* muet(ette) *m,f* **(b)** *Mus* sourdine *f*
   2 *adj* muet(ette)

muted ['mjuːtɪd] *adj (sound)* assourdi(e); *(applause)* faible; *(protest, criticism)* voilé(e); *(color)* sourd(e)

mutilate ['mjuːtɪleɪt] *vt also Fig* mutiler

mutilation [mju:tɪˈleɪʃən] *n* mutilation *f*

mutineer [mju:tɪˈnɪə(r)] *n* mutiné(e) *m,f*

mutinous [ˈmju:tɪnəs] *adj* rebelle

mutiny [ˈmju:tɪnɪ] **1** *n* (*pl* **mutinies**) *(on ship)* mutinerie *f*; *(of workers)* révolte *f*
2 *vi* (*pt & pp* **mutinied**) *(of crew, soldiers)* se mutiner; *(of workers)* se révolter

mutt [mʌt] *n Fam (dog)* clébard *m*

mutter [ˈmʌtə(r)] **1** *n* murmure *m*
2 *vt & vi* marmonner

mutton [ˈmʌtən] *n* mouton *m*

mutual [ˈmju:tʃʊəl] *adj (reciprocal)* mutuel(elle), réciproque; *(shared)* commun(e); **the feeling is m.** c'est réciproque; *Fin* **m. fund** fonds *m* commun de placement, SICAV *f*

mutually [ˈmju:tʃʊəlɪ] *adv* mutuellement, réciproquement; **to be m. exclusive** s'exclure mutuellement

Muzak® [ˈmju:zæk] *n* musique *f* de fond, fond *m* sonore

muzzle [ˈmʌzəl] **1** *n* (**a**) *(dog's nose)* museau *m*; *(guard)* muselière *f* (**b**) *(of gun)* canon *m*
2 *vt also Fig* museler

MW (**a**) (*abbr* **Medium Wave**) OM (**b**) *Elec* (*abbr* **Megawatts**) MW

my [maɪ] **1** *possessive adj* (**a**) *(singular)* mon (ma); *(plural)* mes; **my job** mon travail; **my wife** ma femme; **my parents** mes parents; **it wasn't MY idea!** ce n'est pas moi qui en ai eu l'idée! (**b**) *(with parts of body)* **I hit my head** je me suis cogné la tête
2 *exclam* oh là là!

Myanmar [maɪænˈmɑ:(r)] *n* le Myanmar

mynah [ˈmaɪnə] *n* **m. (bird)** mainate *m*

myopia [maɪˈəʊpɪə] *n* myopie *f*; *Fig* manque *m* de perspicacité

myopic [maɪˈɒpɪk] *adj* myope; *Fig* à courte vue

myriad [ˈmɪrɪəd] *adj Lit* innombrable

myrrh [mɜ:(r)] *n* myrrhe *f*

myrtle [ˈmɜ:təl] *n* myrte *m*

myself [maɪˈself] *pron* (**a**) *(reflexive)* **I hurt m.** je me suis blessé (**b**) *(emphatic)* moi-même; **I m. have never...** moi-même je n'ai jamais...; **I told her m.** je lui ai dit moi-même; **I'm not m. today** je ne suis pas dans mon état normal aujourd'hui (**c**) *(after preposition)* moi; **I live by m.** je vis seul; **I bought it for m.** je me le suis acheté; **I talk to m.** je parle tout seul

mysterious [mɪsˈtɪərɪəs] *adj* mystérieux(euse)

mysteriously [mɪsˈtɪərɪəslɪ] *adv* mystérieusement

mystery [ˈmɪstərɪ] **1** *n* (*pl* **mysteries**) mystère *m*; **m. tour** voyage *m* surprise
2 *adj (guest, prize)* surprise *inv*; *(benefactor, witness)* mystérieux(euse)

mystic [ˈmɪstɪk] *n & adj* mystique *mf*

mystical [ˈmɪstɪkəl] *adj (person)* mystique; *(power, ceremony)* occulte

mysticism [ˈmɪstɪsɪzəm] *n* mysticisme *m*

mystify [ˈmɪstɪfaɪ] (*pt & pp* **mystified**) *vt* déconcerter

mystique [mɪsˈti:k] *n* mystère *m*

myth [mɪθ] *n* mythe *m*

mythical [ˈmɪθɪkəl] *adj* mythique

mythological [mɪθəˈlɒdʒɪkəl] *adj* mythologique

mythology [mɪˈθɒlədʒɪ] (*pl* **mythologies**) *n* mythologie *f*

myxomatosis [mɪksəməˈtəʊsɪs] *n* myxomatose *f*

N

N, n [en] *n* (**a**) *(letter)* N, n *m inv* (**b**) *(abbr* **north**) N
NAACP [eneIeIsi:'pi:] *n Pol* *(abbr* **National Association for the Advancement of Colored People**) = association pour la défense des droits des personnes de couleur
naan [nɑ:n] *n* **n. (bread)** = pain plat indien
nab [næb] *(pt & pp* **nabbed**) *vt Fam* (**a**) *(catch, arrest)* choper (**b**) *(steal)* piquer, faucher
nadir ['neIdIə(r)] *n Astron* nadir *m*; *Fig* **to reach a n.** atteindre son niveau le plus bas
NAFTA ['næftə] *n* (*abbr* **North American Free Trade Agreement**) ALENA *m*
nag¹ [næg] *n Fam (horse)* carne *f*
nag² [næg] **1** *n (person)* enquiquineur(euse) *m,f*
   2 *vt (pt & pp* **nagged**) *(of person)* être sur le dos de; *(of doubt, conscience)* tourmenter; **to n. sb into doing sth** harceler qn pour qu'il fasse qch
   3 *vi* **he's always nagging** il est tout le temps sur mon dos
nagging ['nægIŋ] **1** *n* harcèlement *m*; **I've had enough of your n.** arrête de me harceler
   2 *adj (pain, doubt, worry)* tenace
nail [neIl] **1** *n* (**a**) *(in carpentry)* clou *m*; *Fig* **it was another n. in his coffin** c'était un pas de plus vers la fin; *Fig* **the final n. in the coffin** la goutte d'eau qui fait déborder le vase; *Fig* **to hit the n. on the head** mettre le doigt dessus (**b**) *(of person)* ongle *m*; **n. file** lime *f* à ongles; **n. salon** salon *m* de manucure; **n. scissors** ciseaux *mpl* à ongles; **n. polish** vernis *m* à ongles; **n. polish remover** dissolvant *m*
   2 *vt* (**a**) *(fasten)* clouer; **to n. sth shut** clouer qch; *Fig* **to stand nailed to the spot** rester cloué(e) sur place (**b**) *(idioms)* *Fam* **to n. sb** *(for crime)* coincer qn; *Fam* **to n. a lie** dénoncer un mensonge
▸**nail down** *vt sep (fasten)* clouer, fixer avec des clous; *Fam Fig* **to n. sb down to a date/price** obtenir de qn qu'il fixe une date/un prix
nail-biting ['neIlbaItIŋ] *adj Fam (contest, finish)* palpitant(e); *(wait)* angoissant(e)
nailbrush ['neIlbrʌʃ] *n* brosse *f* à ongles
naive [naI'i:v] *adj* naïf(ïve)
naively [naI'i:vlI] *adv* naïvement
naivety [naI'i:vətI] *n* naïveté *f*
naked ['neIkId] *adj (body, flame)* nu(e); *Fig (aggression, exploitation)* délibéré(e); **visible to the n. eye** visible à l'œil nu
namby-pamby ['næmbI'pæmbI] *Pej* **1** *n (pl* **namby-pambies**) mollasson(onne) *m,f*
   2 *adj* gnangnan *inv*
name [neIm] **1** *n* (**a**) *(in general)* nom *m*; **my n. is...** je m'appelle...; **what's your n.?** comment t'appelles-tu?; **to mention sb by n.** désigner nommément qn; **a big n. in the theater** un grand nom du théâtre; **to put one's n. down (for sth)** s'inscrire (pour qch); **to go by** *or* **under the n. of...** être connu(e) sous le nom de...; **in the n. of...** au nom de...; **in the n. of God** *or* **Heaven!** au nom du Ciel!; **he was President in all but n.** c'était lui le président, même s'il n'en

avait pas le titre; **to call sb names** insulter qn; **he hasn't got a penny to his n.** il n'a pas un sou (**b**) *(reputation)* réputation *f*; **to have a good/bad n.** avoir (une) bonne/mauvaise réputation; **to have a n. for** être réputé(e) pour; **to make a n. for oneself** se faire un nom
   2 *vt* (**a**) *(give name to, appoint)* nommer; **a boy named John** un garçon prénommé John; **to n. sb for sb** donner à qn le nom de qn (**b**) *(designate, identify)* citer; **to n. names** donner des noms; **n. your price** dites votre prix
name-calling ['neImkɔ:lIŋ] *n* insultes *fpl*
name-dropper ['neImdrɒpə(r)] *n Fam* = personne qui se vante de connaître des gens célèbres
name-dropping ['neImdrɒpIŋ] *n Fam* = fait de se vanter de connaître des gens célèbres
nameless ['neImlIs] *adj (person)* anonyme; **someone who shall remain n.** quelqu'un que je ne nommerai pas
namely ['neImlI] *adv* c'est-à-dire, à savoir
nameplate ['neImpleIt] *n* plaque *f*
namesake ['neImseIk] *n* homonyme *mf*
Namibia [nə'mIbIə] *n* la Namibie
Namibian [nə'mIbIən] **1** *n* Namibien(enne) *m,f*
   2 *adj* namibien(enne)
nan = **naan**
nancy ['nænsI] *(pl* **nancies**), **nance** [næns] *n very Fam* **n. (boy)** *(homosexual)* tapette *f*, pédale *f*; *(effeminate man)* chochotte *f*
nanny ['nænI] *(pl* **nannies**) *n* (**a**) *(for children)* jeune fille *f* au pair (**b**) **n. goat** chèvre *f*
nanosecond ['nænəʊsekənd] *n Phys* nanoseconde *f*
nanotechnology ['nænəʊtek'nɒlədʒI] *n* nanotechnologie *f*
nap¹ [næp] **1** *n (sleep)* (petit) somme *m*; **to take** *or* **to have a n.** faire un (petit) somme
   2 *vi (pt & pp* **napped**) faire un (petit) somme; *Fig* **to be caught napping** être pris(e) au dépourvu
nap² [næp] *n (of cloth)* poil *m*
napalm ['neIpɑ:m] *n* napalm *m*
nape [neIp] *n* **n. (of the neck)** nuque *f*
naphthalene ['næfθəli:n] *n* naphtaline *f*
napkin ['næpkIn] *n* (**a**) **(table) n.** serviette *f* (de table); **n. ring** rond *m* de serviette (**b**) **(sanitary) n.** serviette *f* hygiénique
Naples ['neIpəlz] *n* Naples
Napoleonic [nəpəʊlɪ'ɒnɪk] *adj* napoléonien(enne)
narc [nɑ:k] *n Fam* agent *m* de la brigade des stups
narcissus [nɑ:'sɪsəs] *(pl* **narcissi** [nɑ:'sɪsaɪ]) *n* narcisse *m*
narcosis [nɑ:'kəʊsɪs] *n* narcose *f*
narcotic [nɑ:'kɒtɪk] **1** *n (medicine)* narcotique *m*; *(illegal drug)* stupéfiant *m*; **narcotics agent** agent *m* de la brigade des stupéfiants; **narcotics squad** brigade *f* des stupéfiants
   2 *adj* narcotique
narrate [nə'reɪt] *vt* raconter
narrative ['nærətɪv] **1** *n* récit *m*
   2 *adj* narratif(ive)

narrator [nə'reɪtə(r)] *n* narrateur(trice) *m,f*

narrow ['nærəʊ] **1** *adj* étroit(e); *(majority)* faible; **to grow** *or* **to become n.** se rétrécir; **to have a n. mind** avoir l'esprit étroit; **to have a n. escape** l'échapper belle; **to win/lose by a n. margin** gagner/perdre de justesse; **to take a n. view of sth** adopter un point de vue étroit sur qch

2 *vt* **to n. one's eyes** *(in suspicion, anger)* froncer les sourcils

3 *vi (of road)* se rétrécir, se resserrer

▸**narrow down** *vt sep* limiter, réduire

narrowly ['nærəʊlɪ] *adv (only just)* de peu; **she n. missed being run over** elle a failli se faire écraser

narrow-minded [nærəʊ'maɪndɪd] *adj* étroit(e) d'esprit, borné(e)

NASA ['næsə] *n (abbr* **National Aeronautics and Space Administration***)* NASA *f*

nasal ['neɪzəl] *adj* nasal(e); **to have a n. voice** parler du nez

nastily ['nɑːstɪlɪ] *adv* méchamment

nastiness ['nɑːstɪnɪs] *n (of person, remark)* méchanceté *f*

nasturtium [nə'stɜːʃəm] *n* capucine *f*

nasty ['nɑːstɪ] *adj* mauvais(e); *(crime)* ignoble; *(shock, business)* sale; *(accident)* grave; **to be n. to sb** être méchant(e) avec qn; **to have a n. mind** penser toujours à mal; **to turn n.** *(of situation, weather)* se dégrader, se gâter; **that was a really n. thing to do** c'était vraiment ignoble de sa/ta/*etc.* part; *Fig* **it left a n. taste in my mouth** ça m'a laissé un arrière-goût désagréable

nation ['neɪʃən] *n* nation *f*

national ['næʃənəl] **1** *n* **(a)** *(person)* ressortissant(e) *m,f* **(b)** *(newspaper)* journal *m* national

2 *adj* national(e); **n. anthem** hymne *m* national; **n. debt** dette *f* publique; **n. grid** réseau *m* national (d'électricité); **n. park** parc *m* national; **n. service** service *m* militaire

nationalism ['næʃənəlɪzəm] *n* nationalisme *m*

nationalist ['næʃənəlɪst] *n & adj* nationaliste *mf*

nationalistic [næʃənə'lɪstɪk] *adj* nationaliste

nationality [næʃə'nælɪtɪ] *(pl* **nationalities***) n* nationalité *f*

nationalization [næʃənəlaɪ'zeɪʃən] *n* nationalisation *f*

nationalize ['næʃənəlaɪz] *vt* nationaliser

nationally ['næʃənəlɪ] *adv* nationalement

nationwide ['neɪʃənwaɪd] **1** *adj* national(e)

2 *adv* dans tout le pays

native ['neɪtɪv] **1** *n (person)* natif(ive) *m,f*; *(plant)* plante *f* indigène; *(animal)* animal *m* indigène; **to be a n. of** être originaire de; **she speaks English like a n.** elle parle anglais comme si c'était sa langue maternelle

2 *adj* natal(e); **he returned to his n. London** il est retourné à Londres, sa ville natale; **N. American** Indien(enne) *m,f* d'Amérique; **n. land** pays *m* natal; **n. language** langue *f* maternelle; **I'm not a n. speaker of Spanish** ma langue maternelle n'est pas l'espagnol

Nativity [nə'tɪvɪtɪ] *n Rel* **the N.** la Nativité *f*; **N. play** mystère *m* de la Nativité

NATO ['neɪtəʊ] *n Mil (abbr* **North Atlantic Treaty Organization***)* l'OTAN *f*

natty ['nætɪ] *adj Fam* chic *inv*

natural ['nætʃərəl] **1** *adj* **(a)** *(color, taste)* naturel(elle); *(gift, talent)* inné(e); **to die from n. causes** mourir de mort naturelle; **n. childbirth** accouchement *m* naturel; **n. disaster** catastrophe *f* naturelle; **n. gas** gaz *m* naturel; **n. history** histoire *f* naturelle; **n. mother** mère *f* naturelle; **n. resources** ressources *fpl* naturelles; **n. sciences** sciences *fpl* naturelles; **n. yoghurt** yaourt *m* nature **(b)** *(normal)* naturel(elle); **it's only n.** c'est tout à fait naturel **(c)** *(unaffected)* naturel(elle)

2 *n* **he's a n. as an actor** c'est un acteur né

naturalism ['nætʃərəlɪzəm] *n* naturalisme *m*

naturalist ['nætʃərəlɪst] *n* naturaliste *mf*

naturalistic ['nætʃərəlɪstɪk] *adj* naturaliste

naturalization [nætʃərələ'zeɪʃən] *n* naturalisation *f*

naturalize ['nætʃərəlaɪz] *vt* naturaliser

naturally ['nætʃərəlɪ] *adv* **(a)** *(unaffectedly)* naturellement; *(by nature)* de nature; **to come n. to sb** être un don chez qn **(b)** *(of course)* naturellement

nature ['neɪtʃə(r)] *n* **(a)** *(the natural world)* nature *f*; **to let n. take its course** laisser faire la nature; **n. reserve** réserve *f* naturelle; *Sch* **n. study** sciences *fpl* naturelles; **n. trail** = sentier aménagé doté d'explications concernant la faune et la flore **(b)** *(character)* nature *f*; **to have a jealous n.** être d'une nature jalouse; **it's not in her n.** ça n'est pas dans sa nature; **to be shy by n.** être timide de nature **(c)** *(sort)* nature *f*, genre *m*; **problems of this n.** des problèmes de cette nature; *Formal* **what is the n. of your complaint?** quelle est la nature de votre réclamation?

naturist ['neɪtʃərɪst] *n & adj* naturiste *mf*

naught [nɔːt] *n (nothing)* zéro *m*; *Litt* **to come to n.** se réduire à néant

naughties ['nɔːtɪz] *npl Fam* années *fpl* deux mille à deux mille dix

naughtily ['nɔːtɪlɪ] *adv* **to behave n.** être vilain(e)

naughty ['nɔːtɪ] *adj (child)* méchant(e), vilain(e); *(book, picture)* coquin(e)

nausea ['nɔːzɪə] *n* nausée *f*

nauseate ['nɔːzɪeɪt] *vt* donner la nausée à; *Fig* écœurer

nauseating ['nɔːzɪeɪtɪŋ] *adj also Fig* écœurant(e)

nauseous ['nɔːzɪəs] *adj (disgusting)* écœurant(e); **to feel n.** avoir envie de vomir

nautical ['nɔːtɪkəl] *adj* nautique; **n. mile** mille *m* marin *ou* nautique

naval ['neɪvəl] *adj* naval(e); **n. battle** bataille *f* navale; **n. college** école *f* navale; **n. officer** officier *m* de marine

nave [neɪv] *n (of church)* nef *f*

navel ['neɪvəl] *n* nombril *m*

navel-gazing ['neɪvəlgeɪzɪŋ] *n* nombrilisme *m*

navigable ['nævɪɡəbəl] *adj* navigable

navigate ['nævɪɡeɪt] **1** *vt* **(a)** *(seas)* naviguer sur; *(ship, plane)* piloter **(b)** *Comput (website)* naviguer sur

2 *vi (in ship, plane)* naviguer; *(in car)* faire le pilote

navigation [nævɪ'ɡeɪʃən] *n* navigation *f*

navigational [nævɪ'ɡeɪʃənəl] *adj* de navigation

navigator ['nævɪɡeɪtə(r)] *n (in ship, plane)* navigateur(trice) *m,f*; *(in car)* copilote *mf*

navy ['neɪvɪ] *(pl* **navies***) n* marine *f*; **n. (blue)** bleu marine *m inv*

Nazi ['nɑːtsɪ] **1** *n* Nazi(e) *m,f*

2 *adj* nazi(e)

Nazism ['nɑːtsɪzəm] *n* nazisme *m*

NB [en'biː] *(abbr* **nota bene***)* NB

NBA [enbiː'eɪ] *n (abbr* **National Basketball Association***)* = fédération américaine de basket-ball

NCO [ensiː'əʊ] *n Mil (abbr* **non-commissioned officer***)* sous-officier *m*

NE *(abbr* **northeast***)* N-E

Neanderthal [nɪ'ændətɑːl] **1** *n* **(a)** *(during Stone Age)* homme *m* de Neandertal **(b)** *Fig (uncivilized man)* homme *m* des cavernes

2 *adj* **(a)** *(during Stone Age)* **N. man** homme *m* de Neandertal **(b)** *Fig (attitude, behavior)* d'homme des cavernes

Neapolitan [nɪːə'pɒlɪtən] **1** *n* Napolitain(e) *m,f*

2 *adj* napolitain(e)

near [nɪə(r)] **1** *adj* proche; **to the nearest meter** au mètre près; **in the n. future** dans un avenir proche; **it was a n. thing** il s'en est fallu de peu; **the N. East** le Proche-Orient

2 *adv* près; **to be n. to sth** *(in space)* être près de qch; *(in time)* être proche de qch; **n. at hand** tout près; *(of thing)* tout proche; **to be n. to doing sth** être sur le point de faire qch; **n. to tears/despair** au bord des larmes/du désespoir;

she's nowhere n. finished elle est loin d'avoir fini; a n. total failure un échec presque total

3 *prep* près de; he came n. to being run over il a failli se faire écraser; nobody comes anywhere n. her *(in skill, performance)* il n'y a personne à son niveau

4 *n Fam* my nearest and dearest mes plus proches parents
5 *vt* (s')approcher de; to be nearing completion être presque terminé(e)

nearby 1 *adj* ['nɪəbaɪ] proche
2 *adv* [nɪə'baɪ] tout près

nearly ['nɪəlɪ] *adv* presque; we're n. there *(finished)* nous y sommes presque; *(at destination)* nous sommes presque arrivés; he n. died il a failli mourir; not n. enough money/time vraiment pas assez d'argent/de temps; not n. so beautiful bien moins beau (belle)

nearly-new ['nɪəlɪ'nju:] *adj* = d'occasion mais en parfait état
near-sighted [nɪə'saɪtɪd] *adj* myope

neat [ni:t] *adj* (a) *(in habits)* ordonné(e); *(in appearance)* soigné(e); *(work, handwriting)* soigné; *(room, house)* bien rangé(e); to make a n. job of doing sth faire qch très bien (b) *(undiluted)* pur(e) (c) *Fam (good)* super *inv*

▶**neaten up** ['ni:tən] *vt sep (hair, garden)* arranger; *(piece of work)* peaufiner

neatly ['ni:tlɪ] *adv* (a) *(carefully)* soigneusement (b) *(skillfully)* habilement, adroitement

neatness ['ni:tnɪs] *n (of appearance)* aspect *m* soigné; *(of work)* soin *m*; *(of handwriting)* netteté *f*; *(of room, house)* ordre *m*

nebula ['nebjʊlə] (*pl* nebulas or nebulae ['nebjʊlaɪ]) *n Astron* nébuleuse *f*

nebulous ['nebjʊləs] *adj (vague)* nébuleux(euse)

necessarily [nesɪ'serəlɪ] *adv* nécessairement, forcément

necessary ['nesɪsərɪ] *adj* nécessaire; it is n. to remind them il faut le leur rappeler; to do what is n. faire le nécessaire; when(ever) n. si nécessaire, si besoin est; a n. evil un mal nécessaire

necessitate [nɪ'sesɪteɪt] *vt Formal* nécessiter, rendre nécessaire

necessity [nɪ'sesɪtɪ] (*pl* necessities) *n* nécessité *f*; out of n. par nécessité; the necessities *(things needed)* le nécessaire; *Prov* n. is the mother of invention en cas de besoin, on trouve toujours une solution

neck [nek] **1** *n* (a) *(of person, animal)* cou *m*; *(of dress)* encolure *f*, col *m*; *(of bottle)* goulot *m*; *(of guitar, violin)* manche *m*; *(of land)* langue *f*; *(of lamb, beef)* collier *m* (b) *(idioms) Fam* to risk one's n. risquer sa peau; *Fam* he got it in the n. il s'est pris un savon; *Fam* he's in it up to his n. il est impliqué là-dedans jusqu'au cou; to finish n. and n. finir au coude à coude; *Fam* to stick one's n. out se lancer; *Fam* in this n. of the woods dans le coin
2 *vi Fam (of couple)* se bécoter

necklace ['neklɪs] *n* collier *m*
neckline ['neklaɪn] *n* encolure *f*
necktie ['nektaɪ] *n* cravate *f*

necromancy ['nekrəʊmænsɪ] *n Formal* nécromancie *f*
nectar ['nektə(r)] *n* nectar *m*

nectarine ['nektəri:n] *n* nectarine *f*, brugnon *m*

née [neɪ] *adj* née; Mrs Richardson, n. Johnston Mme Richardson, née Johnston

need [ni:d] **1** *n* besoin *m* (for de); there is no n. to shout/worry inutile de crier/de t'inquiéter; if n. be en cas de besoin; to be in n. *(poor)* être dans le besoin; to be in n. of sth avoir besoin de qch; in time of n. dans les moments difficiles; their n. is greater than mine ils en ont plus besoin que moi

2 *vt* to n. sth/to do sth avoir besoin de qch/de faire qch; n. more time il me faut plus de temps; you'll n. to take more money il te faudra prendre plus d'argent, il faudra que tu prennes plus d'argent; I didn't n. to be reminded of it je

n'avais pas besoin qu'on me le rappelle, il était inutile de me le rappeler; his hair needs cutting il a besoin d'une coupe de cheveux; the flashlight needs a new battery la lampe a besoin d'une nouvelle pile; this work needs a lot of patience ce travail demande beaucoup de patience; *Ironic* that's all I n.! il ne (me) manquait plus que ça!

3 *modal aux v* you needn't worry inutile de t'inquiéter; you needn't wait tu n'as pas besoin d'attendre; n. I say more? ai-je besoin d'en dire plus?

needle ['ni:dəl] **1** *n* aiguille *f*; it's like looking for a n. in a haystack c'est comme chercher une aiguille dans une botte de foin
2 *vt Fam* asticoter

needlecraft ['ni:dəlkrɑ:ft] *n* travaux *mpl* d'aiguille

needless ['ni:dlɪs] *adj (waste, suffering, worry)* inutile; *(remark)* déplacé(e); n. to say... il va de soi que...

needlessly ['ni:dlɪslɪ] *adv* inutilement

needlework ['ni:dəlwɜ:k] *n (sewing)* couture *f*; *(embroidery)* broderie *f*

need-to-know [ni:dtə'nəʊ] *adj* information is given on a n. basis les renseignements ne sont donnés qu'aux personnes concernées

needy ['ni:dɪ] **1** *npl* the n. les nécessiteux *mpl*
2 *adj (person) (financially)* nécessiteux(euse), dans le besoin; *(emotionally)* en manque d'affection

nefarious [nɪ'feərɪəs] *adj* infâme, ignoble

negate [nɪ'geɪt] *vt (effect)* annuler; *(work, efforts)* anéantir

negation [nɪ'geɪʃən] *n (of work, efforts)* anéantissement *m*

negative ['negətɪv] **1** *n* (a) *Gram* the n. la forme négative; to answer in the n. répondre par la négative (b) *(of photo)* négatif *m*
2 *adj* négatif(ive); don't be so n. ne sois pas si négatif; n. feedback réaction *f* négative

negatively ['negətɪvlɪ] *adv* négativement

negativity [negə'tɪvɪtɪ] *n* négativité *f*

neglect [nɪ'glekt] **1** *n (of person)* négligence *f*; *(of machine, garden)* manque *m* d'entretien; *(of duties, responsibilities)* manquement *m*; from or through n. par négligence
2 *vt* (a) *(not care for)* négliger; to n. oneself se négliger (b) *(ignore) (duties, responsibilities)* manquer à; *(post)* abandonner; to n. to do sth négliger de faire qch

neglectful [nɪ'glektfʊl] *adj* négligent(e); to be n. of sb/sth négliger qn/qch

negligée, negligee ['neglɪʒeɪ] *n* négligé *m*, déshabillé *m*

negligence ['neglɪdʒəns] *n* négligence *f*; *(of duties, responsibilities)* manquement *m* (of à)

negligent ['neglɪdʒənt] *adj* négligent(e)

negligently ['neglɪdʒəntlɪ] *adv* négligemment

negligible ['neglɪdʒɪbəl] *adj* négligeable

negotiable [nɪ'gəʊʃəbəl] *adj (demand, salary)* négociable; *(price)* à débattre; *(obstacle)* franchissable; *(road)* praticable

negotiate [nɪ'gəʊʃɪeɪt] **1** *vt* (a) *(price, treaty, salary, contract)* négocier (b) *(obstacle)* franchir; *(difficulty)* surmonter; *(bend)* négocier
2 *vi* négocier

negotiation [nɪgəʊʃɪ'eɪʃən] *n* négociation *f*; under n. en négociation

negotiator [nɪ'gəʊʃɪeɪtə(r)] *n* négociateur(trice) *m,f*

Negress ['ni:grɪs] *n Old-fashioned* négresse *f*

Negro ['ni:grəʊ] *Old-fashioned* **1** *n* (*pl* Negroes) nègre *m*
2 *adj* nègre; N. spiritual *(song)* Negro spiritual *m*

neigh [neɪ] **1** *n* hennissement *m*
2 *vi* hennir

neighbor ['neɪbə(r)] *n* voisin(e) *m,f*; to be a good n. être bon voisin

neighborhood ['neɪbəhʊd] *n* (a) *(district)* quartier *m*; *(people)* voisinage *m* (b) *(vicinity)* voisinage *m*, environs *mpl*; in the n.

dans les environs; **a figure in the n. of $2,000** un chiffre avoisinant les 2000 dollars

neighboring ['neɪbərɪŋ] *adj* voisin(e)

neighborliness ['neɪbəlɪnɪs] *n* (relations *fpl* de) bon voisinage *m*

neighborly ['neɪbəlɪ] *adj* **they're very n.** ce sont de très bons voisins

neither ['naɪðə(r), 'niːðə(r)] **1** *conj* **n.... nor...** ni... ni...; **n. you nor your brother** ni toi ni ton frère; **he n. drinks nor smokes** il ne boit pas et ne fume pas non plus; *Fig* **that's n. here nor there** là n'est pas la question

2 *adv* **n. do I** moi non plus; **if you don't go n. shall I** si tu n'y vas pas, moi non plus; **the workers aren't happy and n. is the management** les ouvriers ne sont pas contents et la direction non plus

3 *adj* **n. driver was injured** aucun des deux conducteurs n'a été blessé

4 *pron* **n. (of them) will do** aucun (des deux) ne fera l'affaire; **n. of my two brothers can come** aucun de mes deux frères ne peut venir

neo- ['niːəʊ] *pref* néo-

neoclassical [niːəʊ'klæsɪkəl] *adj* néoclassique

neofascist [niːəʊ'fæʃɪst] *n & adj* néofasciste *mf*

neolithic [niːəʊ'lɪθɪk] *adj* néolithique

neon ['niːɒn] *n* néon *m*; **n. light** lumière *f* au néon; **n. sign** enseigne *f* au néon

Nepal [nɪ'pɔːl] *n* le Népal

Nepalese [nepə'liːz], **Nepali** [ne'pɔːlɪ] **1** *n* (*pl* **Nepalese** or **Nepalis**) **(a)** *(person)* Népalais(e) *m,f* **(b)** *(language)* népalais *m*
2 *adj* népalais(e)

nephew ['nefjuː] *n* neveu *m*

nepotism ['nepətɪzəm] *n* népotisme *m*

Neptune ['neptjuːn] *n* (*planet*) Neptune *f*

nerd [nɜːd] *n Fam Pej* (*stupid person*) crétin(e) *m,f*; (*unfashionable person*) ringard(e) *m,f*

nerdy ['nɜːdɪ] *adj Fam Pej* ringard(e)

nerve [nɜːv] **1** *n* **(a)** (*in body*) nerf *m*; *Fam* **to get on sb's nerves** taper sur les nerfs à qn; **her nerves were in a terrible state** elle était à bout de nerfs; *Anat* **n. cell** cellule *f* nerveuse; *Fig* **n. center** (*of organization*) centre *m* nerveux; **n. gas** gaz *m* neurotoxique **(b)** (*courage*) courage *m*; **to have nerves of steel** avoir des nerfs d'acier; **to keep/lose one's n.** garder/perdre son sang-froid **(c)** *Fam* (*cheek*) culot *m*; **to have the n. to do sth** avoir le culot de faire qch
2 *vt* **to n. oneself to do sth** s'armer de courage pour faire qch

nerve-(w)racking ['nɜːvrækɪŋ] *adj* éprouvant(e)

nervous ['nɜːvəs] *adj* **(a)** (*apprehensive*) nerveux(euse), anxieux(euse); **to be n. about sth/doing sth** être nerveux *ou* anxieux à l'idée de qch/de faire qch **(b)** (*energy, exhaustion*) nerveux(euse); **n. breakdown** dépression *f* nerveuse; **n. system** système *m* nerveux

nervously ['nɜːvəslɪ] *adv* nerveusement

nervousness ['nɜːvəsnɪs] *n* nervosité *f*

nervy ['nɜːvɪ] *adj Fam* (*bold*) culoté(e)

nest [nest] **1** *n* (*of bird, insects*) nid *m*; *Fig* (*of criminals*) repaire *m*; *Fig* **to fly the n.** quitter le nid; **n. of tables** tables *fpl* gigognes; *Fig* **n. egg** pécule *m*
2 *vi* (*of bird*) faire son nid

nestle ['nesəl] *vi* se pelotonner, se blottir; **to n. up to sb** se blottir contre qn

nestling ['neslɪŋ] *n* oisillon *m*

Net [net] *n Fam Comput* **the N.** le Net; **N. user** internaute *mf*

net¹ [net] **1** *n* filet *m*; *Fig* **to slip through the n.** passer à travers les mailles du filet; **n. curtain** voilage *m*
2 *vt* (*pt & pp* **netted**) (*animals, fish*) prendre au filet; *Fig* (*drugs, criminals*) mettre la main sur; (*donations, contracts*) récolter

net² [net] **1** *adj* (*weight, price, profit*) net (nette)
2 *vt* (*earn*) **to n. $2,000** gagner 2000 dollars net

nethead ['nethed] *n Fam Comput* accro *mf* de l'Internet

Netherlands ['neðələndz] *npl* **the N.** les Pays-Bas *mpl*

netiquette ['netɪket] *n Fam Comput* netiquette *f*

netsurfer ['netsɜːfə(r)] *n Comput* internaute *mf*

netting ['netɪŋ] *n* filet *m*

nettle ['netəl] **1** *n* (*plant*) ortie *f*
2 *vt* (*irritate*) irriter, énerver

network ['netwɜːk] **1** *n* réseau *m*
2 *vi* (*make contacts*) établir un réseau de contacts

networking ['netwɜːkɪŋ] *n* (*making contacts*) établissement *m* d'un réseau de contacts

neural ['njʊərəl] *adj Anat* neural(e)

neuralgia [njʊ'rældʒə] *n* névralgie *f*

neurologist [njʊə'rɒlədʒɪst] *n* neurologue *mf*

neurology [njʊə'rɒlədʒɪ] *n* neurologie *f*

neuron ['njʊərɒn] *n Anat* neurone *m*

neurosis [njʊə'rəʊsɪs] (*pl* **neuroses** [njʊə'rəʊsiːz]) *n* névrose *f*

neurosurgery ['njʊərəʊ'sɜːdʒərɪ] *n* neurochirurgie *f*

neurotic [njʊ'rɒtɪk] **1** *n* névrosé(e) *m,f*
2 *adj* névrosé(e); **to be n. about sth** être obsédé(e) par qch

neuter ['njuːtə(r)] **1** *n Gram* neutre *m*
2 *adj Gram* neutre
3 *vt* (*animal*) castrer, châtrer

neutral ['njuːtrəl] **1** *n* **(a)** (*country*) pays *m* neutre; (*person*) personne *f* neutre **(b)** (*of car*) point *m* mort; **in n.** au point mort
2 *adj* (*country, color*) neutre

neutrality [njuː'trælɪtɪ] *n* neutralité *f*

neutralize ['njuːtrəlaɪz] *vt* neutraliser

neutrino [njʊ'triːnəʊ] (*pl* **neutrinos**) *n Phys* neutrino *m*

neutron ['njuːtrɒn] *n Phys* neutron *m*; **n. bomb** bombe *f* à neutrons

never ['nevə(r)] *adv* **(a)** (*not once*) jamais; **I've n. met him** je ne l'ai jamais rencontré; **n. again!** plus jamais!; **he's n. yet been beaten** il n'a encore jamais été battu; **I've n. understood why** je n'ai jamais compris pourquoi **(b)** (*emphatic negative*) **she n. said a word** elle n'a pas dit un mot; **I n. expected this** je ne m'attendais vraiment pas à ça; **he n. even congratulated me** il ne m'a même pas félicité

never-ending [nevər'endɪŋ] *adj* interminable

nevertheless [nevəðə'les] *adv* néanmoins, cependant

new [njuː] *adj* nouveau(elle); (*not used*) neuf (neuve); **what's n.?** quoi de neuf?; **that's nothing n.!** ça n'est pas nouveau!; **she's n. to this work** elle débute dans ce travail; **to be n. to a town** être nouveau dans une ville; **N. Age** (*music, thinking*) new age *inv*; **N. Brunswick** le Nouveau-Brunswick; **N. Caledonia** la Nouvelle-Calédonie; **N. Delhi** New Delhi; **N. England** la Nouvelle-Angleterre; **N. Guinea** la Nouvelle-Guinée; **N. Mexico** le Nouveau-Mexique; **n. moon** nouvelle lune *f*; **N. Orleans** la Nouvelle-Orléans; **N. South Wales** la Nouvelle-Galles du Sud; **the N. Testament** le Nouveau Testament; **n. wave** (*trend*) Nouvelle Vague *f*; **the N. World** le Nouveau Monde; **N. Year** Nouvel An *m*; **N. Year's Day** le jour de l'an; **N. Year's Eve** la Saint-Sylvestre; **N. Year's resolution** résolution *f* du jour de l'an; **N. York** New York; **N. Yorker** New-Yorkais(e) *m,f*

newbie ['njuːbɪ] *n Fam* **(a)** (*new recruit*) bleu(e) *m,f* **(b)** *Comput* (*Internet user*) internaute *mf* novice

newborn ['njuːbɔːn] *adj* nouveau-né(e); **n. baby** nouveau-né(e) *m,f*

newcomer ['njuːkʌmə(r)] *n* nouveau(elle) venu(e) *m,f* (**to** dans)

newfangled [njuː'fæŋgəld] *adj Pej* (*idea*) nouveau(elle); (*gadget*) dernier cri *inv*

Newfoundland ['njuːfəndlænd] *n* Terre-Neuve *f*

newly ['njuːlɪ] *adv* nouvellement, récemment

newlyweds ['nju:lɪwedz] *npl* jeunes mariés *mpl*

newness ['nju:nɪs] *n (of design)* nouveauté *f; (of clothing)* état *m* neuf

news [nju:z] *n* nouvelles *fpl; (on TV, radio)* informations *fpl*; **a piece of n.** une nouvelle; **in the n.** sous les feux de l'actualité; *Fam* **he's bad n.** il n'est pas fréquentable; *Fam* **that's n. to me!** première nouvelle!; *Prov* **no n. is good n.** pas de nouvelles, bonnes nouvelles; **n. agency** agence *f* de presse; **n. bulletin** bulletin *m* d'informations; **n. conference** conférence *f* de presse; **n. item** information *f*, nouvelle *f*

newscaster ['nju:zkɑ:stə(r)] *n* présentateur(trice) *m,f* du journal

newsdealer ['nju:zdi:lə(r)] *n* marchand(e) *m,f* de journaux

newsflash ['nju:zflæʃ] *n* flash *m* d'informations

newsgroup ['nju:zgru:p] *n Comput* newsgroup *m*, forum *m* de discussion

newsletter ['nju:zletə(r)] *n* bulletin *m*

newspaper ['nju:zpeɪpə(r)] *n* journal *m*; **n. report** reportage *m*

newspaperman ['nju:zpeɪpəmæn] *n (reporter)* journaliste *m; (owner)* propriétaire *m* d'un journal

newsprint ['nju:zprɪnt] *n* papier *m* journal

newsreel ['nju:zri:l] *n* actualités *fpl*

newsroom ['nju:zru:m] *n* (salle *f* de) rédaction *f*

newsstand ['nju:zstænd] *n* kiosque *m* à journaux

newsworthy ['nju:zwɜ:ðɪ] *adj* d'un intérêt médiatique

newt [nju:t] *n* triton *m*

New Zealand [nju:'zi:lənd] *n* la Nouvelle-Zélande

New Zealander [nju:'zi:ləndə(r)] *n* Néo-Zélandais(e) *m,f*

next [nekst] **1** *adj* **(a)** *(in space)* d'à côté; **n. door** à côté **(b)** *(in time, order)* prochain(e); *(subsequent)* suivant(e), d'après; **n. week** la semaine prochaine; **the n. week** la semaine suivante *ou* d'après; **the year after n.** dans deux ans; **the n. time** la prochaine fois; **your name is n. on the list** votre nom est le suivant sur la liste; **the n. but one** pas le prochain, mais celui d'après; **(the) n. to arrive was Carmen** Carmen est arrivée ensuite; **who's n.?** c'est à qui?; **n., please!** au suivant!; **the n. size up/down** la taille au-dessus/au-dessous

2 *adv* **(a)** *(in space)* **n. to** à côté de **(b)** *(in time, order)* ensuite, après; *Fam* **what will they think of n.?** qu'est-ce qu'ils vont encore inventer?; **n. to Paris I like Madrid best** après Paris, la ville que je préfère, c'est Madrid; **when shall we meet n.?** quand nous reverrons-nous?; **the n. best thing would be to...** à défaut, le mieux serait de...; **the n. fastest after the Ferrari was...** la voiture la plus rapide après la Ferrari était...; **who is the n. oldest/youngest after Mark?** qui est le plus âgé/le plus jeune après Mark?; **n. to nothing** quasiment rien; **there is n. to no evidence** il n'y a pratiquement aucune preuve; **in n. to no time** en un rien de temps

next-door [neks'dɔ:(r)] *adj* d'à côté; **n. neighbor** voisin(e) *m,f* d'à côté

next-of-kin [nekstəv'kɪn] *n* plus proche parent *m*

NFL [enef'el] *n (abbr* **National Football League**) = fédération nationale de football américain

NGO [endʒi:'əʊ] *n (abbr* **non-governmental organization**) ONG *f*

nib [nɪb] *n* plume *f*

nibble ['nɪbəl] **1** *n* **to have a n. at sth** grignoter qch; **nibbles** *(snacks)* amuse-gueule *mpl*

2 *vt* grignoter

Nicaragua [nɪkə'ræɡjʊə] *n* le Nicaragua

Nicaraguan [nɪkə'ræɡjʊən] **1** *n* Nicaraguayen(enne) *m,f*

2 *adj* nicaraguayen(enne)

nice [naɪs] *adj* **(a)** *(pleasant)* agréable; *(physically attractive)* beau (belle); *(tasty)* bon (bonne); **a n. idea** une bonne idée; **to be n.**

to sb se montrer aimable avec qn; **to have a n. time** bien s'amuser; **have a n. day!** bonne journée!; **it was n. of her to...** c'était gentil de sa part de...; *Ironic* **that's a n. way to behave!** en voilà des manières! **(b)** *(intensive)* **n. and easy** très facile; **n. and handy** bien commode; **a n. warm bath** un bain bien chaud

nice-looking ['naɪslʊkɪŋ] *adj* beau (belle)

nicely ['naɪslɪ] *adv (ask)* gentiment; *(behave, sit)* bien; **to be doing n.** aller bien; **to do n. for oneself** bien se débrouiller

niceties ['naɪsɪtɪz] *npl* subtilités *fpl*

niche [ni:ʃ] *n (in wall)* niche *f; (in market)* créneau *m*; **to find one's n. (in life)** trouver sa voie

nick [nɪk] **1** *n (in wood, on face)* entaille *f*

2 *vt (cut)* entailler

nickel ['nɪkəl] *n* **(a)** *(metal)* nickel *m* **(b)** *(coin)* pièce *f* de cinq cents

nickname ['nɪkneɪm] **1** *n* surnom *m*

2 *vt* surnommer

nicotine ['nɪkəti:n] *n* nicotine *f*; **n. patch** patch *m* anti-tabac

niece [ni:s] *n* nièce *f*

nifty ['nɪftɪ] *adj Fam* **(a)** *(idea, device)* génial(e) **(b)** *(agile)* vif (vive)

Niger *n* **(a)** [ni:'ʒeə(r)] *(country)* Niger *m* **(b)** ['naɪdʒə(r)] *(river)* le Niger

Nigeria [naɪ'dʒɪərɪə] *n* le Nigéria

Nigerian [naɪ'dʒɪərɪən] **1** *n* Nigérian(e) *m,f*

2 *adj* nigérian(e)

niggardly ['nɪɡədlɪ] *adj (person)* avare, pingre; *(sum, portion)* maigre

nigger ['nɪɡə(r)] *n very Fam Pej* nègre (négresse) *m,f*, = terme raciste désignant un Noir

niggle ['nɪɡ(ə)l] *vi (be overfussy)* couper les cheveux en quatre

niggling ['nɪɡəlɪŋ] *adj (detail)* insignifiant(e); *(pain, doubt)* persistant(e); **I have a n. feeling that...** je ne peux pas m'empêcher de penser que...

nigh [naɪ] *adv* **(a)** *Lit (near)* près, proche; **the end is n.!** la fin est proche! **(b)** **well n.** *(almost)* presque

night [naɪt] *n* nuit *f; (evening)* soir *m*; **at n.** la nuit; *(in the evening)* le soir; **late at n.** tard dans la nuit; **all n.** toute la nuit; **last n.** la nuit dernière; *(evening)* hier soir; **tomorrow n.** demain soir; **on Thursday n.** jeudi soir; **good n.!** *(when going to bed)* bonne nuit!, bonsoir!; *(when leaving)* bonsoir!; **to work nights** travailler la nuit; **to have a n. out** sortir; **let's make a n. of it** et si on continuait la soirée?; **n. flight** vol *m* de nuit; *Fam* **n. owl** couche-tard *mf inv*, oiseau *m* de nuit; **n. school** cours *m* du soir; **n. table** table *f* de chevet; **n. watchman** veilleur *m* de nuit

nightcap ['naɪtkæp] *n* **(a)** *(hat)* bonnet *m* de nuit **(b)** *(drink)* petit verre *m (avant d'aller se coucher)*

nightclub ['naɪtklʌb] *n* boîte *f* de nuit, *Can* club *m* de nuit

nightdress ['naɪtdres] *n* chemise *f* de nuit

nightfall ['naɪtfɔ:l] *n* tombée *f* de la nuit; **at n.** à la nuit tombante

nightgown ['naɪtgaʊn] *n* chemise *f* de nuit

nightie ['naɪtɪ] *n Fam* chemise *f* de nuit

nightingale ['naɪtɪŋgeɪl] *n* rossignol *m*

nightjar ['naɪtdʒɑ:(r)] *n* engoulevent *m* (d'Europe)

nightlife ['naɪtlaɪf] *n* vie *f* nocturne; **there's not much n.** il n'y a pas grand-chose à faire le soir

nightlong ['naɪtlɒŋ] *adj* qui dure toute la nuit

nightly ['naɪtlɪ] **1** *adj* de toutes les nuits; *(in the evening)* du soir

2 *adv* toutes les nuits; *(in the evening)* tous les soirs

nightmare ['naɪtmeə(r)] *n also Fig* cauchemar *m*

nightmarish ['naɪtmeərɪʃ] *adj* cauchemardesque

nightshirt ['naɪtʃɜ:t] *n* chemise *f* de nuit

nightstick ['naɪtstɪk] *n* matraque *f (de policier)*

night-time ['naɪttaɪm] **1** *n* nuit *f*; **at n.** la nuit

2 *adj* nocturne

nihilistic [naɪ(h)ɪ'lɪstɪk] *adj* nihiliste

nil [nɪl] *n* néant *m*; *(in sports)* zéro *m*; **two n.** deux à zéro

Nile [naɪl] *n* **the N.** le Nil

nimble ['nɪmbəl] *adj (person)* souple; *(leap, movement)* leste; *(fingers)* preste; *(mind)* vif (vive)

nimbly ['nɪmbəlɪ] *adv* avec souplesse

nincompoop ['nɪŋkəmpu:p] *n Fam* nigaud(e) *m,f*

nine [naɪn] **1** *n* neuf *m inv*; *Fam* **dressed up to the nines** sur son trente et un; **n. eleven** = le onze septembre; **ever since n. eleven, I've been afraid to fly** depuis les attentats du onze septembre, j'ai peur de prendre l'avion

2 *adj* neuf; **n. times out of ten** neuf fois sur dix; **a n.-to-five job** un travail de bureau; **to have n. lives** *(of person)* avoir l'âme chevillée au corps; *see also* **eight**

nineteen [naɪn'ti:n] **1** *n* dix-neuf *m inv*

2 *adj* dix-neuf; *see also* **eight**

nineteenth [naɪn'ti:nθ] **1** *n* **(a)** *(fraction)* dix-neuvième *m* **(b)** *(in series)* dix-neuvième *mf* **(c)** *(of month)* dix-neuf *m inv*

2 *adj* dix-neuvième; *Fam Hum* **the n. hole** *(of golf course)* le bar du golf; *see also* **eighth**

ninetieth ['naɪntɪɪθ] **1** *n* **(a)** *(fraction)* quatre-vingt-dixième *m* **(b)** *(in series)* quatre-vingt-dixième *mf*

2 *adj* quatre-vingt-dixième; *see also* **eighth**

ninety ['naɪntɪ] **1** *n* quatre-vingt-dix *m inv*, *Belg & Suisse* nonante

2 *adj* quatre-vingt-dix, *Belg & Suisse* nonante; **n. nine times out of a hundred** quatre-vingt-dix-neuf fois sur cent; *see also* **eighty**

ninth [naɪnθ] **1** *n* **(a)** *(fraction)* neuvième *m* **(b)** *(in series)* neuvième *mf* **(c)** *(of month)* neuf *m inv*

2 *adj* neuvième; **n. floor** huitième étage; *Scol* **n. grade** = classe de lycée pour les 13–14 ans; *see also* **eighth**

nip [nɪp] **1** *n* **(a)** *(pinch)* pincement *m*; *(bite)* morsure *f* légère **(b)** *(of cold, frost)* **there's a n. in the air** il fait frisquet **(c)** *Fam (of drink)* petit verre *m*

2 *(pt & pp nipped)* *vt* **(a)** *(pinch)* pincer; *(bite)* mordre légèrement; *Fam Fig* **to n. sth in the bud** étouffer qch dans l'œuf **(b)** *(of cold, frost)* pincer, piquer

3 *vi (sting)* piquer

nipple ['nɪp(ə)l] *n (on breast)* mamelon *m*; *(on baby's bottle)* tétine *f*; *(pacifier)* tétine *f*

nippy ['nɪpɪ] *adj Fam (cold)* vif (vive); **it's a bit n. today** il fait plutôt frisquet aujourd'hui

nit [nɪt] *n (in hair)* lente *f*; **to have nits** avoir des poux

nit-picker ['nɪtpɪkə(r)] *n Fam* chipoteur(euse) *m,f*

nit-picking ['nɪtpɪkɪŋ] *Fam* **1** *n* chipotage *m*

2 *adj* chipoteur(euse)

nitrate ['naɪtreɪt] *n* nitrate *m*

nitric ['naɪtrɪk] *adj* nitrique

nitrogen ['naɪtrədʒən] *n* azote *m*

nitroglycerine ['naɪtrəʊ'glɪsəri:n] *n* nitroglycérine *f*

nitrous ['naɪtrəs] *adj* nitreux(euse)

nitty-gritty ['nɪtɪ'grɪtɪ] *n Fam* **to get down to the n.** entrer dans le vif du sujet

nitwit ['nɪtwɪt] *n Fam* crétin(e) *m,f*

NNE *(abbr* **north-northeast)** NNE

NNW *(abbr* **north-northwest)** NNO

No., no. *(abbr* **number)** n°

no [nəʊ] **1** *n (pl* **noes** *or* **nos)** non *m*; **she won't take no for an answer** elle n'accepte pas qu'on lui dise non

2 *adj* **(a)** *(not any)* pas de; **there's no bread** il n'y a pas de pain; **of no importance** sans importance; **I am in no way surprised** je ne suis pas du tout surpris; **he's no friend of mine** je ne le compte certainement pas au nombre de mes amis; *Fam* **no way!** pas question!

(b) *(with gerund)* **there's no denying it** on ne peut pas le nier; **there's no pleasing him** il n'est jamais satisfait; **no smoking** *(sign)* interdiction de fumer

3 *adv* **(a)** *(interjection)* non

(b) *(not any)* **no richer/poorer** pas plus riche/pauvre; **no more/less than $100** pas plus/moins de 100 dollars; **he no longer lives there** il n'habite plus là

Noah ['nəʊə] *n* Noé; **N.'s ark** l'arche *f* de Noé

Nobel Prize [nəʊ'bel'praɪz] *n* prix *m* Nobel

nobility [nəʊ'bɪlɪtɪ] *n* noblesse *f*

noble ['nəʊbəl] **1** *n* noble *mf*

2 *adj* noble; *Fig (building)* majestueux(euse)

nobleman ['nəʊbəlmən] *n* noble *m*

nobleminded [nəʊbəl'maɪndɪd] *adj (person)* au cœur noble, magnanime; *(sentiment, action)* noble

noblewoman ['nəʊbəlwʊmən] *n* noble *f*

nobly ['nəʊbəlɪ] *adv* avec noblesse

nobody ['nəʊbədɪ] **1** *pron* personne; **n. spoke to me** personne ne m'a parlé; **n. else** personne d'autre; **she's n.'s fool** elle n'est pas née de la dernière pluie; **if you don't have money, you're n.** si on n'a pas d'argent on est un moins que rien

2 *n (pl* **nobodies)** **a n.** un(e) moins que rien

no-brainer [nəʊ'breɪnə(r)] *n Fam* **(a)** *(stupid thing)* truc *m* pour débiles **(b)** *(easy)* **it's a n.** c'est simplissime

nocturnal [nɒk'tɜ:nəl] *adj* nocturne

nod [nɒd] **1** *n (in greeting, as signal)* signe *m* de tête; *(in agreement)* signe de tête affirmatif; *Fig* **to give sb/sth the n.** donner le feu vert à qn/qch

2 *vt (pt & pp* **nodded)** **to n. one's head** *(in greeting, as signal)* faire un signe de tête; *(in agreement)* faire oui de la tête; **to n. one's agreement/approval** consentir/approuver d'un signe de tête

3 *vi* **to n. in agreement/approval** consentir/approuver d'un signe de tête

▸**nod off** *vi Fam* s'assoupir

node [nəʊd] *n (of curve, plant)* nœud *m*; *Med* ganglion *m*; *Comput* noyau *m*

nodule ['nɒdju:l] *n* nodule *m*

no-fault [nəʊ'fɒlt] *adj* **n. divorce** divorce *m* par consentement mutuel; **n. insurance** assurance *f* à remboursement automatique

no-fly zone [nəʊ'flaɪzəʊn] *n Mil* zone *f* d'exclusion aérienne

no-frills [nəʊ'frɪlz] *adj (wedding)* tout(e) simple; *(airline, travel)* sans prestation de services; *(car, bicycle)* sans gadgets

no-good ['nəʊgʊd] *adj Fam* **a n. idiot** un imbécile propre à rien; **that n. husband of hers** son bon à rien de mari

no-hoper [nəʊ'həʊpə(r)] *n* tocard(e) *m,f*

noise [nɔɪz] *n* bruit *m*; *Fig* **to make noises about doing sth** parler de faire qch

noiselessly ['nɔɪzlɪslɪ] *adv* sans bruit, silencieusement

noisily ['nɔɪzɪlɪ] *adv* bruyamment

noisy ['nɔɪzɪ] *adj* bruyant(e)

nomad ['nəʊmæd] *n & adj* nomade *mf*

nomadic [nəʊ'mædɪk] *adj* nomade

no man's land ['nəʊmænz'lænd] *n Fig* no man's land *m*

nomenclature [nəʊ'menklətʃə(r)] *n* nomenclature *f*

nominal ['nɒmɪnəl] *adj* nominal(e); *(damages)* symbolique; *(rent)* insignifiant(e)

nominally ['nɒmɪnəlɪ] *adv* nominalement

nominate ['nɒmɪneɪt] *vt (propose)* proposer **(for/as** pour/comme); *(appoint)* nommer **(to/as** à/comme)

nomination [nɒmɪ'neɪʃən] *n (a) (proposal)* candidature *f*; *(for film, TV awards)* nomination *f* **(b)** *(appointment)* nomination *f*

nominee [nɒmɪ'ni:] *n (proposed)* candidat(e) *m,f*; *(appointed)* personne *f* nommée

non- [nɒn] *pref* non(-)

non-aggression pact [nɒnə'greʃən'pækt] *n Pol* pacte *m* de non-agression

nonalcoholic [nɒnælkə'hɒlɪk] *adj* sans alcool

nonaligned [nɒnə'laɪnd] *adj Pol* non-aligné(e)

nonattendance [nɒnə'tendəns] *n* absence *f*

nonchalance ['nɒnʃələns] *n* désinvolture *f*

nonchalant ['nɒnʃələnt] *adj* désinvolte

nonchalantly [nɒnʃə'lɒntlɪ] *adv* avec désinvolture

noncombatant [nɒn'kɒmbətənt] *n & adj Mil* non-combattant(e) *m,f*

non-commissioned officer ['nɒnkə'mɪʃənd'ɒfɪsə(r)] *n Mil* sous-officier *m*

noncommittal [nɒnkə'mɪtəl] *adj (answer)* de Normand; **to be n.** ne pas s'engager

nonconformist [nɒnkən'fɔːmɪst] *n & adj* non-conformiste *mf*

non-denominational [nɒndɪ'nɒmɪ'neɪʃənəl] *adj (school, education)* non confessionel(elle)

nondescript ['nɒndɪskrɪpt] *adj* banal(e); *(color)* fade

none [nʌn] **1** *pron* aucun(e) *m,f*; **n. of you/us** aucun d'entre vous/nous; **n. of my friends** aucun de mes amis; **n. of this concerns me** rien de tout cela ne me concerne; **it was n. other than the President** c'était le Président, rien de moins; **there was/were n. left** il n'en restait plus; *Fam* **we'll have n. of that!** pas de ça!

  2 *adv* **his answer left me n. the wiser** sa réponse ne m'a pas avancé; **n. too happy** pas très satisfait(e); **n. too soon** pas trop tôt

nonentity [nɒ'nentɪtɪ] (*pl* **nonentities**) *n* personne *f* sans intérêt

nonessential [nɒnɪ'senʃəl] *adj* qui n'est pas essentiel(elle)

nonetheless [nʌnðə'les] *adv* néanmoins, cependant

nonevent [nɒnɪ'vent] *n* **to be a n.** être décevant(e)

nonexistent [nɒnɪg'zɪstənt] *adj* inexistant(e)

nonfat ['nɒn'fæt] *adj* sans matière grasse *ou* matières grasses; **n. milk** lait *m* écrémé

non-fiction [nɒn'fɪkʃən] *n* ouvrages *mpl* généraux

nonflammable [nɒn'flæməbəl] *adj* ininflammable

non-linear [nɒn'lɪnɪə(r)] *adj Comput* non linéaire

non-negotiable [nɒnnɪ'gəʊʃəbəl] *adj* non négociable

non-nuclear [nɒn'njuːklɪə(r)] *adj (country)* non nucléarisé(e); *(war, defense)* non nucléaire

no-no ['nəʊnəʊ] (*pl* **no-nos** *or* **no-noes**) *n Fam* **that's a n.** c'est à ne pas faire

no-nonsense [nəʊ'nɒnsəns] *adj* direct(e)

non-partisan [nɒn'pɑːtɪzæn] *adj* impartial(e)

non-payment [nɒn'peɪmənt] *n* non-paiement *m*

non-person ['nɒn'pɜːsən] *n* proscrit(e) *m,f*

nonplussed [nɒn'plʌst] *adj* interloqué(e)

non-profit [nɒn'prɒfɪt] *adj* à but non lucratif

non-racist [nɒn'reɪsɪst] *adj* non raciste

nonresident [nɒn'rezɪdənt] *n (of country)* non-résident(e) *m,f*

nonreturnable [nɒnrɪ'tɜːnəbəl] *adj (bottle)* non consigné(e); *(deposit)* non remboursable

nonsense ['nɒnsəns] *n* bêtises *fpl*, idioties *fpl*; **n.!** n'importe quoi!; **to talk (a lot of) n.** dire des bêtises

nonsensical [nɒn'sensɪkəl] *adj* absurde, qui n'a pas de sens

non sequitur [nɒn'sekwɪtə(r)] *n* absurdité *f*

non-sexist [nɒn'seksɪst] *adj* non sexiste

non-smoker [nɒn'sməʊkə(r)] *n* non-fumeur(euse) *m,f*

non-smoking [nɒn'sməʊkɪŋ] *adj (area, train car)* non-fumeur; *(seat)* non-fumeur

non-specialist [nɒn'speʃəlɪst] **1** *n* non-spécialiste *mf*
  2 *adj* non spécialisé(e)

nonstarter [nɒn'stɑːtə(r)] *n* **to be a n.** *(of plan)* être fichu(e) d'avance

nonstick ['nɒn'stɪk] *adj (surface)* anti-adhésif(ive); *(frying pan)* qui n'attache pas

non-stop ['nɒn'stɒp] **1** *adj (journey)* sans arrêt; *(flight)* sans escale
  2 *adv* sans arrêt; *(fly)* sans escale

non-tariff barrier ['nɒn'tærɪf'bærɪə(r)] *n Econ* barrière *f* non tarifaire

nontransferable ['nɒntræns'fɜːrəbəl] *adj (ticket, membership)* nominatif(ive); *(property, right)* incessible

nonverbal [nɒn'vɜːbəl] *adj* non-verbal(e)

nonviolent [nɒn'vaɪələnt] *adj* non-violent(e)

noodles ['nuːdəlz] *npl* nouilles *fpl*

nook [nʊk] *n (corner)* recoin *m*; *(retreat)* coin *m*; **every n. and cranny** le moindre recoin

nookie, nooky ['nʊkɪ] *n Fam* crac-crac *m*; **to have a bit of n.** faire une partie de jambes en l'air

noon [nuːn] *n* midi *m*; **at n.** à midi

noonday ['nuːndeɪ] *n Lit* midi *m*; **the n. sun** le soleil de midi

no-one ['nəʊwʌn] = **nobody**

noose [nuːs] *n* nœud *m* coulant; *Fig* **to put one's head in a n.** signer son arrêt de mort

nope [nəʊp] *adv Fam* non

nor [nɔː(r)] **1** *conj* **neither you n. your brother** ni toi ni ton frère; **neither... n.** ni... ni; **he neither drinks n. smokes** il ne boit pas et ne fume pas non plus
  2 *adv* **n. do I** moi non plus; **if you don't go n. shall I** si tu n'y vas pas, moi non plus

Nordic ['nɔːdɪk] *adj* nordique

norm [nɔːm] *n* norme *f*

normal ['nɔːməl] **1** *n* **above/below n.** *(temperature, rate)* au-dessus/au-dessous de la normale; **to get back to n.** redevenir normal(e)
  2 *adj* normal(e)

normalcy ['nɔːməlsɪ], **normality** [nɔː'mælɪtɪ] *n* normalité *f*; **a return to n.** un retour à la normale

normalization [nɔːməlaɪ'zeɪʃən] *n* normalisation *f*

normalize ['nɔːməlaɪz] **1** *vt* normaliser
  2 *vi* redevenir normal(e)

normally ['nɔːməlɪ] *adv* normalement

Norman ['nɔːmən] **1** *n* Normand(e) *m,f*
  2 *adj* normand(e)

Normandy ['nɔːməndɪ] *n* la Normandie

north [nɔːθ] **1** *n* nord *m*; **to the n. (of)** au nord (de)
  2 *adj (coast, side)* nord; *(wind)* du nord; **N. Africa** Afrique *f* du Nord; **N. African** nord-africain(e); *(person)* Nord-Africain(e) *m,f*; **N. America** Amérique *f* du Nord; **N. American** nord-américain(e); *(person)* Nord-Américain(e) *m,f*; **N. Carolina** la Caroline du Nord; **N. Dakota** le Dakota du Nord; **N. Korea** Corée *f* du Nord; **N. Korean** nord-coréen(enne); *(person)* Nord-Coréen(enne) *m,f*; **the N. Pole** le Pôle Nord; **the N. Sea** la mer du Nord
  3 *adv* au nord; *(travel)* vers le nord; **to face n.** *(of house)* être exposé(e) au nord

northbound ['nɔːθbaʊnd] *adj (train, traffic)* en direction du nord; **n. road** voie *f* nord

northeast [nɔːθ'iːst] **1** *n* nord-est *m*
  2 *adj (side)* nord-est; *(wind)* du nord-est
  3 *adv* au nord-est; *(travel)* vers le nord-est

northeasterly [nɔːθ'iːstəlɪ] **1** *n (wind)* vent *m* du nord-est
  2 *adj (direction)* vers le nord-est; *(wind)* du nord-est

northeastern [nɔːθ'iːstən] *adj (region)* (du) nord-est

northerly ['nɔːðəlɪ] **1** *n (pl* **northerlies**) *(wind)* vent *m* du nord
  2 *adj (direction)* vers le nord; *(wind)* du nord; **the most n. point** le point le plus au nord

northern ['nɔːðən] *adj (region, accent)* du nord; **n. France** le nord de la France; **n. hemisphere** hémisphère *m* nord; **N.**

Ireland l'Irlande f du Nord; **N. Irish** de l'Irlande du Nord; **the N. Irish** les Irlandais mpl du Nord; **N. Lights** aurore f boréale

northerner ['nɔ:ðənə(r)] n habitant(e) m,f du Nord

north-facing ['nɔ:θ'feɪsɪŋ] adj exposé(e) au nord

north-northeast [nɔ:θnɔ:θ'i:st] adv au nord-nord-est; (travel) vers le nord-nord-est

north-northwest [nɔ:θnɔ:θ'west] adv au nord-nord-ouest; (travel) vers le nord-nord-ouest

northward ['nɔ:θwəd] **1** adj au nord
2 adv vers le nord

northwards ['nɔ:θwədz] adv = northward

northwest [nɔ:θ'west] **1** n nord-ouest m
2 adj (side) nord-ouest; (wind) du nord-ouest
3 adv au nord-ouest; (travel) vers le nord-ouest

northwesterly [nɔ:θ'westəlɪ] **1** n (pl **northwesterlies**) (wind) vent m du nord-ouest
2 adj (direction) vers le nord-ouest; (wind) du nord-ouest

northwestern [nɔ:θ'westən] adj (region) (du) nord-ouest

Northwest Territories ['nɔ:θ'west'terɪtri:z] npl les Territoires mpl du Nord-Ouest

Norway ['nɔ:weɪ] n la Norvège

Norwegian [nɔ:'wi:dʒən] **1** n (a) (person) Norvégien(enne) m,f (b) (language) norvégien m
2 adj norvégien(enne)

nose [nəʊz] n (a) (of person, animal, airplane) nez m; **her n. is bleeding** elle saigne du nez; **to blow one's n.** se moucher (le nez); **to hold one's n.** se boucher le nez; Fam **to have a n. job** se faire refaire le nez (b) (idioms) **it's under your n.** vous l'avez sous le nez; **to turn one's n. up at sth** dédaigner qch; **she walked by with her n. in the air** elle passa, l'air dédaigneux; **to look down one's n. at sb** prendre qn de haut; **to pay through the n. for sth** payer qch une fortune; **to lead sb by the n.** mener qn par le bout du nez; **to keep one's n. clean** se tenir à carreau; **to have a n. for sth** savoir flairer qch; **to poke one's n. into other people's business** fourrer son nez dans les affaires des autres; Fam **on the n.** (spot on) dans le mille

▸**nose about, nose around** vi Fam fouiner

nosebleed ['nəʊzbli:d] n **to have a n.** saigner du nez

nose-dive ['nəʊzdaɪv] **1** n (of plane) (vol m en) piqué m; Fig (of prices) chute f rapide
2 vi (of plane) piquer du nez; Fig (of prices) chuter fortement

nosh [nɒʃ] Fam **1** n (food) bouffe f
2 vi (eat) bouffer

no-show [nəʊ'ʃəʊ] n défection f

nosiness ['nəʊzɪnəs] n curiosité f

no-smoking [nəʊ'sməʊkɪŋ] adj (car, area) non-fumeurs; (seat) non-fumeur

nostalgia [nɒs'tældʒɪə] n nostalgie f

nostalgic [nɒs'tældʒɪk] adj nostalgique

nostalgically [nɒs'tældʒɪklɪ] adv avec nostalgie

nostril ['nɒstrɪl] n narine f

nosy ['nəʊzɪ] adj Fam fouineur(euse); (questions) indiscret(ète)

not [nɒt] adv **n. me/him** pas moi/lui; **I don't know** je ne sais pas; **don't move!** ne bouge pas!; **whether she likes it or n.** que ça lui plaise ou non; **I think/hope n.** je pense/j'espère que non; **she asked me n. to tell him** elle m'a demandé de ne pas le lui dire; **n. wishing to cause an argument, he said nothing** ne voulant pas provoquer de dispute, il s'est tu; **you understand, don't you?** tu comprends, n'est-ce pas?; **n. at all** pas du tout; (you're welcome) je vous en prie; **n. any more** plus maintenant; **n. even** pas même, même pas; **n. only..., but also...** non seulement..., mais encore...; **n. yet** pas encore; **n. that I minded** non pas que ça me dérangeait; **n. that it matters** non pas que ça ait de l'importance; **n. that I know of** pas que je sache

notable ['nəʊtəbəl] adj (person, thing) notable; (achievement, success) remarquable; **with a few n. exceptions** à quelques exceptions près, et non des moindres

notably ['nəʊtəblɪ] adv notamment

notary ['nəʊtərɪ] (pl **notaries**) n Law **n. (public)** notaire m

notation [nəʊ'teɪʃən] n notation f

notch [nɒtʃ] **1** n (a) (in stick) encoche f; (in belt) cran m (b) (grade, level) cran m
2 vt encocher

▸**notch up** vt sep (victory, sale) remporter; (points) marquer

note [nəʊt] **1** n (a) (information, reminder) note f; (short letter) mot m; (lecture) **notes** notes (de cours); **to take** or **to make (a) n. of sth** prendre note de qch; **to take n. of sb/sth** remarquer qn/qch (b) (musical) note f; Fig (of impatience, anger) pointe f; **on a lighter/more serious n.** pour en venir à un sujet moins/plus sérieux (c) (money) billet m (d) (significance) **of n.** (event) remarquable; (person) éminent(e)
2 vt noter, remarquer; (error) relever; (fact) constater

▸**note down** vt sep prendre note de, noter

notebook ['nəʊtbʊk] n carnet m; (larger) cahier m; Comput agenda m

noted ['nəʊtɪd] adj éminent(e); **to be n. for sth** être réputé(e) pour qch

notepad ['nəʊtpæd] n bloc-notes m

notepaper ['nəʊtpeɪpə(r)] n papier m à lettres

noteworthy ['nəʊtwɜ:ðɪ] adj remarquable

nothing ['nʌθɪŋ] **1** pron rien; **n. happened** il ne s'est rien passé; **I have n. to do** je n'ai rien à faire; **to have n. to do with sb/sth** (be unconnected to) n'avoir rien à voir avec qn/qch; (not get involved with) n'avoir rien à faire avec qn/qch; **to say n. of...** sans parler de...; **she was n. if not discreet** elle a été très discrète; **n. new/remarkable** rien de nouveau/d'exceptionnel; **n. but** rien que; **n. else** rien d'autre; **n. much** pas grand-chose; **there is n. more to be said** il n'y a plus rien à dire; **there's n. like a nice steak!** rien de tel qu'un bon steak!; **as a pianist, he has n. on his brother** en tant que pianiste, son frère n'a rien à lui envier; **there's n. in it** (it's untrue) il n'y a rien de vrai dans tout ça; **to think n. of doing sth** trouver normal de faire qch; Fam **there's n. to it** ce n'est pas sorcier; **$2,000 is n. to her** 2000 dollars, ce n'est rien pour elle; **to get angry/worried for** or **about n.** se fâcher/s'inquiéter pour un rien; **to do sth for n.** (in vain, free of charge) faire qch pour rien
2 n **to come to n.** être anéanti(e); **$100? – a mere n.!** cent dollars? – une bagatelle!
3 adv **she looks n. like her sister** elle ne ressemble pas du tout à sa sœur; **it was n. like as difficult as they said** c'était loin d'être aussi difficile qu'on le disait

notice ['nəʊtɪs] **1** n (a) (warning) avertissement m; (of resignation, dismissal) préavis m; **to give sb n. (of sth)** avertir qn (de qch); (of resignation, dismissal) donner un préavis à qn (pour qch); **until further n.** jusqu'à nouvel ordre; **at short n.** au pied levé; **at a moment's n.** sur-le-champ; **to give in** or **to hand in one's n.** (resign) donner sa démission, démissionner; **to give sb n.** (of employer) licencier qn
(b) (attention) **to take n. of sb/sth** faire ou prêter attention à qn/qch; **to take no n. of sb/sth** ne pas prêter la moindre attention à qn/qch; **the fact escaped everyone's n.** ce fait a échappé à tout le monde; **it has come to my n. that...** (I was told) on m'a signalé que...; (I read it) je me suis rendu compte que...
(c) (sign) écriteau m, pancarte f; (poster) affiche f
(d) (criticism of play, film) critique f
2 vt remarquer, s'apercevoir de; **to be noticed, to get oneself noticed** se faire remarquer
3 vi remarquer

noticeable ['nəʊtɪsəbəl] adj (change, difference) sensible, perceptible; **it was n. that...** il était évident que...

noticeably ['nəʊtɪsəblɪ] *adv* sensiblement

notification [nəʊtɪfɪ'keɪʃən] *n* avis *m*, notification *f*; **to give sb n. of sth** avertir qn de qch

notify ['nəʊtɪfaɪ] (*pt & pp* **notified**) *vt* annoncer, notifier; **to n. sb of sth** avertir qn de qch

notion ['nəʊʃən] *n* notion *f*; **to have a n. that...** avoir dans l'idée que...; **to have a n. to do sth** avoir envie de faire qch

notoriety [nəʊtə'raɪətɪ] *n* notoriété *f*; **to achieve** *or* **to gain n.** se rendre célèbre

notorious [nəʊ'tɔːrɪəs] *adj* tristement célèbre; *(criminal)* notoire; *(place)* mal famé(e); *(liar)* fieffé(e)

notoriously [nəʊ'tɔːrɪəslɪ] *adv* **to be n. tactless/rude** être bien connu(e) pour son manque de tact/son impolitesse; **Scottish weather is n. unpredictable** il est bien connu qu'en Écosse, le temps est très changeant

notwithstanding [nɒtwɪθ'stændɪŋ] *Formal* **1** *prep* en dépit de, malgré
  2 *adv* néanmoins; **difficulties n.,...** ces difficultés mises à part,...

nougat ['nuːgət] *n* nougat *m*

nought, noughties = **naught, naughties**

noun [naʊn] *n* nom *m*

nourish ['nʌrɪʃ] *vt* nourrir

nourishing ['nʌrɪʃɪŋ] *adj* nourrissant(e)

nourishment ['nʌrɪʃmənt] *n* nourriture *f*; *(nourishing quality)* richesse *f* nutritive

Nov. *(abbr* **November)** novembre

Nova Scotia ['nəʊvə'skəʊʃə] *n* la Nouvelle-Écosse

novel ['nɒvəl] **1** *n* roman *m*
  2 *adj (original)* nouveau(elle), original(e)

novelist ['nɒvəlɪst] *n* romancier(ère) *m,f*

novelty ['nɒvəltɪ] *(pl* **novelties)** *n (newness)* nouveauté *f*; *(cheap object)* bricole *f*; **the n. will soon wear off** l'attrait de la nouveauté ne tardera pas à s'estomper; **n. value** attrait *m* de la nouveauté

November [nəʊ'vembə(r)] *n* novembre *m; see also* **May**

novice ['nɒvɪs] *n (beginner)* débutant(e) *m,f* (**at** en); *Rel* novice *mf*

now [naʊ] **1** *adv* (**a**) *(at this moment, these days)* maintenant; **it's n. or never** c'est maintenant ou jamais; **that'll do for n.** ça suffit pour le moment; **it's two years n. since his mother died** ça fait maintenant deux ans que sa mère est morte; **she won't be long n.** elle ne va plus tarder; **any minute/day n.** d'une minute/d'un jour à l'autre; **n. is the time to...** c'est le moment de...; **right n.** *(immediately)* tout de suite; *(at the moment)* pour le moment; **(every) n. and then, (every) n. and again** de temps en temps, de temps à autre; **up to** *or* **until n.** jusqu'à présent *ou* maintenant; **from n. on** dorénavant; **in three days from n.** dans trois jours; **she ought to be here by n.** elle devrait déjà être ici; **and n. for some music** et maintenant, un peu de musique (**b**) *(before statement, argument)* bon; **n., there are two ways of interpreting this** bon, il y a deux interprétations possibles; **come n.!** allons!; **n., n.! stop quarreling!** allons, allons! arrêtez de vous disputer!
  2 *conj* **n. (that)...** maintenant que...; **n. (that) you mention it,...** maintenant que tu le dis,...

nowadays ['naʊədeɪz] *adv* de nos jours

nowhere ['nəʊweə(r)] **1** *adv* nulle part; **n. else** nulle part ailleurs; **she was n. to be found** elle était introuvable; **qualifications alone will get you n.** les diplômes seuls ne servent à rien; **to be n. near as nice/stupid (as)** être loin d'être aussi agréable/stupide (que); **it's n. near the shopping center** c'est à des kilomètres du centre commercial; **to finish n.** *(in contest)* finir loin derrière les autres; *Fam* **we're getting n. fast** on perd notre temps
  2 *n* **in the middle of n.** dans un coin paumé; **he came from n. to win the race** il a gagné la course après une remontée spectaculaire

noxious ['nɒkʃəs] *adj* nocif(ive)

nozzle ['nɒzəl] *n (of gas pump)* pistolet *m*; *(of vacuum cleaner)* suceur *m*; *(of pipe)* jet *m*; *(for icing)* douille *f*

nr *(abbr* **near)** près de

NRA [enɑː'reɪ] *n (abbr* **National Rifle Association)** = association américaine favorable à la généralisation des armes à feu

nth [enθ] *adj Fam* énième

nuance ['njuːɒns] *n* nuance *f*

nub [nʌb] *n (of question, argument)* cœur *m*

nubile ['njuːbaɪl] *adj* désirable

nuclear ['njuːklɪə(r)] *adj* nucléaire; **n. bomb** bombe *f* atomique; **n. disarmament** désarmement *m* nucléaire; **n. energy** énergie *f* nucléaire *ou* atomique; **n. family** famille *f* nucléaire; **n. physics** physique *f* nucléaire; **n. power** énergie *f* nucléaire; **n. power station** centrale *f* atomique *ou* nucléaire; **n. reactor** réacteur *m* nucléaire; **n. warfare** guerre *f* atomique *ou* nucléaire; **n. waste** déchets *mpl* nucléaires; **n. weapon** arme *f* atomique *ou* nucléaire; **n. winter** hiver *m* nucléaire

nuclear-free zone ['njuːklɪə'friː'zəʊn] *n* zone *f* dénucléarisée

nucleus ['njuːklɪəs] *(pl* **nuclei** ['njuːklɪaɪ]) *n also Fig* noyau *m*

nude [njuːd] **1** *n* nu *m*; **in the n.** tout(e) nu(e)
  2 *adj* nu(e)

nudge [nʌdʒ] **1** *n* coup *m* de coude
  2 *vt* donner un coup de coude à

nudist ['njuːdɪst] *n* nudiste *mf*; **n. camp** *or* **colony** camp *m* de nudistes

nudity ['njuːdɪtɪ] *n* nudité *f*

nugatory ['njuːgətɒrɪ] *adj* sans valeur

nugget ['nʌgɪt] *n (of gold)* pépite *f*; *Fig* **a n. of information** un renseignement précieux

nuisance ['njuːsəns] *n* **to be a n.** *(of person, situation)* être embêtant(e); **to make a n. of oneself** embêter le monde

nuke [njuːk] *vt Fam* lâcher la bombe sur

null [nʌl] *adj* nul (nulle); **n. and void** nul et non avenu

nullify ['nʌlɪfaɪ] (*pt & pp* **nullified**) *vt* annuler; *(decree)* invalider

numb [nʌm] **1** *adj* engourdi(e); **to go n.** s'engourdir; **n. with cold** engourdi par le froid; **n. with fear** paralysé(e) par la peur
  2 *vt (of cold)* engourdir; *(of fear)* paralyser

number ['nʌmbə(r)] **1** *n* (**a**) *(numeral)* nombre *m*; *(when written)* chiffre *m*; *Comput* **n. crunching** calculs *mpl* (rapides); **numbers game** loterie *f* clandestine
  (**b**) *(of house, page, telephone)* numéro *m*; **I live at n. 40** j'habite au (numéro) 40; **(telephone) n.** numéro de téléphone; *Fam* **to look after n. one** s'occuper de sa petite personne
  (**c**) *(quantity)* nombre *m*; **a large n. of** un grand nombre de; **in small/great numbers** en petit/grand nombre
  (**d**) *(song)* chanson *f*
  (**e**) *(idioms)* **he's my n. two** *(subordinate)* c'est mon adjoint; *Fam* **I've got your n.!** je sais ce que tu as en tête!; *Fam* **his n.'s up** son compte est bon; *Fam* **that car/dress is a nice little n.** c'est une jolie petite voiture/robe; *Fam* **she's got a nice little n. there** *(situation)* elle s'est dégoté un bon plan
  2 *vt* (**a**) *(assign number to)* numéroter
  (**b**) *(count)* compter; **his days are numbered** ses jours sont comptés; **to n. sb among one's friends** compter qn parmi *ou* au nombre de ses amis

numbly ['nʌmlɪ] *adv (say, react)* mollement; *(stare)* d'un air hébété

numbness ['nʌmnɪs] *n (in body)* engourdissement *m*; *(of emotions)* torpeur *f*

numbskull ['nʌmskʌl] *n Fam* bêta(asse) *m,f*

numeracy ['njuːmərəsɪ] *n* degré *m* d'aptitude en calcul

numeral ['njuːmərəl] *n* chiffre *m*

numerate ['njuːmərət] *adj* **to be n.** savoir compter

numerator ['njuːməreɪtə(r)] *n Math* numérateur *m*

numerical [njuːˈmerɪkəl] *adj* numérique

numerically [njuːˈmerɪklɪ] *adv* numériquement

numerous [ˈnjuːmərəs] *adj* nombreux(euse); **on n. occasions** en de nombreuses occasions

nun [nʌn] *n* religieuse *f*, nonne *f*; **to become a n.** prendre la voile

nunnery [ˈnʌnərɪ] (*pl* **nunneries**) *n* couvent *m*

nuptial [ˈnʌpʃəl] **1** *npl Hum or Lit* **nuptials** noces *fpl*
2 *adj Lit* nuptial(e)

nurse [nɜːs] **1** *n* (**a**) *(medical)* infirmière *f*; **(male) n.** infirmier *m* (**b**) *(looking after children)* nurse *f*
2 *vt (look after)* soigner; *(suckle)* allaiter; *Fig (feeling, hope)* nourrir; *(grievance)* entretenir; **to n. sb back to health** faire recouvrer la santé à qn

nursery [ˈnɜːsərɪ] (*pl* **nurseries**) *n* (**a**) *(for children) (establishment)* garderie *f*; *(room in house)* chambre *f* d'enfants; **n. education** enseignement *m* en maternelle; **n. rhyme** comptine *f*; **n. (school)** maternelle *f* (**b**) *(for plants)* pépinière *f*

nursing [ˈnɜːsɪŋ] *n (profession)* profession *f* d'infirmière; *(care)* soins *mpl*; **n. home** *(for old people)* maison *f* de retraite; *(for convalescents)* maison *f* de repos; **n. mother** mère *f* qui allaite; **n. staff** personnel *m* soignant

nurture [ˈnɜːtʃə(r)] *vt* (**a**) *(feed) (children, plants)* nourrir; *(plan, idea)* élaborer (**b**) *(bring up)* faire l'éducation de

nut [nʌt] *n* (**a**) *(food)* = noix, noisette, cacahuète, pistache ou autre fruit sec de cette nature; *Fig* **he's a hard** *or* **tough n.** c'est un dur; *Fig* **a tough** *or* **hard n. to crack** *(problem)* un problème difficile à résoudre (**b**) *Fam (head)* caboche *f* (**c**) *Fam (mad person)* dingue *mf*; **a tennis n.** un dingue de tennis (**d**) *(for fastening bolt)* écrou *m*; *Fig* **the nuts and bolts** les notions de base (**e**) *very Fam* **nuts** *(testicles)* couilles *fpl* (**f**) *Fam* **n.!** mince !

nutcase [ˈnʌtkeɪs] *n Fam* cinglé(e) *m,f*

nutcrackers [ˈnʌtkrækəz] *npl* **(pair of) n.** casse-noisettes *m inv*, casse-noix *m inv*

nuthouse [ˈnʌthaʊs] *n Fam* maison *f* de fous

nutmeg [ˈnʌtmeg] *n (noix f de)* muscade *f*

nutrient [ˈnjuːtrɪənt] **1** *n* élément *m* nutritif
2 *adj* nutritif(ive)

nutrition [njuːˈtrɪʃən] *n* nutrition *f*

nutritional [njuːˈtrɪʃənəl] *adj* nutritionnel(elle); *(value)* nutritif(ive)

nutritious [njuːˈtrɪʃəs] *adj* nutritif(ive)

nuts [nʌts] *adj Fam (mad)* dingue; **to be n. about sb/sth** être dingue de qn/qch

nutshell [ˈnʌtʃel] *n* coquille *f* de noix/noisette/*etc*; *Fig* **in a n.,...** bref,...

nutty [ˈnʌtɪ] *adj* (**a**) *(in taste)* au goût de noisette/noix/*etc*; *(containing nuts)* aux noisettes/noix/*etc.* (**b**) *Fam (mad)* dingue

nuzzle [ˈnʌzəl] **1** *vt (push with nose)* pousser du nez; *(sniff)* renifler
2 *vi* (**a**) **to n. against sb** *(push with nose)* pousser qn du nez; *(sniff)* renifler qn (**b**) *(nestle)* se blottir; **to n. (up) against sb** se blottir contre qn

NW *(abbr* **northwest***)* N-O

NY [enˈweɪ] *n (abbr* **New York***)* New York

nylon [ˈnaɪlɒn] *n* Nylon® *m*; **nylons** *(stockings)* bas *mpl* Nylon®

nymph [nɪmf] *n* nymphe *f*

nymphomania [nɪmfəʊˈmeɪnɪə] *n* nymphomanie *f*

nymphomaniac [nɪmfəʊˈmeɪnɪæk] *n* nymphomane *f*

NZ *(abbr* **New Zealand***)* la Nouvelle-Zélande

O, o [əʊ] *n* (**a**) *(letter)* O, o *m inv* (**b**) *(zero)* zéro *m*

oaf [əʊf] *n* lourdaud *m*

oak [əʊk] *n (tree, wood)* chêne *m*; **o. apple** noix *f* de galle

oar [ɔ:(r)] *n* aviron *m*, rame *f*; *Fig* **to put** *or* **to stick one's o. in** mettre son grain de sel

oarsman ['ɔ:zmən] *n* rameur *m*

oarswoman ['ɔ:zwʊmən] *n* rameuse *f*

OAS [əʊeɪ'es] *n (abbr* **Organization of American States**) OEA *f*

oasis [əʊ'eɪsɪs] *(pl* **oases** [əʊ'eɪsi:z]*) n also Fig* oasis *f*

oatcake ['əʊtkeɪk] *n* galette *f* d'avoine

oath [əʊθ] *n* (**a**) *(pledge)* serment *m*; **o. of allegiance** serment d'allégeance; **to take** *or* **to swear an o.** prêter serment; **on** *or* **under o.** sous serment (**b**) *(swear word)* juron *m*

oatmeal ['əʊtmi:l] *n* (**a**) *(flakes)* flocons *mpl* d'avoine; *(flour)* farine *f* d'avoine; *(porridge)* bouillie *f* d'avoine (**b**) *(color)* beige *m*

oats [əʊts] *npl (plant)* avoine *f*; **(porridge) o.** *(food)* flocons *mpl* d'avoine

OAU [əʊeɪ'ju:] *n (abbr* **Organization of African Unity**) OUA *f*

obdurate ['ɒbdjʊrɪt] *adj* obstiné(e)

obedience [ə'bi:dɪəns] *n* obéissance *f*

obedient [ə'bi:dɪənt] *adj* obéissant(e)

obelisk ['ɒbəlɪsk] *n* obélisque *m*

obese [əʊ'bi:s] *adj* obèse

obesity [əʊ'bi:sɪtɪ] *n* obésité *f*

obey [ə'beɪ] **1** *vt* obéir à
　2 *vi* obéir

obfuscation [ɒbfʌ'skeɪʃən] *n* obscurcissement *m*

obituary [ə'bɪtjʊərɪ] *(pl* **obituaries***) n* nécrologie *f*; **o. column** rubrique *f* nécrologique; **o. notice** nécrologie *f*

object 1 *n* ['ɒbdʒɪkt] (**a**) *(thing, recipient)* objet *m*; **an o. of contempt/desire** un objet de mépris/de désir; **an o. lesson in** un parfait exemple de (**b**) *(aim)* objet *m*, but *m*; **the o. of the exercise is to...** cet exercice a pour objet *ou* but de... (**c**) *(obstacle)* **money/distance is no o.** le prix/la distance importe peu (**d**) *Gram* complément *m* d'objet
　2 *vi* [əb'dʒekt] émettre une objection; **to o. to sth/to doing sth** ne pas être d'accord avec qch/pour faire qch

objectify [əb'dʒektɪfaɪ] *(pt & pp* **objectified***) vt* objectiver

objection [əb'dʒekʃən] *n* (**a**) *(protest)* objection *f*; **to have no o. to sth** ne voir aucune objection à qch; **I have no o. to going** ça ne me dérange pas d'y aller (**b**) *(reason for objecting)* inconvénient *m* (**to** de)

objectionable [əb'dʒekʃənəbəl] *adj (unpleasant)* déplaisant(e)

objective [əb'dʒektɪv] **1** *n (aim, goal)* objectif *m*
　2 *adj (impartial)* objectif(ive)

objectively [əb'dʒektɪvlɪ] *adv* objectivement

objectivity [ɒbdʒek'tɪvɪtɪ] *n* objectivité *f*

obligation [ɒblɪ'geɪʃən] *n* obligation *f*; **to be under an o. to sb** avoir une dette envers qn; **to be under an o. to do sth** être dans l'obligation de faire qch

obligatory [ɒ'blɪgətɒrɪ] *adj* obligatoire

oblige [ə'blaɪdʒ] *vt* (**a**) *(compel)* obliger; **to be obliged to do sth** être obligé(e) de faire qch (**b**) *(do a favor for)* rendre service à (**c**) *(be grateful)* **to be obliged to sb** être reconnaissant(e) à qn; **I'd be obliged if you'd...** ça me rendrait service si vous pouviez...; **much obliged** merci infiniment

obliging [ə'blaɪdʒɪŋ] *adj* serviable; **it was very o. of her** c'était très aimable de sa part

oblique [ə'bli:k] *adj (line, angle)* oblique; *(reference, hint)* indirect(e)

obliterate [ə'blɪtəreɪt] *vt* (**a**) *also Fig (erase)* effacer (**b**) *(destroy)* détruire; *(town)* rayer de la carte

oblivion [ə'blɪvɪən] *n* oubli *m*; **to sink into o.** sombrer dans l'oubli

oblivious [ə'blɪvɪəs] *adj* **to be o. to sth** ne pas avoir conscience de qch

oblong ['ɒblɒŋ] **1** *n* rectangle *m*
　2 *adj* rectangulaire

obnoxious [əb'nɒkʃəs] *adj (person, action)* odieux(euse); *(smell)* repoussant(e)

oboe ['əʊbəʊ] *n* hautbois *m*

oboist ['əʊbəʊɪst] *n* hautboïste *mf*

obscene [əb'si:n] *adj* obscène; *Fig (profits, prices)* scandaleux(euse)

obscenely [əb'si:nlɪ] *adv* d'une manière obscène; *Fig (rich)* scandaleusement

obscenity [əb'senɪtɪ] *(pl* **obscenities***) n* obscénité *f*

obscure [əb'skjʊə(r)] **1** *adj* obscur(e)
　2 *vt* (**a**) *(hide from view)* cacher (**b**) *(make unclear)* obscurcir

obscurity [əb'skjʊərɪtɪ] *n* obscurité *f*; **to fall into o.** tomber dans l'oubli

obsequious [əb'si:kwɪəs] *adj Formal* obséquieux(euse)

observable [əb'zɜ:vəbəl] *adj* observable; *(change, difference)* perceptible

observance [əb'zɜ:vəns] *n (of law, custom)* observation *f*

observant [əb'zɜ:vənt] *adj* observateur(trice)

observation [ɒbzə'veɪʃən] *n* observation *f*; *(by police)* surveillance *f*; **to keep sb under o.** surveiller qn; *(in hospital)* garder qn en observation; **to escape o.** passer inaperçu(e); **to make an o.** faire une observation; *Mil* **o. post** poste *m* d'observation

observatory [əb'zɜ:vətɒrɪ] *(pl* **observatories***) n* observatoire *m*

observe [əb'zɜ:v] *vt* observer

observer [əb'zɜ:və(r)] *n* observateur(trice) *m,f*

obsess [əb'ses] *vt* obséder; **to be obsessed with** *or* **by sb** faire une fixation sur qn; **to be obsessed with** *or* **by sth** être obsédé(e) par qch

obsession [əb'seʃən] *n* obsession *f*; **to become an o.** tourner à l'obsession

obsessive [əb'sesɪv] *adj (person)* à tendances obsessionnelles; *(fear, hatred, behavior)* obsessionnel(elle)

obsessive-compulsive disorder [əb'sesɪvkəm'pʌlsɪv-dɪsɔ:də(r)] *n Psy* névrose *f* obsessionnelle

obsolescence [ɒbsə'lesəns] *n* obsolescence *f*

obsolete ['ɒbsəli:t] *adj* obsolète; *(design, model)* dépassé(e), démodé(e)

obstacle ['ɒbstəkəl] *n* obstacle *m*; **to put obstacles in sb's way** mettre des bâtons dans les roues à qn; *also Fig* **o. course** course *f* d'obstacles

obstetrician [ɒbste'trɪʃən] *n* obstétricien(enne) *m,f*

obstetrics [ɒb'stetrɪks] *n* obstétrique *f*

obstinacy ['ɒbstɪnəsɪ] *n* obstination *f*

obstinate ['ɒbstɪnɪt] *adj* obstiné(e); **to be o. about doing sth** s'obstiner à vouloir faire qch

obstreperous [əb'strepərəs] *adj Formal* tapageur(euse); **to get o. (about sth)** faire un scandale (à propos de qch)

obstruct [əb'strʌkt] *vt* **(a)** *(block) (road, pipe)* obstruer; *(view)* boucher, cacher **(b)** *(hinder)* gêner; *(in sport)* faire obstruction à; *Pol* **to o. a bill** faire de l'obstruction; *Law* **to o. the course of justice** entraver le cours de la justice

obstruction [əb'strʌkʃən] *n* **(a)** *(action) (of street, in sport)* obstruction *f* **(b)** *(blockage) (in road)* encombrement *m*; *(in pipe)* engorgement *m*; *Med* obstruction *f*; **to cause an o.** *(on road)* entraver la circulation

obstructive [əb'strʌktɪv] *adj* **to be o.** faire de l'obstruction

obtain [əb'teɪn] **1** *vt* obtenir

2 *vi Formal (of practice)* avoir cours; *(of rule)* être en vigueur

obtainable [əb'teɪnəbəl] *adj* que l'on peut se procurer; **easily o.** facile à obtenir

obtrusive [əb'tru:sɪv] *adj* *(person, behavior)* importun(e); *(smell)* pénétrant(e)

obtuse [əb'tju:s] *adj* obtus(e)

obverse ['ɒbvɜ:s] **1** *n* **(a)** *(of medal)* avers *m* **(b)** *(opposite)* contraire *m*

2 *adj* **o. side** *(of medal)* avers *m*

obviate ['ɒbvɪeɪt] *vt Formal (difficulty, danger)* parer à

obvious ['ɒbvɪəs] **1** *n* **to state the o.** enfoncer une porte ouverte

2 *adj* évident(e)

obviously ['ɒbvɪəslɪ] *adv* **(a)** *(in an obvious way)* manifestement **(b)** *(of course)* évidemment; **o. not** certainement pas

occasion [ə'keɪʒən] **1** *n* **(a)** *(time)* occasion *f*; **on one o.** une fois; **on several occasions** plusieurs fois, à plusieurs reprises; **on o.** parfois, de temps en temps **(b)** *(event)* occasion *f*, événement *m*; **on the o. of...** à l'occasion de...; **to have a sense of o.** savoir marquer le coup **(c)** *(opportunity)* occasion *f*; **I'd like to take this o. to...** j'aimerais profiter de cette occasion pour... **(d)** *Formal (cause)* sujet *m*, cause *f*; **to have o. for complaint** avoir des raisons de se plaindre; **to have o. to do sth** avoir lieu de faire qch

2 *vt Formal (cause)* occasionner, causer

occasional [ə'keɪʒənəl] *adj* occasionnel(elle); *(showers)* intermittent(e); **I have the o. cigar** il m'arrive de fumer un cigare de temps en temps; **o. table** table *f* d'appoint

occasionally [ə'keɪʒənəlɪ] *adv* occasionnellement, de temps en temps

occidental [ɒksɪ'dentəl] *adj* occidental(e)

occult [ɒ'kʌlt] **1** *n* **the o.** l'occulte *m*

2 *adj* occulte

occupant ['ɒkjupənt] *n (of house, car)* occupant(e) *m,f*; *(of bus, plane)* passager(ère) *m,f*

occupation [ɒkjʊ'peɪʃən] *n* **(a)** *(profession)* métier *m*, profession *f*; *(pastime)* occupation *f* **(b)** *(of house, land)* occupation *f*

occupational [ɒkjʊ'peɪʃənəl] *adj* **o. disease** maladie *f* professionnelle; **o. hazard** risque *m* du métier; **o. therapist** ergothérapeute *mf*; **o. therapy** ergothérapie *f*

occupied ['ɒkjupaɪd] *adj* occupé(e); **to be o. with sth** être occupé à qch; **to keep sb o.** occuper qn

occupier ['ɒkjupaɪə(r)] *n (of house)* occupant(e) *m,f*

occupy ['ɒkjupaɪ] *(pt & pp* **occupied**) *vt (house, attention)* occuper; **to o. one's time (in doing sth)** occuper son temps (à faire qch)

occur [ə'kɜ:(r)] *(pt & pp* **occurred**) *vi* **(a)** *(happen) (of event)* avoir lieu; *(of opportunity)* se présenter; *(of problem)* surgir **(b)** *(be present)* apparaître **(c)** *(of idea)* **to o. to sb** venir à l'esprit de qn

occurrence [ə'kʌrəns] *n* **(a)** *(event)* événement *m* **(b)** *(of disease)* incidence *f*; **to be a regular o.** se produire régulièrement

OCD ['əʊsi:'di:] *n Psy (abbr* **obsessive-compulsive disorder**) névrose *f* obsessionnelle

ocean ['əʊʃən] *n* océan *m*; **the o.** *(the sea)* la mer; *Fam* **oceans of** plein de; *Fig* **o. liner** paquebot *m*

oceanfront ['əʊʃənfrʌnt] **1** *n* bord *m* de mer

2 *adj* au bord de la mer, en bord de mer

ocean-going ['əʊʃəngəʊɪŋ] *adj* de haute mer

Oceania [əʊʃɪ'eɪnɪə] *n* l'Océanie *f*

oceanic [əʊʃɪ'ænɪk] *adj* océanique

ocelot ['ɒsəlɒt] *n* ocelot *m*

ocher ['əʊkə(r)] **1** *n* ocre *m*

2 *adj* ocre *inv*

o'clock [ə'klɒk] *adv* **(it's) one o.** (il est) une heure; **two o.** deux heures

OCR [əʊsi:'ɑ:(r)] *n Comput* **(a)** *(abbr* **optical character reader**) lecteur *m* optique **(b)** *(abbr* **optical character recognition**) ROC *f*

Oct. *(abbr* **October**) octobre

octagon ['ɒktəgən] *n* octogone *m*

octagonal [ɒk'tægənəl] *adj* octogonal(e)

octane ['ɒkteɪn] *n Chem* octane *m*; **o. number** indice *m* d'octane

octave ['ɒktɪv] *n* octave *f*

October [ɒk'təʊbə(r)] *n* octobre *m*; *see also* **May**

octogenarian [ɒktədʒɪ'neərɪən] *n & adj* octogénaire *mf*

octopus ['ɒktəpəs] *n* pieuvre *f*, poulpe *m*

OD [əʊ'di:] *(pt & pp* **OD'd, OD'ed**) *vi Fam (abbr* **overdose**) faire une overdose *(* **on** de); *Fig* **I think I've OD'd a bit on pizzas** je crois que j'y suis allé un peu fort sur les pizzas

odd [ɒd] **1** *adj* **(a)** *(strange)* bizarre, curieux(euse) **(b)** *(number)* impair(e); **to be the o. man out** être à part; **I felt the o. one out** je ne me suis pas senti à ma place **(c)** *(one of a pair)* dépareillé(e) **(d)** *(occasional)* **I smoke the o. cigarette** il m'arrive de fumer une cigarette de temps en temps; **you've made the o. mistake** tu as fait deux ou trois fautes; **o. jobs** petits travaux *mpl*

2 *adv* **a hundred o. sheep** cent et quelques moutons; **she must be thirty o.** elle doit avoir trente ans ou plus

oddball ['ɒdbɔ:l] *n & adj Fam* excentrique *mf*

oddity ['ɒdɪtɪ] *(pl* **oddities**) *n* **(a)** *(strangeness)* bizarrerie *f* **(b)** *(person) (strange)* excentrique *mf*; *(exceptional)* cas *m* à part; *(thing)* curiosité *f*

oddly ['ɒdlɪ] *adv* bizarrement, curieusement; **o. enough,...** chose curieuse,...

oddness ['ɒdnɪs] *n* bizarrerie *f*

odds [ɒdz] *npl* **(a)** *(probability)* chances *fpl*; *(in betting)* cote *f*; **the o. are that...** il y a de grandes chances pour que... + *subjunctive*; **the o. are against her/in her favor** il y a peu de chance(s)/de grosses chances qu'elle réussisse; **against the o.** contre toute attente **(b)** **to be at o. (with sb)** *(of person)* être en désaccord (avec qn); **to be at o. with sth** *(of thing)* contredire qch **(c)** *Fam* **o. and ends** bricoles *fpl*

odds-on [ɒd'zɒn] *adj (horse)* **o. favorite** grand favori *m*; *Fam* **it's o. that...** il y a gros à parier que...

ode [əʊd] *n* ode *f*

odious ['əʊdɪəs] *adj* odieux(euse)

odor ['əʊdə(r)] *n* odeur *f*

odorless ['əʊdəlɪs] *adj* inodore

odyssey ['ɒdɪsɪ] (*pl* **odysseys**) *n* odyssée *f*

OECD [əʊiːsiːˈdiː] *n* (*abbr* **Organization for Economic Co-operation and Development**) OCDE *f*

Oedipal ['iːdɪpəl] *adj* oedipien(enne)

of [ɒv, *unstressed* əv] *prep* (**a**) (*belonging to*) de; **a friend of mine** un de mes amis; **a car of her own** une voiture à elle; **the University of California** l'université de Californie

(**b**) (*with amount, quantity*) **two pints of milk** ≃ un litre de lait; **a bottle of wine** une bouteille de vin; **a year of her life** un an de sa vie; **many of us** beaucoup d'entre nous; **there are six of us** nous sommes six; **hundreds of people** des centaines de gens; **a girl of ten** une fille de dix ans; **you of all people should know that** si quelqu'un doit le savoir, c'est bien toi

(**c**) (*indicating agency*) **it was nice/clever of you to...** c'était gentil/intelligent de ta part de...

(**d**) (*with material*) **made of wood/glass** en bois/verre

(**e**) (*with dates, time*) **the 4th of October** le 4 octobre; **a quarter of one** une heure moins le quart

off [ɒf] **1** *adj* (**a**) (*not functioning*) (*light, TV*) éteint(e); (*water, electricity*) coupé(e); **o. and on, on and o.** (*intermittently*) par intermittence

(**b**) (*canceled*) annulé(e); **the deal is o.** l'affaire ne se fera pas

(**c**) (*absent from work, school*) absent(e)

(**d**) (*unsuccessful*) **I'm having an o. day** c'est un jour sans; **the o. season** (*in tourism*) la morte-saison

(**e**) **to be well/badly o.** être aisé(e)/pauvre; **you'd be better o. staying where you are** tu ferais mieux de rester où tu es

2 *adv* (**a**) (*away*) **two weeks o.** dans deux semaines; **five miles o.** ≃ à huit kilomètres; **to be o.** (*leave*) s'en aller; **I'm o. to London** je pars pour Londres; **o. you go!** allez, file maintenant!

(**b**) (*indicating removal*) **to take o. one's coat** enlever son manteau; **the handle has come o.** la poignée est partie

(**c**) (*with prices*) **20 percent/$5 o.** 20 pour cent/5 dollars de réduction

(**d**) (*away from work, school*) **to have a day/week o.** avoir un jour/une semaine de congé; **to take some time o.** prendre des vacances

3 *prep* (**a**) (*away from*) **o. the coast** au large de la côte; **o. the main road** qui donne dans la rue principale; **o. the record** officieusement

(**b**) (*indicating removal from*) **to fall/to jump o. sth** tomber/sauter de qch; **the handle has come o. the saucepan** la poignée s'est détachée de la casserole

(**c**) (*with prices*) **20 percent/$5 o. the price** 20 pour cent/5 dollars de réduction sur le prix

(**d**) (*absent from*) **to be o. work/school** être absent(e) de son travail/de l'école

offal ['ɒfəl] *n* abats *mpl*

offbeat ['ɒfbiːt] *adj Fam* original(e)

off-chance ['ɒftʃɑːns] *n* **on the o.** à tout hasard; **on the o. that...** en espérant que...

off-color [ɒf'kʌlə(r)] *adj* (**a**) (*joke*) d'un goût douteux (**b**) (*unwell*) **to be o.** ne pas se sentir dans son assiette

off-duty ['ɒf'djuːtɪ] *adj* qui n'est pas de service

offend [ə'fend] **1** *vt* (*of person, remark*) vexer; (*of book, film*) choquer; **to be offended at** *or* **by sth** mal prendre qch

2 *vi Law* commettre une infraction; (*more serious*) commettre un délit; **to o. against good taste** être une insulte au bon goût

offended [ə'fendɪd] *adj* vexé(e)

offender [ə'fendə(r)] *n Law* délinquant(e) *m,f*

offending [ə'fendɪŋ] *adj* fautif(ive)

offense [ə'fens] *n* (**a**) *Law* infraction *f*; (*more serious*) délit *m*

(**b**) (*displeasure*) **to cause sb o.** (*of person, remark*) vexer qn;

(*of film, book*) choquer qn; **to take o.** se vexer; **to take o. at sth** mal prendre qch; **no o., but...** ne le prends pas mal, mais...

offensive [ə'fensɪv] **1** *n also Fig* offensive *f*; **to be on/to take the o.** être passé(e)/passer à l'attaque

2 *adj* choquant(e); (*smell*) repoussant(e); **to be o. to sb** se montrer blessant(e) envers qn; **o. weapon** arme *f* offensive

offer ['ɒfə(r)] **1** *n* offre *f*, proposition *f*; **to make sb an o.** faire une offre *ou* une proposition à qn; **on special o.** en promotion; **o. of marriage** demande *f* en mariage

2 *vt* offrir; (*explanation*) donner; (*apologies*) présenter; **to o. sb sth, to o. sth to sb** offrir qch à qn; **to o. to do sth** offrir *ou* proposer de faire qch

▸**offer up** *vt sep* offrir

offering ['ɒfərɪŋ] *n* offre *f*; (*in church*) offrande *f*

offhand [ɒf'hænd] **1** *adj* (*nonchalant*) désinvolte; (*abrupt*) brusque, abrupt(e)

2 *adv* (*immediately*) au pied levé; (*at a rough guess*) à première vue

office ['ɒfɪs] *n* (**a**) (*place*) bureau *m*; **o. boy** garçon *m* de bureau; **o. building** immeuble *m* de bureaux; **o. hours** heures *fpl* de bureau; **o. manager** chef *m* de bureau; **o. worker** employé(e) *m,f* de bureau (**b**) (*position*) charge *f*, fonctions *fpl*; **to hold o.** être au pouvoir; **to be out of o.** ne plus être au pouvoir; **to run for** *or* **to seek o.** se présenter aux élections

officeholder ['ɒfɪshəʊldə(r)] *n* responsable *mf*

officer ['ɒfɪsə(r)] *n* (*in army*) officier *m*; (*in police*) agent *m* de police; (*in local government*) fonctionnaire *mf* municipal(e)

official [ə'fɪʃəl] **1** *n* (*in public sector*) fonctionnaire *mf*; (*of political party*) responsable *mf*

2 *adj* officiel(elle)

officialdom [ə'fɪʃəldəm] *n Pej* bureaucratie *f*

officialese [əfɪʃə'liːz] *n Pej* jargon *m* administratif

officially [ə'fɪʃəlɪ] *adv* officiellement

officiate [ə'fɪʃɪeɪt] *vi Rel* officier

officious [ə'fɪʃəs] *adj* trop zélé(e)

officiously [ə'fɪʃəslɪ] *adv* avec trop de zèle

offing ['ɒfɪŋ] *n* **in the o.** en perspective, en vue

off-key [ɒf'kiː] **1** *adj* faux (fausse); *Fig* (*remark*) déplacé(e)

2 *adv* faux

off-line, offline ['ɒflaɪn] *adj Comput* (*processing*) en différé; (*printer*) déconnecté(e)

off-load [ɒf'ləʊd] *vt* (*surplus goods*) écouler; **to o. sth onto sb** (*task*) se décharger de qch sur qn; (*blame, responsibility*) rejeter qch sur qn

off-peak ['ɒf'piːk] *adj* (*electricity*) consommé(e) pendant les heures creuses; (*vacation*) en basse saison; (*telephone call, travel*) en dehors des heures de pointe

offprint ['ɒfprɪnt] *n Typ* tirage *m* à part

off-putting ['ɒfpʊtɪŋ] *adj* peu engageant(e)

off-season ['ɒfsiːzən] *adj* hors saison, en basse saison

offset ['ɒfset] **1** *n Typ* offset *m*

2 *vt* (*pt & pp* **offset**) compenser

offshoot ['ɒfʃʊt] *n* (*of tree*) rejeton *m*; (*of family*) branche *f*; (*of political party, artistic movement*) ramification *f*

offshore 1 *adj* ['ɒfʃɔː(r)] (*island*) proche de la côte; (*oil rig*) offshore *inv*; *Fin* **o. investment** placement *m* offshore *ou* extraterritorial

2 *adv* [ɒf'ʃɔː(r)] au large, en mer

offside [ɒf'saɪd] *adj* (*in sports*) hors jeu

offspring ['ɒfsprɪŋ] *n* progéniture *f*

offstage [ɒf'steɪdʒ] *adj & adv* dans les coulisses

off-the-cuff [ɒfðə'kʌf] **1** *adj* impromptu(e)

2 *adv* au pied levé

off-the-record [ɒfðə'rekɔːd] *adj* officieux(euse)

off-the-wall [ɒfðə'wɔːl] *adj Fam* loufoque

off-white ['ɒf'waɪt] **1** *n* blanc *m* cassé

2 *adj* blanc cassé *inv*

often ['ɒfən, 'ɒftən] *adv* souvent; **how o.?** *(how many times?)* combien de fois?; *(how frequently?)* tous les combien?; **as o. as not** très souvent; **more o. than not** le plus souvent; **every so o.** de temps en temps, de temps à autre

ogle ['əʊɡəl] *vt* lorgner, reluquer

ogre ['əʊɡə(r)] *n* ogre *m*

ogress ['əʊɡrɪs] *n* ogresse *f*

oh [əʊ] *exclam* oh!

ohm [əʊm] *n* ohm *m*

oho [əʊ'həʊ] *exclam* ah ah!

OHP [əʊeɪtʃ'pi:] *n* (*abbr* **overhead projector**) rétroprojecteur *m*

oil [ɔɪl] **1** *n (for cooking, lubricating)* huile *f*; *(petroleum)* pétrole *m*; *(for heating)* mazout *m*; *Fig* **to pour o. on troubled waters** apaiser les esprits; **o. company** compagnie *f* pétrolière; **o. crisis** choc *m* pétrolier; **o. drum** bidon *m* à pétrole; **o. lamp** lampe *f* à pétrole; **o. painting** peinture *f* à l'huile; *Fig Hum* **she's no o. painting** ce n'est pas une beauté; **o. refinery** raffinerie *f* de pétrole; **o. rig** *(on land)* derrick *m*; *(offshore)* plateforme *f* pétrolière *ou* de forage; **o. slick** *(on sea)* nappe *f* de pétrole; *(on shore)* marée *f* noire; **o. spill** *(event)* marée *f* noire; *(result)* nappe *f* de pétrole; **o. tanker** pétrolier *m*; **o. well** puits *m* de pétrole
2 *vt* huiler, lubrifier; *Fig* **to o. the wheels** faciliter les choses

oilcan ['ɔɪlkæn] *n (for applying oil)* burette *f*; *(large container)* bidon *m* à huile

oilfield ['ɔɪlfi:ld] *n* gisement *m* de pétrole

oil-fired ['ɔɪlfaɪəd] *adj (heating)* au mazout

oilskin ['ɔɪlskɪn] *n (fabric)* toile *f* cirée; **oilskins** *(garment)* ciré *m*

oily ['ɔɪlɪ] *adj* **(a)** *(hands, rag)* graisseux(euse); *(skin, hair)* gras (grasse); *(food)* huileux(euse) **(b)** *Pej (manner)* onctueux(euse)

oink [ɔɪŋk] *vi* grogner

ointment ['ɔɪntmənt] *n* pommade *f*

OK, okay ['əʊ'keɪ] *Fam* **1** *adj (in order)* correct(e), exact(e); *(acceptable)* pas mal; **that's OK by** *or* **with me** ça me va; **is it OK to wear jeans?** ça va si on vient en jean?; **no, it is** NOT **OK** (il n'en est) pas question; **she was OK about it** elle n'a pas fait d'histoires; **he's an OK sort of guy** c'est un type plutôt bien; **are we OK for time?** est-ce qu'on a assez de temps?
2 *exclam* OK!; **OK, OK! I'll do it now** OK, ça va, je vais le faire
3 *n* **to give (sb) the OK** donner le feu vert (à qn)
4 *vt (pt & pp* **OK'd** *or* **okayed**) donner le feu vert à

okra ['ɒkrə] *n* gombo *m*, okra *m*

old [əʊld] **1** *adj* **(a)** *(aged) (person)* vieux (vieille), âgé(e); *(car)* vieux; **to grow** *or* **to get older** vieillir; **o. people** personnes *fpl* âgées; **o. people's home** maison *f* de retraite; **o. age** vieillesse *f*; **to go over o. ground** revenir sur des choses qui ont déjà été dites; **to be an o. hand at sth** être rompu(e) à qch; **o. maid** vieille fille *f*; **to be o. hat** être démodé(e); *Fig* **to be one of the o. school** être de la vieille école; **the O. Testament** l'Ancien Testament *m*; **o. wives' tale** conte *m* de bonne femme
(b) *(with specific age)* **how o. are you?** quel âge avez-vous?; **to be five years o.** avoir cinq ans; **when you're older** *(to child)* quand tu seras plus grand; **at six years o.** à (l'âge de) six ans; **a two-year-o. (child)** un enfant (âgé) de deux ans; **you're o. enough to do that yourself** tu es assez grand pour le faire toi-même
(c) *(former)* ancien(enne); **in the o. days** autrefois; **o. boy/girl** *(of school)* ancien(enne) élève *mf*; **the o. boy network** = la franc-maçonnerie des écoles privées et des universités; **an o. flame** un(e) ancien(enne) amoureux(euse)
(d) *(longstanding)* **an o. friend** un(e) vieil (vieille) ami(e); **o. habits die hard** il n'est pas facile de se défaire de ses habitudes
(e) *Fam (intensifier)* **any o. how** n'importe comment; **any o. thing** n'importe quoi

(f) *Fam (affectionate)* **o. Fred** ce vieux Fred; **the poor o. thing** le (la) pauvre vieux (vieille); **my** *or* **the o. man** *(father)* le pater; *(husband)* mon homme; **my** *or* **the o. woman** *(mother)* la mater; *(wife)* la bourgeoise
2 *npl* **the o.** les personnes *fpl* âgées

old-fashioned [əʊld'fæʃənd] *adj* **(a)** *(outdated)* démodé(e); *(person)* vieux jeu *inv* **(b)** *(traditional)* à l'ancienne

old-timer [əʊld'taɪmə(r)] *n Fam* **(a)** *(experienced person)* ancien(enne) *m,f* **(b)** *(form of address)* vieux *m*

old-world ['əʊld'wɜːld] *adj (atmosphere, elegance)* suranné(e); *(furnishings)* à l'ancienne

oleander [əʊlɪ'ændə(r)] *n* laurier-rose *m*

olfactory [ɒl'fæktərɪ] *adj* olfactif(ive)

oligarchy ['ɒlɪɡɑːkɪ] *(pl* **oligarchies**) *n* oligarchie *f*

olive ['ɒlɪv] **1** *n* olive *f*; *Fig* **to hold out the o. branch** proposer la paix; **o. grove** oliveraie *f*; **o. oil** huile *f* d'olive; **o. tree** olivier *m*
2 *adj (skin)* olivâtre; **o. (green)** *(vert)* olive *inv*

Olympic [ə'lɪmpɪk] **1** *n* **the Olympics** les Jeux *mpl* olympiques
2 *adj* olympique; **the O. Games** les Jeux *mpl* olympiques

Oman [əʊ'mæn] *n* Oman

Omani [əʊ'mænɪ] **1** *n* Omanais(e) *m,f*
2 *adj* omanais(e)

ombudsman ['ɒmbʊdzmən] *n* ≃ médiateur *m* de la République

omelet ['ɒmlɪt] *n* omelette *f*; **ham o.** omelette au jambon

omen ['əʊmən] *n* présage *m*, augure *m*

ominous ['ɒmɪnəs] *adj* inquiétant(e); *(event)* de mauvais augure; **an o.-looking sky** un ciel menaçant; **an emergency meeting? – that sounds o.** une réunion d'urgence? – ça ne présage rien de bon

ominously ['ɒmɪnəslɪ] *adv* **she spoke o.** ce qu'elle a dit ne présage rien de bon; **it was o. quiet** il régnait un silence inquiétant

omission [əʊ'mɪʃən] *n* omission *f*

omit [əʊ'mɪt] *(pt & pp* **omitted**) *vt* omettre; **to o. to do sth** omettre de faire qch

omnibus ['ɒmnɪbəs] **1** *n* **(a)** *(book)* recueil *m* **(b)** *Old-fashioned (bus)* omnibus *m*
2 *adj* **o. edition** *(of stories, poems)* recueil *m*

omnipotence [ɒm'nɪpətəns] *n* omnipotence *f*, toute-puissance *f*

omnipotent [ɒm'nɪpətənt] *adj* omnipotent(e), tout-puissant (toute-puissante)

omnipresent [ɒmnɪ'prezənt] *adj* omniprésent(e)

omniscient [ɒm'nɪsɪənt] *adj* omniscient(e)

omnivorous [ɒm'nɪvərəs] *adj* omnivore; *Fig (reader)* qui lit de tout

on [ɒn] **1** *adv* **(a)** *(in operation) (light, television)* allumé(e); *(engine)* en marche; **the "on" position** la position marche
(b) *(taking place)* **what's on?** *(on TV)* qu'est-ce qu'il y a à la télé?; *(at movies)* qu'est-ce qui passe au cinéma?; **is the meeting still on?** la réunion doit-elle toujours avoir lieu?; **I've got a lot on** j'ai beaucoup de choses à faire; **on and off, off and on** *(intermittently)* par intermittence
(c) *(on duty) (in hospital, consultation)* de garde; *(in store)* de service
(d) *(with clothing)* **to have sth on** porter qch; **to put sth on** mettre qch; **to have nothing on** être nu(e)
(e) *(in time)* **earlier on** plus tôt; **later on** plus tard; **from that day on** à dater *ou* à partir de ce jour
(f) *(expressing continuation)* **to read/talk/work on** continuer à lire/bavarder/travailler; **he went on and on about it** il n'en finissait pas
2 *prep* **(a)** *(expressing position)* sur; **on the table** sur la table; **on the second floor** au deuxième étage; **on the wall** sur le

mur; *(hanging)* au mur; **on page four** à la page quatre; **on the right/left** à droite/gauche; **on foot** à pied; **on horseback** à cheval; **on (the) television** à la télévision; **to be on a committee** faire partie d'un comité; **I don't have any money on me** je n'ai pas d'argent sur moi

(b) *(with time)* **on the 15th** le 15; **on Sunday** dimanche; **on the hour** à l'heure pile; **on that occasion** à cette occasion

(c) *(about)* sur; **a book on France** un livre sur la France; *Fam* **the police have nothing on him** la police n'a rien sur lui

(d) *(introducing a gerund)* **on completing the test, you should...** une fois l'examen terminé, les candidats devront...; **on discovering the corpse, she screamed** elle hurla lorsqu'elle découvrit le corps

(e) *(expressing use, support)* **to live on $200 a week** vivre avec 200 dollars par semaine; **the drinks are on me** c'est ma tournée; **to be on antibiotics** prendre des antibiotiques; **to be on drugs** se droguer

once [wʌns] **1** *adv* **(a)** *(on one occasion)* une fois; **not o.** jamais; **o. a week** une fois par semaine; **o. or twice** une ou deux fois, une fois ou deux; **o. in a while** une fois de temps en temps; **o. more, o. again** encore une fois; **o. too often** une fois de trop; **o. and for all** une fois pour toutes; **a o.-in-a-lifetime opportunity** une occasion qui ne se présente qu'une fois **(b)** *(formerly)* autrefois; **o. upon a time there was a princess** il était une fois une princesse **(c) at o.** *(immediately)* immédiatement, tout de suite; *(at the same time)* à la fois, en même temps

2 *conj* **o. he reached home, he collapsed** une fois arrivé chez lui, il s'effondra; **o. he finishes, we can leave** une fois qu'il aura terminé, nous pourrons partir

once-over ['wʌnsəʊvə(r)] *n Fam* **to give sb/sth the o.** jeter un coup d'œil à qn/qch

oncoming ['ɒnkʌmɪŋ] *adj (traffic)* venant en sens inverse

one [wʌn] **1** *n (number)* un (une) *m,f;* **in ones and twos** par petits groupes; *Fam* **to get o. up on sb** prendre l'avantage sur qn

2 *pron* **(a)** *(identifying)* **this o.** celui-ci (celle-ci); **that o.** celui-là (celle-là); **these ones** ceux-ci (celles-ci); **those ones** ceux-là (celles-là); **which o. do you want?** lequel veux-tu?; **the o. I told you about** celui dont je t'ai parlé; **the big o.** le (la) grand(e); **the ones with the long sleeves** ceux qui ont les manches longues; **that's a difficult o.!** *(question)* c'est une question difficile!

(b) *(indefinite)* un (une); **have you got o.?** tu en as un?; **any o. of us** n'importe lequel d'entre nous; **o. of my friends** un de mes amis; **she's o. of the family** elle fait partie de la famille; **o. of these days** un de ces jours; **it was just o. of those things** on n'y peut rien; **o. after the other** l'un après l'autre; **o. at a time** un à la fois; **o. by o.** un par un; **to have had o. too many** *(drinks)* avoir bu un coup de trop

(c) *(particular person)* **to act like o. possessed** se conduire comme un (une) possédé(e); **I, for o., do not believe it** quant à moi, je n'y crois pas; **I'm not o. to complain** je ne suis pas du genre à me plaindre; **she's not a great o. for parties** les soirées, ce n'est pas son fort

(d) *(people in general) (subject)* on; *(object)* vous; **o. never knows** on ne sait jamais; **it can make o. unhappy** cela peut vous rendre malheureux; **to do o.'s best** faire de son mieux

3 *adj* **(a)** *(number)* un (une); **page/number o.** page/numéro un; **o. o'clock** une heure; **to be o. (year old)** avoir un an; **o. day/evening** un jour/soir; **o. or two people** une ou deux personnes; **for o. thing...** d'abord...; **o. American in two thinks that...** un Américain sur deux pense que...

(b) *(single)* un (une) seul(e); **I have just o. thing to say** je n'ai qu'une seule chose à dire; **my o. regret** mon seul regret; **the o. person who...** la seule personne qui...; **my o. and only suit** mon seul et unique costume

(c) *(same)* le même (la même); **they all live in the o. house** ils habitent dans la même maison; **they are o. and the same thing/person** ils ne font qu'un; *Fam* **it's all o. to me** ça m'est égal

one-armed ['wʌnɑːmd] *adj (person)* manchot(e); **o. bandit** *(machine)* machine *f* à sous

one-eyed ['wʌnaɪd] *adj* borgne

one-horse town ['wʌnhɔːs'taʊn] *n Fam* trou *m* perdu

one-legged [wʌn'legɪd] *adj* unijambiste

one-liner [wʌn'laɪnə(r)] *n Fam* bon mot *m*

one-man ['wʌnmæn] *adj (job)* pour un seul homme; **o. band** homme-orchestre *m;* **o. show** *(by performer)* spectacle *m* solo, one-man-show *m inv;* *(by artist)* exposition *f* individuelle

one-night stand ['wʌnnaɪt'stænd] *n Fam (sexual encounter)* rencontre *f* sans lendemain *ou* d'un soir

one-off [wʌn'ɒf] *Fam* **1** *n (object)* objet *m* unique; *(event)* événement *m* unique; **it was a o.** *(mistake, success)* ça ne se reproduira pas

2 *adj* unique

one-on-one ['wʌnɒn'wʌn] **1** *adj (talk, meeting)* seul à seul, en tête-à-tête; **o. tuition** cours *mpl* particuliers

2 *adv Sport* **he was o. with the goalkeeper** il était seul face au gardien de but

one-parent family ['wʌnpeərənt'fæmɪlɪ] *n* famille *f* monoparentale

one-party [wʌn'pɑːtɪ] *adj* à parti unique

one-piece swimsuit ['wʌnpiːs'swɪmsuːt] *n* maillot *m* de bain une pièce

onerous ['əʊnərəs] *adj Formal* lourd(e)

oneself [wʌn'self] *pron* **(a)** *(reflexive)* se; **to look after o.** *(when ill)* se soigner; *(generally)* s'occuper de soi; **to feel o. again** se sentir complètement rétabli(e) **(b)** *(emphatic)* soi-même; **to do sth all by o.** faire qch tout(e) seul(e); **to see for o.** regarder soi-même

one-sided [wʌn'saɪdɪd] *adj* **(a)** *(unequal) (contest)* inégal(e); *(relationship)* à sens unique **(b)** *(biased)* partial(e)

one-time [wʌntaɪm] *adj* ancien(enne)

one-track ['wʌntræk] *adj* **to have a o. mind** *(be obsessed with one thing)* avoir une idée fixe; *(be obsessed with sex)* être obsédé(e), ne penser qu'à ça

one-upmanship [wʌn'ʌpmənʃɪp] *n Fam* ≃ tendance à s'affirmer supérieur aux autres

one-way ['wʌnweɪ] *adj (street, traffic)* à sens unique; **o. ticket** aller *m* (simple)

ongoing ['ɒngəʊɪŋ] *adj* en cours; *(situation, problem)* qui dure

onion ['ʌnjən] *n* oignon *m*

online, on-line [ɒn'laɪn] *adj & adv Comput* en ligne; **o. bank** banque *f* en ligne; **o. banking** transactions *fpl* bancaires en ligne; **o. dating** rencontres *fpl* en ligne; **o. dating agency** agence *f* de rencontres en ligne; **o. help** aide *f* en ligne; **o. shopping** achats *mpl* par Internet

onlooker ['ɒnlʊkə(r)] *n* spectateur(trice) *m,f;* *(at accident)* badaud *m*

only ['əʊnlɪ] **1** *adj* seul(e), unique; **o. child** *(boy)* fils *m* unique; *(girl)* fille *f* unique; **you're not the o. one** tu n'es pas le seul

2 *adv* seulement, ne... que; **I was o. joking** c'était (uniquement) pour rire; **permit holders o.** *(sign)* stationnement réservé; **o. an expert could advise us** seul un expert pourrait nous conseiller; **I o. touched it** je n'ai fait que le toucher; **I shall be o. too pleased to come** je serais ravi de venir; **if o. they knew!, if they o. knew!** s'ils savaient!; **not o...., but also...** non seulement..., mais encore...; **I saw her o. yesterday** je l'ai vue pas plus tard qu'hier; **o. just** de justesse; **it's o. me** ce n'est que moi

3 *conj* mais

on-off switch ['ɒn'ɒfswɪtʃ] *n* interrupteur *m* marche-arrêt

onomatopoeic [ɒnəmætə'piːɪk] *adj* onomatopéique

onrush ['ɒnrʌʃ] *n (of emotions)* vague *f;* *(of people)* ruée *f*

onset ['ɒnset] *n* début *m*, commencement *m*

on-site ['ɒnsaɪt] *adj & adv* sur place

onslaught ['ɒnslɔːt] *n* assaut *m*, attaque *f* (**on** contre)

onto ['ɒntʊ, *unstressed* 'ɒntə] *prep* (**a**) *(with direction)* sur (**b**) *(idioms)* **to be o. sb** être sur la piste de qn; **to be o. a good thing** avoir tiré le gros lot

onus ['əʊnəs] *n* responsabilité *f*, obligation *f*; **the o. is on the government to resolve the problem** il incombe au gouvernement de résoudre ce problème; *Law* **o. of proof** charge *f* de la preuve

onward ['ɒnwəd] **1** *adj* en avant

2 *adv* **from tomorrow o.** à partir de demain; **from now o.** désormais, dorénavant; **from then o.** à partir de ce moment-là

onwards ['ɒnwədz] *adv* = **onward**

onyx ['ɒnɪks] *n* onyx *m*

oodles ['uːdəlz] *npl Fam* **o. of** des tonnes de; **to have o. of time** avoir largement le temps

oomph [ʊmf] *n Fam (energy)* punch *m*; **to have plenty of o.** avoir du punch

oops [uːps] *exclam* houp là!

ooze [uːz] **1** *n* (**a**) *(mud)* vase *f* (**b**) *(flow)* suintement *m*

2 *vt (liquid)* laisser suinter; *Fig (confidence)* déborder de; **to o. charm** avoir un charme fou

3 *vi (of liquid)* suinter (**from** de); *Fig* **to o. with confidence** déborder d'assurance

op [ɒp] *n Fam (medical operation)* opération *f*

opal ['əʊpəl] *n* opale *f*

opaque [əʊ'peɪk] *adj* opaque; *Fig (difficult to understand)* obscur(e)

OPEC ['əʊpek] *n (abbr* **Organization of Petroleum-Exporting Countries***)* OPEP *f*

open ['əʊpən] **1** *n* (**a**) **in the o.** *(outside)* dehors; *(not hidden)* sur la place publique; **to bring sth out into the o.** étaler qch au grand jour; **to come out into the o. about sth** révéler qch (**b**) *(sporting competition)* open *m*

2 *adj* (**a**) *(not shut)* ouvert(e); **o. to the public** ouvert au public; **o. late** ouvert en nocturne; **to be o. to sb/sth** *(accessible to)* être ouvert à qn/qch; **to be o. to doubt** être sujet(ette) à caution; **to be o. to ridicule** s'exposer à être ridiculisé(e); **to be o. to suggestions** être ouvert à toute suggestion; **in the o. air** au grand air; **to welcome sb with o. arms** accueillir qn à bras ouverts; **o. country** rase campagne *f*; *Law* **in o. court** en audience publique; **o. house** journée *f* portes ouvertes; **o. invitation** invitation *f* permanente; *Fig (to thieves)* invitation; **o. letter** lettre *f* ouverte; *Econ* **o. market** marché *m* libre; **to keep an o. mind (on sth)** réserver son jugement (sur qch); **o. prison** prison *f* ouverte; **o. sandwich** canapé *m*; **the o. sea** le large, la haute mer; **o. season** *(for hunting)* saison *f* de la chasse; *Fig* **to declare o. season on sb/sth** partir en guerre contre qn/qch; **o. spaces** *(parks)* espaces *mpl* verts; **o. ticket** billet *m* open; **o. wound** plaie *f* béante

(**b**) *(person, manner)* ouvert(e), franc (franche); *(conflict)* ouvert; **to be o. with sb** être franc avec qn; **to be o. about sth** être franc sur qch; **o. letter** *(in newspaper)* lettre *f* ouverte; **o. secret** secret *m* de Polichinelle

3 *adv* **to cut/to break sth o.** couper/casser qch; **the door flew o.** la porte s'ouvrit brusquement

4 *vt* ouvrir; *(legs, arms)* écarter; *(negotiations, conversation)* entamer; **to o. fire (on sb)** ouvrir le feu (sur qn); **to o. one's heart to sb** ouvrir son cœur à qn, s'ouvrir à qn

5 *vi (of door, window, flower)* s'ouvrir; *(of store, bank)* ouvrir; *(of movie)* sortir; *(of meeting, negotiations)* commencer; **to o. late** *(of store)* ouvrir en nocturne; **to o. onto sth** donner sur qch; **the play opens with a death scene** la pièce s'ouvre sur une scène de mort

▸**open out 1** *vt sep (paper, map)* ouvrir, déplier

2 *vi (of flower)* s'ouvrir; *(of wings)* se déployer; *(of view)* s'étendre; *(of road, valley)* s'élargir

▸**open up 1** *vt sep (store, business, area)* ouvrir (**to** à); *(possibility, opportunity)* offrir

2 *vi (of storekeeper, new store)* ouvrir; *(of flower)* s'ouvrir; *Fig (of person)* s'ouvrir, s'épancher

open-air [əʊpə'neə(r)] *adj (restaurant, market)* en plein air; *(swimming pool)* découvert(e)

open-and-shut case [əʊpənən'ʃʌt'keɪs] *n* **to be an o.** ne pas faire l'ombre d'un doute

open-door policy ['əʊpən'dɔːpɒlɪsɪ] *n (for immigrants)* politique *f* d'ouverture des frontières; *(for university)* politique non sélective

open-ended ['əʊpən'endɪd] *adj (contract)* à durée indéterminée; *(question)* ouvert(e); *(discussion)* sans cadre strict

open-heart surgery ['əʊpən'hɑːt'sɜːdʒərɪ] *n* opération *f* à cœur ouvert

opening ['əʊpənɪŋ] **1** *n* (**a**) *(of play, new era)* commencement *m*; *(of negotiations, Congress)* ouverture *f* (**b**) *(gap)* ouverture *f*, trou *m* (**c**) *(of cave, tunnel)* entrée *f* (**d**) *(opportunity)* occasion *f* favorable; *(job)* débouché *m*

2 *adj* **o. address** *or* **speech** *(in court case)* déclaration *f* préliminaire; **o. ceremony** cérémonie *f* d'ouverture, inauguration *f*; **o. gambit** *(in chess)* gambit *m*; *(in conversation, negotiation)* manœuvre *f* d'approche; **o. hours** heures *fpl* d'ouverture; *Theat* **o. night** première *f*

openly ['əʊpənlɪ] *adv* ouvertement; **she wept o.** elle a pleuré sans retenue

open-minded [əʊpən'maɪndɪd] *adj* **to be o.** avoir l'esprit ouvert

open-mouthed [əʊpən'maʊðd] *adj & adv* bouche bée *inv*

openness ['əʊpənnɪs] *n* franchise *f*

open-plan ['əʊpənplæn] *adj (office)* paysager(ère); *(house)* sans cloisons; **o. kitchen** coin-cuisine *m*

opera ['ɒpərə] *n* opéra *m*; **o. glasses** jumelles *fpl* de théâtre; **o. house** opéra; **o. singer** chanteur(euse) *m,f* d'opéra

operable ['ɒpərəbəl] *adj* opérable

operate ['ɒpəreɪt] **1** *vt (machine)* faire fonctionner; *(bus service)* assurer; **to be operated by electricity** fonctionner à l'électricité

2 *vi* (**a**) *(of machine)* fonctionner; *(of company)* opérer, travailler (**b**) *(of surgeon)* opérer; **to o. on sb (for)** opérer qn (de); **to be operated on** se faire opérer

operatic [ɒpə'rætɪk] *adj* d'opéra

operating ['ɒpəreɪtɪŋ] *adj* **o. costs** coûts *mpl ou* frais *mpl* d'exploitation; *Comput* **o. system** système *m* d'exploitation; **o. table** table *f* d'opération; **o. room** salle *f* d'opération

operation [ɒpə'reɪʃən] *n* (**a**) *(of machine)* fonctionnement *m*; **to be in o.** *(of machine)* être en service; *(of law)* être en vigueur; **to come into o.** *(of law)* entrer en vigueur (**b**) *(process)* opération *f* (**c**) *(of company)* activité *f* (**d**) *(military, surgical)* opération *f*; **to have an o. (for sth)** se faire opérer (de qch); *Mil* **operations room** salle *f* d'opérations *(d'un état-major)*

operational [ɒpə'reɪʃənəl] *adj (system, factory)* opérationnel(elle)

operative ['ɒpərətɪv] **1** *n (manual worker)* ouvrier(ère) *m,f*; *(of machine)* opérateur(trice) *m,f*; *(spy)* agent *m*

2 *adj (law, rule)* en vigueur; **to become o.** entrer en vigueur; **the o. word** le mot-clé

operator ['ɒpəreɪtə(r)] *n* (**a**) *(of machine)* opérateur(trice) *m,f* (**b**) *Tel* opérateur(trice) *m,f*; **(switchboard) o.** standardiste *mf* (**c**) *Fam* **a smooth o.** un petit finaud

operetta [ɒpə'retə] *n* opérette *f*

ophthalmology [ɒfθæl'mɒlədʒɪ] *n* ophtalmologie *f*

opinion [ə'pɪnjən] *n* opinion *f*; **in my o.** à mon avis; **to be of the o. that...** être d'avis *ou* estimer que...; **to ask sb's o.** demander l'avis *ou* l'opinion de qn; **to form an o. of sb/sth** se faire une opinion sur qn/qch; **to have a high/low o. of sb** avoir une haute/mauvaise opinion de qn; **o. poll** sondage *m* (d'opinion)

opinionated [ə'pɪnjəneɪtɪd] *adj* dogmatique

opium ['əʊpɪəm] *n* opium *m*; **o. addict** opiomane *mf*; **o. den** fumerie *f* d'opium

opossum [ɒ'pɒsəm] *n* opossum *m*

opp. (*abbr* **opposite**) ci-contre

opponent [ə'pəʊnənt] *n* adversaire *mf*; (*of government*) opposant(e) *m,f* (**of** à)

opportune ['ɒpətjuːn] *adj* opportun(e)

opportunism [ɒpə'tjuːnɪzəm] *n* opportunisme *m*

opportunist [ɒpə'tjuːnɪst] *n & adj* opportuniste *mf*

opportunity [ɒpə'tjuːnɪtɪ] (*pl* **opportunities**) *n* occasion *f*; **to have the o. of doing** *or* **to do sth** avoir l'occasion de faire qch; **at every o.** à la moindre occasion; **at the first** *or* **earliest o.** à la première occasion; **if you get an o.** si tu en as l'occasion; **the o. of a lifetime** la chance de sa/ta/*etc.* vie; **a job with opportunities** un emploi qui offre des perspectives

oppose [ə'pəʊz] *vt* s'opposer à; **to be opposed to sth** être opposé(e) à qch; **as opposed to...** par opposition à...

opposing [ə'pəʊzɪŋ] *adj* (*characters, viewpoints*) opposé(e); (*armies*) ennemi(e); (*team*) adverse

opposite ['ɒpəzɪt] **1** *n* **the o.** le contraire
   2 *adj* (**a**) (*side, shore*) opposé(e); (*page*) d'en face; **on the o. side of the street** de l'autre côté de la rue (**b**) (*opinion*) contraire; **in the o. direction** en sens inverse, dans le sens opposé; **the o. sex** l'autre sexe
   3 *adv* en face; **the house o.** la maison d'en face
   4 *prep* en face de

opposition [ɒpə'zɪʃən] *n* (**a**) (*resistance*) opposition *f* (**to** à); **to meet with o.** (*of idea, plan*) être contesté(e) (**b**) (*contrast*) **in o. to** contre (**c**) (*opponents*) **the o.** le camp adverse

oppress [ə'pres] *vt* opprimer

oppressed [ə'prest] **1** *npl* **the o.** les opprimés *mpl*
   2 *adj* opprimé(e)

oppression [ə'preʃən] *n* oppression *f*

oppressive [ə'presɪv] *adj* (**a**) (*law, regime*) oppressif(ive) (**b**) (*atmosphere, heat*) oppressant(e), étouffant(e)

opt [ɒpt] **1** *vt* **to o. to do sth** choisir de faire qch
   2 *vi* **to o. for sth** opter pour qch
▸**opt in** *vi* choisir de participer
▸**opt out** *vi* se désengager

optic ['ɒptɪk] *adj* optique; **o. nerve** nerf *m* optique

optical ['ɒptɪkəl] *adj* optique; (*instrument*) d'optique; *Comput* **o. character reader** lecteur *m* optique de caractères; *Comput* **o. character recognition** reconnaissance *f* optique de caractères; *Comput* **o. disk** disque *m* optique; **o. fiber** fibre *f* optique; **o. illusion** illusion *f* d'optique

optician [ɒp'tɪʃən] *n* (*prescribing*) ophtalmologue *mf*; (*dispensing*) opticien(enne) *m,f*

optics ['ɒptɪks] *n* optique *f*

optimism ['ɒptɪmɪzəm] *n* optimisme *m*

optimist ['ɒptɪmɪst] *n* optimiste *mf*

optimistic [ɒptɪ'mɪstɪk] *adj* optimiste (**about** quant à)

optimize ['ɒptɪmaɪz] *vt* optimiser

optimum ['ɒptɪməm] **1** *n* optimum *m*
   2 *adj* optimum *inv*, optimal(e)

option ['ɒpʃən] *n* (**a**) (*choice*) option *f*, choix *m*; **to have the o. of doing sth** avoir la possibilité de faire qch; **to have no o. (but to do sth)** ne pas pouvoir faire autrement (que de faire qch); **an easy o.** une solution de facilité; **to leave** *or* **to keep one's options open** ne pas prendre de décision tout de suite (**b**) *Fin* option *f* (**c**) (*school or university subject*) option *f*

optional ['ɒpʃənəl] *adj* facultatif(ive); **o. extra** (accessoire *m* en) option *f*; **o. subject** (*at school, university*) matière *f* à option

opulent ['ɒpjʊlənt] *adj* opulent(e)

OR [əʊ'ɑː(r)] *n* (*abbr* **operating room**) salle *f* d'opération

or [ɔː(r), *unstressed* ə(r)] *conj* (**a**) (*in general*) ou; **an hour or so** une heure environ; **in a day or two** dans un jour ou deux; **did**

she do it or not? est-ce qu'elle l'a fait ou pas?; **snow or no snow, I'm going!** qu'il neige ou pas, j'y vais! (**b**) (*otherwise*) sinon; **stop it or I'll tell mom!** arrête, sinon je vais le dire à maman! (**c**) (*with negative*) ni; **she didn't write or phone** elle n'a ni écrit ni téléphoné

oracle ['ɒrəkəl] *n* oracle *m*

oral ['ɔːrəl] **1** *n* (*exam*) oral *m*
   2 *adj* (*tradition, contraception*) oral(e); (*medication*) par voie orale; (*hygiene*) buccal(e); **o. examination** (examen *m*) oral *m*; **o. sex** rapports *mpl* bucco-génitaux

orally ['ɔːrəlɪ] *adv* oralement, de vive voix; (*take medicine*) par voie orale

orange ['ɒrɪndʒ] **1** *n* (*fruit*) orange *f*; (*color*) orange *m*; **o. blossom** fleurs *fpl* d'oranger; **o. grove** orangeraie *f*; **o. juice** jus *m* d'orange; **o. peel** peau *f* ou écorce *f* d'orange; **o. tree** oranger *m*
   2 *adj* (*color*) orange *inv*

orang-outan(g) [ɔː'ræŋuːtæŋ] *n* orang-outan(g) *m*

oration [ɔː'reɪʃən] *n* allocution *f*

orator ['ɒrətə(r)] *n* orateur(trice) *m,f*

oratory ['ɒrətərɪ] (*pl* **oratories**) *n* (**a**) (*art of speaking*) art *m* oratoire, éloquence *f* (**b**) *Rel* (*chapel*) oratoire *m*

orb [ɔːb] *n* (*of regalia*) globe *m*; *Lit* (*sphere*) orbe *m*

orbit ['ɔːbɪt] **1** *n* (**a**) (*of planet*) orbite *f*; **in o.** en orbite; **to go into o.** se mettre en orbite (**b**) (*scope*) domaine *m*
   2 *vt* être en orbite *ou* décrire une orbite autour de
   3 *vi* être en orbite, décrire une orbite

orchard ['ɔːtʃəd] *n* verger *m*

orchestra ['ɔːkɪstrə] *n* orchestre *m*; **o. pit** fosse *f* d'orchestre

orchestral [ɔː'kestrəl] *adj* orchestral(e)

orchestrate ['ɔːkɪstreɪt] *vt also Fig* orchestrer

orchid ['ɔːkɪd] *n* orchidée *f*

ordain [ɔː'deɪn] *vt* (**a**) *Formal* (*decree*) ordonner; (*measure*) décréter; *Fig* **fate ordained that we should meet** il était écrit que nous devions nous rencontrer (**b**) (*priest*) ordonner

ordeal [ɔː'diːl] *n* épreuve *f*; **it was a bit of an o.** ça a été éprouvant

order ['ɔːdə(r)] **1** *n* (**a**) (*instruction*) ordre *m*; **to give sb an o.** donner un ordre à qn; **to be under orders (to do sth)** avoir reçu des ordres (pour faire qch); **to take orders from sb** recevoir des ordres de qn; *Fin* **pay to the o. of S. Fraser** payer à l'ordre de S. Fraser
   (**b**) *Com* commande *f*; **to place an o. (with sb)** passer (une) commande (à qn); **to make sth to o.** faire qch sur commande; **o. book** carnet *m* de commandes; **o. form** bon *m* de commande
   (**c**) (*peace, tidiness*) ordre *m*; *Fig* **to put one's own house in o.** faire le ménage chez soi
   (**d**) (*condition*) **out of o.** (*elevator, toilet, machine*) hors service; (*telephone*) en dérangement; **in (good) working** *or* **running o.** en (bon) état de fonctionnement
   (**e**) (*in meeting*) **o. of the day** ordre *m* du jour; **to call sb to o.** rappeler qn à l'ordre; *Fig* **I think a celebration is in o.** je pense que ça mérite d'être fêté; *Fam* **that's out of o.!** ça ne se fait vraiment pas!; *Rel* **o. of service** office *m*
   (**f**) (*system*) ordre *m*; **the new world o.** le nouvel ordre mondial
   (**g**) (*sequence*) ordre *m*; **in the right/wrong o.** dans le bon ordre/le désordre; **in o.** en ordre; **out of o.** en désordre; **in o. of age/size** par ordre d'âge/de taille
   (**h**) (*degree*) ordre *m*; **of the highest o.** de premier ordre; **the higher/lower orders** (*social classes*) les classes *fpl* supérieures/inférieures
   (**i**) *Rel* ordre *m*; **to take holy orders** entrer dans les ordres
   (**j**) **in o. to do sth** afin de *ou* pour faire qch; **in o. that...** afin *ou* pour que... + *subjunctive*
   2 *vt* (**a**) (*instruct*) **to o. sb to do sth** ordonner à qn de faire qch; **to be ordered to do sth** recevoir l'ordre de faire qch;

Law **to be ordered to pay costs** être condamné(e) aux dépens

(**b**) *Com & (in restaurant)* commander

(**c**) *(arrange) (papers, books)* classer, ranger; *(one's thoughts)* mettre de l'ordre dans; **to o. sth according to size** classer *ou* ranger qch par taille

3 *vi (in restaurant)* commander; **are you ready to o.?** vous avez choisi?

▸**order about, order around** *vt sep (person)* commander

▸**order in** *vt sep (supplies)* commander; *(troops)* faire venir

ordered ['ɔ:dəd] *adj (organized)* ordonné(e); *(life)* régulier(ère)

orderly ['ɔ:dəlɪ] **1** *n (pl* **orderlies)** *(in army)* planton *m*; *(in hospital)* aide-soignant(e) *m,f*

2 *adj* (**a**) *(tidy)* méthodique; *(life, room)* rangé(e) (**b**) *(well-behaved)* discipliné(e); **in an o. fashion** avec calme

ordinal ['ɔ:dɪnəl] **1** *n* (nombre *m*) ordinal *m*

2 *adj* ordinal(e)

ordinance ['ɔ:dɪnəns] *n Formal (decree)* ordonnance *f*

ordinarily ['ɔ:dɪnərɪlɪ] *adv* normalement

ordinary ['ɔ:dɪnərɪ] **1** *n* **out of the o.** qui sort de l'ordinaire, exceptionnel(elle)

2 *adj* ordinaire; **she was just an o. tourist** c'était une touriste comme une autre

ordination [ɔ:dɪ'neɪʃən] *n Rel* ordination *f*

ordnance ['ɔ:dnəns] *n Mil (supplies)* matériel *m*; *(guns)* artillerie *f*; **o. factory** manufacture *f* d'artillerie

ore [ɔ:(r)] *n* minerai *m*

oregano [ɒrɪ'gɑ:nəʊ] *n* origan *m*

organ ['ɔ:gən] *n* (**a**) *(part of body, newspaper)* organe *m*; **o. donor** donneur(euse) *m,f* d'organe; **o. transplant** greffe *f* d'organe (**b**) *(musical instrument)* orgue *m*

organ-grinder ['ɔ:gəngraɪndə(r)] *n* joueur(euse) *m,f* d'orgue de Barbarie

organic [ɔ:'gænɪk] *adj (disease, chemistry)* organique; *(food, farming)* biologique, *Fam* bio *inv*; **an o. whole** un tout

organism ['ɔ:gənɪzəm] *n* organisme *m*

organist ['ɔ:gənɪst] *n* organiste *mf*

organization [ɔ:gənaɪ'zeɪʃən] *n* organisation *f*

organize ['ɔ:gənaɪz] **1** *vt* (**a**) *(put into order)* organiser; **to o. one's time** s'organiser (**b**) *(take care of)* s'occuper de

2 *vi (of workers)* se syndiquer

organized ['ɔ:gənaɪzd] *adj (trip)* organisé(e); **o. crime** le crime organisé, le grand banditisme; **o. labor** main-d'œuvre *f* syndiquée

organizer ['ɔ:gənaɪzə(r)] *n (person)* organisateur(trice) *m,f*; *(datebook)* agenda *m*; *(electronic)* agenda *m* électronique

orgasm ['ɔ:gæzəm] *n* orgasme *m*; **to have an o.** avoir un orgasme

orgy ['ɔ:dʒɪ] *(pl* **orgies)** *n* orgie *f*; *Fig* **an o. of violence** un déchaînement de violence

orient ['ɔ:rɪənt] **1** *n* **the O.** l'Orient *m*

2 *vt* = **orientate**

oriental [ɔ:rɪ'entəl] **1** *n Old-fashioned* **O.** Oriental(e) *m,f*

2 *adj* oriental(e)

orientate ['ɔ:rɪənteɪt] *vt* orienter (**to** *or* **towards** vers); **to o. oneself** s'orienter; **to be orientated toward sb/sth** *(aimed at)* être destiné(e) à qn/qch

orientation [ɔ:rɪən'teɪʃən] *n* orientation *f*; **o. course** stage *m* d'initiation

orienteering [ɒrɪən'tɪərɪŋ] *n* course *f* d'orientation

orifice ['ɒrɪfɪs] *n* orifice *m*

origin ['ɒrɪdʒɪn] *n* origine *f*; **country of o.** pays *m* d'origine; **of Greek o.** d'origine grecque

original [ə'rɪdʒɪnəl] **1** *n (painting, document)* original *m*

2 *adj* (**a**) *(not copied, innovative)* original(e) (**b**) *(first)* d'origine; *Rel* **o. sin** péché *m* originel

originality [ərɪdʒɪ'nælɪtɪ] *n* originalité *f*

originally [ə'rɪdʒɪnəlɪ] *adv* (**a**) *(initially)* à l'origine, au départ; **where do you come from o.?** d'où êtes-vous originaire? (**b**) *(in an innovative way)* d'une façon originale

originate [ə'rɪdʒɪneɪt] **1** *vt* être à l'origine de

2 *vi (of fire)* prendre naissance; **to o. from** *(of person)* être originaire de; **to o. in** *(of custom)* être originaire de

ornament 1 *n* ['ɔ:nəmənt] ornement *m*

2 *vt* ['ɔ:nəment] orner

ornamental [ɔ:nə'mentəl] *adj* ornemental(e), décoratif(ive); **o. lake** pièce *f* d'eau

ornate [ɔ:'neɪt] *adj (building, surroundings)* orné(e), ornementé(e); *(style)* fleuri(e)

ornithology [ɔ:nɪ'θɒlədʒɪ] *n* ornithologie *f*

orphan ['ɔ:fən] **1** *n* orphelin(e) *m,f*; **to be left an o.** devenir orphelin

2 *adj* **an o. child** un (une) orphelin(e)

3 *vt* **to be orphaned** devenir orphelin(e)

orphanage ['ɔ:fənɪdʒ] *n* orphelinat *m*

orthodontist [ɔ:θəʊ'dɒntɪst] *n* orthodontiste *mf*

orthodox ['ɔ:θədɒks] *adj* orthodoxe

orthodoxy ['ɔ:θədɒksɪ] *n* orthodoxie *f*

orthopedic [ɔ:θə'pi:dɪk] *adj* orthopédique; **o. surgeon** (chirurgien *m*) orthopédiste *mf*

orthopedics [ɔ:θə'pi:dɪks] *n* orthopédie *f*

Oscar ['ɒskə(r)] *n Cin* oscar *m*; **O. Night, the Oscars** la cérémonie des oscars, les oscars *mpl*

Oscar-winning ['ɒskəwɪnɪŋ] *adj* oscarisé(e)

oscillate ['ɒsɪleɪt] *vi* osciller

osmosis [ɒz'məʊsɪs] *n also Fig* osmose *f*

osprey ['ɒspreɪ] *(pl* **ospreys)** *n* balbuzard *m*, *Can* aigle *m* pêcheur

ossify ['ɒsɪfaɪ] *(pt & pp* **ossified)** *vi Anat* s'ossifier; *Fig (of person)* se fossiliser; *(of system, organization)* se scléroser

ostensible [ɒs'tensɪbəl] *adj* soi-disant *inv*

ostensibly [ɒs'tensɪblɪ] *adv* soi-disant

ostentation [ɒsten'teɪʃən] *n* ostentation *f*

ostentatious [ɒsten'teɪʃəs] *adj (person)* m'as-tu-vu *inv*; *(thing)* prétentieux(euse)

osteoarthritis [ɒstɪəʊɑ:'θraɪtɪs] *n* ostéoarthrite *f*

osteopath ['ɒstɪəpæθ] *n* ostéopathe *mf*

osteopathy [ɒstɪ'ɒpəθɪ] *n* ostéopathie *f*

osteoplasty ['ɒstɪəʊplæstɪ] *n Med* ostéoplastie *f*

osteoporosis [ɒstɪəʊpə'rəʊsɪs] *n Med* ostéoporose *f*

ostracism ['ɒstrəsɪzəm] *n* ostracisme *m*

ostracize ['ɒstrəsaɪz] *vt* mettre en quarantaine

ostrich ['ɒstrɪtʃ] *n* autruche *f*

other ['ʌðə(r)] **1** *adj* autre; **the o. one** l'autre; **every o. day/week** un jour/une semaine sur deux; **the o. day/week** l'autre jour/semaine; **the o. four** les quatre autres; **o. people seem to like it** d'autres ont l'air de bien aimer ça; **any o. book** n'importe quel autre livre; **somebody o. than me** quelqu'un d'autre que moi

2 *pron* autre; **others** d'autres; **the others** les autres; **one after the o.** l'un(e) après l'autre; **one or o. of us** l'un d'entre nous; **somewhere or o.** quelque part; **somebody or o.** quelqu'un; **some woman or o.** une femme

3 *adv* **the color's odd, but o. than that, it's perfect** la couleur est bizarre mais à part cela, il est très bien; **she never speaks of him o. than admiringly** elle ne parle jamais de lui autrement qu'avec admiration

otherwise ['ʌðəwaɪz] **1** *adv* autrement; **to be o. engaged** avoir d'autres engagements; **except where o. stated** sauf indication contraire

2 *conj* autrement, sinon

other-worldly [ʌðə'wɜ:ldlɪ] *adj (person)* détaché(e) de ce monde

Ottawa [ˈɒtəwə] *n* Ottawa

otter [ˈɒtə(r)] *n* loutre *f*

Ottoman [ˈɒtəmən] *Hist* **1** *n* Ottoman(e) *m,f*
 2 *adj* ottoman(e)

ottoman [ˈɒtəmən] *n (furniture)* ottomane *f*

ouch [aʊtʃ] *exclam (expressing pain)* aïe!, ouïe!

ought [ɔːt] *v aux* (**a**) *(expressing obligation, desirability)* **I o. to be going** je devrais m'en aller; **you oughtn't to worry so much** vous ne devriez pas vous inquiéter autant; **he had drunk more than he o. to** il n'aurait pas dû boire autant; **this o. to have been done before** on aurait dû le faire avant; **they o. not to have waited** ils n'auraient pas dû attendre (**b**) *(expressing probability)* **they o. to be in Paris by now** ils ont dû arriver à Paris maintenant; **you o. to be able to get $400 for the painting** vous devriez pouvoir tirer 400 dollars de ce tableau

oughtn't [ˈɔːtənt] = **ought not**

ounce [aʊns] *n (unit of weight)* = 28,35 g, once *f*; *Fig* **an o. of** une once de

our [ˈaʊə(r)] *possessive adj* (**a**) *(singular)* notre; *(plural)* nos; **o. job** notre travail; **o. wives** nos femmes; **it wasn't OUR idea!** ce n'est pas nous qui en avons eu l'idée! (**b**) *(for parts of body)* **we hit o. heads** nous nous sommes cogné la tête

ours [ˈaʊəz] *possessive pron* (**a**) *(singular)* le nôtre (la nôtre) *m,f*; *(plural)* les nôtres; **their house is big but o. is bigger** leur maison est grande, mais la nôtre est plus grande encore (**b**) *(used attributively)* **this book is o.** ce livre est à nous; **a friend of o.** un de nos amis; **where's that brother of o.?** où notre frère a-t-il bien pu passer?

ourselves [aʊəˈselvz] *pron* (**a**) *(reflexive)* **we hurt o.** nous nous sommes blessés (**b**) *(emphatic)* nous-mêmes; **we o. have never...** nous-mêmes n'avons jamais...; **we told you o.** nous vous l'avons dit nous-mêmes; **we're not o. today** nous ne sommes pas dans notre état normal aujourd'hui (**c**) *(after preposition)* **we live by o.** nous vivons seuls; **we bought it for o.** nous nous le sommes acheté; **we talk to o.** nous parlons tout seuls

oust [aʊst] *vt* évincer (**from** de)

out [aʊt] **1** *adv* (**a**) *(outside)* dehors; **to go o.** sortir; **o. here** ici; **o. there** dehors; **o.!** *(in tennis)* faute!
 (**b**) *(not at home, not in)* **to be o.** être sorti(e); **to stay o. late** rentrer tard
 (**c**) *(not concealed)* **the secret is o.** on a révélé le secret; **he's o.** *(openly gay)* il a révélé son homosexualité; **the sun is o.** il y a du soleil; **the moon is o.** la lune est levée
 (**d**) *(published)* sorti(e)
 (**e**) *(not in fashion)* passé(e) de mode
 (**f**) *(indicating aim)* **to be o. to do sth** chercher à faire qch; **to be o. for money** vouloir à tout prix de l'argent; *Fam* **to be o. to get sb** chercher la perte de qn
 (**g**) *(unconscious, asleep)* **to be o. cold** *or* **for the count** être K-O; *Fam* **to go o. like a light** s'endormir comme une masse
 (**h**) *(extinguished)* éteint(e)
 (**i**) **to be o. (on strike)** faire grève
 (**j**) *(inaccurate)* faux (fausse); **I was $25 o.** *(over)* j'avais 25 dollars de trop; *(under)* il me manquait 25 dollars
 (**k**) *(indicating completion)* **before the week is o.** avant la fin de la semaine
 (**l**) *(in phrases with of)* **o. of** *(outside)* hors de; **to go o. of the office** sortir du bureau; **to look o. of the window** regarder par la fenêtre; **to be o. of the country** être en voyage à l'étranger; **o. of reach/danger** hors de portée/danger; **to be o. of cash/ideas** ne plus avoir de liquide/d'idées; **to do sth o. of friendship/curiosity** faire qch par amitié/curiosité; **she paid for it o. of her own money** elle l'a payé de ses propres deniers; **20 o. of 20** 20 sur 20; **three days o. of four** trois jours sur quatre; *Fam* **to feel o. of it** ne pas se sentir dans le coup

 2 *prep (through)* **to look o. the window** regarder par la fenêtre

 3 *vt Fam (expose)* dénoncer; **to o. sb** *(reveal to be homosexual)* outer qn, révéler que qn est homosexuel

outage [ˈaʊtɪdʒ] *n (breakdown)* panne *f*; *(of service)* interruption; *Elec* **a power o.** une coupure ou une panne de courant

out-and-out [aʊtəˈnaʊt] *adj (villain, liar)* fieffé(e); *(failure)* total(e); *(disgrace, scandal)* véritable

outback [ˈaʊtbæk] *n (in Australia)* **the o.** l'intérieur *m*

outbid [aʊtˈbɪd] *(pt & pp* **outbid***) vt* enchérir avec succès sur

outboard [ˈaʊtbɔːd] **1** *n (motor)* moteur *m* hors-bord
 2 *adj* **o. motor** moteur *m* hors-bord

outbox [ˈaʊtbɒks] *n Comput (for e-mail)* corbeille *f* de départ

outbreak [ˈaʊtbreɪk] *n (of hostilities, war)* déclenchement *m*; *(of rioting, violence)* flambée *f*; *(of disease)* épidémie *f*

outbuilding [ˈaʊtbɪldɪŋ] *n* dépendance *f*

outburst [ˈaʊtbɜːst] *n éclat m*; *(of activity, temper)* accès *m*; *(of hatred, violence)* explosion *f*; *(of enthusiasm)* élan *m*

outcast [ˈaʊtkɑːst] *n* paria *m*

outclass [aʊtˈklɑːs] *vt* surclasser

outcome [ˈaʊtkʌm] *n* résultat *m*, issue *f*

outcrop [ˈaʊtkrɒp] *n* affleurement *m*

outcry [ˈaʊtkraɪ] *(pl* **outcries***) n (protest)* tollé *m*; **public o.** tollé général

outdated [aʊtˈdeɪtɪd] *adj* démodé(e)

outdid [aʊtˈdɪd] *pt of* **outdo**

outdistance [aʊtˈdɪstəns] *vt* distancer, dépasser

outdo [aʊtˈduː] *(pt* **outdid** [aʊtˈdɪd]*, pp* **outdone** [aʊtˈdʌn]*) vt* surpasser; **not to be outdone,...** pour ne pas être en reste,...

outdoor [ˈaʊtdɔː(r)] *adj (life)* au grand air; *(activities, games)* de plein air; *(swimming pool)* découvert(e); **she's an o. person** elle aime le grand air

outdoors [aʊtˈdɔːz] **1** *n* **the great o.** les grands espaces *mpl*
 2 *adv* dehors

outer [ˈaʊtə(r)] *adj* extérieur(e); **O. Mongolia** Mongolie-Extérieure *f*; **o. space** espace *m* intersidéral

outermost [ˈaʊtəməʊst] *adj (nearest the outside)* le (la) plus à l'extérieur; *(most remote)* le (la) plus reculé(e)

outfit [ˈaʊtfɪt] *n* (**a**) *(clothes)* ensemble *m*, tenue *f* (**b**) *Fam (organization)* boîte *f*

outflank [aʊtˈflæŋk] *vt Mil* déborder; *Fig* prendre par surprise

outflow [ˈaʊtfləʊ] *n (of liquid)* écoulement *m*; *(of capital)* fuite *f*

outgoing [ˈaʊtgəʊɪŋ] *adj* (**a**) *(departing)* sortant(e) (**b**) *(sociable)* extraverti(e)

outgrow [aʊtˈgrəʊ] *(pt* **outgrew** [aʊtˈgruː]*, pp* **outgrown** [aʊtˈgrəʊn]*) vt (habit, behavior, toys)* passer l'âge de; **she's outgrown her jacket** son blouson est devenu trop petit pour elle

outhouse [ˈaʊthaʊs] *n (toilet)* toilettes *fpl* extérieures

outing [ˈaʊtɪŋ] *n* (**a**) *(excursion)* excursion *f*, sortie *f* (**b**) *(of homosexual)* = fait, principalement pour une organisation militante, de rendre publique l'homosexualité d'une personne connue

outlandish [aʊtˈlændɪʃ] *adj* incongru(e), bizarre

outlast [aʊtˈlɑːst] *vt (object)* durer plus longtemps que; *(person)* survivre à

outlaw [ˈaʊtlɔː] **1** *n* hors-la-loi *m inv*
 2 *vt (practice)* rendre illégal(e); *(person)* mettre hors la loi

outlay [ˈaʊtleɪ] *n (expense)* frais *mpl*, dépenses *fpl*

outlet [ˈaʊtlet] *n* (**a**) *(for water, steam)* orifice *m* de sortie; *(for emotions, energy)* exutoire *m* (**b**) *(store)* point *m* de vente

outline [ˈaʊtlaɪn] **1** *n* (**a**) *(shape)* silhouette *f*; *(drawing)* tracé *m* (**b**) *(summary)* *(of play, novel)* résumé *m*; *(of plan, policy)* grandes lignes *fpl*; **in o.** en gros, dans les grandes lignes
 2 *vt* (**a**) *(shape)* repasser les contours de; **her figure was outlined against the sky** sa silhouette se découpait sur le ciel (**b**)

(plot of novel) résumer; *(plan, policy)* donner les grandes lignes de

outlive [aʊt'lɪv] *vt* survivre à; **she will o. us all** elle nous enterrera tous; **to have outlived its usefulness** *(of machine, theory)* ne plus servir (à rien)

outlook ['aʊtlʊk] *n* (**a**) *(prospect)* perspectives *fpl*; *(of weather)* prévisions *fpl* (**b**) *(attitude)* façon *f* de voir les choses; **o. on life** conception *f* de la vie (**c**) *(view)* vue *f* (**over** sur)

outlying ['aʊtlaɪɪŋ] *adj* éloigné(e), isolé(e)

outmaneuver [aʊtmə'nuːvə(r)] *vt Mil* l'emporter tactiquement sur; *(in politics, sport)* déjouer les tactiques de

outmoded [aʊt'məʊdɪd] *adj* démodé(e)

outnumber [aʊt'nʌmbə(r)] *vt* l'emporter en nombre sur; **we were outnumbered** ils étaient plus nombreux (que nous)

out-of-date [aʊtəv'deɪt] *adj (idea, attitude, clothes)* démodé(e); *(passport)* périmé(e)

out-of-doors [aʊtəv'dɔːz] *adv* = **outdoors**

out-of-pocket expenses [aʊtəv'pɒkɪt'ɪk'spensɪz] *npl* menues dépenses *fpl*

out-of-the-way [aʊtəvðə'weɪ] *adj (remote)* écarté(e), loin de tout; *(unusual)* insolite, qui sort de l'ordinaire

outpatient ['aʊtpeɪʃənt] *n* malade *mf* en consultation externe; **outpatients' (department)** service *m* des consultations externes

outplacement ['aʊtpleɪsmənt] *n* = aide à la recherche d'un nouvel emploi, fournie par l'employeur lors d'un licenciement

outpost ['aʊtpəʊst] *n Mil* poste *m* avancé; *Fig* bastion *m*

output ['aʊtpʊt] **1** *n (of goods)* production *f*; *(of data, information)* sortie *f*; *(of generator, machine)* débit *m*
2 *vt (pt & pp* **output**) produire; *(data, information)* sortir

outrage ['aʊtreɪdʒ] **1** *n* (**a**) *(act)* atrocité *f*; **it's an o.!** c'est un scandale! (**b**) *(indignation)* indignation *f* (**at** face à)
2 *vt (make indignant)* scandaliser, outrer

outrageous [aʊt'reɪdʒəs] *adj (shocking)* scandaleux(euse); *(clothes, haircut)* extravagant(e)

outrageously [aʊt'reɪdʒəslɪ] *adv (expensive)* scandaleusement; *(behave)* de façon scandaleuse; *(dressed)* de façon extravagante

outreach worker ['aʊtriːtʃwɜːkə(r)] *n* = employé d'une association travaillant sur le terrain

outright1 *adv* [aʊt'raɪt] (**a**) *(completely)* **to buy sth o.** acheter qch au comptant; **he was killed o.** il fut tué sur le coup (**b**) *(ask, tell)* franchement; *(refuse)* catégoriquement
2 *adj* ['aʊtraɪt] *(refusal)* catégorique; *(failure)* total(e); *(winner)* incontesté(e)

outrun [aʊt'rʌn] *(pt* **outran** [aʊt'ræn], *pp* **outrun**) *vt* courir plus vite que

outsell [aʊt'sel] *(pt & pp* **outsold** [aʊt'səʊld]) *vt* se vendre mieux que

outset ['aʊtset] *n* **at the o.** au départ; **from the o.** dès le départ

outshine [aʊt'ʃaɪn] *(pt & pp* **outshone** [aʊt'ʃɒn]) *vt (surpass)* éclipser

outside ['aʊtsaɪd, aʊt'saɪd] **1** *n* extérieur *m*, dehors *m*; **on the o.** à l'extérieur; *Fig* extérieurement; **from the o.** du dehors, de l'extérieur; **at the o.** *(of estimate)* tout au plus
2 *adj (influence)* extérieur(e); *Rad & TV* **o. broadcast** reportage *m*; **o. lane** file *f* de gauche; **the o. world** le monde extérieur; **an o. chance** une petite chance
3 *adv* dehors, à l'extérieur; **to go o.** sortir
4 *prep* (**a**) *(physically)* en dehors de, à l'extérieur de; *(in front of)* devant; **o. office hours** en dehors des heures de bureau (**b**) *(apart from)* en dehors de; **o. (of) a few friends** en dehors de quelques amis

outsider [aʊt'saɪdə(r)] *n* (**a**) *(socially)* étranger(ère) *m,f* (**b**) *(in race, election)* outsider *m*

outsize ['aʊtsaɪz], **outsized** ['aʊtsaɪzd] *adj (clothes)* très grande taille; *(appetite, ego)* démesuré(e)

outskirts ['aʊtskɜːts] *npl* **the o.** la banlieue

outsmart [aʊt'smɑːt] *vt* se montrer plus fin(e) que

outsource ['aʊtsɔːs] *vt Com* externaliser

outsourcing ['aʊtsɔːsɪŋ] *n Com* externalisation *f*

outspoken [aʊt'spəʊkən] *adj* franc (franche)

outstanding [aʊt'stændɪŋ] *adj* (**a**) *(remarkable)* exceptionnel(elle) (**b**) *(unresolved) (business)* en suspens (**c**) *(unpaid) (amount, debt)* impayé(e); *(payment)* en retard; *(interest)* échu(e)

outstay [aʊt'steɪ] *vt* **I hope I haven't outstayed my welcome** j'espère ne pas avoir abusé de votre hospitalité

outstretched ['aʊtstretʃt] *adj (leg, arm)* tendu(e)

outstrip [aʊt'strɪp] *(pt & pp* **outstripped**) *vt* dépasser

outtake ['aʊtteɪk] *n Cin & TV* coupure *f*

out-tray ['aʊttreɪ] *n* courrier *m* à expédier

outward ['aʊtwəd] **1** *adj* (**a**) *(external)* extérieur(e) (**b**) **o. voyage** *or* **journey** voyage *m* aller
2 *adv* vers l'extérieur

outwardly ['aʊtwədlɪ] *adv* en apparence

outwards ['aʊtwədz] *adv* = **outward**

outweigh [aʊt'weɪ] *vt (be more important than)* l'emporter sur

outwit [aʊt'wɪt] *(pt & pp* **outwitted**) *vt* se montrer plus malin(igne) que

outworn [aʊt'wɔːn] *adj (theory, idea)* périmé(e)

ova ['əʊvə] *pl of* **ovum**

oval ['əʊvəl] **1** *n* ovale *m*
2 *adj* ovale; **the O. Office** *(office)* le Bureau ovale; *(authority)* la présidence des États-Unis

ovarian [əʊ'veərɪən] *adj Anat* ovarien(enne)

ovary ['əʊvərɪ] *(pl* **ovaries**) *n Anat* ovaire *m*

ovation [əʊ'veɪʃən] *n* ovation *f*; **to give sb a standing o.** se lever pour applaudir qn

oven ['ʌvən] *n* four *m*; **o. glove** gant *m* isolant

oven-proof ['ʌvənpruːf] *adj* qui va au four

oven-ready ['ʌvənredɪ] *adj* prêt(e) à rôtir

ovenware ['ʌvənweə(r)] *n* vaisselle *f* allant au four

over ['əʊvə(r)] **1** *prep* (**a**) *(above)* au-dessus de; **the plane flew o. our heads** l'avion est passé au-dessus de nos têtes; **I couldn't hear her o. the noise** impossible de l'entendre avec tout ce bruit; *Fig* **her talk was way o. my head** son exposé m'est passé complètement au-dessus de la tête
(**b**) *(on top of)* sur; **to put a blanket o. sb** mettre une couverture sur qn
(**c**) *(from one side to the other of)* par-dessus; **to throw sth o. the wall** jeter qch par-dessus le mur; **to read o. sb's shoulder** lire par-dessus l'épaule de qn
(**d**) *(across)* **to go o. the road** traverser la rue; **to live o. the road** habiter en face; **o. the border** de l'autre côté de la frontière; **the bridge o. the river** le pont qui traverse la rivière
(**e**) *(about)* **to laugh o. sth** rire de qch; **to fight o. sth** se battre pour qch
(**f**) *(more than)* plus de; **he's o. fifty** il a plus de cinquante ans; **children o. five** les enfants de plus de cinq ans; **o. and above** en plus de
(**g**) *(during)* pendant; **o. the last three years** les trois dernières années; **o. lunch** en déjeunant
(**h**) *(recovered from)* **to be o. sth** *(illness, disappointment)* s'être remis(e) de qch; **to be o. sb** ne plus penser à qn
2 *adv* (**a**) *(across)* **o. here** ici; **o. there** là-bas; **to cross o.** *(the street)* traverser; **to ask** *or* **to invite sb o.** **(to one's house)** inviter qn (chez soi)
(**b**) *(down)* **to fall o.** tomber; **to bend o.** se pencher; **to push sb/sth o.** faire tomber qn/qch
(**c**) *(everywhere)* **famous the world o.** célèbre dans le monde entier
(**d**) *(expressing repetition)* **three times o.** trois fois de suite; **o.**

and o. again encore et encore; to do sth all o. again refaire qch; to start o. recommencer

(e) (in excess) children of five and o. les enfants de cinq ans et plus; there were $5 left o. il restait 5 dollars

(f) (on radio) o.! à vous!; o. and out! terminé!

3 adj to be (all) o. être fini(e); to get sth o. (and done) with en finir avec qch

overabundant [əʊvərə'bʌndənt] adj surabondant(e)

overactive [əʊvər'æktɪv] adj (imagination) débridé(e)

overall ['əʊvərɔːl] 1 adj global(e); (size, area) total(e); she has o. responsibility for sales elle est responsable de l'ensemble du service des ventes

2 adv dans l'ensemble; $10 o. 10 dollars en tout; third o. troisième au classement général

overalls ['əʊvərɔːlz] npl (dungarees) salopette f

overanxious [əʊvər'æŋkʃəs] adj trop inquiet(ète)

overawe [əʊvər'ɔː] vt to be overawed by sb/sth se laisser impressionner par qn/qch

overbearing [əʊvə'beərɪŋ] adj autoritaire

overblown [əʊvə'bləʊn] adj (style) ampoulé(e)

overboard ['əʊvəbɔːd] adv par-dessus bord; man o.! un homme à la mer!; Fig to go o. (about) s'emballer (pour)

overbook [əʊvə'bʊk] vt faire de la surréservation ou du surbooking sur

overbooking [əʊvə'bʊkɪŋ] n surréservation f, surbooking m

overcapacity ['əʊvəkə'pæsɪti] n Ind surcapacité f

overcast ['əʊvəkɑːst] adj (sky, day) nuageux(euse)

overcautious [əʊvə'kɔːʃəs] adj trop prudent(e)

overcharge [əʊvə'tʃɑːdʒ] vt to o. sb for sth faire payer qch trop cher à qn; he overcharged me by a dollar il m'a fait payer un dollar en trop

overcoat ['əʊvəkəʊt] n pardessus m

overcome [əʊvə'kʌm] (pt overcame [əʊvə'keɪm], pp overcome) vt (opponent, one's fears) vaincre; (problem, obstacle) surmonter; to be overcome with or by grief être accablé(e) de chagrin; I was quite overcome j'ai été bouleversé

overcompensate [əʊvə'kɒmpenseɪt] vi to o. for sth surcompenser qch

overconfident [əʊvə'kɒnfɪdənt] adj trop confiant(e)

overcook [əʊvə'kʊk] vt (faire) trop cuire

overcooked [əʊvə'kʊkd] adj trop cuit(e)

overcrowded [əʊvə'kraʊdəd] adj bondé(e)

overcrowding [əʊvə'kraʊdɪŋ] n surpeuplement m

overdeveloped [əʊvədɪ'veləpt] adj trop développé(e)

overdo [əʊvə'duː] (pt overdid [əʊvə'dɪd], pp overdone [əʊvə'dʌn]) vt exagérer; to o. it (work too hard) se surmener; to o. the salt/make-up forcer sur le sel/le maquillage

overdone [əʊvə'dʌn] adj (food) trop cuit(e)

overdose [əʊvə'dəʊs] 1 n overdose f

2 vi faire une overdose (on de); Fig to o. on chocolate exagérer avec le chocolat

overdraft ['əʊvədrɑːft] n Fin découvert m

overdrawn [əʊvə'drɔːn] adj à découvert

overdressed [əʊvə'drest] adj trop habillé(e)

overdrive ['əʊvədraɪv] n Fig to go into o. passer à la vitesse supérieure

overdue [əʊvə'djuː] adj (person, train) en retard; (bill) impayé(e); (library book) qui n'a pas été rendu(e); this measure is long o. cette mesure aurait dû être prise il y a longtemps

overeat [əʊvə'riːt] (pt overate [əʊvə'reɪt], pp overeaten [əʊvə'riːtən]) vi trop manger

overemphasize [əʊvər'emfəsaɪz] vt trop mettre l'accent sur

overenthusiastic ['əʊvərɪnθjuːzɪ'æstɪk] adj trop enthousiaste

overestimate [əʊvə'restɪmeɪt] vt surestimer; (danger) exagérer

overexcited [əʊvərɪk'saɪtɪd] adj surexcité(e)

overexpose [əʊvərɪks'pəʊz] vt Phot surexposer

overexposed ['əʊvərɪk'spəʊzd] adj Phot surexposé(e); Fig (in the media) surmédiatisé(e)

overextend ['əʊvərɪk'stend] vt Fin to o. oneself s'engager au-dessus de ses moyens

overextended [əʊvərɪk'stendɪd] adj Fin incapable de faire face à ses engagements

overfishing [əʊvə'fɪʃɪŋ] n surpêche f

overflow 1 n ['əʊvəfləʊ] (liquid) trop-plein m; o. (pipe) trop-plein

2 vi [əʊvə'fləʊ] déborder; his desk was overflowing with papers son bureau disparaissait sous la paperasse

overgrown [əʊvə'grəʊn] adj (garden) envahi(e) par les mauvaises herbes; he's like an o. schoolboy il se conduit comme un collégien

overhang 1 n ['əʊvəhæŋ] (of roof, cliff) surplomb m

2 vt [əʊvə'hæŋ] (pt & pp overhung [əʊvə'hʌŋ]) surplomber

overhaul 1 n ['əʊvəhɔːl] also Fig révision f

2 vt [əʊvə'hɔːl] (a) (machine, policy) réviser (b) (overtake) dépasser

overhead 1 n ['əʊvəhed] Com frais mpl généraux

2 adj ['əʊvəhed] (cable) aérien(enne); o. projector rétroprojecteur m

3 adv [əʊvə'hed] au-dessus; a plane flew o. un avion passa au-dessus de nos têtes

overhear [əʊvə'hɪə(r)] (pt & pp overheard [əʊvə'hɜːd]) vt (person) entendre (par hasard); (words) surprendre

overheat [əʊvə'hiːt] vi (of engine) chauffer; (of economy) être en surchauffe

overindulge [əʊvərɪn'dʌldʒ] 1 vt (child) trop gâter; to o. oneself (drink, eat to excess) faire des excès

2 vi faire des excès

overjoyed [əʊvə'dʒɔɪd] adj absolument ravi(e) (at de)

overkill ['əʊvəkɪl] n it's o. c'est exagéré, c'est trop; media o. matraquage m

overland ['əʊvəlænd] adv & adj par voie de terre

overlap 1 n ['əʊvəlæp] (between planks, tiles) chevauchement m

2 vi [əʊvə'læp] (pt & pp overlapped) (of planks, tiles, periods) se chevaucher; (of theories) avoir des points communs (with avec); to o. with (in time) empiéter sur

overleaf [əʊvə'liːf] adv au verso; see o. voir au verso

overload 1 n ['əʊvələʊd] Elec surcharge f

2 vt [əʊvə'ləʊd] also Fig surcharger (with de)

overlong [əʊvə'lɒŋ] adj trop long (longue)

overlook [əʊvə'lʊk] vt (a) (of building, window) donner sur; the castle overlooks the town le château surplombe la ville (b) (fail to notice) oublier (c) (disregard) fermer les yeux sur

overly ['əʊvli] adv excessivement, trop

overmanning [əʊvə'mænɪŋ] n sureffectifs mpl

overmuch [əʊvə'mʌtʃ] adv outre mesure, trop

overnight 1 adv [əʊvə'naɪt] (a) (during the night) (pendant) la nuit; to stay o. passer la nuit; leave to soak o. laisser tremper toute la nuit (b) (suddenly) du jour au lendemain

2 adj ['əʊvənaɪt] (a) (for one night) o. train/flight train m/vol m de nuit; o. bag petit sac m de voyage; o. stay séjour m d'une nuit; (in hotel) nuit f (b) (sudden) soudain(e)

overoptimistic [əʊvərɒptɪ'mɪstɪk] adj trop optimiste (about quant à)

overpaid [əʊvə'peɪd] adj trop payé(e)

overpass ['əʊvəpɑːs] n (road) pont m routier; (for pedestrians) passerelle f

overpayment [əʊvə'peɪmənt] n (of taxes) trop-perçu m; (of employee) rémunération f excessive

overpopulation [əʊvəpɒpjʊ'leɪʃən] n surpopulation f, surpeuplement m

overpower [əʊvə'paʊə(r)] *vt* maîtriser

overpowering [əʊvə'paʊərɪŋ] *adj (heat, smell)* suffocant(e); *(taste)* qui prend à la gorge; *(desire)* irrépressible

overpriced [əʊvə'praɪst] *adj* trop cher(ère)

overproduction [əʊvəprə'dʌkʃən] *n Econ* surproduction *f*

overrated [əʊvə'reɪtɪd] *adj* surfait(e)

overreach [əʊvə'riːtʃ] *vt* **to o. oneself** trop présumer de ses forces

overreact [əʊvərɪ'ækt] *vi* réagir de façon excessive

override [əʊvə'raɪd] *vt (pt* **overrode** [əʊvə'rəʊd], *pp* **overridden** [əʊvə'rɪdən]) **(a)** *(objections, wishes, regulations)* passer outre à; *(decision)* annuler **(b)** *(take precedence over)* avoir la priorité sur; *Tech (device)* annuler

overriding [əʊvə'raɪdɪŋ] *adj (importance)* capital(e); *(factor)* prépondérant(e)

overrule [əʊvə'ruːl] *vt (opinion)* rejeter; *(decision)* annuler; **she was overruled by her boss** son patron a rejeté sa proposition

overrun 1 *vt* [əʊvə'rʌn] *(pt* **overran** [əʊvə'ræn], *pp* **overrun)** **(a)** *(country)* envahir; **the house was overrun with mice** la maison était infestée de souris **(b)** *(allotted time)* dépasser

2 *vi* [əʊvə'rʌn] *(of TV, radio program)* déborder sur l'horaire

3 *vt* [əʊvərʌn] *Com* **(cost) o.** dépassement *m* du budget

oversaw [əʊvə'sɔː] *pt of* **oversee**

overseas 1 *adj* ['əʊvəsiːz] d'outre-mer; *(trade, debt)* extérieur(e)

2 *adv* [əʊvə'siːz] à l'étranger

oversee [əʊvə'siː] *(pt* **oversaw** [əʊvə'sɔː], *pp* **overseen** [əʊvə'siːn]) *vt* superviser

overseer ['əʊvəsɪə(r)] *n Old-fashioned* contremaître *m*

oversensitive [əʊvə'sensɪtɪv] *adj* hypersensible

oversexed [əʊvə'sekst] *adj* qui a une libido démesurée

overshadow [əʊvə'ʃædəʊ] *vt Fig (of atmosphere, threat)* planer sur; *(of person)* éclipser

overshoe ['əʊvəʃuː] *n* caoutchouc *m*

overshoot [əʊvə'ʃuːt] *(pt & pp* **overshot** [əʊvə'ʃɒt]) *vt* dépasser

oversight ['əʊvəsaɪt] *n* oubli *m*, omission *f*

oversimplify [əʊvə'sɪmplɪfaɪ] *(pt & pp* **oversimplified)** *vt* simplifier à outrance

oversized ['əʊvəsaɪzd] *adj (very big)* énorme; *(clothes)* trop grand(e)

oversleep [əʊvə'sliːp] *(pt & pp* **overslept** [əʊvə'slept]) *vi* ne pas se réveiller à temps

overspend [əʊvə'spend] *(pt & pp* **overspent** [əʊvə'spent]) **1** *vt* **to o. one's budget** dépasser son budget

2 *vi* trop dépenser

overstaffing [əʊvə'stɑːfɪŋ] *n* sureffectifs *mpl*

overstate [əʊvə'steɪt] *vt* exagérer

overstay [əʊvə'steɪ] = **outstay**

overstep [əʊvə'step] *(pt & pp* **overstepped)** *vt* outrepasser; *Fig* **to o. the mark** dépasser les bornes

oversubscribed [əʊvəsəb'skraɪbd] *adj Fin* sursouscrit(e)

overt [əʊ'vɜːt] *adj* manifeste

overtake [əʊvə'teɪk] *(pt* **overtook** [əʊvə'tʊk], *pp* **overtaken** [əʊvə'teɪkən]) *vt & vi* dépasser, doubler; **to be overtaken by events** être dépassé(e) par les événements

overthrow 1 *n* ['əʊvəθrəʊ] renversement *m*

2 *vt* [əʊvə'θrəʊ] *(pt* **overthrew** [əʊvə'θruː], *pp* **overthrown** [əʊvə'θrəʊn]) renverser

overtime ['əʊvətaɪm] **1** *n* heures *fpl* supplémentaires

2 *adv* **to work o.** faire des heures supplémentaires; *Fig (of imagination)* s'emballer

overtly [əʊ'vɜːtlɪ] *adv* ouvertement

overtone ['əʊvətəʊn] *n (of sadness, bitterness)* pointe *f*; *(of vio-*

lence, racism) relent *m*; **his speech was full of racist overtones** son discours était truffé de sous-entendus racistes

overtook [əʊvə'tʊk] *pt of* **overtake**

overture ['əʊvətjʊə(r)] *n Mus* ouverture *f*; *Fig* **to make overtures to sb** *(sexually)* faire des avances à qn; *(in business, politics)* faire des démarches auprès de qn

overturn [əʊvə'tɜːn] **1** *vt (table, government)* renverser; *(boat)* faire chavirer; *(decision)* annuler

2 *vi* se renverser; *(of boat)* chavirer

overuse 1 *n* [əʊvə'juːs] emploi *m* excessif

2 *vt* [əʊvə'juːz] abuser de

overvalue [əʊvə'væljuː] *vt (currency)* surévaluer; *(ability)* surestimer

overview ['əʊvəvjuː] *n* vue *f* d'ensemble

overweight [əʊvə'weɪt] *adj* trop gros (grosse); **to be 10 pounds o.** ≃ avoir 4,5 kilos de trop

overwhelm [əʊvə'welm] *vt (enemy, opponent)* écraser; **overwhelmed with joy** au comble de la joie; **overwhelmed by grief/with work** accablé(e) de chagrin/de travail

overwhelming [əʊvə'welmɪŋ] *adj (need, desire)* irrépressible; *(pressure, defeat, majority)* écrasant(e)

overwhelmingly [əʊvə'welmɪŋlɪ] *adv* massivement

overwork *n* ['əʊvəwɜːk] surmenage *m*

2 *vt* [əʊvə'wɜːk] *(person)* surcharger de travail

3 *vi* [əʊvə'wɜːk] se surmener

overwrite [əʊvə'raɪt] *(pt* **overwrote** [əʊvə'rəʊt], *pp* **overwritten** [əʊvə'rɪtən]) *vt Comput (file)* écraser; **o. mode** mode *m* de superposition

overwrought [əʊvə'rɔːt] *adj* à bout; **to get o. (about sth)** se mettre dans tous ses états (à propos de qch)

ovulate ['ɒvjʊleɪt] *vi Biol* ovuler

ovulation [ɒvjʊ'leɪʃən] *n Biol* ovulation *f*

ovum ['əʊvəm] *(pl* **ova** ['əʊvə]) *n Biol* ovule *m*

ow [aʊ] *exclam* aïe!, ouïe!

owe [əʊ] *vt also Fig* devoir; **to o. sb sth, to o. sth to sb** devoir qch à qn; **to o. sb an apology** devoir des excuses à qn; **to o. it to oneself to do sth** se devoir de faire qch

owing ['əʊɪŋ] *adj* **(a)** **the money o. to me** l'argent qui m'est dû **(b)** **o. to** *(because of)* en raison de, à cause de

owl [aʊl] *n* hibou *m*, chouette *f*

own [əʊn] **1** *adj* propre; **her o. money** son propre argent; **I saw it with my o. eyes** je l'ai vu de mes propres yeux; **I do my o. accounts** je fais mes comptes moi-même; **she's famous in her o. right** elle est célèbre elle aussi; **o. goal** *(in soccer)* = but marqué contre son propre camp; *Fig* **to score an o. goal** apporter de l'eau au moulin de l'adversaire

2 *pron* **(a)** **my o.** le mien (la mienne); **the house is my o.** la maison est à moi; **I have money of my o.** j'ai de l'argent à moi; **to make sth one's o.** s'approprier qch; **for reasons of her o.** pour des raisons qui ne regardent qu'elle

(b) **to do sth on one's o.** *(without company)* faire qch tout(e) seul(e); **I am (all) on my o.** je suis seul; **you're on your o.!** *(I won't support you)* débrouille-toi tout seul!

(c) *(idioms)* **to come into one's o.** montrer ce dont on est capable; **to get one's o. back (on sb)** se venger (de qn); **to hold one's o.** se maintenir

3 *vt* **(a)** *(property)* posséder, être propriétaire de; **who owns this sweater?** à qui est ce pull?; **he behaves as if he owns the place** il se conduit comme en pays conquis

(b) *Old-fashioned (admit)* avouer

▸**own up** *vi (confess)* avouer; **to o. up to sth** avouer qch

own-brand ['əʊn'brænd] *adj Com* vendu(e) sous la marque du distributeur

owner ['əʊnə(r)] *n* propriétaire *mf*

ownership ['əʊnəʃɪp] *n* propriété *f*; **under new o.** *(sign)* changement de propriétaire; **to be in private/public o.** appartenir au secteur privé/public

ox [ɒks] (*pl* **oxen** [ˈɒksən]) *n* bœuf *m*

oxide [ˈɒksaɪd] *n Chem* oxyde *m*

oxidize [ˈɒksɪdaɪz] *Chem* **1** *vt* oxyder
  2 *vi* s'oxyder

oxtail [ˈɒksteɪl] *n* queue *f* de bœuf

oxyacetylene [ɒksɪəˈsetɪliːn] *n Chem* **o. torch** chalumeau *m* oxyacétylénique

oxygen [ˈɒksɪdʒən] *n* oxygène *m*; **o. bottle** *or* **cylinder** bouteille *f* d'oxygène; **o. mask** masque *m* à oxygène

oxymoron [ɒksɪˈmɔːrɒn] (*pl* **oxymora** [ɒksɪˈmɔːrə]) *n* oxymore *m*, oxymoron *m*

oyster [ˈɔɪstə(r)] *n* huître *f*; *Fig* **the world's your o.** le monde t'appartient; **o. bed** parc *m* à huîtres; **o. farming** ostréiculture *f*

oystercatcher [ˈɔɪstəkætʃə(r)] *n* huîtrier *m*

Oz [ɒz] *n Fam* l'Australie *f*

oz (*abbr* **ounce(s)**) once *f*

ozone [ˈəʊzəʊn] *n Chem* ozone *m*; **o. depletion** diminution *f* de la couche d'ozone; **the o. layer** la couche d'ozone

ozone-friendly [ˈəʊzəʊnˈfrendlɪ] *adj* qui préserve la couche d'ozone

P

P, p [piː] *n (letter)* P, p *m inv; Fam* **to mind one's P's and Q's** bien se tenir

P2P [ˈpiːtuːˈpiː] *adj Comput (abbr* **peer to peer)** P2P

PA [ˈpiːˈeɪ] *n* **(a)** *(abbr* **public address)** PA (system) (système *m* de) sonorisation *f* **(b)** *Com (abbr* **personal assistant)** secrétaire *mf* de direction

pa [pɑː] *n Fam (dad)* papa *m*

p.a. *(abbr* **per annum)** par an

pace [peɪs] **1** *n* **(a)** *(step)* pas *m; Fig* **to put sb through his/her paces** mettre qn à l'épreuve **(b)** *(speed)* vitesse *f*, allure *f;* **at a slow/fast p.** à petite/vive allure; **to set the p.** donner l'allure; *Fig* montrer la voie; **to keep p. with sb** suivre qn; *Fig (in activity)* suivre le rythme de qn; **the slower p. of country life** le rythme plus paisible de la vie à la campagne
2 *vt (room, street)* arpenter; **to p. oneself** *(in race, work)* trouver son rythme
3 *vi* **to p. up and down** faire les cent pas

pacemaker [ˈpeɪsmeɪkə(r)] *n* **(a)** *(in race)* meneur(euse) *m,f* de train **(b)** *(for heart)* stimulateur *m* cardiaque

Pacific [pəˈsɪfɪk] *adj* **the P. (Ocean)** le Pacifique, l'océan *m* Pacifique; **the P. Rim** les pays *mpl* de l'Asie Pacifique; **P. Standard Time** heure *f* de la côte ouest de l'Amérique du Nord

pacifier [ˈpæsɪfaɪə(r)] *n* tétine *f*

pacifism [ˈpæsɪfɪzəm] *n* pacifisme *m*

pacifist [ˈpæsɪfɪst] *n & adj* pacifiste *mf*

pacify [ˈpæsɪfaɪ] *(pt & pp* **pacified)** *vt (country)* pacifier; *(person)* apaiser, calmer

pack [pæk] **1** *n* **(a)** *(rucksack)* sac *m* à dos
(b) *(of cigarettes, detergent)* paquet *m; (of beer)* pack *m; (of playing cards)* jeu *m*
(c) *(of thieves, photographers)* bande *f; (of runners, cyclists)* peloton *m; (in rugby)* pack *m; (of wolves)* meute *f;* **a p. of lies** un tissu de mensonges; **p. animal** animal *m* de bât; **p. ice** banquise *f*
2 *vt* **(a)** *(in box, suitcase)* mettre (dans sa valise/son sac/sa malle/*etc.*)
(b) *(cram) (earth into hole)* tasser; *(passengers into bus, train)* entasser
(c) *(fill) (hole, box)* bourrer **(with** de); *also Fig* **to p. one's bags** faire ses valises
(d) **to p. a punch** *(of fighter)* cogner dur; *(of drink)* être costaud
3 *vi* **(a)** *(prepare luggage)* faire ses valises *ou* bagages; *Fam Fig* **to send sb packing** envoyer promener qn
(b) *(cram)* **to p. into a room/bus** s'entasser dans une pièce/un bus

▸**pack off** *vt sep Fam (send away)* expédier

▸**pack up 1** *vt sep (tidy away)* ranger
2 *vi Fam (finish work)* arrêter

package [ˈpækɪdʒ] **1** *n (parcel)* paquet *m*, colis *m; (of measures, laws)* ensemble *m; (contract)* contrat *m* global; **p. deal** *or* **vacation** forfait *m (comprenant au moins transport et logement)*
2 *vt* emballer, conditionner; *Fig* **to p. sb** *(pop star, politician)* créer l'image de marque de qn

packaging [ˈpækɪdʒɪŋ] *n* emballage *m*

packed [pækt] *adj (crowded)* bondé(e)

packer [ˈpækə(r)] *n (person)* emballeur(euse) *m,f*

packet [ˈpækɪt] *n* paquet *m*

packhorse [ˈpækhɔːs] *n* cheval *m* de bât

packing [ˈpækɪŋ] *n* **(a)** *(packing material)* emballage *m;* **p. case** caisse *f* d'emballage **(b)** *(for trip)* **to do one's p.** faire ses valises *ou* bagages

pact [pækt] *n* pacte *m*

pad [pæd] **1** *n* **(a)** *(for protection)* protection *f; (of dog's, cat's paw)* coussinet *m; (of cotton wool)* tampon *m; (for helicopters)* aire *f* d'atterrissage; **(writing) p.** bloc *m* **(b)** *Fam (home)* piaule *f*
2 *vt (pt & pp* **padded)** *(furniture)* capitonner **(with** avec)
3 *vi* **to p. about** aller et venir à pas feutrés

▸**pad out** *vt sep (speech, essay)* étoffer

padded [ˈpædɪd] *adj (furniture, wall, cell)* capitonné(e); *(jacket)* matelassé(e); **p. shoulders** épaulettes *fpl*

padding [ˈpædɪŋ] *n (for clothes)* ouate *f; Fig (in speech, essay)* remplissage *m*

paddle [ˈpædəl] **1** *n* **(a)** *(for canoe)* pagaie *f; (of paddle boat)* aube *f;* **p. boat** bateau *m* à aubes **(b)** *(walk in water)* **to have a p.** patauger **(c)** *(for table tennis)* raquette *f*
2 *vt* **to p. a canoe** pagayer
3 *vi* **(a)** *(in canoe)* pagayer; *(of duck)* nager **(b)** *(walk in water)* patauger

paddock [ˈpædək] *n* paddock *m*

paddy [ˈpædɪ] *n (pl* **paddies)** **p. (field)** rizière *f*

padlock [ˈpædlɒk] **1** *n* cadenas *m*
2 *vt* cadenasser

padre [ˈpɑːdreɪ] *n* aumônier *m (militaire)*

pagan [ˈpeɪgən] *n & adj* païen(enne) *m,f*

paganism [ˈpeɪgənɪzəm] *n* paganisme *m*

page¹ [peɪdʒ] *n (of book, on Internet)* page *f;* **on p. six** (à la) page six

page² [peɪdʒ] **1** *n (servant, at wedding)* page *m*
2 *vt (call) (by loudspeaker)* appeler par haut-parleur; *(by electronic device)* biper

pageant [ˈpædʒənt] *n (procession)* spectacle *m* grandiose; *(historical)* spectacle *m* historique

pageantry [ˈpædʒəntrɪ] *n* pompe *f*, apparat *m*

pageboy [ˈpeɪdʒbɔɪ] *n* page *m;* **p. (haircut)** coiffure *f* à la Jeanne d'Arc

pager [ˈpeɪdʒə(r)] *n* récepteur *m* d'appel

pagination [pædʒɪˈneɪʃən] *n Typ* pagination *f*

pagoda [pəˈgəudə] *n* pagode *f*

paid [peɪd] **1** *adj* **(a)** *(person, work)* rémunéré(e), payé(e) **(b)** **to put p. to sb's chances/hopes** réduire les chances/espoirs de qn à néant
2 *pt & pp of* **pay**

paid-up [ˈpeɪdʌp] *adj (member)* qui a payé sa cotisation

pail [peɪl] *n* seau *m*

pain [peɪn] **1** *n* **(a)** *(physical)* douleur *f; (emotional)* peine *f;* **to**

cause sb p. *(physical)* faire souffrir qn; *(emotional)* faire de la peine à qn; **to be in p.** souffrir; **I have a p. in my leg** j'ai une douleur à la jambe

(**b**) *(trouble)* **to take pains** *or* **to be at great pains to do sth** se donner du mal pour faire qch; **for my pains** pour ma peine

(**c**) *Formal* **under p. of death** sous peine de mort

(**d**) *(idioms) Fam* **he's a p. (in the neck)** il est casse-pieds; *Vulg* **it's a p. in the ass** c'est chiant; *Fam* **cooking is such a p.!** c'est tellement casse-pieds de faire la cuisine!

2 *vt* peiner

pained [peɪnd] *adj (look, expression)* peiné(e), affligé(e)

painful ['peɪnfʊl] *adj (physically)* douloureux(euse); *(emotionally)* pénible; **it's p. to watch** c'est un spectacle pénible

painfully ['peɪnfʊlɪ] *adv (walk)* avec difficulté; **she fell p.** elle s'est fait mal en tombant; *Fig* **p. shy** d'une timidité maladive

painkiller ['peɪnkɪlə(r)] *n* analgésique *m*

painless ['peɪnlɪs] *adj (not painful)* indolore; *Fig (easy)* facile

painstaking ['peɪnzteɪkɪŋ] *adj* minutieux(euse)

paint [peɪnt] **1** *n* peinture *f*; **wet p.** *(sign)* peinture fraîche; **p. gun** pistolet *m* à peinture; **p. remover** décapant *m*

2 *vt* peindre; *Fam* **to p. one's face** *(put on make-up)* se maquiller; **to p. one's nails** se faire les ongles; *Fig* **to p. a favorable picture of a situation** brosser un tableau favorable d'une situation; *Fig* **to p. the town red** faire la noce

3 *vi* peindre

paintball ['peɪntbɔːl] *n (game)* paintball *m*

paintballing ['peɪntbɔːlɪŋ] *n* **to go p.** faire du paintball

paintbox ['peɪntbɒks] *n* boîte *f* de couleurs

paintbrush ['peɪntbrʌʃ] *n* pinceau *m*

painter ['peɪntə(r)] *n* peintre *m*; **p. and decorator** peintre-tapissier *m*

painting ['peɪntɪŋ] *n (picture)* tableau *m*, peinture *f*; *(activity)* la peinture

paintwork ['peɪntwɜːk] *n* peinture *f*

pair [peə(r)] **1** *n* paire *f*; **in pairs** deux par deux; **a p. of glasses** une paire de lunettes; **a p. of scissors** une paire de ciseaux; **a p. of pants** un pantalon

2 *vt* **to p. sb with sb** mettre qn avec qn

▶**pair off 1** *vt sep (people)* mettre deux par deux

2 *vi (of people)* se mettre deux par deux

▶**pair up** *vi* se mettre ensemble

pajamas [pəˈdʒɑːməz] *npl* pyjama *m*; **a pair of p.** un pyjama

Pakistan [pækɪˈstæn] *n* le Pakistan

Pakistani [pækɪˈstɑːnɪ] **1** *n* Pakistanais(e) *m,f*

2 *adj* pakistanais(e)

PAL [pæl] *n TV (abbr* **phase alternation line***)* PAL

pal [pæl] *n Fam* copain (copine) *m,f*; **listen, p.!** fais gaffe, mon vieux!

palace ['pælɪs] *n* palais *m*

palatable ['pælətəbəl] *adj (food)* agréable au palais; *Fig (suggestion)* acceptable

palate ['pælɪt] *n (in mouth)* palais *m*

palatial [pəˈleɪʃəl] *adj (impressive)* grandiose; *(luxurious)* luxueux(euse)

palaver [pəˈlɑːvə(r)] *n Fam (fuss)* histoire *f*

pale¹ [peɪl] **1** *adj* pâle; **to turn p.** pâlir; **p. with fright** blanc de peur

2 *vi (of person)* pâlir; **to p. into insignificance** être insignifiant(e)

pale² [peɪl] *n* **beyond the p.** *(behavior)* inacceptable; *(person)* infréquentable

paleness ['peɪlnɪs] *n* pâleur *f*

Palestine ['pælɪstaɪn] *n* la Palestine

Palestinian [pælɪˈstɪnɪən] **1** *n* Palestinien(enne) *m,f*

2 *adj* palestinien(enne)

palette ['pælɪt] *n Art* palette *f*; **p. knife** couteau *m* à palette

palings ['peɪlɪŋz] *npl (fence)* palissade *f*

palisade [pælɪˈseɪd] *n* palissade *f*

pall¹ [pɔːl] *n* (**a**) *(of smoke)* voile *m* (**b**) *(coffin)* cercueil *m*

pall² [pɔːl] *vi (become uninteresting)* perdre son attrait

pallbearer ['pɔːlbeərə(r)] *n* porteur *m* (du cercueil)

pallet ['pælɪt] *n* palette *f*

palliative ['pælɪətɪv] *n* palliatif *m*

pallid ['pælɪd] *adj* blême, blafard(e)

palm¹ [pɑːm] *n* **p. (tree)** palmier *m*; **p. (leaf)** palme *f*; **p. oil** huile *f* de palme; **P. Sunday** Dimanche *m* des Rameaux

palm² [pɑːm] *n (of hand)* paume *f*; *Fig* **to have sb in the p. of one's hand** avoir qn dans sa poche

▶**palm off** *vt sep* **to p. sth off on sb** refiler qch à qn

palmistry ['pɑːmɪstrɪ] *n* chiromancie *f*

palmtop ['pɑːmtɒp] *n Comput* **p. (computer)** ordinateur *m* de poche

palomino [pæləˈmiːnəʊ] *(pl* **palominos***) n (horse)* palomino *m*

palpable ['pælpəbəl] *adj (atmosphere)* palpable; *(lie)* manifeste; *(difference)* sensible

palpate ['pælpeɪt] *vt Med* palper

palpitate ['pælpɪteɪt] *vi also Fig* palpiter

palpitations [pælpɪˈteɪʃənz] *npl* palpitations *fpl*

paltry ['pɔːltrɪ] *adj (amount, sum)* dérisoire; *(excuse)* piètre

pamper ['pæmpə(r)] *vt (person)* dorloter; **to p. oneself** se faire plaisir

pamphlet ['pæmflɪt] *n (informative)* brochure *f*; *(political)* pamphlet *m*

pan¹ [pæn] **1** *n (saucepan)* casserole *f*; *(frying pan)* poêle *f*; *(of scales)* plateau *m*

2 *vi (pt & pp* **panned***)* **to p. for gold** faire de l'orpaillage

pan² [pæn] *(pt & pp* **panned***) vt Fam (criticize)* descendre en flammes

▶**pan out** *vi Fam (turn out)* marcher, se dérouler; **it depends how things p. out** ça dépend de comment les choses vont s'arranger

panacea [pænəˈsɪə] *n* panacée *f*

panache [pəˈnæʃ] *n* panache *m*

Pan-African [pænˈæfrɪkən] *adj* panafricain(e)

Panama ['pænəmɑː] *n* le Panama; **the P. Canal** le canal de Panama; **P. (hat)** panama *m*

Panamanian [pænəˈmeɪnɪən] **1** *n* Panaméen(enne) *m,f*

2 *adj* panaméen(enne)

Pan-American [pænəˈmerɪkən] *adj* panaméricain(e)

pancake ['pænkeɪk] *n* crêpe *f*

pancreas ['pæŋkrɪəs] *n Anat* pancréas *m*

panda ['pændə] *n* panda *m*

pandemonium [pændɪˈməʊnɪəm] *n (confusion)* chaos *m*; *(uproar)* vacarme *m* assourdissant

pander ['pændə(r)] *vi* **to p. to sb/sth** flatter qn/qch

pane [peɪn] *n* **p. (of glass)** vitre *f*

panel ['pænəl] *n* (**a**) *(of wood, metal)* panneau *m* (**b**) *(of switches, lights)* tableau *m* de bord (**c**) *(of experts)* comité *m*; **p. discussion** table *f* ronde; *(on radio, TV program)* invités *mpl*

paneling ['pænəlɪŋ] *n* lambris *m*

panelist ['pænəlɪst] *n (on radio, TV program)* invité(e) *m,f*

pang [pæŋ] *n (of guilt, jealousy)* accès *m*; **pangs of hunger** tiraillements *mpl* d'estomac

panhandle ['pænhændəl] **1** *n* langue *f* de terre

2 *vt Fam* **to p. money from sb** taper qn

3 *vi Fam* faire la manche

panic ['pænɪk] **1** *n* panique *f*, affolement *m*; **in a p.** paniqué(e), affolé(e); **to get into a p.** paniquer, s'affoler; **p. attack** crise *f* d'angoisse; **p. button** bouton *m* déclencheur du signal d'alarme; *Fin* **p. buying/selling** achat *m*/vente *f* sous le coup de la panique

2 *vt* (*pt & pp* **panicked**) affoler

3 *vi* paniquer, s'affoler

panicky ['pænɪkɪ] *adj Fam* **to be/get p.** paniquer, s'affoler

panic-stricken ['pænɪkstrɪkən] *adj* pris(e) de panique, affolé(e)

pannier ['pænɪə(r)] *n* (*on bicycle*) sacoche *f*; (*on animal*) panier *m* de bât

panoply ['pænəplɪ] *n* panoplie *f*

panorama [pænə'rɑ:mə] *n* panorama *m*

panoramic [pænə'ræmɪk] *adj* panoramique

panpipes ['pænpaɪps] *npl Mus* flûte *f* de Pan

pansy ['pænzɪ] (*pl* **pansies**) *n* (**a**) (*flower*) pensée *f* (**b**) *Fam* (*effeminate man*) tante *f*

pant [pænt] *vi* haleter; **to p. for breath** chercher son souffle

panther ['pænθə(r)] *n* panthère *f*

pantihose = **pantyhose**

panties ['pæntɪz] *npl* (*petite*) culotte *f*, slip *m*

pantomime ['pæntəmaɪm] *n* (*mime*) mime *m*

pantry ['pæntrɪ] (*pl* **pantries**) *n* garde-manger *m inv*

pants [pænts] *npl* (**a**) (*trousers*) pantalon *m* (**b**) (*idioms*) *Fam* **to scare the p. off sb** flanquer la trouille à qn; *Fam* **to wear the p.** porter la culotte; *Fam* **to be caught with one's p. down** être pris(e) en flagrant délit

pantsuit ['pæntsu:t] *n* tailleur-pantalon *m*

pantyhose ['pæntɪhəʊz] *n* collant *m*

Pap [pæp] *adj Med* **P. smear**, **P. test** frottis *m* vaginal

pap [pæp] *n Fam Pej* (*nonsense*) idioties *fpl*

papa ['pɑpə] *n Old-fashioned* papa *m*

papacy ['peɪpəsɪ] *n* papauté *f*

papal ['peɪpəl] *adj* papal(e)

paparazzi ['pæpə'rætsɪ] *npl* paparazzi *mpl*

papaya [pə'paɪə] *n* (*fruit*) papaye *f*; (*tree*) papayer *m*

paper ['peɪpə(r)] **1** *n* (**a**) (*material*) papier *m*; **a piece of p.** un bout *ou* un morceau de papier; *Fig* **on p.** (*in theory*) sur le papier; **p. airplane** avion *m* en papier; **p. bag** sac *m* en papier; **p. cup** gobelet *m* en carton; *Comput* **p. feed** alimentation *f* en papier; **p. mill** papeterie *f*; **p. money** papier-monnaie *m*; **p. plate** assiette *f* en carton; **p. towel** essuie-tout *m inv*; *Comput* **p. tray** chariot *m* d'alimentation en papier

(**b**) **papers** (*documents*) papiers *mpl*

(**c**) (*examination*) épreuve *f* écrite

(**d**) (*scholarly study, report*) article *m*; **to read** *or* **to give a p.** faire un exposé

(**e**) (*newspaper*) journal *m*; **p. boy/girl** livreur *m*/livreuse *f* de journaux

2 *vt* (*wall, room*) tapisser

▶**paper over** *vt sep Fig* **to p. over the cracks** masquer les problèmes

paperback ['peɪpəbæk] *n* livre *m* de poche

paperclip ['peɪpəklɪp] *n* trombone *m*

paperknife ['peɪpənaɪf] (*pl* **paperknives** ['peɪpənaɪvz]) *n* coupe-papier *m*

paperweight ['peɪpəweɪt] *n* presse-papiers *m inv*

paperwork ['peɪpəwɜ:k] *n* travail *m* administratif, paperasserie *f*; (*documentation*) documents *mpl*

papery ['peɪpərɪ] *adj* (*skin*) parcheminé(e)

papier-mâché ['pæpjeɪ'mæʃeɪ] *n* papier *m* mâché

paprika ['pæprɪkə] *n* paprika *m*

Papuan ['pæpjʊən] **1** *n* Papou(e) *m,f*

2 *adj* papou(e)

Papua New Guinea ['pæpjʊənju:'gɪnɪ:] *n* Papouasie-Nouvelle-Guinée *f*

papyrus [pə'paɪrəs] *n* papyrus *m*

par [pɑ:(r)] *n* (**a**) (*equality*) égalité *f*, pair *m*; **to be on a p. with sb/sth** être au même niveau que qn/qch (**b**) (*in golf*) par *m*; **a p.-three (hole)** un par trois; *Fig* **to be p. for the course**

n'avoir rien de surprenant (**c**) *Fin* (*of bills, shares*) pair *m*; **above/below p.** au-dessus/au-dessous du pair; *Fig* **to feel below p.** ne pas être dans son assiette

parable ['pærəbəl] *n* parabole *f*

parabolic [pærə'bɒlɪk] *adj* parabolique

paracetamol [pærə'si:təmɒl] *n* paracétamol *m*

parachute ['pærəʃu:t] **1** *n* parachute *m*; **p. jump** saut *m* en parachute; **to make a p. jump** sauter en parachute

2 *vt* parachuter

3 *vi* sauter en parachute

parachuting ['pærəʃu:tɪŋ] *n* parachutisme *m*; **to go p.** faire du parachutisme

parachutist ['pærəʃu:tɪst] *n* parachutiste *mf*

parade [pə'reɪd] **1** *n* (*procession*) défilé *m*; **on p.** (*troops*) à l'exercice; **p. ground** terrain *m* de manœuvres

2 *vt* (*troops*) faire défiler; *Fig* (*wealth, knowledge*) faire étalage de

3 *vi* (*of troops*) défiler; **to p. about** *or* **around** (*of person*) se pavaner

paradigm ['pærədaɪm] *n* paradigme *m*

paradise ['pærədaɪs] *n* paradis *m*

paradox ['pærədɒks] *n* paradoxe *m*

paradoxical [pærə'dɒksɪkəl] *adj* paradoxal(e)

paraffin ['pærəfɪn] *n* paraffine *f*; **p. heater** chauffage *m* à pétrole; **p. lamp** lampe *f* à pétrole; **p. wax** paraffine

paragliding ['pærəglaɪdɪŋ] *n* parapente *m*; **to go p.** faire du parapente

paragon ['pærəgən] *n* modèle *m*; **a p. of virtue** un modèle de vertu

paragraph ['pærəgræf] *n* paragraphe *m*

Paraguay ['pærəgwaɪ] *n* le Paraguay *m*

Paraguayan [pærə'gwaɪən] **1** *n* Paraguayen(enne) *m,f*

2 *adj* paraguayen(enne)

parakeet ['pærəki:t] *n* perruche *f*

parallel ['pærəlel] **1** *n Math* parallèle *f*; *Fig* (*analogy*) parallèle *m*; **to draw a p. between two things** établir un parallèle entre deux choses; **without p.** sans égal, sans pareil

2 *adj Math* parallèle; *Fig* (*analogous*) pareil(eille), semblable; **to be** *or* **to run p. to sth** être parallèle à qch; **p. bars** barres *fpl* parallèles; **p. lines** lignes *fpl* parallèles; *Comput* **p. processing** traitement *m* en simultanéité

3 *vt* (*be similar to*) être analogue à; (*be equal to*) égaler

parallelogram [pærə'leləgræm] *n* parallélogramme *m*

paralysis [pə'ræləsɪs] (*pl* **paralyses** [pə'ræləsi:z]) *n* paralysie *f*

paralytic [pærə'lɪtɪk] **1** *n* paralytique *mf*

2 *adj* paralytique

paralyze ['pærəlaɪz] *vt also Fig* paralyser

paramedic [pærə'medɪk] *n* auxiliaire *mf* médical(e)

parameter [pə'ræmɪtə(r)] *n* paramètre *m*

paramilitary [pærə'mɪlɪtərɪ] **1** *adj* paramilitaire

2 *n* (*pl* **paramilitaries**) paramilitaire *mf*

paramount ['pærəmaʊnt] *adj* primordial(e); **of p. importance** d'une importance capitale

paranoia [pærə'nɔɪə] *n* paranoïa *f*

paranoid ['pærənɔɪd] *adj* paranoïaque; **to be p. about sth** être obsédé(e) par qch

paranormal [pærə'nɔ:məl] **1** *n* **the p.** le paranormal

2 *adj* paranormal(e)

parapet ['pærəpet] *n* parapet *m*

paraphernalia [pærəfə'neɪlɪə] *n* (*equipment*) attirail *m*; (*things*) affaires *fpl*; (*clutter*) bazar *m*

paraphrase ['pærəfreɪz] **1** *n* paraphrase *f*

2 *vt* paraphraser

paraplegic [pærə'pli:dʒɪk] *n & adj* paraplégique *mf*

parascending ['pærəsendɪŋ] *n* parachute *m* ascensionnel

parasite ['pærəsaɪt] *n also Fig* parasite *m*

parasitic [pærə'sıtık] *adj also Fig* parasite; *(existence)* de parasite

parasol ['pærəsɒl] *n* ombrelle *f*

paratrooper ['pærətru:pə(r)] *n* parachutiste *m*

parboil ['pa:bɔɪl] *vt* faire cuire à demi

parcel ['pɑ:səl] **1** (**a**) *(package)* colis *m*, paquet *m*; **p. bomb** colis piégé; **p. post** service *m* de colis postaux (**b**) *(of land)* parcelle *f*

▸**parcel out** *vt sep* répartir

▸**parcel up** *vt sep* empaqueter, emballer

parchment ['pɑ:tʃmənt] *n* parchemin *m*; **p. paper** papier *m* parchemin

pardon ['pɑ:dən] **1** *n (forgiveness)* pardon *m*; *Law* grâce *f*; **(I beg your) p.?** *(what did you say?)* pardon?, comment?; **I beg your p.!** *(in apology)* je vous demande pardon!
2 *vt (action, person)* pardonner; *Law* grâcier; **to p. sb for sth** pardonner qch à qn; **p. me?** *(what did you say?)* (je vous demande) pardon?; **p. me!** *(in apology)* pardonnez-moi!

pardonable ['pɑ:dənəbəl] *adj* pardonnable, excusable

pare [peə(r)] *vt (vegetable)* éplucher; *(apple)* peler; *(nails)* rogner; *(expenses)* réduire

▸**pare down** *vt sep (expenses)* réduire

parent ['peərənt] *n (father)* père *m*; *(mother)* mère *f*; **parents** parents *mpl*; **p. company** société *f* ou maison *f* mère; **p.-teacher association** = association des parents d'élèves et des professeurs

parentage ['peərəntıdʒ] *n* origine *f*

parental [pə'rentəl] *adj* parental(e)

parenthesis [pə'renθəsɪs] *(pl* **parentheses** [pə'renθəsi:z]*) n* parenthèse *f*; **in parentheses** entre parenthèses

parenthood ['peərənhʊd] *n (gen)* parentalité *f*; *(fatherhood)* paternité *f*; *(motherhood)* maternité *f*; **the joys of p.** le bonheur d'être parent; **single p.** monoparentalité *f*

parenting ['peərəntıŋ] *n* art *m* d'être parent; **p. skills** capacité *f* à élever des enfants

pariah [pə'raɪə] *n* paria *m*

Paris ['pærɪs] *n* Paris

parish ['pærɪʃ] *n* paroisse *f*; **p. church** église *f* paroissiale; **p. priest** *(Catholic)* curé *m*; *(Protestant)* pasteur *m*

parishioner [pə'rɪʃənə(r)] *n* paroissien(enne) *m,f*

Parisian [pə'rɪzɪən] **1** *n* Parisien(enne) *m,f*
2 *adj* parisien(enne)

parity ['pærɪtɪ] *n* égalité *f*; **to achieve p.** *(of pay)* obtenir l'égalité

park [pɑ:k] **1** *n* (**a**) jardin *m* public, parc *m* (**b**) *(on automatic gearbox)* position *f* (de) stationnement
2 *vt (car)* garer; *Fam* **to p. oneself in a chair/in front of the TV** s'installer dans un fauteuil/devant la télé

parka ['pɑ:kə] *n* parka *f*

parking ['pɑ:kıŋ] *n* stationnement *m*; **no p.** *(sign)* défense de stationner; **p. attendant** gardien(enne) *m,f* de parking; **p. brake** frein *m* à main; **p. lights** *(on car)* feux *mpl* de position; **p. lot** parking *m*; **p. meter** parcmètre *m*, *Can* compteur *m* de stationnement; **p. space** place *f* (de parking); **p. ticket** contravention *f*

Parkinson's disease ['pɑ:kınsənzdı'zi:z] *n* la maladie de Parkinson

parkland ['pɑ:klænd] *n* espace(s) *m(pl)* vert(s)

parkway ['pɑ:kweɪ] *n* route *f* bordée d'arbres et de verdure

parlance ['pɑ:ləns] *n* langage *m*; **in legal/political p.** en termes juridiques/politiques; **in common p.** en langage ordinaire

parlay ['pɑ:leɪ] *vt (winnings)* remettre en jeu; *Fig (money)* faire fructifier

parley ['pɑ:lɪ] *vi* parlementer (**with** avec); *(more officially)* être en pourparlers (**with** avec)

parliament ['pɑ:ləmənt] *n* parlement *m*

parliamentarian [pɑ:ləmen'teərɪən] *n* parlementaire *mf*

parliamentary [pɑ:lə'mentərɪ] *adj* parlementaire; **p. privilege** immunité *f* parlementaire

parlor ['pɑ:lə(r)] *n* salon *m*

Parmesan [pɑ:mɪ'zæn] *n* **P. (cheese)** parmesan *m*

parochial [pə'rəʊkɪəl] *adj Rel* paroissial(e); *Fig Pej* de clocher; **to be p.** *(of person)* avoir l'esprit de clocher; **p. school** école *f* religieuse

parody ['pærədɪ] **1** *n (pl* **parodies)** parodie *f* (**of** de)
2 *vt (pt & pp* **parodied)** parodier

parole [pə'rəʊl] **1** *n* liberté *f* conditionnelle; **to be (out) on p.** être en liberté conditionnelle; **p. officer** contrôleur *m* judiciaire
2 *vt* mettre en liberté conditionnelle

paroxysm ['pærəksızəm] *n (of anger, guilt, jealousy)* crise *f*; **to be in paroxysms of laughter** avoir le fou rire

parquet ['pɑ:keɪ] *n* **p. (floor)** parquet *m*

parrot ['pærət] **1** *n also Fig* perroquet *m*
2 *vt* répéter comme un perroquet

parrot-fashion ['pærətfæʃən] *adv* comme un perroquet

parry ['pærɪ] *(pt & pp* **parried)** *vt (blow)* parer; *(question)* éluder

parsimonious [pɑ:sɪ'məʊnɪəs] *adj* parcimonieux(euse)

parsley ['pɑ:slɪ] *n* persil *m*

parsnip ['pɑ:snɪp] *n* panais *m*

parson ['pɑ:sən] *n* pasteur *m*

parsonage ['pɑ:sənɪdʒ] *n* presbytère *m*

part [pɑ:t] **1** *n* (**a**) *(portion, component)* partie *f*; **p. of the body** partie du corps; **p. of speech** partie du discours; **(spare) parts** pièces *fpl* détachées; **p. two** *(of TV series, story)* deuxième partie; **in that p. of the world** dans cette région du monde; **in these parts** dans ces régions; **good in parts** bon (bonne) en partie; **the best/worst p. was when...** le meilleur/le pire ça a été quand...; **the difficult p. is remembering** ce qui est difficile, c'est de se souvenir; **for the best** *or* **greater p. of five years** pendant presque cinq ans; **the greater p. of the population** la plus grande partie de la population; **to be p. of sth** faire partie de qch; **it's all p. of growing up** c'est ce qui arrive quand on grandit; **it is p. and parcel of...** c'est une partie intégrante de...; **in p.** en partie; **for the most p.** pour la plupart; **p. exchange** reprise *f* (en compte); **p. owner** copropriétaire *mf*
(**b**) *(role)* rôle *m*; **to take p. (in sth)** prendre part (à qch); **to have** *or* **to play a p. in sth** jouer un rôle dans qch; **I want no p. in it** je ne veux rien avoir à faire là-dedans
(**c**) *(side)* **to take sb's p.** prendre le parti de qn; **on the p. of...** de la part de...; **for my p.** pour ma part
(**d**) *(in hair)* raie *f*
2 *adv* **she's p. French** elle est en partie française; **p. silk p. cotton** soie et coton
3 *vt (fighters, lovers)* séparer; **to p. one's hair** se faire une raie; **to p. company** se séparer
4 *vi* (**a**) *(leave one another)* se quitter; *(split up)* se rompre; **to p. (as) friends** se séparer (en) bons amis; **to p. with sth** se défaire de qch
(**b**) *(of curtains, lips)* s'entrouvrir; *(of crowd)* s'ouvrir

partake [pɑ:'teɪk] *(pt* **partook** [pɑ:'tʊk]*, pp* **partaken** [pɑ:'teɪkən]*) vi Formal* (**a**) **to p. of** *(eat, drink)* prendre (**b**) *(have quality)* **to p. of** relever de

partial ['pɑ:ʃəl] *adj* (**a**) *(incomplete)* partiel(elle) (**b**) *(biased)* partial(e) (**c**) *(fond)* **to be p. to sb/sth** avoir un faible pour qn/qch

partially ['pɑ:ʃəlɪ] *adv* (**a**) *(in part)* en partie, partiellement (**b**) *(with bias)* avec partialité

participant [pɑ:'tɪsɪpənt] *n* participant(e) *m,f*

participate [pɑ:'tɪsɪpeɪt] *vi* participer (**in** à)

participation [pɑ:tɪsɪ'peɪʃən] *n* participation (**in** à)

participle ['pɑ:tɪsɪpəl] *n Gram* participe *m*

particle ['pɑ:tɪkəl] *n (of matter)* particule *f*; *(of dust, sand)* grain *m*; *Fig (of truth)* once *f*

particular [pə'tɪkjʊlə(r)] **1** *n* détail *m*; **in p.** en particulier; **I didn't see anything in p.** je n'ai rien vu de particulier; **to go into particulars** entrer dans les détails; **to take down sb's particulars** noter les coordonnées de qn

2 *adj* (**a**) *(specific)* particulier(ère); *(reason, case, example)* précis(e); **which p. thing/person did you have in mind?** à quoi/à qui pensiez-vous en particulier?; **on that p. day** ce jour-là (**b**) *(special)* particulier(ère); **a p. favorite of mine** (*une*) de mes favoris *(favorites)*; **she is a p. friend of mine** c'est une de mes meilleures amies; **to take p. care over sth** mettre un soin particulier à qch (**c**) *(exacting)* méticuleux(euse); **to be p. about sth** être exigeant(e) pour qch; **I'm not p.** ça m'est égal

particularly [pə'tɪkjʊləlɪ] *adv (especially)* particulièrement, spécialement

parting ['pɑːtɪŋ] *n (separation)* séparation *f*; **the p. of the ways** la croisée des chemins; **p. shot** pique *f (lancée en partant)*; **p. words** mots *mpl* d'adieu

partisan [pɑːtɪ'zæn] *n & adj* partisan(e) *m,f*

partition [pɑː'tɪʃən] **1** *n (in room)* cloison *f*
2 *vt (country)* partager
▸**partition off** *vt sep (room)* cloisonner

partly ['pɑːtlɪ] *adv* partiellement, en partie

partner ['pɑːtnə(r)] **1** *n (in games)* partenaire *mf*; *(in business)* associé(e) *m,f*; *(in dancing)* cavalier(ère) *m,f*; *(in relationship)* compagnon (compagne) *m,f*; **p. in crime** complice *mf*
2 *vt (in games)* faire équipe avec; *(in dancing)* être le (la) cavalier(ère) de

partnership ['pɑːtnəʃɪp] *n* association *f*; **to enter** *or* **to go into p. (with sb)** s'associer (avec qn)

partridge ['pɑːtrɪdʒ] *n* perdrix *f*

part-time [pɑːt'taɪm] *adj & adv* à temps partiel

part-timer [pɑːt'taɪmə(r)] *n* travailleur(euse) *m,f* à temps partiel

partway ['pɑːtweɪ] *adv* **to be p. through sth** ne pas avoir complètement terminé qch; **this will go p. toward covering the costs** cela couvrira en partie les dépenses

party ['pɑːtɪ] **1** *n (pl parties)* (**a**) *(political)* parti *m*; **to follow** *or* **to toe the p. line** suivre la ligne du parti; **p. member** membre *m* du parti; **p. politics** politique *f* de parti; *Pej* politique politicienne (**b**) *(celebration)* fête *f*; **to have** *or* **to give** *or* **to throw a p.** organiser *ou* faire une fête; *Fig* **the p.'s over** la fête est finie; *Fam* **p. animal** fêtard(e) *m,f*; **p. pooper** rabat-joie *m inv* (**c**) *(group)* groupe *m*; *(of workers)* équipe *f*; *Tel* **p. line** ligne *f* commune (à plusieurs abonnés); **p. wall** mur *m* mitoyen (**d**) *Law (participant)* partie *f*; **to be (a) p. to sth** se faire complice de qch
2 *vi (pt & pp partied) Fam (celebrate)* faire la fête

pass¹ [pɑːs] *n (over mountains)* col *m*

pass² [pɑːs] **1** *n* (**a**) *(permit)* laissez-passer *m inv*; *Mil* sauf-conduit *m*; *(for travel)* carte *f* d'abonnement
(**b**) *(in examination)* **to get a p.** avoir la moyenne; **p. mark** moyenne *f*
(**c**) *(in sport)* passe *f*
(**d**) *Fam* **to make a p. at sb** faire des avances à qn
2 *vt* (**a**) *(go past) (person)* croiser; *(destination)* dépasser; *(frontier)* traverser; *(car, runner)* dépasser, doubler
(**b**) *(exam, test)* réussir
(**c**) *(bill, resolution)* voter
(**d**) *(give)* passer; **p. (me) the salt, please** passe-moi le sel, s'il te plaît
(**e**) **to p. the time** *(of person)* passer le temps; **it passes the time** ça fait passer le temps
(**f**) *Law* **to p. sentence** prononcer le verdict; **to p. judgment on sb** porter un jugement sur qn
(**g**) **to p. water** uriner; **to p. wind** avoir des vents
3 *vi* (**a**) *(go past)* passer; *(overtake)* dépasser, doubler; **to p. unobserved** passer inaperçu(e); **to let sth p.** laisser tomber

qch; *also Fig* **p.!** je passe!; **I think I'll p. on the onions** je crois que je ne prendrai pas d'oignons
(**b**) *(of time)* s'écouler, (se) passer; **the weekend passed uneventfully** le week-end s'est passé sans surprises
(**c**) *(go away)* passer
(**d**) *(in exam)* avoir la moyenne
(**e**) *Lit (take place)* **it came to p. that...** c'est alors qu'il arriva que...
▸**pass away** *vi Euph* décéder
▸**pass down** *vt sep (knowledge, tradition)* transmettre
▸**pass for** *vt insep* passer pour; **she'd p. for 25** on pourrait lui donner 25 ans
▸**pass off** *vt sep* **to p. oneself off as sb** se faire passer pour qn; **to p. sth off as sth** faire passer qch pour qch; **she passed it off as a joke** elle a prétendu que c'était une plaisanterie
▸**pass on 1** *vt sep (object)* faire passer; *(news, information)* faire circuler; *(disease)* passer
2 *vi Euph* décéder
▸**pass out** *vi (faint)* perdre connaissance
▸**pass over** *vt sep* **to p. sb over (for promotion)** ignorer qn au moment d'une promotion
▸**pass through 1** *vt insep* traverser
2 *vi* passer
▸**pass up** *vt sep (opportunity)* laisser passer

passable ['pɑːsəbəl] *adj* (**a**) *(of acceptable quality)* passable (**b**) *(road, bridge)* praticable; *(river)* franchissable

passage ['pæsɪdʒ] *n* (**a**) *(journey)* passage *m*; **with the p. of time** avec le temps; **to work one's p.** *(on ship)* travailler pour payer sa traversée (**b**) *(corridor)* couloir *m*, corridor *m*; *(alley)* passage *m* (**c**) *(extract)* passage *m*

passageway ['pæsɪdʒweɪ] *n (corridor)* couloir *m*, corridor *m*; *(alley)* passage *m*

passé [pæ'seɪ] *adj* dépassé(e)

passenger ['pæsəndʒə(r)] *n* passager(ère) *m,f*; **p. seat** place *f* du passager

passer-by ['pɑːsə'baɪ] *(pl passers-by) n* passant(e) *m,f*

passing ['pɑːsɪŋ] **1** *n* (**a**) *(going past)* passage *m*; **to say sth in p.** dire qch en passant; **p. place** *(on road)* aire *f* de croisement (**b**) *(of time)* écoulement *m* (**c**) *(death)* décès *m*
2 *adj (car, motorist)* qui passe; *(remark)* en passant; *(whim, attraction)* passager(ère)

passion ['pæʃən] *n (desire)* passion *f*; *(anger, vehemence)* emportement *m*, colère *f*; **to have a p. for sth** adorer qch; **in a fit of p.** sous le coup de la passion; **she hates him with a p.** elle le hait de toute son âme; **crime of p.** crime *m* passionnel; *Rel* **the P. (of Christ)** la Passion (du Christ); **p. fruit** fruit *m* de la passion

passionate ['pæʃənɪt] *adj (lover, embrace)* passionné(e); *(plea, speech)* véhément(e); *(believer, defender)* fervent(e); **to make p. love** faire l'amour avec passion

passive ['pæsɪv] **1** *n Gram* **the p.** le passif; **in the p.** au passif
2 *adj* passif(ive); **p. resistance** résistance *f* passive; **p. smoking** tabagisme *m* passif

passive-aggressive ['pæsɪvə'gresɪv] *adj Psy* passif-agressif (passive-aggressive)

passively ['pæsɪvlɪ] *adv* passivement, avec passivité

passkey ['pɑːskiː] *(pl passkeys) n* passe-partout *m*

Passover ['pɑːsəʊvə(r)] *n Rel* la Pâque (Juive)

passport ['pɑːspɔːt] *n* passeport *m*; **p. control** contrôle *m* des passeports; **p. photo** photo *f* d'identité

password ['pɑːswɜːd] *n* mot *m* de passe

past [pɑːst] **1** *n* passé *m*; **in the p.** autrefois; **a thing of the p.** une chose qui appartient au passé; **to live in the p.** vivre dans le passé
2 *adj* passé(e); **those days are p.** ces jours sont révolus; **in times p.** autrefois; **to be a p. master at sth** être passé(e) maître dans l'art de qch; **the p. week** la semaine dernière;

the p. few days ces derniers jours; *Gram* **p. participle** participe *m* passé; **in the p. tense** au passé

3 *prep (beyond)* au-delà de; **to walk p. the house** passer devant la maison; **it's p. four (o'clock)** il est quatre heures passées; **ten p. four** quatre heures dix; **I'm p. caring** je n'en ai plus rien à faire; *Fam* **to be p. it** avoir fait son temps; *Fam* **I wouldn't put it p. her** elle en est bien capable

4 *adv* **to walk** *or* **to go p.** passer; **to run p.** passer en courant

pasta ['pæstə] *n* pâtes *fpl*

paste [peɪst] **1** *n* (**a**) *(substance)* pâte *f* (**b**) *(pâté)* mousse *f* (**c**) *(glue)* colle *f*
2 *vt (glue)* coller

pastel ['pæstəl] **1** *n* pastel *m*
2 *adj* pastel *inv*; **p. shades** tons *mpl* pastel

pasteurize ['pæstjʊraɪz] *vt* pasteuriser; **pasteurized milk** lait *m* pasteurisé

pastiche [pæ'stiːʃ] *n* pastiche *m*

pastille ['pæstɪl] *n* pastille *f*

pastime ['pɑːstaɪm] *n* passe-temps *m inv*

pasting ['peɪstɪŋ] *n Fam (beating)* raclée *f*; **to give sb a p.** flanquer une raclée à qn

pastor ['pɑːstə(r)] *n Rel* pasteur *m*

pastoral ['pɑːstərəl] *adj* (**a**) *(rural)* pastoral(e) (**b**) *(work, activities)* de conseiller(ère)

pastry ['peɪstrɪ] *(pl* **pastries**) *n (dough)* pâte *f*; *(cake)* pâtisserie *f*; **p. chef** pâtissier(ère) *m,f*

pasture ['pɑːstʃə(r)] *n* pâture *f*, pré *m*; **to be put out to p.** *(of animals)* être mis(e) au pré; *Fig (of person)* être mis au vert; *Fig* **to move on to pastures new** aller vers de nouveaux horizons

pasty ['peɪstɪ] *adj (face, complexion)* terreux(euse); **p.-faced** au teint terreux

pat [pæt] **1** *n* (**a**) *(tap)* petite tape *f*; *(on animal)* caresse *f*; *Fig* **to give sb a p. on the back** féliciter qn (**b**) *(of butter)* médaillon *m*
2 *adj (answer, explanation)* tout(e) prêt(e)
3 *adv* **to know sth down p.** savoir qch par cœur
4 *vt (pt & pp* **patted**) *(tap)* tapoter; *(animal)* caresser; **to p. sb on the head/shoulder** donner une tape sur la tête/l'épaule de qn; *Fig* **to p. sb on the back** féliciter qn

Patagonia [pætə'gəʊnɪə] *n* la Patagonie

patch [pætʃ] **1** *n* (**a**) *(of cloth)* pièce *f*; **(eye) p.** bandeau *m* (**b**) *(of color, light)* tache *f*; *(of fog, mist)* nappe *f*; *(of ice)* plaque *f*; **a p. of blue sky** un coin de ciel bleu; *Fam Fig* **to be going through a bad p.** traverser une mauvaise passe (**c**) *(of land)* lopin *m*; *(of prostitute, salesperson)* secteur *m*; *Fam* **keep off my p.!** hors de mon territoire!
2 *vt (hole, garment)* rapiécer

▸**patch up** *vt sep Fam (wounded person)* donner les premiers soins à; *(marriage, friendship)* raccommoder; **to p. things up** *(after argument)* se raccommoder

patchwork ['pætʃwɜːk] *n also Fig* patchwork *m*; **p. quilt** couvre-lit *m* en patchwork

patchy ['pætʃɪ] *adj* inégal(e)

pâté ['pæteɪ] *n* pâté *m*

patent ['peɪtənt] **1** *n (license)* brevet *m* d'invention; **to take out a p. on sth** faire breveter qch; *Com* **p. applied for, p. pending** demande de brevet déposée
2 *adj* (**a**) *(patented)* breveté(e); **p. medicine** spécialité *f* pharmaceutique (**b**) *(evident)* manifeste (**c**) **p. leather** cuir *m* verni
3 *vt (of authorities)* breveter; *(of inventor)* faire breveter

patently ['peɪtəntlɪ] *adv* manifestement

paternal [pə'tɜːnəl] *adj (feelings)* paternel(elle); *(duty, responsibilities)* de père

paternally [pə'tɜːnəlɪ] *adv* paternellement

paternity [pə'tɜːnɪtɪ] *n* paternité *f*; **p. leave** congé *m* de paternité; *Law* **p. suit** action *f* en recherche de paternité; **p. test** test *m* de recherche de paternité

path [pɑːθ] *n* (**a**) *(track)* chemin *m*; *(narrow)* sentier *m*; *(in garden)* allée *f*; **their paths had crossed before** leurs chemins s'étaient croisés auparavant (**b**) *(of rocket, planet)* trajectoire *f*; *(of inquiry, to success)* voie *f*; **the storm destroyed everything in its p.** la tempête a tout détruit sur son passage (**c**) *Comput* chemin *m*

pathetic [pə'θetɪk] *adj (useless)* lamentable; *(touching)* attendrissant(e)

pathetically [pə'θetɪklɪ] *adv (uselessly)* lamentablement; *(touchingly)* de manière attendrissante

pathological [pæθə'lɒdʒɪkəl] *adj* pathologique

pathologist [pə'θɒlədʒɪst] *n* pathologiste *mf*

pathology [pə'θɒlədʒɪ] *n* pathologie *f*

pathos ['peɪθɒs] *n* pathétique *m*

pathway ['pɑːθweɪ] *n* sentier *m*

patience ['peɪʃəns] *n (quality)* patience *f*; **to try** *or* **to tax sb's p.** mettre la patience de qn à l'épreuve; **to exhaust sb's p.** abuser de la patience de qn; **to lose one's p. (with sb)** perdre patience (avec qn); **I've no p. with him** il m'énerve

patient ['peɪʃənt] **1** *n* patient(e) *m,f*
2 *adj* patient(e)

patiently ['peɪʃəntlɪ] *adv* patiemment

patio ['pætɪəʊ] *(pl* **patios**) *n* patio *m*; **p. doors** porte-fenêtre *f*

patriarch ['peɪtrɪɑːk] *n* patriarche *m*

patriarchal [peɪtrɪ'ɑːkəl] *adj* patriarcal(e)

patriarchy ['peɪtrɪɑːkɪ] *(pl* **patriarchies**) *n* patriarcat *m*

patrimony ['pætrɪmənɪ] *n* patrimoine *m*, héritage *m*

patriot ['peɪtrɪət] *n* patriote *mf*

patriotic [peɪtrɪ'ɒtɪk] *adj* patriotique

patriotism ['peɪtrɪətɪzəm] *n* patriotisme *m*

patrol [pə'trəʊl] **1** *n* patrouille *f*; **to be on p.** être de patrouille; **p. car** voiture *f* de police
2 *vt (pt & pp* **patrolled**) patrouiller dans
3 *vi* patrouiller; **to p. up and down** faire les cent pas

patrolman [pə'trəʊlmæn] *n* agent *m* de police

patron ['peɪtrən] *n* (**a**) *(of arts)* protecteur(trice) *m,f*, mécène *m*; *(of charity)* patron(onne) *m,f*; **p. saint** (saint(e)) patron(onne) *m,f* (**b**) *(of store)* client(e) *m,f*

patronage ['pætrənɪdʒ] *n* (**a**) *(of arts, charity)* patronage *m*; **under the p. of** sous le patronage de (**b**) *Pej (in politics)* copinage *m*

patronize ['pætrənaɪz] *vt* (**a**) *(arts)* protéger; *(store, restaurant)* fréquenter (**b**) *(treat condescendingly)* traiter avec condescendance

patronizing ['pætrənaɪzɪŋ] *adj* condescendant(e)

patter[1] ['pætə(r)] **1** *n (of footsteps)* petit bruit *m*; *(of rain)* crépitement *m*
2 *vi (of rain)* crépiter; **she pattered along the corridor** elle trottinait le long du couloir

patter[2] ['pætə(r)] *n Fam (talk)* boniment *m*, baratin *m*

pattern ['pætən] **1** *n* (**a**) *(design)* dessin *m*, motif *m*; **p. book** catalogue *m* d'échantillons (**b**) **p. of behavior** comportement *m* type; **a normal p. of events** une suite typique d'événements; **the evening followed the usual p.** la soirée s'est déroulée comme d'habitude; **some clear patterns emerge from the statistics** des tendances nettes ressortent des statistiques (**c**) *(in sewing)* patron *m*; *(in knitting)* modèle *m* (**d**) *(norm)* modèle *m*; **to set a p.** créer un modèle
2 *vt (model)* **to p. sth on sth** modeler qch sur qch

patterned ['pætənd] *adj* à motifs

paunch [pɔːntʃ] *n* ventre *m*; **to have a p.** avoir du ventre

pauper ['pɔːpə(r)] *n* indigent(e) *m,f*; **p.'s grave** fosse *f* commune

pause [pɔːz] **1** *n (in conversation)* silence *m*; *(rest)* pause *f*; *(in music)* point *m* d'orgue
2 *vi* faire une pause; **to p. for breath** reprendre son souffle

pave [peɪv] *vt (road)* paver (**with** de); *Fig* **to p. the way for sth** ouvrir la voie à qch

pavement ['peɪvmənt] *n (roadway)* chaussée *f*

pavilion [pə'vɪlɪən] *n* pavillon *m*

paving ['peɪvɪŋ] *n (with tiles)* carrelage *m*; *(with slabs)* dallage *m*; **p. stone** pavé *m*

paw [pɔː] **1** *n* patte *f*; *Fam* **paws off!** bas les pattes!
2 *vt (of animal)* donner un coup/des coups de patte à; **to p. the ground** frapper le sol du sabot

pawn[1] [pɔːn] *vt* mettre au mont-de-piété *ou* en gage

pawn[2] [pɔːn] *n (in chess) & Fig* pion *m*

pawnbroker ['pɔːnbrəʊkə(r)] *n* prêteur(euse) *m,f* sur gage

pawnshop ['pɔːnʃɒp] *n* mont-de-piété *m*, bureau *m* de prêt sur gage

pawpaw ['pɔːpɔː] *n (fruit)* papaye *f*; *(tree)* papayer *m*

pay [peɪ] **1** *n* paie *f*, salaire *m*; **the p.'s good/bad** ça paie bien/mal; **to be in sb's p.** être à la solde de qn; **p. TV** chaîne *f* à péage
2 *vt (pt & pp* **paid** [peɪd]) (**a**) *(person, money, bill)* payer; **I paid ten dollars for it** je le ai payé dix dollars; **to be well/badly paid** être bien/mal payé(e); **I wouldn't do it if you paid me** je ne le ferais pas même si on me payait; **to p. one's way** payer son écot; **to p. cash** payer (argent) comptant; **to p. money into sb's account** verser de l'argent sur le compte de qn
(**b**) *(give)* **to p. sb a compliment** faire un compliment à qn; **to p. sb a visit** rendre visite à qn; **to p. tribute to sb** rendre hommage à qn; **to p. one's respects to sb** présenter ses respects à qn
(**c**) *(profit)* **it will p. you to do it** c'est dans votre intérêt de le faire
3 *vi* (**a**) *(give payment)* payer; **to p. through the nose** payer le prix fort; **to p. by check** payer par chèque
(**b**) *(be profitable)* être rentable; **crime doesn't p.** le crime ne paie pas; **it pays to be honest** l'honnêteté est toujours récompensée

▸**pay back** *vt sep (loan, person)* rembourser; *Fig* **I'll p. you back for this!** tu me le paieras!

▸**pay off 1** *vt sep (debt)* régler; *(mortgage)* purger; *Fam* **to p. sb off** *(bribe)* soudoyer qn
2 *vi (of work, efforts)* porter ses fruits

▸**pay out 1** *vt sep* (**a**) *(money)* débourser, dépenser (**b**) *(pt* **payed**) *(rope)* laisser filer
2 *vi* payer

▸**pay up** *vi* payer

payable ['peɪəbəl] *adj* payable; **to make a check p. to sb** libeller un chèque à l'ordre de qn

pay-as-you-talk ['peɪəzjuː'tɔːk] *n Tel* paiement *m* par carte prépayée

paycheck ['peɪtʃek] *n* chèque *m* de paie

payday ['peɪdeɪ] *n* jour *m* de paie

payee [peɪ'iː] *n* bénéficiaire *mf*

paying ['peɪɪŋ] *adj* payant(e); **p. guest** hôte *m* payant

payload ['peɪləʊd] *n* charge *f* utile

paymaster ['peɪmɑːstə(r)] *n* caissier *m*

payment ['peɪmənt] *n* paiement *m*; **to make a p.** effectuer un versement; **to stop p. (on a check)** faire opposition sur un chèque; **on p. of $100** contre paiement de 100 dollars; **p. by installments** paiement par acomptes; **p. in full** paiement intégral

payoff ['peɪɒf] *n Fam* (**a**) *(bribe)* pot-de-vin *m* (**b**) *(reward)* récompense *f*

pay-per-view [peɪpə'vjuː] **1** *n* = système de télévision à la carte
2 *adj* à la carte

payphone ['peɪfəʊn] *n* téléphone *m* public

payroll ['peɪrəʊl] *n Com* liste *f* du personnel; **to be on the p.** faire partie du personnel

PBS [piːbiː'es] *n TV (abbr* **Public Broadcasting Service**) = société américaine de production télévisuelle

PC ['piː'siː] **1** *n Comput (abbr* **personal computer**) PC *m*
2 *adj (abbr* **politically correct**) politiquement correct(e)

PDA [piːdiː'eɪ] *n (abbr* **personal digital assistant**) ADP *m*

PDQ [piːdiː'kjuː] *adv Fam (abbr* **pretty damn quick**) illico

pea [piː] *n* pois *m*; **like two peas in a pod** comme deux gouttes d'eau

peace [piːs] *n* paix *f*; **at p.** en paix; **to make (one's) p. with sb** faire la paix avec qn; **p. of mind** tranquillité *f* d'esprit; *Law* **to disturb the p.** troubler l'ordre public; **p. campaigner** militant(e) *m,f* pour la paix; **P. Corps** = organisation américaine d'aide aux pays du tiers-monde, composée de bénévoles intervenant sur le terrain; **p. movement** mouvement *m* pour la paix; **p. offering** cadeau *m* de réconciliation; **p. process** processus *m* de paix; **p. talks** pourparlers *mpl* de paix; **p. treaty** traité *m* de paix

peaceable ['piːsəbəl] *adj* pacifique

peaceful ['piːsfʊl] *adj (calm)* paisible; *(non-violent)* pacifique

peacekeeping ['piːskiːpɪŋ] *n* maintien *m* de la paix; **p. force** force *f* de maintien de la paix

peace-loving ['piːslʌvɪŋ] *adj* pacifique

peacetime ['piːstaɪm] *n* temps *m* de paix

peach [piːtʃ] *n (fruit)* pêche *f*; *Fam* **she's a p.** elle est canon; *Fam* **a p. of a goal** un but de toute beauté; **p. Melba** pêche Melba; **p. tree** pêcher *m*

peacock ['piːkɒk] *n* paon *m*

peak [piːk] **1** *n* (**a**) *(summit of mountain)* sommet *m*; *(mountain)* pic *m*; *Fig (of success, career)* apogée *m* (**b**) *(of price, inflation, fitness)* maximum *m*; **in p. condition** dans une forme excellente; **p. period** *(for traffic)* heures *fpl* de pointe; *(in store)* heures d'affluence; **p. season** haute saison *f* (**c**) *(of cap)* visière *f*
2 *vi* culminer (**at** à)

peal [piːl] *n (of bells)* sonnerie *f*; *(of thunder)* coup *m*; **peals of laughter** éclats *mpl* de rire

▸**peal out** *vi (of bells)* sonner à toute volée

peanut ['piːnʌt] *n* cacah(o)uète *f*; *Fam Fig* **peanuts** *(small sum of money)* clopinettes *fpl*; **p. butter** beurre *m* d'arachide; **p. oil** huile *f* d'arachide

pear [peə(r)] *n* poire *f*; **p. tree** poirier *m*

pearl [pɜːl] *n* (**a**) *(jewel)* perle *f*; **p. diver** pêcheur(euse) *m,f* de perles; **p. necklace** collier *m* de perles (**b**) *(idioms)* **pearls of wisdom** paroles *fpl* pleines de sagesse; **to cast pearls before swine** jeter des perles aux cochons

pearly ['pɜːlɪ] *adj* nacré(e); **the P. Gates** les portes *fpl* du paradis

pear-shaped ['peəʃeɪpt] *adj* en forme de poire; *(female figure)* plus fort(e) au niveau des hanches

peasant ['pezənt] *n* paysan(anne) *m,f*; *Pej (ignorant person)* péquenaud(e) *m,f*

peashooter ['piːʃuːtə(r)] *n* petite sarbacane *f*

peat [piːt] *n* tourbe *f*; **p. bog** tourbière *f*

pebble ['pebəl] *n* caillou *m*; *(on beach)* galet *m*; **p. beach** plage *f* de galets

pebbly ['peblɪ] *adj* caillouteux(euse); *(beach)* de galets

pecan ['piːkən] *n* **p. (nut)** noix *f* de pecan

peccary ['pekərɪ] *(pl* **peccaries**) *n* pécari *m*

peck [pek] **1** *n* (**a**) *(of bird)* coup *m* de bec (**b**) *(kiss)* bise *f*; **to give sb a p. on the cheek** faire une bise à qn
2 *vt* (**a**) *(of bird) (grain)* picorer; *(person)* donner un coup/des coups de bec à (**b**) *(kiss)* **to p. sb on the cheek** faire une bise à qn

pecs [peks] *npl Fam (pectoral muscles)* pectoraux *mpl*

pectin ['pektɪn] *n Chem* pectine *f*

pectoral ['pektərəl] **1** *n* **pectorals** pectoraux *mpl*
2 *adj* pectoral(e)

peculiar [pɪ'kju:lɪə(r)] *adj* (a) *(strange)* curieux(euse), bizarre (b) *(particular)* **p. to** particulier(ère) à, propre à; **this species is p. to France** cette espèce n'existe qu'en France

peculiarity [pɪkju:lɪ'ærɪtɪ] (*pl* **peculiarities**) *n (strangeness)* singularité *f*, bizarrerie *f*; *(unusual characteristic)* particularité *f*

peculiarly [pɪ'kju:lɪəlɪ] *adv* (a) *(strangely)* singulièrement (b) *(especially)* particulièrement

pecuniary [pɪ'kju:nɪərɪ] *adj Formal* pécuniaire

pedagogic [pedə'gɒdʒɪk], **pedagogical** [pedə'gɒdʒɪkəl] *adj* pédagogique

pedagogy ['pedəgɒdʒɪ] *n* pédagogie *f*

pedal ['pedəl] **1** *n* pédale *f*; **p. boat** Pédalo® *m*
2 *vt* **to p. a bicycle** être à bicyclette
3 *vi* pédaler

pedant ['pedənt] *n* pédant(e) *m,f*

pedantic [pɪ'dæntɪk] *adj* pédant(e)

pedantry ['pedəntrɪ] *n* pédantisme *m*, pédanterie *f*

peddle ['pedəl] *vt (goods, ideas, theories)* colporter; *(drugs)* faire du trafic de

peddler ['pedlə(r)] *n (of goods, ideas, theories)* colporteur(euse) *m,f*; *(of drugs)* trafiquant(e) *m,f*

pederast ['pedəræst] *n Formal* pédéraste *m*

pedestal ['pedɪstəl] *n* piédestal *m*; *Fig* **to put sb on a p.** mettre qn sur un piédestal; **p. lamp** lampe *f* sur piédestal

pedestrian [pɪ'destrɪən] **1** *n* piéton(onne) *m,f*; **p. area, p. zone** zone *f* piétonnière
2 *adj (unimaginative)* banal(e)

pedestrianize [pɪ'destrɪənaɪz] *vt* transformer en zone piétonnière

pediatric [pi:dɪ'ætrɪk] *adj Med (ward)* de pédiatrie; *(specialist, nurse)* en pédiatrie

pediatrician [pi:dɪə'trɪʃən] *n Med* pédiatre *mf*

pediatrics [pi:dɪ'ætrɪks] *n Med* pédiatrie *f*

pedicure ['pedɪkjʊə(r)] *n* **to have a p.** se faire soigner les pieds

pedigree ['pedɪgri:] **1** *n* (a) *(of animal)* pedigree *m* (b) *(of person)* ascendance *f*, généalogie *f*; *Fig (background)* passé *m*, antécédents *mpl*
2 *adj (animal)* de race

peddler ['pedlə(r)] *n* colporteur(euse) *m,f*

pedometer [pɪ'dɒmɪtə(r)] *n* pédomètre *m*, podomètre *m*

pedophile ['pi:dəfaɪl] *n* pédophile *mf*

pedophilia [pi:də'fɪlɪə] *n* pédophilie *f*

pee [pi:] *Fam* **1** *n* pipi *m*; **to have a p.** faire pipi
2 *vi* faire pipi

peek [pi:k] **1** *n* coup *m* d'œil furtif; **to take** *or* **to have a p. (at)** jeter un coup d'œil furtif (à)
2 *vi* jeter un coup d'œil furtif (**at** à)

peel [pi:l] **1** *n (of apple, vegetable)* peau *f*; *(of orange, lemon)* écorce *f*
2 *vt (fruit)* peler; *(vegetable)* éplucher; *Fam* **to keep one's eyes peeled** ouvrir l'œil
3 *vi (of paint)* s'écailler; *(of skin, person)* peler

►**peel off 1** *vt sep* enlever
2 *vi (of paint)* s'écailler; *(of skin)* peler; *(of label)* s'enlever

peeler ['pi:lə(r)] *n (for vegetables)* éplucheur *m*

peelings ['pi:lɪŋz] *npl (of potato, carrot)* épluchures *fpl*

peep[1] [pi:p] **1** *n (furtive glance)* coup *m* d'œil furtif; **to have** *or* **to take a p. (at)** jeter un coup d'œil furtif (à)
2 *vi* **to p. at sb/sth** jeter un coup d'œil furtif à qn/qch; **to p. through the keyhole** regarder par le trou de la serrure

peep[2] [pi:p] *n (sound) (of bird)* pépiement *m*; *(of mouse)* cri *m*; *Fam* **I don't want to hear another p. out of you** je ne veux plus entendre un mot

peephole ['pi:phəʊl] *n* judas *m*

Peeping Tom ['pi:pɪŋ'tɒm] *n Fam* voyeur *m*

peer[1] [pɪə(r)] *n (equal)* pair *m*; **p. group** pairs *mpl*; **p. pressure** influence *f* du groupe

peer[2] [pɪə(r)] *vi* **to p. at sb/sth** scruter qn/qch du regard; **to p. over sth** jeter un coup d'œil par-dessus qch

peerless ['pɪəlɪs] *adj* sans pareil(eille), hors pair

peer-to-peer ['pɪətə'pɪə(r)] *adj Comput* peer-to-peer

peeve [pi:v] *vt Fam* mettre en rogne; **to be peeved (at)** être en rogne (à cause de)

peevish ['pi:vɪʃ] *adj* irritable, maussade

peewit ['pi:wɪt] *n* vanneau *m* (huppé)

peg [peg] **1** *n (wooden)* cheville *f*; *(metal)* fiche *f*; *(for coat, hat)* patère *f*; **(clothes) p.** pince *f* à linge; **(tent) p.** piquet *m* de tente; **to buy clothes off the p.** acheter du prêt-à-porter; *Fig* **to take sb down a p. (or two)** remettre qn à sa place
2 *vt (pt & pp* **pegged**) (a) **to p. sth in place** fixer qch avec des piquets; **to p. the washing on the line** étendre le linge *(en utilisant des pinces à linge)* (b) *(set) (prices)* fixer; *(tie) (currency)* indexer; **to p. sth to the rate of inflation** indexer qch sur le taux de l'inflation

pejorative [pɪ'dʒɒrətɪv] *adj* péjoratif(ive)

Pekinese [pi:kɪ'ni:z] *n (dog)* pékinois *m*

Peking [pi:'kɪŋ] *n* Pékin *m*

pelican ['pelɪkən] *n* pélican *m*

pellet ['pelɪt] *n (of paper, bread, clay)* boulette *f*; *(for gun)* plomb *m*

pell-mell ['pel'mel] *adv (run)* de façon désordonnée

pelmet ['pelmɪt] *n* cantonnière *f*

pelt[1] [pelt] *n (animal skin)* peau *f*, fourrure *f*

pelt[2] [pelt] **1** *vt* bombarder (**with** de)
2 *vi Fam* (a) *(rain)* **it was pelting down** il pleuvait à verse (b) *(go fast)* aller à toute allure; **to p. upstairs** grimper l'escalier quatre à quatre; **she came pelting along the corridor** elle a déboulé du fond du couloir

pelvic ['pelvɪk] *adj* pelvien(enne)

pelvis ['pelvɪs] *n* pelvis *m*

pen[1] [pen] **1** *n (for writing)* stylo *m*; **to put p. to paper** prendre la plume; **p. pal** correspondant(e) *m,f*; **p. name** nom *m* de plume; **p. pusher** gratte-papier *m inv*
2 *vt (pt & pp* **penned**) écrire, rédiger

pen[2] [pen] *n (for sheep, cattle)* enclos *m*

pen[3] [pen] *n Fam (prison)* taule *f*

►**pen in** *vt sep (animals, people)* parquer

penal ['pi:nəl] *adj* pénal(e); **p. code** code *m* pénal; **p. colony** colonie *f* pénitentiaire; **p. servitude** travaux *mpl* forcés

penalize ['pi:nəlaɪz] *vt* pénaliser

penalty ['penəltɪ] (*pl* **penalties**) *n* (a) *(punishment)* peine *f*; **to impose a p. (on sb)** prendre une sanction (contre qn); **on** *or* **under p. of death** sous peine de mort; *Fig* **to pay the p. for sth** subir les conséquences de qch; *Com* **p. clause** clause *f* pénale (b) *(in soccer)* penalty *m*; *(in rugby)* pénalité *f*; **p. area** surface *f* de réparation; **p. kick** penalty

penance ['penəns] *n also Fig* pénitence *f*; **to do p. (for sth)** faire pénitence (pour qch)

pence [pens] *pl of* **penny (b)**

pencil ['pensəl] **1** *n* crayon *m*; **p. case** trousse *f*; **p. drawing** dessin *m* au crayon; **p. sharpener** taille-crayon *m*
2 *vt (draw)* dessiner au crayon; *(write)* écrire au crayon

►**pencil in** *vt sep (date)* fixer provisoirement; **to p. sb in** fixer provisoirement un rendez-vous à qn

pendant ['pendənt] *n* pendentif *m*

pending ['pendɪŋ] **1** *adj (trial)* en instance; *(negotiations)* en cours; *(documents)* en souffrance, en attente
2 *prep* en attendant

pendulum ['pendjʊləm] *n* pendule *m*

penetrate ['penɪtreɪt] *vt & vi* pénétrer

penetrating ['penɪtreɪtɪŋ] *adj (sound, wind, cold)* pénétrant(e); *(voice, scream, stare)* perçant(e)

penetration [penɪ'treɪʃən] *n* pénétration *f*

penguin ['peŋgwɪn] *n* manchot *m*

penicillin [penɪ'sɪlɪn] *n* pénicilline *f*

peninsula [pɪ'nɪnsjʊlə] *n* péninsule *f*; *(smaller)* presqu'île *f*

peninsular [pɪ'nɪnsjʊlə(r)] *adj* péninsulaire

penis ['piːnɪs] *n* pénis *m*

penitence ['penɪtəns] *n* pénitence *f*, repentir *m*

penitent ['penɪtənt] *n & adj* pénitent(e) *m,f*

penitentiary [penɪ'tenʃərɪ] (*pl* **penitentiaries**) *n* pénitencier *m*

penknife ['pennaɪf] (*pl* **penknives** ['pennaɪvz]) *n* canif *m*

pennant ['penənt] *n* (**a**) *Naut* flamme *f* (**b**) *Fig Sport* **to win the p.** remporter le championnat

penne ['peneɪ] *npl (pasta)* penne *mpl*

penniless ['penɪlɪs] *adj* sans le sou

Pennsylvania [pensɪl'veɪnɪə] *n* la Pennsylvanie

penny ['penɪ] *n* (**a**) (*pl* **pennies**) *(cent)* cent *m* (**b**) (*pl* **pence**) *(British currency)* penny *m* (**c**) *(idioms)* **they haven't a p. to their name** il n'ont pas un sou vaillant; **the p. dropped** ça a fait tilt; **a p. for your thoughts** à quoi penses-tu?; **a bad p.** un(e) bon (bonne) à rien

penny-pinching ['penɪpɪntʃɪŋ] *adj (person)* pingre; *(ways, habits)* de radin

pension ['penʃən] *n* pension *f*; *(after retirement)* (pension de) retraite *f*; **to be on a p.** recevoir une pension; *(after retirement)* recevoir une retraite; **p. fund** caisse *f* de retraite; **p. scheme** plan *m* de retraite

▸**pension off** *vt sep* mettre à la retraite

pensioner ['penʃənə(r)] *n* retraité(e) *m,f*

pensive ['pensɪv] *adj* pensif(ive), songeur(euse)

pensively ['pensɪvlɪ] *adv* pensivement

pentagon ['pentəgən] *n* pentagone *m*; **the P.** *(building)* le Pentagone

pentathlon [pen'tæθlən] *n* pentathlon *m*

Pentecost ['pentɪkɒst] *n* la Pentecôte

penthouse ['penthaʊs] *n* = appartement de standing au dernier étage d'un immeuble

pent-up [pen'tʌp] *adj (desire)* refoulé(e); *(rage, energy)* contenu(e)

penultimate [pe'nʌltɪmɪt] *adj* pénultième, avant-dernier(ère)

penury ['penjʊrɪ] *n* indigence *f*

peony ['piːənɪ] (*pl* **peonies**) *n* pivoine *f*

people ['piːpəl] **1** *npl* (**a**) *(as group)* gens *mpl*; *(as individuals)* personnes *fpl*; **most p.** la plupart des gens; **old p.** les personnes âgées; **he's one of those p. who think (that)...** c'est le genre de type qui pense que...; **p. say (that)...** les gens disent que...; *Aut* **p. carrier, p. mover** monospace *m* (**b**) *(citizens)* peuple *m*; **the common p.** le peuple; **a man of the p.** un homme du peuple; **p. power** pouvoir *m* populaire; **P.'s Republic** République *f* populaire (**c**) *Fam (family)* **my/his p.** ma/sa famille

2 *n (nation)* peuple *m*; **the Scottish p.** les Écossais *mpl*

3 *vt* peupler

pep [pep] *n Fam* entrain *m*, allant *m*; **p. pill** excitant *m*; **p. talk** petit discours *m* d'encouragement

▸**pep up** (*pt & pp* **pepped**) *vt sep Fam (person)* ragaillardir, revigorer; *(event)* animer; *(dish)* relever

pepper ['pepə(r)] **1** *n (spice)* poivre *m*; *(vegetable)* poivron *m*; **p. mill** moulin *m* à poivre

2 *vt* (**a**) *(in cooking)* poivrer (**b**) *Fig (speech, essay)* parsemer (**with** de); **to p. sb with bullets** cribler qn de balles

pepperbox ['pepəbɒks] *n* poivrière *f*

peppercorn ['pepəkɔːn] *n* grain *m* de poivre

peppermint ['pepəmɪnt] *n (plant)* menthe *f* poivrée; *(sweet)* bonbon *m* à la menthe; **p. tea** thé *m* à la menthe

peppery ['pepərɪ] *adj* (**a**) *(dish)* poivré(e) (**b**) *(irritable)* irascible, colérique

peptic ulcer ['peptɪk'ʌlsə(r)] *n* ulcère *m* gastro-duodénal

per [pɜː(r)] *prep* par; **p. day** par jour; **50 miles p. hour** ≃ 80 km à l'heure; *Formal* **as p. your instructions** conformément à vos instructions; **as p. usual** comme d'habitude; **p. annum** par an; **p. capita** par habitant; **p. se** en soi

perceive [pə'siːv] *vt* percevoir

percent [pə'sent] **1** *n* pourcentage *m*

2 *adv* pour cent

percentage [pə'sentɪdʒ] *n* pourcentage *m*

perceptible [pə'septɪbəl] *adj* perceptible

perceptibly [pə'septɪblɪ] *adv* sensiblement

perception [pə'sepʃən] *n* perception *f*

perceptive [pə'septɪv] *adj (person, remark)* perspicace; *(analysis, article)* pertinent(e)

perch¹ [pɜːtʃ] **1** *n (for bird) & Fig* perchoir *m*; *Fam Fig* **to knock sb off his p.** détrôner qn

2 *vi* se percher

perch² [pɜːtʃ] *n (fish)* perche *f*

percolate ['pɜːkəleɪt] **1** *vt (coffee)* passer; **percolated coffee** = café préparé dans une cafetière à pression

2 *vi (of liquid)* passer; *Fig (of information)* filtrer

percolator ['pɜːkəleɪtə(r)] *n* cafetière *f* à pression

percussion [pə'kʌʃən] *n* percussion *f*; **p. instrument** instrument *m* à percussion

percussionist [pə'kʌʃənɪst] *n* percussionniste *mf*

peregrine falcon ['perɪgrɪn'fɔːlkən] *n* faucon *m* pèlerin

peremptory [pə'remptərɪ] *adj* péremptoire; *(refusal)* absolu(e)

perennial [pə'renɪəl] **1** *n (plant)* plante *f* vivace

2 *adj (plant)* vivace; *(problem, beauty)* éternel(elle); *(worry)* perpétuel(elle)

perfect 1 *adj* ['pɜːfɪkt] (**a**) *(ideal)* parfait(e); **nobody's p.** personne n'est parfait; **Tuesday would be p.** mardi me conviendrait parfaitement; **to have p. pitch** avoir l'oreille absolue (**b**) *(complete)* **it makes p. sense** c'est parfaitement logique; **she's a p. stranger** je ne la connais pas du tout; **he's a p. gentleman/fool** c'est un parfait homme du monde/imbécile (**c**) *Gram* **the p. (tense)** le passé composé

2 *vt* [pə'fekt] parfaire

perfection [pə'fekʃən] *n* perfection *f*

perfectionist [pə'fekʃənɪst] *n* perfectionniste *mf*

perfectly ['pɜːfɪktlɪ] *adv (faultlessly)* à la perfection; *(completely)* parfaitement

perfidious [pə'fɪdɪəs] *adj Lit* perfide

perforate ['pɜːfəreɪt] *vt* perforer

perforated ['pɜːfəreɪtɪd] *adj* perforé(e); **p. ulcer** perforation *f* ulcéreuse

perforation [pɜːfə'reɪʃən] *n (hole)* perforation *f*; *(on stamp)* dentelure *f*

perform [pə'fɔːm] **1** *vt (play, role, piece of music)* jouer; *(miracle)* faire; *(one's duty)* remplir; **to p. an operation on sb** opérer qn

2 *vi (of machine, car)* marcher; *(of actor)* jouer; *(of singer)* chanter

performance [pə'fɔːməns] *n* (**a**) *(of task, duty)* accomplissement *m*; **p. appraisal** appréciation *f*, évaluation *f* (**b**) *(of athlete)* performance *f*; *(of actor)* interprétation *f*; *(of pupil, economy)* résultats *mpl*, performance; *(of machine, car)* performances *fpl* (**c**) *(of play)* représentation *f*; *Fig* **to make a p.** faire toute une histoire; **p. art** performance *f*, action *f*; **p. artist** = artiste spécialisé dans la performance

performance-enhancing [pə'fɔːmənsen'hɑːnsɪŋ] *adj (drug)* qui améliore les performances

performance-related [pə'fɔːmənsrɪ'leɪtɪd] *adj* en fonction du mérite *ou* résultat; **p. pay** salaire *m* au mérite

performer [pə'fɔːmə(r)] *n* artiste *mf (des arts du spectacle)*

performing [pə'fɔːmɪŋ] *adj (dog, seal)* savant(e); **p. arts** arts *mpl* du spectacle

perfume 1 *n* ['pɜːfjuːm] parfum *m*; **p. counter** rayon *m* parfumerie

2 *vt* [pə'fjuːm] parfumer

perfumed ['pɜːfjuːmd] *adj* parfumé(e)

perfunctory [pə'fʌŋktərɪ] *adj (examination, glance)* rapide; *(smile)* mécanique; *(letter, instructions)* sommaire

perhaps [pə'hæps] *adv* peut-être; **p. so/not** peut-être que oui/non; **p. she'll come** elle viendra peut-être, peut-être qu'elle viendra

peril ['perəl] *n* péril *m*, danger *m*; **at one's p.** à ses risques et périls

perilous ['periləs] *adj* dangereux(euse)

perilously ['periləslɪ] *adv* dangereusement

perimeter [pə'rɪmɪtə(r)] *n* périmètre *m*; **p. fence** clôture *f*

period ['pɪərɪəd] *n* (**a**) *(stretch of time)* période *f*; **within the agreed p.** dans les délais convenus; **sunny periods** intervalles *mpl* ensoleillés (**b**) *(in school)* heure *f* de cours; **a French/math p.** un cours de français/maths (**c**) *(menstruation)* règles *fpl*; **to have one's p.** avoir ses règles; **p. pains** règles douloureuses (**d**) *(historical age)* époque *f*; **p. drama** *(on TV)* drame *m* historique; **p. dress** costume(s) *m(pl)* d'époque; **p. furniture** meubles *mpl* d'époque (**e**) *(full stop)* point *m*

periodic [pɪərɪ'ɒdɪk] *adj* périodique; *Chem* **p. table** classification *f* périodique

periodical [pɪərɪ'ɒdɪkəl] *n* périodique *m*

periodically [pɪərɪ'ɒdɪklɪ] *adv* périodiquement

peripheral [pə'rɪfərəl] **1** *n Comput* périphérique *m*

2 *adj (area, vision)* périphérique; *(issue, importance)* accessoire

periphery [pə'rɪfərɪ] *(pl* **peripheries)** *n* périphérie *f*

periscope ['perɪskəʊp] *n* périscope *m*

perish ['perɪʃ] *vi* (**a**) *(of person)* périr; **p. the thought!** loin de moi cette pensée! (**b**) *(of rubber, leather)* se détériorer; *(of food)* s'avarier

perishable ['perɪʃəbəl] **1** *n* **perishables** denrées *fpl* périssables

2 *adj* périssable

peritonitis [perɪtə'naɪtɪs] *n* péritonite *f*

perjure ['pɜːdʒə(r)] *vt Law* **to p. oneself** faire un faux témoignage

perjury ['pɜːdʒərɪ] *n Law* faux témoignage *m*; **to commit p.** faire un faux témoignage

perk [pɜːk] *n Fam* avantage *m*, à-côté *m*

▶**perk up** *Fam* **1** *vt sep (revive)* requinquer, ragaillardir; *(cheer up)* remonter le moral à

2 *vi (revive)* se requinquer, se ragaillardir; *(cheer up)* retrouver sa bonne humeur

perky ['pɜːkɪ] *adj Fam (lively)* plein(e) d'entrain; *(cheerful)* guilleret(ette)

perm [pɜːm] **1** *n* permanente *f*; **to have a p.** se faire faire une permanente

2 *vt* **to have one's hair permed** se faire faire une permanente

permanence ['pɜːmənəns] *n* permanence *f*

permanent ['pɜːmənənt] *adj* permanent(e); *(ink, stain)* indélébile; *(residence, address)* fixe

permeate ['pɜːmɪeɪt] **1** *vt* **to be permeated with sth** *(liquid)* être saturé(e) de qch; *(smell)* être rempli(e) de qch; *Fig (feeling)* être imprégné(e) de qch

2 *vi* **to p. through sth** *(of liquid)* passer à travers qch; *(of smell)* se répandre dans qch; *Fig (of feeling)* imprégner qch

permissible [pə'mɪsɪbəl] *adj* admissible, acceptable

permission [pə'mɪʃən] *n* permission *f*, autorisation *f*; **to ask for p. to do sth** demander la permission de faire qch; **to give sb p. to do sth** donner à qn la permission de faire qch, autoriser qn à faire qch

permissive [pə'mɪsɪv] *adj* permissif(ive)

permit 1 *n* ['pɜːmɪt] permis *m*; **p. holders only** *(sign)* réservé aux personnes autorisées

2 *vt* [pə'mɪt] *(pt & pp* **permitted)** permettre; **to p. sb to do sth** permettre à qn de faire qch, autoriser qn à faire qch

3 *vi* [pə'mɪt] **weather permitting** si le temps le permet

permutation [pɜːmjʊ'teɪʃən] *n* permutation *f*

pernicious [pə'nɪʃəs] *adj* pernicieux(euse)

pernickety [pə'nɪkɪtɪ] *adj Fam (person)* tatillon(onne), pointilleux(euse); *(task)* délicat(e), minutieux(euse)

peroxide [pə'rɒksaɪd] *n Chem* peroxyde *m*; **p. blonde** blonde *f* décolorée

perpendicular [pɜːpən'dɪkjʊlə(r)] **1** *n* perpendiculaire *f*

2 *adj* perpendiculaire

perpetrate ['pɜːpɪtreɪt] *vt (crime)* perpétrer; *(fraud, error)* commettre

perpetrator ['pɜːpɪtreɪtə(r)] *n* auteur *m*

perpetual [pə'petjʊəl] *adj (eternal)* perpétuel(elle), éternel(elle); *(constant)* incessant(e), continuel(elle); *Phys* **p. motion** mouvement *m* perpétuel

perpetually [pə'petjʊəlɪ] *adv* perpétuellement

perpetuate [pə'petjʊeɪt] *vt* perpétuer

perpetuity [pɜːpɪ'tjuːɪtɪ] *n Formal* perpétuité *f*; **in p.** à perpétuité

perplex [pə'pleks] *vt* rendre *ou* laisser perplexe

perplexing [pə'pleksɪŋ] *adj* difficile; *(person)* déconcertant(e)

perplexity [pə'pleksɪtɪ] *n* perplexité *f*

persecute ['pɜːsɪkjuːt] *vt* persécuter

persecution [pɜːsɪ'kjuːʃən] *n* persécution *f*; *Psy* **p. complex** délire *m* de persécution

persecutor ['pɜːsɪkjuːtə(r)] *n* persécuteur(trice) *m,f*

perseverance [pɜːsɪ'vɪərəns] *n* persévérance *f*

persevere [pɜːsɪ'vɪə(r)] *vi* persévérer (**with** dans); **to p. in doing sth** persister à faire qch

Persia ['pɜːʒə] *n Hist* la Perse

Persian ['pɜːʒən] **1** *n* (**a**) *(person) Hist* Perse *mf; (after 7th century)* Persan(e) *m,f* (**b**) *(language)* persan *m*

2 *adj Hist* perse; *(after 7th century)* persan(e); **P. carpet** tapis *m* persan; **P. cat** chat *m* persan; **the P. Gulf** le golfe Persique

persimmon [pɜː'sɪmən] *n (arbre)* plaqueminier *m*; *(fruit)* kaki *m*

persist [pə'sɪst] *vi* persister; **to p. in doing sth** s'obstiner à faire qch; **to p. in one's belief that...** persister à croire que...

persistence [pə'sɪstəns] *n (of person)* ténacité *f*, obstination *f*; *(of fog, belief)* persistance *f*

persistent [pə'sɪstənt] *adj (person)* tenace; *(problems, pain)* incessant(e), continuel(elle); *(rumors)* persistant(e); **p. offender** récidiviste *mf; Med* **p. vegetative state** état *m* végétatif chronique

persistently [pə'sɪstəntlɪ] *adv* continuellement

person ['pɜːsən] *(pl* **people** ['piːpəl], *Formal* **persons)** *n* personne *f*; **in p.** en personne; **on one's p.** sur soi; *Gram* **in the first/second/third p.** à la première/deuxième/troisième personne; *Law* **by a p. or persons unknown** par un ou plusieurs inconnus

personable ['pɜːsənəbəl] *adj* charmant(e)

personage ['pɜːsənɪdʒ] *n* personnage *m*

personal ['pɜːsənəl] **1** *adj* personnel(elle); **to make a p. appearance** venir *ou* apparaître en personne; **for p. reasons** pour des raisons personnelles; **don't be p.** ne parle pas des choses aussi personnelles; **it's nothing p., but...** ça n'a rien de personnel, mais...; **p. friend** ami(e) *m,f* personnel(elle); **p. ad** petite annonce *f*; **p. assistant** secrétaire *mf* de direction; **p. best** *(in sports)* record *m* personnel; **p. column** petites annonces; **p. computer** ordinateur *m* individuel; **p. effects** effets *mpl* personnels; **p. growth** développement *m* personnel;

p. hygiene hygiène *f*; **p. loan** prêt *m* personnel; **p. organizer** *(book)* agenda *m*; *(electronic)* agenda électronique; *Gram* **p. pronoun** pronom *m* personnel; **p. stereo** baladeur *m*
2 *n (personal ad)* petite annonce *f*

personality [pɜːsəˈnælɪtɪ] *(pl* **personalities**) *n* personnalité *f*; **p. cult** culte *m* de la personnalité; *Psy* **p. disorder** trouble *m* de la personnalité

personally [ˈpɜːsənəlɪ] *adv* personnellement; **don't take it p.** n'en faites pas une affaire personnelle

personification [pɜːsɒnɪfɪˈkeɪʃən] *n* incarnation *f*; **to be the p. of meanness** être l'avarice incarnée

personify [pɜːˈsɒnɪfaɪ] *(pt & pp* **personified**) *vt* personnifier

personnel [pɜːsəˈnel] *n* personnel *m*; **p. department** service *m* du personnel; **p. manager** directeur(trice) *m,f* du personnel

perspective [pəˈspektɪv] *n* perspective *f*; **to see things in p.** relativiser les choses; **to put sth in(to) p.** relativiser qch

perspicacious [pɜːspɪˈkeɪʃəs] *adj Formal* perspicace

perspiration [pɜːspəˈreɪʃən] *n* transpiration *f*

perspire [pəˈspaɪə(r)] *vi* transpirer

persuade [pəˈsweɪd] *vt* persuader, convaincre; **to p. sb to do sth** persuader *ou* convaincre qn de faire qch; **to p. sb not to do sth** dissuader qn de faire qch

persuasion [pəˈsweɪʒən] *n* **(a)** *(act, ability)* persuasion *f*; **powers of p.** pouvoir *m* de persuasion **(b)** *(beliefs)* **political p.** opinions *fpl* politiques; **religious p.** religion *f*, confession *f*

persuasive [pəˈsweɪzɪv] *adj (person)* persuasif(ive); *(argument)* convaincant(e)

persuasively [pəˈsweɪzɪvlɪ] *adv (say)* d'un ton persuasif; *(argue)* de façon convaincante

pert [pɜːt] *adj* **(a)** *(cheeky)* espiègle; *(reply)* direct(e) **(b)** *(nose, breasts)* pointu(e); *(bottom)* petit(e) et ferme

pertain [pəˈteɪn] *vi Formal* **to p. to** *(belong to)* appartenir à; *(be relevant to)* se rapporter à

pertinent [ˈpɜːtɪnənt] *adj* pertinent(e); **to be p. to** avoir rapport à

perturb [pəˈtɜːb] *vt* inquiéter, troubler

Peru [pəˈruː] *n* le Pérou

perusal [pəˈruːzəl] *n Formal* lecture *f*

peruse [pəˈruːz] *vt Formal (read carefully)* lire attentivement; *(read quickly)* feuilleter; *(article)* survoler

Peruvian [pəˈruːvɪən] **1** *n* Péruvien(enne) *m,f*
2 *adj* péruvien(enne)

pervade [pɜːˈveɪd] *vt* imprégner

pervasive [pɜːˈveɪsɪv] *adj (feeling)* général(e); *(smell)* envahissant(e)

perverse [pəˈvɜːs] *adj* **(a)** *(contrary)* contrariant(e); **he's just being p.** il fait ça pour contrarier; **to take a p. pleasure in doing sth** prendre un malin plaisir à faire qch **(b)** *(sexually deviant)* pervers(e)

perversely [pəˈvɜːslɪ] *adv (contrarily)* par pur esprit de contradiction

perversion [pəˈvɜːʃən] *n (sexual)* perversion *f*; *(of truth, justice)* travestissement *m*

pervert 1 *n* [ˈpɜːvɜːt] *(sexual deviant)* pervers(e) *m,f*
2 *vt* [pəˈvɜːt] *(corrupt)* pervertir; *(distort)* altérer, dénaturer; *Law* **to p. the course of justice** entraver le bon fonctionnement de la justice

peseta [pəˈseɪtə] *n* peseta *f*

pesky [ˈpeskɪ] *adj Fam* embêtant(e), empoisonnant(e)

peso [ˈpeɪsəʊ] *(pl* **pesos**) *n* peso *m*

pessary [ˈpesərɪ] *(pl* **pessaries**) *n* ovule *m*

pessimism [ˈpesɪmɪzəm] *n* pessimisme *m*

pessimist [ˈpesɪmɪst] *n* pessimiste *mf*

pessimistic [pesɪˈmɪstɪk] *adj* pessimiste

pest [pest] *n* **(a)** *(animal)* animal *m* nuisible; *(insect)* insecte *m* nuisible; **p. control** *(of rats)* dératisation *f*; *(of insects)* désinsectisation *f* **(b)** *Fam (nuisance)* poison *m*, plaie *f*

pester [ˈpestə(r)] *vt* tourmenter, importuner; **to p. sb to do sth** harceler qn pour qu'il fasse qch; **to p. sb into doing sth** harceler qn jusqu'à ce qu'il fasse qch

pesticide [ˈpestɪsaɪd] *n* pesticide *m*

pestilence [ˈpestɪləns] *n Lit* peste *f*

pestle [ˈpesəl] *n* pilon *m*; **p. and mortar** pilon et mortier

pet [pet] **1** **(a)** *(animal)* animal *m* familier *ou* domestique; **p. food** nourriture *f* pour animaux familiers; **p. store** animalerie *f* **(b)** *(favorite)* **the teacher's p.** le chouchou du professeur; **p. hate** bête *f* noire; **p. name** surnom *m*; **p. subject** dada *m* **(c)** *(term of address)* mon petit chou
2 *vt (pt & pp* **petted**) *(person, dog)* caresser, câliner
3 *vi Fam (sexually)* se peloter

petal [ˈpetəl] *n* pétale *m*

▸**peter out** [ˈpiːtə(r)] *vi (of conversation, enthusiasm)* tarir; *(of scheme)* n'aboutir à rien; *(of path, stream)* disparaître

petite [pəˈtiːt] *adj* menu(e)

petition [pɪˈtɪʃən] **1** *n* pétition *f*
2 *vt (court, sovereign)* adresser *ou* présenter une pétition à
3 *vi* **to p. for sth** faire une pétition pour qch; *Law* **to p. for divorce** faire une demande de divorce

petitioner [pɪˈtɪʃənə(r)] *n Law (for divorce)* pétitionnaire *mf*, requérant(e) *m,f*

petrify [ˈpetrɪfaɪ] *(pt & pp* **petrified**) *vt* pétrifier

petrochemical [petrəʊˈkemɪkəl] **1** *n* produit *m* pétrochimique
2 *adj* pétrochimique

petrol [ˈpetrəl] *n* essence *f*; **p. can** bidon *m* d'essence; **p. pump** pompe *f* à essence; **p. station** station *f* d'essence, station-service *f*; **p. tank** réservoir *m* d'essence

petroleum [pəˈtrəʊlɪəm] *n* pétrole *m*; **p. jelly** vaseline *f*

petticoat [ˈpetɪkəʊt] *n (from waist)* jupon *m*; *(full-length)* combinaison *f*

petty [ˈpetɪ] *adj* **(a)** *(insignificant)* insignifiant(e); **p. cash** petite caisse *f*; **p. crime** petite délinquance *f*; *Naut* **p. officer** second maître *m* **(b)** *(small-minded)* mesquin(e)

petulance [ˈpetjʊləns] *n* irascibilité *f*

petulant [ˈpetjʊlənt] *adj* irascible

petunia [pɪˈtjuːnɪə] *n* pétunia *m*

pew [pjuː] *n* banc *m* d'église

pewter [ˈpjuːtə(r)] *n* étain *m*

pH [piːˈeɪtʃ] *n Chem* pH *m*

phalanx [ˈfælæŋks] *n Mil Hist* phalange *f*; *Fig (of officials, journalists)* armée *f*

phallic [ˈfælɪk] *adj* phallique; **p. symbol** symbole *m* phallique

phallus [ˈfæləs] *n* phallus *m*

phantom [ˈfæntəm] *n* fantôme *m*, spectre *m*; **p. pregnancy** grossesse *f* nerveuse

Pharaoh [ˈfeərəʊ] *n* pharaon *m*

pharmaceutical [fɑːməˈsjuːtɪkəl] **1** *n* **pharmaceuticals** produits *mpl* pharmaceutiques
2 *adj* pharmaceutique

pharmacist [ˈfɑːməsɪst] *n* pharmacien(enne) *m,f*

pharmacology [fɑːməˈkɒlədʒɪ] *n* pharmacologie *f*

pharmacy [ˈfɑːməsɪ] *(pl* **pharmacies**) *n* pharmacie *f*

phase [feɪz] *n* phase *f*; **it's just a p. (he's going through)** ça lui passera; *Fig* **out of p.** déphasé(e)

▸**phase in** *vt sep* mettre en place progressivement

▸**phase out** *vt sep* éliminer progressivement

phased [feɪzd] *adj* progressif(ive)

PhD [piːeɪtʃˈdiː] *n Univ (abbr* **Doctor of Philosophy**) *(person)* docteur *m*; *(degree)* doctorat *m* (**in** de)

pheasant [ˈfezənt] *n* faisan *m*

phenomenal [fɪˈnɒmɪnəl] *adj* phénoménal(e)

phenomenally [fɪˈnɒmɪnəlɪ] *adv* prodigieusement

phenomenon [fɪˈnɒmɪnən] (*pl* **phenomena** [fɪˈnɒmɪnə]) *n* phénomène *m*

phew [fjuː] *exclam (when hot)* pfff!; *(in relief)* ouf!

phial [ˈfaɪəl] *n* fiole *f*

Philadelphia [fɪləˈdelfɪə] *n* Philadelphie

philanderer [fɪˈlændərə(r)] *n Pej* coureur *m* de jupons

philanthropic [fɪlənˈθrɒpɪk] *adj* philanthropique; *(person)* philanthrope

philanthropist [fɪˈlænθrəpɪst] *n* philanthrope *mf*

philanthropy [fɪˈlænθrəpɪ] *n* philanthropie *f*

philately [fɪˈlætəlɪ] *n* philatélie *f*

philharmonic [fɪləˈmɒnɪk] *Mus* **1** *n* (orchestre *m*) philharmonique *m*
  2 *adj* philharmonique

Philippines [ˈfɪlɪpiːnz] *npl* **the P.** les Philippines *fpl*

philology [fɪˈlɒlədʒɪ] *n* philologie *f*

philosopher [fɪˈlɒsəfə(r)] *n* philosophe *mf*

philosophic [fɪləˈsɒfɪk], **philosophical** [fɪləˈsɒfɪkəl] *adj* philosophique; *(person, attitude)* philosophe

philosophize [fɪˈlɒsəfaɪz] *vi* philosopher

philosophy [fɪˈlɒsəfɪ] (*pl* **philosophies**) *n* philosophie *f*

phishing [ˈfɪʃɪŋ] *n Fam Comput* phishing *m*, = extorsion de données confidentielles par e-mail

phlegm [flem] *n* flegme *m*

phlegmatic [flegˈmætɪk] *adj* flegmatique

phobia [ˈfəʊbɪə] *n* phobie *f*; **to have a p. about sth** avoir la phobie de qch

phoenix [ˈfiːnɪks] *n* phénix *m*; **to rise like a p.** renaître tel un phénix

phone [fəʊn] **1** *n* téléphone *m*; **to be on the p.** être au téléphone; **p. bill** facture *f* de téléphone; **p. book** annuaire *m* (du téléphone); **p. booth** cabine *f* téléphonique; **p. call** coup *m* de téléphone; **p. number** numéro *m* de téléphone
  2 *vt* téléphoner à
  3 *vi* téléphoner

phonecard [ˈfəʊnkɑːd] *n* carte *f* de téléphone

phone-in [ˈfəʊnɪn] *n* **p. (program)** = émission au cours de laquelle les téléspectateurs ou les auditeurs peuvent intervenir par téléphone

phoneme [ˈfəʊniːm] *n* phonème *m*

phonetic [fəˈnetɪk] *adj* phonétique

phonetics [fəˈnetɪks] **1** *n (science)* phonétique *f*
  2 *npl (symbols)* symboles *mpl* phonétiques

phony [ˈfəʊnɪ] (*pl* **phonies**) *Fam* **1** *n (impostor)* imposteur *m*; *(insincere person)* faux jeton *m*; *(thing)* faux *m*
  2 *adj* bidon

phosphate [ˈfɒsfeɪt] *n* phosphate *m*

phosphorescent [fɒsfəˈresənt] *adj* phosphorescent(e)

phosphorus [ˈfɒsfərəs] *n* phosphore *m*

photo [ˈfəʊtəʊ] (*pl* **photos**) *n* photo *f*; **to take sb's p.** prendre qn en photo; **p. album** album *m* (de) photos; **p. booth** Photomaton® *m*; **p. finish** photo-finish *f*; **it's just another p. opportunity** *or Fam* **p. op** ce n'est qu'un nouveau prétexte pour se faire photographier

photocopier [ˈfəʊtəʊkɒpɪə(r)] *n* photocopieuse *f*

photocopy [ˈfəʊtəʊkɒpɪ] **1** *n* (*pl* **photocopies**) photocopie *f*
  2 *vt* (*pt & pp* **photocopied**) photocopier

photoelectric [fəʊtəʊɪˈlektrɪk] *adj* photoélectrique; **p. cell** cellule *f* photoélectrique

photogenic [fəʊtəˈdʒenɪk] *adj* photogénique

photograph [ˈfəʊtəgrɑːf] **1** *n* photographie *f*; **to take sb's p.** prendre qn en photo; **p. album** album *m* de photographies
  2 *vt* photographier, prendre en photo

photographer [fəˈtɒgrəfə(r)] *n* photographe *mf*

photographic [fəʊtəˈɡræfɪk] *adj* photographique; **to have a p. memory** avoir une mémoire photographique

photography [fəˈtɒgrəfɪ] *n* photographie *f*

photosensitive [fəʊtəʊˈsensɪtɪv] *adj* photosensible

Photostat® [ˈfəʊtəʊstæt] *n* photostat *m*

photosynthesis [fəʊtəʊˈsɪnθɪsɪs] *n Bot* photosynthèse *f*

photosynthesize [fəʊtəʊˈsɪnθɪsaɪz] *vt Bot* fabriquer par photosynthèse

phrasal verb [ˈfreɪzəlˈvɜːb] *n Gram* verbe *m* à particule

phrase [freɪz] **1** *n* phrase *f*; **p. book** manuel *m* ou guide *m* de conversation
  2 *vt* **(a)** *(verbally)* exprimer; *(in writing)* tourner **(b)** *Mus* phraser

phraseology [freɪzɪˈɒlədʒɪ] *n* phraséologie *f*

Phys Ed [ˈfɪzˈed] *n (abbr* **physical education***)* EPS *f*

physical [ˈfɪzɪkəl] **1** *n (examination)* visite *f* médicale
  2 *adj* physique; **p. education** éducation *f* physique; **p. exercise** *or* **training** (exercices *mpl* de) gymnastique *f*; **p. fitness** forme *f* physique; **p. geography** géographie *f* physique; **p. impossibility** impossibilité *f* physique *ou* matérielle; **p. sciences** sciences *fpl* physiques

physically [ˈfɪzɪklɪ] *adv* physiquement; **p. fit** en bonne forme physique; **p. handicapped** handicapé(e) physique

physician [fɪˈzɪʃən] *n* médecin *m*

physicist [ˈfɪzɪsɪst] *n* physicien(enne) *m,f*

physics [ˈfɪzɪks] *n* physique *f*

physiognomy [fɪzɪˈɒnəmɪ] *n Formal* physionomie *f*

physiological [fɪzɪəˈlɒdʒɪkəl] *adj* physiologique

physiology [fɪzɪˈɒlədʒɪ] *n* physiologie *f*

physiotherapist [fɪzɪəˈθerəpɪst] *n* kinésithérapeute *mf*

physiotherapy [fɪzɪəʊˈθerəpɪ] *n* kinésithérapie *f*

physique [fɪˈziːk] *n* physique *m*

pianist [ˈpɪənɪst] *n* pianiste *mf*

piano [pɪˈænəʊ] (*pl* **pianos**) *n* piano *m*; **p. concerto** concerto *m* pour piano; **p. stool** tabouret *m* de piano; **p. tuner** accordeur *m* de pianos

piccolo [ˈpɪkələʊ] (*pl* **piccolos**) *n* piccolo *m*

pick [pɪk] **1** *n* **(a)** *(tool)* pic *m*, pioche *f* **(b)** *(choice)* **to take one's p.** choisir; **the p. of the bunch** le (la) meilleur(e) du lot
  2 *vt* **(a)** *(choose)* choisir; **to p. a fight (with sb)** chercher la bagarre (avec qn) **(b)** *(flowers, fruit)* cueillir **(c)** *(other uses)* **to p. a lock** crocheter une serrure; **to p. a guitar** pincer la guitare; **to p. one's nose** mettre les doigts dans le nez; **to p. one's teeth** se curer les dents; **to p. a pimple** tripoter un bouton; **to p. sb's pocket** voler dans les poches de qn; **to p. a hole in sth** faire un trou à qch en tirant dessus; *Fig* **to p. holes in sth** trouver des failles dans qch; **to p. sb's brains** soumettre quelque chose à la sagacité de qn
  3 *vi* **to p. and choose** se permettre de choisir

▸**pick off** *vt sep (remove)* enlever, ôter; *(of gunman, sniper)* éliminer

▸**pick on** *vt insep* utiliser comme souffre-douleur

▸**pick out** *vt sep* **(a)** *(remove)* retirer **(b)** *(select)* choisir **(c)** *(recognize)* repérer

▸**pick up 1** *vt sep* **(a)** *(lift up)* ramasser; *(to upright position)* relever; **to p. up the phone** décrocher (le téléphone); *Fig* **to p. oneself up** se remettre, se reprendre; *Fig* **to p. up the pieces** ramasser les morceaux; *Fig* **to p. up the bill** payer l'addition **(b)** *(collect)* prendre; *(arrest)* arrêter; **to p. up survivors** recueillir des survivants **(c)** *Fam (sexually)* ramasser **(d)** *(learn)* apprendre; *(acquire)* acquérir; **to p. up speed** prendre de la vitesse **(e)** *(radio station, message)* capter **(f)** *(notice)* relever **(g)** *(discussion)* reprendre **(h)** *(make better)* remonter
  2 *vi* **(a)** *(improve)* s'améliorer; *(after illness)* se remettre; *(of match, party)* s'animer; **business is picking up** les affaires reprennent **(b)** *(continue)* **let's p. up where we left off** reprenons (là où nous en étions restés)

pickax [ˈpɪkæks] *n* pioche *f*, pic *m*

picket ['pɪkɪt] **1** n (a) (in strike) piquet m de grève; **p. line** piquet de grève (b) (stake) piquet m, pieu m; **p. fence** palissade f
2 vt (during strike) former un piquet de grève aux portes de

pickings ['pɪkɪŋz] npl bénéfices mpl; **rich p.** gros bénéfices

pickle ['pɪkəl] **1** n cornichon m; Fam Fig **to be in a p.** être dans le pétrin
2 vt conserver dans du vinaigre; **pickled cabbage/onions** chou m rouge/oignons mpl au vinaigre

pick-me-up ['pɪkmɪʌp] n Fam remontant m

pickpocket ['pɪkpɒkɪt] n pickpocket m, voleur(euse) m,f à la tire

pick-up ['pɪkʌp] n (a) **p. (arm)** (on record player) lecteur m (phonographique); **p. (truck)** pick-up m inv (petite camionnette à plateau); Fam **p. line** = formule d'entrée en matière pour commencer à draguer quelqu'un; **p. point** (for goods, passengers) point m de ramassage (b) Fam (improvement) amélioration f; (of business) reprise f

picky ['pɪkɪ] adj Fam difficile (**about** sur)

picnic ['pɪknɪk] **1** n pique-nique m; **to go on a p.** aller faire un pique-nique, aller pique-niquer; Fam Fig **it was no p.** ça n'a pas été une partie de plaisir; **p. basket** panier m à pique-nique
2 vi (pt & pp **picnicked**) pique-niquer, faire un pique-nique

picnicker ['pɪknɪkə(r)] n pique-niqueur(euse) m,f

Pict [pɪkt] n Hist Picte mf

pictorial [pɪk'tɔːrɪəl] adj (magazine) illustré(e); (representation) en images

picture ['pɪktʃə(r)] **1** n (a) (painting) tableau m; (drawing) dessin m; (in book, on TV) image f; (photograph) photo f; Fig (situation) situation f; **to be the p. of health** respirer la santé; **her face was a p.** elle a fait une de ces têtes; Fig **to put sb in the p.** mettre qn au courant; Fam Fig **I get the p.** je pige; **p. book** livre m d'images; **p. frame** cadre m; **p. gallery** galerie f de peintures; **p. library** banque f d'images; **p. postcard** carte f postale illustrée; **p. window** baie f vitrée (b) Fam (film) film m
2 vt (a) (imagine) **to p. sth (to oneself)** s'imaginer qch; **to p. sb/sth as sth** s'imaginer qn/qch en qch; **to p. sb doing sth** s'imaginer qn en train de faire qch (b) (in photo, painting) représenter; Fig (in words) dépeindre, décrire

picturesque [pɪktʃə'resk] adj pittoresque

pidgin ['pɪdʒɪn] n pidgin m; **p. English/French** ≃ petit nègre m

pie [paɪ] n (sweet) tarte f; (savory) tourte f; Fam **p. in the sky** des châteaux en Espagne; **p. chart** camembert m; **p. dish** plat m à tarte; **p. plate** plat m allant au four

piece [piːs] n (a) (in general) morceau m; (smaller) bout m; (of cake) part f; (newspaper article) article m; **p. of land** (parcelle f de) terrain m; **a p. of furniture** un meuble; **a p. of luggage** (suitcase) une valise; (bag) un sac; **a p. of advice** un conseil; **a p. of luck** un coup de chance; **a p. of news** une nouvelle; **p. rate** (pay) salaire m à la pièce
(b) (in chess, of jigsaw puzzle) pièce f; (in dominoes) domino m; (in checkers) pion m
(c) (coin) pièce f
(d) (of music) morceau m
(e) (of artillery) pièce f; (firearm) arme f
(f) (idioms) **to be still in one p.** être encore entier(ère); **to give sb a p. of one's mind** dire ses quatre vérités à qn; **to say one's p.** dire ce qu'on a à dire; **p. by p.** par morceaux; Fig **to go to pieces** s'effondrer (complètement); **to fall to pieces** tomber en morceaux; (of house) se délabrer, crouler; (of garment) partir en morceaux; **to take sth to pieces** démonter qch; **to be a p. of cake** être facile comme tout

▶**piece together** vt sep (parts) assembler les morceaux de; (something broken) recoller les morceaux de; (facts) reconstituer

piecemeal ['piːsmiːl] **1** adj fragmentaire, parcellaire; (work) fait(e) petit à petit
2 adv petit à petit

piecework ['piːswɜːk] n travail m à la tâche ou à la pièce

Piedmont ['piːdmɒnt] n le Piémont

pier [pɪə(r)] n (landing stage) embarcadère m; (at seaside resort) jetée f; (of bridge) pilier m

pierce [pɪəs] vt percer, transpercer; **to have pierced ears/a pierced nose** avoir les oreilles percées/le nez percé

piercing ['pɪəsɪŋ] **1** adj (cry, look) perçant(e); (cold) vif (vive)
2 n (body piercing) piercing m

piety ['paɪətɪ] n piété f

pig [pɪg] **1** n (a) (animal) cochon m, porc m (b) Fam (greedy person) goinfre m, glouton(onne) m,f; (unpleasant man) salaud m; (unpleasant woman) salope f (c) Fam (policeman) poulet m (d) Fam (idioms) **to buy a p. in a poke** acheter chat en poche; **pigs might fly!** on peut toujours rêver!; **to make a p.'s ear of sth** bousiller qch, saloper qch; **to make a p. of oneself** s'en mettre plein la lampe
2 vt (pt & pp **pigged**) Fam **to p. oneself** s'en mettre plein la lampe

▶**pig out** vi Fam s'en mettre plein la lampe

pigeon ['pɪdʒɪn] n pigeon m

pigeonhole ['pɪdʒɪnhəʊl] **1** n casier m
2 vt (person) étiqueter, mettre une étiquette à

piggy ['pɪgɪ] Fam **1** n (pl **piggies**) petit cochon m; **p. bank** tirelire f, Can cochon m
2 adj (eyes) de cochon

piggyback ['pɪgɪbæk] n **to give sb a p. (ride)** porter qn sur son dos

pig-headed [pɪg'hedɪd] adj entêté(e), têtu(e)

piglet ['pɪglɪt] n porcelet m

pigment ['pɪgmənt] n pigment m

pigmentation [pɪgmən'teɪʃən] n pigmentation f

pigmy ['pɪgmɪ] (pl **pigmies**) n Pigmée mf

pigsty ['pɪgstaɪ] (pl **pigsties**) n also Fig porcherie f

pigtail ['pɪgteɪl] n natte f

pike¹ [paɪk] n (weapon) pique f

pike² [paɪk] n (fish) brochet m

Pilates [pɪ'lɑːteɪz] n Pilates m, méthode f Pilates; **to do P.** pratiquer la méthode Pilates

pilchard ['pɪltʃəd] n pilchard m

pile [paɪl] **1** n (a) (heap) tas m; (stack) pile f; **to put things in(to) a p.** (heap) mettre des choses en tas; (stack) empiler des choses; Fam **to make one's p.** faire fortune; Fam **to have piles of** or **a p. of things/work to do** avoir un tas de choses/des tonnes de travail à faire; Fam Fig **to be at the top/bottom of the p.** être favorisé(e)/défavorisé(e) (b) (of carpet) poils mpl (c) Phys (atomic) **p.** pile f atomique (d) (building) édifice m; (column, pillar) pieu m
2 vt entasser; (stack) empiler; **to p. food onto one's plate** bien remplir son assiette
3 vi Fam **to p. into a car** s'entasser dans une voiture

▶**pile in** vi s'entasser

▶**pile on** vt sep **to p. on the pressure** faire monter la pression; **to p. on the agony** dramatiser; Fam **to p. it on** en rajouter

▶**pile out** vi sortir en masse

▶**pile up** vi s'accumuler

pile-driver ['paɪldraɪvə(r)] n sonnette f

piles [paɪlz] npl (hemorrhoids) hémorroïdes fpl; **to have p.** avoir des hémorroïdes

pile-up ['paɪlʌp] n Fam carambolage m

pilfer ['pɪlfə(r)] vt & vi chaparder

pilgrim ['pɪlgrɪm] n pèlerin(e) m,f

pilgrimage ['pɪlgrɪmɪdʒ] n pèlerinage m; **to go on** or **make a p.** aller en pèlerinage, faire un pèlerinage

pill [pɪl] n pilule f; **the p.** (contraceptive) la pilule; **to be on the p.** prendre la pilule

pillage ['pɪlɪdʒ] **1** n pillage m
  2 vt & vi piller

pillar ['pɪlə(r)] n also Fig pilier m; **to go from p. to post** courir à droite et à gauche; **a p. of society** un pilier de la société; **to be a p. of strength** être d'un grand soutien

pillion ['pɪljən] **1** n **p. (seat)** siège m arrière
  2 adv **to ride p.** monter derrière

pillory ['pɪlərɪ] **1** n (pl **pillories**) pilori m
  2 vt (pt & pp **pilloried**) mettre au pilori

pillow ['pɪləʊ] n oreiller m

pillowcase ['pɪləʊkeɪs], **pillowslip** ['pɪləʊslɪp] n taie f d'oreiller

pilot ['paɪlət] **1** n (of plane, ship) pilote m; **p. (program)** (on TV) émission f pilote; **p. light** veilleuse f; **p. scheme** projet-pilote m; **p. study** étude-pilote f
  2 vt (plane, ship) piloter

pimp [pɪmp] n souteneur m, proxénète m

pimple ['pɪmpəl] n bouton m

pimply ['pɪmplɪ] adj boutonneux(euse)

PIN [pɪn] n (abbr **personal identification number**) code m confidentiel

pin [pɪn] **1** n (for sewing) épingle f; (for surgery) broche f; (in grenade) goupille f; (brooch) broche f; **three-p. plug** prise f à trois broches; **(firing) p.** percuteur m; **(safety) p.** épingle à nourrice; Fam **to have pins and needles** avoir des fourmis; **you could have heard a p. drop** on aurait entendu une mouche voler; **p. money** argent m de poche
  2 vt (pt & pp **pinned**) (fasten with pin) épingler; (with thumbtack, safety pin) attacher; **to p. sth against** or **to a wall** plaquer qn contre un mur; **to p. the blame on sb** rejeter la responsabilité sur qn; **to p. one's hopes on sb/sth** mettre tous ses espoirs en qn/qch

▸**pin down** vt sep (a) (trap) coincer (b) (identify) mettre le doigt sur (c) (force to be definite) **to p. sb down** obliger qn à s'engager; **to p. sb down to a date** obliger qn à donner une date

▸**pin up** vt sep (notice) fixer ou accrocher au mur; (hair) relever; (hem) rabattre avec des épingles

pinafore ['pɪnəfɔː(r)] n (apron) tablier m; **p. (dress)** robe f chasuble

pinball ['pɪnbɔːl] n flipper m

pincer ['pɪnsə(r)] n (of crab, insect) pince f; Mil **p. movement** mouvement m en tenailles

pincers ['pɪnsəz] npl (tool) tenailles fpl, pince f

pinch [pɪntʃ] **1** n (a) (action) pincement m; **to give sb a p.** pincer qn; Fam Fig **to feel the p.** être gêné(e); **in a p.** à la rigueur (b) (of salt, herbs) pincée f
  2 vt (a) (nip) pincer; **these shoes p. my feet** ces chaussures me serrent (b) Fam (steal) piquer, faucher
  3 vi (of shoes) serrer

pincushion ['pɪnkʊʃən] n pelote f à épingles

pine[1] [paɪn] n (tree, wood) pin m; **p. cone** pomme f de pin, Can cocotte f; **p. forest** pinède f; **p. needle** aiguille f de pin; **p. nut** pignon m

pine[2] [paɪn] vi **to p. for sb/sth** se languir de qn/qch
▸**pine away** vi languir

pineapple ['paɪnæpəl] n ananas m

ping [pɪŋ] **1** n tintement m
  2 vi tinter

ping-pong ['pɪŋpɒŋ] n ping-pong m

pinion ['pɪnjən] **1** n pignon m
  2 vt (restrain) **to p. sb (to/against)** clouer ou plaquer qn (à/contre)

pink [pɪŋk] **1** n (a) (color) rose m; Fam **to be in the p.** être en parfaite santé (b) (flower) œillet m
  2 adj rose; **to turn p.** rosir; Fam **p. slip** lettre f ou avis m de licenciement

pinkeye ['pɪŋkaɪ] n conjonctivite f infectieuse

pinky ['pɪŋkɪ] (pl **pinkies**) n petit doigt m

pinnacle ['pɪnəkəl] n sommet m; Fig (of fame, career) apogée m

pinpoint ['pɪnpɔɪnt] vt déterminer, identifier; (place) localiser exactement

pinprick ['pɪnprɪk] n piqûre f d'aiguille

pinstripe ['pɪnstraɪp] n rayures fpl fines; **p. suit** costume m rayé

pint [paɪnt] n (unit of measurement) = 0,473l, pinte

pinto bean ['pɪntəʊ'biːn] n haricot m pinto

pint-size ['paɪntsaɪz], **pint-sized** ['paɪntsaɪzd] adj Fam minuscule

pin-up ['pɪnʌp] n Fam pin-up f inv

pioneer [paɪə'nɪə(r)] **1** n also Fig pionnier(ère) m,f
  2 vt **to p. sth** être le (la) premier(ère) à mettre au point qch

pioneering [paɪə'nɪərɪŋ] adj (work) innovateur(trice); (person) qui fait œuvre de pionnier

pious ['paɪəs] adj pieux(euse)

piously ['paɪəslɪ] adv pieusement, avec piété

pip [pɪp] n (a) (of fruit) pépin m (b) (on card, die) point m

pipe [paɪp] **1** n (a) (tube) tuyau m, canalisation f; (musical instrument) chalumeau m; **the pipes** la cornemuse; **p. band** orchestre m de cornemuses (b) (for smoking) pipe f; **to smoke a p.** fumer la pipe; Fam Fig **put that in your p. and smoke it!** mettez ça dans votre poche et votre mouchoir par-dessus!; **p. cleaner** cure-pipe m; **p. dream** chimère f
  2 vt (water, oil) canaliser; Fam **piped music** musiquette f

▸**pipe down** vi Fam (make less noise) faire moins de bruit; (not talk so much) se taire

▸**pipe up** vi (of person) risquer un commentaire; (of voice) se faire entendre

pipeline ['paɪplaɪn] n (for oil) pipeline m, oléoduc m; (for gas) gazoduc m; Fig **to be in the p.** être en préparation

piper ['paɪpə(r)] n (bagpipe player) joueur(euse) m,f de cornemuse; Prov **he who pays the p. calls the tune** il est normal que celui qui paie ait le droit de choisir

pipette [pɪ'pet] n pipette f

piping ['paɪpɪŋ] **1** n (a) (pipes) tuyauterie f, canalisations fpl (b) (sound of bagpipes) son m de la cornemuse (c) (on uniform) passepoil m
  2 adj (sound, voice) flûté(e)
  3 adv **p. hot** tout(e) chaud(e)

pipsqueak ['pɪpskwiːk] n Fam minus m

piquant ['piːkənt] adj piquant(e)

pique [piːk] **1** n dépit m; **in a fit of p.** dans un accès de dépit
  2 vt piquer

piracy ['paɪrəsɪ] n (a) (of ships) piraterie f (b) (of videos, software) piratage m

piranha [pɪ'rɑːnə] n piranha m

pirate ['paɪrət] n pirate m; **p. edition** édition f pirate; **p. radio** radio f pirate

pirouette [pɪrʊ'et] **1** n pirouette f
  2 vi pirouetter

Pisa ['piːzə] n Pise

Pisces ['paɪsiːz] n les Poissons mpl; **to be (a) P.** être Poissons

piss [pɪs] very Fam **1** n (urine) pisse f; **to have** or **to take a p.** pisser
  2 vi pisser; **to p. in one's pants** pisser dans son froc

▸**piss off** very Fam **1** vt sep (annoy) faire chier; **to be pissed off** en avoir plein le cul
  2 vi (go away) foutre le camp

pissed [pɪst] adj very Fam (angry) en rogne

pisser ['pɪsə(r)] n very Fam (a) (annoying situation) **what a p.!** quel merde!; **it was a real p. that the weather wasn't better** c'était vraiment chiant qu'il fasse pas plus beau (b) (annoying person) emmerdeur(euse) m,f

pistachio [pɪ'stæʃɪəʊ] (pl **pistachios**) n (nut) pistache f; (tree) pistachier m

pistol ['pɪstəl] *n* pistolet *m*; **p. shot** coup *m* de pistolet

piston ['pɪstən] *n* piston *m*

pit¹ [pɪt] *n* (**a**) *(hole in ground)* fosse *f*; *(coal mine)* mine *f*; **in the p. of one's stomach** au creux de l'estomac; *Fam* **to be the pits** être nul (nulle) (**b**) *(in theater)* parterre *m*; **the pits** *(in motor racing)* les stands *mpl* de ravitaillement; **p. stop** *(in motor racing)* arrêt *m* au stand; *Fam Hum* arrêt *m* pipi (**c**) *(on metal, glass)* piqûre *f*; *(on skin)* marque *f*, cicatrice *f*

pit² [pɪt] *n (of cherry, olive)* noyau *m*

pit³ [pɪt] *(pt & pp* **pitted**) *vt* **to p. sb against sb** mettre qn aux prises avec qn, opposer qn à qn; **to p. oneself against sb** se mesurer à qn; **to p. one's wits against sb** se mesurer intellectuellement à qn

pit-a-pat ['pɪtə'pæt] **1** *n (of rain)* crépitement *m*; *(of feet)* trottinement *m*; *(of heart)* battement *m*
2 *adv* **to go p.** *(of rain)* crépiter; *(of feet)* trottiner; *(of heart)* palpiter

pitch¹ [pɪtʃ] **1** *n* (**a**) *(for sport)* terrain *m* (**b**) *(in music)* hauteur *f*; *Fig* **to reach such a p. that…** atteindre un tel point que… (**c**) *(talk)* (**sales**) **p.** baratin *m* publicitaire (**d**) *(slope)* inclinaison *f*
2 *vt* (**a**) *(throw)* lancer (**b**) *(aim)* adapter (**at** à) (**c**) *(tent)* monter, dresser
3 *vi (of ship, plane)* tanguer

▸**pitch in** *vi* mettre du sien

pitch² [pɪtʃ] *n (tar)* poix *f*

pitch-black [pɪtʃ'blæk] *adj* noir(e) comme dans un four; **it's p. outside** il fait nuit noire

pitched [pɪtʃt] *adj* (**a**) *(sloping)* en pente (**b**) **p. battle** bataille *f* rangée

pitcher¹ ['pɪtʃə(r)] *n (jug)* cruche *f*, pichet *m*

pitcher² ['pɪtʃə(r)] *n (in baseball)* lanceur *m*

pitchfork ['pɪtʃfɔːk] *n* fourche *f*

piteous ['pɪtɪəs] *adj* pitoyable

pitfall ['pɪtfɔːl] *n* piège *m*

pith [pɪθ] *n (of orange)* peau *f* blanche; *(of argument, idea)* essence *f*; **p. helmet** casque *m* colonial (en sola)

pithy ['pɪθɪ] *adj* concis(e)

pitiable ['pɪtɪəbəl] *adj* pitoyable

pitiful ['pɪtɪfʊl] *adj* pitoyable

pitifully ['pɪtɪfʊlɪ] *adv* pitoyablement

pitiless ['pɪtɪlɪs] *adj* impitoyable

pitta bread ['pɪtəbred] *n* pita *m*

pittance ['pɪtəns] *n* salaire *m* de misère

pituitary gland [pɪ'tjuːɪtərɪ'glænd] *n* hypophyse *f*

pity ['pɪtɪ] **1** *n* (**a**) *(compassion)* pitié *f*; **to take** *or* **to have p. on sb** prendre qn en pitié; **for p.'s sake!** par pitié! (**b**) *(misfortune)* **it's a p. (that…)** c'est dommage (que… + *subjunctive*); **what a p.!** quel dommage!; **more's the p.** c'est bien dommage
2 *vt (pt & pp* **pitied**) plaindre, avoir pitié de

pitying ['pɪtɪɪŋ] *adj* compatissant(e)

pivot ['pɪvət] **1** *n also Fig* pivot *m*
2 *vi* pivoter (**on** sur); *Fig (of plan)* reposer (**on** *or* **around** sur)

pivotal ['pɪvətəl] *adj (position)* clef; *(importance)* capital(e)

pixel ['pɪksəl] *n Comput* pixel *m*

pixelize ['pɪksəlaɪz] *vt TV (to hide identity)* mosaïquer

pixellated ['pɪksəleɪtɪd] *adj Comput* pixelisé(e)

pixie ['pɪksɪ] *n* lutin *m*

pizza ['piːtsə] *n* pizza *f*; **p. parlor** pizzeria *f*

pizzazz [pi'zæz] *n (liveliness)* punch *m*; *(style)* panache *m*

Pk. *abbr* **Park**

pkt *(abbr* **packet**) paquet

Pl. *abbr* **Place**

placard ['plækɑːd] *n* pancarte *f*

placate [plə'keɪt] *vt* apaiser, calmer

place [pleɪs] **1** *n* (**a**) *(location)* endroit *m*, lieu *m*; *(in street names)* rue *f*; **a p. to live/eat** un logement/un restaurant; **I can't be in two places at once** je ne peux pas être à deux endroits à la fois; *Fam* **all over the p.** *(everywhere)* un peu partout; **my hair was all over the p.** j'étais coiffé n'importe comment; **at the interview he was all over the p.** à l'entretien, il a raconté n'importe quoi; *Fam Fig* **to go places** réussir (dans la vie); **p. of birth/death/business** lieu de naissance/décès/travail; **p. of residence** domicile *m*; **p. of worship** lieu *m* de culte; **p. name** nom *m* de lieu
(**b**) *(assigned to person, thing)* place *f*; **to find a p. for sb** *(job)* trouver une place pour qn; **to get a p. at the university** être admis(e) à l'université; **there's a time and a p. for everything** il y a un temps pour tout; **to hold sth in p.** tenir qch en place; **to lose one's p.** *(in a book)* perdre sa page; **to take p.** avoir lieu; **to take sb's p.** remplacer qn; *(oust)* prendre la place de qn; *Fig* **out of p.** *(remark)* déplacé(e); **to feel out of p.** ne pas se sentir à sa place
(**c**) *Fam (residence)* chez soi; **my parents' p.** chez mes parents; **your p. or mine?** on va chez toi ou chez moi?
(**d**) *(seat, position in line)* place *f*; **to set an extra p. at the table** mettre un couvert de plus; **to change places with sb** changer de place avec qn; *Fig* être à la place de qn; *Fig* **put yourself in my p.** mettez-vous à ma place; **p. mat** set *m* de table
(**e**) *(in competition, society)* place *f*, rang *m*; **in first/second p.** à la première/seconde place; **in the first p…., in the second p….** *(parts of an argument)* en premier lieu…, en second lieu…; **you shouldn't have said it in the first p.** d'abord, tu n'aurais pas dû le dire; **to know one's p.** savoir où est sa place; **to put sb in his p.** remettre qn à sa place
(**f**) *Math* **to three decimal places** à trois décimales
2 *vt* (**a**) *(put)* placer, mettre; **the house is well placed** la maison est bien située; **to be well placed to do sth** être bien placé(e) pour faire qch; **I know her face but I can't p. her** je l'ai déjà vue mais je ne sais pas où
(**b**) *Com & Fin (order)* passer (**with** à); *(contract)* adjuger (**with** à); **to p. a bet (on sth)** parier (sur qch)
(**c**) *(find a job for)* placer
(**d**) *(classify)* classer; **to be placed third** se classer troisième

placebo [plə'siːbəʊ] *(pl* **placebos**) *n also Fig* placebo *m*; **p. effect** effet *m* placebo

placenta [plə'sentə] *n* placenta *m*

placid ['plæsɪd] *adj* placide, calme

plagiarism ['pleɪdʒərɪzəm] *n* plagiat *m*

plagiarize ['pleɪdʒəraɪz] *vt* plagier

plague [pleɪg] **1** *n (disease)* peste *f*; *(of insects, frogs)* invasion *f*; **to avoid sb/sth like the p.** éviter qn/qch comme la peste
2 *vt (of person)* harceler; *(of problem)* tourmenter; **to p. sb with questions** harceler qn de questions

plaice [pleɪs] *n* carrelet *m*

plaid [plæd] **1** *n (fabric)* tissu *m* écossais; *(garment)* plaid *m*
2 *adj* en tissu écossais

plain [pleɪn] **1** *n* plaine *f*
2 *adj* (**a**) *(clear, unambiguous)* clair(e), évident(e); **to make sth p. to sb** faire comprendre qch à qn; **I'll be quite p. with you** je vais être franc avec vous; *Fam* **it's as p. as the nose on your face** ça se voit comme le nez au milieu de la figure; **in p. English** clairement; *Fig* **to be p. sailing** aller tout seul; **p. speaking** franc-parler *m* (**b**) *(simple)* simple; *Fam* **that's just p. foolishness/ignorance** c'est de la pure bêtise/ignorance; **one p., one purl** *(in knitting)* une maille à l'endroit, une maille à l'envers; **a p.-clothes policeman** un agent en civil (**c**) *(not beautiful)* quelconque; **a p. Jane** une jeune fille plutôt quelconque

plainly ['pleɪnlɪ] *adv* (**a**) *(clearly)* clairement, nettement; **to speak p.** parler franchement *ou* sans détours (**b**) *(simply)* simplement

plain-spoken [pleɪn'spəʊkən] *adj* franc (franche)

plaintiff ['pleɪntɪf] *n Law* plaignant(e) *m,f*

plaintive ['pleɪntɪv] *adj* plaintif(ive)

plaintively ['pleɪntɪvlɪ] *adv* d'un ton plaintif

plait [plæt] **1** *n* natte *f*, tresse *f*
  2 *vt* natter, tresser

plan [plæn] **1** *n* (**a**) *(proposal, intention)* projet *m*; **to go according to p.** marcher comme prévu; **the best p. would be to...** le mieux serait de... (**b**) *(of building, city, essay)* plan *m*
  2 *vt (pt & pp* **planned**) (**a**) *(arrange)* projeter; *(crime)* comploter, tramer; **to p. to do sth** projeter de faire qch; **to go as planned** marcher comme prévu (**b**) *(building, city)* faire le plan de; *(economy)* planifier
  3 *vi* faire des projets; **to p. for the future** faire des projets d'avenir
▸**plan out** *vt sep* prévoir (en détail)

plane¹ [pleɪn] *n (surface)* plan *m*

plane² [pleɪn] *n (airplane)* avion *m*; **by p.** en avion; **p. ticket** billet *m* d'avion

plane³ [pleɪn] **1** *n (tool)* rabot *m*
  2 *vt* raboter, aplanir

plane⁴ [pleɪn] *n* **p. (tree)** platane *m*

planet ['plænɪt] *n* planète *f*

planetarium [plænɪ'teərɪəm] *(pl* **planetariums** *or* **planetaria** [plænɪ'teərɪə]) *n* planétarium *m*

planetary ['plænɪtərɪ] *adj* planétaire

plank [plæŋk] *n (of wood)* planche *f*; *Fig (policy)* point *m*

plankton ['plæŋktən] *n* plancton *m*

planner ['plænə(r)] *n* planificateur(trice) *m,f*; *(for towns)* urbaniste *mf*

planning ['plænɪŋ] *n* conception *f*, élaboration *f*; **it's still at the p. stage** c'est encore à l'état de projet; **p. permission** permis *m* de construire

plant [plɑːnt] **1** *n* (**a**) *(living thing)* plante *f*; **p. life** flore *f* (**b**) *Ind (equipment)* matériel *m*; *(factory)* usine *f*; **p. maintenance** entretien *m* du matériel
  2 *vt (tree, flower)* planter; *(crops, field)* semer; *(bomb)* poser; **to p. an idea in sb's mind** mettre une idée dans l'esprit de qn; *Fam* **to p. sth on sb** cacher qch dans les affaires de qn *(pour le/la compromettre en cas de découverte)*

plantain ['plæntɪn] *n* (**a**) *(wild plant)* plantain *m* (**b**) *(fruit)* banane *f* des Antilles; *(tree)* bananier *m* du paradis

plantation [plæn'teɪʃən] *n* plantation *f*

planter ['plɑːntə(r)] *n (person)* planteur(euse) *m,f*; *(machine)* planteuse

plaque [plɑːk] *n* (**a**) *(sign)* plaque *f* (commémorative) (**b**) *(on teeth)* plaque *f* dentaire

plasma ['plæzmə] *n* plasma *m*

plaster ['plɑːstə(r)] **1** *n (on wall)* plâtre *m*; **p. of Paris** plâtre de Paris; **to put sb's leg in p.** mettre la jambe de qn dans le plâtre; **p. cast** *(for broken bone)* plâtre; *(in art)* moulage *m* en plâtre
  2 *vt* (**a**) *(wall)* plâtrer (**b**) *(cover)* tapisser (**with** de); **plastered with mud** couvert(e) de boue; **her name was plastered over the front pages** son nom s'étalait en première page (**c**) *(make stick)* coller; **the rain had plastered his shirt to his back** la pluie lui avait plaqué la chemise sur le dos

plasterboard ['plɑːstəbɔːd] *n* placoplâtre® *m*

plastered ['plɑːstəd] *adj Fam (drunk)* beurré(e)

plasterer ['plɑːstərə(r)] *n* plâtrier *m*

plastic ['plæstɪk] **1** *n* (**a**) *(material)* plastique *m* (**b**) *Fam (credit cards)* cartes *fpl* de crédit; **do they take p.?** est-ce qu'ils acceptent les cartes de crédit?
  2 *adj (cup, bag)* en plastique; *(bullet)* de plastique; **p. explosive** plastic *m*; **p. surgeon** chirurgien(enne) *m,f* esthétique; **p. surgery** *(cosmetic)* chirurgie *f* esthétique; *(after accident)* chirurgie réparatrice; **p. wrap** film *m* alimentaire

plate [pleɪt] **1** *n* (**a**) *(for food)* assiette *f*; *(for church offering)* plateau *m* de quête; *Fam Fig* **to have a lot on one's p.** avoir du

pain sur la planche; *Fam Fig* **to hand sth to sb on a p.** apporter qch à qn sur un plateau; **p. rack** égouttoir *m* (**b**) *(sheet of glass, plastic)* lamelle *f*; *(sheet of metal)* plaque *f*; **p. glass** vitrage *m* très épais
  2 *vt (with gold)* plaquer en or; *(with silver)* plaquer en argent

plateau ['plætəʊ] *(pl* **plateaux** ['plætəʊz] *or* **plateaus**) *n Geog* plateau *m*; *Fig* **to reach a p.** *(of career, economy)* atteindre un palier

platform ['plætfɔːm] *n* (**a**) *(raised flat surface)* plate-forme *f*; *(in train station) (where passengers stand)* quai *m*; *(where train stops)* voie *f*; **p. 4** *(in train station)* quai n° 4; **p. shoes** chaussures *fpl* à semelles compensées (**b**) *(at meeting)* estrade *f*, tribune *f*; *(political program)* programme *m* (**c**) *Comput* plate-forme *f*

platform-independent ['plætfɔːmɪndɪ'pendənt] *adj Comput* indépendant(e) de la plate-forme

platinum ['plætɪnəm] *n Chem* platine *m*; **p. blond hair** cheveux blond platine

platitude ['plætɪtjuːd] *n* platitude *f*

platonic [plə'tɒnɪk] *adj* platonique

platoon [plə'tuːn] *n Mil* section *f*, peloton *m*

platter ['plætə(r)] *n (serving plate)* plat *m*

platypus ['plætɪpəs] *n* ornithorynque *m*

plausible ['plɔːzəbəl] *adj (excuse, argument)* plausible; *(person)* convaincant(e)

play [pleɪ] **1** *n* (**a**) *(drama)* pièce *f* (de théâtre)
  (**b**) *(of children)* **at p.** en train de jouer; **p. on words** jeu *m* de mots
  (**c**) *(in sports)* jeu *m*; **in p.** en jeu; **out of p.** hors jeu; *Fig* **to come into p.** entrer en jeu; *Fig* **to make a p. for sth** tenter sa chance à qch
  (**d**) *Tech* jeu *m*
  2 *vt* (**a**) *(game, sports)* jouer à; *(opponent)* affronter; *(shot, card, position)* jouer; **to p. soccer/chess** jouer au football/aux échecs; *Fig* **stop playing games!** arrête de te moquer de moi!; *Fig* **to p. ball** *(cooperate)* coopérer; *Fig* **to p. the Stock Exchange** jouer à la Bourse; **to p. a joke** *or* **a trick on sb** jouer un tour à qn
  (**b**) *(in play, movie)* jouer; **to p. Macbeth** jouer le rôle de Macbeth; *Fig* **to p. an important part in sth** jouer un rôle important dans qch; *Fig* **to p. no part in sth** ne pas intervenir dans qch; *Fig* **to p. the fool** faire l'idiot
  (**c**) *(musical instrument)* jouer de; *(piece, tune)* jouer; *(CD, tape, record)* mettre; **to p. the piano/the flute** jouer du piano/de la flûte
  3 *vi* (**a**) *(of children)* jouer; *(of animals)* folâtrer; **to p. with sth** *(pen, hair)* tripoter qch; *Fig* **to p. with fire** jouer avec le feu; *Fam Fig* **what's she playing at?** à quoi elle joue?
  (**b**) *(of athlete)* jouer; **to p. fair/dirty** jouer franc jeu/en traître; *Fig* **to p. for time** essayer de gagner du temps; *Fig* **to p. into sb's hands** faire le jeu de qn; *Fig* **to p. safe** ne pas prendre de risques
  (**c**) *(of musician)* jouer
  (**d**) *(of actor)* jouer; *(of movie, play)* être à l'affiche
▸**play about, play around** *vi* jouer, s'amuser
▸**play along** *vi* coopérer
▸**play back** *vt sep (tape, recording) (for first time)* écouter; *(replay)* réécouter
▸**play down** *vt sep* minimiser
▸**play off** *vt sep* **to p. sb off against sb** monter qn contre qn
▸**play on 1** *vt insep (feelings, fears)* jouer sur
  2 *vi (of musician, athlete)* continuer à jouer
▸**play out** *vt sep* **the drama being played out before them** le drame qui se déroule sous leurs yeux

play-acting ['pleɪæktɪŋ] *n* comédie *f*

playboy ['pleɪbɔɪ] *n* play-boy *m*

player ['pleɪə(r)] *n (of game, instrument)* joueur(euse) *m,f*; *(actor)* acteur(trice) *m,f*; *Fig* **the key players** les acteurs principaux

playful ['pleɪfʊl] *adj (person, animal)* joueur(euse); *(mood, tone)* enjoué(e); *(remark)* espiègle

playground ['pleɪgraʊnd] *n (at school)* cour *f* de récréation; *(in park)* aire *f* de jeu

playhouse ['pleɪhaʊs] *n* (a) *(theater)* théâtre *m* (b) *(children's)* maison *f* de poupée

playing ['pleɪɪŋ] *n* **p. card** carte *f* à jouer; **p. field** terrain *m* de jeu

playmate ['pleɪmeɪt] *n* camarade *mf* de jeu

play-off ['pleɪɒf] *n Sport* match *m* de barrage

playpen ['pleɪpen] *n* parc *m (pour bébé)*

playroom ['pleɪru:m] *n* salle *f* de jeu

plaything ['pleɪθɪŋ] *n* jouet *m*

playtime ['pleɪtaɪm] *n (at school)* récréation *f*

playwright ['pleɪraɪt] *n* auteur *m* dramatique

plaza ['plɑ:zə] *n (shopping center)* centre *m* commercial

PLC, plc [pi:el'si:] *n Com (abbr* **public limited company)** ≃ SA *f*

plea [pli:] *n* (a) *(appeal)* appel *m* (**for** à) (b) *(excuse)* excuse *f* (c) *Law* **to enter a p. of guilty/not guilty** plaider coupable/non coupable; **p. bargaining** = possibilité donnée à l'accusé de voir ses charges réduites s'il plaide coupable

plead [pli:d] **1** *vt Law* **to p. sb's case** *(of lawyer)* plaider la cause de qn; *Law* **to p. insanity** plaider la démence; **to p. ignorance** faire l'ignorant(e)
2 *vi* **to p. with sb (to do sth)** supplier qn (de faire qch); *Law* **to p. guilty/not guilty** plaider coupable/non coupable

pleasant ['plezənt] *adj* agréable

pleasantly ['plezəntlɪ] *adv (smile, behave)* aimablement; *(surprised)* agréablement

pleasantry ['plezəntrɪ] *(pl* **pleasantries)** *n (joke)* plaisanterie *f*; **to exchange pleasantries** *(polite remarks)* échanger des politesses

please [pli:z] **1** *adv* s'il vous/te plaît; **come in, p.** entrez, je vous prie; **p. don't cry** s'il te plaît, ne pleure pas; **p. tell me the truth** dis-moi la vérité(, je t'en prie); **may I? — p. do** puis-je? — je vous en prie; **p. sit down** asseyez-vous, je vous en prie; **yes, p.** oui, s'il te plaît
2 *vt* faire plaisir à; **you can't p. everybody** on ne peut pas contenter tout le monde; **p. yourself!** fais comme tu voudras!; **to be easy/hard to p.** être facile/difficile à contenter; **p. God!** plaise à Dieu!
3 *vi* (a) *(like)* **to do as one pleases** faire ce que l'on veut; **this way, if you p.** par ici, s'il vous plaît; **and then, if you p., he blamed me for it!** et le comble, c'est qu'il a dit que c'était de ma faute! (b) *(give pleasure)* **to be eager to p.** vouloir plaire

pleased [pli:zd] *adj* content(e) (**with** de); **to be p. to do sth** faire qch avec plaisir; **to be p. for sb** être content pour qn; **to be as p. as Punch** être content comme tout; **he's very p. with himself** il est très content de lui; **p. to meet you!** enchanté!; **I'm p. to say that...** je suis heureux de vous dire que...

pleasurable ['pleʒərəbəl] *adj* agréable

pleasure ['pleʒə(r)] *n* (a) *(contentment, enjoyment)* plaisir *m*; **to take p. in doing sth** prendre plaisir à faire qch; **with p.** avec plaisir; **my p.!** je t'en prie!; *Formal* **I have p. in informing you that...** j'ai le plaisir de vous informer que...; **p. boat** bateau *m* de plaisance; **p. trip** excursion *f* (b) *(will)* **at your p.** à votre gré

pleat [pli:t] *n* pli *m*

pleated ['pli:tɪd] *adj* plissé(e)

plebeian [plə'bi:ən] *n & adj* plébéien(enne) *m,f*

plebiscite ['plebɪsɪt] *n* plébiscite *m*

plectrum ['plektrəm] *n Mus* médiator *m*

pledge [pledʒ] **1** *n* (a) *(promise)* promesse *f* (b) *(object)* gage *m*
2 *vt (promise)* **to p. to do sth** s'engager à faire qch; **to p. one's loyalty/support** accorder sa loyauté/son soutien; **to**

p. money *(in radio, television appeal)* faire une promesse de don

plenary ['pli:nərɪ] *adj* plénier(ère); **p. session** séance *f* plénière

plentiful ['plentɪfʊl] *adj* abondant(e)

plenty ['plentɪ] **1** *n* abondance *f*; **a land of p.** un pays d'abondance
2 *pron* **p. of** beaucoup de; **you've got p. of time** tu as largement le temps; **that's p.** *(of food)* merci, j'en ai assez
3 *adv Fam* **it's p. big enough** c'est bien assez grand

plethora ['pleθərə] *n* pléthore *f*

pleurisy ['plʊərɪsɪ] *n* pleurésie *f*

pliable ['plaɪəbəl] *adj (wood, plastic)* souple; *(person)* malléable

pliers ['plaɪəz] *npl* pince *f*, tenaille *f*; **a pair of p.** une pince, une tenaille

plight [plaɪt] *n* situation *f* critique; *(of refugees)* détresse *f*

plinth [plɪnθ] *n* socle *m*

PLO [pi:e'ləʊ] *n (abbr* **Palestine Liberation Organization)** OLP *f*

plod [plɒd] *(pt & pp* **plodded)** *vi* (a) *(walk)* marcher péniblement (b) *(work)* **to p. (away)** trimer

plonk [plɒŋk] **1** *n (sound)* bruit *m* sourd
2 *vt Fam* **just p. it down there** tu n'as qu'à le poser là; **to p. oneself down in an armchair** s'affaler dans un fauteuil

plop [plɒp] **1** *n* plouf *m*
2 *vi (pt & pp* **plopped)** faire plouf

plot [plɒt] **1** *n* (a) *(conspiracy)* complot *m* (b) *(of play, novel)* intrigue *f*; *Fig* **the p. thickens** l'affaire se corse (c) *(land)* parcelle *f*; **(vegetable) p.** potager *m*
2 *vt (pt & pp* **plotted)** (a) *(plan)* comploter; **to p. to do sth** comploter de faire qch (b) *(position, course)* déterminer; *(progress, development)* suivre de près (c) *Math* tracer

plotter ['plɒtə(r)] *n (conspirator)* conspirateur(trice) *m,f*

plover ['plʌvə(r)] *n* pluvier *m*

plow [plaʊ] **1** *n* charrue *f*; **the P.** *(constellation)* le Grand Chariot
2 *vt (field)* labourer; *Fig (profits)* réinvestir
3 *vi* labourer; *Fig* **to p. through sth** *(work, reading)* avancer péniblement dans qch; *Fig* **to p. into sth** *(of vehicle)* rentrer dans qch

▸**plow on with** *vt insep* poursuivre laborieusement

▸**plow up** *vt sep (field)* labourer

plowman ['plaʊmən] *n* laboureur *m*

ploy [plɔɪ] *n* stratagème *m*, ruse *f*

pluck [plʌk] **1** *n (courage)* courage *m*
2 *vt (hair, feathers)* arracher; *(flower)* cueillir; *(chicken, turkey)* plumer; *(string of guitar)* pincer; **to p. one's eyebrows** s'épiler les sourcils; **they were plucked from danger by a helicopter** un hélicoptère les a sauvés du danger
3 *vt* **to p. at sb's sleeve** tirer qn par la manche

▸**pluck up** *vt sep* **to p. up the courage to do sth** trouver le courage de faire qch

plucky ['plʌkɪ] *adj* courageux(euse)

plug [plʌg] **1** *n* (a) *(for sink)* bonde *f* (b) *(electrical) (on device)* fiche *f*; *(socket)* prise *f* (de courant); *Fam Fig* **to pull the p. on sth** *(put a stop to)* mettre le holà à qch; *(stop funding)* arrêter de financer qch (c) *Aut* **(spark) p.** bougie *f* (d) *Fam (publicity)* pub *f*
2 *vt (pt & pp* **plugged)** (a) *(gap, hole)* boucher; *(leak)* colmater (b) *Fam (promote)* faire de la pub pour

▸**plug away** *vi Fam* s'acharner (**at** sur)

▸**plug in** *vt sep* brancher

plughole ['plʌghəʊl] *n* trou *m* d'écoulement

plug-in ['plʌgɪn] *n Comput* module *m* externe, *Can* plugiciel *m*

plum [plʌm] **1** *n (fruit)* prune *f*; **p. pudding** plum-pudding *m*; **p. tomato** olivette *f*; **p. tree** prunier *m*
2 *adj* (a) *(color)* prune *inv* (b) *Fam (very good)* **a p. job** un boulot en or

plumage ['plu:mɪdʒ] n plumage m

plumb [plʌm] **1** n **p. (line)** fil m à plomb; **to be out of p.** ne pas être d'aplomb

2 adv (exactly) **p. in the center** en plein centre

3 vt Fig **to p. the depths** toucher le fond; **that's really plumbing the depths!** c'est vraiment le comble du mauvais goût!

plumber ['plʌmə(r)] n plombier m

plumbing ['plʌmɪŋ] n (job, system) plomberie f

plume [plu:m] n (feather) plume f; (on hat) aigrette f; Fig (of smoke) volute f

plummet ['plʌmɪt] vi (of morale, standards) chuter; (of prices) s'effondrer; **the plane plummeted to the ground** l'avion a piqué et s'est écrasé au sol

plump [plʌmp] adj dodu(e); (cheeks, face) rond(e)

▸**plump down** vt sep Fam laisser tomber lourdement

▸**plump for** vt insep Fam (choose) se décider pour

plunder ['plʌndə(r)] **1** n (action) pillage m; (loot) butin m

2 vt piller

plunge [plʌndʒ] **1** n (dive) plongeon m; Fig (decrease) chute f; Fam Fig **to take the p.** se jeter à l'eau

2 vt plonger (**into** dans)

3 vi (fall) plonger; Fig (decrease) chuter; **she plunged to her death** elle a fait une chute mortelle

plunger ['plʌndʒə(r)] n (of coffeepot, syringe) piston m; (for clearing sink) ventouse f

plunging ['plʌndʒɪŋ] adj (prices) en chute libre; **p. neckline** décolleté m plongeant

pluperfect ['plu:'pɜ:fɪkt] n Gram **the p.** le plus-que-parfait

plural ['plʊərəl] Gram **1** adj pluriel(elle)

2 n pluriel m

pluralism ['plʊərəlɪzəm] n pluralisme m

plurality [plʊə'rælɪtɪ] n pluralité f

plus [plʌs] **1** n (pl **plusses** ['plʌsɪz]) **(a) p. (sign)** (signe m) plus m; **(b)** (advantage) plus m **(c) p. fours** pantalon m de golf

2 adj **but on the p. side...** mais d'un autre côté...; **fifteen p.** plus de quinze

3 prep plus; **7 p. 9** 7 plus 9

plush [plʌʃ] **1** n Tex peluche f

2 adj Fam luxueux(euse)

Pluto ['plu:təʊ] n (planet) Pluton f

plutonium [plu:'təʊnɪəm] n Chem plutonium m

ply¹ [plaɪ] n **three-p.** (wood, paper handkerchief) triple épaisseur; (wool) à trois fils

ply² [plaɪ] (pt & pp **plied**) **1** vt (trade) exercer; **to p. sb with questions** assaillir qn de questions; **to p. sb with drink** ne pas arrêter de verser à boire à qn

2 vi (of ship, bus) **to p. between** faire la navette entre

plywood ['plaɪwʊd] n contreplaqué m

PM [pi:'em] n (abbr **Prime Minister**) Premier ministre m

p.m. ['pi:em] adv (abbr **post meridiem**) **6 p.m.** 18h

PMS [pi:em'es] n (abbr **premenstrual syndrome**) syndrome m prémenstruel

pneumatic [nju:'mætɪk] adj pneumatique; **p. drill** marteau m piqueur

pneumonia [nju:'məʊnɪə] n pneumonie f

PO [pi:'əʊ] n **(a)** (abbr **Post Office**) poste f; **PO Box** BP **(b)** (abbr **postal order**) mandat m postal

poach¹ [pəʊtʃ] vt Culin (eggs, fish) pocher

poach² [pəʊtʃ] vt **(a)** (catch illegally) (fish) pêcher sans permis; (game) chasser sans permis **(b)** (employee) débaucher

poacher ['pəʊtʃə(r)] n (of fish, game) braconnier m

pocket ['pɒkɪt] **1** n **(a)** (of clothes, bag) poche f; **to go through sb's pockets** faire les poches à qn; **prices to suit every p.** des prix pour toutes les bourses; **to be out of p.** en être de sa poche; **to pay for sth out of one's own p.** payer qch de sa poche; Fig **to line one's pockets** se remplir les poches; Fig **to**

have sb in one's p. avoir qn dans sa poche; **p. calculator** calculette f; **p. money** argent m de poche **(b)** (in pool) poche f, blouse f **(c)** (of gas, air, resistance) poche f

2 vt (put in pocket) empocher; Fam (steal) rafler

pocketbook ['pɒkɪtbʊk] n (wallet) portefeuille m; (handbag) sac m à main

pocketknife ['pɒkɪtnaɪf] (pl **pocketknives** ['pɒkɪtnaɪvz]) n couteau m de poche

pockmarked ['pɒkmɑːkt] adj grêlé(e)

pod [pɒd] n (of plant) gousse f

podgy ['pɒdʒɪ] adj grassouillet(ette)

podiatrist [pə'daɪətrɪst] n pédicure mf

podium ['pəʊdɪəm] n (for speaker, conductor) estrade f; (for winner) podium m

poem ['pəʊɪm] n poème m

poet ['pəʊɪt] n poète m

poetic [pəʊ'etɪk] adj poétique; **it's p. justice that...** ça n'est que justice que...; **p. license** licence f poétique

poetical [pəʊ'etɪkəl] adj poétique

poetry ['pəʊɪtrɪ] n poésie f; **p. in motion** un véritable plaisir; **p. reading** lecture f de textes poétiques

poignancy ['pɔɪnjənsɪ] n caractère m poignant

poignant ['pɔɪnjənt] adj poignant(e)

point [pɔɪnt] **1** n **(a)** (location) endroit m; **the highest p.** le point le plus haut; **p. of sale** point m de vente; **p. of view** point m de vue

(b) (in time) moment m; **at this p. in time** actuellement; **at this p. the phone rang** à ce moment le téléphone a sonné; **to be on the p. of doing sth** être sur le point de faire qch; **to reach the p. of no return** arriver au point de non-retour; **outspoken to the p. of rudeness** d'une franchise qui frise l'impolitesse

(c) (of argument, discussion) point m; **the p. is that...** le fait est que...; **I take your p.** je vois ce que tu veux dire; **she has a p.** elle a raison; **to make a p.** faire une remarque; **to get to the p.** en arriver au fait; **that's beside the p.** ça n'a rien à voir; **that's not the p.** il ne s'agit pas de cela; **what's the p.?** à quoi bon?; **to make a p. of doing sth** mettre un point d'honneur à faire qch; **there is no p. in waiting any longer** cela ne sert à rien d'attendre plus longtemps; **in p. of fact** en fait; **to the p.** (relevant) pertinent(e); **it has its good points** ça a ses avantages; **up to a p.** jusqu'à un certain point; **not to put too fine a p. on it...** pour parler franchement...; **p. of grammar/of law** question f de grammaire/de droit; **p. of order** question f de procédure

(d) (punctuation mark) point m; Math (decimal) **p.** virgule f (décimale); **three p. five** trois virgule cinq

(e) (in game, exam, on scale) point m; **to win on points** gagner aux points

(f) (on compass) point m

(g) (of needle, pencil, sword) pointe f; **to end in a p.** avoir un bout pointu

(h) (plug socket) prise f (de courant)

(i) (of land) pointe f

2 vt (camera, gun) braquer (**at** sur); Fig **to p. the finger at sb** montrer qn du doigt; **can you p. me in the right direction?** pouvez-vous me dire quelle direction je dois prendre?; **to p. the way (to)** montrer le chemin (à); Fig montrer la voie (à)

3 vi **to p. at** or **to sb/sth** (with finger) montrer qn/qch du doigt; **to p. north** (of arrow, compass needle) indiquer le nord; **to be pointing toward sth** (of car, chair) être face à qch; **this points to the fact that...** ceci montre ou indique que...; **all the evidence points to suicide** tout laisse penser à un suicide

▸**point out** vt sep (with finger) montrer; (error, fact) signaler

▸**point up** vt sep (highlight) mettre en évidence

point-blank ['pɔɪnt'blæŋk] **1** adj (refusal, denial) catégorique; **at p. range** à bout portant

2 *adv (fire)* à bout portant; *(ask)* de but en blanc; *(refuse, deny)* catégoriquement

pointed ['pɔɪntɪd] *adj* **(a)** *(sharp)* pointu(e) **(b)** *(remark)* mordant(e)

pointedly ['pɔɪntɪdlɪ] *adv* ostensiblement

pointer ['pɔɪntə(r)] *n* **(a)** *(indicator)* aiguille *f*; *(stick)* baguette *f* **(b)** *Fam (advice)* tuyau *m* **(c)** *(dog)* pointer *m*

pointless ['pɔɪntlɪs] *adj* inutile; *(life)* absurde; **it would be p.** ça ne servirait à rien

poise [pɔɪz] *n (composure)* assurance *f*; *(balance)* équilibre *m*

poised [pɔɪzd] *adj* **(a)** *(composed)* posé(e) **(b)** *(ready)* **to be p. to do sth** être prêt(e) à faire qch **(c)** *(suspended)* suspendu(e)

poison ['pɔɪzən] **1** *n* poison *m*; *Fam* **what's your p.?** qu'est-ce que tu veux boire?; **p. gas** gaz *m* toxique; **p. ivy** sumac *m* vénéneux; **p. pen letter** lettre *f* anonyme malfaisante
2 *vt* **(a)** *(person, food)* empoisonner; **to p. sb's mind against sb** monter qn contre qn **(b)** *(pollute)* contaminer

poisoning ['pɔɪzənɪŋ] *n* **(a)** *(of person, food)* empoisonnement *m*; **to die of p.** mourir empoisonné(e) **(b)** *(pollution)* contamination *f*

poisonous ['pɔɪzənəs] *adj (snake, remark)* venimeux(euse); *(chemical, fumes)* toxique; *(plant, mushroom)* vénéneux(euse); *Fig (rumor, doctrine)* pernicieux(euse)

poke [pəʊk] **1** *n* coup *m* léger
2 *vt (person)* donner un coup à; *(object)* tâter; *(fire)* attiser; **to p. sb in the eye** mettre le doigt dans l'œil à qn; **to p. sb in the ribs** *(with elbow)* donner un coup de coude à qn; **to p. a hole in sth** faire un trou dans qch; **to p. one's nose into other people's business** mettre son nez dans les affaires des autres; **to p. one's head out of the window** passer la tête par la fenêtre; **to p. fun at** se moquer de
3 *vi* **to p. at sth (with one's finger/a stick)** tâter qch (du doigt/avec le bout d'un bâton)

▸**poke about, poke around** *vi (search) (of person)* fouiller; *(be nosy)* fourrer son nez partout

▸**poke out 1** *vt sep* **you nearly poked my eye out!** un peu plus et tu me crevais l'œil!
2 *vi (protrude)* sortir, dépasser

poker¹ ['pəʊkə(r)] *n (for fire)* tisonnier *m*

poker² ['pəʊkə(r)] *n (card game)* poker *m*

poker-faced ['pəʊkəfeɪst] *adj* au visage impassible

poky ['pəʊkɪ] *adj* **a p. little apartment** un appartement exigu

Poland ['pəʊlənd] *n* la Pologne

polar ['pəʊlə(r)] *adj* polaire; **p. bear** ours *m* polaire *ou* blanc

polarity [pəʊ'lærɪtɪ] *n* polarité *f*

polarization [pəʊləraɪ'zeɪʃən] *n (of opinion, country)* division *f*

polarize ['pəʊləraɪz] *vt (opinion, country)* diviser

Polaroid® ['pəʊlərɔɪd] *n (camera, photo)* polaroid® *m*

Pole [pəʊl] *n* Polonais(e) *m,f*

pole¹ [pəʊl] *n (post, stick)* perche *f*; *(for flag)* hampe *f*; **the p. vault** le saut à la perche; **p. dancer** = danseuse qui pratique le "pole dancing"; **p. dancing** = style de danse de strip-tease qui s'exécute autour d'une barre verticale

pole² [pəʊl] *n Elec & Geog* pôle *m*; *Fig* **to be poles apart** être diamétralement opposés; **the P. Star** l'étoile *f* polaire

poleax ['pəʊlæks] *vt (physically)* assommer; *(emotionally)* abasourdir

polecat ['pəʊlkæt] *n* putois *m*

polemic [pə'lemɪk] *n* polémique *f*

polemical [pə'lemɪkəl] *adj* polémique

police [pə'liːs] **1** *npl* **the p.** la police; **two hundred p.** deux cents policiers; **p. captain** ≃ commissaire *m* de police; **p. car** voiture *f* de police; **p. chief** ≃ préfet *m* de police; **p. department** service *m* de police; **p. dog** chien *m* policier; **p. force** police; **p. inspector** inspecteur(trice) *m,f* de police; **p. officer** policier *m*; **p. record** casier *m* judiciaire; **p. state** État *m* poli-

cier; **p. station** poste *m* de police; **p. wagon** fourgon *m* cellulaire
2 *vt (area, city)* maintenir l'ordre dans; *Fig* réglementer

policeman [pə'liːsmən] *n* agent *m* de police

policewoman [pə'liːswʊmən] *n* femme *f* agent de police

policy ['pɒlɪsɪ] *(pl* **policies)** *n* **(a)** *(of government, personal)* politique *f*; **it's a matter of p.** c'est une question de principe; **a good/bad p.** une bonne/mauvaise idée **(b)** *Fin* **(insurance) p.** police *f* (d'assurance); *Fin* **p. holder** assuré(e) *m,f*

polio ['pəʊlɪəʊ] *n* polio *f*

Polish ['pəʊlɪʃ] **1** *n (language)* polonais *m*
2 *adj* polonais(e)

polish ['pɒlɪʃ] **1** *n* **(a)** *(for shoes)* cirage *m*; *(for furniture, floors)* cire *f*; *(for metal)* pâte *f* à polir; *(for nails)* vernis *m* à ongles **(b)** *(finish, shine)* éclat *m*, brillant *m*; **to give sth a p.** faire briller qch **(c)** *(refinement)* raffinement *m*
2 *vt (silver, brass)* astiquer; *(shoes, furniture, floor)* cirer; *(stone, metal)* polir

▸**polish off** *vt sep Fam (food)* avaler; *(drink)* descendre; *(work)* expédier; *(opponent)* liquider

▸**polish up** *vt sep (improve)* perfectionner

polished ['pɒlɪʃt] *adj (shoes, furniture, floor)* ciré(e); *(metal, stone, glass)* poli(e); *Fig (manners, style)* raffiné(e)

polite [pə'laɪt] *adj* poli(e) (**to** avec); **in p. society** chez les gens bien

politely [pə'laɪtlɪ] *adv* poliment

politeness [pə'laɪtnɪs] *n* politesse *f*

politic ['pɒlɪtɪk] *adj Formal* sage; **it would not be p. to refuse** ce ne serait pas prudent de refuser

political [pə'lɪtɪkəl] *adj* politique; **she isn't very p.** elle ne s'intéresse pas beaucoup à la politique; **p. asylum** asile *m* politique; **p. correctness** le politiquement correct; **p. prisoner** prisonnier(ère) *m,f* politique; **p. science** sciences *fpl* politiques

politically [pə'lɪtɪklɪ] *adv* politiquement; **p. correct** politiquement correct(e)

politician [pɒlɪ'tɪʃən] *n* homme *m*/femme *f* politique

politicize [pə'lɪtɪsaɪz] *vt* politiser

politics ['pɒlɪtɪks] **1** *n* politique *f*
2 *npl* **(a)** *(views)* opinions *fpl* politiques **(b)** **office p.** intrigues *fpl* de bureau

polka ['pɒlkə] *n* polka *f*; **p. dot** pois *m*

polka-dot ['pɒlkədɒt] *adj* à pois; **a p. necktie** une cravate à pois

poll [pəʊl] **1** *n (votes cast)* scrutin *m*; **(opinion) p.** *(survey)* sondage *m*; **to go to the polls** aller aux urnes
2 *vt (votes)* obtenir; *(people)* sonder

pollen ['pɒlən] *n* pollen *m*; **p. count** taux *m* de pollen dans l'atmosphère

pollinate ['pɒlɪneɪt] *vt* polliniser

polling ['pəʊlɪŋ] *n* élections *fpl*, scrutin *m*; **p. booth** isoloir *m*; **p. place** bureau *m* de vote

pollutant [pə'luːtənt] *n* polluant *m*

pollute [pə'luːt] *vt* polluer

polluter [pə'luːtə(r)] *n* pollueur(euse) *m,f*

pollution [pə'luːʃən] *n* pollution *f*

polo ['pəʊləʊ] *n* **(a)** *Sport* polo *m* **(b)** **p. neck (sweater)** (pull *m* à) col *m* roulé

poltergeist ['pɒltəgaɪst] *n* esprit *m* frappeur

polyester [pɒlɪ'estə(r)] *n* polyester *m*

polyethylene [pɒlɪ'eθɪliːn] *n* polyéthylène *m*, Polythène *m*

polygamy [pə'lɪɡəmɪ] *n* polygamie *f*

polyglot ['pɒlɪɡlɒt] *n & adj* polyglotte *mf*

polygon ['pɒlɪɡən] *n* polygone *m*

polymer ['pɒlɪmə(r)] *n Chem* polymère *m*

Polynesia [pɒlɪ'niːzɪə] *n* la Polynésie

Polynesian [pɒlɪˈniːzɪən] **1** *n* Polynésien(enne) *m,f*
2 *adj* polynésien(enne)

polyp [ˈpɒlɪp] *n Med* polype *m*

polyphonic [pɒlɪˈfɒnɪk] *adj Mus* polyphonique; *Tel* **p. ring-tone** sonnerie *f* polyphonique

polystyrene [pɒlɪˈstaɪriːn] *n* polystyrène *m*

polyunsaturated [pɒlɪʌnˈsætjʊreɪtɪd] *adj* polyinsaturé(e)

polyurethane [pɒlɪˈjʊərɪθeɪn] *n* polyuréthane *m*

pomegranate [ˈpɒmɪɡrænɪt] *n (fruit)* grenade *f*; **p. (tree)** grenadier *m*

pomp [pɒmp] *n* pompe *f*; **p. and circumstance** grand appa-rat *m*

pompom [ˈpɒmpɒm] *n* pompon *m*

pomposity [pɒmˈpɒsɪtɪ] *n* suffisance *f*

pompous [ˈpɒmpəs] *adj* pompeux(euse)

poncho [ˈpɒntʃəʊ] *(pl* **ponchos)** *n* poncho *m*

pond [pɒnd] *n* étang *m*; *(smaller)* mare *f*

ponder [ˈpɒndə(r)] **1** *vt* réfléchir à, considérer
2 *vi* réfléchir (**on** *or* **over** à)

ponderous [ˈpɒndərəs] *adj (movement, person)* lourd(e); *(pro-gress, piece of writing)* laborieux(euse)

pontiff [ˈpɒntɪf] *n* pontife *m*

pontificate [pɒnˈtɪfɪkeɪt] *vi* pontifier (**about** sur)

pontoon¹ [pɒnˈtuːn] *n (float)* ponton *m*; **p. bridge** pont *m* flottant

pontoon² [pɒnˈtuːn] *n (card game)* vingt-et-un *m*

pony [ˈpəʊnɪ] *(pl* **ponies)** *n* poney *m*; **p. trekking** randonnée *f* à dos de poney

ponytail [ˈpəʊnɪteɪl] *n* queue *f* de cheval

poo [puː] *n Fam* caca *m*; **to do a p.** faire caca

poodle [ˈpuːdəl] *n* caniche *m*

poof [pʊf], **poofter** [ˈpʊftə(r)] *n very Fam* pédé *m*, = terme injurieux désignant un homosexuel

pooh [puː] *exclam* bah!

pooh-pooh [ˈpuːˈpuː] *vt* rejeter

pool¹ [puːl] *n (pond, of blood)* mare *f*; *(puddle)* flaque *f*; **(swimming) p.** piscine *f*

pool² [puːl] **1** *n (of money, helpers)* réserve *f*; *(of knowledge)* mine *f*; **car p.** parc *m* de voitures
2 *vt (ideas, resources)* mettre en commun, grouper

pool³ [puːl] *n (game)* billard *m* américain; **p. table** (table *f* de) billard

poop [puːp] **1** *n Fam* caca *m*; **to take a p.** faire caca
2 *vi* faire caca

pooped [puːpt] *adj Fam* vanné(e)

poor [pʊə(r)] **1** *adj* **(a)** *(not rich)* pauvre; **the p. man's cham-pagne** le champagne du pauvre **(b)** *(bad)* mauvais(e); *(chances)* faible; *(harvest, reward)* maigre; **to be in p. health** ne pas bien se porter; **to have a p. memory** ne pas avoir une bonne mém-oire; **to be p. at math** être faible en maths; **p. loser** mau-vais(e) perdant(e) *m,f*; **in p. taste** de mauvais goût **(c)** *(expressing sympathy)* **you p. thing!** pauvre petit(e)!; **p. (old) Simon** le pauvre Simon
2 *npl* **the p.** les pauvres *mpl*

poorly [ˈpʊəlɪ] **1** *adv* mal; *(dressed)* pauvrement; **to be p. off** être pauvre
2 *adj* malade, souffrant(e)

pop¹ [pɒp] **1** *n (music)* pop *f*
2 *adj* **p. art** pop art *m*; **p. group** groupe *m* de pop; **p. music** musique *f* pop; **p. singer** chanteur(euse) *m,f* pop; **p. song** chanson *f* pop; **p. star** chanteur(euse) *m,f* pop

pop² [pɒp] *n Fam (father)* papa *m*

pop³ [pɒp] **1** *n* **(a)** *(sound)* bruit *m* sec **(b)** *Fam (fizzy drink)* soda *m*
2 *vt (pt & pp* **popped)** **(a)** *(burst)* faire éclater **(b)** *Fam (put quickly)* mettre; **to p. one's head out of the window** passer la tête par la fenêtre; *Fam* **to p. the question** faire sa demande en mariage; **to p. pills** se bourrer de comprimés
3 *vi* **(a)** *(burst)* éclater; *(of cork)* sauter; *(of ears)* se déboucher **(b)** *Fam (go quickly)* **I'm just popping next door** je fais juste un saut chez les voisins

▸**pop in** *vi Fam* passer

▸**pop off** *vi very Fam (die)* claquer

▸**pop out** *vi Fam (go out)* sortir; **I'm just popping out to the grocery store** je fais juste un saut à l'épicerie

pop. *(abbr* **population)** population *f*

popcorn [ˈpɒpkɔːn] *n* pop-corn *m*

pope [pəʊp] *n* pape *m*

popgun [ˈpɒpɡʌn] *n* pistolet *m* à bouchon

poplar [ˈpɒplə(r)] *n* peuplier *m*

poplin [ˈpɒplɪn] *n* popeline *f*

poppy [ˈpɒpɪ] *(pl* **poppies)** *n* coquelicot *m*; **p. seed** graine *f* de pavot

poppycock [ˈpɒpɪkɒk] *n Fam (nonsense)* bêtises *fpl*

Popsicle® [ˈpɒpsɪkəl] *n* glace *f* à l'eau

populace [ˈpɒpjʊləs] *n Formal* **the p.** la population

popular [ˈpɒpjʊlə(r)] *adj* populaire; *(fashionable)* à la mode; *(restaurant, film)* qui a beaucoup de succès; **to make oneself p.** se faire bien voir; **she is p. with her colleagues** elle est appréciée par ses collègues; **by p. demand** à la demande gé-nérale; **contrary to p. belief** contrairement à ce que les gens croient

popularity [pɒpjʊˈlærɪtɪ] *n* popularité *f*; **p. rating** cote *f* de popularité

popularize [ˈpɒpjʊləraɪz] *vt* populariser

popularly [ˈpɒpjʊləlɪ] *adv* communément; **it is p. believed that...** les gens croient généralement que...

populate [ˈpɒpjʊleɪt] *vt* peupler

population [pɒpjʊˈleɪʃən] *n* population *f*; **p. explosion** ex-plosion *f* démographique

populous [ˈpɒpjʊləs] *adj* populeux(euse)

pop-up [ˈpɒpʌp] **1** *adj* **(a)** *(book, card)* en relief **(b)** *Comput* **p. ad** pop-up *m*; **p. menu** menu *m* local
2 *n Comput (advert)* pop-up *m*

porcelain [ˈpɔːslɪn] *n* porcelaine *f*; **p. ware** porcelaine

porch [pɔːtʃ] *n (veranda)* véranda *f*

porcupine [ˈpɔːkjʊpaɪn] *n* porc-épic *m*

pore [pɔːr] *n* pore *m*

▸**pore over** *vt insep (examine closely)* étudier soigneusement

pork [pɔːk] *n* porc *m*; **p. chop** côte *f* de porc

porn [pɔːn] *n & adj Fam* porno *m*

pornographic [pɔːnəˈɡræfɪk] *adj* pornographique

pornography [pɔːˈnɒɡrəfɪ] *n* pornographie *f*

porous [ˈpɔːrəs] *adj* poreux(euse)

porpoise [ˈpɔːpəs] *n* marsouin *m*

porridge [ˈpɒrɪdʒ] *n* porridge *m*

port¹ [pɔːt] *n* **(a)** *(harbor, town)* port *m*; **in p.** au port; *also Fig* **p. of call** escale *f*; *Prov* **any p. in a storm** nécessité fait loi **(b)** *Comput* port *m*

port² [pɔːt] *n Naut (left-hand side)* bâbord *m*

port³ [pɔːt] *n (drink)* porto *m*

portable [ˈpɔːtəbəl] *adj* portable

portal [ˈpɔːtəl] *n Archit & Comput* portail *m*

Port-au-Prince [pɔːtəʊˈprɛ̃s] *n* Port-au-Prince

portcullis [pɔːtˈkʌlɪs] *n* sarrasine *f*

portend [pɔːˈtend] *vt Formal* présager

portent [ˈpɔːtent] *n Formal* présage *m*

portentous [pɔːˈtentəs] *adj Formal* majeur(e)

porter [ˈpɔːtə(r)] *n (for carrying luggage)* porteur *m*, bagagiste *m*; *(door attendant)* chasseur *m*; *(in hospital)* brancardier *m*

portfolio [pɔːtˈfəʊlɪəʊ] *(pl* **portfolios)** *n (for documents)* porte-documents *m*; *(for drawings)* carton *m*; *(of shares, govern-*

ment minister) portefeuille *m*; *(of model, artist)* portfolio *m*

porthole ['pɔːthəʊl] *n* hublot *m*

portion ['pɔːʃən] *n* part *f*, partie *f*; *(of food)* portion *f*

▶**portion out** *vt sep* partager

portly ['pɔːtlɪ] *adj* corpulent(e)

portrait ['pɔːtreɪt] *n also Fig* portrait *m*; **to have one's p. painted** faire faire son portrait; **p. gallery** galerie *f* de portraits; *Comput* **p. (orientation)** (orientation *f*) portrait; **p. painter** portraitiste *mf*

portray [pɔː'treɪ] *vt (describe)* dépeindre; *(of actor)* interpréter

portrayal [pɔː'treɪəl] *n (description)* tableau *m*; *(by actor)* interprétation *f*

Portugal ['pɔːtjʊɡəl] *n* le Portugal

Portuguese [pɔːtjʊˈɡiːz] **1** *npl* **the P.** *(people)* les Portugais *mpl*
2 *n* (**a**) *(person)* Portugais(e) *m,f* (**b**) *(language)* portugais *m*
3 *adj* portugais(e)

POS [piːəʊˈes] *n Com (abbr* **point of sale**) PDV *m*

pose [pəʊz] **1** *n* (**a**) *(position)* pose *f* (**b**) *Pej (affectation)* **it's just a p.** c'est pour épater la galerie
2 *vt (problem, question)* poser; *(danger, threat)* représenter
3 *vi also Pej* poser; **to p. as** *(pretend to be)* se faire passer pour

poser ['pəʊzə(r)] *n Fam* (**a**) *Pej (affected person)* poseur(euse) *m,f* (**b**) *(difficult question)* colle *f*

posh [pɒʃ] *adj (person)* huppé(e); *(accent)* snob *inv*; *(restaurant, area, clothes)* chic *inv*

position [pəˈzɪʃən] **1** *n* (**a**) *(of person) (posture, opinion)* position *f* (**b**) *(of object)* emplacement *m*; *(of enemy, plane, in team sport)* position *f*; **in the on/off p.** *(of switch, lever)* en position marche/arrêt; **in p.** en place; **out of p.** déplacé(e) (**c**) *(situation)* situation *f*; **to be in a strong p.** être dans une position forte; **put yourself in my p.** mets-toi à ma place; **to be in a p. to do sth** être en mesure de faire qch; **to be in no p. to do sth** être mal placé(e) pour faire qch (**d**) *(job)* poste *m*; **a p. of responsibility** un poste à responsabilité
2 *vt (object)* placer; *(town)* situer; *(troops)* poster; **to p. oneself** se placer; **to be well/poorly positioned to do sth** être bien/mal placé(e) pour faire qch

positioning [pəˈzɪʃənɪŋ] *n Com* positionnement *m*

positive ['pɒzɪtɪv] *adj* (**a**) *(person, answer, test)* positif(ive); *(evidence, proof)* formel(elle); **to be p. about sth** être optimiste à propos de qch; **on the p. side,...** le bon côté des choses, c'est que...; **p. discrimination** = mesures antidiscriminatoires favorisant les groupes minoritaires (**b**) *(certain)* certain(e), sûr(e) (**about** de) (**c**) *Fam (for emphasis)* véritable (**d**) *Math & Elec* positif(ive)

positively ['pɒzɪtɪvlɪ] *adv* (**a**) *(identify)* formellement (**b**) *(think, react)* de façon positive (**c**) *(for emphasis)* absolument

posse ['pɒsɪ] *n (to catch criminal)* = dans le Far West, groupe d'hommes commandé par un shérif, lancé à la poursuite d'un criminel; *Fam (of friends)* bande *f*

possess [pəˈzes] *vt* (**a**) *(property)* posséder; *(quality, faculty)* avoir (**b**) *(of evil spirit)* posséder; **possessed by fear** pris(e) de terreur; **what possessed you to do that?** qu'est-ce qui t'a pris de faire ça?

possession [pəˈzeʃən] *n (ownership)* possession *f*; *(thing possessed)* bien *m*; **to be in p. of sth** être en possession de qch; **in full p. of one's faculties** en pleine possession de ses facultés

possessive [pəˈzesɪv] **1** *n Gram* **the p.** le possessif
2 *adj* possessif(ive); **she's very p. about** *or* **of her children** c'est une mère possessive

possessor [pəˈzesə(r)] *n* possesseur *m*

possibility [pɒsɪˈbɪlɪtɪ] *(pl* **possibilities**) *n* possibilité *f*; **to be within/outside the bounds of p.** être dans la limite du possible/au delà des limites du possible; **it's a distinct p.** c'est bien possible

possible ['pɒsɪbəl] *adj* possible; **it's p. that...** il est possible

que... + subjunctive; **as soon as p.** dès que possible; **as much as p.** autant que possible; **anything's p.** tout est possible

possibly ['pɒsɪblɪ] *adv* (**a**) *(perhaps)* peut-être; **p. not** peut-être pas (**b**) *(for emphasis)* **I can't p. accept it** je ne peux vraiment pas l'accepter; **I'll do all I p. can** je ferai tout mon possible

post¹ [pəʊst] **1** *n* (**a**) *(wooden stake)* piquet *m*; *(of goal)* poteau *m* (**b**) *(job, military position)* poste *m*
2 *vt (assign)* affecter

post² [pəʊst] *vt (affix)* afficher; **p. no bills** *(sign)* défense d'afficher

post³ [pəʊst] **1** *n (mail)* courrier *m*; **p. office** (bureau *m* de) poste *f*
2 *vt (letter)* poster; *Fam Fig* **to keep sb posted** tenir qn au courant

postage ['pəʊstɪdʒ] *n* affranchissement *m*; **p. and packing** frais *mpl* de port et d'emballage; **p. paid** port *m* payé; **p. stamp** timbre-poste *m*

postal ['pəʊstəl] *adj* postal(e)

postbox ['pəʊstbɒks] *n* boîte *f* aux lettres

postcard ['pəʊstkɑːd] *n* carte *f* postale

postdate [pəʊstˈdeɪt] *vt* postdater

post-doctorate ['pəʊstˈdɒktərət] *Univ* **1** *n* post-doctorat *m*
2 *adj* post-doctoral(e)

poster ['pəʊstə(r)] *n (for advertising)* affiche *f*; *(for decoration)* poster *m*; **p. advertising** publicité *f* par affichage; **p. paint** gouache *f*

posterior [pɒsˈtɪərɪə(r)] *n Hum (buttocks)* postérieur *m*

posterity [pɒsˈterɪtɪ] *n* postérité *f*

postgraduate [pəʊstˈɡrædjʊɪt] **1** *n* étudiant(e) *m,f* de troisième cycle
2 *adj* de troisième cycle

posthaste [pəʊstˈheɪst] *adv* en toute hâte

posthumous ['pɒstjʊməs] *adj* posthume

posthumously ['pɒstjʊməslɪ] *adv* à titre posthume

posting ['pəʊstɪŋ] *n (assignment)* affectation *f*

postman ['pəʊstmən] *n* facteur *m*

postmark ['pəʊstmɑːk] *n* cachet *m* de la poste

postmaster ['pəʊstmɑːstə(r)] *n* (**a**) *(in post office)* receveur *m* des postes (**b**) *Comput (for e-mail)* maître *m* de poste

postmistress ['pəʊstmɪstrɪs] *n* receveuse *f* des postes

postmortem [pəʊstˈmɔːtəm] *n* autopsie *f*

postnatal [pəʊstˈneɪtəl] *adj* postnatal(e)

postoperative [pəʊstˈɒpərətɪv] *adj* postopératoire

postpone [pəʊstˈpəʊn] *vt* reporter

postponement [pəʊstˈpəʊnmənt] *n* report *m*

postscript ['pəʊsskrɪpt] *n* post-scriptum *m*

postulate ['pɒstjʊleɪt] *vt* poser comme hypothèse

posture ['pɒstʃə(r)] **1** *n* (**a**) *(physical)* posture *f*; **to have good/bad p.** se tenir bien/mal (**b**) *Fig (attitude)* position *f*
2 *vi* prendre des poses

postwar ['pəʊstˈwɔː(r)] *adj* d'après-guerre; **the p. period** l'après-guerre *m*

posy ['pəʊzɪ] *(pl* **posies**) *n* petit bouquet *m*

pot [pɒt] **1** *n* (**a**) *(container)* pot *m*; *(saucepan)* casserole *f*; *(for tea)* théière *f*; *(for coffee)* cafetière *f*; **pots and pans** casseroles *fpl*; **a p. of tea** un thé; *Fam* **to have pots of money** avoir plein de fric; *Fam* **to go to p.** aller à la ruine; **to take a p. shot at sth** tirer à vue sur qch; *Prov* **it's a case of the p. calling the kettle black** c'est l'hôpital qui se moque de la charité; **p. roast** rôti *m* à la cocotte (**b**) *Fam (marijuana)* hasch *m*
2 *vt (pt & pp* **potted**) (**a**) *(butter, meat)* mettre en pot; *(plant)* empoter (**b**) *(in pool)* blouser

potash ['pɒtæʃ] *n* potasse *f*

potassium [pəˈtæsɪəm] *n* potassium *m*

potato [pəˈteɪtəʊ] *(pl* **potatoes**) *n* pomme *f* de terre; **p. chips**

chips *mpl*; **p. peeler** épluche-légumes *m*; **p. salad** salade *f* de pommes de terre

potbellied [pɒt'belɪd] *adj (from overeating)* bedonnant(e); *(from malnourishment)* au ventre ballonné; **p. stove** poêle *m*

potency ['pəʊtənsɪ] *n* puissance *f*; *(virility)* virilité *f*

potent ['pəʊtənt] *adj* puissant(e); *(drink)* fort(e)

potentate ['pəʊtənteɪt] *n* potentat *m*

potential [pə'tenʃəl] **1** *n* potentiel *m*; **to have p.** avoir du potentiel; **to fulfill one's p.** aller au maximum de ses capacités **2** *adj* potentiel(elle)

potentially [pə'tenʃəlɪ] *adv* potentiellement

pothole ['pɒthəʊl] *n (cave)* marmite *f* torrentielle; *(in road)* nid *m* de poule

potholer ['pɒthəʊlə(r)] *n* spéléologue *mf*

potholing ['pɒthəʊlɪŋ] *n* spéléologie *f*; **to go p.** faire de la spéléologie

potion ['pəʊʃən] *n* potion *f*

potluck ['pɒt'lʌk] *n Fam* **to take p.** prendre ce que l'on trouve; **p. lunch/supper** déjeuner *m*/dîner *m* où chacun apporte un plat

potpourri [pəʊ'pʊərɪ] *n (of flowers, music)* pot-pourri *m*

potted ['pɒtɪd] *adj* **(a)** *(food)* en terrine **(b)** *(description, history)* condensé(e) **(c)** **p. plant** plante *f* en pot

potter ['pɒtə(r)] *n* potier(ère) *m,f*; **p.'s wheel** tour *m* de potier

pottery ['pɒtərɪ] *n (pl **potteries**)* poterie *f*

potty ['pɒtɪ] *(pl **potties**)* *n* pot *m*; **p. training** apprentissage *m* de la propreté

potty-trained ['pɒtɪtreɪnd] *adj* propre

pouch [paʊtʃ] *n* **(a)** *(for money)* bourse *f*; *(for tobacco)* blague *f*; *(for ammunition)* étui *m* **(b)** *(of marsupial)* poche *f*

poulterer ['pəʊltərə(r)] *n* volailler(ère) *m,f*

poultice ['pəʊltɪs] *n* cataplasme *m*

poultry ['pəʊltrɪ] *n* volaille *f*; **p. farm** élevage *m* de volaille; **p. farmer** éleveur(euse) *m,f* de volaille

pounce [paʊns] *vi* **to p. on** *(of animal)* bondir sur; *(of person)* se précipiter sur

pound¹ [paʊnd] *n* **(a)** *(unit of weight)* = 453,6 g, livre *f* **(b)** *(British currency)* livre *f*; **p. sign** *(£)* symbole *m* de la livre sterling; *(on telephone)* dièse *m*; **p. sterling** livre sterling

pound² [paʊnd] *n (for dogs, cars)* fourrière *f*

pound³ [paʊnd] **1** *vt (crush) (spices, garlic)* piler; *(meat)* attendrir; *(with artillery)* pilonner; **to p. sth to pieces** réduire qch en miettes **2** *vi (of heart)* battre à tout rompre; **to p. on the door** cogner à la porte; **my head is pounding** j'ai des élancements dans la tête

pour [pɔː(r)] **1** *vt* verser (**into/down** dans); **to p. sb a drink** verser à boire à qn; **to p. money into sth** investir beaucoup d'argent dans qch **2** *vi* couler; **it's pouring (with rain)** il pleut à verse; **sweat was pouring off him** il ruisselait de sueur; **tourists were pouring into the palace** les touristes entraient en masse dans le palais

▶**pour in 1** *vt sep (liquid)* verser **2** *vi (of liquid)* couler; *Fig (of people, letters)* affluer

▶**pour out 1** *vt sep (tea, coffee)* verser; *Fig (anger, grief)* déverser; *(emotions)* déballer **2** *vi (of liquid)* se déverser; *Fig (of people)* sortir en masse

pouring ['pɔːrɪŋ] *adj (rain)* torrentiel(elle)

pout [paʊt] **1** *n* moue *f* **2** *vi* faire la moue

poverty ['pɒvətɪ] *n* pauvreté *f*; *Fig (of ideas, resources)* pénurie *f*; **to live in p.** vivre dans la misère; **p. line** seuil *m* de pauvreté

poverty-stricken ['pɒvətɪstrɪkən] *adj* très pauvre

POW [piːəʊ'dʌbəljuː] *n (abbr **prisoner of war**)* prisonnier(ère) *m,f* de guerre

powder ['paʊdə(r)] **1** *n* poudre *f*; **p. blue** bleu *m* pastel; *Fig* **p. keg** poudrière *f*; **p. puff** houppe *f*; **p. room** toilettes *fpl* pour dames **2** *vt* saupoudrer (**with** de); **to p. one's face** se poudrer le visage; *Euph* **to p. one's nose** aller se laver les mains

powdered ['paʊdəd] *adj (milk, eggs)* en poudre; **p. sugar** sucre *m* glace

powdery ['paʊdərɪ] *adj* poudreux(euse)

power ['paʊə(r)] **1** *n* **(a)** *(authority, capacity)* pouvoir *m*; **to come to/be in p.** arriver/être au pouvoir; **to have sb in one's p.** tenir qn à sa merci; **to have the p. to do sth** avoir le pouvoir de faire qch; **to do everything in one's p. (to do sth)** faire tout ce qui est en son pouvoir (pour faire qch); **to be at the height** *or* **peak of one's powers** être au sommet de ses capacités; **it is beyond my p. to help you** je ne peux pas t'aider, cela dépasse mes capacités; *Fam* **to do sb a p. of good** faire énormément de bien à qn; **powers of concentration/persuasion** force *f* de concentration/persuasion; **p. of speech** usage *m* de la parole; **p. base** base *f* politique; **p. struggle** lutte *f* pour le pouvoir

(b) *(physical strength)* force *f*, puissance *f*; **p. steering** *(in car)* direction *f* assistée

(c) *(powerful person, group, nation)* puissance *f*; *Fig* **the p. behind the throne** l'éminence *f* grise; **the powers that be** les autorités *fpl*

(d) *Law* pouvoir *m*; **p. of attorney** procuration *f*

(e) *(electricity)* courant *m*; **p. cut** coupure *f* de courant; **p. pack** bloc *m* d'alimentation; **p. plant** centrale *f* électrique; **p. shower** douche *f* à jet puissant; **p. station** centrale *f* électrique

(f) *Math* puissance *f*; **three to the p. of ten** trois (à la) puissance dix

2 *vt (provide with power)* actionner; **powered by two engines** propulsé(e) par deux moteurs

power-assisted steering ['paʊərəsɪstɪd'stɪərɪŋ] *n Aut* direction *f* assistée

powerful ['paʊəfʊl] *adj (muscles, engine, voice, country)* puissant(e); *(politician)* influent(e); *(drug, smell)* fort(e); *(speech, image)* impressionnant(e)

powerhouse ['paʊəhaʊs] *n Fam (person)* moteur *m*

powerless ['paʊəlɪs] *adj* impuissant(e); **to be p. to do sth** être impuissant(e) à faire qch

PR [piː'ɑː(r)] *n* **(a)** *(abbr **public relations**)* RP **(b)** *Pol (abbr **proportional representation**)* représentation *f* proportionnelle

practicable ['præktɪkəbəl] *adj* réalisable

practical ['præktɪkəl] *adj* **(a)** *(mind, solution)* pratique; **she's very p.** elle a l'esprit pratique; **for all p. purposes** dans la pratique; **p. joke** farce *f* **(b)** *(virtual)* **it's a p. certainty** c'est pratiquement certain

practicality [præktɪ'kælɪtɪ] *(pl **practicalities**)* *n (of suggestion, plan)* aspect *m* pratique; **practicalities** détails *mpl* pratiques

practically ['præktɪklɪ] *adv* **(a)** *(in a practical manner)* de façon pratique **(b)** *(almost)* pratiquement, presque

practice ['præktɪs] **1** *n* **(a)** *(action, exercise)* pratique *f*; *(in sport)* entraînement *m*; **in p.** dans la *ou* en pratique; **to put sth into p.** mettre qch en pratique; **to be out of p.** avoir perdu l'habitude; *Prov* **p. makes perfect** c'est en forgeant qu'on devient forgeron; **p. match** *(in soccer, rugby)* match *m* d'entraînement

(b) *(of medicine, law)* exercice *m*

(c) *(doctor's office)* centre *m* médical; *(lawyer's office)* cabinet *m* d'avocat

(d) *(custom)* pratique *f*; **to make a p. of doing sth** se faire une règle de faire qch; **to be good/bad p.** être conseillé(e)/déconseillé(e)

2 *vt* **(a)** *(musical instrument)* travailler; *(language, sport)* pratiquer (**b**) *(medicine, law)* exercer

(**c**) *(religion, custom)* pratiquer; **to p. what one preaches** mettre en pratique ce que l'on prêche

3 *vi* (**a**) *(of musician)* s'exercer; *(of athlete)* s'entraîner

(**b**) *(of doctor, lawyer)* exercer

practiced ['præktɪst] *adj (teacher, nurse, speaker)* expérimenté(e); *(liar)* professionnel(elle); *(eye, ear)* exercé(e); *(charm)* étudié(e)

practicing ['præktɪsɪŋ] *adj (doctor, lawyer)* en exercice; *(Christian)* pratiquant(e)

pragmatic [præg'mætɪk] *adj* pragmatique

pragmatism ['prægmətɪzəm] *n* pragmatisme *m*

pragmatist ['prægmətɪst] *n* pragmatiste *mf*

Prague [prɑːg] *n* Prague

prairie ['preərɪ] *n* prairie *f*; **p. dog** chien *m* de prairie; **p. schooner** chariot *m* bâché

praise [preɪz] **1** *n* éloges *mpl*; **to sing the praises of** faire l'éloge de

2 *vt* faire l'éloge de; *(God)* louer; **to p. sb to the skies** porter qn aux nues

praiseworthy ['preɪzwɜːðɪ] *adj* digne d'éloges

prance [prɑːns] *vi (of horse)* caracoler; *(of person)* sautiller; **to p. in/out** entrer/sortir en sautillant

prank [præŋk] *n* farce *f*; **to play a p. on sb** faire une farce à qn

prattle ['prætəl] **1** *n* papotage *m*

2 *vi* papoter (**about** de)

prawn [prɔːn] *n* crevette *f* rose; **p. cocktail** crevettes à la mayonnaise; **p. cracker** beignet *m* de crevette

pray [preɪ] *vi* prier (**for** pour); **to p. to God** prier Dieu; *Fig* **to p. for good weather/rain** prier pour qu'il fasse beau/qu'il pleuve

prayer [preə(r)] *n* prière *f*; **to say one's prayers** dire ses prières; *Fam Fig* **he doesn't have a p.** il n'a aucune chance; **p. beads** chapelet *m*; **p. book** livre *m* de prières; **p. mat** tapis *m* de prière; **p. meeting** réunion *f* de prière

preach [priːtʃ] **1** *vt* prêcher

2 *vi* prêcher; *Fig (moralize)* faire la morale; *Fig* **to p. to the converted** prêcher un converti

preacher ['priːtʃə(r)] *n* prédicateur(trice) *m,f*

preamble ['priːæmbəl] *n Formal* préambule *m*

prearranged [priːə'reɪndʒd] *adj* convenu(e)

precarious [prɪ'keərɪəs] *adj* précaire

precariously [prɪ'keərɪəslɪ] *adv* de façon précaire; **p. balanced** en équilibre précaire

precaution [prɪ'kɔːʃən] *n* précaution *f*; **to take precautions** prendre des précautions; **as a p.** par précaution

precautionary [prɪ'kɔːʃənərɪ] *adj* préventif(ive)

precede [prɪ'siːd] *vt* précéder

precedence ['presɪdəns] *n* priorité *f*; **in order of p.** par ordre de préséance; **to take p. over sb** avoir la préséance sur qn; **to take p. over sth** passer avant qch

precedent ['presɪdənt] *n* précédent *m*

preceding [prɪ'siːdɪŋ] *adj* précédent(e)

precept ['priːsept] *n* précepte *m*

precinct ['priːsɪŋkt] *n (administrative district)* circonscription *f*; *(police division)* quartier *m*

precious ['preʃəs] **1** *n (term of endearment)* **my p.** mon trésor

2 *adj also Pej* précieux(euse); **that photo is very p. to me** cette photo m'est très chère; *Ironic* **you and your p. books!** toi et tes sacrés bouquins!

3 *adv Fam (for emphasis)* **p. little** très peu; **p. little money** très peu d'argent

precipice ['presɪpɪs] *n* précipice *m*

precipitate1 *n* [prɪ'sɪpɪtɪt] *Chem* précipité *m*

2 *adj* [prɪ'sɪpɪtət] *Formal* précipité(e)

3 *vt* [prɪ'sɪpɪteɪt] *Formal* précipiter

precipitately [prɪ'sɪpɪtətlɪ] *adv* précipitamment

precipitation [prɪsɪpɪ'teɪʃən] *n* précipitation *f*; **annual p.** précipitations annuelles

precipitous [prɪ'sɪpɪtəs] *adj (descent)* à pic; *(steps)* raide

précis ['preɪsiː] *(pl* **précis** ['preɪsiːz]) *n* résumé *m*

precise [prɪ'saɪs] *adj* (**a**) *(exact)* précis(e); **..., to be p.** ..., pour être précis (**b**) *(meticulous)* méticuleux(euse)

precisely [prɪ'saɪslɪ] *adv* exactement, précisément; **at six (o'clock) p.** à six heures précises; **p.!** exactement!

precision [prɪ'sɪʒən] *n* précision *f*; *Mil* **p. bombing** bombardement *m* de précision; **p. instrument** instrument *m* de précision

preclude [prɪ'kluːd] *vt Formal* empêcher; **to p. sb from doing sth** empêcher qn de faire qch

precocious [prɪ'kəʊʃəs] *adj* précoce

precociousness [prɪ'kəʊʃəsnɪs], **precocity** [prɪ'kɒsɪtɪ] *n* précocité *f*

preconceived [priːkən'siːvd] *adj* préconçu(e)

preconception [priːkən'sepʃən] *n* idée *f* préconçue; *(prejudice)* préjugé *m*

precondition [priːkɒn'dɪʃən] *n* condition *f* préalable

precooked [priː'kʊkt] *adj* précuit(e)

precursor [prɪ'kɜːsə(r)] *n* précurseur *m*

predate [priː'deɪt] *vt* (**a**) *(precede)* précéder (**b**) *(put earlier date on)* antidater

predator ['predətə(r)] *n* prédateur *m*

predatory ['predətərɪ] *adj* prédateur(trice); *Fig* avide

predecessor ['priːdɪsesə(r)] *n (person)* prédécesseur *m*; *(object)* précédent(e) *m,f*

predestination [priːdestɪ'neɪʃən] *n* prédestination *f*

predestine [priː'destɪn] *vt* **to be predestined to do sth** être prédestiné(e) à faire qch

predetermine [priːdɪ'tɜːmɪn] *vt* prédéterminer

predicament [prɪ'dɪkəmənt] *n* situation *f* difficile; **to be in a p.** être dans le pétrin

predicate1 *n* ['predɪkət] *Gram* prédicat *m*

2 *vt* ['predɪkeɪt] **to be predicated on sth** être fondé(e) sur qch

predict [prɪ'dɪkt] *vt (from instinct)* prédire; *(from information)* prévoir

predictable [prɪ'dɪktəbəl] *adj* prévisible; *Fam* **you're so p.!** j'aurais pu le deviner!

predictably [prɪ'dɪktəblɪ] *adv* de manière prévisible; **p., he arrived an hour late** comme on pouvait s'y attendre, il est arrivé une heure en retard

prediction [prɪ'dɪkʃən] *n (from instinct)* prédiction *f*; *(from information)* prévision *f*

predictive [prɪ'dɪktɪv] *adj (anticipating)* de prédiction; *(prophetic)* prophétique; **to be p. of sth** être annonciateur de qch; *Tel* **p. texting, p. text input** écriture *f* prédictive, T9 *m*

predispose [priːdɪs'pəʊz] *vt* prédisposer; **to be predisposed to do sth** être prédisposé(e) à faire qch

predisposition [priːdɪspə'zɪʃən] *n* prédisposition *f* (**to** *or* **toward** envers)

predominance [prɪ'dɒmɪnəns] *n* prédominance *f*

predominant [prɪ'dɒmɪnənt] *adj* prédominant(e)

predominantly [prɪ'dɒmɪnəntlɪ] *adv* en majorité, principalement

predominate [prɪ'dɒmɪneɪt] *vi* prédominer

pre-eminence [prɪ'emɪnəns] *n* prééminence *f*

pre-eminent [prɪ'emɪnənt] *adj* prééminent(e)

pre-empt [prɪ'empt] *vt* devancer

pre-emptive [prɪ'emptɪv] *adj* préventif(ive)

preen [priːn] *vt* **to p. itself** *(of bird)* se lisser les plumes; **to p. oneself** *(of person)* se faire beau (belle), se pomponner; *Fig* **to p. oneself on one's success** s'enorgueillir de son succès

pre-established [priːɪs'tæblɪʃt] *adj* préétabli(e)

prefab ['priːfæb] *n Fam (house)* préfabriqué *m*

prefabricated [priːˈfæbrɪkeɪtɪd] *adj* préfabriqué(e)

preface [ˈprefɪs] **1** *n (of book)* préface *f; (to speech)* préambule *m*
2 *vt* commencer (**with** par)

prefer [prɪˈfɜː(r)] *(pt & pp* **preferred**) *vt* (**a**) *(favor)* préférer (**to** à); **to p. to do sth** préférer faire qch (**b**) *Law* **to p. charges** porter plainte

preferable [ˈprefərəbəl] *adj* préférable

preferably [ˈprefərəblɪ] *adv* de préférence

preference [ˈprefərəns] *n* préférence *f;* **to give sth p., to give p. to sth** donner la préférence à qch; **in p. to** plutôt que; **in order of p.** par ordre de préférence

preferential [prefəˈrenʃəl] *adj (treatment)* de faveur; *(tariff)* préférentiel(elle)

preferred [prɪˈfɜːd] *adj* préféré(e)

prefigure [priːˈfɪɡə(r)] *vt* préfigurer

prefix [ˈpriːfɪks] *n* préfixe *m*

pregnancy [ˈpreɡnənsɪ] *(pl* **pregnancies**) *n* grossesse *f;* **p. test** test *m* de grossesse

pregnant [ˈpreɡnənt] *adj* (**a**) *(woman)* enceinte; *(animal)* pleine; **to be three months p.** être enceinte de trois mois (**b**) *Fig (pause, silence)* éloquent(e)

preheat [priːˈhiːt] *vt* préchauffer

prehensile [prɪˈhensaɪl] *adj* préhensile

prehistoric [priːhɪsˈtɒrɪk] *adj* préhistorique

prehistory [priːˈhɪstərɪ] *n* préhistoire *f*

prejudge [priːˈdʒʌdʒ] *vt (actions, motives)* préjuger de; *(person)* juger sans connaître

prejudice [ˈpredʒʊdɪs] **1** *n* (**a**) *(bias)* préjugé *m* (**against/in favor of** contre/en faveur de) (**b**) *Law* **without p. to** sans préjudice de
2 *vt* (**a**) *(bias)* prévenir (**against/in favor of** contre/en faveur de) (**b**) *(harm)* nuire à, faire du tort à

prejudiced [ˈpredʒʊdɪst] *adj* **to be p.** avoir des préjugés (**against/in favor of** contre/en faveur de)

prejudicial [predʒʊˈdɪʃəl] *adj* préjudiciable (**to** à)

preliminary [prɪˈlɪmɪnərɪ] **1** *(pl* **preliminaries**) *n* préliminaire *m;* **preliminaries** *(to investigation, meeting)* préliminaires *mpl*
2 *adj* préliminaire

prelude [ˈpreljuːd] *n* prélude *m*

premarital [priːˈmærɪtəl] *adj* avant le mariage

premature [priːˈemətjʊə(r)] *adj (baby, action, comment)* prématuré(e); *(baldness, senility, ejaculation)* précoce; *Fam* **you're being a bit p.!** tu vas un peu vite!

prematurely [priːməˈtjʊəlɪ] *adv* prématurément

premeditated [priːˈmedɪteɪtɪd] *adj* prémédité(e)

premenstrual [priːˈmenstrʊəl] *adj* prémenstruel(elle); **I'm p.** mes règles ne vont pas tarder à arriver; **p. syndrome** syndrome *m* prémenstruel

premier [ˈpremɪə(r)] **1** *n (prime minister)* Premier ministre *m*
2 *adj* premier(ère)

premiere [prəˈmɪeə(r)] *n (of play, film)* première *f*

premise [ˈpremɪs] **1** *n (of argument, theory)* prémisse *f*
2 *vt* **to be premised on sth** être fondé(e) sur qch

premises [ˈpremɪsɪz] *npl* locaux *mpl;* **business p.** locaux commerciaux; **on the p.** sur place; **off the p.** en dehors de l'établissement; **to see sb off the p.** accompagner qn jusqu'au dehors

premium [ˈpriːmɪəm] *n* (**a**) *Fin (for insurance)* prime *f; (additional sum)* supplément *m;* **at a p.** au prix fort (**b**) *(idioms)* **to be at a p.** être très recherché(e); **to put a p. on sth** accorder de l'importance à qch

premium-rate [ˈpriːmɪəmˈreɪt] *adj Tel (call)* vers un numéro surtaxé; *(number)* surtaxé

premonition [priːməˈnɪʃən] *n* prémonition *f;* **to have a p. that...** avoir le pressentiment que...

prenatal [priːˈneɪtəl] *adj* prénatal(e)

prenuptial agreement [prɪˈnʌpʃələˈɡriːmənt], *Fam* **prenup** [ˈpriːnʌp] *adj* contrat *m* de mariage

preoccupation [priːɒkjʊˈpeɪʃən] *n* préoccupation *f* (**with** pour); **to have a p. with sth** être préoccupé(e) par qch

preoccupied [priːˈɒkjʊpaɪd] *adj* préoccupé(e) (**with** par)

preoccupy [priːˈɒkjʊpaɪ] *(pt & pp* **preoccupied**) *vt* préoccuper au plus haut point

prepaid [priːˈpeɪd] *adj* prépayé(e)

preparation [prepəˈreɪʃən] *n* préparation *f;* **preparations** *(for ceremony, party)* préparatifs *mpl*

preparatory [prɪˈpærətərɪ] *adj* préparatoire; **p. school** école préparatoire

prepare [prɪˈpeə(r)] **1** *vt* préparer
2 *vi* se préparer (**for** à); **to p. to do sth** se préparer à faire qch

prepared [prɪˈpeəd] *adj* (**a**) *(willing)* **to be p. to do sth** être prêt(e) à faire qch (**b**) *(ready)* **to be p. for sth** s'attendre à qch (**c**) *(made in advance)* préparé(e) à l'avance; *(excuse, explanation)* tout(e) prêt(e)

prepayment [priːˈpeɪmənt] *n* paiement *m* d'avance

preponderance [prɪˈpɒndərəns] *n* prépondérance *f*

preposition [prepəˈzɪʃən] *n* préposition *f*

prepositional [prepəˈzɪʃənəl] *adj* prépositif(ive)

prepossessing [priːpəˈzesɪŋ] *adj* avenant(e), engageant(e)

preposterous [prɪˈpɒstərəs] *adj* ridicule

preppy [ˈprepɪ] *adj Fam* ≃ BCBG *inv*

preprogrammed [priːˈprəʊɡræmd] *adj Comput* préprogrammé(e)

prep school [ˈprepskuːl] *n* = école privée qui prépare à l'enseignement supérieur

prequel [ˈpriːkwəl] *n Cin* = film qui reprend les thèmes et les personnages d'un film réalisé précédemment, mais dont l'action est antérieure

prerecorded [priːrɪˈkɔːdɪd] *adj* préenregistré(e)

prerequisite [priːˈrekwɪzɪt] *n* (condition *f)* préalable *m*

prerogative [prɪˈrɒɡətɪv] *n* prérogative *f*

presage [ˈpresɪdʒ] *Lit* **1** *n* présage *m*
2 *vt* présager

Presbyterian [prezbɪˈtɪərɪən] *n & adj* presbytérien(enne) *m,f*

preschool [priːˈskuːl] **1** *n* école *f* maternelle
2 *adj* préscolaire

prescribe [prɪˈskraɪb] *vt (medicine, punishment)* prescrire; *(solution)* préconiser; *(task, rule)* exiger

prescription [prɪˈskrɪpʃən] *n* ordonnance *f;* **available only on p.** délivré(e) seulement sur ordonnance; **p. drug** = médicament délivré seulement sur ordonnance

presence [ˈprezəns] *n* présence *f;* **in the p. of** en présence de; **to have p.** avoir de la présence; **to make one's p. felt** ne pas passer inaperçu(e); **p. of mind** présence d'esprit

present¹ [ˈprezənt] **1** *n* **the p.** le présent; **at p.** en ce moment; **for the p.** pour l'instant
2 *adj* (**a**) *(in attendance)* présent(e) (**at** à) (**b**) *(current)* actuel(elle); **at the p. time** *or* **moment** actuellement; *Gram* **the p. tense** le présent; **p. participle** participe *m* présent

present² **1** *n* [ˈprezənt] *(gift)* cadeau *m;* **to give sb a p.** offrir un cadeau à qn
2 *vt* [prɪˈzent] (**a**) *(introduce, put forward)* présenter; **if the opportunity presents itself** si l'occasion se présente (**b**) *(give) (gift)* donner; *(award, certificate)* remettre; **to p. sth to sb, to p. sb with sth** *(gift)* donner qch à qn; *(award, certificate)* remettre qch à qn (**c**) *Mil* **p. arms!** présentez armes!

presentable [prɪˈzentəbəl] *adj* présentable; **to make oneself p.** s'arranger

presentation [prezənˈteɪʃən] *n* (**a**) *(of person)* présentation *f* (**b**) *(of gift, award)* remise *f;* **to make a p. to sb** *(give present)* offrir un cadeau à qn; *(give award)* remettre un prix à qn (**c**) *(formal talk)* présentation *f; (by student)* exposé *m* (**d**) **on p. of** *(passport, coupon)* sur présentation de

present-day [prezənt'deɪ] *adj* actuel(elle)

presenter [prɪ'zentə(r)] *n (on radio, TV)* présentateur(trice) *m, f*

presentiment [prɪ'zentɪmənt] *n* pressentiment *m*

presently ['prezəntlɪ] *adv* (**a**) *(soon)* bientôt; *(soon afterward)* peu de temps après (**b**) *(now)* actuellement

preservation [prezə'veɪʃən] *n* (**a**) *(maintenance)* maintien *m* (**b**) *(protection) (of species)* protection *f*; *(of building)* conservation *f*

preservative [prɪ'zɜːvətɪv] *n* conservateur *m*

preserve [prɪ'zɜːv] **1** *n* (**a**) *(jam)* confiture *f* (**b**) *(in hunting)* réserve *f* (**c**) *(area of dominance)* domaine *m*; **engineering is no longer a male p.** le métier d'ingénieur n'est plus réservé aux hommes

2 *vt* (**a**) *(custom, belief)* préserver; *(calm, sense of humor)* garder; *(dignity, self-respect)* conserver (**b**) *(leather, wood)* entretenir (**c**) *(fruit)* mettre en conserve (**d**) *(protect)* préserver (**from** de); **saints p. us!** le ciel nous préserve!

preshrunk [priː'ʃrʌŋk] *adj* lavé(e)

preside [prɪ'zaɪd] *vi* présider; **to p. over a meeting** présider une réunion

presidency ['prezɪdənsɪ] *(pl* **presidencies)** *n* présidence *f*

president ['prezɪdənt] *n (of country)* président *m*; *(of company)* P-DG *m*

presidential [prezɪ'denʃəl] *adj* présidentiel(elle)

press [pres] **1** *n* (**a**) *(act of pushing)* pression *f*; **at the p. of a button** en appuyant sur le bouton

(**b**) *(newspapers)* **the p.** la presse; **to get a good/bad p.** avoir bonne/mauvaise presse; **p. agency** agence *f* de presse; **p. box** tribune *f* de la presse; **p. clipping** coupure *f* de presse; **p. conference** conférence *f* de presse; **p. photographer** photographe *mf* de presse; **p. release** communiqué *m* de presse

(**c**) *(machine)* **(printing) p.** presse *f* (typographique); **to go to p.** *(of newspaper)* partir à l'impression

2 *vt* (**a**) *(button, switch)* appuyer sur; *(into clay, cement)* enfoncer; **she pressed the bill into my hand** elle m'a glissé le billet dans la main

(**b**) *(squeeze)* serrer

(**c**) *(grapes, olives, flowers)* presser

(**d**) *(iron)* repasser

(**e**) *(pressure)* faire pression sur; **to p. sb to do sth** presser qn de faire qch; **to be pressed for time/money** être pressé(e) par le temps/l'argent

(**f**) *(force)* **to p. sth on sb** forcer qn à accepter qch; **to p. home one's advantage** profiter de son avantage; **to p. one's attentions on sb** faire des avances à qn

(**g**) *(insist on) Law* **to p. charges (against sb)** porter plainte (contre qn); **I didn't p. the point** je n'ai pas insisté

3 *vi (push)* appuyer; *(of crowd)* se presser

▸**press ahead** = press on

▸**press for** *vt insep (demand)* exiger

▸**press on** *vi* continuer; **to p. on with one's work** continuer de travailler

pressing ['presɪŋ] *adj (urgent)* pressant(e)

pressure ['preʃə(r)] **1** *n* pression *f*; **to put p. on sb (to do sth)** faire pression sur qn (pour qu'il fasse qch); **to be under p.** être stressé(e); **p. of work** stress *m* lié au travail; **p. cooker** Cocotte-Minute® *f*, autocuiseur *m*; **p. gauge** manomètre *m*; **p. group** groupe *m* de pression; *Med* **p. point** point *m* de compression

2 *vt* **to p. sb to do sth** *or* **into doing sth** faire pression sur qn pour qu'il/elle fasse qch

pressurize ['preʃəraɪz] *vt (container)* pressuriser

prestige [pres'tiːʒ] *n* prestige *m*

prestigious [pres'tɪdʒəs] *adj* prestigieux(euse)

presumably [prɪ'zjuːməblɪ] *adv* sans doute; **p. she'll come** je suppose qu'elle viendra

presume [prɪ'zjuːm] **1** *vt* présumer, supposer; **to p. to do sth** se permettre de faire qch; **I p. so** je suppose que oui

2 *vi* abuser; **I don't want to p. on you** je ne voudrais pas abuser

presumption [prɪ'zʌmpʃən] *n* présomption *f*

presumptuous [prɪ'zʌmptjʊəs] *adj* présomptueux(euse)

presuppose [priːsə'pəʊz] *vt* présupposer, supposer

presupposition [priːsʌpə'zɪʃən] *n* présupposition *f*

pretense [prɪ'tens] *n* simulation *f*; **he says he doesn't mind, but it's all a p.** il dit que ça lui est égal, mais il fait semblant; **to make a p. of doing sth** faire semblant de faire qch

pretend [prɪ'tend] **1** *vt* (**a**) *(feign)* feindre, simuler; **to p. to do sth** faire semblant de faire qch; **they pretended that nothing had happened** ils ont fait comme si de rien n'était (**b**) *(claim)* prétendre

2 *vi (put on an act)* faire semblant

3 *adj Fam* **p. money** de l'argent pour faire semblant; **a. p. slap** une gifle pour rire

pretension [prɪ'tenʃən] *n* prétention *f*

pretentious [prɪ'tenʃəs] *adj* prétentieux(euse)

pretentiousness [prɪ'tenʃəsnəs] *n* prétention *f*

preterite ['pretərɪt] *n Gram* **the p.** le prétérit

pretext ['priːtekst] *n* prétexte *m*; **under** *or* **on the p. of doing sth** sous prétexte de faire qch

Pretoria [prɪ'tɔːrɪə] *n* Prétoria

pretty ['prɪtɪ] **1** *adj* joli(e); **it's not a p. sight** ce n'est pas beau à voir; **to cost a p. penny** coûter la peau des fesses

2 *adv* (**a**) *(fairly)* plutôt; **p. certain** pratiquement sûr(e); **they're p. much the same** ils sont pratiquement pareils (**b**) *Fam* **to be sitting p.** ne pas avoir à s'en faire

pretzel ['pretzəl] *n* bretzel *m*

prevail [prɪ'veɪl] *vi* (**a**) *(be successful)* l'emporter (**over** sur) (**b**) *(persuade)* **to p. (up)on sb to do sth** amener qn à faire qch (**c**) *(predominate)* prédominer

prevailing [prɪ'veɪlɪŋ] *adj* prédominant(e); *(wind)* dominant(e)

prevalent ['prevələnt] *adj* très répandu(e)

prevaricate [prɪ'værɪkeɪt] *vi* tergiverser

prevarication [prɪværɪ'keɪʃən] *n* tergiversation *f*

prevent [prɪ'vent] *vt* empêcher, éviter; **to p. sb from doing sth** empêcher qn de faire qch; **to p. sth from happening** empêcher qch n'arrive

preventable [prɪ'ventəbəl] *adj* évitable

preventative [prɪ'ventətɪv] = **preventive**

prevention [prɪ'venʃən] *n* prévention *f*; *Prov* **p. is better than cure** mieux vaut prévenir que guérir

preventive [prɪ'ventɪv] *adj* préventif(ive)

preview ['priːvjuː] **1** *n* (**a**) *(of play, movie) (advance showing)* avant-première *f*; *(trailer)* bande-annonce *f* (**b**) *(of new product)* aperçu *m*

2 *vt* **to be previewed** *(of movie)* sortir en avant-première

previous ['priːvɪəs] **1** *adj* précédent(e); **to have a p. engagement** être déjà pris(e); *Law* **p. conviction** condamnation *f* antérieure

2 *adv* **p. to** avant

previously ['priːvɪəslɪ] *adv* auparavant

prewar ['priːwɔː(r)] *adj* d'avant-guerre

prey [preɪ] *n* proie *f*; *Fig* **to be a p. to** être la proie de; **to fall p. to** devenir la proie de

▸**prey on, prey upon** *vt insep (person)* prendre pour cible; *(fears, doubts)* exploiter; **to p. on sb's mind** tourmenter qn

price [praɪs] *n* prix *m*; **to rise** *or* **to increase in p.** augmenter; **at any p.** à tout prix; **not at any p.** à aucun prix; *Fig* **to pay the p. (for sth)** faire les frais (de qch); *Fig* **it's too high a p. (to pay)** c'est trop cher payé; **to put** *or* **to set a p. on sb's head** mettre la tête de qn à prix; *Fig* **everyone has his p.** il n'y a pas d'homme qu'on ne puisse acheter; *Fam* **what p. patriotism now?** que vaut le patriotisme maintenant?; **p. cut** baisse *f* des prix; **p. freeze** gel *m* des prix; **p. increase** hausse *f* des prix; **p. index** indice *m* des prix; **p. list** liste *f* de prix; **p. range** gamme *f* de prix; *(budget)* budget *m*; **p. tag** étiquette *f* de prix; **p. war** guerre *f* des prix

2 *vt (decide cost of)* fixer le prix de; *(indicate cost of)* mettre le prix sur; **the toy is priced at $10** le prix du jouet est 10 dollars; **to p. oneself out of the market** perdre ses clients en pratiquant des prix trop élevés

price-cutting ['praɪs'kʌtɪŋ] *n Com* baisse *f* des prix
price-fixing ['praɪs'fɪksɪŋ] *n Com* alignement *m* des prix
priceless ['praɪslɪs] *adj* **(a)** *(invaluable)* qui n'a pas de prix **(b)** *Fam (funny)* impayable
pricey ['praɪsɪ] *adj Fam* cher(ère)
prick [prɪk] **1** *n* **(a)** *(of needle)* piqûre *f*; *Fig (of conscience)* remords *m* **(b)** *Vulg (penis)* bite *f*; *(man)* con *m*
2 *vt (sausage, potato)* piquer; *(balloon)* percer; **to p. one's finger** se piquer le doigt; **to p. a hole in sth** percer qch
▸**prick up** *vt sep* **to p. up one's ears** *(of animal)* dresser les oreilles; *(of person)* tendre l'oreille
prickle ['prɪkəl] **1** *n* **(a)** *(of hedgehog)* piquant *m*; *(of plant)* épine *f* **(b)** *(sensation)* picotement *m*
2 *vi (of skin)* picoter
prickly ['prɪklɪ] *adj* **(a)** *(animal)* couvert(e) de piquants; *(plant)* à épines; *Fig (person)* susceptible; **p. pear** *(tree)* figuier *m* de Barbarie; *(fruit)* figue *f* de Barbarie **(b)** *(sensation)* de picotement; **p. heat** miliaire *f*
pride [praɪd] **1** *n* **(a)** *(satisfaction)* fierté *f*; *(self-esteem)* amour-propre *m*; *Pej (vanity)* orgueil *m*; **to take p. in sth** mettre sa fierté dans qch **(b)** *(person, thing)* **she is the p. of the family** elle fait la fierté de la famille; **the p. of my collection** le clou de ma collection; **she's his p. and joy** elle fait son bonheur; **to have p. of place** trôner **(c)** *(of lions)* troupe *f*
2 *vt* **to p. oneself on sth** être fier(ère) de qch
priest [priːst] *n* prêtre *m*
priestess ['priːstɪs] *n* prêtresse *f*
priesthood ['priːsthʊd] *n* prêtrise *f*; **to enter the p.** entrer dans les ordres
prig [prɪg] *n* prêcheur(euse) *m,f*
priggish ['prɪgɪʃ] *adj* prêcheur(euse)
prim [prɪm] *adj* **p. (and proper)** *(person, expression)* collet monté *inv*; *(manner)* guindé(e)
primacy ['praɪməsɪ] *n* primauté *f*
prima facie ['praɪmə'feɪʃɪ] **1** *adj Law* **p. case** = affaire qui, au premier abord, paraît légitime
2 *adv* de prime abord
primarily ['praɪmərɪlɪ] *adv* principalement
primary ['praɪmərɪ] **1** *n (pl* **primaries)** *(election)* primaire *f*
2 *adj* **(a)** *(main)* principal(e); **p. colors** couleurs *fpl* fondamentales **(b)** *(initial)* primaire; **p. education** enseignement *m* primaire; **p. election** (élection *f*) primaire *f*; **p. school** école *f* primaire
primate ['praɪmeɪt] *n* primate *m*
prime [praɪm] **1** *n (best time)* **the p. of life** la fleur de l'âge; **to be in one's p.** être à la fleur de l'âge; **to be past one's p.** ne plus être de première jeunesse
2 *adj* **(a)** *(principal)* principal(e); *(importance)* capital(e); **p. minister** premier ministre *m*; *Math* **p. number** nombre *m* premier; **p. time** *(on TV)* prime time *m*, heures *fpl* de grande écoute **(b)** *(excellent)* excellent(e); **a p. example (of)** un exemple typique (de); **p. quality** de premier choix
3 *vt* **(a)** *(engine, pump)* amorcer; *(surface)* apprêter **(b)** *(provide with information)* **to p. sb for an interview/an exam** préparer qn à un entretien/un examen
primer[1] ['praɪmə(r)] *n (paint)* apprêt *m*
primer[2] ['praɪmə(r)] *n (textbook)* manuel *m* élémentaire

primeval [praɪ'miːvəl] *adj* primitif(ive)
primitive ['prɪmɪtɪv] *adj (original)* primitif(ive); *(basic)* primitif, rudimentaire
primly ['prɪmlɪ] *adv* d'une manière guindée
primordial [praɪ'mɔːdɪəl] *adj* primordial(e); **p. soup** soupe *f* primitive
primrose ['prɪmrəʊz] *n (plant)* primevère *f*; **p. yellow** jaune pâle *inv*
primula ['prɪmjʊlə] *n* primula *f*
primus (stove)® ['praɪməs('stəʊv)] *n* réchaud *m* portatif
prince [prɪns] *n* prince *m*; **the P. of Wales** le prince de Galles; **P. Charming** le prince charmant
princely ['prɪnslɪ] *adj also Fig* princier(ère)
princess [prɪn'ses] *n* princesse *f*
principal ['prɪnsɪpəl] **1** *n (of school)* directeur(trice) *m,f*
2 *adj* principal(e)
principality [prɪnsɪ'pælɪtɪ] *(pl* **principalities)** *n* principauté *f*
principle ['prɪnsɪpəl] *n* principe *m*; **in p.** en principe; **on p.** par principe
principled ['prɪnsɪpəld] *adj (person)* de principes; *(behavior)* dicté(e) par des principes; **to be p.** avoir des principes
print [prɪnt] **1** *n* **(a)** *(of fingers)* empreinte *f* **(b)** *(printed matter)* texte *m*; **in p.** disponible en librairie; **out of p.** épuisé(e); **to appear in p.** être publié(e) **(c)** *(characters)* caractères *mpl*; *Fig* **to read the small p.** *(in contract)* lire ce qu'il y a d'écrit en petits caractères **(d)** *(engraving)* estampe *f*; *(photograph)* épreuve *f*; *(textile)* imprimé *m*
2 *vt* **(a)** *(book, newspaper)* imprimer **(b)** *(write clearly)* écrire en script **(c)** *(in photography)* **to p. a negative** tirer une épreuve d'un négatif
3 *vi (write clearly)* écrire en script
▸**print out** *vt sep Comput* imprimer
printed ['prɪntɪd] *adj* imprimé(e); **p. circuit** circuit *m* imprimé; **p. matter** imprimés *mpl*
printer ['prɪntə(r)] *n (person)* imprimeur *m*; *(machine)* imprimante *f*
printing ['prɪntɪŋ] *n (process, industry)* imprimerie *f*; *(action)* tirage *m*; **p. error** faute *f* d'impression; **p. press** presse *f*
printout ['prɪntaʊt] *n Comput* sortie *f* papier
prior[1] ['praɪə(r)] **1** *adj* antérieur(e); **to have p. knowledge (of sth)** avoir une connaissance préalable (de qch)
2 *adv* **p. to** avant
prior[2] ['praɪə(r)] *n Rel* prieur *m*
prioritize [praɪ'ɒrɪtaɪz] **1** *vt* donner la priorité à
2 *vi* établir ses priorités
priority [praɪ'ɒrɪtɪ] *(pl* **priorities)** *n* priorité *f*; **to have** *or* **to take p. over sb/sth** avoir la priorité sur qn/qch; **to get one's priorities right/wrong** savoir/ne pas savoir ce qui est important
priory ['praɪərɪ] *(pl* **priories)** *n Rel* prieuré *m*
prism ['prɪzəm] *n* prisme *m*
prison ['prɪzən] *n* prison *f*; **p. camp** camp *m* de prisonniers; **p. officer** gardien(enne) *m,f* de prison
prisoner ['prɪzənə(r)] *n* prisonnier(ère) *m,f*; **to take/to hold sb p.** faire/retenir qn prisonnier; *Fig* **to take no prisoners** être impitoyable; **p. of conscience** prisonnier(ère) *m,f* d'opinion; **p. of war** prisonnier(ère) *m,f* de guerre
prissy ['prɪsɪ] *adj Fam* collet monté *inv*
pristine ['prɪstiːn] *adj* impeccable
privacy ['praɪvəsɪ] *n* intimité *f*; **in the p. of one's own home** dans l'intimité de son foyer
private ['praɪvɪt] **1** *adj* **(a)** *(personal)* personnel(elle); **can we go somewhere p.?** est-ce qu'on peut se voir en privé?; **p. life** vie *f* privée; *Fam* **p. parts** parties *fpl* (génitales)
(b) *(secret)* confidentiel(elle); **p. and confidential** *(on letter)* confidentiel

(c) *(for personal use)* privé(e); **p. house** maison *f* particulière; **p. lessons** leçons *fpl* particulières; **p. line** ligne *f* privée; **p. office** bureau *m* personnel; **p. secretary** secrétaire *mf* particulier(ère)

(d) *(not state-run)* privé(e); **p. detective** *or* **investigator** détective *m* privé; **p. education** enseignement *m* privé; **p. enterprise** entreprise *f* privée; **p. health insurance** assurance *f* maladie privée; **p. school** école *f* privée; **p. sector** secteur *m* privé

(e) *(not for the public)* privé(e); **p. party** soirée *f* privée; **p. property** propriété *f* privée; **p. road** voie *f* privée

2 *n* **(a)** **in p.** en privé

(b) *(soldier)* simple soldat *m*

privately ['praɪvɪtlɪ] *adv (in private)* en privé; **to be p. educated** faire sa scolarité dans le privé; **p. owned** *(company)* privé(e); *(hotel)* familial(e)

privation [praɪ'veɪʃən] *n* privation *f*

privatization [praɪvɪtaɪ'zeɪʃən] *n* privatisation *f*

privatize ['praɪvɪtaɪz] *vt* privatiser

privet ['prɪvɪt] *n* troène *m*

privilege ['prɪvɪlɪdʒ] **1** *n* privilège *m*; **to have the p. of doing sth** avoir le privilège de faire qch

2 *vt* **to be privileged to do sth** avoir le privilège de faire qch

privy ['prɪvɪ] **1** *n (pl* **privies)** *Old-fashioned (toilet)* cabinets *mpl*

2 *adj Formal* **to be p. to sth** avoir connaissance de qch

prize[1] [praɪz] **1** *n (award)* prix *m*; **to win a p.** remporter un prix; **p. draw** tombola *f*; **p. money** argent *m* du prix

2 *vt (value)* attacher de la valeur à

prize[2] [praɪz] *vt* **to p. sth off/open** retirer/ouvrir qch en forçant; *Fig* **to p. sth out of sb** *(secret, truth)* soutirer qch à qn

prizefight ['praɪzfaɪt] *n* combat *m* professionnel

prizefighter ['praɪzfaɪtə(r)] *n* boxeur *m* professionnel

prizewinner ['praɪzwɪnə(r)] *n* gagnant(e) *m,f*

pro[1] [prəʊ] *(pl* **pros)** *n Fam (professional)* pro *mf*

pro[2] [prəʊ] **1** *n (advantage)* **the pros and cons** le pour et le contre

2 *prep (in favor of)* pour

proactive [prəʊ'æktɪv] *adj* qui fait preuve d'initiative

pro-am ['prəʊ'æm] *n Sport* tournoi *m* professionnel-amateur

probability [prɒbə'bɪlɪtɪ] *(pl* **probabilities)** *n* probabilité *f*; **in all p....,** il y a de fortes chances que...

probable ['prɒbəbəl] *adj* probable

probably ['prɒbəblɪ] *adv* probablement

probation [prə'beɪʃən] *n (in job)* période *f* d'essai; *Law* mise *f* en liberté surveillée; **on p.** *(in job)* à l'essai; *Law* en liberté surveillée; **p. officer** agent *m* de probation

probationary [prə'beɪʃənərɪ] *adj* d'essai

probationer [prə'beɪʃənə(r)] *n (in job)* personne *f* à l'essai

probe [prəʊb] **1** *n* **(a)** *(instrument)* sonde *f*; **(space) p.** sonde spatiale **(b)** *(inquiry)* enquête *f*

2 *vt* **(a)** *(prod)* sonder **(b)** *(inquire into)* enquêter sur

3 *vi* **to p. into sth** *(past, private life)* fouiller dans qch

probity ['prəʊbɪtɪ] *n Formal* probité *f*

problem ['prɒbləm] *n* problème *m*; *Fam* **no p.!** pas de problème!; **p. area** *(in town)* quartier *m* à problèmes; *(in project)* source *f* de problèmes; **p. child** enfant *mf* à problèmes

problematic [prɒblɪ'mætɪk], **problematical** [prɒblɪ'mætɪkəl] *adj* problématique

procedure [prə'siːdʒə(r)] *n* procédure *f*

proceed [prə'siːd] **1** *vt* **to p. to do sth** se mettre à faire qch

2 *vi* **(a)** *(go on)* se poursuivre; **to p. to sth** passer à qch; **to p. with sth** poursuivre qch; **how shall we p.?** comment allons-nous procéder? **(b)** *(result)* **to p. from** provenir de

proceedings [prə'siːdɪŋz] *npl* **(a)** *(events)* opérations *fpl* **(b)** *Law* poursuites *fpl*; **to take p. (against sb)** engager des poursuites (contre qn)

proceeds ['prəʊsiːdz] *npl* recette *f*

process ['prəʊses] **1** *n* processus *m*; **by a p. of elimination** en procédant par élimination; **she fell down the stairs, breaking her leg in the p.** elle est tombée dans les escaliers, et s'est cassée la jambe; **to be in the p. of doing sth** être en train de faire qch

2 *vt (raw material, information, application)* traiter; *(film)* développer; **processed food** aliments *mpl* conditionnés

processing ['prəʊsesɪŋ] *n (of raw material, information)* traitement *m*; *(of photographs)* développement *m*; *Comput* **p. language** langage *m* de traitement; *Comput* **p. speed** vitesse *f* de traitement

procession [prə'seʃən] *n* défilé *m*; **in p.** en cortège

processor ['prəʊsesə(r)] *n Comput* processeur *m*

pro-choice ['prəʊtʃɔɪs] *adj* partisan(e) de l'avortement

proclaim [prə'kleɪm] *vt* proclamer

proclamation [prɒklə'meɪʃən] *n* proclamation *f*

proclivity [prəʊ'klɪvɪtɪ] *(pl* **proclivities)** *n Formal* tendance *f* (**for** à)

procrastinate [prəʊ'kræstɪneɪt] *vi* atermoyer

procrastination [prəʊkræstɪ'neɪʃən] *n* atermoiements *mpl*

procreate ['prəʊkrɪeɪt] *vi* procréer

procreation [prəʊkrɪ'eɪʃən] *n* procréation *f*

procure [prə'kjʊə(r)] *vt* procurer (**for sb** à qn); **to p. sth (for oneself)** se procurer qch

procurement [prə'kjʊəmənt] *n* acquisition *f*

prod [prɒd] **1** *n* to give sb a p. donner un petit coup à qn; *Fig* pousser qn; **to give sth a p.** donner un petit coup à qch

2 *vt (pt & pp* **prodded)** *(poke)* donner un petit coup dans; *Fig* **to p. sb (into doing sth)** pousser qn (à faire qch)

prodigal ['prɒdɪgəl] *adj* prodigue

prodigious [prə'dɪdʒəs] *adj* prodigieux(euse)

prodigy ['prɒdɪdʒɪ] *(pl* **prodigies)** *n* prodige *m*

produce 1 *n* ['prɒdjuːs] *(products)* produits *mpl*

2 *vt* [prə'djuːs] **(a)** *(create)* produire; *(machine, car)* fabriquer; *(reaction, feeling)* entraîner **(b)** *(present) (ticket, passport)* présenter; *(documents, alibi)* fournir; *(from pocket, bag)* sortir **(c)** *(movie, play, radio, TV program)* produire

producer [prə'djuːsə(r)] *n* **(a)** *(of crops, goods)* producteur(trice) *m,f* **(b)** *(of film, play, radio, TV program)* producteur(trice) *m,f*

product ['prɒdʌkt] *n* produit *m*; *Com* **p. development** mise *f* au point de produit; **p. placement** placement *m* de produit

production [prə'dʌkʃən] *n* **(a)** *(manufacture)* production *f*, fabrication *f*; **to go into/out of p.** être/ne plus être fabriqué(e); **p. costs** coûts *mpl* de production; **p. line** chaîne *f* de fabrication; **p. manager** directeur(trice) *m,f* de production; **p. process** procédé *m* de fabrication; **p. target** cible *f* de production **(b)** *(of document, ticket)* présentation *f*; **on p. of** sur présentation de **(c)** *(movie, play, radio or TV program)* production *f*

productive [prə'dʌktɪv] *adj* productif(ive)

productivity [prɒdʌk'tɪvɪtɪ] *n Ind* productivité *f*; **p. agreement** accord *m* de productivité; **p. bonus** prime *f* de rendement

Prof. *(abbr* **Professor) (a)** *(title)* Professeur **(b)** *Fam* prof *mf*

profane [prə'feɪn] **1** *adj* **(a)** *(language)* grossier(ère) **(b)** *Rel (secular)* profane

2 *vt* profaner

profanity [prə'fænɪtɪ] *(pl* **profanities)** *n* grossièreté *f*

profess [prə'fes] *vt* **(a)** *(declare)* professer **(b)** *(claim)* prétendre

professed [prə'fest] *adj* **(a)** *(self-declared)* avoué(e) **(b)** *(pretended)* prétendu(e)

profession [prə'feʃən] *n* **(a)** *(occupation)* profession *f*; **the medical/teaching p.** le corps médical/enseignant; **by p.** de profession **(b)** *(declaration)* déclaration *f*

professional [prə'feʃənəl] **1** *n* professionnel(elle) *m,f*

2 *adj (paid, competent)* professionnel(elle); *(soldier)* de carrière; *(army)* de métier; **he made a very p. job of it** il a fait du bon travail; **to turn** *or* **to go p.** *(of athlete)* passer en catégorie professionnelle; **to take p. advice on sth** demander l'avis d'un professionnel sur qch; **p. misconduct** faute *f* professionnelle; **p. training** formation *f* professionnelle

professionalism [prə'feʃənəlɪzəm] *n* professionnalisme *m*

professor [prə'fesə(r)] *n Univ* enseignant(e) *m,f* d'université

proffer ['prɒfə(r)] *vt Formal (advice)* offrir; *(opinion)* avancer; *(thanks)* présenter; *(hand, object)* tendre

proficiency [prə'fɪʃənsɪ] *n* compétence *f* (**in** *or* **at** en *ou* dans); *(in language)* maîtrise *f* (**in** en)

proficient [prə'fɪʃənt] *adj* compétent(e) (**in** *or* **at** en *ou* dans)

profile ['prəʊfaɪl] **1** *n* (**a**) *(side view, outline)* profil *m*; **to keep a low p.** garder un profil bas (**b**) *(description)* portrait *m*
2 *vt (describe)* faire le portrait de

profiling ['prəʊfaɪlɪŋ] *n Psy* profilage *m*

profit ['prɒfɪt] **1** *n* (**a**) *(of company, on deal)* bénéfice *m*, profit *m*; **at a p.** à profit; **to make a p.** réaliser un bénéfice; **p. and loss account** compte *m* de pertes et profits; **p. margin** marge *f* bénéficiaire (**b**) *(advantage)* avantage *m*
2 *vi* **to p. by** *or* **from** tirer profit de

profitability [prɒfɪtə'bɪlɪtɪ] *n* rentabilité *f*

profitable ['prɒfɪtəbəl] *adj (company, deal)* rentable; *(experience)* profitable

profitably ['prɒfɪtəblɪ] *adv (trade, operate)* à profit; *(use one's time)* profitablement

profiteer [prɒfɪ'tɪə(r)] *Pej* **1** *n* profiteur(euse) *m,f*
2 *vi* profiter d'une situation pour faire des bénéfices

profit-making ['prɒfɪtmeɪkɪŋ] *adj* rentable

profit-sharing ['prɒfɪtʃeərɪŋ] *n Com* intéressement *m*

profligate ['prɒflɪgət] *adj Formal* prodigue

profound [prə'faʊnd] *adj* profond(e)

profundity [prə'fʌndɪtɪ] *(pl* **profundities**) *n* profondeur *f*

profuse [prə'fjuːs] *adj* abondant(e)

profusely [prə'fjuːslɪ] *adv (sweat, bleed)* abondamment; **to apologize p.** se confondre en excuses; **to thank sb p.** remercier qn avec effusion

profusion [prə'fjuːʒən] *n* profusion *f*

progeny ['prɒdʒɪnɪ] *(pl* **progenies**) *n Formal* progéniture *f*

prognosis [prɒg'nəʊsɪs] *(pl* **prognoses** [prɒg'nəʊsiːz]) *n Med* pronostic *m*; *Fig* pronostics

program¹ ['prəʊgræm] *Comput* **1** *n* programme *m*
2 *vt & vi* programmer

program² ['prəʊgræm] **1** *n (for play, of political party)* programme *m*; *(on TV, radio)* émission *f*
2 *vt (machine)* programmer; **to p. sth to do sth** programmer qch pour faire qch

programmable [prəʊ'græməbəl] *adj* programmable

programmed ['prəʊgræmd] *adj Educ* **p. instruction** *or* **learning** enseignement *m* programmé

programmer ['prəʊgræmə(r)] *n Comput* programmeur(euse) *m,f*

progress 1 *n* ['prəʊgres] (**a**) *(improvement)* progrès *m*; **to make p.** faire des progrès (**b**) *(movement)* marche *f*; **in p.** en cours; **to make p. (in sth)** progresser (dans qch); **p. report** rapport *m*
2 *vi* [prə'gres] (**a**) *(improve)* progresser (**b**) *(advance)* avancer; *(of meeting)* progresser

progression [prə'greʃən] *n* progression *f*

progressive [prə'gresɪv] **1** *adj* (**a**) *(increasing)* progressif(ive); **p. disease** maladie *f* évolutive (**b**) *(radical) (person, idea)* progressiste
2 *n (radical)* progressiste *mf*

progressively [prə'gresɪvlɪ] *adv* progressivement

prohibit [prə'hɪbɪt] *vt* interdire; **to p. sb from doing sth** interdire à qn de faire qch

prohibition [prəʊɪ'bɪʃən] *n* interdiction *f*; *Hist* la Prohibition

prohibitive [prə'hɪbɪtɪv] *adj* prohibitif(ive)

prohibitively [prə'hɪbɪtɪvlɪ] *adv* **p. expensive** à un prix prohibitif

project 1 *n* ['prɒdʒekt] *(undertaking, plan)* projet *m*; *(at school)* dossier *m*; *(at university)* mémoire *m*; *Com* **p. manager** directeur(trice) *m,f* de projet
2 *vt* [prə'dʒekt] (**a**) *(plan)* prévoir (**b**) *(propel)* projeter; **to p. one's voice** projeter sa voix
3 *vi* [prə'dʒekt] *(protrude)* dépasser

projectile [prə'dʒektaɪl] *n* projectile *m*

projection [prə'dʒekʃən] *n* (**a**) *(in general)* projection *f*; **p. room** *(in movie theater)* salle *f* de projection (**b**) *(protruding part)* saillie *f*

projectionist [prə'dʒekʃənɪst] *n* projectionniste *mf*

projector [prə'dʒektə(r)] *n* projecteur *m*

prolapse ['prəʊlæps] *n Med* prolapsus *m*

proletarian [prəʊlɪ'teərɪən] **1** *n* prolétaire *mf*
2 *adj* prolétarien(enne)

proletariat [prəʊlɪ'teərɪət] *n* prolétariat *m*

pro-life ['prəʊlaɪf] *adj* antiavortement, contre l'avortement

proliferate [prə'lɪfəreɪt] *vi* proliférer

proliferation [prəlɪfə'reɪʃən] *n* prolifération *f*

prolific [prə'lɪfɪk] *adj* prolifique

prolix ['prəʊlɪks] *adj Formal* prolixe

prologue ['prəʊlɒg] *n* prologue *m*

prolong [prə'lɒŋ] *vt* prolonger

prom [prɒm] *n (school dance)* soirée *f* dansante

promenade ['prɒmənɑːd] *vi* se promener

prominence ['prɒmɪnəns] *n* (**a**) *(of land)* saillie *f*; *(of physical feature)* proéminence *f* (**b**) *(importance)* importance *f*; **to give sth p.** donner de l'importance à qch; **to come to p.** devenir célèbre

prominent ['prɒmɪnənt] *adj* (**a**) *(peak, landscape)* en saillie; *(physical feature)* proéminent(e); **to be in a p. position** être en évidence (**b**) *(important)* important(e)

prominently ['prɒmɪnentlɪ] *adv* bien en vue; **to figure p. in sth** figurer en bonne place dans qch

promiscuity [prɒmɪs'kjuːɪtɪ] *n* promiscuité *f* sexuelle

promiscuous [prə'mɪskjʊəs] *adj* qui a des partenaires multiples

promise ['prɒmɪs] **1** *n* (**a**) *(pledge)* promesse *f*; **to make a p.** faire une promesse; **to keep/to break one's p.** tenir/ne pas tenir sa promesse (**b**) *(potential)* **to show p.** promettre; **she never fulfilled her early p.** *(as a writer, musician)* elle n'a jamais eu le succès qu'elle promettait d'avoir
2 *vt* promettre (**to do** de faire); **to p. sth to sb, to p. sb sth** promettre qch à qn; **it promises to be hot** le temps promet d'être chaud

promising ['prɒmɪsɪŋ] *adj* prometteur(euse)

promontory ['prɒməntərɪ] *(pl* **promontories**) *n* promontoire *m*

promote [prə'məʊt] *vt* (**a**) *(raise in rank, encourage)* promouvoir; **to be promoted** *(of officer, employee)* être promu(e); **to p. sb's interests** servir les intérêts de qn (**b**) *Com* faire la publicité de

promoter [prə'məʊtə(r)] *n (of theory, cause)* défenseur(euse) *m,f*; *(of boxing match)* organisateur(trice) *m,f*; *(of show)* imprésario *m*

promotion [prə'məʊʃən] *n* promotion *f*

promotional [prə'məʊʃənəl] *adj* promotionnel(elle)

prompt [prɒmpt] **1** *adj* (**a**) *(swift)* rapide; **p. payment** paiement *m* dans les plus brefs délais (**b**) *(punctual)* ponctuel(elle)
2 *adv* **at three o'clock p.** à trois heures précises
3 *vt* (**a**) *(cause)* provoquer; **to p. sb to do sth** pousser qn à faire qch (**b**) **to p. sb** *(encourage to speak)* = aider quelqu'un à répondre en lui suggérant quelque chose; **"was he tall?" the policeman prompted** "est-ce qu'il était grand?" suggéra le policier (**c**) *(in theater)* souffler à

4 *n* (**a**) **to give an actor a p.** souffler sa réplique à un acteur (**b**) *Comput* invite *f*

prompter ['prɒmptə(r)] *n Theat* souffleur(euse) *m,f*

promptly ['prɒmptlɪ] *adv (rapidly, punctually)* rapidement; *(immediately)* immédiatement

prone [prəʊn] *adj* (**a**) *(inclined)* **to be p. to sth** être sujet(ette) à qch; **to be p. to do sth** avoir tendance à faire qch (**b**) *Formal (lying face down)* couché(e) sur le ventre

prong [prɒŋ] *n (of fork)* dent *f*

pronoun ['prəʊnaʊn] *n Gram* pronom *m*

pronounce [prə'naʊns] **1** *vt* (**a**) *(word)* prononcer (**b**) *(declare) (opinion)* émettre; **to p. that...** déclarer que...; **to p. oneself for/against sth** se prononcer en faveur de/contre qch; **he was pronounced dead/innocent** il a été déclaré mort/innocent; *Law* **to p. sentence** rendre le verdict
2 *vi* **to p. on** se prononcer sur

pronounced [prə'naʊnst] *adj* prononcé(e)

pronouncement [prə'naʊnsmənt] *n Formal* déclaration *f*

pronto ['prɒntəʊ] *adv Fam* illico

pronunciation [prənʌnsɪ'eɪʃən] *n* prononciation *f*

proof [pru:f] **1** *n* (**a**) *(evidence)* preuve *f*; **to give p. of sth** prouver qch; **p. of identity** pièce *f* d'identité; **p. of purchase** preuve *f* d'achat; **to put sth to the p.** mettre qch à l'épreuve; *Prov* **the p. of the pudding is in the eating** il faut juger les choses à l'usage (**b**) *Typ* épreuve *f* (**c**) *(of alcohol)* teneur *f* en alcool; **to be 40 percent p.** faire 40 degrés
2 *adj (resistant)* **to be p. against sth** être résistant(e) à qch

proofread ['pru:fri:d] *(pt & pp* **proofread** ['pru:fred]) *vt Typ* relire, corriger

proofreader ['pru:fri:də(r)] *n Typ* correcteur(trice) *m,f*

proofreading ['pru:fri:dɪŋ] *n* correction *f* (d'épreuves)

prop [prɒp] **1** *n* (**a**) *(physical support)* support *m*; *(emotional support)* soutien *m* (**b**) *(in theater)* accessoire *m*
2 *vt (pt & pp* **propped**) **to p. sth against sth** appuyer qch contre qch

▶**prop up** *vt sep (building, tunnel)* étayer; *Fig (economy, regime)* soutenir; **to p. sth up against sth** appuyer qch contre qch

propaganda [prɒpə'gændə] *n* propagande *f*

propagate ['prɒpəgeɪt] **1** *vt* propager
2 *vi* se propager

propagation [prɒpə'geɪʃən] *n* propagation *f*

propane ['prəʊpeɪn] *n Chem* propane *m*

propel [prə'pel] *(pt & pp* **propelled**) *vt* propulser; *Fig* pousser

propellant, propellent [prə'pelənt] *n (for rocket)* propergol *m*; *(for aerosol)* gaz *m* propulseur

propeller [prə'pelə(r)] *n* hélice *f*

propensity [prə'pensɪtɪ] *(pl* **propensities**) *n* propension *f* (**for** à)

proper ['prɒpə(r)] *adj* (**a**) *(correct, real)* vrai(e); *(word)* correct(e); *Gram* **p. noun** nom *m* propre (**b**) *(appropriate)* bon (bonne); *(equipment, clothing)* adéquat(e); *(behavior)* convenable (**c**) *(characteristic)* **p. to** propre à

properly ['prɒpəlɪ] *adv* (**a**) *(correctly)* correctement (**b**) *(suitably)* convenablement

property ['prɒpətɪ] *(pl* **properties**) *n* (**a**) *(possessions)* biens *mpl*; *(land, house)* propriété *f*; **p. developer** promoteur(trice) *m,f* (immobilier(ère)); **p. market** marché *m* immobilier; **p. owner** propriétaire *mf*; **p. tax** impôt *m* foncier (**b**) *(quality)* propriété *f*

prophecy ['prɒfɪsɪ] *(pl* **prophecies**) *n* prophétie *f*

prophesy ['prɒfɪsaɪ] *(pt & pp* **prophesied**) *vt* prédire

prophet ['prɒfɪt] *n* prophète *m*

prophetic [prə'fetɪk] *adj* prophétique

prophylactic [prɒfɪ'læktɪk] *Med* **1** *n* prophylactique *m*; *(condom)* préservatif *m*
2 *adj* prophylactique

propitiate [prə'pɪʃɪeɪt] *vt Formal* gagner les faveurs de

propitious [prə'pɪʃəs] *adj Formal* favorable

proportion [prə'pɔːʃən] **1** *n* (**a**) *(relationship)* proportion *f*; **in p.** proportionné(e); **out of p.** disproportionné(e); **the payment is out of all p. to the work involved** la rétribution n'est pas du tout proportionnelle au travail requis (**b**) *(part, amount)* proportion *f*; **to get sth out of p.** exagérer qch; **try to keep things in p.** essaie de ne pas dramatiser (**c**) **proportions** *(dimensions)* proportions *fpl*
2 *vt* proportionner

proportional [prə'pɔːʃənəl] *adj* proportionnel(elle) (**to** à); *Pol* **p. representation** (représentation *f*) proportionnelle *f*

proportionate [prə'pɔːʃənɪt] *adj* proportionnel(elle) (**to** à)

proposal [prə'pəʊzəl] *n (offer)* proposition *f*; *(plan)* projet *m*; **p. (of marriage)** demande *f* en mariage

propose [prə'pəʊz] **1** *vt* proposer; **to p. a toast** porter un toast; **to p. to do sth, to p. doing sth** *(suggest)* suggérer de faire qch; *(intend)* avoir l'intention de faire qch
2 *vi* **to p. to sb** demander qn en mariage

proposition [prɒpə'zɪʃən] **1** *n* proposition *f*
2 *vt* faire des avances à

propound [prə'paʊnd] *vt Formal* exposer

proprietary [prə'praɪətərɪ] *adj (air, attitude)* possessif(ive); *Com* **p. brand** marque *f* déposée

proprietor [prə'praɪətə(r)] *n* propriétaire *mf*

propriety [prə'praɪətɪ] *(pl* **proprieties**) *n* bienséance *f*

propulsion [prə'pʌlʃən] *n* propulsion *f*

pro rata ['prəʊ'rɑːtə] *adj & adv* au prorata

prosaic [prəʊ'zeɪk] *adj* prosaïque

proscribe [prəʊ'skraɪb] *vt* proscrire

prose [prəʊz] *n* prose *f*

prosecute ['prɒsɪkjuːt] *Law* **1** *vt* poursuivre en justice
2 *vi (of lawyer)* représenter le ministère public

prosecution [prɒsɪ'kjuːʃən] *n Law (proceedings)* poursuites *fpl* judiciaires; **the p.** *(in trial)* les plaignants *mpl*; *(in state)* ≃ le ministère public

prosecutor ['prɒsɪkjuːtə(r)] *n Law* procureur *m*

prospect¹ *n* ['prɒspekt] (**a**) *(expectation, thought)* perspective *f* (**b**) *(chance, likelihood)* perspectives *fpl*; **there is no p. of success** il n'y a aucune chance de réussite; **future prospects** perspectives d'avenir; **a job with prospects** un travail qui offre des perspectives d'avenir (**c**) *(view)* vue *f*
2 *vi* [prə'spekt] **to p. for gold** chercher de l'or

prospective [prə'spektɪv] *adj (future)* futur(e); *(potential)* potentiel(elle)

prospector [prə'spektə(r)] *n* prospecteur(trice) *m,f*; *(for gold)* chercheur(euse) *m,f*

prospectus [prə'spektəs] *n* prospectus *m*

prosper ['prɒspə(r)] *vi* prospérer

prosperity [prɒs'perɪtɪ] *n* prospérité *f*

prosperous ['prɒspərəs] *adj* prospère

prostate ['prɒsteɪt] *n Anat* **p. (gland)** prostate *f*

prosthesis [prɒs'θiːsɪs] *(pl* **prostheses** [prɒs'θiːsiːz]) *n* prothèse *f*

prostitute ['prɒstɪtjuːt] **1** *n* prostituée *f*; **male p.** prostitué *m*
2 *vt also Fig* **to p. oneself** se prostituer

prostitution [prɒstɪ'tjuːʃən] *n* prostitution *f*

prostrate 1 *adj* ['prɒstreɪt] *(lying down)* couché(e); *Fig* **p. with grief** terrassé(e) par le chagrin
2 *vt* [prə'streɪt] **to p. oneself** se prosterner

protagonist [prə'tægənɪst] *n* protagoniste *mf*; *(of idea, theory)* partisan(e) *m,f*

protease ['prəʊtɪeɪz] *n* protéase *f*; **p. inhibitor** antiprotéase *f*, inhibiteur *m* de protéase

protect [prə'tekt] *vt* protéger (**from** *or* **against** de)

protection [prə'tekʃən] *n* protection *f*; **p. money** = argent versé à un racketteur; **p. racket** racket *m*

protectionism [prə'tekʃənɪzəm] n Econ protectionnisme m

protective [prə'tektɪv] adj protecteur(trice); **to put sb in p. custody** mettre qn en lieu sûr

protector [prə'tektə(r)] n (device) protecteur m; (person) protecteur(trice) m,f

protégé ['prɒtəʒeɪ] n protégé(e) m,f

protein ['prəʊtiːn] n protéine f

protest 1 n ['prəʊtest] protestation f; **to do sth under p.** faire qch contre son gré; **to do sth in p.** faire qch en signe de protestation; **p. song** chanson f engagée; **p. vote** vote m de protestation
    2 vt [prə'test] (a) (protest against) protester contre (b) (one's innocence, love) protester de; **to p. that...** protester en disant que...
    3 vi [prə'test] protester (**about/against** à propos de/contre)

Protestant ['prɒtɪstənt] n & adj protestant(e) m,f

Protestantism ['prɒtɪstəntɪzəm] n protestantisme m

protestation [prɒtes'teɪʃən] n protestation f

protester [prə'testə(r)] n protestataire mf

protocol ['prəʊtəkɒl] n protocole m; **the Kyoto P.** le Protocole de Kyoto

proton ['prəʊtɒn] n Phys proton m

prototype ['prəʊtətaɪp] n prototype m

protracted [prə'træktɪd] adj prolongé(e)

protractor [prə'træktə(r)] n rapporteur m

protrude [prə'truːd] vi dépasser (**from** de); (of jaw, teeth) avancer

protruding [prə'truːdɪŋ] adj en saillie; (jaw, teeth) qui avance

protuberance [prə'tjuːbərəns] n protubérance f

proud [praʊd] **1** adj (person) fier(ère) (**of** de); (moment) grand(e); **as p. as a peacock** fier comme un paon
    2 adv **to do sb p.** faire honneur à qn; **to do oneself p.** se distinguer

proudly ['praʊdlɪ] adv fièrement

prove [pruːv] (pp **proven** ['pruːvən] or **proved**) **1** vt (demonstrate) prouver; **to p. sb wrong/guilty** prouver que qn a tort/est coupable; **to p. oneself** faire ses preuves
    2 vi **to p. (to be) correct** se révéler correct(e)

proverb ['prɒvɜːb] n proverbe m

proverbial [prə'vɜːbɪəl] adj proverbial(e)

provide [prə'vaɪd] vt (a) (supply) fournir; (service, support) offrir; **to p. sb with sth** fournir qch à qn (b) (stipulate) stipuler
▸**provide against** vt insep (danger, possibility) parer à
▸**provide for** vt insep (a) (support) pourvoir aux besoins de; **he left his family well provided for** il a laissé sa famille à l'abri du besoin (b) Formal (allow for) parer à

provided [prə'vaɪdɪd] conj **p. (that)** à condition que + subjunctive

providence ['prɒvɪdəns] n providence f

providential [prɒvɪ'denʃəl] adj providentiel(elle)

provider [prə'vaɪdə(r)] n pourvoyeur(euse) m,f

providing [prə'vaɪdɪŋ] conj **p. (that)** à condition que + subjunctive

province ['prɒvɪns] n (a) (of country) province f; **in the provinces** en province (b) Fig (domain) domaine m

provincial [prə'vɪnʃəl] adj de province; Pej (parochial) provincial(e)

provision [prə'vɪʒən] n (a) **provisions** (supplies) provisions fpl (b) (supplying) approvisionnement m (**of** en); (of services) prestation f (**of** de) (c) (allowance) **to make p. for sth** prévoir qch (d) (in treaty) disposition f; (in contract) clause f

provisional [prə'vɪʒənəl] adj provisoire

provisionally [prə'vɪʒənəlɪ] adv provisoirement

proviso [prə'vaɪzəʊ] (pl **provisos** or **provisoes**) n condition f; **with the p. that** à condition que + subjunctive

provocation [prɒvə'keɪʃən] n provocation f; **at the slightest p.** pour un rien

provocative [prə'vɒkətɪv] adj provocateur(trice)

provoke [prə'vəʊk] vt provoquer; **to p. sb into doing sth** pousser qn à faire qch

provoking [prə'vəʊkɪŋ] adj (irritating) agaçant(e)

prow [praʊ] n (of ship) proue f

prowess ['praʊɪs] n (skill) prouesses fpl

prowl [praʊl] **1** n **to be on the p.** (of person, animal) être en chasse; **to be on the p. for sth** être à l'affût de qch
    2 vt (streets, area) rôder dans
    3 vi rôder

prowler ['praʊlə(r)] n rôdeur(euse) m,f

proximity [prɒk'sɪmɪtɪ] n proximité f; **in p. to** à proximité de

proxy ['prɒksɪ] (pl **proxies**) n (power) procuration f; (person) mandataire mf; **by p.** par procuration; Comput **p. server** serveur m proxy; Pol **p. vote** vote m par procuration

Prozac® ['prəʊzæk] n Prozac m

prude [pruːd] n prude f

prudence ['pruːdəns] n prudence f

prudent ['pruːdənt] adj prudent(e)

prudish ['pruːdɪʃ] adj pudibond(e)

prune¹ [pruːn] n (fruit) pruneau m

prune² [pruːn] vt (bush, tree) tailler; Fig (article) élaguer

prurient ['prʊərɪənt] adj malsain(e)

Prussia ['prʌʃə] n la Prusse

Prussian ['prʌʃən] **1** n Prussien(enne) m,f
    2 adj prussien(enne)

pry [praɪ] (pt & pp **pried**) vi être indiscret(ète); **to p. into sth** mettre son nez dans qch
▸**pry open** vt sep ouvrir à l'aide d'un levier; **he tried to p. open the door** il a essayé de forcer la porte

prying ['praɪɪŋ] adj indiscret(ète)

PS ['piː'es] n (abbr **postscript**) PS m

psalm [sɑːm] n psaume m

pseudo- ['suːdəʊ] pref Fam pseudo-

pseudonym ['suːdənɪm] n pseudonyme m

PST [piːes'tiː] n (abbr **Pacific Standard Time**) PST m

psyche ['saɪkɪ] n psychisme m
▸**psyche out** [saɪk] vt sep Fam (unnerve) déstabiliser
▸**psyche up** [saɪk] vt sep Fam **to p. sb up (for sth)** préparer qn psychologiquement (à qch); **to p. oneself up (for sth)** se préparer psychologiquement (à qch)

psyched [saɪkd] adj Fam surexcité(e)

psychedelic [saɪkə'delɪk] adj psychédélique

psychiatric [saɪkɪ'ætrɪk] adj psychiatrique

psychiatrist [saɪ'kaɪətrɪst] n psychiatre mf

psychiatry [saɪ'kaɪətrɪ] n psychiatrie f

psychic ['saɪkɪk] **1** n médium m
    2 adj (a) (paranormal) paranormal(e) (b) (clairvoyant) **to be p., to have p. powers** être médium; Fam **I'm not p.!** je ne suis pas médium!

psycho ['saɪkəʊ] (pl **psychos**) n Fam dingue mf

psychoanalysis [saɪkəʊə'nælɪsɪs] n psychanalyse f

psychoanalyst [saɪkəʊ'ænəlɪst] n psychanalyste mf

psychoanalyze [saɪkəʊ'ænəlaɪz] vt psychanalyser

psychobabble ['saɪkəʊ'bæbəl] n Fam Pej jargon m des psychologues

psychological [saɪkə'lɒdʒɪkəl] adj psychologique; **p. warfare** guerre f psychologique

psychologist [saɪ'kɒlədʒɪst] n psychologue mf

psychology [saɪ'kɒlədʒɪ] n psychologie f

psychometric [saɪkə'metrɪk] adj psychométrique

psychopath ['saɪkəʊpæθ] n psychopathe mf

psychosis [saɪ'kəʊsɪs] (pl **psychoses** [saɪ'kəʊsiːz]) n psychose f

psychosomatic [saɪkəʊsəˈmætɪk] *adj* psychosomatique
psychotherapist [saɪkəʊˈθerəpɪst] *n* psychothérapeute *mf*
psychotherapy [saɪkəʊˈθerəpɪ] *n* psychothérapie *f*
psychotic [saɪˈkɒtɪk] *n & adj* psychotique *mf*
PTA [piːtiːˈeɪ] *n Sch* (*abbr* **Parent-Teacher Association**) ≃ APE *f*
ptarmigan [ˈtɑːmɪgən] *n* lagopède *m*
PTO [piːtiːˈəʊ] (*abbr* **please turn over**) TSVP
pub [pʌb] *n* pub *m*
puberty [ˈpjuːbətɪ] *n* puberté *f*
pubic [ˈpjuːbɪk] *adj* pubien(enne), du pubis
public [ˈpʌblɪk] **1** *n* **the (general) p.** le grand public; **in p.** en public
  2 *adj* public(ique); (*library, swimming pool*) municipal(e); **to go p. with sth** (*reveal information*) révéler qch (*à la presse*); **the company's going p.** la compagnie va être cotée en Bourse; **to make sth p.** rendre qch public; **to make a p. appearance** faire une apparition en public; **to be in the p. domain** être dans le domaine public; **at p. expense** aux frais du contribuable; **to be in the p. eye** être très en vue; **a p. figure** une personnalité en vue; **in the p. interest** dans l'intérêt du public; **p. address system** sonorisation *f*; *Com* **p. enterprise** entreprise *f* publique; **p. health** santé *f* publique; **p. housing** logements *mpl* sociaux, ≃ HLM *f inv*; **p. library** bibliothèque *f* municipale; **p. opinion** l'opinion *f* publique; **p. ownership** nationalisation *f*, étatisation *f*; **to be under p. ownership** appartenir à l'état; *Law* **p. prosecutor** procureur *m*; **p. relations** relations *fpl* publiques; **p. school** école *f* publique; **p. sector** secteur *m* public; **p. spending** dépenses *fpl* publiques; **p. television** (télévision *f* du) service *m* public; **p. transportation** transports *mpl* en commun; *Com* **p. utility** service *m* public
publication [pʌblɪˈkeɪʃən] *n* publication *f*
publicity [pʌbˈlɪsɪtɪ] *n* publicité *f*; **p. campaign** campagne *f* publicitaire; **p. stunt** coup *m* de pub
publicize [ˈpʌblɪsaɪz] *vt* faire connaître au public
publicly [ˈpʌblɪklɪ] *adv* publiquement; **p. owned** à capitaux publics
public-spirited [ˈpʌblɪkˈspɪrɪtɪd] *adj* (*person*) qui a le sens civique; (*gesture, response*) dicté(e) par le sens civique
publish [ˈpʌblɪʃ] *vt* publier
publisher [ˈpʌblɪʃə(r)] *n* (*person*) éditeur(trice) *m,f*; (*company*) maison *f* d'édition
publishing [ˈpʌblɪʃɪŋ] *n* édition *f*; **p. house** maison *f* d'édition
pucker [ˈpʌkə(r)] **1** *vt* (*brow*) froncer; (*lips*) pincer
  2 *vi* (*of face*) se rider; (*lips*) se plisser
pudding [ˈpʊdɪŋ] *n* (*dish*) pudding *m*; **p. basin** *or* **bowl** jatte *f*
puddle [ˈpʌdəl] *n* flaque *f*
pudgy [ˈpʌdʒɪ] *adj* rondelet(ette)
puerile [ˈpjʊəraɪl] *adj Pej* puéril(e)
Puerto Rican [pweətəʊˈriːkən] **1** *n* Portoricain(e) *m,f*
  2 *adj* portoricain(e)
Puerto Rico [pweətəʊˈriːkəʊ] *n* Porto Rico
puff [pʌf] **1** *n* (*of breath, air*) souffle *m*; (*of smoke, cigarette*) bouffée *f*; **p. paste**, **p. pastry** pâte *f* feuilletée
  2 *vt* **to p. smoke into sb's face** envoyer de la fumée à la figure de qn
  3 *vi* (*of person*) souffler; (*of steam engine*) lancer des bouffées de vapeur; **to p. on a cigarette** fumer une cigarette
▶**puff out** *vt sep* (*cheeks, chest*) gonfler
▶**puff up** *vt sep* (*cheeks*) gonfler; **to be puffed up with pride** être gonflé(e) d'orgueil
puffin [ˈpʌfɪn] *n* macareux *m*
puffy [ˈpʌfɪ] *adj* gonflé(e)
pug [pʌg] *n* (*dog*) carlin *m*; **p.-nosed** au nez camus
pugnacious [pʌgˈneɪʃəs] *adj* pugnace

puke [pjuːk] *Fam* **1** *n* dégueulis *m*
  2 *vi* dégueuler
▶**puke up** *Fam* **1** *vt sep* dégueuler, rendre
  2 *vi* dégueuler
pull [pʊl] **1** *n* (**a**) (*act of pulling*) traction *f*; (*of water current*) force *f*; **to give sth a p.** tirer qch; **to take a p. at a bottle** boire une gorgée d'une bouteille; **p. date** date *f* limite de vente
  (**b**) *Fam* (*influence*) influence *f*; **to have a lot of p.** avoir le bras long
  2 *vt* (**a**) (*tug*) tirer; **to p. sth open/shut** ouvrir/fermer qch; **to p. a muscle** se froisser un muscle; **to p. the trigger** appuyer sur la gâchette; *Fig* **to p. sth to pieces** démolir qch; *Fam Fig* **to p. sb's leg** faire marcher qn
  (**b**) (*attract*) attirer
  (**c**) (*extract*) (*cork*) retirer, enlever; (*tooth*) arracher; **to p. a gun on sb** braquer un pistolet sur qn; *Fam Fig* **it's like pulling teeth** il faut t'/lui/*etc.* arracher les vers du nez
  (**d**) (*idioms*) **to p. a face** faire la grimace; *Fam* **to p. a bank job** se faire une banque; *Fam* **to p. a fast one on sb** rouler qn
  3 *vi* tirer (**on** sur); **to p. clear of sth** s'éloigner de qch
▶**pull ahead** *vi* (*in race, election*) prendre la tête (**of** de)
▶**pull apart** *vt sep* (*break up*) séparer; *Fig* (*criticize*) massacrer
▶**pull away** *vi* (*of car, train*) partir; (*from embrace*) s'écarter
▶**pull back 1** *vt sep* (*curtains*) ouvrir
  2 *vi* (*of person*) se retirer
▶**pull down** *vt sep* (*demolish*) démolir
▶**pull in 1** *vt sep* (**a**) (*rope, fishing line*) ramener (**b**) (*money*) gagner; (*of deal*) rapporter; **to p. sb in for questioning** arrêter qn pour l'interroger (**c**) (*attract*) attirer
  2 *vi* (*of car*) s'arrêter; (*of train, bus*) arriver
▶**pull off** *vt sep* (**a**) (*clothes*) retirer (**b**) (*task, deal*) réaliser; (*bank raid, burglary*) réussir; **to p. it off** réussir
▶**pull on** *vt sep* (*clothes*) enfiler, mettre
▶**pull out 1** *vt sep* (*tooth*) arracher; *Fam Fig* **to p. out all the stops** faire tout son possible
  2 *vi* (**a**) (*of car*) déboîter; (*of train*) partir (**b**) (*from race, agreement, deal*) se retirer (**of** de)
▶**pull over** *vi* (*of driver*) s'arrêter
▶**pull through** *vi* (*recover*) s'en sortir
▶**pull together** *vt sep* **to p. oneself together** se ressaisir
▶**pull up** *vi* (*of car*) s'arrêter
pull-by date [ˈpʊlbaɪdeɪt] *n* date *f* limite de vente
pull-down menu [ˈpʊldaʊnˈmenjuː] *n Comput* menu *m* déroulant
pullet [ˈpʊlɪt] *n* poulette *f*
pulley [ˈpʊlɪ] (*pl* **pulleys**) *n* poulie *f*
pull-out [ˈpʊlaʊt] *n* (*in newspaper, magazine*) supplément *m* détachable
pullover [ˈpʊləʊvə(r)] *n* pull-over *m*
pull-up [ˈpʊlʌp] *n* (*exercise*) traction *f*; **to do pull-ups** faire des tractions
pulmonary [ˈpʌlmənərɪ] *adj* pulmonaire
pulp [pʌlp] **1** *n* (*of fruit*) pulpe *f*; **to reduce sth to (a) p.** écraser qch; *Fam* **to beat sb to a p.** mettre qn en bouillie; **p. fiction** romans *mpl* de gare
  2 *vt* écraser
pulpit [ˈpʊlpɪt] *n* chaire *f*
pulsate [pʌlˈseɪt] *vi* (*of vein*) palpiter; (*of room, music*) vibrer; (*of heart*) battre
pulse¹ [pʌls] *n* (*of blood*) pouls *m*; (*of light, sound*) vibration *f*; **to feel** *or* **take sb's p.** prendre le pouls de qn
pulse² [pʌls] *n* (*seed*) légumineuse *f*
pulverize [ˈpʌlvəraɪz] *vt* pulvériser; *Fam Fig* (*beat up*) démolir; (*defeat heavily*) pulvériser
puma [ˈpjuːmə] *n* puma *m*
pumice [ˈpʌmɪs] *n* **p. (stone)** pierre *f* ponce
pummel [ˈpʌməl] *vt* marteler

pump¹ [pʌmp] *n (flat shoe)* escarpin *m*; *(ballet shoe)* ballerine *f*

pump² [pʌmp] **1** *n (machine)* pompe *f*

2 *vt* pomper; **to p. sb's stomach** faire un lavage d'estomac à qn; *Fig* **to p. money into sth** injecter des capitaux dans qch; *Fam* **to p. sb for information** tirer les vers du nez à qn; **to p. sb's hand** *(shake vigorously)* donner une poignée de main vigoureuse à qn; *Fam* **to p. iron** *(do weightlifting)* faire de la gonflette

3 *vi (of heart)* battre; *(of machine)* pomper

▶**pump out** *vt sep* pomper

▶**pump up** *vt sep* gonfler

pumpkin ['pʌmpkɪn] *n* potiron *m*, citrouille *f*; **p. pie** tarte *f* au potiron

pun [pʌn] *n* jeu *m* de mots

punch¹ [pʌntʃ] **1** *n (tool)* poinçon *m*; *(for tickets)* poinçonneuse *f*

2 *vt (metal)* percer; *(ticket)* poinçonner

punch² [pʌntʃ] **1** *n* (a) *(blow)* coup *m* (de poing); *Fig* **she didn't pull her punches** elle n'y est pas allée de main morte (b) *(energy)* punch *m*; **p. line** *(of joke, story)* chute *f*

2 *vt (hit)* donner un coup de poing à; **to p. sb in the face/on the nose** donner un coup de poing à qn dans la figure/dans le nez

punch³ [pʌntʃ] *n (drink)* punch *m*; **p. bowl** coupe *f* à punch

Punch and Judy show ['pʌntʃən'dʒuːdɪ'ʃəʊ] *n* ≃ spectacle *m* de Guignol

punch-drunk ['pʌntʃdrʌŋk] *adj* assommé(e)

punching bag ['pʌntʃɪŋbæg] *n* sac *m* de sable

punching ball ['pʌntʃɪŋbɔːl] *n* punching-ball *m*

punchy ['pʌntʃɪ] *adj Fam* plein(e) de punch

punctilious [pʌŋk'tɪlɪəs] *adj* pointilleux(euse)

punctual ['pʌŋktjʊəl] *adj* ponctuel(elle)

punctuality [pʌŋktjʊ'ælɪtɪ] *n* ponctualité *f*

punctually ['pʌŋktjʊəlɪ] *adv* à l'heure

punctuate ['pʌŋktjʊeɪt] *vt* ponctuer (**with** de)

punctuation [pʌŋktjʊ'eɪʃən] *n* ponctuation *f*; **p. mark** signe *m* de ponctuation

puncture ['pʌŋktʃə(r)] **1** *n (in tire)* crevaison *f*; *(in skin, metal)* perforation *f*; **to have a p.** *(of cyclist, driver)* crever; *(of bicycle, car)* avoir un pneu crevé

2 *vt (tire)* crever; *(metal, lung)* perforer; *(blister, abscess)* percer

pundit ['pʌndɪt] *n* expert(e) *m,f*

pungent ['pʌndʒənt] *adj (smell, taste)* âcre; *(style, wit)* mordant(e)

punish ['pʌnɪʃ] *vt* punir; **to p. sb for doing sth** punir qn pour avoir fait qch

punishment ['pʌnɪʃmənt] *n* punition *f*; *Law* peine *f*; **to make the p. fit the crime** adapter la punition à la faute; **to take a lot of p.** être mis(e) à rude épreuve

punitive ['pjuːnɪtɪv] *adj* punitif(ive)

punk [pʌŋk] *n* (a) punk *mf*; **p. (rock)** punk *m* (b) *very Fam (worthless person)* vaurien(enne) *m,f*; *(hoodlum)* voyou *m*

punt [pʌnt] **1** *n (boat)* barque *f* à fond plat

2 *vi* **to go punting** faire de la barque

puny ['pjuːnɪ] *adj* chétif(ive)

pup [pʌp] *n (of dog)* chiot *m*; *(of seal)* bébé-phoque *m*

pupil¹ ['pjuːpəl] *n (student)* élève *mf*

pupil² ['pjuːpəl] *n (of eye)* pupille *f*

puppet ['pʌpɪt] *n also Fig* marionnette *f*; *Fig* **p. government** gouvernement *m* fantoche; **p. show** (spectacle *m* de) marionnettes *fpl*

puppy ['pʌpɪ] *(pl* **puppies***) n* chiot *m*; **p. fat** rondeurs *fpl* préadolescentes; **p. love** amour *m* d'adolescence

purchase ['pɜːtʃɪs] **1** *n* (a) *(action, thing bought)* achat *m*; **p. price** prix *m* d'achat (b) *(grip)* prise *f*; **to get a p. on sth** trouver une prise sur qch

2 *vt* acheter

purchaser ['pɜːtʃəsə(r)] *n* acheteur(euse) *m,f*

purchasing ['pɜːtʃəsɪŋ] *n* **p. manager** directeur(trice) *m,f* des achats; **p. power** pouvoir *m* d'achat

pure [pjʊə(r)] *adj* pur(e); **by p. chance** par pur hasard; **p. mathematics** mathématiques *fpl* pures

purebred ['pjʊəbred] *adj (dog)* de race pure; *(horse)* pur-sang *inv*

purée ['pjʊəreɪ] **1** *n* purée *f*

2 *vt* réduire en purée

purely ['pjʊəlɪ] *adv* purement; **p. and simply** purement et simplement

purgatory ['pɜːgətərɪ] *n Rel* purgatoire *m*; *Fig* enfer *m*

purge [pɜːdʒ] **1** *n* purge *f*

2 *vt* purger

purification [pjʊərɪfɪ'keɪʃən] *n* purification *f*

purify ['pjʊərɪfaɪ] *(pt & pp* **purified***) vt* purifier

purist ['pjʊərɪst] *n* puriste *mf*

puritan ['pjʊərɪtən] *n* puritain(e) *m,f*

puritanical [pjʊərɪ'tænɪkəl] *adj* puritain(e)

purity ['pjʊərɪtɪ] *n* pureté *f*

purl [pɜːl] **1** *n* maille *f* à l'envers

2 *vt* tricoter à l'envers

purloin [pɜː'lɔɪn] *vt Formal or Hum* dérober

purple ['pɜːpəl] **1** *n* violet *m*

2 *adj* violet(ette); **to turn** *or* **to go p.** *(of person)* devenir cramoisi(e); **pages of p. prose** des pages d'un style ampoulé

purport *Formal* **1** ['pɜːpɔːt] *n* teneur *f*

2 *vt* [pɜː'pɔːt] **to p. to be sth** prétendre être qch

purpose ['pɜːpəs] *n* (a) *(object, aim)* but *m*, objectif *m*; **on p.** exprès; **what is the p. of your visit?** quel est l'objet de votre visite?; **to have a sense of p.** savoir ce que l'on veut; **to be to no p.** ne servir à rien (b) *(use)* utilité *f*; **to serve a p.** servir à quelque chose; **to serve no p.** ne servir à rien; **to serve sb's purpose(s)** faire l'affaire de qn; **for all practical purposes** à toutes fins utiles; **for the purposes of** pour les besoins de

purpose-built ['pɜːpəs'bɪlt] *adj* spécialement construit(e)

purposeful ['pɜːpəsfʊl] *adj* résolu(e)

purposely ['pɜːpəslɪ] *adv* délibérément; **to be p. rude** faire exprès d'être grossier(ère)

purr [pɜː(r)] **1** *n* ronron *m*, ronronnement *m*

2 *vi* ronronner

purse [pɜːs] **1** *n (handbag)* sac *m* à main; *(wallet)* porte-monnaie *m inv*; *Fig* **to hold the p. strings** tenir les cordons de la bourse

2 *vt* **to p. one's lips** pincer les lèvres

pursue [pə'sjuː] *vt* poursuivre; *(pleasure, happiness)* rechercher; *(profession)* exercer

pursuer [pə'sjuːə(r)] *n* poursuivant(e) *m,f*

pursuit [pə'sjuːt] *n* (a) *(of person, animal)* poursuite *f*; *(of pleasure, knowledge, happiness)* quête *f*; **to be in p. of** être à la poursuite de; **in hot p.** à ses trousses (b) *(activity)* activité *f*

purveyor [pə'veɪə(r)] *n Formal* fournisseur(euse) *m,f*

pus [pʌs] *n* pus *m*

push [pʊʃ] **1** *n* (a) *(act of pushing)* poussée *f*; **to give sb/sth a p.** pousser qn/qch; **at a p.** à la rigueur; **when p. comes to shove, if it comes to the p.** dans le pire des cas (b) *Mil (attack)* poussée *f*; **sales p.** campagne *f* de vente; **to make a p. for sth** lutter pour qch

2 *vt* (a) *(in general)* pousser; *(button)* appuyer sur; **to p. the door shut/open** fermer/ouvrir la porte; **p. (sign)** poussez; **to p. sb out of the way** écarter qn; **to p. one's way through the crowd** se frayer un chemin à travers la foule; *Fig* **don't p. yourself too hard** ne force pas trop; *Fig* **to p. sb into doing sth** pousser qn à faire qch; **to p. one's luck** y aller un peu fort; **to be pushed for time** être très pressé(e)

(b) *(promote)* faire la promotion de; *(theory)* promouvoir

(c) *Fam (drugs)* vendre

(d) *Fam* **to be pushing sixty** approcher de la soixantaine

3 *vi (in general)* pousser; *(move forward)* avancer; **to p. past sb** passer devant qn en le bousculant; **to p. forward** pousser en avant

▸**push about, push around** *vt sep Fam Fig (bully)* **to p. sb about** faire de qn ce que l'on veut

▸**push ahead** *vi* continuer; **to p. ahead with sth** continuer qch

▸**push aside** *vt sep also Fig* écarter

▸**push in** *vi (in line)* resquiller

▸**push on** *vi (continue)* continuer; **to p. on with sth** continuer qch

▸**push over** *vt sep* faire tomber

▸**push through** *vt sep (reform, law)* faire passer

push-button ['pʊʃˌbʌtən] *adj* à touches

pusher ['pʊʃə(r)] *n Fam* **(drug) p.** dealer *m*

pushover ['pʊʃəʊvə(r)] *n Fam* **it's a p.** c'est un jeu d'enfant; **she's no p.** elle ne se laisse pas avoir facilement

push-up ['pʊʃʌp] *n (exercise)* pompe *f*

pushy ['pʊʃɪ] *adj Fam* batailleur(euse)

puss [pʊs] *n Fam (cat)* minou *m*

pussy ['pʊsɪ] (*pl* **pussies**) *n* **(a)** *Fam* **p. (cat)** minou *m*; **p. willow** saule *m* blanc **(b)** *Vulg (vagina)* chatte *f*; *(women)* nanas *fpl*, meufs *fpl*

pussyfoot ['pʊsɪfʊt] *vi Fam* **to p. (around** or **about)** tourner autour du pot; *(in one's actions)* toujours remettre les choses à plus tard

pustule ['pʌstjuːl] *n* pustule *f*

put [pʊt] (*pt & pp* **put**) **1** *vt* **(a)** *(place)* mettre; *(on flat surface)* poser; **to p. one's arms around sb** prendre qn dans ses bras; **to p. a man on the moon** envoyer un homme sur la lune; **to p. a limit on sth** mettre une limite à qch; *Fam* **p. it there!** *(shake hands)* tope là!; *Fig* **to p. oneself in sb's hands** s'en remettre à qn; *Fig* **to p. sb in his place** remettre qn à sa place; *Fig* **p. yourself in my position** mets-toi à ma place; **to p. a matter right** mettre les choses au point; **to p. money on a horse** parier sur un cheval; **to p. a lot of work into sth** beaucoup travailler à qch; **to p. a stop to sth** mettre fin à qch; **to p. a child to bed** mettre un enfant au lit; **to p. sb to the test** mettre qn à l'épreuve; *Fam Fig* **I didn't know where to p. myself** je ne savais pas où me mettre

(b) *(present)* **to p. a question to sb** poser une question à qn; **to p. a proposal to sb** soumettre une proposition à qn; **I p. it to you that...** *(in court)* n'est-il pas vrai que...?

(c) *(express)* **to p. sth well** bien tourner qch; **I couldn't have put it better myself** je n'aurais pas mieux dit; **to p. it bluntly** pour parler franchement; **how shall I p. it...?** comment dire...?

(d) *(estimate)* estimer (**at** à); **I would p. her age at forty** je dirais qu'elle a quarante ans

2 *vi* **to p. to sea** prendre la mer

▸**put about** *vt sep (rumor)* faire courir; **to p. it about that...** faire courir le bruit que...

▸**put across** *vt sep (message, idea)* faire comprendre (**to** à); **to p. oneself across well/badly** *(at interview)* se mettre/ne pas se mettre en valeur

▸**put aside** *vt sep* **(a)** *(goods, money)* mettre de côté **(b)** *(problem, fact)* laisser de côté

▸**put away** *vt sep* **(a)** *(tidy away)* ranger **(b)** *Fam (prisoner)* enfermer **(c)** *Fam (eat, drink)* s'enfiler, ingurgiter

▸**put back** *vt sep* **(a)** *(replace)* remettre **(b)** *(postpone)* reporter; *(clock, schedule)* retarder; *Fig* **that puts the clock back ten years** cela nous ramène dix ans en arrière

▸**put by** *vt sep (save)* mettre de côté

▸**put down** *vt sep* **(a)** *(set down)* poser; **I couldn't p. it down** *(book)* je ne pouvais pas m'arrêter de (le) lire **(b)** *(revolt, opposition)* réprimer **(c)** *(write)* écrire, mettre par écrit; **to p. sth down in writing** mettre qch par écrit; **to p. one's name down for sth** s'inscrire à qch **(d)** *(attribute)* **to p. sth down to sb/sth** attribuer qch à qn/qch **(e)** *(animal)* piquer; **to have a cat/dog put down** faire piquer un chat/un chien **(f)** *(criticize)* rabaisser; **to p. oneself down** se rabaisser

▸**put forward** *vt sep* **(a)** *(plan, theory, candidate)* proposer; *(proposal)* faire **(b)** *(clock, time of meeting)* avancer

▸**put in 1** *vt sep* **(a)** *(install)* installer **(b)** *(claim, application)* soumettre; **to p. in a (good) word for sb** dire un mot en faveur de qn **(c)** *(time)* passer; **they've p. in a lot of work** ils ont énormément travaillé

2 *vi (of ship)* faire escale

▸**put off** *vt sep* **(a)** *(postpone)* remettre à plus tard; **to p. off doing sth** retarder le moment de faire qch **(b)** *(cause to dislike)* **to p. sb off sth** dégoûter qn de qch **(c)** *(disturb)* gêner **(d)** *(discourage)* **to p. sb off doing sth** enlever à qn l'envie de faire qch **(e)** *(make wait)* faire patienter

▸**put on** *vt sep* **(a)** *(clothes)* mettre; **to p. on one's make-up** se maquiller; **to p. on an act** jouer la comédie; **to p. on an accent** prendre un accent; *Fam* **she's just putting it on!** elle fait semblant; **to p. on weight** grossir, prendre du poids **(b)** *(light, TV, heating)* allumer; *(music, video)* mettre; **to p. the kettle on** mettre l'eau à chauffer **(c)** *(play, show)* monter **(d)** *(tease)* faire monter

▸**put out 1** *vt sep* **(a)** *(fire, light)* éteindre **(b)** *(place outside)* mettre dehors **(c)** *(extend)* **to p. out one's hand** tendre la main **(d)** *(arrange for use)* sortir **(e)** *(report, statement)* publier **(f)** *(annoy)* **to be put out** être contrarié(e) **(g)** *(inconvenience)* déranger; **to p. oneself out (for sb)** se donner du mal (pour qn) **(h)** *(dislocate)* **to p. one's shoulder/knee out** se démettre l'épaule/le genou

2 *vi Fam* accepter de coucher; **she'd p. out for anybody** elle coucherait avec le premier venu

▸**put through** *vt sep* **(a)** *(on phone)* **to p. sb through to sb** passer qn à qn; **hold on, I'll p. you through** ne quittez pas, je vous le/la passe **(b)** *(subject to)* **to p. sb through sth** faire subir qch à qn; **to p. sb through hell** faire souffrir le martyre à qn

▸**put together** *vt sep (assemble)* assembler; *(file, report)* préparer; *(meal, team)* composer; **she's more intelligent than the rest of them put together** elle est cent fois plus intelligente qu'eux; *Fig* **to p. two and two together** tirer ses conclusions

▸**put up** *vt sep* **(a)** *(tent, fence)* monter; *(ladder)* dresser; *(building)* construire; *(statue)* ériger; *(notice)* afficher; *(painting)* accrocher; *(umbrella)* ouvrir; **to p. up one's hand** lever la main; **to p. one's hair up** relever ses cheveux **(b)** *(provide accommodation for)* loger, héberger **(c)** *(provide) (money)* verser, fournir; *(candidate)* présenter; **to p. sth up for sale** mettre qch en vente; **to p. up a fight** or **a struggle** se défendre

▸**put upon** *vt insep* **to feel p. upon** se sentir exploité(e)

▸**put up to** *vt sep* **to p. sb up to doing sth** pousser qn à faire qch; **he put me up to it** c'est lui qui m'a poussé à le faire

▸**put up with** *vt insep* supporter

putative ['pjuːtətɪv] *adj Formal* putatif(ive)

put-down ['pʊtdaʊn] *n Fam* remarque *f* humiliante

putrefy ['pjuːtrɪfaɪ] (*pt & pp* **putrefied**) *vi* se putréfier

putrid ['pjuːtrɪd] *adj* putride

putsch [pʊtʃ] *n* putsch *m*

putt [pʌt] **1** *n (in golf)* putt *m*

2 *vi (in golf)* putter

putter ['pʌtə(r)] *n (golf club)* putter *m*

▸**putter about, putter around** *vi (do odd jobs)* bricoler; *(spend time leisurely)* traîner

putty ['pʌtɪ] *n* mastic *m*; *Fig* **he's p. in her hands** elle en fait ce qu'elle veut

put-up job ['pʊtʌp'dʒɒb] *n Fam* coup *m* monté

puzzle ['pʌzl] **1** n (**a**) (game) casse-tête m; (mental) devinette f; (jigsaw) puzzle m; **p. book** livre m de devinettes et de jeux (**b**) (mystery) énigme f

2 vt (person) rendre perplexe

▸**puzzle out** vt sep (solution, meaning) trouver; (action, motive) essayer de comprendre

▸**puzzle over** vt insep essayer de comprendre

puzzled ['pʌzld] adj perplexe

puzzling ['pʌzlɪŋ] adj bizarre

PVC [piːviːˈsiː] n (abbr **polyvinyl chloride**) PVC m

pygmy ['pɪgmɪ] (pl **pygmies**) n pygmée m

pylon ['paɪlən] n pylône m

pyramid ['pɪrəmɪd] n pyramide f; Com **p. scheme** plan m commercial en cascade

pyre ['paɪə(r)] n bûcher m (funéraire)

Pyrenean [pɪrəˈnɪən] adj pyrénéen(enne)

Pyrenees [pɪrəˈniːz] npl the P. les Pyrénées fpl

Pyrex® ['paɪreks] n pyrex® m; **P. dish** plat m en pyrex®

pyromaniac [paɪrəʊˈmeɪnɪæk] n pyromane mf

pyrotechnics [paɪrəʊˈtekniks] **1** n (science) pyrotechnie f

2 npl (fireworks display) feu m d'artifice; Fig (in speech, writing) prouesses fpl

python ['paɪθən] n python m

Q

Q, q [kjuː] *n (letter)* Q, q *m inv*

Qatar [kæˈtɑː(r)] *n* le Qatar

QED [kjuːiːˈdiː] *(abbr **quod erat demonstrandum**)* CQFD

Q-tip® [ˈkjuːtɪp] *n* coton-tige® *m*

qty *Com (abbr **quantity**)* qté

quack¹ [kwæk] **1** *n (of duck)* coin-coin *m*
2 *vi (of duck)* faire coin-coin

quack² [kwæk] *n (doctor) Pej* charlatan *m*; *Hum* toubib *m*

quad [kwɒd] *n* (**a**) *Fam (abbr **quadrangle**) (of school, college)* cour *f* (**b**) *Fam (abbr **quadruplet**)* quadruplé(e) *m,f* (**c**) q. **bike** quad *m*; **to go q. biking** faire du quad

quadrangle [ˈkwɒdræŋgəl] *n* (**a**) *(shape)* quadrilatère *m* (**b**) *(of school, college)* cour *f*

quadrant [ˈkwɒdrənt] *n* quart *m* de cercle

quadraphonic [kwɒdrəˈfɒnɪk] *adj* quadriphonique

quadratic equation [kwɒˈdrætɪkɪˈkweɪʒən] *n Math* équation *f* du second degré

quadrilateral [kwɒdrɪˈlætərəl] **1** *n* quadrilatère *m*
2 *adj* quadrilatéral(e)

quadriplegic [kwɒdrɪˈpliːdʒɪk] *n & adj* tétraplégique *mf*

quadruped [ˈkwɒdrʊped] *n* quadrupède *m*

quadruple [kwɒˈdrʊpəl] **1** *adj* quadruple
2 *vt & vi* quadrupler

quadruplet [ˈkwɒdrʊplet] *n* quadruplé(e) *m,f*

quaff [kwɒf] *vt Lit* boire

quagmire [ˈkwægmaɪə(r)] *n also Fig* bourbier *m*

quail¹ [kweɪl] *(pl* **quail)** *n (bird)* caille *f*

quail² [kweɪl] *vi (of person)* avoir un mouvement de recul

quaint [kweɪnt] *adj (picturesque)* pittoresque; *(old-fashioned)* vieillot(otte)

quake [kweɪk] **1** *n Fam (earthquake)* tremblement *m* de terre
2 *vi* trembler; **to q. in one's boots** trembler de peur

Quaker [ˈkweɪkə(r)] *n Rel* quaker(eresse) *m,f*

qualification [kwɒlɪfɪˈkeɪʃən] *n* (**a**) *(diploma)* diplôme *m*; *(skill)* compétence *f* (**b**) *(completion of studies)* **on/after q.** une fois le diplôme obtenu (**c**) *(modification)* précision *f* (**d**) *(for competition)* qualification *f*

qualified [ˈkwɒlɪfaɪd] *adj* (**a**) *(having diploma)* diplômé(e); *(competent)* compétent(e); **to be q. to do sth** *(have diploma)* avoir les diplômes requis pour faire qch; *(be competent)* avoir les compétences requises pour faire qch (**b**) *(modified)* mitigé(e); **a q. success** un demi-succès

qualifier [ˈkwɒlɪfaɪə(r)] *n* (**a**) *(person, team)* qualifié(e) *m,f*; *(match)* match *m* de qualification (**b**) *Gram* qualificatif *m*

qualify [ˈkwɒlɪfaɪ] *(pt & pp* **qualified)** **1** *vt* (**a**) *(make competent)* **to q. sb to do sth** donner les compétences nécessaires à qn pour faire qch (**b**) *(modify)* nuancer
2 *vi* (**a**) *(in competition)* se qualifier; **to q. as a doctor/teacher** obtenir son diplôme de médecin/professeur (**b**) *(be eligible)* **to q. for sth** avoir droit à qch

qualifying [ˈkwɒlɪfaɪɪŋ] *adj* (**a**) *(round, match)* éliminatoire (**b**) *(exam)* d'entrée

qualitative [ˈkwɒlɪtətɪv] *adj* qualitatif(ive)

quality [ˈkwɒlɪtɪ] *(pl* **qualities)** *n* qualité *f*; **of good/poor q.** de bonne/mauvaise qualité; **q. of life** qualité de la vie; **q. circle** cercle *m* de qualité; **q. control** contrôle *m* (de) qualité; **q. goods** marchandises *fpl* de qualité; **she wants to spend more q. time with her children** elle veut passer davantage de temps avec ses enfants

qualm [kwɑːm] *n* doute *m*; **to have no qualms about doing sth** ne pas hésiter une seconde avant de faire qch; *(scruples)* n'avoir aucun scrupule à faire qch

quandary [ˈkwɒndərɪ] *(pl* **quandaries)** *n* dilemme *m*; **to be in a q. (about sth)** être face à un dilemme (à propos de qch)

quantifier [ˈkwɒntɪfaɪə(r)] *n Math* quantificateur *m*

quantify [ˈkwɒntɪfaɪ] *(pt & pp* **quantified)** *vt* évaluer

quantitative [ˈkwɒntɪtətɪv] *adj* quantitatif(ive)

quantity [ˈkwɒntɪtɪ] *(pl* **quantities)** *n* quantité *f*; **q. surveyor** métreur vérificateur *m*

quantum [ˈkwɒntəm] *n Phys* quantum *m*; *Fig* **q. leap** bond *m* en avant; **q. mechanics** mécanique *f* quantique; **q. theory** théorie *f* des quanta

quarantine [ˈkwɒrəntiːn] **1** *n* quarantaine *f*; **to be in q.** être en quarantaine
2 *vt* mettre en quarantaine

quark [kwɑːk] *n Phys* quark *m*

quarrel [ˈkwɒrəl] **1** *n* (**a**) *(argument)* dispute *f*, querelle *f*; **to have a q.** se disputer; **to pick a q. with sb** chercher querelle à qn (**b**) *(disagreement)* désaccord *m*; **to have no q. with sb** n'avoir rien à reprocher à qn
2 *vi* (**a**) *(argue)* se disputer (**with** avec) (**b**) *(disagree)* **to q. with sth** ne pas être d'accord avec qch

quarreling [ˈkwɒrəlɪŋ] *n* disputes *fpl*

quarrelsome [ˈkwɒrəlsəm] *adj* querelleur(euse)

quarry¹ [ˈkwɒrɪ] *(pl* **quarries)** *n (prey) & Fig* proie *f*

quarry² [ˈkwɒrɪ] **1** *n (pl* **quarries)** *(for stone)* carrière *f*
2 *vt (pt & pp* **quarried)** *(hill)* exploiter; *(stone)* extraire

quart [kwɔːt] *n (liquid measurement)* = 0,946 l

quarter [ˈkwɔːtə(r)] **1** *n* (**a**) *(fraction)* quart *m*; *(of orange, moon)* quartier *m*; **a q. of a century** un quart de siècle; **a q. of an hour** un quart d'heure; **a q. (of a pound)** = 113,4 g, un quart de livre; **three quarters** trois quarts; **three and a q.** trois un quart; **three and a q. liters** trois litres un quart; **a q. full** au quart plein(e)
(**b**) *(in telling time)* **a q. to** *or* **of six** six heures moins le quart; **it's a q. to** il est moins le quart; **a q. past** *or* **after six** six heures un *ou* et quart; **it's a q. past** il est le quart
(**c**) *(three-month period)* trimestre *m*
(**d**) *(area)* quartier *m*
(**e**) *(group)* milieu *m*; **help came from an unexpected q.** nous avons reçu une aide inespérée
(**f**) *Mil* **quarters** *(lodgings)* quartiers *mpl*
(**g**) *(coin)* pièce *f* de 25 cents
2 *vt* (**a**) *(divide into four)* partager en quatre (**b**) *Mil (troops)* loger

quarterback ['kwɔːtəbæk] *n* quarterback *m*, *Can* quart-arrière *m*

quarterdeck ['kwɔːtədek] *n (of ship)* plage *f* arrière

quarterfinal [kwɔːtə'faɪnəl] *n* quart *m* de finale

quarterly ['kwɔːtəlɪ] **1** *n (pl* **quarterlies**) publication *f* trimestrielle
   2 *adj* trimestriel(elle)
   3 *adv* tous les trimestres

quartermaster ['kwɔːtəmɑːstə(r)] *n Mil* intendant *m*

quarter-pounder [kwɔːtə'paʊndə(r)] *n* gros hamburger *m*

quartet [kwɔː'tet] *n* quatuor *m*

quarto ['kwɔːtəʊ] *(pl* **quartos**) *n* in-quarto *m*

quartz [kwɔːts] *n* quartz *m*; **q. watch** montre *f* à quartz

quasar ['kweɪzɑː(r)] *n Astron* quasar *m*

quash [kwɒʃ] *vt (objection, plan)* rejeter; *(revolt, feeling)* réprimer; *Law (sentence)* annuler

quaver ['kweɪvə(r)] **1** *n* **(a)** *Mus* croche *f* **(b)** *(in voice)* tremblement *m*
   2 *vi (of voice)* trembler

quay [kiː] *n* quai *m*

quayside ['kiːsaɪd] *n* quai *m*

queasy ['kwiːzɪ] *adj* **to feel q.** avoir mal au cœur

Quebec [kwɪ'bek] *n* le Québec; **Q. City** Québec

queen [kwiːn] *n* **(a)** *(of country, in cards, chess)* reine *f*; *Fam Fig* **she's the q. bee around here** c'est elle la patronne ici; **the Q.'s English** l'anglais *m* correct; **the Q. Mother** la reine mère **(b)** *very Fam (homosexual)* tante *f*, folle *f*, = terme injurieux désignant un homosexuel

queen-size ['kwiːnsaɪz], **queen-sized** ['kwiːnsaɪzd] *adj* **q. bed** grand lit *m* double

queer ['kwɪə(r)] **1** *adj* **(a)** *(strange)* bizarre **(b)** *very Fam (homosexual)* homo, pédé
   2 *n very Fam (male homosexual)* homo *m*, pédé *m*, = terme injurieux désignant un homosexuel

quell [kwel] *vt (revolt)* réprimer; *(doubt, worry)* dissiper

quench [kwentʃ] *vt (thirst)* étancher

querulous ['kwerʊləs] *adj (person)* grincheux(euse); *(tone)* maussade, plaintif(ive)

query ['kwiːərɪ] **1** *n (pl* **queries**) question *f*
   2 *vt (pt & pp* **queried**) mettre en question; **to q. if** *or* **whether...** mettre en question le fait que...

quest [kwest] *Lit* **1** *n* quête *f*, poursuite *f* (**for** de); **to go** *or* **to be in q. of sth** être en quête *ou* à la poursuite de qch
   2 *vi* **to q. after** *or* **for sth** être en quête *ou* à la poursuite de qch

question ['kwestʃən] **1** *n* **(a)** *(query)* question *f*; **to ask (sb) a q.** poser une question (à qn); **q. mark** point *m* d'interrogation; *Fig* **a q. mark hangs over the future of the project** l'avenir du projet reste en suspens
   (b) *(doubt)* doute *m*; **to call sth into q.** mettre qch en doute; **beyond q.** indiscutable; **it's open to q. whether...** reste à savoir si...; **without q.** indiscutablement
   (c) *(matter)* question *f*, problème *m*; **it is a q. of...** il s'agit de...; **there is no q. of our agreeing to that** il n'est pas question que nous acceptions cela; **to be out of the q.** être hors de question; **it's only a q. of time** ce n'est qu'une question de temps; **the matter/person in q.** l'affaire/la personne en question
   2 *vt* **(a)** *(put questions to)* interroger (**on** sur)
   (b) *(cast doubt on)* mettre en doute

questionable ['kwestʃənəbəl] *adj* discutable

questioning ['kwestʃənɪŋ] **1** *n (interrogation)* interrogation *f*; **to be held for q.** *(by police)* être interrogé(e)
   2 *adj (look)* interrogateur(trice); *(mind)* curieux(euse)

questionnaire [kwestʃə'neə(r)] *n* questionnaire *m*

queue [kjuː] **1** *n* queue *f*, file *f* (d'attente); **to jump the q.** resquiller
   2 *vi* faire la queue

quibble ['kwɪbəl] **1** *n* petite question *f*
   2 *vi* chipoter (**about** *or* **over** à propos de)

quiche [kiːʃ] *n* quiche *f*

quick [kwɪk] **1** *adj* **(a)** *(rapid)* rapide; **to take a q. bath/drink** prendre un bain/un verre en vitesse; **to be q.** *(hurry)* faire vite; **that was q.!** tu as fait vite!; **as q. as a flash** *or* **a wink** rapide comme l'éclair; **to be q. to do sth** faire qch vite *ou* rapidement; **to be q. off the mark** *(to act)* réagir vite; *(to understand)* avoir l'esprit vif; **to have a q. temper** s'emporter facilement **(b)** *(clever)* vif (vive)
   2 *adv Fam (run, take, think)* vite
   3 *n* **to bite one's nails to the q.** se ronger les ongles jusqu'au sang; *Fig* **to cut sb to the q.** piquer qn au vif

quicken ['kwɪkən] **1** *vt* **(a)** *(make faster)* accélérer; **to q. one's pace** presser le pas **(b)** *(imagination)* stimuler; *(interest)* éveiller, exciter
   2 *vi (of pace, pulse)* s'accélérer

quickfire ['kwɪkfaɪə(r)] *adj* rapide

quickie ['kwɪkɪ] *Fam* **1** *n* **to have a q.** *(drink)* prendre un verre en vitesse; *(sex)* faire l'amour en vitesse
   2 *adj* **q. divorce** divorce *m* rapide

quicklime ['kwɪklaɪm] *n* chaux *f* vive

quickly ['kwɪklɪ] *adv* vite, rapidement

quickness ['kwɪknɪs] *n (speed)* rapidité *f*; *(of mind)* vivacité *f*

quicksand ['kwɪksænd] *n* sables *mpl* mouvants

quicksilver ['kwɪksɪlvə(r)] *n Old-fashioned (mercury)* vif-argent *m*

quick-tempered ['kwɪk'tempəd] *adj* emporté(e)

quick-witted ['kwɪk'wɪtɪd] *adj* vif (vive)

quiescent [kwaɪ'esənt] *adj Formal* passif(ive)

quiet ['kwaɪət] **1** *n* silence *m*; *Fam* **to do sth on the q.** faire qch en douce
   2 *adj* **(a)** *(not loud)* silencieux(euse); *(voice)* petit(e); *(music)* doux (douce); **to keep sb q.** faire tenir qn tranquille; **to keep q.** *(make no noise)* ne pas faire de bruit; *(say nothing)* se taire; **to keep q. about sth** ne rien dire au sujet de qch; **to keep sth q.** cacher qch; **be q.!** tais-toi!; **as q. as a mouse** *(person)* silencieux **(b)** *(discreet)* discret(ète); **to have a q. laugh at sb/sth** se moquer discrètement de qn/qch **(c)** *(peaceful)* tranquille; **a q. wedding** un mariage célébré dans l'intimité **(d)** *(business, market)* calme

▸**quiet down 1** *vt sep* calmer
   2 *vi* se calmer

quietly ['kwaɪətlɪ] *adv* **(a)** *(silently)* tranquillement, silencieusement **(b)** *(discreetly)* discrètement; **to be q. confident** être optimiste sans excès

quietness ['kwaɪətnɪs] *n (of person, place)* tranquillité *f*; *(of manner)* douceur *f*

quill [kwɪl] *n (feather)* penne *f*; *(pen)* plume *f* d'oie; *(of porcupine)* piquant *m*

quilt [kwɪlt] **1** *n* édredon *m*; *(duvet)* couette *f*
   2 *vt (garment)* matelasser; **quilted jacket** blouson *m* matelassé

quince [kwɪns] *n* coing *m*; **q. jelly** gelée *f* de coing

quinine [kwɪ'niːn] *n* quinine *f*

quintessential [kwɪntɪ'senʃəl] *adj Formal* quintessentiel(elle)

quintessentially [kwɪntɪ'senʃəlɪ] *adv Formal* fondamentalement

quintet [kwɪn'tet] *n* quintette *m*

quintuplet [kwɪn'tʊplɪt] *n* quintuplé(e) *m,f*

quip [kwɪp] **1** *n* boutade *f*
   2 *vi (pt & pp* **quipped**) plaisanter

quirk [kwɜːk] *n* **(a)** *(of character)* particularité *f* **(b)** *(of fate, nature)* caprice *m*; **by a q. of fate** par un caprice du destin

quirky ['kwɜːkɪ] *adj* bizarre, insolite

quisling ['kwɪzlɪŋ] *n* collaborateur(trice) *m,f*

quit [kwɪt] **1** *vt* (*pt & pp* **quit**) (*person, place*) quitter; *Comput* (*program*) sortir de; **to q. one's job** démissionner; **to q. doing sth** arrêter de faire qch
2 *vi* (*give up*) abandonner; (*resign*) démissionner; *Comput* sortir
3 *adj* **to be q. of** être débarrassé(e) de

quite [kwaɪt] *adv* (**a**) (*entirely*) tout à fait; **q. enough** bien assez; **that's q. enough of that!** ça suffit comme ça!; **q. apart from the fact that...** mis à part le fait que...; **q.!** tout à fait!; **that's q. all right** (*it doesn't matter*) ça n'a pas d'importance du tout; (*you're welcome*) mais pas du tout!; **you know q. well what I mean!** vous savez parfaitement ce que je veux dire!; **I q. understand** je comprends parfaitement (**b**) (*fairly*) assez, plutôt; **I q. like him** il me plaît bien; **q. a lot of people** pas mal de monde (**c**) (*for emphasis*) **it was q. a surprise** ça a été une véritable surprise; **it's been q. a day!** quelle journée!; **that movie is q. something** ce film, c'est vraiment quelque chose!

quits [kwɪts] *adj* **to be q. (with sb)** être quitte (envers qn); **let's call it q.** restons-en là

quitter ['kwɪtə(r)] *n Fam* dégonflé(e) *m,f*

quiver[1] ['kwɪvə(r)] *n* (*for arrows*) carquois *m*

quiver[2] ['kwɪvə(r)] **1** *n* (*tremble*) tremblement *m*
2 *vi* (*tremble*) trembler (**with** de); (*of flame*) vaciller

quivering ['kwɪvərɪŋ] *adj* tremblant(e)

quixotic [kwɪk'sɒtɪk] *adj* chimérique

quiz [kwɪz] **1** *n* (*pl* **quizzes**) (**a**) (*on TV*) jeu télévisé; (*on radio*) jeu *m* radiophonique; (*in magazine*) questionnaire *m*; **q. show** jeu *m* télévisé/radiophonique (**b**) *Sch* (*test*) interrogation *f* écrite
2 *vt* (*pt & pp* **quizzed**) interroger

quizzical ['kwɪzɪkəl] *adj* (*look, air*) interrogateur(trice)

quorum ['kwɔːrəm] *n* quorum *m*

quota ['kwəʊtə] *n* (*share*) quota *m*

quotation [kwəʊ'teɪʃən] *n* (**a**) (*from author*) citation *f*; **q. marks** guillemets *mpl*; **in q. marks** entre guillemets (**b**) *Com* (*for work*) devis *m*

quote [kwəʊt] **1** *n Fam* (**a**) (*from author*) citation *f*; **in quotes** (*in quotation marks*) entre guillemets (**b**) *Com* (*for work*) devis *m*
2 *vt* (**a**) (*author, passage*) citer; **she was quoted as saying that...** elle aurait dit que... (**b**) *Com* (*price*) indiquer

quotient ['kwəʊʃənt] *n Math* quotient *m*

R

R¹, r [ɑː(r)] *n (letter)* R, r *m inv*; *Fam* **the three R's** = la lecture, l'écriture et l'arithmétique, fondements de l'enseignement primaire

R² [ɑː(r)] *Pol (abbr* **Republican**) républicain(e)

rabbi ['ræbaɪ] *n* rabbin *m*

rabbit ['ræbɪt] *n* lapin *m*; *TV* **r. ears** antenne *f* téléscopique; **r. hole** terrier *m*; **r. hutch** clapier *m*

rabble ['ræbəl] *n* foule *f* bruyante; **r. rouser** agitateur(trice) *m,f*

rabid ['ræbɪd] *adj (animal) & Fig (person)* enragé(e); *(prejudice)* profondément enraciné(e); *(supporter)* pur et dur

rabies ['reɪbiːz] *n* rage *f*

raccoon [rə'kuːn] *n* raton *m* laveur

race¹ [reɪs] **1** *n (contest)* course *f*; *Fig* **a r. against time** une course contre la montre; **the races** *(horseraces)* les courses; **r. car** voiture *f* de course; **r. driver** pilote *m* de course

2 *vt* **(a)** *(person)* faire la course avec; **I'll r. you home!** on fait la course jusqu'à la maison! **(b)** *(horse)* faire courir

3 *vi* **(a)** *(of athlete, horse)* courir **(b)** *(move quickly)* aller à toute vitesse; **to r. in/out** entrer/sortir à toute vitesse; **to r. down the street** dévaler la rue à toute vitesse; **to r. by** *(of time)* passer vite, filer **(c)** *(of engine)* s'emballer; *(of pulse, heart)* battre la chamade

race² [reɪs] *n (of people, animals)* race *f*; **the human r.** le genre humain; **r. relations** relations *fpl* interraciales

racecourse ['reɪskɔːs] *n* champ *m* de courses

racehorse ['reɪshɔːs] *n* cheval *m* de course

racer ['reɪsə(r)] *n (person)* coureur(euse) *m,f*; *(bicycle)* vélo *m* de course

racetrack ['reɪstræk] *n (for athletes, cars)* piste *f*; *(for horses)* champ *m* de courses

racial ['reɪʃəl] *adj* racial(e); **r. discrimination** discrimination *f* raciale

racing ['reɪsɪŋ] **1** *n* les courses *fpl*

2 *adj* **r. bicycle/car** vélo *m*/voiture *f* de course

racism ['reɪsɪzəm] *n* racisme *m*

racist ['reɪsɪst] *n & adj* raciste *mf*

rack [ræk] **1** *n* **(a)** *(for bottles)* casier *m*; *(for plates)* égouttoir *m*; *(for goods in store)* présentoir *m*; *(for luggage)* porte-bagages *m inv*; **to buy a suit off the r.** acheter un costume en prêt-à-porter; **r. and pinion** crémaillère *f* **(b)** *(for torture)* chevalet *m*; *Fig* **to be on the r.** avoir des ennuis **(c)** *(idiom)* **to go to r. and ruin** aller de mal en pis

2 *vt (torment)* tourmenter; **to be racked with guilt** être rongé(e) par le remords; **to be racked with pain** être tenaillé(e) par la douleur; **to r. one's brains** se creuser la tête

racket¹ ['rækɪt] *n (for tennis)* raquette *f*

racket² ['rækɪt] *n Fam* **(a)** *(noise)* vacarme *m*, tapage *m*; **to make a r.** faire du vacarme *ou* tapage **(b)** *(criminal activity)* racket *m*

racketeer [rækɪ'tɪə(r)] *n* racketteur *m*

racketeering [rækɪ'tɪərɪŋ] *n* racket *m*

racquet ['rækɪt] *n (for tennis)* raquette *f*

racy ['reɪsɪ] *adj (risqué)* osé(e); *(lively)* savoureux(euse), piquant(e)

radar ['reɪdɑː(r)] *n* radar *m*; **r. operator** radariste *mf*; **r. screen** écran *m* radar

radial ['reɪdɪəl] **1** *n (tire)* pneu *m* radial

2 *adj* radial(e)

radiance ['reɪdɪəns] *n* éclat *m*, rayonnement *m*

radiant ['reɪdɪənt] *adj (light)* éclatant(e); *(person)* resplendissant(e)

radiate ['reɪdɪeɪt] **1** *vt (heat, light)* émettre; *Fig (happiness, health)* être rayonnant(e) de; *Fig (optimism, enthusiasm)* être débordant(e) de

2 *vi* rayonner (**from** à partir de)

radiation [reɪdɪ'eɪʃən] *n* radiation *f*

radiator ['reɪdɪeɪtə(r)] *n (heater)* radiateur *m*

radical ['rædɪkəl] *n & adj* radical(e) *m,f*

radicalism ['rædɪkəlɪzəm] *n* radicalisme *m*

radio ['reɪdɪəʊ] **1** *n (pl* **radios**) radio *f*; **r. alarm (clock)** radio-réveil *m*; **r. cassette (recorder** *or* **player)** radiocassette *m*; **r. station** station *f* de radio

2 *vt (pt & pp* **radioed**) *(information)* communiquer par radio; *(person)* contacter par radio

3 *vi* **to r. for help** demander de l'aide par radio

radioactive [reɪdɪəʊ'æktɪv] *adj* radioactif(ive); **r. waste** déchets *mpl* radioactifs

radioactivity [reɪdɪəʊæk'tɪvɪtɪ] *n* radioactivité *f*

radio-controlled [reɪdɪəʊkən'trəʊld] *adj* télécommandé(e)

radiographer [reɪdɪ'ɒgrəfə(r)] *n* radiologue *mf*

radiography [reɪdɪ'ɒgrəfɪ] *n* radiographie *f*

radiologist [reɪdɪ'ɒlədʒɪst] *n* radiologue *mf*

radiology [reɪdɪ'ɒlədʒɪ] *n* radiologie *f*

radiotherapy [reɪdɪəʊ'θerəpɪ] *n* radiothérapie *f*

radish ['rædɪʃ] *n* radis *m*

radium ['reɪdɪəm] *n Chem* radium *m*

radius ['reɪdɪəs] *(pl* **radii** ['reɪdɪaɪ]) *n* rayon *m*; **within a r. of** dans un rayon de

radon ['reɪdɒn] *n Chem* radon *m*

RAF [ɑːreɪ'ef] *n Mil (abbr* **Royal Air Force**) = armée de l'air britannique

raffia ['ræfɪə] *n* raphia *m*

raffish ['ræfɪʃ] *adj* canaille

raffle ['ræfəl] **1** *n* tombola *f*; **r. ticket** billet *m* de tombola

2 *vt* donner comme lot à une tombola

raft [rɑːft] *n* radeau *m*

rafter ['rɑːftə(r)] *n* chevron *m*

rag¹ [ræg] *n* **(a)** *(piece of cloth)* chiffon *m*; **rags** *(clothes)* haillons *mpl*, guenilles *fpl*; **to go from rags to riches** passer de la misère à la richesse; **hers is a rags to riches story** elle est partie de rien; **r. doll** poupée *f* de chiffon; *Fam* **the r. trade** la confection **(b)** *Fam Pej (newspaper)* torchon *m*

rag² [ræg] *vt (pt & pp* **ragged**) *Old-fashioned (tease)* taquiner

ragamuffin ['rægəmʌfɪn] *n* polisson(onne) *m,f*

ragbag ['rægbæg] *n* ramassis *m*

rage [reɪdʒ] **1** *n* (**a**) *(fury)* rage *f*, fureur *f*; **to be in a r.** être furieux(euse) (**b**) *Fam (fashion)* **to be all the r.** faire fureur
2 *vi* (**a**) *(of person)* être furieux(euse) (**against** *or* **at** contre) (**b**) *(of sea)* être démonté(e); *(of epidemic, war)* faire rage

ragga ['rægə] *n Mus* ragga *m*

ragged ['rægɪd] *adj (clothes)* en haillons, en lambeaux; *(edge)* irrégulier(ère); *(person)* en haillons; *Fam* **to run oneself r.** s'épuiser

raging ['reɪdʒɪŋ] *adj* (**a**) *(person)* furieux(euse); **to be in a r. temper** être furieux (**b**) *(sea)* démonté(e); *(fever, headache)* violent(e); *(thirst)* terrible

ragwort ['rægwɜːt] *n Bot* séneçon *m*

raid [reɪd] **1** *n (by army)* raid *m*; *(by police)* descente *f*; *(on bank)* hold-up *m inv*
2 *vt (of army)* faire un raid sur; *(of police)* faire une descente dans; *(of robbers)* attaquer; *Fig & Hum* **to r. the refrigerator** faire la razzia dans le frigo

raider ['reɪdə(r)] *n (criminal)* voleur(euse) *m,f*; *Fin (on Stock Exchange)* raider *m*

rail[1] [reɪl] *n* (**a**) *(of stairway)* rampe *f*; *(of balcony)* balustrade *f* (**b**) *(train system)* chemin de fer; *(track)* rail *m*; **by r.** par le *ou* en chemin de fer; *Fig* **to go off the rails** *(of person)* s'écarter du droit chemin; **r. network** réseau *m* ferroviaire; **r. strike** grève *f* des chemins de fer *ou* des cheminots

rail[2] [reɪl] *vi* **to r. at** *or* **against sth** s'insurger contre qch

railcar ['reɪlkɑː(r)] *n* wagon *m*

railings ['reɪlɪŋz] *npl* grille *f*

railroad ['reɪlrəʊd] **1** *n (system)* chemin *m* de fer; *(track)* voie *f* ferrée; **r. car** voiture *f*; **r. line** ligne *f* de chemin de fer; **r. station** gare *f*
2 *vt Fam* **to r. sb into doing sth** forcer qn à faire qch

railway ['reɪlweɪ] *n* = **railroad**

rain [reɪn] **1** *n* pluie *f*; **in the r.** sous la pluie; **it looks like r.** on dirait qu'il va pleuvoir; **the rains** la saison des pluies; **come r. or shine** *(whatever the weather)* qu'il pleuve ou qu'il vente; *(whatever the circumstances)* quoi qu'il arrive; *Fam Fig* **I'll take a r. check on that** ça sera pour une autre fois; **r. cloud** nuage *m* de pluie; **r. dance** danse *f* de la pluie
2 *vt* **to r. gifts on sb** couvrir qn de cadeaux; **to r. blows on sb** rouer qn de coups
3 *vi* pleuvoir; **it's raining** il pleut; *Prov* **it never rains but it pours** un malheur n'arrive jamais seul

rainbow ['reɪnbəʊ] *n* arc-en-ciel *m*; **r. coalition** coalition *f* des minorités; **r. trout** truite *f* arc-en-ciel

raincoat ['reɪnkəʊt] *n* imperméable *m*

raindrop ['reɪndrɒp] *n* goutte *f* de pluie

rainfall ['reɪnfɔːl] *n* précipitations *fpl*

rainforest ['reɪnfɒrɪst] *n* forêt *f* tropicale humide

rainproof ['reɪnpruːf] *adj* imperméable

rainslicker ['reɪnslɪkə(r)] *n* ciré *m*

rainstorm ['reɪnstɔːm] *n* pluie *f* torrentielle

rainwater ['reɪnwɔːtə(r)] *n* eau *f* de pluie

rainy ['reɪnɪ] *adj* pluvieux(euse); *(day)* de pluie; *Fig* **to save sth for a r. day** mettre qch de côté; **the r. season** la saison des pluies

raise [reɪz] **1** *vt* (**a**) *(lift)* lever; **to r. one's voice** élever la voix; **to r. one's glass to one's lips** porter son verre à ses lèvres; *Fig* **to r. one's hat to sb** tirer son chapeau à qn; *Fam Fig* **to r. the roof** faire du raffut
(**b**) *(price, salary)* augmenter; *(standard)* élever; *Fig* **to r. the stakes** faire monter la mise
(**c**) *(problem, subject)* soulever
(**d**) *(fears, doubts)* faire naître; **to r. a smile/laugh** faire sourire/rire; **to r. sb's hopes** donner trop d'espoir à qn; **to r. the alarm** donner l'alarme; *Fam* **to r. hell** *or* **Cain** faire un foin d'enfer

(**e**) *(money)* rassembler; *(for charity)* collecter
(**f**) *(children, cattle)* élever; *(crops)* cultiver
(**g**) *(statue)* dresser
2 *n (pay increase)* augmentation *f* (de salaire)

raisin ['reɪzən] *n* raisin *m* sec

rake [reɪk] **1** *n* (**a**) *(garden tool)* râteau *m*; **to be as thin as a r.** être maigre comme un clou (**b**) *(dissolute man)* libertin *m*
2 *vt (leaves, soil)* ratisser; **to r. one's memory** fouiller dans sa mémoire

▸**rake about, rake around** *vi (search)* fouiller (**for** pour trouver)

▸**rake in** *vt sep Fam (money)* rapporter; **she's raking it in!** elle s'en met plein les poches!

▸**rake off** *vt sep Fam (money)* empocher

▸**rake over** *vt sep (subject, the past)* ressasser

rakish ['reɪkɪʃ] *adj (dissolute)* libertin(e); *(jaunty)* désinvolte

rally ['rælɪ] **1** *n (pl rallies)* (**a**) *(protest gathering)* manifestation *f* (**b**) *(in tennis)* échange *m* (**c**) *(car race)* rallye *m*; **r. driver** pilote *mf* de rallye
2 *vt (pt & pp rallied) (troops)* rallier; **to r. support for sb/sth** gagner des appuis à la cause de qn/qch; **to r. sb's spirits** redonner courage à qn; **rallying cry** cri *m* de ralliement
3 *vi (of prices)* se redresser; *(of patient)* aller mieux; **to r. to sb's defense** se porter au secours de qn

▸**rally around, rally round 1** *vt insep* soutenir
2 *vi* apporter son soutien

RAM [ræm] *n Comput (abbr random access memory)* mémoire *f* vive

ram [ræm] **1** *n* (**a**) *(animal)* bélier *m* (**b**) *(implement)* (**battering**) **r.** bélier *m*
2 *vt (pt & pp rammed)* (**a**) *(crash into)* percuter; *(of ship)* aborder (**b**) *(force into place)* tasser; *Fam* **to r. one's views down sb's throat** bassiner qn avec ses opinions

Ramadan [ræmə'dɑːn] *n Rel* le ramadan

ramble ['ræmbəl] **1** *n (walk)* randonnée *f* (pédestre)
2 *vi* (**a**) *(walk)* faire une randonnée (**b**) *(digress)* divaguer

▸**ramble on** *vi* divaguer; **to r. on about sth** radoter à propos de qch

rambler ['ræmblə(r)] *n (walker)* randonneur(euse) *m,f*

rambling ['ræmblɪŋ] *n* (**a**) *(walking)* **to go r.** aller en randonnée (**b**) *ramblings (words)* divagations *fpl*
2 *adj* (**a**) *(letter, speech)* décousu(e) (**b**) *(house)* plein(e) de coins et de recoins; **r. rose** rosier *m* grimpant

ramification [ræmɪfɪ'keɪʃən] *n (consequence)* conséquence *f*

ramp [ræmp] *n* rampe *f*; *(to plane)* passerelle *f*; *(on road)* petit dos *m* d'âne; *(to or from highway)* bretelle *f*

rampage 1 ['ræmpeɪdʒ] *n* **to go on a** *or* **the r.** *(lose control)* se déchaîner; *(cause damage)* tout saccager
2 *vi* [ræm'peɪdʒ] **to r. about** se déchaîner

rampant ['ræmpənt] *adj* endémique; **corruption is r.** la corruption sévit

rampart ['ræmpɑːt] *n* rempart *m*

ramrod ['ræmrɒd] *n (for rifle)* écouvillon *m*; *Fig* **r. straight** raide comme un piquet

ramshackle ['ræmʃækəl] *adj (building)* délabré(e); *(economy, organization)* qui s'effondre

ran [ræn] *pt of* **run**

ranch [rɑːntʃ] *n* ranch *m*; **r. dressing** = mayonnaise crémeuse à l'ail; **r. hand** ouvrier(ère) *m,f* agricole; **r. house** *(single story)* maison *f* sans étage; *(on ranch)* maison *f*

rancher ['rɑːntʃə(r)] *n* propriétaire *mf* de ranch

rancid ['rænsɪd] *adj* rance; **to go r.** rancir

rancor ['ræŋkə(r)] *n* rancœur *f*

rand [rænd] *n* rand *m*

random ['rændəm] **1** *n* **at r.** au hasard
2 *adj (choice, sample)* (fait(e)) au hasard; *Comput* **r. access**

memory mémoire *f* vive; **r. sampling** prélèvement *m* d'échantillons au hasard

rang [ræŋ] *pt of* **ring**²

range [reɪndʒ] **1** *n* (a) *(of weapon, telescope)* portée *f*; **within r.** *(of fire)* à portée de tir; *(of hearing)* à portée de la voix; **out of r.** hors de portée

(b) *(of prices, colors, products)* gamme *f*; *(of instrument, voice)* registre *m*; *(of knowledge, research)* étendue *f*; *Mktg* **r. extension** déclinaison *f* de gamme

(c) *(of hills, mountains)* chaîne *f*; *(prairie)* prairie *f*

(d) *(practice area)* **(shooting) r.** champ *m* de tir

(e) *(cooker)* fourneau *m*

2 *vt* (a) *(arrange in row)* ranger; **to r. oneself with sb** se ranger du côté de qn; **to r. oneself against sb** s'opposer à qn

(b) *(travel)* parcourir

3 *vi* (a) *(extend)* **to r. from... to** aller de... à

(b) **to r. over** *(include)* porter sur

rangefinder ['reɪndʒfaɪndə(r)] *n* télémètre *m*

ranger ['reɪndʒə(r)] *n (in forest)* garde *m* forestier; *Mil* commando *m*

rangy ['reɪndʒɪ] *adj* élancé(e)

rank¹ [ræŋk] **1** *n* (a) *(status)* grade *m*; *Fig* **to pull r.** abuser de son rang (b) *(row)* rangée *f*; *Mil* **the ranks** les hommes *mpl* du rang; *Fig* **to rise from the ranks** sortir du rang; *Fig* **the ranks of the unemployed** les rangs des chômeurs; *Fig* **to break ranks (with)** se désolidariser (de); *Fig* **to close ranks** se montrer solidaire

2 *vt* placer (**among** parmi); **to r. sb/sth as** considérer qn/qch comme

3 *vi* compter (**among** parmi); **to r. as** être considéré(e) comme; **to r. above/below sb** être supérieur(e)/inférieur(e) à qn; **this ranks as a major disaster** on peut qualifier ceci de catastrophe majeure

rank² [ræŋk] *adj* (a) *(foul-smelling)* fétide (b) *(absolute)* total(e); **she's a r. outsider** elle n'est vraiment pas dans la course

rank-and-file [ræŋkən'faɪl] *n* **the r.** *(in army)* les hommes *mpl* du rang; *(of political party)* la base

ranking ['ræŋkɪŋ] *n (classification)* classement *m*

rankle ['ræŋkəl] *vi* **it still rankles with me** cela m'est resté sur l'estomac

ransack ['rænsæk] *vt (house, desk)* mettre sens dessus dessous; *(store, town)* piller

ransom ['rænsəm] **1** *n* rançon *f*; **to hold sb to r.** rançonner qn; *Fig* retenir qn en otage

2 *vt* rançonner

rant [rænt] *vi Fam* déblatérer (**about/at** au sujet de/contre); **to r. and rave** tempêter (**about/at** au sujet de/contre)

rap [ræp] **1** *n* (a) *(sharp blow)* coup *m* sec; *Fig* **to take the r. for sth** écoper *ou* trinquer pour qch (b) *(music)* rap *m*

2 *vt (pt & pp* **rapped)** *(window, door)* frapper à; *(table)* frapper sur; *Fig* **to r. sb's knuckles, to r. sb over the knuckles** taper sur les doigts de qn

3 *vi* (a) *(hit)* frapper (**on** à) (b) *(sing)* rapper

rapacious [rə'peɪʃəs] *adj* rapace

rape¹ [reɪp] **1** *n (crime)* viol *m*; *Fig (of countryside, environment)* destruction *f*

2 *vt* violer

rape² [reɪp] *n (crop)* colza *m*

rapid ['ræpɪd] *adj* rapide; **r. reaction force** force *f* d'intervention rapide; **r. transit** transport *m* urbain rapide

rapidity [rə'pɪdɪtɪ] *n* rapidité *f*

rapidly ['ræpɪdlɪ] *adv* rapidement

rapids ['ræpɪdz] *npl (in river)* rapides *mpl*

rapier ['reɪpɪə(r)] *n* rapière *f*

rapist ['reɪpɪst] *n* violeur *m*

rappel [rə'pel] *vi (pt & pp* **rappelled)** descendre en rappel; **to r. down sth** descendre qch en rappel

rappelling [rə'pelɪŋ] *n* rappel *m*, descente *f* en rappel; **to go r.** faire du rappel

rapper ['ræpə(r)] *n (singer)* rappeur(euse) *m,f*

rapport [ræ'pɔː(r)] *n* **to have a good r. (with sb)** avoir de bons rapports (avec qn)

rapt [ræpt] *adj (attention)* profond(e); *(look)* absorbé(e); *(smile)* d'extase

rapture ['ræptʃə(r)] *n* extase *f*; **to be in raptures** être ravi(e); **to go into raptures over sb/sth** s'extasier devant qn/sur qch

rapturous ['ræptʃərəs] *adj (cries)* d'extase; *(applause)* frénétique; *(reception, welcome)* enthousiaste

rare [reə(r)] *adj* (a) *(animal, stamp)* rare; **to have a r. gift (for sth)** être exceptionnellement doué(e) (pour qch) (b) *(steak)* saignant(e)

rarefied ['reərɪfaɪd] *adj (air, gas)* raréfié(e); *Fig (atmosphere, ideas)* fermé(e)

rarely ['reəlɪ] *adv* rarement

raring ['reərɪŋ] *adj* **to be r. to do sth** être impatient(e) de faire qch; **to be r. to go** piaffer d'impatience

rarity ['reərɪtɪ] *(pl* **rarities)** *n* rareté *f*; **to be/to become a r.** être/devenir rare; **r. value** rareté

rascal ['rɑːskəl] *n (child)* coquin(e) *m,f*; *Old-fashioned or Hum (scoundrel)* vaurien(enne) *m,f*

rash¹ [ræʃ] *n* (a) *(on skin) (spots)* éruption *f*; *(red area)* rougeurs *fpl* (b) *(series)* série *f*

rash² [ræʃ] *adj (imprudent)* irréfléchi(e)

rasher ['ræʃə(r)] *n (of bacon)* tranche *f*

rashly ['ræʃlɪ] *adv* sans réfléchir

rasp [rɑːsp] **1** *n* (a) *(tool)* râpe *f* (b) *(sound)* grincement *m*

2 *vt (say hoarsely)* grogner

raspberry ['rɑːzbərɪ] *(pl* **raspberries)** *n (fruit)* framboise *f*; *(plant)* framboisier *m*; *Fam Fig* **to blow a r.** souffler en signe de dérision; **r. jam** confiture *f* de framboises

rat [ræt] **1** *n* (a) *(animal)* rat *m*; **r. poison** mort-aux-rats *f inv*; **r. trap** piège *m* à rats, ratière *f* (b) *Fam (scoundrel)* dégueulasse *mf* (c) *(idioms)* **to smell a r.** flairer quelque chose de louche; **r. race** foire *f* d'empoigne

2 *vi (pt & pp* **ratted)** *Fam (inform)* **to r. on sb** dénoncer qn

ratchet ['rætʃɪt] *n* rochet *m*; **r. (wheel)** roue *f* à rochet

▸**ratchet up 1** *vt sep (prices, inflation)* faire augmenter de façon irréversible

2 *vi (of prices, inflation)* augmenter de façon irréversible

rate [reɪt] **1** *n* (a) *(of inflation, interest)* taux *m*; *Fin* **r. of return** taux de rendement (b) *(speed)* rythme *m*; **at this r.** à ce rythme (c) **at any r.** en tout cas (d) *(price, charge)* tarif *m*

2 *vt* (a) *(classify)* placer (**among** parmi); **to r. sb/sth as** considérer qn/qch comme; **to r. sb/sth highly** tenir qn/qch en haute estime (b) *(deserve)* mériter; **to r. a mention** mériter d'être mentionné(e)

3 *vi* **to r. as** être considéré(e) comme

rather ['rɑːðə(r)] *adv* (a) *(preferably)* **I'd r. stay** j'aimerais mieux rester; **I'd r. not go** j'aimerais mieux ne pas y aller; **I'd r. not** je n'y tiens pas; **r. you than me!** je n'aimerais pas être à ta place (b) *(more exactly)* plutôt; **he sounded surprised or, r., annoyed** il semblait surpris, ou plutôt, fâché (c) *(fairly)* assez; **I r. liked it** j'ai bien aimé (d) **r. than him** plutôt que lui; **r. than staying** plutôt que de rester

ratification [rætɪfɪˈkeɪʃən] *n* ratification *f*

ratify ['rætɪfaɪ] *(pt & pp* **ratified)** *vt* ratifier

rating ['reɪtɪŋ] *n (of popularity)* classement *m*; **the ratings** *(for TV, radio)* l'indice *m* d'écoute, l'Audimat® *m*

ratio ['reɪʃɪəʊ] *(pl* **ratios)** *n* rapport *m*

ration ['reɪʃən] **1** *n* ration *f*; *Fig (dose)* dose *f*; **rations** *(supplies)* provisions *fpl*; **r. book** carte *f* de rationnement

2 *vt* rationner

rational ['ræʃənəl] *adj (sensible)* raisonnable, sensé(e); *(sane)* rationnel(elle)

rationalism [ˈræʃənəlɪzəm] *n* rationalisme *m*

rationalist [ˈræʃənəlɪst] *n* rationaliste *mf*

rationalization [ræʃənəlaɪˈzeɪʃən] *n* (*of company*) rationalisation *f*

rationalize [ˈræʃənəlaɪz] *vt* (**a**) (*action, dislike*) justifier (**b**) (*company*) rationaliser

rationally [ˈræʃənəlɪ] *adv* (*sensibly*) raisonnablement; (*sanely*) rationnellement

rationing [ˈræʃənɪŋ] *n* rationnement *m*

rattle [ˈrætəl] **1** *n* (**a**) (*for baby*) hochet *m* (**b**) (*noise*) (*of train, chains, keys*) cliquetis *m*; (*of gunfire*) crépitement *m*; (*of door, window*) frottement *m*
2 *vt* (**a**) (*chains, keys*) faire cliqueter; (*door, window*) faire vibrer (**b**) *Fam* (*make nervous*) démonter
3 *vi* (*of chains, keys*) cliqueter; (*of door, window*) vibrer

▸**rattle off** *vt sep Fam* (*list, facts*) débiter

▸**rattle on** *vi Fam* parler sans cesse

▸**rattle through** *vt insep Fam* (*work, book*) expédier

rattlesnake [ˈrætəlsneɪk] *n* serpent *m* à sonnette

ratty [ˈrætɪ] *adj Fam* (*shabby*) miteux(euse)

raucous [ˈrɔːkəs] *adj* (*hoarse*) rauque; (*rowdy*) bruyant(e)

raunchy [ˈrɔːntʃɪ] *adj Fam* (*film, scene, lyrics*) osé(e); (*dress*) provocant(e)

ravage [ˈrævɪdʒ] **1** *npl* **ravages** ravages *mpl*
2 *vt* ravager

rave [reɪv] **1** *n* rave *f*
2 *adj* (*review*) dithyrambique
3 *vi* (*deliriously*) délirer; **to r. about sb/sth** (*enthusiastically*) être dithyrambique à propos de qn/qch

raven [ˈreɪvən] **1** *n* (*bird*) grand corbeau *m*
2 *adj* (*color*) noir de jais *inv*

ravenous [ˈrævənəs] *adj* (*animal*) vorace; (*person*) affamé(e)

raver [ˈreɪvə(r)] *n Fam* (*socially active person*) noceur(euse) *m,f*; (*who goes to raves*) raver *mf*

ravine [rəˈviːn] *n* ravin *m*

raving [ˈreɪvɪŋ] *adj* (**a**) (*delirious*) **r. mad** complètement fou (folle); **a r. lunatic** un fou furieux (une folle furieuse) (**b**) (*success*) éclatant(e)

ravish [ˈrævɪʃ] *vt* (**a**) *Lit* (*delight*) enchanter, ravir (**b**) *Old-fashioned* (*rape*) violenter

ravishing [ˈrævɪʃɪŋ] *adj* magnifique

raw [rɔː] *adj* (**a**) (*food*) cru(e); (*silk, sugar, statistics*) brut(e); **r. materials** matières *fpl* premières; **r. recruit** bleu *m* (**b**) (*skin*) écorché(e); *Fig* **to get a r. deal** être mal traité(e); *Fig* **to touch a r. nerve** toucher un point sensible (**c**) (*weather, wind*) glacial(e)

ray¹ [reɪ] *n* (*of light, sun*) rayon *m*; *Fig* (*of hope*) lueur *f*

ray² [reɪ] *n* (*fish*) raie *f*

rayon [ˈreɪɒn] *n* (*fabric*) rayonne *f*

raze [reɪz] *vt* **to r. sth to the ground** raser qch

razor [ˈreɪzə(r)] *n* rasoir *m*; **r. blade** lame *f* de rasoir

razor-sharp [ˈreɪzəʃɑːp] *adj* (*knife*) effilé(e); *Fig* (*intelligence, wit*) vif (vive)

razor-shell [ˈreɪzəʃel] *n* couteau *m*

razzmatazz [ˈræzmətæz] *n Fam* tape-à-l'œil *m inv*

R & B [ɑːrənˈbiː] *n Mus* (*abbr* **rhythm and blues**) R & B *m inv*

RC [ɑːˈsiː] *n & adj* (*abbr* **Roman Catholic**) catholique *mf*

R & D [ɑːrənˈdiː] *n Com* (*abbr* **research and development**) recherche et développement

Rd. (*abbr* **Road**) rue

RDA [ɑːdiːˈeɪ] *n* (*abbr* **recommended daily allowance**) recommandation *f* quotidienne officielle (*en vitamines, sels minéraux, etc.*)

RE [ɑːˈriː] *n* (*abbr* **Religious Education**) instruction *f* religieuse

re¹ [riː] *prep* concernant; **re your letter** suite à votre lettre; **re: 2004 sales figures** Réf: les ventes de 2004

re² [reɪ] *n Mus* ré *m*

reach [riːtʃ] **1** *n* (**a**) (*accessibility*) portée *f*; **within r.** (*thing*) à portée de main; (*location*) tout(e) proche; **out of r.** hors de portée (**b**) (*of river*) **the upper reaches** l'amont *m*
2 *vt* (**a**) (*destination, conclusion*) atteindre, arriver à; (*agreement*) aboutir à; (*decision*) prendre; **the news didn't r. her** les nouvelles ne lui sont pas parvenues (**b**) (*contact*) joindre; **to r. a wider audience** toucher un public plus important (**c**) (*stretch as far as*) (*one's shoulder, waist*) atteindre, arriver jusqu'à
3 *vi* (*extend*) (*of forest, property*) s'étendre (**to** jusqu'à); (*of noise, voice*) porter (**to** jusqu'à); **to r. for sth** tendre le bras pour prendre qch; *Fig* **to r. for the sky** *or* **the stars** viser très haut

▸**reach out** *vi* tendre le bras

reachable [ˈriːtʃəbəl] *adj* accessible

react [rɪˈækt] *vi* réagir (**against/to** contre/à)

reaction [rɪˈækʃən] *n* réaction *f*

reactionary [rɪˈækʃənərɪ] (*pl* **reactionaries**) *n & adj* réactionnaire *mf*

reactivate [rɪˈæktɪveɪt] *vt* réactiver

reactor [rɪˈæktə(r)] *n* réacteur *m*

read [riːd] **1** *n* **to have a r.** lire; **her books are a good r.** ses livres se lisent bien
2 *vt* (*pt & pp* **read** [red]) (**a**) (*book, newspaper, letter*) lire; **do you r. me?** (*on radio*) est-ce que vous me recevez?; *Fig* **to take it as read that...** considérer comme acquis que... (**b**) (*interpret*) interpréter; **to r. sb's mind** lire dans les pensées de qn; **to r. the future** prédire l'avenir (**c**) (*of dial, thermometer*) indiquer; (*of inscription*) être; **the sign read...** sur l'écriteau, on pouvait lire...
3 *vi* (**a**) (*of person*) lire; **to r. aloud** lire à haute voix; **I'd read about it in the newspapers** je l'avais lu dans les journaux; *Fig* **to r. between the lines** lire entre les lignes (**b**) (*of text*) **to r. well/badly** se lire facilement/difficilement

▸**read out** *vt sep* lire (à haute voix)

▸**read up on** *vt sep* étudier

readable [ˈriːdəbəl] *adj* (*book*) facile à lire; (*handwriting*) lisible

reader [ˈriːdə(r)] *n* (**a**) (*of book, newspaper, etc.*) lecteur(trice) *m,f* (**b**) (*reading book*) livre *m* de lecture (**c**) (*device*) lecteur *m* (**d**) *Univ* (*in the US*) ≃ assistant(e) *m,f*; (*in Canada*) ≃ chargé(e) *m,f* de cours

readily [ˈredɪlɪ] *adv* (*willingly*) volontiers; (*easily*) facilement

reading [ˈriːdɪŋ] *n* (**a**) (*action, interpretation, pastime*) lecture *f*; **r. glasses** lunettes *fpl* de lecture (**b**) (*measurement*) relevé *m*

readjust [riːəˈdʒʌst] **1** *vt* (*figures, salaries*) réajuster; (*instrument*) remettre au point; (*clothing*) rajuster
2 *vi* se réadapter (**to** à)

readjustment [riːəˈdʒʌstmənt] *n* (*of figures, salaries*) réajustement *m*; (*of person*) réadaptation *f*

readmit [riːədˈmɪt] (*pt & pp* **readmitted**) *vt* (*to club, party*) réintégrer (**to** à); **to r. sb (to the hospital)** réhospitaliser qn

read-only [ˈriːdˈəʊnlɪ] *adj Comput* (*file*) à lecture seule; **r. memory** mémoire *f* morte

readvertize [riːˈædvətaɪz] *vt* repasser une annonce pour

ready [ˈredɪ] **1** *adj* (**a**) (*prepared*) prêt(e) (**for** pour); **to be r. to do sth** être prêt à faire qch; **to get r.** se préparer; **to get sth r.** préparer qch; **to be r. for bed** être prêt à se coucher; **r. cash** argent *m* liquide (**b**) (*willing*) **to be r. to do sth** être prêt(e) *ou* disposé(e) à faire qch (**c**) (*quick*) **to have a r. wit** avoir l'esprit vif
2 *vt* (*pt & pp* **readied**) (*prepare*) préparer
3 **at the r.** prêt(e)

ready-made [redɪˈmeɪd] *adj* (*food*) tout(e) préparé(e); (*excuse, phrase*) tout(e) fait(e)

reaffirm [riːəˈfɜːm] *vt* réaffirmer

real [rɪəl] **1** *adj* (**a**) (*authentic*) vrai(e); (*gold, leather*) véritable;

(danger, fear, effort) réel(elle) (**b**) *(actual)* réel(elle); **the r. world** la réalité; **what does that mean in r. terms?** qu'est-ce que cela signifie en clair?; *Com* **r. estate** *(property)* biens *mpl* immobiliers; *(profession)* l'immobilier *m* (**c**) *(for emphasis)* **a r. idiot** un véritable idiot

2 *adv Fam (very)* très

realism ['rɪəlɪzəm] *n* réalisme *m*

realist ['rɪəlɪst] *n* réaliste *mf*

realistic [rɪə'lɪstɪk] *adj* réaliste

reality [rɪ'ælɪtɪ] *(pl* **realities**) *n* réalité *f*; **in r.** en réalité; *Fam* **it was a r. check for him** ça l'a ramené à la réalité; *TV* **r. show** reality show *m*; **r. television** télé-réalité *f*, télé-vérité *f*

realize ['rɪəlaɪz] *vt* (**a**) *(become aware of)* se rendre compte de; **I r. he's busy, but…** j'ai bien conscience qu'il est occupé mais… (**b**) *(ambition, dream)* réaliser

really ['rɪəlɪ] *adv* vraiment; *(in actual fact)* en réalité

realm [relm] *n* (**a**) *(kingdom)* royaume *m* (**b**) *(field)* domaine *m*

Realtor ['rɪəltə(r)] *n* agent *m* immobilier

ream [riːm] *n (of paper)* rame *f*; *Fig* **reams of** des quantités de

reanimate [riː'ænɪmeɪt] *vt* r(é)animer

reap [riːp] *vt* moissonner; **to r. the benefits (of)** récolter les bénéfices (de)

reaper ['riːpə(r)] *n (machine)* moissonneuse *f*; *Lit* **the Grim R.** la Faucheuse

reappear [riːə'pɪə(r)] *vi* réapparaître

reappearance [riːə'pɪərəns] *n* réapparition *f*

reapply [riːə'plaɪ] *(pt & pp* **reapplied**) *vi (for job)* poser à nouveau sa candidature (**for** à)

reappraise [riːə'preɪz] *vt* réévaluer; *(policy)* réexaminer

rear¹ [rɪə(r)] *n* (**a**) *(back part)* arrière *m*; **at the r. of** *(inside)* à l'arrière de; *(behind)* derrière; **in the r.** à l'arrière; **to bring up the r.** être en queue; **r. admiral** contre-amiral *m*; **r. entrance** entrée *f* de derrière; **r. legs** pattes *fpl* de derrière; **r. lights** feux *mpl* arrière; **r.-view mirror** rétroviseur *m*; **r. window** vitre *f* arrière (**b**) *Fam (buttocks)* derrière *m*

rear² [rɪə(r)] *vt* (**a**) *(child, livestock)* élever (**b**) *(one's head)* relever; *Fig* **to r. its ugly head** faire son apparition

▸**rear up** *vi (of horse)* se cabrer

rearguard ['rɪəgɑːd] *n Mil* arrière-garde *f*; *also Fig* **r. action** combat *m* d'arrière-garde

rearm [riː'ɑːm] *vt & vi* réarmer

rearmament [riː'ɑːməmənt] *n* réarmement *m*

rearrange [riːə'reɪndʒ] *vt (books, furniture)* changer la disposition de; *(appointment)* changer

reason ['riːzən] **1** *n* (**a**) *(cause, motive)* raison *f* (**for** de); **for no particular r.** sans raison précise; **I don't know the r. why** je ne sais pas pourquoi; *Ironic* **for reasons best known to himself** pour une raison connue de lui seul; **give me one good r. why I should!** donne-moi une raison valable de le faire! (**b**) *(sanity, common sense)* raison *f*; **to listen to** *or* **to see r.** entendre raison; **it stands to r.** il va de soi *ou* sans dire; **within r.** dans des limites raisonnables

2 *vt* **to r. that** estimer que

3 *vi* raisonner (**about/with** sur/avec)

reasonable ['riːzənəbəl] *adj* (**a**) *(fair)* raisonnable; *(excuse)* valable (**b**) *(quite good)* passable

reasonably ['riːzənəblɪ] *adv* (**a**) *(behave, act)* raisonnablement (**b**) *(quite)* plutôt

reasoning ['riːzənɪŋ] *n (thinking)* raisonnement *m*

reassemble [riːə'sembəl] **1** *vt (people)* rassembler; *(machine)* remonter

2 *vi (of people)* se rassembler

reassess [riːə'ses] *vt* (**a**) *(policy, situation)* reconsidérer (**b**) *Fin (tax, property)* réévaluer

reassurance [riːə'ʃʊərəns] *n (comfort)* réconfort *m*; *(guarantee)* assurance *f*

reassure [riːə'ʃʊə(r)] *vt* rassurer

reassuring [riːə'ʃʊərɪŋ] *adj* rassurant(e)

reawaken [riːə'weɪkən] **1** *vt (interest, feeling)* faire renaître

2 *vi (of person)* se réveiller à nouveau

rebate ['riːbeɪt] *n (refund)* remboursement *m*; *(discount)* rabais *m*

rebel 1 *n* ['rebəl] rebelle *mf*

2 *vi* [rɪ'bel] *(pt & pp* **rebelled**) se rebeller (**against** contre)

rebellion [rɪ'beljən] *n* rébellion *f*

rebellious [rɪ'beljəs] *adj* rebelle

rebirth [riː'bɜːθ] *n* renaissance *f*

reboot [riː'buːt] *Comput* **1** *vt* réamorcer

2 *vi* se réamorcer

reborn [riː'bɔːn] *adj* **to be r.** renaître

rebound 1 *n* ['riːbaʊnd] *(of ball)* rebond *m*; *Fig* **she married him on the r.** elle l'a épousé à la suite d'une déception sentimentale

2 *vi* [rɪ'baʊnd] *(of ball)* rebondir; *Fig (of joke, lie)* se retourner (**on** contre)

rebuff [rɪ'bʌf] **1** *n (of person)* rebuffade *f*; *(of suggestion)* refus *m*; **to meet with a r.** *(of person)* essuyer une rebuffade; *(of suggestion)* être repoussé(e)

2 *vt* repousser

rebuild [riː'bɪld] *(pt & pp* **rebuilt** [riː'bɪlt]) *vt* reconstruire

rebuke [rɪ'bjuːk] **1** *n* réprimande *f*

2 *vt* réprimander

rebut [rɪ'bʌt] *(pt & pp* **rebutted**) *vt* réfuter

rebuttal [rɪ'bʌtəl] *n* réfutation *f*

recalcitrant [rɪ'kælsɪtrənt] *adj* récalcitrant(e)

recall 1 *n* ['riːkɔːl] *(memory)* mémoire *f*; **lost beyond r.** irrévocablement perdu(e)

2 *vt* [rɪ'kɔːl] (**a**) *(remember)* se souvenir de, se rappeler; **to r. doing sth** se souvenir d'avoir fait qch, se rappeler avoir fait qch (**b**) *(defective goods)* rappeler; *(library book)* demander le retour de

recant [rɪ'kænt] **1** *vt (opinion)* rétracter

2 *vi* se rétracter

recap ['riːkæp] **1** *n (summary)* récapitulation *f*

2 *vi (pt & pp* **recapped**) récapituler

recapitulate [riːkə'pɪtjʊleɪt] *vt & vi* récapituler

recapture [riː'kæptʃə(r)] **1** *n (of criminal)* capture *f*; *(of town, territory)* reprise *f*

2 *vt* (**a**) *(criminal)* capturer; *(town, territory)* reprendre (**b**) *Fig (memory, atmosphere)* faire revivre; *(one's youth)* retrouver

recede [rɪ'siːd] *vi (of tide)* se retirer; *(of coastline)* reculer; **to have a receding chin** avoir le menton fuyant; **to have receding hair** *or* **a receding hairline** avoir le front qui se dégarnit

receipt [rɪ'siːt] *n* (**a**) *(act of receiving)* réception *f*; **to be in r. of sth** avoir reçu qch (**b**) *(proof of payment)* reçu *m*; **receipts** *(at box office)* recette *f*, entrées *fpl*

receive [rɪ'siːv] *vt* recevoir; *(stolen goods)* receler; **to be well/badly received** *(of film, proposal)* être bien/mal reçu(e); **to r. sb into the Church** admettre qn au sein de l'Église

received [rɪ'siːvd] *adj (idea)* reçu(e); *(opinion)* admis(e)

receiver [rɪ'siːvə(r)] *n* (**a**) *(of stolen goods)* receleur(euse) *m,f* (**b**) *(of telephone, radio set)* récepteur *m*; **to pick up the r.** décrocher; **to replace the r.** raccrocher (**c**) *Fin* administrateur *m* judiciaire

receivership [rɪ'siːvəʃɪp] *n Fin* **to go into r.** être placé(e) sous règlement judiciaire

receiving [rɪ'siːvɪŋ] **1** *n (of stolen goods)* recel *m*

2 *adj Fam* **to be on the r. end (of sth)** faire les frais (de qch)

recent ['riːsənt] *adj* récent(e); *(acquaintance)* nouveau(elle); *(development)* dernier(ère); **in r. months** au cours des derniers mois; **in r. times** récemment

recently ['riːsəntlɪ] *adv* récemment; **as r. as yesterday** pas plus tard qu'hier; **until quite r.** jusqu'à ces derniers temps

receptacle [rɪ'septəkəl] n récipient m

reception [rɪ'sepʃən] n (a) (of guests, announcement, book) accueil m; **to get a warm r.** être accueilli(e) chaleureusement; **r. center** (for refugees) centre m d'accueil; **r. room** (in house) salon m (b) (party) réception f; **(wedding) r.** réception (c) (in hotel) **r. (desk)** réception f (d) (of radio, TV program) réception f

receptionist [rɪ'sepʃənɪst] n réceptionniste mf

receptive [rɪ'septɪv] adj réceptif(ive)

recess ['ri:ses] n (a) (of law courts, Congress) vacances fpl (b) (in wall) renfoncement m; (smaller) niche f; (of mind, past) recoins mpl (c) Sch (between classes) récréation f, Fam récré f

recession [rɪ'seʃən] n récession f

recharge [ri:'tʃɑːdʒ] vt (battery) recharger; Fig **to r. one's batteries** recharger ses batteries

rechargeable [ri:'tʃɑːdʒəbəl] adj rechargeable

recharger [ri:'tʃɑːdʒə(r)] n (for battery) chargeur m

recidivism [rɪ'sɪdɪvɪzəm] n Law récidivisme m

recipe ['resɪpɪ] n also Fig recette f; **a r. for success** le secret de la réussite; **to be a r. for disaster** mener à la catastrophe; **r. book** livre m de recettes

recipient [rɪ'sɪpɪənt] n (of gift, letter) destinataire mf; (of check, money) bénéficiaire mf; (of award, honor) lauréat(e) m,f

reciprocal [rɪ'sɪprəkəl] adj réciproque

reciprocate [rɪ'sɪprəkeɪt] **1** vt retourner
2 vi rendre la pareille

recital [rɪ'saɪtəl] n (of poetry, music) récital m

recitation [resɪ'teɪʃən] n (of poem) récitation f

recite [rɪ'saɪt] **1** vt (poem) réciter; (complaints, details) énumérer
2 vi réciter

reckless ['reklɪs] adj imprudent(e); **r. driver** chauffard m

reckon ['rekən] **1** vt (a) (consider) considérer; **she is reckoned to be...** on la considère comme... (b) (calculate) calculer (c) Fam (think) penser
2 vi compter, calculer

▶**reckon on** vt insep compter sur

▶**reckon up** vt sep calculer

▶**reckon with** vt insep compter avec

reckoning ['rekənɪŋ] n estimation f; **by my r.** d'après mes calculs; **day of r.** moment m de vérité

reclaim [rɪ'kleɪm] vt (lost property, waste materials) récupérer; (expenses) se faire rembourser; **to r. land from the sea/the desert** gagner du terrain sur la mer/le désert

reclamation [reklə'meɪʃən] n (of waste materials) récupération f

recline [rɪ'klaɪn] vi s'allonger

reclining [rɪ'klaɪnɪŋ] adj **in a r. position** (person) en position allongée; **r. seat** siège m à dossier inclinable

recluse [rɪ'kluːs] n reclus(e) m,f

recognition [rekəg'nɪʃən] n reconnaissance f; **to have changed beyond** or **out of all r.** être devenu(e) méconnaissable; **in r. of** en reconnaissance de

recognizable [rekəg'naɪzəbəl] adj reconnaissable

recognize ['rekəgnaɪz] vt reconnaître

recognized ['rekəgnaɪzd] adj reconnu(e); **to be a r. authority (on sth)** faire autorité (en matière de qch)

recoil 1 n ['ri:kɔɪl] (of gun) recul m
2 vi [rɪ'kɔɪl] (of gun) reculer; (of person) avoir un mouvement de recul

recollect [rekə'lekt] vt se souvenir de

recollection [rekə'lekʃən] n souvenir m; **to the best of my r.** autant que je m'en souviens

recommend [rekə'mend] vt (a) (praise) recommander; **to r. sth to sb** recommander qch à qn; **the proposal has a lot to r. it** cette proposition présente de nombreux avantages (b) (advise) recommander, conseiller; **to r. sb to do sth** conseiller à qn de faire qch; Com **recommended retail price** prix m conseillé

recommendation [rekəmen'deɪʃən] n recommandation f

recompense ['rekəmpens] **1** n dédommagement m; **in r. for** en dédommagement de
2 vt dédommager

reconcile ['rekənsaɪl] vt (a) (person) réconcilier; **to be reconciled with sb** s'être réconcilié(e) avec qn; **to be reconciled to sth** se résigner à qch (b) (facts, differences, opinions) concilier

reconciliation [rekənsɪlɪ'eɪʃən] n réconciliation f

reconditioned [ri:kən'dɪʃənd] adj (TV, washing machine) remis(e) à neuf

reconnaissance [rɪ'kɒnɪsəns] n Mil reconnaissance f; **r. flight/mission** vol m/mission f de reconnaissance

reconquer [ri:'kɒŋkə(r)] vt reconquérir

reconquest [ri:'kɒŋkwest] n reconquête f

reconsider [ri:kən'sɪdə(r)] **1** vt réexaminer
2 vi réconsidérer la question

reconstitute [ri:'kɒnstɪtjuːt] vt reconstituer

reconstruct [ri:kən'strʌkt] vt reconstruire; (crime, event) reconstituer

reconstruction [ri:kən'strʌkʃən] n reconstruction f; (of crime, event) reconstitution f

record 1 n ['rekɔːd] (a) (account) rapport m; (file) dossier m; **we have no r. of this** nous n'en avons aucune trace; **to keep a r. of sth** garder une trace écrite de qch; **the coldest winter on r.** l'hiver le plus froid qu'on ait jamais enregistré; **she's on r. as saying that...** elle a déclaré officiellement que...; **(just) for the r.** au passage; **to put** or **to set the r. straight** mettre les choses au point; **r. office** archives fpl
(b) (personal history) passé m; (achievements) résultats mpl; (of criminal) casier m judiciaire; **to have a good/bad safety r.** avoir bonne/mauvaise réputation en matière de sécurité
(c) (musical) disque m; **r. company** maison f de disques; **r. player** tourne-disques m inv
(d) (best performance) record m; **to set/to break a r.** établir/battre un record
(e) Comput enregistrement m
2 adj ['rekɔːd] record inv; **in r. time** en un temps record; **unemployment is at a r. high/low** le chômage a atteint son taux le plus haut/bas
3 vt [rɪ'kɔːd] (a) (on video, cassette) enregistrer
(b) (write down) noter

record-breaking ['rekɔːdbreɪkɪŋ] adj record inv

recorder [rɪ'kɔːdə(r)] n (musical instrument) flûte f à bec

record-holder ['rekɔːdhəʊldə(r)] n détenteur(trice) m,f du record

recording [rɪ'kɔːdɪŋ] n (on tape) enregistrement m; **r. studio** studio m d'enregistrement

recount [rɪ'kaʊnt] vt (relate) raconter

re-count ['ri:kaʊnt] n (in election) deuxième décompte m

recoup [rɪ'kuːp] vt récupérer

recourse [rɪ'kɔːs] n recours m; **to have r. to** avoir recours à

recover [rɪ'kʌvə(r)] **1** vt (territory, customers) & Comput récupérer; (one's appetite, balance) retrouver
2 vi (from illness, setback) se remettre; (after running, traveling) récupérer; Fig (of economy) se redresser; (of sales) reprendre

recoverable [rɪ'kʌvərəbəl] adj (money) recouvrable

recovery [rɪ'kʌvərɪ] n (pl **recoveries**) n (a) (of lost or stolen item) récupération f (b) (from illness) rétablissement m; Fig (of economy) redressement m; (of sales) reprise f; **to make a r.** se rétablir

recreate [ri:krɪ'eɪt] vt recréer

recreation [rekrɪ'eɪʃən] n (leisure) divertissement m; Sch (recess) récréation f; **r. area** aire f de jeux; **r. room** salle f de jeux

recreational [rekrɪ'eɪʃənəl] adj de loisirs; **r. drug** = drogue prise occasionnellement, dans un but récréatif; **r. vehicle** mobile home m

recrimination [rɪkrɪmɪˈneɪʃən] n récrimination f

recruit [rɪˈkruːt] also Mil **1** n recrue f
2 vt recruter

recruitment [rɪˈkruːtmənt] n also Mil recrutement m; **r. consultant** conseil m en recrutement

rectangle [ˈrektæŋgəl] n rectangle m

rectangular [rekˈtæŋgjʊlə(r)] adj rectangulaire

rectify [ˈrektɪfaɪ] (pt & pp **rectified**) vt rectifier

rectitude [ˈrektɪtjuːd] n Formal rectitude f

rector [ˈrektə(r)] n Rel pasteur m anglican

rectory [ˈrektərɪ] (pl **rectories**) n Rel presbytère m

rectum [ˈrektəm] n rectum m

recumbent [rɪˈkʌmbənt] adj Formal allongé(e)

recuperate [rɪˈkuːpəreɪt] vi (from illness) se rétablir

recuperation [rɪkuːpəˈreɪʃən] n (from illness) rétablissement m

recur [rɪˈkɜː(r)] (pt & pp **recurred**) vi (of event, problem) se reproduire; (of theme, illness) revenir, réapparaître

recurrence [rɪˈkʌrəns] n récurrence f

recurring [rɪˈkɜːrɪŋ] adj (problem) récurrent(e); (nightmare) qui revient souvent; **six point six r.** six virgule six à l'infini

recyclable [riːˈsaɪkləbəl] adj recyclable

recycle [riːˈsaɪkəl] vt recycler; Comput **r. bin** corbeille f

recycled [riːˈsaɪkəld] adj recyclé; **r. paper** papier m recyclé

recycling [riːˈsaɪklɪŋ] n recyclage m; **r. plant** usine f de recyclage

red [red] **1** n (color) rouge m; Fam Fig **to see r.** (get angry) voir rouge; **to be in the r.** (in debt) être à découvert ou dans le rouge
2 adj rouge; (hair) roux (rousse); **to turn** or **to go r.** rougir; **to be as r. as a beet** être rouge comme une pivoine; **r. alert** alerte f rouge; **the R. Army** l'Armée f rouge; **r. blood cell** globule m rouge, hématie f; **r. card** (in soccer) carton m rouge; Fig **to roll out the r. carpet** dérouler le tapis rouge; **the R. Cross** la Croix-Rouge; Fig **r. herring** diversion f; (in movie, book) fausse piste f; Old-fashioned **R. Indian** Peau-Rouge mf; **r. light** feu m rouge; **r. meat** viande f rouge; **r. pepper** poivron m rouge; **mentioning her name to him is like a r. rag to a bull** le simple fait d'entendre son nom le met dans une colère noire; **(Little) R. Riding Hood** le Petit Chaperon rouge; **the R. Sea** la mer Rouge; **r. squirrel** écureuil m roux; **r. tape** paperasserie f; **r. wine** vin m rouge

red-blooded [redˈblʌdɪd] adj **a r. male** un homme viril

redbrick [ˈredbrɪk] adj (building) en brique rouge

redcurrant [ˈredkʌrənt] n groseille f

redden [ˈredən] **1** vt rougir
2 vi (of sky) rougeoyer; (of person) rougir

reddish [ˈredɪʃ] adj (light, color) rougeâtre; (hair) légèrement roux (rousse)

redecorate [riːˈdekəreɪt] vt (repaint) refaire la peinture de; (rewallpaper) retapisser

redeem [rɪˈdiːm] vt (a) (pawned item) racheter; (promise) tenir; (gift token, coupon) échanger; (mortgage, loan) rembourser (b) (rescue) racheter; **to r. oneself** se racheter

Redeemer [rɪˈdiːmə(r)] n Rel **the R.** le Rédempteur

redeeming [rɪˈdiːmɪŋ] adj **he has no r. features** il n'a rien pour le racheter; **his one r. feature is...** la seule chose qui le rachète, c'est...

redemption [rɪˈdem(p)ʃən] n Rel rédemption f; also Fig **to be beyond** or **past r.** être irrécupérable

redeploy [riːdɪˈplɔɪ] vt (troops) redéployer; (staff) réaffecter

redeployment [riːdɪˈplɔɪmənt] n (of troops) redéploiement m; (of staff) réaffectation f

redevelop [riːdɪˈveləp] vt réaménager

red-faced [ˈredˈfeɪst] adj (naturally) rougeaud(e); (with anger, embarrassment) rouge

red-handed [ˈredˈhændɪd] adj **to be caught r.** être pris(e) la main dans le sac

redhead [ˈredhed] n roux (rousse) m,f

red-hot [redˈhɒt] adj **(a)** (very hot) brûlant(e) **(b)** Fam (very good) super bon (bonne); **r. news** des nouvelles de dernière minute

redial [riːˈdaɪəl] **1** n **r. button** (on phone) touche f bis
2 vt (phone number) recomposer

redirect [riːdɪˈrekt, riːdaɪˈrekt] vt (letter) faire suivre; (plane, traffic) dévier; (energy) canaliser

rediscover [riːdɪsˈkʌvə(r)] vt redécouvrir

redistribute [riːdɪsˈtrɪbjuːt] vt redistribuer

red-letter day [ˈredˈletədeɪ] n journée f mémorable

red-light district [ˈredˈlaɪtdɪstrɪkt] n quartier m chaud

redo [riːˈduː] (pt **redid** [riːˈdɪd], pp **redone** [riːˈdʌn]) vt refaire

redolent [ˈredələnt] adj **to be r. of** (smell of) sentir; (suggest) avoir un parfum de

redraft [riːˈdrɑːft] vt rédiger de nouveau

redress [rɪˈdres] **1** n (of injustice, grievance) réparation f
2 vt (injustice, grievance) réparer; **to r. the balance** rétablir l'équilibre

redskin [ˈredskɪn] n Old-fashioned Peau-Rouge mf

reduce [rɪˈdjuːs] vt **(a)** (cost, amount, tax) réduire; (importance) minimiser; (price) baisser; (number of people) faire baisser; (sauce) faire réduire; **to r. speed** ralentir **(b)** (bring to a certain state) **to r. sth to ashes/dust** réduire qch en cendres/poussière; **to r. sb to silence** réduire qn au silence; **to r. sb to tears** faire fondre qn en larmes; **to be reduced to doing sth** être réduit(e) à faire qch

reduced [rɪˈdjuːst] adj réduit(e); **to live in r. circumstances** vivre dans la gêne

reduction [rɪˈdʌkʃən] n (of price, temperature) baisse f (**in** de); (of spending, on item) réduction f (**in/on** de/sur)

redundant [rɪˈdʌndənt] adj **(a)** (worker) **to make sb r.** licencier qn; **to be made r.** être licencié(e) **(b)** (superfluous) inutile

reed [riːd] n **(a)** (plant) roseau m **(b)** (of musical instrument) anche f

reef [riːf] n récif m

reek [riːk] **1** n relent m
2 vi also Fig **to r. (of sth)** puer (qch)

reel [riːl] **1** n **(a)** (for film, thread) bobine f; (for fishing line) moulinet m **(b)** (dance, music) quadrille m
2 vi (sway) chanceler; Fig **my head is reeling** la tête me tourne

▶**reel off** vt sep (names, statistics) débiter

re-elect [riːɪˈlekt] vt réélire

re-election [riːɪˈlekʃən] n réélection f

re-enact [riːɪˈnækt] vt reconstituer

re-enter [riːˈentə(r)] **1** vt entrer à nouveau dans
2 vi rentrer

re-establish [riːɪˈstæblɪʃ] vt rétablir

re-examine [riːɪgˈzæmɪn] vt réexaminer

ref [ref] n **(a)** (abbr **reference**) réf **(b)** Fam (abbr **referee**) arbitre m

refectory [rɪˈfektərɪ] (pl **refectories**) n réfectoire m

refer [rɪˈfɜː(r)] (pt & pp **referred**) vt soumettre (**to** à); **to r. a patient to a specialist** envoyer un patient chez un spécialiste

▶**refer to** vt insep **(a)** (mention) parler de; **she never refers to it** elle n'en parle jamais **(b)** (allude to) faire allusion à; **referred to as...** appelé(e)... **(c)** (consult) consulter **(d)** (apply to) s'appliquer à

referee [refəˈriː] **1** n (in sports) arbitre m
2 vt & vi arbitrer

reference [ˈrefərəns] n **(a)** (consultation, source) référence f; **for future r.** à titre d'information; **I can't do it without r. to headquarters** je ne peux pas le faire sans en référer au siège; **r. book** ouvrage m de référence; **r. number** (numéro m de) référence; **r. point, point of r.** point m de repère **(b)** (allusion) allusion f; **with r. to** (in letter) suite à **(c)** (from employer) lettre f de référence

referendum [refə'rendəm] *n* référendum *m*

refill 1 *n* ['ri:fɪl] *(for notebook)* feuillets *fpl* de rechange; *(for pen)* cartouche *f*; *(for lighter)* recharge *f*; **would you like a r.?** *(of drink)* je te ressers?

2 *vt* [ri:'fɪl] *(glass)* remplir à nouveau; *(lighter, pen)* recharger

refine [rɪ'faɪn] *vt* (**a**) *(sugar, petroleum)* raffiner (**b**) *(improve)* perfectionner

refined [rɪ'faɪnd] *adj also Fig* raffiné(e)

refinement [rɪ'faɪnmənt] *n* (**a**) *(of manners, taste, person)* raffinement *m* (**b**) *(improvement)* perfectionnement *m*; **to make refinements to sth** perfectionner qch

refinery [rɪ'faɪnərɪ] (*pl* **refineries**) *n* raffinerie *f*

refit 1 *n* ['ri:fɪt] *(of ship)* remise *f* en état

2 *vt* [ri:'fɪt] *(pt & pp* **refitted**) *(ship)* remettre en état

reflate [ri:'fleɪt] *vt Econ* relancer

reflation [ri:'fleɪʃən] *n Econ* relance *f*

reflect [rɪ'flekt] **1** *vt* (**a**) *(image, light)* réfléchir, refléter; **to be reflected (in)** se réfléchir ou se refléter (dans) (**b**) *Fig (portray)* refléter (**c**) *(think)* **to r. that...** se dire que...

2 *vi* (**a**) *(think)* réfléchir (**on** à) (**b**) **to r. well/badly on sb/sth** faire honneur/du tort à qn/qch

reflection [rɪ'flekʃən] *n* (**a**) *(image, indication)* reflet *m*; *Fig* **it is no r. on your own capabilities** cela ne remet pas en cause vos compétences (**b**) *(thought)* réflexion *f*; **on r.** après réflexion

reflective [rɪ'flektɪv] *adj* (**a**) *(surface)* réfléchissant(e) (**b**) *(person)* réfléchi(e)

reflector [rɪ'flektə(r)] *n* *(on bicycle, vehicle)* catadioptre *m*

reflex ['ri:fleks] **1** *n* réflexe *m*

2 *adj* réflexe; **r. action** réflexe *m*; **r. camera** réflex *m*

reflexive [rɪ'fleksɪv] *adj Gram* **r. pronoun** pronom *m* réfléchi; **r. verb** verbe *m* pronominal réfléchi

reflexologist [ri:flek'splədʒɪst] *n* réflexologiste *mf*

reflexology [ri:flek'splədʒɪ] *n* réflexologie *f*

reforestation [ri:fprɪ'steɪʃən] *n* reboisement *m*

reform [rɪ'fɔ:m] **1** *n* réforme *f*

2 *vt* réformer

3 *vi* se réformer

re-form ['ri:'fɔ:m] *vi (of organization, pop group)* se reformer

re-format ['ri:'fɔ:mæt] *(pt & pp* **re-formatted**) *vt Comput (disk)* reformater

reformation [refə'meɪʃən] *n* réforme *f*; *Hist* **the R.** la Réforme

reformatory [rɪ'fɔ:mətərɪ] (*pl* **reformatories**) *n* ≃ centre *m* d'éducation surveillée

reformed [rɪ'fɔ:md] *adj (alcoholic, drug addict)* ancien(enne); **he's a r. character** il s'est assagi

reformer [rɪ'fɔ:mə(r)] *n* réformateur(trice) *m,f*

reformist [rɪ'fɔ:mɪst] *n & adj* réformiste *mf*

refract [rɪ'frækt] *vt* réfracter

refrain [rɪ'freɪn] **1** *n* *also Fig* refrain *m*

2 *vi* **to r. from sth/doing sth** s'abstenir de qch/de faire qch

re-freeze [ri:'fri:z] *(pt* **re-froze** [ri:'frəʊz], *pp* **re-frozen** [ri:'frəʊzən]) *vt* recongeler

refresh [rɪ'freʃ] *vt (of drink)* rafraîchir; *(of nap, vacation)* reposer; *(bath)* revigorer; *Comput* actualiser; **to r. one's memory** se rafraîchir la mémoire; **to r. sb's glass** *(top up)* resservir à boire à qn

refreshing [rɪ'freʃɪŋ] *adj (breeze, drink)* rafraîchissant(e); *(nap, vacation)* reposant(e); *(bath)* revigorant(e); *Fig (honesty)* qui fait l'effet d'une bouffée d'air frais

refreshments [rɪ'freʃmənts] *npl* rafraîchissements *mpl*

refrigerate [rɪ'frɪdʒəreɪt] *vt* réfrigérer; **r. after opening** *(on package)* à conserver au frais après ouverture

refrigeration [rɪfrɪdʒə'reɪʃən] *n* réfrigération *f*

refrigerator [rɪ'frɪdʒəreɪtə(r)] *n (domestic)* réfrigérateur *m*, frigidaire® *m*; *(industrial)* chambre *f* froide

re-froze [ri:'frəʊz] *pt of* **re-freeze**

re-frozen [ri:'frəʊzən] *pp of* **re-freeze**

refuel [ri:'fjʊəl] **1** *vt (ship, aircraft)* ravitailler en carburant

2 *vi (of ship, aircraft)* se ravitailler en carburant

refuge ['refju:dʒ] *n (from danger, weather)* refuge *m*; *(for battered women)* foyer *m*; **to seek r.** chercher refuge; **to take r.** se réfugier

refugee [refjʊ'dʒi:] *n* réfugié(e) *m,f*; **r. camp** camp *m* de réfugiés; **r. status** statut *m* de réfugié

refund 1 *n* ['ri:fʌnd] remboursement *m*

2 *vt* [ri:'fʌnd] rembourser

refurbish [ri:'fɜ:bɪʃ] *vt* rénover

refusal [rɪ'fju:zəl] *n* refus *m*; **to give a flat r.** refuser catégoriquement; **to have first r. (on sth)** avoir la priorité (pour qch)

refuse[1] ['refju:s] *n (rubbish)* ordures *fpl*

refuse[2] [rɪ'fju:z] **1** *vt (invitation, offer)* refuser; *(request)* rejeter; **to r. to do sth** refuser de faire qch; **to r. sb sth** refuser qch à qn

2 *vi (of person)* refuser; *(of horse)* refuser l'obstacle

refute [rɪ'fju:t] *vt (argument, theory)* réfuter; *(allegation)* nier

regain [rɪ'geɪn] *vt* (**a**) *(get back)* retrouver; *(power, political seat)* reconquérir; **to r. possession of sth** rentrer en possession de qch; **to r. consciousness** revenir à soi; **to r. the lead** *(in contest)* reprendre l'avantage (**b**) *(reach again)* regagner

regal ['ri:gəl] *adj* royal(e)

regale [rɪ'geɪl] *vt* **to r. sb with sth** gratifier qn de qch

regalia [rɪ'geɪlɪə] *npl* insignes *mpl*

regard [rɪ'gɑ:d] **1** *n* (**a**) *(admiration)* respect *m*, estime *f*; **to hold sb in high r.** tenir qn en haute estime (**b**) *(consideration)* égard *m*; **out of r. for** par égard pour; **without r. to** sans tenir compte de (**c**) *(connection)* **in this r.** à cet égard; **in all regards** à tous égards; **with r. to** en ce qui concerne (**d**) **regards** *(good wishes)* amitiés *fpl*; **give her my regards** transmets-lui mes amitiés

2 *vt* (**a**) *(admire, respect)* estimer (**b**) *(consider)* **to r. sb/sth as** considérer qn/qch comme; **to r. sb/sth with suspicion** être soupçonneux(euse) à l'égard de qn/qch (**c**) *(concern)* concerner; **as regards...** en ce qui concerne..., concernant...

regarding [rɪ'gɑ:dɪŋ] *prep* en ce qui concerne, concernant

regardless [rɪ'gɑ:dlɪs] *adv* (**a**) *(despite everything)* quand même (**b**) **r. of** *(without considering)* sans tenir compte de; **r. of the expense** sans regarder à la dépense

regatta [rɪ'gætə] *n* régate *f*

regency ['ri:dʒənsɪ] (*pl* **regencies**) *n* régence *f*

regenerate [rɪ'dʒenəreɪt] **1** *vt (sector, city)* régénérer; *(interest, enthusiasm)* raviver

2 *vi* se régénérer

regeneration [rɪdʒenə'reɪʃən] *n* régénération *f*

regent ['ri:dʒənt] *n & adj* régent(e) *m,f*

reggae ['regeɪ] *n* reggae *m*

regime [reɪ'ʒi:m] *n* régime *m*

regiment ['redʒɪmənt] **1** *n* régiment *m*

2 *vt* enrégimenter

regimental [redʒɪ'mentəl] *adj* du régiment

regimentation [redʒɪmen'teɪʃən] *n* discipline *f* draconienne

regimented ['redʒɪmentɪd] *adj* très strict(e)

region ['ri:dʒən] *n* région *f*; *Fig* **in the r. of** environ

regional ['ri:dʒənəl] *adj* régional(e)

regionalism ['ri:dʒənəlɪzəm] *n* régionalisme *m*

register ['redʒɪstə(r)] **1** *n* registre *m*; *(at school)* cahier *m* d'appel; *(of voters)* liste *f* électorale; **to take the r.** *(at school)* faire l'appel; **r. of births, marriages and deaths** registre de l'état civil; **(cash) r.** caisse *f* (enregistreuse)

2 *vt* (**a**) *(member, student)* inscrire; *(birth, marriage, death)* déclarer; *(complaint)* déposer; **to r. a protest** protester (**b**) *(temperature, speed)* enregistrer; *(astonishment, displeasure)* manifester (**c**) *(realize)* se rendre compte de (**d**) *(achieve) (victory, progress)* enregistrer

3 *vi* (**a**) *(for course)* s'inscrire; *(at hotel)* signer le registre; *(of voter)* s'inscrire sur les listes électorales (**b**) *Fam (of fact)* **I told him but it didn't r.** je lui ai dit mais il n'a pas enregistré

registered ['redʒɪstəd] *adj (letter)* recommandé(e); **r. trademark** marque *f* déposée

registrar ['redʒɪstrɑː(r)] *n* (**a**) *(record keeper)* officier *m* de l'état civil (**b**) *(in university)* responsable *mf* des inscriptions (**c**) *(in hospital)* chef *m* de clinique

registration [redʒɪs'treɪʃən] *n (of student)* inscription *f; (of voter)* inscription sur les listes électorales; *(of birth, death, marriage)* déclaration *f*

regress [rɪ'gres] *vi* régresser

regression [rɪ'greʃən] *n* régression *f*

regressive [rɪ'gresɪv] *adj* régressif(ive)

regret [rɪ'gret] **1** *n* regret *m;* **to send one's regrets** *(apologies)* envoyer ses excuses; *(condolences)* envoyer ses condoléances

2 *vt (pt & pp* **regretted)** regretter; **to r. doing** *or* **having done sth** regretter d'avoir fait qch; **I r. to (have to) inform you that...** j'ai le regret de vous annoncer que...

regretful [rɪ'gretfʊl] *adj (voice, smile)* plein(e) de regret; *(person)* qui a des regrets

regrettable [rɪ'gretəbəl] *adj* regrettable

regroup [riː'gruːp] **1** *vt* regrouper

2 *vi* se regrouper

regular ['regjʊlə(r)] **1** *n (in bar, restaurant)* habitué(e) *m,f*

2 *adj* (**a**) *(features, pulse, verb)* régulier(ère); **on a r. basis** régulièrement; **he comes twice a week, as r. as clockwork** il vient deux fois par semaine, c'est réglé comme du papier à musique (**b**) *(normal, habitual)* habituel(elle); *(in size)* moyen(enne); *(listener, viewer)* fidèle; *(customer)* régulier(ère); **she was a r. visitor to the house** elle venait régulièrement à la maison (**c**) *(army, soldier)* régulier(ère) (**d**) *Fam (pleasant)* sympa; **a r. guy** un type sympa (**e**) *Fam (for emphasis)* vrai(e)

regularity [regjʊ'lærɪtɪ] *n* régularité *f*

regulate ['regjʊleɪt] *vt* (**a**) *(adjust)* régler (**b**) *(control)* réglementer

regulation [regjʊ'leɪʃən] **1** *n* (**a**) *(action)* réglementation *f* (**b**) *(rule)* règlement *m*

2 *adj (statutory)* réglementaire

regulator ['regjʊleɪtə(r)] *n* régulateur *m*

regulatory [regjʊ'leɪtərɪ] *adj* de contrôle

regurgitate [rɪ'gɜːdʒɪteɪt] *vt* régurgiter; *Fig* recracher

rehabilitate [riːhə'bɪlɪteɪt] *vt* réhabiliter

rehabilitation [riːhəbɪlɪ'teɪʃən] *n* réhabilitation *f*

rehash *Fam* **1** *n* ['riːhæʃ] resucée *f*

2 *vt* [riː'hæʃ] *(ideas, proposal)* reprendre; *(film, book)* remanier

rehearsal [rɪ'hɜːsəl] *n* répétition *f*

rehearse [rɪ'hɜːs] *vt & vi* répéter

rehouse [riː'haʊz] *vt* reloger

reign [reɪn] **1** *n* règne *m*

2 *vi also Fig* régner

reigning ['reɪnɪŋ] *adj (monarch)* régnant(e); *(champion)* en titre

reimburse [riːɪm'bɜːs] *vt* rembourser

rein [reɪn] *n also Fig* rêne *f; Fig* **to give sb free r. to do sth** donner carte blanche à qn pour qu'il/elle fasse qch; *Fig* **to give free r. to one's imagination** donner libre cours à son imagination; *Fig* **to keep a tight r. on sb** tenir la bride haute à qn

▸**rein in** *vt sep* (**a**) *(horse) & Fig (person)* ramener au pas (**b**) *(expenses)* maîtriser

reincarnate [riːɪn'kɑːneɪt] *vt* **to be reincarnated** être réincarné(e)

reincarnation [riːɪnkɑː'neɪʃən] *n* réincarnation *f*

reindeer ['reɪndɪə(r)] *n* renne *m*

reinforce [riːɪn'fɔːs] *vt also Fig* renforcer; **reinforced concrete** béton *m* armé

reinforcement [riːɪn'fɔːsmənt] *n* renforcement *m; also Fig* **reinforcements** renforts *mpl*

reinsert [riːɪn'sɜːt] *vt* réinsérer

reinstate [riːɪn'steɪt] *vt* réintégrer

reinsurance [riːɪn'ʃʊərəns] *n* réassurance *f*

reinsure [riːɪn'ʃʊə(r)] *vt* réassurer

reinvent [riːɪn'vent] *vt Fig* **to r. oneself** changer d'image; **to r. the wheel** refaire ce qui a déjà été fait

reinvest [riːɪn'vest] *vt* réinvestir

reissue [riː'ɪʃuː] **1** *n (of book, record)* réédition *f*

2 *vt (book, record)* rééditer

reiterate [riː'ɪtəreɪt] *vt* réitérer

reiteration [riːɪtə'reɪʃən] *n* réitération *f*

reject 1 *n* ['riːdʒekt] *(object)* rebut *m; Fam (person)* inadapté(e) *m,f*

2 *vt* [rɪ'dʒekt] rejeter; *(offer, goods)* refuser

rejection [rɪ'dʒekʃən] *n* rejet *m; (of offer, goods)* refus *m;* **to meet with r.** être rejeté(e)

rejoice [rɪ'dʒɔɪs] *vi* se réjouir

rejoicing [rɪ'dʒɔɪsɪŋ] *n* réjouissance *f*

rejoin[1] [riː'dʒɔɪn] *vt* (**a**) *(group, highway)* rejoindre; *(race)* reprendre (**b**) *(join again)* réintégrer

rejoin[2] [rɪ'dʒɔɪn] *vt & vi (retort)* répliquer, rétorquer

rejoinder [rɪ'dʒɔɪndə(r)] *n* réplique *f*

rejuvenate [rɪ'dʒuːvɪneɪt] *vt* rajeunir

rekindle [riː'kɪndəl] *vt* raviver

relapse 1 *n* ['riːlæps] rechute *f*

2 *vi* [rɪ'læps] rechuter; **to r. into** retomber dans

relate [rɪ'leɪt] **1** *vt* (**a**) *(narrate)* raconter (**b**) *(connect)* mettre en rapport (**to** avec)

2 *vi* (**a**) *(be relevant)* **to r. to** avoir rapport à (**b**) **to r. to** *(understand) (person)* avoir des affinités avec; *(music)* apprécier; *(idea)* comprendre

related [rɪ'leɪtɪd] *adj (people, animals, languages)* apparenté(e); *(ideas, events, activities)* lié(e)

relation [rɪ'leɪʃən] *n* (**a**) *(relative)* parent(e) *m,f* (**b**) *(connection)* rapport *m;* **to bear no r. to** n'avoir aucun rapport avec

relationship [rɪ'leɪʃənʃɪp] *n* (**a**) *(between people)* relation *f; (romantic, sexual)* relation amoureuse; *(between countries)* relations *fpl; (within family)* lien *m* de parenté; **to have a good/bad r. with sb** s'entendre/ne pas bien s'entendre avec qn (**b**) *(connection)* rapport *m*

relative ['relətɪv] **1** *n (person)* parent(e) *m,f*

2 *adj (comparative)* relatif(ive); **r. to** en rapport avec; *Gram* **r. clause** proposition *f* relative; **r. pronoun** pronom *m* relatif

relatively ['relətɪvlɪ] *adv* relativement

relativity [relə'tɪvɪtɪ] *n Phys* relativité *f*

relax [rɪ'læks] **1** *vt (person)* détendre; *(muscles, discipline)* relâcher; *(law, control)* assouplir; **to r. one's grip (on)** relâcher son étreinte (sur); *Fig* relâcher son emprise (sur)

2 *vi (of person)* se détendre; *(of muscles)* se relâcher; **r.!** *(calm down)* du calme!

relaxation [riːlæk'seɪʃən] *n* (**a**) *(of person)* détente *f; (of discipline)* relâchement *m; (of control)* assouplissement *m* (**b**) *(as therapy)* relaxation *f;* **r. exercises/classes** exercices *mpl*/cours *mpl* de relaxation

relaxed [rɪ'lækst] *adj* détendu(e)

relaxing [rɪ'læksɪŋ] *adj* relaxant(e)

relay 1 *n* ['riːleɪ] *(of workers)* équipe *f* de relais; **to work in relays** se relayer; **r. (race)** course *f* de relais *m; Rad & TV* **r. station** relais *m*

2 *vt* [rɪ'leɪ] retransmettre; *(information)* transmettre

release [rɪ'liːs] **1** *n* (**a**) *(of prisoner)* libération *f; (of gas)* émission *f; (emotional)* soulagement *m; (of record, film)* sortie *f;* **to be on general r.** *(of film)* être sorti(e) dans toutes les grandes salles de cinéma

2 *vt* (**a**) *(prisoner)* libérer; *(gas, fumes)* émettre; *(balloon, bomb)*

lâcher; *(funds)* dégager; *(brake)* desserrer; **to r. sb from an obligation** dégager qn d'une obligation; **to r. sb's hand** lâcher la main de qn (**b**) *(record, film)* sortir; *(news, information)* communiquer

relegate ['relɪgeɪt] *vt* reléguer (**to** à)

relegation [relɪ'geɪʃən] *n (of person)* relégation *f* (**to** à)

relent [rɪ'lent] *vi (of storm, wind)* se calmer; *(of person)* céder

relentless [rɪ'lentlɪs] *adj (person, attitude)* implacable; *(rain, criticism)* incessant(e)

relevance ['reləvəns] *n* pertinence *f*; **to have r. to sth** avoir un rapport avec qch

relevant ['reləvənt] *adj* (**a**) *(apt)* pertinent(e); **to be r. (to sth)** avoir un rapport (avec qch) (**b**) *(appropriate) (chapter)* correspondant(e); *(authorities)* compétent(e); *(experience, qualifications)* requis(e) (**c**) *(topical)* d'actualité

reliability [rɪlaɪə'bɪlɪtɪ] *n (of person, information)* sérieux *m*; *(of machine)* sûreté *f*, fiabilité *f*

reliable [rɪ'laɪəbəl] *adj (person, machine)* fiable; *(information)* sûr(e); **from a r. source** de source sûre

reliably [rɪ'laɪəblɪ] *adv* **to be r. informed that...** savoir de source sûre que...

reliance [rɪ'laɪəns] *n* (**a**) *(dependence)* dépendance *f* (**on** vis-à-vis de) (**b**) *(trust)* confiance *f*; **to place r. on sb/sth** faire confiance à qn/qch

reliant [rɪ'laɪənt] *adj* **to be r. on** être dépendant(e) de

relic ['relɪk] *n Rel* relique *f*; *Fig* vestige *m*

relief [rɪ'liːf] *n* (**a**) *(comfort)* soulagement *m*; **to bring r. to sb** soulager qn (**b**) *(help)* secours *m*, aide *f*; **r. fund** fonds *m* d'aide (**c**) *(replacement)* remplaçant(e) *m,f* (**d**) *(of besieged city, troops)* libération *f* (**e**) *(in art)* relief *m*; **in r.** en relief; *Fig* **to throw sth into r.** mettre qch en relief; **r. map** carte *f* en relief

relieve [rɪ'liːv] *vt* (**a**) *(alleviate)* soulager; *(boredom)* tromper; *(pressure)* réduire; *Euph* **to r. oneself** se soulager (**b**) *(replace)* remplacer (**c**) *(liberate)* libérer; **to r. sb of his duties** relever qn de ses fonctions; *Hum* **to r. sb of his wallet** soulager qn de son portefeuille

religion [rɪ'lɪdʒən] *n* religion *f*; **what is your r.?** quelle est votre religion?; *(on form)* à quelle confession appartenez-vous?

religious [rɪ'lɪdʒəs] *adj also Fig* religieux(euse); **r. education, r. instruction** instruction *f* religieuse

religiously [rɪ'lɪdʒəslɪ] *adv also Fig* religieusement

relinquish [rɪ'lɪŋkwɪʃ] *vt (hope, habit, thought)* abandonner; *(claim, share)* renoncer à; *Fig* **to r. one's hold on sb/sth** relâcher son emprise sur qn/qch

relish ['relɪʃ] **1** *n* (**a**) *(pleasure)* goût *m* (**for** pour); **to do sth with r.** faire qch avec délectation (**b**) *(pickle)* condiments *mpl*
2 *vt* savourer; **I didn't r. the idea** l'idée ne m'enthousiasmait guère

relive [riː'lɪv] *vt* revivre

relocate [riːləʊ'keɪt] **1** *vt (company)* transférer; *(person)* muter
2 *vi (of company)* être transféré(e); *(of person)* se déplacer

relocation [riːləʊ'keɪʃən] *n* déménagement *m*

reluctance [rɪ'lʌktəns] *n* réticence *f*; **to do sth with r.** faire qch à contrecœur

reluctant [rɪ'lʌktənt] *adj (smile, promise)* accordé(e) à contrecœur; **to be r. to do sth** être réticent(e) à faire qch

▶**rely on, rely upon** [rɪ'laɪ] *(pt & pp relied) vt insep* (**a**) **to r. on sb (to do sth)** compter sur qn (pour faire qch) (**b**) *(be dependent on)* dépendre de

REM [ɑːriː'em] *n (abbr rapid eye movement)* mouvements *mpl* oculaires rapides

remade [riː'meɪd] *pt & pp of remake*

remain [rɪ'meɪn] *vi* (**a**) *(stay behind, continue to be)* rester (**b**) *(be left)* subsister; **it remains to be seen** cela reste à voir

remainder [rɪ'meɪndə(r)] *n* reste *m*

remaindered [rɪ'meɪndɜːd] *adj (book)* soldé(e)

remaining [rɪ'meɪnɪŋ] *adj* restant(e)

remains [rɪ'meɪnz] *npl (of meal, fortune)* restes *mpl*; *(of civilization, building)* vestiges *mpl*; (**human**) **r.** restes humains

remake 1 *n* ['riːmeɪk] *(of film)* remake *m*
2 *vt* [riː'meɪk] *(pt & pp remade* [riː'meɪd]*) (film)* faire un remake de

remand [rɪ'mɑːnd] *Law* **1** *n* **on r.** en détention préventive
2 *vt* **to r. sb (in custody)** placer qn en détention préventive

remark [rɪ'mɑːk] **1** *n* remarque *f*; **to make** *or* **to pass a r.** faire une remarque
2 *vt* faire remarquer

remarkable [rɪ'mɑːkəbəl] *adj* remarquable

remarkably [rɪ'mɑːkəblɪ] *adv* remarquablement

remarry [riː'mærɪ] *(pt & pp remarried) vi* se remarier

remedial [rɪ'miːdɪəl] *adj* (**a**) *(class)* de rattrapage; **r. education** rattrapage *m* scolaire (**b**) *(corrective)* **to take r. measures** prendre des mesures

remedy ['remɪdɪ] **1** *n (pl remedies) also Fig* remède *m*
2 *vt (pt & pp remedied)* remédier à

remember [rɪ'membə(r)] **1** *vt* (**a**) *(recall)* se souvenir de, se rappeler; **to r. doing sth** se souvenir d'avoir fait qch; **to r. to do sth** penser à faire qch; **a night to r.** une nuit mémorable (**b**) *(commemorate)* commémorer; **to r. the dead** rendre hommage aux disparus (**c**) *(speak of)* **to r. sb to sb** rappeler qn au bon souvenir de qn
2 *vi* se souvenir, se rappeler; **as far as I r.** pour autant que je me souvienne

remembrance [rɪ'membrəns] *n Formal (memory)* souvenir *m*; **in r. of** en souvenir de

remind [rɪ'maɪnd] *vt* **to r. sb of sth** rappeler qch à qn; **to r. sb to do sth** rappeler à qn de faire qch; **that reminds me...** à propos...

reminder [rɪ'maɪndə(r)] *n* rappel *m*

reminisce [remɪ'nɪs] *vi* évoquer des souvenirs; **to r. about sth** évoquer qch

reminiscence [remɪ'nɪsəns] *n* souvenir *m*

reminiscent [remɪ'nɪsənt] *adj* **to be r. of** rappeler

remiss [rɪ'mɪs] *adj* négligent(e); **it was very r. of him not to phone** c'était très négligent de sa part de ne pas téléphoner

remission [rɪ'mɪʃən] *n* (**a**) *Law* remise *f* de peine (**b**) *(of disease)* **to be in r.** être en phase de rémission

remit 1 *n* ['riːmɪt] *(area of authority)* attributions *fpl*
2 *vt* [rɪ'mɪt] *(pt & pp remitted) (payment)* remettre

remittance [rɪ'mɪtəns] *n* versement *m*

remix *Mus* **1** *vt* [riː'mɪks] *(record, recording)* remixer, refaire le mixage de
2 *n* ['riːmɪks] remix *m*

remnant ['remnənt] *n* reste *m*; *(of civilization, building)* vestige *m*; *(of cloth)* coupon *m*

remonstrate ['remənstreɪt] *vi* protester; **to r. with sb** faire des remontrances à qn

remorse [rɪ'mɔːs] *n* remords *m*; **to feel r.** avoir du *ou* des remords

remorseful [rɪ'mɔːsfʊl] *adj* plein(e) de remords

remorseless [rɪ'mɔːslɪs] *adj* impitoyable

remortgage [riː'mɔːgɪdʒ] *vt (house, property)* hypothéquer de nouveau, prendre une nouvelle hypothèque sur

remote [rɪ'məʊt] *adj* (**a**) *(far-off) (in space)* éloigné(e) (**from** de); *(in time)* lointain(e) (**from** de); **r. control** télécommande *f* (**b**) *(aloof)* distant(e) (**c**) *(chance, possibility)* vague; **the remotest chance/idea** la moindre chance/idée

remote-controlled [rɪ'məʊtkən'trəʊld] *adj* télécommandé(e)

remotely [rɪ'məʊtlɪ] *adv* (**a**) *(distantly)* **r. situated** isolé(e) (**b**) *(slightly)* vaguement; **not r.** pas du tout

removal [rɪ'muːvəl] *n (of politician, official)* renvoi *m*; *(of control, doubt, threat)* suppression *f*; *(of stain)* nettoyage *m*

remove [rɪ'muːv] *vt* (**a**) *(take away) (thing)* enlever; *(doubt)* dissiper;

(stain) faire partir; *(politician, official)* renvoyer; **to r. one's child from a school** retirer son enfant d'une école (**b**) *(take off) (coat, hat)* enlever, retirer; *(tire)* démonter

remover [rɪ'muːvə(r)] *n (for paint)* décapant *m*; *(for nail polish)* dissolvant *m*

remunerate [rɪ'mjuːnəreɪt] *vt Formal* rémunérer

remuneration [rɪmjuːnə'reɪʃən] *n Formal* rémunération *f*

remunerative [rɪ'mjuːnərətɪv] *adj Formal* rémunéra-teur(trice)

renaissance [rɪ'neɪsəns] *n* renouveau *m*; **the R.** la Renaissance

renal ['riːnəl] *adj* rénal(e)

rename [riː'neɪm] *vt* rebaptiser

rend [rend] *(pt & pp* **rent** [rent]) *vt Lit (tear)* déchirer

render ['rendə(r)] *vt Formal* rendre; **to r. homage to sb** rendre hommage à qn; **to r. sth into French** rendre qch en français; **for services rendered** pour services rendus; **the news rendered her speechless** la nouvelle l'a laissée sans voix

rendezvous ['rɒndɪvuː] **1** *n (pl* **rendezvous** ['rɒndɪvuːz])* rendez-vous *m inv*
  2 *vi (pt & pp* **rendezvoused** ['rɒndɪvuːd])* se retrouver

rendition [ren'dɪʃən] *n* interprétation *f*

renegade ['renɪɡeɪd] *n* renégat(e) *m,f*

renege [rɪ'neɪɡ] *vi* **to r. on sth** revenir sur qch

renew [rɪ'njuː] *vt (passport, membership)* renouveler; *(activity, negotiations, library book)* reprendre; *(optimism, strength, interest)* raviver; *(speculation)* relancer

renewable [rɪ'njuːəbəl] *adj* renouvelable

renewal [rɪ'njuːəl] *n (of passport, membership)* renouvellement *m*; *(of activity, negotiations)* reprise *f*; *(of library book)* renouvellement de prêt; *(of optimism, interest)* regain *m*

rennet ['renɪt] *n* présure *f*

renounce [rɪ'naʊns] *vt* renoncer à; *(treaty)* dénoncer; *(friends, faith, principles)* renier

renovate ['renəveɪt] *vt* rénover

renovation [renə'veɪʃən] *n* rénovation *f*

renown [rɪ'naʊn] *n* renommée *f*

renowned [rɪ'naʊnd] *adj* renommé(e) (**for** pour)

rent[1] [rent] **1** *n (on apartment, house)* loyer *m*; **for r.** à louer; **r. subsidy** allocation *f* (de) logement
  2 *vt* louer

rent[2] [rent] *pt & pp of* **rend**

rental ['rentəl] *n* (**a**) *(thing or place rented)* location *f* (**b**) *(money) (for house)* loyer *m*; *(for car, equipment, TV)* location *f*; *(for telephone)* abonnement *m*

rent-free [rent'friː] **1** *adj* exempt(e) de loyer
  2 *adv* sans payer de loyer

reopen [riː'əʊpən] **1** *vt* rouvrir; *(talks)* reprendre; *Fig* **to r. old wounds** rouvrir une plaie
  2 *vi (of talks)* reprendre; *(of store, theater)* rouvrir; **school reopens on August 21st** la rentrée des classes aura lieu le 21 août

reorder [riː'ɔːdə(r)] *vt* passer une nouvelle commande de

reorganization [riːɔːɡənaɪ'zeɪʃən] *n* réorganisation *f*

reorganize [riː'ɔːɡənaɪz] *vt* réorganiser

rep [rep] *n Fam (abbr* **representative**) VRP *m*

repaid [riː'peɪd] *pt & pp of* **repay**

repaint [riː'peɪnt] *vt* repeindre

repair [rɪ'peə(r)] **1** *n* réparation *f*; **to be beyond r.** être irréparable; **to be in good/bad r.** être en bon/mauvais état; **to be under r.** être en réparation; **r. shop** atelier *m* de réparations
  2 *vt* réparer

repairman [rɪ'peəmæn] *n* réparateur *m*

reparation [repə'reɪʃən] *n* (**a**) *Formal (compensation)* réparation *f*; **to make r. for sth** réparer qch (**b**) *(after war)* **reparations** réparations *fpl*

repartee [repɑː'tiː] *n* repartie *f*

repast [rɪ'pɑːst] *n Lit* repas *m*

repatriate [riː'pætrɪeɪt] *vt* rapatrier (**to** vers)

repatriation [riːpætrɪ'eɪʃən] *n* rapatriement *m*

repay [riː'peɪ] *(pt & pp* **repaid** [riː'peɪd])* *vt* (**a**) *(reimburse) (person, money)* rembourser (**b**) *(reward) (person)* remercier (**for** de); *(kindness)* payer de retour; *(loyalty)* récompenser

repayable [riː'peɪəbəl] *adj* remboursable

repayment [riː'peɪmənt] *n* remboursement *m*; **r. plan** calendrier *m* des paiements

repeal [rɪ'piːl] *vt* abroger

repeat [rɪ'piːt] **1** *n (of event)* répétition *f*; *(of TV or radio program)* rediffusion *f*; **r. prescription** ≃ ordonnance *f* renouvelable
  2 *vt* répéter; *(attempt)* renouveler; *(TV program)* rediffuser; **to r. oneself** se répéter

repeated [rɪ'piːtɪd] *adj* répété(e)

repeatedly [rɪ'piːtɪdlɪ] *adv* à maintes reprises

repel [rɪ'pel] *(pt & pp* **repelled**)* *vt also Fig* repousser

repellent [rɪ'pelənt] **1** *n (for insects)* anti-moustiques *m inv*
  2 *adj (disgusting)* repoussant(e)

repent [rɪ'pent] **1** *vt* se repentir de
  2 *vi* se repentir (**of** de)

repentance [rɪ'pentəns] *n* repentir *m*

repentant [rɪ'pentənt] *adj* repentant(e) (**of** de)

repercussion [riːpə'kʌʃən] *n* répercussion *f*

repertoire ['repətwɑː(r)] *n* répertoire *m*

repertory ['repətərɪ] *(pl* **repertories**)* *n Theat* répertoire *m*; **r. company** troupe *f* de répertoire

repetition [repɪ'tɪʃən] *n* répétition *f*; *(of attempt)* renouvellement *m*

repetitive [rɪ'petɪtɪv] *adj* répétitif(ive); **r. strain injury** = douleurs dans les bras et les mains dues à la répétition de certains mouvements

rephrase [riː'freɪz] *vt* reformuler

replace [rɪ'pleɪs] *vt* (**a**) *(put back)* **to r. sth** remettre qch à sa place; **to r. the receiver** *(on telephone)* raccrocher (**b**) *(substitute for)* remplacer

replacement [rɪ'pleɪsmənt] *n* (**a**) *(putting back)* remise *f* en place; *(substituting)* remplacement *m*; *Fin* **r. cost** coût *m* de remplacement; **r. parts** pièces *fpl* de remplacement; **r. value** valeur *f* de remplacement (**b**) *(person)* remplaçant(e) *m,f*

replay **1** *n* ['riːpleɪ] *(of match)* nouvelle rencontre *f*; *(on TV)* reprise *f* de l'action; *(at slow speed)* ralenti *m*
  2 *vt* [riː'pleɪ] *(match)* rejouer

replenish [rɪ'plenɪʃ] *vt (cup, tank)* remplir à nouveau (**with** de); **to r. one's supplies** se réapprovisionner

replete [rɪ'pliːt] *adj Formal* rassasié(e) (**with** de)

replica ['replɪkə] *n* réplique *f*; *Fig (of person)* portrait *m*

replicate ['replɪkeɪt] *vt* reproduire

reply [rɪ'plaɪ] **1** *n (pl* **replies**)* réponse *f*; **in r. to your letter** en réponse à votre lettre; **to say sth in r. (to sth)** répondre qch (à qch); **there was no r.** *(on telephone)* ça ne répondait pas
  2 *vt & vi (pt & pp* **replied**)* répondre (**to** à)

report [rɪ'pɔːt] **1** *n* (**a**) *(account)* compte rendu *m*; *(analysis)* rapport *m*; *(in newspaper, on radio, television)* reportage *m*; **there are reports that...** il paraîtrait que...; **r. card** *(for primary school)* carnet *m* de notes; *(for secondary school)* bulletin *m* scolaire (**b**) *(sound)* détonation *f*
  2 *vt (information)* rapporter; *(accident, theft)* signaler; **to r. sb missing** signaler la disparition de qn; **to r. sb to the police/the authorities** dénoncer qn à la police/aux autorités; **to r. one's findings (to sb)** faire un rapport (à qn); **nothing to r.** rien à signaler
  3 *vi* (**a**) *(present oneself)* se présenter (**to** à); **to r. for duty** prendre son service (**b**) *(give account)* faire un rapport (**to** à); *(of journalist)* faire un reportage (**on** sur) (**c**) *(be accountable)* **to r. to sb** rendre compte à qn

▶**report back** vi (**a**) (return) rentrer, être de retour; (of soldier) regagner ses quartiers (**b**) (present report) présenter son rapport (**to** à)

reportedly [rɪ'pɔːtɪdlɪ] adv **he r. said that...** il aurait dit que...; **he is r. resident in Paris** il résiderait à Paris

reporter [rɪ'pɔːtə(r)] n (for newspaper) journaliste mf; (on television, radio) reporter m

repose [rɪ'pəʊz] Formal **1** n repos m
2 vi reposer

repository [rɪ'pɒzɪtərɪ] (pl **repositories**) n (for books, furniture) dépôt m

repossess [riːpə'zes] vt saisir

reprehensible [reprɪ'hensɪbəl] adj répréhensible

represent [reprɪ'zent] vt représenter; (describe) présenter

representation [reprɪzen'teɪʃən] n représentation f

representative [reprɪ'zentətɪv] **1** n représentant(e) m,f
2 adj représentatif(ive)

repress [rɪ'pres] vt réprimer; (memories, feelings) refouler; **to be repressed** (of person) être un(e) refoulé(e)

repression [rɪ'preʃən] n répression f; (of memories, feelings) refoulement m

repressive [rɪ'presɪv] adj répressif(ive)

reprieve [rɪ'priːv] **1** n Law (cancellation) commutation f de la peine capitale; (postponement) sursis m; Fig **to win a r.** (of project, company) bénéficier d'un sursis
2 vt Law **to r. sb** (cancel punishment of) commuer la peine capitale de qn en réclusion à perpétuité; (postpone punishment of) accorder un sursis à qn

reprimand ['reprɪmɑːnd] **1** n (to child) réprimande f; (to employee) avertissement m
2 vt (child) réprimander; (employee) avertir

reprint 1 n ['riːprɪnt] réimpression f
2 vt [riː'prɪnt] réimprimer

reprisal [rɪ'praɪzəl] n représailles fpl; **to take reprisals** exercer des représailles; **in r. for** en représailles à

reproach [rɪ'prəʊtʃ] **1** n reproche m; **a look of r.** un regard plein de reproche; **beyond** or **above r.** irréprochable
2 vt faire des reproches à; **to r. sb for** or **with sth** reprocher qch à qn; **to r. oneself for sth** se reprocher qch

reproachful [rɪ'prəʊtʃfʊl] adj (tone) de reproche; (look) plein(e) de reproche

reprobate ['reprəbeɪt] n réprouvé(e) m,f; Hum dépravé(e) m,f

reproduce [riːprə'djuːs] **1** vt reproduire
2 vi se reproduire

reproduction [riːprə'dʌkʃən] n reproduction f; **r. furniture** copies fpl (de meubles anciens)

reproductive [riːprə'dʌktɪv] adj reproducteur(trice); **r. organs** organes mpl reproducteurs

reproof [rɪ'pruːf] n Formal réprobation f

reprove [rɪ'pruːv] vt Formal (person) réprimander; (action) condamner

reproving [rɪ'pruːvɪŋ] adj Formal réprobateur(trice)

reptile ['reptaɪl] n reptile m

reptilian [rep'tɪlɪən] adj reptilien(enne); Fig (manner, looks) de reptile

republic [rɪ'pʌblɪk] n république f

Republican [rə'pʌblɪkən] n & adj républicain(e) m,f; **the R. Party** le Parti républicain

republican [rə'pʌblɪkən] n & adj républicain(e) m,f

repudiate [rɪ'pjuːdɪeɪt] vt Formal (offer) rejeter; (person, belief) renier; (wife) répudier; (rumor) démentir

repudiation [rɪpjuːdɪ'eɪʃən] n Formal (of offer) rejet m; (of person, belief) reniement m; (of wife) répudiation f; (of rumor) démenti m

repugnant [rɪ'pʌgnənt] adj répugnant(e)

repulse [rɪ'pʌls] vt repousser

repulsive [rɪ'pʌlsɪv] adj repoussant(e)

reputable ['repjʊtəbəl] adj de bonne réputation

reputation [repjʊ'teɪʃən] n réputation f; **to have a good/bad r.** avoir (une) bonne/mauvaise réputation; **to have a r. for doing sth** avoir la réputation de faire qch; **to have a r. for frankness** avoir la réputation d'être franc (franche); **to live up to one's r.** être à la hauteur de sa réputation

repute [rɪ'pjuːt] **1** n Formal réputation f; **to be held in high r.** être estimé(e); **of r.** réputé(e)
2 vt **she is reputed to be wealthy/a genius** on la dit riche/un génie

reputedly [rɪ'pjuːtɪdlɪ] adv à ce qu'on dit

request [rɪ'kwest] **1** n demande f (**for** de); **available on r.** qui peut être obtenu(e) sur simple demande; **to make a r. (for)** faire une demande (de); **at sb's r.** à la demande de qn; **by popular r.** à la demande générale
2 vt demander; **to r. sb to do sth** prier qn de faire qch

requiem ['rekwɪəm] n requiem m; **r. (mass)** messe f de requiem

require [rɪ'kwaɪə(r)] vt (of task, problem, situation) requérir; (of person) avoir besoin de; **to be required to do sth** être tenu(e) de faire qch; **if required** si besoin est/était; **when required** quand il le faut/fallait/faudra

requirement [rɪ'kwaɪəmənt] n (need) exigence f; (condition) condition f (requise); **to meet** or **to satisfy sb's requirements** (needs) correspondre aux besoins de qn; (demands) satisfaire aux exigences de qn

requisite ['rekwɪzɪt] **1** n élément m essentiel
2 adj requis(e)

requisition [rekwɪ'zɪʃən] vt réquisitionner

reran [riː'ræn] pt of **rerun**

rerecord [riːrɪ'kɔːd] vt réenregistrer

rerecordable [riːrɪ'kɔːdəbəl] adj (CD, DVD) réenregistrable

rerun 1 n ['riːrʌn] (on TV) rediffusion f; Fig (of situation, conflict) répétition f
2 vt [riː'rʌn] (pt **reran** [riː'ræn], pp **rerun**) (**a**) (TV program) rediffuser (**b**) (race) courir de nouveau

resale [riː'seɪl] n revente f

reschedule [riː'skedjuːl] vt (**a**) (meeting, flight) (change time of) changer l'heure de; (change date of) changer la date de (**b**) (debt) rééchelonner

rescind [rɪ'sɪnd] vt (law) abroger; (contract) résilier

rescue ['reskjuː] **1** n secours m; (from drowning) sauvetage m; **to come to sb's r.** venir au secours de qn; **r. attempt, r. operation** opération f de sauvetage; **r. services** secours mpl
2 vt (from death) sauver; (from difficulty) secourir

rescuer ['reskjuːə(r)] n sauveteur m

research [rɪ'sɜːtʃ] **1** n recherche f; **to do r.** faire de la recherche; **to do r. into sth** faire des recherches sur qch; **r. and development** recherche et développement m; **r. assistant/laboratory** assistant(e) m,f/laboratoire m de recherche
2 vt faire des recherches sur
3 vi faire des recherches (**into** sur)

researcher [rɪ'sɜːtʃə(r)] n chercheur(euse) m,f

resemblance [rɪ'zembləns] n ressemblance f (**to** avec); **to bear a r. to** ressembler à

resemble [rɪ'zembəl] vt ressembler à

resend [riː'send] vt (e-mail, text message) renvoyer

resent [rɪ'zent] vt (person) en vouloir à; (remark, criticism) ne pas apprécier du tout

resentful [rɪ'zentfʊl] adj plein(e) de ressentiment; **to be** or **to feel r.** éprouver du ressentiment

resentment [rɪ'zentmənt] n ressentiment m; **to feel r. toward sb** éprouver du ressentiment à l'égard de qn

reservation [rezə'veɪʃən] n (**a**) (booking) réservation f; **to make a r.** faire une réservation; **r. desk** bureau m des réservations (**b**) (doubt) réserve f; **to have reservations about** avoir

reserve [rɪ'zɜ:v] **1** n (**a**) (supply) réserve f; **to draw on one's reserves** puiser dans ses réserves; **to keep sth in r.** garder qch en réserve (**b**) (in sports) remplaçant(e) m,f; Mil **the reserves** les réservistes mpl (**c**) (for birds, game) réserve f (**d**) (reticence) réserve f
2 vt (book, keep) réserver; **to r. the right to do sth** se réserver le droit de faire qch; **to r. one's strength** ménager ses forces; **to r. judgment (on sth)** réserver son jugement (sur qch)

reserved [rɪ'zɜ:vd] adj réservé(e)

reservist [rɪ'zɜ:vɪst] n Mil réserviste m

reservoir ['rezəvwɑ:(r)] n (lake) réservoir m; Fig (of strength, courage) réserve f

reset [ri:'set] (pt & pp **reset**) vt (**a**) (clock, watch) mettre à l'heure; (counter) remettre à zéro; **r. button** bouton m de remise à zéro (**b**) (fracture) réduire

reshape [ri:'ʃeɪp] vt réorganiser

reshuffle [ri:'ʃʌfəl] **1** n Pol (of government) remaniement m
2 (**a**) Pol (government) remanier (**b**) (cards) rebattre

reside [rɪ'zaɪd] vi résider (**at/in** à/dans/en)

residence ['rezɪdəns] n (**a**) (stay) séjour m; **to take up r.** s'installer; **place of r.** lieu m de résidence; **r. permit** permis m de séjour (**b**) Formal (home) demeure f

resident ['rezɪdənt] **1** n (of country, street) habitant(e) m,f; **residents only** (sign) (in street) interdit sauf aux riverains; **residents' association** = association de propriétaires ou de locataires d'un immeuble ou d'un quartier
2 adj **to be r. in Boston** résider à Boston

residential [rezɪ'denʃəl] adj (**a**) (neighborhood) résidentiel(elle) (**b**) (staff) à demeure

residual [rɪ'zɪdjʊəl] adj résiduel(elle); Fig (doubt, worry) qui persiste; (income) net (nette)

residue ['rezɪdju:] n (**a**) (remainder) reste m (**b**) Chem résidu m

resign [rɪ'zaɪn] **1** vt (**a**) (job, position) démissionner de (**b**) **to r. oneself to sth/to doing sth** se résigner à qch/à faire qch
2 vi démissionner

resignation [rezɪg'neɪʃən] n (**a**) (from job) démission f; **to hand in one's r.** donner sa démission (**b**) (attitude) résignation f

resilience [rɪ'zɪlɪəns] n (of material, metal) élasticité f; (of person, economy) résistance f

resilient [rɪ'zɪlɪənt] adj (material, metal) élastique; (person) résistant(e)

resin ['rezɪn] n résine f

resist [rɪ'zɪst] **1** vt résister à; Law **to r. arrest** refuser d'obtempérer (lors d'une arrestation); **to r. doing sth** s'empêcher de faire qch
2 vi résister

resistance [rɪ'zɪstəns] n résistance f (**to** à); **to put up** or **to offer r.** offrir une résistance; **to meet with r.** rencontrer une résistance; **to take the line of least r.** adopter la solution de facilité; Hist **the (French) R.** la Résistance (française); **r. fighter** résistant(e) m,f

resistant [rɪ'zɪstənt] adj **to be r. to sth** résister à qch

resistor [rɪ'zɪstə(r)] n Elec résistance f

resolute ['rezəlu:t] adj résolu(e); (refusal, opposition) clair(e)

resolution [rezə'lu:ʃən] n (**a**) (decision, solution) résolution f; **to pass** or **to carry a r.** adopter une résolution (**b**) (firmness) fermeté f (**c**) Comput & TV (of image) résolution f

resolve [rɪ'zɒlv] **1** n résolution f
2 vt (**a**) (decide) **to r. to do sth** (of individual) se résoudre à faire qch; (of committee) décider de faire qch (**b**) (solve) résoudre
3 vi **to r. on/against doing sth** se résoudre à faire/ne pas faire qch

resonance ['rezənəns] n résonance f

resonant ['rezənənt] adj qui résonne

resonate ['rezəneɪt] vi résonner

resort [rɪ'zɔ:t] **1** n (**a**) (recourse) recours m; **without r. to** sans avoir recours à; **as a last r.** en dernier recours (**b**) (vacation place) lieu m de villégiature
2 vi **to r. to sth** recourir à qch; **to r. to doing sth** finir par faire qch

resound [rɪ'zaʊnd] vi résonner (**with** de)

resounding [rɪ'zaʊndɪŋ] adj (crash, applause, failure) retentissant(e); (success) éclatant(e)

resource [rɪ'zɔ:s] **1** n ressource f; **to be left to one's own resources** être livré(e) à soi-même; **r. management** gestion f des ressources
2 vt financer

resourceful [rɪ'zɔ:sfʊl] adj ingénieux(euse)

respect [rɪ'spekt] **1** n (**a**) (admiration, consideration) respect m; **to have r. for** avoir du respect pour; **treat mountains with r.** soyez prudent en montagne; **with all due r.** sauf le respect que je vous dois; **to pay one's last respects to sb** rendre les derniers hommages à qn (**b**) (aspect) égard m; **in many respects** à bien des égards; **in some** or **certain respects** à certains égards; **in all respects** or **every r.** à tous les égards; **with r. to,** **in r. of** concernant
2 vt respecter

respectability [rɪspektə'bɪlɪtɪ] n respectabilité f

respectable [rɪ'spektəbəl] adj (decent, fairly large) respectable; (fairly good) honorable

respectably [rɪ'spektəblɪ] adv (**a**) (honorably, decently) de manière respectable; (dressed) convenablement (**b**) (fairly well) honorablement

respecter [rɪ'spektə(r)] n **to be no r. of** n'avoir aucun respect pour

respectful [rɪ'spektfʊl] adj respectueux(euse)

respective [rɪ'spektɪv] adj respectif(ive)

respectively [rɪ'spektɪvlɪ] adv respectivement

respiration [respɪ'reɪʃən] n respiration f

respirator ['respɪreɪtə(r)] n respirateur m; **to be on a r.** être branché(e) sur un respirateur

respiratory [rɪ'spɪrɪtərɪ] adj respiratoire

respite ['respaɪt] n (rest) répit m; (delay) sursis m

resplendent [rɪ'splendənt] adj resplendissant(e)

respond [rɪ'spɒnd] vi (answer) répondre (**to** à); (react) réagir (**to** à); **to r. (to treatment)** (of patient) bien réagir (au traitement)

respondent [rɪ'spɒndənt] n (**a**) Law défendeur(eresse) m,f (**b**) (to questionnaire) sondé(e) m,f

response [rɪ'spɒns] n (answer) réponse f; (reaction) réaction f; **in r. to** en réponse à; **the appeal met with a generous r.** le public a répondu généreusement à l'appel; **r. time** temps m de réponse

responsibility [rɪspɒnsɪ'bɪlɪtɪ] (pl **responsibilities**) responsabilité f (**for** de); **to take** or **to accept r. for sth** accepter la responsabilité de qch

responsible [rɪ'spɒnsɪbəl] adj responsable (**for** de); (job) à responsabilité; **to hold sb r.** tenir qn pour responsable

responsive [rɪ'spɒnsɪv] adj (to kindness, praise) sensible (**to** à); (to idea, suggestion) réceptif(ive) (**to** à)

rest[1] [rest] **1** n (**a**) (repose) repos m; **to have** or **to take a r.** se reposer; Euph **to be at r.** reposer en paix; **to put** or **to set sb's mind at r.** rassurer qn; Fam **give it a r.!** tu veux bien arrêter cinq minutes!; **to come to r.** (of ball, car) s'arrêter
(**b**) (support) support m
(**c**) Mus (pause) silence m
2 vt (**a**) (cause to repose) **to r. one's eyes/legs** se reposer les yeux/les jambes; **God r. his soul!** que Dieu ait son âme!
(**b**) (lean) poser (**on** sur)
(**c**) (argument, hopes, confidence) fonder (**on** sur); Fig **I r. my case!** sans commentaire!

3 vi **(a)** (repose) se reposer, prendre du repos; **I won't r. until she has been caught** je n'aurai de cesse qu'elle ne soit prise; **r. in peace** (on gravestone) qu'il/elle repose en paix
(b) (lean) être posé(e) (**on** sur)
(c) (remain) **to r. with sb** (of decision, responsibility) incomber à qn; **there the matter rests** l'affaire en est là; **I won't let it r. at that** je n'en resterai pas là; **r. assured...** soyez assuré que...
(d) (of argument, theory) **to r. on** reposer sur

rest² [rest] n **the r.** (remainder) le reste; (others) les autres mfpl; **the r. of the time/the men** le reste du temps/des hommes; **the r. of them will stay here** les autres resteront ici

restaurant ['restərɒnt] n restaurant m; **r. car** (in train) wagon-restaurant m

restful ['restfʊl] adj reposant(e)

restive ['restɪv] adj agité(e)

restless ['restlɪs] adj agité(e); **to have a r. night** passer une nuit agitée

restoration [restə'reɪʃən] n (of furniture, monarchy) restauration f; (of communications, law and order) rétablissement m; (of property) restitution f

restore [rɪ'stɔː(r)] vt (furniture, monarchy, faith, calm) restaurer; (communications, law and order, confidence) rétablir; (property) restituer (**to** à); **to r. sb to health/strength** redonner la santé/des forces à qn

restrain [rɪ'streɪn] vt (person, dog) maîtriser; (passions) refréner; (anger, crowd) contenir; **to r. sb from doing sth** retenir qn pour qu'il/elle ne fasse pas qch; **to r. oneself (from doing sth)** se retenir (de faire qch)

restrained [rɪ'streɪnd] adj (person, manner) réservé(e); (tone, terms) mesuré(e); (style) sobre

restraint [rɪ'streɪnt] n **(a)** (moderation) mesure f, modération f; **to show** or **to exercise great r.** faire preuve d'une grande modération **(b)** (restriction) restriction f; **without r.** sans retenue

restrict [rɪ'strɪkt] vt (person, freedom) restreindre; **to r. oneself to sth/to doing sth** se limiter à qch/à faire qch

restricted [rɪ'strɪktɪd] adj restreint(e), limité(e); (document) secret(ète); **r. area** Mil zone f interdite; (for parking) zone bleue

restriction [rɪ'strɪkʃən] n restriction f; (of speed) limitation f; **to place restrictions on sth** apporter des restrictions à qch

restrictive [rɪ'strɪktɪv] adj restrictif(ive); Ind **r. practices** pratiques fpl restrictives

restroom ['restruːm] n toilettes fpl

restructure [riː'strʌktʃə(r)] vt restructurer

restructuring [riː'strʌktʃərɪŋ] n restructuration f

result [rɪ'zʌlt] **1** n résultat m; **as a r.** en conséquence; **as a r. of** à la suite de; **the r. is that...** il en résulte que...; **to yield** or **to show results** donner des résultats
2 vi **to r. from** résulter de; **to r. in** entraîner

resultant [rɪ'zʌltənt] adj résultant(e)

resume [rɪ'zjuːm] **1** vt reprendre; (relations) renouer; (attempt) renouveler; (interest) retrouver
2 vi reprendre

résumé ['rezjʊmeɪ] n (summary) résumé m; (curriculum vitae) curriculum vitae m inv

resumption [rɪ'zʌmpʃən] n reprise f

resurface [riː'sɜːfɪs] **1** vt (road) refaire le revêtement de
2 vi also Fig refaire surface

resurgent [rɪ'sɜːdʒənt] adj renaissant(e); (economy) qui connaît une reprise

resurrect [rezə'rekt] vt Rel ressusciter; Fig (fashion) remettre au goût du jour; (argument) ressortir; (tradition) faire renaître

resurrection [rezə'rekʃən] n Fig réapparition f; Rel **the R.** la Résurrection (du Christ)

resuscitate [rɪ'sʌsɪteɪt] vt (person) ranimer; Fig (career) redonner un nouvel élan à; (scheme) ressortir

retail ['riːteɪl] **1** n Com (vente f au) détail m; **r. outlet** magasin m de détail; **r. price** prix m de détail; **r. trade** commerce m de détail; Hum **I did a bit of r. therapy this weekend** j'ai fait un peu de shopping pour me remonter le moral ce week-end
2 vt (goods) vendre au détail
3 vi se vendre (**at** à)

retailer ['riːteɪlə(r)] n détaillant(e) m,f

retain [rɪ'teɪn] vt **(a)** (keep) conserver, garder **(b)** (hold in place) maintenir; **retaining wall** mur m de soutènement **(c)** (remember) retenir

retainer [rɪ'teɪnə(r)] n **(a)** (fee) appointements mpl **(b)** (nominal rent) loyer m nominal

retaliate [rɪ'tælɪeɪt] vi riposter

retaliation [rɪtælɪ'eɪʃən] n représailles fpl; **in r. (for sth)** en représailles (à qch)

retard 1 vt [rɪ'tɑːd] retarder
2 n ['riːtɑːd] Fam Pej démeuré(e) m,f

retarded [rɪ'tɑːdɪd] adj **(mentally) r.** arriéré(e)

retch [retʃ] vi avoir des haut-le-cœur

retention [rɪ'tenʃən] n (of custom, practice) maintien m; (of fact, impression) mémorisation f

retentive [rɪ'tentɪv] adj (memory) fidèle; (person) qui a (une) bonne mémoire

rethink 1 n ['riːθɪŋk] **to have a r. (about sth)** réfléchir à nouveau (à qch)
2 vt [riː'θɪŋk] (pt & pp **rethought** [riː'θɔːt]) repenser

reticent ['retɪsənt] adj réservé(e), réticent(e); **to be r. about sth** parler peu de qch

retina ['retɪnə] n rétine f

retinue ['retɪnjuː] n suite f, cortège m

retire [rɪ'taɪə(r)] **1** vt mettre à la retraite
2 vi **(a)** (of employee) prendre sa retraite **(b)** (withdraw) se retirer; (go to bed) (aller) se coucher

retired [rɪ'taɪəd] adj retraité(e), à la retraite

retirement [rɪ'taɪəmənt] n (from work, army) retraite f; **to take early r.** partir en retraite anticipée; **to come out of r.** reprendre sa carrière; **r. age** l'âge m de la retraite; **r. home** maison f de retraite; **r. pension** (pension f de) retraite f

retiring [rɪ'taɪərɪŋ] adj **(a)** (reserved) réservé(e) **(b)** (chairman, congressman) sortant(e); (employee) qui prend sa retraite; **r. age** l'âge m de la retraite

retort [rɪ'tɔːt] **1** n (answer) réplique f
2 vt & vi répliquer

retrace [rɪ'treɪs] vt **to r. one's steps** revenir sur ses pas

retract [rɪ'trækt] **1** vt **(a)** (statement, offer) revenir sur **(b)** (claws, aircraft undercarriage) rentrer
2 vi **(a)** (of person) se rétracter **(b)** (of claws, aircraft undercarriage) rentrer

retractable [rɪ'træktəbəl] adj rétractable; (antenna, aircraft undercarriage) escamotable

retrain [riː'treɪn] **1** vt recycler
2 vi se recycler

retraining [riː'treɪnɪŋ] n recyclage m

retread ['riːtred] n pneu m rechapé

retreat [rɪ'triːt] **1** n **(a)** (withdrawal) retraite f; also Fig **to beat a (hasty) r.** battre en retraite **(b)** (place) retraite f
2 vi battre en retraite; Fig se réfugier

retrial [riː'traɪəl] n Law nouveau procès m

retribution [retrɪ'bjuːʃən] n châtiment m

retrieve [rɪ'triːv] vt récupérer; Comput (file) ouvrir

retriever [rɪ'triːvə(r)] n (dog) retriever m

retroactive [retrəʊ'æktɪv] adj Formal rétroactif(ive)

retrograde ['retrəgreɪd] adj rétrograde

retrospect ['retrəspekt] n **in r.** après coup, rétrospectivement

retrospective [retrə'spektɪv] **1** n (exhibition) rétrospective f
2 adj rétrospectif(ive); (measure, decision) à effet rétroactif

return [rɪ'tɜːn] **1** n (a) (of person, peace, season, tennis service) retour m; (of goods) renvoi m; **on my r.** à mon retour; **in r. (for)** en échange (de); **to do sth in r.** faire qch en retour; **many happy returns (of the day)!** bon anniversaire!; **r. journey** (voyage m de) retour; **r. match** match m retour (b) Fin (profit) rapport m; **to bring a good r.** rapporter un bon bénéfice; **r. on investment** retour m sur investissement
2 vt (a) (give or send back) rendre; **to r. a favor** rendre la pareille; **r. to sender** (on letter) retour à l'envoyeur; **to r. service** (in tennis) renvoyer le service; **to r. sb's call** (on phone) rappeler qn; Law **to r. a verdict of guilty/not guilty** déclarer l'accusé(e) coupable/non coupable (b) Fin (profit) rapporter
3 vi (come back) revenir; (go back) retourner; **to r. to work** reprendre son travail

returnable [rɪ'tɜːnəbəl] adj (bottle) consigné(e)

reunification [riːjuːnɪfɪ'keɪʃən] n réunification f

reunify [riː'juːnɪfaɪ] (pt & pp **reunified**) vt réunifier

reunion [riː'juːnɪən] n réunion f

reunite [riːjʊ'naɪt] vt réconcilier; **to be reunited with sb** retrouver qn

reusable [riː'juːzəbəl] adj réutilisable

reuse [riː'juːz] vt réutiliser

Rev. Rel (abbr **Reverend**) R. Gray le révérend Gray

rev [rev] Fam **1** n (abbr **revolution**) tour m; **r. counter** compte-tours m inv
2 vt (pt & pp **revved**) **to r. the engine** faire monter le régime (du moteur)

revalue [riː'væljuː] vt Fin réévaluer

revamp [riː'væmp] vt Fam (image) rajeunir; (company) restructurer; (house) retaper

reveal [rɪ'viːl] vt révéler

revealing [rɪ'viːlɪŋ] adj (sign, comment) révélateur(trice); (clothing) qui ne cache pas grand-chose

revel ['revəl] vi faire la fête; **to r. in sth** savourer qch

revelation [revə'leɪʃən] n révélation f; **(the Book of) Revelations** l'Apocalypse f

reveler ['revələr] n fêtard(e) m,f

revenge [rɪ'vendʒ] **1** n (punishment) vengeance f; (getting one's own back) revanche f; **to take r. (on sb)** se venger (de qn); Prov **r. is sweet** ça fait du bien de se venger!
2 vt venger

revenue ['revənjuː] n revenu m; (from sales) recettes fpl

reverberate [rɪ'vɜːbəreɪt] vi (a) (of sound) résonner (b) (of news, rumor) se propager

reverberation [rɪvɜːbə'reɪʃən] n (a) (sound) réverbération f (b) (of news, rumor) répercussion f

revere [rɪ'vɪər] vt révérer

reverence ['revərəns] n révérence f

Reverend ['revərənd] adj Rel révérend; **the R. Paul James** le révérend Paul James

reverential [revə'renʃəl] adj révérencieux(euse)

reverie ['revərɪ] n rêverie f

reversal [rɪ'vɜːsəl] n (of opinion, policy) revirement m; (of roles) renversement m; (of fortune) revers m; Law (of decision) annulation f

reverse [rɪ'vɜːs] **1** n (a) (opposite) contraire m; **quite the r.!** bien au contraire! (b) (of coin) revers m; (of fabric) envers m (c) (defeat) échec m; (misfortune) revers m; **to suffer a r.** (defeat) subir un échec; (misfortune) subir un revers (d) (gear) marche f arrière; **to put the car into r.** passer la marche arrière
2 adj inverse; **in r. order** en ordre inverse; **the r. side** (of coin) le revers; (of fabric) l'envers m; **r. gear** marche f arrière
3 vt (a) (order, policy, roles) inverser; (decision) revenir sur; (situation, trend) renverser (b) (vehicle) **to r. the car** faire marche arrière

reversible [rɪ'vɜːsəbəl] adj (a) (jacket) réversible (b) (decree) révocable; (surgery) réversible; **not r.** (decision) irrévocable; (surgery) irréversible

▸**revert to** [rɪ'vɜːt] vt insep revenir à; **to r. to type** reprendre ses vieilles habitudes

review [rɪ'vjuː] **1** n (a) (of policy, salary) révision f; (of situation) examen m; **to be under r.** faire l'objet d'une révision (b) (of book, play, movie) critique f (c) Mil revue f
2 vt (a) (policy, salary) réviser; (situation) faire le point sur (b) (book, play, movie) faire la critique de (c) Mil (troops) passer en revue (d) (notes, school subject) réviser

reviewer [rɪ'vjuːər] n (of book, play, movie) critique mf

revile [rɪ'vaɪl] vt Formal vilipender

revise [rɪ'vaɪz] **1** vt (text, law) réviser; (decision) réexaminer; **to r. one's opinion (of)** changer d'opinion (à l'égard de)
2 vi (for exam) réviser, faire des révisions

revision [rɪ'vɪʒən] n (of text, law) révision f

revisionism [rɪ'vɪʒənɪzəm] n Pol révisionnisme m

revisit [riː'vɪzɪt] vt (place) revisiter; (person) retourner voir

revitalize [riː'vaɪtəlaɪz] vt (person) revigorer; (arts, industry) donner un nouvel essor à

revival [rɪ'vaɪvəl] n (of person) réanimation f; (of hopes) renaissance f; (of industry, custom, fashion) renouveau m; (of play) reprise f

revive [rɪ'vaɪv] **1** vt (person) ranimer; (industry, hopes, custom) faire renaître; (fashion) relancer
2 vi (of person) reprendre connaissance; (of industry) connaître un renouveau; (of hopes) renaître

revoke [rɪ'vəʊk] vt (law) abroger; (decision) revenir sur; (privilege) abolir; **to r. sb's license** retirer son permis à qn

revolt [rɪ'vəʊlt] **1** n révolte f; **to be in r.** être en révolte
2 vt (disgust) dégoûter
3 vi (rebel) se révolter (**against** contre)

revolting [rɪ'vəʊltɪŋ] adj (disgusting) dégoûtant(e)

revolution [revə'luːʃən] n (a) (radical change) révolution f (b) (turn) tour m, révolution f

revolutionary [revə'luːʃənərɪ] (pl **revolutionaries**) n & adj révolutionnaire mf

revolutionize [revə'luːʃənaɪz] vt révolutionner

revolve [rɪ'vɒlv] vi tourner (**around** autour de); Fig **to r. around sth** s'articuler autour de qch

revolver [rɪ'vɒlvər] n revolver m

revolving [rɪ'vɒlvɪŋ] adj (chair) pivotant(e); (platform) tournant(e); Fin (credit) revolving inv; **r. door** porte f à tambour

revue [rɪ'vjuː] n Theat revue f

revulsion [rɪ'vʌlʃən] n dégoût m

reward [rɪ'wɔːd] **1** n récompense f; **as a r. for** en récompense de; Com **rewards card** carte f de fidélité
2 vt récompenser (**for** de ou pour)

rewarding [rɪ'wɔːdɪŋ] adj (experience) enrichissant(e), intéressant(e); (job) gratifiant(e)

rewind [riː'waɪnd] (pt & pp **rewound** [riː'waʊnd]) vt (tape, film) rembobiner

rewire [riː'waɪər] vt refaire l'installation électrique de

reword [riː'wɜːd] vt reformuler

rework [riː'wɜːk] vt retravailler

rewound [riː'waʊnd] pt & pp of **rewind**

rewrite [riː'raɪt] (pt **rewrote** [riː'rəʊt], pp **rewritten** [riː'rɪtən]) vt réécrire

Reykjavik ['rekjəvɪk] n Reykjavik

rhapsodic [ræp'sɒdɪk], **rhapsodical** [ræp'sɒdɪkəl] adj (prose, description) dithyrambique; (person) enthousiaste

rhapsodize ['ræpsədaɪz] vi s'extasier (**over** ou **about** sur)

rhapsody ['ræpsədɪ] (pl **rhapsodies**) n Mus rhapsodie f; **to go into rhapsodies over sth** s'extasier sur qch

rhesus ['riːsəs] n **r. factor** facteur m rhésus; **r. positive/negative** rhésus m positif/négatif; **r. monkey** rhésus m

rhetoric ['retərɪk] n rhétorique f; **the speech was nothing but empty r.** le discours ne consistait qu'en de belles phrases creuses

rhetorical [rɪ'tɒrɪkəl] *adj (style, question)* rhétorique; *(term)* de rhétorique

rheumatic [ru:'mætɪk] *adj (pain)* rhumatismal(e); *(joint)* atteint(e) de rhumatisme; **r. fever** rhumatisme *m* articulaire aigu

rheumatism ['ru:mətɪzəm] *n* rhumatisme *m*

rheumatoid arthritis ['ru:mətɔɪdɑ:θ'raɪtɪs] *n* polyarthrite *f* rhumatoïde

Rhine [raɪn] *n* **the R.** le Rhin

rhinestone ['raɪnstəʊn] *n* faux diamant *m*

rhino ['raɪnəʊ] *(pl* **rhinos)** *n Fam* rhinocéros *m*

rhinoceros [raɪ'nɒsərəs] *n* rhinocéros *m*

Rhodes [rəʊdz] *n* Rhodes

rhododendron [rəʊdə'dendrən] *n* rhododendron *m*

rhomboid ['rɒmbɔɪd] *n* rhomboïde *m*

rhombus ['rɒmbəs] *(pl* **rhombuses** *or* **rhombi** ['rɒmbaɪ]) *n* losange *m*

Rhone [rəʊn] *n* **the R.** le Rhône

rhubarb ['ru:bɑ:b] *n* rhubarbe *f*; **r. jam/tart** confiture *f*/tarte *f* à la rhubarbe

rhyme [raɪm] **1** *n (sound)* rime *f*; *(poem)* vers *mpl*; **without r. or reason** sans rime ni raison
2 *vi* rimer (**with** avec)

rhythm ['rɪðəm] *n* rythme *m*; **r. method** *(of contraception)* méthode *f* du calendrier

rhythmic ['rɪðmɪk], **rhythmical** ['rɪðmɪkəl] *adj* rythmé(e), cadencé(e)

rib [rɪb] **1** *n (a) (of person, animal)* côte *f* **(b)** *(of umbrella)* baleine *f*
2 *vt (pt & pp* **ribbed)** *Fam (tease)* taquiner (**about** à propos de)

ribald ['rɪbəld, 'raɪbəld] *adj* grivois(e), paillard(e)

ribbed [rɪbd] *adj (fabric, sweater)* à côtes

ribbon ['rɪbən] *n (for hair, typewriter)* ruban *m*; *(of land)* bande *f* étroite; **to tear sth to ribbons** déchiqueter qch; *Fig (criticize)* éreinter qch

ribcage ['rɪbkeɪdʒ] *n* cage *f* thoracique

riboflavin(e) [raɪbəʊ'fleɪvɪn] *n Chem* riboflavine *f*

rice [raɪs] *n* riz *m*; **r. field** *or* **paddy** rizière *f*; **r. pudding** riz au lait

rich [rɪtʃ] **1** *npl* **the r.** les riches *mpl*; **riches** *(wealth)* richesses *fpl*
2 *adj* riche; *(harvest, supply)* abondant(e); *(color)* intense; *(voice)* chaud(e); **to be r. in sth** être riche en qch; *Fam* **that's r.!** c'est un peu fort!

richly ['rɪtʃlɪ] *adv* richement; **r. deserved** bien mérité(e)

Richter Scale ['rɪktə'skeɪl] *n* échelle *f* de Richter

rick [rɪk] *n (of hay, straw)* meule *f*

rickets ['rɪkɪts] *npl* rachitisme *m*; **to have r.** être rachitique

rickety ['rɪkɪtɪ] *adj Fam (furniture, staircase)* branlant(e); *(alliance, alibi)* boiteux(euse)

ricochet ['rɪkəʃeɪ] **1** *n* ricochet *m*
2 *vi (pt & pp* **ricochetted** ['rɪkəʃeɪd]) ricocher (**off** sur)

rid [rɪd] *(pt* rid, *pp* rid *or* ridden ['rɪdən]) *vt* **to r. sb of sth** débarrasser qn de qch; **to get r. of sth** se débarrasser de qch

riddance ['rɪdəns] *n Fam* **good r.!** bon débarras!

ridden ['rɪdən] *pp* of **rid, ride**

riddle ['rɪdəl] **1** *n (puzzle)* devinette *f*; *(mystery)* énigme *f*
2 *vt* **to r. sb/sth with bullets** cribler qn/qch de balles; **riddled with mistakes** truffé(e) de fautes

ride [raɪd] **1** *n (a) (on bicycle, in car)* tour *m*; *(on horse)* promenade *f*; **to go for a r.** aller faire un tour; **to give sb a r.** *(in car)* conduire qn en voiture; **it's only a short r. away** ce n'est pas très loin; *Fig* **she was given a rough r.** on lui en a fait voir de toutes les couleurs; *Fig* **to take sb for a r.** mener qn en bateau **(b)** *(at amusement park)* attraction *f*

2 *vt (pt* **rode** [rəʊd], *pp* **ridden** ['rɪdən]) *(horse, bicycle)* monter à; *(bus, train)* prendre

3 *vi (on horse)* faire du cheval; *(on bicycle)* faire de la bicyclette; *Fig* **to be riding high** connaître une période de succès; *Fam Fig* **to let it r.** laisser courir

▸**ride out** *vt sep (problem, crisis)* survivre à; *Fig* **to r. out the storm** surmonter la crise

rider ['raɪdə(r)] *n (a) (on horse)* cavalier(ère) *m,f*; *(on bicycle)* cycliste *mf*; *(on motorcycle)* motocycliste *mf* **(b)** *Law (to document, treaty)* annexe *f*; *(to bill)* clause *f* additionnelle

ridge [rɪdʒ] *n (of mountain)* crête *f*; *(of roof)* faîte *m*; *(on surface)* strie *f*; *Met* **r. of high pressure** dorsale *f* barométrique

ridicule ['rɪdɪkju:l] **1** *n* ridicule *m*; **to hold sb/sth up to r.** tourner qn/qch en ridicule
2 *vt* ridiculiser, tourner en ridicule

ridiculous [rɪ'dɪkjʊləs] *adj* ridicule; **to make sb/sth look r.** rendre qn/qch ridicule; **to make oneself look r.** se rendre ridicule, se ridiculiser

riding ['raɪdɪŋ] *n* équitation *f*; **to go r.** faire du cheval; **r. boots** bottes *fpl* de cheval; **r. crop** *or* **whip** cravache *f*; **r. school** école *f* d'équitation

rife [raɪf] *adj* **to be r.** être très répandu(e); *(of rumors)* aller bon train

riffraff ['rɪfræf] *n* racaille *f*

rifle¹ ['raɪfəl] *n* fusil *m*; **r. range** champ *m* de tir; *(at amusement park)* stand *m* de tir; **r. shot** coup *m* de fusil

rifle² ['raɪfəl] *vt (house, office)* mettre sens dessus dessous; *(pockets, drawer)* fouiller dans

▸**rifle through** *vt insep* fouiller dans

rifleman ['raɪfəlmən] *n Mil* fusilier *m*

rift [rɪft] *n (in earth, rock)* fissure *f*; *(in relationship)* rupture *f*; *(difference of opinion)* désaccord *m*

rig [rɪg] **1** *n (a) (of ship)* gréement *m* **(b)** *(oil)* **r.** derrick *m*; *(at sea)* plate-forme *f* pétrolière **(c)** *Fam (truck)* semi-remorque *m*
2 *vt (pt & pp* **rigged)** **(a)** *(ship)* gréer **(b)** *Fam (election, contest)* truquer

▸**rig out** *vt sep Fam* **to be rigged out in** être attifé(e) de

▸**rig up** *vt sep* monter, installer

Riga ['ri:gə] *n* Riga

rigging ['rɪgɪŋ] *n (of ship)* gréement *m*

right [raɪt] **1** *n (a) (morality)* bien *m*; **to be in the r.** avoir raison; **to set things to rights** arranger les choses
(b) *(entitlement)* droit *m*; **to have the r. to do sth** avoir le droit de faire qch; **to be within one's rights** être dans son droit; **by rights** en principe; **by r.** de droit; **to be famous in one's own r.** être soi-même une célébrité; **the r. to vote** le droit de vote; **r. of way** *(on land)* droit de passage; *(on road)* priorité *f*
(c) *(right-hand side)* droite *f*, côté *m* droit; **on** *or* **to the r.** à droite; **on my r.** à *ou* sur ma droite; **the r.** *(in politics)* la droite
2 *adj* **(a)** *(correct)* exact(e), bon (bonne); *(word)* juste; **to be r.** *(of person)* avoir raison; **to keep on the r. side of sb** veiller à ne pas se mettre qn à dos; **to be on the r. track** être sur la bonne voie
(b) *(morally good)* bien *inv*; **to do the r. thing** faire ce qu'il faut
(c) *(appropriate)* bon (bonne); **the r. thing to do** la meilleure chose à faire; **to know the r. people** connaître les gens qu'il faut; **to be in the r. place at the r. time** se trouver là au bon moment
(d) *(mentally, physically well)* **I'm not feeling quite r.** je ne me sens pas très bien; **to be as r. as rain** être en parfaite santé; **no one in his r. mind would do that** aucune personne sensée ne ferait cela; **he's not quite r. in the head** il n'a pas toute sa tête
(e) *(right-hand)* droit(e); **on the r. side** à *ou* sur la droite; *Pol* **the r. wing** la droite
(f) *Math* **r. angle** angle *m* droit

3 *adv* (**a**) *(straight)* (tout) droit; **to put things r.** arranger les choses; **to put sb r.** détromper qn

(**b**) **r. away** *(immediately)* sur-le-champ, immédiatement; **I'll be r. back** je reviens tout de suite; **r. now** *(immediately)* tout de suite; *(at the moment)* en ce moment

(**c**) *(completely)* **to go r. through sth** traverser qch de part en part; **to go r. up to sb** se diriger (tout) droit vers qn; **to turn r. around** se retourner; **r. at the top/back** tout en haut/à l'arrière

(**d**) *(exactly)* **r. here/there** juste ici/là; **r. in the middle** en plein milieu; **r. behind** juste derrière; *Fig* **to be r. behind sb** soutenir qn à fond

(**e**) *(answer)* correctement; *(guess)* juste; **to understand/to remember r.** bien comprendre/se souvenir

(**f**) *(look, turn)* à droite; *Fig* **r., left and center** de tous les côtés

4 *vt* (**a**) *(put upright)* redresser

(**b**) *(redress)* **to r. a wrong** réparer un tort

right-angled ['raɪtæŋgəld] *adj* à angle droit; *(triangle)* rectangle

righteous ['raɪtʃəs] *adj* *(person)* droit(e), vertueux(euse); *(indignation)* vertueux(euse)

rightful ['raɪtfʊl] *adj* *(heir, owner)* légitime; *(share)* auquel (à laquelle) on a droit

right-hand ['raɪthænd] *adj* de droite; *(corner, side)* droit(e); **r. bend** virage *m* à droite; **r. drive** conduite *f* à droite; **on the r. side** à droite; **to be sb's r. man** être le bras droit de qn

right-handed [raɪt'hændɪd] **1** *adj* droitier(ère)

2 *adv* de la main droite

right-hander [raɪt'hændə(r)] *n* *(person)* droitier/ère *m,f*

rightly ['raɪtlɪ] *adv* *(correctly)* bien; *(justifiably)* à juste titre; **I don't r. know why...** je ne sais pas exactement pourquoi...; **r. or wrongly** à tort ou à raison; **...and r. so** ...et non sans raison

right-minded [raɪt'maɪndɪd], **right-thinking** [raɪt-'θɪŋkɪŋ] *adj* sensé(e)

right-wing [raɪt'wɪŋ] *adj Pol* de droite

right-winger [raɪt'wɪŋə(r)] *n Pol* *(man)* homme *m* de droite; *(woman)* femme *f* de droite

rigid ['rɪdʒɪd] *adj* rigide; *Fig* *(person, ideas)* inflexible

rigidity [rɪ'dʒɪdɪtɪ] *n* rigidité *f*

rigmarole ['rɪgmərəʊl] *n Fam* *(process)* procédure *f* compliquée; *(speech)* long discours *m*

rigor ['rɪgə(r)] *n* rigueur *f*

rigor mortis ['rɪgə'mɔːtɪs] *n* rigidité *f* cadavérique

rigorous ['rɪgərəs] *adj* rigoureux(euse)

rile [raɪl] *vt Fam* agacer

rim [rɪm] *n* *(of cup, bowl)* bord *m*; *(of wheel)* jante *f*; *(of eyeglasses)* monture *f*

rind [raɪnd] *n* *(of fruit)* écorce *f*; *(of cheese)* croûte *f*; *(of bacon)* couenne *f*

ring[1] [rɪŋ] **1** *n* (**a**) *(for finger)* *(with stone)* bague *f*; *(without stone)* anneau *m*; *(for keys)* porte-clés *m inv*; **the rings** *(in gymnastics)* les anneaux; **r. binder** classeur *m* à anneaux; **r. finger** annulaire *m* (**b**) *(of people, chairs)* cercle *m*; *(on stove)* brûleur *m*; *(stain)* marque *f*; **to have rings under one's eyes** avoir des cernes sous les yeux; *Fig* **to run rings around sb** éclipser qn; **r. road** périphérique *m* (**c**) *(for boxing, wrestling)* ring *m* (**d**) *(of criminals)* bande *f*; *(of spies)* réseau *m*

2 *vt* *(surround)* encercler

ring[2] [rɪŋ] **1** *n* *(sound)* *(of doorbell, telephone)* sonnerie *f*; *(of small bell, coins)* tintement *m*; **there was a r. at the door** on sonna à la porte; *Fam* **to give sb a r.** passer un coup de fil à qn; **to have a r. of truth** avoir l'air vrai(e); **the name has a familiar r. to it** ce nom me dit quelque chose

2 *vt* (*pt* **rang** [ræŋ], *pp* **rung** [rʌŋ]) *(bell)* sonner; *(alarm)* déclencher; *(on phone)* appeler; **to r. the doorbell** sonner à la porte; *Fig* **that rings a bell** cela me dit quelque chose; *Fig* **to r. the changes** introduire des changements

3 *vi* (**a**) *(of bell, telephone)* sonner; **to r. at the door** sonner à la porte; *Fig* **to r. true** avoir l'air vrai(e); **to r. false** sonner faux (**b**) *(resonate)* *(of ears)* bourdonner; **to r. with** *(of street, room)* retentir de

▸**ring out** *vi* *(of voice, shout)* retentir

▸**ring up** *vt sep* *(on cash register)* enregistrer; **to r. up a profit** enregistrer un bénéfice

ringleader ['rɪŋliːdə(r)] *n* *(of strike)* meneur(euse) *m,f*; *(of gang)* chef *m* de bande

ringlet ['rɪŋlɪt] *n* anglaise *f*

ringmaster ['rɪŋmɑːstə(r)] *n* ≃ Monsieur *m* Loyal

ringside ['rɪŋsaɪd] *n* **at the r.** près du ring; **to have a r. seat** avoir une place au premier rang; *Fig* être aux premières loges

ringworm ['rɪŋwɜːm] *n Med* teigne *f*

rink [rɪŋk] *n* *(for roller skating)* piste *f*; *(for ice skating)* patinoire *f*

rinse [rɪns] **1** *n* **to give sth a r.** rincer qch

2 *vt* *(clothes, dishes)* rincer; **to r. one's hands/hair** se rincer les mains/les cheveux

▸**rinse out** *vt sep* rincer

Rio (de Janeiro) ['riːəʊ(dɪdʒə'neərəʊ)] *n* Rio (de Janeiro)

riot ['raɪət] **1** *n* *(uprising)* émeute *f*; *Fig* **a r. of color** une explosion de couleurs; **to run r.** se déchaîner; **her imagination was running r.** elle s'imaginait toutes sortes de choses; **to read sb the r. act** passer un savon à qn; **r. police** police *f* anti-émeute, ≃ CRS *mpl*

2 *vi* faire une émeute; *(of prisoners)* se mutiner

rioter ['raɪətə(r)] *n* émeutier(ère) *m,f*

rioting ['raɪətɪŋ] *n* émeutes *fpl*

riotous ['raɪətəs] *adj* *(party, behavior, event)* tapageur(euse); **r. living** vie *f* déréglée

RIP [ɑːraɪ'piː] *(abbr* **Rest In Peace**) qu'il/elle repose en paix

rip [rɪp] **1** *n* déchirure *f*

2 *vt* (*pt & pp* **ripped**) déchirer; **to r. sth to pieces** *(cloth)* mettre qch en lambeaux; *(paper)* déchirer qch en mille morceaux; *Fig* *(criticize)* mettre qch en pièces

3 *vi* (**a**) *(of cloth, paper)* se déchirer (**b**) *Fam* **to let r.** *(in performance)* se déchaîner; **to let r. at sb** s'en prendre violemment à qn

▸**rip off** *vt sep* (**a**) *(tear)* arracher (**b**) *Fam* *(swindle)* arnaquer; *(steal)* piquer

▸**rip open** *vt sep* **to r. open a letter** ouvrir une lettre en déchirant l'enveloppe; **to r. open a package** ouvrir un paquet en le déchirant

▸**rip up** *vt sep* (**a**) *(letter)* déchirer (**b**) *(floorboards)* arracher; *(pavement)* creuser des trous dans

ripe [raɪp] *adj* *(fruit)* mûr(e); *(cheese)* fait(e) à point; **to live to a r. old age** vivre jusqu'à un âge avancé; **the time is r. (to do sth)** le temps est venu (de faire qch)

ripen ['raɪpən] *vi* mûrir; *(of cheese)* se faire

rip-off ['rɪpɒf] *n Fam* arnaque *f*

riposte [rɪ'pɒst] *n* riposte *f*, réplique *f*

ripple ['rɪpəl] **1** *n* *(on water)* ride *f*; *(of applause)* vague *f*; *(of excitement)* frémissement *m*

2 *vi* *(of water)* se rider; **laughter rippled through the audience** des vagues de rires ont parcouru le public

rise [raɪz] **1** *n* (**a**) *(in price, temperature, pressure)* hausse *f*; **to be on the r.** *(of prices)* être en hausse; *(of crime, inflation)* être en augmentation; **the r. and fall of** la grandeur et la décadence de

(**b**) *(of leader, party)* ascension *f*; **r. to power** accession *f* au pouvoir

(**c**) *(in road, ground)* éminence *f*

(**d**) *(idioms)* **to give r. to sth** donner lieu à qch; *Fam* **to get a r. out of sb** faire enrager qn

2 *vi* (*pt* **rose** [rəʊz], *pp* **risen** ['rɪzən]) (**a**) *(get up)* se lever; *(after falling)* se relever; *Fam* **r. and shine!** debout là-dedans!

(**b**) *(of smoke, balloon, ground)* monter; *(of sun, moon)* se lever; *(in career)* monter; **a murmur rose from the crowd** un murmure s'éleva de la foule; **to r. to the occasion** se montrer à la hauteur de la situation; **to r. to the position of managing director** accéder au poste de P-DG; **to r. to power** accéder au pouvoir; **to r. in sb's esteem** monter dans l'estime de qn

(**c**) *(of temperature)* s'élever, monter; *(of price)* augmenter; *(of hope)* grandir; *(of dough)* lever; **my spirits rose** je repris courage; **her voice rose in anger** elle a élevé la voix sous l'effet de la colère

(**d**) *(revolt)* se soulever; **to r. in arms** prendre les armes; **to r. in protest (against sth)** se soulever (contre qch)

▸**rise above** *vt insep (problem, criticism)* surmonter

▸**rise up** *vi (revolt)* se soulever; **to r. up in arms** prendre les armes; **to r. up in protest (against sth)** se soulever (contre qch)

riser ['raɪzə(r)] *n* **to be an early/late r.** être un(e) lève-tôt *inv*/lève-tard *inv*

risible ['rɪzɪbəl] *adj Formal* risible

rising ['raɪzɪŋ] **1** *n (revolt)* soulèvement *m*

2 *adj (sun)* levant; *(temperature)* en hausse; *(prices, inflation)* en augmentation; *(artist, politician)* qui monte; *Fig* **r. star** étoile *f* montante

risk [rɪsk] **1** *n* risque *m*; **to take a r.** prendre un risque; **at r.** *(life, person)* en danger; *(job)* menacé(e); **to put one's health at r.** risquer de s'abîmer la santé; **at the r. of doing sth** au risque de faire qch; **to run the r. of doing sth** courir le risque de faire qch; **at one's own r.** à ses risques et périls; **r. assessment** évaluation *f* des risques; **r. capital** capital *m* à risque; **r. management** gestion *f* des risques

2 *vt* (**a**) *(life, reputation)* risquer; **to r. one's neck** risquer sa peau (**b**) *(take the chance of)* **to r. failure** risquer d'échouer; **to r. death** risquer sa vie; **I can't r. going** je ne peux pas prendre le risque d'y aller; **they r. losing all their money** ils risquent de perdre tout leur argent; **we can't r. it** nous ne pouvons pas courir ce risque

risky ['rɪskɪ] *adj* risqué(e)

risotto [rɪ'zɒtəʊ] (*pl* **risottos**) *n* risotto *m*

risqué ['rɪskeɪ] *adj* osé(e)

rite [raɪt] *n* rite *m*

ritual ['rɪtjʊəl] **1** *n* rituel *m*

2 *adj* rituel(elle)

ritzy ['rɪtsɪ] *adj Fam* chic *inv*

rival ['raɪvəl] **1** *n & adj* rival(e) *m,f*

2 *vt (compete with)* rivaliser avec; *(equal)* égaler

rivalry ['raɪvəlrɪ] *n* rivalité *f*

river ['rɪvə(r)] *n* rivière *f*; *(flowing into sea)* fleuve *m*; *Fig (of blood)* flot *m*

riverbed ['rɪvəbed] *n* lit *m* de la rivière

riverside ['rɪvəsaɪd] *n* bord *m* de l'eau; **r. villa** villa *f* au bord de l'eau

rivet ['rɪvɪt] **1** *n* rivet *m*

2 *vt* river; **to be riveted (by)** être fasciné(e) (par); *Fig* **to be riveted to the spot** *(with fear, surprise)* être cloué(e) sur place

riveting ['rɪvɪtɪŋ] *adj Fig* fascinant(e)

Riviera [rɪvɪ'eərə] *n* **the (French) R.** la Côte d'Azur

RNA [ɑːren'eɪ] *n (abbr* **ribonucleic acid**) ARN *m*

roach [rəʊtʃ] *n* (**a**) *(fish)* gardon *m* (**b**) *Fam (cockroach)* cafard *m*

road [rəʊd] *n* route *f*; *(in town)* rue *f*; **they live across** *or* **over the r.** ils habitent en face; **by r.** par la route; **down/up the r.** un peu plus loin dans la rue; *Fam* **one for the r.** *(final drink)* un petit dernier pour la route; **to be on the r.** *(of salesman)* être sur la route; *(of pop group)* être en tournée; **after three hours on the r.** après trois heures de route; **to be on the r. to**

recovery être en voie de guérison; *Fig* **to be on the right r.** être sur la bonne voie; *Fam* **let's get this show on the r.!** allez, c'est parti, on y va!; **a few years down the r.** dans quelques années; *Fig* **to come to the end of the r.** *(of relationship)* toucher à sa fin; **r. accident** accident *m* de la route; **r. conditions** états *mpl* des routes; *Fam* **r. hog** chauffard *m*; **r. map** carte *f* routière; **r. rage** agressivité *f* au volant; **r. safety** sécurité *f* routière; **r. sign** panneau *m* de signalisation

roadblock ['rəʊdblɒk] *n* barrage *m* routier

roadmap ['rəʊdmæp] *n* carte *f* routière; *Fig* **a r. for peace** un plan de paix

roadside ['rəʊdsaɪd] *n* bord *m* de la route; **r. bar/hotel** bar *m*/hôtel *m* situé en bord de route

road-test ['rəʊdtest] *vt (car)* essayer sur route

roadway ['rəʊdweɪ] *n* chaussée *f*

roadwork ['rəʊdwɜːk] *n* travaux *mpl* de voirie

roadworthy ['rəʊdwɜːðɪ] *adj* en état de rouler

roam [rəʊm] **1** *vt (streets, world)* parcourir; *(seas)* sillonner

2 *vi* **to r. (about)** errer; **to r. about the streets** traîner dans les rues

roaming ['rəʊmɪŋ] **1** *n* (**a**) *(wandering)* vagabondage *m* (**b**) *Tel (of cellphone)* roaming *m*, itinérance *f*; *Comput (on Internet)* roaming

2 *adj* vagabond(e), errant(e)

roar [rɔː(r)] **1** *n (of person, crowd)* hurlement *m*; *(of animal, engine)* rugissement *m*; *(of sea, wind)* mugissement *m*; *(of cars)* vacarme *m*

2 *vi (of person, crowd)* hurler; *(of animal, engine)* rugir; *(of sea, wind)* mugir; *(of cars)* vrombir; **to r. with laughter** hurler de rire

roaring ['rɔːrɪŋ] *adj* **r. drunk** ivre mort(e); **a r. fire** une belle flambée; **a r. success** un succès fou; **to do a r. trade** faire des affaires en or

roast [rəʊst] **1** *n (piece of meat)* rôti *m*

2 *adj* rôti(e)

3 *vt* (**a**) *(meat, potatoes)* faire rôtir; *(nuts, coffee)* faire griller (**b**) *Fam (criticize)* éreinter

roasting ['rəʊstɪŋ] *Fam* **1** *n* **to give sb a r.** *(reprimand)* passer un savon à qn; *(criticize)* descendre qn en flammes

2 *adj* **r.(-hot)** brûlant(e); **it's r. in here** il fait une chaleur à crever ici

rob [rɒb] (*pt & pp* **robbed**) *vt (bank)* dévaliser; *(person)* voler; *(house)* cambrioler; **to r. sb of sth** *(money, jewelry)* voler qch à qn; *Fig (youth, opportunity)* priver qn de qch

robber ['rɒbə(r)] *n* voleur(euse) *m,f*

robbery ['rɒbərɪ] (*pl* **robberies**) *n* vol *m*

robe [rəʊb] *n (of priest, judge)* robe *f*; *(dressing gown)* robe de chambre

robin ['rɒbɪn] *n* rouge-gorge *m*

robot ['rəʊbɒt] *n* robot *m*

robotics [rəʊ'bɒtɪks] *n* robotique *f*

robust [rəʊ'bʌst] *adj (person, economy)* robuste; *(material, suitcase, structure, health)* solide; *(defense, speech)* musclé(e)

rock [rɒk] **1** *n* (**a**) *(substance)* roche *f*; *(large stone)* rocher *m*; *(smaller stone)* pierre *f*; *Fig* **to be on the rocks** *(of marriage, company)* être en pleine débâcle; **on the rocks** *(drink)* avec des glaçons, *Can* sur glace; **the R. of Gibraltar** le Rocher de Gibraltar; **to reach** *or* **to hit r. bottom** toucher le fond; **r. climbing** varappe *f*; **r. face** paroi *f* rocheuse; **r. garden** rocaille *f*; **r. pool** = flaque d'eau dans les rochers à marée basse; **r. salt** sel *m* gemme; **r. solid** solide comme le roc

(**b**) *(rocking motion)* **to give the crib a r.** balancer un peu le berceau

(**c**) *(music)* rock *m*; **r. and roll** rock-and-roll *m*; **r. concert** concert *m* de rock; **r. group** groupe *m* de rock; **r. singer** chanteur(euse) *m,f* de rock

2 *vt (boat, chair)* balancer; *(building)* secouer; **to r. a baby to**

sleep bercer un enfant pour qu'il s'endorme; *Fig* **to r. the boat** faire des histoires; *Fig* **the country has been rocked by these revelations** le pays a été secoué par ces révélations

3 *vi (sway)* se balancer; *(of building)* trembler; **to r. with laughter** être secoué(e) par un fou rire

rock-bottom ['rɒkbɒtəm] *adj* **r. prices** prix *mpl* incroyables

rocker ['rɒkə(r)] *n* **(a)** *(chair)* fauteuil *m* à bascule, *Can* berçante *f*; *Fam* **to be off one's r.** être givré(e) **(b)** *(musician, fan)* rocker(euse) *m,f*

rockery ['rɒkərɪ] *(pl* **rockeries)** *n* rocaille *f*

rocket ['rɒkɪt] **1** *n Aviat & Astron* fusée *f*; **r. launcher** lance-fusées *m inv*

2 *vi (of prices, inflation, unemployment)* monter en flèche

rockfall ['rɒkfɔ:l] *n* éboulement *m*

rock-hard [rɒk'hɑ:d] *adj* dur(e) comme (de la) pierre

Rockies ['rɒkɪz] *npl* **the R.** les Rocheuses *fpl*

rocking chair ['rɒkɪŋtʃeə(r)] *n* fauteuil *m* à bascule, *Can* berçante *f*

rocky ['rɒkɪ] *adj* **(a)** *(path, soil)* rocailleux(euse); **the R. Mountains** les Montagnes *fpl* Rocheuses **(b)** *Fig (economy, relationship)* instable

rod [rɒd] *n (wooden)* baguette *f*; *(metal)* tige *f*; *(for curtain)* tringle *f*; *(for fishing)* canne *f* à pêche; *Fig* **to rule with a r. of iron** gouverner d'une main de fer

rode [rəʊd] *pt of* **ride**

rodent ['rəʊdənt] *n* rongeur *m*

rodeo ['rəʊdɪəʊ] *(pl* **rodeos)** *n* rodéo *m*

roe¹ [rəʊ] *n* **r. (deer)** chevreuil *m*

roe² [rəʊ] *n (of fish)* œufs *mpl* de poisson

roger ['rɒdʒə(r)] *exclam (in radio message)* bien reçu!

rogue [rəʊg] *n (dishonest)* filou *m*; *(mischievous)* coquin(e) *m,f*

roguish ['rəʊgɪʃ] *adj* canaille

role [rəʊl] *n* rôle *m*; *Fig* **to play an important/a leading r. (in sth)** jouer un rôle important/prépondérant (dans qch); **r. model** modèle *m*

role-playing ['rəʊlpleɪɪŋ] *n* jeu *m* de rôle

roll [rəʊl] **1** *n* **(a)** *(of paper)* rouleau *m*; *(of fat)* bourrelet *m*; *(of bills)* liasse *f*; **a r. of film** une pellicule (photo)

(b) *(bread)* petit pain *m*; **cheese r.** ≃ sandwich *m* au fromage

(c) *(of drum, thunder)* roulement *m*

(d) *(movement)* roulis *m*; *Fam* **to be on a r.** avoir la chance de son côté

(e) *(list)* liste *f*; **r. call** appel *m*; *Mil* **r. of honor** liste de ceux qui sont morts pour la patrie

2 *vt* **(a)** *(ball)* faire rouler; **to r. sth along the ground** faire rouler qch sur le sol; **to r. one's eyes** lever les yeux au ciel; **to r. one's r's** rouler les r; **the animal rolled itself into a ball** l'animal se mit en boule

(b) *(lawn)* passer au rouleau; *(road)* cylindrer; *(metal)* laminer

(c) *(cigarette)* rouler

3 *vi* **(a)** *(of ball, ship)* rouler; *(of camera)* tourner; *Fig* **heads will r.** il y a des têtes qui vont tomber; *Fam* **to be rolling in money, to be rolling in it** rouler sur l'or; *Fig* **to start** *or* **to get the ball rolling** mettre les choses en route

(b) *(of thunder)* gronder

▶**roll back** *vt sep* **(a)** *(push back) (object)* reculer; *Fig (time, years)* faire reculer **(b)** *(prices)* casser

▶**roll down 1** *vt sep (sleeves)* redescendre; *(blind, car window)* descendre

2 *vi (of tears, sweat)* couler

▶**roll over** *vi (of person) (once)* se retourner; *(several times)* se rouler; *(of car) (once)* capoter; *(several times)* faire des tonneaux

▶**roll up** *vt sep (newspaper)* rouler; *(sleeves)* retrousser; *(blind, car window)* remonter; **to r. sth up in paper** envelopper qch dans du papier

rolled-up [rəʊl'dʌp] *adj (sleeves, trousers)* retroussé(e); *(umbrella)* replié(e); *(newspaper)* roulé(e)

roller ['rəʊlə(r)] *n (for paint, garden)* rouleau *m*; *(for hair)* bigoudi *m*; **r. blind** store *m* (à cylindre); **r. coaster** montagnes *fpl* russes; **r. skates** patins *mpl* à roulettes

rollerblades ['rəʊləbleɪdz] *npl* rollers *mpl*

rollerblading ['rəʊləbleɪdɪŋ] *n* **to go r.** faire du roller

roller-skate ['rəʊləskeɪt] *vi* faire du patin à roulettes

roller-skating ['rəʊləskeɪtɪŋ] *n* **to go r.** faire du patin à roulettes

rolling ['rəʊlɪŋ] *adj (hills, fields)* ondulant(e); *(sea, waves)* gros (grosse); *(thunder)* qui gronde; **r. mill** *(for steel)* laminoir *m*; **r. pin** rouleau *m* à pâtisserie; *Rail* **r. stock** matériel *m* roulant

roll-on ['rəʊlɒn] *adj* **(a)** **r. (deodorant)** déodorant *m* à bille **(b)** *Naut* **r.-roll-off ferry** ferry *m* de type roll-on-roll-off

Rolls [rəʊlz] *n Fam (Rolls-Royce)* Rolls Royce *f*

roll-top desk ['rəʊltɒp'desk] *n* bureau *m* à cylindre

roly-poly ['rəʊlɪ'pəʊlɪ] *adj Fam (plump)* grassouillet(ette)

ROM [rɒm] *n Comput (abbr* **read only memory)** mémoire *f* morte

Roman ['rəʊmən] **1** *n* Romain(e) *m,f*

2 *adj* romain(e); **R. Catholic** catholique; **R. nose** nez *m* aquilin; **R. numerals** chiffres *mpl* romains

roman ['rəʊmən] *Typ* **1** *n* romain *m*

2 *adj* romain(e)

romance ['rəʊmæns, rə'mæns] *n* **(a)** *(book)* roman *m* d'amour; *(film)* histoire *f* d'amour **(b)** *(love affair)* aventure *f* **(c)** *(charm)* charme *m*

Romania [rə'meɪnɪə] *n* la Roumanie

Romanian [rə'meɪnɪən] **1** *n* **(a)** *(person)* Roumain(e) *m,f* **(b)** *(language)* roumain *m*

2 *adj* roumain(e)

romantic [rəʊ'mæntɪk, rə'mæntɪk] **1** *n* romantique *mf*

2 *adj* romantique; *(scheme, notion)* romanesque

romanticism [rəʊ'mæntɪsɪzəm] *n* romantisme *m*

romanticize [rə'mæntɪsaɪz] *vt (incident)* romancer; *(idea, war)* présenter sous un jour romantique

Romany ['rəʊmənɪ] **1** *n (pl* **Romanies)** **(a)** *(person)* Tzigane *mf* **(b)** *(language)* tzigane *m*

2 *adj* tzigane

Rome [rəʊm] *n* Rome; **R. wasn't built in a day** Paris ne s'est pas fait en un jour; **when in R.(, do as the Romans do)** = il faut adopter les usages de l'endroit où l'on se trouve

romp [rɒmp] **1** *n* **to have a r.** chahuter

2 *vi* **to r. (about** *or* **around)** s'ébattre; **to r. through an exam** réussir un examen les doigts dans le nez; **to r. home** *(candidate, runner)* arriver dans un fauteuil

romper ['rɒmpə(r)] *n* **r. suit, rompers** barboteuse *f*

roof [ru:f] **1** *n (of building, car)* toit *m*; *(of tunnel, cave)* plafond *m*; **to have a r. over one's head** avoir un endroit où vivre; **to live under one** *or* **the same r.** vivre sous le même toit; *Fam* **to hit the r.** sortir de ses gonds; *Fam* **to go through the r.** connaître une flambée; **r. of the mouth** voûte *f* du palais; **r. garden** jardin *m* aménagé sur le toit; **r. rack** galerie *f*

2 *vt* couvrir

roofing ['ru:fɪŋ] *n* toiture *f*; **r. material** matériaux *mpl* de couverture

rooftop ['ru:ftɒp] *n* toit *m*; *Fig* **to shout sth from the rooftops** crier qch sur les toits

rook [rʊk] *n (bird)* freux *m*; *(in chess)* tour *f*

rookery ['rʊkərɪ] *(pl* **rookeries)** *n* colonie *f* de freux

rookie ['rʊkɪ] *n Fam* bleu *m*

room [ru:m] **1** *n* **(a)** *(in house)* pièce *f*; *(bedroom, in hotel)* chambre *f*; *(large, public)* salle *f*; **r. and board** chambre et pension; **r. service** service *m* dans les chambres; **r. temperature** température *f* ambiante **(b)** *(space)* place *f*; **there's no r. to move** il n'y a pas de place; **to make r. (for sb)** faire de la place (pour qn); **there's no r. for doubt** cela ne fait aucun doute; **there is r. for improvement** ça pourrait être mieux

2 vi **to r. with sb** partager une chambre avec qn

roomie ['ruːmɪ] n Fam (at boarding school, college) camarade mf de chambre; (in apartment) colocataire mf, coloc mf

roommate ['ruːmmeɪt] n (at boarding school, college) camarade mf de chambre; (in apartment) colocataire mf

roomy ['ruːmɪ] adj spacieux(euse); (clothes) ample

roost [ruːst] **1** n perchoir m; **to rule the r.** faire la loi

2 vi se percher; Fig **her actions have come home to r.** ses actions se sont retournées contre elle

rooster ['ruːstə(r)] n coq m

root [ruːt] **1** n (a) (of plant, tooth, word, hair) racine f; **to pull up by the roots** (plant) déraciner; also Fig **to take r.** prendre racine; **they destroyed the party r. and branch** ils ont entièrement détruit le parti; Fig **to put down roots** s'intégrer; Fig **to get back to one's roots** retrouver ses racines; **r. beer** = boisson gazeuse aux extraits de plantes; **r. crops** racines comestibles; **r. vegetables** légumes mpl à racine comestible (b) (origin) origine f; Prov **money is the r. of all evil** l'argent est la source de tous les maux

2 vt **to be rooted to the spot** être figé(e) sur place

3 vi (a) **to r. about** or **around (for sth)** fouiller (pour trouver qch) (b) **to r. for sb** appuyer qn

▸**root for** vt insep (support) être pour

▸**root out** vt sep supprimer

rope [rəʊp] **1** n (a) (cord) corde f; (of pearls) sautoir m; (of onions) chapelet m; **r. ladder** échelle f de corde (b) (idioms) **to be on the ropes** (of company) battre de l'aile; **to learn the ropes** apprendre les ficelles; **to show sb the ropes** former qn; **to give sb plenty of r.** donner du mou à qn

2 vt (fasten) lier (avec une corde) (**to** à); **they roped themselves together** (for climbing) ils se sont encordés

▸**rope in** vt sep Fam (recruit) recruter; **to get roped in to do sth** se laisser convaincre de faire qch

▸**rope off** vt sep **to r. sth off** interdire l'accès de qch avec une corde

rosary ['rəʊzərɪ] (pl rosaries) n Rel chapelet m; **to say one's r.** dire son chapelet

rose[1] [rəʊz] **1** n (a) (flower) rose f; (on watering can) pomme f; **r. bed** parterre m de rosiers; **r. bush** rosier m; **r. garden** roseraie f; **r. grower** rosiériste mf; **r. window** rosace f (b) (idioms) **life isn't a bed of roses** tout n'est pas rose dans la vie; **to come up roses** se passer à merveille

2 adj (color) rose

rose[2] [rəʊz] pt of **rise**

rosé ['rəʊzeɪ] n rosé m

rosebud ['rəʊzbʌd] n bouton m de rose

rose-colored ['rəʊzkʌləd], **rose-tinted** ['rəʊztɪntɪd] adj **to see things through r. glasses** voir la vie en rose

rosehip ['rəʊzhɪp] n gratte-cul m

rosemary ['rəʊzmərɪ] n romarin m

rosette [rəʊˈzet] n rosette f

rosewater ['rəʊzwɔːtə(r)] n eau f de rose

rosewood ['rəʊzwʊd] n bois m de rose

roster ['rɒstə(r)] n liste f de service

rostrum ['rɒstrəm] (pl rostrums or rostra ['rɒstrə]) n (for speaker) estrade f; (for prizewinner) podium m

rosy ['rəʊzɪ] adj (pink) rose; (complexion) de rose; Fig (future) prometteur(euse)

rot [rɒt] **1** n (a) (in house, wood) pourriture f; Fig **the r. has set in** ça se gâte; Fig **to stop the r.** empêcher la situation de se dégrader (b) Fam (nonsense) bêtises fpl

2 vt (pt & pp rotted) (faire) pourrir

3 vi pourrir; **to r. in prison** moisir en prison

rotary ['rəʊtərɪ] **1** n (pl rotaries) (traffic circle) rond-point m

2 adj rotatif(ive)

rotate [rəʊˈteɪt] **1** vt (a) (turn) faire tourner (b) (alternate) (duties) remplir à tour de rôle (**c**) (crops) alterner

2 vi (a) (turn) tourner (b) (in job) remplir des fonctions à tour de rôle

rotation [rəʊˈteɪʃən] n (a) (of planet) rotation f (b) (in job) roulement m; (of crops) alternance f; **by** or **in r.** à tour de rôle

rote [rəʊt] n **by r.** par cœur; **r. learning** apprentissage m par cœur

rotor ['rəʊtə(r)] n rotor m

rotten ['rɒtən] adj (a) (wood, egg, fruit) pourri(e) (b) Fam (bad) nul (nulle); (weather) pourri(e); **to feel r.** (ill) ne pas se sentir dans son assiette; (guilty) ne pas être fier(ère) (**about** de); **to have r. luck** avoir la guigne (**c**) (unpleasant) dégueulasse; **a r. trick** un tour de cochon

rottweiler ['rɒtvaɪlə(r)] n rottweiler m

rotund [rəʊˈtʌnd] adj rond(e)

rouge [ruːʒ] n rouge m (à joues)

rough [rʌf] **1** n (a) (in golf) rough m

(b) Fam Old-fashioned (hooligan) voyou m

(**c**) (difficulty) **you have to take the r. with the smooth** on ne peut pas tout avoir dans la vie

2 adj (a) (surface, skin) rugueux(euse); (terrain) accidenté(e)

(b) (unrefined) (manners) fruste; Fig **a r. diamond** un cœur d'or sous des dehors frustes; **r. draft** brouillon m; **r. sketch** ébauche f

(**c**) Fam (ill) **to feel/look r.** se sentir/avoir l'air patraque

(**d**) (violent) brutal(e); (crossing, sea) agité(e)

(**e**) (harsh) (voice) rude; (wine, spirits) âpre; Fam **it was r. on her** c'était dur pour elle; **r. justice** justice f sommaire

(**f**) (approximate) approximatif(ive); **at a r. guess** à vue de nez; **I have a r. idea of what he wants** j'ai une petite idée de ce qu'il veut

3 adv **to play r.** jouer avec brutalité; Fig ne pas faire de cadeaux

4 vt Fam **to r. it** vivre à la dure

▸**rough up** vt sep Fam (beat up) tabasser

roughage ['rʌfɪdʒ] n fibres fpl (alimentaires)

rough-and-ready [rʌfənˈredɪ] adj (meal, accommodations) sommaire; (person) rustre

rough-and-tumble [rʌfənˈtʌmbəl] n bousculade f; Fig **the r. of politics** le monde sans pitié de la politique

roughly ['rʌflɪ] adv (a) (violently) brutalement; **to treat sb r.** rudoyer qn (b) (crudely) grossièrement (**c**) (approximately) à peu près; **r. (speaking)** en gros

roughness ['rʌfnɪs] n (a) (of surface, skin) rugosité f (b) (of behavior) rudesse f

roughshod ['rʌfʃɒd] adv **to ride r. over sth** ne faire aucun cas de qch

rough-spoken [rʌfˈspəʊkən] adj au langage grossier

roulette [ruːˈlet] n roulette f; **r. table** table f de roulette; **r. wheel** roulette

round [raʊnd] **1** n (a) (stage of match) manche f; (stage of tournament) tour m; (in boxing) round m; (of golf) partie f; **to get/to be through to the next r.** se qualifier/s'être qualifié(e) pour le tour suivant

(b) (of talks, visits) série f; (of drinks) tournée f; **r. of applause** applaudissements mpl; **to give sb a r. of applause** applaudir qn

(**c**) **to do one's rounds** (of doctor) faire ses visites; **to do the rounds** (of rumor, illness) circuler; **the daily r.** (of tasks) le train-train quotidien

(**d**) Mil (bullet) balle f

(**e**) Mus canon m

2 adj rond(e); **to have r. shoulders** avoir le dos rond; **a r. dozen** une douzaine exactement; **in r. figures** en arrondissant; **r. table (conference)** table f ronde; **r. trip** aller (et) retour m

3 adv autour; **all (the) year r.** toute l'année; **all r.** (on the *whole)* dans l'ensemble; **the wrong way r.** à l'envers; **the right way r.** *(not back to front)* à l'endroit; *(in the correct order)* dans le bon ordre; **the other way r.** *(in the other direction)* dans l'autre sens; **do it the other way r.** fais l'inverse; **to go r. (to sb's house)** passer (chez qn); **to invite sb r.** inviter qn

4 *prep* **(a)** *(position)* autour de; **r. here** dans le coin

(b) *(motion)* **to look r. a room** parcourir une pièce du regard; **to travel r. the world** parcourir le monde; **to go r. an obstacle** contourner un obstacle; **to go r. the corner** *(of person)* tourner le coin; *(of vehicle)* prendre le virage; **it's just r. the corner** c'est juste au coin (de la rue); *Fig* **to drive** *or* **to send sb r. the bend** rendre qn maboul(e)

(c) *(approximately)* **r. about** environ; **r. about midday** vers midi

5 *vt* **(a)** *(make round)* arrondir

(b) *(obstacle)* contourner; *(corner)* tourner

▶**round down** *vt sep (figure)* arrondir au chiffre inférieur

▶**round off** *vt sep (conclude)* conclure

▶**round up** *vt sep* **(a)** *(cattle)* rassembler; *(criminals, suspects)* ramasser **(b)** *(figure)* arrondir au chiffre supérieur

roundabout ['raʊndəbaʊt] *adj (approach, route)* détourné(e); **to lead up to a question in a r. way** aborder une question de biais

roundly ['raʊndlɪ] *adv (praise, condemn)* vivement; *(beat)* sévèrement

round-trip ['raʊndtrɪp] *adj (ticket)* aller (et) retour

roundup ['raʊndʌp] *n (of criminals)* rafle *f; (of events, news)* résumé *m*

rouse [raʊz] *vt* réveiller; **to r. oneself (to do sth)** se secouer (et faire qch); **to r. sb to action** pousser qn à agir; **to r. sb to anger** susciter la colère de qn

rousing ['raʊzɪŋ] *adj (music, speech)* exaltant(e); *(welcome, cheers)* enthousiaste

rout [raʊt] **1** *n* déroute *f*

2 *vt* mettre en déroute

▶**rout out** *vt sep (discover)* dénicher

route [raʊt] **1** *n* **(a)** *(of traveler)* itinéraire *m; (of plane, ship)* route *f; (of bus, parade)* parcours *m; Fig (to success)* voie *f* (**to** de) **(b)** *(highway)* ≃ route *f* nationale

2 *vt (package, goods)* acheminer; *(bus, train, flight)* faire passer

router ['ru:tə(r)] *n Comput* routeur *m*

routine [ru:'ti:n] **1** *n* **(a)** *(habit)* routine *f;* **the daily r.** le train-train quotidien **(b)** *(of performer, comedian)* numéro *m; Fam Fig* **don't give me that r.** arrête ton numéro **(c)** *Comput* sous-programme *m*

2 *adj* **(a)** *(normal)* de routine **(b)** *(dull)* routinier(ère)

routinely [ru:'ti:nlɪ] *adv* systématiquement

rove [raʊv] **1** *vt* parcourir

2 *vi* rôder, vagabonder; **her eyes roved around the room** son regard parcourait la pièce

roving reporter ['raʊvɪŋrɪ'pɔːtə(r)] *n* reporter *m (qui va sur le terrain)*

row[1] [raʊ] *n (line)* rangée *f;* **in a r.** en rang; **two Sundays in a r.** deux dimanches d'affilée; **in the front r.** *(of seats)* au premier rang

row[2] [raʊ] **1** *n (in boat)* promenade *f* en canot; **to go for a r.** canoter

2 *vt (boat)* faire aller à la rame; *(person)* transporter en canot

3 *vi (in boat)* ramer

row[3] [raʊ] **1** *n* **(a)** *(noise)* vacarme *m; (protest)* tollé *m* **(b)** *(quarrel)* dispute *f;* **to have a r. (with sb)** se disputer (avec qn)

2 *vi (quarrel)* se disputer (**about** à propos de)

rowan ['raʊən] *n* sorbier *m*

rowboat ['raʊbaʊt] *n* bateau *m* à rames

rowdy ['raʊdɪ] **1** *n (pl* **rowdies)** chahuteur(euse) *m,f*

2 *adj (person)* chahuteur(euse); *(event, party)* bruyant(e); **to be r.** chahuter

rower ['raʊə(r)] *n* rameur(euse) *m,f*

rowing ['raʊɪŋ] *n* canotage *m; (as sport)* aviron *m;* **r. machine** rameur *m*

royal ['rɔɪəl] **1** *adj* royal(e); *Fig (splendid)* princier(ère); **His/Her R. Highness** Son Altesse Royale; **r. blue** bleu roi *m inv;* **the R. Family** la famille royale; **r. flush** *(in cards)* quinte *f* royale; **r. jelly** gelée *f* royale

2 *n Fam* membre *m* de la famille royale; **the Royals** la famille royale

royalist ['rɔɪəlɪst] *n & adj* royaliste *mf*

royally ['rɔɪəlɪ] *adv (entertain, welcome)* royalement

royalty ['rɔɪəltɪ] *n* **(a)** *(rank, position)* royauté *f;* **to be r.** faire partie de la famille royale; **to be treated like r.** être traité(e) royalement **(b)** **royalties** *(for author, singer)* droits *mpl* d'auteur

RPI [ɑːpiː'aɪ] *n Econ (abbr* **retail price index**) indice *m* des prix de détail

rpm [ɑːpiː'em] *n Aut (abbr* **revolutions per minute**) tr/min

R & R [ɑːrən'ɑː(r)] *n (abbr* **rest and recreation**) *Mil* permission *f; Fam Fig* **to get some R & R** se reposer un peu

RRP [ɑːrɑː'piː] *n Com (abbr* **recommended retail price**) prix *m* conseillé

RSA [ɑːres'eɪ] *n (abbr* **Republic of South Africa**) Afrique *f* du Sud

RSI [ɑːres'aɪ] *n (abbr* **repetitive strain injury**) lésions *fpl* attribuables au travail répétitif

RSVP [ɑːresviː'piː] *(abbr* **répondez s'il vous plaît**) *(on invitation)* RSVP

rub [rʌb] **1** *n* **to give sth a r.** frotter qch; *Fig* **there's the r.!** voilà le hic!

2 *vt (pt & pp* **rubbed**) frotter; **to r. one's hands together** se frotter les mains; *Fig* **to r. shoulders with sb** côtoyer qn; *Fam* **to r. sb the wrong way** prendre qn à rebrousse-poil

3 *vi (of straps, shoes)* frotter (**against** contre)

▶**rub in** *vt sep (lotion, ointment)* faire pénétrer; *Fam* **to r. it in** retourner le couteau dans la plaie

▶**rub off 1** *vt sep (dirt, stain)* enlever en frottant; *(writing)* effacer

2 *vi* partir, s'enlever; *Fig* **to r. off on sb** *(of manners, enthusiasm)* déteindre sur qn

▶**rub out** *vt sep* **(a)** *(erase)* effacer **(b)** *Fam (murder)* buter

rubber ['rʌbə(r)] *n* **(a)** *(substance)* caoutchouc *m;* **r. ball/gloves** balle *f*/gants *mpl* en caoutchouc; **r. band** élastique *m;* **r. boots** bottes *f* en caoutchouc; **r. check** chèque *f* en bois; **r. dinghy** canot *m* pneumatique; **r. plant** caoutchouc *m;* **r. ring** bouée *f;* **r. stamp** tampon *m* **(b)** *Fam (condom)* capote *f*

rubber-stamp [rʌbə'stæmp] *vt Fig (approve)* approuver sans discussion

rubbery ['rʌbərɪ] *adj* caoutchouteux(euse)

rubbing alcohol ['rʌbɪŋ'ælkəhɒl] *n* alcool *m* à 90 degrés

rubbish ['rʌbɪʃ] *n* **(a)** *(refuse)* détritus *mpl; (from house)* ordures *fpl; (junk)* cochonneries *fpl* **(b)** *Fam (nonsense)* idioties *fpl;* **that book/movie is a load of r.** ce livre/film est nul; **r.!** n'importe quoi!

rubble ['rʌbəl] *n* décombres *mpl*

rubella [ruː'belə] *n* rubéole *f*

ruble ['ruːbəl] *n* rouble *m*

rubric ['ruːbrɪk] *n* instructions *fpl*

ruby ['ruːbɪ] **1** *n (pl* **rubies)** rubis *m*

2 *adj (color)* rubis

ruck [rʌk] *n (in cloth)* faux pli *m*

▶**ruck up** *vt sep (of sheet, cloth)* se froisser

rucksack ['rʌksæk] *n* sac *m* à dos

ructions ['rʌkʃənz] *npl Fam* grabuge *m*

rudder ['rʌdə(r)] *n* gouvernail *m*

ruddy ['rʌdɪ] *adj (complexion)* rose

rude [ruːd] *adj* **(a)** *(impolite)* impoli(e) **(b)** *(vulgar)* grossier(ère); *(gesture)* obscène **(c)** *(primitive)* rudimentaire **(d)** *(shock, surprise)* to receive a r. **awakening** être brutalement rappelé(e) à la réalité (**e**) *(vigorous)* **to be in r. health** jouir d'une santé robuste

rudeness ['ru:dnɪs] *n* (**a**) *(impoliteness)* impolitesse *f* (**b**) *(vulgarity)* grossièreté *f*

rudimentary [ru:dɪ'mentərɪ] *adj* rudimentaire

rudiments ['ru:dɪmənts] *npl* rudiments *mpl*

rue [ru:] *vt Lit* regretter amèrement; **I r. the day I met her** je maudis le jour où je l'ai rencontrée

rueful ['ru:fʊl] *adj (voice, smile)* de regret; *(person)* qui a des regrets

ruff [rʌf] *n (on costume)* fraise *f*

ruffian ['rʌfɪən] *n Old-fashioned* voyou *m*

ruffle ['rʌfəl] *vt (water)* troubler; *(hair)* ébouriffer; **to r. sb's feathers** froisser qn; **to r. sb's composure** faire perdre contenance à qn

rug [rʌg] *n* tapis *m*; *Fig* **to pull the r. from under sb's feet** couper l'herbe sous le pied à qn; *Fig* **to sweep sth under the r.** enterrer qch

rugby ['rʌgbɪ] *n* rugby *m*; **r. ball** ballon *m* de rugby

rugged ['rʌgɪd] *adj (ground, country)* accidenté(e); *(features, manner)* rude; **r. good looks** beauté *f* un peu rude

rugrat ['rʌgræt] *n Fam* môme *mf*

ruin ['ru:ɪn] **1** *n* ruine *f*; **to fall into ruin(s)** tomber en ruine(s); **it will be the r. of him** ça le perdra
2 *vt (suit, shoes)* abîmer; *(person)* ruiner; *(meal, evening, vacation)* gâcher; **to r. one's health** se ruiner la santé; **to r. one's eyesight** s'user la vue; **tourism has ruined the town** le tourisme a défiguré la ville; **a ruined castle** un château en ruine(s)

ruinous ['ru:ɪnəs] *adj (expensive)* ruineux(euse)

rule [ru:l] **1** *n* (**a**) *(principle)* règle *f*; *(regulation)* règlement *m*; **rules** *(of club, school)* règlement; **as a r.** en règle générale; **to make it a r. to do sth** se faire un principe de faire qch; **rules and regulations** règles; *Ind* **to work to r.** faire la grève du zèle; **it's against the r.** c'est contraire au règlement; **as a r. of thumb** pour avoir une idée approximative; **r. book** règlement
(**b**) *(government)* autorité *f*
(**c**) *(for measuring)* règle *f*
2 *vt* (**a**) *(country, people)* gouverner; **to let sth r. one's life** laisser qch dominer toute sa vie; *Fig* **to r. the roost** commander
(**b**) *(decide, decree)* décider; **to be ruled illegal** être décrété(e) illégal(e)
(**c**) *(paper)* régler
3 *vi* (**a**) *(of monarch)* régner
(**b**) *(of judge)* statuer (**on** sur); **to r. in favor of/against sb** décider en faveur de/contre qn

▶**rule out** *vt sep* exclure

ruler ['ru:lə(r)] *n* (**a**) *(of country)* dirigeant(e) *m,f* (**b**) *(for measuring)* règle *f*

ruling ['ru:lɪŋ] **1** *n (of judge, umpire)* décision *f*
2 *adj* (**a**) *(party)* au pouvoir; *(class)* dirigeant(e) (**b**) *(passion)* dominant(e); *(consideration)* premier(ère)

rum [rʌm] *n* rhum *m*

Rumania = Romania

Rumanian = Romanian

rumble ['rʌmbəl] **1** *n* (**a**) *(of thunder, gunfire, traffic)* grondement *m*; *(of voices)* bourdonnement *m*; *(of stomach)* gargouillement *m*; **rumbles of discontent** murmures *mpl* de protestation (**b**) *(fistfight)* baston *m ou f*, rixe *f*
2 *vi (of thunder, traffic)* gronder; *(of stomach)* gargouiller

rumbustious [rʌm'bʌstjəs] *adj* exubérant(e)

ruminant ['ru:mɪnənt] *n Zool* ruminant *m*

ruminate ['ru:mɪneɪt] *vi Formal* **to r. (about** *or* **on sth)** ruminer (qch)

rummage ['rʌmɪdʒ] **1** *vi* **to r. about** *or* **around (for sth)** farfouiller (à la recherche de qch); **to r. through sth** fouiller qch
2 *n* **r. sale** vente *f* de charité

rumor ['ru:mə(r)] **1** *n* rumeur *f*, bruit *m*; **r. has it...** on raconte que...; **there's a r. going around that...** le bruit court que...
2 *vt* **it is rumored that...** le bruit court que...; **he is rumored to be very rich/in hiding** le bruit court qu'il est très riche/qu'il se cache

rump [rʌmp] *n* (**a**) *(of animal)* croupe *f*; *Fam (of person)* postérieur *m*; **r. steak** romsteck *m* (**b**) *(of political party, assembly)* restant *m*; **r. state** état *m* croupion

rumple ['rʌmpəl] *vt (clothes, sheets)* friper, froisser; *(hair)* ébouriffer

rumpus ['rʌmpəs] *n Fam (noise)* chahut *m*; **to kick up** *or* **to cause a r. (about sth)** faire un scandale (à propos de qch); **r. room** salle *f* de jeu

run [rʌn] **1** *n* (**a**) *(act of running)* course *f*; **at a r.** en courant; **to go for a r.** aller courir; **to be on the r.** être en fuite; *Fig* **we've got them on the r.** nous les avons mis en déroute; **to give sb the r. of the house** mettre sa maison à la disposition de qn; *Fam* **to make a r. for it** *(escape)* se tirer; *(to catch train)* grouiller; *Fam* **to give sb a r. for his/her money** donner du fil à retordre à qn; *Fam* **to have the runs** avoir la courante
(**b**) *(trip)* trajet *m*; *(for pleasure)* balade *f*; **to go for a r.** *(in car)* aller se balader en voiture
(**c**) *Com (of book)* tirage *m*; *(of product)* série *f*
(**d**) *(sequence, series)* série *f*; *(in cards)* suite *f*; **a r. of good luck** une période faste; **a r. of bad luck** une série de malheurs; **in the short/long r.** à court/long terme
(**e**) *Fin (on currency, stock exchange)* ruée *f* (**on** sur); *(on bank)* retrait *m* massif
(**f**) *(in stocking)* échelle *f*
(**g**) *(in baseball)* point *m*
(**h**) *(for skier)* piste *f*
(**i**) *(for chickens, rabbits)* enclos *m*
2 *vt (pt* **ran** [ræn]*, pp* **run**) (**a**) *(distance, race)* courir; **to r. an errand** faire une course; **to allow things to r. their course** laisser les choses se faire; **to r. sb close** talonner qn; *Fam* **to be run off one's feet** être débordé(e)
(**b**) *(drive)* **to r. sb to the airport** conduire qn à l'aéroport
(**c**) *(drugs, arms)* faire le trafic de
(**d**) *(machine)* faire fonctionner; *(tests)* effectuer; *Comput (program)* exécuter
(**e**) *(business)* diriger; *(hotel)* tenir; *(car)* avoir; **to r. sb's life for them** dire à qn comment vivre sa vie
(**f**) *(cables, pipes)* faire passer; **to r. one's fingers over/through sth** passer la main sur/dans qch; **to r. one's eye over sth** parcourir qch du regard
(**g**) *(water, bath)* faire couler
(**h**) **to r. a temperature** avoir de la température
(**i**) **to r. a deficit** enregistrer un déficit
(**j**) **to r. an article** publier un article
3 *vi* (**a**) *(of person)* courir; **to r. up/down the street** monter/descendre la rue en courant; **to r. about** courir çà et là; **I'll just r. across/over to the store** je fais un saut à l'épicerie; **to r. after sb** courir après qn; **to r. for help** courir chercher de l'aide; **to r. in/out** entrer/sortir en courant
(**b**) *(flee)* s'enfuir, se sauver; **r. for it!** sauve qui peut!
(**c**) *(compete in race)* courir; **to r. for President** se présenter aux élections présidentielles
(**d**) *(flow)* couler; **the river runs into a lake** la rivière se jette dans un lac; **my nose is running** j'ai le nez qui coule; **my blood ran cold** mon sang se glaça
(**e**) **to r. aground** *(of ship)* s'échouer; *Fig (of project, economy)* échouer
(**f**) *(of contract, lease)* courir; *(of play)* être à l'affiche; **it runs in the family** c'est de famille; **the total ran to $2,000** le montant total s'élevait à 2000 dollars

(**g**) *(of bus, train)* circuler; **to be running late** *(of bus, train)* avoir du retard; *(of person)* être en retard

(**h**) *(operate) (of machine)* marcher, fonctionner; *(of engine)* tourner; **to r. on gas/electricity** marcher *ou* fonctionner au gaz/à l'électricité; **to r. off the mains** marcher *ou* fonctionner sur secteur; **the car runs on unleaded gas** la voiture roule à l'essence sans plomb; **things are running smoothly** tout marche comme sur des roulettes

(**i**) *(of road, railroad)* passer; **the line runs along the coast** la ligne suit *ou* longe la côte

(**j**) **feelings** *or* **tempers are running high** les esprits sont échauffés; **to be running low** *(of funds, supplies)* s'épuiser; **to r. dry** *(of river)* s'assécher

(**k**) *(of color, dye)* déteindre

▸**run away** *vi (of person)* s'enfuir, se sauver (**from** de); **to r. away from home** faire une fugue; *Fig* **to r. away from the facts** refuser l'évidence; *Fig* **don't r. away with the idea that...** ne va pas t'imaginer que...

▸**run down 1** *vt sep* (**a**) *(in car)* renverser (**b**) *(find)* dénicher (**c**) *(criticize)* dénigrer (**d**) *(reduce) (production, stocks)* diminuer, réduire; *(industry, factory)* fermer progressivement

  2 *vi (of battery)* se décharger

▸**run in** *vt sep Fam (arrest)* pincer

▸**run into** *vt insep* (**a**) *(collide with)* rentrer dans; *Fig (difficulties)* rencontrer; **to r. into trouble** s'attirer des ennuis (**b**) *(meet by chance)* tomber sur

▸**run off 1** *vt sep (print)* imprimer; *(photocopy)* photocopier; **to r. off a copy of sth** faire une copie de qch

  2 *vi (of person)* s'enfuir, se sauver (**with** avec)

▸**run on** *vi* (**a**) *(of meeting)* durer (**b**) *Fam (talk a lot)* parler sans arrêt

▸**run out** *vi (of lease, contract)* expirer; *(of money, supplies)* s'épuiser; **to have run out of sth** ne plus avoir de qch; **time is running out** il ne reste plus beaucoup de temps; *Fig* **to r. out of steam** *(of person, project)* s'essouffler

▸**run over 1** *vt sep (in car)* renverser, écraser

  2 *vt insep (speech, lines)* revoir

  3 *vi (of speech, TV program)* déborder

▸**run up** *vt sep* (**a**) *(debts)* accumuler (**b**) *(flag)* hisser (**c**) *(clothes)* confectionner à la hâte

run-around ['rʌnəraʊnd] *n Fam* **to give sb the r.** faire tourner qn en bourrique

runaway ['rʌnəweɪ] **1** *n* fugitif(ive) *m,f*; *(child)* fugueur(euse) *m,f*

  2 *adj (prisoner, slave)* en fuite; *(train, truck)* fou (folle); *(inflation)* galopant(e); *(victory)* remporté(e) haut la main; *(success)* fou (folle)

rundown ['rʌndaʊn] *n (summary)* résumé *m*; **to give sb a r. (on sth)** mettre qn au courant (de qch)

run-down [rʌn'daʊn] *adj (building)* délabré(e); *(person)* fatigué(e)

rung[1] [rʌŋ] *n (of ladder)* échelon *m*; *Fig* **on the bottom/top r.** tout en bas/en haut de l'échelle

rung[2] [rʌŋ] *pp of* **ring**[2]

run-in ['rʌnɪn] *n Fam* **to have a r. with sb** avoir un accrochage avec qn

runner ['rʌnə(r)] *n* (**a**) *(athlete)* coureur(euse) *m,f*; *(messenger)* coursier(ère) *m,f*; *(for film crew)* grouillot *m*; *(for drugs, guns)* passeur(euse) *m,f* (**b**) *(on sleigh)* patin *m*; *(on drawer)* glissière *f*

runner-up [rʌnə'rʌp] *(pl* **runners-up)** *n* suivant(e) *m,f*; *(in second place)* second(e) *m,f*

running ['rʌnɪŋ] **1** *n* (**a**) *(activity)* course *f*; **to go r.** courir; *Fig* **to be out of the r.** *(in competition, race)* n'avoir aucune chance; **to be in the r. for sth** être sur les rangs *ou* dans la course pour qch; *Pol* **r. mate** = candidat à la vice-présidence accompagnant dans sa campagne le candidat à la présidence des États-Unis; **r. shoe** chaussure *f* de course; **r. track** piste *f*

(**b**) *(of machine, car)* **r. costs** frais *mpl* d'entretien

(**c**) *(management)* gestion *f*

  2 *adj (battle, feud)* incessant(e); *Fam* **go take a r. jump!** va voir ailleurs si j'y suis!; **r. board** *(on car)* marchepied *m*; **r. commentary** commentaire *m* en direct; **r. repairs** petites réparations *fpl*; **r. sore** plaie *f* qui suppure; **to keep a r. total (of sth)** comptabiliser (qch) au fur et à mesure; **r. water** eau *f* courante

runny ['rʌnɪ] *adj (liquid)* liquide; **to have a r. nose** avoir le nez qui coule

run-off ['rʌnɒf] *n* (**a**) *(election)* deuxième tour *m*; *(contest)* manche *f* pour départager deux candidats (**b**) *(from fields)* eaux *fpl* de ruissellement

run-of-the-mill [rʌnəvðə'mɪl] *adj* ordinaire

runt [rʌnt] *n* (**a**) *(of litter)* **the r.** le (la) plus faible de la portée (**b**) *(weak person)* avorton *m*

run-up ['rʌnʌp] *n (before jump)* course d'élan; **the r. to the wedding/the election** la période précédant le mariage/les élections

runway ['rʌnweɪ] *n* (**a**) *(for planes)* piste *f* (**b**) *(for fashion show)* passerelle *f*

rupee [ruː'piː] *n* roupie *f*

rupture ['rʌptʃə(r)] **1** *n* rupture *f*

  2 *vt (relations)* rompre; *(container)* faire éclater

  3 *vi also Med* éclater

rural ['rʊərəl] *adj* rural(e)

ruse [ruːz] *n* ruse *f*

rush[1] [rʌʃ] *n (plant)* jonc *m*; **r. matting** natte *f* (de jonc)

rush[2] [rʌʃ] **1** *n* (**a**) *(hurry)* **what's the r.?** pourquoi tant de hâte?; **to be in a r.** être pressé(e); **to do sth in a r.** faire qch à toute vitesse; **there's no r.** il n'y a rien qui presse; **to make a r. for sth** se précipiter vers qch; **r. hour** heures *fpl* de pointe; **a r. job** *(urgent)* un travail urgent; *(hurried)* un travail bâclé

(**b**) *(surge) (of air)* bouffée *f*; *(of water)* flot *m* soudain; *(of requests)* flot

(**c**) *(demand)* ruée *f*; **there's been a r. on tickets** les gens se sont rués sur les billets

(**d**) *Cin* **rushes** rush(e)s *mpl*

  2 *vt* (**a**) *(hurry) (task)* faire à la hâte; *(person)* bousculer; **to r. sb into doing sth** bousculer qn pour qu'elle fasse qch; **to be rushed off one's feet** être débordé(e)

(**b**) *(transport quickly)* transporter d'urgence

(**c**) *(attack)* prendre d'assaut

  3 *vi (move quickly)* se ruer (**at/towards** sur/vers); *(act quickly)* se dépêcher; **the blood rushed to her cheeks** le sang afflua à ses joues; **to r. to do sth** s'empresser de faire qch

▸**rush about, rush around** *vi* courir à droite et à gauche

▸**rush in** *vi (enter)* entrer précipitamment

▸**rush into 1** *vt insep (room)* entrer précipitamment dans; *Fig* **to r. into doing sth** faire qch sans réfléchir; **to r. into marriage** se marier sans réfléchir

  2 *vt sep* **to r. sb into doing sth** bousculer qn pour qu'elle fasse qch

▸**rush off** *vi* partir précipitamment

▸**rush out 1** *vt sep (book)* publier à la hâte

  2 *vi (exit)* sortir précipitamment

▸**rush through 1** *vt sep (bill)* faire passer à la hâte; *(decision)* prendre à la hâte

  2 *vt insep (book)* lire à toute vitesse; *(meal, work)* expédier

rusk [rʌsk] *n* gros biscuit *m (pour bébés)*

russet ['rʌsɪt] **1** *n (color)* brun *m* roux

  2 *adj* brun roux *inv*

Russia ['rʌʃə] *n* la Russie

Russian ['rʌʃən] **1** *n* (**a**) *(person)* Russe *mf* (**b**) *(language)* russe *m*

  2 *adj* russe; **the R. Federation** la Fédération de Russie; **R. roulette** roulette *f* russe

rust [rʌst] **1** *n* rouille *f*
  2 *adj (color)* rouille *inv*
  3 *vi* rouiller
rustic ['rʌstɪk] *adj* rustique
rustle[1] ['rʌsəl] **1** *n (of leaves, paper)* bruissement *m*
  2 *vt (leaves, paper)* faire bruire
  3 *vi (of leaves, paper)* bruire
rustle[2] ['rʌsəl] *vt (cattle)* voler
▸**rustle up** *vt sep Fam (meal, snack)* improviser; **to r. up support** rassembler des partisans
rustler ['rʌslə(r)] *n (cattle thief)* voleur(euse) *m,f* de bétail
rustproof ['rʌstpruːf] *adj (paint)* antirouille *inv*; *(metal)* inoxydable

rusty ['rʌstɪ] *adj also Fig* rouillé(e); *(color)* rouille *inv*
rut[1] [rʌt] *n (groove)* ornière *f*; *Fig* **to be in a r.** être prisonnier(ère) de la routine
rut[2] [rʌt] **1** *n (of stag)* rut *m*
  2 *vi (pt & pp* **rutted**) *(of stag)* être en rut
rutabaga ['ruːtəbeɪgə] *n* rutabaga *m*
ruthless ['ruːθlɪs] *adj* impitoyable
RV [ɑːˈviː] *n (abbr* **recreational vehicle**) mobile home *m*
Rwanda [rəˈwændə] *n* le Rwanda
Rwandan [rəˈwændən] **1** *n* Rwandais(e) *m,f*
  2 *adj* rwandais(e)
rye [raɪ] *n* seigle *m*; **r. bread** pain *m* de seigle

S

S, s [es] *n* (**a**) *(letter)* S, s *m inv* (**b**) *(abbr* **south**) S

Sabbath ['sæbəθ] *n (Jewish)* (jour *m* du) sabbat *m*; *(Christian)* jour du seigneur

sabbatical [sə'bætɪkəl] *Univ* **1** *n* congé *m* sabbatique; **to be on s.** être en congé sabbatique
    2 *adj (term, year)* sabbatique

sable ['seɪbəl] **1** *n (animal)* zibeline *f*; **s. coat** manteau *m* de *ou* en zibeline
    2 *adj Lit (black)* noir(e)

sabotage ['sæbətɑːʒ] **1** *n* sabotage *m*
    2 *vt* saboter

saboteur [sæbə'tɜː(r)] *n* saboteur(euse) *m,f*

saber ['seɪbə(r)] *n* sabre *m*

sac [sæk] *n Biol* sac *m*

saccharin ['sækərɪn] *n* saccharine *f*

saccharine ['sækərɪn] *adj Pej (smile, words)* mielleux(euse); *(movie)* à l'eau de rose

sachet ['sæʃeɪ] *n* sachet *m*

sack¹ [sæk] **1** *n* (**a**) *(bag)* sac *m*; *Fam* **to hit the s.** se pieuter (**b**) *Fam (dismissal)* renvoi *m*; **to give sb the s.** virer qn; **to get the s.** se faire virer
    2 *vt Fam (dismiss)* virer

sack² **1** *n (plundering)* sac *m*
    2 *vt (plunder)* mettre à sac

sacking ['sækɪŋ] *n* (**a**) *(textile)* grosse toile *f* (**b**) *Fam (dismissal)* renvoi *m*

sacrament ['sækrəmənt] *n Rel* sacrement *m*; **to take** *or* **to receive the sacraments** communier

sacred ['seɪkrɪd] *adj* sacré(e); *Fig* **s. cow** *(belief, institution)* véritable institution *f*

sacrifice ['sækrɪfaɪs] **1** *n* sacrifice *m*; **to make sacrifices** faire des sacrifices
    2 *vt* sacrifier (**to** à); **to s. oneself** se sacrifier

sacrificial [sækrɪ'fɪʃl] *adj* sacrificiel(elle); *Fig* **s. lamb** *or* **victim** bouc *m* émissaire

sacrilege ['sækrɪlɪdʒ] *n also Fig* sacrilège *m*

sacrilegious [sækrɪ'lɪdʒəs] *adj also Fig* sacrilège

sacristan ['sækrɪstən] *n Rel* sacristain *m*

sacrosanct ['sækrəʊsæŋkt] *adj* sacro-saint(e)

SAD [sæd] *n Med (abbr* **Seasonal Affective Disorder**) dépression *f* saisonnière

sad [sæd] *adj* (**a**) *(unhappy, depressing)* triste; **to make sb s.** attrister qn (**b**) *Fam (pathetic)* pitoyable; **s. sack** raté(e) *m,f*

sadden ['sædən] *vt* attrister

saddle ['sædəl] **1** *n (on horse, bicycle)* selle *f*; **to be in the s.** être en selle; *Fig* être aux commandes
    2 *vt (horse)* seller; *Fam Fig* **to s. sb with sb/sth** refiler qn/qch à qn; **to get saddled with sb/sth** se retrouver avec qn/qch sur les bras

saddlebag ['sædəlbæg] *n* sacoche *f*

sadism ['seɪdɪzəm] *n* sadisme *m*

sadist ['seɪdɪst] *n* sadique *mf*

sadistic [sə'dɪstɪk] *adj* sadique

sadly ['sædlɪ] *adv* (**a**) *(unhappily)* tristement (**b**) *(unfortunately)* malheureusement (**c**) *(greatly)* **to be s. mistaken** se tromper lourdement; **he is s. missed** il nous/leur/*etc.* manque beaucoup

sadness ['sædnɪs] *n* tristesse *f*

sadomasochism [seɪdəʊ'mæsəkɪzəm] *n* sadomasochisme *m*

sadomasochist [seɪdəʊ'mæsəkɪst] *n* sadomasochiste *mf*

SAE [eseɪ'iː] *n (abbr* **stamped addressed envelope**) enveloppe *f* timbrée

safari [sə'fɑːrɪ] *n* safari *m*; **to go on (a) s.** faire un safari; **s. jacket** saharienne *f*; **s. park** réserve *f* d'animaux sauvages

safe [seɪf] **1** *adj* (**a**) *(not in danger)* en sécurité; *(house, activity)* sûr(e); *(topic of conversation)* sans danger; **s. from sth** à l'abri de qch; **s. and sound** sain et sauf (saine et sauve); *Prov* **better s. than sorry** deux précautions valent mieux qu'une (**b**) *(not dangerous)* **it is s. to say that...** on peut dire sans risque de se tromper que...; **it's a s. bet that...** il y a fort à parier que...; **at a s. distance** à distance respectueuse; **in s. hands** entre de bonnes mains; **to wish sb a s. journey** souhaiter bon voyage à qn; **...to be on the s. side** ...pour plus de sûreté; **s. house** *(for spies)* cachette *f* sûre; **s. sex** rapports *mpl* sexuels protégés
    2 *n (for money)* coffre-fort *m*
    3 *adv* **to play (it) s.** ne pas prendre de risques

safe-conduct [seɪf'kɒndʌkt] *n* sauf-conduit *m*

safeguard ['seɪfgɑːd] **1** *n* garantie *f*
    2 *vt* sauvegarder
    3 *vi* **to s. against sth** se protéger contre qch

safe-keeping [seɪf'kiːpɪŋ] *n* **in s.** en lieu sûr; **to give sth to sb for s.** confier qch à la garde de qn

safely ['seɪflɪ] *adv* (**a**) *(without risk)* en toute sécurité; *(drive)* prudemment; **to arrive s.** *(of person)* bien arriver; *(of goods)* arriver sans dommage (**b**) *(with certainty)* avec certitude

safety ['seɪftɪ] *n* sûreté *f*; **for s.'s sake** pour plus de sûreté; **to be s. conscious** se préoccuper beaucoup de la sécurité; *Prov* **(there's) s. in numbers** plus on est nombreux, moins on court de risques; **s. belt** ceinture *f* de sécurité; **s. catch** cran *m* de sûreté; **s. glass** verre *m* de sécurité; **s. matches** allumettes *fpl* de sûreté; **s. measures** mesures *fpl* de sécurité; **s. net** filet *m*; *Fig* mesure *f* de sécurité; **s. pin** épingle *f* de sûreté; *also Fig* **s. valve** soupape *f* de sûreté

saffron ['sæfrən] **1** *n* safran *m*
    2 *adj* safran *inv*

sag [sæg] *(pt & pp* **sagged**) *vi (of roof, bridge)* s'affaisser; *(of flesh)* être flasque; *(of rope)* pendre; *(of breasts)* être tombant(e); *(of prices, support)* baisser

saga ['sɑːgə] *n also Fig (story)* saga *f*

sagacious [sə'geɪʃəs] *adj Formal* sagace

sagacity [sə'gæsɪtɪ] *n Formal* sagacité *f*

sage¹ [seɪdʒ] **1** *n (wise man)* sage *m*
    2 *adj (person, conduct)* sage

sage² [seɪdʒ] *n (herb)* sauge *f*

Sagittarius [sædʒɪ'teərɪəs] n (sign of zodiac) le Sagittaire; **to be (a) S.** être (du) Sagittaire

Sahara [sə'hɑːrə] n the S. (Desert) le Sahara

said [sed] pt & pp of **say**

sail [seɪl] **1** n (on boat) voile f; (of windmill) aile f; **to set s.** prendre la mer; **to go for a s.** faire un tour en voilier

2 vi (of ship, person) naviguer; (start voyage) prendre la mer; Fig **the clouds sailed by** les nuages passaient dans le ciel; Fig **his book sailed out of the window** son livre vola par la fenêtre; Fig **to s. close to the wind** jouer avec le feu; Fam **to s. through an examination** réussir un examen les doigts dans le nez

sailboat ['seɪlbəʊt] n voilier m

sailing ['seɪlɪŋ] n (activity) voile f; (departure) appareillage m; **to go s.** faire de la voile; **s. ship** grand voilier m

sailor ['seɪlə(r)] n marin m; **to be a good/bad s.** avoir/ne pas avoir le pied marin; **s. suit** costume m marin (d'enfant)

saint [seɪnt] n saint(e) m,f; **All Saints' (Day)** la Toussaint; **S. Bernard** (dog) saint-bernard m inv; **S. Patrick's Day** la Saint Patrick

saintly ['seɪntlɪ] adj (life, behavior) de saint; (smile) d'ange

sake [seɪk] n **for the s. of sb, for sb's s.** (for the good of) pour le bien de qn; (out of respect for) par égard de qn; **for God's or heaven's s.!** mais bon sang!; **for the s. of peace** pour avoir la paix; **for old times' s.** en souvenir du passé; **this is just talking for talking's s.** c'est parler pour parler; **let's say, for the s. of argument...** admettons que...

salacious [sə'leɪʃəs] adj salace

salad ['sæləd] n salade f; **s. bar** (restaurant) = restaurant où l'on mange des salades; (area) salad bar m; **s. bowl** saladier m; Fig **s. days** années fpl de jeunesse; **s. dressing** = vinaigrette ou sauce pour salade; **s. spinner** essoreuse f à salade

salamander ['sæləmændə(r)] n salamandre f

salami [sə'lɑːmɪ] n salami m

salaried ['sælərɪd] adj salarié(e)

salary ['sælərɪ] (pl **salaries**) n salaire m; **s. earner** salarié(e) m,f; **s. grade** échelon m de salaire; **s. scale** échelle f des salaires

sale [seɪl] n (a) (action, event) vente f; **for s.** à vendre; **to put sth up for s.** mettre qch en vente; **on s.** (at a reduced price) en solde; **sales assistant** vendeur(euse) m,f; **sales department** service m commercial; **sales drive** campagne f de vente; **sales force** force f de vente; **sales forecast** prévision f des ventes; **sales manager** directeur(trice) m,f commercial(e); **sales pitch** arguments mpl de vente; **s. price** prix m de vente; **sales slip** ticket m de caisse; **sales target** objectif m de vente; **sales tax** TVA f; **s. of work** vente f de charité (b) (at reduced prices) soldes mpl; **the sales** les soldes

salable ['seɪləbəl] adj vendable

salesclerk ['seɪlzklɜːk] n vendeur(euse) m,f

salesgirl ['seɪlzgɜːl] n vendeuse f

salesman ['seɪlzmən] n (for company) représentant m; (in store) vendeur m

salesmanship ['seɪlzmənʃɪp] n technique f de vente

salesperson ['seɪlzpɜːsən] (pl **salespeople**) n (for company) représentant(e) m,f; (in store) vendeur(euse) m,f

salesroom ['seɪlzruːm] n salle f des ventes

saleswoman ['seɪlzwʊmən] n (for company) représentante f; (in store) vendeuse f

salient ['seɪlɪənt] adj Formal (feature) marquant(e); (point) essentiel(elle)

saline ['seɪlaɪn] adj salin(e); **s. drip** perfusion f de solution saline; **s. solution** solution f saline

saliva [sə'laɪvə] n salive f

salivate ['sælɪveɪt] vi also Fig saliver

sallow ['sæləʊ] adj jaunâtre

▸**sally forth** ['sælɪ] (pt & pp **sallied**) vi Lit partir

salmon ['sæmən] (pl **salmon**) n saumon m; **s. (pink)** (rose m) saumon; **s. trout** truite f saumonée

salmonella [sælmə'nelə] n salmonelle f

salon ['sælɒn] n (beauty) s. institut m de beauté; (hairdressing) s. salon m de coiffure

saloon [sə'luːn] n (room) salle f; (bar) bar m

SALT [sɔːlt] n (abbr **Strategic Arms Limitation Talks**) SALT m

salt [sɔːlt] **1** n (a) (substance) sel m; **s. flat** marais m salant; **s. mine** mine f de sel (b) (idioms) **to be worth one's s.** être à la hauteur; **to rub s. in sb's wounds** remuer le couteau dans la plaie; Fig **that woman is the s. of the earth!** cette femme est la bonté incarnée! (c) Fam **an old s.** (sailor) un vieux loup de mer

2 adj **s. beef** bœuf m salé; **s. cod** morue f salée; **s. water** eau f salée

3 vt (food) saler; (roads) sabler

▸**salt away** vt sep (money) mettre de côté

salt-free ['sɔːltfriː] adj sans sel

saltpeter [sɒlt'piːtə(r)] n salpêtre m

saltshaker ['sɔːltʃeɪkə(r)] n salière f

saltwater ['sɔːltwɔːtə(r)] adj (lake) salé(e); (fish) de mer

salty ['sɔːltɪ] adj salé(e)

salubrious [sə'luːbrɪəs] adj Formal salubre

salutary ['sæljʊtərɪ] adj salutaire

salute [sə'luːt] **1** n salut m; **to take the s.** passer les troupes en revue

2 vt also Fig saluer

3 vi faire un salut

salvage ['sælvɪdʒ] **1** n (of ship) sauvetage m; (of waste material) récupération f; **s. vessel** bateau m de sauvetage

2 vt also Fig sauver

salvation [sæl'veɪʃən] n salut m; **S. Army** Armée f du Salut

salve [sælv] vt **to s. one's conscience** se donner bonne conscience

salver ['sælvə(r)] n (tray) plateau m (de présentation)

salvo ['sælvəʊ] (pl **salvos** or **salvoes**) n also Fig salve f; (of questions) flot m; (of insults) torrent m

Samaritan [sə'mærɪtən] n also Fig **the Good S.** le bon Samaritain; **the Samaritans** ≃ S.O.S. Amitié

same [seɪm] **1** adj **the s. man** le même homme; **the s. woman** la même femme; **the s. children** les mêmes enfants; **in the s. way** de la même façon; Fig **to go the s. way** prendre le même chemin; **the s. day** le même jour; **the** or **that (very) s. day** (for emphasis) le jour même; **it all comes to the s. thing** cela revient au même; **at the s. time** (regularly) au même moment; (simultaneously) en même temps, à la fois

2 pron **the s.** le même, la même; (plural) les mêmes; **I would have done the s.** j'aurais fait la même chose ou pareil; **all the s. to you** si cela vous est égal; Fam **(the) s. again?** (in bar) la même chose?; Fam **s. here!** (so do I) moi aussi!; (neither do I) moi non plus!; (I did the same thing) pareil!; **the house isn't the s. without her** la maison n'est plus la même sans elle

3 adv **to think/feel the s.** penser/ressentir la même chose; **to look the s.** (of two things) sembler pareils; **to taste the s.** avoir le même goût; **all the s.** (nevertheless) tout de même

sameness ['seɪmnɪs] n monotonie f

Samoa [sə'məʊə] n Samoa m

Samoan [sə'məʊən] **1** n (a) (person) Samoan(e) m,f (b) (language) samoan m

2 adj samoan(e)

samosa [səm'əʊsə] n samosa m

sample ['sɑːmpəl] **1** n échantillon m; (of blood, urine) prélèvement m; **to take a blood s.** faire une prise de sang; Comput **s. prices** prix mpl données à titre d'exemple

2 vt (a) (food, experience) goûter (b) (public opinion) sonder (c) (piece of music) sampler

sanatorium [sænə'tɔːrɪəm] (*pl* **sanatoria** [sænə'tɔːrɪə]) *n* sanatorium *m*

sanctify ['sæŋ(k)tɪfaɪ] (*pt & pp* **sanctified**) *vt* sanctifier; *Fig* consacrer

sanctimonious [sæŋ(k)tɪ'məʊnɪəs] *adj* moralisateur(trice)

sanction ['sæŋ(k)ʃən] **1** *n* (**a**) (*penalty*) sanction *f*; **to impose sanctions on a country** imposer des sanctions à un pays (**b**) *Formal (consent)* consentement *m*, accord *m*
2 *vt Formal (consent to)* sanctionner

sanctity ['sæŋ(k)tɪtɪ] *n* sainteté *f*; *Fig (of life, marriage)* caractère *m* sacré

sanctuary ['sæŋ(k)tj(ʊ)ərɪ] (*pl* **sanctuaries**) *n Rel* sanctuaire *m*; *(for fugitive, refugee)* refuge *m*, asile *m*; *(for birds, wildlife)* réserve *f*; **to seek/to find s.** chercher/trouver refuge

sand [sænd] **1** *n* sable *m*; **s. castle** château *m* de sable; **s. dune** dune *f*
2 *vt* (**a**) *(smooth with sandpaper)* poncer (**b**) *(cover with sand)* sabler

sandal ['sændəl] *n* sandale *f*

sandbag ['sændbæg] *n* sac *m* de sable

sandbank ['sændbæŋk] *n* banc *m* de sable

sandblast ['sændblæst] *vt* décaper à la sableuse

sandbox ['sændbɒks] *n* bac *m* à sable

sandpaper ['sændpeɪpə(r)] **1** *n* papier *m* de verre
2 *vt* poncer, passer au papier de verre

sandstone ['sændstəʊn] *n* grès *m*

sandstorm ['sændstɔːm] *n* tempête *f* de sable

sandwich ['sændwɪtʃ] **1** *n* sandwich *m*; **ham s.** sandwich au jambon; **s. loaf** ≃ pain *m* de mie; **s. toaster** appareil *m* à croque-monsieur
2 *vt* **to be sandwiched between** *(of layer)* être intercalé(e) entre; *(of person, building)* être coincé(e) entre

sandy ['sændɪ] *adj* (**a**) *(earth)* sablonneux(euse); *(beach)* de sable (**b**) *(hair)* blond roux *inv*

sane [seɪn] *adj (person)* sain(e) d'esprit; *(action, remark)* sensé(e)

San Franciscan ['sænfrən'sɪskən] **1** *n* habitant(e) *m,f* de San Francisco
2 *adj* de San Francisco

San Francisco ['sænfrən'sɪskəʊ] *n* San Francisco

sang [sæŋ] *pt of* **sing**

sanguine ['sæŋgwɪn] *adj* optimiste

sanitarium [sænɪ'teərɪəm] (*pl* **sanitaria** [sænɪ'teərɪə]) = **sanatorium**

sanitary ['sænɪtərɪ] *adj* (**a**) *(clean)* hygiénique (**b**) *(relating to hygiene)* sanitaire; **s. napkin** serviette *f* hygiénique

sanitation [sænɪ'teɪʃən] *n* installations *fpl* sanitaires; **s. worker** éboueur *m*

sanitize ['sænɪtaɪz] *vt* expurger

sanity ['sænɪtɪ] *n* santé *f* mentale

sank [sæŋk] *pt of* **sink²**

San Marino [sænmə'riːnəʊ] *n* Saint-Marin

Santa (Claus) ['sæntə('klɔːz)] *n* le père Noël

sap¹ [sæp] *n (of plant)* sève *f*

sap² [sæp] *n Fam (gullible person)* andouille *f*

sap³ [sæp] (*pt & pp* **sapped**) *vt (weaken)* saper

sapling ['sæplɪŋ] *n* jeune arbre *m*

sapphire ['sæfaɪə(r)] *n* saphir *m*

Sarajevo [særə'jeɪvəʊ] *n* Sarajevo

Saran wrap® [sə'rænræp] *n* film *m* alimentaire transparent

sarcasm ['sɑːkæzəm] *n* sarcasme *m*

sarcastic [sɑː'kæstɪk] *adj* sarcastique

sarcastically [sɑː'kæstɪklɪ] *adv* de manière sarcastique; *(speak)* d'un ton sarcastique

sarcophagus [sɑː'kɒfəgəs] (*pl* **sarcophagi** [sɑː'kɒfəgaɪ]) *n* sarcophage *m*

sardine [sɑː'diːn] *n* sardine *f*; *Fam Fig* **we were packed in like sardines** nous étions serrés comme des sardines

Sardinia [sɑː'dɪnɪə] *n* la Sardaigne

Sardinian [sɑː'dɪnɪən] **1** *n* Sarde *mf*
2 *adj* sarde

sardonic [sɑː'dɒnɪk] *adj* sardonique

sari ['sɑːrɪ] *n* sari *m*

sarong [sə'rɒŋ] *n* paréo *m*

SARS [sɑːz] *n Med (abbr* **severe acute respiratory syndrome***)* SRAS *m*

sartorial [sɑː'tɔːrɪəl] *adj Formal* vestimentaire

SASE [eseɪes'iː, 'seɪziː] *n (abbr* **self-addressed stamped envelope***)* enveloppe *f* timbrée *(portant l'adresse à laquelle elle doit être renvoyée)*

sash [sæʃ] *n (around waist)* large ceinture *f* de tissu; *(around shoulder)* écharpe *f*; **s. cord** corde *f (actionnant une fenêtre à guillotine)*; **s. window** fenêtre *f* à guillotine

sass [sæs] **1** *n (cheek)* culot *m*
2 *vt* répondre avec impertinence à; **don't you s. me!** ne me réponds pas sur ce ton!

sassy ['sæsɪ] *adj* (**a**) *(stylish)* chic (**b**) *(cheeky)* culotté(e) (**c**) *(lively)* plein(e) de pêche

Sat. (*abbr* **Saturday***)* samedi

sat [sæt] *pt & pp of* **sit**

Satan ['seɪtən] *n* Satan

satanic [sə'tænɪk] *adj* satanique, diabolique

satanism ['seɪtənɪzəm] *n* satanisme *m*

satanist ['seɪtənɪst] **1** *n* sataniste *mf*
2 *adj* sataniste

satchel ['sætʃəl] *n* cartable *m*

sate [seɪt] *vt Formal* assouvir

satellite ['sætəlaɪt] *n* satellite *m*; **s. dish** antenne *f* parabolique; **s. (state)** (État *m*) satellite; **s. television** télévision *f* par satellite; **s. town** ville *f* satellite

satiate ['seɪʃɪeɪt] *vt Formal* assouvir

satin ['sætɪn] *n* satin *m*

satire ['sætaɪə(r)] *n* satire *f*

satirical [sə'tɪrɪkəl] *adj* satirique

satirist ['sætɪrɪst] *n* écrivain *m* satirique

satirize ['sætɪraɪz] *vt* satiriser, faire la satire de

satisfaction [sætɪs'fækʃən] *n* satisfaction *f*; **to have the s. of doing sth** avoir la satisfaction de faire qch

satisfactory [sætɪs'fæktərɪ] *adj* satisfaisant(e)

satisfied ['sætɪsfaɪd] *adj* satisfait(e)

satisfy ['sætɪsfaɪ] (*pt & pp* **satisfied**) *vt* (**a**) *(meet needs of)* (*person, curiosity*) satisfaire; *(condition)* remplir (**b**) *(convince)* convaincre, persuader

saturate ['sætʃəreɪt] *vt* saturer; **to s. the market** saturer le marché; **saturated fats** graisses *fpl* saturées

saturation [sætʃə'reɪʃən] *n* saturation *f*; **to reach s. point** arriver à saturation; *Mil* **s. bombing** bombardement *m* intensif

Saturday ['sætədɪ] *n* samedi *m*; **this S.** samedi prochain *ou* qui vient; **on S.** samedi; **on S. morning/afternoon/evening** samedi matin/après-midi/soir; **on Saturdays** le samedi; **every S.** tous les samedis; **every other S.** un samedi sur deux; **last S.** samedi dernier; **the S. before last** pas samedi dernier mais celui d'avant; **next S.** samedi prochain; **the S. after next** le samedi d'après, samedi en huit; **the following S.** le samedi suivant; **S.'s paper** le journal de samedi; **S. job** petit boulot *m (du samedi)*

Saturn ['sætɜːn] *n (planet)* Saturne *f*

sauce [sɔːs] *n* (**a**) *(for food)* sauce *f*; **tomato/cheese s.** sauce tomate/au fromage; **s. boat** saucière *f* (**b**) *Fam (impudence)* culot *m* (**c**) *Fam (alcohol)* alcool *m*, bibine *f*

sauced [sɔːst] *adj Fam (drunk)* bourré(e), pété(e)

saucepan [ˈsɔːspən] *n* casserole *f*

saucer [ˈsɔːsə(r)] *n* soucoupe *f*, *Belg & Suisse* sous-tasse *f*

saucy [ˈsɔːsɪ] *adj Fam (impertinent)* insolent(e); *(risqué)* coquin(e)

Saudi [ˈsaʊdɪ] **1** *n (person)* Saoudien(enne) *m,f*; *Fam (country)* l'Arabie *f* Saoudite
  2 *adj* saoudien(enne)

Saudi Arabia [ˈsaʊdɪəˈreɪbɪə] *n* l'Arabie *f* Saoudite

Saudi Arabian [ˈsaʊdɪəˈreɪbɪən] **1** *n* Saoudien(enne) *m,f*
  2 *adj* saoudien(enne)

sauna [ˈsɔːnə] *n* sauna *m*; **to have a s.** aller au sauna

saunter [ˈsɔːntə(r)] **1** *n* balade *f*; **to go for a s.** partir en balade
  2 *vi* **to s. (along)** flâner

sausage [ˈsɒsɪdʒ] *n* saucisse *f*; **s. meat** chair *f* à saucisse

sauté [ˈsəʊteɪ] **1** *adj* sauté(e)
  2 *vt (pt & pp* **sautéed)** faire sauter

savage [ˈsævɪdʒ] **1** *n Old-fashioned* sauvage *mf*
  2 *adj (animal, person)* féroce, brutal(e); *(attack, criticism)* violent(e)
  3 *vt (attack physically)* attaquer; *Fig (criticize)* descendre en flammes

savagely [ˈsævɪdʒlɪ] *adv (beat, attack)* sauvagement; *Fig (criticize)* violemment, avec virulence

savanna(h) [səˈvænə] *n* savane *f*

save¹ [seɪv] *prep Formal (except)* hormis

save² [seɪv] **1** *vt* (**a**) *(rescue)* sauver; **to s. sb's life** sauver la vie à qn; *Fam* **she can't sing to s. her life** elle chante comme un pied; *Fam* **to s. one's (own) neck** *or* **skin** sauver sa peau; **to s. sb from falling** empêcher qn de tomber; **to s. a goal** arrêter un but; **God s. the King/the Queen!** vive le Roi/la Reine!
  (**b**) *(keep for future)* garder, conserver; *(money)* mettre de côté; *Comput* sauvegarder; **to s. oneself for sth** se réserver pour qch
  (**c**) *(not waste) (money, space)* économiser; *(time)* gagner; **s. your breath** ne te fatigue pas
  (**d**) *(spare)* **to s. sb sth** éviter qch à qn; **to s. sb (from) doing sth** éviter à qn de faire qch
  2 *vi* faire des économies (**for/on** pour/sur)
  3 *n (of goalkeeper)* arrêt *m*; **to make a s.** arrêter un but
▶**save up** *vi* mettre de l'argent de côté (**for** pour)

saver [ˈseɪvə(r)] *n* épargnant(e) *m,f*

saving [ˈseɪvɪŋ] **1** *n* (**a**) *(economy)* économie *f* (**b**) **savings** *(money saved)* économies *fpl*; **to live off one's savings** vivre sur ses économies; **savings account** compte *m* d'épargne; **savings bank** caisse *f* d'épargne; **savings and loan association** caisse *f* d'épargne logement
  2 *adj* **her/its s. grace** ce qui la/le sauve

savior [ˈseɪvjə(r)] *n* sauveur *m*; **the S.** le Sauveur

savor [ˈseɪvə(r)] **1** *n* saveur *f*
  2 *vt also Fig* savourer
  3 *vi Formal* **to s. of** sentir

savory [ˈseɪvərɪ] *adj* (**a**) *(food)* salé(e) (**b**) *(conduct)* honorable

saw¹ [sɔː] *pt of* **see²**

saw² [sɔː] **1** *n (tool)* scie *f*
  2 *vt (pp* **sawn** [sɔːn] *or* **sawed)** scier
▶**saw off** *vt sep* scier
▶**saw up** *vt sep* découper à la scie

sawdust [ˈsɔːdʌst] *n* sciure *f*

sawed-off shotgun [ˈsɔːdɒfˈʃɒtɡʌn] *n* fusil *m* à canon scié

sawmill [ˈsɔːmɪl] *n* scierie *f*

sawn [sɔːn] *pp of* **saw²**

sax [sæks] *n Fam (saxophone)* sax *m*

Saxon [ˈsæks(ə)n] **1** *n* (**a**) *(person)* Saxon(onne) *m,f* (**b**) *(language)* saxon *m*
  2 *adj* saxon(onne)

Saxony [ˈsæksənɪ] *n* Saxe *f*

saxophone [ˈsæksəfəʊn] *n* saxophone *m*

saxophonist [sækˈsɒfənɪst] *n* saxophoniste *mf*

say [seɪ] **1** *vt (pt & pp* **said** [sed]) dire; *(of clock, watch)* indiquer; **to s. sth to sb** dire qch à qn; **it says that...** *(of text, sign)* il y a écrit que...; **I wouldn't s. no to a cup of tea** je prendrais volontiers une tasse de thé; **I didn't s. a word** je n'ai pas dit un mot; **it's not for me to s.** ce n'est pas à moi de le dire; **there's no saying what might happen if...** inutile de vous dire ce qui se passerait si...; **what have you got to s. for yourself?** as-tu une excuse valable?; **there's a lot to be said for living in the country** il y a bien des avantages à vivre à la campagne; **you're honest, I'll s. that for you** tu es honnête, je te l'accorde; **it says a lot about her** ça en dit long sur sa personne; **don't s. you've forgotten already!** ne me dis pas que tu as déjà oublié!; **you can s. that again!, you said it!** c'est le cas de le dire!, tu l'as dit!; **need I s. more?** ai-je besoin d'en dire plus?; **they s. that..., it is said that...** on dit que...; **s. we won first prize** supposons que nous gagnions le premier prix; **if I had, s., $10,000** si j'avais, mettons, 10 000 dollars
  2 *vi* **I'm not saying** je ne dirai rien; **as they s.** comme on dit; **I'll s.!** absolument!, tout à fait!; *Fam* **you don't s.!** sans blagues!
  3 *n* **to have one's s.** avoir son mot à dire; **to have a s./no s. in sth** avoir/ne pas avoir voix au chapitre concernant qch

saying [ˈseɪɪŋ] *n* maxime *f*; **as the s. goes** comme dit la maxime

say-so [ˈseɪsəʊ] *n Fam (permission)* permission *f*

scab [skæb] *n* (**a**) *(on skin)* croûte *f* (**b**) *Fam (strikebreaker)* jaune *mf*

scabbard [ˈskæbəd] *n* fourreau *m*, gaine *f*

scabies [ˈskeɪbiːz] *n* gale *f*

scaffold [ˈskæfəld] *n (outside building)* échafaudage *m*; *(for execution)* échafaud *m*

scaffolding [ˈskæfəldɪŋ] *n* échafaudage *m*

scalawag [ˈskæləwæɡ] *n Fam* coquin(e) *m,f*

scald [skɔːld] **1** *n* brûlure *f*
  2 *vt* ébouillanter; **to s. one's hand** s'ébouillanter la main

scalding [ˈskɔːldɪŋ] *adj* brûlant(e)

scale¹ [skeɪl] **1** *n (on fish, reptile)* écaille *f*; *(in pipes, kettle)* dépôt *m* calcaire
  2 *vt (fish)* écailler

scale² [skeɪl] *n* (**a**) *(of instrument)* gamme *f*; *(of salaries)* barème *m*; **on a s. of one to ten** sur une échelle allant de un à dix (**b**) *(of map, drawing)* échelle *f*; *Fig (of problem, changes)* étendue *f*; **to s. à la bonne échelle; s. drawing** dessin *m* à l'échelle; **s. model** modèle *m* réduit (**c**) *(of ruler, thermometer)* graduation *f*

scale³ [skeɪl] *vt (climb)* escalader
▶**scale down** *vt sep (reduce)* revoir à la baisse
▶**scale up** *vt sep (increase)* augmenter

scales [skeɪlz] *npl* **(set of) s.** *(for kitchen)* balance *f*; *(for bathroom)* pèse-personne *m*

scallion [ˈskælɪən] *n (spring onion)* oignon *m* blanc; *(leek)* poireau *m*; *(shallot)* échalote *f*

scallop [ˈskæləp, ˈskɒləp] **1** *n* (**a**) *(shellfish)* coquille *f* Saint-Jacques (**b**) *(in sewing)* feston *m*
  2 *vt (in sewing)* festonner

scalp [skælp] **1** *n* cuir *m* chevelu; *(as war trophy)* scalp *m*
  2 *vt* (**a**) *(in war)* scalper (**b**) *Fam (tickets)* = acheter pour revendre au noir (**c**) *Fam (cheat)* arnaquer; **I've been scalped!** je me suis fait avoir *ou* arnaquer!

scalpel [ˈskælpəl] *n* scalpel *m*

scalper [ˈskælpə(r)] *n (ticket seller)* revendeur(euse) *m,f* de billets *(au marché noir)*

scaly [ˈskeɪlɪ] *adj (fish)* écailleux(euse); *(skin)* squameux(euse)

scam [skæm] *n Fam* arnaque *f*, magouille *f*

scamp [skæmp] *n (rascal)* coquin(e) *m,f*

scamper ['skæmpə(r)] *vi* gambader, galoper

▶**scamper away, scamper off** *vi* détaler, partir en courant

scampi ['skæmpɪ] *n* scampi *mpl*

scan [skæn] **1** *vt (pt & pp scanned)* **(a)** *(examine closely)* scruter; *Comput* balayer; *Med* faire une scanographie de; *(with ultrasound)* faire une échographie de **(b)** *(glance at)* parcourir
2 *n Med* scanographie *f*; *(with ultrasound)* échographie *f*

scandal ['skændəl] *n* **(a)** *(outrage)* scandale *m*; **to create** *or* **to cause a s.** créer *ou* provoquer un scandale **(b)** *(gossip)* ragots *mpl*

scandalize ['skændəlaɪz] *vt* scandaliser, choquer

scandalous ['skændələs] *adj* scandaleux(euse)

Scandinavia [skændɪ'neɪvɪə] *n* la Scandinavie

Scandinavian [skændɪ'neɪvɪən] **1** *n* Scandinave *mf*
2 *adj* scandinave

scanner ['skænə(r)] *n Med & Comput* scanner *m*; *(using ultrasound)* échographe *f*

scant [skænt] *adj* insuffisant(e)

scantily ['skæntɪlɪ] *adv* insuffisamment, sommairement; **s. dressed** *or* **clad** légèrement vêtu(e)

scanty ['skæntɪ] *adj (dress)* léger(ère); *(amount, information)* maigre, limité(e)

scapegoat ['skeɪpgəʊt] *n* bouc *m* émissaire

scar [skɑː(r)] **1** *n also Fig* cicatrice *f*; **s. tissue** tissu *m* cicatriciel
2 *vt (pt & pp scarred)* marquer de cicatrices; *Fig* marquer; **to be scarred for life** garder des cicatrices toute sa vie; *Fig* être marqué(e) à vie
3 *vi (of wound)* laisser une cicatrice

scarce ['skeəs] *adj* rare; *Fam* **to make oneself s.** filer

scarcely ['skeəslɪ] *adv* à peine; **she could s. speak** elle pouvait à peine parler; **s. ever/anyone** presque jamais/personne; **it is s. likely that…** il est peu probable que…

scarcity ['skeəsɪtɪ], **scarceness** ['skeəsnɪs] *n* manque *m*, pénurie *f*

scare ['skeə(r)] **1** *n* frayeur *f*; **bomb s.** alerte *f* à la bombe; **you gave me an awful s.** tu m'as fait une belle frayeur
2 *vt* effrayer; *Fam* **to s. the life** *or* **the living daylights out of sb** faire une de ces trouilles à qn
3 *vi* s'effrayer

▶**scare away, scare off** *vt sep* faire fuir

scarecrow ['skeəkrəʊ] *n* épouvantail *m*

scared [skeəd] *adj* effrayé(e); **to be s. of sb/sth** avoir peur de qn/qch; **to be s. stiff** *or* **to death** être mort(e) de peur

scaremongering ['skeəmʌŋgərɪŋ] *n* alarmisme *m*

scarf [skɑːf] *(pl* **scarves** [skɑːvz]) *n (long)* écharpe *f*; *(square)* foulard *m*

scarlet ['skɑːlɪt] **1** *n* écarlate *f*
2 *adj* écarlate; *Fig* **to go** *or* **to turn s.** *(with anger, embarrassment)* devenir rouge; **s. fever** scarlatine *f*

scarves [skɑːvz] *pl of* **scarf**

scary ['skeərɪ] *adj Fam* effrayant(e)

scat [skæt] *exclam Fam* fiche le camp!, dégage!

scathing ['skeɪðɪŋ] *adj (remark, sarcasm)* acerbe; **to be s. about sb/sth** faire des remarques acerbes sur qn/qch

scatological [skætə'lɒdʒɪkəl] *adj* scatologique

scatter ['skætə(r)] **1** *vt (clouds, demonstrators)* disperser, éparpiller; *(corn, seed)* jeter *ou* semer à la volée; *(crumbs, papers)* laisser traîner
2 *vi (of crowd)* se disperser

scatterbrain ['skætəbreɪn] *n Fam* tête *f* de linotte

scavenge ['skævɪndʒ] **1** *vt* récupérer
2 *vi* **to s. for sth** fouiller pour trouver qch; **to s. in the garbage cans** fouiller dans *ou* faire les poubelles

scavenger ['skævɪndʒə(r)] *n (animal)* charognard *m*; *Fig (person)* fouilleur(euse) *m,f* de poubelles

scenario [sɪ'nɑːrɪəʊ] *(pl* **scenarios**) *n* **(a)** *(of movie)* scénario *m* **(b)** *(situation)* hypothèse *f*

scene [siːn] *n* **(a)** *(in book, movie, play)* scène *f*; *also Fig* **a touching/terrifying s.** une scène touchante/terrifiante; *also Fig* **behind the scenes** dans les coulisses; *Theat* **s. shifter** machiniste *mf* **(b)** *(of event)* lieu *m*, endroit *m*; **a change of s.** un changement de décor *ou* d'air; **to arrive** *or* **to come on the s.** *(of police, ambulance)* arriver sur les lieux; *Fig* faire son apparition; **the s. of the crime/accident** le lieu du crime/de l'accident; **a s. of devastation** un spectacle de dévastation; **I can picture the s.** j'imagine la scène; *Fam* **it's not my s.** ce n'est pas mon truc **(c)** *(fuss)* scandale *m*; **to make a s.** faire un scandale

scenery ['siːnərɪ] *n* **(a)** *(in play)* décor(s) *m(pl)* **(b)** *(landscape)* paysage *m*; **a change of s.** un changement de décor *ou* d'air

scenic ['siːnɪk] *adj* pittoresque; **s. railroad** petit train *m* (touristique); **s. route** route *f* touristique

scent [sent] **1** *n* **(a)** *(smell)* odeur *f* **(b)** *(perfume)* parfum *m* **(c)** *(in hunting)* fumet *m*; **to pick up the s.** trouver la piste; **to be on the s. of sth** être sur la trace de qch; **to lose the s.** perdre la trace; **she threw her pursuers off the s.** elle sema ses poursuivants
2 *vt* **(a)** *(smell)* flairer; *Fig* **to s. blood** sentir que sa victime est affaiblie; *Fig* **to s. danger** flairer le danger **(b)** *(perfume)* parfumer

scepter ['septə(r)] *n* sceptre *m*

schedule ['ʃedjuːl] **1** *n* **(a)** *(plan) (for work, project)* planning *m*; *(for events)* programme *m*, calendrier *m*; *(for trains, buses)* horaire *m*; **on s.** *(train, bus)* à l'heure; *(person)* dans les temps; **to be behind/ahead of s.** être en retard/en avance sur le programme; **to go according to s.** se dérouler comme prévu; **to work to a tight s.** avoir un emploi du temps serré **(b)** *Com (list of prices)* barème *m*
2 *vt* prévoir; **we're scheduled to arrive at 9.45** notre arrivée est prévue à 9h45; **the museum is scheduled to open in August** l'ouverture du musée est prévue pour le mois d'août

scheduled ['ʃedjuːld] *adj* prévu(e); **s. flight** vol *m* régulier

schematic [skɪ'mætɪk] *adj* schématique

scheme [skiːm] **1** *n (arrangement, system)* arrangement *m*; *(plan)* plan *m*; *(plot)* machination *f*, complot *m*; **in the (great) s. of things** dans le fond
2 *vi Pej* comploter, intriguer (**against** contre)

schilling ['ʃɪlɪŋ] *n* schilling *m*

schism ['s(k)ɪzəm] *n* schisme *m*

schizoid ['skɪtsɔɪd] *n & adj* schizoïde *mf*

schizophrenia [skɪtsəʊ'friːnɪə] *n* schizophrénie *f*

schizophrenic [skɪtsəʊ'frenɪk] *n & adj* schizophrène *mf*

schmaltzy ['ʃmɔːltsɪ] *adj Fam* à l'eau de rose, cucul *inv*

schmuck ['ʃmʌk] *n Fam* andouille *f*, courge *f*

scholar ['skɒlə(r)] *n (learned person)* érudit(e) *m,f*

scholarly ['skɒləlɪ] *adj* érudit(e)

scholarship ['skɒləʃɪp] *n* **(a)** *(learning)* érudition *f*, savoir *m* **(b)** *(grant)* bourse *f* (d'études)

scholastic [skə'læstɪk] *adj Formal* scolaire

school¹ [skuːl] **1** *n* **(a)** *(for children)* école *f*; **to go to s.** aller à l'école; **s. of art, art s.** école d'art; **of s. age** d'âge scolaire; *Fig* **I went to the s. of hard knocks** j'ai été à rude école; **s. bag** cartable *m*; **s. book** manuel *m ou* livre *m* scolaire; **s. bus** car *m* de ramassage scolaire; **s. day** journée *f* d'école *ou* scolaire; **s. friend** camarade *mf* d'école; **s. uniform** uniforme *m* scolaire; **s. year** année *f* scolaire **(b)** *(college, university)* faculté *f*, université *f* **(c)** *(of artists, thinkers)* école *f*; **s. of thought** école de pensée; *Fig* **he's one of the old s.** il est de la vieille école
2 *vt (educate)* scolariser; *(train)* former, entraîner; **to s. sb in sth** former qn à qch

school² [sku:l] *n (of fish)* banc *m*

schoolboy ['sku:lbɔɪ] *n* écolier *m*, élève *m*

schoolchild ['sku:ltʃaɪld] *n* écolier(ère) *m,f*, élève *mf*

schoolgirl ['sku:lgɜ:l] *n* écolière *f*, élève *f*

schooling ['sku:lɪŋ] *n* scolarité *f*, éducation *f*

schoolmaster ['sku:lmɑ:stə(r)] *n Formal (primary)* instituteur *m*, maître *m* d'école; *(secondary)* professeur *m*

schoolmate ['sku:lmeɪt] *n* camarade *mf* de classe

schoolmistress ['sku:lmɪstrɪs] *n Formal (primary)* institutrice *f*, maîtresse *f* d'école; *(secondary)* professeur *m*

schoolroom ['sku:lru:m] *n* salle *f* de classe

schoolteacher ['sku:lti:tʃə(r)] *n (primary)* instituteur(trice) *m,f*; *(secondary)* professeur *m*

schoolyard ['sku:lja:d] *n* cour *f* de récréation

schooner ['sku:nə(r)] *n (ship)* schooner *m*

sciatica [saɪ'ætɪkə] *n* sciatique *f*

science ['saɪəns] *n* science *f*; **she's good at s.** elle est bonne en sciences; **s. fiction** science-fiction *f*; **s. park** parc *m* scientifique, zone *f* scientifique; **s. teacher** professeur *m* de sciences

scientific [saɪən'tɪfɪk] *adj* scientifique

scientist ['saɪəntɪst] *n* scientifique *mf*

sci-fi ['saɪfaɪ] *Fam* **1** *n* SF *f*
   2 *adj* de SF

Scilly ['sɪlɪ] *n* **the S. Isles, the Scillies** les Sorlingues *fpl*

scimitar ['sɪmɪtə(r)] *n* cimeterre *m*

scintillating ['sɪntɪleɪtɪŋ] *adj* brillant(e)

scissors ['sɪzəz] *npl* ciseaux *mpl*; **a pair of s.** une paire de ciseaux

sclerosis [sklə'rəʊsɪs] *n Med* sclérose *f*

scoff [skɒf] **1** *vt Fam (eat)* bouffer
   2 *vi (mock)* se moquer (**at** de)

scofflaw ['skɒflɔ:] *n* filou *m*

scold [skəʊld] *vt* gronder

scone [skɒn] *n* scone *m*

scoop [sku:p] **1** *n* (**a**) *(device) (for ice cream)* cuillère *f* à glace; *(for flour, sugar)* pelle *f*; *(for mashed potatoes)* cuillère *f* (**b**) *(portion) (of ice cream)* boule *f*; *(of mashed potatoes)* portion *f* (**c**) *Fam (in journalism)* scoop *m*
   2 *vt* (**a**) *(with hands, spoon)* ramasser (**b**) *(story)* publier en exclusivité

▸**scoop up** *vt sep* ramasser

scoot [sku:t] *vi Fam* **to s. (off** *or* **away)** filer

scooter ['sku:tə(r)] *n (for child)* trottinette *f*; *(small motorbike)* scooter *m*

scope [skəʊp] *n (of action)* possibilité *f*; *(of inquiry)* étendue *f*, portée *f*; **to give s. for...** *(interpretation, explanation)* laisser le champ libre à...; **the book is too narrow in s.** le livre est d'une portée trop limitée; **there's plenty of s. for improvement** les possibilités d'amélioration ne manquent pas; **the job gave him little s. to demonstrate his talents** son travail lui fournissait peu d'occasions de montrer ses talents

scorch [skɔ:tʃ] **1** *vt* roussir; **scorched-earth policy** politique *f* de la terre brûlée
   2 *n* **s. mark** brûlure *f*

scorcher ['skɔ:tʃə(r)] *n Fam (hot day)* **it's been a s.** ça a été la canicule

scorching ['skɔ:tʃɪŋ] *adj (day, weather)* torride; *(sun)* brûlant(e)

score [skɔ:(r)] **1** *n* (**a**) *(in sport, quiz)* score *m*; **there was still no s.** personne n'avait encore marqué; **to keep the s.** compter les points; *Fam Fig* **to know the s.** connaître le topo
   (**b**) *(line)* rayure *f*, entaille *f*
   (**c**) *(quarrel)* **to have a s. to settle with sb** avoir un compte à régler avec qn
   (**d**) *(reason, grounds)* **on that s.** à ce sujet, sur ce point
   (**e**) *(in music)* partition *f*

(**f**) *Old-fashioned (twenty)* **a s.** vingt; *Fam* **scores of** *(a lot)* des tas de
   2 *vt* (**a**) *(in sport)* marquer; **to s. a hit** *(hit target)* atteindre la cible; *Fig (of person, movie)* remporter un grand succès; *Fig* **to s. points off sb** avoir le dessus
   (**b**) *(cut line in)* entailler
   (**c**) *Fam (buy)* **to s. drugs** acheter de la drogue
   3 *vi* (**a**) *(score a goal)* marquer un but
   (**b**) *Fam (sexually)* faire une touche; *(buy drugs)* acheter de la drogue

▸**score out** *vt sep (delete)* biffer, barrer

scoreboard ['skɔ:bɔ:d] *n* tableau *m* d'affichage (des scores)

scorecard ['skɔ:kɑ:d] *n* carte *f* de score

scorer ['skɔ:rə(r)] *n* marqueur(euse) *m,f*

scorn [skɔ:n] **1** *n* mépris *m*; **to pour s. on sb/sth** n'avoir que du mépris pour qn/qch
   2 *vt* mépriser

scornful ['skɔ:nfʊl] *adj* méprisant(e); **to be s. of sb/sth** considérer qn/qch avec mépris

Scorpio ['skɔ:pɪəʊ] *n (sign of zodiac)* Scorpion *m*; **to be (a) S.** être (du) Scorpion

scorpion ['skɔ:pɪən] *n* scorpion *m*

Scot [skɒt] *n* Écossais(e) *m,f*

Scotch [skɒtʃ] **1** *n (whiskey)* scotch *m*
   2 *adj* **S. tape®** scotch® *m*; **S. terrier** scotch-terrier *m*; **S. whiskey** scotch *m*

scotch [skɒtʃ] *vt (rumor)* étouffer

scot-free ['skɒt'fri:] *adj Fam* **to get off s.** s'en tirer sans la moindre punition

Scotland ['skɒtlənd] *n* l'Écosse *f*

Scots [skɒts] **1** *n (dialect)* écossais *m*
   2 *adj* écossais(e)

Scotsman ['skɒtsmən] *n* Écossais *m*

Scotswoman ['skɒtswʊmən] *n* Écossaise *f*

Scottie dog ['skɒtɪ'dɒg] *n Fam* scotch-terrier *m*

Scottish ['skɒtɪʃ] *adj* écossais(e); **the S. Parliament** le parlement écossais; **S. terrier** scotch-terrier *m*

scoundrel ['skaʊndr(ə)l] *n* crapule *f*; *Fam (child)* coquin(e) *m,f*

scour ['skaʊə(r)] *vt* (**a**) *(pot, surface)* récurer, frotter (**b**) *(area, house)* ratisser, fouiller

scourer ['skaʊərə(r)] *n* tampon *m* à récurer

scourge [skɜ:dʒ] *n* fléau *m*

scout [skaʊt] **1** *n* (**a**) *(boy)* **s.** (boy-)scout *m*, éclaireur *m*; *(girl)* **s.** éclaireuse *f*; **(talent) s.** dénicheur(euse) *m,f* de talents (**b**) *Mil (searcher)* éclaireur *m* (**c**) *(action)* **to have a s. around (for sth)** chercher (qch)
   2 *vi* **to s. for talent** dénicher des talents

scoutmaster ['skaʊtmɑ:stə(r)] *n* chef *m* scout

scowl [skaʊl] **1** *n* regard *m* noir
   2 *vi* lancer des regards noirs (**at** à)

scrabble ['skræb(ə)l] *vi* **to s. about** *or* **around for sth** chercher qch à tâtons

scraggy ['skrægɪ] *adj* maigre, décharné(e)

scram [skræm] *(pt & pp* **scrammed)** *vi Fam* se tirer

scramble ['skræmb(ə)l] **1** *n* (**a**) *(rush)* ruée *f*; *(struggle)* bousculade *f* (**for** pour)
   2 *vt Tel (signal)* brouiller
   3 *vi* **to s. for sth** se précipiter pour qch; **to s. up a hill** gravir une colline avec les mains

scrambled eggs ['skræmb(ə)ld'egz] *npl* œufs *mpl* brouillés

scrap¹ [skræp] **1** *n* (**a**) *(of material, paper)* bout *m*; *(of information)* bribe *f*; *(of evidence)* semblant *m*; **scraps** *(of food)* restes *mpl*; **a s. of truth** une once de vérité (**b**) **s. (metal)** ferraille *f*; **s. merchant** *or* **dealer** ferrailleur *m*; **to sell sth for s.** vendre qch à la casse
   2 *vt (pt & pp* **scrapped)** *(car)* envoyer à la casse; *(submarine, missile)* mettre au rebut; *(project)* abandonner

scrap² [skræp] *Fam* **1** *n (fight)* bagarre *f*; **to have a s., to get into a s.** se bagarrer

  2 *vi (fight)* se bagarrer

scrapbook ['skræpbʊk] *n* album *m (de coupures de presse etc)*

scrape [skreɪp] **1** *n* **(a)** *(action)* coup *m* de grattoir; *(mark)* éraflure *f*; *(sound)* raclement *m*; **to give sth a s.** donner un coup de grattoir à qch **(b)** *Fam* **to get into a s.** se mettre dans le pétrin

  2 *vt* **(a)** *(skin, side of car)* érafler; *(dirt, wallpaper, vegetables)* gratter; **to s. one's plate clean** nettoyer son assiette; *Fig* **to s. the bottom of the barrel** être tombé(e) bien bas **(b)** *(barely obtain)* **to s. a living** arriver tout juste à vivre

  3 *vi* **(a)** *(make sound)* gratter, grincer **(b)** *(barely manage)* **to s. home** *(in contest)* réussir de justesse; **to s. into college** passer de justesse à l'université

▸**scrape through** *vt insep* passer de justesse

▸**scrape together** *vt sep (money, resources)* parvenir à rassembler

scraper ['skreɪpə(r)] *n (tool)* grattoir *m*

scrapheap ['skræphiːp] *n* tas *m* de ferraille; *Fig* **to be on the s.** être au rebut

scrappy ['skræpɪ] *adj* **(a)** *(performance)* décousu(e); *(knowledge)* limité(e) **(b)** *Fam (quarrelsome)* bagarreur(euse), chamailleur(euse)

scratch [skrætʃ] **1** *n* **(a)** *(on skin)* égratignure *f*; *(on record, furniture)* rayure *f*; *(by claw)* griffure *f*

  (b) *(action)* **to give one's arm a s.** se gratter le bras

  (c) *Fam (idioms)* **to start from s.** partir de rien *ou* de zéro; *(restart)* recommencer à zéro; **to come up** *or* **to be up to s.** être à la hauteur; **to bring sth/sb up to s.** mettre qch/qn à niveau

  2 *adj (meal, team)* improvisé(e)

  3 *vt* **(a)** *(skin) (by accident)* égratigner; *(to relieve itching)* gratter; *(with claw, nail)* griffer; *(glass, record)* rayer; **to s. oneself** se gratter; **to s. one's arm** se gratter le bras; *Fig* **you s. my back and I'll s. yours** un service en vaut un autre; *Fig* **we've only scratched the surface of the problem** nous n'avons fait que survoler le problème

  (b) *(write, draw)* griffonner; **s. paper** *(papier m)* brouillon *m*

  (c) *(in sport)* retirer

  4 *vi* **(a)** *(of person)* se gratter; *(of pen, new clothes)* gratter; *(of thorns)* piquer; **the dog was scratching at the door** le chien grattait à la porte

  (b) *(of DJ)* scratcher

▸**scratch out** *vt sep (number, name)* rayer; *Fig* **to s. sb's eyes out** arracher les yeux à qn

scratchcard ['skrætʃkɑːd] *n (for lottery)* carte *f* à gratter

scratching ['skrætʃɪŋ] *n* **(a)** *(with fingernail)* coups *mpl* d'ongle; *(to relieve itch)* grattement *m*; *(of glass, record)* rayage *m* **(b)** *(sound)* grattement *m*; *(of pen nib)* grincement *m*; *(by DJ)* scratch *m*, scratching *m*

scratchpad ['skrætʃpæd] *n* bloc-notes *m*

scratchy ['skrætʃɪ] *adj (garment, towel)* qui gratte; *(record)* rayé(e)

scrawl [skrɔːl] **1** *n (writing)* gribouillage *m*

  2 *vt & vi* gribouiller

scrawny ['skrɔːnɪ] *adj* maigrelet(ette)

scream [skriːm] **1** *n* **(a)** *(of person)* hurlement *m*; **screams of laughter** éclats *mpl* de rire **(b)** *Fam (good fun)* **it/he was a s.** c'était/il était tordant

  2 *vt* hurler; **the headlines screamed "guilty"** le mot "coupable" s'étalait en gros à la une des journaux

  3 *vi* hurler; **the car screamed past** la voiture est passée en rugissant; **to s. with pain** hurler de douleur; **to s. with laughter** se tordre de rire

screamingly ['skriːmɪŋlɪ] *adv Fam* **s. funny** tordant(e)

scree [skriː] *n* éboulis *m*

screech [skriːtʃ] **1** *n (of bird, person)* cri *m* strident; *(of brakes)* crissement *m*; *(of laughter)* éclat *m*

  2 *vt* hurler

  3 *vi (of bird)* pousser des cris stridents; *(of person)* hurler; *(of brakes)* crisser; **the car screeched to a halt** la voiture s'est arrêtée dans un crissement de pneus

screen [skriːn] **1** *n* **(a)** *(barrier)* écran *m*; *(folding)* paravent *m*; **s. door** porte *f* avec moustiquaire **(b)** *(of TV, computer, in movie theater)* écran *m*; **the big/small s.** le grand/petit écran; **s. actor/actress** acteur *m*/actrice *f* de cinéma; *Comput* **s. saver** économiseur *m* d'écran; *Cin* **s. test** bout *m* d'essai; *Aut* **s. wash** liquide *m* lave-glace

  2 *vt* **(a)** *(protect)* protéger; **to s. sth from view** cacher qch aux regards **(b)** *(movie)* projeter; *(TV program)* diffuser **(c)** *(test)* *(for security)* effectuer une enquête sur; *(for disease)* tester

screening ['skriːnɪŋ] *n* **(a)** *Cin* projection *f* **(b)** *(for security)* enquête *f*; *(for disease)* dépistage *m*

screenplay ['skriːnpleɪ] *n Cin* scénario *m*

screenwriter ['skriːnraɪtə(r)] *n Cin* scénariste *mf*

screw [skruː] **1** *n* **(a)** *(for fixing)* vis *f*; *Fam Fig* **she's got a s. loose** elle a une case en moins; *Fam Fig* **to put the screws on sb** faire pression sur qn; **s. top** *(of bottle, jar)* couvercle *m* qui se visse **(b)** *(propeller)* hélice *f* **(c)** *very Fam (prison officer)* maton(onne) *m,f* **(d)** *Vulg (sex)* **to have a s.** s'envoyer en l'air

  2 *vt* **(a)** *(fix)* visser **(to** à); **to s. one's face into a smile** se forcer à sourire; *Fam* **to s. money out of sb** extorquer de l'argent à qn **(b)** *Vulg (have sex with)* baiser; **s. you!** va te faire foutre!

  3 *vi Vulg (have sex)* baiser

▸**screw around** *vi Vulg* baiser à droite et à gauche

▸**screw on 1** *vt sep (attach)* visser; *Fam* **she's got her head screwed on** elle a la tête sur les épaules

  2 *vi (of lid)* se visser

▸**screw up 1** *vt sep* **(a)** *(paper)* froisser; **to s. up one's face** faire la grimace; *Fig* **to s. up one's courage** prendre son courage à deux mains **(b)** *very Fam (spoil)* foutre en l'air

  2 *vi very Fam (fail)* cafouiller

screwdriver ['skruːdraɪvə(r)] *n* tournevis *m*

screw-up ['skruːʌp] *n very Fam* **(a)** *(person) (bungler)* manche *mf*; *(misfit)* paumé(e) *m,f* **(b)** *(situation)* foirade *f*

screwy ['skruːɪ] *adj Fam* cinglé(e), dingue

scribble ['skrɪbəl] **1** *n* gribouillage *m*

  2 *vt & vi* griffonner

scribe [skraɪb] *n* scribe *m*

scrimmage ['skrɪmɪdʒ] *n* **(a)** *(pushing)* bousculade *f* **(b)** *(in football)* mêlée *f*

scrimp [skrɪmp] *vi* **to s. (and save)** économiser sur tout

script [skrɪpt] *n* **(a)** *(for play)* texte *m*; *(for movie, TV program)* script *m*; *(in exam)* copie *f* d'examen **(b)** *(handwriting)* script *m*

Scripture ['skrɪptʃə(r)] *n* **(Holy) S., the Scriptures** les saintes Écritures *fpl*

scriptwriter ['skrɪptraɪtə(r)] *n Cin & TV* scénariste *mf*

scroll [skrəʊl] **1** *n* **(a)** *(of paper, parchment)* rouleau *m* **(b)** *Archit* volute *f*

  2 *vi Comput* défiler

▸**scroll down** *vi Comput* défiler vers le bas

▸**scroll up** *vi Comput* défiler vers le haut

scrooge [skruːdʒ] *n* avare *mf*

scrotum ['skrəʊtəm] *n* scrotum *m*

scrounge [skraʊndʒ] *Fam* **1** *n* **to be on the s.** venir quémander

  2 *vt* **to s. sth from** *or* **off sb** taper qch à qn

  3 *vi* **to s. off sb** vivre aux crochets de qn

scrounger ['skraʊndʒə(r)] *n Fam* parasite *m*

scrub [skrʌb] **1** *n* **(a)** *(bushes)* broussailles *fpl* **(b)** *(wash)* **to give sth a (good) s.** (bien) frotter qch; **s. brush** brosse *f* en chiendent **(c)** *(for skin, face)* gommage *m*

2 *vt (pt & pp* **scrubbed***)* **(a)** *(floor)* frotter; *(pots)* récurer; **to s. one's hands** bien se frotter les mains **(b)** *Fam (cancel)* annuler

▶**scrub up** *vi Med* se brosser les mains

scrubber ['skrʌbə(r)] *n (for dishes)* tampon *m* à récurer

scrubland ['skrʌblænd] *n* brousse *f*

scruff [skrʌf] *n* **by the s. of the neck** par la peau du cou

scruffily ['skrʌfɪlɪ] *adv* **to be s. dressed** être dépenaillé(e)

scruffy ['skrʌfɪ] *adj (person)* peu soigné(e); *(clothes)* miteux(euse)

scrum [skrʌm] *n (in rugby)* mêlée *f*; *Fig* bousculade *f*

scrumptious ['skrʌm(p)ʃəs] *adj Fam* délicieux(euse)

scrunch [skrʌntʃ] **1** *vt (paper)* froisser en boule; *(can, cigarette)* écraser
2 *vi* crisser

scrunchie ['skrʌntʃɪ] *n (for hair)* chouchou *m*

scruple ['skru:pəl] *n* scrupule *m*; **to have no scruples** n'avoir aucun scrupule

scrupulous ['skru:pjʊləs] *adj* scrupuleux(euse)

scrupulously ['skru:pjʊləslɪ] *adv* scrupuleusement

scrutineer [skru:tɪ'nɪə(r)] *n* scrutateur(trice) *m,f*

scrutinize ['skru:tɪnaɪz] *vt (document, contract)* éplucher; *(votes)* vérifier

scrutiny ['skru:tɪnɪ] *n (of document, votes)* examen *m* minutieux; **to come under s.** être examiné(e)

scuba ['sku:bə] *n* **s. diver** plongeur(euse) *m,f* sous-marin(e); **s. diving** plongée *f* sous-marine

scuff [skʌf] **1** *n* **s. mark** éraflure *f*
2 *vt (shoe)* érafler

scuffle ['skʌfəl] **1** *n* échauffourée *f*
2 *vi* se bagarrer

scull [skʌl] **1** *n (oar)* aviron *m*
2 *vi* ramer

scullery ['skʌlərɪ] *(pl* **sculleries***) n* arrière-cuisine *f*

sculpt [skʌlpt] *vt* sculpter

sculptor ['skʌlptə(r)] *n* sculpteur *m*

sculpture ['skʌlptʃə(r)] **1** *n* sculpture *f*
2 *vt* sculpter

scum [skʌm] *n* **(a)** *(layer of dirt)* crasse *f*; *(froth)* écume *f* **(b)** *very Fam Pej (person)* ordure *f*; *(people)* racaille *f*; **the s. of the earth** le rebut de la société

scupper ['skʌpə(r)] *vt (ship, project)* couler

scurrilous ['skʌrɪləs] *adj* calomnieux(euse)

scurry ['skʌrɪ] *(pt & pp* **scurried***) vi (dash)* courir

▶**scurry away, scurry off** *vi* se sauver

scurvy ['skɜ:vɪ] *n Med* scorbut *m*

scuttle¹ ['skʌtəl] **1** *n* **(coal) s.** seau *m* à charbon
2 *vt (ship, plan)* saborder

scuttle² ['skʌtɪ] *vi (run)* courir

▶**scuttle away, scuttle off** *vi* déguerpir

scuzzy ['skʌzɪ] *adj Fam* dégueulasse, cradingue

scythe [saɪð] **1** *n* faux *f*
2 *vt* faucher

SE [es'i:] *n (abbr* **southeast***)* SE

SEA [esi:'eɪ] *n (abbr* **Single European Act***)* AUE *m*

sea [si:] *n* mer *f*; **by the s.** au bord de la mer; **to go to s.** *(become a sailor)* devenir marin; *Fig* **a s. of people** une marée humaine; **heavy seas** mer démontée; **on the high seas, out at s.** en haute mer; **to find** *or* **to get one's s. legs** s'habituer au roulis; *Fig* **to be all at s.** être complètement perdu(e); **s. air** air *m* marin; **s. anemone** anémone *f* de mer; **s. battle** bataille *f* navale; **s. breeze** brise *f* de mer; **s. change** changement *m* radical; *Fam* **(old) s. dog** (vieux) loup *m* de mer; **s. horse** hippocampe *m*; *Naut* **s. lane** couloir *m* maritime; **s. level** niveau *m* de la mer; **s. lion** otarie *f*; **s. salt** sel *m* de mer; **s. urchin** oursin *m*; **s. voyage** voyage *m* en mer

seaboard ['si:bɔ:d] *n* côte *f*

seaborne ['si:bɔ:n] *adj (trade)* maritime; *(invasion)* naval(e)

seafarer ['si:feərə(r)] *n* marin *m*

seafaring ['si:feərɪŋ] *adj (people)* de navigateurs

seafood ['si:fu:d] *n* fruits *mpl* de mer

seafront ['si:frʌnt] *n* front *m* de mer

seagoing ['si:gəʊɪŋ] *adj (boat)* de mer

seagull ['si:gʌl] *n* mouette *f*

seal¹ [si:l] *n (animal)* phoque *m*

seal² [si:l] **1** *n* **(a)** *(stamp)* sceau *m*; **to give one's s. of approval to sth** donner son approbation à qch; **to set the s. on sth** *(on alliance, friendship)* sceller qch; *(on victory, defeat)* confirmer qch **(b)** *(device)* joint *m* (d'étanchéité); *(on food container)* = fermeture garantissant la fraîcheur d'un produit
2 *vt (document, envelope)* cacheter; *(with official seal)* sceller; *(jar)* fermer hermétiquement; *(joint)* assurer l'étanchéité de; **to s. sb's fate** décider du sort de qn; **my lips are sealed** je ne dirai rien

▶**seal in** *vt sep* enfermer

▶**seal off** *vt sep (area)* boucler; *(people)* isoler

sealing wax ['si:lɪŋ'wæks] *n* cire *f* à cacheter

sealskin ['si:lskɪn] *n* peau *f* de phoque

seam [si:m] *n* **(a)** *(of garment)* couture *f*; *(in metalwork)* soudure *f*; **to be coming apart at the seams** *(of clothing)* craquer de partout; *Fig (of plan, organization)* s'effondrer **(b)** *(of coal)* veine *f*

seaman ['si:mən] *n Naut* marin *m*

seamanship ['si:mənʃɪp] *n Naut* qualités *fpl* de navigateur

seamstress ['semstrɪs] *n* couturière *f*

seamy ['si:mɪ] *adj* sordide

seance ['seɪɒns] *n* séance *f* de spiritisme

seaplane ['si:pleɪn] *n* hydravion *m*

seaport ['si:pɔ:t] *n* port *m* maritime

sear [sɪə(r)] *vt (skin)* brûler; *Fig* **the image was seared on her memory** l'image était gravée dans sa mémoire

search [sɜ:tʃ] **1** *n* recherches *fpl*; *(of building, room)* fouille *f*; **to have a s. for sth** chercher qch; **in s. of** à la recherche de; **to make a s.** faire des recherches; *Comput* **to do a s.** faire une recherche; *Comput* **s. engine** moteur *m* de recherche; **s. party** équipe *f* de secours; *Law* **s. warrant** mandat *m* de perquisition
2 *vt (person, place)* fouiller; *Comput (file, directory)* rechercher dans; *Fam* **s. me!** je n'en ai pas la moindre idée!
3 *vi* chercher; **to s. for sth** chercher qch; *Comput* **s. and replace** rechercher et remplacer

searching ['sɜ:tʃɪŋ] *adj (examination)* minutieux(euse); *(look)* pénétrant(e)

searchlight ['sɜ:tʃlaɪt] *n* projecteur *m*

searing ['sɪərɪŋ] *adj (pain, heat)* fulgurant(e); *(criticism, indictment)* virulent(e)

seascape ['si:skeɪp] *n Art* marine *f*

seashell ['si:ʃel] *n* coquillage *m*

seashore ['si:ʃɔ:(r)] *n* rivage *m*

seasick ['si:sɪk] *adj* **to be s.** avoir le mal de mer

seasickness ['si:sɪknɪs] *n* mal *m* de mer

seaside ['si:saɪd] *n* **the s.** le bord de la mer; **at the s.** au bord de la mer; **s. resort** station *f* balnéaire

season¹ ['si:zən] *n* saison *f*; *(of movies)* cycle *m*; **S.'s Greetings** meilleurs vœux de fin d'année; **the high s.** *(for tourism)* la haute saison; **cherries are out of s.** ce n'est pas la saison des cerises; **s. ticket** abonnement *m*

season² ['si:zən] *vt* **(a)** *(with salt, pepper)* assaisonner; *(with spice)* épicer **(b)** *(wood)* faire sécher

seasonable ['si:zənəbəl] *adj* **s. weather** un temps de saison

seasonal ['si:zənəl] *adj (work, fluctuations)* saisonnier(ère)

seasoned ['si:zənd] *adj* **(a)** *(food)* assaisonné(e); **a highly s. dish** un plat très relevé **(b)** *(wood)* sec (sèche) **(c)** *(person)* expérimenté(e); *(soldier)* aguerri(e)

seasoning ['si:zənɪŋ] *n Culin* assaisonnement *m*

seat [siːt] **1** *n* **(a)** *(chair)* chaise *f*; *(on bus, train, in theater, movies)* place *f*, siège *m*; *(in Parliament)* siège *m*; **to take a s.** s'asseoir; **s. belt** ceinture *f* de sécurité **(b)** *(part of chair, toilet)* siège *m*; *(of trousers)* fond *m* **(c)** *(center)* *(of government)* siège *m*; **a s. of learning** un haut lieu du savoir; **country s.** *(of aristocrat)* demeure *f* familiale

2 *vt* **(a)** *(cause to sit)* *(child)* asseoir; *(guests)* faire asseoir; **to be/to remain seated** être/rester assis(e); *Formal* **please be seated** veuillez vous asseoir **(b)** *(accommodate)* **the bus seats thirty** il y a trente places assises dans le bus; **this table seats twelve** on tient douze à cette table; **the hall seats two hundred** la salle compte deux cents places

seating ['siːtɪŋ] *n* *(seats)* sièges *mpl*; *(positioning)* placement *m*; **s. capacity** nombre *m* de places assises; **s. plan** plan *m* de table

SEATO ['siːtəʊ] *n* *(abbr* **Southeast Asia Treaty Organization**) OTASE *f*

seaway ['siːweɪ] *n* route *f* (maritime)

seaweed ['siːwiːd] *n* algues *fpl*

seaworthy ['siːwɜːðɪ] *adj* en état de naviguer

sebaceous [sɪ'beɪʃəs] *adj* sébacé(e)

sec [sek] *n* *Fam* *(second)* **I'll be there in a s.** j'arrive tout de suite; **wait a s.!** attends une seconde!

sec. *(abbr* **second(s)**) s.

secateurs [sekə'tɜːz] *npl* sécateur *m*

secede [sɪ'siːd] *vi* faire sécession (**from** de)

secession [sɪ'seʃən] *n* sécession *f*

secluded [sɪ'kluːdɪd] *adj* *(place)* reculé(e); *(life)* de reclus(e)

seclusion [sɪ'kluːʒən] *n* isolement *m*

second¹ ['sekənd] *n* *(of time)* seconde *f*; **I won't be a s.** j'en ai pour deux secondes; **s. hand** *(of clock)* trotteuse *f*

second² ['sekənd] **1** *n* **(a)** *(in series)* deuxième *mf*, second(e) *m,f*; **Edward the S.** Edward II; **I was s. in the race** je suis arrivé deuxième à la course

(b) *(of month)* deux *m*; **May s.** le deux mai

(c) *Com* **seconds** articles *mpl* défectueux

(d) *(in duel)* témoin *m*; *(in boxing)* soigneur *m*

(e) **s. (gear)** seconde *f*

(f) *Fam* **anyone for seconds?** *(at meal)* quelqu'un veut du rab?

2 *adj* deuxième, second(e); **twenty-s.** vingt-deuxième; **ninety-s.** quatre-vingt-douzième; **to be s. to none** être sans égal(e); **s. in command** *Mil* commandant *m* en second; *(in organization)* adjoint(e) *m,f*; **the s. largest city in England** la deuxième ville d'Angleterre; **a s. Picasso/Churchill** un nouveau Picasso/Churchill; **on s. thought** tout bien réfléchi; **to have s. thoughts (about sth)** ne plus être très sûr(e) (de qch); *Fig* **to play s. fiddle to sb** être dans l'ombre de qn; **it's s. nature to her** elle le fait automatiquement; **to get one's s. wind** trouver un second souffle; **s. chance** deuxième chance *f*; **to be in one's s. childhood** être retombé(e) en enfance; **s. class** *(on train)* deuxième classe *f*; *Rel* **the S. Coming** le second avènement; **s. cousin** petit(e) cousin(e) *m,f*; **s. floor** premier étage *m*; *Scol* **s. grade** = classe de primaire pour les 6-7 ans; **s. language** seconde langue *f*; **s. name** nom *m* de famille; *Law* **s. offense** récidive *f*; **s. opinion** deuxième avis *m*; *Gram* **s. person** deuxième personne *f*; **s. sight** don *m* de double vue; **s. violin** second violon *m*; **the S. World War** la Seconde Guerre mondiale

second³ ['sekənd] *vt* *(motion)* appuyer

secondary ['sekəndərɪ] *adj* secondaire; **s. school** établissement *m* secondaire, *Can & Suisse* école *f* secondaire

second-best ['sekənd'best] **1** *n* pis-aller *m*; **to be content with s.** se contenter d'un pis-aller

2 *adv* **to come off s.** être battu(e)

second-class ['sekənd'klɑːs] **1** *adj* *(ticket, car)* de deuxième classe; **s. citizen** citoyen(enne) *m,f* de second rang; **s. mail** courrier *m* au tarif lent

2 *adv* **to travel s.** voyager en seconde classe

seconder ['sekəndə(r)] *n* = personne qui appuie une motion

second-guess ['sekənd'ges] *vt* **to s. sb** anticiper ce que qn va faire

second-hand ['sekənd'hænd] **1** *adj* *(car, clothes)* d'occasion; **s. store** magasin *m* d'articles d'occasion

2 *adv* *(buy)* d'occasion; **to hear news s.** avoir des nouvelles de seconde main

secondly ['sekəndlɪ] *adv* deuxièmement

second-rate ['sekəndreɪt] *adj* médiocre

secrecy ['siːkrɪsɪ] *n* secret *m*; **in s.** en secret; **to swear sb to s.** faire jurer le silence à qn

secret ['siːkrɪt] **1** *n* secret *m*; **to do sth in s.** faire qch secrètement; **I make no s. of it** je ne m'en cache pas; **it's no s.** tout le monde le sait

2 *adj* secret(ète); **to keep sth s. from sb** cacher qch à qn; **s. agent** agent *m* secret; **s. police** police *f* secrète; **s. service** services *mpl* secrets; **the S. Service** = service de sécurité du président américain; *also Fig* **s. weapon** arme *f* secrète

secretarial [sekrə'teərɪəl] *adj* *(work)* administratif(ive); *(job, college, course)* de secrétariat

secretariat [sekrə'teərɪət] *n* secrétariat *m*

secretary ['sekrətərɪ] *(pl* **secretaries**) *n* *(in office)* secrétaire *mf*; *Pol* **S. of State** ministre *m* des Affaires étrangères

secretary-general ['sekrətərɪ'dʒenərəl] *n* *Pol* secrétaire *m* général

secrete [sɪ'kriːt] *vt* **(a)** *(discharge)* sécréter **(b)** *(hide)* cacher

secretion [sɪ'kriːʃən] *n* sécrétion *f*

secretive ['siːkrɪtɪv] *adj* secret(ète); **to be s. about sth** faire des cachotteries à propos de qch

secretly ['siːkrɪtlɪ] *adv* secrètement

sect [sekt] *n* secte *f*

sectarian [sek'teərɪən] *adj* sectaire

sectarianism [sek'teərɪənɪzəm] *n* sectarisme *m*

section ['sekʃən] **1** *n* **(a)** *(in general)* partie *f*; *(of road, railroad)* tronçon *m*; *(of machine)* élément *m*; *(of organization)* département *m*; *(in orchestra)* section *f*; *(of law, treaty)* article *m*; **all sections of society** toutes les catégories sociales **(b)** *(of soldiers)* section *f* **(c)** *(cross-section)* coupe *f*

2 *vt* *(cut)* sectionner

sector ['sektə(r)] *n* secteur *m*

secular ['sekjʊlə(r)] *adj* *(history, art)* laïque; *(music)* profane

secure [sɪ'kjʊə(r)] **1** *adj* **(a)** *(free from anxiety)* en sécurité; **s. in the knowledge that...** ayant l'assurance que... **(b)** *(investment, place)* sûr(e); *(foothold)* ferme; *(nomination, future)* assuré(e); *(load, rope)* bien attaché(e); *(foundations, lock)* solide

2 *vt* **(a)** *(make safe)* *(position, future)* assurer **(b)** *(fasten)* *(load)* bien amarrer; *(door, window)* bien fermer **(c)** *(obtain)* *(support, promise, loan)* obtenir

securely [sɪ'kjʊəlɪ] *adv* **(a)** *(stored, hidden)* en toute sécurité; *(protected)* bien **(b)** *(firmly)* solidement; **the door was s. fastened** la porte était bien fermée

security [sɪ'kjʊərɪtɪ] *n* **(a)** *(stability, safety)* sécurité *f*; **s. of tenure** sécurité de l'emploi; **the S. Council** le Conseil de sécurité; **s. forces** forces *fpl* de sécurité; **s. guard** garde *m*; **s. officer** agent *m* de sécurité; **to be a s. risk** être un danger pour la sécurité **(b)** *Fin (for loan)* garantie *f* **(c)** *Fin* **securities** titres *mpl*

sedan [sɪ'dæn] *n* **(a)** *(car)* berline *f* **(b)** **s. chair** chaise *f* à porteurs

sedate [sɪ'deɪt] **1** *adj* tranquille

2 *vt* donner des calmants à

sedately [sɪ'deɪtlɪ] *adv* tranquillement

sedation [sɪ'deɪʃən] *n* **under s.** sous calmants

sedative ['sedətɪv] *n* sédatif *m*, calmant *m*

sedentary ['sedəntərɪ] *adj* sédentaire

sediment ['sedɪmənt] *n* sédiment *m*

sedition [sɪ'dɪʃən] *n* sédition *f*

seditious [sɪ'dɪʃəs] *adj* séditieux(euse)

seduce [sɪ'djuːs] *vt (sexually)* séduire; *Fig* **to s. sb into doing sth** persuader qn de faire qch

seducer [sɪ'djuːsə(r)] *n* séducteur(trice) *m,f*

seduction [sɪ'dʌkʃən] *n* séduction *f*

seductive [sɪ'dʌktɪv] *adj (look)* séducteur(trice); *(argument, offer)* séduisant(e)

see¹ [siː] *n Rel* évêché *m*

see² [siː] *(pt* **saw** [sɔː]*, pp* **seen** [siːn]) **1** *vt* **(a)** *(with eyes, perceive)* voir; **now s. what you've done!** regarde ce que tu as fait!; **s. page 50** voir page 50; **to be seeing things** *(hallucinate)* avoir des visions; **it has to be seen to be believed** il faut le voir pour le croire; **to s. sb do** *or* **doing sth** voir qn faire qch; **I can't s. a way out of this problem** je ne vois pas comment on peut s'en sortir; **could you s. your way to lending me your car?** cela te serait-il possible de me prêter ta voiture?; **to s. sense** *or* **reason** entendre raison; **the city has seen many changes** la ville a connu de grands changements; **I don't know what you s. in her** je ne vois pas ce que tu lui trouves; **it remains to be seen whether...** reste à savoir si...; **I'll s. what I can do** je vais voir ce que je peux faire

(b) *(understand)* voir; **I s. what you mean** je vois ce que tu veux dire; **I don't s. the point** je n'en vois pas l'intérêt

(c) *(envisage, imagine)* imaginer, voir; **what do you s. happening next?** à ton avis, qu'est-ce qui va se passer maintenant?; **I can't s. them arriving before six** ça m'étonnerait qu'ils arrivent avant six heures; **I can't s. you as a boxer** je ne t'imagine pas boxeur

(d) *(make sure)* **I shall s. that he comes** je ferai en sorte qu'il vienne; **s. that this doesn't happen again!** fais en sorte que ça ne se reproduise pas!

(e) *(meet) (person, doctor, lawyer)* voir; **I'm seeing Bill tomorrow** je vois Bill demain; **s. you (soon)!** à bientôt!

(f) *(accompany)* **to s. sb home** accompagner qn chez lui; **to s. sb to the door** accompagner qn jusqu'à la porte

2 *vi* **(a)** *(with eyes)* voir; **s. for yourself** à toi de juger; **we shall s.** nous verrons bien

(b) *(understand)* comprendre; **ah, I s.!** ah, je vois!

(c) *(consider)* **let me s.!, let's s.!** voyons!; **do you have a free room? – let me s.** avez-vous une chambre libre? – voyons voir

(d) *(find out)* **I'll go and s.** je vais voir

▶**see about** *vt insep* **(a)** *(deal with)* s'occuper de **(b)** *(consider)* voir; *Fam* **we'll (soon) s. about that!** c'est ce qu'on va voir!

▶**see in** *vt sep* **to s. the New Year in** fêter le Nouvel An

▶**see off** *vt sep (say goodbye to)* dire au revoir à

▶**see out** *vt sep* accompagner jusqu'à la porte; **I'll s. myself out** inutile de me raccompagner

▶**see through 1** *vt sep (project, policy)* mener à bien
2 *vt insep (person, lie, plan)* percer à jour

▶**see to** *vt insep (deal with)* s'occuper de; **to get sth seen to** *(machine, roof)* faire réparer qch; *(wound, injury)* faire examiner qch; **I'll s. to it that you're not disturbed** je ferai en sorte que tu ne sois pas dérangé

seed [siːd] **1** *n* **(a)** *(for sowing)* graine *f*; *(of fruit)* pépin *m*; **to go** *or* **to run to s.** *(of plant)* monter en graine **(b)** *Sport (in tournament)* tête *f* de série **(c)** *Lit (semen)* semence *f*
2 *vt* **(a)** *(remove seeds from)* épépiner **(b)** *(lawn)* ensemencer **(c)** *(in tournament)* **seeded players** joueurs *mpl* classés tête de série
3 *vi (of plant)* monter en graine

seedless ['siːdlɪs] *adj* sans pépins

seedling ['siːdlɪŋ] *n* plant *m*

seedy ['siːdɪ] *adj* **(a)** *(shabby) (person, hotel, area)* miteux(euse) **(b)** *Fam (unwell)* mal fichu(e)

seeing ['siːɪŋ] **1** *conj* **s. (that** *or* **how)...** étant donné que...
2 *n* **s. is believing** voir c'est croire

seeing-eye dog [siːɪŋ'aɪdɒg] *n* chien *m* d'aveugle

seek [siːk] *(pt & pp* **sought** [sɔːt]) *vt* **(a)** *(look for) (thing lost, job)* chercher; *(someone's friendship, promotion)* essayer d'obtenir **(b)** *(request)* **to s. sth from sb** demander qch à qn; **to s. sb's advice** demander conseil à qn **(c)** *(try)* **to s. to do sth** essayer de faire qch

▶**seek after** *vt insep* **to be much sought after** être très recherché(e)

▶**seek out** *vt sep (person)* dénicher

seem [siːm] *vi* sembler; **to s. tired** avoir l'air fatigué(e); **do what seems best** fais au mieux; **it seemed like a dream** j'avais l'impression de rêver; **I s. to have heard her name somewhere** il me semble avoir entendu son nom quelque part; **I can't s. to get it right** je n'y arrive pas; **it seems (that)..., it would s. that...** il semble que...+ *subjunctive*; **it seems to me that...** il me semble que...; **it seems** *or* **would s. so** il paraît; **it seems** *or* **would s. not** il paraît que non

seeming ['siːmɪŋ] *adj* apparent(e)

seemingly ['siːmɪŋlɪ] *adv* apparemment

seemly ['siːmlɪ] *adj Formal* bienséant(e)

seen [siːn] *pp of* **see**²

seep [siːp] *vi* suinter; **to s. into sth** s'infiltrer dans qch

seepage ['siːpɪdʒ] *n (oozing)* suintement *m*; *(into surface)* infiltration *f*

seer [sɪə(r)] *n Lit* voyant(e) *m,f*

seesaw ['siːsɔː] **1** *n* tapecul *m*
2 *vi Fig (of prices)* être en dents de scie

seethe [siːð] *vi (of liquid)* bouillonner; *(of street)* grouiller **(with** de); **to be seething (with anger)** bouillir (de rage)

see-through ['siːθruː] *adj* transparent(e)

segment 1 *n* ['segmənt] segment *m*; *(of orange)* quartier *m*
2 *vt* [seg'ment] *(line)* segmenter; *(orange)* couper en quartiers

segmentation [segmen'teɪʃən] *n Econ* segmentation *f*

segregate ['segrɪgeɪt] *vt* séparer **(from** de); *(prisoner)* isoler **(from** de)

segregation [segrɪ'geɪʃən] *n* ségrégation *f*; *(of prisoner)* isolement *m*

Seine [seɪn] *n* **the S.** la Seine

seismic ['saɪzmɪk] *adj* sismique

seismograph ['saɪzməgrɑːf] *n* sismographe *m*

seismology [saɪz'mɒlədʒɪ] *n* sismologie *f*

seize [siːz] *vt* **(a)** *(grab) & Fig (opportunity)* saisir; **to s. hold of** saisir **(b)** *(city, territory)* s'emparer de; *(drugs, stolen goods)* saisir

▶**seize on, seize upon** *vt insep* sauter sur

▶**seize up** *vi (of engine, back)* se bloquer

seizure ['siːʒə(r)] *n* **(a)** *(of land, city)* prise *f*; *Law (of property, drugs)* saisie *f* **(b)** *Med* crise *f*

seldom ['seldəm] *adv* rarement; **s. have I seen such courage** j'ai rarement vu un tel courage

select [sɪ'lekt] **1** *adj (exclusive)* sélect(e); **a s. few** quelques privilégiés(ées)
2 *vt* sélectionner

selected [sɪ'lektɪd] *adj* choisi(e)

selection [sɪ'lekʃən] *n* sélection *f*, choix *m*; **to make a s.** faire un choix; **a wide s.** un grand choix

selective [sɪ'lektɪv] *adj* sélectif(ive)

selector [sɪ'lektə(r)] *n (of team)* sélectionneur(euse) *m,f*

self [self] *(pl* **selves** [selvz]) *n* **(a)** **he's quite his old s. again** il est redevenu comme avant; **she was her usual cheerful s.** comme à son habitude, elle était gaie **(b)** *Psy* **the s.** le moi

self-addressed envelope ['selfə'drest'envələʊp] *n* enveloppe *f* libellée à ses nom et adresse

self-appointed ['selfə'pɔɪntɪd] *adj* **he's the s. spokesman** il s'est proclamé porte-parole

self-assessment ['selfə'sesmənt] *n (of person)* auto-évaluation *f*

self-assured ['selfə'ʃʊəd] *adj* plein(e) d'assurance

self-centered ['self'sentəd] *adj* égocentrique

self-confessed ['selfkən'fest] *adj* **he's a s. liar/cheat** il est menteur/tricheur de son propre aveu

self-confidence ['self'kɒnfɪdəns] *n* confiance *f* en soi

self-confident ['self'kɒnfɪdənt] *adj* plein(e) d'assurance

self-conscious ['self'kɒnʃəs] *adj* timide, gêné(e)

self-contained ['selfkən'teɪnd] *adj (person)* réservé(e); *(apartment)* indépendant(e)

self-contradictory ['selfkɒntrə'dɪktərɪ] *adj* qui contient des contradictions

self-control ['selfkən'trəʊl] *n* maîtrise *f* de soi

self-deception ['selfdɪ'sepʃən] *n* aveuglement *m*

self-defeating ['selfdɪ'fiːtɪŋ] *adj* qui va à l'encontre du but recherché

self-defense ['selfdɪ'fens] *n* autodéfense *f; Law* légitime défense *f*; **in s.** en état de légitime défense

self-denial ['selfdɪ'naɪəl] *n* abnégation *f*

self-destruct ['selfdɪ'strʌkt] *vi* s'autodétruire

self-determination ['selfdɪtɜːmɪ'neɪʃən] *n* autodétermination *f*

self-discipline ['self'dɪsɪplɪn] *n* autodiscipline *f*

self-doubt ['self'daʊt] *n* manque *m* de confiance en soi

self-effacing ['selfɪ'feɪsɪŋ] *adj* effacé(e)

self-employed ['selfɪm'plɔɪd] *adj* indépendant(e)

self-esteem [selfə'stiːm] *n* confiance *f* en soi

self-evident ['self'evɪdənt] *adj* évident(e)

self-explanatory ['selfɪk'splænətərɪ] *adj* **to be s.** se passer d'explications

self-expression ['selfɪk'spreʃən] *n* expression *f* individuelle

self-government ['self'gʌvənmənt] *n* autonomie *f*

self-help ['self'help] *n* **s. book** = livre pour apprendre à résoudre ses problèmes par soi-même; **s. group** groupe *m* d'entraide

self-important ['selfɪm'pɔːtənt] *adj* suffisant(e)

self-indulgent ['selfɪn'dʌldʒənt] *adj (person)* qui ne se refuse rien; *(book, movie)* complaisant(e)

self-inflicted ['selfɪn'flɪktɪd] *adj* que l'on s'inflige à soi-même

self-interest ['self'ɪntərest] *n* intérêt *m* personnel

selfish ['selfɪʃ] *adj* égoïste

selfishness ['selfɪʃnɪs] *n* égoïsme *m*

self-knowledge ['self'nɒlɪdʒ] *n* connaissance *f* de soi

selfless ['selflɪs] *adj* désintéressé(e)

self-made man ['selfmeɪd'mæn] *n* self-made-man *m*

self-pity ['self'pɪtɪ] *n* apitoiement *m* sur son propre sort; **to be full of s.** s'apitoyer sur son sort

self-portrait ['self'pɔːtreɪt] *n* autoportrait *m*

self-possessed ['selfpə'zest] *adj* qui a une grande maîtrise de soi

self-preservation ['selfprezə'veɪʃən] *n* **instinct for s.** instinct *m* de conservation

self-reliant ['selfrɪ'laɪənt] *adj* indépendant(e)

self-respect ['selfrɪ'spekt] *n* amour-propre *m*

self-respecting ['selfrɪ'spektɪŋ] *adj* qui se respecte

self-restraint ['selfrɪs'treɪnt] *n* retenue *f*, maîtrise *f* de soi

self-righteous ['self'raɪtʃəs] *adj* suffisant(e)

self-rising flour ['selfraɪzɪŋ'flaʊə(r)] *n* = farine contenant de la levure chimique

selfsame ['selfseɪm] *adj* **the s. day** le même jour exactement; **the s. thing** la même chose exactement

self-satisfied ['self'sætɪsfaɪd] *adj* suffisant(e), content(e) de soi

self-service ['self'sɜːvɪs] **1** *n* self-service *m*
2 *adj* self-service

self-starter ['self'stɑːtə(r)] *n (person)* personne *f* très motivée

self-styled ['selfstaɪld] *adj* prétendu(e), soi-disant *inv*

self-sufficient ['selfsə'fɪʃənt] *adj (person)* indépendant(e); *(country)* auto-suffisant(e)

self-tan ['self'tæn], **self-tanning cream** ['self'tænɪŋkriːm] *n* autobronzant *m*

self-taught ['self'tɔːt] *adj* autodidacte

sell [sel] *(pt & pp* **sold** [səʊld]) **1** *vt* vendre; **to s. sb sth, to s. sth to sb** vendre qch à qn; **scandal sells newspapers** le scandale fait vendre les journaux; *Fig* **to s. oneself** *(present oneself)* se vendre; *Fig* **to s. sb an idea** faire accepter une idée à qn; *Fig* **to s. sb down the river** trahir qn
2 *vi (of product)* se vendre; *(of person)* vendre; **to s. like hot cakes** se vendre comme des petits pains; **s. date** date *f* limite de vente

▸**sell off** *vt sep (at reduced prices)* solder; *(clear)* liquider; *(privatize)* privatiser

▸**sell out 1** *vt sep* **(a) to be sold out** *(of book, item)* être épuisé(e); *(of show, concert)* afficher complet; **the tickets are sold out** il n'y a plus de billets **(b)** *(betray)* trahir, vendre
2 *vi* **(a) to s. out of sth** ne plus avoir de qch **(b)** *(betray beliefs)* renier ses principes

seller ['selə(r)] *n* vendeur(euse) *m,f; Econ* **s.'s market** marché *m* favorable au vendeur

selling ['selɪŋ] *n* vente *f*; **s. point** atout *m*; **s. price** prix *m* de vente

sell-off ['selɒf] *n (of state-owned company)* vente *f*

sellout ['selaʊt] *n* **(a) the play was a s.** il n'y avait plus de places pour cette pièce, la pièce a joué à guichets fermés **(b)** *(betrayal)* trahison *f*

selves [selvz] *pl of* **self**

semantic [sɪ'mæntɪk] *adj* sémantique

semantics [sɪ'mæntɪks] *n* sémantique *f*

semaphore ['seməfɔː(r)] *n* signaux *mpl* à bras

semblance ['sembləns] *n* semblant *m*

semen ['siːmən] *n* sperme *m*

semester [sɪ'mestə(r)] *n* semestre *m*

semi ['semɪ] *n Fam* **(a)** *(abbr* **semitrailer)** semi-remorque *m* **(b)** *(abbr* **semifinal)** demi-finale *f*

semiannual ['semɪ'ænjuːəl] *adj* semestriel(elle)

semiautomatic ['semɪɔːtə'mætɪk] *adj* semi-automatique

semicircle ['semɪsɜːkəl] *n* demi-cercle *m*

semicircular ['semɪ'sɜːkjʊlə(r)] *adj* semi-circulaire, en demi-cercle

semicolon ['semɪ'kəʊlən] *n* point-virgule *m*

semiconductor ['semɪkən'dʌktə(r)] *n Elec* semi-conducteur *m*

semiconscious ['semɪ'kɒnʃəs] *adj* à demi conscient(e)

semifinal ['semɪ'faɪnəl] *n* demi-finale *f*

semifinalist ['semɪ'faɪnəlɪst] *n* demi-finaliste *mf*

seminal ['semɪnəl] *adj* majeur(e), de première importance

seminar ['semɪnɑː(r)] *n* séminaire *m*

semi-precious ['semɪ'preʃəs] *adj* semi-précieux(euse)

semiquaver ['semɪkweɪvə(r)] *n Mus* double croche *f*

semi-skim milk ['semɪskɪm'mɪlk] *n* lait *m* demi-écrémé

Semite ['semaɪt] *n* Sémite *mf*

Semitic [sɪ'mɪtɪk] *adj (language)* sémitique; *(people)* sémite

semitone ['semɪtəʊn] *n Mus* demi-ton *m*

semitrailer ['semɪtreɪlə(r)] *n* semi-remorque *m*

semitropical ['semɪ'trɒpɪkəl] *adj* semi-tropical(e)

semolina [semə'liːnə] *n* semoule *f*

Senate ['senɪt] *n* **the S.** le Sénat

senator ['senətə(r)] *n* sénateur *m*

send [send] *(pt & pp* **sent** [sent]) *vt (letter, message, person)* envoyer; **to s. sb sth, to s. sth to sb** envoyer qch à qn; **to s. sb home** renvoyer qn chez soi; **to s. sb to prison** envoyer qn en prison; **to s. sb on an errand** envoyer qn faire une course; *Fig* **to s. sb/sth flying** envoyer qn/qch valser; **to s. sb into fits of laughter** faire rire qn aux larmes

▸**send away 1** *vt sep (person)* renvoyer
  2 *vi* **to s. away for sth** se faire envoyer qch

▸**send back** *vt sep* renvoyer

▸**send for** *vt insep (help, supplies)* envoyer chercher; *(doctor)* faire venir

▸**send in** *vt sep* envoyer

▸**send off 1** *vt sep (letter, order)* expédier, envoyer
  2 *vi* **to s. off for sth** se faire envoyer qch

▸**send on** *vt sep (ahead)* expédier; *(later)* faire suivre

▸**send out 1** *vt sep* envoyer
  2 *vi* **to s. out for sth** envoyer chercher qch

▸**send up** *vt sep Fam (parody)* se moquer de

sender ['sendə(r)] *n* expéditeur(trice) *m,f*

send-off ['sendɒf] *n Fam* **to give sb a good s.** faire des adieux en règle à qn

send-up ['sendʌp] *n Fam* parodie *f*, pastiche *m*

Senegal [senɪ'gɔːl] *n* le Sénégal

Senegalese [senɪgə'liːz] **1** *n (person)* Sénégalais(e) *m,f*
  2 *adj* sénégalais(e)

senile ['siːnaɪl] *adj* sénile; **s. dementia** démence *f* sénile

senility [sɪ'nɪlɪtɪ] *n* sénilité *f*

senior ['siːnjə(r)] **1** *n* **(a)** *(in age)* **to be sb's s.** être l'aîné(e) de qn; **she's three years his s.** elle est son aînée de trois ans **(b)** *(in rank)* supérieur(e) *m,f*; **(c)** *Sch* élève *mf* de terminale; *Univ* étudiant(e) *m,f* de licence
  2 *adj* **(a)** *(in age)* aîné(e); **Thomas Smith, S.** Thomas Smith père; **he's two years s. to me** il a deux ans de plus que moi; **s. citizen** personne *f* du troisième âge **(b)** *(in rank, position)* supérieur(e); *Sch* **s. high (school)** lycée *m*; **(the) s. management** la direction; **s. officer** officier *m* supérieur; **s. partner** *(in company)* associé(e) *m,f* principal(e); **s. year** *Sch* terminale *f*; *Univ* licence *f*

seniority [siːnɪ'ɒrɪtɪ] *n (in age, length of service)* ancienneté *f*; *(in rank)* supériorité *f*

sensation [sen'seɪʃən] *n* **(a)** *(feeling)* sensation *f*; **a tingling/burning s.** une sensation de picotement/brûlure **(b)** *(excitement)* **to cause a s.** faire sensation

sensational [sen'seɪʃənəl] *adj* sensationnel(elle)

sensationalism [sen'seɪʃənəlɪzəm] *n* sensationnalisme *m*

sense [sens] **1** *n* **(a)** *(faculty)* sens *m*; **to come to one's senses** *(recover consciousness)* revenir à soi; *(see reason)* revenir à la raison; **s. of direction** sens de l'orientation; **s. of duty** sens du devoir; **s. of hearing** ouïe *f*; **s. of humor** sens de l'humour
  (b) *(rationality)* bon sens *m*, intelligence *f*; **there's no s. in staying/leaving** ça ne sert à rien de rester/partir
  (c) *(feeling)* sentiment *m*; **to lose all s. of time/reality** perdre toute notion du temps/de la réalité; **a s. of achievement** un sentiment de satisfaction
  (d) *(meaning)* sens *m*, signification *f*; **to make s.** être logique; **to make no s.** n'avoir aucun sens; **to make s. of sth** comprendre qch; **in a s.** dans un sens
  2 *vt (perceive)* sentir, deviner; **to s. that** sentir que

senseless ['senslɪs] *adj* **(a)** *(unconscious)* sans connaissance **(b)** *(pointless)* absurde

sensibilities [sensɪ'bɪlɪtɪz] *npl* susceptibilité *f*

sensible ['sensɪbəl] *adj* **(a)** *(rational)* sensé(e) **(b)** *(practical)* pratique **(c)** *Formal (aware)* **to be s. of sth** être sensible à qch

sensibly ['sensɪblɪ] *adv (rationally)* raisonnablement

sensitive ['sensɪtɪv] *adj* **(a)** *(person)* sensible (**to** à) **(b)** *(subject, issue)* délicat(e); *(document, information)* confidentiel(elle)

sensor ['sensə(r)] *n* détecteur *m*

sensory ['sensərɪ] *adj* sensoriel(elle); **s. organs** organes *mpl* sensoriels

sensual ['sensjʊəl] *adj* sensuel(elle)

sensuality [sensjʊ'ælɪtɪ] *n* sensualité *f*

sensuous ['sensjʊəs] *adj* sensuel(elle)

sent [sent] *pt & pp of* **send**

sentence ['sentəns] **1** *n* **(a)** *(phrase)* phrase *f* **(b)** *(in prison)* peine *f*; **to pass s.** prononcer la sentence
  2 *vt (criminal)* condamner (**to** à)

sententious [sen'tenʃəs] *adj Formal* sentencieux(euse)

sentient ['sentɪənt] *adj* sensible

sentiment ['sentɪmənt] *n* **(a)** *(opinion)* sentiment *m*; **my sentiments exactly** je suis tout à fait du même avis **(b)** *(sentimentality)* sentimentalité *f*

sentimental [sentɪ'mentəl] *adj* sentimental(e); **to have s. value** avoir une valeur sentimentale

sentimentality [sentɪmen'tælɪtɪ] *n* sentimentalité *f*, sensiblerie *f*

sentry ['sentrɪ] *n (pl* **sentries***)* sentinelle *f*; **to be on s. duty** être de garde; **s. box** guérite *f*

Seoul [səʊl] *n* Séoul

Sep. *(abbr* **September***)* septembre

separable ['sepərəbəl] *adj* séparable

separate 1 *adj* ['sepərət] *(parts)* séparé(e), distinct(e); *(box, room, document)* à part; *(occasion, attempt, entrance)* différent(e); *(organization)* indépendant(e); **fish and meat should be kept s.** le poisson et la viande doivent être gardés séparément; **he was kept s. from the others** on le laissait à l'écart *ou* on l'isolait des autres; **to lead s. lives** avoir chacun sa vie; *also Fig* **they went their s. ways** ils sont partis chacun de leur côté; *Can* **s. school** ≃ école *f* libre
  2 *vt* ['sepəreɪt] séparer (**from** de)
  3 *vi* ['sepəreɪt] se séparer (**from** de)

separation [sepə'reɪʃən] *n* séparation *f*

separatist ['sepərətɪst] *n Pol* séparatiste *mf*

sepia ['siːpɪə] *n* sépia *f*

sepsis ['sepsɪs] *n* infection *f*

Sept. *(abbr* **September***)* septembre

September [sep'tembə(r)] *n* septembre *m*; *see also* **May**

septet [sep'tet] *n* septuor *m*

septic ['septɪk] *adj* septique; **to go s.** s'infecter; **s. tank** fosse *f* septique

septicemia [septɪ'siːmɪə] *n* septicémie *f*

sepulcher ['sepəlkə(r)] *n Formal* sépulcre *m*

sequel ['siːkwəl] *n* **(a)** *(book, movie)* suite *f* (**to** de) **(b)** *(result)* conséquence *f* (**to** de)

sequence ['siːkwəns] *n* **(a)** *(order)* ordre *m*, suite *f*; **in s.** par ordre; **out of s.** dans le désordre **(b)** *(of numbers, events)* suite *f*, série *f*; *(in movie)* séquence *f*

sequencing ['siːkwənsɪŋ] *n Biol & Chem* séquençage *m*

sequential [sɪ'kwenʃəl] *adj* séquentiel(elle)

sequestrate [sɪ'kwestreɪt] *vt Law* séquestrer

sequestration [siːkwe'streɪʃən] *n Law* mise *f* sous séquestre

sequin ['siːkwɪn] *n* paillette *f*

sequined ['siːkwɪnd] *adj* pailleté, à paillettes

sequoia [se'kwɔɪə] *n* séquoia *m*

Serbia ['sɜːbɪə] *n* la Serbie

Serb ['sɜːb], **Serbian** ['sɜːbɪən] **1** *n* Serbe *mf*
  2 *adj* serbe

Serbo-Croat ['sɜːbəʊ'krəʊæt] **1** *n* serbo-croate *m*
  2 *adj* serbo-croate

serenade [serə'neɪd] **1** *n* sérénade *f*
  2 *vt* chanter une sérénade à

serene [sɪ'riːn] *adj* serein(e)

serenity [sɪ'renɪtɪ] *n* sérénité *f*

serf [sɜːf] *n Hist* serf (serve) *m,f*

serfdom ['sɜːfdəm] *n Hist* servage *m*

serge [sɜːdʒ] *n* serge *f*

sergeant ['sɑːdʒənt] *n (in police)* brigadier *m*; *Mil* sergent *m*

sergeant-major ['sɑːdʒənt'meɪdʒə(r)] *n* sergent-major *m*

serial ['sɪərɪəl] **1** *n (in magazine)* roman-feuilleton *m*; *(on TV)* feuilleton *m*

2 *adj* d'une série, en série; **s. killer** tueur(euse) *m,f* en série; **s. number** numéro *m* de série

serialize ['sɪərɪəlaɪz] *vt (in magazine)* publier en feuilleton; *(on TV)* adapter en feuilleton

series ['sɪərɪːz] *(pl* **series)** *n* série *f*

serious ['sɪərɪəs] *adj (person)* sérieux(euse); *(situation, problem, injury)* grave; **to be s. about doing sth** envisager sérieusement de faire qch; **are you s.?** tu parles sérieusement?; *Fam* **s. money** un bon paquet d'argent

seriously ['sɪərɪəslɪ] *adv* **(a)** *(in earnest)* sérieusement; **to take sb/sth s.** prendre qn/qch au sérieux; **to take oneself too s.** se prendre trop au sérieux; **you can't s. expect...** sérieusement, vous ne pensez pas que... **(b)** *(gravely, critically)* gravement

sermon ['sɜːmən] *n also Fig* sermon *m*

serotonin [serə'təʊnɪn] *n* sérotonine *f*

serpent ['sɜːpənt] *n Lit* serpent *m*

serpentine ['sɜːpəntaɪn] *adj Lit* qui serpente, sinueux(euse)

serrated [se'reɪtɪd] *adj* en dents de scie

serum ['sɪərəm] *n* sérum *m*

servant ['sɜːvənt] *n* domestique *mf*

serve [sɜːv] **1** *vt* **(a)** *(country, cause)* servir; **to s. one's own interests** servir ses propres intérêts **(b)** *(be useful to)* servir à, être utile à; **to s. a purpose** avoir une utilité; **it doesn't s. my purpose** cela ne me sert à rien; **it has served me well** ça m'a fait de l'usage; **if my memory serves me right** si ma mémoire est bonne **(c)** *(prison sentence)* purger; *(apprenticeship)* faire **(d)** *(meal, customer, drink)* servir; **s. chilled** *(on wine)* servir frais; **serves four** *(on package, in recipe)* pour quatre personnes **(e)** *Law* **to s. sb with a summons** remettre une assignation à qn **(f)** **(it) serves her right!** bien fait pour elle! **2** *vi* servir; **to s. as** *(be used as)* servir de **3** *n (in tennis)* service *m*; **(it's) your s.!** à toi de servir!

▶**serve up** *vt sep* servir

server ['sɜːvə(r)] *n* **(a)** *(in tennis)* serveur(euse) *m,f* **(b)** *Comput* serveur *m*

service ['sɜːvɪs] **1** *n* **(a)** *(with army, firm)* service *m*; *Mil* **the services** les forces *fpl* armées; **to do sb a s.** rendre un service à qn; **to be at sb's s.** être au service de qn; **to be of s. to sb** être utile à qn; **to offer one's services** offrir ses services; *Comput* **s. provider** *(for Internet)* fournisseur *m* d'accès **(b)** *(in store, restaurant)* service *m*; **s. included/not included** service compris/non compris; **s. charge** service; **s. elevator** ascenseur *m* de service; **s. industry** industrie *f* de services **(c)** *(system)* **postal/air/train s.** service *m* postal/aérien/des trains **(d)** *(maintenance) (of machine)* entretien *m*; *(of car)* révision *f*; **s. area** *(on highway)* aire *f* de service; **s. station** *(on highway)* station-service *f* **(e)** *(in church)* service *m*, office *m* **(f)** *(in tennis)* service *m*; **s. line** ligne *f* de service **(g)** *Old-fashioned* **to be in/go into s.** *(of servant)* être/devenir domestique **2** *vt (machine)* entretenir; *(car)* réviser

serviceable ['sɜːvɪsəbəl] *adj* **(a)** *(in working order)* en état de marche **(b)** *(durable)* résistant(e)

serviceman ['sɜːvɪsmən] *n* militaire *m*

servicewoman ['sɜːvɪswʊmən] *n* femme *f* soldat

servile ['sɜːvaɪl] *adj* servile, obséquieux(euse)

serving ['sɜːvɪŋ] *n (portion)* portion *f*; **s. dish** plat *m*; **s. hatch** passe-plat *m*

servitude ['sɜːvɪtjuːd] *n* servitude *f*, asservissement *m*

servo ['sɜːvəʊ] **1** *n (pl* **servos)** *Fam (servomechanism)* servomécanisme *m* **2** *adj* **s. brake** servofrein *m*

sesame ['sesəmɪ] *n* **(a)** **s. oil** huile *f* de sésame; **s. seeds** graines *fpl* de sésame **(b)** **open s.!** sésame, ouvre-toi!

session ['seʃən] *n* **(a)** *(period of activity)* séance *f*, session *f* **(b)** *(meeting)* séance *f*; **to be in s.** siéger **(c)** *(university, school term)* trimestre *m*; *(university year)* année *f* universitaire; *(school year)* année scolaire

SET® [esiː'tiː] *n Comput (abbr* **secure electronic transaction)** SET® *f*

set [set] **1** *n* **(a)** *(of keys)* jeu *m*; *(of saucepans)* série *f*, assortiment *m*; *(of books)* collection *f*; *(of tires)* train *m*; *(of problems, rules, symptoms)* ensemble *m*; **s. of teeth** dentition *f* **(b)** *(of people)* cercle *m* **(c)** *(TV, radio)* poste *m* **(d)** *(in theater)* décor *m*; *(in movies)* plateau *m* **(e)** *(in tennis)* set *m*; **s. point** balle *f* de set **2** *adj* **(a)** *(fixed) (look)* figé(e); *(ideas)* déterminé(e); *(price)* fixe; **to be s. in one's ways** tenir à ses habitudes; **s. menu** menu *m*; **s. phrase** expression *f* figée; **s. piece** *(in play, movie)* morceau *m* de bravoure; *(in sports)* tactique *f* **(b)** *(ready)* **to be (all) s. for sth/to do sth** être (fin) prêt(e) pour qch/à faire qch **(c)** *(determined)* **to be (dead) s. on sth** avoir fixé son choix sur qch; **to be (dead) s. on doing sth** être fermement décidé(e) à faire qch; **to be dead s. against** être formellement opposé(e) à **3** *vt (pt & pp* **set)** **(a)** *(place)* placer, mettre; *(jewel)* sertir; **to s. the table** mettre la table; **to s. a trap (for sb)** tendre un piège (à qn); **the novel/movie is set in San Francisco** le roman/film se passe à San Francisco **(b)** *(fix) (date, day, limit, price)* fixer, déterminer; *(watch)* régler; *(alarm clock)* mettre; *(record)* établir; **to s. a value on sth** estimer la valeur de qch; **to s. the scene** planter le décor; **the scene was set for the arms negotiations** tout était prêt pour les négociations sur les armements **(c)** *(cause to start)* **to s. sb thinking** faire réfléchir qn; **to s. sb free** libérer qn; **to s. sth on fire** mettre le feu à qch **(d)** *(task)* fixer; *(essay, homework)* donner **(e)** *(bone, fracture)* réduire **4** *vi* **(a)** *(of sun, moon)* se coucher **(b)** *(become firm) (of Jell-O®, concrete)* prendre; *(of broken bone)* se ressouder

▶**set about** *vt insep (task, job)* se mettre à; **to s. about doing sth** se mettre à faire qch

▶**set against** *vt sep* **(a)** *(cause to oppose)* **to s. sb against sb** monter qn contre qn **(b)** *(compare)* **to s. sth against sth** comparer qch à qch **(c)** *(deduct)* **to s. expenses against tax** déduire les dépenses des impôts

▶**set apart** *vt sep* distinguer (**from** de)

▶**set aside** *vt sep* **(a)** *(put down, disregard)* laisser de côté **(b)** *(save) (money)* mettre de côté; *(time)* réserver

▶**set back** *vt sep* **(a)** *(delay)* retarder **(b)** *Fam (cost)* coûter

▶**set down** *vt sep (put down)* poser, laisser; **to s. sth down in writing** coucher qch par écrit

▶**set forth** *vi Lit (depart)* partir, se mettre en route

▶**set in** *vi (of winter, mood)* s'installer; *(of fog, night)* tomber; *(of infection)* se déclarer

▶**set off 1** *vt sep* **(a)** *(bomb, explosion, alarm)* déclencher; *(argument, chain of events)* provoquer; **to s. sb off (laughing)** faire éclater qn de rire; **to s. sb off (crying)** faire éclater qn en sanglots **(b)** *(enhance)* mettre en valeur, rehausser **2** *vi (depart)* partir, se mettre en route

▶**set out 1** *vt sep (arrange)* disposer **2** *vi* **(a)** *(depart)* partir, se mettre en route; *(in job, task)* démarrer **(b)** *(intend)* **to s. out to do sth** avoir l'intention de faire qch

▶**set to** vi (**a**) (start working) s'y mettre (**b**) Fam (start arguing) recommencer à se disputer

▶**set up 1** vt sep (**a**) (statue) ériger; (tent, barrier) monter; (roadblock) mettre en place (**b**) (meeting) arranger; (company) créer, fonder; (system) mettre en place; **to s. up house** or **home** s'installer; **to s. sb up in business (as)** installer qn (comme) (**c**) (trick, frame) monter un coup contre; **to be set up** être victime d'un coup monté

2 vi (establish oneself) s'installer (**as** comme); **to s. up in business (as)** s'installer (comme)

▶**set upon** vt insep (attack) attaquer

setback ['setbæk] n revers m, échec m

settee [se'ti:] n canapé m

setter ['setə(r)] n (dog) setter m

setting ['setɪŋ] **1** n (**a**) (of story, movie) cadre m (**b**) (of sun) coucher m (**c**) (on machine) réglage m (**d**) (of hair) mise f en plis; **s. lotion** lotion f pour mise en plis (**e**) Comput **settings** paramètres mpl

2 adj (sun) couchant(e)

settle ['setəl] **1** vt (**a**) (put in place) installer; **to s. oneself** s'installer (**b**) (nerves) calmer; **to s. one's stomach** calmer ses douleurs d'estomac (**c**) (day, venue) décider, régler (**d**) (problem, dispute, bill) régler; **to s. one's affairs** régler ses affaires; Fam **that settles it!** c'est décidé!; Law **to s. a matter out of court** régler une affaire à l'amiable (**e**) (colonize) coloniser

2 vi (**a**) (of bird, insect) se poser; (of dust, liquid, beer) se déposer (**b**) (of person, family) s'installer, s'établir; (of crowd) se calmer, s'apaiser; **to s. into an armchair** s'installer confortablement dans un fauteuil (**c**) Law **to s. out of court** régler l'affaire à l'amiable

▶**settle down 1** vt sep (**a**) (make comfortable) installer (**b**) (make calm) calmer

2 vi (**a**) (make oneself comfortable) s'installer confortablement; **to s. down to work** se mettre au travail (**b**) (in new home) s'installer; (adopt steady lifestyle) se ranger, s'assagir; **to s. down with sb** se mettre en couple (**c**) (of situation, excitement) se calmer

▶**settle for** vt insep accepter, se contenter de

▶**settle in** vi (in new home) s'installer; (in new school, job) s'adapter

▶**settle on** vt insep se décider pour, choisir

▶**settle up** vi (pay bill) régler

settled ['setəld] adj (person, life) rangé(e), établi(e); (weather) stable

settlement ['setəlmənt] n (**a**) (of problem, dispute, bill) règlement m; **to reach a s.** parvenir à un accord (**b**) (village) village m; (colony) colonie f

settler ['setlə(r)] n colon m

set-to ['set'tu:] n Fam bagarre f

set-top box ['set'tɒpbɒks] n TV décodeur m numérique

setup ['setʌp] n Fam (arrangement) système m

seven ['sevən] **1** n sept m inv

2 adj sept; **the s. deadly sins** les sept péchés capitaux; Lit **to sail the s. seas** parcourir les mers; see also **eight**

seventeen [sevən'ti:n] **1** n dix-sept m inv

2 adj dix-sept; see also **eight**

seventeenth [sevən'ti:nθ] **1** n (**a**) (fraction) dix-septième m (**b**) (in series) dix-septième mf (**c**) (of month) dix-sept m inv

2 adj dix-septième; see also **eighth**

seventh ['sevənθ] **1** n (**a**) (fraction) septième m (**b**) (in series) septième mf (**c**) (of month) sept m inv

2 adj septième; **s. floor** sixième étage m; Scol **s. grade** = classe du primaire pour les 10–11 ans; **to be in s. heaven** être au septième ciel; see also **eighth**

seventieth ['sevəntɪɪθ] **1** n (**a**) (fraction) soixante-dixième m (**b**) (in series) soixante-dixième mf

2 adj soixante-dixième

seventy ['sevəntɪ] **1** n soixante-dix m inv; Belg & Suisse septante m inv

2 adj soixante-dix, Belg & Suisse septante; see also **eighty**

sever ['sevə(r)] vt (arm, finger) couper, trancher; Fig (link, relationship) rompre

several ['sevərəl] **1** adj plusieurs

2 pron plusieurs; **s. of us/them** plusieurs d'entre nous/eux

severance ['sevərəns] n rupture f; **s. pay** indemnité f de licenciement

severe [sɪ'vɪə(r)] adj (person, punishment, criticism) sévère; (pain) vif (vive); (illness, injury) grave; (winter) rude; (weather) très mauvais(e); (style) austère, sévère

severity [sɪ'verɪtɪ] n (of person, punishment, criticism) sévérité f; (of pain) intensité f; (of injury, illness) gravité f; (of winter) rigueur f; (of style) austérité f, sévérité f

sew [səʊ] (pp **sewn** [səʊn]) vt & vi coudre

▶**sew up** vt sep (**a**) (stitch) coudre (**b**) Fam **it's all sewn up** (decided, settled) l'affaire est dans le sac

sewage ['su:ɪdʒ] n eaux fpl usées ou d'égout; **s. disposal** évacuation f des eaux usées; **s. works** champ m d'épandage

sewer ['su:ə(r)] n égout m; Fam **to have a mind like a s.** avoir l'esprit mal tourné

sewing ['səʊɪŋ] n (activity) couture f; (work) ouvrage m; **s. machine** machine f à coudre

sewn [səʊn] pp of **sew**

sex [seks] n sexe m; **to have s. with sb** faire l'amour avec qn; **s. appeal** sex-appeal m; **s. education** éducation f sexuelle; **s. life** vie f sexuelle; **s. maniac** obsédé(e) m,f sexuel(elle); **s. shop** sex-shop m; **s. symbol** sex-symbol m; **s. therapist** sexothérapeute m/f; **s. therapy** sexothérapie f; **s. tourism** tourisme m sexuel; **s. tourist** touriste mf sexuel(elle)

▶**sex up** vt sep (**a**) (image, style) rendre plus sexy; **she's really sexed up her look** elle a adopté un look beaucoup plus sexy; **the company is trying to s. up the cellphone** la société essaie de rendre les portables plus intéressants (**b**) Fig (text, document, story) enjoliver

sexagenarian [seksədʒɪ'neərɪən] n séxagénaire mf

sexism ['seksɪzəm] n sexisme m

sexist ['seksɪst] n & adj sexiste mf

sexologist [sek'sɒlədʒɪst] n sexologue mf

sextant ['sekstənt] n sextant m

sextet [seks'tet] n sextuor m

sexton ['sekstən] n sacristain m, bedeau m

sexual ['seksjʊəl] adj sexuel(elle); **s. assault** agression f sexuelle; **s. discrimination** discrimination f sexuelle; **s. harassment** harcèlement m sexuel; **s. intercourse** rapports mpl sexuels; **s. reproduction** reproduction f sexuée

sexuality [seksjʊ'ælɪtɪ] n sexualité f

sexually ['seksjʊəlɪ] adv sexuellement; **s. transmitted disease** or **infection** maladie f sexuellement transmissible

sexy ['seksɪ] adj Fam sexy inv; Fig (car, hi-fi) branché(e)

Seychelles [seɪ'ʃelz] npl **the S.** les Seychelles fpl

Sgt. (abbr **Sergeant**) Sgt

sh [ʃ] exclam chut!

shabbily ['ʃæbɪlɪ] adv (**a**) (furnished, dressed) pauvrement (**b**) (treat, behave) avec mesquinerie

shabbiness ['ʃæbɪnɪs] n (**a**) (of person, clothes, area) apparence f miteuse (**b**) (of treatment, behavior) mesquinerie f

shabby ['ʃæbɪ] adj (**a**) (dingy, worn out) miteux(euse) (**b**) (behavior, treatment) minable, mesquin(e)

shack [ʃæk] n cabane f, hutte f

▶**shack up** vi Fam **to s. up with sb** se mettre à la colle avec qn

shackle ['ʃækəl] **1** n **shackles** chaînes fpl, fers mpl

2 vt (prisoner) enchaîner

shade [ʃeɪd] **1** n (**a**) (shadow) ombre f; **in the s.** à l'ombre; Fig

to put sb in the s. éclipser qn; **shades of 1968/the Beatles** *(reminders, suggestions)* ça rappelle 1968/les Beatles **(b)** *(of color, meaning, opinion)* nuance *f*, ton *m*; **a s. better/longer** un tout petit peu mieux/plus long **(c)** *Fam* **shades** *(sunglasses)* lunettes *fpl* de soleil

2 *vt (from sun)* **to s. one's eyes** se protéger les yeux

shaded ['ʃeɪdɪd] *adj* **(a)** *(garden, path)* à l'ombre, ombragé(e) **(b)** *(area on diagram, map)* hachuré(e)

shading ['ʃeɪdɪŋ] *n (on drawing)* ombres *fpl*; *(on diagram, map)* hachure *f*

shadow ['ʃædəʊ] **1** *n* ombre *f*; **to cast a s.** projeter une ombre; *Fig* **to cast a s. over sth** jeter une ombre sur qch; **to be a s. of one's former self** n'être plus que l'ombre de soi-même; **without a s. of doubt** sans l'ombre d'un doute; **the s. of death/war** le spectre de la mort/de la guerre; **to have shadows under one's eyes** avoir des cernes, avoir les yeux cernés

2 *vt (follow)* filer, prendre en filature

shadowy ['ʃædəʊɪ] *adj (dark)* ombragé(e); *(form, outline)* vague

shady ['ʃeɪdɪ] *adj* **(a)** *(garden, lane)* ombragé(e) **(b)** *Fam (suspicious)* louche

shaft [ʃɑːft] **1** *n* **(a)** *(of golf club, tool)* manche *m*; *(of light)* rayon *m* **(b)** *(of mine)* puits *m*; *(for elevator)* cage *f*

2 *vt very Fam (cheat)* entuber

shag [ʃæg] *n* **(a)** *(tobacco)* tabac *m* **(b)** **s. (pile) carpet** moquette *f* à poils longs

shaggy ['ʃægɪ] *adj (hairy)* hirsute; *Fam* **s. dog story** histoire *f* sans queue ni tête

shah [ʃɑː] *n* schah *m*

shake [ʃeɪk] **1** *n* **(a)** *(action)* secousse *f*; **to give sb/sth a s.** secouer qn/qch; *Fig* **to give oneself a s.** se secouer; *Fam* **to have the shakes** avoir la tremblote; *Fam* **in two shakes (of a lamb's tail)** en un rien de temps; *Fam* **to be no great shakes** ne pas casser trois pattes à un canard **(b)** **(milk) s.** (milk-)shake *m*

2 *vt (pt* **shook** [ʃʊk], *pp* **shaken** ['ʃeɪkən]) *(person, box, bottle)* secouer; *(building)* faire trembler, ébranler; *Fig* **to s. sb's faith/trust** ébranler la foi/la confiance de qn; **to s. one's head** faire non de la tête; **to s. one's fist at sb** menacer qn du poing; **to s. hands with sb** serrer la main à qn; **to s. hands on a deal** conclure un accord par une poignée de mains

3 *vi* **(a)** *(of person, building, voice)* trembler; **to s. like a leaf** trembler comme une feuille **(b)** *Fam* **to s. on it** *(shake hands)* toper; **s. on it!** tope là!

▸**shake off** *vt sep (illness, depression)* sortir de; *(pursuer)* semer

▸**shake up** *vt sep* **(a)** *(upset)* secouer **(b)** *(reorganize)* réorganiser de fond en comble

shaken ['ʃeɪkən] *pp of* **shake**

Shakespearean [ʃeɪks'pɪərɪən] *adj* shakespearien(enne)

shake-up ['ʃeɪkʌp] *n Fam (reorganization)* chambardement *m*

shakily ['ʃeɪkɪlɪ] *adv (walk)* d'un pas vacillant; *(write)* d'une main tremblante; *(speak)* d'une voix tremblante

shaky ['ʃeɪkɪ] *adj (table, ladder)* branlant(e); *(handwriting)* tremblé(e); *(voice)* tremblant(e); *(health, position)* précaire

shale [ʃeɪl] *n* schiste *m* argileux

shall [stressed ʃæl, unstressed ʃəl] *modal aux v* **(a)** *(with first person)* *(expressing future tense)* **I s. be there** j'y serai; **where s. I sit?** où veux-tu que je m'asseye?; **I shan't say this more than once** je ne le dirai pas plus d'une fois; **as we s. see** comme nous le verrons **(b)** *(making suggestions, offers)* **s. I make some coffee?** veux-tu que je fasse du café?; **let's go in, s. we?** entrons, tu veux bien? **(c)** *Formal (with 2nd and 3rd person) (expressing determination)* **you s. pay for this!** tu me le paieras! **(d)** *(indicating general truth)* **all members s. be entitled to vote** tous les membres auront le droit de vote

shallot [ʃə'lɒt] *n* échalote *f*

shallow ['ʃæləʊ] *adj* **(a)** *(water, dish)* peu profond(e); **s. end** *(of swimming pool)* petit bain *m* **(b)** *Fig (person, mind)* superficiel(elle)

sham [ʃæm] **1** *n (trial, election)* comédie *f*, farce *f*; *(person)* imposteur *m*

2 *adj* feint(e); **a s. election** un simulacre d'élections

3 *vt (pt & pp* **shammed**) feindre, simuler

4 *vi* faire semblant

shamble ['ʃæmbəl] *vi* **to s. along** marcher en traînant les pieds

shambles ['ʃæmbəlz] *n* désordre *m*, pagaille *f*; **this place is a s.!** quel désordre!, quelle pagaille!

shame [ʃeɪm] **1** *n* **(a)** *(disgrace, guilt)* honte *f*; **to my s.** à ma grande honte; **s. on you!** tu devrais avoir honte!; **to put sb to s.** faire honte à qn **(b)** *(pity)* dommage *m*; **it's a s. (that...)** c'est dommage (que... + *subjunctive*); **what a s.!** quel dommage!

2 *vt* **(a)** *(cause to feel ashamed)* faire honte à; **to s. sb into doing sth** obliger qn à faire qch en lui faisant honte **(b)** *(bring shame on)* couvrir de honte

shamefaced ['ʃeɪmfeɪst] *adj* honteux(euse), penaud(e)

shameful ['ʃeɪmfʊl] *adj* honteux(euse), scandaleux (euse)

shamefully ['ʃeɪmfəlɪ] *adv* honteusement

shameless ['ʃeɪmlɪs] *adj* impudique; **to be s. about doing sth** n'avoir aucun scrupule à faire qch

shammy ['ʃæmɪ] *n* **s. (leather)** peau *f* de chamois

shampoo [ʃæm'puː] **1** *n* shampooing *m*

2 *vt (pt & pp* **shampooed**) **to s. one's hair** se faire un shampooing

shamrock ['ʃæmrɒk] *n* trèfle *m*

shandy ['ʃændɪ] *n* panaché *m*

shank [ʃæŋk] *n (of lamb, beef)* jarret *m*

shan't [ʃɑːnt] = **shall not**

shanty¹ ['ʃæntɪ] *n (hut)* baraque *f*, cabane *f*; **s. town** bidonville *m*

shanty² ['ʃæntɪ] *n (song)* chanson *f* de marins

shape [ʃeɪp] **1** *n* **(a)** *(form)* forme *f*; **what s. is it?** quelle forme cela a-t-il?; **to be the same s. as...** avoir la même forme que...; **to take s.** *(of plan)* prendre forme; *Fig* **in any s. or form** quel (quelle) qu'il (elle) soit; *Fig* **in the s. of** sous la forme de; *(person)* en la personne de **(b)** *(condition)* **to be in good/bad s.** *(of person)* être en bonne/mauvaise forme; *(of company, economy)* bien/mal marcher; **to get into/keep in s.** *(of person)* retrouver/garder la forme

2 *vt* **(a)** *(clay)* modeler; *(wood)* façonner **(b)** *Fig (perception, events, future)* influencer; *(character)* former

▸**shape up** *vi (a) (get organized) (of person)* progresser; *(of team, plans)* prendre forme **(b)** *(get fit)* se remettre en forme

shapeless ['ʃeɪplɪs] *adj* informe

shapely ['ʃeɪplɪ] *adj* bien fait(e)

shard [ʃɑːd] *n (of glass)* éclat *m*; *(of pottery)* tesson *m*

share [ʃeə(r)] **1** *n* **(a)** *(portion)* part *f*; **in equal shares** en parts égales; **to have a s. in sth** avoir une part dans qch; **to do one's s.** mettre la main à la pâte; *also Fig* **to get one's fair s. of sth** avoir sa part de qch **(b)** *Fin* action *f*; **s. capital** capital *m* social; **s. certificate** certificat *m* ou titre *m* d'actions; **s. option** option *f* d'achat des actions

2 *vt* partager

3 *vi* partager; **to s. in sth** partager qch; **s. and s. alike!** chacun sa part!

▸**share out** *vt sep* partager, répartir

shareholder ['ʃeəhəʊldə(r)] *n Fin* actionnaire *mf*

shareholding ['ʃeəhəʊldɪŋ] *n Fin* actionnariat *m*

shareware ['ʃeəweə(r)] *n Comput* shareware *m*, partagiciel *m*

shark [ʃɑːk] *n also Fig* requin *m*

sharp [ʃɑːp] **1** *adj* (**a**) *(knife)* bien aiguisé(e); *(pencil)* bien taillé(e); *(scissors, razor)* qui coupe bien; *(point)* aigu(uë); *(claws)* acéré(e)
(**b**) *(features)* anguleux(euse); *(turning, rise, fall)* brusque; *(photo, outline, focus)* net (nette); *(contrast)* marqué(e); *(hearing)* fin(e); *(eyesight)* perçant(e); *Fig* **to be at the s. end** être en première ligne
(**c**) *(intelligent)* vif (vive)
(**d**) *(harsh) (voice, words)* cinglant(e); *(person)* mordant(e); **to have a s. tongue** être mordant
(**e**) *(taste, sauce)* acide; *(sound)* perçant(e); *(pain, wind)* vif (vive)
(**f**) *(in music)* **C s.** do dièse
2 *adv* (**a**) *(punctually)* pile; **at four o'clock s.** à quatre heures pile *ou* précises
(**b**) *(immediately)* **to turn s. left/right** tourner tout de suite à gauche/à droite
(**c**) *(idiom) Fam* **look s.!** grouille-toi!
3 *n (in music)* dièse *m*

sharpen [ˈʃɑːpən] *vt* (**a**) *(knife, tool)* aiguiser; *(pencil)* tailler, *Can* affiler (**b**) *(pain)* accentuer; *(passion, desire)* exacerber; **to s. one's wits** faire travailler sa matière grise

sharpener [ˈʃɑːpənə(r)] *n (for knife)* aiguisoir *m* (à couteaux); *(for pencil)* taille-crayon *m*

sharp-eyed [ˈʃɑːpaɪd] *adj* observateur(trice)

sharply [ˈʃɑːplɪ] *adv* (**a**) *(contrast)* nettement (**b**) *(rise, fall, brake)* brusquement

sharpness [ˈʃɑːpnɪs] *n* (**a**) *(of knife)* tranchant *m* (**b**) *(of outline, photo)* netteté *f* (**c**) *(of mind, hearing, sight)* acuité *f* (**d**) *(of voice, words)* brusquerie *f* (**e**) *(of pain)* acuité *f*; *(of wind)* âpreté *f*

sharpshooter [ˈʃɑːpʃuːtə(r)] *n* tireur *m* d'élite

sharp-sighted [ʃɑːpˈsaɪtɪd] *adj* observateur(trice)

sharp-tongued [ʃɑːpˈtʌŋd] *adj* mordant(e)

shat [ʃæt] *pt of* **shit**

shatter [ˈʃætə(r)] **1** *vt* (**a**) *(glass, bone)* briser en mille morceaux; *Fig (hopes, silence, nerves)* briser; *(health)* ruiner (**b**) *Fam* **to be shattered** *(stunned)* être accablé(e); *(exhausted)* être crevé(e)
2 *vi* se briser en mille morceaux

shattering [ˈʃætərɪŋ] *adj* (**a**) *(defeat)* accablant(e); **it was a s. blow** ça a été un coup terrible (**b**) *Fam (stunning)* accablant(e); *(exhausting)* crevant(e)

shatterproof [ˈʃætəpruːf] *adj (glass)* Sécurit®; *(windshield, door)* en verre Sécurit®

shave [ʃeɪv] **1** *n* **to have a s.** se raser; *Fig* **that was a close s.** il était moins une
2 *vt* (**a**) *(face, legs)* raser; **to s. one's legs/head** se raser les jambes/la tête (**b**) *(wood)* raboter
3 *vi* se raser

▶**shave off** *vt sep (beard, hair, etc.)* se raser

shaven [ˈʃeɪvən] *adj* rasé(e)

shaver [ˈʃeɪvə(r)] *n* rasoir *m* électrique

shaving [ˈʃeɪvɪŋ] *n* (**a**) **s. brush** blaireau *m*; **s. foam** mousse *f* à raser (**b**) *(piece of wood)* copeau *m*; *(piece of metal)* rognure *f*

shawl [ʃɔːl] *n* châle *m*

she [ʃiː] **1** *pron* elle; **she's Scottish** elle est écossaise; SHE **hasn't got it!** ce n'est pas elle qui l'a!
2 *n* **it's a s.** *(of animal)* c'est une femelle

sheaf [ʃiːf] *(pl* **sheaves** [ʃiːvz]*) n (of corn)* gerbe *f*; *(of papers)* liasse *f*

shear [ʃɪə(r)] *(pp* **shorn** [ʃɔːn] *or* **sheared**) **1** *vt (sheep)* tondre; *Fig* **to be shorn of sth** être dépouillé(e) de qch
2 *vi (cut)* **to s. through sth** couper qch

shears [ʃɪəz] *npl* cisailles *fpl*

sheath [ʃiːθ] *n* (**a**) *(for sword, knife)* fourreau *m*; *(for electric cable)* gaine *f*; **s. knife** couteau *m* à gaine (**b**) *(contraceptive)* préservatif *m*

sheaves [ʃiːvz] *pl of* **sheaf**

shed¹ [ʃed] *n (in garden)* abri *m*, remise *f*; *(in factory)* atelier *m*

shed² [ʃed] *(pt & pp* **shed**) *vt (leaves)* perdre; *(tears)* verser; **to s. its skin** *(of snake)* muer; **to s. light on sth** jeter de la lumière sur qch; **to s. weight** perdre du poids; **to s. its load** *(of truck)* perdre son chargement

she'd [ʃiːd] = **she had, she would**

sheen [ʃiːn] *n (on metal, silk)* lustre *m*; *(on hair)* brillant *m*

sheep [ʃiːp] *(pl* **sheep**) *n* mouton *m*

sheepdog [ˈʃiːpdɒg] *n* chien *m* de berger

sheepfold [ˈʃiːpfəʊld] *n* parc *m* à moutons

sheepish [ˈʃiːpɪʃ] *adj* penaud(e)

sheepskin [ˈʃiːpskɪn] *n* peau *f* de mouton; **s. jacket** veste *f* en peau de mouton

sheer [ʃɪə(r)] *adj* (**a**) *(pure)* pur(e); **it's s. madness** c'est de la folie pure; **by s. chance** tout à fait par hasard (**b**) *(steep)* à pic *inv* (**c**) *(stockings, fabric)* très fin(e)

sheet [ʃiːt] *n (on bed)* drap *m*; *(of paper)* feuille *f*; *(of glass, ice, metal)* plaque *f*; *(of flame)* rideau *m*; **s. lightning** éclair *m* en nappe(s); **s. metal** tôle *f*; **s. music** partitions *fpl*

sheetfeed [ˈʃiːtfiːd] *n Comput* avancement *m* du papier

sheik(h) [ʃeɪk] *n* cheikh *m*

shekel [ˈʃekəl] *n* shekel *m*

shelf [ʃelf] *(pl* **shelves** [ʃelvz]*) n* (**a**) *(in cupboard, bookcase)* étagère *f*; (**set of) shelves** étagère; *Fig* **to be left on the s.** rester vieille fille; *Com* **s. life** *(of goods)* durée *f* de conservation avant vente (**b**) *(of cliff, rock face)* rebord *m*

shell [ʃel] **1** *n* (**a**) *(of snail, oyster, egg, nut)* coquille *f*; *(of lobster, tortoise)* carapace *f*; *(on beach)* coquillage *m*; *Fig* **to come out of one's s.** sortir de sa coquille (**b**) *(of building)* carcasse *f* (**c**) *(bomb)* obus *m*; **s. shock** psychose *f* traumatique *(à la suite d'une explosion)*
2 *vt* (**a**) *(nuts)* décortiquer; *(peas)* écosser; *(eggs)* écaler (**b**) *(bombard)* bombarder

▶**shell out** *Fam* **1** *vt sep (money)* casquer
2 *vi* **to s. out (for sth)** casquer (pour qch)

she'll [ʃiːl] = **she will, she shall**

shellfire [ˈʃelfaɪə(r)] *n* tirs *mpl* d'obus

shellfish [ˈʃelfɪʃ] *n (crustacean)* crustacé *m*; *(mollusk)* coquillage *m*; *(as food)* fruits *mpl* de mer

shelling [ˈʃelɪŋ] *n* bombardement *m*

shellshocked [ˈʃelʃɒkt] *adj (soldier)* commotionné(e) *(à la suite d'une explosion)*; *Fig* sous le choc

shelter [ˈʃeltə(r)] **1** *n (place, protection)* abri *m*; **to take s.** se mettre à l'abri, s'abriter
2 *vt* abriter (**from** de); *(criminal, refugee)* accueillir
3 *vi* s'abriter, se mettre à l'abri (**from** de)

sheltered [ˈʃeltəd] *adj (place)* abrité(e); *(life, childhood)* protégé(e); **s. housing** = logements spécialement conçus pour les personnes âgées

shelve [ʃelv] *vt (postpone)* mettre au placard

shelves [ʃelvz] *pl of* **shelf**

shelving [ˈʃelvɪŋ] *n* étagères *fpl*

shepherd [ˈʃepəd] **1** *n* berger *m*; **s.'s pie** ≃ hachis *m* Parmentier
2 *vt (sheep)* garder; *Fig (people)* guider, conduire

shepherdess [ʃepəˈdes] *n* bergère *f*

sherbet [ˈʃɑːbət] *n (sorbet)* sorbet *m*

sheriff [ˈʃerɪf] *n* shérif *m*

sherry [ˈʃerɪ] *n* sherry *m*, xérès *m*

she's [ʃiːz] = **she has, she is**

Shetland [ˈʃetlənd] *n* **the S. Islands, the Shetlands** les (îles *fpl*) Shetland *fpl*; **S. pony** poney *m* des Shetland

shiatsu, shiatzu [ʃɪˈætsuː] *n (massage)* shiatsu *m*

shield [ʃiːld] **1** *n (of knight) & Fig (protection)* bouclier *m*; *(police badge)* badge *m*; *(trophy)* trophée *m* en forme d'écusson

2 *vt (protect)* protéger (**from** de); **to s. one's eyes** se protéger les yeux

shift [ʃɪft] **1** *n* (**a**) *(change of position)* changement *m*; **a s. in meaning** un glissement de sens; **a s. to the right/left** *(in politics)* un revirement à droite/gauche; **s. key** *(on typewriter, computer)* touche *f* des majuscules; *Aut* **s. stick** levier *m* de vitesse (**b**) *(period)* poste *m*; *(workers)* équipe *f*; **to work (in) shifts** avoir un travail posté (**c**) **s. (dress)** robe *f* chasuble

2 *vt (move)* déplacer; *(stain)* enlever, faire partir; **to s. the blame onto sb** rejeter la responsabilité sur qn; *Aut* **to s. gears** changer de vitesse

3 *vi (move)* bouger; *(of stain)* partir

shiftless ['ʃɪftlɪs] *adj* fainéant(e)

shiftwork ['ʃɪftwɜːk] *n* travail *m* posté

shifty ['ʃɪftɪ] *adj (person)* louche; *(look)* fuyant(e)

shilling ['ʃɪlɪŋ] *n* shilling *m*

shimmer ['ʃɪmə(r)] **1** *n (of light)* scintillement *m*; *(of water)* miroitement *m*; *(of silk)* chatoiement *m*

2 *vi (of light)* scintiller; *(of water)* miroiter; *(of silk)* chatoyer

shimmering ['ʃɪmərɪŋ] *adj (light)* scintillant(e); *(water)* miroitant(e); *(silk)* chatoyant(e)

shin [ʃɪn] *n* tibia *m*; **s. guard** *or* **pad** *(in sport)* jambière *f*

▶**shin up** *(pt & pp* **shinned)** *vt insep (climb)* grimper à

shinbone ['ʃɪnbəʊn] *n* tibia *m*

shindy ['ʃɪndɪ] *(pl* **shindies)** *n Fam (din)* boucan *m*; **to kick up a s.** faire du boucan

shine [ʃaɪn] **1** *n* (**a**) brillant *m*, éclat *m* (**b**) *(idioms)* **to take the s. off sth** faire perdre son éclat à qch, ternir qch; *Fam* **to take a s. to sb** *(take a liking to)* se prendre d'amitié pour qn; *(get a crush on)* s'enticher de qn

2 *vt* (**a**) *(pt & pp* **shone** [ʃɒn]) *(light, torch)* braquer (**on** sur) (**b**) *(pt & pp* **shined)** *(polish)* faire briller

3 *vi (pt & pp* **shone** [ʃɒn]) briller; *Fig* **to s. at sth** *(excel)* briller en qch; **her face shone with joy** son visage rayonna de joie

shiner ['ʃaɪnə(r)] *n Fam (black eye)* œil *m* au beurre noir

shingle ['ʃɪŋgəl] *n* (**a**) *(wooden tile)* bardeau *m* (**b**) *(pebbles)* galets *mpl*

shingles ['ʃɪŋgəlz] *n (disease)* zona *m*; **to have s.** avoir un zona

shining ['ʃaɪnɪŋ] *adj* brillant(e); *Fig* **a s. example (of)** un parfait exemple (de)

shiny ['ʃaɪnɪ] *adj* brillant(e)

ship [ʃɪp] **1** *n* navire *m*; *Fig* **when my s. comes in** quand je serai riche

2 *vt (pt & pp* **shipped)** *(transport)* transporter; *(send)* expédier; *(take on board)* embarquer

▶**ship off** *vt sep Fam* expédier

shipboard ['ʃɪpbɔːd] *n Naut* **on s.** à bord

shipbuilder ['ʃɪpbɪldə(r)] *n* constructeur *m* naval

shipbuilding ['ʃɪpbɪldɪŋ] *n* construction *f* navale; **the s. industry** (l'industrie *f* de) la construction navale

shipload ['ʃɪpləʊd] *n* cargaison *f*; *Fig* **by the s.** en masse

shipmate ['ʃɪpmeɪt] *n Naut* camarade *m* de bord

shipment ['ʃɪpmənt] *n* cargaison *f*

shipowner ['ʃɪpəʊnə(r)] *n* armateur *m*

shipping ['ʃɪpɪŋ] *n (ships)* navires *mpl*; **s. agent** *(person)* agent *m* maritime; *(company)* agence *f* maritime; **shipping charges** frais *mpl* d'expédition; **s. lane** voie *f* de navigation

shipshape ['ʃɪpʃeɪp] *adj* rangé(e), en ordre

shipwreck ['ʃɪprek] **1** *n (disaster)* naufrage *m*; *(ship)* épave *f*

2 *vt* **to be shipwrecked** faire naufrage

shipwrecked ['ʃɪprekt] *adj* naufragé(e)

shipwright ['ʃɪpraɪt] *n Naut (company)* constructeur *m* naval; *(worker)* ouvrier(ère) *m,f* de chantier naval

shipyard ['ʃɪpjɑːd] *n* chantier *m* naval

shire ['ʃaɪə(r)] *n (British county)* comté *m*; **s. horse** shire *m*

shirk [ʃɜːk] **1** *vt (task)* éviter de faire; *(obligation, responsibility)* se dérober à

2 *vi (avoid work)* tirer au flanc

shirker ['ʃɜːkə(r)] *n* tire-au-flanc *mf inv*

shirt [ʃɜːt] *n* chemise *f*; *Fam* **keep your s. on!** on se calme!

shirtmaker ['ʃɜːtmeɪkə(r)] *n* fabricant(e) *m,f* de chemises

shirtsleeves ['ʃɜːtsliːvz] *npl* **to be in s.** être en bras de chemise

shirt-tail ['ʃɜːtteɪl] *n* pan *m* de chemise

shit [ʃɪt] *Vulg* **1** *n* (**a**) *(excrement)* merde *f*; *(mess)* bordel *m*; *(nonsense)* conneries *fpl*; **to take a s.** chier (**b**) *(nasty man)* salaud *m*; *(nasty woman)* salope *f* (**c**) *(idioms)* **to talk s.** dire des conneries; **to be in the s.** être dans la merde; **he doesn't give a s.** il n'en a rien à foutre; **to beat the s. out of sb** casser la gueule à qn; **to scare the s. out of sb** foutre une de ces trouilles à qn; **to be up s. creek (without a paddle)** être dans une merde noire

2 *vt (pt & pp* **shitted** *or* **shat** [ʃæt]) **to s. oneself** chier dans son froc

3 *vi* chier

4 *exclam* merde!

shitty ['ʃɪtɪ] *adj Vulg* (**a**) *(diaper, trousers)* dégueulasse (**b**) *(weather, job)* merdique; *(behavior, remark)* dégueulasse; **to feel s.** *(ill)* avoir la tête dans le cul; *(guilty)* se sentir merdeux(euse)

shiver ['ʃɪvə(r)] **1** *n (of cold, fear)* frisson *m*; **to send shivers down sb's spine** donner le frisson à qn

2 *vi* frissonner, trembler (**with** de)

shoal [ʃəʊl] *n (of fish)* banc *m*; *Fig (of people)* foule *f*

shock¹ [ʃɒk] *n (of hair)* crinière *f*

shock² [ʃɒk] **1** *n* (**a**) *(impact)* choc *m*; *(of earthquake)* secousse *f*; **s. absorber** amortisseur *m*; **s. tactics** tactique *f* de choc; *Mil* **s. troops** troupes *fpl* de choc; *also Fig* **s. wave** onde *f* de choc (**b**) *(emotional blow)* choc *m*, coup *m*; **I got a real s. when...** cela m'a vraiment fait un choc quand...; **to be in s.** être en état de choc (**c**) *(electric)* décharge *f* (électrique); **s. therapy** (traitement *m* par) électrochocs *mpl*

2 *vt (surprise, startle)* stupéfier; *(scandalize)* choquer; **to s. sb into doing sth** pousser qn à faire qch en lui faisant peur

shocked [ʃɒkt] *adj (startled)* stupéfié(e); *(scandalized)* choqué(e)

shocking ['ʃɒkɪŋ] *adj* (**a**) *(scandalous)* choquant(e); **s. pink** rose *m* bonbon (**b**) *(very bad)* atroce

shockproof ['ʃɒkpruːf] *adj (watch)* antichoc *inv*

shod [ʃɒd] *pt & pp of* **shoe**

shoddy ['ʃɒdɪ] *adj (goods)* de mauvaise qualité; *(workmanship)* mal fait(e); *(conduct)* méprisable

shoe [ʃuː] **1** *n* chaussure *f*; *(horseshoe)* fer *m* (à cheval); *Fig* **I wouldn't like to be in her shoes** je n'aimerais pas être à sa place; *Fig* **put yourself in my shoes** mets-toi à ma place; **s. polish** cirage *m*; **s. store** magasin *m* de chaussures

2 *vt (pt & pp* **shod** [ʃɒd] *or* **shoed)** *(horse)* ferrer

shoebrush ['ʃuːbrʌʃ] *n* brosse *f* à chaussures

shoehorn ['ʃuːhɔːn] *n* chausse-pied *m*

shoelace ['ʃuːleɪs] *n* lacet *m* (de chaussure)

shoemaker ['ʃuːmeɪkə(r)] *n (manufacturer)* bottier *m*; *(seller)* chausseur *m*

shoeshine ['ʃuːʃaɪn] *n (person)* cireur *m* de chaussures

shoestring ['ʃuːstrɪŋ] *n* (**a**) *Fam* **on a s.** avec trois fois rien; **s. budget** petit budget *m* (**b**) *lacet m* (de chaussure)

shone [ʃɒn] *pt & pp of* **shine**

shoo [ʃuː] *exclam* ouste!

▶**shoo away, shoo off** *vt sep* chasser

shoo-in [ʃuːɪn] *n Fam* **he's/she's a s.** il/elle gagnera à coup sûr; **it's a s.** c'est couru d'avance

shook [ʃʊk] *pt of* **shake**

shoot [ʃuːt] **1** *vt (pt & pp* **shot** [ʃɒt]) (**a**) *(fire)* *(bullet)* tirer; *(arrow)* & *Fig (glance)* lancer (**b**) **to s. sb** *(wound)* blesser qn par balle; *(kill)* tuer qn par balle; *(execute)* fusiller qn; **to be shot in the arm** recevoir une balle dans le bras; **to s. rabbits/grouse** chasser le lapin/la grouse; *Fig* **to s. oneself in the foot** compromettre ses chances; *Fam* **to s. the breeze** *or* **(the) bull** tailler une bavette

(**c**) *(movie, TV program)* tourner

(**d**) *(pass rapidly)* **to s. the rapids** franchir les rapides; **to s. the lights** *(in car)* brûler *ou* griller le feu rouge

(**e**) **to s. dice/pool** jouer aux dés/au billard

2 *vi* (**a**) *(with gun)* tirer (**at** sur); *(in soccer)* tirer, shooter

(**b**) *(move rapidly)* filer; **he shot into/out of the house** il se précipita dans/hors de la maison; **the pain shot up her left side** elle ressentit soudain une vive douleur au côté gauche

(**c**) **can I ask you something? – s.!** je peux te poser une question? – vas-y!

3 *n (of plant)* pousse *f*

4 *exclam Fam* zut!, mince!

▸**shoot down** *vt sep (person)* descendre; *(plane)* abattre

▸**shoot off 1** *vt sep Fam* **to s. one's mouth off** parler à tort et à travers; **he had to go and s. his mouth off** il a fallu qu'il ouvre sa grande gueule

2 *vi (leave quickly)* filer

▸**shoot out** *vi (emerge quickly)* jaillir

▸**shoot up** *vi* (**a**) *(of plant)* pousser vite; *(of child)* monter en graine; *(of buildings)* pousser comme des champignons (**b**) *(of rocket)* s'élever; *(of prices)* monter *ou* grimper en flèche (**c**) *Fam (with drugs)* se shooter

shooting [ˈʃuːtɪŋ] **1** *n* (**a**) *(gunfire)* coups *mpl* de feu; *(incident)* fusillade *f*; **s. stick** canne-siège *f* (**b**) *(of movie, TV program)* tournage *m*

2 *adj* **s. star** étoile *f* filante

shoot-out [ˈʃuːtaʊt] *n* fusillade *f*

shop [ʃɒp] **1** *n* (**a**) *(for goods)* magasin *m* (**b**) *(workshop)* atelier *m*; *Fig* **the s. floor** les ouvriers *mpl* (**c**) *(idiom) Fam* **to talk s.** parler boutique

2 *vi* faire ses courses; **to go shopping** faire des courses; *(for food)* faire ses courses; **to s. around** comparer les prix

shopaholic [ʃɒpəˈhɒlɪk] *n* **he's a real s.** il adore faire les magasins

shopkeeper [ˈʃɒpkiːpə(r)] *n* commerçant(e) *m,f*

shoplifter [ˈʃɒplɪftə(r)] *n* voleur(euse) *m,f* à l'étalage

shoplifting [ˈʃɒplɪftɪŋ] *n* vol *m* à l'étalage

shopper [ˈʃɒpə(r)] *n* personne *f* qui fait ses courses; *(customer)* client(e) *m,f*

shopping [ˈʃɒpɪŋ] *n* courses *fpl*; **to do the s.** faire les courses; **to do one's s.** faire ses courses; **s. bag** sac *m* à provisions, cabas *m*; **s. basket** panier *m* (à provisions); *Econ* panier de la ménagère; **s. cart** chariot *m*; **s. center** *or* **mall** centre *m* commercial; **s. list** liste *f* des courses

shopworn [ˈʃɒpwɔːn] *adj* défraîchi(e)

shore [ʃɔː(r)] *n (of sea)* rivage *m*; *(of lake)* bord *m*; **on s.** à terre; **to go on s.** *(from ship)* débarquer; **s. leave** permission *f* à terre

▸**shore up** *vt sep (house, wall)* étayer; *Fig (reputation)* consolider

shoreline [ˈʃɔːlaɪn] *n* littoral *m*

shorn [ʃɔːn] *pp of* **shear**

short [ʃɔːt] **1** *adj* (**a**) *(physically)* court(e); *(person)* petit(e); **Bill is s. for William** Bill est le diminutif de William; **the s. answer is no** en deux mots la réponse est non; **to have a s. temper** *or* **fuse** être soupe au lait; **s. story** nouvelle *f*

(**b**) *(in time)* court(e), bref (brève); **in s.** en bref; **to make s. work of sb/sth** expédier qn/qch; **s. and sweet** bref (brève)

(**c**) *(abrupt)* brusque, sec (sèche) (**with** avec)

(**d**) *(insufficient, lacking)* insuffisant(e); **to be in s. supply** manquer; **to be s. of sth** être à court *ou* manquer de qch; **I'm 50 cents s.** il me manque 50 cents; **little** *or* **not far s. of** *(almost)* pas loin de; **he's not far s. of forty** il n'est pas loin

de la quarantaine; **it was nothing s. of miraculous that she survived** c'est vraiment un miracle qu'elle ait survécu

2 *adv* (**a**) *(suddenly)* **to stop s.** s'arrêter net; **to bring sb up s.** arrêter net qn

(**b**) *(in length, duration)* **to stop s. of doing sth** se retenir tout juste de faire qch; **to cut sb s.** couper la parole à qn, interrompre qn; **to cut sth s.** abréger qch

(**c**) *(without)* **to go s. (of sth)** se priver (de qch)

(**d**) *(insufficiency)* **to be running s. of sth** n'avoir presque plus de qch; **to fall s. of sth** *(target)* ne pas atteindre qch; *(expectations)* ne pas répondre à qch; *Fig* **to sell sb s.** rouler qn; **to be taken** *or* **caught s.** être pris(e) d'un besoin pressant; **to buy s.** *(on Stock Exchange)* acheter à court terme; **to sell s.** *(on Stock Exchange)* vendre à découvert

3 *n Fam* (**a**) *(short movie)* court-métrage *m*

(**b**) *(short circuit)* court-circuit *m*

shortage [ˈʃɔːtɪdʒ] *n* pénurie *f*; **gas/food s.** pénurie d'essence/de nourriture; **housing s.** crise *f* du logement; **to have no s. of sth** ne pas manquer de qch

shortbread [ˈʃɔːtbred], **shortcake** [ˈʃɔːtkeɪk] *n* sablés *mpl* au beurre

short-change [ʃɔːt'(t)ʃeɪndʒ] *vt (in store)* ne pas rendre assez de monnaie à; *Fig (cheat)* escroquer

short-circuit [ʃɔːt'sɜːkɪt] **1** *n* court-circuit *m*

2 *vt also Fig* court-circuiter

3 *vi* se mettre en court-circuit

shortcomings [ˈʃɔːtkʌmɪŋz] *npl* défauts *mpl*

shorten [ˈʃɔːtən] *vt (skirt, text)* raccourcir; *(visit, task)* abréger

shortfall [ˈʃɔːtfɔːl] *n* manque *m*, insuffisance *f*

shorthaired [ˈʃɔːtheəd] *adj (cat, dog)* à poil(s) court(s); *(person)* aux cheveux courts

shorthand [ˈʃɔːthænd] *n* sténographie *f*, sténo *f*; **s. typist** sténodactylo *mf*

short-haul [ˈʃɔːthɔːl] *adj* moyen-courrier *m*

shortlist [ˈʃɔːtlɪst] **1** *n* = liste de candidats après une première selection

2 *vt* **to be shortlisted (for sth)** être parmi les candidats retenus (à qch)

short-lived [ʃɔːt'lɪvd] *adj* de courte durée

shortly [ˈʃɔːtlɪ] *adv* (**a**) *(soon)* bientôt; **s. after(wards)** peu (de temps) après (**b**) *(abruptly)* sèchement

short-range [ˈʃɔːtreɪndʒ] *adj (missile)* de courte portée

shorts [ʃɔːts] *npl (short trousers)* short *m*; *(underpants)* caleçon *m*

short-sighted [ʃɔːt'saɪtɪd] *adj Fig* peu clairvoyant(e)

short-sleeved [ʃɔːt'sliːvd] *adj* à manches courtes

shortstop [ˈʃɔːtstɒp] *n Sport* bloqueur *m*

short-tempered [ʃɔːt'tempəd] *adj* coléreux(euse)

short-term [ˈʃɔːtɜːm] *adj* à court terme

shot [ʃɒt] **1** *n* (**a**) *(act of firing, sound)* coup *m* (de feu); **to fire a s.** tirer; *Fig* **like a s.** sans hésiter; *Fig* **to take a s. in the dark** tenter le coup; *Fig* **to call the shots** faire la loi; **s. put** lancer *m* du poids (**b**) *(marksman)* tireur *m* (**c**) *(in soccer, rugby)* coup *m* de pied; *(in basketball)* lancer *m*; **good s.!** bien joué! (**d**) *(photograph)* photo *f*; *(of movie, TV program)* prise *f* de vue, plan *m* (**e**) *Fam (injection)* piqûre *f* (**f**) *(attempt)* tentative *f*, essai *m*; **to have a s. at sth/at doing sth, to give sth a s.** essayer qch/de faire qch (**g**) *(drink)* petit verre *m*

2 *pt & pp of* **shoot**

shotgun [ˈʃɒtgʌn] *n* fusil *m* de chasse; *Fam* **s. wedding** mariage *m* en catastrophe

should [ʃʊd] *modal aux v* (**a**) *(expressing obligation, desirability)* **you s. do it at once** vous devriez le faire tout de suite; **you s. have come earlier** vous auriez dû venir plus tôt; **she shouldn't have told them** elle n'aurait pas dû le leur dire

(**b**) *(expressing probability)* **the weather s. improve from now on** le temps devrait s'améliorer à partir de maintenant;

she s. have arrived by this time elle devrait être arrivée à l'heure qu'il est

(c) *(in exclamations, rhetorical questions)* why s. you suspect me? pourquoi me soupçonnez-vous?; who s. I meet but Martin! et qui a-t-il fallu que je rencontre? Martin!; he apologized – I s. think so, too! il s'est excusé – j'espère bien!

(d) *(in subordinate clauses)* he ordered that they s. be released il a ordonné leur libération; she insisted that he s. meet her parents elle a insisté pour qu'il rencontre ses parents

(e) *(in conditional clauses)* if he s. come *or Formal* s. he come, let me know s'il vient, fais-le-moi savoir

(f) *(expressing opinions, preferences)* I s. like a drink je prendrais bien un verre; I s. imagine he was rather angry j'imagine qu'il était plutôt en colère; I shouldn't be surprised if... cela ne m'étonnerait pas si...

shoulder [ˈʃəʊldə(r)] **1** *n (of person, meat)* épaule *f*; to stand s. to s. *(of two people)* se tenir l'un(e) contre l'autre; *Fig* to rub shoulders with sb côtoyer qn; *Fig* to be looking over one's s. être constamment sur ses gardes; *Fig* to cry on sb's s. pleurer sur l'épaule de qn; s. bag (sac *m*) besace *f*; s. blade omoplate *f*; s. pad épaulette *f*; s. strap *(of bag)* bandoulière *f*; *(of garment)* bretelle *f*

2 *vt* (a) *(push)* to s. one's way through a crowd se frayer un passage à travers la foule à coups d'épaule; to s. sb aside écarter qn d'un coup d'épaule (b) *(put on shoulder)* mettre sur son épaule; *Fig* to s. the responsibility endosser la responsabilité

shouldn't [ˈʃʊdənt] = should not

shout [ʃaʊt] **1** *n* cri *m*; shouts of laughter des éclats *mpl* de rire; give me a s. when you're ready appelle-moi quand tu seras prêt

2 *vt* crier; to s. sth at sb crier qch à qn

3 *vi* crier; to s. at sb crier après qn; to s. for help crier au secours; *Fig* to have something to s. about pouvoir être fier(ère) de qch

▶**shout down** *vt sep* to s. sb down huer qn

shouting [ˈʃaʊtɪŋ] *n* cris *mpl*

shove [ʃʌv] **1** *n* poussée *f*; to give sb/sth a s. pousser qn/qch

2 *vt & vi* pousser

▶**shove around** *vt sep Fam (bully)* chahuter

▶**shove off** *vi Fam (leave)* dégager

shovel [ˈʃʌvəl] **1** *n* pelle *f*

2 *vt* pelleter; *Fam* to s. food into one's mouth enfourner de la nourriture

shovelful [ˈʃʌvəlfʊl] *n* pelletée *f*

show [ʃəʊ] **1** *n* (a) *(exhibition)* exposition *f*; to be on s. être exposé(e); to put sth on s. exposer qch; s. jumper = cavalier spécialisé dans le jumping; s. jumping jumping *m*; *Pej* s. trial procès *m* à grand spectacle

(b) *(concert, play)* spectacle *m*; *(on TV, radio)* émission *f*; *Fig* to run the s. commander; s. business show-business *m*, monde *m* du spectacle; s. girl girl *f*; *Fam* to be a s. stopper être le clou du spectacle

(c) *(act of showing)* démonstration *f*, manifestation *f*; s. of hands vote *m* à main levée; it's all s. tout ça, c'est de la comédie; to do sth for s. faire qch pour épater la galerie

2 *vt (pp shown* [ʃəʊn]*)* (a) *(display)* montrer; *(picture)* exposer; *(courage, talent)* faire preuve de; to s. sb sth, to s. sth to sb montrer qch à qn; *Fig* to s. one's cards *or* one's hand abattre ses cartes; they had nothing to s. for all that work ils avaient fait tout ce travail pour rien; he won't s. his face around here again on ne le reverra pas de sitôt; to s. oneself se montrer; to s. a profit/a loss enregistrer un bénéfice/ une perte; you're showing your age ça ne te rajeunit pas!; to s. oneself to be... se révéler...

(b) *(indicate)* montrer, indiquer

(c) *(prove, demonstrate)* démontrer, prouver; it goes to s. that... cela montre bien que...

(d) *(teach)* montrer; to s. sb how to do sth montrer à qn comment faire qch

(e) *(movie)* passer; *(TV program)* diffuser

(f) *(escort, lead)* to s. sb the way montrer le chemin à qn; to s. sb to his/her room conduire qn à sa chambre; to s. sb around the town faire visiter la ville à qn

3 *vi* (a) *(be visible)* se voir (b) *(of movie)* passer

▶**show in** *vt sep (escort in)* faire entrer

▶**show off 1** *vt sep* exhiber

2 *vi* frimer

▶**show out** *vt sep (escort out)* reconduire, raccompagner

▶**show up 1** *vt sep* (a) *(reveal)* révéler (b) *(embarrass)* faire honte à

2 *vi* (a) *(stand out)* ressortir, se voir (b) *Fam (arrive)* se pointer

showbiz [ˈʃəʊbɪz] *n Fam* show-biz *m*, monde *m* du spectacle

showcase [ˈʃəʊkeɪs] *n* vitrine *f*

showdown [ˈʃəʊdaʊn] *n* confrontation *f*

shower [ˈʃaʊə(r)] **1** *n* (a) *(of rain)* averse *f*; *(of stones, insults)* pluie *f* (b) *(for washing)* douche *f*; to take a s. prendre une douche; s. cap bonnet *m* de douche; s. curtain rideau *m* de douche; s. gel gel *m* douche; s. head pomme *f* de douche (c) *(party)* = fête au cours de laquelle les invités offrent des cadeaux; baby s. = fête où les invités apportent des cadeaux pour le bébé

2 *vt* to s. sb with sth, to s. sth on sb couvrir qn de qch

3 *vi (take a shower)* se doucher

showery [ˈʃaʊərɪ] *adj* pluvieux(euse)

showing [ˈʃəʊɪŋ] *n (exhibition)* exposition *f*; *(of movie)* séance *f*

showman [ˈʃəʊmən] *n (at circus)* forain *m*; *Fig* cabotin *m*

showmanship [ˈʃəʊmənʃɪp] *n* sens *m* du spectacle

shown [ʃəʊn] *pp of* show

show-off [ˈʃəʊɒf] *n Fam* frimeur(euse) *m,f*

showpiece [ˈʃəʊpiːs] *n* joyau *m*

showroom [ˈʃəʊruːm] *n* magasin *m*

showstopping [ˈʃəʊstɒpɪŋ] *adj* sensationnel(elle)

showy [ˈʃəʊɪ] *adj* voyant(e)

shrank [ʃræŋk] *pt of* shrink

shrapnel [ˈʃræpnəl] *n* éclats *mpl* d'obus

shred [ʃred] **1** *n* lambeau *m*; in shreds en lambeaux; to tear sth to shreds mettre qch en lambeaux; *Fig (criticize)* mettre qch en pièces; *Fig* there isn't a s. of evidence il n'y a pas l'ombre d'une preuve

2 *vt (pt & pp shredded) (documents)* déchiqueter; *(food)* couper grossièrement

shredder [ˈʃredə(r)] *n (for paper)* déchiqueteuse *f*

shrew [ʃruː] *n* (a) *(animal)* musaraigne *f* (b) *(nagging woman)* mégère *f*

shrewd [ʃruːd] *adj (person)* perspicace; *(decision)* judicieux(euse)

shrewdly [ˈʃruːdlɪ] *adv* judicieusement

shriek [ʃriːk] **1** *n* cri *m* strident; shrieks of laughter hurlements *mpl* de rire; to give a s. pousser un cri strident

2 *vt* hurler

3 *vi* pousser un cri strident; to s. with laughter hurler de rire

shrift [ʃrɪft] *n* to give sb short s. envoyer qn promener

shrill [ʃrɪl] *adj* strident(e), aigu(uë)

shrimp [ʃrɪmp] *n* crevette *f*; s. boat crevettier *m*; s. net haveneau *m*

shrine [ʃraɪn] *n (tomb)* tombeau *m*; *(place)* lieu *m* de pèlerinage; *Fig* haut lieu *m*

shrink [ʃrɪŋk] **1** *vt (pt shrank* [ʃræŋk]*, pp shrunk* [ʃrʌŋk]*)* faire rétrécir

2 *vi* (a) *(of material)* rétrécir; *(of income, budget)* diminuer, se réduire (b) *(move back)* to s. from sth se dérober devant qch; to s. from doing sth répugner à faire qch

3 *n Fam (psychiatrist)* psy *mf*

shrinkage ['ʃrɪŋkɪdʒ] *n (of material)* rétrécissement *m*; *Fig (in sales, profit)* diminution *f*

shrink-wrapped [ʃrɪŋk'ræpt] *adj* emballé(e) sous film plastique

shrivel ['ʃrɪvəl] **1** *vt* dessécher
2 *vi* se dessécher
▸**shrivel up** *vi* se dessécher

shroud [ʃraʊd] **1** *n* linceul *m*; *Fig (of mystery, darkness)* voile *m*
2 *vt Fig* **to be shrouded in sth** être enveloppé(e) de qch

Shrove Tuesday ['ʃrəʊv'tjuːzdɪ] *n* Mardi *m* gras

shrub [ʃrʌb] *n* arbuste *m*

shrubbery ['ʃrʌbərɪ] *(pl* **shrubberies)** *n* jardin *m* d'arbustes

shrug [ʃrʌg] **1** *n* haussement *m* d'épaules
2 *vt (pt & pp* **shrugged) to s. one's shoulders** hausser les épaules
3 *vi* hausser les épaules
▸**shrug off** *vt sep* ignorer

shrunk [ʃrʌŋk] *pp of* **shrink**

shrunken ['ʃrʌŋkən] *adj* rétréci(e)

shudder ['ʃʌdə(r)] **1** *n (of person)* frisson *m*
2 *vi (of person)* frissonner; *(of vehicle)* vibrer; **I s. to think!** j'ai des frissons quand j'y pense!

shuffle ['ʃʌfəl] **1** *n* **(a) to walk with a s.** marcher en traînant les pieds **(b) to give the cards a s.** battre les cartes
2 *vt (papers)* brasser; *(cards)* battre
3 *vi (when walking)* traîner les pieds

shun [ʃʌn] *(pt & pp* **shunned)** *vt* fuir, éviter

shunt [ʃʌnt] *vt (train, railcars)* aiguiller; *Fam Fig (people)* transbahuter

shush [ʃʊʃ] **1** *vt* faire taire
2 *exclam* chut!

shut [ʃʌt] **1** *adj* fermé(e); *Fam* **to keep one's mouth s.** se taire
2 *vt (pt & pp* **shut)** fermer; **to s. the door on sb** fermer la porte au nez de qn; **to s. one's finger in the door** se coincer le doigt dans la porte; *Fam* **s. your mouth!** ferme-la!
3 *vi (of door)* se fermer; *(of store)* fermer
▸**shut down 1** *vt sep* fermer; *(production)* arrêter
2 *vi* fermer
▸**shut in** *vt sep (confine)* enfermer
▸**shut off** *vt sep* **(a)** *(electricity, water, funds)* couper **(b)** *(road, exit)* fermer **(c)** *(isolate)* isoler **(from** de)
▸**shut out** *vt sep* **(a)** *(exclude)* exclure; *(light, view)* bloquer **(b)** *(keep outside)* empêcher d'entrer; **to s. oneself out** s'enfermer dehors
▸**shut up 1** *vt sep* **(a)** *(confine)* enfermer **(b)** *(close)* fermer **(c)** *Fam (silence)* faire taire
2 *vi Fam (be quiet)* se taire

shutdown ['ʃʌtdaʊn] *n (of factory)* fermeture *f*

shut-eye ['ʃʌtaɪ] *n Fam* roupillon *m*; **to get some s.** roupiller

shutter ['ʃʌtə(r)] *n* **(a)** *(on window)* volet *m*; *(of store)* store *m*; **to put up the shutters** *(of store)* fermer le magasin **(b)** *(in camera)* obturateur *m*

shuttle ['ʃʌtəl] **1** *n* **(a)** *(in sewing, train, bus, plane)* navette *f*; **s. service** service *m* de navettes **(b)** *(in badminton)* volant *m*
2 *vt* véhiculer
3 *vi* faire la navette **(between** entre)

shuttlecock ['ʃʌtəlkɒk] *n* volant *m*

shy [ʃaɪ] **1** *adj* timide; **to be s. of sb** être intimidé(e) par qn; **to be s. of doing sth** éviter de faire qch à tout prix
2 *vi (pt & pp* **shied)** *(of horse)* s'effaroucher (**at** devant)
▸**shy away** *vi* **to s. away from sth/from doing sth** éviter qch/de faire qch

shyly ['ʃaɪlɪ] *adv* timidement

Siamese [saɪə'miːz] **1** *n (pl* **Siamese)** *(cat)* siamois *m*
2 *adj* siamois(e); **S. cat** chat *m* siamois; **S. twins** *(boys)* frères *mpl* siamois; *(girls)* sœurs *fpl* siamoises

Siberia [saɪ'bɪərɪə] *n* la Sibérie

Siberian [saɪ'bɪərɪən] **1** *n* Sibérien(enne) *m,f*
2 *adj* sibérien(enne)

sibling ['sɪblɪŋ] *n (brother)* frère *m*; *(sister)* sœur *f*; **s. rivalry** rivalité *f* entre frères et sœurs

sic [sɪk] *adv* sic

Sicilian [sɪ'sɪlɪən] **1** *n* Sicilien(enne) *m,f*
2 *adj* sicilien(enne)

Sicily ['sɪsɪlɪ] *n* la Sicile

sick [sɪk] **1** *adj* **(a)** *(ill)* malade; **to be s.** *(be ill)* être malade; *(vomit)* vomir; **to feel s.** *(ill)* être malade; *(nauseous)* avoir envie de vomir; *Fig* **it makes me s.!** ça me dégoûte!; *Fig* **to be worried s.** se faire un sang d'encre; **s. bay** infirmerie *f*; **s. leave** congé *m* de maladie; **s. pay** indemnité *f* de maladie **(b)** *(fed up)* **to be s. of sb/sth** en avoir assez de qn/qch; **to be s. and tired** *or* **s. to death of sb/sth** en avoir ras le bol de qn/qch **(c)** *(humor, joke)* de mauvais goût; *(person)* malsain(e); **to have a s. mind** avoir l'esprit dérangé
2 *npl* **the s.** les malades *mpl*

sicken ['sɪkən] *vt (make ill)* rendre malade; *Fig (disgust)* écœurer

sickening ['sɪkənɪŋ] *adj* écœurant(e)

sickle ['sɪkəl] *n* faucille *f*

sickly ['sɪklɪ] *adj* **(a)** *(person, complexion)* maladif(ive); *(plant)* rabougri(e); *(color, light, smile)* faible **(b)** *(taste, sentiment)* écœurant(e); **s. sweet** douceâtre

sickness ['sɪknɪs] *n (illness)* maladie *f*; *(nausea)* écœurement *m*

sickroom ['sɪkruːm] *n* chambre *f* de malade

side [saɪd] **1** *n* **(a)** *(of person, animal, object)* côté *m*; *(of mountain)* flanc *m*, versant *m*; **by sb's s.** aux côtés de qn; **s. by s.** côte à côte; *Fam* **to split one's sides (laughing)** se tordre de rire; **s. door/entrance** porte *f*/entrée *f* latérale
(b) *(of record)* face *f*; *(paper)* côté *m*
(c) *(adjacent area)* côté *m*; **on this/that s. (of)** de ce côté (de); **on the other s. (of)** de l'autre côté (de); **from all sides, from every s.** de toutes parts; **to move from s. to s.** osciller; **the left-/right-hand s.** le côté gauche/droit; **to lean to one s.** se pencher sur le côté; **to stand to one s.** se tenir à l'écart; **a pizza with salad on the s.** une pizza avec une salade; **s. dish** plat *m* d'accompagnement; **s. mirror** rétroviseur *m* extérieur; **s. salad** salade *f* *(pour accompagner un plat)*; **s. view** vue *f* latérale
(d) *(aspect)* côté *m*; **to look on the bright/gloomy s. (of things)** voir le bon/mauvais côté (des choses)
(e) *(in game)* camp *m*; *(in dispute)* côté *m*; **to be on sb's s.** être du côté de qn; **to take sides** prendre parti; **to change sides** changer de camp; **he had let the s. down** il nous/les/*etc.* avait fait faux bond
(f) *(secondary)* **s. effects** effets *mpl* secondaires; **s. issue** question *f* d'intérêt secondaire; **s. road** petite route *f*; **s. street** ruelle *f*
(g) *(idioms)* **on his mother's s.** *(of family)* du côté de sa mère; **to put sth to one s.** mettre qch de côté; **to take sb to one s.** prendre qn à part; **to be on the wrong s. of forty** avoir plus de quarante ans; **to get on the right s. of sb** se faire bien voir de qn; **to get on the wrong s. of sb** prendre qn à rebrousse-poil; **it's a bit on the expensive/long s.** c'est un peu cher/long; **to do sth on the s.** *(as extra job)* faire qch pour arrondir ses fins de mois; *Fam* **to have a bit on the s.** *(of man)* avoir une maîtresse; *(of woman)* avoir un amant
2 *vi* **to s. with** prendre le parti de; **to s. against** prendre parti contre

sidebar ['saɪdbɑː] *n Comput* menu *m* latéral

sideboard ['saɪdbɔːd] *n* buffet *m*

sideburns ['saɪdbɜːnz] *npl (facial hair)* pattes *fpl*

sidecar ['saɪdkɑː(r)] *n* side-car *m*

sidekick ['saɪdkɪk] *n Fam* acolyte *m*

sidelight ['saɪdlaɪt] *n* feu *m* de position

sideline ['saɪdlaɪn] **1** *n* (**a**) *(of soccer, football field)* ligne *f* de touche; *Fig* **to sit on the sidelines** rester sur la touche (**b**) *(business, job)* à-côté *m*; **we sell guidebooks as a s.** nous vendons également des guides

2 *vt Sport & Fig* mettre sur la touche

sidesaddle ['saɪdsædəl] *adv* **to ride s.** monter en amazone

sideshow ['saɪdʃəʊ] *n (at amusement park)* attraction *f*; *Fig* événement *m* mineur

side-splitting ['saɪdsplɪtɪŋ] *adj Fam* tordant(e)

sidestep ['saɪdstep] *(pt & pp* **sidestepped**) **1** *vt (tackle, player)* éviter; *Fig (question)* éluder

2 *vi (in boxing)* esquiver

sideswipe ['saɪdswaɪp] *n* remarque *f* désobligeante

sidetrack ['saɪdtræk] *vt* distraire

sidewalk ['saɪdwɔːk] *n* trottoir *m*

sideways ['saɪdweɪz] **1** *adj (look, movement)* de côté

2 *adv (move, walk)* latéralement; *(turn, fall, lean)* sur le côté

siding ['saɪdɪŋ] *n (on railroad)* voie *f* de garage

sidle ['saɪdəl] *vi* **to s. up to sb** se glisser vers qn

siege [siːdʒ] *n* siège *m*; **to lay s. to a town** assiéger une ville; **under s.** assiégé(e); **to have a s. mentality** se sentir persécuté(e)

Sierra Leone [sɪ'erəlɪ'əʊn] *n* la Sierra Leone

sieve [sɪv] **1** *n* crible *m*; *(in kitchen)* passoire *f*; *Fam* **to have a memory like a s.** avoir la tête comme une passoire

2 *vt* tamiser

sift [sɪft] **1** *vt (flour, sugar)* tamiser

2 *vi Fig* **to s. through sth** passer qch au crible

sigh [saɪ] **1** *n* soupir *m*

2 *vi* soupirer; *(of wind)* gémir

sight [saɪt] **1** *n* (**a**) *(faculty)* vue *f*; **to lose one's s.** perdre la vue (**b**) *(act of seeing)* **to catch s. of sb/sth** apercevoir qn/qch; **to lose s. of sb/sth** perdre qn/qch de vue; **I hate the s. of him** je ne peux pas le voir; **I can't stand the s. of blood** je ne supporte pas la vue du sang; **to shoot on s.** tirer à vue; **at first s.** à première vue; **it was love at first s.** ça a été le coup de foudre; **to know sb by s.** connaître qn de vue; **to buy sth s. unseen** acheter qch sans l'avoir vu

(**c**) *(range of vision)* **to come into s.** apparaître; **in s.** en vue; **to keep sb in s.** garder un œil sur qn; **out of s.** caché(e); **to put sth out of s.** cacher qch; **to keep out of s.** se cacher; *Prov* **out of s., out of mind** loin des yeux, loin du cœur

(**d**) *(of instrument, gun)* viseur *m*; *Fig* **to have sb/sth in one's sights** avoir qn/qch en vue; *Fig* **to have** *or* **to set one's sights on sb/sth** avoir des vues sur qn/qch

(**e**) *(spectacle)* spectacle *m*; **you're/it's a s. for sore eyes** c'est un plaisir de te voir/de voir ça; *Fam* **to look a s.** ne pas être beau (belle) à voir; **sights** *(of city)* attractions *fpl* touristiques

(**f**) *Fam (for emphasis)* **a damn s. easier/longer** bien plus facile/long (longue)

2 *vt (see)* apercevoir

sighted ['saɪtɪd] **1** *npl* **the s.** les voyants *mpl*

2 *adj (person)* voyant(e)

sighting ['saɪtɪŋ] *n* **several sightings of the fugitive have been reported** on a aperçu le fugitif à plusieurs reprises; **there have been several UFO sightings in the area** on a aperçu plusieurs ovnis dans les parages

sightless ['saɪtləs] *adj* aveugle

sight-read ['saɪtriːd] *(pt & pp* **sight-read** ['saɪtred]) *vt & vi* déchiffrer

sightseeing ['saɪtsiːɪŋ] *n* tourisme *m*; **to go s.** faire du tourisme

sightseer ['saɪtsiːə(r)] *n* touriste *mf*

sign [saɪn] **1** *n* (**a**) *(gesture, symbol, indication)* signe *m*; **to make**

a s. to sb faire un signe à qn; **it's a sure s. that...** on peut être sûr que...; **a s. of the times** un signe des temps; **there's no s. of an improvement** il n'y a rien qui annonce une quelconque amélioration; **there's no s. of it/him** je ne le vois nulle part; **she gave no s. of having heard** elle n'a pas semblé avoir entendu; **all the signs are that...** tout laisse à penser que...; **the equipment showed signs of having been used** on voyait que l'équipement avait déjà été utilisé; **s. language** langage *m* des sourds-muets

(**b**) *(notice)* panneau *m*; *(of store)* enseigne *f*; *(on road)* panneau de signalisation routière; **follow the signs for Miami** suivre la direction de Miami

2 *vt* (**a**) *(write signature on)* signer

(**b**) *(in sign language)* dire en langage des sourds-muets

(**c**) *(in sports)* engager

3 *vi* (**a**) *(write signature)* signer

(**b**) *(in sports)* signer (**for** avec)

▸**sign away** *vt sep (rights)* renoncer à

▸**sign for** *vt insep (delivery, package)* signer un reçu pour

▸**sign in** *vi (in factory)* pointer; *(in hotel)* signer le registre en arrivant

▸**sign off** *vi* (**a**) *(of radio, TV presenter)* terminer l'émission (**b**) *(close letter)* finir la lettre (**c**) *(approve)* **to s. off on an idea** approuver une idée

▸**sign out 1** *vt sep* **to s. sth out** *(book, equipment)* signer un registre pour emprunter qch

2 *vi (from hotel)* signer le registre à son départ

▸**sign up** *vi* (**a**) *(register)* s'inscrire (**for** à) (**b**) *(of soldier)* s'engager

signal ['sɪgnəl] **1** *n* signal *m*; **radio s.** signal *m* radiophonique; *Fig* **to send the wrong signals** ne pas être clair(e); **s. flare** fusée *f* éclairante; **s. rocket** fusée de signalisation; **s. tower** poste *m* d'aiguillage

2 *vt* (**a**) *(make gesture to)* faire signe à; **to s. sb to do sth** faire signe à qn de faire qch (**b**) *(be sign of)* être le signe de

3 *vi* (**a**) *(make gesture)* faire signe (**to** à) (**b**) *(in car)* clignoter

signalman ['sɪgnəlmən] *(pl* **signalmen**) *n* aiguilleur *m*

signatory ['sɪgnətərɪ] *(pl* **signatories**) *n* signataire *mf*

signature ['sɪgnətʃə(r)] *n* signature *f*; **s. tune** *(of radio, TV program)* indicatif *m*

signboard ['saɪnbɔːd] *n* enseigne *f*

signet ring ['sɪgnɪt'rɪŋ] *n* chevalière *f*

significance [sɪg'nɪfɪkəns] *n* (**a**) *(importance)* importance *f*; **of great s.** d'une grande importance; **of no s.** sans importance (**b**) *(meaning)* signification *f*

significant [sɪg'nɪfɪkənt] *adj (important)* important(e), considérable; *(meaningful)* significatif(ive); **s. other** partenaire *mf* *(dans une relation affective)*; *Psy* = personne dont on se sent très proche

significantly [sɪg'nɪfɪkəntlɪ] *adv* (**a**) *(appreciably)* nettement; **to vary/change s.** varier/changer considérablement (**b**) *(meaningfully)* d'une manière significative; **s., no one mentioned it** fait révélateur, personne n'en a parlé

signify ['sɪgnɪfaɪ] *(pt & pp* **signified**) *vt* signifier

signpost ['saɪnpəʊst] **1** *n* poteau *m* indicateur; *Fig* indice *m*

2 *vt* signaliser

Sikh [siːk] *n & adj* sikh *mf*

silage ['saɪlɪdʒ] *n* ensilage *m*

silence ['saɪləns] **1** *n* silence *m*; **to listen/watch in s.** écouter/regarder en silence; *Prov* **s. is golden** le silence est d'or

2 *vt* faire taire

silencer ['saɪlənsə(r)] *n (on gun)* silencieux *m*

silent ['saɪlənt] *adj (person, place)* silencieux(euse); *(letter)* muet(ette); **to fall s.** se taire; **to remain** *or* **to keep s.** garder le silence; **s. majority** majorité *f* silencieuse; **s. movie** film *m* muet; *Com* **s. partner** associé *(m)* commanditaire *m*; **s. protest** manifestation *f* silencieuse

silently ['saɪləntlɪ] *adv* silencieusement

silhouette [sɪlu:'et] **1** *n* silhouette *f*
2 *vt* **she was silhouetted against the light** sa silhouette se détachait à contre-jour

silica ['sɪlɪkə] *n* silice *f*

silicon ['sɪlɪkən] *n* silicium *m*; **s. chip** puce *f* électronique; **S. Valley** Silicon Valley *f* (centre de l'industrie électronique américaine, situé en Californie)

silicone ['sɪlɪkəʊn] *n* silicone *m*; **s. implants** implants *mpl* mammaires en silicone

silk [sɪlk] *n* soie *f*; **s.-screen printing** sérigraphie *f*

silkworm ['sɪlkwɜːm] *n* ver *m* à soie

silky ['sɪlkɪ] *adj* soyeux(euse); *(voice)* suave

sill [sɪl] *n (of window)* rebord *m*

silliness ['sɪlɪnɪs] *n* stupidité *f*

silly ['sɪlɪ] **1** *adj* idiot(e), stupide; **the s. thing is that...** ce qui est idiot, c'est que...; **to look s.** avoir l'air ridicule; **to say/to do something s.** dire/faire une bêtise; **to laugh/to worry oneself s.** mourir de rire/d'inquiétude; **to knock sb s.** assommer qn
2 *n Fam* bêta(asse) *m,f*

silo ['saɪləʊ] *(pl* **silos)** *n* silo *m*

silt [sɪlt] *n* vase *f*
▶**silt up** *vi* s'envaser

silver ['sɪlvə(r)] **1** *n (a) (metal)* argent *m*; *Prov* **every cloud has a s. lining** à quelque chose malheur est bon; **s. haired** aux cheveux argentés; **s. (medal)** médaille *f* d'argent; **s. paper** papier *m* d'argent; **s. plate** *(coating)* plaqué *m* argent; *(articles)* argenterie *f*; **the s. screen** le grand écran; **s. wedding** noces *fpl* d'argent *(b) (coins)* pièces *fpl* en argent *(c) (silverware)* argenterie *f*
2 *adj (a) (made of silver)* en argent *(b)* **s.(-colored)** argenté(e)

silver-plated [sɪlvə'pleɪtɪd] *adj* plaqué(e) argent

silversmith ['sɪlvəsmɪθ] *n* orfèvre *mf*

silverware ['sɪlvəweə(r)] *n* argenterie *f*

silverwork ['sɪlvəwɜːk] *n* orfèvrerie *f*

silvery ['sɪlvərɪ] *adj (color)* argenté(e); *(sound)* argentin(e)

simian ['sɪmɪən] *adj* simien(enne)

similar ['sɪmɪlə(r)] *adj* semblable, similaire (**to** à); **s. in appearance/size** d'apparence/de taille semblable; **they are very s.** ils se ressemblent beaucoup

similarity [sɪmɪ'lærɪtɪ] *(pl* **similarities)** *n* ressemblance *f*

similarly ['sɪmɪləlɪ] *adv* de la même façon

simile ['sɪmɪlɪ] *n* comparaison *f*

simmer ['sɪmə(r)] **1** *n* **at a s.** à feu doux
2 *vt* mijoter
3 *vi* mijoter; *Fig (of revolt, discontent)* couver; **to s. with rage** bouillonner de rage
▶**simmer down** *vi Fam* se calmer

simper ['sɪmpə(r)] *vi* minauder

simple ['sɪmpəl] *adj (a) (easy)* simple; **in s. terms** dit simplement; **the s. truth** la vérité pure et simple *(b) (unintelligent)* simplet(ette)

simple-minded [sɪmpəl'maɪndɪd] *adj (person)* simple d'esprit; *(ideas, belief)* naïf(ïve)

simpleton ['sɪmpəltən] *n* simple *mf* d'esprit

simplicity [sɪm'plɪsɪtɪ] *n* simplicité *f*

simplification [sɪmplɪfɪ'keɪʃən] *n* simplification *f*

simplify ['sɪmplɪfaɪ] *(pt & pp* **simplified)** *vt* simplifier

simplistic [sɪm'plɪstɪk] *adj* simpliste

simply ['sɪmplɪ] *adv (a) (in simple manner)* simplement *(b) (absolutely)* absolument *(c) (just)* simplement; **it's s. a question of time** c'est une simple question de temps; **she s. had to snap her fingers and...** elle n'avait qu'à claquer des doigts et...

simulate ['sɪmjʊleɪt] *vt* simuler

simulated ['sɪmjʊleɪtɪd] *adj (leather, marble)* faux (fausse); *(surprise, anger)* simulé(e)

simulation [sɪmjʊ'leɪʃən] *n* simulation *f*

simultaneous [saɪməl'teɪnɪəs] *adj* simultané(e); **s. broadcast** retransmission *f* simultanée; **s. translation** traduction *f* simultanée

simultaneously [saɪməl'teɪnɪəslɪ] *adv* simultanément

sin [sɪn] **1** *n* péché *m*; *Old-fashioned or Hum* **to be living in s.** *(of unmarried couple)* vivre dans le péché; *Fam* **it would be a s. to...** ce serait un crime de...
2 *vi (pt & pp* **sinned)** pécher

since [sɪns] **1** *adv* depuis; **long s.** depuis longtemps
2 *prep* depuis; **s. June/1984** depuis le mois de juin/1984; **s. then** depuis
3 *conj (a) (in time)* depuis que; **it's a long time s. I saw her** cela fait longtemps que je ne l'ai pas vue *(b) (because)* puisque

sincere [sɪn'sɪə(r)] *adj* sincère

sincerely [sɪn'sɪəlɪ] *adv* sincèrement; **Yours s.** *(ending letter)* Veuillez agréer, Monsieur/Madame, l'expression de mes salutations distinguées

sincerity [sɪn'serɪtɪ] *n* sincérité *f*; **in all s.** en toute sincérité

sinecure ['saɪnɪkjʊə(r)] *n* sinécure *f*

sinew ['sɪnjuː] *n* tendon *m*

sinewy ['sɪnjuːɪ] *adj* musclé(e)

sinful ['sɪnfʊl] *adj (act, life)* coupable; *(waste)* scandaleux(euse); **s. person** pécheur(eresse) *m,f*

sing [sɪŋ] *(pt* **sang** [sæŋ], *pp* **sung** [sʌŋ]) **1** *vt (song)* chanter
2 *vi (of person, bird, kettle)* chanter
▶**sing out** *vi (sing loudly)* chanter fort

Singapore [sɪŋə'pɔː(r)] *n* Singapour

Singaporean [sɪŋə'pɔːrɪən] **1** *n* Singapourien(enne) *m,f*
2 *adj* singapourien(enne)

singe [sɪndʒ] *vt* roussir

singer ['sɪŋə(r)] *n* chanteur(euse) *m,f*; **s. songwriter** auteur-compositeur-interprète *m*

singing ['sɪŋɪŋ] *n* chant *m*; **his s. is awful** il chante atrocement; **s. lessons** cours *mpl* de chant; **to have a fine s. voice** chanter admirablement

single ['sɪŋgəl] **1** *adj (a) (just one)* seul(e); **every s. day** tous les jours; **not a s. one** pas un(e); **don't say a s. word** ne dis pas un mot; *Fin* **s. currency** monnaie *f* unique; *Econ* **s. European market** marché *m* unique européen *(b) (not double)* **in s. figures** inférieur à dix; **in s. file** en file indienne; **s. bed** lit *m* à une place; **s. room** chambre *f* pour une personne *(c) (not married)* célibataire; **s. mother** mère *f* célibataire; **s. parent** parent *m* isolé; **s. parent family** famille *f* monoparentale
2 *n (a) (record)* single *m* *(b) (hotel room)* chambre *f* pour une personne *(c) (in tennis)* **singles** *(in tennis)* simple *m*
▶**single out** *vt sep* distinguer; **she was singled out for praise** on n'a choisi de faire des compliments qu'à elle

single-breasted ['sɪŋgəl'brestɪd] *adj (jacket, suit)* droit(e)

single-handedly ['sɪŋgəl'hændɪdlɪ] *adv* tout(e) seul(e)

single-income ['sɪŋgəl'ɪŋkʌm] *adj (family)* à salaire unique

single-minded ['sɪŋgəl'maɪndɪd] *adj (person)* résolu(e); *(determination, conviction)* farouche

single-sex school ['sɪŋgəl'seks'skuːl] *n* école *f* non mixte

singsong ['sɪŋsɒŋ] **1** *n (voice, tone)* voix *f* chantante
2 *adj (voice, tone)* chantant(e)

singular ['sɪŋgjʊlə(r)] **1** *n Gram* singulier *m*; **in the s.** au singulier
2 *adj (a) Gram* singulier(ère) *(b) (remarkable)* remarquable

singularly ['sɪŋgjʊləlɪ] *adv* remarquablement

Sinhalese [sɪnə'liːz] **1** *n (pl* **Sinhalese)** *(a) (person)* Cinghalais(e) *m,f* *(b) (language)* cinghalais *m*
2 *adj* cinghalais(e)

sinister ['sɪnɪstə(r)] *adj* sinistre

sink[1] [sɪŋk] *n (in kitchen)* évier *m*; *(in bathroom)* lavabo *m*

sink² (*pt* sank [sæŋk], *pp* sunk [sʌŋk]) **1** *vt* (**a**) (*ship*) couler; **to be sunk in thought** être perdu(e) dans ses pensées; *Fam Fig* **to be sunk** être fichu(e) (**b**) (*well*) creuser; **to s. one's teeth into sth** mordre à pleines dents dans qch; **to s. money into sth** investir des capitaux dans qch

2 *vi* (*in water, mud*) couler; **her heart sank** son cœur s'est serré; **his spirits sank** il a perdu tout son courage; **to s. into sb's memory** (*of information*) se graver dans la mémoire de qn; **to s. into oblivion** tomber dans l'oubli; **to s. into a deep sleep** sombrer dans un profond sommeil; **to s. into an armchair** s'affaler dans un fauteuil; **to s. to the ground** s'effondrer par terre; **to s. in sb's estimation** baisser dans l'estime de qn; **how could you s. so low?** comment peux-tu tomber aussi bas?

▶**sink in** *vi* (*of liquid*) pénétrer; (*of information*) être assimilé(e); *Fig* **it hasn't sunk in yet** je n'ai/il n'a/*etc.* pas encore digéré la nouvelle

sinking ['sɪŋkɪŋ] **1** *n* (**a**) (*of ship*) naufrage *m* (**b**) *Fin* **s. fund** fonds *m* d'amortissement

2 *adj* (*feeling*) d'angoisse; **with a s. heart** avec un serrement de cœur

sinner ['sɪnə(r)] *n* pécheur(eresse) *m,f*

sinuous ['sɪnjʊəs] *adj* (*river, curves*) sinueux(euse); (*snake, dancer*) qui ondule; (*movement*) ondulant(e)

sinus ['saɪnəs] *n* sinus *m*

sinusitis [saɪnə'saɪtɪs] *n* sinusite *f*

sip [sɪp] **1** *n* petite gorgée *f*; **to take a s. (of sth)** boire une petite gorgée (de qch)

2 *vt* (*pt & pp* **sipped**) siroter

3 *vi* **to s. at sth** siroter qch

siphon ['saɪfən] **1** *n* siphon *m*

2 *vt* siphonner

▶**siphon off** *vt sep* (*liquid*) siphonner; *Fig* (*money, supplies*) détourner

sir [sɜː(r)] *n* (**a**) (*form of address*) monsieur *m*; **Dear S./Sirs** (*in letter*) Monsieur/Messieurs (**b**) (*title*) **S. Clyde** sir Clyde (*titre de noblesse masculin*)

sire ['saɪə(r)] **1** *n* (**a**) (*father of animal*) père *m* (**b**) *Old-fashioned* (*address to sovereign*) sire *m*

2 *vt* engendrer

siren ['saɪərən] *n* sirène *f*

sirloin ['sɜːlɔɪn] *n* **s. (steak)** steak *m* d'aloyau

sissy ['sɪsɪ] (*pl* **sissies**) *n Fam* (*weak male*) poule *f* mouillée; (*effeminate male*) garçon *m* efféminé

sister ['sɪstə(r)] *n* (**a**) (*sibling, nun*) sœur *f*; **s. ship** sister-ship *m*, navire *m* jumeau (**b**) (*nurse*) infirmière-chef *f*

sisterhood ['sɪstəhʊd] *n* (**a**) (*community of nuns*) communauté *f* religieuse (**b**) (*solidarity*) solidarité *f* féminine

sister-in-law ['sɪstərɪnlɔː] (*pl* **sisters-in-law**) *n* belle-sœur *f*

sisterly ['sɪstəlɪ] *adj* (*advice, devotion*) de sœur

sit [sɪt] (*pt & pp* **sat** [sæt]) **1** *vt* **to s. a child on one's knee** asseoir un enfant sur ses genoux

2 *vi* (**a**) (*of person*) s'asseoir; **to be sitting** être assis(e); **to be sitting reading** être assis en train de lire; **s.!** (*to dog*) assis!; *Fam* **to s. tight** (*not move*) ne pas bouger de sa place; (*not take action*) ne rien faire (**b**) (*of assembly, court*) siéger; **to s. on a jury** faire partie d'un jury (**c**) (*of object*) **to be sitting on the radiator/outside** être sur le radiateur/dehors

▶**sit about, sit around** *vi* rester assis(e) à ne rien faire

▶**sit back** *vi* (**a**) (*lean back*) **to s. back in one's chair** s'installer confortablement sur sa chaise (**b**) *Fam* (*relax*) se détendre; (*not intervene*) ne rien faire

▶**sit down 1** *vt sep* asseoir; *Fam* **s. yourself down!** assieds-toi donc!

2 *vi* s'asseoir; **to be sitting down** être assis(e)

▶**sit in** *vi* (*at meeting*) assister (**on** à)

▶**sit on** *vt insep Fam* (**a**) (*not deal with*) laisser traîner (**b**) (*repress*) rembarrer

▶**sit out 1** *vt sep* (*not participate in*) ne pas participer à

2 *vi* (*in garden*) s'asseoir dehors

▶**sit through** *vt insep* rester jusqu'au bout de

▶**sit up** *vi* (**a**) (*straighten one's back*) se redresser; (*from lying position*) s'asseoir; *Fig* **to make sb s. up (and take notice)** secouer qn (**b**) (*not go to bed*) veiller

sitar ['sɪtɑː(r)] *n* sitar *m*

sitcom ['sɪtkɒm] *n* sitcom *m*

site [saɪt] **1** *n* (**a**) (*of building*) emplacement *m*; (*archeological*) site *m* (**b**) (**building**) **s.** chantier *m* (de construction) (**c**) *Comput* (*on Internet*) site *m*

2 *vt* situer

sit-in ['sɪtɪn] *n* occupation *f* des locaux

sitting ['sɪtɪŋ] **1** *n* (*of committee, for portrait*) séance *f*; (*for meal*) service *m*; **at one s.** d'un trait; **s. room** (*in house*) salon *m*

2 *adj* (**a**) (*seated*) assis(e); *Fam Fig* **s. duck** *or* **target** cible *f* facile (**b**) (*current*) *Pol* **s. member** député *m* en exercice

situate ['sɪtjʊeɪt] *vt* situer

situated ['sɪtjʊeɪtɪd] *adj* situé(e)

situation [sɪtjʊ'eɪʃən] *n* (**a**) (*circumstances*) situation *f*; **s. comedy** (*on TV*) sitcom *m* (**b**) (*location*) emplacement *m*

sit-up ['sɪtʌp] *n* **to do sit-ups** faire des abdominaux

six [sɪks] **1** *n* six *m inv*; *Fam* **it's s. of one and half a dozen of the other** c'est kif-kif; **at sixes and sevens** sens dessus dessous; *Fam* **s. feet under** six pieds sous terre

2 *adj* six; *see also* **eight**

six-figure ['sɪksfɪgə(r)] *adj* **a s. sum** une somme à six chiffres

six-pack ['sɪkspæk] *n* (**a**) (*of beer*) pack *m* de six (**b**) *Fam Hum* (*stomach muscles*) **to have a s.** avoir les abdos en tablette de chocolat; **he's got a great s.** il a des supers abdos

six-shooter ['sɪksʃuːtə(r)] *n* six-coups *m inv*

sixteen [sɪks'tiːn] **1** *n* seize *m inv*

2 *adj* seize; *see also* **eight**

sixteenth [sɪks'tiːnθ] **1** *n* (**a**) (*fraction*) seizième *m* (**b**) (*in series*) seizième *mf* (**c**) (*of month*) seize *m inv*

2 *adj* seizième; *see also* **eighth**

sixth [sɪksθ] **1** *n* (**a**) (*fraction*) sixième *m* (**b**) (*in series*) sixième *mf* (**c**) (*of month*) six *m inv*

2 *adj* sixième; **s. floor** cinquième étage *m*; *Scol* **s. grade** = classe du primaire pour les 10–11 ans; **s. sense** sixième sens *m*; *see also* **eighth**

sixtieth ['sɪkstɪɪθ] **1** *n* (**a**) (*fraction*) soixantième *m* (**b**) (*in series*) soixantième *mf*

2 *adj* soixantième

sixty ['sɪkstɪ] **1** *n* soixante *m inv*

2 *adj* soixante; *see also* **eighty**

size [saɪz] *n* (*of person, clothes*) taille *f*; (*of shoe*) pointure *f*; (*of place, object*) dimensions *fpl*; (*of country*) superficie *f*; (*of problem, undertaking*) ampleur *f*; *Fam* **that's about the s. of it** c'est à peu près ça; **s. 12 shoes** ≃ des chaussures du 44; **what s. do you take?** (*of clothes*) quelle taille faites-vous?; (*of shoes*) quelle est votre pointure?, vous chaussez du combien?; **to try sth (on) for s.** essayer qch pour voir si la taille convient

▶**size up** *vt sep* (*person*) jauger; (*situation*) évaluer

sizeable ['saɪzəbəl] *adj* non négligeable; (*improvement*) net(nette)

sizzle ['sɪzəl] **1** *n* grésillement *m*

2 *vi* grésiller

skate¹ [skeɪt] *n* (*fish*) raie *f*

skate² [skeɪt] **1** *n* patin *m*; *Fam Fig* **to get one's skates on** se dépêcher

2 *vi* (*on ice skates*) faire du patin à glace; (*on roller skates*) faire du roller; *Fig* **to s. around sth** tourner autour de qch

▶**skate over** *vt insep* (*deal with superficially*) survoler

skateboard ['skeɪtbɔːd] **1** *n* skateboard *m*, planche *f* à roulettes

2 *vi* faire du skate(board) *ou* de la planche à roulettes

skateboarder [ˈskeɪtbɔːdə(r)] *n* skateboardeur(euse) *m,f*, skateur(euse) *m,f*

skatepark [ˈskeɪtpɑːk] *n* skatepark *m*

skater [ˈskeɪtə(r)] *n* (*on ice*) patineur(euse) *m,f*; (*on rollerskates*) patineur(euse) *m,f* à roulettes; (*on skateboard*) skateur(euse) *m,f*

skating [ˈskeɪtɪŋ] *n* patinage *m*; **s. rink** (*for ice skating*) patinoire *f*; (*for roller skating*) piste *f*

skeletal [ˈskelɪtəl] *adj* squelettique

skeleton [ˈskelɪtən] *n* (**a**) (*of person*) squelette *m*; (*of building*) charpente *f*; *Fig* **to have a s. in the cupboard** *or* **closet** avoir un secret honteux; **s. staff/crew** personnel *m*/équipage *m* réduit; **s. key** passe-partout *m inv* (**b**) (*sled, sport*) skeleton *m*

skeptic [ˈskeptɪk] *n* sceptique *mf*

skeptical [ˈskeptɪkəl] *adj* sceptique

skeptically [ˈskeptɪklɪ] *adv* avec scepticisme

skepticism [ˈskeptɪsɪzəm] *n* scepticisme *m*

sketch [sketʃ] **1** *n* (**a**) (*drawing, description*) croquis *m*; **s. pad** bloc *m* à dessin (**b**) (*on stage, TV*) sketch *m*
2 *vt also Fig* esquisser

▸**sketch in** *vt sep also Fig* esquisser

▸**sketch out** *vt sep* ébaucher

sketchbook [ˈsketʃbʊk] *n* carnet *m* de croquis

sketchily [ˈsketʃɪlɪ] *adv* vaguement

sketchy [ˈsketʃɪ] *adj* vague (**about** à propos de)

skew [skjuː] *vt* (*distort*) fausser

skewer [ˈskjuːə(r)] **1** *n* brochette *f*
2 *vt* embrocher

ski [skiː] **1** *n* ski *m*; **s. boots** chaussures *fpl* de ski; **s. instructor** moniteur(trice) *m,f* de ski; **s. jump** saut *m* à skis; **s. jumper** sauteur(euse) *m,f* à ski; **s. lift** remontée *f* mécanique; **s. pants** fuseau *m*; **s. resort** station *f* de ski; **s. run** *or* **slope** piste *f* de ski; **s. stick** bâton *m* de ski; **s. tow** téléski *m*
2 *vi* (*pt & pp* **skied**) skier, faire du ski

skid [skɪd] **1** *n* (**a**) (*of car*) dérapage *m*; **to go into a s.** faire un dérapage (**b**) (*idioms*) *Fam* **to be on the skids** battre de l'aile; *Fam* **to be on s. row** être à la rue
2 *vi* (*pt & pp* **skidded**) déraper

skier [ˈskiːə(r)] *n* skieur(euse) *m,f*

skiing [ˈskiːɪŋ] *n* ski *m*; **to go s.** aller faire du ski; **s. instructor** moniteur(trice) *m,f* de ski

skill [skɪl] *n* (*ability*) qualités *fpl*; (*technique*) compétence *f*, connaissances *fpl*

skilled [skɪld] *adj* (*person, work*) qualifié(e); **to be s. in doing sth** être habile à faire qch; **s. worker** ouvrier(ère) *m,f* qualifié(e)

skillet [ˈskɪlɪt] *n* poêle *f* à frire

skillful [ˈskɪlfʊl] *adj* habile

skillfully [ˈskɪlfʊlɪ] *adv* habilement

skim [skɪm] (*pt & pp* **skimmed**) **1** *vt* (**a**) (*milk*) écrémer; (*soup*) écumer (**b**) (*surface*) effleurer; **to s. stones on water** faire des ricochets
2 *vi* **to s. along** *or* **over the ground** voler au ras du sol; **to s. over the water** raser la surface de l'eau

▸**skim off** *vt sep* (*fat, cream*) enlever; *Fig* (*money*) ponctionner

▸**skim through** *vt insep* (*novel, document*) lire en diagonale

skim milk [ˈskɪmˈmɪlk] *n* lait *m* écrémé

skimp [skɪmp] **1** *vt* lésiner sur; (*work*) bâcler
2 *vi* **to s. on sth** lésiner sur qch

skimpy [ˈskɪmpɪ] *adj* (*meal*) maigre; (*clothes*) étriqué(e)

skin [skɪn] **1** *n* (**a**) (*of person, animal, fruit, on milk, sauce*) peau *f*; **to be all s. and bone** n'avoir que la peau et les os; *Fam* **to jump out of one's s.** sauter au plafond; **by the s. of one's teeth** de justesse; **to save one's (own) s.** sauver sa peau; *Fam* **to get under sb's s.** taper sur les nerfs de qn; *Fam* **it's no s. off my nose** je m'en balance; **s. cancer** cancer *m* de la peau; **s. complaint** problème *m* de peau; **s. cream** crème *f* pour la peau; **s. disease** maladie *f* de peau; **s. diving** plongée *f* sous-marine; *Fam* **s. flick** (*porn movie*) film *m* porno; *Med* **s. graft** greffe *f* de peau; **s. patch** timbre *m* transdermique (**b**) *Fam* (*skinhead*) skin *mf*
2 *vt* (*pt & pp* **skinned**) (*animal*) écorcher; (*tomato*) peler; **to s. one's knees** s'écorcher les genoux

skinflint [ˈskɪnflɪnt] *n Fam* radin(e) *m,f*

skinhead [ˈskɪnhed] *n* skinhead *mf*

skinny [ˈskɪnɪ] *adj* maigre

skintight [ˈskɪntaɪt] *adj* moulant(e)

skip [skɪp] **1** *n* (*jump*) saut *m*
2 *vt* (*pt & pp* **skipped**) (*meal, page, stage*) sauter
3 *vi* (*of lambs, children*) gambader; (*with rope*) sauter à la corde

skipper [ˈskɪpə(r)] **1** *n* (*of ship, team*) capitaine *m*
2 *vt Fam* commander

skipping [ˈskɪpɪŋ] *n* saut *m* à la corde

skirmish [ˈskɜːmɪʃ] **1** *n Mil* escarmouche *f*; *Fig* accrochage *m*
2 *vi* s'engager dans une escarmouche

skirt [skɜːt] **1** *n* jupe *f*
2 *vt* (*village, hill*) contourner; **to s. around a problem** contourner un problème

skit [skɪt] *n* satire *f*

skittish [ˈskɪtɪʃ] *adj* (**a**) (*nervous*) nerveux(euse) (**b**) (*playful*) espiègle

skittle [ˈskɪtəl] *n* quille *f*

skulduggery [skʌlˈdʌgərɪ] *n* magouille *f*

skulk [skʌlk] *vi* rôder

skull [skʌl] *n* crâne *m*; **s. and crossbones** tête *f* de mort

skullcap [ˈskʌlkæp] *n* calotte *f*

skunk [skʌŋk] *n* (**a**) (*animal*) moufette *f*, *Can* bête *f* puante; *Fam Pej* (*person*) mufle *m* (**b**) *Fam* (*cannabis*) skunk *m*

sky [skaɪ] (*pl* **skies**) *n* ciel *m*; *Fam* **the s.'s the limit** tout est possible; *Fam* **to praise sb to the skies** porter qn aux nues; **s. high** (*price, costs*) astronomique

sky-blue [skaɪˈbluː] *adj* bleu ciel *inv*

skydiver [ˈskaɪdaɪvə(r)] *n* parachutiste *mf* (*qui pratique la chute libre*)

skydiving [ˈskaɪdaɪvɪŋ] *n* parachutisme *m* (*en chute libre*)

skylark [ˈskaɪlɑːk] *n* alouette *f* des champs

skylight [ˈskaɪlaɪt] *n* lucarne *f* faîtière

skyline [ˈskaɪlaɪn] *n* (*horizon*) horizon *m*; (*of city*) silhouette *f*

skyscraper [ˈskaɪskreɪpə(r)] *n* gratte-ciel *m inv*; *Mktg* **s. ad** skyscraper *m*

slab [slæb] *n* (**a**) (*of stone, concrete*) dalle *f*; (*of cake*) tranche *f*; (*of meat*) pavé *m*; (*of chocolate*) plaque *f* (**b**) (*in mortuary*) table *f* d'autopsie

slack [slæk] **1** *adj* (**a**) (*not tight*) mou (molle); **trade is s.** le commerce marche mal; **in s. periods** en période creuse (**b**) (*careless*) négligent(e)
2 *n* **to take up the s.** (*in rope*) tendre la corde; *Fig* prendre le relais
3 *vi Fam* se relâcher

▸**slack off** *vi* (*of rain*) se calmer; (*of trade, demand*) se ralentir

slacken [ˈslækən] **1** *vt* (*pace*) ralentir; (*rope*) détendre
2 *vi* (*of person, rope*) se relâcher; (*of speed*) se ralentir; (*of storm, wind*) se calmer; (*of energy, enthusiasm*) retomber

▸**slacken off** *vi* (*of rain*) se calmer; (*of trade, demand*) se ralentir

slacker [ˈslækə(r)] *n Fam* flemmard(e) *m,f*

slackness [ˈslæknɪs] *n* (**a**) (*negligence*) négligence *f*; (*laziness*) fainéantise *f* (**b**) (*of rope*) mou *m* (**c**) (*of business*) stagnation *f*

slacks [slæks] *npl* pantalon *m*

slag [slæg] *n* (*from coalmine*) scories *fpl*; **s. heap** terril *m*

slain [sleɪn] **1** *npl* **the s.** les morts *mpl*
2 *pp of* **slay**

slake [sleɪk] *vt Lit* **to s. one's thirst** étancher sa soif

slalom ['slɑːləm] *n* slalom *m*

slam [slæm] **1** *vt* (*pt & pp* **slammed**) (**a**) (*door*) claquer; (*lid, drawer*) fermer violemment; **to s. the door in sb's face** claquer la porte au nez de qn; **to s. sth down** flanquer qch (**b**) *Fam (criticize)* éreinter
2 *vi* (*of door*) claquer; **to s. on the brakes** freiner à fond
3 *n* (*of door*) claquement *m*

slander ['slɑːndə(r)] **1** *n* calomnie *f*
2 *vt* calomnier

slanderous ['slɑːndərəs] *adj* calomnieux(euse)

slang [slæŋ] *n* argot *m*

slant [slɑːnt] **1** *n* (**a**) (*slope*) pente *f* (**b**) (*point of view*) perspective *f*; (*bias*) parti *m* pris; **to put a s. on sth** présenter qch d'une manière partiale
2 *vt* (**a**) (*set at angle*) incliner (**b**) (*bias*) présenter avec parti pris
3 *vi* (*slope*) être incliné(e)

slanting ['slɑːntɪŋ] *adj* (*roof*) en pente; (*writing*) penché(e)

slap [slæp] **1** *n* (*with hand*) claque *f*; *also Fig* **a s. in the face** une gifle; **to get a s. on the wrist** (*reprimand*) se faire taper sur les doigts
2 *adv* **s. (bang) in the middle** en plein milieu
3 *vt* (*pt & pp* **slapped**) donner une claque à; **to s. sb's face, to s. sb in the face** gifler qn; **to s. sb on the back** donner une tape dans le dos à qn; *Fig* **to s. sb down** remettre qn à sa place; **to s. some paint on sth** passer un coup de peinture sur qch

slapdash ['slæpdæʃ] *adj* (*work*) fait n'importe comment *ou* à la va-vite; (*person*) négligent(e)

slapstick ['slæpstɪk] *n* **s. (comedy)** comique *m* tarte à la crème

slash [slæʃ] **1** *n* (**a**) (*cut*) coupure *f*, balafre *f* (**b**) *Typ* barre *f* oblique
2 *vt* (*cut*) taillader, balafrer; (*reduce*) réduire considérablement; **prices slashed** (*sign*) prix sacrifiés

slat [slæt] *n* latte *f*

slate [sleɪt] **1** *n* (**a**) (*stone*) ardoise *f*; **s. gray** ardoise *m inv*; **s. quarry** ardoisière *f* (**b**) (*idioms*) *Fam* **put it on the s.** mettez-le-moi sur mon ardoise; **to wipe the s. clean** faire table rase
2 *vt Fam (criticize)* éreinter

slaughter ['slɔːtə(r)] **1** *n* (*of animals*) abattage *m*; (*of people*) massacre *m*
2 *vt* (*animals*) abattre; (*people*) massacrer; *Fam (defeat heavily)* massacrer

slaughterhouse ['slɔːtəhaʊs] *n* abattoir *m*

Slav [slɑːv] *n* Slave *mf*

slave [sleɪv] **1** *n* esclave *mf*; *Fam Fig* **s. driver** négrier *m*; **s. labor** travail *m* de forçat; **s. trade** commerce *m* des esclaves
2 *vi* trimer (**over** sur); **I've been slaving over a hot stove all day** j'ai passé ma journée aux fourneaux

slaver ['slævə(r)] *vi* baver

slavery ['sleɪvərɪ] *n* esclavage *m*

Slavic ['slɑːvɪk] *adj* slave

slavish ['sleɪvɪʃ] *adj* servile

Slavonic [slə'vɒnɪk] *adj* slave

slay [sleɪ] (*pt* **slew** [sluː], *pp* **slain** [sleɪn]) *vt Lit (kill)* tuer

sleaze [sliːz] *n Fam* (**a**) (*immorality*) côté *m* scabreux (**b**) (*in politics*) scandales *mpl*

sleazy ['sliːzɪ] *adj Fam (affair, place)* sordide; (*person*) louche

sled [sled] **1** *n* luge *f*; (*for transporting*) traîneau *m*
2 *vi* (*pt & pp* **sledded**) faire de la luge

sledgehammer ['sledʒhæmə(r)] *n* masse *f*; *Fig* **to use a s. to crack a nut** avoir recours à des moyens démesurés

sleek [sliːk] *adj* (*hair*) lisse et brillant(e); (*manner*) mielleux(euse)

▸**sleek down** *vt sep* **to s. down one's hair** se lisser les cheveux

sleep [sliːp] **1** *n* (**a**) (*rest*) sommeil *m*; **to go to s.** s'endormir; **to put sb to s.** (*anesthetize*) endormir qn; **to put an animal to s.** (*kill*) faire piquer un animal; *Fig* **to send sb to s.** (*bore*) endormir qn; **I won't lose any s. over it** cela ne va pas m'empêcher de dormir; **to walk in one's s.** être somnambule; **to talk in one's s.** parler en dormant; **my foot has gone to s.** je ne sens plus mon pied (**b**) (*in eye*) **to have s. in one's eyes** avoir les yeux chassieux
2 *vi* (*pt & pp* **slept** [slept]) dormir; *Euph* **to s. with sb** coucher avec qn; **I slept through the alarm** je n'ai pas entendu le réveil; **I'll s. on it** la nuit porte conseil; **to s. late** ne pas se réveiller à l'heure; **to s. rough** dormir dehors *ou* dans la rue
3 *vt* **the apartment sleeps four** on peut dormir à quatre dans l'appartement; **I haven't slept a wink all night** je n'ai pas fermé l'œil de la nuit

▸**sleep around** *vi Fam* coucher à droite et à gauche

▸**sleep off** *vt sep* **to s. off a hangover** cuver son vin

▸**sleep together** *vi* coucher ensemble

sleeper ['sliːpə(r)] *n* (**a**) (*person*) dormeur(euse) *m,f*; **to be a light/heavy s.** avoir le sommeil léger/lourd (**b**) *Rail (train)* train-couchettes *m* (**c**) (*sofa bed*) canapé-lit *m* (**d**) (*unexpected success*) révélation *f*

sleepily ['sliːpɪlɪ] *adv* d'un air endormi

sleeping ['sliːpɪŋ] **1** *n* **s. arrangements** couchage *m*; **s. bag** sac *m* de couchage; **s. car** (*on train*) wagon-lit *m*; **s. pill** somnifère *m*
2 *adj* endormi(e); *Prov* **let s. dogs lie** ne réveillez pas le chat qui dort

sleepless ['sliːplɪs] *adj* **to have a s. night** passer une nuit blanche, ne pas fermer l'œil de la nuit

sleepover ['sliːpəʊvə(r)] *n* = soirée entre fillettes, où les invitées restent dormir chez leur hôte

sleepwalk ['sliːpwɔːk] *vi* être somnambule

sleepwalker ['sliːpwɔːkə(r)] *n* somnambule *mf*

sleepy ['sliːpɪ] *adj* somnolent(e); **to be** *or* **to feel s.** avoir sommeil

sleet [sliːt] **1** *n* neige *f* fondue
2 *vi* **it's sleeting** il tombe de la neige fondue

sleeve [sliːv] *n* (**a**) (*of shirt, jacket*) manche *f*; *Fig* **he's still got something up his s.** il n'a pas encore dit son dernier mot (**b**) (*of record*) pochette *f*

sleeveless ['sliːvlɪs] *adj* sans manches

sleigh [sleɪ] *n* traîneau *m*

sleight [slaɪt] *n* **s. of hand** tour *m* de passe-passe

slender ['slendə(r)] *adj* (**a**) (*person, figure*) svelte; (*waist*) fin(e) (**b**) (*hope*) mince; (*income*) maigre; (*majority*) faible; **of s. means** qui a peu de moyens

slenderize ['slendəraɪz] *Fam* **1** *vi* maigrir, mincir
2 *vt* amincir

slept [slept] *pt & pp of* **sleep**

sleuth [sluːθ] *n Fam* limier *m*

slew [sluː] *pt of* **slay**

slice [slaɪs] **1** *n* (*of bread, meat, cake*) tranche *f*; (*of pizza*) part *f*; (*of cheese*) lamelle *f*; (*of salami*) rondelle *f*; *Fig* **a s. of the profits** une part des bénéfices
2 *vt* (**a**) (*bread, meat, cake*) couper en tranches; (*cheese*) couper en lamelles; (*salami*) couper en rondelles; **to s. sth in two** *or* **in half** couper qch en deux (**b**) (*in sport*) slicer

▸**slice off** *vt sep* couper

▸**slice through** *vt insep* trancher

▸**slice up** *vt sep* couper en tranches

sliced bread ['slaɪst'bred] *n* pain *m* en tranches; *Fam* **it's the best thing since s.** on n'a rien fait de mieux depuis l'invention du fil à couper le beurre

slick [slɪk] **1** *adj* (**a**) (*campaign, event*) bien mené(e) (**b**) *Pej* (*reply, person, manner*) habile (**c**) (*surface, tire*) lisse
2 *n* (*oil*) **s.** marée *f* noire

▶**slick back** *vt sep* **to s. one's hair back** se lisser les cheveux

slide [slaɪd] **1** *n* (**a**) *(fall) (in prices, popularity)* chute *f*; *Math* **s. rule** règle *f* à calcul (**b**) *(in playground)* toboggan *m* (**c**) *(for microscope)* lame *f*; *(photographic)* diapositive *f*; **s. projector** projecteur *m* de diapositives; **s. show** diaporama *m*

2 *vt* (*pt & pp* **slid** [slɪd]) glisser; **s. the lid off** faites glisser le couvercle

3 *vi* (**a**) *(slip) (of person)* glisser; *(of door, hatch)* coulisser; **the door slid open** la porte coulissante s'est ouverte; *Fig* **to let things s.** laisser les choses se dégrader; **to s. down a rope** glisser le long d'une corde (**b**) *(move quietly)* se glisser

sliding ['slaɪdɪŋ] *adj* coulissant(e); **s. door** porte *f* coulissante; **s. scale** échelle *f* mobile

slight [slaɪt] **1** *adj* (**a**) *(small, unimportant)* léger(ère); **not the slightest danger/interest** pas le moindre danger/intérêt; **not in the slightest** pas du tout (**b**) *(person)* menu(e)

2 *n (affront)* affront *m*

3 *vt* blesser

slightly ['slaɪtlɪ] *adv* (**a**) *(to a small degree)* légèrement (**b**) **s. built** menu(e)

slim [slɪm] **1** *adj (person)* mince, svelte; *(book, chance, hope)* mince; *(majority)* faible

2 *vi* (*pt & pp* **slimmed**) faire un régime

▶**slim down 1** *vt sep Fig (budget, company)* réduire

2 *vi (of person)* perdre du poids; *Fig (of company)* réduire ses effectifs

slime [slaɪm] *n (mud)* vase *f*; *(of snail, slug)* bave *f*

slimmer ['slɪmə(r)] *n* personne *f* qui fait un régime amaigrissant

slimming ['slɪmɪŋ] *n* **s. can be bad for you** les régimes amaigrissants peuvent être dangereux pour la santé; **s. diet** régime *m* amaigrissant; **s. product** produit *m* amaigrissant

slimy ['slaɪmɪ] *adj (frog, snail)* visqueux(euse); *Pej (person)* mielleux(euse)

sling [slɪŋ] **1** *n* (**a**) *(for injured arm)* écharpe *f*; **he had his arm in a s.** il avait le bras en écharpe (**b**) *(weapon)* fronde *f*

2 *vt* (*pt & pp* **slung** [slʌŋ]) *(throw)* lancer; **to s. sth over one's shoulder** mettre qch sur son épaule

slingshot ['slɪŋʃɒt] *n* lance-pierres *m inv*

slink [slɪŋk] (*pt & pp* **slunk** [slʌŋk]) *vi* **to s. off** *or* **away** s'éclipser

slinky ['slɪŋkɪ] *adj (dress)* long (longue) et sexy

slip [slɪp] **1** *n* (**a**) *(fall)* chute *f*; *(of land)* glissement *m*; *(in prices, standards)* chute

(**b**) *(error)* erreur *f*; **a s. of the pen/tongue** un lapsus

(**c**) **to give sb the s.** semer qn

(**d**) *(of paper)* bout *m* de papier; *(printed)* bordereau *m*

(**e**) *(garment)* combinaison *f*; **(pillow) s.** taie *f* d'oreiller

2 *vt* (*pt & pp* **slipped**) (**a**) *(escape)* **her name has slipped my mind** son nom m'échappe; **the ship slipped its moorings** le bateau a quitté son mouillage

(**b**) *(put)* glisser; **to s. sth into the conversation** glisser qch dans la conversation; **to s. a coat on/off** enfiler/quitter un manteau

(**c**) **to s. a disk** se faire une hernie discale

3 *vi* (**a**) *(slide) (of person, foot)* glisser; *(of prices, popularity)* chuter; **to s. from sb's hands** *or* **grasp** glisser des mains de qn; *Fig* **to s. through sb's fingers** glisser entre les doigts de qn; **to let one's guard/concentration s.** relâcher sa vigilance/concentration

(**b**) *(move quickly)* **to s. into sth** *(bed, room, shoes)* se glisser dans qch; *(clothes)* enfiler qch; **to s. out of sth** *(clothes)* quitter qch

(**c**) *(make mistake)* faire une erreur; **you're slipping!** tu baisses!

(**d**) **to let sth s.** *(words, information)* lâcher qch

▶**slip away** *vi (leave)* s'éclipser

▶**slip by** *vi (of time, years)* passer vite

▶**slip out** *vi (escape)* s'échapper; **to s. out to the store** faire un saut au magasin

▶**slip through** *vi (of mistake)* échapper à l'attention

▶**slip up** *vi (make mistake)* se planter

slip-on ['slɪpɒn] **1** *n Fam* **slip-ons** chaussures *fpl* sans lacets

2 *adj (shoes)* sans lacets

slipper ['slɪpə(r)] *n* pantoufle *f*

slippery ['slɪpərɪ] *adj* glissant(e); *(person)* fuyant(e); *Fig* **to be on a s. slope** être sur une pente savonneuse

slippy ['slɪpɪ] *adj* glissant(e)

slipshod ['slɪpʃɒd] *adj (work)* bâclé(e)

slipstream ['slɪpstriːm] *n* sillage *m*

slip-up ['slɪpʌp] *n* bourde *f*

slipway ['slɪpweɪ] *n Naut (for repairs)* cale *f* de construction; *(for launching)* cale de lancement

slit [slɪt] **1** *n* fente *f*

2 *vt* (*pt & pp* **slit**) fendre; **to s. sth open** ouvrir qch; **to s. sb's throat** couper la gorge à qn

slither ['slɪðə(r)] *vi* glisser

sliver ['slɪvə(r)] *n (of ham, cheese)* mince tranche *f*; *(of wood, glass)* éclat *m*

slob [slɒb] *n Fam (untidy person)* dégueulasse *mf*; *(lazy person)* flemmard(e) *m,f*

slobber ['slɒbə(r)] *vi* baver

sloe [sləʊ] *n (fruit)* prunelle *f*; **s. gin** alcool *m* de prunelles

slog [slɒg] *Fam* **1** *vi* (*pt & pp* **slogged**) *(work hard)* trimer, bosser (**at** sur)

2 *n* **it was a bit of a s.** ça a été dur; **it's a long s.** *(walk)* ça fait une trotte

slogan ['sləʊgən] *n* slogan *m*

slo-mo ['sləʊməʊ] *adj Fam (abbr* **slow-motion**) au ralenti

sloop [sluːp] *n (ship)* sloop *m*

slop [slɒp] *n* (**a**) *(pig food)* pâtée *f* (**b**) *Fam Pej (sentimentality)* sensiblerie *f*

2 *vt* (*pt & pp* **slopped**) renverser

3 *vi* se renverser

slope [sləʊp] **1** *n* pente *f*

2 *vi* être en pente

▶**slope off** *vi Fam* se tailler

sloping ['sləʊpɪŋ] *adj (roof, ground)* en pente; *(handwriting)* penché(e); **s. shoulders** épaules *fpl* tombantes

sloppy ['slɒpɪ] *adj* (**a**) *(careless) (person)* sans soin; *(attitude)* négligé(e); *(work)* bâclé(e) (**b**) *Fam Pej (sentimental)* sentimental(e)

slosh [slɒʃ] *vi (of liquid)* clapoter; *(spill)* se renverser

sloshed [slɒʃt] *adj Fam (drunk)* bourré(e); **to get s.** prendre une cuite

slot [slɒt] **1** *n (in box, machine)* fente *f*; *(in schedule, list)* créneau *m*; **s. machine** *(for vending)* distributeur *m* automatique; *(for gambling)* machine *f* à sous

2 *vt* (*pt & pp* **slotted**) *(part)* insérer

▶**slot in 1** *vt sep (into schedule)* caser

2 *vi (of part)* rentrer; *(into team)* s'intégrer

sloth [sləʊθ] *n* (**a**) *(laziness)* paresse *f* (**b**) *(animal)* paresseux *m*

slothful ['sləʊθfʊl] *adj* paresseux(euse)

slouch [slaʊtʃ] **1** *n Fam* **he's no s.** il n'est pas empoté

2 *vi (on chair)* être avachi(e); **she slouched out of the room** elle est sortie de la pièce en traînant les pieds; **don't s.!** tiens-toi droit!

slough [slʌf] *vt* **to s. its skin** *(of reptile)* muer

Slovak ['sləʊvæk] **1** *n* (**a**) *(person)* Slovaque *mf* (**b**) *(language)* slovaque *m*

2 *adj* slovaque

Slovakia [sləʊ'vækɪə] *n* la Slovaquie

Slovakian [sləʊ'vækɪən] **1** n Slovaque mf
2 adj slovaque
Slovene ['sləʊviːn] **1** n (**a**) (person) Slovène mf (**b**) (language) slovène m
2 adj slovène
Slovenia [sləʊ'viːnɪə] n la Slovénie
Slovenian [sləʊ'viːnɪən] **1** n Slovène mf
2 adj slovène
slovenly ['slʌvənlɪ] adj (untidy) négligé(e); (careless) négligent(e); (unkempt) débraillé(e)
slow [sləʊ] **1** adj (not fast, stupid) lent(e); **business is s.** les affaires tournent au ralenti; **my watch is s.** ma montre a du retard; **to be s. to do sth** être lent à faire qch; **to be s. off the mark** (in race) être lent à démarrer; (to understand) être lent à la détente; Culin **in a s. oven** à four doux; **we're making s. progress** nous avançons lentement; **she's a s. worker** elle travaille lentement; Aut **s. lane** voie f lente; Cin & TV **(in) s. motion** (au) ralenti m
2 adv lentement
3 vi ralentir
▸**slow down, slow up** vt sep & vi ralentir
slowly ['sləʊlɪ] adv lentement; **s. but surely** lentement mais sûrement
slowness ['sləʊnɪs] n lenteur f
slowpoke ['sləʊpəʊk] n Fam lambin(e) m,f
slow-witted ['sləʊ'wɪtɪd] adj à l'esprit lent
slow-worm ['sləʊwɜːm] n orvet m
SLR [esel'ɑː(r)] n Phot (abbr **single-lens reflex**) reflex m monoculaire
sludge [slʌdʒ] n vase f, boue f
slug [slʌg] **1** n (**a**) (mollusk) limace f (**b**) Fam (bullet) balle f (**c**) Fam (of drink) goutte f
2 vt (pt & pp **slugged**) Fam (hit) cogner
sluggish ['slʌgɪʃ] adj (person) (lazy) paresseux(euse); (not energetic) léthargique; (business, market) au ralenti
sluice [sluːs] **1** n (**a**) (channel) canal m (**b**) (sluicegate) écluse f
2 vt **to s. sth down/out** laver qch à grande eau
sluicegate ['sluːsgeɪt] n écluse f
slum [slʌm] **1** n (district) quartier m délabré; (shantytown) bidonville m; (house) taudis m
2 vt (pt & pp **slummed**) **to s. it** s'encanailler
slumber ['slʌmbə(r)] **1** n (**a**) Lit sommeil m (**b**) **s. party** = soirée entre fillettes, où les invitées restent dormir chez leur hôte
2 vi dormir
slump [slʌmp] **1** n (in prices, sales) effondrement m; (economic depression) crise f (économique)
2 vi (of person, economy, prices) s'effondrer
slung [slʌŋ] pt & pp of **sling**
slunk [slʌŋk] pt & pp of **slink**
slur [slɜː(r)] **1** n (**a**) (insult) insulte f; **to cast a s. on sb's reputation** entacher la réputation de qn (**b**) (in speech) **there was a s. in her voice** elle avait du mal à articuler
2 vt (pt & pp **slurred**) mal articuler
slurp [slɜːp] vt & vi (drink) boire bruyamment; (eat) manger bruyamment
slush [slʌʃ] n (**a**) (snow) neige f fondue (**b**) Pol **s. fund** caisse f noire (**c**) Fam Pej (sentimentality) sensiblerie f
slushy [slʌʃɪ] adj (**a**) (snow) fondu(e) (**b**) Fam Pej (movie, book) à l'eau de rose
slut [slʌt] n Fam Pej (promiscuous woman) salope f
sluttish ['slʌtɪʃ] adj Fam Pej (slovenly) négligé(e)
slutty ['slʌtɪ] adj Fam Pej (person, clothes) qui fait pute
sly [slaɪ] **1** adj (**a**) (cunning) rusé(e) (**b**) (dishonest) sournois(e) (**c**) (mischievous) espiègle
2 n **on the s.** en douce
smack [smæk] **1** n (**a**) (blow) claque f; (on bottom) fessée f;

(sound) claquement m; **a s. in the face** une gifle (**b**) Fam (heroin) héro f
2 adv Fam **to bump s. into a tree** rentrer en plein dans un arbre
3 vt (hit) donner une claque à; (on bottom) donner une fessée à; **to s. one's lips** faire claquer ses lèvres
▸**smack of** vt insep (suggest) avoir des relents de
smacker ['smækə(r)] n Fam (**a**) (kiss) grosse bise f (**b**) **50 smackers** (dollars) 50 dollars
small [smɔːl] **1** adj (**a**) (not large) petit(e); **to make sth smaller** rapetisser qch; Fig **it made me feel s.** (inconsequential) je me suis senti tout petit; **the s. hours** le petit matin; **s. arms** armes fpl portatives; **s. business** petite entreprise f; **s. businessman** petit entrepreneur m; **s. letters** (not capitals) minuscules fpl; **s. talk** banalités fpl; **to make s. talk** échanger des banalités (**b**) (not important) peu important(e); **it's s. wonder that...** ce n'est pas très étonnant que...; **in a s. way** à sa façon; Fam **to be s. beer** (of money) être que dalle; **s. change** petite monnaie f; **s. fry** menu fretin m
2 adv (chop) menu; (write) petit; **to think s.** voir petit
3 n **the s. of the back** la chute des reins
small-minded [smɔːl'maɪndɪd] adj étroit(e) d'esprit
smallness ['smɔːlnɪs] n petitesse f
smallpox ['smɔːlpɒks] n variole f
small-scale ['smɔːlskeɪl] adj (model) réduit(e); (research, project) à petite échelle
small-time ['smɔːltaɪm] adj Fam (criminal, businessman) petit(e)
smarmy ['smɑːmɪ] adj Pej mielleux(euse)
smart [smɑːt] **1** adj (**a**) (clever, sharp) (person) futé(e); (decision, move) habile; **don't get s. with me** n'essaie pas de faire le malin avec moi; Fam **s. aleck** petit malin m; **s. bomb** bombe f intelligente; **s. card** carte f à puce; **s. drug** psychotrope m; **s. missile** missile m guidé (**b**) (elegant) (clothes) élégant(e); (hotel, area) chic inv; **the s. set** le beau monde; **to be a s. dresser** bien s'habiller (**c**) (quick) (pace, work) rapide; **look s. (about it)!** et que ça saute! (**d**) Fam (excellent) génial(e); (pretty) canon inv
2 vi (sting) (of wound, graze) brûler; (of eyes) piquer; Fig (of person) être piqué(e) au vif
▸**smarten up** ['smɑːtən] **1** vt sep égayer; **to s. oneself up** se faire beau
2 vi (improve) se reprendre
smarty-pants ['smɑːtɪpænts] (pl **smarty-pants**) n Fam Pej petit(e) malin(igne) m,f
smash [smæʃ] **1** n (blow) coup m; (noise) fracas m; (collision) collision f; (in tennis) smash m; **s. (hit)** (record, movie) gros succès m
2 vt (**a**) **to s. sth (to pieces)** fracasser qch; **to s. sth open** défoncer qch; **to s. down a door** défoncer une porte (**b**) (ruin) anéantir; **to s. a drugs ring** démanteler un réseau de trafiquants de drogue; **she smashed the world record** elle a pulvérisé le record du monde
3 vi (**a**) (strike) **to s. into sth** s'écraser contre qch (**b**) **to s. (into pieces)** éclater (en morceaux)
▸**smash up** vt sep (room, car, furniture) saccager
smashed [smæʃt] adj Fam (drunk) pété(e)
smashing ['smæʃɪŋ] adj (blow) violent(e); Fam (success) éclatant(e)
smattering ['smætərɪŋ] n notions fpl
smear [smɪə(r)] **1** n (**a**) (stain) tache f; Med **s. test** frottis m (**b**) (slander) propos m diffamatoire; **s. campaign** campagne f de diffamation
2 vt (**a**) (stain) tacher; (spread) enduire, barbouiller; (smudge) (paint) salir (**b**) (slander) calomnier
smell [smel] **1** n (**a**) (sense) odorat m (**b**) (odor) odeur f; **there's a bad s.** ça sent mauvais; **to have a s. of sth** sentir qch

2 vt (pt & pp **smelled** or **smelt** [smelt]) also Fig sentir; Fig **I s. a rat** ça sent l'embrouille

3 vi sentir; (stink) sentir mauvais; **to s. of sth** sentir qch; **his breath smells** il a mauvaise haleine

smelly ['smelɪ] adj qui sent mauvais

smelt [smelt] **1** vt (ore) fondre

2 pt & pp of **smell**

smile [smaɪl] **1** n sourire m; **to give sb a s.** sourire à qn; **she was all smiles** elle était tout sourire; **to take** or **to wipe the s. off sb's face** passer l'envie de sourire à qn

2 vi sourire (**at** à); **fortune smiled on them** la fortune leur sourit; **s.!** (for photograph) un petit sourire!

smiley ['smaɪlɪ] (pl **smileys**) n Comput souriant m, émoticon m, Can binette f

smiling ['smaɪlɪŋ] adj souriant(e)

smirk [smɜːk] **1** n sourire m en coin

2 vi sourire en coin

smite [smaɪt] (pt **smote** [sməʊt], pp **smitten** ['smɪtən]) vt (**a**) Lit (strike) frapper (**b**) **smitten with terror** terrorisé(e); **smitten with remorse** envahi(e) par les remords

smith [smɪθ] n forgeron m

smithereens [smɪðə'riːnz] npl **to smash/blow sth to s.** réduire qch en miettes

smithy ['smɪðɪ] (pl **smithies**) n forge f

smitten ['smɪtən] **1** adj (in love) très épris(e) (**with** de)

2 pp of **smite**

smock [smɒk] n blouse f

smog [smɒg] n smog m

smoke [sməʊk] **1** n fumée f; **to have a s.** fumer une cigarette; Fig **to go up in s.** partir en fumée; Prov **there's no s. without fire** il n'y a pas de fumée sans feu; **s. bomb** bombe f fumigène; **s. detector** détecteur m de fumée; also Fig **s. screen** rideau m de fumée; **s. signals** signaux mpl de fumée

2 vt (**a**) (cigarette) fumer; **to s. a pipe** fumer la pipe (**b**) (meat, fish) fumer

3 vi (**a**) (of person) fumer (**b**) (of chimney, oil) fumer

▸**smoke out** vt sep (insects) enfumer; Fig (rebels) débusquer

smoked [sməʊkt] adj fumé(e); **s. glass** verre m fumé; **s. salmon** saumon m fumé

smokeless ['sməʊklɪs] adj **s. fuel** combustible m non polluant; **s. zone** = zone où l'usage de combustible polluant n'est pas autorisé

smoker ['sməʊkə(r)] n fumeur(euse) m,f; **to be a cigarette/pipe s.** fumer des cigarettes/la pipe; **to be a heavy s.** être un grand fumeur; **s.'s cough** toux f de fumeur

smoking ['sməʊkɪŋ] n **s. can damage your health** fumer ou le tabac nuit à la santé; **no s.** (sign) défense de fumer; **s. car** (on train) compartiment m fumeurs; Fig **s. gun** (clue) indice m flagrant; **s. jacket** veste f d'intérieur; **s. room** salle f fumeurs

smoky ['sməʊkɪ] adj (atmosphere, room) enfumé(e); (fire) qui dégage de la fumée; (surface) noirci(e) par la fumée; (taste) de fumée

smolder ['sməʊldə(r)] vi (of fire) couver; Fig **to s. with anger/passion** se consumer de colère/passion

smooch [smuːtʃ] vi Fam se bécoter

smooth [smuːð] **1** adj (**a**) (not rough) lisse; (sea) calme; (sauce) homogène; (skin, wine, whiskey) doux (douce); (style) coulant(e); (flight, crossing) calme; **a s. shave** un rasage de près (**b**) (person, manner) onctueux(euse); **he's a s. talker** c'est un beau parleur; **to be a s. operator** savoir y faire (**c**) (without problems) sans problèmes; **to get off to a s. start** commencer sans problèmes

2 vt (feathers, hair) lisser; (pillow, sheet, clothing) défroisser; (surface) égaliser; **to s. the way for sb** faciliter les choses à qn; **to s. the way for sth** faciliter qch

▸**smooth back** vt sep **to s. back one's hair** lisser ses cheveux en arrière

▸**smooth down** vt sep lisser

▸**smooth out** vt sep (map, sheets) défroisser; (crease) faire disparaître; Fig (difficulty) aplanir

▸**smooth over** vt sep (difficulties) aplanir; (differences) atténuer; **to s. things over** arranger les choses

smoothie ['smuːðɪ] n (**a**) Fam (smooth talker) individu m mielleux (**b**) (drink) = boisson à base de jus de fruit mélangé à du yaourt ou à du lait

smoothly ['smuːðlɪ] adv sans problèmes; **to go s.** se passer sans problèmes

smoothness ['smuːðnɪs] n (of skin, wine, whiskey) douceur f; (of surface) aspect m lisse; (of flight, crossing) calme m; (of sauce) homogénéité f

smooth-talking ['smuːð'tɔːkɪŋ] adj mielleux(euse)

smote [sməʊt] pt of **smite**

smother ['smʌðə(r)] vt (**a**) (person, fire, yawn) étouffer; **to s. sb with kisses** couvrir qn de baisers (**b**) (cover) **to s. sth in sth** recouvrir qch de qch

SMS [esem'es] n Tel (abbr **short message service**) service m SMS

smudge [smʌdʒ] **1** n tache f

2 vt (ink, lipstick) étaler; (drawing) maculer

3 vi (of ink, lipstick) s'étaler

smug [smʌg] adj suffisant(e)

smuggle ['smʌgəl] vt (arms, drugs) faire de la contrebande de; **to s. sth in/out** faire entrer/sortir qch en contrebande; **to s. sb in/out** faire entrer/sortir qn clandestinement; **to s. sth through customs** passer qch en fraude à la douane

smuggler ['smʌglə(r)] n contrebandier(ère) m,f; (of drugs) trafiquant(e) m,f

smuggling ['smʌglɪŋ] n contrebande f; (of drugs) trafic m

smut [smʌt] n (**a**) (soot) tache f de suie (**b**) (obscenity) cochonneries fpl

smutty ['smʌtɪ] adj (**a**) (dirty) sale, noirci(e) (**b**) (obscene) cochon(onne)

snack [snæk] **1** n casse-croûte m inv; **to have a s.** grignoter quelque chose; **s. bar** snack-bar m

2 vi **to s. on sth** grignoter qch; **you shouldn't s. between meals** il ne faut pas grignoter entre les repas

snackish ['snækɪʃ] adj **to be feeling s.** (slightly hungry) avoir un petit creux

snag [snæg] **1** n (problem) problème m

2 vt (pt & pp **snagged**) (**a**) (tear) faire un accroc à (**b**) (obtain) dégoter; **I managed to s. a great prize in the raffle** j'ai réussi à décrocher un super lot à la tombola; **he snagged a job as a reporter** il a dégoté un poste de reporter

snail [sneɪl] n escargot m; **at a s.'s pace** (move) comme un escargot; (change, learn, progress) très lentement; Fam **s. mail** courrier m escargot, = courrier postal

snake [sneɪk] **1** n serpent m; Fig **s. in the grass** traître(esse) m,f; **s. charmer** charmeur(euse) m,f de serpent; Fig **s. pit** fosse f aux serpents

2 vi (of road, river) serpenter

snakebite ['sneɪkbaɪt] n (of snake) morsure f de serpent

snakeskin ['sneɪkskɪn] n peau f de serpent

snap [snæp] **1** n (**a**) (bite) coup m de dents

(**b**) (sound) craquement m; **a s. of the fingers** un claquement de doigts; **s. fastener** bouton-pression m

(**c**) (of weather) **a cold s.** une brusque vague de froid

(**d**) Fam (photograph) photo f

(**e**) Fam (simple thing) **it's a s.!** c'est simple comme bonjour!

2 adj (judgment, decision) hâtif(ive); **to call a s. election** procéder à une élection surprise

3 vt (pt & pp **snapped**) (**a**) (break) casser net; **to s. sth in two** casser qch en deux

(**b**) **to s. one's fingers** faire claquer ses doigts

(**c**) (say sharply) dire sèchement

(**d**) *Fam (take photograph of)* prendre en photo
4 *vi* (**a**) *(break cleanly)* casser net; *(break noisily)* casser avec un bruit sec
(**b**) *(bite)* **to s. (at)** essayer de mordre; **to s. shut** *(of jaws, lid)* se refermer avec un bruit sec
(**c**) *(speak abruptly)* parler sèchement (**at** à)
(**d**) *(idioms)* **to s. out of it** *(of depression, apathy)* se secouer; *(of sulk)* arrêter de faire la tête

▸**snap off 1** *vt sep* (**a**) *(break)* casser net (**b**) *Fam* **to s. sb's head off** rembarrer qn
2 *vi* casser net

▸**snap up** *vt sep* (**a**) *(seize in jaws)* attraper (**b**) *(buy, take quickly)* rafler

snapdragon ['snæpdrægən] *n* gueule-de-loup *f*

snappy ['snæpɪ] *adj Fam (style, prose)* vif (vive); *(slogan)* accrocheur(euse); **to be a s. dresser** s'habiller toujours à la mode; **make it s.!** *(be quick)* au trot!

snapshot ['snæpʃɒt] *n Fam (photograph)* photo *f*

snare [sneə(r)] **1** *n* collet *m*; *Fig* piège *m*; **s. drum** caisse *f* claire
2 *vt* prendre au collet; *Fig* prendre au piège

snarl [snɑːl] **1** *n* grognement *m*
2 *vi* grogner (**at** après)

▸**snarl up 1** *vt sep (thread, hair)* emmêler; **to get snarled up** *(thread, hair)* s'emmêler
2 *vi (of thread, hair)* s'emmêler

snarl-up ['snɑːlʌp] *n (of traffic)* bouchon *m*; *(in system)* paralysie *f*

snatch [snætʃ] **1** *n (of conversation)* bribe *f*; **to sleep in snatches** avoir un sommeil fragmenté; **a s. of music** quelques notes de musique
2 *vt* (**a**) *(grab)* saisir; **to s. something to eat** avaler quelque chose à la hâte; **to s. some sleep** dormir un peu (**b**) *(steal, abduct) (wallet, handbag)* arracher; *(person)* enlever
3 *vi* **to s. at sth** essayer de saisir qch

▸**snatch away** *vt sep* arracher

snazzy ['snæzɪ] *adj Fam* chicos, classe

sneak [sniːk] **1** *n* **to get a s. preview of sth** voir qch en avant-première
2 *vt (pt & pp* **sneaked** *or* **snuck** [snʌk]) **to s. sth past sb** passer qch subrepticement devant qn; **to s. sb in/out** faire entrer/sortir qn subrepticement; **to s. a glance at sb** jeter un coup d'œil furtif à qn
3 *vi (move furtively)* se déplacer furtivement; **to s. past sb** passer furtivement devant qn; **to s. in/out** entrer/sortir furtivement

▸**sneak away, sneak off** *vi* s'esquiver

sneaker ['sniːkə(r)] *n (athletic shoe)* chaussure *f* de sport

sneaky ['sniːkɪ] *adj* sournois(e)

sneer [snɪə(r)] **1** *n (expression)* sourire *m* méprisant
2 *vt* **"you couldn't do that," he sneered** "vous n'en seriez pas capable", dit-il d'un air méprisant
3 *vi* ricaner; **to s. at sb/sth** se moquer de qn/qch

sneering ['snɪərɪŋ] **1** *n (laughter)* ricanement *m*; *(remarks)* sarcasmes *mpl*
2 *adj* méprisant(e)

sneeze [sniːz] **1** *n* éternuement *m*
2 *vi* éternuer; *Fam Fig* **it's not to be sneezed at** il ne faut pas cracher dessus

snicker ['snɪkə(r)] **1** *n* ricanement *m*
2 *vi* ricaner

snide [snaɪd] *adj* méprisant(e)

sniff [snɪf] **1** *vt* (**a**) *(smell)* sentir; *(detect)* flairer (**b**) *(inhale) (air)* respirer; *(cocaine, glue)* sniffer
2 *vi* renifler; *(disdainfully)* avoir une moue de dédain; *Fam* **it's not to be sniffed at** il ne faut pas cracher dessus
3 *n* **to take a s. at sth** sentir qch; **with a s. of disgust** avec une moue de dégoût

▸**sniff out** *vt sep (of dog)* découvrir à l'odeur; *Fig (of investigator)* découvrir

sniffer dog ['snɪfədɒg] *n* chien *m* renifleur

sniffle ['snɪfəl] **1** *n (slight cold)* petit rhume *m*; *Fam* **to have the sniffles** avoir un petit rhume
2 *vi* (**a**) *(sniff repeatedly)* renifler (**b**) *(cry quietly)* pleurer (doucement)

sniffy ['snɪfɪ] *adj Fam (disdainful)* dédaigneux(euse); **to be s. about sth** éprouver du dédain pour qch

snigger ['snɪgə(r)] **1** *n* ricanement *m* étouffé
2 *vi* ricaner

snip [snɪp] **1** *n* (**a**) *(cut)* petite entaille *f* (**b**) *(piece cut off)* bout *m*
2 *vt (pt & pp* **snipped**) couper

▸**snip off** *vt sep* couper

snipe[1] [snaɪp] *(pl* **snipe**) *n (bird)* bécassine *f*

snipe[2] [snaɪp] *vi (shoot)* tirer (d'une position cachée); **to s. at sb** tirer sur qn (d'une position cachée); *Fig (criticize)* critiquer qn de façon malveillante

sniper ['snaɪpə(r)] *n* tireur(euse) *m,f* embusqué(e)

snippet ['snɪpɪt] *n (of information, conversation)* bribe *f*; **a s. of news** une nouvelle brève

snitch [snɪtʃ] *Fam* **1** *n (informer)* mouchard(e) *m,f*
2 *vi* moucharder; **to s. on sb** moucharder qn

snivel ['snɪvəl] *vi* pleurnicher

sniveling ['snɪvəlɪŋ] *adj* pleurnicheur(euse)

snob [snɒb] *n* snob *mf*

snobbery ['snɒbərɪ] *n* snobisme *m*

snobbish ['snɒbɪʃ] *adj* snob *inv*

snooker ['snuːkə(r)] *n (game)* snooker *(sorte de billard qui se joue avec vingt-deux billes)*

snoop [snuːp] *Fam* **1** *n* (**a**) *(person)* fouineur(euse) *m,f* (**b**) *(look)* **to have a s. (around)** jeter un coup d'œil
2 *vi* fouiner, fureter

snooper ['snuːpə(r)] *n Fam* fouineur(euse) *m,f*

snooty ['snuːtɪ] *adj Fam* prétentieux(euse)

snooze [snuːz] *Fam* **1** *n* petit somme *m*; **to have a s.** faire un petit somme
2 *vi* faire un petit somme

snore [snɔː(r)] **1** *n* ronflement *m*
2 *vi* ronfler

snoring ['snɔːrɪŋ] *n* ronflements *mpl*

snorkel ['snɔːkəl] **1** *n* tuba *m*
2 *vi* nager sous l'eau avec un tuba

snorkeling ['snɔːklɪŋ] *n* **to go s.** faire de la plongée avec un tuba

snort [snɔːt] **1** *n (of person)* grognement *m*; *(of horse)* ébrouement *m*
2 *vt Fam (drugs)* sniffer
3 *vi (of person)* grogner; *(of horse)* s'ébrouer

snot [snɒt] *n Fam* morve *f*

snotty ['snɒtɪ] *adj Fam* (**a**) *(nose)* qui coule (**b**) *(arrogant)* arrogant(e)

snout [snaʊt] *n (of pig)* groin *m*; *(of other animal)* museau *m*; *Fam (of person)* pif *m*

snow [snəʊ] **1** *n* neige *f*; **s. blindness** cécité *f* des neiges; *Fam* **s. job** baratin *m*; **s. line** limite *f* des neiges éternelles; **s. pea** mange-tout *m inv*
2 *vi* neiger; **it's snowing** il neige

▸**snow in** *vt sep* **to be snowed in** être bloqué(e) par la neige

▸**snow under** *vt sep* **to be snowed under (with)** *(work)* être débordé(e) (de); *(invitations, offers)* être submergé(e) (de)

snowball ['snəʊbɔːl] **1** *n* boule *f* de neige, *Can* balle *f* de neige; **s. fight** bataille *f* de boules de neige; *Fam* **she hasn't a s.'s chance in hell** elle n'a pas la moindre chance
2 *vi Fig* faire boule de neige

snowbike ['snəʊbaɪk] *n* motoski *m*

snowboard ['snəʊbɔːd] **1** *n* planche *f* de snowboard
2 *vi* faire du snowboard

snowboarding ['snəʊbɔːdɪŋ] *n* snowboard *m*; **to go s.** faire du snowboard

snowbound ['snəʊbaʊnd] *adj* bloqué(e) par la neige

snowcapped ['snəʊkæpt] *adj* couronné(e) de neige

snowdome ['snəʊdəʊm] *n (ornament)* boule *f* à neige

snowdrift ['snəʊdrɪft] *n* congère *f*

snowdrop ['snəʊdrɒp] *n (flower)* perce-neige *m ou f inv*

snowfall ['snəʊfɔːl] *n* chute *f* de neige

snowflake ['snəʊfleɪk] *n* flocon *m* de neige

snowglobe ['snəʊɡləʊb] = **snowdome**

snowman ['snəʊmæn] *n* bonhomme *m* de neige

snowmobile ['snəʊməʊbiːl] *n (enclosed)* autoneige *f*; *(open)* motoneige *f*

snowplow ['snəʊplaʊ] *n* chasse-neige *m inv*

snowshoe ['snəʊʃuː] *n* raquette *f*

snowstorm ['snəʊstɔːm] *n* tempête *f* de neige

snowsuit ['snəʊsuːt] *n* combinaison *f* de ski *(pour enfants)*

Snow White ['snəʊ'waɪt] *n* **S. and the Seven Dwarfs** Blanche-Neige et les sept nains

snowy ['snəʊɪ] *adj (landscape, field)* enneigé(e); *(weather)* neigeux(euse); *(day)* de neige

Snr. *(abbr* **Senior)** Thomas Watkins S. Thomas Watkins père

snub [snʌb] **1** *n (refusal)* rebuffade *f*; *(insult)* affront *m*
2 *vt (pt & pp* **snubbed)** snober

snub nose ['snʌb'nəʊz] *n* nez *m* retroussé

snuck [snʌk] *pt & pp of* **sneak**

snuff [snʌf] **1** *n* tabac *m* à priser
2 *vt (candle)* moucher; *Fam* **to s. it** *(die)* casser sa pipe; *Fam Cin* **s. movie** = film pornographique au cours duquel un participant est réellement assassiné

▸**snuff out** *vt sep (candle)* moucher; *(life, opposition)* mettre fin à

snuffbox ['snʌfbɒks] *n* tabatière *f*

snuffle ['snʌfəl] **1** *n (sniff)* reniflement *m*
2 *vi (sniff)* renifler

snug [snʌɡ] *adj* **(a)** *(place)* douillet(ette); *(person)* bien au chaud **(b)** *(tight-fitting)* bien ajusté(e)

▸**snuggle up** ['snʌɡəl] *vi* **to s. up to sb** se blottir contre qn

snugly ['snʌɡlɪ] *adv (comfortably)* confortablement; **to fit s.** être bien ajusté(e)

so [səʊ] **1** *adv* **(a)** *(to such an extent)* tellement, si *(***that** que); **I was so angry (that) I almost hit him** j'étais tellement en colère que j'ai failli le frapper; **he's not so clever as she is** il n'est pas aussi intelligent qu'elle; **it isn't so very old** il n'est pas si vieux; **I'm not so sure of that** je n'en suis pas si sûr; **so much money/many people** tant *ou* autant d'argent/de gens; **it was difficult, so much so that...** c'était difficile, à tel point que...
(b) *(for emphasis)* tellement; **I was so disappointed!** j'étais tellement déçu!; **we enjoyed ourselves so much!** nous nous sommes tellement amusés!; *Fam* **I so don't want to go!** j'ai vraiment pas envie d'y aller!
(c) *(expressing agreement)* **you're late – so I am!** tu es en retard – ah oui, tu as raison!; **that's Johnny Depp – so it is!** c'est Johnny Depp – ah oui, tu as raison!
(d) *(referring to statement already mentioned)* **I hope so** j'espère bien; **I think so** je crois; **I suppose so** je le suppose; **so I believe** c'est ce que je crois; **I told you so!** je vous l'avais bien dit!; **I'm not very organized – so I see!** je ne suis pas très bien organisé – c'est ce que je vois!; **so be it!** soit!
(e) *(also)* **so am I** moi aussi; **so do we** nous aussi; **so can they** eux aussi; **so is my brother** mon frère aussi
(f) *(in this way)* ainsi; **do it (like) so** fais-le comme ça; **and so on, and so forth** et ainsi de suite

(g) *Fam (indeed)* **I didn't say that! – you did so!** je n'ai pas dit ça! – si, tu l'as dit!
2 *conj* **(a)** *(because of this)* donc; **she has a bad temper, so be careful** elle a mauvais caractère, donc fais attention
(b) *(introducing remark)* alors; **so you're not coming?** alors, tu ne viens pas?; **so that's why!** alors, c'est pour ça!; **so (what)?** et alors?, et après?
(c) **so as to** afin de; **we hurried so as not to be late** nous nous sommes dépêchés afin de ne pas être en retard
(d) **so that** pour que + *subjunctive*; **she sat down so that I could see better** elle s'est assise pour que je puisse mieux voir; **we hurried so that we wouldn't be late** nous nous sommes dépêchés pour ne pas arriver en retard

soak [səʊk] **1** *vt (leave in water)* faire *ou* laisser tremper; *(make very wet)* tremper *(***with** de)
2 *vi (of food, clothes)* tremper; **to leave sth to s.** faire *ou* laisser tremper qch

▸**soak in** *vi (of liquid)* pénétrer

▸**soak up** *vt sep (liquid)* absorber; *Fig* **to s. up the sun** prendre un bain de soleil

soaked [səʊkt] *adj* trempé(e); **s. to the skin** trempé(e) jusqu'aux os

so-and-so ['səʊənsəʊ] *n Fam* **(a)** *(unspecified person)* untel (unetelle) *m,f*; **Mr S.** M. Untel; **Mrs S.** Mme Unetelle **(b)** *(unpleasant person)* peau *f* de vache

soap [səʊp] **1** *n* savon *m*; **a bar of s.** un morceau de savon; **s. (opera)** feuilleton *m* populaire; **s. powder** lessive *f* (en poudre)
2 *vt* savonner

soapbox ['səʊpbɒks] *n* tribune *f* improvisée à l'extérieur; **s. orator** harangueur(euse) *m,f*

soapdish ['səʊpdɪʃ] *n* porte-savon *m*

soapflakes ['səʊpfleɪks] *npl* savon *m* en paillettes

soapsuds ['səʊpsʌdz] *npl* mousse *f* de savon

soapy ['səʊpɪ] *adj (water)* savonneux(euse); *(body)* couvert(e) de savon; *(taste, smell)* de savon

soar [sɔː(r)] *vi (of bird, plane) & Fig (of prices)* monter en flèche; *Fig (of building)* se dresser

soaring ['sɔːrɪŋ] *adj Fig (prices)* en forte hausse; *(building)* élancé(e)

sob [sɒb] **1** *n* sanglot *m*; *Fam* **s. story** histoire *f* larmoyante
2 *vi (pt & pp* **sobbed)** sangloter

s.o.b. [esəʊ'biː] *n very Fam (abbr* **son of a bitch)** salaud *m*

sobbing ['sɒbɪŋ] *n* sanglots *mpl*

sober ['səʊbə(r)] *adj* **(a)** *(not drunk)* qui n'a pas bu **(b)** *(sensible)* sobre

▸**sober up** *vt sep & vi* dessoûler

sobering ['səʊbərɪŋ] *adj (news, thought)* qui donne à réfléchir

sobriety [səʊ'braɪətɪ] *n* sobriété *f*

Soc. *n (abbr* **society)** club *m*, société *f*

so-called ['səʊ'kɔːld] *adj* **(a)** *(supposed)* soi-disant *inv*; **his s. aunt** sa soi-disant tante **(b)** *(so named)* appelé(e) ainsi; **the s. temperate zone** la zone dite tempérée

soccer ['sɒkə(r)] *n* football *m*; **s. match** match *m* de football; **s. player** footballeur(euse) *m,f*

sociable ['səʊʃəbəl] *adj* sociable

social ['səʊʃəl] **1** *adj* social(e); **s. class** classe *f* sociale; **s. climber** arriviste *mf*; *Pol* **s. democrat** social(e)-démocrate *m,f*; **s. intercourse** relations *fpl* avec les gens; **s. life** vie *f* sociale; **he doesn't have much of a s. life** il ne sort pas beaucoup; **s. outcast** paria *m*; **s. sciences** sciences *fpl* humaines; **s. security** prestations *fpl* sociales; **the s. services** les services *mpl* sociaux; **s. work** assistance *f* sociale; **s. worker** assistant(e) *m,f* social(e)
2 *n (party)* fête *f*

socialism ['səʊʃəlɪzəm] *n* socialisme *m*

socialist ['səʊʃəlɪst] *n & adj* socialiste *mf*

socialite ['səʊʃəlaɪt] *n* mondain(e) *m,f*

socialize ['səʊʃəlaɪz] *vi* fréquenter des gens; **to s. with sb** fréquenter qn

socially ['səʊʃəlɪ] *adv* socialement; **to see sb s.** fréquenter qn

society [sə'saɪətɪ] (*pl* **societies**) *n* (**a**) *(community)* société *f*; **(high) s.** haute société, (beau) monde *m* (**b**) *(club)* club *m*, société *f*

socioeconomic [səʊsɪəʊiːkə'nɒmɪk] *adj* socio-économique

sociological [səʊsɪə'lɒdʒɪkəl] *adj* sociologique

sociologist [səʊsɪ'ɒlədʒɪst] *n* sociologue *mf*

sociology [səʊsɪ'ɒlədʒɪ] *n* sociologie *f*

sock [sɒk] **1** *n* (**a**) *(garment)* chaussette *f*; *Fam Fig* **to pull one's socks up** se secouer (**b**) *Fam (blow)* coup *m* de poing
2 *vt Fam (hit)* donner un coup de poing à; *Fig* **to s. it to sb** montrer à qn de quoi on est capable

socket ['sɒkɪt] *n (of eye)* orbite *f*; *(for plug)* prise *f* de courant

sod [sɒd] *n (of earth)* motte *f*

soda ['səʊdə] *n* (**a**) **s. (water)** eau *f* de Seltz; **s. fountain** cafétéria *f* (**b**) *(carbonated drink)* boisson *f* gazeuse (**c**) *Chem* soude *f*

sodden ['sɒdən] *adj* trempé(e)

sodium ['səʊdɪəm] *n Chem* sodium *m*; **s. bicarbonate** bicarbonate *m* de soude; **s. chloride** chlorure *m* de sodium

sodomize ['sɒdəmaɪz] *vt* sodomiser

sodomy ['sɒdəmɪ] *n* sodomie *f*

sofa ['səʊfə] *n* canapé *m*; **s. bed** canapé-lit *m*

Sofia [səʊ'fiːə] *n* Sofia

soft [sɒft] *adj* (**a**) *(in texture)* mou (molle); *(ground)* meuble; *(pillow, carpet)* moelleux(euse); *(fabric, skin)* doux (douce); **s. cheese** fromage *m* frais; *Comput* **s. copy** visualisation *f* sur écran; *Comput* **s. return** retour *m* de chariot conditionnel, changement *m* de ligne facultatif; **s. shoulder** *(on road)* accotement *m* non stabilisé; *Anat* **s. tissue** parties *fpl* charnues; **s. toy** peluche *f*
(**b**) *(voice)* doux (douce); *(rain)* léger(ère); *(color)* doux, tendre; **s. currency** devise *f* faible; **s. drinks** boissons *fpl* non alcoolisées; **s. drugs** drogues *fpl* douces; *Phot* **in s. focus** dans le flou artistique; *Fin* **s. loan** prêt *m* offrant des conditions avantageuses; **s. porn** soft *m*; *Comput* **s. sell** méthode *f* de vente non agressive
(**c**) *(not strict)* indulgent(e), faible; **to have a s. spot for sb** avoir un faible pour qn; **to have a s. heart** avoir le cœur tendre
(**d**) *Fam (stupid)* idiot(e)
(**e**) *(easy) (job, life)* facile; *Fam* **to be a s. touch** être bonne pâte; **s. option** solution *f* de facilité

softback ['sɒftbæk] *n* livre *m* broché

softball ['sɒftbɔːl] *n* = sorte de base-ball joué sur un plus petit terrain avec une balle moins dure

soft-boiled ['sɒftbɔɪld] *adj (egg)* à la coque

soften ['sɒfən] **1** *vt (wax, butter)* ramollir; *(leather, fabric)* assouplir; *(skin, light)* adoucir; *Fig* **to s. the blow** amortir le choc
2 *vi (of wax, butter)* ramollir; *Fig (of person)* se radoucir; *(of opinions, resolve, stance)* devenir plus modéré(e)

▸**soften up** *vt sep Fam (before attack)* affaiblir; *(before request)* amadouer

softener ['sɒfənə(r)] *n* adoucissant *m*

softhearted [sɒft'hɑːtɪd] *adj* qui se laisse facilement attendrir

softie = **softy**

softly ['sɒftlɪ] *adv (quietly, gently)* doucement; **to be s. lit** être légèrement éclairé(e)

softly-softly ['sɒftlɪ'sɒftlɪ] *adj Fam (approach, attitude)* en douceur

softness ['sɒftnɪs] *n (of ground)* consistance *f* meuble; *(of fabric, skin, voice)* douceur *f*

soft-pedal [sɒft'pedəl] *vi also Fig* mettre la pédale douce

soft-soap [sɒft'səʊp] *vt Fam* amadouer

soft-spoken [sɒft'spəʊkən] *adj* qui a une voix douce

software ['sɒftweə(r)] *n Comput* logiciel *m*; **a piece of s.** un logiciel; **s. company** éditeur *m* de logiciels; **s. developer** développeur(euse) *m,f*; **s. package** progiciel *m*

softy ['sɒftɪ] (*pl* **softies**) *n Fam (gentle person)* bonne pâte *f*; *(weakling)* mauviette *f*

soggy ['sɒgɪ] *adj* trempé(e)

soh [səʊ] *n Mus* sol *m*

soil [sɔɪl] **1** *n (earth)* terre *f*; **on American s.** sur le sol américain
2 *vt (clothes, sheet)* salir; *Fig* **to s. one's hands** se salir les mains

solace ['sɒləs] *n Lit* réconfort *m*

solar ['səʊlə(r)] *adj* solaire; **s. eclipse** éclipse *f* solaire; **s. plexus** plexus *m* solaire; **s. system** système *m* solaire

sold [səʊld] *pt & pp of* **sell**

solder ['səʊldə(r)] **1** *n* soudure *f*
2 *vt* souder

soldering iron ['səʊdərɪŋ'aɪən] *n* fer *m* à souder

soldier ['səʊldʒə(r)] **1** *n* soldat *m*
2 *vi* être soldat

▸**soldier on** *vi* persévérer

sole¹ [səʊl] **1** *n (of foot)* plante *f*; *(of shoe)* semelle *f*
2 *vt (shoe)* ressemeler

sole² [səʊl] *n (fish)* sole *f*

sole³ [səʊl] *adj (only)* unique; *Com* **s. agent** agent *m* exclusif

solely ['səʊllɪ] *adv* uniquement

solemn ['sɒləm] *adj* solennel(elle)

solemnity [sə'lemnɪtɪ] *n* solennité *f*

sol-fa [sɒl'fɑː] *n Mus* solfège *m*

solicit [sə'lɪsɪt] **1** *vt (request)* solliciter, demander
2 *vi (of prostitute)* racoler

solicitor [sə'lɪsɪtə(r)] *n (in Great Britain) (for property, wills)* notaire *m*; *(in court cases)* avocat(e) *m,f*

solicitous [sə'lɪsɪtəs] *adj Formal* empressé(e); *(caring)* plein(e) de sollicitude; *(concerned)* soucieux(euse) **(for)** de)

solid ['sɒlɪd] **1** *n* solide *m*; **solids** *(food)* aliments *mpl* solides
2 *adj* (**a**) *(not liquid)* solide; **s. food** aliments *mpl* solides; **s. fuel** combustible *m* solide (**b**) *(not hollow)* plein(e); *(gold, silver)* massif(ive); **made of s. brick** construit(e) entièrement en brique (**c**) *(worker)* sérieux(euse)
3 *adv* **ten hours s.** dix heures d'affilée

solidarity [sɒlɪ'dærɪtɪ] *n* solidarité *f*

solidify [sə'lɪdɪfaɪ] (*pt & pp* **solidified**) *vi* se solidifier

solidity [sə'lɪdɪtɪ] *n* solidité *f*

solidly ['sɒlɪdlɪ] *adv (firmly)* solidement; *(without interruption)* sans arrêt

solid-state [sɒlɪd'steɪt] *adj Elec* transistorisé(e)

soliloquy [sə'lɪləkwɪ] (*pl* **soliloquies**) *n* soliloque *m*

solitaire [sɒlɪ'teə(r)] *n (card game)* réussite *f*; *(board game, jewelry)* solitaire *m*

solitary ['sɒlɪtərɪ] *adj* (**a**) *(single)* seul(e) (**b**) *(alone)* solitaire; **s. confinement** isolement *m* cellulaire

solitude ['sɒlɪtjuːd] *n* solitude *f*

solo ['səʊləʊ] **1** *n* (*pl* **solos**) *(musical)* solo *m*
2 *adj (flight, crossing)* en solitaire; *(performance)* solo
3 *adv* en solitaire; **to go s.** *(of musician)* faire une carrière solo; *(of business partner)* s'établir à son compte

soloist ['səʊləʊɪst] *n* soliste *mf*

Solomon Islands ['sɒləmən'aɪləndz] *npl* **the S.** les îles *fpl* Salomon

solstice ['sɒlstɪs] *n* solstice *m*

soluble ['sɒljʊbəl] *adj* soluble

solution [sə'luːʃən] *n* solution *f*

solve [sɒlv] *vt* résoudre

solvency ['sɒlvənsɪ] *n* solvabilité *f*

solvent ['sɒlvənt] **1** *n* solvant *m*, dissolvant *m*; **s. abuse** = utilisation de solvants comme stupéfiants
2 *adj (financially)* solvable

Somali [sə'mɑːlɪ] **1** *n* (a) *(person)* Somalien(enne) *m,f* (b) *(language)* somali *m*
2 *adj* somalien(enne)

Somalia [sə'mɑːlɪə] *n* la Somalie

somber ['sɒmbə(r)] *adj* sombre

some [sʌm] **1** *pron* (a) *(certain quantity or number)* **there is/are s. over there** il y en a là-bas; *(a few)* il y en a quelques-uns là-bas; **give me s. (of them)** donne-m'en; *(a few)* donne-m'en quelques-uns; **do you want s.?** en veux-tu?; *(a few)* en veux-tu quelques-uns?; **s. of my wine** un peu de mon vin; **s. of my toys** quelques-uns de mes jouets; **s. of the time** une partie du temps
(b) *(as opposed to others)* certains *mpl*, certaines *fpl*; **s. say...** certains disent que..., il y en a qui disent que...; **s. of the guests** certains invités; **they went off, s. one way, s. another** ils sont partis, certains par là, d'autres par là-bas
2 *adj* (a) *(certain quantity or number of)* **s. wine** du vin; **s. ice-cream** de la glace; **s. water** de l'eau; **s. books** des livres; *(a few)* quelques livres; **in s. ways** par certains côtés; **to s. extent** jusqu'à un certain point
(b) *(as opposed to other)* certain(e); **s. people say...** certains disent que..., il y a des gens qui disent que...
(c) *(considerable quantity or number of)* **I've been waiting for s. time/hours** ça fait un moment/plusieurs heures que j'attends; **s. distance away** assez loin; **s. miles away** à plusieurs kilomètres
(d) *(unspecified)* **for s. reason or other** pour une raison ou pour une autre; **she'll come s. day** elle viendra un jour (ou l'autre); **at s. time in the future** plus tard; **in s. book or other** dans un livre quelconque; **s. fool left the door open** un imbécile a laissé la porte ouverte
(e) *Fam (for emphasis)* **that was s. storm/meal!** quel orage/repas!; *Ironic* **s. hope!** je peux/il peut/*etc.* toujours y compter!; *Ironic* **s. friend you are!** quel ami tu fais!
3 *adv (approximately)* environ; **s. fifteen minutes** environ quinze minutes

somebody ['sʌmbədɪ] **1** *pron* quelqu'un; **she's s. you can trust** c'est quelqu'un en qui vous pouvez avoir confiance; **s.'s coming** on vient; **s. important/taller** quelqu'un d'important/de plus grand; **s. else** quelqu'un d'autre
2 *n* **she thinks she's s.** elle se croit importante; **I want to be s.** je veux devenir quelqu'un

somehow ['sʌmhaʊ] *adv* (a) *(in some way or other)* d'une façon ou d'une autre (b) *(for some reason or other)* pour une raison ou pour une autre

someone ['sʌmwʌn] = **somebody**

someplace ['sʌmpleɪs] = **somewhere**

somersault ['sʌməsɔːlt] **1** *n (on the ground)* roulade *f*; *(in the air)* saut *m* périlleux
2 *vi (of person) (on the ground)* faire une roulade; *(in the air)* faire un saut périlleux; *(of car)* faire un tonneau

something ['sʌmθɪŋ] **1** *pron* quelque chose; **there's s. about him I don't like** il y a quelque chose chez lui que je n'aime pas; **s. tells me she'll be there** quelque chose me dit qu'elle sera là; **s. to drink/to eat/to read** quelque chose à boire/à manger/à lire; **s. red/different/special** quelque chose de rouge/de différent/de spécial; **he's s. in publishing** il a un poste important dans l'édition; **in nineteen-fifty s.** dans les années cinquante; **she's eighty s.** elle a quatre-vingts ans et quelques; **what's his name? – Simon s.** comment s'appelle-t-il? – Simon quelque chose; **at least he apologized, that's s.!** au moins, il s'est excusé, c'est déjà ça!; **there's s. in what you say** il y a quelque chose d'intéressant dans ce que vous dites; **she has s. to do with what happened** elle y est pour quelque chose dans ce qui s'est passé; **that**

was quite s.! ce n'était pas mal du tout!; **he's a mechanic or s. like that** il est mécanicien ou un truc comme ça; **she has a cold or s. (like that)** elle a un rhume, je crois
2 *adv* (a) *(expressing degree)* **there's been s. of an improvement** il y a eu une certaine amélioration; **she's s. of a miser** elle est plutôt avare; **it's s. like a guinea pig** ça ressemble à un cobaye (b) *(for emphasis)* **it hurt s. awful!** ça faisait mal, quelque chose de bien!
3 *n* **a little s.** un petit quelque chose

sometime ['sʌmtaɪm] *adv* **see you s.** à un de ces jours; **s. last week** la semaine dernière; **s. before Christmas** avant Noël; **you'll have to make up your mind s.** il faudra bien que tu te décides un jour; **s. soon** d'ici peu, bientôt; **s. or other** un jour ou l'autre

sometimes ['sʌmtaɪmz] *adv* quelquefois

someway ['sʌmweɪ] = **somehow**

somewhat ['sʌmwɒt] *adv* quelque peu, un peu

somewhere ['sʌmweə(r)] *adv* (a) *(some place)* quelque part; **s. else** ailleurs; **do you have s. to stay?** est-ce que tu as trouvé à loger?; *Fig* **now we're getting s.!** nous voilà enfin sur la bonne route *ou* voie! (b) *(approximately)* **she's s. around fifty** elle a environ cinquante ans; **it costs s. in the region** *or* **neighborhood of $500** cela coûte environ 500 dollars

somnolent ['sɒmnələnt] *adj Formal* somnolent(e)

son [sʌn] *n* fils *m*; *very Fam* **s. of a bitch** salaud *m*

sonar ['səʊnɑː(r)] *n* sonar *m*

sonata [sə'nɑːtə] *n* sonate *f*

song [sɒŋ] *n* (a) *(music with words)* chanson *f*; **to burst** *or* **to break into s.** se mettre à chanter; **s. book** livre *m* de chansons; **s. thrush** grive *f* musicienne (b) *(idioms)* **to buy sth for a s.** acheter qch pour une bouchée de pain; **to make a s. and dance (about sth)** faire toute une histoire (de qch)

songbird ['sɒŋbɜːd] *n* oiseau *m* chanteur

songwriter ['sɒŋraɪtə(r)] *n* auteur-compositeur *m*

sonic ['sɒnɪk] *adj* sonique; **s. boom** bang *m*

son-in-law ['sʌnɪnlɔː] *n (pl* **sons-in-law***)* gendre *m*

sonnet ['sɒnɪt] *n* sonnet *m*

sonny ['sʌnɪ] *n Fam* fiston *m*

sonorous ['sɒnərəs] *adj (deep)* sonore; *(impressive)* imposant(e)

soon [suːn] *adv* (a) *(within a short time)* bientôt; *(in past)* vite; **it will s. be Friday/Christmas** c'est bientôt vendredi/Noël; **she s. changed her mind** elle a vite changé d'avis; **s. after(wards)** peu après; **s. after four** peu après quatre heures; **no sooner had she left than...** elle n'était pas plus tôt partie que... (b) *(early)* tôt; **none too s.** pas trop tôt; **how s. can you get here?** quand pouvez-vous être ici au plus tôt?; **sooner or later** tôt ou tard; **the sooner the better** le plus tôt sera le mieux; **as s. as** aussitôt que, dès que; **as s. as possible** aussitôt que possible, dès que possible (c) *(expressing preference)* **I would just as s. stay** j'aimerais autant rester; **I would sooner do it alone** je préférerais le faire seul

soot [sʊt] *n* suie *f*

soothe [suːð] *vt* apaiser

soothing ['suːðɪŋ] *adj* apaisant(e)

soothsayer ['suːθseɪə(r)] *n* devin (devineresse) *m,f*

sooty ['sʊtɪ] *adj (covered in soot)* couvert(e) de suie; *(black)* noir(e) comme de la suie

sop [sɒp] *n (concession)* concession *f* (**to** à)

sophist ['sɒfɪst] *n* sophiste *mf*

sophisticated [sə'fɪstɪkeɪtɪd] *adj (person, taste)* raffiné(e); *(style, humor)* recherché(e); *(machinery, technique)* sophistiqué(e)

sophistication [səfɪstɪ'keɪʃən] *n (of person, taste)* raffinement *m*; *(of style, humor)* recherche *f*; *(of machinery, technique)* sophistication *f*

sophistry ['sɒfɪstrɪ] *n (reasoning)* sophistique *f*; *(argument)* sophisme *m*

sophomore ['sɒfəmɔ:(r)] **1** *n Sch* élève *mf* de deuxième année; *Univ* étudiant(e) *m,f* de deuxième année

2 *adj Sch & Univ* **s. year** deuxième année *f*

soporific [sɒpə'rɪfɪk] *adj Formal* soporifique

sopping ['sɒpɪŋ] *adj* **s. (wet)** trempé(e)

soppy ['sɒpɪ] *adj Fam* sentimental(e)

soprano [sɒ'prɑ:nəʊ] (*pl* **sopranos** *or* **soprani** [sɒ'prɑ:ni:]) *n (singer)* soprano *mf*; **s. voice** voix *f* de soprano

sorbet ['sɔ:beɪ] *n* sorbet *m*

sorcerer ['sɔ:sərə(r)] *n* sorcier *m*

sorceress ['sɔ:sərɪs] *n* sorcière *f*

sorcery ['sɔ:sərɪ] *n* sorcellerie *f*

sordid ['sɔ:dɪd] *adj* sordide

sore [sɔ:(r)] **1** *adj* (**a**) *(painful)* douloureux(euse); **to have a s. throat/back** avoir mal à la gorge/au dos; **my feet are s.** mes pieds me font mal (**b**) *Fam (annoyed)* en colère (**about** à propos de); **it's a s. point (with him)** c'est un sujet douloureux (pour lui)

2 *n (wound)* plaie *f*

sorely ['sɔ:lɪ] *adv (greatly)* sérieusement; **she will be s. missed** elle nous/leur manquera beaucoup; **to be s. in need of sth** avoir vraiment besoin de qch; **s. tempted** sérieusement tenté(e)

sorrow ['sɒrəʊ] *n* chagrin *m*; **to my great s.** à mon grand regret

sorrowful ['sɒrəfʊl] *adj* triste

sorry ['sɒrɪ] *adj* (**a**) *(regretful, disappointed)* désolé(e); **to be s. about sth** être désolé de qch; **to be s. one did sth** regretter d'avoir fait qch; **to say s. (to sb)** s'excuser (auprès de qn); **I'm s. you didn't like it** je suis désolé que tu n'aies pas aimé; **s. to keep you waiting** désolé de vous faire attendre; **I'm s. to hear (that)...** je suis désolé d'apprendre que...; *Fam* **you'll be s.!** tu vas le regretter!; **s.?** *(pardon?)* pardon? (**b**) *(sympathetic)* **to feel s. for sb** plaindre qn; **to feel s. for oneself** s'apitoyer sur son propre sort; **I'm just feeling a bit s. for myself** je suis juste un peu déprimé (**c**) *(pathetic)* triste; **to be a s. sight** être dans un triste état; **to be in a s. state** être dans un triste état

sort [sɔ:t] **1** *n* (**a**) *(kind)* sorte *f*; **all sorts of** toutes sortes de; **what s. of tree is it?** qu'est-ce que c'est comme arbre?; **that s. of thing** ce genre de chose; **she's that s. of person** elle est comme ça; **something of the s.** quelque chose de ce genre; **I did nothing of the s.** je n'ai jamais fait ça; **he's so arrogant – he's nothing of the s.!** il est vraiment arrogant – pas du tout!; **it takes all sorts** il faut de tout pour faire un monde; *Fam* **she's a good s.** c'est une brave fille; **she's not the s. to give in easily** elle n'est pas du genre à abandonner facilement; **we don't want your s. here** nous ne voulons pas de personnes de votre genre ici; **to be out of sorts** *(unwell)* ne pas être dans son assiette; *(in a bad mood)* être de mauvaise humeur; **they served us coffee of a s.** ils nous ont servi du café, si on peut appeler ça du café; **an artist of sorts** une espèce d'artiste

(**b**) *Fam* **this is s. of embarrassing** c'est plutôt gênant; **I s. of expected it** je m'y attendais un peu; **do you like it? – s. of** ça te plaît? – oui, plus ou moins

(**c**) *(in order to organize)* **to have a s. through sth** faire du tri dans qch

2 *vt also Comput* trier

▸**sort out** *vt sep* (**a**) *(organize)* ranger; **to s. oneself out** résoudre ses problèmes (**b**) *(problem)* régler

sortie ['sɔ:ti:] *n Mil* sortie *f*; *Fig* escapade *f*

sorting ['sɔ:tɪŋ] *n* tri *m*; **s. office** bureau *m* de tri

SOS [esəʊ'es] *n* S.O.S. *m*; **to send out an S.** lancer un S.O.S.

soufflé ['su:fleɪ] *n* soufflé *m*; **cheese s.** soufflé au fromage

sought [sɔ:t] *pt & pp of* **seek**

sought-after ['sɔ:tɑ:ftə(r)] *adj* recherché(e)

soul [səʊl] *n* (**a**) *(spirit)* âme *f*; **to sell one's s.** vendre son âme au diable; *Fig* **she's the s. of discretion** c'est la discrétion même; *Fig* **it lacks s.** cela n'a pas d'âme; **All Souls' Day** le jour des Morts (**b**) *(person)* âme *f*, personne *f*; **he's a good s.** c'est une bonne personne; **there wasn't a s. in the street** il n'y avait pas âme qui vive dans la rue; **poor s.!** le/la pauvre! (**c**) *(music)* soul *f*

soul-destroying ['səʊldɪstrɔɪɪŋ] *adj* démoralisant(e)

soulful ['səʊlfʊl] *adj (look, eyes)* mélancolique; *(song)* émouvant(e)

soulless ['səʊllɪs] *adj (person)* insensible; *(place)* sans âme

soulmate ['səʊlmeɪt] *n* âme *f* sœur

soul-searching ['səʊlsɜ:tʃɪŋ] *n* examen *m* de conscience

sound¹ [saʊnd] **1** *n* son *m*; *(noise)* bruit *m*; **not a s. could be heard** on n'entendait pas un bruit; **she likes the s. of her own voice** elle aime s'écouter parler; **to turn the s. up/down** *(on TV, radio)* monter/baisser le son; *Fig* **I don't like the s. of it** cela ne me dit rien qui vaille; **she's angry, by the s. of it** elle est en colère, on dirait; **s. barrier** mur *m* du son; **s. bite** petite phrase *f* *(prononcée par un homme politique à la radio ou à la télévision pour frapper les esprits)*; *Comput* **s. card** carte *f* son; **s. effects** bruitage *m*; **s. engineer** ingénieur *m* du son; **s. wave** onde *f* sonore

2 *vt* (**a**) *(bell)* sonner; *also Fig (alarm)* donner; **to s. one's horn** klaxonner (**b**) *(pronounce)* prononcer; **the "h" is not sounded** le "h" ne se prononce pas

3 *vi* (**a**) *(make sound)* *(of trumpet, bell)* sonner (**b**) *(seem)* avoir l'air, sembler; **she sounds French** on dirait qu'elle est française; **that sounds like a good idea** ça me semble une bonne idée; **he sounds like a nice guy** ça a l'air d'être un type bien; **it sounds like Mozart** on dirait du Mozart; **that sounds like trouble!** c'est signe de problèmes!; **how does that s. to you?** *(referring to suggestion)* qu'en pensez-vous?

▸**sound off** *vi Fam* se plaindre (**about** de)

▸**sound out** *vt sep* sonder (**about** à propos de)

sound² [saʊnd] **1** *adj* (**a**) *(healthy)* sain(e); *(in good condition)* en bon état; **to be of s. mind** être sain d'esprit (**b**) *(sensible, logical) (argument)* valable; *(basis)* solide; *(advice)* bon (bonne) (**c**) *(reliable) (investment)* sûr(e); *(business)* sain(e); *(person)* compétent(e)

2 *adv* **to be s. asleep** être profondément endormi(e)

sounding board ['saʊndɪŋbɔ:d] *n (on pulpit, stage)* abat-voix *m*; *Fig* **I use John as a s.** j'utilise John pour tester mes idées

soundings ['saʊndɪŋz] *npl* **to take s.** faire des sondages

soundly ['saʊndlɪ] *adv* (**a**) *(solidly)* solidement (**b**) *(logically)* judicieusement (**c**) *(thoroughly)* **to sleep s.** dormir profondément; **to thrash sb s.** donner une bonne correction à qn

soundproof ['saʊndpru:f] **1** *adj* insonorisé(e)

2 *vt* insonoriser

soundtrack ['saʊndtræk] *n* bande *f* sonore

soup [su:p] *n* soupe *f*; *Fig* **to be in the s.** être dans le pétrin; **s. kitchen** soupe populaire; **s. ladle** louche *f*; **s. plate** assiette *f* creuse; **s. spoon** cuillère *f* à soupe

▸**soup up** *vt sep Fam (engine)* gonfler; *(car)* gonfler le moteur de

sour ['saʊə(r)] **1** *adj (fruit, milk, taste)* aigre; *Fig (person)* aigri(e); **to turn s.** *(of milk)* tourner; *Fig (of situation, relationship)* tourner à l'aigre, mal tourner; **s. cream** crème *f* aigre; *Fig* **it was just s. grapes** c'était par dépit

2 *vt (milk)* faire tourner; *Fig (atmosphere, relationship)* empoisonner

3 *vi (of milk)* tourner; *Fig (of atmosphere, relationship)* détériorer

source [sɔ:s] *n* source *f*; *(of unrest, discontent)* origine *f*; *(of infection)* foyer *m*

sourly ['saʊəlɪ] *adv* avec aigreur

souse [saʊs] *vt* tremper

south [saʊθ] **1** *n* sud *m*; **to the s. of** au sud de
2 *adj (coast, side)* sud; *(wind)* du sud; **S. Africa** Afrique *f* du Sud; **S. African** sud-africain(e); *(person)* Sud-Africain(e) *m,f*; **S. America** Amérique *f* du Sud; **S. American** sud-américain(e); *(person)* Sud-Américain(e) *m,f*; **S. Carolina** la Caroline du Sud; **S. China Sea** mer *f* de Chine du Sud; **S. Dakota** le Dakota du Sud; **S. Korea** Corée *f* du Sud; **S. Korean** sud-coréen(enne); *(person)* Sud-Coréen(enne) *m,f*; **S. Pole** pôle *m* sud
3 *adv* au sud; *(travel)* vers le sud; **to face s.** *(of house)* être exposé(e) au sud

southbound ['saʊθbaʊnd] *adj (train, traffic)* en direction du sud; **s. road** voie *f* sud

southeast [saʊθ'iːst] **1** *n* sud-est *m*
2 *adj (side)* sud-est; *(wind)* du sud-est
3 *adv* au sud-est; *(travel)* vers le sud-est

southeasterly [saʊθ'iːstəlɪ] **1** *n (wind)* vent *m* du sud-est
2 *adj (direction)* vers le sud-est; *(wind)* du sud-est

southeastern [saʊθ'iːstən] *adj (region)* (du) sud-est

southerly ['sʌðəlɪ] **1** *n (wind)* vent *m* du sud
2 *adj (direction)* vers le sud; *(wind)* du sud; **the most s. point** le point le plus au sud

southern ['sʌðən] *adj (region, accent)* du sud; **s. France** le sud de la France; **s. hemisphere** hémisphère *m* sud

southerner ['sʌðənə(r)] *n* habitant(e) *m,f* du Sud

south-facing ['saʊθ'feɪsɪŋ] *adj* exposé(e) au sud

southpaw ['saʊθpɔː] *Fam* **1** *n* gaucher(ère) *m,f*
2 *adj* gaucher(ère)

south-southeast ['saʊθsaʊθ'iːst] *adv* au sud-sud-est; *(travel)* vers le sud-sud-est

south-southwest ['saʊθsaʊθ'west] *adv* au sud-sud-ouest; *(travel)* vers le sud-sud-ouest

southward ['saʊθwəd] **1** *adj* au sud
2 *adv* vers le sud

southwards ['saʊθwədz] *adv* = **southward**

southwest [saʊθ'west] **1** *n* sud-ouest *m*
2 *adj (side)* sud-ouest; *(wind)* du sud-ouest
3 *adv* au sud-ouest; *(travel)* vers le sud-ouest

southwesterly [saʊθ'westəlɪ] **1** *n (wind)* vent *m* du sud-ouest
2 *adj (direction)* vers le sud-ouest; *(wind)* du sud-ouest

southwestern [saʊθ'westən] *adj (region)* (du) sud-ouest

souvenir [suːvə'nɪə(r)] *n* souvenir *m*

sovereign ['sɒvrɪn] *n & adj* souverain(e) *m,f*

sovereignty ['sɒvrəntɪ] *n* souveraineté *f*

Soviet ['səʊvɪət] **1** *n (person)* Soviétique *mf*
2 *adj* soviétique; *Formerly* **the S. Union** l'Union *f* soviétique

sow[1] [səʊ] *(pt* sowed [səʊd], *pp* sown [səʊn] *or* sowed) *vt (seeds) & Fig (discord, doubt)* semer; *(field)* ensemencer (**with** en)

sow[2] [saʊ] *n (female pig)* truie *f*

sown [səʊn] *pp of* **sow**[1]

soya ['sɔɪə] *n* soja *m*; **s. bean** graine *f* de soja; **s. milk** lait *m* de soja

soy sauce [sɔɪ'sɔːs] *n* sauce *f* de soja

sozzled ['sɒzəld] *adj Fam (drunk)* bourré(e); **to get s.** se cuiter

spa [spɑː] *n (place)* ville *f* d'eau; *(spring)* source *f* thermale; *(health club)* spa *m*; **s. bath** spa *m*

space [speɪs] **1** *n* (**a**) *(room)* place *f*; **to stare into s.** regarder dans le vide (**b**) *(individual place)* place *f*; *(on printed form)* espace *m*; **wide open spaces** grands espaces; **s. bar** *(on keyboard)* barre *f* d'espacement (**c**) *(period of time)* espace *m*; **in the s. of a year** en l'espace d'une année (**d**) *(outer space)* espace *m*; **the s. age** l'ère *f* spatiale; *Fam* **to be a s. cadet** planer; **s. rocket** fusée *f* spatiale; **s. shuttle** navette *f* spatiale; **s. station** station *f* spatiale; **s. suit** combinaison *f* spatiale; **s. tourism**

tourisme *m* spatial; **s. travel** voyages *mpl* dans l'espace (**e**) *(gap)* espace *m*, vide *m*; *(in schedule)* trou *m*
2 *vt* espacer

▸**space out** *vt sep* espacer

space-age ['speɪseɪdʒ] *adj* futuriste

spacecraft ['speɪskrɑːft] *n* vaisseau *m* spatial

spaced out ['speɪst'aʊt] *adj Fam* **to be s.** planer complètement

spaceman ['speɪsmæn] *n* astronaute *m*

spaceship ['speɪsʃɪp] *n* vaisseau *m* spatial

spacing ['speɪsɪŋ] *n* espacement *m*; *Typ* **single/double s.** simple/double interligne *m*

spacious ['speɪʃəs] *adj* spacieux(euse)

spade [speɪd] *n* (**a**) *(tool)* bêche *f*; **to call a s. a s.** appeler un chat un chat (**b**) *(in cards)* pique *m*

spaghetti [spə'getɪ] *n* spaghetti *mpl*

Spain [speɪn] *n* l'Espagne *f*

spam [spæm] **1** *n (e-mails)* messages *mpl* publicitaires, *Fam* pourriels *mpl*; **a s. e-mail** un message publicitaire, *Fam* un pourriel
2 *vi (pt & pp* spammed) *Comput* envoyer des messages publicitaires en masse *ou Fam* des pourriels

spammer ['spæmə(r)] *n Comput* spammeur *m*

spamming ['spæmɪŋ] *n Comput* spamming *m*

span [spæn] **1** *n* (**a**) *(of hand)* empan *m*; *(of wing)* envergure *f* (**b**) *(of arch)* portée *f*; *(of bridge)* travée *f* (**c**) *(period of time)* période *f* (**d**) *(of knowledge, interests)* étendue *f*
2 *vt (pt & pp* spanned) *(of bridge)* franchir; *Fig (of life, knowledge)* couvrir

Spaniard ['spænjəd] *n* Espagnol(e) *m,f*

spaniel ['spænjəl] *n* épagneul *m*

Spanish ['spænɪʃ] **1** *n (people)* **the S.** les Espagnols *mpl*
2 *n (language)* espagnol *m*
3 *adj* espagnol(e); **the S. Inquisition** l'Inquisition *f* espagnole; *Culin* **S. omelet** omelette *f* à l'espagnole

spank [spæŋk] **1** *n* **to give sb a s.** donner une fessée à qn
2 *vt* donner une fessée à

spanking ['spæŋkɪŋ] **1** *n* fessée *f*; **to give sb a s.** donner une fessée à qn
2 *adv Fam* **s. new** flambant neuf (neuve); **they had a s. good time** ils se sont rudement bien amusés

spanner ['spænə(r)] *n* clef *f*; *Fig* **to throw a s. in the works** compliquer les choses

spar[1] [spɑː(r)] *n (on ship)* espar *m*

spar[2] [spɑː(r)] *(pt & pp* sparred) *vi* **to s. with sb** *(in boxing)* s'entraîner avec qn; *(argue)* se chamailler avec qn

spare ['speə(r)] **1** *n (spare part)* pièce *f* de rechange; *(tire)* pneu *m* de rechange
2 *adj* (**a**) *(available)* disponible; *(surplus)* en trop, qui reste; *(reserve)* de rechange; **do you have a s. pen?** tu as un stylo à me prêter?; **a s. moment** un moment de libre; **s. part** pièce *f* de rechange; **s. ribs** travers *mpl* de porc; **s. room** chambre *f* d'amis; **s. time** temps *m* (de) libre; **s. tire** pneu *m* de secours *ou* de rechange; *Fam Fig (around waist)* bourrelet *m*; **s. wheel** roue *f* de secours
(**b**) *(frugal) (meal)* frugal(e); *(style)* dépouillé(e); *(room)* austère
3 *vt* (**a**) *(give away, go without) (person)* se passer de; **to have no time to s.** ne pas avoir le temps; **can you s. the time?** avez-vous le temps?; **with five minutes to s.** avec cinq minutes d'avance; **to have a few moments to s.** disposer de quelques minutes; **can you s. me a few moments?** pouvez-vous m'accorder quelques minutes?; **could you s. me some milk?** est-ce que tu peux me donner un peu de lait?; **to s. a thought for sb** penser à qn
(**b**) *(avoid)* **to s. no expense** ne pas regarder à la dépense
(**c**) *(save from)* **to s. sb sth** épargner qch à qn; **s. me the details!** épargnez-moi les détails!

(d) *(show mercy toward)* épargner; **to s. sb's life** épargner la vie de qn; **to s. sb's feelings** ménager les sentiments de qn

sparing ['speərɪŋ] *adj* économe (**with** avec); **to be s. with one's compliments** être avare de compliments

sparingly ['speərɪŋlɪ] *adv* en petite quantité

spark [spɑːk] **1** *n (electrical, from fire)* étincelle *f; Fig (of intelligence, interest)* lueur *f; Fig* **sparks will fly** cela va faire des étincelles; *Fig* **s. plug** bougie *f*
2 *vi* jeter *ou* faire des étincelles

▸**spark off** *vt sep* déclencher

sparkle ['spɑːkəl] **1** *n also Fig* éclat *m*
2 *vi (of light, eyes) & Fig (of person, conversation)* briller; *(of diamond)* scintiller

sparkler ['spɑːklə(r)] *n (firework)* cierge *m* magique

sparkling ['spɑːklɪŋ] *adj (light, eyes) & Fig (person, conversation)* brillant(e); *(diamond)* scintillant(e); *(wine)* pétillant(e)

sparring partner ['spɑːrɪŋ'pɑːtnə(r)] *n (in boxing)* partenaire *mf* d'entraînement; *Fig* adversaire *mf*

sparrow ['spærəʊ] *n* moineau *m*

sparse [spɑːs] *adj* clairsemé(e)

sparsely ['spɑːslɪ] *adv (populated, furnished)* peu; **s. covered with trees** aux arbres clairsemés

spartan ['spɑːtən] *adj also Fig* spartiate

spasm ['spæzəm] *n* spasme *m; Fig (of coughing)* quinte *f; (of jealousy)* crise *f*

spasmodic [spæz'mɒdɪk] *adj (irregular)* irrégulier(ère)

spasmodically [spæz'mɒdɪklɪ] *adv (irregularly)* irrégulièrement

spastic ['spæstɪk] *n* **(a)** *Med* handicapé(e) *m,f* moteur **(b)** *very Fam Pej (clumsy, useless person)* empoté(e) *m,f*

spat¹ [spæt] *n Fam (quarrel)* querelle *f*

spat² [spæt] *pt & pp of* **spit²**

spate [speɪt] *n (of letters, calls)* avalanche *f; (of crimes)* vague *f*

spatial ['speɪʃəl] *adj* spatial(e)

spatter ['spætə(r)] *vt* éclabousser (**with** avec)

spatula ['spætjʊlə] *n* spatule *f*

spawn [spɔːn] **1** *n (of frog, fish)* œufs *mpl*
2 *vt (give rise to)* engendrer
3 *vi (of frog, fish)* frayer

speak [spiːk] *(pt* spoke [spəʊk], *pp* spoken ['spəʊkən]) **1** *vt* **(a)** *(utter)* dire **(b)** *(language)* parler
2 *vi (talk, give a speech)* parler (**to/about** à/de); **they're not speaking** *(to each other)* ils ne se parlent pas; **I know her to s. to** on se parle quelquefois; **legally/morally speaking** légalement/moralement parlant; **so to s.** pour ainsi dire; **who's speaking?** *(on phone)* qui est à l'appareil?; **Mr Curry? – yes, speaking** Mr Curry? – lui-même

▸**speak for** *vt insep* **to s. for sb** *(on behalf of)* parler pour qn; **s. for yourself!** parle pour toi!; **the facts s. for themselves** les faits parlent d'eux-mêmes

▸**speak out** *vi* parler franchement; **to s. out against sth** s'élever contre qch

▸**speak up** *vi* **(a)** *(speak more loudly)* parler plus fort **(b)** *(speak in favor of)* **to s. up for sb/sth** parler en faveur de qn/qch; **to s. up for oneself** se défendre

speaker ['spiːkə(r)] *n* **(a)** *(at meeting)* intervenant(e) *m,f; (at conference)* conférencier(ère) *m,f;* **an Italian s.** une personne qui parle italien; **a French/Spanish/Portuguese s.** un(e) francophone/hispanophone/lusophone; **to be a slow/fast s.** parler lentement/vite; *Pol* **the S.** le Président du Congrès **(b)** *(loudspeaker)* enceinte *f*

speaking ['spiːkɪŋ] *adj (doll, robot)* parlant(e); **s. clock** horloge *f* parlante; **s. part** *(in play, movie)* rôle *m* parlant

spear ['spɪə(r)] **1** *n* lance *f*
2 *vt* transpercer d'un coup de lance

spearhead ['spɪəhed] **1** *n also Fig* fer *m* de lance
2 *vt (attack, campaign)* être le fer de lance de

spearmint ['spɪəmɪnt] *n* menthe *f* verte

spec [spek] *n Fam* **on s.** à tout hasard

special ['speʃəl] **1** *adj* spécial(e); *(friend)* proche; *(reason, effort, attention)* particulier(ère); **what's so s. about November 19th?** qu'est-ce que le 19 novembre a de si spécial?; **s. agent** agent *m* secret; **s. delivery** envoi *m* en exprès; **s. effects** effets *mpl* spéciaux; **s. interest group** groupe *m* d'intérêt commun; *(lobby)* lobby *m*, groupe *m* de pression; *Comput* groupe d'intérêt; **s. needs** difficultés *fpl* d'apprentissage; **s. offer** offre *f* spéciale; *Pol* **s. powers** pouvoirs *mpl* exceptionnels
2 *n (on menu)* plat *m* du jour

specialist ['speʃəlɪst] **1** *n* spécialiste *mf; Med* **heart s.** cardiologue *mf;* **lung s.** pneumologue *mf*
2 *adj (skills, equipment)* d'un spécialiste; *(store)* spécialisé(e)

specialization [speʃəlaɪ'zeɪʃən] *n* spécialisation *f*

specialize ['speʃəlaɪz] *vi* se spécialiser (**in** en)

specially ['speʃəlɪ] *adv (expressly)* spécialement

specialty ['speʃəltɪ] *(pl* **specialties**) *n* spécialité *f*

species ['spiːʃiːz] *(pl* **species**) *n* espèce *f*

specific [spɪ'sɪfɪk] **1** *adj* précis(e) (**about** au sujet de); **to be s.,...** pour être précis,...; *Phys* **s. gravity** densité *f*
2 *npl* **specifics** détails *mpl*

specifically [spɪ'sɪfɪkəlɪ] *adv* **(a)** *(explicitly)* expressément **(b)** *(specially)* spécialement **(c)** *(precisely)* précisément

specification [spesɪfɪ'keɪʃən] *n* spécification *f*

specify ['spesɪfaɪ] *(pt & pp* **specified**) *vt* **(a)** *(state exactly)* préciser **(b)** *(stipulate)* stipuler

specimen ['spesɪmɪn] *n* **(a)** *(sample amount) (of handwriting, blood)* échantillon *m;* **s. copy** spécimen *m* **(b)** *(individual example)* spécimen *m; Fam* **he's an odd s.** c'est un drôle de spécimen

specious ['spiːʃəs] *adj* spécieux(euse)

speck [spek] *n (of dust)* grain *m; (of paint, ink)* petite tache *f;* **a s. of dirt** une poussière

speckled ['spekəld] *adj* tacheté(e) (**with** de)

specs [speks] *npl Fam (spectacles)* lunettes *fpl*

spectacle ['spektəkəl] *n* **(a)** *(show, sight)* spectacle *m;* **to make a s. of oneself** se donner en spectacle **(b)** **spectacles** *(glasses)* lunettes *fpl*

spectacular [spek'tækjʊlə(r)] **1** *n* production *f* à grand spectacle
2 *adj* spectaculaire

spectator [spek'teɪtə(r)] *n* spectateur(trice) *m,f;* **s. sport** sport *m* à grand public

specter ['spektə(r)] *n* spectre *m*

spectrum ['spektrəm] *(pl* **spectra** ['spektrə]) *n* spectre *m; Fig* éventail *m*

speculate ['spekjʊleɪt] *vi* **(a)** *(hypothesize)* faire des suppositions (**about** au sujet de) **(b)** *Fin* **to s. (on the Stock Market)** spéculer (à la Bourse)

speculation [spekjʊ'leɪʃən] *n* suppositions *fpl*

speculative ['spekjʊlətɪv] *adj* spéculatif(ive)

speculator ['spekjʊleɪtə(r)] *n Fin* spéculateur(trice) *m,f*

sped [sped] *pt & pp of* **speed**

speech [spiːtʃ] *n* **(a)** *(faculty)* parole *f;* **s. defect** *or* **impediment** défaut *m* d'élocution; **s. therapist** orthophoniste *mf, Belg & Suisse* logopède *mf;* **s. therapy** orthophonie *f* **(b)** *(address)* discours *m;* **to give** *or* **to make a s.** faire un discours **(c)** *(way of speaking)* langue *f* **(d)** *Gram* **part of s.** partie *f* du discours

speechless ['spiːtʃlɪs] *adj* muet(ette) (**with** de); **to be left s.** rester sans voix

speechwriter ['spiːtʃraɪtə(r)] *n* personne *f* qui écrit des discours

speed [spiːd] **1** *n* **(a)** *(rapidity)* vitesse *f;* **the s. of light/sound** la vitesse de la lumière/du son; **at s.** à toute vitesse; **to gather** *or* **to pick up/lose s.** prendre/perdre de la vitesse; *Fig*

to be up to s. on sth être au courant de qch; **s. bump** ralentisseur *m*; **s. camera** radar *m*; *Fam* **s. cop** motard *m* (de la police); **s. dating** speed dating *m*; **s. dial** numérotation *f* abrégée; **s. limit** limitation *f* de vitesse; **s. skating** patinage *m* de vitesse; **s. trap** contrôle *m* de vitesse

(**b**) *(gear)* vitesse *f*; **five-s. gearbox** boîte *f* à cinq vitesses

(**c**) *Fam (amphetamine)* amphés *fpl*, speed *m*

2 *vi* (**a**) *(pt & pp* **sped** [sped] *or* **speeded**) *(move quickly)* **to s. along** foncer; **to s. away/out** partir/sortir à toute vitesse

(**b**) *(exceed speed limit)* faire un excès de vitesse; **to be caught speeding** être arrêté pour excès de vitesse

(**c**) *Fam* **to be speeding** *(under effect of amphetamines)* être sous amphés

▸**speed off** *vi* partir à toute vitesse

▸**speed up 1** *vt sep (person)* faire aller plus vite; *(work, project, process)* accélérer

2 *vi* aller plus vite

speedboat ['spi:dbəut] *n* vedette *f*; *(with outboard motor)* hors-bord *m inv*

speedily ['spi:dɪlɪ] *adv* vite, rapidement

speeding ['spi:dɪŋ] *n* excès *m* de vitesse

speedometer [spi:'dɒmɪtə(r)] *n* compteur *m* de vitesse

speedway ['spi:dweɪ] *n* speedway *m*

speedy ['spi:dɪ] *adj* rapide

spell¹ [spel] *n (magic words)* formule *f* magique; **to cast a s. on sb** jeter un sort à qn; **to break the s.** rompre le charme; **to be under a s.** être envoûté(e); **to be under sb's s.** être sous le charme de qn

spell² [spel] *(pt & pp* **spelt** [spelt] *or* **spelled**) **1** *vt* (**a**) *(in writing)* écrire, orthographier; *(aloud)* épeler; **how do you s. it?** comment ça s'écrit? (**b**) *(signify)* signifier; **to s. disaster** être un désastre; **to s. trouble** être mauvais signe

2 *vi* **he can s. well** il a une bonne orthographe; **he can't s.** il a une mauvaise orthographe

▸**spell out** *vt sep (address, name)* épeler; *Fig (explain explicitly)* expliquer clairement; **do I have to s. it out for you?** est-ce qu'il faut que je te fasse un dessin?

spell³ [spel] *n (period)* période *f*; **after a s. as a teacher, he...** après avoir été professeur pendant un temps, il...; **a cold s.** une période de froid; **a good/bad s.** une bonne/mauvaise période

spellbound ['spelbaʊnd] *adj* fasciné(e)

spell-checker ['speltʃekə(r)] *n Comput* correcteur *m* d'orthographe

speller ['spelə(r)] *n* manuel *m* d'orthographe

spelling ['spelɪŋ] *n* orthographe *f*; **to be good/bad at s.** être bon (bonne)/mauvais(e) en orthographe; **s. bee** concours *m* d'orthographe; **s. mistake** faute *f* d'orthographe

spelt [spelt] *pt & pp of* **spell²**

spelunker [spɪ'lʌŋkə(r)] *n* spéléologue *mf*

spelunking [spɪ'lʌŋkɪŋ] *n* spéléologie *f*

spend [spend] *(pt & pp* **spent** [spent]) *vt* (**a**) *(money)* dépenser; **to s. money on sb** dépenser de l'argent pour qn; **to s. money on sth** *(object)* dépenser de l'argent en qch; *(vacation, education)* dépenser de l'argent pour qch (**b**) *(time)* passer; **to s. time on sth/doing sth** passer du temps sur qch/à faire qch

spender ['spendə(r)] *n* **to be a big s.** être très dépensier(ère)

spending ['spendɪŋ] *n* dépenses *fpl*; **s. money** argent *m* de poche; **s. power** pouvoir *m* d'achat; **to go on a s. spree** faire des folies

spendthrift ['spendθrɪft] *n* dépensier(ère) *m,f*

spent [spent] **1** *adj (bullet, match)* utilisé(e); **to be a s. force** ne plus avoir d'influence

2 *pt & pp of* **spend**

sperm [spɜːm] *n (semen)* sperme *m*; **s. bank** banque *f* de sperme; **s. donor** donneur *m* de sperme; **s. whale** cachalot *m*

spermicide ['spɜːmɪsaɪd] *n* spermicide *m*

spew [spju:] *vt & vi Fam (vomit)* dégobiller

sphere [sfɪə(r)] *n also Fig* sphère *f*; **that's outside my s.** ce n'est pas dans mes compétences; **s. of influence** sphère d'influence

spherical ['sferɪkəl] *adj* sphérique

sphincter ['sfɪŋktə(r)] *n Anat* sphincter *m*

sphinx [sfɪŋks] *n* sphinx *m*

spice [spaɪs] **1** *n (seasoning)* épice *f*; *Fig (excitement)* sel *m*, piquant *m*; **s. rack** présentoir *m* à épices

2 *vt (food)* épicer; *Fig* **to s. sth (up)** *(make more exciting)* ajouter du piquant à qch

spic, spick [spɪk] *n very Fam* = terme injurieux désignant une personne originaire d'Amérique latine

spick-and-span [spɪkən'spæn] *adj Fam* nickel, impeccable

spicy ['spaɪsɪ] *adj (food)* épicé(e); *Fig (story, gossip)* croustillant(e)

spider ['spaɪdə(r)] *n* araignée *f*; **s.'s web** toile *f* d'araignée; **s. plant** chlorophytum *m*

spiel [ʃpi:l] *n Fam* baratin *m*

spike [spaɪk] **1** *n* pointe *f*; **spikes** *(running shoes)* pointes *fpl*

2 *vt* **to s. sb's guns** mettre des bâtons dans les roues de qn; **to s. sb's drink** ajouter de l'alcool dans la boisson de qn

spiky ['spaɪkɪ] *adj (plant)* couvert(e) de piquants; *(hair)* en épis

spill [spɪl] **1** *n* **to take a s.** *(fall)* faire une chute

2 *vt (pt & pp* **spilt** [spɪlt] *or* **spilled**) renverser; *Fig* **to s. the beans** vendre la mèche

3 *vi (of liquid)* se répandre

▸**spill over** *vi (of liquid)* déborder; *Fig (of conflict)* s'étendre

spillage ['spɪlɪdʒ] *n* déversement *m*

spilt [spɪlt] *pt & pp of* **spill**

spin [spɪn] **1** *n* (**a**) *(turning movement)* tournoiement *m*; **to go into a s.** *(of car)* faire un tête-à-queue; *Fam* **to put the right s. on a story** présenter une affaire sous un angle favorable; *Pej Pol* **s. doctor** = spécialiste en communication chargé de présenter l'information de façon à mettre en valeur un parti politique (**b**) *Fam (in car)* **to go for a s.** aller faire un tour (**c**) *(on ball)* effet *m*; **to put s. on a ball** donner de l'effet à une balle

2 *vt (pt & pp* **spun** [spʌn]) (**a**) *(wool, cotton)* filer (**b**) *(wheel, top)* faire tourner, faire tournoyer; **to s. a coin** jouer à pile ou face

3 *vi* tourner, tournoyer; **my head's spinning** j'ai la tête qui tourne; **the room's spinning** la pièce tourne (autour de moi)

▸**spin out** *vt sep (speech, debate)* faire traîner (en longueur); *(money)* faire durer

spinach ['spɪnɪtʃ] *n* épinards *mpl*

spinal ['spaɪnəl] *adj* vertébral(e); **s. column** colonne *f* vertébrale; **s. cord** moelle *f* épinière; **s. injury** lésion *f* de la colonne vertébrale

spindly ['spɪndlɪ] *adj (person)* chétif(ive); *(arms, legs)* maigre

spin-dry ['spɪndraɪ] *(pt & pp* **spin-dried**) *vt* essorer

spin-dryer ['spɪndraɪə(r)] *n* essoreuse *f*

spine [spaɪn] *n* (**a**) *(backbone)* colonne *f* vertébrale (**b**) *(of book)* dos *m* (**c**) *(of plant, hedgehog)* piquant *m*

spine-chilling ['spaɪntʃɪlɪŋ] *adj* à vous glacer le sang

spineless ['spaɪnlɪs] *adj (weak)* mou (molle)

spinning ['spɪnɪŋ] *n.* **s. top** toupie *f*; **s. wheel** rouet *m*

spin-off ['spɪnɒf] *n* (**a**) *(result)* retombée *f* (**b**) *(TV program)* = feuilleton tiré d'un film ou d'un autre feuilleton

spinster ['spɪnstə(r)] *n* vieille fille *f*

spiny ['spaɪnɪ] *adj* couvert(e) de piquants; **s. lobster** langouste *f*

spiral ['spaɪərəl] **1** *n* spirale *f*; **s. staircase** escalier *m* en colimaçon

2 *vi (of smoke)* s'élever *ou* monter en spirale; *(of prices)* s'envoler

spire ['spaɪə(r)] *n (of church)* flèche *f*

spirit ['spɪrɪt] *n* (**a**) *(soul, being)* esprit *m*; **the Holy S.** le Saint-Esprit (**b**) *(mood, attitude)* esprit *m*; **to enter into the s. of sth** participer de bon cœur à qch; **to take sth in the right/**

wrong s. bien/mal prendre qch; **to be in good/poor spirits** être de bonne humeur/déprimé(e); *Fam* **that's the s.!** à la bonne heure! (**c**) *(determination)* courage *m*; **to break sb's s.** entamer le courage de qn (**d**) **spirits** *(drinks)* spiritueux *mpl*; **s. lamp** lampe *f* à alcool; **s. level** niveau *m* (à bulle)

▶**spirit away, spirit off** *vt sep* faire disparaître (comme par enchantement)

spirited ['spɪrɪtɪd] *adj (person, defense)* courageux(euse); *(reply)* énergique; *(performance)* plein de brio

spiritual ['spɪrɪtjʊəl] **1** *adj* spirituel(elle); **France is my s. home** c'est en France que je me sens vraiment chez moi
2 *n* **(Negro) s.** Negro spiritual *m*

spiritualism ['spɪrɪtjʊəlɪzəm] *n* spiritisme *m*

spirituality [spɪrɪtjʊ'ælɪtɪ] *n* spiritualité *f*

spit¹ [spɪt] *n* (**a**) *(for cooking)* broche *f* (**b**) *(of land)* pointe *f*

spit² [spɪt] **1** *n (saliva)* salive *f*; *(spittle)* crachat *m*; *Fam* **s. and polish** astiquage *m*
2 *vt (pt & pp spat* [spæt]*)* cracher
3 *vi (of person, cat)* cracher; *(of hot fat)* sauter; *Fig* **to be within spitting distance (of)** être à deux pas (de); **it's spitting** *(with rain)* il pleuvote

▶**spit out** *vt sep* cracher; *Fam* **s. it out!** *(say what you want to)* allez, accouche!

spite [spaɪt] **1** *n* (**a**) *(malice)* dépit *m*; **out of s.** par dépit (**b**) **in s. of** malgré; **to do sth in s. of oneself** faire qch malgré soi
2 *vt* vexer

spiteful ['spaɪtfʊl] *adj* vexant(e)

spitting image ['spɪtɪŋ'ɪmɪdʒ] *n Fam* **he's the s. of his father** c'est son père tout craché

spittle ['spɪtəl] *n* crachat *m*

splash [splæʃ] **1** *n* (**a**) *(of liquid)* éclaboussure *f*; *(sound)* plouf *m*; *Fam Fig* **to make a s.** faire sensation; *Comput* **s. page** page *f* de garde (**b**) *(of color, light)* tache *f*
2 *vt* éclabousser (**with** de); **to s. one's face with water** se passer le visage à l'eau; **the photo was splashed across the front page** la photo était étalée à la une
3 *vi (of liquid, waves)* faire des éclaboussures

▶**splash about, splash around** *vi* patauger

▶**splash down** *vi (of spacecraft)* amerrir

▶**splash out** *vt sep Fam* claquer des ronds (**on** en achetant)

splatter ['splætə(r)] **1** *n* éclaboussure *f*; *(sound)* crépitement *m*
2 *vt* éclabousser (**with** de)

splay [spleɪ] *vt* écarter

spleen [spliːn] *n* (**a**) *(part of body)* rate *f* (**b**) *Formal (anger)* mauvaise humeur *f*; **to vent one's s. (on sb)** passer sa mauvaise humeur (sur qn)

splendid ['splendɪd] *adj* magnifique

splendor ['splendə(r)] *n* splendeur *f*

splice [splaɪs] *vt (movie)* coller; *(rope)* épisser; *Fam* **to get spliced** *(marry)* se caser

splint [splɪnt] *n* attelle *f*

splinter ['splɪntə(r)] **1** *n (of wood, glass)* éclat *m*; *(in finger)* écharde *f*; *(of bone)* esquille *f*; *Pol* **s. group** groupe *m* dissident
2 *vt* briser
3 *vi* se briser; *Fig (of political party)* se scinder

split [splɪt] **1** *n (in wood)* fente *f*; *(in group)* division *f*; *(in garment)* *(tear)* déchirure *f*; *(by design)* fente *f*; **to do the splits** faire le grand écart
2 *adj* brisé(e); **s. ends** *(in hair)* fourches *fpl*; **s. peas** pois *mpl* cassés; **s. personality** dédoublement *m* de la personnalité; *Cin & Comput* **s. screen** écran *m* divisé; **in a s. second** en quelques dixièmes de seconde
3 *vt (pt & pp split)* (**a**) *(wood)* fendre; *(cloth)* déchirer; *(seam)* faire craquer; *(group)* diviser; *(political party)* scinder; **to s. one's head open** se fendre le crâne; **to s. the vote** éparpiller les voix; *Fam* **to s. one's sides (laughing)** se tordre de rire; *Fig* **to s. hairs** couper les cheveux en quatre (**b**) *(share)* parta-

ger; **to s. the difference** partager la différence
4 *vi* (**a**) *(of wood)* se fendre; *(of cloth)* se déchirer; *(of seam)* craquer; *(of group)* se diviser; *(of political party)* se scinder; *Fam* **my head's splitting** j'ai un mal de tête atroce (**b**) *very Fam (leave)* se casser

▶**split up 1** *vt sep (share out)* diviser, partager
2 *vi (of couple, group)* se séparer; **to s. up with sb** rompre avec qn

split-second ['splɪtsekənd] *adj (decision)* pris(e) en un rien de temps; *(timing)* au quart de seconde

splitting ['splɪtɪŋ] *adj* **to have a s. headache** avoir un mal de tête atroce

splotch [splɒtʃ] *n Fam* tache *f*

splutter ['splʌtə(r)] *vi (of person)* bredouiller; *(of engine)* tousser; *(of flame, candle)* crépiter

spoil [spɔɪl] *(pt & pp* **spoilt** [spɔɪlt] *or* **spoiled**) **1** *vt* (**a**) *(ruin)* gâcher; **to s. sb's fun** gâcher le plaisir de qn; **to s. sb's appetite** couper l'appétit à qn; *Pol* **spoiled ballot** vote *m* nul (**b**) *(indulge)* gâter; **spoiled child** enfant gâté; **to be spoiled for choice** avoir l'embarras du choix
2 *vi* (**a**) *(of food)* s'abîmer (**b**) **to be spoiling for a fight** chercher la bagarre

spoils [spɔɪlz] *npl (of war, crime)* butin *m*

spoilsport ['spɔɪlspɔːt] *n Fam* rabat-joie *mf inv*

spoilt [spɔɪlt] *pt & pp of* **spoil**

spoke¹ [spəʊk] *n (of wheel)* rayon *m*; *Fig* **to put a s. in sb's wheel** mettre des bâtons dans les roues à qn

spoke² [spəʊk] *pt of* **speak**

spoken ['spəʊkən] *pp of* **speak**

spokesman ['spəʊksmən] *n* porte-parole *m*

spokesperson ['spəʊkspɜːsən] *n* porte-parole *m*

spokeswoman ['spəʊkswʊmən] *n* porte-parole *m*

sponge [spʌndʒ] **1** *n* éponge *f*; *Fig* **to throw in the s.** jeter l'éponge; **s. cake** génoise *f*
2 *vt* (**a**) *(wash)* nettoyer avec une éponge (**b**) *Fam (scrounge)* taper (**off** *or* **from** à)
3 *vi Fam (scrounge)* taper les autres

▶**sponge down** *vt sep (wash)* nettoyer avec une éponge

▶**sponge off 1** *vt sep (stain)* faire partir d'un coup d'éponge
2 *vt insep Fam (scrounge from)* taper

sponger ['spʌndʒə(r)] *n Fam* tapeur(euse) *m,f*

spongy ['spʌndʒɪ] *adj* spongieux(euse)

sponsor ['spɒnsə(r)] **1** *n* sponsor *m*; *(of student, club member)* parrain *m*
2 *vt* sponsoriser; *(student)* financer les études de; *(club member)* parrainer

sponsorship ['spɒnsəʃɪp] *n* sponsoring *m*; *(of student, club member)* parrainage *m*; **s. deal** *(for athlete, team)* contrat *m* de sponsoring

spontaneity [spɒntə'neɪtɪ] *n* spontanéité *f*

spontaneous [spɒn'teɪnɪəs] *adj* spontané(e)

spoof [spuːf] *n Fam* (**a**) *(parody)* parodie *f* (**on** de) (**b**) *(hoax)* canular *m*

spook [spuːk] *Fam* **1** *n* (**a**) *(ghost)* fantôme *m* (**b**) *(spy)* barbouze *f*
2 *vt* ficher la trouille à

spooky ['spuːkɪ] *adj Fam* qui fait froid dans le dos

spool [spuːl] *n* bobine *f*

spoon [spuːn] **1** *n* cuillère *f*
2 *vt* **s. sth onto sth** mettre qch sur qch avec une cuillère

spoon-feed ['spuːnfiːd] *(pt & pp* **spoon-fed** ['spuːnfed]*)* *vt* faire manger à la cuillère; *Fig* mâcher le travail de

spoonful ['spuːnfʊl] *n* cuillerée *f*

sporadic [spə'rædɪk] *adj* sporadique

spore [spɔː(r)] *n* spore *f*

sporran ['spɒrən] *n* = bourse portée sur le devant du kilt

sport [spɔːt] **1** *n* (**a**) *(activity)* sport *m* (**b**) *Fam (person)* **to be a**

(good) s. *(man)* être un chic type; *(woman)* être une chic fille; **to be a bad s.** être mauvais(e) joueur(euse)

2 *vt (wear)* arborer

sporting ['spɔːtɪŋ] *adj* (**a**) *(related to sport)* sportif(ive) (**b**) *(fair)* chic *inv*; **to give sb a s. chance** donner sa chance à qn

sports [spɔːts] *adj (activity)* sport *m*; **s. bra** soutien-gorge *m* de sport; **s. car** voiture *f* de sport; **s. center** complexe *m* sportif; **s. coat** veste *f* sport; **s. ground** terrain *m* de sport; **s. page** page *f* des sports; **s. science** sciences *fpl* du sport; **s. store** magasin *m* de sports

sportsman ['spɔːtsmən] *n* sportif *m*

sportsmanship ['spɔːtsmənʃɪp] *n* esprit *m* sportif

sportsperson ['spɔːtspɜːsən] *n* sportif(ive) *m,f*

sportswoman ['spɔːtswʊmən] *n* sportive *f*

sport-utility vehicle ['spɔːtjuːˈtɪlətɪviːkəl] *n* quatre-quatre *m ou f*

sporty ['spɔːtɪ] *adj (person)* sportif(ive); *(car, clothing)* de sport

spot [spɒt] **1** *n* (**a**) *(place)* endroit *m*; **on the s.** sur place; *Fam* **to put sb on the s.** mettre qn en mauvaise posture; *Fam* **to be in a (tight) s.** être dans le pétrin; **s. check** contrôle *m* surprise

(**b**) *(stain)* tache *f*

(**c**) *(pimple)* bouton *m*

(**d**) *(forming pattern on cloth)* pois *m*; *(on leopard)* tache *f*

(**e**) *Fam (small amount)* goutte *f*; **to have a s. of lunch** manger un morceau; **a s. of trouble** de petits problèmes *mpl*

(**f**) *(spotlight)* projecteur *m*; *(smaller)* spot *m*

(**g**) *(on TV, radio, in show)* numéro *m*

2 *vt (pt & pp* **spotted**) (**a**) *(stain, mark)* tacher

(**b**) *(notice)* remarquer; *(opportunity, opening)* repérer; **to s. sb doing sth** apercevoir qn en train de faire qch; **well spotted!** bien vu!

spotless ['spɒtlɪs] *adj* impeccable; *Fig (reputation)* irréprochable

spotlight ['spɒtlaɪt] *n* projecteur *m*; *(smaller)* spot *m*; *Fig* **to be in the s.** être sous le feu des projecteurs

spot-on ['spɒt'ɒn] *adj Fam* tout à fait exact(e)

spotter plane ['spɒtə'pleɪn] *n* avion-espion *m*

spotty ['spɒtɪ] *adj* (**a**) *(pimply)* boutonneux(euse) (**b**) *(patchy)* irrégulier(ère)

spouse [spaʊz] *n* époux (épouse) *m,f*

spout [spaʊt] **1** *n (of teapot, kettle)* bec *m*

2 *vt (water)* faire jaillir; *Fam Fig (speech, nonsense)* débiter

3 *vi (of liquid)* jaillir; *Fam Fig (of person)* faire des discours

sprain [spreɪn] **1** *n (injury)* entorse *f*

2 *vt* **to s. one's ankle/wrist** se fouler la cheville/le poignet

sprang [spræŋ] *pt of* **spring**

sprat [spræt] *n* sprat *m*

sprawl [sprɔːl] *vi (of person)* s'affaler; *(of town)* s'étendre

sprawling ['sprɔːlɪŋ] *adj (person)* affalé(e); *(town)* tentaculaire

spray¹ [spreɪ] *n (of flowers)* bouquet *m*

spray² **1** *n* (**a**) *(of liquid)* fines gouttelettes *fpl*; *(from sea)* embruns *mpl* (**b**) *(act of spraying)* **to give sth a s.** *(flowers, crops)* pulvériser; *(room)* vaporiser (**c**) *(device)* bombe *f*; *(for perfume)* atomiseur *m*; **s. can** bombe aérosol; **s. gun** *(for paint)* pistolet *m* (à peinture)

2 *vt (flowers, crops)* pulvériser; *(room)* vaporiser; **to s. oneself with perfume** se mettre du parfum *(avec un vaporisateur)*; **to s. sb with sth** asperger qn de qch

spray-on ['spreɪɒn] *adj (product, lotion etc)* en bombe, en aérosol

spray-paint ['spreɪ'peɪnt] **1** *n* peinture *f* en bombe

2 *vt (with spray can)* peindre à la bombe; *(with spray gun)* peindre au pistolet

spread [spred] **1** *n* (**a**) *(of idea, religion, language)* diffusion *f*; *(of disease)* propagation *f* (**b**) *(of products, ages)* éventail *m* (**c**) *(in newspaper)* **full-page s.** pleine page *f*; **two-page s.** double page *f* (**d**) *(paste)* **cheese/chocolate s.** fromage *m*/chocolat

m à tartiner (**e**) *(of wings, sails)* envergure *f* (**f**) *Fam (big meal)* festin *m*

2 *vt (pt & pp* **spread**) (**a**) *(arms, legs)* écarter; *Fig* **to s. one's wings** acquérir de l'indépendance (**b**) *(sand, sawdust, terror)* répandre; *(rumor, disease, germs)* propager; *(payments)* étaler (**c**) *(butter, ointment)* étaler; **to s. a surface with sth** étaler qch sur une surface

3 *vi* se répandre; *(of rumor, disease, fire)* se propager

▸**spread out 1** *vt sep* (**a**) *(map, newspaper)* étaler (**b**) **to be spread out** *(of fields, city)* s'étendre

2 *vi (of person)* s'étendre; *(of search party)* se disperser

spreadsheet ['spredʃiːt] *n Comput* tableur *m*

spree [spriː] *n Fam* **to go on a s.** *(go drinking)* prendre une cuite; **to go on a shopping** *or* **spending s.** faire des folies dans les magasins

sprig [sprɪg] *n (of parsley)* brin *m*; *(of holly, mistletoe)* branche *f*

sprightly ['spraɪtlɪ] *adj* alerte

spring [sprɪŋ] **1** *n* (**a**) *(of water)* source *f* (**b**) *(season)* printemps *m*; **in (the) s.** au printemps; **s. onion** ciboule *f*; **s. roll** rouleau *m* de printemps; **s. tide** grande marée *f* (**c**) *(leap)* bond *m* (**d**) *(elasticity)* élasticité *f*; **to walk with a s. in one's step** marcher d'un pas souple (**e**) *(device)* ressort *m*

2 *vt (pt* **sprang** [spræŋ]*, pp* **sprung** [sprʌŋ]*)* (**a**) *(reveal unexpectedly)* **to s. sth on sb** annoncer qch à qn de but en blanc; **to s. a surprise on sb** faire une surprise à qn (**b**) *(develop)* **to s. a leak** commencer à fuir; *(of boat)* commencer à prendre l'eau (**c**) *Fam (prisoner)* faire évader

3 *vi* (**a**) *(jump)* bondir, sauter; **to s. to one's feet** se lever d'un bond; **to s. into action** passer rapidement à l'action; **to s. to life** *(of person, town)* s'animer; *(of machine)* se mettre en marche; **to s. to sb's defense** prendre vivement la défense de qn; **to s. open/shut** s'ouvrir/se fermer brusquement; **to s. to mind** venir à l'esprit (**b**) *(originate)* **to s. from** venir de; **to s. into existence** voir le jour; *Fam* **where did you s. from?** d'où sortez-vous?

▸**spring up** *vi* (**a**) *(jump to one's feet)* se lever d'un bond (**b**) *(appear suddenly)* surgir; *(of wind)* se lever; *(of feeling)* prendre naissance

springboard ['sprɪŋbɔːd] *n also Fig* tremplin *m*

spring-clean [sprɪŋ'kliːn] **1** *n* grand nettoyage *m*

2 *vt* nettoyer à fond

spring-cleaning [sprɪŋ'kliːnɪŋ] *n* grand nettoyage *m*; **to do the s.** faire le grand nettoyage

springtime ['sprɪŋtaɪm] *n* printemps *m*

springy ['sprɪŋɪ] *adj* souple

sprinkle ['sprɪŋkəl] **1** *n (of salt, flour)* pincée *f*

2 *vt (with liquid)* arroser, asperger (**with** de); *(with salt, flour)* saupoudrer (**with** de); **to s. liquid on sth** arroser *ou* asperger qch de liquide; **to s. salt/flour on sth** saupoudrer qch de sel/farine

sprinkler ['sprɪŋklə(r)] *n (for lawns)* arroseur *m*; **s. system** *(for fire prevention)* installation *f* sprinkler

sprinkling ['sprɪŋklɪŋ] *n* **a s. of** *(liquid)* quelques gouttes de; *(salt, flour)* un peu de; *Fig (people)* quelques

sprint [sprɪnt] **1** *n (fast run)* sprint *m*; *(running race)* course *f* (de vitesse); **to put on a s.** piquer un sprint

2 *vi (run fast)* piquer un sprint; **to s. off** partir en courant

sprinter ['sprɪntə(r)] *n* sprinter(euse) *m,f*

sprocket ['sprɒkɪt] *n* **s. (wheel)** pignon *m*

sprout [spraʊt] **1** *n (of plant)* pousse *f*; **(Brussels) s.** chou *m* de Bruxelles

2 *vt (leaves, shoots)* faire; *Fam (mustache, beard)* se laisser pousser

3 *vi (of leaves, hair)* pousser

▸**sprout up** *vi (of plant, child)* pousser; *(of new buildings, towns)* surgir

spruce¹ [spruːs] *n (tree)* épicéa *m*

spruce² [spru:s] *adj* impeccable

▶**spruce up** *vt sep (room)* bien nettoyer; **to s. oneself up** se faire beau (belle)

sprung [sprʌŋ] *pp of* **spring**

spry [spraɪ] *adj* alerte

spud [spʌd] *n Fam (potato)* patate *f*

spun [spʌn] **1** *adj* **s. silk** schappe *f*
2 *pt & pp of* **spin**

spunk [spʌŋk] *n Fam (courage)* cran *m*

spur [spɜ:(r)] **1** *n* **(a)** *(for riding)* éperon *m*; *Fig (stimulus)* motivation *f*; *Fig* **to win one's spurs** faire ses preuves; **on the s. of the moment** sur un coup de tête **(b)** *(of land, rock)* éperon *m*
2 *vt (pt & pp* **spurred***) (horse)* éperonner; *Fig* **to s. sb on** stimuler qn; **to s. sb on to do sth** inciter qn à faire qch; *Fig* **to s. sb into action** inciter qn à agir

spurious ['spjʊərɪəs] *adj (argument, reasoning)* spécieux(euse); *(claim, story, charge)* sans fondement

spurn [spɜ:n] *vt* repousser, rejeter

spurt [spɜ:t] **1** *n (of liquid)* giclée *f*; *(of activity, energy)* regain *m*; *(increase in speed)* accélération *f*; **to do sth in spurts** faire qch par à-coups; **to put on a s.** accélérer
2 *vt* **the wound was spurting blood** le sang giclait de la blessure; **the pen spurted ink** l'encre giclait du stylo
3 *vi* **(a)** *(of liquid)* gicler **(b)** *(move quickly)* **to s. off** s'élancer brusquement

sputter ['spʌtə(r)] *vi (of engine)* toussoter; *(of flame, candle)* crépiter

spy [spaɪ] **1** *n* espion(onne) *m,f*; **s. plane** avion *m* espion; **s. ring** réseau *m* d'espionnage; **s. satellite** satellite *m* espion
2 *vt (pt & pp* **spied***) (notice)* repérer
3 *vi* espionner, faire de l'espionnage; **to s. on sb** espionner qn

▶**spy out** *vt sep Fig* **to s. out the land** tâter le terrain

spyware ['spaɪweə(r)] *n Comput* logiciel *m* espion

Sq. *(abbr* **Square***)* pl

sq. *(abbr* **square***)* carré; **sq. ft.** ≃ mètres *mpl* carrés

squabble ['skwɒbəl] **1** *n* querelle *f*
2 *vi* se quereller (**about** *or* **over** à propos de)

squabbling ['skwɒblɪŋ] *n* querelles *fpl*

squad [skwɒd] *n (of workers)* équipe *f*; *(of athletes, soccer players)* délégation *f*; *(of soldiers)* section *f*; *(of police)* brigade *f*; **s. car** voiture *f* de patrouille

squadron ['skwɒdrən] *n Mil (of planes)* escadron *m*; *(of ships)* escadrille *f*

squalid ['skwɒlɪd] *adj (dirty)* crasseux(euse); *(sordid)* sordide

squall [skwɔ:l] **1** *n (of wind)* bourrasque *f*
2 *vi (cry)* pousser des hurlements

squalor ['skwɒlə(r)] *n (dirtiness)* crasse *f*; *(poverty)* misère *f* noire

squander ['skwɒndə(r)] *vt (money, resources, talents)* gaspiller; *(time)* perdre; *(fortune, inheritance)* dilapider; *(opportunity)* laisser passer

square [skweə(r)] **1** *n* **(a)** *(shape)* carré *m*; *(on chessboard, map)* case *f*; *Fig* **to be back at s. one** être de retour à la case départ
(b) *Math* carré *m*
(c) *(of town, village)* place *f*
(d) *Fam (unfashionable person)* **to be a s.** être ringard(e)
2 *adj* **(a)** *(in shape)* carré(e)
(b) *(right-angled)* **s. corner** angle *m* droit
(c) *Math* carré(e); **s. root** racine *f* carrée
(d) *Fam (unfashionable)* vieux jeu *inv*; ringard(e)
(e) *(idioms)* **to be s. with sb** être honnête avec qn; **now we're s.** nous sommes quittes; **to feel like a s. peg in a round hole** ne pas se sentir à sa place; **s. dance** quadrille *m* (américain); **s. deal** arrangement *m* équitable; **s. meal** bon repas *m*
3 *adv* **to hit sb s. on the jaw** frapper qn en pleine mâchoire; **to look sb s. in the eye** regarder qn bien en face

4 *vt* **(a)** *(make square)* mettre en forme de carré; *Math (number)* élever au carré; **squared paper** papier *m* quadrillé
(b) *(settle) (account, debt)* régler
(c) *(arrange)* **to s. sth with sb** arranger qch avec qn
5 *vi (agree)* coller; **to s. with** correspondre à

▶**square up** *vi* **(a)** *(settle debts)* régler ses comptes **(b)** *(of fighters)* se mettre en garde; *Fig* **to s. up to a problem/an opponent** faire face à un problème/un adversaire

squarely ['skweəlɪ] *adv* **(a)** *(directly)* **to hit sb s. in the chest/face** frapper qn en pleine poitrine/figure **(b)** *(honestly)* honnêtement

squash¹ [skwɒʃ] **1** *n* **(a)** *(crush)* cohue *f*; **it was a s.** on était serrés comme des sardines **(b)** *(sport)* squash *m*; **s. court** court *m* de squash
2 *vt* écraser
3 *vi* **to s. into a room/car** s'entasser dans une pièce/voiture

squash² [skwɒʃ] *n (vegetable)* courge *f*

▶**squash up** *vi* se serrer

squat [skwɒt] **1** *n (illegally occupied dwelling)* squat *m*
2 *adj (person, object, building)* trapu(e)
3 *vi (pt & pp* **squatted***)* **(a)** *(crouch down) (of person)* s'accroupir; *(of animal)* se tapir **(b)** *(occupy illegally)* squatter

squatter ['skwɒtə(r)] *n* squatter *m*, squatteur(euse) *m,f*

squaw [skwɔ:] *n* squaw *f*

squawk [skwɔ:k] **1** *n (of bird)* cri *m* rauque; *Fam (of person)* braillement *m*
2 *vi (of bird)* pousser un cri rauque; *Fam (of person)* brailler

squeak [skwi:k] **1** *n (of animal, person)* cri *m* aigu; *(of door, hinges)* grincement *m*; *Fam* **I don't want to hear another s. out of you** je ne veux plus t'entendre
2 *vi (of animal, person)* pousser un cri aigu; *(of door, hinges)* grincer; *(of shoes)* craquer

squeaky ['skwi:kɪ] *adj (voice)* aigu(uë); *(door, hinges)* qui grince; *(shoes)* qui craque; **s. clean** impeccable

squeal [skwi:l] **1** *n (of person, animal)* cri *m* perçant; *(of brakes)* crissement *m*
2 *vt* crier
3 *vi* **(a)** *(of person, animal)* pousser un cri perçant; *(of brakes)* crisser; *Fam* **to s. about sth** *(complain)* se lamenter au sujet de qch **(b)** *very Fam (inform)* moucharder; **to s. on sb** balancer qn

squeamish ['skwi:mɪʃ] *adj* de nature délicate; **to be s. about sth** ne pas supporter qch

squeeze [skwi:z] **1** *n* pression *f*; **to give sth a s.** presser qch; **to give sb a s.** *(hug)* serrer qn dans ses bras; **a s. of lemon** quelques gouttes de citron; *Fam* **it was a tight s.** nous étions/ils etaient/*etc.* serrés comme des sardines; *Fam* **to put the s. on sb** *(pressure)* faire pression sur qn
2 *vt* **(a)** *(press)* presser; **to s. sb's hand** serrer la main à qn; *Fig* **to s. sb** *(pressure)* faire pression sur qn **(b)** *(squash)* **to s. sth into sth** faire rentrer qch dans qch; **I think we can just s. you in** je pense qu'on peut vous trouver une place
3 *vi* **to s. into sth** s'entasser dans qch; **to s. past sb** se glisser devant qn; **s. a bit closer!** serrez-vous un peu!

▶**squeeze out** *vt sep (juice)* exprimer

squelch [skweltʃ] **1** *vi (walk)* patauger; *(make noise)* clapoter; **to s. through the mud** avancer en pataugeant dans la boue
2 *vt (crush)* écraser; *(rumor)* étouffer

squib [skwɪb] *n (firework)* pétard *m*

squid [skwɪd] *n (pl* **squid***) n* calmar *m*

squiggle ['skwɪgəl] *n* gribouillis *m*

squint [skwɪnt] **1** *n* **(a)** *(eye defect)* strabisme *m*; **to have a s.** loucher **(b)** *(quick look)* coup d'œil *m*; **to have a s. at** jeter un coup d'œil à
2 *vi* **(a)** *(have eye defect)* loucher **(b)** *(narrow one's eyes)* plisser les yeux; **to s. at** plisser les yeux pour voir

squire ['skwaɪə(r)] *n (landowner)* châtelain *m*; *Hist* écuyer *m*

squirm [skwɜːm] *vi (wriggle)* se tortiller; *Fig* **to s. (with em-barrassment)** être mal à l'aise

squirrel ['skwɪrəl] *n* écureuil *m*

squirt [skwɜːt] **1** *n* (**a**) *(of liquid)* giclée *f* (**b**) *Fam Pej (insignif-icant person)* petit(e) morveux(euse) *m,f*
2 *vt (liquid)* faire gicler; **to s. sth on sb/sth, to s. sb/sth with sth** asperger qn/qch de qch
3 *vi (of liquid)* **to s. out** gicler

Sr. *(abbr* **Senior)** **Thomas Smith, Sr.** Thomas Smith père

Sri Lanka [sriːˈlæŋkə] *n* le Sri Lanka

Sri Lankan [sriːˈlæŋkən] **1** *n* Sri Lankais(e) *m,f*
2 *adj* sri lankais(e)

SSE *(abbr* **south-southeast)** sud-sud-est

SSN [esesˈen] *n (abbr* **social security number)** numéro *m* de sécurité sociale

SSW *(abbr* **south-southwest)** sud-sud-ouest

St. (**a**) *(abbr* **Street)** rue *f* (**b**) *(abbr* **Saint)** st(e); *Bot & Med* **St. John's wort** millepertuis *m; Geog* **St. Kitts and Nevis** Saint-Kitts-et-Nevis; **St. Lucia** Sainte-Lucie; **St. Petersburg** Saint-Petersbourg; **St. Vincent and the Grenadines** Saint-Vin-cent-et-Grenadines; *see also* **saint**

stab [stæb] **1** *n* (**a**) *(with knife)* coup *m* de couteau; *Fig* **a s. of pain** un élancement; **a s. of envy** un pincement de jalousie; **a s. of guilt** un accès de culpabilité (**b**) *Fam (attempt)* **to have a s. at sth/at doing sth** essayer qch/de faire qch
2 *vt (pt & pp* **stabbed)** *(with knife)* poignarder; *(with other weapon)* transpercer; **to s. sb to death** tuer qn d'un coup de couteau; *Fig* **to s. sb in the back** poignarder qn dans le dos

stabbing ['stæbɪŋ] **1** *n (attack)* agression *f* au couteau
2 *adj (pain)* lancinant(e)

stability [stəˈbɪlɪtɪ] *n* stabilité *f*

stabilize ['steɪbɪlaɪz] **1** *vt* stabiliser
2 *vi* se stabiliser

stabilizer ['steɪbɪlaɪzə(r)] *n (on bicycle)* stabilisateur *m*

stable[1] ['steɪbəl] **1** *n* écurie *f; Fig* **to lock the s. door after the horse has bolted** prendre des mesures trop tard
2 *vt* mettre à l'écurie

stable[2] ['steɪbəl] *adj* stable

stack [stæk] **1** *n* (**a**) *(pile)* pile *f; Fam* **stacks of** des tas de (**b**) *(chimney)* cheminée *f*
2 *vt* empiler; **to be stacked with sth** *(full of)* être plein(e) de qch; **the odds were stacked against them** ils n'avaient au-cune chance

▸**stack up 1** *vt sep (pile up)* empiler
2 *vi (measure up)* se comparer; **our product stacks up well against theirs** notre produit soutient bien la comparaison avec le leur

stadium ['steɪdɪəm] *(pl* **stadiums** *or* **stadia** ['steɪdɪə]) *n* stade *m*

staff [stɑːf] **1** *n* (**a**) *(stick)* bâton *m* (**b**) *(personnel)* personnel *m;* **teaching/nursing s.** personnel *m* enseignant/infirmier (**c**) *(pl* **staves** [steɪvz]) *Mus* portée *f*
2 *vt* **the office is staffed by volunteers** le personnel du bureau est composé de volontaires; **the desk is staffed at all times** il y a toujours quelqu'un au bureau

stag [stæg] *n (animal)* cerf *m;* **s. beetle** cerf-volant *m*

stage [steɪdʒ] **1** *n* (**a**) *(platform)* plate-forme *f; (in theater)* scène *f;* **to go on the s.** faire du théâtre; *Fig* **to set the s. for sth** préparer le terrain à qch; **s. directions** indications *fpl* scéni-ques; **s. door** entrée *f* des artistes; **s. fright** trac *m;* **s. man-ager** régisseur *m;* **s. name** nom *m* de scène; **s. whisper** aparté *m* (**b**) *(phase)* stade *m;* **at this s. in...** à ce stade de...; **to do sth in stages** faire qch par étapes (**c**) **s. (coach)** dili-gence *f*
2 *vt (play)* monter, mettre en scène; *Fig (demonstration, inva-sion)* organiser

stagehand ['steɪdʒhænd] *n* machiniste *m*

stage-manage ['steɪdʒˈmænɪdʒ] *vt (play)* s'occuper de la ré-gie de; *Fig (event, demonstration)* mettre en scène

stage-struck ['steɪdʒstrʌk] *adj* fou (folle) de théâtre

stagflation [stægˈfleɪʃən] *n Econ* stagflation *f*

stagger ['stægə(r)] **1** *vt* (**a**) *(astound)* stupéfier (**b**) *(working hours, vacations)* échelonner
2 *vi (stumble)* tituber; **to s. along/in/out** marcher/entrer/sortir en titubant; **to s. to one's feet** se relever péniblement

stagnant ['stægnənt] *adj* stagnant(e)

stagnate [stægˈneɪt] *vi* stagner

stagnation [stægˈneɪʃən] *n* stagnation *f*

staid [steɪd] *adj* collet monté *inv*

stain [steɪn] **1** *n (mark)* tache *f; (dye)* teinture *f;* **s. remover** détachant *m*
2 *vt (mark)* tacher; *(dye)* teindre; *Fig (reputation)* salir

stained-glass ['steɪndɡlɑːs] *n* vitrail *m;* **s. window** vitrail *m*

stainless steel ['steɪnlɪsˈstiːl] *n* acier *m* inoxydable, inox® *m*

stair [steə(r)] *n (single step)* marche *f;* **stairs** *(staircase)* escalier *m*

staircase ['steəkeɪs] *n* escalier *m*

stairway ['steəweɪ] *n* escalier *m*

stairwell ['steəwel] *n* cage *f* d'escalier

stake [steɪk] **1** *n* (**a**) *(piece of wood)* pieu *m; (piece of metal)* pi-quet *m; (for plant)* tuteur *m;* **to be burnt at the s.** périr sur le bûcher (**b**) *(bet)* enjeu *m;* **to be at s.** être en jeu (**c**) *(share)* **to have a s. in sth** avoir des intérêts dans qch; *Fig* être concer-né(e) par qch
2 *vt* (**a**) *(money)* miser (**on** sur); *Fig (one's reputation, job)* ris-quer (**on** sur); **I'd s. my life on it** j'en mettrais ma tête à cou-per (**b**) **to s. a claim (to sth)** revendiquer un droit (à qch)

stakeout ['steɪkaʊt] *n* surveillance *f*

stalactite ['stæləktaɪt] *n* stalactite *f*

stalagmite ['stæləgmaɪt] *n* stalagmite *f*

stale [steɪl] *adj* (**a**) *(bread, cake)* rassis(e); *(air)* confiné(e); *(smell)* âcre (**b**) *Fig (social life, politics)* sans intérêt; *(excuse, joke)* écu-lé(e); *(person)* blasé(e)

stalemate ['steɪlmeɪt] *n (in chess)* pat *m; (in negotiations)* im-passe *f;* **to reach a s.** être dans l'impasse

stalk[1] [stɔːk] **1** *vt (suspect, wild animal)* traquer; *(obsessively)* harceler
2 *vt (of obsessive fan, infatuated person etc)* suivre en perma-nence *(de façon obsessionnelle)*
3 *vi (walk angrily)* **to s. in/out** entrer/sortir d'un air furieux mais digne

stalk[2] [stɔːk] *n (of plant, flower)* tige *f; (of fruit)* queue *f*

stalker ['stɔːkə(r)] *n* = admirateur obsessionnel qui harcèle une de ses connaissances ou une célébrité

stall [stɔːl] **1** *n* (**a**) *(in stable)* stalle *f; (for shower, toilet)* cabine *f* (**b**) *(in market)* étal *m; (at exhibition)* stand *m*
2 *vt (hold up)* faire patienter
3 *vi* (**a**) *(of car)* caler; *Fig (of campaign)* être interrompu(e) (**b**) *(delay)* **to s. (for time)** essayer de gagner du temps

stallion ['stæljən] *n* étalon *m*

stalwart ['stɔːlwət] **1** *n* fidèle *mf*
2 *adj* résolu(e)

stamen ['steɪmən] *n* étamine *f*

stamina ['stæmɪnə] *n* résistance *f* physique

stammer ['stæmə(r)] **1** *n* bégaiement *m;* **to have a s.** bégayer
2 *vi* bégayer
3 *vt* balbutier

▸**stammer out** *vt insep* balbutier

stamp [stæmp] **1** *n (for letter)* timbre *m; (mark)* cachet *m; (de-vice)* tampon *m; Fig* **to bear the s. of sth** porter l'empreinte de qch; *Fig* **s. of approval** aval *m,* approbation *f;* **s. album** al-bum *m* de timbres; **s. collector** philatéliste *mf;* **s. machine** distributeur *m* de timbres-poste
2 *vt* (**a**) *(document)* tamponner; **to s. the date on sth** tam-

ponner la date sur qch; **stamped addressed envelope** enveloppe *f* timbrée libellée à ses noms et adresse (**b**) **to s. one's foot** taper du pied

3 *vi* **to s. on sth** *(on purpose)* écraser qch avec le pied; *(accidentally)* écraser qch du pied; **to s. off/out** partir/sortir en tapant des pieds

▶**stamp out** *vt sep* (**a**) *(resistance, dissent)* anéantir; *(poverty, racism)* éradiquer (**b**) *(fire)* éteindre en piétinant

stampede [stæm'piːd] **1** *n* débandade *f*; **there was a s. for the door** il y a eu une ruée vers la porte

2 *vi* se ruer

stance [stɑːns] *n also Fig* position *f*

stand [stænd] **1** *n* (**a**) *(opinion)* position *f*; **to take a s. (on sth)** prendre position (sur qch)

(**b**) *(of lamp, microphone)* pied *m*; *(for books, postcards)* présentoir *m*

(**c**) *(stall)* *(outside)* étalage *m*; *(at exhibition)* stand *m*

(**d**) *(at sports ground)* tribune *f*

(**e**) *(taxi line)* station *f*

(**f**) *Jur (for witnesses)* barre *f*; **to take the s.** venir à la barre

2 *vt* *(pt & pp* **stood** [stʊd]) (**a**) *(place)* poser; **to s. sth against sth** mettre qch contre qch

(**b**) *(endure)* supporter; **to s. comparison with sb/sth** soutenir la comparaison avec qn/qch; **to s. one's ground** tenir bon

(**c**) *(pay for)* **to s. sb a drink/meal** payer à boire/manger à qn

(**d**) *(have)* **to s. a chance (of doing sth)** avoir des chances (de faire qch); **she doesn't s. a chance** elle n'a aucune chance

(**e**) *Law* **to s. trial** passer en jugement

3 *vi* (**a**) *(of person)* *(get up)* se mettre debout; *(be upright)* être debout; *(remain upright)* rester debout; **to s. on one's head** faire le poirier; **I could hardly s.** je tenais à peine debout; **don't just s. there!** ne reste pas planté là les bras ballants!; **to s. fast** *or* **firm** tenir bon; **to s. still** *(of person)* se tenir immobile; **time seemed to s. still** le temps semblait s'être arrêté

(**b**) *(of building)* se dresser; *(of object)* être, se trouver

(**c**) *(be in situation)* **inflation/unemployment stands at...** le taux d'inflation/de chômage s'élève à...; **to s. in need of sth** avoir besoin de qch; **to s. to do sth** risquer de faire qch; **it stands to reason that...** il est clair que...

(**d**) *(idioms)* **to be standing right behind sb** être avec qn; **to s. on one's own two feet** se débrouiller tout(e) seul(e); **I don't know where I s.** je ne sais pas à quoi m'en tenir; **to know how things s.** savoir où en sont les choses; **I s. corrected** autant pour moi; **to s. for Parliament** se présenter aux élections législatives; **the offer still stands** l'offre tient toujours

▶**stand aside** *vi* s'écarter

▶**stand back** *vi (move away)* reculer (**from** de); *Fig* prendre de la distance (**from** par rapport à)

▶**stand by 1** *vt insep* (**a**) *(person, cause)* défendre, soutenir (**b**) *(promise, decision)* maintenir

2 *vi* (**a**) *(be ready)* **to s. by (for sth/to do sth)** *(of person)* se tenir prêt(e) (pour qch/à faire qch); *(of vehicle)* être prêt (pour qch/à faire qch) (**b**) *(not get involved)* rester sans rien faire

▶**stand down** *vi (retire)* se retirer

▶**stand for** *vt insep* (**a**) *(mean, represent)* vouloir dire (**b**) *(tolerate)* supporter

▶**stand out** *vi* (**a**) *(be prominent)* ressortir; **to s. out in a crowd** se détacher dans la foule; *Fam* **it stands out a mile** ça se voit comme le nez au milieu de la figure (**b**) *(oppose)* **to s. out against sth** résister à qch

▶**stand up 1** *vt sep* (**a**) *(put in upright position)* mettre à la verticale (**b**) *Fam* **to s. sb up** *(on date)* poser un lapin à qn

2 *vi* (**a**) *(get up)* se mettre debout; *(be standing)* être debout; *Fig* **to s. up for sb/sth** défendre qn/qch; *Fig* **to s. up to sb** tenir tête à qn (**b**) *(of argument, theory)* faire le poids; **to s. up to sth**

résister à qch; **it'll never s. up in court** ça ne sera pas valable au tribunal

stand-alone [ˈstændələʊn] *adj* autonome; **s. computer** ordinateur *m* autonome

standard [ˈstændəd] **1** *n* (**a**) *(point of reference)* référence *f*; *(set requirement)* norme *f*; *(for weight, measurement)* étalon *m* (**b**) *(required level)* niveau *m*; **to be up to/below s.** être du/en dessous du niveau requis; **s. of living** niveau de vie; **s. of accommodations** qualité *f* du logement (**c**) **standards** *(morals)* principes *mpl* moraux; **to have high/low standards** être/ne pas être exigeant(e) (**d**) *(flag)* étendard *m; also Fig* **s. bearer** porte-drapeau *m*

2 *adj* (**a**) *(design, size)* standard *inv; Math* **s. deviation** écart *m* type; **s. measure** mesure *f* étalon; **s. time** heure *f* légale (**b**) *(usual)* habituel(elle); **S. English** anglais *m* standard; **s. practice** pratique *f* courante

standardization [stændədaɪˈzeɪʃən] *n* normalisation *f*

standardize [ˈstændədaɪz] *vt* normaliser

stand-by [ˈstændbaɪ] *n* (**a**) *(fuel, food)* réserve *f*; **to have sth as a s.** avoir qch en réserve; **to be on s.** *(of troops, emergency services)* être en état d'alerte (**b**) *(for air travel)* **to be on s.** être en stand-by *ou* en attente; **s. passenger** passager(ère) *m,f* en stand-by; **s. ticket** billet *m* en stand-by

stand-in [ˈstændɪn] *n* remplaçant(e) *m,f*; *(for actor)* doublure *f*

standing [ˈstændɪŋ] **1** *n* (**a**) *(status)* réputation *f* (**b**) *(duration)* **of long s.** de longue date

2 *adj* (**a**) *(upright)* debout; **to give sb a s. ovation** se lever pour applaudir qn (**b**) *(permanent)* permanent(e); **I have a s. invitation** je peux y aller quand je veux; **s. army** armée *f* de métier; **s. joke** plaisanterie *f* classique; *Fin* **s. order** virement *m* automatique

standoffish [stændˈɒfɪʃ] *adj* distant(e)

standpoint [ˈstændpɔɪnt] *n* point *m* de vue

standstill [ˈstændstɪl] *n* **to be at a s.** *(of traffic)* être immobilisé(e); *(of production, economy)* être paralysé(e); **to come to a s.** *(of traffic)* s'immobiliser; *(of production)* s'arrêter; *(of economy)* être paralysé(e)

stand-up [ˈstændʌp] *adj* (**a**) **s. comedian** comique *mf* (qui se produit seul en scène); **s. comedy** spectacle *m* comique (**b**) *(fight, argument)* en règle

stank [stæŋk] *pt of* **stink**

stanza [ˈstænzə] *n* strophe *f*

staple¹ [ˈsteɪpəl] **1** *n* *(for fastening paper)* agrafe *f*; **s. gun** agrafeuse *f*

2 *vt* agrafer

staple² [ˈsteɪpəl] *n* *(basic food)* aliment *m* de base; *(basic product)* principale production *f*; *Fig* **such stories are a s. of the tabloid press** la presse à sensation se nourrit de telles histoires

stapler [ˈsteɪplə(r)] *n* agrafeuse *f*

star [stɑː(r)] **1** *n* (**a**) *(heavenly body)* étoile *f*; **the Stars and Stripes, the Star-Spangled Banner** *(US flag)* la bannière étoilée; *Fig* **to reach for the stars** essayer d'atteindre les sommets; *Fig* **to see stars** *(after blow to head)* voir trente-six chandelles; **s. fruit** carambole *f*; **s. sign** signe *m* du zodiaque (**b**) *(famous person)* star *f*, vedette *f*; **s. player** vedette *f* (**c**) *Fam* **stars** *(horoscope)* horoscope *m*

2 *vt* *(pt & pp* **starred**) *(of movie, play)* avoir pour vedette

3 *vi* **to s. in a movie/play** jouer dans un film/une pièce

starboard [ˈstɑːbəd] *n Naut* tribord *m*

starch [stɑːtʃ] **1** *n* *(for shirts, in food)* amidon *m*

2 *vt* *(shirt)* amidonner

starchy [ˈstɑːtʃɪ] *adj* (**a**) *(food)* riche en féculents (**b**) *Fam (person, manner)* guindé(e)

stardom [ˈstɑːdəm] *n* célébrité *f*

stare [steə(r)] **1** *n* regard *m* fixe

2 *vt* **to be staring sb in the face** *(be obvious)* crever les yeux à qn

3 *vi* **to s. at sb** dévisager qn; **to s. at sth** regarder qch fixement; **to s. into space** regarder dans le vague; **it's rude to s.** ce n'est pas poli de dévisager les gens

starfish ['stɑːfɪʃ] *n* étoile *f* de mer

stark [stɑːk] **1** *adj (contrast)* net (nette); *(light, colors)* cru(e); *(truth, facts)* brut(e); *(landscape)* nu(e)

2 *adv* **s. naked** tout(e) nu(e); *Fam* **s. raving mad** complètement dingue

starlet ['stɑːlɪt] *n (young actress)* starlette *f*

starlight ['stɑːlaɪt] *n* lumière *f* des étoiles

starling ['stɑːlɪŋ] *n* étourneau *m*

starlit ['stɑːlɪt] *adj* étoilé(e)

starry ['stɑːrɪ] *adj* étoilé(e)

starry-eyed [stɑːrɪ'aɪd] *adj* naïf(ïve)

start [stɑːt] **1** *n* **(a)** *(beginning)* début *m*; *(starting place, of journey, race)* départ *m*; **for a s.** pour commencer; **at the s.** au début; **from the s.** dès le départ; **from s. to finish** du début à la fin; **to make a s. on sth** commencer qch; **he lent her $50 to give her a s.** il lui a prêté 50 dollars pour l'aider à démarrer; **to give sb a 60-meter s.** *(in race)* laisser 60 mètres d'avance à qn

(b) *(sudden movement)* sursaut *m*; **to wake with a s.** se réveiller en sursaut; **to give sb a s.** faire sursauter qn

2 *vt* **(a)** *(begin)* commencer; *(conversation, talks)* entamer; *(fire)* déclencher; *(fashion, rumor)* lancer; *(business)* monter; **to s. doing sth, to s. to do sth** commencer de faire qch; **to s. crying/laughing/sneezing** se mettre à pleurer/rire/éternuer; **to get started** démarrer

(b) *(machine, engine)* mettre en marche; *(car)* démarrer

3 *vi* **(a)** *(begin)* commencer; **to s. at the beginning** commencer par le commencement; **to s. by doing sth** commencer par faire qch; **to s. on sth** commencer qch; **she had started as a doctor** elle avait commencé sa carrière comme médecin; **to s. with** au début, d'abord; **now don't you s.!** tu ne vas pas t'y mettre aussi!

(b) *(make sudden movement)* sursauter

(c) *(begin journey)* se mettre en route

(d) *(of car, engine)* démarrer

▸**start off 1** *vt sep (argument, debate)* commencer; **to s. sb off** *(in business)* aider qn à démarrer; *(on a subject)* lancer qn

2 *vi (begin)* commencer; *(on journey)* se mettre en route

▸**start out** *vi (begin)* débuter; *(on journey)* se mettre en route

▸**start up 1** *vt sep (car)* démarrer; *(machine)* mettre en marche; *(business)* monter

2 *vi (of engine)* démarrer; **to s. up in business** monter son entreprise

starter ['stɑːtə(r)] *n* **(a)** *(competitor)* partant(e) *m,f*; *(official)* starter *m* **(b) to be a late s.** *(of child)* ne pas être très précoce; **to be a slow s.** *(of person)* être lent(e) à démarrer **(c)** *(device)* starter *m* **(d)** *(in meal)* hors-d'œuvre *m inv*; *Fig* **for starters** pour commencer

starting ['stɑːtɪŋ] *n* **(a)** *(in sport)* **s. block** starting-block *m*; **s. line** ligne *f* de départ; **s. pistol** pistolet *m* de starter **(b)** *(initial)* **s. point** *or* **place** point *m* de départ; **s. price** *(in betting)* cote *f* au départ; **s. salary** salaire *m* de départ

startle ['stɑːtəl] *vt* faire sursauter

startling ['stɑːtlɪŋ] *adj (noise)* effrayant(e); *(news, event)* incroyable

start-up ['stɑːtʌp] *n* **(a)** *Comput* démarrage *m* **(b)** *Com (of new business)* lancement *m*; **s. costs** coûts *mpl* d'installation **(c)** *(Internet company)* start-up *f*, jeune pousse *f*

starvation [stɑː'veɪʃən] *n* privation *f* totale de nourriture; **to die of s.** mourir de faim; **to be on a s. diet** *(not have enough to eat)* n'avoir presque rien à manger; **s. wages** salaires *mpl* de misère

starve [stɑːv] **1** *vt* priver de nourriture; **to s. sb to death** faire mourir qn de faim; *Fig* **to be starved of sth** être privé(e) de qch

2 *vi (lack food)* souffrir de la faim; **to s. (to death)** mourir de faim; *Fam* **I'm starving!** je meurs de faim!

starving ['stɑːvɪŋ] *adj* famélique

stash [stæʃ] *Fam* **1** *n* réserve *f*

2 *vt* planquer

state [steɪt] **1** *n* **(a)** *(condition)* état *m*; *(situation)* situation *f*; **I'm not in a fit s. to travel** je ne suis pas en état de voyager; **s. of war/emergency** état de guerre/d'urgence; **s. of affairs** situation *f*; **s. of health** état de santé; **s. of mind** état d'esprit; **in a s. of terror** terrifié(e); **in a s. of shock** en état de choc; **to be in a terrible s.** être dans un état lamentable; **to lie in s.** *(of dead person)* être exposé(e) au public

(b) *(country, administrative region)* État *m*; *Fam* **the States** *(the USA)* les États-Unis; **s. control** étatisme *m*; **S. Department** ≃ ministère *m* des Affaires étrangères; **s. occasion** cérémonie *f* officielle; **s. school** école *f* publique; **s. secret** secret *m* d'État; **s. sector** secteur *m* public; **S. Supreme Court** = la plus haute instance judiciaire dans chaque État américain; *Pol* **S. of the Union address** le discours sur l'état de l'Union; **s. visit** visite *f* officielle

2 *vt (declare)* déclarer; *(address, age)* indiquer, préciser; **to s. the obvious** enfoncer une porte ouverte; **as stated earlier/above** comme mentionné précédemment/ci-dessus; **at the stated times** aux heures prévues

stateless ['steɪtlɪs] *adj* apatride

stately ['steɪtlɪ] *adj* imposant(e); **s. home** ≃ château *m*

statement ['steɪtmənt] *n* **(a)** *(of opinion)* déclaration *f*; *(of facts)* exposé *m*; **to make a s.** *(of spokesperson)* faire une déclaration; *(of witness)* faire une déposition; *Fig (of lifestyle, behavior)* faire passer un message **(b)** *(from bank)* relevé *m* de compte

state-of-the-art [steɪtəvðɪ'ɑːt] *adj (technology, computer etc)* de pointe; **it's s.** c'est du dernier cri

state-owned ['steɪt'əʊnd] *adj (company)* d'État; *(property)* de l'État

statesman ['steɪtsmən] *n* homme *m* d'État

statesmanlike ['steɪtsmənlaɪk] *adj* digne d'un homme d'État

static ['stætɪk] **1** *adj* statique; **s. electricity** électricité *f* statique

2 *n* électricité *f* statique

station ['steɪʃən] **1** *n* **(a)** *(for trains)* gare *f*; **s. master** chef *m* de gare; **s. wagon** *(car)* break *m* **(b)** *(post)* poste *m*; **(police) s.** poste (de police); **(radio/television) s.** station *f* de radio/télévision **(c)** *(social condition)* condition *f*; **to have ideas above one's s.** ne pas avoir les moyens de ses ambitions

2 *vt (person)* placer; *(soldier, troops)* poster

stationary ['steɪʃənərɪ] *adj* immobile

stationer ['steɪʃənə(r)] *n* **s.'s (store)** papeterie *f*

stationery ['steɪʃənərɪ] *n (writing materials)* papeterie *f*; *(writing paper)* papier *m* à lettres

statistic [stə'tɪstɪk] *n* chiffre *m* statistique; **statistics** statistiques *fpl*

statistical [stə'tɪstɪkəl] *adj* statistique

statistician [stætɪs'tɪʃən] *n* statisticien(enne) *m,f*

statue ['stætjuː] *n* statue *f*

statuesque [stætjʊ'esk] *adj* sculptural(e)

statuette [stætjʊ'et] *n* statuette *f*

stature ['stætʃə(r)] *n (physical build)* stature *f*; *(reputation)* envergure *f*, réputation *f*

status ['steɪtəs] *n (position, prestige)* statut *m*; *Comput* **s. bar** barre *f* d'état; *Comput* **s. line** ligne *f* d'état; **s. meeting** réunion *f* de bilan; **s. report** rapport *m* de situation; **s. symbol** marque *f* de prestige

status quo ['steɪtəs'kwəʊ] *n* statu quo *m inv*

statute ['stætjuːt] *n* texte *m* de loi; **by s.** par la loi; **s. book** recueil *m* de lois

statutory ['stætjʊtərɪ] *adj* légal(e); **s. duty** obligation *f* légale;

s. holiday jour *m* férié; **s. rape** détournement *m* de mineur

staunch[1] [stɔːntʃ] *adj (resolute)* convaincu(e); *(supporter)* ardent(e)

staunch[2] [stɔːntʃ] *vt (blood)* étancher

staunchly ['stɔːntʃlɪ] *adv* résolument

stave [steɪv] *n* **(a)** *(of barrel)* douve *f* **(b)** *Mus* portée *f*

▶**stave in** *(pt & pp* **staved** *or* **stove** [stəʊv]) *vt sep* défoncer; *(ribs)* enfoncer

▶**stave off** *vt sep (problem, disaster)* éviter; *(hunger)* tromper

stay [steɪ] **1** *vt (endure)* **to s. the course** *or* **distance** tenir la distance

2 *vi* **(a)** *(not move, remain)* rester; *Fam* **to s. put** rester tranquille; **to s. still** rester tranquille; **computers are here to s.** l'informatique est entrée dans les mœurs **(b)** *(reside temporarily)* séjourner; **I stayed five years in the States** j'ai passé cinq ans aux États-Unis; **to s. with sb** loger chez qn

3 *n* **(a)** *(visit)* séjour *m* **(b)** *Law & Fig* **s. of execution** sursis *m*

▶**stay away** *vi* **to s. away from sb/sth** ne pas s'approcher de qn/qch; **to s. away from school** ne pas aller à l'école

▶**stay in** *vi (not go out)* rester chez soi

▶**stay on** *vi* rester

▶**stay out** *vi* **(a)** *(not go home)* ne pas rentrer; **to s. out all night** ne pas rentrer de la nuit; **to s. out late** rentrer tard **(b)** *(of strikers)* continuer la grève **(c)** *(not interfere)* **to s. out of sth** ne pas se mêler de qch

▶**stay up** *vi* ne pas aller se coucher

staying power ['steɪɪŋˌpaʊə(r)] *n* endurance *f*

STD [estiːˈdiː] *n Med (abbr* **sexually transmitted disease)** MST *f*

stead [sted] *n* **to stand sb in good s.** être fort utile à qn; **in sb's s.** à la place de qn

steadfast ['stedfɑːst] *adj* dévoué(e); *(opponent, resistance)* constant(e)

steadily ['stedɪlɪ] *adv (change, grow)* progressivement; *(work)* assidûment; *(walk)* d'un pas régulier; *(look)* fixement; *(breathe, increase)* régulièrement

steady ['stedɪ] **1** *adj* **(a)** *(stable)* stable; **in a s. voice** d'une voix assurée **(b)** *(regular)* régulier(ère); *(progress)* constant(e); *(relationship)* durable; **to have a s. girlfriend** avoir une copine (attitrée); **to drive at a s. 30 mph** ≃ rouler à une vitesse régulière de 50 km/h

2 *adv* **to be going s.** sortir ensemble sérieusement

3 *vt* faire tenir; **to s. oneself** trouver son équilibre; **to s. one's nerves** se calmer; **to s. one's voice** contrôler sa voix

steak [steɪk] *n (beef)* steak *m*; *(of fish)* darne *f*

steal [stiːl] *(pt* **stole** [stəʊl], *pp* **stolen** ['stəʊlən]) **1** *vt* **(a)** *(thieve)* voler; **to s. sth from sb** voler qch à qn **(b)** *(idioms)* **to s. a glance at sb** jeter un coup d'œil à qn; **to s. the show** ravir la vedette

2 *vi* **(a)** *(thieve)* voler **(b)** *(move quietly)* **to s. away/in/out** s'en aller/rentrer/sortir sans faire de bruit; **to s. up on sb** s'approcher de qn sans faire de bruit; *Fig* prendre qn par surprise

stealth [stelθ] *n* ruse *f*

stealthily ['stelθɪlɪ] *adv* furtivement

stealthy ['stelθɪ] *adj* furtif(ive)

steam [stiːm] **1** *n* **(a)** *(water vapor)* vapeur *f*; *(on glass)* buée *f*; **s. bath** bain *m* de vapeur; **s. engine** locomotive *f* à vapeur; **s. iron** fer *m* à vapeur; **s. shovel** pelleteuse *f* **(b)** *(idioms)* **to get up s.** prendre de l'élan; **to run out of s.** s'essouffler; **to let off s.** se défouler; **to do sth under one's own s.** faire qch tout(e) seul(e)

2 *vt (food)* faire cuire à la vapeur

3 *vi (give off steam)* fumer

▶**steam open** *vt sep (envelope)* décacheter à la vapeur

▶**steam up 1** *vt sep* **to get all steamed up (about sth)** *(of person)* se mettre dans tous ses états (à propos de qch)

2 *vi (of window, glasses)* s'embuer

steamer ['stiːmə(r)] *n* **(a)** *(ship)* (bateau *m* à) vapeur *m* **(b)** *(for food)* panier *m* de cuisson à la vapeur

steamroller ['stiːmrəʊlə(r)] **1** *n* rouleau *m* compresseur

2 *vt* **to s. sb into doing sth** forcer qn à faire qch

steamship ['stiːmʃɪp] *n* bateau *m* à vapeur

steamy ['stiːmɪ] *adj* **(a)** *(room)* plein(e) de vapeur; *(mirror)* embué(e) **(b)** *Fam (novel, movie)* torride

steel [stiːl] **1** *n* acier *m*; **nerves of s.** nerfs *mpl* d'acier; **the s. industry** la sidérurgie; **s. band** steel band *m*; **s. mill** aciérie *f*; **s. wool** paille *f* de fer

2 *vt* **to s. oneself to do sth** s'armer de courage pour faire qch; **to s. oneself against sth** se blinder contre qch

steelworker ['stiːlwɜːkə(r)] *n* employé(e) *m,f* de la sidérurgie

steep[1] [stiːp] *adj* **(a)** *(path, hill)* pentu(e), escarpé(e); *(climb)* raide; *Fig (increase)* considérable **(b)** *Fam (expensive)* salé(e); *(unreasonable)* raide

steep[2] [stiːp] *vt (soak)* faire tremper; *Fig* **steeped in history/tradition** imprégné(e) d'histoire/de tradition

steeple ['stiːpəl] *n* clocher *m*

steeplechase ['stiːpəltʃeɪs] *n* steeple-chase *m*

steeplejack ['stiːpəldʒæk] *n* réparateur *m* de clochers et de cheminées d'usines

steer[1] [stɪə(r)] **1** *vt (car)* conduire; *(ship)* barrer; **to s. sb out of trouble** sortir qn du pétrin

2 *vi (of person)* conduire; *(of ship)* se diriger (**for** vers); **to s. clear of sb/sth** éviter qn/qch

steer[2] [stɪə(r)] *n (bull)* bouvillon *m*

steering ['stɪərɪŋ] *n (mechanism)* direction *f*; **s. column** colonne *f* de direction; *Pol* **s. committee** comité *m* d'organisation; **s. wheel** volant *m*

stem [stem] **1** *n (of plant)* tige *f*; *(of glass)* pied *m*; *(of pipe)* tuyau *m*; *(of word)* radical *m*; *Biol* **s. cell** cellule *f* souche

2 *vt (pt & pp* **stemmed)** *(halt)* stopper; **to s. the tide of sth** enrayer le flot de qch

3 *vi* **to s. from** provenir de

stench [stentʃ] *n* puanteur *f*

stencil ['stensəl] **1** *n* pochoir *m*

2 *vt* dessiner au pochoir

stenographer [stəˈnɒɡrəfə(r)] *n* sténographe *mf*

step [step] **1** *n* **(a)** *(movement, sound)* pas *m*; **to take a s.** faire un pas; **s. by s.** pas à pas; *Fig* petit à petit; *also Fig* **to watch one's s.** faire attention où l'on met les pieds; **to keep in s.** *(in dance)* danser en mesure; *Fig* **to be out of s. (with sb)** être en décalage (par rapport à qn)

(b) *(action, measure)* mesure *f*; **to take steps (to do sth)** 7tjl;prendre des mesures (pour faire qch); **the next s. is to...** la prochaine chose à faire, c'est de...; **a s. in the right direction** un pas dans la bonne direction

(c) *(stage)* étape *f*; **at every s.** à chaque étape; **every s. of the way** sur toute la ligne

(d) *(of staircase)* marche *f*; *(of stepladder)* échelon *m*; **(flight of) steps** escalier *m*; *(on outside of building)* perron *m*

(e) *(exercise)* step *m*; **s. class** cours *m* de step

2 *vi (pt & pp* **stepped)** *(take a step)* faire un pas; *(walk)* marcher; **to s. on sth** marcher sur qch; **s. this way** venez par ici; *Fam Fig* **to s. on it** se grouiller

▶**step back** *vi* reculer (**from** de); *Fig* prendre du recul (**from** par rapport à)

▶**step down** *vi (resign)* démissionner

▶**step forward** *vi (volunteer)* se porter volontaire

▶**step in** *vi (intervene)* intervenir

▶**step up** *vt sep (increase)* accélérer; *(pressure)* augmenter

stepbrother ['stepbrʌðə(r)] *n* = fils du conjoint d'un des parents

stepchild ['steptʃaɪld] *n (boy)* beau-fils *m*; *(girl)* belle-fille *f*

stepdaughter ['stepdɔːtə(r)] *n* belle-fille *f*

stepfather ['stepfɑːðə(r)] *n* beau-père *m*

stepladder ['steplædə(r)] *n* escabeau *m*

stepmother ['stepmʌðə(r)] *n* belle-mère *f*

stepparent ['steppeərənt] *n (father)* beau-père *m*; *(mother)* belle-mère *f*

steppe [step] *n* steppe *f*

stepper ['stepə(r)] *n (gym equipment)* stepper *m*

stepsister ['stepsɪstə(r)] *n* = fille du conjoint d'un des parents

stepson ['stepsʌn] *n* beau-fils *m*

stereo ['sterɪəʊ] **1** *n (pl* **stereos)** *(equipment)* chaîne *f* stéréo; *(sound)* stéréo *f*; **in s.** en stéréo

  2 *adj* stéréo *inv*

stereophonic [sterɪə'fɒnɪk] *adj* stéréophonique

stereoscopic [sterɪəʊ'skɒpɪk] *adj* stéréoscopique

stereotype ['sterɪətaɪp] **1** *n* stéréotype *m*

  2 *vt* stéréotyper

stereotyped ['sterɪətaɪpt] *adj* stéréotypé(e)

sterile ['steraɪl] *adj* stérile

sterility [ste'rɪlɪtɪ] *n* stérilité *f*

sterilization [sterɪlaɪ'zeɪʃən] *n* stérilisation *f*

sterilize ['sterɪlaɪz] *vt* stériliser

sterling ['stɜːlɪŋ] **1** *n (British currency)* livre *f* sterling

  2 *adj* **(a)** *(silver)* fin(e) **(b)** *(effort, quality)* remarquable

stern¹ [stɜːn] *adj (person, look)* sévère

stern² [stɜːn] *n (of boat)* poupe *f*

sternum ['stɜːnəm] *(pl* **sternums** *or* **sterna** ['stɜːnə]) *n* sternum *m*

steroid ['stɪərɔɪd] *n* stéroïde *m*

stethoscope ['steθəskəʊp] *n* stéthoscope *m*

stevedore ['stiːvədɔː(r)] *n* docker *m*

stew [stjuː] **1** *n* ragoût *m*

  2 *vt (meat)* faire cuire en ragoût; *(fruit)* faire de la compote de

  3 *vi (of meat)* mijoter; *Fam* **to let sb s. (in his/her own juice)** laisser qn mariner

steward ['stjʊəd] *n (on estate)* régisseur *m*; *(on ship, plane)* steward *m*; *(at sporting event)* organisateur *m*; *(at demonstration)* membre *m* du service d'ordre

stewardess ['stjʊə'des] *n (on ship, plane)* hôtesse *f*

stewed [stjuːd] *adj* **(a)** *Culin* **s. beef** bœuf *m* en ragoût; **s. fruit** compote *f* de fruits **(b)** *Fam (drunk)* bourré(e)

STI [esti:'aɪ] *n Med (abbr* **sexually transmitted infection)** MST *f*

stick¹ [stɪk] *n (of wood, glue, chewing gum)* bâton *m*; *(for walking)* canne *f*; *(of celery, rhubarb)* tige *f*; *Fam Fig* **to get hold of the wrong end of the s.** comprendre de travers; *Fam* **she lives out in the sticks** elle habite dans un trou perdu; **s. insect** phasme *m*; *Aut* **s. shift** levier *m* de vitesse; **to drive a s. shift** conduire une voiture à vitesses manuelles

stick² [stɪk] *(pt & pp* **stuck** [stʌk]) **1** *vt* **(a)** *(insert)* **to s. sth in(to) sth** planter qch dans qch **(b)** *Fam (put)* mettre, poser **(c)** *(attach with glue)* coller **(on/in** sur/dans)

  2 *vi* **(a)** *(adhere)* coller; *Fig* **the name stuck** ce nom lui/leur/ *etc.* est resté; *Fig* **to s. to one's guns** ne pas en démordre; **to s. to the facts** s'en tenir aux faits; **to s. to one's principles** rester fidèle à ses principes **(b)** *(become jammed)* se coincer; *Fig* **it sticks in my throat** c'est dur à avaler

▶**stick around** *vi Fam* attendre

▶**stick at** *vt insep (persevere with)* persévérer dans; **to s. at nothing** ne reculer devant rien

▶**stick by** *vt insep (friend)* soutenir; *(promise, statement)* maintenir

▶**stick out 1** *vt sep* **(a)** *(cause to protrude)* faire sortir; **to s. one's tongue out (at sb)** tirer la langue (à qn); *Fam* **to s. one's neck out (for sb)** prendre des risques (pour qn) **(b)** *Fam (endure)* **to s. it out** tenir bon

  2 *vi* **(a)** *(protrude)* ressortir; *(of ears)* être décollés(ées); *(of teeth)* avancer **(b)** *Fam (be noticeable)* se voir; **it sticks out a mile** *or* **like a sore thumb** ça se voit comme le nez au milieu de la figure

▶**stick together 1** *vt sep* coller

  2 *vi* **(a)** *(with glue)* être collé(e) **(b)** *(of friends)* rester ensemble

▶**stick up 1** *vt sep (sign, poster)* mettre; *Fam* **s. 'em up!** haut les mains!

  2 *vi (of building, hair)* se dresser

▶**stick up for** *vt insep (person, rights)* prendre la défense de

▶**stick with** *vt insep (not give up)* rester avec

sticker ['stɪkə(r)] *n* autocollant *m*; *Mktg* **s. price** prix *m* affiché

stick-in-the-mud ['stɪkɪnðəmʌd] *n Fam* rabat-joie *m inv*

stickleback ['stɪkəlbæk] *n* épinoche *f*

stickler ['stɪklə(r)] *n* **to be a s. for sth** être à cheval sur qch

stick-on ['stɪkɒn] *adj* autocollant(e)

stick-up ['stɪkʌp] *n Fam (robbery)* braquage *m*

sticky ['stɪkɪ] *adj* **(a)** *(substance)* collant(e); *(climate)* humide, moite; *(label)* adhésif(ive); *Fig* **to have s. fingers** avoir une tendance pickpocket; **s. tape** ruban *m* adhésif **(b)** *Fig (awkward)* délicat(e); **to come to a s. end** mal finir

stiff [stɪf] *adj* **(a)** *(rigid)* rigide; *(paste)* ferme; **as s. as a board** tout(e) raide; **to be bored s.** s'ennuyer à mourir; **to be scared s.** avoir une trouille bleue; **to be frozen s.** être frigorifié(e) **(b)** *(joint)* ankylosé(e); **to be s.** *(of person)* avoir des courbatures; **to have a s. neck** avoir un torticolis; **my leg is s.** j'ai la jambe ankylosée **(c)** *(handle, hinge, drawer)* dur(e) **(d)** *(severe)* *(punishment, fine)* sévère; *(resistance)* opiniâtre; *(competition)* rude; *(exam)* dur(e); *(breeze)* fort(e); **a s. drink** une boisson forte **(e)** *(formal)* rigide; *(smile)* forcé(e)

stiffen ['stɪfən] **1** *vt* renforcer; *(paste)* épaissir

  2 *vi* se raidir

stiffly ['stɪflɪ] *adv (bow)* avec raideur; *(answer, greet)* avec froideur

stifle ['staɪfəl] *vt also Fig* étouffer

stifling ['staɪflɪŋ] *adj* étouffant(e)

stigma ['stɪɡmə] *(pl* **stigmas)** *n* honte *f*

stigmata [stɪɡ'mɑːtə] *npl (of saint)* stigmates *mpl*

stigmatize ['stɪɡmətaɪz] *vt* stigmatiser

stile [staɪl] *n* échalier *m*

stiletto [stɪ'letəʊ] *(pl* **stilettos)** *n (dagger)* stylet *m*; *(shoe)* talon *m* aiguille; **s. heels** talons aiguille

still¹ [stɪl] **1** *adj (motionless)* immobile; *(calm)* calme; *(silent)* silencieux(euse); *(drink)* non gazeux(euse); **to stand s.** ne pas bouger; *Art* **s. life** nature *f* morte; *Prov* **s. waters run deep** il faut se méfier de l'eau qui dort

  2 *vt* calmer, apaiser

  3 *n* **(a)** **in the s. of the night** dans le silence de la nuit **(b)** *(photograph)* photo *f* de plateau

still² [stɪl] *adv* **(a)** *(up to given point in time)* toujours, encore; **she's s. alive** elle vit toujours; **I s. think/say that...** je continue de penser/dire que...; **I s. have 25 dollars** il me reste encore 25 dollars **(b)** *(nonetheless)* tout de même; **s., it could have been worse** enfin, ç'aurait pu être pire **(c)** *(even)* encore; **s. more/better** encore plus/mieux

still³ [stɪl] *n (distilling equipment)* alambic *m*

stillbirth ['stɪlbɜːθ] *n* enfant *mf* mort-né(e)

stillborn ['stɪlbɔːn] *adj* mort-né(e)

stillness ['stɪlnɪs] *n* tranquillité *f*

stilt [stɪlt] *n (for walking)* échasse *f*; *(for building)* pilotis *m*

stilted ['stɪltɪd] *adj* guindé(e)

stimulant ['stɪmjʊlənt] *n* stimulant *m*

stimulate ['stɪmjʊleɪt] *vt* stimuler

stimulating ['stɪmjʊleɪtɪŋ] *adj* stimulant(e)

stimulation [stɪmjʊ'leɪʃən] *n* stimulation *f*

stimulus ['stɪmjʊləs] *(pl* **stimuli** ['stɪmjʊlaɪ]) *n* encouragement *m*; *(physiological)* stimulus *m inv*

sting [stɪŋ] **1** *n* **(a)** *(of bee)* dard *m*; *(of scorpion)* aiguillon *m*; *(wound)* piqûre *f* **(b)** *(sensation)* brûlure *f* **(c)** *(idiom)* **to take the s. out of sth** atténuer les effets de qch **(d)** *Fam (police operation)* coup *m* monté

2 *vt* (*pt & pp* **stung** [stʌŋ]) *(of bee, nettle)* piquer; *Fig (of remark)* blesser, piquer au vif; *Fig* **to s. sb into action** inciter qn à agir; *Fam Fig* **they stung him for $30** ils l'ont arnaqué de 30 dollars

3 *vi (of eyes, skin)* piquer

stinging ['stɪŋɪŋ] *adj (pain)* cuisant(e); *(remark, criticism)* cinglant(e); **s. nettle** ortie *f*

stingray ['stɪŋreɪ] *n* pastenague *f*

stingy ['stɪndʒɪ] *adj (person)* pingre; *(portion)* minuscule; **to be s. with one's praise** être avare de compliments

stink [stɪŋk] **1** *n (smell)* puanteur *f*; *Fam Fig* **to kick up a s. (about sth)** faire tout un scandale (à propos de qch)

2 *vi (pt* **stank** [stæŋk] *or* **stunk** [stʌŋk], *pp* **stunk**) **(a)** *(smell)* puer; **to s. of sth** puer qch; *Fam Fig* **to s. of corruption** sentir la corruption à plein nez **(b)** *Fam Fig (be of bad quality)* craindre

stinkbomb ['stɪŋkbɒm] *n* boule *f* puante

stinker ['stɪŋkə(r)] *n Fam (person)* peau *f* de vache; *(difficult task)* casse-tête *m*; **a s. of a cold** un rhume carabiné

stinking ['stɪŋkɪŋ] **1** *adj* puant(e); **a s. cold** un rhume carabiné

2 *adv Fam* **to be s. rich** être bourré(e) de fric

stint [stɪnt] **1** *n (period)* période *f*; *(share of work)* part *f* de travail; **to take a s. at the wheel** prendre le volant; **he had a two-year s. in the army** il a fait deux ans d'armée

2 *vt* épargner; **to s. oneself** se sacrifier

3 *vi* **to s. on sth** lésiner sur qch

stipend ['staɪpend] *n* traitement *m*

stipulate ['stɪpjʊleɪt] *vt* stipuler

stipulation [stɪpjʊ'leɪʃən] *n* stipulation *f*

stir [stɜ:(r)] **1** *vt (pt & pp* **stirred**) **(a)** *(liquid, mixture)* remuer; *(leaves)* agiter **(b)** *Fig (person)* émouvoir, remuer; *(emotion)* réveiller; *(curiosity)* exciter; **to s. sb to do sth** inciter qn à faire qch; *Fam* **to s. oneself** se remuer; *Fam* **to s. it** *(make trouble)* envenimer les choses

2 *vi (move)* bouger, remuer

3 *n* **(a) to give sth a s.** remuer qch **(b)** *Fig* **to cause a s.** faire du bruit

▸**stir up** *vt sep* **(a)** *(dust, leaves)* remuer **(b)** *Fig (rebellion, anger, resentment)* attiser; *(workers, crowd)* inciter à la révolte; **to s. up trouble** semer la zizanie; **to s. things up** envenimer les choses

stir-fry ['stɜ:fraɪ] *Culin* **1** *n* sauté *m*

2 *vt (pt & pp* **stir-fried**) faire sauter

stirrer ['stɜ:rə(r)] *n Fam (troublemaker)* semeur(euse) *m,f* de zizanie

stirring ['stɜ:rɪŋ] **1** *n* **the first stirrings of** les premiers signes de

2 *adj (speech, movie)* poignant(e)

stirrup ['stɪrəp] *n* étrier *m*

stitch [stɪtʃ] **1** *n* **(a)** *(in sewing)* point *m*; *(in knitting)* maille *f*; *Med* point (de suture); *Fam* **she didn't have a s. on** elle était nue comme un ver; *Prov* **a s. in time saves nine** un point à temps en vaut cent **(b)** *(sharp pain)* point *m* (de côté); **to get a s.** prendre un point **(c)** *Fam* **we were in stitches** *(laughing)* on était pliés

2 *vt (clothing)* coudre; *Med* recoudre

▸**stitch up** *vt sep Fam (falsely incriminate)* faire porter le chapeau à

stoat [stəʊt] *n* hermine *f*

stock [stɒk] **1** *n* **(a)** *(supply)* provisions *fpl*; *Com* stock *m*; *Com* **while stocks last** jusqu'à épuisement des stocks; **to have sth in s.** avoir qch en stock; **to be out of s.** être épuisé(e); *Fig* **to take s.** faire le point; *Com* **s. control** gestion *f* des stocks; *Com* **s. list** inventaire *m* des stocks

(b) *(livestock)* bétail *m*

(c) *Fin* valeurs *fpl*, actions *fpl*; *Fig* **her s. is going up/down**

sa cote est en hausse/baisse; **stocks and shares** valeurs mobilières; **s. exchange** Bourse *f* (des valeurs); **s. market** marché *m* des valeurs; **s. option** stock-option *f*, option *f* de titres

(d) *(descent)* **of German s.** de souche allemande

(e) *(of rifle)* fût *m*

(f) **stocks** *(for punishment)* pilori *m*

(g) *(in cooking)* bouillon *m*; **chicken/vegetable stock** bouillon *m* de poulet/légumes **s. cube** bouillon cube *m*

2 *adj (argument, excuse)* classique

3 *vt* **(a)** *(goods)* vendre

(b) *(supply) (store)* approvisionner (**with** en)

▸**stock up** *vi* faire des provisions (**with** de)

stockade [stɒ'keɪd] *n* palissade *f*

stockbroker ['stɒkbrəʊkə(r)] *n Fin* agent *m* de change

stockholder ['stɒkhəʊldə(r)] *n Fin* actionnaire *mf*

Stockholm ['stɒkhəʊm] *n* Stockholm

stocking ['stɒkɪŋ] *n (garment)* bas *m*

stockist ['stɒkɪst] *n Com* stockiste *mf*

stockpile ['stɒkpaɪl] **1** *n* réserves *fpl*

2 *vt* faire des réserves de

stockroom ['stɒkru:m] *n* réserve *f*, magasin *m*

stock-still ['stɒk'stɪl] *adv* **to stand s.** se tenir complètement immobile

stocktaking ['stɒkteɪkɪŋ] *n Com* inventaire *m* des stocks; *Fig* **a s. exercise** un examen de situation

stocky ['stɒkɪ] *adj* trapu(e)

stodgy ['stɒdʒɪ] *adj (food)* bourratif(ive); *(book)* indigeste

stoic ['stəʊɪk] *n & adj* stoïque *mf*

stoical ['stəʊɪkəl] *adj* stoïque

stoicism ['stəʊɪsɪzəm] *n* stoïcisme *m*

stoke [stəʊk] *vt (fire, boiler)* alimenter; *Fig* entretenir

STOL [stɒl] *n Aviat (abbr* **short take-off and landing**) ADAC *m*

stole¹ [stəʊl] *n (garment)* étole *f*

stole² [stəʊl] *pt of* **steal**

stolen ['stəʊlən] **1** *adj* volé(e)

2 *pp of* **steal**

stolid ['stɒlɪd] *adj* impassible

stomach ['stʌmək] **1** *n* ventre *m*; *(organ)* estomac *m*; **on an empty s.** à jeun; *Fig* **it turns my s.** ça m'écœure; *Fig* **I've no s. for his vulgar jokes this evening** je n'ai aucune envie d'écouter ses plaisanteries vulgaires ce soir; **to have a s. ache** avoir mal au ventre; *(in organ)* avoir mal à l'estomac; *Med* **s. pump** pompe *f* stomacale

2 *vt Fig (tolerate)* supporter

stomp [stɒmp] *vi* marcher en tapant des pieds; **to s. in/out** entrer/sortir en tapant des pieds

stomping ground ['stɒmpɪŋ'graʊnd] *n* lieu *m* de prédilection; **this was one of my old stomping grounds** j'y allais tout le temps

stone [stəʊn] **1** *n* **(a)** *(material, piece of rock)* pierre *f*; *(smaller)* caillou *m*; *Fig* **to leave no s. unturned** remuer ciel et terre; *Fig* **a s.'s throw from here** à deux pas d'ici; **the S. Age** l'âge *m* de pierre; *Zool* **s. marten** fouine *f* **(b)** *(of fruit)* noyau *m* **(c)** *(unit of weight)* = 6,35kg

2 *adj* en pierre; *(pitcher)* en grès; *Fam Fig* **to be s. broke** n'avoir pas un rond

3 *vt* **(a)** *(fruit)* dénoyauter **(b)** *(person)* lapider

stone-cold ['stəʊn'kəʊld] *adj* glacé(e)

stoned [stəʊnd] *adj Fam (on drugs)* défoncé(e)

stone-dead ['stəʊn'ded] *adj* raide mort(e)

stone-deaf ['stəʊn'def] *adj* sourd(e) comme un pot

stonemason ['stəʊnmeɪsən] *n* maçon *m*

stonewall [stəʊn'wɔ:l] *vi (in game)* pratiquer un jeu défensif; *(in inquiry)* refuser de répondre

stoneware ['stəʊnweə(r)] *n* poterie *f* en grès

stonework ['stəʊnwɜːk] *n* maçonnerie *f*

stonily ['stəʊnɪlɪ] *adv* froidement

stony ['stəʊnɪ] *adj (ground, beach)* caillouteux(euse); *Fig (look, silence)* glacial(e)

stood [stʊd] *pt & pp of* **stand**

stooge [stuːdʒ] *n (comedian's fall guy)* faire-valoir *m*; *(minion)* larbin *m*

stool [stuːl] *n* (**a**) *(seat)* tabouret *m*; *Fig* **to fall between two stools** être assis(e) entre deux chaises; *Fam* **s. pigeon** balance *f*, indic *m* (**b**) *Med (feces)* selles *fpl*

stoop¹ [stuːp] **1** *n* **to have a s.** être voûté(e); **to walk with a s.** marcher le dos courbé

   2 *vi (bend down)* se pencher; *Fig* **to s. to sth/doing sth** s'abaisser à qch/à faire qch

stoop² [stuːp] *n (of house) (with roof)* véranda *f*; *(without roof)* perron *m*

stop [stɒp] **1** *n* (**a**) *(halt)* arrêt *m*; **to put a s. to sth** mettre fin à qch; **to come to a s.** s'arrêter; *Aut* **s. sign** stop *m* (**b**) *(pause) (in work)* pause *f*; *(in journey)* halte *f*; *(of plane)* escale *f*; *(of train)* arrêt *m* (**c**) *(for bus, train)* arrêt *m* (**d**) *(period)* point *m*; *(in telegram)* stop *m* (**e**) *Mus (on organ)* jeu *m*; *Fig* **to pull out all the stops** remuer ciel et terre

   2 *vt (pt & pp* **stopped**) (**a**) *(halt) (person, vehicle)* arrêter; *(conversation, speaker)* interrompre; *(corruption, abuse)* mettre fin à; *Fin* **to s. a check** faire opposition à un chèque; **s., thief!** au voleur! (**b**) *(cease)* arrêter; **to s. doing sth** arrêter de faire qch (**c**) *(prevent)* empêcher; **to s. sb from doing sth** empêcher qn de faire qch; **I couldn't s. myself** je n'ai pas pu m'en empêcher (**d**) *(fill in) (hole, gap)* boucher

   3 *vi* (**a**) *(halt) (of moving person, vehicle)* s'arrêter (**b**) *(cease) (of speaker, worker)* s'arrêter; *(of pain, bleeding)* cesser; *(of rain)* s'arrêter, cesser; **she'll s. at nothing** rien ne l'arrêtera; **to s. short** s'arrêter net (**c**) *(stay)* rester

▸**stop by** *vi (visit)* passer; **I'll s. by your place tomorrow** je passerai chez toi demain

▸**stop off** *vi* faire une halte

▸**stop over** *vi Aviat* faire escale

▸**stop up** *vt sep (hole, sink, pipe)* boucher

stopcock ['stɒpkɒk] *n* robinet *m* d'arrêt

stopgap ['stɒpgæp] *n (thing, person)* bouche-trou *m*; **s. measure** mesure *f* transitoire

stoplight ['stɒplaɪt] *n Aut* feux *mpl* (tricolores *ou* de signalisation)

stopover ['stɒpəʊvə(r)] *n Aviat* escale *f*

stoppage ['stɒpɪdʒ] *n (of flow, traffic)* arrêt *m*; *(strike)* débrayage *m*

stopper ['stɒpə(r)] *n* bouchon *m*

stopwatch ['stɒpwɒtʃ] *n* chronomètre *m*

storage ['stɔːrɪdʒ] *n* (**a**) *(action)* emmagasinage *m*; *(space available)* rangement *m*; **to put sth into s.** entreposer qch; **s. space** espace *m* de rangement; **s. tank** citerne *f* (**b**) *Comput* mémoire *f*

store [stɔː(r)] **1** *n* (**a**) *(supply) (of goods, food)* provision *f*; *Fig (of knowledge)* fonds *m*; **stores** réserves *fpl* (**b**) *(warehouse)* entrepôt *m* (**c**) *(shop)* magasin *m*; **s. detective** vigile *m*; **s. card** carte *f* de crédit *(d'un grand magasin)* (**d**) *(idioms)* **to hold** *or* **to keep sth in s.** tenir *ou* garder qch en réserve; **I have a surprise in s. for her** je lui réserve une surprise; **to set great s. by sth** faire grand cas de qch

   2 *vt (put in storage)* entreposer; *(food)* ranger; *(electricity, heat)* emmagasiner; **s. in a cool place** conserver au frais

▸**store up** *vt sep* accumuler

storehouse ['stɔːhaʊs] *n* entrepôt *m*

storeroom ['stɔːruːm] *n (in office, factory)* réserve *f*; *(at home)* débarras *m*

stork [stɔːk] *n* cigogne *f*

storm [stɔːm] **1** *n* (**a**) *(bad weather)* tempête *f*; *(thunderstorm)* orage *m*; **s. cloud** nuée *f* d'orage; **s. door** double porte *f* (**b**) *Fig (scandal, of protest)* tempête *f*; *(of abuse)* bordée *f* (**c**) *Mil* **to take sth by s.** prendre qch d'assaut; *Fig* **she/the show took London by s.** elle/le spectacle a eu un succès foudroyant à Londres; **s. troops** troupes *fpl* d'assaut

   2 *vt (town, fortress)* prendre d'assaut

   3 *vi (of person)* tempêter (**at sb** contre qn); **to s. in/out** entrer/sortir comme un ouragan

stormy ['stɔːmɪ] *adj also Fig* orageux(euse)

story¹ ['stɔːrɪ] *(pl* **stories**) *n* (**a**) *(account)* histoire *f*; *Fig* **to tell stories** *(lie)* raconter des histoires (**b**) *(plot) (of novel, play)* intrigue *f*, histoire *f* (**c**) *(in newspaper)* article *m* (**d**) *(idioms)* **that's quite another s.** ça c'est une autre histoire; **it's the same old s.** c'est toujours la même histoire; **or so the s. goes** c'est du moins ce que l'on raconte; *Fam* **it's the s. of my life** je suis le/la spécialiste de ce genre de choses; **it's a long s.** c'est une longue histoire; **to cut a long s. short,...** bref, pour résumer...

story² ['stɔːrɪ] *n* étage *m*; **a four-s. building** un immeuble de quatre étages

storybook ['stɔːrɪbʊk] **1** *n* livre *m* d'histoires

   2 *adj* **a s. ending** une fin digne d'un conte de fées; **a s. romance** une idylle de conte de fées;

storyteller ['stɔːrɪtelə(r)] *n* conteur(euse) *m,f*

stout [staʊt] **1** *n (beer)* stout *f*, bière *f* brune forte

   2 *adj* (**a**) *(fat)* corpulent(e) (**b**) *(solid) (door, shoes)* solide (**c**) *(brave) (person, resistance)* acharné(e)

stouthearted [staʊt'hɑːtɪd] *adj Lit* vaillant(e)

stoutly ['staʊtlɪ] *adv (resist, maintain)* avec fermeté

stove [stəʊv] *n (for cooking)* cuisinière *f*; *(for heating)* poêle *m*

stow [stəʊ] *vt (put away)* ranger; *Naut* arrimer

▸**stow away** *vi (on ship)* s'embarquer clandestinement

stowaway ['stəʊəweɪ] *n* passager(ère) *m,f* clandestin(e)

straddle ['strædəl] *vt (horse)* enfourcher; *(chair)* se mettre à califourchon sur; *Fig (period of time, subject)* couvrir

strafe [streɪf] *vt Mil* mitrailler en rase-mottes

straggle ['strægəl] *vi* (**a**) *(lag behind)* être à la traîne (**b**) *(of hair)* pendouiller

straggler ['stræglə(r)] *n* retardataire *mf*

straggly ['strægli] *adj (hair)* épars(e)

straight [streɪt] **1** *adj* (**a**) *(level, not curved) (line, tie, skirt, picture, back)* droit(e); *(hair)* raide; **to keep a s. face** garder son sérieux; **to put things** *or* **matters s.** arranger les choses; **to put sb s. about sth** éclairer qn sur qch

   (**b**) *(consecutive)* consécutif(ive); **s. flush** *(in cards)* quinte *f* flush

   (**c**) *(honest) (person)* honnête; *(answer)* clair(e); **to be s. with sb** jouer franc jeu avec qn

   (**d**) *(conventional)* conformiste; *Theat* **s. man** faire-valoir *m*

   (**e**) *Fam (heterosexual)* hétéro

   (**f**) *(undiluted)* pur(e)

   2 *adv* (**a**) *(in straight line)* droit; **sit up s.!** tiens-toi droit sur ton siège!; **to see s.** voir bien; **I can't think s.** je n'ai pas les idées claires; **to look s. ahead** regarder droit devant soi; **go s. on** allez tout droit; *Fig* **to go s.** *(of criminal)* se ranger

   (**b**) *(immediately)* immédiatement; **I'll be s. back** je reviens tout de suite; **s. away** *or* **off** tout de suite

   (**c**) *(directly)* directement; **to come** *or* **to get s. to the point** allez droit au fait; **to come s. out with sth** dire qch tout net

   3 *n* (**a**) **to keep to the s. and narrow** rester sur le droit chemin

   (**b**) *(on running track, racecourse)* ligne *f* droite

   (**c**) *(in poker)* quinte *f*

straightaway ['streɪtəweɪ] *adv* tout de suite

straighten ['streɪtən] *vt (bent nail, rod)* redresser; *(picture)* remettre droit; *(tie, hat)* ajuster; **to s. one's back** se redresser

▶**straighten out** *vt sep (problem)* régler; *(one's affairs)* mettre de l'ordre dans

straight-faced ['streɪt'feɪst] *adj* à l'air sérieux

straightforward [streɪt'fɔːwəd] *adj* **(a)** *(honest)* direct(e), franc (franche) **(b)** *(simple)* simple

strain¹ [streɪn] **1** *n* **(a)** *(on rope, beam, economy, friendship)* tension *f*; *(on muscle, ankle)* foulure *f*; **to put a s. on** *(economy)* grever; *(friendship)* éprouver **(b)** *(mental stress)* stress *m*; **to be under a lot of s.** être très stressé(e)

2 *vt* **(a)** *(muscle, ankle)* se fouler; *(economy)* grever; *(friendship)* éprouver; **to s. one's back** se faire mal au dos; **to s. one's ears** tendre l'oreille **(b)** *Culin (liquid)* filtrer, passer; *(vegetables)* égoutter

3 *vi* **to s. at a rope** tirer sur une corde; *Fig* **to s. at the leash** ne plus tenir en place

strain² [streɪn] *n (variety) (of virus)* souche *f*; *(of plant)* variété *f*

strained [streɪnd] *adj (muscle)* froissé(e); *Fig (atmosphere, relationship)* tendu(e)

strainer ['streɪnə(r)] *n* passoire *f*

strait [streɪt] *n* détroit *m*; **the Straits of Gibraltar** le détroit de Gibraltar

straitlaced ['streɪt'leɪst] *adj* collet monté *inv*

strand¹ [strænd] *vt (ship)* échouer; **to be stranded** *(of person)* être bloqué(e)

strand² [strænd] *n (of rope, cotton)* brin *m*; *(of hair)* mèche *f*; *Fig (of plot)* fil *m*

strange [streɪndʒ] *adj* **(a)** *(odd) (person, behavior)* bizarre **(b)** *(unfamiliar)* inconnu(e)

strangely ['streɪndʒlɪ] *adv (behave, dress)* bizarrement; **s. enough,...** chose bizarre,...

strangeness ['streɪndʒnɪs] *n* **(a)** *(oddness)* bizarrerie *f* **(b)** *(unfamiliarity)* étrangeté *f*

stranger ['streɪndʒə(r)] *n (unknown person)* inconnu(e) *m,f*; *(from somewhere else)* étranger(ère) *m,f*; **I'm a s. here myself** je ne suis pas d'ici

strangle ['stræŋgəl] *vt also Fig* étrangler

stranglehold ['stræŋgəlhəʊld] *n Fig* **to have a s. on sth** avoir la mainmise sur qch

strangulation [stræŋgjʊ'leɪʃən] *n* strangulation *f*

strap [stræp] **1** *n (of leather, canvas)* sangle *f*, lanière *f*; *(on dress, bra)* bretelle *f*; *(for watch)* bracelet *m*; *(for shoe)* bride *f*

2 *vt (pt & pp* **strapped)** **to s. sth to sth** sangler qch à qch; *Fam* **to be strapped (for cash)** être un peu juste

▶**strap in** *vt sep* attacher; **to s. oneself in** attacher sa ceinture de securité

strapless ['stræplɪs] *adj (dress, bra)* sans bretelles

strapping ['stræpɪŋ] *adj* costaud(e)

Strasbourg ['stræzbɜːg] *n* Strasbourg

strata ['strɑːtə] *pl of* **stratum**

strategic [strə'tiːdʒɪk] *adj* stratégique

strategist ['strætədʒɪst] *n* stratège *m*

strategy ['strætɪdʒɪ] *(pl* **strategies)** *n* stratégie *f*

stratification [strætɪfɪ'keɪʃən] *n* stratification *f*

stratosphere ['strætəsfɪə(r)] *n* stratosphère *f*

stratum ['strɑːtəm] *(pl* **strata** ['strɑːtə]) *n* strate *f*; *Fig* couche *f*

straw [strɔː] *n* **(a)** *(from wheat, for drinking)* paille *f*; **s. hat** chapeau *m* de paille; *Fig* **s. man** homme *m* de paille; **s. poll** sondage *m* d'opinion **(b)** *(idioms)* **to clutch** *or* **to grasp at straws** se raccrocher à de faux espoirs; **that's the last s.!** ça c'est le comble!

strawberry ['strɔːbərɪ] *(pl* **strawberries)** *n* fraise *f*; **s. jam** confiture *f* de fraises

straw-colored ['strɔːkʌləd] *adj* jaune paille *inv*

stray [streɪ] **1** *n (dog)* chien *m* errant; *(cat)* chat *m* égaré

2 *adj (animal)* égaré(e); *(dog)* errant(e); *(bullet)* perdu(e)

3 *vi (of person, animal)* s'égarer; **to s. from the point** s'écarter du sujet

streak [striːk] **1** *n (stripe) (of paint, dirt)* traînée *f*; *(of light)* rai *m*; *(in hair)* mèche *f*; **a s. of lightning** un éclair; **a s. of luck** une période de chance; **to be on a winning/losing s.** être dans une période de chance/poisse; **to have a mean s.** avoir un côté mesquin

2 *vt* **streaked with dirt** plein(e) de traînées sales; **streaked with tears** strié(e) de larmes; **his hair is streaked with silver** ses cheveux sont parsemés de cheveux gris; **to have one's hair streaked** se faire faire des mèches

3 *vi* **(a)** *(move quickly)* **to s. off** partir à toute vitesse; **to s. past** passer en trombe **(b)** *Fam (run naked)* courir nu(e) (en public)

streaker ['striːkə(r)] *n Fam* = personne qui court nue en public

streaky ['striːkɪ] *adj (surface, pattern)* strié(e)

stream [striːm] **1** *n* **(a)** *(brook)* ruisseau *m* **(b)** *(of light, blood, water)* jet *m*; *(of tears, insults)* torrent *m*; *(of people)* flot *m*; **to come on s.** *(of industrial plant)* entrer en production

2 *vt (spurt)* **to s. blood** ruisseler de sang

3 *vi* **(a)** *(of liquid)* ruisseler; *(of people)* affluer; *(of traffic)* s'écouler; **her eyes were streaming** ses yeux étaient ruisselants de larmes **(b)** *(of hair, banner)* flotter

streamer ['striːmə(r)] *n* banderole *f*

streamline ['striːmlaɪn] *vt (vehicle)* caréner; *Fig (system)* rationaliser; *(department)* dégraisser

streamlined ['striːmlaɪnd] *adj (vehicle)* caréné(e); *Fig (system)* rationalisé(e); *(department)* dégraissé(e)

street [striːt] *n* **(a)** *(road)* rue *f*; **on the s.** dans la rue; **to take to the streets** *(of protesters)* descendre dans la rue; **s. fighting** combats *mpl* de rue; **s. lamp** lampadaire *m*; **s. map** plan *m* (de la ville); **s. market** marché *m* de plein air; **s. sweeper** balayeur(euse) *m,f*; **s. theater** théâtre *m* de rue; **s. value** *(of drugs)* valeur *f* à la revente **(b)** *(idioms)* **to walk the streets** *(of prostitute)* faire le tapin *ou* le trottoir; **the man in the s.** Monsieur Tout-le-Monde; **that's right up my s.** c'est tout à fait mon rayon; *Fam* **to have s. cred** être très branché(e)

streetcar ['striːtkɑː(r)] *n* tramway *m*

streetwalker ['striːtwɔːkə(r)] *n* racoleuse *f*

streetwise ['striːtwaɪz] *adj* dégourdi(e)

strength [streŋθ] *n* **(a)** *(of person, wind, emotion, currency)* force *f*; *(of rope, fabric)* solidité *f*; *(of light, alcohol, army)* puissance *f*; **to be at full s.** *(of department, regiment)* avoir des effectifs complets; **to be under s.** *(of department, regiment)* ne pas avoir des effectifs complets; **in s.** en force; **to go from s. to s.** aller de mieux en mieux; **on the s. of** sur la base de; **on the s. of her qualifications** grâce à ses diplômes **(b)** *(strong point)* point *m* fort

strengthen ['streŋθən] **1** *vt (wall, building)* renforcer, consolider; *(muscle)* affermir; *(friendship)* consolider; *(determination, position)* renforcer

2 *vi (of friendship)* se consolider; *(of determination)* se renforcer; *(of currency)* se raffermir; *(of wind)* souffler plus fort

strenuous ['strenjʊəs] *adj (activity, lifestyle)* fatigant(e); *(effort, opposition)* vigoureux(euse); *(denial)* énergique

strenuously ['strenjʊəslɪ] *adv (campaign, deny)* énergiquement; *(resist)* vigoureusement

strep throat ['strep'θrəʊt] *n Med* gorge *f* atteinte d'une infection streptococcique

stress [stres] **1** *n* **(a)** *(tension) (physical)* tension *f*; *(mental)* stress *m*; **to be under a lot of s.** être très stressé(e); **s. factor** facteur *m* de stress; *Med* **s. fracture** fracture *f* de surmenage **(b)** *(emphasis)* insistance *f*; *Ling* accentuation *f*; **to put s. on sth** insister sur qch

2 *vt (emphasize)* insister sur; *Ling* accentuer

3 *vi Fam* stresser

stressed [strest] *adj* **(a)** *(person)* stressé, tendu **(b)** *Ling* accentué(e)

stressed-out *adj Fam* stressé(e)

stressful ['stresfʊl] *adj* stressant(e)

stretch [stretʃ] **1** *n* (**a**) *(of body)* **to have a s.** s'étirer; *Fig* **by no s. of the imagination** même avec beaucoup d'imagination; **s. marks** vergetures *fpl*

(**b**) *(of water, land)* étendue *f*; *(of road)* tronçon *m*; *(of time, silence)* période *f*; **at one s.** d'une traite

(**c**) **at full s.** *(factory)* au maximum de ses capacités

2 *vt* (**a**) *(elastic)* étirer; *(belt, arm, hand)* tendre; **to s. the truth** exagérer; **to s. one's legs** se dégourdir les jambes

(**b**) *(put demands on) (person)* pousser à son maximum; *(resources)* utiliser au maximum; *(someone's patience)* abuser de; **we're fully stretched at the moment** nous sommes au maximum de notre rendement en ce moment

(**c**) *(make last) (income, supplies)* faire durer

3 *vi* (**a**) *(of elastic)* s'étendre; *(of person, fabric)* s'étirer

(**b**) *(of road, land, years)* s'étendre, s'étaler

(**c**) *(of resources, budget)* **my budget won't s. to a new car** je n'ai pas les moyens de m'acheter une nouvelle voiture

4 *adj* **s. fabric** Stretch *m*; *Aut* **s. limousine**, *Fam* **s. limo** limousine f à la carrosserie allongée

▸**stretch out 1** *vt sep (arm, hand)* tendre

2 *vi* (**a**) *(of person)* s'étirer (**b**) *(of road, land, time)* s'étaler, s'étendre

stretcher ['stretʃə(r)] *n* brancard *m*; **s. bearer** brancardier *m*

stretchy ['stretʃɪ] *adj* extensible

strew [struː] *(pp* strewed *or* strewn [struːn]) *vt (objects)* éparpiller; **to be strewn with sth** *(of surface)* être jonché(e) de qch

stricken ['strɪkən] *adj (with grief, guilt)* accablé(e) (**with** de); *(with illness, by disaster)* frappé(e) (**with** par); **the s. city** la ville sinistrée

strict [strɪkt] *adj* (**a**) *(person, instruction, discipline)* strict(e); **s. morals** morale f sévère; **a s. Muslim** un musulman de stricte obédience (**b**) *(meaning, minimum)* strict(e); **in strictest confidence** en toute confidence

strictly ['strɪktlɪ] *adv* (**a**) *(severely, only)* strictement (**b**) *(exactly)* **s. speaking** à proprement parler; **not s. true** pas tout à fait vrai(e)

strictness ['strɪktnɪs] *n (of discipline, rules)* sévérité *f*

stride [straɪd] **1** *n* (**a**) pas *m*; *(when running)* foulée *f* (**b**) *(idioms)* **to make great strides** faire des pas de géant; **to take sth in one's s.** prendre qch calmement; **to get into one's s.** trouver son rythme

2 *vi (pt* strode [strəʊd], *pp* stridden ['strɪdən]) **to s. in/out** entrer/sortir à grands pas

strident ['straɪdənt] *adj* strident(e)

strife [straɪf] *n* conflits *mpl*

strike [straɪk] **1** *n* (**a**) *(refusal to work)* grève *f*; **to be on s.** être en grève; **s. pay** indemnité f de grève

(**b**) *(discovery) (of ore, oil)* découverte *f*

(**c**) *(blow)* coup *m*; *Mil* attaque *f*, raid *m*

2 *vt (pt & pp* struck [strʌk]) (**a**) *(hit)* frapper; *(collide with)* heurter, taper contre; **to be struck by lightning** être frappé(e) par la foudre; **to s. sb in the face** frapper qn à la figure; **to s. a blow** donner un coup; *Fig* **to s. a blow for freedom** se battre pour défendre sa liberté; **the clock struck ten** l'horloge a sonné dix heures; *Fig* **to s. the right/wrong note** *(of speech, remark)* sonner juste/faux; **to s. terror into sb** frapper qn de terreur; **to be struck dumb/blind** être frappé(e) de mutisme/cécité; **a stray bullet struck him dead** il a été tué par une balle perdue

(**b**) *(match)* craquer

(**c**) *(coin, medal)* frapper

(**d**) *(impress)* frapper; **she strikes me as a reasonable person** elle me paraît raisonnable; **it struck me that...** il m'a semblé que...

(**e**) *(discover) (gold, oil)* découvrir; *Fam* **to s. it rich** faire fortune; *Fam* **to s. it lucky** avoir un coup de chance

(**f**) *(reach) (bargain, deal)* conclure; **to s. a balance** trouver un équilibre

3 *vi* (**a**) *(attack) (of enemy)* attaquer; *(of criminal)* frapper; *(of disaster, earthquake)* se produire; *(of clock)* sonner; **to s. home** *(of criticism)* faire mouche; *Prov* **s. while the iron is hot** il faut battre le fer pendant qu'il est chaud

(**b**) *(of workers)* faire grève

▸**strike back** *vi (retaliate)* riposter

▸**strike down** *vt sep (of disease)* terrasser; *(of bullet)* abattre

▸**strike off** *vt sep (doctor, lawyer)* radier

▸**strike out 1** *vt sep (delete)* rayer

2 *vi* (**a**) *(hit out)* **to s. out at sb** essayer de frapper qn (**b**) *(leave)* s'élancer (**for** vers); **to s. out on one's own** s'établir à son compte (**c**) *(in baseball)* s'éliminer

▸**strike up** *vt sep (song)* entonner; *(conversation)* entamer; **to s. up a friendship (with sb)** se lier d'amitié (avec qn)

strikebreaker ['straɪkbreɪkə(r)] *n* briseur(euse) *m, f* de grève

striker ['straɪkə(r)] *n* (**a**) *(striking worker)* gréviste *mf* (**b**) *(in soccer)* buteur *m*

striking ['straɪkɪŋ] *adj* (**a**) *(similarity, appearance)* frappant(e), saisissant(e) (**b**) *(worker)* en grève (**c**) **she lives within s. distance of New York** elle habite tout près de New York

string [strɪŋ] **1** *n* (**a**) *(for tying)* ficelle *f*; *(of violin, tennis racket, bow)* corde *f*; *(of puppet)* fil *m*; *Mus* **the strings** *(in orchestra)* les cordes; *Fig* **to have more than one s. to one's bow** avoir plus d'une corde à son arc; *Fig* **no strings attached** sans conditions; *Fig* **to pull strings for sb** *(obtain favors)* faire jouer ses relations pour qn; *(get job, promotion)* pistonner qn; *Mus* **s. quartet** quatuor *m* à cordes; **s. vest** maillot *m* de corps à grosses mailles (**b**) *(of onions, islands)* chapelet *m*; *(of words, stores, defeats)* série *f*; *Comput* série

2 *vt (pp & pt* strung [strʌŋ]) (**a**) *(violin)* monter; *(tennis racket)* corder; *(bow)* bander (**b**) *(pearls, beads)* enfiler

▸**string along** *vt sep Fam* mener en bateau

▸**string up** *vt sep Fam (hang) (criminal)* pendre

stringed [strɪŋd] *adj (instrument)* à cordes

stringent ['strɪndʒənt] *adj* rigoureux(euse)

strip¹ [strɪp] *n (of cloth, paper)* bande *f*; *(of metal)* lame *f*; **s. lighting** éclairage *m* au néon; **s. mining** extraction f à ciel ouvert

strip² [strɪp] **1** *n* **to do a s.** *(undress)* se déshabiller; *(for show)* faire un strip-tease; **s. club** boîte f de strip-tease; **s. poker** strip-poker *m*; **s. show** strip-tease *m*

2 *vt (pt & pp* stripped) *(person)* déshabiller; *(bed)* défaire; *(paint)* gratter; *(wallpaper)* décoller; **to s. sb of sth** dépouiller qn de qch

3 *vi (undress)* se déshabiller

▸**strip off 1** *vt sep (paint)* gratter; *(wallpaper)* décoller

2 *vi (undress)* se déshabiller

stripe [straɪp] *n* (**a**) *(on cloth, animal's coat)* rayure *f*, raie *f* (**b**) *(indicating rank)* galon *m*

striped [straɪpt] *adj* à rayures, rayé(e)

stripling ['strɪplɪŋ] *n* tout jeune homme *m*

stripper ['strɪpə(r)] *n (woman)* strip-teaseuse *f*; **(male) s.** strip-teaseur *m*

strip-search ['strɪpsɜːtʃ] **1** *n* fouille f corporelle

2 *vt* **to s. sb** faire subir une fouille corporelle à qn

striptease ['strɪptiːz] *n* strip-tease *m*

strive [straɪv] *(pt* strove [strəʊv], *pp* striven ['strɪvən]) *vi* **to s. to do sth** s'efforcer de faire qch; **to s. for** *or* **after sth** se battre pour obtenir qch

strobe [strəʊb] *n Phys* stroboscope *m*; **s. lighting** lumières *fpl* stroboscopiques

strode [strəʊd] *pt of* **stride**

stroke [strəʊk] **1** *n* (**a**) *(blow, tennis shot)* coup *m*; *(in rowing, swimming) (style)* nage *f*; *(single movement)* mouvement *m*; **a brush s.** un coup de pinceau (**b**) *(of clock, bell)* **on the s. of**

nine à neuf heures sonnantes (**c**) *(caress)* caresse *f*; **to give sb/ sth a s.** caresser qn/qch (**d**) *Med* attaque *f* (**e**) *(idioms)* **she hasn't done a s. of work** elle n'a rien fichu; **a s. of luck** un coup de chance; **a s. of genius** un coup de génie; **at a s.** d'un seul coup

2 *vt (caress)* caresser

stroll [strəʊl] **1** *n* promenade *f*, tour *m*; **to go for a s.** aller se promener *ou* faire un tour

2 *vi* se promener, flâner

stroller ['strəʊlə(r)] *n* poussette *f*

strong [strɒŋ] **1** *adj* (**a**) *(physically, mentally)* fort(e); *(candidate, team)* bon (bonne); *(friendship, argument)* solide; **the pound is s. against the dollar** la livre est solide face au dollar (**b**) *(in degree) (color, light, protest)* vif (vive); *(smell, drink, accent, possibility)* fort(e); *(resemblance)* grand(e); *(measures)* énergique; **s. language** grossièretés *fpl*; **s. point** point *m* fort (**c**) *(sturdy) (rope, chair, shoes)* solide

2 *adv* **to be still going s.** *(band, program)* marcher toujours très bien; *(person)* être toujours d'attaque

3 *npl* **the s.** les forts *mpl*

strong-arm tactics ['strɒŋɑ:m'tæktɪks] *npl* manière *f* forte

strongbox ['strɒŋbɒks] *n* coffre-fort *m*

stronghold ['strɒŋhəʊld] *n (fortress)* forteresse *f*; *Fig (of political party, religion)* bastion *m*

strongly ['strɒŋlɪ] *adv (oppose, endorse)* vigoureusement; *(believe)* fermement; **s. built** solide; **a s. worded letter** une lettre bien sentie; **to feel s. about sth** être convaincu(e) de qch

strongman ['strɒŋmæn] *n (in circus)* hercule *m* (de foire); *Fig (dictator)* homme *m* fort

strong-minded [strɒŋ'maɪndɪd] *adj* résolu(e)

strongroom ['strɒŋru:m] *n* chambre *f* forte

strong-willed [strɒŋ'wɪld] *adj* résolu(e)

strontium ['strɒntɪəm] *n Chem* strontium *m*

strop [strɒp] *n (for razor)* cuir *m* (à rasoir)

strove [strəʊv] *pt of* **strive**

struck [strʌk] *pt & pp of* **strike**

structural ['strʌktʃərəl] *adj* structurel(elle); **s. damage** dégâts *mpl* de structure; **s. survey** = inspection pour vérifier la solidité d'un bâtiment

structurally ['strʌktʃərəlɪ] *adv* structurellement

structure ['strʌktʃə(r)] **1** *n* (**a**) *(of society, language, story)* structure *f* (**b**) *(building, monument)* édifice *m*, construction *f*

2 *vt* structurer

struggle ['strʌgəl] **1** *n* lutte *f* (**for** pour); **without a s.** sans résistance; **life is a s.** la vie est un combat

2 *vi* lutter (**for** pour); **to s. to do sth** lutter pour faire qch; **to be struggling** *(of person, company)* avoir des difficultés *ou* du mal

strum [strʌm] *(pt & pp* **strummed)** *vt (guitar)* gratter

strung [strʌŋ] *pt & pp of* **string**

strut¹ [strʌt] *n (for frame)* étai *m*; *Aviat* pilier *m*

strut² [strʌt] *(pt & pp* **strutted)** **1** *vi* se pavaner

2 *vt Fam* **to s. one's stuff** frimer

strychnine ['strɪkni:n] *n* strychnine *f*

stub [stʌb] **1** *n (of pencil)* bout *m*; *(of cigarette)* mégot *m*; *(of check)* talon *m*

2 *vt (pt & pp* **stubbed) to s. one's toe (on** *or* **against)** se cogner l'orteil (contre)

▶**stub out** *vt sep (cigarette)* écraser

stubble ['stʌbəl] *n* (**a**) *(in field)* chaume *m* (**b**) *(on face)* barbe *f* de plusieurs jours

stubborn ['stʌbən] *adj (person)* têtu(e); *(determination, resistance)* farouche; *(stain, infection)* rebelle

stubbornness ['stʌbənnɪs] *n (of person)* entêtement *m*, obstination *f*; *(of determination, resistance)* inflexibilité *f*

stubby ['stʌbɪ] *adj* court(e) et boudiné(e)

stucco ['stʌkəʊ] *n* stuc *m*

stuck [stʌk] **1** *adj* bloqué(e), coincé(e); **to get s.** être coincé; *(in mud, sand, with problem)* s'enliser; **to be s. for sth** être à court de qch; *Fam* **to be s. with sb/sth** ne pas pouvoir se débarrasser de qn/qch

2 *pt & pp of* **stick²**

stuck-up ['stʌk'ʌp] *adj Fam* snob *inv*

stud¹ [stʌd] *n (fastener)* bouton-pression *m*; *(on soccer boots)* crampon *m*; *(earring)* clou *m* d'oreille

stud² [stʌd] *n* (**a**) *(farm)* haras *m*; *(stallion)* étalon *m* (**b**) *Fam (man)* étalon *m*

student ['stju:dənt] *n (at university)* étudiant(e) *m,f*; *(at school)* élève *mf*; **law s.** étudiant(e) *m,f* en droit; **s. body** *Univ* étudiants *mpl* inscrits; *Sch* élèves *mpl* inscrits; **s. card** carte *f* d'étudiant; **s. driver** apprenti(e) *m,f* conducteur(trice); **s. life** vie *f* étudiante; **s. loan** = prêt bancaire pour étudiants; **s. nurse** élève *mf* infirmier(ère); **s. teacher** enseignant(e) *m,f* stagiaire; **s. union** *(place)* foyer *m* des étudiants

studied ['stʌdɪd] *adj (manner, attitude)* calculé(e)

studio ['stju:dɪəʊ] *(pl* **studios)** *n* studio *m*; *(of artist)* atelier *m*; *TV* **s. audience** public *m* (présent lors de l'enregistrement)

studious ['stju:dɪəs] *adj* studieux(euse)

study ['stʌdɪ] **1** *n (pl* **studies)** (**a**) *(investigation, by artist)* étude *f*; **to make a s. of sth** faire une étude sur qch; **s. group** groupe *m* d'étude; **s. hall** *(room)* salle *f* d'étude; *(period)* heure *f* d'étude; **s. period** heure *f* d'étude; **s. trip** voyage *m* d'études (**b**) *(room)* bureau *m*, cabinet *m* de travail

2 *vt (pt & pp* **studied)** *(facts, evidence)* examiner; *(behavior, school subject)* étudier; *(university subject)* faire des études de

3 *vi (review)* travailler; *(be at university)* faire des études

stuff [stʌf] **1** *n* (**a**) *(objects, possessions)* affaires *fpl*; **some s.** *(substance)* un truc; *Fam* **he reads all that intellectual s.** il lit tous ces trucs intellos; *Fam* **she writes good s.** c'est bien, ce qu'elle écrit; *Fam* **he knows his s.** il s'y connaît; *Fam* **that's the s.!** c'est bien! (**b**) *(cloth)* étoffe *f*

2 *vt (fill) (cushion)* rembourrer; *(chicken, tomatoes)* farcir; *(pocket)* remplir; **to s. sth into sth** fourrer qch dans qch; *Fam* **to s. oneself** s'empiffrer

stuffed [stʌft] *adj (furniture, cushion)* rembourré(e); *(chicken, tomatoes)* farci(e); **s. animal** *(toy)* peluche *f*

stuffing ['stʌfɪŋ] *n (for furniture)* rembourrage *m*; *(for chicken)* farce *f*; *Fam* **to knock the s. out of sb** ficher un coup à qn

stuffy ['stʌfɪ] *adj* (**a**) *(room)* qui sent le renfermé (**b**) *(person)* vieux jeu *inv*

stultifying ['stʌltɪfaɪɪŋ] *adj* abrutissant(e)

stumble ['stʌmbəl] **1** *n* faux-pas *m*

2 *vi (when walking, speaking)* trébucher

▶**stumble across** *vt insep (find)* tomber par hasard sur

stump [stʌmp] **1** *n* (**a**) *(of tree)* souche *f*; *(of arm, leg)* moignon *m* (**b**) *Fam (of politician)* **to be on the s.** être en campagne électorale

2 *vt (baffle)* laisser perplexe; **to be stumped for an answer** ne pas savoir quoi répondre

stumpy ['stʌmpɪ] *adj* court(e) et boudiné(e)

stun [stʌn] *(pt & pp* **stunned)** *vt (make unconscious)* assommer; *Fig (shock)* abasourdir

stung [stʌŋ] *pt & pp of* **sting**

stunk [stʌŋk] *pt & pp of* **stink**

stunning ['stʌnɪŋ] *adj (shocking)* étourdissant(e); *(excellent)* excellent(e); *(beautiful)* superbe

stunt¹ [stʌnt] *vt (person)* ralentir la croissance de; *(growth)* ralentir

stunt² [stʌnt] *n (in movie)* cascade *f*; *(for publicity)* coup *m* de pub; **s. man** cascadeur *m*

stunted [stʌntɪd] *adj (plant, person)* chétif(ive); *(growth)* retardé(e)

stupefy ['stju:pɪfaɪ] *(pt & pp* **stupified)** *vt (of alcohol, drugs)* abrutir; *(of news, behavior)* stupéfier

stupefying ['stjuːpɪfaɪɪŋ] *adj* stupéfiant(e)

stupendous [stjuːˈpendəs] *adj* fantastique

stupid ['stjuːpɪd] *adj* bête, stupide; **the s. TV keeps breaking down** cette saleté de télé est sans arrêt en panne; **what a s. thing to do!** c'est vraiment idiot d'avoir fait ça!

stupidity [stjuːˈpɪdɪtɪ] *n* bêtise *f*, stupidité *f*

stupidly ['stjuːpɪdlɪ] *adv* bêtement

stupor ['stjuːpə(r)] *n* état *m* d'abrutissement

sturdy ['stɜːdɪ] *adj (person, object)* robuste; *(opposition, resistance)* résolu(e)

sturgeon ['stɜːdʒən] *n* esturgeon *m*

stutter ['stʌtə(r)] **1** *n* bégaiement *m*
2 *vi* bégayer

sty¹ [staɪ] *n (for pigs) & Fig* porcherie *f*

sty², stye [staɪ] *n (in eye)* orgelet *m*

style [staɪl] **1** *n* **(a)** *(manner, design)* style *m* **(b)** *(sophistication)* classe *f*; **to live in s.** mener grand train
2 *vt (design)* créer; *(hair)* coiffer

stylish ['staɪlɪʃ] *adj* élégant(e), chic *inv*

stylist ['staɪlɪst] *n (fashion designer)* styliste *mf* (de mode), modéliste *mf*; **(hair) s.** coiffeur(euse) *m,f*

stylistic [staɪˈlɪstɪk] *adj* stylistique

stylized ['staɪəlaɪzd] *adj* stylisé(e)

stylus ['staɪləs] *(pl* **styluses** *or* **styli** ['staɪlaɪ]) *n (for engraving)* style *m*; *(on record player)* pointe *f* de lecture

suave [swɑːv] *adj* affable; *Pej* mielleux(euse)

sub [sʌb] *Fam* **1** *n* **(a)** *(abbr* **substitute)** remplaçant(e) *m,f* **(b)** *(abbr* **submarine)** sous-marin *m*; *(sandwich)* = grand sandwich mixte de forme allongée **(c)** *Journ (abbr* **subeditor)** secrétaire *mf* de rédaction
2 *vt (pt & pp* **subbed)** *Journ (abbr* **subedit)** mettre au point
3 *vi (abbr* **substitute)** **to s. for sb** remplacer qn

subaltern ['sʌbəltən] *n Mil* officier *m* subalterne

subcommittee ['sʌbkəmɪtɪ] *n* sous-comité *m*

subconscious [sʌbˈkɒnʃəs] **1** *n* **the s.** l'inconscient *m*
2 *adj* inconscient(e)

subcontinent [sʌbˈkɒntɪnənt] *n* sous-continent *m*

subcontract 1 *n* [sʌbˈkɒntrækt] sous-traitance *f*
2 *vt* [sʌbkənˈtrækt] sous-traiter

subcontractor ['sʌbkəntræktə(r)] *n* sous-traitant *m*

subculture ['sʌbkʌltʃə(r)] *n* phénomène *m* de groupe

subdivision [sʌbdɪˈvɪʒən] *n* subdivision *f*

subdue [səbˈdjuː] *vt (enemy, rioter)* soumettre; *(emotions)* maîtriser

subdued [səbˈdjuːd] *adj (person, event)* inhabituellement calme; *(light)* tamisé(e); *(sound, voice)* bas (basse)

subedit ['sʌbedɪt] *vt Journ* mettre au point

subeditor ['sʌbedɪtə(r)] *n Journ* secrétaire *mf* de rédaction

subhuman [sʌbˈhjuːmən] **1** *n* sous-homme *m*
2 *adj* inférieur(e) (aux humains)

subject 1 *n* ['sʌbdʒɪkt] **(a)** *(of conversation, book, painting, photograph)* sujet *m*; *(at school, university)* matière *f*; **while we're on the s.** à ce propos; **to change the s.** parler d'autre chose; **s. matter** *(of letter)* contenu *m*; *(of book)* sujet **(b)** *Gram* sujet *m* **(c)** *(of monarch)* sujet(ette) *m,f*
2 *adj* ['sʌbdʒɪkt] **(a)** *(prone)* **to be s. to** *(illness)* être sujet(ette) à; *(fine, taxation)* être passible de; **to be s. to jealousy/depression** avoir tendance à être jaloux(ouse)/dépressif(ive) **(b)** **s. to** *(dependent on)* sous réserve de
3 *vt* [səbˈdʒekt] *(control)* soumettre, assujettir; **to s. sb to sth** *(force to undergo)* soumettre qn à qch

subjective [səbˈdʒektɪv] *adj* subjectif(ive)

subjectivity [sʌbdʒekˈtɪvɪtɪ] *n* subjectivité *f*

sub judice ['sʌb'dʒuːdɪsɪ] *adj Law* en instance

subjugate ['sʌbdʒʊgeɪt] *vt* assujettir

subjunctive [səbˈdʒʌŋktɪv] *Gram* **1** *n* subjonctif *m*
2 *adj* subjonctif(ive)

sublet [sʌbˈlet] *(pt & pp* **sublet)** *vt* sous-louer

sublimate ['sʌblɪmeɪt] *vt* sublimer

sublime [səˈblaɪm] **1** *adj* sublime; *(utter)* suprême
2 *n* **from the s. to the ridiculous** du sublime au ridicule

subliminal [sʌbˈlɪmɪnəl] *adj* subliminal(e)

submachine gun [sʌbməˈʃiːngʌn] *n* mitraillette *f*

submarine [sʌbməˈriːn] *n* **(a)** sous-marin *m* **(b)** **s. sandwich** = grand sandwich mixte de forme allongée

submerge [səbˈmɜːdʒ] **1** *vt (immerse)* immerger; *(cover)* submerger; *Fig* **to be submerged in sth** être submergé(e) par qch
2 *vi* plonger

submersion [səbˈmɜːʃən] *n* submersion *f*

submission [səbˈmɪʃən] *n* **(a)** *(to will, authority)* soumission *f*; **to starve sb into s.** réduire qn à la soumission en le/la privant de nourriture; **to beat sb into s.** battre qn jusqu'à ce qu'il/elle se soumette **(b)** *(of document)* présentation *f* **(c)** *(report)* soumission *f*

submissive [səbˈmɪsɪv] *adj* soumis(e)

submit [səbˈmɪt] *(pt & pp* **submitted)** **1** *vt* soumettre **(for** à)
2 *vi (to person, authority)* se soumettre **(to** à)

subnormal [sʌbˈnɔːməl] *adj* arriéré(e)

subordinate 1 *n* [səˈbɔːdɪnət] subordonné(e) *m,f*
2 *adj* [səˈbɔːdɪnət] *(rank)* subalterne; *(role)* secondaire; **to be s. to sb** être subordonné(e) à qn; *Gram* **s. clause** proposition *f* subordonnée
3 *vt* [səˈbɔːdɪneɪt] subordonner

subordination [səbɔːdɪˈneɪʃən] *n* subordination *f*

subplot ['sʌbplɒt] *n* intrigue *f* secondaire

subpoena [səˈpiːnə] *Law* **1** *n* citation *f ou* assignation *f* à comparaître
2 *vt* citer *ou* assigner à comparaître

subscribe [səbˈskraɪb] *vi* **(a)** *(to newspaper, magazine)* s'abonner **(to** à); *(to charity, organization)* être membre **(to** de) **(b)** **to s. to** *(opinion, theory)* souscrire à

subscriber [səbˈskraɪbə(r)] *n (to newspaper, magazine, telephone, ISP)* abonné(e) *m,f*; *(to charity, organization)* membre *m*

subscript ['sʌbskrɪpt] *n Typ* indice *m*

subscription [sʌbˈskrɪpʃən] *n (to newspaper, magazine, telephone, ISP)* abonnement *m*; *(to charity, organization, club)* cotisation *f*

subsection ['sʌbsekʃən] *n* subdivision *f*

subsequent ['sʌbsɪkwənt] *adj* ultérieur(e)

subsequently ['sʌbsɪkwəntlɪ] *adv* par la suite, ultérieurement

subservient [sʌbˈsɜːvɪənt] *adj* servile

subside [səbˈsaɪd] *vi (of ground, building)* s'affaisser; *(of water)* baisser; *(of bump)* dégonfler; *(of storm, excitement, fever)* s'apaiser; *(of noise, pain)* s'affaiblir

subsidence [səbˈsaɪdəns] *n (of ground, building)* affaissement *m*; *(of water)* baisse *f*

subsidiarity [sʌbsɪdɪˈærɪtɪ] *n* subsidiarité *f*

subsidiary [səbˈsɪdɪərɪ] **1** *n (pl* **subsidiaries)** *(company)* filiale *f*
2 *adj* subsidiaire

subsidize ['sʌbsɪdaɪz] *vt* subventionner

subsidy ['sʌbsɪdɪ] *(pl* **subsidies)** *n* subvention *f*

subsist [səbˈsɪst] *vi* **to s. on** vivre de

subsistence [səbˈsɪstəns] *n* subsistance *f*; **s. allowance** faux frais *mpl*; **s. wage** salaire *m* à peine suffisant pour vivre

substance ['sʌbstəns] *n* **(a)** *(matter)* substance *f*; **s. abuse** usage *m* de stupéfiants **(b)** *(essential element)* fond *m* **(c)** *(solidity, worth)* fondement *m*

substandard [sʌbˈstændəd] *adj* de qualité inférieure

substantial [səbˈstænʃəl] *adj* **(a)** *(significant)* important(e);

(meal) substantiel(elle); **a s. number of** un nombre important de **(b)** *(solid, robust)* solide

substantially [səb'stænʃəlɪ] *adv* **(a)** *(considerably)* considérablement **(b)** *(for the most part)* pour l'essentiel; **they are s. the same** ils sont pareils dans l'ensemble **(c)** *(solidly)* solidement

substantiate [səb'stænʃɪeɪt] *vt (statement)* corroborer; *(claim)* justifier

substantive ['sʌbstəntɪv] **1** *n Gram* substantif *m*
   2 *adj* important(e)

substitute ['sʌbstɪtjuːt] **1** *n (person)* remplaçant(e) *m,f; (foodstuff, drug)* succédané *m;* **to be a s./no s. for** remplacer/ne pas remplacer; **s. teacher** suppléant(e) *m,f*
   2 *vt* **to s. A for B** remplacer B par A
   3 *vi* **to s. for sb** remplacer qn

substitution [sʌbstɪ'tjuːʃən] *n* substitution *f; (of person, player)* remplacement *m*

subsume [sʌb'sjuːm] *vt Formal* subsumer

subterfuge ['sʌbtəfjuːdʒ] *n* subterfuge *m*

subterranean [sʌbtə'reɪnɪən] *adj* souterrain(e)

subtitle ['sʌbtaɪtəl] **1** *n* sous-titre *m*
   2 *vt* sous-titrer

subtle ['sʌtəl] *adj* subtil(e)

subtlety ['sʌtəltɪ] *(pl* **subtleties)** *n* subtilité *f*

subtly ['sʌtəlɪ] *adv* subtilement

subtotal ['sʌbtəʊtəl] *n* sous-total *m*

subtract [səb'trækt] *vt* soustraire **(from** de)

subtraction [səb'trækʃən] *n* soustraction *f*

subtropical [sʌb'trɒpɪkəl] *adj* subtropical(e)

suburb ['sʌbɜːb] *n* banlieue *f;* **the suburbs** la banlieue

suburban [sə'bɜːbən] *adj* **(a)** *(of suburb)* de banlieue; *(population, development)* suburbain(e) **(b)** *Pej (narrow-minded)* étriqué(e)

suburbia [sə'bɜːbɪə] *n* la banlieue

subversion [səb'vɜːʃən] *n* subversion *f*

subversive [səb'vɜːsɪv] *n & adj* subversif(ive) *m,f*

subvert [səb'vɜːt] *vt* renverser, subvertir

subway ['sʌbweɪ] *n* **(a)** *(underground transport)* métro *m;* **s. station** station *f* de métro; **s. train** rame *f* de métro **(b)** *(underpass)* passage *m* souterrain

sub-zero [sʌb'zɪərəʊ] *adj* au-dessous de zéro

succeed [sək'siːd] **1** *vt (follow)* succéder à
   2 *vi* **(a)** *(be successful)* réussir; **to s. in doing sth** réussir à faire qch **(b)** **to s. to the throne** monter sur le trône

succeeding [sək'siːdɪŋ] *adj (following)* suivant(e)

success [sək'ses] *n* réussite *f,* succès *m;* **to be a s.** avoir du succès; **s. story** réussite *f*

successful [sək'sesfʊl] *adj (person)* brillant(e); *(project, application)* couronné(e) de succès; **to be s.** réussir; **to be s. in doing sth** réussir à faire qch

successfully [sək'sesfəlɪ] *adv* avec succès

succession [sək'seʃən] *n* succession *f,* série *f;* **two years in s.** deux années de suite

successive [sək'sesɪv] *adj* successif(ive); **on five s. Sundays** cinq dimanches consécutifs

successor [sək'sesə(r)] *n* successeur *m*

succinct [sʌk'sɪŋ(k)t] *adj* succinct(e)

succulent ['sʌkjʊlənt] **1** *adj (delicious)* succulent(e)
   2 *n (plant)* plante *f* grasse

succumb [sə'kʌm] *vi* succomber **(to** à)

such [sʌtʃ] **1** *pron* tel (telle) *m,f;* **if s. were the case** si tel était le cas; **and s.** et des choses comme ça; **as s.** en tant que tel; **s. is life!** c'est la vie!
   2 *adj* tel (telle), pareil(eille); **s. a question** une telle question, une question pareille; **animals s. as the lion or the tiger** des animaux tels que le lion ou le tigre; **s. books as these, books s. as these** de tels livres, des livres pareils; **here's my bed-room, s. as it is** voici ce qui me sert de chambre; **s. as?** par exemple?; **do you have s. a thing as a screwdriver?** est-ce que tu aurais un tournevis, par hasard?; **there's no s. thing as aliens** les extraterrestres n'existent pas; **I said/did no s. thing** je n'ai rien dit/fait de tel; **in s. a way that** d'une façon telle que; **on s. and s. a day** tel jour
   3 *adv* **(a)** *(in comparisons)* **s. a big house** une si *ou* aussi grande maison; **I had never heard s. good music** je n'avais jamais entendu de si bonne musique **(b)** *(for emphasis)* **we had s. a good time** nous nous sommes tellement bien amusés; **it was s. a long time ago** ça fait tellement longtemps; **s. a lot of people** tant de gens

suchlike ['sʌtʃlaɪk] *pron* **...and s.** ...et autres

suck [sʌk] **1** *vt (lollipop, thumb)* sucer; *(liquid, air)* aspirer; *(mother's milk)* téter
   2 *vi very Fam (be of bad quality)* être nul (nulle); **this bar/movie sucks** ce bar/film est vraiment nul

▸ **suck in** *vt sep* aspirer; *Fig* **to get sucked into sth** se laisser entraîner dans qch

▸ **suck up 1** *vt sep (liquid, dust)* aspirer
   2 *vi Fam* **to s. up to sb** lécher les bottes a qn

sucker ['sʌkə(r)] *n* **(a)** *(of octopus)* suçoir *m; (of plant)* rejeton *m* **(b)** *Fam (gullible person)* niais(e) *m,f;* **to be a s. for sth** craquer pour qch

suckle ['sʌkəl] **1** *vt* allaiter
   2 *vi* téter

sucrose ['suːkrəʊs] *n* saccharose *m*

suction ['sʌkʃən] *n* succion *f*

Sudan [suː'dæn] *n* le Soudan

Sudanese [suːdə'niːz] **1** *npl (people)* **the S.** les Soudanais *mpl*
   2 *n* Soudanais(e) *m,f*
   3 *adj* soudanais(e)

sudden ['sʌdən] *adj* soudain(e), subit(e); **all of a s.** tout à coup; *Fig* **s. death** *(in match, contest)* la mort subite

suddenly ['sʌdənlɪ] *adv* soudain, tout à coup; *(die, happen)* subitement

suddenness ['sʌdənnɪs] *n* soudaineté *f*

suds [sʌdz] *npl (of soap)* mousse *f*

sue [suː] **1** *vt* intenter un procès à **(for** en)
   2 *vi* **to s. for damages** demander des dommages-intérêts

suede [sweɪd] *n* daim *m*

suet ['suːɪt] *n* graisse *f* de rognon

Suez ['suːɪz] *n* **the S. Canal** le canal de Suez

suffer ['sʌfə(r)] **1** *vt* **(a)** *(loss, defeat, consequence)* subir; *(pain)* avoir **(b)** *(tolerate)* supporter; **she doesn't s. fools gladly** elle ne supporte pas les imbéciles
   2 *vi (of person)* souffrir **(from** de); *(of health, work)* en pâtir

sufferance ['sʌf(ə)rəns] *n* **I'm just here on s.** on me tolère tout juste ici

sufferer ['sʌfərə(r)] *n* victime *f*

suffering ['sʌfərɪŋ] *n* souffrance *f*

suffice [sə'faɪs] *vi Formal* suffire

sufficient [sə'fɪʃənt] *adj* suffisant(e); **to be s.** suffire, être suffisant

sufficiently [sə'fɪʃəntlɪ] *adv* suffisamment

suffix ['sʌfɪks] *n Gram* suffixe *m*

suffocate ['sʌfəkeɪt] *also Fig* **1** *vt* étouffer
   2 *vi* suffoquer

suffocating ['sʌfəkeɪtɪŋ] *adj* suffocant(e)

suffocation [sʌfə'keɪʃən] *n* suffocation *f*

suffrage ['sʌfrɪdʒ] *n* droit *m* de vote

suffragette [sʌfrə'dʒet] *n* suffragette *f*

suffuse [sə'fjuːz] *vt Lit (of light, liquid, color)* inonder; *(of heat)* envahir

sugar ['ʃʊgə(r)] **1** *n* **(a)** *(food)* sucre *m;* **two sugars, please** deux sucres, s'il te plaît; **s. almond** dragée *f;* **s. beet** betterave *f* sucrière; **s. bowl** sucrier *m;* **s. cane** canne *f* à sucre; *Fam* **s.**

daddy vieux *m* plein de fric *(qui entretient une jeune femme)*; **s. lump** morceau *m* de sucre; **s. plantation** plantation *f* de canne à sucre; **s. refinery** raffinerie *f* de sucre (**b**) *Fam (term of address)* mon trésor

2 *vt (coffee, tea)* sucrer; *Fig* **to s. the pill** dorer la pilule

sugar-coated [ʃʊgə'kəʊtɪd] *adj* recouvert(e) de sucre

sugar-free [ʃʊgə'friː] *adj* sans sucre

sugary ['ʃʊgərɪ] *adj* (**a**) *(containing sugar)* sucré(e) (**b**) *Fig (smile, tone)* mielleux(euse), doucereux(euse)

suggest [sə'dʒest] *vt* (**a**) *(propose)* suggérer (**b**) *(imply)* indiquer

suggestible [sə'dʒestɪbəl] *adj* influençable

suggestion [sə'dʒestʃən] *n* (**a**) *(proposal)* suggestion *f*; **suggestions box** boîte *f* à idées (**b**) *(insinuation, hint)* indication *f*; **there is no s. that...** rien ne dit que...; **a s. of** une pointe de

suggestive [sə'dʒestɪv] *adj* suggestif(ive); **to be s. of** évoquer

suicidal [sʊɪ'saɪdəl] *adj* suicidaire

suicide ['sʊɪsaɪd] *n* suicide *m*; **to commit s.** se suicider; **s. attack** attentat-suicide *m*; **s. attempt** tentative *f* de suicide; **suicide bomber** auteur *m* d'un attentat-suicide à la bombe; **s. mission** mission *f* suicide; **s. note** lettre *f* *(laissée par un suicidé)*

suit [suːt] **1** *n* (**a**) *(clothing) (man's)* costume *m*, complet *m*; *(woman's)* tailleur *m*; **s. of armor** armure *f* complète (**b**) *(in cards)* couleur *f*; *Fig* **to follow s.** faire de même; *Fig* **politeness is not her strong s.** la politesse n'est pas son fort (**c**) *Law* procès *m*

2 *vt* (**a**) *(of clothes, colors)* aller à (**b**) *(of arrangement, time, job)* convenir à; **to be suited to** *or* **for sth** *(purpose, job)* être fait(e) pour qch; **to s. sb down to the ground** convenir parfaitement à qn; **they are well suited** ils sont vraiment faits l'un pour l'autre; *Fam* **s. yourself** fais comme tu voudras (**c**) *(adapt)* **to s. sth to sth** adapter qch à qch

suitability [suːtə'bɪlɪtɪ] *n (of behavior)* caractère *m* convenable; *(of clothing)* caractère *m* approprié; *(of person)* aptitude *f*

suitable ['suːtəbəl] *adj (behavior, subject)* convenable; *(clothing)* approprié(e); *(candidate, date, title)* adéquat(e); **the movie is not s. for children** ce n'est pas un film pour les enfants

suitably ['suːtəblɪ] *adv (behave, dress)* convenablement; **s. impressed/embarrassed** vraiment impressionné(e)/gêné(e)

suitcase ['suːtkeɪs] *n* valise *f*

suite [swiːt] *n* (**a**) *(of rooms)* suite *f* (**b**) *(of furniture)* **(three-piece) s.** canapé *m* avec deux fauteuils assortis; **bathroom s.** salle *f* de bains; **bedroom s.** chambre *f* à coucher (**c**) *Mus* suite *f*

suitor ['suːtə(r)] *n* *Old-fashioned (admirer)* soupirant *m*

sulfate ['sʌlfeɪt] *n* *Chem* sulfate *m*

sulfide ['sʌlfaɪd] *n* *Chem* sulfure *m*

sulfur ['sʌlfə(r)] *n* *Chem* soufre *m*; **s. dioxide** anhydride *m* sulfureux

sulfuric [sʌl'fjʊərɪk] *adj* *Chem* sulfurique; **s. acid** acide *m* sulfurique

sulk [sʌlk] **1** *n* **to be in a s.** bouder
2 *vi* bouder

sulky ['sʌlkɪ] *adj* boudeur(euse)

sullen ['sʌlən] *adj* renfrogné(e)

sully ['sʌlɪ] *(pt & pp* **sullied)** *vt* *Lit (reputation)* ternir; *Fig* **to s. one's hands (with sth)** se salir les mains (en faisant qch)

sultan ['sʌltən] *n* sultan *m*

sultana [sʌl'tɑːnə] *n* raisin *m* de Smyrne

sultry ['sʌltrɪ] *adj (heat)* étouffant(e); *(weather)* lourd(e); *(look, smile)* sensuel(elle)

sum [sʌm] *n (amount of money)* somme *f*; *(mathematical problem)* problème *m*; **the s. of** la somme de; **s. total** somme totale

▶**sum up** *(pt & pp* **summed) 1** *vt sep* (**a**) *(summarize)* résumer (**b**) *(assess quickly)* jauger, évaluer
2 *vi (summarize)* résumer

summarily ['sʌmərɪlɪ] *adv* sommairement

summarize ['sʌməraɪz] *vt* résumer

summary ['sʌmərɪ] **1** *n (pl* **summaries)** résumé *m*
2 *adj (brief)* sommaire

summer ['sʌmə(r)] **1** *n* été *m*; **in (the) s.** en été; **s. vacation** vacances *fpl* d'été; **s. school** cours *mpl* d'été
2 *vi* passer l'été

summerhouse ['sʌməhaʊs] *n (in garden)* pavillon *m*

summertime ['sʌmətaɪm] *n* été *m*

summery ['sʌmərɪ] *adj* d'été

summing-up [sʌmɪŋ'ʌp] *n Law* résumé *m* des débats

summit ['sʌmɪt] *n* sommet *m*; **to hold a s.** tenir un sommet

summon ['sʌmən] *vt (person, meeting)* convoquer; *(police, doctor, help)* appeler, faire venir; *Law (witness)* assigner *ou* citer à comparaître

▶**summon up** *vt sep* rassembler

summons ['sʌmənz] *Law* **1** *n (pl* **summonses** ['sʌmənzɪz]) assignation *f* ou citation *f* à comparaître
2 *vt* assigner *ou* citer à comparaître

sump [sʌmp] *n* (**a**) *(in engine)* carter *m* à huile (**b**) *(cesspool)* fosse *f* d'aisance

sumptuous ['sʌm(p)tjʊəs] *adj* somptueux(euse)

Sun. *(abbr* **Sunday)** dimanche

sun [sʌn] **1** *n* soleil *m*; **in the s.** au soleil; **to catch the s.** prendre le soleil; **everything under the s.** tout ce qu'il est possible d'imaginer; **s. cream** crème *f* solaire; **s. lamp** lampe *f* à bronzer; **s. lotion** lotion *f* solaire; **s. shield** *or* **visor** *(in car)* pare-soleil *m*
2 *vt (pt & pp* **sunned) to s. oneself** prendre le soleil

sunbathe ['sʌnbeɪð] *vi* se faire bronzer

sunbeam ['sʌnbiːm] *n* rayon *m* de soleil

sunbed ['sʌnbed] *n (on beach)* (fauteuil *m*) relax *m*; *(with UV lamps)* lit *m* à ultraviolets

sunburn ['sʌnbɜːn] *n* coup *m* de soleil; **to have a s.** avoir un coup de soleil

sunburnt ['sʌnbɜːnt], **sunburned** ['sʌnbɜːnd] *adj* **to be s.** avoir un coup de soleil

sundae ['sʌndeɪ] *n* coupe *f* glacée

Sunday ['sʌndeɪ] *n* dimanche *m*; **S. best** habits *mpl* du dimanche; **S. paper** journal *m* du dimanche; **S. school** ≃ catéchisme *m*; *see also* **Saturday**

sundial ['sʌndaɪəl] *n* cadran *m* solaire

sundown ['sʌndaʊn] *n* coucher *m* du soleil

sun-drenched ['sʌndren(t)ʃt] *adj* inondé(e) de soleil

sun-dried ['sʌndraɪd] *adj* séché(e) au soleil

sundry ['sʌndrɪ] **1** *n* (**a**) **all and s.** tout le monde (**b**) **sundries** *(items)* articles *mpl* divers; *(costs)* frais *mpl* divers
2 *adj* divers(e)

sunflower ['sʌnflaʊə(r)] *n* tournesol *m*; **s. oil** huile *f* de tournesol; **s. seeds** *(as snack)* graines *fpl* de tournesol

sung ['sʌŋ] *pp of* **sing**

sunglasses ['sʌnglɑːsɪz] *npl* lunettes *fpl* de soleil, *Belg* lunettes *fpl* solaires

sunhat ['sʌnhæt] *n* chapeau *m* de soleil

sunk ['sʌŋk] *pp of* **sink**²

sunken ['sʌŋkən] *adj (ship)* englouti(e); *(eyes)* enfoncé(e); *(rock)* immergé(e)

sunlight ['sʌnlaɪt] *n* lumière *f* du soleil; **in the s.** au soleil

sunlit ['sʌnlɪt] *adj* éclairé(e) par le soleil

sunny ['sʌnɪ] *adj* (**a**) *(day, place)* ensoleillé(e); **it's s.** il fait du soleil (**b**) *Fig (face)* radieux(euse); **to have a s. personality** être toujours content(e)

sunray lamp ['sʌnreɪ'læmp] *n* lampe *f* à bronzer

sunrise ['sʌnraɪz] *n* lever *m* de soleil; **at s.** au lever du soleil, au soleil levant; *Econ* **s. industry** industrie *f* d'avenir

sunroof ['sʌnruːf] *n* toit *m* ouvrant

sunscreen ['sʌnskriːn] *n (suntan lotion)* écran *m ou* filtre *m* solaire

sunset ['sʌnset] *n* coucher *m* de soleil; **at s.** au coucher du soleil, au soleil couchant

sunshade ['sʌnʃeɪd] *n* parasol *m*

sunshine ['sʌnʃaɪn] *n* soleil *m*

sunspot ['sʌnspɒt] *n* **(a)** *(on sun)* tache *f* solaire **(b)** *Fam (vacation resort)* destination *f* ensoleillée

sunstroke ['sʌnstrəʊk] *n* insolation *f*; **to have s.** avoir une insolation

suntan ['sʌntæn] *n* bronzage *m*; **to have a s.** être bronzé(e); **s. cream** crème *f* solaire; **s. lotion** lotion *f* solaire

sun-up ['sʌnʌp] *n* lever *m* du soleil; **at s.** au lever du soleil, au soleil levant

sup [sʌp] *(pt & pp supped) vt* boire à petites gorgées

super ['suːpə(r)] **1** *adj Fam (excellent)* super *inv*; *Sport* **the S. Bowl** le Superbowl *(finale du championnat des États-Unis de football américain)*
2 *n* **(a)** *(gas)* super *m* **(b)** *Fam (in apartment building)* gardien(enne) *m,f*, concierge *mf*

superb [suːˈpɜːb] *adj* excellent(e)

supercharger ['suːpətʃɑːdʒə(r)] *n Aut & Aviat* compresseur *m*

supercilious [suːpəˈsɪlɪəs] *adj* hautain(e)

superconductor [suːpəkənˈdʌktə(r)] *n Phys* supraconducteur *m*

super-duper ['suːpəˈduːpə(r)] *adj Fam* super, génial(e)

superego ['suːpərɪgəʊ] *n Psy* surmoi *m*

superficial [suːpəˈfɪʃəl] *adj* superficiel(elle)

superficiality [suːpəfɪʃɪˈælɪtɪ] *n* superficialité *f*

superficially [suːpəˈfɪʃəlɪ] *adv* superficiellement

superfluous [suːˈpɜːfluəs] *adj* superflu(e)

superhuman [suːpəˈhjuːmən] *adj* surhumain(e)

superimpose [suːpərɪmˈpəʊz] *vt* superposer

superintend [suːpərɪnˈtend] *vt (run)* diriger; *(supervise)* surveiller

superintendent [suːpərɪnˈtendənt] *n (supervisor)* directeur(trice) *m,f*; *(police officer)* ≃ commissaire *m* de police; *(in apartment building)* gardien(enne) *m,f*, concierge *mf*

superior [suːˈpɪərɪə(r)] **1** *adj* **(a)** *(better, more senior)* supérieur(e) **(b)** *(arrogant) (person)* qui se croit supérieur(e); *(tone, air, smile)* de supériorité
2 *n (senior)* supérieur(e) *m,f*

superiority [suːpɪərɪˈɒrɪtɪ] *n* supériorité *f*

superlative [suːˈpɜːlətɪv] **1** *n Gram* superlatif *m*
2 *adj* **(a)** *(excellent)* excellent(e) **(b)** *Gram* superlatif(ive)

superman ['suːpəmæn] *n* surhomme *m*

supermarket ['suːpəmɑːkɪt] *n* supermarché *m*

supermodel ['suːpəmɒdəl] *n* top model *m*

supernatural [suːpəˈnætʃərəl] **1** *n* **the s.** le surnaturel
2 *adj* surnaturel(elle)

superpower ['suːpəpaʊə(r)] *n* superpuissance *f*

supersede [suːpəˈsiːd] *vt* supplanter, détrôner

supersonic [suːpəˈsɒnɪk] *adj* supersonique

superstar ['suːpəstɑː(r)] *n* superstar *f*

superstition [suːpəˈstɪʃən] *n* superstition *f*

superstitious [suːpəˈstɪʃəs] *adj* superstitieux(euse)

superstore ['suːpəstɔː(r)] *n* hypermarché *m*

superstructure ['suːpəstrʌktʃə(r)] *n* superstructure *f*

supertanker ['suːpətæŋkə(r)] *n* supertanker *m*, pétrolier *m* géant

supervise ['suːpəvaɪz] *vt (children)* surveiller; *(staff)* superviser

supervision [suːpəˈvɪʒən] *n (of children)* surveillance *f*; *(of staff)* supervision *f*

supervisor ['suːpəvaɪzə(r)] *n* **(a)** *(in office)* chef *m* de service; *(in factory)* chef d'équipe **(b)** *(for thesis)* directeur(trice) *m,f* de thèse

supervisory [suːpəˈvaɪzərɪ] *adj* de supervision

supine ['suːpaɪn] **1** *adj* couché(e) sur le dos; *Fig (inactive)* mou (molle)
2 *adv* **to lie s.** être couché(e) sur le dos

supper ['sʌpə(r)] *n (evening meal)* dîner *m*; *(snack before going to bed)* = casse-croûte pris avant d'aller se coucher

supplant [səˈplɑːnt] *vt* supplanter

supple ['sʌpəl] *adj* souple

supplement ['sʌplɪmənt] **1** *n* supplément *m*
2 *vt* compléter

supplementary [sʌplɪˈmentərɪ] *adj* supplémentaire

supplication [sʌplɪˈkeɪʃən] *n* supplication *f*

supplier [səˈplaɪə(r)] *n* fournisseur(euse) *m,f*

supply [səˈplaɪ] **1** *n (pl supplies) (stock)* provision *f*; *(act of supplying)* approvisionnement *m*, fourniture *f*; **a week's/month's s. of sth** une provision de qch pour une semaine/un mois; **gas is in short s.** on manque d'essence; *Econ* **s. and demand** l'offre *f* et la demande; **s. lines** lignes *fpl* de ravitaillement; **s. ship** ravitailleur *m*
2 *vt (pt & pp supplied) (provide)* fournir; **to s. sb with sth** fournir qch à qn

support [səˈpɔːt] **1** *n* **(a)** *(backing)* soutien *m*; **to give sb/sth s.** appuyer qn/qch; **in s. of** *(theory, claim)* à l'appui de; *(cause)* en faveur de; **s. band** *(at concert)* première partie *f*; **s. group** groupe *m* de soutien **(b)** *(person supporting)* soutien *m*; *(thing supporting)* support *m*
2 *vt* **(a)** *(hold up)* supporter, soutenir; **I supported her with my arm** je lui ai donné le bras pour qu'elle s'appuie dessus **(b)** *(encourage, aid)* soutenir, apporter son soutien à; *(team in sport)* supporter **(c)** *(sustain)* pourvoir aux besoins de; **to s. oneself** subvenir à ses propres besoins

supporter [səˈpɔːtə(r)] *n (of opinion, party, policy)* défenseur *m*, sympathisant(e) *m,f*; *(of team)* supporter *m*

supporting [səˈpɔːtɪŋ] *adj (role)* secondaire; *(actor)* qui a un rôle secondaire; **s. movie** film *m* qui passe en première partie; **s. cast** seconds rôles *mpl*

supportive [səˈpɔːtɪv] *adj* d'un grand soutien

suppose [səˈpəʊz] *vt* supposer; **I s. so/not** je suppose que oui/non; **s. or supposing he came back** supposons qu'il revienne; **I don't s. you'd consider sharing it?** je suppose que tu ne veux pas partager?; **s. we change the subject?** et si nous changions de sujet?

supposed [səˈpəʊzd] *adj* **(a)** *(meant)* **to be s. to do sth** être censé(e) faire qch; **there's s. to be a meeting today** il est censé y avoir une réunion aujourd'hui **(b)** *(reputed)* **the movie's s. to be very good** il paraît que c'est un très bon film

supposition [sʌpəˈzɪʃən] *n* supposition *f*; **on the s. that...** en supposant que...

suppository [səˈpɒzɪtrɪ] *n (pl suppositories) n Med* suppositoire *m*

suppress [səˈpres] *vt (revolt)* réprimer; *(fact, evidence)* faire disparaître; *(emotions)* refouler; *(cough, smile)* réprimer

suppressed [səˈprest] *adj (emotion)* refoulé(e)

suppression [səˈpreʃən] *n (of revolt)* répression *f*; *(of fact, evidence)* dissimulation *f*; *(of emotions)* refoulement *m*

suppurate ['sʌpjʊreɪt] *vi* suppurer

supranational [suːprəˈnæʃənəl] *adj* supranational(e)

supremacy [suːˈpreməsɪ] *n* suprématie *f*

supreme [suːˈpriːm] *adj* suprême; **to make the s. sacrifice** se sacrifier; *Fig* **to reign s.** régner; *Mil* **S. Commander** commandant *m* en chef; *Law* **S. Court** Cour *f* suprême

supremely [suːˈpriːmlɪ] *adv* suprêmement

supremo [suːˈpriːməʊ] *n (pl supremos) n Fam* grand chef *m*

surcharge ['sɜːtʃɑːdʒ] **1** *n* supplément *m*
2 *vt* faire payer un supplément à

sure [ʃʊə(r)] **1** *adj* sûr(e); **to be s. of** *or* **about sth** être sûr de qch; **to be s. to do sth** ne pas oublier de faire qch; **to be s. of oneself** être sûr de soi; **to make s. of sth** s'assurer de qch; **to make s. that…** s'assurer que…; **I don't know for s.** je ne suis pas absolument certain(e); **that's for s.** ça, c'est sûr; *Fam* **s. thing!** bien sûr!
2 *adv* (**a**) *Fam (really)* **it s. is cold** il fait vachement froid; **are you tired? – I s. am** tu es fatigué? – ça oui (**b**) *(yes)* bien sûr (**c**) **s. enough he was there** il était bien là

surefooted [ʃʊə'fʊtɪd] *adj* **to be s.** avoir le pied sûr

surely ['ʃʊəlɪ] *adv* (**a**) *(certainly)* sûrement; **s. you don't believe that!** tu ne crois quand même pas ça!; **s. not!** c'est pas vrai! (**b**) *(in a sure manner)* **slowly but s.** lentement mais sûrement

surety ['ʃʊərətɪ] *n Law* caution *f*; **to stand s. (for sb)** se porter caution (pour qn)

surf [sɜːf] **1** *n* surf *m*
2 *vi (go surfing)* faire du surf
3 *vt Comput* **to s. the Net** naviguer sur l'Internet

surface ['sɜːfɪs] **1** *n* surface *f*; *Fig* **on the s.** en apparence; *Fig* **beneath the s.** au fond; **s. mail** courrier *m* par voie de terre; **s. tension** tension *f* de surface; **s. water** eaux *fpl* de surface
2 *vt (road)* revêtir
3 *vi (from water)* & *Fam Hum (from bed)* faire surface; *Fig (of person, emotion)* réapparaître

surface-to-air missile ['sɜːfɪstʊ'eə'mɪsaɪl] *n Mil* missile *m* sol-air

surface-to-surface missile ['sɜːfɪstə'sɜːfɪs'mɪsaɪl] *n Mil* missile *m* sol-sol

surfboard ['sɜːfbɔːd] *n* (planche *f* de) surf *m*

surfeit ['sɜːfɪt] *n Formal* surabondance *f*

surfer ['sɜːfə(r)] *n* (**a**) *(in sea)* surfeur(euse) *m,f* (**b**) *(on Internet)* internaute *mf*

surfing ['sɜːfɪŋ] *n* surf *m*; **to go s.** aller faire du surf

surge [sɜːdʒ] **1** *n (of electricity)* surtension *f*; *(of enthusiasm, support, demand)* sursaut *m*; *(of profits)* hausse *f* soudaine; *(of crowd)* ruée *f*
2 *vi (of water, crowd)* déferler; *(of feeling)* monter

surgeon ['sɜːdʒən] *n* chirurgien *m*

surgery ['sɜːdʒərɪ] *n* chirurgie *f*; *(operation)* intervention *f* chirurgicale; **to perform s. on sb** opérer qn

surgical ['sɜːdʒɪkəl] *adj* chirurgical(e); *Fig* **with s. precision** avec une précision mathématique; **s. instruments** instruments *mpl* de chirurgie; *Mil* **s. strike** frappe *f* chirurgicale

Surinam ['sʊrɪnæm] *n* le Surinam

surly ['sɜːlɪ] *adj* revêche

surmise [sɜː'maɪz] *vt* conjecturer

surmount [sɜː'maʊnt] *vt* surmonter

surname ['sɜːneɪm] *n* nom *m* de famille

surpass [sɜː'pɑːs] *vt (person)* surpasser; *(record)* battre; *(expectation)* dépasser; **to s. oneself** se surpasser

surplice ['sɜːplɪs] *n Rel* surplis *m*

surplus ['sɜːpləs] **1** *n* surplus *m*; *Econ (of trade)* excédent *m*
2 *adj (items)* en trop, en surplus; **to be s. to requirements** être en trop

surprise [sə'praɪz] **1** *n* surprise *f*; **to take sb by s.** prendre qn par surprise; **to give sb a s.** faire une surprise à qn; **it was no s.** cela n'a étonné personne
2 *adj (attack, defeat)* surprise *inv*; **s. party** soirée *f* surprise
3 *vt* surprendre, étonner; **I'm not surprised** ça ne m'étonne pas

surprising [sə'praɪzɪŋ] *adj* surprenant(e), étonnant(e)

surprisingly [sə'praɪzɪŋlɪ] *adv* étonnamment; **not s.** comme il fallait s'y attendre; **s. enough,…** chose surprenante…

surreal [sə'rɪəl] *adj (surrealist)* surréaliste; *(strange)* délirant(e)

surrealism [sə'rɪəlɪzəm] *n Art* surréalisme *m*

surrealist [sə'rɪəlɪst] *n* & *adj Art* surréaliste *mf*

surrender [sə'rendə(r)] **1** *n* (**a**) *(of army, weapons)* reddition *f*; **no s.!** nous ne nous rendrons pas! (**b**) *Fin* **s. value** valeur *f* de rachat
2 *vt (town)* livrer; *(right, possessions)* abandonner; *(advantage)* perdre; **to s. control of sth** abandonner la direction de qch
3 *vi* se rendre

surreptitious [sʌrəp'tɪʃəs] *adj* furtif(ive)

surrogacy ['sʌrəgəsɪ] *n* maternité *f* de substitution

surrogate ['sʌrəgət] *n* substitut *m*; **s. mother** mère *f* porteuse

surround [sə'raʊnd] **1** *vt* entourer; *(of police)* cerner
2 *n* encadrement *m*; *Cin, TV* & *Comput* **s. sound** son *m* 3D

surrounding [sə'raʊndɪŋ] *adj* environnant(e)

surroundings [sə'raʊndɪŋz] *npl* environnement *m*

surtax ['sɜːtæks] **1** *n* surtaxe *f*
2 *vt* surtaxer

surveillance [sə'veɪləns] *n* surveillance *f*; **under s.** sous surveillance

survey 1 *n* ['sɜːveɪ] (**a**) *(of subject, situation)* étude *f*; *(of opinions)* sondage *m* (**b**) *(of house)* expertise *f*; *(of land)* relevé *m*
2 *vt* [sə'veɪ] (**a**) *(look at)* contempler (**b**) *(subject, situation)* étudier, examiner (**c**) *(house)* faire l'expertise de; *(land)* faire un relevé de

surveying [sɜː'veɪɪŋ] *n (of house)* expertise *f*; *(of land)* relevé *m*

surveyor [sə'veɪə(r)] *n (of building)* expert *m*; *(of land)* géomètre *mf*

survival [sə'vaɪvəl] *n* (**a**) *(continued existence)* survie *f*; *also Fig* **the s. of the fittest** la survie du plus apte; **s. kit** équipement *m* de survie (**b**) *(relic)* vestige *m*

survive [sə'vaɪv] **1** *vt (of person)* survivre à; *(of object)* résister à; **he is survived by a wife and son** il laisse une épouse et un fils
2 *vi* survivre

surviving [sə'vaɪvɪŋ] *adj (person)* survivant(e); *(remains, copy)* restant(e)

survivor [sə'vaɪvə(r)] *n* survivant(e) *m,f*

susceptible [sə'septɪbəl] *adj* sensible (**to** à)

suspect 1 *n* ['sʌspekt] suspect(e) *m,f*
2 *adj* ['sʌspekt] suspect(e)
3 *vt* [sə'spekt] (**a**) *(person)* soupçonner (**b**) *(have intuition of)* se douter de; **to s. the truth** soupçonner la vérité (**c**) *(consider likely)* croire

suspend [sə'spend] *vt* (**a**) *(hang)* suspendre (**from** à) (**b**) *(service, employee, player)* suspendre; *(pupil)* renvoyer temporairement

suspended [sə'spendɪd] *adj* suspendu(e); **in s. animation** en hibernation; *Law* **s. sentence** condamnation *f* avec sursis

suspenders [sə'spendəz] *npl* bretelles *fpl*

suspense [sə'spens] *n (uncertainty)* incertitude *f*; *(in movie)* suspense *m*; **to keep sb in s.** tenir qn en haleine

suspension [sə'spenʃən] *n* (**a**) *(of car)* suspension *f*; **s. bridge** pont *m* suspendu (**b**) *(of service, employee)* suspension *f*; *(of pupil)* renvoi *m*

suspicion [sə'spɪʃən] *n* (**a**) *(belief of guilt)* soupçon *m*; **to be under s.** être soupçonné(e); **to be above s.** être au-dessus de tout soupçon; **to have one's suspicions about sb/sth** avoir des doutes sur qn/qch; **to arouse s.** éveiller les soupçons (**b**) *(small amount)* soupçon *m*

suspicious [sə'spɪʃəs] *adj (arousing suspicions)* suspect(e); *(having suspicions)* méfiant(e) (**of** *or* **about** à l'égard de); **to make sb s.** éveiller les soupçons de qn

suspiciously [sə'spɪʃəslɪ] *adv (behave)* d'une manière suspecte; *(ask)* avec méfiance; *Fam* **it looks s. like…** ça ressemble étrangement à…

sustain [sə'steɪn] *vt* (**a**) *(maintain)* soutenir; *(life)* maintenir; **a**

proper breakfast will s. you until lunchtime un bon petit déjeuner vous permettra de tenir jusqu'à midi; *Law* **objection sustained** objection accordée (**b**) *(loss, attack, damage)* subir; **to s. an injury** être blessé(e)

sustainable [sə'steɪnəbəl] *adj (growth, development)* durable

sustained [sə'steɪnd] *adj* soutenu(e); **s. applause** applaudissements *mpl* prolongés

sustenance ['sʌstɪnəns] *n* subsistance *f*

suture ['suːtʃə(r)] *n* suture *f*

SUV [esjuː'viː] *n (abbr* **sport-utility vehicle**) quatre-quatre *m ou f*

svelte [svelt] *adj* svelte

SW *n* (**a**) *(abbr* **southwest**) SO (**b**) *Rad (abbr* **Short Wave**) OC

swab [swɒb] **1** *n (cotton wool)* tampon *m*
2 *vt (pt & pp* **swabbed**) *(wound)* nettoyer; *(floor)* laver

swag [swæg] *n very Fam (of thief)* butin *m*

swagger ['swægə(r)] **1** *n* démarche *f* balancée et crâneuse
2 *vi (strut)* se pavaner

swallow[1] ['swɒləʊ] **1** *n (of drink)* gorgée *f; (of food)* bouchée *f*
2 *vt* (**a**) *(food, drink)* avaler; *Fig (pride, anger)* ravaler; **to s. sth whole** avaler qch tout rond (**b**) *Fam (believe)* gober, avaler
3 *vi* avaler; **to s. hard** *(when nervous, afraid)* avaler sa salive

swallow[2] ['swɒləʊ] *n (bird)* hirondelle *f; Prov* **one s. doesn't make a summer** une hirondelle ne fait pas le printemps

▶**swallow up** *vt sep Fig (company, country)* engloutir

swam [swæm] *pt of* **swim**

swamp [swɒmp] **1** *n* marais *m*
2 *vt (flood)* inonder; *Fig* **to be swamped with sth** être submergé(e) de qch

swan [swɒn] **1** *n* cygne *m; Fig* **s. song** chant *m* du cygne
2 *vi (pt & pp* **swanned**) *Fam* **to s. in/out/off** arriver/sortir/ partir tranquillement

swank [swæŋk] *Fam* **1** *n (ostentation)* épate *f; (ostentatious person)* frimeur(euse) *m,f*
2 *vi* frimer

swanky ['swæŋkɪ] *adj Fam* chic *inv*

swap [swɒp] **1** *n* échange *m;* **to do a s.** faire un échange
2 *vt (pt & pp* **swapped**) **to s. sth for sth** échanger qch contre qch; **to s. places with sb** changer de place avec qn; **to s. insults/ideas** échanger des insultes/idées
3 *vi* échanger

swarm [swɔːm] **1** *n (of bees)* essaim *m; (of people)* nuée *f*
2 *vi (of bees)* essaimer; *(of people)* accourir en masse; **to be swarming with** *(of place)* grouiller de

swarthy ['swɔːðɪ] *adj* basané(e)

swashbuckling ['swɒʃbʌklɪŋ] *adj* de cape et d'épée

swastika ['swɒstɪkə] *n* svastika *m*

SWAT [swɒt] *n (abbr* **Special Weapons and Tactics**) **S. team** = groupe d'intervention d'élite de la police américaine

swat [swɒt] *(pt & pp* **swatted**) *vt* écraser

swatch [swɒtʃ] *n* échantillon *m*

swathe [sweɪð] **1** *n (of grass)* andain *m; (of material, land)* bande *f; Fig* **to cut a s. through sth** *(of fire, storm)* détruire qch sur son passage
2 *vt* envelopper (**in** de)

sway [sweɪ] **1** *n* (**a**) *(movement)* balancement *m* (**b**) *(influence)* influence *f;* **to be under sb's s.** être sous l'influence de qn; **to hold s. over sb/sth** tenir qn/qch sous sa domination
2 *vt (influence)* influencer
3 *vi* se balancer; **to s. from side to side** se balancer d'un côté à l'autre

Swazi ['swɑːzɪ] *n* (**a**) *(person)* Swazi(e) *m,f* (**b**) *(language)* swazi *m*
2 *adj* swazi(e)

Swaziland ['swɑːzɪlænd] *n* le Swaziland

swear [sweə(r)] *(pt* **swore** [swɔː(r)], *pp* **sworn** [swɔːn]) **1** *vt*

(vow) jurer; **to s. to do sth** jurer de faire qch; *Law* **to s. an oath** prêter serment
2 *vi (use swearwords)* jurer; **to s. at sb** injurier qn

▶**swear by** *vt insep (have confidence in)* se fier à

▶**swear in** *vt sep Law (jury, witness)* faire prêter serment à

swearing ['sweərɪŋ] *n* grossièretés *fpl*

swearword ['sweəwɜːd] *n* juron *m*, mot *m* grossier

sweat [swet] **1** *n* transpiration *f*, sueur *f; Fig* **to be in a s. about sth** avoir des sueurs froides à propos de qch; *Fam* **no s.!** pas de problèmes!; **s. gland** glande *f* sudoripare
2 *vt Fam* **to s. buckets** être en nage; *Fig* **to s. blood** suer sang et eau
3 *vi* (**a**) *(perspire)* transpirer, suer; *Fam* **to s. like a pig** suer comme un bœuf (**b**) *Fam Fig (worry)* se faire de la bile; **to make sb s.** laisser mariner qn

sweatband ['swetbænd] *n (on head)* bandeau *m; (on wrist)* poignet *m*

sweater ['swetə(r)] *n* pullover *m*, pull *m*

sweatpants ['swetpænts] *npl* pantalon *m* de survêtement

sweatshirt ['swetʃɜːt] *n* sweatshirt *m*

sweatshop ['swetʃɒp] *n* = atelier de confection où l'on exploite le personnel

sweaty ['swetɪ] *adj (person)* en sueur; *(hands)* moite; *(clothes)* imprégné(e) de sueur; *(work)* qui fait transpirer

Swede [swiːd] *n (person)* Suédois(e) *m,f*

Sweden ['swiːdən] *n* la Suède

Swedish ['swiːdɪʃ] **1** *npl (people)* **the S.** les Suédois *mpl*
2 *n (language)* suédois *m*
3 *adj* suédois(e)

sweep [swiːp] **1** *n* (**a**) *(action)* coup *m* de balai; **to give sth a s.** donner un coup de balai à qch; *Fig* **at one s.** d'un seul coup; *Fig* **to make a clean s.** *(win everything)* tout gagner (**b**) *(movement)* **with a s. of the arm** d'un geste large (**c**) *(of land, hills)* étendue *f; (of road, river)* courbe *f*
2 *vt (pt & pp* **swept** [swept]) (**a**) *(floor, street)* balayer; *(chimney)* ramoner; **to be swept overboard** être emporté(e) par une vague; **the boat was swept out to sea** le bateau a été emporté vers le large (**b**) *(idioms)* **to s. sth under the carpet** tirer le rideau sur qch; **to s. the board** *(in competition)* rafler tous les prix; **the latest craze to s. the country** la dernière folie qui a envahi le pays; *Fig* **he swept her off her feet** elle est tombée follement amoureuse de lui
3 *vi* (**a**) *(with broom)* balayer (**b**) *(move rapidly)* **to s. in/out** faire une entrée/une sortie majestueuse; **to s. to power** être propulsé(e) au pouvoir; **a wave of nationalism swept through the country** une vague de nationalisme a déferlé sur le pays

▶**sweep aside** *vt sep (opposition, criticism)* écarter

▶**sweep away** *vt sep (building)* emporter; *Fig (obstacle, difficulty)* balayer; *Fig* **to be swept away by sth** *(enthusiasm, passion)* être emporté(e) par qch

▶**sweep up** *vt sep & vi* balayer

sweeper ['swiːpə(r)] *n* (**carpet**) **s.** balai *m* mécanique

sweeping ['swiːpɪŋ] *adj (gesture)* large; *(statement)* généralisateur(trice); *(change, proposal)* radical(e)

sweepstake ['swiːpsteɪk] *n* sweepstake *m*

sweet [swiːt] **1** *adj* (**a**) *(sugary)* sucré(e); *(wine)* doux (douce); **to taste s.** avoir un goût sucré; **as s. as honey** doux comme le miel; **to have a s. tooth** aimer les sucreries; **s. pea** pois *m* de senteur; **s. potato** patate *f* douce; **s. william** œillet *m* de poète (**b**) *(smell)* agréable; *(sound)* doux (douce) (**c**) *(pretty, kind)* adorable; **to whisper s. nothings to sb** dire des mots doux à qn
2 *n (dessert)* dessert *m; (piece of confectionery)* bonbon *m*

sweetbreads ['swiːtbredz] *npl* ris *m (de veau, d'agneau)*

sweet-and-sour [swiːtən'saʊə(r)] *adj* aigre-doux (aigre-douce)

sweetcorn ['swiːtkɔːn] *n* maïs *m*

sweeten ['swiːtən] *vt (food)* sucrer; *Fig (task)* adoucir; *(offer)* améliorer; **to s. sb up** amadouer qn

sweetener ['swiːtənə(r)] *n* (**a**) *(in food)* édulcorant *m* (**b**) *Fam (bribe)* pot-de-vin *m*

sweetheart ['swiːthɑːt] *n (term of address) (to woman)* chérie *f*; *(to man)* chéri *m*

sweetie ['swiːtɪ] *n Fam (darling)* chou *m*; **he's such a s.** il est adorable

sweetly ['swiːtlɪ] *adv (sing)* d'une voix douce; *(smile, answer)* gentiment

sweetness ['swiːtnɪs] *n* douceur *f*; **to be all s. and light** être tout sucre tout miel

sweet-talk ['swiːtˈtɔːk] *vt Fam* **to s. sb into doing sth** baratiner qn pour qu'il fasse qch

sweet-tempered [swiːtˈtempəd] *adj* doux (douce)

swell [swel] **1** *vt* (*pp* **swollen** ['swəʊlən] *or* **swelled**) *(numbers, crowd)* gonfler
2 *vi (of part of body)* enfler; *(of number, crowd)* grossir; *(of sea)* se soulever; **to s. with pride** se gonfler d'orgueil
3 *n (of sea)* houle *f*
4 *adj Fam (excellent)* super *inv*

▸**swell up** *vi (part of body)* enfler

swelling ['swelɪŋ] *n* gonflement *m*, enflure *f*; **the s. had gone down** ça avait désenflé

sweltering ['sweltərɪŋ] *adj* étouffant(e)

swept [swept] *pt & pp of* **sweep**

swerve [swɜːv] **1** *n (of car)* embardée *f*; *(of player)* écart *m*
2 *vi (of car, driver)* faire une embardée; *(of player)* faire un écart; *(of ball)* décrire une courbe

swift [swɪft] **1** *n (bird)* martinet *m*
2 *adj* rapide

swift-footed ['swɪftfʊtɪd] *adj* rapide à la course

swiftly ['swɪftlɪ] *adv* rapidement, vite

swiftness ['swɪftnɪs] *n* rapidité *f*

swig [swɪg] *Fam* **1** *n* lampée *f*; **to take a s. from a bottle** boire un coup à une bouteille
2 *vt (pt & pp* **swigged)** boire à grands traits

swill [swɪl] **1** *n (food) (for pigs)* pâtée *f*; *Pej (for people)* nourriture *f* infâme
2 *vt Fam (drink)* écluser

swim [swɪm] **1** *n* **to go for** *or* **to have a s.** aller nager
2 *vt (pt* **swam** [swæm], *pp* **swum** [swʌm]) nager; **to s. the breast stroke** nager la brasse; **to s. the Channel** traverser la Manche à la nage
3 *vi* (**a**) *(in water)* nager; **to go swimming** aller nager; **to s. across sth** traverser qch à la nage; *Fig* **to s. with the tide** suivre le courant (**b**) *(be dizzy)* **my head is swimming** j'ai la tête qui tourne

swimmer ['swɪmə(r)] *n* nageur(euse) *m,f*

swimming ['swɪmɪŋ] *n* natation *f*; **s. cap** bonnet *m* de bain; **s. lesson** cours *m* de natation; **s. pool** piscine *f*; **s. trunks** slip *m* de bain

swimmingly ['swɪmɪŋlɪ] *adv Fam* au mieux; **things are going s.** ça baigne

swimsuit ['swɪmsuːt] *n* maillot *m* de bain

swindle ['swɪndəl] **1** *n* escroquerie *f*
2 *vt* escroquer; **to s. sb out of sth** soutirer qch à qn

swindler ['swɪndlə(r)] *n* escroc *m*

swine [swaɪn] *(pl* **swine)** *n* (**a**) *Lit (pig)* porc *m*; **s. fever** peste *f* porcine (**b**) *Fam (man)* salaud *m*; *(woman)* garce *f*

swing [swɪŋ] **1** *n* (**a**) *(movement) (of rope, chain)* balancement *m*; *(in golf)* swing *m*; *Fam* **to take a s. at sb/sth** balancer un coup de poing à qn/qch; **to be in full s.** battre son plein; *Fam* **to get into the s. of things** se mettre dans le bain
(**b**) *(change) (in opinion)* revirement *m* (**in** de); *(in economy)* fluctuation *f* (**in** de); *(in mood)* saute *f* (**in** de)
(**c**) *(in playground)* balançoire *f*

2 *vt (pt & pp* **swung** [swʌŋ]) *(arms, racket, ax)* balancer; **to s. one's hips** balancer les hanches; **to s. sb/sth onto one's shoulder** hisser qn/qch sur ses épaules; *Fam* **to s. it so that...** arranger les choses de manière à ce que... + *subjunctive*

3 *vi* (**a**) *(move to and fro)* se balancer; **to s. open** *(of door)* s'ouvrir; **to s. into action** passer à l'action; *Fam* **he should s. for this** *(be hanged)* il mérite d'être pendu; *Fam* **the party was really swinging** la fête battait son plein
(**b**) *(change direction)* virer; **to s. around** se retourner

swipe [swaɪp] **1** *vt* (**a**) *(through electronic reader)* passer dans un lecteur de cartes (**b**) *Fam (steal)* faucher
2 *vi (hit)* **to s. at** essayer de frapper
3 *n* (**a**) **to take a s. at** *(aim blow at)* essayer de frapper; *Fig (criticize)* s'en prendre à (**b**) *(for electronic reader)* **s. card** badge *m*

swirl [swɜːl] **1** *n (of cream)* spirale *f*; *(of smoke, leaves, dust)* tourbillon *m*
2 *vt* remuer
3 *vi* tourbillonner, tournoyer

swish [swɪʃ] **1** *n (of cane, whip)* sifflement *m*; *(of dress, silk)* froufrou *m*
2 *vt (cane)* faire siffler; **to s. its tail** *(of animal)* remuer la queue
3 *vi (of cane, whip)* siffler; *(of dress, silk)* froufrouter

Swiss [swɪs] **1** *npl* **the S.** *(people)* les Suisses *mpl*
2 *adj* suisse; **S. army knife** couteau *m* suisse; **S. chard** bette *f*; **S. cheese plant** philodendron *m*

switch [swɪtʃ] **1** *n* (**a**) *(electrical)* interrupteur *m* (**b**) *(change)* revirement *m*; **to make a s.** effectuer un changement (**c**) *(stick)* baguette *f*
2 *vt* (**a**) *(change)* **to s. channels/jobs** changer de chaîne/d'emploi; **they switched their attention to...** leur attention s'est portée sur...; **he's been switched to another department** il a été muté dans un autre service (**b**) *(exchange)* échanger
3 *vi (change)* **to s. to** passer à; *Comput* basculer vers

▸**switch off 1** *vt sep (appliance, heating)* éteindre
2 *vi* (**a**) *(of appliance, heating)* s'éteindre (**b**) *Fam (of person)* décrocher

▸**switch on 1** *vt sep (appliance, heating)* allumer
2 *vi (of appliance, heating)* s'allumer

▸**switch over** *vi (change TV channel)* passer sur une autre chaîne; **to s. over to sth** passer à qch

switchback ['swɪtʃbæk] *n* route *f* en lacets

switchblade ['swɪtʃbleɪd] *n (couteau m à)* cran *m* d'arrêt

switchboard ['swɪtʃbɔːd] *n* standard *m*; **s. operator** standardiste *mf*

Switzerland ['swɪtsələnd] *n* la Suisse

swivel ['swɪvəl] **1** *n* pivot *m*; **s. chair** chaise *f* pivotante
2 *vi* pivoter

swollen ['swəʊlən] **1** *pp of* **swell**
2 *adj* enflé(e)

swoon [swuːn] **1** *n* évanouissement *m*
2 *vi* s'évanouir

swoop [swuːp] **1** *n (of bird, plane)* descente *f* en piqué; *(of police)* descente *f*
2 *vi (of bird, plane)* descendre en piqué; *(of police)* faire une descente

swop = **swap**

sword [sɔːd] *n* épée *f*; **s. dance** danse *f* du sabre

swordfish ['sɔːdfɪʃ] *n* espadon *m*

swore [swɔː(r)] *pt of* **swear**

sworn [swɔːn] **1** *adj* **s. enemy** ennemi(e) *m,f* juré(e)
2 *pp of* **swear**

swum [swʌm] *pp of* **swim**

swung [swʌŋ] *pt & pp of* **swing**

sycamore ['sɪkəmɔː(r)] *n* sycomore *m*

sycophant ['sɪkəfənt] *n* flagorneur(euse) *m,f*

sycophantic [sɪkə'fæntɪk] *adj* flagorneur(euse)

Sydney ['sɪdnɪ] *n* Sydney

syllable ['sɪləbəl] *n* syllabe *f*

syllabus ['sɪləbəs] *n* programme *m*

sylph-like ['sɪlflaɪk] *adj Hum* **a s. woman** une sylphide

symbiotic [sɪmb(a)ɪ'ɒtɪk] *adj* symbiotique

symbol ['sɪmbəl] *n* symbole *m*

symbolic [sɪm'bɒlɪk] *adj* symbolique

symbolism ['sɪmbəlɪzəm] *n Art* symbolisme *m*

symbolist ['sɪmbəlɪst] *n & adj Art* symboliste *mf*

symbolize ['sɪmbəlaɪz] *vt* symboliser

symmetrical [sɪ'metrɪkəl] *adj* symétrique

symmetry ['sɪmɪtrɪ] *n* symétrie *f*

sympathetic [sɪmpə'θetɪk] *adj (understanding)* compréhensif(ive); *(compassionate)* compatissant(e); **to be s. to a proposal/cause** être favorable à une proposition/cause

sympathize ['sɪmpəθaɪz] *vi* (**a**) *(show compassion)* compatir (**with** avec) (**b**) *(show understanding)* **to s. (with sb)** comprendre (qn)

sympathizer ['sɪmpəθaɪzə(r)] *n* sympathisant(e) *m,f*

sympathy ['sɪmpəθɪ] *n* (**a**) *(pity, compassion)* compassion *f*; **to have s. for sb** éprouver de la compassion pour qn; **with deepest s.** avec toutes mes/nos condoléances (**b**) *(understanding, support)* sympathie *f*; **to feel s. for sb** éprouver de la sympathie pour qn; **s. strike** grève *f* de solidarité

symphony ['sɪmfənɪ] *(pl* **symphonies)** *n* symphonie *f*; **s. orchestra** orchestre *m* symphonique

symposium [sɪm'pəʊzɪəm] *(pl* **symposia** [sɪm'pəʊzɪə])* *n* symposium *m*

symptom ['sɪm(p)təm] *n also Fig* symptôme *m*

symptomatic [sɪm(p)tə'mætɪk] *adj* symptomatique

synagogue ['sɪnəgɒg] *n* synagogue *f*

sync, synch [sɪŋk] *n Fam* synchronisation *f*; **in/out of s. (with)** synchrone/pas synchrone (avec)

synchronization [sɪŋkrənaɪ'zeɪʃən] *n* synchronisation *f*

synchronize ['sɪŋkrənaɪz] *vt* synchroniser

syncopation [sɪŋkə'peɪʃən] *n Mus* syncope *f*

syndicalism ['sɪndɪkəlɪzəm] *n Pol* syndicalisme *m*

syndicalist ['sɪndɪkəlɪst] *n & adj Pol* syndicaliste *mf*

syndicate 1 *n* ['sɪndɪkət] syndicat *m*
2 *vt* ['sɪndɪkeɪt] *Journ* publier simultanément dans plusieurs journaux; **syndicated columnist** journaliste *mf* d'agence

syndrome ['sɪndrəʊm] *n Fig* syndrome *m*

synergy ['sɪnədʒɪ] *n* synergie *f*

synod ['sɪnəd] *n Rel* synode *m*

synonym ['sɪnənɪm] *n* synonyme *m*

synonymous [sɪ'nɒnɪməs] *adj* synonyme (**with** de)

synopsis [sɪ'nɒpsɪs] *(pl* **synopses** [sɪ'nɒpsiːz])* *n* résumé *m*; *(of movie)* synopsis *m*

syntax ['sɪntæks] *n Ling* syntaxe *f*; *Comput* **s. error** erreur *f* de syntaxe

synthesis ['sɪnθɪsɪs] *(pl* **syntheses** ['sɪnθɪsiːz])* *n* synthèse *f*

synthesize ['sɪnθəsaɪz] *vt* synthétiser

synthesizer ['sɪnθəsaɪzə(r)] *n* synthétiseur *m*

synthetic [sɪn'θetɪk] **1** *adj* synthétique
2 *n* **synthetics** synthétique *m*

syphilis ['sɪfɪlɪs] *n* syphilis *f*

syphon = **siphon**

Syria ['sɪrɪə] *n* la Syrie

Syrian ['sɪrɪən] **1** *n* Syrien(enne) *m,f*
2 *adj* syrien(enne)

syringe [sɪ'rɪndʒ] **1** *n* seringue *f*
2 *vt (ears)* déboucher

syrup ['sɪrəp] *n* sirop *m*

syrupy ['sɪrəpɪ] *adj (smile, music)* sirupeux(euse)

SYSOP ['sɪsɒp] *n Comput (abbr* **Systems Operator)** sysop *m*, opérateur *m* système

system ['sɪstəm] *n* (**a**) *(structure)* système *m*; **the S.** *(established order)* le système; *Fam* **it was a shock to the s.** ça a été un choc; *Fam* **to get sb out of one's s.** oublier qn; *Fam* **to get sth out of one's s.** se débarrasser de qch (**b**) *Comput* système *m*; **systems analyst** analyste-programmeur(euse) *m,f* (**c**) *(method)* méthode *f*

systematic [sɪstə'mætɪk] *adj* systématique

systematize ['sɪstəmətaɪz] *vt* systématiser

T

T, t¹ [tiː] *n* (**a**) *(letter)* T, t *m inv* (**b**) *(idioms)* **that's you to a T** c'est tout à fait toi; **to suit sb to a T** convenir parfaitement à qn

t² *(abbr* **ton(s))** t

TA [ˈtiːˈeɪ] *n Univ (abbr* **teaching assistant**) = étudiant de deuxième cycle qui assure quelques heures de cours en échange d'une bourse d'études

tab [tæb] *n* (**a**) *(on garment)* étiquette *f; Fam* **to keep tabs on sb/sth** avoir qn/qch à l'œil (**b**) *(on typewriter, word processor)* tabulation *f;* **t. (key)** tabulateur *m* (**c**) *Fam (for meal, drinks)* addition *f; also Fig* **to pick up the t.** payer l'addition (**d**) *(of LSD, ecstasy)* pilule *f*

tabbouleh [tæˈbuːleɪ] *n Culin* taboulé *m*

tabby [ˈtæbɪ] *(pl* **tabbies**) *n* **t. (cat)** chat *m* tigré

tabernacle [ˈtæbənækəl] *n (church)* temple *m; (on altar)* tabernacle *m*

table [ˈteɪbəl] **1** *n* (**a**) *(furniture)* table *f;* **to lay** *or* **to set the t.** mettre *ou* dresser la table; **to clear the t.** débarrasser la table; **t. dancing** danse *f* aux tables; **t. lamp** petite lampe *f;* **t. linen** linge *m* de table; **to have good/bad t. manners** bien/mal se tenir à table; **t. mat** set *m* de table; **t. salt** sel *m* de table; **t. tennis** tennis *m* de table; **t. wine** vin *m* de table (**b**) *(of facts, figures)* tableau *m*, table *f;* **t. of contents** table des matières; **twelve times t.** table de douze (**c**) *(idioms)* **the offer is still on the t.** l'offre tient toujours; **to turn the tables on sb** renverser les rôles

2 *vt* **to t. a motion/proposal** *(postpone)* ajourner une motion/une proposition

tablecloth [ˈteɪbəlklɒθ] *n* nappe *f*

tablespoon [ˈteɪbəlspuːn] *n* cuillère *f* à soupe

tablet [ˈtæblɪt] *n* (**a**) *(pill)* cachet *m* (**b**) *(inscribed stone)* tablette *f* (**c**) *(of soap)* pain *m*

tableware [ˈteɪbəlweə(r)] *n* vaisselle *f*

tabloid [ˈtæblɔɪd] *n (newspaper)* tabloïd *m;* **the t. press** la presse populaire

taboo [təˈbuː] **1** *n* tabou *m*
2 *adj* tabou(e)

tabular [ˈtæbjʊlə(r)] *adj* **in t. form** sous forme de tableau

tabulate [ˈtæbjʊleɪt] *vt* présenter sous forme de tableau

tachometer [tækˈɒmɪtə(r)] *n* compte-tours *m*

tacit [ˈtæsɪt] *adj* tacite

tacitly [ˈtæsɪtlɪ] *adv* tacitement

taciturn [ˈtæsɪtɜːn] *adj* taciturne

tack [tæk] **1** *n* (**a**) *(small nail)* clou *m; (thumbtack)* punaise *f* (**b**) *Naut (course)* bordée *f; Fig* **to change t.** changer de tactique
2 *vt* (**a**) *(fasten)* clouer; *(with thumbtack)* punaiser; *Fig* **to t. sth on** *(add)* rajouter qch (**b**) *(in sewing)* faufiler
3 *vi Naut* louvoyer

tackle [ˈtækəl] **1** *n* (**a**) *(equipment)* matériel *m*, équipement *m* (**b**) *(in soccer)* tacle *m; (in football)* placage *m*
2 *vt* (**a**) *(deal with) (problem)* s'attaquer à; *(subject)* aborder; **to t. sb about sth** *(confront)* confronter qn à propos de qch (**b**) *(in soccer)* tacler; *(in football)* plaquer

tacky [ˈtækɪ] *adj* (**a**) *(sticky)* collant(e) (**b**) *Fam Pej (tasteless)* de mauvais goût; *(person)* vulgaire

tact [tækt] *n* tact *m*

tactful [ˈtæktfʊl] *adj (person)* qui a du tact; *(answer, remark)* diplomatique

tactic [ˈtæktɪk] *n* tactique *f*

tactical [ˈtæktɪkəl] *adj* tactique; *Pol* **t. voting** vote *m* utile

tactician [tækˈtɪʃən] *n* tacticien(enne) *m,f*

tactile [ˈtæktaɪl] *adj* tactile

tactless [ˈtæktlɪs] *adj* dépourvu(e) de tact

tactlessly [ˈtæktlɪslɪ] *adv* sans tact

tad [tæd] *n Fam* **a t.** un tantinet, un peu

tadpole [ˈtædpəʊl] *n* têtard *m*

Tadzhikistan [tædʒɪkɪˈstɑːn] *n* le Tadjikistan

taffeta [ˈtæfɪtə] *n* taffetas *m*

taffy [ˈtæfɪ] *(pl* **taffies**) *n* bonbon *m* au caramel; **t. apple** pomme *f* d'amour

tag [tæg] *n* (**a**) *(label)* étiquette *f; Gram* **t. question** tag *m* (**b**) *(game)* **to play t.** jouer à chat
2 *vt (pt & pp* **tagged**) *(label)* étiqueter

▶ **tag along** *vi* **she always tags along** elle me/le/*etc.* suit partout; **to t. along with sb** venir avec qn

▶ **tag on** *vt sep* **to t. sth on** rajouter qch

Tagus [ˈteɪgəs] *n* **the T.** le Tage

Tahiti [təˈhiːtɪ] *n* Tahiti *f*

Tahitian [təˈhiːʃən] *n* Tahitien(enne) *m,f*
2 *adj* tahitien(enne)

tai chi [taɪˈtʃiː] *n* tai chi *m*

tail [teɪl] **1** *n* (**a**) *(of animal, plane)* queue *f; (of shirt)* pan *m;* **heads or tails?** *(when tossing coin)* pile ou face?; **tails, t. coat** queue-de-pie *f;* **t. end** *(last part)* fin *f; Aut* **t. light** feu *m* arrière (**b**) *(idioms)* **with one's t. between one's legs** la queue entre les jambes; *Fam* **to put a t. on sb** prendre qn en filature; *Fam* **to turn t.** tourner les talons
2 *vt Fam (follow)* filer

▶ **tail away, tail off** *vi* décliner; *(of voice)* baisser

tailgate [ˈteɪlgeɪt] *Aut* **1** *n* hayon *m;* **t. party** pique-nique *m* *(où le hayon de la voiture sert de table)*
2 *vt* **to t. sb** coller au pare-chocs de qn

tailor [ˈteɪlə(r)] **1** *n* tailleur *m;* **t.'s dummy** mannequin *m;* **t.'s shop** atelier *m* de tailleur
2 *vt (suit)* faire; *Fig (speech, policy)* adapter (**to** à)

tailored [ˈteɪləd] *adj* ajusté(e)

tailor-made [ˈteɪləmeɪd] *adj also Fig* fait(e) sur mesure

tailplane [ˈteɪlpleɪn] *n Aviat* stabilisateur *m*

tailspin [ˈteɪlspɪn] *n Aviat* descente *f* en vrille; **to go into a t.** descendre en vrille; *Fig* paniquer

tailwind [ˈteɪlwɪnd] *n* vent *m* arrière

taint [teɪnt] **1** *n* contamination *f; Fig* tare *f*
2 *vt (contaminate)* contaminer; *Fig* souiller

Taiwan [taɪˈwɑːn] *n* Taiwan

Taiwanese [taɪwəˈniːz] **1** *n* Taiwanais(e) *m,f*

2 *adj* taiwanais(e)

Tajikistan = Tadzhikistan

take [teɪk] **1** *vt* (*pt* **took** [tʊk], *pp* **taken** ['teɪkən]) **(a)** *(grasp)* prendre; **to t. hold of** prendre *ou* saisir; **to t. sb by the arm** prendre qn par le bras; **to t. sb in one's arms** prendre qn dans ses bras; **to t. the opportunity to do sth** profiter de l'occasion pour faire qch

(b) *(remove)* prendre; **to t. sth away from sb** prendre qch à qn; **to t. sth out of sth** prendre qch dans qch

(c) *(tolerate)* supporter; **he can't t. a joke** il prend mal la plaisanterie; **I can't t. (it) any more** je n'en peux plus

(d) *(lead, carry)* amener; **to t. sb home/to the station** conduire qn chez lui/à la gare; **to t. sb to court** faire un procès à qn; **to t. the dog for a walk** aller promener le chien; **her job takes her all over the world** son travail l'amène à voyager dans le monde entier; **if you can get the money we'll t. it from there** quand tu auras l'argent on verra comment on procède

(e) *(go by)* *(bus, road, turning)* prendre

(f) *(require)* prendre; **it takes courage (to do)** il faut du courage (pour faire); **how long does it t.?** combien de temps cela prend-il?; **it took me an hour to get here** il m'a fallu une heure pour venir; **that will t. a lot of explaining** ça ne va pas être facile de se faire pardonner

(g) *(adopt)* *(precautions, measures)* prendre; **to t. legal advice** consulter un avocat; **to t. sth as an example** prendre qch comme exemple

(h) *(record)* *(temperature, notes)* prendre

(i) *(capture)* *(power, town, chess piece)* prendre; **to t. first prize** remporter le premier prix

(j) *(assume)* **I t. it (that)...** je suppose que...

(k) *(accept)* *(check, credit card)* accepter; **my car only takes unleaded** ma voiture ne marche qu'à l'essence sans plomb; **t. it or leave it!** c'est à prendre ou à laisser!; **to t. sth well/badly** prendre bien/mal qch; **to t. sth the wrong way** mal comprendre qch; **how much** *or* **what will you t. for it?** combien est-ce que tu en veux?; **you can t. it from me that...** je peux te garantir que...

(l) *(contain)* avoir une capacité de

(m) *(subject)* faire; *(course)* suivre; *(exam)* passer; **he takes them for English** il leur enseigne l'anglais

(n) *(in phrases)* **to t. a bath** prendre un bain; **to t. drugs** se droguer; **to t. fright** prendre peur; **to be taken ill** tomber malade; **to t. a look at sth** jeter un coup d'œil à qch; **to t. a photograph of sb/sth** prendre qn/qch en photo; **to t. a seat** s'asseoir; **to t. a walk** se promener

2 *vi* *(be successful)* *(of fire, plant cutting, dye)* prendre

3 *n* **(a)** *(of movie, music)* prise *f*

(b) *(money)* recette *f*; *Fam* **to be on the t.** toucher des pots-de-vin

▸**take after** *vt insep* ressembler à

▸**take apart** *vt* *(machine, engine)* démonter; *(argument)* démolir

▸**take away 1** *vt sep* *(remove)* enlever, retirer; *(deduct)* ôter; **to t. sth away from sb** enlever qch à qn

2 *vi* **to t. away from the pleasure/value of sth** diminuer le plaisir/la valeur de qch

▸**take back** *vt sep* **(a)** *(return)* ramener, rapporter; **that takes me back to my childhood** cela me rappelle mon enfance **(b)** *(accept)* reprendre **(c)** *(withdraw)* retirer; **t. that back!** retire ce que tu viens de dire!

▸**take down** *vt sep* **(a)** *(remove)* *(from shelf)* prendre; *(downstairs)* descendre; *(poster, decorations)* enlever **(b)** *(lower)* baisser; *Fam* **to t. sb down a peg or two** remettre qn à sa place **(c)** *(dismantle)* *(tent, scaffolding)* démonter; *(wall, barricade)* démolir **(d)** *(record)* noter; *(notes)* prendre

▸**take for** *vt sep* **to t. sb for somebody else** prendre qn pour quelqu'un d'autre; **what do you t. me for?** pour qui est-ce que tu me prends?

▸**take in** *vt sep* **(a)** *(lead, carry)* *(person)* faire entrer; *(harvest)* rentrer **(b)** *(orphan)* recueillir; *(lodger)* prendre **(c)** *(garment)* reprendre **(d)** *(include)* inclure, comprendre **(e)** *(understand)* saisir **(f)** *(deceive)* tromper, rouler

▸**take off 1** *vt sep* **(a)** *(remove)* enlever; **to t. sth off sb's hands** retirer qch des mains de qn; **to t. years off sb** *(of clothes, diet)* rajeunir qn; **he took $10 off (the price)** il a baissé (le prix) de 10 dollars; **he never took his eyes off us** il ne nous a pas quittés des yeux **(b)** *(lead)* *(person)* emmener; **to t. oneself off** s'en aller **(c)** *(mimic)* imiter

2 *vi* **(a)** *(of plane)* décoller **(b)** *Fam (of person)* se casser **(c)** *Fam (succeed)* prendre

▸**take on** *vt sep* **(a)** *(task, responsibility)* assumer; *(problem)* s'occuper de; *(opponent)* défier; *(fuel, supplies)* prendre **(b)** *(employ)* embaucher **(c)** *(acquire)* prendre

▸**take out** *vt sep* **(a)** *(remove)* sortir; *Fam* **to t. it** *or* **a lot out of sb** épuiser qn; **to t. it out on sb** passer sa colère sur qn **(b)** *(person)* inviter (à sortir) **(c)** *(obtain)* *(license)* obtenir; *(insurance policy)* souscrire; *(subscription)* prendre **(d)** *(food)* **sandwiches to t. out** sandwiches à emporter

▸**take over 1** *vt sep* **(a)** *(become responsible for)* *(job, business)* reprendre **(b)** *(take control of)* *(place)* envahir; *(company)* racheter

2 *vi* **(a)** *(assume power)* prendre le pouvoir **(b)** *(relieve)* prendre la relève (**from** de)

▸**take to** *vt insep* **(a)** *(go to)* **to t. to one's heels** prendre ses jambes à son cou; **to t. to one's bed** s'aliter; **to t. to the hills** se réfugier dans les collines **(b)** *(adopt habit)* **to t. to doing sth** se mettre à faire qch **(c)** *(like)* **to t. to sb** se prendre de sympathie pour qn; **to t. to sth** prendre goût à qch

▸**take up 1** *vt sep* **(a)** *(carry)* monter **(b)** *(lead)* *(person)* faire monter **(c)** *(lift)* enlever **(d)** *(shorten)* *(skirt, hem)* raccourcir **(e)** *(challenge)* relever; *(offer, suggestion)* accepter; **to t. sb up on an offer** accepter l'offre de qn **(f)** *(subject, problem)* parler de (**with sb** avec qn) **(g)** *(assume)* *(position, post)* prendre **(h)** *(hobby, studies)* se mettre à; **we t. up the story just after...** nous reprenons l'histoire juste après... **(i)** *(space, time)* prendre

2 *vi* **to t. up with sb** se lier avec qn

▸**take upon** *vt sep* **to t. it upon oneself to do sth** prendre sur soi de faire qch

take-home pay ['teɪkhəʊmpeɪ] *n* salaire *m* net

taken ['teɪkən] **1** *adj* **(a)** *(occupied)* pris(e) **(b)** *(impressed)* **I was very t. with him** il m'a fait très bonne impression

2 *pp of* **take**

takeoff ['teɪkɒf] *n* **(a)** *(imitation)* imitation *f*; **to do a t. of sb** imiter qn **(b)** *(of plane)* décollage *m*

takeout ['teɪkaʊt] **1** *n* *(food)* plat *m* à emporter; *(restaurant)* restaurant *m* qui fait des plats à emporter

2 *adj* *(food)* à emporter

takeover ['teɪkəʊvə(r)] *n* **(a)** *Com (of company)* rachat *m*; **t. bid** offre *f* publique d'achat **(b)** *(of government, country)* prise *f* de pouvoir

taker ['teɪkə(r)] *n (buyer)* acheteur(euse) *m,f*, preneur(euse) *m,f*; **there were no takers** personne n'en voulait; **any takers?** *(for food)* y a-t-il des amateurs?

taking ['teɪkɪŋ] *n* **(a)** **it's yours for the t.** tu n'as plus qu'à accepter **(b)** *Com* **takings** recette *f*

talc [tælk] *n* talc *m*

talcum powder ['tælkəmpaʊdə(r)] *n* talc *m*

tale [teɪl] *n* **(a)** *(story)* histoire *f*; *(legend)* conte *m*; **to live to tell the t.** survivre **(b)** *(lie)* histoire *f*, salades *fpl* **(c)** **to tell tales (on sb)** moucharder (qn)

talent ['tælənt] *n (person, ability)* talent *m*; **t. scout** *or* **spotter** dénicheur(euse) *m,f* de talents

talented ['tæləntɪd] *adj* talentueux(euse)

talisman ['tælɪzmən] *n* talisman *m*

talk [tɔːk] **1** n (**a**) *(conversation)* conversation f; **to have a t. with sb** parler ou s'entretenir avec qn; *Fam* **to be all t. (and no action)** parler beaucoup (et ne pas faire grand-chose); **t. show** *(on TV, radio)* talk-show m
(**b**) **talks** *(negotiations)* pourparlers mpl
(**c**) *(gossip)* **there is some t. of him resigning** le bruit court qu'il va démissionner; **it's the t. of the town** on ne parle que de cela
(**d**) *(lecture)* intervention f
2 vt *(speak)* parler; **to t. nonsense** dire des bêtises; **to t. business/politics** parler affaires/politique; **to t. sense** tenir des propos sensés; **to t. (some) sense into sb** faire entendre raison à qn; **she can t. her way out of anything** avec son bagou elle arrive toujours à se tirer d'affaire; **to t. sb into/out of doing sth** convaincre/dissuader qn de faire qch
3 vi (**a**) *(speak)* parler (**to/about** à/de); **to t. to oneself** parler tout(e) seul(e); **talking of embarrassing situations,...** à propos de situations embarrassantes,...; *Fam* **now you're talking!** voilà qui est mieux!; *Fam* **you can t.!, look who's talking!** tu peux parler!
(**b**) *(gossip)* cancaner, jaser
(**c**) *(give lecture)* faire une intervention (**on** sur)
▸**talk back** vi répondre avec insolence
▸**talk down to** vt insep **to t. down to sb** parler à qn sur un ton de supériorité
▸**talk over** vt sep discuter
▸**talk up** vt sep faire de la publicité pour
talkative ['tɔːkətɪv] adj bavard(e)
talker ['tɔːkə(r)] n **he was never much of a t.** il n'a jamais été très bavard
talking ['tɔːkɪŋ] adj **t. book** livre m enregistré; *TV* **t. head** *(presenter)* présentateur(trice) m,f; *Hum or Pej (interviewee)* = expert qui s'exprime à la télévision; **t. point** sujet m de conversation
talking-to ['tɔːkɪŋtuː] n *Fam* savon m; **to give sb a t.** passer un savon à qn
tall [tɔːl] **1** adj *(person)* grand(e); *(building)* haut(e); **how t. are you?** combien est-ce que tu mesures?; **to be 6 feet t.** *(of person)* ≃ mesurer 1,80 mètres; *(of object)* faire 1,80 mètres de haut; *Fig* **that's a t. order** c'est beaucoup demander; *Fig* **a t. story** une histoire invraisemblable
2 adv **to walk** or **to stand t.** marcher la tête haute
tallboy ['tɔːlbɔɪ] n commode f haute
Tallin(n) ['tælɪn] n Tallinn
tallow ['tæləʊ] n suif m
tally ['tælɪ] **1** n *(pl* **tallies**) compte m; **to keep a t. of sth** tenir le compte de qch
2 vi *(pt & pp* **tallied**) *(of figure, report)* concorder
talon ['tælən] n serre f
tamarind ['tæmərɪnd] n *(fruit)* tamarin m; *(tree)* tamarinier m
tambourine [tæmbə'riːn] n tambourin m
tame [teɪm] **1** adj (**a**) *(not timid or vicious)* familier(ère); *(domesticated)* apprivoisé(e) (**b**) *(unadventurous)* timide; *(speech, attempt)* mou (molle); *(party, evening)* morne
2 vt *(animal)* apprivoiser; *Fig (emotion)* dominer
tamely ['teɪmlɪ] adv *(say, ask)* timidement; *(accept)* docilement
Tamil ['tæmɪl] **1** n (**a**) *(person)* Tamoul(e) m,f (**b**) *(language)* tamoul m
2 adj tamoul(e)
▸**tamper with** ['tæmpə(r)] vt insep toucher à; *(lock)* tripoter; *(documents, records)* trafiquer
tampon ['tæmpɒn] n tampon m *(hygiénique)*
tan[1] [tæn] n *Math (abbr* **tangent**) tan f, tg f
tan[2] [tæn] **1** n (**a**) *(color)* marron m clair (**b**) *(from sun)* bronzage m
2 adj *(color)* marron clair inv

3 vt *(pt & pp* **tanned**) (**a**) *(of sun) (skin)* hâler (**b**) *(leather)* tanner; *Fam* **to t. sb, to t. sb's hide** tanner le cuir à qn
4 vi *(of person, skin)* bronzer
tandem ['tændəm] n (**a**) *(bicycle)* tandem m (**b**) **to do sth in t.** faire qch à deux
tang [tæŋ] n *(taste)* saveur f acidulée; *(smell)* odeur f acidulée
tangent ['tændʒənt] n *Math* tangente f; *Fig* **to go off on** or **at a t.** changer de sujet
tangerine [tændʒə'riːn] **1** n *(fruit, color)* mandarine f
2 adj *(color)* mandarine inv
tangible ['tændʒɪbəl] adj tangible; *Fig (real)* évident(e); *Fin* **t. assets** biens mpl corporels
tangibly ['tændʒɪblɪ] adv manifestement
Tangier [tæn'dʒɪə(r)], **Tangiers** [tæn'dʒɪəz] n Tanger
tangle ['tæŋgəl] **1** n enchevêtrement m; **to be in a t.** être emmêlé(e); *Fig (of person, figures, accounts)* être embrouillé(e); **to get into a t.** s'emmêler; *Fig (of person, figures, accounts)* s'embrouiller
2 vt **to get tangled up in sth** se prendre dans qch; *Fig* se retrouver mêlé(e) à qch
▸**tangle with** vt insep *Fam* s'en prendre à
tangled ['tæŋgəld] adj emmêlé(e); *Fig* embrouillé(e)
tango ['tæŋgəʊ] **1** n *(pl* **tangos**) *(dance)* tango m
2 vi danser le tango; *Fam* **it takes two to t.** chacun a sa part de responsabilité
tangy ['tæŋɪ] adj acidulé(e)
tank [tæŋk] **1** n (**a**) *(container)* réservoir m (**b**) *Mil* tank m (**c**) **t. top** *(garment)* débardeur
2 vi *Fam (fail miserably)* faire fiasco
3 vt *Fam (lose intentionally)* perdre délibérément
tankard ['tæŋkəd] n chope f
tanker ['tæŋkə(r)] n *(ship)* navire-citerne m; *(truck)* camion-citerne m
tanned [tænd] adj bronzé(e)
tanner ['tænə(r)] n tanneur(euse) m,f
tannery ['tænərɪ] *(pl* **tanneries**) n tannerie f
tannin ['tænɪn] n tan(n)in m
tantalize ['tæntəlaɪz] vt allécher (**with** avec)
tantalizing ['tæntəlaɪzɪŋ] adj *(smell)* alléchant(e); *(hint, possibility)* tentant(e)
tantamount ['tæntəmaʊnt] adj **t. to** équivalent(e) à
Tantric ['tæntrɪk] adj tantrique
tantrum ['tæntrəm] n caprice m; **to throw a t.** faire un caprice
Tanzania [tænzə'nɪə] n la Tanzanie
Tanzanian [tænzə'nɪən] **1** n Tanzanien(enne) m,f
2 adj tanzanien(enne)
tap[1] [tæp] **1** n (**a**) *(for water, gas)* robinet m; **to be on t.** *(of beer)* être à la pression; *Fig (of person, information)* être toujours disponible; **t. water** eau f du robinet (**b**) **to put a t. on a phone** mettre un téléphone sur écoute
2 vt *(pt & pp* **tapped**) (**a**) *(tree)* inciser; *(resources)* puiser dans; *Fam* **to t. sb for money** taper de l'argent à qn (**b**) *(phone)* mettre sur écoute
tap[2] [tæp] **1** n (**a**) *(light blow)* petit coup m; *(with hand)* tape f (**b**) **t. dancer** danseur(euse) m,f de claquettes; **t. dancing** claquettes fpl
2 vt *(pt & pp* **tapped**) donner un petit coup à; *(with hand)* donner une tape à
3 vi **to t. (at** or **on)** frapper doucement (à)
tape [teɪp] **1** n (**a**) *(ribbon)* ruban m; *(of paper)* bande f; **(adhesive** or **Scotch®) t.** ruban m adhésif, Scotch® m; *Sport (finishing)* **t.** ligne f d'arrivée; **t. (measure)** mètre m (**b**) *(for recording)* bande f; *(cassette)* cassette f; **t. deck** platine f cassette; **t. recorder** magnétophone m; **t. recording** enregistrement m
2 vt (**a**) *(stick with tape)* scotcher (**b**) *(record)* enregistrer (**c**) *(bandage)* bander

▸**tape up** vt (**a**) (package) attacher avec du ruban adhésif ou du Scotch®; (hole, opening) coller (avec du ruban adhésif ou du Scotch®) (**b**) (bandage) bander

taper ['teɪpə(r)] **1** n (candle) bougie f filée
2 vi s'effiler; **to t. to a point** se terminer en pointe

▸**taper off** vi (of object) s'effiler; Fig (decrease) s'amenuiser

tape-record ['teɪprɪkɔːd] vt enregistrer

tapestry ['tæpɪstrɪ] (pl **tapestries**) n tapisserie f

tapeworm ['teɪpwɜːm] n ver m solitaire

tapioca [tæpɪ'əʊkə] n tapioca m

tapping ['tæpɪŋ] n (sound) petits coups mpl

tar [tɑː(r)] **1** n (**a**) (substance) goudron m (**b**) Fam Old-fashioned (sailor) matelot m
2 vt (pt & pp **tarred**) goudronner; **to t. and feather sb** rouler qn dans le goudron et les plumes; Fig **we've been tarred with the same brush** on nous a mis dans le même sac

tarantula [tə'ræntjʊlə] n tarentule f

tardily ['tɑːdɪlɪ] adv Formal (late) tardivement; (slowly) lentement

tardy ['tɑːdɪ] adj Formal (late) tardif(ive); (slow) lent(e)

target ['tɑːgɪt] **1** n (**a**) (of bullet, missile, joke) cible f; **t. language** (in translating) langue f d'arrivée; **t. practice** exercices mpl de tir (**b**) Fig (goal) objectif m; **to set oneself a t.** se fixer un objectif; **to be on t. (to do sth)** être dans les temps (pour faire qch); **t. audience** type m d'écoute ciblé; **t. market** marché m ciblé
2 vt (**a**) (aim) **to t. sth at sth** (missile) diriger qch sur qch; Fig (campaign, TV program, benefits) destiner qch à qch (**b**) also Fig (aim at) viser

tariff ['tærɪf] n (tax) tarif m, droit m de douane; (price list) tarif; **t. barrier** barrière f douanière

tarmac® ['tɑːmæk] **1** n macadam m; **the t.** (runway) le tarmac
2 vt (pt & pp **tarmacked**) goudronner

tarnish ['tɑːnɪʃ] **1** vt also Fig ternir
2 vi se ternir

tarot ['tærəʊ] n tarot m; **t. card** carte f de tarot

tarpaulin [tɑː'pɔːlɪn] n bâche f

tarragon ['tærəgən] n estragon m

tart [tɑːt] **1** n (**a**) (cake) (large) tarte f; (small) tartelette f (**b**) Fam Pej (promiscuous woman, prostitute) pute f
2 adj (**a**) (in taste) âpre (**b**) (tone, remark) aigrelet(ette)

▸**tart up** vt sep Fam (room, pub) retaper; **to t. oneself up** se faire une beauté

tartan ['tɑːtən] n tartan m, écossais m; **t. tie/jacket** cravate f/ veste f écossaise

Tartar ['tɑːtə(r)] n Tatar(e) m,f

tartar ['tɑːtə(r)] n (on teeth) tartre m

tartar(e) sauce ['tɑːtə'sɔːs] n sauce f tartare

tartly ['tɑːtlɪ] adv avec aigreur

task [tɑːsk] n tâche f; **to take sb to t. for sth/for doing sth** reprocher qch à qn/à qn d'avoir fait qch

task force ['tɑːskfɔːs] n Mil corps m expéditionnaire; Fig commission f

taskmaster ['tɑːskmɑːstə(r)] n **to be a hard t.** être très exigeant(e)

Tasmania [tæz'meɪnɪə] n la Tasmanie

Tasmanian [tæz'meɪnɪən] **1** n Tasmanien(enne) m,f
2 adj tasmanien(enne)

Tasman Sea ['tæzmən'siː] n **the T.** la mer de Tasman

tassel ['tæsəl] n gland m

taste [teɪst] **1** n (**a**) (flavor, sense) goût m; **t. bud** papille f gustative (**b**) (sample) also Fig **to have a t. of sth** goûter à qch; **a t. of things to come** un avant-goût des choses à venir; **to give sb a t. of his own medicine** rendre la pareille à qn (**c**) (liking) goût m (**for** pour); **to acquire** or **to develop a t. for sth** prendre goût à qch; **add sugar to t.** ajouter du sucre à volonté;

violent movies are not to my t. les films violents ne me plaisent pas (**d**) (judgment) goût m; **in good/bad** or **poor t.** de bon/mauvais goût
2 vt (**a**) (detect flavor of) sentir (le goût de) (**b**) (sample) goûter; Fig (happiness, success) goûter à
3 vi **to t. of** or **like sth** avoir un goût de qch; **to t. good/bad** être bon (bonne)/mauvais(e)

tasteful ['teɪstfʊl] adj de bon goût

tastefully ['teɪstfəlɪ] adv avec goût

tasteless ['teɪstlɪs] adj (**a**) (food) insipide (**b**) (remark, clothes) de mauvais goût

taster ['teɪstə(r)] n (**a**) (person) (of food) goûteur(euse) m,f; (of wine) dégustateur(trice) m,f (**b**) (foretaste) avant-goût m

tasting ['teɪstɪŋ] n (of wine, cheese, etc.) dégustation f

tasty ['teɪstɪ] adj (food) savoureux(euse)

tatters ['tætəz] npl also Fig **in t.** en lambeaux

tattered ['tætəd] adj déguenillé(e)

tattle ['tætəl] **1** n potins mpl, commérages mpl
2 vi commérer

tattoo[1] [tə'tuː] n (on drum) retraite f du soir

tattoo[2] [tə'tuː] **1** n (design) tatouage m; **to get a t.** se faire faire un tatouage; **t. artist** tatoueur(euse) m,f; **t. parlor** boutique f de tatouages
2 vt tatouer

tattooist [tə'tuːɪst] n tatoueur(euse) m,f

tatty ['tætɪ] adj Fam minable

taught [tɔːt] pt & pp of **teach**

taunt [tɔːnt] **1** n (words) raillerie f
2 vt railler

Taurus ['tɔːrəs] n le Taureau; **to be (a) T.** être Taureau

taut [tɔːt] adj tendu(e)

tauten ['tɔːtən] **1** vt tendre
2 vi se tendre

tautness ['tɔːtnɪs] n tension f

tautological [tɔːtə'lɒdʒɪkəl] adj tautologique

tautology [tɔː'tɒlədʒɪ] n tautologie f

tavern ['tævən] n taverne f

tawdry ['tɔːdrɪ] adj (**a**) (conduct, motive) lâche (**b**) (decor, jewelry) tape-à-l'œil inv

tawny ['tɔːnɪ] adj fauve; **t. owl** chouette f hulotte

tax [tæks] **1** n impôt m, taxe f; **t. avoidance** = moyen (légal) pour payer moins d'impôts; **t. bracket** tranche f d'imposition; **t. break** allègement m fiscal; **t. collector** percepteur(trice) m,f; **t. cut** réduction f d'impôt; **t. evasion** évasion f fiscale; **t. exemption** exonération f d'impôt; **t. exile** = personne vivant à l'étranger pour échapper au fisc; **t. haven** paradis m fiscal; **t. incentive** incitation f fiscale; **t. inspector** inspecteur(trice) m,f des impôts; **t. relief** dégrèvement m fiscal; **t. return** déclaration f d'impôt
2 vt (**a**) (subject to tax) imposer, frapper d'un impôt (**b**) (put under strain) mettre à l'épreuve (**c**) Formal (accuse) **to t. sb with sth** taxer qn de qch

taxable ['tæksəbl] adj imposable

taxation [tæk'seɪʃən] n imposition f; **an increase in t.** une augmentation des impôts

tax-deductible [tæksdɪ'dʌktɪbəl] adj déductible des impôts

tax-exempt [tæksɪg'zempt] adj (goods) exonéré(e) de taxes; (income) exonéré(e) d'impôts

tax-free [tæks'friː] adj (goods) exonéré(e) de taxes; (income) exonéré(e) d'impôts

taxi ['tæksɪ] **1** n taxi m; **t. driver** chauffeur m de taxi; **t. stand** station f de taxi
2 vi (of aircraft) rouler

taxidermist ['tæksɪdɜːmɪst] n taxidermiste mf

taxing ['tæksɪŋ] adj ardu(e)

taxonomy [tæk'sɒnəmɪ] n taxonomie f

taxpayer ['tækspeɪə(r)] *n* contribuable *mf*

TB [tiː'biː] *n* (*abbr* **tuberculosis**) tuberculose *f*

T-bone steak [tiːbəʊn'steɪk] *n* côte *f* de bœuf à l'os

te [tiː] *n Mus* si *m*

tea [tiː] *n* (*plant, drink*) thé *m*; (*herbal infusion*) tisane *f*; **t. caddy** boîte *f* à thé; **t. cozy** couvre-théière *m*; **t. leaves** feuilles *fpl* de thé; **t. party** goûter *m*; **t. set** service *m* à thé; **t. strainer** passoire *f* à thé; **t. towel** torchon *m* (pour la vaisselle); **t. tray** plateau *m*

teabag ['tiːbæg] *n* sachet *m* de thé

teach [tiːtʃ] (*pt & pp* **taught** [tɔːt]) **1** *vt* enseigner; **to t. sb sth, to t. sth to sb** enseigner qch à qn; **to t. sb (how) to do sth** apprendre à qn à faire qch; **to t. oneself sth** apprendre qch tout seul; **to t. school** enseigner; *Fig* **to t. sb a lesson** donner une leçon à qn; *Fam* **that'll t. him!** ça lui apprendra!
2 *vi* enseigner

teacher ['tiːtʃə(r)] *n* (*at primary school*) instituteur(trice) *m,f*; (*at secondary school*) professeur *m*, enseignant(e) *m,f*; **t.'s pet** chouchou(te) *m,f* du professeur; **t. training** formation *f* pédagogique; **teachers college** ≃ IUFM *m*

teaching ['tiːtʃɪŋ] *n* (**a**) (*profession, action*) enseignement *m*; *Univ* **t. assistant** chargé(e) *m,f* de cours; **t. hospital** CHU *m*; **t. practice** stage *m* pratique d'enseignement; **t. staff** personnel *m* enseignant (**b**) (*doctrine*) doctrine *f*

teacup ['tiːkʌp] *n* tasse *f* à thé

teak [tiːk] *n* teck *m*

team [tiːm] *n* équipe *f*; *Sport & Fig* **to be a t. player** avoir l'esprit d'équipe; **a t. effort** un travail d'équipe; **t. game** jeu *m* d'équipe; **t. spirit** esprit *m* d'équipe
▸**team up** *vi* s'associer (**with** avec)

teammate ['tiːmmeɪt] *n* coéquipier(ère) *m,f*

teamwork ['tiːmwɜːk] *n* travail *m* d'équipe

teamster ['tiːmstə(r)] *n* (*truck driver*) routier *m*

teapot ['tiːpɒt] *n* théière *f*

tear¹ [tɪə(r)] *n* larme *f*; **in tears** en larmes; **t. duct** canal *m* lacrymal; **t. gas** gaz *m* lacrymogène

tear² [teə(r)] **1** *vt* (*pt* **tore** [tɔː(r)], *pp* **torn** [tɔːn]) (*rip*) déchirer; (*snatch*) arracher (**from** à); **to t. sth in two** *or* **in half** déchirer qch en deux; **to t. sth to pieces** déchirer qch en mille morceaux; *Fig* démolir qch; *Fig* **to t. sb to pieces** mettre qn en pièces; **to be torn between two things** se sentir tiraillé(e) entre deux choses
2 *vi* (**a**) (*rip*) se déchirer (**b**) **to t. at sth** déchirer qch (**c**) (*move quickly*) **to t. along/past/away** aller/passer/partir à toute vitesse
3 *n* déchirure *f*
▸**tear apart** *vt sep Fig* déchirer
▸**tear away** *vt sep Fig* **to t. oneself away from sth** s'arracher de qch
▸**tear down** *vt sep* (*building*) démolir; (*statue*) renverser; (*poster*) arracher
▸**tear into** *vt insep* **to t. into sb** (*physically*) se jeter sur qn; (*verbally*) passer un savon à qn
▸**tear off 1** *vt sep* (*remove*) arracher
2 *vi* (*run away*) se sauver à toute vitesse
▸**tear out** *vt sep* arracher; *Fig* **to t. one's hair out** s'arracher les cheveux
▸**tear up** *vt sep* (*document, photo*) déchirer; (*plant*) déraciner; (*floorboards*) enlever

teardrop ['tɪədrɒp] *n* larme *f*

tearful ['tɪəfʊl] *adj* en larmes; **in a t. voice** avec des larmes dans la voix

tearfully ['tɪəfəlɪ] *adv* en pleurant

tearjerker ['tɪədʒɜːkə(r)] *n Fam* (*movie, book*) **it's a real t.** c'est complètement mélo

tearoom ['tiːruːm] *n* salon *m* de thé

tearstained ['tɪəsteɪnd] *adj* barbouillé(e) de larmes

tease [tiːz] **1** *vt* taquiner (**about** sur *ou* à propos de)
2 *vi* plaisanter
3 *n* (*person*) taquin(e) *m,f*
▸**tease out** *vt sep* clarifier

teaser ['tiːzə(r)] *n* (**a**) *Fam* (*problem*) colle *f* (**b**) *Mktg* (*advertisement*) aguiche *f*; **t. advertising** aguichage *m*

teasing ['tiːzɪŋ] *n* taquinerie *f*

teaspoon ['tiːspuːn] *n* cuillère *f* à café

teat [tiːt] *n* (*of animal*) trayon *m*; (*of feeding bottle*) tétine *f*

teatime ['tiːtaɪm] *n* (*for afternoon tea*) l'heure *f* du goûter

technical ['teknɪkəl] *adj* technique; **t. drawing** (*school subject*) dessin *m* industriel; **t. hitch** incident *m* technique

technicality [teknɪ'kælɪtɪ] *n* détail *m* technique

technically ['teknɪkəlɪ] *adv* techniquement

technician [tek'nɪʃən] *n* technicien(enne) *m,f*

technique [tek'niːk] *n* technique *f*

techno ['teknəʊ] *n Mus* techno *f*

technological [teknə'lɒdʒɪkəl] *adj* technologique

technology [tek'nɒlədʒɪ] (*pl* **technologies**) *n* technologie *f*

teddy ['tedɪ] (*pl* **teddies**) *n* **t. (bear)** ours *m* en peluche

tedious ['tiːdɪəs] *adj* ennuyeux(euse); (*task*) fastidieux(euse)

tedium ['tiːdɪəm] *n* ennui *m*

tee [tiː] *n* (*in golf*) tee *m*
▸**tee off** *vi* (*in golf*) jouer le départ

teem [tiːm] *vi* (**a**) (*rain*) **to t. (down)** pleuvoir à verse (**b**) **to be teeming with sth** (*insects, ideas*) grouiller de qch

teeming ['tiːmɪŋ] *adj* grouillant(e)

teen ['tiːn] *adj* adolescent(e); **t. idol** idole *f* des jeunes

teenage ['tiːneɪdʒ] *adj* adolescent(e)

teenager ['tiːneɪdʒə(r)] *n* adolescent(e) *m,f*

teens [tiːnz] *npl* adolescence *f*; **to be in one's t.** être adolescent(e)

teensy(-weensy) ['tiːnzɪ('wiːnzɪ)] *adj Fam* tout(e) petit(e)

teeny-bopper ['tiːnɪbɒpə(r)] *n Fam* petite minette *f*

teeny(-weeny) ['tiːnɪ('wiːnɪ)] *adj Fam* tout(e) petit(e)

teeshirt ['tiːʃɜːt] *n* tee-shirt *m*

teeter ['tiːtə(r)] *vi* chanceler; *Fig* **to t. on the brink of sth** être au bord de qch

teeth [tiːθ] *pl of* **tooth**

teethe [tiːð] *vi* **to be teething** faire ses dents

teething ['tiːðɪŋ] *n* poussée *f* dentaire; *Fig* **t. troubles** (*of project*) difficultés *fpl* initiales

teetotal [tiː'təʊtəl] *adj* qui ne boit jamais d'alcool

teetotaler [tiː'təʊtələ(r)] *n* = personne qui ne boit jamais d'alcool

TEFL ['tefəl] *n* (*abbr* **Teaching of English as a Foreign Language**) enseignement *m* de l'anglais langue étrangère

Teh(e)ran [teə'rɑːn] *n* Téhéran

tel. (*abbr* **telephone**) tél

telebanking ['telɪbæŋkɪŋ] *n* monétique *f*; (*home banking*) banque *f* à domicile

telecommunications [telɪkəmjuːnɪ'keɪʃənz] *npl* télécommunications *fpl*

telecommuting [telɪkə'mjuːtɪŋ] *n* télétravail *m*

teleconference [telɪ'kɒnfərəns] *n* téléconférence *f*

telegenic [telɪ'dʒenɪk] *adj* télégénique

telegram ['telɪgræm] *n* télégramme *m*

telegraph ['telɪgrɑːf] **1** *n* télégraphe *m*; **t. pole/wire** poteau *m*/fil *m* télégraphique
2 *vt* télégraphier

telegraphic [telɪ'græfɪk] *adj* télégraphique

telemarketing [telɪ'mɑːkɪtɪŋ] *n* télémarketing *m*

telepathic [telɪ'pæθɪk] *adj* télépathique

telepathy [tɪ'lepəθɪ] *n* télépathie *f*

telephone ['telɪfəʊn] **1** *n* téléphone *m*; **to be on the t.** être au

téléphone; *Com* **t. banking** opérations *fpl* bancaires par téléphone, banque *f* à domicile; **t. bill** facture *f* de téléphone; **t. booth** cabine *f* téléphonique; **t. call** appel *m* téléphonique, coup *m* de téléphone; **t. directory** *or* **book** annuaire *m* (téléphonique); **t. exchange** central *m* téléphonique; **t. number** numéro *m* de téléphone; **t. pole** poteau *m* télégraphique
2 *vt* téléphoner à
3 *vi* téléphoner

telephoto lens ['telɪfəʊtəʊlenz] *n* téléobjectif *m*

teleport ['telɪpɔːt] *vt* téléporter

teleportation [telɪpɔː'teɪʃən] *n* téléportation *f*

teleprinter ['telɪprɪntə(r)] *n* téléimprimeur *m*

telesales ['telɪseɪlz] *npl Com* téléventes *fpl*

telescope ['telɪskəʊp] *n* télescope *m*

telescopic [telɪs'kɒpɪk] *adj* télescopique; **t. sight** *(of rifle)* lunette *f*

teleshopping ['telɪʃɒpɪŋ] *n* téléachat *m*

teletext ['telɪtekst] *n* Télétexte® *m*

televangelist [telɪ'vændʒəlɪst] *n* = évangéliste qui prêche a la télévision

televise ['telɪvaɪz] *vt* téléviser

television [telɪ'vɪʒən] *n* télévision *f*; **on t.** à la télévision; **t. camera** caméra *f* de télévision; **t. program** émission *f* de télévision; **t. screen** écran *m* de télévision; **t. set** téléviseur *m*, poste *m* de télévision

teleworker ['telɪwɜːkə(r)] *n* télétravailleur(euse) *m,f*

teleworking ['telɪwɜːkɪŋ] *n* télétravail *m*

telex ['teleks] **1** *n* télex *m*
2 *vt (message)* télexer

tell [tel] *(pt & pp* **told** [təʊld]) **1** *vt* **(a)** *(say)* dire; *(story, joke)* raconter; **to t. sb sth, to t. sth to sb** dire qch à qn; **to t. the truth/a lie** dire la vérité/un mensonge; **to t. you the truth, I don't know** je t'avouerai que je ne sais pas; **can you t. me the way to the station?** est-ce que vous pouvez m'indiquer la gare?; **I told you so!** je te l'avais bien dit!; **t. me about it!, you're telling me!** à qui le dis-tu!; **let me t. you, I was frightened** laisse-moi te dire que j'ai eu peur!; **to t. the time** *(of clock)* donner l'heure; **to t. sb the time** *(of person)* donner l'heure à qn; **he can't t. the time** il ne sait pas lire l'heure
(b) *(discern)* **I could t. he was lying** je savais qu'il mentait; **you can t. she's lived abroad** ça se voit qu'elle a vécu à l'étranger; **there's no telling what she'll do next** qui sait ce qu'elle va inventer maintenant
(c) *(distinguish)* **to t. sth from sth** distinguer qch de qch; **to t. two people/things apart** distinguer deux personnes/choses; **to t. right from wrong** discerner le bien du mal; **I can't t. the difference** je ne vois pas la différence
(d) *(order)* **to t. sb to do sth** dire à qn de faire qch; **do as you're told!** fais ce qu'on te dit!; **I'm not asking you, I'm telling you!** ce n'est pas une question, c'est un ordre!; **he wouldn't be told** il refusait d'écouter ce qu'on lui disait
(e) *Pol (votes)* compter; **all told** au total
2 *vi* **(a)** *(say)* dire; **that would be telling!** je ne veux pas cafarder!
(b) *(discern)* dire; **it's difficult** *or* **hard to t.** c'est difficile à dire; **it's too early to t.** il est trop tôt pour se prononcer; **you never can t.** on ne sait jamais
(c) *(have effect)* se faire sentir

▸**tell off** *vt sep (scold)* **to t. sb off** disputer qn

▸**tell on** *vt insep Fam (inform on)* dénoncer, balancer

teller ['telə(r)] *n* **(a)** *(of votes)* scrutateur(trice) *m,f* **(b)** *(in bank)* guichetier(ère) *m,f*

telling ['telɪŋ] **1** *n* **(a)** *(of story)* narration *f* **(b)** **t. off** réprimande *f*; **to give sb a t. off** disputer qn
2 *adj* **(a)** *(revealing)* révélateur(trice) **(b)** *(decisive)* qui porte

telltale ['telteɪl] **1** *n (person)* rapporteur(euse) *m,f*
2 *adj (revealing)* révélateur(trice)

temerity [tɪ'merɪtɪ] *n* témérité *f*, audace *f*; **to have the t. to do sth** avoir l'audace de faire qch

temp [temp] *Fam* **1** *n* intérimaire *mf*; **to be a t.** faire de l'intérim
2 *vi* faire de l'intérim

temper ['tempə(r)] **1** *n (character)* caractère *m*, tempérament *m*; *(mood)* humeur *f*; *(bad mood)* mauvaise humeur *f*; **to be in a good/bad t.** être de bonne/mauvaise humeur; **to have a short t.** être coléreux(euse); **to lose one's t.** se mettre en colère; **to fly into a t.** piquer une colère; *Fam* **t., t.!** on se calme!; **t. tantrum** caprice *m*
2 *vt* **(a)** *(steel)* tremper **(b)** *(action)* tempérer

temperament ['tempərəmənt] *n* tempérament *m*, caractère *m*

temperamental [tempərə'mentəl] *adj* capricieux(euse)

temperance ['tempərəns] *n* **(a)** *(moderation)* modération *f* **(b)** *(abstinence from alcohol)* tempérance *f*; *Hist* **t. movement** mouvement *m* antialcoolique

temperate ['tempərət] *adj* **(a)** *Geog (climate, zone)* tempéré(e) **(b)** *Formal (language, criticism)* mesuré(e)

temperature ['tempərətʃə(r)] *n* température *f*; **to take sb's t.** prendre la température de qn; **to have a t.** avoir de la température

tempered ['tempəd] *adj (steel)* trempé(e)

tempest ['tempɪst] *n Lit* tempête *f*; *Fig* **a t. in a teacup** une tempête dans un verre d'eau

tempestuous [tem'pestjʊəs] *adj* tempétueux(euse)

temping ['tempɪŋ] *n* intérim *m*; **to do t.** faire de l'intérim; **t. agency** agence *f* d'intérim

template ['templeɪt] *n* gabarit *m*; *Comput* modèle *m*

temple¹ ['tempəl] *n (place of worship)* temple *m*

temple² ['tempəl] *n (side of head)* tempe *f*

tempo ['tempəʊ] *(pl* **tempos** *or* **tempi** ['tempiː]) *n Mus* tempo *m*

temporal ['tempərəl] *adj* temporel(elle)

temporarily [tempə'reərɪlɪ] *adv* temporairement

temporary ['tempərərɪ] *adj (accommodations, solution)* temporaire, provisoire; *(employment)* temporaire, intérimaire; *(improvement)* passager(ère)

tempt [tem(p)t] *vt* tenter; **to t. sb to do sth** inciter qn à faire qch; **to be tempted to do sth** être tenté(e) de faire qch; **to t. fate** tenter le diable

temptation [tem(p)'teɪʃən] *n* tentation *f*

tempting ['tem(p)tɪŋ] *adj* tentant(e)

temptress ['tem(p)trɪs] *n Lit* tentatrice *f*

ten [ten] **1** *n* dix *m inv*; **t. to one he'll find out** je te parie qu'il finira par le savoir
2 *adj* dix; **the T. Commandments** les dix commandements; *see also* **eight**

tenable ['tenəbəl] *adj* défendable

tenacious [te'neɪʃəs] *adj* tenace

tenacity [te'næsɪtɪ] *n* ténacité *f*

tenancy ['tenənsɪ] *(pl* **tenancies**) *n* location *f*; **t. agreement** bail *m* (de location)

tenant ['tenənt] *n* locataire *mf*

tend¹ [tend] *vt (look after)* s'occuper de

tend² [tend] *vi* pencher (**towards** vers); **to t. to do sth** avoir tendance à faire qch

▸**tend to** *vt insep (look after)* s'occuper de

tendency ['tendənsɪ] *(pl* **tendencies**) *n* tendance *f* (**toward** à); **to have a t. to do sth** avoir tendance à faire qch

tendentious [ten'denʃəs] *adj Formal* tendancieux(euse)

tender¹ ['tendə(r)] *n Naut* navette *f*; *Rail* tender *m*

tender² ['tendə(r)] *adj* **(a)** *(affectionate)* tendre **(b)** *(sore)* sensible **(c)** *(meat)* tendre **(d)** *(young)* **at the age of...** dès l'âge de...

tender³ ['tendə(r)] **1** *n Com (bid)* offre *f*, soumission *f*; **to make** *or* **to put in a t.** soumissionner

2 *vt* *(services, money)* offrir; *(resignation)* donner; *(apology)* présenter

3 *vi* *Com* **to t. for a contract** soumissionner à un appel d'offres

tenderhearted [tendə'hɑːtɪd] *adj* au cœur tendre

tenderly ['tendəlɪ] *adv* tendrement

tenderness ['tendənɪs] *n* **(a)** *(affection)* tendresse *f* **(b)** *(soreness)* sensibilité *f* **(c)** *(of meat)* tendreté *f*

tendon ['tendən] *n* tendon *m*

tendril ['tendrɪl] *n* vrille *f*

tenement ['tenɪmənt] *n* immeuble *m*

tenet ['tenət] *n* *(principle)* dogme *m*; *(belief)* croyance *f*

tenfold ['tenfəʊld] **1** *adj* décuple

2 *adv* dix fois plus; **to increase t.** être multiplié(e) par dix

tenner ['tenə(r)] *n* *(bill)* billet *m* de dix dollars

tennis ['tenɪs] *n* tennis *m*; **t. ball** balle *f* de tennis; **t. club** club *m* de tennis; **t. court** court *m* de tennis; **t. elbow** tennis-elbow *m*; **t. player** joueur(euse) *m,f* de tennis; **t. racquet** *or* **racket** raquette *f* de tennis; **t. shoe** *(chaussure f de)* tennis *m ou f*

tenor ['tenə(r)] *n* **(a)** *(singer)* ténor *m*; **t. saxophone** saxophone *m* ténor **(b)** *Formal (content, sense)* teneur *f*

tenpins ['tenpɪnz] *n* bowling *m* *(jeu)*

tense¹ [tens] *n* *Gram* temps *m*

tense² [tens] **1** *adj* *(cord, person, situation)* tendu(e); *(voice)* étranglé(e); *(muscle)* contracté(e)

2 *vt* *(cord)* tendre; *(muscle)* contracter; **to t. oneself** se raidir **3** *vi* se tendre, se raidir

▸**tense up** *vi* se crisper

tensely ['tenslɪ] *adv* nerveusement

tension ['tenʃən] *n* tension *f*

tent [tent] *n* tente *f*; **t. pole** mât *m* de tente; **t. stake** piquet *m* de tente

tentacle ['tentəkəl] *n* tentacule *m*

tentative ['tentətɪv] *adj* *(hesitant)* hésitant(e), timide; *(provisional)* provisoire

tentatively ['tentətɪvlɪ] *adv* *(hesitantly)* timidement; *(provisionally)* provisoirement

tenterhooks ['tentəhʊks] *npl* **to be on t.** être sur des charbons ardents; **to keep sb on t.** mettre qn au supplice

tenth [tenθ] *n* **(a)** *(fraction)* dixième *m* **(b)** *(in series)* dixième *mf* **(c)** *(of month)* dix *m inv*

2 *adj* dixième; **t. floor** neuvième étage; *Scol* **t. grade** = classe de lycée pour les 14–15 ans; *see also* **eighth**

tenuous ['tenjʊəs] *adj* *(connection)* ténu(e); *(comparison)* subtil(e); *(argument)* faible

tenure ['tenjə(r)] *n* *(of land)* fermage *m*; *(of office)* occupation *f*; *(of university teaching job)* titularisation *f*

tepid ['tepɪd] *adj* *also Fig* tiède

tequila [tɪ'kiːlə] *n* tequila *f*

term [tɜːm] **1** *n* **(a)** *(word, expression)* terme *m*; **I told her in no uncertain terms** je le lui ai dit carrément

(b) to be on good/bad terms (with sb) *(relations)* être en bons/mauvais termes (avec qn); **to be on friendly terms with sb** avoir des relations amicales avec qn; **to be on speaking terms** *(of two people)* se parler; **to come to terms with sth** accepter qch; **in financial/international terms** sur le plan *ou* d'un point de vue financier/international; **in terms of** en ce qui concerne, du point de vue de; **I was thinking more in terms of a Jaguar** je pensais plutôt à une Jaguar

(c) *Com* **terms** *(conditions)* conditions *fpl*; *(of contract)* termes *mpl*; **terms of reference** *(of commission)* attributions *fpl*; **terms of payment** conditions de paiement

(d) *(at school, university)* trimestre *m*; **t. of office** *(of politician)* mandat *m*; **t. of imprisonment** peine *f* de prison; **in the long/short t.** à long/court terme; **to have reached (full) t.** *(of pregnancy)* arriver à terme

2 *vt* appeler

terminal ['tɜːmɪnəl] **1** *n* **(a)** *(of battery)* pôle *m*, borne *f* **(b)** *(rail, bus)* terminus *m*; *(at airport)* terminal *m* **(c)** *Comput* terminal *m*

2 *adj* terminal(e); *(illness)* en phase terminale

terminally ['tɜːmɪnəlɪ] *adv* **to be t. ill** être condamné(e)

terminate ['tɜːmɪneɪt] **1** *vt* **(a)** *(employment, project)* mettre fin à; *(contract)* résilier **(b)** *(pregnancy)* interrompre

2 *vi* **(a)** *(of contract)* prendre fin **(b)** *(of bus, train)* aller jusqu'à

termination [tɜːmɪ'neɪʃən] *n* **(a)** *(of employment, project)* fin *f*; *(of contract)* résiliation *f* **(b) t. (of pregnancy)** interruption *f* de grossesse

terminology [tɜːmɪ'nɒlədʒɪ] *n* terminologie *f*

terminus ['tɜːmɪnəs] *(pl* **terminuses** *or* **termini** ['tɜːmɪnaɪ]) *n* terminus *m*

termite ['tɜːmaɪt] *n* termite *m*

tern [tɜːn] *n* sterne *f*

Terr. *abbr* **Terrace**

terrace ['terɪs] *n* *(beside house, on hillside)* terrasse *f*

terraced ['terɪst] *adj* *(hillside)* en terrasses

terracotta ['terə'kɒtə] *n* terre *f* cuite

terrain [tə'reɪn] *n* terrain *m*

terrapin ['terəpɪn] *n* tortue *f* d'eau douce

terrestrial [tɪ'restrɪəl] *adj* terrestre; **t. broadcasting, t. television** diffusion *f* hertzienne *ou* terrestre

terrible ['terɪbəl] *adj* *(shocking)* terrible; *(of poor quality)* épouvantable

terribly ['terɪblɪ] *adv* **(a)** *(badly)* affreusement mal; *(injured)* très gravement **(b)** *Fam (very)* extrêmement

terrier ['terɪə(r)] *n* *(dog)* terrier *m*; *Fig* **he's a real t.** il n'abandonne jamais

terrific [tə'rɪfɪk] *adj Fam* **(a)** *(excellent)* super *inv* **(b)** *(enormous)* incroyable

terrifically [tə'rɪfɪklɪ] *adv Fam (very)* extrêmement

terrified ['terɪfaɪd] *adj* terrifié(e); **to be t. of** avoir une peur bleue de

terrify ['terɪfaɪ] *vt* terrifier

terrifying ['terɪfaɪɪŋ] *adj* terrifiant(e)

territorial [terɪ'tɔːrɪəl] *adj* territorial(e); *(animal)* qui défend son territoire; **t. waters** eaux *fpl* territoriales

territory ['terɪtərɪ] *(pl* **territories**) *n* territoire *m*; *Fig (area of activity)* domaine *m*

terror ['terə(r)] *n* terreur *f*; **reign of t.** régime *m* de terreur; *Fam* **that child is a t.** cet enfant est une vraie terreur

terrorism ['terərɪzəm] *n* terrorisme *m*

terrorist ['terərɪst] *n & adj* terroriste *mf*

terrorize ['terəraɪz] *vt* terroriser

terror-stricken ['terəstrɪkən] *adj* terrorisé(e)

terse [tɜːs] *adj* *(person, reply)* sec (sèche); *(style, prose)* concis(e)

terseness ['tɜːsnɪs] *n* *(of person, reply)* brusquerie *f*; *(of style, prose)* concision *f*

tertiary ['tɜːʃərɪ] *adj* tertiaire; **t. education** enseignement *m* supérieur

TESL ['tesəl] *n* *(abbr* **Teaching of English as a Second Language)** enseignement *m* de l'anglais deuxième langue

TESOL ['tiːsɒl] *n* *(abbr* **Teaching of English to Speakers of Other Languages)** enseignement *m* de l'anglais langue étrangère

test [test] **1** *n* **(a)** *(trial, check)* test *m*; **to put sb/sth to the t.** mettre qn/qch à l'épreuve; **to pass the t.** se montrer à la hauteur; **to stand the t. of time** résister à l'épreuve du temps; **t. ban** interdiction *f* des essais nucléaires; **t. bed** banc *m* d'essai; *Law* **t. case** affaire *f* qui fait jurisprudence; **t. drive** essai *m* sur route; **t. flight** vol *m* d'essai; **t. pilot** pilote *m* d'essai; **t. tube** tube *m* à essai, éprouvette *f*; **t. tube baby** bébé-éprouvette *m*

(b) *(examination)* examen *m*; **(driving) t.** examen du permis de conduire; **French/math t.** examen de français/maths (**c**) *(in cricket, rugby)* **t. (match)** match *m* international

2 *vt* (**a**) *(examine) (pupil)* interroger (**on** sur); *(sight, hearing)* examiner; **to t. sb's knowledge** tester les connaissances de qn; **to t. sb for Aids** faire subir à qn le test de dépistage du sida (**b**) *(try out)* tester, mettre à l'épreuve

3 *vi* **to t. for Aids** faire un test de dépistage du sida; **to t. positive/negative** *(for drugs)* être positif(ive)/négatif(ive); *(for Aids)* être séropositif(ive)/séronégatif(ive)

▸**test out** *vt sep* tester

testament ['testəmənt] *n* (**a**) *Law (will)* testament *m* (**b**) *(tribute)* preuve *f* (**to** de)

test-drive ['testdraɪv] *vt* essayer

testes ['testiːz] *pl of* **testis**

testicle ['testɪkəl] *n* testicule *m*

testify ['testɪfaɪ] *(pt & pp* **testified)** *Law* **1** *vt* **to t. that...** attester que...

2 *vi* témoigner (**for/against** en faveur de/contre); *Fig* **to t. to sth** *(be proof of)* témoigner de qch

testily ['testɪlɪ] *adv* d'un ton irrité

testimonial [testɪ'məʊnɪəl] *n (character reference)* références *fpl*

testimony ['testɪmənɪ] *(pl* **testimonies)** *n Law* témoignage *m*, déposition *f*; *Fig* **to be a t. to sth** *(proof of)* témoigner de qch

testing ['testɪŋ] **1** *n* essai *m*; **t. ground** terrain *m* d'essai

2 *adj* éprouvant(e)

testis ['testɪs] *(pl* **testes** ['testiːz]) *n* testicule *m*

testosterone [tes'tɒstərəʊn] *n* testostérone *f*

testy ['testɪ] *adj (person, mood)* irritable; *(tone, manner)* irrité(e)

tetanus ['tetənəs] *n* tétanos *m*

tetchy ['tetʃɪ] *adj Fam* irritable

tether ['teðə(r)] **1** *n (for tying animal)* longe *f*; *Fig* **to be at the end of one's t.** être à bout

2 *vt (animal)* attacher

Texan ['teksən] **1** *n* Texan(e) *m,f*

2 *adj* texan(e)

Texas ['teksəs] *n* le Texas

Tex-Mex [teks'meks] *adj* tex-mex *inv*

text [tekst] **1** *n* texte *f*; *Comput* **t. editor** éditeur *m* de texte; **t. (message)** texto *m*, SMS *m*

2 *vt (send text message to)* envoyer un texto *ou* un SMS à

textbook ['tekstbʊk] *n* manuel *m*; *Fig* **a t. example (of)** un parfait exemple (de)

textile ['tekstaɪl] **1** *n* textile *m*

2 *adj* textile

textual ['tekstjʊəl] *adj* de texte

texture ['tekstʃə(r)] *n* texture *f*

Thai [taɪ] **1** *n* (**a**) *(person)* Thaïlandais(e) *m,f* (**b**) *(language)* thaï *m*

2 *adj* thaïlandais(e)

Thailand ['taɪlænd] *n* la Thaïlande

Thames [temz] *n* **the T.** la Tamise

than [ðæn, *unstressed* ðən] *conj* que; **he's taller t. me** il est plus grand que moi; **he was taller t. I had expected** il était plus grand que je (ne) l'imaginais; **more/less t. ten** plus/moins de dix; **more t. once** plus d'une fois

thank [θæŋk] *vt* remercier; **to t. sb for sth/for doing sth** remercier qn pour qch/d'avoir fait qch; **t. God!** Dieu merci!; **t. you** merci; **t. you very much** merci beaucoup; **no, t. you** non merci; **t. you for coming** merci d'être venu; *also Ironic* **we have Mike to t. for this** c'est à Mike que nous devons cela

thankful ['θæŋkfʊl] *adj* reconnaissant(e) (**for** de); **to be t. that...** être heureux(euse) que...

thankfully ['θæŋkfəlɪ] *adv* (**a**) *(gratefully)* avec gratitude (**b**) *(fortunately)* heureusement

thankless ['θæŋklɪs] *adj* ingrat(e)

thanks [θæŋks] **1** *npl* remerciements *mpl*; **t. to** *(because of)* grâce à; **no t. to you/them!** ce n'est pas grâce à toi/eux!

2 *exclam Fam* **t.!** merci!; *Fam* **no t.** non merci; **t. for coming/your letter** merci d'être venu/pour ta lettre; *Fam Ironic* **t. for nothing!** je te remercie!

thanksgiving [θæŋks'gɪvɪŋ] *n* action *f* de grâces; **T. (Day)** = 4ème jeudi de novembre, fête commémorant la première action de grâce des colons anglais

thank you ['θæŋkjʊ] *n* merci *m*, remerciement *m*; **to say t. to sb** dire merci à qn, remercier qn; **t. letter** lettre *f* de remerciement

that [ðæt] **1** *demonstrative pron (pl* **those** [ðəʊz]) (**a**) *(subject)* ce, cela, ça *(in more informal contexts)*; *(object)* cela, ça *(in more informal contexts)*; **who's t.?** qui est-ce?; **what's t.?** qu'est-ce que c'est?; **t.'s strange** c'est bizarre; **t.'s what she told me** c'est ce qu'elle m'a dit; **is t. all the luggage you're taking?** c'est tout ce que vous prenez comme bagages?; **t.'s where he lives** c'est là qu'il habite; **can you run as fast as t.?** tu peux courir aussi vite que ça?; **t.'s it!** c'est ça!; **and t.'s t.!** un point, c'est tout!

(**b**) *(as opposed to* **this**) celui-là (celle-là) *m,f*; **in a case like t.** dans un cas comme celui-là

2 *demonstrative adj (pl* **those**) (**a**) *(indicating person, thing)* ce (cette); **t. book** ce livre; **t. question** cette question; **t. man** cet homme

(**b**) *(as opposed to* **this**) ce...-là (cette...-là); **I prefer t. movie** je préfère ce film-là; **take t. cup** prends cette tasse-là; **t. one** celui-là (celle-là)

3 *adv* **high/big** haut(e)/grand(e) comme ça; **I tasted it but it wasn't t. good** j'y ai goûté mais ce n'était pas si bon que ça; **I've never seen one t. good** je n'en ai jamais vu d'aussi bon que ça; **he's t. stupid he...** il est tellement stupide qu'il...

4 [*unstressed* ðət] *relative pron* (**a**) *(subject)* qui; *(object)* que; **the letter t. came yesterday** la lettre qui est arrivée hier; **the woman t. I saw** la femme que j'ai vue

(**b**) *(with preposition)* **the person t. I gave it to** la personne à qui je l'ai donné; **the woman t. we're talking about** la femme dont nous parlons; **the room t. he's sleeping in** la chambre où il dort

(**c**) *(when)* où; **the day t. you arrived** le jour où tu es arrivé

5 [*unstressed* ðət] *conj* que; **she said t. she would come** elle a dit qu'elle viendrait

thatch [θætʃ] **1** *n (on roof)* chaume *m*; *Fam (of hair)* tignasse *f*

2 *vt (roof)* couvrir de chaume; **thatched cottage** chaumière *f*; **thatched roof** toit *m* de chaume

thaw [θɔː] **1** *n also Fig* dégel *m*

2 *vt (snow, ice)* faire fondre; *(food)* décongeler

3 *vi (of snow, ice)* fondre; *(of food)* se décongeler; *Fig (of person)* se dérider

▸**thaw out** *vi (of lake)* dégeler; *(of food)* se décongeler; *Fig (of person)* se dérider

the [*before consonant sounds* ðə, *before vowel sounds* ðɪ, *stressed* ðiː] *definite art* (**a**) *(singular)* le (la); *(plural)* les; **t. pen** le stylo; **t. house** la maison; **t. airport** l'aéroport; **in t. summer** *(this summer)* cet été; *(every summer)* l'été; **to have t. measles/flu** avoir la rougeole/la grippe; **at t. time** à ce moment-là; **t. Europe of today** l'Europe d'aujourd'hui; *Fam* **how's t. knee?** et ce genou?

(**b**) *(denoting concept, group)* **t. poor/blind** les pauvres/aveugles; **t. Wilsons** les Wilson

(**c**) *(with titles)* **Edward t. Eighth** Édouard VIII; **Alexander t. Great** Alexandre le Grand; **Catherine t. Great** la Grande Catherine

(**d**) *(with proportions, rates)* **to be paid by t. hour** être payé(e) à l'heure; **the car does 40 miles to the gallon** la voiture consomme 7 litres aux 100

(**e**) *(in exclamations)* **t. arrogance/stupidity of it!** quelle arrogance/stupidité!

(**f**) [*stressed* ðiː] **not THE Professor Branestorm?** pas le célèbre professeur Branestorm?; **it's THE look for the summer** c'est LE look de l'été

(**g**) (*in comparisons*) **t. more I see him, t. more I like him** plus je le vois, plus il me plaît; **t. more I see him, t. less I like him** plus je le vois, moins je l'apprécie; **t. sooner t. better** le plus tôt sera le mieux

(**h**) (*with dates*) **t. sixties** les années soixante; **t. eighteen hundreds** le dix-neuvième siècle

theater [ˈθɪətə(r)] *n* (**a**) (*drama, building*) théâtre *m*; **t. company** compagnie *f* théâtrale, troupe *f* de théâtre (**b**) (*area*) **t. of war** théâtre *m* des hostilités

theater-goer [ˈθɪətəgəʊə(r)] *n* amateur(trice) *m,f* de théâtre

theatrical [θɪˈætrɪkəl] *adj also Fig* théâtral(e); **t. company** compagnie *f* théâtrale, troupe *f* de théâtre

thee [ðiː] *pron Lit or Rel* te; (*after preposition*) toi

theft [θeft] *n* vol *m*

theftproof [ˈθeftpruːf] *adj* (*lock*) antivol *inv*; (*vehicle*) muni(e) d'un dispositif antivol

their [ˈðeə(r)] *possessive adj* (**a**) (*singular*) leur; (*plural*) leurs; **t. job** leur travail; **t. wives** leurs femmes; **it wasn't THEIR idea!** ce n'est pas eux qui en ont eu l'idée! (**b**) (*for parts of body*) **they hit t. heads** ils se sont cogné la tête (**c**) (*indefinite use*) **someone's left t. umbrella** quelqu'un a oublié son parapluie

theirs [ðeəz] *possessive pron* (**a**) (*singular*) le leur (la leur) *m,f*; (*plural*) les leurs; **our house is big, but t. is bigger** notre maison est grande, mais la leur est plus grande encore (**b**) (*used attributively*) **this book is t.** ce livre est à eux/à elles; **a friend of t.** un de leurs amis; **where's that brother of t.?** où leur frère a-t-il bien pu passer? (**c**) (*indefinite use*) **if anyone hasn't got t. they can use mine** si quelqu'un n'a pas le sien, il pourra utiliser le mien

theism [ˈθiːɪzəm] *n Rel* théisme *m*

them [ðem, *unstressed* ðəm] *pron* (**a**) (*direct object*) les; **I hate t.** je les déteste; **I can understand their son but not THEM** je comprends leur fils, mais eux, je ne les comprends pas (**b**) (*indirect object*) leur; **I gave t. the book** je leur ai donné le livre; **I gave it to t.** je le leur ai donné (**c**) (*after preposition*) eux (elles) *mpl,fpl*; **I'm thinking of t.** je pense à eux/elles (**d**) (*as complement of verb* **to be**) eux (elles) *mpl,fpl*; **it's t.!** ce sont eux/elles!; **it was t. who did it** c'est eux/elles qui l'ont fait (**e**) (*indefinite use*) **if anyone comes, tell t....** si quelqu'un vient, dis-lui...

thematic [θiːˈmætɪk] *adj* thématique

theme [θiːm] *n* thème *m*; **t. bar** bar *m* à thème; **t. park** parc *m* à thème; **t. restaurant** restaurant *m* à thème; **t. song** *or* **tune** chanson *f* du générique

themselves [ðəmˈselvz, *stressed* ðemˈselvz] *pron* (**a**) (*reflexive*) **they hurt t.** ils se sont blessés (**b**) (*emphatic*) eux-mêmes (elles-mêmes) *mpl,fpl*; **they t. have never...** eux-mêmes n'ont jamais...; **they told me t.** ils me l'ont dit eux-mêmes; **they're not t. today** ils ne sont pas dans leur état normal aujourd'hui (**c**) (*after preposition*) **they live by t.** ils vivent seuls; **they bought it for t.** ils se le sont acheté; **they talk to t.** ils parlent tout seuls

then [ðen] **1** *adv* (**a**) (*at that time*) alors, à ce moment-là; **since t.** depuis (ce moment-là), depuis (lors); **until t.** (*in future*) jusque-là; (*in past*) jusqu'à ce moment-là; **by t.** (*in future*) d'ici là; (*in past*) entre-temps; **there and t., t. and there** sur-le-champ (**b**) (*next*) ensuite, puis; **what t.?** et alors, qu'est-ce qui va se passer? (**c**) (*in that case*) alors; **if it rains, t. we get wet** s'il pleut, alors on va se mouiller (**d**) (*therefore*) donc; **you already knew, t.?** donc, tu le savais déjà?

2 *adj* **the t. President** le Président de l'époque

thence [ðens] *adv Formal* de là

theologian [θiːəˈləʊdʒ(ɪ)ən] *n* théologien(enne) *m,f*

theological [θiːəˈlɒdʒɪkəl] *adj* théologique

theology [θiːˈɒlədʒɪ] *n* théologie *f*

theorem [ˈθɪərəm] *n* théorème *m*

theoretical [θiːəˈretɪkəl] *adj* théorique

theoretically [θiːəˈretɪkəlɪ] *adv* théoriquement

theoretician [θiːərɪˈtɪʃən] *n* théoricien(enne) *m,f*

theorist [ˈθiːərɪst] *n* théoricien(enne) *m,f*

theorize [ˈθiːəraɪz] *vi* théoriser (**about** sur)

theory [ˈθɪərɪ] (*pl* **theories**) *n* théorie *f*; **in t.** en théorie

therapeutic [θerəˈpjuːtɪk] *adj also Fig* thérapeutique; *Med* **t. cloning** clonage *m* thérapeutique

therapist [ˈθerəpɪst] *n* thérapeute *mf*

therapy [ˈθerəpɪ] (*pl* **therapies**) *n* thérapie *f*; **to be in t.** suivre une thérapie

there [ðeə(r), *unstressed* ðə(r)] **1** *pron* **t. is/are** il y a; **t. was/were** il y avait; **t.'s somebody at the door** il y a quelqu'un à la porte; **t. isn't/aren't any** il n'y en a pas; **t. are** *or Fam* **t.'s two left** il (en) reste deux; **t.'s a page missing** il manque une page; **t. comes a time when...** il arrive un moment où...

2 *adv* (**a**) (*in that place*) là; (*over there*) là-bas; **he isn't t.** il n'est pas là; **the weather's nice t.** il fait beau là-bas; **I'm going t. tomorrow** j'y vais demain; **give me that book t.** donne-moi ce livre-là; **do we have time to get t. and back?** avons-nous le temps d'y aller et de revenir?; **t. it is!** le voilà!; **t. you are!** (*I was looking for you*) te voilà!; (*when handing over something*) voilà!; (*expressing triumph, satisfaction*) tu vois!; **t. and then, then and t.** sur-le-champ; *Fam* **he's not all t.** il n'a pas toute sa tête

(**b**) (*at that point*) là; **t.'s the difficulty** voilà la difficulté; **we'll stop t. for today** nous nous arrêterons là pour aujourd'hui; *Fam* **you've got me t.!** alors là, vous me posez une colle!

3 *exclam* voilà!; **t., t.!** allons, allons!; **t., I told you so!** et voilà, je te l'avais bien dit!; **t. now, that wasn't so bad!** voilà, ce n'était pas si terrible!

thereabouts [ˈðeərəˈbaʊts] *adv* (**a**) (*with place*) dans les environs; **he's from Toronto or t.** il est de Toronto, ou quelque part par là (**b**) (*with number, quantity, distance*) environ, à peu près; **it costs $500 or t.** ça coûte environ *ou* à peu près 500 dollars

thereafter [ðeərˈɑːftə(r)] *adv Formal* après cela, par la suite

thereby [ˈðeəbaɪ] *adv Formal* ainsi; **t. hangs a tale!** c'est une longue histoire!

therefore [ˈðeəfɔː(r)] *adv* donc

thereupon [ðeərəˈpɒn] *adv Formal* sur ce

thermal [ˈθɜːməl] **1** *n Met* ascendance *f* thermique

2 *adj* thermique; **t. energy** énergie *f* thermique; *Comput* **t. paper** papier *m* thermique; **t. springs** sources *fpl* thermales; **t. underwear** sous-vêtements *mpl* en Thermolactyl®

thermodynamics [θɜːməʊdaɪˈnæmɪks] *n* thermodynamique *f*

thermoelectric [θɜːməʊˈlektrɪk] *adj* thermoélectrique

thermometer [θəˈmɒmɪtə(r)] *n* thermomètre *m*

Thermos® [ˈθɜːməs] *n* **T. (flask)** (bouteille *f*) Thermos® *m ou f*

thermostat [ˈθɜːməstæt] *n* thermostat *m*

thesaurus [θɪˈsɔːrəs] (*pl* **thesauruses** *or* **thesauri** [θɪˈsɔːraɪ]) *n* dictionnaire *m* de synonymes

these [ðiːz] **1** *demonstrative pron* ceux-ci (celles-ci) *mpl,fpl*; **in cases like t.** dans des cas comme ceux-ci; **t. are the ones I want** voici ceux que je veux; **t. are my parents** (*introducing*) je te présente mes parents

2 *demonstrative adj* (**a**) (*indicating people or things*) ces; **t. children** ces enfants (**b**) (*as opposed to* **those**) ces...-ci; **I like t. shoes** j'aime bien ces chaussures-ci; **t. ones** ceux-ci (celles-ci) *mpl,fpl*

thesis [ˈθiːsɪs] (*pl* **theses** [ˈθiːsiːz]) *n* thèse *f*

thespian [ˈθespɪən] *n Lit or Hum* comédien(enne) *m,f*

they [ðeɪ] *pron* (**a**) (*subject*) ils (elles) *mpl,fpl*; **they're Scottish** (*masculine*) ils sont écossais; (*feminine*) elles sont écossaises;

THEY **haven't got it!** ce ne sont pas eux/elles qui l'ont!; **(b)** *(indefinite use)* **somebody called – what did t. want?** quelqu'un a appelé – qu'est-ce qu'il voulait?; **t. say that...** on dit que...

they'd [ðeɪd] = **they had, they would**

they'll [ðeɪl] = **they will, they shall**

they're [ðeə(r)] = **they are**

they've [ðeɪv] = **they have**

thick [θɪk] **1** *adj* **(a)** *(in general)* épais(aisse); **to be a meter t.** faire un mètre d'épaisseur; **the air was t. with smoke** l'air était empli d'une épaisse fumée; **the snow was t. on the ground** il y avait une épaisse couche de neige sur le sol
(b) *(voice)* pâteux(euse); *(accent)* fort(e)
(c) *Fam (stupid)* bouché(e)
(d) *(idioms)* **to have a t. skin** ne pas être susceptible; *Fam* **to be as t. as thieves** s'entendre comme larrons en foire
2 *adv* **(a)** *(cut)* en tranches épaisses; *(spread)* en couche épaisse
(b) *(idioms)* **to come t. and fast** *(questions, orders)* pleuvoir; *Fam* **to lay it on a bit t.** exagérer
3 *n* **in the t. of the forest** au beau milieu de la forêt; **to be in the t. of it** *or* **things** être au cœur de l'action; **through t. and thin** quoi qu'il arrive

thicken [θɪkən] **1** *vt* épaissir
2 *vi* s'épaissir; *Hum* **the plot thickens...** les choses se compliquent..., l'histoire se corse...

thicket [θɪkɪt] *n* fourré *m*

thickly [θɪklɪ] *adv* **(a)** *(cut)* en tranches épaisses; *(spread)* en couche épaisse **(b)** *(populated)* fortement **(c)** *(speak)* d'une voix pâteuse

thickness [θɪknɪs] *n* épaisseur *f*

thickset [θɪk'set] *adj* trapu(e)

thick-skinned [θɪk'skɪnd] *adj Fig* peu susceptible

thief [θiːf] *(pl* **thieves** [θiːvz]) *n* voleur(euse) *m,f*

thieve [θiːv] *vt & vi* voler

thieves [θiːvz] *pl of* **thief**

thieving [θiːvɪŋ] **1** *n* vol *m*
2 *adj* voleur(euse)

thigh [θaɪ] *n* cuisse *f*

thighbone [θaɪbəʊn] *n* fémur *m*

thimble [θɪmbəl] *n* dé *m* à coudre

thin [θɪn] **1** *adj* **(a)** *(person, wall)* mince; *(paper, slice, layer)* fin(e), mince; *(blanket, clothing)* léger(ère); *(book)* peu épais(aisse); **to get thinner** *(of person)* maigrir; **he's as t. as a rail** il est maigre comme un clou
(b) *(sparse)* *(hair, crowd, vegetation)* clairsemé(e); *(fog, mist)* léger(ère)
(c) *(soup, sauce)* liquide; *(paint)* dilué(e); *(blood)* appauvri(e)
(d) *(voice)* grêle
(e) *(idioms)* **to vanish into t. air** se volatiliser; **it's just the t. end of the wedge** ce n'est qu'un début
2 *adv* *(cut)* en tranches fines *ou* minces; *Fig* **our forces/resources are spread very t.** nos forces/ressources sont très éparpillées
3 *vt (pt & pp* **thinned)** *(paint)* diluer; *(sauce)* éclaircir
4 *vi (of crowd)* s'éclaircir; *(of fog, mist)* se lever; **his hair is thinning** il perd ses cheveux, il se dégarnit

thing [θɪŋ] *n* **(a)** *(action, remark, fact)* chose *f*; **the important t. is that...** l'important, c'est que...; **it's the only t. we can do** c'est tout ce que nous pouvons faire; **that's another t. altogether** c'est une autre affaire; **the t. is,...** le problème, c'est que...; **that was a silly t. to do/say** c'était stupide de faire/dire ça; **for one t.** d'abord; **what with one t. and another** avec tout ce qui s'est passé; **I don't know a t. about algebra** je n'y connais rien en algèbre; **to know a t. or two (about sth)** s'y connaître (en qch); **to take things too seriously** prendre les choses trop au sérieux; **it's just one of those things** ce sont des choses qui arrivent; **things are going**

well/badly les choses vont bien/mal; *Fam* **how are things?, how's things?** comment ça va?
(b) *(object)* chose *f*; *Fam* **what's that t.?** qu'est-ce que c'est que ce truc?; *Fam* **where's that wrench t. I was using?** où est cette espèce de clé dont je me suis servi tout à l'heure?; **things** *(belongings)* affaires *fpl*
(c) *Fam (person)* **you poor t.!** pauvre de toi!; **you lucky t.!** sacré veinard!; **you silly t.!** espèce d'idiot!
(d) *(idioms)* **to have a t. about sb/sth** *(like)* avoir un faible pour qn/qch; *(dislike)* avoir quelque chose contre qn/qch; **to have a t. about tidiness/punctuality** être très à cheval sur la propreté/la ponctualité; **it's not the done t.** ça ne se fait pas; **the latest t. in shoes** la dernière mode en matière de chaussures

thingamajig, thingumajig [θɪŋəmɪdʒɪg], **thingamabob, thingumabob** [θɪŋəmɪbɒb] *n Fam (object)* truc *m*; *(person)* machin(e) *m,f*

think [θɪŋk] **1** *vt (pt & pp* **thought** [θɔːt]) **(a)** *(have in mind)* **to t. that...** penser que...; **what are you thinking?** à quoi penses-tu?; **to t. evil thoughts** avoir de mauvaises pensées; **to t. to do sth** penser à faire qch
(b) *(believe, have as opinion)* croire, penser; **he thinks he knows everything** il croit tout savoir; **anyone would t. she was asleep** on jurerait qu'elle dort; **who'd have thought it!** qui l'eût cru!; **what do you t.?** qu'en penses-tu?; **I t. so** je pense (que oui); **I don't t. so, I t. not** je ne pense pas, je pense que non; **I thought so, I thought as much** c'est ce que je pensais; **I should t. so, too!** j'espère bien!; **that's what YOU t.!** c'est ce que tu crois!; **what do you t. about that idea?** qu'est-ce que tu penses de cette idée?
(c) *(imagine)* imaginer; **I can't t. why/what/where...** je me demande bien pourquoi/ce que/où...; **t. what we could do with all that money!** imagine ce qu'on pourrait faire avec tout cet argent!; **to t. that he's only twenty!** et dire qu'il n'a que vingt ans
2 *vi* réfléchir, penser; **to t. ahead** voir loin; **to t. aloud** penser tout haut; **to t. long and hard before doing sth** bien réfléchir avant de faire qch; **to t. on one's feet** réagir vite; **it makes you t.** ça fait réfléchir; **you can t. again!** tu te fourres le doigt dans l'œil!
3 *n* **to have a t.** réfléchir; *Fam* **you've got another t. coming!** tu te fourres le doigt dans l'œil!; **t. tank** groupe *m* de réflexion

▸**think about** *vt insep (have in mind, take into account)* penser à; *(consider)* réfléchir à; **to t. about doing sth** songer à faire qch; **it's quite cheap when you t. about it** ça n'est pas très cher quand on y pense; **that will give them something to t. about** voilà qui va leur donner matière à réflexion

▸**think back to** *vt insep* repenser à

▸**think of** *vt insep (have in mind, take into account)* penser à; **to t. of doing sth** songer à faire qch; **come to t. of it, I DID see her that night** maintenant que j'y pense, je l'ai effectivement vue ce soir-là; **what were you thinking of, walking home alone?** qu'est-ce qui t'a pris de rentrer à pied tout seul? **(b)** *(have opinion about)* **what do you t. of this?** qu'est-ce que tu penses de cela?; **to t. well/badly of sb** avoir une bonne/mauvaise opinion de qn; **I don't t. much of the idea** cette idée ne me dit pas grand-chose **(c)** *(recall)* se rappeler; **I can't t. of the right word** le mot m'échappe

▸**think out** *vt sep* réfléchir à

▸**think over** *vt sep* réfléchir à

▸**think through** *vt sep* **to t. sth through** bien réfléchir à qch

▸**think up** *vt sep* imaginer, inventer

thinker [θɪŋkə(r)] *n* penseur *m*

thinking [θɪŋkɪŋ] *n* **(a)** *(process of thought)* réflexion *f*; **to do some t.** réfléchir **(b)** *(opinion)* avis *m*, opinion *f*; **to my (way of) t.** à mon avis

thinly ['θɪnlɪ] *adv* (**a**) *(cut)* en tranches fines *ou* minces; *(spread)* en couche fine *ou* mince (**b**) *(populated)* faiblement

thinner ['θɪnə(r)] *n* diluant *m*

thinness ['θɪnnɪs] *n* *(of person, wall)* minceur *f*; *(of paper, slice, layer)* finesse *f*; *(of liquid)* fluidité *f*; *(of blanket, clothing)* légèreté *f*

third [θɜːd] **1** *n* (**a**) *(fraction)* tiers *m inv* (**b**) *(in series)* troisième *mf* (**c**) *(of month)* trois *m inv* (**d**) *Mus* tierce *f*
2 *adj* troisième; *Fam* **to give sb the t. degree** cuisiner qn; **t. floor** deuxième étage *m*; *Scol* **t. grade** = classe du primaire pour les 7–8 ans; *Law* **t. party** tiers *m*, tierce personne *f*; **t. rate** *(mediocre)* très mauvais(e); **the T. World** le tiers-monde; *see also* **eighth**

third-degree burns ['θɜːdɪɡriːˈbɜːnz] *npl* brûlures *fpl* au troisième degré

thirdly ['θɜːdlɪ] *adv* troisièmement

third-party insurance ['θɜːdpɑːtɪnˈʃʊərəns] *npl* assurance *f* au tiers

thirst [θɜːst] **1** *n* soif *f*; *Fig* **the t. for sth** la soif de qch
2 *vi Fig* être assoiffé(e) (**for** de)

thirsty ['θɜːstɪ] *adj also Fig* assoiffé(e); **to be** *or* **to feel t.** avoir soif; *Fam* **all this talking is t. work** ça donne soif de parler autant

thirteen [θɜːˈtiːn] **1** *n* treize *m inv*
2 *adj* treize; *see also* **eight**

thirteenth [θɜːˈtiːnθ] **1** *n* (**a**) *(fraction)* treizième *m* (**b**) *(in series)* treizième *mf* (**c**) *(of month)* treize *m inv*
2 *adj* treizième; *see also* **eighth**

thirtieth ['θɜːtɪɪθ] **1** *n* (**a**) *(fraction)* trentième *m* (**b**) *(in series)* trentième *mf* (**c**) *(of month)* trente *m inv*
2 *adj* trentième; *see also* **eighth**

thirty ['θɜːtɪ] **1** *n* trente *m inv*
2 *adj* trente; *see also* **eighty**

this [ðɪs] **1** *demonstrative pron* (*pl* **these** [ðiːz]) (**a**) *(subject)* ce, ceci; *(object)* ceci; **who's t.?** qui est-ce?; **what's t.?** qu'est-ce que c'est?; **t. is ridiculous!** c'est ridicule!; **t. leads me to believe that...** ceci me mène à croire que...; **I do it like t.** je le fais comme ceci; **t. is what she told me** voici ce qu'elle m'a dit; **listen to t.** écoute ça; **t. is Sarah Jervis** *(on telephone)* c'est Sarah Jervis à l'appareil; *(introducing another person)* je te présente Sarah Jervis; *Fam* **to talk about t. and that** parler de choses et d'autres
(**b**) *(as opposed to* **that**) celui-ci (celle-ci) *m,f*; **in a case like t.** dans un cas comme celui-ci
2 *demonstrative adj* (*pl* **these**) (**a**) *(indicating person, thing)* ce (cette); **t. book** ce livre; **t. question** cette question; **t. man** cet homme
(**b**) *(as opposed to* **that**) ce...-ci (cette...-ci); **I prefer t. movie** je préfère ce film-ci; **take t. cup** prends cette tasse-ci; **t. one** celui-ci (celle-ci)
3 *adv* **t. high/big** haut(e)/grand(e) comme ça; **I didn't think it would be t. good** je ne pensais pas que ce serait aussi bon; **I've never seen one t. good** je n'en ai jamais vu d'aussi bon que ça; **t. much is certain,...** une chose est sûre,...

thistle ['θɪsəl] *n* chardon *m*

thither ['ðɪðə(r)] *adv Lit* **hither and t.** ça et là

thong [θɒŋ] *n* (**a**) *(strip)* lanière *f* (**b**) *(underwear)* string *m*; *(swimwear)* tanga *m*

thongs [θɒŋz] *npl (sandals)* tongs *fpl*

thorax ['θɔːræks] *n Anat* thorax *m*

thorn [θɔːn] *n* épine *f*; *Fig* **to be a t. in sb's flesh** *or* **side** être une source d'irritation constante pour qn

thorny ['θɔːnɪ] *adj also Fig* épineux(euse)

thorough ['θʌrə] *adj* (**a**) *(search, cleaning, preparation)* minutieux(euse); *(knowledge, examination, revision)* approfondi(e); **to do** *or* **to make a t. job of sth** faire qch très consciencieusement (**b**) *(work, worker)* consciencieux(euse) (**c**) *(complete)* intégral(e)

thoroughbred ['θʌrəbred] **1** *n* pur-sang *m inv*
2 *adj (horse)* pur-sang *inv*

thoroughfare ['θʌrəfeə(r)] *n* rue *f*; **no t.** *(sign) (no entry)* passage interdit; *(cul-de-sac)* voie sans issue

thoroughgoing ['θʌrəɡəʊɪŋ] *adj (search)* minutieux(euse); *(knowledge, revision)* approfondi(e)

thoroughly ['θʌrəlɪ] *adv* (**a**) *(with thoroughness)* à fond (**b**) *(completely)* tout à fait

thoroughness ['θʌrənɪs] *n* minutie *f*

those [ðəʊz] *(plural of* **that***)* **1** *demonstrative pron* ceux-là (celles-là) *mpl,fpl*; **in cases like t.** dans des cas comme ceux-là; **t. are the ones I want** voilà ceux que je veux; **t. of us who...** ceux d'entre nous qui...
2 *demonstrative adj* ces; **t. ones** ceux-là (celles-là) *mpl, fpl*

though [ðəʊ] **1** *conj* bien que + *subjunctive*; **t. I say so myself** sans fausse modestie; **strange t. it may seem** aussi étrange que cela puisse paraître; **even t.** même si; **as t.** comme si
2 *adv* pourtant

thought [θɔːt] **1** *n* (**a**) *(thinking, idea)* pensée *f*; **it's quite a t.!** *(pleasant)* le rêve!; *(unpleasant)* quelle horreur!; **what a kind t.!** quelle délicate attention!; **the very t. of it...** le simple fait d'y penser...; **I didn't give it another t.** je n'y ai plus pensé; **her thoughts were elsewhere** son esprit était ailleurs; **what are your thoughts on the matter?** quelle est votre opinion sur le sujet?
(**b**) *(reflection)* réflexion *f*; **after much t.** après mûre réflexion; **to give some/no t. to sth** réfléchir/ne pas réfléchir à qch; **to be deep** *or* **lost in t.** être perdu(e) *ou* plongé(e) dans ses pensées
(**c**) *(intention)* intention *f*; **to have no t. of doing sth** ne pas avoir l'intention de faire qch; **you must give up all t.** *or* **thoughts of seeing him** tu dois renoncer à le voir
2 *pt & pp of* **think**

thoughtful ['θɔːtfʊl] *adj* (**a**) *(pensive) (person)* pensif(ive); *(book, writer)* sérieux(euse) (**b**) *(considerate) (person)* attentionné(e); *(gesture, remark)* gentil(ille)

thoughtfully ['θɔːtfəlɪ] *adv* (**a**) *(pensively)* pensivement (**b**) *(considerately)* gentiment

thoughtless ['θɔːtlɪs] *adj* irréfléchi(e)

thought-out ['θɔːtˈaʊt] *adj* **well/poorly t.** *(plan, scheme)* bien/mal étudié(e)

thought-provoking ['θɔːtprəvəʊkɪŋ] *adj* qui donne à réfléchir

thousand ['θaʊzənd] **1** *n* mille *m inv*; **one** *or* **a t.** mille; **thousands of people** des milliers de gens; **she's one in a t.** elle est unique
2 *adj* mille *inv*; **a t. years** mille ans; **two t. men** deux mille hommes; *Fam* **to have a t. and one things to do** avoir mille choses à faire

thousandth ['θaʊzənθ] **1** *n* (**a**) *(fraction)* millième *m* (**b**) *(in series)* millième *mf*
2 *adj* millième

thrash [θræʃ] *vt (beat)* battre; *Fam Fig (defeat heavily)* écraser, battre à plate(s) couture(s)

▸**thrash about, thrash around 1** *vt sep* **to t. one's arms and legs about** se débattre
2 *vi (move wildly)* se débattre

▸**thrash out** *vt sep* discuter *ou* débattre de

thread [θred] **1** *n* (**a**) *(for sewing)* fil *m*; *Fig* **his life hung by a t.** sa vie ne tenait qu'à un fil; **to lose the t. (of sth)** perdre le fil (de qch) (**b**) *(of screw, bolt)* filetage *m*
2 *vt* (**a**) *(needle, beads)* enfiler (**b**) *(move)* **to t. one's way between the cars** se faufiler entre les voitures; **to t. one's way through the crowd** se frayer un chemin à travers la foule

threadbare ['θredbeə(r)] *adj (clothes)* élimé(e); *Fig (argument, joke)* éculé(e)

threat [θret] *n* menace *f*

threaten ['θretən] **1** vt menacer; **to t. to do sth** menacer de faire qch; **to t. sb with sth** menacer qn de qch

2 vi menacer

threatening ['θretənɪŋ] adj (look, gesture) menaçant(e); (letter) de menaces

three [θriː] **1** n trois m inv; **come with us – no, (two's company,) t.'s a crowd** viens avec nous – non, je me sentirais de trop

2 adj trois inv; see also **eight**

three-cornered [θriːˈkɔːnəd] adj triangulaire

three-course meal ['θriːkɔːsˈmiːl] n repas m à trois plats (entrée, plat principal, dessert)

three-dimensional [θriːdaɪˈmenʃənəl] adj (object) tridimensionnel(elle), en trois dimensions; (character) qui semble réel; (movie, picture) en relief

threefold ['θriːfəʊld] **1** adj triple

2 adv **to increase t.** être multiplié(e) par trois

three-legged [θriːˈlegɪd] adj (stool) à trois pieds; **t. race** = course dont les participants sont attachés deux à deux par une jambe

three-piece ['θriːpiːs] adj **t. suit** (costume m) trois-pièce m inv; **t. suite** canapé m avec deux fauteuils assortis

three-point turn ['θriːpɔɪntˈtɜːn] n demi-tour m en trois manœuvres

threescore ['θriːskɔː(r)] adj Lit soixante inv; **t. (years) and ten** soixante-dix inv

threesome ['θriːsəm] n **(a)** (group) groupe m de trois personnes **(b)** Fam (for sex) partouze f à trois

three-wheeler [θriːˈwiːlə(r)] n (car) voiture f à trois roues; (tricycle) tricycle m

thresh [θreʃ] vt battre

threshold ['θreʃəʊld] n also Fig seuil m; **to cross the t.** franchir le seuil; Fig **to be on the t. of sth** être au seuil de qch; Fig **to have a high/low pain t.** avoir un seuil de tolérance à la douleur élevé/peu élevé

threw [θruː] pt of **throw**

thrice [θraɪs] adv Lit trois fois

thrift [θrɪft] n économie f, épargne f; **t. shop** = magasin vendant des articles d'occasion au profit d'œuvres charité

thriftless ['θrɪftlɪs] adj dépensier(ère)

thrifty ['θrɪftɪ] adj économe

thrill [θrɪl] **1** n (excitement) sensation f; (trembling) frisson m; **to get a t. out of doing sth** adorer faire qch

2 vt exalter, donner des frissons à; **to be thrilled for sb/with sth** être ravi(e) pour qn/de qch

3 vi Lit tressaillir, frissonner

thriller ['θrɪlə(r)] n thriller m

thrilling ['θrɪlɪŋ] adj (story, movie, match) palpitant(e); (idea, proposal, situation) exaltant(e)

thrive [θraɪv] (pt & pp **thrived** [θraɪvd], pt also **throve** [θrəʊv]) vi (of child, plant) se développer; (of adult) s'épanouir; (of business) prospérer; **to t. on sth** (stress, danger) avoir besoin de qch pour s'épanouir

thriving ['θraɪvɪŋ] adj (plant, person, animal) vigoureux(euse); (business) prospère, florissant(e)

throat [θrəʊt] n **(a)** (part of body) gorge f; **to clear one's t.** se racler la gorge, s'éclaircir la voix **(b)** (idioms) **to ram** or **to shove sth down sb's t.** rebattre les oreilles à qn de qch; **to jump down sb's t.** sauter sur qn; **to be at each other's throats** se battre

throaty ['θrəʊtɪ] adj rauque

throb [θrɒb] **1** n (of heart) battement m; (of pain) élancement m; (of engine) vibration f

2 vi (pt & pp **throbbed**) (of heart) battre; (of engine) vibrer; **my head is throbbing** j'ai une douleur lancinante dans la tête

throes [θrəʊz] npl **t. of death, death t.** affres fpl de la mort,

l'agonie f; **to be in the t. of sth/of doing sth** être en plein qch/en train de faire qch

thrombosis [θrɒmˈbəʊsɪs] (pl **thromboses** [θrɒmˈbəʊsiːz]) n thrombose f

throne [θrəʊn] n trône m

throng [θrɒŋ] **1** n foule f

2 vt se presser dans; **the streets were thronged with people** les rues étaient noires de monde

3 vi affluer, se presser; **to t. around sb** se presser autour de qn

throttle ['θrɒtəl] **1** n (valve) papillon m des gaz; (accelerator) manette f des gaz; **at full t.** à pleins gaz

2 vt also Fig étrangler

through [θruː] **1** prep **(a)** (with place) par, à travers; **to go t. a tunnel** passer par un tunnel; **to look t. a hole** regarder par un trou; **to come in t. the window** entrer par la fenêtre; **we went t. Belgium** nous sommes passés par la Belgique

(b) (in the course of) all t. his life toute sa vie durant; **halfway t. a book/movie** à la moitié d'un livre/film; **to get t. sth** (finish) venir à bout de qch; Fam **he's been t. a lot** il en a bavé

(c) (by means of) par; **to send sth t. the mail** envoyer qch par la poste; **I found out t. my brother/the newspaper** je l'ai appris par mon frère/le journal

(d) (because of) à cause de; **t. ignorance/carelessness** par ignorance/négligence

(e) (up to) **Tuesday t. Thursday** de mardi à jeudi

2 adv **(a)** (to other side) **to go t.** (of bullet, nail) traverser; **to let sb t.** laisser passer qn; **to get t. to the final** être en finale

(b) (from start to finish) **to sleep all night t.** dormir toute la nuit; **to read a book right t.** lire un livre tout entier; **he's bad t. and t.** il est vraiment méchant

(c) (in contact) **to get t. to sb** (on phone) joindre qn; **to put sb t. to sb** (on phone) passer qn à qn; Fam **I just can't get t. to him** (make myself understood) je n'arrive pas à le lui faire comprendre

3 adj **(a)** (finished) fini(e); **to be t. with sb/sth** en avoir fini avec qn/qch

(b) (direct) **t. train** train m direct

throughout [θruːˈaʊt] **1** prep (in every part of) partout dans; (during) tout au long de; **t. the country** dans tout le pays; **t. her life** tout au long de sa vie, pendant toute sa vie

2 adv (everywhere) partout; (the whole time) tout le temps

throughput ['θruːpʊt] n Comput débit m

throve [θrəʊv] pt of **thrive**

throw [θrəʊ] **1** vt (pt **threw** [θruː], pp **thrown** [θrəʊn]) **(a)** (in general) jeter, lancer; (javelin, discus) lancer; **to t. sth at sb/sth** lancer qch à qn/contre qch; **to t. sth in sb's face** lancer qch à la figure de qn; Fig jeter qch à la figure de qn; **to t. sb forward/backward** projeter qn en avant/en arrière; Fig **to t. oneself into sth** (after traumatic event) se jeter dans qch; (enthusiastically) se lancer dans qch; **to t. oneself at sb** se jeter sur qn; **to t. sb into confusion** plonger qn dans l'embarras; **to t. a switch** appuyer sur un interrupteur; Fam **to t. one's weight about** or **around** la ramener

(b) (image, shadow) projeter (**on** sur); Fig **to t. light on sth** éclairer qch

(c) (have) **to t. a fit** piquer une crise; Fam **to t. a party** organiser une fête

(d) (in wrestling) renverser

(e) (of horse) désarçonner

(f) Fam (disconcert) désarçonner, déconcerter

2 n **(a)** (in general) jet m; (of javelin, discus) lancer m; (in wrestling) mise f à terre

(b) (for furniture, bed) jeté m

(c) Fam **$50 a t.** (each) 50 dollars chaque

▸ **throw away** vt sep **(a)** (discard) jeter **(b)** (chance, life) gâcher; (money) gaspiller

▸ **throw in** vt sep **(a)** (in general) jeter; Fig **to t. in the sponge** *or* **the towel** jeter l'éponge; *Fig* **to t. in one's lot with sb** s'associer avec qn (**b**) *(add)* placer; *(give as extra)* ajouter, donner en plus

▸**throw out** *vt sep* (**a**) *(eject) (person)* exclure, mettre à la porte; *(thing)* jeter; *(proposal)* rejeter (**b**) *(emit) (light, heat)* émettre

▸**throw together** *vt sep (assemble or gather hurriedly)* assembler à la hâte; *(make hurriedly)* faire à la hâte; **chance had thrown us together** le hasard nous avait réunis

▸**throw up 1** *vt sep* (**a**) *(raise)* **to t. up one's hands** *(in horror, dismay)* lever les bras au ciel (**b**) *(reveal) (facts, information)* révéler (**c**) *(abandon) (career)* abandonner
  2 *vi Fam (vomit)* vomir

throwaway ['θrəʊəweɪ] *adj* (**a**) *(disposable)* jetable (**b**) *(line, remark)* fait(e) sans y penser

throwback ['θrəʊbæk] *n Biol* régression *f* (**to** à); *Fig* retour *m* (**to** à)

thrown [θrəʊn] *pp of* **throw**

thru = **through**

thrush¹ [θrʌʃ] *n (bird)* grive *f*

thrush² [θrʌʃ] *n (infection)* muguet *m*

thrust [θrʌst] **1** *n* (**a**) *(forward movement)* mouvement *m* en avant; *(of army)* attaque *f* (**b**) *(of argument)* idée *f* principale (**c**) *(force of engine)* poussée *f*
  2 *vt (pt & pp thrust)* **to t. sth into sth** enfoncer qch dans qch; **to t. one's way through the crowd** se frayer un chemin à travers la foule

▸**thrust aside** *vt sep* repousser, écarter

▸**thrust forward** *vt sep* pousser en avant; *Fig* **to t. oneself forward** se mettre en avant

▸**thrust on** *vt sep* **to t. sth on sb** imposer qch à qn; **he thrust himself on them** il s'est imposé

▸**thrust out** *vt sep (arm, leg)* allonger; *(chest)* bomber; *(chin)* avancer

▸**thrust upon** = **thrust on**

thrusting ['θrʌstɪŋ] *adj* entreprenant(e), dynamique

thruway ['θruːweɪ] *n* autoroute *f*

thud [θʌd] **1** *n* bruit *m* sourd
  2 *vi (pt & pp thudded)* faire un bruit sourd; **to t. against sth** frapper qch avec un bruit sourd

thug [θʌɡ] *n* voyou *m*

thumb [θʌm] **1** *n* pouce *m*; *Fig* **she's got him under her t.** il est sous sa coupe; *Fam* **to be all thumbs** être maladroit(e); *Fam* **to give sth the thumbs up/down** accepter/rejeter qch
  2 *vt* **to t. one's nose at sb** faire un pied de nez à qn; *Fam* **to t. a lift** *or* **ride** faire de l'auto-stop; **a well thumbed book/magazine** un livre/magazine qui a beaucoup servi
  3 *vi* **to t. through a book/magazine** feuilleter un livre/magazine

thumbnail ['θʌmneɪl] *n* ongle *m* du pouce; **t. sketch** description *f* rapide

thumbprint ['θʌmprɪnt] *n* empreinte *f* du pouce

thumbtack ['θʌmtæk] *n* punaise *f*

thump [θʌmp] **1** *n (blow)* coup *m*; *(sound)* bruit *m* sourd
  2 *vt (hit)* cogner, frapper; *(put down heavily)* poser lourdement
  3 *vi* (**a**) **to t. on sth** *(table, door)* cogner, frapper qch (**b**) *(walk heavily)* **to t. around** *or* **about** marcher à pas lourds (**c**) *(of heart)* battre la chamade

thumping ['θʌmpɪŋ] *Fam* **1** *adj* (**a**) *(very large)* énorme (**b**) *(headache)* lancinant(e)
  2 *adv* **a t. great book/salary** un livre/un salaire énorme

thunder ['θʌndə(r)] **1** *n* tonnerre *m*; **with a face like t.** le visage déformé par la colère
  2 *vi also Fig* tonner; **to t. along** *(of train, truck)* passer dans un bruit de tonnerre

thunderbolt ['θʌndəbəʊlt] *n* éclair *m* suivi d'un coup de tonnerre

thunderclap ['θʌndəklæp] *n* coup *m* de tonnerre

thundercloud ['θʌndəklaʊd] *n* nuage *m* orageux

thunderous ['θʌndərəs] *adj (voice)* tonitruant(e); **t. applause** un tonnerre d'applaudissements

thunderstorm ['θʌndəstɔːm] *n* orage *m*

thunderstruck ['θʌndəstrʌk] *adj* abasourdi(e)

Thurs. *(abbr* **Thursday)** jeudi

Thursday ['θɜːzdɪ] *n* jeudi *m*; *see also* **Saturday**

thus [ðʌs] *adv Formal* (**a**) *(in this way, therefore)* ainsi (**b**) **t. far** *(in present)* jusqu'ici; *(in past)* jusque-là

thwart [θwɔːt] *vt* contrecarrer

thyme [taɪm] *n* thym *m*

thyroid ['θaɪərɔɪd] **1** *n* thyroïde *f*
  2 *adj* thyroïde; **t. gland** thyroïde *f*

tiara [tɪ'ɑːrə] *n (jewelry)* diadème *m*

Tibet [tɪ'bet] *n* le Tibet

Tibetan [tɪ'betən] **1** *n* (**a**) *(person)* Tibétain(e) *m,f* (**b**) *(language)* tibétain *m*
  2 *adj* tibétain(e)

tibia ['tɪbɪə] *n Anat* tibia *m*

tic [tɪk] *n* tic *m*

tick¹ [tɪk] *n (parasite)* tique *f*

tick² [tɪk] **1** *n* (**a**) *(of clock)* tic-tac *m inv*; *Fam (moment)* instant *m* (**b**) *(mark)* coche *f*; **to put a t. beside sth** cocher qch
  2 *vt (mark)* cocher
  3 *vi (of clock)* faire tic-tac; **the minutes were ticking by** *or* **away** les minutes passaient; *Fam* **I don't know what makes him t.** je ne sais pas ce qui se passe dans sa tête

▸**tick off** *vt sep* (**a**) *(on list)* cocher (**b**) *Fam (irritate)* énerver

▸**tick over** *vi (of engine)* tourner au ralenti; *(of business)* tourner

ticket ['tɪkɪt] **1** *n* (**a**) *(for train, plane, movies, lottery)* billet *m*; *(for subway, bus)* ticket *m*; **(parking) t.** P-V *m*; **t. office** guichet *m*, billetterie *f*; **t. scalper** revendeur(euse) *m,f* de billets (**b**) *(label)* **(price) t.** étiquette *f* (**c**) *Pol (list of candidates)* liste *f* électorale; **she ran on an anti-corruption t.** elle a fondé son programme électoral sur la lutte contre la corruption (**d**) *Fam* **it was just the t.!** c'était juste ce qu'il fallait!
  2 *vt (goods)* étiqueter

ticketless ['tɪkɪtləs] *adj* **t. travel** = vol avec reçu de paiement tenant lieu de billet

ticking ['tɪkɪŋ] *n* (**a**) *(of clock)* tic-tac *m inv* (**b**) *(fabric)* toile *f* à matelas

tickle ['tɪkəl] **1** *n* chatouillement *m*; **to have a t. in one's throat** avoir des picotements dans la gorge
  2 *vt* chatouiller; *Fig (amuse)* amuser; **to t. sb's fancy** plaire à qn; **to be tickled pink** être ravi(e)
  3 *vi* chatouiller

ticklish ['tɪklɪʃ] *adj* (**a**) *(person)* chatouilleux(euse) (**b**) *Fam (situation, problem)* délicat(e)

tic-tac-toe [tɪktæk'təʊ] *n (game)* morpion *m*

tidal ['taɪdəl] *adj* régi(e) par les marées; **t. energy** énergie *f* marémotrice; **t. wave** raz de marée *m inv*

tidbit ['tɪdbɪt] *n (snack)* morceau *m* de choix; *Fig* **t. of gossip** potin *m*; **t. of information** nouvelle *f*

tiddledywinks ['tɪdəldɪwɪŋks] *n* jeu *m* de puce

tide [taɪd] *n* marée *f*; *Fig (of events)* cours *m*; **high/low t.** marée haute/basse; *Fig* **to go against the t.** aller à contre-courant; *Fig* **the t. has turned** le vent a tourné

▸**tide over** *vt sep* **to t. sb over** dépanner qn

tidemark ['taɪdmɑːk] *n (mark left by tide)* laisse *f* de haute mer; *Fam (in bath, around neck)* ligne *f* de crasse

tidings ['taɪdɪŋz] *npl Lit* nouvelles *fpl*

tidy ['taɪdɪ] **1** *adj* (**a**) *(room, house)* rangé(e), en ordre; *(hair)* bien coiffé(e); *(appearance, handwriting)* soigné(e); *(person) (in habits)* ordonné(e); *(in appearance)* soigné (**b**) *Fam (considerable)* joli(e)
  2 *vt* ranger; *(garden)* nettoyer; **to t. one's hair** se recoiffer

▸**tidy up** *vt sep & vi* ranger

tie [taɪ] **1** n (**a**) (link) lien m (**b**) (garment) cravate f; **t. rack** porte-cravates m (**c**) (draw) (in match) match m nul; **there was a t. for second place** (in race, competition) il y a eu égalité pour la deuxième place (**d**) (match) match m (**e**) Rail traverse f, Can dormant m

2 vt (shoelace, string) attacher, nouer; **to t. a knot** faire un nœud; **to t. sth to sth** attacher qch à qch; Fig **to have one's hands tied** avoir les mains liées; Fig **to be tied to one's desk** être cloué(e) à son bureau

3 vi (in race, contest) être à égalité; **to t. for first/second place** être premiers(ères)/deuxièmes ex aequo

▸**tie back** vt sep (hair, curtains) relever

▸**tie down** vt sep (immobilize) attacher; Fig **children t. you down** les enfants sont une contrainte; **she didn't want to feel tied down** elle voulait garder sa liberté

▸**tie in** vi (of facts, story) concorder, cadrer

▸**tie on** vt (**a**) attacher (**b**) Fam **to t. one on** (get drunk) prendre une cuite

▸**tie up** vt sep (**a**) (person, animal) attacher; (package) ficeler; (boat) amarrer (**b**) (deal) conclure; (money) immobiliser (**c**) Fig **to be tied up** (busy) être occupé(e)

tie-break ['taɪbreɪk], **tie-breaker** ['taɪbreɪkə(r)] n (in tennis) tie-break m; (in quiz, competition) question f subsidiaire

tie-in ['taɪɪn] n (link) lien m, rapport m (**with** avec); **a movie/TV t.** = livre, jouet, etc. commercialisé à la suite d'un film ou d'une série télévisée

tier [tɪə(r)] n (of theater, stadium) gradin m; (of wedding cake) étage m; (administrative) échelon m

tiff [tɪf] n Fam querelle f

tiger ['taɪɡə(r)] n tigre m

tight [taɪt] **1** adj (**a**) (clothes, knot, screw) serré(e); **to be a t. fit** (of clothes) être un peu juste; **to keep a t. hold** or **grip on sth** s'agripper à qch; **it was a t. squeeze** il a fallu se serrer un peu; Fig **to be in a t. spot** or **corner** être dans une mauvaise passe; Fig **to run a t. ship** mener son monde à la baguette (**b**) (competition, race, bend, schedule) serré(e); (restrictions) strict(e); **a t. finish** (in race) une arrivée disputée; Fam **money's a bit t. at the moment** je suis un peu à court d'argent en ce moment (**c**) Fam (mean) radin(e) (**d**) Fam (drunk) bourré(e)

2 adv (hold, squeeze) fortement; (seal, shut) bien; **hold t.!** tiens bon!; **sleep t.!** dors bien!

tighten ['taɪtən] **1** vt (screw, knot) serrer; (rope) tendre; (restrictions, security) renforcer; (conditions, rules) durcir; **to t. one's grip on sth** (rope, handle) resserrer sa prise sur qch; Fig (power, organization) renforcer son emprise sur qch; Fig **to t. one's belt** se serrer la ceinture

2 vi (of knot, grip) se resserrer; (of rope) se tendre

▸**tighten up** vt sep (screw) resserrer; (restrictions, security) renforcer

tightfisted [taɪt'fɪstɪd] adj Fam radin(e)

tightknit ['taɪt'nɪt] adj (community) uni(e)

tight-lipped ['taɪtlɪpt] adj (silent) peu bavard(e); (angry) renfrogné(e)

tightly ['taɪtlɪ] adv (hold, squeeze) fortement; (seal, shut) bien

tightness ['taɪtnɪs] n (of link, clothing) étroitesse f; (of regulations, security) rigueur f

tightrope ['taɪtrəʊp] n corde f raide; Fig **to walk a t.** être sur la corde raide; **t. walker** funambule mf

tights [taɪts] npl (garment) collant m

tigress ['taɪɡrɪs] n tigresse f

'til [tɪl] = until

tile [taɪl] **1** n (on roof) tuile f; (on floor, wall) carreau m

2 vt (roof) couvrir de tuiles; (floor, wall) carreler

tiled [taɪld] adj (roof) de tuiles; (floor, wall) carrelé(e)

till[1] [tɪl] vt (field) labourer

till[2] [tɪl] n (cash register) caisse f; Fig **to be caught with one's hand** or **fingers in the t.** être pris(e) la main dans le sac

till[3] [tɪl] = until

tiller ['tɪlə(r)] n (on boat) barre f

tilt [tɪlt] **1** n (**a**) (angle) inclinaison f (**b**) **at full t.** à toute vitesse

2 vt (head, chair) incliner, pencher; **to t. the balance of opinion in favor of** faire pencher l'opinion en faveur de

3 vi (**a**) (incline) pencher; **to t. backward/forward** pencher vers l'arrière/vers l'avant (**b**) Fig **to t. at windmills** se battre contre des moulins à vent

▸**tilt over** vi basculer

timber ['tɪmbə(r)] n (wood) bois m; **t. merchant** marchand m de bois

time [taɪm] **1** n (**a**) (in general) temps m; Fig **to have no t. for sb/sth** ne pas avoir de temps à perdre avec qn/qch; **to take t.** prendre du temps; **to take one's t. (doing sth)** prendre son temps (pour faire qch); **you took your t.!** tu as pris ton temps!; **in t.** (eventually) avec le temps; **in t. for sth/to do sth** à temps pour qch/pour faire qch; **in good t.** (early) à temps; (in due course) en temps voulu; **all in good t.** chaque chose en son temps; **she'll do it in her own good t.** elle fera quand elle le pourra; **now my t. is my own** maintenant, je suis libre de mon temps; **in no t. at all, in next to no t.** en un rien de temps; **on one's own t.** (out of working hours) pendant son temps libre; **t.'s up!** c'est l'heure!; **t. will tell** l'avenir le dira; Prov **t. is money** le temps, c'est de l'argent; Fam **to do t.** (go to prison) faire de la taule; also Fig **t. bomb** bombe f à retardement; **to be in a t. warp** être hors du temps; **t. travel** voyage m dans le temps

(**b**) (period) **in a short/long t.** dans peu de temps/longtemps; **for some t.** pendant quelque temps; **in three weeks' t.** dans trois semaines; **to take a long t. over sth/to do sth** passer beaucoup de temps sur qch/à faire qch; **for the t. being** pour le moment; **to have a good t.** bien s'amuser; **to give sb a hard t.** faire passer un mauvais moment à qn; Fam **long t. no see!** ça faisait longtemps!

(**c**) (age) époque f; **before my t.** avant ma naissance; **to be ahead of one's t.** être en avance sur son temps; **to move with the times** vivre avec son temps; **she was a good singer in her t.** c'était une bonne chanteuse à son époque; **she's seen a few things in her t.** elle a vu pas mal de choses dans sa vie; **t. capsule** capsule f témoin (qui doit servir de témoignage historique aux générations futures)

(**d**) (moment) moment m; **at the t.** à ce moment-là; **at the present t.** en ce moment; **at one t.** à une époque; **at no t.** jamais, à aucun moment; **at the same t.** en même temps; **at times** parfois, par moments; **by the t. you get this, I'll already be in Paris** quand tu recevras cette lettre, je serai déjà à Paris; **this t. next year** l'année prochaine à la même époque; **from t. to t.** de temps en temps; **at this t. of (the) year** à cette époque de l'année; **the t. has come to...** le moment est venu de...; Fam **it's high t. (that)...** il est grand temps que... + subjunctive

(**e**) (on clock) heure f; **what's the t.?** quelle heure est-il?; **to pass the t. of day with sb** parler de la pluie et du beau temps avec qn; Fam **he wouldn't give you the t. of day** il n'est vraiment pas aimable; **this t. tomorrow** demain à la même heure; **on t.** à l'heure; **it's t. we left** il est temps de partir; **t. difference** décalage m horaire; **t. lag** décalage; **t. limit** délai m; Ind **t. sheet** fiche f horaire; **t. switch** minuterie f

(**f**) (occasion) fois f; **five times** cinq fois; **t. and t. again, t. after t.** encore et encore

(**g**) (in multiplication) **4 times 2 is 8** 4 fois 2 égalent 8; **three times as big/expensive as** trois fois plus grand(e)/cher (chère) que

(**h**) (in music) mesure f; **to keep t.** rester en mesure

2 vt (**a**) (meeting, visit) prévoir

(**b**) (remark, action) **well timed** opportun(e); **badly timed** mal venu(e)

(**c**) (athlete, race) chronométrer

time-consuming ['taɪmkənsjuːmɪŋ] *adj* qui prend beaucoup de temps

time-honored ['taɪmɒnəd] *adj* consacré(e) (par l'usage)

timekeeper ['taɪmkiːpə(r)] *n* (*in competition*) chronométreur *m*

timekeeping ['taɪmkiːpɪŋ] *n* (**a**) (*in factory*) contrôle *m* de présence (**b**) (*punctuality*) ponctualité *f*

timeless ['taɪmlɪs] *adj* intemporel(elle)

timely ['taɪmlɪ] *adj* opportun(e)

time-out ['taɪmaʊt] *n* (*in sports*) temps *m* mort; *Fig* pause *f*; **to take t.** faire une pause

timepiece ['taɪmpiːs] *n* (*clock*) pendule *f*; (*watch*) montre *f*

timer ['taɪmə(r)] *n* minuteur *m*

time-saving ['taɪmseɪvɪŋ] *adj* qui permet de gagner du temps

timescale ['taɪmskeɪl] *n* période *f*

time-share ['taɪmʃeə(r)] *n* (*apartment*) appartement *m* en multipropriété; (*house*) maison *f* en multipropriété

timespan ['taɪmspæn] *n* laps *m* de temps

timetable ['taɪmteɪbəl] **1** *n* (*for event, project*) calendrier *m*; (*for trains, buses*) horaire *m*
2 *vt* (*talks, meeting*) fixer une date pour

time-wasting ['taɪmweɪstɪŋ] *n* perte *f* de temps

timid ['tɪmɪd] *adj* timide

timidity [tɪ'mɪdɪtɪ] *n* timidité *f*

timidly ['tɪmɪdlɪ] *adv* timidement

timing ['taɪmɪŋ] *n* (**a**) (*of announcement, election*) moment *m* choisi (**of** pour) (**b**) (*of remark, action*) **good t.** à-propos *m*; **bad t.** manque *m* d'à-propos; **perfect t.!** ça tombe bien! (**c**) (*of musician*) sens *m* du rythme

timorous ['tɪmərəs] *adj* timoré(e)

tin [tɪn] *n* (**a**) (*metal*) étain *m*; **t. mine** mine *f* d'étain; **t. plate** fer-blanc *m*; **t. soldier** soldat *m* de plomb (**b**) (*mold*) moule *m* (**c**) (*container*) boîte *f*; (*for biscuits, cakes*) boîte en fer

tinder ['tɪndə(r)] *n* petit bois *m*

tinderbox ['tɪndəbɒks] *n Fig* poudrière *f*

tinfoil ['tɪnfɔɪl] *n* papier *m* aluminium

ting-a-ling ['tɪŋə'lɪŋ] *n* dring-dring *m inv*

tinge [tɪn(d)ʒ] **1** *n* (*of color, emotion*) pointe *f*
2 *vt* **tinged with** teinté(e) de

tingle ['tɪŋgəl] **1** *n* (*physical sensation*) picotement *m*; (*of fear*) frisson *m*; (*of excitement*) frémissement *m*
2 *vi* picoter; **to t. with fear** frissonner de peur; **to t. with excitement** frémir d'excitation

tingling ['tɪŋglɪŋ] *n* picotement *m*

tinker ['tɪŋkə(r)] **1** *n* (*traveling person*) rétameur *m*
2 *vi* **to t. with sth** bricoler qch

tinkle ['tɪŋkəl] **1** *n* (*of bell*) tintement *m*
2 *vi* tinter

tinned [tɪnd] *adj* (*food*) en boîte

tinnitus ['tɪnɪtəs] *n* acouphène *m*

tinny ['tɪnɪ] *adj* (*sound*) métallique

tinsel ['tɪnsəl] *n* guirlandes *fpl* de Noël

tint [tɪnt] **1** *n* teinte *f*, nuance *f*; (*in hair*) rinçage *m*
2 *vt* teinter

tiny ['taɪnɪ] *adj* minuscule; **a t. bit** un tout petit peu

tip[1] [tɪp] **1** *n* (*end*) bout *m*; **on the tips of one's toes** sur la pointe des pieds; **it's on the t. of my tongue** je l'ai sur le bout de la langue; *Fig* **that's just the t. of the iceberg** ce n'est que la partie visible de l'iceberg
2 *vt* (*pt & pp* **tipped**) **to be tipped with sth** avoir le bout recouvert de qch

tip[2] [tɪp] **1** *n* (**a**) (*payment*) pourboire *m* (**b**) (*piece of advice*) truc *m*
2 *vt* (*pt & pp* **tipped**) (**a**) (*give money to*) donner un pourboire à (**b**) (*predict*) **to t. a winner** (*in horse race*) pronostiquer un cheval gagnant; **to t. sb for success/promotion** prédire à

qn le succès/une promotion; **the movie is tipped to win an Oscar** de l'avis général il y a de fortes chances que le film remporte un Oscar

tip[3] [tɪp] *vt* (*pt & pp* **tipped**) (**a**) (*pour*) verser; **to t. sth over sb/sth** renverser qch sur qn/qch (**b**) **to t. the scales at 150 pounds** ≃ peser 68 kg; *Fig* **to t. the scales** *or* **balance (in sb's favor)** faire pencher la balance (en faveur de qn)
▸**tip off** *vt sep* (*warn*) avertir
▸**tip over 1** *vt sep* renverser
2 *vi* se renverser
▸**tip up 1** *vt sep* renverser
2 *vi* basculer

tip-off ['tɪpɒf] *n Fam* tuyau *m*

tipple ['tɪpəl] *n Fam* **what's your t.?** qu'est-ce que vous buvez habituellement?; **sherry's her favorite t.** ce qu'elle préfère, c'est le sherry

tipsy ['tɪpsɪ] *adj Fam* pompette

tiptoe ['tɪptəʊ] **1** **on t.** sur la pointe des pieds
2 *vi* marcher sur la pointe des pieds; **to t. in/out** entrer/sortir sur la pointe des pieds

tiptop ['tɪptɒp] *adj* excellent(e)

tirade [taɪ'reɪd] *n* diatribe *f*

tire[1] ['taɪə(r)] **1** *vt* fatiguer
2 *vi* se fatiguer; **to t. of sth/of doing sth** se lasser de qch/de faire qch
▸**tire out** *vt sep* (*exhaust*) épuiser

tire[2] ['taɪə(r)] *n* pneu *m*; **t. marks** traces *fpl* de pneu; **t. pressure** pression *f* des pneus

tired ['taɪəd] *adj* fatigué(e); **to be t. of sth/of doing sth** en avoir assez de qch/de faire qch

tireless ['taɪəlɪs] *adj* infatigable

tiresome ['taɪəsəm] *adj* ennuyeux(euse)

tiring ['taɪərɪŋ] *adj* fatigant(e)

tissue ['tɪʃuː] *n* (**a**) *Biol* tissu *m* (**b**) (*paper handkerchief*) mouchoir *m* en papier; *Fig* **a t. of lies** un tissu de mensonges; **t. paper** papier *m* de soie

tit[1] [tɪt] *n* (*bird*) mésange *f*

tit[2] [tɪt] *n* **t. for tat** un prêté pour un rendu; **to give sb t. for tat** rendre à qn la monnaie de sa pièce

tit[3] [tɪt] *n very Fam* (*breast*) nichon *m*

titanic [taɪ'tænɪk] *adj* (*conflict, struggle*) titanesque

titanium [taɪ'teɪnɪəm] *n Chem* titane *m*

tit-for-tat [tɪtfə'tæt] *adj Fam* (*murder*) en représailles; **it's just t.** c'est un prêté pour un rendu

titillate ['tɪtɪleɪt] *vt* titiller

titillation [tɪtɪ'leɪʃən] *n* titillation *f*

title ['taɪtəl] **1** *n* titre *m*; **the titles** le générique; **t. deeds** titres de propriété; **t. fight** combat *m* comptant pour le titre; **t. page** page *f* de titre; **t. role** (*in play, movie*) rôle-titre *m*; **t. track** (*of album*) morceau *m* qui donne son titre à l'album
2 *vt* intituler

titled ['taɪtəld] *adj* (*person*) titré(e)

titleholder ['taɪtəlhəʊldə(r)] *n* (*in sport*) tenant(e) *m,f* du titre

titter ['tɪtə(r)] **1** *n* petit rire *m*
2 *vi* rire bêtement

tittle-tattle ['tɪtəltætəl] *Fam* **1** *n* potins *mpl*, cancans *mpl*
2 *vi* cancaner

titular ['tɪtjʊlə(r)] *adj* en titre

tizzy ['tɪzɪ] *n Fam* **to be in/to get into a t.** être/se mettre dans tous ses états

T-junction ['tiːdʒʌŋkʃən] *n* carrefour *m* en T

TLC [tiːel'siː] *n* (*abbr* **tender loving care**) affection *f*, tendresse *f*

TNT [tiːen'tiː] *n Chem* (*abbr* **trinitrotoluene**) TNT *m*

to [tuː, *unstressed* tə] **1** *prep* (**a**) (*toward*) à; **to go to church/school** aller à l'église/à l'école; **to go to France/Japan/the**

USA aller en France/au Japon/aux États-Unis; **to go to sb's house** aller chez qn; **to the left/right** à gauche/droite

(b) *(until)* jusqu'à; **it's ten to (six)** il est (six heures) moins dix; **to count to ten** compter jusqu'à dix; **a year to the day** un an jour pour jour

(c) *(expressing indirect object)* **to give sth to sb** donner qch à qn; **to speak to sb** parler à qn

(d) *(with result)* **to my surprise/joy** à ma grande surprise/joie; **to my horror, I discovered that…** et, horreur!, je découvris que…

(e) *(expressing proportion)* **six votes to four** six voix contre quatre; **there are two pounds to the dollar** un dollar vaut deux livres

2 *particle* **(a)** *(with infinitive)* **to go** aller; **to have things to do** avoir des choses à faire; **it's too hot to go out** il fait trop chaud pour sortir; **he came to help me** il est venu m'aider; **I want him to know** je veux qu'il sache; **she told me to stay** elle m'a dit de rester

(b) *(representing verb)* **I want/ought to** je veux/devrais le faire; **I was told to** on m'a dit de le faire

toad [təʊd] *n (animal)* crapaud *m*; *Fam Pej (man)* type *m* répugnant

toadstool [ˈtəʊdstuːl] *n* champignon *m* non comestible

toady [ˈtəʊdɪ] *Fam* **1** *n* lèche-bottes *mf inv*
2 *vi* **to t. to sb** lécher les bottes de qn

toast [təʊst] **1** *n* **(a)** *(toasted bread)* pain *m* grillé; **a slice** *or* **piece of t.** un toast; **t. rack** porte-toasts *m inv* **(b)** *(tribute)* toast *m*; **to drink a t. to sb/sth** porter un toast à qn/qch

2 *vt* **(a)** *(bread)* (faire) griller; **toasted cheese** fromage *m* fondu; **toasted sandwich** sandwich *m* grillé **(b)** *(tribute)* porter un toast à

toaster [ˈtəʊstə(r)] *n* grille-pain *m inv*

tobacco [təˈbækəʊ] *(pl* **tobaccos)** *n* tabac *m*; **t. pouch** blague *f* à tabac

tobacconist [təˈbækənɪst] *n* marchand(e) *m,f* de tabac

toboggan [təˈbɒɡən] **1** *n* luge *f*
2 *vi* faire de la luge

today [təˈdeɪ] *adv* aujourd'hui; **a week ago t.** il y a juste une semaine aujourd'hui; **a week from t.** aujourd'hui en huit; **t.'s date** la date d'aujourd'hui; **t.'s paper** le journal du jour

toddle [ˈtɒdəl] *vi (of infant)* commencer à marcher; *Fam* **to t. off** ficher le camp

toddler [ˈtɒdlə(r)] *n* tout-petit *m (qui fait ses premiers pas)*

to-die-for [təˈdaɪfɔː(r)] *adj Fam* craquant(e)

to-do [təˈduː] *n Fam* remue-ménage *m inv*; **what a t.!** quelle histoire!

toe [təʊ] **1** *n* **(a)** *(of foot)* orteil *m*, doigt *m* de pied; *(of sock, shoe)* bout *m*; **big/little t.** gros/petit orteil **(b)** *(idioms)* **to be on one's toes** être en alerte; **to keep sb on his/her toes** ne pas laisser de répit à qn; **to tread on sb's toes** marcher sur les pieds de qn

2 *vt* **to t. the line** bien se tenir

toehold [ˈtəʊhəʊld] *n (in climbing)* prise *f* de pied; *Fig* **to gain a t. in the market** mettre un pied sur le marché

toenail [ˈtəʊneɪl] *n* ongle *m* de pied

toffee [ˈtɒfɪ] *n* caramel *m* (au beurre)

tofu [ˈtəʊfuː] *n* tofu *m*

together [təˈɡeðə(r)] **1** *adv* ensemble; **t. with** ainsi que, en même temps que
2 *adj Fam (person)* équilibré(e)

togetherness [təˈɡeðənɪs] *n* unité *f*, harmonie *f*

toggle [ˈtɒɡəl] **1** *n (on coat)* olive *f*; *Comput & Elec* **t. switch** commande *f* à bascule
2 *vi Comput* basculer

Togo [ˈtəʊɡəʊ] *n* le Togo

Togolese [təʊɡəʊˈliːz] **1** *n* Togolais(e) *m,f*
2 *adj* togolais(e)

togs [tɒɡz] *npl Fam (clothes)* fringues *fpl*

toil [tɔɪl] **1** *n Lit* labeur *m*
2 *vi (work hard)* travailler dur; **to t. away at sth** peiner sur qch; **to t. up a hill** gravir péniblement une colline

toilet [ˈtɔɪlɪt] *n* **(a)** *(bathroom)* toilettes *fpl*; **to go to the t.** aller aux toilettes; **t. paper** papier *m* hygiénique; **t. roll** rouleau *m* de papier hygiénique; **t. seat** siège *m* des toilettes **(b)** *Old-fashioned (washing and dressing)* toilette *f*; **t. bag** trousse *f* de toilette; **t. soap** savon *m* de toilette

toiletries [ˈtɔɪlɪtrɪz] *npl* articles *mpl* de toilette

toilet-trained [ˈtɔɪlɪttreɪnd] *adj* propre

toilet-training [ˈtɔɪlɪttreɪnɪŋ] *n* apprentissage *m* de la propreté

token [ˈtəʊkən] **1** *n* **(a)** *(symbol)* signe *m*, marque *f*; **as a t. of respect** en signe de respect; **by the same t.** de même, pareillement **(b)** *(for vending machine)* jeton *m*
2 *adj (resistance, effort)* symbolique; *(gesture)* symbolique, pour la forme; **I was the t. woman on the committee** j'étais la seule femme de la commission, parce qu'il en fallait une

Tokyo [ˈtəʊkɪəʊ] *n* Tokyo

told [təʊld] *pt & pp of* **tell**

tolerable [ˈtɒlərəbəl] *adj* **(a)** *(bearable)* tolérable, supportable **(b)** *(reasonably good)* acceptable

tolerance [ˈtɒlərəns] *n* tolérance *f*; **to have a high/low t. for sth** bien/mal tolérer qch

tolerant [ˈtɒlərənt] *adj* tolérant(e); **to be t. of sb/sth** tolérer qn/qch

tolerate [ˈtɒləreɪt] *vt* tolérer

toleration [tɒləˈreɪʃən] *n* tolérance *f*

toll[1] [təʊl] *n* **(a)** *(charge)* péage *m*; **t. bridge** pont *m* à péage; **t. road** route *f* à péage **(b)** *(of dead, injured)* nombre *m* de victimes; *Fig* **to take its t.** faire des dégâts

toll[2] [təʊl] **1** *vt (bell)* sonner
2 *vi (of bell)* sonner

toll-free [təʊlˈfriː] **1** *adj* **t. number** ≃ numéro *m* vert
2 *adv (call)* gratuitement

Tom [tɒm] *n Fam* **any T., Dick or Harry** le premier venu

tom [tɒm] *n Fam* matou *m*

tomahawk [ˈtɒməhɔːk] *n* tomahawk *m*

tomato [təˈmeɪtəʊ] *(pl* **tomatoes)** *n* tomate *f*; **t. juice** jus *m* de tomate; **t. ketchup** ketchup *m*; **t. purée** concentré *m* de tomates; **t. sauce** *(for pasta)* sauce *f* tomate; *(ketchup)* ketchup *m*; **t. soup** soupe *f* à la tomate

tomb [tuːm] *n* tombe *f*

tomboy [ˈtɒmbɔɪ] *n* garçon *m* manqué

tombstone [ˈtuːmstəʊn] *n* pierre *f* tombale

tomcat [ˈtɒmkæt] *n* matou *m*

tome [təʊm] *n Formal* gros volume *m*

tomfoolery [tɒmˈfuːlərɪ] *n Fam* bêtises *fpl*

tomorrow [təˈmɒrəʊ] **1** *n* demain *m*; *Fam* **to do sth like there's no t.** faire qch frénétiquement
2 *adv* demain; **t. morning/evening** demain matin/soir

tom-tom [ˈtɒmtɒm] *n* tam-tam *m*

ton [tʌn] *n* **(a)** *(weight)* tonne *f* **(b)** *(idioms) Fam* **to weigh a t.** peser une tonne; *Fam* **tons of** des tonnes de; *Fam* **to come down on sb like a t. of bricks** tomber dessus à qn

tone [təʊn] *n* **(a)** *(of voice)* ton *m*; *(quality of sound)* sonorité *f*; **don't speak to me in that t. of voice** ne me parle pas sur ce ton; **leave your name and number after the t.** *(on answering machine)* laissez votre nom et votre numéro de téléphone après le signal sonore; *Fig* **it set the t. for the evening** et le ton a été donné pour le reste de la soirée; *Fig* **to raise/lower the t. of the neighborhood** améliorer/faire baisser le standing du quartier **(b)** *(color)* ton *m*

▶**tone down** *vt sep (color)* adoucir; *Fig (remarks)* modérer

▶**tone up** *vt sep (muscles)* raffermir, tonifier

tone-deaf [təʊn'def] *adj* **to be t.** ne pas avoir d'oreille

Tonga ['tɒŋgə] *n* les îles *fpl* Tonga

Tongan ['tɒŋgən] **1** *n* **(a)** *(person)* Tonguien(enne) *m,f* **(b)** *(language)* tongan *m*
    2 *adj* tonguien(enne)

tongs [tɒŋz] *npl* **(pair of) t.** pince *f*; **(curling) t.** *(for hair)* fer *m* à friser

tongue [tʌŋ] *n* **(a)** *(in mouth, of land, flame)* langue *f*; *(of shoe)* languette *f*; *(language)* langue *f*; **to stick one's t. out** tirer la langue; **t. twister** = mot ou phrase difficile à prononcer **(b)** *(idioms)* **hold your t.!** tiens ta langue!, tais-toi!; **have you lost your t.?** tu as perdu ta langue?; **to say sth t. in cheek** dire qch en plaisantant

tongue-tied ['tʌŋtaɪd] *adj* muet(ette)

tonic ['tɒnɪk] *n also Fig* tonique *m*, remontant *m*; **t. (water)** Schweppes® *m*

tonight [tə'naɪt] **1** *n (evening)* ce soir *m*; *(night)* cette nuit *f*
    2 *adv (evening)* ce soir; *(night)* cette nuit

tonnage ['tʌnɪdʒ] *n Naut (of ship)* tonnage *m*

tonne [tʌn] *n* tonne *f*

tonsil ['tɒnsəl] *n* amygdale *f*; **to have one's tonsils out** se faire opérer des amygdales

tonsillitis [tɒnsɪ'laɪtɪs] *n* amygdalite *f*; **to have t.** avoir une amygdalite

too [tuː] *adv* **(a)** *(excessively)* trop; **t. many people** trop de gens; **I know her all** *or* **only t. well** je ne la connais que trop; **you're t. kind** vous êtes trop aimable; **he's not t. well today** il ne va pas trop bien aujourd'hui; **t. bad** tant pis **(b)** *(also)* aussi **(c)** *(moreover)* en plus **(d)** *Fam (indeed)* **I never said that! – you did t.!** je n'ai jamais dit ça! – si, tu l'as dit!

took [tʊk] *pt of* **take**

tool [tuːl] *n* **(a)** *(implement)* outil *m*; **(set of) tools** outillage *m*; **t. bag** trousse *f* à outils; *Comput* **t. bar** barre *f* d'outils; *also Comput* **t. box** boîte *f* à outils; **t. kit** trousse *f* à outils; **t. shed** remise *f* **(b)** *(means, instrument)* instrument *m*

toot [tuːt] **1** *n* coup *m* de Klaxon®
    2 *vt* **to t. the horn** klaxonner; **to t. sb** klaxonner qn; *Fig* **to t. one's own horn** se vanter
    3 *vi* klaxonner

tooth [tuːθ] *(pl* **teeth** [tiːθ]*)* *n* **(a)** *(of person, saw, comb)* dent *f*; **to cut a t.** percer une dent; **t. decay** carie *f* **(b)** *(idioms)* **to fight t. and nail** se défendre bec et ongles; **to lie through one's teeth** mentir effrontément; **in the teeth of opposition** malgré l'opposition; **armed to the teeth** armé(e) jusqu'aux dents; *Fam* **to get one's teeth into sth** se mettre à fond dans qch; *Fam* **to be long in the t.** n'être plus tout jeune

toothache ['tuːθeɪk] *n* mal *m* de dents; **to have a t.** avoir mal aux dents

toothbrush ['tuːθbrʌʃ] *n* brosse *f* à dents

toothless ['tuːθlɪs] *adj* édenté(e), sans dents; *Fig (powerless)* sans pouvoir

toothpaste ['tuːθpeɪst] *n* dentifrice *m*

toothpick ['tuːθpɪk] *n* cure-dents *m inv*

toothy ['tuːθɪ] *adj* **t. grin** large sourire *m*

top¹ [tɒp] *n (toy)* toupie *f*

top² [tɒp] **1** *n* **(a)** *(highest part)* *(of tree, mountain, tower, head)* sommet *m*; *(of page, map)* haut *m*; **at the t. of the stairs/street** en haut des escaliers/de la rue; **to be (at the) t. of the class** être premier(ère) de la classe; **from t. to bottom** de haut en bas; *Fig* de fond en comble; **at the t. of one's voice** à tue-tête; **to go over the t.** *Mil* partir à l'assaut; *Fig* aller trop loin; *Fig* **over the t.** *(excessive)* exagéré(e); **to make it to the t.** parvenir au sommet; *Fig* réussir
    (b) *(lid)* *(of box)* couvercle *m*; *(of bottle)* bouchon *m*; *(of pen)* capuchon *m*
    (c) *(surface)* dessus *m*
    (d) *(garment)* haut *m*

(e) **on t.** dessus; **on t. of** sur; *Fig* **to be on t. of sth** maîtriser qch; **you mustn't let things get on t. of you** il ne faut pas te laisser dépasser par les événements; *Fig* **to come out on t.** prendre le dessus; **to feel on t. of the world** se sentir en pleine forme
    2 *adj* **(a)** *(highest)* *(shelf, drawer)* du haut; *(floor)* dernier(ère); **the t. people** *(in society)* les gens *mpl* en vue; *(in an organization)* la direction *f*; *Fam* **the t. brass** les gros bonnets *mpl*; **t. coat** *(of paint)* dernière couche *f*; **t. deck** *(of bus)* impériale *f*; *Fam Fig* **t. dog** chef *m*; **to feel in t. form** se sentir en pleine forme; **t. hat** haut-de-forme *m*; **t. security** haute sécurité *f*; **t. speed** vitesse *f* de pointe; *Fig* **at t. speed** à toute vitesse
    (b) *(best, major)* premier(ère); **the t. ten** les dix premiers
    3 *vt (pt & pp* **topped***)* **(a)** *(place on top of)* couvrir (**with** de); *(cake, ice-cream)* napper; **and to t. it all** et pour couronner le tout
    (b) *(exceed)* dépasser
    (c) *(be at the top of)* être en tête de; **to t. the bill** être la tête d'affiche

▶ **top off** *vt sep (glass, tank)* remplir; *(sum of money)* compléter

top-heavy [tɒp'hevɪ] *adj (structure)* trop lourd(e) du haut, déséquilibré(e); *Fig (organization)* aux dirigeants trop nombreux

topic ['tɒpɪk] *n* sujet *m*, thème *m*

topical ['tɒpɪkəl] *adj* d'actualité

topless ['tɒplɪs] *adj (woman)* aux seins nus; **to go t.** faire du monokini

top-level ['tɒplevəl] *adj* au plus haut niveau

topmost ['tɒpməʊst] *adj* le (la) plus haut(e)

top-notch ['tɒpnɒtʃ] *adj Fam* de première classe

topography [tə'pɒgrəfɪ] *n* topographie *f*

topping ['tɒpɪŋ] *n (for pizza)* garniture *f*; *(for cake, ice-cream)* nappage *m*

topple ['tɒpəl] **1** *vt* faire tomber, renverser
    2 *vi* tomber

top-quality ['tɒpkwɒlətɪ] *adj* de qualité supérieure

top-secret ['tɒpsiːkrɪt] *adj* top secret(ète)

topsoil ['tɒpsɔɪl] *n* couche *f* arable

topsy-turvy [tɒpsɪ'tɜːvɪ] *Fam* **1** *adj (untidy)* sens dessus dessous; *(confused)* tordu(e)
    2 *adv (untidily)* sens dessus dessous

torch [tɔːtʃ] **1** *n* torche *f*; *Fig* **to carry a t. for sb** aimer qn secrètement
    2 *vt* incendier, mettre le feu à

torchlight ['tɔːtʃlaɪt] *n* **by t.** à la lumière d'une torche; **t. procession** retraite *f* aux flambeaux

tore [tɔː] *pt of* **tear²**

torment 1 *n* ['tɔːment] supplice *m*; **to be in t.** être au supplice
    2 *vt* [tɔː'ment] tourmenter

tormentor [tɔː'mentə(r)] *n* bourreau *m*

torn [tɔːn] *pp of* **tear²**

tornado [tɔː'neɪdəʊ] *n* tornade *f*

Toronto [tə'rɒntəʊ] *n* Toronto

torpedo [tɔː'piːdəʊ] **1** *n (pl* **torpedoes***)* torpille *f*; **t. boat** torpilleur *m*, vedette *f* lance-torpilles
    2 *vt also Fig* torpiller

torpid ['tɔːpɪd] *adj* engourdi(e), léthargique

torpor ['tɔːpə(r)] *n* torpeur *f*

torrent ['tɒrənt] *n* torrent *m*; *Fig (of abuse, insults)* flot *m*; **it's raining in torrents** il pleut à torrents

torrential [tə'renʃəl] *adj* torrentiel(elle)

torrid ['tɒrɪd] *adj also Fig* torride

torso ['tɔːsəʊ] *(pl* **torsos***)* *n* torse *m*

tortoise ['tɔːtəs] *n* tortue *f*

tortoiseshell ['tɔːtəsʃel] *n* écaille *f* (de tortue); **t. (cat)** chat *m* noir, blanc et roux

tortuous ['tɔːtjʊəs] *adj* tortueux(euse)

torture ['tɔːtʃə(r)] **1** *n* torture *f*; *Fig* **it was sheer t.!** c'était un vrai supplice!; **t. chamber** chambre *f* de torture
    2 *vt also Fig* torturer

Tory ['tɔːrɪ] (*pl* **Tories**) *n & adj Pol (in Great Britain)* Tory *m*, conservateur(trice) *m,f*

toss [tɒs] **1** *n (of ball)* lancer *m*; *(of head)* mouvement *m* brusque; **to decide sth on the t. of a coin** décider qch à pile ou face; **to argue the t.** discuter inutilement
    2 *vt (throw)* lancer; *(pancake)* faire sauter; *(salad)* remuer; **to t. sth to sb** lancer qch à qn; **to t. a coin** jouer à pile ou face; **to t. one's head** rejeter la tête en arrière; **the ship was tossed by the sea** le bateau était ballotté par la mer
    3 *vi* **to t. (up) for sth** jouer qch à pile ou face; **to t. and turn** *(in bed)* se tourner et se retourner *(pour trouver le sommeil)*
▸**toss about, toss around** *vt sep (ship)* ballotter; *Fig (idea)* lancer
▸**toss off** *vt sep (write)* expédier
▸**toss out** *vt sep* jeter

toss-up ['tɒsʌp] *n* **to have a t.** jouer à pile ou face; *Fam* **it was a t. between the restaurant and the movies** nous n'arrivions pas à nous décider entre le resto et le cinéma; **it's a t. whether or not she'll say yes** je ne sais vraiment pas si elle va dire oui

tot [tɒt] *n* **(a)** *(child)* tout-petit *m* **(b)** *(of drink)* (petite) goutte *f*
▸**tot up** *(pt & pp* **totted**) *vt sep* additionner

total ['təʊtəl] **1** *n* total *m*; **in t.** au total
    2 *adj* total(e); **t. eclipse** éclipse *f* totale
    3 *vt* **(a)** *(sum)* se monter à **(b)** *Fam (wreck)* bousiller

totalitarian [təʊtælɪ'teərɪən] *adj* totalitaire

totality [təʊ'tælɪtɪ] *n* totalité *f*

totally ['təʊtəlɪ] *adv* totalement

tote¹ [təʊt] *n (in betting)* totalisateur *m*, totaliseur *m*

tote² [təʊt] **1** *n* **t. (bag)** grand sac *m*, fourre-tout *m inv*
    2 *vt Fam (carry)* trimbal(l)er

totem pole ['təʊtəm'pəʊl] *n* totem *m*

totter ['tɒtə(r)] *vi also Fig* chanceler; **to t. in/out** entrer/sortir d'un pas chancelant

toucan ['tuːkæn] *n* toucan *m*

touch [tʌtʃ] **1** *n* **(a)** *(act of touching)* toucher *m*, contact *m*; **I felt a t. on my arm** j'ai senti qu'on me touchait le bras; **it was t. and go whether...** il n'était pas certain que... + *subjunctive*
    (b) *(sense)* toucher *m*; *(feel)* contact *m*; **hard/soft to the t.** dur/doux au toucher; **he's lost his t.** il a perdu la main
    (c) *(detail)* **there were some nice touches in the movie** il y avait quelques bons passages dans le film
    (d) *(small amount)* pointe *f*; **a t. (too) strong/short** un peu trop fort(e)/court(e); **to have a t. of flu** être un peu grippé(e)
    (e) *(communication)* **to be/to get in t. with sb** être/se mettre en contact avec qn; **to stay in/to lose t. with sb** rester en/perdre contact avec qn
    2 *vt (physically, emotionally)* toucher; *(interfere with)* toucher à; **to t. bottom** *(of ship, economy)* toucher le fond; **I never t. alcohol** je ne touche jamais à l'alcool; **you haven't touched your meal** tu n'as pas touché à ton repas; **the law can't t. her** la loi ne peut rien contre elle; *Fig* **there's nothing to t. it** c'est sans égal; **there's nothing to t. her** elle est imbattable
▸**touch down** *vi (of plane)* atterrir
▸**touch on** *vt insep* aborder
▸**touch up** *vt sep (picture)* retoucher

touchdown ['tʌtʃdaʊn] *n* **(a)** *(of plane)* atterrissage *m* **(b)** *(in football)* but *m*

touched [tʌtʃt] *adj* **(a)** *(moved)* touché(e), ému(e) **(b)** *Fam (mad)* toqué(e)

touching ['tʌtʃɪŋ] *adj (moving)* touchant(e), émouvant(e)

touchline ['tʌtʃlaɪn] *n* ligne *f* de touche

touch-sensitive screen ['tʌtʃ'sensɪtɪv'skriːn] *n Comput* écran *m* tactile

touchstone ['tʌtʃstəʊn] *n* pierre *f* de touche

touch-tone ['tʌtʃtəʊn] *adj (telephone)* à touches

touch-type ['tʌtʃtaɪp] *vi* taper au toucher

touch-typing ['tʌtʃtaɪpɪŋ] *n* dactylographie *f* au toucher

touchy ['tʌtʃɪ] *adj (subject)* délicat(e); *(person)* susceptible (**about** à propos de)

touchy-feely ['tʌtʃɪ'fiːlɪ] *adj Fam Pej* qui affectionne les contacts physiques

tough [tʌf] **1** *adj* **(a)** *(strict, severe)* dur(e); *(resistant)* résistant(e), solide; *Fam* **a t. guy** un dur à cuire; **to get t. (with sb)** se montrer plus sévère (avec qn) **(b)** *(difficult)* dur(e), difficile; *(unfair)* dur(e); *Fam* **t. luck!** pas de chance!; *Ironic* tant pis!
    2 *adv* **to act t.** jouer au dur
    3 *n* dur(e) *m,f*

toughen ['tʌfən] *vt (person, skin)* endurcir; *(penalties, conditions)* durcir; **toughened glass** verre *m* trempé

toughness ['tʌfnɪs] *n (of meat, skin, conditions)* dureté *f*; *(of task)* difficulté *f*; *(of person) (strength)* force *f*; *(hardness)* dureté *f*

toupee ['tuːpeɪ] *n* postiche *m*

tour [tʊə(r)] **1** *n (by tourist)* voyage *m*; *(of building, town)* visite *f*; *(by pop group, theater company)* tournée *f*; **to go on a t.** *(of tourist)* faire un voyage organisé; **to go on t.** *(of pop group, theater company)* partir en tournée; *Mil* **t. of duty** service *m*; **t. of inspection** tournée *f* d'inspection; **t. guide** *(person)* guide *mf*; **t. operator** voyagiste *m*
    2 *vt (country, hospital)* visiter; *(of pop group, theater company)* être en tournée à/en
    3 *vi (of tourist)* faire du tourisme, voyager; *(of pop group, theater company)* être en tournée

tour de force ['tʊədə'fɔːs] *n* tour *m* de force

tourism ['tʊərɪzəm] *n* tourisme *m*

tourist ['tʊərɪst] *n* touriste *mf*; **t. attraction** site *m* touristique; **t. class** classe *f* touriste; **t. (information) office** syndicat *m* d'initiative, office *m* du tourisme; *Fam* **t. trap** piège *m* à touristes

tournament ['tʊənəmənt] *n* tournoi *m*

tourniquet ['tʊənɪkeɪ] *n Med* garrot *m*

tousle ['taʊzəl] *vt* ébouriffer

tout [taʊt] **1** *n (soliciting business)* rabatteur(euse) *m,f*; **(ticket) t.** revendeur(euse) *m,f* de billets *(au marché noir)*
    2 *vi* **to t. for trade** *or* **custom** racoler des clients

tow [təʊ] **1** *n* **to give sb a t.** remorquer qn; **on t.** en remorque; *Fam* **to have someone in t.** avoir qn dans son sillage; **t. truck** dépanneuse *f*
    2 *vt* remorquer
▸**tow away** *vt sep* **to t. a car away** remorquer une voiture; *(of police)* emmener une voiture à la fourrière

toward [tə'wɔːd], **towards** [tə'wɔːdz] *prep* **(a)** *(in space, time)* vers **(b)** *(directed at) (of feelings, behavior)* envers **(c)** *(contributing to)* **to contribute t. the cost of sth** participer au coût de qch; **15% of the budget will go t. improving safety** 15% du budget sera destiné à l'amélioration de la sécurité

towaway zone ['təʊəweɪzəʊn] *n* = zone de ramassage des véhicules en infraction

towbar ['təʊbɑː(r)] *n* barre *f* de remorquage

towel ['taʊəl] **1** *n* serviette *f* (de toilette); **t. rack** porte-serviette *m*
    2 *vt* **to t. oneself (dry)** se sécher, s'essuyer

toweling ['taʊəlɪŋ] *n* tissu-éponge *m*

tower ['taʊə(r)] **1** *n* tour *f*; *Fig* **a t. of strength** un roc; *Comput* **t. system** tour
    2 *vi* **to t. over sb/sth** dominer qn/qch

towering ['taʊərɪŋ] *adj* immense

town [taʊn] *n* ville *f*; **to go into t.** aller en ville; **to go out on the t.** faire la fête en ville; *Fam Fig* **to go to t. (on sth)** mettre le paquet (sur qch); **t. center** centre-ville *m*; **t. clerk** secrétaire *mf* de mairie; **t. hall** mairie *f*

townsfolk ['taʊnzfəʊk] *npl* citadins *mpl*

township ['taʊnʃɪp] *n (in North America)* municipalité *f; (in South Africa)* township *f*

townspeople ['taʊnzpiːpəl] *npl* citadins *mpl*

towpath ['təʊpɑːθ] *n* chemin *m* de halage

towrope ['təʊrəʊp] *n* câble *m* de remorque

toxic ['tɒksɪk] *adj* toxique

toxin ['tɒksɪn] *n* toxine *f*

toy [tɔɪ] **1** *n* jouet *m*; **t. soldier** petit soldat *m*; **t. store** magasin *m* de jouets; **t. train** train *m* miniature

2 *vi* **to t. with sb** jouer avec qn; **to t. with an idea** caresser une idée; **to t. with sb's affections** jouer avec les sentiments de qn

toyboy ['tɔɪbɔɪ] *n Fam* jeune amant *m (d'une femme plus âgée)*

trace [treɪs] **1** *n* trace *f*; **without t.** sans laisser de traces; *Chem* **t. element** oligo-élément *m*

2 *vt* (**a**) *(diagram, picture)* tracer (**b**) *(person)* retrouver (la trace de); *(development, history)* retracer

trachea [trə'kiːə] *(pl* **tracheae** [trə'kiːɪ]*) n Anat* trachée *f*

track [træk] **1** *n* (**a**) *(mark)* trace *f*; *(trail)* piste *f*
(**b**) *(path)* piste *f*, chemin *m*; *(in athletics)* piste *f*; *Sport* **t. and field** athlétisme *m*; **t.-and-field events** épreuves *fpl* d'athlétisme; *Fig* **t. record** passé *m*; **t. shoes** chaussures *fpl* d'athlétisme
(**c**) *(on record, CD)* morceau *m*, titre *m*
(**d**) *(of tank, tractor)* chenille *f*
(**e**) *(railroad line)* voie *f*
(**f**) *(idioms)* **to be on the right t.** être sur la bonne voie; **to keep t. of sth** surveiller qch; **to lose t. of sb** perdre qn de vue; **I've lost t. of how much money I've spent** je ne sais plus combien d'argent j'ai dépensé; **to stop sb in his/her tracks** stopper qn net; *Fam* **to make tracks** filer, mettre les voiles

2 *vt (animal)* suivre à la trace; *(missile)* suivre la trajectoire de; *(person)* traquer

▸**track down** *vt sep (locate)* trouver

tracked [trækt] *adj (vehicle)* chenillé(e)

tracker dog ['trækə'dɒg] *n* chien *m* policier

tracksuit ['træksuːt] *n* survêtement *m*; **t. top** veste *f* de survêtement; **t. pants** *or* **bottoms** pantalon *m* de survêtement

tract¹ [trækt] *n* (**a**) *(of land)* étendue *f* (**b**) *Anat (respiratory, digestive)* appareil *m*

tract² [trækt] *n (pamphlet)* tract *m*

tractable ['træktəbəl] *adj (person, animal)* docile

traction ['trækʃən] *n (force)* traction *f*; *Med* **to be in t.** être en extension; **t. engine** locomobile *f*; *Fam Fig* **to get t.** *(move forward)* avancer, progresser; **to get t. on sth** *(push it forward)* faire avancer qch

tractor ['træktə(r)] *n (vehicle)* tracteur *m*; *Comput* **t. feed** alimentation *f* par entraînement

trade [treɪd] **1** *n* (**a**) *Com (commerce)* commerce *m*; **t. association** association *f* professionnelle; **t. deficit** déficit *m* commercial; **t. discount** remise *f* professionnelle; **t. embargo** embargo *m* commercial; **t. fair** foire *f ou* exposition *f* commerciale; **t. gap** déficit commercial; **t. name** *(of product)* nom *m* de marque; *(of firm)* raison *f* commerciale; *also Fig* **t. secret** secret *m* de fabrication; *Geog* **t. winds** alizés *mpl* (**b**) *(swap)* échange *m*; **to do a t.** faire un échange (**c**) *(profession)* métier *m*; **he's a plumber by t.** il est plombier (de son métier); **t. union** syndicat *m*; **t. unionist** syndicaliste *mf*

2 *vt* **to t. sth (for sth)** échanger qch (contre qch); **to t. places with sb** changer de place avec qn; **to t. insults/ blows** échanger des insultes/coups

3 *vi* commercer, faire du commerce

▸**trade in** *vt sep* faire reprendre; **I traded my car in for a new one** ils ont repris ma vieille voiture quand j'ai acheté la nouvelle

▸**trade on** *vt insep (exploit)* profiter de

trade-in ['treɪdɪn] *n* reprise *f*

trademark ['treɪdmɑːk] *n* marque *f (de fabrique)*; *Fig* signe *m* distinctif

trade-off ['treɪdɒf] *n* compromis *m*

trader ['treɪdə(r)] *n* commerçant(e) *m,f*, marchand(e) *m,f; (on stock exchange)* opérateur(trice) *m,f*

tradesman ['treɪdzmən] *n* commerçant(e) *m,f*

trading ['treɪdɪŋ] *n* **t. partner** partenaire *m* commercial; **t. post** comptoir *m* commercial; **t. stamp** timbre-prime *m*

tradition [trə'dɪʃən] *n* tradition *f*

traditional [trə'dɪʃənəl] *adj* traditionnel(elle)

traditionalist [trə'dɪʃənəlɪst] *n & adj* traditionaliste *mf*

traffic ['træfɪk] **1** *n* (**a**) *(vehicles)* circulation *f*, trafic *m*; **t. circle** rond-point *m*; **t. cone** cône *m* de signalisation; *Fam* **t. cop** agent *m* de la circulation; **t. island** refuge *m*; **t. jam** embouteillage *m*; **t. lights** feux *mpl* (tricolores *ou* de signalisation); **t. police** police *f* de la route (**b**) *(trade)* trafic *m*

2 *vt* faire le trafic de

3 *vi* faire du trafic (**in** de)

trafficker ['træfɪkə(r)] *n* trafiquant(e) *m,f*

tragedy ['trædʒɪdɪ] *n* tragédie *f*

tragic ['trædʒɪk] *adj* tragique

tragically ['trædʒɪkəlɪ] *adv* tragiquement

trail [treɪl] **1** *n* (**a**) *(of smoke, blood)* traînée *f*; **to be on the t. of sb/sth** être sur les traces *ou* la piste de qn/qch (**b**) *(path)* sentier *m*, piste *f*; **t. bike** moto *f* de cross

2 *vt (drag)* traîner

3 *vi* (**a**) *(drag)* traîner (**b**) *(move slowly)* se traîner (**c**) *(in sport, contest)* être mené(e); **to be trailing (behind)** être mené(e)

▸**trail away, trail off** *vi (of voice)* se taire; *(of sound)* s'arrêter

trailblazer ['treɪlbleɪzə(r)] *n* pionnier(ère) *m,f*

trailer ['treɪlə(r)] *n* (**a**) *(vehicle)* remorque *f; (caravan)* camping-car *m*; **t. park** = terrain aménagé pour les camping-cars; *Fam Pej* **t. trash** prolos *mpl* (qui vivent dans les caravanes) (**b**) *(for movie, TV program)* bande-annonce *f*

train [treɪn] **1** *n* (**a**) *(means of transport)* train *m* (**b**) *(series)* suite *f*, enchaînement *m*; **t. of thought** enchaînement d'idées (**c**) *(retinue)* suite *f* (**d**) *(of dress)* traîne *f*

2 *vt* (**a**) *(person)* former; *(animal)* dresser; **to t. sb for sth/to do sth** former qn à qch/à faire qch (**b**) *(gun, telescope)* braquer (**on** sur)

3 *vi (of athlete, soldier)* s'entraîner; **to t. as a nurse/teacher** suivre une formation d'infirmière/de professeur

trained [treɪnd] *adj* (**a**) *(animal)* dressé(e) (**b**) *(teacher, nurse)* diplômé(e) (**c**) *(eye, ear)* exercé(e)

trainee [treɪ'niː] *n* stagiaire *mf*

traineeship [treɪ'niːʃɪp] *n* stage *m*

trainer ['treɪnə(r)] *n* (**a**) *(of athlete, team, racehorse)* entraîneur *m; (of animals)* dresseur(euse) *m,f* (**b**) *(shoe)* chaussure *f* de sport (**c**) **t. (aircraft)** avion-école *m*

training ['treɪnɪŋ] *n (in sports)* entraînement *m; (for job)* formation *f*; **to be in t. (for)** *(of athlete, team)* s'entraîner (pour); **to be out of t.** manquer d'entraînement; **t. course** stage *m* (de formation); **t. officer** officier *m* instructeur

trainload ['treɪnləʊd] *n* **a t. of** un train plein de

traipse [treɪps] *vi Fam* traîner

trait [treɪt] *n* trait *m* (de caractère)

traitor ['treɪtə(r)] *n* traître(esse) *m,f*

trajectory [trə'dʒektərɪ] *n* trajectoire *f*

tram [træm] *n* tramway *m*

tramp [træmp] **1** *n* (**a**) *(vagabond)* clochard(e) *m,f* (**b**) *very Fam (immoral woman)* traînée *f* (**c**) **t. (steamer)** tramp *m* (**d**) *(walk)* promenade *f*

2 *vt (country)* arpenter, parcourir; **to t. the streets** battre le pavé

3 *vi* marcher (d'un pas lourd)

trample ['træmpəl] **1** vt piétiner; **to t. sth underfoot** fouler qch aux pieds

2 vi **to t. on sb/sth** piétiner qn/qch

trampoline [træmpə'liːn] n trampoline m

trance [trɑːns] n transe f; **to go into a t.** entrer ou se mettre en transe

tranquil ['træŋkwɪl] adj tranquille, calme

tranquility [træŋ'kwɪlɪtɪ] n tranquillité f, calme m

tranquilizer, tranquillizer ['træŋkwɪlaɪzə(r)] n tranquillisant m, calmant m

transaction [træn'zækʃən] n transaction f, opération f

transatlantic [trænzət'læntɪk] adj transatlantique

transcend [træn'send] vt (go beyond) transcender; (be superior to) surpasser

transcendental [trænsen'dentəl] adj transcendantal(e); **t. meditation** méditation f transcendantale

transcontinental [trænzkɒntɪ'nentəl] adj transcontinental(e)

transcribe [træns'kraɪb] vt transcrire

transcript ['trænskrɪpt] n transcription f

transcription [træns'krɪpʃən] n transcription f

transfer 1 n ['trænsfɜː(r)] (move) transfert m; (of employee) mutation f; (of power) passation f; **t. fee** (for sports player) prime f de transfert; **t. lounge** (in airport) salle f de transit; **t. passenger** passager m en transit; Comput **t. speed** vitesse f de transfert

2 vt [træns'fɜː(r)] (pt & pp **transferred**) transférer; (employee) muter; (attention, affection) déplacer

3 vi [træns'fɜː(r)] être transféré(e) (**to** dans); (between planes, trains) changer

transferable [træns'fɜːrəbəl] adj transmissible; **not t.** (on ticket) titre de transport nominal

transfigure [træns'fɪɡə(r)] vt transfigurer

transfix [træns'fɪks] vt transpercer; Fig **to be transfixed with fear** être pétrifié(e) par la peur

transform [træns'fɔːm] vt transformer (**into** en)

transformation [trænsfə'meɪʃən] n transformation f

transformer [træns'fɔːmə(r)] n Elec transformateur m

transfusion [træns'fjuːʒən] n (blood) **t.** transfusion f (sanguine)

transgender [træns'dʒendə(r)] **1** n transsexuel(elle) m,f

2 adj transsexuel(elle)

transgenic [trænz'dʒenɪk] adj transgénique

transgress [trænz'gres] Formal **1** vt (law) transgresser, enfreindre

2 vi (violate law) transgresser la loi; (sin) pécher

transient ['trænzɪənt] adj éphémère

transistor [træn'zɪstə(r)] n Elec transistor m; **t. (radio)** transistor m

transit ['trænzɪt] n transit m; **in t.** en transit; **t. camp** camp m de transit; **t. system** transports mpl en commun; **t. visa** visa m de transit

transition [træn'zɪʃən] n transition f; **the t. from sth to sth** le passage de qch à qch

transitional [træn'zɪʃənəl] adj transitoire, de transition

transitive ['trænzɪtɪv] adj Gram transitif(ive)

transitory ['trænsɪtərɪ] adj transitoire

translate [trænz'leɪt] **1** vt traduire (**from/into** de/en); Fig **to t. one's ideas into action** mettre ses idées en pratique

2 vi (of person) faire de la traduction; (of word, expression) se traduire (**as** par)

translation [trænz'leɪʃən] n (of language) traduction f

translator [trænz'leɪtə(r)] n traducteur(trice) m,f

transliterate [trænz'lɪtəreɪt] vt transcrire

translucent [trænz'luːsənt] adj translucide

transmission [trænz'mɪʃən] n (action) transmission f; (TV, radio program) émission f; Aut transmission f; **t. shaft** (in vehicle) arbre m de transmission

transmit [trænz'mɪt] vt transmettre; (TV, radio program) diffuser

transmitter [trænz'mɪtə(r)] n (emitter) émetteur m; (relay station) réémetteur m

transparent [træns'pærənt] adj (a) (see-through) transparent(e) (b) (obvious) évident(e)

transpire [træns'paɪə(r)] **1** vt (become apparent) **it transpired that...** il s'est avéré que...; **she transpired to be...** elle s'est avérée être...

2 vi (happen) arriver, se passer

transplant 1 n ['trænsplɑːnt] (of organ) transplantation f, greffe f

2 vt [træns'plɑːnt] (a) (organ) transplanter, greffer (b) (population) transplanter

transport 1 n ['trænspɔːt] transport m

2 vt [træns'pɔːt] transporter

transportation [trænspɔː'teɪʃən] n transport m; Hist (as punishment) transportation f

transporter [træns'pɔːtə(r)] n (vehicle) camion m pour transport d'automobiles

transpose [træns'pəʊz] vt transposer

transsexual [træn(z)'seksjʊəl] **1** n transsexuel(elle) m,f

2 adj transsexuel(elle)

Transvaal ['trænzvɑːl] n **the T.** le Transvaal

transverse ['trænzvɜːs] adj transversal(e)

transvestite [trænz'vestaɪt] n travesti m

trap [træp] **1** n (a) (in hunting) & Fig piège m; **to set a t.** tendre un piège; Fig **to walk** or **to fall straight into the t.** tomber en plein dans le piège (b) very Fam (mouth) gueule f; **shut your t.!** ta gueule!

2 vt (pt & pp **trapped**) piéger, prendre au piège; **to t. sb into saying/doing sth** faire dire/faire faire qch à qn en usant de ruse

trapdoor [træp'dɔː(r)] n trappe f

trapeze [trə'piːz] n trapèze m; **t. artist** trapéziste mf

trapper ['træpə(r)] n trappeur m

trappings ['træpɪŋz] npl signes mpl extérieurs

trash [træʃ] **1** n (a) (worthless objects) camelote f; Fam **that book/movie is a load of t.** ce livre/film est nul (b) (refuse) ordures fpl; **t. can** poubelle f

2 vt Fam (a) (vandalize) saccager (b) (criticize) descendre en flammes

trashy ['træʃɪ] adj Fam à la noix

trauma ['trɔːmə] n traumatisme m

traumatic [trɔː'mætɪk] adj traumatisant(e)

traumatize ['trɔːmətaɪz] vt traumatiser

travail ['træveɪl] n Lit labeur m

travel ['trævəl] **1** n voyage m; **on my travels** au cours de mes voyages; **I spend half my money on t.** (to and from work) la moitié de mon argent part dans les transports; **t. agency** agence f de voyages; **t. agent** agent m de voyages; **t. documents** titre m de transport; **t. insurance** assurance-voyage f; **t. writer** auteur m de récits de voyage

2 vt (road, country) parcourir

3 vi (a) (of person) voyager; (vehicle, of light, sound, electricity) se déplacer; **we traveled across France by train** nous avons traversé la France en train; **wine doesn't t. well** le vin supporte mal d'être transporté; Fam **(good) news travels fast** les nouvelles vont vite

traveler ['trævələ(r)] n voyageur(euse) m,f; **t.'s check** chèque m de voyage

traveling ['trævəlɪŋ] **1** n déplacement m; **t. bag** sac m de voyage; **t. companion** compagnon m de voyage; **t. expenses** frais mpl de déplacement

2 adj (performer, circus) itinérant(e); **t. salesman** voyageur m de commerce

traverse [trə'vɜːs] *vt Lit* traverser

travesty ['trævəstɪ] *n* travestissement *m*; **t. of justice** simulacre *m* de justice

trawl [trɔːl] **1** *n* **(a)** *(net)* chalut *m* **(b)** *Fig (search)* **to carry out** *or* **to make a t. through sth** passer qch au crible

2 *vt* **(a)** *(sea)* aller à la pêche au chalut en **(b)** *Fig (search through)* passer au crible

3 *vi* **(a)** *(fish)* pêcher au chalut **(b)** *Fig* **to t. through sth** passer qch au crible

trawler ['trɔːlə(r)] *n (ship)* chalutier *m*

tray [treɪ] *n* plateau *m*; *(in office)* corbeille *f*

treacherous ['tretʃərəs] *adj* traître

treachery ['tretʃərɪ] *n* traîtrise *f*

treacle [triːkəl] *n* mélasse *f*

tread [tred] **1** *vt* (*pt* **trod** [trɒd], *pp* **trodden** ['trɒdən]) marcher sur; **to t. sth underfoot** fouler qch aux pieds; **to t. sth into the carpet** mettre qch sur le tapis (avec ses chaussures); **to t. the boards** *(appear on stage)* monter sur les planches; **to t. grapes** fouler le raisin; **to t. water** faire du surplace; *Fig (of company)* se maintenir à flot

2 *vi* marcher (**on** sur); *also Fig* **to t. on sb's toes** marcher sur les pieds de qn; *Fig* **to t. carefully** *or* **warily** y aller doucement

3 *n* **(a)** *(sound of footstep)* pas *m* **(b)** *(of tire)* chape *f*

treadmill ['tredmɪl] *n (in gym)* tapis *m* roulant de jogging; *Hist (in prison)* = roue ou manège auxquels étaient attachés les prisonniers; *Fig (routine)* routine *f*

treason ['triːzən] *n* trahison *f*

treasonable ['triːzənəbəl] *adj* qui constitue un acte de trahison

treasure ['treʒə(r)] **1** *n also Fig* trésor *m*; **t. hunt** chasse *f* au trésor; **t. trove** *Law* trésor *m*; *Fig* mine *f*

2 *vt (person, possession)* tenir beaucoup à; *(memory)* chérir

treasurer ['treʒərə(r)] *n* trésorier(ère) *m,f*

treasury ['treʒərɪ] (*pl* **treasuries**) *n* trésorerie *f*; **the T.** *(government department)* ≃ le ministère des Finances; *Fin* **t. bond** ≃ bon *m* du Trésor

treat [triːt] **1** *n (pleasure)* plaisir *m*; *(gift)* cadeau *m*; **to give sb a t.** faire plaisir à qn; **it's my t.** *(I'm paying)* c'est moi qui régale; *also Ironic* **you've got a real t. in store** attends-toi à une belle surprise

2 *vt* **(a)** *(person, illness, metal)* traiter; **to t. sb well/badly** bien/mal traiter qn; **to t. sth as a joke** prendre qch à la rigolade **(b)** *(give present to)* **to t. sb to sth** offrir qch à qn; **to t. oneself to sth** s'offrir qch; **I'll t. you** *(pay for you)* je t'invite; *Ironic* **she treated us to one of her tantrums** nous avons eu droit à une de ses colères

3 *vi Formal (negotiate)* **to t. with sb/sth** traiter avec qn/qch

treatise ['triːtɪs] *n* traité *m*

treatment ['triːtmənt] *n* traitement *m*; *Fam* **to give sb the t.** rosser qn

treaty ['triːtɪ] (*pl* **treaties**) *n (international)* traité *m*; *(between individuals)* accord *m*, contrat *m*

treble ['trebəl] **1** *n Mus (person, voice)* soprano *m*

2 *adj (triple)* triple; *Mus* **t. clef** clef *f* de sol

3 *vt & vi* tripler

tree [triː] *n* arbre *m*; *Fig* **at the top of the t.** en haut de l'échelle; *Fam* **to be out of one's t.** débloquer; *Fam* **to be up a t.** être dans l'impasse; *Pej* **t. hugger** écologiste *mf* fanatique; **t. trunk** tronc *m* d'arbre

treetop ['triːtɒp] *n* cime *f* d'un arbre

trek [trek] **1** *n (long walk)* randonnée *f* (pédestre); *Fig* **it's quite a t. to the stores** ça fait loin à pied jusqu'aux magasins

2 *vi* (*pt & pp* **trekked**) faire de la randonnée; *Fig* **to t. to the store/home** se taper le chemin à pied jusqu'au magasin/jusqu'à chez soi

trellis ['trelɪs] *n* treillis *m*, treillage *m*

tremble ['trembəl] **1** *n* tremblement *m*

2 *vi* trembler (**with** de)

tremendous [trɪ'mendəs] *adj* **(a)** *(enormous)* énorme **(b)** *Fam (excellent)* formidable

tremendously [trɪ'mendəslɪ] *adv (very)* extrêmement

tremor ['tremə(r)] *n* tremblement *m*

tremulous ['tremjʊləs] *adj (voice, hand)* tremblant(e); *(person, smile)* timide

trench [trentʃ] *n (ditch)* fossé *m*; *Mil* tranchée *f*; **t. coat** trench-coat *m*; **t. warfare** guerre *f* de tranchées

trenchant ['tren(t)ʃənt] *adj* tranchant(e)

trend [trend] *n (tendency)* tendance *f*; *(fashion)* mode *f*; **to set** *or* **to start a t.** lancer une mode

trendsetter ['trendsetə(r)] *n* lanceur(euse) *m,f* de mode

trendspotter ['trendspɒtə(r)] *n* tendanceur *m*

trendy ['trendɪ] *n & adj Fam* branché(e) *m,f*

trepidation [trepɪ'deɪʃən] *n Formal* inquiétude *f*

trespass ['trespəs] *vi Law* s'introduire illégalement dans une propriété privée

trespasser ['trespəsə(r)] *n Law* intrus(e) *m,f*; **trespassers will be prosecuted** *(sign)* défense d'entrer sous peine de poursuites

tresses ['tresɪz] *npl Lit (hair)* chevelure *f*

trestle ['tresəl] *n* tréteau *m*; **t. table** table *f* à tréteaux

trial ['traɪəl] *n* **(a)** *Law* procès *m*; **to bring sb to t.** traduire qn en justice; **to be on t. (for)** passer en jugement (pour) **(b)** *(test)* essai *m*; **on t.** à l'essai; **by t. and error** par tâtonnements; **t. period** période *f* d'essai; **t. run** essai; **t. separation** *(of couple)* séparation *f* à l'essai **(c)** *(ordeal)* épreuve *f*

triangle ['traɪæŋgəl] *n* triangle *m*

triangular [traɪ'æŋgjʊlə(r)] *adj* triangulaire

triathlon [traɪ'æθlɒn] *n* triathlon *m*

tribal ['traɪbəl] *adj* tribal(e)

tribalism ['traɪbəlɪzəm] *n* tribalisme *m*

tribe [traɪb] *n* tribu *f*

tribesman ['traɪbzmən] *n* membre *m* d'une tribu

tribulation [trɪbjʊ'leɪʃən] *n Formal* malheur *m*

tribunal [traɪ'bjuːnəl] *n Law* tribunal *m*

tributary ['trɪbjʊtərɪ] (*pl* **tributaries**) *n (of river)* affluent *m*

tribute ['trɪbjuːt] *n* **(a)** *(homage)* hommage *m*; **to pay t. to** rendre hommage à **(b)** *(testimony)* **our success is a t. to all your hard work** c'est grâce à vos efforts soutenus que nous avons réussi

trice [traɪs] *n* **in a t.** en un clin d'œil

triceps ['traɪseps] *n Anat* triceps *m*

trick [trɪk] **1** *n* **(a)** *(ruse)* tour *m*; *(practical joke)* farce *f*; **to play a t. on sb** jouer un tour à qn; *(practical joke)* faire une farce à qn; **t. photography** truquage *m*; **t. question** question *f* piège **(b)** *(by magician)* tour *m* **(c)** *(in card game)* pli *m* **(d)** *(idioms)* **to do the t.** marcher; **to know all the tricks** connaître toutes les astuces; **the tricks of the trade** les ficelles du métier; **she doesn't miss a t.** rien ne lui échappe; **he's been up to his old tricks again** il a encore fait des siennes; *Fam* **how's tricks?** comment ça va, quoi de neuf ?

2 *vt (person)* duper; **to t. sb into doing sth** amener qn à faire qch par la ruse

trickery ['trɪkərɪ] *n* duperie *f*, ruse *f*

trickle ['trɪkəl] **1** *vt (liquid)* faire couler goutte à goutte

2 *vi (of liquid)* couler goutte à goutte; **to t. in/out** *(of people)* entrer/sortir au compte-gouttes

3 *n (of liquid)* filet *m*; *(of complaints, letters)* petit nombre *m*; *Econ* **t.-down theory** = théorie selon laquelle la richesse de quelques-uns finira par profiter à toute la société

tricky ['trɪkɪ] *adj* délicat(e)

tricycle ['traɪsɪkəl] *n* tricycle *m*

trident ['traɪdənt] *n* trident *m*

tried-and-tested ['traɪdən'testɪd] *adj* qui a fait ses preuves

trier ['traɪə(r)] *n Fam* **to be a t.** être persévérant(e)

trifle ['traɪfəl] *n* (**a**) *(insignificant thing)* broutille *f*, bagatelle *f* (**b**) **a t. wide/short** un tantinet trop large/court(e)

▸ **trifle with** *vt insep* plaisanter avec

trifling ['traɪflɪŋ] *adj* insignifiant(e)

trigger ['trɪgə(r)] **1** *n (of gun)* détente *f*; *Fig (of change, decision)* élément *m* déclencheur
2 *vt* déclencher

▸ **trigger off** *vt sep* déclencher

trigger-happy ['trɪgəhæpɪ] *adj Fam* **to be t.** avoir la gâchette facile

trigonometry [trɪgə'nɒmɪtrɪ] *n* trigonométrie *f*

trill [trɪl] **1** *n* trille *m*
2 *vi* triller

trillion ['trɪljən] *n* trillion *m*; *Fam* **trillions of** *(lots of)* un milliard de

trilogy ['trɪlədʒɪ] *(pl* **trilogies**) *n* trilogie *f*

trim [trɪm] **1** *adj* (**a**) *(neat)* soigné(e) (**b**) *(slim)* svelte
2 *vt (pt & pp* **trimmed**) (**a**) *(cut) (hair)* rafraîchir; *(hedge)* tailler, élaguer; *(meat)* parer; *(budget)* réduire (**b**) *(decorate)* orner, décorer (**with** de)
3 *n* (**a**) **to give sb's hair a t.** faire une coupe d'entretien à qn; **to give the hedge a t.** tailler la haie (**b**) **to be/keep in t.** *(keep fit)* être en/garder la forme

▸ **trim down** *vt sep (text)* élaguer; *(company, expenditure)* réduire

trimaran ['traɪməræn] *n* trimaran *m*

trimester [trɪ'mestə(r)] *n* trimestre *m*

trimming ['trɪmɪŋ] *n* (**a**) *(on clothes)* garniture *f* (**b**) **trimmings** *(of meal)* accompagnements *mpl* traditionnels

Trinidad and Tobago ['trɪnɪdædəntə'beɪgəʊ] *n* Trinité-et-Tobago

Trinity ['trɪnɪtɪ] *n Rel* **the T.** la Trinité

trinket ['trɪŋkɪt] *n* babiole *f*

trio ['triːəʊ] *(pl* **trios**) *n* trio *m*

trip [trɪp] **1** *n* (**a**) *(journey)* trajet *m*, voyage *m*; *(for one day)* excursion *f* (**b**) *Fam (on drugs)* trip *m* (**c**) *(stumble)* faux pas *m*; **t. wire** *m* de détente
2 *vt (pt & pp* **tripped**) (**a**) *(make stumble)* faire un croche-pied à (**b**) **to t. a switch** déclencher un interrupteur (**c**) *(idiom) Hum* **to t. the light fantastic** danser
3 *vi* (**a**) *(stumble)* trébucher (**b**) *(step lightly)* marcher d'un par léger; **to t. off the tongue** *(of word, name)* être facile à prononcer (**c**) *Fam (on drugs)* **to be tripping** être en plein trip

▸ **trip over 1** *vt insep* trébucher sur
2 *vi* trébucher

▸ **trip up 1** *vt sep (cause to stumble)* faire un croche-pied à; *Fig (cause to make mistake)* désarçonner
2 *vi (stumble)* trébucher

tripe [traɪp] *n (food)* tripes *fpl*; *Fam (nonsense)* foutaises *fpl*

triple ['trɪpəl] **1** *adj* triple; **t. jump** triple saut *m*; *Med* **t. (combination) therapy** trithérapie *f*
2 *adv* **t. the number/amount** trois fois le nombre/la quantité
3 *vt & vi* tripler

triplet ['trɪplɪt] *n* (**a**) *(person)* triplé(e) *m,f* (**b**) *Mus* triolet *m*

triplicate ['trɪplɪkət] *n* **in t.** en trois exemplaires

tripod ['traɪpɒd] *n* trépied *m*

Tripoli ['trɪpəlɪ] *n* Tripoli

trite [traɪt] *adj* banal(e)

triumph ['traɪəmf] **1** *n* triomphe *m*; **in t.** triomphant(e)
2 *vi* triompher (**over** de)

triumphant [traɪ'ʌmfənt] *adj* triomphant(e)

triumvirate [traɪ'ʌmvɪrɪt] *n* triumvirat *m*

trivet ['trɪvɪt] *n (on open fire)* trépied *m*; *(stand)* = support métallique surélevé pour plats chauds

trivia ['trɪvɪə] *npl (unimportant details)* détails *mpl*; *(useless information)* futilités *fpl*

trivial ['trɪvɪəl] *adj (detail, matter)* sans importance, insignifiant(e); *(person)* superficiel(elle)

trivialize ['trɪvɪəlaɪz] *vt* banaliser

trod [trɒd] *pt of* **tread**

trodden ['trɒdən] *pp of* **tread**

Trojan ['trəʊdʒən] *Hist* **1** *n* Troyen(enne) *m,f*
2 *adj* de Troie, troyen(enne); **T. Horse** cheval *m* de Troie; **the T. War** la guerre de Troie

troll [trəʊl] *n also Comput* troll *m*

trolley ['trɒlɪ] *(pl* **trolleys**) *n* **t. car** tramway *m*

trolleybus ['trɒlɪbʌs] *n* trolleybus *m*, trolley *m*

trollop ['trɒləp] *n Old-fashioned or Hum* gourgandine *f*, catin *f*

trombone [trɒm'bəʊn] *n* trombone *m (instrument)*

trombonist [trɒm'bəʊnɪst] *n* trombone *m (musicien)*

troop [truːp] **1** *n* (**a**) **troops** *(soldiers)* troupes *fpl* (**b**) *(of people)* groupe *m*
2 *vi* **to t. in/out** entrer/sortir en groupe

trooper ['truːpə(r)] *n (soldier)* cavalier *m*; *(mounted policeman)* membre *m* de la police montée; *Fam* **to swear like a t.** jurer comme un charretier

trophy ['trəʊfɪ] *(pl* **trophies**) *n* trophée *m*

tropic ['trɒpɪk] *n* tropique *m*; **in the tropics** sous les tropiques

tropical ['trɒpɪkəl] *adj* tropical(e)

trot [trɒt] **1** *n* trot *m*; **at a t.** au trot; *Fam* **on the t.** *(consecutively)* de suite; *Fam* **to have the trots** avoir la courante
2 *vi (pt & pp* **trotted**) *(of horse)* aller au trot; *(of person)* trotter

▸ **trot out** *vt sep Fam* débiter

Trotskyism ['trɒtskɪɪzəm] *n* trotskisme *m*

Trotskyist ['trɒtskɪɪst], **Trotskyite** ['trɒtskɪaɪt] *n & adj* trotskiste *mf*

trotter ['trɒtə(r)] *n (of pig)* pied *m*

trouble ['trʌbəl] **1** *n* (**a**) *(problem)* ennui *m*; **to have t. with sb/sth** avoir des problèmes avec qn/qch; **to have t. doing sth** avoir du mal à faire qch; **to be in/to get into t.** avoir/s'attirer des ennuis; **to get sb into t.** attirer des ennuis à qn; **to get sb out of t.** tirer qn d'affaire; **to make t. (for sb)** créer des ennuis (à qn); **it's more t. than it's worth** le jeu n'en vaut pas la chandelle; *Fam* **man/woman t.** ennuis *mpl* de cœur
(**b**) *(inconvenience)* problème *m*; **to go to the t. of doing sth** se donner la peine de faire qch; **it's not worth the t.** ça n'en vaut pas la peine; **(it's) no t.** *(ça ne pose)* aucun problème
(**c**) *(disorder, unrest)* troubles *mpl*; **t. spot** point *m* chaud
2 *vt (worry)* inquiéter; *(inconvenience)* déranger
3 *vi* **to t. to do sth** se donner la peine de faire qch

troubled ['trʌbəld] *adj (person)* inquiet(ète); *(region)* agité(e) de troubles; *(period)* troublé(e)

trouble-free ['trʌbəlfriː] *adj (life)* sans soucis; *(visit, journey)* sans histoires

troublemaker ['trʌbəlmeɪkə(r)] *n* semeur(euse) *m,f* de troubles

troubleshooter ['trʌbəlʃuːtə(r)] *n (for organizational problems)* expert *m*; *(for industrial disputes)* conciliateur(trice) *m,f*; *(for machines)* dépanneur(euse) *m,f*

troublesome ['trʌbəlsəm] *adj* pénible

trough [trɒf] *n (for food)* mangeoire *f*; *(for drink)* abreuvoir *m*; *(of wave, on graph)* creux *m*; *(in weather front)* dépression *f*

trounce [traʊns] *vt* battre à plates coutures

troupe [truːp] *n* troupe *f*

trouser press ['traʊzə'pres] *n* presse-pantalon *m*

trousers ['traʊzəz] *npl (garment)* pantalon *m*

trousseau ['truːsəʊ] *n* trousseau *m (de jeune mariée)*

trout [traʊt] *(pl* **trout**) *n* truite *f*

trowel ['traʊəl] n truelle f

truancy ['truːənsɪ] n absentéisme m scolaire

truant ['truːənt] n (pupil) élève mf qui fait l'école buissonnière; **to play t.** faire l'école buissonnière

truce [truːs] n also Fig trêve f; **to call a t.** demander une trêve

truck [trʌk] **1** n (a) (vehicle) camion m; **t. driver** conducteur(trice) m,f de camion, camionneur m; **t. farm** jardin m maraîcher; **t. farmer** maraîcher(ère) m,f; **t. stop** relais m routier (b) Fam **to have no t. with sb/sth** ne rien avoir à faire avec qn/qch
 2 vt (goods) acheminer par camion
 3 vi (drive a truck) être conducteur(trice) m,f de camion

trucker ['trʌkə(r)] n (truck driver) camionneur m

truculent ['trʌkjʊlənt] adj agressif(ive)

trudge [trʌdʒ] **1** n trajet m pénible
 2 vi marcher péniblement, se traîner

true [truː] **1** adj (a) (not fictional) vrai(e); **to come t.** se réaliser; **to hold t. (for)** être vrai (de) (b) (genuine) véritable; **t. love** grand amour m; **t. north** le nord géographique (c) (faithful) fidèle; **to be t. to sb** être loyal(e) envers qn; **to be t. to sth** être fidèle à qch; **t. to life** fidèle à la réalité; **t. to form** or **type** fidèle à soi-même (d) (accurate) exact(e)
 2 n **out of t.** hors d'aplomb

truffle ['trʌfəl] n truffe f

truism ['truːɪzəm] n truisme m

truly ['truːlɪ] adv vraiment; **yours t.** (at end of letter) = je vous prie d'agréer, Madame/Monsieur, l'expression de mes sentiments distingués; Fam Hum (myself) mézigue

trump [trʌmp] **1** n atout m; **spades are trumps** c'est atout pique; Fig **to play one's t. card** jouer son atout; Fam Fig **to turn up trumps** sauver la mise
 2 vt couper à l'atout

trumped up ['trʌmptʌp] adj fabriqué(e)

trumpet ['trʌmpɪt] **1** n trompette f
 2 vt (proclaim) claironner
 3 vi (of elephant) barrir

trumpeter ['trʌmpɪtə(r)] n trompettiste mf

truncate [trʌŋ'keɪt] vt tronquer

trundle ['trʌndəl] **1** vt pousser péniblement
 2 vi rouler péniblement

trunk [trʌŋk] n (a) (of tree, body) tronc m (b) (case) malle f (c) (of car) coffre m (d) (of elephant) trompe f (e) **trunks** (swimming costume) slip m de bain

truss [trʌs] **1** n (a) (for hernia) bandage m herniaire (b) (for roof, bridge) ferme f
 2 vt (tie up) ligoter
▸**truss up** vt sep (person) ligoter; (chicken, turkey) trousser

trust [trʌst] **1** n (a) (faith) confiance f (in en); **to put one's t. in sb/sth** se fier à qn/qch; **to take sth on t.** croire qch sur parole (b) Law **in t.** par fidéicommis; Fin **t. fund** fonds m en fidéicommis (c) Com (group of companies) trust m
 2 vt (a) (believe in) faire confiance à; **to t. sb with sth** confier qch à qn; **to t. sb to do sth** laisser à qn le soin de faire qch; Fam **t. him to say that!** c'est bien de lui! (b) Formal (hope) **to t. (that)…** espérer que…
 3 vi **to t. in sb/sth** faire confiance à qn/qch; **to t. to luck** s'en remettre au hasard

trusted ['trʌstɪd] adj de confiance; **t. third party** (for Internet transactions) tierce partie f de confiance

trustee [trʌs'tiː] n Law (of fund, property) fidéicommissaire m; (of charity) administrateur(trice) m,f

trusting ['trʌstɪŋ] adj qui fait confiance aux gens

trustworthy ['trʌstwɜːðɪ] adj (person) digne de confiance; (thing) fiable

trusty ['trʌstɪ] adj fidèle

truth [truːθ] n vérité f; **to tell the t.** dire la vérité; **to tell (you) the t., I don't care** à vrai dire, je m'en moque complètement

truthful ['truːθfʊl] adj (person) sincère; (story) véridique

try [traɪ] **1** vt (pt & pp **tried**) (a) (sample, attempt) essayer; (food, drink) goûter (à); **to t. to do sth** essayer de faire qch; **I'll t. anything once** il faut tout essayer dans la vie (b) Law (case, person) juger (c) (test) tester; (person) mettre à l'épreuve; **to t. sb's patience** mettre la patience de qn à l'épreuve
 2 vi essayer; **to t. harder** faire plus d'efforts; **just you t.!** essaie un peu pour voir!
 3 n (attempt) essai m; **to give sth a t.** essayer qch; **to have a t. at sth/at doing sth** essayer qch/de faire qch; **it's worth a t.** ça vaut le coup d'essayer
▸**try on** vt sep (clothes) essayer
▸**try out 1** vt sep essayer; **to t. sth out on sb** expérimenter qch sur qn
 2 vi **to t. out for a team** faire un essai pour se faire engager dans une équipe

trying ['traɪɪŋ] adj difficile

tryout ['traɪaʊt] n essai m; Sport épreuve f de sélection

tsar [zɑː(r)] n tsar m

tsarist ['zɑːrɪst] n & adj tsariste mf

tsetse ['t(s)etsɪ] n **t. (fly)** (mouche f) tsé-tsé f inv

T-shirt ['tiːʃɜːt] n tee-shirt m

TTP [tiːtiː'piː] n (abbr **trusted third party**) (for Internet transactions) TPC f

tub [tʌb] n (a) (bathtub) baignoire f; (for washing clothes) baquet m (b) (for food, plants) pot m

tuba ['tjuːbə] n tuba m

tubby ['tʌbɪ] adj Fam boulot(otte)

tube [tjuːb] n (a) (cylindrical container) tube m; (pipe) tuyau m; Fam **to go down the tubes** (of money) être foutu en l'air; (of work, plan) tomber à l'eau (b) Fam (TV) télé f

tuber ['tjuːbə(r)] n tubercule m

tuberculosis [tjʊbɜːkjʊ'ləʊsɪs] n tuberculose f

tubing ['tjuːbɪŋ] n tuyaux mpl

tubular ['tjuːbjʊlə(r)] adj tubulaire; **t. bells** carillon m

tuck [tʌk] **1** n (a) (in sewing) pli m (b) (in cosmetic surgery) (for face) lifting m
 2 vt **to t. one's shirt into one's pants** rentrer sa chemise dans son pantalon; **to t. sth under one's arm** mettre qch sous son bras; **to t. sb up in bed** border qn; **to t. sth into a drawer** glisser qch dans un tiroir
▸**tuck in 1** vt sep (sheets, child) border; (clothes) rentrer
 2 vi Fam (start to eat) attaquer
▸**tuck into** vt insep Fam (meal) attaquer

Tudor ['tjuːdə(r)] **1** n Hist **the Tudors** les Tudor
 2 adj des Tudor

Tue(s). (abbr **Tuesday**) mardi

Tuesday ['tjuːzdɪ] n mardi m; see also **Saturday**

tuft [tʌft] n touffe f

tug [tʌg] **1** vt (pt & pp **tugged**) (a) (pull) tirer sur (b) (tow) remorquer
 2 vi **to t. at sth** tirer sur qch
 3 n (a) (pull) **to give sth a t.** tirer sur qch (b) (boat) remorqueur m

tugboat ['tʌgbəʊt] n remorqueur m

tug-of-war [tʌgəv'wɔː(r)] n (game) lutte f (de traction) à la corde; Fig lutte acharnée

tuition [tjʊ'ɪʃən] n (a) (teaching) cours mpl, leçons fpl (b) Univ (fees) frais mpl de scolarité ou d'inscription

tulip ['tjuːlɪp] n tulipe f

tumble ['tʌmbəl] **1** vi (of person) faire une chute; Fig (of prices) chuter; **t. dryer** sèche-linge m inv
 2 n (fall) chute f; **to take a t.** (of person) faire une chute; Fig (of prices) chuter
▸**tumble down** vi s'écrouler

tumbledown ['tʌmbəldaʊn] adj qui tombe en ruines

tumble-dry ['tʌmbəldraɪ] *vt* faire sécher au sèche-linge

tumbler ['tʌmblə(r)] *n* verre *m* droit

tummy ['tʌmɪ] *n Fam* ventre *m*; **to have a t. ache** avoir mal au ventre

tumor ['tju:mə(r)] *n* tumeur *f*

tumult ['tju:mʌlt] *n* tumulte *m*

tumultuous [tjʊ'mʌltjʊəs] *adj* tumultueux(euse)

tuna ['tju:nə] *n* thon *m*

tundra ['tʌndrə] *n* tundra *f*

tune [tju:n] **1** *n* (**a**) *(melody)* air *m*, mélodie *f*; **to be in/out of t.** *(of person)* chanter juste/faux; *(of instrument)* être accordé(e)/ désaccordé(e) (**b**) *(idioms)* **to be in t. with sb/sth** être en harmonie avec qn/qch; **to call the t.** commander; **to change one's t.** changer de discours; **to be in debt to the t. of $2000** avoir 2000 dollars de dettes

2 *vt (musical instrument)* accorder; *(engine, TV, radio)* régler

▸**tune in** *vi* brancher son poste

tuneful ['tju:nfʊl] *adj* mélodieux(euse)

tuneless ['tju:nlɪs] *adj* discordant(e)

tuner ['tju:nə(r)] *n* (**a**) *(person)* accordeur(euse) *m,f* (**b**) *(on TV, radio)* tuner *m*

tungsten ['tʌŋstən] *n* tungstène *m*; **t. steel** acier *m* au tungstène

tunic ['tju:nɪk] *n* tunique *f*

tuning fork ['tju:nɪŋ'fɔ:k] *n* diapason *m*

Tunis ['tju:nɪs] *n* Tunis

Tunisia [tju:'nɪzɪə] *n* la Tunisie

Tunisian [tju:'nɪzɪən] **1** *n* Tunisien(enne) *m,f*

2 *adj* tunisien(enne)

tunnel ['tʌnəl] **1** *n* tunnel *m*; **to have t. vision** souffrir d'un rétrécissement du champ visuel; *Fig* avoir des œillères

2 *vt* **to t. one's way out of prison** s'échapper de prison en creusant un tunnel

3 *vi* creuser un tunnel

turban ['tɜ:bən] *n* turban *m*

turbine ['tɜ:baɪn] *n* turbine *f*

turbo-charged ['tɜ:bəʊtʃɑ:dʒd] *adj* turbocompressé(e)

turbo-charger ['tɜ:bəʊtʃɑ:dʒə(r)] *n* turbocompresseur *m*

turbojet ['tɜ:bəʊdʒet] *n (engine)* turboréacteur *m*; *(plane)* avion *m* à turboréacteur

turboprop ['tɜ:bəʊprɒp] *n (engine)* turbopropulseur *m*; *(plane)* avion *m* à turbopropulseur

turbot ['tɜ:bət] *n* turbot *m*

turbulence ['tɜ:bjʊləns] *n* turbulence *f*

turbulent ['tɜ:bjʊlənt] *adj* agité(e)

turd [tɜ:d] *n very Fam* (**a**) *(excrement)* étron *m* (**b**) *(person)* connard (connasse) *m,f*

tureen [tjʊə'ri:n] *n* soupière *f*

turf [tɜ:f] **1** *n (grass-covered earth)* gazon *m*; *Fam (territory)* territoire *m*

2 *vt* gazonner

Turk [tɜ:k] *n* Turc (Turque) *m,f*

Turkey ['tɜ:kɪ] *n* la Turquie

turkey ['tɜ:kɪ] *(pl* **turkeys***)* *n* (**a**) *(bird)* dinde *f* (**b**) *Fam (bad play, movie)* navet *m*

Turkish ['tɜ:kɪʃ] **1** *n (language)* turc *m*

2 *adj* turc (turque); **T. bath** bain *m* turc; **T. delight** loukoum *m*

Turkmenistan [tɜ:kmenɪ'stɑ:n] *n* le Turkménistan

turmeric ['tɜ:mərɪk] *n* curcuma *m*

turmoil ['tɜ:mɔɪl] *n (of person)* émoi *m*; *(of country)* agitation *f*; **to be in** (**a**) **t.** *(of person)* être dans tous ses états; *(of country)* être en ébullition; **his mind was in t.** il était très troublé

turn [tɜ:n] **1** *n* (**a**) *(of wheel, screw)* tour *m*; **the meat is done to a t.** la viande est cuite à point

(**b**) *(change of direction)* demi-tour *m*; *(in road)* virage *m*; **no right/left t.** *(on sign)* défense de tourner à droite/gauche; *Fig*

at every t. à tout bout de champ; **to take a t. for the better** s'améliorer; **to take a t. for the worse** se détériorer; **events took an unexpected t.** les événements ont pris une tournure inattendue; **the t. of the century** le tournant du siècle; **the t. of the tide** le changement de marée; *Fig* le renversement de tendances; *Aut* **t. signal** clignotant *m*, *Belg* clignoteur *m*, *Suisse* signafil(e) *m*

(**c**) *(in game, line)* tour *m*; **to take turns (to do sth)** se relayer (pour faire qch); **in t.** à tour de rôle

(**d**) *(service)* **to do sb a good t.** rendre un service à qn; **one good t. deserves another** un service en vaut un autre

(**e**) **t. of phrase** tournure *f* de phrase

2 *vt* (**a**) *(cause to move)* tourner; *Fam Fig* **without turning a hair** sans broncher; *Fam Fig* **success has turned her head** le succès lui a tourné la tête; **to t. sb's stomach** soulever le cœur à qn

(**b**) *(direct)* **to t. the conversation to sb/sth** orienter la conversation sur qn/qch

(**c**) *(go around)* **to t. the corner** tourner au coin de la rue; *Fig* passer le moment critique; **she's just turned forty** elle vient d'avoir quarante ans

(**d**) *(change)* **to t. sth into sth** transformer qch en qch; **to t. sth green/black** verdir/noircir qch; **to t. sb against sb** monter qn contre qn

(**e**) *(on lathe)* tourner

3 *vi* (**a**) *(rotate) (of wheel)* tourner; *(of person)* se retourner; **she turned to me** elle s'est tournée vers moi; **to t. to sb (for help/advice)** se tourner vers qn (pour obtenir de l'aide/des conseils); **to t. (to the) right/left** tourner à droite/gauche

(**b**) *(change)* **to t. against sb** se retourner contre qn; **to t. nasty** *(of person)* devenir méchant(e); *(of situation)* mal tourner; **to t. red** devenir rouge; **to t. sour** *(of milk)* tourner; *Fig (of relationship)* tourner au vinaigre

▸**turn around 1** *vt sep (object)* retourner; *(situation)* renverser; *(company, economy)* remettre sur pied

2 *vi (of person)* se retourner

▸**turn away 1** *vt sep (refuse entry, help to)* refuser

2 *vi* se détourner

▸**turn back 1** *vt sep (person)* refouler; *(sheets)* rabattre; **to t. the clocks back** retarder les pendules; *Fig* revenir en arrière

2 *vi* faire demi-tour; **t. back to page 20** revenez à la page 20

▸**turn down** *vt sep* (**a**) *(volume, heat)* baisser (**b**) *(request, application)* rejeter, refuser

▸**turn in 1** *vt sep (lost property)* rapporter à la police; *(person)* livrer à la police

2 *vi Fam (go to bed)* aller se pieuter

▸**turn into** *vt insep (become)* devenir

▸**turn off 1** *vt sep* (**a**) *(water, gas)* fermer; *(light, TV, engine)* éteindre (**b**) *Fam* **to t. sb off** dégoûter qn; *(sexually)* couper l'envie à qn

2 *vt insep* **to t. off the road** quitter la route

3 *vi (leave road)* sortir

▸**turn on 1** *vt sep* (**a**) *(water, gas)* ouvrir; *(light, TV, engine)* allumer (**b**) *Fam* **to t. sb on** *(excite)* brancher qn; *(sexually)* exciter qn

2 *vt insep* (**a**) *(attack)* **to t. on sb** attaquer qn (**b**) *(depend on)* dépendre de

▸**turn out 1** *vt sep* (**a**) *(light)* éteindre; *(gas)* fermer (**b**) *(eject)* mettre à la porte (**c**) *(pocket, container)* vider (**d**) *(produce)* produire, fabriquer; **to be well turned out** *(of person)* être élégant(e)

2 *vi* (**a**) *(appear, attend)* se déplacer (**b**) *(result)* se terminer; **to t. out to be** s'avérer (être); **it turns out that...** il se trouve que...

▸**turn over 1** *vt sep* (**a**) *(change position of)* retourner; **to t. sth over in one's mind** retourner qch dans sa tête; *Fig* **to t. over a new leaf** tourner la page (**b**) *(hand in)* **to t. sb/sth over to sb** remettre qn/qch entre les mains de qn

2 *vi (of person)* se retourner; *(of car)* faire un tonneau, capoter

▶**turn up 1** vt sep **(a)** (collar) relever; (pants) retrousser **(b)** (volume, heat) mettre plus fort

2 vi (of person) arriver; (of lost object) réapparaître; **something is sure to t. up** quelque chose finira bien par se présenter

turnabout ['tɜːnəbaʊt] n (in situation, opinion) revirement m

turnaround ['tɜːnəraʊnd] n **(a)** (in situation, opinion) revirement m **(b)** Comput **t. time** temps m de rotation

turncoat ['tɜːnkəʊt] n renégat(e) m,f

turning ['tɜːnɪŋ] n **t. circle** (of car) rayon m de braquage; Fig **t. point** tournant m

turnip ['tɜːnɪp] n navet m

turn-off ['tɜːnɒf] n **(a)** (on road) sortie f **(b)** Fam **to be a t.** être rébarbatif(ive); (sexually) couper l'envie

turn-on ['tɜːnɒn] n Fam **to be a t.** (sexually) être excitant(e)

turnout ['tɜːnaʊt] n (attendance) assistance f; (at election) taux m de participation

turnover ['tɜːnəʊvə(r)] n **(a)** (of company) chiffre m d'affaires **(b)** (cake) chausson m; **apple t.** chausson m aux pommes

turnpike ['tɜːnpaɪk] n (road) autoroute f

turnstile ['tɜːnstaɪl] n tourniquet m

turntable ['tɜːnteɪbəl] n platine f

turpentine ['tɜːpəntaɪn] n essence f de térébenthine

turquoise ['tɜːkwɔɪz] **1** n **(a)** (stone) turquoise f **(b)** (color) turquoise m

2 adj turquoise inv

turret ['tʌrɪt] n tourelle f; **(gun) t.** (on ship, tank) tourelle f

turtle ['tɜːtəl] n tortue f; **to turn t.** (of ship) chavirer; **t. dove** tourterelle f; **t. soup** potage m à la tortue

turtleneck ['tɜːtəlnek] n col m roulé; **t. sweater** pull m à col roulé

Tuscan ['tʌskən] adj toscan(e)

Tuscany ['tʌskənɪ] n la Toscane

tusk [tʌsk] n défense f

tussle ['tʌsəl] **1** n empoignade f; **to have a t. (with sb)** (physically) se battre (avec qn); (verbally) se disputer (avec qn)

2 vi (physically) se battre; (verbally) se disputer

tutor ['tjuːtə(r)] **1** n professeur m particulier

2 vt **to t. sb (in sth)** donner des leçons particulières (de qch) à qn

tutorial [tjuːˈtɔːrɪəl] n **(a)** Univ travaux mpl dirigés **(b)** Comput didacticiel m

tux [tʌks] n Fam smoking m

tuxedo [tʌkˈsiːdəʊ] n smoking m

TV [tiːˈviː] n (television) télé f, TV f; **TV dinner** plateau m télé; **TV movie** téléfilm m

TVP [tiːviːˈpiː] n (abbr **textured vegetable protein**) protéine f végétale texturée

twang [twæŋ] **1** n (sound) vibration f; (nasal voice) ton m nasillard

2 vi (of string) vibrer

tweak [twiːk] **1** n **to give sth a t.** (nose) pincer qch; (ear) tirer qch; Fam Fig (statistics, mechanism) ajuster légèrement qch

2 vt (nose) pincer; (ear) tirer; Fam Fig (statistics, mechanism) ajuster légèrement

twee [twiː] adj Fam Pej cucul (la praline) inv

tweed [twiːd] n tweed m; **tweeds** (suit) costume m de tweed

tweet [twiːt] **1** n pépiement m

2 vi pépier

tweezers ['twiːzəz] npl pince f à épiler

twelfth [twelfθ] **1** n **(a)** (fraction) douzième m **(b)** (in series) douzième mf **(c)** (of month) douze m inv

2 adj douzième; **t. floor** onzième étage; Scol **t. grade** ≃ (classe f de) terminale f; **T. Night** ≃ la fête des Rois; see also **eighth**

twelve [twelv] **1** n douze m inv; **half past t.** (in the afternoon) douze heures trente, midi et demi; (at night) zéro heures trente, minuit et demi

2 adj douze; see also **eight**

twentieth ['twentɪθ] **1** n **(a)** (fraction) vingtième m **(b)** (in series) vingtième mf **(c)** (of month) vingt m inv

2 adj vingtième; see also **eighth**

twenty ['twentɪ] **1** n vingt m inv

2 adj vingt; **to have t.-t. vision** avoir dix sur dix à chaque œil; see also **eighty**

twenty-first ['twentɪˈfɜːst] **1** n **(a)** (in series) vingt et unième mf **(b)** (of month) vingt et un m inv

2 adj vingt et unième

twenty-one ['twentɪˈwʌn] **1** n vingt et un m inv

2 adj vingt et un

twerp [twɜːp] n Fam crétin(e) m,f

twice [twaɪs] adv deux fois; **t. a week** deux fois par semaine; **t. as big (as)** deux fois plus grand (que); **it would cost t. as much elsewhere** ça coûterait le double ailleurs; **t. over** à deux reprises; **to think t. before doing sth** réfléchir à deux fois avant de faire qch; **he didn't have to be asked t.** il ne s'est pas fait prier

twiddle ['twɪdəl] **1** vt tripoter; **to t. one's thumbs** se tourner les pouces

2 vi **to t. with sth** tripoter qch

twig [twɪg] n (small branch) brindille f

twilight ['twaɪlaɪt] n crépuscule m; **his t. years** les dernières années de sa vie; **t. zone** zone f crépusculaire; Fig zone floue

twin [twɪn] **1** n jumeau(elle) m,f; **t. brother** frère m jumeau; **t. sister** sœur f jumelle

2 adj (paired) jumeau(elle), jumelé(e); **t. beds** lits mpl jumeaux; **t.-engine(d) aircraft** avion m bimoteur

twine [twaɪn] **1** n (string) ficelle f

2 vt **to t. sth around sb/sth** enrouler qch autour de qn/qch

twinge [twɪn(d)ʒ] n (of pain) élancement m; **a t. of conscience** un léger remords

twinkle ['twɪŋkəl] **1** vi (of star, light) scintiller; (of eyes) pétiller

2 n (of star, light) scintillement m; (of eyes) pétillement m

twirl [twɜːl] **1** n (movement) tournoiement m

2 vt faire tournoyer

3 vi (of person) tournoyer

twist [twɪst] n **(a)** (action) tour m; **to give sth a t.** (to open) dévisser qch; (to close) visser qch **(b)** (bend) tortillement m; **twists and turns** (in road) tours mpl et détours; Fig (of events) rebondissements mpl **(c)** (in story, plot) tour m inattendu; **by a strange t. of fate** par un hasard extraordinaire **(d)** **a t. of lemon** une rondelle de citron **(e)** (dance) **the t.** le twist

2 vt (hair, rope, thread) tordre, tortiller; Fig (words, meaning) déformer; **to t. one's ankle** se fouler la cheville; **to t. sb's arm** tordre le bras à qn; Fig forcer la main à qn; Fig **to t. the knife in the wound** retourner ou remuer le couteau dans la plaie

3 vi (of smoke) faire des volutes; (of road) faire des lacets; **to t. and turn** (of road) être en lacets

▶**twist off 1** vt sep (lid) dévisser

2 vi se dévisser

twisted ['twɪstɪd] adj also Fig tordu(e)

twister ['twɪstə(r)] n (tornado) tornade f

twitch [twɪtʃ] **1** n (pull) coup m sec; **to have a nervous t.** avoir un tic (nerveux)

2 vt (pull) tirer d'un coup sec

3 vi (of muscle, limb, face) se contracter nerveusement

twitter ['twɪtə(r)] **1** vi (of bird) gazouiller; Fig (of person) jacasser

2 n (of bird) gazouillis m

two [tuː] **1** n (pl twos) deux m; **to break/to fold sth in t.** casser/plier qch en deux; **to walk in twos** or **t. by t.** marcher deux par deux; Fig **to put t. and t. together** faire le rapprochement; Fam **that makes t. of us** comme ça, on est deux

2 adj deux; see also **eight**

two-bit ['tuːˈbɪt] adj Fam (cheap) de quatre sous

two-dimensional [tuːdaɪˈmenʃənəl] *adj* à deux dimensions; *Fig (character, movie)* simpliste

two-faced [ˈtuːfeɪst] *adj* hypocrite

twofold [ˈtuːfəʊld] *adj* double

two-legged [tuːˈlegɪd] *adj* bipède

two-piece [ˈtuːpiːs] *adj (suit, swimsuit)* deux pièces

two-pin [ˈtuːpɪn] *adj (plug, socket)* à deux fiches

twosome [ˈtuːsəm] *n* couple *m*

two-time [ˈtuːtaɪm] *vt Fam (boyfriend, girlfriend)* tromper

two-way [ˈtuːweɪ] *adj* **t. mirror** miroir *m* sans tain; **t. radio** poste *m* émetteur-récepteur

tycoon [taɪˈkuːn] *n* magnat *m*

type [taɪp] **1** *n* (**a**) *(kind)* type *m*, genre *m*; *Fam* **he's not my t.** ce n'est pas mon genre de mec (**b**) *Typ* caractères *mpl*; **in bold t.** en caractères gras
2 *vt & vi* taper (à la machine)

▸**type up** *vt sep* taper (à la machine)

typecast [ˈtaɪpkɑːst] *(pt & pp* **typecast**) *vt* **to be typecast** être cantonné(e) dans un rôle

typeface [ˈtaɪpfeɪs] *n* police *f* de caractères

typescript [ˈtaɪpskrɪpt] *n* texte *m* dactylographié, tapuscrit *m*

typesetter [ˈtaɪpsetə(r)] *n* typographe *mf*

typewriter [ˈtaɪpraɪtə(r)] *n* machine *f* à écrire

typhoid [ˈtaɪfɔɪd] *n* **t. (fever)** (fièvre *f*) typhoïde *f*; **to have t.** avoir la typhoïde

typhoon [taɪˈfuːn] *n* typhon *m*

typhus [ˈtaɪfəs] *n* typhus *m*

typical [ˈtɪpɪkəl] *adj* typique; **it was t. of him to offer to pay** c'était bien son genre de proposer de payer; *Pej* **that's t. (of him/her)!** ça ne m'étonne pas (de lui/d'elle)!

typically [ˈtɪpɪkəlɪ] *adv* typiquement

typify [ˈtɪpɪfaɪ] *(pt & pp* **typified**) *vt* caractériser

typing [ˈtaɪpɪŋ] *n* dactylographie *f*, frappe *f*; **t. error** faute *f* de frappe; **t. paper** papier *m* machine; **t. pool** équipe *f* de dactylos; **t. speed** vitesse *f* de frappe

typist [ˈtaɪpɪst] *n* dactylo *mf*

typographic [taɪpəˈgræfɪk], **typographical** [taɪpəˈgræfɪkəl] *adj* typographique

typography [taɪˈpɒgrəfɪ] *n* typographie *f*

tyrannical [tɪˈrænɪkəl] *adj* tyrannique

tyrannize [ˈtɪrənaɪz] *vt* tyranniser

tyranny [ˈtɪrənɪ] *n* tyrannie *f*

tyrant [ˈtaɪrənt] *n* tyran *m*

tzar, tzarist = tsar, tsarist

T-zone [tiːˈzəʊn] *n* zones *fpl* graisses du visage *(front, nez, menton)*

U

U, u [juː] *n (letter)* U, u *m inv*; **U bend** tuyau *m* U; **U boat** sous-marin *m* allemand; **U turn** *(in car)* demi-tour *m*; *Fig* virage *m* à 180 degrés

UAE [juːeɪˈiː] *n (abbr* **United Arab Emirates)** EAU *mpl*

ubiquitous [juːˈbɪkwɪtəs] *adj* omniprésent(e)

udder [ˈʌdə(r)] *n* pis *m*, mamelle *f*

UDI [juːdiːˈaɪ] *n Pol (abbr* **Unilateral Declaration of Independence)** déclaration *f* unilatérale d'indépendance

UFO [juːefˈəʊ] *n (abbr* **unidentified flying object)** OVNI *m*

Uganda [juːˈgændə] *n* l'Ouganda *m*

Ugandan [juːˈgændən] **1** *n* Ougandais(e) *m,f*
2 *adj* ougandais(e)

ugh [ʌχ] *exclam* berk!

ugly [ˈʌglɪ] *adj* **(a)** *(in appearance)* laid(e); *Fig* **u. duckling** vilain petit canard *m* **(b)** *(unpleasant)* désagréable, déplaisant(e)

UHF [juːeɪtʃˈef] *n (abbr* **ultra-high frequency)** UHF

UHT [juːeɪtʃˈtiː] *adj (abbr* **ultra-heat-treated)** UHT

UK [juːˈkeɪ] *n (abbr* **United Kingdom)** *(written)* RU; *(spoken)* Royaume-Uni *m*

Ukraine [juːˈkreɪn] *n* **the U.** l'Ukraine *f*

Ukrainian [juːˈkreɪnɪən] **1** *n* **(a)** *(person)* Ukrainien(enne) *m,f* **(b)** *(language)* ukrainien *m*
2 *adj* ukrainien(enne)

ukulele [juːkəˈleɪlɪ] *n* ukulélé *m*

ulcer [ˈʌlsə(r)] *n* ulcère *m*; *(in mouth)* aphte *m*

ulcerate [ˈʌlsəreɪt] **1** *vt* ulcérer
2 *vi* s'ulcérer

ulna [ˈʌlnə] *n* cubitus *m*

Ulster [ˈʌlstə(r)] *n* l'Ulster *m*

ulterior [ʌlˈtɪərɪə(r)] *adj* ultérieur(e); **u. motive** arrière-pensée *f*

ultimate [ˈʌltɪmət] **1** *adj* **(a)** *(last)* final(e) **(b)** *(supreme, best)* absolu(e); **the u. vacation** les vacances idéales
2 *n Fam* **the u. (in)** le summum (de)

ultimately [ˈʌltɪmɪtlɪ] *adv* **(a)** *(finally)* finalement **(b)** *(basically)* en fin de compte

ultimatum [ʌltɪˈmeɪtəm] *n* ultimatum *m*; **to deliver an u. to sb** adresser un ultimatum à qn

ultra- [ˈʌltrə] *pref* ultra-

ultramarine [ʌltrəməˈriːn] *n* bleu *m* outremer

ultramodern [ʌltrəˈmɒdən] *adj* ultramoderne

ultrasound [ˈʌltrəsaʊnd] *n* ultrasons *mpl*

ultraviolet [ʌltrəˈvaɪələt] *adj* ultraviolet(ette)

Ulysses [juːˈlɪsiːz] *n* Ulysse

umbilical cord [ʌmˈbɪlɪkəlkɔːd] *n* cordon *m* ombilical

umbrage [ˈʌmbrɪdʒ] *n* **to take u. (at sth)** prendre ombrage (de qch)

umbrella [ʌmˈbrelə] *n* parapluie *m*; *Fig* **under the u. of** sous les auspices de; **u. organization** organisme *m* de tutelle; **u. stand** porte-parapluie *m*

umpire [ˈʌmpaɪə(r)] **1** *n* arbitre *mf*
2 *vt* arbitrer

umpteen [ʌmpˈtiːn] *adj Fam* je ne sais combien de

umpteenth [ʌmpˈtiːnθ] *adj Fam* énième, ixième

UN [juːˈen] *n (abbr* **United Nations)** ONU *f*

unabashed [ʌnəˈbæʃt] *adj* nullement décontenancé(e)

unable [ʌnˈeɪbəl] *adj* **to be u. to do sth** être incapable de faire qch

unabridged [ʌnəˈbrɪdʒd] *adj* intégral(e)

unacceptable [ʌnəkˈseptəbəl] *adj* inacceptable

unaccompanied [ʌnəˈkʌmpənɪd] **1** *adj (person)* non accompagné(e); *(violin, singer)* sans accompagnement
2 *adv (travel)* seul(e); *(play, sing)* sans accompagnement

unaccomplished [ʌnəˈkʌmplɪʃt] *adj* médiocre

unaccountable [ʌnəˈkaʊntəbəl] *adj* **(a)** *(not answerable)* **to be u. (to sb)** ne pas avoir de comptes à rendre (à qn) **(b)** *(puzzling)* inexplicable

unaccounted [ʌnəˈkaʊntɪd] *adj* **to be u. for** *(of person)* ne pas être retrouvé(e)

unaccustomed [ʌnəˈkʌstəmd] *adj* **(a)** *(not used)* **to be u. to sth/to doing sth** ne pas être habitué(e) à qch/à faire qch **(b)** *(not usual)* inhabituel(elle)

unacknowledged [ʌnəkˈnɒlɪdʒd] **1** *adj* non reconnu(e)
2 *adv* **to go u.** *(of talent, achievement)* ne pas être reconnu(e)

unacquainted [ʌnəˈkweɪntɪd] *adj* **to be u. with sb/sth** ne pas connaître qn/qch

unadulterated [ʌnəˈdʌltəreɪtɪd] *adj* **(a)** *(food)* naturel(elle) **(b)** *(total, sheer)* pur(e)

unadventurous [ʌnədˈventʃərəs] *adj* peu audacieux(euse)

unaffected [ʌnəˈfektɪd] *adj* **(a)** *(sincere)* simple **(b)** *(not touched)* **to be u. (by sth)** ne pas être affecté(e) (par qch)

unaffiliated [ʌnəˈfɪlɪeɪtɪd] *adj* non affilié(e)

unafraid [ʌnəˈfreɪd] *adj* **to be u.** ne pas avoir peur

unaided [ʌnˈeɪdɪd] *adv* sans aide

unaltered [ʌnˈɔːltəd] *adj* inchangé(e)

unambiguous [ʌnæmˈbɪgjʊəs] *adj* sans équivoque

unambitious [ʌnæmˈbɪʃəs] *adj* sans ambition

un-American [ʌnəˈmerɪkən] *adj* **(a)** *(uncharacteristic)* peu américain(e); **that's rather u.** ce n'est pas très américain **(b)** *(anti-American)* antiaméricain(e); *(unpatriotic)* peu patriotique

unanimity [juːnəˈnɪmɪtɪ] *n* unanimité *f*

unanimous [juːˈnænɪməs] *adj* unanime

unanimously [juːˈnænɪməslɪ] *adv* à l'unanimité

unannounced [ʌnəˈnaʊnst] **1** *adj* non annoncé(e)
2 *adv* sans prévenir

unanswerable [ʌnˈɑːnsərəbəl] *adj* irréfutable

unanswered [ʌnˈɑːnsəd] **1** *adj* sans réponse
2 *adv* **to go u.** *(of question, letter)* rester sans réponse

unappealing [ʌnəˈpiːlɪŋ] *adj* peu attrayant(e)

unappetizing [ʌnˈæpɪtaɪzɪŋ] *adj* peu appétissant(e)

unappreciated [ʌnəˈpriːʃieɪtɪd] *adj* non reconnu(e)

unapproachable [ʌnəˈprəʊtʃəbəl] *adj* inaccessible

unarmed [ʌnˈɑːmd] *adj* non armé(e); **u. combat** combat *m* à mains nues

unashamed [ʌnə'ʃeɪmd] *adj (joy, greed)* non dissimulé(e); **he's u.** about **his background** il n'a absolument pas honte de ses origines

unassailable [ʌnə'seɪləbəl] *adj (castle, position)* imprenable; *(argument, theory)* inattaquable

unassuming [ʌnə'sjuːmɪŋ] *adj* sans prétention

unattached [ʌnə'tætʃt] *adj* **(a)** *(not connected)* détaché(e) **(b)** *(without partner)* sans attaches

unattainable [ʌnə'teɪnəbəl] *adj* inaccessible

unattractive [ʌnə'træktɪv] *adj (place, habit, prospect)* peu attrayant(e); *(person, appearance)* sans charme

unauthorized [ʌn'ɔːθəraɪzd] *adj* non autorisé(e)

unavailable [ʌnə'veɪləbəl] *adj* non disponible; **to be u.** ne pas être disponible

unavailing [ʌnə'veɪlɪŋ] *adj* vain(e)

unavoidable [ʌnə'vɔɪdəbəl] *adj* inévitable

unaware [ʌnə'weə(r)] *adj* ignorant(e); **to be u. of sth** ignorer qch

unawares [ʌnə'weəz] *adv* **to catch sb u.** prendre qn au dépourvu

unbalanced [ʌn'bælənst] *adj* **(a)** *(person)* instable **(b)** *(biased)* partial(e)

unbearable [ʌn'beərəbəl] *adj* insupportable

unbeatable [ʌn'biːtəbəl] *adj* imbattable

unbecoming [ʌnbɪ'kʌmɪŋ] *adj (behavior)* inconvenant(e); *(dress)* peu seyant(e)

unbeknown [ʌnbɪ'nəʊn], **unbeknownst** [ʌnbɪ'nəʊnst] *adv* **u.** **to me/him** à mon/son insu

unbelievable [ʌnbɪ'liːvəbəl] *adj* incroyable

unbending [ʌn'bendɪŋ] *adj* inflexible

unbias(s)ed [ʌn'baɪəst] *adj* impartial(e)

unblock [ʌn'blɒk] *vt (sink, pipe)* déboucher; *(road)* dégager

unborn ['ʌnbɔːn] *adj (child)* à naître

unbounded [ʌn'baʊndɪd] *adj* sans bornes

unbreakable [ʌn'breɪkəbəl] *adj* **(a)** *(glass, toy)* incassable **(b)** *(promise, rule)* sacré(e)

unbridled [ʌn'braɪdəld] *adj* débridé(e)

unbroken [ʌn'brəʊkən] *adj* **(a)** *(intact)* intact(e) **(b)** *(uninterrupted)* ininterrompu(e)

unburden [ʌn'bɜːdən] *vt* **to u. oneself to sb** se confier à qn

unbusinesslike [ʌn'bɪznɪslaɪk] *adj* peu professionnel(elle)

unbutton [ʌn'bʌtən] *vt* déboutonner

uncalled-for [ʌn'kɔːldfɔː(r)] *adj (of behavior, remark)* déplacé(e); *(insult)* gratuit(e)

uncanny [ʌn'kænɪ] *adj* étrange, troublant(e)

uncaring [ʌn'keərɪŋ] *adj* indifférent(e)

unceasing [ʌn'siːsɪŋ] *adj* incessant(e)

uncertain [ʌn'sɜːtən] *adj* incertain(e); **to be u. about sth** ne pas être certain(e) de qch; **it is u. if...** on ne sait pas si...; **in no u. terms** en termes on ne peut plus clairs

uncertainty [ʌn'sɜːtəntɪ] *(pl* **uncertainties)** *n* incertitude *f*

unchallenged [ʌn'tʃælɪndʒd] *adj* incontesté(e)

unchanged [ʌn'tʃeɪndʒd] *adj* inchangé(e)

unchanging [ʌn'tʃeɪndʒɪŋ] *adj* immuable

uncharacteristic [ʌnkærəktə'rɪstɪk] *adj* inhabituel(elle)

uncharitable [ʌn'tʃærɪtəbəl] *adj* peu charitable

uncharted [ʌn'tʃɑːtɪd] *adj* inexploré(e)

unchecked [ʌn'tʃekt] **1** *adj* **(a)** *(not restrained)* incontrôlé(e) **(b)** *(not verified)* non vérifié(e)
2 *adv* **to go u.** rester incontrôlé(e)

uncivil [ʌn'sɪvɪl] *adj* impoli(e)

uncivilized [ʌn'sɪvɪlaɪzd] *adj* non civilisé(e)

unclaimed [ʌn'kleɪmd] *adj* non réclamé(e); **to go u.** ne pas être réclamé(e)

uncle ['ʌŋkəl] *n* oncle *m*; **U. Sam** l'oncle Sam

unclean [ʌn'kliːn] *adj* sale, souillé(e)

unclear [ʌn'klɪə(r)] *adj* vague

unclothed [ʌn'kləʊðd] *adj* nu(e)

uncoil [ʌn'kɔɪl] *vt* dérouler

uncombed [ʌn'kəʊmd] *adj* pas peigné(e)

uncomfortable [ʌn'kʌmfətəbəl] *adj* inconfortable; *(silence)* gêné(e); **to feel u.** *(physically)* ne pas être à l'aise; *(ill at ease)* être mal à l'aise

uncommitted [ʌnkə'mɪtɪd] *adj* indécis(e)

uncommon [ʌn'kɒmən] *adj* peu commun(e)

uncommunicative [ʌnkə'mjuːnɪkətɪv] *adj* peu communicatif(ive)

uncomplicated [ʌn'kɒmplɪkeɪtɪd] *adj* simple, non compliqué(e)

uncomplimentary [ʌnkɒmplɪ'mentərɪ] *adj* peu flatteur(euse)

uncomprehending [ʌnkɒmprɪ'hendɪŋ] *adj* **to be u. of sth** ne pas comprendre qch; **with an u. look** l'air perplexe

uncompromising [ʌn'kɒmprəmaɪzɪŋ] *adj (person, opposition)* intransigeant(e)

unconcealed [ʌnkən'siːld] *adj* non dissimulé(e)

unconcerned [ʌnkən'sɜːnd] **1** *adj* indifférent(e); **to be u.** **about sth** ne pas s'inquiéter de qch
2 *adv* avec indifférence

unconditional [ʌnkən'dɪʃənəl] *adj* sans condition

unconfirmed [ʌnkən'fɜːmd] *adj* non confirmé(e)

unconnected [ʌnkə'nektɪd] *adj* sans lien

unconscious [ʌn'kɒnʃəs] **1** *adj* **(a)** *(having fainted)* sans connaissance; *(asleep)* profondément endormi(e) **(b)** *(unaware)* inconscient(e); **to be u. of sth** ne pas avoir conscience de qch
2 *n* **the u.** l'inconscient *m*

unconsciously [ʌn'kɒnʃəslɪ] *adv* inconsciemment

unconstitutional [ʌnkɒnstɪ'tjuːʃənəl] *adj* inconstitutionnel(elle)

uncontaminated [ʌnkən'tæmɪneɪtɪd] *adj* non contaminé(e)

uncontested [ʌnkən'testɪd] *adj* incontesté(e)

uncontrollable [ʌnkən'trəʊləbəl] *adj* incontrôlable

uncontroversial [ʌnkɒntrə'vɜːʃəl] *adj* anodin(e)

unconventional [ʌnkən'venʃənəl] *adj* non-conformiste

unconvinced [ʌnkən'vɪnst] *adj* sceptique

unconvincing [ʌnkən'vɪnsɪŋ] *adj* peu convaincant(e)

uncooked [ʌn'kʊkt] *adj* cru(e)

uncool [ʌn'kuːl] *adj Fam* ringard(e)

uncooperative [ʌnkəʊ'ɒpərətɪv] *adj* peu coopératif(ive)

uncoordinated [ʌnkəʊ'ɔːdɪneɪtɪd] *adj* qui manque de coordination

uncork [ʌn'kɔːk] *vt* déboucher

uncorroborated [ʌnkə'rɒbəreɪtɪd] *adj* non corroboré(e)

uncountable [ʌn'kaʊntəbəl] *adj* indénombrable

uncouth [ʌn'kuːθ] *adj* fruste

uncover [ʌn'kʌvə(r)] *vt also Fig* découvrir

uncritical [ʌn'krɪtɪkəl] *adj* peu critique; **to be u. of sb/sth** ne pas être critique envers qn/qch

UNCTAD ['ʌŋktæd] *n Econ (abbr* **United Nations Conference on Trade and Development)** CNUCED *f*

unction ['ʌŋkʃən] *n Rel* onction *f*

unctuous ['ʌŋktjʊəs] *adj Pej* onctueux(euse)

uncultivated [ʌn'kʌltɪveɪtɪd] *adj* inculte

uncultured [ʌn'kʌltʃəd] *adj* inculte

uncut [ʌn'kʌt] *adj (gem)* brut(e); *(text, movie)* intégral(e)

undamaged [ʌn'dæmɪdʒd] *adj* intact(e)

undated [ʌn'deɪtɪd] *adj* non daté(e)

undaunted [ʌn'dɔːntɪd] *adj* qui n'est pas impressionné(e); **to** **be u. by sth** ne pas se laisser impressionner par qch

undecided [ʌndɪ'saɪdɪd] *adj* **(a)** *(question, problem)* sans réponse; **that's still u.** aucune décision n'a encore été prise **(b)** *(person)* indécis(e) **(about** à propos de)

undefeated [ʌndɪ'fiːtɪd] *adj* invaincu(e)

undefended [ʌndɪ'fendɪd] *adj* sans défense

undemanding [ʌndɪ'mɑːndɪŋ] *adj (job)* peu prenant(e); *(person)* peu exigeant(e)

undemocratic [ʌndemə'krætɪk] *adj* antidémocratique

undemonstrative [ʌndɪ'mɒnstrətɪv] *adj* peu démonstratif(ive)

undeniable [ʌndɪ'naɪəbəl] *adj* indéniable

undeniably [ʌndɪ'naɪəblɪ] *adv* indéniablement

under ['ʌndə(r)] **1** *prep* **(a)** *(beneath)* sous; **u. the table/the stairs** sous la table/l'escalier; *Fam* **to be u. the weather** ne pas être dans son assiette

(b) *(less than)* moins de; **he's u. thirty** il a moins de trente ans; **children u. five** les enfants de moins de cinq ans

(c) *(under the control of)* sous; **he had a hundred men u. him** il avait cent hommes sous ses ordres; **Spain u. Franco** l'Espagne de Franco

(d) *(subject to)* **to be u. orders to do sth** avoir pour ordre de faire qch; **u. the terms of the agreement** d'après les termes de l'accord; **u. these conditions** dans ces conditions; **u. the circumstances** dans ces circonstances

(e) *(in the process of)* **u. repair/observation** en réparation/observation; **to be u. investigation** faire l'objet d'une enquête; **to get u. way** *(of meeting, campaign)* commencer

2 *adv* **(a)** *(underneath)* dessous; *(underwater)* sous l'eau; **to go u.** *(of company)* faire faillite

(b) *(less)* au-dessous; **children of five and u.** les enfants de cinq ans et au-dessous

underachiever [ʌndərə'tʃiːvə(r)] *n* = personne qui ne tire pas profit de ses capacités intellectuelles

under-age [ʌndər'eɪdʒ] *adj* mineur(e); **u. drinking** consommation *f* d'alcool par les mineurs; **u. sex** relations *fpl* sexuelles entre personnes mineures

undercarriage ['ʌndəkærɪdʒ] *n* train *m* d'atterrissage

undercharge [ʌndə'tʃɑːdʒ] *vt* se tromper dans l'addition de *(à l'avantage du client)*; **he undercharged me by $5** il aurait dû me faire payer 5 dollars de plus

underclass ['ʌndəklɑːs] *n* sous-prolétariat *m*

underclothes ['ʌndəkləʊðz] *npl* sous-vêtements *mpl*

underclothing ['ʌndəkləʊðɪŋ] *n* sous-vêtements *mpl*

undercoat ['ʌndəkəʊt] *n* sous-couche *f*

undercook [ʌndə'kʊk] *vt* ne pas faire cuire assez longtemps

undercover ['ʌndəkʌvə(r)] **1** *adj* secret(ète)
2 *adv* clandestinement

undercurrent ['ʌndəkʌrənt] *n (in sea)* courant *m* sous-marin; *Fig (of emotion, unrest)* courant sous-jacent

undercut [ʌndə'kʌt] *(pt & pp* **undercut***) vt* vendre moins cher que

underdeveloped [ʌndədɪ'veləpt] *adj* sous-développé(e)

underdog ['ʌndədɒg] *n* **(a)** *(in contest)* celui *m*/celle *f* qui risque de perdre **(b)** *(in society)* **the u.** les opprimés *mpl*

underestimate 1 *n* [ʌndər'estɪmɪt] sous-estimation *f*
2 *vt* [ʌndər'estɪmeɪt] sous-estimer

underexposed ['ʌndərɪks'pəʊzd] *adj* sous-exposé(e)

underfed [ʌndə'fed] *adj* sous-alimenté(e)

underfoot [ʌndə'fʊt] *adv* sous les pieds; **it's wet u.** le sol est mouillé; **to trample sth u.** piétiner qch

underfunding [ʌndə'fʌndɪŋ] *n* insuffisance *f* de financement

undergarment ['ʌndəgɑːmənt] *n* sous-vêtement *m*

undergo [ʌndə'gəʊ] *(pt* **underwent** [ʌndə'went]*, pp* **undergone** [ʌndə'gɒn]*) vt (change)* connaître; *(test)* subir; **to u. surgery** être opéré(e); **to u. treatment** *(of patient)* suivre un traitement

undergraduate [ʌndə'grædjʊɪt] *n* étudiant(e) *m,f* qui prépare une licence

underground 1 *adj* ['ʌndəgraʊnd] **(a)** *(below ground)* souterrain(e) **(b)** *(clandestine)* clandestin(e)

2 *adv* [ʌndə'graʊnd] **(a)** *(below ground)* sous terre **(b)** **to go u.** *(into hiding)* passer dans la clandestinité

3 *n* ['ʌndəgraʊnd] *(resistance movement)* mouvement *m* de résistance

undergrowth ['ʌndəgrəʊθ] *n* broussailles *fpl*

underhand ['ʌndəhænd] *adj* sournois(e)

underlain ['ʌndə'leɪn] *pp of* **underlie**

underlay ['ʌndəleɪ] *n (for carpet)* thibaude *f*

underlie [ʌndə'laɪ] *(pt* **underlay** [ʌndə'leɪ]*, pp* **underlain** [ʌndə'leɪn]*) vt* sous-tendre

underline [ʌndə'laɪn] *vt also Fig* souligner

underlying [ʌndə'laɪɪŋ] *adj* sous-jacent(e)

undermanning [ʌndə'mænɪŋ] *n* manque *m* de main-d'œuvre

undermentioned ['ʌndəmenʃənd] *adj Formal* ci-dessous

undermine [ʌndə'maɪn] *vt (weaken) (cliff, person, authority)* saper; *(confidence)* ébranler; *(democracy)* fragiliser

underneath [ʌndə'niːθ] **1** *prep* sous
2 *adv* dessous
3 *n* **the u.** le dessous

undernourished [ʌndə'nʌrɪʃt] *adj* sous-alimenté(e)

underpaid [ʌndə'peɪd] *adj* sous-payé(e)

underpants ['ʌndəpænts] *npl* slip *m*

underpass ['ʌndəpɑːs] *n* passage *m* souterrain

underperform [ʌndəpə'fɔːm] *vi Fin (of shares, investment)* ne pas être performant(e)

underpin [ʌndə'pɪn] *(pt & pp* **underpinned***) vt* étayer

underpopulated [ʌndə'pɒpjʊleɪtɪd] *adj* sous-peuplé(e)

underprivileged [ʌndə'prɪvɪlɪdʒd] *adj* défavorisé(e)

underqualified [ʌndə'kwɒlɪfaɪd] *adj* sous-qualifié(e)

underrate [ʌndə'reɪt] *vt* sous-estimer

undersecretary ['ʌndəsekrətərɪ] *(pl* **undersecretaries***) n Pol* sous-secrétaire *m*; **u. of state** sous-secrétaire d'État

undershirt ['ʌndəʃɜːt] *n* maillot *m* de corps

underside ['ʌndəsaɪd] *n* dessous *m*

undersized [ʌndə'saɪzd] *adj* trop petit(e)

underskirt ['ʌndəskɜːt] *n* jupon *m*; *(full-length)* combinaison *f*

understaffed [ʌndə'stɑːft] *adj* **to be u.** manquer de personnel

understand [ʌndə'stænd] *(pt & pp* **understood** [ʌndə'stʊd]*)* **1** *vt* **(a)** *(comprehend)* comprendre; **to make oneself understood** se faire comprendre; **they u. each other** ils se comprennent **(b)** *(believe, assume)* **to u. that** croire que; **I u. that you're coming to work here** j'ai appris que vous venez travailler ici; **to give sb to u. that** laisser entendre à qn que; **are we to u. that...?** devons-nous en conclure que...?

2 *vi* comprendre

understandable [ʌndə'stændəbəl] *adj* compréhensible

understandably [ʌndə'stændəblɪ] *adv* naturellement

understanding [ʌndə'stændɪŋ] **1** *n* **(a)** *(comprehension, sympathy)* compréhension *f* **(b)** *(agreement)* accord *m*; **to come to or to reach an u.** parvenir à un accord; **on the u. that** à condition que + *subjunctive*

2 *adj* compréhensif(ive)

understatement [ʌndə'steɪtmənt] *n* euphémisme *m*; *(in literature)* litote *f*; **that's an u.!** c'est peu dire!

understood [ʌndə'stʊd] *pt & pp of* **understand**

understudy ['ʌndəstʌdɪ] *n* doublure *f*

undertake [ʌndə'teɪk] *(pt* **undertook** [ʌndə'tʊk]*, pp* **undertaken** [ʌndə'teɪkən]*) vt* entreprendre; **to u. to do sth** entreprendre de faire qch

undertaker ['ʌndəteɪkə(r)] *n* entrepreneur *m* de pompes funèbres; **the undertakers** les pompes *fpl* funèbres

undertaking [ʌndə'teɪkɪŋ] *n* **(a)** *(enterprise)* entreprise *f* **(b)** *(promise)* engagement *m*, promesse *f*

undertone ['ʌndətəʊn] *n (low voice)* voix *f* basse; *Fig (hint, suggestion)* fond *m*

undertook [ʌndə'tʊk] *pt of* **undertake**

undertow ['ʌndətəʊ] *n* ressac *m*

undervalue [ʌndə'vælju:] *vt (property)* sous-évaluer; *Fig (person, ability)* sous-estimer

underwater 1 *adj* ['ʌndəwɔ:tə(r)] de plongée
    2 *adv* [ʌndə'wɔ:tə(r)] sous l'eau

underwear ['ʌndəweə(r)] *n* sous-vêtements *mpl*

underweight [ʌndə'weɪt] *adj* trop maigre

underwent [ʌndə'went] *pt of* **undergo**

underworld ['ʌndəwɜ:ld] *n* (**a**) *(in mythology)* **the U.** les Enfers *mpl* (**b**) *(of criminals)* pègre *f*

underwrite ['ʌndəraɪt] (*pt* **underwrote** [ʌndə'rəʊt], *pp* **underwritten** [ʌndə'rɪtən]) *vt* souscrire

underwriter ['ʌndəraɪtə(r)] *n (in insurance)* souscripteur *m*

underwritten [ʌndə'rɪtən] *pp of* **underwrite**

underwrote [ʌndə'rəʊt] *pt of* **underwrite**

undeserved [ʌndɪ'zɜ:vd] *adj* immérité(e)

undeserving [ʌndɪ'zɜ:vɪŋ] *adj* peu méritant(e); **to be u. of sth** ne pas mériter qch

undesirable [ʌndɪ'zaɪərəbəl] *n & adj* indésirable *mf*

undetected [ʌndɪ'tektɪd] **1** *adj* non détecté(e)
    2 *adv* **to go u.** passer inaperçu(e)

undetermined [ʌndɪ'tɜ:mɪnd] *adj* indéterminé(e)

undeterred [ʌndɪ'tɜ:d] **1** *adj* **to be u. (by sth)** ne pas se laisser décourager (par qch)
    2 *adv* sans se laisser décourager

undeveloped [ʌndɪ'veləpt] *adj* non développé(e); *(land)* inexploité(e)

undid [ʌn'dɪd] *pt of* **undo**

undies ['ʌndɪz] *npl Fam* sous-vêtements *mpl*

undigested [ʌndaɪ'dʒestɪd] *adj also Fig* non digéré(e)

undignified [ʌn'dɪgnɪfaɪd] *adj* indigne

undiluted [ʌndaɪ'lu:tɪd] *adj (liquid)* non dilué(e); *Fig (emotion)* pur(e)

undiminished [ʌndɪ'mɪnɪʃt] *adj* intact(e)

undiplomatic [ʌndɪplə'mætɪk] *adj* peu diplomate

undisciplined [ʌn'dɪsɪplɪnd] *adj* indiscipliné(e)

undisclosed [ʌndɪs'kləʊzd] *adj* non révélé(e)

undiscovered [ʌndɪs'kʌvəd] *adj* inconnu(e); **to go/to continue u.** rester ignoré(e)

undiscriminating [ʌndɪs'krɪmɪneɪtɪŋ] *adj* **to be u.** manquer de discernement

undisputed [ʌndɪs'pju:tɪd] *adj* incontesté(e)

undistinguished [ʌndɪs'tɪŋgwɪʃt] *adj* médiocre

undisturbed [ʌndɪs'tɜ:bd] *adj (sleep)* paisible; **to leave sth u.** ne pas toucher à qch

undo [ʌn'du:] (*pt* **undid** [ʌn'dɪd], *pp* **undone** [ʌn'dʌn]) *vt* (**a**) *(mistake, damage)* réparer; *Comput (command)* annuler (**b**) *(knot, button, shoelaces)* défaire; *(package, zip)* ouvrir; *(bra, dress)* dégrafer

undoing [ʌn'du:ɪŋ] *n* ruine *f*; **her pride was her u.** c'est sa fierté qui l'a perdue

undone [ʌn'dʌn] *pp of* **undo**

undoubted [ʌn'daʊtɪd] *adj* indubitable

undoubtedly [ʌn'daʊtɪdlɪ] *adv* indubitablement

undreamed-of ['ʌn'dri:mdɒv], **undreamt-of** [ʌn'dremtɒv] *adj* inimaginable

undress [ʌn'dres] **1** *vt* déshabiller; **to get undressed** se déshabiller
    2 *vi* se déshabiller
    3 *n* **in a state of u.** *(naked)* nu(e); *(nearly naked)* en petite tenue

undue [ʌn'dju:] *adj* excessif(ive)

undulate ['ʌndjʊleɪt] *vi* onduler

undulation [ʌndjʊ'leɪʃən] *n* ondulation *f*

unduly [ʌn'dju:lɪ] *adv* trop

unearned [ʌn'ɜ:nd] *adj (reward, punishment)* immérité(e); *Fin* **u. income** rentes *fpl*

unearth [ʌn'ɜ:θ] *vt (buried object)* déterrer; *Fig (information, secret)* mettre à jour

unearthly [ʌn'ɜ:θlɪ] *adj* (**a**) *(supernatural)* mystérieux(euse) (**b**) *Fam* **at an u. hour** à une heure impossible; **an u. din** or **racket** un vacarme de tous les diables; **for some u. reason** pour une raison étrange

unease [ʌn'i:z] *n* malaise *m*

uneasily [ʌn'i:zɪlɪ] *adv* d'un air gêné

uneasy [ʌn'i:zɪ] *adj (person)* mal à l'aise; *(sleep)* agité(e); *(silence)* gêné(e)

uneconomical [ʌni:kə'nɒmɪkəl] *adj* peu économique

uneducated [ʌn'edjʊkeɪtɪd] *adj* sans instruction; **to be u.** ne pas avoir d'instruction

unemotional [ʌnɪ'məʊʃənəl] *adj* impassible

unemployable [ʌnɪm'plɔɪəbəl] *adj* inemployable

unemployed [ʌnɪm'plɔɪd] **1** *npl* **the u.** les sans-emploi *mpl*, les chômeurs *mpl*
    2 *adj* sans emploi, au chômage

unemployment [ʌnɪm'plɔɪmənt] *n* chômage *m*; **u. compensation** allocation *f* (de) chômage

unending [ʌn'endɪŋ] *adj* interminable

unendurable [ʌnɪn'djʊərəbəl] *adj* insupportable

unenlightened [ʌnɪn'laɪtənd] *adj (person)* peu éclairé(e)

unenlightening [ʌnɪn'laɪtnɪŋ] *adj* obscur(e)

unenterprising [ʌn'entəpraɪzɪŋ] *adj* qui manque d'initiative

unenthusiastic [ʌnɪnθju:zɪ'æstɪk] *adj* peu enthousiaste

unenviable [ʌn'envɪəbəl] *adj* peu enviable

unequal [ʌn'i:kwəl] *adj* inégal(e)

unequivocal [ʌnɪ'kwɪvəkəl] *adj* sans équivoque

unerring [ʌn'ɜ:rɪŋ] *adj* infaillible

UNESCO [ju:'neskəʊ] *n (abbr* **United Nations Educational, Scientific and Cultural Organization**) UNESCO *f*

unethical [ʌn'eθɪkəl] *adj* contraire à l'éthique

uneven [ʌn'i:vən] *adj* inégal(e)

uneventful [ʌnɪ'ventfʊl] *adj* sans histoires

unexceptionable [ʌnɪk'sepʃənəbəl] *adj* tout à fait convenable

unexceptional [ʌnɪk'sepʃənəl] *adj* qui n'a rien d'exceptionnel

unexciting [ʌnɪk'saɪtɪŋ] *adj* peu intéressant(e)

unexpected [ʌnɪks'pektɪd] *adj* inattendu(e), imprévu(e)

unexplained [ʌnɪks'pleɪnd] *adj* inexpliqué(e)

unexplored [ʌnɪks'plɔ:d] *adj* inexploré(e)

unfailing [ʌn'feɪlɪŋ] *adj* à toute épreuve

unfair [ʌn'feə(r)] *adj* injuste; **to be u. to sb** être injuste envers qn; **to have an u. advantage (over sb)** être injustement favorisé(e) (par rapport à qn); *Com* **u. competition** concurrence *f* déloyale; *Law* **u. dismissal** licenciement *m* abusif

unfairly [ʌn'feəlɪ] *adv (act, treat)* injustement; *(share, distribute)* inéquitablement; *(dismiss)* abusivement

unfairness [ʌn'feənɪs] *n* injustice *f*

unfaithful [ʌn'feɪθfʊl] *adj* infidèle

unfamiliar [ʌnfə'mɪlɪə(r)] *adj* (**a**) *(unknown)* inconnu(e) (**b**) *(unacquainted)* **to be u. with** ne pas connaître

unfashionable [ʌn'fæʃənəbəl] *adj* démodé(e)

unfasten [ʌn'fɑ:sən] **1** *vt* défaire
    2 *vi* se défaire

unfathomable [ʌn'fæðəməbəl] *adj* insondable

unfavorable [ʌn'feɪvərəbəl] *adj* défavorable; *(moment)* peu propice

unfazed [ʌn'feɪzd] *adj Fam* **to be u. by sth** n'être pas du tout impressionné(e) par qch

unfeeling [ʌnˈfiːlɪŋ] *adj* insensible

unfinished [ʌnˈfɪnɪʃt] *adj* inachevé(e); **to have (some) u. business (with sb)** avoir des affaires à régler (avec qn)

unfit [ʌnˈfɪt] *adj* (**a**) *(unsuitable)* inapte; **to be u. to do sth** être incapable de faire qch; **he's u. for the job** il est incapable d'assumer ce travail; **u. for human consumption** impropre à la consommation; **u. mother** mère *f* indigne (**b**) *(physically)* qui n'est pas en forme; **to be u.** ne pas être en forme

unflagging [ʌnˈflægɪŋ] *adj* *(optimism, courage, enthusiasm)* inépuisable; *(attention, interest)* sans faille

unflappable [ʌnˈflæpəbəl] *adj* imperturbable

unflattering [ʌnˈflætərɪŋ] *adj* peu flatteur(euse)

unflinching [ʌnˈflɪnʃɪŋ] *adj* *(courage)* inépuisable; *(resolve, loyalty, support)* à toute épreuve

unfold [ʌnˈfəʊld] **1** *vt* (**a**) *(newspaper, map)* déplier (**b**) *(intentions, proposal)* dévoiler
2 *vi* *(of story, events)* se développer, se dérouler

unforced [ʌnˈfɔːst] *adj* naturel(elle)

unforeseeable [ʌnfɔːˈsiːəbəl] *adj* imprévisible

unforeseen [ʌnfɔːˈsiːn] *adj* imprévu(e)

unforgettable [ʌnfəˈgetəbəl] *adj* inoubliable

unforgivable [ʌnfəˈgɪvəbəl] *adj* impardonnable

unforgiving [ʌnfəˈgɪvɪŋ] *adj* implacable, impitoyable

unformatted [ʌnˈfɔːmætɪd] *adj* Comput *(disk)* non formaté(e); *(text)* non mis(e) en forme

unforthcoming [ʌnfɔːθˈkʌmɪŋ] *adj* réticent(e)

unfortunate [ʌnˈfɔːtʃənɪt] *adj* *(person)* malchanceux(euse); *(accident, event)* fâcheux(euse), regrettable; **it is u. that...** il est fâcheux *ou* regrettable que... + *subjunctive*

unfortunately [ʌnˈfɔːtʃənɪtlɪ] *adv* malheureusement

unfounded [ʌnˈfaʊndɪd] *adj* infondé(e), sans fondement

unfriendly [ʌnˈfrendlɪ] *adj* *(person)* peu sympathique; *(reception, tone, look)* froid(e)

unfulfilled [ʌnfʊlˈfɪld] *adj* *(promise)* non tenu(e); *(desire, ambition)* insatisfait(e); *(potential)* non réalisé(e); **to feel u.** se sentir insatisfait

unfunny [ʌnˈfʌnɪ] *adj* qui n'a rien de drôle

unfurl [ʌnˈfɜːl] **1** *vt* déployer
2 *vi* se déployer

unfurnished [ʌnˈfɜːnɪʃt] *adj* non meublé(e)

ungainly [ʌnˈgeɪnlɪ] *adj* disgracieux(euse)

ungenerous [ʌnˈdʒenərəs] *adj* *(person)* qui manque de générosité; *(remark)* pas gentil(ille)

ungodly [ʌnˈgɒdlɪ] *adj* impie; *Fam* **at an u. hour** à une heure impossible

ungovernable [ʌnˈgʌvənəbəl] *adj* *(people, country)* ingouvernable; *(feelings)* irrépressible

ungracious [ʌnˈgreɪʃəs] *adj* peu aimable

ungrateful [ʌnˈgreɪtfʊl] *adj* ingrat(e)

ungrudging [ʌnˈgrʌdʒɪŋ] *adj* accordé(e) de bon cœur; **to be u. in one's praise** être généreux(euse) avec ses compliments

unguarded [ʌnˈgɑːdɪd] *adj* (**a**) *(place)* sans surveillance (**b**) *(remark)* irréfléchi(e); **in an u. moment** dans un moment d'inattention

unhampered [ʌnˈhæmpəd] *adj* non entravé(e) (**by** par)

unhappily [ʌnˈhæpɪlɪ] *adv* (**a**) *(unfortunately)* malheureusement (**b**) *(sadly)* sans joie, sans bonheur

unhappiness [ʌnˈhæpɪnɪs] *n* tristesse *f*

unhappy [ʌnˈhæpɪ] *adj* (**a**) *(sad)* triste, malheureux(euse) (**b**) *(worried)* **to be u. about doing sth** ne pas vouloir faire qch (**c**) *(not pleased)* mécontent(e) (**with** de) (**d**) *(unfortunate)* malheureux(euse), regrettable

unharmed [ʌnˈhɑːmd] *adj* indemne

UNHCR [juːenertʃsiːˈɑː(r)] *n* *(abbr* **United Nations High Commission for Refugees**) HCR *m*

unhealthy [ʌnˈhelθɪ] *adj* (**a**) *(person)* maladif(ive); *(environment, climate)* malsain(e) (**b**) *(unwholesome)* malsain(e)

unheard-of [ʌnˈhɜːdɒv] *adj* (**a**) *(unknown)* inconnu(e) (**b**) *(unprecedented)* inouï(e); **it was u. in my youth!** c'était inconcevable dans ma jeunesse!

unheeded [ʌnˈhiːdɪd] *adj* ignoré(e); **to go u.** rester ignoré

unhelpful [ʌnˈhelpfʊl] *adj* *(person)* peu serviable; *(criticism, advice)* de peu d'utilité

unhesitating [ʌnˈhezɪteɪtɪŋ] *adj* *(support)* résolu(e), ferme; *(reply, reaction)* immédiat(e)

unhindered [ʌnˈhɪndəd] **1** *adj* *(progress)* sans encombres; **to be u. by sth** *(doubts, worry)* ne pas être gêné(e) par qch
2 *adv* sans encombres

unhinged [ʌnˈhɪndʒd] *adj* *(mad)* déséquilibré(e)

unhip [ʌnˈhɪp] *adj* Fam *(unfashionable)* ringard(e)

unholy [ʌnˈhəʊlɪ] *adj* impie; Fam **an u. mess/noise** une pagaille/un bruit invraisemblable; **u. alliance** alliance *f* contre nature

unhurt [ʌnˈhɜːt] *adj* indemne

unhygienic [ʌnhaɪˈdʒiːnɪk] *adj* contraire à l'hygiène; *(person)* qui manque d'hygiène

UNICEF [ˈjuːnɪsef] *n* *(abbr* **United Nations International Children's Emergency Fund**) UNICEF *m*

unicorn [ˈjuːnɪkɔːn] *n* licorne *f*

unidentified [ʌnaɪˈdentɪfaɪd] *adj* non identifié(e); **u. flying object** objet *m* volant non identifié

unification [juːnɪfɪˈkeɪʃən] *n* unification *f*

uniform [ˈjuːnɪfɔːm] **1** *n* uniforme *m*
2 *adj* *(color, size)* uniforme; *(temperature)* constant(e)

uniformity [juːnɪˈfɔːmɪtɪ] *n* uniformité *f*

uniformly [ˈjuːnɪfɔːmlɪ] *adv* uniformément

unify [ˈjuːnɪfaɪ] *(pt & pp* **unified***)* **1** *vt* unifier
2 *vi* s'unifier

unilateral [juːnɪˈlætərəl] *adj* unilatéral(e)

unimaginable [ʌnɪˈmædʒɪnəbəl] *adj* inimaginable

unimaginative [ʌnɪˈmædʒɪnətɪv] *adj* qui manque d'imagination, peu imaginatif(ive)

unimpaired [ʌnɪmˈpeəd] *adj* intact(e)

unimportant [ʌnɪmˈpɔːtənt] *adj* sans importance

unimpressed [ʌnɪmˈprest] *adj* qui n'est pas impressionné(e); *(unconvinced)* qui n'est pas convaincu(e)

uninformed [ʌnɪnˈfɔːmd] *adj* mal informé(e) (**about** sur)

uninhabitable [ʌnɪnˈhæbɪtəbəl] *adj* inhabitable

uninhabited [ʌnɪnˈhæbɪtɪd] *adj* inhabité(e)

uninhibited [ʌnɪnˈhɪbɪtɪd] *adj* *(person)* sans complexes; *(feeling)* non refréné(e)

uninitiated [ʌnɪˈnɪʃɪeɪtɪd] *adj* non initié(e)

uninspiring [ʌnɪnˈspaɪrɪŋ] *adj* peu stimulant(e)

unintelligible [ʌnɪnˈtelɪdʒɪbəl] *adj* inintelligible

unintended [ʌnɪnˈtendɪd] *adj* involontaire

unintentional [ʌnɪnˈtenʃənəl] *adj* involontaire

uninterested [ʌnˈɪntərestɪd] *adj* indifférent(e)

uninteresting [ʌnˈɪntərestɪŋ] *adj* inintéressant(e)

uninterrupted [ʌnɪntəˈrʌptɪd] *adj* ininterrompu(e)

uninvited [ʌnɪnˈvaɪtɪd] **1** *adj* *(comment, advice)* non désiré(e); **u. guest** invité(e)-surprise *m,f*
2 *adv* sans invitation

uninviting [ʌnɪnˈvaɪtɪŋ] *adj* peu attrayant(e); *(food)* peu appétissant(e)

union [ˈjuːnjən] *n* (**a**) *(between countries, people)* union *f*; **the U. Jack** l'Union Jack *m (drapeau du Royaume-Uni)* (**b**) *(trade union)* syndicat *m*

unionist [ˈjuːnjənɪst] *n* (**a**) *(supporter of trade union)* syndicaliste *mf* (**b**) *(in Northern Ireland)* unioniste *mf*

unionize [ˈjuːnjənaɪz] *vt* syndiquer

unique [juːˈniːk] *adj* unique; **to be u. to** être propre à

unisex [ˈjuːnɪseks] *adj* unisexe

unison [ˈjuːnɪsən] *n* **in u.** *(sing, play)* à l'unisson; *(speak, reply)* en même temps

unit [ˈjuːnɪt] *n* (**a**) *(in general)* unité *f*; **u. of measurement** unité de mesure; *Com* **u. price** prix *m* à l'unité (**b**) *(part of system, machine)* bloc *m*, élément *m* (**c**) *(in hospital)* service *m*, département *m*; *(in army)* unité *f* (**d**) *(of furniture)* élément *m*

unitary [ˈjuːnɪtərɪ] *adj* unitaire

unite [juːˈnaɪt] **1** *vt* unir, rassembler
2 *vi* s'unir; **to u. in doing sth** s'unir pour faire qch

united [juːˈnaɪtɪd] *adj* uni(e); **the U. Arab Emirates** les Émirats *mpl* arabes unis; **the U. Kingdom** le Royaume-Uni; **the U. Nations** les Nations *fpl* unies; **the U. States (of America)** les États-Unis *mpl* (d'Amérique)

unity [ˈjuːnɪtɪ] *n* unité *f*

univ. *(abbr* **university)** univ

universal [juːnɪˈvɜːsəl] *adj* universel(elle); **u. suffrage** suffrage *m* universel

universally [juːnɪˈvɜːsəlɪ] *adv* universellement

universe [ˈjuːnɪvɜːs] *n* univers *m*

university [juːnɪˈvɜːsɪtɪ] *n* université *f*; **u. tuition** frais *mpl* d'inscription à l'université; **u. student** étudiant(e) *m,f* à l'université, *Belg & Suisse* universitaire *mf*; **u. town** ville *f* universitaire

UNIX [ˈjuːnɪks] *n* *Comput (abbr* **Uniplexed Information and Computing System)** UNIX *m*

unjust [ʌnˈdʒʌst] *adj* injuste

unjustifiable [ʌndʒʌstɪˈfaɪəbəl] *adj* injustifiable

unjustified [ʌnˈdʒʌstɪfaɪd] *adj* injustifié(e)

unkempt [ʌnˈkem(p)t] *adj* *(appearance)* négligé(e); *(hair)* en bataille

unkind [ʌnˈkaɪnd] *adj* pas gentil(ille); **to be u. to sb** ne pas être gentil avec qn

unkindly [ʌnˈkaɪndlɪ] *adv* méchamment; **to take u. to sth** mal accepter qch

unknowingly [ʌnˈnəʊɪŋlɪ] *adv* inconsciemment

unknown [ʌnˈnəʊn] **1** *adj* inconnu(e); *Fig* **to be an u. quantity** rester une inconnue; **the U. Soldier** le Soldat inconnu
2 *adv* **u. to me/us** à mon/notre insu
3 *n (person)* inconnu(e) *m,f*; **the u.** l'inconnu *m*

unlace [ʌnˈleɪs] *vt* délacer, défaire

unladylike [ʌnˈleɪdɪlaɪk] *adj* *(person)* qui ne se conduit pas comme une jeune fille; *(behavior)* qui n'est pas digne d'une jeune fille

unlawful [ʌnˈlɔːfʊl] *adj* illégal(e), illicite

unleaded [ʌnˈledɪd] **1** *adj* sans plomb
2 *n* sans plomb *m*

unleash [ʌnˈliːʃ] *vt* *(dog)* détacher, lâcher; *Fig (emotion, criticism)* susciter

unleavened [ʌnˈlevənd] *adj* sans levain

unless [ʌnˈles] *conj* à moins que + *subjunctive*; **u. I hear to the contrary** sauf avis contraire

unlike [ʌnˈlaɪk] *prep* **to be u. sb/sth** ne pas être comme qn/qch; **he's not u. his sister** il ressemble assez à sa sœur; **he, u. his father,...** lui, à la différence de son père...; **it's u. her to do such a thing** cela ne lui ressemble pas de faire une chose pareille

unlikely [ʌnˈlaɪklɪ] *adj* improbable; *(story, explanation)* invraisemblable; **it's u. to happen** il est peu probable que cela se produise; **she's u. to do it** il est peu probable qu'elle le fasse; **in the u. event of an accident** dans le cas fort peu probable d'un accident

unlimited [ʌnˈlɪmɪtɪd] *adj* illimité(e), sans limites; *Com* **u. liability** responsabilité *f* illimitée; **u. mileage** *(of rental car)* ≃ kilométrage *m* illimité

unlisted [ʌnˈlɪstɪd] *adj* (**a**) *Fin* non inscrit(e) à la cote (**b**) *Tel (phone number)* qui est sur liste rouge

unlit [ʌnˈlɪt] *adj* *(fire, cigarette)* non allumé(e); *(place)* non éclairé(e)

unload [ʌnˈləʊd] **1** *vt* *(boat, gun, goods)* décharger; *Fig* **to u. one's problems onto sb** se soulager de ses problèmes en en parlant à qn
2 *vi* *(of truck, ship)* décharger

unlock [ʌnˈlɒk] *vt* *(door)* ouvrir; *Fig (mystery)* dévoiler, révéler

unlovable [ʌnˈlʌvəbəl] *adj* peu attachant(e)

unloved [ʌnˈlʌvd] *adj* mal aimé(e)

unlovely [ʌnˈlʌvlɪ] *adj* déplaisant(e)

unluckily [ʌnˈlʌkɪlɪ] *adv* malheureusement

unlucky [ʌnˈlʌkɪ] *adj* *(coincidence, decision)* malheureux(euse); *(day)* de malchance; **to be u.** *(of person)* être malchanceux(euse); *(of thing)* porter malheur

unmanageable [ʌnˈmænɪdʒəbəl] *adj* *(person, situation)* difficile; *(hair)* impossible à coiffer

unmanly [ʌnˈmænlɪ] *adj* *(effeminate)* efféminé(e), peu viril(e); *(cowardly)* lâche

unmanned [ʌnˈmænd] *adj* *(spaceship)* inhabité(e)

unmarked [ʌnˈmɑːkt] *adj* (**a**) *(grave)* sans inscription; **u. (police) car** voiture *f* (de police) banalisée (**b**) *(uncorrected)* non corrigé(e)

unmarried [ʌnˈmærɪd] *adj* non marié(e)

unmask [ʌnˈmɑːsk] *vt* démasquer

unmentionable [ʌnˈmenʃənəbəl] *adj* à ne pas mentionner

unmistakable [ʌnmɪsˈteɪkəbəl] *adj* caractéristique

unmissable [ʌnˈmɪsəbəl] *adj* inratable

unmitigated [ʌnˈmɪtɪgeɪtɪd] *adj* total(e), absolu(e)

unmoved [ʌnˈmuːvd] **1** *adj* **to be u. by sth** rester insensible à qch; **he was u. by her** elle le laissait complètement indifférent
2 *adv* sans broncher

unnamed [ʌnˈneɪmd] *adj* *(person)* anonyme; *(thing)* sans nom

unnatural [ʌnˈnætjərəl] *adj* (**a**) *(abnormal)* anormal(e) (**b**) *(affected)* affecté(e)

unnecessary [ʌnˈnesɪsərɪ] *adj* inutile, superflu(e)

unnerve [ʌnˈnɜːv] *vt* troubler

unnerving [ʌnˈnɜːvɪŋ] *adj* troublant(e)

unnoticed [ʌnˈnəʊtɪst] **1** *adj* inaperçu(e)
2 *adv* **to pass** *or* **to go u.** passer inaperçu(e)

UNO [juːenˈəʊ] *n* *(abbr* **United Nations Organization)** ONU *f*

unobservant [ʌnəbˈzɜːvənt] *adj* peu observateur(trice)

unobserved [ʌnəbˈzɜːvd] **1** *adj* inaperçu(e)
2 *adv* **to do sth u.** faire qch sans être vu(e)

unobstructed [ʌnəbˈstrʌktɪd] *adj* dégagé(e); *(pipe)* non obstrué(e)

unobtainable [ʌnəbˈteɪnəbəl] *adj* impossible à obtenir

unobtrusive [ʌnəbˈtruːsɪv] *adj* discret(ète)

unoccupied [ʌnˈɒkjʊpaɪd] *adj* *(person)* qui n'est pas occupé(e); *(seat)* libre; *(house)* inhabité(e), inoccupé(e)

unofficial [ʌnəˈfɪʃəl] *adj* officieux(euse), non officiel(elle)

unopened [ʌnˈəʊpənd] *adj* non ouvert(e)

unopposed [ʌnəˈpəʊzd] **1** *adj* sans opposition; **to be u.** ne pas rencontrer d'opposition
2 *adv* **to go u.** ne pas rencontrer d'opposition

unorthodox [ʌnˈɔːθədɒks] *adj* peu orthodoxe

unpack [ʌnˈpæk] **1** *vt* (**a**) *(suitcase)* défaire; *(contents)* déballer; *(box)* ouvrir (**b**) *Comput (data)* décompacter
2 *vi* défaire ses bagages

unpaid [ʌnˈpeɪd] *adj* (**a**) *(work, volunteer)* non rémunéré(e) (**b**) *(bill, debt)* impayé(e)

unpalatable [ʌnˈpælətəbəl] *adj* *(food)* qui n'est pas très bon (bonne); *Fig (truth)* désagréable à entendre

unparalleled [ʌnˈpærəleld] *adj* incomparable, sans pareil(eille)

unpardonable [ʌnˈpɑːdənəbəl] *adj* impardonnable

unpatriotic [ʌnpeɪtrɪ'ɒtɪk] *adj (person)* peu patriote; *(song, remark)* antipatriotique

unperturbed [ʌnpə'tɜːbd] **1** *adj* **to be u. by sth** ne pas se laisser perturber par qch
2 *adv* imperturbablement

unplanned [ʌn'plænd] *adj* imprévu(e); *(pregnancy)* accidentel(elle)

unpleasant [ʌn'plezənt] *adj* désagréable, déplaisant(e)

unpleasantness [ʌn'plezəntnɪs] *n* **(a)** *(unpleasant nature)* côté *m* désagréable **(b)** *(ill-feeling)* désagréments *mpl*

unplug [ʌn'plʌg] *(pt & pp* **unplugged)** *vt* débrancher

unpolished [ʌn'pɒlɪʃt] *adj (shoes, surface)* non ciré(e); *Fig (performance, style)* imparfait(e)

unpolluted [ʌnpə'luːtɪd] *adj* non pollué(e)

unpopular [ʌn'pɒpjələ(r)] *adj* impopulaire; **she's very u. with the boss at the moment** elle n'est pas dans les bonnes grâces du patron en ce moment

unpopularity [ʌnpɒpjʊ'lærɪtɪ] *n* impopularité *f*

unpredictability [ʌnprɪdɪktə'bɪlətɪ] *n* imprévisibilité *f*

unpredictable [ʌnprɪ'dɪktəbəl] *adj* imprévisible

unprejudiced [ʌn'predʒʊdɪst] *adj (view, person)* impartial(e)

unprepared [ʌnprɪ'peəd] *adj (speech)* improvisé(e); **to be u. for sth** être mal préparé(e) à qch; *(not expect)* ne pas s'attendre à qch

unprepossessing [ʌnpriːpə'zesɪŋ] *adj* peu avenant(e)

unpresentable [ʌnprɪ'zentəbəl] *adj* qui n'est pas présentable

unpretentious [ʌnprɪ'tenʃəs] *adj* sans prétention(s)

unprincipled [ʌn'prɪnsɪpəld] *adj* sans scrupules

unprintable [ʌn'prɪntəbəl] *adj* licencieux(euse)

unproductive [ʌnprə'dʌktɪv] *adj* improductif(ive)

unprofessional [ʌnprə'feʃənəl] *adj* qui n'est pas professionnel(elle)

unprofitable [ʌn'prɒfɪtəbəl] *adj* peu rentable

Unprofor [ʌn'prəfɔː(r)] *n (abbr* **United Nations Protection Force)** FORPRONU *f*

unpromising [ʌn'prɒmɪsɪŋ] *adj* peu prometteur(euse)

unpronounceable [ʌnprə'naʊnsəbəl] *adj* imprononçable

unprotected [ʌnprə'tektɪd] *adj* sans protection; *(sex)* non protégé(e)

unprovoked [ʌnprə'vəʊkt] *adj* gratuit(e)

unpublished [ʌn'pʌblɪʃt] *adj* inédit(e)

unpunished [ʌn'pʌnɪʃt] **1** *adj* impuni(e)
2 *adv* **to go u.** rester impuni(e)

unqualified [ʌn'kwɒlɪfaɪd] *adj* **(a)** *(doctor, teacher)* non qualifié(e); **to be u. to do sth** ne pas être qualifié pour faire qch **(b)** *(support)* inconditionnel(elle), sans réserve; *(disaster, success)* total(e), complet(ète)

unquestionable [ʌn'kwestjənəbəl] *adj* indubitable, incontestable

unquestioning [ʌn'kwestjənɪŋ] *adj (trust, obedience)* absolu(e), aveugle

unravel [ʌn'rævəl] **1** *vt (wool, knitting)* défaire; *(threads)* démêler; *Fig (plot)* dénouer; *(mystery)* éclaircir
2 *vi (of wool, knitting)* se défaire; *Fig (of plan)* péricliter; *(of mystery)* s'éclaircir

unreadable [ʌn'riːdəbəl] *adj* illisible

unreal [ʌn'rɪəl] *adj* irréel(elle)

unrealistic [ʌnrɪə'lɪstɪk] *adj* irréaliste

unreasonable [ʌn'riːzənəbəl] *adj* déraisonnable

unrecognizable [ʌnrekəg'naɪzəbəl] *adj* méconnaissable

unrecognized [ʌn'rekəgnaɪzd] **1** *adj* méconnu(e)
2 *adv* **to go u.** rester méconnu(e)

unrecorded [ʌnrɪ'kɔːdɪd] *adj* non enregistré(e)

unrefined [ʌnrɪ'faɪnd] *adj* **(a)** *(sugar, gas)* non raffiné(e) **(b)** *(person, taste)* qui manque de raffinement

unregistered [ʌn'redʒɪstəd] *adj (birth)* non déclaré(e)

unrelated [ʌnrɪ'leɪtɪd] *adj* **to be u.** *(of events)* ne pas avoir de rapport; *(of people)* n'avoir aucun lien de parenté

unrelenting [ʌnrɪ'lentɪŋ] *adj* incessant(e); *(person)* tenace

unreliable [ʌnrɪ'laɪəbəl] *adj* peu fiable

unrelieved [ʌnrɪ'liːvd] *adj (pain)* constant(e)

unremarkable [ʌnrɪ'mɑːkəbəl] *adj* quelconque

unremitting [ʌnrɪ'mɪtɪŋ] *adj* inlassable, infatigable

unrepentant [ʌnrɪ'pentənt] *adj* impénitent(e)

unreported [ʌnrɪ'pɔːtɪd] **1** *adj* non signalé(e)
2 *adv* **to go u.** ne pas être signalé(e)

unrepresentative [ʌnreprɪ'zentətɪv] *adj* non représentatif(ive)

unrepresented [ʌnreprɪ'zentɪd] *adj* non représenté(e)

unrequited love ['ʌnrɪkwaɪtɪd'lʌv] *n* amour *m* non partagé

unreserved [ʌnrɪ'zɜːvd] *adj* **(a)** *(praise, support)* sans réserve **(b)** *(seat, table)* non réservé(e)

unresponsive [ʌnrɪ'spɒnsɪv] *adj* sans réaction; **to be u. to sth** être insensible à qch

unrest [ʌn'rest] *n* agitation *f*, troubles *mpl*

unrestricted [ʌnrɪ'strɪktɪd] *adj* illimité(e); *(access)* libre

unrewarding [ʌnrɪ'wɔːdɪŋ] *adj (financially)* qui ne rapporte pas; *(intellectually)* ingrat(e)

unripe [ʌn'raɪp] *adj* qui n'est pas mûr(e)

unrivaled [ʌn'raɪvəld] *adj* sans pareil(eille), incomparable

unromantic [ʌnrə'mæntɪk] *adj* peu romantique

unruffled [ʌn'rʌfəld] *adj* imperturbable

unruly [ʌn'ruːlɪ] *adj (child, hair)* indiscipliné(e); *(crowd)* incontrôlé(e)

unsaddle [ʌn'sædəl] *vt (horse)* desseller

unsafe [ʌn'seɪf] *adj* **(a)** *(in danger)* en danger **(b)** *(dangerous)* dangereux(euse)

unsaid [ʌn'sed] *adj* **to leave sth u.** passer qch sous silence; **it's better left u.** il vaut mieux garder le silence là-dessus

unsalted [ʌn'sɔːltɪd] *adj* sans sel; **u. butter** beurre *m* doux

unsatisfactory [ʌnsætɪs'fæktərɪ] *adj* peu satisfaisant(e)

unsatisfying [ʌn'sætɪsfaɪɪŋ] *adj* peu satisfaisant(e)

unsavory [ʌn'seɪvərɪ] *adj (person, place)* peu recommandable; *(reputation)* sale

unscathed [ʌn'skeɪðd] *adj* indemne

unscheduled [ʌn'skedjuːld] *adj* imprévu(e)

unscientific [ʌnsaɪən'tɪfɪk] *adj* non scientifique

unscramble [ʌn'skræmbəl] *vt* décoder

unscrew [ʌn'skruː] **1** *vt* dévisser
2 *vi* se dévisser

unscrupulous [ʌn'skruːpjʊləs] *adj (person)* sans scrupules; *(action)* malhonnête

unseat [ʌn'siːt] *vt (rider)* désarçonner; *Fig (leader)* faire tomber

unseemly [ʌn'siːmlɪ] *adj* inconvenant(e), indécent(e)

unseen [ʌn'siːn] **1** *adj* invisible; **u. translation** traduction *f* à vue
2 *adv* **to do sth u.** faire qch sans qu'on vous voie

unselfconscious [ʌnself'kɒnʃəs] *adj* naturel(elle); **he's quite u. about it** il n'en est pas du tout complexé

unselfish [ʌn'selfɪʃ] *adj* généreux(euse)

unsentimental [ʌnsentɪ'mentəl] *adj (person)* peu sentimental(e); *(book, movie)* dénué(e) de tout sentimentalisme

unsettle [ʌn'setəl] *vt* troubler, perturber

unshakeable [ʌn'ʃeɪkəbəl] *adj* inébranlable

unshaven [ʌn'ʃeɪvən] *adj* pas rasé(e)

unsightly [ʌn'saɪtlɪ] *adj* laid(e)

unsigned [ʌn'saɪnd] *adj* non signé(e)

unskillful [ʌn'skɪlfʊl] *adj* maladroit(e), malhabile

unskilled [ʌn'skɪld] *adj* non qualifié(e)

unsociable [ʌn'səʊʃəbəl] *adj (by nature)* sauvage; **she's feeling rather u. at the moment** elle n'a pas envie de voir du monde en ce moment

unsold [ʌn'səʊld] *adj* invendu(e)

unsolicited [ʌnsə'lɪsɪtɪd] *adj* non sollicité(e)

unsolved [ʌn'sɒlvd] *adj* non résolu(e)

unsophisticated [ʌnsə'fɪstɪkeɪtɪd] *adj* simple

unsound [ʌn'saʊnd] *adj* **(a)** *(health)* précaire; *Law* **to be of u. mind** ne pas jouir de toutes ses facultés mentales **(b)** *(decision, advice)* peu judicieux(euse); *(investment)* hasardeux(euse); **he's ideologically u.** son idéologie est suspecte

unsparing [ʌn'speərɪŋ] *adj* **to be u. of one's time/with one's advice** ne pas être avare de son temps/de ses conseils

unspeakable [ʌn'spi:kəbəl] *adj* indescriptible

unspecified [ʌn'spesɪfaɪd] *adj* non spécifié(e)

unspoiled [ʌn'spɔɪld], **unspoilt** [ʌn'spɔɪlt] *adj (beach, landscape)* préservé(e)

unspoken [ʌn'spəʊkən] *adj (fear, threat)* inexprimé(e); *(agreement)* tacite

unsporting [ʌn'spɔ:tɪŋ], **unsportsmanlike** [ʌn'spɔ:tsmənlaɪk] *adj* qui n'est pas fair-play

unstable [ʌn'steɪbəl] *adj* instable

unsteady [ʌn'stedɪ] *adj (table, chair)* bancal(e); *(hand, voice)* mal assuré(e); **to be u. on one's feet** ne pas être très solide sur ses jambes

unstinting [ʌn'stɪntɪŋ] *adj (praise, effort)* sans réserve

unstressed [ʌn'strest] *adj Ling* inaccentué(e)

unstuck [ʌn'stʌk] *adj Fam* **to come u.** *(of person)* se casser la figure; *(of plan)* tomber à l'eau

unsubscribe [ʌnsəb'skraɪb] *vi Comput (from ISP)* résilier son abonnement; *(from mailing list)* se désinscrire

unsubstantiated [ʌnsəb'stænʃɪeɪtɪd] *adj (accusation)* sans fondement

unsuccessful [ʌnsək'sesfʊl] *adj* **to be u.** *(of person, project)* ne pas réussir

unsuccessfully [ʌnsək'sesfəlɪ] *adv* en vain, sans succès

unsuitable [ʌn'su:təbəl] *adj (candidate)* inadéquat(e); *(friend)* pas convenable; *(time)* inopportun(e); *(choice)* inapproprié(e); **to be u. for sth** ne pas convenir à qch; **this movie is u. for children** ce n'est pas un film pour les enfants

unsuited [ʌn'su:tɪd] *adj* **to be u. to sth** ne pas être fait(e) pour qch; **to be u.** *(of couple)* être mal assorti(e)

unsupervised [ʌn'su:pəvaɪzd] *adj (child)* non surveillé(e)

unsupported [ʌnsə'pɔ:tɪd] *adj* **(a)** *(statement, charges)* sans fondement **(b)** *(structure)* non soutenu(e)

unsure [ʌn'ʃʊə(r)] *adj* incertain(e), peu sûr(e); **to be u. of** *or* **about sth** ne pas être sûr de qch

unsurpassed [ʌnsə'pɑ:st] *adj* inégalé(e)

unsuspected [ʌnsəs'pektɪd] *adj* insoupçonné(e)

unsuspecting [ʌnsəs'pektɪŋ] *adj* qui ne se doute de rien

unsustainable [ʌnsə'steɪnəbəl] *adj* non viable

unsweetened [ʌn'swi:tənd] *adj* non sucré(e), sans sucre ajouté

unswerving [ʌn'swɜ:vɪŋ] *adj* à toute épreuve

unsympathetic [ʌnsɪmpə'θetɪk] *adj* peu compatissant(e) (**to** à); *(to cause, request)* insensible (**to** à)

unsystematic [ʌnsɪstə'mætɪk] *adj* non systématique

untainted [ʌn'teɪntɪd] *adj (food)* qui n'a pas été contaminé(e); *(reputation)* qui n'a pas été entaché(e)

untalented [ʌn'tæləntɪd] *adj* peu doué(e)

untamed [ʌn'teɪmd] *adj (animal)* sauvage

untangle [ʌn'tæŋgəl] *vt* démêler; *Fig (plot)* dénouer

untapped [ʌn'tæpt] *adj* inexploité(e)

untenable [ʌn'tenəbəl] *adj (position)* intenable; *(theory)* indéfendable

untested [ʌn'testɪd] *adj (drug, product)* non testé(e); *(method, system)* qui n'a pas été mis(e) à l'épreuve

unthinkable [ʌn'θɪŋkəbəl] *adj* impensable, inconcevable

untidiness [ʌn'taɪdɪnɪs] *n* désordre *m*

untidy [ʌn'taɪdɪ] *adj (person)* désordonné(e); *(place)* en désordre

untie [ʌn'taɪ] *vt (knot, shoelaces)* défaire; *(string)* dénouer; *(person, animal)* détacher

until [ʌn'tɪl] **1** *prep* jusqu'à; **u. April** jusqu'en avril; **u. now** jusqu'à présent; **not u. tomorrow** pas avant demain; **I didn't see her u. Sunday** c'est seulement dimanche que je l'ai vue
2 *conj* jusqu'à ce que + *subjunctive*; **u. she gets back** jusqu'à ce qu'elle revienne; **don't move u. I tell you** ne bouge pas avant que je (ne) te le dise

untimely [ʌn'taɪmlɪ] *adj (death)* prématuré(e); *(remark)* inopportun(e); *(moment)* mauvais(e)

untiring [ʌn'taɪərɪŋ] *adj* infatigable, inlassable

untold [ʌn'təʊld] *adj (wealth, beauty)* immense

untouchable [ʌn'tʌtʃəbəl] **1** *n* intouchable *mf*; *Fig* paria *m*
2 *adj* intouchable

untouched [ʌn'tʌtʃt] *adj* qui n'a pas été touché(e); **to leave sth u.** ne pas toucher à qch

untoward [ʌntə'wɔ:d] *adj Formal* fâcheux(euse), malencontreux(euse)

untrained [ʌn'treɪnd] *adj (animal)* non dressé(e); *(person)* sans formation

untranslatable [ʌntræns'leɪtəbəl] *adj* intraduisible

untried [ʌn'traɪd] *adj* **(a)** *(person, system)* qui n'a pas encore fait ses preuves **(b)** *Law (person, case)* non jugé(e)

untroubled [ʌn'trʌbəld] *adj* tranquille, calme; **to be u. by sth** ne pas être perturbé(e) par qch

untrue [ʌn'tru:] *adj* **(a)** *(false)* faux (fausse) **(b)** *(unfaithful)* infidèle (**to** à)

untrustworthy [ʌn'trʌstwɜ:ðɪ] *adj (person)* qui n'est pas digne de confiance; *(information)* qui n'est pas fiable

untruth [ʌn'tru:θ] *n* mensonge *m*

untruthful [ʌn'tru:θfʊl] *adj (person)* menteur(euse); *(story, reply)* mensonger(ère)

unusable [ʌn'ju:zəbəl] *adj* inutilisable

unused *adj* **(a)** [ʌn'ju:zd] *(not in use)* inutilisé(e) **(b)** [ʌn'ju:zd] *(never yet used)* neuf (neuve) **(c)** [ʌn'ju:st] *(unaccustomed)* **to be u. to sth/to doing sth** ne pas avoir l'habitude de qch/de faire qch

unusual [ʌn'ju:ʒʊəl] *adj (not common)* inhabituel(elle); *(strange)* bizarre, étrange; **it's u. of her not to notice** c'est rare qu'elle ne s'en rende pas compte

unusually [ʌn'ju:ʒʊəlɪ] *adv* exceptionnellement

unvaried [ʌn'veərɪd] *adj* monotone

unvarnished [ʌn'vɑ:nɪʃt] *adj* non verni(e); *Fig* **the u. truth** la vérité pure et simple

unveil [ʌn'veɪl] *vt also Fig* dévoiler

unverifiable [ʌn'verɪfaɪəbəl] *adj* invérifiable

unvoiced [ʌn'vɔɪst] *adj* **(a)** *Ling* non voisé(e) **(b)** *(unspoken)* inexprimé(e)

unwaged [ʌn'weɪdʒd] **1** *npl* **the u.** ceux qui n'ont pas d'activité rémunérée
2 *adj* qui n'a pas d'activité rémunérée

unwanted [ʌn'wɒntɪd] *adj* non désiré(e); **to feel u.** se sentir de trop

unwarranted [ʌn'wɒrəntɪd] *adj* injustifié(e)

unwary [ʌn'weərɪ] *adj* sans méfiance

unwashed [ʌn'wɒʃt] **1** *adj (dishes, floor)* non lavé(e); *(person)* qui ne s'est pas lavé(e)
2 *npl Fam Hum* **the great u.** la populace

unwavering [ʌn'weɪvərɪŋ] *adj (devotion)* inébranlable; *(loyalty, support)* à toute épreuve; *(gaze)* fixe

unwelcome [ʌn'welkəm] *adj (visit, visitor)* importun(e); *(news)* fâcheux(euse); **to make sb feel u.** faire sentir à qn qu'il n'est pas le bienvenu

unwell [ʌn'wel] *adj* souffrant(e)

unwholesome [ʌn'həʊlsəm] *adj* malsain(e)

unwieldy [ʌn'wiːldɪ] *adj (object)* difficile à manier; *Fig (system, method)* lourd(e)

unwilling [ʌn'wɪlɪŋ] *adj* réticent(e); **to be u. to do sth** être réticent à faire qch

unwillingness [ʌn'wɪlɪŋnɪs] *n* réticence *f*

unwind [ʌn'waɪnd] (*pt & pp* **unwound** [ʌn'waʊnd]) **1** *vt (string, wool)* dérouler
2 *vi* (**a**) *(of string, wool)* se dérouler (**b**) *Fam (relax)* se détendre, se relaxer

unwise [ʌn'waɪz] *adj (person)* imprudent(e); *(decision, action)* peu judicieux(euse)

unwitting [ʌn'wɪtɪŋ] *adj* involontaire

unworkable [ʌn'wɜːkəbəl] *adj* impraticable

unworthy [ʌn'wɜːðɪ] *adj* indigne (**of** de)

unwrap [ʌn'ræp] (*pt & pp* **unwrapped**) *vt* déballer

unwritten [ʌn'rɪtən] *adj (language)* non écrit(e); *(agreement)* verbal(e); **it's an u. rule that...** il est entendu que...

unyielding [ʌn'jiːldɪŋ] *adj* inflexible

unzip [ʌn'zɪp] (*pt & pp* **unzipped**) *vt* (**a**) *(garment, bag etc)* ouvrir (la fermeture Éclair® de) (**b**) *Comput (file)* décompresser, dézipper

up [ʌp] **1** *adv* (**a**) *(with motion)* **to come/to go up** monter; **to go up to sb** s'approcher de qn; **to go up north** aller au nord; **to put one's hand up** lever la main; **to put a poster up** accrocher un poster; **gas has gone up in price** l'essence a augmenté
(**b**) *(with position)* en haut; **up here** ici; **up there** là-haut; **up above** au-dessus; **further up** plus haut; **gas is up in price** l'essence a augmenté
(**c**) *(ahead)* **to be one goal/five points up** avoir un but/ cinq points d'avance
(**d**) *(in phrases with* **to**) **up to now/the age of seven** jusqu'à maintenant/l'âge de sept ans; **what are the children up to?** que fabriquent les enfants?; **she's up to something** elle manigance quelque chose; **what have you been up to?** qu'est-ce que tu deviens?; **it's up to you to do it** c'est à vous de le faire; **it's up to you** *(you decide)* c'est à vous de décider; **he's not up to the job** il n'est pas à la hauteur de la tâche; **I don't feel up to it** je ne m'en sens pas capable; **it's not up to much** *(not very good)* ce n'est pas extraordinaire
2 *prep* (**a**) *(with motion)* **to go up the stairs/the street** monter les escaliers/la rue; **to run up the stairs/the street** monter les escaliers/la rue en courant; **to climb up a hill** monter à une colline; *Vulg* **up yours!** va te faire foutre!
(**b**) *(with position)* **to be up a tree/ladder** être dans un arbre/sur une échelle; **to live up the street (from sb)** habiter plus haut dans la rue (que qn); *Fig* **to be up against sth** avoir affaire à qch
3 *adj* (**a**) *(out of bed)* levé(e); **I was up at seven** j'étais levé à sept heures; **she was up late last night** elle a veillé tard hier soir; **we were up all night** nous sommes restés debout toute la nuit; **to be up and about** être debout; *(after illness)* être sur pied
(**b**) *(finished)* **the two weeks were up** les deux semaines étaient terminées; **(your) time's up** c'est terminé
(**c**) *Fam (wrong)* **something's up** quelque chose ne va pas; **what's up?** qu'est-ce qu'il y a?; **what's up with her?** qu'est-ce qu'elle a?
(**d**) *(idiom)* **to be up and running** *(of machine, system)* être opérationnel(elle)
4 *n* **to be on the up (and up)** *(market)* être à la hausse; *(price)* être en hausse; *(person, celebrity)* qui monte; **ups and downs** des hauts et des bas
5 *vt* (*pt & pp* **upped**) *Fam (price, offer)* augmenter
6 *vi Fam* **to up and go** *or* **leave** filer

up-and-coming ['ʌpənd'kʌmɪŋ] *adj* qui monte

upbeat [ʌp'biːt] *adj* optimiste

upbraid [ʌp'breɪd] *vt Formal* réprimander; **to u. sb for sth** reprocher qch à qn; **to u. sb for doing sth** reprocher à qn d'avoir fait qch

upbringing ['ʌpbrɪŋɪŋ] *n* éducation *f*

upcoming ['ʌp'kʌmɪŋ] *adj (event)* à venir, prochain(e); *(book)* à paraître, qui va paraître; *(movie)* qui va sortir; **the u. election** l'élection qui va bientôt avoir lieu

update 1 *n* ['ʌpdeɪt] mise *f* à jour, actualisation *f*
2 *vt* [ʌp'deɪt] mettre à jour, actualiser; **to u. sb on sth** mettre qn au courant de qch

upend [ʌp'end] *vt* renverser

upfront [ʌp'frʌnt] **1** *adj Fam (frank)* franc (franche), direct(e)
2 *adv (in advance)* d'avance

upgradable [ʌp'greɪdəbəl] *adj Comput (hardware, system)* évolutif(ive); *(memory)* extensible

upgrade 1 *n* ['ʌpgreɪd] (**a**) *Comput (of hardware)* augmentation *f* de puissance; *(of software)* nouvelle version *f* (**b**) *(on plane)* surclassement *m*
2 *vt* [ʌp'greɪd] (**a**) *(improve)* améliorer; *(promote)* promouvoir; **I was upgraded to business class** *(on plane)* on m'a mis en classe affaires (**b**) *Comput (hardware)* augmenter la puissance de; *(software)* acquérir la dernière version de

upheaval [ʌp'hiːvəl] *n* bouleversement *m*

upheld [ʌp'held] *pt & pp of* **uphold**

uphill ['ʌphɪl] **1** *adj* qui monte; *Fig (struggle)* ardu(e), pénible
2 *adv* **to go u.** monter

uphold [ʌp'həʊld] (*pt & pp* **upheld** [ʌp'held]) *vt (opinion, principle)* soutenir; *(decision)* maintenir; **to u. the law** faire respecter la loi

upholstered [ʌp'həʊlstəd] *adj* tapissé(e)

upholstery [ʌp'həʊlstərɪ] *n* tapisserie *f*; *(in car)* sièges *mpl*

upkeep ['ʌpkiːp] *n* entretien *m*

uplift 1 *n* ['ʌplɪft] élévation *f* morale *ou* spirituelle
2 *vt* [ʌp'lɪft] élever

uplifting [ʌp'lɪftɪŋ] *adj* édifiant(e)

upload [ʌp'ləʊd] *Comput* **1** *vt* télécharger *(vers le serveur)*
2 *vi* effectuer un téléchargement *(vers le serveur)*

upmarket [ʌp'mɑːkɪt] *adj (product)* haut de gamme *inv*; *(area, place)* chic *inv*

upon [ə'pɒn] *prep* sur; **u. my word!** ma parole!

upper ['ʌpə(r)] **1** *adj* supérieur(e); **the u. class** l'aristocratie *f*; **to get/have the u. hand** prendre/avoir le dessus
2 *n (of shoe)* empeigne *f*; *Fam* **to be on one's uppers** manger de la vache enragée; *Fam* **uppers** *(amphetamines)* amphés *fpl*

upper-class ['ʌpəklɑːs] *adj* aristocratique

upper-crust ['ʌpəkrʌst] *adj Fam* aristo

uppermost ['ʌpəməʊst] *adj* le (la) plus haut(e); *Fig* **it was u. in my mind** c'était la première de mes préoccupations

uppity ['ʌpɪtɪ] *adj Fam* crâneur(euse); **to get u.** crâner

upright ['ʌpraɪt] **1** *adj* (**a**) *(vertical)* droit(e); **u. piano** piano *m* droit; **u. vacuum cleaner** aspirateur *m* balai (**b**) *(honest)* droit(e)
2 *adv* droit; **to set** *or* **to stand sth u.** mettre qch debout *ou* d'aplomb
3 *n (beam)* montant *m*

uprising ['ʌpraɪzɪŋ] *n* soulèvement *m*, révolte *f*

uproar ['ʌprɔː(r)] *n (noise, protest)* tumulte *m*; **the house was in an u.** ce fut le tumulte dans la maison

uproarious [ʌp'rɔːrɪəs] *adj (noisy)* tonitruant(e); *(funny)* hilarant(e)

uproot [ʌp'ruːt] *vt* déraciner

upset 1 *vt* [ʌp'set] (*pt & pp* **upset**) (**a**) *(liquid, container)* renverser (**b**) *(person, plans, schedule)* bouleverser
2 *n* ['ʌpset] *(disturbance)* bouleversement *m*; *(surprise)* défaite *f*; **to have a stomach u.** avoir l'estomac dérangé
3 *adj* [ʌp'set] *(unhappy)* bouleversé(e) (**about** par); **to have an u. stomach** avoir l'estomac dérangé

upsetting [ʌpˈsetɪŋ] *adj* bouleversant(e)

upshot [ˈʌpʃɒt] *n* conséquence *f*, résultat *m*

upside down [ˈʌpsaɪdˈdaʊn] **1** *adj* à l'envers
2 *adv* à l'envers; **to turn sth u.** retourner qch; *Fig* mettre qch sens dessus dessous

upstage [ʌpˈsteɪdʒ] **1** *adv Theat (move)* vers le fond de la scène; **u. of sb/sth** à l'arrière-plan par rapport à qn/qch
2 *vt Theat & Fig* éclipser, voler la vedette à

upstairs 1 *n* [ʌpˈsteəz] étage *m*
2 *adj* [ˈʌpsteəz] de l'étage du dessus; **u. neighbors** les voisins du dessus; **the u. bathroom** la salle de bains du haut
3 *adv* [ʌpˈsteəz] en haut; **to come/go u.** monter; **he lives u.** il habite à l'étage au-dessus

upstanding [ʌpˈstændɪŋ] *adj* droit(e)

upstart [ˈʌpstɑːt] *n* parvenu(e) *m,f*

upstream [ʌpˈstriːm] *adv* en amont; *(with movement)* vers l'amont

upsurge [ˈʌpsɜːdʒ] *n (of anger, enthusiasm)* vague *f*; *(of interest)* recrudescence *f*

upswing [ˈʌpswɪŋ] *n* amélioration *f* (**in** de); *(in economy)* redressement *m* (**in** de)

uptake [ˈʌpteɪk] *n Fam* **to be quick on the u.** piger vite; **to be slow on the u.** être lent(e) à la détente

uptight [ʌpˈtaɪt] *adj Fam (nervous)* tendu(e), crispé(e); *(inhibited)* coincé(e)

up-to-date [ʌptəˈdeɪt] *adj* **(a)** *(most recent)* à jour; *(news)* récent(e); **to bring sb u. (on sth)** mettre qn au courant (de qch) **(b)** *(modern)* à la mode

up-to-the-minute [ʌptəðəˈmɪnɪt] *adj (news, information)* de dernière minute; *(style, fashion)* dernier cri *inv*

upturn [ˈʌptɜːn] *n* amélioration *f* (**in** de); *(in economy)* redressement *m* (**in** de)

upturned [ʌpˈtɜːnd] *adj (bucket, box)* retourné(e); *(nose)* retroussé(e)

upward [ˈʌpwəd] **1** *adj* vers le haut; **u. mobility** ascension *f* sociale; **an u. trend** une tendance à la hausse
2 *adv* vers le haut; **from $100 u.** à partir de 100 dollars; **u. of** plus de

upwardly mobile [ˈʌpwədlɪˈməʊbaɪl] *adj* qui connaît une ascension sociale rapide

upwards [ˈʌpwədz] *adv* = **upward**

Urals [ˈjʊərəlz] *npl* **the U.** l'Oural *m*

uranium [jʊˈreɪnɪəm] *n* uranium *m*

Uranus [jʊˈreɪnəs] *n (planet)* Uranus *f*

urban [ˈɜːbən] *adj* urbain(e); **u. legend** *or* **myth** = anecdote souvent inventée mais qui passe pour vraie; **u. renewal** rénovations *fpl* urbaines; **u. sprawl** étalement *m* urbain

urbane [ɜːˈbeɪn] *adj* urbain(e), courtois(e)

urbanization [ɜːbənaɪˈzeɪʃən] *n (process)* urbanisation *f*

urchin [ˈɜːtʃɪn] *n* galopin(e) *m,f*

Urdu [ˈʊəduː] *n* ourdou *m*

urethra [jʊˈriːθrə] *n* urètre *m*

urge [ɜːdʒ] **1** *n* terrible envie *f*; **to have an u. to do sth** avoir très envie de faire qch
2 *vt* **(a)** *(encourage)* **to u. sb to do sth** presser qn de faire qch **(b)** *(recommend)* conseiller; **to u. that sth be done** insister pour que qch soit fait

▸**urge on** *vt sep* encourager; **to u. sb on to do sth** encourager qn à faire qch

urgency [ˈɜːdʒənsɪ] *n* urgence *f*; **it's a matter of u.** il y a urgence

urgent [ˈɜːdʒənt] *adj* urgent(e); **to be in u. need of sth** avoir un besoin urgent de qch

urgently [ˈɜːdʒəntlɪ] *adv* d'urgence

urinal [ˈjʊərɪnəl] *n* urinoir *m*

urinary [ˈjʊərɪnərɪ] *adj* urinaire

urinate [ˈjʊərɪneɪt] *vi* uriner

urine [ˈjʊərɪn] *n* urine *f*

URL [juːɑːˈrel] *n Comput (abbr* **uniform resource locator**) *(adresse f)* URL *m*

urn [ɜːn] *n* urne *f*; **(tea) u.** fontaine *f* (à thé)

urology [jʊˈrɒlədʒɪ] *n Med* urologie *f*

Uruguay [ˈjʊərəgwaɪ] *n* l'Uruguay *m*

Uruguayan [jʊərəˈgwaɪən] **1** *n* Uruguayen(enne) *m,f*
2 *adj* uruguayen(enne)

us [*stressed* ʌs, *unstressed* əs] *pron* **(a)** *(direct object)* nous; **she hates us** elle nous déteste; **she can understand our son but not us** elle comprend notre fils, mais nous, elle ne nous comprend pas **(b)** *(indirect object)* nous; **she gave us the book** elle nous a donné le livre; **she gave it to us** elle nous l'a donné **(c)** *(after preposition)* nous; **she's thinking of us** elle pense à nous **(d)** *(as complement of verb* **to be**) nous; **it's us!** c'est nous!; **it was us who did it** c'est nous qui l'avons fait

US [juːˈes] **1** *n (abbr* **United States**) **the US** les USA *mpl*
2 *adj (forces, officials)* américain(e), des États-Unis

USA [juːesˈeɪ] *n* **(a)** *(abbr* **United States of America**) **the U.** les USA *mpl* **(b)** *(abbr* **United States Army**) = armée de terre des États-Unis

usability [juːzəˈbɪlɪtɪ] *n* facilité *f* d'utilisation

usable [ˈjuːzəbəl] *adj* utilisable

USAF [juːeserˈef] *n (abbr* **United States Air Force**) = armée de l'air des États-Unis

usage [ˈjuːsɪdʒ] *n* usage *m*

use 1 *n* [juːs] **(a)** *(utilization)* utilisation *f*, emploi *m*; **to make (good) u. of sth** faire (bon) usage de qch; **to be in u.** être utilisé(e); **not in u., out of u.** hors d'usage
(b) *(ability, permission to use)* usage *m*; **to have the u. of sth** pouvoir utiliser qch; **she has full u. of her faculties** elle jouit de toutes ses facultés
(c) *(usefulness)* **to be of u.** être utile; **can I be of any u. to you?** puis-je vous être d'une quelconque utilité?; **it's not much u.** cela ne sert pas à grand-chose; **to have no u. for sth** ne pas avoir l'usage de qch; **it's no u.** cela ne sert à rien; **it's no u. crying** cela ne sert à rien de pleurer; **what's the u. of worrying?** à quoi bon s'inquiéter?
2 *vt* [juːz] **(a)** *(utilize)* utiliser, se servir de; *(force, diplomacy)* avoir recours à; *Fam* **u. your head!** réfléchis un peu!; *Fam* **I could u. some sleep** un peu de sommeil ne me ferait pas de mal
(b) *(exploit)* utiliser, se servir de
(c) *(consume) (gas, electricity)* consommer; **who's used all the milk?** qui a pris tout le lait?
3 *v aux* **used to** [ˈjuːstə] *(translated by imperfect of main verb)* **we used to live abroad** (autrefois,) nous vivions à l'étranger; **I didn't u. to like him** avant, je ne l'aimais pas; **do you travel much? – I used to** tu voyages beaucoup? – autrefois, oui

▸**use up** *vt sep (food, fuel)* finir; *(ideas)* épuiser; *(money)* dépenser

use-by date [ˈjuːzbaɪdeɪt] *n* date *f* limite de consommation

used *adj* **(a)** [juːzd] *(second-hand)* d'occasion **(b)** [juːst] *(accustomed)* **to be u. to sth/to doing sth** être habitué(e) à qch/à faire qch; **to get u. to sb/sth** s'habituer à qn/qch

useful [ˈjuːsfʊl] *adj* utile; **to make oneself u.** se rendre utile

usefully [ˈjuːsfʊlɪ] *adv* utilement

usefulness [ˈjuːsfʊlnɪs] *n* utilité *f*

useless [ˈjuːslɪs] *adj* **(a)** *(not useful)* inutile; **to be worse than u.** ne servir strictement à rien **(b)** *(incompetent)* nul (nulle) (**at** en)

user [ˈjuːzə(r)] *n (of road, dictionary)* utilisateur(trice) *m,f*; *(of telephone)* usager *m*; *(of drugs)* consommateur(trice) *m,f*; *Comput* **u. name** nom *m* de l'utilisateur

user-friendly [juːzəˈfrendlɪ] *adj* convivial(e)

usher ['ʌʃə(r)] **1** *n (in court)* huissier *m*; *(in theater, movie theater)* ouvreur *m*; *(at wedding)* placeur *m*
  2 *vt* **to u. sb in/out** faire entrer/sortir qn
usherette [ʌʃə'ret] *n* ouvreuse *f*
USIA [ju:esaɪ'eɪ] *n (abbr* **United States Information Agency**) renseignements *mpl* généraux américains
USN [ju:es'en] *n (abbr* **United States Navy**) = marine de guerre des États-Unis
USP [ju:es'pi:] *n Com (abbr* **unique selling point** *or* **proposition**) avantage *m* unique
USS [ju:es'es] *n (abbr* **United States Ship**) U. Lexington le Lexington *(bâtiment de la marine américaine)*
USSR [ju:eses'ɑ:(r)] *n Formerly (abbr* **Union of Soviet Socialist Republics**) URSS *f*
usual ['ju:ʒʊəl] **1** *adj* habituel(elle); **you're not your u. cheery self today** tu n'es pas aussi gai que d'habitude aujourd'hui; **earlier/later than u.** plus tôt/tard que d'habitude; **as u.** comme d'habitude
  2 *n Fam (drink)* **the u., sir?** comme d'habitude, monsieur?
usually ['ju:ʒʊəlɪ] *adv* habituellement, d'habitude; **he was more than u. polite** il était plus poli que d'habitude
usurer ['ju:ʒərə(r)] *n* usurier(ère) *m,f*
usurp [ju:'zɜ:p] *vt* usurper
usurper [jʊ'zɜ:pə(r)] *n* usurpateur(trice) *m,f*
usury ['ju:ʒʊrɪ] *n* usure *f*
utensil [ju:'tensəl] *n* ustensile *m*
uterus ['ju:tərəs] *(pl* **uteri** ['ju:təraɪ]) *n* utérus *m*

utilitarian [ju:tɪlɪ'teərɪən] **1** *adj (approach, design)* utilitaire; *(in philosophy)* utilitariste
  2 *n (in philosophy)* utilitariste *mf*
utility [ju:'tɪlɪtɪ] *(pl* **utilities**) *n* **(a)** *(usefulness)* utilité *f*; *Comput* **u. program** (programme *m*) utilitaire *m*; **u. room** pièce *f* de rangement **(b) (public) utilities** services *mpl* (publics) **(c) utilities** *(service charges)* charges *fpl*
utilize ['ju:tɪlaɪz] *vt* utiliser, se servir de
utmost ['ʌtməʊst] **1** *n* **to the u.** au plus haut point; **to do one's u. (to do sth)** faire de son mieux (pour faire qch)
  2 *adj* **(a)** *(greatest)* **the u.** le (la) plus grand(e); **it is of the u. importance that...** il est de la plus haute importance que... + *subjunctive* **(b)** *(furthest)* **to the u. ends of the earth** au bout du monde
utopia [ju:'təʊpɪə] *n* utopie *f*
utopian [ju:'təʊpɪən] **1** *n* utopiste *mf*
  2 *adj* utopique
utter¹ ['ʌtə(r)] *adj* total(e); **it's u. madness** c'est de la folie pure; **it's u. nonsense** c'est complètement absurde
utter² ['ʌtə(r)] *vt (cry)* pousser; *(word)* prononcer
utterance ['ʌtərəns] *n (act)* énonciation *f*; *(words spoken)* paroles *fpl*, déclaration *f*
utterly ['ʌtəlɪ] *adv* complètement, tout à fait
uttermost ['ʌtəməʊst] *n & adj =* **utmost**
UV [ju:'vi:] *adj Phys (abbr* **ultra-violet**) UV *inv*; **UV rays** UV *mpl*
uvula ['ju:vjələ] *n* luette *f*
Uzbekistan [ʊzbekɪ'stɑ:n] *n* l'Ouzbékistan *m*

V

V¹, v [vi:] n (a) *(letter)* V, v m *inv;* **V. sign** *(for victory)* signe m de la victoire (b) *(abbr* **very**) t (c) *(abbr* **versus**) contre

V² *(abbr* **volt**) V

VA [vi:'eɪ] n *(abbr* **Veterans Administration**) ≃ ministère m des Anciens Combattants

vacancy ['veɪkənsɪ] n (a) *(position, job)* poste m vacant (b) *(at hotel)* chambre f libre *ou* à louer; **no vacancies** *(sign)* complet

vacant ['veɪkənt] adj (a) *(seat, space)* libre, inoccupé(e); **v. lot** terrain m vague (b) *(expression, look)* absent(e)

vacantly ['veɪkəntlɪ] adv d'un air absent

vacate [və'keɪt] vt *(seat, apartment)* libérer, quitter; *(one's post)* démissionner de

vacation [və'keɪʃən] n vacances fpl; **to take a v.** prendre des vacances; **on v.** en vacances

vacationer [və'keɪʃənə(r)] n vacancier(ère) m,f

vaccinate ['væksɪneɪt] vt vacciner

vaccination [væksɪ'neɪʃən] n vaccination f

vaccine ['væksi:n] n vaccin m

vacillate ['væsɪleɪt] vi hésiter (**between** entre)

vacuous ['vækjʊəs] adj *(person, look)* vide, sans expression; *(book, remark)* dénué(e) de sens

vacuum ['vækjʊm] **1** n *Phys* vacuum m; *Fig* vide m; **v. cleaner** aspirateur m

2 vt *(room)* passer l'aspirateur dans

3 vi passer l'aspirateur

vacuum-packed [vækjʊm'pækt] adj (emballé(e)) sous vide

vagabond ['vægəbɒnd] n vagabond(e) m,f

vagary ['veɪgərɪ] n caprice m

vagina [və'dʒaɪnə] n vagin m

vagrancy ['veɪgrənsɪ] n vagabondage m

vagrant ['veɪgrənt] n vagabond(e) m,f

vague [veɪg] adj *(idea, feeling)* vague; *(shape, outline)* flou(e), indistinct(e); **I haven't the vaguest idea** je n'en ai pas la moindre idée

vaguely ['veɪglɪ] adv vaguement

vagueness ['veɪgnɪs] n imprécision f, flou m

vain [veɪn] **1** adj (a) *(conceited)* vaniteux(euse) (b) *(hopeless)* vain(e)

2 n **in v.** en vain

vale [veɪl] n Lit val m, vallée f; Fig **v. of tears** vallée de larmes

valence ['veɪləns] n *Chem* valence f

valentine ['væləntaɪn] n **v. (card)** carte f de la Saint-Valentin; **V.'s Day** la Saint-Valentin

valet ['væleɪ] n valet m de chambre; **v. parking** *(service)* service m de voiturier

valiant ['vælɪənt] adj Lit vaillant(e)

valiantly ['vælɪəntlɪ] adv vaillamment

valid ['vælɪd] adj valable; **v. for six months** valable six mois; **no longer v.** périmé(e)

validate ['vælɪdeɪt] vt *(document)* valider; *(theory)* confirmer

validation [vælɪ'deɪʃən] n *(of document)* validation f; *(of theory)* confirmation f

validity [və'lɪdɪtɪ] n validité f

valise [væ'li:z] n mallette f

valley ['vælɪ] n vallée f

valor ['vælə(r)] n bravoure f

valuable ['væljʊəbəl] **1** adj *(object)* de valeur; *(advice, time, contribution)* précieux(euse) (**to** à)

2 n **valuables** objets mpl de valeur

valuation [væljʊ'eɪʃən] n (a) *(act)* estimation f (b) *(price)* évaluation f

value ['vælju:] **1** n (a) *(worth)* valeur f; **to be of v.** avoir de la valeur; **to be good/poor v. (for money)** être d'un bon/mauvais rapport qualité-prix; **to set a v. upon sth** estimer la valeur de qch; **to the v. of** pour une valeur de; **to make a v. judgment** faire un jugement de valeur (b) **values** *(principles)* valeurs fpl

2 vt (a) *(evaluate)* estimer (b) *(appreciate)* apprécier

value-added tax ['vælju:ædɪd'tæks] n taxe f sur la valeur ajoutée, Can taxe f sur les ventes

valued ['vælju:d] adj précieux(euse)

valueless ['væljʊlɪs] adj sans valeur

valve [vælv] n (a) Anat valve f (b) Tech *(in pipe, tube, air chamber)* valve f; *(in machine)* soupape f

vampire ['væmpaɪə(r)] n vampire m; **v. bat** vampire

van¹ [væn] n *(vehicle)* camionnette f, fourgonnette f; **v. driver** chauffeur m de camionnette

van² [væn] = **vanguard**

Vancouver [væn'ku:və(r)] n Vancouver

vandal ['vændəl] n vandale mf

vandalism ['vændəlɪzəm] n vandalisme m

vandalize ['vændəlaɪz] vt saccager

vane [veɪn] n girouette f

vanguard ['vængɑ:d] n avant-garde f; **to be in the v. of** être à l'avant-garde de

vanilla [və'nɪlə] n vanille f; **v. essence** extrait m de vanille; **v. ice cream** glace f à la vanille

vanish ['vænɪʃ] vi disparaître

vanishing ['vænɪʃɪŋ] adj **to do a v. act** disparaître dans la nature; **v. point** point m de fuite

vanity ['vænɪtɪ] n (a) *(conceit)* vanité f; **v. case** vanity-case m, mallette f de toilette; **v. plate** plaque f d'immatriculation personnalisée; **v. press** maison f d'édition à compte d'auteur; **v. publishing** publication f à compte d'auteur (b) *(dressing table)* coiffeuse f, table f de toilette

vanquish ['væŋkwɪʃ] vt Lit vaincre

vantage point ['vɑ:ntɪdʒ'pɔɪnt] n point m de vue; Fig position f objective

Vanuatu [vænu:'ætu:] n Vanuatu m

vapid ['væpɪd] adj insipide

vapor ['veɪpə(r)] n vapeur f; **v. trail** traînée f de condensation

vaporize ['veɪpəraɪz] **1** vt vaporiser

2 vi se vaporiser

variable ['veərɪəbəl] **1** n variable f

2 adj variable

variance ['veərıəns] n désaccord m; **to be at v. with sb** être en désaccord avec qn; **to be at v. with sth** ne pas concorder avec qch

variant ['veərıənt] **1** n variante f
2 adj différent(e)

variation [veərı'eıʃən] n variation f

varicose vein ['værıkəʊs'veın] n varice f

varied ['veərıd] adj varié(e)

variegated ['veərıgeıtıd] adj panaché(e)

variety [və'raıətı] (pl **varieties**) n (**a**) (diversity) variété f; **a v. of** toutes sortes de; Prov **v. is the spice of life** la diversité est le sel de la vie (**b**) (of plant) variété f (**c**) (in theater, on TV) variétés fpl; **v. show** spectacle m de variétés

various ['veərıəs] adj (different) divers(e); (several) plusieurs

variously ['veərıəslı] adv **v. described as a hero or a rogue** parfois décrit comme un héros, d'autres fois comme un escroc

varnish ['vɑːnıʃ] **1** n vernis m
2 vt vernir
▸**varnish over** vt sep Fig maquiller, dissimuler

vary ['veərı] **1** vt varier
2 vi varier (**in/with** en/selon)

varying ['veərııŋ] adj qui varie, variable

vase [veız] n vase m

vasectomy [və'sektəmı] n vasectomie f; **to have a v.** subir une vasectomie

Vaseline® ['væsəliːn] n vaseline f

vast [vɑːst] adj immense

vastly ['vɑːstlı] adv à l'extrême; (superior) infiniment

VAT [viːeɪ'tiː] n (abbr **value-added tax**) TVA f

vat [væt] n (container) cuve f, bac m

Vatican ['vætıkən] n **the V.** le Vatican; **V. City** la cité du Vatican, le Vatican

vaudeville ['vɔːdəvıl] n music-hall m

vault[1] [vɔːlt] n (**a**) (roof) voûte f (**b**) (cellar) cave f; (for burial) caveau m; (of bank) chambre f forte, salle f des coffres

vault[2] [vɔːlt] vt & vi sauter

vaulted ['vɔːltıd] adj (ceiling) voûté(e)

vaulting horse ['vɔːltıŋ'hɔːs] n cheval m d'arçons

vaunt [vɔːnt] vt vanter; **his much vaunted reputation as...** sa réputation tant vantée de...

VC [viː'siː] n (abbr **Vice-Chairman**) vice-président m

vCJD [viːsiːdʒeɪ'diː] n Med (abbr **new-variant Creutzfeldt-Jakob disease**) vMCJ m

VCR [viːsiː'ɑː(r)] n (abbr **video cassette recorder**) magnétoscope m

VD [viː'diː] n (abbr **venereal disease**) maladie f vénérienne

VDU [viːdiː'juː] n Comput (abbr **visual display unit**) moniteur m

veal [viːl] n veau m

vector ['vektə(r)] n vecteur m

veer ['vıə(r)] vi virer; **to v. to the left/right** virer à gauche/droit
▸**veer around** vi tourner, changer de direction; Fig **she has veered around to our point of view** elle s'est ralliée à notre point de vue

vegan ['viːgən] n végétalien(enne) m,f

vegetable ['vedʒtəbəl] n (**a**) (food) légume m; **v. garden** potager m (**b**) (brain-damaged person) légume m

vegetarian [vedʒı'teərıən] n & adj végétarien(enne) m,f

vegetarianism [vedʒı'teərıənızəm] n végétarisme m

vegetate ['vedʒıteıt] vi végéter

vegetation [vedʒı'teıʃən] n végétation f

veggie ['vedʒı] n & adj Fam (abbr **vegetarian**) végétarien(enne) m,f

vehemence ['viːıməns] n véhémence f

vehement ['viːımənt] adj véhément(e)

vehicle ['viːıkəl] n also Fig véhicule m

vehicular [vı'hıkjʊlə(r)] adj de véhicules; **v. traffic** circulation f automobile

veil [veıl] **1** n also Fig voile m; Fig **to draw a v. over sth** jeter un voile sur qch; Fig **under a v. of secrecy** sous le voile du secret
2 vt voiler; Fig **veiled in secrecy** secret(ète)

veiled [veıld] adj also Fig voilé(e)

vein [veın] n (**a**) (in body, wood, marble) veine f; (in leaf) nervure f; (in rock) filon m (**b**) (idioms) **and now, in a lighter v....** et maintenant, dans un registre plus léger...; **in a similar v.** de la même veine

Velcro® ['velkrəʊ] n (bande f) Velcro® m

vellum ['veləm] n vélin m; **v. (paper)** papier m vélin

velocity [vı'lɒsıtı] n vélocité f

velvet ['velvıt] n velours m; **v. jacket** veste f en velours; Fig **an iron fist** or **hand in a v. glove** une main de fer dans un gant de velours

velveteen [velvı'tiːn] n velvantine f

velvety ['velvıtı] adj velouté(e)

venal ['viːnəl] adj vénal(e)

vendetta [ven'detə] n vendetta f; **to carry on a v. against sb** mener une vendetta contre qn

vending machine ['vendıŋmə'ʃiːn] n distributeur m automatique

vendor ['vendɔː(r)] n vendeur(euse) m,f

veneer [və'nıə(r)] n placage m; Fig vernis m, apparence f

venerable ['venərəbəl] adj vénérable

venerate ['venəreıt] vt vénérer

veneration [venə'reıʃən] n vénération f

venereal [vı'nıərıəl] adj vénérien(enne); **v. disease** maladie f vénérienne

Venetian [vı'niːʃən] **1** n Vénitien(enne) m,f
2 adj vénitien(enne); **V. blind** store m vénitien

Venezuela [vene'zweılə] n le Venezuela

Venezuelan [vene'zweılən] **1** n Vénézuélien(enne) m,f
2 adj vénézuélien(enne)

vengeance ['vendʒəns] n vengeance f; **to take v. on sb** se venger de qn; Fig **it started to rain with a v.** il s'est mis à pleuvoir de plus belle; **she's back with a v.** elle fait un retour en force

vengeful ['vendʒfʊl] adj vengeur(eresse)

venial ['viːnıəl] adj véniel(elle)

Venice ['venıs] n Venise f

venison ['venısən] n viande f de chevreuil

venom ['venəm] n also Fig venin m

venomous ['venəməs] adj also Fig venimeux(euse)

vent [vent] **1** n conduit m; Fig **to give v. to sth** donner ou laisser libre cours à qch
2 vt **to v. one's anger (on)** décharger sa colère (sur)

ventilate ['ventıleıt] vt ventiler, aérer

ventilation [ventı'leıʃən] n ventilation f, aération f

ventilator ['ventıleıtə(r)] n (**a**) Tech ventilateur m (**b**) Med respirateur m; **to be on a v.** être branché(e) sur respirateur

ventriloquism [ven'trıləkwızəm] n ventriloquie f

ventriloquist [ven'trıləkwıst] n ventriloque mf; **v.'s dummy** marionnette f de ventriloque

venture ['ventʃə(r)] **1** n entreprise f hasardeuse; (in business) entreprise; Fin **v. capital** capital-risque m
2 vt (fortune, life) risquer; (opinion, suggestion) hasarder; **to v. to do sth** se risquer à faire qch; Prov **nothing ventured, nothing gained** qui ne risque rien n'a rien
3 vi s'aventurer
▸**venture on, venture upon** vt insep s'aventurer dans

venue ['venjuː] n (for meeting, concert) salle f; (for sports match) stade m

Venus ['vi:nəs] *n (planet)* Vénus *f*

veracity [və'ræsɪtɪ] *n Formal* véracité *f*

veranda(h) [və'rændə] *n* véranda *f*

verb [vɜːb] *n* verbe *m*

verbal ['vɜːbəl] *adj* verbal(e); **v. abuse** insultes *fpl* verbales

verbalize ['vɜːbəlaɪz] *vt* verbaliser

verbally ['vɜːbəlɪ] *adv* verbalement

verbatim [vɜː'beɪtɪm] **1** *adj* textuel(elle)
2 *adv* mot pour mot

verbiage ['vɜːbɪdʒ] *n* verbiage *m*

verbose [vɜː'bəʊs] *adj* verbeux(euse)

verbosity [vɜː'bɒsɪtɪ] *n* verbosité *f*

verdict ['vɜːdɪkt] *n also Fig* verdict *m*; **to return a v. of guilty/not guilty** rendre un verdict de culpabilité/non-culpabilité; **to give one's v. on sth** se prononcer sur qch

verge [vɜːdʒ] *n Fig* **on the v. of sth** au bord de qch; *(victory, defeat)* à deux doigts de qch; **to be on the v. of doing sth** être sur le point de faire qch

▸ **verge on** *vt insep* friser

verger ['vɜːdʒə(r)] *n (in Church of England)* bedeau *m*

verifiable [verɪ'faɪəbəl] *adj* vérifiable

verification [verɪfɪ'keɪʃən] *n* vérification *f*

verify ['verɪfaɪ] *(pt & pp* **verified**) *vt* vérifier

verisimilitude [verɪsɪ'mɪlɪtjuːd] *n Formal* vraisemblance *f*

veritable ['verɪtəbəl] *adj Formal* véritable

vermilion [və'mɪljən] **1** *n* vermillon *m*
2 *adj* vermillon *inv*

vermin ['vɜːmɪn] *npl also Fig* vermine *f*

vermouth ['vɜːməθ] *n* vermouth *m*

vernacular [və'nækjʊlə(r)] **1** *n* langue *f* vernaculaire
2 *adj* vernaculaire

verruca [ve'ruːkə] *n* verrue *f* plantaire

versatile ['vɜːsətaɪl] *adj (person)* aux talents variés; *(tool)* polyvalent(e)

versatility [vɜːsə'tɪlɪtɪ] *n (of person)* variété *f* de talents; *(of tool)* polyvalence *f*

verse [vɜːs] *n* **(a)** *(poetry)* vers *mpl* **(b)** *(stanza)* strophe *f* **(c)** *(of Bible)* verset *m*

versed [vɜːst] *adj* **to be (well) v. in sth** être versé(e) dans qch

version ['vɜːʃən] *n* version *f*

versus ['vɜːsəs] *prep* **(a)** *(in law, sport)* contre **(b)** *(compared to)* comparé(e) à

vertebra ['vɜːtɪbrə] *(pl* **vertebrae** ['vɜːtɪbriː]) *n* vertèbre *f*

vertebral column ['vɜːtɪbrəl'kɒləm] *n* colonne *f* vertébrale

vertebrate ['vɜːtɪbrɪt] **1** *n* vertébré *m*
2 *adj* vertébré(e)

vertex ['vɜːteks] *(pl* **vertices** ['vɜːtɪsiːz]) *n* sommet *m*

vertical ['vɜːtɪkəl] **1** *n* verticale *f*
2 *adj* vertical(e)

vertically ['vɜːtɪklɪ] *adv* à la verticale

vertices ['vɜːtɪsiːz] *pl of* **vertex**

vertigo ['vɜːtɪgəʊ] *n* vertige *m*

verve [vɜːv] *n* verve *f*

very ['verɪ] **1** *adv* **(a)** *(extremely)* très; **v. little** très peu; **v. much** beaucoup; **are you hungry? – yes, v.** as-tu faim? – oui, très; *Rad* **v. high frequency** hyperfréquences *fpl* **(b)** *(emphatic use)* **the v. first/last** le (la) tout(e) premier(ère)/dernier(ère); **the v. best** tout ce qu'il y a de mieux; **at the v. most/least** tout au plus/moins; **at the v. earliest/latest** au plus tôt/tard; **the v. same** exactement le même; **I v. nearly died** j'ai bien failli mourir; **the v. next day** le lendemain même
2 *adj (emphatic use)* **this v. house** cette maison même; **this v. day** aujourd'hui même; **those were her v. words** c'est ce qu'elle a dit mot pour mot; **at the v. beginning** au tout début; **the v. thought of it!** rien que d'y penser!

vessel ['vesəl] *n* **(a)** *(ship)* vaisseau *m* **(b)** *(container)* récipient *m*

vest [vest] *n (waistcoat)* gilet *m*

vested ['vestɪd] *adj* **to have a v. interest in sth/in doing sth** avoir un intérêt personnel dans qch/à faire qch

vestibule ['vestɪbjuːl] *n* hall *m*

vestige ['vestɪdʒ] *n* vestige *m*

vestments ['vestmənts] *npl Rel* habits *mpl* sacerdotaux

vest-pocket 1 *n* poche *f* de gilet
2 *adj (book, camera)* de poche

vestry ['vestrɪ] *(pl* **vestries**) *n Rel* sacristie *f*

vet¹ [vet] *n Fam (veterinarian)* vétérinaire *mf*

vet² [vet] *(pt & pp* **vetted**) *vt (person)* effectuer une enquête sur; *(application)* examiner minutieusement; *(figures)* vérifier soigneusement

vet³ [vet] *n Fam Mil (veteran)* ancien combattant *m*

veteran ['vetərən] **1** *n Mil* ancien combattant *m*; *Fig* vétéran *m*
2 *adj* de longue date

veterinarian [vetərɪ'neərɪən] *n* vétérinaire *mf*

veterinary ['vetərɪnərɪ] *adj* vétérinaire; **v. medicine** médecine *f* vétérinaire

veto ['viːtəʊ] **1** *n (pl* **vetoes**) veto *m*; **right** *or* **power of v.** droit *m* de veto; **to impose a v. on sth** mettre son veto à qch
2 *vt* mettre son veto à

vetting ['vetɪŋ] *n (of person)* enquête *f* (**of** sur); *(of things)* contrôle *m* (**of** de)

vex [veks] *vt* contrarier

vexation [vek'seɪʃən] *n (annoyance)* contrariété *f*

vexed [vekst] *adj* **(a)** *(annoyed)* très contrarié(e) **(b)** **v. question** question *f* controversée

VHF [viːeɪtʃ'ef] *n (abbr* **very high frequency**) VHF *f*

VHS [viːeɪtʃ'es] *n (abbr* **video home system**) VHS *m*

via ['vaɪə] *prep* par, via

viability [vaɪə'bɪlɪtɪ] *n* viabilité *f*

viable ['vaɪəbəl] *adj* viable

viaduct ['vaɪədʌkt] *n* viaduc *m*

Viagra® ['vaɪægrə] *n* Viagra® *m*

vibe [vaɪb] *n Fam* atmosphère *f*, ambiance *f*; **this bar has a chilled-out v.** l'ambiance est très cool dans ce bar; **their new album has kind of an R&B v.** leur nouvel album a un petit côté R&B; **I got good/bad vibes from her** je me sentais/je ne la sentais pas bien

vibrant ['vaɪbrənt] *adj* très actif(ive)

vibrate [vaɪ'breɪt] *vi* vibrer

vibration [vaɪ'breɪʃən] *n* vibration *f*

vibrator [vaɪ'breɪtə(r)] *n* vibromasseur *m*

vicar ['vɪkə(r)] *n (in Church of England)* pasteur *m*

vicarage ['vɪkərɪdʒ] *n* presbytère *m*

vicarious [vaɪ'keərɪəs] *adj* indirect(e), **to lead a v. existence** vivre par procuration

vice¹ [vaɪs] *n (immorality, immoral activity)* vice *m*; **the V. Squad** ≃ la brigade des mœurs

vice² [vaɪs] *n (tool)* étau *m*

vice-chairman [vaɪs'tʃeəmən] *n* vice-président(e) *m,f*

vice-president [vaɪs'prezɪdənt] *n* vice-président(e) *m,f*

viceroy ['vaɪsrɔɪ] *n* vice-roi *m*

vice versa [vaɪs'vɜːsə] *adv* vice versa

vicinity [vɪ'sɪnɪtɪ] *n (surrounding area)* environs *mpl*; *(proximity)* proximité *f*; **in the v. (of)** dans les alentours (de); **a sum in the v. of \$25,000** un chiffre aux alentours de 25 000 dollars

vicious ['vɪʃəs] *adj (violent)* violent(e); *(malicious, cruel)* malveillant(e); **v. circle** cercle *m* vicieux

vicissitudes [vɪ'sɪsɪtjuːdz] *npl Formal* vicissitudes *fpl*

victim ['vɪktɪm] *n* victime *f*; **to be the v. of sth** être victime de qch

victimization [vɪktɪmaɪ'zeɪʃən] *n* victimization *fpl*

victimize ['vɪktɪmaɪz] *vt (bully)* victimser, prendre comme tête de Turc; *(penalize)* pénaliser

victor ['vɪktə(r)] *n* vainqueur *m*
Victorian [vɪk'tɔːrɪən] **1** *n* Victorien(enne) *m,f*
2 *adj* victorien(enne)
victorious [vɪk'tɔːrɪəs] *adj* victorieux(euse); **to be v. over sb** vaincre qn
victory ['vɪktərɪ] *n* victoire *f*; **v. celebrations** = fêtes pour célébrer une victoire
victuals ['vɪtəlz] *npl Old-fashioned (food)* victuailles *fpl*
video ['vɪdɪəʊ] *n (pl videos) (medium)* vidéo *f*; *(cassette)* (cassette *f*) vidéo; **v. camera** caméra *f* vidéo; **v. cassette** *or* **tape** cassette *f* vidéo; **v. (cassette) recorder** magnétoscope *m*; **v. game** jeu *m* vidéo; **v. installation** installation *f* vidéo; **v. library** vidéothèque *f*; **v. nasty** = film vidéo à contenu très violent ou pornographique; **v. projection** vidéoprojection *f*; **v. projector** vidéoprojecteur *m*; **v. store** magasin *m* vidéo
videotape ['vɪdɪəʊteɪp] **1** *n* bande *f* vidéo
2 *vt* enregistrer (sur magnétoscope); **v. recorder** magnétoscope *m*
vie [vaɪ] *(pt & pp* **vied** [vaɪd]) *vi* **to v. with sb (for sth/to do sth)** rivaliser avec qn (pour qch/pour faire qch)
Vienna [vɪ'enə] *n* Vienne
Viennese [vɪə'niːz] **1** *n* Viennois(e) *m,f*
2 *adj* viennois(e)
Vietnam [vɪet'næm] *n* le Viêt Nam; **the V. War** la guerre du Viêt Nam
Vietnamese [vɪetnə'miːz] **1** *npl (people)* **the V.** les Vietnamiens *mpl*
2 *n* **(a)** *(person)* Vietnamien(enne) *m,f* **(b)** *(language)* vietnamien *m*
3 *adj* vietnamien(enne)
view [vjuː] **1** *n* **(a)** *(sight, scene, prospect)* vue *f*; **a room with a v.** une chambre avec vue; **to have a good v. of sth** avoir une belle vue de qch; **in full v. of** sous les yeux de; *Fig* **in v. of** *(considering)* compte tenu de, étant donné **(b)** *(opinion)* opinion *f*; **in my v.** à mon avis **(c)** *(intention)* intention *f*; **with this in v.** dans cette intention; **with a v. to doing sth** dans l'intention de faire qch
2 *vt* **(a)** *(look at)* voir; *(prospective property, exhibition)* visiter **(b)** *(consider)* voir, considérer; **to v. sth with horror/delight** envisager qch avec horreur/ravissement
viewer ['vjuːə(r)] *n* **(a)** *(of TV)* téléspectateur(trice) *m,f* **(b)** *(for slides)* visionneuse *f*
viewfinder ['vjuːfaɪndə(r)] *n* viseur *m*
viewpoint ['vjuːpɔɪnt] *n* point *m* de vue
vigil ['vɪdʒɪl] *n* veillée *f*; **to keep v.** veiller
vigilance ['vɪdʒɪləns] *n* vigilance *f*
vigilant ['vɪdʒɪlənt] *adj* vigilant(e)
vigilante [vɪdʒɪ'læntɪ] *n* = membre d'une milice privée
vignette [vɪn'jet] *n (photo, picture)* buste *m* sur un fond dégradé; *(short essay)* court portrait *m*
vigor ['vɪgə(r)] *n* vigueur *f*
vigorous ['vɪgərəs] *adj* vigoureux(euse)
Viking ['vaɪkɪŋ] **1** *n* Viking *mf*
2 *adj* viking *inv*
vile [vaɪl] *adj (weather, person, thought)* abominable; *(food, drink)* infecte; *(temper)* exécrable
vilification [vɪlɪfɪ'keɪʃən] *n* calomnie *f*
vilify ['vɪlɪfaɪ] *(pt & pp* **vilified**) *vt* calomnier
villa ['vɪlə] *n* villa *f*
village ['vɪlɪdʒ] *n* village *m*; **v. hall** salle *f* des fêtes; **v. idiot** idiot *m* du village
villager ['vɪlɪdʒə(r)] *n* villageois(e) *m,f*
villain ['vɪlən] *n (scoundrel)* scélérat *m*; *Hum* **the v. of the piece** le/la coupable
villainous ['vɪlənəs] *adj* diabolique
villainy ['vɪlənɪ] *n* infamie *f*
Vilnius ['vɪlnɪʌs] *n* Vilnius

vindicate ['vɪndɪkeɪt] *vt (decision, action)* donner raison à; *(right, claim)* justifier
vindication [vɪndɪ'keɪʃən] *n (of decision, action)* bien-fondé *m*; *(of right, claim)* justification *f*
vindictive [vɪn'dɪktɪv] *adj* vindicatif(ive)
vine [vaɪn] *n* vigne *f*; **v. leaf** feuille *f* de vigne
vinegar ['vɪnɪgə(r)] *n* vinaigre *m*
vineyard ['vɪnjəd] *n* vigne *f*
vintage ['vɪntɪdʒ] **1** *n* **(a)** *(year)* année *f*; *(wine)* cru *m*; *Fig* **a v. year (for)** une grande année (pour); *Fig* **it was v. Agatha Christie** c'était de l'Agatha Christie du meilleur style; **v. car** = voiture construite entre 1919 et 1930; **v. wine** vin *m* de cru **(b)** *(fashion)* vintage
2 *adj (clothes etc.)* vintage
vinyl ['vaɪnɪl] *n* vinyle *m*
viola [vɪ'əʊlə] *n* alto *m*
violate ['vaɪəleɪt] *vt (agreement)* violer; *(rule, law)* enfreindre
violation [vaɪə'leɪʃən] *n* violation *f*
violence ['vaɪələns] *n* violence *f*
violent ['vaɪələnt] *adj* violent(e); **to die a v. death** mourir de mort violente; **to take a v. dislike to sb/sth** se prendre d'une aversion violente pour qn/qch
violently ['vaɪələntlɪ] *adv* violemment; *(die)* de mort violente; **to be v. sick** être pris(e) de violents vomissements
violet ['vaɪələt] **1** *n* **(a)** *(flower)* violette *f* **(b)** *(color)* violet *m*
2 *adj* **v.(-colored)** violet(ette)
violin [vaɪə'lɪn] *n* violon *m*
violinist [vaɪə'lɪnɪst] *n* violoniste *mf*
VIP [viːaɪ'piː] *n (abbr* **very important person**) VIP *mf*; **V. lounge** salon *m* de luxe; **to get V. treatment** recevoir un accueil princier
viper ['vaɪpə(r)] *n* vipère *f*
viral ['vaɪrəl] *adj* viral(e)
virgin ['vɜːdʒɪn] **1** *n* vierge *mf*; **the (Blessed) V.** la Sainte Vierge; **the V. Islands** les îles *fpl* Vierges
2 *adj* vierge
Virginia [vɜː'dʒɪnjə] *n* la Virginie
virginity [və'dʒɪnɪtɪ] *n* virginité *f*
Virgo ['vɜːgəʊ] *n (sign of zodiac)* la Vierge; **to be (a) V.** être Vierge
virile ['vɪraɪl] *adj* viril(e)
virility [vɪ'rɪlɪtɪ] *n* virilité *f*
virology [vaɪ'rɒlədʒɪ] *n* virologie *f*
virtual ['vɜːtjʊəl] *adj* **(a)** *(near)* quasi; **it's a v. impossibility** c'est quasiment impossible **(b)** *Comput* virtuel(elle); **v. reality** réalité *f* virtuelle
virtually ['vɜːtjʊəlɪ] *adv* quasiment, pratiquement
virtue ['vɜːtjuː] *n* **(a)** *(goodness)* vertu *f*; **by v. of** en vertu de; **to make a v. of necessity** faire de nécessité vertu **(b)** *(advantage)* avantage *m*
virtuoso [vɜːtjʊ'əʊzəʊ] *(pl* **virtuosos** *or* **virtuosi** [vɜːtjʊ'əʊziː]) *n* virtuose *mf*
virtuous ['vɜːtjʊəs] *adj* vertueux(euse)
virulent ['vɪr(j)ʊlənt] *adj* virulent(e)
virus ['vaɪrəs] *n Med & Comput* virus *m*
visa ['viːzə] *n* visa *m*
vis-à-vis ['viːzɑːviː] *prep* par rapport à, vis-à-vis de
visceral ['vɪsərəl] *adj* viscéral(e)
viscount ['vaɪkaʊnt] *n* vicomte *m*
viscous ['vɪskəs] *adj* visqueux(euse)
visibility [vɪzɪ'bɪlɪtɪ] *n* visibilité *f*
visible ['vɪzɪbəl] *adj* visible
visibly ['vɪzɪblɪ] *adv* visiblement
vision ['vɪʒən] *n* **(a)** *(eyesight)* vue *f*; **to have good/poor v.** avoir une bonne/mauvaise vue **(b)** *(foresight, imagination)* clairvoyance *f*; **a man of v.** un visionnaire **(c)** *(apparition)* vision *f*;

I had visions of being left homeless je me suis vu devenir sans-abri

visionary ['vɪʒənərɪ] (pl **visionaries**) n & adj visionnaire mf

visit ['vɪzɪt] **1** n visite f; **to pay sb a v.** rendre visite à qn; **to be on a v.** être en visite

2 vt (person) rendre visite à; (museum, monument) visiter

3 vi **to be visiting** être de passage

visiting ['vɪzɪtɪŋ] adj (circus) de passage; (lecturer) invité(e); **v. card** carte f de visite; **v. hours** heures fpl de visite; **v. professor** professeur m invité; **v. rights** (of divorced parent) droits mpl de visite

visitor ['vɪzɪtə(r)] n visiteur(euse) m,f; **visitors' book** livre m d'or

visor ['vaɪzə(r)] n visière f

vista ['vɪstə] n vue f; Fig perspective f

visual ['vɪʒʊəl] adj visuel(elle); **v. aid** support m visuel; **v. arts** arts mpl plastiques; Comput **v. display unit** console f de visualisation

visualize ['vɪʒʊəlaɪz] vt (imagine) visualiser, se représenter; (foresee) envisager

visually ['vɪʒʊəlɪ] adv visuellement; **v. impaired** malvoyant(e)

vital ['vaɪtəl] adj (a) (essential) vital(e); **v. organ** organe m vital; Hum **v. statistics** (of woman) mensurations fpl (b) (vigorous) vigoureux(euse)

vitality [vaɪ'tælɪtɪ] n vitalité f

vitally ['vaɪtəlɪ] adv **supplies are v. needed** on a un besoin vital de vivres; **v. important** d'une importance vitale ou capitale

vitamin ['vaɪtəmɪn] n vitamine f; **v. C/E** vitamine C/E; **with added vitamins** vitaminé(e)

vitreous ['vɪtrɪəs] adj **v. enamel** émail m vitrifié; **v. humor** humeur f vitrée

vitriol ['vɪtrɪəl] n also Fig vitriol m

vitriolic [vɪtrɪ'ɒlɪk] adj Chem de vitriol; Fig au vitriol

vituperative [vɪ'tjuːpərətɪv] adj Formal injurieux(euse)

vivacious [vɪ'veɪʃəs] adj enjoué(e)

vivacity [vɪ'væsɪtɪ] n vivacité f

vivid ['vɪvɪd] adj (a) (vive); (memory) clair(e)

vividly ['vɪvɪdlɪ] adv vivement; (remember) clairement; (describe) de manière vivante

vivisection [vɪvɪ'sekʃən] n vivisection f

vixen ['vɪksən] n renarde f

viz. [vɪz] adv (abbr **videlicet**) à savoir

VOA [viːəʊ'eɪ] n (abbr **Voice of America**) = station de radio américaine de diffusion mondiale

vocabulary [və'kæbjʊlərɪ] n vocabulaire m

vocal ['vəʊkəl] **1** adj (a) (relating to the voice) vocal(e); **v. cords** cordes fpl vocales (b) (outspoken) franc (franche); **to be v. about sth** se faire entendre à propos de qch

2 npl **vocals** chant m; **on vocals** au chant

vocalist ['vəʊkəlɪst] n chanteur(euse) m,f

vocation [və'keɪʃən] n vocation f; **to have a v. (for sth)** avoir une vocation (pour qch)

vocational [və'keɪʃənəl] adj professionnel(elle)

vocative ['vɒkətɪv] n vocatif

vociferous [və'sɪfərəs] adj bruyant(e)

vociferously [və'sɪfərəslɪ] adv bruyamment

vodka ['vɒdkə] n vodka f

vogue [vəʊg] n vogue f; **to be in v.** être en vogue

voice [vɔɪs] **1** n (a) (of person) voix f; **to raise/to lower one's v.** élever/baisser la voix; **at the top of one's v.** à tue-tête; **I've lost my v.** je n'ai plus de voix; **v. box** larynx m; Comput **v. recognition** reconnaissance f de la parole; Mus **v. training** cours mpl de chant (b) Gram **active/passive v.** voix f active/passive (c) (idioms) **the v. of reason** la voix de la raison; **with**

one v. d'une seule voix; **to make one's v. heard** se faire entendre; **these reforms would give small parties a v.** ces réformes donneraient voix au chapitre aux petits partis

2 vt (a) (opinion, feelings) exprimer (b) (consonant) sonoriser

voiced [vɔɪst] adj (consonant) sonore

voiceless ['vɔɪslɪs] adj (consonant) sans voix

voicemail ['vɔɪsmeɪl] n Tel (message service) messagerie f vocale; (message) message m vocal

voice-over ['vɔɪsəʊvə(r)] n voix f off

void [vɔɪd] **1** n vide m; **to fill the v.** combler le vide

2 adj (a) (devoid) **v. of** dépourvu(e) de (b) Law (deed, contract) (null and) **v.** nul (nulle) et non avenu(e)

volatile ['vɒlətaɪl] adj (a) (person) (fickle) inconstant(e); (temperamental) lunatique; (situation) explosif(ive); (economy, market) instable (b) Chem volatil(e)

volcanic [vɒl'kænɪk] adj volcanique

volcano [vɒl'keɪnəʊ] (pl **volcanoes**) n volcan m

vole [vəʊl] n campagnol m

volition [və'lɪʃən] n Formal **of one's own v.** de son propre gré

volley ['vɒlɪ] (pl **volleys**) n (a) (of gunfire, blows, stones) volée f; Fig (of insults) bordée f (b) (in tennis) volée f

volleyball ['vɒlɪbɔːl] n volley(-ball m) m

volt [vəʊlt] n volt m

voltage ['vəʊltɪdʒ] n voltage m; **high/low v.** haute/basse tension f

volte-face ['vɒltfɑːs] n volte-face f inv

voluble ['vɒljʊbəl] adj volubile

volubly ['vɒljʊblɪ] adv avec volubilité

volume ['vɒljuːm] n (a) (book) volume m, tome m; Fig **to speak volumes (about)** (of action, expression) en dire long (sur) (b) (amount, space occupied) volume m; (of work) quantité f (c) (loudness) volume m; **to turn the v. up/down** (on TV, radio) monter/baisser le volume; **v. control** bouton m de réglage du volume (d) (of hair) volume m

voluminous [və'luːmɪnəs] adj (garment) ample; (container) volumineux(euse)

voluntarily [vɒlʌn'terɪlɪ] adv de plein gré

voluntary ['vɒləntərɪ] adj volontaire; **v. work** travail m bénévole

volunteer [vɒlən'tɪə(r)] **1** n volontaire mf; (for charity) bénévole mf

2 vt (information) donner spontanément; (advice) offrir; **to v. to do sth** se porter volontaire pour faire qch

3 vi (a) (for military service) s'engager (b) (to help, for charity) se porter volontaire (**for** pour)

voluptuous [və'lʌptjʊəs] adj voluptueux(euse)

vomit ['vɒmɪt] **1** n vomi m

2 vt & vi vomir

voodoo ['vuːduː] n vaudou m

voracious [və'reɪʃəs] adj vorace

vortex ['vɔːteks] (pl **vortices** ['vɔːtɪsiːz]) n vortex m; Fig tourbillon m

vote [vəʊt] **1** n (choice) vote m; (election) scrutin m; (paper) voix f; **to put sth to the v.** soumettre qch au vote; **to take a v. on sth** voter sur qch; **to have the v.** avoir le droit de vote; **they got 52% of the v.** ils ont remporté 52% des voix; **the party has increased its share of the v.** le parti a amélioré ses résultats aux élections; **v. of confidence** vote de confiance; **v. of no confidence** motion f de censure; **to propose a v. of thanks** faire un discours de remerciement

2 vt **to v. Democrat** voter démocrate; **to v. to do sth** voter pour faire qch; **to v. sth down** voter contre qch; **to v. sb in** élire qn; **to v. sb out** ne pas réélire qn; **I v. (that) we go** je propose qu'on y aille

3 vi voter (**for/against** pour/contre); **to v. on sth** voter sur qch; Fig **to v. with one's feet** manifester son mécontentement en partant

voter ['vəʊtə(r)] n électeur(trice) m,f

voting ['vəʊtɪŋ] **1** n scrutin m; **v. booth** isoloir m
  2 adj (member) votant(e)

votive ['vəʊtɪv] adj Rel votif(ive)

▸**vouch for** [vaʊtʃ] vt insep (person) se porter garant(e) de;
  (quality, truth) attester de

voucher ['vaʊtʃə(r)] n coupon m, bon m; **(gift) v.** chèque-
  cadeau m

vow [vaʊ] **1** n vœu m; **to make a v.** faire un vœu; **to take a v.
  of poverty/silence** faire vœu de pauvreté/silence
  2 vt jurer; **to v. to do sth** jurer de faire qch; **to v. that** jurer
  que

vowel ['vaʊəl] n voyelle f; **v. sound** son m vocalique

voyage ['vɔɪdʒ] n voyage m

voyager ['vɔɪdʒə(r)] n voyageur(euse) m,f

voyeur [vwɑ:'jɜ:(r)] n voyeur(euse) m,f

voyeuristic [vwɑ:jʊə'rɪstɪk] adj voyeuriste

vs. (abbr **versus**) contre

VTOL [vi:ti:əʊ'el] n (abbr **vertical take-off and landing**)
  ADAV m

VTR [vi:ti:'ɑ:(r)] n (abbr **videotape recorder**) magnétoscope m

vulgar ['vʌlgə(r)] adj vulgaire; Math **v. fraction** fraction f ordinaire

vulgarity [vʌl'gærɪtɪ] n vulgarité f

vulnerability [vʌlnərə'bɪlɪtɪ] n vulnérabilité f

vulnerable ['vʌlnərəbəl] adj vulnérable

vulture ['vʌltʃə(r)] n also Fig vautour m

vulva ['vʌlvə] (pl **vulvas** or **vulvae** ['vʌlvi:]) n vulve f

W

W¹, w [ˈdʌbəljuː] n (**a**) (letter) W, w m inv (**b**) (abbr **west**) O

W² n (abbr **watt(s)**) W

wacky [ˈwækɪ] adj Fam farfelu(e)

wad [wɒd] n (of cotton wool) morceau m; (of paper, bills) liasse f

wadding [ˈwɒdɪŋ] n ouate f

waddle [ˈwɒdəl] vi se dandiner

wade [weɪd] vi (in water) marcher dans l'eau; **to w. across a stream** traverser une rivière à gué; Fam Fig **to w. in** intervenir; Fig **it took me a month to w. through that book** il m'a fallu un mois pour venir à bout de ce livre

▸**wade into** vt insep Fam Fig (task) s'attaquer à

wader [ˈweɪdə(r)] n (**a**) (bird) échassier m (**b**) **waders** (boots) bottes fpl de pêcheur

wafer [ˈweɪfə(r)] n (**a**) (biscuit) gaufrette f, Belg galette f (**b**) Rel (for communion) hostie f

wafer-thin [weɪfəˈθɪn] adj ultramince

waffle¹ [ˈwɒfəl] n (food) gaufre f; **w. iron** gaufrier m

waffle² [ˈwɒfəl] Fam **1** n (spoken) baratin m; (written) remplissage m

2 vi (in speaking) baratiner; (in writing) faire du remplissage

waft [wɒft] **1** vt (smell, sound) porter

2 vi (of smell, sound) parvenir

wag¹ [wæg] **1** vt (pt & pp **wagged**) agiter, remuer; **to w. one's finger at sb** menacer qn du doigt; **to w. its tail** (of dog) remuer la queue

2 vi frétiller, remuer; **its tail was wagging** (of dog) il remuait la queue; Fam **tongues will w.** les langues vont aller bon train

3 n (action) frétillement m; **with a w. of its tail** la queue frétillante

wag² [wæg] n Fam (joker) farceur(euse) m,f

wage [weɪdʒ] **1** n (pay) **wage(s)** salaire m, paie f; **w. cut** diminution f de salaire; **w. earner** salarié(e) m,f; **w. freeze** gel m des salaires

2 vt **to w. war (on)** faire la guerre (à); **to w. a campaign against smoking** mener une campagne anti-tabac

wager [ˈweɪdʒə(r)] **1** n pari m

2 vt parier

waggle [ˈwægəl] vt & vi remuer

wagon [ˈwægən] n (horse-drawn) charrette f; Fam Fig **to be on the w.** être au régime sec; Fam Fig **to fall off the w.** se remettre à boire

waif [weɪf] n (abandoned child) enfant mf abandonné(e); (very thin girl) fille f excessivement maigre; **waifs and strays** (children) enfants mpl abandonnés; (animals) animaux mpl abandonnés

wail [weɪl] **1** n (of person) gémissement m; (of siren) hurlement m

2 vi (of person) gémir, pousser des gémissements; (of siren) hurler

waist [weɪst] n taille f; **w. measurement** tour m de taille

waistband [ˈweɪstbænd] n ceinture f

waistline [ˈweɪstlaɪn] n taille f; **to watch one's w.** surveiller sa ligne

wait [weɪt] **1** n attente f; **to have a long w.** attendre longtemps; **to lie in w. for sb** guetter qn

2 vt (**a**) attendre; **to w. one's turn** attendre son tour (**b**) **to w. tables** faire le service

3 vi (**a**) (remain in expectation) attendre; **to w. for sb/sth** attendre qn/qch; **to keep sb waiting** faire attendre qn; **to w. in line** faire la queue; **I can't w. to see her** j'ai vraiment hâte de la voir; **repairs while you w.** (sign) réparations minute; **we must w. and see** on verra bien (**b**) **to w. on table** (serve) faire le service

▸**wait about, wait around** vi attendre

▸**wait on** vt insep (serve) servir; **to w. on sb hand and foot** être aux petits soins pour qn

▸**wait up** vi **to w. up for sb** attendre qn pour aller se coucher

waiter [ˈweɪtə(r)] n serveur m

waiting [ˈweɪtɪŋ] n attente f; **to play the w. game** faire de l'attentisme; **w. list** liste f d'attente; **w. room** salle f d'attente

waitperson [ˈweɪtpɜːsən] n serveur(euse) m,f

waitress [ˈweɪtrɪs] n serveuse f

waitstaff [ˈweɪtstɑːf] n serveurs mpl

waive [weɪv] vt (rights, claim) renoncer à; (rule) ignorer

wake¹ [weɪk] n (of ship) sillage m; Fig **in the w. of sth** à la suite de qch; Fig **to follow in sb's w.** suivre l'exemple de qn

wake² [weɪk] n (on night before funeral) veillée f de corps

wake³ [weɪk] (pt **woke** [wəʊk] or **waked**, pp **woken** [ˈwəʊkən] or **waked**) **1** vt réveiller

2 vi se réveiller

▸**wake up 1** vt sep réveiller

2 vi se réveiller; Fig **to w. up to sth** prendre conscience de qch

wakeboard [ˈweɪkbɔːd] n Sport monoski m nautique

wakeboarding [ˈweɪkbɔːdɪŋ] n Sport monoski m nautique

wakeful [ˈweɪkfʊl] adj (**a**) (sleepless) éveillé(e); **to have a w. night** ne pas fermer l'œil de la nuit (**b**) (vigilant) vigilant(e)

waken [ˈweɪkən] vt réveiller

wake-up call [ˈweɪkʌpkɔːl] n (in hotel) réveil m téléphonique; Fig **the bomb scare was a w. to the government to tighten security** avec cette alerte à la bombe, le gouvernement a compris qu'il devait renforcer les mesures de sécurité

Wales [weɪlz] n le pays de Galles

walk [wɔːk] **1** n (**a**) (short) promenade f; (long) marche f; **it's a long w.** c'est loin à pied; **it's a ten-minute w.** c'est à dix minutes à pied; **to go for a w.** aller se promener (**b**) (gait) démarche f; **I know her by her w.** je la reconnais à sa démarche (**c**) (speed) **at a w.** au pas (**d**) (path) avenue f (**e**) (profession, situation) **people from all walks of life** des gens de tous les milieux

2 vt **to w. the dog** promener le chien; **to w. sb home** raccompagner qn; **to w. the streets** battre le pavé; Euph (of prostitute) faire le trottoir

3 vi (move on foot) marcher; (as opposed to riding, driving) aller à pied; (for exercise, pleasure) se promener (à pied); **to w. home** rentrer à pied

▶**walk away** *vi* s'en aller; *Fig* **to w. away from trouble** éviter les ennuis; *Fig* **to w. away with a prize** remporter un prix

▶**walk in** *vi* entrer

▶**walk into** *vt insep* (**a**) *(enter)* entrer dans (**b**) *(collide with)* rentrer dans

▶**walk off** *vi* s'en aller; **to w. off with sth** *(steal)* partir avec qch; *(win easily)* remporter qch

▶**walk out** *vi* (**a**) *(leave)* sortir; **to w. out on sb** quitter qn (**b**) *(go on strike)* se mettre en grève

▶**walk over** *vt insep Fam* **to w. all over sb** marcher sur les pieds de qn

walker ['wɔːkə(r)] *n* (**a**) *(person)* marcheur(euse) *m, f* (**b**) *(aid) (for invalids)* déambulateur *m*; *(for babies)* trotte-bébé *m*

walkie-talkie [wɔːkɪ'tɔːkɪ] *n* talkie-walkie *m*

walk-in ['wɔːkɪn] **1** *adj* **w. closet** penderie *m*
 2 *n Fam (victory)* victoire *f* dans un fauteuil

walking ['wɔːkɪŋ] **1** *n* marche *f*; **w. shoes** chaussures *fpl* de marche; **w. stick** canne *f*; *Fam* **to give sb his/her w. papers** mettre qn à la porte
 2 *adj* **at a w. pace** au pas; *Fam* **she's a w. encyclopedia** c'est une encyclopédie ambulante; **the w. wounded** les blessés *mpl* en état de marcher

Walkman® ['wɔːkmən] *n* baladeur *m*

walk-on part ['wɔːkɒn'pɑːt] *n (in movie, play)* rôle *m* de figurant(e)

walkout ['wɔːkaʊt] *n (strike)* débrayage *m*; *(from meeting)* départ *m* en signe de protestation

walkover ['wɔːkəʊvə(r)] *n Fam* **it was a w.!** c'était du gâteau!

walkway ['wɔːkweɪ] *n* passage *m* (couvert)

wall [wɔːl] *n* (**a**) *(of building, room)* mur *m*; **the Great W. of China** la grande muraille de Chine; **w. cupboard** placard *m* mural; **w. hanging** tenture *f* murale (**b**) *(idioms)* **a w. of silence** un mur de silence; **to go to the w.** faire faillite; *Fam* **to drive sb up the wall** rendre qn dingue; *Fam* **I could be talking to the w.!** c'est comme parler à un mur; **off the w.** loufoque

▶**wall in** *vt sep* entourer

▶**wall off** *vt sep* séparer

▶**wall up** *vt sep* murer

wallaby ['wɒləbɪ] *(pl* **wallabies**) *n* wallaby *m*

wallet ['wɒlɪt] *n* portefeuille *m*

wallflower ['wɔːlflaʊə(r)] *n (plant)* giroflée *f*; *Fig* **to be a w.** *(of person)* faire tapisserie

Walloon [wɒ'luːn] **1** *n* (**a**) *(person)* Wallon(onne) *m, f* (**b**) *(language)* wallon *m*
 2 *adj* wallon(onne)

wallop ['wɒləp] *Fam* **1** *n* beigne *f*, grand coup *m*
 2 *vt* filer un grand coup à

walloping ['wɒləpɪŋ] *Fam* **1** *n* raclée *f*
 2 *adv (for emphasis)* super; **a w. great lie** un mensonge gros comme ça

wallow ['wɒləʊ] *vi* se vautrer; **to w. in self-pity** s'apitoyer sur son propre sort

wallpaper ['wɔːlpeɪpə(r)] **1** *n* papier *m* peint
 2 *vt* tapisser

wall-to-wall ['wɔːltə'wɔːl] *adj* **w. carpeting** moquette *f*; *Fig* **w. coverage** couverture *f* complète

walnut ['wɔːlnʌt] *n (fruit)* noix *f*; *(tree, wood)* noyer *m*

walrus ['wɔːlrəs] *(pl* **walruses**) *n* morse *m*

waltz [wɔːls] **1** *n* valse *f*
 2 *vi* (**a**) *(dance)* valser (**b**) *Fam (move confidently)* **to w. in/out** entrer/sortir avec désinvolture; *Fam* **to w. off with sth** partir avec qch

WAN [dʌbəljuːeɪ'en] *n Comput (abbr* **wide area network**) grand réseau *m*

wan [wɒn] *adj* blême

wand [wɒnd] *n* baguette *f*

wander ['wɒndə(r)] **1** *vt (streets)* traîner dans; *(world)* courir
 2 *vi* (**a**) *(roam)* errer; **to w. around the town** se promener dans la ville; **she had wandered from the path** elle s'était éloignée du chemin (**b**) *(verbally)* radoter; *(mentally)* dérailler; **to w. from the subject** s'écarter du sujet
 3 *n* balade *f*; **to go for a w.** aller faire un tour

wanderer ['wɒndərə(r)] *n* vagabond(e) *m, f*

wandering ['wɒndərɪŋ] *adj (person, life)* errant(e); *(tribe)* nomade

wanderlust ['wɒndəlʌst] *n* soif *f* de voyages

wane [weɪn] **1** *vi (of moon)* décroître; *(of popularity, enthusiasm, power)* décliner
 2 *n* **to be on the w.** *(of moon)* décroître; *(of popularity, enthusiasm, power)* être en déclin

wangle ['wæŋɡəl] *vt Fam* se débrouiller pour avoir; **to w. sth for sb** se débrouiller pour avoir qch à qn; **to w. it so that** se débrouiller pour que + *subjunctive*

wanna ['wɒnə] *Fam* (**a**) = **want to** (**b**) = **want a**

want [wɒnt] **1** *vt* (**a**) *(wish, desire)* vouloir; **to w. to do sth** vouloir faire qch; **to w. sb to do sth** vouloir que qn fasse qch; **that's the last thing we w.** nous ne voulons surtout pas cela; **I know when I'm not wanted** je sais quand je suis de trop; **what does she w. with me?** qu'est-ce qu'elle me veut?
 (**b**) *Fam (need)* avoir besoin de; **the lawn wants cutting** la pelouse a besoin d'être tondue; **you w. to be careful with him** il faut que tu fasses attention avec lui
 (**c**) *(seek)* **to be wanted by the police** être recherché(e) par la police; **you're wanted on the phone** on te demande au téléphone; **accommodations wanted** *(in advertisement)* cherche appartement
 2 *vi* **to w. for nothing** ne manquer de rien
 3 *n* (**a**) *(need)* besoin *m*; **w. ad** petite annonce *f*
 (**b**) *(lack)* manque *m* (**of** de); **for w. of sth/of doing sth** faute de qch/de faire qch; **for w. of anything better** faute de mieux

wanting ['wɒntɪŋ] *adj* **to be w. in sth** manquer de qch; **to be found w.** *(of person)* se révéler incapable; *(of thing)* laisser à désirer

wanton ['wɒntən] *adj* (**a**) *(unjustified)* gratuit(e) (**b**) *(unrestrained)* dévergondé(e); *(sexually)* licencieux(euse)

WAP [wæp] *n Comput & Tel (abbr* **wireless application protocol**) WAP *m*

war [wɔː(r)] *n* guerre *f*; **to be at w. (with)** être en guerre (avec); **to go to w. (with/over)** entrer en guerre (contre/à propos de); *Fig* **w. of words** altercation *f*; *Fam Fig* **you look as if you've been through the wars** tu es dans un bel état!; **w. cabinet** cabinet *m* de guerre; **w. correspondent** correspondant(e) *mf* de guerre; **w. crime** crime *m* de guerre; **w. criminal** criminel *m* de guerre; **w. cry** cri *m* de guerre; **w. games** *Mil* manœuvres *fpl*; *(with model soldiers)* wargame *m*; **w. memorial** monument *m* aux morts

warble ['wɔːbəl] **1** *n* gazouillement *m*
 2 *vi* gazouiller

warbler ['wɔːblə(r)] *n* fauvette *f*

ward [wɔːd] *n* (**a**) *(in hospital)* salle *f* (**b**) *(electoral division)* circonscription *f* (**c**) *Law* **w. of court** pupille *mf* sous tutelle judiciaire

▶**ward off** *vt sep (blow)* éviter; *(danger)* chasser

warden ['wɔːdən] *n (of prison)* directeur(trice) *m,f*; *(of park)* gardien(enne) *m,f*

wardrobe ['wɔːdrəʊb] *n* (**a**) *(closet)* armoire *f* (**b**) *(clothes)* garde-robe *f*; **to have a large w.** avoir une garde-robe importante (**c**) *(theatrical costumes)* costumes *mpl*

warehouse ['weəhaʊs] *n* entrepôt *m*

wares [weə(r)z] *npl* articles *mpl*

warfare ['wɔːfeə(r)] *n* guerre *f*; **class w.** lutte *f* des classes

warhead ['wɔːhed] *n* ogive *f*

warhorse ['wɔːhɔːs] *n Fig* **an old w.** un vétéran

warily ['weərɪlɪ] *adv* avec une prudence circonspecte

wariness ['weərɪnɪs] *n* prudence *f* circonspecte

warlike ['wɔːlaɪk] *adj* guerrier(ère)

warm [wɔːm] **1** *adj* (a) *(in temperature)* chaud(e); **to be w.** *(of person)* avoir chaud; *(of object, water, clothing)* être chaud(e); **it's w.** *(of weather)* il fait chaud; **you're getting warmer** *(in guessing game)* tu chauffes (b) *(kind, friendly)* chaleureux(euse)
  2 *vt* chauffer; **to w. oneself by the fire** se chauffer près du feu
  3 *vi* **to w. to sb** se prendre de sympathie pour qn; **to w. to sth** se laisser séduire par qch

▸**warm over** *vt sep (food)* réchauffer

▸**warm up 1** *vt sep (food)* réchauffer
  2 *vi* (a) *(of person, room)* se réchauffer (b) *(of dancer, athlete)* s'échauffer (c) *(of engine)* chauffer

warm-blooded [wɔːm'blʌdɪd] *adj* à sang chaud

warm-hearted [wɔːm'hɑːtɪd] *adj* chaleureux(euse)

warmly ['wɔːmlɪ] *adv* (a) *(dress)* chaudement (b) *(applaud, thank)* chaleureusement

warmonger ['wɔːmʌŋgə(r)] *n* belliciste *mf*

warmth [wɔːmθ] *n* chaleur *f*

warm-up ['wɔːmʌp] *n (of dancer, athlete)* échauffement *m*

warn [wɔːn] *vt* avertir, prévenir; **to w. sb about sb/sth** mettre qn en garde contre qn/qch; **to w. sb about doing sth** dire à qn de ne pas faire qch; **to w. sb not to do sth** déconseiller à qn de faire qch; **you have been warned!** te voilà prévenu!

warning ['wɔːnɪŋ] *n* (a) *(caution)* avertissement *m*; *(against danger)* mise *f* en garde; **to give sb a w.** donner un avertissement à qn; *(against danger)* mettre qn en garde; *Fig* **w. sign** signe *m* (b) *(advance notice)* avis *m*; **without w.** sans prévenir

warp [wɔːp] **1** *vt* (a) *(wood, metal)* gauchir (b) *(person, mind)* pervertir
  2 *vi (of wood, metal)* gauchir

warpath ['wɔːpɑːθ] *n Fam* **to be on the w.** en vouloir à tout le monde

warped [wɔːpt] *adj* (a) *(wood, metal)* gauchi(e) (b) *(person)* perverti(e); *(mind)* tordu

warrant ['wɒrənt] **1** *n Law* mandat *m*; *Mil* **w. officer** adjudant *m*
  2 *vt* (a) *(justify)* justifier (b) *(guarantee)* garantir

warranty ['wɒrəntɪ] *(pl* **warranties)** *n* garantie *f*; **under w.** sous garantie

warren ['wɒrən] *n (of rabbit)* garenne *f*; *Fig (of streets)* labyrinthe *m*

warring ['wɔːrɪŋ] *adj* en guerre

warrior ['wɒrɪə(r)] *n* guerrier(ère) *m,f*

Warsaw ['wɔːsɔː] *n* Varsovie; *Formerly* **the W. Pact** le pacte de Varsovie

warship ['wɔːʃɪp] *n* navire *m* de guerre

wart [wɔːt] *n* verrue *f*; **warts and all** *(biography, portrait)* sans complaisance

warthog ['wɔːthɒg] *n* phacochère *m*

wartime ['wɔːtaɪm] *n* temps *m* de guerre; **in w.** en temps de guerre

wary ['weərɪ] *adj* méfiant(e); **to be w. of sb/sth** se méfier de qn/qch

was [wɒz] *pt of* **be**

wash [wɒʃ] **1** *n* (a) *(action)* lavage *m*; **to give sth a w.** laver qch; **your jeans are in the w.** ton jean est au lavage; *Fig* **it will all come out in the w.** tout va s'arranger (b) *(of ship)* remous *m*
  2 *vt* (a) *(clean)* laver; **to w. oneself** se laver; **to w. one's face/one's hands** se laver la figure/les mains; *Fig* **to w. one's hands of sth** se laver les mains de qch; **to wash one's hands of sb** ne plus se préoccuper de qn (b) *(carry)* **to w. sb/sth**

ashore rejeter qn/qch sur le rivage; **he was washed overboard** une vague l'a emporté par-dessus bord
  3 *vi (wash oneself)* se laver

▸**wash away** *vt sep* emporter

▸**wash down** *vt sep* (a) *(walls, car)* laver à grande eau (b) *(pill)* faire descendre (**with** avec); **to w. down one's dinner with a bottle of wine** arroser son dîner d'une bouteille de vin

▸**wash off 1** *vt sep* enlever
  2 *vi* partir

▸**wash out 1** *vt sep* (a) *(cup, bottle)* rincer (b) *(stain, dirt)* faire partir; **to be completely washed out** *(exhausted)* être complètement lessivé(e)
  2 *vi (of stain, dirt)* partir

▸**wash over** *vt insep (of waves)* balayer; *Fig (have no effect on)* ne faire aucun effet à

▸**wash up 1** *vt sep* (a) *(clean)* laver (b) *(carry ashore)* rejeter sur le rivage
  2 *vi (freshen up)* se débarbouiller

washboard ['wɒʃbɔːd] *n* planche *f* à laver; *Fam* **w. stomach** ventre *m* plat

washbowl ['wɒʃbəʊl] *n (small)* cuvette *f*; *(large)* bassine *f*

washcloth ['wɒʃklɒθ] *n (face cloth)* lingette *f*

washer ['wɒʃə(r)] *n* (a) *Fam (for clothes)* machine *f* à laver (b) *(for screw)* rondelle *f*; *(made of rubber)* joint *m*

washer-dryer [wɒʃə'draɪə(r)] *n* machine *f* à laver qui fait sèche-linge

washing ['wɒʃɪŋ] *n* (a) *(action)* lavage *m*; **to do the w.** faire la lessive; **w. machine** machine *f* à laver (b) *(dirty clothes)* linge *m* sale; *(clean clothes)* linge (propre)

Washington ['wɒʃɪŋtən] *n* Washington; **W. (State)** l'État *m* de Washington; **W. DC** Washington

washout ['wɒʃaʊt] *n Fam* bide *m*

washroom ['wɒʃruːm] *n* toilettes *fpl*

wasn't [wɒzənt] = **was not**

Wasp, WASP [wɒsp] *n (abbr* **White Anglo-Saxon Protestant)** = Blanc d'origine anglo-saxonne et protestante, appartenant aux classes aisées et influentes

wasp [wɒsp] *n* guêpe *f*; **w.'s nest** guêpier *m*

waspish ['wɒspɪʃ] *adj* hargneux(euse)

wastage ['weɪstɪdʒ] *n* gaspillage *m*

waste [weɪst] **1** *n* (a) *(of food, effort)* gaspillage *m*; *(of time, money)* perte *f*; **to go to w.** être gaspillé(e) (b) *(rubbish)* déchets *mpl*; **w. disposal unit** broyeur *m* d'ordures (c) **wastes** *(desert)* étendues *fpl* désertiques
  2 *adj (heat, fuel)* gaspillé(e); *(water)* usé(e)
  3 *vt (money)* gaspiller; *(time)* perdre; *(opportunity)* gâcher; **to w. no time doing sth** ne pas perdre de temps pour faire qch; *Prov* **w. not, want not** = il ne faut pas gaspiller

▸**waste away** *vi* dépérir

wastebasket ['weɪstbɑːskɪt] *n* corbeille *f* à papier

wasted ['weɪstɪd] *adj* (a) *(effort)* gaspillé(e); *(opportunity)* gâché(e) (b) *Fam (drunk)* bourré(e), pété(e)

wasteful ['weɪstfʊl] *adj* **to be w.** *(of process, practice)* ne pas être rentable; *(of person)* être gaspilleur(euse)

wasteland ['weɪstlænd] *n (of desert, snow)* désert *m*; *(disused land)* terrain *m* vague

wastepaper [weɪst'peɪpə(r)] *n* vieux papiers *mpl*; **w. basket** corbeille *f* à papier

wasting disease ['weɪstɪŋdɪ'ziːz] *n* maladie *f* dégénérative

watch [wɒtʃ] **1** *n* (a) *(timepiece)* montre *f* (b) *(period of guard duty)* garde *f*; *(guard)* sentinelle *f*; **to be on w.** monter la garde; **to keep a close w. on sb/sth** surveiller qn/qch de près; *Fig* **it won't happen on my w.** ça n'arrivera pas tant que ce sera moi le responsable
  2 *vt* (a) *(observe)* regarder; **to w. television** regarder la télévision; **to w. sb doing sth** regarder qn faire qch (b) *(keep an eye on)* surveiller (c) *(be careful of)* faire attention à; **w. your lan-**

guage! surveille ton langage!; *Fam* **w. it!** attention!

3 *vi* regarder

▶**watch out** *vi* faire attention; **w. out!** attention!

▶**watch out for** *vt insep* (**a**) *(look for) (person)* guetter; *(thing)* chercher (**b**) *(be on guard for)* faire attention à

▶**watch over** *vt insep* veiller sur

watchdog ['wɒtʃdɒg] *n* chien *m* de garde; *Fig (organization)* organisme *m* de contrôle

watchful ['wɒtʃfʊl] *adj* vigilant(e)

watchmaker ['wɒtʃmeɪkə(r)] *n* horloger(ère) *m,f*

watchman ['wɒtʃmən] *n* gardien *m*

watchstrap ['wɒtʃstræp] *n* bracelet *m* de montre

watchtower ['wɒtʃtaʊə(r)] *n* tour *f* de guet

watchword ['wɒtʃwɜːd] *n* mot *m* d'ordre

water ['wɔːtə(r)] **1** *n* (**a**) *(substance)* eau *f*; **to pass w.** *(urinate)* uriner; **w. bed** matelas *m* d'eau; **w. bottle** gourde *f*; **w. chestnut** macre *f*; *Old-fashioned* **w. closet** waters *mpl*; **w. cooler** distributeur *m* d'eau fraîche; **w. heater** chauffe-eau *m inv*; **w. level** niveau *m* d'eau; **w. lily** nénuphar *m*; **w. meter** compteur *m* d'eau; **w. pistol** pistolet *m* à eau; **w. polo** water-polo *m*; **w. rat** rat *m* d'eau; **w. skiing** ski *m* nautique; **w. tank** réservoir *m* d'eau; **w. tower** château *m* d'eau; **w. wings** brassards *mpl* de natation

(**b**) *(idioms)* **to spend money like w.** jeter l'argent par les fenêtres; **the argument doesn't hold w.** cet argument ne tient pas debout; **to keep one's head above w.** garder la tête hors de l'eau; **that's all w. under the bridge now** c'est de l'histoire ancienne; **a lot of w. has passed under the bridge since then** il a coulé beaucoup d'eau sous les ponts depuis

2 *vt* (**a**) *(fields, plants)* arroser

(**b**) *(horse)* donner à boire à

3 *vi (of eyes)* pleurer; **it makes my mouth w.** ça me met l'eau à la bouche; **my mouth is watering** j'en ai l'eau à la bouche

▶**water down** *vt sep (liquid, chemical)* diluer; *Fig (criticism, legislation)* atténuer

waterborne ['wɔːtəbɔːn] *adj (goods)* transporté(e) par voie d'eau; *(disease)* d'origine hydrique

watercolor ['wɔːtəkʌlə(r)] *n (paint, painting)* aquarelle *f*

watercourse ['wɔːtəkɔːs] *n* cours *m* d'eau

watercress ['wɔːtəkres] *n* cresson *m* (de fontaine)

waterfall ['wɔːtəfɔːl] *n* cascade *f*

waterfowl ['wɔːtəfaʊl] *(pl* **waterfowl***)* *n* gibier *m* d'eau

waterfront ['wɔːtəfrʌnt] *n (by river)* bord *m* de l'eau; *(by sea)* front *m* de mer

watering ['wɔːtərɪŋ] *n (of garden, plant)* arrosage *m*; **w. can** arrosoir *m*; **w. hole** *(for animals)* point *m* d'eau; *Fam (bar)* bar *m*

waterlogged ['wɔːtəlɒgd] *adj (shoes, clothes)* trempé(e); *(land)* détrempé(e)

watermark ['wɔːtəmɑːk] *n* filigrane *m*

watermelon ['wɔːtəmelən] *n* pastèque *f*

waterproof ['wɔːtəpruːf] **1** *adj* imperméable; *(watch, joint, seal)* étanche; *(make-up)* waterproof *inv*; *(sun lotion)* résistant(e) à l'eau

2 *vt* imperméabiliser

water-resistant ['wɔːtərɪzɪstənt] *adj (watch)* étanche; *(fabric)* qui résiste à l'eau

watershed ['wɔːtəʃed] *n Geog* ligne *f* de partage des eaux; *Fig (turning point)* tournant *m*

waterside ['wɔːtəsaɪd] *n* bord *m* de l'eau

water-ski ['wɔːtəskiː] *vi* faire du ski nautique

watertight ['wɔːtətaɪt] *adj (seal)* hermétique; *(compartment)* étanche; *Fig (argument, alibi)* inattaquable

waterway ['wɔːtəweɪ] *n* voie *f* navigable

waterworks ['wɔːtəwɜːks] *n* station *f* hydraulique; *Fam* **to turn on the w.** *(cry)* se mettre à pleurer comme une madeleine

watery ['wɔːtərɪ] *adj (soup)* trop liquide; *(beer, tea, coffee)* insipide, fade; *(eyes)* qui pleure; *(color)* délavé(e)

watt [wɒt] *n* watt *m*

wattage ['wɒtɪdʒ] *n* puissance *f* en watts

wave [weɪv] **1** *n* (**a**) *(of water, dislike, crime)* vague *f*; *Fig* **to make waves** faire des vagues (**b**) *(gesture)* signe *m* (de la main); **to give sb a w.** faire signe à qn (**c**) *(in hair)* ondulation *f* (**d**) *(in physics)* onde *f*

2 *vt (arm, flag)* agiter; *(stick)* brandir; **to w. one's arms about** agiter les bras; **to w. goodbye to sb** faire au revoir de la main à qn

3 *vi* (**a**) *(of person)* faire signe; **to w. to sb** faire signe à qn (**b**) *(of flag)* flotter au vent

▶**wave aside** *vt insep Fig (objection, criticism)* écarter

waveband ['weɪvbænd] *n* bande *f* de fréquences

wavelength ['weɪvleŋθ] *n* longueur *f* d'ondes; *Fig* **to be on the same w.** être sur la même longueur d'ondes

waver ['weɪvə(r)] *vi (of person)* vaciller; *(of voice)* trembler; *(of courage)* faiblir

waverer ['weɪvərə(r)] *n* indécis(e) *m,f*

wavy ['weɪvɪ] *adj* ondulé(e)

wax¹ [wæks] **1** *n (for candles, polishing, hair removal)* cire *f*; *(in ear)* cérumen *m*; **w. crayons** crayons *mpl* gras

2 *vt (polish)* cirer; *(remove hair from)* épiler à la cire; **to w. one's legs** s'épiler les jambes (à la cire)

wax² [wæks] *vi* (**a**) *(of moon)* croître (**b**) *(become)* **to w. lyrical (about sth)** devenir lyrique (à propos de qch)

waxed [wækst] *adj* ciré(e); **w. paper** papier *m* sulfurisé

waxen ['wæksən] *adj (complexion)* de cire

waxwork ['wækswɜːk] *n* **w. (dummy)** mannequin *m* de cire; **waxworks** musée *m* de cire

way [weɪ] **1** *n* (**a**) *(route) & Fig* chemin *m*; **the w. in** l'entrée *f*; **the w. out** la sortie *f*; **the w. to the station** le chemin pour aller à la gare; **to ask sb the w.** demander son chemin à qn; **to show sb the w.** montrer le chemin à qn; **to lose one's w.** se perdre; **to know one's w. about** savoir se débrouiller; **on the w.** en chemin, en route; *Fam* **they've got a baby on the w.** ils ont un bébé en route; **I must be on my w.** je dois partir; **out of the w.** isolé(e); *Fig* **to go out of one's w. to help sb** se mettre en quatre pour aider qn; *Fig* **to find a w. out of a problem** trouver une issue à un problème; *Fig* **she is well on the w. to success** elle est bien partie pour réussir; **to make one's w. to a place** se diriger vers un endroit; **to make one's w. through the crowd** se frayer un chemin à travers la foule; *Fig* **to make w. for sb** laisser la place à qn; *Fig* **to make one's w. in the world** réussir dans la vie; *also Fig* **to stand in sb's w.** barrer le passage à qn; *also Fig* **to be/to get in the w.** gêner; *also Fig* **to get out of the w.** s'écarter; *also Fig* **to keep out of the w.** se tenir à l'écart

(**b**) *(manner)* manière *f*, façon *f*; **in this w.** de cette manière; **to do things in one's own w.** faire les choses à sa manière; **I don't like the w. things are going** je n'aime pas la façon dont les choses tournent; *Fam* **w. to go!** bravo!; **one w. or another** d'une manière ou d'une autre; **to find a w. of doing sth** trouver un moyen de faire qch; **to have a w. with children/animals** savoir s'y prendre avec les enfants/animaux; **to get one's (own) w.** arriver à ses fins; **he's used to getting his own w.** il n'a pas l'habitude qu'on le contrarie; **to get used to sb's ways** se faire aux habitudes de qn

(**c**) *(distance)* **to go a part of the w.** faire un bout de chemin; **to go all the w.** aller jusqu'au bout; *Fig* **I'm with you all the w.** je suis tout à fait d'accord avec toi; **San Francisco is a long w. from New York** San Francisco est loin de New York; **we've still got a long w. to go** nous avons encore du chemin à faire; **to be a little/long w. off** être proche/loin

(**d**) *(direction)* direction *f*, sens *m*; **which w. ...?** dans quel sens...?; **this/that w.** par ici/là; *Fig* **to look the other w.** se boucher les yeux; *Fam* **down our w.** chez nous; *Fig* **it works both ways** cela marche dans les deux sens; **to split sth three ways** partager qch en trois

(e) *(street)* rue *f*

(f) *(respect)* égard *m*; **in a w.** d'une certaine manière; **in every w.** en tous points; **in no w.** en aucune façon; *Fam* **no w.!** pas question!

(g) *(state, condition)* **to be in a good w.** bien aller; **to be in a bad w.** être mal en point

2 *adv Fam* **w. back in the 1920s** dans les années vingt; **Lucy and I go w. back** Lucy et moi sommes des amis de longue date; **w. ahead** devant tout le monde; **w. down south** tout au sud; **your guess was w. out** tu étais loin de la vérité

wayfarer ['weɪfeərə(r)] *n* voyageur(euse) *m,f*

waylay [weɪ'leɪ] *(pt & pp* **waylaid** [weɪ'leɪd]) *vt (attack)* agresser; *Fig (stop)* arrêter au passage

way-out [weɪ'aʊt] *adj Fam (person)* excentrique; *(ideas, beliefs)* bizarre, curieux(euse)

wayside ['weɪsaɪd] *n* bord *m* de la route; *Fig* **to fall by the w.** se retrouver à la traîne

wayward ['weɪwəd] *adj* difficile

WBA [dʌbəlju:bi:'eɪ] *n (abbr* **World Boxing Association**) WBA, = association mondiale de boxe

WC [dʌbəlju:'si:] *n (abbr* **water closet**) WC *mpl*

we [wi:] *pron* nous; **we're American** nous sommes américains; ᴡᴇ **haven't got it!** ce n'est pas nous qui l'avons!; **as we say in the States** comme on dit aux États-Unis; **we French are…** nous autres Français, nous sommes…

weak [wi:k] *adj (person, currency, character)* faible; *(heart)* fragile; *(argument, excuse)* peu convaincant(e); *(tea, coffee)* peu fort(e); **to grow w.** s'affaiblir; **to be w. at sth** *(school subject)* être faible en qch; *Fig* **to go w. at the knees** avoir les jambes en coton; *Fig* **w. spot** point *m* faible

weaken ['wi:kən] **1** *vt* affaiblir
2 *vi* s'affaiblir

weak-kneed [wi:k'ni:d] *adj Fig* mou (molle)

weakling ['wi:klɪŋ] *n* mauviette *f*, faible *mf*

weakly ['wi:klɪ] *adv* faiblement

weakness ['wi:knɪs] *n* faiblesse *f*; **to have a w. for sb/sth** avoir un faible pour qn/qch

weak-willed [wi:k'wɪld] *adj* sans volonté

weal [wi:l] *n (mark)* trace *f* de coup

wealth [welθ] *n* richesse *f*; *Fig* **a w. of sth** une abondance de qch

wealthy ['welθɪ] **1** *npl* **the w.** les riches
2 *adj* riche

wean [wi:n] *vt (baby)* sevrer; *Fig* **to w. sb off sth** *(bad habit)* faire passer qch à qn; *(alcohol, drugs)* sevrer qn de qch

weapon ['wepən] *n* arme *f*; **weapons inspector** inspecteur *m* du désarmement; **weapons of mass destruction** armes *fpl* de destruction massive

wear [weə(r)] **1** *vt (pt* **wore** [wɔ:(r)], *pp* **worn** [wɔ:n]) **(a)** *(garment, glasses)* porter; **to w. black** porter du noir; **to w. one's hair up** avoir les cheveux relevés **(b)** *(erode)* user; **to w. a hole in sth** faire un trou dans qch
2 *vi (of clothing)* s'user; **to w. thin** s'user; *Fig* **that excuse is wearing thin** cette excuse ne prend plus; **my patience is wearing thin** je suis à bout de patience; **to w. smooth** devenir lisse; **to w. well** *(of clothing, person, movie)* bien vieillir
3 *n* **(a)** *(clothing)* vêtements *mpl*; **evening w.** habits *mpl* de soirée; **children's w.** vêtements pour enfants **(b)** *(use)* usure *f*; **to get a lot of w. out of sth** porter qch longtemps; *Fam* **to be the worse for w.** être bien éméché(e); **w. and tear** usure *f* naturelle

▸**wear away 1** *vt sep* user
2 *vi* s'user

▸**wear down 1** *vt sep* user; *Fig* **to w. sb down** avoir qn à l'usure
2 *vi* s'user

▸**wear off** *vi (of pain)* disparaître; *(of effect)* cesser; *(of anes-*

thetic) cesser de faire effet; **the novelty soon wore off** l'attrait de la nouveauté n'a pas duré

▸**wear on** *vi (of time)* s'écouler

▸**wear out** *vt sep* user; **to w. sb out** épuiser qn; **to w. oneself out** s'épuiser

wearily ['wɪərɪlɪ] *adv* avec lassitude

weariness ['wɪərɪnɪs] *n* lassitude *f*

wearing ['weərɪŋ] *adj* lassant(e)

wearisome ['wɪərɪsəm] *adj* fatigant(e)

weary ['wɪərɪ] **1** *adj* las (lasse); **to be w. of sth/of doing sth** être las de qch/de faire qch; **to grow w. of sth** se lasser de qch
2 *vt* fatiguer, lasser
3 *vi* se lasser **(of** de)

weasel ['wi:zəl] *n* belette *f*

weather ['weðə(r)] **1** *n* **(a)** *(atmospheric conditions)* temps *m*; **what's the w. like?** quel temps fait-il?; **the w. is good/bad** il fait beau/mauvais; **in this w.** par un temps pareil; **w. permitting** si le temps le permet; **w. forecast** prévisions *fpl* météorologiques; **w. map** *or* **chart** carte *f* météorologique **(b)** *(idioms)* **to make heavy w. of sth** faire tout un plat de qch; **to be under the w.** se sentir patraque
2 *vt* **(a)** *(rock)* éroder **(b)** *(problem, situation)* surmonter; *Fig* **to w. the storm** tenir le coup
3 *vi (of rock)* s'éroder

weatherbeaten ['weðəbi:tən] *adj (person, face)* hâlé(e); *(cliff, rock)* battu(e) par les vents

weathercock ['weðəkɒk] *n* girouette *f*

weathergirl ['weðəgɜ:l] *n* présentatrice *f* de la météo

weatherman ['weðəmæn] *n* présentateur *m* de la météo

weatherproof ['weðəpru:f] *adj* résistant(e) aux intempéries

weave [wi:v] **1** *vt (pt* **wove** [wəʊv] *or* **weaved**, *pp* **woven** ['wəʊvən]) tisser; *Fig* **a skillfully woven plot** une intrigue bien ficelée
2 *vi* tisser; *Fig* **to w. through the traffic** se faufiler parmi les voitures
3 *n (pattern)* tissage *m*

weaver ['wi:və(r)] *n* tisserand(e) *m,f*

weaving ['wi:vɪŋ] *n* tissage *m*

web [web] *n* **(a)** *(of spider)* toile *f*; *Fig (of lies)* tissu *m*; *(of intrigue)* nid *m* **(b)** *(of duck, frog)* palmure *f* **(c)** *Comput* **the W.** le Web; **W. design** conception *f* de sites Web; **W. designer** concepteur(trice) *m,f* de sites Web; **W. page** page *f* Web; **W. site** site *m* Web

webbed [webd] *adj (foot)* palmé(e)

webbing ['webɪŋ] *n (on chair, bed)* sangles *fpl*

webcam ['webkæm] *n Comput* webcam *f*, caméra *f* Internet

webcast ['webkɑ:st] *Comput* **1** *n* webcast *m*
2 *vt* diffuser sur Internet

web-footed [web'fʊtɪd] *adj* palmipède

weblog ['weblɒg] *n Comput* weblog *m*

webmaster ['webmɑ:stə(r)] *n Comput* webmestre *m*, webmaster *m*

website ['websaɪt] *n* site *m* Web

webzine ['webzi:n] *n Comput* webzine *m*

we'd [wi:d] = **we had, we would**

wed [wed] *(pt & pp* **wedded**) **1** *vt* épouser; *Fig* **to be wedded to sth** être totalement dévoué(e) à qch
2 *vi* se marier

Wed. *(abbr* **Wednesday**) mercredi

wedding ['wedɪŋ] *n* mariage *m*; **w. anniversary** anniversaire *m* de mariage; **w. band** alliance *f*; **w. breakfast** repas *m* de noces; **w. cake** gâteau *m* de mariage; **w. day** jour *m* du mariage; **w. dress** robe *f* de mariée; **w. night** nuit *f* de noces; **w. planner** organisateur(trice) *m,f* de mariages; **w. singer** = chanteur qui anime les mariages; **w. ring** alliance *f*

wedge [wedʒ] **1** *n (for door, wheel)* cale *f*; *(of cake)* part *f*; *(of* *cheese)* morceau *m; Fig* **it has driven a w. between them** ça les a éloignés l'un de l'autre; **w. heel** semelle *f* compensée

2 *vt* coincer; **to w. a door open** maintenir une porte ouverte avec une cale

wedlock ['wedlɒk] *n Law* mariage *m;* **to be born out of w.** naître de parents non mariés

Wednesday ['wenzdɪ] *n* mercredi *m; see also* **Saturday**

wee [wi:] *adj (small)* petit(e); **a w. bit** un petit peu

weed [wi:d] **1** *n (plant)* mauvaise herbe *f*

2 *vt* désherber

▶ **weed out** *vt sep Fig* éliminer

weedkiller ['wi:dkɪlə(r)] *n* désherbant *m*

weeds [wi:dz] *npl (mourning clothes)* vêtements *mpl* de deuil; **in widow's w.** en deuil

week [wi:k] *n* semaine *f;* **next/last w.** la semaine prochaine/dernière; **once/twice a w.** une fois/deux fois par semaine; **in a w., in a w.'s time** dans huit jours; **within a w.** sous huitaine; **w. in w. out** chaque semaine

weekday ['wi:kdeɪ] *n* jour *m* de semaine

weekend [wi:k'end] *n* week-end *m,* fin *f* de semaine; **at** *or* **on the w.** ce week-end; *(every weekend)* le week-end; **w. break** week-end

weekly ['wi:klɪ] **1** *n (magazine)* hebdomadaire *m*

2 *adj* hebdomadaire

3 *adv* chaque semaine; **twice w.** deux fois par semaine

weeknight ['wi:knaɪt] *n* soir *m* de semaine

weep [wi:p] **1** *n* **to have a w.** pleurer un coup

2 *vt & vi (pt & pp* **wept** [wept]) pleurer

weeping ['wi:pɪŋ] **1** *n* pleurs *mpl*

2 *adj* qui pleure; **w. willow** saule *m* pleureur

weepy ['wi:pɪ] *adj Fam (book, movie)* mélo; **to be w.** *(of person)* avoir envie de pleurer

weft [weft] *n* trame *f*

weigh [weɪ] **1** *vt* **(a)** *(measure)* peser; **to w. oneself** se peser **(b)** *(consider)* mesurer; **to w. sth against sth** mettre qch en balance avec qch **(c)** *Naut* **to w. anchor** lever l'ancre

2 *vi (of person, package)* peser; **how much do you w.?** combien tu pèses?; **it's weighing on my conscience** ça me pèse sur la conscience; **her experience weighed in her favor** son expérience a fait pencher la balance en sa faveur

▶ **weigh down** *vt sep* lester; *Fig* **to be weighed down with sth** *(grief, responsibilities)* être accablé(e) de qch

▶ **weigh in** *vi* **(a)** *(of boxer, jockey)* être pesé(e); **to w. in at 180 pounds** ≃ peser 82 kilos **(b)** *(join in)* intervenir; **he always has to w. in with his opinions** il faut toujours qu'il intervienne pour imposer ses opinions

▶ **weigh out** *vt sep* peser

▶ **weigh up** *vt sep (consider)* mesurer; **to w. up the pros and cons** peser le pour et le contre

weighbridge ['weɪbrɪdʒ] *n* pont-bascule *m*

weight [weɪt] **1** *n* **(a)** *(of person, thing)* poids *m;* **they're the same w.** ils font le même poids; **to lose/to put on w.** perdre/prendre du poids; **to have a w. problem** avoir un problème de poids; **weights and measures** poids et mesures; **w. training** entraînement *m* aux haltères **(b)** *(idioms)* **to throw one's w. about** *or* **around** affirmer son autorité; **to pull one's w.** faire sa part de travail; **that's a w. off my mind** ça m'ôte un poids; **to carry w.** avoir du poids

2 *vt Fig* **to be weighted in favor of sb/sth** favoriser/ne pas favoriser qn/qch

▶ **weight down** *vt sep (to keep in place)* maintenir avec un poids; *(to make sink)* lester

weighting ['weɪtɪŋ] *n Fin* pondération *f*

weightless ['weɪtlɪs] *adj (astronaut)* en apesanteur; *(conditions)* d'apesanteur

weightlifter ['weɪtlɪftə(r)] *n* haltérophile *mf*

weightlifting ['weɪtlɪftɪŋ] *n* haltérophilie *f*

weighty ['weɪtɪ] *adj (heavy)* lourd(e); *Fig (serious, important)* grave

weird [wɪəd] *adj* bizarre

weirdo ['wɪədəʊ] *(pl* **weirdos)** *n Fam* type *m* bizarre

welcome ['welkəm] **1** *adj (person, news, change)* bienvenu(e); **to make sb w.** faire un bon accueil à qn; **to feel w.** se sentir le (la) bienvenu(e); **she's always w.** elle est toujours la bienvenue; **w. home!** ça fait plaisir de te revoir!; **w. to Texas!** bienvenue au Texas!; **you're w!** *(acknowledgment of thanks)* je vous en prie!, *Suisse* service!; **you're w. to borrow it** n'hésite pas à l'emprunter si tu veux

2 *vt (person)* souhaiter la bienvenue à; *(news, change)* accueillir favorablement; *(opportunity)* profiter de

3 *n* accueil *m;* **to give sb a warm w.** faire un accueil chaleureux à qn

welcoming ['welkəmɪŋ] *adj* accueillant(e)

weld [weld] **1** *n* soudure *f*

2 *vt* souder

welder ['weldə(r)] *n* soudeur(euse) *m,f*

welding ['weldɪŋ] *n* soudure *f*

welfare ['welfeə(r)] *n* **(a)** *(wellbeing)* bien-être *m;* **w. work** assistance *f* sociale **(b)** *(social security)* **to be on w.** recevoir l'aide sociale; **the W. State** l'État *m* providence

well¹ [wel] *n (for water, oil)* puits *m; (for elevator, stairwell)* cage *f*

▶ **well up** *vi (of tears)* monter

well² [wel] *(comparative* **better** ['betə(r)]*, superlative* **best** [best]) **1** *adj* bien; **to be w.** aller bien; **to get w.** se remettre; **get w. soon!** bon rétablissement!; **it's just as w....** heureusement...; **that's all very w., but...** tout ça, c'est très bien, mais...; **it's all very w. for you to say that** c'est facile pour toi de dire ça

2 *adv* **(a)** *(satisfactorily)* bien; **to speak w. of sb** dire du bien de qn; **I did as w. as I could** j'ai fait de mon mieux; **w. done!** bravo!; **you would do w. to keep quiet about it** vous feriez bien de vous taire à ce sujet; **he apologized, as w. he might** il s'est excusé, et c'était la bien la moindre des choses; **very w.!** *(OK)* très bien!

(b) *(for emphasis)* **to be w. able to do sth** être parfaitement capable de faire qch; **to be w. aware of sth** avoir parfaitement conscience de qch; **to leave w. enough alone** ne pas s'en mêler; *Fam* **to be w. in with sb** être dans les petits papiers de qn; **it is w. known that...** il est bien connu que...; **it's w. worth the effort** ça vaut vraiment la peine; **I can w. believe it** je n'ai aucun mal à le croire; **w. before/after** bien avant/après

(c) **as w.** *(also)* aussi, également; **she has an apartment in town as w. as a house in the country** elle a un appartement en ville ainsi qu'une maison à la campagne

3 *exclam (expressing surprise, inquiry)* eh bien!; *(expressing resignation, qualifying previous remark)* enfin; **w., who would have believed it!** eh bien, qui l'eût cru!; **w., who was it?** eh bien, qui était-ce?; **w., if you must!** enfin, si tu es vraiment obligé!; **he's nice, w. sometimes** il est gentil, enfin quelquefois

we'll [wi:l] = **we will, we shall**

well-adjusted [welə'dʒʌstɪd] *adj* équilibré(e)

well-advised [weləd'vaɪzd] *adj* sage; **you'd be w. to stay indoors today** tu ferais bien de ne pas sortir aujourd'hui

well-appointed [welə'pɔɪntɪd] *adj* bien équipé(e)

well-argued [wel'ɑ:gju:d] *adj* bien argumenté(e)

well-balanced [wel'bælənst] *adj* équilibré(e)

well-behaved [welbɪ'heɪvd] *adj* sage

wellbeing ['welbi:ɪŋ] *n* bien-être *m*

well-built [wel'bɪlt] *adj (building)* solide; *(person)* bien bâti(e)

well-chosen [wel'tʃəʊzən] *adj* bien choisi(e)

well-disposed [weldɪs'pəʊzd] *adj* **to be w. toward sb** être bien disposé(e) envers qn; **to be w. toward sth** être favorable à qch

well-dressed [wel'drest] *adj* bien habillé(e)

well-earned [wel'ɜ:nd] *adj* bien mérité(e)

well-fed [wel'fed] *adj* bien nourri(e)

well-founded [wel'faʊndɪd] *adj* fondé(e)

well-heeled [wel'hi:ld] *adj Fam* cossu(e)

well-informed [welɪn'fɔ:md] *adj* bien informé(e)

well-intentioned [welɪn'tenʃənd] *adj* bien intentionné(e)

well-kept [wel'kept] *adj* (garden) bien entretenu(e); (secret) bien gardé(e)

well-known [wel'nəʊn] *adj* connu(e)

well-loved [wel'lʌvd] *adj* très aimé(e)

well-made [wel'meɪd] *adj* bien fait(e)

well-meaning [wel'mi:nɪŋ] *adj* bien intentionné(e)

well-nigh ['welnaɪ] *adv* pratiquement

well-off [wel'ɒf] *adj* (wealthy) riche; *Fig* **you don't know when you're w.** tu ne connais pas ton bonheur

well-paid [wel'peɪd] *adj* bien payé(e)

well-read [wel'red] *adj* cultivé(e)

well-spoken [wel'spəʊkən] *adj* qui s'exprime bien

well-timed [wel'taɪmd] *adj* opportun(e)

well-to-do [weltə'du:] *adj* aisé(e)

wellwisher ['welwɪʃə(r)] *n* sympathisant(e) *m,f*

well-worn [wel'wɔ:n] *adj* (garment) très usé(e); (argument) éculé(e)

well-written [wel'rɪtən] *adj* bien écrit(e)

Welsh [welʃ] **1** *npl* (people) **the W.** les Gallois *mpl*
2 *n* (language) gallois *m*
3 *adj* gallois(e); **W. dresser** vaisselier *m*

Welshman ['welʃmən] *n* Gallois *m*

Welshwoman ['welʃwʊmən] *n* Galloise *f*

welt [welt] *n* trace *f* de coup

welter ['weltə(r)] *n* (of forms, details) masse *f*; (of ideas, activities) multitude *f*

welterweight ['weltəweɪt] *n Sport* poids *m* welter

wench [wentʃ] *n* Old-fashioned or Hum jeune fille *f*, jeune femme *f*

wend [wend] *vt Lit* **to w. one's way homewards** prendre le chemin du retour

went [went] *pt of* **go**

wept [wept] *pt & pp of* **weep**

we're [wɪə(r)] = **we are**

were [wɜ:(r)] *pt of* **be**

weren't [wɜ:nt] = **were not**

werewolf ['wɪəwʊlf] (*pl* **werewolves** ['wɪəwʊlvz]) *n* loup-garou *m*

west [west] **1** *n* ouest *m*; **to the w. (of)** à l'ouest (de); **the W.** l'Occident *m*, l'Ouest *m*
2 *adj* (coast, side) ouest *inv*; (wind) d'ouest; **W. Africa** l'Afrique *f* de l'Ouest; **the W. Bank** la Cisjordanie; **the W. End** (of London) = quartier chic de Londres où l'on trouve théâtres et restaurants; *Formerly* **W. Germany** l'Allemagne *f* de l'Ouest; **W. Indian** antillais(e); (person) Antillais(e) *m,f*; **the W. Indies** les Antilles *fpl*; **the W. Side** = les quartiers ouest de New York; **W. Virginia** la Virginie occidentale
3 *adv* à l'ouest; (travel) vers l'ouest; *Fam Fig* **to go w.** (of TV, car) rendre l'âme

westbound ['westbaʊnd] *adj* (train, traffic) en direction de l'ouest

westerly ['westəlɪ] **1** *n* (wind) vent *m* d'ouest
2 *adj* (point) à l'ouest; (wind) d'ouest, qui vient de l'ouest; **in a w. direction** vers l'ouest

western ['westən] **1** *n* (movie) western *m*; (novel) roman-western *m*
2 *adj* (region) de l'ouest; (in politics, sociology) occidental(e); **w. France** l'ouest *m* de la France; **W. Europe** l'Europe *f* de l'Ouest; **the W. Isles** (of Scotland) les Hébrides *fpl*; **W. Samoa**

les Samoa *fpl* occidentales; **W. Samoan** samoan(e); (person) Samoan(e) *m,f*

westernized ['westənaɪzd] *adj* occidentalisé(e)

westward ['westwəd] **1** *adj* (in the west) à l'ouest, dans l'ouest
2 *adv* (face, point) à l'ouest; (go, travel) vers l'ouest

westwards ['westwədz] *adv* = **westward**

wet [wet] **1** *adj* (not dry) mouillé(e); (weather) pluvieux(euse); **to get w.** se mouiller; **the ink/paint was still w.** l'encre/la peinture n'était pas sèche; *Fam Fig* **to be still w. behind the ears** manquer d'expérience; *Fig* **w. blanket** rabat-joie *mf*; **w. dream** pollution *f* nocturne; **w. paint** (sign) peinture fraîche; **w. suit** combinaison *f* de plongée
2 *vt* (pt & pp **wet** or **wetted**) mouiller; **to w. the bed** faire pipi au lit; **to w. oneself** mouiller sa culotte
3 *n* (dampness) humidité *f*; (rain) pluie *f*

WEU [dʌbəlju:i:'u:] *n* (abbr **Western European Union**) UEO *f*

we've [wi:v] = **we have**

whack [wæk] *Fam* **1** *n* (a) (blow) grand coup *m*; **to give sb/sth a w.** donner un grand coup à qn/qch (b) (share) part *f* (c) *Fam* (idioms) **the price is out of w. with the marketplace** le prix ne correspond pas au cours du marché; **to be out of w. with reality** ne pas être en phase avec la réalité
2 *vt* (a) (hit) donner un grand coup à; **to w. sb on** or **over the head** donner un grand coup sur la tête de qn (b) very *Fam* (murder) liquider

whacked [wækt] *adj Fam* (exhausted) nase, vanné(e)

whacking ['wækɪŋ] *adv Fam* **a w. great increase/fine** une vache d'augmentation/d'amende

whale [weɪl] *n* baleine *f*; *Fam* **to have a w. of a time** s'éclater

whaler ['weɪlə(r)] *n* baleinier *m*

whaling ['weɪlɪŋ] *n* pêche *f* ou chasse *f* à la baleine

wharf [wɔ:f] (*pl* **wharves** [wɔ:vz]) *n* quai *m*

what [wɒt] **1** *pron* (a) (in questions) (subject) qu'est-ce qui; (object) qu'est-ce que, que; (after preposition) quoi; **w.'s happening?** qu'est-ce qui se passe?; **w. do you want?** qu'est-ce que tu veux?, que veux-tu?; **w. are you thinking about?** à quoi penses-tu?; **w.'s that?** qu'est-ce que c'est?; **w.'s that to you?** qu'est-ce que ça peut vous faire?; **w. for?** (for what purpose?) pour quoi faire?; (why) pourquoi?; **w.'s a modem for?** à quoi ça sert, un modem?; **w. did he do that for?** pourquoi est-ce qu'il a fait ça?; **w.'s French for "dog"?** comment dit-on "dog" en français?; **w.'s he like?** comment est-il?; **w. about the money I lent you?** et l'argent que je vous ai prêté?; **w. about a game of tennis?** et si on faisait une partie de tennis?; **w. about me?** et moi?; **if that doesn't work, w. then?** si ça ne marche pas, qu'est-ce qui reste?; *Fam* **w. of it?** et alors?; *Fam* **are you coming or w.?** tu viens ou quoi?
(b) (in relative constructions) (subject) ce qui; (object) ce que; **I don't know w. has happened** je ne sais pas ce qui s'est passé; **I can't remember w. you told me** je ne me souviens plus de ce que tu m'as dit; **w. is surprising is that...** ce qu'il y a de surprenant, c'est que...; **w. I like is...** ce que j'aime, c'est...; *Fam* **he knows w.'s w.** il sait ce qu'il en est
2 *adj* (a) (in questions) quel (quelle); (plural) quels (quelles); **w. time is it?** quelle heure est-il?; **tell me w. time it is** dis-moi l'heure qu'il est; **show me w. books you want** montre-moi quels livres tu veux
(b) (in relative constructions) **I'll give you w. money I have** je vais vous donner l'argent que j'ai; **he took w. little food was left** il a pris le peu de nourriture qui restait
(c) (in exclamations) **w. an idea!** quelle idée!; **w. a fool he is!** qu'il est bête!; **w. a lot of people!** quel monde!
3 *exclam* quoi?; **w. next!** et quoi encore!

what-d'ye-call-her ['wɒtjəkɔ:lə(r)] *n Fam* (person) Machine *f*

what-d'ye-call-him ['wɒtjəkɔ:lɪm] *n Fam* (person) Machin *m*

what-d'ye-call-it ['wɒtjəkɔːlɪt] n Fam (thing) machin m, truc m

whatever [wɒt'evə(r)] **1** pron (a) (no matter what) quoi que + subjunctive; **w. it is, w. it may be** quoi que ce soit; **w. happens** quoi qu'il arrive (**b**) (anything) ce que; **do w. you like** fais ce que tu veux; **give him w. he wants** donne-lui tout ce qu'il veut; **w. you say** comme tu voudras (**c**) (in questions) **w. does that mean?** qu'est-ce que ça peut bien vouloir dire?

2 adj (**a**) (no matter what) **take w. food you want** prends toute la nourriture que tu veux; **pay w. price they ask** donne-leur le prix qu'ils en demandent, quel qu'il soit (**b**) (emphatic) **for no reason w.** sans aucune raison; **nothing w.** absolument rien

what's-her-name ['wɒtsəneɪm], **what's-his-name** ['wɒtsɪzneɪm], **what's-its-name** ['wɒtsɪtsneɪm] = **what-d'ye-call-her/him/it**

whatsit ['wɒtsɪt] n Fam machin m, truc m

whatsoever [wɒtsəʊ'evə(r)] adj **for no reason w.** sans aucune raison; **none w.** aucun(e); **nothing w.** absolument rien

wheat [wiːt] n blé m; **w. germ** germe m de blé

wheaten ['wiːtən] adj (loaf, roll) de blé ou froment

wheatfield ['wiːtfiːld] n champ m de blé

wheedle ['wiːdəl] vt **to w. sth out of sb** soutirer qch à qn par des cajoleries; **to w. sb into doing sth** amadouer qn pour qu'il/elle fasse qch

wheel [wiːl] **1** n (**a**) (on car, bike, stroller) roue f; (on shopping cart, suitcase) roulette f (**b**) (steering wheel) volant m; **to be at the w.** être au volant

2 vt (push) pousser

3 vi (turn) **to w. (about** or **around)** (of person) se retourner brusquement; (of plane) tourner; (of bird) tournoyer

wheelbarrow ['wiːlbærəʊ] n brouette f

wheelbase ['wiːlbeɪs] n empattement m

wheelchair ['wiːltʃeə(r)] n fauteuil m roulant

-wheeled [wiːld] suff **two/three/four-w.** à deux/trois/quatre roues

wheeling and dealing ['wiːlɪŋəndiːlɪŋ] n tractations fpl

wheeze [wiːz] **1** n (**a**) (noise) respiration f sifflante (**b**) Fam (trick) astuce f, combine f

2 vi (breathe heavily) respirer péniblement

whelk [welk] n bulot m

whelp [welp] n petit m

when [wen] **1** adv (in questions) quand; **w. will you come?** quand viendras-tu?; **tell me w. it happened** dis-moi quand cela s'est produit; Fam **say w.!** (when pouring drink) tu me dis stop!

2 conj (**a**) (with time) quand, lorsque; **w. I came into the room** quand ou lorsque je suis entré dans la pièce; **tell me w. you've finished** dis-moi quand tu auras terminé; **what's the good of talking w. you never listen?** à quoi sert de parler puisque tu n'écoutes jamais? (**b**) (whereas) alors que

whence [wens] adv Lit d'où

whenever [wen'evə(r)] **1** conj (**a**) (every time that) chaque fois que; **I go w. I can** j'y vais aussi souvent que je peux (**b**) (no matter when) n'importe quand; **come w. you like** viens quand tu veux

2 adv (**a**) (referring to unspecified time) n'importe quand; **Sunday, Monday or w.** dimanche, lundi ou n'importe quel autre jour (**b**) (in questions) **w. did you do that?** quand est-ce que tu as fait ça?

where [weə(r)] **1** adv (in questions) où; **w. are you going?** où vas-tu?; **w. does he come from?** d'où vient-il?; **tell me w. she is** dis-moi où elle est; **w. would we be if…?** que serions-nous devenus si…?

2 conj où; **I'll stay w. I am** je reste (là) où je suis; **that's w. he lives** c'est là qu'il habite; **that is w. you are mistaken** c'est là que vous vous trompez; **they went to Paris, w. they**

stayed a week ils sont allés à Paris, où ils ont séjourné une semaine

whereabouts 1 npl ['weərəbaʊts] **nobody knows her w., her w. are unknown** personne ne sait où elle est

2 adv [weərə'baʊts] (where) où

whereas [weə'ræz] conj alors que, tandis que

whereby [weə'baɪ] adv Formal par lequel (laquelle)

whereupon [weərə'pɒn] conj Lit sur quoi

wherever [weə'revə(r)] **1** conj (**a**) (everywhere that) où que; **I see him w. I go** où que j'aille, je le vois; **w. possible** partout où cela est possible (**b**) (no matter where) n'importe où; **we'll go w. you want** nous irons où tu veux

2 adv (**a**) (referring to unknown or unspecified place) **at home, in the office or w.** chez soi, au bureau ou n'importe où; **it's in Eagleton, w. that is** c'est à Eagleton, mais je ne sais pas où se trouve Eagleton (**b**) (in questions) **w. can she be?** où peut-elle bien être?

wherewithal ['weərwɪðɔːl] n **to have the w. (to do sth)** avoir les moyens (de faire qch)

whet [wet] (pt & pp **whetted**) vt (tool, blade, appetite) aiguiser

whether ['weðə(r)] conj (**a**) (with indirect questions) si; **I don't know w. it's true** je ne sais pas si c'est vrai (**b**) (conditional) **w. she comes or not we shall leave** qu'elle vienne ou non, nous partirons

whew [hjuː] exclam (of relief) ouf!; (of fatigue) pff!; (of astonishment) dis donc!

whey [weɪ] n petit-lait m

which [wɪtʃ] **1** pron (**a**) (in questions) lequel (laquelle) m,f; (plural) lesquels (lesquelles) mpl,fpl; **w. (one) is better?** lequel est le meilleur?; **w. of you is going?** qui d'entre vous y va?; **I can never remember w. is w.** je ne me rappelle jamais la différence

(**b**) (relative) (subject) qui; (object) que; **the house w. is for sale** la maison qui est à vendre; **the movie w. I saw last week** le film que j'ai vu la semaine dernière

(**c**) (referring back to whole clause) (subject) ce qui; (object) ce que; **he's getting married, w. surprises me** il va se marier, ce qui m'étonne; **she was back in London, w. I didn't know** elle était de retour à Londres, ce que je ne savais pas

(**d**) (with prepositions) **behind/in front of w.** derrière/devant lequel (laquelle); **beside/above w.** à côté/au-dessus duquel (de laquelle); **the countries w. we are going to** les pays où nous allons; **the town w. we live in** la ville où nous habitons; **after w. he went out** après quoi, il est sorti

2 adj (**a**) (in questions) quel (quelle); (plural) quels (quelles); **w. color do you like best?** quelle couleur préférez-vous?; **w. way do we go?** de quel côté allons-nous?; **w. one?** lequel (laquelle)?; **w. ones?** lesquels (lesquelles)?

(**b**) (in relative constructions) **I was there for a week, during w. time…** j'y suis resté une semaine, période pendant laquelle…; **she came at noon, by w. time I had left** elle est arrivée à midi, heure à laquelle j'étais déjà parti

whichever [wɪtʃ'evə(r)] **1** pron (**a**) (no matter which) quel (quelle) que soit celui (celle) qui; **w. you choose, I'm sure she'll like it** quel que soit celui que tu choisisses, je suis sûr que ça lui plaira (**b**) (any) **take w. you want** prends celui (celle) que tu voudras (**c**) (according to which) **come on Saturday or Sunday, w. suits you** viens samedi ou dimanche, suivant ce qui t'arrange

2 adj (no matter which) **take w. book you like best** choisis le livre que tu préfères

whiff [wɪf] n odeur f; **to catch a w. of sth** sentir qch; Fig **a w. of scandal** un parfum de scandale

while [waɪl] **1** n (**a**) (time) **a w.** un moment; **after/in a w.** après/dans un moment; **a short** or **little w. ago** il y a un petit moment; **a good w., quite a w.** un bon moment; **a long w.** longtemps; **once in a w.** de temps en temps

(**b**) **it's not worth my w.** ça n'en vaut pas la peine; **it's not** worth my w. **going** ça ne vaut pas la peine que j'y aille; **I'll make it worth your w.** vous serez récompensé de votre peine

2 *conj* (**a**) *(during the time that)* pendant que; **w. reading I fell asleep** je me suis endormi en lisant

(**b**) *(as long as)* tant que; **it won't happen w. I'm in charge!** ça ne se produira pas tant que ce sera moi le responsable!

(**c**) *(although)* bien que + *subjunctive;* **w. I admit it's difficult,...** bien que j'admette que ce soit difficile...

(**d**) *(whereas)* alors que; **one wore white, w. the other was in black** l'un portait du blanc, alors que l'autre était en noir

▶**while away** *vt sep* **to w. away the time** passer le temps

whilst [waɪlst] *conj* = while

whim [wɪm] *n* lubie *f*, fantaisie *f*; **to do sth on a w.** faire qch sur un coup de tête

whimper ['wɪmpə(r)] **1** *n* gémissement *m*, geignement *m*; *Fig* **without a w.** sans broncher

2 *vi* gémir, geindre

whimsical ['wɪmzɪkəl] *adj (person, behavior)* fantasque; *(remark, story)* saugrenu(e)

whine [waɪn] **1** *n (of person, animal)* gémissement *m*; *(of machine)* grincement *m*

2 *vi also Fig* gémir (**about** à propos de)

whinny ['wɪnɪ] **1** *n* hennissement *m*

2 *vi* hennir

whip [wɪp] **1** *n* (**a**) *(for punishment)* fouet *m* (**b**) *Pol* chef *m* de file *(chargé de la discipline de son parti)*

2 *vt* (*pt & pp* **whipped**) (**a**) *(beat with whip)* fouetter; **whipped cream** crème *f* fouettée; *Fig* **she whipped the crowd into a frenzy** son discours rendit la foule frénétique (**b**) *Fam (defeat)* battre à plates coutures

▶**whip around** *vi Fam (turn quickly)* se retourner brusquement

▶**whip off** *vt sep Fam (clothes)* ôter rapidement

▶**whip out** *vt sep Fam* sortir soudainement

▶**whip up** *vt sep* (**a**) *(support, enthusiasm)* susciter; *(audience)* galvaniser (**b**) *(prepare quickly) (dish, meal)* préparer vite fait

whiplash ['wɪplæʃ] *n* lésion *f* des cervicales

whippersnapper ['wɪpəsnæpə(r)] *n Fam* garnement *m*

whippet ['wɪpɪt] *n* whippet *m*

whirl [wɜːl] **1** *n also Fig* tourbillon *m*; **the social w.** le tourbillon de la vie mondaine; **my head's in a w.** j'ai la tête qui tourne; *Fam* **let's give it a w.** on va tenter le coup

2 *vt* **to w. sb/sth around** faire tournoyer qn/qch

3 *vi* tourbillonner; **my head's whirling** j'ai la tête qui tourne

▶**whirl along** *vi (of car, train)* filer à toute vitesse

▶**whirl around** *vi* se retourner brusquement

whirlpool ['wɜːlpuːl] *n* tourbillon *m*; **w. bath** bain *m* à remous, Jacuzzi® *m*

whirlwind ['wɜːlwɪnd] *n* tourbillon *m*; **w. romance** passion *f* enivrante; **w. tour** visite *f* éclair

whirr [wɜː(r)] **1** *n* ronflement *m*

2 *vi* ronfler

whisk [wɪsk] **1** *n* batteur *m*, fouet *m*

2 *vt* (**a**) *(eggs)* battre (**b**) *(move quickly)* **to w. sb to the hospital** transporter qn d'urgence à l'hôpital

3 *vi (move quickly)* **she whisked past me** elle est passée devant moi comme un éclair

▶**whisk away, whisk off** *vt sep (person)* emmener rapidement; *(object)* enlever rapidement

whisker ['wɪskə(r)] *n* **whiskers** *(of cat, mouse)* moustaches *fpl*; *(of man)* favoris *mpl*; *Fam* **to win by a w.** gagner de justesse

whiskey ['wɪskɪ] *n* whisky *m*

whisper ['wɪspə(r)] **1** *n* chuchotement *m*; **to speak in a w.** chuchoter

2 *vt* chuchoter; **to w. sth to sb** chuchoter qch à qn; **it's being whispered that...** le bruit court que...

3 *vi* chuchoter; **to w. to sb** chuchoter à l'oreille de qn

whist [wɪst] *n* whist *m*

whistle ['wɪsəl] **1** *n* (**a**) *(noise)* sifflement *m* (**b**) *(musical instrument)* flageolet *m*; *(of referee, policeman)* sifflet *m*

2 *vt (tune)* siffler

3 *vi* siffler; *Fam* **he can w. for his money** s'il compte récupérer son argent, il peut toujours courir

whistle-stop tour ['wɪsəlstɒp'tʊə(r)] *n* tournée *f* rapide

whit [wɪt] *n* **it doesn't matter a w.** ça n'a aucune importance; **it won't make a w. of difference** ça ne changera absolument rien

white [waɪt] **1** *n* (**a**) *(color, of egg, eye)* blanc *m*; **w. doesn't suit her** le blanc ne lui va pas (**b**) *(person)* Blanc (Blanche) *m,f*

2 *adj* blanc (blanche); **a w. man** un Blanc; **a w. woman** une Blanche; **to turn** *or* **to go w.** *(person)* devenir blême; *(object, hair)* blanchir; **w. with fear** vert(e) de peur; **w. as a ghost/sheet** pâle comme la mort/un linge; *Biol* **w. blood cell** globule *m* blanc; **w. chocolate** chocolat *m* blanc; *Fig* **w. elephant** = chose coûteuse et peu rentable; **w. fish** poisson *m* à chair blanche; **w. flag** drapeau *m* blanc; **w. flour** farine *f* blanche; **the W. House** la Maison-Blanche; **w. lie** pieux mensonge *m*; **w. meat** viande *f* blanche; **W. Out®** correcteur *m* liquide; *Pol* **w. paper** livre *m* blanc; **w. sauce** sauce *f* blanche; **w. spirit** white-spirit *m*; **w. stick** canne *f* blanche; **w. supremacist** partisan(e) *m,f* de la suprématie blanche; **w. tie** *(formal dress)* tenue *f* de soirée; *Pej* **w. trash** pauvres blancs *mpl*; **w. wedding** mariage *m* en blanc; **w. wine** vin *m* blanc

whitebait ['waɪtbeɪt] *n* friture *f*

whitecaps ['waɪtkæps] *npl (waves)* moutons *mpl*

white-collar worker ['waɪt'kɒlə'wɜːkə(r)] *n* col *m* blanc

white-haired ['waɪt'heəd] *adj* aux cheveux blancs

white-hot ['waɪt'hɒt] *adj* chauffé(e) à blanc

whiteness ['waɪtnɪs] *n* blancheur *f*

whitewash ['waɪtwɒʃ] **1** *n (paint)* badigeon *m* à la chaux; *Fig (cover-up)* blanchiment *m*

2 *vt (paint)* badigeonner à la chaux; *Fig (cover up)* blanchir

whitewater rafting ['waɪtwɔːtə'rɑːftɪŋ] *n* descente *f* en eau vive, rafting *m*

whither ['wɪðə(r)] *adv Lit* **w. this country/education?** où va ce pays/l'enseignement?

whiting ['waɪtɪŋ] *n (fish)* merlan *m*

whitish ['waɪtɪʃ] *adj* blanchâtre

Whitsun ['wɪtsən] *n* Pentecôte *f*

whittle ['wɪtəl] *vt* tailler (au couteau); *Fig* **to w. sth down** réduire qch

▶**whittle away** *vt sep Fig* **to w. sth away** réduire qch à presque rien

whiz [wɪz] **1** *n Fam (expert)* crack *m*; **w. kid** jeune prodige *m*

2 *vi (of bullet)* siffler; *(of person, car)* passer à toute vitesse; **to w. through a book/meal** lire un livre/manger à toute vitesse

WHO [dʌbəlju:'eɪtʃ'əʊ] *n (abbr* **World Health Organization)** OMS *f*

who [huː] *pron* (**a**) *(in questions)* qui; **w. is it?** qui est-ce?; **w. with?** avec qui?; **do you know w. she is?** sais-tu qui elle est?; **w.'s speaking?** *(on phone)* qui est à l'appareil?; **w. did you say was there?** qui était là, déjà?; **w. does he think he is?** pour qui se prend-il? (**b**) *(relative)* qui; **the people w. came yesterday** les gens qui sont venus hier; **those w. have already paid can leave** ceux qui ont déjà payé peuvent s'en aller; **Louise's father, w. is a doctor, was there** le père de Louise, qui est médecin, était là

whodun(n)it [huː'dʌnɪt] *n Fam* polar *m*

whoever [huː'evə(r)] *pron* (**a**) *(no matter who)* qui que + *subjunctive;* **w. you are** qui que vous soyez; **w. wrote that letter** la personne qui a écrit cette lettre; *Fam* **ask Simon or Chris or w.** demande à Simon ou à Chris ou à n'importe qui d'autre (**b**) *(anyone that)* celui (celle) qui; **w. finds it may keep it** celui qui le trouvera pourra le garder (**c**) (*in questions*) **w. can that be?** qui cela peut-il être?

whole [həʊl] **1** *adj* (**a**) (*entire, intact*) entier(ère); **the w. truth** toute la vérité; **the w. world** le monde entier; **a w. week** toute une semaine, une semaine entière; **to swallow sth w.** avaler qch sans le mâcher; *Fig* avaler qch; **w. milk** lait *m* entier (**b**) *Fam* (*for emphasis*) **a w. lot of** tout un tas de; **the w. lot of you** vous tous

2 *n* totalité *f*, ensemble *m*; **the w. of the village/the money** tout le village/l'argent; **as a w.** dans sa totalité; **on the w.** dans l'ensemble

wholefood ['həʊlfuːd] *n* aliments *mpl* complets; **w. restaurant** restaurant *m* bio

wholehearted [həʊl'hɑːtɪd] *adj* sans réserve, total(e)

wholesale ['həʊlseɪl] **1** *adj* de gros; *Fig* (*large-scale*) à grande échelle

2 *adv* en gros; *Fig* (*on a large scale*) à grande échelle

3 *n* (vente *f* en) gros *m*

wholesaler ['həʊlseɪlə(r)] *n* grossiste *mf*

wholesome ['həʊlsəm] *adj* (*food, entertainment*) sain(e); (*air, climate*) salubre; (*person*) comme il faut

wholewheat ['həʊlwiːt] *adj* (*bread, flour*) complet(ète)

wholly ['həʊllɪ] *adv* entièrement

whom [huːm] *pron Formal* (**a**) (*in questions*) qui; **w. did you see?** qui avez-vous vu?; **for/to/of w.?** pour/à/de qui? (**b**) (*relative*) que; **the woman w. you saw** la femme que vous avez vue; **the man w. you gave the money to** l'homme à qui vous avez donné l'argent; **the person of w. we were speaking** la personne dont nous parlions; **the men, both of w. were quite young,...** les hommes, tous deux assez jeunes,...

whoop [wuːp] **1** *n* cri *m* de joie

2 *vi* crier de joie

whoopee 1 *n* ['wʊpiː] *Fam* **to make w.** (*have fun*) faire la bombe; (*have sex*) faire crac-crac

2 *exclam* [wʊ'piː] youpi!

whooping cough ['huːpɪŋ'kɒf] *n* coqueluche *f*

whoops [wuːps] *exclam* houp-là!

whopper ['wɒpə(r)] *n Fam* (**a**) (*huge thing*) truc *m* énorme (**b**) (*lie*) gros bobard *m*

whopping ['wɒpɪŋ] *adj Fam* **w. (great)** énorme

whore [hɔː(r)] *n very Fam* putain *f*

whorehouse ['hɔːhaʊs] *n* bordel *m*

whose [huːz] **1** *possessive pron* (*in questions*) à qui; **w. are these gloves?** à qui sont ces gants?; **w. is this?** à qui est-ce?; **tell me w. they are** dis-moi à qui ils sont

2 *possessive adj* (**a**) (*in questions*) à qui; **w. gloves are these?** à qui sont ces gants?; **w. daughter are you?** de qui es-tu la fille? (**b**) (*relative*) dont; **the pupil w. work I showed you** l'élève dont je t'ai montré le travail; **the man to w. wife I gave the money** l'homme à la femme de qui j'ai donné l'argent

why [waɪ] **1** *adv* (**a**) (*in questions*) pourquoi; **w. didn't you say so?** pourquoi ne l'as-tu pas dit?; **w. get angry?** pourquoi se mettre en colère?; **w. not?** pourquoi pas? (**b**) (*in suggestions*) **w. don't you phone him?** pourquoi ne lui téléphones-tu pas?; **w. don't I come with you?** pourquoi est-ce que je ne viendrais pas avec toi?; **w. not sell the car?** pourquoi ne pas vendre la voiture?

2 *conj* pourquoi; **I'll tell you w. I don't like her** je vais vous dire pourquoi je ne l'aime pas; **that's w....** voilà pourquoi...; **the reason w....** la raison pour laquelle...

3 *n* **the whys and wherefores (of sth)** le pourquoi et le comment (de qch)

4 *exclam* **w., it's David!** mais voilà David!

wick [wɪk] *n* (*of lamp, candle*) mèche *f*

wicked ['wɪkɪd] *adj* (**a**) (*evil*) méchant(e); *Fig* (*dreadful*) affreux(euse) (**b**) *Fam* (*excellent*) génial(e)

wickedness ['wɪkɪdnɪs] *n* méchanceté *f*

wicker ['wɪkə(r)] *n* osier *m*

wickerwork ['wɪkəwɜːk] *n* vannerie *f*

wide [waɪd] **1** *adj* (**a**) (*broad*) large; **to be 10 feet w.** ≃ faire 3 mètres de large; **in the whole w. world** dans le monde entier; *Cin* **w. screen** écran *m* panoramique (**b**) (*extensive*) vaste

2 *adv* **w. open** (*eyes, mouth, door*) grand ouvert(e); **to be w. open to criticism** prêter le flanc à la critique; **w. apart** très espacé(e); (*legs*) très écarté(e); **w. awake** complètement réveillé(e); **the shot went w.** la balle est passée à côté; *Fig* **w. of the mark** loin de la vérité

wide-angle ['waɪdæŋɡəl] *adj* grand angle *inv*

wide-eyed ['waɪdaɪd] *adj* aux yeux écarquillés

widely ['waɪdlɪ] *adv* (**a**) (*extensively*) largement; **it is w. believed that...** beaucoup de gens pensent que...; **w. known** connu(e) de tout le monde (**b**) (*at a distance*) **w. spaced** très espacé(e)

widen ['waɪdən] **1** *vt* agrandir; (*garment*) élargir; *Fig* (*influence, scope*) étendre; **to w. one's horizons** élargir son horizon

2 *vi* s'élargir; (*of gap, eyes*) s'agrandir

▸ **widen out** *vi* s'élargir

widespread ['waɪdspred] *adj* répandu(e)

widow ['wɪdəʊ] **1** *n* veuve *f*; **w.'s pension** allocation *f* veuvage

2 *vt* **to be widowed** devenir veuf (veuve)

widowed ['wɪdəʊd] *adj* veuf (veuve)

widower ['wɪdəʊə(r)] *n* veuf *m*

width [wɪdθ] *n* largeur *f*

wield [wiːld] *vt* (**a**) (*sword, pen*) manier (**b**) (*power, influence*) exercer

wife [waɪf] (*pl* **wives** [waɪvz]) *n* femme *f*, épouse *f*

wife-beater ['waɪfbiːtə(r)] *n* (*man*) = homme qui bat sa femme; *Fam* (*T-shirt*) marcel *m*

wifely ['waɪflɪ] *adj* de bonne épouse

WiFi ['waɪfaɪ] *Comput* (*abbr* **wireless fidelity**) **1** *n* WiFi *m*

2 *adj* WiFi

wig [wɪɡ] *n* perruque *f*

wiggle ['wɪɡəl] **1** *n* trémoussement *m*

2 *vt* remuer

3 *vi* se trémousser

wiggly ['wɪɡlɪ] *adj Fam* (*line*) ondulé(e)

wigwam ['wɪɡwæm] *n* wigwam *m*

wild [waɪld] **1** *adj* (**a**) (*not domesticated*) (*animal, flower, countryside*) sauvage; *Fig* **it was a w. goose chase** ça n'a rien donné; *Fam* **w. horses wouldn't drag it out of me** rien au monde ne me le ferait dire; *Fig* **to sow one's w. oats** jeter sa gourme; **the W. West** le Far West

(**b**) (*unrestrained*) (*wind*) violent(e); (*weather*) très mauvais(e); (*hair*) en bataille; (*child*) turbulent(e); (*enthusiasm*) délirant(e); (*promise, rumor*) insensé(e); **w. eyes** regard *m* fou; **to be w.** (*person*) mener une vie agitée; **to drive sb w.** rendre qn fou (folle)

(**c**) (*random*) **it was just a w. guess** j'ai dit ça au hasard; *Comput & Fig* **w. card** joker *m*

(**d**) *Fam* (*enthusiastic*) **to be w. about sb/sth** être dingue de qn/qch

(**e**) *Fam* (*excellent*) génial(e)

2 *adv* **to grow w.** (*of plant*) pousser à l'état sauvage; **to run w.** être livré(e) à soi-même; **the audience went w.** le public s'est déchaîné

3 *n* **in the w.** à l'état sauvage; **in the wilds** en pleine brousse

wildcat ['waɪldkæt] *n* chat *m* sauvage; *Ind* **w. strike** grève *f* sauvage

wilderness ['wɪldənɪs] *n* région *f* sauvage; *Fig* (*overgrown garden*) jungle *f*; *Fig* **to be in the w.** être en pleine traversée du désert

wildfire ['waɪldfaɪə(r)] *n* **to spread like w.** se répandre comme une traînée de poudre

wildfowl ['waɪldfaʊl] (*pl* **wildfowl**) *n* gibier *m* d'eau

wildlife ['waɪldlaɪf] *n* nature *f*; **w. program** (*on TV*) émission *f* sur les animaux

wildly ['waɪldlɪ] *adv* (**a**) (*cheer, applaud*) frénétiquement; **to rush about w.** courir dans tous les sens (**b**) (*guess*) au hasard (**c**) (*for emphasis*) extrêmement; (*inaccurate, exaggerated*) complètement

wildness ['waɪldnɪs] *n* (*of countryside, animal*) état *m* sauvage; (*of wind, waves*) fureur *f*; (*of applause*) frénésie *f*; (*of ideas, words*) extravagance *f*

will¹ [wɪl] **1** *n* (**a**) (*resolve, determination*) volonté *f* (**to do de** faire); **at w.** à volonté!; (*cry*) à la demande; (*fire*) au hasard; *Mil* **fire at w.!** feu à volonté; **to show good w.** faire preuve de bonne volonté; **with the best w. in the world** avec la meilleure volonté du monde; *Prov* **where there's a w. there's a way** vouloir, c'est pouvoir (**b**) (*document*) testament *m*; **the last w. and testament of...** les dernières volontés de...; **to make one's w.** faire son testament

2 *vt* (**a**) **to w. sb to do sth** souhaiter ardemment que qn fasse qch; **to w. oneself to do sth** faire un effort de volonté pour faire qch (**b**) (*leave in one's will*) **to w. sth to sb** léguer qch à qn par testament

will² [wɪl] *modal aux v* (**a**) (*expressing future tense*) **I'll do it tomorrow** je le ferai demain; **it won't take long** ça ne prendra pas longtemps; **when w. he be coming?** quand viendra-t-il?; **I'll have finished by five** j'aurai fini avant cinq heures; **w. you be there? – yes I w./no I won't** tu seras là? – oui/non; **you'll write to me, won't you?** tu m'écriras, n'est-ce pas?

(**b**) (*expressing wish, determination*) **I won't allow it!** je ne le permettrai pas!; **w. you help me?** tu veux bien m'aider?; **she won't let me see him** elle refuse que je le voie; **won't you sit down?** vous ne voulez pas vous asseoir?; **be quiet, w. you!** tais-toi, s'il te plaît!; **if she WILL insist on doing everything herself...** si elle continue à tout vouloir faire elle-même...; **WILL you go away!** va-t'en, je te dis!; **it won't open** ça ne s'ouvre pas

(**c**) (*expressing general truth*) **these things w. happen** ça arrive parfois; **the restaurant w. seat a hundred people** le restaurant peut accueillir cent personnes

(**d**) (*expressing conjecture*) **you'll be tired** vous devez être fatigué; **they'll be home by now** ils ont dû arriver chez eux maintenant

willful ['wɪlfʊl] *adj* (**a**) (*stubborn*) têtu(e) (**b**) (*deliberate*) délibéré(e); *Law* **w. murder** homicide *m* volontaire

willfully ['wɪlfəlɪ] *adv* (**a**) (*stubbornly*) avec entêtement (**b**) (*deliberately*) délibérément

William ['wɪljəm] *pr n* **W. the Conqueror** Guillaume le Conquérant

willies ['wɪlɪz] *npl Fam* **to have the w.** avoir la trouille; **to give sb the w.** flanquer la trouille à qn

willing ['wɪlɪŋ] *adj* (*assistant, participant*) plein(e) de bonne volonté; **he was a w. accomplice** c'est de son plein gré qu'il est devenu complice; **to be w. to do sth** bien vouloir faire qch; **to show w.** faire preuve de bonne volonté

willingly ['wɪlɪŋlɪ] *adv* (*voluntarily*) de son plein gré; (*with pleasure*) volontiers

willingness ['wɪlɪŋnɪs] *n* bonne volonté *f*

will-o'-the-wisp [wɪləðə'wɪsp] *n also Fig* feu *m* follet

willow ['wɪləʊ] *n* **w. (tree)** saule *m*

willowy ['wɪləʊɪ] *adj* (*person, figure*) élancé(e)

willpower ['wɪlpaʊə(r)] *n* volonté *f*

willy-nilly [wɪlɪ'nɪlɪ] *adv* bon gré, mal gré

wilt [wɪlt] *vi* (*of plant*) se flétrir; *Fig* (*of person*) fatiguer

wily ['waɪlɪ] *adj* rusé(e)

wimp [wɪmp] *n Fam* mauviette *f*

wimpish ['wɪmpɪʃ] *adj Fam* mauviette

win [wɪn] **1** *n* victoire *f*

2 *vt* (*pt & pp* **won** [wʌn], *continuous* **winning**) (**a**) (*battle, race, prize*) gagner; **to w. an argument** avoir le dernier mot; *Fam* **you can't w. them all, you w. some, you lose some** on ne peut pas toujours être gagnant (**b**) (*popularity, recognition*) acquérir; (*confidence, love*) gagner (**c**) (*congressional seat, election*) remporter

3 *vi* gagner; *Fam* **you can't w.** j'aurai/tu auras/*etc.* toujours tort; **OK, you w.!** bon, d'accord!

▸**win around** *vt sep* persuader

▸**win back** *vt sep* reconquérir

▸**win out** *vi* triompher

▸**win over** = **win around**

▸**win through** *vi* réussir

wince [wɪns] **1** *n* grimace *f*

2 *vi* **to w. (with pain/embarrassment)** grimacer de douleur/d'embarras

winch [wɪntʃ] **1** *n* treuil *m*

2 *vt* hisser

wind¹ [wɪnd] **1** *n* (**a**) (*air current*) vent *m*; **to sail into** *or* **against the w.** naviguer vent debout; *Fig* **to sail close to the w.** (*take risks*) jouer avec le feu; (*be risqué*) friser l'indécence; **w. energy** *or* **power** énergie *f* éolienne; **w. instrument** instrument *m* à vent; **w. pump, w. turbine** aéolienne *f*; **w. tunnel** soufflerie *f*

(**b**) (*breath*) souffle *m*; **let me get my w. back** laisse-moi reprendre mon souffle

(**c**) (*abdominal*) gaz *m*, vent *m*; **to have w.** avoir des gaz; **break w.** lâcher un vent

(**d**) (*idioms*) **to take the w. out of sb's sails** couper l'herbe sous le pied à qn; **to get w. of sth** avoir vent de qch; **to be scattered to the four winds** être éparpillés aux quatre vents

2 *vt* **to w. sb** (*with punch*) couper la respiration à qn

wind² [waɪnd] (*pt & pp* **wound** [waʊnd]) **1** *vt* (**a**) (*thread, string*) enrouler (**around** autour de) (**b**) (*clock, watch*) remonter; **to w. a cassette on/back** faire avancer/rembobiner une cassette

2 *vi* (*of path, river*) serpenter

▸**wind down 1** *vt sep* (**a**) (*car window*) baisser (**b**) (*reduce*) (*production*) réduire progressivement; (*company*) fermer progressivement

2 *vi* (*of party*) se calmer; (*of meeting*) tirer à sa fin; *Fam* (*of person*) se détendre, décompresser

▸**wind up 1** *vt sep* (**a**) (*car window*) remonter (**b**) (*finish*) (*speech, meeting*) terminer

2 *vi* (**a**) (*end speech, meeting*) terminer (**b**) *Fam* (*end up*) finir; **w. up doing sth** finir par faire qch; **she'll w. up in prison** elle va finir en prison

windbag ['wɪndbæg] *n Fam Pej* moulin *m* à paroles

windbreak ['wɪndbreɪk] *n* brise-vent *m inv*

Windbreaker® ['wɪndbreɪkə(r)] *n* (*jacket*) coupe-vent *m inv*

windchill factor ['wɪndtʃɪlfæktə(r)] *n* = abaissement de la température dû au vent

winder ['waɪndə(r)] *n* (*on watch*) remontoir *m*

windfall ['wɪndfɔːl] *n* (*fruit*) fruit *m* abattu par le vent; *Fig* (*money*) aubaine *f*; *Fin* **w. profits** (*of company*) bénéfices *mpl* exceptionnels; **w. tax** impôt *m* sur les bénéfices exceptionnels

winding ['waɪndɪŋ] *adj* (*path, stream*) sinueux(euse); (*staircase*) en colimaçon

windmill ['wɪndmɪl] *n* moulin *m* à vent

window ['wɪndəʊ] *n* (**a**) (*of house*) & *Comput* fenêtre *f*; (*of vehicle*) vitre *f*, glace *f*; (*of store*) vitrine *f*; **w. box** jardinière *f*; **w. cleaner** laveur(euse) *m,f* de carreaux; **w. display** étalage *m*; **w. frame** châssis *m*; **w. ledge** rebord *m* de fenêtre; **w. seat** (*in vehicle, plane*) place *f* côté fenêtre; **w. shade** store *m*; **w. washer** laveur(euse) *m,f* de carreaux (**b**) (*idioms*) **to provide a w. on sth** procurer une ouverture sur qch; **w. of opportu-**

nity ouverture *f*; *Fam* **that's my vacation out of the w.** voilà mes vacances fichues en l'air

window-dressing ['wɪndəʊdresɪŋ] *n (in store)* présentation *f* de l'étalage; *Fig* façade *f*

windowpane ['wɪndəʊpeɪn] *n* vitre *f*, carreau *m*

window-shopping ['wɪndəʊʃɒpɪŋ] *n* **to go w.** faire du lèche-vitrines

windowsill ['wɪndəʊsɪl] *n* rebord *m* de fenêtre

windpipe ['wɪndpaɪp] *n* trachée *f*

windshield ['wɪndʃiːld] *n* pare-brise *m inv*; **w. wiper** essuie-glace *m inv*

windsock ['wɪndsɒk] *n Aviat* manche *f* à air

windsurf ['wɪndsɜːf] *vi* faire de la planche à voile

windsurfing ['wɪndsɜːfɪŋ] *n* planche *f* à voile; **to go w.** faire de la planche à voile

windswept ['wɪndswept] *adj (hillside, scene)* balayé(e) par le vent; *(hair)* décoiffé(e) par le vent; *(person)* échevelé(e)

windward ['wɪndwəd] *adj* au vent; **the W. Islands** les îles *fpl* du Vent

windy[1] ['wɪndɪ] *adj (day)* venteux(euse); *(place)* venté(e); **I hate w. weather** je déteste le vent

windy[2] ['waɪndɪ] *adj (road)* sinueux(euse)

wine [waɪn] **1** *n* vin *m*; **w. bar** bar *m* à vin; **w. bottle** bouteille *f* de vin; **w. box** Cubitainer®; **w. cellar** cave *f* à vin; **w. list** carte *f* des vins; **w. tasting** dégustation *f* (de vins); **w. vinegar** vinaigre *m* de vin
2 *vt* **to w. and dine sb** inviter qn dans de bons restaurants

wineglass ['waɪnglɑːs] *n* verre *m* à vin

wing [wɪŋ] **1** *n* **(a)** *(of bird, plane)* aile *f*; *Fig* **to take sb under one's w.** prendre qn sous son aile; *Fig* **to spread** *or* **to stretch one's wings** élargir son horizon; *Tech* **w. nut** papillon *m*
(b) *(of building, hospital)* aile *f*
(c) *(in soccer) (player)* ailier *m*; *(area)* aile *f*
(d) the wings *(in theater)* les coulisses *fpl*; *Fig* **to be waiting in the wings** attendre son heure
(e) *Pol* **the left/right w.** la gauche/la droite
2 *vt* **(a)** *(injure) (bird)* blesser à l'aile; *(person)* blesser au bras
(b) *Fam (improvise)* **to w. it** improviser
(c) *(fly)* **to w. its way toward sth** *(of bird)* voler vers qch; *Fig* **my report should be winging its way toward you** j'ai posté mon rapport, tu devrais l'avoir bientôt

winger ['wɪŋə(r)] *n (in soccer)* ailier *m*

wingspan ['wɪŋspæn] *n* envergure *f*

wink [wɪŋk] **1** *n* clin *m* d'œil; **to give sb a w.** faire un clin d'œil à qn; *Fam* **I didn't sleep a w.** je n'ai pas fermé l'œil
2 *vi* cligner de l'œil; *(of star, light)* clignoter

▶**wink at** *vt insep (person)* faire un clin d'œil à; *Fig (offense, illegal practice)* fermer les yeux sur

winkle ['wɪŋkəl] *n (mollusk)* bigorneau *m*

winner ['wɪnə(r)] *n* gagnant(e) *m,f*; **this book will be a w.** ce livre est assuré d'avoir du succès

winning ['wɪnɪŋ] **1** *npl* **winnings** gains *mpl*
2 *adj* **(a)** *(victorious)* gagnant(e); **w. post** poteau *m* d'arrivée
(b) *(attractive)* charmant(e)

winnow ['wɪnəʊ] *vt* vanner

wino ['waɪnəʊ] *(pl* **winos)** *n Fam (alcoholic)* poivrot(e)

winsome ['wɪnsəm] *adj* charmant(e)

winter ['wɪntə(r)] **1** *n* hiver *m*; **in (the) w.** en hiver; **w. break** vacances *fpl* d'hiver; **w. clothing** vêtements *mpl* d'hiver; **w. sports** sports *mpl* d'hiver
2 *vi* passer l'hiver

wintertime ['wɪntətaɪm] *n* hiver *m*

wintery ['wɪntərɪ], **wintry** ['wɪntrɪ] *adj (weather)* d'hiver; *Fig (hostile)* glacial(e)

wipe [waɪp] **1** *n* **(a)** *(action)* **to give sth a w.** essuyer qch **(b)** *(moist tissue)* lingette *f*
2 *vt* **(a)** *(table, plate)* essuyer; **to w. one's nose** s'essuyer le

nez; **to w. one's hands (on)** s'essuyer les mains (avec); **to w. one's shoes (on)** s'essuyer les pieds (sur); *Fam Fig* **to w. the floor with sb** ne faire qu'une bouchée de qn **(b)** *(recording, tape)* effacer

▶**wipe away** *vt sep (tears)* essuyer; *(mark)* enlever

▶**wipe off 1** *vt sep* effacer; *Fam* **that'll w. the smile off his face!** ça lui fera passer l'envie de rire!
2 *vi (of stain)* partir

▶**wipe out** *vt sep* **(a)** *(erase)* effacer; *(debt)* liquider **(b)** *(destroy)* décimer

▶**wipe up** *vt sep* essuyer

wiper ['waɪpə(r)] *n* essuie-glace *m inv*

wire ['waɪə(r)] **1** *n* **(a)** *(of metal)* fil *m* de fer; *(electrical)* fil *m* (électrique); **w. brush** brosse *f* métallique; **w. fence** clôture *f* en fil de fer; **w. mesh** toile *f* métallique; **w. wool** paille *f* de fer **(b)** *(telegram)* télégramme *m* **(c)** *(idioms) Fam* **to get one's wires crossed** s'emmêler les pinceaux; **the tournament went right down to the w.** l'issue du tournoi a été incertaine jusqu'au bout
2 *vt* **(a)** *(house)* faire l'installation électrique de; **to w. sth to sth** *(connect electrically)* relier qch à qch; *(attach with wire)* attacher qch à qch avec du fil de fer **(b)** *(send telegram to)* télégraphier à

▶**wire up** *vt sep (attach with wire)* attacher avec du fil à fer

wirecutters ['waɪəkʌtəz] *npl* **(pair of) w.** pince *f* coupante

wireless ['waɪəlɪs] *adj Comput* sans fil

wiretapping ['waɪətæpɪŋ] *n* mise *f* sur écoute d'une ligne téléphonique

wiring ['waɪərɪŋ] *n* installation *f* électrique

wiry ['waɪərɪ] *adj (hair)* crépu(e); *(person)* petit(e) et musclé(e)

wisdom ['wɪzdəm] *n* sagesse *f*; **w. tooth** dent *f* de sagesse

wise [waɪz] *adj (knowledgeable)* sage; *(advisable)* prudent(e); *Fam Pej* **a w. guy** un gros malin; **the Three W. Men** les Rois *mpl* mages; **it's easy to be w. after the event** c'est facile de savoir ce qui est bien ou pas bien après coup; **to be none the wiser** ne pas être plus avancé(e); *Fam* **to get w. to sth** se rendre compte de qch; *Fam* **to get w. to sb** percer qn à jour

▶**wise up** *vi Fam* **to w. up to sb** voir qn sous son vrai jour; **to w. up to sth** se rendre compte de qch; **w. up!** ouvre les yeux!

-wise [waɪz] *suff Fam (as regards)* **health-/salary-/etc./w.** du point de vue de la santé/du salaire/*etc.*

wisecrack ['waɪzkræk] *Fam* **1** *n* vanne *f*, blague *f*
2 *vi* sortir des vannes

wisely ['waɪzlɪ] *adv* sagement

wish [wɪʃ] **1** *n* **(a)** *(desire)* désir *m*; *(thing desired)* vœu *m*; **to make a w.** faire un vœu; **to do sth against sb's wishes** faire qch contre le souhait de qn; **w. list** liste *f* de vœux
(b) *(greeting)* **best wishes** meilleurs vœux; *(in letter)* amicalement
2 *vt* **(a)** *(want)* désirer; **to w. to do sth** désirer faire qch; **to w. sb well** souhaiter à qn que tout se passe bien; **to w. sb luck/a pleasant journey** souhaiter bonne chance/bon voyage à qn; **to w. sth on sb** souhaiter qch à qn
(b) *(want something impossible, unlikely)* **I w. she could come** j'aurais bien aimé qu'elle vienne; **I w. I had seen it!** j'aurais bien voulu voir ça!; **I w. I hadn't left so early** je regrette d'être parti aussi tôt; **I w. she wouldn't say things like that** je préférerais qu'elle s'abstienne de dire des choses pareilles; **w. you were here!** *(on postcard)* je pense/nous pensons bien à toi
3 *vi* **to w. for sth** souhaiter qch; **what more could you w. for?** que souhaiter de plus?; **as you w.** comme tu voudras

wishbone ['wɪʃbəʊn] *n* bréchet *m*

wishful ['wɪʃfʊl] *adj* **that's w. thinking** tu te fais/il se fait/*etc.* des illusions

wishy-washy ['wɪʃɪwɒʃɪ] *adj Fam* mou (molle); *(couleur)* délavé(e)

wisp [wɪsp] *n (of straw, wool)* brin *m; (of hair)* mèche *f; (of smoke, cloud)* traînée *f*

wistful ['wɪstfʊl] *adj* nostalgique

wit [wɪt] *n* (**a**) *(intelligence, presence of mind)* esprit *m;* **to have the w. to do sth** être assez intelligent(e) pour faire qch; **to have quick wits** avoir l'esprit vif; **to have lost one's wits** avoir perdu l'esprit; **to have/keep one's wits about one** être/rester très vigilant(e); **to be at one's wits' end** ne plus savoir que faire; **to live by one's wits** vivre d'expédients; **to scare sb out of their wits** faire une peur bleue à qn (**b**) *(humor)* esprit *m* (**c**) *(witty person) (man)* homme *m* d'esprit; *(woman)* femme *f* d'esprit

witch [wɪtʃ] *n* sorcière *f;* **w. doctor** sorcier *m*

witchcraft ['wɪtʃkrɑːft] *n* sorcellerie *f*

witch-hunt ['wɪtʃhʌnt] *n Pol* chasse *f* aux sorcières

with [wɪð] *prep* (**a**) *(expressing accompaniment)* avec; **w. me/him** avec moi/lui; **to live w. one's parents** vivre chez ses parents; **I was left w. nobody to talk to** je me suis retrouvé sans personne à qui parler

(**b**) *(having)* **the girl w. glasses/blue eyes** la fille aux lunettes/aux yeux bleus; **w. one's hands in one's pockets** les mains dans les poches

(**c**) *(expressing association)* **to be pleased w. sb** être content(e) de qn; **to be angry w. sb** être en colère contre qn; **to fight/compete w. sb** se battre/être en concurrence avec qn; **to be in love w. sb** être amoureux(euse) de qn; **covered w. mud** couvert(e) de boue

(**d**) *(expressing manner)* **w. pleasure/difficulty** avec plaisir/difficulté; **to say sth w. a smile** dire qch avec un sourire

(**e**) *(expressing instrument, agent)* **to hit sb w. sth** frapper qn avec qch; **to cut sth w. a knife** couper qch avec un couteau; **it's pouring w. rain** il pleut à verse

(**f**) *(because of)* **to tremble w. rage** trembler de rage; **to cry w. laughter** pleurer de rire; **w. her money, she can surely afford it** avec l'argent qu'elle a, elle peut bien se permettre ça

(**g**) *(expressing simultaneity)* **to improve w. age** s'améliorer avec l'âge; **w. those words, he left** sur ces mots, il partit; **w. Christmas coming,...** puisque c'est bientôt Noël,...

(**h**) *(idioms)* **to be w. it** être dans le vent; **get w. it!** *(wake up)* réveille-toi!; *(face reality)* ouvre les yeux!; **I'm w. you** *(I support you)* je suis avec vous; **I'm not w. you** *(I don't understand)* je ne vous suis pas

withdraw [wɪð'drɔː] *(pt* **withdrew** [wɪð'druː], *pp* **withdrawn** [wɪð'drɔːn]) **1** *vt* retirer (**from** de)

2 *vi* se retirer (**from** de); **to w. in favor of sb** se désister en faveur de qn; **to w. into oneself** se replier sur soi-même

withdrawal [wɪð'drɔːəl] *n* retrait *m;* **to make a w.** *(from bank)* faire un retrait; **w. symptoms** symptômes *mpl* de manque; **to have w. symptoms** être en (état de) manque

withdrawn [wɪð'drɔːn] *adj* replié(e) sur soi-même

withdrew [wɪð'druː] *pt of* **withdraw**

wither ['wɪðə(r)] *vi (of plant)* se flétrir; *(of limb)* s'atrophier

withered ['wɪðəd] *adj (plant)* flétri(e); *(limb)* atrophié(e)

withering ['wɪðərɪŋ] *adj (look)* foudroyant(e); *(tone)* cinglant(e)

withhold [wɪð'həʊld] *(pt & pp* **withheld** [wɪð'held]) *vt (consent, help)* refuser; *(money)* retenir; *(truth)* cacher; *(information)* faire de la rétention de

within [wɪð'ɪn] **1** *prep* (**a**) *(inside)* à l'intérieur de; **problems w. the company** des problèmes au sein de l'entreprise

(**b**) *(not beyond)* **w. 10 miles of the town** ≃ à moins de 16 km de la ville; **w. a radius of** dans un rayon de; **w. limits** jusqu'à un certain point; **w. reason** dans des limites raisonnables; **to stay w. budget** rester dans les limites du budget; **to come w. an inch of doing sth** bien faillir faire qch

(**c**) *(with expressions of time)* **w. an hour/a week** en moins d'une heure/d'une semaine; **w. minutes** en quelques minutes; **w. the next five years** *(in the space of) (in future)* au cours des

cinq années à venir; *(in past)* au cours des cinq années suivantes; *(before the end of) (in future)* avant cinq ans; *(in past)* en moins de cinq ans; **they died w. a few days of each other** ils sont morts à quelques jours d'intervalle

2 *adv* à l'intérieur; **from w.** de l'intérieur

without [wɪð'aʊt] **1** *prep* sans; **w. any money/difficulty** sans argent/difficulté; **w. doing sth** sans faire qch; **do it w. him knowing** fais-le sans qu'il le sache; **it goes w. saying that...** il va sans dire que...; **to do** *or* **to go w. sth** se passer de qch

2 *adv* **to do** *or* **to go w.** se priver

withstand [wɪð'stænd] *(pt & pp* **withstood** [wɪð'stʊd]) *vt* supporter

witless ['wɪtlɪs] *adj (person, remark)* stupide; **to scare sb w.** faire une peur bleue à qn

witness ['wɪtnɪs] **1** *n* (**a**) *(person)* témoin *m;* **to call sb as w.** citer qn comme témoin; **w. for the defense/prosecution** témoin à décharge/charge; **w. stand** barre *f* des témoins (**b**) *(testimony)* **to bear w. (to sth)** témoigner (de qch)

2 *vt* être témoin de; **I witnessed the whole thing** j'ai assisté à tout ce qui s'est passé; *Fig* **this town has witnessed many battles** cette ville a été le théâtre de nombreuses batailles

3 *vi Law* **to w. to sth** témoigner de qch

witticism ['wɪtɪsɪzəm] *n* mot *m* d'esprit

wittily ['wɪtɪlɪ] *adv* avec esprit

wittingly ['wɪtɪŋlɪ] *adv* sciemment

witty ['wɪtɪ] *adj* spirituel(elle), plein(e) d'esprit

wives [waɪvz] *pl of* **wife**

wizard ['wɪzəd] *n* magicien *m; Fig* as *m*

wizened ['wɪzənd] *adj* ratatiné(e)

wk. *(abbr* **week***)* semaine

WMD [dʌbəlju:em'diː] *npl (abbr* **weapons of mass destruction***)* ADM *fpl*

wobble ['wɒbəl] *vi (of chair, table)* branler; *(of building, Jell-O®)* trembler; *(of person)* être chancelant(e)

wobbly ['wɒblɪ] *adj (chair, table)* bancal(e); *(shelf, ladder)* branlant(e); *(person)* chancelant(e)

woe [wəʊ] *n Lit* malheur *m; Hum* **w. betide you if you're late** malheur à toi si tu es en retard

woebegone ['wəʊbɪgɒn] *adj* abattu(e)

woeful ['wəʊfʊl] *adj* (**a**) *(sad)* affligé(e) (**b**) *(very bad)* déplorable

wok [wɒk] *n* wok *m,* poêle *f* chinoise

woke [wəʊk] *pt of* **wake³**

woken ['wəʊkən] *pp of* **wake³**

wolf [wʊlf] *(pl* **wolves** [wʊlvz]) *n* (**a**) loup *m;* **w. cub** louveteau *m;* **w. whistle** = sifflement admiratif au passage de quelqu'un (**b**) *(idioms)* **to keep the w. from the door** je ne gagne pas beaucoup mais ça me met à l'abri du besoin; **to throw sb to the wolves** abandonner qn à son sort; **a w. in sheep's clothing** un loup déguisé en brebis; **to cry w.** crier au loup

▸ **wolf down** *vt sep* engloutir

woman ['wʊmən] *(pl* **women** ['wɪmɪn]) *n* femme *f;* **women's magazine** magazine *m* féminin; **women's lib, women's liberation** mouvement *m* de libération de la femme; **women's movement** mouvement *m* féministe; **women's page** page *f* des lectrices; **women's refuge, women's shelter** centre *m* d'accueil pour les femmes; **w. doctor** femme médecin *f;* **w. driver** conductrice *f*

womanizer ['wʊmənaɪzə(r)] *n* coureur *m* (de jupons)

womanly ['wʊmənlɪ] *adj* féminin(e)

womb [wuːm] *n* utérus *m*

women ['wɪmɪn] *pl of* **woman**

womenfolk ['wɪmɪnfəʊk] *n* femmes *fpl*

won [wʌn] *pt & pp of* **win**

wonder ['wʌndə(r)] **1** *n* (**a**) *(miracle)* miracle *m*, merveille *f*; **to work** *or* **to do wonders** faire des miracles; **it's a w. (that)...** c'est un miracle que... + *subjunctive*; **(it's) no w....** ce n'est pas étonnant que... + *subjunctive*; **w. drug** remède *m* miracle (**b**) *(astonishment)* émerveillement *m*; **in w.** avec émerveillement

2 *vt* se demander; **one wonders whether...** c'est à se demander si...; **I was wondering if you were free tonight** je voulais savoir si tu étais libre ce soir

3 *vi* (**a**) *(be curious)* se demander; *Fam* **I w. about her sometimes!** je me pose parfois des questions à son sujet! (**b**) *Lit (be amazed)* s'étonner (**at** de)

wonderful ['wʌndəfʊl] *adj* merveilleux(euse), formidable

wonk [wɒŋk] *n Fam (expert)* intello *mf*; *(studious person)* bûcheur(euse) *m,f*

wont [wəʊnt] *Formal* **1** *n* habitude *f*; **as is her w.** comme à son habitude

2 *adj* **to be w. to do sth** avoir l'habitude de faire qch

won't [wəʊnt] = **will not**

woo [wuː] *(pt & pp* **wooed**) *vt* (**a**) *Lit (woman)* courtiser (**b**) *Fig (supporters, investors)* attirer

wood [wʊd] *n* (**a**) *(forest, material)* bois *m*; **w. carving** sculpture *f* sur bois (**b**) *(idioms)* **she can't see the w. for the trees** elle se perd dans les détails; **we're not out of the woods yet** nous ne sommes pas encore tirés d'affaire; **knock on w.!** je touche du bois!

woodbine ['wʊdbaɪn] *n (plant)* vigne *f* vierge

woodcock ['wʊdkɒk] *n* bécasse *f*

woodcut ['wʊdkʌt] *n* gravure *f* sur bois

woodcutter ['wʊdkʌtə(r)] *n* bûcheron *m*

wooded ['wʊdɪd] *adj* boisé(e)

wooden ['wʊdən] *adj (made of wood)* en bois; *Fig (unexpressive)* impassible; **w. spoon** cuillère *f* de bois; *Fig* **to get the w. spoon** *(in contest)* arriver dernier au classement

woodland ['wʊdlənd] *n (woods)* bois *mpl*; *(wooded area)* région *f* boisée

woodlouse ['wʊdlaʊs] *(pl* **woodlice** ['wʊdlaɪs]) *n* cloporte *m*

woodpecker ['wʊdpekə(r)] *n* pic *m*

woodpile ['wʊdpaɪl] *n* tas *m* de bois

woodshed ['wʊdʃed] *n* remise *f* à bois

woodwind ['wʊdwɪnd] *n Mus* **the w.** *(instruments)* les bois *mpl*; **w. instrument** bois *m*

woodwork ['wʊdwɜːk] *n (craft)* travail *m* du bois; *(in house)* boiserie *f*; *Fig* **to come** *or* **to crawl out of the w.** faire soudain surface

woodworm ['wʊdwɜːm] *n* ver *m* à bois

woof [wʊf] **1** *n* aboiement *m*

2 *exclam* ouah!

wool [wʊl] *n* laine *f*; *Fam* **to pull the w. over sb's eyes** embobiner qn

woolen ['wʊlən] **1** *n* **woolens** lainages *mpl*

2 *adj (garment)* en laine

wooly ['wʊlɪ] *adj (garment)* en laine; *Fig (idea, theory)* nébuleux(euse)

woozy ['wuːzɪ] *adj Fam* dans les vapes

word [wɜːd] **1** *n* (**a**) *(in general)* mot *m*; **w. for w.** mot pour mot; **in a w.** en un mot; **in other words** autrement dit; **not in so many words** pas en ces termes-là; **not a w.** pas un mot; **in one's own words** à sa façon; **I can't put it into words** je n'arrive pas à trouver les mots; **he's a man of few words** c'est un homme qui parle peu; **I couldn't get a w. in (edgeways)** je n'ai pas pu placer un mot; **the w. of God** la parole de Dieu; **I'll take your w. for it** je te crois sur parole; **to take sb at his/her w.** prendre qn au mot; **it was too ridiculous for words** c'était d'un ridicule sans nom; **my w.!** ma parole!; *Comput* **w. count** nombre *m* des mots

(**b**) *(remarks, conversation)* **to have a w. with sb** parler à qn;

to have words with sb avoir des mots avec qn; **just say the w.** tu n'as qu'à me faire signe; **you're putting words into my mouth** tu me fais dire des choses que je n'ai pas voulu dire; **you took the words right out of my mouth** c'est justement ce que j'allais dire; **to put in a good w. for sb** glisser un mot en faveur de qn; **he never has a good w. for anyone** il ne peut pas s'empêcher de dire du mal des gens; **a w. of warning** une mise en garde; **a w. of advice** un petit conseil

(**c**) *(news)* **to receive w. from sb** avoir des nouvelles de qn; **to send sb w. of sth** faire part à qn de qch; **the w. is that...** on raconte que...; **by w. of mouth** de bouche à oreille

(**d**) *(promise)* parole *f*; **w. of honor** parole d'honneur; **to give sb one's w.** donner sa parole à qn; **to keep one's w.** tenir sa promesse; **to go back on one's w.** manquer à sa parole

(**e**) **words** *(lyrics)* paroles *fpl*

2 *vt (express in words)* formuler

wording ['wɜːdɪŋ] *n* formulation *f*

wordprocessing [wɜːd'prəʊsesɪŋ] *n Comput* traitement *m* de texte

wordprocessor [wɜːd'prəʊsesə(r)] *n Comput (machine)* machine *f* à traitement de texte; *(software)* logiciel *m* de traitement de texte

wordy ['wɜːdɪ] *adj* prolixe

wore [wɔː(r)] *pt of* **wear**

work [wɜːk] **1** *n* (**a**) *(labor)* travail *m*; **to be at w. on sth** travailler à *ou* sur qch; **to get to w.** se mettre au travail; **w. in progress** *(sign)* travaux

(**b**) *(task)* travail *m*; **to put a lot of w. into sth** beaucoup travailler à qch; **to have one's w. cut out (to do sth)** avoir du mal (à faire qch); **to make quick** *or* **short w. of sth** venir rapidement à bout de qch; **good w.!** c'est du bon travail!

(**c**) *(literary, artistic)* œuvre *f*; **a w. of art** une œuvre d'art

(**d**) *(employment)* travail *m*; **to be out of w.** être sans travail; **w. experience** stage *m* (en entreprise); **w. permit** permis *m* de travail

(**e**) **works** *(construction)* travaux *mpl*; **road works ahead** *(sign)* attention travaux

(**f**) **works** *(mechanism)* mécanisme *m*

(**g**) *Fam* **the works** *(everything)* le grand jeu; **to give sb the works** *(beating)* passer qn à tabac; *(luxury treatment)* jouer le grand jeu à qn

2 *vt* (**a**) *(person)* **to w. sb hard** exiger beaucoup de qn; **to w. oneself to death** se tuer à la tâche

(**b**) *(operate) (machine)* faire fonctionner

(**c**) *(bring about) (miracle, cure, change)* opérer; **to w. it** *or* **things so that** faire en sorte que

(**d**) *(move)* **to w. one's hands free** se libérer les mains; **to w. one's way through a book/list** avancer progressivement dans la lecture d'un livre/dans une liste

(**e**) *(exploit) (mine, quarry)* exploiter; *(land)* travailler

3 *vi* (**a**) *(of person)* **to w. against sb/in sb's favor** jouer en la défaveur/la faveur de qn

(**b**) *(function) (of machine, system)* marcher, fonctionner

(**c**) *(have effect) (of medicine)* faire effet; *(of plan, method)* marcher

▸ **work in** *vt sep (include)* introduire, glisser

▸ **work off** *vt sep (anger)* évacuer; **he worked off 10 pounds** ≃ il a perdu 4,5 kilos en faisant de l'exercice

▸ **work on 1** *vt insep* **to w. on sth** travailler à *ou* sur qch

2 *vi (continue to work)* continuer à travailler

▸ **work out 1** *vt sep (cost, total)* calculer; *(answer)* trouver; **to w. out how to do sth** trouver comment faire qch; **I'm sure we can w. this thing out** je suis sûr qu'on peut arranger ça

2 *vi* (**a**) *(turn out)* **to w. out well/badly (for sb)** bien/mal se passer (pour qn); **it all worked out in the end** finalement, tout s'est arrangé (**b**) *(total)* **to w. out to** revenir à (**c**) *(exercise)* s'entraîner

▸ **work up** *vt sep* (**a**) *(develop)* **to w. up enthusiasm/interest**

for sth s'enthousiasmer pour/s'intéresser à qch; **I worked up an appetite** ça m'a ouvert l'appétit (**b**) *(excite)* **to get worked up (about sth)** se mettre dans tous ses états (à propos de qch)

▸**work up to** *vt insep* se préparer à

workable ['wɜːkəbəl] *adj* possible

workaday ['wɜːkədeɪ] *adj* de tous les jours

workaholic [wɜːkə'hɒlɪk] *n Fam* bourreau *m* de travail

workbench ['wɜːkbentʃ] *n* établi *m*

workday ['wɜːkdeɪ] *n* jour *m* ouvrable

worker ['wɜːkə(r)] *n* travailleur(euse) *m,f*; *(in industry)* ouvrier(ère) *m,f*; **to be a fast/slow w.** travailler vite/lentement; **w. bee** ouvrière *f*; **w. participation** participation *f* des travailleurs à la gestion

workfare ['wɜːkfeə(r)] *n Pol* = principe selon lequel les bénéficiaires de l'allocation de chômage doivent fournir un travail en échange

workforce ['wɜːkfɔːs] *n* main-d'œuvre *f*

workhouse ['wɜːkhaʊs] *n Hist* asile *m* des pauvres

working ['wɜːkɪŋ] **1** *n* (**a**) *(operation) (of machine)* fonctionnement *m* (**b**) **workings** *(mechanism)* mécanisme *m*
2 *adj (person)* qui travaille; **to have a w. knowledge of sth** avoir de bonnes bases en qch; **in w. order** en état de marche; **w. capital** capital *m* de roulement; **the w. class(es)** la classe ouvrière; **w. clothes** vêtements *mpl* de travail; **w. hours** heures *fpl* de travail; **w. lunch** déjeuner *m* d'affaires; **w. majority** majorité *f* suffisante; **w. model** maquette *f* animée

working-class ['wɜːkɪŋ'klɑːs] *adj* ouvrier(ère); *(accent)* prolétaire

workload ['wɜːkləʊd] *n* charge *f* de travail

workman ['wɜːkmən] *n* ouvrier *m*

workmanlike ['wɜːkmənlaɪk] *adj* de professionnel

workmanship ['wɜːkmənʃɪp] *n* travail *m*; **a fine piece of w.** du beau travail

workout ['wɜːkaʊt] *n* séance *f* d'entraînement

workplace ['wɜːkpleɪs] *n* lieu *m* de travail

workshop ['wɜːkʃɒp] *n* atelier *m*

workshy ['wɜːkʃaɪ] *adj* fainéant(e)

workstation [wɜːksteɪʃən] *n Comput* poste *m ou* station *f* de travail

worktop ['wɜːktɒp] *n (in kitchen)* plan *m* de travail, *Can* comptoir *m* de cuisine

work-to-rule [wɜːktə'ruːl] *n Ind* grève *f* du zèle

workweek ['wɜːkwiːk] *n* semaine *f* du travail

world [wɜːld] *n* (**a**) *(the earth)* monde *m*; **the best/biggest in the w.** le (la) meilleur(e)/plus grand(e) du monde; **the w. over, all over the w.** dans le monde entier; **the W. Bank** la Banque mondiale; **w. champion** champion(onne) *m,f* du monde; **the W. Cup** la Coupe du monde; **the W. Health Organization** l'Organisation *f* mondiale de la santé; **w. map** mappemonde *f*; **w. music** world music *f*; **w. record** record *m* du monde; **W. Series** = championnat national américain de base-ball; **the W. Trade Organization** l'Organisation *f* mondiale du commerce; **W. War One/Two** la Première/Seconde *ou* Deuxième Guerre mondiale
(**b**) *(sphere of activity)* **the literary/political/business w.** le monde littéraire/politique/des affaires
(**c**) *(society)* **man of the w.** homme *m* d'expérience; **to go up in the w.** faire du chemin; **to come down in the w.** déchoir; **to have the w. at one's feet** avoir le monde à ses pieds
(**d**) *(for emphasis)* **to do sb a w. of good** faire le plus grand bien à qn; **a w. of difference** une différence énorme; **to think the w. of sb** admirer énormément qn; **they carried on for all the w. as if nothing had happened** ils ont continué comme si de rien n'était
(**e**) *(idioms)* **she's not long for this w.** elle n'en a plus pour longtemps; **to bring a child into the w.** mettre un enfant au monde; **to have the best of both worlds** avoir tous les

avantages et aucun des inconvénients; **she lives in a w. of her own** elle vit dans un monde à elle; *Fam* **it's out of this w.** c'est extraordinaire; **not for (anything in) the w.** pour rien au monde; **it's a small w.!** le monde est petit!; **what is the w. coming to?** où va-t-on?

world-beater ['wɜːldbiːtə(r)] *n* leader *m* mondial

world-famous ['wɜːld'feɪməs] *adj* célèbre dans le monde entier

worldly ['wɜːldlɪ] *adj (pleasure, goods)* matériel(elle)

worldly-wise ['wɜːldlɪ'waɪz] *adj* qui a de l'expérience

world-weary ['wɜːldwɪərɪ] *adj* désabusé(e)

worldwide ['wɜːldwaɪd] **1** *adj* mondial(e); *Comput* **the W. Web** le Worldwide Web
2 *adv* dans le monde entier

WORM [wɜːm] *Comput (abbr* **write once read many times)** WORM

worm [wɜːm] **1** *n* (**a**) ver *m*; *(maggot)* asticot *m*; **to have worms** *(of person, animal)* avoir des vers; *Fig* **the w. has turned** il/elle/*etc.* a fini par se rebiffer
2 *vt* (**a**) *(animal)* traiter contre les vers (**b**) **to w. one's way out of a situation** réussir à se tirer d'une situation; **to w. oneself into sb's favor/confidence** s'insinuer dans les bonnes grâces/la confiance de qn; **to w. a secret out of sb** arracher un secret à qn

wormeaten ['wɜːmiːtən] *adj (wood)* vermoulu(e); *(fruit)* véreux(euse)

worn [wɔːn] *pp of* wear

worried ['wʌrɪd] *adj* inquiet(ète); **to be w. about sb** être inquiet pour qn; **I'm w. about his safety** je m'inquiète pour sa sécurité; **he's w. about losing his job** il a peur de perdre son emploi

worrier ['wʌrɪə(r)] *n* anxieux(euse) *m,f*

worry ['wʌrɪ] **1** *n (pl* **worries)** souci *m*; **that's the least of my worries** c'est le cadet de mes soucis
2 *vt (pt & pp* **worried)** *(cause anxiety to)* inquiéter; **to w. oneself sick (about sth)** se faire un sang d'encre (à propos de qch)
3 *vi* s'inquiéter, se faire du souci; **to w. about sb** s'inquiéter pour qn; **to w. about the future** s'inquiéter pour l'avenir; **to w. about doing sth** avoir peur de faire qch; **not to w.!** ce n'est pas grave!; **there's/it's nothing to w. about** il n'y a pas de quoi s'inquiéter

worrying ['wʌrɪɪŋ] *adj* inquiétant(e)

worse [wɜːs] **1** *adj (comparative of* **bad)** pire (**than** que); **there's nothing w. than...** il n'y a rien de pire que...; **to get w.** aller en empirant; **things could be w.** les choses pourraient aller plus mal; **and to make matters w.,...** et, pour tout arranger...; **to go from bad to w.** aller de mal en pis; **I'm none the w. for it** je ne m'en porte pas plus mal; **to be the w. for drink** être éméché(e); *Fam* **to be the w. for wear** *(of car, book)* être en mauvais état; *(of drunk person)* être dans un sale état
2 *adv (comparative of* **badly)** plus mal; **you could do w.** tu aurais pu tomber plus mal; **I don't think any w. of her for it** elle n'a pas pour autant baissé dans mon estime; **he is w. off than before** sa situation a empiré
3 *n* **there was w. to come** le pire restait à venir; **I've seen w.** j'ai vu pire; **a change for the w.** une détérioration

worsen ['wɜːsən] **1** *vt* aggraver
2 *vi* empirer

worship ['wɜːʃɪp] **1** *n (of deity)* vénération *f*, culte *m*; *(of person)* adoration *f*; **place of w.** lieu *m* de culte
2 *vt (pt & pp* **worshiped)** *(deity)* vénérer; *(person)* adorer

worst [wɜːst] **1** *adj (superlative of* **bad)** **the w.** le (la) pire; **the w. book I've ever read** le plus mauvais livre que j'aie jamais lu; **her w. mistake** sa plus grave erreur; **the w. thing was...** le pire, c'était que...

2 *adv (superlative of badly)* le plus mal; **the elderly are the w. off** ce sont les personnes âgées qui sont le plus mal loties

3 *n* the w. le pire; **the w. that could happen** le pire qui puisse arriver; **the w. of it is that...** le pire dans tout ça, c'est que...; **if w. comes to w.** au pire; **the w. is over** on a passé le plus dur; **at (the) w.** au pire

worst-case scenario ['wɜːstkeɪsɪ'nɑːrɪəʊ] *(pl* **worst-case scenarios**) *n* le pire qui puisse se produire

worsted ['wʊstɪd] *n* peigné *m*

worth [wɜːθ] **1** *prep* (**a**) *(having a value of)* **to be w. sth** valoir qch; **how much is it w.?** combien est-ce que cela vaut?; **that's my opinion, for what it's w.** c'est mon opinion, elle vaut ce qu'elle vaut; **he's w. millions** il est millionnaire; **he was pulling for all he was w.** il tirait de toutes ses forces (**b**) *(meriting)* **the museum is w. a visit** le musée vaut le détour; **this book is not w. buying** ce livre ne vaut pas la peine d'être acheté; **it's w./it isn't w. it** ça en vaut/ça n'en vaut pas la peine; **it's w. thinking about** ça vaut le coup d'y réfléchir

2 *n* valeur *f*; **give me $30 w. of gas** donnez-moi pour 30 dollars d'essence; **to get one's money's w.** en avoir pour son argent

worthless ['wɜːθlɪs] *adj* **to be w.** *(of object)* ne rien valoir; *(of person)* être un(e) bon (bonne) à rien

worthwhile [wɜːθ'waɪl] *adj* **to be w.** valoir la peine *ou* le coup

worthy ['wɜːðɪ] **1** *adj (person, life)* digne; **to be w. of sth** être digne de qch

2 *n* notable *m*

would [wʊd] *modal aux v* (**a**) *(expressing conditional tense)* **she w. come if you invited her** elle viendrait si vous l'invitiez; **if he had let go, he w. have fallen** s'il avait lâché prise, il serait tombé; **if she had asked me, I w. have refused** si elle m'avait demandé, j'aurais refusé; **w. you do it? – yes, I w./ no, I wouldn't** le ferais? – oui/non; **you wouldn't do it, w. you?** tu ne le ferais pas, dis? (**b**) *(expressing wish, determination)* **w. you pass the salt, please?** pourrais-tu passer le sel, s'il te plaît?; **w. you like a drink?** tu veux boire quelque chose?; **she wouldn't let me speak to him** elle m'empêchait de lui parler; **be quiet, w. you!** tais-toi, s'il te plaît!; **the car wouldn't start** la voiture ne démarrait pas (**c**) *(for emphasis)* **you** WOULD **insist on going!** il fallait que tu insistes pour y aller!; **I forgot – you w.!** j'ai oublié – c'est bien (de) toi! (**d**) *(expressing past habit)* **she w. often return home exhausted** il lui arrivait souvent de rentrer épuisée; **there w. always be some left over** il en restait toujours (**e**) *(in reported speech)* **she told me she w. be there** elle m'a dit qu'elle serait là; **I said I w. do it** j'ai dit que je le ferais (**f**) *(expressing conjecture)* **w. that be my pen you're using?** est-ce que, par hasard, ce serait mon stylo que vous utilisez?; **they w. have been tired after their journey** ils devaient être fatigués après leur voyage; **I wouldn't know** je n'en ai aucune idée

would-be ['wʊdbiː] *adj* (**a**) *(aspiring)* **a w. writer** une personne qui veut être écrivain (**b**) *Pej (so-called)* prétendu(e), soi-distant *inv*

wouldn't ['wʊdənt] = **would not**

wound¹ [wuːnd] **1** *n* blessure *f*

2 *vt also Fig* blesser; **to w. sb's feelings** blesser qn, heurter la sensibilité de qn

wound² [waʊnd] *pt & pp of* **wind²**

wounded ['wuːndɪd] **1** *adj* blessé(e)

2 *npl* **the w.** les blessés *mpl*

wounding ['wuːndɪŋ] *adj* blessant(e)

wove [wəʊv] *pt of* **weave**

woven ['wəʊvən] *pp of* **weave**

wow [waʊ] *Fam* **1** *vt* séduire, emballer

2 *exclam* la vache!

WP [dʌbəljuː'piː] *n Comput* (**a**) *(abbr* **wordprocessor**) *(machine)* machine *f* à traitement de texte; *(software)* logiciel *m* de traitement de texte (**b**) *(abbr* **wordprocessing**) *(skill)* traitement *m* de texte

wpm [dʌbəljuːpiː'em] *(abbr* **words per minute**) mots par minute

wrangle ['ræŋɡəl] **1** *n* dispute *f*

2 *vi* se disputer (**about** *or* **over** à propos de)

wrap [ræp] **1** *n* (**a**) *(shawl)* châle *m*; *Fig* **to keep sth under wraps** garder qch secret (**b**) *Culin (sandwich)* = tortilla fourrée

2 *vt (pt & pp* **wrapped**) envelopper, emballer (**in** dans); **to w. sth around sth** enrouler qch autour de qch; *Fig* **wrapped in mystery** enveloppé(e) de mystère

▸**wrap up 1** *vt sep* (**a**) *(package, present)* envelopper; *Fig* **to be wrapped up in sth** être absorbé(e) par qch (**b**) *Fam (bring to an end)* conclure

2 *vi (dress warmly)* s'emmitoufler

wraparound sunglasses ['ræpəraʊnd'sʌnɡlɑːsɪz] *npl* lunettes *fpl* de soleil panoramiques

wrapper ['ræpə(r)] *n (of candy)* papier *m*

wrapping ['ræpɪŋ] *n* emballage *m*; **w. paper** papier *m* d'emballage

wrath [rɒθ] *n Lit* courroux *m*

wreak [riːk] *vt* **to w. havoc** faire des ravages; **to w. vengeance on sb** assouvir sa vengeance sur qn

wreath [riːθ] *n* couronne *f*

wreathe [riːð] *vt Lit* couronner

wreck [rek] **1** *n (ship, car, train, plane)* épave *f*; *Fig* **to be a physical/nervous w.** être physiquement/nerveusement au bout du rouleau

2 *vt (ship)* faire faire naufrage à; *(car)* démolir; *(room, house)* saccager; *Fig (plans, hopes, happiness)* ruiner, anéantir; *(marriage, career)* ruiner; **to w. one's health** se ruiner la santé

wreckage ['rekɪdʒ] *n (debris) (of plane, car, ship)* débris *mpl*; *(of building)* décombres *mpl*

wrecked [rekt] *adj (ship)* naufragé(e); *(car, plane)* complètement détruit(e)

wrecker ['rekə(r)] *n (tow truck)* dépanneuse *f*

wren [ren] *n* roitelet *m*

wrench [rentʃ] **1** *n* (**a**) *(pull) (to ankle, shoulder)* faux mouvement *m*; *Fig (emotional)* déchirement *m* (**b**) *(tool)* clef *f*

2 *vt* **to w. one's ankle/shoulder** se fouler la cheville/l'épaule; **to w. sth out of sb's hands** arracher qch des mains de qn

wrest [rest] *vt* **to w. sth from sb** arracher qch à qn

wrestle ['resəl] *vi (with person)* lutter (**with** contre); *Fig* **to w. with sth** se débattre avec qch

wrestler ['reslə(r)] *n* lutteur(euse) *m,f*

wrestling ['reslɪŋ] *n* lutte *f*, catch *m*; **w. match** match *m* de catch

wretch [retʃ] *n* malheureux(euse) *m,f*

wretched ['retʃɪd] *adj* (**a**) *(very bad)* atroce (**b**) *(unhappy)* démoralisé(e) (**c**) *Fam (for emphasis)* **I can't find the w. umbrella!** je ne trouve pas ce maudit parapluie!

wriggle ['rɪɡəl] **1** *vt* **to w. one's way out of a situation** se sortir d'une situation

2 *vi* **to w. (about)** gigoter, se tortiller; **to w. out of sth** couper à qch; **he managed to w. out of paying me back** il s'est débrouillé pour ne pas me rembourser

wring [rɪŋ] *vt (pt & pp* **wrung** [rʌŋ]) *(clothes)* essorer; **to w. one's hands** se tordre les mains; **to w. sb's neck** tordre le cou à qn; *Fam* **I'd like to w. his neck** j'ai envie de lui tordre le cou; *Fig* **to w. sth from sb** réussir à arracher qch à qn

▸**wring out** *vt sep (clothes)* essorer

wringer ['rɪŋə(r)] *n* essoreuse *f*; *Fam Fig* **to put sb through the w.** faire passer un mauvais quart d'heure à qn

wringing ['rɪŋɪŋ] *adj* **w. (wet)** trempé(e)

wrinkle ['rɪŋkəl] **1** *n (on skin, paper)* ride *f*; *(in cloth)* faux pli *m* **2** *vi* se froisser

wrinkled ['rɪŋkəld] *adj (skin)* ridé(e); *(clothes, fabric)* froissé(e)

wrinkly ['rɪŋklɪ] *adj* fripé(e)

wrist [rɪst] *n* poignet *m*; *Comput* **w. rest** repose-poignets *m*

wristwatch ['rɪstwɒtʃ] *n* montre-bracelet *f*

writ [rɪt] *n Law* ordre *m*, assignation *f*; **to serve a w. on sb** assigner qn en justice

write [raɪt] *(pt* **wrote** [rəʊt], *pp* **written** ['rɪtən]) **1** *vt (answer, name)* écrire; *(check)* faire; **to w. sb** écrire à qn; **she had guilt written all over her face** la culpabilité se lisait sur son visage
  2 *vi* écrire; **to w. to sb** écrire à qn; *Fam* **it's nothing to w. home about** ça n'a rien d'extraordinaire

▸ **write away for** *vt insep* **to w. away for sth** écrire pour recevoir qch

▸ **write back** *vi* répondre

▸ **write down** *vt sep* noter

▸ **write in 1** *vt sep (insert)* inscrire
  2 *vi (send letter)* écrire

▸ **write off 1** *vt sep* **(a)** *(debt)* annuler **(b)** *Fam (person)* enterrer; **to w. sb off as a has-been** considérer qn comme un(e) ringard(e)
  2 *vi* **to w. off for sth** écrire pour recevoir qch

▸ **write out** *vt sep (instructions, recipe)* noter; *(check)* faire

▸ **write up** *vt sep (notes, thesis)* rédiger; *(diary, journal)* tenir

write-off ['raɪtɒf] *n (of debt)* annulation *f*

write-protected ['raɪtprə'tektɪd] *adj Comput* protégé(e) en écriture

writer ['raɪtə(r)] *n (by profession)* écrivain *m*, auteur *m*; *(of article, book)* auteur *m*; **w.'s block** angoisse *f* de la page blanche

write-up ['raɪtʌp] *n (of play)* critique *f*

writhe [raɪð] *vi* se tordre (**in** de)

writing ['raɪtɪŋ] *n* **(a)** *(action, profession)* écriture *f*; **w. desk** bureau *m*, secrétaire *m*; **w. pad** bloc-notes *m*; **w. paper** papier *m* à lettres **(b)** *(handwriting)* écriture *f*; **in w.** par écrit **(c)** *(thing written)* écrit *m*; *Fig* **the w. is on the wall** la fin est proche

written ['rɪtən] **1** *adj* écrit(e); **w. consent** consentement *m* par écrit; **w. examination** écrit *m*, épreuve *f* écrite
  2 *pp of* **write**

wrong [rɒŋ] **1** *n (immoral action)* mal *m*; **to know right from w.** distinguer le bien du mal; *Ironic* **he can do no w.** il est parfait; **to do sb w.** faire du tort à qn; *Prov* **two wrongs don't make a right** on ne répare pas le mal par le mal; **to be in the w.** être dans son tort
  2 *adj* **(a)** *(morally bad)* mauvais(e); **stealing is w.** c'est mal de voler; **it was w. of you not to tell me** ce n'est pas bien de ta part de ne pas me l'avoir dit
  (b) *(incorrect, mistaken)* mauvais(e); **to be w.** *(of person)* avoir tort; **my watch is w.** ma montre n'est pas à l'heure; **don't get the w. idea** ne te fais pas de fausses idées; **I did/said the w. thing** j'ai fait/dit ce qu'il ne fallait pas; *Fig* **to go the w. way about doing sth** mal s'y prendre pour faire qch; *Fig* **to get on the w. side of sb** se faire mal voir de qn; **you've got the w. number** *(on phone)* vous vous êtes trompé de numéro
  (c) *(amiss)* **what's w.?** qu'est-ce qui ne va pas?; **what's w. with you?** qu'est-ce que tu as?; **is anything w.?** quelque chose ne va pas?; **there's something w. with the car** il y a quelque chose qui ne va pas dans cette voiture; *Fam* **he's w. in the head** il ne tourne pas rond
  3 *adv* **(a)** *(morally)* mal; **to do w.** mal agir
  (b) *(incorrectly)* mal; **to go w.** se gâter; **where did I go w.?** qu'est-ce que j'ai fait qui n'allait pas?; **don't get me w., I like her** je n'ai pas dit que je ne l'aimais pas
  4 *vt* faire du tort à, léser

wrongdoer ['rɒŋduːə(r)] *n* auteur *m* d'un tort

wrongdoing ['rɒŋduːɪŋ] *n (immoral action)* méfait *m*; *(crime)* infraction *f*

wrongful ['rɒŋfʊl] *adj* arbitraire; **w. dismissal** licenciement *m* abusif

wrong-headed [rɒŋ'hedɪd] *adj* buté(e), borné(e)

wrongly ['rɒŋlɪ] *adv* **(a)** *(unjustly)* à tort **(b)** *(incorrectly)* incorrectement

wrote [rəʊt] *pt of* **write**

wrought-iron ['rɔːt'aɪən] *adj* en fer forgé

wrought-up ['rɔːt'ʌp] *adj* **to be w.** être dans tous ses états

wrung [rʌŋ] *pt & pp of* **wring**

wry [raɪ] *adj* ironique

wt. *(abbr* **weight***)* p.

WTO [dʌbəljuːtiː'əʊ] *n (abbr* **World Trade Organization***)* OMC *f*

WW *(abbr* **World War***)* **WWI/II** la Première/Deuxième *ou* Seconde Guerre mondiale

WWF [dʌbəljuːdʌbəljuː'ef] *n (abbr* **World Wildlife Fund, Worldwide Fund for Nature***)* WWF *m*

WWW ['dʌbəljuː'dʌbəljuː'dʌbəljuː] *n Comput (abbr* **worldwide web***)* WWW, W3

WYSIWYG ['wɪzɪwɪg] *n Comput (abbr* **what you see is what you get***)* WYSIWYG *m*

X

X, x [eks] *n* (**a**) *(letter)* X, x *m inv*; **for x number of years** pendant x années (**b**) *(abbr* **ecstasy**) X *f*, ecsta *f*
xenon ['zenɒn] *n Chem* xénon *m*
xenophobia [zenə'fəʊbɪə] *n* xénophobie *f*
xenophobic [zenə'fəʊbɪk] *adj* xénophobe
Xerox® ['zɪərɒks] **1** *n (machine)* photocopieur *m*; *(copy)* photocopie *f*
   2 *vt* photocopier
XL ['eks'el] *(abbr* **extra large**) XL

Xmas ['eksməs] *n (abbr* **Christmas**) Noël *m*
X-rated [eks'reɪtɪd] *adj (movie)* interdit aux mineurs *ou* aux moins de dix-huit ans; *Fam* **some of the stuff she told me was pretty X.** elle m'a dit des choses assez corsées
X-ray ['eksreɪ] **1** *n (radiation)* rayon *m* X; *(picture)* radio *f*; **to have an X.** passer une radio
   2 *vt* radiographier
xylophone ['zaɪləfəʊn] *n* xylophone *m*

Y

Y, y [waɪ] *n (letter)* Y, y *m inv;* **Y-fronts** slip *m* ouvert

yacht [jɒt] *n (sailing boat)* voilier *m; (large private boat)* yacht *m;* **y. club** club *m* de voile; **y. race** régate *f*

yachting [ˈjɒtɪŋ] *n* voile *f;* **to go y.** faire de la voile

yachtsman [ˈjɒtsmən] *n* navigateur *m*

yachtswoman [ˈjɒtswʊmən] *n* navigatrice *f*

yack [jæk] *Fam* **1** *n* papotage *m*

    2 *vi* papoter

yak [jæk] *n* (**a**) *Zool* yack *m* (**b**) = yack *(pt & pp* **yakked)**

yam [jæm] *n* patate *f* douce

Yank [jæŋk], **Yankee** [ˈjæŋkɪ] *n Fam (person from northeastern states of the USA)* habitant(e) *m,f* des États du Nord

yank [jæŋk] *Fam* **1** *n* **to give sth a y.** tirer qch d'un coup sec

    2 *vt* tirer d'un coup sec; **to y. sth open/out** ouvrir/arracher qch d'un coup sec

yap [jæp] *(pt & pp* **yapped)** *vi (of dog)* japper; *Fam (of person)* jacasser

yard¹ [jɑːd] *n (unit of measurement)* = 0,914 m, yard *m*

yard² [jɑːd] *n* (**a**) *(garden)* jardin *m; (of school, farm)* cour *f;* **y. sale** vide-grenier *m* (**b**) *(for working)* chantier *m;* **(builder's) y.** chantier de construction (**c**) *(for storage)* dépôt *m* de marchandises

yardstick [ˈjɑːdstɪk] *n (standard)* point *m* de référence

yarn [jɑːn] *n* (**a**) *(thread, wool)* fil *m* (à tricoter) (**b**) *Fam (story)* histoire *f* à dormir debout; **to spin a y.** raconter une histoire

yawn [jɔːn] **1** *n* bâillement *m; Fam (boring thing)* plaie *f*

    2 *vi* (**a**) *(of person)* bâiller (**b**) *(of chasm)* béer

yd. *(abbr* **yard(s))** yard *m*

ye [jiː] **1** *pron Lit =* **you**

    2 *definite art Lit or Hum =* **the**

yea [jeɪ] **1** *n* **yeas and nays** voix *fpl* pour et voix contre

    2 *adv Lit =* **yes**

yeah [jeə] *adv Fam* ouais

year [jɪə(r)] *n (twelve-month period)* an *m; (referring to duration)* année *f;* **in the y. 1931** en 1931; **this y.** cette année; **last/next y.** l'année dernière/prochaine; **every y.** chaque année, tous les ans; **twice a y.** deux fois par an; **to earn $50,000 a y.** gagner 50 000 dollars par an; **to be ten years old** avoir dix ans; **he got five years** *(prison sentence)* il en a pris pour cinq ans; **for many years** pendant des années; **y. in y. out** chaque année; **over the years** au fil des ans, avec les années; **years ago** il y a des années; **it's years since I saw him, I haven't seen him for** *or* **in years** ça fait des années que je ne l'ai pas vu; **from her earliest years** dès son plus jeune âge; **to be getting on in years** prendre de l'âge

yearbook [ˈjɪəbʊk] *n* almanach *m*

yearlong [ˈjɪəlɒŋ] *adj* d'un an

yearly [ˈjɪəlɪ] **1** *adj* annuel(elle)

    2 *adv* annuellement; **twice y.** deux fois par an

yearn [jɜːn] *vi* **to y. for sth** désirer qch ardemment; **to y. to do sth** brûler de faire qch

yearning [ˈjɜːnɪŋ] *n* désir *m* ardent

yeast [jiːst] *n* levure *f*

yell [jel] **1** *n* hurlement *m;* **to give a y.** pousser un hurlement

    2 *vt & vi* hurler

yellow [ˈjeləʊ] **1** *n* jaune *m*

    2 *adj* (**a**) *(in color)* jaune; **to turn** *or* **to go y.** jaunir; **y. card** *(in soccer)* carton *m* jaune, *Belg* carte *f* jaune; **y. fever** fièvre *f* jaune; **the Y. Pages**® les Pages *fpl* Jaunes; **the Y. River** le fleuve Jaune (**b**) *Fam (cowardly)* trouillard(e)

    3 *vi* jaunir

yelp [jelp] **1** *n* jappement *m*

    2 *vi* japper

Yemen [ˈjemən] *n* le Yémen

Yemeni [ˈjemənɪ] **1** *n* Yéménite *mf*

    2 *adj* yéménite

yen¹ [jen] *n (Japanese currency)* yen *m*

yen² [jen] *n Fam* **to have a y. for sth/to do sth** avoir envie de qch/de faire qch

Yerevan [jerəˈvæn] *n* Erevan

yes [jes] **1** *adv* oui; *(after negative question)* si; **haven't you seen the movie? – y.(, I have)** tu n'as pas vu ce film? – mais si

    2 *n* oui *m inv*

yes-man [ˈjesmæn] *n Fam* béni-oui-oui *m inv*

yesterday [ˈjestədeɪ] **1** *n* hier *m*

    2 *adv* hier; **y. morning/evening** hier matin/soir

yet [jet] **1** *adv* (**a**) *(still)* encore; **I haven't finished y.** je n'ai pas encore fini; **don't go y.** ne pars pas tout de suite; **I'll catch her y.!** je finirai bien par l'attraper!; **as y.** jusqu'à présent; **not y.** pas encore; **y. again** encore une fois; **y. more** encore plus; **y. another mistake** encore une erreur (**b**) *(in questions)* **have they decided y.?** est-ce qu'ils ont décidé?

    2 *conj* cependant; **small y. strong** petit(e) mais fort(e); **and y. I like her** et pourtant, je l'aime bien

yeti [ˈjetɪ] *n* yéti *m*

yew [juː] *n* if *m*

Yiddish [ˈjɪdɪʃ] **1** *n* yiddish *m*

    2 *adj* yiddish *inv*

yield [jiːld] **1** *n (of field, shares)* rendement *m; (of mine)* production *f*

    2 *vt* (**a**) *(interest)* rapporter; *(results)* donner; **to y. a profit** rapporter (**b**) *(territory, right)* céder

    3 *vi (surrender)* se rendre; **to y. to force** céder devant la force; **to y. to reason** se rendre à la raison; **to y. to temptation** céder à la tentation

yippee [jɪˈpiː] *exclam* youpi!

YMCA [waɪemsiːˈeɪ] *n (abbr* **Young Men's Christian Association)** = association chrétienne proposant hébergement et activités sportives

yo [jəʊ] *exclam Fam* salut!

yodel [ˈjəʊdəl] *vi* iodler

yoga [ˈjəʊɡə] *n* yoga *m;* **y. mat** tapis *m* de yoga

yoghurt, yogurt [ˈjəʊɡət] *n* yaourt *m*

yoke [jəʊk] **1** *n* (**a**) *(for oxen) & Fig* joug *m* (**b**) *(for carrying)* palanche *f*

2 vt (oxen) atteler; Fig **to be yoked to sth** être lié(e) à qch

yokel [ˈjəʊkəl] n Pej or Hum péquenaud(e) m,f

yolk [jəʊk] n jaune m (d'œuf)

yonder [ˈjɒndə(r)] adv **(over) y.** là-bas

Yorkshire pudding [ˈjɔːkʃɪəˈpʊdɪŋ] n = croquette de pâte à frire servie avec le rosbif

you [juː] pron (**a**) (subject) (familiar) tu; (formal, familiar plural) vous; **you're late** tu es/vous êtes en retard; **have YOU got it?** c'est toi qui l'as/vous qui l'avez?

(**b**) (direct object) (familiar) te; (formal, familiar plural) vous; **I hate y.** je te/vous déteste; **I love y.** je t'aime/je vous aime; **I can understand your son but not YOU** je comprends ton fils, mais toi, je ne te comprends pas

(**c**) (indirect object) (familiar) te; (formal, familiar plural) vous; **I gave y. the book** je t'ai/vous ai donné le livre; **I gave it to y.** je te/vous l'ai donné

(**d**) (after preposition) (familiar) toi; (formal, familiar plural) vous; **I'm thinking of y.** je pense à toi/vous

(**e**) (as complement of verb to be) (familiar) toi; (formal, familiar plural) vous; **it's y.** c'est toi/vous; **it was y. who did it** c'est toi qui l'as fait/vous qui l'avez fait

(**f**) (impersonal) on; **y. never know** on ne sait jamais; **y. have to be careful with her** il faut faire attention avec elle; **smoking is bad for y.** fumer est mauvais pour la santé

(**g**) (in apposition) **y. men/French** vous les hommes/les Français; **y. idiot!** espèce d'idiot!

(**h**) (with imperative) **y. sit down here** toi, tu t'assois ici; **don't y. dare!** je t'interdis de le faire!

(**i**) (with interjections) **silly y.!** que tu es bête!; **poor y.!** pauvre de toi!

you'd [juːd] = **you had, you would**

you-know-who [juːnəʊˈhuː] n qui-tu-sais

you'll [juːl] = **you will, you shall**

young [jʌŋ] **1** adj jeune; **she's younger than me** elle est plus jeune que moi; **she's two years younger than me** elle a deux ans de moins que moi; **you're only y. once** on n'a qu'une jeunesse; **when I was a y. man/woman** quand j'étais jeune; **in his younger days** dans sa jeunesse; **the night is y.!** la soirée ne fait que commencer!; **y. people** les jeunes mpl; **she's y. for her age** elle fait plus jeune que son âge; **y. in spirit** or **at heart** jeune d'esprit

2 npl (**a**) (people) **the y.** les jeunes mpl (**b**) (animals) petits mpl

youngster [ˈjʌŋstə(r)] n jeune mf

your [jɔː(r)] possessive adj (**a**) (with singular possession) (familiar) ton (ta); (formal, familiar plural) votre; (with plural possession) (familiar) tes; (formal, familiar plural) vos; **y. job** ton/votre travail; **y. wife** ta/votre femme; **y. parents** tes/vos parents; **it wasn't YOUR idea!** ce n'est pas toi qui en as eu l'idée! (**b**) (for parts of body) **did you hit y. head?** vous vous êtes cogné la tête? (**c**) (impersonal) **you should buy y. ticket first** on doit acheter son billet d'abord; **smoking is bad for y. health** fumer est mauvais pour la santé; Fam **y. average Frenchman** le Français moyen

you're [jɔː(r)] = **you are**

yours [jɔːz] possessive pron (**a**) (replacing singular possession) (familiar) le tien (la tienne) m,f; (formal, familiar plural) le vôtre (la vôtre) m,f; (replacing plural possession) (familiar) les tiens (les tiennes) mpl,fpl; (formal, familiar plural) les vôtres mfpl; **my house is big, but y. is bigger** ma maison est grande, mais la tienne est plus grande encore (**b**) (used attributively) **this book is y.** ce livre est à toi/à vous; **a friend of y.** un de tes/vos amis; **where's that brother of y.?** où ton frère a-t-il bien pu passer?

yourself [jɔːˈself] pron (**a**) (reflexive) **did you hurt y.?** (familiar) tu t'es blessé?; (formal) vous vous êtes blessé? (**b**) (emphatic) (familiar) toi-même; (formal) vous-même; **you y. have never...** vous-même n'avez jamais...; **you told me y.** vous me l'avez dit vous-même; **you're not y. today** tu n'es pas dans ton état normal aujourd'hui (**c**) (after preposition) **do you live by y.?** vous vivez seul(e)?; **did you buy it for y.?** vous l'avez acheté pour vous-même?; **are you talking to y.?** tu parles tout(e) seul(e)?

yourselves [jɔːˈselvz] pron (**a**) (reflexive) **did you hurt y.?** vous vous êtes blessés(ées)? (**b**) (emphatic) vous-mêmes; **you y. have never...** vous-mêmes n'avez jamais...; **you told me y.** vous me l'avez dit vous-mêmes; **you're not y. today** vous n'êtes pas dans votre état normal aujourd'hui (**c**) (after preposition) **do you live by y.?** vous vivez seuls(es)?; **did you buy it for y.?** vous l'avez acheté pour vous-mêmes?; **do you talk to y.?** vous parlez tout(es) seuls(es)?

youth [juːθ] n (**a**) (period) jeunesse f (**b**) (young man) adolescent m, jeune m (**c**) (young people) jeunes mpl; **y. club** centre m de loisir pour les jeunes; **y. hostel** auberge f de jeunesse; **y. worker** éducateur(trice) m,f

youthful [ˈjuːθfʊl] adj (person, looks) jeune; (enthusiasm) juvénile

you've [juːv] = **you have**

yowl [jaʊl] **1** n hurlement m
2 vi hurler

yo-yo® [ˈjəʊjəʊ] (pl **yo-yos**) n yo-yo® m

yr. (abbr **year**) année f

yuan [juːˈæn] n yuan m

yucca [ˈjʌkə] n yucca m

yuck [jʌk] exclam Fam berk!

yucky [ˈjʌkɪ] adj Fam dégoûtant(e)

Yugoslav [ˈjuːgəʊslɑːv] **1** n Yougoslave mf
2 adj yougoslave

Yugoslavia [juːgəʊˈslɑːvɪə] n la Yougoslavie

Yugoslavian [juːgəʊˈslɑːvɪən] adj yougoslave

yuletide [ˈjuːltaɪd] n Noël m

yummy [ˈjʌmɪ] adj Fam délicieux(euse)

yuppie [ˈjʌpɪ] n yuppie mf; **y. area** quartier m riche et branché; Fam **y. flu** syndrome m de la fatigue chronique

yuppify [ˈjʌpɪfaɪ] (pt & pp **yuppified**) vt **to become yuppified** s'embourgeoiser

YWCA [waɪdʌbəljuːsiːˈeɪ] n (abbr **Young Women's Christian Association**) = association chrétienne proposant hébergement et activités sportives

Z

Z, z [zi:] *n (letter)* Z, z *m inv*; *Fam* **to catch some z's** *(take a nap)* piquer un roupillon

Zaire [zɑːˈɪə(r)] *n Formerly* le Zaïre

Zairean [zɑːˈɪərɪən] **1** *n* Zaïrois(oise) *m,f*
2 *adj* zaïrois(oise)

Zambia [ˈzæmbɪə] *n* la Zambie

Zambian [ˈzæmbɪən] **1** *n* Zambien(enne) *m,f*
2 *adj* zambien(enne)

zany [ˈzeɪnɪ] *adj* loufoque

zap [zæp] *(pt & pp* **zapped)** *Fam* **1** *vt* **(a)** *(destroy, disable)* éliminer **(b)** *Comput (delete)* effacer
2 *vi* **(a)** *(change TV channel)* zapper **(b)** *(move quickly)* **to z. in/out/off** entrer/sortir/partir à toute pompe

zapper [ˈzæpə(r)] *n Fam (TV remote control)* télécommande *f*

zeal [ziːl] *n* zèle *m*

zealot [ˈzelət] *n* fanatique *mf*

zealous [ˈzeləs] *adj* zélé(e); *(campaigner, supporter)* fervent(e)

zebra [ˈziːbrə] *n* zèbre *m*

zenith [ˈziːnɪθ] *n also Fig* zénith *m*; **at the z. of her powers/influence** au sommet de son pouvoir/influence

zephyr [ˈzefə(r)] *n* zéphyr *m*

zero [ˈzɪərəʊ] **1** *n (pl* **zeros)** zéro *m*; **22 degrees below z.** 22 degrés en dessous de zéro
2 *adj Fam* aucun(e); **to have z. charm** n'avoir aucun charme; **z. tolerance** tolérance *f* zéro
3 *vi* **to z. in on sb** foncer sur qn; **to z. in on sth** se concentrer sur qch

zest [zest] *n* **(a)** *(enjoyment)* enthousiasme *m* **(b)** *(of orange, lemon)* zeste *m*

zigzag [ˈzɪgzæg] **1** *n* zigzag *m*
2 *vi (pt & pp* **zigzagged)** zigzaguer

zilch [zɪltʃ] *n Fam* que dalle

Zimbabwe [zɪmˈbɑːbweɪ] *n* le Zimbabwe

Zimbabwean [zɪmˈbɑːbweɪən] **1** *n* Zimbabwéen(enne) *m,f*
2 *adj* zimbabwéen(enne)

zinc [zɪŋk] *n* zinc *m*

Zionism [ˈzaɪənɪzəm] *n* sionisme *m*

Zionist [ˈzaɪənɪst] *n & adj* sioniste *mf*

zip [zɪp] **1** *n* **(a)** *Fam (vigor)* punch *m* **(b)** **z. code** code *m* postal
2 *vt Comput (file)* zipper, compresser
3 *vi (pt & pp* **zipped)** **to z. past** *(of car)* passer en trombe; *(of bullet)* passer en sifflant

▶ **zip through** *vt insep Fam* **I zipped through the book** j'ai lu le livre à toute vitesse; **we zipped through the work** nous avons fait le travail à toute vitesse

▶ **zip up 1** *vt sep (clothes)* remonter la fermeture Éclair® de
2 *vi* se fermer par une fermeture Éclair®

Zip® disk [ˈzɪpˈdɪsk] *n Comput* cartouche *f* Zip®

Zip® drive [ˈzɪpˈdraɪv] *n Comput* lecteur *m* Zip®

zipper [ˈzɪpə(r)] *n* fermeture *f* Éclair®

zippy [ˈzɪpɪ] *adj Fam* plein(e) de punch

zit [zɪt] *n Fam* bouton *m*

zither [ˈzɪðə(r)] *n* cithare *f*

zodiac [ˈzəʊdɪæk] *n* zodiaque *m*

zombie [ˈzɒmbɪ] *n* zombi(e) *m*

zone [zəʊn] **1** *n* zone *f*
2 *vt* diviser en zones

zonked (out) [zɒŋkt(ˈaʊt)] *adj Fam (exhausted)* cassé(e); *(drugged)* défoncé(e); *(drunk)* pété(e)

zoo [zuː] *n* zoo *m*

zoological [zəʊəˈlɒdʒɪkəl] *adj* zoologique; **z. garden(s)** jardin *m* zoologique

zoologist [zəʊˈɒlədʒɪst] *n* zoologiste *mf*

zoology [zəʊˈɒlədʒɪ] *n* zoologie *f*

zoom [zuːm] **1** *n* **(a)** *(noise)* vrombissement *m* **(b)** **z. lens** zoom *m*
2 *vi Fam* **(a)** *(move quickly)* **to z. in/out/past** entrer/sortir/passer comme une flèche **(b)** *(increase quickly)* monter en flèche

▶ **zoom in** *vi (of camera)* faire un zoom avant (**on** sur)

zucchini [zuːˈkiːnɪ] *(pl* **zucchini** *or* **zucchinis)** *n* courgette *f*

Zulu [ˈzuːluː] **1** *n* Zoulou *mf*
2 *adj* zoulou(e)